P9-DIB-528

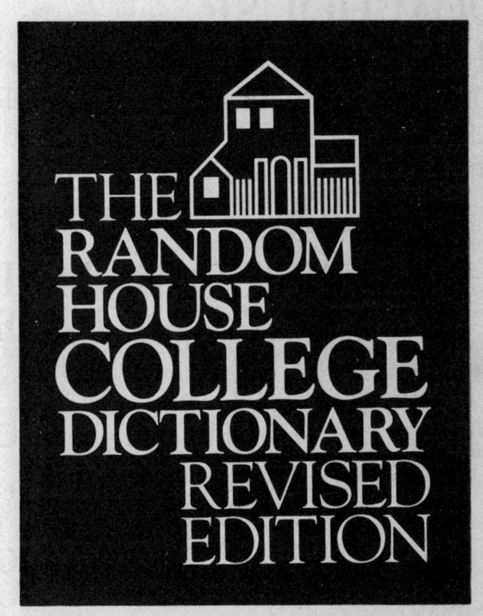
THE
RANDOM
HOUSE
COLLEGE
DICTIONARY
REVISED
EDITION

RANDOM HOUSE DICTIONARIES
A WIDELY ACCLAIMED SERIES OF MODERN AUTHORITATIVE DICTIONARIES SUITABLE FOR MANY DIFFERENT NEEDS AND LEVELS
STUART B. FLEXNER, EDITORIAL DIRECTOR

THE **RANDOM HOUSE COLLEGE DICTIONARY**

FIRST EDITION
LAURENCE URDANG, EDITOR IN CHIEF
STUART B. FLEXNER, MANAGING EDITOR

REVISED EDITION
JESS STEIN, EDITOR IN CHIEF
LEONORE C. HAUCK, MANAGING EDITOR
P.Y. SU, SENIOR DEFINING EDITOR

BASED ON **THE RANDOM HOUSE DICTIONARY OF THE ENGLISH LANGUAGE**
THE UNABRIDGED EDITION
JESS STEIN, EDITOR IN CHIEF

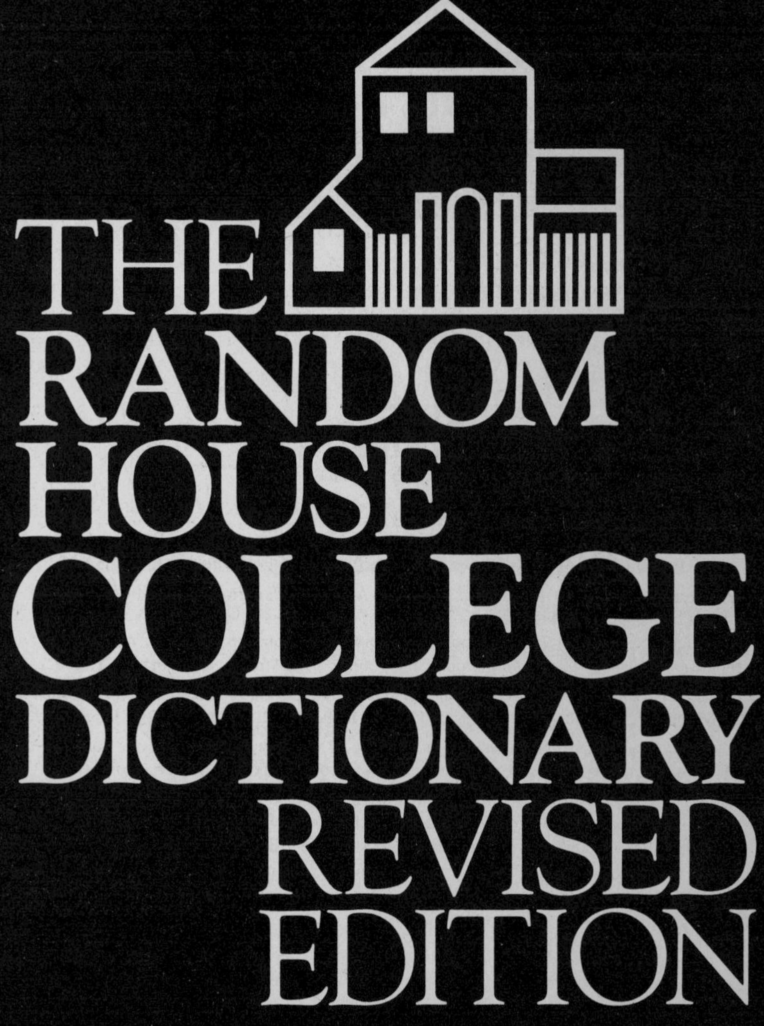
THE
RANDOM
HOUSE
COLLEGE
DICTIONARY
REVISED
EDITION

Table of Contents

REVISED EDITION

PUBLISHED IN THE UNITED STATES OF AMERICA BY RANDOM HOUSE, INC., NEW YORK AND SIMULTANEOUSLY IN CANADA BY RANDOM HOUSE OF CANADA LIMITED, TORONTO

LIBRARY OF CONGRESS CATALOGING IN PUBLICATION DATA
Main entry under title:
The Random House college dictionary.
Based on the Random House dictionary of the English language, unabridged ed.
Published in 1968 under title: The Random House dictionary of the English language, college ed.
1. English language—Dictionaries.
PE1625.R34 1975 423 75-4858 ISBN 0-394-43500-1
ISBN 0-394-43600-8 thumb-indexed ed.
ISBN 0-394-51192-1 deluxe ed.
ISBN 0-394-57350-1 leather ed.
ISBN 0-679-72720-5 trade paperback ed.

Manufactured in the United States of America

Preface to the Revised Edition

WHEN THE FIRST edition of *The Random House College Dictionary* appeared seven years ago, it was immediately received with widespread approval for its complete, authoritative, and up-to-date coverage of the English language. To maintain this position of leadership, the permanent lexicographic staff of Random House has prepared this newly revised edition.

While we have retained those qualities and features that have served the users well, we have now expanded and revised our coverage significantly to make the dictionary even more helpful. Many recent words have been included, as have new meanings of old words. Definitions have often been modernized or improved, frequently as a result of the good-willed suggestions and comments of users.

We have avoided making changes simply for the sake of change itself or as a calculated means of drawing public attention. Our guiding policy on all Random House dictionaries, from the time the program began more than a generation ago, has been to give the user the information he wants and needs as reliably, clearly, and quickly as possible. Our dictionaries have always enjoyed the warm approval and preference of discerning and demanding users. It is our sincere hope that this revision will continue to warrant the reputation of the *RHCD* as the most complete and authoritative dictionary of its kind ever published.

JESS STEIN

Preface to the First Edition

IN THE DECADES recently past, especially since World War II, the educational standards of the world have been extended to embrace more people than ever before. Literacy has increased enormously. Coupled with the technological advances of the period, the necessity for reading and study has resulted in an unprecedented interest in words.

The dictionary has traditionally been the only source of information on language for the majority of people. In it they expect to find how a word is spelled, how it may be hyphenated, how it is pronounced, what its various forms are, what its meanings are, and what its origins and history are. They also expect to find whether a word is technical or general, whether it can be used in polite company or not, and even whether someone who is called a certain word is justified in feeling offended. They want unfamiliar objects illustrated and particular places pinpointed on maps; they want biographical information, geographical, demographic, and political data, abbreviations, symbols, synonyms, antonyms, usage notes—in short, people expect to find condensed between the covers of a dictionary the knowledge of the world as reflected in their language. Above all, they demand that this knowledge be accurate and up to date. Indeed, why not? The dictionary is often the only reference book of any kind that many people ever own.

That these prodigious demands are met is, of course, no accident. A dictionary is the product of specialists, linguists, and highly trained editors who are devoted to researching language and information and to interpreting it and presenting it in understandable form.

The Random House College Dictionary is an abridgment of *The Random House Dictionary of the English Language—The Unabridged Edition*, and its style follows that of the *RHD*. No dictionary, no matter how extensive, could record the entire English language. It is obvious, then, that the editors of any dictionary are compelled to exercise discretion in what is to be included. The goal cannot be completeness: the goal must be judicious selectivity. There is no dearth of resources on language. In fact, the question is not Where do you begin? it is How, when, and where do you stop?

The Reference Department at Random House has been actively engaged in lexicographic research for more than twenty years. In the past ten years, through the use of electronic data processing equipment, it has been possible to pursue research programs in language that far outstrip those accessible to old-fashioned methods of handling information. The results yielded by this research have provided more comprehensive and more accurate information on words than was ever before available. It has been possible, for example, to acquire texts of every kind of written material imaginable—newspaper and magazine articles, stories, textbooks, novels, even specialized texts ranging from parts catalogs through articles in technical and scholarly journals to court decisions. These sources are vital to the study of the frequencies of the words used and to the analysis of their forms and meanings. Two dozen years ago, such research would have been time-consuming and prohibitively expensive; today, thousands of words can be processed in microseconds—in nanoseconds—with an accuracy and uniformity unattainable by manual techniques. Further, it is possible to collate and sort, compare and contrast, and manipulate data in many ways not dreamed of before.

But its written form yields only part of the story of a language, for, when necessary, tape recordings of radio and television programs must be analyzed not only for regional, dialectal variants of word forms, but particularly for the accurate transcription of pronunciations.

The Random House College Dictionary is the product of its editors' analysis and synthesis of more information on the words of English than has ever been collected for any dictionary of similar size. It is their sincere hope that the efforts to make it the best dictionary available will be repaid by its greater usefulness to a greater number of people.

LAURENCE URDANG

Staff

STUART B. FLEXNER	Editor in Chief
JESS STEIN	Editor in Chief Emeritus
LEONORE C. HAUCK	Managing Editor
P.Y. SU	Senior Defining Editor

EDITOR IN CHIEF (First Edition): Laurence Urdang
MANAGING EDITOR (First Edition): Stuart B. Flexner
SENIOR EDITORS: Walter C. Kidney • Thomas Hill Long • Enid Pearsons • Salvatore Ramondino • Edwin M. Ripin • Eugene F. Shewmaker • Sidney E. Zimmerman

EDITORS: Suzanne Grossman Berger • Harvey L. Bilker • Elizabeth G. Christensen • Andrea C. Denson • Robert M. Friedberg • Janet R. Goldstein • Hazel G. Kahn • Richard McDougall • Margaret Miner • Bar-Kochba Shur

ASSISTANT EDITORS: Antoinette R. Baicich • Valerie J. Clift • James DeMetro • Keith Hollaman • Alice Kovac • Suzanne Osgood • Constance Baboukis Padakis • June Rephan • Anne Ross • Martha Shrier • Dorothy Gerner Stein • Virginia Swisshelm • Anne L. Topham

EDITORIAL ASSISTANTS: Pauline G. Demetri • David S. Disenhouse • Rima Elkin • Kevin Gleason • Daniel L. Heiple • Jean Bearn Henrickson • Carolyn R. Herzog • Paul Merrill • Patricia J. Napolin • Lawrence E. Patterson • Leonard Potash • Sally G. Raymond • Lynn St. C. Strong • Robert B. Williams

ADMINISTRATIVE SUPERVISOR: Gunilla Kronvall • ADMINISTRATIVE ASSISTANTS: Rona S. Goodman • Marianne E. Gregory • Xenia Keblis • Brian Philpotts • Susan Ratzker • Mary Sapounakis

ARTISTS: Ben Feder, Inc.: George Buctel • Albert J. Carreno • Don Spaulding

CARTOGRAPHER (Spot Maps): Clare O. Ford

ART DIRECTOR: Robert D. Scudellari

DESIGNER: Tracey M. Penton

PRODUCTION MANAGERS: Otto Barz • Howard Goldstein • Robert Spencer

PRODUCTION ASSOCIATES: Michael Fragnito • Cornelia Hall • Mark Roland

Consultant Staff

Robert W. Abbett, Partner, Tippetts-Abbett-McCathy-Stratton, Consulting Engineers.

Loraine Alterman, Contemporary Music Critic.

American Telephone and Telegraph Company, Staff.

Frank C. Andrews, Professor of Chemistry, Merrill College, University of California, Santa Cruz.

Edmund C. Arnold, Professor and Chairman, Graphic Arts Department, Syracuse University.

J. G. Aston, Professor of Chemistry and Director, Cryogenic Laboratory, Pennsylvania State University.

Walter S. Avis, Professor of English, Royal Military College of Canada.

John A. Bailey, Director, The Transportation Center, Northwestern University.

Robert H. Ball, Professor of English, Queens College of the City University of New York; formerly, Curator, William Seymour Theatre Collection, Princeton University.

Stanley S. Ballard, Professor of Physics and Chairman, Department of Physics and Astronomy, University of Florida.

Theodore X. Barber, Director of Psychological Research, Medfield Foundation, Medfield State Hospital, Medfield, Mass.

Philip Bard, Professor and Director, Department of Physiology, School of Medicine, Johns Hopkins University.

Duncan Barnes, Writer-Reporter, *Sports Illustrated*.

Roy P. Basler, Director, Reference Department, Library of Congress.

Virginia A. Basler, Editorial Researcher.

Caroline Bates, Senior Editor, *Gourmet Magazine*.

Ned D. Bayley, Assistant Director, Animal Husbandry Research Division, U.S. Department of Agriculture.

W.C. Benzer, Metallurgical Engineer, American Iron and Steel Institute.

Peter L. Bernstein, President, Peter L. Bernstein, Inc.; Visiting Professor of Economics, Graduate Faculty, The New School.

Theodore M. Bernstein, Assistant Managing Editor, *The New York Times*.

Raymond C. Binder, Professor of Mechanical Engineering, University of Southern California.

Max Birnbaum, Educational Consultant; Training Associate, Human Relations Center, Boston University.

Cyril E. Black, Professor of History, Princeton University.

Max Black, Professor, Sage School of Philosophy, Cornell University.

A. Harold Blatt, Professor and Chairman, Department of Chemistry, Queens College of the City University of New York.

Herbert Blumer, Professor of Sociology and Director, Institute of Social Sciences, University of California.

Ralph Philip Boas, Jr., Professor and Chairman, Department of Mathematics, Northwestern University.

Philip K. Bock, Professor of Anthropology, The University of New Mexico.

Winthrop S. Boggs, H. R. Harmer, Inc. International Philatelic Auctioneers; formerly, Director, Philatelic Foundation.

J. T. Bonner, Professor of Biology, Princeton University.

Alfred Bornemann, Professor of Metallurgy, Stevens Institute of Technology.

B. A. Botkin, formerly, President, American Folklore Society; Associate Professor of English, University of Oklahoma; Chief, Archive of Folk Song, and Fellow in Folklore, Library of Congress.

Jerald C. Brauer, Professor and Dean, Divinity School, University of Chicago.

Theodore M. Brody, Professor of Pharmacology, University of Michigan.

Arthur J. Bronstein, Professor of Speech, Queens College of the City University of New York.

Dirk Brouwer, Professor and Chairman, Department of Astronomy, Yale University; Director, Yale University Observatory.

Dorsey W. Bruner, Professor and Chairman, Department of Veterinary Microbiology, New York State Veterinary College, Cornell University.

Ralph Buchsbaum, Professor of Biology, University of Pittsburgh.

Arthur H. Burr, Sibley Professor of Mechanical Engineering and Head, Department of Machine Design, College of Engineering, Cornell University.

Meredith F. Burrill, Director, Office of Geography, U.S. Department of the Interior.

Meribeth E. Cameron, Professor of History and Dean, Mount Holyoke College.

William Card, Professor of English, Illinois Teachers College: Chicago —South.

James Cass, Associate Education Editor, *Saturday Review*.

Elliott E. Cheatham, Frank C. Rand Professor of Law, Vanderbilt University; Charles Evans Hughes Professor Emeritus of Law, Columbia University.

John E. Chrisinger, Major USAF, retired; formerly, Associate Professor of Aeronautics, U.S. Air Force Academy.

Anatole Chujoy, Editor and Publisher, *Dance News*.

Craig Claiborne, Food Editor, *The New York Times*.

Gerson D. Cohen, Chancellor, Jewish Theological Seminary of America.

Henry Steele Commager, Professor of American History, Amherst College.

Edward U. Condon, Professor of Physics and Fellow of the Joint Institute for Laboratory Astrophysics, University of Colorado.

Carleton S. Coon, Professor of Anthropology, retired, and Research Curator of Ethnology, University Museum, University of Pennsylvania.

Edward M. Crane, Jr., President, Pitman Publishing Corporation.

Charles R. Dahlberg, Associate Professor and Chairman, Department of English, Queens College of the City University of New York.

Russell E. Davis, Assistant Chief, Beef Cattle Research Branch, U.S. Department of Agriculture.

John P. Dawson, Professor of Law, Harvard University.

Arthur Gerard DeVoe, M.D.; Professor of Ophthalmology, Medical School, Columbia University.

Emery M. Dieffenbach, Assistant to Chief, Crop Production Engineering Research Branch, U.S. Department of Agriculture.

David Diringer, Professor, University of Florence, Italy; Lecturer, University of Cambridge, England.

Mario Einaudi, Walter Carpenter Professor of International and Comparative Politics, Cornell University.

Maximilian Ellenbogen, Professor of Classical and Oriental Languages, Queens College of the City University of New York.

John R. Elting, Colonel, USA; Deputy Chief of Staff for Intelligence, Military District of Washington; formerly, Acting Professor of Military Art and Engineering, U.S. Military Academy.

Erik H. Erikson, Professor of Human Development Emeritus, Harvard University.

Vincent J. Esposito, Brigadier General, USA; Head, Department of Military Art and Engineering, U.S. Military Academy.

Thomas H. Everett, Assistant Director (Horticulture) and Senior Curator of Education, New York Botanical Garden.

William L. Everitt, Professor and Dean, College of Engineering, University of Illinois.

Dorothy Fey, Executive Director, The United States Trademark Association.

Andreas Feininger, Photographer.

Donald Finkel, Poet-in-Residence, Washington University.

Louis Finkelstein, Professor and Chancellor, Jewish Theological Seminary of America.

Sydney N. Fisher, Professor of History, Ohio State University.

Georges Florovsky, Professor Emeritus of Eastern Church History, Divinity School, Harvard University; Visiting Professor of History, Princeton University.

Food and Nutrition Service, U.S. Department of Agriculture.

Henry B. Fried, Technical Director, American Watchmakers Institute; Teacher, Watch and Clock Mechanics, George Westinghouse Vocational and Technical High School.

Clifford Frondel, Professor of Mineralogy, Harvard University.

Bil Gilbert, Writer.

Bruce Gilchrist, Director, Columbia University Center for Computing Activities.

Wilbur E. Gilman, Professor and Chairman, Department of Speech, Queens College of the City University of New York.

Cyrus H. Gordon, Professor and Chairman, Department of Mediterranean Studies, Brandeis University.

Charles M. Goren, Author-Lecturer.

Stephen V. Grancsay, Curator Emeritus of Arms and Armor, The Metropolitan Museum of Art.

Joseph H. Greenberg, Professor of Anthropology, Stanford University.

Charles H. Greene, Professor and Chairman, Department of Glass Science, Alfred University.

Konrad Gries, Professor and Chairman, Department of Classical and Oriental Languages, Queens College of the City University of New York.

Harold J. Grossman, Harold J. Grossman Associates; Consultant, American Hotel and Motel Association.

Harry G. Guthmann, Professor Emeritus of Finance, School of Business, Northwestern University.

Sherman P. Haight, Jr., Chairman of Advisory Committee, formerly President, U.S. Pony Clubs; Joint Master, Litchfield County Hounds.

Livingston Hall, Roscoe Pound Professor of Law, Harvard University.

Robert A. Hall, Jr., Professor of Linguistics, Cornell University.

H. George Hamilton, Director, Fels Planetarium, The Franklin Institute Science Museum and Planetarium.

Eric P. Hamp, Professor of Linguistics, University of Chicago.

Kelsie B. Harder, Professor and Chairman, Department of English, State University of New York.

Henry N. Harkins, M.D.; Professor of Surgery, School of Medicine, University of Washington.

Anna Granville Hatcher, Professor of Romance Languages, Johns Hopkins University.

Gene R. Hawes, Reference book Author and Editor.

W. W. Hay, Professor of Railway Civil Engineering, University of Illinois.

Richard Heffner, University Professor of Communications and Public Policy, Rutgers—The State University of New Jersey.

Louis G. Heller, Assistant Professor of Classical Languages and Hebrew, City College of the City University of New York.

Rhoda A. Hendricks, Instructor in Greek and Latin, Westover School.

Nat Hentoff, Jazz Critic, *The New Yorker;* Novelist.

Fred C. Hess, Associate Astronomer, Hayden Planetarium, The American Museum.

Gilbert Highet, Anthon Professor of the Latin Language and Literature, Columbia University.

Ralph Hodges, Associate Technical Editor, *Stereo Review.*

Robert D. Hodgson, Assistant Geographer, U.S. Department of State.

Lamar Hoover, Managing Editor, *Gourmet Magazine.*

Adrian Horne, Head of Advertising and Information, Dolby Laboratories, Inc.

J. E. Householder, Associate Professor of Mathematics, Humboldt State College.

Carl L. Hubbs, Professor of Biology, Scripps Institution of Oceanography, University of California.

Frederick S. Hulse, Professor of Anthropology, University of Arizona.

Charles F. Hummel, Associate Curator, Henry Francis du Pont Winterthur Museum.

Cornelius S. Hurlbut, Jr., Professor of Mineralogy, Harvard University.

Ralph E. Huschke, Physical Scientist, The RAND Corporation.

Joan S. Hyman, Educational Consultant.

Fred L. Israel, Professor of American History, City College of the City University of New York.

Harold K. Jacobson, Professor of Political Science, University of Michigan.

William S. Janney, Publisher, *Bicycle Spokesman.*

H. W. Janson, Professor and Chairman, Department of Fine Arts, Washington Square College of Arts and Science, New York University.

Assar Janzén, Professor of Scandinavian, University of California.

Eunice W. Johnson, Fashion Editor, *Ebony.*

John H. Johnson, Administrative Officer, Office of Commissioner of Baseball.

Lewis V. Judson, Physicist, Office of Weights and Measures, National Bureau of Standards, Retired.

Edward J. Jurji, Professor of the History of Religions, Princeton Theological Seminary.

Braj B. Kachru, Professor and Head, Department of Linguistics, University of Illinois.

C. M. Kahler, Professor of Insurance, Wharton School of Finance and Commerce, University of Pennsylvania; formerly, President, American Risk and Insurance Association, Inc.

Charles J. Kelly, Detective, 40th Precinct of the New York Police Force.

G. C. Kent, Professor and Chairman, Department of Plant Pathology, New York State College of Agriculture, Cornell University.

Michael Kirby, Editor, *The Drama Review;* Chairman, Graduate Drama Department, New York University.

Philip Kissam, Professor of Civil Engineering, Princeton University.

John H. Knowles, M.D.; President, The Rockefeller Foundation.

John Knox, Professor of Sacred Literature, Union Theological Seminary.

Jerry J. Kollros, Professor and Chairman, Department of Zoology, State University of Iowa.

I. M. Kolthoff, Professor Emeritus, Department of Chemistry, University of Minnesota.

Samuel Noah Kramer, Professor of Oriental Studies, University of Pennsylvania.

William M. Kunstler, Partner, Kunstler Kunstler & Kinoy; Adjunct Assistant Professor of Law, Pace College.

Hans Kurath, Professor Emeritus of English, University of Michigan.

Robert V. Langmuir, Professor of Electrical Engineering, California Institute of Technology.

Arthur M. Lassek, M.D.; Professor Emeritus of Anatomy, School of Medicine, Boston University.

Chester F. Lay, Professor and Chairman, Department of Business and Economics, Florida Southern College.

W. P. Lehmann, Ashbel Smith Professor of Germanic Languages and Linguistics, University of Texas.

Robert Lekachman, Professor and Chairman, Department of Economics, State University of New York.

Morton A. Lieberman, Professor and Acting Chairman, Department of Behavioral Sciences (Human Development) and Department of Psychiatry, University of Chicago.

George E. Linton, Professor Emeritus of Textiles, Fashion Institute of Technology.

Bertram Lippman, Author, Editor.

Robert C. Lusk, Director, Educational Services, Automobile Manufacturers Association, Inc.

E. A. Lycett, Department Head, Special Photographic Effects, Walt Disney Productions.

Earle R. MacAusland, Editor and Publisher, *Gourmet Magazine.*

Curtis D. MacDougall, Professor of Journalism, Northwestern University.

Kemp Malone, Professor Emeritus of English Literature, Johns Hopkins University.

James W. Marchand, Professor of German, Cornell University.

John H. Martin, Collaborator, Crops Research Division, U.S. Department of Agriculture.

Kirtley F. Mather, Professor Emeritus of Geology, Harvard University.

Raven I. McDavid, Professor of English, University of Chicago.

Virginia McDavid, Professor of English, Illinois Teachers College: Chicago—South.

Gordon McLintock, Rear Admiral, USMS, Superintendent, U.S. Merchant Marine Academy.

Arthur T. von Mehren, Professor of Law, Harvard University.

Robert C. Mellors, M.D.; Professor of Pathology, Hospital for Special Surgery; School of Medicine, Cornell University.

J. I. Miller, Professor of Animal Husbandry, New York State College of Agriculture, Cornell University.

David R. Mitchell, Dean, College of Mineral Industries, Pennsylvania State University.

Therald Moeller, Professor of Chemistry, University of Illinois.

E. G. Moore, Director, Agricultural Research Service Information Division, U.S. Department of Agriculture.

Toni Morrison, Author and Editor.

Philip M. Morse, Professor of Physics; Director, Computation Center; Director, Operations Research Center, Massachusetts Institute of Technology.

Motor Vehicle Manufacturers Association of the United States, Inc., Staff.

Ernest Nagel, John Dewey Professor of Philosophy, Columbia University.

C. B. Neblette, Professor and Dean, College of Graphic Arts and Photography, Rochester Institute of Technology.

Norman D. Newell, Chairman, Department of Fossil Invertebrates, The American Museum of Natural History.

Robert Earl Nixon, M.D.; Psychiatrist, Mary Conover Mellon Foundation, Vassar College.

Sydney P. Noe, Chief Curator Emeritus, American Numismatic Society.

F. H. Norton, Professor Emeritus, Department of Ceramics, Massachusetts Institute of Technology.

John B. Oakes, Editor of the Editorial Page, *The New York Times.*

William B. Ober, M.D.; Attending Pathologist and Director of Laboratories, Knickerbocker Hospital.

Frederick I. Ordway, III, President and Director, General Astronautics Research Corp.

Raúl Ortiz y Ortiz, Dean of the School for Foreign Students, National Autonomous University of Mexico.

George P. Oslin, Director, Public Relations, The Western Union Telegraph Company.

Sidney R. Packard, Professor Emeritus of History, Smith College.

George C. Pappageotes, Lecturer in Greek, Columbia University.

Kenneth C. Parkes, Curator of Birds, Carnegie Museum.

Bradley M. Patten, Professor Emeritus of Anatomy, School of Medicine, University of Michigan.

G. Etzel Pearcy, The Geographer, U.S. Department of State.

Thomas M. Peery, M.D.; Professor and Chairman, Department of Pathology, School of Medicine, George Washington University.

Michael J. Pelczar, Jr., Professor of Microbiology, University of Maryland.

Herbert Penzl, Professor of Germanic Philology, University of California.

George E. Pettengill, Librarian, American Institute of Architects.

Walter Piston, Professor Emeritus of Music, Harvard University.

David D. Polon, SETI/Western (Scientist Engineer Technological Institute).

Clifford H. Pope, formerly, Curator, Division of Amphibians and Reptiles, Chicago Natural History Museum.

Consultant Staff

Frederick H. Pough, Director, Santa Barbara Museum of Natural History.

James W. Poultney, Professor of Classics, Johns Hopkins University.

Steven D. Price, Author.

W. A. Ramey, Soil Scientist, Soil and Water Conservation Research Division, U.S. Department of Agriculture.

Allen Walker Read, Professor of English, Columbia University.

Joseph P. Reddy, Public Relations Director, Walt Disney Productions.

Charles M. Rehmus, Co-Director, Institute of Labor and Industrial Relations, University of Michigan.

Herbert W. Reich, Managing Editor, Odyssey Scientific Library.

Martin Reich, Specialist in Instrumental Music Education, Board of Education, New York City.

Fred Reinfeld, Chess Editor, Sterling Publishing Company.

M. M. Rhoades, Professor and Chairman, Department of Botany, Indiana University.

Ring Magazine, Staff.

C. A. Robinson, Jr., Professor of Classics, Brown University.

Saul Rosenzweig, Professor of Psychology and Psychiatry, Washington University.

Sigmund Rothschild, Lecturer, New York University; Consultant, Fashion Industry Foundation and Fashion Institute of Technology.

G. H. Russell, Professor of English, University of Sydney, Australia.

Pat Ryan, Writer-Reporter, *Sports Illustrated.*

Edward A. Saibel, Professor and Chairman, Department of Mechanics, Rensselaer Polytechnic Institute.

E. B. Sandell, Professor of Chemistry, University of Minnesota.

Louis Sas, Professor of Romance Languages, City College of the City University of New York.

David Schapiro, Department of Psychiatry, University of California, Los Angeles.

Harold Schonberg, Senior Music Critic, *The New York Times.*

John H. Schruben, FAIA; Executive Vice President, Production Systems for Architects and Engineers, Inc.

G. W. Schulz, Lieutenant Colonel, USA; formerly, Associate Professor, Department of Military Art and Engineering, U.S. Military Academy.

Charles H. Seevers, Professor and Chairman, Department of Biology, Roosevelt University; Research Associate in Entomology, Chicago Natural History Museum.

M. H. Seevers, M.D.; Associate Dean, School of Medicine, University of Michigan.

Richard Sennett, Professor of Sociology, New York University.

Charles E. Sheedy, C.S.C., Dean, College of Arts and Letters, University of Notre Dame.

Roger L. Shinn, Professor of Applied Christianity, Union Theological Seminary; Adjunct Professor of Religion, Columbia University.

Chester B. Slawson, Professor of Mineralogy, University of Michigan.

William G. Steere, Director, New York Botanical Garden; Professor of Botany, Columbia University.

Paula E. Stephan, Assistant Professor of Economics, Georgia State University.

DeWitt Stetten, Jr., M.D.; Dean, School of Medicine, Rutgers, The State University.

Lindley J. Stiles, Professor and Dean, School of Education, University of Wisconsin.

Hugh Stubbins, Hugh Stubbins and Associates, Inc.

Marie H. Suthers, Registered Parliamentarian; Member and Secretary, Board of Election Commissioners of Chicago.

Carl P. Swanson, William D. Gill Professor in Biology, Johns Hopkins University.

Gay Talese, Author.

Vernon D. Tate, Professor and Librarian, U.S. Naval Academy.

Maurice F. Tauber, Melvil Dewey Professor of Library Service, Columbia University.

Laurance Taylor, Director of Advertising and Publicity, Vidal Sassoon, Inc.

Samuel Terrien, Davenport Professor of Hebrew and the Cognate Languages, Union Theological Seminary.

Alvin Toffler, Author.

Henry M. Truby, Chairman, Division of Newborn Infant and Phonetic Studies, Communication Research Institute.

Arnold S. Turetsky, Rabbi, Temple Israel Center, White Plains, N.Y.

U.S. Department of Defense, Staff.

U.S. Department of Health, Education, and Welfare, Education Division, Staff.

Francis Lee Utley, Professor of English, Ohio State University.

Jack J. Valenti, President, Motion Picture Association of America, Inc.

W. J. G. Verco, M.V.O., Chester Herald of Arms, College of Arms, England.

Arthur P. Wade, Colonel, USA; Associate Professor, Department of Military Art and Engineering, U.S. Military Academy.

Miles Waggoner, Director of Public Information, National Aeronautics and Space Administration.

Donald T. Wallace, Vice President and Executive Producer, Television Programming, Benton & Bowles, Inc.

Harland W. Warner, Consumer Program Manager, Public Relations Department, Corning Glass Works.

Donald Washburn, Director, Bureau of Library and Indexing Services, American Dental Association.

Josephine Jay Watkins, Director of Community Resources and Professor of Apparel Design, Fashion Institute of Technology.

James D. Watson, Professor of Molecular Biology, Harvard University; Director, Cold Spring Harbor Laboratory.

H. Marguerite Webb, Associate Professor of Biology, Goucher College.

Ferris Webster, Associate Director for Research, Woods Hole Oceanographic Institution.

Edwin P. Weigel, Public Affairs Officer, National Weather Service.

Herman Weiskopf, Writer-Reporter, *Sports Illustrated.*

John Arch White, Dean, College of Business Administration and Dean, Graduate School of Business, University of Texas.

Lou White, Supervisor, Still Photography Color Laboratory, Walt Disney Productions.

Leon F. Whitney, D.V.M.; Clinical Instructor in Pathology, School of Medicine, Yale University.

C. R. Whittlesey, Professor of Finance and Economics, University of Pennsylvania.

Nancy P. Williamson, Writer-Reporter, *Sports Illustrated.*

Emanuel Winternitz, Curator of Musical Collections, The Metropolitan Museum of Art.

W. G. Wolfgang, Professor of Textiles, Philadelphia College of Textiles and Science.

Les Woodcock, Associate Editor, *Sports Illustrated.*

Herbert L. Wurth, General Manager, Public Affairs Division, United States Postal Service.

David C. Yu, Professor of History of Religions, Colorado Women's College.

Beatrice Zelin, Associate Professor of Apparel Design and Assistant Director of Placement, Fashion Institute of Technology.

Mark W. Zemansky, Professor of Physics, City College of the City University of New York.

SPECIAL ACKNOWLEDGMENTS

Robert L. Bernstein • Anita Bretzfield • José Burke • Murray Curtin • David C. Follmer • Ashbel Green • William P. Hansen • Gerald Harrison • Alex Keeney • Alexander C. Kliger • Edward Kline • Paul Shensa • Howard A. Stern

INDO-EUROPEAN LANGUAGES

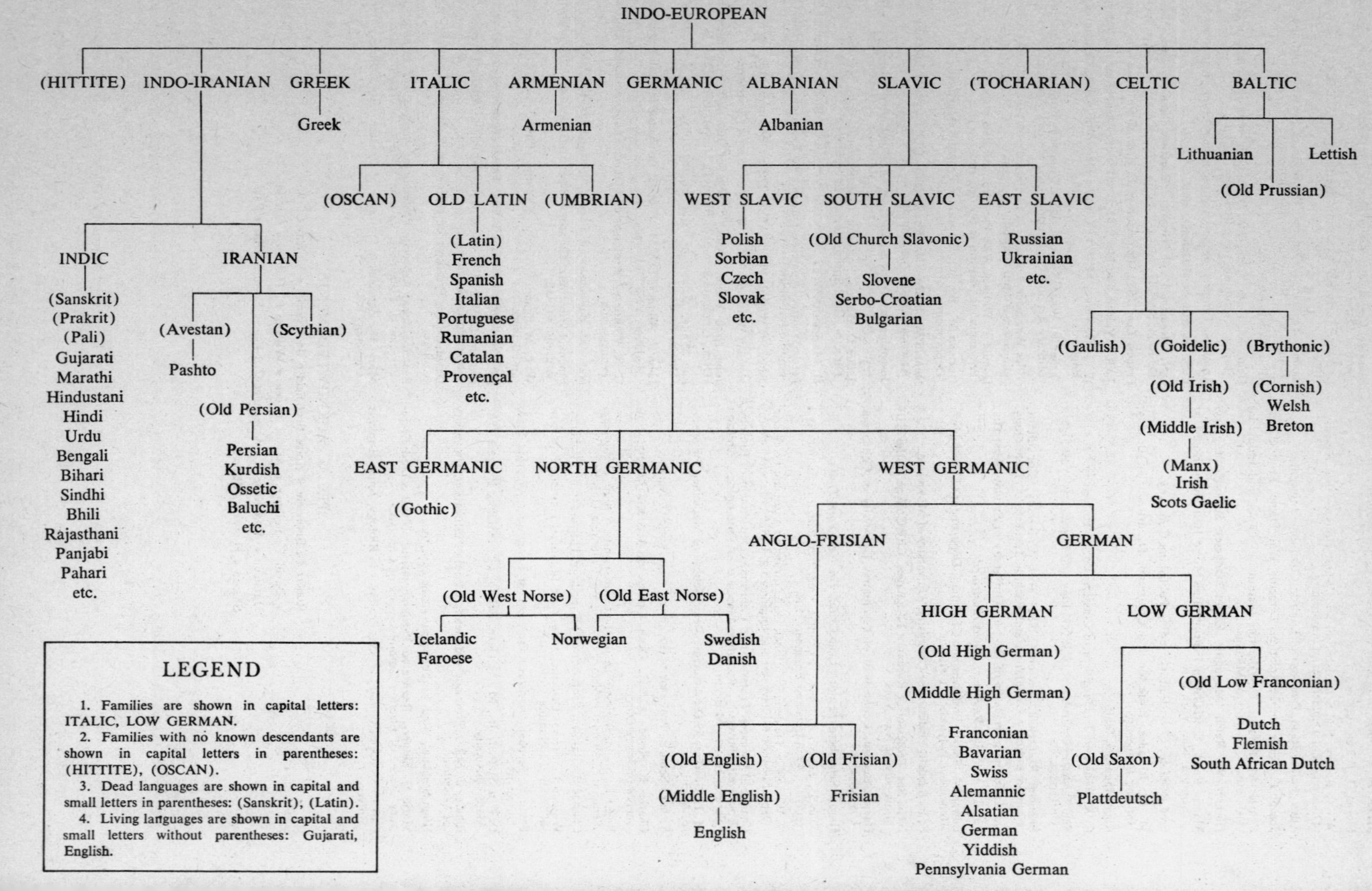

Historical Sketch of the English Language

I. THE INDO-EUROPEAN LANGUAGE FAMILY

The English language is only one of more than three thousand languages in use in the world. It is related to about a hundred of these, which together constitute the Indo-European (IE) family, one of the largest and most widely distributed of the world's language families. Some of the languages of the IE family may seem to have little resemblance to one another; many are written in alphabets different from our own. Yet all are descendants of a single ancestral language now lost.

The term Indo-European is expressive of the geographical extent of the family, from India to western Europe (including Britain and Iceland), an area later expanded with the European settlement of the New World. The original home of the Indo-Europeans is believed to have been somwhere in east central Europe. Because there is a common IE word for copper (seen in Latin *aes*) but none for bronze or iron, it is thought that the Indo-Europeans lived through the New Stone Age as a single tribe speaking a common language. Some time before the beginning of the Bronze Age, the tribal unity came to an end, and portions of the tribe migrated at first probably southeast from central Europe and later across all of Europe and into western Asia as far as India. The discovery of Tocharian, an IE language, showed that at least one group migrated as far east as Chinese Turkestan. The date of the dispersal of the original IE tribe is assumed to be about 2500 B.C. From then on, because each group was in relative isolation, the original IE language was broken up into various dialects which underwent separate linguistic development. Later, these emerged as subgroups of the IE family. (See the IE Language Chart, page x.)

Since there are no written records to tell us what the original IE language was like, it is supposed that the original speakers of IE did not know the art of writing. By using comparative methods, historical linguists have been able to make a plausible reconstruction of the original language. Toward the end of the 18th century, European scholars studying Sanskrit noted its resemblance to the classical languages, Latin and Greek, with which they were familiar. The comparison was extended to other languages, and soon the theory of a common origin was established. The words for common concepts such as "eat" and "five" illustrate the kinds of evidence that were used to establish the kinship of the IE languages. For example:

IE	Skt	Gk	L	Arm
*ed-	atti	édō	edō	utem
*peŋque	páñca	pénte (dial. pémpe)	quīnque	hing

Lith	OIr	OCS	Goth	OE	ModE
ėsti	ithim	jasti	itan	etan	eat
penkì	cōic	pęt'	fimf	fīf	five

Examination of long lists of such comparisons shows that, despite differences of detail, original IE sounds changed predictably and consistently in each of the languages and language groups.

The Germanic Branch of Indo-European. The characteristics English shares with Dutch, Flemish, Frisian, German, Gothic, and the Scandinavian languages point to their origin in a single dialect of the IE family which is reconstructed as **Proto-Germanic**. The word *mead*, as a name for honey, illustrates this kinship:

IE	Proto-Gmc	Goth	ON
*medhu-	*meduz	*midus	mjǫðr

Dan	D	OHG	OE	ModE
mjød	mee	metu	medu	mead

With the scattering of the Germanic tribes, Proto-Germanic broke up into three branches: East Germanic, North Germanic, and West Germanic, to which English belongs. (See the language chart, page x.)

II. OLD ENGLISH (c450-c1150)

The Beginnings of English. The tribes inhabiting Roman Britain were chiefly of Celtic or pre-Celtic stock. Many place-names still show traces of their languages. In the 5th century A.D., Britain was invaded by Germanic tribes from the mainland, who moved into the vacuum created by the withdrawal of the Roman legions. These tribes, of which the best known were the Angles, the Saxons, and the Jutes, displaced the earlier Celtic-speaking inhabitants and established Germanic as the principal language of Britain. The majority of our texts of the languages which developed there come from the West Saxon area, the dialect of which in time became the dominant one. The Angles, however, were the most numerous, and they gave their name to the language that has since been called English (in OE *englisc* or *ænglisc*). The Latin name for the Angles was *Angli*, reflected in the modern combining element **Anglo-**.

The English spoken in Britain from the Germanic invasions of the 5th century up to about the end of the 11th century is now usually called *Old English* (OE), though a learned coinage, *Anglo-Saxon*, is also in use. The term OE has the advantage, when used together with *Middle English* (ME) and *Modern English* (ModE), of pointing up the continuous historical development of the English language.

OE Inflection. As an IE language and a member of the Germanic branch as well, OE shares certain features of both groups. One feature that distinguishes OE markedly from ModE is its fullness of inflection in adjectives and demonstrative pronouns. The inflection of verbs in OE was considerably more complex than in ModE, and OE had many more strong verbs, usually reckoned at 365. Many of them have been leveled out in ModE to conform to the weak pattern of inflection, now regarded as the regular pattern. IE nouns had three grammatical genders—masculine, feminine, and neuter—a feature true also of the Germanic languages, in some of which, like modern German and Icelandic, the three genders are preserved to the present day. In grammatical gender, nouns and adjectives are classified by the type of inflectional endings they take, without regard to sex. Thus OE *wīf* wife, woman, is neuter, but the compound *wīfmann*, also meaning woman, is masculine. By contrast, in natural gender, as in ModE, only animate beings are considered masculine or feminine, according to sex, and all inanimate things, with a few notable exceptions, are neuter.

Germanic nouns fell into five major declensions and five minor ones, each with its own set of endings to show number and case. This number was greatly lessened in OE inflected patterns, which had only three major declensions and a few relics, some kept to this day. Furthermore, Germanic nouns had a five-case system of inflection (nominative, accusative, genitive, dative, instrumental), but this was much simplified in OE, with the falling together of the nominative and accusative and of the dative and instrumental in the chief declension. The result was a three-case system. The masculine noun *fox* fox and the neuter nouns *hūs* house and *col* coal illustrate this:

	Sing.			Pl.		
Nom.-Acc.	fox	hūs	col	foxas	hūs	colu
Gen.	foxes	hūses	coles	foxa	hūsa	cola
Dat.-Instr.	foxe	hūse	cole	foxum	hūsum	colum

Adjectives in OE were inflected to show agreement with the nouns in gender, number, and case. This system of inflection was drastically reduced in ME and given up altogether in ModE, and the only endings an adjective now takes are the comparative *-er* and the superlative *-est* (in OE *-ra* and *-ost*).

Personal pronouns still behave much as they did in OE, marking gender in the third person singular, and case and number in all persons. Here are the first and second person singular and plural pronouns of OE:

	1st sing.	**2nd sing.**	**1st pl.**	**2nd pl.**
Nom.	ic, ih	thū	wē	gē
Dat.-Instr.-Acc.	mē	thē	ūs	ēow
Gen.	mīn	thīn	ūre	ēower

Greater changes have taken place in the third person pronoun, as the OE paradigm shows:

	masc. sing.	**fem. sing.**	**neut. sing.**	**pl. (all genders)**
Nom.	hē	hēo	hit	hīe
Acc.	hine	hīe	hit	hīe
Dat.	him	hi(e)re	him	him, heom
Gen.	his	hi(e)re	his	hi(e)ra

In early ME many variants of *hēo* arose, one of which, *she*, in time became standard. The accusatives *hine* (sing.) and *hīe* (sing. and pl.) gradually went out of use, the corresponding datives serving for both cases. The OE plural forms eventually yielded to *they*, *their*, *them*, taken from the speech of the Scandinavian north (Danelaw). Another northernism in origin is the suffix *-s* added to possessives to mark them as pronouns, whence ModE *ours*, *yours*, *hers*, *theirs*. The singulars *him* and *his* have become exclusively masculine in ModE, *hit* has lost its *h*, and a neuter genitive singular has been made by adding *s* to *it*.

The Germanic verb was inflected for number, person, mode, and tense, but most of these inflections either do not appear at all in OE or are much reduced. The passive voice was expressed in OE, as today, with the help of an auxiliary verb. The OE verb had no dual number and the persons were distinguished in the indicative singular only. The tenses of Indo-European had been reduced in Germanic to two: present and past, the present serving also as a future. Verbal inflection in OE, as in ModE, falls into a system for the present and one for the past. The present system is comprised of an infinitive, a participle, and three present-tense modes: indicative, subjunctive, and imperative. The past system is comprised of a participle and two past-tense modes: indicative and subjunctive.

Nearly all Germanic verbs distinguished past from present in one of two ways. The two types of verbs are traditionally called *strong* and *weak*. The past of a strong verb is marked by changing the root vowel; that of a weak verb, by adding a dental suffix, whence ModE *-(e)d*, *-t*. Reflexes of this difference are seen in ModE in strong verbs—often referred to as "irregular" verbs—like *sing* (*sang*, *sung*), *give* (*gave*, *given*), and *grow* (*grew*, *grown*), and in weak verbs like *talk* (*talked*, *talked*), *buy* (*bought*, *bought*), and *make* (*made*, *made*).

Further losses and simplifications of endings reduced conjugation proper to very small proportions: present and past were systematically marked, and *-s* marked the third singular of the present indicative, but number, person, and mode were otherwise left unmarked. The infinitive might be marked by setting *to* before it, the grammatical construction determining whether the marker was used or not. Throughout the history of the language strong verbs have tended to become weak, but what is today left of the strong conjugation holds its own; indeed, a weak verb may become strong, as *dig*, with past tense and past participle *dug*, or the often encountered *dive*, *dove* for traditional *dive*, *dived*.

OE Word Formation. OE formed new words from other words and word stems in much the same way as ModE. Many of the OE prefixes and suffixes are now used rarely or not at all, while many in common use today were unknown to OE. For examples of OE prefixes, see in the dictionary the entries **a-**[1], **a-**[2], **a-**[3], **after-**, **arch-**, **be-**, **by-**, **for-**, **fore-**, **in-**[1], **mid-**, **mis-**[1], **off-**, **out-**, **over-**, **twi-**, **un-**[1], **un-**[2], **under-**, **up-**, **with-**; for the noun suffixes, **-dom**, **-en**[5], **-er**[1], **-hood**, **-ing**[1], **-ling**[1], **-ness**, **-red**, **-ship**, **-ster**, **-teen**, **-th**[1], **-ty**[1]; for the adjectival suffixes, **-ed**[3], **-en**[2], **-ern**, **-eth**[2], **-fold**, **-ful**, **-ish**[1], **-ly**, **-th**[2], **-some**[1], **-ward**, **-y**[1]; and for the verbal suffixes, **-en**[1], **-er**[6], **-le**.

Besides the use of prefixes and suffixes, English has at all periods made abundant use of compounding in order to form new words. Many of the OE compounds are no longer in use, but ModE has more than made up for the loss by creating an enormous number of new compounds, and the process goes on at an accelerated pace.

Foreign Influences on OE. When the Angles, Saxons, and Jutes migrated from the Continent to Britain, they found a native British population Celtic in speech. Modern representatives of this speech are Welsh, Cornish (now extinct), and Breton, the speech of Brittany, where fugitives from war-torn Britain had settled. Scots (Gaels) from Ireland invaded western Britain at about the same time that Germanic tribesmen were invading eastern and southern Britain, and they made permanent settlements in the north (Scotland). Their speech was also Celtic, though very different from that of the Britons.

There is surprisingly little influence of the Celtic languages on English itself. They left their mark chiefly in place-names. The Celtic *cumb* valley, which survives in *cwm* as a technical geological term, is seen in the place-names *Duncombe*, *Holcombe*, etc.; *torr* peak, surviving in *tor*, is seen in *Torcross*, *Torhill*, etc. The names of some cities such as *London*, *Carlisle*, *Dover*, and *York* are of Celtic origin, as are the names of many rivers: *Thames*, *Cam*, *Dee*, *Avon*, *Aire*, *Severn*, *Trent*, *Wye*, etc. A few common nouns also are Celtic: *bin*, *crag*, *curse*, *dun* (the color). Most of the other words of Celtic etymology in English are recent borrowings from modern Irish, Gaelic, Welsh, and so on.

The Latin influence on OE may be regarded as falling into three distinct periods. The first is the pre-English period which represents the influence of Latin on the languages of the Germanic tribes while they were still on the Continent. The borrowings from Latin reflect the relations of the Romans with the Germanic speakers in such areas as trade, warfare, and the domestic arts. English *wall*, *street*, *mile*, *cheap*, *monger*, *pound*, *mint*, *wine*, *kitchen*, *cup*, *dish*, *cheese*, *spelt*, *pepper*, *cherry*, *butter*, *plum*, *pea*, *chalk*, *pitch*, *pipe*, *tile*, *church*, *bishop* are all words that can be traced back to early Continental borrowings from Latin.

The second period of Latin influence came with the Roman occupation, lasting from about the middle of the 1st century A.D. to the end of the 4th century. During this period there was extensive Romanization among the then Celtic inhabitants of Britain, but Latin did not succeed in displacing the Celtic languages. Thus, the sole opportunity for direct contact between living, spoken Latin and Old English failed to materialize. The few Latin words that can be traced to this period are those passed on by the Celts. Latin *castra* (camp) is reflected in a number of place-names, evidently of towns that sprang up around the old Roman garrisons: *Winchester*, *Manchester*, *Lancaster*, *Gloucester*, *Worcester*, etc. Other Latin words that are believed to have entered the language at this time are *port*, *mount* (mountain), and the element *-wick* (from L *vicus* village), all found in place-names.

The third period of Latin influence, from about A.D. 600 on, produced greater and more lasting effects on the development of the English language. The Christianization of England at this time wrought sweeping changes throughout Anglo-Saxon culture, including the language. Many terms pertaining to religious life were taken over from Latin: *abbot*, *alms*, *altar*, *anthem*, *ark*, *candle*, *canon*, *cowl*, *deacon*, *disciple*, *epistle*, *hymn*, *litany*, *martyr*, *mass*, *nun*, *pope*, *priest*, *psalm*, *shrine*, *shrive*, *stole*, *temple*. The Church also deeply affected the domestic life of the people as can be seen from words for articles of clothing and household use that came in at this time: *cap, sock, chest, mat, sack;* and names of foods and herbs: *beet, pear, radish, mussel, aloes, balsam, fennel, mallow, myrrh.* The influence of the Church on education and learning is seen in *school, master, grammatic, verse, meter, notary.*

The Germanic invasions of the 5th century had already taken place before this period of Latin influence, and English soon displaced both Celtic and Latin as the chief language of Britain. The next important foreign influence on the English language came in the 9th century with the invasions by the Scandinavians, or Vikings, in OE times called Danes. As the Vikings were also of Germanic stock, their language was related to that of the Anglo-Saxons, and consequently the influence on OE went beyond vocabulary to affect the very structure of the language. By the latter half of the 9th century the Danes had taken control of the eastern half of England. Alfred, king of the Saxons, held them off and managed to retain the sovereignty of Wessex, but the invaders were ceded Northumbria, part of Mercia, and East Anglia, a region which came to be called *Danelaw*, that is, the country under the law of the Danes. But they did not impose their own language on the speakers of English, who were culturally more advanced. Instead, they adopted the culture, religion, and language of the Anglo-Saxons and by intermarrying were gradually absorbed.

The large number of place-names from the Scandinavian attests to its pervasive influence. For example, the element *-by* (from Scand *bȳr* town, village) is seen in such names as *Derby, Rugby,* and *Whitby* and in the word *bylaw.* Common nouns, as *law, fellow, husband, hustings, band, booth, bull, dirt, egg, gap, girth, keel, leg, root, skill, skin, skirt, sky, window,* and a large number of common verbs, as *bask, crawl, die, get, give, raise, take, thrust,* are all taken from Scandinavian. Many Scandinavian words that were closely related to English words but differed from them slightly in form were in use side by side with the corresponding English forms. In some cases the Scandinavian words prevailed, as when *egg, sister, boon, loan,* and *weak* replaced the native forms *ey, sweostor, bēn, læn, wāc.* In some instances, a Scandinavian word, synonymous with but not a cognate of the English word, supplanted the native form: *take* replaced OE *niman; cast* replaced OE *weorpan; cut* replaced OE *snīthan; anger* replaced several OE synonyms that had been in use (*torn, grama, irre*); *sky* replaced OE *wolcen* (surviving in the poetic word *welkin*); and *window* (lit., wind eye) replaced OE *ēagthȳrel* (lit., eyehole). Some competing forms remained, along with the native forms, usually with differentiated sense. In the following list the first of each pair is from Scandinavian, the second is native: *nay—no, raise—rear, fro—from, skill—craft, skin—hide, ill—sick.*

In morphology, the influence of Scandinavian is seen in certain fundamental changes in inflection and usage. The pronouns *they* (ON *þeir*), *their* (ON *þeirra*), and *them* (ON *þeim*) are Scandinavian, replacing OE *hīe, hiera, him.* The present plural *are* of the verb *to be,* reflecting a northern OE form *aron,* was doubtless aided in prevailing over its West Saxon rival *syndon* by the similar Scandinavian form. The two important words *both* and *same,* used as adjectives and pronouns, are likewise of Scandinavian origin. In addition, many turns of phrase and peculiarities of word order found in ModE can probably be traced back to Scandinavian influence.

III. MIDDLE ENGLISH (c1150-c1475)

The most important changes affecting the language during this period were the further leveling of OE inflectional endings (which were much reduced in both number and complexity), the change in vocabulary due to the introduction of words of French origin, the loss of grammatical gender, and the adoption of a more fixed word order similar to that of ModE. It should be emphasized that these changes occurred gradually and at different rates in different dialect areas of England. For example, the influx of French words did not begin precisely with the Norman Conquest (1066): there was some French influence before that time, under the reign of Edward the Confessor. On the other hand, borrowing from French did not reach its peak until long after the Conquest. Furthermore, the OE dialects, from which developed roughly corresponding ME dialects, underwent these changes at different times. Thus, even in 1150 what was basically OE was still being written in the south, while in the north, where the dialect changed more rapidly, ME was probably being spoken before 1100.

The ultimate effect of the Norman Conquest was to facilitate changes in English that had already begun. The immediate effect was the temporary displacement of English by French as the language of the ruling class—of the Court, the nobility, the Church, and the schools. This was the result of circumstances and not due to a deliberate plan. There was at first no compelling need for the new rulers of England to learn English, for they retained their ties with the Continent and continued to speak and write French. At the same time, English remained the only language of the vast majority of the people and from about 1200 began to reemerge as the national tongue. The reasons for its reinstatement are many and complex. One important reason was that after the loss of Normandy to the French in 1204, the nobility came to identify itself more closely with England. Thereafter, there was a greater feeling of national unity in England, and differences that had separated Norman and Englishman gradually disappeared. The rivalry with France that culminated in the period of the Hundred Years' War (1337–1453) as well as social changes within England, such as the rise of the middle class, contributed to the eventual decline of French. A few of the events that reflect this process were the production, about 1200, of two major literary works in English, Layamon's *Brut* and the *Ormulum,* the first royal proclamation, in 1258, in both French and English, the Statute of Pleading, in 1362, requiring that lawsuits be in English, and, for the first time, the opening of Parliament with a speech in English.

As English reemerged, it retained the three major dialects reflected in OE. Of the three, the Northern dialect, which corresponded to OE Northumbrian, had been subjected to the most extensive changes. Having already been influenced by Scandinavian, it was losing its inflectional endings even in the OE period. Southern ME, the slowest to change, corresponded to West Saxon, the language of King Alfred. Midland, a development of OE Mercian, was divided into East and West Midland. A form of East Midland, specifically the dialect of London and the language of the great 14th-century poets Gower and Chaucer, was gradually established as a standard and thus became the ancestor of ModE.

A major difference between OE and ME was the simplification and reduction of inflections, and the most important cause of this and of other significant formal changes in the language was the leveling of unstressed vowels. In late OE unstressed *a, o, u,* and *e* had been reduced to *schwa* [ə]. The results can easily be seen in the adjective declensions. In OE, a weak adjective had five distinct singular and plural forms which indicated both case and gender by means of the endings *-a, -e, -an, -ena,* and *-um.* All were leveled to *-e.* The same process affected the noun, with the result that, when the development was complete, most nouns were reduced to two forms: one with *-s* for the genitive singular and the plural, and one without *-s* for the rest of the singular. The leveling of unstressed vowels also brought about the loss of grammatical gender. For example, OE nominative and accusative plural (short-stem nouns) distinguished the three genders: *-as* (masc.), *-a* (fem.), and *-u* (neut.). In late OE, *-as* was changed to *-es* by the leveling of the vowel, and this ending was eventually generalized to serve as the plural for all nouns (except those mutated nouns having plurals like *feet, geese,* etc.).

With the loss of grammatical gender and the drastic reduction of inflections, word order took on a much more significant function in ME. In some cases, the object of a verb preceded it, and frequent use was made of certain impersonal constructions, but generally word order became fixed in patterns not unlike those of ModE.

Although a few French words had come into English before the Conquest, the borrowing of French words reached its height between 1250 and 1400. After the Conquest but before the period of heaviest borrowing, the French of Paris, or Central French, had become established as standard in France. Consequently, when English began extensive borrowing from French, there was a high incidence of "doublets"—words which entered the language in both their Norman and Central French forms. Of Norman origin are *cattle* and *warranty;* of Central French origin *chattel* and *guarantee*. The influence of French is most evident in those fields in which the Norman conquerors were dominant: (in law and government) *attorney, judge, jury, crime, court, country;* (in the Church) *preach, clergy, vestment, sacrament;* (in the nobility) *prince, duke, baron*—though it is worth noting that *king, queen, lord,* and *lady* are all OE; (in the army) *soldier, sergeant, lieutenant, captain.* In the basic word stock, however, OE words remained dominant. Of the 1,000 most frequent words in ModE, we find that about 60% are of OE, 30% of French origin. There is, finally, no better example of the extensive influence of French borrowings than in the well-known opening 18 lines of Chaucer's *Canterbury Tales,* in which we find 10 words of French origin (*perced, veyne, licour, vertu, engendred, flour, tendre, corages, palmeres,* and *straunge*). Along with this expansion of the vocabulary, French influence introduced into the language new resources for the formation of words. Some of the most common affixes, as *-ance, -ant, -ity, -ment, -tion, con-, de-, dis-, ex-, pre-*, became formative as English affixes through the influence of French models.

IV. MODERN ENGLISH (c1475 to the present)

The first important development of English in the modern period was the *Great Vowel Shift*, which radically altered the ME vowel system, so that toward the end of the 15th century a new system of vowels may be said to have emerged. The Great Vowel Shift affected principally the long vowels of ME, beginning with *ou* (in ME pronounced as in ModE *you*) and *ī* (in ME pronounced as in ModE *machine*). An on-glide developed before each of these vowels, which finally became full-fledged diphthongs, *ou* as in ModE *loud*, *ī* as in ModE *ride*. This left a pair of gaps in the vowel pattern which were then filled by raising the other long vowels in succession, so that the pronunciation of ME *ō* changed from ō to o͞o, ME *ē* changed from ā to ē, and ME *ā* went from ä to ā, etc. Although these sounds have changed, the ME spelling for the most part persists, a cause of the difficulty beginners and foreigners have in learning English spelling today.

In morphology, ModE has dropped all inflections of nouns except for marking the plural and the possessive singular. The plural in *-s* has become the only regular form, with other forms surviving as anomalous remnants: plurals in *-en* or *-n* (*oxen, children, brethren,* etc.), unchanged plurals (*sheep, swine,* etc.), plurals with internal vowel change (*mice, feet,* etc.). Inflections of adjectives have been entirely lost, so that adjectives no longer show distinctions of gender, number, or case. In the 16th century the personal pronouns became fixed in the forms that they have today: *thou, thee,* and *thy* fell into disuse except in poetry and ritual use and among the Quakers; *you* became generalized as the nominative and objective singular and plural form, displacing the earlier plural nominative *ye; its* supplanted the earlier form *his* as the possessive of *it.* In the inflection of verbs, the ModE period saw the change of many strong verbs to weak, and the almost complete loss of the subjunctive as a distinctive form. The ending *-s* or *-es* for the present 3rd person singular began to compete with *-eth* in the 15th century. In Shakespeare's period both endings were common, but by the middle of the 17th century *-eth* had fallen out of use.

Regarding syntax, the further loss of inflectional endings has caused greater dependence on fixed word order and prepositional phrases. The main sentence scheme consists of subject + verb + object. This has come to be regarded as the "natural" word order for declarative sentences though other orderings are far from uncommon. A second principle is that related words in a sentence must stand close together, since the possibility of connecting words through their distinctive endings is limited. Modern syntactical rules also forbid the use of double negatives, in Shakespeare's time regarded merely as intensive forms of expression.

One of the most outstanding features of Modern English is its large and varied vocabulary. Perhaps no other language has borrowed so many words from so many other languages and made them its own. In the modern period a large number of new affixes have been taken from French, Latin, Greek, and a few others.

Whereas in OE and ME most borrowings had been made by direct contact of English with other languages, in the 16th century there began the large-scale adoption of foreign words from the literary forms of languages, either living or extinct, as Latin, Greek, Hebrew, French, and the other Romance Languages. Interest in the classics prompted the adoption of thousands of Latin and Greek words which have been in common use since. In addition, English continues to form new words from foreign stems, sometimes using affixes that are taken from our own native stock. Many of these formations, created wholly out of stems existing in the classical languages, result in words which could be taken for Latin or Greek, but were in fact unknown to the ancient speakers of those languages. Finally, beginning with the middle of the 19th century and still going on apace is the fertile coinage of scientific, technical, scholarly, commercial, and political terms that have swelled the English vocabulary to such proportions that even the largest unabridged dictionaries can select and define only a small portion of the total number of words that actually exist.

In the course of three centuries or so, English has expanded geographically from its original home in Britain to become the most far-flung language of the globe, spoken and understood by over 300 million of the earth's inhabitants. Colonial expansion established the English language as official in most of North America, in parts of South America, and in Australia, New Zealand, and South Africa. In these major areas distinct national standards have evolved which enjoy the same prestige as British English. Furthermore, English serves as an auxiliary language or lingua franca in India, Pakistan, Burma, Ceylon, Cyprus, Malaya, Hong Kong, Israel, Singapore, and Puerto Rico, and as a language of culture and of international communication in almost all countries of the western hemisphere and large areas of Asia.

ETYMOLOGY KEY

<	descended from, derived from, from
<<	descended, derived from, through intermediate stages not shown
>	whence
=	equivalent to
?	origin unknown, perhaps
*	hypothetical
abbr.	abbreviation
abl.	ablative
acc.	accusative
adj.	adjective
adv.	adverb
alter.	alteration
aph.	aphetic
appar.	apparently
assoc.	association
aug.	augmentative
b.	blend of, blended
c.	cognate with
cf.	compare
comb. form	combining form
comp.	comparative
contr.	contraction
decl.	declension
dial.	dialect, dialectal
dat.	dative
deriv.	derivative
dim.	diminutive
eccl.	ecclesiastical
etc.	etcetera
etym.	etymology, etymological
fem.	feminine
fig.	figurative
freq.	frequentative
fut.	future
gen.	genitive
ger.	gerund, gerundive
i.e.	that is
imit.	imitative
impv.	imperative
indic.	indicative
inf.	infinitive
irreg.	irregularly
lit.	literally
m.	modification of
masc.	masculine
mod.	modern
n.	noun
nom.	nominative
north.	northern
obl.	oblique
obs.	obsolete
orig.	origin, originally
pass.	passive
perh.	perhaps
pl.	plural
prep.	preposition
pres.	present
prob.	probably
prp.	present participle
ptp.	past participle
r.	replacing
redupl.	reduplication
repr.	representing
s.	stem
sing.	singular
sp.	spelling
subj.	subjunctive
superl.	superlative
syll.	syllable
trans.	translation
transit.	transitive
ult.	ultimate, ultimately
uncert.	uncertain
v.	verb, verbal
var.	variant
voc.	vocative

LANGUAGES

AF	Anglo-French
Afr	African
AInd	Anglo-Indian
AL	Anglo-Latin
Amer	American
AmerInd	American Indian
AmerSp	American Spanish
Ar	Arabic
Aram	Aramaic
Arm	Armenian
Austral	Australian
Bulg	Bulgarian
CanF	Canadian French
Celt	Celtic
Chin	Chinese
D	Dutch
Dan	Danish
E	English
EGmc	East Germanic
Egypt	Egyptian
F	French
Finn	Finnish
Flem	Flemish
Fris	Frisian
G	German
Gael	Gaelic
Gk	Greek
Gmc	Germanic
Goth	Gothic
Heb	Hebrew
HG	High German
Hind	Hindustani
Hung	Hungarian
Icel	Icelandic
IE	Indo-European
Ind	Indian
Ir	Irish
IrGael	Irish Gaelic
It	Italian
Jap	Japanese
L	Latin
LaF	Louisiana French
LG	Low German
LGk	Late Greek
Lith	Lithuanian
LL	Late Latin
ME	Middle English
Mex	Mexican
MexSp	Mexican Spanish
MF	Middle French
MGk	Medieval Greek
MHG	Middle High German
MPers	Middle Persian
ML	Medieval Latin
ModGk	Modern Greek
ModHeb	Modern Hebrew
NL	Neo-Latin
Norw	Norwegian
OBulg	Old Bulgarian
OCS	Old Church Slavonic
ODan	Old Danish
OE	Old English
OF	Old French
OFris	Old Frisian
OHG	Old High German
OIcel	Old Icelandic
OIr	Old Irish
OIt	Old Italian
OL	Old Latin
OLG	Old Low German
ON	Old Norse
ONF	Old North French
OPers	Old Persian
OPr	Old Provençal
OPruss	Old Prussian
ORuss	Old Russian
OS	Old Saxon
OSlav	Old Slavic
OSp	Old Spanish
PaG	Pennsylvania German
Pers	Persian
Pg	Portuguese
Pol	Polish
Pr	Provençal
Pruss	Prussian
Rom	Romance
Rum	Rumanian
Russ	Russian
SAfrD	South African Dutch (Afrikaans)
Scand	Scandinavian
Scot	Scottish
ScotGael	Scots Gaelic
Sem	Semitic
Skt	Sanskrit
Slav	Slavic
Sp	Spanish
SpAr	Spanish Arabic
Sw	Swedish
SwissF	Swiss French
Turk	Turkish
VL	Vulgar Latin
WFlem	West Flemish
WGmc	West Germanic

PRONUNCIATION KEY

The symbol (ʹ), as in **moth•er** (muṯẖʹər), **blueʹ devʹils,** is used to mark primary stress; the syllable preceding it is pronounced with greater prominence than the other syllables in the word or phrase. The symbol (ʹ), as in **grand•moth•er** (grandʹmuṯẖʹər), **buzzʹ bombʹ**, is used to mark secondary stress; a syllable marked for secondary stress is pronounced with less prominence than one marked (ʹ) but with more prominence than those bearing no stress mark at all.

a act, bat, marry
ā aid, cape, way
â(r) air, dare, Mary
ä alms, art, calm

b back, cabin, cab

ch chief, butcher, beach

d do, rudder, bed

e ebb, set, merry
ē equal, seat, bee, mighty
ēr ear, mere

f fit, differ, puff

g give, trigger, beg

h hit, behave, hear
hw white, nowhere

i if, big, mirror, furniture
ī ice, bite, pirate, deny

j just, badger, fudge

k kept, token, make

l low, mellow, all

m my, simmer, him

n now, sinner, on
ng sing, Washington

o ox, box, wasp
ō over, boat, no
ô ought, ball, raw
oi oil, joint, joy
o͝o book, poor
o͞o ooze, fool, too
ou out, loud, prow

p pot, supper, stop

r read, hurry, near

s see, passing, miss
sh shoe, fashion, push

t ten, butter, bit
th thin, ether, path
ṯẖ that, either, smooth

u up, love
û(r) urge, burn, cur

v voice, river, live

w west, away

y yes, lawyer

z zeal, lazy, those
zh vision, mirage

ə occurs only in unaccented syllables and indicates the sound of
a *in* alone
e *in* system
i *in* easily
o *in* gallop
u *in* circus

ᵊ occurs in unaccented syllables before **l** preceded by **t, d,** or **n,** or before **n** preceded by **t** or **d** to show syllabic quality, as in
cra•dle (krādʹᵊl)
red•den (redʹᵊn)
met•al (metʹᵊl)
men•tal (menʹtᵊl)
and in accented syllables between **ī** and **r** to show diphthongal quality, as in **fire** (fīᵊr) **hire** (hīᵊr)

FOREIGN SOUNDS

A as in French **a•mi** (A mēʹ) [a vowel intermediate in quality between the **a** of *cat* and the **ä** of *calm,* but closer to the former]

KH as in German **ach** (äKH) or **ich** (iKH); Scottish **loch** (lôKH) [a consonant made by bringing the tongue into the position for **k** as in *key, coo,* while pronouncing a strong, rasping **h**]

N as in French **bon** (bôN) [used to indicate that the preceding vowel is nasalized. Four such vowels are found in French: **un bon vin blanc** (ŒN bôN vaN bläN)]

Œ as in French **feu** (fŒ); German **schön** (shŒn) [a vowel made with the lips rounded in the position for **o** as in *over,* while trying to say **a** as in *able*]

R as in French **rouge** (Ro͞ozh), German **rot** (Rōt), Italian **ma•re** (mäʹRe), Spanish **pe•ro** (peʹRô) [a symbol for any non-English **r,** including a trill or flap in Italian and Spanish and a sound in French and German similar to KH but pronounced with voice]

Y as in French **tu** (tY); German **ü•ber** (Yʹbər) [a vowel made with the lips rounded in position for **o͞o** as in *ooze,* while trying to say **ē** as in *east*]

ᵊ as in French **Bas•togne** (bA-stônʹyᵊ) [a faint prolongation of the preceding voiced consonant or glide]

The Pronunciation of English

ARTHUR J. BRONSTEIN

People do not speak "language" but *a* language. Each language, in turn, is usually made up of a variety of dialects. To the linguist, a dialect is not a provincial deviation from the standard language, but simply a group of characteristics peculiar to a language in a specific locality or social group. No dialect may properly be singled out as "better than" or "preferable to" another, except as it manages to communicate meaning with effectiveness, ease, and appropriateness to the situation in which it is used.

Despite an apparent conformity to group or regional usage, each individual still retains certain speech patterns—subtle variations of pronunciation, vocabulary, and syntax—that are uniquely his own. The sum of these individual characteristics is described as an *idiolect*.

In determining which speech patterns are socially acceptable, the terms *standard* and *nonstandard* have been widely adopted. *Standard* is used to describe the varieties of speech used by the educated people of any community, *nonstandard* to describe the deviations therefrom.

In England, standard pronunciation is often referred to as Received Pronunciation, or simply RP. Formerly the dialect of the upper class of London, it became the speech fostered by the most prestigious English universities and schools. It is now the speech of most of England's political, commercial, cultural, and social leaders. The reason for the wide acceptance of RP in England was one of practical necessity: the dialects of England are numerous and differ markedly from one region to the next. By adopting a variety or pattern of speech generally recognized as desirable, a twofold purpose was served of facilitating communication throughout the country and establishing a criterion of social acceptability. To a greater or lesser extent RP has been an influence on all English-speaking nations of the British Commonwealth.

In the United States there has been much less need for a single prestigious pronunciation standard. Although American English is made up of a large number of local and regional types of speech, the differences among them are relatively minor and constitute no appreciable barrier to communication. No one regional dialect has gained ascendancy here as more desirable than any other. It is accepted here that cultivated speech can and does exist in all regions, with many regional differences quite readily noticeable to the sophisticated listener.

Within any geographical area will be found a variety of socially defined dialects reflecting different levels of educational and sometimes social attainment. Urban dwellers—especially those of greatest influence—who have a college education and enjoy many cultural advantages are generally characterized as having *cultivated* speech. Contrasted with this is *folk* speech, usually characteristic of inhabitants of remote or isolated rural areas who have had little education and cultural contact. Between the two extremes and constituting the great majority of speakers in any region are those with *common* speech, who may or may not hold important positions and usually have less formal education than speakers of the *cultivated* variety of speech. Needless to say, these three varieties are not mutually exclusive compartments.*

Every person uses different styles or varieties of speech. The most commonly identified are the *formal* and *informal* styles. In the case of speakers of *cultivated* English, *cultivated formal* is the language style reserved for the more formal occasions, for public speeches, scholarly reports, and the like. Its tone most nearly approaches writing in its careful structure of sentences, its avoidance of contractions, etc. *Cultivated informal* is the language style of the same speakers in most other situations. It may range from the near-formal constructions to the more casual if not intimate expressions and forms that may even include slang and folk forms. It is this language style that most nearly reflects everyday living. There is a good deal of overlapping, of course, between what we consider *cultivated* standard speech and *common* or even *folk* speech.

Available evidence identifies a number of major regional speech areas. In the eastern part of the United States and Canada, where the greatest amount of investigation has been undertaken, three large regional areas have been separately identified, each quite distinctive from the other. These are known as the *Northern, Middle Atlantic* or *Midland*, and *Southern* areas. In turn, these larger areas possess reasonably distinct subareas, thus separating eastern New England from western New England; New York City from the Hudson Valley, upstate New York, Vermont, and eastern Canada; the more northern Midland regions (eastern Pennsylvania, New Jersey, and the Delaware Valley south to the Delmarva peninsula) from the southern Midland regions (the upper Potomac and Ohio Valleys, western North and South Carolina, West Virginia and eastern Tennessee and eastern Kentucky); and the Piedmont section of Virginia from North Carolina, the low country of South Carolina and Georgia, the Florida peninsula, and the Gulf States of Alabama, Mississippi, Louisiana, and Texas. As the listener travels west, the lines separating speech areas from each other are less distinct, yet sufficient evidence is available to identify such larger regional areas as the *Central Midland* area (perhaps the largest regional speech area, since it seems to extend from Ohio and the *Southern Mountain* regions west to the *Rocky Mountain* areas of Colorado, Utah, and Wyoming and south to the northwest tip of Texas and to New Mexico, with many regional subareas); the *North Central* area (spreading from east of the Great Lakes to the Dakotas); the *Pacific* and *Southwestern* areas (California, Nevada, Arizona); and the *Northwest* (Washington, Oregon, Idaho, and Montana). Detailed studies have not been completed in most of these areas, but there seems to be little doubt that many subareas exist within each of the larger speech areas mentioned.

Geographical divisions are most clearly defined along the Atlantic coast, the earliest area of settlement; but to the west, the boundaries between speech areas are harder to determine because the westward migrations of the 19th century often crossed and intermingled, and the areas never knew the relative isolation of the 17th and 18th centuries in the Atlantic colonies.

The speech patterns of present-day American English have their origin in the language of the colonies along the eastern seaboard during the 17th century. Since there was relatively little communication between the colonies for nearly a century, the diverse speech patterns of the colonial settlers had a chance to develop their own distinctive forms prior to the time of increased contacts between the seaboard settlements and the beginnings of the inland expansion to the West.

The regional dialects of the interior correspond closely to the waves of settlers during the 18th century. Large migrations moved westward from western New England into the Great Lakes basin, and from Pennsylvania southward into the Carolinas and Georgia, and later into Kentucky, Tennessee, and the southern parts of Ohio, Indiana, and Illinois. Other Pennsylvanians and New Jerseyites settled in the Ohio Valley and West Virginia. Another large migration from the southern colonies settled in the Gulf States and eastern Texas. The westward settlement into the interior of the country stemmed mostly from the former inhabitants of the south Midland areas and the more northern inland sections (western New England,

*The labels *cultivated, folk,* and *common* were first applied by Professor Hans Kurath, Director of the Linguistic Atlas of the United States.

upper New York State, etc.), with very few settlers from the South Atlantic, the northern Midland, or eastern New England joining the large westward migrations of the 18th century. Later, these streams of migrations continued, crossing a number of times, as people moved into the Great Plains, the Rocky Mountain States, and the west coast areas.

By the 19th century, many sections of the country had developed distinctive speech patterns, but, since the differences were more of flavor than of substance, communication between speakers of different dialects never became a problem and the need for a single, accepted standard pronunciation never developed here as it did in England.

Systems for pronunciation transcription vary in detail according to the purposes for which they are used. Such pronunciation systems must contain symbols for the representation of each of the distinctive sounds in a language. The most widely known and used phonetic system is the International Phonetic Alphabet (IPA), a system used for the transcription of many of the languages of the world. This system contains symbols not only for the transcription of significant or distinctive sounds of languages, but also for the indication or transcription of many phonetic variations of these sounds. The detail available in this system makes it suitable for the representation of both the significant and nonsignificant spoken features of many languages.

A different type of pronunciation representation uses symbols only for what is known as phonemic or broad transcription. In this system, each symbol represents a sound that is significantly different from all other sounds in a given language. In English we recognize the initial sounds of *bat* and *pat* as completely different because they serve to change the meaning of a word and to distinguish one word from another. If, however, we compare the *p*-sound in *peak* with the *p*-sound in *speak*, we may notice that they are not phonetically identical: the first *p* is pronounced with aspiration, the second without. Thus, while the English speaker recognizes *b* and *p* as separate sounds that can distinguish similar words from each other, the presence and absence of aspiration in the *p*'s of *peak* and *speak* constitute only phonetic variations, or allophones, of the same sound in English. The speaker of the language does not recognize them as significantly different. They are, to him, simply (p).

A broad transcription presents the sounds of a language as a pattern of phonemic oppositions characteristic of that language, each language having its own pattern of phonemes, each with its allophonic variants. A narrow transcription provides a stock of symbols attempting to cover other identifiable sound features of the language, thus allowing for greater phonetic accuracy when needed. In order to present a simple yet comprehensive pronunciation key, this dictionary utilizes a type of broad transcription modified when necessary by additional phonetic detail.

In this dictionary, the basic principle has been that each distinctive sound in our language should be represented by only one symbol. The initial sound of *fine* and the final sound of *enough* are both transcribed as (f). In addition to these easily distinguishable phonemic units, there are certain nonphonemic features which the reader can hear and distinguish. These nondistinctive but phonically important features are shown in order to provide the speaker with a smooth and realistic guide to pronunciation. Thus, for example, the symbol (ᵊ) is used before syllabic consonants in words like *button* (but′ᵊn) and *channel* (chan′ᵊl) to indicate that the vocalic quality is transferred to the final consonant. The same symbol is used to indicate the gliding, diphthongal quality of the vowel sounds of *fire* (fīᵊr) and *tire* (tīᵊr).

In using an essentially broad transcription, the symbols chosen must be those most likely to lead the user to a phonetically accurate pronunciation. Thus, this dictionary uses the symbol (ē) rather than the traditional (i) in the less stressed syllables of *city* (sit′ē) and *funny* (fun′ē). Many phoneticians in the United States agree that the vowel of this less stressed syllable varies from (ē) to (i), with perhaps greater use of (ē) by most speakers. The use of (ē) gives the reader a close phonetic approximation of the sound and allows him to make his own adjustment in pronunciation more accurately than he can with the (i) as a guide.

Among educated speakers of American English—and indeed in the English-speaking world—there are few differences in the system of phonemes. Among them are the following:

In eastern New England and western Pennsylvania there is general homophony of the vowel sounds in such words as *tot* and *taught*, *collar* and *caller*, resulting in (o)—IPA [ɒ]—for most speakers in those areas. In other areas a distinction is made between *cot* (kät) or (kot) and *caught* (kôt), etc.

In words like *sister*, *dinner*, and *milk*, many speakers use a high, central vowel, IPA [ɨ], where others retain (i). For many speakers, [ɨ] and (i) are in free variation; for others, the use of [ɨ] is of such consistency that some linguists believe it should be accorded phonemic status. Whether it is considered a separate phoneme or an allophone of (i), there can be no question about its use by many educated speakers.

The loss of final (r) is common in the eastern United States at every level of speech. Bostonians, New Yorkers, and Southern coastal speakers either replace the dropped (r) with a (ə), as in *pair*, *for* (pā′ə, fô′ə), or drop it completely, as in *car* (kä), with simultaneous vowel lengthening. A phenomenon that often occurs along with "r-dropping" is the addition of a "linking-r." Certain speakers who drop postvocalic (r) in such expressions as *He's not here* (. . . hē′ə), reinsert the (r) when it becomes intervocalic. This change occurs, for example, in *He's not here anymore* (. . . hē′ər en′ē . . .). Linking-r is not commonly used by r-dropping speakers of the South.

An added, unhistorical (r) may appear in the speech of many people. This (r), which usually intrudes intervocalically, is common to those people, especially Bostonians, New Yorkers, and others in the Northeast, who lose final (r) sounds. Thus we may hear *Whose idea is that?* (. . . ī-dē′ər iz . . .), *I saw a star* (. . . sôr′ə . . .). The phenomenon is uncommon among Southern coastal speakers who also lose final (r), and is, of course, uncommon to speakers in the rest of the country, who typically do not lose final (r). Attitudes toward the use of this (r) range from disdain through indifference to acceptance. It is not uncommon in casual, educated speech, and will probably remain in those regions in which it is heard.

Since each speaker is usually consistent in his use of (o) or (ô), in his dropping of (r), etc., the pronunciation key of a dictionary will automatically guide him to his own, consistent pronunciation of each sound. Similarly, differences in the actual sounds of the phonemes do not need to be shown in pronunciation keys, although they do exist; the *a* as in *date* is not pronounced identically in Boston, Charleston, Chicago, and Pittsburgh.

In some instances, however, it seems important to indicate those major dialect differences which cannot be accommodated automatically in a pronunciation key. These variations are either regional, as in the pronunciation of *dance* (dans, däns), or a result of language change, as in *tune* (to͞on, tyo͞on), and are in common use among educated speakers.

Many speakers pronounce such pairs as *weather-whether* and *wear-where* quite differently as (weth′ər, hweth′ər) and (wâr, hwâr). Other speakers pronounce the pairs as homonyms with an initial (w). The loss of initial (h) and a merger of (hw) and (w) is found in at least three regions of the United States: the coastal Middle Atlantic, coastal New England, and the coast of South Carolina and Georgia. Among speakers from these areas an initial (hw) does not occur. Among others, a phonemic contrast (hw)-(w) is present, as in *wear* (wâr) and *where* (hwâr). Both types of speech may be heard throughout the country at all social levels, although the use of (w) for these *wh-* words is growing, especially in urban areas.

The use of initial (hy) and (y) may be described in much the same way as that of (hw) and (w). In words like *huge* and *humor*, we may hear two possible forms: (hyo͞oj, yo͞oj) and (hyo͞o′mər, yo͞o′mər). Although speakers throughout the country use initial (hy) in *human, hue,* and *huge,* and distinguish between *hue* (hyōō) and *you* (yōō), the number of speakers who omit (h) in *hue* is sufficiently large to warrant showing both varieties in a dictionary. The use of (hy), like that of (hw), is regional only to a certain extent: the merger of (hy) and (y) is increasing at all levels, although it is not as commonly heard among educated speakers as the merger of (hw) and (w).

Another example of common phonetic variation is heard in the pronunciations of *tune* (tōōn, tyōōn), *dune* (dōōn, dyōōn), and *news* (nōōz, nyōōz). The (y) after (t, d, *and* n) survives to some extent in New England and in the New York City area and is the common pronunciation in the South. In all other areas (y) drops out after these consonants, although individual speakers may retain it to a greater or lesser degree. The pronunciations (tōōn), (dōōn), and (nōōz), with (ōō) or a somewhat centralized (ōō)—IPA [ü]—are normal for most Americans.

In words like *hurry, worry,* and *courage,* central and western speakers and some speakers in the southern Midlands have the pronunciations (hûr′ē), (wûr′ē), and (kûr′ij). They use the same vowel in *fur* (fûr). In the East and South, most speakers distinguish between the vowels of *fur* (fûr) and *hurry, worry,* and *courage* (hur′ē), (wur′ē), and (kur′ij). To accommodate both widely heard pronunciations, *The Random House College Dictionary* shows both the (hûr′ē) and the (hur′ē) varieties.

The distribution of the vowels (ō), (ô), and (o) is an important part of American dialect division. The distinction between *horse* (hôrs) and *hoarse* (hōrs) has been lost by most speakers in the north central and southwestern areas of the country, in western New England and upstate New York, and in metropolitan New York. The resulting vowel is (ô) in both words and in such pairs as *for-four* and *morning-mourning.* The rest of the country generally maintains the distinction in these words. The pronunciation of *territory* (ter′i tōr′ē, -tôr′ē) also reflects this regional division. Before intersyllabic (r), as in *orange* and *tomorrow,* variants ranging from (ä) to (ô) appear in all areas of the country; (o) and (ä) occur regularly in the Northeast and in the eastern coastal areas, with (o) predominating in eastern New England. The most common form in the South is (ä). In the rest of the country (ô) is heard regularly, although (o) is also frequent. In words like *hog, mock,* and *prong,* (ä) predominates in western New England and in upstate and metropolitan New York, (o) in eastern New England and western Pennsylvania, and (ô) in the rest of the country. Lastly, the word *dog* and words like *song, long,* and *strong* are said with either (ô) or (o) in all areas of the country.

The words *glass, dance,* and *aunt* are pronounced with the vowel (ä) by many in eastern New England, in eastern Virginia, and along the Georgia and South Carolina coast. In the rest of the country the vowel is (a), or in the South, the diphthongal variant (aᵊ). Although certain individuals imitate the "broad a" (ä) for its supposed prestige value, the pronunciation with (a) is actually becoming more frequent in the areas where (ä) has predominated.

The obscuring of vowels as they lose stress is an extremely common phenomenon in English and results in the presence of weak vowels, most often the schwa (ə). Vowel obscuration occurs both within the word, as in *above* (ə buv′), *circus* (sûr′kəs), and within the phrase. Thus many function words have two levels of pronunciation, a stressed and an unstressed one. The forms *her* (hûr) and *them* (t͟hem) become (hər *or* ər), (t͟həm *or* əm) when unstressed, as *her* in *Did′ you see′ her?* Other words affected by weak stress are prepositions, such as *from* (frum, from; *unstressed* frəm) and *at* (at; *unstressed* ət, it); conjunctions, such as *and* (and; *unstressed* ənd, ən) and *but* (but; *unstressed* bət); and auxiliaries, such as *have* (hav; *unstressed* həv, əv), *has* (haz; *unstressed* həz, əz), and *was* (wuz, woz; *unstressed* wəz). The use of unstressed vowels is normal and expected in English, and both stressed and unstressed forms are recorded in the dictionary.

A final important feature of this dictionary is the large body of foreign words and phrases that form an active part of the English lexicon. Each borrowed term occupies a place on a continuum stretching from the point where it is still considered foreign to the point where it has been completely assimilated into English. The foreign word is recognized as such by speakers of English but is used frequently enough to warrant inclusion in an English dictionary. For these words and phrases, such as the phrases of greeting in French, Spanish, German, etc., only a foreign pronunciation is given. At the other extreme is the loan word. Although etymologically from another language, it is almost always thought of as English, and given an English pronunciation by speakers. Words such as *ski* and *sauerkraut* are typical loan words.

Between these two extremes fall words which have been assimilated into English to different extents. Their degree of "Englishness" is determined by how most speakers pronounce them. The more foreign a word is, the more we tend to mark its difference by putting it in italics or, in a less formal situation, quotation marks, and by giving it a foreign or at least a hybrid pronunciation. When a word is thought of as English, we write it normally, sometimes with an Anglicized spelling, omitting accents, and give it an Anglicized pronunciation.

The dictionary entry reflects the current general status of the foreign word in English. If a word is considered foreign, only a foreign pronunciation is shown. If it is completely English, it receives only an English pronunciation. If it is at an in-between point on the continuum, the more common pronunciation—English or foreign—is shown first.

The pronunciation key on the inside of the front of the dictionary (repeated on page xvi) is the central point of departure for those who wish to make maximum use of the pronunciations given in the entries. Each symbol described is followed by common sample words. The user of the dictionary who is unfamiliar with the sound represented by a certain symbol should find the symbol in the key and pronounce the sample words aloud in order to hear the sound itself. That sound will be the one appropriate in the speaker's own dialect for the word he is looking up.

Usage, Dialects, and Functional Varieties

RAVEN I. MCDAVID, JR.

SINCE LANGUAGE is the most habitual form of human behavior, the details of usage often become class markers. Social anthropologists have noted that the more ostensibly "open" a society happens to be, the more tolerant it is of the rise of its members to higher class status and the more subtle are the values used for setting one group above another. In the United States, where it is accepted that the grandsons of immigrants and laborers may fill the highest offices in the land, concern with acquiring certain forms of usage as indications of social status is likely to replace the slow acculturation to upper-class mores that has characterized older and more traditionally oriented societies.

Although actually there are subtle distinctions in usage which will determine the appropriateness of a given form on a particular occasion, and which can be appreciated only by long observation and intuitive experience, the prevailing public attitude is that certain forms of usage are "correct" and others are "incorrect." Teachers, especially of English, are supposed to know the difference between "right" and "wrong" in language. And entrepreneurs who make fortunes out of public anxieties stand ready to provide what the schools haven't given, by warning against "common mistakes" in the language of even the best educated. Furthermore, "right" usage is supposed to be stable, as opposed to "wrong" usage which is changing, while in fact some widely spread forms, favored by authoritarians, are clearly innovations and are still regarded by many cultivated speakers as pretentious affectations of the half-educated.

The cold fact about usage in natural languages is that it is diverse and is subject to change. Essentially, in the usage of native speakers, whatever is, is right; but some usages may be more appropriate than others, at least socially. It is not merely the number of speakers and writers that determines the appropriateness, but their age, education, sophistication, and social position. Within any living language there will be varieties of usage associated with geographical origin (*regional dialects* or simply *dialects*), social status (*social dialects* or *social levels*), and relationships (*styles* or *functional varieties*), as well as such special varieties as *slang*, *argot*, and *technical language*. All of these arise out of the normal interactions of human beings in a complex society.

Regional dialects originate in a variety of ways. Most commonly they come about from settlement, whether old, as of the Germanic tribes between the Rhine and the Elbe, or recent, as of Southern Englishmen in eastern Virginia and Ulster Scots (more commonly called Scotch-Irish) west of the Blue Ridge. Dialects spread along routes of migration and communication. For example, words and pronunciations characteristic of western New England mark the progress of Yankees across New York State and the Great Lakes Basin. In this Northern dialect area we find such grammatical forms as *dove* for the past tense of *dive*, "sick *to* the stomach" for "nauseated," and *darning needle* as the popular name of the dragonfly. Settlements by speakers of other languages may leave their mark. In the Hudson Valley, which was settled by the Dutch, *stoop*, derived from *stoep*, is commonly used for "porch." In Pennsylvania and settlements elsewhere by Pennsylvania Germans, *smearcase*, modified from *Schmierkäse*, denotes "cottage cheese" or any soft cheese suitable for spreading. The Scandinavian loan translation, to *cook coffee*, is used in place of to *make*, *brew*, or *fix* it in the Upper Midwest. The Spanish *frijoles*, plural of *frijol*, is used to denote the kidney beans widely used in Texas and other parts of the Southwest.

A dialect area with an important cultural center, whose characteristic speech forms tend to spread, is a *focal area*. Older focal areas in the United States are southeastern New England (Boston), the Delaware Valley (Philadelphia), the Upper Ohio Valley (Pittsburgh), the Virginia Piedmont (Richmond and its neighboring cities), and the South Carolina Low Country (Charleston). Among newer focal areas that have been identified are the Carolina-Georgia Piedmont (Atlanta-Charlotte), Metropolitan Chicago, New Orleans, Salt Lake City, and the San Francisco Bay area. Others are in process of developing, even as older areas like Richmond and Charleston have lost their preeminence.

An area lacking an important center, whose characteristic speech forms are preserved mainly by the older and less educated, is a *relic area*. Among the more noticeable relic areas are northeastern New England (Maine and New Hampshire), Delmarva (the eastern shore of Chesapeake Bay), the North Carolina Coast, and the Southern Appalachians. Similar regional dialects are found in other parts of the English-speaking world. They are much more sharply defined in the British Isles, much less sharply in Australia. In Canada, as in the United States, regional and local differences are sharpest in the older coastal settlements (New Brunswick, Nova Scotia, Prince Edward Island, and especially in Newfoundland), least sharp in the prairie and Rocky Mountain areas where there was almost no permanent settlement before the building of the transcontinental railroads. But no geographic region is without its local subtypes, and in the United States there is nothing that qualifies as a mythically uniform General American Speech.

Cutting across regional distinctions are social ones. In every linguistic community there are certain people whose speech and writing is admired as a model of *cultivated usage*, because of their wealth, education, family connections, or social position. In sharp contrast is the usage of those with little formal education, experience acquired from travel, or other marks of sophistication, and this we would call *folk usage*. In between is *common usage*. How distant from each other the three types are depends, essentially, on the social structure of a particular community.

What is standard usage may sometimes be determined by an official body charged with setting the standard. In England in the 17th and 18th centuries there was a movement toward setting up an academy for the English language, a manifestation of the appeal of the idea of linguistic legislation to the neoclassical era. The movement drew its strength in part from the classical model of Plato's Academy, but more from the example of the extant academies on the Continent, the Italian Academia della Crusca (1592) and especially the Académie Française (1635), founded by Richelieu. Other academies developed in Europe, notably in Spain and Russia, but no English academy ever arose. Although Dryden, Defoe, Pope, Swift, and Addison and Steele, among others, viewed with alarm the "decay" of the English language and agreed that only an academy could set things right, they could not agree on who was to head it, and the Royal Society, the one learned body that might have assumed the role, confined its interest to the physical sciences. Samuel Johnson originally proposed to set himself up as the arbiter of the English language through his dictionary, but the result of his labors was to convince him that such a role was impracticable.

Nevertheless, the learned of Johnson's day vested in his dictionary the authority of the academy that Johnson had eschewed, and established the Anglo-American tradition of dictionary worship, which assumes that a dictionary must and does include within its covers more accurate information on any word than any layman could possibly have. The yearning for an academy is not a thing of the past; laymen are far less likely to criticize a dictionary or a grammar for unwarranted assumptions of authority than for abdicating its responsibility to make decisions the public are bound to obey.

Academies usually select one local variety of educated speech to impose as an official standard: Roman-Florentine in Italy, Parisian in France, Castilian in Spain, and Moscovian in Russia. Their legislative power induces a conservatism that prevents their decisions from accurately representing cultivated usage. If the Académie Française overlooks or rejects a word or meaning at its weekly meeting, no reconsideration is possible for several decades, until the rest of the dictionary has been revised and the same part of the alphabet comes up again. As a result, there is a growing split between academic usage, subservient to the Academy, and popular educated usage, defiant of it.

Inasmuch as the academy-sponsored prestige dialects of Italy, France, Spain, and Russia had achieved their positions before the academies were set up, essentially the academies merely recognized accomplished facts. In Great Britain the grammar and pronunciation used by educated men from the south of England, called Received Standard, have informally achieved highest status without an academy. Fostered by the "public schools," Winchester, Eton, and the like, and by the two great universities, Oxford and Cambridge, Received Standard has long been a badge of office for those who handle the affairs of church and state. Used normally by upper-class families, Received Standard as taught in the public schools to children of the newly rich has been one of the ways for the established order to accommodate the new wealth. A merchant or manufacturer who has risen in society cannot acquire the accent or forms of usage of his new class, but his children can—and the status that goes with it. Yet even in its heyday Received Standard was never uniform or unchanging. Observers have commented on many changes over the past two generations. Today, with the expansion of education under the welfare state, it is no longer possible to bestow Received Standard on every recruit to the intellectual elite, and it has consequently lost much of its glamour.

Until the 1920's, Received Standard was the usual model for teaching English to native speakers of other languages. It is the basis for the local varieties of English that have arisen in the new nations developing out of the Commonwealth in Asia and Africa. The educational systems of these countries have been modeled on British practice, and some of their institutions of higher education are still affiliated with British universities. In Europe there is still a notion in some quarters that Received Standard is "better" or "more elegant" than any variety of American English. However, as overseas students come to the United States in increasing numbers, and as American commercial and educational operations develop overseas, the prestige of Received Standard is no longer unquestioned.

The American criteria for separating standard from nonstandard usage are of yet another sort. On the one hand, a predominantly middle-class society, believing in the importance of formal education, is likely to accept authoritarian judgments; on the other, Americans have inherited traditions of democratic individualism, and are likely to resent the proscription of habitual pronunciations, words, and even grammatical forms. But contributing most to the American multivalued standard is the history of strong local cultural traditions. Before the American Revolution and for some time thereafter, communication between the colonies, or the new states, was difficult. In Boston, New York, Philadelphia, Richmond, and Charleston, indigenous cultivated English developed in different ways. In the new cities to the west similar developments took place. In some rural areas and in a few cities, notably New York, the rapid assimilation of large numbers of immigrants with languages other than English has almost swamped traditional local educated usage and pronunciation.

Throughout the English-speaking world and particularly in America, the grammar of the educated is much more uniform than their pronunciation. In fact, grammar is the surest linguistic index of a speaker's education and general culture. There are almost no structural differences from region to region. The familiar use of such verb phrases as *might could* and *used to could* by educated Southerners stands almost alone. Even in matters of incidence there are few regional differences in the grammar of educated people. One of these is the Northern use of *dove* (dov) for the past tense of *dived.*

As we might expect, grammatical variations are greater in folk and common usage than among the cultivated. Alongside the standard past tense *saw* we find *see, seed,* and *seen.* The last is common everywhere but in New England, the two others are restricted regionally. Beside the standard *climbed,* we have *clam, clim, clom, clome, cloom,* and *clum,* with fairly clear regional patterns, though the last is the most common.

In vocabulary, the sharpest regional distinctions concern matters of humble and rustic life before the mechanization of agriculture. Many such words are only faintly remembered as supermarkets and mass advertising substitute national terms for local ones. But at the same time, new local and regional terms are developing. A dry-cleaning establishment is a *cleanser* in Boston; a rubber band is a *rubber binder* in Minnesota. The grass strip between sidewalk and street is a *boulevard* in Minneapolis, a *devil strip* in Akron, a *tree lawn* in Cleveland, and a *tree belt* in Springfield, Massachusetts; a sandwich of many ingredients, in a small loaf of bread, is a *poor boy* in New Orleans, a *submarine* in Boston, a *hoagy* in Philadelphia, a *hero* in New York City, and a *grinder* in upstate New York.

Regional and social differences are not to be confused with style. Both educated and uneducated usage, wherever encountered, have formal and informal modes though the educated speaker has more gradations at his command. Informal usage is neither better nor worse than the formal usage of the same speaker. What really matters is that each usage should be appropriate for the situation. An educated speaker will transfer from informal *haven't* to formal *have not.* The uneducated speaker who informally uses *I seen* or *I done gone* may adjust to the formal mode with *I have saw* and *I have went.*

Slang is usually but not inevitably associated with the informal style. Characterized by novelty and impermanence, it is used to indicate that one is up to date, but it often merely indicates that one is dated. Within a few years *hot* as a general adjective of approbation gave way to *cool,* and *cool* in turn to *boss.* Recently, however, old slang terms have been temporarily revivified by the rerunning of old movies on television.

Slang was once a synonym for argot, the ingroup language used by those who participate in a particular activity, especially a criminal one. In fact, much slang still derives from small, specialized groups, some of it nursed along tenderly by press agents. Popular musicians have originated many slang expressions now in general use. The word *jazz* itself is a good example: a Southern term meaning to copulate, it was used by the musicians who entertained in New Orleans brothels to describe their kinds of musical improvisations and soon came into general use despite the horror of Southerners who had previously known the word as a taboo verb. Today much slang originates with narcotic addicts, spreads to popular musicians, and then gains vogue among the young, while falling into disuse among its inventors. Other argot, however, is restricted to the practitioners of a particular field: *boff,* meaning variously "a humorous line," "a belly laugh," or "a box-office hit," seems restricted in its use to theatrical circles; *snow,* as it means "cocaine or heroin," is a common term only among drug addicts.

The fate of slang and argot terms is unpredictable. Most of them disappear rapidly, some win their way into standard use, and still others remain what they were to begin with. *Mob,* deplored by Swift and other purists of 1700, would never be questioned today, but *moll,* meaning "a prostitute" or "the mistress of a gangster," has been in use since the early 1600's, and is still slang.

Technical terms arise because it is necessary for those who share a scientific or technical interest to have a basis for discussion. The difference between scientific and popular usage may be seen most strikingly in the biological sciences. A Latin term like *Panthera leo* (lion) has a specific reference, while *cougar* may refer to any large wild American feline predator, or *partridge* may designate the bobwhite quail, a kind of grouse, or some other game bird, according to local usage. Common words may be used with specific reference in a given field: *fusion* denotes one thing in politics, another in nuclear physics. As a field of inquiry becomes a matter of general interest, its technical terms will be picked up and used with less precision. Because of popular interest in Freudian psychology, such terms as *complex, fixation,* and *transference* are bandied about in senses Freud would never have sanctioned.

Despite some yearnings for authorities who would prescribe how people should use their language, the tendency in the English-speaking world is toward teaching based on objective description of the language. This does not mean an abandonment of standards. Indeed, in some situations this approach may call for rigorous drill so as to make habitual the features which everywhere set off standard usage from other varieties. It may also lead to systematic and rigorous drill to impart a fuller command of the rhetorical possibilities of standard English. At the same time, it should provide a more flexible attitude, an acceptance of varieties of cultivated speech other than one's own, and an understanding of the ways in which varieties of a language arose.

A Guide to the Dictionary

I. ENTRY WORD OR WORDS

A. Typeface

1. The main entry word appears in large boldface type, usually roman, flush left to the margin of the column.

bak·er (bā′kər), *n.* **1.** a person who bakes, esp. one who makes and sells bread, cake, etc. **2.** a small portable oven. [ME *baker(e)*, OE *bæcere*]

2. Foreign words and phrases and other entries that are usually italicized in printing and underlined in typewriting are shown in large boldface italic type.

bas·so-ri·lie·vo (bäs′sô rē lye′vô), *n., pl.* **bas·si-ri·lie·vi** (bäs′sē rē lye′vē). *Italian.* bas-relief.

hô·tel de ville (ō tel′ də vēl′), *pl.* **hô·tels de ville** (ō tel′ də vēl′). *French.* a city hall. [lit., mansion of the city]

When one, but not all, of the definitions of an entry requires the entry to be italicized, an (*italics*) label is placed immediately after the definition number.

Il·i·ad (il′ē əd), *n.* **1.** (*italics*) a Greek epic poem describing the siege of Troy, ascribed to Homer. **2.** (*sometimes l.c.*) any similar poem; long narrative. **3.** (*often l.c.*) a long

B. Syllabification

[For syllabification of pronunciation, see below II, C and G.]

Words are syllabified in this dictionary according to the usual American principles of word division, as observed, with certain modifications, in printing and typing.

1. Single-word entries of more than one syllable are shown with syllables set off by a boldface centered dot.

ac·claim (ə klām′), *v.t.* **1.** to salute with shouts or

ac·com·plish (ə kom′plish), *v.t.* **1.** to bring to a success-

2. Since syllable divisions for the spelled entry word and syllable divisions in the pronunciation parentheses are determined by entirely different sets of rules, they will not necessarily correspond in number or placement.
   a. Most words contain the same number of syllables in the spelled form as in the pronunciation. Certain words, in which a single consonant represents an entire spoken syllable, are conventionally shown with one syllable less in the boldface spelling than in the pronunciation.

A·mer·i·can·ism (ə mer′i kə niz′əm), *n.* **1.** devotion

rhythm (rith′əm), *n.* **1.** movement or procedure with

   b. The American system of syllabifying is primarily a phonetic one. The division usually occurs after the vowel for a long syllable or for an unstressed syllable and after the consonant for a short syllable. Certain affixes, however, as *-cious*, *-gion*, and *-tion*, are never divided.

pre·var·i·cate (pri var′ə kāt′), *v.i.*, **-cat·ed, -cat·ing.**

but

na·tion·al (nash′ə nəl), *adj.* **1.** of, pertaining to, or

3. With the exception of some loan words, entries are syllabified according to the first pronunciation given, since only one division may be shown in the boldface spelling.

sta·tus (stā′təs, stat′əs), *n.* **1.** the position of an individual in relation to another or others. **2.** a state or

re·cord (*v.* ri kôrd′; *n., adj.* rek′ərd), *v.t.* **1.** to set down

When pronounced according to the second pronunciation shown, the word *status* would logically be syllabified as **stat·us.** Similarly, when used as a noun or adjective, the word *record* would appropriately be syllabified as **rec·ord.**

4. In all hyphenated entries the hyphen replaces a centered dot as a syllable divider. Syllables that are not separated by a hyphen are separated by a centered dot.

in-law (in′lô′), *n.* a relative by marriage. [back

moth·er-in-law (muth′ər in lô′), *n., pl.* **moth·ers-in-law.** the mother of one's husband or wife. [late ME

5. With the exception of foreign words, certain loan words, some homograph entries (see below, I, D), and certain chemical compounds (see below II), words are completely syllabified only once, usually the first time they appear.

Bar·ba·ry (bär′bə rē), *n.* a region in N Africa, extending

Bar′bary States′, Morocco, Algiers, Tunis, and

but

non com·pos men·tis (nōn kōm′pōs men′tis; *Eng.* non kom′pəs men′tis), *Latin.* not of sound mind;

non ob·stan·te (nōn ōb stän′te; *Eng.* non ob stan′tē), *Latin.* notwithstanding. [late ME < AL: short for

non pos·su·mus (nōn pō′sŏŏ mŏŏs′; *Eng.* non pos′ə-məs), *Latin.* we cannot.

C. Stress

[For stress in the pronunciation, see below II, D and H.]

Entries consisting of two or more words are shown with a pattern of stress in the boldface that reveals the prosodic relationship of each word to the others in the entry. This pattern is not meant to show the relationship of one syllable to another within an individual word.

elemen′tary school′, the lowest school giving

A primary stress mark (′) follows the syllable or syllables that normally have greater stress than those marked with a secondary stress (′). The absence of a stress mark indicates that the syllable or word receives less stress than those marked (′) or (′).

1. In two-word entries, for example, the pattern —′ —′ is used to show relationships of approximately equal stress.

good′ will′, **1.** friendly disposition; benevolence; kind-

Babylo′nian captiv′ity, **1.** the period of the exile

2. Some people may hear, in their own speech, slightly less stress on the first words of the preceding phrases. This dictionary, however, has reserved the pattern —′ —′ for entries where the first words have considerably less stress than the second, but more than would an article, preposition, auxiliary verb, etc.

New′ Lon′don, **1.** a seaport in SE Connecticut, on

Mount′ Leb′anon, a town in SW Pennsylvania, SW of Pittsburgh. 35,361 (1960).

Ad′miral of the Fleet′, an officer of the highest rank

3. The pattern ——′ ——′, rather than ——′ ——′ is shown for **walk′ing pa′pers** and **char′ley horse′**. This is to distinguish them from **walk′ing pa′pers** and **char′ley horse′**, which might be construed to mean "papers that are walking" and "a man whose first name is Charley and whose last name is Horse."
4. The stress pattern shown in the boldface indicates how the entry phrase is usually stressed in a simple, declarative sentence like "Here is the **wa′ter glass′**," not a contrastive sentence like "I said **wa′ter glass′**, not **wa′ter gas′**."
5. The stress for a word in a phrase is shown as part of the prosodic pattern of that phrase, and may be different from the stress the word would have in isolation.

Mon·te·rey (mon′tə rā′), *n.* **1.** a city in W California,

but

Mon′terey Bay′, an inlet of the Pacific in W Califor-

con·ti·nen·tal (kon′tənen′təl), *adj.* **1.** of or of the

but

con′tinen′tal divide′, **1.** a divide separating river

6. Entries with stress patterns that vary from region to region or person to person are given the stress considered to be in most frequent use. Other stress patterns, although not shown, may also be widely used.

cot′tage cheese′, a loose, white, mild-flavored cheese

cream′ so′da, a soft drink made with vanilla-flavored

hot′ rod′, *U.S. Slang.* a car, esp. an old one whose

7. Entries with stress patterns that vary with individual definitions, as *party line*, show their various stress patterns in the pronunciation parentheses.

par·ty line (pär′tē līn′ *for 1, 2;* pär′tē līn′ *for 3, 4*), **1.** a telephone line connecting the telephones of a number of subscribers. **2.** the boundary line separating adjoining properties. **3.** the authoritatively announced policies and practices of a political party or group, esp. of the Communist party. **4.** the guiding policy, tenets, or practices of a political party: *The delegates voted along party lines.*

8. Relative stress is not shown in the spelled main entry when the entry is pronounced in its entirety or when

it contains Roman numerals, abbreviations, or letters of the alphabet.

> ***de·us ex ma·chi·na*** (de′o͝os eks mä′ki nä′; *Eng.* dē′əs eks mak′ə nə, dā′-), *Latin.* **1.** (in Greek drama) a god who resolves the entanglements of the play by his
>
> **Henry V,** 1387–1422, king of England 1413–22 (son of
>
> **St. George's Channel,** a channel between Wales
>
> **K ration,** *U.S. Army.* one of the emergency field rations

D. Homographs

1. Separate main entries are made for all words in the general language that are spelled identically but are of different derivation. When these words appear in boldface roman type, when they are spelled with lower-case rather than capital letters, and when they have no distinguishing diacritical markings, each one is followed by a small superscript number.

> **pat**[1] (pat), *v.*, **pat·ted, pat·ting,** *n.* —*v.t.* **1.** to strike lightly or gently with something flat, usually in order to
>
> **pat**[2] (pat), *adj.* **1.** exactly to the point or purpose. **2.** excessively glib. **3.** learned, known, or mastered perfectly
>
> **bow**[1] (bou), *v.i.* **1.** to bend the knee or body or incline the head, as in submission, salutation, or acknowledgment.
>
> **bow**[2] (bō), *n.* **1.** a flexible strip of wood or other material, bent by a string stretched between its ends, esp. for pro-
>
> **bow**[3] (bou), *n.* **1.** *Naut., Aeron.* **a.** the forward end of a vessel or airship. **b.** either side of this forward end, esp.

2. No entry that is capitalized, spelled with a diacritical mark, or shown in italic type is given a homograph number.

> **Dra·co** (drā′kō), *n.* a late 7th-century B.C. Athenian statesman noted for the severity of his code of laws. Also called
>
> **Dra·co** (drā′kō), *n.*, *gen.* **Dra·co·nis** (drā kō′nis). *Astron.* the Dragon, a northern circumpolar constellation between
>
> **thorn** (t̲h̲ôrn), *n.* **1.** a sharp excrescence on a plant, esp. a sharp-pointed aborted branch; spine; prickle. **2.** any of
>
> **Thorn** (tôRN), *n.* German name of **Torun.**
>
> **mate**[1] (māt), *n.*, *v.*, **mat·ed, mat·ing.** —*n.* **1.** one of a pair: *I can't find the mate to this glove.* **2.** a counterpart. **3.** husband or wife; spouse. **4.** one of a pair of mated animals. **5.** a habitual associate; fellow worker; comrade; partner (often used in combination): *classmate.* **6.** *Naut.*
>
> **mate**[2] (māt), *n.*, *v.*, **mat·ed, mat·ing,** *interj.* *Chess.* checkmate (def. 1). [ME *mat* defeated (adj.), defeat (n.) < OF << Pers; see CHECKMATE]
>
> **ma·te**[3] (mä′tā, mat′ā), *n.* maté.
>
> **ma·té** (mä′tā, mat′ā), *n.* a tealike South American beverage made from the leaves of a species of holly. Also, **mate.** [< Sp *mate,* orig. the vessel in which the herb is steeped < Quechua *mâti* calabash]
>
> **beg** (beg), *v.*, **begged, beg·ging.** —*v.t.* **1.** to ask for as a gift, as charity, or as a favor: *to beg alms; to beg forgiveness.*
>
> ***beg*** (bāg; *Eng.* beg), *n.* *Turkish.* bey.

II. PRONUNCIATION

Pronunciations are shown in this dictionary in parentheses immediately following the entry word. For the entries of some chemical compounds, however, the pronunciation and syllabification of the first word of the compound will be found at the end of the entry where this word is used alone as a run-on.

> **hy′drochlo′ric ac′id,** *Chem.* a corrosive and fuming liquid, HCl, used chiefly in chemical and industrial processes. —**hy·dro·chlo·ric** (hī′drə klōr′ik, -klôr′-), *adj.*
>
> **hydrocinnam′oyl group′,** *Chem.* the univalent group, $C_6H_5CH_2CH_2CO-$. Also called **hydrocinnam′oyl rad′ical.** [HYDRO-[2] + CINNAMO(N) + -YL] —**hy·dro·cin·nam·o·yl** (hī′drō si nam′ō il), *adj.*

The first pronunciation shown is generally the one considered to be in most frequent use, although there may be very little difference in usage between any two consecutive pronunciations. Occasionally, when there is some disagreement about how widespread a certain pronunciation is among educated speakers, that pronunciation may be preceded by a qualifying label, as "*often*" or "*sometimes.*" Other more specific labels, as those restricting a pronunciation to a certain part of speech, to certain definitions of a word, or to particular areas, are self-explanatory.

While assuming that any pronunciation shown is common to many educated speakers of the language, the reader should be aware that no dictionary, whatever its size, can possibly record every pronunciation used among educated speakers for each word it lists. An omitted pronunciation does not necessarily imply its absence in the educated community.

A. The Pronunciation of English

The system of pronunciation symbols used in this dictionary has been devised to represent major sound divisions in English. Just as, on a color wheel, the shadings that we conventionally name *red* and *orange* have between them and around them infinite gradations of color, so certain sounds in the English language have between and around them infinite gradations of sound coloration. We may well regard certain sounds, then, not as points but as areas in a continuum. It will be seen from the description of individual sounds below that many of the varied ways of pronouncing a given sound, although not made explicit by the use of a cumbersome number of symbols, are to be considered implicit in the symbols that are shown. The Pronunciation Key is so constructed that the user of the dictionary, by pronouncing the key words given for each symbol, will automatically produce the variety or varieties of each sound appropriate to his own dialect.

B. A Guide to the Symbols for the Sounds of English

NOTE: In the following descriptions the terms *front, central, back, high, mid,* and *low* refer to the approximate area of the mouth in which a portion of the tongue is raised during the pronunciation of a given *vowel.* The blade of the tongue is raised for front vowels, the central portion for central vowels, and the dorsum for back vowels.

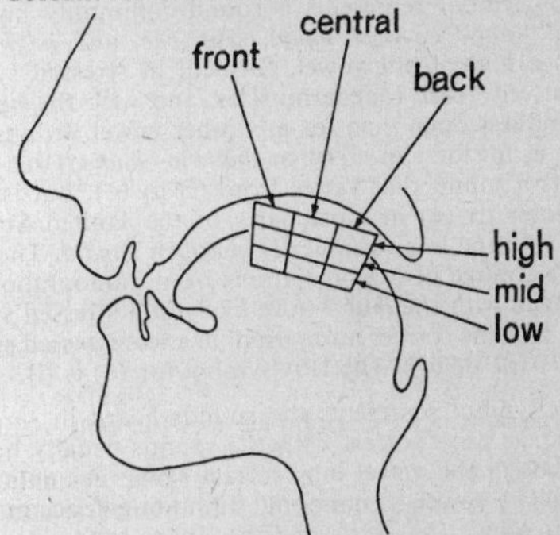

Explanations of the terms used to describe consonants may be found in the vocabulary.

a This symbol represents a sound commonly known as the "short" or "flat" *a,* as in *act, nap,* and *bat.* The sound is typically a low, front vowel, made with relatively lax tongue muscles and with the lips and mouth more open than for (e), but less open than for (ä). In the speech of many the sound may be raised toward (â), esp. in certain words, as *marry, dance, ham, hag,* and others. When shown in variation with the sound (ä), as in the pronunciations of *ask* (ask, äsk) or *half* (haf, häf), the two symbols represent a range of pronunciations, any one of which may be heard in educated speech. The IPA symbol is [æ].

ā This symbol represents a sound commonly known as the "long" *a,* as in *aid, cape,* and *way.* The sound is typically a mid, front vowel, formed with relatively tense tongue muscles, and with the lips slightly more open and less spread than for (ē) or (i), but less open and more spread than for (e) or (a). The sound may have a range of pronunciations from monophthongal to diphthongal, with the latter more likely in a stressed syllable, as in *way,* and the former more usual in a less stressed syllable, as in the first syllable of *vacation* (vā kā′s̲h̲ən). Before *l* the (ā) may be raised toward (â) by some speakers, or may be followed by a faint schwa. The IPA symbol is [e] for the monophthongal variant, [eɪ] for the diphthongal one.

â This symbol, shown with an *r* in the pronunciation key, represents the sound most commonly heard before *r* in *air, dare,* and *Mary.* Typically, it is a mid, front vowel with a range extending from (ä) through (e) to (a). When the (âr) is final, it is commonly diphthongal, pronounced with a faint schwa intervening before the *r,* as in *care* and *spare.* When not final, as in *Mary* or *careful,* it is usually monophthongal. In dialects where the *r* is dropped, the sound is normally followed by a schwa. The usual IPA symbol for (â) is [ɛə].

ä This symbol represents the relatively long sound of *a* in *alms, art,* and *calm,* a low, back vowel formed with the tongue muscles quite lax and with the lips more open than for any other vowel. In certain words it appears in variation with the sound (a) (see above). For words like *hot* and *watch,* spelled with *o* or an initial *wa-,* see the discussion below for the symbol (o). The IPA symbol for (ä) is [ɑ].

b This symbol represents the voiced, bilabial, plosive consonant sound heard in *back, cabin,* and *cab.* Its voiceless counterpart is (**p**), and its IPA symbol [b].

ch This symbol represents the voiceless, affricate consonant sound heard in *chief, butcher,* and *beach.* It is a combination of the plosive (**t**) and the fricative (**sh**), blended to form a single sound, and is formed with the tip and blade of the tongue behind the alveolar ridge. Its voiced counterpart is (**j**), and its IPA symbol [tʃ].

d This symbol represents the voiced, alveolar, plosive consonant sound heard in *do, rudder,* and *bed.* Intervocalically, before a relatively unstressed vowel, as in *rudder, daddy,* or *leader,* the sound is often flapped. The voiceless counterpart of (**d**) is (**t**), and its IPA symbol [d].

e This symbol represents a sound commonly known as the "short" *e,* as in *ebb, set,* and *merry.* The sound is typically a mid, front vowel, formed with relatively lax tongue muscles, and with the lips slightly more open and less spread than for (**ā**), but less open and more spread than for (**a**). Before *r,* in some dialects, the sound may resemble the (**â**). The IPA symbol is [ɛ].

ē This symbol represents a sound commonly known as the "long" *e,* as in *equal, seat, bee,* and *mighty.* The sound is a high, front vowel, formed, in stressed syllables, with relatively tense tongue muscles, and with the lips quite spread and less open than for any other vowel. In unstressed syllables, as for the *y* in *pretty* or the *ie* in *candied,* this symbol represents a sound that varies from (**i**) to (**ē**), but is acoustically closer to (**ē**) in most parts of the United States, in contrast with the less variable (**i**) heard in *candid.* The sound may have a range of pronunciations from monophthongal to diphthongal, with the latter more likely in a stressed syllable, as in *bee,* and the former more usual in a less stressed syllable, as in *radio* (rā′dē ō′). The IPA symbol for (**ē**) is [i].

ēr This symbol represents the sounds heard in *ear, mere, here,* etc., in contrast with the sounds usually heard in *mirror,* though the vowel may in fact range in quality from (**ē**) to (**i**). The vowel is commonly diphthongal, accompanied by a faint schwa, as (**ēᵊr**) or (**iᵊr**). In dialects where the *r* is dropped, the vowel is normally followed by a schwa.

f This symbol represents the voiceless, labiodental, fricative consonant sound heard in *fit, differ,* and *puff.* Its voiced counterpart is (**v**), and its IPA symbol [f].

g This symbol represents the voiced, velar, plosive consonant sound commonly known as the "hard" *g* and heard in *give, trigger,* and *beg.* Its voiceless counterpart is (**k**) and its IPA symbol [g].

h This symbol represents the usually voiceless, glottal, fricative consonant heard in *hit, behave,* and *hear.* In combination with *y,* as in *huge* (hyo͞oj), it may represent either a genuine combination of the two sounds or a voiceless *y,* a palatal fricative sound. The combination (**hl**) represents the voiceless *l* used in Welsh. The IPA symbol for (**h**) is [h].

hw This symbol represents either the sound combination (**h** + **w**), usually symbolized in IPA as [hw], or a voiceless *w,* usually symbolized in IPA as [ʍ]. Either sound may be heard in *which, when, where,* etc., when spoken by those who do not pronounce these words with the *w* of *witch, wen,* and *wear.*

i This symbol represents a sound known as the "short" *i,* as heard in *if, big,* and *mirror.* The sound is a high, front vowel, formed with relatively lax tongue muscles, and with the lips slightly more open and less spread than for (**ē**). In initial, unstressed syllables, as in *event,* the (**i**) represents a sound that may vary from (**i**) to (**ē**). Its IPA symbol is [ɪ].

In this dictionary the (**i**) also represents the unstressed vowel heard in the second syllables of *furniture, citizen,* and other words, where the sound may be considered to vary between (**i**) and (**ə**).

ī This symbol represents a sound commonly known as the "long" *i,* as heard in *ice, bite, pirate,* and *deny.* The sound is a diphthong, with the first element in the position of (**ä**) or, more usually, a sound between (**ä**) and (**a**), and the second element varying between (**i**) and (**ē**), but usually closer to (**i**). The IPA symbol is [aɪ].

j This symbol represents the voiced, affricate consonant sound heard in *just, badger,* and *fudge.* It is a combination of the plosive (**d**) and the fricative (**zh**), blended to form a single sound, and is formed with the tip and blade of the tongue behind the alveolar ridge. Its voiceless counterpart is (**ch**), and its IPA symbol [dʒ].

k This symbol represents the voiceless, velar, plosive consonant sound heard in *kept, keep, coop, scoop, token,* and *make.* Its voiced counterpart is (**g**), and its IPA symbol [k].

l This symbol represents the voiced, alveolar, lateral consonant sound heard in *low, mellow,* and *all.* The sound ranges in quality from the "light" or "clear" *l* heard usually when (**l**) is in initial position, preceding a front vowel, as in *leaf* and *list,* or followed by (**y**), as in *value,* to the "dark" *l* heard usually when (**l**) is in final or preconsonantal position or precedes a back vowel, as in *call, silk,* or *low.* When preceded by the homorganic sounds (**t**), (**d**), or (**n**), the (**l**) may constitute a syllable, as in *battle* (bat′ᵊl), *ladle* (lād′ᵊl), and *funnel* (fun′ᵊl). Its IPA symbol is [l].

m This symbol represents the voiced, bilabial, nasal consonant sound heard in *my, simmer,* and *him.* The (**m**) may constitute a syllable in some pronunciations of words in which the (**m**) is preceded by (**z**), as in *chasm* and *schism.* More frequently the latter class of words, as shown in this dictionary, would be pronounced with a full schwa between the (**z**) and the (**m**). The (**m**) is homorganic with the plosives (**p**) and (**b**), and its IPA symbol is [m].

n This symbol represents the voiced, alveolar, nasal consonant sound heard in *now, sinner,* and *on.* When preceded by the homorganic sounds (**t**) and (**d**), the (**n**) may constitute a syllable, as in *button* (but′ᵊn) and *Sweden* (swēd′ᵊn). Its IPA symbol is [n].

ng This symbol represents the voiced, velar, nasal consonant sound heard in *sing* and *Washington.* The sound is pronounced without an accompanying homorganic (**g**) or (**k**) in *ring* (ring), *ringing* (ring′ing), *Springfield* (spring′fēld′), and *gingham* (ging′əm). It is followed by a (**g**) in *wrangle* (rang′gəl), *finger* (fing′gər), *youngest* (yung′gist), and *elongate* (i lông′gāt, -long′-), and by a (**k**) in *sink* (singk), *anchor* (ang′kər), and one pronunciation of *lengthen* (lengk′thən). The (**ng**) is homorganic with the plosives (**k**) and (**g**), and its IPA symbol is [ŋ].

o This symbol represents a sound commonly known as the "short" *o,* as in *ox, box,* and *wasp.* Found only in words spelled with *o* or with an initial *wa-,* this variable symbol reflects differences between regional dialects. For many speakers in the United States the normal vowel in *bomb, ox,* and *hot* is the same as the vowel in *balm, alms,* and *father.* The traditional use of (**o**) in words like *hot* allows a dictionary to accommodate with a single symbol the pronunciations of different dialect areas. These pronunciations range from the sound of (**ä**) to a sound almost like that of the (**ô**) in *paw.* As found, for example, in eastern New England, where the pronunciations of *bomb* and *balm* are not identical, the sound is typically a low, back vowel, made with relatively lax tongue muscles and with the lips slightly less open and more rounded than for (**ä**), but more open and less rounded than for (**ô**). In this dialect its IPA symbol is [ɒ].

ō This symbol represents a sound commonly known as the "long" *o,* as in *over, boat,* and *no.* The sound is typically a mid, back vowel, made with relatively tense tongue muscles and lips more rounded and less open than for (**ô**), and less rounded and more open than for (**o͞o**). The sound may have a range of pronunciations from monophthongal to diphthongal, with the latter more likely in a stressed syllable, as in *toe,* and the former more usual in a less stressed syllable, as in *obey* (ō bā′). The IPA symbol is [o] for the monophthongal variant, [oʊ] for the diphthongal one. Before *r,* in the speech of those who distinguish between the (-ōr-) of *borne* and the (-ôr-) of *born,* the (ō) is often followed by a faint schwa, as (bōᵊrn).

ô This symbol represents the relatively long sound heard in *ought, ball,* and *raw.* It is typically a low, back vowel, formed with slightly tense tongue muscles and the lips less rounded and more open than for (**ō**). Before *r* this symbol may be shown in variation with (**ōr**) to represent the sound used by those who do not distinguish between the sounds of *borne* and *born.* The IPA symbol for (**ô**) is [ɔ].

oi This symbol represents the vowel sound heard in *oil, point,* and *joy.* The sound is a diphthong, with the first element in the position of (**ô**) or, sometimes, a similar sound closer to (**o**), and the second element approaching (**ē**), but normally closer to (**i**). The IPA symbol is [ɔɪ].

o͝o This symbol represents the high, back vowel heard in *book* and *foot.* The sound is formed with relatively lax tongue muscles and with lips less rounded and more open than for (**o͞o**). Before *r,* this symbol represents the sound between (**ōō**) and (**o͞o**) heard in *pure* and *touring.* Its IPA symbol is [ʊ].

o͞o This symbol represents the high, back vowel heard in *ooze, fool,* and *too.* The sound is formed with relatively tense tongue muscles and with lips more rounded and less open than for (o͝o). Its IPA symbol is [u].

ou This symbol represents the vowel sound heard in *out, loud,* and *prow.* The sound is a diphthong, with the first element in the position of (ä) or, more usually, a sound between (ä) and (a), and the second element approaching (o͞o), but normally closer to (o͝o). Before *r* this sound may become triphthongal, pronounced with either a faint or full schwa. The IPA symbol is [aʊ].

p This symbol represents the voiceless, bilabial, plosive consonant sound heard in *pool, spool, supper,* and *stop.* Its voiced counterpart is (b) and its IPA symbol [p].

r This symbol represents a major sound division that includes a multiplicity of *r*-sounds, ranging from a vowellike *r,* as often heard in American English, to a more consonantal sound, as often heard in British English. The vowellike, sounded, frictionless or retroflex *r* is heard in American pronunciations of *red* and *rich.* Similar to it is the postvocalic *r* heard as an *r*-colored vowel in one American pronunciation of *fair* and *bird.* A consonantal fricative, voiced or voiceless, may be heard in *dress* and *try* respectively, while a consonantal flapped *r* is often heard intervocalically in the British pronunciations of *very* and *worry.* In some loan words or in certain biographical and geographical entries in which all the sounds would be recorded identically for the English and foreign pronunciations, either an English or non-English *r* may be assumed when (r) is shown.

In some dialects a final, postvocalic *r* or a preconsonantal *r* may be omitted entirely, being replaced with either a lengthened vowel or a faint schwa, as in *car* (kä̤ä̤) or (käᵊ), *carp* (kä̤ä̤p) or (käᵊp), or *dear* (dēᵊ). The dropped *r* may be reinserted when a final *r* becomes intervocalic, as in the phrase *dear Anne.* Among the IPA symbols that may be used to represent various *r*-sounds are: [ɾ] flapped *r;* [ɹ] fricative and vowellike *r;* [r] trilled *r.*

s This symbol represents the voiceless, sibilant, fricative consonant sound heard in *see, passing,* and *miss.* The sound is formed usually with the blade of the tongue held close to the alveolar ridge. The breath stream is forced through a groove formed by the tongue, striking the teeth to produce a hissing sound. The voiced equivalent of (s) is (z), and its IPA symbol [s].

sh This symbol represents the voiceless, sibilant, fricative consonant sound heard in *shoe, fashion,* and *push.* It is formed with the blade of the tongue held farther back than for (s) and with the breath stream forced through a broader groove formed by the tongue, striking the teeth to produce a hushing sound. Its voiced equivalent is (zh) and its IPA symbol [ʃ].

t This symbol represents the voiceless, alveolar, plosive consonant sound heard in *team, steam, butter,* and *bit.* Intervocalically, before a relatively unstressed vowel, as in *matter* and *lettuce,* or before syllabic *l,* as in *settle,* the sound may vary from a voiced quality almost identical to that of the intervocalic *d* of *rudder* to a voiceless flapped sound that distinguishes between *butter* and *budder, matter* and *madder.* The voiced equivalent of (t) is (d), and its IPA symbol [t].

th This symbol represents the voiceless, dental or interdental, fricative consonant sound heard in *thin, ether,* and *path.* Its voiced equivalent is (t͟h) and its IPA symbol [θ].

t͟h This symbol represents the voiced, dental or interdental, fricative consonant sound heard in *that, either,* and *smooth.* Its voiceless equivalent is (th) and its IPA symbol [ð].

u This symbol represents a sound commonly known as the "short" *u,* as in *up* and *love.* It is typically a low, central vowel formed with relatively lax tongue muscles and with unrounded lips. The IPA symbol is [ʌ].

û This symbol is shown with an *r* in the pronunciation key to represent the stressed, *r*-colored vowel heard in *urge, burn,* and *cur.* It is typically a mid, central vowel, formed with relatively tense tongue muscles and, except in *r*-dropping dialects, some degree of retroflexion of the tongue tip toward the hard palate. It is often symbolized in American phonetic transcription as [ɝ] or, in *r*-dropping dialects, [ɜ].

v This symbol represents the voiced, labiodental, fricative consonant sound heard in *voice, river,* and *live.* Its voiceless counterpart is (f), and its IPA symbol [v].

w This symbol represents the voiced, bilabial-velar semivowel heard in *west* and *away.* It is produced as the lips and tongue move from the position of an (o͞o) to the position of a following vowel. Its IPA symbol is [w].

y This symbol represents the voiced, palatal semivowel heard in *yes* and *beyond.* It is produced as the tongue moves from the position of an (ē) to the position of a following vowel. Its IPA symbol is [j].

z This symbol represents the voiced, sibilant, fricative consonant sound heard in *zeal, lazy,* and *those.* The sound is formed usually with the blade of the tongue held close to the alveolar ridge. The breath stream is forced through a groove formed by the tongue, striking the teeth to produce a vibrating, hissing sound. The voiceless equivalent of (z) is (s), and its IPA symbol [z].

zh This symbol represents the voiced, sibilant, fricative consonant sound heard in *vision* and *mirage.* It is formed with the blade of the tongue held farther back than for (z) and with the breath stream forced through a broader groove formed by the tongue, striking the teeth to produce a vibrating, hushing sound. Its voiceless equivalent is (sh) and its IPA symbol [ʒ].

ə This symbol, the schwa, represents the unstressed vowel commonly heard as the sound of *a* in *alone, e* in *system, i* in *easily, o* in *gallop,* and *u* in *circus.* It is typically a mid, central vowel, formed with lax tongue muscles and with the lips open, but neither spread nor rounded. The sound of schwa is variable to the extent that it may, while remaining unstressed, move in the direction of any one of the surrounding vowels. Its IPA symbol is [ə].

ᵊ The superscript schwa is used in unaccented syllables to represent the syllabic quality of an *l* or *n* that is preceded by a homorganic sound, as *t* or *d.* The symbol is shown in circumstances where the *l* or *n* most frequently constitutes a syllable, as in *cradle* (krād′ᵊl), *metal* (met′ᵊl), and *redden* (red′ᵊn).

In such words as *competence* (kom′pi tᵊns), *president* (prez′i dənt), and *distance* (dis′təns), the pronunciation is indicated by either a full or superscript schwa, but rarely both. The choice has been made on the basis of frequency and does not imply that the alternative pronunciation is not used by educated speakers.

In accented syllables the (ᵊ) is used between the diphthong (ī) and an (r) in the same syllable to show triphthongal quality, as in *lyre* (līᵊr), *fire* (fīᵊr), and *tiring* (tīᵊr′ing), in contrast with the sounds in *liar* (lī′ər) and *irate* (ī rāt′).

In certain loan words, as *Mbutu* (ᵊmbo͞o′to͞o), (ᵊ) before the nasals (m), (n), or (ng) may represent pronunciations ranging from those in which the nasal consonant initiates the first syllable to those in which the consonant is preceded by a vowel ranging from (ᵊ) or (ə) to (e) or (i).

C. Syllabification

[For syllabification of main entry words, see above, I, B; for syllabification of foreign pronunciations, see below, II, G.]

Pronunciations are divided into syllables within the parentheses as a visual aid in sounding out a word as well as an aid in producing the appropriate phonetic variant of a given sound. Although it is customary in dictionaries to show most short syllables, which contain checked vowels, closed by the following consonants and most syllables containing free vowels left open, certain modifications are made in this dictionary, among them the following:

1. Words like *mistake* are recorded as (mi stāk′) so as to avoid the aspiration of the voiceless plosive that might be indicated by the pronunciation (mis tāk′), a pronunciation that might sound as if the word were *mis-take,* "take badly."

2. Words like *atrophy,* in which the stressed, checked vowel would normally be closed by the following (t), are shown in this dictionary with (t) and (r) kept together, as in (a′trə fē). Showing this syllabification rather than (at′rə fē) in words of this type aids the user in producing the phonetic variants of the adjacent (t) and (r) usually heard in educated speech. It does so by helping him to avoid the possibility of a pronunciation in which the (t), as the final consonant in a syllable, might not be exploded, or might even be said as a glottal stop. The difference in question may best be illustrated by comparing the pronunciation of the word *citric* with that of the sentence *Sit, Rick.*
Since words with the analogous combinations of (k) plus (r) and (p) plus (r) do not present the same problems, all stressed, checked syllables followed by these combinations are closed in the usual way, as *acrid* (ak′rid) and *reciprocate* (ri sip′rə kāt′).

3. Lengthened consonants, which are single sounds, are recorded as double symbols, one ending one syllable and one beginning the next, as in *roommate* (ro͞om′māt′, ro͞om′-), *sackcloth* (sak′klôth′, -kloth′), and *misspell* (mis-spel′).

None of these syllable divisions necessarily reflects those shown in the spelled main entry word.

D. Stress

[For stress of main entry words, see above, I, C; for stress in foreign pronunciations, see below, II, H.]

Relative differences in stress between syllables in a word may be indicated in the pronunciations.

1. In words of two or more syllables a primary stress mark (′) follows the syllable having greatest stress.

ex·act·ly (ig zakt′lē), *adv.* **1.** in an exact manner; pre-

2. A secondary stress mark (′) follows a syllable having slightly less stress, particularly in a word of three or more syllables in which marked, stressed syllables alternate with unmarked, weaker ones.

peek·a·boo (pēk′ə bo͞o′), *n.* **1.** a game played by very

3. An unmarked syllable, when adjacent to a stressed syllable, may sometimes be spoken with secondary stress if shown with a full vowel.

va·cate (vā′kāt), *v.*, **-cat·ed, -cat·ing.** **—***v.t.* **1.** to cause

4. Relatively weak stress in a word is always unmarked.

an·i·mal (an′ə məl), *n.* **1.** any living being typically
in·tu·i·tion (in′to͞o ish′ən, -tyo͞o-), *n.* **1.** direct percep-

5. Monosyllables are unmarked and are considered to have primary stress unless a pronunciation specifically labeled *unstressed* is shown.

bread (bred), *n.* **1.** a food made of baked dough or batter

but

and (and; *unstressed* ənd, ən), *conj.* **1.** (used to connect
her (hûr; *unstressed* hər, ər), *pron.* **1.** the objective case

E. The Pronunciation of Foreign Sounds

Foreign sounds are represented, for the most part, by the symbols shown above (II, B), although it must be understood that the quality of these sounds varies from language to language. Symbols that will most help a native speaker of English to produce appropriate sounds are shown. Thus both the Spanish *b* and *v* are shown as (**b**) when initial or after *m*, as in *vaquero* (bä ke′ʀô) or *hombre* (ôm′bʀe), and as (**v**) when intervocalic, as in *Ribera* (ʀē ve′ʀä). Similarly, Spanish *d* at word beginning or after *n* or *l* is shown as (**d**), as in *Diego* (dye′gô) or *San Fernando* (sän feʀ nän′dô), but as (*th*) when intervocalic or final, as in *Granada* (gʀä nä′*th*ä) or *Valladolid* (bä′lyä dô lēth′). In Spanish, though, both of these sets of sounds, (**b**)/(**v**) and (**d**)/(*th*), are part of larger sound units, or phonemes.

Additional symbols, shown below (II, F), are used only for those sounds that cannot be approximated by symbols in the English key.

F. A Guide to the Symbols for Foreign Sounds

A This symbol represents the low vowel heard in French *ami.* It is slightly to the front of (ä) in the French vowel system and is made with the lips open and somewhat spread. The sound may be thought of by the English speaker as roughly intermediate in quality between the (**a**) of *cat* and the (ä) of *calm.* Its IPA symbol is [a].

KH This symbol represents a range of voiceless fricative consonants heard in Arabic, German, Scottish, Hebrew, Russian, etc. When produced with back articulation, as in German *ach* and Scottish *loch,* it is usually described as a velar fricative. This consonant and similar varieties of it or similar consonants, as in Arabic, may have uvular vibration or pharyngeal constriction. When produced with articulation that is farther forward, as heard in German *ich,* it is described as a palatal fricative. The former sound may be articulated by bringing the tongue almost into the position of (**k**), as in *coo,* while pronouncing a strong, rasping (**h**); the latter sound may be articulated by bringing the tongue almost into the position of (**k**), as in *key,* while pronouncing a strong, rasping (**h**) similar to the initial sound in *human* when it is pronounced with a greater than usual degree of friction. Among the IPA symbols used for the various sounds symbolized in this dictionary by (KH) are [x] for the voiceless velar fricative and [ç] for the voiceless palatal fricative.

N This symbol, as in French *bon* (bôɴ), is used to indicate that the preceding vowel is nasalized; it does not stand for a type of *n*-sound. There are four nasalized vowels in French, found in the phrase *un bon vin blanc* (œɴ bôɴ vaɴ bläɴ). In Portuguese both vowels and diphthongs may be nasalized. The usual IPA symbol is a tilde (~) over the nasalized vowel.

Œ This symbol represents either the vowel sound heard in German *schön* (shœn) and French *feu* (fœ), usually transcribed in IPA as [ø], or the vowel sound heard in the initial syllables of German *öffnen* (œf′nən) and French *neuvième* (nœ vyem′), usually transcribed in IPA as [œ]. They are both rounded, front vowels.

The former sound is made with relatively tense tongue muscles and with the lips rounded in the position for (ō), as in *over,* while trying to say (ā), as in *able.* The latter sound is made with relatively lax tongue muscles and with the lips rounded in the position for (ô), as in *ought,* while trying to say (**e**), as in *get.*

An approximation for the English speaker may be achieved by pronouncing the vowel in the word *fir* (fûr) without any *r*-color.

R This symbol represents any non-English *r,* and therefore does not stand for a sound with any one specific point of articulation. Since the *r* varies from language to language to a greater extent than any other consonant, the symbol (ʀ) has been introduced to obviate the tendency of an American speaker of English to substitute his own *r* in an otherwise foreign pronunciation. An (ʀ), therefore, should be interpreted as an instruction to use whatever sound is appropriate in a given foreign language. Someone who is not familiar with the language in question, or who feels more comfortable with the sound qualities of English, will of course use his own *r.*

Among the sounds the (ʀ) may represent are a flap, as in Spanish *pero* (pe′ʀô), a uvular sound, as in the Parisian French pronunciation of *rouge* (ʀo͞ozh), and a trill, as in Italian *mare* (mä′ʀe) and Scottish *harst* (häʀst, hâʀst). [Note that the (ʀ) has been used in Scottish pronunciations, where the sound is always consonantal, but not in British-English pronunciations, where the *r* may sometimes be vocalic or dropped entirely.] Where the (ʀ) appears in Chinese pronunciations, it represents a sound similar to a uvular, (Parisian) French *r,* used in Chinese for the sound usually transliterated as *j.* Various IPA symbols for the variant sounds of (ʀ) may be seen above under English sounds.

Y This symbol represents either the vowel sound heard in the initial syllable of German *fühle* (fʏ′lə) and French *lumière* (lʏ myeʀ′), usually transcribed in IPA as [y], or the one heard in the initial syllable of German *Fülle* (fʏ′lə), usually transcribed in IPA as [ʏ]. They are both rounded, front vowels.

The former sound is made with relatively tense tongue muscles and with the lips rounded in the position for (o͞o), as in *boot,* while trying to say (ē), as in *meet.* The latter sound is made with relatively lax tongue muscles and with the lips rounded in the position for (o͝o), as in *book,* while trying to say (i), as in *sit.*

ə A superscript schwa has been used in foreign pronunciations to represent a sound ranging from a short, faint schwa immediately following a consonant or glide to a faint prolongation of the preceding consonant or glide, voiced or unvoiced, as in French *Bastogne* (bᴀ stôn′yə) or *boulevard* (bo͞olə vᴀʀ′).

G. Syllabification of Foreign Pronunciations

[For syllabification of main entry words, see above, I, B; for syllabification of English pronunciations, see above, II, C.]

Rules for syllabifying the pronunciations of foreign words often differ from the rules applicable to English. Pronunciations are divided into syllables according to the specific requirements of each individual language. While English contains some free vowels (vowels that may occur in both open and closed syllables) and some checked vowels (vowels that may occur only in closed syllables) certain languages, as Italian and Spanish, contain only free vowels. Certain other languages, as the Slavic languages, contain consonant clusters not encountered in English. Some languages, as German, contain familiar clusters in unfamiliar places. The syllable divisions shown for a pronunciation in a given language are those that will most help the reader to produce sound combinations appropriate to that language.

bo·de·ga (bô *th*e′gä; *Eng.* bō dā′gə), *n., pl.* **-gas** (-gäs; *Eng.* -gəz). *Spanish.* **1.** (esp. among Spanish-speaking Americans) a grocery store. **2.** a warehouse, esp. for wine.

Dvo·řák (*Eng.* dvôr′zhäk, -zhak; *Czech.* dvô′rzhäk), *n.* **An·ton** (*Eng.* an′tən, -ton; *Czech.* än′tôn), 1841–1904,

Schutz·staf·fel (shōōts′shtä′fəl), *n.* *German.* See **SS Troops.**

H. Stress in Foreign Pronunciations

[For stress of main entry words, see above, I, C; for stress in English pronunciations, see above, II, D.]

Different languages have different patterns of stress. In some languages the major stress is fixed on a certain syllable in words; in others stress is variable; in still others, at least to the native speaker, stress appears to be level. The stress patterns shown in this dictionary are those that are likely to aid the speaker of English in approximating appropriate patterns of speech.

1. In the Modern Greek pronunciation of *antidoron* (än dē′-thô rôn), for example, where an English speaker might expect a stress pattern alternating between weak and strong syllables, no stress is shown on the final syllable. The native speaker of Greek would be more likely to give secondary stress to (-thô-) than to (-rôn).
2. In French pronunciations, although stress is relatively level, a stress mark on the final syllable of an entry word or phrase shown in isolation indicates where a slight rise or fall in pitch or a slight increase in force is possible. In French speech individual words are not stressed. Instead there is probably a rise in pitch at the end of each phrase and a fall in pitch at the end of each declarative sentence.

The user of a dictionary compiled for English speakers should be aware that no series of stress marks or other visual symbols can adequately substitute for firsthand knowledge of a foreign language, encounters with a native speaker, or even for a recording. The less like English a given language is—with regard to its patterns of intonation, with regard to the interrelationships within it among force, duration, and pitch, or with regard to the function in the language of any of these—the more likelihood there is that a written transcription of its pronunciation, with or without stress marks, will be somewhat deceptive.

III. PARTS OF SPEECH

A. A part-of-speech label for each main entry that consists of a single word is given as an italicized abbreviation preceding the definition or definitions for that part of speech.

big·ot (big′ət), *n.* a person who is utterly intolerant of

B. If the entry word is used in more than one grammatical form, the appropriate italicized part-of-speech label precedes each set of definitions given for that part of speech. Part-of-speech labels subsequent to the first are preceded by a boldface dash.

in·tro·vert (*n., adj.* in′trə vûrt′; *v.* in′trə vûrt′), *n.* **1.** *Psychol.* a person characterized by concern primarily with his own thoughts and feelings. **2.** *Informal.* a shy person. **3.** *Zool.* a part that is or can be introverted. **—*adj.* 4.** *Psychol.* marked by introversion. **—*v.t.* 5.** to turn inward:

C. If the entry word shows irregularly spelled inflected forms (see below, IV, A), a summary of all the parts of speech for the entry is given with the inflected forms following the pronunciation. The part-of-speech labels are listed in the same order as they appear in the definition text, where they are all preceded by a boldface dash.

brave (brāv), *adj.*, **brav·er, brav·est,** *n., v.*, **braved, brav·ing.** **—*adj.* 1.** possessing or exhibiting courage or courageous endurance. **2.** making a fine appearance. **3.** *Archaic.* excellent; fine; admirable. **—*n.* 4.** a brave person. **5.** a warrior, esp. among North American Indian tribes. **—*v.t.* 6.** to meet or face courageously. **7.** to defy; challenge; dare. **8.** *Obs.* to make splendid. **—*v.i.* 9.** *Obs.* to

D. If an entry word with more than one grammatical form is given a usage, area, subject, or other label that applies to all its parts of speech (see below, V, A, B), a boldface dash precedes the first part-of-speech label as well as the others.

Pa·le·o·zo·ic (pā′lē ə zō′ik, pal′ē-), *Geol.* **—*adj.* 1.** noting or pertaining to an era occurring between 220,000,000 and 600,000,000 years ago, characterized by the appearance of fish, insects, and reptiles. See table at **era.** **—*n.* 2.** the Paleozoic era or group of systems. Also, **Palae-**

IV. INFLECTED FORMS

Inflected forms are shown primarily for those entry words that form inflections in some way other than by the simple addition of appropriate inflectional endings. Certain additional plurals are shown to avoid possible confusion, although they are formed by the simple addition of *-s* or *-es*.

A. Inflected forms generally shown include those for:

1. nouns, adjectives, and verbs ending in a consonant plus a *y*, where the *y* changes to *i* before an inflectional ending is added.

stead·y (sted′ē), *adj.*, **stead·i·er, stead·i·est,** *interj., n., pl.* **stead·ies,** *v.*, **stead·ied, stead·y·ing,** *adv.* **—*adj.* 1.** firm-

2. adjectives and verbs ending in *e*, where the *e* is dropped before the inflectional ending is added.

fine[1] (fīn), *adj.*, **fin·er, fin·est,** *adv., v.*, **fined, fin·ing.** **—*adj.* 1.** of superior or best quality; of high or highest

3. adjectives and verbs doubling the consonant before adding inflectional endings.

big (big), *adj.*, **big·ger, big·gest,** *adv.* **—*adj.* 1.** large, as

ad·mit (ad mit′), *v.*, **-mit·ted, -mit·ting.** **—*v.t.* 1.** to

4. nouns and verbs changing an internal spelling to form inflections.

half (haf, häf), *n., pl.* **halves** (havz, hävz), *adj., adv.*

mouse (*n.* mous; *v.* mouz), *n., pl.* **mice** (mīs), *v.*, **moused,**

steal (stēl), *v.*, **stole, sto·len, steal·ing,** *n.* **—*v.t.* 1.** to

5. adjectives changing their roots to form the comparative and superlative.

good (gŏŏd); *adj.*, **bet·ter, best,** *n., interj., adv.* **—*adj.***

6. nouns having plurals that are not native English formations.

phe·nom·e·non (fi nom′ə non′), *n., pl.* **-na** (-nə) for 1, 3, **-nons** for 2. **1.** a fact, occurrence, or circumstance

a·lum·na (ə lum′nə), *n., pl.* **-nae** (-nē). a girl or woman

a·lum·nus (ə lum′nəs), *n., pl.* **-ni** (-nī). a male graduate

7. nouns having the plural and singular spelled identically.

Chin·ese (chī nēz′, -nēs′), *n., pl.* **-nese,** *adj.* **—*n.* 1.** the standard language of China, based on the speech of

8. Latin names of constellations, which show the genitive form, as used in naming stars.

O·ri·on (ō rī′ən, ô rī′-), *n., gen.* **Or·i·o·nis** (ôr′ē ō′nis, or′-, ə rī′ə nis) for 2. **1.** *Class. Myth.* a giant-sized hunter who pursued the Pleiades, was eventually slain by Artemis, and was then placed in the sky as a constellation. **2.** *Astron.* the Hunter, a constellation lying on

The star Betelgeuse, for instance, the brightest star in the constellation Orion, is also known as Alpha Orionis.

9. nominative pronouns, which show their declensions.

I (ī), *pron., nom.* **I,** *poss.* **my** or **mine,** *obj.* **me;** *pl. nom.* **we,** *poss.* **our** or **ours,** *obj.* **us;** *n., pl.* **I's.** **—*pron.* 1.** the nominative singular pronoun, used by a speaker in referring to himself. **—*n.* 2.** (used to denote the narrator of a literary work written in the first person singular.) **3.**

B. To avoid possible confusion as to their spellings, certain plural forms are also shown, including those for:

1. nouns ending in *-o*, *-ful*, *-ey*, or *-us*.

po·ta·to (pə tā′tō), *n., pl.* **-toes.** **1.** Also called **Irish potato, white potato.** the edible tuber of a cultivated

bra·vo (brä′vō, brä vō′), *interj., n., pl.* **-vos** for 2, 3, **-voes** for 3, *v.*, **-voed, -vo·ing.** **—*interj.* 1.** well done!

cup·ful (kup′fŏŏl′), *n., pl.* **-fuls.** **1.** the amount that a cup can hold. **2.** *Cookery.* a half pint; eight fluid ounces.

mon·key (mung′kē), *n., pl.* **-keys,** *v.*, **-keyed, -key·ing.** **—*n.* 1.** any mammal of the order *Primates,* including the

pro·spec·tus (prə spek′təs), *n., pl.* **-tus·es.** a report de-

2. nouns ending in elements resembling words that form their plurals in a different way.

mon·goose (mong′gōōs′, mon′-), *n., pl.* **-goos·es.** **1.** a slender, ferretlike carnivore, *Herpestes edwardsii,* of India,

3. nouns about which there might be confusion as to the pronunciation of the plural.

house (*n., adj.* hous; *v.* houz), *n., pl.* **hous·es** (hou′ziz), *v.*, **housed, hous·ing,** *adj.* **—*n.* 1.** a building in which people

path (path, päth), *n., pl.* **paths** (pathz, päthz, paths, päths). **1.** a way beaten or trodden by the feet of men or

pet·it four (pet′ē fôr′, fôr′; *Fr.* pə tē fōōr′), *pl.* **pet·its fours** (pet′ē fôrz′, fôrz′; *Fr.* pə tē fōōr′). a small teacake, variously frosted and decorated. [< F:

pe·so (pā′sō; *Sp.* pe′sô), *n., pl.* **-sos** (-sōz; *Sp.* -sôs). **1.** a silver and copper coin and monetary unit of Mexico,

4. entries of two or more words about which there might be confusion as to which element is pluralized.

ad′jutant gen′eral, *pl.* **adjutants general. 1. the Adjutant General,** the chief administrative officer of the U.S. Army. **2.** (in the U.S. Army) an adjutant of a unit

C. Where variant inflected forms occur, all forms are shown, with labels when appropriate.

la·bel (lā′bəl), *n., v.,* **-beled, -bel·ing** or (*esp. Brit.*) **-belled, -bel·ling.** —*n.* **1.** a slip of paper or other mate-

break (brāk), *v.,* **broke** or (*Archaic*) **brake; bro·ken** or (*Archaic*) **broke; break·ing;** *n.* —*v.t.* **1.** to injure so as to

bass[2] (bas), *n., pl.* (*esp. collectively*) **bass,** (*esp. referring to two or more kinds or species*) **bass·es. 1.** any of numerous

D. Where two inflected forms are given for a verb, the first is the past tense and the past participle and the second is the present participle.

love (luv), *n., v.,* **loved, lov·ing.** —*n.* **1.** a profoundly

E. Where three inflected forms are given for a verb, the first is the past tense, the second is the past participle, and the third is the present participle.

run (run), *v.,* **ran, run, run·ning,** *n., adj.* —*v.i.* **1.** to go

F. Inflected forms are not generally shown for:

1. nouns whose plural is formed by the addition of *-s* (dog, dogs) or *-es* (class, classes).
2. verbs whose past tense is formed by the addition of *-ed* with no alteration of the spelling, whose past participle is formed by the addition of *-ed* with no alteration of the spelling, and whose present participle is formed by the addition of *-ing* with no alteration of the spelling (*talk, talked, talking*).
3. the third person singular, present tense of verbs, with the exception of auxiliary verbs.

V. DEFINITIONS

A. Definitions within an entry are individually numbered in a single sequence, regardless of any division according to part of speech. The most common part of speech is listed first, and the most frequently encountered meaning appears as the first definition for each part of speech. Specialized senses follow, and rare, archaic, and obsolete senses are usually listed at the end of their part-of-speech group. This order is changed in those cases where it is desirable to group related meanings together.

B. Idioms appear in boldface type under the main entry word whose use in the idiom is least clear or denotative, unless that word is a preposition or an adverbial particle. When more than one such word is used, the idiom is usually listed under the entry for the first word, with a cross reference under the other or others. One-word cross references to idiom definitions appear in boldface and are preceded by "See."

tide[1] (tīd), *n., v.,* **tid·ed, tid·ing.** —*n.* **1.** the periodic rise and fall of the waters of the ocean and its inlets, produced by the attraction of the moon and sun, and occurring about every 12 hours. **2.** the inflow, outflow, or current of water at any given place resulting from the waves of tides. **3.** See **flood tide. 4.** a stream or current. **5.** anything that alternately rises and falls, increases and decreases, etc.: *the tide of the seasons.* **6.** current, tendency, or drift, as of events, ideas, action, etc.: *the tide of international events.* **7.** any extreme or critical period or condition: *The tide of her illness is at its height.* **8.** a season or period in the course of the year, day, etc. (now used chiefly in combination): *wintertide; eventide.* **9.** *Eccles.* a period of time that includes and follows an anniversary, festival, etc. **10.** *Archaic.* a suitable time or occasion. **11.** *Obs.* an extent of time. **12. turn the tide,** to reverse the course of events, esp. from one extreme to another. —*v.i.* **13.** to flow as the tide; flow to and fro. **14.** to float

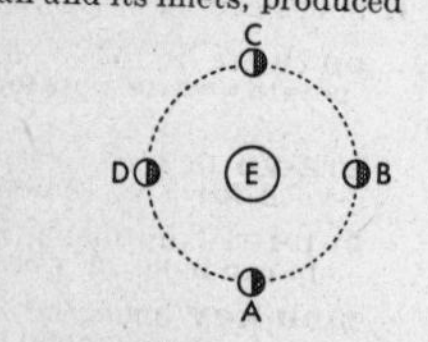

Tide
S, Sun; E, Earth;
A, C, Moon at neap tide;
B, D, Moon at spring tide

turn . . . 60. turn the tide. See **tide**[1] (def. 12).

C. The part of speech under which an idiom appears depends on the grammatical function of the main entry word in the idiom, and not on the grammatical function of the idiom in a sentence. Idioms are listed in alphabetical order after the definitions for the part of speech under which they appear. However, no distinction is made between transitive and intransitive verbs, and verbal idioms are listed after the last verb definition. Idiom definitions may be given the same types of restrictive labels as any other definitions.

sack[1] (sak), *n.* **1.** a large bag of strong, coarsely woven material, as for grain, potatoes, coal, etc. **2.** the amount such a bag can hold. **3.** *U.S.* any bag: *a sack of candy.* **4.** Also, **sacque. a.** a loose-fitting dress, fashionable esp. in the early 18th century. **b.** a loose-fitting coat, jacket, or cape. **5.** *U.S. Slang.* bed: *I bet he's still in the sack.* **6.** *Slang.* dismissal or discharge, as from a job. **7.** *Baseball Slang.* a base. **8. hit the sack,** *U.S. Slang.* to go to bed. **9. hold the sack.** See **bag** (def. 12). —*v.t.* **10.** to put into a

D. Where two or more definitions belong to the same labeled subject field, they may be marked with boldface letters under the same definition number.

re·treat (ri trēt′), *n.* **1.** the forced or strategic withdrawal of a military force before an enemy. **2.** the act of withdrawing, as into safety or privacy; retirement; seclusion. **3.** a place of refuge, seclusion, or privacy. **4.** an asylum, as for the insane. **5.** a retirement or a period of retirement for religious exercises and meditation. **6.** *Mil.* **a.** a flag-lowering ceremony held at sunset at a military installation. **b.** the bugle call or drumbeat played at this ceremony. **7. beat a retreat,** to withdraw or retreat, esp.

E. Where an idiomatic phrase has two or more meanings, each meaning is marked with a boldface letter and the idiom itself is listed only once.

break . . . 55. break in, a. to enter enclosed property by force or cunning. **b.** to train: *The boss is breaking in a new assistant.* **c.** to begin to wear or use: *to break in a new pair of shoes.* **56. break into, a.** to enter (a profession

F. For meanings using the entry word in a form slightly different from that shown at the main entry, as with a capital letter or a lower-case letter or in italic type, the changed form is indicated at the beginning of the definition.

pa·cif·ic (pə sif′ik), *adj.* **1.** tending to make peace; conciliatory. **2.** not warlike; peaceable; mild. **3.** at peace; peaceful: *a pacific era in history.* **4.** calm; tranquil: *The Wabash is a pacific river.* **5.** (*cap.*) of or pertaining to the Pacific Ocean. **6.** (*cap.*) of or pertaining to the region bordering on the Pacific Ocean: *the Pacific states.* —*n.* **7.** (*cap.*) See **Pacific Ocean.** [< L *pācific(us),* lit., peace-

G. For meanings using a singular entry in the plural form or a plural entry in the singular form, the changed form is spelled out at the beginning of the definition.

ten·pin (ten′pin′), *n.* **1.** one of the pins used in tenpins. **2. tenpins,** (*construed as sing.*) a form of bowling, played with ten wooden pins at which a ball is bowled to knock

H. When there is some question as to whether an entry that is plural in form is used with a singular verb or a plural verb, an appropriate statement, in parentheses and italics, follows the entry. A similar statement may follow the changed form of an entry that appears at the beginning of a specific definition. (See above, V, G.)

pros·tho·don·tics (pros′thə don′tiks), *n.* (*construed as sing.*) the branch of dentistry that deals with the restora-

VI. RESTRICTIVE LABELS

Entries that are limited, in whole or in part, to a particular region, time, subject, or level of usage, are marked with appropriate labels, as *U.S., Brit., Australian, Canadian; Archaic, Obs.; Physics, Chem.; Slang, Informal.* Sometimes labels are combined: *Railroads Slang.*

A. If the label applies to the entire entry, it appears before the first part-of-speech label if there is more than one part of speech and after it if there is only one part of speech.

la·bi·o·ve·lar (lā′bē ō vē′lər), *Phonet.* —*adj.* **1.** pronounced with simultaneous bilabial and velar articulations, as *w.* —*n.* **2.** a labiovelar speech sound.

fi·ne[3] (fē′nā), *n.* *Music.* the end of a repeated section,

B. If the label applies to a certain part of speech only, it follows the part-of-speech label and precedes the subsequent definition numbers.

maim (mām), *v.t.* **1.** to deprive of the use of some part of the body by wounding or the like; cripple. **2.** to impair; make essentially defective. —*n. Obs.* **3.** a physical injury, esp. a loss of a limb. **4.** an injury or defect; blemish; lack.

C. If the label applies to a certain definition only, it follows the definition number and precedes the text of the definition.

a·vun·cu·lar (ə vuŋg′kyə lər), *adj.* **1.** of, pertaining to, or characteristic of an uncle: *avuncular affection.* **2.** *Obs.* of or pertaining to a pawnbroker. [< L *avuncul(us)* a mother's

D. If a definition has two or more lettered parts and the label applies to both, it precedes the first letter.

hi·lum (hī′ləm), *n.* **1.** *Bot.* **a.** the mark or scar on a seed produced by separation from its funicle or placenta. **b.** the nucleus of a granule of starch. **2.** *Anat.* the region at

E. If the label applies to only one of the lettered parts, it follows that letter.

high′ sea′, 1. the sea or ocean beyond the three-mile limit or territorial waters of a country. 2. Usually, **high seas. a.** the open, unenclosed waters of any sea or ocean. **b.** *Law.* the area within which transactions are subject

F. If the label applies to a definition that consists of two or more lettered parts, and one of them has an additional label, the subject label follows the number and the additional label follows the letter.

mass (mas), *n.* **1.** a body of coherent matter, usually of indefinite shape and often of considerable size: *a mass of dough.* **2.** a collection of incoherent particles, parts, or objects regarded as forming one body: *a mass of sand.* **3.** a considerable assemblage, number, or quantity. **4.** *Fine Arts.* **a.** *Painting.* an expanse of color or tone that defines form or shape in general outline rather than in detail. **b.** a three-dimensional shape or volume that has or gives the illusion of having great density and bulk. **5.** the

VII. CROSS REFERENCES

Main entries are defined under the form most commonly encountered in contemporary English, and therefore most likely to be looked up by the user of the dictionary. Other forms, as less common terms, other names for an entry, or shortened forms, may be listed in their own alphabetical places and may also be shown at the entry that is defined. Various kinds of relationships between entries may also be indicated. Single-word cross references are usually shown in regular body type and cross references of two or more words in boldface preceded by "See." For cross references to idiom definitions see above V, B.

A. Variants

1. Common variant spellings appear in boldface type at the form of the entry that is defined. Variants are usually shown in alphabetical order, unless one form is preferred to the others, in which case the preferred form will be shown first. They are preceded by "Also," and followed by a period. Variant names for an entry may be similarly shown, preceded by "Also called." Either kind of variant may be shown with an appropriate restrictive label.

pre·em·i·nence (prē em′ə nəns), *n.* state or character of being preeminent . . . Also, **pre-em′i·nence, pre·ëm′i·nence.** [ME < LL *praeēminentia*]

Ched·dar (ched′ər), *n.* a hard, smooth-textured cheese. Also called **Ched′dar cheese′.** [after *Cheddar,* village

val·or (val′ər), *n.* boldness or determination in facing great danger, as in a battle. Also, *esp. Brit.*, **val′our.**

2. If a variant applies to all the definitions in an entry or to two or more specifically numbered definitions that do not constitute one entire part-of-speech group, it is shown after the last definition and before the etymology if there is one.

cab·a·la (kab′ə lə, kə bä′-), *n.* **1.** a system of esoteric theosophy and theurgy developed by rabbis from about the 7th to 18th centuries, reaching its peak about the 12th and 13th centuries, and based on a mystical method of interpreting the Scriptures . . . **2.** any occult or secret doctrine or science. Also, **cabbala, kabala, kabbala.** [< ML

swad′dling clothes′, **1.** clothes consisting of long, narrow strips of cloth for swaddling an infant. **2.** long garments for an infant. **3.** the period of infancy or immaturity, as of a person, or incipience, as of a thing. **4.** rigid supervision or restriction of actions or movements, as of the immature. Also called **swad′dling bands′** (for defs. 1, 2).

3. If a variant applies to a certain part of speech only, it follows the part-of-speech label and precedes the subsequent definition numbers.

en·do·crine (en′də krin, -krīn′, -krēn′), *Anat., Physiol.* —*adj.* Also, **en·do·cri·nal** (en′də krīn′əl), **en′do·crin′ic, en·doc·rin·ous** (en dok′rə nəs). **1.** secreting internally. **2.** of or pertaining to an endocrine gland or its secretion: *an endocrine imbalance.* —*n.* **3.** an internal secretion;

4. If a variant applies to a certain definition only, it follows the definition number and precedes the text of the definition.

Brah·man (brä′mən), *n., pl.* **-mans.** *Hinduism.* **1.** Also, **Brahmin.** a member of the highest, or priestly, caste among the Hindus. Cf. **Kshatriyya, Sudra, Vaisya. 2.** Also, **Brahma.** the impersonal supreme being, the primal

5. When a less common form of an entry, as a spelling or other type of variant, appears as a main entry, it is not defined. Instead it is followed by a cross reference guiding the user to the entry where the definition appears.

nick·nack (nik′nak′), *n.* knickknack.

black′ flag′. See **jolly roger.**

B. Alternative Names

1. Alternative names may be shown at the main entry that is defined. In geographical entries, they appear in boldface specifically labeled and placed in the entry as if they were variants. In biographical entries, such alternative names are most often shown in italic type, enclosed in parentheses, following the given name. Nicknames and assumed names follow this style and also are within quotation marks.

Czech·o·slo·va·ki·a (chek′ə slə vä′kē ə, -vak′ē ə), *n.* a republic in central Europe: formed after World War I; comprises the former countries of Bohemia, Moravia, Silesia, and Slovakia. 13,951,473 (est. 1963); 49,379 sq. mi. *Cap.:* Prague. Also, **Czech′o-Slo·va′ki·a.** Official name, **Czech′o·slo′vak So′cialist Repub′lic.** —**Czech′o·slo·va′ki·an, Czech′o-Slo·va′ki·an,** *adj., n.*

Charles′ Lou′is, (*Karl Ludwig Johann*) 1771–1847, archduke of Austria.

Mar·i·on (mar′ē ən, mâr′-), *n.* **1. Francis** ("*the Swamp Fox*"), 1732?–95, American Revolutionary general. **2.** a

Len·in·grad (len′in grad′; *Russ.* le′nin gʀät′), *n.* a seaport in the NW RSFSR, in the NW Soviet Union in Europe, on the Gulf of Finland, off the Baltic Sea: founded by Peter the Great 1703; capital of the Russian Empire 1712–1917. 3,636,000 (1965). Formerly, **St. Petersburg** (1703–1914); **Petrograd** (1914–24).

2. Cross references with specific designations may be given, particularly following certain biographical and geographical main entries, to guide the user to the name by which a person or place is most commonly known. A cross reference of this type appears in boldface only when it duplicates exactly the form under which it is elsewhere defined. Otherwise it appears in regular body type.

Haag (häᴋʜ), *n.* **Den** (den), a Dutch name of The Hague.

Swamp′ Fox′. See **Marion, Francis.**

Nya·sa·land (nyä′sä land′, nī as′ə-), *n.* former name of **Malawi.**

Fi·ren·ze (fē ʀen′dze), *n.* Italian name of **Florence.**

Clem·ens (klem′ənz), *n.* **Samuel Lang·horn** (laṅg′hôrn, -ərn). See **Twain, Mark.**

C. Inflected Forms

When an inflected form (see above, IV), is given its own main entry, it is cross-referred to the defined entry of which it is a part.

ran (ran), *v.* pt. of **run.**

o·per·a² (ō′pər ə, op′ər ə), *n.* *Chiefly Music.* a pl. of **opus.**

D. Abbreviations, Symbols

1. Certain definitions, as those in the sciences, may show an abbreviated form, symbol, atomic number, etc., at the end of a definition.

avoirdupois′ weight′, the system of weights in Britain and the U.S. for goods other than gems, precious metals, and drugs. *Abbr.:* av.; avdp.; avoir.

2. When abbreviations, symbols, etc., have their own main entries, they are followed by their full, expanded forms, which are shown in alphabetical order, unless the abbreviation given is that of the etymology of the full form.

N.Y.C., New York City.

ca., **1.** cathode. **2.** centiare. **3.** Also, **ca** (with a year) about: *ca. 1872.* [< L *circā*]

E. Hidden entries

1. A hidden entry may be implicitly or explicitly defined or named within the text of a broader definition in the same field. It is shown in boldface, enclosed in parentheses.

stand′ard time′, the civil time officially adopted for a country or region, usually the civil time of some specific meridian lying within the region. The standard time zones in the U.S. (**Eastern time, Central time, Mountain time, Pacific time, Yukon time, Alaska time,** and **Bering time**) use the civil times of the 75th, 90th, 105th, 120th, 135th, 150th, and 165th meridians respectively, the dif-

2. When a hidden entry is given its own main entry, it is followed by a cross reference to the broad definition in which it is contained. This cross reference, shown in boldface, is preceded by the words "See under."

Moun′tain time′. See under **standard time.**

F. Comparisons

1. Cross-reference information preceded by "Cf." may be shown in boldface following a definition to guide the user to related material in another definition.

ni·dic·o·lous (nī dik′ə ləs), *adj.* *Ornith.* remaining in the nest for a period after hatching. Cf. **nidifugous.**

ni·dif·u·gous (nī dif′yə gəs), *adj.* *Ornith.* leaving the nest shortly after hatching. Cf. **nidicolous.** [< L *nīd-*

2. Similar cross references are used to pinpoint specific relationships between definitions. The words expressing the relationship, in regular body type, and the cross reference to another entry, in italic type, are enclosed in parentheses following a definition. The three types of relationships are expressed by the phrases (opposed to . . .), (contrasted with . . .), and (distinguished from . . .).

pos·i·tive (poz′i tiv), *adj.* . . . **10.** consisting in or characterized by the presence or possession of distinguishing or marked qualities or features (opposed to *negative*): *Light is positive, darkness negative.* **11.** noting the presence of such

neg·a·tive (neg′ə tiv), *adj., n., v.,* **-tived, -tiv·ing.** —*adj.* . . . **5.** characterized by the absence of distinguishing or marked qualities or features; lacking positive attributes (opposed to *positive*): *a dull, lifeless, negative character.* **6.** lacking in constructiveness, helpfulness, optimism, co-

cir′cumstan′tial ev′idence, proof of facts offered as evidence from which other facts are to be inferred (contrasted with *direct evidence*).

direct′ ev′idence, evidence of a witness who testifies to the truth of the fact to be proved (contrasted with *circumstantial evidence*).

cook·ing (ko͝ok′ing), *n.* **1.** the act of a person or thing that cooks. **2.** cookery (def. 1). —*adj.* **3.** used in preparing foods. **4.** fit to eat when cooked (distinguished from *eating*): *cooking apples.*

eat·ing (ē′ting), *n.* **1.** the act of a person or thing that eats. **2.** food with reference to the quality it displays when eaten: *This fish is delicious eating.* —*adj.* **3.** good or fit to eat, esp. raw (distinguished from *cooking*): *eating apples.* **4.** used in eating: *eating utensils.* [ME]

G. Illustrations

When additional useful information is given in an illustration, map, diagram, or table, a definition may be followed by an instruction guiding the user to the main entry under which the information may be found.

North·um·bri·a (nôr thum′brē ə), *n.* an early English kingdom extending N from the Humber to the Firth of Forth. See map at **Mercia.**

VIII. ETYMOLOGIES

Etymologies in this dictionary appear in square brackets after the definitions or, when they occur, after the variant spellings of the entry word. Etymologies are not given for words formed in Modern English from constituents that should be obvious to the user. Thus, etymologies are not given for words such as DEVELOPER and CAMPFIRE, since the constituents—[DEVELOP + -ER¹] and [CAMP¹ + FIRE]—were felt to be readily apparent or inferable from the definition. On the other hand, all words bearing homograph numbers, even when formed in Modern English, have been etymologized. Etymologies have also been given for a number of Modern English formations when it was felt that the constituents were not immediately obvious, as for **lunacy** [LUNA(TIC) + -CY] or **wherewithal,** which is [WHERE + WITHAL] and not [WHEREWITH + ALL]. A full key to the etymologies appears on page xv.

A. Symbols

The following are the most important symbols in the etymologies and occur with great frequency.

< This symbol, meaning "from," is used to show descent from one language or group of languages to another, or to show that a word is derived from another word. It is placed before a language label (e.g., < OF, < L, < Gk) in order to indicate from what source and in what form a word enters English and to trace, in turn, the line of descent from one pre-English source to another.

diadem . . . [ME *diademe* < L *diadēma* < Gk *diádēma* . . .]
negative . . . [< L *negātīv(us)* denying (see NEGATE, -IVE); r. ME *negatif* < MF]

This symbol is not used between words that belong merely to different historical stages of the same language. It is omitted, for example, between ME and OE forms, AF and OF forms, and LL and L forms.

madder¹ . . . [ME *mad(d)er,* OE *mæd(e)re;* c. Icel *madhra* . . .]
moratorium . . . [< NL, LL . . .]

It is also omitted before the analysis of a word—that is, before the breaking down of a word into its constituent morphemes. See = below.

<< This symbol is used to show descent from one language to another but with an intermediate stage omitted. It may be read as "goes back to."

tick³ . . . [ME *tikke, teke, tyke* (c. D *tijk,* G *Zieche*) << L *thēca, thēca* . . .]
kitchen . . . [ME *kichene,* OE *cycene* << L *coquīna* . . .]

> This symbol, meaning "whence," is used to indicate that the word following it is descended from the word preceding it. It serves the general purpose of citing a modern foreign language word that is akin to the entry word.

yet . . . [ME *yet(e),* OE *gīet(a);* c. MHG *ieze* yet, now > G *jetzt* now]

= This symbol of equivalence precedes the analysis of a word. It is used to show that a word is made up of the words or morphemes that follow it.

ferreous . . . [< L *ferreus* = *ferr(um)* iron + *-eus* -EOUS]
billiard . . . [< F *billard* cue = *bille* stick (see BILLET²) + *-ard* -ARD]

\+ This symbol is used between morphemes, the members of a compound or a blend, etc., in order to indicate that these are the immediate constituents of the word being analyzed.

wherewithal . . . [WHERE + WITHAL]
boron . . . [BOR(AX + CARB)ON]
iniquity . . . [ME < L *inīquitās* unevenness, unfairness = *inīqu(us)* uneven, unfair (*in-* IN-³ + *-īquus,* var. of *aequus* EQUI-) + *-itās* -ITY]

B. Parentheses

Parentheses are used in the etymologies to set off the analysis of a preceding word which is itself part of a larger analysis (as *orbiculus* in the following example).

bequest . . . [ME *biqueste* = *be-* BE- + *-queste* (*-ques-* (OE *-cwiss-;* akin to BEQUEATH) + *-te,* var. of -TH¹)]

Parentheses frequently are used to enclose grammatical or other comments on a preceding form.

inherent . . . [< L *inhaerent-* (s. of *inhaerēns*) . . .]
divan . . . [< Turk < Pers *dīwān,* orig. *dēvan* booklet (whence the meanings account book, office . . .)]

Parentheses are used to set off parts of the etymons that are felt not to require analysis or that do not have any bearing on the entry word. They are also used to show various kinds of ellipsis or omission, as in blends and acronyms (see below), variant spellings, etc.

inoculate . . . [ME < L *inoculāt(us)* . . .]
bathe . . . [ME *bath(i)e(n),* OE *bathian* = *bæth* BATH¹ + *-ian* inf. suffix]

C. Language Labels

Language labels, as given in the Etymology Key, precede the italicized etymons. Before an English form, the language label is omitted when the form is "obs." (obsolete), "dial." (dialect), or "earlier," or when it has some other special relationship to the entry word.

unkempt . . . [var. of *unkembed* = UN-¹ + *kembed,* ptp. of obs. *kemb* to comb . . .]

A language label is shown before the initial form in a given language but is not repeated before subsequent forms in the same language if the series is continuous.

bomb . . . [earlier *bom(b)e* < Sp *bomba* (*de fuega*) ball (of fire), akin to *bombo* drum . . .]

A language label is shown alone without an accompanying italicized form when there is no significant difference in form or meaning between the word in the given language and the preceding word. In some cases an italicized word is not shown after a language label when the word is identical to one immediately following.

base¹ . . . [ME < MF < L *basis* . . .]
dart . . . [ME < MF < Gmc]
wintertime . . . [ME; r. ME, OE *wintertīd* . . .]

A language label is followed by a colon and a translation when there is a difference in meaning but none in form between a word in a given language and the preceding word.

incentive . . . [ME < LL *incentīv(us)* provocative, L: setting the tune = *incent(us)* . . .]

D. Typeface

Three styles of type are used in the etymologies. Roman type is used for translations, definitions, comments on grammar, and other explanatory matter.

Italic type is used for all words or parts of words (usually not entries in the dictionary) from which the entry words are formed by derivation or composition. Foreign words, those labeled ME, OE, "obs.," "earlier," "dial.," and those, including proper names, that are not otherwise entries in the dictionary are italicized.

Small capitals indicate a cross reference to another entry in the dictionary where further information may be obtained. Especially frequent reference is made to numerous affixes or combining forms which correspond to common elements in pre-English words, as -ATE¹, -ION, -IVE, etc., for L *-ātus, -iōn-, -īvus,* etc.

E. Special Types of Etymologies

In addition to the etymologies concerned with tracing words to their pre-English sources, there are those that require only simple cross references to their parts. These are chiefly compounds composed in English.

lunacy . . . [LUNA(TIC) + -CY]
batfowl . . . [late ME *batfowlyn.* See BAT², FOWL (V.)]

Acronyms are shown in italics with parentheses enclosing all parts but those composing the entry word.

NATO . . . [*N(orth) A(tlantic) T(reaty) O(rganization)*]

TASS . . . [< Russ *T(elegraphnoye) A(genstvo) S(ovyetskovo) S(oyuza)*]

scuba . . . [*s(elf)-c(ontained) u(nderwater) b(reathing) a(pparatus)*]

Blends are shown in small capitals.

flurry . . . [b. FLUTTER and HURRY]

smog . . . [SM(OKE + F)OG[1]]

Biographical and other explanatory matter is included in the etymologies when the entry word contains a proper name, an allusion or metaphor, etc., that requires elucidation.

Boyle's law . . . [named after R. BOYLE]

Flathead . . . [so called from their supposed practice of flattening their children's heads]

willemite . . . [named after King WILLEM I; see -ITE[1]]

magnolia . . . [< NL, named after Pierre *Magnol* (1638–1715), French botanist; see -IA]

Literal translations are given, without analysis, for some entries set in boldface italics when there is a difference between the definition and the literal meaning.

shibah . . . [lit., seven (days)]

maftir . . . [lit., dismisser]

In uncertain and unknown etymologies, the symbol [?] is used to mean either "perhaps" or "unknown," depending on the context.

beach . . . [?]

bird . . . [ME *byrd, bryd,* OE *brid(d)* young bird, chick < ?]

dickens . . . [prob. substitute for *devil; ?* special use of *Dicken,* earlier form of *Dick,* proper name]

The following examples show several other obvious formula etymologies which occur occasionally.

swish . . . [imit.] (*Note:* The abbreviation "imit." (imitative) is used in a large sense and frequently implies conventional symbolism rather than merely the reproduction of a sound. See the etymology for **bobwhite.**)

boom[1] . . . [late ME *bombon, bummyn* to buzz; c. D *bommen,* G *bummen,* orig. imit.]

castoff . . . [adj., n. use of v. phrase *cast off*]

rep[2] . . . [by shortening]

back[2] . . . [aph. var. of ABACK]

headquarter . . . [back formation from HEADQUARTERS]

IX. RUN-ON ENTRIES

Derivatives of the main entry word may be formed by adding a suffix to the root of the main entry. When their meanings are manifestly clear from the combined senses of the root word and the suffix, these derivatives can be run on at the end of the entry.

A. The run-on entry appears in boldface type at the end of the entry as part of a sequential order that includes, in a complete entry, the last definition, any variant spellings, the etymology, run-on entries, and synonym, antonym, or usage studies. The run-on entry is usually preceded by a lightface dash and is followed by an italicized, abbreviated part-of-speech label or labels.

bear·a·ble (bâr′ə bəl), *adj.* capable of being borne; endurable. —**bear′a·ble·ness,** *n.* —**bear′a·bly,** *adv.*

Mon·tan·a (mon tan′ə), *n.* a state in the NW United States. 674,767 (1960); 147,138 sq. mi. *Cap.:* Helena. *Abbr.:* Mont. —**Mon·tan′an,** *adj., n.*

In the entry for *bearable* the first run-on entry is implicitly defined as "*n.* the quality or state of being bearable," and the second as "*adv.* in a bearable manner."
In the entry for *Montana* the run-on entry is implicitly defined first as "*adj.* of, pertaining to, or characteristic of Montana," and second as "*n.* a native or inhabitant of Montana."

B. Run-on entries are usually shown in alphabetical order. However, if two or more are variant spellings of one another, they are shown in sets within which the most commonly used form is given first. Each set is preceded by a lightface dash and followed by a part-of-speech label indicating the shared grammatical function of the run-on entries in the set.

de·lec·ta·ble (di lek′tə bəl), *adj.* **1.** delightful; highly pleasing. **2.** delicious. [ME < L *dēlectābil(is)* delightful = *dēlect(āre)* to delight + *-ābilis* -ABLE] —**de·lec′ta·ble·ness, de·lec′ta·bil′i·ty,** *n.* —**de·lec′ta·bly,** *adv.* —**Ant.**

C. If the pronunciation of a one-word run-on entry is clearly derivable from that of the main entry, a preceding variant of the main entry, or a preceding run-on entry, the run-on entry is syllabified with centered dots and appropriately stressed in the boldface spelling.

bi·o·met·rics (bī′ə me′triks), *n.* (*construed as sing.*) **1.** *Biol.* the application of mathematical-statistical theory to biology. **2.** biometry (def. 1). —**bi′o·met′ric, bi′o·met′ri·cal,** *adj.* —**bi′o·met′ri·cal·ly,** *adv.*

D. If the pronunciation of a run-on entry is not clearly derivable from that of the main entry, a preceding variant of the main entry, or a preceding run-on entry, the run-on entry is syllabified with centered dots in the boldface spelling, with the pronunciation and stress shown in parentheses following.

de·clared (di klârd′), *adj.* avowed; professed: *a declared liberal.* —**de·clar·ed·ly** (di klâr′id lē), *adv.*

E. When two or more variant run-on entries requiring pronunciation are pronounced similarly but not identically, the first is syllabified in the boldface and followed by a pronunciation while subsequent ones are syllabified and given stress in the boldface spelling.

ba·rom·e·ter (bə rom′i tər), *n.* **1.** *Meteorol.* any instrument that measures atmospheric pressure, esp. an aneroid or mercury barometer. Cf. **hypsometer. 2.** anything that indicates changes. —**bar·o·met·ric** (bar′ə me′trik), **bar′o·met′ri·cal,** *adj.* —**bar′o·met′ri·cal·ly,** *adv.*

F. When two or more variant run-on entries requiring pronunciation are pronounced identically, they are syllabified with centered dots in the boldface spelling and followed by the shared pronunciation.

pre·empt (prē empt′), *v.t.* **1.** to occupy (land) in order to establish a prior right to buy. **2.** to acquire or appropriate before someone else: *to preempt the choicest cut of meat.* —*v.i.* **3.** *Bridge.* to make a preemptive bid. —*n.* **4.** *Bridge.* a preemptive bid. Also, **pre-empt′, pre·ëmpt′.** [back formation from PREEMPTION] —**pre·emp·tor, pre-emp·tor, pre·ëmp·tor** (prē emp′tôr), *n.*

G. When a run-on entry consists of two or more words, it is preceded by a lightface dash and followed by a period. Such an entry is given relative stress in the boldface spelling (see above, I, C.)

toe-dance (tō′dans′, -däns′), *v.i.,* **-danced, -danc·ing.** to perform a toe dance. —**toe′ danc′er.**

X. SYNONYMS

A. At the ends of many entries synonym lists appear, preceded by **—Syn.** They are keyed to the entry definitions to which they relate. These lists are general in nature, with semicolons separating clusters of words that are somewhat more closely connected in denotation and connotation.

B. At the ends of many entries synonym studies appear, set flush left to the margin and preceded by **—Syn.** Keyed to the entry definitions to which they relate and often accompanied by a synonym list, the studies describe meaning discriminations of a more detailed nature than is possible either in synonym lists or in the definitions themselves.

C. At the ends of some entries, either set off alone or following a synonym list, cross references are shown to entries where synonym studies appear.

XI. ANTONYMS

At the ends of many entries antonym lists appear, preceded by **—Ant.** These are generally brief and the user is guided to the entries of the antonyms themselves where *their* synonym lists and studies, in turn, will provide full coverage of antonyms of the original word.

XII. USAGE NOTES

At the ends of a number of entries usage notes and comments appear, set flush left to the margin and preceded by **—Usage.** These describe many of the problems that arise in matters of grammar and usage, and they are intended to reflect the opinions of educated users of English, particularly editors and teachers.

In cases where the note contrasts or compares the usage of two or more words, the note appears under only one of them, with appropriate cross references under the others.

Table of English Sounds and Their Common Spellings

This table may be used to find the spelling of a word when only its pronunciation is known. For example, using the boldface, italicized equivalents in the Spellings column, the word pronounced (bit) would most likely be spelled bit. At the left, the first two columns show the relationships between the symbols used in this dictionary and those in the International Phonetic Alphabet (IPA). Under the Examples column are listed words that have in at least one of their pronunciations the symbol listed under the Dictionary Symbol column. For a complete table of IPA symbols, see page 697.

Dictionary Symbol	IPA Symbol	Spellings	Examples
a	[æ]	***a***, a'a, ach, ag, ai, au, ui	hat, ma'am, drachm, diaphragm, plaid, draught, guimpe
ā	[eɪ, e]	***a***, ae, ag, ai, aig, ao, au, ay, é, è, ê, ea, ee, ée, eg, eh, ei, eig, eige, eigh, eilles, es, et, ey, ez	ate, Gael, champagne, rain, arraign, gaol, gauge, ray, exposé, suède, tête-à-tête, steak, matinee, née, thegn, eh, veil, feign, greige, sleigh, Marseilles, demesne, beret, obey, laissez faire
ä	[ɑ]	***a***, à, aa, ah, al, as, at, e, ea, oi, ua	father, à la mode, bazaar, hurrah, calm, faux pas, éclat, sergeant, hearth, reservoir, guard
â(r)	[ɛː(r)]	air, aire, ***are***, ayer, ear, eer, e'er, eir, er, ere, ère, ert, ey're, uerre	chair, doctrinaire, dare, prayer, wear, Mynheer, ne'er, their, mal de mer, there, étagère, Camembert, they're, nom de guerre
b	[b]	***b***, bb, bh	bed, hobby, bheesty
ch	[tʃ]	c, ***ch***, che, tch, te, ti, tu	cello, chief, niche, catch, righteous, question, natural
d	[d]	***d***, 'd, dd, de, ed, ld	do, we'd, ladder, fade, pulled, should
e	[ɛ]	a, ae, ai, ay, ***e***, è, ê, ea, eg, ei, eo, ie, oe, u, ue	any, aesthetic, said, says, ebb, manège, bête-noir, leather, phlegm, heifer, leopard, friend, foetid, bury, guest
ē	[i]	ae, ay, ***e***, ea, ***ee***, e'e, ei, eip, eo, es, ey, i, ie, is, oe, uay, y	Caesar, quay, equal, team, see, e'en, deceive, receipt, people, demesne, key, machine, field, debris, amoeba, quay, pity
f	[f]	***f***, ff, gh, lf, ph	feed, muffin, tough, calf, physics
g	[g]	***g***, gg, gh, gu, gue	give, egg, ghost, guard, plague
h	[h]	***h***, wh	hit, who
hw	[hw, ʍ]	wh	where
i	[ɪ]	a, e, ee, ei, ***i***, ia, ie, o, u, ui, y	damage, England, been, counterfeit, if, carriage, sieve, women, busy, build, sylph
ī	[aɪ]	ai, ais, aye, ei, eigh, eye, ***i***, ie, igh, is, uy, y, ye	faille, aisle, aye, stein, height, eye, ice, tie, high, island, buy, sky, lye
j	[dʒ]	ch, d, dg, dge, di, ge, gg, gi, ***j***, jj	Greenwich, graduate, judgment, bridge, soldier, sage, exaggerate, magic, just, Hajji
k	[k]	***c***, cc, cch, ch, ck, cq, cqu, cque, cu, gh, ***k***, ke, kh, lk, q, qu	car, account, bacchanal, character, back, acquaint, lacquer, sacque, biscuit, lough, kill, rake, Sikh, walk, Iraq, liquor
l	[l]	***l***, le, ll, 'll, 'lle, sl	live, mile, call, she'll, faille, lisle
m	[m]	chm, gm, lm, ***m***, 'm, mb, me, mh, mm, mn	drachm, paradigm, calm, more, I'm, limb, home, mho, hammer, hymn
n	[n]	gn, kn, mn, ***n***, ne, nn, pn	gnat, knife, mnemonic, not, done, runner, pneumatic
ng	[ŋ]	n, ***ng***, ngg, ngue	pink, ring, mahjongg, tongue
o	[ɒ]	a, ach, au, ***o***, ou	wander, yacht, astronaut, box, cough
ō	[oʊ, o]	au, aut, aux, eau, eaux, eo, ew, ho, ***o***, oa, oe, oh, ol, oo, os, ot, ou, ow, owe	mauve, hautboy, faux pas, beau, Bordeaux, yeoman, sew, mho, note, road, toe, oh, yolk, brooch, dos-a-dos, depot, soul, flow, owe
ô	[ɔ]	***a***, ah, al, as, au, augh, aw, ***o***, oa, ou, ough	tall, Utah, talk, Arkansas, fault, caught, raw, alcohol, broad, sought, fought
oi	[ɔɪ]	aw, eu, ***oi***, ois, oy, uoy	lawyer, Freud, oil, Iroquois, toy, buoy
o͝o	[ʊ]	o, ***oo***, ou, oul, u	wolf, look, would, could, pull
o͞o	[u]	eu, ew, ieu, o, oe, oeu, ***oo***, ou, u, ue, ug, ui	maneuver, grew, lieu, move, canoe, manoeuvre, ooze, troupe, rule, flue, impugn, fruit
ou	[aʊ]	au, ***ou***, ough, ***ow***	landau, out, bough, brow
p	[p]	***p***, pp	pen, stopper
r	[r]	***r***, re, 're, rh, rr, rrh, wr	red, pure, we're, rhythm, carrot, catarrh, wrong
s	[s]	c, ce, ps, ***s***, 's, sc, sch, se, ss	city, mice, psychology, see, it's, scene, schism, mouse, loss
sh	[ʃ]	ce, ch, chsi, ci, psh, s, sch, sci, se, ***sh***, si, ss, ssi, ti	ocean, machine, fuchsia, special, pshaw, sugar, schist, conscience, nauseous, ship, mansion, tissue, mission, mention
t	[t]	bt, cht, ct, ed, ght, phth, ***t***, 't, te, th, tt	doubt, yacht, ctenophore, talked, bought, phthisic, toe, 'twas, bite, thyme, bottom
th	[θ]	chth, ***th***	chthonian, thin
t͟h	[ð]	***th*** the	then, bathe
u	[ʌ]	o, oe, oo, ou, ***u***	son, does, flood, couple, cup
û(r)	[ɜr, ɝ]	ear, ***er***, err, eur, ir, or, our, ***ur***, urr, yr, yrrh	learn, term, err, poseur, thirst, worm, scourge, hurt, purr, myrtle, myrrh
v	[v]	f, ph, ***v***, ve, 've, vv	of, Stephen, visit, have, we've, flivver
w	[w]	o, ou, u, ***w***	choir, ouija, quiet, well
y	[j]	i, j, ***y***	union, hallelujah, yet
yo͞o	[ju, ɪu]	eau, eu, ew, ieu, iew, ***u***, ue, ueue, yew, you, yu	beauty, feud, few, purlieu, view, use, cue, queue, yew, you, yule
z	[z]	s, 's, sc, se, ss, x, ***z***, ze, zz	has, who's, discern, raise, scissors, anxiety, zone, raze, dazzle
zh	[ʒ]	ge, s, ***si***, z, zi	garage, measure, division, azure, brazier
ə	[ə]	***a***, à, ai, ***e***, ei, eo, ***i***, ia, io, ***o***, oi, ou, ***u***, y	alone, tête-à-tête, mountain, system, mullein, dungeon, easily, parliament, legion, gallop, porpoise, curious, circus, Abyssinia
ər	[ər, ɚ]	ar, ***er***, ir, or, our, ur, ure, yr	liar, father, elixir, labor, labour, augur, future, martyr

DEVELOPMENT OF MAJUSCULE								
NORTH SEMITIC	GREEK		ETR.	LATIN		MODERN		
						GOTHIC	ITALIC	ROMAN
K	Δ	A	A	A	A	𝔄	*A*	A

DEVELOPMENT OF MINUSCULE					
ROMAN CURSIVE	ROMAN UNCIAL	CAROL. MIN.	MODERN		
			GOTHIC	ITALIC	ROMAN
λ	λ	a	𝔞	*a*	a

The first letter of the English alphabet developed from North Semitic *aleph* and Greek *alpha* (α, A) through Etruscan and Latin. The capital (A) goes back to North Semitic *aleph,* which acquired its modern form in Greek and was retained in the Latin monumental script. The minuscule (a) derives from Latin cursive *a,* a variant form of A, through Anglo-Irish, Carolingian, and Florentine influence to yield both italic and roman forms.

A, a (ā), *n., pl.* **A's** or **As, a's** or **as.** **1.** the first letter of the English alphabet, a vowel. **2.** any spoken sound represented by the letter *A* or *a,* as in *pale, hat,* or *small.* **3.** something having the shape of an A. **4.** a written or printed representation of the letter *A* or *a.* **5.** a device, as a printer's type, for reproducing the letter *A* or *a.* **6. from A to Z,** from the beginning to the end.

a[1] (ə; *when stressed* ā), *indefinite article.* **1.** any one of some class or group: *a man.* **2.** any certain one: *one thing at a time; A Miss Johnson called.* **3.** one (used before a noun expressing quantity): *a score of times.* **4.** (used with adjectives and nouns expressing indefinite amounts to suggest quantity): *a great many years.* **5.** any single: *not a one.* **6.** (used before the name of a person or thing used as a typical example): *a Cicero in eloquence.* [ME; phonetic var. of AN[1]]

a[2] (ə; *when stressed* ā), *prep.* for or in each; for or in every; per: *ten cents a ride; three times a day.* [orig. *a,* prep. var. of ON (see A-[1]); confused with A[1]]

a[3] (ə), *prep. Informal except Eye Dial.* of (often written as an unhyphenated element): *time a day; kinda.* [var. of OF[1]]

A, 1. *Elect.* ampere; amperes. **2.** *Physics.* angstrom unit. **3.** answer.

A, 1. the first in order or in a series. **2.** (*sometimes l.c.*) (in some grading systems) a grade or mark that indicates something of the highest quality. **3.** *Music.* **a.** the sixth tone in the scale of C major or the first tone in the relative minor scale of A minor. **b.** a string, key, or pipe tuned to this tone. **c.** a written or printed note representing this tone. **d.** the tonality having A as the tonic note. **4.** a major blood group usually enabling a person whose blood is of this group to donate blood to persons of group A or AB and to receive blood from persons of O or A. **5.** *Chem.* argon. **6.** *Chem., Physics.* See **mass number.**

a, *Metric System.* are; ares.

Å, *Physics.* angstrom unit.

a' (ä, ô), *adj. Scot.* all: *for a' that.*

a-[1], a reduced form of Old English prep. *on,* meaning "on," "in," "into," "to," "toward," preserved before a noun in a prepositional phrase, forming a predicate adjective or an adverbial element (*afoot; abed; ashore; aside*), and in archaic and dialectal use before a present participle in *-ing* (*set the bells aringing*). [ME, late OE]

a-[2], a reduced form of Old English prep. *of: akin; afresh; anew.* [ME]

a-[3], an old point-action prefix, not referring to an act as a whole, but only to the beginning or end: *She awoke* (became awake). *They abided by these conclusions* (remained faithful to the end). [ME; OE *ā-;* in some cases confused with A-[5], as in ABRIDGE]

a-[4], var. of **ab-** before *p* and *v: aperient; avert.* [ME < L *ā-, a-* (var. of *ab-* AB-); in some words < F *a-* < L *ab-,* as in ABRIDGE]

a-[5], var. of **ad-,** used: (1) before *sc, sp, st* (*ascend*) and (2) in words of French derivation (often with the sense of increase, addition): *amass.* [ME, in some words < MF *a-* < L *ad-* prefix or *ad* prep. (see AD-), as in ABUT; in others < L *a-* (var. of *ad-* AD-), as in ASCEND]

a-[6], var. of **an-**[1] before a consonant: *achromatic.*

A-, atomic (used in combination): *A-plant; A-ship.*

-a, a plural ending of nouns borrowed from Greek and Latin: *phenomena; criteria; data; errata.*

A., 1. Absolute. **2.** Academy. **3.** acre; acres. **4.** America. **5.** American. **6.** angstrom unit. **7.** year. [< L *annō,* abl. of *annus*] **8.** answer. **9.** before. [< L *ante*] **10.** April. **11.** Artillery.

a., 1. about. **2.** acre; acres. **3.** active. **4.** adjective. **5.** alto. **6.** ampere. **7.** year. [< L *annō,* abl. of *annus*] **8.** anonymous. **9.** answer. **10.** before. [< L *ante*] **11.** *Metric System.* are; ares. **12.** *Baseball.* assist; assists.

A-1, See **A one.**

a·a (ä′ä), *n.* basaltic lava having a rough surface. [< Hawaiian *a′ā*]

AA, See **Alcoholics Anonymous.**

A.A., 1. See **Alcoholics Anonymous. 2.** antiaircraft. **3.** antiaircraft artillery.

AAA, 1. Amateur Athletic Association. **2.** American Automobile Association. Also, **A.A.A.**

AAAA, Amateur Athletic Association of America.

A.A.A.L., American Academy of Arts and Letters.

A.A.A.S., American Association for the Advancement of Science. Also, **AAAS.**

Aa·chen (ä′kən; *Ger.* ä′ᴋʜən), *n.* a city in W West Germany. 174,300 (1963). French, **Aix-la-Chapelle.**

AAF, 1. Allied Air Forces. **2.** (formerly) Army Air Forces.

Aal·borg (ôl′bôrg), *n.* Ålborg.

Aa·le·sund (ô′lə so͞on′), *n.* Ålesund.

aa·li·i (ä lē′ē), *n.* a bushy shrub, *Dodonaea viscosa,* of Australia, Hawaii, Africa, and tropical America, having sticky foliage. [< Hawaiian]

Aalst (älst), *n.* Flemish name of **Alost.**

Aal·to (äl′tô), *n.* **Al·var** (äl′vär), 1898–1976, Finnish architect and furniture designer.

AAM, air-to-air missile.

A and M, Agricultural and Mechanical. Also, **A. and M.**

A & R, artists and repertory (used to refer to the profession of selecting recording artists, approving their music, and arranging its distribution and promotion).

Aar (är), *n.* a river in central Switzerland, flowing N to the Rhine. 175 mi. long. Also, **Aare.**

aard·vark (ärd′värk′), *n.* a large, nocturnal, burrowing mammal, *Orycteropus afer,* of Africa, feeding on ants and termites and having a long, extensile tongue, strong claws, and long ears. [< obs. SAfrD (replaced by *erdvark*) = *aarde* EARTH + *vark* pig; see FARROW[1]]

Aardvark
(2 ft. high at shoulder; total length 5½ ft.; tail to 2½ ft.)

aard·wolf (ärd′wo͝olf′), *n., pl.* **-wolves.** a striped, hyenalike African mammal, *Proteles cristatus,* that feeds chiefly on insects. [< SAfrD = *aarde* EARTH + *wolf* WOLF]

Aar·hus (ôr′ho͞os′), *n.* Århus.

Aar·on (âr′ən, ar′-), *n.* **1.** the brother of Moses, usually regarded as first high priest of Hebrews. Ex. 28; 40:13–16. **2. Henry (Louis)** ("*Hank*"), born 1934, U.S. baseball player.

Aa·ron·ic (â ron′ik), *adj.* of or pertaining to Aaron or to the order of Jewish priests descended from him. Also, **Aaronical.**

Aa·ron·i·cal (â ron′i kəl), *adj.* **1.** Aaronic. **2.** pontifical.

Aar′on's rod′, 1. a rod, inscribed with the name of Aaron, that miraculously blossomed and yielded almonds. Num. 17:8. **2.** any of various plants having a tall, flowering stem, as the goldenrod or mullein.

A.A.U., Amateur Athletic Union.

A.A.U.P., American Association of University Professors.

A.A.U.W., American Association of University Women.

Ab (ôv; *Heb.* äb), *n.* the eleventh month of the Jewish calendar. Also, **Av.** Cf. **Jewish calendar.** [< Heb *ābh*]

AB, a major blood group or type usually enabling a person whose blood is of this group to donate blood to persons of group AB and to receive blood from persons of group O, A, B, or AB.

Ab, *Chem.* alabamine.

ab-, a formal element occurring in loan words from Latin, where it meant "away from": *abdicate; abolition.* Also, **a-, abs-.** [< L *ab* prep. and prefix, from, away, c. Gk *apó,* Skt *apa,* G *ab,* E OF[1], OFF]

ab., 1. about. **2.** *Baseball.* (times) at bat.

A.B., 1. *Naut.* See **able seaman. 2.** See **Bachelor of Arts.** [< L *Artium Baccalaureus*]

a·ba (ə bä′, ä′bə), *n.* **1.** a fabric woven of camel's or goat's hair. **2.** a sleeveless outer garment made of this fabric or silk, worn by Arabs. [< Ar *ʻabā'(ah)*]

A.B.A., 1. American Bar Association. **2.** American Basketball Association.

a·ba·ca (ä′bä kä′, ä′bə-), *n.* **1.** a Philippine plant, *Musa textilis.* **2.** the fiber of this plant, used in making rope. [< Sp < Tagalog *abakā*]

a·back (ə bak′), *adv.* **1.** *Naut.* so that the wind presses against the forward side of the sail or sails. **2.** toward the back. **3. taken aback,** surprised and disconcerted. **—***adj.* **4.** *Naut.* (of a sail) in such a position that the wind presses against the forward side. [ME *abak,* OE *on bæc* to the rear]

ab·a·cus (ab′ə kəs, ə bak′əs), *n., pl.* **ab·a·cus·es, ab·a·ci** (ab′ə sī′, -kī′, ə bak′ī). **1.** a device for making arithmetic calculations, consisting of a frame set with rods on which balls or beads are moved. **2.** *Archit.* a slab forming the top of a capital. [< L; re-formed < Gk *ábax* board, counting board]

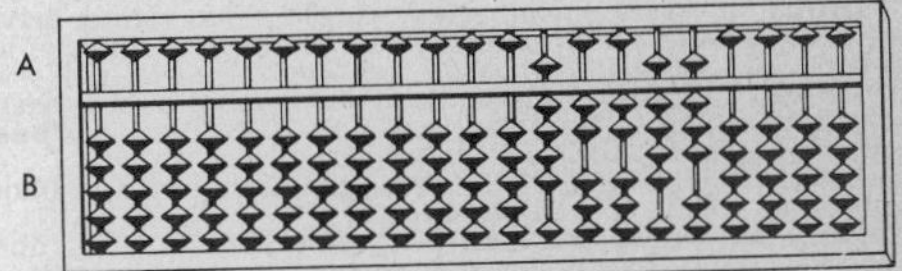

Abacus (Japanese)
Each vertical column = one integer: each bead in group A = 5 when lowered; each bead in group B = 1 when raised; value of this setting is 922,980,000

A·ba·dan (ä′bä dän′), *n.* a city in SW Iran, on the Shatt-al-Arab: oil refineries. 270,726 (est. 1967).

A·bad·don (ə bad′ən), *n.* **1.** Apollyon. **2.** a place of destruction; depths of hell. [< Heb *avhaddōn* destruction]

a·baft (ə baft′, ə bäft′), *Naut.* **—***prep.* **1.** to the rear of; aft of; behind. **—***adv.* **2.** in the direction of the stern; astern; aft. [ME *on baft, abaft* = *on* ON + *baft,* OE *bæftan.* See BY, AFT]

A·bai·lard (ᴀ bā ʟᴀʀ′), *n.* **Pierre** (pyeʀ), Abélard.

ab·a·lo·ne (ab′ə lō′nē), *n.* a large snail of the genus *Haliotis*, the flesh of which is used for food and the shell for ornament and as a source of mother-of-pearl. Also called **ear shell, sea ear.** [< AmerSp, var. of *abulón* < ?]

ab·am·pere (ab am′pēr, ab′am pēr′), *n.* *Elect.* the centimeter-gram-second unit of electromagnetic current, equivalent to 10 amperes. [*ab-* (prefix abstracted from ᴀʙsᴏʟᴜᴛᴇ, used for a cgs. electromagnetic unit) + ᴀᴍᴘᴇʀᴇ]

a·ban·don[1] (ə ban′dən), *v.t.* **1.** to leave or forsake completely and finally: *to abandon a sinking ship; to abandon a child.* **2.** to give up; discontinue; withdraw from: *to abandon a research project.* **3.** to give up the possession or control of: *to abandon a city to a conqueror.* **4.** to yield (oneself) utterly to one's emotions or to an impulse. **5.** *Law.* to cast away, leave, or desert, as property or a child. **6.** *Insurance.* to relinquish (insured property) to the underwriter in case of partial loss, thus enabling the insured to claim a total loss. **7.** *Obs.* to banish. [ME *abando(u)ne* < MF *abandon(er)* for OF *(mettre) a bandon* (put) under ban = *a* at, to (< L *ad;* see ᴀᴅ-) + *bandon* < LL *bandum*, var. of *bannum* interdict < Gmc; see ʙᴀɴ[2]] **—a·ban′don·a·ble,** *adj.* **—a·ban′don·er,** *n.* **—a·ban′don·ment,** *n.*
—Syn. 2. Aʙᴀɴᴅᴏɴ, ʀᴇʟɪɴǫᴜɪsʜ, ʀᴇɴᴏᴜɴᴄᴇ mean to give up all concern in something. Aʙᴀɴᴅᴏɴ means to give up or discontinue any further interest in something because of discouragement, weariness, distaste, or the like: *to abandon one's efforts.* Rᴇʟɪɴǫᴜɪsʜ implies being or feeling compelled to give up something one would prefer to keep: *to relinquish a long-cherished desire.* Rᴇɴᴏᴜɴᴄᴇ implies making (and perhaps formally stating) a voluntary decision to give something up: *to renounce worldly pleasures.* See also **desert**[2]. **3.** yield, surrender, resign, abdicate.

a·ban·don[2] (ə ban′dən), *n.* a complete surrender to natural impulses without restraint or moderation; freedom from constraint or conventionality: *to dance with reckless abandon.* [< F, back formation from *abandonner* to ᴀʙᴀɴᴅᴏɴ[1]]

a·ban·doned (ə ban′dənd), *adj.* **1.** forsaken; deserted: *an abandoned child; an abandoned cabin.* **2.** unrestrained; uncontrolled. **3.** utterly lacking in moral restraints; shameless. [ME] **—a·ban′doned·ly,** *adv.* **—Syn. 3.** See **immoral.**

à bas (ᴀ bä′), *French.* down with. [lit., to the bottom]

a·base (ə bās′), *v.t.*, **a·based, a·bas·ing.** **1.** to reduce or lower, as in rank, office, reputation, or estimation; humble; degrade. **2.** *Archaic.* to lower; put or bring down. [ᴀ-[5] + ʙᴀsᴇ[2]; r. late ME *abaisse, abesse* < MF *abaiss(ier)* = *a-* ᴀ-[5] + *baissier* to make low; see ʙᴀss[1]] **—a·base′ment,** *n.* **—a·bas′er,** *n.* **—Syn. 1.** humiliate. **—Ant. 1.** elevate, exalt.

a·bash (ə bash′), *v.t.* to make ashamed or embarrassed. [ME *aba(i)sshe* < AF *abaiss-*, var. of MF *esbaiss-*, long s. of *esbair* (F *ébahir*) to be surprised (*es-* ᴇx-[1] + *bair* to gape)] **—a·bash·ed·ly** (ə bash′id lē), *adv.* **—a·bash′ed·ness,** *n.* **—a·bash′ment,** *n.* **—Syn.** shame, discompose.

a·bate (ə bāt′), *v.*, **a·bat·ed, a·bat·ing.** **—***v.t.* **1.** to reduce in amount, degree, intensity, worth, etc.; lessen; diminish. **2.** *Law.* **a.** to put an end to or suppress (a nuisance). **b.** to annul (a writ). **3.** to deduct or subtract. **4.** to omit. **5.** to remove or hammer down (a portion of a surface) in order to produce a figure or pattern in low relief. **—***v.i.* **6.** to decrease or diminish in intensity, amount, worth, etc. [late ME < MF *abat(re)* = *a-* ᴀ-[5] + *batre* < LL *batere* for L *batuere* to beat] **—a·bat′a·ble,** *adj.* **—a·bat′er;** *Law.* **a·ba′tor,** *n.* **—Syn. 6.** subside. **—Ant. 1, 6.** increase, intensify.

a·bate·ment (ə bāt′mənt), *n.* **1.** the act or state of abating. **2.** the state of being abated. **3.** suppression or termination: *abatement of a nuisance.* **4.** an amount deducted or subtracted, as from the usual price, the full tax, etc. **5.** *Law.* **a.** a decrease in the legacies of a will when the assets of an estate are insufficient to pay all general legacies in full. **b.** a reduction of a tax assessment. [< MF] **—Syn. 1.** lessening, letup, diminution. **3.** end, cessation. **—Ant. 1, 2.** intensification, increase.

ab·a·tis (ab′ə tē′, -tis, ə bat′ē, ə bat′is), *n.*, *pl.* **ab·a·tis** (ab′ə tēz′, ə bat′ēz), **ab·a·tis·es** (ab′ə tis′iz, ə bat′i siz). an obstacle of trees with bent or sharpened branches directed toward an enemy, now often interlaced with barbed wire. [< F; OF *abateis* < LL **abateticius*]

A battery, *Electronics.* an electric battery for heating the filament or cathode heater of an electron tube. Cf. **B battery, C battery.**

ab·at·toir (ab′ə twär′), *n.* a slaughterhouse. [< F = *abatt(re)* (to) slaughter (see ᴀʙᴀᴛᴇ) + *-oir* -ᴏʀʏ[2]]

ab·ax·i·al (ab ak′sē əl), *adj.* being or situated away from the axis: *the abaxial surface of a leaf.*

Ab·ba (ab′ə), *n.* (*sometimes l.c.*) **1.** a title of reverence for bishops and patriarchs in certain Eastern churches. **2.** *New Testament.* a title of reverence for God, used esp. in prayers; Father. Mark 14:36; Rom. 8:15; Gal. 4:6. [< Aram *abbā* father]

ab·ba·cy (ab′ə sē), *n.*, *pl.* **-cies.** **1.** the rank, rights, privileges, or jurisdiction of an abbot. **2.** the term of office of an abbot. [< LL *abbātia* = *abbāt-* (see ᴀʙʙᴏᴛ) + *-ia* -ɪᴀ]

Ab·bas·id (ab′ə sid, ə bas′id), *n.* a member of a dynasty of caliphs ruling at Baghdad, ᴀ.ᴅ. 750–1258. Also, **Ab′bas·sid, Ab·bas·side** (ab′ə sīd′, ə bas′īd).

ab·ba·tial (ə bā′shəl), *adj.* of or pertaining to an abbot, abbess, or abbey. [< LL *abbātiāl(is)*]

ab·bé (a bā′, ab′ā; *Fr.* ᴀ bā′), *n.*, *pl.* **ab·bés** (a bāz′, ab′āz; *Fr.* ᴀ bā′). (esp. in France) **1.** an abbot. **2.** a title of respect for any ecclesiastic or clergyman. [< F < LL *abbāt-* ᴀʙʙᴏᴛ]

ab·bess (ab′is), *n.* the female superior of a convent of nuns. [ME *abbesse* < OF *abbesse, abaesse* < LL *abbātissa*, fem. of *abbāt-* ᴀʙʙᴏᴛ]

Ab·be·ville (ab′ē vil′; *Fr.* ᴀb vēl′), *n.* a town in N France, on the Somme River. 22,816 (1962).

Abbe·vill·i·an (ab vil′ē ən, -vil′yən, ab′ə vil′-), *adj.* of, pertaining to, or characteristic of a Paleolithic culture in which crude stone hand axes were produced; Chellean. Also, **Abbe·vil′e·an.**

ab·bey (ab′ē), *n.*, *pl.* **-beys.** **1.** a monastery under the supervision of an abbot or a convent under the supervision of an abbess. **2.** the group of buildings comprising such a monastery or convent. **3.** the church of an abbey. **4.** *Brit.* a country residence that was formerly an abbatial house: *Newstead Abbey.* [ME < OF *abeie* < LL *abbātia* ᴀʙʙᴀᴄʏ]

Ab′bey The′atre, a theater in Dublin associated with the Irish National Theatre Society (founded 1901) and the dramas of Synge, Yeats, and Lady Gregory.

ab·bot (ab′ət), *n.* the head or superior of a monastery. [ME, var. of *abbat* < L *abbāt-* (s. of *abbās*) < Gk < Aram *abbā* ᴀʙʙᴀ; r. ME, OE *abbod* < LL *abbād-* for L *abbāt-*] **—ab′bot·cy, ab′bot·ship′,** *n.*

Ab·bots·ford (ab′əts fərd), *n.* Sir Walter Scott's residence from 1812 to 1832, near Melrose, in SE Scotland.

Ab·bott (ab′ət), *n.* **1. Edith,** 1876–1957, and her sister, **Grace,** 1878–1939, U.S. social reformers. **2. Jacob,** 1803–1879, and his son, **Ly·man** (lī′mən), 1835–1922, U.S. clergymen and writers.

abbr., abbreviation. Also, **abbrev.**

ab·bre·vi·ate (ə brē′vē āt′), *v.t.*, **-at·ed, -at·ing.** **1.** to shorten (a word or phrase) by omitting letters, substituting shorter forms, etc., as *ft.* for *foot, ab.* for *about, R.I.* for *Rhode Island, NW* for *Northwest,* or *Xn* for *Christian.* **2.** to reduce (anything) in length, duration, etc.; make briefer. [< L *abbreviāt(us)* shortened (ptp. of *abbreviāre*) = *ad-* ᴀᴅ- + *breviātus* (*brevi(s)* short + *-ātus* -ᴀᴛᴇ[1])] **—ab·bre′vi·a′tor,** *n.* **—Syn.** See **shorten.**

ab·bre·vi·at·ed (ə brē′vē ā′tid), *adj.* **1.** shortened; made briefer. **2.** (of clothing) scanty; barely covering the body. **3.** constituting a shorter form of: *an abbreviated ladder.*

ab·bre·vi·a·tion (ə brē′vē ā′shən), *n.* **1.** a shortened or contracted form of a word or phrase, used to represent the whole. **2.** the act of abbreviating. **3.** the state or result of being abbreviated. [< L *abbreviātiōn-* (s. of *abbreviātiō*)]

ABC, atomic, biological, and chemical: *ABC warfare.*

ab·cou·lomb (ab ko͞o′lom, ab′ko͞o lom′), *n.* *Elect.* the centimeter-gram-second unit of quantity of electricity, equivalent to 10 coulombs. [*ab-* (see ᴀʙᴀᴍᴘᴇʀᴇ) + ᴄᴏᴜʟᴏᴍʙ]

ABC's (ā′bē′sēz′), *n.pl.* **1.** the basic or elementary facts, principles, etc., of a subject: *the ABC's of electricity.* **2.** the alphabet. Also, **ABCs.**

Abd-el-Ka·dir (äb′del kä′dēr), *n.* 1807?–83, Algerian leader. Also, **Abd·al·Ka·dir** (äb′dal kä′dēr).

Abd-el Krim (äb′del krēm′, krim′), 1881?–1963, Moroccan chief: leader of the Riffian revolts 1921, 1924.

ab·di·cate (ab′də kāt′), *v.*, **-cat·ed, -cat·ing.** **—***v.i.* **1.** to renounce or relinquish a throne, right, power, claim, or the like, esp. in a formal manner. **—***v.t.* **2.** to give up or renounce (authority, duties, an office, etc.), esp. in a voluntary, public, or formal manner. [< L *abdicāt(us)* renounced (ptp. of *abdicāre*) = *ab-* ᴀʙ- + *dicātus* dedicated (*dic-* (see ᴅɪᴄᴛᴜᴍ) + *-ātus* -ᴀᴛᴇ[1])] **—ab·di·ca·ble** (ab′də kə bəl), *adj.* **—ab·di·ca·tive** (ab′də kā′tiv, -kə-), *adj.* **—ab′di·ca′tor,** *n.* **—Syn. 2.** abandon, repudiate.

ab·di·ca·tion (ab′də kā′shən), *n.* the act or state of abdicating, esp. of sovereign power. [< L *abdicātiōn-* (s. of *abdicātiō*)]

ab·do·men (ab′də mən, ab dō′-), *n.* **1.** *Anat., Zool.* **a.** the part of the body of a mammal between the thorax and the pelvis; belly. **b.** the cavity of this part of the body, containing most of the digestive organs. **2.** (in vertebrates below mammals) a region of the body corresponding to, but not coincident with, this part or cavity. **3.** *Entomol.* the posterior section of the body of an arthropod, behind the thorax or the cephalothorax. [< L: belly < ?]

ab·dom·i·nal (ab dom′ə nᵊl), *adj.* of, in, on, or for the abdomen. [< L *abdomin-* (s. of *abdōmen*) ᴀʙᴅᴏᴍᴇɴ + -ᴀʟ[1]] **—ab·dom′i·nal·ly,** *adv.*

ab·dom·i·nous (ab dom′ə nəs), *adj.* having a large belly; potbellied. [< L *abdomin-* (see ᴀʙᴅᴏᴍɪɴᴀʟ) + -ᴏᴜs]

ab·duce (ab do͞os′, -dyo͞os′), *v.t.*, **-duced, -duc·ing.** to draw or take away; abduct. [< L *abdūc(re)* = *ab-* ᴀʙ- + *dūcere* to lead]

ab·du·cent (ab do͞o′sənt, -dyo͞o′-), *adj.* *Physiol.* drawing away, as by the action of a muscle; abducting. [< L *abdūcent-* (s. of *abdūcens*)]

ab·duct (ab dukt′), *v.t.* **1.** to carry off or lead away (a person) illegally and in secret or by force, esp. to kidnap. **2.** *Physiol.* to move or draw away from the axis of the body or from one of its parts (opposed to *adduct*). [< L *abduct(us)*, ptp. of *abdūcere* to ᴀʙᴅᴜᴄᴇ]

ab·duc·tion (ab duk′shən), *n.* **1.** act of abducting. **2.** the state of being abducted. [< F < L *abduct(us)* (see ᴀʙᴅᴜᴄᴛ) + F *-ion* -ɪᴏɴ]

ab·duc·tor[1] (ab duk′tər), *n.* any muscle that abducts (opposed to *adductor*). [< NL; see ᴀʙᴅᴜᴄᴛ, -ᴏʀ[2]]

ab·duc·tor[2] (ab duk′tər), *n.* a person who abducts. [ᴀʙᴅᴜᴄᴛ + -ᴏʀ[2]]

Ab·dul-Ha·mid II (äb′do͝ol hä mēd′), 1842–1918, sultan of Turkey 1876–1909.

a·beam (ə bēm′), *adv., adj.* *Naut., Aeron.* at right angles to the fore-and-aft line: *to sail with the wind directly abeam.*

a·be·ce·dar·i·an (ā′bē sē dâr′ē ən), *n.* **1.** a person who is learning the letters of the alphabet. **2.** a beginner in any field of learning. **—***adj.* **3.** of or pertaining to the alphabet. **4.** in alphabetical order. **5.** rudimentary; elementary; primary. [< ML *abecedāriān(us)* = LL *abecedāri(us)* (*a be ce d(e)* + *-ārius* -ᴀʀʏ) + *-ānus* -ᴀɴ]

a·bed (ə bed′), *adv.* **1.** in bed: *to stay abed late on Sundays.* **2.** confined to bed.

A·bed·ne·go (ə bed′nə gō′), *n.* a companion of Daniel. Cf. **Shadrach.**

A·bel (ā′bəl; *for 4 also Norw.* ä′bəl), *n.* **1.** the second son of Adam and Eve, slain by his brother, Cain. Gen. 4. **2. Sir Frederick Augustus,** 1827–1902, English chemist. **3. I. W.,** born 1908, U.S. labor leader: president of the United Steelworkers of America since 1965. **4. Niels Hen·rik** (nēls hen′ʀik), 1802–29, Norwegian mathematician.

Ab·é·lard (ab′ə lärd′; *Fr.* ᴀ bā ʟᴀʀ′), *n.* **Pierre** (pyeʀ), (*Peter Abelard*), 1079–1142, French scholastic philosopher, teacher, and theologian. Also, **Abailard.** Cf. **Héloïse.**

a·bele (ə bēl′, ā′bəl), *n.* the white poplar tree, *Populus alba.* [< D *abeel* < north F *a(u)biel*, irreg. < L *albus* white]

A·be·li·an (ə bē′lē ən, ə bēl′yən), *adj.* *Math.* **1.** of or pertaining to Niels Henrik Abel or his theorems. **2.** pertaining to an algebraic system in which an operation is commutative: *an Abelian group.* **3.** pertaining to such an operation.

a·bel·mosk (ā′bəl mosk′), *n.* a tropical, malvaceous plant, *Hibiscus Abelmoschus*, cultivated for its musky seeds, which yield a valuable oil. [< NL *abelmosch(us)* < Ar *abu'l misk* father of musk]

A·be·o·ku·ta (ä′bā ō′kŏŏ tä), *n.* a city in SW Nigeria. 187,292 (1963).

Ab·er·deen (ab′ər dēn′; *also, for 1, 2,* ab′ər dēn′), *n.* **1.** Also called **Ab·er·deen·shire** (ab′ər dēn′shēr, -shər). a county in NE Scotland. 298,503 (1961); 1974 sq. mi. **2.** its county seat, a seaport on the North Sea. 185,034 (est. 1964). **3.** a city in NE South Dakota. 26,476 (1970). **—Ab·er·do·ni·an** (ab′ər dō′nē ən), *adj., n.*

Ab′erdeen An′gus, one of a breed of hornless beef cattle raised originally in Scotland and having a smooth, black coat.

Ab′erdeen ter′rier. See **Scottish terrier.**

Ab·er·na·thy (ab′ər nath′ē), *n.* **Ralph David,** born 1926, U.S. pastor: president of the Southern Christian Leadership Conference 1968–77.

ab·er·rant (ə ber′ənt, ab′ər-), *adj.* **1.** straying from the right, normal, or usual course. **2.** deviating from the ordinary, usual, or normal type; exceptional; abnormal. [< L *aberrant-* (s. of *aberrāns*, prp. of *aberrāre* to deviate)] **—ab·er′rance, ab·er′ran·cy,** *n.* **—Syn. 1.** wandering. **2.** divergent, unusual.

ab·er·ra·tion (ab′ə rā′shən), *n.* **1.** deviation from what is common, normal, or right. **2.** deviation from truth or moral rectitude. **3.** mental irregularity or disorder, esp. of a minor nature. **4.** *Astron.* apparent displacement of a heavenly body owing to the motion of the earth in its orbit. **5.** *Optics.* any disturbance of the rays of a pencil of light such that they can no longer be brought to a sharp focus or form a clear image. [< L *aberrātiōn-* (s. of *aberrātiō*) = *aberrāt(us)* (ptp. of *aberrāre*; see ABERRANT) + *-iōn-* -ION] **—ab′er·ra′tion·al,** *adj.* **—Syn. 1.** divergence. **3.** illusion, delusion.

a·bet (ə bet′), *v.t.*, **a·bet·ted, a·bet·ting.** to encourage, support, or countenance by aid or approval, usually in wrongdoing. [ME *abette* (whence OF *abeter*), OE **abǣtan* to hound on = *ā-* A-³ + *bǣtan* to bait, akin to BITE] **—a·bet′ment, a·bet′tal,** *n.* **—a·bet′tor, a·bet′ter,** *n.* **—Syn.** help, aid, assist.

ab ex·tra (äb ek′strä; *Eng.* ab ek′strə), *Latin.* from outside; from without.

a·bey·ance (ə bā′əns), *n.* **1.** temporary inactivity, cessation, or suspension: *to hold a problem in abeyance.* **2.** *Law.* a state or condition of real property in which title is not yet vested in a known titleholder: *an estate in abeyance.* [< AF (= OF *abeance*) aspiration, lit., a gaping toward]

a·bey·ant (ə bā′ənt), *adj.* temporarily inactive or suspended. [ABEY(ANCE) + -ANT]

ab·far·ad (ab far′ad, -əd), *n.* *Elect.* the centimeter-gram-second unit of capacitance, equivalent to 10^9 farads. [*ab-* (see ABAMPERE) + FARAD]

ab·hen·ry (ab hen′rē), *n., pl.* **-ries.** *Elect.* the centimeter-gram-second unit of inductance, equivalent to 10^{-9} henry. [*ab-* (see ABAMPERE) + HENRY]

ab·hor (ab hôr′), *v.t.*, **-horred, -hor·ring.** to regard with extreme repugnance; detest utterly; loathe. [< L *abhorr(ēre)* (to) shrink back from, shudder at = *ab-* AB- + *horrēre* to bristle, tremble] **—ab·hor′rer,** *n.* **—Syn.** despise. See **hate.**

ab·hor·rence (ab hôr′əns, -hor′-), *n.* **1.** a feeling of extreme repugnance; utter loathing; detestation. **2.** something or someone abhorred. [ABHORR(ENT) + -ENCE]

ab·hor·rent (ab hôr′ənt, -hor′-), *adj.* **1.** feeling extreme repugnance (usually fol. by *of*). **2.** utterly opposed or in conflict (usually fol. by *to*): *abhorrent to reason.* **3.** causing repugnance or loathing; abominable: *an abhorrent deed.* **4.** remote in character (usually fol. by *from*): *abhorrent from the principles of law.* [< L *abhorrent-* (s. of *abhorrēns*, prp. of *abhorrēre*)] **—ab·hor′rent·ly,** *adv.*

A·bib (ā′bib; *Heb.* ä bēb′), *n.* *Chiefly Biblical.* the month equivalent to Nisan of the modern Jewish calendar. Ex. 34:18. [< Heb *ābhībh*: lit., ear of grain]

a·bid·ance (ə bīd′ᵊns), *n.* **1.** the act or state of abiding. **2.** conformity; compliance (usually fol. by *by*).

a·bide (ə bīd′), *v.*, **a·bode** or **a·bid·ed, a·bid·ing.** **—***v.i.* **1.** to remain; continue; stay: *Abide with me.* **2.** to have one's abode; dwell; reside. **3.** to continue in a particular condition, attitude, relationship, etc.; last. **—***v.t.* **4.** to wait for; await: *to abide the coming of the Lord.* **5.** to endure, tolerate, sustain, or withstand. **6.** to accept without opposition or question. **7.** to pay the price or penalty of; suffer for. **8.** **abide by, a.** to act in accord with. **b.** to submit to; agree to. **c.** to remain steadfast or faithful to: *If you make a promise, abide by it.* [ME *abide(n)*, OE *ābīdan*] **—a·bid′er,** *n.* **—Syn. 1.** tarry. **2.** live. **5.** bear.

a·bid·ing (ə bī′diŋ), *adj.* continuing without change; enduring; steadfast: *an abiding faith.* [ME] **—a·bid′ing·ly,** *adv.* **—a·bid′ing·ness,** *n.*

Ab·i·djan (ab′i jän′; *Fr.* A bē jäN′), *n.* a seaport in and capital of the Ivory Coast. 850,000.

ab′i·et′ic ac′id (ab′ē et′ik, ab′-), *Chem.* a water-insoluble acid, $C_{19}H_{29}COOH$, obtained from a species of pine: used chiefly in varnishes and soaps. [< L *abiet-* (s. of *abiēs*) fir + -IC]

ab·i·gail (ab′ə gāl′), *n.* a lady's maid. [after *Abigail*, name of attendant in play *The Scornful Lady* (1610), by Francis Beaumont and John Fletcher]

Ab·i·gail (ab′ə gāl′), *n.* the wife of Nabal and later of David. I Sam. 25.

Ab·i·lene (ab′ə lēn′), *n.* **1.** a city in central Texas. 89,653 (1970). **2.** a town in central Kansas: childhood home of Dwight Eisenhower. 6661 (1970).

a·bil·i·ty (ə bil′i tē), *n., pl.* **-ties.** **1.** power or capacity to act physically, mentally, legally, morally, financially, etc. **2.** competence in an activity or occupation. **3.** **abilities,** talents; special skills or aptitudes. [ME *(h)abilite* < MF < L *habilitās* aptitude = *habili(s)* handy (see ABLE) + *-tās* -TY²; r. ME *ablete* < F < L] **—Syn. 1.** capability; proficiency, expertness, dexterity. **2.** ABILITY, FACULTY, TALENT denote mental qualifications or powers. ABILITY is a general word for mental power, native or acquired, enabling one to do things well: *a person of great ability; ability in mathematics.* FACULTY denotes a natural ability for a particular kind of action: *a faculty of saying what he means.* TALENT is often used to mean a native ability or aptitude in a special field: *a talent for music or art.*

-ability, a combination of **-able** and **-ity,** used to form nouns from stems in **-able:** *capability.* [ME *-abilite* << L *-abilitās*]

A·bim·e·lech (ə bim′ə lek′), *n.* either of two kings of Gerar. Gen. 20:1–18; 26:1–33.

Ab·ing·don (ab′iŋ dən), *n.* a town in N Berkshire, in S England, on the Thames: site of Benedictine abbey founded 7th century A.D. 14,283 (1961).

ab in·i·ti·o (äb i nit′ē ō′; *Eng.* ab i nish′ē ō′), *Latin.* from the beginning.

ab in·tra (äb in′trä; *Eng.* ab in′trə), *Latin.* from inside; from within.

a·bi·o·gen·e·sis (ā′bī ō jen′i sis, ab′ē ō-), *n.* *Biol.* the production of living organisms from inanimate matter; spontaneous generation. [< NL] **—a·bi·og·e·nist** (ā′bī oj′ə nist, ab′ē-), *n.*

a·bi·o·ge·net·ic (ā′bī ō jə net′ik, ab′ē ō-), *adj.* *Biol.* of or pertaining to abiogenesis. Also, **a′bi·o·ge·net′i·cal.** [< NL *abiogenetic(us)*] **—a′bi·o·ge·net′i·cal·ly,** *adv.*

a·bi·o·sis (ā′bī ō′sis, ab′ē-), *n.* the absence or lack of life; a nonviable state. [A-⁶ + Gk *bíōsis* way of life; see BIO-, -OSIS]

a·bi·ot·ic (ā′bī ot′ik), *adj.* pertaining to or characterized by the absence of life or living organisms. Also, **a′bi·ot′i·cal.** **—a′bi·ot′i·cal·ly,** *adv.*

ab·ir·ri·tant (ab ir′i tᵊnt), *n.* *Med.* a soothing agent.

ab·ir·ri·tate (ab ir′i tāt′), *v.t.*, **-tat·ed, -tat·ing.** *Med.* to make less irritable. **—ab·ir′ri·ta′tion,** *n.* **—ab·ir′ri·ta′tive,** *adj.*

ab·ject (ab′jekt, ab jekt′), *adj.* **1.** utterly hopeless, humiliating, or wretched: *abject poverty.* **2.** contemptible; despicable; base-spirited: *an abject coward.* **3.** shamelessly servile. **4.** *Obs.* cast aside. [< L *abject(us)* thrown down (ptp. of *abicere, abjicere*) = *ab-* AB- + *-jec-* throw + *-tus* ptp. suffix] **—ab·jec′tion,** *n.* **—ab·ject·ly** (ab jekt′lē, ab′jekt lē), *adv.* **—ab·ject′ness, ab·ject′ed·ness,** *n.* **—Syn. 1.** miserable. **2.** base, mean, low, vile.

ab·ju·ra·tion (ab′jŏŏ rā′shən), *n.* **1.** the act of abjuring. **2.** renunciation upon oath. [< ML *abjūrātiōn-* (s. of *abjūrātiō*) = *abjūrāt(us)* denied on oath (ptp. of *abjūrāre*; see ABJURE, -ATE¹) + *-iōn-* -ION]

ab·jure (ab jŏŏr′), *v.t.*, **-jured, -jur·ing.** **1.** to renounce, repudiate, or retract, esp. with solemnity. **2.** to renounce or give up under oath. **3.** to avoid or shun. [late ME < L *abjūr(āre)* (to) deny on oath = *ab-* AB- + *jūrāre* to swear; see JURY¹] **—ab·jur′a·to′ry,** *adj.* **—ab·jur′er,** *n.*

Ab·kha·zi·a (äb khä′zē ä; *Eng.* ab kā′zhə, -zē ə), *n.* an administrative division of NW Georgia, in the SE Soviet Union, on the E coast of the Black Sea. 507,000; 3360 sq. mi. *Cap.:* Sukhum. Also, **Ab·kha′si·a.** Official name, **Ab′khaz Auton′omous So′viet So′cialist Repub′lic** (ab′kaz; *Russ.* äb khäz′).

abl., ablative.

ab·la·tion (ab lā′shən), *n.* **1.** removal, esp. of organs, abnormal growths, or harmful substances, from the body by mechanical means, as by surgery. **2.** *Rocketry.* burning away of parts of a nose cone by heat generated in reentry. [< LL *ablātiōn-* (s. of *ablātiō*) = *ablāt(us)* carried away (ptp. of *auferre*; see AB-, BEAR¹, -ATE¹) + *-iōn-* -ION]

ab·la·tive¹ (ab′lə tiv), *Gram.* **—***adj.* **1.** (in some inflected languages) noting a case that has among its functions the indication of place from which, or, as in Latin, place in which, manner, means, instrument, agent, etc. **—***n.* **2.** the ablative case. **3.** a word in that case. [< L *ablātīv(us)*. See ABLATION, -IVE] **—ab·la·ti·val** (ab′lə tī′vəl), *adj.*

ab·la·tive² (ab lā′tiv), *adj.* capable of or susceptible to ablation.

ab′lative ab′solute, *Latin Gram.* a construction not dependent upon any other part of the sentence, consisting of a noun and a participle, noun and adjective, or two nouns, in which both members are in the ablative case, as Latin *viā factā*, "the road having been made."

ab·laut (äb′lout, ab′-; *Ger.* äp′lout), *n.* *Gram.* (in Indo-European languages) regular alternation of a word element, esp. of a vowel, indicating a change in grammatical function, as in English *sing, sang, sung, song.* [< G = *ab-* off + *Laut* sound]

a·blaze (ə blāz′), *adj.* **1.** burning; on fire. **2.** gleaming or brilliant, as with bright lights, bold colors, etc. **3.** excited; eager; zealous; ardent.

a·ble (ā′bəl), *adj.*, **a·bler, a·blest,** *n.* **—***adj.* **1.** having necessary power, skill, resources, or qualifications: *able to lift a trunk; able to write music; able to vote.* **2.** having or showing confidence, intelligence, skill, etc.: *an able minister; an able speech.* **—***n.* **3.** (*usually cap.*) a code word formerly used in communications to represent the letter *A*. [ME < MF < L *habil(is)* handy = *hab(ēre)* (to) have, hold + *-ilis* -ILE] **—Syn. 1.** fit, fitted. ABLE, CAPABLE, COMPETENT all mean possessing adequate power for doing something. ABLE implies power equal to effort required: *able to finish in time.* CAPABLE implies power to meet or fulfill ordinary, usual requirements: *a capable workman.* COMPETENT suggests power to meet demands in a completely satisfactory manner: *a competent nurse.* **2.** talented; skilled.

-able, a suffix, associated in meaning with the word **able,** occurring in loan words from Latin (*laudable*); used in English as a highly productive suffix to form adjectives by addition to stems of any origin (*teachable; photographable*). Also, **-ble, -ible.** [ME < OF < L *-ābilis* adj. suffix]

a·ble-bod·ied (ā′bəl bod′ēd), *adj.* having a strong, healthy body; physically fit. **—a′ble-bod′ied·ness,** *n.*

ab·le·gate (ab′lə gāt′), *n.* a papal envoy to a newly appointed church dignitary. [< L *ablēgāt(us)* sent away (ptp. of *ablēgāre*) = *ab-* AB- + *-lēg-* send (on a mission) + *-ātus* -ATE¹]

a′ble sea′man, a member of the deck department of a merchant vessel, certified to have certain skills. *Abbr.:* A.B. Also called **a′ble-bodied sea′man.**

a·blins (ā′blinz), *adv.* *Scot.* perhaps. Also, **a′blings, aiblins.** [ABLE + -LING² + -S¹]

ab·lu·tion (ab lo͞o′shən, ə blo͞o′-), *n.* **1.** a cleansing with water or other liquid, esp. as a religious ritual. **2.** the liquid used. **3.** a washing of the hands, body, etc. [ME < L *ablūtiōn-* (s. of *ablūtiō*) = *ablūt(us)* washed away, ptp. of *ablūere* (*ab-* AB- + *-lū-* wash + *-tus* ptp. suffix) + *-iōn-* -ION] —**ab·lu′tion·ar′y,** *adj.*

a·bly (ā′blē), *adv.* in an able manner; with skill.

-ably, a combination of **-able** and **-ly** used to form adverbs by addition to stems in **-able:** *probably.* Also, **-bly, -ibly.**

ABM, antiballistic missile.

ab·mho (ab′mō), *n., pl.* **-mhos.** *Elect.* the centimeter-gram-second unit of conductance, equivalent to 10^9 mhos. [*ab-* (see ABAMPERE) + MHO]

ab·ne·gate (ab′nə gāt′), *v.t.,* **-gat·ed, -gat·ing.** **1.** to refuse or deny oneself (rights, conveniences, etc.); reject; renounce. **2.** to relinquish; give up. [< L *abnegāt(us)* denied (ptp. of *abnegāre*)] —**ab′ne·ga′tion,** *n.* —**ab′ne·ga′tor,** *n.*

ab·nor·mal (ab nôr′məl), *adj.* **1.** not average, typical, or usual; deviating from the normal. **2.** extremely or excessively large: *abnormal profit.* [AB- + NORMAL; r. *anormal* < ML *anōrmāl(us),* var. of *anōmālus* ANOMALOUS] —**ab·nor′mal·ly,** *adv.* —**ab·nor′mal·ness,** *n.* —**Syn. 1.** anomalous, aberrant, deviant, unnatural. See **irregular.**

ab·nor·mal·i·ty (ab′nôr mal′i tē), *n., pl.* **-ties.** **1.** an abnormal thing or event. **2.** an abnormal condition, state, or quality; deviation. —**Syn.** anomaly, aberration, peculiarity.

abnor′mal psychol′ogy, the branch of psychology that deals with modes of behavior, mental phenomena, etc., that deviate widely from the average.

ab·nor·mi·ty (ab nôr′mi tē), *n., pl.* **-ties.** **1.** an abnormal condition, quality, etc. **2.** a malformation or monstrosity. [< LL *abnōrmitās* = *abnōrm(is)* (*ab-* AB- + *nōrm(a)* rule + *-is* adj. suffix) + *-itās* -ITY]

ab·o (ab′ō), *n., pl.* **ab·os,** *adj.* *Australian.* —*n.* **1.** an aborigine. —*adj.* **2.** aboriginal. [by shortening]

Å·bo (ô′bo͞o), *n.* Swedish name of **Turku.**

a·board (ə bōrd′, ə bôrd′), *adv.* **1.** on board; on, in, or into a ship, train, etc. **2.** alongside; to the side. —*prep.* **3.** on board of; on, in, or into: *to come aboard a ship.*

a·bode¹ (ə bōd′), *n.* **1.** a place in which one resides; dwelling; habitation; home. **2.** an extended stay in a place. [ME *abood* a waiting, delay, stay; akin to ABIDE]

a·bode² (ə bōd′), *v.i., v.t.* a pt. and pp. of **abide.**

ab·ohm (ab ōm′, ab′ōm′), *n.* *Elect.* the centimeter-gram-second unit of resistance, equivalent to 10^{-9} ohm. [*ab-* (see ABAMPERE) + OHM]

a·bol·ish (ə bol′ish), *v.t.* **1.** to do away with; put an end to: *to abolish slavery.* **2.** to destroy totally. [late ME < MF *aboliss-* (long s. of *abolir*) < L *abolēsc(ere)* (to) wither = *abolē(re)* (to) efface (*ab-* AB- + *-ol-* grow) + *-sc-* inchoative suffix] —**a·bol′ish·a·ble,** *adj.* —**a·bol′ish·er,** *n.* —**a·bol′ish·ment,** *n.*

—**Syn.** suppress, nullify, cancel; annihilate, obliterate, extinguish; exterminate, extirpate, eliminate. ABOLISH, STAMP OUT, ERADICATE mean to do away completely with something. To ABOLISH is to cause to cease, often by a summary order: *to abolish a requirement.* STAMP OUT, stronger though less formal, implies forcibly making an end to something considered undesirable or harmful: *to stamp out the opium traffic.* ERADICATE, a formal word, suggests extirpation, leaving no vestige or trace: *to eradicate the dandelions in the lawn.*

ab·o·li·tion (ab′ə lish′ən), *n.* **1.** the act of abolishing. **2.** the state of being abolished; annulment; abrogation. **3.** (*often cap.*) the legal termination of Negro slavery in the U.S. [< L *abolitiōn-* (s. of *abolitiō*) = *abolit(us)* effaced, destroyed, ptp. of *abolēre* (*ab-* AB- + *-ol-* grow + *-itus* -ITE²) + *-iōn-* -ION] —**ab′o·li′tion·ar′y,** *adj.* —**Syn. 2.** annihilation, eradication, elimination, extinction; nullification, repeal.

ab·o·li·tion·ism (ab′ə lish′ə niz′əm), *n.* the principle or policy of abolition, esp. of Negro slavery in the U.S. —**ab′o·li′tion·ist,** *n.*

ab·o·ma·sum (ab′ə mā′səm), *n., pl.* **-sa** (-sə). the fourth or true stomach of cud-chewing animals, lying next to the omasum. [< NL]

A-bomb (ā′bom′), *n.* See **atomic bomb.**

a·bom·i·na·ble (ə bom′ə nə bəl), *adj.* **1.** repugnantly hateful; detestable; loathsome. **2.** very unpleasant; disagreeable: *abominable weather.* **3.** very bad, poor, or inferior: *She has abominable taste in clothes.* [late ME < L *abōminābil(is)* = *abōminā(rī)* (to) loathe as of ill omen (see AB-, OMEN) + *-bilis* -BLE] —**a·bom′i·na·ble·ness,** *n.* —**a·bom′i·na·bly,** *adv.* —**Syn. 1.** abhorrent, horrible, revolting, foul.

Abom′inable Snow′man, a large, hairy, manlike creature reported to inhabit the Himalayas. Also called **yeti.** [trans. of Tibetan *metohkangmi* = *metoh* foul + *kangmi* snowman]

a·bom·i·nate (ə bom′ə nāt′), *v.t.,* **-nat·ed, -nat·ing.** **1.** to regard with intense aversion or loathing; abhor. **2.** to dislike strongly. [< L *abōmināt(us)* loathed, ptp. of *abōminārī.* See ABOMINABLE, -ATE¹] —**a·bom′i·na′tor,** *n.* —**Syn. 1.** loathe, execrate. See **hate.**

a·bom·i·na·tion (ə bom′ə nā′shən), *n.* **1.** anything abominable; anything greatly disliked or abhorred. **2.** intense aversion or loathing; detestation. **3.** a vile, shameful, or detestable action, condition, habit, etc. [< LL *abōminātiōn-* (s. of *abōminātiō*)] —**Syn. 2.** hatred. **3.** depravity.

a·boon (ə bo͞on′), *adv., prep.* *Scot. and Brit. Dial.* above. [ME *abone, abowne*]

ab·o·ral (ab ōr′əl, -ôr′-), *adj.* *Anat., Zool.* opposite to or away from the mouth.

ab·o·rig·i·nal (ab′ə rij′ə nəl), *adj.* **1.** of or pertaining to aborigines; primitive: *aboriginal customs.* **2.** native; indigenous; original. —*n.* **3.** an aborigine. —**ab′o·rig′i·nal′i·ty,** *n.* —**ab′o·rig′i·nal·ly,** *adv.*

ab·o·rig·i·ne (ab′ə rij′ə nē), *n.* **1.** one of the original or earliest known inhabitants of a country or region, as a primitive tribesman of Australia. **2. aborigines,** the original fauna or flora of a region. [< L, based on phrase *ab origine* from the very first]

a·born·ing (ə bôr′ning), *adj.* being born; coming into being, fruition, realization, etc. [A-¹ + BORN + -ING²]

a·bort (ə bôrt′), *v.i.* **1.** to bring forth a fetus from the uterus before the fetus is viable; miscarry. **2.** to be developed incompletely. **3.** to fail, cease, or stop at an early or premature stage. **4.** *Mil.* (of an aircraft or missile) to fail to accomplish its purpose for any reason other than enemy action. **5.** *Rocketry.* to terminate a scheduled missile flight before it is completed. —*v.t.* **6.** to cause to bring forth a fetus from the uterus before the fetus is viable. **7.** to cause to cease or end at an early or premature stage, as a missile flight. [< L *abort(us)* miscarried (ptp. of *aborīrī* to disappear, miscarry) = *ab-* AB- + *-or-* come into being + *-tus* ptp. suffix]

a·bor·ti·cide (ə bôr′ti sīd′), *n.* **1.** destruction of a fetus in the uterus; feticide. **2.** an agent that causes abortion; abortifacient.

a·bor·ti·fa·cient (ə bôr′tə fā′shənt), *adj.* **1.** causing abortion. —*n.* **2.** a drug or other agent used to cause abortion.

a·bor·tion (ə bôr′shən), *n.* **1.** the expulsion of a human fetus within the first 12 weeks of pregnancy, before it is viable. Cf. **miscarriage** (def. 3). **2.** an immature and nonviable fetus. **3.** any malformed or monstrous person, thing, etc. **4.** *Biol.* the arrested development of an embryo or an organ at a more or less early stage. **5.** anything that fails to develop, progress, or mature, as a design or project. **6.** the stopping of an illness, infection, etc., at a very early stage. [< L *abortiōn-* (s. of *abortiō*)] —**a·bor′tion·al,** *adj.*

a·bor·tion·ist (ə bôr′shə nist), *n.* a person who performs or induces abortions illegally.

a·bor·tive (ə bôr′tiv), *adj.* **1.** failing to succeed; unsuccessful. **2.** born prematurely. **3.** imperfectly developed; rudimentary. **4.** *Med.* **a.** producing or intended to produce abortion; abortifacient. **b.** acting to halt progress of a disease. **5.** *Pathol.* (of the course of a disease) short and mild without the usual, pronounced clinical symptoms. [< L *abortīv(us)*] —**a·bor′tive·ly,** *adv.* —**a·bor′tive·ness,** *n.*

a·bought (ə bôt′), *v.* pt. and pp. of **aby.**

A·bou·kir (ä′bo͞o kēr′, ə bo͞o′kər), *n.* Abukir.

a·bound (ə bound′), *v.i.* **1.** to occur or exist in great quantities or numbers: *Trout abound in that brook.* **2.** to be rich or well supplied (usually fol. by *in*). **3.** to be filled; teem (usually fol. by *with*): *The brook abounds with trout.* [late ME *abounde* < L *abund(āre)* (to) overflow = *ab-* AB- + *undāre* to move in waves; see UNDULATE] —**a·bound′ing·ly,** *adv.*

a·bout (ə bout′), *prep.* **1.** of; concerning; in regard to: *instructions about the work; a movie about Pasteur.* **2.** connected or associated with: *There was an air of mystery about her.* **3.** in, on, or somewhere near: *He is about the house.* **4.** near; close to; more or less: *about my height.* **5.** on every side of; around: *the railing about the tower.* **6.** so as to be of use to: *Keep your wits about you.* **7.** on the verge or point of (usually fol. by an infinitive): *about to leave.* **8.** here or there; in or on: *to wander about the place.* **9.** engaged in doing: *while you're about it.* —*adv.* **10.** nearly; approximately: *to drive about a hundred miles.* **11.** nearly; almost: *He is about ready.* **12.** nearby; not far off: *He is somewhere about.* **13.** on every side; in every direction; around: *Look about and see if you can find it.* **14.** halfway around; in the opposite direction: *to turn a car about.* **15.** from one place to another; in this place or that: *to move furniture about; his papers strewn about.* **16.** in rotation or succession; alternately: *Turn about is fair play.* **17.** in circumference: *a wheel two inches about.* —*adj.* **18.** moving around; astir: *He was up and about while the rest of us still slept.* **19.** in existence; current; prevalent: *Smallpox is about.* **20.** *Naut.* **a.** onto a new tack. **b.** onto a new course. [ME *aboute(n),* OE *abūtan, onbūtan* on the outside of (*on* + *b(e)* BY + *ūtan,* c. Icel *ūtan,* OHG *ūzan(a)* outside)]

about′ face′, *U.S.* a military command to face to the rear in a prescribed manner while standing. Also called, *Brit.,* **about′ turn′.**

a·bout-face (*n.* ə bout′fās′, ə bout′fās′; *v.* ə bout′fās′), *n., v.,* **-faced, -fac·ing.** —*n.* **1.** a complete, sudden change in position, direction, principle, attitude, etc. —*v.i.* **2.** to turn in the opposite direction, switch to an opposite opinion, etc.

a·bout-ship (ə bout′ship′), *v.i.,* **-shipped, -ship·ping.** *Naut.* to tack.

a·bove (ə buv′), *adv.* **1.** in or to a higher place. **2.** overhead, upstairs, or in the sky: *My brother lives in the apartment above. A flock of birds circled above.* **3.** higher in rank, authority, or power: *appeal to the courts above.* **4.** higher in quantity or number: *books with 100 pages and above.* **5.** before or earlier, esp. in a book or other piece of writing: *the remark quoted above.* Cf. **below** (def. 5). **6.** in or to heaven: *gone to her eternal rest above.* **7.** *Zool.* on the upper or dorsal side. —*prep.* **8.** in or to a higher place than; over: *to fly above the clouds.* **9.** more in quantity or number than; in excess of: *all boys above 10 years of age.* **10.** superior in rank, authority, or standing to: *A captain is above a lieutenant.* **11.** not subject or liable to; not capable of (some undesirable action, thought, etc.): *above suspicion.* **12.** of too fine a character for: *above trickery.* **13.** in preference to: *to favor one son above another.* **14.** north of: *six miles above Baltimore.* **15.** *Theat.* upstage of. **16. above all,** most important of all; principally: *charity above all.* —*adj.* **17.** written above: *the above explanation.* —*n.* **18.** that which was written above: *to refer to the above.* **19.** the person or persons previously indicated: *The above will all stand trial.* **20.** heaven: *a gift from above.* [ME *above(n),* OE *abufan, onbufan* (*on* + *b(e)* BY + *ufan,* c. Icel *ofan,* G *oben* above)]

a·bove·board (ə buv′bōrd′, -bôrd′), *adv., adj.* in open sight; without tricks or disguise. [ABOVE + BOARD; so called from the requirement of keeping the hands above the table or board in order to discourage possible cheating at cards]

a·bove·ground (ə buv′ground′), *adj.* situated on or above the ground.

ab o·vo (äb ō′wō; *Eng.* ab ō′vō), *Latin.* from the beginning. [lit., from the egg]

abp., archbishop. Also, **Abp.**

abr., **1.** abridge. **2.** abridged. **3.** abridgment.

ab·ra·ca·dab·ra (ab′rə kə dab′rə), *n.* **1.** a mystical word used in incantations, on amulets, etc., as a magical means of warding off misfortune, harm, or illness. **2.** any charm or incantation using nonsensical or supposedly magical words. **3.** gibberish; jargon; nonsense. [< L]

a·bra·dant (ə brād′ənt), *n.* an abrasive.

a·brade (ə brād′), *v.t., v.i.,* **a·brad·ed, a·brad·ing.** **1.** to wear off or down by friction; erode. **2.** to scrape off. [< L *abrādere* = *ab-* AB- + *rādere* to scrape] —**a·brad′er,** *n.*

A·bra·ham (ā′brə ham′, -həm), *n.* the first of the great postdiluvian patriarchs, father of Isaac, and traditional founder of the ancient Hebrew nation.

A′braham's bos′om, heaven, considered as the reward of the righteous. Luke 16:22.

a·bran·chi·ate (ā braŋ′kē it, -āt′), *adj. Zool.* having no gills. Also, **a·bran·chi·al** (ā braŋ′kē əl). [A-[6] + Gk *bránchi(a)* (neut. pl.) gills + -ATE[1]]

a·bra·sion (ə brā′zhən), *n.* **1.** a scraped spot or area; the result of rubbing or abrading. **2.** the act or process of abrading. [< ML *abrāsiōn-* (s. of *abrāsiō*) = *abrās(us)* scraped off (ptp. of *abrādere;* see ABRADE) + *-iōn-* -ION]

a·bra·sive (ə brā′siv, -ziv), *n.* **1.** any material or substance used for grinding, polishing, or smoothing, as emery, pumice, or sandpaper. **—*adj.* 2.** tending to abrade; causing abrasion; abrading. [< L *abrās(us)* (see ABRASION) + -IVE]

ab·re·act (ab′rē akt′), *v.t. Psychoanal.* to remove by abreaction. [AB- + REACT, modeled on G *abreagieren*]

ab·re·ac·tion (ab′rē ak′shən), *n. Psychoanal.* the release of psychic tension through verbalizing or acting out an adequate resolution of a repressed traumatic experience, with the appropriate emotion or affect. [AB- + REACTION, modeled on G *Abreagierung*]

a·breast (ə brest′), *adv., adj.* **1.** side by side; beside each other in a line: *They walked two abreast.* **2.** equal to or alongside in progress, attainment, or awareness (usually fol. by *of* or *with*): *to keep abreast of the times.*

a·bri (a brē′, ä brē′; *Fr.* A BRĒ′), *n., pl.* **a·bris** (a brēz′, ä brēz′; *Fr.* A BRĒ′). a shelter or place of refuge, esp. a dugout. [< F < L *apri(cum)* open place]

a·bridge (ə brij′), *v.t.,* **a·bridged, a·bridg·ing. 1.** to shorten by condensation or omission while retaining the basic contents: *to abridge a long novel.* **2.** to reduce or lessen in duration, scope, etc.; diminish; curtail. **3.** to deprive; cut off. [ME *abregge, abrigge* < MF *abreg(i)er* < LL *abbreviāre* to shorten. See ABBREVIATE] **—a·bridg′a·ble;** *esp. Brit.,* **a·bridge′a·ble,** *adj.* **—a·bridg′er,** *n.* **—Syn. 1.** condense, abstract. See **shorten. 2.** contract.

a·bridg·ment (ə brij′mənt), *n.* **1.** a shortened or condensed form of a book, speech, etc., that still retains the basic contents. **2.** the act or process of abridging. **3.** the state of being abridged. Also, *esp. Brit.,* **a·bridge′ment.** [late ME *abrygement* < MF *abregement*] **—Syn. 1.** digest; synopsis, abstract, précis. **2.** reduction, shortening.

a·broach (ə brōch′), *adv., adj.* **1.** opened or tapped so that the contents can flow out; broached. **2.** astir; in circulation. [late ME *abroche*]

a·broad (ə brôd′), *adv.* **1.** in or to a foreign country or countries; overseas: *famous at home and abroad.* **2.** *Chiefly U.S.* to or in Europe. **3.** outside of a usual abode or shelter, esp. out of doors: *The owl ventures abroad at night.* **4.** in general circulation, as a rumor. **5.** broadly; widely; far and wide. **6.** astray; in error. [ME *abrod*]

ab·ro·gate (ab′rə gāt′), *v.t.,* **-gat·ed, -gat·ing. 1.** to abolish or nullify by formal or official means. **2.** to put aside; put an end to. [< L *abrogāt(us)* repealed (ptp. of *abrogāre*). See AB-, ROGATION, -ATE[1]] **—ab·ro·ga·ble** (ab′rə gə bəl), *adj.* **—ab′ro·ga′tion,** *n.* **—ab′ro·ga′tive,** *adj.* **—ab′ro·ga′tor,** *n.* **—Syn. 1.** cancel, revoke, rescind, void.

ab·rupt (ə brupt′), *adj.* **1.** sudden; quick and unexpected: *an abrupt departure.* **2.** curt or brusque in speech, manner, etc.: *an abrupt reply.* **3.** terminating or changing suddenly: *an abrupt turn in a road.* **4.** lacking in continuity or smoothness. **5.** steep; precipitous: *an abrupt descent.* **6.** *Bot.* truncate (def. 3). [< L *abrupt(us)* broken off (ptp. of *abrumpere*) = *ab-* AB- + *-rup-* break + *-tus* ptp. suffix] **—ab·rupt′ly,** *adv.* **—ab·rupt′ness,** *n.* **—Syn. 1, 3.** quick, sharp. See **sudden. 2.** hurried, hasty, blunt. **4.** broken.

ab·rup·tion (ə brup′shən), *n.* a sudden breaking off. [< L *abruptiōn-* (s. of *abruptiō*)]

A·bruz·zi (ä brōōt′tsē), *n.* **Duke of the** (*Prince Luigi Amedeo of Savoy-Aosta*), 1873–1933, Italian naval officer, mountain climber, and arctic explorer.

abs-, var. of **ab-:** *abscond; abstract.*

abs., 1. absent. **2.** absolute. **3.** absolutely. **4.** abstract.

Ab·sa·lom (ab′sə ləm), *n.* the third son of David: he rebelled against his father and was slain by Joab. II Sam. 13–18.

Ab·scam (ab′skam′), *n.* the code name for an FBI investigation (1979–80) of bribe-taking among members of Congress, in which government agents posed as Arab businessmen and attempted to gain illegal favors by the payment of large sums of money. [b. A(RA)B + SCAM]

ab·scess (ab′ses), *n. Pathol.* a localized collection of pus in the tissues of the body, often accompanied by swelling and inflammation and often caused by bacteria. [< L *abscess(us)* a going away, abscess, n. use of ptp. of *abscēdere* = *abs-* ABS- + *cessus* (see CEDE)] **—ab′scessed,** *adj.*

ab·scise (ab sīz′), *v.i.,* **-scised, -scis·ing.** *Bot.* to separate by abscission, as a leaf from a stem. [< L *abscīs(us)* cut off (ptp. of *abscīdere*) = *abs-* ABS- + *-cīdere* (for *caedere* to cut)]

ab·scis·sa (ab sis′ə), *n., pl.* **-scis·sas, -scis·sae** (-sis′ē). *Math.* (in plane Cartesian coordinates) the horizontal or *x*-coordinate of a point: its distance from the *y*-axis measured parallel to the *x*-axis. Cf. **ordinate.** [fem. of L *abscissus* (ptp. of *abscindere* to cut off, sever) = *ab-* AB- + *scissus* (*scid-* cut apart + *-tus* ptp. suffix)]

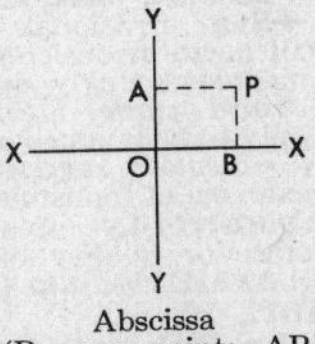

Abscissa (P, any point; AP or OB, abscissa of P; XX, axis of abscissas; YY, axis of ordinates)

ab·scis·sion (ab sizh′ən, -sish′-), *n.* **1.** the act of cutting off; sudden termination. **2.** *Bot.* the normal separation of flowers, fruit, and leaves from plants, usually caused by the development and disintegration of specialized cells. [< L *abscissiōn-*]

ab·scond (ab skond′), *v.i.* to depart in a sudden and secret manner, esp. to avoid detection or capture. [< L *abscond(ere)* (to) hide or stow away = *abs-* ABS- + *condere* to stow (*con-* CON- + *-dere* to put; see DO[1])] **—ab·scond′er,** *n.*

ab·sence (ab′səns), *n.* **1.** state of being away or of not being present. **2.** a period of being away: *an absence of several weeks.* **3.** failure to attend or appear when expected. **4.** lack, deficiency, or nonexistence: *the absence of proof.* [late ME < MF < L *absentia.* See ABSENT, -IA] **—Ant. 1.** presence.

ab′sence without′ leave′, *Mil.* See **A.W.O.L.**

ab·sent (*adj.* ab′sənt; *v.* ab sent′), *adj.* **1.** not in a certain place at a given time (opposed to *present*). **2.** lacking; nonexistent. **3.** not attentive; preoccupied; absent-minded: *an absent look on his face.* **—*v.t.* 4.** to take or keep (oneself) away. [late ME < L *absent-* (s. of *absēns,* prp. of *abesse* to be away) = *ab-* AB- + *-s-* be (see IS) + *-ent-* -ENT] **—ab·sen·ta·tion** (ab′sən tā′shən), *n.* **—ab·sent′er,** *n.* **—ab′sent·ness,** *n.*

ab·sen·tee (ab′sən tē′), *n.* **1.** a person who is absent. **2.** a person who absents himself from his property, duty, etc. **—ab′sen·tee′ism,** *n.*

ab′sentee bal′lot, the ballot used for an absentee vote.

ab′sentee land′lord, a landlord who lives in a place other than that in which his property is located.

ab′sentee vote′, a vote cast by a person who, because of illness, military service, or the like, has been permitted to vote by mail. **—ab′sentee vot′er.**

ab·sent-mind·ed (ab′sənt mīn′did), *adj.* preoccupied with one's thoughts so as to be unaware or forgetful of other matters: *an absent-minded professor.* **—ab′sent-mind′ed·ly,** *adv.* **—ab′sent-mind′ed·ness,** *n.*

ab′sent without′ leave′, *Mil.* See **A.W.O.L.**

ab·sinthe (ab′sinth), *n.* **1.** a green, bitter, licorice-flavored liqueur now made with wormwood substitutes and other herbs. **2.** wormwood (def. 2). **3.** *U.S.* sagebrush. Also, **ab′sinth.** [< F < L *absinth(ium)* wormwood < Gk *apsínthion*] **—ab·sin′thi·al, ab·sin′thi·an,** *adj.*

ab·sit o·men (äb′sit ō′men; *Eng.* ab′sit ō′men), *Latin.* may it bear no ill omen. [lit., may omen be wanting]

ab·so·lute (ab′sə lōōt′), *adj.* **1.** being fully or perfectly as indicated: *an absolute correspondence between two parts.* **2.** free from any restriction, limitation, or exception: *an absolute denial.* **3.** independent of any arbitrary standard; not comparative or relative: *a search for absolute values.* **4.** utter; outright: *an absolute lie.* **5.** unrestrained in the exercise of governmental power; without constitutional or parliamentary restraint: *an absolute monarch.* **6.** positive; certain: *absolute in opinion.* **7.** not mixed or adulterated; pure. **8.** *Gram.* **a.** relatively independent in its syntactic relation to other elements, as *It being Sunday* in *It being Sunday, the family went to church.* **b.** (of a usually transitive verb) used without an object, as *give* in *The solicitors for the community chest asked him to give.* **c.** (of an adjective) functioning as a noun, as *poor* in *The poor are always with us.* **9.** *Physics.* **a.** independent of arbitrary standards or of particular properties of substances or systems: *absolute humidity.* **b.** pertaining to a system of units, as the centimeter-gram-second system, based on some primary units, esp. units of length, mass, and time. **c.** pertaining to a measurement based on an absolute zero or unit: *absolute temperature.* **10.** *Educ.* noting or pertaining to the scale of a grading system based solely on an individual's performance considered as representing his personal knowledge of a given subject regardless of the performance of others in a group. Cf. **curve** (def. 9). **11.** *Math.* (of an inequality) indicating that the expression is true for all values of the variable, as $x^2 + 1 < 0$ for all real numbers x; unconditional. **—*n.* 12.** something that is not dependent upon external conditions for existence or for its specific nature, size, etc. (opposed to *relative*). **13. the absolute, a.** something that is independent of any restriction or condition, or some or all relations. **b.** (in Hegel) the world process operating in accordance with the absolute idea. [< L *absolūt(us)* free, unrestricted, unconditioned (ptp. of *absolvere* to ABSOLVE) = *ab-* AB- + *solū-* loose + *-tus* ptp. suffix] **—ab′so·lute′ness,** *n.*
—Syn. 2. total, unconditional; categorical. ABSOLUTE, UNQUALIFIED, UTTER all mean unmodified. ABSOLUTE implies an unquestionable finality: *an absolute coward.* UNQUALIFIED means without reservations or conditions: *an unqualified success.* UTTER expresses totality or entirety: *an utter failure.* **6.** unequivocal, definite, sure. **7.** unadulterated, unmixed. **—Ant. 2.** qualified. **3.** relative. **7.** mixed.

ab′solute al′cohol, ethyl alcohol containing less than one percent by weight of water.

ab′solute humid′ity, the ratio of the mass of water vapor to the volume of moist air within which it is contained. Cf. **relative humidity.**

ab′solute ide′a, *Hegelianism.* the spiritual principle of which the world process is the expression and fulfillment.

ab′solute ide′alism, *Philos.* any of various doctrines, esp. Hegel's, that reality is based on an absolute idea or principle.

ab·so·lute·ly (ab′sə lōōt′lē, ab′sə lōōt′-), *adv.* **1.** completely; wholly; fully: *He is absolutely wrong.* **2.** positively; certainly. **3.** (of a transitive verb) without an object. **—*interj.* 4.** (used to express complete agreement or unqualified assent.) **—Syn. 1.** entirely, totally, unqualifiedly. **2.** unquestionably, unequivocally, definitely.

ab′solute mag′nitude, *Astron.* the magnitude of a star as it would appear to a hypothetical observer at a distance of 10 parsecs or 32.6 light years.

ab′solute major′ity, a majority of votes representing more than half of those voting or eligible to vote.

ab′solute max′imum, *Math.* the largest value a given function assumes on a specified set. Cf. **maximum** (def. 2a).

ab′solute min′imum, *Math.* the smallest value a given function assumes on a specified set. Cf. **minimum** (def. 3a).

ab′solute mon′archy, a monarchy that is not limited by laws or a constitution.

ab′solute mu′sic, music whose patterns in sound are not illustrative of or dependent on a literary work, historical theme, etc. (distinguished from *program music*).

ab′solute pitch′, *Music.* **1.** the exact pitch of a tone in terms of vibrations per second. **2.** Also called **perfect pitch.** the ability to sing or recognize the pitch of a tone by ear. Cf. **relative pitch.**

ab′solute scale′, *Physics.* a temperature scale in which zero corresponds to absolute zero. Cf. **Kelvin** (def. 2), **Rankine** (def. 2).

ab′solute tem′perature, *Physics.* temperature measured on an absolute scale.

ab′solute val′ue, *Math.* the magnitude of a quantity, irrespective of sign; the distance of a quantity from zero. The absolute value of a number is symbolized by two parallel lines, as |3| or |−3| is 3.

ab′solute ze′ro, *Physical Chem.* the lowest possible temperature that the nature of matter admits; the temperature at which the particles whose motion constitutes heat would be at rest, being a hypothetical point 273° below the zero of the Celsius scale. Cf. **absolute** (def. 9c).

ab·so·lu·tion (ab′sə lo͞o′shən), *n.* **1.** act of absolving; release from consequences, obligations, or penalties. **2.** the state of being absolved. **3.** *Rom. Cath. Theol.* a remission of sin or of the punishment due to sin, made by a priest in the sacrament of penance. **4.** *Prot. Theol.* a declaration or assurance of divine forgiveness to penitent believers, made after confession of sins. [ME *absolucion* < L *absolūtiōn-* (s. of *absolūtiō*) acquittal]

ab·so·lut·ism (ab′sə lo͞o tiz′əm), *n.* **1.** the principle or the exercise of complete and unrestricted power in government. **2.** *Philos.* the doctrine of an absolute or nonrelative being. —**ab′so·lut′ist,** *n.* —**ab′so·lu·tis′tic,** *adj.* —**ab′so·lu·tis′ti·cal·ly,** *adv.*

ab·sol·u·to·ry (ab sol′yə tôr′ē, -tōr′ē), *adj.* giving absolution. [< L *absolūtōri(us)*]

ab·solve (ab zolv′, -solv′), *v.t.*, **-solved, -solv·ing. 1.** to free from the consequences or penalties resulting from actions (usually fol. by *from*): *to absolve a person from blame.* **2.** to set free or release, as from some duty, obligation, or responsibility (usually fol. by *from*). **3.** to grant pardon for. **4.** *Eccles.* **a.** to grant or pronounce remission of sins to. **b.** to remit (a sin) by absolution. [< L *absolve(re)* = *ab-* AB- + *solvere* to loose] —**ab·solv′a·ble,** *adj.* —**ab·sol′vent,** *adj., n.* —**ab·solv′er,** *n.*

—**Syn. 1.** pardon, clear. ABSOLVE, ACQUIT, EXONERATE all mean to free from blame. ABSOLVE is a general word for this idea. To ACQUIT is to release from a specific and usually formal accusation: *The court must acquit the accused if there is not enough evidence of guilt.* To EXONERATE is to consider a person clear of blame or consequences for an act (even when the act is admitted), or to justify him for having done it: *to exonerate one for a crime committed in self-defense.*

ab·so·nant (ab′sə nənt), *adj.* dissonant; discordant (usually fol. by *from* or *to*). [AB- + *-sonant*, as in *consonant*]

ab·sorb (ab sôrb′, -zôrb′), *v.t.* **1.** to suck up or drink in (a liquid). **2.** to incorporate or assimilate (something). **3.** to engross or engage wholly: *He was absorbed in his reading.* **4.** to occupy (an amount of time). **5.** to take up or receive by chemical or molecular action. **6.** to take in without echo, recoil, or reflection: *The bumper absorbed most of the shock of impact.* **7.** to accept or purchase in quantity. **8.** to assume (an expense). **9.** *Archaic.* to swallow up. [< L *absorb(ēre)* = *ab-* AB- + *sorbēre* to suck in, swallow] —**ab·sorb′a·ble,** *adj.* —**ab·sorb′a·bil′i·ty,** *n.*

ab·sorbed (ab sôrbd′, -zôrbd′), *adj.* deeply engrossed. —**ab·sorb·ed·ly** (ab sôr′bid lē, -zôr′-), *adv.*

ab·sor·be·fa·cient (ab sôr′bə fā′shənt, -zôr′-), *adj.* causing absorption. [ABSORB + *-e-* (as in *liquefy, liquefaction*) + -FACIENT]

ab·sorb·ent (ab sôr′bənt, -zôr′-), *adj.* **1.** capable of or tending to absorb: *absorbent material.* —*n.* **2.** a thing or material that absorbs. [< L *absorbent-* (s. of *absorbēns*, prp. of *absorbēre*)] —**ab·sorb′en·cy,** *n.*

absorb′ent cot′ton, raw cotton for surgical dressings, cosmetic purposes, etc., made absorbent by chemically removing the natural wax. Also called, *Brit.*, **cotton wool.**

ab·sorb·er (ab sôr′bər, -zôr′-), *n.* **1.** a person or thing that absorbs. **2.** See **shock absorber. 3.** *Physics.* a material in a nuclear reactor which absorbs neutrons.

ab·sorb·ing (ab sôr′biŋ, -zôr′-), *adj.* extremely interesting; engrossing. —**ab·sorb′ing·ly,** *adv.*

ab·sorp·tance (ab sôrp′təns, -zôrp′-), *n.* *Physics, Optics.* the ratio of the amount of radiation absorbed by a surface to the amount of radiation incident upon it. Cf. **reflectance, transmittance** (def. 2). [trans. of G *Absorptionsvermögen*]

ab·sorp·tion (ab sôrp′shən, -zôrp′-), *n.* **1.** the act of absorbing. **2.** the state or process of being absorbed. **3.** assimilation; incorporation. **4.** passage of substances to the blood, lymph, and cells, as from the alimentary canal or from the tissues. **5.** a taking in or reception by molecular or chemical action, as of gases or liquids. **6.** *Physics.* the reduction of energy in the form of electromagnetic radiation by a medium or by a reflecting surface. **7.** complete preoccupation; deep engrossment. [< L *absorptiōn-* (s. of *absorptiō*) = *absorpt(us)* (ptp.) (*absorb-* (see ABSORB) + *-tus* ptp. suffix) + *-iōn-* -ION] —**ab·sorp′tive,** *adj.* —**ab·sorp′tive·ness,** *n.*

absorp′tion coeffi′cient, *Physics, Optics.* a measure of the rate of decrease in the intensity of electromagnetic radiation, such as light, as it passes through a given substance.

ab·stain (ab stān′), *v.i.* **1.** to refrain voluntarily, esp. from something regarded as improper or unhealthy (usually fol. by *from*): *to abstain from smoking.* **2.** *Parl. Proc.* to refrain from voting either for or against a motion. [late ME *abste(i)ne* < MF *absten(ir)* < L *abstinēre* = *abs-* ABS- + *tinēre*, comb. form of *tenēre* to hold, keep]

ab·stain·er (ab stā′nər), *n.* **1.** a person who abstains from something regarded as improper or unhealthy, esp. the drinking of alcoholic beverages: *a total abstainer.* **2.** a person who abstains from anything.

ab·ste·mi·ous (ab stē′mē əs), *adj.* **1.** sparing or moderate in eating and drinking. **2.** characterized by abstinence. **3.** sparing: *an abstemious diet.* [< L *abstēmius* = *abs-* ABS- + *tēm-* (root of *tēmētum* intoxicating drink) + *-ius* -IOUS] —**ab·ste′mi·ous·ly,** *adv.* —**ab·ste′mi·ous·ness,** *n.*

ab·sten·tion (ab sten′shən), *n.* **1.** the act or an instance of abstaining. **2.** *Parl. Proc.* a declaration to vote neither for nor against a motion. [< LL *abstentiōn-* (s. of *abstentiō*) = L *abstent(us)* (ptp.) (see ABSTAIN) + *-iōn-* -ION] —**ab·sten′tious,** *adj.*

ab·sterge (ab stûrj′), *v.t.*, **-sterged, -sterg·ing. 1.** *Med.* to purge. **2.** to make clean by wiping. [< L *absterg(ēre)* = *abs-* ABS- + *tergēre* to wipe]

ab·ster·gent (ab stûr′jənt), *adj.* **1.** cleansing. —*n.* **2.** a cleansing agent, as a detergent or soap. [< L *abstergent-* (s. of *abstergēns* (prp.) wiping off)]

ab·sti·nence (ab′stə nəns), *n.* **1.** forbearance from any indulgence of appetite, esp. from the use of alcoholic liquors: *total abstinence.* **2.** self-restraint; self-denial; forbearance. **3.** *Eccles.* the refraining from certain kinds of food on certain days, as from flesh on Fridays. Also, **ab′sti·nen·cy.** [ME < MF < L *abstinentia.* See ABSTAIN, -ENCE] —**ab′sti·nent,** *adj.* —**Syn. 1.** abstemiousness, teetotalism.

abstr., 1. abstract. **2.** abstracted.

ab·stract (*adj.* ab′strakt, ab strakt′; *n.* ab′strakt; *v.* ab strakt′ *for 12–15,* ab′strakt *for 16*), *adj.* **1.** conceived apart from any concrete realities, specific object, or actual instance: *an abstract idea.* **2.** expressing a quality or characteristic apart from any specific object or instance. **3.** theoretical; not applied or practical: *abstract science.* **4.** abstruse: *abstract speculations.* **5.** *Fine Arts.* **a.** of or pertaining to the formal aspect of art, emphasizing lines, colors, generalized or geometrical forms, etc., esp. with reference to their relationship to one another. **b.** (*often cap.*) pertaining to the nonrepresentational art styles of the 20th century. —*n.* **6.** a summary of a statement, document, speech, etc.; epitome. **7.** something that concentrates in itself the essential qualities of anything more extensive or more general, or of several things; essence. **8.** an idea or term considered apart from some material basis or object. **9.** an abstract work of art. **10. in the abstract,** without reference to practical considerations or applications; in theory: *beauty in the abstract.* **11. the abstract,** something that exists only as an idea: *the abstract versus the concrete.* —*v.t.* **12.** to draw or take away; remove. **13.** to divert or draw away the attention of. **14.** to steal. **15.** to consider as a general quality or characteristic apart from specific objects or instances: *to abstract the notions of time, space, and matter.* **16.** to summarize. [< L *abstract(us)* drawn off (ptp. of *abstrahere*). See ABS-, TRACT[1]] —**ab·stract′er,** *n.* —**ab′stract·ly,** *adv.* —**ab′stract·ness,** *n.*

ab′stract al′gebra, the branch of mathematics that deals with the extension of algebraic concepts usually associated with the real number system to other, more general systems.

ab·stract·ed (ab strak′tid), *adj.* lost in thought; deeply engrossed or preoccupied. —**ab·stract′ed·ly,** *adv.* —**ab·stract′ed·ness,** *n.*

Ab′stract Expres′sionism, (*sometimes l.c.*) *Fine Arts.* a style of painting in which paint is applied in an apparently random manner producing images that may or may not have reference to forms exterior to the picture.

ab·strac·tion (ab strak′shən), *n.* **1.** an abstract or general idea or term. **2.** an idea that cannot lead to any practical result; something visionary and unrealistic. **3.** the act of considering something as a general quality or characteristic, apart from any concrete realities, specific object, or actual instance. **4.** the act of taking away or separating. **5.** the state of being lost in thought. **6.** *Fine Arts.* **a.** the abstract qualities or characteristics of a work of art. **b.** a nonrepresentational work of art. [< LL *abstractiōn-* (s. of *abstractiō*) separation] —**ab·strac′tion·al,** *adj.*

ab·strac·tion·ism (ab strak′shə niz′əm), *n.* *Fine Arts.* the practice and theory of abstract art.

ab·strac·tion·ist (ab strak′shə nist), *n.* **1.** a person who paints abstract paintings. —*adj.* **2.** of or pertaining to abstract art.

ab·strac·tive (ab strak′tiv), *adj.* **1.** having the power of abstracting. **2.** pertaining to an abstract or summary. [< ML *abstractīv(us)*] —**ab·strac′tive·ly,** *adv.* —**ab·strac′tive·ness,** *n.*

ab′stract noun′, *Gram.* a noun having an abstract or general rather than a concrete or specific referent, as *dread* or *grayness.* Cf. **concrete noun.**

ab′stract of ti′tle, *Law.* an outline history of the title to a parcel of real estate, showing the original grant, subsequent conveyances, mortgages, etc.

ab·stric·tion (ab strik′shən), *n.* *Bot.* a method of spore formation in fungi in which successive portions of the sporophore are cut off through the growth of septa.

ab·struse (ab stro͞os′), *adj.* **1.** hard to understand; recondite; esoteric: *abstruse theories.* **2.** *Obs.* secret; hidden. [< L *abstrūs(us)* thrust away, concealed (ptp. of *abstrūdere*) = *abs-* ABS- + *trūd-* thrust + *-tus* ptp. suffix] —**ab·struse′ly,** *adv.* —**ab·stru′si·ty, ab·struse′ness,** *n.*

ab·surd (ab sûrd′, -zûrd′), *adj.* contrary to all reason or common sense; illogical, ridiculous, or untrue: *an absurd explanation.* [< L *absurd(us)* dissonant] —**ab·surd′ly,** *adv.* —**ab·surd′ness,** *n.*

—**Syn.** irrational. ABSURD, RIDICULOUS, PREPOSTEROUS all mean inconsistent with reason or common sense. ABSURD means glaringly opposed to manifest truth or reason: *an absurd claim.* RIDICULOUS implies that something is fit only to be laughed at, perhaps contemptuously or derisively: *a ridiculous suggestion.* PREPOSTEROUS implies an amazing extreme of foolishness: *a preposterous proposal.*

ab·surd·i·ty (ab sûr′di tē, -zûr′-), *n., pl.* **-ties. 1.** the state or quality of being absurd. **2.** something absurd. [late ME *absurdite* (< MF) < L *absurditāt-* (s. of *absurditās*)]

abt., about.

A·bu-Bekr (ə bo͞o′bek′ər), *n.* A.D. 573–634, Muhammad's father-in-law and successor: first caliph of Mecca 632–634. Also, **A·bu-Bakr** (ə bo͞o′bak′ər).

A·bu Dha·bi (ä′bo͞o dä′bē, dab′ē), **1.** a sheikdom on the S coast of the Persian Gulf in N United Arab Emirates. 235,662. **2.** the capital of this sheikdom. 95,000.

A·bu·kir (ä′bo͞o kēr′, ə bo͞o′kər), *n.* a bay in the N Arab Republic of Egypt, at the mouth of the Nile: French fleet defeated here by British fleet 1798. Also, **Aboukir.**

a·bu·li·a (ə byo͞o′lē ə), *n.* *Psychiatry.* a form of mental disorder in which volition is impaired or lost. [< NL < Gk *aboulia* irresolution. See A-[6], -BULIA] —**a·bu′lic,** *adj.*

A·bu·me·ron (ä bo͞o′mə ron′), *n.* Avenzoar.

a·bun·dance (ə bun′dəns), *n.* **1.** an extremely plentiful or oversufficient quantity or supply: *an abundance of grain.* **2.** affluence; wealth. [ME < MF < L *abundantia*] —**Syn. 1.** copiousness, plenteousness. See **plenty.** —**Ant. 1.** scarcity.

a·bun·dant (ə bun′dənt), *adj.* **1.** present in great quantity; more than adequate: *an abundant supply of water.* **2.** having in great quantity; abounding (usually fol. by *in*). **3.** richly supplied; having an abundance of good things: *an abundant land.* [late ME (< MF) < L *abundant-* (s. of *abundāns*) overflowing] —**a·bun′dant·ly,** *adv.* —**Syn. 1.** copious, profuse, overflowing. See **plentiful. 2.** teeming. —**Ant. 1, 2.** sparse, scarce.

abun′dant year′. See under **Jewish Calendar.**

ab ur·be con·di·ta (äb o͝or′be kōn′di tä′; *Eng.* ab ûr′bē kon′di tə), *Latin.* from the founding of the city (Rome, c753 B.C.). *Abbr.:* A.U.C. [lit., from the built city]

a·buse (*v.* ə byo͞oz′; *n.* ə byo͞os′), *v.,* **a·bused, a·bus·ing,** *n.* —*v.t.* **1.** to use wrongly or improperly; misuse: *to abuse one's authority.* **2.** to treat in a harmful, injurious, or offensive way: *to abuse a horse; to abuse one's eyesight.* **3.** to speak insultingly, harshly, and unjustly to or about. **4.** *Obs.* to deceive; cheat. **5. abuse oneself,** to masturbate. —*n.* **6.** wrong or improper use; misuse: *the abuse of privileges.* **7.** harshly or coarsely insulting language. **8.** bad or improper treatment; maltreatment. **9.** a corrupt or improper practice or custom: *the abuses of bad government.* **10.** *Obs.* deception; misrepresentation. [late ME < MF *abuse(r)* < L *abūs(us)* misused (ptp. of *abūtī*). See AB-, USE] —**a·bus′a·ble,** *adj.* —**a·bus′er,** *n.*
—**Syn. 1.** misapply, mistreat. **2.** maltreat, injure, harm, hurt. **3.** vilify, berate, slander, defame. **7.** slander, aspersion. ABUSE, CENSURE, INVECTIVE all mean strongly expressed disapproval. ABUSE implies an outburst of harsh and scathing words against another (often one who is defenseless): *abuse directed against an opponent.* CENSURE implies blame, adverse criticism, or hostile condemnation: *severe censure of acts showing bad judgment.* INVECTIVE applies to strong but formal denunciation in speech or print, often in the public interest: *invective against graft.* —**Ant. 3.** praise, compliment, eulogize, laud.

A·bu Sim·bel (ə bo͞o′ sim′bel, -bəl), a village in the S United Arab Republic, on the Nile: site of two temples of Ramses II which were moved to higher ground to save them from the backwater of the Aswan Dam. Also, **Abu′ Sim′bil** (sim′bil). Also called **Ipsambul.**

a·bu·sive (ə byo͞o′siv), *adj.* **1.** using, containing, or characterized by harshly or coarsely insulting language: *abusive remarks.* **2.** treating badly or injuriously; mistreating, esp. physically. **3.** wrongly used; corrupt: *an abusive exercise of power.* [< L *abūsīv(us).* See ABUSE, -IVE] —**a·bu′sive·ly,** *adv.* —**a·bu′sive·ness,** *n.*

a·but (ə but′), *v.,* **a·but·ted, a·but·ting.** —*v.i.* **1.** to touch or join at the edge or border; to be adjacent (often fol. by *on, upon,* or *against*). —*v.t.* **2.** to border on, end at, or be adjacent to. **3.** to support by an abutment. [late ME < MF *about(er)* (to) join end to end (*a-* A-[5] + *bout* end) and *abut(er)* (to) touch at one end (*a-* A-[5] + *but* end)]

a·bu·ti·lon (ə byo͞ot′ᵊlon′), *n.* a shrub of the genus *Abutilon,* comprising the flowering maples. [< NL < Ar *awbūtīlōn*]

a·but·ment (ə but′mənt), *n.* **1.** *Archit., Civ. Eng.* **a.** a masonry mass supporting and receiving the thrust of part of an arch or vault. **b.** a force that serves to abut an arch or vault. **c.** a mass, as of masonry, receiving the arch, beam, truss, etc., at each end of a bridge. **2.** the place where projecting parts meet; junction.

a·but·tal (ə but′ᵊl), *n.* **1. abuttals, a.** those parts of one piece of land that abut on adjacent lands; boundaries. **b.** Also, **buttals.** *Law.* the boundary lines of a piece of land in relation to adjacent lands. **2.** the act or state of abutting.

a·but·ter (ə but′ər), *n.* a person who owns adjacent land.

abv., above.

ab·volt (ab vōlt′), *n.* *Elect.* the centimeter-gram-second unit of electromotive force, equivalent to 10^{-8} volt. [*ab-* (see ABAMPERE) + VOLT[1]]

ab·watt (ab wot′), *n.* *Elect.* the centimeter-gram-second unit of electrical power, equivalent to 10^{-7} watt. [*ab-* (see ABAMPERE) + WATT]

a·by (ə bī′), *v., pt. and pp.* **a·bought.** —*v.t.* **1.** *Archaic.* to pay the penalty of. —*v.i. Obs.* **2.** to endure; continue. **3.** to undergo suffering as a penalty. Also, **abye.** [ME *abye(n).* OE *ābycgan.* See A-[3], BUY]

A·by·dos (ə bī′dos), *n.* **1.** an ancient ruined city in central Egypt; temples and necropolis. **2.** an ancient town in NW Asia Minor, at the narrowest part of the Hellespont.

a·bye (ə bī′), *v.t., v.i., pt. and pp.* **a·bought.** aby.

a·bysm (ə biz′əm), *n.* an abyss. [ME *abi(s)me* < VL **abyssim(us),* a superl. of LL *abyssus* ABYSS]

a·bys·mal (ə biz′məl), *adj.* of or like an abyss; immeasurably deep or great: *abysmal ignorance; abysmal poverty.* —**a·bys′mal·ly,** *adv.*

a·byss (ə bis′), *n.* **1.** a deep, immeasurable space, gulf, or cavity; vast chasm. **2.** anything profound, unfathomable, or infinite: *the abyss of time.* **3.** (in ancient cosmogony) **a.** the primal chaos before Creation. **b.** the infernal regions; hell. **c.** a subterranean ocean. [< LL *abyss(us)* < Gk *ábyssos* bottomless = *a-* A-[6] + *byssós* bottom of the sea]

Abyss., **1.** Abyssinia. **2.** Abyssinian.

a·byss·al (ə bis′əl), *adj.* **1.** of or like an abyss; immeasurable; unfathomable. **2.** of or pertaining to the lowest depths of the ocean, esp. the stratum of bottom waters. [< ML *abyssāl(is)*]

Ab·ys·sin·i·a (ab′i sin′ē ə), *n.* former name of **Ethiopia.** —**Ab′ys·sin′i·an,** *adj., n.*

AC, *Elect.* alternating current: an electric current that reverses direction at regular intervals, having a magnitude that varies continuously in a sinusoidal manner. Also, **A.C., ac, a-c, a.c.** Cf. **DC** (def. 2).

Ac, *Chem.* **1.** acetate. **2.** acetyl.

Ac, *Chem.* actinium.

ac-, var. of **ad-** before *c* and *qu: accede; acquire.*

-ac, a suffix used in forming adjectives: *elegiac; cardiac.* [comb. form repr. L *-acus,* Gk *-akos,* r. *-ikos* -IC when the base ended in *-i-*]

A/C, *Bookkeeping.* **1.** account. **2.** account current. Also, **a/c**

A.C., **1.** before Christ. [< L *ante Christum*] **2.** See **AC**

a.c., **1.** (in prescriptions) before meals. [< L *ante cibum*] **2.** See **AC**

a·ca·cia (ə kā′shə), *n.* **1.** any mimosaceous tree or shrub of the genus *Acacia,* of warm regions. **2.** one of several other plants, as the locust tree. **3.** See **gum arabic.** [< L < Gk *akakía* Egyptian thorn]

acad., **1.** academic. **2.** academy.

ac·a·deme (ak′ə dēm′), *n.* **1.** (*cap.*) the public grove in Athens in which Plato taught. **2.** (*sometimes cap.*) any place of instruction; a school. **3.** the environment of a college or university. **4.** academic. [< L *Acadēm(us)* < Gk *Akádēmos* name of an Arcadian at whose estate Athenian philosophers met]

ac·a·dem·ic (ak′ə dem′ik), *adj.* **1.** of or pertaining to a school, esp. one for higher education. **2.** *U.S.* pertaining to areas of study that are not vocational or technical, as the humanities, pure mathematics, etc. **3.** theoretical; not practical or directly useful: *an academic discussion.* **4.** learned or scholarly but lacking in worldliness, common sense, or practicality. **5.** conforming to set rules, standards, or traditions; conventional: *academic painting style.* **6.** acquired by formal education, esp. at a college or university: *academic preparation for the ministry.* —*n.* **7.** a student or teacher at a college or university. [< L *Acadēmic(us)* < Gk *Akadēmeikós.* See ACADEMY, -IC] —**Syn. 2.** humanistic, liberal. **5.** See **formal**[1].

ac·a·dem·i·cal (ak′ə dem′i kəl), *adj.* academic. [ACADEMIC + -AL[1]] —**ac′a·dem′i·cal·ly,** *adv.*

ac′adem′ic free′dom, **1.** freedom of a teacher to discuss social, economic, or political problems without interference from officials, organized groups, etc. **2.** freedom of a student to explore any field or hold any belief without interference or penalty from a teacher, school authorities, etc.

a·cad·e·mi·cian (ə kad′ə mish′ən, ak′ə də-), *n.* **1.** a member of an association or institution for the advancement of arts, sciences, or letters. **2.** a follower or promoter of the traditional in philosophy, art, or literature. [< F *académicien* = *académic-* ACADEMIC + *-ien* -IAN]

ac·a·dem·i·cism (ak′ə dem′i siz′əm), *n.* traditionalism or conventionalism in art, literature, etc. Also **academism.**

A·ca·dé·mie Fran·çaise (A KA dā mē fräN sez′), *French.* See **French Academy.**

a·cad·e·mism (ə kad′ə miz′əm), *n.* **1.** academicism. **2.** *Philos.* the philosophy of the school founded by Plato.

a·cad·e·my (ə kad′ə mē), *n., pl.* **-mies. 1.** a secondary or high school, esp. a private one. **2.** a school or college for special instruction or training: *a military academy.* **3.** an association or institution for the advancement of art, literature, or science: *the National Academy of Arts and Letters.* **4.** a group of acknowledged authorities and leaders in a field of scholarship, art, etc., esp. when considered as influential in maintaining traditional standards, dictating methods, etc. **5. the Academy,** the Platonic school of philosophy or its adherents. [< L *acadēmīa* < Gk *akadḗmeia* = *Akádēm(os)* (see ACADEME) + *-eia* adj. suffix]

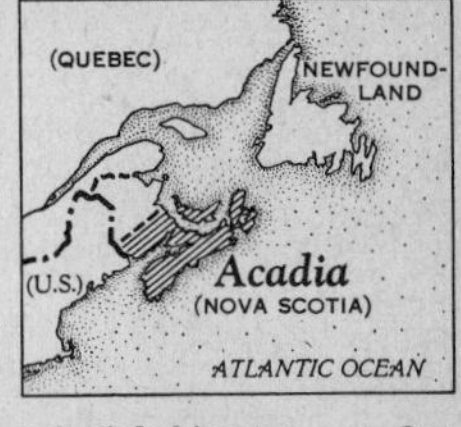

A·ca·di·a (ə kā′dē ə), *n.* a former French colony in SE Canada: ceded to Great Britain 1713. French, **A·ca·die** (A KA dē′).

A·ca·di·an (ə kā′dē ən), *adj.* **1.** of or pertaining to Acadia or its inhabitants. —*n.* **2.** a native or inhabitant of Acadia, or a descendant of such natives or inhabitants who lives in Louisiana.

ac·a·leph (ak′ə lef′), *n.* (in former classifications) any coelenterate of the group *Acalephae,* including the sea nettles and jellyfishes. Also, **ac·a·lephe** (ak′ə lēf′). [< NL *acaleph(a)* < Gk *akalḗphē* stinging nettle, sea anemone]

ac·an·tha·ceous (ak′ən thā′shəs), *adj.* **1.** having prickly growths. **2.** belonging to the *Acanthaceae,* or acanthus family. [< NL *Acanthace(ae)* (see ACANTH-, -ACEAE) + -OUS]

acantho-, a learned borrowing from Greek meaning "spiny," used in the formation of compound words: *acanthocephalan.* Also, *esp. before a vowel,* **acanth-.** [< Gk *akantho-,* comb. form of *ákantha* thorn]

a·can·tho·ceph·a·lan (ə kan′thə sef′ə lən), *n.* **1.** any parasitic worm of the phylum or class *Acanthocephala,* having a proboscis covered with recurved hooks and a hollow body without a digestive tract, found in the intestine of vertebrates. —*adj.* **2.** belonging or pertaining to the *Acanthocephala.*

a·can·thoid (ə kan′thoid), *adj.* spiny; spinous.

ac·an·thop·ter·yg·i·an (ak′ən thop′tə rij′ē ən), *adj.* **1.** belonging or pertaining to the *Acanthopterygii* (*Acanthopteri*), the group of spiny-finned fishes, including the bass and perch. —*n.* **2.** an acanthopterygian fish. [< NL *Acanthopterygi(ī)* (*acantho-* ACANTHO- + Gk *pterýgi(on)* small wing, fin + L *-ī-* masc. pl. ending) + -AN]

a·can·thous (ə kan′thəs), *adj.* spinous.

a·can·thus (ə kan′thəs), *n., pl.* **-thus·es, -thi** (-thī). **1.** any of several herbs of the genus *Acanthus,* of the Mediterranean region, having spiny or toothed leaves. **2.** an architectural ornament, as in the Corinthian capital, resembling the leaves of this plant. [< L < Gk *ákanthos* bearsfoot] —**a·can·thine** (ə kan′thin, -thīn), *adj.*

A B
Acanthus
A, Leaf of plant, *Acanthus mollis;* B, Architectural ornament, front and side views

a cap·pel·la (ä′ kə pel′ə; *It.* ä′ käp pel′lä), *Music.* **1.** without instrumental accompaniment. **2.** in the style of church or chapel music. [< It: according to chapel]

A·ca·pul·co (ak′ə po͞ol′kō; *Sp.* ä′kä po͞ol′kô), *n.* a seaport in SW Mexico, on the Pacific. 58,870 (1960).

ac·a·ri·a·sis (ak′ə rī′ə sis), *n.* *Pathol.* **1.** infestation with acarids, esp. mites. **2.** a skin disease caused by such infestation. [< NL; see ACARUS, -IASIS]

ac·a·rid (ak′ə rid), *n.* **1.** an acarine, esp. of the family *Acaridae.* —*adj.* **2.** pertaining to an acarid. [ACAR(US) + -ID[2]]

a·car·i·dan (ə kar′i dən), *adj.* **1.** belonging or pertaining to the order *Acarina.* —*n.* **2.** an acarine.
ac·a·rine (ak′ə rīn′, -rēn′, -rin), *n.* **1.** any of numerous arachnids of the order *Acarina,* comprising the mites and ticks. —*adj.* **2.** belonging or pertaining to the order *Acarina.* [< NL *Acarina.* See ACARUS, -INE[1]]
ac·a·roid (ak′ə roid′), *adj.* resembling a mite or tick.
ac′aroid res′in, a red or yellow resin obtained from the trunks of several grass trees, esp. *Xanthorrhoea hastilis,* used chiefly in varnishes and lacquers and as a substitute for rosin.
ac·a·rol·o·gy (ak′ə rol′ə jē), *n.* the branch of zoology dealing with mites and ticks. [< NL *acar(us)* ACARUS + -O- + -LOGY] —**ac′a·rol′o·gist,** *n.*
a·car·pel·ous (ā kär′pə ləs), *adj.* *Bot.* having no carpels. Also, **a·car′pel·lous.**
a·car·pous (ā kär′pəs), *adj.* *Bot.* not producing fruit; sterile; barren. [< Gk *ákarpos* = *a-* A-[6] + *karpós* fruit; see -OUS]
ac·a·rus (ak′ər əs), *n., pl.* **-a·ri** (-ə rī′). a mite, esp. of the genus *Acarus.* [< NL < Gk *akarí* mite]
a·cat·a·lec·tic (ā kat′əlek′tik), *Pros.* —*adj.* **1.** not catalectic; complete. —*n.* **2.** a verse having the complete number of syllables in the last foot. Cf. **catalectic, hypercatalectic.** [< LL *acatalectic(us)*]
a·cau·dal (ā kôd′əl), *adj.* *Zool.* tailless. Also, **a·cau·date** (ā kô′dāt).
a·cau·les·cent (ā′kô les′ənt), *adj.* *Bot.* not caulescent; without a visible stem. Also, **a·cau·line** (ā kô′lin), **a·cau·lose** (ā kô′lōs), **a·cau·lous** (ā kô′ləs). —**a′cau·les′cence,** *n.*
acc., **1.** accelerate. **2.** acceleration. **3.** accept. **4.** acceptance. **5.** accompanied. **6.** accompaniment. **7.** according. **8.** account. **9.** accountant. **10.** accusative.
Ac·cad (ak′ad, ä′käd), *n.* one of the four cities of Nimrod's kingdom. Gen. 10:10. Also, **Akkad.**
ac·cede (ak sēd′), *v.i.,* **-ced·ed, -ced·ing.** **1.** to give consent, approval, or adherence; agree; assent: *to accede to a request; He acceded under pressure.* **2.** to attain, assume, or succeed to an office, title, or dignity (usually fol. by *to*): *to accede to the throne.* **3.** *Internat. Law.* to become a party to by way of accession. [< L *accēde(re)* (to) approach, assent = *ac-* AC- + *cēdere* to go] —**ac·ced′ence,** *n.* —**ac·ced′er,** *n.* —**Syn. 1.** See **agree.**
ac·cel·er·an·do (ak sel′ə rän′dō; *It.* ät che′le rän′dô), *adv., adj.* *Music.* gradually increasing in tempo. [< It < L *accelerand(us),* ger. of *accelerāre* to speed up. See ACCELERATE]
ac·cel·er·ant (ak sel′ər ənt), *n.* *Chem.* accelerator (def. 3). [< L *accelerant-* (s. of *accelerāns*) hastening (prp. of *accelerāre*). See ACCELERATE]
ac·cel·er·ate (ak sel′ə rāt′), *v.,* **-at·ed, -at·ing.** —*v.t.* **1.** to cause faster or greater activity, progress, advancement, etc., in: *to accelerate economic growth.* **2.** to hasten the occurrence of: *to accelerate the fall of a government.* **3.** to increase the velocity or rate of motion of. **4.** to reduce the time required for (a course of study) by intensifying the work, eliminating detail, etc. —*v.i.* **5.** to move or go faster; increase in speed. [< L *accelerāt(us)* speeded up (ptp. of *accelerāre*) = *ac-* AC- + *celer* swift + *-ātus* -ATE[1]] —**ac·cel′er·a·ble,** *adj.* —**ac·cel′er·at′ed·ly,** *adv.* —**ac·cel·er·a·tive** (ak sel′ə rā′tiv, -ər ə-tiv), **ac·cel′er·a·to′ry,** *adj.*
ac·cel·er·a·tion (ak sel′ə rā′shən), *n.* **1.** the act or an instance of accelerating. **2.** the state of being accelerated. **3.** a change in velocity with reference to an increase: *negative acceleration.* **4.** the time rate of change of velocity with respect to magnitude or direction; the derivative of velocity. [< L *accelerātiōn-* (s. of *accelerātiō*)]
accelera′tion of grav′ity, *Physics.* the acceleration of a falling body in the earth's gravitational field: an increase in velocity of approximately 32 feet per second per second. *Symbol:* g
ac·cel·er·a·tor (ak sel′ə rā′tər), *n.* **1.** a person or thing that accelerates. **2.** a throttle, as the gas pedal of an automobile, for controlling the speed of an engine. **3.** *Chem.* any substance that increases the speed of a chemical change. **4.** *Anat.* any muscle, nerve, or activating substance that quickens a movement. **5.** Also called **atom smasher.** *Physics.* an electrostatic or electromagnetic device, as a cyclotron, that produces high-energy particles and focuses them on a target.
ac·cel·er·om·e·ter (ak sel′ə rom′i tər), *n.* an instrument for measuring acceleration, as of aircraft.
ac·cent (*n.* ak′sent; *v.* ak′sent, ak sent′), *n.* **1.** prominence of a syllable in terms of differential loudness, pitch, length, or a combination of these. **2.** degree of prominence of a syllable within a word and sometimes of a word within a phrase: *primary accent; secondary accent.* **3.** a mark indicating stress, as (**′**) (′), or (ˈ) (″), or (ˈ) (ˌ), either following or preceding a syllable. **4.** *Pros.* regularly recurring stress. **5.** a musical tone or pattern of pitch inherent in a particular language either as a feature essential to the identification of a vowel or a syllable or to the general acoustic character of the language. Cf. **pitch**[1] (def. 21), **tone** (def. 7). **6.** Often, **accents.** speech patterns, inflections, choice of words, etc., that are characteristic of a particular speaker or of speech expressing a particular emotion. **7.** a mode of pronunciation, as pitch or tone, emphasis pattern, or intonation, characteristic of or peculiar to the speech of a particular person, group, or locality: *foreign accent; a Southern accent.* Cf. **tone** (def. 5). **8.** such a mode of pronunciation recognized as being of foreign origin: *He still speaks with an accent.* **9.** *Music.* **a.** a stress or emphasis given to certain notes. **b.** a mark noting this. **c.** stress or emphasis regularly recurring as a feature of rhythm. **10.** *Math.* **a.** a symbol used to distinguish similar quantities that differ in value, as in b′, b″, b‴ (called *b prime, b second* or *b double prime,* and *b third* or *b triple prime,* respectively). **b.** a symbol used to indicate a particular unit of measure, as feet (′) or inches (″), minutes (′) or seconds (″). **c.** a symbol used to indicate the order of a derivative of a function in calculus, as *f′* (called *f prime*) is the first derivative of a function *f.* **11.** a distinctive but subordinate pattern, motif, color, flavor, or the like: *The salad dressing had an accent of garlic.* —*v.t.* **12.** to pronounce with prominence (a syllable within a word or a word within a phrase): *Accent the first syllable.* **13.** to mark with a written accent or accents. **14.** to give emphasis or prominence to; accentuate. [< L *accent(us)* speaking tone = *ac-* AC- + *-centus,* comb. form of *cantus* song (see CANTO); trans. of Gk *prosōidía* PROSODY] —**ac′cent·less,** *adj.*

ac′cent mark′, a mark used to indicate an accent, stress, etc., as for pronunciation or in musical notation. Cf. **diacritic** (def. 1).
ac·cen·tu·al (ak sen′cho͞o əl), *adj.* **1.** of or pertaining to accent or stress; rhythmical. **2.** *Pros.* of or pertaining to poetry based on the number of stresses, as distinguished from poetry depending on the number of syllables or quantities. [< L *accentu(s)* (see ACCENT) + -AL[1]] —**ac·cen′tu·al′i·ty,** *n.* —**ac·cen′tu·al·ly,** *adv.*
ac·cen·tu·ate (ak sen′cho͞o āt′), *v.t.,* **-at·ed, -at·ing.** **1.** to give emphasis or prominence to; emphasize. **2.** to mark or pronounce with an accent. [< ML *accentuāt(us)* intoned (ptp. of *accentuāre*). See ACCENT, -ATE[1]] —**ac·cen·tu·a·ble** (ak sen′cho͞o ə bəl), *adj.* —**ac·cen′tu·a′tion,** *n.* —**ac·cen′tu·a′tor,** *n.*
ac·cept (ak sept′), *v.t.* **1.** to take or receive (something offered). **2.** to agree, consent, or accede to: *to accept an apology.* **3.** to respond or answer affirmatively to: *to accept an invitation.* **4.** to undertake the duties, honors, etc., of: *to accept the office of treasurer.* **5.** to receive or admit formally, as to membership. **6.** to accommodate or reconcile oneself to: *to accept a situation.* **7.** to regard as true or valid; believe. **8.** to regard as normal, suitable, or usual. **9.** to understand as having a certain meaning. **10.** *Com.* to acknowledge as calling for payment, and thus to agree to pay, as a draft. **11.** (of a deliberative body) to receive as an adequate performance of the duty with which an officer or a committee has been charged; receive for further action: *Congress accepted the committee's report.* **12.** to receive or contain (something attached, inserted, etc.): *This socket won't accept a three-pronged plug.* —*v.i.* **13.** to accept an invitation, gift, position, etc. (sometimes fol. by *of*). [late ME *accepte* < L *accept(āre)* = *ac-* AC- + *-cep-* take + *-t-* freq. suffix] —**ac·cep′ter,** *n.* —**Syn. 7.** acknowledge. —**Ant. 1.** reject.
—**Usage.** ACCEPT and EXCEPT are sometimes confused as verbs because of their similarity in sound. ACCEPT means "to take or receive," *I accept this trophy,* while EXCEPT means "to exclude," *They excepted him from the membership list.*
ac·cept·a·ble (ak sep′tə bəl), *adj.* **1.** capable or worthy of being accepted; satisfactory. **2.** pleasing to the receiver; agreeable; welcome. **3.** meeting only minimum requirements; barely adequate: *acceptable applicants.* [late ME < L *acceptābil(is)*] —**ac·cept′a·bil′i·ty, ac·cept′a·ble·ness,** *n.* —**ac·cept′a·bly,** *adv.*
ac·cept·ance (ak sep′təns), *n.* **1.** the act of taking or receiving something offered. **2.** favorable reception; approval; favor. **3.** the act of assenting or believing: *acceptance of a theory.* **4.** the fact or state of being accepted or acceptable. **5.** acceptation (def. 3). **6.** *Com.* **a.** an engagement to pay an order, draft, etc., when due. **b.** an order, draft, etc., that a person has accepted as calling for payment and has thus promised to pay.
ac·cept·an·cy (ak sep′tən sē), *n., pl.* **-cies.** **1.** act of accepting; acceptance. **2.** willingness to accept or receive; receptiveness.
ac·cept·ant (ak sep′tənt), *adj.* willingly accepting or receiving; receptive.
ac·cep·ta·tion (ak′sep tā′shən), *n.* **1.** favorable regard; approval. **2.** belief. **3.** the usual or accepted meaning of a word, phrase, etc. [late ME < MF]
ac·cept·ed (ak sep′tid), *adj.* generally approved; usually regarded as normal, right, etc.: *an accepted pronunciation.* —**ac·cept′ed·ly,** *adv.*
ac·cept·ee (ak′sep tē′), *n.* a person who is accepted, as for military service.
ac·cep·tor (ak sep′tər), *n.* *Finance.* a person who accepts a draft or bill of exchange, esp. the drawee who signs the draft or bill, confirming his willingness to pay it when due. [< L]
ac·cess (ak′ses), *n.* **1.** ability or permission to approach, enter, speak with, or use; admittance: *They have access to the files.* **2.** state or quality of being approachable: *The house was difficult of access.* **3.** a way or means of approach. **4.** *Theol.* approach to God through Jesus Christ. **5.** an attack or onset, as of a disease. **6.** a sudden and strong emotional outburst. **7.** accession. —*v.t.* **8.** *Computer Technol.* to retrieve (data) from the memory of a computer. [late ME *accesse* < L *accessus* an approach; ME *acces* attack (of illness, anger, etc.)]
ac·ces·sa·ry (ak ses′ə rē), *n., pl.* **-ries,** *adj.* *Chiefly Law.* accessory (defs. 3, 5). —**ac·ces′sa·ri·ly,** *adv.*
ac·ces·si·ble (ak ses′ə bəl), *adj.* **1.** easy to approach, enter, speak with, or use. **2.** able to be used, entered, reached, etc. **3.** obtainable; attainable: *accessible evidence.* **4.** open to the influence of (usually fol. by *to*): *accessible to bribery.* [< L *accessibil(is)*] —**ac·ces′si·bil′i·ty,** *n.* —**ac·ces′si·bly,** *adv.*
ac·ces·sion (ak sesh′ən), *n.* **1.** act of coming into the possession of a right, title, office, etc.: *accession to the throne.* **2.** an increase by the addition of something: *an accession of territory.* **3.** something added: *accessions to a library.* **4.** *Law.* addition to property by growth or improvement. **5.** consent; agreement; approval: *accession to a demand.* **6.** *Internat. Law.* formal acceptance of a treaty, international convention, or other agreement between states. —*v.t.* **7.** to make a record of (a book, painting, etc.) in the order of acquisition. **8.** to acquire (a book, pamphlet, etc.), esp. for a permanent collection. [< L *accessiōn-* (s. of *accessiō*) an approach, addition] —**ac·ces′sion·al,** *adj.*
ac·ces·so·ry (ak ses′ə rē), *n., pl.* **-ries,** *adj.* —*n.* **1.** a subordinate or supplementary part, object, etc., used mainly for convenience, attractiveness, safety, etc., as an automobile spotlight or a camera tripod. **2.** an article or set of articles of dress, as gloves, earrings, or scarf, that adds completeness, convenience, attractiveness, etc., to one's basic apparel. **3.** *Law.* **a.** Also called **acces′sory before′ the fact′.** a person who, though not present during the commission of a felony, is guilty of having aided and abetted another who has committed a felony. **b.** Also called **acces′sory af′ter the fact′.** a person who knowingly conceals or assists another who has committed a felony. —*adj.* **4.** Also, **ac·ces·so·ri·al** (ak′si sōr′ē əl, -sôr′-). contributing to a general effect; supplementary. **5.** *Law.* giving aid as an accessory. [< ML *accessōri(us)*] —**ac·ces′so·ri·ly,** *adv.*
ac′cess time′, *Computer Technol.* the elapsed time from the instant that information is called from a storage unit to the instant it is received.

ac·ciac·ca·tu·ra (ä chä′kə to͝or′ə; *It.* ät chäk′kä to͞o′rä), *n., pl.* **-tu·ras, -tu·re** (-to͝or′ā, -to͝or′ē; *It.* -to͞o′re). *Music.* **1.** a short appoggiatura. **2.** a short grace note one half step below, and struck at the same time as, a principal note. [< It: lit., a pounding, crushing = *acciaccat(o)* (*acciacc-* crush, pound < ? + *-ato* -ATE[1]) + *-ura* -URE]

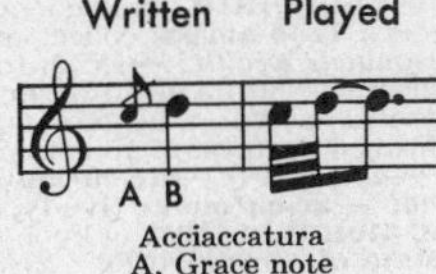

Acciaccatura
A, Grace note
B, Principal note

ac·ci·dence (ak′si dəns), *n.* **1.** the rudiments or essentials of a subject. **2.** *Gram.* the study of inflection and word order as grammatical devices. [< L *accidentia*, neut. pl. of *accidēns* (prp. of *accidere* to fall, befall). See ACCIDENT]

ac·ci·dent (ak′si dənt), *n.* **1.** an unintentional or unexpected happening that is undesirable or unfortunate, esp. one resulting in injury, damage, harm, or loss. **2.** any event that happens unexpectedly. **3.** chance; fortune; luck: *I was there by accident.* **4.** *Philos.* any entity or event contingent upon the existence of something else. **5.** *Geol.* an unexplained, usually small, surface irregularity. [< L *accident-* (s. of *accidēns* happening, prp. of *accidere* to befall) = *ac-* AC- + *-cid-*, var. of *-cad-* fall + *-ent-* -ENT] **—Syn. 1.** mischance, misfortune, misadventure, contingency, disaster, calamity, catastrophe. **—Ant. 3.** design, intent.

ac·ci·den·tal (ak′si den′tᵊl), *adj.* **1.** happening by chance or accident. **2.** nonessential; incidental: *accidental benefits.* **3.** *Music.* relating to or indicating sharps, flats, or naturals. **—***n.* **4.** a nonessential or subsidiary circumstance, characteristic, or feature. **5.** *Music.* a sign placed before a note indicating a chromatic alteration of its pitch. [< ML *accidentāl(is).* See ACCIDENT, -AL[1]] **—ac′ci·den′tal·ly,** *adv.* **—ac′ci·den′tal·ness, ac′ci·den·tal′i·ty,** *n.*
—Syn. 1. unintentional, unplanned, contingent. ACCIDENTAL, CASUAL, FORTUITOUS all describe something outside the usual course of events. ACCIDENTAL implies occurring unexpectedly or by chance: *an accidental blow.* CASUAL describes a passing event of slight importance: *a casual reference.* FORTUITOUS is applied to events occurring without known cause: *a fortuitous shower of meteors.* **—Ant. 1.** planned.

ac·cip·i·ter (ak sip′i tər), *n.* any hawk of the genus *Accipiter*, of the family *Accipitridae*, having short, rounded wings and a long tail and feeding chiefly on small mammals and birds. [< L: hawk]

ac·cip·i·tral (ak sip′i trəl), *adj.* accipitrine. [< L *accipitr-* (s. of *accipiter*) ACCIPITER + -AL[1]]

ac·cip·i·trine (ak sip′i trin, -trīn′), *adj.* **1.** of, pertaining to, or belonging to the family *Accipitridae*, comprising the hawks, Old World vultures, kites, harriers, and eagles. **2.** raptorial; like or related to birds of prey. Also, **accipitral.** [< L *accipitr-* (s. of *accipiter*) ACCIPITER + -INE[1]]

ac·claim (ə klām′), *v.t.* **1.** to salute with shouts or sounds of joy and approval; applaud: *to acclaim the conquering heroes.* **2.** to announce or proclaim by acclamation: *to acclaim someone king.* **—***v.i.* **3.** to make acclamation; applaud. **—***n.* **4.** acclamation (defs. 1, 2). [< L *acclām(āre)*] **—ac·claim′er,** *n.*

ac·cla·ma·tion (ak′lə mā′shən), *n.* **1.** a loud shout or other demonstration of welcome, good will, or applause. **2.** act of acclaiming. **3.** an affirmative vote made by shouts, hand-clapping, etc., rather than by formal ballot. [< L *acclāmātiōn-* (s. of *acclāmātiō*) a shouting = *acclāmāt(us)* (ptp. of *acclāmāre*; see ACCLAIM, -ATE[1]) + *-iōn-* -ION] **—ac·clam·a·to·ry** (ə klam′ə tôr′ē, -tōr′ē), *adj.*

ac·cli·mate (ə klī′mit, ak′lə māt′), *v.t., v.i.,* **-mat·ed, -mat·ing.** to accustom or become accustomed to a new climate or environment; adapt. [< F *acclimat(er)*] **—ac·cli·mat·a·ble** (ə klī′mi tə bəl), *adj.* **—ac·cli·ma·tion** (ak′lə mā′shən), *n.*

ac·cli·ma·tise (ə klī′mə tīz′), *v.t., v.i.,* **-tised, -tis·ing.** *Chiefly Brit.* acclimatize. **—ac·cli′ma·tis′a·ble,** *adj.* **—ac·cli′ma·ti·sa′tion,** *n.* **—ac·cli′ma·tis′er,** *n.*

ac·cli·ma·tize (ə klī′mə tīz′), *v.t., v.i.,* **-tized, -tiz·ing.** to acclimate. **—ac·cli′ma·tiz′a·ble,** *adj.* **—ac·cli′ma·ti·za′tion, ac·cli′ma·ta′tion,** *n.* **—ac·cli′ma·tiz′er,** *n.*

ac·cliv·i·ty (ə kliv′i tē), *n., pl.* **-ties.** an upward slope, as of ground; an ascent (opposed to *declivity*). [< L *acclīvitās* = *acclīv(is)* steep (*ac-* AC- + *-clīvis*, alter. of *clīvus* slope) + *-itās* -ITY] **—ac·cliv′i·tous, ac·cli·vous** (ə klī′vəs), *adj.*

ac·co·lade (ak′ə lād′; ak′ə läd′), *n.* **1.** any award, honor, or laudatory notice. **2.** a light blow upon the shoulder, given with the flat of a sword in the act of conferring knighthood upon a person. **3.** *Music.* a brace joining several staves. [< F < It *accollat(a)*, fem. of *accollato* (ptp. of *accollāre* to hug around the neck). See AC-, COLLAR, -ATE[1]] **—ac·co·lad·ed** (ak′ə lā′did), *adj.*

ac·com·mo·date (ə kom′ə dāt′), *v.,* **-dat·ed, -dat·ing.** **—***v.t.* **1.** to do a kindness or a favor for; oblige. **2.** to provide suitably; supply. **3.** to lend money. **4.** to provide with lodging, or food and lodging. **5.** to afford space for: *This elevator accommodates 12 persons.* **6.** to make suitable or consistent; adapt: *to accommodate oneself to circumstances.* **7.** to bring into harmony; adjust; reconcile: *to accommodate differences.* **—***v.i.* **8.** to become or be conformable; act conformably; agree. [< L *accommodāt(us)* adjusted (ptp. of *accommodāre*) = *ac-* AC- + *commod(us)* fitting, suitable (*com-* COM- + *modus* measure, manner) + *-ātus* -ATE[1]] **—ac·com′mo·da·ble,** *adj.* **—ac·com′mo·da′tive,** *adj.* **—ac·com′mo·da′tive·ness,** *n.* **—ac·com′mo·da′tor,** *n.* **—Syn. 1.** serve, aid, assist, help. See **oblige. 5.** See **contain.**

ac·com·mo·dat·ing (ə kom′ə dā′ting), *adj.* easy to deal with; eager to help or please; obliging. **—ac·com′mo·dat′ing·ly,** *adv.*

ac·com·mo·da·tion (ə kom′ə dā′shən), *n.* **1.** the act of accommodating. **2.** the state or process of being accommodated. **3.** adjustment of differences; reconciliation. **4.** *Sociol.* a process of mutual adaptation between persons or groups, usually achieved by eliminating or reducing hostility, as by compromise, arbitration, etc. **5.** anything that supplies a need, want, convenience, etc. **6.** Usually, **accommodations. a.** lodging. **b.** food and lodging. **c.** a seat, berth, or other facilities for a passenger on a train, plane, etc. **7.** readiness to aid others; obligingness. **8.** a loan. **9.** *Ophthalm.* the automatic adjustment by which the eye adapts itself to distinct vision at different distances. **10.** See **accommodation bill.** [< L *accommodātiōn-* (s. of *accommodātiō*)] **—ac·com′mo·da′tion·al,** *adj.*

accommoda′tion bill′, a bill, draft, or note made, drawn, accepted, or endorsed by one person for another without consideration, to enable the second person to obtain credit or raise money.

accommoda′tion lad′der, a portable flight of steps suspended at the side of a vessel to give access to and from boats, a wharf, etc.

ac·com·pa·ni·ment (ə kum′pə ni mənt, ə kump′ni-), *n.* **1.** something incidental or added for ornament, symmetry, etc. **2.** *Music.* a part in a composition designed to serve as background and support for more important parts: *a piano accompaniment.*

ac·com·pa·nist (ə kum′pə nist, ə kump′nist), *n. Music.* a person who plays an accompaniment, esp. on the piano. Also, **accompanyist.**

ac·com·pa·ny (ə kum′pə nē), *v.t.,* **-nied, -ny·ing. 1.** to go along or in company with; join in action: *to accompany a friend on a walk.* **2.** to be or exist in association with: *Thunder accompanies lightning.* **3.** to put something else in association or together with (usually fol. by *with*): *He accompanied his speech with gestures.* **4.** *Music.* to play or sing an accompaniment to. [late ME *accompanye* < MF *accompagni(er)*] **—ac·com′pa·ni·er,** *n.*
—Syn. 1. ACCOMPANY, ATTEND, CONVOY, ESCORT mean to go along with someone (or something). To ACCOMPANY is to go along as an associate on equal terms: *to accompany a friend on a shopping trip.* ATTEND implies going along with, usually to render service or perform duties: *to attend one's employer on a business trip.* To CONVOY is to accompany (esp. ships) with an armed guard for protection: *to convoy a fleet of merchant vessels.* To ESCORT is to accompany in order to protect, guard, honor, or show courtesy: *to escort a visiting dignitary.*

ac·com·pa·ny·ist (ə kum′pə nē ist), *n.* accompanist.

ac·com·plice (ə kom′plis), *n.* a person who helps another in a crime or wrongdoing; accessory. [AC- + late ME *complice* < MF < ML *complici-* (s. of *complex*) partner; see COMPLEX]

ac·com·plish (ə kom′plish), *v.t.* **1.** to bring to a successful conclusion; perform fully; fulfill: *to accomplish one's mission.* **2.** to complete (a distance or period of time). [late ME, earlier *accomplice* < MF *acompliss-* (s. of *acomplir*) = *a-* AC- + L *complē(re)* (to) fill up (*com-* COM- + *plere* to FILL) + *-sc-* -ISH[2]] **—ac·com′plish·a·ble,** *adj.* **—ac·com′plish·er,** *n.* **—Syn. 1.** complete, execute, effect. See **do**[1].

ac·com·plished (ə kom′plisht), *adj.* **1.** completed; effected: *an accomplished fact.* **2.** perfected by practice, experience, or training; expert: *an accomplished scholar.* **3.** having all the social graces, manners, and other attainments of polite society.

ac·com·plish·ment (ə kom′plish mənt), *n.* **1.** the act of carrying into effect; fulfillment. **2.** anything accomplished; achievement. **3.** Often, **accomplishments. a.** a grace, skill, or knowledge expected in polite society. **b.** any acquired ability or knowledge. [late ME] **—Syn. 1.** completion, execution, consummation. **—Ant. 1.** failure.

ac·cord (ə kôrd′), *n.* **1.** proper relationship or proportion; harmony. **2.** a harmonious union of sounds. **3.** consent or concurrence of opinions or wills; agreement. **4.** an international agreement. **—***v.t.* **5.** to make to agree or correspond; adapt. **6.** to grant; bestow: *to accord due praise.* **—***v.i.* **7.** to be in agreement or correspondence; agree. [late OE *ācordian* < VL **acordāre* = L *ac-* AC- + *cord-* heart, mind + *-āre* inf. suffix (translated *-ian* in OE)] **—ac·cord′a·ble,** *adj.* **—ac·cord′er,** *n.* **—Syn. 5.** reconcile. **7.** concur. See **correspond.**

ac·cord·ance (ə kôr′dᵊns), *n.* **1.** agreement; conformity: *in accordance with the rules.* **2.** act of according or granting: *the accordance of all rights and privileges.* [ME *acordance* < OF]

ac·cord·ant (ə kôr′dᵊnt), *adj.* agreeing; conformable. [ME *acordant* < OF] **—ac·cord′ant·ly,** *adv.*

ac·cord·ing (ə kôr′ding), *adj.* **1.** agreeing. **2.** *Informal.* depending: *It's all according what you want to do.* Cf. **according to.** [ME]

ac·cord·ing·ly (ə kôr′ding lē), *adv.* **1.** in accordance; correspondingly. **2.** therefore; so; in due course. [ME] **—Syn. 1, 2.** consequently, hence, thus. See **therefore.**

accord′ing to′, 1. in accordance or accord with: *according to his judgment.* **2.** consistent with; contingent on or in proportion to: *You'll be taxed according to your income level.* **3.** as stated by; on the authority of: *According to the weather report, it will rain today.*

Accordion

ac·cor·di·on (ə kôr′dē ən), *n. Music.* **1.** Also called **piano accordion.** a portable wind instrument having a large bellows for forcing air through small metal reeds, a keyboard for the right hand, and buttons for sounding either single bass notes or chords for the left hand. **2.** a similar instrument having single-note buttons instead of a keyboard for the right hand. **—***adj.* **3.** having folds like the bellows of an accordion: *accordion pleat.* [ACCORD + -ION, modeled on *clarion*] **—ac·cor′di·on·ist,** *n.*

ac·cost (ə kôst′, ə kost′), *v.t.* **1.** to confront boldly. **2.** to approach, esp. with a greeting or remark. **3.** (of prostitutes, procurers, etc.) to solicit (someone) for immoral purposes. **—***n.* **4.** a greeting. [< LL *accost(āre)* (to) be or put side by side. See AC-, COAST] **—ac·cost′a·ble,** *adj.*

ac·couche·ment (A ko͞osh mäN′; *Eng.* ə ko͞osh′mänt, -mənt), *n., pl.* **-ments** (-mäN′; *Eng.* -mänts, -mənts). *French.* **1.** period of confinement in childbirth. **2.** childbirth; parturition. [lit., a going to bed]

ac·cou·cheur (A ko͞o shœr′), *n., pl.* **-cheurs** (-shœr′). *French.* a man who assists during childbirth; obstetrician. [lit., he who is present at the bedside]

ac·cou·cheuse (A ko͞o shœz′), *n., pl.* **-cheuses** (-shœz′). *French.* a midwife. [lit., she who is present at the bedside]

ac·count (ə kount′), *n.* **1.** a verbal or written description of particular transactions or events; narrative. **2.** an explanatory statement of conduct, as to a superior. **3.** a statement of reasons, causes, etc., explaining some event. **4.** reason; basis; consideration: *On this account I'm refusing your offer.* **5.** importance; worth; value; consequence: *things of no account.* **6.** estimation; judgment: *In his account it was an excellent piece of work.* **7.** *Business, Banking, and Finance.* **a.** an official business relation, as with a bank, store, or stockbroker, allowing a depositor, customer, or client certain banking or credit privileges. **b.** the money or credit available to such a depositor, customer, or client, as the amount of money deposited in a checking or a savings account at a bank. **c.** a banking or credit privilege or service extended by a bank, store, or the like, to customers or clients. **8.** a statement of pecuniary transactions. **9.** *Bookkeeping.* **a.** a formal record of the debits and credits relating to the person named, or caption placed, at the head of the ledger account. **b.** a balance of receipts and expenditures for a specified period. **10.** *Com.* **a.** any customer or client. **b.** the business assigned to an advertising agency by a client: *The toothpaste account was awarded to a new agency.* **11. give a good (bad,** etc.) **account of,** to conduct oneself in a certain manner: *She gave a good account of herself in the tennis tournament.* **12. on account of, a.** by reason of; because of. **b.** for the sake of: *She saw it through on account of me.* **13. on (someone's) account,** in the interest or for the sake of someone: *She left her native land on her husband's account.* **14. take account of,** to make allowance for; consider: *One must take account of the difficult circumstances.* Also, **take into account.** —*v.i.* **15.** to give an explanation (usually fol. by *for*). **16.** to answer concerning one's conduct, duties, etc. (usually fol. by *for*): *to account for shortages.* **17.** to provide a report on money received, kept, and spent. **18.** to cause (usually fol. by *for*): *Reckless driving accounted for the accident.* —*v.t.* **19.** to count; consider as: *I account myself well paid.* **20.** to assign or impute (usually fol. by *to*): *the many virtues accounted to him.* [ME *acunt(en)* < OF *acunt(er).* See AC-, COUNT[1]] —**Syn. 1.** report, chronicle. See **narrative.**

ac·count·a·ble (ə koun′tə bəl), *adj.* **1.** subject to the obligation to report, explain, or justify something; responsible; answerable. **2.** capable of being explained; explicable. —**ac·count′a·bil′i·ty, ac·count′a·ble·ness,** *n.* —**ac·count′a·bly,** *adv.*

ac·count·an·cy (ə koun′tᵊn sē), *n.* the art or practice of an accountant.

ac·count·ant (ə koun′tᵊnt), *n.* a person whose profession is inspecting and auditing personal or commercial accounts. [ACCOUNT + -ANT; r. late ME *accomptant* < MF; OF *acuntant,* prp. of *acunter* to ACCOUNT] —**ac·count′ant·ship′,** *n.*

account′ exec′utive, an executive responsible for managing a client's account, esp. in an advertising agency.

ac·count·ing (ə koun′ting), *n.* the theory or system of organizing, maintaining, and auditing the books of a firm; art of analyzing the financial position and operating results of a business house from a study of its sales, purchases, overhead, etc. (distinguished from *bookkeeping*). [ME]

account′ pay′able, *pl.* **accounts payable.** a liability or record of liability to a creditor, carried on open account, usually for purchases of goods and services.

account′ receiv′able, *pl.* **accounts receivable.** a claim or record of a claim against a debtor, carried on open account, usually limited to debts due from the sale of goods and services.

ac·cou·ter (ə ko͞o′tər), *v.t.* to equip or outfit, esp. with military accouterments. Also, *esp. Brit.,* **accoutre.** [earlier *accou(s)tre* < MF *accoustre(r)* (*ac-* AC- + *coustre* attendant who robes clergy in vestry)]

ac·cou·ter·ment (ə ko͞o′tər mənt), *n.* **1.** equipage; trappings. **2.** the equipment, excluding arms and clothing, of a soldier. Also, *esp. Brit.,* **ac·cou·tre·ment** (ə ko͞o′tər mənt, -trə-). [< MF *accou(s)trement*]

ac·cou·tre (ə ko͞o′tər), *v.t.,* **-tred, -tring.** *Chiefly Brit.* accouter.

Ac·cra (ak′rə, ə krä′), *n.* a seaport in and the capital of Ghana, on the Gulf of Guinea. 700,000. Also, **Akkra.**

ac·cred·it (ə kred′it), *v.t.* **1.** to ascribe or attribute to; credit: *a discovery accredited to Edison.* **2.** to provide or send with credentials: *to accredit an envoy.* **3.** to certify (a school or college) as meeting all formal requirements, as of academic excellence, facilities, etc. **4.** to make authoritative, creditable, or reputable; sanction. **5.** to believe. [earlier *acredit* < MF *acredit(er)*] —**ac·cred′i·ta′tion, ac·cred′it·ment,** *n.*

ac·crete (ə krēt′), *v.,* **-cret·ed, -cret·ing,** *adj.* —*v.i.* **1.** to grow together; adhere (usually fol. by *to*). —*v.t.* **2.** to add, as by growth. —*adj.* **3.** *Bot.* grown together. [back formation from ACCRETION]

ac·cre·tion (ə krē′shən), *n.* **1.** an increase by natural growth or by gradual external addition. **2.** the result of this process. **3.** an extraneous addition. **4.** the growing together of separate parts into a single whole. **5.** *Law.* increase of property by gradual additions caused by acts of nature, as of land by alluvion. [< L *accrētiōn-* (s. of *accrētiō*) = *accrēt(us)* increased, ptp. of *accrēscere* to grow (*ac-* AC- + *crē-* grow + *-tus* ptp. suffix) + *-iōn-* -ION] —**ac·cre′tive, ac·cre′tion·ar′y,** *adj.*

ac·cru·al (ə kro͞o′əl), *n.* **1.** the act or process of accruing. **2.** something accrued; accretion.

ac·crue (ə kro͞o′), *v.i.,* **-crued, -cru·ing. 1.** to happen or result as a natural growth, addition, etc. **2.** to be added as a matter of periodic gain or advantage, as interest on money. **3.** *Law.* to become an enforceable right. [late ME *acrewe* < MF *acreue* growth] —**ac·cru′al,** *adj.* —**ac·crue′ment,** *n.*

acct., account.

ac·cul·tur·a·tion (ə kul′chə rā′shən), *n.* **1.** *Sociol.* the process of adopting the cultural traits or social patterns of another group. **2.** the result of this process. —**ac·cul′tur·a′tion·al,** *adj.* —**ac·cul′tur·a′tion·ist,** *n.* —**ac·cul′tur·a′·tive,** *adj.*

ac·cul·tur·ize (ə kul′chə rīz′), *v.t.,* **-ized, -iz·ing.** to cause (an ethnic group) to adopt the culture of another people. [ACCULTUR(ATION) + -IZE]

accum., accumulative.

ac·cum·bent (ə kum′bənt), *adj.* **1.** reclining: *accumbent posture.* **2.** *Bot.* lying against something. [< L *accumbent-* (s. of *accumbēns,* prp. of *accumbere*) = *ac-* AC- + *cumb-* (nasalized var. of *cub-* lie, recline; see COVEY) + *-ent-* -ENT] —**ac·cum′ben·cy,** *n.*

ac·cu·mu·late (ə kyo͞o′myə lāt′), *v.,* **-lat·ed, -lat·ing.** —*v.t.* **1.** to amass; collect or gather, as into a mass: *to accumulate wealth.* —*v.i.* **2.** to increase in amount or number; grow, as into a heap or mass. **3.** to develop, combine, or gather, as into a heap or mass; collect. [< L *accumulāt(us)* heaped up (ptp. of *accumulāre*) = *ac-* AC- + *cumul(us)* heap + *-ātus* -ATE[1]] —**ac·cu′mu·la·ble,** *adj.* —**ac·cu′mu·la′tive,** *adj.* —**ac·cu′mu·la′tive·ly,** *adv.* —**ac·cu′mu·la′tive·ness,** *n.*

ac·cu·mu·la·tion (ə kyo͞o′myə lā′shən), *n.* **1.** the act or state of accumulating. **2.** the state of being accumulated. **3.** something that is accumulated; an accumulated amount, number, or mass. **4.** growth by continuous additions. [< L *accumulātiōn-* (s. of *accumulātiō*)]

ac·cu·mu·la·tor (ə kyo͞o′myə lā′tər), *n.* **1.** a person or thing that accumulates. **2.** a register or electric device on an arithmetic machine, as an adding machine, cash register, digital computer, etc., that receives a number and produces and stores the results of arithmetic operations of the given number with other numbers. **3.** an apparatus for storing the fluid in a hydraulic or pneumatic system to assure a constant supply at working pressure. **4.** *Brit.* a storage battery or storage cell. [< L *accumulātor*]

ac·cu·ra·cy (ak′yər ə sē), *n., pl.* **-cies. 1.** condition or quality of being true, correct, or exact; precision, exactness, or correctness. **2.** *Chem., Physics.* the extent to which a given measurement agrees with the standard value for that measurement. Cf. **precision** (def. 5). **3.** *Math.* the degree of correctness of a quantity, expression, etc. Cf. **precision** (def. 4). [ACCUR(ATE) + -ACY]

ac·cu·rate (ak′yər it), *adj.* **1.** conforming to truth; free from error. **2.** consistent with a standard, rule, or model; free from defect. **3.** precise; careful or meticulous; not making mistakes: *an accurate typist.* [< L *accūrāt(us)* carefully prepared (ptp. of *accūrāre*) = *ac-* AC- + *cūr(a)* care + *-ātus* -ATE[1]] —**ac′cu·rate·ly,** *adv.* —**ac′cu·rate·ness,** *n.* —**Syn. 1.** true, unerring. See **correct.**

ac·curs·ed (ə kûr′sid, ə kûrst′), *adj.* **1.** subject to a curse; ruined. **2.** deserving to be cursed; damnable. Also, **ac·curst** (ə kurst′). [ME *acursed,* OE *ācursod,* ptp. of *ācursian*] —**ac·curs·ed·ly** (ə kûr′sid lē), *adv.* —**ac·curs′ed·ness,** *n.*

accus., accusative.

ac·cu·sa·tion (ak′yo͝o zā′shən), *n.* **1.** a charge of wrongdoing; imputation of guilt or blame. **2.** the specific offense charged: *an accusation of murder.* **3.** the act of accusing or charging. Also, **ac·cus·al** (ə kyo͞o′zəl). [late ME *accusacion* < L *accūsātiōn-* (s. of *accūsātiō*) = *accūsāt(us)* (ptp.) called to account (see ACCUSE, -ATE[1]) + *-iōn-* -ION]

ac·cu·sa·tive (ə kyo͞o′zə tiv), *Gram.* —*adj.* **1.** noting a case that indicates the direct object of a verb or preposition. **2.** accusatory. —*n.* **3.** the accusative case. **4.** a word in the accusative case. [< L *accūsātīv(us)* = *ac-* AC- + *cūsātīvus,* var. of *causātīvus;* see CAUSATIVE (*accūsātīvus* is a loan transl. of Gk *aitiatikḗ,* in the sense of causing)] —**ac·cu·sa·ti·val** (ə kyo͞o′zə tī′vəl), *adj.* —**ac·cu′sa·tive·ly,** *adv.*

ac·cu·sa·to·ri·al (ə kyo͞o′zə tôr′ē əl, -tôr′-), *adj.* pertaining to an accuser. —**ac·cu′sa·to′ri·al·ly,** *adv.*

ac·cu·sa·to·ry (ə kyo͞o′zə tôr′ē, -tôr′ē), *adj.* containing an accusation; accusing. Also, **accusative.** [< L *accūsātōri(us)* = *accūsāt(us)* (ptp. of *accūsāre* to ACCUSE) + *-ōrius* -ORY[1]]

ac·cuse (ə kyo͞oz′), *v.,* **-cused, -cus·ing.** —*v.t.* **1.** to charge with a fault, offense, or crime. **2.** to blame. —*v.i.* **3.** to make an accusation. [ME *ac(c)use* < OF *acuse(r)* < L *accūs(āre)* (to) call to account (*ac-* AC- + *cūs-,* var. of *caus-;* see CAUSE)] —**ac·cus′a·ble,** *adj.* —**ac·cus′a·bly,** *adv.* —**ac·cus′er, ac·cus′ant,** *n.* —**ac·cus′ing·ly,** *adv.* —**Syn. 1.** arraign, indict; incriminate, impeach. —**Ant. 1, 2.** exonerate.

ac·cused (ə kyo͞ozd′), *adj.* **1.** charged with a fault, offense, or crime. —*n.* **2.** the defendant or defendants in a trial. **3.** a person or persons charged with a mistake, fault, offense, etc.

ac·cus·tom (ə kus′təm), *v.t.* to familiarize by custom or use; habituate: *to accustom oneself to cold weather.* [late ME < MF *acoustume(r).* See AC-, CUSTOM]

ac·cus·tomed (ə kus′təmd), *adj.* **1.** customary; habitual: *in their accustomed manner.* **2.** in the habit of (usually fol. by *to* or an infinitive): *He is accustomed to staying up late.* [ME] —**ac·cus′tomed·ly,** *adv.* —**ac·cus′tomed·ness,** *n.* —**Syn. 1.** usual, characteristic. **2.** used (to).

AC/DC, *Elect.* alternating current or direct current. Also, **A.C./D.C., ac/dc, a-c/d-c, a.c.-d.c.**

ace (ās), *n.* **1.** a playing card or a die face bearing a single pip or spot. **2.** (in tennis, badminton, handball, etc.) **a.** Also called **service ace.** a placement made on a service. **b.** any placement. **c.** a successful serve that the opponent fails to touch. **d.** the point thus scored. **3.** a very skilled person; expert. **4.** a fighter pilot credited with downing a prescribed number or more of enemy aircraft, usually five. **5.** Also called **hole in one.** *Golf.* a shot in which the ball is driven from the tee into the hole in one stroke. **6. ace in the hole,** an advantage or a resource kept until the proper opportunity presents itself: *His strength in a crisis is an ace in the hole.* **7. have** or **keep an ace up one's sleeve,** to be in possession of the most important information, argument, etc. —*adj.* **8.** excellent; first in quality; outstanding. [ME *as, aas* < OF *as* < L *as* the whole, a unit, perh. < dial. Gk *ás* one (Gk *heîs*)]

-acea, *Zool.* a learned borrowing from Latin, used in the formation of names of classes and orders: *Crustacea.* [< L, neut. pl. of *-āceus.* See -ACEOUS]

-aceae, *Bot.* a learned borrowing from Latin, used in the formation of names of families: *Rosaceae.* [< L, fem. pl. of *-āceus.* See -ACEOUS]

A·cel·da·ma (ə sel′də mə), *n.* the place near Jerusalem purchased with the bribe Judas took for betraying Jesus. Acts 1:18, 19. [< L < Gk *Akeldamá* < Aram *hăqēl dămā* field of blood]

a·cen·tric (ā sen′trik), *adj.* **1.** not centered. **2.** having no center.

-aceous, a suffix of adjectives, used in scientific terminology and in the formation of adjectives from stems ending in **-acea** and **-aceae:** *cretaceous; herbaceous.* [< L *-āceus* of the nature of]

a·ceph·a·lous (ā sef′ə ləs), *adj.* **1.** headless or lacking a distinct head. **2.** without a leader or ruler.

a·ce·quia (ə sā′kyə; *Sp.* ä se′kyä), *n., pl.* **-quias** (-kyəz; *Sp.* -kyäs). *Southwestern U.S.* an irrigation ditch. [< Sp < Ar *as sāqiyah* the irrigating stream]

ac·er·ate (as′ə rāt′, -ər it), *adj.* acerose[1]. [< L *ācer* sharp + -ATE[1]]

a·cerb (ə sûrb′), *adj.* **1.** sour or astringent in taste. **2.** harsh or severe, as of temper or expression. Also, **a·cer·bic** (ə sûr′bik). [< L *acerb(us)* bitter, morose]

ac·er·bate (*v.* as′ər bāt′; *adj.* ə sûr′bit), *v.*, **-bat·ed, -bat·ing,** *adj.* —*v.t.* **1.** to make sour or bitter. **2.** to exasperate. —*adj.* **3.** embittered. [< L *acerbāt(us)* (ptp. of *acerbāre*)]

a·cer·bi·ty (ə sûr′bi tē), *n.* **1.** sourness, with astringency of taste. **2.** harshness or severity, as of temper or expression. [< L *acerbitās*]

ac·er·ose[1] (as′ə rōs′), *adj.* *Bot.* needle-shaped, as the leaves of the pine. Also, **acerate, ac·er·ous** (as′ər əs). [special sense of ACEROSE[2], by confusion of *acer-* with L *acus* needle]

ac·er·ose[2] (as′ə rōs′), *adj.* **1.** resembling chaff. **2.** mixed with chaff. [< L *acerōs(us)* = *acer-* (s. of *acus*) chaff + *-ōsus* -OSE[1]]

a·cer·vate (ə sûr′vit, -vāt), *adj.* *Bot.* growing in heaps or in closely compacted clusters. [< L *acervāt(us)* heaped up (ptp. of *acervāre*) = *acerv(us)* heap + *-ātus* -ATE[1]] —**a·cer′vate·ly,** *adv.*

a·ces·cent (ə ses′ənt), *adj.* turning sour; slightly sour; acidulous. [< L *acēscent-* (s. of *acēscēns* souring, prp. of *acēscere*) = *ac-* sharp + *-ēscent-* -ESCENT] —**a·ces′cence, a·ces′cen·cy,** *n.*

acet-, var. of **aceto-,** esp. before a vowel.

ac·e·tab·u·lum (as′i tab′yə ləm), *n., pl.* **-la** (-lə). **1.** *Anat.* the socket in the hipbone, which receives the head of the thighbone. **2.** *Zool.* any of the suction appendages of a leech, octopus, etc. [< L: vinegar cup = *acēt(um)* vinegar + *-abulum* suffix denoting instrument or vessel] —**ac′e·tab′u·lar,** *adj.*

ac·e·tal (as′i tal′), *n.* *Chem.* **1.** a volatile liquid, $CH_3CH(OC_2H_5)_2$, having a nutlike aftertaste: used as a solvent, in perfumery, in organic synthesis, and as a hypnotic. **2.** any of a class of compounds of aldehydes with alcohols.

ac·et·al·de·hyde (as′i tal′də hīd′), *n.* *Chem.* a water-soluble liquid, CH_3CHO, having a fruitlike odor: used chiefly in the silvering of mirrors and in organic synthesis.

ac·et·am·ide (as′i tam′īd, -id; ə set′ə mīd′, -mid), *n.* *Chem.* a water-soluble solid, CH_3CONH_2, used chiefly in organic synthesis. Also, **ac·et·am·id** (as′i tam′id, ə set′ə-mid). Also called **ace′tic ac′id am′ide.**

ac·et·an·i·lide (as′i tan′ᵊlīd′, -ᵊlid), *n.* *Chem., Pharm.* a white powder, $CH_3CONHC_6H_5$, used chiefly in organic synthesis and in the treatment of fever, headache, and rheumatism. Also, **ac·et·an·i·lid** (as′i tan′ᵊlid).

ac·e·tate (as′i tāt′), *n.* **1.** *Chem.* a salt or ester of acetic acid. **2.** a synthetic filament, yarn, or fabric composed of a derivative of the acetic ester of cellulose. —**ac′e·tat′ed,** *adj.*

a·ce·tic (ə sē′tik, ə set′ik), *adj.* pertaining to, derived from, or producing vinegar or acetic acid.

ace′tic ac′id, *Chem.* a water-miscible liquid, CH_3COOH, the essential constituent of vinegar: used chiefly in the manufacture of acetate fibers and in other organic syntheses.

ace′tic anhy′dride, *Chem.* a colorless liquid, $(CH_3CO)_2O$, the anhydride of acetic acid: used chiefly as a reagent and in the production of plastics and synthetic fibers.

a·cet·i·fy (ə set′ə fī′), *v.t., v.i.*, **-fied, -fy·ing.** to turn into vinegar; make or become acetous. —**a·cet′i·fi·ca′tion, ac·e·ta·tion** (as′i tā′shən), *n.* —**a·cet′i·fi′er,** *n.*

aceto-, a combining form indicating the presence of acetic acid or the acetyl group (*acetophenetidin*), used esp. before a consonant. Also, *esp. before a vowel,* **acet-.** [< L *acēt(um)* vinegar + -o-]

ac·e·tom·e·ter (as′i tom′i tər), *n.* *Chem.* an instrument for measuring the amount of acetic acid present in a solution. Also, **ac·e·tim·e·ter** (as′i tim′i tər). —**ac·e·to·met·ri·cal, ac·e·ti·met·ri·cal** (as′i tə me′tri kəl), **ac·e·to·met·ric, ac·e·ti·met·ric** (as′i tə me′trik), *adj.* —**ac′e·to·met′ri·cal·ly, ac′e·ti·met′ri·cal·ly,** *adv.* —**ac′e·tom′e·try, ac′e·tim′e·try,** *n.*

ac·e·tone (as′i tōn′), *n.* *Chem.* a volatile, flammable liquid, $(CH_3)_2CO$, used chiefly in paints and varnishes, as a solvent, and in organic synthesis. —**ac·e·ton·ic** (as′i ton′ik), *adj.*

ac·e·to·phe·net·i·din (as′i tō fə net′i din, ə sē′tō-), *n.* *Pharm.* a crystalline solid, $CH_3CONHC_6H_4OC_2H_5$: used chiefly as an agent for decreasing fever or for relieving pain. Also, **ac·e·to·phe·net·i·dine** (as′i tō fə net′i dēn′, -din, ə sē′tō-). Also called **phenacetin.**

ac·e·to·phe·none (as′i tō fə nōn′, ə sē′tō-), *n.* *Chem.* a colorless liquid, $C_6H_5COCH_3$, having a sweet odor: used chiefly as a scent in the manufacture of perfume. Also called **phenyl methyl ketone.**

ac·e·tous (as′i təs, ə sē′-), *adj.* **1.** containing or producing acetic acid. **2.** sour; vinegary. Also, **ac·e·tose** (as′i tōs′). [< LL *acētōs(us)* = *acēt(um)* vinegar + *-ōsus* -OSE[1]]

a·ce·tum (ə sē′təm), *n.* a preparation having vinegar or dilute acetic acid as the solvent. [< L: vinegar]

a·ce·tyl (ə sēt′ᵊl, ə set′-, as′i tᵊl), *adj.* *Chem.* containing the acetyl group.

a·cet·y·late (ə set′ᵊlāt′), *v.*, **-lat·ed, -lat·ing.** *Chem.* —*v.t.* **1.** to introduce one or more acetyl groups into (a compound). —*v.i.* **2.** to become acetylated. Also, **acetylize.** —**a·cet′y·la′tion,** *n.*

a·ce·tyl·cho·line (ə sēt′ᵊl kō′lēn, -lin, -kol′ēn, -in, as′i-til-), *n.* **1.** *Biochem.* the acetic acid ester of choline, $(CH_3)_3N(OH)(CH_2)_2OCOCH_3$, released and hydrolyzed during nerve conduction and causing muscle action by transmitting nerve impulses across synapses. **2.** *Pharm.* a commercial form of this compound: used chiefly as its hydrochloride or hydrobromide in medicine to decrease blood pressure or initiate peristalsis.

a·cet·y·lene (ə set′ᵊlēn′, -ᵊlin), *n.* *Chem.* a colorless gas, $HC{\equiv}CH$: used esp. in metal cutting and welding, as an illuminant, and in organic synthesis. Also called **ethyne.** —**a·cet·y·len·ic** (ə set′ᵊlen′ik), *adj.*

ace′tyl group′, *Chem.* the univalent group, CH_3CO-, derived from acetic acid. Also called **ace′tyl rad′ical.** —**ac·e·tyl·ic** (as′i til′ik), *adj.*

a·cet·y·lide (ə set′ᵊlīd′), *n.* *Chem.* **1.** any compound derived from acetylene by the replacement of one or both of its hydrogen atoms by a metal, as silver acetylide, Ag_2Cl_2. **2.** any of a class of compounds having the general formula RC≡CM, where R is an organic group and M is a metal.

a·cet·y·lize (ə set′ᵊlīz′), *v.t., v.i.*, **-lized, -liz·ing.** acetylate. —**a·cet′y·li·za′tion,** *n.* —**a·cet′y·liz′er,** *n.*

a·ce′tyl·sal·i·cyl′ic ac′id (ə sēt′ᵊl sal′i sil′ik, ə set′-, as′i tᵊl-), *Pharm.* aspirin (def. 1).

ace·y-deuc·y (ā′sē dōō′sē, -dyōō′-), *n.* a form of backgammon.

A·chae·a (ə kē′ə), *n.* an ancient district in S Greece, on the Gulf of Corinth. Also, **A·cha·ia** (ə kā′ə, ə kī′ə).

A·chae·an (ə kē′ən), *adj.* **1.** of or pertaining to Achaea or the Achaeans. **2.** (in the *Iliad*) Greek. —*n.* **3.** an inhabitant of Achaea. **4.** a Greek, esp. a member of the Achaean League. **5.** a member of one of the four main divisions of prehistoric Greeks. Cf. **Aeolian** (def. 2), **Dorian** (def. 2), **Ionian** (def. 3). Also, **A·cha·ian** (ə kā′ən, ə kī′ən).

Achae′an League′, a political confederation of Achaean and other Greek cities, established in the late 3rd century B.C. and dissolved by the Romans in 146 B.C.

A·chae·me·nid (ə kē′mə nid, ə kem′ə-), *n., pl.* **A·chae·me·nids, Ach·ae·men·i·dae** (ak′ə men′i dē′), **Ach·ae·men·i·des** (ak′ə men′i dēz′). a member of the dynasty of kings in ancient Persia that ruled from c550 B.C. to 331 B.C. [named after *Achaemenes* (fl. 7th century B.C.), traditional founder of the dynasty]

A·cha·tes (ə kā′tēz), *n.* (in the *Aeneid*) the companion and friend of Aeneas.

ache (āk), *v.*, **ached, ach·ing,** *n.* —*v.i.* **1.** to have or suffer a continuous, dull pain. **2.** to feel sympathy, pity, or the like: *Her heart ached for the orphans.* **3.** *Informal.* to feel eager; yearn; long: *He's just aching to get even.* —*n.* **4.** a continuous, dull pain. [(v.) ME *ake(n),* OE *acan;* (n.) late ME *ake* < v.; r. ME *ache, eche,* OE *æce, ece*] —**ach′ing·ly,** *adv.* —**Syn. 1.** hurt. **4.** See **pain.**

Ach·e·lo·us (ak′ə lō′əs), *n.* *Class. Myth.* a river god, defeated by Hercules in a struggle over Deianira.

a·chene (ā kēn′), *n.* *Bot.* a small, dry, hard, one-seeded, indehiscent fruit. Also, **akene.** [< NL *achaen(ium)* = *a-* A-[6] + Gk *chain-* (s. of *chaínein* to gape) + NL *-ium* n. suffix] —**a·che′ni·al,** *adj.*

A, Achene of strawberry (1) and of fruit of sunflower (2); B, Seed

Ach·er·on (ak′ə ron′), *n.* **1.** *Class. Myth.* a river in Hades over which Charon ferried the souls of the dead. **2.** the infernal regions; hell; Hades.

Ach·e·son (ach′i sən), *n.* **Dean (Good·er·ham)** (gŏŏd′ər ham′, -əm), 1893–1971, U.S. statesman: Secretary of State 1949–53.

A·cheu·le·an (ə shōō′lē ən), *adj.* of, pertaining to, or characteristic of the Lower Paleolithic Age, during which time finely made bifacial tools were produced. Also, **A·cheu′li·an.** [< F *Acheuléen,* named after *St. Acheul* (where remains were found) + *-é* (see -EE) + *-en* -AN]

à cheval (A shə VAL′), *French.* by horse; on horseback.

a·chieve (ə chēv′), *v.*, **a·chieved, a·chiev·ing.** —*v.t.* **1.** to bring to a successful end; accomplish. **2.** to get or attain by effort: *to achieve victory.* —*v.i.* **3.** to bring about an intended result; accomplish some purpose. [ME *acheve(n)* < OF *achever* to finish, from phrase *a chef* to (the) head (i.e., to conclusion). See CHIEF] —**a·chiev′a·ble,** *adj.* —**a·chiev′er,** *n.* —**Syn. 1.** complete; effect; realize, reach. See **do**[1].

a·chieve·ment (ə chēv′mənt), *n.* **1.** something accomplished, as by superior ability, special effort, or great valor. **2.** act of achieving; accomplishment. **3.** *Heraldry.* the full display of the armorial bearings of an individual or corporation, consisting of an escutcheon, usually with a crest, helmet, mantling, and motto, and often with supporters and a badge; coat of arms. [late ME < MF *achevement* conclusion] —**Syn. 2.** attainment, realization.

achieve′ment age′, *Psychol.* the level of educational development of an individual as determined by comparing his score on an achievement test with the average score of individuals of the same chronological age.

achieve′ment quo′tient, *Psychol.* achievement age divided by chronological age, usually expressed as a multiple of 100. The achievement quotient of a ten-year-old child whose achievement age equals that of the average twelve-year-old is 1.2, or 120. *Abbr.:* AQ Cf. **intelligence quotient.**

achieve′ment test′, *Psychol.* a test designed to measure the knowledge or proficiency of an individual in something that has been learned or taught. Cf. **intelligence test.**

A·chil·les (ə kil′ēz), *n.* *Class. Myth.* the greatest Greek warrior in the Trojan War and hero of Homer's *Iliad,* killed when Paris wounded him in the heel, his one vulnerable spot. —**Ach·il·le·an** (ak′ə lē′ən), *adj.*

Achil′les heel′, an area, part, feature, trait, etc., that is solely or especially vulnerable. Also, **Achil′les' heel′.**

Achil′les ten′don, *Anat.* the tendon joining the calf muscles to the heel bone. Also, **Achil′les' ten′don.**

ach·la·myd·e·ous (ak′lə mid′ē əs), *adj.* *Bot.* having neither calyx nor corolla.

a·chlor·hy·dri·a (ā′klôr hī′drē ə, ā′klōr-), *n.* *Pathol.* absence of hydrochloric acid in the gastric juice. [< NL; see A-[6], CHLOR-[2], HYDR-[2], -IA] —**a′chlor·hy′dric,** *adj.*

a·chon·dro·pla·sia (ā kon′drə plā′zhə, -zhē ə, -zē ə), *n.* *Pathol.* defective conversion of cartilage into bone, producing dwarfism. —**a·chon·dro·plas·tic** (ā kon′drə plas′tik), *adj.*

a·choo (ä chōō′), *interj.* ahchoo.

ach·ro·mat·ic (ak′rə mat′ik), *adj.* **1.** *Optics.* **a.** free from color or chromatic aberration. **b.** able to emit, transmit, or receive light without separating it into colors. **2.** *Biol.* **a.** containing or consisting of achromatin. **b.** (of a cell structure) difficult to stain. **3.** *Music.* without accidentals or changes in key. **—ach′ro·mat′i·cal·ly,** *adv.*

a·chro·ma·tin (ā krō′mə tin), *n.* *Biol.* the portion of the nucleus of a cell not easily stainable by the usual dyes.

a·chro·ma·tise (ə krō′mə tīz′), *v.t.,* **-tised, -tis·ing.** *Chiefly Brit.* achromatize. **—a·chro′ma·ti·sa′tion,** *n.*

a·chro·ma·tism (ā krō′mə tiz′əm), *n.* *Optics.* freedom from color or chromatic aberration. Also, **ach·ro·ma·tic·i·ty** (ak′rō mə tis′i tē, ā krō′-). [ACHROMAT(IC) + -ISM]

a·chro·ma·tize (ā krō′mə tīz′), *v.t.,* **-tized, -tiz·ing.** *Optics.* to make achromatic. Also, *esp. Brit.* **achromatise.** [ACHROMAT(IC) + -IZE] **—a·chro′ma·ti·za′tion,** *n.*

a·chro·ma·tous (ā krō′mə təs), *adj.* **1.** without color. **2.** having little or inadequate color; lighter in color than normal. [ACHROMAT(IC) + -OUS]

a·chro·mic (ā krō′mik), *adj.* colorless; without coloring matter. Also, **a·chro′mous.**

a·cic·u·la (ə sik′yə lə), *n., pl.* **-lae** (-lē′). a needlelike part; spine, bristle, or needlelike crystal. [< NL, LL: small pin for a headdress = L *aci-* (var. s. of *acus*) needle + *-cula* -CULE]

a·cic·u·lar (ə sik′yə lər), *adj.* needle-shaped. **—a·cic·u·lar·i·ty** (ə sik′yə lar′i tē), *n.* **—a·cic′u·lar·ly,** *adv.*

a·cic·u·late (ə sik′yə lit, -lāt′), *adj.* **1.** having aciculae. **2.** acicular. Also, **a·cic′u·lat′ed.**

ac·id (as′id), *n.* **1.** *Chem.* a compound, usually having a sour taste and capable of neutralizing alkalis and reddening blue litmus paper, containing hydrogen that can be replaced by a metal or an electropositive group to form a salt, or containing an atom that can accept a pair of electrons from a base. **2.** a substance with a sour taste. **3.** *U.S. Slang.* See **LSD** (def. 1). **—***adj.* Also, **acidic** (for defs. 5, 7). **4.** *Chem.* **a.** belonging or pertaining to acids or the anhydrides of acids. **b.** having only a part of the hydrogen of an acid replaced by a metal or its equivalent: *an acid phosphate.* **5.** sharp or biting to the taste; tasting like vinegar; sour: *acid fruits.* **6.** sharp, biting, or ill-natured in mood, manner, etc.: *an acid remark; an acid wit.* **7.** *Geol.* containing much silica. **8.** *Metall.* noting, pertaining to, or made by a process in which the lining of the furnace or the slag that is present, usually a siliceous material, as sand or ganister, functions as an acid in high-temperature reactions in taking electrons from oxide ions. Cf. **basic** (def. 3). [< L *acid(us)* sour, akin to *ācer* sharp, *acētum* vinegar] **—ac′id·ly,** *adv.* **—ac′id·ness,** *n.*

Ac·i·dal·i·um (as′i dal′ē əm), *n.* **Mare.** See **Mare Acidalium.**

ac·id-fast (as′id fast′, -fäst′), *adj.* (of bacteria and tissues) resistant to decolorizing by acidified alcohol after staining. **—ac′id-fast′ness,** *n.*

ac·id-form·ing (as′id fôr′ming), *adj.* yielding acid in chemical reaction; acidic.

ac′id head′, *U.S. Slang.* a habitual user of LSD. Also, **ac·id·head** (as′id hed′).

a·cid·ic (ə sid′ik), *adj.* **1.** acid (def. 5). **2.** *Geol.* acid (def. 7). **3.** acid-forming.

a·cid·i·fy (ə sid′ə fī′), *v.,* **-fied, -fy·ing.** **—***v.t.* **1.** to make or convert into acid. **—***v.i.* **2.** to become or convert into acid. **—a·cid′i·fi′a·ble,** *adj.* **—a·cid′i·fi·ca′tion,** *n.* **—a·cid′i·fi′er,** *n.*

ac·i·dim·e·ter (as′i dim′i tər), *n.* *Chem.* an instrument for measuring the amount of acid in a solution. **—ac·i·di·met·ric** (as′i də me′trik), **ac′i·di·met′ri·cal,** *adj.* **—ac′i·di·met′ri·cal·ly,** *adv.* **—ac′i·dim′e·try,** *n.*

a·cid·i·ty (ə sid′i tē), *n.* **1.** the quality or state of being acid. **2.** sourness; tartness. **3.** excessive acid quality, as of the gastric juice. [< LL *aciditās*]

ac·i·do·phil (as′i dō fil′, ə sid′ə-), *Biol.* **—***adj.* **1.** acidophilic. **—***n.* **2.** an acidophilic cell, tissue, organism, or substance; eosinophil. Also, **ac·i·do·phile** (as′i dō fīl′, ə sid′ə-).

ac·i·do·phil·ic (as′i dō fil′ik, ə sid′ə-), *adj.* *Biol.* staining easily with acid stains; eosinophilic. Also, **ac·i·doph·i·lus** (as′i dof′ə ləs).

acidoph′ilus milk′, a fermented milk typically produced by growing the bacterium *Lactobacillus acidophilus* in milk, used in medicine to alter the microbial flora of the intestinal tract. [< NL; see ACID, -O-, -PHILOUS]

ac·i·do·sis (as′i dō′sis), *n.* *Pathol.* a blood condition in which the bicarbonate concentration is below normal. [< NL] **—ac·i·dot·ic** (as′i dot′ik), *adj.*

ac′id rain′, rain containing large amounts of acid-bearing chemicals, such as the pollutants from coal smoke, vehicle exhaust, or chemical manufacturing, that have been released into the atmosphere and combined with water vapor: regarded as harmful to the environment.

ac′id test′, a severe, conclusive test to establish genuineness, worth, etc.

a·cid·u·late (ə sij′ə lāt′, ə sid′yə-), *v.t.,* **-lat·ed, -lat·ing.** to make acid. [ACIDUL(OUS) + -ATE] **—a·cid′u·la′tion,** *n.*

a·cid·u·lous (ə sij′ə ləs, ə sid′yə-), *adj.* **1.** slightly sour. **2.** sharp; caustic. **3.** moderately acid or tart; subacid. Also, **a·cid′u·lent.** [< L *acidulus*]

ac·id·y (as′i dē), *adj.* acid (def. 5).

ac·i·er·ate (as′ē ə rāt′), *v.t.,* **-at·ed, -at·ing.** to convert (iron) into steel. [< F *acier* steel (< VL **aciār(ium)*] **—ac′i·er·a′tion,** *n.*

ac·i·form (as′ə fôrm′), *adj.* needle-shaped; acicular. [< L *ac-* (s. of *acus*) needle + -I- + -FORM]

ac·i·nac·i·form (as′ə nas′ə fôrm′), *adj.* *Bot.* scimitar-shaped, as a leaf. [< L *acīnac-* (s. of *acīnacēs* < Gk *akinákēs* short sword) + -I- + -FORM]

Acinaciform leaf

a·cin·i·form (ə sin′ə fôrm′), *adj.* **1.** clustered like grapes. **2.** acinous.

ac·i·nous (as′ə nəs), *adj.* consisting of acini. Also, **ac·i·nose** (as′ə nōs′). [< L *acinōs(us).* See ACINUS, -OUS]

ac·i·nus (as′ə nəs), *n., pl.* **-ni** (-nī′). **1.** *Bot.* one of the small drupelets or berries of an aggregate, baccate fruit, as the blackberry. **2.** a berry, as a grape, currant, etc. **3.** *Anat.* **a.** a minute rounded lobule. **b.** the smallest secreting portion of a gland. [< L: grape, berry, seed of a berry] **—a·cin·ic** (ə sin′ik), *adj.*

-acious, a form resulting from the addition of the adjectival suffix **-ous** to stems ending in **-acity** or **-acy:** *audacious; fallacious.* [< L *-āci-* (s. of *-āx*) adj. suffix + -OUS]

-acity, a formal element meaning "quality of" or "abounding in," appearing in loan words from Latin: *tenacity.* [ME *-acite* << L *-ācitāt-* (s. of *-ācitās*). See -AC, -ITY]

ack-ack (ak′ak′), *n.* **1.** antiaircraft fire. **2.** antiaircraft arms. Also, **Ack′-Ack′.** [for A.A. (abbreviation) as said by British signalmen, by assoc. with *aircraft* and *attack*]

ac·knowl·edge (ak nol′ij), *v.t.,* **-edged, -edg·ing.** **1.** to admit to be real or true; recognize the existence, truth, or fact of: *to acknowledge that the earth is round.* **2.** to admit or show recognition or realization of. **3.** to recognize the authority, validity, or claims of. **4.** to show or express appreciation or gratitude for: *I acknowledge your recommendation with thanks.* **5.** to make known the receipt of, as with a response or reply: *to acknowledge a greeting.* **6.** *Law.* to confirm as binding or of legal force. [late ME *acknowleche*] **—ac·knowl′edge·a·ble,** *adj.* **—ac·knowl′·edged·ly,** *adv.* **—ac·knowl′edg·er,** *n.*

—Syn. 1. concede, grant. ACKNOWLEDGE, ADMIT, CONFESS agree in declaring something to be true. ACKNOWLEDGE implies making a statement, often reluctantly, about something previously doubted or denied: *to acknowledge a fault.* ADMIT especially implies acknowledging something under pressure: *to admit a charge.* CONFESS usually means stating somewhat formally an admission of wrongdoing, crime, or shortcoming: *to confess guilt; to confess an inability to understand.*

ac·knowl·edg·ment (ak nol′ij mənt), *n.* **1.** the act of acknowledging or admitting. **2.** recognition of the existence or truth of anything. **3.** an expression of appreciation. **4.** a thing done or given in appreciation or gratitude. **5.** *Law.* declaration by a person before an official that he has executed a legal document. Also, *esp. Brit.,* **ac·knowl′edge·ment.**

a·clin′ic line′ (ā klin′ik), an imaginary line on the surface of the earth, close and approximately parallel to the equator, connecting all points over which a magnetic needle shows no inclination from the horizontal. Also called **magnetic equator.** [< Gk *aklin(ḗs)* not bending]

A.C.L.U., American Civil Liberties Union.

ac·me (ak′mē), *n.* the highest point; summit. [< Gk *akmḗ* point, highest point, extremity] **—ac·mic** (ak′mik), **ac·mat·ic** (ak mat′ik), *adj.*

ac·ne (ak′nē), *n.* *Pathol.* an inflammatory disease of the sebaceous glands, characterized by an often pustular eruption of the skin, esp. of the face. [< Gk *aknḗ* facial eruption]

a·cock (ə kok′), *adv., adj.* cocked.

ac·o·lyte (ak′ə līt′), *n.* **1.** an altar attendant in public worship; altar boy. **2.** *Rom. Cath. Ch.* **a.** a member of the highest-ranking of the four minor orders. **b.** the order itself. Cf. **exorcist** (def. 2), **lector** (def. 2), **ostiary** (def. 1). **3.** any attendant, assistant, or follower. [< ML *acolyt(us)* < Gk *akólouthos* follower, attendant = *a-* prefix denoting association + *-kolouthos,* var. of *kéleuthos* road, journey]

A·con·ca·gua (ä′kông kä′gwä), *n.* a mountain in W Argentina, in the Andes: the highest peak in the Western Hemisphere. 22,834 ft.

ac·o·nite (ak′ə nīt′), *n.* any ranunculaceous plant of the genus *Aconitum,* including species with poisonous and medicinal properties. Also, **a·co·ni·tum** (ak′ə nī′təm). Cf. **monkshood, wolfsbane.** [< L *aconīt(um)* < Gk *akóniton* leopard's bane, wolfsbane] **—ac·o·nit·ic** (ak′ə nit′ik), *adj.*

a·corn (ā′kôrn, ā′kərn), *n.* the typically ovoid fruit or nut of an oak, enclosed at the base by a cupule. [ME *acorne,* r. *akern,* OE *æcern, æcren* mast, oak **mast;** c. Icel *akarn,* Goth *akran* fruit, yield]

A, Acorn
C, Cupule

a′corn bar′nacle. See under **barnacle.**

a′corn squash′, an acorn-shaped variety of winter squash, dark-green to orange-yellow in color.

a′corn tube′, *Electronics.* a vacuum tube, resembling an acorn in size and shape, used chiefly in ultrahigh-frequency electronic devices.

a·cot·y·le·don (ā′kot^əlēd′^ən, ā kot′-), *n.* any plant without cotyledons, therefore any plant belonging to a group lower than the seed plants. **—a·cot·y·le·don·ous** (ā′kot^əlēd′^ənəs, ā kot′^əlēd′-; ā′kot^əled′^ənəs, ā kot′^əled′-), *adj.*

a·cous·tic (ə ko͞o′stik *or, esp. Brit.,* ə kou′-), *adj.* **1.** pertaining to the sense or organs of hearing, to sound, or to the science of sound. **2.** (of a building material) designed for controlling sound: *acoustic tile.* **3.** activated or operated by sound waves: *an acoustic mine.* **4.** using, measuring, or recording sound waves: *Sonar is an acoustic device.* Also, **a·cous′ti·cal.** [< Gk *akoustik(ós)* = *akous-* (< *akoúesthai* to listen) + *-tikos* -TIC] **—a·cous′ti·cal·ly,** *adv.*

acous′tical cloud′, an acoustic panel suspended from the ceiling of a concert hall to reflect sound and improve the acoustic quality of music.

ac·ous·ti·cian (ak′o͞o stish′ən *or, esp. Brit.,* ak′ou-), *n.* a specialist in acoustics.

acous′tic phonet′ics, the study or branch of phonetics dealing with the sounds of speech in terms of their acoustic properties, as loudness, pitch, duration, etc., esp. as analyzed by such instruments as the sound spectrograph, oscillograph, etc. Cf. **articulatory phonetics.**

a·cous·tics (ə ko͞o′stiks *or, esp. Brit.,* ə kou′-), *n.* **1.** (*construed as sing.*) *Physics.* the branch of physics that deals with sound and sound waves. **2.** (*construed as pl.*) the qualities or characteristics of a room, auditorium, stadium, etc., that determine the audibility or fidelity of sounds in it. [see ACOUSTIC, -ICS]

à cou·vert (A ko͞o VER′), *French.* under cover; sheltered.

A.C.P., American College of Physicians.

ac·quaint (ə kwānt′), *v.t.* **1.** to make familiar or conversant; accustom to (usually fol. by *with*): *She acquainted her daughter with good music.* **2.** to furnish with knowledge; inform (usually fol. by *with*): *I'm not acquainted with the facts of the case.* **3.** to bring into social contact; introduce (usually fol. by *with*): *I'll acquaint you with my sister when she arrives.* [ME *acointe(n)* < OF *acoint(i)er* < ML *accognitāre* < L *accognitus* made known to (ptp. of *accognoscere*) = *ac-* AC- + *co-* co- + *gni-* know + *-tus* ptp. suffix]

ac·quaint·ance (ə kwān′t^əns), *n.* **1.** a person whom one knows but who is not a close personal friend. **2.** Also, **ac·quaint′ance·ship′.** the state of being acquainted. **3.** personal knowledge: *a good acquaintance with opera.* **4.** (*construed*

as pl.) the persons with whom one is acquainted. [ME *acoyntaunce* < OF *acointance*]
—Syn. 1. ACQUAINTANCE, ASSOCIATE, COMPANION, FRIEND refer to a person with whom one is in contact. An ACQUAINTANCE is a person known, though not intimately: *a casual acquaintance.* An ASSOCIATE is a person who is often in one's company, usually because of some work, enterprise, or pursuit in common: *a business associate.* A COMPANION is a person who shares one's activities, fate, or condition: *a traveling companion; companion in despair.* A FRIEND is a person with whom one is on intimate terms and for whom one feels a warm affection: *a trusted friend.*

ac·quaint·ed (ə kwān′tid), *adj.* **1.** having personal knowledge; informed (usually fol. by *with*): *to be acquainted with law.* **2.** having been brought into social contact; introduced. [ME] **—ac·quaint′ed·ness,** *n.*

ac·quest (ə kwest′), *n.* *Law.* property acquired other than by inheritance, as by purchase or gift. [< obs. F < VL **acquaesit(um)* that which has been acquired, n. use of *acquaesitus* (ptp. of *acquaerere* to acquire, alter. of L *acquīrere* to ACQUIRE)]

ac·qui·esce (ak′wē es′), *v.i.*, **-esced, -esc·ing.** to assent tacitly; consent or comply. [< L *acquiēsce(re)* (to) find rest in = *ac-* AC- + *quiēt-* (see QUIET[1]) + *-sce-* inchoative suffix] **—ac′qui·esc′ing·ly,** *adv.* **—Syn.** accede, concur.

ac·qui·es·cence (ak′wē es′əns), *n.* **1.** act or condition of acquiescing or giving tacit assent; submission implying consent; compliance (usually fol. by *to* or *in*): *acquiescence to his boss's demands.* **2.** *Law.* neglect to take legal proceedings for such a long time as to imply the abandonment of a right.

ac·qui·es·cent (ak′wē es′ənt), *adj.* disposed to acquiesce or yield; submissive; compliant. [< L *acquiēscent-* (s. of *acquiēscēns,* prp. of *acquiēscere*)] **—ac′qui·es′cent·ly,** *adv.*

ac·quire (ə kwīər′), *v.t.*, **-quired, -quir·ing. 1.** to come into possession of; get as one's own. **2.** to gain for oneself through one's actions or efforts: *to acquire learning.* [< L *acquīre(re)* (to) get besides (*ac-* AC- + *quīr-,* var. of *quaer-* get); r. late ME *aquere* < MF *aquer(re)* < L] **—ac·quir′a·bil′i·ty,** *n.* **—ac·quir′a·ble,** *adj.* **—ac·quir′er,** *n.* **—Syn. 1.** See **get.**

acquired′ char′acter, *Genetics.* a noninheritable character that results from certain environmental influences.

acquired′ immunodefi′ciency syn′drome. See **AIDS.** Also, **acquired′ immune′ defi′ciency syn′drome.**

ac·quire·ment (ə kwīər′mənt), *n.* **1.** act of acquiring, esp. the gaining of knowledge or mental attributes. **2.** Often, **acquirements.** something that is acquired; an attainment.

ac·qui·si·tion (ak′wi zish′ən), *n.* **1.** the act or an instance of acquiring possession. **2.** something acquired: *a recent acquisition to the library.* [< L *acquīsītiōn-* (s. of *acquīsītiō*) = *acquīsīt(us)* gotten (ptp. of *acquīrere* to ACQUIRE) + *-iōn-* -ION]

ac·quis·i·tive (ə kwiz′i tiv), *adj.* tending or seeking to acquire and own, often greedily. [ACQUISIT(ION) + -IVE] **—ac·quis′i·tive·ly,** *adv.* **—ac·quis′i·tive·ness,** *n.*

ac·quit (ə kwit′), *v.t.*, **-quit·ted, -quit·ting. 1.** to relieve from a charge of fault or crime. **2.** to release or discharge (a person) from an obligation. **3.** to settle or satisfy (a debt, obligation, claim, etc.). **4.** to bear or conduct (oneself) as specified; behave: *He acquitted himself well in battle.* **5.** to free or clear (oneself), as of an accusation or suspicion. [ME *aquit(en)* < OF *aquite(r)* = *a-* (< L *ac-* AC-) + *quiter* to QUIT] **—ac·quit′ter,** *n.* **—Syn. 1.** exculpate. See **absolve.**

ac·quit·tal (ə kwit′əl), *n.* **1.** the act of acquitting; discharge. **2.** the state of being acquitted; release. **3.** discharge or settlement of a debt, obligation, etc. **4.** *Law.* judicial deliverance from a criminal charge on a verdict of not guilty.

ac·quit·tance (ə kwit′əns), *n.* **1.** the act of acquitting. **2.** discharge of or from debt or obligation. **3.** a document or receipt as evidence of the discharge of debt, obligation, etc. [late ME *aquitance* < OF]

acr-, var. of **acro-** before a vowel: *acronym.*

a·cre (ā′kər), *n.* **1.** a common variable unit of land measure, now equal in the U.S. and Great Britain to 43,560 square feet or 1/640 square mile. **2. acres, a.** lands; land in general: *the fertile acres of Kentucky.* **b.** *Informal.* large quantities: *a library with acres of books.* [ME *aker,* OE *æcer;* c. Icel *akr,* Goth *aker(s),* OHG *ackar* (G *Acker*), L *ager,* Gk *agrós*(s), Skt *ájra*]

A·cre (ä′krə *for 1;* ä′kər, ā′kər *for 2*), *n.* **1.** a state in W Brazil. 160,208 (1960); 58,899 sq. mi. *Cap.:* Rio Branco. **2.** a seaport in NW Israel. 28,100 (est. 1963).

a·cre·age (ā′kər ij), *n.* extent or area in acres; acres collectively.

a·cred (ā′kərd), *adj.* owning many acres; landed.

a·cre-foot (ā′kər fo͝ot′), *n.* a unit of volume of water in irrigation: the volume that would cover one acre to a depth of one foot, equal to 43,560 cubic feet.

a·cre-inch (ā′kər inch′), *n.* one-twelfth of an acre-foot.

ac·rid (ak′rid), *adj.* **1.** sharp or biting to the taste or smell; bitterly pungent; irritating to the eyes, nose, etc. **2.** extremely or sharply stinging or caustic: *acrid remarks.* [< L *ācr-* (s. of *ācer*) sharp, sour + -ID[4], perh. through influence of ACID] **—a·crid·i·ty** (ə krid′i tē), **ac′rid·ness,** *n.* **—ac′rid·ly,** *adv.*

ac·ri·dine (ak′ri dēn′, -din), *n.* *Chem.* a colorless, crystalline solid, $C_{13}H_9N$: used in the synthesis of dyes and drugs.

ac·ri·fla·vine (ak′rə flā′vin, -vēn), *n.* *Chem.* a granular solid, $C_{14}H_{14}N_3Cl$, usually in mixture with another acridine derivative, proflavine: used chiefly in medicine as an antiseptic. Also called **neutral acriflavine, trypaflavine neutral.** [ACRI(DINE) + -FLAVIN]

Ac·ri·lan (ak′rə lan′), *n.* *Trademark.* an acrylic fiber used in textiles, characterized chiefly by softness, strength, and wrinkle-resistant properties.

ac·ri·mo·ni·ous (ak′rə mō′nē əs), *adj.* caustic, stinging, or bitter in nature, speech, behavior, etc.: *an acrimonious answer.* [< ML *ācrimōniōs(us)*] **—ac′ri·mo′ni·ous·ly,** *adv.* **—ac′ri·mo′ni·ous·ness,** *n.*

ac·ri·mo·ny (ak′rə mō′nē), *n.* sharpness, harshness, or bitterness of nature, speech, disposition, etc. [< L *ācrimōnia* = *ācri-* (s. of *ācer*) sharp, sour + *-mōnia* -MONY]

acro-, a learned borrowing from Greek meaning "extremity" or "height," used in the formation of compound words: *acrophobia.* Also, *esp. before a vowel,* **acr-.** [< Gk *ákro(s)* topmost, highest; akin to L *ācer* sharp. Cf. ACME, EAR[2]]

ac·ro·bat (ak′rə bat′), *n.* **1.** a skilled performer of gymnastic feats. **2.** a person who makes sudden changes or reversals in his opinions, relationships, etc. [back formation from NL *acrobatēs* rope-dancers < Gk *akrobatos* going aloft = *akro-* ACRO- + *-batos,* verbal adj. of *bainein* to go]

ac·ro·bat·ic (ak′rə bat′ik), *adj.* of or pertaining to an acrobat or acrobatics. Also, **ac′ro·bat′i·cal.** [< Gk *akrobatik(ós)*] **—ac′ro·bat′i·cal·ly,** *adv.*

ac·ro·bat·ics (ak′rə bat′iks), *n.* **1.** (*construed as pl.*) the feats of an acrobat; gymnastics. **2.** (*construed as sing.*) the art of performing acrobatic feats. **3.** any remarkably agile feat or performance. [see ACROBAT, -ICS]

ac·ro·car·pous (ak′rə kär′pəs), *adj.* *Bot.* having the fruit at the end of the primary axis, as in ferns or mosses. [< NL *acrocarpus* < Gk *akrókarpos*]

ac·ro·dont (ak′rə dont′), *adj.* *Anat., Zool.* having rootless teeth fastened to the alveolar ridge of the jaws. **—ac′ro·dont′ism,** *n.*

ac·ro·gen (ak′rə jən), *n.* *Bot.* a flowerless plant growing and producing its reproductive structures at the apex only, as a fern or moss. **—ac·ro·gen·ic** (ak′rə jen′ik), **a·crog·e·nous** (ə kroj′ə nəs), *adj.* **—a·crog′e·nous·ly,** *adv.*

a·cro·le·in (ə krō′lē in), *n.* *Chem.* a flammable liquid, $CH_2{=}CHCHO$, having a stifling odor: used chiefly in the synthesis of dyes and pharmaceuticals. [< L *ācr-* (s. of *ācer*) sharp + *olē(re)* (to) smell + -IN[2]]

ac·ro·me·gal·ic (ak′rō mə gal′ik), *adj.* **1.** pertaining to or suffering from acromegaly. **—***n.* **2.** a person suffering from acromegaly.

ac·ro·meg·a·ly (ak′rə meg′ə lē), *n.* *Pathol.* a chronic disease characterized by enlargement esp. of the bones of the head and of the soft parts of the feet and hands, due to pituitary dysfunction. [< NL *acromegalia*]

a·cro·mi·on (ə krō′mē ən), *n.*, *pl.* **-mi·a** (-mē ə). *Anat.* the outward end of the spine of the scapula or shoulder blade. [< NL < Gk *akrōmion* = *akro-* ACRO- + *ōm(os)* shoulder + *-ion* dim. suffix] **—a·cro′mi·al,** *adv.*

a·cron·i·cal (ə kron′i kəl), *adj.* occurring at sunset, as the rising or setting of a star. Also, **a·cron′y·cal.** [alter. of *acronychal* < Gk *akrónych(os)* vespertine (*akro-* ACRO- + *nych-,* var. s. of *nýx* night + *-os* adj. suffix) + -AL[1]] **—a·cron′i·cal·ly, a·cron′y·cal·ly,** *adv.*

ac·ro·nym (ak′rə nim), *n.* **1.** a word formed from the initial letters or groups of letters of words in a set phrase, as *WAC* from *Women's Army Corps* or *loran* from *long-range navigation.* **2.** an acrostic. **—ac′ro·nym′ic, a·cron·y·mous** (ə kron′ə məs), *adj.*

a·crop·e·tal (ə krop′i təl), *adj.* *Bot.* (of an inflorescence) developing upward, toward the apex. **—a·crop′e·tal·ly,** *adv.*

ac·ro·pho·bi·a (ak′rə fō′bē ə), *n.* *Psychiatry.* a pathological dread of high places. [< NL]

a·crop·o·lis (ə krop′ə lis), *n.* **1.** a fortified hill in an ancient Greek city. **2. the Acropolis,** the citadel of Athens and the site of the Parthenon. [< Gk *akrópolis*] **—ac·ro·pol·i·tan** (ak′rə pol′i tən), *adj.*

a·cross (ə krôs′, ə kros′), *prep.* **1.** from one side to the other of: *a bridge across a river.* **2.** on or to the other side of: *across the sea.* **3.** into contact with or into the presence of, usually by accident: *to come across an old friend.* **4.** so as to be crosswise of or transverse to the length of something. **—***adv.* **5.** from one side to another. **6.** on the other side: *We'll soon be across.* **7.** crosswise; transversely: *with arms across.* **8.** so as to be understood or learned: *He couldn't get the idea across to the class.*

a·cross-the-board (ə krôs′thə bōrd′, -bôrd′, ə kros′-), *adj.* **1.** applying to all: *an across-the-board pay increase.* **2.** (of a bet) covering all possibilities of winning on a given result, esp. by placing a combination bet on one horse in a race for win, place, and show.

a·cros·tic (ə krô′stik, ə kros′tik), *n.* **1.** a series of written lines or verses in which the first, last, or other particular letters form a word, phrase, the alphabet, etc. **—***adj.* **2.** Also, **a·cros′ti·cal.** of, like, or forming an acrostic. [< Gk *akrostich(ís)* = *ákro(s)* ACRO- + *stích(os)* STICH + *-is* dim. suffix] **—a·cros′ti·cal·ly,** *adv.*

a·cryl·ic (ə kril′ik), *adj.* **1.** of, pertaining to, or characteristic of acrylic acid or its derivatives. **—***n.* **2.** See **acrylic resin.** [ACR(OLEIN) + -YL + -IC]

acryl′ic ac′id, *Chem.* a corrosive liquid, $CH_2{=}CHCOOH$, used esp. in the synthesis of acrylic resins.

acryl′ic fi′ber, *Chem.* any of a group of synthetic textile fibers, as Orlon, made by polymerizing acrylonitrile with one or more other monomers.

acryl′ic res′in, *Chem.* any of a group of thermoplastic resins formed by polymerizing the esters of amides of acrylic or methacrylic acid: used chiefly where transparency is desired. Also called **ac′rylate res′in.**

ac·ry·lo·ni·trile (ak′rə lō nī′tril, -trēl, -trīl), *n.* *Chem.* a poisonous liquid, $CH_2{=}CHCN$, used chiefly in the polymerization or copolymerization of rubber, textile fibers, and plastics. [*acryl(ic)* (see ACRYLIC ACID) + -O- + NITRILE]

A.C.S., American Chemical Society.

A/cs pay., accounts payable. Also, **a/cs pay.**

A/cs rec., accounts receivable. Also, **a/cs rec.**

act (akt), *n.* **1.** anything done, being done, or to be done; performance; deed. **2.** the process of doing: *caught in the act.* **3.** a formal decision, law, or the like, by a legislature, ruler, court, or other authority; decree or edict; statute; judgment, resolve, or award: *an act of Congress.* **4.** an instrument or document stating something done or transacted. **5.** one of the main divisions of a play or opera. **6.** a short performance by one or more entertainers, usually part of a variety show, television program, etc. **7.** two or more entertainers in partnership to present such performances. **8.** a piece of insincere conduct, pretended manner, or the like: *Her tearful farewell was all an act.* **9.** *Philos.* (in scholasticism) **a.** activity in process; operation. **b.** the principle or power of operation. **c.** form as determining essence. **d.** a state of realization, as opposed to potentiality. **—***v.i.* **10.** to do something; exert energy or force; be employed or operative. **11.** to reach, make, or issue a decision on some matter. **12.** to operate, function, or serve in a particular way: *to* *act as chairman.* **13.** to produce an effect; perform a function: *The medicine failed to act.* **14.** to behave or conduct oneself in a particular fashion: *to act well under all conditions.* **15.** to pretend or feign something false, not felt, etc.: *Try to act interested.* **16.** to perform on a stage as an actor. **17.** to be capable of being performed on the stage as specified: *His plays don't act well.* **—*v.t.* 18.** to represent (a fictitious or historical character) with one's person: *to act Macbeth.* **19.** to feign; counterfeit: *to act outraged virtue.* **20.** to behave as: *He acted the fool.* **21.** *Obs.* to actuate. **22. act on** or **upon, a.** to act in accordance with; follow: *He acted on my advice.* **b.** to bring about a change in; affect: *The stirring music acted on the emotions of the audience.* **23. act one's age,** to behave in a manner suitable to one's maturity. **24. act out, a.** to demonstrate or illustrate by pantomime or by words and gestures. **b.** *Psychol.* to behave in an inappropriate, harmful, or antisocial manner in a subconscious effort to alleviate psychic tension by the gratification of repressed desires. **25. act up,** *Informal.* **a.** to exhibit unusual or unexpected behavior: *The vacuum cleaner is acting up again.* **b.** to behave willfully: *If you're going to act up, you can't go to Grandma's.* [< L *āct(a)* (pl.) things done, and *āct(us)* a doing, n. use of ptp. of *agere* to do (*āg-* ptp. s. + *-tus* ptp. suffix); r. late ME *acte* < MF] **—Syn. 1.** feat, exploit; achievement; transaction; accomplishment. See **action. 4.** record. **6.** routine. **10, 13, 14.** perform, function, work. **16, 17.** play.

act., active.

act·a·ble (ak′tə bəl), *adj.* **1.** capable of being acted on the stage. **2.** capable of being carried out in practice. **—act′a·bil′i·ty,** *n.*

Ac·tae·on (ak tē′ən), *n.* *Class. Myth.* a hunter who, for having seen Diana bathing, was changed by her into a stag and was torn to pieces by his own hounds.

ACTH, **1.** *Biochem.* a hormone, produced by the anterior lobe of the pituitary gland, that stimulates the cortical substance of the adrenal glands. **2.** *Pharm.* this substance, extracted from the pituitary glands of animals, used in the treatment of rheumatic fever, rheumatoid arthritis, and allergic disorders. Also called **adrenocorticotropic hormone.** [*a(dreno)c(ortico)t(ropic) h(ormone)*]

ac·tin (ak′tən), *n.* *Biochem.* a globulin in muscle plasma, important in muscle contraction. [ACT + -IN[2]]

actin-, var. of **actino-** before a vowel: *actinism.*

ac·ti·nal (ak′tə nəl, ak tīn′əl), *adj.* *Zool.* **1.** having tentacles or rays. **2.** pertaining to the oral area from which the arms or tentacles radiate. [ACTIN- + -AL[1]] **—ac′ti·nal·ly,** *adv.*

act·ing (ak′ting), *adj.* **1.** serving temporarily, esp. as a substitute during another's absence; not permanent: *the acting mayor.* **2.** that acts; functioning. **3.** designed, adapted, or suitable for stage performance. **4.** provided with stage directions: *an acting version of a play.* **—*n.* 5.** the art or profession of an actor. **6.** pretending or pretense.

ac·tin·i·a (ak tin′ē ə), *n., pl.* **-tin·i·ae** (-tin′ē ē′), **-tin·i·as.** a sea anemone, esp. of the genus *Actinia.* [< NL; see ACTIN-, -IA]

ac·tin·ic (ak tin′ik), *adj.* pertaining to actinism. **—ac·tin′i·cal·ly,** *adv.*

actin′ic ray′, *Physics.* a ray of light of short wavelengths that produces photochemical effects.

ac′ti·nide se′ries (ak′tə nīd′), *Chem.* the series of radioactive elements that starts with actinium and ends with lawrencium.

ac·tin·ism (ak′tə niz′əm), *n.* the property of radiation by which chemical effects are produced.

ac·tin·i·um (ak tin′ē əm), *n.* *Chem.* a radioactive element, resembling the rare earths in chemical behavior and valence. *Symbol:* Ac; *at. no.:* 89; *at. wt.:* 227; *halflife:* 13.5 years.

actin′ium se′ries, *Chem.* the radioactive series that starts with uranium 235 and ends with a stable isotope of lead of mass number 207.

actino-, **1.** *Physical Chem.* a combining form indicating actinic radioactivity, used esp. before a consonant: *actinometer.* **2.** a combining form meaning "radiate in structure," "raylike": *actinozoan.* Also, *esp. before a vowel,* **actin-.** [< Gk, comb. form of *aktin-*, s. of *aktís* ray]

ac·tin·o·graph (ak tin′ə graf′, -gräf′), *n.* a recording actinometer. **—ac·tin·o·graph·ic** (ak tin′ə graf′ik), *adj.* **—ac·ti·nog·ra·phy** (ak′tə nog′rə fē), *n.*

ac·ti·noid (ak′tə noid′), *adj.* raylike; radiate.

ac·tin·o·lite (ak tin′əlīt′), *n.* *Mineral.* a greenish variety of amphibole. **—ac·tin·o·lit·ic** (ak′ti nəlit′ik, ak tin′əlit′-), *adj.*

ac·ti·nom·e·ter (ak′tə nom′i tər), *n.* a photochemical device for measuring radiation intensity. Cf. **actinograph. —ac·ti·no·met·ric** (ak′tə nō me′trik), **ac′ti·no·met′ri·cal,** *adj.* **—ac′ti·nom′e·try,** *n.*

ac·ti·no·mor·phic (ak′tə nō môr′fik), *adj.* **1.** *Biol.* having radial symmetry. **2.** *Bot.* (of certain flowers, as the buttercup) divisible vertically into similar halves by each of a number of planes passing through the axis. Also, **ac′ti·no·mor′phous. —ac′ti·no·mor′phy,** *n.*

ac·ti·no·my·cete (ak′tə nō mī sēt′), *n.* *Bacteriol.* any of several rod-shaped or filamentous, aerobic or anaerobic bacteria of the family *Actinomycetaceae,* of the order *Actinomycetales,* certain species of which are pathogenic for man and animals. [prob. back formation from NL *actinomycētēs* = *actino-* ACTINO- + *mycētēs,* pl. of *mycēs* < Gk *mýkēs* fungus] **—ac′tin·o·my·cet′ous,** *adj.*

ac·ti·no·my·co·sis (ak′tə nō mī kō′sis), *n.* *Vet. Pathol., Pathol.* an infectious, inflammatory disease of animals and of man, due to parasites and causing lumpy, often suppurating tumors, esp. about the jaws. Also called **lumpy jaw.** [< NL *actinomyc(ēs)* (see ACTINOMYCETE) + -OSIS] **—ac·ti·no·my·cot·ic** (ak′tə nō mī kot′ik), *adj.*

ac·ti·non (ak′tə non′), *n.* *Chem.* a chemically inert, gaseous, radioactive element isotopic with radon. It is a member of the actinium series. *Symbol:* An; *at. no.:* 86; *at. wt.:* 219. [< NL; see ACTINIUM, -ON[2]]

ac·ti·no·u·ra·ni·um (ak′tə nō yŏŏ rā′nē əm), *n.* *Chem.* a radioactive isotope of uranium having an atomic mass of 235.

ac·ti·no·zo·an (ak′tə nə zō′ən), *n., adj.* *Zool.* anthozoan.

ac·tion (ak′shən), *n.* **1.** the process or state of acting or of being active. **2.** something performed; act; deed: *Actions are more important than words.* **3.** a consciously willed act or activity (contrasted with *passion*): *a problem that demands action instead of debate.* **4. actions,** conduct; habitual or usual acts: *He is responsible for his actions.* **5.** energetic activity: *a man of action.* **6.** an exertion of power or force: *the action of wind upon a sail.* **7.** effect or influence: *the action of morphine.* **8.** *Physiol.* a change in organs, tissues, or cells leading to performance of a function, as in muscular contraction. **9.** a way or manner of moving: *the action of a machine.* **10.** a mechanism by which something is operated, as that of a breechloading rifle. **11.** a military encounter or engagement. **12.** combat, esp. military or naval combat. **13.** *Slang.* exciting activity, as a gambling game. **14.** *Literature.* the main subject or story, as distinguished from an incidental episode. **15.** *Theat.* **a.** an event or series of events that form part of a dramatic plot: *the action of a scene.* **b.** one of the three unities. Cf. **unity** (def. 8). **16.** *Law.* **a.** a proceeding instituted by one party against another. **b.** the right of bringing it. **17. in action, a.** performing or taking part in a characteristic act: *Our baseball team is in action tonight.* **b.** functioning; working: *The motor is not yet in action.* [< L *āctiōn-* (s. of *āctiō*) = *āct(us)* (see ACT) + *-iōn-* -ION; r. late ME *accioun* < AF] **—ac′tion·less,** *adj.*

—Syn. 2. ACTION, ACT, DEED mean something done. ACTION applies esp. to the doing; ACT to the result of the doing. An ACTION usually lasts through some time and consists of more than one act: *to take action on a petition.* An ACT is single and of slight duration: *an act of kindness.* DEED emphasizes the finished or completed quality of an act; it may imply an act of some note, good or bad: *an irrevocable deed; a deed of daring.* **4.** behavior. **11.** See **battle. 14.** plot. **16a.** process, case, suit, lawsuit. **—Ant. 1.** rest.

ac·tion·a·ble (ak′shə nə bəl), *adj.* furnishing grounds for a lawsuit. **—ac′tion·a·bly,** *adv.*

Ac·ti·um (ak′tē əm, -shē əm), *n.* a promontory in NW ancient Greece: site of Antony's defeat by Octavian in a naval battle 31 B.C.

ac·ti·vate (ak′tə vāt′), *v.t.,* **-vat·ed, -vat·ing. 1.** to make active. **2.** *Physics.* **a.** to render more reactive; excite: *to activate a molecule.* **b.** to induce radioactivity. **3.** to aerate (sewage) in order to accelerate decomposition of impure organic matter by microorganisms. **4.** *Chem.* **a.** to make (carbon, a catalyst, molecules, etc.) more active. **b.** to hasten (reactions) by various means, such as heating. **5.** *Mil.* to place (a military unit or station) on an active status in an assigned capacity. **—ac′ti·va′tion,** *n.*

ac′tivated sludge′, sludge (def. 5).

ac·ti·va·tor (ak′tə vā′tər), *n.* **1.** a person or thing that activates. **2.** *Chem., Biochem.* a catalyst. **3.** any impurity in a mineral that causes luminescence. Cf. **inhibitor** (def. 2).

ac·tive (ak′tiv), *adj.* **1.** constantly engaged in action; busy: *an active life.* **2.** in actual existence, progress, or motion: *active hostilities.* **3.** involving physical action: *active sports.* **4.** agile; nimble. **5.** characterized by considerable current activity: *an active market in wheat.* **6.** capable of exerting influence (opposed to *passive*): *active treason.* **7.** effective (opposed to *inert*): *active ingredients.* **8.** *Gram.* noting or pertaining to a voice of verbal inflection in which the subject performs the action expressed by the verb (opposed to *passive*): *Writes* in *He writes a letter every day* is an active verb. **9.** requiring or giving rise to action; practical. **10.** *Accounting.* profitable; busy: *active accounts.* **11.** *Mil.* serving on or pertaining to full active duty. **—*n.* 12.** *Gram.* the active voice. [< L *āctīv(us)* (see ACT, -IVE); r. ME *actif* < MF] **—ac′tive·ly,** *adv.* **—ac′tive·ness,** *n.*

—Syn. 1, 3. ACTIVE, ENERGETIC, STRENUOUS, VIGOROUS imply a liveliness and briskness in accomplishing something. ACTIVE suggests quickness and diligence as opposed to laziness or dilatory methods: *an active and useful person.* ENERGETIC suggests forceful and intense, sometimes nervous, activity: *conducting an energetic campaign.* STRENUOUS implies arduous and zealous activity with a sense of urgency: *making a strenuous effort.* VIGOROUS suggests strong, effective activity: *using vigorous measures to accomplish an end.* **4.** sprightly. **—Ant. 1.** lazy. **5.** sluggish.

ac′tive du′ty, *Mil.* **1.** the status of full duty: *on active duty.* **2.** full duty. Also called **ac′tive serv′ice.**

ac′tive immu′nity, *Immunol.* immunity resulting from the production of antibodies within an organism.

ac·tiv·ism (ak′tə viz′əm), *n.* **1.** *Philos.* **a.** a theory that the essence of reality is pure activity, esp. spiritual activity, or process. **b.** a theory that the relationship between the mind and the objects of perception depends upon the action of the mind. **2.** the doctrine or practice of vigorous action or involvement as a means of achieving political goals. [< G *Aktivismus*]

ac·tiv·ist (ak′tə vist), *n.* an especially vigorous or militant advocate of a cause.

ac·tiv·i·ty (ak tiv′i tē), *n., pl.* **-ties. 1.** the state or quality of being active. **2.** the quality of acting vigorously. **3.** a specific deed, action, function, or sphere of action: *social activities.* **4.** work, esp. in elementary grades, that involves learning by direct experience rather than by textbook study. **5.** a use of energy or force; an active movement or operation. **6.** normal mental or bodily action or vigor. **7.** liveliness, alertness, or vigorous action. **8.** *Physical Chem.* the capacity of a substance to react corrected for the loss of reactivity due to the interaction of its constituents. **9.** *Physics.* **a.** the number of atoms of a radioactive substance that disintegrate per unit of time, usually expressed in curies. **b.** radioactivity. **10.** *U.S.* an organizational unit or the function it performs. [< ML *activitāt-* (s. of *activitās*)]

act′ of faith′, **1.** an act that demonstrates or tests the strength of a person's convictions, as an important personal sacrifice. **2.** *Theol.* an act of the will, made possible by God's grace, whereby one assents to divine truth.

act′ of God′, *Law.* a direct, sudden, and irresistible action of natural forces, such as could not reasonably have been foreseen or prevented, as a flood, hurricane, earthquake, or other natural catastrophe.

act′ of war′, any act of aggression by a country against another with which it is nominally at peace.

ac·to·my·o·sin (ak′tə mī′ə sin), *n.* *Biochem.* a complex protein that is the major constituent of skeletal muscle and is thought to interact with ATP to cause muscle contraction. [ACT(IN) + -O- + MYOSIN]

Ac·ton (ak′tən), *n.* **1.** Lord (*John Emerich Edward Dalberg-Acton,* 1st Baron), 1834–1902, English historian. **2.** a city in SE England, near London: center of Puritanism at time of Cromwell. 67,274 (1961).

ac·tor (ak′tər), *n.* **1.** a person, usually a male, who acts in stage plays, motion pictures, television broadcasts, etc., esp. professionally. **2.** a person who does something; doer; participant. [< L *āctor*]

Ac′tors′ Eq′uity Associa′tion, a labor union for actors, founded in 1912 and affiliated with the AFL-CIO.

ac·tress (ak′tris), *n.* a female actor.

Acts′ of the Apos′tles, a book of the New Testament. Also called **Acts.**

ac·tu·al (ak′cho͞o əl), *adj.* **1.** existing in act or fact; real. **2.** existing at present; current; real as of now: *the actual position of the moon.* **3.** *Obs.* pertaining to or involving acts or action. [< LL *āctuāl(is)* = L *āctu-* (s. of *āctus;* see ACT) + *-ālis* -AL[1]; r. ME *actuel* < MF] —**ac′tu·al·ness,** *n.* —**Syn. 1.** genuine, veritable. —**Ant. 1.** unreal.

ac·tu·al·ise (ak′cho͞o ə līz′), *v.t.,* **-ised, -is·ing.** *Chiefly Brit.* actualize. —**ac′tu·al·i·sa′tion,** *n.*

ac·tu·al·ism (ak′cho͞o ə liz′əm), *n.* *Philos.* the doctrine that all reality is animate or in motion. —**ac′tu·al·ist,** *n., adj.* —**ac′tu·al·is′tic,** *adj.*

ac·tu·al·i·ty (ak′cho͞o al′i tē), *n., pl.* **-ties. 1.** actual existence; reality. **2. actualities,** actual conditions or circumstances; facts. [late ME *actualite* < ML *actuālitāt-* (s. of *actuālitās*)]

ac·tu·al·ize (ak′cho͞o ə līz′), *v.t.,* **-ized, -iz·ing.** to make actual; realize in action or fact. Also, *esp. Brit.,* **actualise.** —**ac′tu·al·i·za′tion,** *n.*

ac·tu·al·ly (ak′cho͞o ə lē), *adv.* as an actual or existing fact; really.

ac′tual sin′, *Theol.* any sin committed by an individual of his free will, as contrasted with original sin.

ac·tu·ar·y (ak′cho͞o er′ē), *n., pl.* **-ar·ies. 1.** *Insurance.* a person who computes premium rates, dividends, risks, etc., according to probabilities based on statistical records. **2.** (formerly) a registrar or clerk. [< L *āctuāri(us)* shorthand writer, clerk, var. (with *u* < *āctus* ACT) of *āctārius* = *āct(a)* deeds, documents + *-ārius* -ARY] —**ac·tu·ar·i·al** (ak′cho͞o-âr′ē əl), **ac′tu·ar′i·an,** *adj.* —**ac′tu·ar′i·al·ly,** *adv.*

ac·tu·ate (ak′cho͞o āt′), *v.t.,* **-at·ed, -at·ing. 1.** to incite to action; motivate: *actuated by selfish motives.* **2.** to put into action: *to actuate a machine.* [< ML *actuāt(us)* reduced to action (ptp. of *actuāre*) = L *āctu(s)* (see ACT) + *-ātus* -ATE[1]] —**ac′tu·a′tion,** *n.* —**ac′tu·a′tor,** *n.*

a·cu·i·ty (ə kyo͞o′i tē), *n.* sharpness; acuteness; keenness: *acuity of vision.* [< MF *acuite* irreg. < L *acū(tus)* sharp, ACUTE + MF *-ite* -ITY; r. OF *agüete* < *agu* sharp (< L *acūtus*)]

a·cu·le·ate (ə kyo͞o′lē it, -lē āt′), *adj.* **1.** *Bot., Zool.* having or being any sharp-pointed structure. **2.** *Entomol.* having a slender ovipositor or sting, as the hymenopterous insects. **3.** pointed; stinging. Also, **a·cu′le·at′ed.** [< L *acūleāt(us)* = *acūle(us)* (*acu(s)* needle + *-leus* dim. suffix) + *-ātus* -ATE[1]]

a·cu·men (ə kyo͞o′mən, ak′yə-), *n.* superior mental acuteness and discernment; keen insight. [< L: sharpness = *acū-* (ptp. s. of *acuere* to sharpen; see ACUTE) + *-men* n. suffix] —**a·cu·mi·nous** (ə kyo͞o′mə nəs), *adj.*

a·cu·mi·nate (*adj.* ə kyo͞o′mə nit, -nāt′; *v.* ə kyo͞o′mə nāt′), *adj., v.,* **-nat·ed, -nat·ing.** —*adj.* **1.** *Bot., Zool.* pointed; tapering to a point. —*v.t.* **2.** to make sharp or keen. [< L *acūmināt(us)* (ptp. of *acūmināre*) = *acūmin-* (s. of *acūmen*) ACUMEN + *-ātus* -ATE[1]] —**a·cu′mi·na′tion,** *n.*

Acuminate leaf

ac·u·punc·ture (*n.* ak′yo͝o pungk′chər; *v.* ak′yo͝o pungk′chər), *n., v.,* **-tured, -tur·ing.** —*n.* **1.** a traditional practice in Chinese folk medicine of attempting to cure illness by puncturing specified areas of the skin with needles. **2.** *Med.* the puncture of a tissue with a needle, as for drawing off fluids or relieving pain. —*v.t.* **3.** to perform an acupuncture on. [< L *acu-* (s. of *acus*) needle + PUNCTURE]

a·cut·ance (ə kyo͞ot′əns), *n.* *Photog.* a measure of the sharpness with which a film can reproduce the edge of an object.

a·cute (ə kyo͞ot′), *adj.* **1.** sharp at the end; ending in a point. **2.** severe in effect; intense; poignant: *acute sorrow.* **3.** extremely severe; crucial: *an acute shortage.* **4.** (of disease) brief and severe (opposed to *chronic*): *an acute attack of gout.* **5.** sharp or penetrating in intellect, insight, or perception. **6.** highly sensitive even to slight details or impressions: *acute eyesight.* **7.** *Geom.* **a.** (of an angle) less than 90°. See diag. at **angle. b.** (of a triangle) containing only acute angles. See diag. at **triangle. 8.** consisting of, indicated by, or bearing the mark "´", usually placed over vowels to indicate quality or length of the vowel or stress or pitch of the syllable (opposed to *grave*). —*n.* **9.** the acute accent. [< L *acūt(us)* sharpened (ptp. of *acuere*) = *acū-* (ptp. s., akin to *acus* needle, *ācer* sharp) + *-tus* ptp. suffix] —**a·cute′ly,** *adv.* —**a·cute′ness,** *n.* —**Syn. 2.** sudden, violent. **3.** critical. **5.** astute, perceptive. **6.** keen.

-acy, a suffix of nouns of quality, state, office, etc., many of which accompany adjectives in *-acious* or nouns or adjectives in *-ate: fallacy; papacy; legacy; delicacy; piracy.* [< L *-ācia,* ML *-ācia* (< L *-ātia*), ML *-ātia.* Cf. -CRACY]

a·cy·clic (ā sī′klik, ā sik′lik), *adj.* not cyclic.

ac·yl·ate (as′ə lāt′), *v.t.,* **-at·ed, -at·ing.** *Chem.* to introduce the acyl group into (a compound). —**ac′yl·a′tion,** *n.*

ac′yl group′, *Chem.* the univalent group, RCO–, where R is any organic group attached to one bond of the carbonyl group. Also called **ac′yl rad′ical.** [AC(ID) + -YL] —**ac·yl** (as′il, -ēl), *adj.*

ad[1] (ad), *n.* **1.** advertisement. —*adj.* **2.** advertising: *an ad director.* [by shortening]
—**Usage.** AD is not used in formal writing or speech, but there is no objection to its use in informal contexts.

ad[2] (ad), *n.* *Tennis.* **1.** advantage (def. 4). **2. ad in,** the advantage scored by the server. **3. ad out,** the advantage scored by the receiver. [by shortening]

ad-, a formal element occurring in loan words from Latin, where it meant "toward" and indicated direction, tendency, or addition; attached chiefly to stems not found as words themselves: *adjective.* Also **a-, ac-, af-, ag-, al-, an-, ap-, ar-, as-, at-.** [< L *ad, ad-* prep. and prefix: to, toward, at, about; c. AT[1]]

-ad[1], **1.** a suffix occurring in loan words from Greek denoting a numerical group: *dyad; triad.* **2.** a suffix meaning "derived from," "related to," introduced in loan words from Greek (*Olympiad*) and used sporadically in imitation of Greek models, as *Dunciad,* after *Iliad.* [comb. form repr. Gk *-ad-,* specialization of adjective-forming suffix, often used substantively]

-ad[2], var. of **-ade**[1]: *ballad.*

ad., 1. adverb. **2.** advertisement.

A.D., in the year of our Lord; since Christ was born (used in reckoning dates): *From 20* B.C. *to* A.D. *50 is 70 years.* [< L *annō Dominī*]

A.D.A., 1. American Dental Association. **2.** Americans for Democratic Action. Also, **ADA**

ad ab·sur·dum (ad ab sûr′dəm), to the point of ridiculousness. [< L: to (the) absurd]

a·dac·ty·lous (ā dak′tᵊləs), *adj.* *Zool.* having no fingers or toes. [A-[6] + DACTYL + -OUS]

ad·age (ad′ij), *n.* a traditional saying expressing a common experience or observation; proverb. [< F < L *adag(ium)* = *ad-* AD- + *agi-* (for **agi-,* s. of *āio* I say) + *-um* n. suffix] —**a·da·gi·al** (ə dā′jē əl), *adj.*

a·da·gio (ə dä′jō, -zhē ō′; *It.* ä dä′jô), *adv., adj., n., pl.* **-gios.** —*adv.* **1.** *Music.* in a leisurely manner; slowly. —*adj.* **2.** *Music.* slow. —*n.* **3.** *Music.* an adagio movement or piece. **4.** *Dance.* a duet by a man and a woman or mixed trio emphasizing difficult technical feats. [< It, for *ad agio* at ease < L *ad-* AD- + Pr *aize;* see EASE]

Ad·am (ad′əm), *n.* **1.** the name of the first man: progenitor of the human race. Gen. 2:7; 5:1–5. **2.** man. **3. James,** 1730–94, and his brother, **Robert,** 1728–92, British architects and furniture designers. —*adj.* **4.** noting or pertaining to the style of architecture, decoration, or furnishings associated with Robert and James Adam.

Ad·am-and-Eve (ad′əm ən ēv′, -ənd-), *n.* *U.S.* the puttyroot.

ad·a·mant (ad′ə mənt, -mant′), *n.* **1.** a legendary stone of extreme hardness, sometimes identified with the diamond. **2.** any impenetrably or unyieldingly hard substance. —*adj.* **3.** impenetrably or unyieldingly hard; adamantine. **4.** utterly unyielding in attitude or opinion. [< L *adamant-* (s. of *adamas*) < Gk = *a-* A-[6] + *-damant-* verbal adj. of *damân* to conquer; r. OE *athamans* (< ML) and ME *aymont* < MF *aimant* < VL **adimant-*]

ad·a·man·tine (ad′ə man′tin, -tēn, -tīn), *adj.* **1.** impenetrably or unyieldingly hard. **2.** utterly unyielding or firm in attitude or opinion. **3.** like a diamond in luster. [late ME < L *adamantin(us)* < Gk *adamántinos.* See ADAMANT, -INE[1]]

Ad·am·ic (ad′ə mik), *adj.* pertaining to or suggestive of Adam. Also, **A·dam·i·cal** (ə dam′i kəl). —**A·dam′i·cal·ly,** *adv.*

Ad·am·ite (ad′ə mīt′), *n.* **1.** a descendant of Adam; human being. **2.** a nudist. —**Ad·am·it·ic** (ad′ə mit′ik), **Ad′am·it′i·cal,** *adj.*

Ad·ams (ad′əmz), *n.* **1. Charles Francis,** 1807–86, U.S. statesman: minister to Great Britain 1861–68 (son of John Quincy Adams). **2. Henry (Brooks),** 1838–1918, U.S. historian, writer, and teacher (son of Charles Francis Adams). **3. James Trus·low** (trus′lō), 1878–1949, U.S. historian. **4. John,** 1735–1826, 2nd president of the U.S. 1797–1801: a leader in the American Revolution. **5. John Quin·cy** (kwin′zē, -sē), 1767–1848, 6th president of the U.S. 1825–29; Secretary of State 1817–25 (son of John Adams). **6. Lé·o·nie (Fuller)** (lā ō′nē), born 1899, U.S. poet. **7. Maude** (*Maude Kiskadden*), 1872–1953, U.S. actress. **8. Samuel,** 1722–1803, American statesman: a leader in the American Revolution. **9. Samuel Hopkins,** 1874–1958, U.S. journalist and novelist. **10. Mount,** a mountain in SW Washington, in the Cascade Range. 12,307 ft.

Ad′am's ap′ple, a projection of the thyroid cartilage at the front of the neck, conspicuous in men.

ad·ams·ite (ad′əm zīt′), *n.* *Chem., Mil.* a yellow irritant compound of arsenic, dispersed as a harassing agent. [named after Roger *Adams* (b. 1889), U.S. chemist; see -ITE[1]]

Ad·am's-nee·dle (ad′əmz nēd′ᵊl), *n.* *U.S.* a yucca, *Yucca filamentosa,* grown as an ornamental.

Ad′ams-Stokes′ syn′drome (ad′əmz stōks′), *Pathol.* See **Stokes-Adams syndrome.** Also called **Ad′ams-Stokes′ disease′.**

A·da·na (ä′dä nä′), *n.* a city in S Turkey. 290,515 (1965). Also called **Seyhan.**

a·dapt (ə dapt′), *v.t.* **1.** to make suitable to requirements or conditions; adjust or modify fittingly. —*v.i.* **2.** to adjust oneself to a new environment, different conditions, etc. [< L *adapt(āre)* (to) fit, adjust] —**a·dapt′ed·ness,** *n.* —**Syn. 1.** fit, accommodate, reconcile. See **adjust.**

a·dapt·a·ble (ə dap′tə bəl), *adj.* **1.** capable of being adapted. **2.** able to adjust readily to different conditions: *an adaptable person.* —**a·dapt′a·bil′i·ty, a·dapt′a·ble·ness,** *n.*

ad·ap·ta·tion (ad′əp tā′shən), *n.* **1.** the act of adapting. **2.** the state of being adapted; adjustment. **3.** something produced by adapting: *an adaptation of an opera for television.* **4.** *Biol.* **a.** any alteration in the structure or function of an organism or any of its parts by which the organism becomes better fitted to survive in its environment. **b.** a form or structure modified to fit changed environment. **5.** *Physiol.* a change, usually a decrease, in response of sensory receptor organs following an alteration in intensity or frequency of environmental stimuli. **6.** *Ophthalm.* regulation by the pupil of the quantity of light entering the eye. **7.** Also, **a·dap·tion** (ə dap′shən). *Sociol.* a slow modification of individual and social activity in adjustment to cultural surroundings. [< ML *adaptātiōn-* (s. of *adaptātiō*) = L *adaptāt(us)* fitted (ptp. of *adaptāre* to ADAPT; see -ATE[1]) + *-iōn-* -ION] —**ad′ap·ta′tion·al,** *adj.* —**ad′ap·ta′tion·al·ly,** *adv.*

a·dapt·er (ə dap′tər), *n.* **1.** a person or thing that adapts. **2.** a device for connecting parts having different sizes or designs, enabling them to be fitted together. **3.** an accessory to convert a machine, tool, etc., to a new or modified use. Also, **a·dap′tor.**

a·dap·tive (ə dap′tiv), *adj.* serving or able to adapt. —**a·dap′tive·ly,** *adv.* —**a·dap′tive·ness,** *n.*

A·dar (ə där′; *Heb.* ä dän′), *n.* the sixth month of the Jewish calendar. Cf. **Jewish calendar.** [< Heb]

Adar′ She′ni (shā′nē; *Heb.* shā nē′), an intercalary month of the Jewish calendar, added between Adar and Nisan; Veadar. Cf. **Jewish calendar.** [< Heb: Adar the Second]

ad a·stra per a·spe·ra (äd ä′strä pen ä′spe rä′; *Eng.* ad as′trə pər as′pər ə), *Latin.* to the stars through difficulties: motto of Kansas.

A.D.C., aide-de-camp.

add (ad), *v.t.* **1.** to unite or join to another or others so as to produce a greater number, quantity, size, or degree of importance. **2.** to find the sum of (often fol. by *up*). **3.** to say or write further. **4.** to include (usually fol. by *in*). —*v.i.* **5.** to perform the arithmetic operation of addition. **6.** to be or serve as an addition (usually fol. by *to*): *His illness added to the family's troubles.* **7. add up, a.** to make the desired or expected total. **b.** to seem reasonable or consistent: *There were aspects of the story that didn't add up.* **8. add up to,** to indicate by implication: *The evidence adds up to a case of murder.* [< L *add(ere)* = *ad-* AD- + *-dere* to put (see DO[1])] —**add′a·ble, add′i·ble,** *adj.* —**add′ed·ly,** *adv.* —**Syn. 1.** affix, append, attach, adjoin. **2.** total.

Addax
(3½ ft. high at shoulder; horns 3½ ft.; length 6½ ft.)

add., **1.** addenda. **2.** addition. **3.** additional. **4.** address.

Ad·dams (ad′əmz), *n.* **Jane,** 1860–1935, U.S. social worker and writer: Nobel peace prize 1931.

ad·dax (ad′aks), *n.* a large, pale-colored antelope, *Addax nasomaculatus,* of North Africa, with loosely spiral horns. [< L < some language of ancient North Africa]

ad·dend (ad′end, ə dend′), *n. Math.* any of a group of numbers or terms added together to form a sum. Cf. **augend.** [shortening of ADDENDUM]

ad·den·dum (ə den′dəm), *n., pl.* **-da** (-də). **1.** a thing to be added; an addition. **2.** an appendix or supplement to a book. [neut. sing. of L *addendus* to be added, ger. of *addere* to ADD]

add·er[1] (ad′ər), *n.* a person or thing that adds. [ADD + -ER[1]]

ad·der[2] (ad′ər), *n.* **1.** the common European viper, *Vipera berus.* **2.** any of various other venomous or harmless snakes resembling the viper. [late ME; r. ME *nadder* (*a nadder* becoming *an adder*), OE *nædre;* c. OHG *nātara* (G *Natter*), Icel *nathr(a),* Goth *nadr(s),* OIr *nathir*]

ad·der's-tongue (ad′ərz tung′), *n.* **1.** a fern of the genus *Ophioglossum,* having a fruiting spike. **2.** *U.S.* any of several American dogtooth violets.

ad·dict (*n.* ad′ikt; *v.* ə dikt′), *n.* **1.** a person who is addicted: *a drug addict.* —*v.t.* **2.** to cause addiction in. [< L *addict(us)* assigned, surrendered (ptp. of *addīcere*) = *ad-* AD- + *dic-* (ptp. s. of *dīcere* to fix, determine) + *-tus* ptp. suffix]

ad·dict·ed (ə dik′tid), *adj.* devoted or given up to a practice or habit or to something habit-forming, as a narcotic, cigarettes, etc. (usually fol. by *to*): *to be addicted to heroin.* —**ad·dict′ed·ness,** *n.*

ad·dic·tion (ə dik′shən), *n.* the state of being addicted, esp. to a habit-forming drug, to such an extent that cessation causes severe trauma. [< L *addictiōn-* (s. of *addictiō*) a giving over, surrender]

ad·dic·tive (ə dik′tiv), *adj.* **1.** producing or tending to cause addiction. **2.** more than normally susceptible to becoming addicted: *an addictive personality.*

add′ing machine′, a business machine, typically for adding, but often also capable of subtracting, multiplying, and dividing.

Ad·dis A·ba·ba (ad′is ab′ə bə, ä′dis ä′bə bä′), a city in and the capital of Ethiopia. 1,161,267.

Ad·di·son (ad′i sən), *n.* **1. Joseph,** 1672–1719, English essayist and poet. **2. Thomas,** 1793–1860, English physician.

Ad′dison's disease′, *Pathol.* a disease characterized by asthenia, low blood pressure, and a brownish skin coloration, due to disturbance of the suprarenal glands. [named after T. ADDISON, who described it]

ad·dit·a·ment (ə dit′ə mənt), *n.* something added; an addition. [< L *additāment(um)* = *addit(us)* (ptp.) added (see ADDITION) + *-ā-* connective + *-mentum* -MENT] —**ad·dit·a·men·ta·ry** (ə dit′ə men′tə rē), *adj.*

ad·di·tion (ə dish′ən), *n.* **1.** the act or process of adding or uniting. **2.** the process of uniting two or more numbers into one sum, represented by the symbol +. **3.** something that is added. **4.** *U.S.* a wing, room, etc., added to a building. **5. in addition to,** as well as; besides. [< L *additiōn-* (s. of *additiō*) = *addit(us)* added (ptp. of *addere* to ADD) + *-iōn-* -ION] —**ad·di·to·ry** (ad′i tôr′ē, -tōr′ē), *adj.* —**Syn. 1.** joining. **3.** increment; accession, supplement; appendix. ADDITION, ACCESSORY, ADJUNCT, ATTACHMENT mean something joined onto or used with something else. ADDITION is the general word, carrying no implication of size, importance, or kind, but merely that of being joined to something previously existing: *an addition to an income, to a building, to one's cares.* An ACCESSORY is a subordinate addition to a more important thing, for the purpose of aiding, completing, ornamenting, etc.: *accessories to a costume.* An ADJUNCT is a subordinate addition that aids or assists a main thing or person but is often separate: *a second machine as an adjunct to the first.* An ATTACHMENT is an accessory part that may be easily connected and removed: *a sewing-machine attachment for making pleats.*

ad·di·tion·al (ə dish′ə nəl), *adj.* added; supplementary: *additional information.* —**ad·di′tion·al·ly,** *adv.*

addi′tion pol′ymer, *Chem.* a polymer formed by the direct reaction of two or more monomers, and with no resulting water or other by-product.

ad·di·tive (ad′i tiv), *adj.* **1.** characterized or produced by addition; cumulative. **2.** *Math.* (of a function) having the property that the function of the union or sum of two quantities is equal to the sum of the functional values of each quantity; linear. —*n.* **3.** something that is added, as one substance to another, to alter or improve the general quality or to counteract undesirable properties: *an additive in food to improve its color and retard spoilage.* [< LL *additīv(us)* = *addit(us)* (ptp. of *addere* to ADD) + *-īvus* -IVE] —**ad′di·tive·ly,** *adv.*

ad·dle (ad′əl), *v.t., v.i.,* **-dled, -dling. 1.** to make or become muddled or confused. **2.** to make or become spoiled or rotten, as eggs. [ME *adel,* OE *adel(a)* liquid, filth; c. G *Adel* liquid manure, Sw (dial.) *adel* urine]

ad·dle·brained (ad′əl brānd′), *adj.* having or revealing a muddled or confused mind.

ad·dle·pat·ed (ad′əl pā′tid), *adj.* foolish; silly; addlebrained.

ad·dress (*n.* ə dres′, ad′res; *v.* ə dres′), *n., v.,* **-dressed** or **-drest, -dress·ing.** —*n.* **1.** a formal speech or statement directed to a person or group of persons. **2.** the designation of a place where a person, organization, or the like, may be found or will receive letters, parcels, etc. **3.** such a designation along with the name of the recipient or sender, placed on a letter, parcel, etc. **4.** the conversational manner of a person. **5.** skillful and expeditious management; ready skill. **6.** *Computer Technol.* a label, as an integer, symbol, or other set of characters, designating a location, register, etc., where information is stored. **7.** Usually, **addresses.** attentions paid by a lover; courtship. **8.** *Obs.* preparation. —*v.t.* **9.** to direct a speech or statement to. **10.** to call (a person or persons) by a specific name or title, as in greeting or talking. **11.** to direct (a communication) to. **12.** to direct the speech of (used reflexively, usually fol. by *to*): *He addressed himself to the chairman.* **13.** to put the directions for delivery on: *to address a letter.* **14.** to direct the energy or attention of (used reflexively, usually fol. by *to*): *He addressed himself to the task.* **15.** to woo; court. **16.** *Golf.* to take a stance and place the head of the club behind (the ball) preparatory to hitting it. **17.** *Obs.* to give direction to; aim. [late ME *adresse(n)* (to) adorn < MF *adress(er).* See AD-, DRESS] —**ad·dress′er, ad·dres′sor,** *n.* —**Syn. 1.** discourse, lecture. See **speech. 5.** adroitness, cleverness.

ad·dress·ee (ad′re sē′, ə dre sē′), *n.* a person, company, or the like, to whom a letter, package, etc., is addressed.

Ad·dres·so·graph (ə dres′ə graf′, -gräf′), *n. Trademark.* a machine designed for the rapid, automatic addressing of mail in large quantities.

ad·duce (ə do͞os′, ə dyo͞os′), *v.t.,* **-duced, -duc·ing.** to bring forward in argument or as evidence. [< L *addūce(re)* (to) bring into = *ad-* AD- + *dūcere* to lead] —**ad·duce′a·ble, ad·duc′i·ble,** *adj.* —**ad·duc′er,** *n.*

ad·du·cent (ə do͞o′sənt, ə dyo͞o′-), *adj. Physiol.* drawing toward, as by the action of a muscle; adducting. [< L *addūcent-,* s. of *addūcēns,* prp. of *addūcere* to ADDUCE]

ad·duct (ə dukt′), *v.t. Physiol.* to move or draw toward the axis of the body or one of its parts (opposed to *abduct*). [< L *adduct(us)* drawn to, ptp. of *addūcere*] —**ad·duc′tive,** *adj.*

ad·duc·tion (ə duk′shən), *n.* **1.** *Physiol.* the action of an adducent muscle. **2.** the act of adducing. [< ML *adductiōn-* (s. of *adductiō*)]

ad·duc·tor (ə duk′tər), *n.* any muscle that adducts (opposed to *abductor*). [< NL, LL: conductor]

Ade (ād), *n.* **George,** 1866–1944, U.S. humorist.

-ade[1], **1.** a suffix found in nouns denoting action or process or a person or persons acting, appearing in loan words from French and sometimes from Spanish (*cannonade; fusillade; renegade*), often irregularly attached (*blockade; masquerade*). **2.** a noun suffix indicating a drink made of a particular fruit: *lemonade.* [< F < (It or) L *-āta* (fem. of *-ātus*); < Sp *-ado* < L *-ātus* -ATE[1]]

-ade[2], a collective suffix like **-ad**[1]: *decade.* [< F < Gk *-ada,* acc. to nom. *-ás*]

Ad·e·laide (ad′əlād′), *n.* a city in and the capital of South Australia, in Australia. 899,300.

A·dé′lie Coast′ (ə dā′lē; *Fr.* A dā lē′), a coastal region of Antarctica, south of Australia: claimed by France.

-adelphous, *Bot.* a word element meaning "having stamens growing together in bundles," of the number specified by the prefix: *monadelphous.* [< Gk *adelph(ós)* brother + -OUS]

a·demp·tion (ə demp′shən), *n. Law.* the failure of a specific legacy by the disposal of it before the testator's death. [< L *ademptiōn-* (s. of *ademptiō*) a taking away = *adempt(us)* (*ad-* AD- + *em(p)-,* s. of *emere* to take + *-tus* ptp. suffix) + *-iōn-* -ION]

A·den (äd′ən, ād′ən), *n.* **1.** a seaport in and the capital of the People's Republic of Yemen. 225,000. **2. Colony of,** a former British colony on the Gulf of Aden and member of the Federation of South Arabia, now part of Southern Yemen. 75 sq. mi. **3.** Also called **Aden Protectorate.** former name of the Protectorate of South Arabia. **4. Gulf of,** an arm of the Arabian Sea between the E tip of Africa and the Arabian Peninsula.

aden-, var. of **adeno-** before a vowel: *adenine.*

A·de·nau·er (ad′nou ər, ad′ənou′-; *Ger.* äd′ənou′ən), *n.* **Kon·rad** (kon′rad; *Ger.* kōn′rät), 1876–1967, chancellor of the West German Federal Republic 1949–63.

ad·e·nine (ad′ənin, -ənēn′, -ənīn′), *n. Chem.* alkaloid, obtained from tea or by synthesis: used chiefly in medicine.

adeno-, a learned borrowing from Greek meaning "gland," used in the formation of compound words: *adenocarcinoma.* Also, *esp. before a vowel,* **aden-.** [< Gk, comb. form of *adḗn;* akin to L *inguen* groin]

ad·e·no·car·ci·no·ma (ad′ənō kär′sə nō′mə), *n., pl.* **-mas, -ma·ta** (-mə tə). *Pathol.* a malignant tumor arising in a secretory gland. —**ad·e·no·car·ci·nom·a·tous** (ad′ənō kär′sə nom′ə təs, -nō′mə-), *adj.*

ad·e·noid (ad′ənoid′), *n.* **1.** Usually, **adenoids.** an enlarged mass of lymphoid tissue in the upper pharynx. —*adj.* Also, **ad′e·noi′dal. 2.** of or pertaining to the adenoids. [< Gk *adenoeid(ḗs)*]

ad·e·noid·ec·to·my (ad′ᵊnoi dek′tə mē), *n., pl.* **-mies.** *Surg.* the operation of removing the adenoids.

ad·e·no·ma (ad′ᵊnō′mə), *n., pl.* **-mas, -ma·ta** (-mə tə). *Pathol.* **1.** a benign tumor originating in a secretory gland. **2.** a benign tumor of glandlike structure. [< NL; see ADEN-, -OMA] —**ad·e·nom·a·tous** (ad′ᵊnom′ə təs, -ᵊnō′mə-), *adj.*

a·den·o·sine (ə den′ə sēn′, -sin), *n. Chem.* a powder, $C_{10}H_{13}N_5O_4$, obtained from the nucleic acid of yeast, which upon hydrolysis produces adenine and ribose. [irreg. b. ADENINE and RIBOSE]

aden′osine triphos′phate, *Biochem.* See **ATP.** Also called **a·den′o·sine·tri·phos·phor′ic ac′id.** (ə den′ə sēn-trī′fos fôr′ik, -for′-, -sin-).

A′den Protec′torate, Aden (def. 2).

A·de·od·a·tus I (ā′dē od′ə təs), Deusdedit.

Adeodatus II, Saint, died A.D. 676, pope 672–676.

ad·ept (*adj.* ə dept′; *n.* ad′ept, ə dept′), *adj.* **1.** very skilled; proficient; expert. —*n.* **2.** a skilled or proficient person; expert. [< ML *adept(us)* one who has attained (the secret of transmuting metals), n. use of L ptp. of *adipiscī* to attain to (*ad-* AD- + *-ep-*, var. of *ap-* in *aptus* APT + *-tus* ptp. suffix)] —**a·dept′ly,** *adv.* —**a·dept′ness,** *n.*

ad·e·qua·cy (ad′ə kwə sē), *n.* the state or quality of being adequate; sufficiency for a particular purpose.

ad·e·quate (ad′ə kwit), *adj.* **1.** equal to the requirement or occasion; fully sufficient, suitable, or fit. **2.** barely sufficient or suitable: *The violinist gave only an adequate performance.* **3.** *Law.* reasonably sufficient for legal action: *adequate grounds.* [< L *adaequāt(us)* matched (ptp. of *adaequāre*). See AD-, EQUAL, -ATE[1]] —**ad′e·quate·ly,** *adv.* —**ad′e·quate·ness,** *n.* —**Syn. 1.** satisfactory, enough.

à deux (A dœ′), *French.* of or for two; two at a time.

ad ex·tre·mum (äd ek strā′mŏŏm; *Eng.* ad ek strē′məm), *Latin.* to the extreme; at last; finally.

ad fin., *Latin.* to, toward, or at the end. [< *ad fīnem*]

ad·here (ad hēr′), *v.i.,* **-hered, -her·ing. 1.** to stick fast; cleave; cling (usually fol. by *to*): *The mud adhered to his shoes.* **2.** to be devoted; be attached as a follower or upholder (usually fol. by *to*). **3.** to hold closely or firmly (usually fol. by *to*): *to adhere to a plan.* **4.** *Physics.* (of dissimilar substances) to be united by a molecular force acting in the area of contact. **5.** *Obs.* to be consistent. [< ML *adhēr(ēre)* for L *adhaerēre* (*ad-* AD- + *haerēre* to stick, cling)] —**ad·her′er,** *n.* —**Syn. 1.** See **stick.**

ad·her·ence (ad hēr′əns, -her′-), *n.* **1.** fidelity, as to a party or principle. **2.** the act or state of adhering or clinging. [< ML *adhērentia.* See ADHERE, -ENCE]

ad·her·ent (ad hēr′ənt, -her′-), *n.* **1.** a person who follows or upholds a leader, cause, etc.; supporter (usually fol. by *of*). —*adj.* **2.** sticking; clinging; adhering. **3.** *Bot.* adnate. [< ML *adhērent-* for L *adhaerent-* (s. of *adhaerēns,* prp. of *adhaerēre*)] —**ad·her′ent·ly,** *adv.* —**Syn. 1.** disciple, fan.

ad·he·sion (ad hē′zhən), *n.* **1.** the act or state of adhering or clinging. **2.** intellectual or emotional attachment, as to a party or principle. **3.** assent; concurrence. **4.** *Physics.* the molecular force of attraction in the area of contact between unlike bodies that acts to hold them together. Cf. **cohesion** (def. 2). **5.** *Pathol.* **a.** the abnormal union of adjacent tissues. **b.** the tissue involved. [< ML *adhēsiōn-* for L *adhaesiōn-* (s. of *adhaesiō*) a clinging = *adhaes(us)* clung (*ad-* AD- + *haes-,* perf. s. of *haerēre* to cling + *-sus* ptp. suffix) + *-iōn-* -ION] —**ad·he′sion·al,** *adj.*

ad·he·sive (ad hē′siv), *adj.* **1.** clinging; tenacious. **2.** adhering; gummed; sticky: *an adhesive surface.* **3.** *Physics.* of or pertaining to the molecular force that exists in the area of contact between unlike bodies and that acts to unite them. —*n.* **4.** an adhesive material or substance. **5.** a substance that causes something to adhere, such as glue, rubber cement, etc. **6.** *Philately.* a postage stamp with a gummed back, as distinguished from one embossed or printed on an envelope or card. [ADHES(ION) + -IVE] —**ad·he′sive·ly,** *adv.* —**ad·he′sive·ness,** *n.*

adhe′sive tape′, a strip of flexible material, as cotton, plastic, or the like, coated on one side with an adhesive substance, used esp. for holding a bandage in place.

ad·hib·it (ad hib′it), *v.t.* **1.** to take or let in; admit. **2.** to use or apply. **3.** to attach. [< L *adhibit(us)* brought (ptp. of *adhibēre* to bring to) = *ad-* AD- + *hibi-* (var. s. of *habēre* to hold, have) + *-tus* ptp. suffix] —**ad·hi·bi·tion** (ad′hə bish′ən), *n.*

ad hoc (ad hok′; *Lat.* äd hōk′), for this (special purpose) only; with respect to this (subject or thing).

ad ho·mi·nem (äd hō′mi nem′; *Eng.* ad hom′ə nem′), *Latin.* **1.** appealing to a prejudice, emotion, or a special interest rather than to intellect or reason. **2.** against an opponent rather than against his arguments. [lit., to the man]

ad·i·a·bat·ic (ad′ē ə bat′ik, ā′dī ə-), *adj.* occurring without gain or loss of heat: *an adiabatic process.* [< Gk *adiábat(os)* incapable of being crossed (*a-* A-[6] + *dia-* DIA- + *ba-* (s. of *baínein* to cross) + *-tos* verbal adj. suffix) + -IC] —**ad′i·a·bat′i·cal·ly,** *adv.*

ad·i·aph·or·ism (ad′ē af′ə riz′əm), *n.* tolerance of actions or beliefs not specifically prohibited in the Scriptures. [ADIAPHOR(OUS) + -ISM] —**ad′i·aph′o·rist,** *n.* —**ad′i·aph′o·ris′tic,** *adj.*

ad·i·aph·o·rous (ad′ē af′ər əs), *adj.* doing neither good nor harm, as a medicine. [< Gk *adiáphoros* = *a-* A-[6] + *diáphoros* different (*dia-* DIA- + *phor-* (var. s. of *phérein* to carry, bring) + *-os* adj. suffix)]

a·dieu (ə dōō′, ə dyōō′; *Fr.* A dyœ′), *interj., n., pl.* **a·dieus, a·dieux** (ə dōōz′, ə dyōōz′; *Fr.* A dyœ′). —*interj.* **1.** good-by; farewell. —*n.* **2.** the act or form of taking one's leave. [late ME < MF = *a* (< L *ad* to) + *dieu* (< L *deu-,* obl. s. of *deus* god)]

A·di·ge (ä′dē je), *n.* a river in N Italy, flowing SE to the Adriatic Sea. 220 mi. long.

ad inf., See **ad infinitum,** Also, **ad infin.**

ad in·fi·ni·tum (ad in′fə nī′təm), to infinity; endlessly; without limit. [< L: lit., to the endless]

ad init., See **ad initium.**

ad i·ni·ti·um (ad i nish′ē əm), at the beginning. [< L]

ad int., See **ad interim.**

ad in·te·rim (ad in′tə rim), in the meantime. [< L: lit., for the time between]

ad·i·os (ad′ē ōs′, ä′dē-; *Sp.* ä thyôs′), *interj.* good-by; farewell. [< Sp: lit., to God]

ad·i·pose (ad′ə pōs′), *adj.* **1.** resembling, containing, or pertaining to fat; fatty. —*n.* **2.** animal fat stored in the fatty tissue of the body. [< NL *adipōs(us)* (L *adip-* (s. of *adeps*) fat, suet + *-ōsus* -OSE[1])] —**ad′i·pose′ness, ad·i·pos·i·ty** (ad′ə pos′i tē), **ad′i·po′sis,** *n.*

Ad·i·ron·dack (ad′ə ron′dak), *n., pl.* **-dacks,** (*esp. collectively*) **-dack. 1.** a member of an Algonquian people living mainly north of the St. Lawrence River. **2. Adirondacks.** See **Adirondack Mountains.**

Ad′iron′dack Moun′tains, a mountain range in NE New York. Highest peak, Mt. Marcy, 5344 ft. Also called **Adirondacks.**

ad·it (ad′it), *n.* **1.** *Mining.* a nearly horizontal passage leading into a mine. **2.** an approach or access. [< L *adit(us)* an approach = *ad-* AD- + *-i-* (s. of *īre* to go) + *-tus* suffix marking n. denoting action or the means of action]

adj., **1.** adjective. **2.** adjoining. **3.** adjourned. **4.** adjudged. **5.** *Banking.* adjustment. **6.** adjutant.

ad·ja·cen·cy (ə jā′sən sē), *n., pl.* **-cies. 1.** Also, **ad·ja′cence.** the state of being adjacent. **2.** Usually, **adjacencies.** things, places, etc., that are adjacent. [< LL *adjacentia.* See ADJACENT, -ENCY]

ad·ja·cent (ə jā′sənt), *adj.* **1.** near or close; next or contiguous: *a field adjacent to the highway.* **2.** *Geom.* (of two angles) having a common vertex and one common side. [< L *adjacent-* (s. of *adjacēns,* prp. of *adjacēre* to adjoin) = *ad-* AD- + *jac-* lie + *-ent-* -ENT] —**ad·ja′cent·ly,** *adv.* —**Syn. 1.** abutting, touching. See **adjoining.**

ad·jec·ti·val (aj′ik tī′vəl), *adj.* **1.** of, pertaining to, or used as an adjective. **2.** depending for effect on intensive qualification of subject matter, as a writer or his writings. —**ad′jec·ti′val·ly,** *adv.*

ad·jec·tive (aj′ik tiv), *n.* **1.** *Gram.* any member of a class of words functioning as modifiers of nouns, as *good, wise, perfect.* —*adj.* **2.** pertaining to or functioning as an adjective; adjectival. **3.** not able to stand alone; dependent. **4.** *Law.* concerning methods of enforcement of legal rights, as pleading and practice (opposed to *substantive*). **5.** (of dye colors) requiring a mordant or the like to render them permanent (opposed to *substantive*). [late ME < LL *adjectīv(um),* neut. of *adjectīvus* = *adject(us)* added to, ptp. of *adicere* (*ad-* AD- + *jec-* lay + *-tus* ptp. suffix) + *-īvus* -IVE] —**ad′jec·tive·ly,** *adv.*

ad·join (ə join′), *v.t.* **1.** to be next to or in contact with; abut on: *His house adjoins the lake.* —*v.i.* **2.** to be connected or in contact. [late ME *a(d)joine(n)* < MF *ajoindre*]

ad·join·ing (ə joi′ning), *adj.* being in contact at some point or line; bordering; contiguous: *the adjoining room.* —**Syn.** ADJOINING, ADJACENT, BORDERING all mean near or close to something. ADJACENT implies being nearby or next to: *adjacent angles.* ADJOINING implies touching at a common point or line: *an adjoining yard.* BORDERING means having a common boundary with: *the farm bordering on the river.* —**Ant.** separated.

ad·journ (ə jûrn′), *v.t.* **1.** to suspend the meeting of (a club, legislature, committee, etc.) to a future time, another place, or indefinitely: *to adjourn the court.* **2.** to defer or postpone (a matter) to a future meeting of the same body. —*v.i.* **3.** to postpone, suspend, or transfer proceedings. [ME *ajo(u)rn(en)* < MF *ajo(u)rn(er)* = *a-* AD- + *jorn-* < L *diurn(us)* daily; see JOURNAL, JOURNEY]

ad·journ·ment (ə jûrn′mənt), *n.* **1.** the act of adjourning. **2.** the state or period of being adjourned. [< AF (legal) *adjournement,* MF]

adjt., adjutant.

ad·judge (ə juj′), *v.t.,* **-judged, -judg·ing. 1.** to pronounce formally; decree: *The will was adjudged void.* **2.** to award judicially; assign: *The prize was adjudged to him.* **3.** to decide by a judicial opinion or sentence. **4.** to sentence or condemn. **5.** to deem; consider; think. [late ME *ajuge* < MF *ajug(i)e(r)* < L *adjūdicāre.* See ADJUDICATE]

ad·ju·di·cate (ə jōō′də kāt′), *v.,* **-cat·ed, -cat·ing.** —*v.t.* **1.** to pronounce or decree by judicial sentence; settle judicially; pass judgment on. —*v.i.* **2.** to sit in judgment (usually fol. by *upon*). [< L *adjūdicāt(us)* (ptp. of *adjūdicāre*). See AD-, JUDGE, -ATE[1]] —**ad·ju·di·ca·tive** (ə jōō′də kā′tiv, -kə tiv), *adj.* —**ad·ju′di·ca′tor,** *n.*

ad·ju·di·ca·tion (ə jōō′də kā′shən), *n.* **1.** the act of adjudicating. **2.** *Law.* a judicial decision or sentence. [< LL *adjūdicātiōn-* (s. of *adjūdicātiō*)]

ad·junct (aj′ungkt), *n.* **1.** something added to another thing but not essentially a part of it. **2.** a person joined to another in some duty or service; assistant. **3.** *Gram.* a modifying form, word, phrase, etc., depending on some other form, word, phrase, etc. —*adj.* **4.** joined or associated, esp. in an auxiliary or subordinate relationship. **5.** attached or belonging without full or permanent status: *an adjunct surgeon on the hospital staff.* [< L *adjunct(us)* joined to (ptp. of *adjungere*) = *ad-* AD- + *jung-* (nasal var. of *jug-* YOKE[1]) + *-tus* ptp. suffix] —**ad′junct·ly,** *adv.* —**Syn. 1.** appendix, supplement. See **addition. 2.** aide, attaché.

ad·junc·tion (ə jungk′shən), *n.* the act or process of adjoining. [< L *adjunctiōn-* (s. of *adjunctiō*)]

ad·junc·tive (ə jungk′tiv), *adj.* forming an adjunct. [< LL *adjunctīv(us)*] —**ad·junc′tive·ly,** *adv.*

ad·jure (ə jŏŏr′), *v.t.,* **-jured, -jur·ing. 1.** to charge, bind, or command solemnly, as under oath or the threat of a curse. **2.** to entreat or request earnestly. [late ME < L *adjūr(āre)* = *ad-* AD- + *jūrāre* to swear] —**ad·ju·ra·tion** (aj′ŏŏ rā′shən), *n.* —**ad·jur·a·to·ry** (ə jŏŏr′ə tōr′ē, -tôr′ē), *adj.* —**ad·jur′er, ad·ju′ror,** *n.*

ad·just (ə just′), *v.t.* **1.** to fit, as one thing to another; make correspondent or conformable; adapt; accommodate: *to adjust expenses to income.* **2.** to put in working order; regulate; bring to a proper state or position: *to adjust an instrument.* **3.** to settle or bring to a satisfactory state, so that parties are agreed in the result: *to adjust differences.* **4.** *Insurance.* to determine the amount to be paid in settlement of (a claim). **5.** to systematize. —*v.i.* **6.** to adapt one-

self; become adapted. [< OF *a(d)juster* = *a(d)-* AD- + *just(e)* right, JUST + *-er* inf. suffix] —**ad·just′a·ble,** *adj.* —**ad·just′a·bly,** *adv.* —**ad·just′er, ad·jus′tor,** *n.*
—**Syn. 2.** set, fix. ADJUST, ADAPT, ALTER in their literal meanings imply making necessary or desirable changes (as in position, shape, or the like). To ADJUST is to move into proper position for use: *to adjust the eyepiece of a telescope.* To ADAPT is to make a change in character, to make something useful in a new way: *to adapt a paper clip for a hairpin.* To ALTER is to change the appearance but not the use: *to alter the height of a table.* **3.** arrange; rectify; reconcile.

adjust′able span′ner, *Brit.* See **monkey wrench** (def. 1).

ad·just·ment (ə just′mənt), *n.* **1.** the act of adjusting; adaptation to a particular purpose. **2.** the state of being adjusted. **3.** a device, as a knob or lever, for adjusting: *the adjustments on a television set.* **4.** the act of bringing something into conformity with external requirements: *the adjustment of one's view of reality.* **5.** a harmonious reconciliation of a dispute or of disputed matters. **6.** *Sociol.* a process of modifying, adapting, or altering individual or collective patterns of behavior so as to bring them into conformity with other such patterns, as with those provided by a cultural environment. **7.** *Insurance.* the act of ascertaining the amount to be paid in settlement of a claim. **8.** a settlement of a disputed account or claim. **9.** a change or concession, as in price or other terms, in view of special circumstances. —**ad·just·ment·al** (ə just men′tᵊl), *adj.*

ad·ju·tant (aj′ə tənt), *n.* **1.** *Mil.* a staff officer who assists the commanding officer in issuing orders. **2.** *Mil. Brit.* an executive officer. **3.** an assistant. **4.** See **adjutant stork.** [< L *adjūtant-* (s. of *adjūtāns,* prp. of *adjūtāre*) = *ad-* AD- + *jū-* (perf. s. of *juvāre* to help) + *-t-* freq. suffix + *-ant-* -ANT] —**ad′ju·tan·cy,** *n.*

ad′jutant gen′eral, *pl.* **adjutants general. 1. the Adjutant General,** the chief administrative officer of the U.S. Army. **2.** (in the U.S. Army) an adjutant of a unit having a general staff, usually an officer of the Adjutant General's Corps.

ad′jutant stork′, a stork of the genus *Leptoptilus.* Also called **adjutant, ad′jutant bird′, ad′jutant crane′.**

ad·ju·vant (aj′ə vənt), *adj.* **1.** serving to help or assist; auxiliary. —*n.* **2.** a person or thing that aids or helps. **3.** anything that aids in removing or preventing a disease, esp. a substance added to a prescription to aid the effect of the main ingredient. [< L *adjuvant-* (s. of *adjuvāns,* prp. of *adjuvāre*) = *ad-* AD- + *juv-* (s. of *juvāre* to help) + *-ant-* -ANT]

Ad·ler (ad′lər), *n.* **1. Alfred,** 1870–1937, Austrian psychiatrist and psychologist. **2. Felix,** 1851–1933, U.S. educator, reformer, and writer. **3. Mortimer (Jerome),** born 1902, U.S. philosopher and educator.

Ad·le·ri·an (ad lēr′ē ən), *adj.* of or pertaining to Alfred Adler or his doctrines, esp. to the belief that behavior is determined by compensation for feelings of inferiority.

ad lib (ad lib′, ad′), an ad-libbed remark, esp. a humorous one. [see AD LIBITUM]

ad-lib (ad lib′, ad′-), *v.,* **-libbed, -lib·bing.** —*v.t.* **1.** to improvise (a speech, music, etc.). —*v.i.* **2.** to act, speak, etc., without preparation.

ad lib. See **ad libitum.**

ad lib·i·tum (ad lib′i təm; *Lat.* äd lib′i to͝om′), **1.** at one's pleasure. **2.** *Music.* not so important that it cannot be omitted (opposed to *obbligato*). *Abbr.:* ad lib. [< L]

ad loc., at or to the place. [< L *ad locum*]

Adm., **1.** Admiral. **2.** Admiralty.

adm., **1.** administration. **2.** administrator. **3.** admission.

ad ma·jo·rem De·i glo·ri·am (äd mä yō′rem de′ē glō′rē äm′), *Latin.* for the greater glory of God.

ad·man (ad′man′, -mən), *n., pl.* **-men** (-men′, -mən). See **advertising man.**

ad·meas·ure (ad mezh′ər), *v.t.,* **-ured, -ur·ing.** to measure off or out; apportion. [AD- + MEASURE; r. late ME *amesure* < MF *amesure(r)*] —**ad·meas′ur·er,** *n.*

ad·meas·ure·ment (ad mezh′ər mənt), *n.* **1.** the process of measuring. **2.** the number, dimensions, or measure of anything. **3.** apportionment.

Ad·me·tus (ad mē′təs), *n.* *Class. Myth.* a Thessalian king, one of the Argonauts and husband of Alcestis.

ad·min·i·cle (ad min′i kəl), *n.* an aid; auxiliary. [< L *adminicul(um)* prop, support (*ad-* AD- + *-min-* uphold *min* (c. *moenia* walls) + *-i-* -I- + *-culum* -CLE)] —**ad·mi·nic·u·lar** (ad′mə nik′yə lər), **ad′mi·nic′u·lar′y,** *adj.*

ad·min·is·ter (ad min′i stər), *v.t.* **1.** to manage (affairs, a government, etc.); have executive charge of: *to administer laws.* **2.** to bring into use or operation; dispense: *to administer justice.* **3.** to make application of; give: *to administer medicine.* **4.** to tender or impose: *to administer an oath.* **5.** *Law.* to manage or dispose of, as a decedent's estate by an executor or administrator or a trust estate by a trustee. —*v.i.* **6.** to act usefully or helpfully (usually fol. by *to*): *to administer to the poor.* **7.** to perform the duties of an administrator. [< L *administrāre* (see AD-, MINISTER); r. late ME *amynistre* < MF *aministre(r)*] —**ad·min·is·tra·ble** (ad min′i strə bəl), *adj.* —**ad·min·is·trant** (ad min′i-strənt), *adj.* —**Syn. 1.** conduct, control, execute; direct, superintend, supervise, oversee. See **rule.**

ad·min·is·trate (ad min′i strāt′), *v.t.,* **-trat·ed, -trat·ing.** to administer. [< L *administrāt(us),* ptp. of *administrāre* to ADMINISTER; see -ATE[1]]

ad·min·is·tra·tion (ad min′i strā′shən), *n.* **1.** the act of administering. **2.** the management of any office, employment, or organization; direction. **3.** the duty or duties of an administrator. **4.** an official body serving as an administrator. **5.** the members of such a body at a given time, as the officials appointed by a U.S. president. **6.** the period during which an administrator or body of administrators serves. **7.** *Law.* management of a decedent's estate by an executor or administrator, or of a trust estate by a trustee. [late ME *administracio(u)n* < L *administrātiōn-* (s. of *administrātiō*) service. See ADMINISTRATE, -ION] —**ad·min′is·tra′tion·al,** *adj.*

ad·min·is·tra·tive (ad min′i strā′tiv, -strə-), *adj.* pertaining to administration; executive: *administrative ability.* [< L *administrātīv(us).* See ADMINISTRATE, -IVE] —**ad·min′is·tra′tive·ly,** *adv.*

ad·min·is·tra·tor (ad min′i strā′tər), *n.* **1.** a person or body of persons that administers or manages affairs of any kind. **2.** *Law.* a person appointed by a court to take charge of the estate of a decedent. [< L *administrātor*] —**ad·min′is·tra′tor·ship′,** *n.*

ad·min·is·tra·trix (ad min′i strā′triks, ad′min i-), *n., pl.* **-is·tra·tri·ces** (-i strā′tri sēz′, -i strə trī′sēz). *Law.* a female administrator. [< ML; fem. of ADMINISTRATOR; see -TRIX]

ad·mi·ra·ble (ad′mər ə bəl), *adj.* worthy of admiration; exciting approval, reverence, or affection. [< L *admīrābil(is).* See ADMIRE, -ABLE] —**ad′mi·ra·ble·ness, ad′mi·ra·bil′i·ty,** *n.* —**ad′mi·ra·bly,** *adv.* —**Syn.** estimable, praiseworthy.

ad·mi·ral (ad′mər əl), *n.* **1.** the commander in chief of a fleet. **2.** a naval officer of the highest rank. **3.** a naval officer of a high rank: the grades in the U.S. Navy are fleet admiral, admiral, vice-admiral, and rear admiral. **4.** any of several brightly colored butterflies of the family *Nymphalidae,* as *Vanessa atalanta.* **5.** *Obs.* the flagship of an admiral. [ME, var. of *amiral* < OF < Ar *amīr al* commander of; *-d-* < ML *admirābilis mundi* for Ar *amīr al mūminīn* commander of the faithful] —**ad′mi·ral·ship′,** *n.*

Ad′miral of the Fleet′, an officer of the highest rank in the British navy.

ad·mi·ral·ty (ad′mər əl tē), *n., pl.* **-ties, 1.** the office or jurisdiction of an admiral. **2.** a department having charge of naval affairs, as in Great Britain. **3.** a court dealing with maritime questions, offenses, etc. **4.** maritime law. [ME *amiralty* < MF. See ADMIRAL, -TY[2]]

Ad′miralty Is′lands, a group of islands in the SW Pacific, N of New Guinea: under Australian administration. 19,017 (1964); ab. 800 sq. mi. Also called **Ad′mi·ral·ties.**

Ad′miralty Range′, a mountain range in Antarctica, NW of the Ross Sea.

ad·mi·ra·tion (ad′mə rā′shən), *n.* **1.** a feeling of wonder and approbation. **2.** the act of admiring. **3.** an object of wonder or approbation: *She was the admiration of everyone.* **4.** *Archaic.* wonder; astonishment. [< L *admīrātiōn-* (s. of *admīrātiō*)] —**ad·mi·ra·tive** (ad mī′rə tiv, ad′mə rā′-), *adj.* —**ad·mi′ra·tive·ly,** *adv.* —**Syn. 1.** esteem, regard. —**Ant. 1, 2.** disapproval.

ad·mire (ad mīᵊr′), *v.,* **-mired, -mir·ing.** —*v.t.* **1.** to regard with wonder, pleasure, and approval. **2.** to regard with wonder or surprise (usually used ironically or sarcastically): *I admire your audacity.* —*v.i.* **3.** to feel or express admiration. **4.** *Chiefly Southern and Midland U.S.* to take pleasure; like or desire: *I would admire to go.* [< L *admīr(ārī)* = *ad-* AD- + *mīrārī* (in ML *mīrāre*) to wonder at, admire] —**ad·mir′er,** *n.* —**ad·mir′ing·ly,** *adv.* —**Syn. 1.** esteem. —**Ant. 1.** despise.

ad·mis·si·ble (ad mis′ə bəl), *adj.* **1.** that may be allowed or conceded; allowable. **2.** capable or worthy of being admitted: *admissible evidence.* [< ML *admissibil(is)* = L *admiss-* (see ADMISSION) + *-ibilis* -IBLE] —**ad·mis′si·bil′i·ty, ad·mis′si·ble·ness,** *n.* —**ad·mis′si·bly,** *adv.*

ad·mis·sion (ad mish′ən), *n.* **1.** the act of admitting. **2.** the right or means of entering. **3.** the price paid for entrance, as to a theater, ball park, etc. **4.** the act or condition of being received or accepted in a position or office; appointment: *admission to the bar.* **5.** confession of a charge, an error, or a crime; acknowledgment: *His admission of the theft solved the mystery.* **6.** an acknowledgment of the truth of something. [< L *admissiōn-* (s. of *admissiō*) = *admiss(us)* admitted, ptp. of *admittere* (*ad-* AD- + *mitt-* let go + *-tus* ptp. suffix) + *-iōn-* -ION] —**Syn. 2.** access. See **entrance[1].**

Admis′sion Day′, *U.S.* a legal holiday in some states commemorating the day of admission into the Union.

ad·mis·sive (ad mis′iv), *adj.* tending to admit. [< L *admiss(us)* (see ADMISSION) + -IVE]

ad·mit (ad mit′), *v.,* **-mit·ted, -mit·ting.** —*v.t.* **1.** to allow to enter; grant or afford entrance to: *to admit a student to college.* **2.** to give right or means of entrance to: *This ticket admits two people.* **3.** to permit to exercise a certain function or privilege: *admitted to the bar.* **4.** to permit; allow. **5.** to acknowledge; confess: *He admitted his guilt.* **6.** to concede as true or valid. —*v.i.* **7.** to permit entrance; give access. **8.** to grant opportunity or permission (usually fol. by *of*): *Circumstances do not admit of this.* [< L *admitt(ere)* = *ad-* AD- + *mittere* to send, let go; r. late ME *amitte,* with *a-* (instead of *ad-*) < MF *amettre*] —**ad·mit′ta·ble, ad·mit′ti·ble,** *adj.* —**ad·mit′ter,** *n.* —**Syn. 1.** receive. **5.** own, avow. See **acknowledge.**

ad·mit·tance (ad mit′ᵊns), *n.* **1.** the right or means of entrance. **2.** act of admitting. **3.** the act or fact of entering. **4.** *Elect.* the measure of the ability of a circuit to conduct an alternating current, consisting of two components, conductance and susceptance; the reciprocal of impedance, expressed in mhos. *Symbol:* Y —**Syn. 1.** access. See **entrance[1].**

ad·mit·ted·ly (ad mit′id lē), *adv.* by acknowledgment; as confessed or conceded willingly.

ad·mix (ad miks′), *v.t., v.i.* to mingle with or add to something else. [AD- + MIX, modeled on L *admīscēre* (*admixtus* ptp.)]

ad·mix·ture (ad miks′chər), *n.* **1.** the act of mixing. **2.** the state of being mixed. **3.** an alien or added element or ingredient. **4.** a compound containing such an element or ingredient. [< L *admixt(us).* See ADMIX, -URE]

ad·mon·ish (ad mon′ish), *v.t.* **1.** to caution, advise, or encourage. **2.** to reprove or warn, esp. in a mild manner. **3.** to urge to duty or remind of an obligation. [alter. of late ME *amonyssche* (with *ad-* for *a-*), itself alter. of ME *amoneste* < MF *amoneste(r).* See AD-, MONISH] —**ad·mon′ish·er,** *n.* —**ad·mon′ish·ing·ly,** *adv.* —**ad·mon′ish·ment,** *n.* —**Syn. 1.** See **warn. 2.** rebuke, censure.

ad·mo·ni·tion (ad′mə nish′ən), *n.* **1.** the act of admonishing. **2.** counsel, advice, or caution. **3.** a gentle reproof or warning. [< L *admonitiōn-* (s. of *admonitiō*); see AD-, MONITION; r. late ME *amonicioun* < AF]

ad·mon·i·tor (ad mon′i tər), *n.* an admonisher. [< L; see ADMONIT(ION), -OR[2]] —**ad·mon·i·to·ri·al** (ad mon′i tōr′ē əl, -tôr′-), *adj.*

ad·mon·i·to·ry (ad mon′i tōr′ē, -tôr′ē), *adj.* tending or serving to admonish. [< ML *admonitōri(us).* See ADMONIT(ION), -ORY] —**ad·mon′i·to′ri·ly,** *adv.*

admov., (in prescriptions) **1.** apply. [< L *admovē*] **2.** let it be applied. [< L *admoveātur*]

ad·nate (ad′nāt), *adj. Biol.* grown fast to something; congenitally attached. [< L *adnāt(us)*, var. of *agnātus* AGNATE]

ad nau·se·am (ad nô′zē əm, -am′, -zhē-, -sē-, -shē-), to a sickening or disgusting degree. [< L: lit., to seasickness]

ad·noun (ad′noun), *n. Gram.* an adjective, esp. one used as a noun, as *meek* in *Blessed are the meek.* [AD- + NOUN, modeled on *adverb*] —**ad·nom·i·nal** (ad nom′ə nəl), *adj.*

A, Adnate stipule

a·do (ə do͞o′), *n.* busy activity: bustle; fuss. [ME (north) *at do* = *at* to (< Scand) + *do* DO[1]]
—**Syn.** flurry; confusion, upset, excitement; hubbub. ADO, TO-DO, COMMOTION, STIR, TUMULT suggest a great deal of fuss and noise. ADO implies a confused bustle of activity, a considerable emotional upset, and a great deal of talking: *much ado about nothing.* TO-DO may mean merely excitement and noise: *a great to-do over a movie star.* COMMOTION suggests a noisy confusion and babble: *commotion at the scene of an accident.* STIR suggests excitement and noise, with a hint of emotional cause: *The report was followed by a tremendous stir in the city.* TUMULT suggests disorder with noise and violence: *a tumult as the mob stormed the Bastille.*

a·do·be (ə dō′bē), *n.* **1.** sun-dried brick. **2.** a yellow silt or clay, deposited by rivers, used to make bricks. **3.** a building constructed of such bricks. **4.** a dark, heavy soil, containing clay. [< Sp < Ar *aṭ-ṭōb*, by assimilation from *al ṭōb* the brick < Coptic *tōōb* brick]

ado′be flat′, a plain consisting of adobe deposited by short-lived rainfall or thaw streams.

ad·o·les·cence (ad′əles′əns), *n.* **1.** the transitional period between puberty and adulthood in human development, extending mainly over the teen years. **2.** the quality or state of being adolescent. [late ME < MF < L *adolēscentia*]

ad·o·les·cent (ad′əles′ənt), *adj.* **1.** growing to adulthood; approaching maturity. **2.** having the characteristics of adolescence. —*n.* **3.** an adolescent person. [< L *adolēscent-* (s. of *adolēscēns* growing up, prp. of *adolēscere*) = *adol-* (see ADULT) + *-ēsc-* -ESCE + *-ent-* -ENT] —**ad′o·les′cent·ly,** *adv.* —**Syn. 1.** immature. **3.** youth, teen-ager, minor.

A·do·nai (ä dô nī′; *Eng.* ä′dō noi′), *n. Hebrew.* a title of reverence for God. Also, **A·do·noy** (ä dô nī′; *Eng.* ä′dō noi′). Cf. **Tetragrammaton.** [lit., my Lord; spoken in place of the ineffable name YAHWEH]

A·don·ic (ə don′ik), *adj.* **1.** *Pros.* noting a verse consisting of a dactyl (— ◡ ◡) followed by a spondee (— —) or trochee (— ◡). **2.** of or like Adonis. —*n.* **3.** *Pros.* an Adonic verse or line. [< ML *Adōnic(us)*. See ADONIS, -IC]

A·do·nis (ə don′is, ə dō′nis), *n. Class. Myth.* a youth whom Aphrodite loved for his beauty.

a·dopt (ə dopt′), *v.t.* **1.** to choose or take as one's own: *to adopt a new name.* **2.** to become the legal parent or parents of (another person's child). **3.** to accept into a close, dependent relationship. **4.** to accept into or act in accordance with (a plan, principle, etc.). **5.** to accept formally: *to adopt a report.* **6.** *Brit.* to nominate a candidate for office, esp. for political office. [< L *adopt(āre)* = *ad-* AD- + *optāre* to OPT] —**a·dopt′a·bil′i·ty,** *n.* —**a·dopt′a·ble,** *adj.* —**a·dopt′er,** *n.* —**a·dop′tion,** *n.* —**a·dop′tion·al,** *adj.*

a·dop·tee (ə dop′tē, ə dop tē′), *n.* a person who is adopted.

a·dop·tive (ə dop′tiv), *adj.* **1.** of or involving adoption. **2.** related by adoption. **3.** tending to adopt. [< L *adoptīv(us)*; see ADOPT, -IVE; r. late ME *adoptife* < MF *adoptif*] —**a·dop′tive·ly,** *adv.*

a·dor·a·ble (ə dôr′ə bəl, ə dôr′-), *adj.* **1.** worthy of being adored. **2.** very delightful; charming. [< L *adōrābil(is)*] —**a·dor′a·ble·ness, a·dor′a·bil′i·ty,** *n.* —**a·dor′a·bly,** *adv.*

ad·o·ra·tion (ad′ə rā′shən), *n.* **1.** act of paying honor, as to a divine being; worship. **2.** reverent homage. **3.** fervent and devoted love. [< L *adōrātiōn-* (s. of *adōrātiō*) worship]

a·dore (ə dôr′, ə dōr′), *v.,* **a·dored, a·dor·ing.** —*v.t.* **1.** to regard with the utmost esteem, love, and respect. **2.** to pay divine honor to; worship: *to adore God.* **3.** to like very much: *I adore pizza.* —*v.i.* **4.** to worship. [< L *adōr(āre)* (to) speak to, pray, worship = *ad-* AD- + *ōrāre* to speak, beg (see ORAL); r. ME *aour(i)e* < OF *aourer*] —**a·dor′er,** *n.* —**a·dor′ing·ly,** *adv.* —**Syn. 1.** idolize; revere, venerate.

a·dorn (ə dôrn′), *v.t.* **1.** to decorate or add beauty to, as by ornaments: *garlands of flowers adorning her hair.* **2.** to make pleasing, more attractive, or more impressive. [late ME *adorne* < L *adōrnāre* = *ad-* AD- + *ōrnāre* to dress (see ORNATE); r. late ME *aourne* < MF] —**a·dorn′er,** *n.* —**a·dorn′ing·ly,** *adv.* —**Syn. 1.** beautify; deck, bedeck.

a·dorn·ment (ə dôrn′mənt), *n.* **1.** the act of adorning. **2.** an ornament or scheme of ornamentation. [ADORN + -MENT; r. late ME *aournement* < MF]

A·do·wa (ä′do͝o wä′), *n.* Aduwa.

ADP, 1. *Biochem.* an ester of adenosine and pyrophosphoric acid, $C_{10}H_{12}N_5O_3H_3P_2O_7$, derived from ATP, and serving to transfer energy during glycolysis. **2.** See **automatic data processing.**

ad pa·tres (äd pä′tʀes; *Eng.* ad pā′trēz), *Latin.* dead. [lit., to the fathers]

A·dras·tus (ə dras′təs), *n. Class. Myth.* a king of Argos and leader of the Seven against Thebes. Also, **A·dras′tos.**

ad rem (äd ʀem′; *Eng.* ad rem′), *Latin.* **1.** pertinent: *an* ad rem *remark.* **2.** without digressing; in a straightforward manner: *to reply* ad rem. [lit., to the thing]

ad·re·nal (ə drēn′əl), *Anat., Zool.* —*adj.* **1.** situated near or on the kidneys. **2.** of or produced by the adrenal glands. —*n.* **3.** See **adrenal gland.** [AD- + L *rēn-* (s. of *rēnēs* kidneys) + -AL[1]]

adre′nal gland′, *Anat., Zool.* one of a pair of ductless glands, located above the kidneys, consisting of a cortex and a medulla. Also called **suprarenal gland.**

A·dren·al·in (ə dren′əlin), *n. Pharm., Trademark.* epinephrine (def. 2).

a·dren·a·line (ə dren′əlin, -əlēn′), *n. Biochem.* epinephrine. (def. 1).

a·dre·no·cor·ti·co·trop·ic (ə drē′nō kôr′tə kō trop′ik), *adj.* stimulating the adrenal cortex. Also, **a·dre·no·cor·ti·co·troph·ic** (ə drē′nō kôr′tə kō trof′ik). [ADREN(AL) + -O- + *cortic-* (see CORTICAL) + -O- + -TROPIC]

adre′nocorticotrop′ic hor′mone, *Biochem.* See **ACTH.**

A·dri·an (ā′drē ən), *n.* **1. Edgar Douglas,** 1889–1977, English physiologist: Nobel prize for medicine 1932. **2.** Hadrian.

Adrian I, died A.D. 795, pope 772–795. Also, **Hadrian I.**

Adrian II, Italian ecclesiastic: pope A.D. 867–872. Also, **Hadrian II.**

Adrian III, Saint, Italian ecclesiastic: pope A.D. 884–885. Also, **Hadrian III.**

Adrian IV, (*Nicholas Breakspear*) c1100–59, only Englishman to become pope, 1154–59. Also, **Hadrian IV.**

Adrian V, died 1276, Italian ecclesiastic: pope 1276. Also, **Hadrian V.**

Adrian VI, 1459–1523, Dutch ecclesiastic: pope 1522–23. Also, **Hadrian VI.**

A·dri·an·o·ple (ā′drē ə nō′pəl), *n.* Edirne.

A·dri·an·op·o·lis (ā′drē ə nop′ə lis), *n.* former name of **Edirne.**

A′dri·at′ic Sea′ (ā′drē at′ik, ad′rē-), an arm of the Mediterranean between Italy and Yugoslavia. Also called **A′dri·at′ic.**

a·drift (ə drift′), *adj., adv.* **1.** not fastened by a mooring; without anchor; drifting. **2.** swaying indecisively from one idea or course of action to another.

a·droit (ə droit′), *adj.* **1.** expert or nimble in the use of the hands. **2.** cleverly skillful or resourceful. [< F, orig. phrase *à droit* rightly << L *ad* according to + *dīrectum*, neut. of *dīrectus* right; see DIRECT] —**a·droit′ly,** *adv.* —**a·droit′ness,** *n.* —**Syn. 1.** dexterous, deft, adept. —**Ant.** clumsy.

ad·sci·ti·tious (ad′si tish′əs), *adj.* added or derived from without; supplemental. [< L *adscīt(us)* derived, assumed, foreign (ptp. of *adscīscī*) = *ad-* AD- + *scī-* (s. of *scīre* to know) + *-t(us)* ptp. suffix + -ITIOUS] —**ad′sci·ti′tious·ly,** *adv.*

ad·script (ad′skript), *adj.* **1.** written after (distinguished from *superior, subscript*). —*n.* **2.** an adscript character. Cf. **inferior** (def. 9), **superior** (def. 13). [< L *a(d)script(us)* (ptp. of *ascrībere* to ASCRIBE) = *ad-* AD- + *scrīptus* written]

ad·sorb (ad sôrb′, -zôrb′), *v.t. Physical Chem.* to gather (a gas, liquid, or dissolved substance) on a surface in a condensed layer, as when charcoal adsorbs gases. [AD- + (AB)SORB] —**ad·sorb′a·bil′i·ty,** *n.* —**ad·sorb′a·ble,** *adj.* —**ad·sorb′ent,** *adj., n.* —**ad·sorp·tion** (ad sôrp′shən, -zôrp′-), *n.* —**ad·sorp′tive,** *adj., n.* —**ad·sorp′tive·ly,** *adv.*

ad·sorb·ate (ad sôr′bāt, -bit, -zôr′-), *n.* the substance adsorbed.

ad·su′ki bean′ (ad so͞o′kē, -zo͞o′-). See **adzuki bean.**

ad·u·lar·i·a (aj′ə lâr′ē ə), *n. Mineral.* a sometimes opalescent variety of orthoclase formed at a low temperature. [< It < F *adulaire*, named after *Adula* name of mountain group in Switzerland; see -ARY]

ad·u·late (aj′ə lāt′), *v.t.,* **-lat·ed, -lat·ing.** to show excessive devotion to; flatter or admire servilely. [back formation from *adulation* < L *adūlātiōn-* (s. of *adūlātiō*) a fawning, = *adūlāt(us)*, ptp. of *adūlārī*, *-āre* (*ad-* AD- + *-ūl-* fawn (< ?) + *-ātus* -ATE[1]) + *-iōn-* -ION] —**ad′u·la′tion,** *n.* —**ad′u·la′tor,** *n.* —**ad·u·la·to·ry** (aj′ə lə tōr′ē, -tôr′ē), *adj.*

a·dult (ə dult′, ad′ult), *adj.* **1.** having attained maturity. **2.** of, pertaining to, or befitting adults: *adult education.* **3.** intended for adults only: *adult magazines; adult movies.* —*n.* **4.** a person who has attained maturity. **5.** a person who has attained the legal age of majority. **6.** a full-grown animal or plant. [< L *adult(us)* grown (ptp. of *adolēre* to make grow) = *ad-* AD- + *ul-* (identical with root *al-* in ALIMENT, *ol-* in PROLIFIC) + *-tus* ptp. suffix] —**a·dult′hood,** *n.* —**a·dult′ness,** *n.* —**Syn. 1.** mature; grown.

a·dul·ter·ant (ə dul′tər ənt), *n.* **1.** a substance that adulterates. —*adj.* **2.** adulterating. [< L *adulterant-* (s. of *adulterāns*, prp. of *adulterāre*) = *ad-* AD- + *ulter* (see ADULTERATE) + *-ant-* -ANT]

a·dul·ter·ate (*v.* ə dul′tə rāt′; *adj.* ə dul′tər it, -tə rāt′), *v.,* **-at·ed, -at·ing,** *adj.* —*v.t.* **1.** to debase by adding inferior materials or elements. **2.** to make impure by admixture. —*adj.* **3.** adulterated. **4.** adulterous (def. 1). [< L *adulterāt(us)* altered (ptp. of *adulterāre*) = *ad-* AD- + *ulter* (var. of *alter* other; see ALTER) + *-ātus* -ATE[1]] —**a·dul′ter·a′tor,** *n.*

a·dul·ter·a·tion (ə dul′tə rā′shən), *n.* **1.** the act or process of adulterating. **2.** the state of being adulterated. **3.** something adulterated. [< L *adulterātiōn-* (s. of *adulterātiō*)]

a·dul·ter·er (ə dul′tər ər), *n.* a person, esp. a man, who commits adultery. [earlier *adulter* adulterer (< L, akin to *adulterāre* to defile; see ADULTERATE) + -ER[1]]

a·dul·ter·ess (ə dul′tər is, -tris), *n.* a woman who commits adultery.

a·dul·ter·ine (ə dul′tər in, -tə rēn′, -tə rīn′), *adj.* **1.** characterized by adulteration; spurious. **2.** born of adultery. **3.** of or involving adultery. [< L *adulterīn(us)* = *adulter* adulterer, counterfeiter (see ADULTERER) + *-īnus* -INE[1]]

a·dul·ter·ous (ə dul′tər əs), *adj.* **1.** characterized by or given to adultery; illicit. **2.** spurious (def. 1). —**a·dul′ter·ous·ly,** *adv.*

a·dul·ter·y (ə dul′tə rē), *n., pl.* **-ter·ies** for 2. **1.** voluntary sexual intercourse of a married person with someone other than his or her lawful spouse. **2.** an instance of this. [< L *adulteri(um)* = *adulter* (see ADULTERER) + *-ium* -Y[3]]

ad·um·bral (ad um′brəl), *adj.* shadowy; shady. [AD- + L *umbr(a)* shade, shadow + -AL[1]]

ad·um·brate (ad um′brāt, ad′əm brāt′), *v.t.,* **-brat·ed, -brat·ing. 1.** to give a faint shadow or resemblance of; to outline or sketch. **2.** to foreshadow; prefigure. **3.** to darken or conceal partially; overshadow. [< L *adumbrāt(us)* shaded (ptp. of *adumbrāre*) = *ad-* AD- + *umbr(a)* shade, shadow + *-ātus* -ATE[1]] —**ad′um·bra′tion,** *n.* —**ad·um′bra·tive,** *adj.* —**ad·um′bra·tive·ly,** *adv.*

a·dust (ə dust′), *adj.* **1.** dried or darkened, as by heat; burned; scorched. **2.** gloomy in appearance or mood. [< L *adust(us)* (ptp. of *adūrere*) = *ad-* AD- + *us-* (var. s. of *ūrere* to burn) + *-tus* ptp. suffix]

A·du·wa (ä′do͝o wä′), *n.* a town in N Ethiopia: Italians defeated 1896. 5000 (est. 1948). Also, **Adowa.**
Adv., **1.** Advent. **2.** Advocate.
adv., **1.** ad valorem. **2.** advance. **3.** adverb. **4.** adverbial. **5.** adverbially. **6.** adversus. **7.** advertisement.
ad val., See **ad valorem.**
ad va·lo·rem (ad və lōr′əm, -lôr′-), in proportion to the value (applied esp. to duties on imports that are fixed at a percentage of the value as stated on the invoice). [< L: lit., according to the worth]
ad·vance (ad vans′, -väns′), *v.*, **-vanced, -vanc·ing,** *n.*, *adj.* **—***v.t.* **1.** to bring or send forward. **2.** to present for consideration, as an opinion. **3.** to further the development or prospects of. **4.** to promote, as to a higher rank. **5.** to increase (a rate or figure). **6.** to accelerate. **7.** to furnish or supply (money or goods) on credit. **8.** *Archaic.* to raise (a banner, flag, etc.). **—***v.i.* **9.** to come or go forward. **10.** to make progress or show improvement. **11.** to increase in price, value, quantity, etc. **—***n.* **12.** a forward movement. **13.** a noticeable progress or improvement. **14.** a promotion, as in rank or status. **15.** Usually, **advances. a.** attempts at forming an acquaintance, reaching an agreement, etc., made by one party. **b.** actions or words intended to be sexually inviting. **16.** an increase in a rate or figure. **17.** *Com.* **a.** a sum of money or quantity of goods furnished on credit. **b.** the act of furnishing this sum or quantity. **c.** the total number of sales, as of tickets to a play or of an item of merchandise, made before a play begins its run or the item is available. **d.** the sum of money collected through such sales. **18. in advance, a.** in front (often fol. by *of*). **b.** beforehand. **—***adj.* **19.** before all others: *an advance section of a train.* **20.** made beforehand: *an advance booking of tickets.* **21.** issued beforehand: *an advance copy.* [ME *avaunce(n)* < OF *avanc(i)e(r)* < VL **abanteāre* = LL *abante* away before (see AB-, ANTE-) + *-āre* v. and inf. suffix; *ad-* by confusion of prefixes] **—ad·vanc′er,** *n.* **—ad·vanc′ing·ly,** *adv.*
—Syn. 2. adduce, propound; offer. **3.** forward, promote. **6.** quicken, hasten, speed up. **7.** loan. **9.** ADVANCE, PROCEED imply movement forward. ADVANCE applies to forward movement, esp. toward an objective: *to advance to a platform.* PROCEED emphasizes movement, as from one place to another, and often implies continuing after a halt: *to proceed on one's journey.* **15.** overture, proposal. **—Ant. 1, 2, 9.** withdraw. **9.** retreat. **11.** decrease.
ad·vanced (ad vanst′, -vänst′), *adj.* **1.** placed ahead or forward: *with one foot advanced.* **2.** beyond or past the beginning or elementary; past some specific initial stage. **3.** being greater than another or others in development, growth, progress, etc. **4.** relatively old or very old: *advanced in years.* **5.** reflecting or being an enlightened or liberal idea, attitude, practice, etc.
advanced′ stand′ing, 1. credit for studies completed elsewhere, granted to a student by the college or university to which he has been admitted. **2.** the higher academic status of a student granted such credit.
advance′ guard′, a body of troops going before the main force.
ad·vance·ment (ad vans′mənt, -väns′-), *n.* **1.** the act of moving forward. **2.** promotion, as in rank. **3.** *Law.* money or property given during his lifetime by a person subsequently dying intestate and deducted from the intestate share of the recipient. [ME *avauncement* < OF *avancement*]
ad·van·tage (ad van′tij, -vän′-), *n.*, *v.*, **-taged, -tag·ing.** **—***n.* **1.** anything that is of benefit or gain to someone or something. **2.** benefit or gain. **3.** a superior or dominating position (often fol. by *of* or *over*): *to have the advantage of someone; advantage over an opponent.* **4.** *Tennis.* the first point scored after deuce. **5. take advantage of, a.** to make use of (an opportunity). **b.** to exploit the ignorance or weakness of. **6. to advantage,** usefully or profitably. **—***v.t.* **7.** to be of benefit or gain to. [late ME *avantage* < MF = *avant* before (< LL *abante*; see ADVANCE) + *-age* -AGE]
—Syn. 2. ADVANTAGE, BENEFIT, PROFIT all mean something that is of use or value. ADVANTAGE is anything that places one in an improved position, esp. in coping with competition or difficulties: *It is to one's advantage to have traveled widely.* BENEFIT is anything that promotes the welfare or improves the state of a person or group: *a benefit to society.* PROFIT is any valuable, useful, or helpful gain: *profit from trade or experience.* **7.** serve, avail, help, aid.
ad·van·ta·geous (ad′vən tā′jəs), *adj.* providing an advantage; profitable; beneficial. **—ad′van·ta′geous·ly,** *adv.*
ad·vec·tion (ad vek′shən), *n.* **1.** *Meteorol.* the horizontal transport of atmospheric properties (distinguished from *convection*). **2.** the horizontal movement of air. [< L *advectiōn-* (s. of *advectiō*) = *advect(us)*, ptp. of *advehere* (*ad-* AD- + *vec-* (var. s. of *vehere* to carry, bring) + *-tus* ptp. suffix) + *-iōn-* -ION] **—ad·vec′tive,** *adj.*
ad·vent (ad′vent), *n.* **1.** arrival or coming into being: *the advent of spring.* **2.** (*usually cap.*) the coming of Christ into the world. **3.** (*cap.*) the penitential period beginning four Sundays before Christmas, commemorating this. **4.** (*usually cap.*) See **Second Coming.** [early ME < L *advent(us)* a coming to = *ad-* AD- + *ven-* (s. of *venīre* to come) + *-tus* suffix marking n. denoting action]
Ad·vent·ist (ad′ven tist, ad ven′-), *n.* a member of any of certain Christian denominations that maintain that the Second Coming is imminent. Also called **Second Adventist.** **—Ad′vent·ism,** *n.*
ad·ven·ti·ti·a (ad′ven tish′ē ə, -tish′ə), *n.* *Anat.* the external covering of an organ or other structure, esp. the covering of a blood vessel. [< L *adventīcia*, neut. pl. of *adventīcius* ADVENTITIOUS] **—ad′ven·ti′tial,** *adj.*
ad·ven·ti·tious (ad′vən tish′əs), *adj.* **1.** associated with something incidentally or extrinsically rather than as an integral part; nonessential. **2.** *Bot., Zool.* appearing in an abnormal or unusual position or place, as a root. [< L *adventīcius* coming from outside = *ad-* AD- + *ven-* (s. of *venīre* to come) + *-t(us)* ptp. suffix + *-īcius* -ITIOUS] **—ad′ven·ti′tious·ly,** *adv.* **—ad′ven·ti′tious·ness,** *n.*
ad·ven·tive (ad ven′tiv), *Bot., Zool.* **—***adj.* **1.** not native and usually not yet well established, as exotic plants. **—***n.* **2.** an adventive plant or animal. [< L *advent(us)* (ptp. of *advenīre*; see ADVENT) + -IVE] **—ad·ven′tive·ly,** *adv.*
Ad′vent Sun′day, the first Sunday in Advent.
ad·ven·ture (ad ven′chər), *n.*, *v.*, **-tured, -tur·ing.** **—***n.* **1.** an undertaking involving risk, unforeseeable danger, or unexpected excitement. **2.** an exciting or remarkable experience. **3.** participation in exciting undertakings or enterprises: *the spirit of adventure.* **4.** a venture involving great financial risk; speculation. **5.** *Obs.* **a.** peril; danger. **b.** chance. **—***v.t.* **6.** to risk or hazard. **7.** to take the chance of; dare. **8.** to venture to say. **—***v.i.* **9.** to take the risk involved in something. **10.** to engage in an adventure or venture. [partly Latinized from ME *aventure* < OF < L (*rēs*) *adventūra* (thing) about to happen (to someone), fem. fut. participle of *advenīre* to arrive. See ADVENT, -URE] **—ad·ven′ture·ful,** *adj.*
ad·ven·tur·er (ad ven′chər ər), *n.* **1.** a person who adventures. **2.** a seeker of fortune in daring enterprises; soldier of fortune. **3.** a person who undertakes any great commercial risk; speculator. **4.** a person who seeks power or wealth by underhand or questionable means.
ad·ven·ture·some (ad ven′chər səm), *adj.* bold; daring. **—ad·ven′ture·some·ly,** *adv.* **—ad·ven′ture·some·ness,** *n.*
ad·ven·tur·ess (ad ven′chər is), *n.* **1.** a female adventurer. **2.** a woman who schemes to win social position, wealth, etc., by unscrupulous or questionable means. [ADVENTUR(ER) + -ESS]
ad·ven·tur·ism (ad ven′chə riz′əm), *n.* rash or irresponsible policies, methods, or actions, in defiance or disregard of accepted policies in financial, political, or international affairs. **—ad·ven′tur·ist,** *n.* **—ad·ven′tur·ist′ic,** *adj.*
ad·ven·tur·ous (ad ven′chər əs), *adj.* **1.** inclined or willing to engage in adventures. **2.** full of adventure; exciting or risky. [late ME *aventurous* < MF *aventur(e)os*. See ADVENTURE, -OUS] **—ad·ven′tur·ous·ly,** *adv.* **—ad·ven′tur·ous·ness,** *n.* **—Syn. 1.** daring, venturous, venturesome.
ad·verb (ad′vûrb), *n.* *Gram.* any member of a class of words that function as modifiers of verbs, adjectives, or other adverbs or adverbial phrases, and typically express time, place, manner, degree, etc., as *very, well, now, quickly.* [< L *adverb(ium)* = *ad-* AD- + *verb(um)* word, verb + *-ium* n. suffix; loan trans. of Gk *epírrhēma*] **—ad′verb·less,** *adj.*
ad·ver·bi·al (ad vûr′bē əl), *adj.* of, pertaining to, or functioning as an adverb. **—ad·ver′bi·al·ly,** *adv.*
ad ver·bum (äd wer′bo͝om; *Eng.* ad vûr′bəm), *Latin.* to the word; exactly according to an original in wording; verbatim.
ad·ver·sar·y (ad′vər ser′ē), *n.*, *pl.* **-sar·ies.** **1.** a person or group that opposes another; opponent; foe. **2.** an opponent in a contest; contestant. **3. the Adversary,** the devil; Satan. [late ME *adversarie* < L *adversāri(us)* = *advers(us)* (see ADVERSE) + *-ārius* -ARY; r. ME *adversere* < AF]
—Syn. 1. ADVERSARY, ANTAGONIST mean a person, a group, or a personified force, contending against another. ADVERSARY suggests an enemy who fights determinedly, continuously, and relentlessly: *a formidable adversary.* ANTAGONIST suggests one who, in hostile spirit, opposes another: *a duel with an antagonist.* **—Ant. 1.** ally.
ad·ver·sa·tive (ad vûr′sə tiv), *adj.* **1.** expressing contrariety, opposition, or antithesis: "*But*" *is an adversative conjunction.* **—***n.* **2.** an adversative word or proposition. [< LL *adversātīv(us)* = *adversāt(us)* (ptp. of *adversārī* to resist; see ADVERSE, -ATE[1]) + *-īvus* -IVE] **—ad·ver′sa·tive·ly,** *adv.*
ad·verse (ad vûrs′, ad′vûrs), *adj.* **1.** antagonistic in purpose or effect: *adverse criticism.* **2.** opposing one's interests or desires: *adverse circumstances.* **3.** being or acting in a contrary direction: *adverse winds.* **4.** opposite; confronting: *the adverse page.* **5.** *Bot.* turned toward the axis, as a leaf (opposed to *averse*). [late ME < L *advers(us)* hostile (ptp. of *advertere*) = *ad-* AD- + *vert-* turn + *-tus* ptp. suffix] **—ad·verse′ly,** *adv.* **—ad·verse′ness,** *n.* **—Syn. 1.** hostile, inimical, unfriendly. **2.** unfavorable; unlucky, unfortunate. See **contrary.** **—Ant. 1, 2.** favorable.
ad·ver·si·ty (ad vûr′si tē), *n.*, *pl.* **-ties.** **1.** adverse fortune or fate; a condition marked by misfortune, calamity, etc. **2.** an unfortunate or adverse event. [ME *adversite* < L *adversitāt-* (s. of *adversitās*)] **—Syn. 1.** catastrophe, disaster; trouble, misery.
ad·vert (ad vûrt′), *v.i.* **1.** to remark or comment about or in relation to (usually fol. by *to*). **2.** to turn the attention (usually fol. by *to*). [late ME < L *advert(ere)* (to) pay attention = *ad-* AD- + *vertere* to turn] **—Syn. 1.** allude.
ad·vert·ent (ad vûr′tənt), *adj.* attentive; heedful. [< L *advertent-* (s. of *advertēns*, prp. of *advertere*) = *ad-* AD- + *vert-* turn + *-ent-* -ENT] **—ad·vert′ence, ad·vert′en·cy,** *n.* **—ad·vert′ent·ly,** *adv.*
ad·ver·tise (ad′vər tīz′, ad′vər tīz′), *v.*, **-tised, -tis·ing.** **—***v.t.* **1.** to describe or present (a product, organization, idea, etc.) in some medium of communication in order to induce the public to buy, support, or approve of it. **2.** to call public attention to: *to advertise a reward.* **3.** to call attention to (oneself) in an ostentatious manner. **4.** *Obs.* to give notice or advice to. **—***v.i.* **5.** to seek to acquire something by placing an advertisement (often fol. by *for*). **6.** to use advertising, esp. as a part of one's business methods. Also, **advertize.** [late ME < MF *avertiss-*, long s. of *avertir* << L *advertere* to ADVERT] **—ad·ver·tis·a·ble** (ad′vər tī′zə bəl, ad′vər tī′-), *adj.* **—ad′ver·tis′er,** *n.*
ad·ver·tise·ment (ad′vər tīz′mənt, ad vûr′tis mənt, -tiz-), *n.* **1.** an announcement, description, or presentation of something, as of goods for sale, in newspapers, magazines, on television, etc. **2.** a public notice, esp. in print. **3.** the act of making generally known. Also, **ad′ver·tize′ment.** [late ME < MF *avertissement*]
ad·ver·tis·ing (ad′vər tī′zing), *n.* **1.** the act of producing or placing advertisements. **2.** anything used in or formed of advertisements. **3.** the profession and business of producing and placing advertisements. Also, **ad′ver·tiz′ing.**
ad′vertising a′gency, an agency employed by advertisers to plan, design, and supervise their advertisements.
ad′vertising man′, a person whose profession is writing, designing, or selling advertisements. Also called **adman.**
ad·ver·tize (ad′vər tīz′, ad′vər tīz′), *v.t.*, *v.i.*, **-tized, -tiz·ing.** advertise. **—ad·ver·tiz·a·ble** (ad′vər tī′zə bəl, ad′vər tī′-), *adj.* **—ad′ver·tiz′er,** *n.*
ad·vice (ad vīs′), *n.* **1.** an opinion or recommendation

offered as a guide to action, conduct, etc. **2.** a communication containing information: *Advice from abroad informs us that the government has fallen.* [late ME *advise;* r. ME *avis* < OF *a vis* (in phrase *ce m'est a vis* that is my impression) < L *ad* (see AD-) + *vīs(us)* (see VISAGE)]
—**Syn. 1.** admonition, caution; guidance; urging. ADVICE, COUNSEL, RECOMMENDATION, SUGGESTION refer to opinions urged as worthy bases for thought, opinion, conduct, or action. ADVICE is a practical recommendation as to action or conduct: *advice about purchasing land.* COUNSEL is weighty and serious advice, given after careful deliberation: *counsel about one's career.* RECOMMENDATION is weaker than advice and suggests an opinion that may or may not be acted upon: *Do you think that he'll follow my recommendation?* SUGGESTION implies something more tentative than a recommendation: *He did not expect his suggestion to be taken seriously.*

ad·vis·a·ble (ad vī′zə bəl), *adj.* **1.** proper to be advised or recommended; desirable; prudent: *Is it advisable to write to him?* **2.** open to advice. —**ad·vis′a·bil′i·ty, ad·vis′a·ble·ness,** *n.* —**ad·vis′a·bly,** *adv.* —**Syn. 1.** politic, proper.

ad·vise (ad vīz′), *v.,* **-vised, -vis·ing.** —*v.t.* **1.** to give advice to. **2.** to recommend (an action, policy, etc.) in giving advice: *to advise secrecy.* **3.** to give information or notice to (often fol. by *of*). —*v.i.* **4.** to give advice. **5.** to take counsel (usually fol. by *with*). [late ME; r. ME *avise(n)* < OF *aviser* < VL *advīsāre = ad- AD- + *vīsāre, alter. of L *vīsere* to view, freq. of *vidēre* to see] —**Syn. 1.** counsel, admonish, caution. **2.** suggest. **3.** inform. **5.** confer, consult.

ad·vised (ad vīzd′), *adj.* **1.** considered (usually used in combination): *ill-advised; well-advised.* **2.** informed: *to be kept thoroughly advised.* [ME] —**ad·vis·ed·ness** (ad vī′zid nis), *n.*

ad·vis·ed·ly (ad vī′zid lē), *adv.* after due consideration; deliberately.

ad·vis·ee (əd vī zē′, ad′-), *n.* *Educ.* one of a group of students supervised by a faculty adviser.

ad·vise·ment (ad vīz′mənt), *n.* careful deliberation or consideration. [ADVISE + -MENT; r. ME *avisement* < OF]

ad·vis·er (ad vī′zər), *n.* **1.** a person who gives advice. **2.** *Educ.* a teacher responsible for advising students on academic matters. Also, **ad·vi′sor.** —**ad·vis′er·ship′,** *n.*

ad·vi·so·ry (ad vī′zə rē), *adj.* **1.** of, giving, or containing advice. **2.** having the power or duty to advise: *an advisory council.* —**ad·vi′so·ri·ly,** *adv.*

ad·vo·ca·cy (ad′və kə sē), *n., pl.* **-cies.** an act of pleading for or giving verbal support to a cause. [late ME *advocacye* < ML *advocātia.* See ADVOCATE, -ACY]

ad·vo·cate (*v.* ad′və kāt′; *n.* ad′və kit, -kāt′), *v.,* **-cat·ed, -cat·ing,** *n.* —*v.t.* **1.** to plead in favor of; support or urge by argument; recommend publicly. —*n.* **2.** a person who defends, vindicates, or espouses a cause by argument (usually fol. by *of*). **3.** a person who pleads for or in behalf of another; intercessor. **4.** a person who pleads the cause of another in a court of law. [< L *advocāt(us)* legal counselor (orig. ptp. of *advocāre* to call to one's aid) = *ad-* AD- + *voc-* (s. of *vox* voice) + *-ātus* -ATE[1]; r. ME *avocat* < MF] —**ad·voc·a·to·ry** (ad vok′ə tōr′ē, -tôr′ē), *adj.* —**Syn. 4.** lawyer, attorney, counselor, counsel; barrister.

ad·vo·ca·tion (ad′və kā′shən), *n.* **1.** *Scot. Law.* the action of a superior court in calling before itself or reviewing an action originally brought before an inferior court. **2.** *Obs.* advocacy. **3.** *Obs.* the act of summoning. [late ME < L *advocātiōn-* (s. of *advocātiō*)]

ad·vo·ca·tus di·a·bo·li (äd′vō kä′to͝os dē ä′bə lē′), *Medieval Latin.* See **devil's advocate** (def. 2).

ad·vow·son (ad vou′zən), *n.* *Eng. Eccles. Law.* the right of presentation to a benefice or church office. [< AF; r. ME *avoweisoun* < AF, OF *avoeson* << L *advocātiōn-*. See ADVOCATION]

advt., advertisement.

A·dy·ghe (ä′də gā′, ä′də gā′, ä di ge′), *n.* Circassian (def. 1).

ad·y·nam·ic (ad′ᵊnam′ik, ā′dī nam′-), *adj.* *Pathol.* lacking strength; asthenic. [< NL *adynam(ia)* weakness (< Gk = *a-* A-[6] + *dýnam(is)* force, power) + -IC (prob. by assoc. with DYNAMICS)]

ad·y·tum (ad′i təm), *n., pl.* **-ta** (-tə). (in an ancient temple) a sacred interior shrine accessible only to the priests. [< L < Gk *ádyton* (place) not to be entered = *a-* A-[6] + *dy-* (s. of *dýein* to enter) + *-ton* adj. suffix]

adz (adz), *n., pl.* **adz·es.** a heavy, curved tool, for dressing timbers or planks, with a broad, chisellike steel end mounted on a wooden handle. Also, **adze.** [ME *ad(e)se,* OE *adesa* < ?]

ad·zu′ki bean′ (ad zo͞o′kē), an annual, bushy bean, *Phaseolus angularis,* grown chiefly in Asia, the seeds of which are used for food. Also, **adsuki bean.** [< Jap]

A B

Adzes
A, Cooper's adz
B, Carpenter's adz

ae (ā), *adj.* *Scot.* one. [ME (Scot) *ā-,* OE *ān* ONE]

ae, a digraph appearing in Latin and in English words of Latin and Greek origin.

Æ (ā′ē′), *n.* See **Russell, George William.** Also, **AE, A.E.**

æ, an early English ligature representing a vowel sound like that of *a* in modern *bad;* ash.

ae-, for words with initial **ae-,** see also **e-.**

ae., at the age of; aged. [< L *aetātis*]

A.E. and P., Ambassador Extraordinary and Plenipotentiary.

AEC, See **Atomic Energy Commission.**

ae·cid·i·um (ē sid′ē əm), *n., pl.* **ae·cid·i·a** (ē sid′ē ə). *Bot.* an aecium in which the spores are always formed in chains and enclosed in a cup-shaped peridium. [< NL; see AECIUM, -IDIUM]

ae·ci·um (ē′shē əm, ē′sē-), *n., pl.* **ae·ci·a** (ē′shē ə, ē′sē ə). *Bot.* the sorus of rust fungi that arises from the haploid mycelium, commonly accompanied by spermogonia and bearing chainlike or stalked spores. [< NL < Gk *aik(íā)* assault, injury; see -IUM] —**ae·ci·al** (ē′shē əl, ē′sē-), *adj.*

a·e·des (ā ē′dēz), *n.* See **yellow-fever mosquito.** Also, **a·ë′des.** [< NL < Gk *aēdḗs* distasteful, unpleasant = *a-* A-[6] + *-ēdēs,* akin to *hēdos* pleasure, *hēdýs* sweet, *hēdonḗ* pleasure. See SWEET]

ae·dile (ē′dīl), *n.* *Rom. Hist.* a magistrate in charge of public buildings, streets, markets, games, etc. Also, **edile.** [< L *aedīl(is)* = *aedi-* (s. of *aedēs* temple, shrine) + *-īlis* -ILE] —**ae′dile·ship′,** *n.*

Ae·ë·tes (ē ē′tēz), *n.* *Class. Myth.* a king of Colchis, father of Medea and custodian of the Golden Fleece.

A.E.F., See **American Expeditionary Forces.**

Ae·gae·on (i jē′on), *n.* *Class. Myth.* Briareus.

Ae·ge·an (i jē′ən), *adj.* **1.** of or pertaining to the Aegean Sea. **2.** of or pertaining to the Bronze Age culture that flourished in the region of the Aegean Sea. —*n.* **3.** See **Aegean Sea.** [< L *Aegae(us)* (< Gk *Aigaîos*) + -AN]

Aege′an Is′lands, the islands of the Aegean Sea, including the Dodecanese, Cyclades, and Sporades.

Aege′an Sea′, an arm of the Mediterranean Sea between Greece and Turkey. Also called **Aegean.**

Ae·ge·us (ē′jē əs, ē′jo͞os), *n.* *Class. Myth.* a king of Athens and the father of Theseus.

Ae·gi·na (i jī′nə), *n.* **1. Gulf of.** See **Saronic Gulf.** **2.** an island in the Saronic Gulf: seaport. 10,000 (est. 1960); 32 sq. mi. —**Ae·gi·ne·tan** (ē′jə nēt′ᵊn), *adj.*

Ae·gir (ē′jir), *n.* *Scand. Myth.* the sea-god, the husband of Ran.

ae·gis (ē′jis), *n.* **1.** *Class. Myth.* the shield or breastplate of Zeus or Athena, bearing at its center the head of the Gorgon. **2.** protection or sponsorship: *under the imperial aegis.* Also, **egis.** [< L < Gk *aigís* shield of Zeus or Athena, prob. from *aig-* (s. of *aíx* goat) + *-is* n. suffix, from a type of shield made of goatskin]

Ae·gis·thus (i jis′thəs), *n.* *Class. Myth.* a cousin of Agamemnon who seduced Agamemnon's wife, Clytemnestra, and was later killed by Orestes, her son.

Ae·gos·pot·a·mi (ē′gəs pot′ə mī′), *n.* a river in ancient Thrace, flowing into the Hellespont: site of the last battle of the Peloponnesian War.

Ae·gyp·tus (ē jip′təs), *n.* *Class. Myth.* a king of Egypt and twin brother of Danaüs.

Æl·fric (al′frik), *n.* ("*Ælfric Grammaticus*") A.D. c955–c1020, English abbot and writer.

-aemia, var. of **-emia:** *anaemia.*

-aena, var. of **-ena:** *hyaena.*

Ae·ne·as (i nē′əs), *n.* *Class. Myth.* a Trojan hero, the son of Anchises and Venus, and ancestor of the Romans.

Aene′as Sil′vi·us (sil′vē əs), literary name of **Pius II.** Also, **Aene′as Syl′vius.**

Ae·ne·id (i nē′id), *n.* a Latin epic poem by Vergil about the adventures of Aeneas after the fall of Troy.

A·e·ne·o·lith·ic (ā ē′nē ō lith′ik), *adj.* Chalcolithic. Also, **Eneolithic.** [< L *aēne(us)* (see AENEOUS) + -O- + -LITHIC]

a·e·ne·ous (ā ē′nē əs), *adj.* bronze-colored: *an aeneous beetle.* Also, **a·ë′ne·ous.** [< L *aēneus* = *aēn(us)* of bronze (*ae(s)* bronze + *-n-* adj. suffix) + *-eus* -EOUS]

Ae·o·li·a (ē ō′lē ə), *n.* Aeolis.

Ae·o·li·an (ē ō′lē ən), *adj.* **1.** Also, **Aeolic.** belonging to a branch of the Greek people named after Aeolus. —*n.* **2.** a member of one of the four main divisions of the prehistoric Greeks. Cf. **Achaean** (def. 5), **Dorian** (def. 2), **Ionian** (def. 3). **3.** Aeolic (def. 1). Also, **Eolian.** [< L *Aeoli(i)* (< Gk *Aioleîs* the Aeolians, with change of suffix) + -AN]

Ae·o·li·an (ē ō′lē ən), *adj.* **1.** pertaining to Aeolus, or to the winds in general. **2.** (*usually l.c.*) of or caused by the wind; wind-blown.

aeo′lian harp′, a box equipped with a number of strings of equal length, tuned in unison and sounded by the wind. Also called **aeo′lian lyre′, wind harp.**

Ae·ol·ic (ē ol′ik), *n.* **1.** a group of related Greek dialects of ancient Aeolis, Thessaly, Lesbos, Boeotia, and other regions occupied by the Aeolians. —*adj.* **2.** Aeolian (def. 1). Also, **Eolic.** [< L *Aeolic(us)* < Gk *Aiolikós* = *Aiol(eús),* pl. *Aioleîs* the Aeolians + *-ikos* -IC]

ae·ol·i·pile (ē ol′ə pīl′), *n.* a round vessel caused to rotate by the force of tangentially escaping steam. Also, **ae·ol′i·pyle′, eolipile.** [< L *aeolīpilae* balls of AEOLUS, alter. of *aeolīpylae* gates of AEOLUS = *Aeolī* (gen. sing. of AEOLUS) + *pylae,* pl. of *pyla* < Gk *pýlē* gate]

Ae·o·lis (ē′ə lis), *n.* an ancient coastal region and Greek colony in NW Asia Minor. Also, **Aeolia.**

ae·o·lo·trop·ic (ē′ə lō trop′ik), *adj.* *Physics.* not isotropic; anisotropic. [< Gk *aiólo(s)* fickle, changeful + -TROPIC] —**ae·o·lot·ro·py** (ē′ə lo′trə pē), **ae′o·lot′ro·pism,** *n.*

Ae·o·lus (ē′ə ləs), *n.* *Class. Myth.* the ruler of the winds and the eponymous founder of the Aeolian nation.

ae·on (ē′ən, ē′on), *n.* **1.** Also, **eon.** an indefinitely long period of time; age. **2.** *Geol.* eon (def. 1). [< LL < Gk *aiṓn* space of time, age]

ae·o·ni·an (ē ō′nē ən), *adj.* everlasting. Also, **eonian.** [< Gk *aiṓni(os)* (*aiṓn* AEON + *-ios* adj. suffix) + -AN]

aer-, var. of **aero-** before a vowel: *aerate.*

aer·ate (âr′āt, ā′ə rāt′), *v.t.,* **-at·ed, -at·ing.** **1.** to expose to or supply with air. **2.** to charge or treat with air or a gas, esp. with carbon dioxide. **3.** *Physiol.* to supply (the blood) with oxygen, as in respiration. Also, **aër′ate.** —**aer·a′tion, aër·a′tion,** *n.*

aer·a·tor (âr′ā tər, ā′ə rā′tər), *n.* an apparatus for aerating water, milk, etc. Also, **aër′a·tor.**

aeri-, var. of **aero-** before an element of Latin origin: *aeriferous.*

aer·i·al (*adj.* âr′ē əl, ā ēr′ē əl; *n.* âr′ē əl), *adj.* **1.** of, in, or produced by the air. **2.** inhabiting or frequenting the air. **3.** operating above ground on an elevated track or cable: *an aerial ski lift.* **4.** rising far into the air; lofty. **5.** of the nature of air. **6.** unsubstantial; visionary. **7.** having a light and graceful beauty. **8.** *Biol.* growing in the air, as the adventitious roots of some trees. **9.** pertaining to aircraft. **10.** supplied, performed, or carried by means of aircraft. —*n.* **11.** *Radio.* an antenna. Also, **aër′i·al.** [< L *āeri(us)* of the air (< Gk *āérios* = *āer-* AER- + *-ios* adj. suffix) + -AL[1]] —**aer′i·al·ly, aër′i·al·ly,** *adv.*

aer·i·al·ist (âr′ē ə list, ā ēr′ē-), *n.* a trapeze artist or a tightrope walker. Also, **aër′i·al·ist.**

aer·i·al·i·ty (âr′ē al′i tē, ā ēr′ē-), *n.* unsubstantiality. Also, **aër′i·al′i·ty.**

aer′ial lad′der, a long, extensible ladder, esp. from a hook-and-ladder truck.

aer′ial perspec′tive, a technique of rendering distance in painting by modifying the color and distinctness of objects.

aer·ie (âr′ē, ēr′ē), *n.* **1.** the nest of a large bird, esp. a bird of prey, high on a mountain or cliff. **2.** a dwelling or stronghold on a height. **3.** *Rare.* the brood in a nest, esp. of a bird of prey. Also, **aery, eyrie, eyry.** [< ML *aeria* < OF *aire* < L *ātrium* ATRIUM]

aer·if·er·ous (â rif′ər əs), *adj.* conveying air, as the bronchial tubes. Also, **aër·if′er·ous.**

aer·i·fi·ca·tion (âr′ə fə kā′shən, ā ēr′-), *n.* **1.** the act of combining with air. **2.** the state of being filled with air. Also, **aër′i·fi·ca′tion.**

aer·i·form (âr′ə fôrm′, ā ēr′-), *adj.* having the form or nature of air; gaseous. Also, **aër′i·form′.**

aer·i·fy (âr′ə fī′, ā ēr′-), *v.t.*, **-fied, -fy·ing. 1.** to aerate. **2.** to make aeriform. Also, **aër′i·fy′.**

aero-, a learned borrowing from Greek meaning "air," used in formation of compound words: *aerodrome.* Also, **aer-, aeri-.** [comb. form < Gk = *āer-* (s. of *āḗr* AIR[1]) + *-o-* -O-]

aer·o·bal·lis·tics (âr′ō bə lis′tiks), *n.* (*construed as sing.*) the science of ballistics combined with that of aerodynamics, dealing primarily with the flight paths of rockets, guided missiles, etc. —**aer′o·bal·lis′tic,** *adj.*

aer·o·bat·ics (âr′ə bat′iks), *n.* **1.** (*construed as pl.*) stunts performed by an airplane, glider, or the like. **2.** (*construed as sing.*) the art of performing such stunts. [AERO- + (ACRO)-BATICS] —**aer′o·bat′ic,** *adj.*

aer·obe (âr′ōb), *n.* an organism, esp. a bacterium, that requires air or free oxygen for life (opposed to *anaerobe*). [AERO- + *-be* (< Gk *bíos* life) as in MICROBE]

aer·o·bic (â rō′bik), *adj.* **1.** (of an organism or tissue) requiring air or free oxygen for life. **2.** pertaining to or caused by the presence of oxygen. **3.** of or utilizing the principles of aerobics: *aerobic dancing.* —**aer·o′bi·cal·ly,** *adv.*

aer·o·bics (â rō′biks), *n.* **1.** Also called **aero′bic ex′ercises.** (*construed as pl.*) any of various sustained exercises, as jogging, rowing, swimming, or cycling, that stimulate and strengthen the heart and lungs, thereby improving the body's utilization of oxygen. **2.** (*construed as sing.*) a physical fitness program based on such exercises.

aer·o·bi·o·sis (âr′ō bī ō′sis), *n.* *Biol.* life in an environment containing oxygen or air. [< NL] —**aer·o·bi·ot·ic** (âr′ō bī ot′ik), *adj.* —**aer′o·bi·ot′i·cal·ly,** *adv.*

aer·o·drome (âr′ə drōm′), *n.* *Chiefly Brit.* airdrome.

aer·o·dy·nam·ics (âr′ō dī nam′iks), *n.* (*construed as sing.*) the branch of mechanics that deals with the motion of air and other gases and with the effects of such motion on objects in such media. Cf. **aerostatics** (def. 1). —**aer′o·dy·nam′ic, aer′o·dy·nam′i·cal,** *adj.* —**aer′o·dy·nam′i·cal·ly,** *adv.* —**aer′o·dy·nam′i·cist,** *n.*

aer·o·dyne (âr′ə dīn′), *n.* any heavier-than-air craft. [back formation from AERODYNAMIC; see DYNE]

aer·o·em·bo·lism (âr′ō em′bə liz′əm), *n.* *Pathol.* a condition caused by a substantial decrease in atmospheric pressure, as in high-altitude flying, and characterized by the formation of nitrogen bubbles in the blood, pains in the lungs, etc. Cf. **caisson disease.**

aer·o·gram (âr′ə gram′), *n.* **1.** a radiogram. **2.** an airmail letter.

aer·og·ra·phy (â rog′rə fē), *n.* the description of the air or atmosphere. —**aer·og′ra·pher,** *n.* —**aer·o·graph·ic** (âr′ə graf′ik), **aer′o·graph′i·cal,** *adj.*

aer·o·lite (âr′ə līt′), *n.* a meteorite consisting mainly of stony matter. Also, **aer·o·lith** (âr′ə lith). —**aer·o·lit·ic** (âr′ə lit′ik), *adj.*

aer·o·me·chan·ic (âr′ō mə kan′ik), *n.* **1.** an aviation mechanic. —*adj.* **2.** of or pertaining to aeromechanics.

aer·o·me·chan·ics (âr′ō mə kan′iks), *n.* (*construed as sing.*) the mechanics of air or gases. —**aer′o·me·chan′i·cal,** *adj.*

aer·o·med·i·cine (âr′ə med′i sən), *n.* See **aviation medicine.**

aer·o·me·te·or·o·graph (âr′ə mē′tē ər ə graf′, -gräf′, -mē′tē ôr′ə-, -or′ə-), *n.* a meteorograph for use in aircraft.

aer·om·e·ter (â rom′i tər), *n.* an instrument for determining the weight, density, etc., of air or other gases. —**aer·o·met·ric** (âr′ə me′trik), *adj.* —**aer·om·e·try** (â rom′i trē), *n.*

aeron., aeronautics.

aer·o·naut (âr′ə nôt′, -not′), *n.* **1.** the pilot of a balloon or other lighter-than-air craft. **2.** a traveler in an airship. [AERO- + (ARGO)NAUT; cf. F *aéronaute*]

aer·o·nau·tic (âr′ə nô′tik, -not′ik), *adj.* of aeronautics or aeronauts. Also, **aer′o·nau′ti·cal.** —**aer′o·nau′ti·cal·ly,** *adv.*

aer·o·nau·tics (âr′ə nô′tiks, -not′iks), *n.* (*construed as sing.*) the science or art of flight. [see AERONAUTIC, -ICS]

aer·o·neu·ro·sis (âr′ō nŏŏ rō′sis, -nyŏŏ-), *n.* *Psychiatry.* a psychoneurotic condition that occurs in aviators and is characterized by worry, loss of self-confidence, mild depression, and usually various physical symptoms.

aer·o·pause (âr′ə pôz′), *n.* *Aeron.* (not used scientifically) the region above the earth's surface where the atmosphere becomes too thin for airplanes to function properly.

aer·o·phyte (âr′ə fīt′), *n.* *Bot.* epiphyte.

aer·o·plane (âr′ə plān′), *n.* *Chiefly Brit.* airplane.

aer·o·sol (âr′ə sōl′, -sôl′, -sol′), *n.* **1.** *Physical Chem.* a system of colloidal particles dispersed in a gas; smoke or fog. **2.** a liquid substance, as a disinfectant, deodorant, etc., sealed in a container under pressure with an inert gas or other activating agent for dispensing, as a spray. **3.** a container for such a substance. **4.** See **aerosol bomb.**

aer′osol bomb′, a container filled with an aerosol, as an insecticide, disinfectant, etc., that is released as a spray when a mechanism, as a button, is actuated.

aer·o·space (âr′ə spās′), *n.* **1.** the atmosphere and the space beyond considered as a whole. —*adj.* **2.** of, pertaining to, or concerned with the design and manufacture of vehicles, missiles, and the like, that operate in aerospace.

aer·o·sphere (âr′ə sfēr′), *n.* *Aeron.* (not used scientifically) the region above the earth's atmosphere.

aer·o·stat (âr′ə stat′), *n.* any lighter-than-air craft, as a balloon or dirigible.

aer·o·stat·ics (âr′ə stat′iks), *n.* (*construed as sing.*) **1.** the branch of statics that deals with gases in equilibrium and with gases and bodies in them. Cf. **aerodynamics. 2.** the science of lighter-than-air craft. [see AEROSTAT, -ICS] —**aer′o·stat′ic, aer′o·stat′i·cal,** *adj.*

aer·o·sta·tion (âr′ə stā′shən), *n.* *Aeron.* the science or art of operating aerostats.

aer·o·ther·mo·dy·nam·ics (âr′ō thûr′mō dī nam′iks), *n.* (*construed as sing.*) aerodynamics dealing with situations in which there are significant heat exchanges in gases or significant thermal effects between gas and solid surfaces, as in supersonic flight. —**aer′o·ther′mo·dy·nam′ic,** *adj.*

aer·y[1] (âr′ē, ā′ə rē), *adj.* ethereal; aerial. Also, **aër′y.** [< L *āeri(us)* < Gk *āérios* = *āer-* AER- + *-ios* adj. suffix]

aer·y[2] (âr′ē, ēr′ē), *n.*, *pl.* **aer·ies.** aerie.

aes-, for words with initial **aes-,** see also **es-.**

Aes·chi·nes (es′kə nēz′ *or, esp. Brit.,* ēs′-), *n.* 389–314 B.C., Athenian orator: rival of Demosthenes.

Aes·chy·lus (es′kə ləs *or, esp. Brit.* ē′skə-), *n.* 525–456 B.C., Greek poet and dramatist. —**Aes·chy·le·an** (es′kə-lē′ən *or, esp. Brit.,* ēs′-), *adj.*

Aes·cu·la·pi·an (es′kyə lā′pē ən *or, esp. Brit.,* ēs′-), *adj.* **1.** pertaining to Aesculapius. **2.** medical; medicinal. —*n.* **3.** a physician; doctor. Also, **Esculapian.**

Aes·cu·la·pi·us (es′kyə lā′pē əs *or, esp. Brit.,* ēs′-), *n.* the ancient Roman god of medicine and healing, identified with the Greek Asclepius.

Ae·sir (ē′sir), *n.* (*often l.c.*) (*construed as pl.*) *Scand. Myth.* a superior race of gods, led by Odin and living at Asgard. Cf. **Vanir.** [< Icel, pl. of *āss* god; c. OE *ōs* god, *Os-* in proper names (as *Oswald*), OHG *Ans-* in proper names (as *Anselm*); akin to Skt *asura* lord]

Ae·sop (ē′səp, ē′sop), *n.* c620–c560 B.C., Greek writer of fables. —**Ae·so·pi·an** (ē sō′pē ən), **Ae·sop·ic** (ē sop′ik), *adj.*

aes·the·sia (es thē′zhə, -zhē ə, -zē ə), *n.* esthesia.

aes·thete (es′thēt *or, esp. Brit.,* ēs′-), *n.* a person who has or affects a high degree of sensitivity toward the beautiful, esp. in art, music, poetry, etc. Also, **esthete.** [< Gk *aisthētḗs* one who perceives = *aisthē-* + *-tēs* agent suffix]

aes·thet·ic (es thet′ik *or, esp. Brit.,* ēs-), *adj.* **1.** pertaining to a sense of the beautiful or to aesthetics. **2.** having a sense of the beautiful or characterized by a love of beauty. **3.** pertaining to, involving, or concerned with pure emotion and sensation as opposed to pure intellectuality. —*n.* **4.** aesthetics. **5.** a theory or idea of what is aesthetically valid. Also, **esthetic.** [< NL *aesthetic(us)* < Gk *aisthētikós* = *aisthē-* (var. s. of *aisthánesthai* to perceive) + *-tikos* -TIC]

aes·thet·i·cal (es thet′i kəl *or, esp. Brit.,* ēs-), *adj.* of or pertaining to aesthetics. Also, **esthetical.**

aes·thet·i·cal·ly (es thet′ik lē *or, esp. Brit.,* ēs-), *adv.* **1.** according to aesthetics or its principles. **2.** in an aesthetic manner. Also, **esthetically.**

aes·the·ti·cian (es′thi tish′ən *or, esp. Brit.,* ēs′-), *n.* a person versed in aesthetics. Also, **esthetician.**

aes·thet·i·cism (es thet′i siz′əm *or, esp. Brit.,* ēs-), *n.* **1.** the acceptance of aesthetic standards as of supreme importance. **2.** an exaggerated devotion to the artistic or beautiful. Also, **estheticism.**

aes·thet·ics (es thet′iks *or, esp. Brit.,* ēs-), *n.* (*construed as sing.*) **1.** *Philos.* the study of the qualities perceived in works of art, with a view to the abstraction of principles. **2.** the study of the mind and emotions in relation to the sense of beauty. Also, **esthetics.** [see AESTHETIC, -ICS]

aes·ti·val (es′tə vəl, e stī′- *or, esp. Brit.,* ē′stə-, ē stī′-), *adj.* estival.

aes·ti·vate (es′tə vāt′ *or, esp. Brit.,* ēs′-), *v.i.*, **-vat·ed, -vat·ing.** estivate. —**aes′ti·va′tion,** *n.* —**aes′ti·va′tor,** *n.*

aet., at the age of. [< L *aetātis*]

ae·ta·tis su·ae (ī tä′tis sōō′ī; *Eng.* ē tā′tis sōō′ē), *Latin.* in a certain year of one's age.

Æth·el·bert (eth′əl bərt, ath′-), *n.* old spelling of **Ethelbert.**

ae·ther (ē′thər), *n.* ether (defs. 3–5). —**ae·the·re·al** (i thēr′ē əl), **ae·ther·ic** (i ther′ik), *adj.*

aetio-, var. of **etio-.**

ae·ti·ol·o·gy (ē′tē ol′ə jē), *n.*, *pl.* **-gies.** etiology. —**ae·ti·o·log·i·cal** (ē′tē ə loj′i kəl), *adj.* —**ae′ti·o·log′i·cal·ly,** *adv.* —**ae′ti·ol′o·gist,** *n.*

Aet·na (et′nə), *n.* **Mount.** See **Etna, Mount.**

Ae·to·li·a (ē tō′lē ə), *n.* an ancient district in W Greece. —**Ae·to′li·an,** *adj.*

AF, 1. Air Force. **2.** Anglo-French (def. 3).

af-, var. of **ad-** before *f: affect.*

Af., 1. Africa. **2.** African.

A.F., 1. Air Force. **2.** Anglo-French. **3.** audio frequency.

a.f., audio frequency.

A.F.A.M., Ancient Free and Accepted Masons.

a·far (ə fär′), *adv.* **1.** from, at, or to a distance; far away. —*n.* **2. from afar,** from a long way off. [ME *a fer*]

A·fars and Is·sas (ə färz′ ənd ē′säz), **French Territory of the,** a former name of **Djibouti** (def. 1).

AFB, Air Force Base.

AFC, 1. automatic flight control. **2.** automatic frequency control.

a·feard (ə fērd′), *adj.* *Dial.* afraid. Also, **a·feared′.** [ME *afered,* OE *āfǣred* frightened (ptp. of *āfǣran*)]

af·fa·ble (af′ə bəl), *adj.* **1.** pleasantly easy to talk to; cordial. **2.** showing warmth and friendliness. [< L *affābil(is)* that can be spoken to, courteous = *af-* AF- + *fā-* speak (see FATE) + *-bilis* -BLE] —**af′fa·bil′i·ty, af′fa·ble·ness,** *n.* —**af′fa·bly,** *adv.* —**Syn. 1.** amiable, courteous.

af·fair (ə fâr′), *n.* **1.** anything done or to be done; anything requiring action or effort; business. **2. affairs,** matters of commercial or public interest or concern; the transactions of public or private business: *affairs of state; to put one's affairs in order.* **3.** an event or a performance; a particular action, operation, or proceeding: *When did this affair happen?* **4.** an object, process, etc., not specifically described; thing: *This machine is a complicated affair.* **5.** a private or personal concern. **6.** an illicit amorous relationship; liaison. **7.** a disputed, notorious, or scandalous event. **8.** a party or social gathering. [earlier *affaire* < MF, OF *afaire* for *a faire* to do = *a* (see AD-) + *faire* < L *facere;* r. ME *afere* < OF]

af·faire d'hon·neur (A FER′ dô NŒR′), *pl.* **af·faires d'hon·neur** (A FER′ dô NŒR′). *French.* a duel. [lit., affair of honor]

af·fect[1] (*v.* ə fekt′; *n.* af′ekt, ə fekt′), *v.t.* **1.** to produce an effect or change in. **2.** to impress the mind or move the feelings of. **3.** (of pain, disease, etc.) to attack or lay hold of. **—***n.* **4.** *Psychol.* feeling or emotion. **5.** *Obs.* a person's inward disposition. [< L *affect(us)* acted upon, subjected to (ptp. of *afficere*) = *af-* AF- + *fec-* (var. s. of *facere* to make, do) + *-tus* ptp. suffix] **—Syn. 1.** influence. **2.** touch, stir.

af·fect[2] (ə fekt′), *v.t.* **1.** to give a false appearance of; feign. **2.** to assume pretentiously: *to affect a Boston accent.* **3.** to use or favor as a matter of personal preference. **4.** to tend toward habitually or naturally. **5.** (of animals and plants) to live in or on. **6.** *Archaic.* to have affection for; fancy. **7.** *Archaic.* to aim at; aspire to. **—***v.i.* **8.** *Obs.* to incline, tend (usually fol. by *to*). [late ME < L *affect(āre)* (to) strive after, feign (freq. of *afficere* to do to) = *af-* AF- + *fec-* (see AFFECT[1]) + *-t-* freq. suffix] **—af·fect′er,** *n.* **—Syn. 1.** See **pretend.**

af·fec·ta·tion (af′ek tā′shən), *n.* **1.** a false appearance or assumption of a state, quality, or manner. **2.** conspicuous artificiality of manner or appearance. **3.** a trait or action characterized by such artificiality. **4.** *Obs.* strenuous pursuit or aspiration. [< L *affectātiōn-* (s. of *affectātiō*) a striving after = *affectāt(us)* (ptp. of *affectāre* to AFFECT[2]) + *-iōn-* -ION] **—Syn. 2.** pretension, airs, pose, affectedness, insincerity.

af·fect·ed[1] (ə fek′tid), *adj.* **1.** acted upon; influenced. **2.** influenced injuriously. **3.** (of the mind or feelings) impressed or moved. [AFFECT[1] + -ED[2]]

af·fect·ed[2] (ə fek′tid), *adj.* **1.** falsely assumed: *affected piety.* **2.** unnatural in quality or appearance, esp. because of preciosity. **3.** inclined or disposed: *well affected toward the speaker's cause.* **4.** held in affection; fancied. [AFFECT[2] + -ED[2]] **—af·fect′ed·ly,** *adv.* **—af·fect′ed·ness,** *n.* **—Syn. 1.** pretended, feigned.

af·fect·ing (ə fek′ting), *adj.* moving the feelings or emotions. **—af·fect′ing·ly,** *adv.* **—Syn.** touching, stirring.

af·fec·tion[1] (ə fek′shən), *n.* **1.** fondness for or devotion to a person or thing. **2.** Often, **affections. a.** emotion; sentiment. **b.** love. **c.** the emotional realm of one's love: *a place in someone's affections.* **3.** *Pathol.* a disease or diseased condition. **4.** the act of affecting. **5.** the state of being affected. **6.** *Philos.* a contingent, alterable, and accidental state or quality of being. **7.** the affective aspect of a mental process. **8.** a bent or disposition of mind. [ME < L *affectiōn-* (s. of *affectiō*) disposition or state of mind or body. See AFFECT[1], -ION] **—Syn. 1.** liking, amity, fondness. See **love.**

af·fec·tion[2] (ə fek′shən), *n.* *Obs.* affectation (defs. 1–3). [AFFECT[2] + -ION]

af·fec·tion·al (ə fek′shə nəl), *adj.* relating to or implying affection. **—af·fec′tion·al·ly,** *adv.*

af·fec·tion·ate (ə fek′shə nit), *adj.* **1.** showing or characterized by affection or tenderness. **2.** having great affection or love. **3.** *Obs.* strongly disposed or inclined. [AFFECTION + -ATE[1], modeled after *passionate*] **—af·fec′tion·ate·ly,** *adv.* **—af·fec′tion·ate·ness,** *n.* **—Syn. 1.** loving. **2.** devoted.

af·fec·tive (ə fek′tiv), *adj.* **1.** of, caused by, or expressing emotion or feeling. **2.** causing emotion or feeling. **3.** *Psychol.* pertaining to feeling or emotion. [< ML *affectīv(us)*] **—af·fec·tiv·i·ty** (af′ek tiv′i tē), *n.*

af·fen·pin·scher (af′ən pin′shər), *n.* one of a breed of toy dogs having a dense, wiry, red or gray coat with tufts of hair around the eyes, nose, and chin, cropped ears, and a docked tail. [< G = *Affen* (inflected form of *Affa* APE) + *Pinscher* breed of dogs]

af·fer·ent (af′ər ənt), *adj.* *Physiol.* bringing to or leading toward an organ or part, as a nerve or vein (opposed to *efferent*). [< L *afferent-* (s. of *afferēns*, prp. of *afferre*) = *af-* AF- + *fer-* (s. of *ferre* to carry) + *-ent-* -ENT]

af·fet·tuo·so (a fech′o͞o ō′sō; *It.* äf′fet two′zô), *n., pl.* **-sos.** *Music.* a composition or movement of gentle, tender character. [< It: affecting, moving < L *affectuōsus* = *affectu(s)* AFFECT[1] + *-ōsus* -OUS]

af·fi·ance (ə fī′əns), *v.,* **-anced, -anc·ing,** *n.* **—***v.t.* **1.** to pledge by promise of marriage; betroth. **—***n.* *Archaic.* **2.** a pledging of faith, as a marriage contract. **3.** trust; confidence; reliance. [ME < MF *afiance* = *afi(er)* (to) trust to (< ML *affīdāre: ad-* AD- + **fīdāre*, alter. of L *fīdere* to trust; see CONFIDE) + *-ance* -ANCE]

af·fi·ant (ə fī′ənt), *n.* *Law.* a person who makes an affidavit. [obs. v. *affy* (< MF *afi(er)*; see AFFIANCE) + -ANT]

af·fiche (A fēsh′), *n., pl.* **af·fiches** (A fēsh′). *French.* a notice posted in a public place; poster. [lit., something affixed]

af·fi·da·vit (af′i dā′vit), *n.* *Law.* a written declaration upon oath made before an authorized official. [< ML: he has made oath (perf. 3rd sing. of *affīdāre*). See AFFIANCE]

af·fil·i·ate (*v.* ə fil′ē āt′; *n.* ə fil′ē it, -āt′), *v.,* **-at·ed, -at·ing,** *n.* **—***v.t.* **1.** to bring into close association or connection. **2.** to attach or unite on terms of fellowship; associate (usually fol. by *with* in U.S. usage, by *to* in Brit. usage). **3.** to trace the descent, derivation, or origin of. **4.** to adopt. **5.** *Law.* to fix the paternity of, as a bastard child. **—***v.i.* **6.** to be intimately united in action or interest. **—***n.* **7.** *Com.* a business concern owned or controlled in whole or in part by another concern; subsidiary. **8.** an affiliated person [< L *affīliāt(us)* adopted as son (ptp. of *affīliāre*) = *af-* AF- + *fīli (us)* son + *-ātus* -ATE[1]] **—af·fil·i·a·ble** (ə fil′ē ə bəl), *adj.*

af·fil·i·a·tion (ə fil′ē ā′shən), *n.* **1.** the act of affiliating. **2.** the state of being affiliated or associated. [< ML *affīliātiōn-* (s. of *affīliātiō* adoption)]

af·fine (a fīn′, ə fīn′, af′īn), *adj.* *Math.* of or pertaining to a transformation that maps parallel lines to parallel lines and finite points to finite points. [< F *affin* related < L *affin(is)* a relative] **—af·fine′ly,** *adv.*

af·fined (ə fīnd′), *adj.* **1.** closely related. **2.** obligated.

af·fin·i·tive (ə fin′i tiv), *adj.* characterized by affinity; closely related or associated.

af·fin·i·ty (ə fin′i tē), *n., pl.* **-ties.** **1.** a natural liking or attraction. **2.** the object of such a liking or attraction. **3.** relationship by marriage or by ties other than those of blood. **4.** inherent likeness or agreement. **5.** *Biol.* the phylogenetic relationship between two organisms or groups of organisms resulting in a resemblance in general plan or structure. **6.** *Chem.* the force by which atoms are held together in chemical compounds. [ME *affinite* < MF < L *affīnitāt-* (s. of *affīnitās* connection by marriage). See AFFINE, -ITY]

af·firm (ə fûrm′), *v.t.* **1.** to state or assert positively; maintain as true. **2.** to confirm or ratify. **3.** to declare positively; assert solemnly. **4.** *Law.* **a.** to declare solemnly before a court or magistrate, but without oath. **b.** to ratify and accept (a voidable transaction). **c.** (of an appellate court) to determine (that the action of the lower court shall stand). [< L *affirm(āre)* = *af-* AF- + *firmāre* to make firm (see FIRM[1]); r. late ME *aferme* < MF *afermer* < L] **—af·firm′a·ble,** *adj.* **—af·firm′a·bly,** *adv.* **—af·firm′er,** *n.* **—af·firm′ing·ly,** *adv.* **—Syn. 1.** aver, asseverate, depose, testify. See **declare. 2.** approve, endorse. **—Ant. 1.** deny.

af·firm·ant (ə fûr′mənt), *n.* a person who affirms.

af·fir·ma·tion (af′ər mā′shən), *n.* **1.** the act of affirming. **2.** the state of being affirmed. **3.** an assertion of the truth or existence of something. **4.** a proposition or idea supported by such an assertion. **5.** a confirmation or ratification. **6.** *Law.* a solemn declaration accepted instead of a statement under oath. Also, **af·firm·ance** (ə fûr′məns). [< L *affirmātiōn-* (s. of *affirmātiō*) = *affirmāt(us)* (ptp. of *affirmāre* to AFFIRM) + *-iōn-* -ION]

af·firm·a·tive (ə fûr′mə tiv), *adj.* Also, **af·firm·a·to·ry** (ə fûr′mə tôr′ē, -tōr′ē). **1.** affirming or asserting something as true or real. **2.** assenting; indicating assent. **3.** *Logic.* noting a proposition in which a property is affirmed of a subject, as "All men are happy." **—***n.* **4.** a positive statement or proposition. **5.** a reply indicating assent. **6.** the state of assenting: *a reply in the affirmative.* **7.** the side, as in a debate, that affirms or defends a proposition. [< L *affirmātīv(us)* = *affirmāt-* (see AFFIRMATION) + *-īvus* -IVE; r. late ME *affirmatyff* < MF] **—af·firm′a·tive·ly,** *adv.*

affirm′ative ac′tion, encouragement for increased representation of women and minority-group members, esp. in employment.

af·fix (*v.* ə fiks′; *n.* af′iks), *v.t.* **1.** to fasten, join, or attach (usually fol. by *to*): *to affix stamps to a letter.* **2.** to put or add on; append: *to affix a signature to a contract.* **3.** to impress (a seal or stamp). **4.** to attach (blame, reproach, ridicule, etc.). **—***n.* **5.** something that is joined or attached. **6.** *Gram.* a bound element, as a prefix or suffix, added to a base or stem to form a fresh stem or a word, as *-ed* added to *want* to form *wanted,* or *im-* added to *possible* to form *impossible.* [< L *affīx(us)* fastened to (ptp. of *affīgere*) = *af-* AF- + *fig-* fasten + *-sus,* var. of *-tus* ptp. suffix] **—af·fix·al** (a fik′səl), **af·fix·i·al** (a fik′sē əl), *adj.* **—af·fix′er,** *n.*

af·fix·ture (ə fiks′chər), *n.* **1.** the act of affixing. **2.** the state of being affixed. Also, **af·fix·a·tion** (af′ik sā′shən). [b. obs. *affixion* (see AFFIX, -ION) and FIXTURE]

af·fla·tus (ə flā′təs), *n.* **1.** inspiration. **2.** divine communication of knowledge. [< L: a breathing on = *af-* AF- + *flā-* (s. of *flāre* to blow) + *-tus* n. suffix, r. *-tus* ptp. suffix]

af·flict (ə flikt′), *v.t.* **1.** to distress with mental or bodily pain. **2.** *Obs.* **a.** to overthrow; defeat. **b.** to humble. [< L *afflīct(us)* distressed (ptp. of *afflīgere* to cast down) = *af-* AF- + *flīg-* knock + *-tus* ptp. suffix; r. late ME *aflight* < MF *aflit* < L; see INFLICT] **—af·flict′ed·ness,** *n.* **—af·flict′er,** *n.* **—Syn. 1.** vex, harass, torment, plague.

af·flic·tion (ə flik′shən), *n.* **1.** a state of pain, distress, or grief. **2.** a cause of continued mental or bodily pain. [ME *affliccioun* < L *afflīctiōn-* (s. of *afflīctiō*)] **—af·flic′tion·less,** *adj.* **—Syn. 1.** misery, woe. **2.** trouble, tribulation.

af·flic·tive (ə flik′tiv), *adj.* characterized by or causing pain; distressing. **—af·flic′tive·ly,** *adv.*

af·flu·ence (af′lo͞o əns, *sometimes* ə flo͞o′-), *n.* **1.** abundance of money, property, etc.; wealth. **2.** abundance of thoughts, words, etc. **3.** an afflux. [late ME < MF < L *affluentia* = *af-* AF- + *flu-* flow + *-entia* -ENCE]

af·flu·ent (af′lo͞o ənt, *sometimes* ə flo͞o′-), *adj.* **1.** prosperous; wealthy. **2.** abounding in anything; abundant. **3.** conditioned by or based on prosperity or wealth: *an affluent society.* **4.** flowing freely. **—***n.* **5.** a tributary stream. [late ME < L *affluent-* (s. of *affluēns* rich; orig. prp. of *affluere*) = *af-* AF- + *flu-* flow + *-ent-* -ENT] **—af′flu·ent·ly,** *adv.* **—Syn. 1.** See **rich. 2.** teeming.

af·flux (af′luks), *n.* **1.** something that flows to or toward a point. **2.** the act of flowing to or toward. [< ML *afflux(us)* = *af-* AF- + *fluxus* FLUX]

af·ford (ə fōrd′, ə fôrd′), *v.t.* **1.** to do without serious or adverse consequences: *She can't afford to miss another day at school.* **2.** to meet the expense of. **3.** to spare or bear the loss of. **4.** to furnish or supply (something). **5.** to give as a yield or profit. **6.** to confer or impress upon someone, as a feeling or sensation. [ME *aforthen, iforthen,* OE *geforthian* to further, accomplish = *ge-* Y- + *forth* FORTH + *-ian* inf. suffix] **—af·ford′a·ble,** *adj.*

af·for·est (ə fôr′ist, ə for′-), *v.t.* to convert (bare or cultivated land) into forest. [< ML *afforest(āre)* = *af-* AF- + *forest(is)* FOREST + *-āre* inf. suffix] **—af·for′est·a′tion, af·for′est·ment,** *n.*

af·fran·chise (ə fran′chīz), *v.t.,* **-chised, -chis·ing.** to free from a state of dependence, servitude, or obligation. [late ME < MF *afranchiss-* (long s. of *afranchir*) = *a-* A-[5] + *franch-* free (see FRANK[1]) + *-iss-* -ISE[2]] **—af·fran′chise·ment,** *n.*

af·fray (ə frā′), *n.* **1.** a public fight or a noisy quarrel; brawl. **2.** *Law.* the fighting of two or more persons in a public place. **—***v.t.* **3.** *Archaic.* to frighten. [ME < AF *afray* (n.), *afray(er)* (v.), OF *esfrei* (n.), *esfreer* (v.) < VL **exfridāre* to break the peace = *ex-* EX-[1] + *-frid-* peace (< Gmc; cf. G *Friede*) + *-āre* inf. suffix] **—af·fray′er,** *n.*

af·fri·cate (af′rə kit), *n.* *Phonet.* a speech sound comprising occlusion, plosion, and frication, as either of the *ch* sounds in *church.* Also called **affricative.** [< L *affricāt(us)* rubbed against (ptp. of *affricāre*) = *af-* AF- + *fric-* (see FRICTION) + *-ātus* -ATE]

af·fri·ca·tion (af′rə kā′shən), *n.* *Phonet.* **1.** act or process of changing a stop sound to an affricate. **2.** the result of such a change, as *pf-* in German.

af·fric·a·tive (ə frik′ə tiv, af′rə kā′-), *Phonet.* —*n.* **1.** affricate. —*adj.* **2.** of or pertaining to an affricate. **3.** articulated as an affricate.

af·fright (ə frīt′), *Archaic.* —*v.t.* **1.** to frighten. —*n.* **2.** sudden fear or terror; fright. [ME *afright(en)*, OE *āfyrhtan* = *ā-* A-[3] + *fyrhtan* to FRIGHT]

af·front (ə frunt′), *n.* **1.** a personally offensive act or remark. **2.** an offense to one's dignity or self-respect. —*v.t.* **3.** to offend by a show of disrespect. **4.** to confuse or make ashamed. **5.** to encounter face to face; confront. **6.** *Archaic.* to front; face. [ME *afrounte(n)* < MF *afronter, affronter* to strike in the face < VL **affrontāre* < L phrase *ad frontem* at the face. See AD-, FRONT] —**af·front′ed·ly,** *adv.* —**af·front′ed·ness,** *n.* —**af·front′er,** *n.* —**af·front′ing·ly,** *adv.* —**Syn. 1.** impertinence; indignity, abuse, outrage. See **insult. 3.** insult, slight, abuse. **4.** shame, disconcert, abash. —**Ant. 1.** compliment.

af·fu·sion (ə fyo͞o′zhən), *n.* the pouring on of water or other liquid, as in the rite of baptism. [< LL *affūsiōn-* (s. of *affūsiō* a pouring upon) = *affūs(us)* (ptp. of *affundere;* see AF-, FUSE[2]) + *-iōn-* -ION]

Afgh., Afghanistan. Also, **Afg.**

Af·ghan (af′gən, -gan), *n.* **1.** a native of Afghanistan. **2.** Pashto. **3.** (*l.c.*) a woolen blanket, knitted, crocheted, or woven, usually in a geometric pattern. **4.** Also called **Af′ghan hound′.** one of a breed of hounds having a long head and a long, silky coat. —*adj.* **5.** of Afghanistan or its people.

af·ghan·i (af gan′ē, -gä′nē), *n.* a coin and monetary unit of Afghanistan, equal to 100 puls. *Abbr.:* Af. [< Pushtu]

Af·ghan·i·stan (af gan′i stan′), *n.* a republic in S Asia, NW of India, E of Iran, and S of the Soviet Union. 12,700,000; 250,000 sq. mi. *Cap.:* Kabul.

a·fi·cio·na·do (ə fish′yə nä′dō; *Sp.* ä fē′thyô nä′thô), *n., pl.* **-dos** (-dōz; *Sp.* -thôs). an ardent devotee; fan; enthusiast. [< Sp: lit., affectionate = *afición* AFFECTION[1] + *-ado* -ATE[1]]

a·field (ə fēld′), *adv.* **1.** away from home; abroad. **2.** away from what is relevant, as in an argument. **3.** away from what is known or familiar. **4.** in or to the field or countryside. [ME *afelde*, OE *on felda*]

a·fire (ə fīər′), *adj.* on fire: *to set a house afire.* [ME]

AFL, 1. See **American Federation of Labor. 2.** American Football League.

A.F.L., See **American Federation of Labor.** Also, **A.F. of L.**

a·flame (ə flām′), *adj.* **1.** ablaze. **2.** eager and excited.

AFL-CIO, American Federation of Labor and Congress of Industrial Organizations.

a·float (ə flōt′), *adv., adj.* **1.** borne on the water; floating. **2.** on board a ship, boat, raft, etc. **3.** flooded with water; awash. **4.** drifting without guidance. **5.** in general circulation, as a rumor. **6.** financially solvent. [ME, OE *on flote*]

a·flut·ter (ə flut′ər), *adj.* in a flutter.

AFM, American Federation of Musicians.

a·foot (ə fo͝ot′), *adv., adj.* **1.** on foot; walking. **2.** astir; in progress. [ME *a fote, on fote*]

a·fore (ə fōr′, ə fôr′), *adv., prep., conj.* *Dial.* before. [late ME; ME *aforne, aforen,* OE *on foran*]

a·fore·men·tioned (ə fōr′men′shənd, ə fôr′-), *adj.* cited or mentioned earlier or previously.

a·fore·said (ə fōr′sed′, ə fôr′-), *adj.* said or mentioned earlier or previously.

a·fore·thought (ə fōr′thôt′, ə fôr′-), *adj.* premeditated (usually used predicatively): *with malice aforethought.*

a·fore·time (ə fōr′tīm′, ə fôr′-), *adv.* **1.** formerly. —*adj.* **2.** former; previous.

a for·ti·o·ri (ä fōr′ti ō′rē; *Eng.* ā fōr′shē ōr′ī, ā fôr′-shē ôr′ī), *Latin.* for a still stronger reason; all the more.

a·foul (ə foul′), *adv., adj.* **1.** in a state of collision or entanglement: *a ship with its shrouds afoul.* **2. run afoul of, a.** to come into conflict with: *to run afoul of the law.* **b.** to become entangled with.

Afr, African. Also, **Afr.**

Afr-, var. of **Afro-** before a vowel: *Afric.*

Afr., 1. Africa. **2.** African.

A.-Fr., Anglo-French.

a·fraid (ə frād′), *adj.* **1.** feeling fear or apprehension. **2.** politely regretful, as in declining a request. **3.** deeply reluctant, as through fear. [var. sp. of *affrayed*, ptp. of AFFRAY to disturb, frighten]
—**Syn. 1.** scared, fearful, disquieted, apprehensive, timid, timorous. AFRAID, ALARMED, FRIGHTENED, TERRIFIED all indicate a state of fear. AFRAID implies inner apprehensive disquiet: *afraid of* (or *in*) *the dark.* ALARMED implies that the feelings are aroused through realization of some imminent or unexpected danger to oneself or others: *alarmed by* (or *about*) *someone's illness.* FRIGHTENED means shocked with sudden, but usually short-lived, fear, esp. that arising from apprehension of physical harm: *frightened by* (or *about*) *an accident.* TERRIFIED suggests the emotional reaction when one is struck with a violent, overwhelming fear: *terrified by an earthquake.* —**Ant. 1.** bold, confident.

A-frame (ā′frām′), *n.* any upright, rigid supporting frame in the form of a triangle or an inverted V, as Λ.

Af·ra·mer·i·can (af′rə mer′i kən), *adj., n.* Afro-American.

Af·ra·sia (af rā′zhə, -shə), *n.* *Chiefly Geol.* N Africa and SW Asia considered together.

Af·ra·sian (af rā′zhən, -shən), *adj.* **1.** of Afrasia. **2.** of mixed African and Asian descent. —*n.* **3.** the offspring of an African and an Asian.

af·reet (af′rēt, ə frēt′), *n.* *Arabian Myth.* a powerful evil demon or monster. Also, **afrit.** [< Ar *'ifrīt*]

a·fresh (ə fresh′), *adv.* anew; again.

Af·ric (af′rik), *adj.* African (def. 1). [< L *Afric(us)*]

Af·ri·ca (af′ri kə), *n.* a continent S of Europe and between the Atlantic and Indian oceans. 401,000,000; ab. 11,700,000 sq. mi.

Af·ri·can (af′ri kən), *adj.* **1.** Also, **Afric.** of or from Africa; belonging to the black race of Africa; Negro. —*n.* **2.** a native or inhabitant of Africa. [< L *Africān(us)*]

Af·ri·can·der (af′ri kan′dər), *n.* Afrikander.

Af·ri·can·ist (af′ri kə nist), *n.* a person who specializes in the culture of Africa. —**Af′ri·can·ism,** *n.*

Af·ri·can·ize (af′ri kə nīz′), *v.t.,* **-ized, -iz·ing.** to bring under African, esp. African Negro, influence or to adapt to African needs. —**Af′ri·can·i·za′tion,** *n.*

Af′rican sleep′ing sick′ness, *Pathol.* See **sleeping sickness** (def. 1). Also called **Af′rican trypanosomi′asis.**

Af′rican vi′olet, a popular house plant, *Saintpaulia ionantha*, having violet, pink, or white flowers.

Af·ri·kaans (af′rə käns′, -känz′), *n.* a language of South Africa, developed from 17th-century Dutch. Also called **the Taal.** [var. sp. of D *Afrikaansch* = *Afrikaan* AFRICAN + *-sch* -ISH[1]]

Af·ri·kan·der (af′rə kan′dər), *n.* **1.** Also, **Af·ri·ka·ner** (af′rə kä′nər, -kan′ər). an Afrikaans-speaking native of Cape Province or the neighboring regions of Africa who is born of white, esp. Dutch or Huguenot parents. **2.** one of a breed of red beef cattle, raised originally in southern Africa. Also, **Africander.** [by alter. from SAfrD *Afrikaander* < *Africaaner* (*Afrikaan* AFRICAN + *-er* -ER[1])]

af·rit (af′rēt, ə frēt′), *n.* afreet.

Af·ro (af′rō), *adj.* **1.** of or pertaining to Afro-Americans or to black traditions, culture, etc.: *Afro societies; Afro hair styles.* —*n.* **2.** a hair style of black persons in which the hair is allowed to grow naturally and to acquire a bushy appearance.

Afro-, a combining form of **Africa:** *Afro-American; Afro-Asiatic.* Also, *esp. before a vowel,* **Afr-.** [< L *Afr-* (s. of *Afer* an African) + -o-]

Af·ro-A·mer·i·can (af′rō ə mer′i kən), *adj.* **1.** of or pertaining to black Americans. —*n.* **2.** a black American of African origin or descent. Also, **Aframerican.**

Af·ro-A·sian (af′rō ā′zhən, -shən), *adj.* of or pertaining to the countries or peoples of Africa and Asia.

Af·ro-A·si·at·ic (af′rō ā′zhē at′ik, -ā′shē-), *adj.* **1.** of, belonging to, or pertaining to Afro-Asiatic; Hamito-Semitic. —*n.* **2.** Also called **Hamito-Semitic.** a family of languages including as subfamilies Semitic, Egyptian, Berber, Cushitic, and Chad. Cf. **family** (def. 11). Also, **Af′ro·a′si·at′ic.**

aft (aft, äft), *Naut., Aeron.* —*adv.* **1.** at, close to, or toward the stern or tail. —*adj.* **2.** situated toward or at the stern. [OE *æft(an)* from behind = *æf-* OFF + *-t-* superl. suffix + *-an* suffix marking motion from; c. Goth *aftana,* Icel *aptan*]

aft., afternoon.

A.F.T., American Federation of Teachers.

af·ter (af′tər, äf′-), *prep.* **1.** behind in place or position. **2.** later in time than: *a concert after dinner.* **3.** as a conclusion to: *defeat after all one's struggles.* **4.** as a consequence of: *After that remark, there's nothing more to say.* **5.** below in rank or excellence. **6.** in imitation of or as a copy from. **7.** in search or pursuit of. **8.** concerning; about: *He inquired after your health.* **9.** with the name of: *He was named after his father.* **10.** in accordance or sympathy with: *a man after my own heart.* —*adv.* **11.** behind. **12.** later; afterward. —*adj.* **13.** happening later; subsequent. **14.** *Naut., Aeron.* **a.** farther aft. **b.** located closest to the stern or tail; aftermost. **c.** including the stern or tail. —*conj.* **15.** subsequent to the time that: *after the boys left.* [ME; OE *æfter* = *æf-* OFF + *-ter* comp. suffix (c. Gk *-teros*)] —**Syn. 1.** See **behind.**

af·ter·birth (af′tər bûrth′, äf′-), *n.* the placenta and fetal membranes expelled from the uterus after childbirth.

af·ter·bod·y (af′tər bod′ē, äf′-), *n., pl.* **-bod·ies. 1.** *Naut.* the portion of a ship's hull aft of the middle body. **2.** *Rocketry.* the part of a guided missile behind the nose cone.

af·ter·brain (af′tər brān′, äf′-), *n.* the metencephalon.

af·ter·burn·er (af′tər bûr′nər, äf′-), *n.* **1.** *Aeron.* a device used to produce afterburning. **2.** a device for burning exhaust fumes from an internal-combustion engine.

af·ter·burn·ing (af′tər bûr′ning, äf′-), *n.* **1.** *Aeron.* combustion in an afterburner that results from the injection of fuel into the exhaust gases of a jet engine to produce additional thrust. **2.** *Rocketry.* an irregular burning of residual fuel in some rocket motors after the cessation of the main burning.

af·ter·care (af′tər kâr′, äf′-), *n.* *Med.* the care and treatment of a convalescent patient.

af·ter·damp (af′tər damp′, äf′-), *n.* an irrespirable mixture of gases, chiefly carbon dioxide and nitrogen, left in a mine after an explosion or fire.

af·ter·deck (af′tər dek′, äf′-), *n.* *Naut.* the weather deck of a vessel abaft the bridge house or midship section.

af·ter·ef·fect (af′tər i fekt′, äf′-), *n.* **1.** an effect that follows at some interval after its stimulus. **2.** *Med.* a result appearing after the first effect due to an agent, usually a drug, has gone.

af·ter·glow (af′tər glō′, äf′-), *n.* **1.** the glow frequently seen in the sky after sunset. **2.** the pleasant remembrance of a past experience.

af·ter·growth (af′tər grōth′, äf′-), *n.* a second growth, as of crops after one harvest.

af·ter·im·age (af′tər im′ij, äf′-), *n.* *Psychol.* a visual image or other sense impression that persists after the stimulus is no longer operative. [trans. of G *Nachbild*]

af·ter·life (af′tər līf′, äf′-), *n.* **1.** Also called **future life.** the life after death. **2.** the latter part of one's life.

af·ter·math (af′tər math′, äf′-), *n.* **1.** that which results or follows from an event, esp. one of a disastrous or violent nature. **2.** a new growth of grass following one or more mowings. [AFTER + *math* a mowing, OE *mǣth,* c. OHG *mād* (G *Mahd*); akin to MOW[1]]

af·ter·most (af′tər mōst′, äf′- *or, esp. Brit.,* äf′tər məst), *adj.* **1.** *Naut.* farthest aft. **2.** last or hindmost. [AFTER + -MOST; r. ME *aftermest*, itself r. OE *æftemest* = *æfte* (see AFT) + *-m-* superl. suffix + *-est* -EST[1]]

af·ter·noon (*n.* af′tər no͞on′, äf′-; *adj.* af′tər no͞on′, äf′-, af′-, äf′-), *n.* **1.** the time from noon until evening. **2.** a relatively late period or part: *the afternoon of life.* —*adj.* **3.** pertaining to the afternoon. [ME]

af·ter·noons (af′tər no͞onz′, äf′-), *adv.* in or during any or every afternoon.

af·ter·shaft (af′tər shaft′, äf′tər shäft′), *n.* *Ornith.* a supplementary feather, usually small, arising from the underside of the base of certain feathers in many birds. —**af′ter·shaft′ed,** *adj.*

af·ter·taste (af′tər tāst′, äf′-), *n.* **1.** a taste lingering in the mouth. **2.** the remaining sensation following an unpleasant experience.

af·ter·thought (af′tər thôt′, äf′-), *n.* **1.** a second or later thought. **2.** a belated idea. **3.** an addition not originally planned for.

af·ter·time (af′tər tīm′, äf′-), *n.* future time.

af·ter·ward (af′tər wərd, äf′-), *adv.* in later or subsequent time; subsequently. Also, **af′ter·wards.** [ME; OE *æfterweard,* alter. (with *-r-* of *æfter* AFTER) of *æfteweard*]

af·ter·word (af′tər wûrd′, äf′-), *n.* a concluding section, commentary, etc., as of a book. Cf. **foreword.**

af·ter·world (af′tər wûrld′, äf′-), *n.* the future world, esp. the world after death.

af·ter·years (af′tər yērz′, äf′-), *n.pl.* the years following an event.

Ag, *Chem.* silver. [< L *argentum*]

ag-, var. of **ad-** before *g: agglutinate.*

Ag., August.

ag., agriculture.

A.G., **1.** Adjutant General. **2.** Attorney General.

a·ga (ä′gə), *n.* (in Turkey) **1.** a title of honor, usually implying respect for age. **2.** a general. Also, **agha.** [< Turk *ağa* lord]

A·ga·dir (ä′gä dēr′), *n.* a seaport in SW Morocco: destroyed by earthquake in 1960; new town rebuilt S of original site. 1,220,600.

a·gain (ə gen′ *or, esp. Brit.,* ə gān′), *adv.* **1.** once more. **2.** additionally (used with expressions of proportion and quantity): *half again as much.* **3.** doubly (used with an expression of quantity): *as much again as I have.* **4.** furthermore. **5.** as an alternative possibility. **6. again and again,** repeatedly. [ME *agayn, ageyn,* OE *ongegn* opposite (to)]

a·gainst (ə genst′ *or, esp. Brit.,* ə gānst′), *prep.* **1.** in a contrary direction to. **2.** close beside or in front of. **3.** in or into contact or collision with. **4.** in or into opposition to or hostility toward. **5.** as a protection from. **6.** in or into competition or conflict with. **7.** in anticipation of: *to save money against retirement.* **8.** in payment for. **9.** as contrasted with. —*conj.* **10.** *Archaic.* before; by the time that. [late ME; ME *agens, ageynes* = *ageyn* AGAIN + *-es* -s[1]; for *-t* cf. WHILST, AMONGST]

A·ga Khan III (ä′gə kän′), (*Aga Sultan Sir Mahomed Shah*) 1877–1957, leader of the Ismaili sect of Muslims in India 1885–1957.

Aga Khan IV, (*Shah Karim al-Husainy*) born 1936, leader of the Ismaili sect of Muslims in India since 1957 (grandson of Aga Khan III).

ag·a·ma (ag′ə mə), *n.* any of numerous lizards of the genus *Agama,* many of which are brilliantly colored and have the ability to change the color of the skin. [< Carib]

Ag·a·mem·non (ag′ə mem′non, -nən), *n.* *Class. Myth.* a king of Mycenae, a son of Atreus and brother of Menelaus, who led the Greeks in the Trojan War and who was murdered by Clytemnestra, his wife, upon his return from Troy.

a·gam·ete (ə gam′ēt, ā′gə mēt′), *n.* *Biol.* an asexual reproductive cell, as a spore. [< Gk *agámet(os)* unmarried]

a·gam·ic (ə gam′ik), *adj.* **1.** *Biol.* **a.** asexual. **b.** occurring without sexual union; germinating without impregnation; not gamic. **2.** *Bot.* cryptogamic. Also, **ag·a·mous** (ag′ə məs). [< Gk *ágam(os)* unwed (*a-* A-[6] + *gámos* marriage) + -IC] —**a·gam′i·cal·ly,** *adv.*

ag·a·mo·gen·e·sis (ag′ə mō jen′i sis), *n.* *Biol.* asexual reproduction. [< Gk *ágamo(s)* (see AGAMIC) + -GENESIS] —**ag·a·mo·ge·net·ic** (ag′ə mō jə net′ik), *adj.* —**ag′a·mo·ge·net′i·cal·ly,** *adv.*

A·ga·ña (ä gä′nyä), *n.* a seaport in and the capital of Guam. 2119 (1970).

a·gape[1] (ə gāp′, ə gap′), *adv., adj.* **1.** with the mouth wide open; in an attitude of wonder or eagerness. **2.** wide open. [A-[1] + GAPE]

a·ga·pe[2] (ä gä′pā, ä′gə pā′, ag′ə-), *n., pl.* **-pae** (-pī, -pī′, -pē′), **-pai** (-pī, -pī′) for 4. **1.** the love of God or Christ for mankind. **2.** the brotherly or spiritual love of one Christian for another. Cf. **Eros** (def. 4). **3.** unselfish, platonic love of one person for another; brotherly love. **4.** See **love feast** (defs. 1, 2). [< Gk *agápē* love]

Ag·a·pe·tus I (ag′ə pē′təs), **Saint,** died A.D. 536, Italian ecclesiastic: pope 535–536.

Agapetus II, died A.D. 955, Italian ecclesiastic: pope 946–955.

a·gar (ä′gär, ag′ər), *n.* **1.** Also, **a′gar-a′gar.** a gelatinlike product of certain seaweeds, used for solidifying certain culture media, as a thickening agent for foods, as an emulsifier, and as a sizing for paper and silk. **2.** *Biol.* a culture medium having an agar base. [short for *agar-agar* < Malay]

ag·a·ric (ag′ə rik, ə gar′ik), *n.* an agaricaceous fungus; mushroom. [< NL *Agaric(us)* genus name < Gk *agarikós* (adj.) pertaining to *Agaría,* a town in Sarmatis; neut. *agarikón* used as n., name of some fungi]

a·gar·i·ca·ceous (ə gar′ə kā′shəs), *adj.* belonging to the *Agaricaceae,* a family of fungi including mushrooms having blade-shaped gills on the underside of the cap. [< NL *Agaric(aceae)* (see AGARIC, -ACEAE) + -ACEOUS]

A·gar·ta·la (ə gûr′tə lə, u′gər tə lä′), *n.* a city in and the capital of Tripura, in the W part. 100,264.

Ag·as·siz (ag′ə sē; *for 2 also Fr.* A GA SĒ′), *n.* **1. Alexander,** 1835–1910, U.S. oceanographer and marine zoologist, born in Switzerland. **2.** his father, **(Jean) Louis (Ro·dolphe)** (zhäN lwē RÔ dôlf′), 1807–73, U.S. zoologist and geologist, born in Switzerland.

ag·ate (ag′it), *n.* **1.** a variegated chalcedony with curved, colored bands or other markings. **2.** a playing marble made of this substance, or of glass in imitation of it. **3.** *Print.* a 5½-point type of a size between pearl and nonpareil. Cf. **ruby** (def. 4). [earlier *agat,* appar. < It *agat(a)* << L *achātēs* < Gk *achā́tēs*] —**ag′ate·like′, ag′a·toid′,** *adj.*

ag′ate line′, a measure of advertising space, 1/14 of an inch deep and one column wide.

ag·ate·ware (ag′it wâr′), *n.* **1.** steel or iron household ware enameled in an agatelike pattern. **2.** pottery variegated to resemble agate.

Ag·a·tho (ag′ə thō′), *n.* **Saint,** died A.D. 681, Sicilian ecclesiastic: pope 678–681.

A·gath·o·cles (ə gath′ə klēz′), *n.* 361–289 B.C., tyrant of Syracuse 317–289.

a·ga·ve (ə gā′vē, ə gä′-), *n.* any of numerous American, amaryllidaceous plants of the genus *Agave.* Cf. **century plant, maguey, sisal.** [< NL < Gk *agauḗ,* fem. of *agauós* noble, brilliant]

a·gaze (ə gāz′), *adj.* gazing.

agcy., agency.

age (āj), *n., v.,* **aged, ag·ing** or **age·ing.** —*n.* **1.** the length of time during which a being or thing has existed. **2.** any period of human life regarded as having specific characteristics or as involving certain privileges or responsibilities. **3.** the latter period of a natural term of existence. **4.** the influences operating on the body and mind during this period. **5.** the life expectancy of an average being of some kind: *The age of the horse is from 25 to 30 years.* **6.** a distinctive period of history; era. **7.** the contemporary world: *What is the spirit of the age?* **8.** the world contemporary to any person: *a novel portraying Shelley against the background of his age.* **9.** an indefinitely long time. **10.** *Psychol.* the level of mental, emotional, or educational development of an individual. **11.** *Geol.* **a.** a period of the history of the earth distinguished by some special feature: *Ice Age.* **b.** a period during which one particular stage of rock formation takes place: shorter than an epoch. **12. of age,** *Law.* being any of several ages, usually 21 or 18, at which certain legal rights, as voting, marriage, etc., are acquired. —*v.i.* **13.** to grow old. **14.** to mature, as wine, cheese, wood, etc. —*v.t.* **15.** to make old; cause to grow or seem old. **16.** to cause or allow to stand until transformations have taken place; mature: *to age wine.* [ME < OF *aage, eage* < VL **aetāticum* < L *ae(vi)tāt-* (s. of *ae(vi)tās* = *aev(um)* lifetime (akin to AY[1]) + *-itāt-* -ITY + *-icum* neut. of *-icus* -IC]

—**Syn. 6.** AGE, ERA, EPOCH, PERIOD all refer to an extent of time. AGE usually implies a considerable extent of time, esp. one associated with a dominant personality, influence, characteristic, or institution: *the age of chivalry.* ERA and EPOCH are often used interchangeably, but an ERA is an extent of time characterized by changed conditions and new undertakings: *an era of invention.* An EPOCH is properly the beginning of an era: *an epoch of armed aggression.* A PERIOD may be long or short, but usually has a marked condition or feature: *the glacial period; a period of expansion.* **14.** ripen.

-age, a formal element meaning "pertaining to," occurring in loan words from French (*language; voyage*); used also as a noun-forming suffix to stems of native origin (*fruitage; bondage*). [ME < OF < L *-āticum,* neut. of *-āticus* adj. suffix]

a·ged (ā′jid *for 1, 2, 5, 6;* ājd *for 1, 3, 4*), *adj.* **1.** having lived long; old. **2.** characteristic of old age. **3.** of the age of: *aged 40 years.* **4.** having been improved by aging, as a food or drink. **5.** *Phys. Geog.* old; approaching the state of peneplain. —*n.* **6.** (*construed as pl.*) old persons collectively (usually prec. by *the*). —**a′ged·ly,** *adv.* —**a′ged·ness,** *n.*

a·gee (ə jē′), *adv.* *Brit. Dial.* to one side; awry. Also, **ajee.** [A-[1] + GEE]

A·gee (ā′jē), *n.* **James,** 1909–55, U.S. author and film critic.

age-group (āj′gro͞op′), *n.* persons of approximately the same age and often of the same sex, as of a nation, school system, community, etc.

age·ism (āj′iz əm), *n.* discrimination or prejudice against persons of a certain age, esp. the old. [AGE + -ISM, modeled on *sexism*] —**age′ist,** *adj., n.*

age·less (āj′lis), *adj.* never growing old or outdated. —**age′less·ness,** *n.*

age·long (āj′lông′, -long′), *adj.* lasting for an age.

a·gen·cy (ā′jən sē), *n., pl.* **-cies.** **1.** an organization that provides some service. **2.** a company having a franchise to represent another. **3.** the place of business of an agent. **4.** a government bureau or administrative division. **5.** the duty or function of an agent. **6.** the relationship between a principal and his agent. **7.** the state of being in action or of exerting power. **8.** a means of exerting power or influence; instrumentality. [< ML *agentia* < L *ag-* (s. of *agere* to do) + *-entia* -ENCY] —**Syn. 8.** intercession.

A′gency for Interna′tional Devel′opment. See **AID.**

a·gen·da (ə jen′də), *n., formally a pl. of* **agendum,** *but usually used as a sing. with pl.* **-das** *or* **-da.** a list, plan, outline, or the like, of things to be done, matters to be acted or voted upon, etc. [< L, pl. of *agendum* that which is to be done, ger. of *agere* to do]

a·gen·dum (ə jen′dəm), *n., pl.* **-da** (-də), **-dums.** an agenda. [< L, ger. of *agere* to do]

a·gen·e·sis (ā jen′i sis), *n.* *Med.* **1.** defective development or absence, as of a limb. **2.** sterility; impotence. Also, **a·ge·ne·sia** (ā′jə nē′zhə, -zhē ə, -sē ə). [< NL; see A-[6], GENESIS] —**a·ge·net·ic** (ā′jə net′ik), *adj.*

a·gent (ā′jənt), *n.* **1.** a person authorized by another to act on his behalf. **2.** a person or thing that acts or has the power to act. **3.** a natural force or object producing or used for obtaining specific results. **4.** an active cause; an efficient cause. **5.** a person who works for or manages an agency. **6.** a law-enforcement officer. **7.** a spy. **8.** a representative of a business firm, esp. a traveling salesman. **9.** *Chem.* a substance that causes a reaction. —*adj.* **10.** *Rare.* acting; exerting power. [< L *agent-* (s. of *agēns* (prp.) doing) = *ag-* (s. of *agere* to do) + *-ent-* -ENT] —**Syn. 1.** representative, deputy.

a·gen·tial (ā jen′shəl), *adj.* of an agent or agency.

a′gent noun′, *Gram.* a noun denoting the doer of an action, as *actor, bearer.*

a·gent pro·vo·ca·teur (A zhäN PRÔ VÔ KA TŒR′), *pl.* **a·gents pro·vo·ca·teurs** (A zhäN PRÔ VÔ KA TŒR′). *French.* a secret agent hired to incite suspected persons to an act that will make them liable to prosecution.

A′gent Or′ange, a powerful herbicide and defoliant, containing a toxic impurity, dioxin, and used by U.S. armed forces during the Vietnam War to defoliate jungles concealing enemy troops and supply bases and now believed to cause serious health damage, including cancer, to those exposed to it and birth defects in their offspring.

age′ of consent′, the legal age at which a person, esp. a female, is considered competent to give consent to marriage or sexual intercourse.

age′ of discre′tion, *Law.* the age at which a person becomes legally responsible for certain acts and competent to exercise certain powers.

Age′ of Rea′son, any historical period characterized by rationalism, esp. the period of the Enlightenment.

age-old (āj′ōld′), *adj.* ancient; from time immemorial.

ag·er·a·tum (aj′ə rā′təm, ə jer′ə-), *n.* any of several composite plants of the genus *Ageratum,* esp. *A. Houstonianum,* having small, dense, blue or white flower heads, often grown in gardens. [< NL < L *agēraton* < Gk *agḗraton,* neut. of *agḗratos* unaging = *a-* A-^{6} + *gērat-* (s. of *gêras*) old age + *-os* adj. suffix]

A·ges·i·la·us II (ə jes′ə lā′əs), 444?–c360 B.C., king of Sparta c400–c360.

Ag·ga·dah (ə gä′də; *Heb.* ä gä dä′), *n.* the nonlegal or narrative material, as parables, maxims, or anecdotes, in the Talmud and other rabbinical literature. Also, **Ag·ga′da, Haggadah.** [< Heb *haggādhāh* < *higgīdh* to narrate] —**Ag·gad·ic, ag·gad·ic** (ə gad′ik, ə gä′dik), *adj.*

ag·ger (aj′ər), *n.* a low tide in which the water recedes to a certain level, rises slightly, then recedes again. Also called **double tide.** [< L: heap, pile = *ag-* AG- + *ger-* s. of *gerere* to carry, bring]

ag·gie^1 (ag′ē), *n.* agate (def. 2). [by alter.; see -IE]

ag·gie^2 (ag′ē), *n. Slang.* a student at an agricultural college. [*ag-* (from *agricultural*) + -IE]

ag·glom·er·ate (*v.* ə glom′ə rāt′; *adj., n.* ə glom′ər it, -ə rāt′), *v.,* **-at·ed, -at·ing,** *adj., n.* —*v.t., v.i.* **1.** to collect or gather into a cluster or mass. —*adj.* **2.** gathered together into a cluster or mass. —*n.* **3.** a mass of things clustered together. **4.** rock composed of rounded or angular volcanic fragments. [< L *agglomerāt(us)* (ptp. of *agglomerāre*) = *ag-* AG- + *glomer-* (s. of *glomus* ball of yarn) + *-ātus* -ATE^1] —**ag·glom·er·a·tive** (ə glom′ə rā′tiv, -ər ə tiv), *adj.* —**ag·glom′er·a′tor,** *n.*

ag·glom·er·a·tion (ə glom′ə rā′shən), *n.* **1.** a jumbled cluster or mass. **2.** the act or process of agglomerating.

ag·glu·ti·nant (ə gloot′ənənt), *adj.* **1.** uniting, as glue; causing adhesion. —*n.* **2.** an agglutinating agent. [< L *agglūtinant-* (s. of *agglūtināns,* prp. of *agglūtināre*) = *agglūtin-* (see AGGLUTINATE) + *-ant-* -ANT]

ag·glu·ti·nate (*v.* ə gloot′ənāt′; *adj., n.* ə gloot′ənit, -ənāt′), *v.,* **-nat·ed, -nat·ing,** *adj., n.* —*v.t., v.i.* **1.** to unite, as with glue. **2.** *Linguistics.* to form by agglutination. —*adj.* **3.** united, as by glue. **4.** agglutinative. —*n.* **5.** something that has agglutinated. [< L *agglūtināt(us)* (ptp. of *agglūtināre*) = *ag-* AG- + *glūtin-* (s. of *glūten* glue) + *-ātus* -ATE^1] —**ag·glu·tin·a·bil·i·ty** (ə gloot′ənə bil′i tē), *n.* —**ag·glu′tin·a·ble,** *adj.*

ag·glu·ti·na·tion (ə gloot′ənā′shən), *n.* **1.** the act or process of uniting by glue or other tenacious substance. **2.** the state of being so united. **3.** a mass or group cemented together. **4.** *Immunol.* the clumping of bacteria, erythrocytes, or other cells, due to the introduction of an antibody. **5.** *Linguistics.* a process of word formation in which morphemes, each having one relatively constant shape, are combined without fusion or morphophonemic change.

ag·glu·ti·na·tive (ə gloot′ənā′tiv, ə gloot′ənə-), *adj.* **1.** tending or having power to agglutinate or unite. **2.** *Linguistics.* (of a language or construction) characterized by agglutination: *Hungarian is agglutinative.*

ag·glu·ti·nin (ə gloot′ənin), *n. Immunol.* an antibody that causes agglutination. [AGGLUTIN(ATE) + -IN^2]

ag·glu·tin·o·gen (ag′lo͝o tin′ə jən), *n. Immunol.* an antigen, present in a bacterial body, that, when injected into an animal, causes the production of agglutinins. [AGGLUTIN(ATE) + -O- + -GEN] —**ag·glu·tin·o·gen·ic** (ag′lo͝o tin′ə jen′ik, ə gloot′ənə-), *adj.*

ag·grade (ə grād′), *v.t.,* **-grad·ed, -grad·ing.** *Phys. Geog.* to raise the grade or level of (a river valley, a stream bed, etc.) by depositing detritus, sediment, or the like (opposed to *degrade*). —**ag·gra·da·tion** (ag′rə dā′shən), *n.* —**ag′gra·da′tion·al,** *adj.*

ag·gran·dise (ə gran′dīz, ag′rən dīz′), *v.t.,* **-dised, -dis·ing.** *Chiefly Brit.* aggrandize. —**ag·gran·dise·ment** (ə gran′diz mənt), *n.* —**ag·gran′dis·er,** *n.*

ag·gran·dize (ə gran′dīz, ag′rən dīz′), *v.t.,* **-dized, -diz·ing. 1.** to widen in scope; increase in size or intensity; enlarge; extend. **2.** to make great or greater in power, wealth, rank, or honor; exalt. **3.** to make (something) appear greater; magnify. [< MF *aggrandiss-* (long s. of *aggrandir* to magnify) = *ag-* AG- + *grand* (see GRAND) + *-iss* irregularly equated with -IZE] —**ag·gran·dize·ment** (ə gran′diz mənt), *n.* —**ag·gran′diz·er,** *n.*

ag·gra·vate (ag′rə vāt′), *v.t.,* **-vat·ed, -vat·ing. 1.** to make worse or more severe. **2.** to annoy; irritate; exasperate: *His questions aggravate her.* **3.** to cause to become irritated or inflamed. [< L *aggravāt(us)* (ptp. of *aggravāre*) = *ag-* AG- + *grav-* (see GRAVE^2) + *-ātus* -ATE^1] —**ag′gra·vat′ing·ly,** *adv.* —**ag′gra·va′tive,** *adj.* —**ag′gra·va′tor,** *n.*
—**Syn. 1.** heighten, increase. AGGRAVATE, INTENSIFY mean to increase in degree. To AGGRAVATE is to make graver or more serious: *to aggravate a danger, a wound.* To INTENSIFY is perceptibly to increase intensity, force, energy, vividness, etc.: *to intensify heat, color, rage.* —**Ant. 1.** alleviate.
—**Usage.** AGGRAVATE, in the sense of "to annoy or irritate," is avoided in formal contexts by many precise writers and speakers, but its use is now widespread.

ag·gra·va·tion (ag′rə vā′shən), *n.* **1.** an increase in intensity, seriousness, or severity. **2.** state of being aggravated. **3.** something that increases the intensity, degree, or severity of something. **4.** irritation; annoyance: *Johnny causes me so much aggravation!* **5.** a source of irritation or annoyance: *Johnny's an aggravation to her!* [< ML *aggravātiōn-* (s. of *aggravātiō*)]
—**Usage.** AGGRAVATION, in the sense of defs. 4 and 5, follows the same usage pattern as AGGRAVATE.

ag·gre·gate (*adj., n.* ag′rə git, -gāt′; *v.* ag′rə gāt′), *adj., n., v.,* **-gat·ed, -gat·ing.** —*adj.* **1.** formed by the conjunction or collection of particulars into a mass or sum; total; combined. **2.** *Bot.* **a.** (of a flower) formed of florets collected in a dense cluster but not cohering, as in composite plants. **b.** (of a fruit) composed of a cluster of carpels belonging to the same flower, as the raspberry. —*n.* **3.** a sum, mass, or assemblage of particulars; a total or gross amount: *the aggregate of all past experience.* **4.** *Geol.* a mixture of different mineral substances separable by mechanical means, as granite. **5.** any of various hard, inert materials, as sand, gravel, or pebbles, added to a cementing agent to make concrete, plaster, etc. —*v.t.* **6.** to bring together; collect into one sum, mass, or body. **7.** to amount to (the number of). —*v.i.* **8.** to combine into a collection or mass. [< L *aggregāt(us)* (ptp. of *aggregāre*) = *ag-* AG- + *greg-* (s. of *grex* flock) + *-ātus* -ATE^1] —**ag·gre·ga·ble** (ag′rə gə bəl), *adj.* —**ag′gre·gate·ly,** *adv.* —**ag′gre·gate·ness,** *n.* —**ag·gre·ga·tive** (ag′rə gā′tiv), *adj.* —**ag·gre·ga·to·ry** (ag′rə gə tōr′ē, -tôr′ē), *adj.* —**Syn. 1.** added, complete, whole. **6.** amass, accumulate, assemble, gather.

ag·gre·ga·tion (ag′rə gā′shən), *n.* **1.** a group or mass of distinct or varied things, persons, etc. **2.** collection into an unorganized whole. **3.** the state of being so collected. **4.** *Biol., Ecol.* a group of organisms of the same or different species living closely together but less integrated than a society. [< ML *aggregātiōn-* (s. of *aggregātiō*)]

ag·gress (ə gres′), *v.i.* **1.** to commit the first act of hostility or offense; attack first. **2.** to begin to quarrel. [< ML *aggress(āre)* (to) attack < L *agress(us)* (ptp. of *aggredī* to attack) = *ag-* AG- + *gred-* (see GRADE) + *-tus* ptp. suffix]

ag·gres·sion (ə gresh′ən), *n.* **1.** the action of a state in violating by force the rights of another state, particularly its territorial rights; an unprovoked offensive, attack, invasion, or the like. **2.** any offensive action or procedure; an inroad or encroachment: *an aggression upon one's rights.* **3.** the practice of making assaults or attacks; offensive action in general. **4.** *Psychol.* outwardly or inwardly directed, overt or suppressed hostility. [< L *aggressiōn-* (s. of *aggressiō*)]

ag·gres·sive (ə gres′iv), *adj.* **1.** characterized by or tending toward aggression. **2.** vigorously energetic, esp. in the use of initiative and forcefulness; boldly assertive. [AGGRESS(ION) + -IVE] —**ag·gres′sive·ly,** *adv.* —**ag·gres′sive·ness,** *n.* —**Syn. 1.** pugnacious, militant. **2.** pushing, enterprising, assertive. —**Ant. 2.** retiring.

ag·gres·sor (ə gres′ər), *n.* a person, nation, or group that attacks first or initiates hostilities; an assailant or invader. [< LL, L *aggress(us)* (see AGGRESS) + *-or* -OR^2]

ag·grieve (ə grēv′), *v.t.,* **-grieved, -griev·ing. 1.** to oppress or wrong grievously; injure by injustice (usually used passively). **2.** to afflict with pain, anxiety, etc.; trouble sorely. [ME *agreve(n)* < MF *agrever* < L *aggravāre* to make heavy, worsen = *ag-* AG- + *grav-* (see GRAVE^2) + *-āre* inf. suffix]

ag·grieved (ə grēvd′), *adj.* **1.** wronged, offended, or injured. **2.** *Law.* deprived of legal rights or claims. **3.** worried; disturbed. —**ag·griev·ed·ly** (ə grē′vid lē), *adv.* —**ag·griev′ed·ness,** *n.* —**Syn. 1.** abused, harmed, wounded.

Agh., afghani.

a·gha (ä′gə), *n.* aga.

a·ghast (ə gast′, ə gäst′), *adj.* struck with overwhelming shock, amazement, fright, or horror. [ME *agast* frightened, ptp. of *agasten* = *a-* A-^{3} + *gasten* < OE *gæstan* to frighten]

ag·ile (aj′əl *or, esp. Brit.,* aj′īl), *adj.* **1.** quick and well-coordinated: *an agile leap.* **2.** active; lively: *an agile person.* **3.** mentally acute or aware. [earlier *agil* < L *agil(is)* = *ag-* (s. of *agere* to do) + *-ilis* -ILE] —**ag′ile·ly,** *adv.* —**ag′ile·ness,** *n.* —**Syn. 1.** nimble, sprightly. **2.** brisk, spry. —**Ant. 1.** awkward. **2.** sluggish.

a·gil·i·ty (ə jil′i tē), *n.* **1.** the power of moving quickly and easily; nimbleness. **2.** intellectual acuity. [late ME *agilite* < MF < L *agilitāt-* (s. of *agilitās*)]

Ag·in·court (aj′in kōrt′, -kôrt′; *Fr.* A zhan ko͞or′), *n.* a village in N France, near Calais: victory of the English over the French 1415. 207 (1962).

ag·i·o (aj′ē ō′), *n., pl.* **-os. 1.** a premium on money in exchange. **2.** an allowance for the difference in value of two currencies. [< It *a(g)gio* exchange, premium < ?]

ag·i·o·tage (aj′ē ə tij), *n.* **1.** the business of dealing in foreign exchange. **2.** speculative dealing in securities. [< F = *agiot(er)* to speculate (*agiot* exchange < It *aggio* AGIO) + *-age* -AGE]

agit., (in prescriptions) shake; stir. [< L *agitā*]

ag·i·tate (aj′i tāt′), *v.,* **-tat·ed, -tat·ing.** —*v.t.* **1.** to move or force into violent, irregular action. **2.** to shake or move briskly: *The machine agitated the mixture.* **3.** to move to and fro with a regular motion. **4.** to disturb or excite emotionally; arouse; perturb. **5.** to call attention to by speech or writing; discuss; debate. —*v.i.* **6.** to arouse or attempt to arouse public interest, as in a proposal (usually fol. by *for*): *to agitate for the repeal of a tax.* [< L *agitāt(us)* (ptp. of *agitāre* to set in motion) = *ag-* (s. of *agere* to drive) + *-it-* freq. suffix + *-ātus* -ATE^1] —**ag·i·ta·ble** (aj′i tə bəl), *adj.* —**ag′i·tat′ed·ly,** *adv.* —**ag′i·ta′tive,** *adj.* —**Syn. 1.** disturb. **3.** wave. **5.** dispute. —**Ant. 1.** calm.

ag·i·ta·tion (aj′i tā′shən), *n.* **1.** act or process of agitating. **2.** the state of being agitated. **3.** persistent or emotional urging of a political or social cause or theory before the public. [< L *agitātiōn-* (s. of *agitātiō*)] —**ag′i·ta′tion·al,** *adj.*
—**Syn. 2.** unrest, disquiet. AGITATION, DISTURBANCE, EXCITEMENT, TURMOIL imply inner unrest, uneasiness or apprehension. AGITATION implies a shaken state of emotions, usually perceptible in the face or movements: *With evident agitation she opened the telegram.* DISTURBANCE implies an inner disquiet caused by worry, indecision, apprehension, and the like: *Long-continued mental disturbance is a cause of illness.* EXCITEMENT implies a highly emotional state caused by either agreeable or distressing circumstances: *excitement*

over a proposed trip. TURMOIL suggests such a struggle or conflict of emotions that one is unable to think consecutively: *Her thoughts were in a turmoil.*

a·gi·ta·to (aj′i tä′tō; *It.* ä′jē tä′tô), *adj. Music.* agitated; restless or hurried in movement or style. [< It < L *agitāt(us).* See AGITATE]

ag·i·ta·tor (aj′i tā′tər), *n.* **1.** a person who stirs up others in favor of a cause or urges them to militant action. **2.** a machine or device for agitating and mixing. [< L: one who sets in motion] —**ag·i·ta·to·ri·al** (aj′i tə tōr′ē əl, -tôr′-), *adj.*

ag·it·prop (aj′it prop′), *n.* agitation and propaganda, esp. for the cause of communism. [short for Russ *Agitpropbyuro* = *agit(atsiya)* agitation + *prop(aganda)* propaganda + *byuro* bureau] —**ag′it·prop′ist,** *n.*

a·gleam (ə glēm′), *adj.* gleaming; bright; radiant.

ag·let (ag′lit), *n.* **1.** a metal tag or sheath at the end of a lace used for tying, as of a shoelace. **2.** an ornamental fastening on a garment. **3.** aiguillette. Also, **aiglet.** [late ME < MF *aiguillette* = *aiguille* needle (see AIGUILLE) + *-ette* -ET]

a·gley (ə glē′, ə glī′), *adv. Chiefly Scot. and North Eng.* awry; wrong. Also, **a·gly′.** [A-[1] + *gley* GLEE[2]]

a·glim·mer (ə glim′ər), *adj.* glimmering; shining faintly or unsteadily.

a·glit·ter (ə glit′ər), *adj.* glittering; sparkling.

a·glow (ə glō′), *adj.* glowing.

AGM, air-to-ground missile.

ag·ma (ag′mə), *n.* eng. [< LGk, Gk: fracture]

AGMA, American Guild of Musical Artists. Also, **A.G.M.A.**

ag·mi·nate (ag′mə nit, -nāt′), *adj.* aggregated or clustered together. Also, **ag′mi·nat′ed.** [< L *agmin-* (s. of *agmen*) army on march, throng, crowd + -ATE[1]]

ag·nail (ag′nāl′), *n.* **1.** hangnail. **2.** whitlow. [ME; OE *angnægl* = *ang-* tight, painful + *nægl* corn (on foot), NAIL]

ag·nate (ag′nāt), *n.* **1.** a kinsman whose connection is traceable exclusively through males. **2.** any male relative on the father's side. —*adj.* **3.** related or akin through males or on the father's side. **4.** allied or akin. [< L *agnāt(us)* paternal kinsman, var. of *ad(g)nātus* born to (ptp. of *adgnāscī*) = *ad-* AD- + *-gnā-* be born + *-tus* ptp. suffix] —**ag·nat·ic** (ag nat′ik), **ag·nat′i·cal,** *adj.* —**ag·nat′i·cal·ly,** *adv.* —**ag·na·tion** (ag nā′shən), *n.*

Ag·nes (ag′nis), *n.* **Saint,** A.D. 292?–304?, Roman Catholic child martyr.

Ag·new (ag′nōō, -nyōō), *n.* **Spi·ro T(heodore)** (spēr′ō), born 1918, U.S. politician: vice president 1969–73 (resigned).

Ag·ni (ug′nē; *Eng.* ag′nē), *n. Hindu Myth.* the god of fire, one of the three chief divinities of the Vedas. [< Skt: fire, the fire-god; akin to L *ignis,* Russ *ogon′* fire]

ag·no·men (ag nō′mən), *n., pl.* **-nom·i·na** (-nom′ə nə). **1.** an additional name given to a person by the ancient Romans, as in allusion to some achievement. **2.** a nickname. [< LL = *ad-* AD- + *nōmen* name, with alter. to *ag-* through influence of *agnōscere* to recognize] —**ag·nom·i·nal** (ag nom′ə nəl), *adj.*

ag·nos·tic (ag nos′tik), *n.* **1.** a person who holds that the ultimate cause (God) and the essential nature of things are unknown and unknowable. **2.** a person who denies or doubts the possibility of ultimate knowledge in some area of study. —*adj.* **3.** of or pertaining to agnostics or agnosticism. **4.** asserting the uncertainty of all claims to knowledge. [< Gk *agnōst(os)* not known, incapable of being known (*a-* A-[6] + *gnōs-,* var. of *gnō-* (s. of *gignṓskein* to KNOW) + *-tos* adj. suffix) + -TIC, after GNOSTIC] —**ag·nos′ti·cal·ly,** *adv.* —**Syn. 1.** See **atheist.**

ag·nos·ti·cism (ag nos′ti siz′əm), *n.* **1.** the doctrine or belief of an agnostic. **2.** an intellectual doctrine or attitude affirming the uncertainty of all claims to ultimate knowledge.

Ag·nus De·i (ag′nəs dē′ī, än′yōōs de′ē), **1.** *Eccles.* a figure of a lamb as emblematic of Christ. **2.** *Rom. Cath. Ch.* **a.** a triple chant preceding the communion in the Mass. **b.** the music accompanying this prayer. **3.** (*italics*) *Anglican Ch.* **a.** an invocation beginning "O Lamb of God," said or sung in the communion service. **b.** a musical setting for this. [< L]

a·go (ə gō′), *adj.* **1.** gone; gone by; past (prec. by a noun): *five days ago.* —*adv.* **2.** in the past: *It happened long ago.* [ME *ago, agoon,* OE *āgān,* ptp. of *āgān* to go by, pass = *ā-* A-[3] + *gān* to GO]

a·gog (ə gog′), *adj.* **1.** highly excited by eagerness, curiosity, anticipation, etc. —*adv.* **2.** in a state of eager desire; excitedly. [var. of *on gog* (in phrase *set on gog* rouse, stir up); *gog* perh. akin to GOGGLE]

-agog, var. of **-agogue.**

à go·go (ä gō′gō′, ə gō′gō′), as much as you like; to your heart's content; galore (used esp. in the names of cabarets, discotheques, etc.). Also, **à Go′go′, à go′-go′, au gogo.** [< F]

-agogue, a suffix occurring in loan words from Greek where it meant "leading," "leader," "course," "withdrawing agent." Also, **-agog.** [< Gk *-agōg(ós)* akin to *ágein* to lead, c. L *agere* to lead, drive, Icel *aka* to carry, convey]

ag·on (ag′ōn, -on), *n., pl.* **a·go·nes** (ə gō′nēz). **1.** (in ancient Greece) a contest in which prizes were awarded in a number of events, as athletics, dramatics, music, and poetry. **2.** *Literature.* conflict, esp. between the protagonist and the antagonist. [< Gk *agṓn* struggle, contest]

a·gone (ə gôn′, ə gon′), *adj., adv. Archaic.* ago.

a·gon·ic (ā gon′ik), *adj.* not forming an angle. [< Gk *ágōn(os)* (*a-* A-[6] + *gōn-* (s. of *gōnía* angle) + *-os* adj. suffix) + -IC]

agon′ic line′, an imaginary line on the surface of the earth connecting all points at which the declination of the magnetic field of the earth is zero.

ag·o·nise (ag′ə nīz′), *v.i., v.t.,* **-nised, -nis·ing.** *Chiefly Brit.* agonize. —**ag′o·nis′ing·ly,** *adv.*

ag·o·nist (ag′ə nist), *n.* **1.** a person engaged in a contest, conflict, struggle, etc., esp. the protagonist in a literary work. **2.** a person who is torn by inner conflict. **3.** *Physiol.* a contracting muscle whose action is opposed by another muscle. Cf. **antagonist** (def. 3). [< LL *agonist(a)* < Gk *agōnistḗs* contestant]

ag·o·nis·tic (ag′ə nis′tik), *adj.* **1.** combative; striving to overcome in argument. **2.** straining for effect: *agonistic humor.* **3.** *Gk. Antiq.* of or pertaining to athletic contests. Also, **ag′o·nis′ti·cal.** [< Gk *agōnistik(ós)*] —**ag′o·nis′ti·cal·ly,** *adv.*

ag·o·nize (ag′ə nīz′), *v.,* **-nized, -niz·ing.** —*v.i.* **1.** to suffer extreme pain or anguish. **2.** to put forth great effort. —*v.t.* **3.** to distress with extreme pain; torture. Also, *esp. Brit.,* **agonise.** [< ML *agōniz(āre)* < Gk *agōnízesthai* (to) struggle (for a prize) = *agōn-* AGON + *-ize(sthai)* -IZE]

ag·o·nized (ag′ə nīzd′), *adj.* involving or accompanied by agony or severe struggle: *an agonized effort.* —**ag·o·niz·ed·ly** (ag′ə nī′zid lē), *adv.*

ag·o·niz·ing (ag′ə nī′zing), *adj.* causing or revealing agony. —**ag′o·niz′ing·ly,** *adv.*

ag·o·ny (ag′ə nē), *n., pl.* **-nies.** **1.** extreme and generally prolonged pain or suffering. **2.** a display of intense mental or emotional excitement. **3.** the struggle preceding natural death: *mortal agony.* **4.** a violent struggle. [ME *agonye* < LL *agōnia* < Gk = *agṓn* AGON + *-ia* -Y[3]] —**Syn. 1.** anguish, torment. See **pain. 2.** paroxysm, pang.

ag′ony col′umn, *Informal.* a section or column in a newspaper containing personal advertisements by people seeking missing relatives, announcing the end of a marriage, etc.

ag·o·ra (ag′ər ə), *n., pl.* **-o·rae** (-ə rē′). (in ancient Greece) **1.** a popular political assembly. **2.** the place where such an assembly met, originally a marketplace or public square. [< Gk *agorá* marketplace = *agor-* (var. s. of *ageírein* to gather together) + *-ā* n. suffix]

ag·o·ra·pho·bi·a (ag′ər ə fō′bē ə), *n. Psychiatry.* an abnormal fear of being in an open space.

a·gou·ti (ə gōō′tē), *n., pl.* **-tis, -ties.** **1.** any of several short-haired, short-eared, rabbitlike rodents of the genus *Dasyprocta,* of South and Central America and the West Indies, destructive to sugar cane. **2.** an irregularly barred pattern of the fur of certain rodents. [< F < Sp *agutí* < Guarani *acutí*]

Agouti,
Dasyprocta aguti
(Length 20 in.)

agr., **1.** agricultural. **2.** agriculture.

A·gra (ä′grə), *n.* a city in W Uttar Pradesh, in N India: a former capital of the Mogul empire; site of the Taj Mahal. 517,699 (est. 1965).

a·graffe (ə graf′), *n.* a clasp, often richly ornamented, for clothing or armor. Also, **a·grafe** (ə graf′). [< F, var. of *agrafe,* back formation from *agrafer* to hook = *a-* A-[5] + *grafe* hook, cramp iron, prob. < Gmc; see GRAPE]

A·gram (ä′gräm), *n.* German name of **Zagreb.**

a·gran·u·lo·cy·to·sis (ə gran′yə lō sī tō′sis), *n. Pathol.* a serious, often fatal blood disease, characterized by a great reduction of the leucocytes. [A-[6] + GRANULOCYTE + -OSIS]

ag·ra·pha (ag′rə fə), *n.* (*construed as sing. or pl.*) the sayings of Jesus as recorded in the writings of the early Christians and in parts of the New Testament other than the Gospels. [< Gk, neut. pl. of *ágraphos* = *a-* A-[6] + *-graph* (s. of *gráphein* to write) + *-os* adj. suffix]

a·grar·i·an (ə grâr′ē ən), *adj.* **1.** relating to land, land tenure, or the division of landed property: *agrarian laws.* **2.** pertaining to the advancement of agricultural groups: *an agrarian movement.* **3.** composed of or pertaining to farmers: *an agrarian co-op.* **4.** rural; agricultural. —*n.* **5.** a person who favors the equal division of landed property and the advancement of agricultural groups. [< L *agrāri(us)* (*agr-* s. of *ager* field + *-ārius* -ARY) + -AN] —**a·grar′i·an·ism,** *n.* —**a·grar′i·an·ly,** *adv.*

a·gree (ə grē′), *v.,* **a·greed, a·gree·ing.** —*v.i.* **1.** to be of one mind; harmonize in opinion or feeling (often fol. by *with*): *I don't agree with you.* **2.** to have the same opinion (often fol. by *on* or *upon*): *We don't agree on politics.* **3.** to give consent; assent (often fol. by *to* or an infinitive): *Do you agree to the conditions?* **4.** to live in concord or without contention; harmonize in action. **5.** to reach an agreement or state of agreement upon something. **6.** to be suitable to or in harmony with something or with each other (usually fol. by *with*). **7.** to be consistent; conform (often fol. by *with*): *Does her account agree with yours?* **8.** to be in harmony with one's preferences (usually fol. by *with*). **9.** (of food or drink) to admit of digestion or absorption without difficulty (usually fol. by *with*). **10.** to present no obstruction to one's health, comfort, or the like (often fol. by *with*): *The climate of Jamaica did not agree with him.* **11.** *Gram.* to correspond in inflectional form, as in number, case, gender, or person; to show agreement. In *The boy runs, boy* is a singular noun and *runs* agrees with it in number. —*v.t.* **12.** to concede; grant (usually fol. by a noun clause): *I agree that he is the ablest of us.* **13.** *Chiefly Brit.* to consent to or concur with: *We agree the stipulations. I must agree your plans.* [late ME *agre* < MF *agre(e)r* from phrase *a gre* at pleasure. See A-[5], GREE[2]] —**a·gree′ing·ly,** *adv.*

—**Syn. 3.** AGREE, CONSENT, ACCEDE, ASSENT, CONCUR all imply complying with the idea, sentiment, or action of someone. AGREE, the general term, suggests compliance in response to any degree of persuasion or opposition: *to agree to go; to agree to a meeting, to a request or demand.* CONSENT, applying to rather important matters, conveys an active and positive idea; it implies making a definite decision to comply with someone's expressed wish: *to consent to become engaged.* ACCEDE, a more formal word, also applies to important matters and implies a degree of yielding to conditions: *to accede to terms.* ASSENT conveys a more passive idea; it suggests agreeing intellectually or merely verbally with someone's assertion, request, etc.: *to assent to a speaker's theory.* To CONCUR is to show accord in matters of opinion, as of minds independently running along the same channels: *to concur in a judgment about an art exhibit.* **7.** See **correspond.** —**Ant. 1–3, 5–9.** disagree.

a·gree·a·ble (ə grē′ə bəl), *adj.* **1.** to one's liking; pleasing: *agreeable manners.* **2.** willing or ready to agree or consent: *Are you agreeable to my plans?* **3.** suitable; conformable (usually fol. by *to*): *practice agreeable to theory.* [late ME *agreable* < MF] —**a·gree′a·bil′i·ty, a·gree′a·ble·ness,** *n.* —**a·gree′a·bly,** *adv.* —**Syn. 1.** pleasant, likable, amiable.

a·greed (ə grēd′), *adj.* arranged or set by common consent: *They met at the agreed time.*

a·gree·ment (ə grē′mənt), *n.* **1.** the act of agreeing or of coming to a mutual arrangement. **2.** the state of being in accord. **3.** an arrangement that is accepted by all parties to a transaction. **4.** a contract or other document delineating such an arrangement. **5.** unanimity of opinion; harmony in feeling: *agreement among the members.* **6.** *Gram.* correspondence in number, case, gender, person, etc., between syntactically connected words, esp. between one or more subordinate words and the word or words upon which they depend. **7.** *Law.* an expression of assent by two or more parties to the same object. [late ME *agrement* < MF] **—Syn. 3.** understanding. AGREEMENT, BARGAIN, COMPACT, CONTRACT all suggest a binding arrangement between two or more parties. AGREEMENT ranges in meaning from mutual understanding to binding obligation. BARGAIN applies particularly to agreements about buying and selling. COMPACT applies to treaties or alliances between nations or to solemn personal pledges. CONTRACT is used especially in law and business for such agreements as are legally enforceable.

a·gres·tic (ə gres′tik), *adj.* **1.** rural; rustic. **2.** unpolished; awkward: *agrestic behavior.* [< L *agrest(is)* = *agr-* (s. of *ager* field) + *-estis* adj. suffix + -IC]

ag·ri·busi·ness (ag′rə biz′nis), *n.* farming and related food-processing and marketing businesses, operated as a large-scale modern industry. [AGRI(CULTURE) + BUSINESS]

agric., **1.** agricultural. **2.** agriculture.

A·gric·o·la (ə grik′ə lə), *n.* **1. Geor·gi·us** (jôr′jē əs, jē ôr′-), (*Georg Bauer*), 1494–1555, German historian, physician, and pioneer in mineralogy. **2. Gnae·us Julius** (nē′əs), A.D. 37–93, Roman general: governor of Britain.

agricul′tural a′gent, *U.S.* See **county agent.**

ag·ri·cul·ture (ag′rə kul′chər), *n.* **1.** the science or art of cultivating land in the raising of crops; husbandry; farming. **2.** the production of crops, livestock, or poultry. [< L *agricultūra* = *agrī* (gen. sing. of *ager*) field + *cultūra* CULTURE] **—ag′ri·cul′tur·al,** *adj.* **—ag′ri·cul′tur·al·ly,** *adv.*

ag·ri·cul·tur·ist (ag′rə kul′chər ist), *n.* **1.** a farmer. **2.** an expert in agriculture. Also, **ag′ri·cul′tur·al·ist.**

A·gri·gen·to (ä′grē jen′tô), *n.* a city in S Italy. 47,094 (1961). Formerly, **Girgenti.**

ag·ri·mo·ny (ag′rə mō′nē), *n., pl.* **-nies. 1.** any rosaceous plant of the genus *Agrimonia,* esp. the perennial *A. Eupatoria,* having pinnate leaves and small, yellow flowers. **2.** any of certain other plants, as hemp agrimony or bur marigold. [late ME < L *agrimōnia,* metathetic var. of *argemōnia* < Gk *argemṓnē* poppy; r. ME *egremoyne* < MF *aigremoine*]

A·grip·pa (ə grip′ə), *n.* **Marcus Vip·sa·ni·us** (vip sā′nē əs), 63–12 B.C., Roman statesman, general, and engineer: defeated Antony and Cleopatra at Actium.

agro-, a learned borrowing from Greek meaning "soil," "crop production," used in the formation of compound words: *agronomy.* [comb. form of Gk *agrós* tilled land. See ACRE]

ag·ro·bi·ol·o·gy (ag′rō bī ol′ə jē), *n.* the quantitative science of plant life and plant nutrition. **—ag·ro·bi·o·log·ic** (ag′rō bī′ə loj′ik), **ag′ro·bi′o·log′i·cal,** *adj.* **—ag′ro·bi′o·log′i·cal·ly,** *adv.* **—ag′ro·bi·ol′o·gist,** *n.*

a·grol·o·gy (ə grol′ə jē), *n.* the branch of soil science dealing esp. with the production of crops. **—ag·ro·log·ic** (ag′rə loj′ik), **ag′ro·log′i·cal,** *adj.*

agron., agronomy.

ag·ro·nom·ics (ag′rə nom′iks), *n.* (*construed as sing.*) the art or science of managing land or crops; agronomy.

a·gron·o·my (ə gron′ə mē), *n.* the science of soil management and the production of field crops. **—ag·ro·nom·ic** (ag′rə nom′ik), **ag′ro·nom′i·cal,** *adj.* **—a·gron′o·mist,** *n.*

a·ground (ə ground′), *adv., adj.* **1.** on or onto the ground. **2.** (of a ship) with the bottom stuck or wedged on the ground or rocks beneath a body of water so as to be stranded.

Agt., agent. Also, **agt.**

A·guas·ca·lien·tes (ä′gwäs kä lyen′tes), *n.* **1.** a state in central Mexico. 263,334 (est. 1963); 2499 sq. mi. **2.** a city in and the capital of this state. 147,727 (est. 1965).

a·gue (ā′gyo͞o), *n.* **1.** *Pathol.* a malarial fever characterized by regularly returning paroxysms, marked by successive cold, hot, and sweating fits. **2.** a fit of fever, shivering, or shaking chills, accompanied by malaise, pains in the bones and joints, etc. [late ME < MF, short for *fievre ague* acute fever < L *febris acūta.* See ACUTE] **—a′gue·like′, a′gu·ish,** *adj.* **—a′gu·ish·ly,** *adv.*

a·gue·weed (ā′gyo͞o wēd′), *n.* *U.S.* **1.** a boneset, *Eupatorium perfoliatum.* **2.** a gentian, *Gentiana quinquefolia.*

A·gui·nal·do (ä′gē näl′dô), *n.* **E·mi·lio** (e mē′lyô), 1869–1964, Filipino leader during the Spanish-American War.

A·gul·has (ə gul′əs; *Port.* ä go͞o′lyəsh), *n.* **Cape,** the southernmost point of Africa.

ah (ä), *interj.* (used as an exclamation to express pain, surprise, appreciation, pity, complaint, dislike, joy, etc., according to the manner of utterance.) [ME *a!* which survives in dial. *eh!, ay!*]

Ah, *Elect.* ampere-hour. Also, **a.h.**

A.H., in the year of the Hegira (A.D. 622). [< L *annō Hejirae*]

a·ha (ä hä′), *interj.* (used as an exclamation to express triumph, mockery, contempt, irony, surprise, etc., according to the manner of utterance.) [var. of HA]

A.H.A., **1.** American Historical Association. **2.** American Hospital Association.

A·hab (ā′hab), *n.* a king of Israel and husband of Jezebel, reigned 874?–853? B.C. I Kings 16–22.

A·has·u·e·rus (ə haz′yo͞o ēr′əs, ə has′-, ə hazh′o͞o-), *n.* a king of ancient Persia, known to the Greeks as Xerxes: the husband of the Biblical Esther.

ah·choo (ä cho͞o′), *interj.* (used to represent the sound of a sneeze.) Also, **achoo, kerchoo.**

a·head (ə hed′), *adv.* **1.** in front of or in advance of a person or thing: *Breakers ahead! Go on ahead and say that I'll be late.* **2.** in a forward direction; onward. **3.** in the future: *There are grim days ahead.* **4.** into or for the future: *Plan ahead.* **5.** to or at an earlier time: *to put one's departure ahead.* **6.** on with one's activities or intentions: *to go ahead with a plan.* **7.** in or into a situation more advantageous than the previous or present one: *sure to get ahead in business.* **8. ahead of, a.** in front of. **b.** earlier than. **c.** in the future for. **d.** in or into a more advantageous situation than: *ahead of all competitors.*

a·hem (ə hem′), *interj.* (used as an utterance to attract attention, express doubt, etc.) [var. of HEM]

a·him·sa (ə him′sä, ə hiṅg′sä), *n.* *Hinduism.* the principle of nonviolence. [< Skt = *a-* not, without (c. A-[6]) + *himsā* injury, akin to *hanti* he slays, Gk *phónos* murder]

Ah·med·a·bad (ä′məd ä bäd′), *n.* a city in W India, N of Bombay. 1,149,900 (1961). Also, **Ah′mad·a·bad′.**

Ah·med·na·gar (ä′məd nug′ər), *n.* a city in W Maharashtra, in W India, E of Bombay. 119,000 (1961). Also, **Ah′mad·na′gar.**

a·hold (ə hōld′), *n.* *Informal.* **1.** a hold or grasp upon something (often fol. by *of*): *Grab ahold! Get ahold of that handle.* **2. get ahold of, a.** to succeed in communicating with: *I've been trying to get ahold of you for days.* **b.** to acquire: *I'm trying to get ahold of a copy of the book.*

A horizon, *Geol.* the topsoil in a soil profile. Cf. **B horizon, C horizon.**

a·horse (ə hôrs′), *adj., adv.* mounted on a horse.

a·hoy (ə hoi′), *interj.* *Naut.* (used as a call to hail another ship, attract attention, etc.) [var. of HOY. Cf. AHA, AHEM]

Ah·ri·man (ä′ri mən), *n.* *Zoroastrianism.* See **Angra Mainyu.**

a·hull (ə hul′), *adj.* *Naut.* **1.** having all sails furled and the helm lashed to head into the wind, as in heavy weather. **2.** (of a sailing vessel) abandoned, with decks awash.

A·hu·ra Maz·da (ä′ho͝o rə maz′də), *Zoroastrianism.* the supreme creative deity, the creator of Gayomart and the opponent of Angra Mainyu. Also called **Mazda, Ohrmazd, Ormazd, Ormuzd.**

Ah·ve·nan·maa (äkн′ve nän mä′), *n.* (*construed as pl.*) Finnish name of the **Åland Islands.**

Ah·waz (ä wäz′), *n.* a city in W Iran. 155,054 (est. 1963). Also, **Ah·vaz′.**

ai[1] (ī), *interj.* (used as an utterance to express pity, pain, anguish, etc.)

a·i[2] (ä′ē), *n., pl.* **a·is** (ä′ēz). a large sloth, *Bradypus tridactylus,* of Central and South America, having three toes on each forelimb. [< Pg < Tupi]

A.I.A., See **American Institute of Architects.**

ai·blins (ā′blinz), *adv.* *Scot.* ablins.

aid (ād), *v.t.* **1.** to provide support for or relief to; help. **2.** to promote the progress or accomplishment of; facilitate. **—*v.i.*** **3.** to give help or assistance. **—*n.*** **4.** help; support; assistance. **5.** a person or thing that aids or furnishes assistance; helper; auxiliary. Cf. **aide. 6. aids,** *Manège.* the means, including the hands, legs, voice, and weight, and the devices, as the spurs and whip, by which a rider controls his horse. **7.** *U.S.* aide-de-camp. **8.** See **foreign aid. 9.** a payment made by feudal vassals to their lord on special occasions. **10.** *Eng. Hist.* (after 1066) any of several revenues received by the king from his vassals and other subjects. [late ME *ayde* < MF *aid(i)er* < L *adjūtāre* to help (freq. of *adjuvāre*) = *ad-* AD- + *-jū-* help + *-tā-* freq. suffix + *-re* inf. suffix] **—aid′er,** *n.* **—aid′ful,** *adj.* **—aid′less,** *adj.* **—Syn. 1.** See **help. 2.** abet, back. **4.** succor; relief; subsidy; subvention. **—Ant. 2.** hinder.

AID (ād), *n.* *U.S. Govt.* the division of the Department of State that coordinates the various foreign-aid programs with U.S. foreign policy: established in 1961. [*A(gency for) I(nternational) D(evelopment)*]

AID, American Institute of Decorators.

aid-de-camp (ād′də kamp′), *n., pl.* **aids-de-camp.** *Chiefly U.S.* aide-de-camp.

aide (ād), *n.* **1.** an aide-de-camp. **2.** any official, confidential assistant.

aide-de-camp (ād′də kamp′), *n., pl.* **aides-de-camp.** a subordinate military or naval officer acting as a confidential assistant to a superior, usually to a general officer or admiral. Also, **aid-de-camp.** [< F: lit. camp helper]

aide-mé·moire (ād′mem wär′; *Fr.* ed mā mwar′), *n., pl.* **aides-mé·moire** (ādz′mem wär′; *Fr.* ed mā mwar′). *French.* a memorandum of discussion, agreement, or action.

AIDS (ādz), *n.* a serious, often fatal, disorder of the immune system that diminishes the body's resistance to infectious organisms and certain cancers, caused by the HIV virus and transmitted chiefly by sexual contact and contaminated hypodermic needles and by infected pregnant women to their fetuses. [*a(cquired) i(mmuno) d(eficiency) s(yndrome)*]

aid′ sta′tion, *Mil.* a medical installation in the field for providing medical treatment to the troops.

A.I.E.E.E., American Institute of Electrical and Electronic Engineers. Also, **AIEEE**

ai·glet (ā′glit), *n.* aglet.

ai·grette (ā′gret, ā gret′), *n.* a tuft or plume of feathers, esp. of a heron, worn as a head ornament. [< F = *aigr-* (< Gmc; cf. OHG *heiger* heron) + *-ette* -ETTE. See EGRET]

ai·guille (ā gwēl′, ā′gwēl), *n.* a needlelike rock mass or mountain peak. [< F < VL **acūcula* (r. *acicula*) = *acu(s)* needle + *-cula* -CULE]

ai·guil·lette (ā′gwi let′), *n.* an ornamental tagged cord or braid on a uniform; aglet. [< F; see AIGUILLE, -ETTE] **—ai′guil·let′ted,** *adj.*

Ai·ken (ā′kən), *n.* **Conrad (Pot·ter)** (pot′ər), 1889–1973, U.S. poet.

ai·ki·do (ī′kē dô, ī kē′dō), *n.* a Japanese form of self-defense utilizing wrist, joint, and elbow grips to immobilize or throw one's opponent. [< Jap = *ai* to coordinate + *ki* breath control + *do* way]

ail (āl), *v.t.* **1.** to cause pain, uneasiness, or trouble to. **—*v.i.*** **2.** to be unwell; feel pain; be ill. [ME *ail, eilen,* OE *eglan* to afflict (c. Goth *-agljan*) < *egle* painful; akin to Goth *agls* shameful]

ai·lan·thus (ā lan′thəs), *n., pl.* **-thus·es.** any simaroubaceous tree of the genus *Ailanthus,* esp. *A. altissima.* Cf. **tree of heaven.** [< NL < Amboinese *ai lanto,* lit., tree (of) the gods] **—ai·lan′thic,** *adj.*

ai·ler·on (ā′lə ron′), *n.* *Aeron.* a movable surface, usually near the trailing edge of a wing, that controls the roll of the airframe or effects maneuvers, as banks and the like. [< F = *ail(e)* (see AISLE) + *-eron* dim. suffix]

ail·ing (ā′ling), *adj.* **1.** suffering from ill health, pain, or physical weakness; sickly. **2.** sick; ill. **—Syn.** See **sick**[1].

ail·ment (āl′mənt), *n.* a physical disorder or illness.

aim (ām), *v.t.* **1.** to position (something that shoots a projectile) so that the projectile will strike its target. **2.** to position (something to be thrown or fired) so that it will travel along a certain path. **3.** to direct (a rocket, missile, etc.) toward its target through use of its internal guidance system: *to aim a rocket at the moon.* **4.** to intend or direct for a particular effect or purpose: *to aim a satire at snobbery.* **—***v.i.* **5.** to strive; try (usually fol. by *at* or an infinitive): *We aim to please.* **6.** *Chiefly Dial.* to intend: *She aims to go tomorrow.* **7.** to direct efforts toward an object: *The book aimed at the approval of the intelligentsia.* **8.** *Obs.* to estimate; guess. **—***n.* **9.** act of aiming or directing anything at or toward a particular point or target. **10.** the direction in which a weapon or missile is pointed; the line of sighting. **11.** something intended or desired to be attained by one's efforts; purpose. **12.** *Obs.* conjecture; guess. **13. take aim,** to sight a weapon or missile at a target: *to take aim and fire.* [late ME *aime(n)* < MF *aesmer* < LL *adaestimāre* = L *ad-* AD- + *aestimāre* (see ESTIMATE); r. ME *ame(n)* < OF (dial.) *amer* < L *aestimāre*] **—aim′er,** *n.* **—aim′ful,** *adj.* **—aim′ful·ly,** *adv.* **—aim′less,** *adj.* **—aim′less·ly,** *adv.* **—aim′less·ness,** *n.* **—Syn. 1.** point. **9.** sighting. **11.** goal; intent, design. AIM, END, OBJECT all imply something that is the goal of one's efforts. AIM implies that toward which one makes a direct line, refusing to be diverted from it: *a nobleness of aim; one's aim in life.* END emphasizes the goal as a cause of efforts: *the end for which one strives.* OBJECT emphasizes the goal as that toward which all efforts are directed: *the object of years of study.*

ain (ān), *adj. Scot.* own. [OE *ǣgen*]

ai·né (e nā′), *adj. French.* elder; eldest. Also, *referring to a woman,* ***aî·née′.*** [lit., born before]

ain't (ānt), **1.** *Nonstandard in U.S. except in some dialects. Informal in Brit.* am not. **2.** *Nonstandard.* are not, is not, have not, or has not. [var. of AMN'T (contr. of AM NOT) by loss of *m* and raising with compensatory lengthening of *a*]
—Usage. AIN'T is so traditionally and widely regarded as a nonstandard form that it should be shunned by all who prefer to avoid being considered illiterate. AIN'T occurs occasionally in the informal speech of some educated users, esp. in self-consciously folksy, humorous contexts (*Ain't it the truth! She ain't what she used to be!*), but it is completely unacceptable in formal writing and speech.

Ain·tab (*Turk.* īn täb′), *n.* former name of **Gaziantep.** Also, **Antep, Ayntab.**

Ai·nu (ī′no͞o), *n., pl.* **-nus,** (*esp. collectively*) **-nu. 1.** a member of an aboriginal race of the northernmost islands of Japan, having Caucasoid or Australoid features, light skin, and more body hair than Mongoloids. **2.** the language of the Ainus, of uncertain relationship.

air[1] (âr), *n.* **1.** a mixture of oxygen, nitrogen, and other gases that surrounds the earth and forms its atmosphere. **2.** a stir in the atmosphere; a light breeze. **3.** the apparent character assumed by a person, object, act, situation, etc. **4. airs,** affected or haughty conduct or manners. **5.** *Music.* **a.** a tune; melody. **b.** the soprano or treble part. **c.** an aria. **6.** transportation or travel by airplane: *to arrive by air.* **7.** *Obs.* breath. **8. clear the air,** to eliminate dissension, ambiguity, or tension from a discussion, situation, etc. **9. get the air,** *Slang.* **a.** to be rejected, as by a lover. **b.** to be dismissed, as by an employer. **10. give (someone) the air, a.** to reject, as a lover. **b.** to dismiss, as an employee. **11. in the air,** in circulation; current: *a rumor in the air.* **12. into thin air,** completely or entirely out of sight or reach: *He vanished into thin air.* **13. off the air, a.** not broadcasting: *He goes off the air at midnight.* **b.** no longer being broadcast: *The program went off the air years ago.* **14. on the air,** in the act of broadcasting; being broadcast: *The program will be going on the air in a few seconds.* **15. take the air,** to go out of doors, as for a short walk or ride. **16. tread** or **walk on air,** to feel very happy; be elated. **17. up in the air,** undecided or unsettled: *The contract is still up in the air.* **—***v.t.* **18.** to expose to the air; give access to the open air; ventilate. **19.** to bring to public attention, as an opinion or sentiment. **—***v.i.* **20.** to be exposed to the open air, as in order to be cooled, dried, or ventilated (often fol. by *out*). **—***adj.* **21.** operating by means of air pressure: *an air brake.* **22.** acting upon air: *an air pump.* **23.** of or pertaining to airplanes or to aviation. **24.** taking place in the air; aerial: *air war.* [ME *eir* < OF *air* < L *āer-* < Gk *āer-* (s. of *āḗr*) the lower atmosphere, akin to *áein* to blow] **—air′less,** *adj.* **—air′like′,** *adj.* **—Syn. 2.** See **wind**[1]. **3.** See **manner.**

air[2] (âʀ), *Scot.* **—***adj.* **1.** early. **—***adv.* **2.** *Obs.* before; previously. [var. of ERE]

A·ïr (ä′ēr), *n.* a region in N Niger, in the Sahara: low massif and oases. ab. 30,000 sq. mi. Also called **Asben.**

air′ bag′, a large plastic bag so mounted in a car that it inflates automatically upon impact in order to protect passengers from injury in a collision. Also called **air cushion.**

air′ base′, an operations center for units of an air force.

air′ blad′der, 1. a vesicle or sac containing air. **2.** Also called **gas bladder, swim bladder.** *Ichthyol.* a gas-filled sac located against the roof of the body cavity of most bony fishes, originally functioning only as a lung, now serving in many higher fishes to regulate hydrostatic pressure.

air·borne (âr′bōrn′, -bôrn′), *adj.* **1.** carried by the air, as pollen or dust. **2.** in flight; aloft. **3.** *Mil.* (of ground forces) carried in airplanes or gliders: *airborne infantry.*

air-bound (âr′bound′), *adj.* stopped up by air.

air′ brake′, 1. a brake or system of brakes operated by compressed air. **2.** *Aeron.* (not used scientifically) a device for reducing the air speed of an aircraft by increasing its drag.

air·brush (âr′brush′), *n.* an atomizer for spraying paint.

air·burst (âr′bûrst′), *n.* the explosion of a bomb or shell in midair.

air′ cav′alry, an infantry or reconnaissance unit transported by air to combat areas. Also called **sky cavalry.**

air′ cham′ber, a chamber containing confined air, as in a pump, a lifeboat, or an organic body.

air′ coach′, *U.S.* coach (def. 4).

air′ command′, *U.S. Air Force.* a unit of command that is higher than an air force.

air-con·di·tion (âr′kən dish′ən), *v.t.* **1.** to furnish with an air-conditioning system. **2.** to treat (air) with such a system.

air′ condi′tioner, an air-conditioning device.

air′ condi′tioning, 1. a system that controls or reduces the temperature and humidity of the air in an office, dwelling, theater, etc. **2.** the act or process of such controlling. **—air′-con·di′tion·ing,** *adj.*

air-cool (âr′ko͞ol′), *v.t.* to cool with circulated air.

Air′ Corps′, *U.S. Army.* **1.** (before July 26, 1947) a branch of the U.S. Army concerned with military aviation. **2.** (before May 1, 1942) the name for the Army Air Forces.

air·craft (âr′kraft′, -kräft′), *n., pl.* **-craft.** any machine supported for flight in the air by buoyancy or by the dynamic action of air on its surfaces, esp. powered airplanes, gliders, and helicopters.

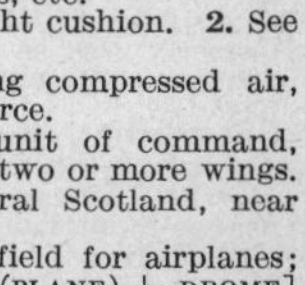
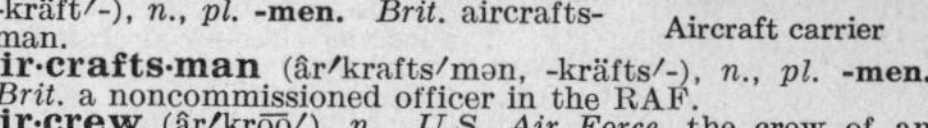

Aircraft carrier

air′craft car′rier, a warship designed mainly with a large deck for the taking off and landing of aircraft and with storage space for aircraft.

air·craft·man (âr′kraft′mən, -kräft′-), *n., pl.* **-men.** *Brit.* aircraftsman.

air·crafts·man (âr′krafts′mən, -kräfts′-), *n., pl.* **-men.** *Brit.* a noncommissioned officer in the RAF.

air·crew (âr′kro͞o′), *n. U.S. Air Force.* the crew of an aircraft. Also, **air′ crew′.**

air′ cur′tain, compressed air directed across a doorway to form a shield to exclude drafts, insects, etc.

air′ cush′ion, 1. an inflatable, airtight cushion. **2.** See **air bag.**

air′ cyl′inder, a cylinder containing compressed air, esp. one used as a reservoir or power source.

air′ divi′sion, *U.S. Air Force.* a unit of command, within an air force, usually composed of two or more wings.

Air·drie (âʀ′drē), *n.* a city in central Scotland, near Glasgow. 33,620 (1961).

air·drome (âr′drōm′), *n.* a landing field for airplanes; airport. Also, *esp. Brit.,* **aerodrome.** [AIR(PLANE) + -DROME]

air·drop (âr′drop′), *v.,* **-dropped, -drop·ping,** *n.* **—***v.t.* **1.** to drop (persons, equipment, etc.) by parachute from an aircraft in flight. **—***n.* **2.** the act or process of airdropping.

air-dry (âr′drī′), *v.,* **-dried, -dry·ing,** *adj.* **—***v.t.* **1.** to dry by exposure to the air. **—***adj.* **2.** dry beyond further evaporation.

Airedale (23 in. high at shoulder)

Aire·dale (âr′dāl′), *n.* one of a breed of large terriers having a wiry, black-and-tan coat and a docked tail.

air·field (âr′fēld′), *n.* a level area, usually equipped with hard-surfaced runways, on which airplanes take off and land. [AIR(PLANE) + FIELD]

air·flow (âr′flō′), *n.* air currents caused by a moving aircraft, automobile, etc.

air·foil (âr′foil′), *n. Aeron.* any surface, as a wing, aileron, or stabilizer, designed to aid in lifting or controlling an aircraft by making use of the air currents through which it moves.

Air′ Force′, 1. *U.S.* the department consisting of practically all military aviation forces, established July 26, 1947. **2.** (*l.c.*) *U.S.* a unit of Air Force command between an air division and an air command. **3.** (*often l.c.*) the military organization of any nation that is mainly responsible for its military operations in the air.

air·frame (âr′frām′), *n.* the framework and external covering of an airplane, rocket, etc. [AIR(PLANE) + FRAME]

air′ freight′, 1. a system of transporting freight by aircraft. **2.** freight transported by aircraft.

air·glow (âr′glō′), *n.* a nighttime glow from the upper atmosphere, occurring over middle and low latitudes.

air′ gun′, a gun operated by compressed air.

air′ ham′mer, a pneumatic hammer, usually portable.

air′ hole′, 1. an opening to admit or discharge air. **2.** a natural opening in the frozen surface of a river or pond. **3.** See **air pocket.**

air·i·ly (âr′ə lē), *adv.* **1.** in a gay or breezy manner; jauntily. **2.** lightly; delicately.

air·ing (âr′ing), *n.* **1.** an exposure to the air, as for drying. **2.** a public discussion, as of ideas, opinions, proposals, etc. **3.** a walk, drive, etc., in the open air.

air′ jack′et, *Brit.* See **life jacket.**

air′ lane′, a route regularly used by airplanes; airway.

air·less (âr′lis), *adj.* **1.** lacking air. **2.** without fresh air; stuffy: *a dark, airless hallway.* **3.** without a breeze.

air′ let′ter, 1. an air-mail letter. **2.** a sheet of extremely lightweight stationery for use in air mail.

air·lift (âr′lift′), *n.* Also, **air′ lift′. 1.** a system for transporting persons or cargo by aircraft, esp. in an emergency. **2.** act or process of transporting such a load. **—***v.t.* **3.** to transport (persons or cargo) by airlift.

air-line (âr′līn′), *adj.* via airplane: *the air-line distance between Detroit and Washington.*

air·line (âr′līn′), *n. Aeron.* **1.** a system furnishing air transport, usually scheduled, between specified points. **2.** the airplanes, airports, etc., of such a system. **3.** Often, **airlines.** a company that owns or operates such a system. **4.** a tube or hose used to pipe air to a deep-sea diver, pneumatic drill, etc.

air·lin·er (âr′lī′nər), *n. Aeron.* a passenger aircraft operated by an airline. Also, **air′ lin′er.**

air′ lock′, 1. *Civ. Eng.* an airtight chamber permitting passage to or from a space, as in a caisson, in which the air is kept under pressure. **2.** the impedance in the functioning

of a pump or a system of piping caused by the presence of an air bubble; vapor lock.
air′ log′, *Aeron.* a device for recording the distance traveled by an aircraft, relative to the air through which it moves.
air′ mail′, 1. the system of transmitting mail by airplane. 2. mail transmitted by airplane. Also called, *Brit.*, **air post.**
air-mail (âr′māl′), *adj.* 1. of or pertaining to air mail. —*n.* 2. an air-mail letter. 3. an air-mail stamp. —*adv.* 4. by air mail: *Send all the letters air-mail.* —*v.t.* 5. to send via air mail. Also, **air′mail′.**
air·man (âr′mən), *n., pl.* **-men.** 1. an aviator. 2. *U.S. Air Force.* an enlisted man of one of the four lowest ranks (**basic airman, air′man third′ class′, air′man sec′ond class′,** and **air′man first′ class′**). 3. *U.S. Navy.* an enlisted man with duties relating to aircraft. —**air′man·ship′,** *n.*
air′ mass′, a body of air covering a relatively wide area, exhibiting approximately uniform properties through any horizontal section.
air′ med′al, *U.S.* a decoration awarded for meritorious achievement in aerial duty.
air′ mile′, mile (def. 3).
air-mind·ed (âr′mīn′did), *adj.* 1. interested in aviation or aeronautics. 2. favoring increased use of aircraft. —**air′-mind′ed·ness,** *n.*
Air′ Na′tional Guard′, a national guard organization similar to and coordinate with the U.S. Air Force.
air′ observ′er, *U.S. Army.* observer (def. 3).
air·plane (âr′plān′), *n.* 1. a heavier-than-air aircraft kept aloft by the upward thrust exerted by the passing air on its fixed wings and driven by propellers, jet propulsion, etc. 2. any similar aircraft, as a glider or helicopter. Also, *esp. Brit.*, **aeroplane.** [< late Gk *āer(ó)plan(os)* wandering in air = *āero-* AERO- + *plan-* (s. of *planâsthai* to wander) + *-os* adj. suffix; see PLANET]
air′plane cloth′, 1. a cotton fabric of plain weave formerly used as a covering for the wings and fuselages of airplanes. 2. a similar, lighter-weight fabric for shirts and pajamas.
air′ plant′, an epiphyte.
air′ pock′et, (not in technical use) a nearly vertical air current that can cause an aircraft to experience a sudden change in altitude, usually a decrease. Also called **air hole.**
Air′ Police′, an organization of personnel in the U.S. Air Force or Air National Guard serving as police. *Abbr.:* AP, A.P.
air·port (âr′pōrt′, -pôrt′), *n.* a tract of land or water with facilities for the landing, takeoff, shelter, supply, and repair of aircraft, esp. one for commercial aircraft and having a passenger terminal. [AIR(CRAFT) + PORT[1]]
air′ post′, *Brit.* See **air mail.**
air′ pres′sure. See **atmospheric pressure.**
air′ raid′, a raid by aircraft, esp. for bombing a particular area. —**air′-raid′,** *adj.* —**air′ raid′er.**
air′-raid shel′ter, an area specifically designated as a shelter during an air raid. Cf. **bomb shelter.**
air′-raid ward′en, a civilian having police duties during an air-raid alert.
air′ ri′fle, an air gun with rifled bore.
air′ right′, 1. a right of way in the air space owned by a person over his land. 2. such a right sold or leased for use or occupation, esp. on a support elevated above an immovable property, as for the erection of an office building over a railroad track.
air′ sac′, any of certain cavities in a bird's body connected with the lungs.
air·screw (âr′skrōō′), *n.* *Brit.* an airplane propeller.
air′ shaft′, a ventilating shaft.
air·ship (âr′ship′), *n.* a self-propelled, lighter-than-air aircraft, usually classed as rigid, semirigid, or nonrigid, with means of controlling the direction of flight.
air·sick (âr′sik′), *adj.* ill with airsickness.
air·sick·ness (âr′sik′nis), *n.* motion sickness resulting from air travel.
air′ space′, 1. a space occupied by air. 2. the amount of breathing air in a room or other enclosed space. 3. Also, **air′space′.** the region of the atmosphere above a plot of ground, municipality, state, or nation.
air·speed (âr′spēd′), *n.* the forward speed of an aircraft relative to the air through which it moves. Also, **air′ speed′.** Cf. **groundspeed.**
air-spray (âr′sprā′), *adj.* pertaining to compressed-air spraying devices or to liquids in them. —**air′-sprayed′,** *adj.*
air′ sta′tion, an airfield having facilities for sheltering and servicing aircraft.
air·strip (âr′strip′), *n.* *Aeron.* runway (def. 2).
airt (ârt; *Scot.* ārt), *Chiefly Scot.* —*n.* 1. a direction. —*v.t.* 2. to point out the way; direct. Also, **airth** (ârth; *Scot.* ārth). [< Gael *aird* a high point, quarter of the compass]
air′ tax′i, a small aircraft for passengers, cargo, and mail, operated, either on a scheduled or nonscheduled basis, along routes not serviced by regular airlines.
air·tight (âr′tīt′), *adj.* 1. constructed or sealed to prevent the entrance or escape of air. 2. having no weak points of which an opponent may take advantage: *an airtight contract.* —**air′tight′ly,** *adv.* —**air′tight′ness,** *n.*
air-to-air (âr′tōō âr′, -tə-), *adj.* operating between flying aircraft or directed from one flying aircraft to another.
air-to-sur·face (âr′tə sûr′fəs), *adj.* operating or directed from a flying aircraft to the surface of the earth.
air·waves (âr′wāvz′), *n.pl.* the media of radio and television broadcasting.
air·way (âr′wā′), *n.* 1. an air route fully equipped with emergency landing fields, beacon lights, radio beams, etc. 2. any passage in a mine used for ventilating purposes. 3. **airways, a.** the band of frequencies, taken collectively, used by radio broadcasting stations. **b.** airline (def. 3).
air·wor·thy (âr′wûr′thē), *adj.* *Aeron.* meeting accepted standards for safe flight. —**air′wor′thi·ness,** *n.*
air·y (âr′ē), *adj.*, **air·i·er, air·i·est.** 1. open to a free current of air: *airy rooms.* 2. consisting of or having the character of air. 3. light in appearance; thin: *airy garments.* 4. light in manner; sprightly; lively: *airy songs.* 5. light in movement; graceful; delicate: *an airy step.* 6. unsubstantial as air; unreal; imaginary: *airy dreams.* 7. visionary; speculative. 8. performed in the air; aerial. 9. high in the air; lofty. [late ME *ayery*] —**air′i·ness,** *n.*
A·i·sha (ä′ē shä′), *n.* A.D. 613?–678, favorite wife of Muhammad (daughter of Abu-Bekr). Also, **Ayesha.**
aisle (īl), *n.* 1. a passageway between sections of seats, as in a theater. 2. *Archit.* **a.** a longitudinal division of an interior area, as in a church, separated from the main area by an arcade or the like. **b.** any of the longitudinal divisions of a church, auditorium, theater, or the like. 3. **in the aisles,** (of an audience) convulsed with laughter. [alter. (with *ai* < F *aile* wing) of earlier *isle, ile;* r. ME *ele* < MF < L *āla* wing. See ALA] —**aisled,** *adj.*
Aisne (ān; *Fr.* en), *n.* a river in N France, flowing NW and W to the Oise. 175 mi. long.
ait (āt), *n.* *Brit. Dial.* a small island, esp. in a river. [ME *eyt* < OE *ȳgett,* dim. of *īeg* island, c. Icel *ey.* See ISLAND]
aitch (āch), *n.* the letter *H, h.* [ME *ache* < OF *ache* < VL **hacca* or **accha;* r. *ha*]
aitch·bone (āch′bōn′), *n.* 1. the rump bone, as of beef. 2. the cut of beef that includes this bone. [late ME *hach-boon* (with spurious *h-*); *(h)ach* var. of *nache* rump < MF < VL **natica,* fem. of **naticus* of the rump < L *nati(s)* rump + *-cus* adj. suffix]
Ait·ken (āt′kən), *n.* 1. **Robert Grant,** 1864–1951, U.S. astronomer. 2. **William Maxwell.** See **Beaverbrook, William Maxwell Aitken.**
Aix-en-Pro·vence (eks än prô väns′), *n.* a city in SE France, N of Marseilles. 72,696 (1962). Also called **Aix** (eks).
Aix-la-Cha·pelle (eks lȧ shȧ pel′; *Eng.* āks′lä shä pel′), *n.* French name of **Aachen.**
Aix-les-Bains (eks lā baN′; *Eng.* āks′lā bānz′), *n.* a town in SE France, N of Chambéry: mineral springs.
A·jac·cio (ä yät′chô), *n.* a seaport in and the capital of Corsica: the birthplace of Napoleon I. 42,282 (1962).
a·jar[1] (ə jär′), *adj., adv.* (of a door, hinged window, or lid) partly open. [ME *on char* on the turn; see CHAR[3]]
a·jar[2] (ə jär′), *adj., adv.* at variance with: *a story ajar with the facts.* [for *at jar* at discord; cf. JAR[3] (n.)]
A·jax (ā′jaks), *n.* *Class. Myth.* 1. Also called **Telamonian Ajax.** a Greek hero in the Trojan War who rescued the body of Achilles and killed himself out of jealousy when Odysseus was awarded the armor of Achilles. 2. Also **A′jax the Less′er.** a Locrian king, noted for his valor in the Trojan War, said to have been killed in a shipwreck as a punishment for violating a shrine of Athena.
a·jee (ə jē′), *adv.* *Brit. Dial.* agee.
a·ji·va (ə jē′və), *n.* *Jainism.* all in the universe that is not jiva, as space, time, and matter. [< Skt *ajīva* without life = *a-* A-[6] + *jīva* living]
Aj·mer (uj mēr′), *n.* a city in central Rajasthan, in NW India. 231,200 (1961).
A·jodh·ya (ə yōd′yə), *n.* a city in central Uttar Pradesh, in N India; a suburb of Fyzabad: sacred Hindu center.
AK, Alaska (approved esp. for use with zip code).
Ak·bar (ak′bär), *n.* ("*the Great*") (*Jalal-ud-Din Mohammed*) 1542–1605, Mogul emperor of India 1556–1605.
A.K.C., American Kennel Club.
a·ke·la (ə kē′lə), *n.* (in the Cub Scouts) a pack leader. [after *Akela,* leader of the wolfpack in *The Jungle Book* (1894, 1895), a series of stories by Kipling]
a·kene (ā kēn′), *n.* achene.
Akh·na·ton (äk nät′ən), *n.* See **Amenhotep IV.**
A·ki·ba ben Jo·seph (ä kē′bä ben jō′zəf, -səf, ə kē′və), A.D. c50–c135, Hebrew scholar: compiler of Jewish oral law on which the Mishnah is based. Also called **A·ki′ba.**
A·ki·hi·to (ä′kē hē′tô; *Eng.* ä′ki hē′tō), *n.* born 1933, crown prince of Japan (son of Hirohito).
a·kim·bo (ə kim′bō), *adj., adv.* with hand on hip and elbow bent outward: *to stand with arms akimbo.* [late ME *in kenebowe,* appar., in keen bow, in a sharp bent]
a·kin (ə kin′), *adj.* 1. (used predicatively) related by blood. 2. allied by nature; having some of the same properties, characteristics, or the like. —**Syn.** 2. cognate; analogous.
A·ki·ta (ä′kē tä′), *n.* a seaport on N Honshu, in N Japan, on the Sea of Japan. 211,866 (1964).
Ak·kad (ak′ad, ä′käd), *n.* 1. Accad. —*adj.* 2. Akkadian.
Ak·ka·di·an (ə kā′dē ən, ə kä′-), *n.* 1. the eastern Semitic language, now extinct, of Assyria and Babylonia, written with a cuneiform script. 2. one of the people of Accad. —*adj.* 3. of or belonging to Accad. 4. of or pertaining to the eastern Semitic language called Akkadian. 5. *Obs.* Sumerian.
Ak·ker·man (ä′kər män′), *n.* former name of **Belgorod-Dnestrovski.**
Ak·kra (ak′rə, ə krä′), *n.* Accra.
Ak·mo·linsk (ak′mō linsk′; *Russ.* äk mô′linsk), *n.* former name of **Tselinograd.**
Ak·ron (ak′rən), *n.* a city in NE Ohio. 275,425 (1970).
Ak·sum (äk′sōōm), *n.* the capital of an ancient Ethiopian kingdom, ruled by Himyaritics from Arabia.
ak·va·vit (äk′vä vēt′), *n.* a dry, ginlike, Scandinavian spirit, flavored with caraway seeds. Also, **aquavit.** [< Scand < L *aqua vit(ae)* water of life]
Ak·yab (ak yab′, ak′yab), *n.* a seaport in W Burma. 42,329 (1953).
à l′, form of **à la** used for either gender before a vowel or *h.*
al (äl), *n.* See **Indian mulberry.** [< Hindi]
AL, 1. Alabama (approved esp. for use with zip code). 2. Also, **AL., A.L.** Anglo-Latin.
Al, *Chem.* aluminum.
al-, var. of **ad-** before *l: allure.*
-al[1], an adjectival suffix occurring in loan words from Latin (*regal; equal*); on this model, used in the formation of adjectives from other sources (*typical*). [< L *-ālis, -āle* pertaining to; often r. ME *-el* < OF]
-al[2], a suffix forming nouns from verbs of French or Latin origin: *denial; refusal.* [< L *-āle* (sing.), *-ālia* (pl.), neut. of *-ālis* -AL[1]; often r. ME *-aille* < OF]
-al[3], *Chem.* a suffix indicating that a compound contains an aldehyde group: *chloral.* [short for ALDEHYDE]
al., 1. other things. [< L *alia*] 2. other persons. [< L *alii*]

A.L., 1. *Baseball.* American League. 2. American Legion. 3. Anglo-Latin.

à la (ä′ lä, ä′ lə; *Fr.* A LA), 1. *Cookery.* **a.** prepared in the manner of, to the taste of, or to celebrate (a person or place): *cutlet à la Kiev.* **b.** prepared with the ingredient of. 2. according to; in the manner of: *a poetic tragedy à la Maxwell Anderson.* Also, **a la.** [< F: short for *à la mode (de)* in the style (of)]

a·la (ā′lə), *n., pl.* **a·lae** (ā′lē). 1. a wing. 2. a winglike part, process, or expansion, as of a bone, shell, seed, stem, etc. 3. one of the two side petals of a papilionaceous flower. [< L: wing, armpit, shoulder = *a(x)-* (see AXIS) + *-la* dim. suffix]

Ala., Alabama.

A.L.A., American Library Association. Also, **ALA**

Al·a·bam·a (al′ə bam′ə), *n.* 1. a state in the SE United States. 3,444,165 (1970); 51,609 sq. mi. *Cap.:* Montgomery. *Abbr.:* AL, Ala. 2. a river flowing SW from central Alabama to the Mobile River. 315 mi. long. —**Al·a·bam·i·an** (al′ə-bam′ē ən), **Al′a·bam′an,** *adj., n.*

al·a·bam·ine (al′ə bam′ēn, -in), *n.* *Chem.* (formerly) astatine. *Symbol:* Ab [ALABAM(A) + -INE²]

al·a·bas·ter (al′ə bas′tər, -bä′stər), *n.* 1. a finely granular variety of gypsum, often white and translucent, used for ornamental objects, lamp bases, figurines, etc. 2. a variety of calcite, often banded, used as alabaster. —*adj.* Also, **al·a·bas·trine** (al′ə bas′trin, -bä′strin). 3. made of alabaster: *an alabaster column.* 4. resembling alabaster; smooth and white as alabaster: *her alabaster throat.* [< L < Gk *alábastros;* r. late ME *alabastre* < MF < L]

à la carte (ä′ lə kärt′, al′ ə; *Fr.* A LA KART′), with a stated price for each dish offered: *dinner à la carte.* Cf. **prix fixe, table d'hôte.** [< F: according to the card; see CARTE²]

a·lack (ə lak′), *interj.* *Archaic.* (used as an exclamation of sorrow, regret, or dismay.) Also, **a·lack·a·day** (ə lak′ə dā′). [var. of old exclamation *lack!* Cf. AHA, AHEM, and OE *læccung* reproach]

a·lac·ri·ty (ə lak′ri tē), *n.* 1. cheerful readiness, promptness, or willingness. 2. liveliness or briskness. [< L *alacritāt-* (s. of *alacritās*) = *alacri(s)* lively + *-tāt-* -TY²] —**a·lac′ri·tous,** *adj.*

a·lae (ā′lē), *n.* pl. of **ala.**

A·la·go·as (ä′lä gô′äs; *Eng.* ä′lə gō′əs), *n.* a state in NE Brazil. 1,271,062 (1960); 10,674 sq. mi. *Cap.:* Maceió.

A·la·göz (ä′lä gœz′), *n.* Turkish name of Mount Aragats.

A·lai′ Moun′tains (ä lī′), a mountain range in the SW Soviet Union in Asia: highest peak, ab. 19,000 ft.

à la king (ä′ lə king′, al′ ə), noting a dish of diced, cooked fowl, fish, etc., creamed with pimiento or green pepper: *chicken à la king.*

Al·a·man·ni (al′ə man′ī), *n.pl.* Alemanni.

al·a·me·da (al′ə mē′də, -mā′-), *n.* *Chiefly Southwestern U.S.* a public walk shaded with poplar or other trees. [< Sp = *álam(o)* poplar + *-eda* < L *-ētum* suffix marking provision]

Al·a·me·da (al′ə mē′də, -mā′-), *n.* a city in W California. 70,968 (1970).

A·la·mein (ä′lä mān′, -lə-), *n.* See **El Alamein.**

Al·a·mo (al′ə mō′), *n.* a Franciscan mission in San Antonio, Texas: taken by Mexicans on March 6, 1836, during the Texan war for independence.

a·la·mode¹ (ä′lə mōd′, al′ə-), *adj., adv.* See **à la mode.**

al·a·mode² (al′ə mōd′), *n.* a lightweight, glossy silk fabric used for scarfs, hoods, etc. [from À LA MODE]

à la mode (ä′ lə mōd′, al′ ə; *Fr.* A LA môd′), 1. in or according to the prevailing fashion. 2. *Cookery.* **a.** (of pie or other dessert) served with a portion of ice cream. **b.** (of beef) larded and braised or stewed with vegetables, herbs, etc., and served with a rich brown gravy. Also, **a′ la mode′, alamode.** [< F: in the manner]

Al·a·mo·gor·do (al′ə mə gôr′dō), *n.* a city in S New Mexico, near site of first atomic bomb explosion. 23,035 (1970).

Å′land Is′lands (ä′lənd, ō′lənd; *Swed.* ō′länd′), a group of Finnish islands in the Baltic Sea, between Sweden and Finland. 21,319 (est. 1965); 572 sq. mi. Finnish, **Ahvenanmaa.**

al·a·nine (al′ə nēn′, -nin), *n.* *Chem., Biochem.* any of several isomers of an amino acid, $CH_3CH(NH_2)COOH$, found in many proteins and used chiefly in research. [AL(DEHYDE) + *-an-* (arbitrarily inserted) + -INE²]

a·lar (ā′lər), *adj.* 1. pertaining to or having wings. 2. winglike; wing-shaped. [< L *ālār(is).* See ALA, -AR¹]

A·lar·cón (ä′lär kôn′), *n.* **Pe·dro An·to·nio** (pe′thrô än tô′nyô), (*Pedro Antonio Alarcón y Ariza*), 1833–91, Spanish novelist, short-story writer, and diplomat.

Al·a·ric (al′ər ik), *n.* A.D. c370–410, king of the Visigoths: captured Rome 410.

a·larm (ə lärm′), *n.* 1. a sudden fear or distressing suspense excited by an awareness of danger; apprehension; fright. 2. any call, sound, or other signal for giving notice of an emergency, rousing from sleep, etc. 3. any device for giving such a signal. 4. a call to arms. 5. *Fencing.* a challenge made by a step or stamp with the advancing foot. —*v.t.* 6. to make fearful or apprehensive. 7. to warn of an emergency. [ME *alarme* < MF < It *allarme* < *all'arme* to (the) arms. See ARM²] —**a·larm′a·ble,** *adj.* —**a·larm·ed·ly** (ə lär′mid lē), *adv.* —**a·larm′ing·ly,** *adv.* —**Syn.** 1. consternation; terror, panic. See **fear.** 6. See **frighten.**

alarm′ clock′, a clock having an alarm that can be set to operate at a given time.

a·larm·ist (ə lär′mist), *n.* 1. a person who tends to raise alarms, as by exaggerating dangers, prophesying calamities, etc. —*adj.* 2. characteristic of an alarmist. —**a·larm′ism,** *n.*

a·lar·um (ə lar′əm, ə lär′-), *n.* *Archaic.* alarm. [ME *alarom*]

alar′ums and excur′sions, (in early modern English drama) military action, represented by sound effects of trumpets, clash of arms, etc.: used as a stage direction.

a·las (ə las′, ə läs′), *interj.* (used to express sorrow, grief, pity, concern, or apprehension of evil.) [ME < OF *(h)a las!* = *(h)a* AH + *las* wretched < L *lass(us)* weary]

Alas., Alaska.

A·las·ka (ə las′kə), *n.* 1. a state of the United States in NW North America. 302,173 (1970); 586,400 sq. mi. *Cap.:* Juneau. *Abbr.:* Alas., AK 2. **Gulf of,** a gulf of the Pacific, on the coast of S Alaska. —**A·las′kan,** *adj., n.*

Alas′ka High′way, a highway in NW Canada and Alaska, extending from E British Columbia to Fairbanks. 1523 mi. long. Also called **Alcan Highway.**

Alas′kan crab′. See **king crab** (def. 2).

Alas′kan mal′amute, one of an Alaskan breed of large dogs having a dense, coarse coat, raised originally for drawing sleds. Also, **Alas′kan Mal′amute.**

Alas′ka Penin′sula, a peninsula in SW Alaska. 500 mi. long.

Alas′ka Range′, a mountain range in S Alaska. Highest peak, Mount McKinley, 20,300 ft.

Alas′ka time′. See under **standard time.**

a·late (ā′lāt), *adj.* 1. having wings; winged. 2. having membranous expansions like wings. Also, **a′lat·ed.** [< L *ālāt(us).* See ALA, -ATE¹]

alb (alb), *n.* *Eccles.* a long-sleeved linen vestment, worn chiefly by priests. [ME, OE *albe* < L *alba (vestis)* white (garment)]

Alb

Alb., 1. Albania. 2. Albanian. 3. Alberta.

Al·ba (al′bə; *Sp.* äl′vä), *n.* **Duke of.** See **Alva, Fernando Álvarez de Toledo.**

Alba., Alberta.

Al·ba·ce·te (äl′bä the′te), *n.* a city in SE Spain. 79,875 (est. 1960).

al·ba·core (al′bə kōr′, -kôr′), *n., pl.* (*esp. collectively*) **-core,** (*esp. referring to two or more kinds or species*) **-cores.** 1. a long-finned edible tuna, *Germa alalunga,* found in all warm or temperate seas. 2. any of various tunalike fishes. [< Pg *albacor(a)* < Ar *al bakūrah* the tuna]

Al·ba Lon·ga (al′bə lông′gə, long′-), a city of ancient Latium, SE of Rome: legendary birthplace of Romulus and Remus.

Al·ba·ne·se (al′bə nā′zə, -sə, äl′-; *It.* äl′bä ne′ze), *n.* **Li·cia** (lē′chə ə; *It.* lē′chä), born 1913, Italian operatic soprano.

Al·ba·ni·a (al bā′nē ə, -bān′yə), *n.* 1. **People's Republic of,** a republic in S Europe, in the Balkan Peninsula between Yugoslavia and Greece. 2,400,000; 10,632 sq. mi. *Cap.:* Tirana. 2. *Obs.* Scotland.

Al·ba·ni·an (al bā′nē ən, -bān′yən), *adj.* 1. of or pertaining to Albania, its inhabitants, or their language. —*n.* 2. a native or inhabitant of Albania. 3. the Indo-European language of Albania.

Al·ba·ny (ôl′bə nē), *n.* 1. a city in and the capital of New York, on the Hudson. 115,781 (1970). 2. a city in SW Georgia. 72,623 (1970). 3. a river in central Canada, flowing E from W Ontario to James Bay. 610 mi. long.

Al′bany Con′gress, *Amer. Hist.* a meeting of delegates from seven American colonies, held in 1754 at Albany, New York, at which Benjamin Franklin proposed a plan (**Al′bany Plan′ of Un′ion**) for unifying the colonies.

al·ba·tross (al′bə trôs′, -tros′), *n.* any of several large, webfooted sea birds of the family *Diomedeidae,* that have the ability to remain aloft for long periods. [var. of *algatross* frigate bird < Pg or Sp *alcatraz* pelican; *-b-* for *-g-* perh. by assoc. with L *alba* white (the bird's color)]

Wandering albatross, *Diomedea exulans* (Length 4 ft.; wingspread 12 ft.)

al·be·do (al bē′dō), *n.* *Astron.* the ratio of the light reflected by a planet or satellite to that received by it. [< LL: whiteness = *alb(us)* white + *-ēdō* n. suffix as in TORPEDO]

Al·bee (ôl′bē), *n.* **Edward (Franklin),** born 1928, U.S. playwright.

al·be·it (ôl bē′it), *conj.* although; even if: *a peaceful, albeit inglorious retirement.* [ME *al be it* al(though) it be]

Al′be·marle Sound′ (al′bə märl′), an inlet of the Atlantic Ocean, in NE North Carolina. 60 mi. long.

Al·bé·niz (äl ve′nēth; *Eng.* äl bā′nēs, al-), *n.* **I·sa·ac** (ē′sä-äk′; *Eng.* ī′zək), 1860–1909, Spanish composer and pianist.

Al·ber·ich (al′bə rik), *n.* *Teutonic Legend.* a king of the dwarfs, the possessor of the treasure of the Nibelungs.

Al·bert (al′bərt), *n.* 1. **Prince** (*Albert Francis Charles Augustus Emanuel, Prince of Saxe-Coburg-Gotha*), 1819–61, consort of Queen Victoria. 2. **Lake.** Also called **Albert Nyanza.** a lake in central Africa: 100 mi. long; 2064 sq. mi.; 2030 ft. above sea level.

Albert I, 1875–1934, king of the Belgians 1909–34.

Al·ber·ta (al bûr′tə), *n.* a province in W Canada. 1,451,000 (1965); 255,285 sq. mi. *Cap.:* Edmonton. *Abbr.:* Alta.

Al·bert, d' (dal′bərt; *Ger.* däl′bert; *Fr.* dal ber′), **Eu·gen** (*Ger.* oi gān′) or **Eu·gène** (*Fr.* œ zhen′) **Francis Charles,** 1864–1932, German-French pianist and composer, born in Scotland.

Al′bert Ed′ward, a mountain in SE New Guinea, in the Owen Stanley Range. 13,030 ft.

Al·ber·ti (äl ber′tē), *n.* **Le·on Bat·ti·sta** (le ôn′ bät tē′-stä), 1404–72, Italian architect, artist, musician, and poet.

al·bert·ite (al′bər tīt′), *n.* an asphaltlike, bituminous mineral. [after *Albert* county, N.B., Canada, where it is mined; see -ITE¹]

Al′bert Ny·an′za (nī an′zə, nyän′zä). See **Albert, Lake.**

Al·ber·tus Mag·nus (al bûr′təs mag′nəs), **Saint** (*Albert von Böllstadt*), 1193?–1280, German scholastic philosopher: teacher of Saint Thomas Aquinas. —**Al·ber·tist** (al bûr′tist, al′bər-), *n.*

Al·bert·ville (*Fr.* al ber vēl′), *n.* former name of **Kalemi.**

al·bes·cent (al bes′ənt), *adj.* becoming white; whitish. [< L *albēscent-* (s. of *albēscēns,* prp. of *albēscere*) = *alb(us)* white + *-ēscent-* -ESCENT] —**al·bes′cence,** *n.*

Al·bi (AL bē′), *n.* a city in S France. 41,268 (1962).

Al·bi·gen·ses (al′bi jen′sēz), *n.pl.* members of an ascetic Christian sect that arose in Albi in the 11th century and was exterminated in the 13th century by a crusade (**Albigen′sian Crusade′**) and the Inquisition. [< L *Albig(a)* ALBI + *-enses* -ESE] —**Al·bi·gen·si·an** (al′bi jen′sē ən, -shən), *adj., n.* —**Al′bi·gen′si·an·ism,** *n.*

al·bi·nism (al′bə niz′əm), *n.* the state or condition of being an albino. —**al′bi·nis′tic,** *adj.*

al·bi·no (al bī′nō *or, esp. Brit.,* -bē′-), *n., pl.* **-nos.** a person, animal, or plant deficient in pigmentation, esp. a person with a pale, milky skin, light hair, and pink eyes. [< Pg = *alb(o)* white (< L *albus*) + *-ino* -INE[1]] —**al·bin·ic** (al bin′ik), **al·bi·nal** (al′bə nəl), *adj.*

Al·bi·nus (al bī′nəs), *n.* Alcuin.

Al·bi·on (al′bē ən), *n.* *Archaic.* Britannia (def. 1).

al·bite (al′bīt), *n.* *Mineral.* the light-colored, sodium-bearing member of the plagioclase feldspar group. [< L *alb(us)* white + -ITE[1]] —**al·bit·ic** (al bit′ik), *adj.*

Al·boin (al′boin, -bō in), *n.* died A.D. 573?, king of the Langobards 561?–573?.

Al·borg (ôl′bôrg), *n.* a seaport in NE Jutland, in Denmark. 96,438 (1960). Also, **Aalborg.**

al·bum (al′bəm), *n.* **1.** a book consisting of blank leaves, pockets, envelopes, etc., for keeping photographs, stamps, or the like. **2.** a long-playing phonograph record or set of records. **3.** the container for such a record or records. **4.** a visitors' register. [< L: neut. sing. of *albus* white]

al·bu·men (al byōō′mən), *n.* **1.** the white of an egg. **2.** *Bot.* the nutritive matter around the embryo in a seed. **3.** *Biochem.* albumin. [< L = *alb(us)* white + *-ū-* connective + *-men* n. suffix]

al·bu·me·nize (al byōō′mə nīz′), *v.t.,* **-nized, -niz·ing.** to treat with an albuminous solution. —**al·bu′me·ni·za′tion,** *n.* —**al·bu′me·niz′er,** *n.*

al·bu·min (al byōō′mən), *n.* *Biochem.* any of a class of water-soluble proteins composed of nitrogen, carbon, hydrogen, oxygen, and sulfur, occurring in animal and vegetable juices and tissues. Also, **albumen.** [ALBUM(EN) + -IN[2]] —**al·bu·mi·nous** (al byōō′mə nəs), **al·bu·mi·nose** (al byōō′mə nōs′), *adj.*

al·bu·mi·nate (al byōō′mə nāt′), *n.* *Biochem.* a compound resulting from the action of an alkali or an acid upon albumin.

al·bu·mi·noid (al byōō′mə noid′), *Biochem.* —*n.* **1.** any of a class of simple proteins, as keratin or gelatin, that are insoluble in all neutral solvents. **2.** scleroprotein. —*adj.* **3.** resembling albumen or albumin. —**al·bu′mi·noi′dal,** *adj.*

al·bu·mi·nu·ri·a (al byōō′mə nŏŏr′ē ə, -nyŏŏr′-), *n.* *Pathol.* albumin in the urine. —**al·bu′mi·nu′ric,** *adj.*

al·bu·mose (al′byə mōs′), *n.* *Biochem.* any of a class of compounds derived from proteins by enzymatic hydrolysis. [ALBUM(IN) + -OSE[2]]

Al·bu·quer·que (al′bə kûr′kē; *for 1 also Port.* ôl′bŏŏ kerʹ-kə), *n.* **1. Af·fon·so de** (ə fôn′sŏŏ də), 1453–1515, founder of the Portuguese empire in the East. **2.** a city in central New Mexico. 243,751 (1970).

al·bur·num (al bûr′nəm), *n.* *Bot.* sapwood. [< L = *alb(us)* white + *-urnum* neut. n. suffix] —**al·bur′nous,** *adj.*

Al·cae·us (al sē′əs), *n.* fl. c600 B.C., Greek poet of Mytilene.

al·ca·hest (al′kə hest′), *n.* alkahest.

Al·ca·ic (al kā′ik), *adj.* **1.** pertaining to Alcaeus or to metrical and strophic forms used by him. —*n.* **2. Alcaics,** verses or strophes written in the Alcaic form. [< LL *Alcaic(us)* < Gk *Alkaïkós*]

al·cai·de (al kī′dē; *Sp.* äl kī′the), *n., pl.* **-cai·des** (-kī′dēz; *Sp.* -kī′thes). (in Spain, Portugal, Southwestern U.S., etc.) **1.** a commander of a fortress. **2.** a jailer or prison warden. [< Sp < Ar *al-qā'id* the chief]

al·cal·de (al kal′dē; *Sp.* äl käl′de), *n., pl.* **-des** (-dēz; *Sp.* -des). (in Spain and Southwestern U.S.) a mayor having judicial powers. Also, **al·cade** (al kād′). [< Sp < Ar *al qāḍī* the judge]

Al′can High′way (al′kan). See **Alaska Highway.**

Al·ca·traz (al′kə traz′), *n.* an island in W California, in San Francisco Bay: former site of a U.S. penitentiary.

Al·cá·zar (al′kə zär′, al kaz′ər; *Sp.* äl kä′thär), *n.* **1.** the palace of the Moorish kings at Seville. **2.** (*l.c.*) a castle or fortress of the Spanish Moors. [< Sp < Ar *al* the + *qaṣr* < L *castr(um)* CASTLE, stronghold]

Al·ces·tis (al ses′tis), *n.* *Class. Myth.* the wife of Admetus who agreed to die in place of her husband and later was brought back from Hades by Hercules.

alchem., alchemy.

al·che·mise (al′kə mīz′), *v.t.,* **-mised, -mis·ing.** *Chiefly Brit.* alchemize.

al·che·mist (al′kə mist), *n.* a person who is versed in or practices alchemy. [prob. < ML *alchymist(a)*]

al·che·mize (al′kə mīz′), *v.t.,* **-mized, -miz·ing.** to change by alchemy; transmute, as metals. Also, *esp. Brit.,* **alchemise.**

al·che·my (al′kə mē), *n., pl.* **-mies** for 2. **1.** a medieval form of chemistry, aiming chiefly at discovering methods for transmuting baser metals into gold and finding a universal solvent and an elixir of life. **2.** magic or a magic appeal. [earlier *alchimie* < ML *alchymia* < Ar *al* the + *kīmiyā'* < Gk *kēmeîa* transmutation; r. ME *alconomye* = *alk(imie)* + *(astr)onomye* ASTRONOMY] —**al·chem·ic** (al kem′ik), **al·chem′i·cal, al·che·mis·tic** (al′kə mis′tik), **al′che·mis′ti·cal,** *adj.* —**al·chem′i·cal·ly,** *adv.*

Al·chuine (al′kwin), *n.* Alcuin.

Al·ci·bi·a·des (al′sə bī′ə dēz′), *n.* 450?–404 B.C., Athenian politician and general. —**Al′ci·bi′a·de′an,** *adj.*

Al·cin·o·üs (al sin′ō əs), *n.* (in the *Odyssey*) king of the Phaeacians and father of Nausicaä.

Alc·me·ne (alk mē′nē), *n.* *Class. Myth.* the mother of Hercules.

al·co·hol (al′kə hôl′, -hol′), *n.* **1.** Also called **ethyl alcohol, grain alcohol, ethanol.** a colorless, volatile, flammable liquid C_2H_5OH, the intoxicating principle of fermented liquors, produced by fermentation of certain carbohydrates, as grains, molasses, starch, or sugar, or obtained synthetically by hydration of ethylene or as a by-product of certain hydrocarbon syntheses: used chiefly as a solvent, in beverages, medicines, organic synthesis, lotions, colognes, as an antifreeze, and as a rocket fuel. **2.** any intoxicating liquor containing this liquid. **3.** *Chem.* any of a class of chemical compounds having the general formula ROH, where R represents an alkyl group and –OH a hydroxyl group, as in methyl alcohol, CH_3OH, or ethyl alcohol, C_2H_5OH. Also called, *esp. Brit.,* **spirit.** [< NL < ML < Ar *al-kuḥul* the powdered antimony, the distillate]

al·co·hol·ic (al′kə hô′lik, -hol′ik), *adj.* **1.** of, pertaining to, or caused by alcohol. **2.** containing, using, or preserved in alcohol. **3.** suffering from alcoholism. —*n.* **4.** *Pathol.* a person suffering from alcoholism. **5.** a person addicted to intoxicating drinks. —**al′co·hol′i·cal·ly,** *adv.*

al·co·hol·ic·i·ty (al′kə hô lis′i tē, -ho-), *n.* alcoholic quality or strength.

Alcohol′ics Anon′ymous, *U.S.* a fellowship formed by alcoholics to achieve sobriety. *Abbr.:* AA, A.A.

al·co·hol·ise (al′kə hô līz′, -ho-), *v.t.,* **-ised, -is·ing.** *Chiefly Brit.* alcoholize. —**al′co·hol′i·sa′tion,** *n.*

al·co·hol·ism (al′kə hô liz′əm, -ho-), *n.* *Pathol.* a diseased condition due to the excessive use of alcoholic beverages.

al·co·hol·ize (al′kə hô līz′, -ho-), *v.t.,* **-ized, -iz·ing.** to place under the influence of alcoholic beverages; besot. Also, *esp. Brit.,* **alcoholise.** —**al′co·hol′i·za′tion,** *n.*

al·co·hol·om·e·ter (al′kə hô lom′i tər, -ho-), *n.* an instrument for measuring the alcoholic content of a liquid.

Al·co·ran (al′kō rän′, -ran′, -kô-), *n.* Alkoran. —**Al′co·ran′ic,** *adj.*

Al·cott (ôl′kət, -kot), *n.* **1. (Amos) Bron·son** (bron′sən), 1799–1888, U.S. philosopher, writer, and reformer. **2.** his daughter, **Louisa May,** 1832–88, U.S. writer.

al·cove (al′kōv), *n.* **1.** a recess adjacent to or opening out of a room. **2.** a recess in a room for a bed, bookcase, etc. **3.** any recessed space, as in a garden. [< F *alcôve* < Sp *alcoba* < Ar *al* the + *qobbah,* var. of *qubbah* arch, vaulted room]

Al·cuin (al′kwin), *n.* (*Ealhwine Flaccus*) A.D. 735–804, English theologian and scholar: teacher and adviser of Charlemagne. Also, **Alchuine.** Also called **Albinus.**

Al·cy·o·ne (al sī′ə nē′), *n.* **1.** a third-magnitude star, the brightest star in the Pleiades. **2.** Also, **Halcyon.** *Class. Myth.* a daughter of Aeolus, transformed into a kingfisher.

Ald., alderman. Also, **ald.**

Al·dan (äl dän′), *n.* a river in the Soviet Union in Asia. ab. 1500 mi. long.

Al·deb·a·ran (al deb′ər ən), *n.* a first-magnitude star, orange in color, in the constellation Taurus. [< Ar *al* the + *dabarān* follower (of the Pleiades)]

al·de·hyde (al′də hīd′), *n.* *Chem.* any of a class of organic compounds containing the group –CHO, which yields acids when oxidized and alcohols when reduced. [< NL *al(cohol) dehyd(rogenātum)* dehydrogenated alcohol] —**al′de·hy′dic,** *adj.*

Al·den (ôl′dən, -dən), *n.* **John,** 1599?–1687, Pilgrim settler in Plymouth, Massachusetts, 1620.

al dente (äl′ den′te), *Italian.* neither too soft nor too firm to the bite. [lit., to the tooth.]

al·der (ôl′dər), *n.* any betulaceous shrub or tree of the genus *Alnus,* growing in moist places in northern or colder regions. [ME *alder, aller,* OE *alor, al(e)r;* akin to OHG *elira, erila* (G *Erle*), Russ *ólicha,* L *alnus*]

al·der·man (ôl′dər mən), *n., pl.* **-men.** **1.** a member of a municipal legislative body; councilman. **2.** (in England) one of the members in a borough or county council. **3.** *Early Eng. Hist.* a chief. [ME; OE *(e)aldormann* = *ealdor* chief, patriarch (*eald* OLD + *-or* n. suffix) + *mann* MAN[1]] —**al′der·man·cy, al′der·man·ship′,** *n.*

al·der·man·ic (ôl′dər man′ik), *adj.* of or characteristic of an alderman or aldermen.

Al·der·ney (ôl′dər nē), *n.* one of the Channel Islands in the English Channel. 1449 (1961); 3 sq. mi.

Al·der·shot (ôl′dər shot′), *n.* a city in S England, SW of London. 33,690 (est. 1964): military training center.

Al·dine (ôl′dīn, -dēn), *adj.* **1.** of or from the press of Aldus Manutius and his family in Venice, c1490–1597, noted chiefly for compactly printed editions of the classics. —*n.* **2.** an Aldine or other early edition. **3.** any of several styles of printing types modeled on those designed by Aldus, esp. italic. [< It *aldin(o),* named after *Ald(o Manuzio);* see MANUTIUS, ALDUS, -INE[1]]

Al·ding·ton (ôl′ding tən), *n.* **Richard,** 1892–1962, English poet and novelist.

Aldm., alderman. Also, **aldm.**

al·dol (al′dôl), *n.* *Chem.* a syrupy liquid, $CH_3CHOHCH_2CHO$, used chiefly in the manufacture of vulcanizers and in perfumery. [ALD(EHYDE) + -OL]

al·dose (al′dōs), *n.* *Chem.* a sugar containing the aldehyde group or its equivalent. [ALD(EHYDE) + -OSE[2]]

al·do·ste·rone (al′dō sti rōn′, al′dō sti rōn′, al dos′tə-rōn′), *n.* *Biochem.* a hormone produced by the cortex of the adrenal gland, instrumental in the regulation of sodium and potassium reabsorption by the cells of the tubular portion of the kidney. [ALD(EHYDE) + -O- + STER(OL) + -ONE]

Al·drich (ôl′drich), *n.* **Thomas Bai·ley** (bā′lē), 1836–1907, U.S. writer.

al·drin (ôl′drin), *n.* *Chem.* a toxic solid more than 95 percent of which is the chlorinated hydrocarbon $C_{12}H_8Cl_6$: used as an insecticide. [named after Kurt *Alder* (1902–58), German chemist; see -IN[2]]

Al·dus Ma·nu·ti·us (ôl′dəs mə nōō′shē əs, -nyōō′-, al′-dəs). See **Manutius, Aldus.**

ale (āl), *n.* a malt beverage, darker, heavier, and more bitter than beer, containing about 6 percent alcohol by volume. [ME; OE *(e)alu;* c. OS *alu,* Icel *öl*]

a·le·a·tor·ic (ā′lē ə tôr′ik, -tor′-), *adj.* **1.** *Music.* employing elements of chance or indeterminacy in the choice of notes. **2.** aleatory (def. 2).

a·le·a·to·ry (ā′lē ə tōr′ē, -tôr′ē), *adj.* **1.** *Law.* (of a contract) depending on a contingent event. **2.** by or employing or pertaining to luck or chance; unpredictable. **3.** aleatoric (def. 1). [< L *āleātōri(us)* = *āleātor-* (s. of *āleātor*) gambler (*ālea* game of dice + *-āt-* -ATE[1] + *-ōr-* -OR[2]) + *-ius* adj. suffix]

al·ec (al′ik), *n.* *Obs.* **1.** a herring. **2.** a sauce or relish made from small herring or anchovies. [< L]

A·lec·to (ə lek′tō), *n.* *Rom. Myth.* one of the Furies.

a·lee (ə lē′), *adv., adj.* *Naut.* upon or toward the lee side of a vessel (opposed to *aweather*).

al·e·gar (al′ə gər, ā′lə-), *n.* *Brit. Informal.* ale vinegar; sour ale. [ALE + (VIN)EGAR]

ale·house (āl′hous′), *n., pl.* **-hous·es** (-hou′ziz). a tavern where ale is sold.

A·lei·chem (ä lā′KHem), *n.* **Sho·lom** (shô′ləm) or **Sho·lem** shō′lem, -ləm) or **Sha·lom** (shä lōm′), (pen name of *Solomon Rabinowitz*), 1859–1916, Russian author of Yiddish novels, plays, and short stories; in the U.S. from 1906.

A·le·ksan·dro·pol (*Russ.* ä le′ksän drô′pol), *n.* former name of **Leninakan.**

A·le·ksan·drovsk (*Russ.* ä′le ksän′drofsk), *n.* former name of **Zaporozhe.**

A·le·mán (ä′le män′), *n.* **1. Ma·te·o** (mä te′ô), 1547?–1610, Spanish novelist. **2. Mi·guel** (mē gel′), born 1902, president of Mexico 1946–52.

Al·e·man·ni (al′ə man′ī), *n.pl.* a confederation of Germanic tribes, first recorded in the 3rd century A.D., that settled in the area between the Rhine, Main, and Danube rivers. Also, **Alamanni.** [< L, of Gmc orig.; c. Goth *alamans* totality of mankind]

Al·e·man·nic (al′ə man′ik), *n.* **1.** the high German speech of Switzerland, Alsace, and southwestern Germany. Cf. **Bavarian** (def. 3). —*adj.* **2.** of, pertaining to, or belonging to Alemannic or the Alemanni. [< L *Alamannic(us)*]

A·lem·bert, d' (dal′əm bâr′; *Fr.* dA-läN beR′), **Jean Le Rond** (zhäN lə rôN′), 1717?–83, French mathematician, philosopher, and writer.

a·lem·bic (ə lem′bik), *n.* **1.** a vessel with a beaked cap or head, formerly used in distilling. **2.** anything that transforms, purifies, or refines. [ME, var. of *alambic* < ML *alambic(us)* < Ar *al* the + *anbīq* still < Gk *ámbix* cup]

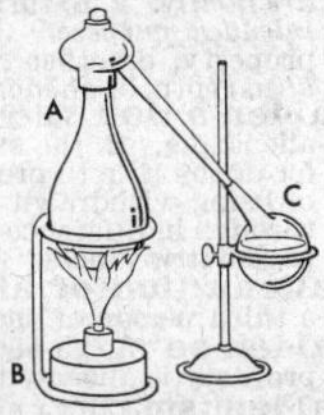

A, Alembic
B, Lamp
C, Receiver

A·len·çon (A läN sôN′; *Eng.* ə len′sən, -son), *n.* a city in NW France: lace manufacture. 27,024 (1962).

Alen′çon lace′ (ə len′sən, -son; *Fr.* A läN sôN′), a delicate lace having a solid design on a background of hexagonal mesh. Also called **point d'Alençon.**

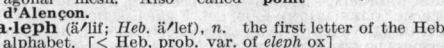

a·leph (ä′lif; *Heb.* ä′lef), *n.* the first letter of the Hebrew alphabet. [< Heb, prob. var. of *eleph* ox]

a·leph-null (ä′lef nul′, ä′lif-), *n.* *Math.* the cardinal number of the set of all positive integers; the smallest infinite cardinal number. *Symbol:* $\aleph_0$ Also called **a·leph-ze·ro** (ä′lef zēr′ō, ä′lif-).

A·lep·po (ə lep′ō), *n.* a city in NW Syria. 425,000 (est. 1960). French, **A·lep** (A lep′).

a·lert (ə lûrt′), *adj.* **1.** vigilantly attentive; keen: *an alert mind.* **2.** agile; nimble: *alert movements.* —*n.* **3.** an attitude of vigilance or caution, as before an expected attack. **4.** a warning or alarm of an impending military attack, storm, etc. **5.** the period during which such a warning or alarm is in effect. **6. on the alert,** on guard against danger; vigilant: *on the alert for an escaped convict.* —*v.t.* **7.** to warn (troops, ships, etc.) to prepare for action. **8.** to warn of an impending attack, storm, etc. **9.** to advise or warn; cause to be on guard (often fol. by *to*): *to alert a community to the dangers of inflation.* [< It *all'erta* = *all(a)* to the + *erta* lookout, watchtower, orig. fem. of *erto,* ptp. of *ergere* < L *ērigere* to ERECT] —**a·lert′ly,** *adv.* —**a·lert′ness,** *n.*
—**Syn. 1.** aware, wary, observant. ALERT, VIGILANT, WATCHFUL imply a wide-awake attitude, as of someone keenly aware of his surroundings. ALERT describes a ready and prompt attentiveness together with a quick intelligence: *The visitor was alert and eager to see the points of interest.* VIGILANT suggests necessity for keen, active observation, and for continuing alertness: *Knowing the danger, the scout was unceasingly vigilant.* WATCHFUL suggests carefulness and preparedness: *watchful waiting.* **2.** brisk, lively, quick.

-ales, *Bot.* a suffix of names of orders: *Cycadales.* [< L, pl. of *-ālis* -AL[1]]

A·les·san·dria (ä′les sän′drYä), *n.* a city in NW Italy, in Piedmont. 92,291 (1961).

Å·le·sund (ô′lə sŏŏn′), *n.* a seaport in W Norway. 18,883 (est. 1965). Also, **Aalesund.**

al·eu·rone (al′yə rōn′, ə lŏŏr′ōn), *n.* (in the seeds of cereal plants) protein granules **(al′eurone grains′)** found in a single layer of cells **(al′eurone lay′er)** in the outermost portion of the endosperm. Also, **al·eu·ron** (al′yə ron′, ə lŏŏr′on). [< Gk *áleuron* flour, meal] —**al·eu·ron·ic** (al′yŏŏ ron′ik), *adj.*

Al·eut (ə lōōt′, al′ē ōōt′), *n.* **1.** Also, **Aleutian.** a native of the Aleutian Islands. **2.** either of two related languages spoken by the Aleuts.

A·leu·tian (ə lōō′shən), *adj.* **1.** of or pertaining to the Aleutian Islands. —*n.* **2.** Aleut (def. 1).

Aleu′tian cur′rent, a current in the Pacific Ocean that flows eastward between latitudes 40° and 50° N.

Aleu′tian Is′lands, an archipelago extending SW from the Alaska Peninsula: part of Alaska. Also called **A·leu′tians.**

ale·wife[1] (āl′wīf′), *n., pl.* **-wives.** a North American fish, *Pomolobus* (or *Alosa*) *pseudoharengus,* resembling a small shad. [?]

ale·wife[2] (āl′wīf′), *n., pl.* **-wives.** a woman who owns or operates an alehouse. [ALE + WIFE]

al·ex·an·der (al′ig zan′dər, -zän′-), *n.* (*often cap.*) a cocktail made with crème de cacao, gin or brandy, and cream. [prob. after the proper name]

Al·ex·an·der (al′ig zan′dər, -zän′-), *n.* **1.** See **Alexander the Great. 2. Earl Harold R. L. G.** (*Alexander of Tunis*), 1891–1969, English field marshal: governor general of Canada 1946–52; minister of defense 1952–54. **3. Hartley Burr,** 1873–1939, U.S. philosopher and educator.

Alexander I, 1. Saint, pope A.D. 106?–115. **2.** (*Aleksandr Pavlovich*) 1777–1825, czar of Russia 1801–25. **3.** 1888–1934, king of Yugoslavia 1921–34 (son of Peter I of Serbia).

Alexander I Island, an island off Antarctica.

Alexander II, 1. died 1073, Italian ecclesiastic: pope 1061–73. **2.** (*Aleksandr Nikolaevich*) 1818–81, czar of Russia 1855–81.

Alexander III, 1. died 1181, Italian ecclesiastic: pope 1159–81. **2.** (*Aleksandr Aleksandrovich*) 1845–94, czar of Russia 1881–94.

Alexander IV, (*Rinaldo Conti*) died 1261, Italian ecclesiastic: pope 1254–61.

Alexander V, 1340?–1410, Cretan ecclesiastic: pope 1409–10.

Alexander VI, (*Rodrigo Borgia*) 1431?–1503, Spanish ecclesiastic: pope 1492–1503 (father of Cesare and Lucrezia Borgia).

Alexander VII, (*Fabio Chigi*) 1599–1667, Italian ecclesiastic: pope 1655–67.

Alexander VIII, (*Pietro Ottoboni*) 1610–91, Italian ecclesiastic: pope 1689–91.

Alexan′der Archipel′ago, an archipelago off the coast of SE Alaska.

Alexan′der Nev′ski (nev′skē, nef′-), 1220?–63, Russian prince, national hero, and saint.

Alexan′der the Great′, 356–323 B.C., king of Macedonia 336–323: conqueror of Greek city-states and of the Persian empire.

Al·ex·an·dra (al′ig zan′drə, -zän′-), *n.* 1844–1925, queen consort of Edward VII of England.

Al·ex·an·dret·ta (al′ig zan dret′ə, -zän-), *n.* former name of **Iskenderun.**

Al·ex·an·dri·a (al′ig zan′drē ə, -zän′-), *n.* **1.** Arabic, **Al-Iskandarīyah.** a seaport in N Egypt, on the Nile Delta: founded by Alexander the Great in 332 B.C. 1,587,700 (est. 1962). **2.** a city in NE Virginia, S of the District of Columbia. 110,938 (1970). **3.** a city in central Louisiana, on the Red River. 41,557 (1970).

Al·ex·an·dri·an (al′ig zan′drē ən, -zän′-), *adj.* **1.** of Alexandria, Egypt. **2.** Alexandrine. —*n.* **3.** a native or inhabitant of Alexandria, Egypt.

Al·ex·an·drine (al′ig zan′drin, -drēn, -zän′-), (*often l.c.*) *Pros.* —*n.* **1.** a verse or line of poetry of twelve syllables. —*adj.* **2.** of or pertaining to such a verse or line. [< MF *alexandrin,* after *Alexandre,* from the use of this meter in an Old French poem on Alexander the Great; see -INE[1]]

Al·ex·an·drine (al′ig zan′drin, -drēn, -zän′-,) *adj.* of or pertaining to Alexandria, Egypt. [ALEXANDR(IA) + -INE[1]]

al·ex·an·drite (al′ig zan′drīt, -zän′-), *n.* a variety of chrysoberyl, green by daylight and red-violet by artificial light, used as a gem. [named after ALEXANDER I of Russia; see -ITE[1]]

A·le·xan·drou·po·lis (ä′le ksän drōō′pô lēs), *n.* a seaport in W Thrace, in NE Greece. 18,453 (1950). Formerly, **Dede Agach.**

a·lex·i·a (ə lek′sē ə), *n.* *Psychiatry.* a cerebral disorder marked by inability to understand written matter. [A-[6] + Gk *léx(is)* speech (*lég-* s. of *légein* to speak + *-sis* -SIS) + -IA; altered meaning by assoc. of *-lex-* with LEXICON, etc.]

a·lex·i·phar·mic (ə lek′sə fär′mik), *Med.* —*adj.* **1.** warding off poisoning or infection; prophylactic. —*n.* **2.** an alexipharmic agent. [obs. *alexipharm(ac)* antidote (< Gk *alexiphármakon* = *alexi-* averter + *phármakon* poison + -IC]

A·lex·is Mi·khai·lo·vich (ə lek′sis mə kī′lə vich; *Russ.* mi KHī′lo vich), (*Aleksey Mikhailovich*) 1629–76, czar of Russia 1645–76.

A·lex·i·us I (ə lek′sē əs), (*Alexius Comnenus*) 1048–1118, emperor of the Byzantine Empire 1081–1118.

alfa (al′fə), *n.* a word used in communications to represent the letter *A.* [var. spelling of ALPHA]

al·fal·fa (al fal′fə), *n.* a European leguminous plant, *Medicago sativa,* grown for forage in the U.S. [< Sp, var. of *alfalfez* < SpAr *al* the + *faṣfaṣah* lucerne]

Al·fie·ri (äl fye′Rē), *n.* **Count Vit·to·rio** (vēt tô′Ryô), 1749–1803, Italian dramatist and poet.

al·fil·a·ri·a (al fil′ə rē′ə), *n.* a geraniaceous herb, *Erodium cicutarium,* grown for forage. [< Sp *alfilerillo* = *alfiler* pin (< Ar *al khilāl* the thorn) + *-illo* dim. suffix]

Al·fon·so X (al fon′sō, -zō; *Sp.* äl fôn′sô), ("*Alfonso the Wise*") 1221–84, king of Castile and León 1252–84.

Alfonso XIII, 1886–1941, king of Spain 1886–1931.

al·for·ja (al fôr′jə; *Sp.* äl fôR′hä), *n., pl.* **-jas** (-jəz; *Sp.* -häs). *Southwestern U.S.* a leather bag; saddlebag. [< Sp < Ar *al* the + *khorj,* var. of *khurj* pair of saddlebags]

Al′fred the Great′ (al′fred, -frid), A.D. 849–899, king of the West Saxons 871–899.

al·fres·co (al fres′kō), *adv., adj.* out-of-doors; open air: *to dine alfresco; an alfresco café.* Also, **al fres′co.** [< It: in the cool. See FRESH]

Alg., **1.** Algerian. **2.** Algiers.

alg., algebra.

ALG, See **antilymphocyte globulin.**

al·ga (al′gə), *n., pl.* **-gae** (-jē). any of numerous chlorophyll-containing plants of the phylum *Thallophyta,* ranging from unicellular to multicellular forms, occurring in fresh or salt water. [< L: seaweed] —**al′gal,** *adj.* —**al·goid** (al′goid), *adj.*

al·gar·ro·ba (al′gə rō′bə), *n.* **1.** any of certain mesquites, esp. *Prosopis juliflora.* **2.** the beanlike pod of this plant. **3.** the carob tree or fruit. Also, **al′ga·ro′ba.** [< Sp < Ar *al* the + *kharrūba* CAROB]

Al-Ga·zel (al′gə zel′), *n.* Ghazzali.

al·ge·bra (al′jə brə), *n.* **1.** the branch of mathematics that deals with general statements of relations, utilizing letters and other symbols to represent specific numbers, values, vectors, etc., in the description of such relations. **2.** any special system of notation adapted to the study of a special system of relationship: *algebra of classes.* [< ML < Ar *al* the + *jebr*, var. of *jabr* bonesetting]

al·ge·bra·ic (al′jə brā′ik), *adj.* of, occurring in, or utilizing algebra or the symbols of algebra. Also, **al′ge·bra′i·cal.** —**al′ge·bra′i·cal·ly,** *adv.*

algebra′ic equa′tion, *Math.* an equation in the form of a polynomial having a finite number of terms and equated to zero, as $3x^3 + 2x^2 + x = 0$.

al′gebra′ic num′ber, *Math.* **1.** a root of an algebraic equation with integral coefficients. **2.** root[1] (def. 10b).

al·ge·bra·ist (al′jə brā′ist), *n.* an expert in algebra.

Al·ge·ci·ras (al′ji sir′əs; *Sp.* äl′he thē′räs), *n.* a seaport in S Spain, on the Strait of Gibraltar. 42,728 (est. 1960).

Al·ger (al′jər), *n.* **Ho·ra·ti·o** (hə rā′shē ō′, ho-, hô-), 1834–1899, U.S. author of a series of books for boys.

Al·ge·ri·a (al jēr′ē ə), *n.* a republic in NW Africa: formerly part of France; gained independence 1962. 16,200,000; 919,595 sq. mi. *Cap.:* Algiers.

Al·ge·ri·an (al jēr′ē ən), *adj.* **1.** of or pertaining to Algeria or its inhabitants. —*n.* **2.** a native or inhabitant of Algeria.

al·ge·rine (al′jə rēn′), *n.* a pirate. [ALGER(IA) + -INE[1]]

Al·ghe·ro (äl gâr′ō), *n.* a seaport in W Sardinia. 26,666.

Al-Ghaz·za·li (al′ga zä′lē), *n.* Ghazzali.

-algia, var. of **algo-** as final element of a compound word: *neuralgia.* Also, **-algy.** [< NL < Gk; see ALGO-, -IA]

al·gid (al′jid), *adj.* cold; chilly. [< L *algid(us)* cold] —**al·gid′i·ty, al′gid·ness,** *n.*

Al·giers (al jērz′), *n.* **1.** a seaport in and the capital of Algeria, in the N part. 1,839,000. **2.** one of the former Barbary States in N Africa: now modern Algeria.

al·gin (al′jin), *n. Chem.* any hydrophilic, colloidal substance found in or obtained from various kelps. [ALG(A) + -IN[2]]

algo-, a learned borrowing from Greek meaning "pain," used in the formation of compound words: *algophobia.* [comb. form repr. Gk *álgos*]

Al·gol (al′gol), *n.* an eclipsing binary star of the second magnitude in the constellation Perseus. [< Ar = *al* the + *ghūl* GHOUL]

ALGOL (al′gol, -gôl), *n. Computer Technol.* a programming language for the explicit formulation of algorithms and with extensive algebraic notation. [*Algo(rithmic) L(anguage)*]

al·go·lag·ni·a (al′gə lag′nē ə), *n. Psychiatry.* sexual pleasure derived from enduring or inflicting pain, as in masochism or sadism. [< NL] —**al′go·lag′nic,** *adj.* —**al′go·lag′nist,** *n.*

al·gol·o·gy (al gol′ə jē), *n.* the branch of botany dealing with algae. —**al·go·log·i·cal** (al′gə loj′i kəl), *adj.* —**al·gol′o·gist,** *n.*

al·gom·e·ter (al gom′i tər), *n.* a device for measuring sensitivity to pain produced by pressure. —**al·go·met·ric** (al′gə me′trik), **al′go·met′ri·cal,** *adj.* —**al′go·met′ri·cal·ly,** *adv.* —**al·gom′e·try,** *n.*

Al·gon·ki·an (al goṅg′kē ən), *adj.* **1.** *Geol.* Proterozoic (def. 1). **2.** Algonquian. —*n.* **3.** *Geol.* Proterozoic (def. 2). **4.** Algonquian.

Al·gon·kin (al goṅg′kin), *n., pl.* **-kins,** (*esp. collectively*) **-kin,** *adj.* —*n.* **1.** Algonquin. **2.** Algonquian. —*adj.* **3.** Algonquian. **4.** Algonquin.

Al·gon·qui·an (al goṅg′kē ən, -kwē ən), *n., pl.* **-ans,** (*esp. collectively*) **-an** for 2, *adj.* —*n.* **1.** a family of languages spoken by North American Indians in an area extending from Labrador to Cape Hatteras and westward to the Rocky Mountains and including Arapaho, Blackfoot, Cheyenne, Cree, Fox, Massachuset, Micmac, and Ojibwa. **2.** a member of an Algonquian tribe. —*adj.* **3.** of or pertaining to Algonquian. Also, **Algonkian, Algonkin, Algonquin.**

Al·gon·quin (al goṅg′kin, -kwin), *n., pl.* **-quins,** (*esp. collectively*) **-quin** for 1, 3, *adj.* —*n.* **1.** a member of a group of Algonquian-speaking tribes formerly along the Ottawa River and the northern tributaries of the St. Lawrence. **2.** their speech, a dialect of Ojibwa. **3.** Algonquian. —*adj.* **4.** Algonquian. Also, **Algonkin.** [< F, var. of *algoumaqin* after native place-name; cf. Micmac *algūmaking* fishing-place]

Algon′quin Park′, a provincial park in S Canada, in SE Ontario. 2741 sq. mi.

al·go·pho·bi·a (al′gə fō′bē ə), *n. Psychiatry.* an abnormal dread of pain.

al·gor (al′gôr), *n. Pathol.* chill, esp. at the onset of fever. [< L: coldness = *alg-* (base of *algidus* algid) + *-or* -OR[1]]

al·go·rism (al′gə riz′əm), *n.* **1.** the Arabic system of arithmetical notation (with the figures 1, 2, 3, etc.). **2.** the method of computation with Arabic figures, 1 to 9, plus the zero; arithmetic. **3.** algorithm. [< ML *algorism(us)* < Ar *al* the + *kh(u)wārizmī* (surname of a 9th-century Muslim mathematician) = *khwārizm* KHIVA + *-ī* -AN; r. ME *augrim*, etc. < MF] —**al′go·ris′mic,** *adj.*

al·go·rithm (al′gə rith′əm), *n.* a set of rules for solving a problem in a finite number of steps, as for finding the greatest common divisor. Also, **algorism.** [var. of ALGORISM, by assoc. with Gk *arithmós* number. See ARITHMETIC] —**al′go·rith′mic,** *adj.*

-algy, var. of **-algia.**

Al·ham·bra (al ham′brə), *n.* **1.** a palace of the Moorish kings in Granada, Spain: completed in the 14th century. **2.** a city in SW California, near Los Angeles. 62,125 (1970).

A·li (ä′lē, ä lē′ *for 1,2;* ä lē′ *for 3*), *n.* **1.** (*Ali ibn-abu-Talib*) ("*the Lion of God*") A.D. c600–661, Arab caliph (cousin and son-in-law of Muhammad). **2.** See **Mehemet Ali. 3. Muhammad** (*Cassius Marcellus Clay, Jr.*), born 1942, U.S. boxer: world heavyweight champion 1964–67, 1974–78, 1978–79.

a·li·as (ā′lē əs), *n., pl.* **-as·es,** *adv.* —*n.* **1.** an assumed name, esp. as used by a criminal; another name: *Simpson used "Smith" as an alias.* —*adv.* **2.** at another time; in another place; in other circumstances; otherwise. "Simpson *alias* Smith" means that Simpson in other circumstances has called himself Smith. [< L (adv.)]

al·i·bi (al′ə bī′), *n., pl.* **-bis,** *v.* —*n.* **1.** *Law.* the defense by an accused person that he was elsewhere at the time the offense with which he is charged was committed. **2.** *U.S. Informal.* an excuse. —*v.i.* **3.** *Informal.* to give an excuse; offer a defense: *to alibi for being late.* —*v.t.* **4.** *Informal.* to provide an alibi for (someone): *He alibied his friend out of a fix.* [< L (adv.): in or at another place]

Al·i·can·te (al′ə kan′tē; *Sp.* ä′lē kän′te), *n.* a seaport in SE Spain, on the Mediterranean. 111,875 (est. 1960).

al·i·dade (al′i dād′), *n. Survey.* **1.** (in plane-tabling) a straightedge having a telescopic sight or other means of sighting parallel to it. **2.** *U.S.* the entire upper part of a theodolite or transit. Also, **al·i·dad** (al′i dad′). [var. of *alhidade* < ML *alhidada* < Ar *al* the + *'idadah* turning radius; r. late ME *allydatha* (? < Sp *alhidada*)]

al·ien (āl′yən, ā′lē ən), *n.* **1.** a person born in and owing allegiance to a country other than the one in which he lives (distinguished from *citizen*). **2.** a foreign-born inhabitant of a nation. **3.** a person who has been estranged or excluded. **4.** a nonterrestrial being. —*adj.* **5.** residing in a country other than that of one's birth without having or obtaining rights of citizenship there. **6.** belonging or relating to aliens: *alien property.* **7.** foreign; strange: *alien philosophy.* **8.** nonterrestrial. [ME < L *aliēn(us)* = *ali(us)* other + *-ēnus* adj. suffix; see -ENE] —**Syn. 2.** See **stranger. 3.** outcast.

al·ien·a·ble (āl′yə nə bəl, ā′lē ə-), *adj. Law.* capable of being sold or transferred. —**al′ien·a·bil′i·ty,** *n.*

al·ien·age (āl′yə nij, ā′lē ə-), *n.* **1.** the state of being an alien. **2.** the legal status of an alien. Also called **alienism.**

al·ien·ate (āl′yə nāt′, ā′lē ə-), *v.t.,* **-at·ed, -at·ing. 1.** to make indifferent or hostile; estrange: *He has alienated his entire family.* **2.** to turn away; divert: *to alienate funds from their intended purpose.* **3.** *Law.* to transfer or convey, as title, property, or other right, to another. [late ME < L *aliēnāt(us)* (ptp. of *aliēnāre*)] —**al′ien·a′tor,** *n.*

al·ien·a·tion (āl′yə nā′shən, ā′lē ə-), *n.* **1.** the act of alienating. **2.** the state of being alienated. **3.** *Law.* a transfer of the title to property to another; conveyance. **4.** state of being withdrawn or isolated from the objective world, as through indifference or disaffection. **5.** *Psychiatry.* mental or psychiatric illness. [late ME < L *aliēnātiōn-* (s. of *aliēnātiō*)]

aliena′tion of affec′tions, *Law.* the estrangement by a third person of one spouse from the other.

al·ien·ee (āl′yə nē′, ā′lē ə-), *n. Law.* a person to whom property is alienated. [obs. *alien* (v.) < ME *aliene(n)* + -EE]

al·ien·ism (āl′yə niz′əm, ā′lē ə-), *n.* **1.** alienage. **2.** the study or treatment of mental diseases, esp. with relation to legal problems.

al·ien·ist (āl′yə nist, ā′lē ə-), *n.* a physician who treats mental disorders; esp. one who specializes in related legal matters. [ALIEN(ATION) + -IST; cf. F *aliéniste* in same sense]

al·ien·or (āl′yə nər, ā′lē ə-, āl′yə nôr′, ā′lē ə-), *n. Law.* a person who transfers property. Also, **al·i·en·er** (āl′yə nər, ā′lēə-). [obs. *alien* (v.) < ME *aliene(n)* + -OR[2]; r. *alienour* < AF (c. F *aliéneur*) < L *aliēnātor.* See ALIENATE, -OR[2]]

a·lif (ä′lif), *n.* **1.** the first letter of the Arabic alphabet. **2.** *Phonet.* the glottal-stop consonant or, alternatively, long vowel represented by this letter. [< Ar; see ALEPH]

al·i·form (al′ə fôrm′, ā′lə-), *adj.* wing-shaped.

A·li·garh (ä′lē gur′, al′ə gär′), *n.* a city in W Uttar Pradesh, in N India. 185,000 (1961).

a·light[1] (ə līt′), *v.i.,* **a·light·ed** or **a·lit, a·light·ing. 1.** to dismount from a horse, descend from a vehicle, etc. **2.** to settle or stay after descending: *A bird alights on a tree.* **3.** to encounter or notice something accidentally or without design. [ME *alighte(n)*, OE *ālīhtan* = *ā-* A-[3] + *līhtan* to relieve of weight, descend (< *lēoht, līht* LIGHT[2])]

a·light[2] (ə līt′), *adv., adj.* provided with light; lighted. [now taken as A-[1] + LIGHT[1]; orig. ptp. of *alight* to light up (ME *alihte(n)*, OE *onlīhtan* = *on* A-[1] + *līhtan* to LIGHT[1])]

a·lign (ə līn′), *v.t.* **1.** to arrange or adjust in a straight line. **2.** to bring into a line. **3.** to ally (oneself) with a group, cause, etc.: *He aligned himself with the liberals.* **4.** to adjust (components of an electronic circuit) for coordinated performance. —*v.i.* **5.** to fall or come into line. **6.** to join with others in a cause. Also, **aline.** [< F *align(er)* = *a-* A-[5] + *ligner* < L *līneāre* < *līnea* LINE[1]] —**a·lign′er,** *n.*

a·lign·ment (ə līn′mənt), *n.* **1.** the act of aligning or of forming in a straight line. **2.** the line or lines so formed. **3.** the state of being aligned; arrangement in a straight line, logical sequence, etc. **4.** the proper adjustment of the components of an electronic circuit, machine, etc., for coordinated performance. **5.** the proper, logical, or expected relation of one thing to another. **6.** a ground plan, as of a highway (opposed to *profile*). Also, **alinement.** [ALIGN + -MENT; r. earlier *alignement* < F]

a·like (ə līk′), *adv.* **1.** in the same manner, form, or degree; in common; equally. —*adj.* **2.** having resemblance or similarity; having or showing no marked or important difference. [late ME *alyke* < Scand; cf. Icel *ālīkr*, c. OE *onlīc*; r. ME *ilich*, OE *gelīc*, c. G *gleich*, Icel *glīkr*] —**a·like′ness,** *n.* —**Syn. 1.** identically. **2.** akin. —**Ant. 1.** differently.

al·i·ment (*n.* al′ə mənt; *v.* al′ə ment′), *n.* **1.** something that nourishes; food. **2.** something that sustains. —*v.t.* **3.** to support. [< L *aliment(um)* = *al(ere)* to feed + *-i-* -I- + *-mentum* -MENT] —**al′i·men′tal,** *adj.* —**al′i·men′tal·ly,** *adv.* —**Syn. 1.** nourishment. **1, 2.** sustenance.

al·i·men·ta·ry (al′ə men′tə rē, -trē), *adj.* **1.** concerned with the function of nutrition. **2.** providing sustenance. [< L *alimentāri(us)*]

alimen′tary canal′, a tubular passage functioning in the digestion and absorption of food, in most animals beginning at the mouth and terminating at the anus.

al·i·men·ta·tion (al′ə men tā′shən, -mən-), *n.* **1.** nourishment; nutrition. **2.** maintenance; support. [< ML *alimentātiōn-* (s. of *alimentātiō*)]

al·i·men·ta·tive (al′ə men′tə tiv), *adj.* nourishing; nutritive. —**al′i·men′ta·tive·ly,** *adv.* —**al′i·men′ta·tive·ness,** *n.*

al·i·mo·ny (al′ə mō′nē), *n.* **1.** *Law.* an allowance paid to a person by a spouse or former spouse, granted by a court upon a legal separation or a divorce or while action is pending. **2.** supply of the means of living; maintenance. [< L *alimōnia* nourishment, sustenance = *ali-* (see ALIMENT) + *-mōnia* -MONY] —**al′i·mo′nied,** *adj.*

A′li Muham′mad of Shiraz′, Báb.

a·line (ə līn′), *v.t., v.i.*, **a·lined, a·lin·ing.** align. —**a·line′ment,** *n.* —**a·lin′er,** *n.*

A·li Pa·sha (ä′lē pä shä′), (*Arslan*) 1741–1822, Turkish pasha and ruler of Albania 1787?–1820.

al·i·ped (al′ə ped′), *Zool.* —*adj.* **1.** having the toes connected by a winglike membrane, as a bat. —*n.* **2.** an aliped animal. [< L *ālipēd-* (s. of *ālipēs* wing-footed)]

al·i·phat·ic (al′ə fat′ik), *adj. Chem.* noting organic compounds in which the carbon atoms form open chains. [< Gk *aleiphat-* (s. of *áleiphar* oil, fat) + -IC]

al·i·quant (al′ə kwənt), *adj. Math.* contained in a number or quantity, but not dividing it evenly: *An aliquant part of 16 is 5.* [< L *aliquant(us)* more or less great = *ali-* differently + *quantus* great]

al·i·quot (al′ə kwət), *adj.* **1.** *Math.* forming an exact proper divisor: *An aliquot part of 15 is 5.* **2.** *Chem.* comprising a definite part of a whole: *an aliquot quantity of acid for analysis.* —*n.* **3.** an aliquot part. [< L: some, several = *ali-* some other + *quot* as many as]

-alis, a suffix occurring in scientific names from Latin: *borealis.* [< L *-ālis;* see -AL[1]]

Al-Is·kan·da·rî·yah (äl′is kän drē′yä), *n.* Arabic name of **Alexandria.**

a·list (ə list′), *adj. Naut.* (of a vessel) heeling or listing.

a·lit (ə lit′), *v.* a pt. and pp. of **alight**[1].

Al It·ti·had (äl it′ē häd′), former name of **Medina as-Shaab.**

a·li·un·de (ā′lē un′dē), *adv., adj. Chiefly Law.* not part of or derivable from the document itself: *evidence aliunde.* [< L: from another place = *ali(us)* other + *unde* whence]

a·live (ə līv′), *adj.* **1.** having life; existing; not dead or lifeless. **2.** living (used for emphasis): *the proudest man alive.* **3.** in force or operation; active: *to keep hope alive.* **4.** full of life; lively: *She's more alive than most of her contemporaries.* **5.** full of verve; vivid; vibrant: *The room was alive with color.* **6. alive to,** alert or sensitive to; aware of: *City planners are alive to the necessity of eradicating slums.* **7. alive with,** swarming or teeming with: *The room was alive with mosquitoes.* **8. look alive!** pay attention! move quickly!: *Look alive! We don't have all day.* [ME; OE *on līfe* in LIFE] —**a·live′ness,** *n.* —**Syn. 4.** active. —**Ant. 1.** dead. **3.** defunct.

a·li·yah (ä lē′ô, ä′lē ä′), *n., pl.* **a·li·yahs, a·li·yos** (ä lē′ôs), **a·li·yot** (ä′lē ôt′). **1.** the act of proceeding to the reading table in a synagogue to recite the blessings before and after the reading of a portion from the Torah. **2.** the immigration of Jews to Israel, either as individuals or in groups. **3.** any of the major waves of Jewish immigration to Palestine and later to Israel. [< Heb: lit., act of going up]

a·liz·a·rin (ə liz′ər in), *n. Chem.* a reddish-orange or brownish-yellow solid, $C_6H_4(CO)_2C_6H_2(OH)_2$, one of the earliest known dyes: used chiefly in the synthesis of other dyes. Also, **a·liz·a·rine** (ə liz′ə rin, -rēn′). [< F *alizarine* = *alizar(i)* (< Sp < Ar *al* the + *'aṣārah* juice) + *-ine* -INE[1]]

alk-, var. of **alka-,** esp. before a vowel.

alk., alkali.

alka-, a combining form of the alkane series, used esp. before a consonant.

al·ka·hest (al′kə hest′), *n.* the universal solvent sought by the alchemists. Also, **alcahest.** [< late ML; prob. coinage of Paracelsus] —**al′ka·hes′tic, al′ka·hes′ti·cal,** *adj.*

al·ka·le·mi·a (al′kə lē′mē ə), *n. Pathol.* a condition of abnormal alkalinity of the blood. —**al′ka·les′cence, al′ka·les′cen·cy,** *n.*

al·ka·li (al′kə lī′), *n., pl.* **-lis, -lies. 1.** *Chem.* **a.** any of various bases, the hydroxides of the alkali metals and of ammonium, that neutralize acids to form salts and turn red litmus paper blue. **b.** any of various other bases, as calcium hydroxide. **c.** *Obs.* any of various other compounds, as the carbonates of sodium and potassium. **2.** *Agric.* a soluble salt in some soils, detrimental to most crops. [late ME *alkaly* < MF *alcali* < Ar *al* the + *qalīy,* var. of *qilīy* saltwort ashes]

al′kali met′al, *Chem.* any of the group of univalent metals including potassium, sodium, lithium, rubidium, cesium, and francium, whose hydroxides are alkalis.

al·ka·lim·e·ter (al′kə lim′i tər), *n. Physical Chem.* an instrument for determining the quantity of carbon dioxide. —**al·ka·li·met·ric** (al′kə lə me′trik), **al′ka·li·met′ri·cal,** *adj.* —**al′ka·li·met′ri·cal·ly,** *adv.* —**al′ka·lim′e·try,** *n.*

al·ka·line (al′kə līn′, -lin), *adj.* of, containing, or like an alkali.

al′kaline earth′, *Chem.* any of the oxides of barium, strontium, calcium, and, sometimes, magnesium.

al·ka·lin·ise (al′kə li nīz′), *v.t.,* **-ised, -is·ing.** *Chiefly Brit.* alkalinize. —**al′ka·lin′i·sa′tion,** *n.*

al·ka·lin·i·ty (al′kə lin′i tē), *n. Chem.* alkaline condition; the quality that constitutes an alkali.

al·ka·lin·ize (al′kə li nīz′), *v.t.,* **-ized, -iz·ing.** to make into an alkali. —**al′ka·lin′i·za′tion,** *n.*

al·ka·lise (al′kə līz′), *v.t.,* **-lised, -lis·ing.** *Chiefly Brit.* alkalize. —**al′ka·lis′a·ble,** *adj.* —**al′ka·li·sa′tion,** *n.*

al′kali soil′, soil that has either a high degree of alkalinity or a high percentage of sodium, or both, so that most crops cannot be grown in it profitably.

al·ka·lize (al′kə līz′), *v.t.,* **-lized, -liz·ing.** *Chem.* alkalinize. Also, *esp. Brit.,* **alkalise.** —**al′ka·liz′a·ble,** *adj.* —**al′ka·li·za′tion,** *n.* —**al′ka·liz′er,** *n.*

al·ka·loid (al′kə loid′), *Biochem., Chem., Pharm.* —*n.* **1.** any of a large class of organic, nitrogen-containing ring compounds that have a bitter taste, that are usually water-insoluble and alcohol-soluble, that form water-soluble salts, and usually exhibit pharmacological action, as nicotine, morphine, or quinine. —*adj.* **2.** alkaline. —**al′ka·loi′dal,** *adj.*

al·ka·lo·sis (al′kə lō′sis), *n. Pathol.* a condition of the blood and other body fluids in which the bicarbonate concentration is above normal, tending toward alkalemia.

al·kane (al′kān), *n. Chem.* any member of the alkane series. [ALK(YL) + -ANE]

al′kane se′ries, *Chem.* the homologous series of saturated, aliphatic hydrocarbons having the general formula, C_nH_{2n+2}, as methane, CH_4, or ethane, C_2H_6. Also called **methane series, paraffin series.**

al·ka·net (al′kə net′), *n.* **1.** a European, boraginaceous plant, *Alkanna tinctoria,* the root of which yields a red dye. **2.** any of several similar plants, as the bugloss, *Anchusa officinalis.* [ME < Sp *alcanet(a)* = *alcan(a)* henna (plant) (< ML *alchanna* < Ar *al* the + *hinnā'* henna) + *-eta* dim. suffix]

al·kene (al′kēn), *n. Chem.* any member of the alkene series. [ALK(YL) + -ENE]

al′kene se′ries, *Chem.* the homologous series of unsaturated, aliphatic hydrocarbons containing one double bond and having the general formula C_nH_{2n}, as ethylene, $H_2C{=}CH_2$. Also called **ethylene series, olefin series.**

Alk·maar (älk′mär), *n.* a city in the W Netherlands. 45,479 (1962).

Al·ko·ran (al′kō rän′, -ran′, -kô-), *n.* the Koran. Also, **Alcoran.** [< Ar *al* the + *qor'ān,* var. of *qur'ān* reading (aloud); r. ME *alkaro(u)n* < MF or ML]

Al Ku·fa (al ko͞o′fə, -fa), Kufa.

al′kyd res′in (al′kid), *Chem.* any of a group of sticky resins, used chiefly in adhesives and paints. Also called **al′kyd.** [ALKY(L + ACI)D]

al·kyl·a·tion (al′kə lā′shən), *n. Chem.* **1.** the replacement of a hydrogen atom in an organic compound by an alkyl group. **2.** the addition of a paraffin to an olefin.

al′kyl group′, *Chem.* any of a series of univalent groups of the general formula C_nH_{2n+1}, derived from aliphatic hydrocarbons, as the methyl group, CH_3–. Also called **al′kyl rad′ical.** [< G = *Alk(ohol)* ALC(OHOL) + *-yl* -YL] —**al·kyl** (al′kil, -kəl), *adj.* —**al·kyl·ic** (al kil′ik), *adj.*

al·kyne (al′kīn), *n. Chem.* any member of the alkyne series. [ALK(YL) + -INE[2], altered to *-yne*]

al′kyne se′ries, *Chem.* the homologous series of unsaturated, aliphatic hydrocarbons containing one triple bond with the general formula, C_nH_{2n-2}, as acetylene, $HC{\equiv}CH$.

all (ôl), *adj.* **1.** the whole of (a quantity, extent, or duration): *all the cake; all the way; all year.* **2.** the whole number of (individuals or particulars, taken collectively): *all men.* **3.** the greatest possible (quality or degree): *with all due respect; with all speed.* **4.** every: *all manner of men.* **5.** any; any whatever: *beyond all doubt.* —*pron.* **6.** the whole quantity or amount: *He ate all of the peanuts. All are gone.* **7.** the whole number: *all of us.* **8.** everything: *Is that all you want to say? All is lost.* —*n.* **9.** (*often cap.*) everything; all matter; the universe. **10.** one's whole interest, energy, or property: *to give one's all.* **11. above all,** before everything else; chiefly: *Above all, the little girl wanted a giant teddy bear.* **12. after all,** in spite of the circumstances; notwithstanding. **13. all in all,** everything considered; in general: *All in all, her condition is greatly improved.* **14. and all,** *Informal.* together with every other associated or connected attribute or object: *What with the snow and all, we may be a little late.* **15. at all, a.** in the slightest degree: *I wasn't surprised at all.* **b.** for any reason: *Why bother at all?* **c.** in any way: *no offense at all.* **16. for all (that),** in spite of; notwithstanding: *For all that, it was a good year.* **17. in all,** all included; all together: *a hundred guests in all.* **18. once and for all,** for the last time; finally. —*adv.* **19.** wholly; entirely: *all alone.* **20.** exclusively: *He spent his income all on pleasure.* **21.** each; apiece: *The score was one all.* **22.** *Archaic.* even; just. **23. all at once.** See **once** (def. 13). **24. all but,** almost; very nearly: *She is all but dead.* **25. all in,** *U.S. Informal.* tired; exhausted: *We were all in at the end of the day.* **26. all the better,** more advantageous: *If the sun shines, it will be all the better for our excursion.* **27. all the more so,** the more reason for (doing, saying, believing, etc., something). **28. be not all there,** *Informal.* to be feeble-minded or insane. [ME; OE *(e)all;* c. Goth *all(s),* Icel *all(r),* OHG, G *all*]

—**Usage.** Such expressions as ALL THE FARTHER (*This is all the farther the elevator goes*) and ALL THE FASTER (*This is all the faster I can run*) are generally avoided in both formal and informal English in favor of AS FAR AS (*This is as far as the elevator goes*) and AS FAST AS (*This is as fast as I can run*). Although some people object to ALL OF (*All of the students will attend*), preferring to drop OF (*All the students will attend*), both forms are so commonly met in educated usage that there need be no hesitation in using ALL OF. See also **altogether, alright, already.**

all-, var. of **allo-** before a vowel: *allonym.*

al·la bre·ve (ä′lə brev′ā; *It.* äl′lä bre′ve), *Music.* using the half note as the basic time unit; 2/2 or 4/2 time. *Symbol:* ₵ Also called **cut time.** Cf. **common time.** [< It: lit., to the breve. See BRIEF]

Al·lah (al′ə, ä′lə), *n. Islam.* the Supreme Being. [< Ar = *al* the + *ilāh* God, akin to Heb *elōah*]

Al·lah·a·bad (al′ə hə bad′, ä′lə hä bäd′), *n.* a city in SE Uttar Pradesh, on the Ganges. 430,700 (1961).

all-A·mer·i·can (ôl′ə mer′i kən), *adj.* **1.** representing the entire United States. **2.** composed exclusively of American members. **3.** representing the best in any field of U.S. sport. **4.** typically American. —*n.* **5.** an all-American player. **6.** a typical American youth. Also, **All′-Amer′ican.**

Al·lan-a-Dale (al′ən ə dāl′), *n.* (in English balladry) a member of Robin Hood's band who carried off his bride just before she was to be forced into marriage with an aged knight.

al·lan·ite (al′ə nīt′), *n.* a mineral, a silicate of calcium, cerium, aluminum, and iron. [named after Thomas *Allan* (1777–1833), English mineralogist; see -ITE[1]]

al·lan·toid (ə lan′toid), *adj.* **1.** Also, **al·lan·toi·dal** (al′ən toid′əl). allantoic. —*n.* **2.** the allantois. [< Gk *allantoeid(ēs)* = *allant-* (s. of *allâs* sausage) + *-oeidēs* -OID]

al·lan·to·is (ə lan′tō is, -tois), *n. Embryol., Zool.* a vascular, extraembryonic membrane of birds, reptiles, and certain mammals, that develops as a sac or diverticulum from the ventral wall of the hindgut. [< NL < Gk *allantoeidēs,* taken for pl. and given a sing., on model of words like *hērōis* (sing.), *hērōides* (pl.)] —**al·lan·to·ic** (al′ən tō′ik), *adj.*

al·lar·gan·do (ä′lär gän′dō; *It.* äl′lär gän′dô), *adj. Music.* becoming slower and broader. [< It: *al* to the + *largando* broadening. See LARGE]

all-a·round (ôl′ə round′), *adj.* **1.** versatile: *an all-around player.* **2.** inclusive; comprehensive.

al·lay (ə lā′), *v.t.,* **-layed, -lay·ing. 1.** to put (fear, doubt, suspicion, anger, etc.) to rest; calm; quiet. **2.** to lessen or relieve; mitigate; alleviate: *to allay pain.* [ME *aleye(n),* OE

ālecgan to put down, allay (*ā-* A-[3] + *lecgan* to LAY[1]); sp. *-ll-* shows influence of the now obs. *allege* (< F *allēger*) to alleviate, allay] —**al·lay′er,** *n.*
—**Syn. 1.** soften, assuage. ALLAY, SOOTHE mean to reduce excitement or emotion. To ALLAY is to lay to rest or lull to a sense of security, possibly by making the emotion seem unjustified: *to allay suspicion, anxiety, fears.* To SOOTHE is to exert a pacifying or tranquilizing influence: *to soothe a terrified child.* **2.** lighten, mollify, temper, ease. —**Ant. 1.** excite.

all′ clear′, the signal that an air raid or air-raid drill is over.

all-day (ôl′dā′), *adj.* extending or lasting throughout a day, esp. the hours of daylight; daylong: *an all-day tour.*

al·le·ga·tion (al′ə gā′shən), *n.* **1.** the act of alleging; affirmation. **2.** a statement offered as a plea, excuse, or justification. **3.** an assertion made without substantial proof. **4.** an assertion made by a party in a legal proceeding, which he undertakes to prove. [late ME < L *allēgātiōn-* (s. of *allēgātiō*) = *allēgāt(us)* (ptp. of *allēgāre*) adduced (*al-* AL- + *lēg-* ordain by law (see LEX) + *-ātus* -ATE[1]) + *-iōn-* -ION]

al·lege (ə lej′), *v.t.*, **-leged, -leg·ing. 1.** to declare with positiveness; assert. **2.** to declare before a court or elsewhere as if under oath. **3.** to assert without proof. **4.** to plead in support of; urge as a reason or excuse. **5.** *Archaic.* to cite or quote in confirmation. [ME *alegge(n)* < AF *alegier* (<< VL **exlītigāre*; see EX-, LITIGATE) with sense of L *allēgāre* to adduce] —**al·lege′a·ble,** *adj.* —**al·leg′er,** *n.*
—**Syn. 1.** state, aver. **2.** attest. —**Ant. 1.** deny.

al·leged (ə lejd′), *adj.* **1.** declared or stated to be as described; asserted: *an alleged murderer.* **2.** doubtful; suspect; supposed: *an alleged cure-all.* —**al·leg·ed·ly** (ə lej′id lē), *adv.*

Al·le·ghe·ny (al′ə gā′nē), *n.* a river flowing from Pennsylvania into SW New York and then S through W Pennsylvania, joining the Monongahela at Pittsburgh to form the Ohio River. 325 mi. long. —**Al′le·ghe′ni·an, Al′le·gha′ni·an,** *adj.*

Al′leghe′ny Moun′tains, a mountain range in Pennsylvania, Maryland, West Virginia, and Virginia: a part of the Appalachian Mountains. Also called **Al′le·ghe′nies.**

al·le·giance (ə lē′jəns), *n.* **1.** the loyalty of a citizen to his government or of a subject to his sovereign. **2.** loyalty or devotion to some person, group, cause, or the like. [late ME *aliegiaunce* = *a-* (< ?) + *liege* LIEGE + *-aunce* -ANCE; cf. MF *ligeance*] —**Syn.** See **loyalty.** —**Ant. 1.** treason.

al·le·gor·i·cal (al′ə gôr′i kəl, -gor′-), *adj.* **1.** consisting of or pertaining to allegory: *an allegorical poem.* **2.** figurative. Also, **al′le·gor′ic.** [< L *allēgoric(us)* (< Gk *allēgorikós*; see ALLEGORY, -IC) + -AL[1]] —**al′le·gor′i·cal·ly,** *adv.*

al·le·go·rise (al′ə gə rīz′), *v.t., v.i.*, **-rised, -ris·ing.** *Chiefly Brit.* allegorize. —**al′le·gor′i·sa′tion,** *n.* —**al′le·go·ris′er,** *n.*

al·le·go·rist (al′ə gôr′ist, -gōr′-, al′ə gər ist), *n.* a person who uses or writes allegory. [ALLEGOR(IZE) + -IST]

al·le·go·ris·tic (al′ə gə ris′tik), *adj.* writing or using allegory; interpreting in an allegorical sense.

al·le·go·rize (al′ə gə rīz′), *v.*, **-rized, -riz·ing.** —*v.t.* **1.** to make into an allegory. **2.** to understand in an allegorical sense. —*v.i.* **3.** to use allegory. Also, *esp. Brit.*, **allegorise.** [< LL *allēgorīzāre*] —**al′le·gor′i·za′tion,** *n.*

al·le·go·ry (al′ə gôr′ē, -gōr′ē), *n., pl.* **-ries. 1.** a representation of an abstract or spiritual meaning through concrete or material forms; figurative treatment of one subject under the guise of another. **2.** a symbolic narrative. **3.** emblem (def. 3). [late ME *allegorie* < Gk *allēgoría* < *allēgorein* so to speak as to imply something other. See ALLO-, AGORA]

al·le·gret·to (al′ə gret′ō; *It.* äl′le greт′tô), *adj., n., pl.* **-tos.** *Music.* —*adj.* **1.** light, graceful, and moderately fast in tempo. —*n.* **2.** an allegretto movement. [< It = *allegr(o)* cheerful + *-etto* -ET]

al·le·gro (ə lā′grō, ə leg′rō; *It.* äl le′grô), *adj., n., pl.* **-gros.** *Music.* —*adj.* **1.** brisk or rapid in tempo. —*n.* **2.** an allegro movement. [< It < L *alacer* brisk. See ALACRITY]

al·lele (ə lēl′), *n.* *Genetics.* any of several forms of a gene, usually arising through mutation, that are responsible for hereditary variation. [short for ALLELOMORPH] —**al·lel·ic** (ə lē′lik), *adj.* —**al·lel′ism,** *n.*

al·le·lo·morph (ə lē′lə môrf′, ə lel′ə-), *n.* *Genetics.* allele. [< Gk *allēlo-* (s. of *allḗlōn* of one another = *áll(os)* other + *állōn*, gen. pl. of *állos*) + -MORPH] —**al·le′lo·mor′phic,** *adj.* —**al·le′lo·mor′phism,** *n.*

al·le·lu·ia (al′ə lo͞o′yə), *interj.* **1.** praise ye the Lord; hallelujah. —*n.* **2.** a song of praise to God. [< LL < Gk *allēloúïa* < Heb *hallĕlūyāh* praise ye Yahweh] —**al·le·lu·iat·ic** (al′ə lo͞o yat′ik), *adj.*

al·le·mande (al′ə mand′, -mänd′, al′ə mand′, -mänd′; *Fr.* al[a] mäɴd′), *n., pl.* **-mandes** (-mandz′, -mändz′, -mandz′, -mändz′; *Fr.* -mäɴd′). **1.** a 17th- and 18th-century dance in slow duple time. **2.** a piece of music based on this rhythm. **3.** a figure in a quadrille. **4.** a German folk dance in triple meter. [< F, short for *danse allemande* German dance]

Al·len (al′ən), *n.* **1. (Charles) Grant (Blair·fin·die)** (blâr-fin′dē), (pen names: *Cecil Power, J. Arbuthnot Wilson*), 1848–99, British philosophical writer and novelist. **2. Ethan,** 1738–89, American soldier in the Revolutionary War: leader of the "Green Mountain Boys" of Vermont.

Al·len·by (al′ən bē), *n.* **Edmund Henry Hyn·man** (hin′mən), **1st Viscount,** 1861–1936, British field marshal: commander of British forces in Egypt in World War I; conquered Jerusalem 1917.

Al′len Park′, a city in SE Michigan. 40,747 (1970).

Al′len screw′, a screw having an axial hexagonal hole in its head for turning. [formerly a trademark]

Al·len·town (al′ən toun′), *n.* a city in E Pennsylvania. 109,527 (1970).

Al′len wrench′, a wrench for Allen screws, formed from a piece of hexagonal bar stock bent to a right angle. See illus. at **wrench.** [formerly a trademark]

al·ler·gen (al′ər jen′), *n.* *Immunol.* any substance inducing or capable of inducing an allergy.

al·ler·gen·ic (al′ər jen′ik), *adj.* causing allergic sensitization. —**al·ler·gen·ic·i·ty** (al′ər jə nis′i tē), *n.*

al·ler·gic (ə lûr′jik), *adj.* **1.** of or pertaining to allergy: *an allergic reaction to wool.* **2.** having an allergy. **3.** excessively sensitive: *allergic to criticism.*

al·ler·gist (al′ər jist), *n.* a physician specializing in the diagnosis and treatment of allergies.

al·ler·gy (al′ər jē), *n., pl.* **-gies. 1.** a state of hypersensitivity, as hay fever or asthma, to certain things, as pollen, foods, animals, etc., characterized by difficult respiration, skin rashes, etc. **2.** altered susceptibility due to a first inoculation, treatment, or the like, as exhibited in reaction to a subsequent one of the same nature. Cf. **anaphylaxis.** [< Gk *áll(os)* other + *-ergy* < *-ergia* = *érg(on)* activity + *-ia* -Y[3]]

al·le·thrin (al′ə thrin), *n.* *Chem.* a clear, amber, viscous liquid, $C_{19}H_{26}O_3$, used as an insecticide. [ALL(YL) + (*pyr*)*ethrin* = *pyrethr(um)* plant genus + -IN[2]]

al·le·vi·ate (ə lē′vē āt′), *v.t.*, **-at·ed, -at·ing.** to make easier to endure; lessen; mitigate: *to alleviate sorrow; to alleviate pain.* [< LL *alleviāt(us)* (ptp. of *alleviāre*) = *al-* AL- + *levi(s)* light, not heavy + *-ātus* -ATE[1]] —**al·le′vi·a′tor,** *n.* —**Syn.** lighten, diminish, abate, relieve, assuage.

al·le·vi·a·tion (ə lē′vē ā′shən), *n.* **1.** the act of alleviating. **2.** something that alleviates or palliates. [< ML *alleviātiōn-* (s. of *alleviātiō*)]

al·le·vi·a·tive (ə lē′vē ā′tiv, -ə tiv), *adj.* **1.** Also, **al·le·vi·a·to·ry** (ə lē′vē ə tôr′ē, -tōr′ē). serving to alleviate; palliative. —*n.* **2.** *Obs.* alleviation (def. 2).

al·ley[1] (al′ē), *n., pl.* **-leys. 1.** a narrow back street. **2.** a walk, as in a garden, enclosed with hedges or shrubbery. **3.** a passage, as through a continuous row of houses, permitting access from the street to backyards, garages, etc. **4.** *Bowling.* **a.** a long, narrow, wooden lane or floor along which the ball is rolled. **b.** See **bowling green. 5.** *Tennis.* the space on each side of a tennis court between the doubles sideline and the service or singles sideline. **6.** *Rare.* an aisle. **7. up one's alley,** *Slang.* in keeping with one's natural abilities or interests. [ME *al(e)y* < MF *alee* walk, passage < fem. of *ale*, ptp. of *aler* to walk < ?] —**Syn. 1.** See **street.**

al·ley[2] (al′ē), *n., pl.* **-leys.** a choice, large playing marble. [alter. and shortening of ALABASTER]

al·ley·way (al′ē wā′), *n.* an alley or other narrow passageway.

all-fired (ôl′fī[ə]rd′), *adj., superl.* **-fired·est,** *adv.* *Chiefly U.S. Informal.* —*adj.* **1.** tremendous; extreme; excessive: *He had the all-fired gall to quit in the middle of the job.* —*adv.* **2.** Also, **all-fired·ly** (ôl′fī[ə]rd′lē, -fī′rid-). extremely; excessively: *Don't be so all-fired sure of yourself.*

All′ Fools′ Day′. See **April Fools' Day.**

all′ fours′, 1. all four limbs or extremities; the four legs of an animal or both arms and both legs of a man: *to land on all fours.* **2.** (*construed as sing.*) Also called **high-low-jack, pitch, seven-up.** *Cards.* a game for two or three players or two partnerships, the object of which is to win special scoring values for certain cards, as the highest or lowest trump.

all′ get′-out (get′out′), *Informal.* to an extreme degree, condition, etc. (usually prec. by *as*): *The wind was cold as all get-out.*

all′ hail′, *Archaic.* a salutation of greeting or welcome.

All·hal·low·mas (ôl′hal′ō məs), *n.* *Archaic.* Allhallows. [ME *alhalwemesse*, OE *ealra hālgena mæsse* mass of all saints]

All·hal·lows (ôl′hal′ōz), *n.* See **All Saints' Day.**

Allhal′lows Eve′, Halloween. Also called **All′ Hal′low E′ven.**

all·heal (ôl′hēl′), *n.* **1.** valerian (def. 1). **2.** a selfheal.

al·li·a·ceous (al′ē ā′shəs), *adj.* **1.** *Bot.* belonging to the genus *Allium*, comprising the garlic, onion, leek, etc. **2.** having the odor or taste of garlic, onion, etc. [< L *alli(um)* garlic + -ACEOUS]

al·li·ance (ə lī′əns), *n.* **1.** the act of allying. **2.** the state of being allied. **3.** marriage or the relationship created by marriage between two families. **4.** a formal agreement between two or more nations. **5.** a merging of efforts or interests by persons, families, states, or organizations: *an alliance between church and state.* **6.** correspondence in basic characteristics; affinity: *the alliance between logic and metaphysics.* [ME *aliance* < OF = *ali(er)* (to) ALLY + *-ance* -ANCE]
—**Syn. 2, 5.** association; coalition; partnership; affiliation. **4.** ALLIANCE, LEAGUE, CONFEDERATION, UNION all mean the joining of states for mutual benefit or to permit the joint exercise of functions. An ALLIANCE may apply to any connection entered into for mutual benefit. LEAGUE usually suggests closer combination or a more definite object or purpose. CONFEDERATION applies to a permanent combination for the exercise in common of certain governmental functions. UNION implies an alliance so close and permanent that the separate states or parties become essentially one. **4.** treaty, pact, compact.

Al·li·ance (ə lī′əns), *n.* a city in NE Ohio. 26,547 (1970).

al·lied (ə līd′, al′īd), *adj.* **1.** joined by treaty: *allied nations.* **2.** related; kindred: *allied species.* **3.** (*cap.*) of or pertaining to the Allies. [ME]

Al·lier (ᴀ lyā′), *n.* a river flowing N from S France to the Loire. ab. 250 mi. long.

al·lies (al′īz, ə līz′), *n.* **1.** pl. of **ally. 2.** (*cap.*) (in World War I) the powers of the Triple Entente (Great Britain, France, and Russia), with the nations allied with them (Belgium, Serbia, Japan, Italy, etc., not including the United States), or loosely, with all the nations (including the United States) allied or associated with them as opposed to the Central Powers. **3.** (*cap.*) the 26 nations that fought against the Axis in World War II. **4.** (*cap.*) the member nations of NATO.

Alligator,
Alligator mississipiensis
(Length 11 ft.)

al·li·ga·tor (al′ə gā′tər), *n.* **1.** either of two broad-snouted crocodilians of the genus *Alligator*, found in the southeastern U.S. and eastern China. **2.** (loosely) any broad-snouted crocodilian, as a caiman. [< Sp *el lagarto* the lizard << L *lacertus* lizard]

al′ligator clip′, *Elect.* a cliplike device with long, narrow jaws for making temporary electrical connections.

al′ligator pear′, avocado (def. 1). [*alligator*, alter. by folk etym. of Sp *avocado, abogado* or AmerSp *aguacate* (see AVOCADO)]

al·lit·er·ate (ə lit′ə rāt′), *v.*, **-at·ed, -at·ing.** —*v.i.* **1.** to show alliteration. **2.** to use alliteration. —*v.t.* **3.** to compose or arrange with alliteration. [back formation from ALLITERATION] —**al·lit′er·a′tive,** *adj.* —**al·lit′er·a′tive·ly,** *adv.* —**al·lit′er·a′tive·ness,** *n.* —**al·lit′er·a′tor,** *n.*

al·lit·er·a·tion (ə lit′ə rā′shən), *n.* **1.** the commencement of two or more stressed syllables of a word group either with the same consonant sound or sound group, as in *from stem to stern,* or with a vowel sound that may differ from syllable to syllable, as in *each to all.* Cf. **consonance** (def. 4a). **2.** the commencement of two or more words of a word group with the same letter, as in *apt alliteration's artful aid.* [< ML *alliterātiōn-* (s. of *alliterātiō*) = *al-* AL- + *literātiōn-;* modeled after *obliterātiō* OBLITERATION]

al·li·um (al′ē əm), *n.* any bulbous, liliaceous plant of the genus *Allium,* including the onion, leek, shallot, garlic, and chive. [< L: garlic]

all-night (ôl′nīt′), *adj.* **1.** extending through a night. **2.** open all night, as for business.

allo-, a learned borrowing from Greek meaning "other," used in the formation of compound words (*allotrope*) and in chemistry to denote the more stable of two geometric isomers. Also (except in chemistry), *esp. before a vowel,* **all-.** [< Gk, comb. form of *állos* other; c. L *alius,* ELSE]

al·lo·bar·ic (al′ə bar′ik), *adj. Meteorol.* of or pertaining to change in barometric pressure: *allobaric wind.*

al·lo·cate (al′ə kāt′), *v.t.*, **-cat·ed, -cat·ing.** **1.** to set apart for a particular purpose; assign or allot: *to allocate funds for new projects.* **2.** to fix the place of; locate. [< ML *allocāt(us)* (ptp. of *allocāre*) = *al-* AL- + *loc(us)* place + *-ātus* -ATE[1]] —**al·lo·ca·ble** (al′ə kə bəl), *adj.*

al·lo·ca·tion (al′ə kā′shən), *n.* **1.** the act of allocating; apportionment. **2.** the state of being allocated. **3.** the share or portion allocated. **4.** *Accounting.* a system of dividing expenses and incomes among the various branches, departments, etc., of a business. [< ML *allocātiōn-* (s. of *allocātiō*)]

al·loch·tho·nous (ə lok′thə nəs), *adj.* **1.** *Geol.* (of rocks, minerals, etc.) formed elsewhere than in the region where found and moved by tectonic forces. **2.** *Physiol.* foreign in origin; introduced. Cf. **autochthonous** (def. 2). [ALLO- + *-chthonous,* modeled after AUTOCHTHONOUS]

al·lo·cu·tion (al′ə kyōō′shən), *n.* **1.** a formal speech, esp. an incontrovertible or hortatory speech. **2.** a pronouncement delivered by the pope to a secret consistory. [< L *allocūtiōn-* (s. of *allocūtiō*) = *allocūt(us),* ptp. of *alloquī* (*al-* AL- + *loquī* to speak) + *-iōn-* -ION]

al·lo·di·al (ə lō′dē əl), *adj.* free from the tenurial rights of a feudal overlord. [< ML *allodiāl(is).* See ALLODIUM, -AL[1]] —**al·lo′di·al′i·ty,** *n.* —**al·lo′di·al·ly,** *adv.*

al·lo·di·um (ə lō′dē əm), *n., pl.* **-di·a** (-dē ə). land owned absolutely, not subject to any rent, service, or other tenurial right of an overlord. Also called **al·lod** (al′od). [< ML < OG *allōd* (*all* ALL + *-ōd* patrimony, c. Icel *ōth-,* OE *ēth-* in *ēthel,* akin (by gradation) to *ath-* of ATHELING)]

al·log·a·my (ə log′ə mē), *n.* cross-fertilization in plants (opposed to *autogamy*). —**al·log′a·mous,** *adj.*

al·lo·graft (al′ə graft′, -gräft′), *n.* homograft. [ALLO- + GRAFT[1]]

al·lo·graph (al′ə graf′, -gräf′), *n.* **1.** writing or a signature inscribed by one person for another, as distinguished from autograph. **2.** a deed or other legal document not in the writing of any of the persons who are party to it. **3.** *Linguistics.* a variant form of a grapheme that is in complementary distribution or free variation with another form of the same grapheme; an orthographic contextual variant.

al·lom·er·ism (ə lom′ə riz′əm), *n. Chem.* variability in chemical constitution without change in crystalline form. —**al·lom′er·ous,** *adj.*

al·lom·e·try (ə lom′i trē), *n. Biol.* **1.** growth of a part of an organism in relation to the growth of the whole organism or some other part of it. **2.** the measurement or study of this growth. Also, **al·loi·om·e·try** (al′oi om′i trē). —**al·lo·met·ric** (al′ə me′trik), **al·loi·o·met·ric** (ə loi′ə me′trik), *adj.*

al·lo·morph (al′ə môrf′), *n.* **1.** any of two or more different forms of the same chemical compound. **2.** *Linguistics.* one of the alternate contextually determined phonological shapes of a morpheme, as *en* in *oxen,* which is an allomorph of the English plural morpheme. Cf. **morph.** —**al′lo·mor′phic,** *adj.*

al·lo·mor·phism (al′ə môr′fiz əm), *n. Chem.* change in crystalline form without change in chemical constitution.

al·lo·nym (al′ə nim), *n.* **1.** the name of another person taken by an author as a pen name. Cf. **pseudonym. 2.** a work published under a name other than that of the author. —**al·lon·y·mous** (ə lon′ə məs), *adj.* —**al·lon′y·mous·ly,** *adv.*

al·lo·path (al′ə path′), *n.* a person who practices or favors allopathy. Also, **al·lop·a·thist** (ə lop′ə thist). [< G, back formation from *Allopathie* ALLOPATHY]

al·lop·a·thy (ə lop′ə thē), *n.* the method of treating disease by the use of agents, producing effects different from those of the disease treated (opposed to *homeopathy*). [< G *Allopathie*] —**al·lo·path·ic** (al′ə path′ik), *adj.* —**al′lo·path′i·cal·ly,** *adv.*

al·lo·pat·ric (al′ə pa′trik), *adj. Biol., Ecol.* originating in or occupying different geographical areas. [ALLO- + Gk *pátr(iā)* fatherland + -IC] —**al′lo·pat′ri·cal·ly,** *adv.*

al·lo·phane (al′ə fān′), *n.* a mineral, an amorphous hydrous silicate of aluminum, occurring in blue, green, or yellow masses. [< Gk *allophan(ēs)* = *allo-* ALLO- + *phan-* (s. of *phaínesthai* to appear) + *-ēs* adj. suffix]

al·lo·phone (al′ə fōn′), *n. Phonet.* a speech sound constituting one of the phonetic variants of a given phoneme, as each of the *t*-sounds in *top, stop, metal,* etc. —**al·lo·phon·ic** (al′ə fon′ik), *adj.* —**al′lo·phon′i·cal·ly,** *adv.*

al·lo·plasm (al′ə plaz′əm), *n. Biol.* a part of protoplasm that is differentiated to perform a special function, as that of the flagellum. —**al′lo·plas·mat′ic, al′lo·plas′mic,** *adj.*

al·lot (ə lot′), *v.t.*, **-lot·ted, -lot·ting.** **1.** to divide or distribute by or as by lot; apportion: *to allot portions.* **2.** to appropriate for a special purpose: *to allot money for a park.* **3.** to assign as a portion; set apart; dedicate. [earlier *alot* < MF *alot(er)* = *a-* A-[5] + *lot* LOT + *-er* inf. suffix] —**al·lot′ta·ble,** *adj.* —**al·lot′ter,** *n.* —**Syn. 1.** See **assign.**

al·lot·ment (ə lot′mənt), *n.* **1.** the act of allotting. **2.** something that is allotted. **3.** a portion or thing allotted; a share granted. **4.** (in U.S. military use) the portion of the pay of an officer or enlisted person that he authorizes to be paid directly to another party. **5.** *Brit.* a plot of land rented to a gardener.

al·lo·trope (al′ə trōp′), *n. Chem.* one of two or more existing forms of an element: *Lampblack, graphite, and diamond are allotropes of carbon.*

al·lo·trop·ic (al′ə trop′ik), *adj.* pertaining to or characterized by allotropy. Also, **al′lo·trop′i·cal.** —**al′lo·trop′i·cal·ly,** *adv.* —**al·lo·tro·pic·i·ty** (al′ə trə pis′i tē), *n.*

al·lot·ro·py (ə lo′trə pē), *n. Chem.* a property of certain elements, as carbon, sulfur, and phosphorus, of existing in two or more distinct forms. Also, **al·lot′ro·pism.**

all' ot·ta·va (äl′ ə tä′və; *It.* äl′ lôt tä′vä), *Music.* a direction (8va), placed above or below the staff to indicate that the passage covered is to be played one octave higher or lower than written. [< It: lit., at the octave]

al·lot·tee (ə lot ē′), *n.* a person to whom something is allotted.

all-out (ôl′out′), *adj.* using all one's resources; complete; total: *an all-out effort.*

all·ov·er (ôl′ō′vər), *adj.* extending or repeated over the entire surface, as a decorative pattern.

al·low (ə lou′), *v.t.* **1.** to give permission to or for; permit: *to allow a student to be absent.* **2.** to grant (a sum of money, period of time for action, etc.) to a person or group of persons at one's discretion. **3.** to permit by neglect, oversight, or the like: *to allow a door to remain open.* **4.** to acknowledge; concede: *to allow a claim.* **5.** to take into consideration, as by adding or subtracting: *to allow an hour for changing trains.* **6.** *U.S. Dial.* to say; think. —*v.i.* **7.** to permit something to happen or exist; admit (sometimes fol. by *of*): *to spend more than one's budget allows; a premise that allows of only one conclusion.* **8. allow for,** to make concession or provision for. [ME *alowe(n)* < MF *alouer* to assign < LL *allocāre.* See AL-, LOCUS]
—**Syn. 1.** ALLOW, PERMIT, LET imply granting the right to do something. ALLOW and PERMIT are often interchangeable, but PERMIT is the more positive. ALLOW implies absence of an attempt, or even an intent, to hinder. PERMIT suggests formal or implied assent. LET is the conversational term for both. —**Ant. 1.** forbid.

al·low·a·ble (ə lou′ə bəl), *adj.* that may be allowed; legitimate; permissible: *an allowable tax deduction.* [late ME < MF *alouable*] —**al·low′a·ble·ness,** *n.* —**al·low′a·bly,** *adv.*

al·low·ance (ə lou′əns), *n., v.,* **-anced, -anc·ing.** —*n.* **1.** the act of allowing. **2.** something allotted or granted. **3.** a sum of money allotted or granted for a particular purpose, as for expenses: *Her allowance for groceries was $25.* **4.** an addition or deduction based on an extenuating or qualifying circumstance: *an allowance for depreciation.* **5.** acknowledgment; concession: *the allowance of a claim.* **6.** sanction; tolerance: *the allowance of slavery.* **7. make allowance** or **allowances (for), a.** to take mitigating factors or circumstances into consideration. **b.** to pardon; excuse. —*v.t.* **8.** to place on a fixed allowance, as of food or drink. **9.** to allocate (supplies, rations, etc.) in fixed or regular amounts. [late ME *alouance* < MF] —**Syn. 2.** allotment. **3.** stipend.

Al·lo·way (al′ə wā′), *n.* a hamlet in SW Scotland, near Ayr: birthplace of Robert Burns.

al·low·ed·ly (ə lou′id lē), *adv.* permissibly.

al·loy (*n.* al′oi, ə loi′; *v.* ə loi′), *n.* **1.** a substance composed of two or more metals, or of a metal or metals with a nonmetal, intimately mixed as by fusion, electrodeposition, etc. **2.** a less costly metal mixed with a more valuable one. **3.** standard, quality, or fineness, as of gold or silver. **4.** admixture, as of good with evil. **5.** anything added that serves to reduce quality or purity. —*v.t.* **6.** to mix (metals or metal with nonmetal) so as to form an alloy. **7.** to debase, impair, or thin by admixture; adulterate. [< MF *aloi,* OF *alei,* back formation from *aleier* to combine < L *alligāre* to bind up = *al-* AL- + *ligāre* to bind. See LIGAMENT]

al′loy steel′, carbon steel to which various elements, as chromium, cobalt, copper, manganese, molybdenum, nickel, tungsten, or vanadium have been added to obtain desirable properties.

all′ right′, 1. safe or unharmed: *Are you all right?* **2.** yes; very well: *All right, I'll go with you.* **3.** satisfactory: *His performance was all right, but I've seen better.* **4.** satisfactorily: *His work is coming along all right.* **5.** without fail: *You'll hear about this, all right!* —**Usage.** See **alright.**

all-round (ôl′round′), *adj.* all-around. Also, **all′ round′.** —**all′-round′er,** *n.*

All′ Saints′′ Day′, a church festival celebrated November 1 in honor of all the saints; Allhallows.

All′ Souls′′ Day′, a day of solemn prayer for all dead persons, usually on November 2.

all·spice (ôl′spīs′), *n.* **1.** Also called **all′spice tree′.** an aromatic, myrtaceous tree, *Pimenta officinalis,* of tropical America. **2.** the brown berry of this tree. **3.** a mildly sharp spice made from this berry, having a scent and flavor resembling a mixture of cloves, cinnamon, and nutmeg.

all-star (ôl′stär′), *adj.* **1.** consisting entirely of star performers. —*n.* **2.** a player selected for an all-star team.

all′-terrain′ ve′hicle, a small, rugged automobile capable of going over any nonroad surface including water, for recreational or industrial use.

al·lude (ə lōōd′), *v.i.*, **-lud·ed, -lud·ing.** to mention briefly or incidentally (usually fol. by *to*). [< L *allūde(re)* = *al-* AL- + *lūdere* to play]

al·lure (ə lŏŏr′), *v.,* **-lured, -lur·ing,** *n.* —*v.t.* **1.** to attract by the offer of something flattering or desirable. **2.** to fascinate; charm. —*n.* **3.** power of fascination; charm; appeal. [late ME *alure* < MF *alure(r)* = *a-* A-[5] + *lurer* to LURE] —**al·lur′er,** *n.* —**Syn. 1.** entice, lure. **2.** enchant, entrance.

al·lure·ment (ə lo͝or′mənt), *n.* **1.** the power of alluring; charm. **2.** the act, means, or process of alluring.

al·lur·ing (ə lo͝or′ing), *adj.* **1.** tempting; enticing. **2.** fascinating; charming. —**al·lur′ing·ly,** *adv.* —**al·lur′ing·ness,** *n.*

al·lu·sion (ə lo͞o′zhən), *n.* **1.** a passing or casual reference; an incidental mention: *an allusion to Shakespeare.* **2.** *Obs.* a metaphor; parable. [< LL *allūsiōn-* (s. of *allūsiō*) = *allūs(us)* played with, ptp. of *allūdere* to ALLUDE (*al-* AL- + *lūd-* play + *-tus* ptp. suffix) + *-iōn-* -ION]

al·lu·sive (ə lo͞o′siv), *adj.* **1.** having reference to something implied or inferred. **2.** containing, abounding in, or characterized by allusions. [ALLUS(ION) + -IVE] —**al·lu′sive·ly,** *adv.* —**al·lu′sive·ness,** *n.*

al·lu·vi·al (ə lo͞o′vē əl), *adj.* **1.** of or pertaining to alluvium. —*n.* **2.** alluvial soil. **3.** *Australian.* gold-bearing alluvial soil. [ALLUVI(UM) + -AL[1]]

allu′vial fan′, *Phys. Geog.* a fan-shaped alluvial deposit formed by a stream where its velocity is abruptly decreased. Also called **allu′vial cone′.**

al·lu·vi·on (ə lo͞o′vē ən), *n.* **1.** alluvium. **2.** *Law.* a gradual increase of land on a shore or river bank by the action of water, from natural or artificial causes. **3.** flood. [< L *alluviōn-* (s. of *alluviō* an overflowing) = *al-* AL- + *luv-* (s. of *luere* to wash) + *-iōn-* -ION]

al·lu·vi·um (ə lo͞o′vē əm), *n., pl.* **-vi·ums, -vi·a** (-vē ə). **1.** a deposit of sand, mud, etc., formed by flowing water. **2.** the sedimentary matter so deposited within recent times, esp. in the valleys of large rivers. Also, **alluvion.** [< L, n. use of neut. of *alluvius* washed against = *alluv-* (see ALLUVION) + *-ius, -ium* adj. suffix]

al·ly (*v.* ə lī′; *n.* al′ī, ə lī′), *v.,* **-lied, -ly·ing,** *n., pl.* **-lies.** —*v.t.* **1.** (used passively or reflexively) to unite formally, as by treaty, league, marriage, or the like (usually fol. by *to* or *with*). **2.** to associate or connect by some mutual relationship, as resemblance or friendship. —*v.i.* **3.** to enter into an alliance; join; unite. —*n.* **4.** a person or thing that is united with another, as by treaty. **5.** something akin to or resembling another. **6.** a person who collaborates, cooperates, or associates with another. [ME *alie(n)* < OF *alier,* var. of *aleier* < L *alligāre* to bind to. See ALLOY] —**al·li′a·ble,** *adj.* —**Syn. 1.** join, combine. **4.** partner, confederate. **6.** friend, accomplice, colleague. —**Ant. 4, 6.** enemy, foe, adversary.

-ally, an adverbial suffix attached to certain adjectives with stems in *-ic* which have no forms ending in *-ical: terrifically.* [-AL[1] + -LY]

all-year (ôl′yēr′), *adj.* **1.** extending through a year. **2.** open all year, as for business. **3.** usable or productive throughout the year.

al·lyl (al′il), *adj.* *Chem.* containing the allyl group. [< L *all(ium)* garlic + -YL]

al′lyl al′cohol, *Chem.* a liquid, $CH_2{=}CHCH_2{=}OH$: used in organic synthesis in the manufacture of resins, plasticizers, and pharmaceuticals. Also called **propenol.**

al′lyl chlo′ride, *Chem.* a flammable liquid, $CH_2{=}CHCH_2Cl$: used chiefly in the synthesis of resins and pharmaceuticals.

al′lyl group′, *Chem.* the univalent group, $CH_2{=}CHCH_2{,}{=}$ derived from propylene. Also called **al′lyl rad′ical.**

al′lyl res′in, *Chem.* any of a class of thermosetting resins made from allyl alcohol and a dibasic acid, used chiefly as adhesives for laminated materials.

al′lyl sul′fide, *Chem.* a water-insoluble liquid, $(CH_2{=}CHCH_2)_2S$, having a garliclike odor, used chiefly in flavoring. Also called **diallyl sulfide, thioallyl ether.**

Al·ma A·ta (äl′mä ä′tä, ä tä′), *n.* a city in and the capital of Kazakstan, in the S Soviet Union in Asia. 617,000 (1965). Formerly, **Vyernyi.**

Al·ma·dén (äl′mä then′), *n.* a town in Spain: mercury mines. 12,998 (1950).

Al·ma·gest (al′mə jest′), *n.* any of various medieval works on astrology or alchemy. [late ME *almageste* < MF < Ar *al* the + *majistī* < Gk *megístē* greatest (composition); so called after the title of a treatise on astronomy by Ptolemy]

al·mah (al′mə), *n.* (in Egypt) a girl who dances or sings professionally. Also, **al′ma, alme, almeh.** [< Ar *'almah* trained (lit., knowledgeable)]

al·ma ma·ter (äl′mə mä′tər, al′-; al′mə mā′tər), a school, college, or university at which a person has studied and, usually, from which he has been graduated. [< L: nourishing (i.e., dear) mother]

al·ma·nac (ôl′mə nak′), *n.* **1.** an annual publication containing a calendar for the coming year, the times of such events and phenomena as sunrises and sunsets, phases of the moon, and other statistical information. **2.** a publication containing astronomical or meteorological data, usually including future positions of celestial objects, star magnitudes, and culmination dates of constellations. **3.** a compendium of useful and interesting facts relating to countries of the world, sports, etc. [late ME *almenak* < ML *almanac(h)* < SpAr *al* the + *'manākh* calendar < ?]

Al·ma-Tad·e·ma (al′mə tad′ə mə), *n.* **Sir Lawrence,** 1836–1912, English painter, born in the Netherlands.

al·me (al′me), *n.* almah. Also, **al′meh.**

al·me·mar (al mē′mär), *n.* bimah. [< Heb < Ar *al* the + *minbar* stand, platform]

Al·me·rí·a (äl′me rē′ä), *n.* a seaport in S Spain, on the Mediterranean. 89,470 (est. 1963). —**Al·me·ri·an** (al′mə rē′ən), *adj., n.*

al·might·y (ôl mī′tē), *adj.* **1.** having unlimited power; omnipotent, as God or a deity. **2.** having very great power, influence, etc. **3.** *Informal.* extreme; terrible: *He's in an almighty fix.* —*adv.* **4.** *Slang.* extremely. —*n.* **5. the Almighty,** God. [ME; OE *ælmihtig, ealmihtig* = *æl-, eal-* ALL + *mihtig* MIGHTY] —**al·might′i·ly,** *adv.* —**al·might′i·ness,** *n.*

al·mond (ä′mənd, am′ənd; *spelling pron.* al′mənd), *n.* **1.** the nutlike stone or kernel of the fruit of a tree, *Amygdalus Prunus,* of warm temperate regions. **2.** the tree itself. —*adj.* **3.** of the taste or shape of an almond. **4.** made or flavored with almonds: *almond cookies.* [ME *almande* < MF, OF *alemandle* = *al-* (< Ar *al* the) + *emandle* < Pr *amandola* << L *amygdala* < Gk *amygdálē*; r. OE *amigdal* < L]

al·mond-eyed (ä′mənd īd′, am′ənd-; *spelling pron.* al′mənd īd′), *adj.* having narrow, oval-shaped eyes.

al·mon·er (al′mə nər, ä′mə-), *n.* **1.** a person who distributes alms on behalf of an institution, a royal personage, etc. **2.** *Brit.* a social worker in a hospital. [ME *aumoner* < OF << LL *eleēmosynār(ius)* ELEEMOSYNARY]

al·mon·ry (al′mən rē, ä′mən-), *n., pl.* **-ries.** a place where an almoner resides or where alms are distributed. [ALMON(ER) + -RY; r. late ME *almonesrie* (? mistake for *almonerrie*)]

al·most (ôl′mōst, ôl mōst′), *adv.* very nearly: *almost every house.* [ME; OE *(e)al māst,* var. of *æl mǣst* nearly]

—**Syn.** ALMOST (MOST), NEARLY, WELL-NIGH all mean within a small degree of or short space of. ALMOST implies very little short of: *almost exhausted; almost home.* MOST is colloquial for ALMOST. NEARLY implies a slightly greater distance or degree than ALMOST: *nearly to the city.* WELL-NIGH, a more literary word, implies a barely appreciable distance or extent: *well-nigh forgotten.*

alms (ämz), *n.* (*construed as sing. or pl.*) money or other donations given to the poor or needy. [ME *almes,* OE *ælmysse* << LL *eleēmosyna* < Gk *eleēmosýnē* compassion, alms. See ELEEMOSYNARY]

alms·house (ämz′hous′), *n., pl.* **-hous·es** (-hou′ziz). *Chiefly Brit.* a poorhouse.

alms·man (ämz′mən), *n., pl.* **-men. 1.** a person supported by or receiving alms. **2.** *Archaic.* a person who gives alms.

alms·wom·an (ämz′wo͝om′ən), *n., pl.* **-wom·en. 1.** a woman supported by or receiving alms. **2.** *Archaic.* a woman who gives alms.

Al·ni·co (al′ni kō′), *n.* *Trademark.* a permanent-magnet alloy having aluminum, nickel, and cobalt as its principal ingredients.

al·oe (al′ō), *n., pl.* **-oes. 1.** any chiefly African, liliaceous plant of the genus *Aloe,* certain species of which yield a drug and a fiber. **2.** Often, **aloes.** (*construed as sing.*) *Pharm.* a bitter purgative drug, the inspissated juice of several species of *Aloe.* **3.** See **century plant.** [ME; OE *alu(w)e* < L *aloē* < Gk *alóē*] —**al·o·et·ic** (al′ō et′ik), *adj.*

a·loft (ə lôft′, ə loft′), *adv.* **1.** high up; in or into the air. **2.** *Naut.* on the masts or in the rigging; overhead. [A-[1] + LOFT; cf. Icel *ā lopt* in the air]

a·lo·ha (ə lō′ə, ä lō′hä), *n., interj.* (in Hawaii) **1.** hello; welcome. **2.** farewell. [< Hawaiian]

Alo′ha State′, Hawaii (used as a nickname).

al·o·in (al′ō in), *n.* *Pharm.* a bitter powder obtained from aloe, used chiefly as a purgative. [ALO(E) + -IN[2]]

a·lone (ə lōn′), *adj.* **1.** apart from any other. **2.** with nothing else besides: *to live for money alone.* **3.** unique, as in excellence or poorness. **4. leave alone,** to allow (someone) to be solitary or free from disturbance. **5. let alone, a.** to refrain from annoying or interfering with. **b.** not to mention: *He was too tired to walk, let alone run.* —*adv.* **6.** solitarily; solely. **7.** only; exclusively. **8.** without aid or help. [ME *al one* ALL (wholly) ONE] —**a·lone′ness,** *n.*

—**Syn. 1.** single, solitary, isolated. ALONE, LONE imply being without companionship or association. ALONE suggests solitariness or desolation: *alone in the house.* LONE is somewhat poetic or is intended humorously: *a lone sentinel.*

a·long (ə lông′, ə long′), *prep.* **1.** through, on, beside, over, or parallel to the length or direction of; from one end to the other of: *to walk along a highway.* **2.** during: *Somewhere along the journey I lost my hat.* **3.** in conformity or accordance with: *Along the lines just stated, I suggest we start the new project.* —*adv.* **4.** by the length; lengthwise; parallel to or in a line with the length or direction: *He ran along beside me.* **5.** onward: *to move along.* **6.** *U.S. Informal.* (of time) some way on: *along toward evening.* **7.** in company or in agreement (usually fol. by *with*): *He planned the project along with his associates.* **8.** *Chiefly U.S.* as a companion: *He took his sister along.* **9.** from one person or place to another: *Pass the word along.* **10.** at or to an advanced place or state: *Work on the new ship is quite far along.* **11.** as an accompanying item: *Take your umbrella along.* **12. all along,** all the time; throughout: *He knew all along that it was a lie.* **13. be along,** *Informal.* to arrive at a place: *He will be along soon.* [ME; OE *andlang* = *and-* (c. OS, Icel *and-,* Goth *and(a)-,* OHG *ant-,* prefix) + *lang* LONG[1]]

along′ of′, *Dial.* owing to; because of. [ME *along on,* alter. of *ilong on,* OE *gelang on* (*ge-* associative prefix + *lang* LONG[1])]

a·long·side (ə lông′sīd′, ə long′-), *adv.* **1.** along, by, at, or to the side of something: *We brought the boat alongside.* —*prep.* **2.** beside; by the side of.

a·loof (ə lo͞of′), *adv.* **1.** at a distance, esp. in feeling or interest: *He stood aloof from their arguments.* —*adj.* **2.** reserved or indifferent. [A-[1] + *loof* LUFF windward] —**a·loof′ly,** *adv.* —**a·loof′ness,** *n.* —**Syn. 1.** apart. **2.** impartial, uninvolved. —**Ant. 2.** involved.

al·o·pe·ci·a (al′ə pē′shē ə), *n.* *Pathol.* baldness. [late ME < L < Gk *alōpekía* mange in foxes = *alōpek-* (s. of *alṓpex*) fox + *-ia* -IA] —**al·o·pe·cic** (al′ə pē′sik), *adj.*

A·lost (*Fr.* A lôst′), *n.* a city in central Belgium, NW of Brussels. 45,476 (est. 1964). Flemish, **Aalst.**

a·loud (ə loud′), *adv.* **1.** with the natural tone and volume of the speaking voice, as distinguished from whisperingly: *They could not speak aloud in the library.* **2.** vocally or orally, as distinguished from silently: *to read aloud.* **3.** with a loud voice; loudly: *to cry aloud.* [ME]

a·low (ə lō′), *adv.* *Naut.* **1.** near the deck; in the lower rigging. **2. alow and aloft,** everywhere.

alp (alp), *n.* a high mountain. [back formation from ALPS]

A.L.P., See **American Labor party.** Also, **ALP**

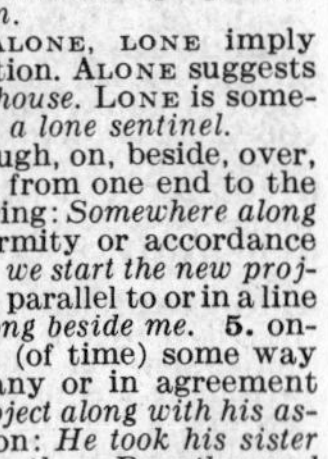

Alpaca, *Lama pacos* (3½ ft. high at shoulder; total height 5 ft.; length 3½ ft.)

al·pac·a (al pak′ə), *n.* **1.** a domesticated, South American animal of the genus *Lama,* having long, soft, silky hair or wool, believed to be a variety of the guanaco. **2.** the hair of this animal. **3.** a fabric made of it. **4.** a cotton or rayon fabric simulating it. [< Sp < Aymara]

al·pen·glow (al′pən glō′), *n.* a reddish glow often seen on the summits of mountains just before sunrise or just after sunset. [< G *Alpenglühen*, with GLOW r. G *glühen*]

al·pen·horn (al′pən hôrn′), *n.* a long, powerful horn of wood or bark, used by Swiss herdsmen and mountaineers. Also called **alphorn.** [< G = *Alpen* ALP(S) + *Horn* HORN]

al·pen·stock (al′pən stok′), *n.* a strong staff with an iron point, used by mountain climbers. [< G = *Alpen* ALP(S) + *Stock* staff]

al·pes·trine (al pes′trin), *adj.* *Bot.* subalpine (def. 2). [< ML *alpestr(is)* (*Alp(ēs)* the Alps + *-estris* adj. suffix) + -INE[1]]

al·pha (al′fə), *n.* **1.** the first letter of the Greek alphabet (A, α). **2.** the first; beginning. **3.** (*cap.*) *Astron.* the brightest star in a constellation. **4.** *Chem.* **a.** one of the possible positions of an atom or group in a compound. **b.** one of two or more isomeric compounds. [< L < Gk < a Phoenician word; cf. Heb *āleph* ox]

al′pha and ome′ga, the beginning and the end.

al·pha·bet (al′fə bet′), *n.* **1.** the letters of a language in their customary order. **2.** any system of characters or signs with which a language is written: *the Greek alphabet.* **3.** the basic facts of a subject of study; rudiments. [< LL *alphabēt(um)*, alter. of Gk *alphábētos.* See ALPHA, BETA]

al·pha·bet·i·cal (al′fə bet′i kəl), *adj.* **1.** in the order of the letters of the alphabet. **2.** pertaining to, expressed by, or using an alphabet. Also, **al′pha·bet′ic.** —**al′pha·bet′i·cal·ly,** *adv.*

al·pha·bet·ise (al′fə bi tīz′), *v.t.*, **-ised, -is·ing.** *Chiefly Brit.* alphabetize. —**al·pha·bet·i·sa·tion** (al′fə bet′i zā′shən), *n.* —**al′pha·bet·is′er,** *n.*

al·pha·bet·ize (al′fə bi tīz′), *v.t.*, **-ized, -iz·ing.** **1.** to put or arrange in alphabetical order. **2.** to express by or furnish with an alphabet. —**al·pha·bet·i·za·tion** (al′fə bet′i zā′shən), *n.* —**al′pha·bet·iz′er,** *n.*

Al′pha Centau′ri, a first-magnitude star in the constellation Centaurus, and the star closest to the sun.

al′pha decay′, *Physics.* a radioactive process in which an alpha particle is emitted from the nucleus of an atom, decreasing its atomic number by two.

al·pha·nu·mer·ic (al′fə nōō mer′ik, -nyōō-), *adj.* *Computer Technol.* (of a set of characters) including both letters and numbers. Also, **al·pha·mer·ic** (al′fə mer′ik), **al′pha·mer′i·cal, al′pha·nu·mer′i·cal.** [ALPHA(BET) + NUMERIC(AL)] —**al′pha·nu·mer′i·cal·ly, al′pha·mer′i·cal·ly,** *adv.*

al′pha par′ticle, *Physics.* a positively charged particle consisting of two protons and two neutrons, emitted in radioactive decay or nuclear fission; the nucleus of a helium atom.

al′pha priv′ative, the prefix *a-*, used in Greek grammar to express negation.

al′pha ray′, *Physics.* a stream of alpha particles.

Al·phe·us (al fē′əs), *n.* *Class. Myth.* a river god, son of Oceanus and Tethys, who fell in love with the nymph Arethusa and, when she became a spring to escape him, changed into a river and mingled with her.

alp·horn (alp′hôrn′), *n.* alpenhorn.

al·pine (al′pīn, -pin), *adj.* **1.** of or pertaining to lofty mountains. **2.** very high; elevated. **3.** (*cap.*) of, pertaining to, or on the Alps. **4.** *Bot.* growing on mountains above the limit of tree growth: *alpine plants.* **5.** (*cap.*) *Anthropol.* having the features characteristic of an Alpine. —*n.* **6.** (*cap.*) *Anthropol.* a Caucasoid people found in central Europe and characterized by heavy body build, a medium complexion, and straight to wavy hair. [< L *Alpīn(us).* See ALPS, -INE[1]] —**al′pine·ly,** *adv.*

al·pin·ism (al′pə niz′əm), *n.* (*often cap.*) mountain climbing, esp. in the Alps. —**al′pin·ist, Al′pin·ist,** *n.*

Alps (alps), *n.* (*construed as pl.*) a mountain range in S Europe, extending from France through Switzerland and Italy into Austria and Yugoslavia. Highest peak, Mont Blanc, 15,781 ft. [< L *Alp(ēs)*]

al·read·y (ôl red′ē), *adv.* **1.** previous to a given or implied time. **2.** so soon; so early: *Is it noon already?* [ME *alredy*] —**Usage.** ALREADY is sometimes confused with ALL READY, although they are far apart in meaning. ALREADY means "previously": *The plane had already left the airport.* ALL READY means "completely prepared or ready": *The troops were all ready to attack.*

al·right (ôl rīt′), *adv.* *Nonstandard.* all right. —**Usage.** The form ALRIGHT is occasionally seen as a variant of ALL RIGHT, probably by analogy with ALREADY and ALTOGETHER, but it is not considered acceptable in standard English.

Al·sace (al sās′, al′sas; *Fr.* AL ZAS′), *n.* a region and former province of France between the Vosges and the Rhine. Ancient, **Al·sa·tia** (al sā′shə). Cf. **Alsace-Lorraine.**

Al·sace-Lor·raine (al′sās lō rān′, -lô-, -sas-; *Fr.* AL ZAS lô REN′), *n.* a region in NE France, including the former provinces of Alsace and Lorraine: part of Germany 1871–1919, 1940–45. 5607 sq. mi. —**Al′sace-Lor·rain′er,** *n.*

BELGIUM
PRUSSIA
LUX.
HESSE
PALATINATE
Metz
Strasbourg
Alsace-Lorraine 1871-1919
WURTTEMBERG
BADEN
FRANCE
SWITZERLAND

Al·sa·tian (al sā′shən), *adj.* **1.** of or pertaining to Alsace or its inhabitants. —*n.* **2.** a native or inhabitant of Alsace. **3.** Also called **Alsa′tian dog′.** *Brit.* the German shepherd dog.

al′sike clo′ver, (al′sīk, -sik, ôl′-), a European clover, *Trifolium hybridum*, having whitish or pink flowers, grown in the U.S. for forage. Also called **al′sike.** [after *Alsike*, near Uppsala, Sweden]

Al Si·rat (al si rät′), *Islam.* **1.** the correct path of religion. **2.** the bridge, fine as a razor's edge, over which all who enter paradise must pass. [< Ar = *al* the + *ṣirāṭ* road < L (*via*) *strāta* paved (way)]

al·so (ôl′sō), *adv.* **1.** in addition; too; besides: *He was thin, and he was also tall.* **2.** likewise: *Since you're having another cup of coffee, I'll also have one.* —*conj.* **3.** and. [ME; OE (*e*)*alswā* ALL (wholly or quite) so[1]] —**Syn. 1.** moreover.

al·so-ran (ôl′sō ran′), *n.* **1.** *Sports.* **a.** (in a race) a contestant who fails to win or to place among the first three finishers. **b.** an athlete or team that rarely wins. **2.** *Informal.* **a.** a person who is defeated in any competition. **b.** a person who attains little or no success.

alt (alt), *Music.* —*adj.* **1.** high. —*n.* **2. in alt,** in the first octave above the treble staff. [< Pr < L *alt(um)*, n. use of neut. of *altus* high]

alt., 1. alternate. **2.** altitude. **3.** alto.

Alta., Alberta.

Al·ta·de·na (al′tə dē′nə), *n.* a town in SW California, near Los Angeles. 42,415 (1970).

Al·ta·ic (al tā′ik), *n.* **1.** a family of languages made up of the Turkic, Mongolian, Tungusic, and Korean subfamilies. —*adj.* **2.** of or belonging to Altaic. **3.** of or pertaining to the Altai Mountains. Also, **Al·ta·ian** (al tā′ən, tī′-).

Al′tai Moun′tains (al tī′, äl-; al′tī, äl′-), a mountain range mostly in Outer Mongolia and the S Soviet Union. Highest peak, Belukha, 15,157 ft.

Al·tair (al′târ), *n.* a first-magnitude star in the constellation Aquila. [< Ar = *al* the + *ṭā'ir* bird (lit., flyer)]

Al·ta·mi·ra (al′tə mēr′ə; *Sp.* äl′tä mē′rä), *n.* a cave in N Spain, near Santander, noted for its Stone Age color drawings of animals.

al·tar (ôl′tər), *n.* **1.** an elevated place or structure, as a mound or platform, at which religious rites are performed or on which sacrifices are offered to gods, ancestors, etc. **2. lead to the altar,** *Informal.* to wed. [ME, OE *alter* (OE also *altar*) < L *altāria* (pl.) = *alt(us)* high + *-āria*, pl. of *-āre* -AR[2]]

al′tar boy′, acolyte (def. 1).

al·tar·piece (ôl′tər pēs′), *n.* a painted or carved screen behind or above the altar in Christian churches; reredos.

al′tar rail′, the rail in front of an altar, separating the sanctuary from those parts of the church in front of it.

al′tar stone′, mensa. Also called **al′tar slab′.**

alt·az·i·muth (al taz′ə məth), *n.* *Astron.* an instrument for determining both the altitude and the azimuth of a heavenly body. [ALT(ITUDE) + AZIMUTH]

Alt·dorf (ält′dôrf′), *n.* a town in central Switzerland, near Lucerne: legendary home of William Tell. 7477 (1960).

al·ter (ôl′tər), *v.t.* **1.** to make different in some particular, as size, style, course, or the like; modify: *to alter a coat; to alter course.* **2.** to castrate or spay (used euphemistically). —*v.i.* **3.** to change; become different or modified. [late ME < OF *alter(er)* < LL *alterāre* to change, worsen < L *alter* other] —**al′ter·a·ble,** *adj.* —**al′ter·a·bil′i·ty, al′ter·a·ble·ness,** *n.* —**al′ter·a·bly,** *adv.*

alter., alteration.

al·ter·ant (ôl′tər ənt), *adj.* **1.** producing alteration. —*n.* **2.** something that produces alteration. [< L *alterant-* (s. of *alterāns* changing, prp. of *alterāre*) = *alter* other + *-ant-* -ANT]

al·ter·a·tion (ôl′tə rā′shən), *n.* **1.** the act or state of altering. **2.** the state of being altered. **3.** a change; modification. [late ME < ML *alterātiōn-* (s. of *alterātiō*)]

al·ter·a·tive (ôl′tə rā′tiv, -tər ə tiv), *adj.* tending to alter. [< ML *alterātīv(us).* See ALTER, -ATIVE]

al·ter·cate (ôl′tər kāt′, al′-), *v.i.*, **-cat·ed, -cat·ing.** to argue with zeal, heat, or anger; wrangle. [< L *altercāt(us)* (ptp. of *altercārī* to quarrel) = **alterc(us)* a disputing (*alter* other + *-cus* formative suffix) + *-ātus* -ATE[1]]

al·ter·ca·tion (ôl′tər kā′shən, al′-), *n.* a heated or angry dispute; noisy argument or controversy. [< L *altercātiōn-* (s. of *altercātiō*)] —**Syn.** quarrel, contention.

al·ter e·go (ôl′tər ē′gō, eg′ō, al′-), **1.** a second self. **2.** an inseparable friend. [< L]

al·ter i·dem (äl′teʀ ē′dem; *Eng.* ôl′tər ī′dem, al′-), *Latin.* another exactly the same.

al·ter·nant (ôl′tûr nənt, al′- *or, esp. Brit.*, ôl tûr′nənt, al-), *adj.* alternating; alternate. [< L *alternant-* (s. of *alternāns*, prp. of *alternāre.* See ALTERNATION, -ANT]

al·ter·nate (*v.* ôl′tər nāt′, al′-; *adj.*, *n.* ôl′tər nit, al′-), *v.*, **-nat·ed, -nat·ing,** *adj.*, *n.* —*v.i.* **1.** to interchange repeatedly and regularly with one another in time or place (usually fol. by *with*). **2.** to change back and forth between conditions, actions, etc.: *He alternates between hope and despair.* **3.** *Elect.* to reverse direction or sign periodically. —*v.t.* **4.** to perform in succession or one after another. **5.** to interchange successively or regularly: *to alternate hot and cold compresses.* —*adj.* **6.** being in a constant state of succession or rotation; interchanged repeatedly one for another: *Winter and summer are alternate seasons.* **7.** reciprocal; mutual: *alternate acts of kindness.* **8.** every second one of a series: *Read only the alternate lines.* **9.** alternative (def. 4). **10.** *Bot.* placed singly at different heights on the axis, on each side in succession, or at definite angular distances from one another, as leaves. —*n.* **11.** *U.S.* a person authorized to fill the position, exercise the duties, etc., of another in his absence. **12.** alternative (defs. 1–3). [< L *alternāt(us)* (ptp.) = *altern(āre)* (to) alternate (< *altern(us)* by turns) + *-ātus* -ATE[1]] —**al′ter·nate·ness,** *n.* —**al′ter·nat′ing·ly,** *adv.*

Alternate leaves

al′ternate an′gles, *Geom.* two nonadjacent angles made by the crossing of two lines by a third line, both angles being either interior or exterior, and being on opposite sides of the third line.

al·ter·nate·ly (ôl′tər nit lē, al′-), *adv.* **1.** in alternate order; by rotation. **2.** in alternate position: *Dark stripes were spaced alternately with light ones.*

al′ternating cur′rent. See AC.

al·ter·na·tion (ôl′tər nā′shən, al′-), *n.* **1.** the act of alternating. **2.** the state of being alternated. **3.** alternate succession; repeated rotation. **4.** one half of an alternating cycle. [< LL *alternātiōn-* (s. of *alternātiō*)]

alterna′tion of genera′tions, *Biol.* the alternation in the life cycle of an organism of forms produced in a different manner, esp. the alternation of sexual with asexual generations.

al·ter·na·tive (ôl tûr′nə tiv, al-), *n.* **1.** a choice limited to one of two or more possibilities: *You have the alternative of riding or walking.* **2.** one of these choices: *The alternative to riding is walking.* **3.** a necessary or remaining choice: *There was no alternative but to walk.* —*adj.* **4.** affording a choice between two things. **5.** (of two choices) mutually exclusive so that if one is chosen the other must be rejected: *The alternative possibilities are neutrality or war.* **6.** *Logic.* (of a proposition) asserting two or more choices, at least one of which is true. Also, **alternate** (for defs. 1–4). —**al·ter′na·tive·ly,** *adv.* —**al·ter′na·tive·ness, al·ter′na·tiv′i·ty,** *n.* —**Syn. 1.** option, selection. See **choice.**

al·ter·na·tor (ôl′tər nā′tər, al′-), *n.* *Elect.* a generator of alternating current.

Alt·geld (ôlt′geld), *n.* **John Peter,** 1847–1902, U.S. politician: governor of Illinois 1892–96.

Al·thae·a (al thē′ə), *n.* *Class. Myth.* wife of Oeneus and mother of Tydeus, Meleager, and Deianira.

al·the·a (al thē′ə), *n.* **1.** any plant of the genus *Althaea,* comprising the hollyhocks, marsh mallows, etc. **2.** the rose of Sharon, *Hibiscus syriacus.* Also, **al·thae′a.** [< L *althaea* < Gk *althaíā* marsh mallow]

alt·horn (alt′hôrn′), *n.* a valved brass musical instrument, varying in shape, that is the alto member of the cornet family. Also called **alto horn.**

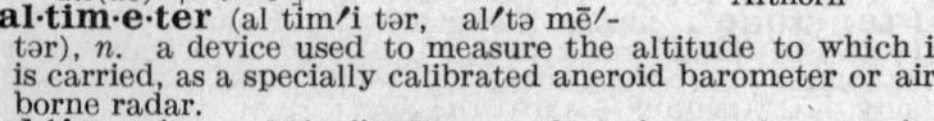

Althorn

al·though (ôl thō′), *conj.* in spite of the fact that; even though; though. Also, **al·tho′.** [ME *al thogh* ALL (adv.) even + THOUGH] —**Syn.** notwithstanding (that), even if, albeit (that).

alti-, a prefix occurring in loan words from Latin where it meant "high" (*altitude*), used in the formation of compound words: *altimeter.* [ME < L = *alt(us)* + *-i-* -I-]

al·tim·e·ter (al tim′i tər, al′tə mē′tər), *n.* a device used to measure the altitude to which it is carried, as a specially calibrated aneroid barometer or airborne radar.

al·tim·e·try (al tim′i trē), *n.* the science of measuring altitudes, as by altimeters. —**al·ti·metri·cal** (al′tə me′tri kəl), *adj.* —**al′ti·met′ri·cal·ly,** *adv.*

al·tis·si·mo (al tis′ə mō′; *It.* äl tēs′sē mô′), *Music.* —*adj.* **1.** very high. —*n.* **2. in altissimo,** in the second octave above the treble staff. [< It: lit., highest]

al·ti·tude (al′ti to͞od′, -tyo͞od′), *n.* **1.** the height above sea level of a given point. **2.** extent or distance upward. **3.** *Astron.* the angular distance of a heavenly body above the horizon. **4.** *Geom.* **a.** the perpendicular distance from the vertex of a figure to the side opposite it. **b.** the line through the vertex of a figure perpendicular to the base. **5.** Usually, **altitudes.** a high point or region: *mountain altitudes.* [< L *altitūd(ō)*] —**Syn. 2.** See **height.** —**Ant. 2.** depth.

al′titude sick′ness, dizziness and nausea, often accompanied by breathlessness, due to insufficient oxygen in the blood, as affecting some people at high altitudes.

al·ti·tu·di·nal (al′ti to͞od′ənəl, -tyo͞od′-), *adj.* relating to altitude or height. [< L *altitūdin-* (s. of *altitūdō*) ALTITUDE + -AL[1]]

al·to (al′tō), *n., pl.* **-tos,** *adj.* *Music.* —*n.* **1.** the lowest female voice; contralto. **2.** the highest male voice; countertenor. **3.** a singer with such a voice. **4.** a musical part for such a voice. **5.** the second highest of the four parts of a mixed vocal chorus, or the voices or persons singing this part. **6.** the second highest instrument in a family of musical instruments. —*adj.* **7.** of, noting, pertaining to, or having the tonal range of the alto. **8.** (of a musical instrument) second highest in a family of musical instruments. [< It *alto* < L *alt(us)* high]

alto-, var. of **alti-:** *altostratus.*

al′to clef′, *Music.* a sign locating middle C on the third line of the staff. Also called **viola clef.** See illus. at **clef.**

al·to·cu·mu·lus (al′tō kyo͞o′myə ləs), *n., pl.* **-lus.** *Meteorol.* a cloud of a class characterized by globular masses or rolls in layers or patches: of medium altitude, ab. 8000–20,000 ft.

al·to·geth·er (ôl′tə geth′ər, ôl′tə geth′ər), *adv.* **1.** wholly; completely; entirely. **2.** with all or everything included: *a debt of ten dollars altogether.* **3.** with all or everything considered; on the whole: *Altogether, I'm glad it's over.* —*n.* **4. in the altogether,** *Informal.* nude. [var. of ME *altogeder*] —**Usage.** ALTOGETHER and ALL TOGETHER are sometimes confused. As an adverb, ALTOGETHER means "wholly, completely, entirely": *an altogether confused report,* while ALL TOGETHER, as an adjective phrase, means "in a group": *They were all together in the kitchen.*

al′to horn′, althorn.

Al·ton (ôl′tən), *n.* a city in SW Illinois. 39,700 (1970).

Al·too·na (al to͞o′nə), *n.* a city in central Pennsylvania. 63,115 (1970).

al·to-re·lie·vo (al′tō ri lē′vō), *n., pl.* **-vos.** See **high relief.** Italian, **alto-rilievo.**

al·to-ri·lie·vo (äl′tô rē lye′vô), *n., pl.* **al·ti-ri·lie·vi** (äl′tē rē lye′vē). *Italian.* See **high relief.**

al·to·stra·tus (al′tō strā′təs, -strat′əs), *n., pl.* **-tus.** *Meteorol.* a cloud of a class characterized by a generally uniform gray sheet or layer: of medium altitude, ab. 8000–20,000 ft.

al·tri·cial (al trish′əl), *adj.* *Ornith.* helpless at hatching and requiring parental care for a period of time. Cf. **precocial.** [< NL *altriciāl(is),* L *altrīci-* (s. of *altrix*) nourisher = *al-* feed (see ALIMENT) + *-trīci-* fem. suffix of agency + *-ālis* -AL[1]]

al·tru·ism (al′tro͞o iz′əm), *n.* the principle or practice of unselfish concern for or devotion to the welfare of others (opposed to *egoism*). [< F *altruisme* = It *altrui* others (alter. of L *alterī*) + F *-isme* -ISM]

al·tru·ist (al′tro͞o ist), *n.* a person unselfishly concerned for or devoted to the welfare of others (opposed to *egoist*). [back formation from ALTRUISTIC]

al·tru·is·tic (al′tro͞o is′tik), *adj.* unselfishly concerned for or devoted to the welfare of others (opposed to *egoistic*). [AL-TRU(ISM) + -ISTIC] —**al′tru·is′ti·cal·ly,** *adv.*

al·u·del (al′yo͝o del′), *n.* *Chem.* one of a series of pear-shaped vessels, open at both ends and fitted one above the other, for recovering the sublimates produced during sublimation. [< MF < Sp < Ar *al* the + *uthāl,* var. of *ithāl,* pl. of *athla* piece of apparatus]

al·u·la (al′yə lə), *n., pl.* **-lae** (-lē′). the group of three to six small, rather stiff feathers growing on the first digit, pollex, or thumb of a bird's wing. Also called **bastard wing.** [< NL = L *āl(a)* wing + *-ula* -ULE] —**al′u·lar,** *adj.*

al·um (al′əm), *n.* **1.** *Chem.* **a.** a solid, $K_2SO_4 \cdot Al_2(SO_4)_3 \cdot 24H_2O$, used as an astringent and styptic, and in dyeing and tanning. **b.** one of class of double sulfates having the general formula $R_2SO_4 \cdot X_2(SO_4)_3 \cdot 24H_2O$, where R is a univalent alkali metal or ammonium, and X one of a number of trivalent metals. **2.** (not in technical use) aluminum sulfate, $Al_2(SO_4)_3$. [ME < MF < L *alūm(en)*; r. OE *alefne* for **alymne* < L *alūmni-* (s. of *alūmen*)]

alum., *Chem.* aluminum.

alumin-, var. of **alumino-,** esp. before a vowel.

a·lu·mi·na (ə lo͞o′mə nə), *n.* the natural or synthetic oxide of aluminum, occurring in nature as corundum. Also called **aluminum oxide.** [pl. of L *alūmen* ALUM]

a·lu·mi·nate (ə lo͞o′mə nāt′), *n.* **1.** *Chem.* a salt of the acid form of aluminum hydroxide, containing the group AlO_2^- or AlO_3^{-3}. **2.** *Mineral.* a metallic oxide combined with alumina.

a·lu·mi·nif·er·ous (ə lo͞o′mə nif′ər əs), *adj.* containing or yielding aluminum.

a·lu·mi·nise (ə lo͞o′mə nīz′), *v.t.,* **-nised, -nis·ing.** *Chiefly Brit.* aluminize.

al·u·min·i·um (al′yə min′ ē əm), *n., adj.* *Chiefly Brit.* aluminum.

a·lu·mi·nize (ə lo͞o′mə nīz′), *v.t.,* **-nized, -niz·ing.** to treat with aluminum. Also, *esp. Brit.,* **aluminise.**

alumino-, a combining form of **aluminum,** used esp. before a consonant: *aluminothermy.* Also, *esp. before a vowel,* **alumin-.**

a·lu·mi·no·sil·i·cate (ə lo͞o′mə nō sil′ə kit, -kāt′), *n.* any aluminum silicate containing alkali-metal or alkaline-earth metal ions, as a feldspar or zeolite.

a·lu·mi·no·ther·my (ə lo͞o′mə nō thûr′mē), *n.* *Metall.* a process of producing high temperatures by causing finely divided aluminum to react with the oxygen from another metallic oxide. Also, **a·lu′mi·no·ther′mics.**

a·lu·mi·nous (ə lo͞o′mə nəs), *adj.* of the nature of or containing alum or alumina. [< L *alūminōs(us)* = *alūmin-* (s. of *alūmen* ALUM) + *-ōsus* -OUS] —**a·lu·mi·nos·i·ty** (ə lo͞o′mə-nos′i tē), *n.*

a·lu·mi·num (ə lo͞o′mə nəm), *n.* **1.** *Chem.* a silver-white metallic element, light in weight, ductile, malleable, and not readily corroded or tarnished, occurring combined in clay, rocks, and soil: used in alloys and for utensils. airplane parts, etc. *Abbr.:* alum. *Symbol:* Al; *at. wt.:* 26.98; *at. no.:* 13; *sp. gr.:* 2.70 at 20°C. —*adj.* **2.** of, pertaining to, made of, or containing aluminum. Also, *esp. Brit.,* **aluminium.** [< NL, alter. of *alumium.* See ALUMINA, -IUM] —**al·u·min·ic** (al′yə-min′ik), *adj.*

alu′minum chlo′ride, *Chem.* a yellow-white solid, $AlCl_3$, in its hydrated form used chiefly as a wood preservative and in its anhydrous form as a catalyst.

alu′minum hydrox′ide, *Chem.* a water-insoluble powder, $Al(OH)_3$ or $Al_2O_3 \cdot H_2O$, used in the manufacture of glass, in dyeing, and as an antacid. Also called **alu′minum hy′drate, hydrated alumina.**

alu′minum ox′ide, alumina.

alu′minum sul′fate, *Chem.* a water-soluble solid, $Al_2(SO_4)_3$, used chiefly as a water-purifying agent, as a mordant, and in the manufacture of paper.

a·lum·na (ə lum′nə), *n., pl.* **-nae** (-nē). a girl or woman who is a graduate or former student of a specific school, college, or university. [< L: foster daughter, pupil; fem. of ALUMNUS] —**Usage.** See **alumnus.**

a·lum·nus (ə lum′nəs), *n., pl.* **-ni** (-nī). a male graduate or former student of a specific school, college, or university. [< L: foster son, pupil = *al-* (s. of *alere* to feed, support) + *-u-* + *-mnus,* orig. passive participial suffix, akin to Gk *-menos;* see PHENOMENON]
—**Usage.** A male graduate is an ALUMNUS (plural ALUMNI) and a female graduate is an ALUMNA (plural ALUMNAE). When referring to male and female graduates together, the masculine form ALUMNI is used.

al·um·root (al′əm ro͞ot′, -ro͝ot′), *n.* **1.** any of several North American, saxifragaceous herbs of the genus *Heuchera,* esp. *H. americana,* the root of which is used as an astringent.

al·u·nite (al′yə nīt′), *n.* a mineral, a hydrous sulfate of potassium and aluminum, $KAl_3(SO_4)_2(OH)_6$. [< F *alun* (< L *alūmen* ALUM) + -ITE[1]]

Al·va (al′və; *Sp.* äl′vä), *n.* **Fer·nan·do Ál·va·rez de To·le·do** (fer nän′dô äl′vä reth′ de tô le′thô), **Duke of,** 1508–1582, Spanish general who suppressed a Protestant rebellion in the Netherlands in 1567. Also, **Alba.**

Al·va·ra·do (äl′vä rä′thô), *n.* **1. A·lon·so de** (ä lôn′sô the), c1490–1554, Spanish soldier in the conquests of Mexico and Peru: governor of Cuzco 1552?–54. **2. Pe·dro de** (pe′thrô the), 1495–1541, Spanish soldier: chief aide of Cortés in conquest of Mexico; governor of Guatemala 1530–34.

alveol-, a combining form of **alveolus:** *alveolar.*

al·ve·o·lar (al vē′ə lər), *adj.* **1.** *Anat., Zool.* of or pertaining to an alveolus or to alveoli. **2.** *Phonet.* articulated with the tongue touching or close to the alveolar ridge, as *t, d, n;* gingival. —*n.* **3.** *Phonet.* an alveolar sound. —**al·ve′o·lar·ly,** *adv.*

alve′olar arch′, the part of the upper or lower jawbone in which the teeth are set.

alve′olar ridge′, the ridgelike border of the upper and lower jaws containing the sockets of the teeth. Also called **alve′olar proc′ess.**

al·ve·o·late (al vē′ə lit, -lāt′), *adj.* having alveoli; pitted. Also, **al·ve′o·lat′ed** [< L *alveolāt(us)*]. —**al·ve′o·la′tion,** *n.*

al·ve·o·lus (al vē′ə ləs), *n., pl.* **-li** (-lī′). *Anat., Zool.* **1.** a little cavity, pit, or cell, as a cell of a honeycomb. **2.** an air cell of the lungs, formed by the terminal dilation of tiny air passageways. **3.** one of the terminal secretory units of a racemose gland. **4.** the socket within the jawbone in which the root or roots of a tooth are set. [< L = *alve(us)* concave vessel + *-olus,* var. of *-ulus* -ULE]

al·way (ôl′wā), *adv.* *Archaic.* always. [ME; OE *ealneweg* = *ealne* (acc. sing. masc. of *eal* ALL) + *weg* WAY]

al·ways (ôl′wāz, -wēz), *adv.* **1.** every time; on every occasion; without exception: *He always works on Saturday.* **2.** forever: *Will you love me always?* **3.** in any event; if necessary: *She can always move back with her parents.* **4.** continually; uninterruptedly: *The light is always burning.* [ME *alles weis,* gen. of *all wei*]
—**Syn. 2, 4.** perpetually, everlastingly. Both ALWAYS and EVER refer to uniform or perpetual continuance. ALWAYS often expresses or implies repetition as producing the uniformity or continuance: *The sun always rises in the east.* EVER implies an unchanging sameness throughout: *Natural law is ever to be reckoned with.*

a·lys·sum (ə lis′əm), *n.* **1.** any of several brassicaceous herbs of the genus *Alyssum,* having small, yellow or white, racemose flowers. **2.** See **sweet alyssum.** [< L *alysson* < Gk, neut. of *ályssos* curing (canine) madness = *a-* A-[6] + *lýss(a)* madness + *-os* adj. suffix]

am (am; *unstressed* əm, m) *v.* 1st pers. sing. pres. indic. of **be.** [ME; OE *am, eam, eom;* c. Goth *im,* Icel *em,* Ir *am,* Gk *eimí,* Skt *asmi*]

AM, 1. *Electronics.* amplitude modulation: a method of impressing a signal on a radio carrier wave by varying its amplitude. **2.** *Radio.* a system of broadcasting by means of amplitude modulation. **3.** of, pertaining to, or utilizing such a system. Cf. **FM.**

Am, *Chem.* americium.

Am., 1. America. **2.** American.

A/m, ampere per meter.

A.M., 1. See **a.m. 2.** See **Master of Arts.** [< L *Artium Magister*]

a.m., the period from 12 midnight to 12 noon. Cf. **p.m.** [< L *ante meridiem*]

A.M.A., American Medical Association.

Am·a·dis (am′ə dis), *n.* *Medieval Romance.* a knight-errant, model of the chivalric hero.

am·a·dou (am′ə dōō′), *n.* a spongy substance prepared from fungi, *Polyporus* (*Fomes*) *fomentarius,* and allied species, used as tinder and in surgery. [< F < Pr: lover (< L *amātor*); so called from its being flammable]

A·ma·ga·sa·ki (ä′mä gä sä′kē), *n.* a city on SW Honshu, in S Japan. 484,885 (1964).

a·mah (ä′mə, am′ə), *n.* (in India and the Orient) **1.** a nurse, esp. a wet nurse. **2.** a maidservant. [< Pg *ama* nurse, governess < ML *amma* wet nurse]

a·main (ə mān′), *adv.* *Archaic.* **1.** with full force. **2.** at full speed. **3.** suddenly. **4.** exceedingly. [A-[1] + MAIN[1]]

amal., amalgamated. Also, **amalg.**

Am·a·lek·ite (am′ə lek′īt, ə mal′ə kīt′), *n.* a member of a tribe descended from Esau. Gen. 36:12. [*Amalek* (< Heb *'Amālēq(ī)*) grandson of Esau + -ITE[1]]

a·mal·gam (ə mal′gəm), *n.* **1.** an alloy of mercury with another metal or metals. **2.** a rare mineral, an alloy of silver and mercury. **3.** a combination: *His character is a strange amalgam of traits.* [late ME *amalgam(a)* (in pl. *amalgame*) < ML < Ar *al* the + Gk *málagma* softening agent = *malak-* (s. of *malássein* to soften) + *-ma* n. suffix]

a·mal·ga·mate (ə mal′gə māt′), *v.,* **-mat·ed, -mat·ing.** —*v.t.* **1.** to make into a combination; blend: *to amalgamate two companies.* **2.** *Metall.* to mix or alloy (a metal) with mercury. —*v.i.* **3.** to combine or coalesce. —**a·mal′ga·ma·ble,** *adj.* —**a·mal′ga·ma′tive,** *adj.* —**a·mal′ga·ma′tor,** *n.* —**Syn. 1.** mingle, commingle, unify.

a·mal·ga·ma·tion (ə mal′gə mā′shən), *n.* **1.** the act or process of amalgamating. **2.** the state or result of being amalgamated. **3.** *Com.* a consolidation of two or more corporations. **4.** *Ethnol.* the biological fusion of diverse racial stocks. **5.** *Metall.* the extraction of the precious metals from their ores by treatment with mercury.

Am·al·thae·a (am′əl thē′ə), *n.* *Class. Myth.* the goat that brought up the infant Zeus. Also, **Am′al·the′a.**

A·man′a Church′ Soci′ety (ə man′ə), a religious group founded in Germany in 1714, moved to New York State in 1843, and then to Iowa in 1855. —**A·man′ist,** *n.*

a·man·dine (ä′mən dēn′, am′ən-), *adj.* (of food) served or prepared with almonds. [< F; see ALMOND, -INE[2]]

am·a·ni·ta (am′ə nī′tə), *n.* any agaricaceous fungus of the genus *Amanita,* comprised chiefly of poisonous species. [< Gk *amanîta(i)* (pl.) kind of fungi]

a·man·u·en·sis (ə man′yōō en′sis), *n., pl.* **-ses** (-sēz). a secretary. [< L = *ā-* A-[4] + *manū,* abl. of *manus* hand + *-ēnsis* -ESE]

A·ma·pá (ä′mä pä′), *n.* a federal territory in N Brazil. 68,889 (1960); 51,177 sq. mi. *Cap.:* Macapá.

am·a·ranth (am′ə ranth′), *n.* **1.** a legendary, undying flower. **2.** any plant of the genus *Amaranthus,* certain species of which are cultivated for their showy flowers or for their colored foliage. **3.** *Chem.* a purplish-red powder, $C_{20}H_{11}N_2O_{10}Na_3$, an azo dye. [< L *amarant(us),* alter. of Gk *amáranton* unfading flower, n. use of neut. sing. of *amárantos* = *a-* A-[6] + *maran-* (s. of *maraínein* to fade) + *-tos* verbal adj. suffix]

am·a·ran·tha·ceous (am′ə ran thā′shəs), *adj.* belonging to the family *Amaranthaceae* (or *Amarantaceae*), comprising mostly herbaceous or shrubby plants, as the cockscomb, pigweed, or amaranth. [< NL *Amaranthāce(ae)* (see AMARANTH, -ACEAE) + -OUS]

am·a·ran·thine (am′ə ran′thin, -thīn), *adj.* **1.** of or like the amaranth. **2.** unfading; everlasting. **3.** of purplish-red color.

am·a·relle (am′ə rel′), *n.* any variety of the sour cherry, *Prunus Cerasus.* [< G < ML *amarell(um)* = L *amār(us)* bitter + *-ellum* dim. suffix]

Am·a·ril·lo (am′ə ril′ō), *n.* a city in NW Texas. 127,010 (1970).

A·mar·na (ə mär′nə), *adj.* (*sometimes l.c.*) of or pertaining to the period in ancient Egypt described on cuneiform tablets, found at Tell el Amarna, that contain correspondence from neighboring kings and governors to Amenhotep III and IV.

am·a·ryl·li·da·ceous (am′ə ril′i dā′shəs), *adj.* belonging to the *Amaryllidaceae,* or amaryllis family of plants, including the amaryllis and narcissus. [< NL *Amaryllidāc(ae)* (*amaryllid-,* s. of *amaryllis* AMARYLLIS + *-āceae* -ACEAE) + -OUS]

am·a·ryl·lis (am′ə ril′is), *n.* **1.** Also called **belladonna lily.** a bulbous plant, *Amaryllis Belladonna,* having large, lilylike, usually rose-colored flowers. **2.** any of several related plants formerly included in the genus *Amaryllis.* **3.** (*cap.*) a shepherdess or country girl, esp. in pastoral poetry. [< L: name of a shepherdess in Vergil's *Eclogues*]

Amaryllis, *Amaryllis Belladonna*

a·mass (ə mas′), *v.t.* **1.** to gather for oneself: *to amass a fortune.* **2.** to collect into a mass or pile: *He amassed his papers for burning.* —*v.i.* **3.** to come together. [< F *amass(er)* = *a-* A-[5] + *mass(e)* MASS + *-er* inf. suffix] —**a·mass′a·ble,** *adj.* —**a·mass′er,** *n.* —**a·mass′ment,** *n.* —**Syn. 1.** accumulate. **2.** aggregate. **2, 3.** assemble.

am·a·teur (am′ə chŏŏr′, -tyŏŏr′, am′ə tûr′), *n.* **1.** a person who engages in an activity for pleasure rather than for financial benefit. Cf. **professional. 2.** an athlete who has never competed for payment or for a monetary prize. **3.** a person inexperienced or unskilled in a particular activity: *Hunting lions is not for amateurs.* **4.** a lover or devotee of an art, activity, etc. —*adj.* **5.** characteristic of an amateur; nonprofessional. [< F, alter. of L *amātor* lover = *amā-* (s. of *amāre* to love) + *-t-* ptp. suffix + *-or* -OR[2]] —**Syn. 2.** nonprofessional. **3.** tyro, novice.

am·a·teur·ish (am′ə chŏŏr′ish, -tyŏŏr′-, -tûr′-), *adj.* characteristic of an amateur, esp. in having faults or deficiencies. —**am′a·teur′ish·ly,** *adv.* —**am′a·teur′ish·ness,** *n.* —**am′a·teur·ism,** *n.*

A·ma·ti (ä mä′tē), *n.* **1. Ni·co·lò** (nē′kô lô′), 1596–1684, Italian violinmaker. **2.** a violin made by him or a member of his family.

am·a·tive (am′ə tiv), *adj.* amorous. [< ML *amātīv(us)* = *amāt(us)* (ptp. of *amāre* to love) + *-īvus* -IVE] —**am′a·tive·ly,** *adv.* —**am′a·tive·ness,** *n.*

am·a·tol (am′ə tol′, -tôl′, -tōl′), *n.* *Chem.* an explosive mixture of ammonium nitrate and TNT. [AM(MONIUM) + *-a-* connective + (TRINITRO)TOL(UENE)]

am·a·to·ry (am′ə tōr′ē, -tôr′ē), *adj.* of or pertaining to lovers, love-making, or expressions of love. Also, **am′a·to′ri·al.** [< L *amātōri(us)* = *amāt(us)* (ptp. of *amāre* to love) + *-ōrius* -ORY[1]] —**am′a·to′ri·al·ly,** *adv.*

am·au·ro·sis (am′ô rō′sis), *n.* partial or total loss of sight. [< Gk: darkening = *amaur(ós)* dim, dark + *-ōsis* -OSIS] —**am·au·rot·ic** (am′ô rot′ik), *adj.*

a·maze (ə māz′), *v.,* **a·mazed, a·maz·ing,** *n.* —*v.t.* **1.** to overwhelm with surprise or wonder. **2.** *Obs.* to bewilder; perplex. —*n.* **3.** *Archaic.* amazement. [ME *amase(n),* OE *āmasian* to confuse, stun, astonish. See A-[3], MAZE] —**Syn. 1.** astound, dumfound. See **surprise.**

a·mazed (ə māzd′), *adj.* filled with wonder; astounded. [ME] —**a·maz·ed·ly** (ə mā′zid lē), *adv.* —**a·maz′ed·ness,** *n.*

a·maze·ment (ə māz′mənt), *n.* overwhelming surprise or astonishment.

a·maz·ing (ə mā′zing), *adj.* causing great surprise or wonder. —**a·maz′ing·ly,** *adv.*

Am·a·zon (am′ə zon′, -zən), *n.* **1.** a river in N South America, flowing E from the Peruvian Andes through N Brazil to the Atlantic Ocean: the largest river in the world in volume of water carried. ab. 3900 mi. long. **2.** *Class. Myth.* one of a race of female warriors said to dwell near the Black Sea. **3.** one of a fabled tribe of female warriors in South America. **4.** (*often l.c.*) a tall, powerful, aggressive woman. [< L *Amazōn* < Gk < ?] —**Am·a·zo·ni·an** (am′ə zō′nē ən), *adj.*

A·ma·zo·nas (am′ə zō′nəs), *n.* a state in NW Brazil. 721,215 (1960); 601,769 sq. mi. *Cap.:* Manáos.

am·a·zon·ite (am′ə zə nīt′), *n.* *Mineral.* a green feldspar, a variety of microcline. Also called **Am′azon stone′.** [AMAZON (river) + -ITE[1]]

am·ba·ges (am bā′jēz), *n.* (*construed as pl.*) *Archaic.* winding, roundabout paths or ways. [late ME < L *ambāgēs* (pl.) circuits = *amb(i)-* AMBI- + *āg-* (var. s. of *agere* to move) + *-ēs* pl. ending]

am·ba·gious (am bā′jəs), *adj.* roundabout; circuitous. [< L *ambāgiōs(us)* = *ambāgi-* (s. of *ambāgēs* AMBAGES) + *-ōsus* -OUS] —**am·ba′gious·ly,** *adv.* —**am·ba′gious·ness,** *n.*

am·ba·ry (am bär′ē), *n.* an East Indian plant, *Hibiscus cannabinus,* yielding a fiber used in canvas and cordage. Also, **am·ba′ri.** Also called **kenaf.** [< Hindi *ambārī*]

am·bas·sa·dor (am bas′ə dər), *n.* **1.** a diplomatic official of the highest rank, esp. a person sent by one sovereign or state to another as its resident representative (**ambas′sador extraor′dinary and plenipoten′tiary**), or appointed on a temporary or special mission. **2.** a diplomatic official serving as permanent head of his country's mission to the United Nations or some other international organization. **3.** an authorized representative. Also, *Archaic,* **embassador.** [late ME *am-, embass(i)adour, imbassadore,* etc. < MF *ambassadeur* < Pr *ambassador* = *ambass-* (see EMBASSY) + *-ador* < L *-ātor* -ATOR] —**am·bas·sa·do·ri·al** (am bas′ə dōr′ē əl, -dôr′-), *adj.* —**am·bas′sa·do′ri·al·ly,** *adv.* —**am·bas′sa·dor·ship′,** *n.*

am·bas·sa·dor-at-large (am bas′ə dər ət lärj′), *n., pl.* **am·bas·sa·dors-at-large.** an ambassador who is not assigned to a particular diplomatic post.

am·bas·sa·dress (am bas′ə dris), *n.* **1.** a female ambassador. **2.** the wife of an ambassador.

am·ber (am′bər), *n.* **1.** a pale yellow, sometimes reddish or brownish, fossil resin, translucent, brittle, and capable of gaining a negative electrical charge by friction. **2.** a yellowish brown. —*adj.* **3.** of the color of amber; yellowish brown. [ME *ambra* < ML < Ar *'anbar* ambergris]

am·ber·gris (am′bər grēs′, -gris), *n.* an opaque, ash-colored, morbid secretion of the sperm whale intestine, fragrant when heated: used in perfumery. [< F *ambre gris* gray amber (see AMBER); r. late ME *imbergres*]

am·ber·jack (am′bər jak′), *n., pl.* (*esp. collectively*) **-jack,** (*esp. referring to two or more kinds or species*) **-jacks.** any of several carangoid fishes of the genus *Seriola,* as *S. dumerili,* a game fish found in warmer waters of the Atlantic Ocean. [AMBER (color) + *jack* (kind of fish)]

am·ber·oid (am′bə roid′), *n.* synthetic amber made by compressing pieces of various resins at a high temperature. Also, **ambroid.**

ambi-, a prefix occurring in loan words from Latin where it meant "both" (*ambiguous*); used in the formation of compound words: *ambidextrous.* [< L; akin to OE *ymb(e)*-around. Cf. AMPHI-]

am·bi·ance (am′bē əns; *Fr.* äN byäNs′), *n., pl.* **-bi·anc·es** (-bē ən siz; *Fr.* -byäNs′). ambience.

am·bi·dex·ter·i·ty (am′bi dek ster′i tē), *n.* **1.** ambidextrous skill or facility. **2.** unusual cleverness. **3.** deceitfulness.

am·bi·dex·trous (am′bi dek′strəs), *adj.* **1.** able to use both hands equally well. **2.** unusually skillful; facile. **3.** double-dealing; deceitful. —**am′bi·dex′trous·ly,** *adv.* —**am′bi·dex′trous·ness,** *n.*

am·bi·ence (am′bē əns; *Fr.* äN byäNs′), *n., pl.* **-bi·enc·es** (-bē ən siz; *Fr.* -byäNs′). **1.** that which surrounds or encompasses; environment. **2.** the mood, character, atmosphere, etc., of an environment or milieu. Also, **ambiance.** [< F; see AMBIENT, -ENCE]

am·bi·ent (am′bē ənt), *adj.* **1.** completely surrounding; encompassing: *ambient noises.* **2.** circulating: *ambient air.* [< L *ambient-* (s. of *ambiēns,* prp. of *ambīre* to go around) = *amb-* AMBI- + *-i-* go + *-ent-* -ENT]

am·bi·gu·i·ty (am′bə gyōō′i tē), *n., pl.* **-ties.** **1.** doubtfulness or uncertainty in meaning or intention: *to speak with ambiguity.* **2.** the condition of admitting more than one meaning. **3.** an equivocal or ambiguous expression, term, etc. [late ME *ambiguite* < L *ambiguitāt-* (s. of *ambiguitās*) = *ambigu-* (see AMBIGUOUS) + *-itāt-* -ITY] —**Syn. 1.** vagueness. **2.** equivocation. —**Ant. 1.** explicitness.

am·big·u·ous (am big′yōō əs), *adj.* **1.** having several possible meanings or interpretations: *an ambiguous answer.* **2.** difficult to comprehend, distinguish, or classify. **3.** lacking clearness or definiteness; obscure; indistinct. [< L *ambigu(us)* (*ambig(ere)* = *amb-* AMBI- + *-igere,* var. of *agere* to drive, lead, act + *-uus* adj. suffix) + -OUS] —**am·big′u·ous·ly,** *adv.* —**am·big′u·ous·ness,** *n.*
—**Syn. 1.** AMBIGUOUS, EQUIVOCAL describe that which is not clear in meaning. That which is AMBIGUOUS leaves the intended sense doubtful; it need not be purposely deceptive. That which is EQUIVOCAL is equally capable of two of more interpretations, and is usually intended to be so for the purpose of mystifying or confusing. **2.** vague, indeterminate, unclassifiable, anomalous. —**Ant. 1.** explicit. **3.** clear.

am·bit (am′bit), *n.* **1.** circumference. **2.** boundary. [ME < L *ambit(us)* a going around = *amb-* AMBI- + *-itus* a going (*-i-* (s. of *īre* to go) + *-tus* verbal n. suffix)]

am·bi·tend·en·cy (am′bi ten′dən sē), *n., pl.* **-cies.** *Psychol.* the coexistence within an individual of positive and negative feelings toward a person or object.

am·bi·tion (am bish′ən), *n.* **1.** an earnest desire for some type of achievement or distinction, as power, fame, wealth, etc. **2.** an object of such desire. —*v.t.* **3.** to seek after earnestly; aspire to. [ME *ambicion* < L *ambitiōn-* (s. of *ambitiō*) = *amb-* AMBI- + *-i-* go + *-t-* ptp. suffix + *-iōn-* -ION] —**am·bi′tion·less,** *adj.* —**am·bi′tion·less·ly,** *adv.* —**Syn. 1.** aspiration, yearning, longing. **2.** goal, aim.

am·bi·tious (am bish′əs), *adj.* **1.** having ambition; eagerly desirous of achieving or obtaining power, superiority, or distinction: *ambitious students.* **2.** showing or caused by ambition. **3.** requiring exceptional effort, ability, etc. [< L *ambitiōs(us)* = *ambiti(ō)* AMBITION + *-ōsus* -OUS] —**am·bi′tious·ly,** *adv.* —**am·bi′tious·ness,** *n.*
—**Syn. 1.** AMBITIOUS, ENTERPRISING, ASPIRING describe a person who wishes to rise above his present position or condition. The AMBITIOUS man wishes to attain worldly success and puts forth effort toward this end: *ambitious for social position.* The ENTERPRISING man, interested especially in wealth, is characterized by energy and daring in undertaking projects. The ASPIRING man wishes to rise (mentally or spiritually) to a higher level or plane, or to attain some end that he feels to be above his ordinary expectations.

am·biv·a·lence (am biv′ə ləns), *n.* **1.** uncertainty or fluctuation, esp. when caused by inability to make a choice or by a simultaneous desire to say or do two opposite things. **2.** *Psychol.* the coexistence of positive and negative feelings toward the same person, object, or action. —**am·biv′a·lent,** *adj.*

am·bi·vert (am′bə vûrt′), *n.* *Psychol.* a person whose personality type is intermediate between extravert and introvert. [AMBI- + *-vert,* as in EXTRAVERT, INTROVERT]

am·ble (am′bəl), *v.,* **-bled, -bling,** *n.* —*v.i.* **1.** to walk at an easy pace; stroll; saunter. **2.** (of a horse) to move at a pace. —*n.* **3.** an ambling gait. **4.** an easy walk or gentle pace. [late ME < MF *amble(r)* < L *ambulāre* to walk = *amb-* AMBI- + *-ulāre* to step (< ?)] —**am′bler,** *n.* —**am′bling·ly,** *adv.*

am·blyg·o·nite (am blig′ə nīt′), *n.* a mineral, a lithium aluminum fluophosphate, $Li(AlF)PO_4$. [< Gk *amblygṓn(ios)* (*amblý(s)* blunt, obtuse + *gōní(ā)* angle + *-os* adj. suffix) + -ITE[1]]

am·bly·o·pi·a (am′blē ō′pē ə), *n.* *Ophthalm.* dimness of sight, without apparent organic defect. [< NL < Gk *amblyōpíā* = *amblý(s)* dull + *-ōpiā* -OPIA] —**am·bly·op·ic** (am′blē op′ik), *adj.*

am·bo (am′bō), *n., pl.* **-bos.** (in an early Christian church) a raised desk from which the Gospels or Epistles were read or chanted. [< ML < Gk *ámbō(n)* edge, rim, pulpit]

am·bo·cep·tor (am′bə sep′tər), *n.* *Immunol.* a substance that develops during infection in the blood, believed to have affinities for both the bacterial cell or erythrocytes and the complement. [< L *ambō* both (akin to AMBI-) + (RE)CEPTOR]

Am·boi·na (am boi′nə), *n.* **1.** an island in the central Moluccas, in E Indonesia. 64,486 (est. 1954); 314 sq. mi. **2.** Also, **Am·bon** (äm′bôn). a seaport on this island. 55,263 (est. 1961). —**Am·boi·nese** (am′boi nēz′, -nēs′), *adj., n.*

Amboi′na wood′. See **padouk wood.** Also, **Am·boy′na wood′.**

am·broid (am′broid), *n.* amberoid.

Am·brose (am′brōz), *n.* **Saint,** A.D. 340?–397, bishop of Milan 374–397.

am·bro·sia (am brō′zhə), *n.* **1.** *Class. Myth.* the food, drink, or perfume of the gods. Cf. **nectar** (def. 2). **2.** something especially delicious to taste or smell. [< L < Gk: immortality, food of the gods, n. use of fem. of *ambrósios* = *a-* A-[6] + *-mbros-* (var. s. of *brotós* mortal; akin to L *mortuus* dead) + *-ios* adj. suffix] —**am·bro′sial, am·bro′sian,** *adj.* —**am·bro′sial·ly,** *adv.*

am·bro·si·a·ceous (am brō′zē ā′shəs), *adj.* *Bot.* belonging to the *Ambrosiaceae,* or ragweed family of plants, which includes the ragweed, marsh elder, etc. [< NL *Ambrosiāce(ae)* (see AMBROSIA, -ACEAE) + -OUS]

Am·bro′sian chant′ (am brō′zhən), the liturgical chant, established by St. Ambrose, characterized by ornamental, often antiphonal, singing. Also called **Milanese chant.**

am·bro·type (am′brə tīp′), *n.* *Photog. Obs.* a glass negative with a thin density made to give the impression of a positive when placed against a dark background. [< Gk *ámbro(tos)* immortal (see AMBROSIA) + -TYPE]

am·bry (am′brē), *n., pl.* **-bries.** **1.** *Eccles.* a recess or a cupboard where sacred vessels, books, vestments, etc., are kept. **2.** *Obs.* any of various types of closet or cupboard. [late ME *almerie, almarie* (also *armarie*) < ML *almāri(um),* dissimilated var. of *armārium* < L; see ARM[2], -ARY]

ambs·ace (āmz′ās′, amz′-), *n.* **1.** the lowest throw at dice, the double ace. **2.** bad luck. **3.** the smallest amount or distance. Also, **amesace.** [ME *ambes as* < OF < L *ambas* both + *as* unit; see ACE]

am·bu·lac·rum (am′byə lak′rəm, -lā′krəm), *n., pl.* **-lac·ra** (-lak′rə, -lā′krə). one of the radial areas in an echinoderm, bearing the tubular protrusions by which locomotion is accomplished. [< NL, L: alley, walking place = *ambulā-* (s. of *ambulāre* to walk) + *-crum* n. suffix denoting means] —**am′bu·lac′ral,** *adj.*

am·bu·lance (am′byə ləns), *n.* a vehicle equipped for transporting sick or injured people. [< F = (*hôpital*) *ambul(ant)* traveling (hospital) + *-ance* -ANCE. See AMBULANT]

am′bulance chas′er, *U.S. Informal.* a lawyer who seeks accident victims as clients and encourages them to sue for damages. —**am′bulance chas′ing.**

am·bu·lant (am′byə lənt), *adj.* **1.** moving from place to place; shifting. **2.** *Med.* ambulatory (def. 4). [< L *ambulant-* (s. of *ambulāns,* prp. of *ambulāre* to walk)]

am·bu·late (am′byə lāt′), *v.i.,* **-lat·ed, -lat·ing.** to walk about or move from place to place. [< L *ambulāt(us)* (ptp. of *ambulāre* to walk) = *ambul-* (see AMBLE) + *-ātus* -ATE[1]] —**am′bu·la′tion,** *n.* —**am′bu·la′tor,** *n.*

am·bu·la·to·ry (am′byə lə tôr′ē, -tōr′ē), *adj., n., pl.* **-ries.** —*adj.* **1.** of or pertaining to walking. **2.** adapted for walking, as the limbs of many animals. **3.** moving about; not stationary: *an ambulatory tribe.* **4.** Also, **ambulant.** *Med.* not confined to bed; able or strong enough to walk: *an ambulatory patient.* **5.** *Law.* not fixed; alterable or revocable. —*n.* *Archit.* **6.** an aisle surrounding the end of the choir or chancel of a church. **7.** the covered walk of a cloister. [< L *ambulātōri(us)*]

am·bus·cade (am′bə skād′), *n., v.,* **-cad·ed, -cad·ing.** —*n.* **1.** an ambush. —*v.i.* **2.** to lie in ambush. —*v.t.* **3.** to attack from a concealed position; ambush. [< F < Pg *embuscada* (or Sp *emboscada*) = *embusc-* (see AMBUSH) + *-ada* -ADE[1]] —**am′bus·cad′er,** *n.*

am·bus·ca·do (am′bə skā′dō), *n., pl.* **-dos.** *Obs.* ambuscade. [pseudo-Sp alter. of AMBUSCADE]

am·bush (am′bōōsh), *n.* Also, **am′bush·ment.** **1.** the act or an instance of lying concealed so as to attack by surprise. **2.** the act or an instance of attacking unexpectedly from a concealed position. **3.** the concealed position itself: *A clump of trees was their ambush.* **4.** those who attack suddenly and unexpectedly from a concealed position. —*v.t.* **5.** to attack from ambush. [ME *enbuss(h)e* < MF *embusch(ier)* (to) set in the woods = *em-* IM-[1] + *busch-* < LL *bosc(um)* wood (< Gmc; see BUSH[1]) + *-ier* verbal and inf. suffix] —**am′bush·er,** *n.* —**am′bush·like′,** *adj.*

A.M.D.G., to the greater glory of God. Also, **AMDG** [< L *ad majorem Dei gloriam*]

A.M.E., African Methodist Episcopal.

a·me·ba (ə mē′bə), *n., pl.* **-bas, -bae** (-bē). amoeba. —**a·me′ba·like′,** *adj.*

a·me·bic (ə mē′bik), *adj.* amoebic.

a·me·bo·cyte (ə mē′bə sīt′), *n.* *Zool.* amoebocyte.

a·me·boid (ə mē′boid), *adj.* amoeboid. —**a·me′boid·ism,** *n.*

a·meer (ə mēr′), *n.* amir. —**a·meer·ate** (ə mēr′it, -āt), *n.*

a·mel·io·rate (ə mēl′yə rāt′), *v.t., v.i.,* **-rat·ed, -rat·ing.** to make or become better; improve; meliorate. —**a·mel′io·ra·ble** (ə mēl′yər ə bəl), *adj.* —**a·mel·io·rant** (ə mēl′yər-ənt), *n.* —**a·mel·io·ra·tive** (ə mēl′yə rā′tiv, -yər ə tiv), *adj.* —**a·mel′io·ra′tor,** *n.* —**Syn.** amend, better. See **improve.** —**Ant.** worsen.

a·mel·io·ra·tion (ə mēl′yə rā′shən), *n.* the act or an instance of ameliorating; improvement.

a·men (ā′men′, ä′men′), *interj.* **1.** it is so; so be it (used after a prayer, creed, or other formal statement to express solemn ratification or agreement). —*adv.* **2.** verily; truly. —*n.* **3.** an utterance of the interjection "Amen." [ME, OE < LL < Gk < Heb *āmēn* certainty, certainly]

A·men (ä′mən), *n.* *Egyptian Myth.* a primeval deity worshiped, esp. at Thebes, as the personification of air or breath and represented either as a ram or a goose: later identified with Amen-Ra. Also, **Amon.**

a·me·na·ble (ə mē′nə bəl, ə men′ə-), *adj.* **1.** ready or willing to answer, act, agree, or yield; agreeable; tractable: *an amenable servant.* **2.** accountable or liable, as in law. **3.** capable of or agreeable to being criticized, tested, etc. [< AF = MF *amen(er)* (to) lead to (*a-* A-[5] + *mener* < L *mināre* to drive) + *-able* -ABLE] —**a·me′na·bil′i·ty, a·me′na·ble·ness,** *n.* —**a·me′na·bly,** *adv.*

a′men′ cor′ner, *U.S.* **1.** a place in a church, usually at one side of the pulpit, occupied by worshipers who lead the responsive amens during the service. **2.** any special place in a church occupied by zealous worshipers.

a·mend (ə mend′), *v.t.* **1.** to modify, rephrase, or add to or subtract from (a motion, bill, constitution, etc.) by formal procedure: *Congress may amend the tax bill.* **2.** to change for the better; improve. **3.** to rectify. —*v.i.* **4.** to become bet-

ter by reforming oneself. [ME *amende(n)* < OF *amende(r)* < L *ēmend(āre)* (to) correct = *ē-* E- + *menda* blemish] —**a·mend′a·ble,** *adj.* —**a·mend′er,** *n.*
—**Syn. 2.** ameliorate, better. **3.** AMEND, EMEND both mean to improve by correcting or by freeing from error. AMEND is the general term, used of any such correction in detail: *to amend spelling.* EMEND usually applies to the correction of a text in the process of editing or preparing for publication; it implies improvement in the sense of greater accuracy: *He emended the text of the play by restoring the original reading.*

a·mend·a·tory (ə men′də tōr′ē, -tôr′ē), *adj. U.S.* serving to amend; corrective. [< LL *emendātōri(us)* (with *e-* for *a-* from AMEND). See EMENDATOR, -Y[1]]

a·mend·ment (ə mend′mənt), *n.* **1.** the act of amending. **2.** the state of being amended. **3.** an alteration of or addition to a bill, constitution, etc. **4.** a change made by correction, addition, or deletion. [ME < OF *amendement*]

a·mends (ə mendz′), *n.* (*construed as sing. or pl.*) **1.** reparation or compensation for a loss, damage, or injury of any kind; recompense. **2.** *Obs.* improvement or recovery, as of health. **3. make amends,** to attempt to compensate for offensive conduct, as by making an apology. [ME *amendes* < MF, pl. of *amende* reparation < *amender* to AMEND]

A·men·ho·tep III (ä′mən hō′tep, am′ən-), king of Egypt 1411?–1375 B.C. Also called **Am·e·no·phis III** (am′ə-nō′fis).

Amenhotep IV, died 1357? B.C., king of Egypt 1375?–1357?: reformer of ancient Egyptian religion (son of Amenhotep III). Also called **Amenophis IV, Akhnaton, Ikhnaton.**

a·men·i·ty (ə men′i tē, ə mē′ni-), *n., pl.* **-ties. 1. amenities,** agreeable ways or manners; courtesies; civilities. **2.** the quality of being pleasing or agreeable in situation, prospect, disposition, etc. [late ME *amenite* < L *amoenitāt-* (s. of *amoenitās*) = *amoen(us)* pleasing + *-itāt-* -ITY]

a·men·or·rhe·a (ā men′ə rē′ə), *n. Pathol.* absence of the menses. Also, **a·men′or·rhoe′a.** [A-[6] + MENO- + -RRHEA] —**a·men′or·rhe′al, a·men′or·rhoe′al, a·men′or·rhe′ic, a·men′or·rhoe′ic,** *adj.*

A·men-Ra (ä′mən rä′), *n. Egyptian Myth.* a god in whom Amen and Ra were combined. Also, **Amon-Ra.**

a men·sa et tho·ro (ā men′sə et thōr′ō, thôr′ō), *Law.* pertaining to or noting a divorce that forbids husband and wife to live together but does not dissolve the marriage bond. [< L: lit., from board and bed]

am·ent (am′ənt, ā′mənt), *n. Bot.* a spike of unisexual, apetalous flowers having scaly, usually deciduous bracts; catkin. [< L *ament(um)* strap, thong] —**am·en·ta·ceous** (am′ən tā′shəs), *adj.* —**am·en·tif·er·ous** (am′ən tif′ər əs), *adj.*

A, Ament

a·men·tia (ā men′shə), *n. Psychiatry.* lack of intellectual development. [< L = *āment-* (s. of *āmēns* mad: *ā-* A-[4] + *mēns* mind) + *-ia* -IA]

Amer., 1. America. **2.** American.

A·mer·a·sian (am′e rā′zhən, shən), *n.* **1.** the offspring of an American and an Asian, esp. one whose father is American. —*adj.* **2.** of or pertaining to an Amerasian. [AMER(ICAN) + ASIA(N), modeled on EURASIAN]

a·merce (ə mûrs′), *v.t.,* **a·merced, a·merc·ing.** to punish by inflicting any discretionary or arbitrary penalty, esp. a fine not fixed by statute. [late ME *amercy* < AF *amerci(er)* (to) fine, repr. (*estre*) *a merci* (to be) at (someone's) mercy. See A-[5], MERCY] —**a·merce′a·ble,** *adj.* —**a·merce′ment,** *n.*

A·mer·i·ca (ə mer′i kə), *n.* **1.** See **United States. 2.** See **North America. 3.** See **South America. 4.** Also called **the Americas.** North and South America, considered together. [named after *Americus* Vespucius. See VESPUCCI]

Amer′ica First′ par′ty, *U.S.* a political party formed in 1942, advocating isolationism, racism, etc.

A·mer·i·can (ə mer′i kən), *adj.* **1.** of or pertaining to the United States of America or its inhabitants. **2.** of or pertaining to North or South America. **3.** of or pertaining to the aboriginal Indians of North and South America. —*n.* **4.** a citizen of the United States of America. **5.** a native or an inhabitant of the Western Hemisphere. **6.** an Indian of North or South America.

A·mer·i·ca·na (ə mer′i kan′ə, -kä′nə, -kā′nə), *n.* **1.** (*often construed as pl.*) books, maps, etc., relating to America, esp. to its history. **2.** (*construed as sing.*) a collection of such materials.

Amer′ican al′oe. See **century plant.**

Amer′ican Beau′ty, an American variety of rose, periodically bearing large crimson blossoms.

Amer′ican chame′leon. See under **chameleon** (def. 2).

Amer′ican cheese′, a type of Cheddar made in America, usually as a mild processed cheese.

Amer′ican cow′slip. See **shooting star** (def. 2).

Amer′ican Dream′, the ideals of freedom, equality, and opportunity traditionally stressed as available to individuals in the United States.

Amer′ican ea′gle, the bald eagle, esp. as depicted on the great seal of the United States.

Amer′ican elm′, an elm, *Ulmus americana,* of North America, cultivated for shade and ornament: state tree of Massachusetts, Nebraska, and North Dakota.

Amer′ican Eng′lish, the English language as used in the U.S.

Amer′ican Expedi′tionary Forc′es, troops sent to Europe by the U.S. Army during WW I. *Abbr.:* A.E.F.

Amer′ican Federa′tion of La′bor, a federation of trade unions organized in 1886; united with C.I.O., 1955. *Abbr.:* AFL, A.F.L., A.F. of L.

Amer′ican In′dian, Indian (def. 1). *Abbr.:* AmerInd

Amer′ican In′stitute of Ar′chitects, the principal association of architects in the U.S. *Abbr.:* A.I.A.

A·mer·i·can·ise (ə mer′i kə nīz′), *v.t., v.i.,* **-ised, -is·ing.** *Chiefly Brit.* Americanize. —**A·mer′i·can·i·sa′tion,** *n.* —**A·mer′i·can·is′er,** *n.*

A·mer·i·can·ism (ə mer′i kə niz′əm), *n.* **1.** devotion to or preference for the United States of America and its institutions. **2.** a custom, trait, or thing peculiar to the U.S. or its citizens. **3.** a word or other language feature especially characteristic of the English language as spoken in the U.S.

A·mer·i·can·ist (ə mer′i kə nist), *n.* **1.** a student of America, esp. of its history and geography. **2.** a specialist in the cultures or languages of American Indians. —**A·mer′i·can·is′tic,** *adj.*

Amer′ican i′vy. See **Virginia creeper.**

A·mer·i·can·ize (ə mer′i kə nīz′), *v.t., v.i.,* **-ized, -iz·ing.** to make or become American in character; assimilate to U.S. customs and institutions. Also, *esp. Brit.,* **Americanise.** —**A·mer′i·can·i·za′tion,** *n.* —**A·mer′i·can·iz′er,** *n.*

Amer′ican La′bor par′ty, *U.S.* a former political party (1936–56), comprising certain labor and liberal factions largely from the Democratic party.

Amer′ican lan′guage, English as used in the U.S.

Amer′ican Le′gion, a society, organized in 1919, now composed of veterans of the armed forces of the U.S. in World Wars I and II and the Korean and Vietnam Wars.

Amer′ican plan′, *U.S.* a hotel rate covering lodging, service, and meals. Cf. **European plan.**

Amer′ican Revised′ Ver′sion, a revision of the Bible, based chiefly on the Revised Version of the Bible, published in the U.S. in 1901. Also called **Amer′ican Stand′ard Ver′sion.**

Amer′ican Revolu′tion, the war between Great Britain and her American colonies, 1775–83, by which the colonies won their independence.

Amer′ican sad′dle horse′, one of a breed of horses, raised originally in the U.S., that have high-stepping gaits and are bred to the three-gaited or five-gaited type. Also called **saddle horse.**

Amer′ican Samo′a, the part of Samoa belonging to the U.S., comprising mainly Tutuila and the Manua Islands. 27,159 (1970); 76 sq. mi. *Cap.:* Pago Pago. Cf. **Samoa, Western Samoa.**

Amer′ican Span′ish, Spanish as used in Latin America.

am·er·i·ci·um (am′ə rish′ē əm), *n. Chem.* a radioactive element produced by helium bombardment of uranium and plutonium. *Symbol:* Am; *at. no.:* 95. [AMERIC(A) + -IUM]

A·me·ri·go Ves·puc·ci (ə mer′ə gō′ ve spo͞o′chē, -spyo͞o′-; *It.* ä′me rē′gō ves po͞ot′chē). See **Vespucci.**

Am·er·ind (am′ə rind), *n.* **1.** a member of any of the aboriginal Indian or Eskimo peoples of North or South America. **2.** any of the indigenous languages of the American Indians. [AMER(ICAN) IND(IAN)] —**Am′er·in′di·an,** *adj., n.* —**Am′er·in′dic,** *adj.*

AmerInd, Amerind (def. 2).

A·mers·foort (ä′mərz fōrt′, -fôrt′, -mərs-), *n.* a city in the central Netherlands. 71,416 (1962).

AmerSp, American Spanish.

Ames (āmz), *n.* a city in central Iowa. 39,505 (1970).

ames·ace (āmz′ās′, amz′-), *n.* ambsace.

am·e·thyst (am′i thist), *n.* **1.** a purple or violet quartz, used as a gem. **2.** a purplish tint. —*adj.* **3.** containing or set with amethysts. [ME *ametist* < L *amethyst(us)* < Gk *améthystos* not intoxicating (from a belief that it prevented drunkenness) = *a-* A-[6] + *methys-* (var. s. of *methýein* to intoxicate) + *-tos* verbal adj. suffix] —**am·e·thys·tine** (am′i-this′tin, -tīn), *adj.* —**am′e·thyst·like′,** *adj.*

am·e·tro·pi·a (am′i trō′pē ə), *n. Ophthalm.* an abnormal condition of the eye causing faulty refraction of light rays, as in astigmatism or myopia. [< Gk *ámetr(os)* unmeasured (*a-* A-[6] + *métr(on)* measure + *-os* adj. suffix) + -OPIA] —**am·e·trop·ic** (am′i trop′ik), *adj.*

Am·ha·ra (äm här′ə), *n.* a former kingdom in E Africa: now a province in NW Ethiopia. *Cap.:* Gondar.

Am·har·ic (am har′ik, äm här′ik), *n.* **1.** the official language of Ethiopia, a Semitic language —*adj.* **2.** of or pertaining to this language.

Am·herst (am′ərst), *n.* **1. Jeffrey, Baron,** 1717–97. British field marshal: governor general of British North America 1760–63. **2.** a town in central Massachusetts. 26,331 (1970).

a·mi (A mē′), *n., pl.* **a·mis** (A mē′). *French.* friend.

a·mi·a·ble (ā′mē ə bəl), *adj.* **1.** having or showing a friendly, willing disposition. **2.** free of rancor, as a contest or discussion. [ME < MF < L *amīcābil(is)* AMICABLE] —**a′mi·a·bil′i·ty, a′mi·a·ble·ness,** *n.* —**a′mi·a·bly,** *adv.* —**Syn. 1.** gracious. **2.** amicable. —**Ant. 1.** unfriendly.

am·i·an·thus (am′ē an′thəs), *n. Mineral.* a fine variety of asbestos, with delicate, flexible filaments. [< L *amiantus* < Gk *amíantos* = *a-* A-[6] + *mian-* (s. of *miaínein* to defile, make impure) + *-tos* verbal adj. suffix] —**am·i·an·thine** (am′ē-an′thən, -thīn), *adj.* —**am′i·an′thoid,** *adj.*

am·i·ca·ble (am′ə kə bəl), *adj.* characterized by or exhibiting good will; friendly. [< LL *amīcābil(is)* = *amīc(us)* friend, friendly + *-ābilis* -ABLE] —**am′i·ca·bil′i·ty, am′i·ca·ble·ness,** *n.* —**am′i·ca·bly,** *adv.* —**Syn.** agreeable.

am·ice (am′is), *n. Eccles.* an oblong vestment, usually of white linen for wearing under the alb about the neck and shoulders. [late ME *amyse,* perh. < MF *amis,* pl. of *amit* < L *amict(us)* wrap = *amic(īre)* (to) wrap around (*am-* AMBI- + *-ic-* var. s. of *iacere* to throw) + *-tus* n. suffix]

a·mi·cus cu·ri·ae (ə mī′kəs kyo͝or′ē ē′), *pl.* **a·mi·ci cu·ri·ae** (ə mī′kī kyo͝or′ē ē′). *Law.* a person, not a party to the litigation, who volunteers advice to the court. [< L: lit., friend of the court]

a·mid (ə mid′), *prep.* **1.** in the midst of or surrounded by; among. **2.** in or throughout the course of; during. Also, **amidst.** [ME *amidde,* OE *amidd(an)* for *on middan* in (the) middle. See MID[1]] —**Syn. 1.** See **among.**

amid-, var. of **amido-** before a vowel: *amidol.*

am·ide (am′īd, -id), *n. Chem.* **1.** a metallic derivative of ammonia in which the $-NH_2$ group is retained, as potassium amide, KNH_2. **2.** an organic compound formed from ammonia by replacing a hydrogen atom by an acyl group. [AM(MONIA) + -IDE] —**a·mid·ic** (ə mid′ik), *adj.*

am·i·din (am′i din), *n.* the soluble matter of starch. [< ML *amid(um)* starch (alter. of L *amylum;* see AMYL) + -IN[2]]

amido-, **1.** a combining form indicating the $-NH_2$ group united with an acid radical. **2.** (erroneously) **amino-.** Also, *esp. before a vowel,* **amid-.**

am·i·dol (am′i dōl′, -dôl′, -dol′), *n. Chem.* a powder, $HOC_6H_4(NH_2)_2 \cdot 2HCl$, used as a photographic developer.

a·mid·ships (ə mid′ships), *Naut., Aeron.* **—adv. 1.** in or toward the middle part of a vessel or aircraft; midway between the ends. **2.** along the central fore-and-aft line of a vessel or aircraft. **—adj. 3.** of, pertaining to, or located in the middle part of a ship or aircraft. Also, **a·mid′ship.**

a·midst (ə midst′), *prep.* amid. [ME *amiddes;* see AMID, -S[1]; for *-t* see AGAINST]

a·mie (A mē′), *n., pl.* ***a·mies*** (A mē′). *French.* fem. form of **ami.**

Am·i·ens (am′ē ənz; *Fr.* A myaN′), *n.* a city in N France: cathedral; battles 1914, 1918, 1944. 109,869 (1962).

a·mi·ga (ə mē′gə; ä mē′-; *Sp.* ä mē′gä), *n., pl.* **-gas** (-gəz; *Sp.* -gäs). a female friend. [< Sp]

a·mi·go (ə mē′gō, ä mē′-; *Sp.* ä mē′gô), *n., pl.* **-gos** (-gōz; *Sp.* -gôs). a friend. [< Sp < L *amīcus*]

amin-, var. of **amino-** before a vowel.

a·mine (ə mēn′, am′in), *n. Chem.* any of a class of compounds derived from ammonia by replacement of one or more hydrogen atoms with organic groups. [AM(MONIUM) + -INE[2]] **—a·min·ic** (ə mē′nik, ə min′ik), *adj.*

-amine, var. of **amino-** as final element of a compound word: *Dramamine.*

a·mi·no (ə mē′nō, am′ə nō′), *adj. Chem.* containing the amino group. [independent use of AMINO-]

amino-, a combining form of the amino group, used esp. before a consonant: *aminobenzoic.* Also, **-amine;** *esp. before a vowel,* **amin-.**

ami′no ac′id, *Chem.* any of a class of organic compounds that contains at least one carboxyl group and one amino group: the alpha-amino acids, $RCH(NH_2)COOH$, are the building blocks of proteins.

a·mi′no·ben·zo′ic ac′id (ə mē′nō ben zō′ik, am′ə nō-, ə mē′nō-, am′ə nō-), *Chem.* any of three isomers having the formula $H_2NC_6H_4COOH$, derived from benzoic acid, esp. the para isomer, para-aminobenzoic acid.

ami′no group′, *Chem.* the univalent group, $-NH_2$. Also called **ami′no rad′ical.**

a·mir (ə mēr′), *n.* **1.** a Muslim prince, lord, or nobleman. **2.** (*cap.*) the former title of the ruler of Afghanistan. Also, **ameer.** [< Ar: commander; see EMIR] **—a·mir·ate** (ə mēr′it, -āt), *n.*

A·mish (ä′mish, am′ish, ā′mish), *adj.* **1.** of or pertaining to any of the strict Mennonite groups descended from the followers of Jakob Ammann, a Swiss Mennonite bishop of the 17th century. **—n. 2.** the Amish people. [< G *amisch,* after Jakob *Ammann;* see -ISH[1]]

a·miss (ə mis′), *adv.* **1.** out of the proper course, order, or condition: *Did I speak amiss?* **2. take amiss,** to be offended at (an action or remark), esp. through a misunderstanding. **—adj. 3.** (usually used predicatively) improper; wrong; faulty. [ME *amis* = *a-* A-[1] + *mis* wrong. See MISS[1]]

am·i·to·sis (am′i tō′sis), *n. Biol.* the direct method of cell division, characterized by simple cleavage of the nucleus without the formation of chromosomes. **—am·i·tot·ic** (am′i tot′ik), *adj.* **—am′i·tot′i·cal·ly,** *adv.*

am·i·ty (am′i tē), *n.* friendship; peaceful harmony; mutual understanding. [late ME *amit(i)e* < MF *amitie,* OF *amiste(t)* < VL **amīcitāt-* = L *amīc(us)* friend + *-itāt-* -ITY]

Am·man (äm män′), *n.* a city in and the capital of Jordan, in the N central part: the ancient Biblical city of Rabbath Ammon. 615,000.

am·me·ter (am′mē′tər), *n. Elect.* an instrument for measuring current in amperes. [AM(PERE) + -METER]

am·mine (am′ēn, ə mēn′), *n. Chem.* **1.** a compound containing one or more ammonia molecules in coordinate linkage. **2.** any coordination compound containing one or more ammonia molecules bonded to a metal ion. [AMM(ONIA) + -INE[2]]

am·mo (am′ō), *n. Informal.* ammunition. [by shortening and alter.]

am·mo·cete (am′ə sēt′), *n.* the larval stage of a lamprey. Also, **am′mo·coete′.** [< NL *ammocoetē(s)*: lit., something bedded in sand < Gk *ámmo(s)* sand + *koítē* bed]

Am·mon (am′ən), *n.* **1.** the classical name of the Egyptian divinity Amen, whom the Greeks identified with Zeus, the Romans with Jupiter. **2.** the ancient country of the Ammonites, east of the Jordan River.

am·mo·nia (ə mōn′yə, ə mō′nē ə), *n. Chem.* **1.** a pungent, suffocating, gaseous compound, NH_3, usually produced by the direct combination of nitrogen and hydrogen gases: used chiefly for refrigeration and in the manufacture of chemicals and reagents. **2.** Also called **ammonia solution, ammonia water, aqua ammoniae, aqueous ammonia.** this gas dissolved in water; ammonium hydroxide. [< NL, so called as being obtained from sal ammoniac. See AMMONIAC]

am·mo·ni·ac (ə mō′nē ak′), *n.* **1.** Also, **am·mo·ni·a·cum** (am′ə nī′ə kəm). See **gum ammoniac.** **—adj. 2.** ammoniacal. [< L *ammōniac(um)* < Gk *ammōniakón* (neut. of *ammōniakós* of AMMON; see -I-, -AC), applied to a salt and a gum resin said to come from near the Shrine of Ammon in Libya]

am·mo·ni·a·cal (am′ə nī′ə kəl), *adj.* **1.** consisting of, containing, or using ammonia. **2.** like ammonia.

ammo′nia solu′tion, *Chem.* ammonia (def. 2).

am·mo·ni·ate (ə mō′nē āt′), *v.t.,* **-at·ed, -at·ing.** *Chem.* to treat or cause to unite with ammonia. **—am·mo′ni·a′tion,** *n.*

ammo′nia wa′ter, *Chem.* ammonia (def. 2).

am·mon·ic (ə mon′ik, ə mō′nik), *adj.* of or pertaining to ammonia or ammonium. Also, **am·mon′i·cal.**

am·mon·i·fi·ca·tion (ə mon′ə fə kā′shən, ə mō′nə-), *n.* **1.** the act of impregnating with ammonia, as in the manufacture of fertilizer. **2.** the state of being so impregnated. **3.** the formation of ammonia or its compounds, as in soil by soil organisms.

am·mo·nite[1] (am′ə nīt′), *n.* one of the coiled, chambered fossil shells of a cephalopod mollusk of the extinct order *Ammonoidea.* [< NL *Ammōnītes* < ML (*cornū*) *Ammōn(is)* (horn) of Ammon + *-ītes* -ITE[1]; fossil so called from resemblance to horn of Jupiter AMMON] **—am·mo·nit·ic** (am′ə nit′ik), *adj.* **—am·mon·i·toid** (ə mon′i toid′), *adj.*

Ammonite[1]

am·mo·nite[2] (am′ə nīt′), *n.* a nitrogenous mixture consisting chiefly of dried animal fats, usually obtained from livestock carcasses, and used as a fertilizer. [AMMO(NIUM) + NI(TRA)TE]

am·mo·ni·um (ə mō′nē əm), *n. Chem.* the univalent ion, NH_4^+, or group, NH_4, which plays the part of a metal in the salt formed when ammonia reacts with an acid. [< NL]

ammo′nium car′bamate, *Chem.* a volatile powder, $H_2NCOONH_4$, used as a fertilizer.

ammo′nium car′bonate, *Chem.* a mixture of ammonium bicarbonate and ammonium carbamate, used chiefly in the manufacture of smelling salts and baking powder. Also called **sal volatile.**

ammo′nium chlo′ride, *Chem., Pharm.* a crystalline powder, NH_4Cl, used chiefly in dry cells, in electroplating, and as an expectorant. Also called **sal ammoniac.**

ammo′nium hydrox′ide, *Chem.* a basic compound, NH_4OH, existing only in solution, formed by dissolving ammonia gas in water. Cf. **ammonia.**

ammo′nium ni′trate, *Chem.* a water-soluble powder, NH_4NO_3, used chiefly in explosives, fertilizers, and in the manufacture of nitrous oxide.

ammo′nium salt′, *Chem.* any salt containing the NH_4^+ ion, formed by the neutralization of ammonium hydroxide by an acid.

ammo′nium sul′fate, *Chem.* a water-soluble solid $(NH_4)_2SO_4$, used chiefly as a fertilizer.

am·mu·ni·tion (am′yə nish′ən), *n.* **1.** the material fired, scattered, dropped, or detonated from any weapon, as bombs or rockets, and esp. shot, shrapnel, bullets, or shells fired by guns. **2.** the means of igniting or exploding such material, as primers, fuzes, and gunpowder. **3.** any material, means, information, or the like, used in any conflict: *Give me some ammunition for the debate.* **4.** *Obs.* military supplies generally. [< F *amunition* (now obs.) for *la munition* the munition]

am·ne·sia (am nē′zhə), *n.* complete or partial loss of memory. [< NL < Gk *amnēsía,* var. of *amnēstía* oblivion. See AMNESTY] **—am·nes·tic** (am nes′tik), *adj.*

am·ne·si·ac (am nē′zhē ak′, -zē-), *n.* **1.** a person affected by amnesia. **—adj. 2.** Also, **am·ne·sic** (am nē′sik, -zik). displaying the symptoms of amnesia.

am·nes·ty (am′ni stē), *n., pl.* **-ties,** *v.,* **-tied, -ty·ing.** **—n. 1.** a general pardon for offenses against a government. **2.** *Law.* an act of forgiveness for past offenses, esp. to a class of persons as a whole. **—v.t. 3.** to grant amnesty to; pardon. [< Gk *amnēstía* oblivion = *ámnēst(os)* forgetting (*a-* A-[6] + *mnēs-* remember + *-tos* verbal suffix) + *-ia* -Y[3]]

am·ni·o·cen·te·sis (am′nē ō sen tē′sis), *n.* a surgical procedure for obtaining a sample of amniotic fluid from the uterus of a pregnant woman by inserting a hollow needle through the abdominal wall, used in diagnosing possible obstetric complications or genetic defects. [AMNIO(N) + NL *centesis,* puncture]

am·ni·on (am′nē ən), *n., pl.* **-ni·ons, -ni·a** (-nē ə). *Anat., Zool.* the innermost of the embryonic or fetal membranes of reptiles, birds, and mammals; the sac in which the embryo is suspended. [< Gk = *amn(ós)* lamb + *-ion* dim. suffix]

am·ni·ot·ic (am′nē ot′ik), *adj. Anat., Zool.* of, pertaining to, or having an amnion. Also, **am·ni·on·ic** (am′nē-on′ik), **am·nic** (am′nik). [*amnio(s)* (pseudo-Gk var. of AMNION) + -TIC]

amn't (ant, am′ənt), *Dial.* contraction of *am not.* **—Usage.** See **ain't.**

a·moe·ba (ə mē′bə), *n., pl.* **-bae** (-bē), **-bas.** *Zool.* **1.** a microscopic, one-celled animal consisting of a naked mass of protoplasm constantly changing in shape as it moves and engulfs food. **2.** a protozoan of the genus *Amoeba.* Also, **ameba.** [< NL < Gk *amoibḗ* change, alternation, akin to *ameíbein* to exchange] **—a·moe′ba·like′,** *adj.*

Amoeba (def.1) A, Pseudopodia; B, Food vacuole; C, Nucleus; D, Contractile vacuole

a·moe·bic (ə mē′bik), *adj.* **1.** of, pertaining to, or like an amoeba. **2.** characterized by or due to the presence of amoebae, as certain diseases. Also, **amebic.**

amoe′bic dys′entery, a variety of dysentery caused by a protozoan, *Endamoeba histolytica,* characterized esp. by intestinal ulceration.

a·moe·bo·cyte (ə mē′bə sīt′), *n. Zool.* a migratory, amoeboid cell, found in many invertebrates, that functions in excretion, assimilation, etc. Also, **amebocyte.**

a·moe·boid (ə mē′boid), *adj. Biol.* resembling or related to amoebae. Also, **ameboid.** **—a·moe′boid·ism,** *n.*

a·mok (ə muk′, ə mok′), *n.* **1.** (among Malays) a psychic disturbance characterized by depression followed by an overwhelming desire to murder. **—adv. 2. run amok.** See **amuck** (def. 1). Also, **amuck.** [< Malay *amoq*]

a·mo·le (ə mō′lā; *Sp.* ä mô′le), *n., pl.* **-les** (-lāz; *Sp.* -les). *Southwestern U.S.* **1.** the root of any of several plants, as Mexican species of agaves, used as a substitute for soap. **2.** any such plant. [< Sp < Nahuatl *amolli* soap]

a·mong (ə mung′), *prep.* **1.** in or into the midst of. **2.** with a portion for each of: *Divide this among you.* **3.** in the group or class of: *the least among one's worries.* **4.** in the midst of, so as to have an influence upon: *missionary work among the people.* **5.** familiar to or characteristic of: *a proverb among the Spaniards.* **6.** in, with, or through the general mass of: *a man popular among the people.* **7.** by the joint or reciprocal action of: *Settle it among yourselves.* **8.** each with the other; mutually: *They quarreled among themselves.* [ME; OE *amang, onmang* for *on gemang* in (the) group (of); akin to MINGLE] **—Syn.** AMONG and BETWEEN suggest a relationship that is not necessarily physical: *among the crowd; Between you and me, I don't like any of them.* AMID, a more literary word, im-

plies being in the middle of a place or surrounded by something: *to stand amid ruins.*
—**Usage.** Precise users of English use AMONG when more than two persons or things are involved: *The winnings were divided among the six men* and use BETWEEN chiefly when only two persons or things are involved: *to decide between tea and coffee.* This distinction is not very widely maintained in the case of BETWEEN, which is often used when more than two persons or things are involved in individual or reciprocal relationships: *a contract between five companies.*

a·mongst (ə mungst′), *prep.* among. [earlier *amongs*, ME *amonges* = *among* AMONG + *-es* -S[1]; excrescent *-t* as in AGAINST]

A·mon-Ra (ä′mən rä′), *n. Egyptian Myth.* Amen-Ra.

a·mon·til·la·do (ə mon′tᵊlä′dō; *Sp.* ä mōn′tē lyä′thō), *n.* a pale, dry Spanish sherry. [< Sp = *a* to, near (< L *ad*) + *Montill(a)* Spanish town + *-ado* -ATE[1]]

a·mor·al (ā môr′əl, a môr′-, ā mor′-, a mor′-), *adj.* **1.** without moral quality; neither moral nor immoral. **2.** lacking or indifferent to moral standards, principles, or criteria. —**a·mo·ral·i·ty** (ā′mə ral′i tē, am′ə-), *n.* —**a·mor′al·ly,** *adv.* —**Syn. 1, 2.** See **immoral.**

am·o·ret·to (am′ə ret′ō; *It.* ä′mô ret′tô), *n., pl.* **-ret·ti** (-ret′ē; *It.* -ret′tē). a little cupid. [< It = *amor(e)* love + *-etto* -ET]

a·mo·ri·no (ä′mô rē′nô), *n., pl.* **-ni** (-nē). *Fine Arts.* a putto represented as an infant cupid. [< It = *amor(e)* love + *-ino* dim. suffix]

am·o·rist (am′ə rist), *n.* **1.** a lover; gallant. **2.** a person who writes about love. [< L *amor* love + -IST] —**am′o·ris′tic,** *adj.*

am·o·rous (am′ər əs), *adj.* **1.** inclined or disposed to love, esp. sexual love. **2.** being in love; enamored (usually fol. by *of*): *to be amorous of someone.* **3.** showing, expressing, or pertaining to love: *an amorous sigh.* [ME < MF < L *amōrōs(us)* = *amor* love + *-ōsus* -OSE[1], -OUS] —**am′o·rous·ly,** *adv.* —**am′o·rous·ness, am·o·ros·i·ty** (am′ə ros′i tē), *n.* —**Syn. 1.** loving; amatory. —**Ant. 1.** cold.

a·mor pa·tri·ae (ä′mōr pä′trē ī′; *Eng.* ā′môr pā′tri ē′), *Latin.* love of country; patriotism.

a·mor·phism (ə môr′fiz əm), *n.* the state or quality of being amorphous. [< G *Amorphism(us)* < Gk *ámorph(os)* AMORPHOUS + *-ismos* -ISM]

a·mor·phous (ə môr′fəs), *adj.* **1.** lacking definite form: *amorphous clouds.* **2.** of no particular kind or character; indeterminate; unorganized. **3.** *Petrol.* occurring in a mass, as without stratification or cystalline structure. **4.** *Chem.* not crystalline. [< Gk *ámorphos* shapeless. See A-[6], -MORPHOUS] —**a·mor′phous·ly,** *adv.* —**a·mor′phous·ness,** *n.*

a·mort (ə môrt′), *adj. Archaic.* spiritless; lifeless. [< F *à mort* at (the point of) death]

am·or·tise (am′ər tīz′, ə môr′tīz), *v.t.,* **-tised, -tis·ing.** *Chiefly Brit.* amortize. —**am′or·tis′a·ble,** *adj.*

am·or·ti·za·tion (am′ər ti zā′shən, ə môr′-), *n.* **1.** the act of amortizing a debt. **2.** the sums devoted to this purpose. Also, **amortizement; amortissement;** *esp. Brit.,* **am′or·ti·sa′tion.** [< ML *a(d)mortizātiōn-* (s. of *admortizātiō*)]

am·or·tize (am′ər tīz′, ə môr′tīz), *v.t.,* **-tized, -tiz·ing.** *Finance.* to liquidate or extinguish (a mortgage, debt, or other obligation), esp. by periodic payments to the creditor or to a sinking fund. Also, *esp. Brit.,* **amortise.** [< ML *a(d)mortiz(āre)* (to) bring to death < MF *amortiss-* (var. s. of *amortir;* see AMORT) + *-āre* inf. suffix; r. ME *amortisse(n)* < MF] —**am′or·tiz′a·ble,** *adj.*

am·or·tize·ment (am′ər tīz′mənt, ə môr′tiz-), *n.* amortization. Also, **a·mor·tisse·ment** (ə môr′tiz mənt).

A·mos (ā′məs), *n.* **1.** a minor Prophet of the 8th century B.C. **2.** a book of the Bible bearing his name.

a·mount (ə mount′), *n.* **1.** the sum total of two or more quantities or sums. **2.** the sum of the principal and interest of a loan. **3.** quantity; measure: *a great amount of resistance.* **4.** the full effect, value, or significance. **5.** a sum of money. —*v.i.* **6.** to combine to yield a sum; total (usually fol. by *to*): *His debts amount to $5000.* **7.** to have a value, effect, or extent (usually fol. by *to*): *All his fine words amount to nothing.* [ME *amount(en)* < OF *amonte(r)* (to) go up < *amont* upward, for *a mont* < L *ad montem* to the mount]

a·mour (ə mŏŏr′), *n.* **1.** a love affair. **2.** an illicit love affair. [ME < L *amōr-* (s. of *amor*) love]

a·mour-pro·pre (A mōōr prô′prᵊ), *n. French.* self-esteem; self-respect. [lit., self-love]

A·moy (ä moi′), *n.* **1.** an island in the Formosa Strait. **2.** a seaport on this island. 224,300 (1953).

amp[1] (amp), *n. Elect.* ampere. [by shortening]

amp[2] (amp), *n. Informal.* amplifier. [by shortening]

amp., **1.** amperage. **2.** *Elect.* ampere; amperes.

am·per·age (am′pər ij, am pēr′-), *n. Elect.* the strength of an electric current measured in amperes.

am·pere (am′pēr, am pēr′), *n. Elect.* the meter-kilogram-second unit of electric current, equal to the current that passes in a resistance of one ohm when a potential difference of one volt is applied: equivalent to one coulomb per second. *Abbr.:* A, amp, amp. Also, **am′père.** [named after A. M. AMPÈRE]

Am·père (am′pēr; *Fr.* äN per′), *n.* **An·dré Ma·rie** (äN′drā mə rē′; *Fr.* äN drā′ mA rē′), 1775–1836, French physicist.

am·pere-hour (am′pēr our′, -ou′ər), *n. Elect.* a unit of electric charge indicating the amount of electricity transferred by a current of one ampere in one hour: equal to 3600 coulombs. *Abbr.:* Ah, amp-hr

am·pere-turn (am′pēr tûrn′), *n. Elect.* the magnetomotive force produced by a current of one ampere passing in one complete turn of a coil. *Abbr.:* At

am·per·sand (am′pər sand′, am′pər sand′), *n.* a character or symbol (& or &) for *and.* [contr. of *and per se and,* lit., (the symbol) & by itself (stands for) and; see PER SE]

am·phet·a·mine (am fet′ə mēn′, -min), *n. Pharm.* a drug, $C_6H_5CH_2CH(NH_2)CH_3$, that stimulates the central nervous system: used chiefly to lift the mood or to control the appetite. [A(LPHA) + M(ETHYL) + PH(ENYL) + ET(HYL) + AMINE]

amphi-, a prefix occurring in loan words from Greek (*amphibious*); on this model, used with the meaning "two," "both," "on both sides," in the formation of compound words: *amphiaster.* [< Gk, comb. form of *amphí* on both sides; akin to Skt *abhitas,* G *-um,* OE *ymb(e)-* around. Cf. AMBI-]

Am·phi·a·ra·us (am′fē ə rā′əs), *n. Class Myth.* a hero who joined the Seven against Thebes, although he knew that his death was fated: deified after death.

am·phi·ar·thro·sis (am′fē är thrō′sis), *n., pl.* **-ses** (-sēz). *Anat.* an articulation permitting only slight motion, as that between the vertebrae. [AMPHI- + Gk *árthrōsis* articulation. See ARTHRO-, -OSIS] —**am′phi·ar·thro′di·al,** *adj.*

am·phi·as·ter (am′fē as′tər), *n. Biol.* the achromatic spindle with two asters that forms during mitosis.

Am·phib·i·a (am fib′ē ə), *n.* the class comprising the amphibians. [< NL < Gk *amphíbia* (*zōia*) (animals) living a double life, neut. pl. of *amphíbios*]

am·phib·i·an (am fib′ē ən), *n.* **1.** any cold-blooded vertebrate of the class *Amphibia,* comprising the frogs, salamanders, and caecilians, the larva of which are typically aquatic, breathing by gills, and the adult of which are terrestrial, breathing by lungs and through the moist, glandular skin. **2.** an amphibious plant. **3.** an airplane designed for taking off from and landing on both land and water. **4.** Also called **amtrac.** a flat-bottomed, armed, military vehicle equipped to move on land or water. —*adj.* **5.** belonging or pertaining to the *Amphibia.* **6.** amphibious (def. 2).

am·phi·bi·ot·ic (am′fə bī ot′ik), *adj. Zool.* living on land during the adult stage and in water during a larval stage.

am·phib·i·ous (am fib′ē əs), *adj.* **1.** living or able to live both on land and in water. **2.** Also, **amphibian.** capable of operating on both land and water: *amphibious vehicles.* **3.** of or pertaining to military operations by both land and naval forces against the same object, esp. to a military attack by troops landed by naval ships. **4.** trained or organized to fight, or fighting, on both land and sea. [< L *amphibius* < Gk *amphíbios* living a double life. See AMPHI-, BIO-, -OUS] —**am·phib′i·ous·ly,** *adv.* —**am·phib′i·ous·ness,** *n.*

am·phi·bole (am′fə bōl′), *n. Mineral.* any of a complex group of hydrous silicate minerals, containing chiefly calcium, magnesium, sodium, iron, and aluminum, and including hornblende, asbestos, etc. [< F < LL *amphibol(us)* < Gk *amphíbolos* ambiguous, lit., thrown on both sides < *amphibállein* to throw or put round (see AMPHI-); so called from its numerous varieties]

am·phi·bol·ic (am′fə bol′ik), *adj.* equivocal; uncertain; ambiguous.

am·phib·o·lite (am fib′ə līt′), *n. Petrol.* a metamorphic rock composed basically of an amphibole, usually hornblende. —**am·phib·o·lit·ic** (am fib′ə lit′ik), *adj.*

am·phi·bol·o·gy (am′fə bol′ə jē), *n., pl.* **-gies.** **1.** ambiguity of speech, esp. from uncertainty of the grammatical construction rather than of the meaning of the words. **2.** an instance of this, as *The Duke yet lives that Henry shall depose.* [ME *amphibologie* < LL *amphibologia.* See AMPHIBOLY, -LOGY] —**am·phib·o·log·i·cal** (am fib′ə loj′i kəl), *adj.* —**am·phib′o·log′i·cal·ly,** *adv.*

am·phib·o·ly (am fib′ə lē), *n., pl.* **-lies.** amphibology. [< L *amphibolia* < Gk. See AMPHIBOLE, -Y[3]]

am·phi·brach (am′fə brak′), *n. Pros.* a trisyllabic foot, the arrangement of the syllables of which is short, long, short in quantitative meter, or unstressed, stressed, unstressed in accentual meter. [< L *amphibrach(us)* < Gk *amphíbrachys* short before and after (*amphi-* AMPHI- + *brachýs* short)] —**am′phi·brach′ic,** *adj.*

am·phi·chro·ic (am′fə krō′ik), *adj. Chem.* giving either of two colors, one with acids and one with alkalis. Also, **am·phi·chro·mat·ic** (am′fi krō mat′ik, -krə-).

am·phic·ty·on (am fik′tē ən), *n.* a deputy to the council of an amphictyony. [back formation from *amphictyons* < Gk *amphiktýones,* orig. *amphiktíones* neighbors = *amphi-* AMPHI- + *-kti-* inhabit + *-ones* n. suffix (pl.)]

am·phic·ty·o·ny (am fik′tē ə nē), *n., pl.* **-nies.** (in ancient Greece) any of the leagues of states, esp. the league at Delphi, united for mutual protection and the worship of a common deity. [< Gk *Amphiktyonía* = *amphiktýon(es)* (pl.; see AMPHICTYON) + *-ia* -Y[3]] —**am·phic·ty·on·ic** (am fik′tē on′ik), *adj.*

am·phi·dip·loid (am′fi dip′loid), *n. Biol.* a plant having the sum of the chromosome numbers of two parental species, owing to the doubling of the chromosomes in a hybrid of two species.

am·phi·go·ry (am′fə gōr′ē, -gôr′ē), *n., pl.* **-ries.** **1.** a meaningless rigamarole, as of nonsense verses. **2.** a nonsensical parody. [< F *amphigouri* = *amphi-* AMPHI- + *gouri* < ?] —**am·phi·gor·ic** (am′fə gôr′ik, -gor′-), *adj.*

am·phi·gou·ri (am′fə gŏŏr′ē), *n., pl.* **-ris.** amphigory.

am·phim·a·cer (am fim′ə sər), *n. Pros.* a trisyllabic foot, the arrangement of the syllables of which is long, short, long in quantitative meter, or stressed, unstressed, stressed in accentual meter. [< L *amphimacr(us)* < Gk *amphímakros* long at both ends. See AMPHI-, MACRO-]

am·phi·mix·is (am′fə mik′sis), *n., pl.* **-mix·es** (-mik′sēz). **1.** *Biol.* the merging of the germ plasm of two organisms in sexual reproduction. **2.** *Embryol., Genetics.* the combining of paternal and maternal hereditary substances. [AMPHI- + Gk *míxis* a mingling]

Am·phi·on (am fī′ən), *n. Class. Myth.* a son of Zeus and the husband of Niobe. With his twin brother, Zethus, he built the walls of Thebes, charming the stones into place with his lyre.

am·phi·ox·us (am′fē ok′səs), *n., pl.* **-ox·i** (-ok′sī), **-ox·us·es.** a lancelet of the genus *Branchiostoma,* having such vertebrate characteristics as a notochord and a dorsal cord of nerve tissue. [< NL: lit., sharp at both ends < Gk *amphi-* AMPHI- + *oxýs* pointed]

am·phi·pod (am′fə pod′), *n.* **1.** any of numerous small crustaceans of the group *Amphipoda,* including the beach fleas, sand hoppers, etc. —*adj.* **2.** of or pertaining to the amphipods.

am·phip·ro·style (am fip′rə stīl′, am′fə prō′stīl), *adj.* (of a classical temple) prostyle on both fronts. [< L *amphiprostȳl(us)* < Gk *amphipróstȳlos*] —**am·phip′ro·sty′lar,** *adj.*

am·phis·bae·na (am′fis bē′nə), *n., pl.* **-nae** (-nē), **-nas.** **1.** any of numerous worm lizards of the genus *Amphisbaena.* **2.** *Class. Myth.* a serpent having a head at each end of its body. [< L < Gk *amphísbaina* a serpent that moves forward or backward = *amphís* both ways + *baín(ein)* (to) go + *-a* n. suffix] —**am′phis·bae′ni·an, am′phis·bae′nic,** *adj.*

am·phi·sty·lar (am′fi stī′lər), *adj.* *Archit.* **1.** (of a classical temple) having columns on both fronts. **2.** having columns at both sides. [AMPHI- + STYL-[2] + -AR[1]]

am·phi·the·a·ter (am′fə thē′ə tər, -thēə′tər), *n.* **1.** a building with tiers of seats around a central area, as those used in ancient Rome for gladiatorial contests. **2.** any similar place for public contests, games, performances, exhibitions, etc.; an arena, stadium, or auditorium. **3.** a room having tiers of seats arranged around a central area, in which students and other observers can view surgery, hear lectures, etc. **4.** a level area surrounded by rising ground. Also, **am′phi·the′a·tre.** [< L *amphitheātr(um)* < Gk *amphithéātron*] —**am·phi·the·at·ric** (am′fə thē a′trik), **am′phi·the·at′ri·cal,** *adj.* —**am′phi·the·at′ri·cal·ly,** *adv.*

Am·phi·tri·te (am′fə trī′tē), *n.* an ancient Greek sea goddess, a daughter of Nereus and the wife of Poseidon.

Am·phit·ry·on (am fi′trē ən), *n.* *Class. Myth.* the husband of Alcmene killed in a war against Erginus.

am·pho·ra (am′fər ə), *n., pl.* **-pho·rae** (-fə rē′), **-pho·ras.** *Gk. and Rom. Antiq.* a large, oval, two-handled vase, used for storage, as a trophy, etc. [< L < Gk *amphor-(eýs)* = *am(phi)-* AMPHI- + *phoreýs* bearer (i.e., handle), akin to *phérein* to bear] —**am′pho·ral,** *adj.*

Amphora

am·pho·ter·ic (am′fə ter′ik), *adj.* *Chem.* capable of functioning either as an acid or as a base. [< Gk *amphóter(os)* (comp. of *ámphō* both; c. L *ambō*) + -IC]

amp-hr, *Elect.* ampere-hour.

am·pi·cil·lin (am′pi sil′in), *n.* a semisynthetic penicillin effective against Gram-positive and Gram-negative bacteria. [AM(INO) (BENZYL) P(EN)ICILLIN]

am·ple (am′pəl), *adj.,* **-pler, -plest.** of adequate or more than adequate extent, size, or amount. [late ME < L *ampl(us)* wide] —**am′ple·ness,** *n.*
—**Syn.** extensive, vast; generous, lavish; plentiful. AMPLE, LIBERAL, COPIOUS, PROFUSE describe degrees of abundant provision. AMPLE implies a plentiful provision: *to give ample praise.* LIBERAL implies provision from a generous supply (more than AMPLE but less than COPIOUS): *Liberal amounts of food were distributed to the needy.* COPIOUS implies an apparently inexhaustible and lavish abundance: *a copious flow of tears.* PROFUSE implies a still more unrestrained abundance of provision or flow: *profuse in his apologies.* —**Ant.** scanty, meager.

am·plex·i·caul (am plek′sə kôl′), *adj.* *Bot.* clasping the stem, as some leaves do at their base. [< NL *amplexicaul(is)* = *amplexi-* (comb. form of L *amplexus* a clasping, n. use of ptp. of *amplectī* to clasp) + *caulis* stem (see COLE)]

Amplexicaul leaf

am·pli·dyne (am′pli dīn′), *n.* *Elect.* a direct-current generator with a rotating armature, capable of magnifying a small amount of power supplied to the field winding of the device and using the amplified power to operate an attached, direct-current motor. [AMPLI(FIER) + DYNE]

am·pli·fi·ca·tion (am′plə fə kā′shən), *n.* **1.** the act of amplifying. **2.** the state of being amplified. **3.** expansion of a statement, narrative, etc., as for rhetorical purposes: *The story underwent considerable amplification.* **4.** a statement, narrative, etc., so expanded. **5.** the matter or substance used to expand an idea, statement, or the like. **6.** *Elect.* increase in the strength of current, voltage, or power. [< L *amplificātiōn-* (s. of *amplificātiō*). See AMPLE, -I-, -FICATION]

am·plif·i·ca·to·ry (am plif′ə kə tōr′ē, -tôr′ē), *adj.* used for amplification, as of a statement or narrative. [< L *amplificātor* amplifier + -Y[1]. See AMPLIFY, -ATORY]

am·pli·fi·er (am′plə fī′ər), *n.* **1.** a person or thing that amplifies or enlarges. **2.** an electronic component or circuit for amplifying power, current, or voltage.

am·pli·fy (am′plə fī′), *v.,* **-fied, -fy·ing.** —*v.t.* **1.** to make larger or greater; enlarge; extend. **2.** to expand in stating or describing, as by details or illustrations; clarify by expanding. **3.** to exaggerate. **4.** *Elect.* to increase the amplitude of; cause amplification in. —*v.i.* **5.** to discourse at length; expatiate or expand one's remarks, speech, ideas, or the like. [late ME *amplifye* < MF *amplifie(r)* << L *amplificāre* to extend. See AMPLE, -IFY] —**am′pli·fi′a·ble,** *adj.*

am·pli·tude (am′pli to͞od′, -tyo͞od′), *n.* **1.** the state or quality of being ample, esp. as to breadth or width; largeness; greatness of extent. **2.** large or full measure; abundance. **3.** *Physics.* the absolute value of the maximum displacement from a zero value during one period of an oscillation. **4.** *Elect.* the maximum deviation of an alternating current from its average value during its cycle. **5.** *Astron.* the arc of the horizon measured from the east or west point to the point where a vertical circle through a heavenly body would intersect the horizon. **6.** *Math.* argument (def. 8b). [< L *amplitūdō.* See AMPLE, -I-, -TUDE]

am′plitude modula′tion, *Electronics, Radio.* See **AM.**

am·ply (am′plē), *adv.* in an ample manner; sufficiently.

am·pule (am′pyo͞ol), *n.* *Med.* a sealed glass or plastic bulb containing solutions for hypodermic injection. Also, **am′pul, am′poule.** [< F < L *ampull(a)* AMPULLA; r. ME *ampulle* < OF < L *ampull(a)*]

am·pul·la (am pul′ə, -po͝ol′ə), *n., pl.* **-pul·lae** (-pul′ē, -po͝ol′ē). **1.** *Anat.* a dilated portion of a canal or duct, esp. of the semicircular canals of the ear. **2.** a two-handled, globular bottle used by the ancient Romans for holding oil, wine, or perfumes. [< L = *amp(hora)* AMPHORA + *-ulla* dim. suffix]

am·pul·la·ceous (am′pə lā′shəs), *adj.* bottle-shaped. Also, **am·pul·lar** (am pul′ər, -po͝ol′-), **am·pul·la·ry** (am-pul′ə rē, -po͝ol′-, am′pə ler′ē). [< L *ampullāceus*]

am·pu·tate (am′pyo͝o tāt′), *v.t.,* **-tat·ed, -tat·ing.** to cut off (all or part of a limb or digit of the body), as by surgery. [< L *amputāt(us)* pruned, trimmed (ptp. of *amputāre*) = *am(bi)* around + *put-* trim + *-ātus* -ATE[1]] —**am′pu·ta′tion,** *n.*

am·pu·tee (am′pyo͝o tē′), *n.* a person who has lost an arm, hand, leg, etc., by amputation. [AMPUT(ATED) + -EE, modeled on F *amputé,* ptp. of *amputer* to amputate]

Am·rit·sar (əm rit′sər), *n.* a city in NW Punjab, in NW India. 418,690 (est. 1964).

Am·ster·dam (am′stər dam′; *Du.* äm′stər däm′), *n.* **1.** a city in and the nominal capital of the Netherlands. 752,500. Cf. **Hague, The. 2.** a city in E New York. 25,524 (1970).

amt., amount.

am·trac (am′trak′), *n.* amphibian (def. 4). Also, **am′-track′.** [AM(PHIBIOUS) + TRAC(TOR)]

Am·trak (am′trak′), *n.* *U.S.* a public corporation created by Congress in 1970 to operate the national rail-passenger system through contracts with existing railroads. [AM(ERICAN) + TRA(C)K, as a nickname for *National Railroad Passenger Corp.*]

amu, See **atomic mass unit.**

a·muck (ə muk′), *adv.* **1. run amuck, a.** to rush about in a murderous frenzy. **b.** to lose self-control, as in panic. —*n.* **2.** amok. [var. of AMOK]

A·mu Dar·ya (ä mo͞o′ där′yä), a river in central Asia. ab. 1400 mi. long. Also called **Oxus.**

am·u·let (am′yə lit), *n.* a charm worn to ward off evil or to bring good fortune; talisman. [< L *amulēt(um)*]

A·mund·sen (ä′mənd sən; *Norw.* ä′mo͝on sən), *n.* **Ro·ald** (rō′äl), 1872–1928, Norwegian explorer: discovered the South Pole 1911.

A·mur (ä mo͝or′), *n.* a river in E Asia, forming most of the boundary between N Manchuria and the SE Soviet Union, flowing into the Sea of Okhotsk. ab. 2700 mi. long.

a·muse (ə myo͞oz′), *v.t.,* **a·mused, a·mus·ing. 1.** to hold the attention of (someone) agreeably; entertain or divert in a pleasant manner. **2.** to excite mirth or the like in. **3.** *Archaic.* to delude by flattery, pretenses, etc. **4.** *Obs.* to engross; absorb. [late ME < MF *amuse(r)* (to) cause to MUSE; see A-[5]] —**a·mus′a·ble,** *adj.* —**a·mus′er,** *n.*
—**Syn. 1.** please, charm, cheer. AMUSE, DIVERT, ENTERTAIN mean to occupy the attention with something pleasant. That which AMUSES dispels the tedium of idleness or pleases the fancy. DIVERT implies turning the attention from serious thoughts or pursuits to something light, amusing, or lively. That which ENTERTAINS usually does so because of a plan or program that engages the attention by being pleasing and sometimes instructive.

a·mused (ə myo͞ozd′), *adj.* **1.** pleasurably occupied. **2.** displaying amusement: *an amused expression.* **3.** aroused to mirth. —**a·mus·ed·ly** (ə myo͞o′zid lē), *adv.*

a·muse·ment (ə myo͞oz′mənt), *n.* **1.** something that amuses; pastime; entertainment. **2.** the act of amusing. **3.** the state of being amused; enjoyment. [< MF]

amuse′ment park′, a park equipped with such recreational devices as a Ferris wheel, roller coaster, etc., and usually having vendors of toys, food, and beverages.

amuse′ment tax′, a tax levied on such forms of entertainment as motion pictures, the theater, etc.

a·mus·ing (ə myo͞o′zing), *adj.* **1.** pleasantly entertaining or diverting. **2.** exciting laughter or gentle mirth; delighting the fancy. —**a·mus′ing·ly,** *adv.* —**a·mus′ing·ness,** *n.*
—**Syn. 1.** charming, cheering, lively. **2.** laughable, delightful, funny. AMUSING, COMICAL, DROLL describe that which causes mirth. That which is AMUSING is quietly humorous or funny in a gentle, good-humored way: *The baby's attempts to talk were amusing.* That which is COMICAL causes laughter by being incongruous, witty, or ludicrous: *His huge shoes made the clown look comical.* DROLL adds to COMICAL the idea of strange or peculiar, and sometimes that of sly or waggish humor: *droll antics of a kitten; a droll imitation.*

a·mu·sive (ə myo͞o′ziv), *adj.* *Rare.* amusing. —**a·mu′-sive·ly,** *adv.* —**a·mu′sive·ness,** *n.*

Am·y·cus (am′ə kəs), *n.* *Class. Myth.* a son of Poseidon and one of the Meliae, known for his ruthlessness and his skill at boxing.

a·myg·da·la (ə mig′də lə), *n., pl.* **-lae** (-lē′). **1.** an almond. **2.** *Anat.* **a.** an almond-shaped part. **b.** a tonsil. [< ML: almond, tonsil, L: almond < Gk *amygdálē;* r. ME *amygdal,* OE *amigdal* almond < L *amygdal(on)* < Gk *amýgdalon*]

a·myg·da·la·ceous (ə mig′də lā′shəs), *adj.* belonging or pertaining to the *Amygdalaceae,* a family of plants bearing fruit containing a single hard seed. [< NL *Amygdalāce(ae)* (see AMYGDALA, -ACEAE) + -OUS]

a·myg·da·late (ə mig′də lit, -lāt′), *adj.* of, pertaining to, or resembling almonds. [< L *amygdal-* ALMOND + -ATE[1]]

a·myg·da·lin (ə mig′də lin), *n.* a bitter-tasting powder, $C_6H_5CHCNOC_{12}H_{21}O_{10}$: an expectorant. [< L *amygdal-* ALMOND + -IN[2]]

a·myg·da·loid (ə mig′də loid′), *n.* *Petrog.* **1.** an igneous rock in which rounded cavities formed by the expansion of steam have later become filled with deposits of various minerals. —*adj.* Also, **a·myg′da·loi′dal. 2.** (of rocks) containing amygdules. **3.** almond-shaped. [< L *amygdal-* ALMOND + -OID]

a·myg·dule (ə mig′do͞ol, -dyo͞ol), *n.* *Petrog.* one of the mineral nodules in amygdaloid. [AMYGD(ALA) + -ULE]

am·yl (am′il), *adj.* *Chem.* containing an amyl group; pentyl. [b. AM(YL)- and -YL]

amyl-, var. of **amylo-,** esp. before a vowel.

am·y·la·ceous (am′ə lā′shəs), *adj.* of the nature of starch.

am′yl ac′etate, *Chem.* See **banana oil.** Also called **am′yl·a·ce′tic e′ther** (am′il ə sē′tik, -set′ik, am′-).

am′yl al′cohol, *Chem.* a liquid, $C_5H_{11}OH$, consisting of a mixture of two or more isomeric alcohols: a solvent and intermediate for organic synthesis.

am·yl·ase (am′ə lās′), *n.* *Biochem.* **1.** a starch-splitting enzyme that hydrolyzes complex sugars to glucose, present in the blood and in certain plants. **2.** any of several digestive enzymes that break down starches.

am·yl·ene (am′ə lēn′), *n. Chem.* any of five unsaturated isomeric hydrocarbons having the formula C_5H_{10}.

am′yl group′, *Chem.* any of several univalent, isomeric groups having the formula C_5H_{11}–, esp. $CH_3CH_2C(CH_3)_2$– whose derivatives are found in fruit extracts, etc. —**a·myl·ic,** (ə mil′ik), *adj.*

am′yl ni′trite, *Pharm.* a flammable liquid, $(CH_3)_2CHCH_2CH_2ONO$, a vasodilator, used esp. in the treatment of angina pectoris.

amylo-, a combining form of **amylum,** used esp. before a consonant: *amylolysis.* Also, *esp. before a vowel,* **amyl-.** [comb. form of Gk *ámylon,* starch, n. use of neut. of *ámylos* not milled (*a-* A-[6] + *mýl(ē)* mill + *-os* adj. suffix)]

am·y·loid (am′ə loid′), *n.* **1.** *Chem.* any gelatinous hydrate formed by the interaction of sulfuric acid and cellulose. **2.** a nonnitrogenous food consisting esp. of starch. —*adj.* **3.** Also, **am′y·loi′dal.** of, resembling, or containing amylum.

am·y·lol·y·sis (am′ə lol′i sis), *n. Biochem.* the conversion of starch into sugar. —**am·y·lo·lyt·ic** (am′ə lō lit′ik), *adj.*

am·y·lo·pec·tin (am′ə lō pek′tin), *n.* the insoluble or gel component of starch that forms a paste with water, but does not solidify. Cf. **amylose.**

am·y·lop·sin (am′ə lop′sin), *n. Biochem.* an enzyme of the pancreatic juice, capable of converting starch into sugar. [AMYLO(LYSIS + PE)PSIN]

am·yl·ose (am′ə lōs′), *n.* the soluble or sol component of starch that forms a stiff gel at ordinary temperatures. Cf. **amylopectin.**

am·y·lum (am′ə ləm), *n.* starch (def. 1). [< L < Gk *ámylon*]

an[1] (ən; *when stressed* an), *indefinite article.* the form of **a** before an initial vowel sound and sometimes, esp. in British English, before an initial *h* that is normally pronounced but is part of an unstressed syllable: *an arch; an event; an honor; an historian.* Cf. **a**[1]. [ME; OE *ān* ONE]

an[2] (ən; *when stressed* an), *conj.* **1.** Also, **'n, 'n'.** *Informal.* and. **2.** *Archaic.* if. Also, **an'.**

An (än), *n.* the Sumerian god of heaven: the counterpart of the Akkadian Anu.

AN, Anglo-Norman. Also, **A.N., A.-N.**

An, *Chem.* actinon.

an-[1], a prefix occurring in loan words from Latin or Greek where it meant "not," "without," "lacking" (*anarchy; anecdote*); used in the formation of compound words: *anaerobe.* Also, *esp. before a consonant,* **a-.** [< L, Gk; see A-[6], UN-[1]]

an-[2], var. of **ad-** before *n: announce.*

an-[3], var. of **ana-** before a vowel: *anion.*

-an, **1.** a suffix occurring in adjectives borrowed from Latin (*republican*); on this model, used with the meaning "belonging to," "pertaining to," "adhering to," and commonly expressing connection with a place, person, doctrine, etc.; serving to form adjectives many of which are also used as nouns (*American; Christian*), and hence used to form other nouns of the same type (*historian; theologian*). **2.** *Zool.* a suffix meaning "relating to a certain class": *mammalian.* Also, *esp. after a vowel,* **-n.** [< L *-ānus, -āna, -ānum;* in some words r. *-ain, -en* < OF]

an., in the year. [< L *anno*]

a·na[1] (ä′nə, ä′nə), *n.* **1.** a collection of miscellaneous information about a particular subject. **2.** an item in such a collection. [independent use of -ANA]

an·a[2] (an′ə), *adv.* (of ingredients in pharmaceutical prescriptions) of each. [< ML < Gk *aná*]

ana-, a first element in loan words from Greek where it meant "up," "again," "throughout," "back" (*anabasis*); used in the formation of compound words: *anacardiaceous.* [< Gk, comb. form of *anā́;* akin to Skt *ā-,* L *an-;* cf. ON]

-ana, a noun suffix denoting a collection of material on a certain subject: *Americana.* [< L, neut. pl. of *-ānus* -AN]

an·a·bae·na (an′ə bē′nə), *n.* any of the fresh-water algae of the genus *Anabaena,* commonly occurring in masses and often contaminating drinking water, giving it a fishy odor and taste. [< NL < Gk *anabaín(ein)* (to) go up (*ana-* ANA- + *baínein* to go) + L *-a* n. suffix]

An·a·bap·tist (an′ə bap′tist), *n.* **1.** a member of any of various Protestant sects, formed in Europe after 1520, that denied the validity of infant baptism, baptized believers only, and advocated the complete separation of church and state. —*adj.* **2.** of or pertaining to Anabaptists or Anabaptism. [< NL *anabaptist(a)* < ML *anabapt(izāre)* (to) rebaptize (< LGk *anabaptízein;* see ANA-, BAPTIZE) + *-ista* -IST] —**An′a·bap′tism,** *n.* —**An′a·bap·tis′ti·cal·ly,** *adv.*

an·a·bas (an′ə bas′), *n.* any fish of the genus *Anabas,* found in Africa and southeastern Asia. [< NL < Gk, aorist participle of *anabaínein* to go up. See ANABAENA]

a·nab·a·sis (ə nab′ə sis), *n., pl.* **-ses** (-sēz′). **1.** a march from the coast into the interior. **2.** *Literary.* any military expedition. Cf. **katabasis.** [< Gk: a going up (used as the title of a historical work by Xenophon). See ANA-, BASIS]

an·a·bat·ic (an′ə bat′ik), *adj. Meteorol.* pertaining to an uphill wind produced by the effects of local heating. Cf. **katabatic.** [< Gk *anabatik(ós)* pertaining to climbing or to a climber = *anaba-* (s. of *anabaínein;* see ANABAENA) + *-tikos* -TIC]

an·a·bi·o·sis (an′ə bī ō′sis), *n.* reanimation after apparent death. [< NL < Gk *anabíōsis* a coming back to life = *anabi-* (s. of *anabióein* to return to life; see ANA-, BIO-) + *-ōsis* -OSIS] —**an·a·bi·ot·ic** (an′ə bī ot′ik), *adj.*

a·nab·o·lism (ə nab′ə liz′əm), *n. Biol., Physiol.* the synthesis in living organisms of more complex substances from simpler ones (opposed to *catabolism*). [ANA- + (META)BOLISM] —**an·a·bol·ic** (an′ə bol′ik), *adj.*

a·nab·o·lite (ə nab′ə līt′), *n.* a product of anabolism.

an·a·branch (an′ə branch′, -bränch′), *n.* a stream branching off from a river and rejoining it further downstream. [short for *anastomotic branch.* See ANASTOMOSIS]

an·a·car·di·a·ceous (an′ə kär′dē ā′shəs), *adj.* belonging to the *Anacardiaceae,* a family of trees and shrubs including the cashew, mango, etc. [< NL *Anacardiāce(ae)* (see ANA-, CARDI-, -ACEAE) + -OUS]

a·nach·ro·nism (ə nak′rə niz′əm), *n.* **1.** a person, object, thing, or event that is chronologically out of place, esp. one appropriate to an earlier period. **2.** an error in chronology in which a person, object, or event is assigned an incorrect date or period. Cf. **parachronism, prochronism.** [< L *anachronism(us)* < Gk *anachronismós* a wrong time reference = *anachron(ízein)* (to) make a wrong time reference (see ANA-, CHRON-, -IZE) + *-ismos* -ISM] —**an·a·chron·i·cal·ly** (an′ə kron′ik lē), *adv.* —**a·nach′ro·nis′tic, a·nach′ro·nis′ti·cal,** *adj.* —**a·nach′ro·nis′ti·cal·ly,** *adv.* —**a·nach′ro·nous,** *adj.* —**a·nach′ro·nous·ly,** *adv.*

An·a·cle·tus (an′ə klē′təs), *n.* fl. 1st century A.D., pope 76–88.

an·a·cli·nal (an′ə klīn′əl), *adj. Geol.* descending in a direction opposite to the dip of the surrounding strata. Cf. **cataclinal.** [< Gk *anaklín(ein)* (to) lean (something) upon]

an·a·cli·sis (an′ə klī′sis), *n. Psychoanal.* the choice of an object of libidinal attachment on the basis of a resemblance to early childhood protective and parental figures. [< Gk *anáklisis* a reclining = *anakli-,* var. s. of *anaklínein* to lean (something) upon (*ana-* ANA- + *klínein* to lean) + *-sis* -SIS]

an·a·clit·ic (an′ə klit′ik), *adj. Psychoanal.* exhibiting or pertaining to anaclisis. [< Gk *anáklit(os)* for reclining (*anakli-* (see ANACLISIS) + *-tos* verbid suffix) + -IC]

an·a·co·lu·thi·a (an′ə kə lōō′thē ə), *n. Rhet.* lack of grammatical sequence or coherence. [< L < Gk *anakolouthía.* See ANACOLUTHON, -IA] —**an′a·co·lu′thic,** *adj.* —**an′a·co·lu′thi·cal·ly,** *adv.*

an·a·co·lu·thon (an′ə kə lōō′thon), *n., pl.* **-tha** (-thə). *Rhet.* a case of anacoluthia. [< Gk *anakólouthon,* neut. of *anakólouthos* not following = *an-* AN-[1] + *akólouthos* marching together (*a-* together + *kolouth-,* gradative var. of *keleuth-* road, march + *-os* adj. suffix)]

an·a·con·da (an′ə kon′də), *n.* **1.** a South American boa, *Eunectes murinus,* that often grows to more than 20 feet. **2.** any large boa. [? < Singhalese *henakandayā* kind of snake = *hena* lightning + *kanda* stem + *-yā* nominal suffix]

An·a·con·da (an′ə kon′də), *n.* a city in SW Montana: largest copper smelter in the world. 9,771 (1970).

An·a·cos·ti·a (an′ə kôs′tē ə, -kos′-), *n.* a section of the District of Columbia, in the SE part.

Anacos′tia Riv′er, a river in the District of Columbia flowing into the Potomac River. ab. 24 mi. long.

an·a·cous·tic (an′ə kōō′stik), *adj.* of or pertaining to the region beyond the earth's atmosphere where sound waves cannot travel due to the lack of a transmitting medium.

A·nac·re·on (ə nak′rē ən), *n.* c570–c480 B.C., Greek writer, esp. of love poems and drinking songs.

A·nac·re·on·tic (ə nak′rē on′tik), *adj.* **1.** (*sometimes l.c.*) of or in the manner of Anacreon. **2.** (*sometimes l.c.*) convivial; amatory. —*n.* **3.** (*l.c.*) an Anacreontic poem. [< L *Anacreōntic(us)* = *Anacreōnt-* (< Gk *Anakreōnt-,* s. of *Anakréōn*) ANACREON + *-icus* -IC] —**A·nac′re·on′ti·cal·ly,** *adv.*

an·a·cru·sis (an′ə krōō′sis), *n., pl.* **-cru·ses** (-krōō′sēz). **1.** *Pros.* an unstressed syllable or syllable group that begins a line of verse but is not counted as part of the first foot. **2.** *Music.* the note or notes preceding a downbeat. [< L < Gk *anákrousis* = *anakroú(ein)* (to) strike up, push back (*ana-* ANA- + *kroúein* to strike, push) + *-sis* -SIS] —**an·a·crus·tic** (an′ə krus′tik), *adj.* —**an′a·crus′ti·cal·ly,** *adv.*

an·a·dem (an′ə dem′), *n. Literary.* a garland or wreath for the head. [< L *anadēm(e)* headband < Gk = *anadé(ein)* (to) bind up (*ana-* ANA- + *déein* to bind) + *-ēma* -EME]

an·a·di·plo·sis (an′ə di plō′sis), *n. Rhet.* repetition in the first part of a clause or sentence of a prominent word from the latter part of the preceding clause or sentence, usually with a change or extension of meaning. [< L < Gk = *anadiplō(esthai)* (to) be doubled back + *-ōsis* -OSIS]

a·nad·ro·mous (ə nad′rə məs), *adj.* (of fish) migrating from the sea up a river to spawn (opposed to *catadromous*). [< Gk *anádromos* running upward. See ANA-, -DROMOUS]

a·nae·mi·a (ə nē′mē ə), *n. Pathol.* anemia.

a·nae·mic (ə nē′mik), *adj. Pathol.* anemic.

an·aer·obe (an âr′ōb, an′ə rōb), *n.* an organism, esp. a bacterium, that does not require air or free oxygen to live (opposed to *aerobe*).

an·aer·o·bic (an′â rō′bik, an′ə-), *adj.* **1.** (of an organism or tissue) living in the absence of air or free oxygen. **2.** pertaining to or caused by the absence of oxygen. —**an′aer·o′bi·cal·ly,** *adv.*

an·aes·the·sia (an′is thē′zhə), *n. Med., Pathol.* anesthesia. —**an·aes·thet·ic** (an′is thet′ik), *adj., n.* —**an·aes·the·tist** (ə nes′thi tist), *n.*

an·aes·the·si·ol·o·gy (an′is thē′zē ol′ə jē), *n.* anesthesiology. —**an′aes·the′si·ol′o·gist,** *n.*

an·aes·the·tize (ə nes′thi tīz′), *v.t.,* **-tized, -tiz·ing.** anesthetize. —**an·aes′the·ti·za′tion,** *n.*

an·a·glyph (an′ə glif), *n.* an ornament sculptured or embossed in low relief, as a cameo. [< Gk *anáglyph(os)* wrought in low relief. See ANA-, GLYPH] —**an′a·glyph′ic, an′a·glyph′i·cal, an·a·glyp·tic** (an′ə glip′tik), **an′a·glyp′ti·cal,** *adj.* —**a·nag·ly·phy** (ə nag′lə fē, an′ə glif′ē), *n.*

an·a·go·ge (an′ə gō′jē, an′ə gō′jē), *n.* a spiritual interpretation or application of words, as of Scriptures. [< LL < Gk *anagōgē* an uplifting = *an-* AN-[3] + *agōgē,* fem. of *agōgós* leading < *ágein* to lead, c. L *agere* to do] —**an·a·gog·ic** (an′ə goj′ik), **an′a·gog′i·cal,** *adj.* —**an′a·gog′i·cal·ly,** *adv.*

an·a·gram (an′ə gram′), *n.* **1.** a transposition of the letters of a word or phrase to form a new word or phrase. **2.** the new word or phrase so formed. [< NL *anagramm(a).* See ANA-, -GRAM[1]] —**an·a·gram·mat·ic** (an′ə grə mat′ik), **an′a·gram·mat′i·cal,** *adj.* —**an′a·gram·mat′i·cal·ly,** *adv.*

an·a·gram·ma·tise (an′ə gram′ə tīz′), *v.t.,* **-tised, -tis·ing.** *Chiefly Brit.* anagrammatize.

an·a·gram·ma·tize (an′ə gram′ə tīz′), *v.t.,* **-tized, -tiz·ing.** to transpose into an anagram. [< Gk *anagrammatíz(ein)* (to) transpose letters = *ana-* ANA- + *grammat-* (s. of *grámma*) letter + *-izein* -IZE] —**an·a·gram·ma·tism** (an′ə gram′ə tiz′əm), *n.* —**an′a·gram′ma·tist,** *n.*

An·a·heim (an′ə hīm′), *n.* a city in SW California, SE of Los Angeles. 166,408 (1970).

a·nal (ān′ᵊl), *adj.* **1.** of, pertaining to, involving, or near the anus. **2.** *Psychoanal.* of or pertaining to libidinal development in which attention is centered on the anal region. [< NL *ānāl(is)*] —**a′nal·ly,** *adv.*

anal., **1.** analogous. **2.** analogy. **3.** analysis.

a·nal·cite (ə nal′sīt, an′ᵊl sīt′), *n.* a white or slightly colored zeolite mineral, generally found in crystalline form. Also, **a·nal·cime** (ə nal′sēm, -sīm, -sim). [< Gk *analk(imos)* weak (*an-* AN-¹ + *álkimos* strong) + -ITE¹]

an·a·lects (an′ᵊlekts′), *n.pl.* selected passages from the writings of one or more authors. Also, **an·a·lec·ta** (an′ᵊlek′tə). [< L *analect(a)* < Gk *análekta,* neut. pl. of *análektos* (ptp. of *analégein* to gather up) = *ana-* ANA- + *-lek-* gather (var. of *-leg-*) + *-tos* ptp. suffix] —**an′a·lec′tic,** *adj.*

an·a·lem·ma (an′ᵊlem′ə), *n., pl.* **-a·lem·mas, -a·lem·ma·ta** (-ᵊlem′ə tə). a scale shaped like the figure 8, showing the declination of the sun and the equation of time for each day of the year. [< L: pedestal of a sundial, sundial < Gk *análēmma* support] —**an·a·lem·mat·ic** (an′ᵊle mat′ik), *adj.*

an·a·lep·tic (an′ᵊlep′tik), *adj.* *Med.* **1.** invigorating; giving strength after disease. **2.** awakening, esp. from drug stupor. [< NL *analēptic(us)* < Gk *analēptikós* restorative = *analēp-,* var. s. of *analambánein* to restore (*ana-* ANA- + *lambánein* to take) + *-tikos* -TIC]

a′nal fin′, the median, unpaired fin on the ventral margin between the anus and the caudal fin in fishes.

an·al·ge·si·a (an′ᵊl jē′zē ə, -sē ə), *n.* *Med.* absence of sense of pain. [< NL < Gk *analgēsía* painlessness = *analgēs* painless (see AN-¹, -ALGIA) + *-ia* -IA]

an·al·ge·sic (an′ᵊl jē′zik, -sik), *Med.* —*n.* **1.** a remedy that relieves or allays pain. —*adj.* **2.** of, pertaining to, or causing analgesia.

an·a·log (an′ᵊlôg′, -ᵊlog′), *n.* analogue.

an′alog comput′er, a computer that solves a given mathematical problem by using physical analogues, as electric voltages or shaft rotations, of the numerical variables in the problem. Also, **analogue computer.** Cf. **digital computer.**

an·a·log·i·cal (an′ᵊloj′i kəl), *adj.* based on, involving, or expressing an analogy. Also, **an′a·log′ic.** [< L *analogic(us)* (< Gk *analogikós;* see ANALOGY, -IC) + -AL¹] —**an′a·log′i·cal·ly,** *adv.* —**an′a·log′i·cal·ness,** *n.*

a·nal·o·gise (ə nal′ə jīz′), *v.i., v.t.,* **-gised, -gis·ing.** *Chiefly Brit.* analogize.

a·nal·o·gism (ə nal′ə jiz′əm), *n.* reasoning or argument by analogy. —**a·nal′o·gist,** *n.* —**a·nal′o·gis′tic,** *adj.*

a·nal·o·gize (ə nal′ə jīz′), *v.,* **-gized, -giz·ing.** —*v.i.* **1.** to make use of analogy in reasoning, argument, etc. **2.** to be analogous; exhibit analogy. —*v.t.* **3.** to make analogous; show an analogy between. Also, *esp. Brit.,* **analogise.**

a·nal·o·gous (ə nal′ə gəs), *adj.* **1.** having analogy; corresponding in some particular: *The two poems are analogous in mood.* **2.** *Biol.* corresponding in function, but not evolved from corresponding organs, as the wings of a bee and those of a hummingbird. [< L *analogus* < Gk *análogos* proportionate = *ana-* ANA- + *lóg(os)* ratio + *-os* adj. suffix; see -OUS] —**a·nal′o·gous·ly,** *adv.* —**a·nal′o·gous·ness,** *n.* —**Syn. 1.** similar, alike, akin. —**Ant. 1.** dissimilar.

an·a·logue (an′ᵊlôg′, -ᵊlog′), *n.* **1.** something having analogy to something else. **2.** *Biol.* an organ or part analogous to another. Also, **analog.** [< F < Gk *análog(on),* neut. of *análogos* ANALOGOUS; r. earlier *analog(on)* < Gk]

an′alogue comput′er. See **analog computer.**

a·nal·o·gy (ə nal′ə jē), *n., pl.* **-gies. 1.** a partial similarity between like features of two things, on which a comparison may be based: *the analogy between the heart and a pump.* **2.** similarity: *I see no analogy between your problem and mine.* **3.** *Linguistics.* **a.** the process by which words or phrases are created or re-formed according to existing patterns in the language, as when *shoon* was re-formed as *shoes* or when a child says *foots* for *feet.* **b.** a form resulting from such a process. **4.** *Logic.* a form of reasoning in which one thing is inferred to be similar to another thing in a certain respect on the basis of the known similarity in other respects. [< L *analogia* < Gk; see ANALOGOUS, -Y³] —**Syn. 1.** comparison, kinship.

an·al·pha·bet·ic (an′al fə bet′ik, an al′-), *adj.* **1.** not alphabetic. **2.** unable to read or write; illiterate. —*n.* **3.** a person who cannot read or write; illiterate. [< Gk *analphábēt(os)* not knowing the alphabet (*an-* AN-¹ + *alphábēt(os)* ALPHABET + *-os* adj. suffix) + -IC]

a·nal·y·sand (ə nal′i sand′, -zand′), *n.* *Psychiatry.* a person undergoing psychoanalysis. [ANALYSE + *-and* as in MULTIPLICAND]

an·a·lyse (an′ᵊlīz′), *v.t.,* **-lysed, -lys·ing.** *Chiefly Brit.* analyze. —**an′a·lys′a·bil′i·ty,** *n.* —**an′a·lys′a·ble,** *adj.* —**an′a·ly·sa′tion,** *n.* —**an′a·lys′er,** *n.*

a·nal·y·sis (ə nal′i sis), *n., pl.* **-ses** (-sēz′). **1.** the separating of any material or abstract entity into its constituent elements (opposed to *synthesis*). **2.** this process as a method of studying the nature of something or of determining its essential features and their relations. **3.** *Math.* **a.** an investigation based on the properties of numbers. **b.** the discussion of a problem by algebra, as opposed to geometry. **c.** the branch of mathematics consisting of calculus and its higher developments. **4.** *Chem.* **a.** intentionally produced decomposition or separation of materials into their ingredients to find their kind or quantity. **b.** the ascertainment of the kind or amount of one or more of the constituents of materials. Cf. **qualitative analysis, quantitative analysis. 5.** psychoanalysis. [< ML < Gk = *analý(ein)* (to) loosen up (*ana-* ANA- + *lýein* to loosen) + *-sis* -SIS]

anal′ysis si′tus, *Math.* topology.

an·a·lyst (an′ᵊlist), *n.* **1.** a person who analyzes or who is skilled in analysis. **2.** a psychoanalyst.

analyt., analytical.

an·a·lyt·ic (an′ᵊlit′ik), *adj.* **1.** pertaining to or proceeding by analysis (opposed to *synthetic*). **2.** skilled in or habitually using analysis. **3.** (of a language) characterized by a relatively frequent use of function words, auxiliary verbs, and changes in word order to express syntactic relations, rather than of inflected forms. Cf. **synthetic** (def. 3), **polysynthetic. 4.** *Logic.* (of a proposition) necessarily true because its denial involves a contradiction, as "All spinsters are unmarried." **5.** *Math.* **a.** (of a function of a complex variable) having a first derivative at all points of a given domain. **b.** (of a curve) having parametric equations that represent analytic functions. Also, **an′a·lyt′i·cal.** [< ML *analytic(us)* < Gk *analytikós* = *analy-* (see ANALYSIS) + *-tikos* -TIC] —**an′a·lyt′i·cal·ly,** *adv.*

analyt′ic geom′etry, a branch of mathematics in which algebraic procedures are applied to geometry and position is represented analytically by coordinates.

an·a·lyt·ics (an′ᵊlit′iks), *n.* (*construed as sing.*) *Logic.* the science of logical analysis.

an·a·lyze (an′ᵊlīz′), *v.t.,* **-lyzed, -lyz·ing. 1.** to separate into constituent parts; determine the elements of (opposed to *synthesize*). **2.** to examine critically, so as to give the essence of: *to analyze a poem.* **3.** to subject to analysis. Also, *esp. Brit.,* **analyse.** [back formation from ANALYSIS] —**an′a·lyz′a·bil′i·ty,** *n.* —**an′a·lyz′a·ble,** *adj.* —**an′a·ly·za′tion,** *n.* —**an′a·lyz′er,** *n.* —**Syn. 1.** reduce. **2.** explicate.

A·nam (ə nam′), *n.* Annam.

an·am·ne·sis (an′am nē′sis), *n., pl.* **-ses** (-sēz). **1.** reminiscence. **2.** *Psychiatry.* a case history. [< NL < Gk *anámnēsis* remembrance = *ana(mi)mnē(skein)* (to) remember (*ana-* ANA- + *mimnḗskein* to call to mind) + *-sis* -SIS] —**an·am·nes·tic** (an′am nes′tik), *adj.* —**an′am·nes′ti·cal·ly,** *adv.*

an·a·mor·phic (an′ə môr′fik), *adj.* *Optics.* having or producing unequal magnifications along two axes perpendicular to each other.

an·a·mor·pho·scope (an′ə môr′fə skōp′), *n.* an optical device for correcting an image distorted by anamorphosis. [ANAMORPHO(SIS) + -SCOPE]

an·a·mor·pho·sis (an′ə môr′fə sis, -môr fō′sis), *n., pl.* **-ses** (-sēz′, -sēz). **1.** a drawing presenting a distorted image that appears in natural form under certain conditions, as when reflected from a mirror. **2.** the method of producing such a drawing. [< Gk = *anamorphō-* (verbid s. of *anamorphōein* to transform; see ANA-, MORPHO-) + *-sis* -SIS]

A·nan·da (ä′nən də), *n.* fl. early 5th century B.C., favorite disciple of Gautama Buddha.

An·a·ni·as (an′ə nī′əs), *n.* a man who was struck dead for lying. Acts. 5:1–5.

an·a·pest (an′ə pest′), *n.* *Pros.* a foot of three syllables, two short followed by one long in quantitative meter, and two unstressed followed by one stressed in accentual meter. Also, **an′a·paest′.** [< L *anapaest(us)* < Gk *anápaistos* struck back, reversed (as compared with a dactyl) = *ana-* ANA- + *pais-* (verbid s. of *paíein* to strike) + *-tos* ptp. suffix] —**an′a·pes′tic, an′a·paes′tic,** *adj.* —**an′a·pes′ti·cal·ly, an′a·paes′ti·cal·ly,** *adv.*

an·a·phase (an′ə fāz′), *n.* *Biol.* the stage in mitosis following metaphase in which the divided chromosomes move away from each other to opposite ends of the cell.

a·naph·o·ra (ə naf′ər ə), *n.* **1.** *Rhet.* repetition of a word or words at the beginning of two or more successive verses, clauses, or sentences. **2.** *Gram.* the use of a word as a regular grammatical substitute for a preceding word or group of words, as the use of *it* and *do* in *I know it and he does, too.* [< L < Gk: a bringing back, repeating = *ana-* ANA- + *-phora,* akin to *phérein* to carry] —**a·naph′o·ral,** *adj.*

an·aph·ro·dis·i·ac (an af′rə diz′ē ak′), *Med.* —*adj.* **1.** capable of diminishing sexual desire. —*n.* **2.** an anaphrodisiac agent.

an·a·phy·lax·is (an′ə fə lak′sis), *n.* *Pathol.* increased susceptibility to a foreign protein resulting from previous exposure to it, as in serum treatment. [ANA- + (PRO)PHYLAXIS] —**an·a·phy·lac·tic** (an′ə fə lak′tik), *adj.* —**an′a·phy·lac′ti·cal·ly,** *adv.*

an·a·plas·tic (an′ə plas′tik), *adj.* **1.** *Surg.* replacing lost tissue or parts, as by transplanting. **2.** *Pathol.* **a.** (of cells) having reverted to a more primitive form. **b.** (of tumors) having a high degree of malignancy.

an·a·plas·ty (an′ə plas′tē), *n.* See **plastic surgery.** [< Gk *anáplast(os)* remolded (see ANA-, -PLAST) + -Y³]

A·ná·po·lis (ä nä′pŏŏ lis), *n.* a city in central Brazil. 51,169 (1960).

an·ap·tyx·is (an′əp tik′sis), *n., pl.* **-tyx·es** (-tik′sēz). epenthesis of a vowel. [< NL < Gk = *anaptyk-* (verbid s. of *anaptýssein* to unfold = *ana-* ANA- + *ptýssein* to fold) + *-sis* -SIS] —**an·ap·tyc·tic** (an′ap tik′tik), **an′ap·tyc′ti·cal,** *adj.*

an·arch (an′ärk), *n.* *Archaic.* anarchist. [back formation from ANARCHY]

an·ar·chism (an′ər kiz′əm), *n.* **1.** a doctrine advocating the abolition of government or governmental restraint as the indispensable condition for full social and political liberty. **2.** the methods or practices of anarchists.

an·ar·chist (an′ər kist), *n.* **1.** a person who advocates or believes in anarchy or anarchism. **2.** a person who seeks to overturn by violence all constituted forms and institutions of society and government, with no purpose of establishing any other system of order. **3.** a person who promotes disorder or excites revolt against any established order. —**an′ar·chis′tic,** *adj.*

an·ar·chy (an′ər kē), *n.* **1.** a state of society without government or law. **2.** lawlessness or political and social disorder due to the absence of governmental control: *The death of the king was followed by a year of anarchy.* **3.** a theory that proposes the cooperative and voluntary association of individuals and groups as the principal mode of organized society. **4.** confusion; chaos; disorder. [< ML *anarchia* < Gk = *ánarch(os)* leaderless (*an-* AN- + *arch(ós)* leader + *-os* adj. suffix) + *-ia* -Y³] —**an·ar′chic** (an är′kik), **an·ar′chi·cal,** *adj.* —**an·ar′chi·cal·ly,** *adv.*

an·ar·throus (an är′thrəs), *adj.* (esp. in Greek grammar) used without the article. [< Gk *ánarthros* jointless. See AN-¹, ARTHR-, -OUS] —**an·ar′throus·ly,** *adv.* —**an·ar′throus·ness,** *n.*

an·a·sar·ca (an′ə sär′kə), *n.* *Pathol.* a pronounced, generalized dropsy. [< NL; see ANA-, SARC-] —**an′a·sar′cous,** *adj.*

An·a·sta·sia (an′ə stä′zhə, än′ə stä′shə), *n.* **Ni·ko·la·iev·na Ro·ma·nov** (*Russ.* ni ko lä′yəv nə ro mä′nof), **Grand Duchess,** 1901–?, daughter of Nicholas II: believed executed by the Bolsheviks in 1918.

An·as·ta·sius I (an′ə stā′shəs, -shē əs), A.D. c430–518, emperor of the Eastern Roman Empire 491–518.

an·as·tig·mat (ə nas′tig mat′, an′ə stig′mat), *n. Optics.* a compound lens corrected for the aberrations of astigmatism and curvature of field. [< G, back formation from *anastigmatisch* ANASTIGMATIC]

an·as·tig·mat·ic (an′ə stig mat′ik, a nas′tig-), *adj. Optics.* (of a lens) not having astigmatism; forming point images of a point object located off the axis of the lens; stigmatic.

a·nas·to·mose (ə nas′tə mōz′), *v.t., v.i.,* **-mosed, -mos·ing.** *Physiol., Anat.* to communicate or connect by anastomosis. [back formation from ANASTOMOSIS]

a·nas·to·mo·sis (ə nas′tə mō′sis), *n., pl.* **-ses** (-sēz). **1.** *Anat., Biol.* connection between parts of any branching system, as of blood vessels. **2.** *Surg., Pathol.* communication between two organs or spaces normally not connected. [< NL < Gk: opening] **—a·nas·to·mot·ic** (ə nas′tə mot′ik), *adj.*

a·nas·tro·phe (ə nas′trə fē), *n. Rhet.* inversion of the usual order of words. [< Gk: a turning back]

anat., **1.** anatomical. **2.** anatomy.

an·a·tase (an′ə tās′), *n. Mineral.* a form of titanium dioxide, occurring as tetragonal crystals. Also called **octahedrite.** [< F < Gk *anátasis* a stretching out]

a·nath·e·ma (ə nath′ə mə), *n., pl.* **-mas. 1.** a person or thing detested or loathed. **2.** a person or thing accursed or condemned to damnation or destruction. **3.** a formal ecclesiastical curse involving excommunication. **4.** any imprecation of divine punishment. **5.** a curse or execration. [< L < Gk: a thing accursed, devoted to evil, orig. devoted = *ana(ti)thé(nai)* to set up + *-ma* n. suffix]

a·nath·e·mat·ic (ə nath′ə mat′ik), *adj.* loathsome; hateful. Also, **a·nath′e·mat′i·cal.** [< Gk *anathemat-* (s. of *anáthema* ANATHEMA) + -IC] **—a·nath′e·mat′i·cal·ly,** *adv.*

a·nath·e·ma·tise (ə nath′ə mə tīz′), *v.t., v.i.,* **-tised, -tis·ing.** *Chiefly Brit.* anathematize. **—a·nath′e·ma·ti·sa′tion,** *n.* **—a·nath′e·ma·tis′er,** *n.*

a·nath·e·ma·tize (ə nath′ə mə tīz′), *v.,* **-tized, -tiz·ing.** **—***v.t.* **1.** to pronounce an anathema against. **—***v.i.* **2.** to pronounce anathemas. [< LL *anathematiz(āre)* (to) curse, detest < Gk *anathematíz(ein)* (to) bind by a curse = *anathemat-* (s. of *anáthema*) + *-izein* -IZE] **—a·nath′e·ma·ti·za′tion,** *n.* **—a·nath′e·ma·tiz′er,** *n.*

An·a·to·li·a (an′ə tō′lē ə), *n.* a vast plateau between the Black and the Mediterranean seas: in ancient usage, the peninsula of Asia Minor; in modern usage, Turkey in Asia. Cf. **Asia Minor.**

An·a·to·li·an (an′ə tō′lē ən), *adj.* **1.** of or pertaining to Anatolia, its inhabitants, or their language. **2.** of, pertaining to, or belonging to a group or family of languages that includes cuneiform Hittite and its nearest congeners. **—***n.* **3.** a native or inhabitant of Anatolia. **4.** any of various Turkish dialects spoken in Anatolia. **5.** a group or family of extinct languages that includes cuneiform Hittite and its nearest congeners. Also, **An·a·tol·ic** (an′ə tol′ik).

an·a·tom·i·cal (an′ə tom′i kəl), *adj.* of or pertaining to anatomy. Also, **an′a·tom′ic.** [< LL *anatomic(us)* (< Gk *anatomikós*; see ANATOMY, -IC) + -AL[1]] **—an′a·tom′i·cal·ly,** *adv.*

a·nat·o·mise (ə nat′ə mīz′), *v.t.,* **-mised, -mis·ing.** *Chiefly Brit.* anatomize. **—a·nat′o·mi·sa′tion,** *n.* **—a·nat′o·mis′er,** *n.*

a·nat·o·mist (ə nat′ə mist), *n.* a specialist in anatomy. [ANATOM(IZE) + -IST]

a·nat·o·mize (ə nat′ə mīz′), *v.t.,* **-mized, -miz·ing. 1.** to cut apart (an animal or plant) to show or examine the position, structure, and relation of the parts; dissect. **2.** to examine in detail. Also, *esp. Brit.,* **anatomise.** [< ML *anatomīz(āre)*] **—a·nat′o·mi·za′tion,** *n.* **—a·nat′o·miz′er,** *n.*

a·nat·o·my (ə nat′ə mē), *n., pl.* **-mies. 1.** the science dealing with the structure of animals and plants. **2.** the structure of an animal or plant, or of any of its parts. **3.** dissection of all or part of an animal or plant in order to study its structure. **4.** an anatomical model. **5.** a skeleton. **6.** an analysis or minute examination. [< L *anatomia* < Gk *anatom(ḗ)* a cutting up. See ANA-, -TOMY]

a·nat·ro·pous (ə na′trə pəs), *adj. Bot.* (of an ovule) inverted at an early stage of growth, so that the micropyle is turned toward the funicle, the chalaza being situated at the opposite end.

a·nat·to (ə nat′ō, ä nä′tō), *n., pl.* **-tos.** annatto.

An·ax·ag·o·ras (an′ak sag′ər əs), *n.* 500?–428 B.C., Greek philosopher. **—An·ax·ag·o·re·an** (an′ak sag′ə rē′ən), *adj.*

A·nax·i·man·der (ə nak′sə man′dər), *n.* 611?–547? B.C., Greek astronomer and philosopher. **—A·nax·i·man·dri·an** (ə nak′sə man′drē ən), *adj.*

An·ax·im·e·nes (an′ak sim′ə nēz′), *n.* fl. 6th century B.C., Greek philosopher at Miletus.

anc., ancient.

-ance, a suffix used to form nouns either from adjectives in **-ant** or from verbs: *brilliance; appearance.* [ME < OF < L *-antia* -ANCY]

an·ces·tor (an′ses tər), *n.* **1.** a person from whom others are descended; forefather; progenitor. **2.** *Biol.* the form or stock from which an organism has developed or descended. **3.** an object, idea, style, or occurrence serving as a prototype, forerunner, or inspiration to a later one: *the ancestor of the modern bicycle.* **4.** a person from whom mental, artistic, or spiritual descent is claimed: *Dryden is his spiritual ancestor.* **5.** *Law.* a person from whom an heir derives an inheritance. Also, *referring to a woman,* **an′ces·tress.** [ME *ancestre* < OF < L *antecēssor* ANTECESSOR]

an·ces·tral (an ses′trəl), *adj.* **1.** pertaining to ancestors. **2.** descending or claimed from ancestors. [earlier *ancestrel* < MF = *ancestre* ANCESTOR + *-el* -AL[1]] **—an·ces′tral·ly,** *adv.*

an·ces·try (an′ses trē), *n., pl.* **-tries. 1.** ancestral descent; lineage. **2.** honorable or distinguished descent: *famous ancestry.* **3.** a series of ancestors. **4.** the origin of a phenomenon, object, idea, or style. **5.** the history or developmental process of a phenomenon, object, idea, or style. [late ME = *ancestre* ANCESTOR + -Y[3]; r. ME *aunce(s)trie* < AF]

An·chi·ses (an kī′sēz), *n. Class. Myth.* a prince of Troy, crippled as a punishment for boasting of his intimacy with Aphrodite, and later carried away from burning Troy by their son Aeneas.

an·chor (aŋ′kər), *n.* **1.** any of various devices for dropping by a chain, cable, or rope to the bottom of a body of water to prevent or restrict the motion of a vessel or other floating object. **2.** any similar device for holding fast or checking motion. **3.** a means of stability of any kind. **4.** *Mil.* a key position in defense lines. **5.** Also called **anchorman.** *Sports.* the person on a team, esp. a relay team, who performs his assignment last. **6.** *Radio & TV.* anchorman (def. 1). **7. at anchor,** (of a vessel) held in place by an anchor. **8. drop anchor,** to anchor a vessel: *They dropped anchor in a bay to escape the storm.* **9. weigh anchor,** to take up the anchor: *We will weigh anchor at dawn.* **—***v.t.* **10.** to hold fast by an anchor. **11.** to fix or fasten; affix firmly. **12.** *Sports, Radio & TV.* to serve as anchor or anchorman for. **—***v.i.* **13.** to drop anchor; lie or ride at anchor. **14.** to keep hold or be firmly fixed. [ME *anker, ancre,* OE *ancor* < L *ancora* < Gk *ánkyra*] **—an′chor·a·ble,** *adj.* **—an′chor·less,** *adj.* **—an′chor·like′,** *adj.*

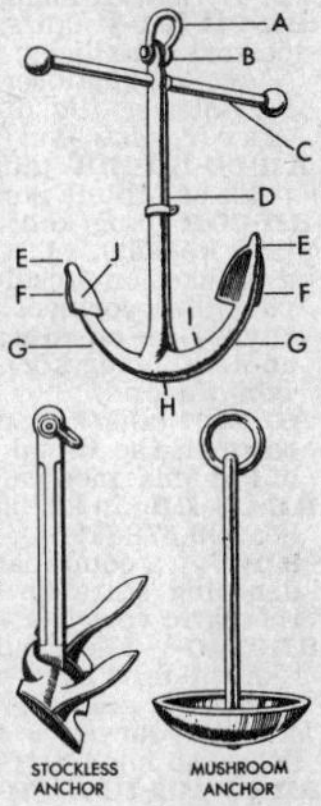

STOCKLESS ANCHOR — MUSHROOM ANCHOR

Anchor
A, Ring; B, Eye; C, Stock; D, Shank; E, Bill; F, Fluke; G, Arm; H, Crown; I, Throat; J, Palm

an·chor·age (aŋ′kər ij), *n.* **1.** a place for anchoring. **2.** a charge for occupying such a place. **3.** the act of anchoring. **4.** the state of being anchored. **5.** that to which anything is fastened. **6.** a means of anchoring or making fast. **7.** a source of stability or support.

An·chor·age (aŋ′kər ij), *n.* a seaport in S Alaska: earthquake 1964. 48,081 (1970).

an′chor escape′ment, *Horol.* an escapement in which wedge-shaped pallets engage with an escape wheel having pointed teeth, usually facing in the direction of revolution, so that the escape wheel recoils slightly at every release. Also called **recoil escapement.** See diag. at **escapement.**

an·cho·ress (aŋ′kər is), *n.* a female anchorite. [ME *ankres* = *ancre* ANCHORITE + *-es* -ESS]

an·cho·ret (aŋ′kər it, -kə ret′), *n.* anchorite. [< L *anachōrēta* < Gk *anachōrētḗs* = *anachōré(ein)* (to) retire (*ana-* ANA- + *chōréein* to withdraw) + *-tēs* suffix] **—an·cho·ret·ic** (aŋ′kə ret′ik), *adj.* **—an′cho·ret′ism,** *n.*

an·cho·rite (aŋ′kə rīt′), *n.* a person who has retired to a solitary place for a life of religious seclusion; hermit. Also, **anchoret.** [late ME *ancorite* < ML *anachōrīta,* var. of *anachōrēta* ANCHORET] **—an·cho·rit·ic** (aŋ′kə rit′ik), *adj.* **—an·chor·it·ism** (aŋ′kə rī tiz′əm), *n.*

an·chor·man (aŋ′kər man′, -mən), *n., pl.* **-men** (-men′, -mən). **1.** Also called **anchor.** *Radio & TV.* a person who is the main broadcaster on a program of news, sports, or the like, and who usually also serves as coordinator of all participating broadcasters while the program is on the air. **2.** *Sports.* anchor (def. 5). **3.** a person upon whose reliable performance an organization, business, or other activity depends; mainstay. Also called **an·chor·per·son** (aŋ′kər pûr′sən) [ANCHOR + MAN] **—an·chor·wom·an** (aŋ′kər wo͝om′ən), *n. fem.*

an′chor ring′, *Geom.* torus (def. 2a).

an·cho·vy (an′chō vē, -chə vē, an chō′vē), *n., pl.* **-vies.** any small, marine, herringlike fish of the family *Engraulidae,* esp. *Engraulis encrasicholus,* found in the Mediterranean Sea, used as food. [< Sp *ancho(v)a* < Genoese *ancioa* < ?]

an′chovy pear′, 1. the fruit of a West Indian tree, *Grias cauliflora,* resembling the mango. **2.** the tree itself.

anchylo-, var. of **ancylo-.**

an·chy·lose (aŋ′kə lōs′), *v.t., v.i.,* **-losed, -los·ing.** ankylose. **—an′chy·lo′sis,** *n.* **—an·chy·lot·ic** (aŋ′kə lot′ik), *adj.*

an·cien ré·gime (äɴ syaɴ′ ʀā zhēm′), *pl.* **an·ciens ré·gimes** (äɴ syaɴ′ ʀā zhēm′). *French.* the political and social system of France before the revolution of 1789.

an·cient[1] (ān′shənt), *adj.* **1.** of or in time long past, esp. before the end of the Western Roman Empire A.D. 476. **2.** dating from a remote period; of great age: *ancient rocks.* **3.** old; aged. **4.** old in wisdom and experience; venerable. **5.** old-fashioned or antique. **—***n.* **6.** a person who lived in ancient times, esp. a Greek, Roman, or Hebrew. **7.** one of the classical writers of antiquity. **8.** a very old person, esp. a venerable or patriarchal one. [ME *auncien* < AF; OF *ancien* < VL **anteanus* = L *ante(ā)* before + *-ānus* -AN] **—an′cient·ness,** *n.*

—Syn. 2. ANCIENT, ANTIQUATED, ANTIQUE, OLD-FASHIONED refer to something dating from the past. ANCIENT implies existence or first occurrence in a distant past: *an ancient custom.* ANTIQUATED connotes something too old or no longer useful: *an antiquated building.* ANTIQUE suggests a curious or pleasing quality in something old: *antique furniture.* OLD-FASHIONED may disparage something as being out of date or may approve something old as being superior: *an old-fashioned hat; old-fashioned courtesy.* **—Ant. 2.** new.

an·cient[2] (ān′shənt), *n. Obs.* **1.** the bearer of a flag. **2.** a flag, banner, or standard; ensign. [var. of ENSIGN]

An′cient Ar′abic Or′der of No′bles of the Mys′tic Shrine′. See under **Shriner.**

an′cient his′tory, 1. the study or a course of study of history before the end of the Western Roman Empire A.D. 476. **2.** *Informal.* recent information or events that are common knowledge or are no longer pertinent.

an·cient·ly (ān′shənt lē), *adv.* in ancient times; of old.

An′cient Mys′tic Or′der Ro′sae Cru′cis (rō′zē kro͞o′sis). See under **Rosicrucian** (def. 2).

An′cient of Days′, the Supreme Being; God.

an·cient·ry (ān′shən trē), *n. Archaic.* **1.** ancient character or style. **2.** ancient times.

an·cil·la (an sil′ə), *n., pl.* **-las.** **1.** an accessory; adjunct. **2.** *Archaic.* a maidservant. [see ANCILLARY]
an·cil·lar·y (an′sə ler′ē *or, esp. Brit.*, an sil′ə rē), *adj.* accessory; auxiliary. [< L *ancillāri(us)* relating to maidservants = *ancill(a)* maidservant (*anc(ula)* maidservant + *-illa* dim. suffix) + *-ārius* -ARY (r. *-āris* -AR[1])]
An·co·hu·ma (äng′kō o͞o′mä), *n.* a peak of Mount Sorata. Cf. **Sorata.**
an·con (ang′kon), *n., pl.* **an·co·nes** (ang kō′nēz). **1.** the elbow. **2.** *Arch.* a bracket or console, as one supporting part of a cornice. [< L < Gk *ankṓn* elbow] —**an·co·nal** (ang kōn′əl), **an·co·ne·al** (ang kō′nē əl), *adj.* —**an′-con·oid′,** *adj.*

A, Ancon

An·cón (ang′kon; *Sp.* äng kôn′), *n.* a town in the Canal Zone, near the city of Panama: medical center. 1151 (1970).
An·co·na (än kô′nä), *n.* a seaport in E Italy, on the Adriatic Sea. 99,678 (1961).
-ancy, a combination of **-ance** and **-y,** used to form nouns denoting state or quality: *brilliancy.* [< L *-antia* = *-ā-* thematic vowel + *-nt-* prp. suffix + *-ia* -Y[3]]
ancylo-, a learned borrowing from Greek meaning "hook," "joint," used in the formation of technical terms: *ancylostomiasis.* Also, **anchylo-, ankylo-.** [< Gk *ankylo-* (s. of *ankýlos*) crooked, curved = *ánk(os)* bend (c. L *uncus* bent, E *angle* to fish with hook and line) + *-ylos* adjective-forming suffix]
an·cy·los·to·mi·a·sis (an′sə los′tə mī′ə sis), *n.* *Pathol.* hookworm (def. 2). Also, **ankylostomiasis.** [< NL = *Ancylostom(a)* a genus of hookworms (see ANCYLO-, STOMA) + *-iasis* -IASIS]
and (and; *unstressed* ənd, ən), *conj.* **1.** (used to connect grammatically coordinate words, phrases, or clauses) with; along with; together with; added to; in addition to: *pens and pencils.* **2.** as well as: *nice and warm.* **3.** then: *He read for an hour and went to bed.* **4.** also, at the same time: *to sleep and dream.* **5.** then again: *He coughed and coughed.* **6.** (used to imply different qualities in things having the same name): *There are bargains and bargains, so watch out.* **7.** (used to introduce a sentence, implying continuation) also; then: *And he said unto Moses.* **8.** to (used between two finite verbs): *Try and do it.* **9.** *Archaic.* if: *and you please.* Cf. **an**[2]. **10. and so forth** or **on, a.** with other things of the same kind. **b.** with the remainder as one would expect: *one, three, five, seven, and so forth.* —*n.* **11.** Often, **ands.** an added condition or stipulation: *no ifs, ands, or buts.* [ME; OE *and, ond;* c. OS, OHG *ant,* OFris, Goth *and,* Icel *and-;* akin to G *und,* D *en,* Skt *anti,* etc.]
—**Usage.** Since ETC. is an abbreviation for ET CETERA which means "and others," the form AND ETC. is redundant. Use ETC., or AND OTHERS, or AND SO FORTH instead.
and., *Music.* andante.
An·da·lu·sia (an′dᵊlo͞o′zhə, -shē ə), *n.* a region in S Spain, bordering on the Atlantic Ocean and the Mediterranean Sea. 33,712 sq. mi. Spanish, **An·da·lu·cí·a** (än′dä lo͞o thē′ä). —**An′da·lu′sian,** *adj., n.*
an·da·lu·site (an′dᵊlo͞o′sīt), *n.* *Mineral.* an orthorhombic form of aluminum silicate, Al_2SiO_5, found in schistose rocks. [named after ANDALUSIA, where first found; see -ITE[1]]
An′daman and Nic′o·bar Is′lands (nik′ə bär′, nik′ə bär′), a centrally administered territory of India, comprising two groups of islands in the E Bay of Bengal. 63,548 (1961); 3143 sq. mi. *Cap.:* Port Blair.
An′daman Is′lands, a group of islands in the E Bay of Bengal. 18,939 (1951); 2508 sq. mi. Also called **An′da·mans.** —**An·da·man** (an′də mən), **An′da·man·ese′,** *adj.*
An′daman Sea′, a part of the Bay of Bengal, E of the Andaman and Nicobar islands. 300,000 sq. mi.
an·dan·te (an dan′tē, än dän′tā; *It.* än dän′te), *Music.* —*adj., adv.* **1.** moderately slow and even. —*n.* **2.** an andante movement or piece. *Abbr.:* and. [< It: lit., walking (prp. of *andare* to walk); see -ANT]
an·dan·ti·no (an′dan tē′nō, än′dän-; *It.* än′dän tē′nô), *adj., adv., n., pl.* **-nos,** *It.* **-ni** (-nē). *Music.* —*adj., adv.* **1.** slightly faster than andante. —*n.* **2.** an andantino piece. [< It = *andan(te)* walking + *-ino* dim. suffix]
An·de·an (an dē′ən, an′dē-), *adj.* of or like the Andes.
An·der·lecht (än′dər lekht′), *n.* a city in central Belgium, near Brussels. 99,485 (est. 1964).
An·der·sen (an′dər sən), *n.* **Hans Christian** (hanz), 1805–75, Danish author, esp. of fairy tales.
An·der·son (an′dər sən), *n.* **1. Carl David,** born 1905, U.S. physicist; discoverer of the positron: Nobel prize 1936. **2. Dame Judith,** born 1898, Australian actress in the U.S. **3. Marian,** born 1908, U.S. contralto. **4. Maxwell,** 1888–1959, U.S. dramatist. **5. Sherwood,** 1876–1941, U.S. novelist and short-story writer. **6.** a city in central Indiana. 70,787 (1970). **7.** a city in NW South Carolina. 27,556 (1970).
An·der·son·ville (an′dər sən vil′), *n.* a village in SW Georgia: site of a Confederate military prison. 274 (1970).
An·des (an′dēz), *n.* (*construed as pl.*) a mountain range in W South America, extending ab. 4500 mi. from N Colombia and Venezuela S to Cape Horn. Highest peak, Aconcagua, 22,834 ft.
an·des·ite (an′di zīt′), *n.* a volcanic rock composed essentially of plagioclase feldspar, resembling trachyte in appearance. [named after ANDES; see -ITE[1]] —**an·de·sit·ic** (an′di zit′ik), *adj.*
An·dhra Pra·desh (än′drə prə dāsh′), a state in SE India, formed from portions of Madras and Hyderabad states 1956. 35,983,447 (1961); 105,963 sq. mi. *Cap.:* Hyderabad.
and·i·ron (and′ī ərn), *n.* one of a pair of metal supports for logs in a fireplace. [ME *aundyr(n)e* < OF *andier,* ? < Gaulish **andera* heifer (through use of cows' heads as decorations on andirons); *-iron* by assoc. with IRON]

Andirons

An·di·zhan (än′di zhän′), *n.* a city in E Uzbekistan, in the SW Soviet Union in Asia. 154,000 (est. 1964).
and/or, (used to imply that any or all of the things named may be affected): *insurance covering fire and/or wind damage.*
An·dor·ra (an dôr′ə, -dor′ə; *Sp.* än dôr′rä), *n.* **1.** a republic in the E Pyrenees between France and Spain, under the joint suzerainty of France and the Spanish Bishop of Urgel. 11,000 (est. 1963); 191 sq. mi. **2.** Also called **An·dor·ra la Ve·lla** (*Catalan.* än dôr′rä lä ve′lyä). a city in and the capital of this republic. 2500 (est. 1963). French, **An·dorre** (äN dôr′). —**An·dor′ran,** *adj., n.*
andr-, var. of **andro-** before a vowel: *androecium.*
An·drás·sy (an dras′ē; *Hung.* on′dräsh shē), *n.* **1. Count Julius,** 1823–90, Hungarian statesman. **2.** his son, **Count Julius** (*Gyula*), 1860–1929, Hungarian statesman.
An·dré (än′drā, an′drē), *n.* **John,** 1751–80, British major hanged as a spy by the Americans in the Revolutionary War.
An·dre·a·nof Is′lands (an′drē an′of; *Russ.* än′dre-ä′nof), a group of islands in the W part of the Aleutian Islands. 1432 sq. mi.
An·drew (an′dro͞o), *n.* one of the 12 apostles of Jesus. Mark 3:18; John 1:40–42.
An·drewes (an′dro͞oz), *n.* **Lancelot,** 1555–1626, English theologian: one of the translators of the Authorized Version of the Bible.
An·drews (an′dro͞oz), *n.* **1. Charles Mc·Lean** (mə klān′), 1863–1943, U.S. historian. **2. Roy Chapman,** 1884–1960, U.S. naturalist, explorer, and author.
An·dre·yev (än dre′yəf), *n.* **Le·o·nid Ni·ko·la·e·vich** (le-o nēt′ ni ko lä′yə vich), 1871–1919, Russian novelist, short-story writer, and playwright.
An·drić (än′drich), *n.* **I·vo** (ē′vô), 1892–1975, Yugoslavian poet, novelist, and short-story writer: Nobel prize 1961.
andro-, a learned borrowing from Greek meaning "male," used in the formation of compound words: *androsterone.* Also, *esp. before a vowel,* **andr-.** [< Gk *andrό(s),* gen. of *anḗr* old man; akin to Skt *nara-,* L *Nero*]
An·dro·cles (an′drə klēz′), *n.* a legendary Roman slave, spared in the arena by a lion from whose foot he had long before extracted a thorn. Also, **An·dro·clus** (an′drə kləs).
an·droe·ci·um (an drē′shē əm), *n., pl.* **-ci·a** (-shē ə). *Bot.* the stamens of a flower collectively. [< NL < Gk *andr-* ANDR- + *oikíon,* dim. of *oîkos* house] —**an·droe·cial** (an-drē′shəl), *adj.*
an·dro·gen (an′drə jən), *n.* *Biochem.* any substance that promotes masculine characteristics. —**an·dro·gen·ic** (an′-drə jen′ik), *adj.*
an·drog·y·nous (an droj′ə nəs), *adj.* **1.** *Bot.* having staminate and pistillate flowers in the same inflorescence. **2.** hermaphroditic. [< MF *androgyne* androgenous organism < L *androgyn(us)* < Gk *andrógynos* hermaphrodite (*andro-* ANDRO- + *gyn-* GYN- + *-os* masc. n. suffix) + -OUS] —**an·drog′y·ny,** *n.*
an·droid (an′droid), *n.* an automaton in the form of a human being. [ANDR- + -OID]
An·drom·a·che (an drom′ə kē′), *n.* *Class. Myth.* the wife of Hector and mother of Astyanax.
an·drom·e·da (an drom′i də), *n.* See **Japanese andromeda.** [special use of ANDROMEDA]
An·drom·e·da (an drom′i də), *n., gen.* **-dae** (-dē′) for 2. **1.** *Class Myth.* the daughter of Cassiopeia and wife of Perseus, by whom she was rescued from a sea monster. **2.** *Astron.* the Chained Lady, a northern constellation between Pisces and Cassiopeia.
An·dro·pov (än drô′pof), *n.* **Yu·ri** (yo͞o′ri), 1914–84, Soviet political leader: general secretary of the Communist party 1982–84.
An·dros (an′drəs), *n.* **1. Sir Edmund,** 1637–1714, British governor in the American colonies, 1686–89, 1692–98. **2.** an island in the Bahamas, in the N West Indies. 7461 (est. 1963); 1600 sq. mi.
An·dros·cog·gin (an′drə skog′in), *n.* a river flowing from NE New Hampshire through SW Maine into the Kennebec River. 171 mi. long.
an·dro·sphinx (an′drə sfingks′), *n., pl.* **-sphinx·es, -sphin·ges** (-sfin′jēz). a sphinx with the head of a man. [< Gk]
an·dros·ter·one (an dros′tə rōn′), *n.* *Biochem.* a sex hormone, $C_{19}H_{30}O_2$, usually present in male urine. [ANDRO- + STER(OL) + -ONE]
-androus, a word element meaning "male," occurring as final element of a compound word: *polyandrous.* [< NL *-andrus.* See ANDR-, -OUS]
-andry, a word element referring to males, occurring as final element of a compound word: *polyandry.* [< Gk *-andria.* See ANDR-, -Y[3]]
An·dva·ri (än′dwä rē), *n.* (in the *Volsunga Saga*) a dwarf from whom Loki extorted a treasure, including a magic ring. Andvari then cursed all those who would possess the treasure: corresponds to Alberich in Teutonic legend. Also, **An·dvar** (än′dwär), **An′dva·re.**
ane (ān), *adj., n., pron.* *Dial.* one [ME *an,* var. of *on* ONE]
-ane, *Chem.* a suffix used in names of hydrocarbons of the methane or paraffin series: *propane.* [< L *-ānus* -AN]
a·near (ə nēr′), *adv., prep.* *Dial.* near.
an·ec·dot·age (an′ik dō′tij), *n.* anecdotes collectively.
an·ec·do·tal (an′ik dōt′ᵊl, an′ik dōt′ᵊl), *adj.* pertaining to, marked by, or consisting of anecdotes. Also, **anecdotic, anecdotical.** —**an′ec·do′tal·ism,** *n.* —**an′ec·do′tal·ist,** *n.* **an′ec·do′tal·ly,** *adv.*
an·ec·dote (an′ik dōt′), *n.* a short narrative concerning an interesting or amusing incident or event. [earlier *anecdota* (pl.) < ML < Gk *anékdota* things unpublished, neut. pl. of *anékdotos* = *an-* AN-[1] + *ékdotos* given out, ptp. of *ekdídonai* to give out, publish (*ek-* EC- + *didónai* to give)]
an·ec·dot·ic (an′ik dot′ik), *adj.* **1.** anecdotal. **2.** given to relating anecdotes. Also, **an′ec·dot′i·cal.** —**an′ec·dot′i-cal·ly,** *adv.*
an·ec·dot·ist (an′ik dō′tist), *n.* a relator of anecdotes.
an·e·cho·ic (an′e kō′ik), *adj.* (of a recording chamber, television studio, or the like) having sound reverberation reduced to the lowest possible level.
a·nele (ə nēl′), *v.t.,* **a·neled, a·nel·ing.** *Archaic.* to administer extreme unction to. [ME *anelien* = *an-* ON + *elien* to oil = *el-* (OE *ele* oil < L *oleum*) + *-i-* thematic vowel + *-en* (OE *-an*) inf. ending]
a·ne·mi·a (ə nē′mē ə), *n.* **1.** *Pathol.* a quantitative deficiency of the hemoglobin, often accompanied by a reduced number of red blood cells, and causing pallor, weakness,

and breathlessness. **2.** a lack of vigor, creativity, forcefulness, or the like. Also, **anaemia.** [< NL < Gk *anaimía* want of blood. See AN-[1], -EMIA]

a·ne·mic (ə nē′mik), *adj.* **1.** *Pathol.* suffering from anemia. **2.** lacking vigor or vitality: *an anemic novel.* Also, **anaemic.**

anemo-, a learned borrowing from Greek meaning "wind": *anemograph.* [< Gk, comb. form of *ánemos;* akin to Skt *anilas,* L *animus* breath]

a·nem·o·graph (ə nem′ə graf′, -gräf′), *n.* a recording anemometer. —**a·nem·o·graph·ic** (ə nem′ə graf′ik), *adj.* —**a·nem′o·graph′i·cal·ly,** *adv.*

an·e·mom·e·ter (an′ə mom′i tər), *n.* *Meteorol.* any instrument for measuring the speed of the wind.

a·nem·o·ne (ə nem′ə nē′), *n.* **1.** any ranunculaceous plant of the genus *Anemone,* esp. *A. quinquefolia.* **2.** See **sea anemone.** [< L < Gk: lit., daughter of the wind = *ánem(os)* wind + *-ōnē* fem. patronymic suffix; see -ONE]

an·e·moph·i·lous (an′ə mof′ə ləs), *adj.* (of seed plants) pollinated by wind-borne pollen. —**an′e·moph′i·ly,** *n.*

a·nem·o·scope (ə nem′ə skōp′), *n.* *Meteorol.* any device showing the existence and direction of the wind.

a·nent (ə nent′), *prep.* **1.** in regard to. **2.** *Brit.* beside; in line with. [ME var. (with excrescent *-t*) of *anen,* OE *on emn, on efen* on EVEN[1] (ground), with, beside]

an·er·gy (an′ər jē), *n.* *Immunol.* lack of immunity to an antigen. [< NL *anergia.* See AN-[1], ERG-, -Y[3]] —**a·ner·gic** (a nûr′jik, an′ər-), *adj.*

an·er·oid (an′ə roid′), *adj.* using no fluid. [A-[6] + Gk *nēr(ós)* wet, fluid (akin to *náein* to flow) + -OID]

an′eroid barom′eter, a device for measuring atmospheric pressure, consisting of a box or chamber containing a partial vacuum and having an elastic top and a pointer to indicate the degree to which the top is compressed by the external air.

an·es·the·sia (an′is thē′zhə), *n.* *Med.* general or local insensibility to pain and other sensation, induced by certain drugs. Also, **anaesthesia.** [< NL < Gk *anaisthēsía* want of feeling]

an·es·the·si·ol·o·gist (an′is thē′zē ol′ə jist), *n.* a physician who specializes in anesthesiology. Also, **anaesthesiologist.**

an·es·the·si·ol·o·gy (an′is thē′zē ol′ə jē), *n.* the science of administering anesthetics. Also, **anaesthesiology.**

an·es·thet·ic (an′is thet′ik), *n.* **1.** a drug that produces anesthesia. —*adj.* **2.** of, pertaining to, or capable of causing anesthesia. **3.** physically insensitive. Also **anaesthetic.** [< Gk *anaísthēt(os)* without feeling, senseless + -IC] —**an′es·thet′i·cal·ly,** *adv.*

an·es·the·tist (ə nes′thi tist), *n.* a person who administers anesthetics, usually a specially trained doctor or nurse. Also, **anaesthetist.** [ANESTHET(IZE) + -IST]

an·es·the·tize (ə nes′thi tīz′), *v.t.,* **-tized, -tiz·ing.** to render insensible to pain or other physical sensation, as by an anesthetic. Also, **anaesthetize.** [< Gk *anaísthēt(os)* (see ANESTHETIC) + -IZE] —**an·es′the·ti·za′tion,** *n.*

an·e·thole (an′ə thōl′), *n.* *Chem., Pharm.* a powder, $CH_3CH{=}CHC_6H_4OCH_3$, used in perfumes, flavoring, and as an antiseptic and carminative. [< Gk *ánēth(on)* dill, anise + -OLE]

A·ne·to (ä ne′tô), *n.* **Pi·co de** (pē′kô the), Spanish name of Pic de Néthou.

an·eu·rysm (an′yə riz′əm), *n.* *Pathol.* a permanent cardiac or arterial dilatation usually caused by weakening of the vessel wall by diseases such as syphilis or arteriosclerosis. Also, **an′eu·rism.** [< Gk *aneúrysma* dilation = *aneurys-* (var. s. of *aneurýnein* to dilate; see AN-[3], EURY-) + *-ma* n. suffix] —**an′eu·rys′mal, an′eu·ris′mal,** *adj.* —**an′eu·rys′mal·ly, an′eu·ris′mal·ly,** *adv.*

a·new (ə nōō′, ə nyōō′), *adv.* **1.** over again; once more: *to play the tune anew.* **2.** in a new form or manner: *to write the story anew.* [ME *onew,* OE *of niowe;* r. OE *edniwe* once more]

an·frac·tu·os·i·ty (an frak′chōō os′i tē), *n.* **1.** the state or quality of being anfractuous. **2.** a channel, crevice, or passage that is anfractuous. [< LL *anfrāctuōs(us)* winding (L *anfrāctu(s)* a bend (see AMBI-, FRACTO-) + *-ōsus* -OSE[1]) + -ITY]

an·frac·tu·ous (an frak′chōō əs), *adj.* characterized by windings and turnings: *an anfractuous passage.* [back formation from ANFRACTUOSITY]

an·ga (ung′gə), *n.* any of the eight practices of Yoga, namely the abstentions, mandatory actions, posture, breath control, control of the senses, concentration, meditation, and contemplation. [< Skt: discipline]

An·ga·ra (än′gä rä′), *n.* a river in the S Soviet Union, flowing NW from Lake Baikal: called Upper Tunguska in its lower course. 1151 mi. long.

An·garsk (än gärsk′), *n.* a city in the S RSFSR, in the S Soviet Union in Asia. 160,000 (est. 1962).

an·ga·ry (ang′gə rē), *n.* *Internat. Law.* the right of a belligerent state to seize and use the property of neutrals, subject to payment of full compensation. [< LL *angaria* service to a lord < Gk *angareía* couriership = *ángar(os)* official courier (< Pers) + *-eia* -Y[3]]

an·gel (ān′jəl), *n.* **1.** one of a class of spiritual beings; a celestial attendant of God. In medieval angelology, angels constituted the lowest of the nine celestial orders (seraphim, cherubim, thrones, dominations or dominions, virtues, powers, principalities or princedoms, archangels, and angels). **2.** a conventional representation of such a being, in human form, with wings. **3.** a messenger, esp. of God. **4.** an attendant or guardian spirit. **5.** a deceased person whose soul is regarded as being in heaven. **6.** a person who performs acts of great kindness. **7.** a person whose actions and thoughts are undeviatingly virtuous. **8.** *Informal.* a person who provides financial backing for some undertaking, esp. a play. [ME, OE < L *angel(us)* < eccl. Gk *ángelos* messenger of God, special use of Gk *ángelos* messenger; r. OE *engel* < L, as above] —**an·gel·ic** (an jel′ik), **an·gel′i·cal,** *adj.* —**an·gel′i·cal·ly,** *adv.*

An·ge·la Me·ri·ci (än′je lä me rē′chē), **Saint,** 1474–1540, Italian ecclesiastic, founder of the Ursuline order.

an′gel dust′, *Slang.* a powerful hallucinogenic drug made from phencyclidine, widely used as an illicit human narcotic, often causing bizarre behavior.

an·gel·fish (ān′jəl fish′), *n., pl.* (*esp. collectively*) **-fish,** (*esp. referring to two or more kinds or species*) **-fish·es.** any of several brightly colored, spiny-headed butterflyfishes of the genera *Holocanthus* and *Pomacanthus,* which have a compressed body and are found in tropical shore waters.

an′gel food′ cake′, a light, white cake made with stiffly beaten egg whites and cream of tartar. Also called **an′gel cake′.** [after the white color of the cake]

an·gel·i·ca (an jel′ə kə), *n.* any umbelliferous plant of the genus *Angelica,* esp. *A. Archangelica,* cultivated in Europe for its scent, medicinal root, and edible stalks. Also called **archangel.** [< ML (*herba*) *angelica* angelic (herb)]

angel′ica tree′, **1.** *U.S.* Hercules'-club (def. 2). **2.** See **prickly ash.**

An·ge·li·co (an jel′ə kō′; *It.* än je′lē kô), *n.* **Fra** (frä; *It.* frä), (*Giovanni da Fiesole*), 1387–1455, Italian painter. —**An·gel·i·can** (an jel′ə kən), *adj.*

An·gell (ān′jəl), *n.* **1. James Row·land** (rō′lənd), 1869–1949, U.S. educator. **2. Norman** (*Sir Ralph Norman Angell Lane*), 1874–1967, English pacifist, economist, and writer: Nobel peace prize 1933.

an·gel·ol·o·gy (ān′jə lol′ə jē), *n.* a doctrine or theory concerning angels.

An·ge·lus (an′jə ləs), *n.* *Rom. Cath. Ch.* **1.** a devotion in memory of the Annunciation. **2.** Also called **An′gelus bell′.** the bell tolled in the morning, at noon, and in the evening to indicate the time the Angelus is to be recited. Also, **an′ge·lus.** [< LL, from the first word of the service: *Angelus (domini nuntiavit Mariae).* See ANGEL]

an·ger (ang′gər), *n.* **1.** a strong feeling of displeasure and belligerence aroused by a real or supposed wrong. **2.** *Dial.* pain or smart, as of a sore. **3.** *Obs.* grief; trouble. —*v.t.* **4.** to excite to anger or wrath. **5.** *Dial.* to cause to smart; inflame. —*v.i.* **6.** to become angry. [ME < Scand; cf. Icel *angr* sorrow, grief, akin to OHG *angust* (G *Angst* fear), L *angor* anguish]
—**Syn. 1.** resentment, exasperation; choler, bile, spleen. ANGER, INDIGNATION, RAGE, FURY imply deep and strong feelings aroused by injury, injustice, wrong, etc. ANGER is a sudden violent displeasure accompanied by an impulse to retaliate: *a burst of anger.* INDIGNATION, a more formal word, implies deep and justified anger, often directed against something unworthy: *indignation at cruelty or against corruption.* RAGE is vehement anger: *rage at being frustrated.* FURY is rage so great that it resembles insanity: *the fury of a woman scorned.* **4.** vex, irritate, exasperate, infuriate, enrage.

An·gers (an′jərz, ang′gərz; *Fr.* äN zhā′), *n.* a city in W France. 122,269 (1962).

An·ge·vin (an′jə vin), *adj.* **1.** of or pertaining to Anjou or its inhabitants. **2.** relating to the counts of Anjou or their descendants, esp. those who ruled in England, or to the period of their rule. —*n.* **3.** an inhabitant of Anjou. **4.** a member of an Angevin royal house, esp. a Plantagenet. Also, **An·ge·vine** (an′jə vin, -vīn′).

angi-, var. of **angio-** before a vowel.

an·gi·na (an jī′nə; *in Med. often* an′jə nə), *n.* *Pathol.* **1.** any inflammatory affection of the throat or fauces, as quinsy, croup, mumps, etc. **2.** See **angina pectoris.** [< L: quinsy = *ang(ere)* (to) throttle, torture (see ANGER) + *-ina* n. use of fem. of *-inus* adj. suffix] —**an·gi′nal, an·gi·nose** (an′jə nōs′, an jī′nōs), **an·gi′nous,** *adj.*

angi′na pec′to·ris (pek′tə ris), *Pathol.* a syndrome characterized by constricting paroxysmal pain below the sternum, most easily precipitated by exertion or excitement and caused by ischemia of the heart muscle, usually due to a coronary artery disease, such as arteriosclerosis. [< NL: angina of the chest]

angio-, a learned borrowing from Greek meaning "vessel," "container," used in the formation of compound words: *angiosperm.* Also, *esp. before a vowel,* **angi-.** [< Gk, comb. form repr. *angeîon* = *áng(os)* vessel, vat, shell + *-eion* dim. suffix]

an·gi·o·car·di·og·ra·phy (an′jē ō kär′dē og′rə fē), *n., pl.* **-phies.** x-ray examination of the heart and its blood vessels following intravenous injection of radiopaque fluid. —**an·gi·o·car·di·o·graph·ic** (an′jē ō kär′dē ə graf′ik), *adj.*

an·gi·o·carp (an′jē ə kärp′), *n.* a plant bearing an angiocarpous fruit.

an·gi·o·car·pous (an′jē ō kär′pəs), *adj.* **1.** (of a fruit) partially or wholly enclosed in a shell, involucre, or husk. **2.** (of a fungus or lichen) having the ascocarp immersed or enclosed in the thallus. Also, **an′gi·o·car′pic.**

an·gi·ol·o·gy (an′jē ol′ə jē), *n.* the branch of anatomy dealing with blood vessels and lymphatics.

an·gi·o·ma (an′jē ō′mə), *n., pl.* **-mas, -ma·ta** (-mə tə). *Pathol.* a tumor consisting chiefly of dilated or newly formed blood vessels or lymph vessels. —**an·gi·om·a·tous** (an′jē-om′ə təs, -ō′mə-), *adj.*

an·gi·o·plas·ty (an′jē ə plas′tē), *n., pl.* **-ties.** *Surg.* the repair of a blood vessel, esp. by inserting a balloon-tipped catheter to unclog it: *coronary angioplasty to widen an artery blocked by plaque.*

an·gi·o·sperm (an′jē ə spûrm′), *n.* a plant having its seeds enclosed in an ovary; a flowering plant. Cf. **gymnosperm.** —**an′gi·o·sper′mous,** *adj.*

Ang·kor (ang′kōr, -kôr), *n.* a vast assemblage of ruins of the Khmer empire, near modern Siem Reap in NW Cambodia: elaborately carved temples, statues, etc.

Ang′kor Wat′ (wät, vät), the largest and best-preserved temple in the Angkor ruins. Also, **Ang′kor Vat′** (vät).

Angl., **1.** Anglican. **2.** Anglicized.

an·gle[1] (ang′gəl), *n., v.,* **-gled, -gling.** —*n.* **1.** *Geom.* **a.** the space within two lines or three or more planes diverging from a common point, or within two planes diverging from a common line. **b.** the figure so formed. **c.** the amount of rotation needed to bring one line or plane into coincidence with another. (See illustration on the following page.) **2.** an angular projection; a projecting corner. **3.** a viewpoint; standpoint: *He looked at all new problems only from his own selfish angle.* **4.** *Journalism.* **a.** slant (def. 10).

b. the point of view from which copy is written, esp. when the copy is intended to interest a particular audience: *the investor's angle; the society angle.* **5.** an aspect of an event or situation; side; phase. **6.** *U.S Informal.* opportunity for gain; advantage: *What was his angle in buying up cheap stocks?* **7.** See **angle iron** (def. 2). **—*v.t.*** **8.** to move or bend in an angle. **9.** to set, fix, direct, or adjust at an angle. **10.** *Journalism.* to write or edit in such a way as to appeal to a particular audience; slant. **—*v.i.*** **11.** to turn sharply in a different direction: *The road angles to the right.* **12.** to move or go in angles or at an angle. [ME < MF < L *angulus;* akin to ANKLE, ANGLE[2]]

Angle[1] (def. 1)

an·gle[2] (ang′gəl), *v.i.,* **-gled, -gling. 1.** to fish with hook and line. **2.** to attempt to get something by artful means; fish: *to angle for a compliment.* [ME *angel,* OE *angul;* fishhook; c. G *Angel,* Icel *öngull.* See ANGLE[1]]

an·gled (ang′gəld), *adj.* having an angle or angles.

an′gle i′ron, 1. an iron or steel bar, brace, or cleat in the form of an angle. **2.** Also called **angle, an′gle bar′.** a piece of structural iron or steel having a cross section in the form of an L. See illus. at **shape.**

an′gle of attack′, the acute angle between the chord of an aircraft wing or other airfoil and the direction of the relative wind.

an′gle of devia′tion, *Optics.* the angle equal to the difference between the angle of incidence and the angle of refraction of a ray of light passing through the surface between one medium and another of different refractive index.

an′gle of in′cidence, 1. Also called **incidence.** the angle that a straight line, ray of light, etc., meeting a surface, makes with a normal to the surface at the point of meeting. **2.** (on an airplane) the angle, usually fixed, between a wing or tail chord and the axis of the fuselage.

an′gle of reflec′tion, the angle that a straight line, ray of light, or the like, reflected from a surface, makes with a normal to the surface at the point of reflection.

ECD, Angle of incidence on surface AB; CD, Normal; E′CD, Angle of reflection

an′gle of refrac′tion, *Physics, Optics.* the angle between a refracted ray and a line drawn normal to the interface between two media at the point of refraction.

an′gle of view′, *Optics.* the angle formed at a nodal point of a lens by the intersection of two lines drawn from the opposite ends of an image produced by the lens.

an·gle·pod (ang′gəl pod′), *n.* an asclepiadaceous plant, *Vincetoxicum* (or *Gonolobus*) *Gonocarpas,* of the southern and central U.S. [ANGLE[1] + POD[1] (from its shape)]

an·gler (ang′glər), *n.* **1.** a person who fishes with hook and line as a hobby or sport. **2.** any large pediculate fish of the family *Lophiidae,* esp. *Lophius americanus,* having an immense mouth and a large, depressed head to which is attached a wormlike filament for luring prey. **3.** any of various related fishes of the order *Pediculati.*

An·gles (ang′gəlz), *n.pl.* a West Germanic people that migrated from Schleswig to Britain in the 5th century A.D. and founded the kingdoms of East Anglia, Mercia, and Northumbria. [OE *Angle,* pl. (var. of *Engle*), tribal name of disputed orig.]

An·gle·sey (ang′gəl sē), *n.* an island and county in NW Wales. 51,700 (1961); 276 sq. mi. *Co. seat:* Holyhead.

an·gle·worm (ang′gəl wûrm′), *n.* an earthworm, as used for bait in angling.

An·gli·a (ang′glē ə), *n.* Latin name of **England.**

An·gli·an (ang′glē ən), *adj.* **1.** Also, **An·glic** (ang′glik). of or pertaining to the Angles or to East Anglia. **—*n.* 2.** a member of the Angles. **3.** the northern and central group of Old English dialects, spoken in Northumbria and Mercia. [< L *Anglī* the ANGLES + -AN]

An·gli·can (ang′glə kən), *adj.* **1.** of or pertaining to the Church of England. **2.** related in origin to and in communion with the Church of England, as various Episcopal churches. **3.** *Chiefly U.S.* English (def. 1). **—*n.* 4.** a member of the Church of England or of a church in communion with it in other parts of the world. **5.** a person who upholds the teaching of the Church of England. [< ML *anglicān(us)* = *anglic(us)* English + *-ānus* -AN] **—An′gli·can·ism′,** *n.* **—An′gli·can·ly,** *adv.*

An′glican Church′, the Church of England and those churches in communion with it.

An·gli·ce (ang′gli sē), *adv.* in English; as the English would say it; according to the English way: *Córdoba, Anglice "Cordova."* [< ML = *anglic(us)* English + *-ē* adv. suffix]

An·gli·cise (ang′gli sīz′), *v.t., v.i.,* **-cised, -cis·ing.** *Chiefly Brit.* Anglicize. Also, **an′gli·cise′. —An′gli·ci·sa′tion, an′gli·ci·sa′tion,** *n.*

An·gli·cism (ang′gli siz′əm), *n.* **1.** the state of being English; characteristic English quality. **2.** a word, idiom, or characteristic feature of the English language occurring in or borrowed by another language. **3.** *U.S.* a Briticism. **4.** any custom, manner, idea, etc., characteristic of the English people. [< ML *anglic(us)* English + -ISM]

An·gli·cist (ang′gli sist), *n.* an authority on the English language or English literature. [< ML *anglic(us)* English + -IST]

An·gli·cize (ang′gli sīz′), *v.t., v.i.,* **-cized, -ciz·ing. 1.** to make or become English in customs, manners, etc. **2.** to conform to the usage of the English language: *to Anglicize the pronunciation of a Russian name.* Also, **an′gli·cize′;** *esp. Brit.,* **Anglicise, anglicise.** [< ML *anglic(us)* English + -IZE] **—An′gli·ci·za′tion, an′gli·ci·za′tion,** *n.*

An·gli·fy (ang′glə fī′), *v.t.,* **-fied, -fy·ing.** to Anglicize. [< ML *Anglī* the English + -FY] **—An′gli·fi·ca′tion,** *n.*

an·gling (ang′gling), *n.* the act or art of fishing with a hook and line, usually attached to a rod.

An·glist (ang′glist), *n.* an authority on England, its language, or its literature. [< G < ML *Angl(ia)* England + G *-ist* -IST]

Anglo-, a combining form of **English:** *Anglo-Norman.* [< ML *Angl(ī)* the English + -o-]

An·glo-A·mer·i·can (ang′glō ə mer′i kən), *adj.* **1.** of, pertaining to, or involving England and America, esp. the United States, or their peoples. **—*n.* 2.** a native or descendant of a native of England who has settled in or become a citizen of America, esp. of the United States. **—An′glo-A·mer′i·can·ism,** *n.*

An·glo-Cath·o·lic (ang′glō kath′ə lik, -kath′lik), *n.* **1.** a person who emphasizes the Catholic character of the Anglican Church. **—*adj.* 2.** of or pertaining to Anglo-Catholics or Anglo-Catholicism. **—An·glo-Ca·thol·i·cism** (ang′glō kə thol′i siz′əm), *n.*

An′glo-E·gyp′tian Sudan′ (ang′glō i jip′shən), former name of **Sudan.**

An·glo-French (ang′glō french′), *adj.* **1.** of, pertaining to, or involving England and France, or the people of the two countries. **2.** of or pertaining to the Anglo-French dialect. **—*n.* 3.** Also called **Anglo-Norman.** the dialect of French current in England from the Norman Conquest to the end of the Middle Ages. *Abbr.:* AF

An·glo-In·di·an (ang′glō in′dē ən), *adj.* **1.** of, pertaining to, or involving England and India, esp. as politically associated: *Anglo-Indian treaties.* **2.** of or pertaining to Anglo-Indians or their speech. **—*n.* 3.** a person of English and Indian ancestry. **4.** the speech of such persons. *Abbr.:* AInd **5.** a person of English birth or citizenship in India.

An·glo-I·rish (ang′glō ī′rish), *n.* **1.** the English or their descendants living in Ireland. **—*adj.* 2.** of or pertaining to the Anglo-Irish or their speech.

An·glo-Lat·in (ang′glō lat′ən, -in), *n.* Medieval Latin as used in England. *Abbr.:* AL, AL., A.L.

An·glo·ma·ni·a (ang′glə mā′nē ə, -mān′yə), *n.* an excessive devotion to English institutions, manners, customs, etc. **—An′glo·ma′ni·ac,** *n.* **—An·glo·ma·ni·a·cal** (ang′glō mə nī′ə kəl), *adj.*

An·glo-Nor·man (ang′glō nôr′mən), *adj.* **1.** pertaining to the period, 1066–1154, when England was ruled by Normans. **2.** of or pertaining to Anglo-Normans or the Anglo-Norman dialect. **—*n.* 3.** a Norman who settled in England after 1066, or one of his descendants. **4.** Anglo-French (def. 3).

An·glo·phile (ang′glə fīl′, -fil), *n.* a person who greatly admires England or anything English. Also, **An·glo·phil** (ang′glə fil). **—An·glo·phil·i·a** (ang′glə fil′ē ə, -fēl′yə), *n.* **—An·glo·phil·i·ac** (ang′glə fil′ē ak′, -fēl′yak), **An·glo·phil·ic** (ang′glə fil′ik), *adj.*

An·glo·phobe (ang′glə fōb′), *n.* a person who hates or fears England or anything English. **—An′glo·pho′bi·a,** *n.* **—An·glo·pho·bi·ac** (an′glə fō′bē ak′), **An′glo·pho′bic,** *adj.*

An·glo-Sax·on (ang′glō sak′sən), *n.* **1.** a person whose native language is English. **2.** an Englishman of the period before the Norman Conquest. **3.** a person of English descent. **4.** *U.S.* a person of colonial descent or British origin. **5.** See **Old English** (def. 1). **6.** plain and simple English. **7.** the original Germanic element in the English language. **—*adj.* 8.** of, pertaining to, or characteristic of the Anglo-Saxons. **9.** pertaining to Anglo-Saxon. **10.** (of words, speech, or writing) frank, direct, or blunt. [< NL *Anglo-Saxonēs* (pl.) the English people (i.e., Angles and Saxons taken as one), ML *Anglī Saxonēs,* Latinizations of OE *Angle* ANGLES and OE *Seaxan* SAXONS]

An·go·la (ang gō′lə), *n.* a republic in SW Africa, formerly an overseas province of Portugal; gained independence 1975. 5,500,000; 481,226 sq. mi. *Cap.:* Luanda. Formerly, **Portuguese West Africa.**

An·go·ra (ang gōr′ə, -gôr′ə, an-, *or, for 3,* ang′gər ə), *n.* **1.** Also called **Ango′ra wool′.** the hair of the Angora goat or of the Angora rabbit. **2.** yarn, fabric, or a garment made from this hair. **3.** Ankara. **4.** See **Angora cat. 5.** See **Angora goat. 6.** See **Angora rabbit. —*adj.* 7.** made from a yarn or fabric of the hairs of the Angora goat or Angora rabbit: *an Angora sweater.* [var. of ANKARA]

Ango′ra cat′, a long-haired variety of the domestic cat. Also called **Angora.**

Ango′ra goat′, a variety of domestic goat, having long, silky hair called mohair. Also called **Angora.**

Ango′ra rab′bit, one of a breed of rabbits raised for its long, silky hair. Also called **Angora.**

an′gos·tu′ra bark′ (ang′gə stŏŏr′ə, -styŏŏr′ə, ang′-), the bitter, aromatic bark of either of two South American rutaceous trees, *Galipea officinalis* or *G. cusparia,* used in medicine and in the preparation of liqueurs and bitters. Also called **an′gostu′ra.** [after *Angostura* (now Ciudad Bolívar), town in central Venezuela]

An·gou·mois (äng′gōōm wä′; *Fr.* äɴ gōō mwa′), *n.* a region and former province of W France.

An·gra do He·ro·is·mo (*Port.* äɴng′grə dōō e′rōō ēzh′mōō), a seaport on and the capital of the island of Terceira in the Azores: former capital of the Azores. 85,650.

An·gra Main·yu (ang′rə mīn′yōō), *Zoroastrianism.* the evil spirit who contends against Spenta Mainyu. Also called **Ahriman.** [Avestan]

an·gry (ang′grē), *adj.,* **-gri·er, -gri·est. 1.** feeling anger or resentment: *to be angry at the dean; to be angry about the snub.* **2.** revealing or characterized by anger: *angry words.* **3.** (of an object or phenomenon) exhibiting a quality suggesting anger: *an angry sea.* **4.** *Med.* inflamed, as a sore. [ME] **—an′gri·ly,** *adv.* **—an′gri·ness,** *n.* **—Syn. 1.** irate, incensed, enraged, infuriated, furious. **—Ant. 1.** calm.

an′gry young′ man′, one of a group of British writers since the late 1950's whose works reflect rebellion against tradition and society. Also, **An′gry Young′ Man′.**

ang·strom (ang′strəm), *n.* a unit of length, equal to one tenth of a millimicron or one ten-millionth of a millimeter, primarily used to express electromagnetic wavelengths. *Abbr.:* A, Å, A., A.U., a.u., Å.U. Also, **Ang′strom.** Also called **Ang′strom u′nit, ang′strom u′nit,** [named after A. J. *Ångström* (1814–74), Swedish physicist]

An·guil·la (an̄g gwil′ə), *n.* one of the Leeward Islands, in the E West Indies: a member of the West Indies Associated States; formerly a British colony. 5810 (1960); 34 sq. mi. Cf. **St. Kitts-Nevis-Anguilla.**

an·guine (an̄g′gwin), *adj.* pertaining to or resembling a snake. [< L *anguīn(us)* pertaining to a snake = *angu(is)* snake, serpent + *-īnus* -INE[1]]

an·guish (an̄g′gwish), *n.* **1.** acute pain, suffering, or distress. —*v.t.* **2.** to inflict with pain, suffering, or distress. [ME *anguisse* < OF < L *angustia* tight place = *angust(us)* narrow + *-ia* -IA; akin to ANGER] —**Syn. 1.** agony, torment. See **pain.**

an·guished (an̄g′gwisht), *adj.* **1.** feeling, showing, or accompanied by anguish. **2.** produced by anguish.

an·gu·lar (an̄g′gyə lər), *adj.* **1.** having an angle or angles. **2.** consisting of, situated at, or forming an angle. **3.** of, pertaining to, or measured by an angle. **4.** *Physics.* pertaining to quantities related to a revolving body that are measured in reference to its axis of revolution. **5.** bony or gaunt: *a tall, angular man.* **6.** acting or moving awkwardly. Also, **angulous, angulose.** [< L *angulār(is)* having angles. See ANGLE[1], -AR[1]] —**an′gu·lar·ly,** *adv.* —**an′gu·lar·ness,** *n.* —**Ant. 1.** curved. **5.** rotund. **6.** graceful.

an′gular accelera′tion, *Physics.* the time rate of change of angular velocity of a rotating body.

an·gu·lar·i·ty (an̄g′gyə lar′i tē), *n., pl.* **-ties. 1.** the quality of being angular. **2. angularities,** sharp corners; angular outlines.

an·gu·late (an̄g′gyə lit, -lāt′), *adj.* of angular form; angled: *angulate stems.* Also, **an′gu·lat′ed.** [< L *angulāt(us)* having angles. See ANGLE[1], -ATE[1]] —**an′gu·late·ly,** *adv.* —**an′gu·late·ness,** *n.*

an·gu·la·tion (an̄g′gyə lā′shən), *n.* **1.** an angular formation. **2.** the exact measurement of angles.

an·gu·lous (an̄g′gyə ləs), *adj.* angular. Also, **an·gu·lose** (an̄g′gyə lōs′). [< L *angulōs(us).* See ANGLE[1], -OUS] —**an·gu·los·i·ty** (an̄g′gyə los′i tē), *n.*

An·gur·bo·da (äng′gər bô′də), *n.* *Scand. Myth.* Angerboda.

An·gus (an̄g′gəs), *n.* **1.** Formerly, **Forfar.** a county in E Scotland. 278,370 (est. 1961); 873 sq. mi. *Co. seat:* Forfar. **2.** See **Aberdeen Angus.**

An′gus Og′ (ōg), *Irish Myth.* the god of love and beauty, the patron deity of young men and women.

An·halt (än′hält), *n.* a former state in central Germany.

An·hwei (än′hwā′), *n.* a province in E China. 33,560,000 (est. 1957); 54,015 sq. mi. *Cap.:* Hofei. Also, **Nganhwei.**

anhydr-, **1.** a combining form meaning "waterless." **2.** a combining form of **anhydride.** [< Gk *ánydr(os)* waterless (with *h* as in *hydro-*). See AN-[1], HYDRO-[1]]

an·hy·dride (an hī′drīd, -drid), *n.* *Chem.* **1.** a compound that forms an acid or a base when united with water. **2.** a compound from which water has been abstracted.

an·hy·drite (an hī′drīt), *n.* a mineral, calcium sulfate, $CaSO_4$, occurring in masses.

an·hy·drous (an hī′drəs), *adj.* *Chem.* with all water removed, esp. water of crystallization. [< Gk *ánydros*]

a·ni (ä′nē), *n., pl.* **a·nis.** any of several black, tropical American cuckoos of the genus *Crotophaga,* having a compressed, bladelike bill. [< Sp or Pg < Tupi]

An·i·ce·tus (an′i sē′təs), *n.* **Saint,** pope A.D. 155?–166?.

an·il (an′əl), *n.* **1.** a fabaceous shrub, *Indigofera suffruticosa,* of the West Indies, yielding indigo. **2.** indigo; deep blue. [< Pg < Ar *an-nīl* = *al* the + *nīl* indigo < Skt *nīlī* indigo (*nīl(a)* dark blue + *-ī* fem. suffix)]

an·ile (an′īl, ā′nīl), *adj.* of or like a weak old woman. [< L *anīl(is)* pertaining to an old woman = *an(us)* old woman + *-īlis* -ILE] —**a·nil·i·ty** (ə nil′i tē), *n.*

an·i·line (an′əlin, -əlīn′), *n.* **1.** Also called **an′iline oil′, phenylamine.** a colorless liquid, $C_6H_5NH_2$, used chiefly in the synthesis of dyes and drugs. —*adj.* **2.** pertaining to or derived from aniline. Also, **an·i·lin** (an′əlin). [ANIL + -INE[2]]

an′iline dye′, *Chem.* any of a large number of dyes derived from aniline, usually obtained from coal tar.

anim., *Music.* animato.

an·i·ma (an′ə mə), *n.* soul or consciousness; life. [< L: lit., air, breath]

an·i·mad·ver·sion (an′ə mad vûr′zhən, -shən), *n.* **1.** a censorious remark; criticism or adverse comment. **2.** the act or fact of criticizing. [< L *animadversiōn-* (s. of *animadversiō*) a heeding, censure = *animadvers(us)* (ptp. of *animadvertere;* see ANIMADVERT) + *-iōn-* -ION] —**an′i·mad·ver′sion·al,** *adj.* —**Syn. 1.** aspersion, derogation.

an·i·mad·vert (an′ə mad vûrt′), *v.i.* to comment critically; make remarks by way of criticism or censure (usually fol. by *on* or *upon*). [< L *animadvert(ere)* (to) heed, censure = *anim(um),* acc. of *animus* (see ANIMUS) + *advertere* to ADVERT] —**an′i·mad·vert′er,** *n.*

an·i·mal (an′ə məl), *n.* **1.** any living being typically differing from a plant in having the ability to move voluntarily, the presence of a nervous system and a greater ability to respond to stimuli, the need for complex organic materials for nourishment, and the delimitation of cells usually by a membrane rather than a cellulose wall. **2.** any such being other than man. **3.** a mammal, as opposed to a fish, bird, etc. **4.** the physical or carnal nature of man: *the animal in every man.* **5.** an inhuman or brutish person. **6.** *Facetious.* a thing: *A perfect vacation?—there's no such animal!* —*adj.* **7.** of, pertaining to, or derived from animals: *animal fats.* **8.** pertaining to the physical or carnal nature of man, rather than his spiritual or intellectual nature. [< L *animāl(e),* neut. of *animālis* living (lit., breathing) = *anim(a)* air, breath + *-ālis* -AL[1]] —**an·i·mal·ic** (an′ə mal′ik), **an·i·ma·li·an** (an′ə mā′lē ən, -māl′yən), *adj.*

—**Syn. 1, 2.** ANIMAL, BEAST, BRUTE refer to sentient creatures as distinct from minerals and plants; figuratively, they usually connote qualities and characteristics below the human level. ANIMAL is the general word; figuratively, it applies merely to the body or to animallike characteristics: *An athlete is a magnificent animal.* BEAST refers to four-footed animals; figuratively, it suggests a base, sensual nature: *A glutton is a beast.* BRUTE implies absence of ability to reason; figuratively, it connotes savagery as well: *a drunken brute.* **8.** fleshly, physical.

an′imal crack′er, a small cookie in the shape of an animal.

an·i·mal·cule (an′ə mal′kyōōl), *n.* **1.** a minute or microscopic animal. **2.** *Rare.* a tiny animal. [< NL *animalcul(um)*] —**an·i·mal·cu·lar** (an′ə mal′kyə lər), **an·i·mal·cu·line** (an′ə mal′kyə lin′, -lin), **an′i·mal′cu·lous,** *adj.*

an′imal heat′, *Physiol.* heat produced in a living animal by any of various metabolic activities.

an′imal hus′bandry, the science of breeding, feeding, and tending domestic animals, esp. farm animals. —**an′imal hus′bandman.**

an·i·mal·ise (an′ə mə līz′), *v.t.,* **-ised, -is·ing.** *Chiefly Brit.* animalize. —**an′i·mal·i·sa′tion,** *n.*

an·i·mal·ism (an′ə mə liz′əm), *n.* **1.** preoccupation with or motivation by physical appetites rather than moral, spiritual, or intellectual forces. **2.** the theory that human beings lack a spiritual nature. [ANIMAL(IZE) + -ISM] —**an′i·mal·ist,** *n.* —**an′i·mal·is′tic,** *adj.*

an·i·mal·i·ty (an′ə mal′i tē), *n.* **1.** the state of being an animal. **2.** the animal nature in man.

an·i·mal·ize (an′ə mə līz′), *v.t.,* **-ized, -iz·ing.** to excite the animal passions of; brutalize; sensualize. Also, *esp. Brit.,* **animalise.** —**an′i·mal·i·za′tion,** *n.*

an′imal king′dom, the animals of the world collectively. Cf. **mineral kingdom, plant kingdom.**

an·i·mal·ly (an′ə mə lē), *adv.* physically.

an′imal mag′netism, **1.** the power that enables a person to induce hypnosis. **2.** physical attractiveness to members of the opposite sex. Also called **biomagnetism.**

an′imal spir′its, exuberance arising from good health, good humor, and energy.

an′imal starch′, *Biochem.* glycogen.

an·i·mate (*v.* an′ə māt′; *adj.* an′ə mit), *v.,* **-mat·ed, -mat·ing,** *adj.* —*v.t.* **1.** to give life to; make alive. **2.** to make lively, vivacious, or vigorous; give zest or spirit to: *Her presence animated the party.* **3.** to encourage. **4.** to move to action; actuate: *He was animated by religious zeal.* —*adj.* **5.** alive; possessing life. **6.** lively. **7.** of or relating to animal life. **8.** able to move voluntarily. [< L *animāt(us)* filled with breath or air, quickened, animated (ptp. of *animāre*). See ANIMA, -ATE[1]] —**an′i·mate·ly,** *adv.* —**an′i·mate·ness,** *n.* —**an′i·mat′ing·ly,** *adv.* —**Syn. 1.** vivify, quicken, vitalize. **2.** energize. **3.** hearten, arouse. **4.** inspire, excite, incite, fire, urge, prompt. —**Ant. 1.** kill. **5.** dead.

an·i·mat·ed (an′ə mā′tid), *adj.* **1.** full of life, action, or spirit; lively: *an animated debate.* **2.** made or equipped to move as if animate: *an animated puppet.* —**an′i·mat′ed·ly,** *adv.*

an′imated cartoon′, a motion picture consisting of a sequence of drawings, each slightly different from the preceding one so that, when filmed and run through a projector, the figures seem to move.

an·i·ma·tion (an′ə mā′shən), *n.* **1.** liveliness or vivacity: *to talk with animation.* **2.** the act or an instance of animating or enlivening. **3.** the state or condition of being animated. **4.** the process of preparing animated cartoons. [< L *animātiōn-* (s. of *animātiō* a bestowing of life)] —**Syn. 1.** vigor, energy; enthusiasm, exhilaration.

a·ni·ma·to (ä′nə mä′tō, an′ə-; *It.* ä′nē mä′tô), *adj.* *Music.* animated (def. 1). *Abbr.:* anim. [< It]

an·i·ma·tor (an′ə mā′tər), *n.* **1.** a person or thing that animates. **2.** a person who draws or prepares animated cartoons. Also, **an′i·mat′er.** [< LL]

an·i·mé (an′ə mā′, -mē), *n.* any of various resins or copals, esp. that from *Hymenaea Courbaril,* a tree of tropical America, used in making varnish, scenting pastilles, etc. Also, **a·ni·mi** (ə nē′mē). [< F < Sp or Pg *anime* < Tupi *an(an)im* resin + excrescent *-e*]

an·i·mism (an′ə miz′əm), *n.* **1.** the belief that natural objects, natural phenomena, and the universe itself possess souls or consciousness. **2.** the belief that souls may exist apart from bodies. **3.** the doctrine that the soul is the principle of life and health. **4.** belief in spiritual beings or agencies. [< L *anim(a)* air, the breath of life, spirit, soul + -ISM] —**an′i·mist,** *n.* —**an′i·mis′tic,** *adj.*

an·i·mos·i·ty (an′ə mos′i tē), *n., pl.* **-ties.** a feeling of ill will that tends to display itself in action (usually fol. by *between* or *against*): *a deep-seated animosity between two sisters; animosity against one's neighbor.* [late ME *animosite* < LL *animōsitās.* See ANIMUS, -OSE[1], -ITY] —**Syn.** hostility, antagonism, animus, hatred.

an·i·mus (an′ə məs), *n.* **1.** hostile feeling or attitude; antagonism. **2.** animating spirit. [< L: soul, feeling, spirit, courage, passion, wrath; akin to ANIMA]

an·i·on (an′ī′ən), *n.* *Physical Chem.* **1.** a negatively charged ion, as one attracted to the anode in electrolysis. **2.** any negatively charged atom or group of atoms (opposed to *cation*). [< Gk, neut. of *aniṓs* going up (prp. of *aniénai* to go up) = *an-* AN-[3] + *-i-* go + *-os* adj. suffix] —**an·i·on·ic** (an′ī on′ik), *adj.*

an·ise (an′is), *n.* **1.** a herbaceous plant, *Pimpinella Anisum,* of Mediterranean regions, yielding aniseed. **2.** aniseed. [ME *anis* < OF < L *anīsum* < Gk *ánīson*] —**a·nis·ic** (ə nis′ik), *adj.*

an·i·seed (an′i sēd′, an′is sēd′), *n.* the aromatic seed of the anise, used in medicine, in cookery, etc., for its licoricelike flavor. [late ME *annes sede*]

an·is·ei·ko·ni·a (an′ī sī kō′nē ə), *n.* *Ophthalm.* a defect of vision in which the images at the retinas are unequal in size. Also, **an·i·so·i·co·ni·a** (an ī′sō ī kō′nē ə, an′ī-), **an·i·so·ko·ni·a** (an ī′sə kō′nē ə, an′ī-). [< NL; see ANISO-, EIKON, -IA] —**an·is·ei·kon·ic** (an′ī sī kon′ik), *adj.*

an·i·sette (an′i set′, -zet′, an′i set′, -zet′), *n.* a cordial or liqueur flavored with aniseed. [< F, short for *anisette de Bordeaux.* See ANISE, -ETTE]

aniso-, a learned borrowing from Greek meaning "unequal," "uneven," used in the formation of compound words: *anisogamous.* [< Gk *ániso(s).* See AN-[1], ISO-]

an·i·sog·a·mous (an′ī sog′ə məs), *adj. Biol.* reproducing by the fusion of dissimilar gametes or individuals, usually differing in size. Also, **an·i·so·gam·ic** (an ī′sə gam′ik, an′ī-). —**an′i·sog′a·my,** *n.*

an·i·sole (an′i sōl′), *n. Chem.* a liquid, $C_6H_5OCH_3$, having a pleasant, aromatic odor: used chiefly in perfumery and organic synthesis, and as a vermicide. [ANISE + -OLE]

an·i·so·met·ric (an ī′sə me′trik, an′ī-), *adj.* **1.** not isometric; of unequal measurement. **2.** (of a crystal) having axes of different lengths.

an·i·so·me·tro·pi·a (an ī′sə mə trō′pē ə, an′ī-), *n. Ophthalm.* inequality in the power of the two eyes to refract light. —**an·i·so·me·trop·ic** (an ī′sə mə trop′ik, an′ī-), *adj.*

an·i·so·trop·ic (an ī′sə trop′ik, an′ī-), *adj.* **1.** *Physics.* of unequal physical properties along different axes. Cf. **isotropic. 2.** *Bot.* of different dimensions along different axes. —**an·i·sot·ro·py** (an′ī so′trə pē), *n.*

An·jou (an′jo͞o; *Fr.* äN zho͞o′), *n.* a region and former province in W France, in the Loire valley.

An·ka·ra (aNG′kər ə; *Turk.* äNG′kä rä′), *n.* a city in and the capital of Turkey, in the central part. 1,522,350. Also, **Angora.**

ankh (aNGk), *n. Egyptian Art.* a tau cross with a loop at the top, used as a symbol of generation or enduring life. [< Egypt]

Ankh

an·kle (aNG′kəl), *n.* **1.** the joint between the foot and the leg, in which movement occurs in two planes. **2.** the slender part of the leg above the foot. [ME *ankel,* perh. < Scand (cf. Dan, Sw *ankel;* c. MLG *enkel,* OHG *anchal, enchil*); r. ME *anclowe,* OE *ancleow(e)* ankle, c. OHG *anchlāo*]

an·kle·bone (aNG′kəl bōn′), *n.* the talus. [ME]

an·klet (aNG′klit), *n.* **1.** a sock that reaches just above the ankle. **2.** an ornamental circlet worn around the ankle. [ANKLE + -LET, modeled on *bracelet*]

an·kus (aNG′kəs, uNG′kəsh), *n., pl.* **-kus, -kus·es.** an elephant goad, as used in India [< Hindi; akin to ANGLE²]

ankylo-, var. of **ancylo-:** *ankylosis.*

an·ky·lo·saur (aNG′kə lō sôr′), *n.* any of several herbivorous dinosaurs of the suborder *Ankylosauria,* from the Cretaceous period, having the body covered with thick, bony plates. [< NL *Ankylosaur(ia).*]

an·ky·lose (aNG′kə lōs′), *v.t., v.i.,* **-losed, -los·ing.** to unite or grow together, as the bones of a joint or the root of a tooth and its surrounding bone. Also, **anchylose.** [back formation from ANKYLOSIS]

an·ky·lo·sis (aNG′kə lō′sis), *n. Anat.* the union or consolidation of two or more bones or other hard tissues into one. Also, **anchylosis.** [< Gk: a stiffening of the joints. See ANKYLO-, -OSIS] —**an·ky·lot·ic** (aNG′kə lot′ik), *adj.*

an·ky·los·to·mi·a·sis (aNG′kə los′tə mī′ə sis), *n. Pathol.* hookworm (def. 2). Also, **ancylostomiasis.**

an·la·ge (än′lä gə), *n., pl.* **-gen** (-gən), **-ges.** (*sometimes cap.*) **1.** *Embryol.* primordium. **2.** *Psychol.* an inherited predisposition to certain traits or to a particular character development. [< G: setup, layout = *an-* ON + *Lage* position, akin to LAY¹]

ann., **1.** years. [< L *annī*] **2.** annual. **3.** annuity.

an·na (an′ə), *n.* a former cupronickel coin of Pakistan and India, the 16th part of a rupee. [< Hindi *ānā*]

An·na·ba (än′nä bä), *n.* a seaport in NE Algeria: site of Hippo Regius. 164,844 (1960). Formerly, **Bône.**

An·na I·va·nov·na (ä′nä ē vä′nov nä), 1693–1740, empress of Russia 1730–40.

an·nal (an′ᵊl), *n. Archaic.* a record, as annals, esp. of a single year, people, etc. [back formation from ANNALS]

an·nal·ist (an′ᵊlist), *n.* a chronicler of yearly events. [*annal* (v., now obs.) + -IST] —**an′nal·is′tic,** *adj.* —**an′nal·is′ti·cal·ly,** *adv.*

an·nals (an′ᵊlz), *n.* (*construed as pl.*) **1.** a record of events, esp. a yearly record, usually in chronological order. **2.** historical records generally: *the annals of war.* **3.** a periodical publication containing the formal reports of an organization. [< L *annālēs* (*librī*), lit., yearly (books), pl. of *annālis* continuing for a year, annual = *ann(us)* a year + *-ālis* -AL¹]

An·nam (ə nam′), *n.* a former kingdom and French protectorate along the E coast of French Indochina: now part of Vietnam. Also, **Anam.**

An·na·mese (an′ə mēz′, -mēs′), *adj., n., pl.* **-mese.** —*adj.* **1.** of or pertaining to Annam, its people, or their language. —*n.* Also, **An·nam·ite** (an′ə mīt′). **2.** a native of Annam. **3.** former name of the Vietnamese language.

An·nan·dale (an′ən dāl′), *n.* a town in E Virginia, near Washington, D.C. 27,405 (1970).

An·nap·o·lis (ə nap′ə lis), *n.* a seaport in and the capital of Maryland, in the central part, on Chesapeake Bay: U.S. Naval Academy. 30,095 (1970).

Annap′olis Roy′al, a town in W Nova Scotia, in SE Canada, on an arm of the Bay of Fundy: the first settlement in Canada 1605. 800 (1961). Formerly, **Port Royal.**

An·na·pur·na (an′ə po͝or′nə, -pûr′-; *also, for 1, Skt.* un′nə po͞or′nä), *n.* **1.** *Hinduism.* Devi (def. 2). **2.** a mountain in N Nepal, in the Himalayas. 26,503 ft.

Ann Ar·bor (an är′bər), a city in SE Michigan. 99,797 (1970).

an·nat·to (ə nat′ō, ə nä′tō), *n., pl.* **-tos. 1.** a small tree, *Bixa Orellana,* of tropical America. **2.** Also, **arnatto.** a yellowish-red dye obtained from the pulp enclosing the seeds of this tree. Also, **anatto.** [< Carib]

Anne (an), *n.* 1665–1714, queen of England 1702–14 (daughter of James II of England).

an·neal (ə nēl′), *v.t.* **1.** to free (glass, earthenware, metals, etc.) from internal stress by heating and gradually cooling. **2.** to toughen or temper, as the mind. **3.** *Obs.* to fuse colors onto (a vitreous or metallic surface) by heating. [ME *anele(n),* OE *anǣlan* to kindle = *an-* ON + *ǣlan* to burn, akin to *āl* fire] —**an·neal′er,** *n.*

An·ne·cy (anᵊ sē′), *n.* a city in SE France. 45,715 (1962).

an·ne·lid (an′ᵊlid), *n.* **1.** any segmented worm of the phylum *Annelida,* including the earthworms, leeches, and various marine forms. —*adj.* **2.** belonging or pertaining to the *Annelida.* Also, **an·nel·i·dan** (ə nel′i dᵊn). [back formation from ANNELIDA]

An·nel·i·da (ə nel′i də), *n.* the phylum comprising the annelids. [< NL = *annel-* (< F *annel(és),* lit., ringed ones, pl. ptp. of *anneler* to ring < OF *an(n)el* ring < L *annell(us),* dim. of *anus* anus, orig. ring) + *-ida* -ID²]

Anne′ of Aus′tria, 1601–66, queen consort of Louis XIII of France: regent during minority of her son, Louis XIV.

Anne′ of Bohe′mia, 1366–94, queen consort of Richard II of England.

Anne′ of Brit′tany, 1477–1514, wife of Maximilian I of Austria 1490–91; queen consort of Charles VIII of France 1491–98; queen consort of Louis XII of France 1499–1514. French, **Anne de Bre·tagne** (An də brə tAnyᵊ).

Anne′ of Cleves′ (klēvz), 1515–57, fourth wife of Henry VIII of England.

Anne′ of France′, (*Anne de Beaujeu*) 1460–1522, daughter of Louis XI of France: regent during the minority of her brother, Charles VIII, 1483–91.

an·nex (*v.* ə neks′; *n.* an′eks), *v.t.* **1.** to attach, subjoin, append, or add, esp. to something larger or more important: *Germany annexed part of Czechoslovakia.* **2.** to attach as an attribute, concomitant, or consequence. —*n.* Also, *esp. Brit.,* **an′nexe. 3.** something annexed. **4.** a subsidiary building, either attached to or separate from the main building. **5.** something added to a document; appendix; supplement. [late ME < ML *annex(āre)* < L *annexus* tied to, ptp. of *annectere* = *an-* AN-² + *nect-* bind] —**an·nex′a·ble,** *adj.*

an·nex·a·tion (an′ək sā′shən, -ek-), *n.* **1.** the act or an instance of annexing, esp. new territory. **2.** the fact of being annexed. **3.** something annexed. [< ML *annexātiōn-* (s. of *annexātiō*) = *annexāt(us)* joined to (ptp. of *annexāre;* see ANNEX, -ATE¹) + *-iōn-* -ION] —**an′nex·a′tion·al,** *adj.* —**an′nex·a′tion·ism,** *n.* —**an′nex·a′tion·ist,** *n.*

An·nie Oak·ley (an′ē ōk′lē), *U.S. Slang.* a free ticket of admittance, as to a theater. [after similarity between a punched ticket and a playing card shot through by *Annie Oakley* (1860–1926), American sharpshooter]

an·ni·hi·late (ə nī′ə lāt′), *v.t.,* **-lat·ed, -lat·ing. 1.** to reduce to utter ruin or nonexistence; destroy utterly: *The bombing annihilated the city.* **2.** to destroy the collective existence or main body of: *to annihilate an army.* **3.** to annul or nullify. [< LL *annihilāt(us)* brought to nothing, annihilated (ptp. of *annihilāre*) (L *an-* AN-² + *nihil* nothing + *-ātus* -ATE¹)] —**an·ni·hi·la·tive** (ə nī′ə lā′tiv, -ə lə-), **an·ni·hi·la·to·ry** (ə nī′ə lə tôr′ē, -tōr′ē), *adj.* —**an·ni′hi·la′tor,** *n.* —**Syn. 1.** devastate, desolate. **1, 2.** obliterate, demolish.

an·ni·hi·la·tion (ə nī′ə lā′shən), *n.* **1.** the act or an instance of annihilating. **2.** the state of being annihilated. **3.** *Physics.* **a.** Also called **pair annihilation.** the process in which a particle and antiparticle unite, annihilate each other, and produce one or more photons. Cf. **positronium. b.** the conversion of rest mass into energy in the form of electromagnetic radiation. [< LL *annihilātiōn-* (s. of *annihilātiō*)]

An·nis·ton (an′i stən), *n.* a city in E Alabama. 31,533 (1970).

anniv., anniversary.

an·ni·ver·sa·ry (an′ə vûr′sə rē), *n., pl.* **-ries,** *adj.* —*n.* **1.** the yearly recurrence of the date of a past event, esp. the date of a wedding. **2.** the celebration or commemoration of such a date. —*adj.* **3.** returning or recurring each year; annual. **4.** pertaining to an anniversary. [ME < L *anniversāri(us)* returning every year = *anni-* (comb. form of *annus* year) + *vers(us)* turned, ptp. of *vertere* (*vert-* turn + *-tus* ptp. suffix) + *-ārius* -ARY]

an·no Dom·i·ni (an′ō dom′ə nī′, -nē′, ä′nō). See **A.D.**

an·no He·ji·rae (an′ō hi jī′rē, hej′ə rē′, ä′nō). See **A.H.**

an·no mun·di (än′nō mo͞on′dē; *Eng.* an′ō mun′dī), *Latin.* in the year of the world.

an·no reg·ni (än′nō reg′nē; *Eng.* an′ō reg′nī), *Latin.* in the year of the reign.

annot., **1.** annotated. **2.** annotation. **3.** annotator.

an·no·tate (an′ō tāt′), *v.,* **-tat·ed, -tat·ing.** —*v.t.* **1.** to supply (a text) with critical or explanatory notes. —*v.i.* **2.** to make annotations. [< L *annotāt(us)* noted down (ptp. of *annotāre*) = *an-* AN-² + *notātus* noted, marked; see NOTE, -ATE¹] —**an′no·ta′tive, an·no·ta·to·ry** (an′ə tā′tə rē, -tə-tôr′ē, -tōr′ē; ə nō′tə tôr′ē, -tōr′ē), *adj.* —**an′no·ta′tor,** *n.*

an·no·ta·tion (an′ō tā′shən), *n.* **1.** the act of annotating. **2.** a critical or explanatory note added to a text. **3.** note (def. 1). *Abbr.:* annot. [< L *annotātiōn-* (s. of *annotātiō*)]

an·nounce (ə nouns′), *v.,* **-nounced, -nounc·ing.** —*v.t.* **1.** to declare or make known publicly, openly, or officially; give notice of. **2.** to make known to the mind or senses. **3.** to state the approach or presence of. **4.** to serve as an announcer for. —*v.i.* **5.** to be employed or serve as an announcer, esp. of a radio or television broadcast. **6.** to declare one's candidacy, as for a public office (usually fol. by *for*). [late ME *anounce* < MF *anoncer* < L *annūntiāre* = *an-* AN-² + *nūntiāre* to announce < *nūntius* messenger] —**an·nounce′a·ble,** *adj.*

—**Syn. 1.** declare, report, promulgate. ANNOUNCE, PROCLAIM mean to communicate something in a formal or public way. To ANNOUNCE is to give out news, often of something expected in the future: *to announce a lecture series.* To PROCLAIM is to make a widespread and general announcement of something of public interest: *to proclaim a holiday.*

an·nounce·ment (ə nouns′mənt), *n.* **1.** public or formal notice announcing something. **2.** the act of announcing. **3.** a short message or commercial, esp. as spoken on radio or television. **4.** a card or piece of formal stationery containing a formal declaration of an event, as of a wedding. [< MF *anoncement*]

an·nounc·er (ə noun′sər), *n.* a person who announces, esp. one who introduces programs, reads advertisements, etc., over radio or television.

an·no ur·bis con·di·tae (än′nō o͞or′bis kōn′di tī′; *Eng.* an′ō ûr′bis kon′di tē′), *Latin.* See **A.U.C.** (def. 2).

an·noy (ə noi′), *v.t.* **1.** to disturb (a person) in a way that displeases, troubles, or slightly irritates. **2.** *Mil.* to molest; harm. —*v.i.* **3.** to be hateful or troublesome. [ME *anoi* < OF, var. of *enui* < L phrase *in odiō* in ill will; see IN-², ODIUM, ENNUI] —**an·noy′er,** *n.* —**Syn. 1.** See **bother, worry.**

an·noy·ance (ə noi′əns), *n.* **1.** a person or thing that annoys; nuisance. **2.** the act or an instance of annoying. **3.** the feeling of being annoyed. [ME < MF]

an·noy·ing (ə noiʹing), *adj.* causing annoyance. [ME] —**an·noyʹing·ly,** *adv.*

an·nu·al (anʹyo͞o əl), *adj.* **1.** of, for, or pertaining to a year; yearly: *the annual enrollment in high schools.* **2.** occurring or returning once a year: *an annual celebration.* **3.** performed or executed during a year: *the annual course of the sun.* **4.** *Bot.* living only one growing season, as beans or corn. **5.** *Entomol.* living or lasting but one season or year, as certain insects. —*n.* **6.** a plant living only one year or season. **7.** a book, report, etc., published annually. [< LL *annuāl(is)* = L *annu(us)* yearly (< *annus* circuit of the sun, year) + *-ālis* -AL[1]; r. ME *annuel* < MF] —**anʹnu·al·ly,** *adv.*

anʹnual parʹallax. See under **parallax** (def. 2).

anʹnual ringʹ, an annual formation of two concentric layers of wood in plants, one springwood and one summerwood.

an·nu·i·tant (ə no͞oʹi tənt, ə nyo͞oʹ-), *n.* a person who receives an annuity.

an·nu·it coep·tis (änʹno͞o it koipʹtis; *Eng.* anʹyo͞o it sepʹtis), *Latin.* He (God) has favored our undertakings: a motto on the reverse of the great seal of the U.S. (adapted from Vergil's *Aeneid* IX: 625).

an·nu·i·ty (ə no͞oʹi tē, ə nyo͞oʹ-), *n., pl.* **-ties. 1.** a specified income payable at stated intervals for a fixed or a contingent period, often for the recipient's life, in consideration of a stipulated premium paid either in prior installment payments or in a single payment. **2.** the right to receive such an income, or the duty to make such a payment or payments. [late ME *annuitee* < MF *annuite* < ML *annuitāt-* (s. of *annuitās*) = L *annu(us)* yearly + *-itāt-* -ITY]

an·nul (ə nulʹ), *v.t.,* **-nulled, -nul·ling. 1.** (esp. of laws or other established rules, usages, etc.) to make void or null; abolish; invalidate: *to annul a marriage.* **2.** to reduce to nothing; obliterate. [late ME < LL *annull(āre)* = *an-* AN-[2] + *nullāre* to reduce to nothing < L *nūllum* nothing, neut. of *nūllus* none] —**an·nulʹla·ble,** *adj.*

an·nu·lar (anʹyə lər), *adj.* having the form of a ring. [< L *annulār(is)* = *annul(us)* ring (var. of *ānulus*) + *-āris* -AR[1]] —**an·nu·lar·i·ty** (anʹyə larʹi tē), *n.* —**anʹnu·lar·ly,** *adv.*

anʹnular eclipseʹ, *Astron.* an eclipse of the sun in which a portion of its surface is visible as a ring surrounding the dark moon. Cf. **total eclipse.**

anʹnular ligʹament, *Anat.* the ligamentous envelope surrounding a part, as the joints of the wrist or ankle.

an·nu·late (anʹyə lit, -lātʹ), *adj.* **1.** formed of ringlike segments, as an annelid. **2.** having rings or ringlike bands. Also, **anʹnu·latʹed.** [< L *annulāt(us),* var. of *ānulātus* ringed = *annul(us),* var. of *ānul(us)* ring + *-ātus* -ATE[1]]

an·nu·la·tion (anʹyə lāʹshən), *n.* **1.** formation with or into rings. **2.** a ringlike formation or part.

an·nu·let (anʹyə lit), *n.* **1.** *Archit.* an encircling band, molding, or fillet, as on the shaft of a column. **2.** *Heraldry.* a ring, represented as a voided roundel, used esp. as the cadency mark of a fifth son. [< L *annul(us)* ring + -ET; r. earlier *anlet* < MF *anelet,* dim. of OF *anel* ring < L *anell(us)* ring]

an·nul·ment (ə nulʹmənt), *n.* **1.** the act of annulling, esp. the formal declaration that annuls a marriage. **2.** *Psychoanal.* a mental process by which painful ideas are abolished.

an·nu·lose (anʹyə lōsʹ), *adj.* having a part, structure, or markings composed of or resembling rings or bands: *annulose animals.* [< NL *annulōs(us)*]

an·nu·lus (anʹyə ləs), *n., pl.* **-li** (-līʹ), **-lus·es. 1.** a ring or ringlike part, band, or space. **2.** *Geom.* the space between two concentric circles on a plane. [< L, var. of *ānulus* = *ān(us)* ring + *-ulus* -ULE]

an·nun·ci·ate (ə nunʹsē ātʹ, -shē-), *v.t.,* **-at·ed, -at·ing.** to announce. [< ML *annunciātus,* sp. var. of L *annuntiātus,* ptp. of *annuntiāre* to make known. See ANNOUNCE, -ATE[1]] —**an·nunʹci·a·ble,** *adj.* —**an·nunʹci·aʹtive, an·nun·ci·a·to·ry** (ə nunʹsē ə tôrʹē, -tōrʹē), *adj.*

an·nun·ci·a·tion (ə nunʹsē āʹshən, -shē-), *n.* **1.** (*cap.*) the announcement by the angel Gabriel to the Virgin Mary of the incarnation of Christ. **2.** (*cap.*) Also called **Lady Day.** the church festival on March 25 in memory of this. **3.** the act or an instance of announcing. [late ME < eccl. L *annunciātiōn-* (s. of *annunciātiō*)]

an·nun·ci·a·tor (ə nunʹsē āʹtər, -shē-), *n.* **1.** an announcer. **2.** *U.S.* an electrical signaling apparatus that displays a visual indication, usually when a buzzer is rung. [ANNUNCIATE + -OR[2]; r. earlier *annuntiator* < L]

An·nun·zio, d' (dän no͞onʹtsyô), **Ga·bri·e·le** (gäʹbrē eʹle). See **D'Annunzio, Gabriele.**

an·nus mi·ra·bi·lis (änʹno͝os mi räʹbi lis; *Eng.* anʹəs mə rabʹə lis), *pl.* **an·ni mi·ra·bi·les** (änʹnē mi räʹbi lesʹ; *Eng.* anʹī mə rabʹə lēzʹ). *Latin.* year of wonders.

ano-[1], a combining form of **anus** or **anal.**

ano-[2], a learned borrowing from Greek meaning "up," "upper," "upward": *anoopsia.* [< Gk, comb. form of *ánō*]

an·ode (anʹōd), *n.* **1.** the electrode or terminal by which current enters an electrolytic cell, voltaic cell, battery, etc. **2.** the negative terminal of a voltaic cell or battery. **3.** the positive terminal, electrode, or element of an electron tube or electrolytic cell. [< Gk *ánod(os)* way up = *an-* AN-[3] + *hodós* a way, path, road]

an·od·ic (an odʹik), *adj.* pertaining to an anode or the phenomena in its vicinity. —**an·odʹi·cal·ly,** *adv.*

an·o·dize (anʹə dīzʹ), *v.t.,* **-dized, -diz·ing.** *Chem.* to coat a metal, esp. magnesium or aluminum, with a protective film by chemical or electrolytic means.

an·o·dyne (anʹə dīn), *n.* **1.** a medicine that relieves or allays pain. **2.** anything that relieves distress. —*adj.* **3.** relieving pain. **4.** soothing to the mind or feelings. [< L *anōdyn(us)* < Gk *anṓdynos* painless = *an-* AN-[1] + *ōdyn-* (akin to *odýnē* pain) + *-os* adj. suffix]

a·noint (ə nointʹ), *v.t.* **1.** to put oil on; apply an unguent or oily liquid to. **2.** to smear with any liquid. **3.** to consecrate by applying oil. [ME *anoynte(n)* < *anoynt,* var. of *enoynt* (ptp.) < F *enoint* < L *inunct(us)* anointed (ptp. of *inungere*) = *in-* IN-[2] + *ung-* smear with oil + *-tus* ptp. suffix] —**a·nointʹer,** *n.* —**a·nointʹment,** *n.*

an·o·lyte (anʹə lītʹ), *n.* the portion of the electrolyte in the immediate vicinity of the anode during electrolysis. [ANO(DE) + (ELECTRO)LYTE]

a·nom·a·lism (ə nomʹə lizʹəm), *n.* *Rare.* **1.** the state or quality of being anomalous. **2.** an anomaly. [< L *anōmal(us)* (see ANOMALOUS) + -ISM]

a·nom·a·lis·tic (ə nomʹə lisʹtik), *adj.* of or pertaining to an anomaly. [< L *anōmal(us)* (see ANOMALOUS) + -ISTIC] —**a·nomʹa·lisʹti·cal·ly,** *adv.*

a·nom·a·lous (ə nomʹə ləs), *adj.* **1.** deviating from the common rule, method, or form; abnormal. **2.** deviating from the common type; inconsistent with the accepted or expected: *He held an anomalous position in the world of art.* **3.** incongruous or inconsistent. [< L *anōmalus* < Gk *anṓmalos* irregular = *an-* AN-[1] + *homalós* even; see HOMO-, -OUS] —**a·nomʹa·lous·ly,** *adv.* —**a·nomʹa·lous·ness,** *n.*

a·nom·a·ly (ə nomʹə lē), *n., pl.* **-lies. 1.** a deviation from the common rule, type, or form. **2.** someone or something anomalous. **3.** an odd, peculiar, or strange condition, situation, quality, or the like. **4.** an incongruity or inconsistency. **5.** *Astron.* the angular distance of an orbiting planet from its perihelion. [< L *anōmalia* < Gk *anōmalía* = *anōmal-* (see ANOMALOUS) + *-ia* -IA] —**Syn. 1, 2.** abnormality.

an·o·mie (anʹə mēʹ), *n.* *Sociol.* a state or condition of individuals or society characterized by a breakdown or absence of social norms and values, as in the case of uprooted people. Also, **anʹo·myʹ.** [< F < Gk *anomía* lawlessness. See A-[6], -NOMY] —**a·nom·ic** (ə nomʹik), *adj.*

a·non (ə nonʹ), *adv.* *Archaic.* **1.** soon. **2.** at another time. **3.** immediately. **4. ever and anon,** now and then. [ME *anon, anoon,* OE *on āne* in ONE (course), i.e., straightway]

anon., anonymous.

an·o·nym (anʹə nim), *n.* **1.** an assumed or false name. **2.** an anonymous person or publication. [back formation from ANONYMOUS]

a·non·y·mous (ə nonʹə məs), *adj.* **1.** without any name acknowledged, as that of author, contributor, or the like: *an anonymous pamphlet.* **2.** of unknown name; whose name is withheld: *an anonymous author.* [< L *anōnymus* < Gk *anṓnymos* = *an-* AN-[1] + *ónym(a)* -ONYM + *-os* adj. suffix; see -OUS] —**an·o·nym·i·ty** (anʹə nimʹi tē), **a·nonʹy·mous·ness,** *n.* —**a·nonʹy·mous·ly,** *adv.*

an·o·op·si·a (anʹō opʹsē ə), *n.* *Ophthalm.* *Rare.* strabismus in which one or both eyes are turned upward. Also, **anʹo·öpʹsi·a, anopia, a·nop·si·a** (ən opʹsē ə). [< NL; see ANO-[2], -OPSIS, -IA]

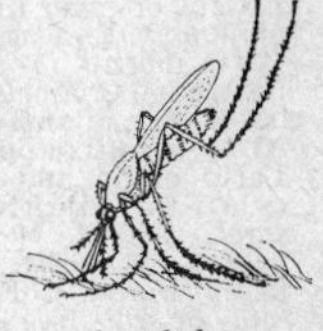
Anopheles, *Anopheles punctipennis* (Length ¼ in.)

a·noph·e·les (ə nofʹə lēzʹ), *n., pl.* **-les.** any mosquito of the genus *Anopheles,* certain species of which are vectors of the parasite causing malaria in man. [< NL < Gk *anōphelḗs* useless, hurtful, harmful = *an-* AN-[1] + *ōphelḗ(ein)* (to) help + *-ēs* adj. suffix]

an·o·pi·a (an ōʹpē ə), *n.* *Ophthalm.* **1.** absence of sight, esp. when due to a structural defect in or absence of an eye. **2.** anoopsia. [< NL < Gk *an-* AN[1]- + *ōp-* (s. of *ṓps*) eye + *-ia* -IA]

a·no·rak (äʹnə räkʹ), *n.* a jacket with a hood, as worn in the arctic. [< Eskimo *anoraq*]

an·o·rex·i·a (anʹə rekʹsē ə), *n.* **1.** lack of appetite and inability to eat. **2.** an eating disorder characterized by compulsive dieting and emaciation. [< NL < Gk = *an-* AN-[1] + *órex(is)* longing (*oreg-* reach after + *-sis* -SIS) + *-ia* -IA] —**an·o·rec·tic** (anʹə rekʹtik), **an·o·ret·ic** (anʹə retʹik), *adj.* —**anʹo·rexʹic,** *n., adj.*

an·or·thic (an ôrʹthik), *adj.* *Crystall.* triclinic. [AN-[1] + ORTH- + -IC]

an·or·thite (an ôrʹthīt), *n.* *Mineral.* the calcium end member of the plagioclase group, a rare mineral that alters easily. [AN-[1] + ORTH- + -ITE[1]] —**an·or·thit·ic** (anʹôr thitʹik), *adj.*

an·os·mi·a (an ozʹmē ə, -osʹ-), *n.* *Pathol.* loss of the sense of smell. [< NL < Gk *an-* AN-[1] + *osm(ḗ)* smell (akin to *ózein* to smell) + *-ia* -IA] —**an·os·mat·ic** (anʹoz matʹik), **an·osʹmic,** *adj.*

an·oth·er (ə nuthʹər), *adj.* **1.** being one more or more of the same; further; additional: *another piece of cake.* **2.** different; distinct; of a different kind: *at another time; another man.* —*pron.* **3.** one more; an additional one: *Try another.* **4.** a different one; something different: *going from one house to another.* **5.** a person other than oneself or the one specified: *He told her he loved another.* **6. one another,** one (person or thing) in relation to another; each other: *Love one another.* [ME; see AN[1], OTHER]

an·oth·er-guess (ə nuthʹər gesʹ), *adj.* *Archaic.* of another kind. [var. of *anothergets, anothergates.* See *another*]

A·nouilh (A nweʹ), *n.* **Jean** (zhäN), 1910–1987, French dramatist.

an·o·vu·lant (anʹov yə lənt), *n.* a drug that inhibits ovulation. [AN-[1] + OVUL(ATE) + -ANT]

an·ox·e·mi·a (anʹok sēʹmē ə), *n.* *Med.* a deficiency of oxygen in the arterial blood. Also, **anʹox·aeʹmi·a.** [AN-[1] + OX(YGEN) + -EMIA] —**anʹox·eʹmic, anʹox·aeʹmic,** *adj.*

an·ox·i·a (an okʹsē ə, ə nokʹ-), *n.* *Med.* **1.** an abnormally low amount of oxygen in the body tissues. **2.** the mental and physical disturbances that occur as a result of hypoxia. [AN-[1] + OX(YGEN) + -IA] —**an·oxʹic,** *adj.*

ans., answer.

an·sate (anʹsāt), *adj.* having a handle or handlelike part. [< L *ansātus* = *ansa* handle + *-ātus* -ATE[1]]

anʹsate crossʹ, ankh.

An·schluss (änʹshlo͝os), *n.* union, esp. the forced political union of Austria with Germany in 1938. [< G: consolidation, joining together = *an-* on, to + *Schluss* a closing]

An·selm (anʹselm), *n.* **Saint,** 1033–1109, archbishop of Canterbury: scholastic theologian and philosopher.

an·ser·ine (anʹsə rīnʹ, -rin), *adj.* **1.** of or pertaining to the subfamily *Anserinae,* of the family *Anatidae,* comprising the true geese. **2.** resembling a goose. Also, **anʹser·ous.** [< L *anserīn(us)* of geese = *anser* a goose + *-īnus* -INE[1]]

an·swer (anʹsər, änʹ-), *n.* **1.** a spoken or written reply or response to a question, request, accusation, or communication. **2.** a correct response to a question asked to test one's knowledge. **3.** an action serving as a reply or response: *The answer was a volley of fire.* **4.** a solution to a problem, esp. in mathematics. **5.** *Law.* the defense by a defendant to a plaintiff's charge. **6.** *Music.* the imitation or exact repetition by one voice or instrument of a theme or phrase introduced by another. **—*v.i.*** **7.** to make answer; reply or respond by word or act. **8.** to be or declare oneself responsible or accountable (usually fol. by *for*): *I will answer for his safety.* **9.** to be satisfactory or serve (usually fol. by *for*): *to answer for a purpose.* **10.** to conform; correspond (usually fol. by *to*): *to answer to a description.* **—*v.t.*** **11.** to make answer to; reply or respond to: *to answer a person; to answer a question.* **12.** to act in reply or response to: *to answer the bell.* **13.** to solve or present a solution of. **14.** to serve or fulfill: *This will answer the purpose.* **15.** to conform or correspond to: *to answer a description.* **16.** to atone for; make amends for. [ME *andswerien,* OE *andswerian, andswarian* < *andswaru* an answer] **—an′swer·er,** *n.*

—Syn. 1. riposte. ANSWER, REJOINDER, REPLY, RESPONSE, RETORT are all words used to meet a question, remark, charge, etc. An ANSWER is a return remark: *an answer giving the desired information.* A REJOINDER is a quick, usually clever answer or remark made in reply to another's comment, not to a question. REPLY is somewhat more formal than ANSWER: *a reply to a letter.* A RESPONSE often suggests an answer to an appeal, exhortation, etc., or an expected or fixed reply: *a response to inquiry; a response in a church service.* A RETORT implies a keen, prompt answer, esp. one that turns a remark upon the person who made it: *a sharp retort.* **5.** plea.

an·swer·a·ble (an′sər ə bəl, än′-), *adj.* **1.** responsible, as to a person, for an act, etc.; liable. **2.** capable of being answered. **—an′swer·a·bil′i·ty, an′swer·a·ble·ness,** *n.* **—an′swer·a·bly,** *adv.*

ant (ant), *n.* **1.** any hymenopterous insect of the family *Formicidae,* comprising thousands of widely distributed species, all of which exhibit some degree of social organization. **2. have ants in one's pants,** *Slang.* to be impatient or eager to act or speak. [ME *am(e)te,* OE *ǣmette;* c. MLG *āmete,* OHG *āmeiza* (*ā-* prefix + *meizan* to beat, cut), G *Ameise*] **—ant′like′,** *adj.*

Ant, *Monomorium minimum* A, Male; B, Female

ant-, var. of **anti-** before a vowel or *h: antacid; anthelmintic.*

-ant, a suffix appearing in adjectives formed from verbs of Latin origin and in nouns formed from those adjectives (when the adjective form may not survive): *pleasant; constant; servant.* [< L *-ant-,* prp. s. of verbs in *-āre;* in many words < F *-ant* < L *-ant-* or *-ent-* (see -ENT); akin to ME, OE *-and-, -end-,* prp. suffix]

ant., antonym.

an't (ant, änt, ānt), **1.** *Chiefly Brit. Dial.* contraction of *am not.* **2.** *Dial.* ain't.

an·ta (an′tə), *n., pl.* **-tae** (-tē). *Archit.* a rectangular pier or pilaster, esp. one formed by thickening the end of a masonry wall. [deduced < L *antae* pilasters (in pl. only); akin to ANTE-]

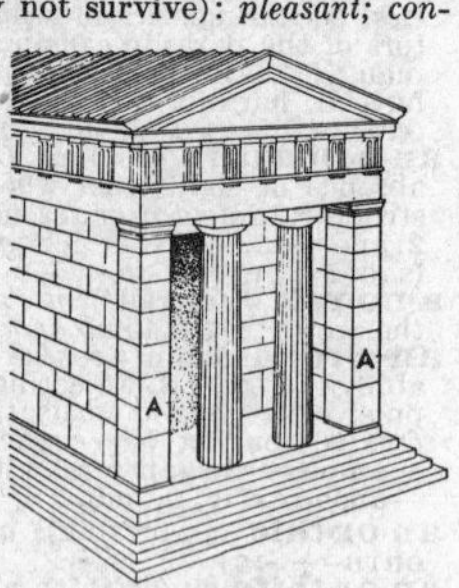

A, Anta

ANTA (an′tə), *n.* American National Theatre and Academy: a privately supported organization chartered by Congress 1935.

ant·ac·id (ant as′id), *adj.* **1.** neutralizing acidity, as of the stomach. **—*n.*** **2.** an antacid agent.

An·tae·us (an tē′əs), *n. Class. Myth.* a giant, invincible when in contact with the earth: crushed by Hercules when lifted into the air. **—An·tae′an,** *adj.*

an·tag·o·nise (an tag′ə nīz′), *v.t.,* **-nised, -nis·ing.** *Chiefly Brit.* antagonize. **—an·tag′o·nis′a·ble,** *adj.*

an·tag·o·nism (an tag′ə niz′əm), *n.* **1.** actively expressed hostility or opposition. **2.** an opposing force, principle, or tendency. [< Gk *antagōnism(a).* See ANTAGONIZE, -ISM]

an·tag·o·nist (an tag′ə nist), *n.* **1.** a person who is opposed to another; opponent; adversary. **2.** *Literature.* the adversary of the hero or of the protagonist. **3.** *Physiol.* a muscle that acts in opposition to another. Cf. **agonist** (def. 3). [< LL *antagōnist(a)* < Gk *antagōnistḗs.* See ANTAGONIZE, -IST] **—Syn. 1.** enemy, foe. See **adversary. —Ant. 1.** ally, friend.

an·tag·o·nis·tic (an tag′ə nis′tik), *adj.* **1.** acting in opposition; mutually opposing. **2.** hostile; unfriendly. **—an·tag′o·nis′ti·cal·ly,** *adv.*

an·tag·o·nize (an tag′ə nīz′), *v.t.,* **-nized, -niz·ing. 1.** to provoke or incur the hostility of; make an enemy or antagonist of: *His speech antagonized many voters.* **2.** to act in opposition to; oppose. Also, *esp. Brit.,* **antagonise.** [< Gk *antagōníz(esthai)* contend against. See ANT-, AGONIZE] **—an·tag′o·niz′a·ble,** *adj.*

An·ta·ki·ya (än tä kē′yä), *n.* Arabic name of **Antioch.**

ant·al·ka·li (ant al′kə lī′), *n., pl.* **-lis, -lies.** something that counteracts alkalis or alkalinity. Also, **antalkaline.**

ant·al·ka·line (ant al′kə lin′, -lin), *adj.* **1.** preventing or counteracting alkalinity. **—*n.*** **2.** antalkali.

An·tal·ya (än täl′yä), *n.* a seaport in SW Turkey. 71,632 (1965).

An·ta·na·na·ri·vo (än′tə nä′nə rē′vō, an′-), *n.* Tananarive.

ant·arc·tic (ant ärk′tik, -är′-), *adj.* **1.** of, at, or near the South Pole. **—*n.*** **2. the Antarctic,** the Antarctic Ocean and Antarctica. [< L *antarctic(us)* < Gk *antarktikós* (see ANT-, ARCTIC); r. ME *antartik* < ML *antartic(us)*]

Ant·arc·ti·ca (ant ärk′ti kə, -är′-), *n.* the continent surrounding the South Pole. ab. 5,000,000 sq. mi.

Antarc′tic Cir′cle, an imaginary line drawn parallel to the equator, at 23°28′ N of the South Pole.

Antarc′tic O′cean, the waters surrounding Antarctica, comprising the southernmost parts of the Pacific, Atlantic, and Indian Oceans.

Antarc′tic Penin′sula, a peninsula in Antarctica, S of South America. Cf. **Graham Land, Palmer Land.**

Antarc′tic Zone′, the section of the earth's surface lying between the Antarctic Circle and the South Pole.

An·tar·es (an târ′ēz), *n. Astron.* a red supergiant star of the first magnitude in the constellation Scorpius. [< Gk = *ant-* ANT- (in the sense of simulating) + *Ares* (Gk name of planet Mars); so called because it is like Mars in color]

ant′ bear′, 1. Also called **great anteater.** a large, terrestrial, tropical American edentate, *Myrmecophaga jubata,* feeding on ants and termites, and having a long, tapering snout and extensile tongue, powerful front claws, and a shaggy gray coat marked with a conspicuous black band. **2.** the aardvark.

Ant bear (2 ft. high at shoulder; total length 6 ft.; tail about 2 ft.)

an·te (an′tē), *n., v.,* **-ted** or **-teed, -te·ing. —*n.*** **1.** *Poker.* a fixed but arbitrary stake put into the pot by each player before the deal. **2.** *Slang.* the price or cost of something, as for membership in a group or enterprise. **—*v.t.*** **3.** *Poker.* to put (one's initial stake) into the pot. **4.** *Informal.* to produce or pay (usually fol. by *up*): *He anted up his half of the bill.* **—*v.i.*** **5.** *Poker.* to put one's initial stake into the pot. **6.** *Informal.* to pay (usually fol. by *up*). [< ANTE-]

ante-, a learned borrowing from Latin meaning "before," used in the formation of compound words: *anteroom; antebellum; antedate.* [< L, comb. form of prep. and adv. *ante;* akin to Gk *antí,* OE *and-* against, toward, opposite. See ANTI-]

ant·eat·er (ant′ē′tər), *n.* **1.** any of several mammals, esp. certain tropical American edentates feeding chiefly on ants and termites. Cf. **ant bear, tamandua. 2.** the aardvark. **3.** a pangolin. **4.** an echidna.

an·te·bel·lum (an′tē bel′əm), *adj.* **1.** before the war. **2.** *U.S.* before or existing before the American Civil War. [< L *ante bellum*]

an·te·cede (an′ti sēd′), *v.t.,* **-ced·ed, -ced·ing.** to go before, in time, order, etc.; precede: *Shakespeare antecedes Milton.* [< L *antecēd(ere)* (to) go before, precede, excel, surpass. See ANTE-, CEDE]

an·te·ced·ence (an′ti sēd′ᵊns), *n.* **1.** the act of going before; precedence. **2.** priority. **—an′te·ced′en·cy,** *n.*

an·te·ced·ent (an′ti sēd′ᵊnt), *adj.* **1.** existing, being, or going before; preceding; prior: *an antecedent event.* **—*n.*** **2.** a preceding circumstance, event, object, style, phenomenon, etc. **3. antecedents, a.** ancestors. **b.** the history, events, characteristics, etc., of one's earlier life. **4.** *Gram.* a word, phrase, or clause, usually a substantive, that is replaced by a pronoun usually at a later point, in a sentence or in a subsequent sentence. In *Jack lost his hat, Jack* is the antecedent of *his.* **5.** *Math.* the first term of a ratio; the first or third term of a proportion. **6.** *Logic.* the conditional element in a proposition. [ME < L *antecēdent-* (s. of *antecēdēns*) going before, prp. of *antecēd(ere)* (to) ANTECEDE; see -ENT] **—an′te·ced′ent·ly,** *adv.*

an·te·ces·sor (an′ti ses′ər), *n.* a person who goes before; predecessor. [late ME *antecessour* < L *antecessor* a predecessor = *antecess(us)* (ptp. of *antecēdere*) preceded (*ante-* ANTE- + *cēd-* go + *-tus* ptp. suffix) + *-or* -OR[2]]

an·te·cham·ber (an′tē chām′bər), *n.* a chamber or room that serves as a waiting room and entrance to a larger room or an apartment. [earlier *antichamber* < MF *antichambre* < It *anticamera* = *anti-* (< L *anti-,* var. of *ante-* ANTE-) + *camera* CHAMBER]

an·te-Chris·tum (an′tē kris′təm), *adj. Latin.* before Christ. *Abbr.:* A.C.

an·te·date (*v.* an′ti dāt′, an′ti dāt′; *n.* an′ti dāt′), *v.,* **-dat·ed, -dat·ing,** *n.* **—*v.t.*** **1.** to be of older date than; precede in time. **2.** predate (def. 1). **3.** to assign to an earlier date: *to antedate a historical event.* **4.** to cause to happen sooner; accelerate: *The cold weather antedated their departure from the country.* **5.** *Archaic.* to take or have in advance; anticipate. **—*n.*** **6.** a prior date.

an·te·di·lu·vi·an (an′tē di lo͞o′vē ən), *adj.* **1.** belonging to the period before the Flood. Gen. 7, 8. **2.** antiquated or primitive: *antediluvian ideas.* **—*n.*** **3.** a person who lived before the Flood. **4.** a very old or old-fashioned person. [ANTE- + L *dīluvi(um)* a flood + -AN]

ante′dilu′vian pa′triarch. See **patriarch** (def. 1).

an·te·fix (an′tə fiks′), *n., pl.* **-fix·es, -fix·a** (-fik′sə). *Archit.* an upright ornament at the eaves of a tiled roof. [< L *antefix(a),* neut. pl. of *antefixus* fastened in front = *ante-* ANTE- + *fixus* ptp. of *fīgere* to FIX] **—an′te·fix′al,** *adj.*

an·te·lope (an′tᵊlōp′), *n., pl.* **-lopes,** (*esp. collectively*) **-lope. 1.** any of several ruminants of the family *Bovidae,* found chiefly in Africa and Asia, having permanent, hollow, unbranched horns. **2.** leather made from the hide of such an animal. **3.** *U.S.* pronghorn. [late ME *antelop* < MF < ML *antalopus* < MGk *anthólops* fabulous beast] **—an′te·lo′pi·an, an·te·lo·pine** (an′tᵊlō′pin, -pīn), *adj.*

an·te·me·rid·i·an (an′tē mə rid′ē ən), *adj.* **1.** occurring before noon. **2.** of or pertaining to the forenoon.

an·te me·rid·i·em (an′tē mə rid′ē əm). See **a.m.**

an·te·mor·tem (an′tē môr′təm), *adj.* before death. [< L]

an·te·mun·dane (an′tē mun′dān), *adj.* before the creation of the world.

an·te·na·tal (an′tē nāt′ᵊl), *adj.* prenatal.

an·ten·na (an ten′ə), *n., pl.* **-ten·nas** for 1, **-ten·nae** (-ten′ē) for 2. **1.** *Radio.* a conductor by which electromagnetic waves are sent out or received; aerial. **2.** *Zool.* one of the jointed, movable, sensory appendages occurring in pairs on the heads of insects and most other arthropods. [< L: a sailyard] **—an·ten′nal,** *adj.*

an·ten·nule (an ten′yo͞ol), *n. Zool.* a small antenna. **—an·ten·nu·lar** (an ten′yə lər), **an·ten·nu·lar·y** (an ten′yə ler′ē), *adj.*

An·tep (än tep′), *n.* Aintab.

an·te par·tum (an′tē pär′təm), *Obstet.* of or noting the period prior to childbirth; before delivery. Also, **an′te·par′·tum, an′te-par′tum.** Cf. **post partum.** [< L]

an·te·pen·di·um (an′ti pen′dē əm), *n., pl.* **-di·a** (-dē ə). the decoration of the front of an altar, as a covering of silk or a painted panel. [< ML < L *ante* before + *pend(ēre)* (to) hang + *-ium* -IUM]

an·te·pe·nult (an′tē pē′nult, -pi nult′), *n.* the last syllable but two in a word, as *te* in *antepenult.* [< L *(syllaba) antepaenult(ima)* the second (syllable) from the last, fem. of *antepaenultimus* standing before the penult. See ANTE-, PENULT] —**an·te·pe·nul·ti·mate** (an′tē pi nul′tə mit), *adj., n.*

an·te·ri·or (an tēr′ē ər), *adj.* **1.** situated in or toward the front (opposed to *posterior*). **2.** going before in time: *an anterior age.* [< L, comp. of *ante* before, formed on model of POSTERIOR] —**an·te·ri·or·i·ty** (an tēr′ē ôr′i tē, -or′-), *n.* —**an·te′ri·or·ly,** *adv.*

antero-, a learned borrowing from Latin meaning "front," "fore." [< L **anter(us)* assumed positive of *anterior* + -o-; cf. ANTE-]

an·te·room (an′tē ro͞om′, -ro͝om′), *n.* **1.** a room that admits to a larger room. **2.** a waiting room.

an·te·type (an′tē tīp′), *n.* an earlier form; prototype.

an·te·vert (an′tē vûrt′), *v.t. Pathol.* to displace (the uterus) by tipping forward. [< L *antevert(ere)* (to) go before, precede = *ante* ANTE- + *vert(ere)* (to) turn] —**an·te·ver·sion** (an′tē vûr′zhən, -shən), *n.*

anth-, var. of **antho-,** esp. before a vowel.

An·theil (an′tīl), *n.* **George,** 1900–59, U.S. composer.

ant·he·li·on (ant hē′lē ən, an thē′-), *n., pl.* **-li·a** (-lē ə). a luminous, white spot occasionally appearing at the sun's elevation but in the opposite part of the sky. [< LGk *anthḗlion,* neut. of *anthḗlios* opposite the sun = *ant-* ANT- + *hḗli(os)* the sun + *-os* adj. suffix]

an·thel·min·tic (an′thel min′tik), *Med.* —*adj.* **1.** destroying or expelling intestinal worms. —*n.* **2.** an anthelmintic drug or medicine. [ANT- + HELMINT(H)IC]

an·them (an′thəm), *n.* **1.** a hymn, as of praise, devotion, or patriotism: *the national anthem of Spain.* **2.** a piece of sacred vocal music, usually with words taken from the Scriptures. **3.** a hymn sung alternately by different sections of a choir or congregation. —*v.t.* **4.** to celebrate with or in an anthem. [ME *antem,* OE *antemn(e), antefne* < VL *antefna* < LL *antifona* < Gk *antíphōna* ANTIPHON]

an·the·mi·on (an thē′mē ən), *n., pl.* **-mi·a** (-mē ə). an ornament of floral forms in a flat radiating cluster, as in architectural decoration, vase painting, etc. Also called **honeysuckle ornament.** [< Gk *anthémion* = *ánthem(on)* flower + *-ion* dim. suffix; see ANTHO-]

an·ther (an′thər), *n. Bot.* the pollen-bearing part of a stamen. [< NL *anthēr(a)* < L < Gk, fem. of *anthērós* flowery; see ANTHESIS] —**an′ther·al,** *adj.* —**an′ther·less,** *adj.*

an·ther·id·i·um (an′thə rid′ē əm), *n., pl.* **-ther·id·i·a** (-thə rid′ē ə). *Bot.* a male reproductive organ containing motile male gametes. [< NL] —**an′ther·id′i·al,** *adj.*

an·the·sis (an thē′sis), *n. Bot.* the period or act of expansion in flowers, esp. the maturing of the stamens. [< NL < Gk *ánthēsis* full bloom = *anthē(ein)* to bloom + *-sis* -SIS]

ant′ hill′, a mound of dirt, mud, leaves, etc., formed by a colony of ants in constructing their nest.

antho-, an element occurring in loan words from Greek (*anthology*); used with the meaning "flower" to form compound words: *anthocyanin.* Also, *esp. before a vowel,* **anth-.** [< Gk, comb. form of *ánthos* flower; akin to Skt *andha* herb, OIr *ainder* maiden]

an·tho·cy·a·nin (an′thə sī′ə nin), *n. Biochem.* any of a class of pigments, including most that give red and blue flowers their colors. Also, **an·tho·cy·an** (an′thə sī′ən).

an·tho·di·um (an thō′dē əm), *n., pl.* **-di·a** (-dē ə). *Bot.* a flower head or capitulum, esp. the head of a composite plant. [< NL < Gk *anthṓd(ēs)* flowerlike (*ánth(os)* a flower + *-ōdēs* -ODE[1]) + L *-ium* -IUM]

anthol., anthology.

an·thol·o·gise (an thol′ə jīz′), *v.i., v.t.,* **-gised, -gis·ing.** *Chiefly Brit.* anthologize.

an·thol·o·gize (an thol′ə jīz′), *v.,* **-gized, -giz·ing.** —*v.i.* **1.** to compile an anthology. —*v.t.* **2.** to include in an anthology.

an·thol·o·gy (an thol′ə jē), *n., pl.* **-gies. 1.** a book or other collection of selected writings by various authors, usually in the same literary form or on the same subject: *an anthology of drama; an anthology of philosophy.* **2.** a collection of selected writings by one author. [< L *anthologia* < Gk: collection of poems, lit., collection of flowers. See ANTHO-, -LOGY] —**an·tho·log·i·cal** (an′thə loj′i kəl), *adj.* —**an′·tho·log′i·cal·ly,** *adv.* —**an·thol′o·gist,** *n.*

An·tho·ny (an′tə nē, -thə- *for 1, 2;* an′thə nē *for 3*), *n.* **1.** See **Antony, Mark. 2. Saint,** A.D. 251?–356?, Egyptian hermit: founder of Christian monasticism. **3. Susan B(row·nell)** (brou nel′, brou′nel), 1820–1906, U.S. suffragist.

An′tho·ny of Pad′ua (an′tə nē, -thə-), **Saint,** 1195–1231, Franciscan monk and preacher in Italy and France.

an·tho·phore (an′thə fōr′, -fôr′), *n. Bot.* a form of floral stipe, produced by the elongation of the internode between the calyx and the corolla, and bearing the corolla, stamens, and pistil. [< Gk *anthophóros* flower-bearing, blooming. See ANTHO-, -PHORE]

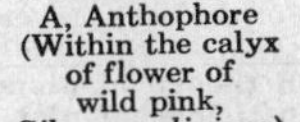

A, Anthophore (Within the calyx of flower of wild pink, *Silene caroliniana*)

-anthous, a combining form meaning "-flowered," used in the formation of compound adjectives. [< Gk *ánth(os)* flower + -OUS]

An·tho·zo·a (an′thə zō′ə), *n.* the class comprising the corals, sea anemones, sea pens, etc. [< NL]

an·tho·zo·an (an′thə zō′ən), *n.* **1.** any marine coelenterate of the class *Anthozoa,* comprising colonial and solitary polyps and including corals, sea anemones, sea pens, etc. —*adj.* **2.** Also, **an′tho·zo′ic.** belonging or pertaining to the *Anthozoa.*

anthrac-, a learned borrowing from Greek meaning "coal," "carbon," "carbuncle," used in the formation of compound words: *anthracnose; anthracoid.* Also, *esp. before a consonant,* **anthraco-.** [< L *anthrac-* < Gk *anthrak-* (s. of *ánthrax*). See ANTHRAX]

an·thra·cene (an′thrə sēn′), *n. Chem.* a powder, $C_6H_4(CH_2)C_6H_4$, used chiefly as a source of anthraquinone and alizarin, and in the process of measuring radioactive materials.

an·thra·cite (an′thrə sīt′), *n.* a mineral coal containing little of the volatile hydrocarbons and burning almost without flame; hard coal. Also called **an′thracite coal′.** Cf. **bituminous coal.** [< L *anthracītes* a kind of bloodstone < Gk *anthrakítēs,* lit., coallike] —**an·thra·cit·ic** (an′thrə sit′ik), **an·thra·cit·ous** (an′thrə sī′təs), *adj.*

an·thrac·nose (an thrak′nōs), *n. Plant Pathol.* a disease of plants, characterized by discolored lesions, caused by a fungus. [< F; see ANTHRAC-, NOS(O)-]

anthraco-, var. of **anthrac-** before a consonant.

an·thra·coid (an′thrə koid′), *adj.* **1.** resembling anthrax. **2.** resembling coal or charcoal.

an·thra·qui·none (an′thrə kwə nōn′, -kwē′nōn, -kwin′ōn), *n. Chem.* a yellow powder, $C_6H_4(CO_2)_2C_6H_4$, usually derived from anthracene or phthalic anhydride: used chiefly in the manufacture of dyes. [ANTHRA(CENE) + QUINONE]

an·thrax (an′thraks), *n., pl.* **-thra·ces** (-thrə sēz′). *Pathol.* **1.** a malignant, infectious disease of cattle, sheep, and other mammals, including man, caused by *Bacillus anthracis.* **2.** a malignant carbuncle that is the diagnostic lesion of anthrax in man. [< L *anthrax* carbuncle < Gk *ánthrax* (live) coal, carbuncle]

anthrop., 1. anthropological. **2.** anthropology.

anthropo-, a learned borrowing from Greek meaning "human," used in the formation of compound words: *anthropometry.* Also, *esp. before a vowel,* **anthrop-.** [< Gk *ánthrōpo(s)* man]

an·thro·po·cen·tric (an′thrə pō sen′trik), *adj.* **1.** regarding man as the central fact of the universe. **2.** assuming man to be the final aim of the universe. **3.** viewing and interpreting everything in terms of human experience and values. —**an′thro·po·cen′trism,** *n.*

an·thro·po·gen·e·sis (an′thrə pō jen′i sis), *n.* the genesis or development of the human race, esp. as a subject of scientific study. Also, **an·thro·pog·e·ny** (an′thrə poj′ə nē). —**an·thro·po·ge·net·ic** (an′thrə pō jə net′ik), **an′thro·po·gen′ic,** *adj.*

an·thro·pog·ra·phy (an′thrə pog′rə fē), *n.* the branch of anthropology that describes the varieties of mankind and their geographical distribution. —**an·thro·po·graph·ic** (an′·thrə pə graf′ik), *adj.*

an·thro·poid (an′thrə poid′), *adj.* **1.** Also, **an′thro·poi′·dal.** resembling man. —*n.* **2.** See **anthropoid ape.** [< Gk *anthrōpoeidḗs* in the shape of a man]

an′thropoid ape′, any tailless ape of the family *Pongidae,* anatomically resembling man, comprising the gorillas, chimpanzees, orangutans, and gibbons.

anthropol., anthropology.

an·thro·pol·o·gist (an′thrə pol′ə jist), *n.* a person who specializes in anthropology. [ANTHROPOLOG(Y) + -IST]

an·thro·pol·o·gy (an′thrə pol′ə jē), *n.* the science that deals with the origins, physical and cultural development, racial characteristics, and social customs and beliefs of mankind. —**an·thro·po·log·i·cal** (an′thrə pə loj′i kəl), **an′·thro·po·log′ic,** *adj.* —**an′thro·po·log′i·cal·ly,** *adv.*

an·thro·pom·e·try (an′thrə pom′i trē), *n.* the measurement of the size and proportions of the human body. —**an·thro·po·met·ric** (an′thrə pə me′trik, -pō-), **an′thro·po·met′ri·cal,** *adj.* —**an′thro·po·met′ri·cal·ly,** *adv.* —**an′thro·pom′e·trist,** *n.*

an·thro·po·mor·phic (an′thrə pə môr′fik, -pō-), *adj.* **1.** ascribing human form or attributes to a being or thing not human, esp. to a deity. **2.** resembling or made to resemble a human form: *an anthropomorphic carving.* Also, **anthropomorphous.** —**an′thro·po·mor′phi·cal·ly,** *adv.*

an·thro·po·mor·phise (an′thrə pə môr′fīz, -pō-), *v.t., v.i.,* **-phised, -phis·ing.** *Chiefly Brit.* anthropomorphize. —**an′thro·po·mor′phi·sa′tion,** *n.*

an·thro·po·mor·phism (an′thrə pə môr′fiz əm, -pō-), *n.* an anthropomorphic conception or representation, as of a deity. —**an′thro·po·mor′phist,** *n.*

an·thro·po·mor·phize (an′thrə pə môr′fīz, -pō-), *v.t., v.i.,* **-phized, -phiz·ing.** to ascribe human form or attributes to (an animal, plant, material object, or the like). [ANTHROPOMORPH(OUS) + -IZE] —**an′thro·po·mor′phi·za′tion,** *n.*

an·thro·po·mor·pho·sis (an′thrə pə môr′fə sis, -pō-), *n.* transformation into human form. [ANTHROPO- + (META)-MORPHOSIS]

an·thro·po·mor·phous (an′thrə pə môr′fəs, -pō-), *adj.* anthropomorphic. [< Gk *anthrōpómorphos* shaped like a man] —**an′thro·po·mor′phous·ly,** *adv.*

an·thro·pop·a·thy (an′thrə pop′ə thē), *n.* ascription of human passions or feelings to a being or beings not human, esp. to a deity. Also, **an′thro·pop′a·thism.** [< ML *anthropopatheia* < Gk *anthrōpopátheia* humanness] —**an·thro·po·path·ic** (an′thrə pə path′ik), *adj.*

an·thro·poph·a·gi (an′thrə pof′ə jī′), *n.pl., sing.* **-a·gus** (-ə gəs). cannibals. [< L, pl. of *anthrōpophagus* cannibal < Gk *anthrōpophágos* man-eating]

an·thro·poph·a·gite (an′thrə pof′ə jīt′), *n.* a cannibal. [< L *anthrōpophag(us)* + -ITE[1]]

an·thro·poph·a·gy (an′thrə pof′ə jē), *n.* the eating of human flesh; cannibalism. [< Gk *anthrōpophagía*] —**an·thro·po·phag·ic** (an′thrə pə faj′ik), **an′thro·po·phag′i·cal, an·thro·poph·a·gous** (an′thrə pof′ə gəs), *adj.* —**an′thro·poph′a·gous·ly,** *adv.*

an·thro·pos·co·py (an′thrə pos′kə pē), *n.* physiognomy (def. 2).

an·thro·pos·o·phy (an′thrə pos′ə fē), *n.* a spiritual and mystical philosophy based on the teachings of Rudolf Steiner. —**an·thro·po·soph·i·cal** (an′thrə pə sof′i kəl), **an′thro·po·soph′ic,** *adj.*

an·thu·ri·um (an tho͝or′ē əm), *n.* any tropical American, araceous plant of the genus *Anthurium,* certain species of which are cultivated for their showy leaves and flowers. [< NL *Anthurium* = *anth-* ANTH- + *-urium* < Gk *our(á)* tail + NL *-ium* n. suffix]

an·ti (an′tī, an′tē), *n., pl.* **-tis.** *Informal.* a person opposed to a particular practice, policy, action, etc. [< ANTI-]

anti-, a prefix from Greek meaning "against," "opposite of," freely combining with elements of any origin and used with the following particular meanings: "opposed," "in opposition to" (*antislavery*); "rival," "spurious," "pseudo-" (*antipope*); "opposite of," "reverse of" (*anti-hero*); "not," "un-" (*antispiritual*); "placed opposite" (*antipole*); "moving in a reverse direction" (*anticyclone*); "corrective," "preventive," "curative" (*antipyretic*). Also, *before a vowel,* **ant-.** [ME < L < Gk, comb. form of *antí;* akin to Skt *anti,* L *ante,* E *an-* in *answer.* Cf. ANTE-]

an·ti·air·craft (an′tē âr′kraft′, -kräft′, an′tī-), *adj.* **1.** designed for or used in defense against enemy aircraft. —*n.* **2.** artillery used against enemy aircraft.

an·ti·al·co·hol·ism (an′tē al′kə hô liz′əm, -ho-, an′tī-), *n.* opposition to excessive use of alcoholic beverages. —**an′ti·al′co·hol′ic,** *adj.*

an·ti-A·mer·i·can (an′tē ə mer′i kən, an′tī-), *adj.* **1.** opposed or hostile to the U.S., its principles, or its policies. —*n.* **2.** an anti-American person. —**An′ti-A·mer′i·can·ism,** *n.*

an·ti·ar (an′tē är′), *n.* **1.** the upas tree. **2.** Also, **an·ti·a·rin** (an′tē ər in). an arrow poison prepared from the sap of the upas tree. [< Javanese]

an·ti·bac·chi·us (an′ti bə kī′əs), *n., pl.* **-chi·i** (-kī′ī). *Pros.* a foot of three syllables that in quantitative meter consists of two long syllables followed by a short one, and that in accentual meter consists of two stressed syllables followed by an unstressed one. Cf. **bacchius.** [< L < Gk *antibák-cheios*] —**an·ti·bac·chic** (an′ti bak′ik), *adj.*

An·tibes (äɴ tēb′), *n.* a seaport in SE France, SW of Nice: resort; ruins of 4th century B.C. Roman town. 35,976 (1962).

an·ti·bi·o·sis (an′tē bī ō′sis, an′tī-), *n. Biol.* an association between organisms that is injurious to one of them.

an·ti·bi·ot·ic (an′ti bī ot′ik, -bē-, an′tē-, -tī-), *n.* **1.** *Biochem.* any of a large group of chemical substances, as penicillin or streptomycin, produced by various microorganisms and fungi, having the capacity in dilute solutions to inhibit the growth of or to destroy bacteria and other microorganisms: used in the treatment of infectious diseases. —*adj.* **2.** of or involving antibiotics. —**an′ti·bi·ot′i·cal·ly,** *adv.*

an·ti·blas·tic (an′tē blas′tik, an′tī-), *adj. Biol.* antagonistic to growth.

an·ti·bod·y (an′ti bod′ē, an′tē-), *n., pl.* **-bod·ies.** a protein naturally existing in blood serum or produced in response to stimulation by an antigen, that reacts to overcome the toxicity of a specific antigen.

an·tic (an′tik), *n., adj., v.,* **-ticked, -tick·ing.** —*n.* **1.** Usually, **antics. a.** playful tricks or pranks. **b.** grotesque, fantastic, or ludicrous gestures or postures. **2.** *Archaic.* **a.** an actor in a grotesque or ridiculous presentation. **b.** a buffoon; clown. **3.** *Obs.* **a.** a grotesque theatrical presentation; ridiculous interlude. **b.** a grotesque or fantastic sculptured figure, as a gargoyle. —*adj.* **4.** *Archaic.* fantastic; odd; whimsical. —*v.i.* **5.** to perform antics; caper. [earlier *antike* < L *antīc(us)* primitive = *anti-* (var. of *ante* before) + *-icus* -IC. See ANTIQUE] —**an′tic·ly,** *adv.*

an·ti·cat·a·lyst (an′tē kat′əlist, an′tī-), *n. Chem.* an inhibitor. —**an′ti·cat′a·lyt′ic,** *adj.*

an·ti·cath·ode (an′tē kath′ōd, an′tī-), *n.* the positive plate of an electron tube, serving as the target for electrons coming from the cathode.

an·ti·chlor (an′ti klōr′, -klôr′), *n. Chem.* any of various substances, esp. sodium thiosulfate, used for removing excess chlorine from paper pulp, textile fiber, etc., after bleaching. [ANTI- + CHLOR(INE)] —**an·ti·chlo·ris·tic** (an′ti klō ris′tik, -klô-), *adj.*

an·ti·cho·lin·er·gic (an′ti kō′li nûr′jik), *Med.* —*adj.* **1.** preventing the action of acetylcholine. —*n.* **2.** an anticholinergic substance. [ANTI- + *cholinergic* = CHOLIN(E) + ERG- + -IC]

An·ti·christ (an′ti krīst′), *n. Theol.* **1.** a personage or power conceived of as appearing in the world as the principal antagonist of Christ. **2.** (*sometimes l.c.*) any opponent of Christ. **3.** a false Christ. [< LL *Antichrīst(us)* < LGk *Antíchrīstos* the Antichrist] —**an·ti·chris·tian** (an′tē-kris′chən, an′tī-), *adj., n.* —**an′ti·chris′tian·ly,** *adv.*

an·tic·i·pant (an tis′ə pənt), *adj.* **1.** anticipative. —*n.* **2.** a person who anticipates. [< L *anticipant-* (s. of *anticipāns,* prp. of *anticipāre*) taking before = *anti-* (var. of *ante* before) + *-cip-* (var. of *cap-* take) + *-ant-* -ANT]

an·tic·i·pate (an tis′ə pāt′), *v.t.,* **-pat·ed, -pat·ing. 1.** to realize beforehand; foresee. **2.** to expect: *to anticipate a favorable decision.* **3.** to perform (an action) before another has had time to act. **4.** to foresee and act in advance of. **5.** to cause to occur earlier than in the normal course of events. **6.** to nullify, prevent, or forestall by taking countermeasures in advance: *to anticipate a blow.* [< L *anticipāt(us)* taken before, anticipated (ptp. of *anticipāre*) = *anti-* (var. of *ante* before) + *-cip-* (var. of *cap-* take) + *-ātus* -ATE[1]] —**an·tic′i·pat′a·ble,** *adj.* —**an·tic′i·pa′tive,** *adj.* —**an·tic′i·pa′tive·ly,** *adv.* —**an·tic′i·pa′tor,** *n.* —**Syn. 1.** See **expect.**

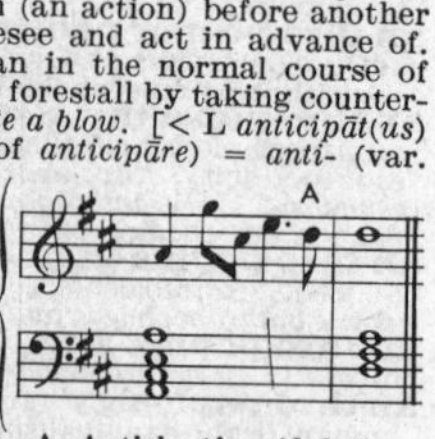

A, Anticipation (def. 5)

an·tic·i·pa·tion (an tis′ə pā′shən), *n.* **1.** the act of anticipating. **2.** the state of being anticipated. **3.** realization in advance; expectation; hope. **4.** intuition, foreknowledge, or prescience. **5.** *Music.* a tone introduced in advance of its harmony so that it sounds against the preceding chord. [< L *anticipātiōn-* (s. of *anticipātiō*) = *anticipāt(us)* (ptp.; see ANTICIPATE) + *-iōn-* -ION]

an·tic·i·pa·to·ry (an tis′ə pə tōr′ē, -tôr′ē), *adj.* of, showing, or expressing anticipation. [< L *anticipātor* (see ANTICIPATE, -OR[2]) + -Y[1]; see -ORY[1]] —**an·tic′i·pa·to′ri·ly,** *adv.*

an·ti·clas·tic (an′tē klas′tik, an′tī-), *adj. Math.* (of a surface) having principal curvatures of opposite sign at a given point. Cf. **synclastic.**

an·ti·cler·i·cal (an′tē kler′i kəl, an′tī-), *adj.* opposed to the influence and activities of the clergy in public affairs. —**an′ti·cler′i·cal·ism,** *n.*

an·ti·cli·max (an′ti klī′maks), *n.* **1.** an event, conclusion, statement, or the like, that is far less important, powerful, or striking than expected. **2.** a noticeable or ludicrous descent in discourse from lofty ideas or expressions to banalities or commonplace remarks. —**an·ti·cli·mac·tic** (an′ti klī mak′tik), *adj.* —**an′ti·cli·mac′ti·cal·ly,** *adv.*

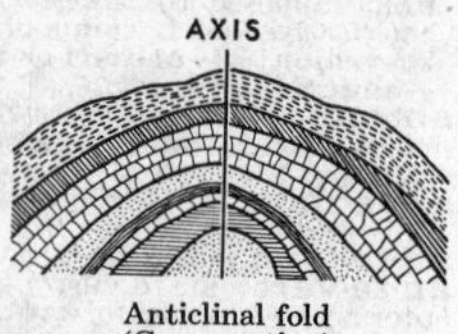

AXIS

Anticlinal fold (Cross section)

an·ti·cli·nal (an′ti klīn′əl) *adj. Geol.* **1.** inclining downward on both sides from a median line or axis, as a fold of rock strata. **2.** pertaining to such a fold. [< Gk *antiklīn(ein)* (to) lean against each other (*anti-* ANTI- + *klīnein* to lean) + -AL[1]]

an·ti·cline (an′ti klīn′), *n. Geol.* an anticlinal rock structure. [back formation from ANTICLINAL]

an·ti·co·ag·u·lant (an′tē kō ag′yə lənt, an′tī-), *Med.* —*adj.* **1.** Also, **an·ti·co·ag·u·la·tive** (an′tē kō ag′yə lā′-tiv, an′tī-). preventing coagulation, esp. of blood. —*n.* **2.** an anticoagulant agent, as heparin.

An′ti-Com′in·tern Pact′ (an′tē kom′in tûrn′, -kom′-in tûrn′, an′tī-), an agreement in 1936 between Germany, Japan, and Italy to oppose the Comintern.

an·ti·com·mu·ta·tive (an′tē kə myōō′tə tiv, -kom′yə-tā′-, an′tī-), *adj. Math.* (of a binary operation) having the property that one term operating on a second is equal to the negative of the second operating on the first, as $ab = -ba$.

an·ti·cor·ro·sive (an′tē kə rō′siv, an′tī-), *n.* **1.** something that prevents or counteracts corrosion. —*adj.* **2.** preventing or counteracting corrosion. —**an′ti·cor·ro′sive·ly,** *adv.* —**an′ti·cor·ro′sive·ness,** *n.*

An·ti·cos·ti (an′tə kô′stē, -kos′tē), *n.* an island at the head of the Gulf of St. Lawrence in E Canada, in E Quebec province. 135 mi. long; 3043 sq. mi.

an·ti·cy·clone (an′ti sī′klōn), *n. Meteorol.* a circulation of winds around a central region of high atmospheric pressure, clockwise in the Northern Hemisphere, counterclockwise in the Southern Hemisphere. Cf. **cyclone** (def. 1), **high** (def. 38). —**an·ti·cy·clon·ic** (an′tē sī klon′ik, an′tī-), *adj.*

an·ti·de·pres·sant (an′tē di pres′ənt, an′tī-), *n. Med.* any of a class of drugs used in the treatment of mental depression for raising the spirits; psychic energizer. Also, **an′ti·de·pres′sant.**

an·ti·de·riv·a·tive (an′tē də riv′ə tiv, an′tī-), *n.* See **indefinite integral.**

an·ti·dis·es·tab·lish·men·tar·i·an·ism (an′tē dis′e-stab′lish mən târ′ē ə niz′əm, an′tī-), *n.* opposition to the withdrawal of state support or recognition from an established church, esp. the Anglican church in 19th-century England.

an·ti·do·ron (än dē′thô rôn; *Eng.* an′tē dōr′on, -dôr′-), *n.* **1.** Also called **holy bread.** *Gk. Orth. Ch.* bread blessed and distributed to the congregation at the end of the liturgy. **2.** *Eastern Ch.* eulogia (def. 1). [< LGk *antídōron* return gift = *anti-* ANTI- + *dōron* gift < *didónai* to give]

an·ti·dote (an′ti dōt′), *n.* **1.** a medicine or other remedy for counteracting the effects of poison, disease, etc. **2.** something that prevents or counteracts: *Hard work is the best antidote to sorrow.* [< L *antidotum* < Gk *antídoton* something given against (i.e., for counteracting) = *anti-* ANTI- + *dotón* (akin to DATUM), neut. of *dotós* given, verbid of *didónai* to give] —**an′ti·dot′al,** *adj.* —**an′ti·dot′al·ly,** *adv.*

An·tie·tam (an tē′təm), *n.* a creek flowing from S Pennsylvania through NW Maryland into the Potomac: Civil War battle fought near here at Sharpsburg, Maryland, in 1862.

An·ti·fed·er·al·ist (an′tē-fed′ər ə list, -fed′rə-, an′tī-), *n.* **1.** *U.S. Hist.* a member or supporter of the Antifederal party. **2.** (*l.c.*) an opponent of federalism. —**An′ti·fed′er·al·ism,** *n.*

An′ti·fed′er·al par′ty (an′tē fed′ər əl, -fed′rəl, an′tī-, an′tē-, an′tī-), *U.S. Hist.* the party which, before 1789, opposed the adoption of the proposed Constitution.

an·ti·fer·ro·mag·net·ic (an′tē fer′ō mag net′ik, an′tī-), *adj. Physics.* noting or pertaining to a substance in which, at sufficiently low temperatures, the magnetic moments of adjacent atoms point in opposite directions. Cf. **diamagnetic, ferromagnetic, paramagnetic.** —**an·ti·fer·ro·mag·ne·tism** (an′tē fer′ō mag′ni tiz′əm, an′tī-), *n.*

an·ti·foul·ing (an′tē fou′ling, an′tī-), *adj.* (of a coating or the like) preventing the accumulation of barnacles, algae, etc., on underwater surfaces.

---

an′ti·a·ris′to·crat′ic, *adj.*
an′ti·bac·te′ri·al, *adj.*
an′ti·bal·lis′tic, *adj.*
an′ti-Bib′li·cal, *adj.;* **-ly,** *adv.*
an′ti-Bol′she·vik, *n., adj.*
an′ti-Bol′she·vism, *n.*
an′ti-Bol′she·vist, *n., adj.*
an′ti-Bol′she·vis′tic, *adj.*
an′ti·cap′i·tal·ist, *n., adj.*
an′ti·cap′i·tal·is′tic, *adj.*
an′ti-Cath′o·lic, *adj., n.*
an′ti-Ca·thol′i·cism, *n.*
an′ti·cen′sor·ship′, *adj.*
an′ti·church′, *adj.*
an′ti·clas′si·cal, *adj.*
an′ti·clas′si·cism, *n.*
an′ti·clas′si·cist, *adj., n.*
an′ti·co·ag′u·lat′ing, *adj.*
an′ti·com′mu·nism, *n.*
an′ti·com′mu·nist, *n., adj.*
an′ti·com′mu·nis′tic, *adj.*
an′ti·con′sti·tu′tion·al, *adj.*
an′ti-Dar·win′i·an, *n., adj.*
an′ti-Dar′win·ism, *n.*
an′ti·dem′o·crat′ic, *adj.*
an′ti·di′u·ret′ic, *adj., n.*
an′ti·draft′, *adj.*
an′ti·ec·cle′si·as′ti·cal, *adj.;* **-ly,** *adv.*
an′ti·em·pir′i·cal, *adj.;* **-ly,** *adv.*
an′ti·ev′o·lu′tion, *adj.*
an′ti·ev′o·lu′tion·ist, *n., adj.*
an′ti·ex·pan′sion·ist, *n., adj.*
an′ti·fas′cism, *n.*
an′ti·fas′cist, *n., adj.*

an·ti·freeze (an′ti frēz′, an′tē-), *n.* a liquid used in the radiator of an internal-combustion engine to lower the freezing point of the cooling medium.

an·ti·fric·tion (an′tē frik′shən, an′tī-), *adj.* tending to prevent or reduce friction. —**an′ti·fric′tion·al,** *adj.*

an·ti·gen (an′ti jən, -jen′), *n.* *Biochem.* any of a class of substances that stimulate production of antibodies. [ANTI-(BODY) + -GEN] —**an·ti·gen·ic** (an′ti jen′ik), *adj.*

An·tig·o·ne (an tig′ə nē′), *n.* *Class. Myth.* a daughter of Oedipus and Jocasta who defied her uncle, King Creon, by performing funeral rites over her brother, Polynices, and was condemned to be immured alive in a cave.

An·tig·o·nus I (an tig′ə nəs), (*Cyclops*) 382?–301 B.C., Macedonian general under Alexander the Great.

Antigonus II, (*Gonatus*) c319–239 B.C., king of Macedonia 283–239.

an·ti·gov·ern·ment (an′tē guv′ərn mənt, -ər mənt), *adj.* **1.** opposed to or in rebellion against an existing government. **2.** of or pertaining to a political group, military force, etc., seeking to replace or overthrow an existing government. —**an′ti·gov′ern·men′tal,** *adj.*

an·ti·grav·i·ty (an′tē grav′i tē, an′tī-), *n.* **1.** *Physics.* a hypothetical force by which a body of positive mass would repel a body of negative mass. **2.** (not in technical use) a controllable force that can be made to act against gravity. —*adj.* **3.** (not in technical use) counteracting gravity.

an·ti-G′ suit′ (an′tē jē′, an′tī-), *Aeron.* a garment for fliers, designed to exert pressure on the abdomen and thighs to prevent or retard the pooling of blood below the heart under the influence of excessive head-to-toe acceleration forces. Also called **G-suit.**

An·ti·gua (an tē′gə, -gwə), *n.* one of the central Leeward Islands, in the E West Indies: member of the West Indies Associated States; formerly a British colony. 54,304 (est. 1964); 108 sq. mi. *Cap.:* St. John's. —**An·ti′guan,** *adj., n.*

an·ti·he·lix (an′tē hē′liks, an′tī-), *n., pl.* **-hel·i·ces** (-hel′i sēz′), **-he·lix·es.** *Anat.* the inward curving ridge of the auricle, or projecting outer portion, of the ear. [ANTI- + HELIX; r. *anthelix* < Gk]

an·ti·he·ro (an′tē hēr′ō, an′tī-), *n., pl.* **-he·roes.** *Literature.* a protagonist who lacks the attributes that would make him a heroic figure, as nobility of mind and spirit, a life or attitude marked by action or purpose, and the like. —**an·ti·he·ro·ic** (an′tē hi rō′ik, an′tī-), *adj.*

an·ti·his·ta·mine (an′ti his′tə mēn′, -min), *n.* *Med.* any of certain compounds or medicines that neutralize or inhibit the effect of histamine in the body, used chiefly in the treatment of allergic disorders and colds. —**an·ti·his·ta·min·ic** (an′tē his′tə min′ik, an′tī-), *adj.*

an·ti·ic·er (an′tē ī′sər), *n.* **1.** a device used to prevent the forming of ice, as on an airplane propeller. **2.** a fluid used in such a device.

an·ti·in·tel·lec·tu·al (an′tē in′tᵊlek′cho͞o əl, an′tī-), *adj.* **1.** opposed to or distrustful of intellectuals, their culture, and theoretical intellectual concerns. **2.** of or pertaining to instinct, emotion, and behavior that is not based on conscious thought. —*n.* **3.** a person who is characterized by distrust of intellectuals, their culture, and theoretical, intellectual concerns. Also, **an′ti-in′tel·lec′tu·al·ist.** —**an′ti-in′tel·lec′tu·al·ism,** *n.* —**an′ti-in′tel·lec′tu·al·ist′ic,** *adj.* —**an′ti-in′tel·lec′tu·al′i·ty,** *n.*

an·ti·knock (an′tē nok′, an′tī-), *adj.* noting or pertaining to any material added to fuel for an internal-combustion engine to eliminate or minimize knock.

An·til·les (an til′ēz), *n.* (*construed as pl.*) a chain of islands in the West Indies, divided into two parts, the one including Cuba, Hispaniola, Jamaica, and Puerto Rico **(Greater Antilles),** the other including a group of smaller islands to the SE **(Lesser Antilles).** —**An·til·le·an** (an′tə lē′ən, an til′ē-), *adj.*

An·til·o·chus (an til′ə kəs), *n.* *Class. Myth.* a son of Nestor and a trusted friend of Achilles.

an·ti·log (an′ti lôg′, -log′), *n.* antilogarithm.

an·ti·log·a·rithm (an′ti lô′gə rith′əm, -log′ə-), *n.* *Math.* the number of which a given number is the logarithm. *Symbol:* antilog —**an′ti·log′a·rith′mic,** *adj.*

an·til·o·gy (an til′ə jē), *n., pl.* **-gies.** a contradiction in terms or ideas. [< Gk *antilogía* controversy]

antilym′phocyte glob′ulin, a serum acting on lymphocytes to prevent the body's rejection of a newly transplanted organ. Also called **ALG.**

an·ti·ma·cas·sar (an′ti mə kas′ər), *n.* a covering, usually ornamental, placed on the backs and arms of upholstered furniture to prevent wear or soiling; tidy. [ANTI- + MACASSAR (OIL)]

an·ti·mag·net·ic (an′tē mag net′ik, an′tī-), *adj.* **1.** resistant to magnetization. **2.** (of a precision instrument, watch, etc.) having the critical parts composed of materials resistant to magnetization, and hence not seriously affected in accuracy by exposure to magnetic fields.

An′ti-Mason′ic par′ty, *U.S.* a political party (1826–1835) that opposed Freemasonry in civil affairs.

an·ti·masque (an′ti mask′, -mäsk′), *n.* a comic or grotesque performance, as a dance, presented before or between the acts of a masque. Also, **an′ti·mask′.** [ANTI- + MASQUE; r. earlier *antemask*] —**an′ti·mas′quer, an′ti·mask′er,** *n.*

an·ti·mat·ter (an′tē mat′ər, an′tī-), *n.* *Physics.* matter composed of particles analogous to but having charges opposite to those of common particles of matter, as positrons, antiprotons, etc. Cf. **annihilation** (def. 3).

an·ti·mere (an′tə mēr′), *n.* *Zool.* a segment or division of the body in the direction of one of the secondary or transverse axes, as either half of a bilaterally symmetrical animal or a radiating part of a radially symmetrical animal. —**an·ti·mer·ic** (an′tə mer′ik), *adj.* —**an·tim·er·ism** (an tim′ə riz′əm), *n.*

an·ti·mis·sile (an′tē mis′əl, an′tī- *or, esp. Brit.,* -mis′īl), *Mil.* —*adj.* **1.** designed or used in defense against guided missiles. —*n.* **2.** a ballistic device for seeking and destroying enemy missiles. Also, **an′ti·mis′sile.**

antimis′sile mis′sile, a ballistic missile for seeking and destroying other missiles in flight.

an·ti·mo·nic (an′tə mō′nik, -mon′ik), *adj.* *Chem.* of or containing antimony, esp. in the pentavalent state.

an·ti·mo·nous (an′tə mō′nəs, an′tə mə nəs), *adj.* *Chem.* of or containing antimony, esp. in the trivalent state. Also, **an·ti·mo·ni·ous** (an′tə mō′nē əs).

an·ti·mon·soon (an′tē mon so͞on′), *n.* *Meteorol.* a current of air lying above a monsoon and moving in an opposite direction.

an·ti·mo·ny (an′tə mō′nē), *n.* *Chem.* a brittle, lustrous, white metallic element occurring in nature free or combined, used chiefly in alloys and in compounds in medicine. *Symbol:* Sb; *at. no.:* 51; *at. wt.:* 121.75. [late ME < ML *antimōni(um)*] —**an′ti·mo′ni·al,** *adj., n.*

an′timony glance′, *Obs.* stibnite.

an·ti·mo·nyl (an′tə mə nil, an tim′ə-), *n.* *Chem.* the univalent group, –SbO, believed to exist in certain compounds, as in antimony potassium tartrate, $K(SbO)C_4H_4O_6$.

an′timony potas′sium tar′trate, *Chem.* See **tartar emetic.** Also, **an′timonyl potas′sium tar′trate.**

an·ti·neu·tri·no (an′tē no͞o trē′nō, -nyo͞o-, an′tī-), *n., pl.* **-nos.** *Physics.* the antiparticle of the neutrino.

an·ti·neu·tron (an′tē no͞o′tron, -nyo͞o′-, an′tī-), *n.* *Physics.* an elementary uncharged particle having a mass and spin equal to that of the neutron but with an opposite magnetic moment.

an·ti·node (an′ti nōd′), *n.* *Physics.* the region of maximum amplitude between two adjacent nodes in a standing wave. —**an′ti·nod′al,** *adj.*

an·ti·no·mi·an (an′ti nō′mē ən), *n.* a person who maintains that Christians are freed from the moral law by virtue of grace as set forth in the gospel. [< ML *Antinomī* name of sect (pl. of *Antinomus* opponent of (the moral) law < Gk *antí* ANTI- + *nómos* law) + -AN] —**an′ti·no′mi·an·ism,** *n.*

an·tin·o·my (an tin′ə mē), *n., pl.* **-mies.** **1.** opposition between one law, principle, rule, etc., and another. **2.** *Philos.* a contradiction between two statements, both apparently obtained by correct reasoning. [< L *antinomia* < Gk *antinomía* a contradiction between laws. See ANTI-, -NOMY] —**an·ti·nom·ic** (an′ti nom′ik), **an′ti·nom′i·cal,** *adj.* —**an′ti·nom′i·cal·ly,** *adv.*

An·tin·o·us (an tin′ō əs), *n.* **1.** *Class. Myth.* the chief suitor of Penelope, killed by Odysseus upon his return from Troy. **2.** A.D. 117–138, favorite of the emperor Hadrian.

an·ti·nov·el (an′tē nov′əl, an′tī-), *n.* a literary work in which the author rejects the use of traditional elements of novel structure, esp. in regard to development of plot. —**an′ti·nov′el·ist,** *n.*

an·ti·nu·cle·on (an′tē no͞o′klē on′, -nyo͞o′-, an′tī-), *n.* *Physics.* an antiproton or an antineutron.

An·ti·och (an′tē ok′), *n.* **1.** Arabic, **Antakiya.** a city in S Turkey: capital of the ancient kingdom of Syria 300–64 B.C. 57,584 (1965). **2.** a city in W California, NE of Oakland. 28,060 (1970).

An·ti·o·chus (an tī′ə kəs), *n.* *Class. Myth.* a son of Hercules.

Antiochus III, ("*the Great*") 241?–187 B.C., king of Syria 223–187.

Antiochus IV, (*Antiochus Epiphanes*) died 164? B.C., king of Syria 175–164?.

an·ti·ox·i·dant (an′tē ok′si dənt, an′tī-), *n.* *Chem.* **1.** any substance inhibiting oxidation. **2.** any of a group of substances that inhibit deterioration of rubber, gasoline, soaps, etc. [ANTI- + *oxidant* (OXID(IZE) + -ANT)]

an·ti·par·ti·cle (an′tē pär′ti kəl, an′tī-), *n.* *Physics.* either of two particles that annihilate each other upon collision, as an electron and a positron.

an·ti·pas·to (an′ti pä′stō, -pas′tō; *It.* än′tē pä′stô), *n., pl.* **-pas·tos, -pas·ti** (-pä′stē, -pas′tē; *It.* -pä′stē). *Italian Cookery.* a course of assorted appetizers, as of olives, anchovies, salami, celery, etc. [< It: lit., before (the) meal = *anti-* (< L, var. of *ante-* ANTE-) + *pasto* < L *pāst(us)* food]

An·tip·a·ter (an tip′ə tər), *n.* 398?–319 B.C., Macedonian statesman and general: regent of Macedonia 334–323.

an·ti·pa·thet·ic (an′ti pə thet′ik, an tip′ə-), *adj.* **1.** having antipathy for or a basic aversion to something or someone. **2.** causing or likely to cause antipathy. Also, **an′ti·pa·thet′i·cal.** [< Gk *antipathḗ(s)* opposed in feeling (*antipathé(ein)* (to) have feelings of aversion = *anti-* ANTI- + *pathe-*, var. s. of *páthos* feeling) + -TIC] —**an′ti·pa·thet′i·cal·ly,** *adv.*

an·tip·a·thy (an tip′ə thē), *n., pl.* **-thies.** **1.** a basic or habitual repugnance; aversion. **2.** an object of repugnance. [< L *antipathīa* < Gk *antipátheia*] —**Syn. 1.** See **aversion.**

an·ti·pe·ri·od·ic (an′tē pēr′ē od′ik, an′tī-), *adj.* **1.** efficacious against periodic diseases, as intermittent fever. —*n.* **2.** an antiperiodic agent.

an·ti·per·son·nel (an′tē pûr′sə nel′, an′tī-), *adj.* *Mil.* used against enemy personnel rather than against mechanized vehicles, matériel, etc.: *antipersonnel bombs.*

an·ti·per·spi·rant (an′ti pûr′spər ənt), *n.* any preparation for retarding perspiration.

an′ti-Freud′i·an, *adj., n.*
an′ti-Freud′i·an·ism, *n.*
an′ti·fun′da·men′tal·ist, *n., adj.*
an′ti·fun′gal, *adj.*
an′ti·gam′bling, *adj., n.*
an′ti·hi′er·ar′chic, *adj.*
an′ti·hi′er·ar′chi·cal, *adj.*
an′ti·hu′man, *adj.*
an′ti·hu′man·ism, *n.*
an′ti·hu′man·ist, *n., adj.*
an′ti·hu′man·is′tic, *adj.*
an′ti·i′so·la′tion·ist, *n., adj.*
an′ti·la′bor, *adj.*
an′ti·lib′er·al, *adj., n.;* **-ly,** *adv.*
an′ti·lib′er·al·ism, *n.*
an′ti·ma·te′ri·al·is′tic, *adj.*
an′ti·ma·te′ri·al·is′ti·cal·ly, *adv.*
an′ti·mech′a·nis′tic, *adj.*
an′ti·mi·cro′bi·al, *adj.*
an′ti·mil′i·ta·rism, *n.*
an′ti·mil′i·ta·ris′tic, *adj.*
an′ti·mod′ern·ist, *n., adj.*
an′ti·mo·nar′chic, *adj.*
an′ti·mon′ar·chist, *n., adj.*
an′ti·mo·nop′o·lis′tic, *adj.*
an′ti·nar·cot′ic, *adj., n.*
an′ti·na′tion·al·ism, *n.*
an′ti·na′tion·al·ist, *n., adj.*
an′ti·na′tion·al·is′tic, *adj.*
an′ti-Ne′gro, *adj.*
an′ti·neu′tral·ism, *n.*
an′ti·noise′, *adj.*
an′ti·pac′i·fist, *n., adj.*
an′ti·pac′i·fis′tic, *adj.*
an′ti·path′o·gen, *n.*
an′ti·path′o·gen′ic, *adj.*
an′ti·pa′tri·ar′chal, *adj.*

an·ti·phlo·gis·tic (an′tē flō jis′tik, an′tī-), *adj.* **1.** acting against inflammation. —*n.* **2.** an antiphlogistic agent.

an·ti·phon (an′tə fon′), *n.* **1.** a verse or song to be chanted or sung in response. **2.** *Eccles.* **a.** a psalm, hymn, or prayer sung in alternate parts. **b.** a verse or a series of verses sung as a prelude or conclusion to some part of the service. [< ML *antiphōna* responsive singing < Gk (*tà*) *antíphōna,* neut. pl. of *antíphōnos* sounding in answer = *anti-* ANTI- + *phōn(ḗ)* sound + *-os* adj. suffix]

an·tiph·o·nal (an tif′ə nəl), *adj.* **1.** pertaining to antiphons or antiphony; responsive. —*n.* **2.** an antiphonary. —**an·tiph′o·nal·ly,** *adv.*

an·tiph·o·nar·y (an tif′ə ner′ē), *n., pl.* **-nar·ies.** a book of antiphons. [< ML *antiphōnāri(um)*]

an·tiph·o·ny (an tif′ə nē), *n., pl.* **-nies. 1.** alternate or responsive singing by a choir in two divisions. **2.** a psalm, verse, etc., so sung; antiphon. **3.** a responsive musical utterance. [ANTIPHON + -Y[3], modeled on *symphony*] —**an·ti·phon·ic** (an′tə fon′ik), *adj.* —**an′ti·phon′i·cal·ly,** *adv.*

an·tiph·ra·sis (an tif′rə sis), *n.* *Rhet.* the use of a word in a sense opposite to its proper or common meaning. [< L < Gk = *antiphráz(ein)* (to) speak the opposite (*anti-* ANTI- + *phrázein* to speak) + *-sis* -SIS; see PHRASE] —**an·ti·phras·tic** (an′ti fras′tik), **an′ti·phras′ti·cal,** *adj.* —**an′ti·phras′ti·cal·ly,** *adv.*

an·ti·plas·tic (an′tē plas′tik, an′tī-), *adj.* allaying or preventing the growth of new tissue.

an·tip·o·dal (an tip′ə dəl), *adj.* **1.** *Geog.* on the opposite side of the globe; pertaining to the antipodes. **2.** diametrically opposite: *twin brothers with antipodal personalities.*

an·ti·pode (an′ti pōd′), *n.* a direct or exact opposite. [back formation from ANTIPODES]

an·tip·o·des (an tip′ə dēz′), *n.pl.* places diametrically opposite to each other on the globe. [ME < L < Gk (*hoi*) *antípodes* (those) with the feet opposite (pl. of *antípous*) = *anti-* ANTI- + *-podes,* nom. pl. of *poûs* foot] —**an·tip·o·de·an** (an tip′ə dē′ən), *adj., n.*

An·tip·o·des (an tip′ə dēz′), *n.* (*construed as pl.*) a group of islands SE of and belonging to New Zealand. 24 sq. mi.

an·ti·pole (an′ti pōl′), *n.* the opposite pole.

an·ti·pope (an′ti pōp′), *n.* a person who claims to be pope in opposition to the one canonically chosen. [ANTI- + POPE; r. *antipape* < ML *antipāpa,* modeled on *Antichrīstus*]

an·ti·pov·er·ty (an′tē pov′ər tē, an′tī-), *adj.* aimed at relieving or eliminating poverty.

an·ti·pro·ton (an′tē prō′ton, an′tī-), *n.* *Physics.* an elementary particle having a negative charge equal to the electron but with the same mass and spin as a proton; the antiparticle of the proton.

an·ti·py·ret·ic (an′tē pī ret′ik, an′tī-), *Med.* —*adj.* **1.** checking or preventing fever. —*n.* **2.** an antipyretic agent. —**an·ti·py·re·sis** (an′tē pī rē′sis, an′tī-), *n.*

an·ti·py·rine (an′tē pī′rēn, -rin, an′tī-), *n.* *Pharm.* a white powder, $C_{11}H_{12}N_2O$, used as a sedative, antipyretic, etc. [< G *Antipyrin* a trademark. See ANTI-, PYR-, -INE[2]]

antiq., antiquity.

an·ti·quar·i·an (an′tə kwâr′ē ən), *adj.* **1.** pertaining to antiquaries or to the study of antiquities. **2.** dealing in or pertaining to old or rare books. —*n.* **3.** an antiquary. [< L *antīquāri(us)* (see ANTIQUARY) + -AN] —**an′ti·quar′i·an·ism,** *n.*

an·ti·quar·y (an′tə kwer′ē), *n., pl.* **-quar·ies. 1.** an expert on or student of antiquities. **2.** a collector of antiquities. [< L *antīquāri(us)* of, belonging to antiquity = *antīqu(us)* ancient + *-ārius* -ARY]

an·ti·quate (an′tə kwāt′), *v.t.,* **-quat·ed, -quat·ing.** to make obsolete by replacing with something newer or better. [< L *antīquāt(us)* (ptp. of *antīquāre*) made old]

an·ti·quat·ed (an′tə kwā′tid), *adj.* **1.** obsolete or obsolescent. **2.** aged; old. **3.** adhering to the past; outmoded. —**an′ti·qua′ted·ness,** *n.* —**Syn. 2.** See **ancient**[1].

an·tique (an tēk′), *adj.* **1.** of or belonging to the past; not modern. **2.** dating from an early period: *antique furniture.* **3.** in the tradition or style of an earlier period. **4.** ancient. —*n.* **5.** any work of art, piece of furniture, or the like, created or produced in a former period, or, according to U.S. customs laws, 100 years before date of purchase. [< MF < L *antīqu(us)* (var. of *anticus* old, primitive; see ANTIC); r. *antike* < L] —**an·tique′ly,** *adv.* —**an·tique′ness,** *n.* —**Syn. 1.** archaic. **2.** See **ancient**[1].

an·tiq·ui·ty (an tik′wi tē), *n., pl.* **-ties. 1.** the quality of being ancient. **2.** ancient times; former ages. **3.** the time before the Middle Ages. **4.** the ancients collectively; the peoples, nations, tribes, or cultures of ancient times. **5.** Usually, **antiquities.** something of ancient times, as monuments, relics, customs, etc. [ME *antiquite* < MF < L *antīquitāt-* (s. of *antīquitās*) = *antīqu(us)* old (see ANTIQUE) + *-itāt-* -ITY]

an·ti·re·mon·strant (an′tē ri mon′strənt, an′tī-), *n.* **1.** a person opposed to remonstrance or to remonstrators. **2.** (*cap.*) a member or supporter of the faction in the Dutch Calvinistic Church which opposed the Remonstrants or Arminians.

An·ti·sa·na (än′tē sä′nä), *n.* **Mount,** an active volcano in N central Ecuador, near Quito. 18,885 ft.

an·ti-Sem·ite (an′tē sem′īt, an′tī- *or, esp. Brit.,* -sē′mīt), *n.* a person who is hostile to Jews. —**an·ti-Se·mit·ic** (an′tē sə mit′ik, an′tī-), *adj.* —**an′ti-Se·mit′i·cal·ly,** *adv.* —**an·ti-Sem·i·tism** (an′tē sem′i tiz′əm, an′tī-), *n.*

an·ti·sep·sis (an′ti sep′sis), *n.* destruction of the microorganisms that produce sepsis or septic disease.

an·ti·sep·tic (an′ti sep′tik), *adj.* **1.** pertaining to or affecting antisepsis. **2.** free from or cleaned of germs and other microorganisms. **3.** exceptionally clean or neat. —*n.* **4.** an antiseptic agent. —**an′ti·sep′ti·cal·ly,** *adv.*

an·ti·se·rum (an′ti sēr′əm), *n., pl.* **-se·rums, -se·ra** (-sēr′ə). a serum containing antibodies, as antitoxins or agglutinins, obtained by inoculation of animals and used for injection into other animals to provide immunity to a specific disease.

an·ti·slav·er·y (an′tē slā′və rē, -slāv′rē, an′tī-), *n.* **1.** opposition to slavery, esp. Negro slavery. —*adj.* **2.** of or pertaining to antislavery.

an·ti·so·cial (an′tē sō′shəl, an′tī-), *adj.* **1.** unwilling or unable to associate with other people. **2.** antagonistic, hostile, or unfriendly toward others. **3.** opposed or hostile to social order or the principles on which society is constituted: *antisocial behavior; an antisocial movement in art.* Also, **an′ti·so′cial·is′tic.** —**an·ti·so·ci·al·i·ty** (an′tē sō′shē al′i tē, an′tī-), *n.* —**an′ti·so′cial·ly,** *adv.*

an·ti·spas·mod·ic (an′tē spaz mod′ik, an′tī-), *adj.* **1.** relieving or preventing spasms. —*n.* **2.** an antispasmodic agent.

An·tis·the·nes (an tis′thə nēz′), *n.* 444?–365? B.C., Greek philosopher: founder of the Cynic school.

an·tis·tro·phe (an tis′trə fē), *n.* **1.** the part of an ancient Greek choral ode answering a previous strophe, sung by the chorus when returning from left to right. **2.** the movement performed by the chorus while singing an antistrophe. **3.** *Pros.* the second of two metrically corresponding systems in a poem. Cf. **strophe** (def. 3). [< Gk: a turning about] —**an·ti·stroph·ic** (an′ti strof′ik, -strō′fik), **an·tis′tro·phal,** *adj.* —**an′ti·stroph′i·cal·ly,** *adv.*

an·ti·tank (an′tē taŋk′, an′tī-), *adj.* *Mil.* for use against tanks or other armored vehicles: *antitank gun.*

an·tith·e·sis (an tith′i sis), *n., pl.* **-ses** (-sēz′). **1.** opposition; contrast: *the antithesis of right and wrong.* **2.** the direct opposite (usually fol. by *of* or *to*). **3.** *Rhet.* **a.** the placing of a sentence or one of its parts against another to which it is opposed, as in "Give me liberty or give me death." **b.** the second sentence or part thus set in opposition, as "or give me death." **4.** *Philos.* See under **Hegelian dialectic.** [< L < Gk: opposition = *anti(ti)thé(nai)* (to) oppose + *-sis* -SIS. See ANTI-, THESIS] —**an·ti·thet·ic** (an′tə thet′ik), **an′ti·thet′i·cal,** *adj.* —**an′ti·thet′i·cal·ly,** *adv.*

an·ti·tox·in (an′ti tok′sin, an′tē-), *n.* **1.** a substance, formed in the body, that counteracts a specific toxin. **2.** the antibody formed in immunization with a given toxin, used in treating certain infectious diseases or in immunizing against them. Also, **an·ti·tox·ine** (an′ti tok′sin, -sēn, an′tē-). —**an′ti·tox′ic,** *adj.*

an·ti·trade (an′ti trād′), *n.* **1. antitrades,** westerly winds lying above the trade winds in the tropics. —*adj.* **2.** noting or pertaining to such a wind.

an·tit·ra·gus (an ti′trə gəs), *n., pl.* **-gi** (-jī′). *Anat.* a process of the external ear. [< NL < Gk *antítragos*]

an·ti·trust (an′tē trust′, an′tī-), *adj.* opposing or intended to restrain trusts or large combinations of business and capital, esp. for promoting competition: *antitrust legislation.*

an·ti·type (an′ti tīp′), *n.* something that is foreshadowed by a type or symbol, as a New Testament event prefigured in the Old Testament. [< ML *antityp(us)* < LGk *antítypos* (impression) answering to a die] —**an·ti·typ·ic** (an′ti tip′ik), **an′ti·typ′i·cal,** *adj.* —**an′ti·typ′i·cal·ly,** *adv.*

an·ti·un·ion (an′tē yōōn′yən, an′tī-), *adj.* *U.S.* opposed to trade unions or unionism. —**an′ti·un′ion·ist,** *n.*

an·ti·ven·in (an′tē ven′in, an′tī-), *n.* **1.** an antitoxin present in the blood of an animal following repeated injections of venom. **2.** the antitoxic serum obtained from such blood. [*antiven(ene)* (ANTI- + *venene* < L *venēnum* love-potion, poison + -IN[2]]

an·ti·world (an′tē wûrld′, an′tī-), *n.* Often, **antiworlds.** *Physics.* a hypothetical world composed of antimatter.

ant·ler (ant′lər), *n.* one of the solid deciduous horns, usually branched, of an animal of the deer family. [late ME *aunteler* < MF *antoillier* < VL **anteoculār(em)* (*rāmum*), acc. sing. of **anteoculāris* (*rāmus*) branch of a stag's horn before the eyes. See ANTE-, OCULAR] —**ant′lered,** *adj.*

Antler of a stag
A, Brow antler
B, Bay antler
C, Royal antler
D, Crown antler

ant·li·on (ant′lī′ən), *n.* any of several neuropterous insects of the family *Myrmeleontidae,* the larva of which digs a pit in sand where it lies in wait for ants or other insects.

An·to·fa·gas·ta (än′tō fə gä′stə; *Sp.* än′tô fä gäs′tä), *n.* a seaport in N Chile. 104,559 (est. 1963).

An·toine (äN twaN′), *n.* **Père** (peR) (*Francisco Ildefonso Mareno*), 1748–1829, Spanish priest who tried to establish Inquisition in Louisiana.

An·toi·nette (an′twə net′; *Fr.* äN twa net′), *n.* **Ma·rie** (mə rē′; *Fr.* ma Rē′), 1755–93, queen of France 1774–93: wife of Louis XVI.

An·to·ni·nus (an′tə nī′nəs), *n.* **Marcus Aurelius.** See **Marcus Aurelius.**

Antoni′nus Pi′us (pī′əs), A.D. 86–161, emperor of Rome 138–161.

An·to·ni·us (an tō′nē əs), *n.* **Marcus.** See **Antony, Mark.**

an·to·no·ma·sia (an′tə nə mā′zhə), *n.* **1.** *Rhet.* the substitution of an epithet or appellative for an individual's name, as *his lordship.* **2.** the use of the name of a person who was distinguished by a particular characteristic, as Don Juan, to designate a person or group of persons having the same characteristic. [< L < Gk < *antonomas-* (var. s. of *antonomázein* to name anew = *ant-* ANT- + *onomázein* to name < *ónoma* name) + *-ia* -IA] —**an·to·no·mas·tic** (an′tə nō mas′tik), **an′to·no·mas′ti·cal,** *adj.* —**an′to·no·mas′ti·cal·ly,** *adv.*

An·to·ny (an′tə nē), *n.* **Mark** (*Marcus Antonius*), 83?–30

an′ti·po·lit′i·cal, *adj.;* **-ly,** *adv.*
an′ti·pol·lu′tion, *adj., n.*
an′ti·prag·mat′ic, *adj.*
an′ti·prag′ma·tism, *n.*
an′ti·pro′hi·bi′tion, *adj.*
an′ti·pro′hi·bi′tion·ist, *n., adj.*
an′ti-Prot′es·tant, *n., adj.*
an′ti-Prot′es·tant·ism, *n.*
an′ti·pu′ri·tan, *n., adj.*
an′ti·ra·chit′ic, *adj.*
an′ti·rad′i·cal, *n., adj.*
an′ti·rad′i·cal·ism, *n.*
an′ti·ra′tion·al, *adj.;* **-ly,** *adv.*
an′ti·ra′tion·al·ism, *n.*
an′ti·ra′tion·al·is′tic, *adj.*
an′ti·re·li′gious, *adj.;* **-ly,** *adv.*
an′ti·re·pub′li·can, *adj., n.*
an′ti·rev′o·lu′tion·ar′y, *n., pl.* **-ar·ies,** *adj.*
an′ti-Rus′sian, *adj., n.*
an′ti·spir′it·u·al, *adj.*
an′ti·sub′ma·rine′, *adj.*
an′ti·su·dor·if′ic, *n., adj.*
an′ti·tar′nish·ing, *adj.*
an′ti·tra·di′tion·al, *adj.*
an′ti·vi′rus, *adj.*
an′ti·war′, *adj.*
an′ti-Zi′on·ism, *n.*
an′ti-Zi′on·ist, *n., adj.*

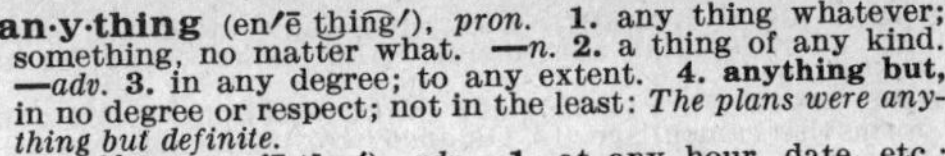

B.C., Roman general: friend of Caesar; member of the second triumvirate and rival of Octavian. Also, **Anthony.**

an·to·nym (an′tə nim), *n.* a word opposite in meaning to another. "*Fast*" is an antonym of "*slow.*" Cf. **synonym** (def. 1). [back formation from Gk *antōnymí(ein)* (to) have an opposite denomination. See ANT-, SYNONYM] —**an·ton·y·mous** (an ton′ə məs), *adj.*

An·trim (an′trim), *n.* a county in NE Northern Ireland. 273,905 (1961); 1098 sq. mi. *Co. seat:* Belfast.

an·trorse (an trôrs′), *adj. Bot., Zool.* bent or directed forward or upward. [< NL *antrors(us)* = *antr-* (var. of *antero-* ANTERO-) + *-orsus* abstracted from L *introrsus* INTRORSE] —**an·trorse′ly,** *adv.*

an·trum (an′trəm), *n., pl.* **-tra** (-trə). *Anat.* a cavity in a bone, esp. that in the maxilla. [< L < Gk *ántron* cave] —**an′tral,** *adj.*

Ant·si·ra·ne (änt′sə rä′nā), *n.* Diego-Suarez.

An·tung (an′tōōng′; *Chin.* än′dōōng′), *n.* **1.** a seaport in S Manchuria, in NE China, at the mouth of the Yalu. 360,000 (1953). **2.** a former province of China, in Manchuria.

Ant·werp (an′twərp), *n.* a seaport in N Belgium, on the Scheldt. 247,156 (est. 1964). French, **Anvers.** Flemish, **Antwer·pen** (änt′vᴇʀ pən).

A·nu (ä′nōō), *n.* the Akkadian god of heaven: the counterpart of the Sumerian An.

A·nu·bis (ə nōō′bis, ə nyōō′-), *n. Egyptian Religion.* a deity, the god of tombs and embalming and weigher of the hearts of the dead: represented as having the head of a jackal.

Anubis

-anum, a suffix occurring in scientific words of Latin origin: *laudanum.* [< L, neut. of *-ānus* -AN]

A number 1. See **A one** (def. 1).

A·nu·ra·dha·pu·ra (ə nōōr′ə də pōōr′ə, un′ōō rä′də-), *n.* a city in central Ceylon: ruins of ancient Buddhist temples. 77,632 (1963).

an·u·ri·a (ə nōōr′ē ə, ə nyōōr′-), *n. Med.* the absence or suppression of urine. [< NL; see AN-[1], UR(O)-[1], -IA] —**an·u′ric, an·u·ret·ic** (an′yə ret′ik), *adj.*

a·nus (ā′nəs), *n., pl.* **a·nus·es.** *Anat.* the opening at the lower end of the alimentary canal, through which the solid refuse of digestion is excreted. [< L *ānus* ring, anus]

-anus, a suffix occurring in scientific words of Latin origin: *Platanus.* [< L; see -AN]

An·vers (äɴ vᴇʀ′), *n.* French name of **Antwerp.**

an·vil (an′vil), *n.* **1.** a heavy iron block, frequently faced with steel, on which metals, usually heated until soft, are hammered into desired shapes. **2.** the fixed jaw in certain measuring instruments. **3.** *Anat.* the incus. **4.** Also called **an′vil cloud′, an′vil top′.** incus (def. 2). **5.** a percussion instrument having steel bars that are struck with a wooden or metal beater. [ME *anvelt, anfelt,* OE *anfilt(e), anfealt;* c. MD *anvilte,* OHG *anafalz.* See ON, FELT[2]]

Anvil (def. 1)

anx·i·e·ty (ang zī′i tē), *n., pl.* **-ties.** **1.** distress or uneasiness caused by danger or misfortune. **2.** solicitous desire; eagerness: *his keen anxiety about his promotion.* **3.** *Psychiatry.* a state of apprehension and psychic tension found in most forms of mental disorder. [< L *anxietāt-* (s. of *anxietās*) = *anxi(us)* ANXIOUS + *-etāt-,* var. of *-itāt-* -ITY] —**Syn. 1.** fear, worry, disquiet. See **apprehension.** —**Ant. 1.** certainty.

anx·ious (angk′shəs, ang′-), *adj.* **1.** full of anxiety or worry due to apprehension or anticipation of danger or misfortune: *Her parents were anxious about her poor health.* **2.** full of eagerness; earnestly desirous (usually fol. by an infinitive or *for*): *anxious to please.* [< L *anxius* troubled in mind; akin to ANGER] —**anx′ious·ly,** *adv.* —**anx′ious·ness,** *n.* —**Syn. 1.** concerned, disturbed, apprehensive, fearful, uneasy. —**Ant. 1.** calm, confident.
—**Usage.** Precise writers and speakers generally avoid the use of ANXIOUS for EAGER in formal contexts.

an·y (en′ē), *adj.* **1.** one, a, an, or some; one or more without specification or identification: *If you have any witnesses, produce them. Pick out any six you like.* **2.** whatever or whichever it may be: *at any price.* **3.** in whatever quantity or number, great or small; some: *Have you any butter?* **4.** every; all: *Read any books you find on the subject.* **5.** (following a negative) even the slightest amount of: *She can't endure any criticism.* —*pron.* **6.** an unspecified person or persons; anybody: *He does better than any before him.* **7.** a single one or ones; an unspecified thing or things; a quantity or number: *We don't have any left.* —*adv.* **8.** in whatever degree; to some extent; at all: *Do you feel any better?* [ME *eni, ani,* OE *ǣnig* (ān ONE + *-ig* -Y[1])] —**Syn. 3.** See **some.** —**Usage.** See **anyone.**

an·y·bod·y (en′ē bod′ē, -bud′ē), *pron., n., pl.* **-bod·ies.** —*pron.* **1.** any person. —*n.* **2.** a person of some importance.

an·y·how (en′ē hou′), *adv.* **1.** in any way whatever. **2.** in any case; under any circumstances. **3.** carelessly.

an·y·one (en′ē wun′, -wən), *pron.* any person at all; anybody.
—**Usage.** ANYONE, SOMEONE, and EVERYONE are accepted as either one-word or two-word forms. A convenient distinction is often made so that the one-word form means "any person" (*Is anyone home?*) while the two-word form means "any specific or single person" (*Can any one of the boys play the flute?*).

an·y·place (en′ē plās′), *adv. Informal.* anywhere.
—**Usage.** ANYPLACE (or, occasionally, ANY PLACE), when adverbial, is usually regarded as suitable only in informal usage: *We couldn't find the book anyplace.* Precise speakers or writers prefer ANYWHERE. The two-word form, when PLACE is a noun, is acceptable in formal usage as well: *I will go to any place you order me.* Similarly, EVERYWHERE is preferred to EVERYPLACE, NOWHERE to NOPLACE, and SOMEWHERE to SOMEPLACE.

an·y·thing (en′ē thing′), *pron.* **1.** any thing whatever; something, no matter what. —*n.* **2.** a thing of any kind. —*adv.* **3.** in any degree; to any extent. **4. anything but,** in no degree or respect; not in the least: *The plans were anything but definite.*

an·y·time (en′ē tīm′), *adv.* **1.** at any hour, date, etc.; whenever. **2.** invariably; without doubt or exception; always: *I can do better than that anytime.*

an·y·way (en′ē wā′), *adv.* **1.** in any way or manner. **2.** in any case; anyhow. **3.** carelessly; haphazardly: *Don't do the job just anyway.*

an·y·ways (en′ē wāz′), *adv. Dial. or Nonstandard.* anyway.

an·y·where (en′ē hwâr′, -wâr′), *adv.* **1.** in, at, or to any place. **2.** to any extent; to some degree: *Does my answer come anywhere near the correct one?* **3. get anywhere,** *Informal.* to achieve success: *You'll never get anywhere with that attitude!* —**Usage.** See **anyplace.**

an·y·wheres (en′ē hwârz′, -wârz′), *adv. Dial. or Nonstandard.* anywhere.

an·y·wise (en′ē wīz′), *adv.* in any way or respect.

An·zac (an′zak), *n.* **1.** a member of the Australian and New Zealand Army Corps during World War I. **2.** a soldier from Australia or New Zealand.

An·zhe·ro-Sud·zhensk (än zhe′ʀo sōōd zhensk′), *n.* a city in the S RSFSR, in the central Soviet Union in Asia. 120,000 (est. 1962).

An·zi·o (an′zē ō′; *It.* än′tsyô), *n.* a town in Italy, S of Rome on the Tyrrhenian coast: site of Allied landing and beachhead in World War II. 15,217 (1961).

A/O, account of. Also, **a/o**

A-O.K. (ā′ō kā′), *adj.* perfect; great; A one: *an A-O.K. rocket launching.* Also, **A-OK, A-O·kay′.**

A·o·mo·ri (ä′ô mô′rē), *n.* a seaport on N Honshu, in N Japan. 232,000 (est. 1963).

A one (ā′ wun′), **1.** Also, **A number 1.** *Informal.* first-class; excellent; superior: *The meals there are A one.* **2.** noting a vessel equipped to the highest standard and maintained in first-class condition. Also, **A-one, A 1, A-1**

A·o·ran·gi (ä′ō räng′gē), *n.* See **Cook, Mount.**

a·o·rist (ā′ə rist), *Gram.* —*n.* **1.** a verb tense, as in Classical Greek, expressing action or, in the indicative mood, past action, without further limitation or implication. —*adj.* **2.** of or in this tense. [< Gk *aóríst(os)* unlimited = *a-* A-[6] + *horistós* limited (*horis-* (var. s. of *horízein* to bound, limit) + *-tos* ptp. suffix)]

a·o·ris·tic (ā′ə ris′tik), *adj.* **1.** *Gram.* aorist. **2.** indefinite; indeterminate. —**a′o·ris′ti·cal·ly,** *adv.*

a·or·ta (ā ôr′tə), *n., pl.* **-tas, -tae** (-tē). *Anat.* the main trunk of the arterial system, conveying blood from the left ventricle of the heart to all of the body except the lungs. [< ML < Gk *aortḗ* the great artery, lit. something hung, carried; akin to *aeírein* to lift, raise, bear, carry] —**a·or′tic, a·or′tal,** *adj.*

aor′tic valve′, *Anat.* a semilunar valve between the aorta and the left ventricle of the heart that prevents the blood from flowing back into the left ventricle.

aou·dad (ou′dad′), *n.* a wild sheep, *Ammotragus lervia,* of northern Africa, having a long fringe of hairs on the throat, chest, and forelegs. Also called **Barbary sheep.** [< F < Berber *audad*]

AP, 1. Associated Press. **2.** See **Air Police.** Also, **A.P.**

ap-[1], var. of **ad-** before *p: appear.*

ap-[2], var. of **apo-** before a vowel or *h: aphelion.*

Ap., 1. Apostle. **2.** Apothecaries'. **3.** April.

a·pace (ə pās′), *adv.* with speed; quickly; swiftly. [ME *a pas(e)* at a (good) pace]

a·pache (ə pash′, ə pash′; *Fr.* A pASH′), *n., pl.* **a·pach·es** (ə pä′shiz, ə pash′iz; *Fr.* A pASH′). a Parisian gangster or ruffian. [< F: APACHE]

A·pach·e (ə pach′ē), *n., pl.* **A·pach·es,** (*esp. collectively*) **A·pach·e. 1.** a member of an Athapaskan people of the southwestern U.S. **2.** any of the several Athapaskan languages of Arizona and the Rio Grande basin. [< Sp, perh. < Zuñi *Apachu,* lit., enemy]

apache′ dance′, a violent dance, usually performed by a man and a woman, originated by the Parisian apaches.

Ap·a·lach·i·co·la (ap′ə lach′ə kō′lə), *n.* a river flowing S from NW Florida into the Gulf of Mexico. 90 mi. long.

ap·a·nage (ap′ə nij), *n.* appanage.

a·pa·re·jo (ap′ə rā′ō, -rā′hō, ä′pə-; *Sp.* ä′pä ʀe′hô), *n., pl.* **-jos** (-ōz, -hōz; *Sp.* -hôs). *Southwestern U.S.* a Mexican packsaddle formed of stuffed leather cushions. [< Sp: lit., preparation (i.e., equipment); see APPAREL]

a·part (ə pärt′), *adv.* **1.** into pieces or parts; to pieces: *falling apart from decay.* **2.** separately in place, time, motion, etc.: *New York and Tokyo are thousands of miles apart. Our birthdays are three days apart.* **3.** to or at one side, with respect to place, purpose, or function: *to keep apart from the group.* **4.** separately or individually in consideration: *each viewed apart from the other.* **5.** aside (used with a gerund or noun): *Joking apart, what do you think?* **6. apart from,** aside from; besides: *Apart from other considerations, time is a factor.* **7. take apart, a.** to disassemble: *to take a clock apart.* **b.** to criticize harshly. **c.** to beat (someone) up. —*adj.* **8.** having independent or unique qualities, features, or characteristics (usually used following the noun it modifies): *a class apart.* [ME < OF *a part* to one side] —**a·part′ness,** *n.*

a·part·heid (ə pärt′hāt, -hīt), *n.* (in the Republic of South Africa) racial segregation and discrimination against Negroes. [< SAfrD = *apart* APART + *-heid* -HOOD]

a·part·ment (ə pärt′mənt), *n.* **1.** a room or a combination of rooms, among similar sets in one building, designed for use as a dwelling. **2.** a building containing such rooms. **3.** any room in a dwelling. **4. apartments,** *Brit.* a set of rooms used as a dwelling by one person or one family. [syncopated var. of *appartiment* < ML *appartīment(um)* = *apparti(re)* (to) divide (see AP-[1], PART) + *-mentum* -MENT] —**a·part·men·tal** (ə pärt men′tᵊl), *adj.*
—**Syn. 1.** APARTMENT, COMPARTMENT agree in denoting a space enclosed by partitions or walls. APARTMENT, however, emphasizes the idea of separateness or privacy: *one's own apartment.* COMPARTMENT suggests a section of a larger space: *compartments in a ship's hold.*

a·part′ment house′, *U.S.* a building containing a number of residential apartments. Also called **apart′ment build′ing.**

ap·a·tet·ic (ap′ə tet′ik), *adj.* *Zool.* assuming colors and forms that camouflage. [< Gk *apatētik(ós)* fallacious = *apatē-* (var. s. of *apateúein* to deceive) + *-tikos* -TIC]

ap·a·thet·ic (ap′ə thet′ik), *adj.* **1.** having or showing little or no emotion. **2.** having or showing little interest or concern. Also, **ap′a·thet′i·cal.** [APATH(Y) + (PATH)ETIC] —**ap′a·thet′i·cal·ly,** *adv.* —**Syn. 1.** impassive. **2.** uninterested, unresponsive. —**Ant. 1.** excited. **2.** concerned.

ap·a·thy (ap′ə thē), *n.* **1.** absence of emotion. **2.** lack of interest or concern. [< L *apathīa* < Gk *apátheia* insensibility to suffering = *apathe-* (s. of *apathḗs*) unfeeling (*a-* A-[6] + *pathe-* (s. of *páthos*) suffering) + *-ia* -IA] —**Syn. 1.** coolness. **2.** indifference. —**Ant. 1.** ardor.

ap·a·tite (ap′ə tīt′), *n.* a common mineral, calcium fluorophosphate, $Ca_5FP_3O_{12}$, used in the manufacture of phosphate fertilizers. [< Gk *apát(ē)* trickery, fraud, deceit + -ITE[1]; so called from its being mistaken for other minerals]

APC, *Pharm.* a compound consisting of aspirin, phenacetin, and caffeine, used to relieve the pain of headache or neuralgia and the symptoms of a cold.

ape (āp), *n., v.,* **aped, ap·ing.** —*n.* **1.** a tailless monkey or a monkey with a very short tail. **2.** any monkey. **3.** See **anthropoid ape. 4.** an imitator; mimic. —*v.t.* **5.** to imitate; mimic. [ME; OE *apa;* c. OS *apo,* Icel *api,* OHG *affo* (> G *Affe*)] —**ape′like′,** *adj.*

a·peak (ə pēk′), *Naut.* —*adj.* **1.** more or less vertical. **2.** (of a dropped anchor) as nearly vertical as possible without being free of the bottom. —*adv.* **3.** vertically. Also, **a·peek′.**

A·pel·doorn (ä′pəl dōrn′, -dôrn′), *n.* a city in the central Netherlands. 109,037 (1962).

ape-man (āp′man′), *n., pl.* **-men.** a primate representing a transitional point between true man and the higher anthropoid apes. Cf. **missing link** (def. 1).

Ap·en·nines (ap′ə nīnz′), *n.* (*construed as pl.*) a mountain range in Italy, traversing the length of the peninsula. Highest peak, Monte Corno, 9585 ft. Also called **Ap′ennine Moun′tains.**

a·per·çu (A PER SY′), *n., pl.* **-çus** (-SY′). *French.* **1.** a hasty glance; glimpse. **2.** an insight. **3.** an outline or summary. [lit., perceived]

a·per·i·ent (ə pēr′ē ənt), *Med.* —*adj.* **1.** purgative; laxative. —*n.* **2.** a medicine or food that acts as a mild laxative. [< L *aperient-* (s. of *aperiēns* opening, prp. of *aperīre* to make open). See APERTURE, -ENT]

a·pe·ri·od·ic (ā′pēr ē od′ik), *adj.* not periodic; irregular. —**a′pe·ri·od′i·cal·ly,** *adv.* —**a·pe·ri·o·dic·i·ty** (ā pēr′ē ə-dis′i tē), *n.*

a·pé·ri·tif (ä per′i tēf′, ə per′-; *Fr.* A pā RE tēf′), *n., pl.* **-tifs** (-tēfs′; *Fr.* -tēf′). a small drink of alcoholic liquor taken to stimulate the appetite before a meal. [< F: lit., for opening < ML *aperitīvus,* LL *apertīvus.* See APERTURE, -IVE]

ap·er·ture (ap′ər chər), *n.* **1.** an opening, as a hole, slit, gap, etc. **2.** Also called **ap′erture stop′.** *Optics.* an opening that limits the quantity of light that can enter an optical instrument. [< L *apertūra* an opening = *apert(us)* opened, ptp. of *aperīre* (*ap-* var. of *ab-* away, from + **(v)er-(īre)* (to) close, cover + *-tus* ptp. suffix) + *-ūra* -URE] —**ap·er·tur·al** (ap′ər choor′əl), *adj.* —**ap′er·tured,** *adj.*

a·pet·al·ous (ā pet′əl əs), *adj.* *Bot.* having no petals. [< NL *apetalus*] —**a·pet′a·ly,** *n.*

a·pex (ā′peks), *n., pl.* **a·pex·es, a·pi·ces** (ap′i sēz′, ā′pi-). **1.** the tip, point, or vertex; summit. **2.** climax; acme. **3.** *Astron.* See **solar apex.** [< L: conical cap; tip, point, summit]

aph., aphetic.

a·phaer·e·sis (ə fer′i sis), *n.* apheresis. —**aph·ae·ret·ic** (af′ə ret′ik), *adj.*

aph·a·nite (af′ə nīt′), *n.* *Petrog.* a fine-grained igneous rock whose constituent minerals cannot be detected with the naked eye. [< Gk *aphan(ḗs)* unseen, hidden, invisible (*a-* A-[6] + *phan-,* s. of *phaínein* to bring to light, disclose) + -ITE[1]] —**aph·a·nit·ic** (af′ə nit′ik), *adj.* —**aph′a·nit′ism,** *n.*

a·pha·sia (ə fā′zhə), *n.* *Pathol.* impairment or loss of the faculty of using or understanding spoken or written language. [< Gk: speechlessness = *a-* A-[6] + *phas-* (var. s. of *phánai* to speak) + *-ia* -IA] —**a·pha·si·ac** (ə fā′zē ak′), *n.* —**a·pha·sic** (ə fā′zik, -sik), *adj., n.*

a·phe·li·on (ə fē′lē ən, ə fēl′yən, ap-hē′lē ən), *n., pl.* **a·phe·li·a** (ə fē′lē ə, ə fēl′yə, ap hē′lē ə). the point in the orbit of a planet or a comet farthest from the sun. Cf. **perihelion.** [Hellenized form of NL *aphēlium* < Gk **aphḗlion* (*diástēma*) off-sun (distance), neut. of **aphḗlios* (adj.) = *ap-* AP-[2] + *hḗli(os)* sun + *-os* adj. suffix. See APOGEE] —**a·phe′li·an,** *adj.*

Aphelion and perihelion

a·pher·e·sis (ə fer′i sis), *n.* the loss or omission of one or more letters or sounds at the beginning of a word, as in *squire* for *esquire,* or *count* for *account.* Also, **aphaeresis.** [< L *aphaeresis* < Gk *aphaíresis* a taking away = *aphairé-(ein)* (to) take away (*ap-* AP-[2] + *hairé-ein* to snatch) + *-sis* -SIS] —**aph·e·ret·ic** (af′ə ret′ik), *adj.*

aph·e·sis (af′i sis), *n.* *Historical Linguistics.* the disappearance or loss of an unstressed initial vowel or syllable. [< Gk *áphesis* a letting go = *aphe-* (var. s. of *aphiénai* to let go, set free: *ap-* AP-[2] + *hiénai* to send) + *-sis* -SIS] —**a·phet·ic** (ə fet′ik), *adj.* —**a·phet′i·cal·ly,** *adv.*

a·phid (ā′fid, af′id), *n.* any of numerous soft-bodied homopterous insects of the family *Aphididae* that suck the sap from the stems and leaves of various plants. Also called **plant louse.** [back formation from APHIDES, pl. of APHIS] —**a·phid·i·an** (ə fid′ē ən), *adj., n.* —**a·phid′i·ous,** *adj.*

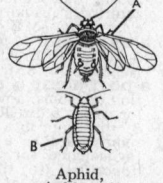

Aphid, *Aphis mali*
A, Male; B, Female
(Length ⅛ in.)

a·phid·li·on (ā′fid lī′ən, af′id-), *n.* the larva of a lacewing, usually predaceous on aphids. Also, **a′phid li′on, a′phid-li′on, a·phis·li·on** (ā′fis lī′ən, af′is-), **a′phis li′on, a′phis-li′on.**

a·phis (ā′fis, af′is), *n., pl.* **aph·i·des** (af′i dēz′). an aphid. [< NL; coined by Linnaeus]

a·pho·ni·a (ā fō′nē ə), *n.* *Pathol.* loss of voice due to an organic or functional disturbance of the vocal organs. [< NL < Gk: speechlessness. See A-[6], PHON-, -IA]

a·phon·ic (ā fon′ik), *adj.* **1.** *Phonet.* **a.** lacking phonation; unvoiced. **b.** without voice; voiceless. **2.** *Pathol.* affected with aphonia. —*n.* **3.** *Pathol.* a person affected with aphonia. [< Gk *áphōn(os)* voiceless (see APHONIA) + -IC]

aph·o·rise (af′ə rīz′), *v.i.,* **-rised, -ris·ing.** *Chiefly Brit.* aphorize. —**aph′o·ris′er,** *n.*

aph·o·rism (af′ə riz′əm), *n.* a terse saying embodying a general truth, as "Art is long, and life is short." [< ML *aphorism(us)* < Gk *aphorismós* definition = *aphor(ízein)* (to) define (see APHORIZE) + *-ismos* -ISM] —**aph′o·ris′-mic, aph·o·ris·mat·ic** (af′ə riz mat′ik), *adj.*

aph·o·rist (af′ə rist), *n.* a person who makes or uses aphorisms. [APHOR(IZE) + -IST]

aph·o·ris·tic (af′ə ris′tik), *adj.* **1.** of, like, or containing aphorisms. **2.** given to making or quoting aphorisms. [< Gk *aphoristik(ós)*] —**aph′o·ris′ti·cal·ly,** *adv.*

aph·o·rize (af′ə rīz′), *v.i.,* **-rized, -riz·ing.** to write or speak in aphorisms. Also, *esp. Brit.,* **aphorise.** [< Gk *aphoríz(ein)* (to) mark off, define, determine = *ap-* AP-[2] + *horízein* to limit, define] —**aph′o·riz′er,** *n.*

a·pho·tic (ā fō′tik), *adj.* lightless; dark.

aph·ro·di·sia (af′rə dizh′ə, -diz′ē ə), *n.* sexual desire. [< NL < Gk, neut. pl. of *aphrodísios* of Aphrodite]

aph·ro·dis·i·ac (af′rə diz′ē ak′), *n.* **1.** an agent, as a drug, arousing sexual desire. —*adj.* **2.** arousing sexual desire. [< Gk *aphrodisiak(ós)* relating to love or desire = *aphrodísi(os)* of Aphrodite + *-akos* -AC]

Aph·ro·di·te (af′rə dī′tē), *n.* the ancient Greek goddess of love and beauty, identified by the Romans with Venus. Also called **Cytherea.**

a·phyl·lous (ā fil′əs), *adj.* *Bot.* naturally leafless. [< NL *aphyllus* < Gk *áphyllos* leafless] —**a′phyl·ly,** *n.*

A·pi·a (ä pē′ä, ä′pē ä′), *n.* a seaport in and the capital of Western Samoa, on N Upolu. 30,593.

a·pi·a·ceous (ā′pē ā′shəs), *adj.* pertaining to the umbelliferous plants of the genus *Apium,* as parsley, celery, etc. [< NL *Api(āciae)* plant family name (L *api(um)* celery + *-āceae* -ACEAE) + -ACEOUS]

a·pi·an (ā′pē ən), *adj.* of or pertaining to bees. [< L *apiān(us)* = *api(s)* a bee + *-ānus* -AN]

a·pi·ar·i·an (ā′pē âr′ē ən), *adj.* of or pertaining to bees or to the breeding and care of bees.

a·pi·ar·y (ā′pē er′ē), *n., pl.* **-ar·ies.** a place in which a colony or colonies of bees are kept; a bee house containing a number of beehives. [< L *apiārium* a beehive = *api(s)* a bee + *-ārium* -ARY] —**a′pi·a·rist,** *n.*

ap·i·cal (ap′i kəl, ā′pi-), *adj.* **1.** of, at, or forming the apex. **2.** *Phonet.* (of a speech sound) articulated principally with the tip of the tongue, as *t, d,* etc. [< L *apic-* (s. of *apex*) APEX + -AL[1]] —**ap′i·cal·ly,** *adv.*

ap·i·ces (ap′i sēz′, ā′pi-), *n.* a pl. of **apex.**

a·pic·u·late (ə pik′yə lit, -lāt′), *adj.* *Bot.* tipped with a short, abrupt point, as a leaf. [< NL *apiculāt(us)* = L *apicul(us),* dim. of *apex* (see APEX, -ULE) + *-ātus* -ATE[1]]

a·pi·cul·ture (ā′pə kul′chər), *n.* beekeeping, esp. on a commercial scale for the sale of honey. [< L *api(s)* bee + CULTURE] —**a′pi·cul′tur·al,** *adj.* —**a′pi·cul′tur·ist,** *n.*

a·piece (ə pēs′), *adv.* for each: *Oranges are 10 cents apiece. We have one orange apiece.* [ME *a pece.* See A-[2], PIECE]

à pied (A pyā′), *French.* afoot; walking; on foot.

a·pi·ol·o·gy (ā′pē ol′ə jē), *n.* the scientific study of bees, esp. honeybees. [< L *api(s)* bee + -O- + -LOGY] —**a′pi·ol′-o·gist,** *n.*

A·pis (ā′pis), *n.* *Egyptian Religion.* a sacred bull, worshiped at Memphis. Also called **Hapi, Hap.**

ap·ish (ā′pish), *adj.* **1.** having the characteristics or appearance of an ape. **2.** slavishly imitative. **3.** foolishly affected. —**ap′ish·ly,** *adv.* —**ap′ish·ness,** *n.*

a·piv·or·ous (ā piv′ər əs), *adj.* *Zool.* feeding on bees, as certain birds. [< L *api(s)* bee + -VOROUS]

Apl., April.

a·pla·cen·tal (ā′plə sen′təl, ap′lə-), *adj.* *Zool.* having or forming no placenta, as the lowest mammals.

ap·la·nat·ic (ap′lə nat′ik), *adj.* *Optics.* free from spherical aberration and coma. [A-[6] + Gk *planá(ein)* (to) wander + -TIC. See PLANET] —**ap′la·nat′i·cal·ly,** *adv.*

a·pla·sia (ə plā′zhə), *n.* *Pathol.* defective development or congenital absence of an organ or tissue. —**a·plas·tic** (ā plas′-tik), *adj.*

a·plen·ty (ə plen′tē), *Informal.* —*adj.* **1.** in sufficient quantity; in generous amounts (usually used following the noun it modifies): *He had troubles aplenty.* —*adv.* **2.** sufficiently; enough; more than sparingly. [A-[1] + PLENTY]

a·plomb (ə plom′, ə plum′), *n.* imperturbable self-possession, poise, or assurance. [< F *à plomb* according to the plummet, i.e., straight up and down, vertical position]

ap·ne·a (ap nē′ə, ap′nē ə), *n.* *Pathol.* **1.** temporary suspension of respiration. **2.** asphyxia. Also, **ap·noe′a.** [< NL *apnoea* < Gk *ápnoia* = *ápno(os)* breathless (*a-* A-[6] + *pno-,* var. s. of *pneîn* to breathe + *-os* adj. suffix) + *-ia* -IA] —**ap·ne′al, ap·ne′ic, ap·noe′al, ap·noe′ic,** *adj.*

A·po (ä′pô), *n.* an active volcano in the S Philippines, on S Mindanao: highest peak in the Philippines. 9690 ft.

apo-, a learned borrowing from Greek, occurring in direct loan words where the meaning is often no longer clear (*apodosis*) and used with the meaning "away," "from," "off," "asunder," as an element in the formation of compound words (*apomorphine*). Also, *esp. before a vowel,* **ap-.** [< Gk, comb. form of *apó;* akin to Skt *apa,* L *ab,* OFF]

A.P.O., Army Post Office. Also, **APO**

Apoc., **1.** Apocalypse. **2.** Apocrypha. **3.** Apocryphal.

a·poc·a·lypse (ə pok′ə lips), *n.* **1.** See **Revelation of St. John the Divine. 2.** any of a class of Jewish or Christian writings on divine revelation that appeared from about 200 B.C. to A.D. 350. **3.** revelation; discovery; disclosure. [ME < LL *apocalyps(is)* < Gk *apokálypsis* revelation = *apokalýp(tein)* to uncover, reveal (*apo-* APO- + *kalýptein* to cover, conceal) + *-sis* -SIS]

a·poc·a·lyp·tic (ə pok′ə lip′tik), *adj.* **1.** of or like an apocalypse; affording a revelation or prophecy. **2.** pertaining to the Apocalypse or biblical book of Revelations. Also, **a·poc′a·lyp′ti·cal.** [< LGk *apokalyptik(os)* = *apokalýpt(ein)* (to) uncover, disclose (see APOCALYPSE) + *-ikos* -IC] **—a·poc′a·lyp′ti·cal·ly,** *adv.*

ap·o·carp (ap′ə kärp′), *n. Bot.* a gynoecium having separate carpels.

ap·o·car·pous (ap′ə kär′pəs), *adj. Bot.* having the carpels separate. **—ap′o·car′py,** *n.*

Apocarpous
C, Carpels

ap·o·chro·mat·ic (ap′ə krō mat′ik, -ō krə-), *adj. Optics.* corrected for spherical and chromatic aberration. **—ap·o·chro·ma·tism** (ap′ə krō′mə tiz′əm), *n.*

a·poc·o·pate (ə pok′ə pāt′), *v.t.*, **-pat·ed, -pat·ing.** to shorten by apocope. [v. use of *apocopate* (adj.) curtailed, docked] **—a·poc′o·pa′tion,** *n.*

a·poc·o·pe (ə pok′ə pē), *n.* loss or omission of the last letter, syllable, or part of a word. [< LL < Gk *apokopḗ* a cutting off = *apokóp(tein)* (to) cut off (*apo-* APO- + *kóptein* to cut) + *-ē* n. suffix] **—ap·o·cop·ic** (ap′ə kop′ik), *adj.*

a·poc·ry·pha (ə pok′rə fə), *n.* (*often construed as sing.*) **1.** a group of 14 books, not considered canonical, included in the Septuagint and the Vulgate as part of the Old Testament. **2.** various religious writings of uncertain origin regarded by some as inspired, but rejected by most authorities. **3.** works of doubtful authorship or authenticity. Cf. **canon**[1] (defs. 5–7). [ME < LL < Gk, neut. pl. of *apókryphos* hidden, unknown, spurious = *apokryph-* (var. s. of *apokrýptein* to hide away; see APO-, CRYPT) + *-os* adj. suffix]

a·poc·ry·phal (ə pok′rə fəl), *adj.* **1.** *Eccles.* **a.** (*cap.*) of or pertaining to the Apocrypha. **b.** of doubtful sanction; uncanonical. **2.** false; spurious. **—a·poc′ry·phal·ly,** *adv.*

ap·o·dal (ap′ə dᵊl), *adj. Zool.* having no distinct feet or footlike members. Also, **ap′o·dous.** [< Gk *apod-*, s. of *ápous* footless (see A-[6], -POD) + -AL[1]]

ap·o·dic·tic (ap′ə dik′tik), *adj.* **1.** incontestable because demonstrated or demonstrable. **2.** *Logic.* (of a proposition) necessarily true or logically certain. Also, **ap·o·deic·tic** (ap′ə dīk′tik), **ap′o·dic′ti·cal.** [< L *apodīctic(us)* < Gk *apodeiktikós* proving fully. See APO-, DEICTIC] **—ap′o·dic′ti·cal·ly, ap′o·deic′ti·cal·ly,** *adv.*

a·pod·o·sis (ə pod′ə sis), *n., pl.* **-ses** (-sēz′). the clause expressing the consequence in a conditional sentence, often beginning with *then*, as "then I will" in "If you go, then I will." Cf. **protasis** (def. 1). [< LL < Gk: a returning, answering clause = *apo(di)dó(nai)* to give back (*apo-* APO- + *didónai* to give) + *-sis* -SIS. See DOSE]

ap·o·en·zyme (ap′ō en′zīm), *n. Biochem.* the protein component that with a coenzyme forms a complete enzyme.

a·pog·a·my (ə pog′ə mē), *n. Bot.* the development of a sporophyte from a cell or cells of the gametophyte other than the egg. **—ap·o·gam·ic** (ap′ə gam′ik), **a·pog′a·mous,** *adj.* **—ap′o·gam′i·cal·ly, a·pog′a·mous·ly,** *adv.*

ap·o·gee (ap′ə jē′), *n.* **1.** *Astron.* the point in the orbit of a heavenly body, esp. of the moon or of a man-made satellite at which it is farthest from the earth. Cf. **perigee. 2.** the highest point; climax. [alter. (after F *apogée*) of earlier *apogaeum* < L < Gk *apógaion* (*diástema*) off-earth (distance), neut. of *apógaios* adj. = *apo-* APO- + *gâios* of the earth < *gaîa*, var. of *gê* the earth] **—ap′o·ge′al, ap′o·ge′an, ap′o·ge′ic,** *adj.*

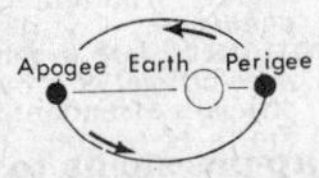

Apogee and perigee

a·po·lit·i·cal (ā′ pə lit′i kəl), *adj.* **1.** not political; of no political significance. **2.** politically indifferent. **—a′po·lit′i·cal·ly,** *adv.*

A·pol·li·naire (ᴀ pô lē neʀ′), *n.* **Guil·laume** (gē yōm′), (*Wilhelm Apollinaris de Kostrowitzki*), 1880–1918, French poet, novelist, and dramatist.

A·pol·lo (ə pol′ō), *n., pl.* **-los** for 2, 3. **1.** the ancient Greek and Roman god of light, healing, music, poetry, prophecy, and manly beauty; the son of Leto and brother of Artemis. **2.** a very handsome young man. **3.** *U.S.* a three-man spacecraft designed to travel to and land on the moon.

Apollo

Ap·ol·lo·ni·an (ap′ə lō′nē ən), *adj.* **1.** pertaining to the cult of Apollo. **2.** (*l.c.*) serene, calm, or well-balanced; poised and disciplined. Cf. **Dionysian.** [< Gk *apollṓni(os)* of APOLLO + -AN]

A·pol·lyon (ə pol′yən), *n.* the destroyer; the angel of the bottomless pit; Abaddon. Rev. 9:11. [< Gk *apollýōn* (prp. of *apollýnai* to destroy utterly) = *ap-* AP-[2] + *olly-* destroy + *-ōn* prp. suffix]

a·pol·o·get·ic (ə pol′ə jet′ik), *adj.* **1.** containing or making an apology: *an apologetic letter.* **2.** willing or eager to apologize. **3.** defending by speech or writing. [< L *apologēticus* < Gk *apologētikós* fit for defense = *apologē-* (verbid s. of *apologéesthai* to speak in defense) + *-tikos* -TIC] **—a·pol′o·get′i·cal·ly,** *adv.*

a·pol·o·get·ics (ə pol′ə jet′iks), *n.* (*construed as sing.*) the branch of theology concerned with the defense or proof of Christianity. [see APOLOGETIC, -ICS]

ap·o·lo·gi·a (ap′ə lō′jē ə), *n. Literature.* a work written as an explanation or justification of one's motives, convictions, or acts. [< LL < Gk: a speaking in defense. See APO-, LOG-, -IA]

a·pol·o·gise (ə pol′ə jīz′), *v.i.*, **-gised, -gis·ing.** *Chiefly Brit.* apologize. **—a·pol′o·gis′er,** *n.*

a·pol·o·gist (ə pol′ə jist), *n.* **1.** a person who makes an apology or defense in speech or writing. **2.** *Eccles.* **a.** Also, **a·pol·o·gete** (ə pol′ə jēt′). a person skilled in apologetics. **b.** one of the authors of the early Christian apologies in defense of the faith.

a·pol·o·gize (ə pol′ə jīz′), *v.i.*, **-gized, -giz·ing. 1.** to offer an apology. **2.** to make a formal defense in speech or writing. Also, *esp. Brit.*, **apologise. —a·pol′o·giz′er,** *n.*

ap·o·logue (ap′ə lôg′, -log′), *n.* **1.** a moral fable. **2.** an allegory. [< L *apolog(us)* < Gk *apólogos* story, fable. See APO-, -LOGUE] **—ap′o·log′al,** *adj.*

a·pol·o·gy (ə pol′ə jē), *n., pl.* **-gies. 1.** an expression of one's regret for having injured, insulted, or wronged another. **2.** a defense or justification in speech or writing, as for a cause or doctrine. [earlier *apologie* < LL *apologia* < Gk. See APOLOGIA] **—Syn. 1.** plea. **2.** vindication, explanation. See **excuse.**

ap·o·lune (ap′ə lo͞on′), *n.* the point of a lunar orbit that is farthest from the moon. [APO- + *lune* < L *lūna* moon]

ap·o·mix·is (ap′ə mik′sis), *n., pl.* **-mix·es** (-mik′sēz). any of several types of asexual reproduction, as apogamy or parthenogenesis. [< NL < Gk *apo-* APO- + *mîxis* a mixing = *mig(nýnai)* to mix + *-sis* -SIS]

ap·o·mor·phine (ap′ə môr′fēn, -fin), *n. Pharm.* an alkaloid, $C_{17}H_{17}NO_2$, derived from morphine: used, usually in the form of its hydrochloride, as an emetic and expectorant. Also, **ap·o·mor·phin** (ap′ə môr′fin).

ap·o·neu·ro·sis (ap′ə no͝o rō′sis, -nyo͝o-), *n., pl.* **-ses** (-sēz). *Anat.* a whitish, fibrous membrane formed by the expansion of a tendon. [< Gk *aponeúrōsis* the part of a muscle becoming a tendon = *aponeur(óein)* to change to tendon (see APO-, NEURO-) + *-ōsis* -OSIS] **—ap·o·neu·rot·ic** (ap′ə no͝o rot′ik, -nyo͝o-), *adj.*

ap·o·pemp·tic (ap′ə pemp′tik), *adj.* **1.** pertaining to leave-taking or departing; valedictory. **—*n.* 2.** *Obs.* a farewell address; valedictory. [< Gk *apopemptik(ós)* of, pertaining to sending away = *apopémp(ein)* to send away (*apo-* APO- + *pémpein* to send) + *-tikos* -TIC]

a·poph·a·sis (ə pof′ə sis), *n. Rhet.* denial of one's intention to speak of a subject that is at the same time named or insinuated, as "I shall not mention Caesar's avarice, nor his cunning, nor his morality." [< LL < Gk: a denial = *apópha(nai)* to say no, deny (*apo-* APO- + *phánai* to say) + *-sis* -SIS]

ap·o·phthegm (ap′ə t͟hem′), *n.* apothegm. **—ap·o·phtheg·mat·ic** (ap′ə t͟heg mat′ik), **ap′o·phtheg·mat′i·cal,** *adj.*

a·poph·y·ge (ə pof′i jē′), *n. Archit.* **1.** a small, concave, outward curve joining the shaft of a column to its base. **2.** Also called **hypophyge.** a similar curve joining the shaft of a column to its capital. Also, **apophysis.** [< Gk: escape, apophyge = *apophyg-* (var. s. of *apopheúgein* to flee away: *apo-* APO- + *pheúgein* to flee; akin to -FUGE) + *-ē* n. suffix]

a·poph·y·sis (ə pof′i sis), *n., pl.* **-ses** (-sēz′). **1.** *Anat., Bot.* an outgrowth; process; projection or protuberance. **2.** *Archit.* apophyge. [< NL < Gk: offshoot = *apo-* APO- + *phýsis* growth (*phý(ein)* to bring forth + *-sis* -SIS)] **—a·poph·y·sate** (ə pof′i sit, -sāt′), *adj.* **—ap·o·phys·e·al, ap·o·phys·i·al** (ap′ə fiz′ē əl), **a·poph·y·sar·y** (ə pof′i ser′ē), *adj.*

ap·o·plec·tic (ap′ə plek′tik), *adj.* **1.** Also, **ap′o·plec′ti·cal.** of, pertaining to, or inclined to apoplexy. **—*n.* 2.** a person having or predisposed to apoplexy. [< LL *apoplēctic(us)* < Gk *apoplēktikós* pertaining to a (paralytic) stroke = *apóplēkt(os)* struck down (verbid of *apoplḗssein*; see APOPLEXY) + *-ikos* -IC] **—ap′o·plec′ti·cal·ly,** *adv.*

ap·o·plex·y (ap′ə plek′sē), *n. Pathol.* **1.** a sudden, usually marked loss of bodily function due to rupture or occlusion of a blood vessel. **2.** hemorrhage into the tissue of any organ, esp. the brain. [ME *apoplexia* < LL < Gk = *apoplēk-* (var. s. of *apoplḗssein* to strike down: *apo-* APO- + *plḗssein* to strike) + *-s(is)* -SIS + *-ia* -Y[3]] **—ap·o·plec·ti·form** (ap′ə plek′tə fôrm′), **ap′o·plec′toid,** *adj.*

a·port (ə pōrt′, ə pôrt′), *adv. Naut.* upon or toward the port side.

ap·o·si·o·pe·sis (ap′ə sī′ə pē′sis), *n., pl.* **-ses** (-sēz). *Rhet.* a sudden breaking off in the midst of a sentence, as if from inability or unwillingness to proceed. [< LL < Gk: lit., a full silence = *aposiōpē-* (var. s. of *aposiōpáein* to be fully silent: *apo-* APO- + *siōpáein* to be silent) + *-sis* -SIS] **—ap·o·si·o·pet·ic** (ap′ə sī′ə pet′ik), *adj.*

a·pos·ta·sy (ə pos′tə sē), *n., pl.* **-sies.** a desertion of or departure from one's religion, principles, cause, etc. [ME *apostasye* < LL *apostasia* < Gk: a standing away, withdrawing = *apóstas(is)* (*apo-* APO- + *sta-* stand + *-sis* -SIS) + *-ia* -IA]

a·pos·tate (ə pos′tāt, -tit), *n.* **1.** a person who forsakes his religion, principles, cause, etc. **—*adj.* 2.** of or characterized by apostasy. [ME < LL *apostat(a)* < Gk *apostátēs* = *aposta-* (see APOSTASY) + *-t-* verbid suffix + *-ēs* n. suffix] **—ap·o·stat·i·cal·ly** (ap′ə stat′ik lē), *adv.*

a·pos·ta·tise (ə pos′tə tīz′), *v.i.*, **-tised, -tis·ing.** *Chiefly Brit.* apostatize.

a·pos·ta·tize (ə pos′tə tīz′), *v.i.*, **-tized, -tiz·ing.** to commit apostasy. [< LL *apostatizāre*] **—a·pos·ta·tism** (ə pos′tə tiz′əm), *n.*

a pos·te·ri·o·ri (ā′ po stēr′ē ōr′ī, -ôr′ī, -ōr′ē, -ôr′ē), **1.** from effect to cause; based upon actual observation or upon experimental data. Cf. **a priori** (def. 1). **2.** not existing in the mind prior to or independent of experience. Cf. **a priori** (def. 2). [< L: lit., from the one behind]

a·pos·til (ə pos′til), *n.* a marginal annotation or note. Also, **a·pos′tille.** [< F *apostille* < (*l*)*a postille* (the) marginal note < ML *postilla* = L *post* after + *illa* those things]

a·pos·tle (ə pos′əl), *n.* **1.** one of the 12 disciples sent forth by Christ to preach the gospel. **2.** the first or the best-known Christian missionary in any region or country. **3.** *Eastern Ch.* one of the 70 disciples of Jesus. **4.** the title of the highest ecclesiastical official in some Protestant sects. **5.** one of the 12 administrative officials of the Mormon Church. **6.** a pioneer of any reform movement. [ME, var. of *apostel*, OE *apostol* < LL *apostol(us)* < Gk *apóstolos*, lit., one who is sent out; akin to *apostéllein* to send off; see APO-] **—a·pos′tle·hood′, a·pos′tle·ship′,** *n.*

Apos′tles' Creed′, a creed dating from about A.D. 500, traditionally ascribed to Christ's apostles, and beginning with "I believe in God the Father Almighty."

a·pos·to·late (ə pos′tᵊlit, -tᵊlāt′), *n.* **1.** the dignity or office of an apostle. **2.** *Rom. Cath. Ch.* the dignity and office of the pope as head of the Apostolic See. [< LL *apostolāt(us)*]

ap·os·tol·ic (ap′ə stol′ik), *adj.* **1.** of or pertaining to an apostle. **2.** derived from the apostles in regular succession. **3.** of or pertaining to the pope; papal. Also, **ap′os·tol′i·cal.** [< LL *apostolic(us)* < Gk *apostolikós.* See APOSTLE, -IC] —**ap′os·tol′i·cal·ly,** *adv.* —**ap·os·tol·i·cism** (ap′ə stol′i-siz′əm), *n.* —**a·pos·to·lic·ity** (ə pos′t^{ə}lis′i tē), **ap′os·tol′i·cal·ness,** *n.*

Ap′ostol′ic Fa′thers, the fathers of the early Christian church whose lives overlapped those of any of the apostles.

Ap′ostol′ic See′, the Roman see, traditionally founded by St. Peter.

ap′ostol′ic succes′sion, *Rom. Cath. Ch., Orth. Ch., Anglican Ch.* the unbroken line of succession beginning with the apostles and perpetuated through bishops.

a·pos·tro·phe[1] (ə pos′trə fē), *n.* the sign ('), as used to indicate the omission of one or more letters in a word, as in *o'er* for *over;* to indicate the possessive case, as in *man's;* or to indicate plurals of abbreviations and symbols, as in *several M.D.'s.* [alter. (by confusion with APOSTROPHE[2]) of earlier *apostrophus* < LL < Gk *apóstrophos (prosōidía)* eliding (mark), lit., (mark) of turning away, verbid of *apostréphein* to turn away = *apo-* APO- + *stréphein* to turn; see STROPHE] —**ap·os·troph·ic** (ap′ə strof′ik), *adj.*

a·pos·tro·phe[2] (ə pos′trə fē), *n. Rhet.* a digression in the form of an address to someone not present, or to a personified object or idea. [< LL < Gk: a turning away = *apostroph-* (var. s. of *apostréphein;* see APOSTROPHE[1]) + *-ē* n. suffix] —**ap·os·troph·ic** (ap′ə strof′ik), *adj.*

a·pos·tro·phise (ə pos′trə fīz′), *v.t., v.i.,* **-phised, -phising.** *Chiefly Brit.* apostrophize.

a·pos·tro·phize (ə pos′trə fīz′), *v.,* **-phized, -phiz·ing.** *Rhet.* —*v.t.* **1.** to address by apostrophe. —*v.i.* **2.** to utter an apostrophe.

apoth′ecaries′ meas′ure, a system of units used chiefly in compounding and dispensing liquid drugs.

apoth′ecaries′ weight′, a system of weights used chiefly in compounding and dispensing drugs.

a·poth·e·car·y (ə poth′ə ker′ē), *n., pl.* **-car·ies.** **1.** a pharmacist licensed to fill prescriptions; druggist. **2.** a pharmacy or drugstore. **3.** (esp. in England and Ireland) a druggist licensed to prescribe medicine. [ME < ML *apothēcāri(us)* shopkeeper = *apothēc(a)* shop, storehouse (< Gk *apothḗkē;* see APO-, THECA) + *-ārius* -ARY]

apoth′ecary jar′, a small, covered jar, formerly used by druggists to hold pharmaceuticals.

ap·o·the·ci·um (ap′ə thē′shē əm, -sē-), *n., pl.* **-ci·a** (-shē ə, -sē ə). *Bot.* the fruit of certain lichens and fungi: usually an open, saucer-shaped or cup-shaped body, the inner surface of which is covered with a layer that bears asci. [< NL < Gk *apo-* APO- + *thēkíon* = *thḗk(ē)* case (see THECA) + *-ion* dim. suffix] —**ap·o·the·cial** (ap′ə thē′shəl), *adj.*

ap·o·thegm (ap′ə them′), *n.* a short, pithy, instructive saying; a terse remark or aphorism. Also, **apophthegm.** [earlier *apothegm(a)* < Gk *apóphthegma* = *apophtheg-* (var. s. of *apophthéng(esthai)* (to) speak out: *apo-* APO- + *phthéngesthai* to speak) + *-ma* n. suffix] —**ap·o·theg·mat·ic** (ap′ə theg mat′ik), **ap′o·theg·mat′i·cal,** *adj.* —**ap′o·theg·mat′i·cal·ly,** *adv.*

ap·o·them (ap′ə them′), *n. Geom.* a perpendicular from the center of a regular polygon to one of its sides. [< Gk *apo(ti)thé(nai)* (to) set off + *-m(a)* n. suffix]

AB, Apothem

a·poth·e·o·sis (ə poth′ē ō′sis, ap′ə thē′ə-sis), *n., pl.* **-ses** (-sēz, -sēz′). **1.** the exaltation of a person to the rank of a god. **2.** the glorification of a person, act, principle, etc., as an ideal. **3.** a deified or glorified ideal. [< LL < Gk. See APO-, THEO-, -OSIS]

a·poth·e·o·sise (ə poth′ē ə sīz′, ap′ə thē′ə sīz′), *v.t.,* **-sised, -sis·ing.** *Chiefly Brit.* apotheosize.

a·poth·e·o·size (ə poth′ē ə sīz′, ap′ə thē′ə sīz′), *v.t.,* **-sized, -siz·ing.** to deify; glorify.

ap·o·tro·pa·ic (ap′ə trə pā′ik), *adj.* intended to ward off evil. [< Gk *apotrópai(on)* something that averts evil (neut. of *apotrópaios* turning away; see APO-, TROPE) + -IC]

app., **1.** apparent. **2.** appendix. **3.** applied. **4.** appointed. **5.** apprentice. **6.** approved. **7.** approximate.

ap·pal (ə pôl′), *v.t.,* **-palled, -pal·ling.** appall.

Ap·pa·la·chi·a (ap′ə lā′chē ə, -chə, -lach′ē ə, -lach′ə), *n.* **1.** *Geol.* a Paleozoic land mass, the erosion of which provided the sediments to form the rocks of the Appalachian Mountains. **2.** a region in the E United States, in the area of the S Appalachian Mountains, usually including NE Alabama, NW Georgia, NW South Carolina, E Tennessee, W Virginia, E Kentucky, West Virginia, and SW Pennsylvania. [back formation from APPALACHIAN]

Ap·pa·la·chi·an (ap′ə lā′chē ən, -chən, -lach′ē ən, lach′-ən), *adj.* **1.** of or pertaining to the Appalachian Mountains. **2.** *Geol.* of or pertaining to the orogeny and accompanying intrusion that occurred during the Pennsylvanian and Permian periods. [perh. < *Apalachee* tribal name + -AN]

Ap′pala′chian Moun′tains, a mountain range in E North America, extending from S Quebec province to N Alabama. Highest peak, Mt. Mitchell, 6684 ft. Also called **Ap′pa·la′chi·ans.**

Ap′pala′chian tea′, **1.** the leaves of any of certain plants of the genus *Ilex* of the eastern U.S., as the shrub or small tree *I. vomitoria,* sometimes used as a tea. **2.** a shrub, *Viburnum cassinoides,* of the eastern U.S.

Ap′pala′chian trail′, a hiking trail extending through the Appalachian Mountains from central Maine to N Georgia. 2050 mi. long.

ap·pall (ə pôl′), *v.t.* to fill or overcome with horror or dismay. Also, **appal.** [ME < MF *ap(p)all(ir)* (to) grow or make pale = *a-* A-[5] + *pal(l)ir* in same sense; see PALE[1]] —**Syn.** horrify, daunt. See **frighten.**

Ap·pa·loo·sa (ap′ə lo͞o′sə), *n.* one of a hardy breed of riding horses, developed in the American West, having a mottled hide, vertically striped hoofs, and eyes that show a relatively large proportion of white. [prob. alter. of *Palouse,* name of an Indian tribe]

ap·pa·nage (ap′ə nij), *n.* **1.** land or revenue granted to a member of a royal family. **2.** whatever belongs rightfully to one's rank or station in life. **3.** a natural or necessary accompaniment; adjunct. Also, **apanage.** [< MF < ML *appanāg(ium)* = *appān(āre)* (to) endow with a maintenance (< L *ap-* AP-[1] + *pān-* bread + *-āre* inf. suffix) + *-āgium* -AGE]

appar., **1.** apparent. **2.** apparently.

ap·pa·rat·us (ap′ə rat′əs, -rā′təs), *n., pl.* **-tus, -tus·es.** **1.** a group or aggregate of instruments, machinery, tools, materials, etc., intended for a specific use. **2.** any complex instrument or machine for a particular purpose. **3.** any system of activities, functions, etc., directed toward a specific goal: *the apparatus of government.* **4.** *Physiol.* a group of structurally different organs performing a particular function. [< L < *apparātus* (ptp. of *apparāre*) provided = *ap-* AP-[1] + *par-* prepare + *-ātus* -ATE[1]]

ap·par·el (ə par′əl), *n., v.,* **-eled, -el·ing** or (*esp. Brit.*) **-elled, -el·ling.** —*n.* **1.** clothing; garments. **2.** anything that decorates or covers. **3.** *Naut.* the masts, sails, anchor, etc., used to equip a vessel. —*v.t.* **4.** to dress or clothe. **5.** to adorn. [ME *appareill(en)* < OF *apareillie(r)* (to) make fit, fit out < VL **appariculāre* = *ap-* AP-[1] + **paricul(us)* a fit (see PAR, -CULE) + *-āre* inf. suffix] —**Syn.** **1.** clothes, dress, garb, costume, habiliments, vesture. **2.** attire. **4.** outfit; array.

ap·par·ent (ə par′ənt, ə pâr′-), *adj.* **1.** exposed to sight; visible. **2.** capable of being easily perceived or understood; obvious. **3.** according to appearances, initial evidence, incomplete results, etc.; ostensible rather than actual: *He was the apparent winner of the election.* **4.** absolutely entitled to succeed to a throne, title, or other estate. Cf. **heir apparent, heir presumptive.** [< L *appārent-* (s. of *appārēns* appearing; see APPEAR, -ENT); r. ME *aparant* < MF] —**ap·par′ent·ly,** *adv.* —**ap·par′ent·ness,** *n.*
—**Syn.** **1.** discernible. **2.** open, manifest, unmistakable. APPARENT, EVIDENT, OBVIOUS, PATENT all refer to something easily perceived. APPARENT applies to that which can readily be seen or perceived: *an apparent effort.* EVIDENT applies to that which facts or circumstances make plain: *His innocence was evident.* OBVIOUS applies to that which is unquestionable, because completely manifest or noticeable: *an obvious change of method.* PATENT, a more formal word, applies to that which is open to view or understanding by all: *a patent error.* —**Ant.** **2.** concealed, obscure.

appar′ent hori′zon, horizon (def. 1).

ap·pa·ri·tion (ap′ə rish′ən), *n.* **1.** a ghostly appearance; a specter or phantom. **2.** anything that appears, esp. something remarkable or startling: *the apparition of cowboys in New York City.* **3.** act of appearing; manifestation. **4.** *Astron.* the appearance of a comet or the time when it is visible: *the 1910 apparition of Halley's Comet.* [late ME < L *appāritiōn-* (s. of *appāritiō*) attendance = *appārit(us)* appeared in public (ptp. of *appārēre;* see APPEAR, -ITE[2]) + *-iōn* -ION] —**ap′pa·ri′tion·al,** *adj.*
—**Syn.** **1.** ghost, spirit, shade. APPARITION, PHANTASM, PHANTOM are terms for a supernatural appearance. An APPARITION of a person or thing is an immaterial appearance that seems real, and is generally sudden or startling in its manifestation: *an apparition of a headless horseman.* Both PHANTOM and PHANTASM denote an illusory appearance, as in a dream; the former may be pleasant, while the latter is usually frightening: *a phantom of a garden; a monstrous phantasm.*

ap·par·i·tor (ə par′i tər), *n.* (in ancient Rome) a subordinate official of a magistrate or court. [< L: servant, esp. an official's attendant in public < *appārit(us)* (ptp.; see APPARITION) + *-or* -OR[2]]

ap·pas·sio·na·to (ə pä′sē ə nä′tō; *It.* äp päs′syô nä′tô), *adj. Music.* impassioned; with passion or strong feeling. [< It; see AP-[1], PASSION, -ATE[1]]

appd., approved.

ap·peal (ə pēl′), *n.* **1.** an earnest request for aid, mercy, etc.; entreaty. **2.** a request or reference to some person or authority for a decision, corroboration, judgment, etc. **3.** *Law.* **a.** an application or proceeding for review by a higher tribunal. **b.** (in a legislative body or assembly) a formal question as to the correctness of a ruling by a presiding officer. **c.** *Obs.* a formal charge or accusation. **4.** the power to attract, interest, amuse, or stimulate the mind or emotions: *The game has lost its appeal.* **5.** *Obs.* a summons or challenge. —*v.i.* **6.** to ask earnestly, as for mercy or aid. **7.** *Law.* to apply for review of a case or particular issue to a higher tribunal. **8.** to have need of or ask for proof, a decision, corroboration, etc. **9.** to attract, be of interest, etc.: *The red hat appeals to me.* —*v.t.* **10.** *Law.* **a.** to apply for review of (a case) to a higher tribunal. **b.** *Obs.* to charge with a crime before a tribunal. **11. appeal to the country,** *Brit.* See **country** (def. 9). [ME *a(p)pel(en)* < MF *a(p)pele(r)* < L *appellāre* to speak to, appeal to (lit., approach) = *ap-* AP-[1] + *pell-* move, go + *-āre* inf. suffix] —**ap·peal′a·bil′i·ty,** *n.* —**ap·peal′a·ble,** *adj.* —**ap·peal′er,** *n.*
—**Syn.** **1.** plea, petition. **2.** suit, solicitation. **4.** attraction. **6.** request, ask. APPEAL, PETITION, ENTREAT, SUPPLICATE mean to ask for something wished for or needed. APPEAL and PETITION may concern groups and formal or public requests. ENTREAT and SUPPLICATE are usually more personal and emotional. To APPEAL is to ask earnestly for help or support, on grounds of reason, justice, common humanity, etc.: *to appeal for contributions to a charity.* To PETITION is to ask by written request, by prayer, or the like, that something be granted: *to petition for more playgrounds.* ENTREAT suggests pleading: *The child entreated his father not to punish him.* To SUPPLICATE is to beg humbly, usually from a superior, powerful, or stern (official) person: *to supplicate that the lives of prisoners be spared.*

ap·peal·ing (ə pē′ling), *adj.* evoking or attracting interest, desire, curiosity, sympathy, or the like; attractive. —**ap·peal′ing·ly,** *adv.* —**ap·peal′ing·ness,** *n.*

ap·pear (ə pēr′), *v.i.* **1.** to come into sight; become visible: *A man appeared in the doorway.* **2.** to seem; give an impression: *to appear wise.* **3.** to be obvious or easily perceived; be made clear by evidence: *It appears to me that you are right.* **4.** to come or be placed before the public: *His biography appeared last year.* **5.** to perform publicly, as in a play, dance, etc. **6.** to attend or be present, esp. to arrive late or stay but a short time: *He appeared at the party but left quickly.* **7.** to come into being; be created, invented, or developed: *Speech appears in the child's first or second year.* **8.** *Law.* to come formally before a tribunal, authority, etc., as defendant, plaintiff, counsel, etc. [ME *a(p)pere* < OF *aper-* (tonic

s. of *apareir*) < L *appār(ēre)* (to) appear, attend, attend in public = *ap-* AP-[1] + *pārēre* to appear] **—Syn. 1.** emerge. **2.** See **seem.**

ap·pear·ance (ə pēr′əns), *n.* **1.** the act or fact of appearing, as to the eye or mind or before the public. **2.** the state, condition, manner, or style in which a person or object appears: *a man of noble appearance.* **3.** outward show or seeming; semblance: *to avoid the appearance of coveting an honor.* **4.** *Law.* the coming into court of either party to a suit or action. **5. appearances,** outward impressions, indications, or circumstances: *To all appearances, he enjoyed himself.* **6.** an apparition. **7.** *Philos.* the sensory, or phenomenal, aspect of existence to an observer. **8. keep up appearances,** to maintain a public impression of decorum, prosperity, etc., despite reverses, unfavorable conditions, or the like. [APPEAR + -ANCE; r. ME *aparance* < MF < *apareir* to APPEAR] **—Syn. 1.** arrival, coming, advent. **2.** demeanor, presence. APPEARANCE, ASPECT, GUISE refer to the way in which something outwardly presents itself to view. APPEARANCE refers to the outward look: *the shabby appearance of his car.* ASPECT refers to the appearance at some particular time or in special circumstances; it often has emotional implications: *In the dusk the forest had a terrifying aspect.* GUISE suggests a misleading appearance, assumed for an occasion or a purpose: *under the guise of friendship.*

ap·pease (ə pēz′), *v.t.*, **-peased, -peas·ing.** **1.** to bring to a state of peace or contentment; pacify. **2.** to satisfy or relieve: *to appease hunger.* **3.** to yield or concede to the belligerent demands of (a nation, group, person, etc.) in a conciliatory effort. [ME *apese* < OF *apais(i)er* = *a-* A-[5] + *pais-* PEACE + *-ier* inf. suffix] **—ap·peas′a·ble,** *adj.* **—ap·pease′ment,** *n.* **—ap·peas′er,** *n.* **—ap·peas′ing·ly,** *adv.* **—Syn. 1.** calm, placate. **—Ant. 1.** enrage. **3.** defy.

ap·pel (ə pel′, a pel′; *Fr.* A pel′), *n., pl.* **ap·pels** (ə pelz′, a pelz′; *Fr.* A pel′). *Fencing.* **1.** a tap or stamp of the foot, formerly serving as a warning of one's intent to attack. **2.** a smart stroke with the blade, used to gain an opening. [< F: APPEAL]

ap·pel·lant (ə pel′ənt), *n.* **1.** a person who appeals. **2.** *Law.* the party that appeals to a higher tribunal. [late ME *appellaunt* < AF, OF *apelant,* prp. of *apeler* to APPEAL; see -ANT]

ap·pel·late (ə pel′it), *adj. Law.* **1.** pertaining to appeals. **2.** having the authority to review and decide appeals, as a court. [< L *appellāt(us)* called upon, named, appealed to (ptp. of *appellāre*). See APPEAL, -ATE[1]]

ap·pel·la·tion (ap′ə lā′shən), *n.* **1.** a name, title, or designation. **2.** act of naming. [< L *appellātiōn-* (s. of *appellātiō*) a naming]

ap·pel·la·tive (ə pel′ə tiv), *n.* **1.** a common noun. **2.** a descriptive name or designation, as *Simple* in *Simple Simon.* **—***adj.* **3.** pertaining to a common noun. **4.** designative; descriptive. [< LL *appellātīv(us)*] **—ap·pel′la·tive·ly,** *adv.* **—ap·pel′la·tive·ness,** *n.*

ap·pel·lee (ap′ə lē′), *n. Law.* the defendant or respondent in an appellate proceeding. [< AF *appelle,* OF *apele,* ptp. of *apeler* to APPEAL; see -EE]

ap·pend (ə pend′), *v.t.* **1.** to add as a supplement, accessory or appendix. **2.** to attach as a pendant. [< LL *append(ere)* (to) make hang to. See AP-[1], PEND]

ap·pend·age (ə pen′dij), *n.* **1.** a subordinate part attached to something. **2.** *Biol.* any member of the body diverging from the axial trunk. **3.** *Bot.* any subsidiary part superadded to another part. **4.** a person in a subordinate or dependent position. **—ap·pend′aged,** *adj.*

ap·pend·ant (ə pen′dənt), *adj.* **1.** attached; annexed. **2.** associated as an accompaniment or consequence: *the salary appendant to a position.* **3.** *Law.* pertaining to a legal appendant. **—***n.* **4.** a person or thing attached or added. **5.** *Law.* any subordinate possession or right dependent on a greater one and automatically passing with it, as by sale or inheritance. Also, **ap·pend′ent.** [ME < MF: belonging to (prp. of *appendre* to APPEND). See -ANT] **—ap·pend′ance, ap·pend′an·cy, ap·pend′ence, ap·pend′en·cy,** *n.*

ap·pen·dec·to·my (ap′ən dek′tə mē), *n., pl.* **-mies.** *Surg.* excision of the vermiform appendix.

ap·pen·di·ci·tis (ə pen′di sī′tis), *n. Pathol.* inflammation of the vermiform appendix. [< NL < L *appendic-* (s. of *appendix*) APPENDIX + *-ītis* -ITIS]

ap·pen·di·cle (ə pen′di kəl), *n.* a small appendage. [< L *appendicul(a)* small appendage = *appendic-* (see APPENDIX) + *-ula* -ULE] **—ap·pen·dic·u·lar** (ap′ən dik′yə lər), *adj.*

ap·pen·dix (ə pen′diks), *n., pl.* **-dix·es, -di·ces** (-di sēz′). **1.** supplementary material at the end of a book, article, or other text, usually of an explanatory, statistical, or bibliographic nature. **2.** an appendage. **3.** *Anat.* **a.** a process or projection. **b.** See **vermiform appendix.** [< L: appendage = *append(ere)* (to) APPEND + *-ix* (= *-ic-* n. suffix + *-s* nom. sing. ending)]

ap·per·ceive (ap′ər sēv′), *v.t.*, **-ceived, -ceiv·ing.** *Psychol.* **1.** to be conscious of perceiving. **2.** to comprehend (a new idea) by assimilation with one's previous knowledge and experience. [ME < OF *aperceiv(re).* See AP-[1], PERCEIVE]

ap·per·cep·tion (ap′ər sep′shən), *n. Psychol.* **1.** conscious perception. **2.** the act or process of apperceiving. [< NL *apperceptiōn-,* s. of *apperceptiō.* See AP-[1], PERCEPTION] **—ap′per·cep′tive,** *adj.* **—ap′per·cep′tive·ly,** *adv.*

ap·per·tain (ap′ər tān′), *v.i.* to belong as a part, right, possession, attribute, etc.; pertain or relate (usually fol. by *to*). [ME *a(p)perte(y)ne* < OF *aperten(ir).* See AP-[1], PERTAIN]

ap·pe·stat (ap′i stat′), *n.* a region in the human brain that functions to adjust appetite. [APPE(TITE) + (THERMO)STAT, by analogy]

ap·pe·tence (ap′i təns), *n.* **1.** intense natural craving. **2.** instinctive inclination or natural tendency. **3.** material or chemical attraction or affinity. Also, **ap′pe·ten′cy.** [obs. *appete* to seek for, long for (< L *appete(re)* = *ap-* AP-[1] + *petere* to seek) + -ENCE]

ap·pe·tite (ap′i tīt′), *n.* **1.** a desire for food or drink. **2.** any bodily need or craving. **3.** a desire, fondness, or inclination for something. [ME *appetit* < L *appetīt(us)* a craving < *appetītus* craved (ptp. of *appetere*). See APPETENCE, -ITE[2]]

ap·pe·tiz·er (ap′i tī′zər), *n.* a portion of food or drink served before a meal to stimulate the desire to eat. [APPETIZ(ING) + -ER[1]]

ap·pe·tiz·ing (ap′i tī′zing), *adj.* appealing to or stimulating the appetite. [APPET(ITE) + -IZE + -ING[2], modeled on F *appétissant*] **—ap′pe·tiz′ing·ly,** *adv.*

Ap′pi·an Way′ (ap′ē ən), an ancient Roman highway extending from Rome to Brundisium (now Brindisi): begun 312 B.C. by Appius Claudius Caecus. ab. 350 mi. long.

ap·plaud (ə plôd′), *v.i.* **1.** to clap the hands as an expression of approval, acclamation, etc. **2.** to render praise or acclaim in any way. **—***v.t.* **3.** to clap the hands so as to show approval, appreciation, etc., of. **4.** to praise or express approval of. [< L *applaud(ere)* = *ap-* AP-[1] + *plaudere* to clap the hands] **—ap·plaud′a·ble,** *adj.* **—ap·plaud′a·bly,** *adv.* **—ap·plaud′er,** *n.* **—ap·plaud′ing·ly,** *adv.*

ap·plause (ə plôz′), *n.* **1.** the act or fact of applauding. **2.** the sound made by persons in applauding. [< L *applaus(us)* struck upon, applauded (ptp. of *applaudere* to APPLAUD)] **—ap·plau·sive** (ə plô′siv, -ziv), *adj.* **—Syn. 1.** acclaim.

ap·ple (ap′əl), *n.* **1.** the usually round, red or yellow, edible fruit of a rosaceous tree, *Malus pumila.* **2.** any of various other similar fruits, or fruitlike products or plants, as the custard apple. **3.** *Informal.* a baseball. [ME; OE *æppel;* c. OE *appel,* Icel *apal(l),* OHG *apful* (> G *Apfel*)]

ap′ple blos′som, the flower of the apple tree: the state flower of Arkansas and Michigan.

ap′ple but′ter, apples stewed to a paste, sweetened, spiced, and served as a spread or condiment.

ap·ple·cart (ap′əl kärt′), *n.* **1.** a pushcart used by a vendor of apples. **2. upset the** or **one's applecart,** to ruin plans or arrangements; spoil something.

ap′ple green′, a clear, light green.

ap·ple·jack (ap′əl jak′), *n. U.S.* **1.** a brandy distilled from fermented cider. **2.** fermented cider.

ap′ple of dis′cord, *Class. Myth.* a golden apple inscribed "For the fairest," thrown by Eris, goddess of discord, among the gods and awarded by Paris to Aphrodite.

ap′ple of one's eye′, something very precious or dear to a person.

ap′ple pan·dow′dy, pandowdy.

ap′ple-pie or′der, *Informal.* excellent or perfect order.

ap·ple-pol·ish (ap′əl pol′ish), *v.i. Informal.* to curry favor with someone, esp. in an obsequious or flattering manner. **—ap′ple-pol′ish·er,** *n.*

ap·ple·sauce (ap′əl sôs′), *n.* **1.** apples stewed to a soft pulp and sweetened. **2.** *Slang.* nonsense; bunk.

Ap·ple·seed (ap′əl sēd′), *n.* **Johnny** (*John Chapman*), 1774–1845, American pioneer and orchardist: prototype for a character in American folklore.

Ap·ple·ton (ap′əl tən), *n.* **1. Sir Edward Victor,** 1892–1965, British physicist: Nobel prize 1947. **2.** a city in E Wisconsin. 57,143 (1970).

ap·pli·ance (ə plī′əns), *n.* **1.** an apparatus for a particular purpose or use. **2.** a piece of equipment, usually electrical, esp. for use in the home, as a refrigerator, washing machine, etc. **3.** the act of applying; application. **4.** *Obs.* compliance.

ap·pli·ca·ble (ap′lə kə bəl, ə plik′ə-), *adj.* applying or capable of being applied; relevant; appropriate. [< L *applic(āre)* (to) APPLY + -ABLE] **—ap′pli·ca·bil′i·ty, ap′pli·ca·ble·ness,** *n.* **—ap′pli·ca·bly,** *adv.* **—Syn.** fitting, suitable, germane, pertinent.

ap·pli·cant (ap′lə kənt), *n.* a person who applies for or requests something: *an applicant for a position.* [< L *applicant-* (s. of *applicāns* applying, prp. of *applicāre*). See APPLY, -ANT]

ap·pli·ca·tion (ap′lə kā′shən), *n.* **1.** the act of applying or putting to use. **2.** the quality of being usable for a particular purpose or in a special way; relevance. **3.** the act or an instance of spreading on, rubbing in, or bringing into contact: *a second application of varnish.* **4.** a salve or healing agent. **5.** the act of requesting. **6.** a written or spoken request or appeal: *to file an application.* **7.** close attention; persistent effort: *application to one's studies.* [late ME < L *applicātiōn-* (s. of *applicātiō*) = *applicāt(us)* applied (ptp. of *applicāre* to APPLY) + *-iōn-* -ION] **—Syn. 2.** suitability, pertinence. **6.** petition. **7.** assiduity, industry. See **effort.**

ap·pli·ca·tive (ap′lə kā′tiv, ə plik′ə-), *adj.* usable or capable of being used; applicatory. [obs. *applicate* to apply (see APPLICATION) + -IVE] **—ap′pli·ca′tive·ly** *adv.*

ap·pli·ca·tor (ap′lə kā′tər), *n.* a simple device, as a rod, spatula, or the like, for applying a substance not usually touched with the fingers. [obs. *applicate* + -OR[2]]

ap·pli·ca·to·ry (ap′lə kə tōr′ē, -tôr′ē, ə plik′ə-), *adj.* fitted for application or use; practical. [obs. *applicate* (see APPLICATIVE) + -ORY[1]] **—ap′pli·ca·to′ri·ly,** *adv.*

ap·plied (ə plīd′), *adj.* having a practical purpose or involved with actual phenomena (distinguished from *theoretical,* opposed to *pure*): *applied mathematics.*

ap·pli·qué (ap′lə kā′), *adj., n., v.,* **-quéd, -qué·ing.** **—***adj.* **1.** ornamented by a different material or a piece of the same type, sewn on or otherwise applied. **—***n.* **2.** the ornamentation so used. **3.** work so created. **—***v.t.* **4.** to apply as appliqué to. [< F: applied, fastened to, ptp. of *appliquer* to APPLY]

ap·ply (ə plī′), *v.*, **-plied, -ply·ing.** **—***v.t.* **1.** to make practical or active use of; use for a particular purpose: *to apply a theory to a problem; to apply pressure to open the door.* **2.** to bring into action; employ: *He applied the brakes and skidded to a stop.* **3.** to assign to a specific purpose: *He applied a portion of his salary each week to savings.* **4.** to put into effect: *They applied the rules to new members only.* **5.** to lay or spread on: *to apply paint to a wall.* **6.** to bring into physical contact with or close proximity to: *to apply a match to gunpowder.* **7.** to devote or employ diligently: *to apply one's mind to a problem.* **8.** to credit to, as an account: *to apply $10 to his account at the store.* **—***v.i.* **9.** to be pertinent, suitable, or relevant: *The theory doesn't apply.* **10.** to make an application or request: *to apply for a job.* **11.** to lay or spread on: *A new paint is easy to apply on any surface.* [ME *applie* < MF *aplie(r)* < L *applicāre* = *ap-* AP-[1] + *plicāre* to fold; see PLY[2]] —**ap·pli′a·ble,** *adj.* —**ap·pli′a·ble·ness,** *n.* —**ap·pli′a·bly,** *adv.* —**ap·pli′er,** *n.* —**Syn. 2.** utilize. **3.** appropriate, allot, assign. **10.** petition, sue.

ap·pog·gia·tu·ra (ə poj′ə-to͝or′ə, -tyo͝or′ə; *It.* äp pôd′jä to͞o′rä), *n., pl.* **-tu·ras,** *It.* **-tu·re** (-to͞o′RE). *Music.* a short or long note of embellishment preceding another note and taking a portion of its time. [< It: a propping = *appoggiat(o),* ptp. of *appoggiare* to support (see AP-[1], PODIUM, -ATE[1]) + *-ura* -URE]

Appoggiatura
A, Short; B, Long

ap·point (ə point′), *v.t.* **1.** to name or assign to a position, office, or the like; designate: *to appoint a judge to the bench.* **2.** to determine by authority or agreement; fix; set: *to appoint a time for a meeting.* **3.** *Law.* to designate (a person) to take the benefit of an estate created by a deed or will. **4.** *Archaic.* to order or establish by decree or command. **5.** *Obs.* to equip; furnish. [ME *apoint(en)* < MF *apointe(r)* = *a-* A-[5] + *pointer* to POINT] —**ap·point′a·ble,** *adj.* —**ap·point′er,** *n.* —**Syn. 1.** name, select. **2.** prescribe, establish.

ap·point·ee (ə poin tē′, ap′oin tē′), *n.* **1.** a person who is appointed. **2.** a beneficiary under a legal appointment. [APPOINT + -EE, modeled on F *appointé*]

ap·poin·tive (ə poin′tiv), *adj.* **1.** of or pertaining to appointment. **2.** filled by appointment: *an appointive office in the government.*

ap·point·ment (ə point′mənt), *n.* **1.** the act of appointing, as to an office or position. **2.** an office, position, or the like, to which a person is appointed. **3.** an agreement to meet at a certain place and time. **4.** the meeting itself. **5.** Usually, **appointments.** equipment, furnishings, or accouterments. [late ME *apoynt(e)ment* < MF *ap(p)ointement*] —**Syn. 2.** APPOINTMENT, OFFICE, POST, STATION mean a place of duty or employment. APPOINTMENT refers to a position for which special qualifications are required. OFFICE often suggests a position of trust or authority. POST in the U.S. is usually restricted to military or other public positions; in England it may be used of any position. STATION means a sphere of duty or occupation; it emphasizes the location of work to be done. See also **position. 3.** assignation, date.

Ap·po·mat·tox (ap′ə mat′əks), *n.* **1.** a town in central Virginia where Lee surrendered to Grant, ending the Civil War. See map at **Antietam. 2.** a river flowing E from E central Virginia to the James River. 137 mi. long.

ap·por·tion (ə pôr′shən, ə pôr′-), *v.t.* to distribute or divide and assign proportionately. [< MF *apportionn(er)*] —**ap·por′tion·a·ble,** *adj.* —**ap·por′tion·er,** *n.*

ap·por·tion·ment (ə pôr′shən mənt, ə pôr′-), *n.* **1.** act of apportioning. **2.** *U.S.* **a.** the determination of the number of members of the U.S. House of Representatives according to the proportion of the population of each state to the total population of the U.S. **b.** the apportioning of members of any other legislative body.

ap·pose (ə pōz′), *v.t.,* **-posed, -pos·ing. 1.** to place side by side or next to. **2.** to put or apply (one thing) to or near to another. [< MF *a(p)pose(r)* (to) set before, beside, or upon = A-[5] + *poser* to POSE[1]] —**ap·pos′a·bil′i·ty,** *n.* —**ap·pos′a·ble,** *adj.* —**ap·pos′er,** *n.*

ap·po·site (ap′ə zit, ə poz′it), *adj.* suitable; pertinent; apt. [< L *apposit(us)* applied to, added to, put near (ptp. of *appōnere*) = *ap-* AP-[1] + *positus* placed (*posi-* place + *-tus* ptp. suffix)] —**ap′po·site·ly,** *adj.* —**ap′po·site·ness,** *n.*

ap·po·si·tion (ap′ə zish′ən), *n.* **1.** the act of placing together; juxtaposition. **2.** the application of one thing to another. **3.** *Gram.* a syntactic relation between two expressions having the same function and relation to other elements in the sentence, the second expression identifying or supplementing the first. In *Washington, our first President,* the phrase *our first President* is in apposition to *Washington.* **4.** *Biol.* growth of a cell wall by the deposition of new particles in layers on the wall. Cf. **intussusception** (def. 2). [< LL *appositiōn-* (s. of *appositiō*). See APPOSITE, -ION] —**ap′po·si′tion·al,** *adj.* —**ap′po·si′tion·al·ly,** *adv.*

ap·pos·i·tive (ə poz′i tiv), *Gram.* —*n.* **1.** a word or phrase in apposition. —*adj.* **2.** placed in apposition. **3.** (of an adjective or adjectival phrase) directly following the noun it modifies. [APPOSIT(ION) + -IVE] —**ap·pos′i·tive·ly,** *adj.*

ap·prais·al (ə prā′zəl), *n.* **1.** the act of estimating or judging the nature or value of someone or something. **2.** an estimate or considered opinion of the nature or value of someone or something: *the critics' appraisal of modern art.* **3.** an estimate of value of property, as for sale, assessment, or taxation; valuation. Also, **ap·praise′ment.**

ap·praise (ə prāz′), *v.t.,* **-praised, -prais·ing. 1.** to estimate the nature or value of. **2.** to estimate the monetary value of; assess: *He appraised the diamond ring at $500.* [AP(PRIZE) + PRAISE (in obs. sense to PRIZE[2])] —**ap·prais′a·ble,** *adj.* —**ap·prais′er,** *n.* —**ap·prais′ing·ly,** *adv.* —**ap·prais′ive,** *adj.*

ap·pre·ci·a·ble (ə prē′shē ə bəl, -shə bəl), *adj.* capable of being readily perceived or estimated; considerable. [AP-PRECI(ATE) + -ABLE] —**ap·pre′ci·a·bly,** *adv.*

ap·pre·ci·ate (ə prē′shē āt′), *v.,* **-at·ed, -at·ing.** —*v.t.* **1.** to be grateful for: *They appreciated his thoughtfulness.* **2.** to value highly; place a high estimate on. **3.** to be fully aware of: *to appreciate the dangers of a situation.* **4.** to raise in value. —*v.i.* **5.** to increase in value: *Property values appreciated yearly.* [< ML *appreciāt(us)* valued, appraised, LL *appretiātus* (ptp. of *appretiāre*) appraised = L *ap-* AP-[1] + *preti(um)* PRICE + *-ātus* -ATE[1]] —**ap·pre′ci·at′ing·ly,** *adv.* —**ap·pre′ci·a′tor,** *n.*
—**Syn. 2.** APPRECIATE, ESTEEM, VALUE, PRIZE imply holding something in high regard. To APPRECIATE is to exercise wise judgment, delicate perception, and keen insight in realizing the worth of something. To ESTEEM is to feel respect combined with a warm, kindly feeling. To VALUE is to attach importance to a thing because of its worth (material or otherwise). To PRIZE is to value highly and cherish.

ap·pre·ci·a·tion (ə prē′shē ā′shən), *n.* **1.** gratitude: *They showed their appreciation by giving him a gold watch.* **2.** the act of estimating the qualities of things according to their true worth. **3.** clear perception or recognition, esp. of aesthetic quality. **4.** an increase in the value of property, goods, etc. **5.** critical notice; evaluation; opinion, as of a situation, person, etc. **6.** a critique or written evaluation, esp. when favorable. [earlier *appretiation* < LL *appretiāt(us)* (see APPRECIATE) + -ION] —**ap·pre′ci·a′tion·al,** *adj.*

ap·pre·cia·tive (ə prē′shə tiv, -shē ā′-), *adj.* **1.** feeling or showing appreciation. **2.** capable of appreciation. —**ap·pre′cia·tive·ly,** *adv.* —**ap·pre′cia·tive·ness,** *n.*

ap·pre·cia·to·ry (ə prē′shə tôr′ē, -tôr′ē, -shē ə-), *adj.* appreciative. —**ap·pre′cia·to′ri·ly,** *adv.*

ap·pre·hend (ap′ri hend′), *v.t.* **1.** to take into custody; arrest by legal warrant or authority. **2.** to grasp the meaning of, esp. intuitively; perceive. **3.** to expect with anxiety, suspicion, or fear. —*v.i.* **4.** to understand. **5.** to be apprehensive; fear. [ME *apprehend(en)* < L *apprehende(re)* (to) grasp = *ap-* AP-[1] + *prehendere* to seize; see PREHENSION] —**ap′pre·hend′er,** *n.*

ap·pre·hen·si·ble (ap′ri hen′sə bəl), *adj.* capable of being understood. [< LL *apprehensibil(is)* < L *apprehens(us)* grasped (ptp. of *apprehendere*) = *apprehend-* (see APPREHEND) + *-t(us)* ptp. suffix + *-ibilis* -IBLE] —**ap′pre·hen′si·bil′i·ty,** *n.* —**ap′pre·hen′si·bly,** *adv.*

ap·pre·hen·sion (ap′ri hen′shən), *n.* **1.** suspicion or fear of future trouble or evil. **2.** the faculty or act of apprehending, esp. intuitive understanding. **3.** a view, opinion, or idea on any subject. **4.** the act of arresting; seizure. [ME < LL *apprehensiōn-* (s. of *apprehensiō*) = *apprehens-* (see APPREHENSIBLE) + *-iōn-* -ION]
—**Syn. 1.** alarm, worry, uneasiness; suspicion. APPREHENSION, ANXIETY, MISGIVING imply an unsettled and uneasy state of mind. APPREHENSION is an active state of fear, usually of some danger or misfortune: *apprehension before opening a telegram.* ANXIETY is a somewhat prolonged state of apprehensive worry: *anxiety because of a reduced income.* MISGIVING implies a dubious uncertainty or suspicion, as well as uneasiness: *to have misgivings about the investment.* **4.** capture. —**Ant. 1.** composure. **4.** release.

ap·pre·hen·sive (ap′ri hen′siv), *adj.* **1.** uneasy or fearful about something that might happen. **2.** quick to learn or understand. **3.** perceptive; discerning (usually fol. by *of*). [< ML *apprehensīv(us).* See APPREHENSIBLE, -IVE] —**ap′pre·hen′sive·ly,** *adv.* —**ap′pre·hen′sive·ness,** *n.*

ap·pren·tice (ə pren′tis), *n., v.,* **-ticed, -tic·ing.** —*n.* **1.** a person who works for another in order to learn a trade: *an apprentice to a plumber.* **2.** *Hist.* a person legally bound through indenture to a master craftsman in order to learn a trade. **3.** a learner; novice. **4.** *U.S. Navy.* an enlisted man receiving specialized training. **5.** a jockey with less than one year's experience who has won fewer than 40 races. —*v.t.* **6.** to bind to or place with an employer for instruction in a trade. [ME *aprentis* < MF = *aprentif* for **aprendif* (*aprend-* < L *apprend-* APPREHEND + *-if* < L *-īvus* -IVE) + *-s* nom. suffix] —**ap·pren′tice·ship′,** *n.*

ap·pressed (ə prest′), *adj.* pressed closely against or fitting closely to something. [< L *appress(us)* pressed to (ptp. of *apprimere*) = *ap-* AP-[1] + *pressus* (see PRESS[1]) + -ED[2]]

ap·prise (ə prīz′), *v.t.,* **-prised, -pris·ing.** to give notice to; inform; advise (often fol. by *of*): *to be apprised of the situation by a friend.* Also, **apprize.** [< F *appris* taught, informed, ptp. of *apprendre;* see APPREHEND]

ap·prize[1] (ə prīz′), *v.t.,* **-prized, -priz·ing.** *Obs.* appraise. [ME *aprise* < MF *apris(i)er* = *a-* A-[5] + *prisier* to PRIZE[2]] —**ap·priz′er,** *n.*

ap·prize[2] (ə prīz′), *v.t.,* **-prized, -priz·ing.** apprise.

ap·proach (ə prōch′), *v.t.* **1.** to come near or nearer to: *to approach the city.* **2.** to come near to in quality, character, time, or condition: *As a poet he hardly approaches Keats.* **3.** to solicit the interest or favor of, as for a proposal: *to approach the president with a suggestion.* **4.** to begin work on; set about: *to approach a problem.* —*v.i.* **5.** to come nearer. **6.** to come near in character, time, amount, etc.; approximate. —*n.* **7.** the act of coming nearer: *the approach of a horseman.* **8.** nearness or close approximation: *a fair approach to accuracy.* **9.** any means of access, as a road, ramp, etc.: *the approaches to a city.* **10.** the method used or steps taken in setting about a task, problem, etc.: *His approach to all problems was to prepare an outline.* **11.** the course followed by an aircraft in landing or in joining a traffic pattern: *The plane's approach to the airport was hazardous.* **12. approaches,** *Mil.* works for protecting forces in an advance against a fortified position. **13.** *Golf.* a stroke made after teeing off, by which a player attempts to get the ball onto the putting green. [ME *a(p)proche(n)* < MF *a(p)proch(i)e(r)* < LL *adpropiāre* = L *ad-* AD- + *propi(us)* nearer (comp. of *prope* near) + *-āre* inf. suffix] —**ap·proach′er,** *n.* —**ap·proach′less,** *adj.*

ap·proach·a·ble (ə prō′chə bəl), *adj.* **1.** capable of being approached; accessible. **2.** (of a person) easy to talk with or know. —**ap·proach′a·bil′i·ty, ap·proach′a·ble·ness,** *n.*

ap·pro·bate (ap′rə bāt′), *v.t.,* **-bat·ed, -bat·ing.** *Chiefly U.S.* to approve officially. [late ME < L *approbāt(us)* approved (ptp. of *approbāre*) = *ap-* AP-[1] + *probātus* proved] —**ap′pro·ba′tor,** *n.*

ap·pro·ba·tion (ap′rə bā′shən), *n.* **1.** approval; commendation. **2.** sanction. **3.** *Obs.* conclusive proof. [ME < L *approbātiōn-* (s. of *approbātiō*)] —**ap·pro·ba·tive** (ap′rə-bā′tiv, ə prō′bə-), **ap·pro·ba·to·ry** (ə prō′bə tôr′ē, -tôr′ē), *adj.* —**ap′pro·ba′tive·ness,** *n.*

ap·pro·pri·a·ble (ə prō′prē ə bəl), *adj.* capable of being appropriated.

ap·pro·pri·ate (*adj.* ə prō′prē it; *v.* ə prō′prē āt′), *adj., v.,* **-at·ed, -at·ing.** —*adj.* **1.** suitable or fitting for a particular purpose, occasion, person, etc. —*v.t.* **2.** to set apart or authorize for some specific purpose or use: *The legislature appropriated funds for the university.* **3.** to take to or for oneself; take possession of. [< LL *appropriāt(us)* made one's own (ptp. of *appropriāre*) = L *ap-* AP-[1] + *propri(us)* one's own + *-ātus* -ATE[1]] —**ap·pro′pri·ate·ly,** *adv.* —**ap-**

pro′pri·ate·ness, *n.* —**ap·pro·pri·a·tive** (ə prō′prē ā′tiv, -ə tiv), *adj.* —**ap·pro′pri·a′tive·ness,** *n.* —**ap·pro′pri·a′tor,** *n.* —**Syn. 1.** befitting, apt, proper, pertinent. **2.** allocate, assign. —**Ant. 1.** unsuitable, inept.

ap·pro·pri·a·tion (ə prō′prē ā′shən), *n.* **1.** the act of appropriating. **2.** anything appropriated for a special purpose, esp. money authorized to be paid from a treasury. [ME < LL *appropriātiōn-* (s. of *appropriātiō*)]

ap·prov·al (ə pro͞o′vəl), *n.* **1.** the act of approving. **2.** formal permission or sanction. **3. on approval,** without obligation to buy unless satisfactory to the customer upon trial or examination (and, otherwise, returnable): *We ship merchandise on approval.*

ap·prove (ə pro͞ov′), *v.*, **-proved, -prov·ing.** —*v.t.* **1.** to speak or think favorably of. **2.** to confirm or sanction formally; ratify: *The Senate approved the bill.* **3.** *Obs.* to demonstrate. **4.** *Obs.* to make good; attest. —*v.i.* **5.** to speak or think favorably of someone or something. **6.** to give one's sanction or confirmation. [ME *a(p)prove* < OF *aprove(r)* < L *approbāre* = *ap-* AP-[1] + *probāre* to PROVE] —**ap·prov′a·bil′i·ty,** *n.* —**ap·prov′a·ble,** *adj.* —**ap·prov′a·bly,** *adv.* —**ap·prov·ed·ly** (ə pro͞o′vid lē), *adv.* —**ap·prov′ed·ness,** *n.* —**ap·prov′er,** *n.* —**ap·prov′ing·ly,** *adv.*

approx., approximately.

ap·prox·i·mate (*adj.* ə prok′sə mit; *v.* ə prok′sə māt′), *adj.*, *v.*, **-mat·ed, -mat·ing.** —*adj.* **1.** being nearly, or more or less, as specified: *an approximate right angle.* **2.** nearly exact: *The approximate time is 10 o'clock.* **3.** near; close together. **4.** very similar: *an approximate situation.* —*v.t.* **5.** to come near to in quantity, quality, or condition. **6.** to estimate roughly: *We approximated the distance as three miles.* **7.** to simulate more or less accurately; imitate closely. **8.** to bring near. —*v.i.* **9.** to come near in quantity, quality, or condition. [< LL *approximāt(us)* drawn near to, approached (ptp. of *approximāre*). See AP-[1], PROXIMATE] —**ap·prox′i·mate·ly,** *adv.*

ap·prox·i·ma·tion (ə prok′sə mā′shən), *n.* **1.** a guess or estimate. **2.** nearness in space, position, degree, or relation. **3.** *Math., Physics.* a result that is not necessarily exact, but is within the limits of accuracy required.

ap·pulse (ə puls′), *n.* *Astron.* the approach or occurrence of conjunction between two celestial bodies. [< L *appuls(us)* driven to, landed (ptp. of *appellere*) = *ap-* AP-[1] + *pul-* (past s. of *pellere* to drive, push) + *-sus*, var. of *-tus* ptp. suffix] —**ap·pul′sive,** *adj.* —**ap·pul′sive·ly,** *adv.*

ap·pur·te·nance (ə pûr′tᵊnəns), *n.* **1.** something subordinate to another, more important thing. **2.** *Law.* a right, privilege, or improvement belonging to and passing with a principal property. **3. appurtenances,** apparatus; instruments. [ME < AF = *ap-* AP-[1] + *-purtenance* a belonging; see APPERTAIN, -ANCE]

ap·pur·te·nant (ə pûr′tᵊnənt), *adj.* **1.** appertaining or belonging; pertaining. —*n.* **2.** an appurtenance. [ME (see APPURTENANCE, -ANT) < LL *appertinent-* (s. of *appertinēns*, prp. of *appertinēre*). See AP-[1], PERTINENT]

Apr., April.

a·prax·i·a (ə prak′sē ə, ā prak′-), *n.* *Pathol.* a disorder of the nervous system, characterized by an inability to perform purposeful movements. [< NL; see A-[6], PRAXIS, -IA] —**a·prax′ic,** *adj.*

après-ski (a′pre skē′, ä′-), *n.* **1.** the period of relaxation that follows skiing. —*adj.* **2.** pertaining to or suitable for such a time: *après-ski clothes.*

ap·ri·cot (ap′rə kot′, ā′prə-), *n.* **1.** the downy, yellow, sometimes rosy fruit of the tree *Prunus Armeniaca.* **2.** the tree. **3.** a pinkish yellow or yellowish pink. [alter. of earlier *apricock*, var. of *abrecock* < Pg *albricoque* << Ar *al* the + *birqūq* << L *praecoquum*, short for *persicum praecox* early-ripening peach; see PRECOCIOUS]

A·pril (ā′prəl), *n.* the fourth month of the year, containing 30 days. [ME, OE *Aprīl(is)* < L; r. ME *averil* < OF *avrill* < L *Aprīl(is)*]

A′pril fool′, **1.** a joke played on April Fools' Day. **2.** the victim of such a joke.

A′pril Fools′′ Day′, April 1, when jokes are played on unsuspecting people. Also called **All Fools' Day.**

a pri·o·ri (ā′ prī ôr′ī, -ōr′ī, ā′ prē ôr′ē, -ōr′ē, ä′ prē-ôr′ē, -ōr′ē), **1.** from cause to effect; from a general law to a particular instance; valid independently of observation. Cf. **a posteriori** (def. 1). **2.** existing in the mind prior to and independent of experience, as a faculty or character trait. Cf. **a posteriori** (def. 2). **3.** not based on prior study or examination. [< L: lit., from the one before. See A-[4], PRIOR] —**a·pri·or·i·ty** (ā′prī ôr′i tē, -or′-), *n.*

a·pron (ā′prən), *n.* **1.** an article of apparel covering part of the front of the body and tied at the waist, for protecting the wearer's clothing. **2.** a metal plate or cover, usually vertical, for a machine, mechanism, artillery piece, etc., to protect those who operate it. **3.** a paved or hard-packed area abutting the buildings and hangars of an airfield, where planes are parked, loaded, or the like. **4.** *Civ. Eng.* **a.** any device for protecting a surface of earth, such as a river bank, from the action of moving water. **b.** a platform to receive the water falling over a dam. **5.** the part of a stage floor in front of the curtain line. **6.** *Furniture.* skirt (def. 5). **7.** the outer border of a green of a golf course. **8.** the part of the floor of a boxing ring outside of the ropes. **9.** *Geol.* a deposit of gravel and sand extending forward from a moraine. **10. tied to someone's apron strings,** dependent on or dominated by someone, esp. one's mother or wife. [ME *napron* (later *a napron* < *an apron*; see ADDER) < MF *naperon* = *nape* tablecloth (< L *mappa* napkin) + *-ron* dim. suffix]

ap·ro·pos (ap′rə pō′), *adv.* **1.** to the purpose; opportunely. **2.** with reference or regard; in respect (usually fol. by *of*): *apropos of the preceding statement.* **3.** *Obs.* by the way. —*adj.* **4.** opportune or pertinent. [< F *à propos*, lit., to purpose < L *ad prōpositum.* See AD-, PROPOSITION]

A.P.S., **1.** American Philatelic Society. **2.** American Philosophical Society. **3.** American Physical Society.

apse (aps), *n.* **1.** *Archit.* a vaulted semicircular or polygonal recess in a building, esp. at the end of the choir of a church. **2.** *Astron.* an apsis. [var. of APSIS] —**ap·si·dal** (ap′si dᵊl), *adj.*

ap·sis (ap′sis), *n.*, *pl.* **-si·des** (-si dēz′). *Astron.* either of two points in an eccentric orbit, one **(higher apsis)** farthest from the center of attraction, the other **(lower apsis)** nearest to the center of attraction. [< L < Gk *hapsís* (felloe of) a wheel, arch, vault]

apt (apt), *adj.* **1.** inclined; disposed; given; prone: *too apt to slander others.* **2.** likely: *Am I apt to find him at home?* **3.** unusually intelligent; quick to learn: *an apt pupil.* **4.** suited to the purpose or occasion: *an apt metaphor.* **5.** *Archaic.* prepared; ready; willing. [ME < L *apt(us)* fastened, fitted, fitting, appropriate = *ap-* fasten, attach + *-tus* ptp. suffix] —**apt′ly,** *adv.* —**apt′ness,** *n.*
—**Syn. 1.** liable. **2.** See **likely. 3.** clever, adaptable; adroit. **4.** appropriate, fitting, germane. APT, PERTINENT, RELEVANT all refer to something suitable or fitting. APT means to the point and particularly appropriate: *an apt comment.* PERTINENT means pertaining to the matter in hand: *a pertinent remark.* RELEVANT means directly related to and important to the subject: *a relevant opinion.*

apt., *pl.* **apts.** apartment.

ap·ter·al (ap′tər əl), *adj.* *Archit.* (of a classical temple) not having a surrounding colonnade; not peripteral. [< Gk *ápter(os)* APTEROUS + -AL[1]]

ap·ter·ous (ap′tər əs), *adj.* **1.** *Zool.* wingless, as some insects. **2.** *Bot.* without membranous expansions, as a stem. [< Gk *ápteros* wingless. See A-[6], -PTEROUS]

ap·ter·yx (ap′tə riks), *n.* kiwi (def. 1). [< NL = A-[6] + Gk *ptéryx* wing]

ap·ti·tude (ap′ti to͞od′, -tyo͞od′), *n.* **1.** capability; innate or acquired capacity for something; talent: *an aptitude for music.* **2.** readiness in learning; intelligence. **3.** the state or quality of being apt. [late ME < LL *aptitūdō.* See APT, -I-, -TUDE] —**ap′ti·tu′di·nal,** *adj.* —**ap′ti·tu′di·nal·ly,** *adv.*

Ap·u·le·ius (ap′yə lē′əs), *n.* **Lucius,** born A.D. 125?, Roman philosopher and satirist.

A·pu·lia (ə pyo͞ol′yə), *n.* a department in SE Italy. 3,409,687 (1961); 7442 sq. mi. *Cap.:* Bari. Italian, **Puglia.** —**A·pu′lian,** *adj.*

a·py·ret·ic (ā′pī ret′ik), *adj.* *Pathol.* free from fever.

AQ, *Psychol.* See **achievement quotient.**

Aq., water. Also, **aq.** [< L *aqua*]

A·qa·ba (ä′kä bä′), *n.* **1.** a seaport in SW Jordan, at the N end of the Gulf of Aqaba. 9722 (est. 1965). **2. Gulf of,** an arm of the Red Sea, between Saudi Arabia and the Arab Republic of Egypt. 100 mi. long.

aq·ua (ak′wə, ä′kwə), *n.*, *pl.* **aq·uae** (ak′wē, ä′kwē), **aq·uas. 1.** *Chiefly Pharm.* **a.** water. **b.** a liquid. **c.** a solution, esp. in water. **2.** a light greenish blue. [< L: water]

aq′ua am·mo′ni·ae (ə mō′nē ē′), ammonia (def. 2). Also, **aq′ua ammo′nia.** [< NL: lit., water of ammonia]

aq·ua·cade (ak′wə kād′, ä′kwə-; ak′wə kād′, ä′kwə-), *n.* an aquatic exhibition consisting of swimming, diving, etc., usually accompanied by music. [AQUA + (CAVAL)CADE]

aq·ua·cul·ture (ak′wə kul′chər, ä′kwə-), *n.* the cultivation of sea animals and plants in controlled marine environments; underwater agriculture. Also, **aquiculture.** [AQUA + (AGRI)CULTURE]

aq′ua for′tis, *Chem.* See **nitric acid.** [< L: lit., strong water]

Aq·ua-Lung (ak′wə lung′, ä′kwə-), *n.* *Trademark.* an underwater breathing apparatus for a swimmer or skin-diver, consisting of a cylinder of compressed air for strapping to the back and a flexible tube leading from the cylinder through an automatic pressure regulator that forces air into the lungs.

aq·ua·ma·rine (ak′wə mə rēn′, ä′kwə-), *n.* **1.** a transparent, light-blue or greenish-blue variety of beryl, used as a gem. **2.** light blue-green or greenish blue. [< L *aqua marīna* sea water (named from its color)]

aq·ua·naut (ak′wə nôt′, -not′, ä′kwə-), *n.* **1.** an underseas explorer, esp. one who skin-dives from or lives for an extended period of time in a submerged dwelling to observe and study man's ability to live and work under the sea. **2.** a skin-diver. [AQUA + (AERO)NAUT]

aq·ua·plane (ak′wə plān′, ä′kwə-), *n.*, *v.*, **-planed, -plan·ing.** —*n.* **1.** a board that skims over water when towed at high speed by a motorboat, used to carry a rider in aquatic sports. —*v.i.* **2.** to ride an aquaplane. [AQUA + (AIR)PLANE] —**aq′ua·plan′er,** *n.*

aq′ua pu′ra (pyo͝or′ə), pure water. [< L]

aq′ua re′gi·a (rē′jē ə), *Chem.* a liquid composed of one part of nitric acid and three to four of hydrochloric acid: used to dissolve gold and platinum. [< NL: lit., royal water]

aq·ua·relle (A KWA REL′; *Eng.* ak′wə rel′, ä′kwə-), *n.*, *pl.* **-relles** (-REL′; *Eng.* -relz′). *French.* watercolor. —**aq′ua·rel′list,** *n.*

a·quar·ist (ə kwâr′ist, ə kwer′-), *n.* a curator, collector, or ichthyologist associated with an aquarium. [AQUAR(IUM) + -IST]

a·quar·i·um (ə kwâr′ē əm), *n.*, *pl.* **a·quar·i·ums, a·quar·i·a** (ə kwâr′ē ə). **1.** a pond, tank, bowl, or the like, in which living aquatic animals or plants are kept, as for exhibition. **2.** a building or institution in which aquatic animals or plants are kept for exhibit, study, etc. [< L: watering place for cattle, n. use of neut. of *aquārius* of water = *aqu(a)* water + *-ārius* -ARY] —**a·quar′i·an, a·quar′i·al,** *adj.*

A·quar·i·us (ə kwâr′ē əs), *n.*, *gen.* **A·quar·i·i** (ə kwâr′ē ī′) for 1. **1.** *Astron.* the Water Bearer, a zodiacal constellation between Pisces and Capricornus. **2.** *Astrol.* the eleventh sign of the zodiac. See diag. at **zodiac.** —**A·quar′i·an,** *adj.*

a·quat·ic (ə kwat′ik, ə kwot′-), *adj.* **1.** living or growing in water: *aquatic plant life.* **2.** practiced on or in water: *aquatic sports.* —*n.* **3. aquatics,** sports practiced on or in water. [< L *aquātic(us)* = *aqu(a)* water + *-āticus* (see -ATE[1], -IC); r. late ME *aquatyque* < MF < L] —**a·quat′i·cal·ly,** *adv.*

aq·ua·tint (ak′wə tint′, ä′kwə-), *n.* **1.** a process imitating the broad flat tints of ink or wash drawings by etching a microscopic crackle on the copperplate intended for printing. **2.** an etching made by this process. —*v.t.*, *v.i.* **3.** to etch in aquatint. [var. of *aqua-tinta* < It *acqua tinta*, lit., tinted water] —**aq′ua·tint′er,** *n.*

aq·ua·tone (ak′wə tōn′, ä′kwə-), *n.* **1.** a lithographic process for printing by offset from a metal plate coated with photosensitized gelatin. **2.** a print so produced.

aq·ua·vit (ä′kwə vēt′, ak′wə-), *n.* akvavit.
aq′ua vi′tae (vī′tē), **1.** alcohol. **2.** spirituous liquor, as brandy or whiskey. [< L: water of life]
aq·ue·duct (ak′wi dukt′), *n.* **1.** *Civ. Eng.* **a.** a conduit or artificial channel for conducting water from a distance, usually by means of gravity. **b.** a structure that carries a conduit or canal across a valley or over a river. **2.** *Anat.* a canal or passage through which liquids pass. [< ML *aquēduct(us)*, L *aquae ductus* a drawing off of water]
a·que·ous (ā′kwē əs, ak′wē-), *adj.* **1.** of, like, or containing water; watery. **2.** (of rocks) formed by matter deposited in or by water. **—a′que·ous·ly,** *adv.* **—a′que·ous·ness,** *n.*
a′queous ammo′nia, ammonia (def. 2).
a′queous hu′mor, *Anat.* the limpid, watery fluid that fills the space between the cornea and the lens in the eye.
aq·ui·cul·ture (ak′wə kul′chər), *n.* **1.** hydroponics. **2.** aquaculture. [< L *aqui-* (comb. form of *aqua* water) + (AGRI)CULTURE] **—aq′ui·cul′tur·al,** *adj.* **—aq′ui·cul′tur·ist,** *n.*
aq·ui·fer (ak′wə fər), *n.* any geological formation containing water, esp. one that supplies the water for wells, springs, etc. [< L *aqui-* (comb. form of *aqua* water) + -FER] **—a·quif·er·ous** (ə kwif′ər əs), *adj.*
Aq·ui·la (ak′wə lə), *n.*, *gen.* **-lae** (-lē′). the Eagle, a northern constellation south of Cygnus.
Aq·ui·la (ak′wə lə; *It.* ä′kwē lä), *n.* a city in central Italy. 300,950. Also called **Aq·ui·la de·gli A·bruz·zi** (ä′kwē lä de′lyē ä brōōt′tsē).
aq·ui·line (ak′wə līn′, -lin), *adj.* **1.** of or like the eagle. **2.** (of the nose) shaped like an eagle's beak; hooked. [< L *aquilīn(us)*. See AQUILA, -INE[1]]
A·qui·nas (ə kwī′nəs), *n.* **Saint Thomas** ("*the Angelic Doctor*"), 1225?–74, Italian scholastic philosopher: a major theologian of the Roman Catholic Church. **—A·qui′nist,** *n.*
A·qui·no (ä kē′nō), *n.* **Co·ra·zon C.** (kôr′ə zon′, kor′-), born 1933, Philippine political leader: president since 1986.
Aq·ui·taine (ak′wi tān′; *Fr.* A kē ten′), *n.* a lowland region in SW France, formerly an ancient Roman province and medieval duchy. Latin, **Aq·ui·ta·ni·a** (ak′wi tā′nē ə). 
a·quiv·er (ə kwiv′ər), *adj.* in a state of trepidation or vibrant agitation; quivering.
AR, Arkansas (approved esp. for use with zip code).
Ar, Arabic (def. 3).
Ar, *Chem.* argon.
ar-, var. of **ad-** before *r: arrear.*
-ar[1], a formal element meaning "pertaining to," appearing in adjectives borrowed from Latin: *regular; singular.* [< L = *-ār(is)* (used instead of *-ālis* when the preceding syllable had an *l*); r. ME *-er* < AF, OF]
-ar[2], a noun suffix borrowed from Latin, denoting one connected with something: *vicar.* Also, **-er.** [< L *-ār(ius)* or *-ār(is)*]
-ar[3], var. of **-er**[1] on the model of **-ar**[2], used in the formation of nouns of agency: *liar; beggar.*
Ar., **1.** Arabic. **2.** Aramaic. **3.** argentum.
ar., **1.** arrival. **2.** arrive; arrives.
Ar·ab (ar′əb), *n.* **1.** a member of a Semitic people inhabiting Arabia and parts of northern Africa. **2.** See **Arabian horse. 3.** See **street Arab.** **—***adj.* **4.** Arabian. [back formation from L *Arabs* (taken as pl.) < Gk *Áraps* Arabian]
Arab., **1.** Arabia. **2.** Arabian. **3.** Arabic.
ar·a·besque (ar′ə besk′), *n.* **1.** any ornament or ornamental object in which plant forms, vases, and figures are represented in a fancifully interlaced pattern. **2.** *Fine Arts.* a sinuous, spiraling, undulating, or serpentine line or linear motif. **3.** a pose in ballet in which the dancer stands on one leg with one arm extended in front and the other leg and arm extended behind. **4.** a short, fanciful musical piece, typically for piano. **—***adj.* **5.** decorated with or characterized by arabesques. [< F: Arabian < It *arabesc(o)* = *Arab(o)* Arab + *-esco* -ISH[1]] **—ar′a·besque′ly,** *adv.*
A·ra·bi·a (ə rā′bē ə), *n.* a peninsula in SW Asia, including Saudi Arabia, Yemen, Oman, and South Yemen: divided in ancient times into Arabia Deserta, Arabia Petraea, and Arabia Felix. 17,800,000; ab. 1,000,000 sq. mi.
Ara′bia De·ser′ta (di zûr′tə), an ancient division of Arabia, in the N part between Syria and Mesopotamia.
Ara′bia Fe′lix (fē′liks), an ancient division of Arabia, in the S part: sometimes restricted to Yemen.
A·ra·bi·an (ə rā′bē ən), *adj.* **1.** of or pertaining to Arabia or the Arabs. **—***n.* **2.** an Arab. **3.** See **Arabian horse.**
Ara′bian Des′ert, **1.** a desert in the Arab Republic of Egypt between the Nile valley and the Red Sea. ab. 80,000 sq. mi. **2.** the desert region in the N part of the Arabian peninsula.
Ara′bian horse′, one of a breed of horses, raised originally in Arabia, noted for their speed. Also called **Arab, Arabian.**
Ara′bian Penin′sula, Arabia.
Ara′bian Sea′, the NW arm of the Indian Ocean between India and Arabia.
Ara′bia Pe·trae′a (pi trē′ə), an ancient division of Arabia, in the NW part.
Ar·a·bic (ar′ə bik), *adj.* **1.** of, belonging to, or derived from, Arabia or the Arabs. **2.** noting, pertaining to, or in the alphabetical script used for the writing of Arabic probably since about the fourth century A.D., and adopted with modifications by Persian, Urdu, and many other languages. **—***n.* **3.** any of the Semitic languages spoken in North Africa, Egypt, Arabia, Palestine, Syria, and Iraq. *Abbr.:* Ar **4.** the standard literary and classical language established by the Koran. [ME *arabik* < L *arabic(us)* = *Arab(ia)* + *-icus* -IC]
Ar′abic nu′merals, the numbers 0, 1, 2, 3, 4, 5, 6, 7, 8, 9. Also called **Ar′abic fig′ures.**
a·rab·i·nose (ə rab′ə nōs′, ar′ə bə-), *n.* *Chem.* a water-soluble carbohydrate, $C_5H_{10}O_5$, used chiefly as a culture medium in bacteriology. [*arabin* the soluble essence of certain gums ((GUM) ARAB(IC) + -IN[2]) + -OSE[2]]
Ar·ab·ist (ar′ə bist), *n.* a person who specializes in or studies the Arabic language or Arabic culture.
ar·a·ble (ar′ə bəl), *adj.* **1.** capable of producing crops; suitable for farming: *arable land.* **—***n.* **2.** land that can be or is cultivated. [< L *arābil(is)* = *arā(re)* (to) plow + *-bilis* -BLE; r. late ME *erable*] **—ar′a·bil′i·ty,** *n.*
Ar′ab League′, a confederation formed in 1945 by Egypt, Iraq, Lebanon, Saudi Arabia, Syria, and Jordan and later joined by Libya, Sudan, Morocco, Tunisia, Algeria, Yemen, and Kuwait.
Ar′ab Repub′lic of E′gypt, a republic in NE Africa. 40,000,000; 386,198 sq. mi. *Cap.:* Cairo.
Ar·a·by (ar′ə bē), *n.* *Archaic.* Arabia. [ME *Arabye* < OF *Arabie* < L *Arabia*]
A·ra·ca·ju (ä′RƏ kä′zhōō), *n.* a seaport in E Brazil. 179,512.
a·ra·ceous (ə rā′shəs), *adj.* *Bot.* belonging to the *Araceae,* or arum family of plants, which includes the arums, calla lily, taro, etc. [AR(UM) + -ACEOUS]
ar′achid′ic ac′id, *Chem.* a water-insoluble solid, $CH_3(CH_2)_{18}COOH$, used chiefly in the manufacture of lubricants, plastics, and waxes. [< NL *Arachid-* (s. of *Arachis* genus name < Gk *arakís* kind of plant) + -IC] **—ar·a·chid·ic** (ar′ə kid′ik), *adj.*
A·rach·ne (ə rak′nē), *n.* *Class. Myth.* a Lydian woman who challenged Athena to a weaving contest and was changed into a spider for her presumption.
a·rach·nid (ə rak′nid), *n.* any arthropod of the class *Arachnida,* comprising the spiders, scorpions, mites, ticks, etc. [< NL *Arachnid(a)* = Gk *aráchn(ē)* spider, spider's web; see -ID[2]] **—a·rach·ni·dan** (ə rak′ni dən), *adj., n.*
a·rach·noid (ə rak′noid), *n.* **1.** an arachnid. **2.** *Anat.* the serous membrane forming the middle of the three coverings of the brain and spinal cord. Cf. **dura mater, meninges, pia mater.** **—***adj.* **3.** resembling a spider's web. **4.** of or belonging to the arachnids. **5.** *Anat.* of or pertaining to the arachnoid membrane. **6.** *Bot.* formed of or covered with long, delicate hairs or fibers. [< NL *arachnoīdes* < Gk *arachnoeidḗs* cobweblike. See ARACHNID, -OID]
A·rad (ä räd′, är′äd), *n.* a city in W Rumania, on the Mures River. 147,145.
A′ra·fu′ra Sea′ (är′ə fōōr′ə, är′ə-), a part of the Pacific between N Australia and SW New Guinea. 
Ar·a·gats (ar′ə gats′), *n.* **Mount,** an extinct volcano in NW Armenia, in the S Soviet Union in Europe. 13,435 ft. Turkish, **Alagöz.**
A·ra·gon (A RA gôN′ *for 1;* ar′ə gon′ *for 2*), *n.* **1. Louis** (lwē), 1897–1982, French novelist, poet, and journalist. **2.** Spanish, **A·ra·gón** (äR′ä·gôn′), a region in NE Spain: formerly a kingdom; later a province. 18,181 sq. mi. **—Ar·a·go·nese** (ar′ə gə nēz′, -nēs′), *adj., n.*
A·ra·gua·ya (ä′RƏ gwä′yä), *n.* a river flowing N from central Brazil to the Tocantins River. ab. 1100 mi. long.
ar·ak (ar′ik, -ak), *n.* arrack.
a·ra·li·a·ceous (ə rā′lē ā′shəs), *adj.* *Bot.* belonging to the *Araliaceae,* a large family of plants usually bearing flowers or a fruit or berry. [< NL *Arali(a)* genus name (< ?) + -ACEOUS]
Ar′al Sea′ (ar′əl), an inland sea in the SW Soviet Union in Asia, E of the Caspian Sea. 26,166 sq. mi. Also called **Lake Aral.**
A·ram (ā′ram, âr′əm), *n.* Biblical name of ancient Syria. See map at **Philistia.**
Aram, Aramaic (def. 1).
Aram., Aramaic.
Ar·a·ma·ic (ar′ə mā′ik), *n.* **1.** Also, **Aramean, Aramaean.** a northwest Semitic language that from c300 B.C.–A.D. 650 was a lingua franca for nearly all of SW Asia and was the everyday speech of Syria, Mesopotamia, and Palestine. *Abbr.:* Aram **—***adj.* **2.** pertaining to Aram, or to the languages spoken there. **3.** noting or pertaining to the alphabetical, or perhaps syllabic, script used for the writing of Aramaic from which were derived the Hebrew, Arabic, and many other scripts. [< Gk *aramaî(os)* of ARAM + -IC, modeled on *Hebraic*]
Ar·a·me·an (ar′ə mē′ən), *n.* **1.** a Semite of the division associated with Aram. **2.** Aramaic (def. 1). Also, **Ar′a·mae′an.** [< L *Aramae(us)* (< Gk *aramaîos* of ARAM) + -AN]
A·ran·da (ə ran′də, ə rän′-), *n., pl.* **-das,** (*esp. collectively*) **-da.** Arunta.
A·ran·ya·ka (ä run′yə kə), *n.* *Hinduism.* one of a class of the Vedic texts that, with the Upanishads, make up the closing portions of the Brahmanas. [< Skt: a forest book]
A·rap·a·ho (ə rap′ə hō′), *n., pl.* **-hos,** (*esp. collectively*) **-ho. 1.** a member of a tribe of North American Indians of Algonquian speech stock, now in Oklahoma and Wyoming. **2.** an Algonquian language, the language of the Arapaho.
A·rap·a·hoe (ə rap′ə hō′), *n., pl.* **-hoes,** (*esp. collectively*) **-hoe.** Arapaho.
ar·a·pai·ma (ar′ə pī′mə), *n.* a large, fresh-water fish, *Arapaima gigas,* found in Brazil and Guinea. [< Pg < Tupi]
Ar·a·rat (ar′ə rat′), *n.* a mountain in E Turkey, near the borders of Iran and the Soviet Union. 16,945 ft.: traditionally considered the landing place of Noah's Ark. Also called **Mount Ararat.**
a·ra·ro·ba (ar′ə rō′bə), *n.* *Pharm.* See **Goa powder.** [< Pg < Tupi, perh. var. of *araribá*]
A·ras (ä räs′), *n.* a river flowing from E Turkey along the boundary between NW Iran and SW Soviet Union into the Kura River. ab. 660 mi. long. Ancient, **Araxes.**
A·rau·can (ə rô′kən), *n., pl.* **-cans,** (*esp. collectively*) **-can.** *adj.* Araucanian.
Ar·au·ca·ni·a (ar′ô kā′nē ə; *Sp.* ä′ROU kä′nyä), *n.* a region in central Chile.
Ar·au·ca·ni·an (ar′ô kā′nē ən), *n.* **1.** a member of an

Indian people of central Chile. 2. the language of the Araucanians, spoken in central Chile and northern Argentina. —*adj.* 3. of Araucania, its people, or their language.

Ar·a·wak (ar′ə wäk′, -wak′), *n., pl.* **-waks,** (*esp. collectively*) **-wak.** 1. a member of an Indian people once widespread in the Antilles but now confined to northeastern South America. 2. the language of the Arawaks.

Ar·a·wak·an (ar′ə wä′kən, -wak′ən), *n.* a family of South American Indian languages.

A·rax·es (ə rak′sēz), *n.* ancient name of **Aras.**

ar·ba·lest (är′bə list, -lest′), *n.* a powerful medieval crossbow. Also, **ar·ba·list** (ar′bə list). [var. of *arbalist, arblast* (late OE *arblast*) < OF *arbaleste* < LL *arcuballista.* See ARC, BALLISTA] —**ar′ba·lest′er, ar′ba·list′er,** *n.*

Ar·be·la (är bē′lə), *n.* an ancient city of Assyria, E of the Tigris, on the site of modern Erbil, Iraq.

Ar·bil (ir′bil), *n.* Erbil.

ar·bi·ter (är′bi tər), *n.* a person who has the power to judge or decide a matter. [late ME < L: judge in equity, umpire; r. late ME *arbitre* < MF < L *arbiter*]

ar·bi·trage (är′bi träzh′), *n.* *Finance.* the simultaneous purchase and sale of the same securities, commodities, or foreign exchange in different markets to profit from unequal prices. [< F = *arbitr(er)* (to) arbitrate, regulate (< L *arbitrārī;* see ARBITRATE) + *-age* -AGE]

ar·bi·tral (är′bi trəl), *adj.* pertaining to an arbiter or to arbitration. [< LL *arbitrāl(is)*]

ar·bit·ra·ment (är bi′trə mənt), *n.* 1. arbitration. 2. the decision of an arbiter. 3. the power of final decision. Also, **ar·bit′re·ment.** [late ME < ML *arbitrāment(um)* < L *arbitrā(rī)* (to) ARBITRATE + *-mentum* -MENT]

ar·bi·trar·y (är′bi trer′ē), *adj.* 1. subject to individual will or judgment without restriction; contingent solely upon one's discretion: *an arbitrary choice.* 2. decided by a judge or arbiter rather than by a law or statute. 3. using or abusing unlimited power; uncontrolled or unrestricted by law; despotic. 4. capricious; unreasonable. 5. *Math.* not assigned a specific value: *an arbitrary constant.* [late ME < L *arbitrāri(us)* uncertain (i.e., depending on an arbiter's decision). See ARBITER, -ARY] —**ar·bi·trar·i·ly** (är′bi trer′ə lē, är′bə trâr′-), *adv.* —**ar′bi·trar′i·ness,** *n.*

ar·bi·trate (är′bi trāt′), *v.,* **-trat·ed, -trat·ing.** —*v.t.* 1. to decide as arbiter or arbitrator. 2. to submit to or settle by arbitration. —*v.i.* 3. to act as arbiter; decide between opposing or contending parties or sides. 4. to submit a matter to arbitration. [< L *arbitrāt(us)* decided, judged (ptp. of *arbitrārī*). See ARBITER, -ATE[1]] —**ar·bi·tra·ble** (är′bi trə bəl), *adj.* —**ar′bi·tra′tive,** *adj.* —**ar′bi·tra′tor,** *n.*

ar·bi·tra·tion (är′bi trā′shən), *n.* 1. the hearing and determining of a dispute between parties by a person or persons chosen or agreed to by them. 2. a hearing given disputants by an arbitrator with the view of reaching a settlement. [ME < L *arbitrātiōn-* (s. of *arbitrātiō*)] —**ar′bi·tra′tion·al,** *adj.* —**ar′bi·tra′tion·ist,** *n.* —**Syn.** 1. See **mediation.**

Ar·blay, d' (där′blā; *Fr.* DAR blā′), **Madame Frances.** See **Burney, Frances.**

ar·bor[1] (är′bər), *n.* 1. a leafy, shady recess formed by tree branches, shrubs, etc. 2. a latticework bower intertwined with climbing vines and flowers. 3. *Obs.* a lawn, garden, or orchard. Also, *esp. Brit.,* **arbour.** [ME *(h)erber* < AF, OF *(h)erbier* HERBARIUM] —**ar′bored, ar′boured,** *adj.*

ar·bor[2] (är′bər), *n.* 1. *Mach.* a bar, shaft, or axis that holds, turns, or supports rotating cutting tools. Cf. **mandrel.** 2. *Obs.* a beam, shaft, axle, or spindle. [< L: beam, pole, gallows; r. earlier *arber, arbre* < F]

ar·bor[3] (är′bər), *n., pl.* **ar·bo·res** (är′bə rēz′). *Bot.* a tree. [< NL, L: tree, beam, etc.] —**ar′bo·resque′,** *adj.*

Ar′bor Day′, a day, varying in date but always in the spring, observed in certain states of the U.S. by the planting of trees.

ar·bo·re·al (är bōr′ē əl, -bôr′-), *adj.* 1. of or pertaining to trees; treelike. 2. living in or among trees. [< L *arbore(us)* of trees + -AL[1]] —**ar·bo′re·al·ly,** *adv.*

ar·bo·re·ous (är bōr′ē əs, -bôr′-), *adj.* 1. abounding in trees; wooded. 2. arborescent. [< L *arboreus* of trees = *arbor* tree + *-eus* -EOUS]

ar·bo·res·cent (är′bə res′ənt), *adj.* treelike in size and form. [< L *arborēscent-* (s. of *arborēscēns*), prp. of *arborēscere* to grow into a tree] —**ar′bo·res′cence,** *n.* —**ar′bo·res′cent·ly,** *adv.*

ar·bo·re·tum (är′bə rē′təm), *n., pl.* **-tums, -ta** (-tə). a plot of land on which trees or shrubs are grown for study or display. [< L: a place grown with trees = *arbor* tree + *-ētum* suffix denoting place]

ar·bor·i·cul·ture (är′bər ə kul′chər), *n.* the cultivation of trees and shrubs. [< L *arbori-* (s. of *arbor* tree) + CULTURE] —**ar′bor·i·cul′tur·al,** *adj.* —**ar′bor·i·cul′tur·ist,** *n.*

ar·bor·i·za·tion (är′bər i zā′shən *or, esp. Brit.,* -bə rī-), *n.* a treelike appearance, as in certain minerals or fossils.

ar·bor vi·tae (är′bər vī′tē), *Anat.* a treelike appearance in a vertical section of the cerebellum, due to the arrangement of the white and gray nerve tissues. [< L: tree of life]

ar·bor·vi·tae (är′bər vī′tē), *n.* any of several pinaceous trees of the genus *Thuja,* of North America and eastern Asia.

ar·bour (är′bər), *n.* *Chiefly Brit.* arbor[1].

ar·bo·vi·rus (är′bə vī′rəs), *n.* any of several groups of viruses which are transmitted by arthropods, some of which cause encephalitis, yellow fever, and dengue fever. [AR(THROPOD-)BO(RNE) VIRUS]

Ar·buth·not (är buth′nət, är′bəth not′), *n.* **John,** 1667–1735, Scottish satirist and physician.

ar·bu·tus (är byōō′təs), *n., pl.* **-tus·es.** 1. any of the evergreen ericaceous shrubs or trees of the genus *Arbutus,* esp. *A. unedo,* of southern Europe, with scarlet berries. 2. Also called **trailing arbutus.** a creeping, ericaceous herb, *Epigaea repens,* of eastern North America, having fragrant white or pink flowers: the state flower of Massachusetts. [< L: the wild strawberry tree]

arc (ärk), *n., v.,* **arced** (ärkt) or **arcked, arc·ing** (är′king) or **arck·ing.** —*n.* 1. *Geom.* any unbroken part of the circumference of a circle or other curved line. 2. *Elect.* a luminous bridge formed in a gap between two conductors or terminals when they are separated. Cf. **spark**[1] (def. 2). 3. *Astron.* the part of a circle representing the apparent course of a heavenly body. 4. anything bow-shaped. —*v.i.* 5. to form an electric arc. 6. to move in a curve suggestive of an arc. [ME *ark* < L *arc(us)* bow, arch, curve]

ARC, American Red Cross. Also, **A.R.C.**

ar·cade (är kād′), *n.* 1. *Archit.* **a.** a series of arches supported on piers or columns. **b.** an arched, roofed-in gallery. 2. an arched or covered passageway, usually with shops on each side. [< F < It *arcata* arch (c. ML *arcāta*) = *arc(o)* arch (see ARC) + *-āta* -ADE[1]]

Ar·ca·di·a (är kā′dē ə), *n.* 1. a city in SW California, E of Los Angeles. 43,237 (1970). 2. a mountainous region of ancient Greece, traditionally known for the pastoral innocence of its people.

Ar·ca·di·an (är kā′dē ən), *adj.* 1. of Arcadia. 2. pastoral; rustic; simple; innocent. —*n.* 3. a native of Arcadia. —**Ar·ca′di·an·ism,** *n.* —**Ar·ca′di·an·ly,** *adv.*

Ar·ca·dy (är′kə dē), *n.* *Literary.* Arcadia.

ar·cane (är kān′), *adj.* mysterious; secret; obscure. [< L *arcān(us)* = *arc(ēre)* (to) shut up, keep (< *arca* a chest, box) + *-ānus* -ANE]

ar·ca·num (är kā′nəm), *n., pl.* **-na** (-nə). 1. Often, **arcana.** a secret; mystery. 2. a supposed great secret of nature that the alchemists sought to discover. 3. a secret and powerful remedy, esp. a universal cure for all diseases. [< L, neut. (used as n.) of *arcānus* ARCANE]

arc-bou·tant (AR bōō täN′), *n., pl.* **arcs-bou·tants** (AR bōō täN′). *French.* See **flying buttress.** [lit., thrusting arch]

arc′ cos′, See **arc cosine.**

arc′ cose′cant, *Trig.* the angle, measured in radians, that has a cosecant equal to a given number. *Abbr.:* arc csc; *Symbol:* $\csc^{-1}$.

arc′ co′sine, *Trig.* the angle, measured in radians, that has a cosine equal to a given number. *Abbr.:* arc cos; *Symbol:* $\cos^{-1}$.

arc′ cotan′gent, *Trig.* the angle, measured in radians, that has a contangent equal to a given number. *Abbr.:* arc cot; *Symbol:* $\cot^{-1}$.

Arc, d' (DARK), **Jeanne** (zhän). See **Joan of Arc.**

Arc de Tri·omphe (ARK də trē ôNf′), the triumphal arch, located in Paris, begun in 1806 by Napoleon and completed in 1836. Also called **Arc de Tri·omphe′ de l'É·toile′** (də lā twAl′). [< F: arch of triumph]

arch[1] (ärch), *n.* 1. *Archit.* a curved masonry construction for spanning an opening, consisting of a number of wedgelike stones, bricks, or the like, set with the narrower side toward the opening. 2. a doorway, gateway, etc., having a curved head; archway. 3. any curvature in the form of an arch: *the arch of the heavens.* 4. something bowed or curved; any bowlike part: *the arch of the foot.* 5. a device in shoes for supporting the arch of the foot. —*v.t.* 6. to cover with a vault, or span with an arch. 7. to throw or make into the shape of an arch; curve: *A horse arches its neck.* —*v.i.* 8. to form an arch. [ME *arch(e)* < OF *arche* < VL **arca,* fem. var. of L *arcus* ARC]

Arch
A, Abutment; S, Springer; V, Voussoir; K, Keystone; Ex., Extrados; P, Pier; I, Impost; In, Intrados

arch[2] (ärch), *adj.* 1. chief; most important; principal: *the arch rebel.* 2. cunning, roguish, or mischievous: *an arch smile.* [see ARCH-] —**arch′ly,** *adv.* —**arch′ness,** *n.*

arch-, a learned borrowing from Greek meaning "chief," used in the formation of compound words: *archbishop; archfiend.* Also, **-arch, archi-, -archy.** [ME; OE *arce-, erce-* < L *arch(e)-, archi-* < Gk *arch-* (s. of *archḗ* beginning)]

-arch, var. of **arch-** as final element of a compound word: *monarch; heresiarch.* [late ME *-arch(a)* < L < Gk *-archēs* = *árch(ein)* to be first, rule + *-ēs* n. suffix]

Arch., Archbishop.

arch., 1. archaic. 2. archaism. 3. archery. 4. archipelago. 5. architect. 6. architectural. 7. architecture. 8. archive; archives.

Ar·chae·an (är kē′ən), *adj., n.* Archean.

archaeo-, var. of **archeo-:** *archaeopteryx.*

archaeol., 1. archaeological. 2. archaeology.

ar·chae·o·log·i·cal (är′kē ə loj′i kəl), *adj.* 1. of or pertaining to archaeology. 2. of or pertaining to historic or prehistoric peoples or their dwellings and artifacts: *an important archaeological site.* Also, **ar′chae·o·log′ic, archeological, archeologic.** [< Gk *archaiologik(ós)* (see ARCHAEOLOGY, -IC) + -AL[1]] —**ar′chae·o·log′i·cal·ly,** *adv.*

ar·chae·ol·o·gy (är′kē ol′ə jē), *n.* the scientific study of historic or prehistoric peoples and their cultures by analysis of their artifacts, inscriptions, and monuments. Also, **archeology.** [< Gk *archaiologia* the discussion of antiquities] —**ar′chae·ol′o·gist,** *n.*

ar·chae·op·ter·yx (är′kē op′tə riks), *n.* a fossil bird of the genus *Archaeopteryx,* from the late Jurassic period, having teeth and a long, feathered, vertebrate tail; the oldest known avian type. [ARCHAEO- + Gk *ptéryx* wing]

Archaeopteryx

ar·chae·or·nis (är′kē ôr′nis), *n.* an extinct bird of the genus *Archaeornis,* from the late Jurassic period, similar to the archaeopteryx. [< NL = *archae(o)-* ARCHAEO- + Gk *órnis* bird]

Ar·chae·o·zo·ic (är′kē ə zō′ik), *adj., n.* Archeozoic.

ar·cha·ic (är kā′ik), *adj.* 1. marked by the characteristics of an earlier period; antiquated. 2. (of a linguistic form) current in an earlier time but rare in present usage. **3.** (*cap.*) pertaining to or designating the style of the fine arts, esp. painting and sculpture, developed in Greece from the middle 7th to the early 5th century B.C. Cf. **classical** (def. 2), **Hellenistic** (def. 5). **4.** primitive. [< Gk *archaïk(ós)* antiquated, old-fashioned = *archaî(os)* old + *-ikos* -IC] —**ar·cha′i·cal·ly,** *adv.*

ar·cha·ise (är′kē īz′, -kā-), *v.t., v.i.*, **-ised, -is·ing.** *Chiefly Brit.* archaize. —**ar′cha·is′er,** *n.*

ar·cha·ism (är′kē iz′əm, -kā-), *n.* **1.** something archaic, as a word, expression, or mannerism. **2.** the use of something archaic. Also, **ar·cha·i·cism** (är kā′i siz′əm). [earlier *archaism(us)* < L < Gk *archaïsmós.* See ARCHAIZE, -ISM] —**ar′cha·ist,** *n.* —**ar′cha·is′tic,** *adj.*

ar·cha·ize (är′kē īz′, -kā-), *v.*, **-ized, -iz·ing.** —*v.t.* **1.** to give an archaic appearance or quality to. —*v.i.* **2.** to use archaisms. Also, *esp. Brit.*, **archaise.** [< Gk *archaïz(ein)* (to) imitate the language of ancient authors. See ARCHAEO-, -IZE] —**ar′cha·iz′er,** *n.*

arch·an·gel (ärk′ān′jəl), *n.* **1.** *Theol.* a chief or principal angel; in medieval angelology one of the nine orders of celestial attendants on God. Cf. **angel** (def. 1). **2.** angelica. [early ME < LL *archangel(us)* < Gk *archángelos.* See ARCH-, ANGEL] —**arch·an·gel·ic** (ärk′an jel′ik), **arch′an·gel′i·cal,** *adj.*

Arch·an·gel (ärk′ān′jəl), *n.* **1.** Russian, **Arkhangelsk.** a seaport in the NW Soviet Union in Europe, on Dvina Bay. 298,000 (est. 1964). **2. Gulf of,** former name of **Dvina Bay.**

arch·bish·op (ärch′bish′əp), *n.* a bishop of the highest rank who presides over an archbishopric or archdiocese. [ME, OE *arcebiscop*, modeled on LL *archiepiscopus* < Gk *archiepískopos;* r. OE *hēahbiscop* (see HIGH)]

arch·bish·op·ric (ärch′bish′əp rik), *n.* the see, diocese, or office of an archbishop. [ME *archebischopric*, OE *arcebiscoprīce* = *arcebiscop* ARCHBISHOP + *rīce* region, realm; c. Icel *rīki*, Goth *reiki*, OHG *rīhki* (> G *Reich*)]

Archbp., Archbishop.

archd., **1.** archdeacon. **2.** archduke. Also, **Archd.**

arch·dea·con (ärch′dē′kən), *n.* **1.** an ecclesiastic, ranking next below a bishop, charged with administrative responsibility for a diocese. **2.** *Rom. Cath. Ch.* a title of honor conferred only on a member of a cathedral chapter. [ME *archideken*, OE *arcediacon* < LL *archidiācon(us)* < Gk *archidiákonos*] —**arch′dea′con·ate, arch′dea′con·ry, arch′dea′con·ship′,** *n.*

arch·di·o·cese (ärch′dī′ə sēs′, -sis), *n.* the diocese of an archbishop. —**arch·di·oc·e·san** (ärch′dī os′i sən), *adj.*

arch·du·cal (ärch′dōō′kəl, -dyōō′-), *adj.* of or pertaining to an archduke or an archduchy. [earlier *archiducal* < F]

arch·duch·ess (ärch′duch′is), *n.* **1.** the wife of an archduke. **2.** a princess of the Austrian imperial family. [ARCH- + DUCHESS, modeled on F *archiduchesse*]

arch·duch·y (ärch′duch′ē), *n., pl.* **-duch·ies.** the domain of an archduke or an archduchess. [ARCH- + DUCHY, modeled on F *archeduché* (now *archiduché*)]

arch·duke (ärch′dōōk′, -dyōōk′), *n.* a title of the sovereign princes of the former ruling house of Austria. [earlier *archeduke* < F *archeduc* (now *archiduc*)]

arche-[1], var. of **archi-:** *archespore.*

arche-[2], var. of **archeo-** before a vowel.

Arch. E., Architectural Engineer.

Ar·che·an (är kē′ən), *Geol. Obs.* —*adj.* **1.** noting or pertaining to the Precambrian era, esp. the oldest part; Archeozoic. —*n.* **2.** the Archeozoic period. Also, **Archaean.**

arched (ärcht), *adj.* **1.** made, covered, or spanned with an arch or arches. **2.** having the form of an arch.

ar·che·go·ni·um (är′kə gō′nē əm), *n., pl.* **-ni·a** (-nē ə). *Bot.* the female reproductive organ in ferns, mosses, etc. [< NL = *archegon-* (< Gk *archegon(os)* first of a race; see ARCHE-[1], GONO-) + *-ium* < Gk *-ion* dim. suffix] —**ar′che·go′ni·al, ar·che·go·ni·ate** (är′kə gō′nē it, -āt′), *adj.*

arch·en·e·my (ärch′en′ə mē), *n., pl.* **-mies.** **1.** a chief enemy. **2.** Satan.

ar·chen·ter·on (är ken′tə ron′), *n.* *Embryol.* the primitive enteron or digestive cavity of a gastrula. [ARCH(EO)- + ENTERON] —**ar·chen·ter·ic** (är′kən ter′ik), *adj.*

archeo-, a learned borrowing from Greek meaning "primitive," used in the formation of compound words: *Archeozoic.* Also, **archaeo-, archi-;** *esp. before a vowel,* **arche-.** [earlier *archaio-* < Gk *archaîo(s)* old]

ar·che·ol·o·gy (är′kē ol′ə jē), *n.* archaeology. —**ar·che·o·log·i·cal** (är′kē ə loj′i kəl), **ar′che·o·log′ic,** *adj.* —**ar′che·o·log′i·cal·ly,** *adv.* —**ar′che·ol′o·gist,** *n.*

Ar·che·o·zo·ic (är′kē ə zō′ik), *Geol.* —*adj.* **1.** noting or pertaining to a period of the Precambrian era, occurring from about 1,000,000,000 to perhaps 3,000,000,000 years ago, during which the earliest datable rocks were formed and the earliest known life, algae and fungi, came into being. See table at **era.** —*n.* **2.** the Archeozoic period or rock system. Also, **Archaeozoic.** [ARCHEO- + Gk *zō(ē)* life + -IC]

arch·er (är′chər), *n.* **1.** a person who shoots with a bow and arrow; bowman. **2.** (*cap.*) *Astron., Astrol.* the constellation or sign of Sagittarius. [ME < AF; OF *archier* < L *arcār(ius)* = *arc(us)* bow (see ARC) + *-ārius* -ARY]

Ar·cher (är′chər), *n.* **William,** 1856–1924, Scottish critic, playwright, and translator.

ar·cher·y (är′chə rē), *n.* **1.** the art, practice, or skill of an archer. **2.** archers collectively, as in an army. **3.** the equipment of an archer, as bows, arrows, etc. [ME *archerye* < MF *archerie* = *arch(i)er* ARCHER + *-ie* -Y[3]]

ar·che·spore (är′ki spōr′, -spôr′), *n.* *Bot.* the primitive cell or group of cells which give rise to the cells from which spores are derived. Also, **archesporium.** —**ar′che·spo′ri·al,** *adj.*

ar·che·spo·ri·um (är′ki spōr′ē əm, -spôr′-), *n., pl.* **-spo·ri·a** (-spōr′ē ə, -spôr′-). *Bot.* archespore. [< NL]

ar·che·type (är′ki tīp′), *n.* the original pattern or model after which a thing is made; a model or first form; prototype. [< L *archetyp(um)* an original < Gk *archétypon* a model, pattern (neut. of *archétypos* of the first mold = *arche-* ARCHE-[1] + *týp(os)* mold, TYPE + *-os* adj. suffix)] —**ar·che·typ·al** (är′ki tī′pəl), **ar·che·typ·i·cal** (är′ki tip′i kəl), **ar′che·typ′ic,** *adj.* —**ar′che·typ′al·ly, ar′che·typ′i·cal·ly,** *adv.*

arch·fiend (ärch′fēnd′), *n.* **1.** a chief fiend. **2.** Satan.

archi-, **1.** var. of **arch-:** *archiepiscopal.* **2.** var. of **archeo-:** *archiplasm.* [< L < Gk: foremost, early, old; akin to *árchein* to begin, lead]

ar·chi·carp (är′kə kärp′), *n.* *Bot.* the female reproductive organ in various ascomycetous fungi.

ar·chi·di·ac·o·nal (är′ki dī ak′ə nəl), *adj.* of or pertaining to an archdeacon or his office. [< LL *archidiācon(us)*]

ar·chi·e·pis·co·pal (är′kē i pis′kə pəl), *adj.* of or pertaining to an archbishop or his office. [< ML *archiepiscopāl(is)* = LL *archiepiscop(us)* ARCHBISHOP + *-ālis* -AL[1]] —**ar′chi·e·pis′co·pal′i·ty;** *Obs.* **ar·chi·e·pis·co·pate** (är′kē ə pis′kə pit, -pāt′), *n.* —**ar′chi·e·pis′co·pal·ly,** *adv.*

ar·chil (är′kil), *n.* orchil.

ar·chi·man·drite (är′kə man′drīt), *n.* *Eastern Ch.* **1.** the head of a monastery or group of monasteries; abbot. **2.** a title given to distinguished celibate priests. [< ML *archimandrīt(a)* < LGk *archimandrī́t(ēs)* abbot = Gk *archi-* ARCHI- + LGk *mándr(a)* monastery (orig., fold, enclosure) + *-ītēs* -ITE[1]]

Ar·chi·me·des (är′kə mē′dēz), *n.* 287?–212 B.C., Greek mathematician, physicist, and inventor: discoverer of the principles of specific gravity and of the lever. —**Ar·chi·me·de·an** (är′kə mē′dē ən, -mi dē′ən), *adj.*

Ar′chime′des′ prin′ciple, *Physics.* the law that a body immersed in a fluid is buoyed up by a force (**buoyant force**) equal to the weight of the fluid displaced by the body.

Ar′chime′des′ screw′, a device consisting essentially of a spiral passage within an inclined cylinder for raising water to a height when rotated. Also, **Ar′chime′dean screw′.**

arch·ing (är′ching), *n.* arched work or formation.

ar·chi·pel·a·go (är′kə pel′ə gō′), *n., pl.* **-gos, -goes.** **1.** any large body of water with many islands. **2.** an island group. **3. the Archipelago,** the Aegean Sea. [< It *arcipelago* = *arci-* ARCHI- + *pelago* < L *pelag(us)* < Gk *pélagos* sea] —**ar·chi·pe·lag·ic** (är′kə pə laj′ik), **ar·chi·pe·la·gi·an** (är′kə pə lā′jē ən, -jən), *adj.*

Ar·chi·pen·ko (är′kə peng′kō; *Russ.* är кнē′pen kô), *n.* **Al·ex·an·der Por·fir·ie·vich** (al′ig zan′dər pər fēr′ə vich, -zän′-; *Russ.* ä′le ksän′dər por fēr′yə vich), 1887–1964, U.S. sculptor born in Russia.

ar·chi·pho·neme (är′kə fō′nēm, är′kə fō′nēm), *n.* *Linguistics.* **1.** an abstract phonological unit consisting of the distinctive features common to two phonemes that differ only in that one has a distinctive feature lacking in the other. **2.** such a unit occurring in a position where the contrast between two or more phonemes is neutralized.

ar·chi·plasm (är′kə plaz′əm), *n.* **1.** the most basic or primitive living substance; protoplasm. **2.** *Cytology.* (in cell division) the substance surrounding the centrosome. Also, **archoplasm.** [ARCHI- + -PLASM, modeled on G *Archiplasma*] —**ar′chi·plas′mic,** *adj.*

archit., architecture.

ar·chi·tect (är′ki tekt′), *n.* **1.** a person engaged in the profession of architecture. **2.** a person who designs large constructions other than buildings: *naval architect.* **3.** the deviser, maker, or creator of anything: *the architects of the Constitution.* [< L *architect(us)* < Gk *architéktōn* = *archi-* ARCHI- + *-tektōn* worker]

ar·chi·tec·ton·ic (är′ki tek ton′ik), *adj.* of, pertaining to, or resembling the structural principles of architecture. [< L *architectonic(us)* < Gk *architektonikós* of, belonging to architecture] —**ar′chi·tec·ton′i·cal·ly,** *adv.*

ar·chi·tec·ton·ics (är′ki tek ton′iks), *n.* the science of planning and constructing buildings. [see ARCHITECTONIC, -ICS]

ar·chi·tec·ture (är′ki tek′chər), *n.* **1.** the profession of designing buildings, open areas, communities, etc., usually with some regard to aesthetic effect. **2.** the character or style of building: *the architecture of Paris.* **3.** the result or product of architectural work, as a building. **4.** buildings collectively. **5.** the structure of anything: *the architecture of a novel.* [< L *architectūr(a)*] —**ar′chi·tec′tur·al,** *adj.* —**ar′chi·tec′tur·al·ly,** *adv.*

ar·chi·trave (är′ki trāv′), *n.* *Archit.* **1.** the lowermost member of a classical entablature, resting originally upon columns. **2.** a molded or decorated band framing a panel or an opening, esp. a rectangular one, as of a door or window. [< It] —**ar′chi·tra′val,** *adj.* —**ar′chi·traved′,** *adj.*

ar·chive (är′kīv), *n.* **1.** Usually, **archives.** documents or records relating to the activities, rights, claims, treaties, constitutions, etc., of a family, corporation, community, nation, or historical figure. **2. archives,** a place where such records or documents are kept. [< LL *archī(v)(um)* < Gk *archeîon* government building (where records were kept) = *arche-* (s. of *archḗ*) government, rule + *-ion* suffix of place] —**ar·chi′val,** *adj.*

ar·chi·vist (är′kə vist), *n.* a custodian of archives. [< ML *archivist(a)*]

ar·chi·volt (är′kə vōlt′), *n.* *Archit.* a molded or decorated band around an arch. [< It *archivolt(o)* < ML *archivolt(um).* See ARCHI-, VAULT[1]]

Arch′ of Tri′umph. See **Arc de Triomphe.**

ar·chon (är′kon), *n.* a chief magistrate in ancient Athens. [< Gk *árchōn* magistrate, ruler (n. use of prp. of *árchein* to be first, rule) = *arch-* ARCH- + *-ōn* prp. suffix] —**ar′chon·ship′,** *n.*

ar·cho·plasm (är′kə plaz′əm), *n.* archiplasm. —**ar′cho·plas′mic,** *adj.*

arch·priest (ärch′prēst′), *n.* **1.** a priest holding first rank, as in a cathedral chapter. **2.** *Rom. Cath. Ch.* a priest acting as superior of the Roman Catholic secular clergy in England, first appointed in 1598 and superseded by a vicar apostolic in 1623. [late ME *archeprest* (modeled on LL *archipresbyter* < Gk *archipresbýter(os)*)] —**arch′priest′hood,** *n.* —**arch′priest′ship,** *n.*

archt., architect.

arch·way (ärch′wā′), *n.* *Archit.* **1.** an entrance or passage under an arch. **2.** a covering or enclosing arch.

-archy, a word element meaning "rule," "government," used in the formation of abstract nouns from stems in **-arch:** *monarchy.* [ME *-archie* < L *-archia* < Gk]

Ar·ci·nie·gas (äʀ sē nye′gäs), *n.* **Ger·mán** (heʀ män′), born 1900, Colombian author, editor, and diplomat.

arc′ light′, **1.** Also called **arc′ lamp′.** a lamp in which the light source of high intensity is an electric arc, usually between carbon rods. **2.** the light produced.

arc·o·graph (är′kə graf′, -gräf′), *n. Geom.* an instrument for drawing arcs, having a flexible arc-shaped part adjusted by an extensible straight bar connecting its sides. Also called **cyclograph.**

A.R.C.S., **1.** Associate of the Royal College of Science. **2.** Associate of the Royal College of Surgeons.

arc′ sec′, See **arc secant.**

arc′ se′cant, *Trig.* the angle, measured in radians, that has a secant equal to a given number. *Abbr.:* arc sec; *Symbol:* sec^{-1}.

arc′ sin′, See **arc sine.**

arc′ sine′, *Trig.* the angle, measured in radians, of which a given number is the sine. *Abbr.:* arc sin; *Symbol:* sin^{-1}.

arc′ tan′, See **arc tangent.**

arc′ tan′gent, *Trig.* the angle, measured in radians, that has a tangent equal to a given number. *Abbr.:* arc tan; *Symbol:* tan^{-1}.

arc·tic (ärk′tik *or, esp. for* 7, är′tik), *adj.* **1.** (*often cap.*) of, at, or near the North Pole: *the arctic region.* **2.** characteristic of the weather at or near the North Pole; frigid; bleak: *an arctic winter; an arctic wind.* **3.** suitable for or resembling that which is used in the arctic: *arctic boots.* **4.** *Astron. Rare.* of, near, or lying under the Great and the Little Bear. —*n.* **5.** (*often cap.*) the region lying north of the Arctic Circle. **6.** the polar area north of the timber line. **7. arctics,** warm, waterproof overshoes. [< L *arctic(us)* < Gk *arktikós* northern, lit., of the Bear = *árkt(os)* bear (see URSA MAJOR) + *-ikos* -IC; r. ME *artik* < MF *artique* < L *ar(c)ticus*] —**arc′ti·cal·ly,** *adv.*

Arc′tic Cir′cle, an imaginary line drawn parallel to the equator, at 23°28′ S of the North Pole.

arc′tic fox′, a thickly furred, foxlike canine, *Alopex lagopus,* of the arctic regions, brownish gray in summer and white in winter. Also called **white fox.**

Arc′tic O′cean, an ocean N of North America, Asia, and the Arctic Circle. ab. 5,540,000 sq. mi.

Arc′tic Zone′, the section of the earth's surface lying between the Arctic Circle and the North Pole.

Arc·to·gae·a (ärk′tə jē′ə), *n.* a biogeographical division comprising the Holarctic and Paleotropical regions. Also, **Arc′to·ge′a.** [< NL = *arcto-* (< L < Gk *arkto-* comb. form of *árktos;* see ARCTIC) + *gaea* (< Gk *gaîa* land, earth)] —**Arc′to·gae′an, Arc′to·ge′an, Arc′to·gae′al, Arc′to·ge′al, Arc′to·gae′ic, Arc′to·ge′ic,** *adj.*

Arc·tu·rus (ärk tŏŏr′əs, -tyŏŏr′-), *n. Astron.* a first-magnitude star in the constellation Boötes. [< L < Gk *Arktoûros* = *árkt(os)* bear + *-oûros* keeper; r. ME *arture* < MF] —**Arc·tu′ri·an,** *adj.*

ar·cu·ate (är′kyōō it, -āt′), *adj.* bent or curved like a bow. Also, **ar′cu·at′ed.** [< L *arcuāt(us)* bent like a bow, curved (ptp. of *arcuāre*) = *arcu(s)* a bow + *-ātus* -ATE¹] —**ar′cu·ate·ly,** *adv.*

ar·cu·a·tion (är′kyōō ā′shən), *n.* **1.** state of being bent or curved. **2.** the use of arches in building. **3.** a system or grouping of arches. [< L *arcuātiōn-* (s. of *arcuātiō*) a curving. See ARCUATE, -ION]

ar·cus (är′kəs), *n., pl.* **-cus.** a dense, arch-shaped cloud, often occurring at the lower front portion of a cumulonimbus. [< L: bow, arch]

-ard, a noun suffix, orig. intensive but now pejorative or without special force: *coward; drunkard; wizard.* Also, **-art.** [ME < OF < Gmc *-hard* (c. OE *-heard*) in men's names, as *Bernhard* Bernard; cf. OHG *-(h)ard, -(h)art* hardy]

ar·deb (är′deb), *n.* a unit of capacity in Egypt and neighboring countries, officially equivalent in Egypt to 5.62 U.S. bushels. [< Ar *ardabb* < Gk *artábē* < OPers *artaba*]

Ar·den (är′dᵊn), *n.* **Forest of,** a forest district in central England, in N Warwickshire: scene of Shakespeare's comedy *As You Like It* (1599?).

Ar·den-Ar·cade (är′dən är kād′), *n.* a town in central California, near Sacramento. 82,492 (1970).

ar·den·cy (är′dᵊn sē), *n.* passion; ardor; fervor. [ARD(ENT) + ENCY]

Ar·dennes (är den′), *n.* **Forest of,** a wooded plateau region in NE France, SE Belgium, and Luxembourg: World War I battle 1914; World War II battles 1944–45.

ar·dent (är′dᵊnt), *adj.* **1.** having, expressive of, or characterized by intense emotion; fervent: *an ardent patriot; an ardent vow.* **2.** vehement; fierce. **3.** *Obs.* burning; fiery. [< L *ārdent-* (s. of *ārdēns,* prp. of *ārdēre* to burn) = *ārd-* burn + *-ent-* -ENT; r. ME *ardant* < MF] —**ar′dent·ly,** *adv.* —**Syn. 1.** fervid, enthusiastic.

ar′dent spir′its, strong alcoholic liquors.

ar·dor (är′dər), *n.* **1.** great warmth of feeling; fervor; zeal; passion: *He spoke persuasively and with ardor.* **2.** *Obs.* burning heat. Also, *esp. Brit.,* **ar′dour.** [< L = *ārd(ēre)* (to) burn + *-or* -OR²; r. ME *ardure* < OF *ardur* < L; 17th century *ardour* < AF < L]

ar·du·ous (är′jōō əs *or, esp. Brit.,* är′dyōō-), *adj.* **1.** involving great hardship or exertion; laborious; difficult: *an arduous undertaking.* **2.** energetic; vigorous; strenuous: *making an arduous effort.* **3.** hard to climb; steep: *an arduous path.* [< L *arduus* erect, steep, laborious; see -OUS] —**ar′du·ous·ly,** *adv.* —**ar′du·ous·ness,** *n.* —**Syn. 1.** hard, burdensome.

are¹ (är; *unstressed* ər), *v.* pres. indic. pl. and 2nd pers. sing. of **be.** [ME, OE (Northumbrian) *aron;* c. Icel *eru,* 3rd pers. pl. See ART²]

are² (âr, är), *n. Metric System.* a surface measure equal to 100 square meters, or 119.6 square yards; ¹/₁₀₀ of a hectare. *Abbr.:* a [< F < L *ārea*). See AREA]

ar·e·a (âr′ē ə), *n.* **1.** any particular extent of space or surface, as a geographical region: *the Chicago area.* **2.** any section reserved for a specific function: *the business area of a town; the dining area of a house.* **3.** extent, range, or scope: *the whole area of science.* **4.** field of study, or a branch of a field of study: *Related areas of inquiry often reflect borrowed notions.* **5.** a piece of unoccupied ground; an open space. **6.** the space or site on which a building stands or the yard or ground attached to or surrounding it. **7.** the quantitative measure of a plane or curved surface; two-dimensional extent. **8.** *Anat.* a zone of the cerebral cortex having a specific function. [< L *ārea* vacant piece of level ground, open space in a town, courtyard, playground, orig. dry place, suitable for games, etc.; akin to *ārēre* to be dry. See ARID] —**ar′e·al,** *adj.*

ar′ea code′, a three-digit code that identifies one of the telephone areas into which a country is divided.

ar·e·a·way (âr′ē ə wā′), *n.* **1.** a sunken area leading to a cellar or basement entrance, or in front of basement or cellar windows. **2.** *U.S.* a passageway.

ar·e·ca (ar′ə kə, ə rē′-), *n.* **1.** any palm of the genus *Areca,* of tropical Asia and the Malay Archipelago, esp. *A. Catechu,* the betel palm, which bears a nut. **2.** Also called **ar′eca nut′.** the nut of the betel palm. **3.** any of various palms formerly referred to the genus *Areca.* Also called **ar′eca palm′** (for defs. 1, 3). [< Pg < Malayalam *aḍekka, aṭekka*]

A·re·ci·bo (är′i sē′bō; *Sp.* ä′re sē′bô), *n.* a seaport in N Puerto Rico. 35,484 (1970).

a·re·na (ə rē′nə), *n.* **1.** the oval space in the center of a Roman amphitheater for combats or other performances. **2.** a platform, ring, area, or the like, used for sports or other forms of entertainment, surrounded by seats for spectators: *a boxing arena; a circus arena.* **3.** a building housing an arena. **4.** a field of conflict, activity, or endeavor: *the political arena.* [< L *(h)arēna* sand, sandy place, area sanded for combat]

ar·e·na·ceous (ar′ə nā′shəs), *adj.* **1.** sandlike; sandy. **2.** (of plants) having a sandy habitat. [< L *(h)arēnaceus.* See ARENA, -ACEOUS]

are′na the′ater, a theater with seats arranged on at least three sides around a central stage.

ar·e·nic·o·lous (ar′ə nik′ə ləs), *adj.* inhabiting sand. [< NL: lit., living in sand. See ARENA, -I-, -COLOUS]

ar·e·nose (ar′ə nōs′), *adj.* sandy; gritty. Also, **ar·e·nous** (ar′ə nəs), **a·ren·u·lous** (ə ren′yə ləs). [< L *(h)arēnōs(us)* sandy. See ARENA, -OSE¹] —**ar·e·nos·i·ty** (ar′ə nos′i tē), *n.*

A·ren·sky (ə ren′skē; *Russ.* ä ren′ski), *n.* **An·ton Ste·pa·no·vich** (än tôn′ sti pä′no vich), 1861–1906, Russian composer.

aren't (ärnt, är′ənt), **1.** contraction of *are not.* **2.** contraction of *am not.*
—**Usage.** AREN'T, in the sense of "am not" in such questions as *I'm doing well, aren't I?,* is generally acceptable but is questioned by precise grammarians and is regarded as cute or affected by many users of English.

areo-, a learned borrowing from Greek meaning "the planet Mars," used in the formation of compound words: *areocentric.* [< Gk *Āreo(s),* gen. of *Árēs* ARES]

ar·e·o·cen·tric (âr′ē ō sen′trik), *adj. Astron.* having the planet Mars as center.

a·re·o·la (ə rē′ə lə), *n., pl.* **-lae** (-lē′), **-las.** *Biol.* **1.** a ring of color, as around a pustule or the human nipple. **2.** a small interstice, as between the fibers of connective tissue. [< L = *āre(a)* AREA + *-ola* dim. suffix] —**a·re′o·lar,** *adj.* —**a·re·o·late** (ə rē′ə lit, -lāt′), **a·re·o·lat·ed** (ə rē′ə lā′tid), *adj.* —**ar·e·o·la·tion** (âr′ē ə lā′shən), *n.*

ar·e·ole (âr′ē ōl′), *n. Biol.* an areola. [< F *aréole*]

ar·e·ol·o·gy (âr′ē ol′ə jē), *n. Astron.* the observation and study of the planet Mars. —**ar·e·o·log·ic** (âr′ē ə loj′ik), **ar′e·o·log′i·cal,** *adj.* —**ar′e·o·log′i·cal·ly,** *adv.* —**ar′e·ol′o·gist,** *n.*

Ar·e·op·a·gite (ar′ē op′ə jīt′, -gīt′), *n. Gk. Hist.* a member of the council of the Areopagus. [< L *Areopagītē(s)* < Gk *Areiopagī́tēs* a member of the AREOPAGUS; see -ITE¹] —**Ar·e·op·a·git·ic** (ar′ē op′ə jit′ik), *adj.*

Ar·e·op·a·gus (ar′ē op′ə gəs), *n.* **1.** a hill in Athens, Greece, W of the Acropolis. **2.** *Gk. Hist.* the high tribunal of Athens which met on this hill. [< L < Gk *Áreio(s)* *págos* hill of Ares]

A·re·qui·pa (ar′ə kē′pə; *Sp.* ä′re kē′pä), *n.* a city in S Peru. 156,657 (1961).

Ar·es (âr′ēz), *n.* the ancient Greek god of war, a son of Zeus and Hera, identified by the Romans with Mars.

a·rête (ə rāt′), *n. Phys. Geog.* a sharp rugged ridge on a mountain. [< F; OF *areste* sharp ridge < L *arist(a)* awn, ear of wheat, spine of fish]

ar·e·thu·sa (ar′ə thōō′zə), *n.* any of several plants of the genus *Arethusa,* esp. *A. bulbosa,* of North America, a small orchid having a pink or white flower. [< NL]

Ar·e·thu·sa (ar′ə thōō′zə), *n. Class. Myth.* a nymph who was changed into a spring to save her from the river god Alpheus, who was pursuing her.

A·re·ti·no (är′i tē′nō; *It.* ä′re tē′nô), *n.* **Pie·tro** (pye′trô), 1492–1556, Italian satirist and dramatist.

A·rez·zo (ə ret′sō; *It.* ä ret′tsô), *n.* a city in central Italy. 74,245 (1961).

arf (ärf), *interj.* (used to express the bark of a dog.)

Arg., Argentina.

arg., argentum.

ar·gal¹ (är′gəl), *n.* argol.

ar·gal² (är′gəl), *n.* argali.

ar·ga·li (är′gə lē), *n., pl.* **-li.** a wild sheep, *Ovis ammon,* of Asia, having long, thick, spirally curved horns. Also, **argal.** [< Mongolian]

Argali (4 ft. high at shoulder; horns 20 in.)

Ar·gall (är′gôl, -gəl), *n.* **Sir Samuel,** 1572–1639, explorer, colonial governor in America 1617–19.

Ar′gand burn′er (är′gand, -gänd, -gənd), a type of oil or gas burner in which air is fed directly into the flame through a metal tube inside a cylindrical wick. [named after Aimé *Argand* (1750–1803), Swiss scientist]

Ar′gand di′agram, *Math.* a Cartesian coordinate system for graphing complex numbers, the real part being plotted along the horizontal axis and the imaginary part being plotted along the vertical axis. Also called **Ar′gand plane′.** [named after Jean-Robert *Argand* (1768–1822), Swiss mathematician]

ar·gent (är′jənt), *n.* **1.** *Heraldry.* the tincture or metal silver. **2.** *Archaic.* **a.** silver. **b.** something silvery or white. —*adj.* **3.** like silver; silvery-white. **4.** *Heraldry.* of the tincture or metal silver: *a lion argent.* [late ME *argent(um)* < L: silver, money]

argent-, a learned borrowing from Latin meaning "silver," used in the formation of compound words: *argentic.* Also, **argenti-, argento-.** [< L *argentum*]

ar·gen·te·ous (är jen′tē əs), *adj.* silvery. Also, **ar·gen·tate** (är′jən tāt′). [< L *argenteus*]

Ar·gen·teuil (AR zhäN tœ′yᵊ), *n.* a city in N France, on the Seine near Paris. 82,458 (1962).

ar·gen·tic (är jen′tik), *adj.* *Chem.* of or containing silver and having a valence greater than the corresponding argentous compound.

ar·gen·tif·er·ous (är′jən tif′ər əs), *adj.* silver-bearing.

Ar·gen·ti·na (är′jən tē′nə; *Sp.* äR′hen tē′nä), *n.* a republic in S South America. 26,056,000; 1,084,120 sq. mi. *Cap.:* Buenos Aires. Also called **the Argentine.** Official name, **Ar′gentine Repub′lic.**

ar·gen·tine (är′jən tin, -tīn′), *adj.* pertaining to or resembling silver. [late ME < L *argentīn(us)* silvery]

Ar·gen·tine (är′jən tēn′, -tīn′), *n.* **1.** a native or inhabitant of Argentina. **2.** Argentina (usually prec. by *the*): *They vacationed in the Argentine.* —*adj.* **3.** of or pertaining to Argentina. Also, **Ar·gen·tin·e·an** (är′jən tin′ē ən).

ar·gen·tite (är′jən tīt′), *n.* a dark lead-gray mineral, silver sulfide, Ag_2S, an ore of silver.

argento-, var. of **argent-,** esp. before a consonant.

ar·gen·tous (är jen′təs), *adj.* *Chem.* containing univalent silver.

ar·gen·tum (är jen′təm), *n.* *Chem.* silver. [< L]

ar·gil·la·ceous (är′jə lā′shəs), *adj.* **1.** of the nature of or resembling clay. **2.** containing clay matter. [< L *argillāceus* clayish = *argill(a)* clay + *-āceus* -ACEOUS]

ar·gil·lite (är′jə līt′), *n.* any compact sedimentary rock composed mainly of clay materials; clay stone. [< L *argill(a)* < Gk *árgill(os)* clay + -ITE[1]] —**ar·gil·lit·ic** (är′jə lit′ik), *adj.*

ar·gi·nine (är′jə nīn′), *n.* *Biochem.* one of the essential amino acids, $C_6H_{14}O_2N_4$, that make up plant and animal proteins. [< Gk *argin(óeis)* bright-shining + -INE[2]]

Ar·give (är′jīv, -gīv), *adj.* **1.** of or pertaining to Argos. **2.** Greek. —*n.* **3.** a native of Argos. **4.** any Greek. [< L *Argīv(us)* < Gk *Argeîos* of Argos]

Ar·go (är′gō), *n., gen.* **Ar·gus** (är′gəs) for 1. **1.** *Astron.* a very large southern constellation, now divided into four, lying south of Canis Major. **2.** *Class. Myth.* the ship in which Jason sailed in quest of the Golden Fleece. [constellation named after ship] —**Ar·go′an,** *adj.*

ar·gol (är′gəl), *n.* a crude tartar, produced as a by-product in casks by the fermentation of wine grapes, used as a mordant in dyeing, in the manufacture of tartaric acid, and in fertilizers. Also, **argal.** [ME *argul, argoile* (c. AF *argoil*) < ?]

Ar·go·lis (är′gə lis), *n.* **1.** an ancient district in SE Greece. **2. Gulf of,** a gulf of the Aegean, in SE Greece. ab. 30 mi. long. —**Ar·gol·ic** (är gol′ik), **Ar·go·li·an** (är gō′lē ən), **Ar′·go·lid,** *adj.*

ar·gon (är′gon), *n.* *Chem.* a chemically inactive, gaseous element: used for filling lamps and electron tubes. *Symbol:* Ar; *at. no.:* 18; *at. wt.:* 39.948. [< Gk, neut. of *argós* not working, idle = *a-* A-[6] + (*é*)*rg(on)* work + *-os* adj. suffix]

Ar·go·naut (är′gə nôt′), *n.* **1.** *Class. Myth.* a member of the band that sailed to Colchis with Jason in the ship Argo in search of the Golden Fleece. **2.** (*sometimes l.c.*) one in search of something, esp. of something dangerous and rewarding; an adventurer. **3.** (*l.c.*) See **paper nautilus.** [< L *Argonaut(a)* < Gk *Argo-naút(ēs)* crewman of the ship ARGO; see NAUTICAL] —**Ar′·go·nau′tic,** *adj.*

NORTH SEA
NETHERLANDS
Brussels
WEST
Bonn
BELGIUM
GERMANY
LUXEMBOURG
Argonne Forest
Paris
FRANCE

Ar′gonne For′est (är′gon; *Fr.* AR gôn′), a wooded region in NE France: battles, World War I, 1918; World War II, 1944. Also called **Ar′gonne.**

Ar·gos (är′gos, -gəs), *n.* an ancient city in SE Greece, on the Gulf of Argolis.

ar·go·sy (är′gə sē), *n., pl.* **-sies.** **1.** a large merchant ship, esp. one with a rich cargo. **2.** a fleet of such ships. **3.** an opulent supply. [earlier *ragusy* < It *Ragusea* (ship) of *Ragusa*]

ar·got (är′gō, -gət), *n.* the vocabulary peculiar to a particular class or group of people, esp. that of an underworld group, as thieves, devised for private communication and identification. [< F < ?] —**ar·got·ic** (är got′ik), *adj.*

ar·gue (är′gyōō), *v.,* **-gued, -gu·ing.** —*v.i.* **1.** to present reasons for or against a thing: *He argued for an allowance and received one.* **2.** to contend in argument; dispute: *He argued with his parents about his allowance.* —*v.t.* **3.** to state the reasons for or against; debate: *The lawyers argued the case.* **4.** to maintain in reasoning: *to argue that something must be so.* **5.** to persuade, drive, etc., by reasoning. **6.** to show; prove; imply; indicate. [ME < L *argue(re)* (to) make clear, prove, declare, accuse, etc.] —**ar′gu·a·ble,** *adj.* —**ar′·gu·er,** *n.*

ar·gu·fy (är′gyə fī′), *v.t., v.i.,* **-fied, -fy·ing.** to argue or wrangle, esp. over something insignificant. —**ar′gu·fi′er,** *n.*

ar·gu·ment (är′gyə mənt), *n.* **1.** disagreement; verbal opposition or contention; altercation: *a violent argument.* **2.** a discussion involving differing points of view; debate. **3.** a process of reasoning; series of reasons: *I did not follow his argument.* **4.** a statement or fact for or against a point: *This is a strong argument in favor of the theory.* **5.** an address or composition intended to convince or persuade. **6.** subject matter; theme: *the central argument of a book.* **7.** an abstract or summary of the major points in a work of prose or poetry, or of sections of such a work. **8.** *Math.* **a.** an independent variable of a function. **b.** Also called **amplitude.** the angle made by a given vector with the reference axis. **c.** the angle corresponding to a point representing a given complex number in polar coordinates. **9.** *Obs.* **a.** evidence or proof. **b.** a matter of contention. [ME < L *argūment(um)*] —**Syn. 2.** ARGUMENT, CONTROVERSY, DISPUTE imply the expression of opinions for and against some idea. An ARGUMENT usually arises from a disagreement between two persons, each of whom advances facts supporting his own point of view. A CONTROVERSY or a DISPUTE may involve two or more persons. A CONTROVERSY is an oral or written expression of contrary opinions, and may be dignified and of some duration: *a political controversy.* A DISPUTE is an oral contention, usually brief, and often of a heated, angry, or undignified character: *a violent dispute over a purchase.*

ar·gu·men·ta·tion (är′gyə men tā′shən), *n.* **1.** the process of developing an argument; reasoning. **2.** discussion; debate; disputation. **3.** a discussion dealing with a controversial point. **4.** the setting forth of reasons together with the conclusion drawn from them. **5.** the premises and conclusion so set forth. **6.** argument (def. 5). [late ME < L *argūmentātiōn-* (s. of *argūmentātiō*)] —**ar′gu·men·ta′·tious,** *adj.*

ar·gu·men·ta·tive (är′gyə men′tə tiv), *adj.* **1.** fond of or given to argument and dispute; disputatious; contentious. **2.** controversial. —**ar′gu·men′ta·tive·ly,** *adv.* —**ar′gu·men′ta·tive·ness,** *n.*

ar·gu·men·tum (äR′gōō men′tŏŏm; *Eng.* är′gyə men′·təm), *n., pl.* **-ta** (-tä; *Eng.* -tə). *Latin.* argument.

argumen′tum ad ho′minem, *Latin.* See **ad hominem.**

Ar·gus (är′gəs), *n.* **1.** *Class. Myth.* a giant with 100 eyes, set to guard the heifer Io: his eyes were transferred after his death to the peacock's tail. **2.** an observant, vigilant person; guardian. [< L < Gk *Árgos* < *argós* bright, shining]

Ar·gyle (är′gīl), (*sometimes l.c.*) —*adj.* **1.** (of knitted articles) having a diamond-shaped pattern in two or more colors. —*n.* **2.** a diamond-shaped pattern of two or more colors, used in knitting socks, sweaters, etc. **3.** a sock having this pattern. [var. of ARGYLL; so called because patterned after tartan of this clan]

Ar·gyll (är gīl′), *n.* a county in W Scotland. 59,390 (1961); 3110 sq. mi. *Co. seat:* Inverary. Also called **Ar·gyll·shire** (är gīl′shēr, -shər).

Ar·gy·rol (är′jə rōl′, -rôl′, -rol′), *n.* *Pharm., Trademark.* See **mild silver protein.**

Ar·hat (är′hət), *n.* a Buddhist who has attained Nirvana. Cf. **Bodhisattva.** [< Skt: meriting respect < *arhati* he merits] —**Ar′hat·ship′,** *n.*

År·hus (ôR′hōōs′), *n.* a seaport in E Jutland, in Denmark. 177,234 (1960). Also, **Aarhus.**

a·rhyth·mi·a (ə rith′mē ə, ə rith′-), *n.* *Pathol.* arrhythmia. —**a·rhyth′mic, a·rhyth′mi·cal,** *adj.* —**a·rhyth′mi·cal·ly,** *adv.*

a·ri·a (är′ē ə, âr′ē ə), *n.* **1.** an air or melody. **2.** an elaborate melody for a single voice, with accompaniment, in an opera, oratorio, etc. [< It; see AIR[1]]

-aria, a suffix occurring in scientific terms of Latin origin, esp. in names of biological genera and groups: *filaria.* [< L: neut. pl. of *-ārius* -ARY]

a·ri·a da ca·po (är′ē ə də kä′pō), *pl.* **arias da capo.** an operatic aria in three sections, with the first and third sections alike and the middle section contrasting. [< It: lit., air from the head, i.e., beginning]

Ar·i·ad·ne (ar′ē ad′nē), *n.* *Class. Myth.* a daughter of Minos and Pasiphaë who gave Theseus the thread by which he escaped from the labyrinth: deserted by Theseus on Naxos, she became the bride of Dionysus.

Ar·i·an (âr′ē ən, ar′-), *adj.* **1.** of or pertaining to Arius or Arianism. —*n.* **2.** an adherent of Arianism. [< LL *Ariān(us)*]

Ar·i·an (âr′ē ən, ar′-), *adj., n.* Aryan.

-arian, **1.** a combination of **-aria** and **-an,** used in the formation of adjectives from stems in **-aria:** *filarian.* **2.** a combination of **-ary** and **-an,** used in the formation of personal nouns from stems in **-ary:** *librarian.* **3.** a suffix, modeled on def. 2, used in the formation of personal nouns from stems other than **-ary:** *vegetarian.* **4.** a formal element resulting from the combination of **-an** with stems in "-ari-": *riparian.* [< L *-āri(us)* -ARY + -AN]

Ar·i·an·ism (âr′ē ə niz′əm, ar′-), *n.* *Theol.* the doctrine of Arius that Christ the Son was not consubstantial with God the Father. —**Ar′i·an·is′tic, Ar′i·an·is′ti·cal,** *adj.*

A·ri·ca (ə rē′kə; *Sp.* ä Rē′kä), *n.* **1.** a seaport in N Chile. 46,542 (1960). **2.** See under **Tacna-Arica.**

ar·id (ar′id), *adj.* **1.** without moisture; extremely dry; parched: *arid land; an arid plain.* **2.** barren from lack of moisture; unproductive: *arid farmland.* **3.** unimaginative, uninteresting, or dull: *an arid subject.* [< L *ārid(us)* = *ār-(ēre)* (to) be dry + *-idus* -ID[4]] —**a·rid·i·ty** (ə rid′i tē), **ar′·id·ness,** *n.* —**ar′id·ly,** *adv.* —**Syn. 1.** See **dry.**

ar·i·el (âr′ē əl), *n.* an Arabian gazelle, *Gazella arabica.* Also, **ar′iel gazelle′.** [< Ar *aryal*]

Ar·i·el (âr′ē əl), *n.* *Astron.* one of the five satellites of Uranus.

Ar·ies (âr′ēz, -ē ēz′), *n., gen.* **A·ri·e·tis** (ə rī′i tis) for 1. **1.** *Astron.* the Ram, a zodiacal constellation between Pisces and Taurus. **2.** *Astrol.* the first sign of the zodiac. See diag. at **zodiac.** [< L: ram]

ar·i·et·ta (ar′ē et′ə; *It.* ä′Rē et′tä), *n., pl.* **-et·tas, -et·te** (-et′ə; *It.* -et′te). *Music.* a short aria. Also, **ar·i·ette** (ar′ē et′). [< It; see ARIA, -ETTE]

A·rif (ä′rif, ä′rēf) *n.* **Ab·dul Rah·man Mo·ham·med** (äb′·dŏŏl räh′män mô häm′med), born 1916, Iraqi army officer and public official: president 1966–68.

a·right (ə rīt′), *adv.* rightly; correctly: *to set things aright.* [ME; OE *ariht*]

ar·il (ar′il), *n.* *Bot.* an accessory covering or appendage of certain seeds, esp. one arising from the placenta, funicle, or hilum. [short for *arillus* < NL, ML *arill(ī)* dried grapes] —**ar′il·loid′,** *adj.*

ar·il·late (ar′ə lāt′, -lit), *adj.* *Bot.* having an aril. [< NL *arill(us)* ARIL + -ATE[1]]

ar·il·lode (ar′ə lōd′), *n.* *Bot.* a false aril; an aril that originates from the micropyle instead of at or below the hilum, as in the nutmeg. [< NL *arill(us)* ARIL + -ODE[1]]

Ar·i·ma·thae·a (ar′ə mə thē′ə), *n.* a town in ancient Palestine. Matt. 27:57. Also, **Ar′i·ma·the′a.** —**Ar′i·ma·thae′an, Ar′i·ma·the′an,** *adj.*

ar·i·ose (ar′ē ōs′, ar′ē ōs′), *adj.* characterized by melody; songlike. [Anglicized var. of ARIOSO]

a·ri·o·so (är′ē ō′sō, ar′-; *It.* ä Rē ô′sō), *adj., adv.* *Music.* in the manner of an air or melody. [< It: lit., songlike. See ARIA, -OSE¹]

A·ri·os·to (är′ē os′tō, -ō′stō, ar′-; *It.* ä RĒ ôs′tô), *n.* **Lu·do·vi·co** (lo͞o′dô vē′ko), 1474–1533, Italian poet.

-arious, 1. a combination of **-aria** and **-ous,** used in the formation of adjectives from stems in **-aria:** *urticarious.* **2.** a formal element resulting from the combination of **-ous** with stems in "-ari-": *precarious.*

-aris, an element occurring in scientific terms in Latin: *polaris.* [< L *-āris;* see -AR¹]

a·rise (ə rīz′), *v.i.*, **a·rose, a·ris·en** (ə riz′ən), **a·ris·ing.** **1.** to come into being, action, or notice; originate; appear; spring up: *New problems arise daily.* **2.** to result or proceed; issue (sometimes fol. by *from*): *the consequences that may arise from this action.* **3.** to move upward; ascend. **4.** to get up from sitting, lying, or kneeling; rise. **5.** to get up from sleep or rest. **6.** to rise in rebellion; revolt. [ME *arise(n),* OE *ārīsan* = *ā-* up + *rīsan* to RISE]

a·ris·ta (ə ris′tə), *n., pl.* **-tae** (-tē). **1.** *Bot.* a bristlelike appendage of grain, etc.; an awn. **2.** *Entomol.* a prominent bristle on the antenna of some dipterous insects. [< L: awn, beard or ear of grain]

Ar·is·tae·us (ar′i stē′əs), *n. Class. Myth.* a son of Apollo and Cyrene, the god of beekeeping, wine-making, and other forms of husbandry.

Ar·is·tar·chus (ar′i stär′kəs), *n.* **of Samos,** late 3rd century B.C., Greek astronomer. **—Ar′i·star′chi·an,** *adj.*

a·ris·tate (ə ris′tāt), *adj.* **1.** *Bot.* having aristae; awned. **2.** *Zool.* tipped with a thin spine. [< LL *aristāt(us)* awned]

Ar·is·ti·des (ar′i stī′dēz), *n.* ("*the Just*") 530?–468? B.C., Athenian statesman and general.

Ar·is·tip·pus (ar′i stip′əs), *n.* 435?–356? B.C., Greek philosopher: founder of the Cyrenaic school of philosophy.

aristo-, a learned borrowing meaning "best," occurring in loan words from Greek: *aristocratic.* [< Gk, comb. form of *áristos*]

ar·is·toc·ra·cy (ar′i stok′rə sē), *n., pl.* **-cies.** **1.** a class of persons holding exceptional rank and privileges, esp. the hereditary nobility. **2.** a government or state ruled by an aristocracy, elite, or privileged class. **3.** government by the best or most able men. **4.** a governing body composed of the best or most able men in a state. **5.** any class or group considered to be superior. [< ML *aristocracia* (var. of *aristocratia*) < Gk *aristokratía* rule of the best]

a·ris·to·crat (ə ris′tə krat′, ar′i stə′-), *n.* **1.** a member of an aristocracy, esp. a nobleman. **2.** a person who has the tastes, manners, etc., characteristic of members of an aristocracy. **3.** an advocate of an aristocratic form of government. [back formation from ARISTOCRATIC, modeled on F *aristocrate*] **—Syn. 1.** noble, peer, lord.

a·ris·to·crat·ic (ə ris′tə krat′ik, ar′i stə-), *adj.* **1.** of or pertaining to government by an aristocracy. **2.** belonging to or favoring the aristocracy. **3.** characteristic of an aristocrat; having the manners, values, or qualities of the aristocracy: *aristocratic bearing.* Also, **a·ris′to·crat′i·cal.** [< Gk *aristokratik(ós)*] **—a·ris′to·crat′i·cal·ly,** *adv.*

Ar·is·toph·a·nes (ar′i stof′ə nēz′), *n.* 448?–385? B.C., Athenian comic dramatist. **—A·ris·to·phan·ic** (ə ris′tə-fan′ik), *adj.*

Ar·is·to·te·lian (ar′i stə tēl′yən, -tē′lē ən, ə ris′tə-), *adj.* **1.** of, pertaining to, based on, or derived from Aristotle or his theories. **—***n.* **2.** a follower of Aristotle.

Ar·is·to·te·lian·ism (ar′i stə tēl′yə niz′əm, -tē′lē ə-, ə-ris′tə-), *n.* the philosophy of Aristotle or philosophical principles and methods derived from his writings.

Ar′istote′lian log′ic, **1.** the logic of Aristotle, esp. in the modified form taught in the Middle Ages. **2.** traditional formal logic based on the categorial propositions of the forms: *All S is P; no S is P; some S is P; some S is not P.*

Ar·is·tot·le (ar′i stot′ᵊl), *n.* 384–322 B.C., Greek philosopher: pupil of Plato; tutor of Alexander the Great.

arith., **1.** arithmetic. **2.** arithmetical.

ar·ith·man·cy (ar′ith man′sē), *n.* divination by the use of numbers, esp. by the number of letters that make up a name. [alter. of NL *arithmomantia* = Gk *arithmó(s)* number + *manteía* -MANCY]

a·rith·me·tic (*n.* ə rith′mə tik; *adj.* ar′ith met′ik), *n.* **1.** the method or process of computation with figures: the most elementary branch of mathematics. **2.** Also called **theoretical arithmetic.** the theory of numbers; the study of the divisibility of whole numbers, the remainders after division, etc. **3.** a book on this subject. **—***adj.* **4.** Also, **ar′ith·met′i·cal.** of or pertaining to arithmetic. [< L *arithmētic(a),* neut. pl. of *arithmēticus* < Gk *arithmētikós* of numbers = *arithmé(ein)* (to) reckon + *-tikos* -TIC; r. ME *arsmet(r)ike* < OF *arismetique* < ML *arismētica*] **—ar′ith·met′i·cal·ly,** *adv.*

a·rith·me·ti·cian (ə rith′mi tish′ən, ar′ith-), *n.* an expert in arithmetic. [ARITHMETIC + -IAN, modeled on MF *arithméticien*]

ar′ithmet′ic mean′, *Math.* the mean obtained by adding several quantities together and dividing the sum by the number of quantities; average.

arithmet′ic progres′sion, *Math.* a sequence in which each term is obtained by the addition of a constant number to the preceding term, as 1, 4, 7, 10, 13. Also called **ar′ithmet′ic se′ries.**

-arium, var. of **-orium:** *aquarium.*

A·ri·us (ə rī′əs, âr′ē-), *n.* died A.D. 336, Christian priest at Alexandria, founder of Arianism.

-arius, a suffix occurring in scientific words from Latin: *denarius.* [< L: -ARY]

a ri·ve·der·ci (ä′ RĒ ve DER′chē), *Italian.* arrivederci.

Ariz., Arizona.

Ar·i·zo·na (ar′i zō′nə), *n.* a state in SW United States. 1,772,482 (1970); 113,909 sq. mi. *Cap.:* Phoenix. *Abbr.:* Ariz., AZ **—Ar′i·zo′nan, Ar·i·zo·ni·an** (ar′i zō′nē ən), *adj., n.*

Ar·ju·na (är′jə nə; *Skt.* UR′jo͝o nə), *n. Hinduism.* the chief hero of the *Bhagavad-Gita.*

ark (ärk), *n.* **1.** (*sometimes cap.*) the vessel built by Noah for safety during the Flood. Gen. 6–9. **2.** Also called **ark′ of the cov′enant.** a chest or box symbolizing the presence of the Deity, carried by the Israelites after the Exodus: the most sacred object of the tabernacle and the temple in Jerusalem. **3.** a refuge or place of security. **4.** (*cap.*) *Judaism.* See **Holy Ark.** **5.** *Archaic.* a chest or box. [ME; OE *arc, earc* < L *arca* chest, coffer]

Ark., Arkansas.

Ar·kan·sas (är′kən sô′; *for 2 also* ar kan′zəs), *n.* **1.** a state in S central United States. 1,923,295 (1970); 53,104 sq. mi. *Cap.:* Little Rock. *Abbr.:* Ark., AR **2.** a river flowing E and SE from central Colorado into the Mississippi in SE Arkansas. 1450 mi. long. **—Ar·kan·san** (är kan′zən), **Ar·kan·si·an** (är kan′zē ən), *n., adj.*

Ar·khan·gelsk (äR KHän′gelsk), *n.* Russian name of **Archangel.**

ark·wright (ärk′rīt′), *n.* a maker of arks or chests.

Ark·wright (ärk′rīt′), *n.* **Sir Richard,** 1732–92, English inventor of the spinning jenny.

Arl·berg (äRL′beRK′), *n.* **1.** a mountain pass in W Austria. 5946 ft. high. **2.** a tunnel beneath this pass.

Ar·len (är′lən), *n.* **Michael** (*Dikran Kouyoumdjian*), 1895–1956, English novelist, born in Bulgaria.

Arles (ärlz; *Fr.* ARL), *n.* a city in SE France, on the Rhone River: Roman ruins. 42,353 (1962).

Ar·ling·ton (är′ling tən), *n.* **1.** a county in NE Virginia, opposite Washington, D.C.: national cemetery. 174,284 (1970). **2.** a town in E Massachusetts. 53,524 (1970). **3.** a city in N Texas. 89,723 (1970).

Ar′lington Heights′, a city in NE Illinois, near Chicago. 64,884 (1970).

Ar′lington Na′tional Cem′etery, a national cemetery located in Arlington, Virginia.

arm¹ (ärm), *n.* **1.** the upper limb of the human body, esp. the portion extending from the shoulder to the wrist. **2.** *Anat.* the upper limb of man from the shoulder to the elbow. **3.** the forelimb of any vertebrate. **4.** some part of an organism like or likened to an arm. **5.** any armlike part or attachment, as a lever on a machine: *the arm of a record player.* **6.** a covering for the arm, esp. a sleeve of a garment: *the arm of a coat.* **7.** an administrative or operational branch of an organization: *a special arm of the government.* **8.** *Naut.* any of the curved or bent pieces of an anchor, terminating in the flukes. **9.** Also called **armrest.** a projecting support for the forearm at the side of a chair, sofa, etc. **10.** an inlet or cove: *an arm of the sea.* **11.** *Mil.* a combat branch of the military service, as the infantry. **12.** power; might; authority: *the long arm of the law.* **13. arm in arm,** with arms intertwined: *They walked along arm in arm.* **14. at arm's length,** at a distance; not on familiar or friendly terms: *to keep at arm's length.* **15. in the arms of Morpheus,** asleep. **16. put the arm on,** *Slang.* **a.** to try to get money from, as for a donation. **b.** to restrain or detain, as by force. **17. with open arms,** cordially; with warm hospitality: *He greeted us with open arms.* [ME; OE *arm, earm;* c. Goth *arms,* G *Arm,* L *armus* shoulder, Gk *harmós* joint] **—arm′less,** *adj.*

arm² (ärm), *n.* **1.** Usually, **arms.** weapons, esp. firearms. **2. arms,** *Heraldry.* the escutcheon, with its divisions, charges, and tinctures, and the other components forming an achievement that symbolizes and is reserved for a person, family, or corporate body; armorial bearings; coat of arms. **3. bear arms, a.** to carry weapons. **b.** to serve as a member of the military or of contending forces. **4. To arms!** Prepare to fight! **5. up in arms,** indignant; ready to take hostile action: *There is no need to get up in arms over such a trifle.* **—***v.i.* **6.** to enter into a state of hostility or of readiness for war. **—***v.t.* **7.** to equip with weapons: *to arm the troops.* **8.** to provide or set the fuze or initiating or destructive element of (a bomb, shell, or missile) so that it can be exploded: *The missile was armed with an atomic warhead.* **9.** to cover protectively. **10.** to provide with whatever will add strength, force, or security; support; fortify: *He was armed with statistics and facts.* **11.** to equip or prepare for any specific purpose or effective use; furnish: *My lawyer is well armed with the facts.* **12.** to prepare for action; make fit; ready. **13.** *Naut.* to fill (a sounding lead) with arming. [(n.) back formation from *arms* (pl.), ME *armes* << L *arma;* (v.) ME *arm(en)* < OF *arme(r)* < L *armāre* to arm < *arma* (pl.) tools, weapons] **—arm′less,** *adj.* **—Syn. 11.** ready, outfit. **—Ant. 8.** disarm.

Arm, Armenian (def. 3).

Arm., **1.** Armenian. **2.** Armoric.

Ar·ma·da (är mä′də, -mā′-), *n.* **1.** Also called **Spanish Armada.** the fleet sent against England by Philip II of Spain in 1588, defeated by the English navy. **2.** (*l.c.*) any fleet of warships. **3.** (*l.c.*) a large group or force of vehicles, airplanes, etc. [< Sp < L *armāta* armed forces, neut. pl. of *armātus* (ptp. of *armāre* to equip with arms). See ARM², -ATE¹]

ar·ma·dil·lo (är′mə dil′ō), *n., pl.* **-los.** any of several burrowing, chiefly nocturnal, edentate mammals of the family *Dasypodidae,* ranging from the southern U.S. through South America, having strong claws and a jointed protective covering of bony plates. [< Sp = *armad(o)* armed (< L *armātus;* see ARM², -ATE¹) + *-illo* < L *-illus* dim. suffix]

Armadillo, *Dasypus novemcinctus* (8 in. high at shoulder; total length 2½ ft.; tail 1 ft.)

Ar·ma·ged·don (är′mə ged′ᵊn), *n.* **1.** the place where the final battle will be fought between the forces of good and evil (probably so called in reference to the battlefield of Megiddo. Rev. 16:16). **2.** a great and decisive battle.

Ar·magh (är mä′), *n.* a county in S Northern Ireland. 118,600 (est. 1963); 489 sq. mi. *Co. seat:* Armagh.

Ar·ma·gnac (är′mən yak′; *Fr.* AR mä nyAK′), *n.* a dry brandy distilled in the Gers department in SW France. [< F, after *Armagnac* the district]

ar·ma·ment (är′mə mənt), *n.* **1.** the weapons with which a military unit, esp. a combat airplane, armored vehicle, or warship, is equipped. **2.** a land, sea, or air force equipped for war. **3.** armor (def. 4). **4.** Usually, **armaments.** military strength collectively. **5.** the process of equipping or arming for war. [< L *armāment(a)* fittings = *armā(re)* (to) fit out (see ARM²) + *-menta* (pl.) -MENT]

ar·ma·ture (är′mə chər), *n.* **1.** armor. **2.** *Biol.* the protective covering of an animal or plant, or any part serving for defense or offense. **3.** *Elect.* **a.** the part of an electric machine that includes the main current-carrying winding and in which the electromotive force is induced. **b.** the pivoted part of an electric device, as a buzzer or relay, that is activated by a magnetic field. **c.** the iron or steel applied across the poles of a permanent magnet to close it, or across the poles of an electromagnet to transmit a mechanical force. **4.** *Sculpture.* a skeletal framework built as a support on which a clay, wax, or plaster figure is constructed. [< L *armātūr(a)* an outfit, armor = *armāt(us)* equipped (see ARM², -ATE¹) + *-ūra* -URE]

Ar·ma·vir (är′mə vēr′; *Russ.* är mä vēr′), *n.* a city in the SW RSFSR, in Europe. 123,000 (est. 1962).

arm·chair (ärm′châr′), *n.* **1.** a chair with sidepieces or arms to support a person's forearms or elbows. —*adj.* **2.** of or characterized by a lack of practical experience: *an armchair strategist.*

armed (ärmd), *adj.* **1.** carrying or bearing arms, esp. firearms; having weapons. **2.** supported or maintained by arms: *armed peace.* **3.** involving the use of weapons: *armed conflict.* **4.** equipped or prepared for any specific purpose: *The students came armed with pencils and notebooks.* **5.** (esp. of an animal) covered protectively, as by a shell. **6.** (of a bomb, shell, or missile) having the fuze or other initiating element in place and ready to operate: *The plane carried an armed atomic bomb.*

armed′ forc′es, military, naval, and air forces, esp. of a nation or of a number of nations. Also called **armed′ serv′ices.**

armed′ neutral′ity, readiness to counter with force an invasion of rights by any belligerent power, esp. as the expressed policy of a neutral nation in wartime.

Ar·me·ni·a (är mē′nē ə, -mēn′yə; *for 3 also Sp.* är me′nyä), *n.* **1.** an ancient country in W Asia: now a region in the Soviet Union, E Turkey, and NW Iran. **2.** Official name, **Arme′nian So′viet So′cialist Repub′lic.** a constituent republic of the Soviet Union, in S Caucasia. 2,100,000 (est. 1965); ab. 11,500 sq. mi. *Cap.:* Erivan. **3.** a city and coffee center in W central Columbia. 107,150 (est. 1964).

Ar·me·ni·an (är mē′nē ən, -mēn′yən), *adj.* **1.** of or pertaining to Armenia, its inhabitants, or their language. —*n.* **2.** a native of Armenia. **3.** the Indo-European language of the Armenians, written in a distinctive script derived from the Aramaic alphabet. *Abbr.:* Arm

Ar·men·tières (ar män tyer′), *n.* a city in N France: World War I battles 1914, 1918. 27,254 (1962).

arm·ful (ärm′fŏŏl′), *n., pl.* **-fuls.** the amount that can be held by the arm or both arms; a large quantity.

arm·hole (ärm′hōl′), *n.* an opening for the arm in a garment.

ar·mi·ger (är′mi jər), *n.* **1.** a person entitled to armorial bearings. **2.** an armorbearer to a knight; a squire. [< ML: squire, L: armorbearer (n.), armorbearing (adj.) = *armi-* (comb. form of *arma* arms) + *-ger* bearing < *gerere* to carry, wear] —**ar·mig·er·ous** (är mij′ər əs), *adj.*

ar·mil·lar·y (är′mə ler′ē, är mil′ə rē), *adj.* consisting of hoops or rings. [< L *armill(a)* bracelet, hoop (*arm(us)* shoulder + *-illa* dim. suffix) + -ARY]

ar′millary sphere′, *Astron.* an ancient instrument consisting of an arrangement of rings, all of which are circles of the same sphere, used to show the relative positions of the celestial equator, ecliptic, and other circles on the celestial sphere.

arm·ing (är′ming), *n.* *Naut.* tallow or a similar soft substance placed in a sounding lead to pick up samples of the ground under the water to show the nature of the bottom.

Ar·min·i·an·ism (är min′ē ə niz′əm), *n.* *Theol.* the doctrinal teachings of Jacobus Arminius or his followers, esp. that Christ died for all men and not only for the elect. Cf. **Calvinism** (def. 1). —**Ar·min′i·an,** *adj., n.*

Ar·min·i·us (är min′ē əs), *n.* **1.** (*Hermann*) 17? B.C.–A.D. 21, Germanic hero who defeated Roman army A.D. 9. **2. Ja·co·bus** (jə kō′bəs), (*Jacob Harmensen*), 1560–1609, Dutch Protestant theologian.

ar·mip·o·tent (är mip′ə tənt), *adj.* strong in battle or possessing powerful weapons. [< L *armipotent-* (s. of *armipotēns* potent in arms). See ARM², -I-, POTENT] —**ar·mip′o·tence,** *n.*

ar·mi·stice (är′mi stis), *n.* a temporary suspension of hostilities by agreement of the warring parties; truce: *The armistice ended World War I.* [< NL *armistitium* = L *armi-* (comb. form of *arma* ARMS) + *-stitium* a stopping (*stit-* (var. s. of *sistere* to stop; see STAND) + *-ium* n. suffix)]

Ar′mistice Day′, former name of **Veterans Day.**

arm·let (ärm′lit), *n.* *Chiefly Brit.* an ornamental band worn on the arm, esp. a bracelet worn high on the arm, rather than on the wrist.

arm·load (ärm′lōd′), *n.* the quantity a person can hold or carry in an arm or both arms.

ar·moire (ärm wär′), *n.* a large wardrobe or movable cupboard, with doors and shelves. [< MF; OF *ar(maire)* + *(au)moire* AMBRY]

ar·mor (är′mər), *n.* **1.** any covering used as a defense against weapons. **2.** a suit of armor. **3.** mechanized units of military forces, as armored divisions. **4.** any protective covering, as on certain animals. —*v.t.* **5.** to cover or equip with armor or armor plate. Also, *esp. Brit.,* **armour.** [ME *armo(u)r,* var. of *armure* < OF *arm(e)ure* < L *armātūr(a)* ARMATURE]

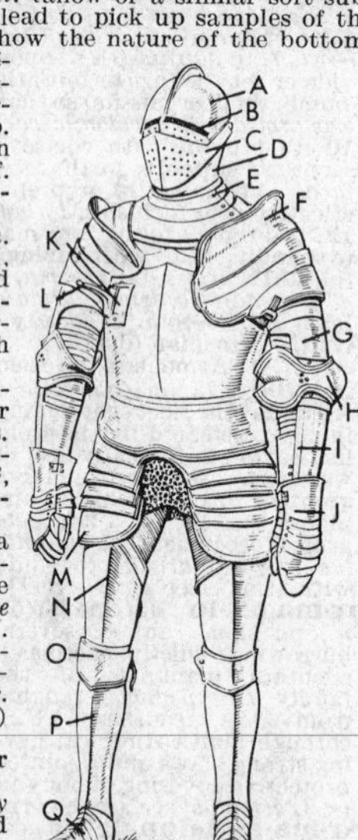

Armor (Full plate, 16th century)
A, Helmet; B, Visor; C, Ventail; D, Beaver; E, Gorget; F, Pauldron; G, Rerebrace; H, Couter; I, Vambrace; J, Gauntlet; K, Breastplate; L, Lance rest; M, Fauld; N, Cuisse; O, Poleyn; P, Greave; Q, Sabaton

armor., arms and armor.

ar·mor·bear·er (är′mər bâr′er), *n.* a retainer bearing the armor or arms of a warrior.

ar·mored (är′mərd), *adj.* **1.** protected by armor or armor plate. **2.** provided with or using armored equipment, as tanks, armored cars, etc.: *an armored patrol.*

ar′mored car′, **1.** a military combat vehicle with wheels, light armor, and usually machine guns. **2.** an armor-plated truck with strong locks and doors for transporting money and valuables.

ar′mored forc′es, military forces composed of tank units and their supporting troops and artillery.

ar·mor·er (är′mər ər), *n.* **1.** a maker or repairer of arms or armor. **2.** a manufacturer of firearms. [late ME; r. ME *armurer* < AF, MF, OF *armurier*]

ar·mo·ri·al (är mōr′ē əl, -môr′-), *adj.* **1.** of or pertaining to heraldry or heraldic bearings. —*n.* **2.** a book containing heraldic bearings and devices.

Ar·mor·i·ca (är môr′i kə, -mor′-), *n.* an ancient region in NW France, corresponding generally to Brittany.

Ar·mor·i·can (är môr′i kən, -mor′-), *adj.* **1.** of or pertaining to Armorica. —*n.* **2.** a native of Armorica. **3.** Breton (def. 2). Also, **Ar·mor′ic.**

ar·mor·y (är′mə rē), *n., pl.* **-mor·ies.** **1.** a storage place for weapons and other war equipment. **2.** *U.S. Army.* a headquarters building and drill center of a National Guard or Army Reserve unit. **3.** *U.S.* arsenal. **4.** *Heraldry.* the art of blazoning arms. **5.** heraldry. **6.** *Archaic.* heraldic bearings or arms. **7.** *Archaic.* arms or armor collectively. Also, *esp. Brit.,* **ar′mour·y** (for defs. 1, 7). [ME *armurie* = *armure* ARMOR + *-ie* -Y³]

ar·mour (är′mər), *n.* *Chiefly Brit.* armor.

arm·pit (ärm′pit′), *n.* *Anat.* the hollow under the arm at the shoulder; axilla.

arm·rest (ärm′rest′), *n.* arm¹ (def. 9).

Arm·strong (ärm′strông′), *n.* **1. (Daniel) Louis** ("*Satchmo*"), 1900–71, U.S. jazz trumpeter and bandleader. **2. Edwin Howard,** 1890–1954, U.S. electrical engineer and inventor: developed frequency modulation.

Arm·strong-Jones (ärm′strông′jōnz′, -strong′-), *n.* **Antony Charles Robert, Earl of Snow·don** (snōd′ᵊn), born 1930, ex-husband of Princess Margaret of England.

ar·mure (är′myər), *n.* a woolen or silk fabric woven with a small, raised pattern. [< F; see ARMOR]

ar·my (är′mē), *n., pl.* **-mies.** **1.** the military forces of a nation, esp. those trained and equipped to fight on land. **2.** (in large military land forces) the second largest unit, consisting of two or more corps. **3.** a large body of men trained and armed for war. **4.** a very large number or group of something; a great multitude: *the army of the unemployed.* [ME *armee* < MF < L *armāta.* See ARMADA]

Ar′my Air′ Forc′es, *U.S. Army.* a unit comprising almost all aviation, with its personnel, equipment, etc.: it became part of the Air Force on July 26, 1947.

ar′my ant′, any of the chiefly tropical ants of the suborder *Dorylinae* that travel in vast swarms, preying mainly on arthropods. Also called **driver ant.**

Ar′my of the Unit′ed States′, the army or armies referred to in the U.S. Consitution, esp. consisting of the Regular Army, National Guard, and Army Reserve. Cf. **United States Army.**

ar·my·worm (är′mē wûrm′), *n.* the caterpillar of a noctuid moth, *Pseudaletia unipuncta,* that often travels in large numbers over a region, destroying crops.

ar·nat·to (är nat′ō, -nä′tō), *n., pl.* **-tos.** annatto (def. 2).

Arne (ärn), *n.* **Thomas (Augustine),** 1710–78, English composer.

Arn·hem (ärn′hem), *n.* a city in the central Netherlands, on the Rhine River: battle 1944. 127,955 (1962).

ar·ni·ca (är′nə kə), *n.* **1.** any asteraceous plant of the genus *Arnica,* esp. *A. montana* of Europe. **2.** a tincture of the flowers of *A. montana* and other species of *Arnica,* used as an external application for sprains and bruises. [< NL < ?]

Ar·no (är′nō; *also It.* är′nô), *n.* a river flowing W from central Italy to the Ligurian Sea. 140 mi. long.

Ar·nold (är′nᵊld), *n.* **1. Benedict,** 1741–1801, American general in the Revolutionary War who became a traitor. **2. Sir Edwin,** 1832–1904, English poet and journalist. **3. Henry H.** ("*Hap*"), 1886–1950, U.S. general. **4. Matthew,** 1822–88, English essayist, poet, and literary critic. **5.** his father, **Thomas,** 1795–1842, English clergyman, educator, historian, and writer.

Ar·nold·son (är′nᵊld sən; *Sw.* är′nŏŏld sôn′), *n.* **Klas Pon·tus** (kläs pôn′təs), 1844–1916, Swedish author and politician: Nobel peace prize 1908.

ar·oid (ar′oid, âr′-), *Bot.* —*adj.* **1.** Also, **a·roi·de·ous** (ə roi′dē əs). araceous. —*n.* **2.** an araceous plant. [< NL *Ar(um)* type genus (see ARUM) + -OID]

a·roint′ thee′ (ə roint′), *Archaic.* avaunt! begone! [?]

a·ro·ma (ə rō′mə), *n.* **1.** an odor arising from spices, plants, etc., esp. an agreeable odor; fragrance. **2.** (of wines and spirits) the odor or bouquet. **3.** a pervasive characteristic. [< L < Gk: spice; r. ME *aromat* < OF < L *arōmat-* (s. of *arōma*)] —**Syn. 1.** See **perfume.**

ar·o·mat·ic (ar′ə mat′ik), *adj.* **1.** having an aroma; fragrant; sweet-scented; odoriferous. **2.** *Chem.* of or pertaining to an aromatic compound or compounds. —*n.* **3.** a plant, drug, or medicine that yields a fragrant smell. [ME *aromatyk* < LL *arōmatic(us)* < Gk *arōmatikós.* See AROMA, -IC] —**ar′o·mat′i·cal·ly,** *adv.* —**ar′o·mat′ic·ness,** *n.*

ar·o·ma·tic·i·ty (ar′ə mə tis′i tē, ə rō′mə-), *n.* **1.** the quality or state of being aromatic. **2.** *Chem.* the property of being or resembling any of the aromatic compounds.

ar′omat′ic spir′its of ammo′nia, *Pharm.* a nearly colorless liquid that yellows on standing and contains ammonia, ammonium carbonate, alcohol, and aromatic oils: used orally as an antacid and carminative and, by inhalation, as a stimulant in the treatment of faintness. Also, **ar′omat′ic spir′it of ammo′nia.**

a·ro·ma·tise (ə rō′mə tīz′), *v.t.,* **-tised, -tis·ing.** *Chiefly Brit.* aromatize. —**a·ro′ma·tis′er,** *n.*

a·ro·ma·ti·za·tion (ə rō′mə ti zā′shən *or, esp. Brit.,* -tī-), *n. Chem.* the conversion of aliphatic or alicyclic compounds to aromatic hydrocarbons. Also, *esp. Brit.,* **a·ro′ma·ti·sa′tion.** [< ML *arōmatizātiōn-* (s. of *arōmatizātiō*)]

a·ro·ma·tize (ə rō′mə tīz′), *v.t.,* **-tized, -tiz·ing.** to make aromatic or fragrant. Also, *esp. Brit.,* **aromatise.** [late ME < LL *arōmatizāre* < Gk *arōmatízein* to spice. See AROMA, -IZE] —**a·ro′ma·tiz′er,** *n.*

A·ron Ko·desh (ä RŌN′ kô′desh), *Hebrew.* See **Holy Ark.**

A·roos·took (ə ro͞os′to͝ok, -tik), *n.* a river flowing NE from N Maine to the St. John River. 140 mi. long.

a·rose (ə rōz′), *v.* pt. of **arise.**

a·round (ə round′), *adv.* **1.** in a circle, ring, or the like; so as to surround: *The crowd gathered around.* **2.** on all sides: *His land is fenced all around.* **3.** in all directions from a center or point of reference: *He owns the land for miles around.* **4.** in a region about a place: *all the country around.* **5.** in circumference: *The tree was 40 inches around.* **6.** in a circular or rounded course: *to fly around and around.* **7.** through a sequence or series, as of places or persons: *to show someone around.* **8.** through a recurring period, as of time, esp. to the present or a particular time: *when spring rolls around again.* **9.** by a circuitous or roundabout course: *The driveway to the house goes around by the stables.* **10.** with a rotating course or movement: *The wheels turned around.* **11.** in or to another or opposite direction, course, opinion, etc.: *Sit still and don't look around. After our arguments, she finally came around.* **12.** back into consciousness: *The smelling salts brought her around.* **13.** *Chiefly U.S.* in circulation, action, etc.; about: *When will she be up and around?* **14.** *U.S. Informal.* somewhere about or near; nearby: *I'll be around if you need me.* **15.** to a specific place: *He came around to see me.* **16. have been around,** *Informal.* to have had much worldly experience; be sophisticated or experienced. —*prep.* **17.** about; on all sides; encircling; encompassing: *a halo around his head.* **18.** so as to encircle, surround, or envelop: *to tie paper around a package.* **19.** on the edge, border, or outer part of: *a skirt with braid around the bottom.* **20.** from place to place in; about: *to get around town.* **21.** in all or various directions from: *to look around one.* **22.** in the vicinity of; within the area that surrounds: *the country around Boston.* **23.** approximately; about: *around five o'clock.* **24.** here and there in: *There are mailboxes all around the city.* **25.** somewhere in or near: *to stay around the house.* **26.** to all or various parts of: *to wander around the country.* **27.** so as to make a circuit about or partial circuit to the other side of: *to row around the lake.* **28.** beyond the turn of, or reached by making a partial circuit about: *the church around the corner.* **29.** so as to revolve or rotate about a center or axis: *the earth's motion around its axis.* **30.** personally close to: *Only the few men around the dictator understood his motives.*

a·rouse (ə rouz′), *v.,* **a·roused, a·rous·ing.** —*v.t.* **1.** to stir to action; awaken: *to arouse one from sleep.* **2.** to provoke; excite: *to arouse anger.* —*v.i.* **3.** to awake or become aroused. [A-[3] + ROUSE[1], modeled on ARISE] —**a·rous′a·ble,** *adj.* —**a·rous′al,** *n.* —**a·rous′er,** *n.* —**Syn. 1.** animate; inspire. **2.** incite. —**Ant. 1.** calm.

Arp (ärp), *n.* **Hans** (häns) or **Jean** (zhäN), 1888?–1966, French painter and sculptor.

Ár·pád (äR′päd), *n.* died A.D. 907, Hungarian national hero.

ar·peg·gi·o (är pej′ē ō′, -pej′ō), *n., pl.* **-gi·os.** *Music.* **1.** the sounding of the notes of a chord in rapid succession instead of simultaneously. **2.** a chord thus sounded. [< It: lit., a harping = *arpeggi(are)* (to) play on the harp (< Gmc; cf. OE *hearpi(g)an* to harp) + *-o* n. suffix] —**ar·peg·gi·at·ed** (är pej′ē ā′tid), **ar·peg′gi·oed′,** *adj.*

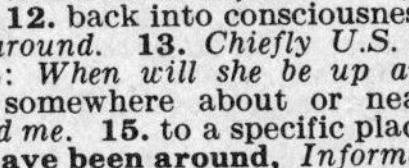

Arpeggio

ar·pent (är′pənt; *Fr.* AR-päN′), *n., pl.* **-pents** (-pənts; *Fr.* -päN′). an old French unit of area equal to about one acre. [< MF < LL *arepennis* half-acre < Gaulish; akin to MIr *airchenn* unit of area]

ar·que·bus (är′kwə bəs), *n., pl.* **-bus·es.** harquebus.

arr., **1.** arranged. **2.** arrangement. **3.** arrival. **4.** arrive.

ar·rack (ar′ək), *n.* any of various spirituous liquors distilled in the East and Middle East from the fermented sap of toddy palms, or from fermented molasses, rice, or other materials. Also, **arak.** [< Ar *'araq* sweat, juice, liquor]

ar·raign (ə rān′), *v.t.* **1.** *Law.* to call or bring before a court to answer to an indictment. **2.** to accuse or charge in general; criticize adversely; censure. [ME *araine(n)* < AF *araine(r),* OF *araisnier* = *a-* A-[5] + *raisnier* < VL **ratiōnāre* to talk, reason; see RATIO] —**ar·raign′er,** *n.*

ar·raign·ment (ə rān′mənt), *n.* **1.** *Law.* the act of arraigning. **2.** the state of being arraigned. [late ME *arainement* < MF *araisnement*]

Ar·ran (ar′ən, aR′ən), *n.* an island in SW Scotland, in the Firth of Clyde. 4300 (est. 1956); 166 sq. mi.

ar·range (ə rānj′), *v.,* **-ranged, -rang·ing.** —*v.t.* **1.** to place in proper, desired, or convenient order. **2.** to come to an agreement or understanding regarding. **3.** to prepare, plan, or schedule: *to arrange a meeting.* **4.** *Music.* to adapt (a composition) for a particular style of performance by voices or instruments. —*v.i.* **5.** to make preparations: *They arranged for a concert on Wednesday.* **6.** to make a settlement; come to an agreement (usually fol. by *for*): *to arrange with the grocer for regular deliveries.* [ME *arayngе(n)* < MF *arangie(r)* = *a-* A-[5] + *rangier* to RANGE] —**ar·range′a·ble,** *adj.* —**ar·rang′er,** *n.* —**Syn. 1.** array. **2.** settle, establish.

ar·range·ment (ə rānj′mənt), *n.* **1.** the act of arranging. **2.** the state of being arranged. **3.** the manner in which things are arranged. **4.** a final settlement; adjustment by agreement. **5.** Usually, **arrangements.** preparatory measures; preparations: *They made arrangements for an early departure.* **6.** something arranged in a particular way: *a floral arrangement.* **7.** *Music.* the adaptation of a composition to voices or instruments, or to a new purpose. [< F]

ar·rant (ar′ənt), *adj.* **1.** downright; thorough; unmitigated: *an arrant fool.* **2.** *Obs.* wandering; errant. [var. of ERRANT] —**ar′rant·ly,** *adv.*

ar·ras (ar′əs), *n.* **1.** a rich tapestry. **2.** a tapestry weave. **3.** a wall hanging, as a tapestry or similar object. [named after ARRAS] —**ar′rased,** *adj.*

Ar·ras (ar′əs; *Fr.* A räs′), *n.* a city in N France: battles in World War I. 45,643 (1962).

ar·ray (ə rā′), *v.t.* **1.** to place in proper or desired order, as troops for battle. **2.** to clothe, esp. with ornamental attire. —*n.* **3.** order, as of troops drawn up for battle. **4.** a military force, esp. a body of troops. **5.** a large and impressive grouping or organization: *an array of facts.* **6.** a regular order or arrangement: *an array of figures.* **7.** attire; dress: *in fine array.* **8.** *Math., Statistics.* an arrangement of a series of terms in some geometric pattern, as in a matrix. [ME *arraye(n)* < AF *araye(r),* OF *are(y)er* < Gmc; cf. OE *arǣdan* to prepare = *ā-* A-[3] + *rǣde* ready] —**Syn. 1.** arrange, dispose. **2.** attire; adorn. **3.** disposition, arrangement. **7.** raiment.

ar·ray·al (ə rā′əl), *n.* **1.** act of arraying. **2.** something that is arrayed.

ar·rear (ə rēr′), *n.* **1.** Usually, **arrears.** the state of being behind or late, esp. in the fulfillment of a promise, obligation, or the like. **2.** Often, **arrears.** something that is behind in being paid. **3. in** or **into arrears,** behind in payment of a debt. Also, **in arrear.** [n. use of *arrear* (adv., now obs.), ME *arere* behind < MF << L *ad retrō.* See AD-, RETRO-]

ar·rear·age (ə rēr′ij), *n.* **1.** the state or condition of being in arrears. **2.** Often, **arrearages.** an amount or amounts overdue. **3.** *Archaic.* something kept in reserve. [ME *arerage* < OF]

ar·rest (ə rest′), *v.t.* **1.** to seize (a person) by legal authority or warrant. **2.** to attract and hold: *to arrest the attention.* **3.** to check the course of; stop or slow down: *to arrest progress.* —*n.* **4.** the act of taking a person into legal custody, as by officers of the law. **5.** the state of being taken into legal custody (sometimes prec. by *under*). **6.** any act of taking by force. **7.** the act of stopping or slowing. **8.** the state of being stopped or slowed. [ME *areste(n)* < MF *areste(r)* = *a-* A-[5] + *rester* to REST; ME *arest(e)* (n.) < OF (v.)] —**ar·rest′a·ble,** *adj.* —**ar·rest′er,** *n.* —**ar·rest′ment,** *n.* —**Syn. 1.** apprehend. **2.** secure, occupy. **3.** stay. See **stop. 4.** detention, apprehension. **7.** stoppage, stay, check. —**Ant. 1-4.** release.

ar·rest·ing (ə res′ting), *adj.* **1.** attracting or capable of attracting attention, interest, or the like: *an arresting smile.* **2.** making or having made an arrest: *the arresting officer.* —**ar·rest′ing·ly,** *adv.*

ar·res·tive (ə res′tiv), *adj.* tending to arrest or take hold of the attention, interest, etc.

arrgt., arrangement.

Ar·rhe·ni·us (äR rā′nē o͝os′), *n.* **Svan·te Au·gust** (svän′te ou′go͝ost), 1859–1927, Swedish physicist and chemist: Nobel prize for chemistry 1903.

ar·rhyth·mi·a (ə rith′mē ə, ə rith′-), *n. Pathol.* any disturbance in the rhythm of the heartbeat. Also, **arhythmia, arythmia, arrythmia.** [< NL < Gk *arrhythmía.* See A-[6], RHYTHM, -IA] —**ar·rhyth′mic, ar·rhyth′mi·cal,** *adj.* —**ar·rhyth′mi·cal·ly,** *adv.*

ar·ri·ère-ban (ar′ē er′ban′; *Fr.* A RYER bäN′), *n., pl.* **-bans** (-banz′; *Fr.* -bäN′). **1.** a group of vassals who owed military service, esp. to French kings. **2.** the message calling on this group for duty. [< F, alter. of OF *(h)arban* < ML *(h)aribannum* < Gmc; cf. OHG *hari* army, *ban* BAN[2]]

ar·rière-pen·sée (A RYER päN sā′), *n., pl.* **-pen·sées** (-päN-sā′). *French.* a mental reservation; hidden motive. [lit., behind thought]

Ar Ri·mal (är′ ri mäl′). See **Rub' al Khali.**

ar·ris (ar′is), *n. Archit.* **1.** a sharp ridge, as between adjoining channels of a Doric column. **2.** the line, ridge, or hip formed by the meeting of two surfaces at an exterior angle. [< MF *areste*]

ar·ri·val (ə rī′vəl), *n.* **1.** the act or an instance of arriving: *His arrival was delayed by traffic.* **2.** the attainment of any object or condition: *arrival at a conclusion.* **3.** the person or thing that arrives or has arrived: *First arrivals will be the first seated.* [ARRIVE + -AL[2]; r. ME *arivaille* < MF]

ar·rive (ə rīv′), *v.,* **-rived, -riv·ing.** —*v.i.* **1.** to come to a certain point in the course of travel; reach one's destination: *He finally arrived in Rome.* **2.** to come to be present: *The time has arrived.* **3.** to attain a position of success in the world. **4.** to reach or attain any conclusion, final state, or the like: *to arrive at an agreement.* **5.** *Archaic.* to happen: *It arrived that the master had already departed.* **6.** *Obs.* to come to shore. —*v.t.* **7.** *Obs.* to reach; come to. [ME *a(r)rive(n)* < OF *a(r)rive(r)* < VL **arrīpāre* to come to land = L *ad rīp(am)* to the riverbank + *-ā-* thematic vowel + *-re* inf. suffix] —**ar·riv′er,** *n.*

—**Syn. 1.** ARRIVE, COME both mean to reach a stopping place. ARRIVE directs the attention to the final point of an activity or state: *The train arrived at noon.* COME rarely refers to the actual moment of arrival but refers instead to the progress toward it.

ar·ri·ve·der·ci (äR′Rē ve deR′chē), *interj. Italian.* until we see each other again. Also, **a rivederci.**

ar·ri·viste (ar′ē vēst′; *Fr.* A Rē vēst′), *n., pl.* **-vistes** (-vēsts′; *Fr.* -vēst′). a person who has recently acquired status, wealth, or success by questionable or unscrupulous means. [< F; see ARRIVE, -IST]

ar·ro·ba (ə rō′bə; *Sp., Port.* äR Rō′bä), *n., pl.* **-bas** (-bəz; *Sp., Port.* -bäs). **1.** a Spanish and Portuguese unit of weight of varying value, equal to 25.37 pounds avoirdupois in Mexico and to 32.38 pounds avoirdupois in Brazil. **2.** a unit of liquid measure of varying value, used esp. in Spain and commonly equal (when used for wine) to 4.26 U.S. gallons. [< Sp < Ar *al rub'* the fourth part, i.e., a quarter of the *qintār*; see QUINTAL]

ar·ro·gance (ar′ə gəns), *n.* **1.** a feeling of superiority or an offensive exhibition of it. **2.** presumptuous or overbearing conduct, statements, etc., resulting from such a feeling. Also, **ar′ro·gan·cy.** [ME < MF < L *arrogantia* presumption. See ARROGANT, -ANCE] —**Syn. 1.** haughtiness, disdain. —**Ant. 1.** humility.

ar·ro·gant (ar′ə gənt), *adj.* **1.** making unwarrantable claims or pretensions to superior importance or rights. **2.**

characterized by or proceeding from arrogance. [ME < L *arrogant-* (s. of *arrogāns*) presuming, prp. of *arrogāre*. See ARROGATE, -ANT] —**ar′ro·gant·ly,** *adv.* —**Syn. 1.** See **proud.**

ar·ro·gate (ar′ə gāt′), *v.t.*, **-gat·ed, -gat·ing. 1.** to claim or appropriate to oneself presumptuously or without right. **2.** to attribute or assign to another without just reason. [< L *arrogāt(us)* appropriated, assumed, questioned (ptp. of *arrogāre*) = *arrog-* (*ar-* var. of *ad-* AD- + *rog(āre)* (to) ask, propose) + *-ātus* -ATE[1]] —**ar′ro·gat′ing·ly,** *adv.* —**ar′ro·ga′tion,** *n.* —**ar′ro·ga′tor,** *n.*

ar·ron·disse·ment (ə ron′dis mənt, ar′ən dēs′mənt; *Fr.* A RôN dēs mäN′), *n.*, *pl.* **-ments** (-mənts; *Fr.* -mäN′). **1.** the largest administrative division of a French department, comprising a number of cantons. **2.** an administrative district of certain large cities in France. [< F = *arrondiss-* (long s. of *arrondir* to round out; see A-[5], ROUND) + *-ment* -MENT]

ar·row (ar′ō), *n.* **1.** a straight, slender, generally pointed missile equipped with feathers at the end of the shaft, made to be shot from a bow. **2.** anything resembling this in form, function, or character. **3.** a linear figure having a wedge-shaped end, used on signs, maps, drawings, and the like, to indicate direction or placement. **4.** See **broad arrow.** —*v.t.* **5.** to indicate the proper position of (an insertion) by means of an arrow (often fol. by *in*). [ME *arewe*, OE *arwe;* c. Icel *ör* (pl. *örvar*); akin to L *arcus* bow] —**ar′row·less,** *adj.* —**ar′row·like′,** *adj.*

ar·row·head (ar′ō hed′), *n.* **1.** the pointed head or tip of an arrow. **2.** anything resembling an arrowhead. **3.** any plant of the genus *Sagittaria*, usually aquatic, species of which have arrowhead-shaped leaves. [late ME]

ar·row·root (ar′ō rōōt′, -rŏŏt′), *n.* **1.** a tropical American plant, *Maranta arundinacea*, or related species, whose rhizomes yield a nutritious starch. **2.** the starch itself. **3.** a similar starch from other plants, used in light puddings, cookies, etc. [named from use of its root in treatment of wounds made by poisoned arrows]

ar·row·wood (ar′ō wŏŏd′), *n.* any of several shrubs and small trees, as the wahoo and certain viburnums, with tough, straight shoots. [named from use in making arrows]

ar·row·worm (ar′ō wûrm′), *n.* any small, elongated, translucent, marine worm of the phylum or class *Chaetognatha*, having lateral and caudal fins. [named from fancied resemblance to arrow]

ar·roy·o (ə roi′ō), *n.*, *pl.* **-os** (-ōz). (chiefly in southwest U.S.) a small steep-sided watercourse or gulch with a nearly flat floor: usually dry except after heavy rains. [< Sp; akin to L *arrūgia* mine shaft]

Ar′ru Is′lands (ä′rōō). See **Aru Islands.**

ar·ryth·mi·a (ə rith′mē ə, ə rith′-), *n.* *Pathol.* arrhythmia. —**ar·ryth′mic, ar·ryth′mi·cal,** *adj.* —**ar·ryth′mi·cal·ly,** *adv.*

ars-, a combining form of **arsenic:** *arsine.*

Ar·sa·ces I (är′sə sēz′, är sā′sēz), founder of the Parthian empire c250 B.C.

arse (ärs), *n.* *Slang.* ass[2] (defs. 1, 2).

arsen-, var. of **arseno-,** esp. before a vowel: *arsenate.*

ar·se·nal (är′sə nᵊl), *n.* **1.** a place of storage for arms and military equipment. **2.** a building used mainly for the training of troops. **3.** a factory for manufacturing military equipment or munitions. **4.** a collection or supply of weapons or munitions. [< It *arsenale* dockyard, alter. of Ar *dār ṣinā'a* workshop (lit., house of handwork)]

ar·se·nate (är′sə nāt′, -nit), *n.* *Chem.* a salt or ester of arsenic acid.

ar·se·nic (*n.* är′sə nik, ärs′nik; *adj.* är sen′ik), *n.* **1.** a grayish-white element, volatilizing when heated, and forming poisonous compounds. *Symbol:* As; *at. wt.:* 74.92; *at. no.:* 33. **2.** See **arsenic trioxide. 3.** a mineral, the native element, occurring in white or gray masses. —*adj.* **4.** of or containing arsenic, esp. in the pentavalent state. [ME *arsenic(um)* < L < Gk *arsenikón* orpiment, n. use of neut. of *arsenikós* virile (*ársēn* male, strong + *-ikos* -IC), prob. alter. of oriental word (? **arznig*, metathetic var. of Syriac *zarnig*) by folk etym.]

arsen′ic ac′id, *Chem.* a water-soluble powder, $H_3AsO_4\cdot\frac{1}{2}H_2O$, used chiefly in the manufacture of arsenates.

ar·sen·i·cal (är sen′i kəl), *adj.* **1.** containing or relating to arsenic. —*n.* **2.** any of a group of pesticides, or other compounds containing arsenic.

ar′senic trichlo′ride, *Chem.* a poisonous liquid, $AsCl_3$, used chiefly as an intermediate in the manufacture of organic arsenicals. Also called **butter of arsenic.**

ar′senic triox′ide, *Chem.* a poisonous powder, As_2O_3, used in the manufacture of pigments and glass, as an insecticide, weed-killer, etc.; arsenous acid; arsenic.

ar·se·nide (är′sə nīd′, -nid), *n.* *Chem.* a compound containing two elements of which arsenic is the negative one, as silver arsenide, Ag_3As.

ar·se·nite (är′sə nīt′), *n.* *Chem.* a salt or ester of arsenous acid.

arseno-, a combining form of the arseno group, used esp. before a consonant: *arsenopyrite.* Also, *esp. before a vowel,* **arsen-.** [ARSEN(IC) + -O-]

ar′seno group′, *Chem.* the bivalent group, –As=As–. Also called **ar′seno rad′ical.** —**ar·se·no** (är′sə nō′), *adj.*

ar·se·no·py·rite (är′sə nō pī′rīt, är sen′ə-), *n.* a common mineral, iron arsenic sulfide, FeAsS: an ore of arsenic. Also called **mispickel.**

ar·se·nous (är′sə nəs), *adj.* *Chem.* containing arsenic in the trivalent state, as arsenous chloride, $AsCl_3$. Also, **ar·se·ni·ous** (är sē′nē əs).

ar′senous ac′id, *Chem.* See **arsenic trioxide.**

arsin-, var. of **arsino-,** esp. before a vowel.

ar·sine (är sēn′, är′sēn, -sin), *n.* *Chem.* **1.** AsH_3, having a fetid, garliclike odor, used in chemical warfare. **2.** any derivative of this compound in which one or more hydrogen atoms are replaced by organic groups. [ARS(ENIC) + -INE[2]]

arsino-, a combining form of the arsino group. Also, *esp. before a vowel,* **arsin-.**

arsi′no group′, *Chem.* the univalent group, H_2As–. Also called **arsi′no rad′ical.** —**ar·si·no** (är sē′nō), *adj.*

ar·sis (är′sis), *n.*, *pl.* **-ses** (-sēz). **1.** *Music.* the upward stroke in conducting; upbeat. Cf. **thesis** (def. 4). **2.** *Pros.* **a.** the part of a metrical foot that bears the ictus or stress. **b.** (less commonly) a part of a metrical foot that does not bear the ictus. Cf. **thesis** (def. 5). [< L < Gk = *ar-* (s. of *aírein* to raise, lift) + *-sis* -SIS]

ars lon·ga, vi·ta bre·vis (ärs lōng′gä wē′tä bre′wis; *Eng.* ärz lông′gə vī′tə brē′vis, ärs), *Latin.* art is long, life is short.

ar·son (är′sən), *n.* *Law.* the malicious burning of another's house or property, or in some statutes, the burning of one's own house, as for revenge, to collect insurance, etc. [< AF OF < LL *ārsiōn-* (s. *ārsiō*) a burning = *ārs-* (L *ārd(ere)* to burn + *-t(us)* ptp. suffix) + *-iōn-* -ION] —**ar′son·ist,** *n.*

ars·phen·a·mine (ärs fen′ə mēn′, -min), *n.* *Pharm.* a yellow powder, $C_{12}H_{12}N_2O_2As_2\cdot 2HCl\cdot 2H_2O$, subject to rapid oxidation, formerly used to treat syphilis and trench mouth: first known as "606." [ARS(ENIC) + PHEN(YL) + AMINE]

ars po·e·ti·ca (ärz′ pō et′i kə, ärs′), the art of poetry.

art[1] (ärt), *n.* **1.** the quality, production, expression, or realm of what is beautiful, or of more than ordinary significance. **2.** the class of objects subject to aesthetic criteria; works or objects belonging to this realm, as paintings, drawings, etc.: *a museum of art.* **3.** a field, genre, or category of this realm: *Dance is an art.* **4.** the fine arts collectively, often excluding architecture: *art and commerce.* **5.** any field using the skills or techniques of art: *advertising art.* **6.** illustrative or decorative material. **7.** the principles or methods governing any craft, skill, or branch of learning: *the art of baking; the art of sailing.* **8.** the craft or trade using these principles or methods. **9.** skill in conducting any human activity: *a master at the art of conversation.* **10.** a branch of learning or university study, esp. one of the fine arts or the humanities. **11. arts, a.** (*construed as sing.*) the humanities: *a college of arts and sciences.* **b.** (*construed as pl.*) See **liberal arts. 12.** skilled workmanship, execution, or agency, as distinguished from nature. **13.** studied action; artificiality in behavior. **14.** an artifice or artful device: *the innumerable arts and wiles of politics.* **15.** *Archaic.* science; learning. [ME < OF, oblique form of *ars* < L *ars* (nom.), *artem* (acc.)]

art[2] (ärt), *v.* *Archaic or Literary.* 2nd pers. sing. pres. indic. of **be.** [ME; OE *eart* = *ear-* (see ARE[1]) + *-t* ending of 2nd pers. sing.]

-art, var. of **-ard:** *braggart.*

art., *pl.* **arts.,** for 1. **1.** article. **2.** artillery. **3.** artist.

ar·tal (är′täl), *n.* pl. of **rotl.**

Ar·ta·xerx·es I (är′tə zûrk′sēz), ("*Longimanus*"), died 424 B.C., king of Persia 464–24.

Artaxerxes II, ("*Mnemon*") died 359? B.C., king of Persia 404?–359?.

Art Deco (är′dā′kō′), (*sometimes l.c.*) *Fine Arts.* a style of fine and applied art that developed in the 1920's and continued into the 1930's (and has been revived since 1966), characterized chiefly by vivid colors and geometric motifs, often using the new synthetic materials and the techniques of mass production. [shortened form of F *Art Décoratif*, lit., decorative art]

art′ direc′tor, 1. *Motion Pictures, Television.* a person responsible for designing all visual aspects of a production, including settings, costumes, lighting, etc. **2.** Also called **art′ ed′itor.** a person responsible for the graphic art for a publication, advertising agency, or the like.

Ar·te·mis (är′tə mis), *n.* an ancient Greek goddess, the daughter of Leto and the sister of Apollo, characterized as a virgin huntress and associated with the moon: identified by the Romans with Diana. Also called **Cynthia.**

ar·te·mis·i·a (är′tə miz′ē ə, -mish′-), *n.* **1.** any of several composite plants of the genus *Artemisia*, abundant in dry regions, esp. of the Northern Hemisphere. **2.** a North American species, *A. tridentata*, the sagebrush of the western plains. [ME < L < Gk]

Ar·te·movsk (äR te′mofsk), *n.* a city in the E Ukraine, in the SW Soviet Union in Europe. 61,000 (1959). Formerly, **Bakhmut.**

ar·te·ri·al (är tēr′ē əl), *adj.* **1.** *Physiol.* pertaining to the blood in the pulmonary vein, the left side of the heart, and in most arteries, which has been oxygenated during its passage through the lungs and which in man is normally bright red. **2.** *Anat.* of, pertaining to, or resembling the arteries. **3.** of or pertaining to a major highway or channel or connecting major highways or channels. [late ME < ML *arteriālis*] —**ar·te′ri·al·ly,** *adv.*

ar·te·ri·al·ise (är tēr′ē ə līz′), *v.t.*, **-ised, -is·ing.** *Chiefly Brit.* arterialize. —**ar·te′ri·al·i·sa′tion,** *n.*

ar·te·ri·al·ize (är tēr′ē ə līz′), *v.t.*, **-ized, -iz·ing.** *Physiol.* to convert (venous blood) into arterial blood by the action of oxygen in the lungs. —**ar·te′ri·al·i·za′tion,** *n.*

arterio-, a learned borrowing from Greek meaning "artery," used in the formation of compound words: *arteriosclerosis.* [< Gk *artērio-*, comb. form of *artēría*]

ar·te·ri·o·scle·ro·sis (är tēr′ē ō sklə rō′sis), *n.* *Pathol.* an arterial disease occurring esp. in the elderly, characterized by inelasticity and thickening of the vessel walls, with lessened blood flow. [< NL] —**ar·te·ri·o·scle·rot·ic** (är tēr′ē ō sklə rot′ik), *adj.*

ar·te·ri·tis (är′tə rī′tis), *n.* *Pathol.* inflammation of an artery.

ar·ter·y (är′tə rē), *n.*, *pl.* **-ter·ies. 1.** *Anat.* a blood vessel that conveys blood from the heart to any part of the body. **2.** a main highway or channel. [ME < L *artēria* < Gk: windpipe, artery. See AORTA]

ar·te′sian well′ (är tē′zhən), a deep-bored well in which water rises under pressure from a permeable stratum overlaid by impermeable rock. [< F *artésien* pertaining to *Artois*, former province in N France where many wells of this kind are found]

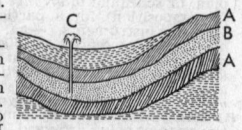

Artesian well (cross section) A, Impermeable strata; B, Permeable strata; C, Artesian boring and well

art·ful (ärt′fəl), *adj.* **1.** crafty; cunning; tricky: *artful schemes.* **2.** skillful in adapting means to ends; ingenious: *an artful choice of metaphors.* **3.** done with or characterized by art or skill. **4.** *Archaic.* artificial. —**art′ful·ly,** *adv.* —**art′ful·ness,** *n.*

art′ glass′, 1. (in the late 19th and early 20th centuries) any of the several varieties of glass using combinations of colors, special effects of opaqueness and transparency, etc., to create an aesthetic effect. **2.** objects made of such glass.

ar·thral·gia (är thral′jə), *n. Pathol.* pain in a joint. **—ar·thral′gic,** *adj.*

ar·thri·tis (är thrī′tis), *n. Pathol.* inflammation of a joint, as in gout or rheumatism. [< L < Gk: gout] **—ar·thrit·ic** (är thrit′ik), **ar·thrit′i·cal,** *adj.*

arthro-, a learned borrowing from Greek meaning "joint," "jointed," used in the formation of compound words: *arthropod.* Also, *esp. before a vowel,* **arthr-.** [< L < Gk *árthro(n)* a joint]

ar·thro·mere (är′thrə mēr′), *n. Zool.* one of the segments or parts into which the body of articulate animals is divided. **—ar·thro·mer·ic** (är′thrə mer′ik), *adj.*

ar·thro·pod (är′thrə pod′), *n.* **1.** any segmented invertebrate of the phylum *Arthropoda,* having jointed legs and including the insects, arachnids, crustaceans, and myriapods. **—*adj.* 2.** Also, **ar·throp·o·dal** (är throp′ə d^{ə}l), **ar·throp·o·dan** (är throp′ə d^{ə}n), **ar·throp·o·dous** (är throp′ə dəs). belonging or pertaining to the *Arthropoda.* [back formation < NL *Arthropoda.* See ARTHRO-, -PODA]

ar·thro·spore (är′thrə spōr′, -spôr′), *n.* **1.** *Bacteriol.* an isolated vegetative cell that has passed into a resting state, occurring in bacteria and not regarded as a true spore. **2.** *Bot.* one of a number of spores of various low fungi and algae, united in the form of a string of beads, formed by fission. **—ar′thro·spor′ic, ar′thro·spor′ous,** *adj.*

Ar·thur (är′thər), *n.* **1. Chester A(lan),** 1830–86, 21st president of the U.S. 1881–85. **2.** a legendary king in ancient Britain: leader of the Knights of the Round Table.

Ar·thu·ri·an (är tho͝or′ē ən), *adj.* of or pertaining to King Arthur, who, with his knights, was the subject of a large part of medieval romance.

Artichoke, *Cynara Scolymus*

ar·ti·choke (är′ti chōk′), *n.* **1.** a herbaceous, thistlelike plant, *Cynara Scolymus,* having an edible flower head. **2.** See **Jerusalem artichoke.** [< It (north) *articiocco,* var. (by dissimilation) of *arciciocco, arcicioffo* < **arcarcioffo* < OSp *alcarchofa* < Ar *al kharshuf* the artichoke]

ar·ti·cle (är′ti kəl), *n., v.,* **-cled, -cling.** **—*n.* 1.** a factual piece of writing on a specific topic. **2.** an individual object, member, or portion of a class; an item or particular: *an article of clothing.* **3.** an indefinite or unnamed object. **4.** *Gram.* a member of a small class of words found in certain languages, as English, French, and Arabic, which are linked to nouns and which typically have a grammatical function identifying the noun as a noun rather than describing it. In English the definite article is *the,* the indefinite article is *a,* or *an,* and their force is generally to impart specificity to the noun or to single out the referent from the class named by the noun. **5.** a clause, item, point, or particular in a contract, treaty, or other formal agreement; a condition or stipulation in a contract or bargain. **6.** *Archaic.* a subject or matter of interest. **7.** *Obs.* a specific or critical point of time: *the article of death.* **—*v.t.* 8.** to charge or accuse, as of specific offenses. **9.** to bind by articles of covenant or stipulation: *to article an apprentice.* **10.** to bind by articles of agreement. [ME < eccl. L *articulus* article of faith, L: limb, member, part; lit., little joint = *arti-* (comb. form of *artus* joint) + *-culus* -CULE]

Ar′ticles of Confedera′tion, the constitution of the 13 American colonies, adopted in 1781 and replaced in 1789 by the Constitution of the United States.

Ar′ticles of War′, the body of laws and legal procedures of the U.S. Army and Air Force, replaced in 1951 by the Uniform Code of Military Justice.

ar·tic·u·lar (är tik′yə lər), *adj.* of or pertaining to the joints. [late ME < L *articulār(is).* See ARTICLE, -AR[1]]

ar·tic·u·late (*adj., n.* är tik′yə lit; *v.* är tik′yə lāt′), *adj., v.,* **-lat·ed, -lat·ing,** *n.* **—*adj.* 1.** uttered clearly in distinct syllables. **2.** capable of speech. **3.** using language easily and fluently; having facility with words: *an articulate person.* **4.** expressed, formulated, or presented with clarity and effectiveness: *an articulate speech.* **5.** clear, distinct, and precise in relation to other parts: *an articulate form.* **6.** organized into a coherent or meaningful whole: *an articulate system of philosophy.* **7.** *Zool.* having joints or articulations; composed of segments. **—*v.t.* 8.** to pronounce clearly and distinctly. **9.** *Phonet.* to make the movements and adjustments of the speech organs necessary to utter (a speech sound). **10.** to give clarity or distinction to: *to articulate an idea.* **11.** to bring the various parts of (a work of art, a field of perception, a system of thought, etc.) into a meaningful or coherent relationship. **12.** to unite by a joint or joints. **—*v.i.* 13.** to pronounce clearly each of a succession of speech sounds, syllables, or words. **14.** *Phonet.* to articulate a speech sound. **15.** *Anat., Zool.* to form a joint. **—*n.* 16.** a segmented invertebrate [< L *articulātus* distinct; lit., jointed (ptp. of *articulāre*). See ARTICLE, -ATE[1]] **—ar·tic′u·la·bil′i·ty,** *n.* **—ar·tic·u·la·ble** (är tik′yə lə bəl), *adj.* **—ar·tic′u·late·ly,** *adv.* **—ar·tic′u·late·ness, ar·tic·u·la·cy** (är tik′yə lə sē), *n.* **—ar·tic·u·la·tive** (är tik′yə lā′tiv, -lə tiv), *adj.*

ar·tic·u·la·tion (är tik′yə lā′shən), *n.* **1.** act or process of articulating. **2.** the state of being articulated. **3.** *Phonet.* **a.** act or process of articulating speech. **b.** the adjustments and movements of speech organs involved in pronouncing a particular sound, taken as a whole. **c.** any one of these adjustments and movements. **d.** any speech sound, esp. a consonant. **4.** act of jointing. **5.** a jointed state or formation; a joint. **6.** *Bot.* **a.** a joint or place between two parts where separation may take place spontaneously, as at the point of attachment of a leaf. **b.** a node in a stem, or the space between two nodes. **7.** *Anat., Zool.* a joint, as the joining or juncture of bones or of the movable segments of an arthropod. [< anatomical L *articulātiōn-,* s. of *articulātiō*] **—ar·tic·u·la·to·ry** (är tik′yə lə tōr′ē, tôr′ē), *adj.* **—ar·tic′u·la·to′ri·ly,** *adv.*

ar·tic·u·la·tor (är tik′yə lā′tər), *n.* **1.** a person or thing that articulates. **2.** *Phonet.* a movable organ of speech, as the tongue, lips, or uvula.

artic′ulatory phonet′ics, the branch of phonetics dealing with the motive processes and anatomy involved in the production of the sounds of speech. Cf. **acoustic phonetics, physiological phonetics.**

ar·ti·fact (är′tə fakt′), *n.* **1.** any object made or modifed by man. **2.** *Biol.* a substance, structure, or the like, not naturally present in tissue but formed by artificial means, as chemicals. [var. of *artefact* < L phrase *arte factum* something made with skill. See ART[1], FACT] **—ar·ti·fac·ti·tious** (är′tə fak tish′əs), *adj.*

ar·ti·fice (är′tə fis), *n.* **1.** a clever trick or stratagem. **2.** cunning; ingenuity; guile; craftiness. **3.** *Archaic.* a skillful or artful contrivance. [back formation from ARTIFICER] **—Syn. 1.** subterfuge. See **trick. 2.** See **cunning.**

ar·tif·i·cer (är tif′i sər), *n.* **1.** a person who is skillful or clever in devising ways of making things; inventor. **2.** a skillful or artistic worker; craftsman. [ME < L *artific-* (s. of *artificium* a work of art; see ART[1], -FIC) + -ER[1]]

ar·ti·fi·cial (är′tə fish′əl), *adj.* **1.** produced by man. **2.** made in imitation or as a substitute; simulated: *artificial flowers.* **3.** lacking naturalness or spontaneity; contrived, affected, or feigned: *an artificial smile.* **4.** stilted. **5.** *Biol.* based on arbitrary, superficial characteristics rather than natural, organic relationships. [ME < L *artificiāl(is)* = *artifici(um)* skilled workmanship + *-ālis* -AL[1]] **—ar·ti·fi·ci·al·i·ty** (är′tə fish′ē al′i tē), *n.* **—ar′ti·fi′cial·ly,** *adv.* **—ar′ti·fi′cial·ness,** *n.* **—Syn. 1.** synthetic. **2, 3.** counterfeit. **Ant. 2.** genuine, real.

artifi′cial hori′zon, 1. a level reflector, as a surface of mercury, used in determining the altitudes of stars. **2.** the bubble in a sextant or octant for aerial use. **3.** Also called **gyro horizon.** *Aeron.* an instrument making use of a gyroscope, which indicates the banking and pitch of an aircraft.

artifi′cial insemina′tion, the injection of semen into the vagina or uterus by means other than coitus in order to induce pregnancy.

artifi′cial intel′ligence, the capacity of a computer to perform operations analogous to learning and decision making in humans.

ar′tifi′cial lan′guage, 1. an invented language, as opposed to a hereditary one. **2.** See **machine language. 3.** code (def. 2).

artifi′cial respira′tion, the stimulation of natural respiratory functions in persons whose breathing has failed or in newborn infants by artificially forcing air into and out of the lungs.

ar·til·ler·y (är til′ə rē), *n.* **1.** mounted projectile-firing guns or missile launchers. **2.** the troops or the branch of an army concerned with such weapons. **3.** the science that treats of the use of such weapons. [ME *artellery, artyllery* = *arteller, artiller* bowyer < MF *art(e)iller* weapon maker (*arteil* ARTICLE + *-(i)er* -ER[2]) + *-y* -Y[3]]

ar·til·ler·y·man (är til′ə rē mən), *n., pl.* **-men.** a soldier in an army artillery unit. Also, **ar·til·ler·ist** (är til′ər ist).

artio-, a learned borrowing from Greek meaning "even number," used in the formation of compound words: *artiodactyl.* [< Gk *ártio(s)* even (in number), perfect; akin to L *ars* art, Skt *arthya* suitable, rich]

ar·ti·o·dac·tyl (är′tē ō dak′til), *adj.* **1.** *Zool.* having an even number of toes or digits on each foot. **—*n.* 2.** a hoofed, even-toed mammal of the order *Artiodactyla,* comprising the pigs, hippopotamuses, camels, deer, giraffes, pronghorns, sheep, goats, antelope, and cattle. Cf. **perissodactyl.** [< NL] **—ar′ti·o·dac′ty·lous,** *adj.*

ar·ti·san (är′ti zən), *n.* **1.** a person skilled in an applied art; craftsman. **2.** *Obs.* an artist. [< F < It *artigian(o)* = L *artīt(us)* trained in arts and crafts (ptp. of *artīre;* see ART[1], -ITE[2]) + It *-iano* (< L *-iānus*) -IAN] **—ar′ti·san·ship′,** *n.* **—Syn. 1.** See **artist.**

art·ist (är′tist), *n.* **1.** a person who practices one of the fine arts, esp. a painter or sculptor. **2.** a person who works in one of the performing arts, as an actor or musician. **3.** a person whose trade or profession requires a knowledge of design, drawing, painting, etc.: *a commercial artist.* **4.** a person who exhibits exceptional skill, manual dexterity, cleverness, or the like. **5.** *Obs.* an artisan. [< ML *artist(a)* master of arts]
—Syn. 1. ARTIST, ARTISAN are persons having superior skill or ability or capable of a superior kind of workmanship. An ARTIST is a person engaged in some type of fine art. An ARTISAN is one engaged in a craft or applied art.

ar·tiste (är tēst′; *Fr.* AR tēst′), *n., pl.* **-tistes** (-tēsts′; *Fr.* -tēst′). an artist, esp. an actor, singer, dancer, or other public performer. [< F; see ARTIST]

ar·tis·tic (är tis′tik), *adj.* **1.** conforming to the standards of art; satisfying aesthetic requirements. **2.** showing skill or excellence in execution. **3.** exhibiting taste, discriminating judgment, or sensitivity. **4.** of or pertaining to the appreciation of art: *artistic interests.* **5.** of or pertaining to an artist. Also, **ar·tis′ti·cal.** **—ar·tis′ti·cal·ly,** *adv.*

art·ist·ry (är′ti strē), *n.* **1.** artistic workmanship, effect, or quality. **2.** artistic pursuits.

art·less (ärt′lis), *adj.* **1.** free from deceit, cunning, or craftiness. **2.** not artificial; natural: *artless beauty.* **3.** lacking art, knowledge, or skill. **4.** poorly made; clumsy. **—art′less·ly,** *adv.* **—art′less·ness,** *n.* **—Syn. 1, 2.** candid, sincere, open. **—Ant. 1.** cunning.

Art Nou·veau (är′ no͞o vō′, ärt′; *Fr.* AR no͞o vō′), (*sometimes l.c.*) *Fine Arts.* a style of fine and applied art current in the late 19th and early 20th centuries, characterized chiefly by curvilinear motifs derived from natural forms. [< F: lit., new art]

arts′ and crafts′, decoration and craftsmanship conceived as a single entity and applied esp. to making or decorating utilitarian objects by hand.

art′ the′ater, a motion-picture theater specializing in foreign and experimental films.

art·work (ärt′wûrk′), *n.* illustrative, artistic, or decorative work, as illustrations for a publication.

art·y (är′tē), *adj.,* **art·i·er, art·i·est.** *Informal.* characterized by an ostentatious display of artistic interest, manner, or mannerism. **—art′i·ness,** *n.*

Arty., Artillery.

Ar·tzy·ba·shev (äʀ′tsi bä′shef), *n.* **Mi·kha·il** (mi кнä-ēl′), 1878–1927, Russian writer. Also, **Ar′tsy·ba′shev.**

A·ru·ba (ä ro͞o′bä, ə ro͞o′bə), *n.* an island in the Netherlands Antilles, in the SE West Indies, off the NW coast of Venezuela. 53,199 (1960); 69 sq. mi.

A′ru Is′lands (är′o͞o), an island group in Indonesia, SW of New Guinea. 3306 sq. mi. Also, **Arru Islands.**
ar·um (âr′əm), *n.* **1.** any plant of the genus *Arum*, having an inflorescence consisting of a spadix enclosed in a large spathe, as the cuckoopint. **2.** any of various allied plants in cultivation, as the calla lily. [< L < Gk *âron* wake-robin]
Ar·un·del (ar′ən dəl; *local* ärn′dəl), *n.* a town in S West Sussex, in S England: castle. 2614 (1961).
a·run·di·na·ceous (ə run′də nā′shəs), *adj. Bot.* pertaining to or like a reed or cane; reedlike; reedy. [< NL = L (*h*)*arundin-* (s. of *harundō* reed) + *-āceus* -ACEOUS]
A·run·ta (ə run′tə), *n., pl.* **-tas,** (*esp. collectively*) **-ta.** a member of an aboriginal desert people of north-central Australia. Also, **Aranda.**
A·ru·wi·mi (ä′ro͞o wē′mē), *n.* a river in the N Republic of the Congo, flowing SW and W into the Congo River. ab. 800 mi. long.
A.R.V., See **American Revised Version.**
Ar·vad·a (är vad′ə), *n.* a city in central Colorado, near Denver. 46,814 (1970).
ar·vo (är′vō), *n. Australian Slang.* afternoon. [?]
-ary, a noun and adjective suffix meaning "pertaining to," "connected with," sometimes referring to a person connected with or engaged in (something), and sometimes indicating a location or repository: *honorary; voluntary; functionary; dictionary; granary.* [< L *-ārius, -āria, -ārium;* in some words < L *-āris;* see -AR[1]]
Ar·y·an (âr′ē ən, âr′yən, ar′-), *n.* **1.** *Ethnol.* a member or descendant of the prehistoric people who spoke Indo-European. **2.** (in Nazi doctrine) a non-Jewish Caucasian. **3.** Nordic. **—***adj.* **4.** of or pertaining to an Aryan or the Aryans. Also, **Arian.** [< Skt *ārya* of high rank (adj.), aristocrat (n.) + -AN]
ar′yl group′ (ar′il), *Chem.* any organic group derived from an aromatic hydrocarbon by the removal of a hydrogen atom, as phenyl, C_6H_5–, from benzene, C_6H_6. Also called **ar′yl rad′i·cal.** [AR(OMATIC) + -YL] **—ar·yl** (ar′il), *adj.*
ar·y·te·noid (ar′i tē′noid, ə rit′ənoid′), *Anat.* **—***adj.* **1.** of or pertaining to either of two small cartilages on top of the cricoid cartilage at the upper back part of the larynx. **—***n.* **2.** an arytenoid cartilage. [< NL *arytaenoīd(es)* < Gk *arytainoeid(ēs)*, lit., ladle-shaped = *arýtain(a)* ladle, pitcher, funnel + *-oeidēs* -OID] **—ar·y·te·noi·dal** (ar′i tənoid′əl, ə rit′ənoid′-), *adj.*
a·ryth·mi·a (ə rith′mē ə, ə rith′-), *n. Pathol.* arrhythmia. —**a·ryth′mic, a·ryth′mi·cal,** *adj.*
as[1] (az; *unstressed* əz), *adv.* **1.** to such a degree or extent; similarly; equally: *I think the temperature is as high today as it was yesterday.* **2.** for example: *Some flowers, as the rose, require special care.* **3.** thought to be or considered to be: *the square as distinct from the rectangle.* **4.** in the manner directed, agreed, promised, etc.: *She sang as promised. He left as agreed.* **5. as well.** See **well**[1] (def. 11). **6. as well as.** See **well**[1] (def. 12). **—***conj.* **7.** (used correlatively after an adjective or adverb prec. by an adverbial phrase, the adverbial *as*, or another adverb) to such a degree or extent that: *You are as good as you think you are.* **8.** (without antecedent) in the degree, manner, etc., of or that: *Do as we do.* **9.** at the same time that; while; when: *Pay as you enter.* **10.** since; because: *As you are leaving last, lock up.* **11.** though: *Strange as it seems, it is so.* **12.** *Informal.* (in independent clauses) that: *I don't know as I do.* **13.** *Brit. Dial.* than. **14. as . . . as,** similarly or equally to: *as rich as Croesus.* **15. as for,** with respect to; in reference to: *As for staying away, I wouldn't think of it.* **16. as good as, a.** equivalent to: *as good as new.* **b.** true to; trustworthy as: *as good as his word.* **17. as if,** as it would be if: *It was as if the world had come to an end.* **18. as is,** *Informal.* in whatever condition something happens to be: *We bought the table as is.* **19. as it were,** in a way; so to speak: *He became, as it were, a man without a country.* **20. as long as,** provided that; since: *As long as you feel that way, we'll forget it.* **21. as regards,** with regard or reference to. **22. as such, a.** as being what is indicated; in that capacity: *The officer of the law, as such, is entitled to respect.* **b.** in itself or in themselves: *The job, as such, does not appeal to him.* **23. as yet,** up to the present time. **—***pron.* **24.** (used relatively) that; who; which (usually prec. by *such* or *the same*): *I have the same trouble as you had.* **25.** a fact that: *She did her job well, as can be proved by the records.* **—***prep.* **26.** in the role, function, or status of: *to act as chairman.* [ME *as, als, alse, also* < OE *alswā, ealswā* ALL so (see ALSO), quite so, quite as, as] **—Syn. 10.** See **because.**
—Usage. As is usually considered less desirable than SINCE or BECAUSE because it seems weaker and less explicit: *Because* (not *As*) *the train was late, we missed the show.* Although educated usage now accepts AS . . . AS in both positive and negative comparisons, some people still restrict AS . . . AS to positive comparisons and SO . . . AS to negative comparisons: *He is as fat as I am. She is not so smart as her sister.* AS TO is generally less acceptable than ABOUT, OF, ON, or UPON: *They argued about* (not *as to*) *the price.* When followed by *whether*, it is redundant to use AS TO: *I will notify him whether* (not *as to whether*) *to leave.* There is no objection to AS TO at the beginning of a sentence when it introduces an element that would otherwise have less emphasis: *As to his performance, there is no room for improvement.* See also **like.**
as[2] (as), *n., pl.* **as·ses** (as′iz). **1.** a copper coin and early monetary unit of ancient Rome, originally having a nominal weight of a pound of 12 ounces. **2.** a unit of weight: 12 ounces: the pound, equal to 327.4 grams or 5153 grains. [< L: a unit, unity, a copper coin]
AS, Anglo-Saxon. Also, **AS., A.-S., A.S.**
As, *Chem.* arsenic (def. 1).
as-, var. of **ad-** before *s: assert.*
ASA, American Standards Association.
as·a·fet·i·da (as′ə fet′i də), *n. Chem.* a gum resin having a bitter, acrid taste and an obnoxious odor, obtained from the roots of several umbelliferous plants of the genus *Ferula.* Also, **a′sa·foet′i·da, assafetida, assafoetida.** [< ML *asafoetida* = *asa* (< Pers *azā* mastic, gum) + L *foetida*, fem. of *foetidus* FETID]
A·sa·hi·ka·wa (ä′sä hē′kä wä), *n.* a city on central Hokkaido, in N Japan. 246,867 (1964). Also, **A·sa·hi·ga·wa** (ä′sä hē′gä wä).
asb., asbestos.
As·ben (äs ben′), *n.* Aïr.
as·bes·tos (as bes′təs, az-), *n.* **1.** *Mineral.* **a.** a fibrous amphibole, used for making fireproof articles. **b.** the mineral chrysotile, similarly used. **2.** a fabric woven from asbestos fibers, used for theater curtains, firemen's gloves, etc. Also, **as·bes′tus.** [< L < Gk: lit., unquenched = *a-* A-[6] + *sbestōs* (*sbes-* var. s. of *sbennýnai* to quench + *-tos* ptp. suffix); r. ME *asbeston*, etc. < MF] **—as·bes·tine** (as bes′tin, az-), **as·bes′tous,** *adj.* **—as·bes′toid, as′bes·toi′dal,** *adj.*
as·bes·to·sis (as′be stō′sis, az′-), *n. Pathol.* a lung condition caused by the inhalation of asbestos dust. [< NL]
As·bur·y (az′bə rē), *n.* **Francis,** 1745–1816, English missionary: first bishop of the Methodist Church in America.
As′bur·y Park′ (az′ber′ē, -bə rē), a city in E New Jersey: seashore resort. 16,533 (1970).
As·ca·ni·us (a skā′nē əs), *n. Class. Myth.* the son of Aeneas and Creusa, and founder of Alba Longa. Also called **Iulus.** **—As·ca′ni·an,** *adj.*
ASCAP (as′kap), *n.* American Society of Composers, Authors, and Publishers.
as·ca·ri·a·sis (as′kə rī′ə sis), *n. Pathol.* infestation with ascarids, esp. *Ascaris lumbricoides.* [< NL; see ASCAR(ID), -IASIS]
as·ca·rid (as′kə rid), *n.* any nematode of the family *Ascaridae*, including the roundworms and pinworms. [< NL *ascarid(ae)* < Gk *askarid(es)* threadworms, pinworms (pl. of *askarís*)]
as·cend (ə send′), *v.i.* **1.** to move, climb, or go upward. **2.** to slant upward. **3.** to rise to a higher point, degree, rank, or the like. **4.** to go toward the source or beginning; go back in time. **5.** *Music.* to rise in pitch. **—***v.t.* **6.** to go or move upward upon or along; climb. **7.** to succeed to; acquire: *to ascend the throne.* [ME *ascende(n)* < L *ascende(re)* (to) climb up = *a-* A-[5] + *-scendere*, var. of *scandere* to climb. See SCAN] **—as·cend′a·ble, as·cend′i·ble,** *adj.* **—Syn. 1.** soar. **6.** See **climb.** **—Ant. 1, 6.** descend.
as·cend·an·cy (ə sen′dən sē), *n.* state of being in a position of dominance. Also, **as·cend′en·cy, as·cend′ance, as·cend′ence.** [ASCEND(ANT) + -ANCY] **—Syn.** mastery.
as·cend·ant (ə sen′dənt), *n.* **1.** a position of dominance, controlling influence, superiority, or preeminence. **2.** an ancestor; forebear. **3.** *Astrol.* the point of the ecliptic or the sign of the zodiac rising above the horizon at the time of a birth, etc. **4. in the ascendant,** increasing in prosperity, influence, authority, or renown. **—***adj.* **5.** ascending; rising. **6.** superior; predominant. **7.** *Bot.* directed or curved upward. Also, **as·cend′ent.** [ME *ascendent* < L *ascendent-* (s. of *ascendēns*) climbing up. See ASCEND, -ENT, -ANT]
as·cend·er (ə sen′dər), *n.* **1.** a person or thing that ascends or causes ascension. **2.** *Print.* **a.** the part of a lower-case letter, as *b, d, f, h,* that rises above the body. **b.** a letter having such a part.
as·cen·sion (ə sen′shən), *n.* **1.** the act of ascending; ascent. **2. the Ascension,** the bodily ascending of Christ from earth to heaven. **3.** (*cap.*) See **Ascension Day.** [ME *ascencion* < L *ascēnsiōn-* (s. of *ascēnsiō*) = *ascēns(us)* risen up (ptp. of *ascendere*) + *-iōn-* -ION] **—as·cen′sion·al,** *adj.*
As·cen·sion (ə sen′shən), *n.* a British island in the S Atlantic Ocean: part of St. Helena. 478 (1963); 34 sq. mi.
Ascen′sion Day′, the 40th day after Easter, commemorating the Ascension of Christ; Holy Thursday.
as·cen·sive (ə sen′siv), *adj.* ascending; rising. [ASCENS(ION) + -IVE]
as·cent (ə sent′), *n.* **1.** the act or movement of a person or thing that ascends. **2.** movement upward from a lower to a higher state, degree, grade, or status; advancement. **3.** a way or means of ascending, as a stair or slope. **4.** a procedure toward a source. **5.** a degree of inclination. [< ASCEND, on the model of DESCENT]
as·cer·tain (as′ər tān′), *v.t.* **1.** to find out definitely; learn with certainty or assurance; determine. **2.** *Archaic.* to make certain, clear, or definitely known. [late ME, var. of *assertain, acertain* < MF *acertain* (tonic s. of *acertener* to make certain). See A-[5], CERTAIN] **—as′cer·tain′a·ble,** *adj.* **—as′cer·tain′a·ble·ness,** *n.* **—as′cer·tain′a·bly,** *adv.* **—as′cer·tain′ment,** *n.* **—Syn. 1.** See **learn.**
as·cet·ic (ə set′ik), *n.* **1.** a person who practices extreme self-denial or self-mortification for religious reasons. **2.** any person who abstains from the normal pleasures of life or denies himself material satisfaction. **3.** (in the early Christian church) a monk; hermit. **—***adj.* **4.** pertaining to asceticism. **5.** rigorously abstinent; austere. **6.** exceedingly strict or severe in religious exercises or self-mortification. [< Gk *askētik(ós)* rigorous, hardworking = *askē-* (var. s. of *askéein* to work hard, discipline oneself) + *-tikos* -TIC] **—Syn. 3.** anchorite, recluse; cenobite. **5.** strict. **—Ant. 5.** self-indulgent.
as·cet·i·cal (ə set′i kəl), *adj.* pertaining to or suggesting ascetic discipline or practice. **—as·cet′i·cal·ly,** *adv.*
as·cet·i·cism (ə set′i siz′əm), *n.* **1.** the manner of life, practices, or principles of an ascetic. **2.** austerity of taste, living, etc., that suggests the practices of an ascetic.
Asch (ash), *n.* **Sho·lom** (shô′ləm) or **Sho·lem** (shô′ləm, -lem), 1880–1957, U.S. author, born in Poland.
As·cham (as′kəm), *n.* **Roger,** 1515–68, English scholar and writer: tutor of Queen Elizabeth.
Asch′heim-Zon′dek test′ (äsh′hīm tson′dek, -zon′-), a test for determining the pregnancy of a woman. [named after S. *Aschheim* (b. 1878), German gynecologist, and B. *Zondek* (b. 1891), Israeli gynecologist born in Germany]
as·ci (as′ī), *n.* pl. of **ascus.**
as·cid·i·an (ə sid′ē ən), *Zool.* **—***n.* **1.** any solitary or colonial tunicate of the class *Ascidiacea*, exhibiting the vertebrate characteristics of nerve cord and notochord in the larvae only. **—***adj.* **2.** belonging or pertaining to the class *Ascidiacea.* [ASCIDI(UM) + -AN]
as·cid·i·um (ə sid′ē əm), *n., pl.* **-cid·i·a** (-sid′ē ə). *Bot.* a baglike or pitcherlike part. [< NL < Gk *askídion* a small bag = *ask(ós)* bag + *-idion* -IDIUM]
as·ci·tes (ə sī′tēz), *n. Pathol.* an accumulation of serous fluid in the peritoneal cavity; dropsy of the peritoneum. [< L < Gk *askítēs (hydrōps)* abdominal (dropsy) = *ask(ós)* belly + *-ītēs* -ITE[1]] **—as·cit·ic** (ə sit′ik), **as·cit′i·cal,** *adj.*
as·cle·pi·a·da·ceous (ə sklē′pē ə dā′shəs), *adj.* belonging to the *Asclepiadaceae*, or milkweed family of plants. [< NL *Asclēpiad-* (s. of *Asclēpias* genus name, L: swallow-

wort < Gk *asklēpiás*, a plant named after *Asklēpiós* ASCLEPIUS) + -ACEOUS]

As·cle·pi·a·de·an (ə sklē′pē ə dē′ən), *Class. Pros.* —*adj.* **1.** noting or pertaining to a verse consisting of a spondee, two or three choriambi, and an iamb. —*n.* **2.** an Asclepiadean verse. [< Gk *Asklēpiádei(os)* pertaining to *Asclepiades*, third-century Greek poet to whom the verse was attributed + -AN]

As·cle·pi·us (ə sklē′pē əs), *n.* a son of Apollo and the ancient Greek god of medicine and healing, identified by the Romans with Aesculapius.

asco-, a learned borrowing from Greek meaning "sac," used in the formation of compound words: *ascomycete.* [< Gk *asko-*, comb. form of *askós* wineskin, bladder, belly]

as·co·carp (as′kə kärp′), *n. Bot.* (in ascomycetous fungi) the fructification bearing the asci, as an apothecium, perithecium, etc. —**as′co·carp′ous,** *adj.*

as·co·go·ni·um (as′kə gō′nē əm), *n., pl.* **-ni·a** (-nē ə). *Bot.* **1.** the female reproductive organ in certain ascomycetous fungi. **2.** the portion of the archicarp in certain ascomycetous fungi that receives the antheridial nuclei and puts out the hyphae bearing the asci. —**as′co·go′ni·al,** *adj.*

as·co·my·cete (as′kə mī sēt′), *n. Bot.* a fungus of the class *Ascomycetes*, including the yeasts, mildews, truffles, etc., characterized by bearing the sexual spores in a sac, the ascus. —**as′co·my·ce′tous,** *adj.*

a·scor′bic ac′id (ə skôr′bik, ā skôr′-), *Biochem.* a water-soluble vitamin, $C_6H_8O_6$, occurring in citrus fruits, green vegetables, etc., essential for normal metabolism: used in the prevention and treatment of scurvy. Also called **vitamin C.** [A-[6] + SCORB(UT)IC]

as·co·spore (as′kə spōr′, -spôr′), *n. Bot.* a spore formed within an ascus. —**as·co·spor·ic** (as′kə spôr′ik, -spor′-), **as·cos·po·rous** (as kos′pər əs, as′kə spōr′-, -spôr′-), *adj.*

as·cot (as′kət), *n.* a broad scarf or necktie worn looped under the chin so that the ends are laid flat, one across the other. [so called from the fashionable dress worn at the Ascot races]

Ascot

As·cot (as′kət), *n.* a village in SE Berkshire, in S England: annual horse races.

as·cribe (ə skrīb′), *v.t.*, **-cribed, -crib·ing.** **1.** to credit or assign, as to a cause or source. **2.** to attribute or think of as belonging, as a quality or characteristic. [late ME < L *ascrībe(re)* = *a-* A-[5] + *scrībere* SCRIBE[2]; r. ME *ascrive* < MF. See SHRIVE] —**a·scrib′a·ble,** *adj.* —**Syn. 1.** See **attribute.**

as·crip·tion (ə skrip′shən), *n.* **1.** the act of ascribing. **2.** a statement ascribing something, esp. praise to the Deity. [< L *ascrīptiōn-* (s. of *ascrīptiō*) a written addition. See A-[5], SCRIPT, -ION]

as·cus (as′kəs), *n., pl.* **as·ci** (as′ī). *Bot.* the sac in ascomycetes in which the sexual spores are formed. [< NL < Gk *askós* bag, sac]

-ase, *Chem.* a suffix used in the names of enzymes: *oxidase.* [abstracted from DIASTASE]

a·sep·sis (ə sep′sis, ā-), *n.* **1.** absence of the microorganisms that produce sepsis or septic disease. **2.** *Med.* methods or treatment that are free from such microorganisms.

a·sep·tic (ə sep′tik, ā sep′-), *adj.* free from the living germs of disease, fermentation, or putrefaction. —**a·sep′ti·cal·ly,** *adv.* —**a·sep·ti·cism** (ə sep′ti siz′əm, ā sep′-), *n.*

a·sex·u·al (ā sek′shōō əl), *adj. Biol.* **1.** not sexual. **2.** having no sex or no sexual organs. **3.** independent of sexual processes. —**a·sex·u·al·i·ty** (ā sek′shōō al′i tē), *n.* —**a·sex′u·al·ly,** *adv.*

asex′ual reproduc′tion, *Biol.* reproduction, as budding, fission, spore formation, etc., not involving the union of gametes.

As·gard (äs′gärd, as′-), *n. Scand. Myth.* the home of the Aesir, where Valhalla and the palaces of the individual gods were: connected with the earth by the rainbow bridge, Bifrost. Also, **As·garth** (äs′gärth), **As·gar·dhr** (äs′gär′thər). [< Icel *Asgarthr*, lit., god-courtyard = *ās* god (c. OE *ōs*) + *garthr* yard; see GARTH]

Ás·geirs·son (äs′gâr sən), *n.* **Ás·geir** (äs′gâr), 1894–1972, Icelandic statesman: president 1952–68.

ash[1] (ash), *n.* **1.** the powdery residue of matter that remains after burning. **2.** See **sodium carbonate** (def. 1). **3.** *Geol.* finely pulverized lava thrown out by a volcano in eruption. **4.** a light, silvery-gray color. **5. ashes, a.** mortal remains. **b.** the residue or remains of something destroyed or extinct: *the ashes of his love.* [ME *asche*, OE *asce*, *æsce*; c. Icel *aska*, OHG *asca* (G *Asche*), Goth *azgo*] —**ash′less,** *adj.*

ash[2] (ash), *n.* **1.** any oleaceous tree of the genus *Fraxinus*, esp. *F. excelsior*, of Europe and Asia, or *F. americana* **(white ash),** of North America. **2.** the wood, tough, straight-grained, and elastic, and valued as timber. [ME *asch*, OE *æsc*; c. OHG *ask* (> G *Esche*), Icel *ask(r)*; akin to L *ornus*, Lith *ūosis*]

ash[3] (ash), *n.* the ligature *æ.*

a·shamed (ə shāmd′), *adj.* **1.** feeling shame; distressed or embarrassed by feelings of guilt, foolishness, or disgrace. **2.** unwilling because of the fear of ridicule or disapproval: *They were ashamed to show their work.* [orig. ptp. of earlier *ashame* (v.) to be ashamed, OE *a-scamian* = *ā-* A-[3] + *scamian* to SHAME] —**a·sham·ed·ly** (ə shā′mid lē), *adv.* —**a·sham′ed·ness,** *n.*

—**Syn. 1.** ASHAMED, HUMILIATED, MORTIFIED refer to a condition or feeling of discomfort or embarrassment. ASHAMED focuses on the sense of one's own responsibility for a foolish, improper, or immoral act: *He was ashamed of his dishonesty.* HUMILIATED stresses a feeling of being humbled or disgraced, without any necessary implication of guilt: *He was humiliated by the king.* Both words are used equally in situations in which one is felt to be responsible for the actions of another: *Robert felt humiliated by his daughter's behavior. Mom was ashamed of the way I looked.* MORTIFIED represents an intensification of the feelings implied by the other two words: *She was mortified by her clumsiness.*

A·shan·ti (ə shan′tē), *n.* **1.** a former native kingdom and British colony in W Africa: now a region of Ghana. 1,108,548 (1960); 9700 sq. mi. *Cap.:* Kumasi. **2.** a native or inhabitant of this kingdom or region.

Ash·bur·ton (ash′bûr′tən, -bər tən), *n.* **1st Baron.** See **Baring, Alexander.**

ash·can (ash′kan′), *n.* **1.** a can or metal receptacle for ashes, garbage, or refuse. **2.** *Informal.* a depth charge.

Ash′can School′, (*sometimes l.c.*) *Fine Arts.* a group of American painters of the early 20th century whose genre paintings were derived from city life.

ash·en[1] (ash′ən), *adj.* **1.** ash-colored; gray. **2.** extremely pale, as the complexion. **3.** consisting of ashes. —**Syn. 1.** ashy. **2.** pasty, colorless. [ASH[1] + -EN[2]]

ash·en[2] (ash′ən), *adj.* **1.** pertaining to the ash tree or its timber. **2.** made of wood from the ash tree. [OE *æscen* (c. MLG *eschen*, MHG *eschin*) = *æsc* ASH[2] + *-en* -EN[2]]

Ash·er (ash′ər), *n.* **1.** a son of Jacob and Zilpah. Gen. 30:12–13. **2.** one of the 12 tribes of Israel.

Ashe·ville (ash′vil), *n.* a city in W North Carolina. 57,681 (1970).

Ash·ke·naz·im (äsh′kə nä′zim), *n.pl., sing.* **-naz·i** (-nä′ zē). Jews of central and eastern Europe, or their descendants. Cf. **Sephardim.** —**Ash′ke·naz′ic,** *adj.*

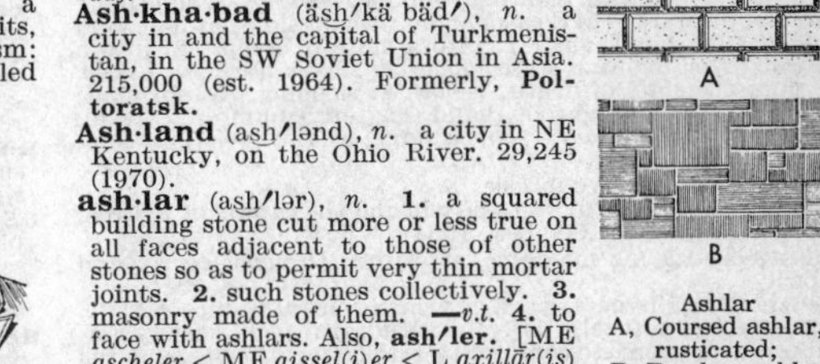

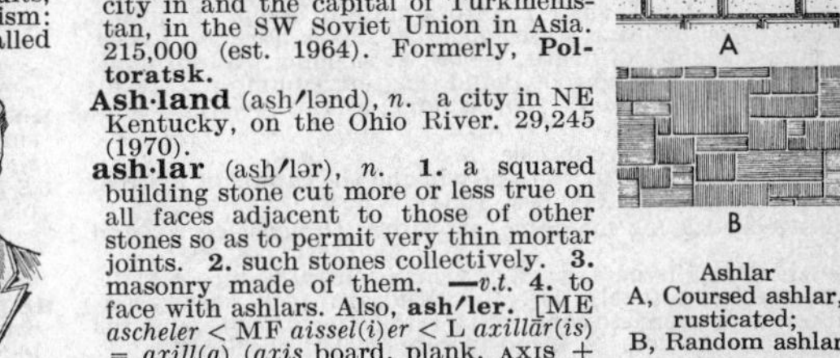

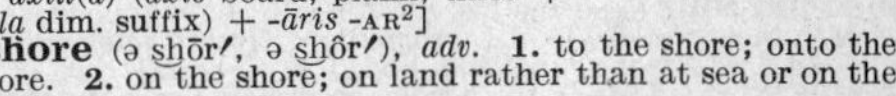

Ashlar
A, Coursed ashlar, rusticated;
B, Random ashlar

Ash·kha·bad (äsh′kä bäd′), *n.* a city in and the capital of Turkmenistan, in the SW Soviet Union in Asia. 215,000 (est. 1964). Formerly, **Poltoratsk.**

Ash·land (ash′lənd), *n.* a city in NE Kentucky, on the Ohio River. 29,245 (1970).

ash·lar (ash′lər), *n.* **1.** a squared building stone cut more or less true on all faces adjacent to those of other stones so as to permit very thin mortar joints. **2.** such stones collectively. **3.** masonry made of them. —*v.t.* **4.** to face with ashlars. Also, **ash′ler.** [ME *ascheler* < MF *aissel(i)er* < L *axillār(is)* = *axill(a)* (*axis* board, plank, AXIS + *-illa* dim. suffix) + *-āris* -AR[2]]

a·shore (ə shōr′, ə shôr′), *adv.* **1.** to the shore; onto the shore. **2.** on the shore; on land rather than at sea or on the water.

ash·ram (äsh′rəm), *n. Hinduism.* a place in which people meet for religious instruction or exercises in common. Also, **asrama.** [< Skt *āśrama* (place) for religious exercise = *ā* towards + *śrama* exertion, fatigue]

Ash·ta·bu·la (ash′tə byōō′lə), *n.* a port in NE Ohio, on Lake Erie. 24,313 (1970).

Ash·ton-un·der-Lyne (ash′tən un′dər līn′), *n.* a city in E Lancashire, in W England, near Manchester. 50,165 (1961).

Ash·to·reth (ash′tə reth′), *n.* an ancient Semitic goddess, the counterpart of the Phoenician Astarte.

ash·tray (ash′trā′), *n.* a receptacle for tobacco ashes.

A·shur (ä′shŏŏr), *n.* Assur.

A·shur·ba·ni·pal (ä′shŏŏr bä′nē päl′), *n.* died 626? B.C., king of Assyria 668?–626? B.C. Also, **Assurbanipal.**

A·shur·na·sir·pal II (ä′shŏŏr nä′zir päl′), (*"the Merciless"*) died 859? B.C., warrior king of Assyria 884?–859 B.C. Also, **A·shur-na·sir-a·pal II** (ä′shŏŏr nä′zir ä päl′). Cf. **Sardanapalus.**

Ash′ Wednes′day, the first day of Lent.

ash·y (ash′ē), *adj.*, **ash·i·er, ash·i·est.** **1.** ash-colored; pale; wan. **2.** of or resembling ashes. **3.** sprinkled or covered with ashes.

A·sia (ā′zhə, ā′shə), *n.* a continent bounded by Europe and the Arctic, Pacific, and Indian Oceans. 2,256,000,000; ab. 16,000,000 sq. mi.

A′sia Mi′nor, a peninsula in W Asia between the Black and Mediterranean seas, including most of Asiatic Turkey. Cf. **Anatolia.**

A·sian (ā′zhən, ā′shən), *adj.* **1.** of, belonging to, or characteristic of Asia or its inhabitants. —*n.* **2.** a native of Asia. [< L *Asiān(us)* < Gk *Asiānós*]

A′sian chol′era, *Pathol.* cholera (def. 1).

A′sian flu′, *Pathol.* a form of influenza caused by a virus believed to have been carried from Asia. Also called **A′sian influen′za.**

A·si·at·ic (ā′zhē at′ik, ā′shē-, ā′zē-), *n.* **1.** *Sometimes Offensive.* Asian. —*adj.* **2.** of or pertaining to Asia or Asians; Asian. [< L *Asiātic(us)* < Gk *Asiātikós*] —**A′si·at′i·cal·ly,** *adv.*

A′siat′ic flu′, *Pathol.* See **Asian flu.** Also called **Asiat′ic influen′za.**

a·side (ə sīd′), *adv.* **1.** on or to one side; away from some position or direction: *to turn aside.* **2.** away from one's thoughts or consideration: *to put one's cares aside.* **3.** in reserve; in a separate place, as for safekeeping; apart: *to lay money aside.* **4.** away from a present group, esp. for reasons of privacy; off to another part, as of a room; into or to a separate place: *He took him aside and talked business.* **5.** in spite of; notwithstanding: *all kidding aside.* **6. aside from,** *U.S. Informal.* **a.** apart from; besides: *Aside from his salary, he receives money from investments.* **b.** except for: *They had no more food, aside from a few rolls.* —*n.* **7.** *Theat.* a comment by an actor intended for the audience and supposedly not heard by others on stage. **8.** words spoken so as not to be heard by others present. **9.** a temporary departure from a main theme or topic, esp. a parenthetical comment or remark; digresssion.

as·i·nine (as′ə nīn′), *adj.* **1.** stupid; unintelligent; silly: *asinine statements.* **2.** of or like an ass. [< L *asinīn(us)* = *asin(us)* ASS[1] + *-īnus* -INE[1]] —**as′i·nine′ly,** *adv.* —**as·i·nin·i·ty** (as′ə nin′i tē), *n.* —**Syn. 1.** See **foolish.**

-asis, an element occurring in scientific, esp. medical, words from Greek: *psoriasis.* [< L < Gk *-āsis* state of, act of, result of]

ask (ask, äsk), *v.t.* **1.** to put a question to; inquire of: *I asked him.* **2.** to request information about: *to ask the way.* **3.** to try to get by using words; request: *to ask a favor; to ask advice.* **4.** to solicit from; request of: *I ask you a great favor. Ask him for advice.* **5.** to demand, expect, or desire: *What price are they asking? A little silence is all I ask.* **6.** to call for; require: *This experiment asks patience.* **7.** to invite: *to ask guests to dinner.* **8.** *Archaic.* to publish (banns); publish the banns of (persons). **—***v.i.* **9.** to make inquiry; inquire: *to ask about a person.* **10.** to request or petition (usually fol. by *for*): *to ask for leniency.* **11. ask for it,** to persist in something that probably leads to trouble. [ME *ask(en), axe(n),* OE *āscian, āxian;* c. OS *ēscon,* OHG *eiscōn* (> G *heischen*), Skt *icch(ati)* seeks] **—ask′er,** *n.* **—Syn. 1.** question, interrogate. **3.** sue. **4.** beseech, beg, entreat. **9.** See **inquire. 10.** appeal. **—Ant. 1, 9.** answer.

Ask (äsk), *n. Scand. Myth.* the first man, made by the gods from an ash tree. Also, **Askr** (äs′kər). Cf. **Embla.** [< Icel; see ASH[2]]

a·skance (ə skans′), *adv.* **1.** with suspicion, mistrust, or disapproval: *He looked askance at my offer.* **2.** with a side glance; sidewise; obliquely. Also, **a·skant** (ə skant′). [ME *asca(u)nce* as if, as much as to say < ?]

a·skew (ə skyo͞o′), *adv.* **1.** to one side; out of line: *to wear one's hat askew.* **—***adj.* **2.** crooked; awry.

a·slant (ə slant′, ə slänt′), *adv.* **1.** at a slant; slantingly; obliquely. **—***adj.* **2.** slanting; oblique. **—***prep.* **3.** slantingly across; athwart. [ME *on slont, on slent* on slope, at a SLANT]

a·sleep (ə slēp′), *adv.* **1.** into a state of sleep. **2.** into a dormant or inactive state: *Their anxieties were put asleep.* **3.** into the state of death. **—***adj.* **4.** sleeping. **5.** dormant; inactive. **6.** (of the foot, hand, leg, etc.) numb. **7.** dead.

a·slope (ə slōp′), *adv.* **1.** at a slope; aslant. **—***adj.* **2.** sloping. [ME]

ASM, air-to-surface missile.

As·ma·ra (äs mär′ə), *n.* a city in and the capital of Eritrea, in N Ethiopia. 131,800 (est. 1964).

As·mo·de·us (az′mə dē′əs, as′-), *n. Demonology.* an evil spirit.

As·nières (ä nyer′), *n.* a city in N central France. 82,201.

a·so·cial (ā sō′shəl), *adj.* **1.** withdrawn from society; indifferent or averse to conformity with conventional standards of social behavior. **2.** inconsiderate of others; selfish.

a·so·ma·tous (ā sō′mə təs, ə sō′-), *adj.* having no material body; incorporeal. [< LL *asōmatus* < Gk *asṓmatos* bodiless = *a-* A-[6] + *sōmat-* (s. of *sôma* body) + *-os* -OUS]

A·so·san (ä′sô sän′), *n.* a volcano in SW Japan, in central Kyushu. 5225 ft.; crater 12 mi. across.

asp[1] (asp), *n.* **1.** any of several venomous snakes, esp. the Egyptian cobra or the horned viper. **2.** the common European viper, *Vipera berus.* **3.** *Archaeol.* uraeus. [back formation from ME *aspis* (taken as pl.) < L < Gk]

asp[2] (asp), *n., adj.* aspen. [ME *aspe,* OE *æspe;* akin to G *Espe,* Icel *ösp*]

as·par·a·gine (ə spar′ə jēn′, -jin), *n. Biochem.* an amino acid, $NH_2COCH_2CH(NH_2)COOH$, obtained from plants, esp. legumes, and used chiefly as a nutrient in culture media. [< F; see ASPARAG(US), -INE[2]]

as·par·a·gus (ə spar′ə gəs), *n.* any liliaceous plant of the genus *Asparagus,* esp. *A. officianalis,* cultivated for its edible shoots. [< L < Gk *asp(h)áragos;* r. OE *sparagi* (< ML) and later *sperage, sparrowgrass,* etc.]

as·par·tame (ə spär′tām, a spär′-, as′pər tām′), *n.* a noncarbohydrate sweetening agent, $C_{14}H_{18}N_2O_5$, synthesized from amino acids: used as a low-calorie substitute for sugar in soft drinks, table sweeteners, and other food products. [ASPART(IC ACID) + (PHENYL)A(LANINE) M(ETHYL) E(STER)]

as·par′tic ac′id (ə spär′tik), *Biochem.* an amino acid, $HOOCCH(NH_2)CH_2COOH$, used in preparing culture media and as a dietary supplement. [ASPAR(AGUS) + -TIC]

A.S.P.C.A., American Society for Prevention of Cruelty to Animals.

as·pect (as′pekt), *n.* **1.** appearance of something to the eye or mind: *the physical aspect of the country.* **2.** a way in which a thing may be viewed or regarded; view: *both aspects of a decision.* **3.** a distinct part, feature, or phase, as of something under consideration. **4.** an apparent attitude, character trait, etc.; mien. **5.** a view in a certain direction, as from a building. **6.** the side or surface facing a given direction: *the dorsal aspect of a fish.* **7.** *Gram.* **a.** a category or set of verb inflections that indicates the duration, repetition, completion, or quality of the action or state denoted by the verb. **b.** a set of syntactic devices, as in the English perfect with *have* in *I have gone,* that has a similar function. **8.** *Astrol.* the relative position of planets as determining their influence. **9.** *Archaic.* a look; glance. [ME < L *aspect(us)* sight, look, appearance, n. use of *aspectus* (ptp. of *aspicere*) = *a-* A-[5] + *spec-* look + *-tus* ptp. suffix] **—Syn. 1.** See **appearance. 5.** prospect, outlook.

as′pect ra′tio, 1. *Aeron.* the ratio of the span of an airfoil to its mean chord. **2.** *Television.* the ratio of the width of an image to its height, usually 4 to 3. **3.** *Rocketry.* the ratio of the mean diameter of the body of a rocket or missile to its length.

as·pen (as′pən), *n.* **1.** any of several poplars, as *Populus tremula,* of Europe, and *P. tremuloides* **(quaking aspen),** of America, having leaves that tremble in the slightest breeze. **—***adj.* **2.** of or pertaining to the aspen. [ME *aspen* (adj.), OE *æspen.* See ASP[2], -EN[2]]

As·pen (as′pən), *n.* a village in central Colorado: ski resort. 2404 (1970).

As·per·ges (ə spûr′jēz), *n. Rom. Cath. Ch.* the rite of sprinkling the altar, clergy, and people with holy water before High Mass. [< L: thou shalt sprinkle (2nd pers. sing. fut. of *aspergere*). See ASPERSE]

as·per·gil·lo·sis (as′pər jə lō′sis), *n., pl.* **-ses** (-sēz). *Vet. Pathol.* disease in an animal caused by a mold fungus of the genus *Aspergillus.* [< NL; see ASPERGILLUS, -OSIS]

as·per·gil·lum (as′pər jil′əm), *n., pl.* **-gil·la** (-jil′ə), **-gil·lums.** *Rom. Cath. Ch.* a brush or instrument for sprinkling holy water; aspersorium. [< L *asperg(ere)* (to) besprinkle + *-illum* dim. suffix]

as·per·gil·lus (as′pər jil′əs), *n., pl.* **-gil·li** (-jil′ī). *Bot.* any fungus of the genus *Aspergillus,* family *Aspergillaceae,* whose sporophores are distinguished by a bristly, knoblike top. [< NL: alter. of ASPERGILLUM]

as·per·i·ty (ə sper′i tē), *n., pl.* **-ties** for 4. **1.** roughness or sharpness of tone, temper, or manner; harshness; severity. **2.** hardship; difficulty. **3.** roughness of surface. **4.** something rough or harsh. [< L *asperitāt-* (s. of *asperitās*) = *asper* rough + *-itāt-* -ITY; r. ME *asprete* < OF < L] **—Syn. 1.** acerbity, bitterness, astringency.

as·perse (ə spûrs′), *v.t.,* **-persed, -pers·ing. 1.** to attack with false, malicious, and damaging charges or insinuations. **2.** to sprinkle; bespatter. [late ME < L *aspers(us)* besprinkled (ptp. of *aspergere*) = *a-* A-[5] + *spēr-* (comb. form of *spār-,* var. of *sparg-* SPARGE) + *-sus* var. of *-tus* ptp. suffix] **—as·pers′er,** *n.* **—as·per′sive,** *adj.* **—as·per′sive·ly,** *adv.*

as·per·sion (ə spûr′zhən, -shən), *n.* **1.** a derogatory, malicious, or damaging remark or statement. **2.** the act of slandering. **3.** the act of sprinkling, as in baptism. [< L *aspersiōn-* (s. of *aspersiō*) a sprinkling] **—Syn. 1.** reproach.

as·per·so·ri·um (as′pər sôr′ē əm, -sōr′-), *n., pl.* **-so·ri·a** (-sôr′ē ə, -sōr′-), **-so·ri·ums.** *Rom. Cath. Ch.* **1.** a vessel for holding holy water. **2.** aspergillum. [< ML; see ASPERSE, -ORIUM]

as·phalt (as′fôlt, -falt), *n.* Also, **as·phal·tum** (as fôl′təm, -fal′-). **1.** any of various dark-colored, solid, bituminous substances, native in various areas of the earth and composed mainly of hydrocarbon mixtures. **2.** a similar substance artificially produced, as a by-product of petroleum-cracking. **3.** a mixture of such substances with gravel, crushed rock, or the like, esp. as used for paving. **—***v.t.* **4.** to cover or pave with asphalt. **—***adj.* **5.** of, pertaining to, or containing asphalt: *asphalt tile.* [earlier *asphaltos, -um* < L < Gk *ásphaltos, -on,* ? akin to *asphalízein* to make firm; r. ME *asphalt(oun)* << Gk *ásphalton*] **—as·phal′tic,** *adj.*

a·spher·i·cal (ā sfer′i kəl), *adj. Optics.* (of a reflecting surface or lens) deviating slightly from an exactly spherical shape and relatively free from aberrations. Also, **a·spher′ic.**

as·pho·del (as′fə del′), *n.* **1.** any of various liliaceous plants of the genera *Asphodelus* and *Asphodeline,* native to southern Europe, having white, pink, or yellow flowers. **2.** any of various other plants, as the daffodil. [< L *asphodel(us)* < Gk *asphódelos* the asphodel. See DAFFODIL]

as·phyx·i·a (as fik′sē ə), *n. Pathol.* the extreme condition caused by lack of oxygen and excess of carbon dioxide in the blood, produced by interference with respiration. [< NL < Gk *asphyxía* a stopping of the pulse = *a-* A-[6] + *sphýx(is)* pulse + *-ia* -IA] **—as·phyx′i·al,** *adj.*

as·phyx·i·ant (as fik′sē ənt), *adj.* **1.** asphyxiating or tending to asphyxiate. **—***n.* **2.** an asphyxiating agent or substance. **3.** an asphyxiating condition.

as·phyx·i·ate (as fik′sē āt′), *v.,* **-at·ed, -at·ing. —***v.t.* **1.** to produce asphyxia in. **2.** to cause to die or lose consciousness by impairing normal breathing, as by gas or other noxious agents; choke; suffocate; smother. **—***v.i.* **3.** to become asphyxiated. **—as·phyx′i·a′tion,** *n.* **—as·phyx′i·a′tor,** *n.*

as·pic[1] (as′pik), *n.* a gelatin usually made with meat or fish stock or tomato juice, chilled and used as a garnish and coating for meats, seafoods, eggs, etc., or as a salad. [< F: said to be so called because cold like an asp]

as·pic[2] (as′pik), *n.* the great lavender, *Lavandula latifolia,* yielding an oil used in perfumery. [< F; OF *espic* < ML *spīc(us)* spikenard, L *spīcus,* var. of *spīca, spīcum* SPIKE[2]]

as·pi·dis·tra (as′pi dis′trə), *n.* a smooth, stemless, Asian herb, *Aspidistra elatior,* having large evergreen leaves often striped with white, grown as a house plant. [< NL = *aspid-* (< Gk: s. of *aspís* shield) + *-istra,* abstracted from *Tupistra* genus of liliaceous plants < Gk *typís* mallet + L *-tra* pl. of *-trum* n. suffix denoting instrument]

as·pir·ant (ə spīər′ənt, as′pər ənt), *n.* **1.** a person who aspires, esp. toward a career, position, etc. **—***adj.* **2.** aspiring. [< L *aspīrant-* (s. of *aspīrāns,* prp. of *aspīrāre*)]

as·pi·ra·ta (as′pə rā′tə), *n., pl.* **-tae** (-tē). *Gk. Grammar.* a strongly fricated, voiceless plosive, as ϕ, θ, χ. [< NL = L *aspīrāt(us)* (see ASPIRATE) + *-a* fem. adj. suffix]

as·pi·rate (*v.* as′pə rāt′; *n., adj.,* as′pər it), *v.,* **-rat·ed, -rat·ing,** *n., adj.* **—***v.t.* **1.** *Phonet.* **a.** to articulate (a speech sound, esp. a stop) so as to produce audible frication, as with the *t* of *time.* **b.** to articulate (the beginning of a word or syllable) with an *h*-sound, as in *which* (hwich) and *hitch* as opposed to *witch* and *itch.* **2.** *Med.* **a.** to remove (a fluid) from a body cavity by use of an aspirator. **b.** to inhale (fluid) into the bronchi and lungs, often after vomiting. **3.** to draw or remove by suction. **—***n.* **4.** *Phonet.* a speech sound having as an obvious concomitant audible frication, as initial stop consonants, initial *h*-sounds, etc. **—***adj.* **5.** *Phonet.* (of a speech sound) pronounced with or accompanied by aspiration; aspirated. [< L *aspīrāt(us)* breathed upon (ptp. of *aspīrāre*)]

as·pi·ra·tion (as′pə rā′shən), *n.* **1.** strong desire, longing, or aim; ambition: *intellectual aspirations.* **2.** a goal or objective desired. **3.** act of aspirating; breath. **4.** *Phonet.* **a.** articulation accompanied by audible frication. **b.** the use of an aspirate in pronunciation. **5.** *Med.* **a.** the act of removing a fluid, as pus or serum, from a cavity of the body, by a hollow needle or trocar connected with a suction syringe. **b.** the act of inhaling fluid into the bronchi and lungs, often after vomiting. [< L *aspīrātiōn-* (s. of *aspīrātiō*)] **—as·pir·a·to·ry** (ə spīər′ə tôr′ē, -tōr′ē), *adj.*

as·pi·ra·tor (as′pə rā′tər), *n.* **1.** an apparatus or device employing suction. **2.** a suction pump operated by the pressure differential created by the high-speed flow of a fluid past an intake orifice. **3.** *Med.* an instrument for removing body fluids by suction.

as·pire (ə spīər′), *v.i.,* **-pired, -pir·ing. 1.** to be eagerly desirous, esp. for something great or of high value (usually fol. by *to, after,* or an infinitive): *to aspire after immortality; to aspire to be a doctor.* **2.** *Archaic.* to rise up; soar; tower. [late ME < L *aspīr(āre)* (to) breathe upon, pant after = *a-* A-[5] + *spīrāre* to breathe, blow] **—as·pir′er,** *n.* **—as·pir′ing·ly,** *adv.* **—Syn. 1.** yearn. See **ambitious.**

as·pi·rin (as′pə rin, -prin), *n., pl.* **-rin, -rins. 1.** *Pharm.* a derivative of salicylic acid, $C_9H_8O_4$, used to relieve pain; acetylsalicylic acid. **2.** an aspirin tablet. [orig. G trademark = *A(cetyl)* ACETYL + *Spir(säure)* salicylic acid (see SPIRAEA) + -IN[2]]

a·squint (ə skwint′), *adv., adj.* with an oblique glance or squint; askance; slyly; dubiously. [A-[1] + *squint* (< ?); akin to D *schuinte* slope]

As·quith (as′kwith), *n.* **Herbert Henry** (*1st Earl of Oxford and Asquith*), 1852–1928, British statesman: prime minister 1908–16.

a·sra·ma (ä′shrə mə), *n.* *Hinduism.* **1.** any of the four phases of the ideally conducted life: education, work, withdrawal from society, or life as a hermit. **2.** ashram. [< Skt *āśrama.* See ASHRAM]

ass[1] (as), *n.* **1.** a long-eared, sure-footed domesticated mammal, *Equus asinus,* related to the horse, used chiefly as a beast of burden. **2.** any wild species of the genus *Equus,* as the onager. **3.** a fool; blockhead. [ME *asse,* OE *assa,* prob. hypocoristic form based on OIr *asan* < L *asinus;* akin to Gk *ónos* ass] —**ass′like′,** *adj.*

Ass, *Equus asinus* (3½ ft. high at shoulder)

ass[2] (as), *n.* **1.** *Slang.* the buttocks. **2.** *Slang* (*vulgar*). the anus. **3.** *Slang* (*vulgar*). sexual intercourse. [ME *ars, ers,* OE *ærs, ears;* akin to OIcel *ars,* G *Arsch,* Gk *órrhos*]

as·sa·fet·i·da (as′ə fet′i də), *n.* *Chem.* asafetida. Also, **as′sa·foet′i·da.**

as·sa·gai (as′ə gī′), *n., pl.* **-gais.** assegai.

as·sa·i[1] (ə sä′ē; *It.* äs sä′ē), *adv.* *Music.* very: *allegro assai* (very quick). [< It: lit., enough << L *ad* (up) to + *satis* enough. See ASSET]

as·sa·i[2] (ə sä′ē), *n.* any of several slender Brazilian palms of the genus *Euterpe,* esp. *E. edulis,* a species bearing a purple fruit from which a beverage is made by infusion. [< Pg < Tupi]

as·sail (ə sāl′), *v.t.* **1.** to set upon with violence; assault. **2.** to attack with criticism, ridicule, abuse, etc. **3.** to impinge upon; make an impact on; beset: *His mind was assailed by conflicting arguments.* [ME *asayle(n)* < OF *asali(r)* < LL *assalīre* = L *as-* AS- + *salīre* to leap, spring] —**as·sail′a·ble,** *adj.* —**as·sail′er,** *n.* —**as·sail′ment,** *n.* —**Syn. 2.** malign.

as·sail·ant (ə sā′lənt), *n.* **1.** a person who attacks. —*adj.* **2.** *Archaic.* assailing or attacking; hostile. [< MF *assaillant*]

As·sam (as sam′), *n.* a state in NE India. 12,209,330 (1961); 85,012 sq. mi. *Cap.:* Shillong.

As·sa·mese (as′ə mēz′, -mēs′), *adj., n., pl.* **-mese.** —*adj.* **1.** of or pertaining to Assam, its inhabitants, or their language. —*n.* **2.** a native or inhabitant of Assam. **3.** an Indic language of Assam.

Assam′ States′, a group of former states in NE India, most of which are now part of the present state of Assam.

as·sas·sin (ə sas′in), *n.* **1.** a murderer or killer, esp. a fanatic who kills a prominent person. **2.** a person who destroys or denigrates: *a character assassin.* **3.** (*cap.*) one of an order of Muslim fanatics, active in Persia and Syria from about 1090 to 1272, whose chief object was to assassinate Crusaders. [< ML *assassīnī* (pl.) < Ar *hashshāshīn* eaters of HASHISH]

as·sas·si·nate (ə sas′ə nāt′), *v.t.,* **-nat·ed, -nat·ing. 1.** to murder premeditatedly and treacherously. **2.** to destroy or denigrate treacherously and viciously. —**as·sas′si·na′tion,** *n.* —**as·sas′si·na′tive,** *adj.* —**as·sas′si·na′tor,** *n.* —**Syn. 1.** slay.

assas′sin bug′, any of numerous hemipterous insects of the family *Reduviidae,* feeding chiefly on other insects but including some bloodsucking parasites of mammals.

as·sault (ə sôlt′), *n.* **1.** a violent attack; onslaught. **2.** *Mil.* the stage of close combat in an attack. **3.** *Law.* an attempt or threat to do violence to another, with or without battery, as by holding a stone or club in a threatening manner. **4.** rape[1]. —*v.t.* **5.** to make an assault upon; attack. [ME *asaut* < OF < ML *assalt(us)* (r. L *assultus*) = L *as-* AS- + *saltus* a leap, n. use of ptp. of *salīre* (*sal-* leap + *-tus* ptp. suffix)] —**as·sault′a·ble,** *adj.* —**as·sault′er,** *n.* —**Syn. 1.** onset, charge; invasion, aggression.

assault′ and bat′tery, *Law.* an assault with an actual touching or other violence upon another.

assault′ boat′, *Mil.* a portable boat used for landing troops on beaches and for crossing rivers.

as·say (*v.* ə sā′; *n.* ə sā′, as′ā), *v.t.* **1.** to try or test; put to trial: *to assay one's strength.* **2.** *Metall.* to analyze (an ore, alloy, etc.) in order to determine the quantity of gold, silver, or other metal in it. **3.** *Pharm.* to subject (a drug) to an analysis for the determination of its potency. **4.** to examine or analyze (a situation, event, etc.); assess; evaluate. **5.** to attempt; endeavor; try. —*v.i.* **6.** *U.S.* to contain, as shown by analysis, a certain proportion of usually precious metal. —*n.* **7.** *Metall.* determination of the amount of metal, esp. gold or silver, in an ore, alloy, etc. **8.** a substance undergoing analysis or trial. **9.** a detailed report of the findings in assaying a substance. **10.** *Obs.* examination or trial; attempt; essay. [ME < MF; var. of ESSAY] —**as·say′a·ble,** *adj.* —**as·say′er,** *n.*

as·se·gai (as′ə gī′), *n., pl.* **-gais. 1.** a slender javelin or spear of the Bantu of southern Africa. **2.** a South African cornaceous tree, *Curtisia faginea,* from whose wood such spears are made. Also, **assagai.** [earlier *azagaia* < Pg < Ar *az zaghāyah* = *al* the + Berber *zaghāyah* assegai]

as·sem·blage (ə sem′blij; *for 4 also Fr.* A SÄN blAzh′), *n.* **1.** a number of persons or things assembled; an assembly, collection, or aggregate. **2.** the act of assembling. **3.** the state of being assembled. **4.** *Fine Arts.* **a.** a sculptural technique of composing into a unified whole a group of unrelated and often fragmentary or discarded objects. **b.** a work of art produced by this technique. Cf. **collage** (def. 2). [< F]

as·sem·ble (ə sem′bəl), *v.,* **-bled, -bling.** —*v.t.* **1.** to bring together; gather into one place, company, body, or whole. **2.** to put or fit together; put together the parts of: *to assemble information; to assemble a toy.* **3.** *Computer Technol.* compile (def. 4). —*v.i.* **4.** to come together; gather; meet. [ME < OF *assemble(r)* < VL **assimulāre* to bring together = L *as-* AS- + *simul* together + *-āre* inf. suffix] —**as·sem′bler,** *n.* —**Syn. 1.** convene. See **gather. 2.** connect. See **manufacture.** —**Ant. 1.** disperse.

as·sem·bly (ə sem′blē), *n., pl.* **-blies. 1.** a body of persons gathered together, usually for a particular purpose. **2.** (*cap.*) *Govt.* a legislative body, esp. a lower house of a legislature. **3.** the act of assembling. **4.** the state of being assembled. **5.** *Mil.* **a.** a signal, as by drum or bugle, for troops to fall into ranks or otherwise assemble. **b.** the movement of tanks, soldiers, etc., scattered by battle or battle drill, toward and into a small area. **6.** the putting together of complex machinery, as airplanes, from interchangeable parts of standard dimensions. **7.** a group of machine parts, esp. one forming a self-contained, independently mounted unit. Cf. **sub assembly.** [ME *assemblee* < MF, lit., (that which is) assembled, fem. ptp. of *assembler* to ASSEMBLE] —**Syn. 1.** assemblage, throng, gathering, mob, meeting. **2.** congress, representatives.

assem′bly dis′trict, *U.S. Govt.* one of a fixed number of districts into which some states are divided, each district electing one member to the lower house of the state legislature. Cf. **Congressional district, senatorial district.**

assem′bly line′, an arrangement of machines, tools, and workers in which a product is assembled by having each perform a specific, successive operation on an incomplete unit as it passes by in a series of stages.

as·sem·bly·man (ə sem′blē mən), *n., pl.* **-men.** *U.S.* a member of a state legislature, esp. of a lower house.

as·sent (ə sent′), *v.i.* **1.** to agree or concur (often fol. by *to*): *to assent to a statement.* **2.** to give in; yield; concede. —*n.* **3.** agreement, as to a proposal; concurrence. **4.** acquiescence or compliance. [ME *asente(n)* < OF *asente(r)* < L *assentārī* = *as-* AS- + *sent-* (see SCENT) + *-t-* freq. suffix + *-āre* inf. suffix] —**as·sen·ta·tion** (as′en tā′shən), *n.* —**as·sent′ing·ly,** *adv.* —**as·sen′tive,** *adj.* —**Syn. 1.** acquiesce. See **agree.**

as·sen·tor (ə sen′tər), *n.* **1.** Also, **as·sent′er.** a person who assents. **2.** *Brit. Govt.* one of the eight voters who endorse the nomination of a candidate for Parliament.

as·sert (ə sûrt′), *v.t.* **1.** to state with assurance, confidence, or force; affirm. **2.** to maintain or defend (claims, rights, etc.). **3.** to put (oneself) forward boldly and insistently. **4.** to state as having existence; postulate: *to assert a first cause as necessary.* [< L *assert(us)* joined to, defended, claimed (ptp. of *asserere*) = *as-* AS- + *ser-* (see SERIES) + *-tus* ptp. suffix] —**as·sert′er, as·ser′tor,** *n.* —**as·sert′i·ble, as·ser·to·ry** (ə sûr′tə rē), *adj.* —**Syn. 1.** avow, maintain. See **declare. 2.** uphold, support. **3.** press. —**Ant. 1.** deny.

as·ser·tion (ə sûr′shən), *n.* **1.** a positive statement or declaration, often without support or reason. **2.** the act of asserting. [late ME *assercion* < L *assertiōn-* (s. of *assertiō*)]

as·ser·tive (ə sûr′tiv), *adj.* given to asserting; positive or aggressive: *He is overly assertive in his selling efforts.* —**as·ser′tive·ly,** *adv.* —**as·ser′tive·ness,** *n.*

as·sess (ə ses′), *v.t.* **1.** to estimate officially the value of (property, income, etc.) as a basis for taxation. **2.** to fix or determine the amount of (damages, a tax, a fine, etc.); appraise. **3.** to impose a tax or other charge on. **4.** to estimate or judge the value, character, etc., of; evaluate: *to assess one's efforts.* [late ME *assesse* < ML *assessā(re)* (to) assess a tax < L *assess(us)* seated beside (a judge) (ptp. of *assidēre*) = *as-* AS- + *sed-* (perf. s. of *sedēre* to SIT) + *-tus* ptp. suffix] —**as·sess′a·ble,** *adj.*

as·sess·ment (ə ses′mənt), *n.* **1.** the act of assessing; appraisal; evaluation. **2.** an amount assessed as payable; an official valuation of taxable property.

as·ses·sor (ə ses′ər), *n.* **1.** a person who makes assessments for purposes of taxation. **2.** an advisor or assistant to a judge, esp. one serving as a specialist in some field. **3.** *Archaic.* **a.** a person who shares another's position, rank, or dignity. **b.** a person sitting beside another in an advisory capacity; an advisory associate. [ME *assessour* < ML *assessor* one who assesses taxes, L: a judge's helper. See ASSESS, -OR[2]] —**as·ses·so·ri·al** (as′i sōr′ē əl, -sôr′-), *adj.*

as·set (as′et), *n.* **1.** a useful thing or quality: *Organizational ability is an asset.* **2.** a single item of ownership having exchange value. **3. assets, a.** items of ownership convertible into cash; total resources of a person or business, as cash, accounts receivable, fixtures, real estate, etc. (opposed to *liabilities*). **b.** *Accounting.* the items detailed on a balance sheet, esp. in relation to liabilities and capital. **c.** all property available for the payment of debts, esp. of a bankrupt. **d.** *Law.* property in the hands of an heir, executor, or administrator, that is sufficient to pay the debts or legacies of a deceased person. [back formation from *assets,* in phrase *have assets,* lit., have enough (to pay obligations) < AF; OF *asez* enough. See ASSAI[1]]

as·sev·er·ate (ə sev′ə rāt′), *v.t.,* **-at·ed, -at·ing.** to declare earnestly or solemnly; aver. [< L *asseverāt(us)* spoken in earnest (ptp. of *asseverāre*) = *as-* AS- + *sever-* (see SEVERE) + *-ātus* -ATE[1]] —**as·sev′er·a′tion,** *n.*

ass·hole (as′hōl′), *n.* *Slang* (*vulgar*). **1.** the anus. **2.** a mean or contemptible person or thing.

As·shur (ä′shŏŏr), *n.* Assur.

as·sib·i·late (ə sib′ə lāt′), *v.t.,* **-lat·ed, -lat·ing.** *Phonet.* to change into or pronounce with the accompaniment of a sibilant sound or sounds. [< L *assībilāt(us)* murmured, whispered at, hissed (ptp. of *assībilāre*). See AS-, SIBILATE] —**as·sib′i·la′tion,** *n.*

as·si·du·i·ty (as′i dōō′i tē, -dyōō′-), *n., pl.* **-ties. 1.** constant application; diligence or industry. **2. assiduities,** devoted or solicitous attentions. [< L *assiduitāt-* (s. of *assiduitās*). See ASSIDUOUS, -ITY]

as·sid·u·ous (ə sij′ōō əs), *adj.* **1.** constant or unremitting: *assiduous reading.* **2.** persevering or industrious. [< L *assiduus,* lit., sitting down to = *as-* AS- + *sidu-* (var. s. of *sede-* SIT) + *-us* -OUS] —**as·sid′u·ous·ly,** *adv.* —**as·sid′u·ous·ness,** *n.* —**Syn. 1.** tireless, persistent. **2.** diligent.

as·sign (ə sīn′), *v.t.* **1.** to designate, give, or reserve (something) for a specific person or purpose. **2.** to appoint, as to a post or duty: *Assign him to guard duty.* **3.** to name; specify:

to assign a day for a meeting. **4.** to ascribe; attribute: *to assign a cause.* **5.** *Law.* to transfer. **6.** *Mil.* to place permanently on duty with a unit or under a commander. **—*v.i.*** **7.** *Law.* to transfer property, esp. in trust or for the benefit of creditors. **—*n.*** **8.** *Law.* assignee. [ME *assigne(n)* < OF *assigne(r)* < L *assignāre.* See AS-, SIGN] **—as·sign′a·bil′i·ty,** *n.* **—as·sign′a·ble,** *adj.* **—as·sign′a·bly,** *adv.* **—as·sign′er;** *Chiefly Law,* **as·sign·or** (ə sī nôr′, as′ə nôr′), *n.* **—Syn. 1.** ASSIGN, ALLOCATE, ALLOT mean to apportion or measure out. To ASSIGN is to distribute available things, designating them to be given to or reserved for specific persons or purposes: *to assign duties.* To ALLOCATE is to earmark or set aside parts of things available or expected in the future, each for a specific purpose: *to allocate income to various types of expenses.* To ALLOT implies making restrictions as to amount, size, purpose, etc., and then apportioning or assigning: *to allot spaces for parking.* **3.** fix, determine.

as·sig·nat (as′ig nat′; *Fr.* A sē nyA′), *n., pl.* **as·sig·nats** (as′ig nats′; *Fr.* A sē nyA′). *Fr. Hist.* one of the notes issued as paper currency by the revolutionary government from 1789 to 1796. [< F < L *assignāt(us)* assigned (ptp. of *assignāre*)]

as·sig·na·tion (as′ig nā′shən), *n.* **1.** an appointment for a meeting, esp. a rendezvous or tryst. **2.** the act of assigning; assignment. [late ME *assignacion* < L *assignātiōn-* (s. of *assignātiō*) assignment]

as·sign·ee (ə sī nē′, as′ə nē′), *n.* *Law.* one to whom some right or interest is transferred. [late ME *assigne* < MF, n. use of ptp. of *assigner* to ASSIGN; see -EE]

as·sign·ment (ə sīn′mənt), *n.* **1.** something assigned, as a particular task or duty. **2.** a position of responsibility or the like to which one is appointed. **3.** the act of assigning. **4.** *Law.* **a.** the transference of a right, interest, or title, or the instrument of transfer. **b.** a transference of property to assignees for the benefit of creditors. [late ME *assignament* < ML *assignāment(um)*] **—Syn. 1.** obligation, job.

as·sim·i·la·ble (ə sim′ə lə bəl), *adj.* capable of being assimilated. [< ML *assimilābil(is)* = L *assimilā(re)* (see ASSIMILATE) + *-bilis* -BLE] **—as·sim′i·la·bil′i·ty,** *n.*

as·sim·i·late (ə sim′ə lāt′), *v.,* **-lat·ed, -lat·ing.** **—*v.t.*** **1.** to take in and incorporate as one's own; absorb: *He assimilated many new experiences in Europe.* **2.** *Physiol.* to convert (food) into a substance suitable for absorption into the system. **3.** to bring into conformity; adapt or adjust (usually fol. by *to* or *with*): *They assimilated their customs to the new environment.* **4.** to make like; cause to resemble (usually fol. by *to* or *with*). **5.** to compare; liken (usually fol. by *to* or *with*). **6.** *Phonet.* to modify by assimilation. **—*v.i.*** **7.** to be or become absorbed. **8.** *Physiol.* (of food) to be converted into the substance of the body; be absorbed into the system. **9.** to become or be like; resemble (usually fol. by *to* or *with*). **10.** to adjust: *The immigrants assimilated easily and quickly.* **11.** *Phonet.* to become modified by assimilation. [< L *assimilāt(us)* likened to, made like (ptp. of *assimilāre*) = *as-* AS- + *simil-* (see SIMILAR) + *-ātus* -ATE[1]] **—as·sim′i·la′tive, as·sim·i·la·to·ry** (ə sim′ə lə tôr′ē, -tōr′ē), *adj.* **—as·sim′i·la′tor,** *n.*

as·sim·i·la·tion (ə sim′ə lā′shən), *n.* **1.** act or process of assimilating. **2.** the state or condition of being assimilated. **3.** *Physiol.* the conversion of absorbed food into the substance of the body. **4.** *Bot.* the total process of plant nutrition, including absorption of external foods and photosynthesis. **5.** *Sociol.* the merging of cultural traits from previously distinct cultural groups, not involving biological amalgamation. **6.** *Phonet.* act or process by which a sound becomes identical with or similar to a neighboring sound, as in (gram′pä) for *grandpa.* Cf. **dissimilation** (def. 2). [< L *assimilātiōn-* (s. of *assimilātiō*)]

as·sim·i·la·tion·ist (ə sim′ə lā′shə nist), *n.* a person who believes in or advocates social assimilation.

As·sin·i·boin (ə sin′ə boin′), *n., pl.* **-boins,** (*esp. collectively*) **-boin.** a member of a Siouan people of northeastern Montana and adjacent parts of Canada. [appar. < CanF *assiniboi* (< Ojibwa *asini* stone + **bwa* < ?) + -(A)N]

As·sin·i·boine (ə sin′ə boin′), *n.* a river in S Canada, flowing S and E from SE Saskatchewan into the Red River in S Manitoba. 450 mi. long.

As·si·si (ə sē′zē; *It.* äs sē′zē), *n.* a town in central Italy: birthplace of Saint Francis of Assisi. 24,400 (1961).

as·sist (ə sist′), *v.t.* **1.** to give support or aid to; help. **2.** to be associated with as an assistant. **—*v.i.*** **3.** to give aid or help. **4.** to be present, as at a meeting, ceremony, etc. **—*n.*** **5.** *Sports.* **a.** *Baseball.* a play that helps to put out a batter or base runner. **b.** a play that helps a teammate in gaining a goal. **6.** aid or a helpful act: *She finished her homework without an assist from her father.* [< L *assist(ere)* (to) stand by, help = *as-* AS- + *sistere* to (cause to) stand (*si-* reduplicative prefix + *-ste-* var. of *sta-* STAND + *-re* inf. suffix)] **—as·sist′er;** *Chiefly Law,* **as·sis·tor,** *n.* **—Syn. 1.** See **help.** **—Ant. 1.** hinder, frustrate.

as·sis·tance (ə sis′təns), *n.* the act of assisting; help; aid; support. [ME *assistence* < ML *assistentia*]

as·sis·tant (ə sis′tənt), *n.* **1.** a person who assists or gives aid and support; helper. **2.** a person subordinate to another in rank, function, etc.; one holding a secondary rank in an office or post: *He served as assistant to the office manager.* **3.** a faculty member of a college or university who ranks below an instructor and whose responsibilities usually include grading papers, supervising laboratories, and assisting in teaching. **—*adj.*** **4.** assisting; helpful. **5.** serving in an immediately subordinate position: *an assistant manager.* [late ME *assistent* < L *assistent-* (s. of *assistēns,* prp. of *assistere* to ASSIST); see -ENT, -ANT] **—Syn. 2.** aide, adjutant.

assis′tant profes′sor, a college or university teacher who ranks above an instructor and below an associate professor.

as·sist·ant·ship (ə sis′tənt ship′), *n.* a form of financial aid awarded to a student studying for a graduate degree at a college or university in which he assists a professor, usually in academic or laboratory work.

As·siut (ä syo͞ot′), *n.* Asyut.

as·size (ə sīz′), *n.* **1.** Usually, **assizes.** *Brit.* a trial session, civil or criminal, held periodically in specific locations. **2.** an edict, ordinance, or enactment made at a session of a legislative assembly. **3.** an inquest or a judicial inquiry. **4.** an action, writ, or verdict of an assize. **5.** judgment (def. 8): *the last assize.* [ME *asise* < OF: a sitting, n. use of fem. of *asis* seated at (ptp. of *aseeir*) = *a-* A-[5] + *-sis* < L *sēss(um)* (*sēd-* perf. s. of *sedēre* to SIT + *-tus* ptp. suffix)]

assn., association. Also, **Assn.**

assoc., **1.** associate. **2.** associated. **3.** association.

as·so·ci·a·ble (ə sō′shē ə bəl, -shə bəl, -sē-), *adj.* capable of being associated. [ASSOCI(ATE) + -ABLE, modeled on *sociable*] **—as·so′ci·a·bil′i·ty, as·so′ci·a·ble·ness,** *n.*

as·so·ci·ate (*v.* ə sō′shē āt′, -sē-; *n., adj.,* ə sō′shē it, -āt′, -sē-), *v.,* **-at·ed, -at·ing,** *n., adj.* **—*v.t.*** **1.** to connect or bring into relation, as thought, feeling, memory, etc.: *to associate peace with prosperity.* **2.** to join as a companion, partner, or ally: *to associate oneself with a cause.* **3.** to unite; combine. **—*v.i.*** **4.** to enter into union; unite. **5.** to keep company, as a comrade or intimate: *to associate with prestigious people.* **—*n.*** **6.** a person who shares actively in a business, enterprise, or other undertaking; partner; colleague. **7.** **associates,** (*cap.*) *U.S.* the members or partners of a business concern, as an engineering or public-relations firm, who are not specifically designated in the concern's name: *C. A. Platt & Associates.* **8.** a companion or comrade. **9.** anything usually accompanying or associated with another; an accompaniment or concomitant. **10.** a person who is admitted to a subordinate degree of membership in an association or institution: *an associate of the Royal Academy.* **—*adj.*** **11.** connected, joined, or related, esp. as a companion or colleague; having equal or nearly equal responsibility. **12.** having subordinate status; without full rights and privileges. **13.** allied; concomitant. [< L *associāt(us)* joined to (ptp. of *associāre*) = *as-* AS- + *soci-* (see SOCIAL) + *-ātus* -ATE[1]] **—Syn. 8.** See **acquaintance.**

asso′ciate profes′sor, a college or university teacher who ranks above an assistant professor and below a professor.

as·so·ci·a·tion (ə sō′sē ā′shən, -shē-), *n.* **1.** an organization of people with a common purpose. **2.** act of associating. **3.** the state of being associated. **4.** friendship; companionship: *Their close association did not last long.* **5.** connection or combination. **6.** the connection or relation of ideas, feelings, sensations, etc. **7.** an idea, image, feeling, etc., suggested by or connected with something other than itself; an accompanying thought, emotion, or the like; an overtone or connotation: *My associations with that painting are of springlike days.* **8.** *Ecol.* a group of plants of one or more species living together under uniform environmental conditions and having a uniform and distinctive aspect. **9.** *Brit.* soccer. **10.** See **free association.** [< ML *associātiōn-* (s. of *associātiō*)] **—as·so′ci·a′tion·al,** *adj.* **—Syn. 1.** alliance, society, company. **4.** fellowship.

associa′tion foot′ball, *Brit.* soccer.

as·so·ci·a·tive (ə sō′shē ā′tiv, -sē-, -shə tiv), *adj.* **1.** pertaining to or resulting from association. **2.** tending to associate or unite. **3.** *Math., Logic.* **a.** (of an operation on a set of elements) giving an equivalent expression when elements are grouped without change of order, as $(a + b) + c = a + (b + c)$. **b.** having reference to this property: *associative law of multiplication.* **—as·so·ci·a·tive·ly** (ə sō′shē ā′tiv lē, -ə tiv-, -sē-), *adv.* **—as·so′ci·a′tive·ness,** *n.*

as·so·nance (as′ə nəns), *n.* **1.** the resemblance of sounds. **2.** *Pros.* rhyme in which the same vowel sounds are used with different consonants in the stressed syllables of the rhyming words, as in *penitent* and *reticence.* **3.** partial agreement or correspondence. [< F = *asson(ant)* sounding in answer (see AS-, SONANT) + *-ance* -ANCE] **—as′so·nant,** *adj., n.*

as·sort (ə sôrt′), *v.t.* **1.** to distribute, place, or arrange according to kind or class; classify; sort. **2.** to furnish with a suitable assortment or variety of goods. **3.** *Archaic.* to group with others of the same or similar kind; associate (usually fol. by *with*). **—*v.i.*** **4.** to agree in sort or kind; be matched or suited. **5.** to associate; consort. [late ME *assorte* < MF *assorte(r).* See AS-, SORT] **—as·sort′a·tive, as·sort′ive,** *adj.* **—as·sort′a·tive·ly,** *adv.* **—as·sort′er,** *n.*

as·sort·ed (ə sôr′tid), *adj.* **1.** consisting of selected kinds; arranged in sorts or varieties: *rows of assorted vegetables.* **2.** consisting of various kinds: *assorted chocolates.* **3.** matched; suited: *a perfectly assorted pair.*

as·sort·ment (ə sôrt′mənt), *n.* **1.** the act of assorting; distribution; classification. **2.** a collection of various kinds of things; a mixed collection.

ASSR, Autonomous Soviet Socialist Republic. Also, **A.S.S.R.**

asst., assistant.

as·suage (ə swāj′), *v.t.,* **-suaged, -suag·ing.** **1.** to make milder or less severe: *to assuage one's grief.* **2.** to appease; satisfy: *to assuage one's hunger.* **3.** to mollify; pacify; calm. [ME *aswage(n)* < OF *asouagie(r)* < VL **assuāviāre* = L *as-* AS- + *suāvi(s)* SUAVE + *-ā-* thematic vowel + *-re* inf. ending] **—as·suage′ment,** *n.* **—Syn. 1.** alleviate. **2.** relieve.

As·suan (äs wän′), *n.* Aswan. Also, **As·souan′.**

as·sua·sive (ə swā′siv), *adj.* soothing; alleviative. [AS- + (PER)SUASIVE]

as·sume (ə so͞om′), *v.t.,* **-sumed, -sum·ing.** **1.** to take for granted or without proof; suppose; postulate: *to assume a principle in reasoning.* **2.** to take upon oneself; undertake: *to assume an obligation.* **3.** to take over the duties or responsibilities of: *to assume office.* **4.** to take on (a particular character, quality, mode of life, etc.); adopt: *The situation assumed a threatening character. He assumed the customs of his new country.* **5.** to pretend to have or be; feign: *He assumed interest and stifled a yawn.* **6.** to appropriate or arrogate: *to assume a right to oneself.* **7.** *Archaic.* to take into relation or association; adopt. [< L *assūme(re)* (to) take to, adopt = *as-* AS- + *sūmere* to take up (*sub-* SUB- + *emere* to take)] **—as·sum′a·ble,** *adj.* **—as·sum′a·bly,** *adv.* **—as·sum′er,** *n.* **—Syn. 1.** presuppose. **5.** See **pretend.**

as·sumed (ə so͞omd′), *adj.* **1.** adopted to deceive; pretended; feigned. **2.** taken for granted. **3.** usurped. **—as·sum·ed·ly** (ə so͞o′mid lē), *adv.*

as·sum·ing (ə so͞o′ming), *adj.* arrogant; presumptuous.

as·sump·sit (ə sump′sit), *n.* *Law.* **1.** a legal action for a breach of contract or promise not under seal. **2.** an actionable promise. [< L: he has taken upon himself]

as·sump·tion (ə sump′shən), *n.* **1.** the act of taking for granted or supposing. **2.** something taken for granted; a supposition: *a correct assumption.* **3.** act of taking to or upon oneself. **4.** act of taking possession of something: *the assumption of power.* **5.** arrogance or presumption. **6.** *Eccles.* **a.** (*often cap.*) the bodily taking up into heaven of the Virgin Mary. **b.** (*cap.*) a feast commemorating this, celebrated on August 15. [ME < L *assūmptiōn-* (s. of *assūmptiō*) = *assūmpt(us)* taken up (ptp. of *assūmere;* see ASSUME) + *-iōn-* -ION] **—Syn. 2.** conjecture, guess. **5.** forwardness.

as·sump·tive (ə sump′tiv), *adj.* **1.** taken for granted. **2.** characterized by assumption. **3.** presumptuous. [< L *assūmptīv(us)* = *assūmpt(us)* (ptp.; see ASSUMPTION) + *-īvus* -IVE] **—as·sump′tive·ly,** *adv.*

As·sur (as′ər), *n.* the god of war and supreme national god of Assyria. Also, **Ashur, Asshur, Asur.**

as·sur·ance (ə sho͝or′əns), *n.* **1.** a positive declaration intended to give confidence. **2.** pledge; guaranty; surety: *He gave his assurance that the job would be done.* **3.** full confidence; freedom from doubt; certainty: *to act in the assurance of success.* **4.** freedom from timidity; self-confidence; self-possession; courage: *He acted with speed and assurance.* **5.** presumptuous boldness; impudence. **6.** *Brit.* insurance. [ME *ass(e)ura(u)nce* < MF *ass(e)urance*] **—Syn. 3.** See **trust. 4.** See **confidence. 5.** effrontery, impertinence, nerve.

As·sur·ba·ni·pal (ä′so͝or bä′nē päl′), *n.* Ashurbanipal.

as·sure (ə sho͝or′), *v.t.,* **-sured, -sur·ing. 1.** to declare earnestly to; inform or tell positively. **2.** to cause to know surely; reassure: *He assured himself that they did as they were told.* **3.** to pledge or promise; guarantee: *He was assured a job in the spring.* **4.** to make (a future event) sure; ensure: *This contract assures the company's profit this month.* **5.** to secure or confirm; render safe or stable: *to assure a person's position.* **6.** to give confidence to; encourage. **7.** to insure, as against loss. [ME *as(e)ure,* assure < OF *aseure(r)* < LL *assēcūrāre* = L *as-* AS- + *sēcūr-* (see SECURE) + *-āre* inf. suffix] **—as·sur′er, as·su′ror,** *n.*

as·sured (ə sho͝ord′), *adj.* **1.** guaranteed; certain; secure: *an assured income.* **2.** bold; confident. **3.** boldly presumptuous. **—***n.* **4.** *Insurance.* **a.** the beneficiary under a policy. **b.** the person whose life or property is covered by a policy. [ME] **—as·sur·ed·ly** (ə sho͝or′id lē), *adv.* **—as·sur′ed·ness,** *n.*

as·sur·gent (ə sûr′jənt), *adj. Bot.* curving upward, as leaves; ascending. [< L *assurgent-* (s. of *assurgēns* rising up, prp. of *assurgere*). See AS-, SURGENT] **—as·sur′gen·cy,** *n.*

Seventh Century B.C.

Assyr., Assyrian.

As·syr·i·a (ə sir′ē ə), *n.* an ancient empire in SW Asia.

As·syr·i·an (ə sir′ē ən), *adj.* **1.** of or pertaining to Assyria, its inhabitants, or their language. **—***n.* **2.** a native or an inhabitant of Assyria. **3.** the dialect of Akkadian spoken in Assyria. Cf. **Akkadian** (def. 1).

As·syr·i·ol·o·gy (ə sir′ē ol′ə jē), *n.* the study of the history, language, etc., of the ancient Assyrians. **—As·syr·i·o·log·i·cal** (ə sir′ē ə loj′i kəl), *adj.* **—As·syr′i·ol′o·gist,** *n.*

a·star·board (ə stär′bərd), *adv. Naut.* toward or on the starboard side.

As·tar·te (a stär′tē), *n.* an ancient Semitic deity, goddess of fertility and reproduction.

a·stat·ic (ā stat′ik), *adj.* **1.** unstable; unsteady. **2.** *Physics.* having no tendency to take a definite position or direction. [< Gk *ástat(os)* not steadfast, unstable (*a-* A-[6] + *statós* standing) + -IC; see STATIC] **—a·stat′i·cal·ly,** *adv.* **—a·stat·i·cism** (ā stat′i siz′əm), *n.*

as·ta·tine (as′tə tēn′, -tin), *n. Chem.* a rare element of the halogen family. *Symbol:* At; *at. no.:* 85. [< Gk *ástat(os)* not steadfast, unstable + -INE[2]]

as·ter (as′tər), *n.* **1.** any composite plant of the genus *Aster,* having rays varying from white or pink to blue around a yellow disk. **2.** a plant of some allied genus, as the China aster. **3.** *Biol.* a structure formed in a cell during mitosis, composed of protoplasmic fibers radiating about the centrosome. [< L < Gk *astḗr* star]

Aster,
Aster novae-angliae

aster-, var. of **astro-** before a vowel: *asteroid.*

-aster[1], a diminutive or pejorative suffix noting something that imperfectly resembles or merely apes the true thing: *criticaster; poetaster; oleaster.* [< L]

-aster[2], *Chiefly Biol.* var. of **astro-** as final element in a compound word: *diaster.* [repr. Gk *astḗr*]

as·ter·a·ceous (as′tə rā′shəs), *adj. Bot.* belonging to the *Asteraceae* or *Carduaceae,* the aster family of plants, usually included in the *Compositae.*

as·te·ri·at·ed (a stēr′ē ā′tid), *adj. Crystall.* exhibiting asterism. [< Gk *astéri(os)* starry (see ASTER-) + -ATE[1] + -ED[2]]

as·ter·isk (as′tə risk), *n.* **1.** the figure of a star (*), used in writing and printing as a reference mark or to indicate omission, doubtful matter, etc. **—***v.t.* **2.** to mark with an asterisk: *to asterisk a word that requires a footnote.* [< L *asteriscus* < Gk *asterískos* small star = *aster-* ASTER- + *-iskos* dim. suffix]

as·ter·ism (as′tə riz′əm), *n.* **1.** *Crystall.* a property of some crystallized minerals of showing a starlike luminous figure. **2.** *Astron. Rare.* **a.** a group of stars. **b.** a constellation. [< Gk *asterism(ós)* a marking with stars]

a·stern (ə stûrn′), *adv. Naut., Aeron.* **1.** in a backward direction. **2.** at or toward the stern. **3.** in a position behind a specified vessel or aircraft: *The cutter was close astern.*

a·ster·nal (ā stûr′nəl), *adj. Anat., Zool.* not reaching to or connected with the sternum.

as·ter·oid (as′tə roid′), *n.* **1.** *Astron.* any of the thousands of small bodies of from 480 miles to less than one mile in diameter that revolve about the sun in orbits lying mostly between those of Mars and Jupiter. **2.** *Zool.* an asteroidean; starfish. **—***adj.* **3.** starlike. [< Gk *asteroeid(ḗs)* starry, starlike. See ASTER-, -OID] **—as′ter·oi′dal,** *adj.*

as·ter·oi·de·an (as′tə roi′dē ən), *n.* **1.** an echinoderm of the class *Asteroidea,* comprising the starfishes. **—***adj.* **2.** belonging or pertaining to the *Asteroidea.* [< NL *Aster(ias)* starfish genus (< Gk *asterías* starry; see ASTER-) + -OIDEA + -AN]

as·the·ni·a (as thē′nē ə, as′thə nī′ə), *n. Pathol.* lack or loss of strength; debility. [< NL < Gk *asthéneia* weakness = *asthene-,* s. of *asthenḗs* (*a-* A-[6] + *sthene-,* var. s. of *sthénos* strength) + *-ia* -IA]

as·then·ic (as then′ik), *adj.* **1.** of, pertaining to, or characterized by asthenia; weak. **2.** *Psychol.* (of a physical type) having a slight build or slender body structure. Cf. **athletic** (def. 4), **pyknic** (def. 1). **—***n.* **3.** an asthenic person. [< Gk *asthenik(ós)* = *asthen-* (see ASTHENIA) + *-ikos* -IC)]

asth·ma (az′mə, as′-), *n.* a paroxysmal, often allergic disorder of respiration, characterized by wheezing, difficulty in expiration, and a feeling of constriction in the chest. [< Gk: a panting (akin to *aázein* to breathe hard); r. ME *asma* < ML < Gk *ásthma*] **—asth·ma·toid** (az′mə toid′), *adj.*

asth·mat·ic (az mat′ik, as-), *adj.* Also, **asth·mat′i·cal. 1.** suffering from asthma. **2.** pertaining to asthma. **—***n.* **3.** a person who suffers from asthma. [< L *asthmaticus(us)* < Gk *asthmatikós* = *asthmat-* (s. of *ásthma*) ASTHMA + *-ikos* -IC] **—asth·mat′i·cal·ly,** *adv.*

As·ti (ä′stē), *n.* a city in central Piedmont, in NW Italy. 60,217 (1961).

as·tig·mat·ic (as′tig mat′ik), *adj. Ophthalm.* pertaining to, exhibiting, or correcting astigmatism. [A-[6] + STIGMATIC] **—as′tig·mat′i·cal·ly,** *adv.*

a·stig·ma·tism (ə stig′mə tiz′əm), *n.* **1.** *Optics.* an aberration of a lens or optical system that causes lines in some directions to be focused less sharply than lines in other directions. **2.** *Ophthalm.* a defect in vision due to such an aberration in the eye. Also called **a·stig·mi·a** (ə stig′mē ə).

a·stir (ə stûr′), *adj.* **1.** in motion; active; stirring: *The very field was astir with insects.* **2.** up and about; out of bed.

As·ti spu·man·te (ä′stē spo͞o män′te; *Eng.* as′tē spə män′tē, spyə-), a sweet, sparkling Italian white wine with a muscat flavor. Also, **As′ti Spuman′te.** [< It lit., effervescent Asti; see SPUME, -ANT]

a·stom·a·tous (ā stom′ə təs, ā stō′mə-), *adj. Zool., Bot.* having no mouth, stoma, or stomata.

As·ton (as′tən), *n.* **Francis William,** 1877–1945, English physicist and chemist: Nobel prize for chemistry 1922.

as·ton·ied (ə ston′ēd), *adj. Archaic.* bewildered or dismayed. [ME < *astonyen* to ASTONISH; see -ED[2]]

as·ton·ish (ə ston′ish), *v.t.* to strike with sudden and overpowering wonder; amaze. [ME *astony(en)* (? OE *āstunian;* see STUN) + -ISH[2]] **—as·ton′ished·ly,** *adv.* **—as·ton′ish·ing·ly,** *adv.* **—as·ton′ish·ment,** *n.* **—Syn.** astound, startle, shock. See **surprise.**

As·tor (as′tər), *n.* **1. John Jacob,** 1763–1848, U.S. capitalist and fur merchant. **2. Nancy (Lang·horne),** (lang′hôrn′, -ərn), **Viscountess,** 1879–1964, first woman Member of Parliament in England.

as·tound (ə stound′), *v.t.* **1.** to overwhelm with amazement; shock with wonder or surprise. **—***adj.* **2.** *Archaic.* astonished; astounded. [ME *astoun(e)d,* ptp. of *astonen,* var. of *astonyen* to ASTONISH] **—as·tound′ing·ly,** *adv.* **—Syn. 1.** See **surprise.**

as·tra·chan (as′trə kən, -kan′), *n.* astrakhan.

a·strad·dle (ə strad′əl), *adv., adj.* with one leg on each side; astride.

As·trae·a (a strē′ə), *n. Class. Myth.* the goddess of justice and the daughter of Zeus and Themis.

as·tra·gal (as′trə gəl), *n. Archit., Furniture.* **1.** a small convex molding in the form of a string of beads. Cf. **bead and reel. 2.** a plain convex molding; bead. [< L *astragal(us)* < Gk *astrágalos* a vertebra, a molding, a kind of vetch; in pl., dice]

a·strag·a·lus (a strag′ə ləs), *n., pl.* **-li** (-lī′). *Zool.* one of the proximal bones of the tarsus in higher vertebrates. [< NL; see ASTRAGAL] **—as·trag′a·lar,** *adj.*

as·tra·khan (as′trə kən, -kan′), *n.* **1.** a fur of young lambs, with lustrous, closely curled wool, from Astrakhan. **2.** Also called **as′trakhan cloth′.** a fabric with curled pile resembling astrakhan fur. Also, **astrachan.**

As·tra·khan (as′trə kan′; *Russ.* ä′strä khän′yə), *n.* a city in the S RSFSR, in the SE Soviet Union in Europe, at the mouth of the Volga. 332,000 (est. 1964).

as·tral (as′trəl), *adj.* **1.** of, pertaining to, or proceeding from the stars; stellar. **2.** *Biol.* pertaining to or resembling an aster; star-shaped. **3.** *Theosophy.* noting a supersensible substance pervading all space and forming the substance of a second body **(as′tral bod′y)** belonging to each individual through life and surviving him in death. [< LL *astrāl(is)* = L *ast(rum)* star (< Gk *ástron*) + *-ālis* -AL[1]] **—as′tral·ly,** *adv.*

a·stray (ə strā′), *adv., adj.* **1.** out of the right way; off the correct or known road or path. **2.** away from what is right; in or into error. [ME *astraye* < MF *estraié* strayed, ptp. of *estraier* to STRAY]

as·trict (ə strikt′), *v.t.* **1.** to bind fast; confine; constrain or restrict. **2.** to bind morally or legally. [< L *astrīct(us)* drawn together, bound, tightened (ptp. of *astringere*) = *a-* A-[5] + *strīg-* (var. s. of *stringere* to draw) + *-tus* ptp. suffix. See ASTRINGE] **—as·tric′tion,** *n.*

as·tric·tive (ə strik′tiv), *adj., n.* astringent. **—as·tric′tive·ly,** *adv.* **—as·tric′tive·ness,** *n.*

a·stride (ə strīd′), *prep.* **1.** with a leg on each side of; straddling. **2.** on both sides of: *The town lay astride the main road.* **—***adv., adj.* **3.** in a posture of striding or straddling; with legs apart or with one leg on each side.

as·tringe (ə strinj′), *v.t.,* **-tringed, -tring·ing.** to compress; constrict. [< L *astringe(re)* (to) draw together = *a-* A-[5] + *stringere* to draw; see STRINGENT]

as·trin·gent (ə strin′jənt), *adj.* **1.** *Med.* contracting; constrictive; styptic. **2.** stern or severe; austere. —*n.* **3.** *Med.* a substance that contracts the tissues or canals of the body, thereby diminishing discharges, as of mucus or blood. **4.** a cosmetic that cleans the skin and constricts the pores. [< L *astringent-* (s. of *astringēns*), prp. of *astringere* to ASTRINGE; see -ENT] —**as·trin′gen·cy,** *n.* —**as·trin′gent·ly,** *adv.* —**Syn. 2.** sharp, harsh, rigorous.

astro-, a learned borrowing from Greek meaning "star," used in the formation of compound words: *astrophotography.* Also, **aster-, -aster.** [< Gk, comb. form of *ástron* a star, constellation]

as·tro·dome (as′trə dōm′), *n.* *Aeron.* a transparent dome on top of the fuselage of an aircraft, through which observations are made for celestial navigation.

as·tro·gate (as′trə gāt′), *v.i., v.t.,* **-gat·ed, -gat·ing.** to navigate in outer space. [ASTRO- + (NAVI)GATE] —**as′tro·ga′tion,** *n.* —**as′tro·ga′tor,** *n.*

as·tro·ge·ol·o·gy (as′trō jē ol′ə jē), *n.* the science dealing with the structure and composition of planets and other bodies in the solar system.

astrol., **1.** astrologer. **2.** astrological. **3.** astrology.

as·tro·labe (as′trə lāb′), *n.* an astronomical instrument used by the ancient Greeks for determining the position of the sun or stars. [ME, var. of *astrolabie* < ML *astrolabi(um)* < LGk *astrolábion,* Gk *astrolábon* (neut. of *astrolábos,* adj. used as n.) = *ástro(n)* star + *lab-* (var. s. of *lambánein* to take) + *-on* neut. suffix]

as·trol·o·gy (ə strol′ə jē), *n.* **1.** the study that assumes, and professes to interpret, the influence of the heavenly bodies on human affairs. **2.** *Obs.* the science of astronomy. [ME < L *astrologia* < Gk] —**as·trol′o·ger, as·trol′o·gist,** *n.* —**as·tro·log·i·cal** (a′strə loj′i kəl), *adj.* —**as′tro·log′i·cal·ly,** *adv.*

astron., **1.** astronomer. **2.** astronomical. **3.** astronomy.

as·tro·naut (as′trə nôt′), *n.* a person engaged in or trained for space flight. [ASTRO- + (AERO)NAUT]

as·tro·nau·ti·cal (as′trə nô′ti kəl), *adj.* of or pertaining to astronautics or astronauts. [*astronautic* (modeled on F *astronautique;* see ASTRONAUT, -IC) + -AL[1]] —**as′tro·nau′ti·cal·ly,** *adv.*

as·tro·nau·tics (as′trə nô′tiks), *n.* (*construed as sing.*) the science of travel beyond the earth's atmosphere, including interplanetary and interstellar flights. [see ASTRONAUTICAL, -ICS]

as·tro·nav·i·ga·tion (as′trō nav′ə gā′shən), *n.* See **celestial navigation.** —**as′tro·nav′i·ga′tor,** *n.*

as·tron·o·mer (ə stron′ə mər), *n.* an expert in astronomy; a scientific observer of the celestial bodies. [earlier *astronomyer.* See ASTRONOMY, -ER[1]]

as·tro·nom·i·cal (as′trə nom′i kəl), *adj.* **1.** of, pertaining to, or connected with astronomy. **2.** extremely large; enormous: *an astronomical sum.* Also, **as′tro·nom′ic.** [< L *astronomic(us)* (< Gk *astronomikós;* see ASTRONOMY, -IC) + -AL[1]] —**as′tro·nom′i·cal·ly,** *adv.*

as′tronom′ical u′nit, *Astron.* a unit of length, equal to the mean distance of the earth from the sun: approximately 93 million miles. *Abbr.:* AU

as′tronom′ical year′, year (def. 3b).

as·tron·o·my (ə stron′ə mē), *n.* the science that deals with the material universe beyond the earth's atmosphere. [ME *astronomie* < L *astronomia* < Gk]

as·tro·pho·tog·ra·phy (as′trō fə tog′rə fē), *n.* the photography of stars and other celestial objects. —**as·tro·pho·to·graph·ic** (as′trō fō′tə graf′ik), *adj.*

as·tro·phys·ics (as′trō fiz′iks), *n.* (*construed as sing.*) the branch of astronomy that deals with the physical properties of celestial bodies, and with the interaction between matter and radiation in the interior of celestial bodies and in interstellar space. —**as′tro·phys′i·cal,** *adj.* —**as·tro·phys·i·cist** (as′trō fiz′i sist), *n.*

as·tro·sphere (as′trə sfēr′), *n.* *Biol.* **1.** the central portion of an aster, in which the centrosome lies. **2.** the whole aster exclusive of the centrosome.

As·tu·ri·as (a stŏŏr′ē əs, a-styŏŏr′-; *Sp.* äs tōōr′yäs), *n.* a former kingdom and province in NW Spain. —**As·tu′ri·an,** *adj., n.*

as·tute (ə stōōt′, ə styōōt′), *adj.* **1.** of keen penetration or discernment; sagacious: *an astute scholar.* **2.** shrewd; ingenious. [< L *astūt(us)* shrewd, sly, cunning = *astū-* (s. of *astus*) cleverness + *-tus* adj. suffix] —**as·tute′ly,** *adv.* —**as·tute′ness,** *n.*

As·ty·a·nax (a stī′ə naks′), *n.* *Class. Myth.* the young son of Hector and Andromache, thrown from the walls of Troy by the victorious Greeks so that he would not grow up to avenge the Trojan defeat.

A·sun·ción (ä′sōōn syôn′, -thyôn′), *n.* a city in and the capital of Paraguay, in the S part. 400,000.

a·sun·der (ə sun′dər), *adv., adj.* **1.** into separate parts; in or into pieces: *to tear asunder.* **2.** apart or widely separated. [ME; OE *on sundrum* apart. See A-[1], SUNDRY]

A·sur (as′ər), *n.* Assur.

As·wan (as′wän; *Arab.* äs wän′), *n.* **1.** Ancient, **Syene.** a city in SE Egypt, on the Nile. 246,000. **2.** a dam near this city, extending across the Nile. 6400 ft. long. Also, **As·wân′, Assuan, Assouan.**

a·swarm (ə swôrm′), *adj.* filled, as by objects, organisms, etc., esp. in motion; teeming (usually used predicatively): *The garden was aswarm with bees.*

a·sy·lum (ə sī′ləm), *n.* **1.** an institution for the maintenance and care of the blind, the insane, orphans, etc. **2.** an inviolable refuge, as formerly for criminals and debtors; sanctuary. **3.** *Internat. Law.* a temporary refuge granted political offenders, esp. in a foreign embassy. **4.** the protection afforded by one nation to exiled political offenders of another nation. **5.** any secure retreat. [< L < Gk *ásȳlon* sanctuary = *a-* A-[6] + *sȳlon* right of seizure] —**Syn. 1.** See **hospital. 2.** haven, shelter, retreat.

a·sym·met·ric (ā′sə me′trik, as′ə-), *adj.* **1.** not identical on both sides of a central line; lacking symmetry. **2.** *Chem.* **a.** having an unsymmetrical arrangement of atoms in the molecule. **b.** noting a carbon atom bonded to four different atoms or groups. Also, **a′sym·met′ri·cal.** —**a′sym·met′ri·cal·ly,** *adv.*

a·sym·me·try (ā sim′i trē), *n.* quality or state of being asymmetric. [< Gk *asymmetría* lack of proportion]

a·symp·to·mat·ic (ā simp′tə mat′ik), *adj.* showing no evidence of disease. —**a·symp′to·mat′i·cal·ly,** *adv.*

as·ymp·tote (as′im tōt′), *n.* *Math.* a straight line approached by a given curve as one of the variables in the equation of the curve approaches infinity. [< Gk *asýmptōt(os)* = *a-* A-[6] + *sýmptōtos* falling together (*sym-* SYM- + *ptōtós* falling < *ptō-,* var. s. of *píptein* to fall, + *-tos* verbid suffix)]

as·ymp·tot·ic (as′im tot′ik), *adj.* *Math.* **1.** of or pertaining to an asymptote. **2.** (of a function) approaching a given value as an expression containing a variable tends to infinity. Also, **as′ymp·tot′i·cal.** —**as′ymp·tot′i·cal·ly,** *adv.*

a·syn·chro·nism (ā sing′krə niz′əm, ā sin′-), *n.* want of synchronism, or coincidence in time. —**a·syn′chro·nous,** *adj.* —**a·syn′chro·nous·ly,** *adv.*

a·syn·de·ton (ə sin′di ton′, -tən), *n.* *Rhet.* the omission of conjunctions, as in "He has provided the poor with jobs, with opportunity, with self-respect." [< L < Gk, n. use of neut. of *asýndetos* not linked (*a-* A-[6] + *syndé(ein)* (to) link + *-tos* verbid suffix)] —**as·yn·det·ic** (as′in det′ik), *adj.* —**as′yn·det′i·cal·ly,** *adv.*

A·syut (ä syōōt′), *n.* a city in central Egypt, on the Nile. 284,000. Also, **A·syût′, Assiut.**

at[1] (at; *unstressed* ət, it), *prep.* **1.** (used to indicate a point or place occupied in space) in, on, or near: *to stand at the door; at the bottom of the barrel.* **2.** (used to indicate a location or position, as in time, on a scale, or in order): *at noon; at age 65.* **3.** (used to indicate presence or location): *at home; at hand.* **4.** (used to indicate amount, degree, or rate): *at great speed; at high altitudes.* **5.** (used to indicate a goal or objective) toward: *Aim at the mark. Look at that!* **6.** (used to indicate occupation or involvement): *at work; at play.* **7.** (used to indicate a state or condition): *at ease; at peace.* **8.** (used to indicate a cause): *She was annoyed at his stupidity.* **9.** (used to indicate a method or manner): *He spoke at length.* **10.** (used to indicate relative quality or value): *at one's best; at cost.* [ME; OE *æt;* c. Icel, OS, Goth *at,* OHG *az,* L *ad*] —**Usage.** See **about.**

at[2] (ät, at), *n., pl.* **at.** a money of account of Laos, the 100th part of a kip. [< Siamese]

at-, var. of **ad-** before *t: attend.*

AT, *Mil.* antitank.

At, *Elect.* ampere-turn.

At, *Chem.* astatine.

at., **1.** atmosphere. **2.** atomic. **3.** attorney.

-ata[1], a plural suffix occurring in loan words from Latin, used esp. in names of zoological groups. [< L, neut. pl. of *-ātus* -ATE[1]]

-ata[2], a plural suffix occurring in loan words from Greek: *stomata.* [< Gk *t*-stems, *-(m)ata* result of, state of, act of; cf. -MENT]

At·a·brine (at′ə brin, -brēn′), *n.* *Pharm., Trademark.* quinacrine.

at·a·ghan (at′ə gan′), *n.* yataghan.

A·ta·hual·pa (ä′tä wäl′pä), *n.* c1500–33, last Incan king of Peru (son of Huayna Capac).

At·a·lan·ta (at′ᵊlan′tə), *n.* *Class. Myth.* a virgin huntress who promised to marry the man who could win a foot race against her: she finally lost to Hippomenes, who distracted her attention by dropping three golden apples given to him by Aphrodite. Also, **At·a·lan·te** (at′ᵊlan′tē).

at·a·man (at′ə mən), *n., pl.* **-mans.** a chief of Cossacks, elected by the whole group; hetman. [< Russ]

at′a·mas′co lil′y (at′ə mas′kō, at′-), **1.** an amaryllidaceous plant, *Zephyranthes atamasco,* of the southeastern U.S., bearing a single white lilylike flower. **2.** any species of this genus. Also called **at′a·mas′co.** [< AmerInd (Virginia)]

at·a·rax·i·a (at′ə rak′sē ə), *n.* a state of tranquillity, free from emotional disturbance and anxiety. Also, **at·a·rax·y** (at′ə rak′sē). [< L < Gk: calmness = *atarak(tós)* unmoved (*a-* A-[6] + *tarak-,* var. s. of *tarássein* to disturb + *-tos* verbid suffix) + *-s(is)* -SIS + *-ia* -IA] —**at·a·rac·tic** (at′ə rak′tik), **at′a·rax′ic,** *adj., n.*

A·ta·türk (at′ə tûrk′, ä tä tûrk′), *n.* See **Kemal Atatürk.**

at·a·vism (at′ə viz′əm), *n.* **1.** *Biol.* the reappearance in a plant or animal of characteristics of some remote ancestor that have been absent in intervening generations. **2.** a plant or animal embodying such a reversion. **3.** reversion to an earlier type. [< L *atav(us)* remote ancestor (*at-* father + *avus* grandfather, forefather) + -ISM] —**at′a·vist,** *n.*

at·a·vis·tic (at′ə vis′tik), *adj.* of, pertaining to, or characterized by atavism; reverting to or suggesting the characteristics of a remote ancestor or a primitive or earlier type: *Hitler's attack on Russia was prompted by the atavistic impulse to go east.* —**at′a·vis′ti·cal·ly,** *adv.*

a·tax·i·a (ə tak′sē ə), *n.* *Pathol.* loss of coordination of the muscles, esp. of the extremities. Also, **a·tax·y** (ə tak′sē, a tak′-). Cf. **tabes dorsalis.** [< NL < Gk = *a-* A-[6] + *táx(is)* -TAXIS + *-ia* -IA] —**a·tax′ic,** *adj.*

At·ba·ra (ät′bə rə, at′-), *n.* **1.** a river in NE Africa, flowing NW from NW Ethiopia to the Nile in E Sudan. ab. 500 mi. long. **2.** a city in NE Sudan. 45,000 (est. 1964).

ATC, **1.** Air Traffic Control. **2.** Air Transport Command.

ate (āt; *Brit.* et), *v.* a pt. of **eat.**

A·te (ā′tē), *n.* an ancient Greek goddess personifying the fatal blindness or recklessness that produces crime and the divine punishment that follows it. [< Gk, special use of *átē* reckless impulse, ruin, akin to *aáein* to mislead, harm]

-ate[1], a suffix occurring in loan words from Latin, its English distribution paralleling that of Latin. The form originated as a suffix added to *a*-stem verbs to form adjectives (*separate*). The resulting form could also be used independently as a noun (*magistrate; advocate*) and came to be used as a stem on which a verb could be formed (*separate; advocate; agitate*). In English the use as a verbal suffix has been extended to stems of non-Latin origin: *calibrate.* [< L *-ātus* (masc.), *-āta* (fem.), *-ātum* (neut.) = *-ā-* thematic vowel + *-tus, -ta, -tum* ptp. suffix]

-ate[2], *Chem.* a specialization of **-ate**[1], used to indicate a salt of an acid ending in **-ic,** added to a form of the stem of the element or group: *sulfate.* Cf. **-ite**[3]. [< L *-ātum,* neut. of *-ātus* -ATE[1]]

-ate[3], a suffix forming nouns indicating condition, estate, office, group, etc.: *episcopate; consulate; senate.* [< L *-ātus* (gen. *-ātūs*) 4th-decl. n. suffix]

at·e·brin (at′ə brin, -brēn′), *n. Pharm.* quinacrine.

a·tel·ic (a tel′ik), *adj.* imperfective. Cf. **telic** (def. 3).

at·el·ier (at′^{ə}l yā′; *Fr.* A T^{ə} lyā′), *n., pl.* **at·el·iers** (at′^{ə}l-yāz′; *Fr.* A T^{ə} lyā′). a workshop or studio, esp. of an artist, artisan, or craftsman. [< F: lit., pile of chips (hence, workshop); OF *astele* chip (< LL *astella,* dim. of L *astula,* var. of *assula* splinter = *ass(is)* plank + *-ula* -ULE) + *-ier* < L *-iārium;* see -ARY]

a tem·po (ä tem′pō; *It.* ä tem′pô), *Music.* resuming the speed that obtained preceding a ritardando or accelerando. [< It: in (the regular) time]

A·ten (ät′^{ə}n), *n.* Aton.

a ter·go (ä teR′gō), *Latin.* at the back; from behind.

à terre (*Fr.* A teR′), *Ballet.* on the ground. [< F]

Ath·a·bas·can (ath′ə bas′kən), *n., adj.* Athapaskan. Also, **Ath′a·bas′kan.**

Ath·a·bas·ka (ath′ə bas′kə), *n.* **1. Lake,** a lake in W Canada, in NW Saskatchewan and NE Alberta. ab. 200 mi. long; ab. 3000 sq. mi. **2.** a river in W Canada flowing NE from W Alberta to Lake Athabaska. 765 mi. long.

ath·a·na·sia (ath′ə nā′zhə), *n.* deathlessness; immortality. [< Gk *athanā(tos)* deathless (*a-* A-[6] + *thánatos* death) + *-sia* (*-s(is)* -SIS + *-ia* -IA)]

Athana′sian Creed′, a creed or formulary of Christian faith, formerly ascribed to Athanasius.

Ath·a·na·sius (ath′ə nā′shəs), *n.* **Saint,** A.D. 296?–373, Greek bishop of Alexandria: opponent of Arianism. **—Ath·a·na·sian** (ath′ə nā′zhən), *adj., n.*

Ath·a·pas·kan (ath′ə pas′kən), *n.* **1.** a family of languages spoken by American Indians in Canada, Alaska, Oregon, California, Arizona, and the Rio Grande basin, including esp. Navaho, Apache, etc. **2.** a member of any of various American Indian peoples speaking Athapaskan. **—***adj.* **3.** belonging to or characteristic of the Athapaskans. Also, **Ath′a·pas′can, Athabascan, Athabaskan.** [*Athapask(a),* name of an aboriginal N American people + -AN]

A·thar·va-Ve·da (ə tär′və vā′də, -vē′də), *n. Hinduism.* one of the Samhitas, a collection of mantras and formulas, some showing pre-Vedic influence. Cf. **Veda.**

a·the·ism (ā′thē iz′əm), *n.* **1.** the doctrine or belief that there is no God or gods (opposed to *theism*). **2.** ungodliness, immorality, or wickedness. [< Gk *áthe(os)* godless + -ISM]

a·the·ist (ā′thē ist), *n.* a person who denies or disbelieves the existence of God or gods. [< Gk *áthe(os)* godless + -IST] **—a′the·is′tic, a′the·is′ti·cal,** *adj.* **—a′the·is′ti·cal·ly,** *adv.* **—Syn.** ATHEIST, AGNOSTIC, INFIDEL refer to persons not inclined toward religious belief or a particular form of religious belief. An ATHEIST is one who denies the existence of a Deity or of divine beings. An AGNOSTIC is one who believes it impossible to know anything about God or about the creation of the universe and refrains from committing himself to any religious doctrine. INFIDEL means an unbeliever, esp. a nonbeliever in Islam or Christianity.

ath·el·ing (ath′ə ling, ath′-), *n. Early Eng. Hist.* a man of royal blood; a prince. [ME; OE *ætheling* (c. OHG *ediling, adalung,* OS *ethiling*) = *æthel(u)* noble family + *-ing* suffix of appurtenance]

Ath·el·stan (ath′əl stan′), *n.* A.D. 895?–940, king of England 925–940.

a·the·mat·ic (ā′thē mat′ik), *adj.* inflected without a thematic vowel.

A·the·na (ə thē′nə), *n.* the ancient Greek goddess of wisdom, fertility, the useful arts, and prudent warfare: identified by the Romans with Minerva. Also, **A·the·ne** (ə thē′nē). Also called **Pallas, Pallas Athena.**

Athena

ath·e·nae·um (ath′ə nē′əm), *n.* **1.** an institution or society for the promotion of literary or scientific learning. **2.** a library. Also, **ath′e·ne′um.** [< L < Gk *Athḗnaion* temple of Athena, where poets read their works]

Ath·e·nag·o·ras I (ath′ə nag′ər əs; *Gk.* ä thē′nä gô′räs), (*Aristocles Spyrou*) 1886–1972, archbishop ecumenical of Constantinople and ecumenical patriarch of the Greek Orthodox Church 1948–1972.

A·the·ni·an (ə thē′nē ən) *adj.* **1.** pertaining to Athens, Greece. **—***n.* **2.** a native or citizen of Athens, Greece. [< L *Athēni(ēnsis)* of Athens + -AN; see -ESE]

Ath·ens (ath′inz), *n.* **1.** Greek, **A·the·nai** (ä thē′ne). a city in and the capital of Greece, in the SE part. 867,000; with suburbs, 2,540,000. **2.** a city in N Georgia. 44,342 (1970).

ath·er·o·ma (ath′ə rō′mə), *n., pl.* **-mas, -ma·ta** (-mə tə). *Pathol.* **1.** a sebaceous cyst. **2.** a condition characterized by the deposit of fat in the inner linings of the arterial walls. [< L: a tumor filled with matter < Gk *atherōma* = *athḗr(ē),* var. of *athár(ē)* gruel + *-ōma* -OMA]

ath·er·o·scle·ro·sis (ath′ə rō sklə rō′sis, ath′-), *n. Pathol.* a form of arteriosclerosis in which fatty substances deposit in and beneath the intima. [< NL < Gk *athḗr(ē)* (see ATHEROMA) + -o- + SCLEROSIS] **—ath·er·o·scle·rot·ic** (ath′ə rō sklə rot′ik, ath′-), *adj.*

Ath·er·ton (ath′ər tən), *n.* **Gertrude Franklin,** nee **Horn,** 1857–1948, U.S. novelist.

a·thirst (ə thûrst′), *adj.* **1.** having a keen desire; eager (often fol. by *for*). **2.** thirsty. [ME *athurst, ofthurst,* OE *ofthyrst,* ptp. of *ofthyrstan.* See A-[2], THIRST]

ath·lete (ath′lēt), *n.* **1.** a person trained to compete in contests involving physical agility, stamina, or strength; a trained competitor in a sport, exercise, or game requiring physical skill. **2.** *Brit.* (traditionally) a person trained for and competing in track-and-field events. [< L *āthlēt(a)* < Gk *āthlētḗ(s)* = *āthlē-* (var. s. of *āthléein* to contend for a prize < *âthlos* a contest) + *-tēs* suffix of agency]

ath′lete's foot′, *Pathol.* a contagious disease, caused by a fungus that thrives on moist surfaces.

ath′lete's heart′, *Pathol.* enlargement of the heart resulting from excessive exercise. Also, **athlet′ic heart′.**

ath·let·ic (ath let′ik), *adj.* **1.** physically active and strong. **2.** of, like, or befitting an athlete. **3.** of or pertaining to athletics. **4.** *Psychol.* (of a physical type) having a sturdy build or well-proportioned body structure. Cf. **asthenic** (def. 2), **pyknic** (def. 1). [< L *athletic(us)* < Gk *āthlētikós*] **—ath·let′i·cal·ly,** *adv.*

ath·let·ics (ath let′iks), *n.* **1.** (*usually construed as pl.*) athletic sports, as running, rowing, boxing, etc. **2.** *Brit.* (traditionally) track-and-field events. **3.** (*usually construed as sing.*) the practice of athletic exercises; the principles of athletic training. [see ATHLETIC, -ICS]

athlet′ic support′er, jockstrap.

ath·o·dyd (ath′ə did), *n.* a ramjet. [*a(ero)-th(erm)ody(namic) d(uct)*]

at-home (at hōm′), *n.* a reception of visitors at one's home during certain announced hours. Also, **at home′.**

Ath·os (ath′ōs, ā′thos; *Gk.* ä′thôs), *n.* **Mount,** the easternmost of three prongs of the peninsula of Chalcidice, in NE Greece: site of an autonomous republic constituted of 20 monasteries. 2687 (1961). 131 sq. mi.; ab. 35 mi. long.

a·thwart (ə thwôrt′), *adv.* **1.** from side to side; crosswise. **2.** perversely; awry; wrongly. **3.** *Naut.* **a.** at right angles to the fore-and-aft line; across. **b.** broadside to the wind because of equal and opposite pressures of wind and tide: *a ship riding athwart.* **—***prep.* **4.** from side to side of; across. **5.** in opposition to. **6.** *Naut.* across the direction or course of.

a·thwart·ships (ə thwôrt′ships), *adv. Naut.* from one side of a ship to the other.

a·tilt (ə tilt′), *adj., adv.* **1.** at a tilt; inclined. **2.** in a tilting encounter.

a·tin·gle (ə ting′gəl), *adj.* tingling.

-ation, a combination of **-ate**[1] and **-ion,** used to form nouns from stems in **-ate**[1] (*separation*); on this model, used independently to form nouns from stems of other origin: *flirtation.* [< L *-ātiōn-* (s. of *-ātiō*) = *-āt(us)* -ATE[1] + *-iōn-* -ION; identical with G *-ation,* F *-ation,* etc.]

-ative, a combination of **-ate**[1] and **-ive,** used to form adjectives from stems in **-ate**[1] (*regulative*); on this model, used independently to form adjectives from stems of other origin: *explanative.* [< L *-ātīv(us)* = *-āt(us)* -ATE[1] + *-īvus* -IVE]

At·kins (at′kinz), *n., pl.* **-kins.** See **Tommy Atkins.**

At·lan·ta (at lan′tə), *n.* a city in and the capital of Georgia, in the N part. 497,421 (1970).

At·lan·te·an (at′lan tē′ən, -lən-), *adj.* **1.** pertaining to the demigod Atlas. **2.** having the strength of Atlas. **3.** pertaining to Atlantis. [< L *Atlantē(us)* (< Gk *Atlánteios* of ATLAS = *Atlant-,* s. of *Átlas,* + *-eios* adj. suffix) + -AN]

at·lan·tes (at lan′tēz), *n.* pl. of **atlas** (def. 8).

At·lan·tic (at lan′tik), *adj.* **1.** of or pertaining to the Atlantic Ocean. **—***n.* **2.** See **Atlantic Ocean.** [< L *Atlantic(um)* (*mare*) the Atlantic (ocean), neut. of *Atlanticus* < Gk *Atlantikós* of (Mount) ATLAS = *Atlant-* (s. of *Átlas*) + *-ikos* -IC]

Atlan′tic Char′ter, the joint declaration of President Roosevelt and Prime Minister Churchill (August 14, 1941), setting forth the postwar aims of their respective governments.

Atlan′tic Cit′y, a city in SE New Jersey: seashore resort. 47,859 (1970).

At·lan·ti·cist (at lan′ti sist′), *n.* an adherent or supporter of close military, political, and economic cooperation between Western Europe and the United States. [(NORTH) ATLANTIC (TREATY ORGANIZATION) + -IST]

Atlan′tic O′cean, an ocean bounded by North America and South America in the Western Hemisphere and by Europe and Africa in the Eastern Hemisphere. ab. 31,530,000 sq. mi.; with connecting seas, ab. 41,000,000 sq. mi.; greatest known depth, 30,246 ft. Also called **the Atlantic.**

Atlan′tic Prov′inces, the Canadian provinces bordering the Atlantic Ocean: New Brunswick, Newfoundland, Nova Scotia, and Prince Edward Island.

At·lan·tis (at lan′tis), *n.* a mythical island in the Atlantic Ocean west of Gibraltar, said to have sunk into the sea.

at·las (at′ləs), *n., pl.* **at·las·es** for 1–3, 5, 7, **at·lan·tes** (at lan′tēz) for 8. **1.** a bound collection of maps. **2.** a bound volume of charts, plates, or tables illustrating any subject. **3.** *Anat.* the first cervical vertebra, which supports the head. **4.** (*cap.*) *Class. Myth.* a Titan, a brother of Prometheus, condemned to support the sky on his shoulders. **5.** (*cap.*) a person who bears a heavy burden; mainstay. **6.** a size of drawing or writing paper, 26 × 34 or 33 inches. **7.** (*cap.*) *U.S.* a liquid-propelled intercontinental ballistic missile. **8.** Also called **telamon.** *Archit.* a figure of a man used as a column. Cf. **caryatid.** [< L < Gk; akin to *tlênai* to suffer, endure, bear]

At′las Moun′tains, a mountain range in NW Africa, extending through Morocco, Algeria, and Tunisia. Highest peak, Mt. Tizi, 14,764 ft.

At·li (ät′lē), *n. Scand. Legend.* Attila, king of the Huns: represented in the *Volsunga Saga* as the brother of Brynhild and the second husband of Gudrun, whose brothers he kills in order to get the Nibelung treasure. Cf. **Etzel.**

atm., **1.** atmosphere (def. 5). **2.** atmospheric.

at. m., See **atomic mass.**

at·man (ät′mən), *n. Hinduism.* **1.** the individual self, known after enlightenment to be identical with Brahman. **2.** (*cap.*) the World Soul, from which all souls derive and to which they return as the supreme goal of existence. Also, **at·ma** (ät′mə). [< Skt *ātman* breath. See ATMO-]

at·mo-, a learned borrowing from Greek meaning "air," used in the formation of compound words: *atmosphere.* [< Gk *atmó(s)* vapor, smoke; c. Skt *ātman*, OE *ǣthm* breath]

at·mol·y·sis (at mol′i sis), *n., pl.* **-ses** (-sēz′). a process for separating gases or vapors of different molecular weights by transmission through a porous substance.

at·mom·e·ter (at mom′i tər), *n.* an instrument for measuring the rate of water evaporation. Also called **evaporimeter, evaporometer, evaporation gauge.**

at·mos·phere (at′məs fēr′), *n.* **1.** the gaseous envelope surrounding the earth; the air. **2.** this medium at a given place. **3.** *Astron.* the gaseous envelope surrounding a celestial body. **4.** *Chem.* any gaseous envelope or medium. **5.** a conventional unit of pressure, the normal pressure of the air at sea level, about 14.7 pounds per square inch. *Abbr.:* atm. **6.** a pervading influence; environment: *an atmosphere of peace.* **7.** the dominant mood or emotional tone of a work of art, as of a play or novel. **8.** a distinctive quality, as of a place. [< NL *atmosphaer(a)*] **—at′mos·phere′less,** *adj.*

at·mos·pher·ic (at′məs fer′ik), *adj.* **1.** pertaining to, existing in, or consisting of the atmosphere: *atmospheric vapors.* **2.** caused, produced, or operated on by the atmosphere: *atmospheric storms.* **3.** resembling or suggestive of the atmosphere; having muted tones and softened or indistinct outlines; hazy: *atmospheric effects.* **4.** having or producing an emotional atmosphere: *atmospheric lighting.* Also, **at′mos·pher′i·cal. —at′mos·pher′i·cal·ly,** *adv.*

at′mospher′ic pres′sure, *Meteorol.* **1.** the pressure exerted by the earth's atmosphere at any given point. **2.** a value of standard or normal atmospheric pressure, equivalent to the pressure exerted by a column of mercury 760 millimeters (29.92 inches) high, or 1013.2 millibars. Also called **barometric pressure.**

at·mos·pher·ics (at′məs fer′iks), *n.* (*construed as pl.*) *Radio.* **1.** noise caused in a radio receiver by natural electromagnetic disturbances in the atmosphere. **2.** natural phenomena causing this interference. Also called **spherics.** [see ATMOSPHERIC, -ICS]

at. no., See **atomic number.**

at·oll (at′ôl, -ol, -ōl, ə tôl′, ə tol′, ə tōl′), *n.* a ring-shaped coral reef or a string of closely spaced small coral islands, enclosing or nearly enclosing a shallow lagoon. [var. of *atollon*, native name in Maldive Islands]

at·om (at′əm), *n.* **1.** *Physics.* the smallest component of an element having all the properties of the element, consisting of an aggregate of protons, neutrons, and electrons such that the number of protons determines the element. **2.** a hypothetical particle of matter so minute as to admit of no division. **3.** anything extremely small; a minute quantity. [ME *attomos, athomus* < L *atomus* < Gk *ătomos*, n. use of *ătomos* undivided = *a-* A-[6] + *tomós* divided, verbal of *témnein* to cut] **—Syn. 3.** iota, jot, whit.

at′om bomb′. See **atomic bomb.**

a·tom·ic (ə tom′ik), *adj.* **1.** of, pertaining to, resulting from, using, or operated by atoms, atomic energy, or atomic bombs: *an atomic explosion; an atomic submarine.* **2.** *Chem.* existing as free, uncombined atoms. **3.** extremely minute. Also, **a·tom′i·cal. —a·tom′i·cal·ly,** *adv.*

atom′ic age′, the period in history initiated by the first use of the atomic bomb (1945) and characterized by atomic energy as a military, political, and industrial factor.

atom′ic bomb′, a bomb whose explosive force comes from a chain reaction based on the nuclear fission of atoms of U-235 or plutonium with the consequent conversion of part of their mass into energy. Also, **atom bomb.** Also called **A-bomb, fission bomb.**

atom′ic clock′, *Physics.* an extremely accurate electric clock regulated by the resonance frequency of atoms or molecules of certain substances, as cesium.

atom′ic cock′tail, *Slang.* an oral dose of a radioactive substance used in the treatment or diagnosis of cancer.

atom′ic en′ergy, energy released by rearrangements of atomic nuclei, as in nuclear fission or fusion. Also called **nuclear energy.**

Atom′ic En′ergy Commis′sion, *U.S. Govt.* the board administering all federal programs dealing with nonmilitary uses of atomic energy. *Abbr.:* AEC

at·o·mic·i·ty (at′ə mis′i tē), *n.* *Chem.* **1.** the number of atoms in the molecule of a gas. **2.** valence.

atom′ic mass′, *Chem.* the mass of an isotope of an element measured in units formerly based on the weight of one hydrogen atom taken as a unit or on $^1/_{16}$ the weight of one oxygen atom, but after 1961 based on $^1/_{12}$ the weight of the carbon-12 atom. *Abbr.:* at. m.

atom′ic mass′ u′nit, *Physics.* **1.** a unit of mass, equal to $^1/_{12}$ the mass of a carbon-12 atom and used to express the mass of atomic and subatomic particles. **2.** (formerly) a unit of mass equal to $^1/_{16}$ the mass of an oxygen (isotope 16) atom. *Abbr.:* amu

atom′ic num′ber, the number of positive charges or protons in the nucleus of an atom of a given element, and therefore also the number of electrons normally surrounding the nucleus. *Abbr.:* at. no.; *Symbol:* Z

atom′ic pile′, *Physics.* reactor (def. 4).

a·tom·ics (ə tom′iks), *n.* (*construed as sing.*) *Informal.* the branch of physics that deals with atoms, esp. atomic energy. [see ATOMIC, -ICS]

atom′ic struc′ture, *Physics.* the structure of an atom, theoretically consisting of a positively charged nucleus surrounded and neutralized by negatively charged electrons revolving in orbits at varying distances from the nucleus.

atom′ic the′ory, *Physics, Chem.* any of several theories describing the structure, behavior, and other properties of the atom and its component parts.

atom′ic vol′ume, *Chem.* the atomic weight of an element divided by its density. *Abbr.:* at. vol.

atom′ic weight′, *Chem.* the average weight of an atom of an element, formerly based on the weight of one hydrogen atom taken as a unit or on $^1/_{16}$ the weight of an oxygen atom, but after 1961 based on $^1/_{12}$ the weight of the carbon-12 atom. *Abbr.:* at. wt.

at·om·ise (at′ə mīz′), *v.t.,* **-ised, -is·ing.** *Chiefly Brit.* atomize. **—at′om·i·sa′tion,** *n.*

at·om·ism (at′ə miz′əm), *n.* *Philos.* the theory that minute, discrete, finite, and indivisible elements are the ultimate constituents of all matter. **—at′om·ist,** *n.* **—at′om·is′tic, at′om·is′ti·cal,** *adj.* **—at′om·is′ti·cal·ly,** *adv.*

at·om·ize (at′ə mīz′), *v.t.,* **-ized, -iz·ing. 1.** to reduce to atoms. **2.** to reduce to fine particles or spray. **3.** to destroy (a target) by bombing, esp. with an atomic bomb. Also, *esp. Brit.,* **atomise. —at′om·i·za′tion,** *n.*

at·om·iz·er (at′ə mī′zər), *n.* an apparatus for reducing liquids to a fine spray, as for medicinal or perfumery application.

at′om smash′er, *Physics.* accelerator (def. 5).

at·o·my[1] (at′ə mē), *n., pl.* **-mies.** *Archaic.* **1.** an atom; mote. **2.** a small creature; pygmy. [< L *atomī*, pl. of *atomus* ATOM used as sing.]

at·o·my[2] (at′ə mē), *n., pl.* **-mies.** *Obs.* a skeleton. [var. of ANATOMY (taken as *an atomy*)]

A·ton (ä′tən), *n.* *Egyptian Religion.* a solar deity declared by Amenhotep IV to be the only god: represented as a solar disk with rays ending in human hands. Also, **Aten.**

a·ton·al (ā tōn′əl), *adj.* *Music.* having no key; twelve-tone. **—a·ton′al·ism,** *n.* **—a·ton′al·is′tic,** *adj.* **—a·to·nal·i·ty** (ā′tō nal′i tē), *n.* **—a·ton′al·ly,** *adv.*

a·tone (ə tōn′), *v.,* **a·toned, a·ton·ing.** **—***v.i.* **1.** to make amends or reparation, as for an offense or a crime (usually fol. by *for*): *to atone for one's sins.* **2.** to make up, as for errors or defiencies (usually fol. by *for*): *to atone for one's failings.* **3.** *Obs.* to become reconciled; agree. **—***v.t.* **4.** to make amends for; expiate. **5.** *Obs.* to bring into unity, harmony, concord, etc. [back formation from ATONEMENT] **—a·ton′a·ble, a·tone′a·ble,** *adj.* **—a·ton′er,** *n.* **—a·ton′ing·ly,** *adv.*

a·tone·ment (ə tōn′mənt), *n.* **1.** satisfaction or reparation for a wrong or injury; amends. **2.** (*sometimes cap.*) *Theol.* the doctrine that the reconciliation of God and man will be accomplished through Christ. **3.** *Christian Science.* the state in which man exemplifies the attributes of God. **4.** *Archaic.* reconciliation; agreement. [from phrase *at onement* at unity (AT[1] + ME *onement*, now obs.); see ONE, -MENT]

a·ton·ic (ə ton′ik, ā ton′-), *adj.* **1.** *Phonet.* **a.** unaccented. **b.** *Obs.* voiceless. **2.** *Pathol.* characterized by atony. **—***n.* **3.** *Gram.* an unaccented word, syllable, or sound. [< medical L *atonic(us)* = *aton(ia)* ATONY + *-icus* -IC]

at·o·nic·i·ty (at′ənis′i tē, ā′tō nis′-), *n.* *Pathol.* lack of tone; atony.

at·o·ny (at′ənē), *n.* **1.** *Pathol.* lack of tone or energy; muscular weakness, esp. in a contractile organ. **2.** *Phonet.* lack of stress accent. [< medical L *atonia* < Gk < *átonos* unaccented, languid, lit., toneless]

a·top (ə top′), *adj., adv.* **1.** on or at the top. **—***prep.* **2.** on the top of: *atop the flagpole.*

-ator, a combination of **-ate**[1] and **-or**[2], used to form agent nouns from stems in **-ate**[1] (*separator*); on this model, used independently to form agent nouns from stems of other origin: *cinerator.* Cf. **-atrix.** [< L = *-āt(us)* -ATE[1] + *-or* -OR[2]]

-atory, a combination of **-ate**[1] and **-ory,** used to form nouns or adjectives from stems in **-ate**[1] (*oratory; migratory*); on this model, used independently to form nouns or adjectives from stems of other origin: *reformatory; explanatory.* [< L *-ātōri(us)* = *-ātōr-* (s. of *-ātor* -ATOR) + *-ius* adj. suffix]

ATP, *Biochem.* an ester of adenosine and triphosphoric acid, $C_{10}H_{12}N_5O_3H_4P_3O_9$, serving as a source of energy for physiological reactions, esp. muscle contraction. Also called **adenosine triphosphate.**

at·ra·bil·ious (a′trə bil′yəs), *adj.* **1.** sad; gloomy. **2.** irritable; bad-tempered. Also, **at′ra·bil′iar.** [< L *ātra bīli(s)* black bile + -OUS] **—at′ra·bil′ious·ness,** *n.*

a·trem·ble (ə trem′bəl), *adv.* in a trembling state.

A·tre·us (ā′trē əs, ā′trōōs), *n.* *Class. Myth.* the father of Plisthenes, Agamemnon, and Menelaus, upon whose house Thyestes pronounced a curse.

a·tri·o·ven·tric·u·lar (ā′trē ō ven trik′yə lər), *adj.* *Anat.* of or pertaining to the atria and ventricles of the heart. [< NL *atrio-* (comb. form of *atrium* heart chamber; see ATRIUM) + VENTRICULAR]

a·trip (ə trip′), *adj.* *Naut.* (of an anchor) clear of the bottom; aweigh. [A-[1] + TRIP]

a·tri·um (ā′trē əm), *n., pl.* **a·tri·a** (ā′trē ə). **1.** *Archit.* **a.** the main or central room of an ancient Roman house, open to the sky at the center. **b.** a courtyard, flanked or surrounded by porticoes, in front of an early or medieval Christian church. **2.** *Anat.* either of the two upper chambers on each side of the heart that receive blood from the veins and in turn force it into the ventricles. [< L (anatomical sense in NL)] **—a′tri·al,** *adj.*

-atrix, a suffix used as the feminine form of **-ator:** *aviatrix.* [< L = *-āt(o)r* -ATOR+ *-īx* fem. suffix]

a·tro·cious (ə trō′shəs), *adj.* **1.** extremely or shockingly wicked, cruel, or brutal: *atrocious behavior; an atrocious crime.* **2.** *Informal.* in shockingly bad taste; dreadful: *an atrocious painting.* [ATROCI(TY) + -OUS] **—a·tro′cious·ly,** *adv.* **—a·tro′cious·ness,** *n.* **—Syn. 1.** diabolical. **2.** tasteless.

a·troc·i·ty (ə tros′i tē), *n., pl.* **-ties** for 2, 4. **1.** the quality or state of being atrocious. **2.** an atrocious act, thing, or circumstance. **3. atrocities,** savagely cruel acts toward enemy civilians or prisoners by a military force. **4.** *Informal.* something in shockingly bad taste. [< L *atrōcitāt-* (s. of *atrōcitās*) = *atrōci-* (s. of *atrōx*) fierce + *-tāt-* -TY[2]]

à trois (A trwä′), *French.* for, among, or composed of three persons collectively: *a secret shared* à trois.

at·ro·phied (a′trə fēd), *adj.* exhibiting or affected with atrophy; wasted.

at·ro·phy (a′trə fē), *n., v.,* **-phied, -phy·ing.** **—***n.* **1.** Also, **a·tro·phi·a** (ə trō′fē ə). *Pathol.* a wasting away of the body or of an organ or part, as from defective nutrition or other cause. **2.** degeneration; decline; decrease, as from disuse: *an atrophy of talent.* **—***v.t., v.i.* **3.** to affect with or undergo atrophy. [earlier *atrophie* < medical L *atrophia* < Gk = *átroph(os)* not fed (see A-[6], TROPHO-) + *-ia* -IA] **—a·troph·ic** (ə trof′ik), *adj.*

at·ro·pine (a′trə pēn′, -pin), *n.* *Pharm.* a poisonous alkaloid, $C_{17}H_{23}NO_3$, obtained from belladonna and other solanaceous plants, that prevents the response of various body structures to certain types of nerve stimulation: used chiefly to relieve spasms, lessen secretions, and to dilate the pupil of the eye. [< NL *Atrop(a)* belladonna genus (< Gk *átropos*; see ATROPOS) + -INE[2]]

at·ro·pism (a′trə piz′əm), *n. Pathol.* poisoning resulting from atropine or belladonna. [ATROP(INE) + -ISM]
At·ro·pos (a′trə pos′), *n. Class. Myth.* the Fate who cuts the thread of life. Cf. **Clotho, Lachesis.** [< Gk: lit., not turning, hence, inflexible. See A-6, -TROPE]
att., attorney.
at·tach (ə tach′), *v.t.* **1.** to fasten or affix; join; connect. **2.** to join in action or function; make part of: *to attach oneself to a group.* **3.** *Mil.* to place on temporary duty with a military unit. **4.** to include as a quality or condition of something: *One proviso is attached to this legacy.* **5.** to assign or attribute: *to attach significance to a gesture.* **6.** to bind by ties of affection or regard. **7.** *Law.* to take (persons or property) by legal authority. —*v.i.* **8.** to adhere; pertain; belong (usually fol. by *to* or *upon*): *No blame attaches to him.* [ME *atache(n)* < AF *atache(r)* (to) seize, OF *atachier* to fasten, alter. of *estachier* to fasten with or to a stake = *estach(e)* (< Gmc **stakka* a STAKE) + *-ier* inf. suffix; prefix *a-* (see A-5) r. supposed prefix *es-* (see EX-1)] —**at·tach′a·ble,** adj. —**Syn. 1.** append, add, annex. —**Ant. 1.** detach.
at·ta·ché (at′ə shā′, a ta- *or, esp. Brit.,* ə tash′ā; *Fr.* A TA-SHĀ′), *n., pl.* **at·ta·chés** (at′ə shāz′, a ta- *or, esp. Brit.,* ə tash′āz; *Fr.* A TA SHĀ′). a diplomatic official or military officer attached to an embassy or legation, esp. in a technical capacity: *a cultural attaché; a naval attaché.* [< F: lit., attached, ptp. of *attacher* to ATTACH]
attaché′ case′, a briefcase with square corners and rigid sides. Also called **dispatch case.**
at·tached (ə tacht′), *adj.* **1.** joined; connected; bound. **2.** having a wall in common with another building (opposed to *detached*): *an attached house.* **3.** *Zool.* permanently fixed to the substratum; sessile.
at·tach·ment (ə tach′mənt), *n.* **1.** the act of attaching. **2.** the state of being attached. **3.** a feeling that binds one to a person, thing, cause, ideal, etc.; devotion; regard: *a close attachment to her sister.* **4.** something that attaches; a fastening or tie. **5.** an additional or supplementary device: *attachments for an electric mixer.* **6.** *Law.* seizure of property or person by legal authority, esp. seizure of a defendant's property to prevent its dissipation before trial or to acquire jurisdiction over it. [late ME *attachment* seizure < AF] —**Syn. 3.** love, devotedness. **5.** See **addition.**
at·tack (ə tak′), *v.t.* **1.** to set upon forcefully, violently, hostilely, or aggressively with or without a weapon: *He attacked him with his bare hands.* **2.** to begin hostilities against: *to attack the enemy.* **3.** to blame or abuse violently or bitterly. **4.** to direct unfavorable criticism against. **5.** to set about (a task) vigorously: *to attack housecleaning.* **6.** (of disease, destructive agencies, etc.) to begin to affect. **7.** to assault sexually; rape or attempt to rape. —*v.i.* **8.** to make an attack; begin hostilities. —*n.* **9.** the act of attacking; onslaught; assault. **10.** a military offensive against an enemy or enemy position. **11.** *Pathol.* a seizure by disease or illness: *an attack of indigestion.* **12.** the beginning or initiating of any action; onset. **13.** an aggressive move in a performance or contest. **14.** a sexual assault; rape or an attempted rape. [earlier *atta(c)que* < MF *atta(c)quer* < It *attaccare* to attack, ATTACH] —**at·tack′er,** *n.* —**Syn. 1.** storm, charge, set upon. **4.** criticize, censure; impugn. **9.** onset, encounter. —**Ant. 1.** defend. **9.** defense.
at·tain (ə tān′), *v.t.* **1.** to reach, achieve, or accomplish; gain; obtain: *to attain one's goals.* **2.** to come to or arrive at, esp. after some labor or tedium; reach: *to attain the mountain peak.* —*v.i.* **3.** to arrive at or succeed in reaching or obtaining something (usually fol. by *to* or *unto*): *to attain to knowledge.* [ME *atei(g)ne* < OF *ateign-* (s. of *ateindre*) < VL **attange(re)* (var. of L *attingere*) = L *at-* AT- + *tangere* to touch] —**at·tain′a·ble,** *adj.* —**at·tain′a·bil′i·ty, at·tain′a·ble·ness,** *n.* —**at·tain′er,** *n.* —**Syn. 1.** secure. See **gain**1.
at·tain·der (ə tān′dər), *n.* **1.** the loss of all civil rights as a result of a sentence of death or outlawry, esp. for conviction of treason or a felony. **2.** *Obs.* dishonor. [late ME, n. use of AF *attaindre* to convict, OF *ataindre* to convict, ATTAIN]
at·tain·ment (ə tān′mənt), *n.* **1.** the act of attaining. **2.** something attained; achievement. [ME *attenement*] —**Syn. 2.** accomplishment.
at·taint (ə tānt′), *v.t.* **1.** *Law.* to condemn by a sentence or a bill or act of attainder. **2.** to disgrace. **3.** *Archaic.* to accuse. **4.** *Obs.* to prove the guilt of. —*n.* **5.** attainder. **6.** a disgrace; taint. **7.** *Obs.* a touch or hit, esp. in tilting. [ME *ataynte* < *ataynt* convicted < AF, OF, ptp. of *ataindre* to convict, ATTAIN]
at·tar (at′ər), *n.* a perfume or essential oil obtained from flowers or petals. Also, **ottar, otto.** [short for Pers *'atar-gūl* attar of roses, akin to *'atara* to smell sweet, *'itr* fragrance (< Ar)]
at·tempt (ə tempt′), *v.t.* **1.** to make an effort at; try; undertake; seek: *to attempt a debate; to attempt to walk six miles.* **2.** to attack; make an effort against. **3.** *Archaic.* to tempt. —*n.* **4.** an effort made to accomplish something. **5.** an attack or assault: *an attempt upon one's life.* [< L *attempt(āre)* (to) test, tamper with. See AT-, TEMPT] —**at·tempt′a·bil′i·ty,** *n.* —**at·tempt′a·ble,** *adj.* —**at·tempt′er,** *n.* —**Syn. 1.** See **try. 4.** undertaking, endeavor.
at·tend (ə tend′), *v.t.* **1.** to be present at: *to attend a lecture; to attend church.* **2.** to go with; accompany: *a cold attended with fever.* **3.** to take care of or wait upon; minister to: *The nurse attended the patient daily.* **4.** to take charge of or watch over: *to attend one's health.* **5.** to listen to; give heed to. **6.** *Archaic.* to wait for; expect. —*v.i.* **7.** to take care or charge: *to attend to a sick person.* **8.** to apply oneself: *to attend to one's work.* **9.** to pay attention; listen or watch attentively. **10.** to be present: *She was invited to the wedding but did not attend.* **11.** to follow; be consequent (usually fol. by *on* or *upon*). [ME *atende(n)* < OF *atend(re)* < L *attendere* to bend to, notice. See AT-, TEND1] —**at·tend′er,** *n.*
at·tend·ance (ə ten′dəns), *n.* **1.** the act of attending. **2.** the persons or number of persons present. **3.** *Obs.* attendants collectively. [ME < MF]
at·tend·ant (ə ten′dənt), *n.* **1.** a person who attends another, as for service or company. **2.** *Chiefly Brit.* an usher or clerk. **3.** that which follows from or accompanies something; a corollary or concomitant thing or quality. **4.** a person who is present, as at a meeting. —*adj.* **5.** being present or in attendance; accompanying. **6.** associated; related: *war and its attendant evils.* [ME < MF, prp. of *attendre* to notice, await, etc.] —**at·tend′ant·ly,** *adv.* —**Syn. 1.** escort, companion; retainer. **3.** accompaniment, consequence.
at·ten·tion (*n.* ə ten′shən; *interj.* ə ten′shun′), *n.* **1.** the act or faculty of attending, esp. by directing the mind to an object. **2.** *Psychol.* **a.** a concentration of the mind on a single object or thought. **b.** a state of consciousness characterized by such concentration. **3.** observant care; consideration; notice: *Individual attention is given each child.* **4.** civility or courtesy: *attention to a stranger.* **5. attentions,** acts of courtesy indicating affection, as in courtship. **6.** *Mil.* **a.** a command to stand or sit in an erect position with eyes to the front, arms to the sides, and heels together. **b.** the act or state of so standing or sitting: *at attention.* —*interj.* **7.** (used to call one to attention, as in the military services or in school.) [ME *attencioun* < L *attentiōn-* (s. of *attentiō*) = *attent(us)* attentive + *-iōn-* -ION] —**at·ten′tion·al,** *adj.* —**Syn. 1.** awareness, watchfulness, alertness. **4.** deference, politeness.
at·ten·tive (ə ten′tiv), *adj.* **1.** characterized by or giving attention; observant. **2.** thoughtful of others; considerate; polite; courteous. —**at·ten′tive·ly,** *adv.* —**at·ten′tive·ness,** *n.* —**Syn. 1.** mindful, aware, alert, watchful.
at·ten·u·ant (ə ten′yo͞o ənt), *adj.* **1.** diluting, as a liquid. —*n.* **2.** a medicine or agent that thins the blood. [< L *attenuant-* (s. of *attenuāns* thinning, prp. of *attenuāre*). See AT-, TENUIS, -ANT]
at·ten·u·ate (*v.* ə ten′yo͞o āt′; *adj.* ə ten′yo͞o it, -āt′), *v.,* **-at·ed, -at·ing,** *adj.* —*v.t.* **1.** to make thin; make slender or fine. **2.** to weaken or reduce in force, intensity, effect, quantity, or value. —*v.i.* **3.** to become thin or fine; lessen. —*adj.* **4.** attenuated; thin. **5.** *Bot.* tapering gradually to a narrow extremity. [< L *attenuāt(us)* (ptp. of *attenuāre* to thin, reduce). See AT-, TENUIS, -ATE1] —**at·ten′u·a′tion,** *n.*
at·ten·u·a·tor (ə ten′yo͞o ā′tər), *n. Elect.* a device for decreasing the amplitude of an electric signal.
at·test (ə test′), *v.t.* **1.** to bear witness to; certify; declare to be correct, true, or genuine, esp. in an official capacity: *to attest the truth of a statement.* **2.** to give proof or evidence of; manifest: *His works attest his industry.* —*v.i.* **3.** to testify or bear witness (often fol. by *to*): *to attest to the truth of a statement.* —*n.* **4.** *Archaic.* attestation. [< L *attest(ārī)* (to) bear witness to = *at-* AT- + *testārī* (*test(is)* a witness + *-āre* inf. suffix)] —**at·test′a·ble,** *adj.* —**at·test′ant,** *n.* —**at·test′er, at·tes′tor, at·tes·ta·tor** (ə tes′tā tər, at′is tā′-), *n.* —**at·tes′tive,** *adj.*
at·tes·ta·tion (at′ə stā′shən), *n.* **1.** the act of attesting. **2.** testimony; evidence. [< L *attestātiōn-* (s. of *attestātiō*)] —**at·tes·ta·tive** (ə tes′tə tiv), *adj.*
Att. Gen., Attorney General.
at·tic (at′ik), *n.* **1.** the part of a building, esp. of a house, directly under a roof; garret. **2.** a room or rooms in that part. **3.** a low story or decorative wall above an entablature or the main cornice of a building. [special use of ATTIC]
At·tic (at′ik), *adj.* **1.** of, pertaining to, or characteristic of Attica or Athens and its culture. **2.** (*often l.c.*) displaying simple elegance, incisive intelligence, and delicate wit. —*n.* **3.** a native or inhabitant of Attica; an Athenian. **4.** the dialect of Attica, which became the standard language of Classical Greek literature in the 5th and 4th centuries B.C. [< L *Attic(us)* < Gk *Attikós* (adj.)]
At·ti·ca (at′ə kə), *n.* a region in SE Greece, surrounding Athens: under Athenian rule in ancient times.
At·ti·cism (at′i siz′əm), *n.* **1.** the style or idiom of Attic Greek. **2.** attachment to Athens or to the style, customs, etc., of the Athenians. **3.** concise and elegant expression, diction, or the like. Also, **at′ti·cism.** [< Gk *Attikism(ós)* a siding with Athens, an Attic expression] —**At′ti·cist, at′ti·cist,** *n.*
At·ti·la (at′ələ, ə til′ə), *n.* ("*Scourge of God*") A.D. 406?–453, king of the Huns who invaded Europe: defeated by the Romans and Visigoths in 451 at Châlons-sur-Marne.
at·tire (ə tīər′), *v.,* **-tired, -tir·ing,** *n.* —*v.t.* **1.** to dress, array, or adorn. —*n.* **2.** clothes or apparel, esp. rich or splendid garments. **3.** the horns of a deer. [ME *atire* < OF *atir(i)e(r)* (to) arrange < phrase *a tire* into a row or rank. See A-5, TIER1] —**at·tire′ment,** *n.*
at·ti·tude (at′i to͞od′, -tyo͞od′), *n.* **1.** manner, disposition, feeling, position, etc., toward a person or thing. **2.** position or posture of the body appropriate to or expressive of an action, emotion, etc.: *a threatening attitude.* **3.** *Aeron.* the inclination of an aircraft relative to the wind, to the ground, etc. [< F < It *attitud(ine)* < LL *aptitūdini-* (s. of *aptitūdō*) APTITUDE] —**at′ti·tu′di·nal,** *adj.* —**Syn. 2.** See **position.**
at·ti·tu·di·nise (at′i to͞od′ənīz′, -tyo͞od′-), *v.i.,* **-nised, -nis·ing.** *Chiefly Brit.* attitudinize. —**at′ti·tu′di·nis′er,** *n.*
at·ti·tu·di·nize (at′i to͞od′ənīz′, -tyo͞od′-), *v.i.,* **-nized, -niz·ing.** to assume attitudes; pose for effect. [< It *attitudin(e)* ATTITUDE + -IZE] —**at′ti·tu′di·niz′er,** *n.*
At·tle·bor·o (at′əl bûr′ō, -bur′ō), *n.* a city in SE Massachusetts. 32,907 (1970).
Att·lee (at′lē), *n.* **Clement Richard,** 1883–1967, British statesman: prime minister 1945–51.
at·torn (ə tûrn′), *Law.* —*v.i.* **1.** to acknowledge the relation of a tenant to a new landlord. —*v.t.* **2.** to turn over to another; transfer. [late ME *attourne* < AF *attourne(r),* OF *atourner* to turn over to. See AT-, TURN] —**at·torn′ment,** *n.*
at·tor·ney (ə tûr′nē), *n., pl.* **-neys.** a lawyer; attorney-at-law. [ME < AF *attourne,* lit., one (who is) turned to, i.e., appointed, ptp. of *attourner* to ATTORN] —**at·tor′ney·ship′,** *n.*
at·tor·ney-at-law (ə tûr′nē ət lô′), *n., pl.* **at·tor·neys-at-law.** *Law.* a legal agent authorized to appear before a court as a representative of a party to a legal controversy.

attor′ney gen′eral, *pl.* **attorneys general, attorney generals. 1.** the chief law officer of a country or state and head of its legal department. **2.** (*caps.*) the head of the U.S. Department of Justice: a member of the president's cabinet.

at·tract (ə trakt′), *v.t.* **1.** to cause to approach, adhere, or unite (opposed to *repel*): *The gravitational force of the earth attracts smaller bodies to it.* **2.** to draw by appealing to emotion, stimulating interest, etc.; allure. —*v.i.* **3.** to possess or exert the power of attraction. [< L *attract(us)* drawn to (ptp. of *attrahere*) = *at-* AT- + *trac-* (perf. s. of *trahere* to draw) + *-tus* ptp. suffix] —**at·tract′a·ble,** *adj.* —**at·tract′a·ble·ness,** *n.* —**at·tract′ant,** *n.* —**at·tract′ing·ly,** *adv.* —**at·trac′tor, at·tract′er,** *n.*

at·trac·tion (ə trak′shən), *n.* **1.** the act, power, or property of attracting. **2.** attractive quality; fascination; allurement; enticement. **3.** a person or thing that attracts: *The main attraction was the after-dinner speaker.* **4.** *Physics.* the electric or magnetic force that acts between oppositely charged bodies, tending to draw them together. [< ML *attractiōn-* (s. of *attractiō*)] —**at·trac′tion·al·ly,** *adv.* —**Syn. 2.** lure.

at·trac·tive (ə trak′tiv), *adj.* **1.** appealing to one's sense of beauty; providing pleasure or delight, esp. in appearance or manner; pleasing; charming; alluring: *an attractive woman.* **2.** arousing interest or engaging one's thought, consideration, etc.; *an attractive idea.* **3.** having the quality of attracting. [< LL *attractīv(us)* (medical L) with drawing power] —**at·trac′tive·ly,** *adv.* —**at·trac′tive·ness,** *n.*

attrib., 1. attribute. **2.** attributive. **3.** attributively.

at·trib·ute (*v.* ə trib′yo͞ot; *n.* a′trə byo͞ot′), *v.,* **-ut·ed, -ut·ing,** *n.* —*v.t.* **1.** to regard as resulting from; consider as caused by. **2.** to consider as belonging, as a quality or characteristic: *He attributed intelligence to his colleagues.* **3.** to regard as produced by or originating in or with; credit; assign: *The critics attribute the unsigned painting to Raphael.* —*n.* **4.** something seen as belonging to or representing someone or something: *Sensitivity is one of his attributes.* **5.** *Gram.* a word or phrase that is syntactically subordinate to another and serves to limit, identify, particularize, describe, or supplement the meaning of the form with which it is in construction. In *the red house, red* is an attribute of *house.* **6.** *Obs.* distinguished character; reputation. [ME < L *attribūt(us)* allotted, assigned, imputed to (ptp. of *attribuere*) = *at-* AT- + *tribū-* (ptp. s. of *tribuere* to assign (to tribes), classify, ascribe; see TRIBE) + *-tus* ptp. suffix] —**at·trib′ut·a·ble,** *adj.* —**at·trib′ut·er, at·trib′u·tor,** *n.* —**at′tri·bu′tion,** *n.* —**Syn. 1.** ATTRIBUTE, ASCRIBE, IMPUTE imply definite origin. ATTRIBUTE and ASCRIBE are often used interchangeably, to imply that something originates with a definite person or from a definite cause. Possibly because of an association with tribute, ATTRIBUTE is coming to have a complimentary connotation, whereas ASCRIBE has neutral implications: *to attribute one's success to a friend's encouragement; to ascribe an accident to carelessness.* IMPUTE has gained uncomplimentary connotations, and usually means to accuse or blame someone or something as a cause or origin: *to impute an error to him.* **4.** See **quality.**

at·trib·u·tive (ə trib′yə tiv), *adj.* **1.** pertaining to or having the character of attribution or an attribute. **2.** *Gram.* expressing an attribute, applied in English esp. to adjectives and adverbs preceding the words which they modify, as *first* in *the first day.* —*n.* **3.** *Gram.* an attributive word or phrase. [ATTRIBUTE or ATTRIBUT(ION) + -IVE] —**at·trib′u·tive·ly,** *adv.* —**at·trib′u·tive·ness,** *n.*

at·tri·tion (ə trish′ən), *n.* **1.** a wearing down or away by friction. **2.** a rubbing against; friction. **3.** a wearing down or weakening of resistance, esp. as a result of continuous pressure or harassment: *The enemy surrounded the town and conducted a war of attrition.* **4.** a natural or expected decrease in numbers or size. [L *attrītiōn-* (s. of *attrītiō*) friction = *-attrīt(us)* rubbed against, worn away + *-iōn-* -ION] —**at·tri′tion·al,** *adj.* —**at·tri·tive** (ə trī′tiv), *adj.*

At·tu (at′to͞o′), *n.* the westernmost of the Aleutian Islands: Japanese occupation 1942–43.

at·tune (ə to͞on′, ə tyo͞on′), *v.t.,* **-tuned, -tun·ing.** to adjust; bring into accord, harmony, or sympathetic relationship: *He has attuned himself to living in the country.*

atty., attorney.

Atty. Gen., Attorney General.

ATV, See **all-terrain vehicle.**

at. vol., See **atomic volume.**

a·twain (ə twān′), *adv. Archaic.* in two; apart. [ME]

At/Wb, ampere-turns per weber.

a·twit·ter (ə twit′ər), *adj.* excited; nervous; aflutter; twittering.

at. wt., See **atomic weight.**

a·typ·i·cal (ā tip′i kəl), *adj.* not typical; not conforming to the type; irregular; abnormal: *a flower atypical of the species.* Also, **a·typ′ic.** —**a·typ′i·cal·ly,** *adv.*

AU, See **astronomical unit.**

Au, *Chem.* gold. [< L *aurum*]

A.U., angstrom unit. Also, **a.u., Å.U.**

au·bade (ō bad′, ō bäd′; *Fr.* ō BAD′), *n., pl.* **au·bades** (ō badz′, ō bädz′; *Fr.* ō BAD′). *Music.* a piece sung or played outdoors at dawn, usually as a compliment to someone. [MF < Pr *aubada* = *aub(a)* dawn (< VL *alba,* n. use of fem. of L *albus* white) + *-ada* -ADE[1]]

Aube (ōb), *n.* a river in N France, flowing NW to the Seine. ab. 125 mi. long.

Au·ber (ō BER′), *n.* **Da·niel Fran·çois Es·prit** (DA nyel′ FRÄN SWA′ es PRĒ′), 1782–1871, French composer.

au·berge (ō berzh′), *n., pl.* **-berges** (-berzh′). *French.* an inn; tavern.

Au·ber·vil·liers (ō BER vē lyā′), *n.* a town in N France, a suburb of Paris. 70,836 (1962).

Au·brey (ô′brē), *n.* **John,** 1626–97, English antiquary.

au·burn (ô′bərn), *n.* **1.** a reddish-brown or golden-brown color. —*adj.* **2.** having auburn color: *auburn hair.* [late ME *abo(u)rne* blond < MF, OF *auborne,* early OF *alborne* < L *alburn(us)* whitish]

Au·burn (ô′bərn), *n.* a city in central New York. 34,599 (1970).

Au′bus·son rug′ (ō′bə sən, -sôN′; *Fr.* ō BY sôN′), an ornate rug constructed in a flat tapestry weave. [after *Aubusson,* town in central France where made]

A.U.C., 1. from the founding of the city (of Rome in 753? B.C.). [< L *ab urbe conditā*] **2.** in the year from the founding of the city (of Rome) (used in reckoning dates). [< L *annō urbis conditae*]

Auck·land (ôk′lənd), *n.* a seaport on N North Island, in New Zealand. 143,583 (1961).

au con·traire (ō kôN TRER′), *French.* **1.** on the contrary. **2.** on the opposite or adverse side.

au cou·rant (ō ko͞o RäN′), *French.* up-to-date. [lit., in the current]

auc·tion (ôk′shən), *n.* **1.** a public sale at which property or goods are sold to the highest bidder. **2.** *Cards.* **a.** See **auction bridge. b.** (in bridge or certain other games) the act or period of bidding. —*v.t.* **3.** to sell by auction (often fol. by *off*): *He auctioned off his furniture.* [< L *auctiōn-* (s. of *auctiō*) an increase, esp. in the bidding at a sale = *auct(us)* increased, ptp. of *augēre* (*aug-* increase + *-tus* ptp. suffix) + *-iōn-* -ION] —**auc′tion·ar′y,** *adj.*

auc′tion bridge′, a variety of bridge in which tricks won in excess of the contract are scored toward game.

auc·tion·eer (ôk′shə nēr′), *n.* **1.** a person who conducts sales by auction. —*v.t.* **2.** to auction (something).

auc·to·ri·al (ôk tōr′ē əl, -tôr′-, ouk-), *adj.* of, by, or pertaining to an author. [< L *auctor* AUTHOR + -IAL]

au·da·cious (ô dā′shəs), *adj.* **1.** extremely bold or daring; recklessly brave; fearless: *an audacious warrior.* **2.** extremely original; without restriction to prior ideas; highly inventive: *an audacious vision of the future.* **3.** defiant of convention, propriety, law, or the like; impudent; insolent; brazen. [AUDACI(TY) + -OUS] —**au·da′cious·ly,** *adv.* —**au·da′cious·ness,** *n.* —**Syn. 1.** venturesome. **3.** unabashed.

au·dac·i·ty (ô das′i tē), *n., pl.* **-ties. 1.** boldness or daring, esp. with confident or arrogant disregard for personal safety, conventional beliefs, etc. **2.** effrontery or insolence. **3.** Usually, **audacities.** audacious acts or statements. [late ME < L *audāci(a)* daring (*aud(ēre)* (to) dare + *-ācia* = *-āci-* adj. suffix + *-a* n. suffix) + -TY[2]] —**Syn. 1.** temerity, foolhardiness.

Au·den (ôd′ən), *n.* **W(ys·tan) H(ugh)** (wis′tən), 1907–1973, English poet in the U.S.

au·di·ble (ô′də bəl), *adj.* actually heard or capable of being heard; loud enough to be heard. [< LL *audībil(is)* = L *audī(re)* (to) hear + *-bilis* -BLE] —**au′di·bil′i·ty, au′di·ble·ness,** *n.* —**au′di·bly,** *adv.*

au·di·ence (ô′dē əns), *n.* **1.** the group of spectators at a public event; listeners or viewers collectively, as at a theater, concert, or the like. **2.** the persons reached by a book, radio or television broadcast, etc.; public. **3.** a regular public that manifests interest, support, enthusiasm, or the like; a following: *Every art form has its own audience.* **4.** opportunity of being heard; hearing. **5.** a formal interview, esp. with a high official of a church or government. **6.** the act of hearing. [ME < MF < L *audientia.* See AUDIENT, -ENCE]

au·di·ent (ô′dē ənt), *adj.* hearing; listening. [< L *audient-* (s. of *audiēns,* prp. of *audīre* to hear) = *audi-* hear + *-ent-* -ENT]

au·dile (ô′dil, -dīl), *n. Psychol.* a person who forms in his mind auditory rather than visual or motor images. [AUD(ITORY) + -ILE]

au·di·o (ô′dē ō′), *adj.* **1.** *Electronics.* of, pertaining to, or using sound or audio frequencies. **2.** of, pertaining to, or used in the transmission, reception, or reproduction of sound or audio frequencies. —*n. Television.* **3.** the audio elements of television (distinguished from *video*). **4.** the circuits in a receiver for reproducing sound. [independent use of AUDIO-]

audio-, a combining form meaning "hearing," "sound," "of or for hearing": *audiometer.* [comb. form repr. L *audīre* to hear]

au′dio fre′quency, *Acoustics, Electronics.* a frequency between 15 and 20,000 cycles per second, within the range of normally audible sound.

au·di·ol·o·gy (ô′dē ol′ə jē), *n.* the science of hearing that includes the treatment and rehabilitation of persons with impaired hearing. [AUDIO- + -LOGY] —**au·di·o·log·i·cal** (ô′dē ə loj′i kəl), *adj.* —**au′di·ol′o·gist,** *n.*

au·di·om·e·ter (ô′dē om′i tər), *n. Med.* an instrument for gauging and recording the power of hearing.

au·di·o·phile (ô′dē ə fīl′), *n.* a person who is especially interested in the high-fidelity sound reproduction of radios, phonographs, tape recorders, etc.

au·di·o·tape (ô′dē ō tāp′), *n.* a type of magnetic tape for recording or reproducing sound.

au·di·o·vis·u·al (ô′dē ō vizh′o͞o əl), *adj.* **1.** using media of sound and sight (other than printed materials), such as films, recordings, television, etc., for education: *audiovisual aids.* **2.** of both hearing and sight. —*n.* **3.** Usually, **audiovisuals.** audiovisual materials or equipment. Also, **au′di·o-vis′u·al.**

au·dit (ô′dit), *n.* **1.** an official examination and verification of accounts and records, esp. of financial accounts. **2.** a report or statement reflecting an audit; a final statement of account. **3.** *Archaic.* a judicial hearing. **4.** *Obs.* an audience. —*v.t.* **5.** to make an audit of; examine (accounts, records, etc.) for purposes of verification: *The accountants audited the company's books at the end of the fiscal year.* **6.** *U.S.* to attend (classes, lectures, etc.) as an auditor —*v.i.* **7.** to examine and verify an account or accounts by reference to vouchers. [late ME *audite* < L *audīt(us)* a hearing, report, n. use of ptp. of *audīre* = *audī-* hear + *-tus* ptp. suffix]

au·di·tion (ô dish′ən), *n.* **1.** the act of hearing. **2.** the sense or power of hearing. **3.** a trial hearing given to an actor, musician, speaker, etc., to test voice qualities, performance, stage presence, or the like. **4.** a reading or other simplified rendering of a theatrical work, performed before a potential backer, producer, etc. **5.** *Rare.* something that is heard. —*v.t., v.i.* **6.** to try in an audition: *The producer plans to audition dancers tomorrow. Do you plan to audition for the part?* [< L *audītiōn-* (s. of *audītiō* hearing)]

au·di·tive (ô′di tiv), *adj.* auditory.

au·di·tor (ô′di tər), *n.* **1.** a hearer; listener. **2.** a person appointed and authorized to examine accounting records, compare the charges with the vouchers, and state the result. **3.** *U.S.* a university student registered for a course without credit. [< L; see AUDIT, -OR[2]] —**au′di·tor·ship′,** *n.*

au·di·to·ri·um (ô′di tōr′ē əm, -tôr′-), *n., pl.* **-to·ri·ums, -to·ri·a** (-tōr′ē ə, -tôr′-). **1.** the space set apart for the audience in a public building. **2.** a building for public gatherings. [< L: lecture hall, n. use of neut. of *audītōrius* AUDITORY]

au·di·to·ry (ô′di tōr′ē, -tôr′ē), *adj., n., pl.* **-ries.** **—***adj.* **1.** *Anat., Physiol.* of or pertaining to hearing, to the sense of hearing, or to the organs of hearing. **2.** perceived through or resulting from the sense of hearing: *auditory hallucinations.* **—***n. Archaic.* **3.** an assembly of hearers; an audience. **4.** an auditorium, esp. the nave of a church. [< L *audītōri(us)* relating to hearing. See AUDIT, -ORY[1]] **—au′di·to′ri·ly, au′di·to′ri·al·ly,** *adv.*

au′ditory nerve′, *Anat.* either one of the eighth pair of cranial nerves, consisting of sensory fibers that conduct impulses from the organs of hearing and from the semicircular canals to the brain.

au′ditory phonet′ics, the branch of phonetics dealing with the physiological processes involved in the hearing of speech. Cf. **articulatory phonetics, physiological phonetics.**

Au·du·bon (ô′də bon′, -bən), *n.* **John James,** 1785–1851, U.S. naturalist who painted and wrote about the birds of North America.

au fait (ō fe′), *French.* having experience or practical knowledge of a thing; expert; versed. [lit., to the fact]

Auf·klä·rung (ouf′kle′RŏŏNG), *n. German.* **1.** enlightenment. **2.** *Eur. Hist.* the Enlightenment.

au fond (ō fôN′), *French.* at bottom or to the bottom; basically; in reality.

auf Wie·der·seh·en (ouf vē′dəR zā′ən), *German.* until we meet again; good-by for the present.

Aug., August.

aug., **1.** augmentative. **2.** augmented.

Au·ge·an (ô jē′ən), *adj.* **1.** resembling the Augean stables in filth or degradation. **2.** difficult and unpleasant. [< L *augē(us)* of AUGEAS (Gk *Augeí(ās)* + *-us* adj. suffix) + -AN]

Auge′an sta′bles, *Class. Myth.* the stables in which King Augeas kept 3000 oxen, and which had not been cleaned for 30 years: Hercules diverted the river Alpheus through them and cleaned them in a day.

Au·ge·as (ô′jē əs, ô jē′əs), *n.* king of the Epeans in Elis and one of the Argonauts. Cf. **Augean stables.**

au·gend (ô′jend, ô jend′), *n. Math.* a number to which another is added in forming a sum. Cf. **addend** (def. 2). [< L *augend(um)* a thing to be increased, n. use of neut. of *augendus* to be increased, ger. of *augēre* to increase]

au·ger (ô′gər), *n. Carpentry.* **1.** a bit, as for a brace. **2.** a boring tool, similar to but larger than a gimlet, consisting of a bit rotated by a transverse handle. [ME *nauger* (a *nauger* taken as *an auger;* cf. ADDER, APRON), OE *nafogār* nave-piercer (c. Icel *nafar(r),* OHG *nabagēr*) = *nafa* NAVE[2] + *gār* spear; see GORE[3]]

au′ger bit′, an auger having a square tang at its upper end and rotated by a brace, used for boring through wood. See illus. at **bit**[1].

aught[1] (ôt), *n.* **1.** anything whatever; any part: *for aught I know.* **—***adv.* **2.** in any degree; at all; in any respect. Also, **ought.** [ME *aught, ought,* OE *āht, āwiht, ōwiht* = *ā, ō* ever + *wiht* thing, WIGHT[1]]

aught[2] (ôt), *n.* a cipher (0); zero. Also, **ought.** [*a naught,* taken as *an aught* (cf. AUGER). See NAUGHT]

Au·gier (ō zhyā′), *n.* **Guil·laume Vic·tor É·mile** (gē yōm′ vēk tôR′ ā mēl′), 1820–89, French dramatist.

au·gite (ô′jīt), *n.* a mineral, a silicate, chiefly of calcium, magnesium, iron, and aluminum: a dark-green to black variety of monoclinic pyroxene, characteristic of basic rocks. [< L *augītēs* < Gk = *aug(ḗ)* bright light + *-ītēs* -ITE[1]] **—au·git·ic** (ô jit′ik), *adj.*

aug·ment (*v.* ôg ment′; *n.* ôg′ment), *v.t.* **1.** to increase or intensify, as in size, degree, or effect: *His small salary is augmented by a commission.* **2.** *Gram.* to add an augment to. **3.** *Music.* **a.** to raise (the upper note of an interval or chord) by a half step. **b.** to double the note values of (a theme). **4.** *Heraldry.* to grant an augmentation to (a coat of arms). **—***v.i.* **5.** to become greater. **—***n.* **6.** *Gram.* a prefixed vowel or a lengthening of the initial vowel that characterizes certain forms in the non-present inflection of verbs in Greek, Sanskrit, Armenian, and Phrygian. [< LL *augment(āre)* (to) increase < *augment(um)* an increase (*aug(ēre)* (to) increase (akin to EKE[1]) + *-mentum* -MENT); r. ME *aument* < MF *aument(er)* < LL, as above] **—aug·ment′a·ble,** *adj.* **—aug·ment′er, aug·men′tor,** *n.* **—Syn. 1.** See **increase.**

aug·men·ta·tion (ôg′men tā′shən), *n.* **1.** the act of augmenting. **2.** the state of being augmented. **3.** the amount by which anything is augmented. **4.** *Music.* modification of a theme by increasing the time value of all its tones. **5.** *Heraldry.* an addition to a coat of arms granted to a person, or to him and his descendants, by a sovereign power in recognition of a notable action. [late ME < LL *augmentātiōn-* (s. of *augmentātiō*); r. late ME *aumentacion* < MF]

aug·ment·a·tive (ôg men′tə tiv), *adj.* **1.** serving to augment. **2.** *Gram.* pertaining to or productive of a form denoting increased size or intensity. In Spanish the augmentative suffix *-ón* is added to a word, as *silla* "chair" to indicate increased size, as in *sillón* "armchair." **—***n.* **3.** *Gram.* an augmentative element or formation. [r. earlier *augmentatif* < MF] **—aug·men′ta·tive·ly,** *adv.*

au go·go (ō gō′gō′). See **à gogo.**

au grat·in (ō grät′ən, ō grat′ən; *Fr.* ō GRA taN′), *Cookery.* cooked or baked with a topping of either browned crumbs and butter or grated cheese, or with both. [< F: lit., with the scraping, i.e., the burnt part]

Augs·burg (ôgz′bûrg; *Ger.* ouks′bŏŏRk), *n.* a city in Bavaria, in S West Germany. 210,500 (1963).

Augs′burg Confes′sion, the statement of beliefs and doctrines of the Lutherans, formulated by Melanchthon and presented at the Diet of Augsburg in 1530.

au·gur (ô′gər), *n.* **1.** one of a body of ancient Roman officials charged with observing and interpreting omens for guidance in public affairs. **2.** any soothsayer; prophet. **—***v.t.* **3.** to divine or predict, as from omens; prognosticate. **4.** to afford an omen of; foreshadow; betoken: *mounting sales that augur a profitable year.* **—***v.i.* **5.** to conjecture from signs or omens; presage. **6.** to be a sign; bode (usually fol. by *well* or *ill*). [< L *augur* (var. of *auger*) a diviner, soothsayer < ?]

au·gu·ry (ô′gyə rē), *n., pl.* **-ries.** **1.** the art or practice of an augur; divination. **2.** the rite or ceremony of an augur. **3.** an omen, token, or indication. [ME < L *auguri(um)* soothsaying = *augur* AUGUR + *-ium* n. suffix denoting office] **—au′gu·ral,** *adj.*

au·gust (ô gust′), *adj.* inspiring reverence or admiration; of supreme dignity or grandeur; majestic. [< L *august(us)* sacred, grand, akin to *augēre* to increase. See EKE[1]] **—au·gust′ly,** *adv.* **—au·gust′ness,** *n.*

Au·gust (ô′gəst), *n.* the eighth month of the year, containing 31 days. [early ME < L *August(us)* (named after AUGUSTUS); r. OE *Agustus* < LL]

Au·gus·ta (ô gus′tə), *n.* **1.** a city in E Georgia, on the Savannah River. 59,864 (1970). **2.** a city in and the capital of Maine, on the Kennebec River. 21,945 (1970).

Au·gus·tan (ô gus′tən), *adj.* **1.** of or pertaining to Augustus Caesar or to the age (**Augus′tan Age′**) in which he flourished and which marked the golden age of Latin literature. **2.** of or pertaining to the neoclassic period, esp. of 18th-century English literature. **—***n.* **3.** an author in an Augustan age.

Au·gus·tine (ô′gə stēn′, ô gus′tin), *n.* **1. Saint,** A.D. 354–430, one of the Latin fathers in the early Christian church; author; bishop of Hippo in N Africa. **2. Saint** (*Austin*), died A.D. 604, Roman monk who began the conversion of the English to Christianity; first archbishop of Canterbury 601–604.

Au·gus·tin·i·an (ô′gə stin′ē ən), *adj.* **1.** pertaining to St. Augustine of Hippo, to his doctrines, or to any religious order following his rule. **—***n.* **2.** *Rom. Cath. Ch.* a member of any of the Augustinian orders. **3.** a follower of St. Augustine. **—Au′gus·tin′i·an·ism, Au·gus·tin·ism** (ô gus′tə niz′əm), *n.*

Au·gus·tus (ô gus′təs), *n.* (*Gaius Julius Caesar Octavianus, Augustus Caesar*) 63 B.C.–A.D. 14, first Roman emperor 27 B.C.–A.D. 14: heir and successor to Julius Caesar. Also called **Octavian** (before 27 B.C.).

au jus (ō zhōōs′, ō jōōs′; *Fr.* ō zhY′), (of meat) served in its natural juices obtained from cooking. [< F: lit., with the gravy]

auk (ôk), *n.* any of several, usually black-and-white diving birds of the family *Alcidae,* of northern seas, having webbed feet and small wings. Cf. **razor-billed auk.** [< Scand; cf. Icel *alka*]

auk·let (ôk′lit), *n.* any of several small auks of the coasts of the north Pacific.

Razor-billed auk, *Alca torda* (Length 1½ ft.)

au lait (ō lā′; *Fr.* ō le′), *French Cookery.* prepared or served with milk.

auld (ôld), *adj. Scot. and North Eng.* old.

auld lang syne (ôld′ lang zīn′, sīn′), *Scot. and North Eng.* **1.** old times, esp. times fondly remembered. **2.** old or long friendship. [lit., old long since]

au·lic (ô′lik), *adj.* pertaining to a royal court. [< L *aulic(us)* < Gk *aulikós* courtly = *aul(ḗ)* hall, court + *-ikos* -IC]

Au′lic Coun′cil, a privy council of the Holy Roman Emperor.

AUM, air-to-underwater missile.

au na·tu·rel (ō NA tY REL′), *French.* **1.** in the natural state, esp. nude. **2.** uncooked or cooked simply.

aunt (ant, änt), *n.* **1.** the sister of one's father or mother. **2.** the wife of one's uncle. **3.** a benevolent elderly woman. [ME *aunte* < OF, var. of *ante* < L *amita* father's sister]

aunt·ie (an′tē, än′-), *n.* a familiar or diminutive form of **aunt.**

aunt·y (an′tē, än′-), *n., pl.* **aunt·ies.** auntie.

au pair (ō PER′), *French.* exchanging services as a governess, companion, or the like, for board and room, usually by a young foreign visitor or student: *She advertised for an* au pair *girl to care for the children.*

aur-[1], var. of **auri-**[1], esp. before a vowel.

aur-[2], var. of **auri-**[2], esp. before a vowel.

au·ra (ôr′ə), *n., pl.* **au·ras** or, for 2, **au·rae** (ôr′ē). **1.** a subtly pervasive quality or atmosphere seen as emanating from a person, place, or thing: *an aura of friendliness.* **2.** *Pathol.* a sensation, as of a current of cold air, or other sensory experience preceding an attack of epilepsy, hysteria, etc. [< L < Gk: breath (of air)]

au·ral[1] (ôr′əl), *adj.* of or pertaining to an aura. [AUR(A) + -AL[1]]

au·ral[2] (ôr′əl), *adj.* of or pertaining to the ear or to the sense of hearing. [< L *aur(is)* ear + -AL[1]] **—au′ral·ly,** *adv.*

Au·rang·zeb (ôr′əng zeb′), *n.* 1618–1707, Mogul emperor of Hindustan 1658–1707. Also, **Aurungzeb.**

au·rar (oi′rär), *n.* pl. of **eyrir.**

au·re·ate (ôr′ē it, -āt′), *adj.* **1.** golden. **2.** brilliant or splendid. [late ME *aureat* < LL *aureāt(us)* decorated with gold = L *aure(us)* golden, of gold (*aur(um)* gold + *-eus* adj. suffix) + *-ātus* -ATE[1]] **—au′re·ate·ly,** *adv.* **—au′re·ate·ness,** *n.*

Au·re·li·an (ô rē′lē ən, ô rēl′yən), *n.* (*Lucius Domitius Aurelianus*) A.D. 212?–275, Roman emperor 270–275.

Au·re·li·us (ô rē′lē əs, ô rēl′yəs), *n.* **Marcus.** See **Marcus Aurelius.**

au·re·ole (ôr′ē ōl′), *n.* **1.** a radiance surrounding the head or the whole figure in the representation of a sacred personage. **2.** any encircling ring of light or color; a halo. **3.** *Astron.* corona (def. 3). Also, **au·re·o·la** (ô rē′ə lə). [ME < L *aureola (corona)* golden (crown) = *aure(us)* golden (see AUREATE) + *-ola,* fem. of *-olus* dim. suffix]

Au·re·o·my·cin (ôr′ē ō mī′sin), *n. Pharm., Trademark.* chlortetracycline.

au·re·us (ôr′ē əs), *n., pl.* **au·re·i** (ôr′ē ī′). a gold coin and monetary unit of ancient Rome, from Caesar to Constantine I. [< L: lit., golden]

au re·voir (ō RƏ VWAR′; *Eng.* ō′ rə vwär′), *French.* until we see each other again; good-by for the present.

auri-[1], a combining form meaning "gold": *auriferous.* Also, *esp. before a vowel,* **aur-.** [< L *aur(um)* + -I-]

auri-[2], a combining form meaning "ear," used esp. before a consonant: *auricle.* Also, *esp. before a vowel,* **aur-.** [< L *auri(s)* ear]

au·ric (ôr′ik), *adj.* *Chem.* of or containing gold, esp. in the trivalent state.

au·ri·cle (ôr′i kəl), *n.* **1.** *Anat.* **a.** the projecting outer portion of the ear; pinna. **b.** Also called **auric′ular append′age.** an ear-shaped appendage projecting from each atrium of the heart. **c.** (loosely) the atrium. **2.** *Bot., Zool.* a part like or likened to an ear. [< L *auricul(a)* the (external) ear, ear lobe. See AURI-², -CLE] —**au′ri·cled,** *adj.*

au·ric·u·la (ô rik′yə lə), *n., pl.* **-lae** (-lē′), **-las.** a yellow primrose, *Primula Auricula,* native in the Alps. Also called **bear's-ear.** [< NL, special use of L *auricula* AURICLE]

au·ric·u·lar (ô rik′yə lər), *adj.* **1.** of or pertaining to the ear or to the sense of hearing. **2.** perceived by or addressed to the ear: *auricular evidence.* **3.** shaped like an ear; auriculate. **4.** *Anat.* pertaining to an auricle of the heart. [< LL *auriculār(is)* of, pertaining to the ear] —**au·ric′u·lar·ly,** *adv.*

au·ric·u·late (ô rik′yə lit, -lāt′), *adj.* **1.** having auricles or earlike parts. **2.** shaped like an ear. [< L *auricul-* AURICLE + -ATE¹] —**au·ric′u·late·ly,** *adv.*

au·rif·er·ous (ô rif′ər əs), *adj.* yielding or containing gold. [< L *aurifer* gold-bearing (see AURI-¹, -FER) + -OUS]

Au·ri·ga (ô rī′gə), *n., gen.* **-gae** (-jē). *Astron.* the Charioteer, a northern constellation between Perseus and Gemini. [late ME < L: charioteer]

Au·ri·gna·cian (ôr′in yā′shən), *adj.* of, belonging to, or characteristic of a sequence of related Upper Paleolithic cultures. [*Aurignac,* village in S France where remains were found + -IAN]

Aurochs, *Bos primigenius* (6 ft. high at shoulder)

Au·riol (ôr′ē ōl′, -ōl′; *Fr.* ō ʀyôl′), *n.* **Vin·cent** (vin′sənt; *Fr.* vaN säN′), 1884–1966, French statesman; president 1947–54.

au·rochs (ôr′oks), *n., pl.* **-rochs.** **1.** a European wild ox, *Bos primigenius,* now extinct. **2.** (not used scientifically) the European bison. [< G, var. (now obs.) of *Auerochs* << OHG *ūrohso* = *ūr* (c. OE *ūr* bison) + *ohso* ox]

Au·ro·ra (ô rōr′ə, ô rôr′ə, ə rōr′ə, ə rôr′ə), *n.* **1.** the ancient Roman goddess of the dawn, identified by the Greeks with the goddess Eos. **2.** (*l.c.*) the rise or dawn of something. **3.** (*l.c.*) a radiant emission from the upper atmosphere that occurs sporadically over the middle and high latitudes of both hemispheres in the form of luminous bands, streamers, or the like, caused by the bombardment of the atmosphere with charged solar particles that are being guided along the earth's magnetic lines of force. **4.** a city in NE Illinois. 74,182 (1970). **5.** a city in central Colorado, near Denver. 74,974 (1970). [late ME < L: dawn, dawn goddess, EAST]

auro′ra aus·tra′lis (ô strā′lis), *Meteorol.* the aurora of the Southern Hemisphere. [< NL: southern aurora]

auro′ra bo·re·al′is (bōr′ē al′is, -ā′lis, bôr′-), *Meteorol.* the aurora of the Northern Hemisphere. Also called **northern lights, auro′ra polar′is.** [< NL: northern aurora]

au·ro·ral (ô rōr′əl, ô rôr′-), *adj.* **1.** of or like the dawn. **2.** pertaining to a polar aurora. —**au·ro′ral·ly,** *adv.*

aur·ous (ôr′əs), *adj.* **1.** *Chem.* of or containing gold in the univalent state. **2.** of or containing gold.

Au·rung·zeb (ôr′ə̄ng zeb′), *n.* Aurangzeb.

Aus., **1.** Austria. **2.** Austrian.

Au·sa·ble (ô sā′bəl), *n.* a river in NE New York, flowing NE through a gorge **(Ausa′ble Chasm′),** into Lake Champlain. 20 mi. long.

Ausch·witz (oush′vits), *n.* a town in SW Poland: site of Nazi concentration camp during World War II. 34,000 (est. 1963). Polish, **Oświęcim.**

aus·cul·tate (ô′skəl tāt′), *v.t., v.i.,* **-tat·ed, -tat·ing.** *Med.* to examine by auscultation. [back formation from AUSCULTATION] —**aus·cul·ta·tive** (ô′skəl tā′tiv, ô skul′tə-), **aus·cul·ta·to·ry** (ô skul′tə tōr′ē, -tôr′ē), *adj.* —**aus′cul·ta′tor,** *n.*

aus·cul·ta·tion (ô′skəl tā′shən), *n.* **1.** *Med.* the act of listening, either directly or through a stethoscope or other instrument, to sounds within the body, as a method of diagnosis. **2.** act of listening. [< L *auscultātiōn-* (s. of *auscultātiō*) a listening, attending to = *auscultāt(us)* listened to (ptp. of *auscultāre: aus-* (var. s. of *auris* ear) + *-cultā-* (< ?) + *-tus* ptp. suffix) + *-iōn-* -ION]

Aus·gleich (ous′glīkʜ), *n., pl.* **-gleich·e** (-glī′kʜə). *German.* **1.** an arrangement or compromise between parties. **2.** the agreement made between Austria and Hungary in 1867, regulating the relations between the countries and setting up the Dual Monarchy. [lit., equalization]

Aus·länd·er (ous′len′dər; *Eng.* ous′lan′dər, ô′slan′-), *n., pl.* **Aus·länd·er.** *German.* a foreigner; an alien or outlander.

aus·pi·cate (ô′spə kāt′), *v.t.,* **-cat·ed, -cat·ing.** to initiate with ceremonies calculated to ensure good luck; inaugurate. [< L *auspicāt(us)* consecrated by auguries (ptp. of *auspicārī*) = *auspic-* (s. of *auspex* soothsayer) + *-ātus* -ATE¹]

aus·pice (ô′spis), *n., pl.* **aus·pic·es** (ô′spi siz). **1.** Usually, **auspices.** patronage; support; sponsorship: *under the auspices of the king.* **2.** Often, **auspices.** a favorable sign or propitious circumstance. **3.** divination, esp. from birds. [< F < L *auspicium* a bird-watching, divination from flight of birds = *auspic-* (s. of *auspex* one who observes birds, soothsayer) + *-ium* n. suffix]

aus·pi·cial (ô spish′əl), *adj.* **1.** of or pertaining to auspices. **2.** auspicious. [< L *auspici(um)* AUSPICE + -AL¹]

aus·pi·cious (ô spish′əs), *adj.* **1.** promising success; propitious; opportune; favorable: *an auspicious occasion.* **2.** *Archaic.* favored by fortune; prosperous. [< L *auspici(um)* AUSPICE + -OUS] —**aus·pi′cious·ly,** *adv.* —**aus·pi′cious·ness,** *n.*

Aus·sie (ô′sē), *n. Slang.* an Australian. [AUS(TRALIAN) + -IE]

Aust., **1.** Austria. **2.** Austrian.

Aus·ten (ô′stən), *n.* **Jane,** 1775–1817, Engish novelist.

aus·ten·ite (ô′stə nīt′), *n.* *Metall.* a solid solution of carbon or of carbon and other elements in iron, having a face-centered cubic lattice at all temperatures. [named after Sir W. C. Roberts-*Austen* (1843–1902), English metallurgist]

Aus·ter (ô′stər), *n.* *Literary.* the south wind personified. Cf. **Notus.** [< L]

aus·tere (ô stēr′), *adj.* **1.** severe in manner or appearance; stern; solemn. **2.** rigorously self-disciplined; living without excess, luxury, or ease: *an austere life.* **3.** severely simple; without ornament: *austere writing.* [ME < L *austēr(us)* < Gk *austērós* harsh, rough, bitter] —**aus·tere′ly,** *adv.* —**aus·tere′ness,** *n.*

aus·ter·i·ty (ô ster′i tē), *n., pl.* **-ties.** **1.** austere quality; severity of manner, life, etc. **2.** Usually, **austerities.** ascetic practices. **3.** *Chiefly Brit.* a national policy of curbing inflation, bolstering the national monetary unit, and decreasing foreign debt by levying high taxes, freezing wages, restricting imports, etc. [ME *austerite* < OF *austerite* < L *austēritāt-* (s. of *austēritās*)] —**Syn. 1.** harshness. —**Ant. 1.** leniency.

Aus·ter·litz (ô′stər lits; *Ger.* ous′tər lits), *n.* a town in S Moravia, in central Czechoslovakia: Russian and Austrian armies defeated by Napoleon I 1805.

Aus·tin (ô′stən), *n.* **1. Alfred,** 1835–1913, English poet: poet laureate 1896–1913. **2. Mary (Hun·ter)** (hun′tər), 1868–1934, U.S. writer. **3. Stephen Fuller,** 1793–1836, American pioneer in Texas. **4.** See **Augustine, Saint** (def. 2). **5.** a city in and the capital of Texas, in the central part, on the Colorado River. 251,808 (1970). **6.** a city in SE Minnesota. 25,074 (1970).

Aus·tin·town (ô′stən toun′), *n.* a town in NE Ohio, near Youngstown. 29,393 (1970).

austr-, var. of **austro-** before a vowel.

aus·tral (ô′strəl), *adj.* **1.** southern. **2.** (*cap.*) Australian. [< L *austrāl(is).* See AUSTR-, -AL¹]

Austral, Australian (def. 6).

Austral., **1.** Australasia. **2.** Australia. **3.** Australian.

Aus·tral·a·sia (ô′strə lā′zhə, -shə), *n.* Australia, New Zealand, and neighboring islands in the S Pacific Ocean. [AUSTRAL(IA) + ASIA] —**Aus′tral·a′sian,** *adj., n.*

Aus·tral·ia (ô strāl′yə), *n.* **1.** a continent SE of Asia, between the Indian and the Pacific Oceans. 13,232,600; 2,948,366 sq. mi. **2. Commonwealth of,** a member of the British Commonwealth of Nations, consisting of the federated states and territories of Australia and Tasmania. 13,642,800; 2,974,581 sq. mi. *Cap.:* Canberra.

Aus·tral·ian (ô strāl′yən), *adj.* **1.** of or pertaining to Australia. **2.** *Zoogeog.* belonging to a geographical division comprising Australia, New Zealand, Tasmania, Celebes, the Moluccas, New Guinea, and adjacent smaller islands. **3.** *Phytogeog.* belonging or pertaining to a geographical division comprising Australia and Tasmania. —*n.* **4.** a native or inhabitant of Australia. **5.** an Australian aborigine. **6.** the speech of the aborigines of Australia, belonging to any of more than a hundred languages. *Abbr.:* Austral, Austral.

Austral′ian aborig′ine, one of the original natives of Australia, having dark skin, nearly straight to frizzy hair, and quite pronounced supraorbital ridges.

Austral′ian Alps′, a mountain range in SE Australia. Highest peak, Mt. Kosciusko, 7328 ft.

Austral′ian bal′lot, a ballot to be marked in secret containing the names of all the candidates for public office.

Austral′ian Cap′ital Ter′ritory, a federal territory in New South Wales, on the continent of Australia in the SE part: includes Canberra, capital of the Commonwealth of Australia. 191,900; 939 sq. mi.

Austral′ian crawl′, *Swimming.* a crawl in which the swimmer kicks twice with one leg for each stroke of the opposite arm.

Aus·tra·loid (ô′strə loid′), *n.* **1.** a racial division of mankind consisting principally of the Australian aborigines and sometimes including Papuans, Melanesians, dwarf peoples, as Negritos, of the Philippines, Malay Peninsula, and Andaman Islands, and some of the tribes of central and southern India. —*adj.* **2.** pertaining to or having the characteristics of the Australoids. Also, **Aus·tra·li·oid** (ô strā′lē oid′). [var. of *Australioid.* See AUSTRALIA, -OID]

Aus·tra·lo·pith·e·cine (ô strā′lō pith′i sīn, -sin, -pə thē′-), *n.* **1.** a primate of the extinct genus *Australopithecus,* of the Pleistocene epoch, found mainly in southern Africa. —*adj.* **2.** belonging or pertaining to the genus *Australopithecus.* [< NL *Australopithec(us)* (*austral(is)* austral + *-o-* -O- + *pithēcus* < Gk: ape) + -INE¹]

Aus·tra·sia (ô strā′zhə, -shə), *n.* the E part of the former kingdom of the Franks, comprising parts of what is now NE France, W Germany, and Belgium. *Cap.:* Metz.

Aus·tri·a (ô′strē ə), *n.* a republic in central Europe. 7,520,000; 32,381 sq. mi. *Cap.:* Vienna. German, **Österreich.** —**Aus′tri·an,** *adj., n.*

Aus·tri·a-Hun·ga·ry (ô′strē ə hung′gə rē), *n.* a monarchy (1867–1918) in central Europe that included the empire of Austria, the kingdom of Hungary, and various crown lands. —**Aus·tro-Hun·gar·i·an** (ô′strō hung gâr′ē ən), *adj., n.*

austro-, a learned borrowing from Latin meaning "south," used in the formation of compound words: *Austronesia.* Also, *esp. before a vowel,* **austr-.** [< L *aust(e)r* the south, the south wind + -o-]

Austro-, a combining form of **Austria:** *Austro-Hungarian.*

Aus·tro·a·si·at·ic (ô′strō ā′zhē at′ik, -shē-), *n.* a family of languages spoken in SE Asia, consisting principally of Vietnamese, Khmer, and the Mon languages.

Aus·tro·ne·sia (ô′strō nē′zhə), *n.* the islands of the central and S Pacific. [AUSTRO- + Gk *nēs(os)* island + *-ia* -IA]

Aus·tro·ne·sian (ô′strō nē′zhən, -shən), *adj.* **1.** of or pertaining to Austronesia or the Austronesian family of languages. **2.** Malayo-Polynesian. —*n.* **3.** Malayo-Polynesian.

aut-, var. of **auto-¹** before a vowel: *autacoid.*

au·ta·coid (ô′tə koid′), *n.* *Physiol.* a substance secreted by one organ into the blood stream or lymph, which controls organic processes elsewhere in the body; hormone. [AUT- + Gk *ák(os)* remedy + -OID] —**au′ta·coi′dal,** *adj.*

au·tar·chy (ô′tär kē), *n., pl.* **-chies. 1.** absolute sovereignty. **2.** an autocratic government. **3.** autarky. [< Gk *autarchía* self-rule] —**au·tar′chic, au·tar′chi·cal,** *adj.* —**au·tar′chi·cal·ly,** *adv.* —**au′tar·chist,** *n.*

au·tar·ky (ô′tär kē), *n., pl.* **-kies. 1.** national economic self-sufficiency. **2.** a national policy of economic independence. Also, **autarchy.** [< Gk *autárkeia* = *aut-* AUT- + *arkê(ein)* (to) suffice + *-ia* -IA] —**au·tar′kic, au·tar′ki·cal,** *adj.* —**au·tar′ki·cal·ly,** *adv.* —**au′tar·kist,** *n.*

au·te·cism (ô tē′siz əm), *n.* autoecism. —**au·te·cious** (ô tē′shəs), *adj.* —**au·te′cious·ly,** *adv.* —**au·te′cious·ness,** *n.*

aut·e·col·o·gy (ô′tə kol′ə jē), *n.* the branch of ecology dealing with the individual organism and its environment. Cf. **synecology.** —**aut·ec·o·log·ic** (ôt′ek ə loj′ik, -ē kə-), **aut′ec·o·log′i·cal,** *adj.* —**aut′ec·o·log′i·cal·ly,** *adv.*

Au·teuil (ō tœ′yə), *n.* a former town, now part of Paris, France.

auth., 1. author. **2.** authorized.

au·then·tic (ô then′tik), *adj.* **1.** entitled to acceptance or belief because of agreement with known facts or experience; reliable; trustworthy: *an authentic portrayal of the past.* **2.** not false or copied; genuine; real: *an authentic antique.* **3.** *Law.* executed with all due formalities. **4.** *Music.* **a.** (of a church mode) having a range extending from the final to the octave above. Cf. **plagal. b.** (of a cadence) consisting of a dominant harmony followed by a tonic. [< LL *authenticus* < Gk *authentikós* original, primary, at first hand = *authént(ēs)* one who does things himself (*aut-* AUT- + *-hentēs* doer) + *-ikos* -IC; r. ME *autentik* < ML *autenticus*] —**au·then′ti·cal·ly,** *adv.*

au·then·ti·cate (ô then′tə kāt′), *v.t.,* **-cat·ed, -cat·ing.** to establish as genuine, valid, or authoritative. [< ML *authenticātus* made authentic (ptp. of *authenticāre*)] —**au·then′ti·ca′tion,** *n.* —**au·then′ti·ca′tor,** *n.* —**Syn.** confirm, validate, substantiate.

au·then·tic·i·ty (ô′thin tis′i tē, -then-), *n.* the quality of being authentic; genuineness.

au·thor (ô′thər), *n.* **1.** a person who writes a novel, poem, essay, etc.; the composer of a literary work, as distinguished from a compiler, translator, editor, or copyist. **2.** the literary production or productions of a writer: *to find a passage in an author.* **3.** the maker of anything; creator. —*v.t.* **4.** to be the author of. Also, *referring to a woman,* **auth′or·ess.** [earlier *auct(h)or* < L *auctor* writer, progenitor < *auctus* magnified (ptp. of *augēre* to increase: *aug-* augment + *-tus* ptp. suffix) + *-or* -OR²; r. ME *auto(u)r* < AF; OF *autor* < L] —**au·tho·ri·al** (ô thôr′ē əl, ô thōr′-), *adj.*

au·thor·i·sa·tion (ô′thər i zā′shən), *n. Chiefly Brit.* authorization.

au·thor·ise (ô′thə rīz′), *v.t.,* **-ised, -is·ing.** *Chiefly Brit.* authorize. —**au′thor·is′a·ble,** *adj.* —**au′thor·is′er,** *n.*

au·thor·ised (ô′thə rīzd′), *adj. Chiefly Brit.* authorized.

au·thor·i·tar·i·an (ə thôr′i târ′ē ən, ə thor′-), *adj.* **1.** favoring complete subjection to authority. **2.** domineering; autocratic. **3.** of or pertaining to a governmental or political system, principle, or practice in which individual freedom is completely subordinate to the power or authority of the state, centered either in one person or a small group that is not constitutionally accountable to the people. Cf. **totalitarian.** (def. 1). —*n.* **4.** a person who favors or acts according to authoritarian principles. —**au·thor′i·tar′i·an·ism,** *n.*

au·thor·i·ta·tive (ə thôr′i tā′tiv, ə thor′-), *adj.* **1.** having due authority; having the sanction or weight of authority: *an authoritative opinion.* **2.** substantiated or supported by documentary evidence and accepted by most authorities in a field: *an authoritative edition of Keats.* **3.** peremptory; dictatorial. —**au·thor′i·ta′tive·ly,** *adv.* —**au·thor′i·ta′tive·ness,** *n.* —**Syn. 1.** official. **3.** dogmatic, authoritarian.

au·thor·i·ty (ə thôr′i tē, ə thor′-), *n., pl.* **-ties. 1.** the power to judge, act, or command. **2.** a power or right delegated or given; authorization: *He has the authority to grant permission.* **3.** a person or body of persons in whom authority is vested. **4.** Usually, **authorities.** persons having the legal power to make and enforce the law. **5.** an accepted source of information, advice, etc. **6.** a quotation or citation from such a source. **7.** an expert on a subject. **8.** persuasive force; conviction: *He spoke with authority.* **9.** judicial precedent; legal power. **10.** right to respect or acceptance of one's word, command, thought, etc.; commanding influence: *the authority of a parent.* **11.** mastery in execution or performance, as of a work of art or literature, piece of music, etc. **12.** a warrant for action; justification. **13.** testimony; witness. [earlier *auct(h)oritie* < L *auctōritāt-* (s. of *auctōritās*); r. ME *autorite* < OF < L. See AUTHOR, -ITY]
—**Syn. 1.** rule, power, sway. AUTHORITY, CONTROL, INFLUENCE denote a power or right to direct the actions or thoughts of others. AUTHORITY is a power or right, usually because of rank or office, to issue commands and to punish for violations: *to have authority over subordinates.* CONTROL is either power or influence applied to the complete and successful direction or manipulation of persons or things: *to be in control of a project.* INFLUENCE is a personal and unofficial power derived from deference of others to one's character, ability, station, or importance: *to have influence over one's friends.* **3.** sovereign, arbiter.

au·thor·i·za·tion (ô′thər i zā′shən), *n.* act of authorizing; permission or power granted by an authority; sanction. Also, *esp. Brit.,* **authorisation.**

au·thor·ize (ô′thə rīz′), *v.t.,* **-ized, -iz·ing. 1.** to give authority or official power to; empower: *to authorize a detective to make arrests.* **2.** to give authority for; formally sanction (an act or usage). **3.** to warrant or justify. Also, *esp. Brit.,* **authorise.** [earlier *auctorize* < ML *auctōriz(āre)*; r. ME *autorise* < MF *autorise(er)* < ML. See AUTHOR, -IZE] —**au′thor·iz′a·ble,** *adj.* —**au′thor·iz′er,** *n.*

au·thor·ized (ô′thə rīzd′), *adj.* **1.** given or endowed with authority: *an authorized agent.* **2.** legally or duly sanctioned. Also, *esp. Brit.,* **authorised.**

Au′thorized Ver′sion, an English version of the Bible prepared under James I and published in 1611. Also called **King James Version.**

au·thor·ship (ô′thər ship′), *n.* **1.** the occupation or career of writing books, articles, etc. **2.** origin of a work, esp. with reference to an author, creator, producer, etc.

Auth. Ver., See **Authorized Version.**

au·tism (ô′tiz əm), *n. Psychol.* self-absorption, esp. extreme withdrawal into fantasy. —**au·tis·tic** (ô tis′tik), *adj.*

au·to (ô′tō), *n., pl.* **-tos.** automobile. [shortened form]

auto-¹, a word element meaning "self," "same," used in the formation of compound words: *autograph.* Also, *esp. before a vowel,* **aut-.** [< Gk, comb. form of *autós* self]

auto-², a combining form of **automobile:** *autobus.*

auto., 1. automatic. **2.** automobile. **3.** automotive.

au·to·bahn (ô′tə bän′; *Ger.* ou′tō bän′), *n., pl.* **-bahns, -bahn·en** (-bä′nən). (in Germany) a superhighway. [< G: path for cars = *auto-* AUTO-¹ + *Bahn* track, road]

au·to·bi·o·graph·i·cal (ô′tə bī′ə graf′i kəl), *adj.* marked by or dealing with one's own experiences or life history; of or in the manner of an autobiography. Also, **au′to·bi′o·graph′ic.** —**au′to·bi′o·graph′i·cal·ly,** *adv.*

au·to·bi·og·ra·phy (ô′tə bī og′rə fē, -bē-), *n., pl.* **-phies.** an account of a person's life written by himself. —**au′to·bi·og′ra·pher,** *n.*

au·to·bus (ô′tə bus′), *n., pl.* **-bus·es, -bus·ses.** bus (def. 1).

au·to·ca·tal·y·sis (ô′tō kə tal′i sis), *n., pl.* **-ses** (-sēz′). *Chem., Biochem.* catalysis caused by a catalytic agent formed during a reaction. —**au·to·cat·a·lyt·ic** (ô′tō kat′əlit′ik), *adj.* —**au′to·cat′a·lyt′i·cal·ly,** *adv.*

au·to·ceph·a·lous (ô′tə sef′ə ləs), *adj. Eastern Ch.* **1.** (of a church) having its own head or chief bishop, though in communion with other Orthodox churches. **2.** (of a bishop) subordinate to no superior authority. [< LGk *autoképhalos* having its own head]

au·toch·thon (ô tok′thən), *n., pl.* **-thons, -tho·nes** (-thə nēz′). **1.** an aboriginal inhabitant. **2.** *Ecol.* one of the native animals or plants of a region. [< Gk *autóchthōn* of the land itself = *auto-* AUTO-¹ + *chthṓn* the earth, land, ground]

au·toch·tho·nous (ô tok′thə nəs), *adj.* **1.** pertaining to autochthons; aboriginal; indigenous (opposed to *heterochthonous*). **2.** native to a place or thing. Also, **au·toch′tho·nal, au·toch·thon·ic** (ô′tok thon′ik). —**au·toch′tho·nism, au·toch′tho·ny,** *n.* —**au·toch′tho·nous·ly,** *adv.*

au·to·clave (ô′tə klāv′), *n., v.,* **-claved, -clav·ing.** —*n.* **1.** an apparatus using steam under pressure, esp. for sterilizing medical equipment. —*v.t.* **2.** to place in an autoclave. [< F = *auto-* AUTO-¹ + *clave* < L *clāv-*, s. of *clāvis* key and *clāvus* nail]

au·toc·ra·cy (ô tok′rə sē), *n., pl.* **-cies. 1.** uncontrolled or unlimited authority over others, invested in a single person; the government or power of an absolute monarch. **2.** a nation, state, or community ruled by an autocrat. [< Gk *autokráteia* power over oneself, sole power = *autokrat(ḗs)* AUTOCRAT + *-eia* -IA; see -CY]

au·to·crat (ô′tə krat′), *n.* **1.** a ruler who holds unlimited powers. **2.** a person invested with, or claiming to exercise, absolute authority. **3.** a domineering person. [< Gk *autokrat(ḗs)* self-ruling, ruling alone = *auto-* AUTO-¹ + *krate-* (s. of *krátos* power) + *-ēs* adj. suffix]

au·to·crat·ic (ô′tə krat′ik), *adj.* **1.** pertaining to or of the nature of autocracy or of an autocrat; absolute: *autocratic government.* **2.** like an autocrat; tyrannical; despotic; domineering: *autocratic behavior; an autocratic person.* Also, **au′to·crat′i·cal.** —**au′to·crat′i·cal·ly,** *adv.*

au·to-da-fé (ô′tō də fā′), *n., pl.* **au·tos-da-fé.** the public declaration of the judgment passed by the courts of the Spanish Inquisition, and the execution of it by the secular authorities, esp. the burning of condemned heretics at the stake. [< Pg: act of the faith]

au·to de fe (ou′tō the fe′), *pl.* **au·tos de fe** (ou′tôs the fe′). *Spanish.* auto-da-fé.

au·to·dyne (ô′tə dīn′), *n. Electronics.* a type of heterodyne circuit containing a vacuum tube or transistor that acts simultaneously as a detector and oscillator.

au·toe·cism (ô tē′siz əm), *n. Bot.* the development of the entire life cycle of a parasitic fungus on a single host or group of hosts. Also, **autecism.** [AUT- + *oec-* (< Gk *oik-*, s. of *oikos* house) + -ISM] —**au·toe·cious** (ô tē′shəs), *adj.* —**au·toe′cious·ly,** *adv.* —**au·toe′cious·ness,** *n.*

au·to·er·o·tism (ô′tō er′ə tiz′əm), *n. Psychoanal.* the arousal and satisfaction of sexual emotion within or by oneself, usually by masturbation. Also, **au·to·e·rot·i·cism** (ô′tō i rot′i siz′əm). —**au′to·e·rot′ic,** *adj.* —**au′to·e·rot′i·cal·ly,** *adv.*

au·tog·a·my (ô tog′ə mē), *n.* **1.** *Bot.* self-fertilization of a flower (opposed to *allogamy*). **2.** (in certain protozoans) conjugation by division of the nucleus into two parts that reunite to form a zygote. —**au·tog′a·mous, au·to·gam·ic** (ô′tō gam′ik), *adj.*

au·to·gen·e·sis (ô′tō jen′i sis), *n. Biol.* abiogenesis. Also, **au·tog·e·ny** (ô toj′ə nē). —**au·to·ge·net·ic** (ô′tō jə net′ik), *adj.* —**au′to·ge·net′i·cal·ly,** *adv.*

au·tog·e·nous (ô toj′ə nəs), *adj.* **1.** self-produced; self-generated. **2.** *Physiol.* pertaining to substances generated in the body. [< Gk *autogen(ḗs)* self-produced. See AUTO-¹, -GEN, -OUS] —**au·tog′e·nous·ly,** *adv.*

au·to·gi·ro (ô′tə jī′rō), *n., pl.* **-ros.** an aircraft having a conventional propeller for forward motion and a horizontal rotor, rotated by airflow, for lift. Also, **au′to·gy′ro.** Also called **gyroplane.** [after *Autogiro,* a trademark]

au·to·graft (ô′tə graft′, -gräft′), *n. Surg.* a tissue or organ grafted onto another part of the body from which it was removed. Also called **autoplast.** Cf. **homograft.**

au·to·graph (ô′tə graf′, -gräf′), *n.* **1.** a person's signature, esp. a signature of a famous person for keeping as a memento. **2.** anything written in one's own hand. —*adj.* **3.** written by a person's own hand: *an autograph letter.* **4.** containing autographs: *an autograph album.* —*v.t.* **5.** to write one's name on or in; sign, esp. as a memento: *to autograph a book.* **6.** to write with one's own hand. [< LL *autograph(um),* n. use of neut. of L *autographus* written with one's own hand < Gk *autógraphos*] —**au·to·graph·ic** (ô′tə graf′ik), **au′to·graph′i·cal,** *adj.* —**au′to·graph′i·cal·ly,** *adv.* —**au·tog·ra·phy** (ô tog′rə fē), *n.*

au·to·harp (ô′tō härp′), *n.* a zither having buttons which, when depressed by the finger, dampen all the strings necessary to the chord desired.

au·to·hyp·no·sis (ô′tō hip nō′sis), *n.* self-induced hypnosis or hypnotic state. —**au·to·hyp·not·ic** (ô′tō hip not′ik), *adj.* —**au′to·hyp·not′i·cal·ly,** *adv.*

au·toi·cous (ô toi′kəs), *adj.* *Bot.* having antheridia and archegonia on the same plant. [AUT- + *oic-* (< Gk *oik-*, s. of *oikos* house) + -OUS]

au·to·ig·ni·tion (ô′tō ig nish′ən), *n.* See **spontaneous combustion.**

au·to·in·fec·tion (ô′tō in fek′shən), *n.* *Pathol.* infection from within the body.

au·to·in·oc·u·la·tion (ô′tō i nok′yə lā′shən), *n.* inoculation of a healthy part with an infective agent from a diseased part of the same body. —**au·to·in·oc·u·la·ble** (ô′tō i-nok′yə lə bəl), *adj.* —**au′to·in·oc′u·la·bil′i·ty,** *n.*

au·to·in·tox·i·ca·tion (ô′tō in tok′sə kā′shən), *n.* *Pathol.* poisoning with toxic substances formed within the body, as during intestinal digestion. Also called **autotoxemia.** —**au·to·tox·ic** (ô′tō tok′sik), *adj.*

au·to·ly·sin (ôt′ᵊlī′sin, ô tol′i-), *n.* any agent producing autolysis. [AUTOLYS(IS) + -IN[2]]

au·tol·y·sis (ô tol′i sis), *n.* *Biochem.* the breakdown of plant or animal tissue by the action of enzymes contained in the tissue affected; self-digestion. —**au·to·lyt·ic** (ôt′ᵊlit′ik), *adj.*

au·to·lyze (ôt′ᵊlīz′), *v.*, **-lyzed, -lyz·ing.** *Biochem.* —*v.t.* **1.** to cause autolysis in. —*v.i.* **2.** to undergo autolysis. [back formation from AUTOLYSIS, modeled on ANALYZE]

au·to·mat (ô′tə mat′), *n.* a restaurant using coin-operated equipment to dispense food. [short for AUTOMATON]

au·tom·a·ta (ô tom′ə tə), *n.* a pl. of **automaton.**

au·to·mate (ô′tə māt′), *v.*, **-mat·ed, -mat·ing.** —*v.t.* **1.** to apply the principles of automation to (a mechanical process, industry, office, or the like). **2.** to operate or control by automation. —*v.i.* **3.** to install automatic procedures, as for manufacturing, servicing, etc.; follow or utilize the principles of automation: *Many banks have begun to automate.* [back formation from AUTOMATION]

au·to·mat·ic (ô′tə mat′ik), *adj.* **1.** having the power of self-motion; self-moving or self-acting: *an automatic device.* **2.** *Physiol.* occurring independently of volition, as certain muscular actions; involuntary. **3.** (of a firearm, pistol, etc.) utilizing the recoil or part of the force of the explosive to eject the spent cartridge shell, introduce a new cartridge, cock the arm, and fire it repeatedly. **4.** done unconsciously or from force of habit; mechanical. **5.** occurring spontaneously: *automatic enthusiasm.* —*n.* **6.** a machine that operates automatically. **7.** See **automatic rifle. 8.** See **automatic pistol.** [< Gk *autómat(os)* self-moving (see AUTOMATON) + -IC] —**au′to·mat′i·cal·ly,** *adv.* —**au·to·ma·tic·i·ty** (ô′tə mə tis′i tē), *n.*
—**Syn. 2.** AUTOMATIC, INVOLUNTARY both mean not under the control of the will. That which is AUTOMATIC, however, is an invariable reaction to a fixed type of stimulus: *The patellar reflex is automatic.* That which is INVOLUNTARY is an unexpected response that varies according to the occasion, circumstances, mood, etc.: *an involuntary cry of pain.*

au′tomat′ic da′ta proc′essing, the processing of information by electronic computers or the like, using techniques which reduce human intervention to a minimum. *Abbr.:* ADP Cf. **integrated data processing.**

au′tomat′ic pi′lot, *Aeron.* a control system that automatically maintains an aircraft on a preset heading and altitude. Also called **gyropilot.**

au′tomat′ic pis′tol, a pistol having a mechanism that throws out the empty shell, puts in a new one, and prepares the pistol to be fired again. Also called **automatic.**

au′tomat′ic ri′fle, a light machine gun capable of firing automatically or in single shots. Also called **machine rifle.**

automat′ic transmis′sion, an automotive transmission requiring either very little or no manual shifting of gears. Also called **au′tomat′ic drive′.**

au·to·ma·tion (ô′tə mā′shən), *n.* **1.** the technique, method, or system of operating or controlling a mechanical or productive process by highly automatic means, as by electronic devices, reducing human intervention to a minimum. **2.** act or process of automating. **3.** the state of being automated. [AUTOMAT(IC) + -ATION]

au·tom·a·tism (ô tom′ə tiz′əm), *n.* **1.** action or condition of being automatic; mechanical or involuntary action. **2.** *Philos.* the doctrine that all activities of men and animals are entirely controlled by physical or physiological causes in which consciousness takes no part. **3.** *Physiol.* the involuntary functioning of an organic process, esp. muscular, without apparent neural stimulation. **4.** *Psychol.* **a.** performance of acts by an individual without his awareness or conscious volition. **b.** such an act, as sleepwalking. **5.** the act or doctrine, esp. of the Surrealists, of allowing the unconscious mind to find expression through uncontrolled or uncensored images. [< Gk *automatism(ós)* a happening of itself. See AUTOMATON, -ISM] —**au·tom′a·tist,** *n.*

au·tom·a·ton (ô tom′ə ton′, -tᵊn), *n.*, *pl.* **-tons, -ta** (-tə). **1.** a mechanical figure or contrivance constructed to act as if by its own motive power; robot. **2.** a person who acts in a monotonous, routine manner, without active intelligence. [< L: a self-moving machine < Gk, n. use of neut. of *autómatos* self-moving = *auto-* AUTO-[1] + *-matos* (*ma-* strive after, move + *-tos* adj. suffix)] —**au·tom′a·tous,** *adj.*

au·to·mo·bile (ô′tə mə bēl′, ô′tə mə bēl′, ô′tə mō′bēl, -bil), *n.* **1.** *Chiefly U.S.* a passenger vehicle designed for operation on ordinary roads for the convenience of an individual or family and typically having four wheels and an internal-combustion gasoline engine. —*adj.* **2.** automotive. [< F: lit., self-movable (vehicle)] —**au·to·mo·bil·ist** (ô′tə-mə bē′list, -mō′bi list), *n.*

au·to·mo·tive (ô′tə mō′tiv, ô′tə mō′tiv), *adj.* **1.** pertaining to the design, operation, manufacture, or sale of automobiles: *automotive parts.* **2.** propelled by a self-contained motor, engine, or the like.

au·to·nom·ic (ô′tə nom′ik), *adj.* **1.** autonomous. **2.** of or pertaining to the autonomic nervous system. **3.** *Bot.* produced by internal forces or causes; spontaneous. Also, **au′to·nom′i·cal.** [AUTONOM(Y) + -IC] —**au′to·nom′i·cal·ly,** *adv.*

au′tonom′ic nerv′ous sys′tem, the system of nerves and ganglia that innervates the blood vessels, heart, smooth muscles, viscera, and glands and controls their involuntary functions, consisting of a sympathetic and parasympathetic division.

au·ton·o·mous (ô ton′ə məs), *adj.* **1.** self-governing. **2.** of or pertaining to a self-governing or independent state, community, organization, etc. **3.** *Biol.* existing as an independent organism and not as a form or state of development of an organism. **4.** *Bot.* spontaneous. [< Gk *autónomos* with laws of one's own, independent = *auto-* AUTO-[1] + *nóm(os)* law, custom + *-os* adj. suffix] —**au·ton′o·mous·ly,** *adv.*

au·ton·o·my (ô ton′ə mē), *n.*, *pl.* **-mies. 1.** independence or freedom: *the autonomy of the individual.* **2.** the condition of being autonomous; the right of self-government; independence. **3.** a self-governing community. [< Gk *autonomía* independence = *autónom(os)* AUTONOMOUS + *-ia* -Y[3]] —**au·ton′o·mist,** *n.*

au·to·phyte (ô′tə fīt′), *n.* any plant that produces its own food. —**au·to·phyt·ic** (ô′tə fit′ik), *adj.* —**au′to·phyt′i·cal·ly,** *adv.*

au·to·plast (ô′tə plast′), *n.* *Surg.* autograft.

au·to·plas·ty (ô′tə plas′tē), *n.* *Surg.* the repair of defects with tissue from another part of the patient's body. —**au′to·plas′tic,** *adj.*

au·top·sy (ô′top sē, ô′təp-), *n.*, *pl.* **-sies. 1.** inspection and dissection of a body after death, as for determination of the cause of death; post-mortem examination. **2.** a highly critical analysis of something past or completed. [< Gk *autopsía* a seeing with one's own eyes = *aut-* AUT- + *óps(is)* -OPSIS + *-ia* -Y[3]] —**au·top′sic, au·top′si·cal,** *adj.* —**au′top·sist,** *n.*

au·to·ra·di·o·graph (ô′tə rā′dē ə graf′, -gräf′), *n.* a picture revealing the presence of radioactive material, the film being laid directly on the object to be tested. Also called **radioautograph.** —**au·to·ra·di·og·ra·phy** (ô′tō rā′dē og′rə fē), *n.*

au·to·some (ô′tə sōm′), *n.* *Genetics.* any chromosome other than a sex chromosome. Also called **euchromosome.** [AUTO-[1] + -SOME[3]]

au·to·sug·ges·tion (ô′tō səg jes′chən, -jesh′-, -sə-), *n.* *Psychol.* suggestion arising from oneself, esp. the repetition of verbal formulas in the hope of changing behavior. —**au·to·sug·gest·i·bil·i·ty** (ô′tō səg jes′tə bil′i tē), *n.* —**au′to·sug·gest′i·ble,** *adj.* —**au′to·sug·ges′tive,** *adj.*

au·tot·o·mise (ô tot′ə mīz′), *v.t.*, **-mised, -mis·ing.** *Chiefly Brit.* autotomize.

au·tot·o·mize (ô tot′ə mīz′), *v.*, **-mized, -miz·ing.** —*v.i.* **1.** to undergo autotomy. —*v.t.* **2.** to effect autotomy of (a part).

au·tot·o·my (ô tot′ə mē), *n.*, *pl.* **-mies.** *Zool.* self-amputation or shedding of a damaged or trapped appendage, as tails by lizards, legs by spiders and crabs, etc. [AUTO-[1] + -TOMY] —**au·to·tom·ic** (ô′tə tom′ik), *adj.*

au·to·tox·e·mi·a (ô′tō tok sē′mē ə), *n.* *Pathol.* autointoxication. Also, **au′to·tox·ae′mi·a.**

au·to·tox·in (ô′tə tok′sin), *n.* *Pathol.* a toxin or poisonous substance formed within the body and acting against it. —**au′to·tox′ic,** *adj.*

au·to·trans·form·er (ô′tō trans fôr′mər), *n.* *Elect.* a transformer having a single coil that serves as both primary and secondary.

au·to·troph (ô′tə trof′, -trôf′), *n.* an organism utilizing inorganic materials as food, as most plants and certain bacteria and protozoans. Cf. **heterotroph.** [back formation from AUTOTROPHIC. See AUTO-[1], -TROPHIC] —**au·to·troph·ic** (ô′tə trof′ik), *adj.* —**au′to·troph′i·cal·ly,** *adv.* —**au·tot·ro·phy** (ô to′trə fē), *n.*

au·to·type (ô′tə tīp′), *n.* **1.** facsimile (defs. 1, 2). **2.** *Photog.* a process for producing permanent prints in a carbon pigment. —**au·to·typ·ic** (ô′tə tip′ik), *adj.* —**au·to·typ·y** (ô′tə tī′pē), *n.*

au·tox·i·da·tion (ô tok′si dā′shən), *n.* *Chem.* the oxidation of a compound by exposure to air.

au·tumn (ô′təm), *n.* the season between summer and winter; fall: in the Northern Hemisphere, from the September equinox to the December solstice; in the Southern Hemisphere, from the March equinox to the June solstice. [< L *autumn(us)*; r. ME *autumpne* < MF *autompne* < L]

au·tum·nal (ô tum′nᵊl), *adj.* **1.** belonging to or suggestive of autumn; produced or gathered in autumn. **2.** past maturity or middle life. [< L *autumnāl(is)*] —**au·tum′nal·ly,** *adv.*

autum′nal e′quinox, 1. See under **equinox** (def. 1). **2.** Also called **autum′nal point′.** the position of the sun at the time of the autumnal equinox.

au′tumn cro′cus, any of several liliaceous herbs of the genus *Colchicum,* esp. *C. autumnale,* bearing showy white, pink, or purple flowers in autumn.

au·tun·ite (ôt′ᵊnīt′, ō tun′īt), *n.* a yellow mineral, a hydrous calcium uranium phosphate, $CaU_2P_2O_{12}\cdot 8H_2O$, occurring in crystals as nearly square tablets: a minor ore of uranium; lime uranite. [named after *Autun,* city in E France near source of supply; see -ITE[1]]

Au·vergne (ō vârn′, ō vûrn′; *Fr.* ō verN′yᵊ), *n.* a former province in central France. See map at **Gascony.**

aux-, var. of **auxo-,** esp. before a vowel: *auxin.*

aux., auxiliary. Also, **auxil.**

Aux Cayes (ō kā′), former name of **Les Cayes.**

aux·e·sis (ôg zē′sis, ôk sē′-), *n.* *Biol.* growth, esp. that resulting from an increase in cell size. Cf. **merisis.** [< Gk: increase = *aúx(ein)* (to) increase + *-sis* -SIS]

aux·et·ic (ôg zet′ik, ôk set′-), *Biol.* —*adj.* **1.** pertaining to or promoting auxesis. —*n.* **2.** an auxetic agent. [< Gk *auxētik(ós)* increasing = *auxēt(ós)* increased + *-ikos* -IC]

aux·il·ia·ry (ôg zil′yə rē, -zil′ə-), *adj.*, *n.*, *pl.* **-ries.** —*adj.* **1.** subsidiary; additional; supplementary: *auxiliary troops.* **2.** used as a reserve: *an auxiliary engine.* **3.** giving support; serving as an aid; helpful. —*n.* **4.** a person or thing that gives aid of any kind; helper. **5.** an organization allied with, but subsidiary to, a main body of restricted membership, esp. one composed of members' wives, mothers, etc. **6.** See **auxiliary verb. 7. auxiliaries,** foreign troops in the service of a nation at war. **8.** *Navy.* a naval vessel designed for other than combat purposes, as a tug, supply ship, transport, etc. **9.** a sailing vessel with one or more propulsion engines. [< L *auxiliāri(us)* assisting, aiding, helping = *auxili(um)* aid, help (*aux(us)* increased, augmented (ptp. of *augēre; aug-* augment + *-sus*, var. of *-tus* ptp. suffix) + *-ilium* n. suffix) + *-ārius* -ARY] **—Syn. 1.** abetting. **2.** ancillary, secondary. **4.** aide, assistant; help.

auxil′iary verb′, a word used in construction with and preceding a certain form of a main verb, as an infinitive or participle, to express distinctions of tense, aspect, mood, etc., as *do* in *I do think; am* in *I am going; have* in *We have spoken; may* in *May we go?; can* in *They can see; shall* in *We shall work.*

aux·in (ôk′sin), *n. Bot., Chem.* a class of substances that in minute amounts regulate or modify the growth of plants.

auxo-, a learned borrowing from Greek meaning "growth," "increase," used in the formation of compound words: *auxochrome.* Also, *esp. before a vowel,* **aux-.** [< Gk *aûx(ein)* (to) grow, increase (var. of *auxánein*) + -o-]

aux·o·chrome (ôk′sə krōm′), *n. Chem.* any group of atoms that intensifies the color of a substance. **—aux′o·chrom′ic,** *adj.*

Av (ôv; *Heb.* äb), *n.* Ab.

av., **1.** avenue. **2.** average. **3.** See **avoirdupois weight.**

A/V, ad valorem. Also, **a.v.**

A.V., 1. Artillery Volunteers. **2.** See **Authorized Version.**

a·va (ə vä′, ə vô′), *adv. Scot.* of all; at all. Also, **a·va′.**

a·vail (ə vāl′), *v.t.* **1.** to be of use or value to; profit; advantage: *All our efforts availed us little.* **—***v.i.* **2.** to be of use; have force or efficacy; serve; help. **3.** to be of value or profit. **4. avail oneself of,** to use to one's advantage. **—***n.* **5.** advantage; effective use in the achievement of some goal or objective: *of little or no avail.* **6. avails,** *Archaic.* profits or proceeds. [ME *availe* = *a-* A-[2] + *vaile* < OF *vail-* (s. of *valoir*) < L *val(ēre)* (to) be of worth] **—a·vail′ing·ly,** *adv.*

a·vail·a·bil·i·ty (ə vā′lə bil′i tē), *n., pl.* **-ties. 1.** the state of being available. **2.** a person or thing that is available.

a·vail·a·ble (ə vā′lə bəl), *adj.* **1.** suitable or ready for use; usable; at hand: *He used whatever excuse seemed available.* **2.** readily obtainable; accessible: *available resources.* **3.** having sufficient power or efficacy; valid. **4.** *Archaic.* efficacious; profitable; advantageous. [late ME; see AVAIL, -ABLE] **—a·vail′a·ble·ness,** *n.* **—a·vail′a·bly,** *adv.*

avail′able light′, *Photog., Fine Arts.* the natural or usual light on a subject.

av·a·lanche (av′ə lanch′, -länch′), *n., v.,* **-lanched, -lanch·ing. —***n.* **1.** a large mass of snow, ice, etc., detached from a mountain slope and sliding or falling suddenly downward. **2.** anything like an avalanche in suddenness and destructiveness: *an avalanche of misfortunes.* **—***v.i.* **3.** to come down in, or like, an avalanche. **—***v.t.* **4.** to overwhelm with an extremely large amount of anything; swamp. [< F < *la valanche* (taken as *l'avalanche*) = *la* the + *valanche* metathetic var. of dial. *lavantse,* akin to OPr *lavanca* avalanche]

Av·a·lon (av′ə lon′), *n. Celtic Legend.* an island, represented as an earthly paradise in the western seas, to which King Arthur and other heroes were carried at death. Also, **Av′al·lon′.** [< ML (*insula*) *avallonis* (island) of Avallon (Geoffrey of Monmouth), lit., apple (island) < OWelsh *aballon* APPLE]

a·vant-garde (ə vänt′gärd′, ə vant′-; *Fr.* A VÄN GARD′), *n.* **1.** the advance group in any field, esp. in the visual, literary, or musical arts, whose works are characterized chiefly by unorthodox and experimental methods. **—***adj.* **2.** of or pertaining to the experimental treatment of artistic, musical, or literary material. **3.** belonging to the avant-garde. [< F: lit., fore-guard. See VANGUARD] **—a·vant′-gard′ism,** *n.* **—a·vant′-gard′ist,** *n.*

av·a·rice (av′ər is), *n.* insatiable greed for riches; inordinate desire to gain and hoard wealth. [ME < OF < L *avāritia* = *avār(us)* greedy + *-itia* -ICE]

av·a·ri·cious (av′ə rish′əs), *adj.* characterized by avarice; covetous. [late ME] **—av′a·ri′cious·ly,** *adv.* **—av′a·ri′cious·ness,** *n.*

a·vast (ə vast′, ə väst′), *interj. Naut.* stop! cease!: *Avast heaving!* [perh. < D *hou(d) vast* HOLD[1] FAST[1]]

av·a·tar (av′ə tär′), *n.* **1.** *Hindu Myth.* the descent of a deity to the earth in an incarnate form or some manifest shape; the incarnation of a god. **2.** an embodiment or concrete manifestation of an abstract concept. [< Skt *avatāra* a passing down = *ava* down + *-tāra* a passing over]

a·vaunt (ə vônt′, ə vänt′), *interj. Archaic.* away! go! [ME < MF *avant* to the front < LL *ab ante* before (L: from before). See AB-, ANTE-]

avdp., See **avoirdupois weight.**

a·ve (ä′vā, ā′vē), *interj.* **1.** hail! welcome! **2.** farewell! good-by! **—***n.* **3.** the salutation "ave." **4.** (*cap.*) See **Ave Maria.** [< L: impv. sing. of *avēre* to be well, fare well]

Ave., avenue. Also, **ave.**

Ave·bur·y (āv′bə rē), *n.* **Baron.** See **Lubbock, Sir John.**

A·vel·la·ne·da (ä ve′yä ne′thä), *n.* a city in E Argentina, near Buenos Aires. 329,626 (1960).

A·ve Ma·ri·a (ä′vā mə rē′ə, ä′vē), a prayer in the Roman Catholic Church, based on the salutation of the angel Gabriel to the Virgin Mary and the words of Elizabeth to her, meaning "Hail Mary." Also, **A·ve Mar·y** (ä′vē mâr′ē, ä′vā). Also called **Hail Mary.**

av·e·na·ceous (av′ə nā′shəs), *adj. Bot.* of or like oats. [< L *avēnāceus* = *avēn(a)* oats + *-āceus* -ACEOUS]

a·venge (ə venj′), *v.,* **a·venged, a·veng·ing. —***v.t.* **1.** to take vengeance or exact satisfaction for: *to avenge the death of a brother.* **2.** to take vengeance on behalf of: *to avenge one's brother.* **—***v.i.* **3.** to take vengeance. [ME *avenge(n)* < OF *avengie(r)* = *a-* A-[5] + *vengier* < L *vindicāre;* see VINDICATE] **—a·venge′ful,** *adj.* **—a·veng′er,** *n.*

—Syn. 1, 2. vindicate. AVENGE, REVENGE both mean to inflict pain or harm in return for pain or harm inflicted on oneself or those persons or causes to which one feels loyalty. The two words were formerly interchangeable, but have been differentiated until they now convey widely diverse ideas. AVENGE is now restricted to inflicting punishment as an act of retributive justice or as a vindication of propriety: *to avenge a murder by bringing the criminal to trial.* REVENGE implies inflicting pain or harm to retaliate for wrongs; a reflexive pronoun is often used with this verb: *He revenged himself upon his tormentors.* **—Ant. 1, 3.** forgive.

av·ens (av′inz), *n., pl.* **-ens.** any perennial, rosaceous herb of the genus *Geum,* having yellow, white, or red flowers. [ME *avence* < OF < ML *avencia* kind of clover]

av·en·tail (av′ən tāl′), *n. Armor.* **1.** Also called **camail.** a mail tippet suspended from the lower edges of a 14th-century basinet as a protection for the neck, throat, and shoulders. **2.** ventail. [ME = *a-* (< ?) + VENTAIL]

Av·en·tine (av′ən tin′, -tin), *n.* one of the seven hills on which ancient Rome was built.

a·ven·tu·rine (ə ven′chə rin), *n.* **1.** an opaque, brown glass containing fine, gold-colored particles. **2.** any of several varieties of minerals, esp. quartz or feldspar, spangled with bright particles of mica, hematite, or other minerals. Also, **a·ven′tu·rin.** Also called **goldstone.** [< F < It *avventurin(a)* = *avventur(a)* chance (see ADVENTURE) + *-ina* -INE[2]; so called because rare and found by chance]

av·e·nue (av′ə nyōō′, -nōō′), *n.* **1.** a wide street or main thoroughfare. **2.** means of access or attainment: *avenues of escape.* **3.** a wide, often tree-lined road, path, or driveway, etc., esp. one leading to a building, monument, etc. [< F, lit., approach, n. use of fem. ptp. of *avenir* < L *advenīre* to come to. See A-[5], VENUE] **—Syn. 1.** See **street.**

A·ven·zo·ar (ä′vən zō′är), *n.* 1091?–1162, Arab physician in Spain. Also called **Abumeron.**

a·ver (ə vûr′), *v.t.,* **a·verred, a·ver·ring. 1.** to affirm with confidence; declare positively. **2.** *Law.* to allege as a fact. [ME < MF *aver(er)* < ML *adverāre* = *ad-* AD- + *-vēr-* (< L *vērus* true) + *-ā-* thematic vowel + *-re* inf. suffix]

av·er·age (av′ər ij, av′rij), *n., adj., v.,* **-aged, -ag·ing. —***n.* **1.** a typical amount, rate, quality, etc.; norm; mean. **2.** *Math.* a quantity intermediate to a set of quantities. **3.** See **arithmetic mean. 4.** *Com.* **a.** an expense, partial loss, or damage to a ship or cargo. **b.** an equitable apportionment among all interested parties of such an expense or loss. **5.** Often, **averages.** *Stock Exchange.* the mean value of a number of stocks or securities as an indication of current price levels: *Industrial averages were up.* **6. on the** or **an average,** usually; typically. **—***adj.* **7.** of or pertaining to an average. **8.** typical; common; ordinary. **—***v.t.* **9.** to find an average value for; reduce or divide to a mean. **10.** to amount to, as a mean quantity: *Wheat averages 56 pounds to a bushel.* **—***v.i.* **11.** *U.S.* to have, show, or reach an average: *to average as expected.* [late ME *averay* charge on goods shipped, orig. duty (< MF *avarie* < ?) + -AGE] **—av′er·age·ly,** *adv.*

av′erage devia′tion. See **mean deviation.**

a·ver·ment (ə vûr′mənt), *n.* **1.** the act of averring. **2.** a positive statement. [late ME *averrement* < MF]

A·ver·nus (ə vûr′nəs), *n.* **1.** a lake near Naples, Italy: crater of extinct volcano, in classical mythology believed to be the entrance to Hades. **2.** hell. [< L < Gk *áornos* birdless = *a-* A-[6] + *órn(is)* bird + *-os* adj. suffix] **—A·ver′nal,** *adj.*

A·ver·ro·ës (ə ver′ō ēz′), *n.* 1126?–98, Arab philosopher in Spain. Also, **A·ver′rho·ës′. —Av·er·ro·ism, Av·er·rho·ism** (av′ə rō′iz əm, ə ver′ō-), *n.* **—Av′er·ro′ist, Av′er·rho′ist,** *n.* **—Av′er·ro·is′tic, Av′er·rho·is′tic,** *adj.*

a·verse (ə vûrs′), *adj.* **1.** having a strong feeling of opposition, antipathy, repugnance, etc.; opposed. **2.** *Bot.* turned away from the central axis (opposed to *adverse*). [< L *āvers-(us)* turned away, averted (ptp. of *āvertere*) = *ā-* A-[4] + *vert-* turn + *-sus* ptp. suffix] **—a·verse′ly,** *adv.* **—a·verse′ness,** *n.* **—Syn. 1.** unwilling, loath. See **reluctant. —Ant. 1.** eager.

a·ver·sion (ə vûr′zhən, -shən), *n.* **1.** a strong desire to avoid because of dislike; repugnance: (usually fol. by *to*). **2.** a cause or object of dislike; person or thing that causes antipathy: *a pet aversion.* **3.** *Obs.* the act of averting; a turning away or preventing. [< L *āversiōn-* (s. of *āversiō*)] **—a·ver·sive** (ə vûr′siv, -ziv), *adj.*

—Syn. 1. distaste, abhorrence, disgust. AVERSION, ANTIPATHY, LOATHING connote strong dislike or detestation. AVERSION is an unreasoning desire to avoid that which displeases, annoys, or offends: *an aversion to* (or *toward*) *cats.* ANTIPATHY is a distaste, dislike, or disgust toward something: *an antipathy toward* (or *for*) *braggarts.* LOATHING connotes a combination of hatred and disgust, or detestation: *a loathing for* (or *toward*) *venison.* **—Ant. 1.** predilection.

a·vert (ə vûrt′), *v.t.* **1.** to turn away or aside: *to avert one's eyes.* **2.** to ward off; prevent: *to avert evil.* [late ME < MF *avert(ir)* << L *āvertere* = *ā-* A-[4] + *vertere* to turn] **—a·vert′ed·ly,** *adv.* **—a·vert′i·ble, a·vert′a·ble,** *adj.*

A·ver·y (ā′və rē), *n.* **Milton,** 1893–1965. U.S. painter.

A·ves (ā′vēz), *n.* (*construed as pl.*) the class comprising the birds. [L, pl. of *avis* bird]

A·ves·ta (ə ves′tə), *n.* a collection of sacred Zoroastrian writings, including the Gathas.

A·ves·tan (ə ves′tən), *n.* **1.** an ancient East Iranian language of the Indo-European family, the language of all the Avesta but the Gathas. **—***adj.* **2.** of or pertaining to the Avesta or its language.

avg., average.

avi-, a learned borrowing from Latin meaning "bird," used in the formation of compound words: *aviculture.* [< L, comb. form of *avis*]

a·vi·an (ā′vē ən), *adj.* of or pertaining to birds.

a·vi·ar·y (ā′vē er′ē), *n., pl.* **-ar·ies.** a large enclosure in which birds are kept. [< L *aviāri(um)* a place where birds are kept, n. use of neut. of *aviārius* pertaining to birds.

a·vi·ate (ā′vē āt′, av′ē-), *v.i.,* **-at·ed, -at·ing.** to fly in an aircraft. [back formation from AVIATION]

a·vi·a·tion (ā′vē ā′shən, av′ē-), *n.* **1.** the act, method, or science of flying by mechanical means, esp. with heavier-than-air craft. **2.** the design, development, and production of aircraft: *advances in American aviation.* [< F = L *avi(s)* bird + *-ation* -ATION]

avia′tion med′icine, the branch of medicine dealing with the psychological, physiological, and pathological effects on man of flying in airplanes.

a·vi·a·tor (ā′vē ā′tər, av′ē-), *n.* a pilot of an airplane or other heavier-than-air craft. [AVI- + -ATOR, modeled on F *aviateur*]

a·vi·a·trix (ā′vē ā′triks, av′ē-), *n., pl.* **-a·tri·ces** (-ā′tri-sēz′, -ə trī′sēz). a female pilot. Also, **a′vi·a′tress.** [AVI-AT(OR) + -TRIX]

Av·i·cen·na (av′i sen′ə), *n.* A.D. 980–1037, Islamic physician and philosopher.

a·vi·cul·ture (ā′vi kul′chər), *n.* the rearing or keeping of birds. —**a′vi·cul′tur·ist,** *n.*

av·id (av′id), *adj.* **1.** keenly desirous; eager; greedy. **2.** enthusiastic; ardent; dedicated; keen: *an avid moviegoer.* [< L *avid(us)* = *av(ēre)* (to) crave + *-idus* -ID^4] —**av′id·ly,** *adv.*

av·i·din (av′i din, ə vid′in), *n. Biochem.* a protein, found in the white of egg, that combines with and prevents the action of biotin, thus injuring the animal that consumes it in excess by producing biotin deficiency. [AVID + (BIOT)IN]

a·vid·i·ty (ə vid′i tē), *n.* eagerness; greediness. [late ME *avidite* < MF < L *aviditāt-* (s. of *aviditās*)]

a·vi·fau·na (ā′və fô′nə), *n.* the birds of a given region, considered as a whole. —**a′vi·fau′nal,** *adj.*

av·i·ga·tion (av′ə gā′shən), *n.* aerial navigation. [AVI- + (NAVI)GATION] —**av′i·ga′tor,** *n.*

A·vi·gnon (A vē nyôN′), *n.* a city in SE France, on the Rhone River: papal residence 1309–77. 93,024.

Á·vi·la Ca·ma·cho (ä′vē lä′ kä mä′chô), **Ma·nuel** (mä-nwel′), 1897–1955, Mexican revolutionary leader: president of Mexico 1940–46.

a·vi·on·ics (ā′vē on′iks, av′ē-), *n.* (*construed as sing.*) the science and technology of electrical and electronic devices in aviation. [*avi(ation electr)onics*]

a·vi·so (ə vī′zō), *n., pl.* **-sos.** information; advice; dispatch. [< Sp = *avis(ar)* (to) ADVISE + *-o* n. suffix]

a·vi·ta·min·o·sis (ā vī′tə mə nō′sis, ā′vi tam′ə nō′sis), *n. Pathol.* any disease caused by a lack of one or more vitamins. [A-^{6} + VITAMIN + -OSIS] —**a·vi·ta·min·ot·ic** (ā vī′tə mə not′ik), *adj.*

Av·lo·na (äv lô′nä), *n.* Valona.

avn., aviation.

av·o·ca·do (av′ə kä′dō, ä′və-), *n., pl.* **-dos.** **1.** Also called **alligator pear.** a tropical American fruit, green to black in color and commonly pear-shaped, borne by the lauraceous tree, *Persea americana,* and eaten raw, esp. as a salad fruit. **2.** the tree. [alter. of Sp *abogado,* lit., lawyer (see ADVOCATE), r. AmerSp *aguacate* < Nahuatl *ahuacatl,* lit., testicle. See ALLIGATOR PEAR]

Avocado, *Persea americana*

av·o·ca·tion (av′ə kā′shən), *n.* **1.** a minor or occasional occupation; hobby. **2.** a person's regular occupation, calling, or vocation. **3.** *Archaic.* diversion or distraction. [< L *āvocātiōn-* (s. of *āvocātiō*) a calling away]

a·voc·a·to·ry (ə vok′ə tôr′ē, -tōr′ē), *adj.* calling away, off, or back. [< ML *āvocātōri(us)* calling away = L *āvocāt(us)* called away (ptp. of *āvocāre*) + *-ōrius* -ORY^1]

av·o·cet (av′ə set′), *n.* any of several long-legged, web-footed shore birds of the genus *Recurvirostra,* having a long, slender bill that curves upward. Also, **avoset.** [earlier *avoset* < It *avosett(a),* var. of *avocetta* < ?]

A′vo·ga′dro's law′ (ä′və gä′drōz, ä′və-), *Chem.* the principle that equal volumes of all gases at the same temperature and pressure contain the same number of molecules. [named after Count Amadeo *Avogadro* (1776–1856), Italian physicist and chemist]

A′voga′dro's num′ber, *Chem.* the constant, 6.02×10^{23}, representing the number of atoms in a gram atom or the number of molecules in a gram molecule. *Symbol:* N Also, **A′voga′dro num′ber.** Also called **A′voga′dro con′stant.** [see AVOGADRO'S LAW]

a·void (ə void′), *v.t.* **1.** to keep away from; keep clear of; shun: *to avoid danger.* **2.** *Law.* to make void or of no effect; invalidate. **3.** *Obs.* to empty; eject or expel. [ME *avoide* < AF *avoide(r)* = *a-* A-^{4} + *voider* to VOID] —**a·void′a·ble,** *adj.* —**a·void′a·bly,** *adv.* —**a·void′er,** *n.* —**Syn. 1.** elude.

a·void·ance (ə void′ᵊns), *n.* **1.** the act of keeping away from: *avoidance of scandal.* **2.** *Law.* a making void; annulment. [ME]

avoir., See **avoirdupois weight.**

av·oir·du·pois (av′ər də poiz′), *n.* See **avoirdupois weight.** [ME *avoir de pois,* lit., property of weight < OF = *avoir* (var. of *aveir* < L *habēre*) + *de* (< L *dē*) + *pois* (var. of *peis* < L *pēnsum*)]

avoirdupois′ weight′, the system of weights in Britain and the U.S. for goods other than gems, precious metals, and drugs. *Abbr.:* av., avdp., avoir.

A·von (ā′vən, av′ən), *n.* **1.** a river in central England, flowing SE past Stratford-on-Avon to the Severn. 96 mi. long. **2.** a river in S England, flowing W to the mouth of the Severn. ab. 75 mi. long. **3.** a river in S England, flowing S to the English Channel. ab. 60 mi. long.

a·vo·set (av′ə set′), *n.* avocet.

à vo·tre san·té (A vô′trᵊ säN tā′), *French.* to your health.

a·vouch (ə vouch′), *v.t.* **1.** to make frank acknowledgment or affirmation of. **2.** to assume responsibility for; guarantee. **3.** to admit; confess. [ME *avouche* < MF *avouchie(r)* < L *advocāre.* See A-^{5}, VOUCH, ADVOCATE] —**a·vouch′er,** *n.* —**a·vouch′ment,** *n.*

a·vow (ə vou′), *v.t.* to declare frankly or openly; acknowledge; confess; admit: *to avow one's principles.* [ME *avowe(n)* < OF *avoue(r)* < L *advocāre.* See ADVOCATE] —**a·vow′a·ble,** *adj.* —**a·vow′er,** *n.*

a·vow·al (ə vou′əl), *n.* an open statement of affirmation; frank acknowledgment or admission.

a·vowed (ə voud′), *adj.* acknowledged; declared: *an avowed enemy.* —**a·vow·ed·ly** (ə vou′id lē), *adv.* —**a·vow′ed·ness,** *n.*

a·vul·sion (ə vul′shən), *n.* **1.** a tearing away. **2.** *Law.* the sudden removal of soil from the land of one owner to that of another, caused by flood or by change in a river's course. **3.** a part torn off. [< L *āvulsiōn-* (s. of *āvulsiō*) = *āvuls(us)* torn off (ptp. of *āvellere* = *ā-* A-^{4} + *vul-* (perf. s. of *vellere* to pluck) + *-sus* ptp. suffix) + *-iōn-* -ION]

a·vun·cu·lar (ə vuŋ′kyə lər), *adj.* **1.** of, pertaining to, or characteristic of an uncle: *avuncular affection.* **2.** *Obs.* of or pertaining to a pawnbroker. [< L *avuncul(us)* a mother's brother = *av(us)* a forefather + *-uncul(us)* dim. suffix + -AR^1]

aw (ô), *interj.* (used as an exclamation expressing protest, disbelief, disgust, or the like): *Aw, gee, why do that?*

a.w., **1.** actual weight. **2.** (in shipping) all water. **3.** atomic weight. Also, **aw**

a·wa (ə wô′, ə wä′), *adv. Scot.* away.

AWACS (ā′waks), *n.* a U.S. military surveillance aircraft fitted with long-range radar and sophisticated computer equipment to detect and monitor hostile air and ground activity and to direct combat forces: identified by a radome atop the plane's superstructure. Also, **A′wacs.** [*A(irborne) W(arning) a(nd) C(ontrol) S(ystem)*]

a·wait (ə wāt′), *v.t.* **1.** to wait for; expect; look for. **2.** to be in store for; be ready for. **3.** *Obs.* to lie in wait for. —*v.i.* **4.** to wait, as in expectation. [ME *awaite(n)* < OF (north) *awaitier* = *a-* A-^{5} + *waitier* to WAIT] —**a·wait′er,** *n.*

a·wake (ə wāk′), *v.,* **a·woke** or **a·waked, a·wak·ing,** *adj.* —*v.t., v.i.* **1.** to wake up; rouse from sleep. **2.** to rouse to action; become active. **3.** to come or bring to an awareness (often fol. by *to*): *He awoke to the realities of life.* —*adj.* **4.** not sleeping. **5.** alert: *He was awake to the danger.* [OE *awacen,* ptp. of *awæcnan*]

a·wak·en (ə wā′kən), *v.t., v.i.* **1.** to awake; waken. **2.** to make or become aware or active. [ME *awak(e)n(en),* OE *awæcnian.* See A-^{1}, WAKEN] —**a·wak′en·er,** *n.*

a·wak·en·ing (ə wā′kə niŋ), *adj.* **1.** rousing; quickening: *an awakening interest.* —*n.* **2.** the act of awaking from sleep. **3.** a revival of interest or attention. **4.** a recognition, realization, or coming into awareness of something: *a rude awakening to the disagreeable facts.* —**a·wak′en·ing·ly,** *adv.*

a·ward (ə wôrd′), *v.t.* **1.** to give as due or merited; assign or bestow: *to award prizes.* **2.** to bestow or assign by judicial decree. —*n.* **3.** something awarded as a prize. **3.** *Law.* the decision of an arbitrator. [ME *award(en)* < AF *awarde(r)* = *a-* A-^{4} + *warder* << Gmc; cf. OE *weardian* to WARD] —**a·ward′a·ble,** *adj.* —**a·ward′er,** *n.*

a·ware (ə wâr′), *adj.* **1.** having knowledge; conscious; cognizant: *aware of the danger.* **2.** informed; alert; knowledgeable: *He is one of the most politically aware young men around.* [ME, var. of *iwar,* OE *gewær* watchful (c. OHG, G *gewahr*) = *ge-* prefix + *wær* WARE^2] —**a·ware′ness,** *n.*

a·wash (ə wosh′, ə wôsh′), *adj., adv.* **1.** *Naut.* **a.** just level or scarcely above the surface of the water, so that waves break over the top. **b.** overflowing with water, as the upper deck of a ship in a heavy sea. **2.** covered with water; flooded. **3.** washing about; tossed about by waves.

a·way (ə wā′), *adv.* **1.** from this or that place; off: *to go away.* **2.** far; apart: *away back; away from the subject.* **3.** aside; to another place; in another direction: *to turn your eyes away.* **4.** out of one's possession or use: *to give money away.* **5.** out of existence or notice; into extinction: *to fade away.* **6.** continuously; repeatedly; on: *He kept on hammering away.* **7.** without hesitation: *Fire away.* **8. away with, a.** take away: *Away with him!* **b.** go away! leave!: *Away with you!* **9. do away with, a.** to get rid of; abolish; stop. **b.** to kill. —*adj.* **10.** absent: *to be away from home.* **11.** distant: *six miles away.* **12.** immediately off and on the way: *The order was given and he was away.* [ME; OE *aweg* < *on weg.* See ON, WAY]

awe (ô), *n., v.,* **awed, aw·ing.** —*n.* **1.** an overwhelming feeling of reverence, admiration, fear, etc., produced by that which is grand, sublime, extremely powerful, or the like. **2.** *Archaic.* power to inspire fear or reverence. **3.** *Obs.* fear or dread. —*v.t.* **4.** to inspire with awe. **5.** to influence or restrain by awe. [ME *aghe, awe* < Scand; cf. Icel *agi* fear, c. Goth *agis,* OE *ege,* Gk *áchos* pain]

a·weath·er (ə weth′ər), *adv., adj. Naut.* upon or toward the windward side of a vessel; in the direction of the wind (opposed to *alee*).

a·weigh (ə wā′), *adj. Naut.* (of an anchor) just free of the bottom. [A-^{1} + WEIGH^2]

awe·less (ô′lis), *adj.* awless. —**awe′less·ness,** *n.*

awe·some (ô′səm), *adj.* **1.** inspiring awe: *an awesome sight.* **2.** characterized by awe. —**awe′some·ly,** *adv.* —**awe′some·ness,** *n.*

awe-struck (ô′struk′), *adj.* filled with awe. Also, **awe′struck′, awe-strick·en, awe·strick·en** (ô′strik′ən).

aw·ful (ô′fəl), *adj.* **1.** inspiring fear; dreadful; terrible. **2.** extremely bad; unpleasant; ugly. **3.** full of awe; reverential. **4.** solemnly impressive; inspiring awe. —*adv.* **5.** *Informal.* very; extremely: *He did an awful good job of painting the corncrib.* [ME; r. OE *egefull* dreadful] —**aw′ful·ness,** *n.*
—**Usage.** In informal use, there is no objection to AWFUL in the sense of "very bad, ugly, etc.," but it has been so overworked that it is ineffective. The word is still limited in strict formal use to the sense of "awe-inspiring."

aw·ful·ly (ô′fə lē, ôf′lē), *adv.* **1.** very; extremely: *That was awfully nice of you.* **2.** in a manner provoking censure, disapproval, or the like. **3.** *Archaic.* **a.** in a manner inspiring awe. **b.** in a manner expressing awe.

a·while (ə hwīl′, ə wīl′), *adv.* for a short time or period.
—**Usage.** AWHILE is an adverb meaning "for a short time" and should not be confused with the article and noun A WHILE, usually used in a prepositional phrase: *Stay awhile. Stay for a while.*

a·whirl (ə hwûrl′, ə wûrl′), *adj.* rotating rapidly; spinning; whirling (usually used predicatively): *dancers awhirl to the strains of a lively waltz.*

awk·ward (ôk′wərd), *adj.* **1.** lacking skill or dexterity; clumsy; inept. **2.** ungraceful; ungainly: *an awkward gesture.* **3.** ill-adapted for use or handling; unwieldy; unmanageable: *an awkward instrument.* **4.** requiring caution; somewhat hazardous; dangerous: *There's an awkward step there.* **5.** hard to deal with: *an awkward customer.* **6.** embarrassing or inconvenient; inopportune: *an awkward moment.* **7.** *Obs.* untoward; perverse. [ME *awk, auk* backhanded (< Scand; cf. Icel *öfug(r)* turned the wrong way) + -WARD] —**awk′ward·ly,** *adv.* —**awk′ward·ness,** *n.* —**Syn. 1.** unskillful, unhandy, inexpert. —**Ant. 1.** deft, adroit. **2.** graceful.

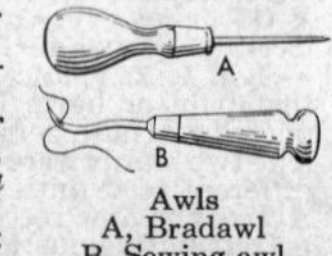

Awls
A, Bradawl
B, Sewing awl

awk′ward age′, early adolescence.

awl (ôl), *n.* a pointed instrument for piercing small holes in leather, wood, etc. [ME *al,* OE *æl;* akin to OHG *āla* (> G *Ahle*), Icel *al(r),* Skt *ārā*]

aw·less (ô′lis), *adj.* without awe; fearless; not to be awed. Also, **aweless.** —**aw′less·ness,** *n.*

awn (ôn), *n. Bot.* **1.** a bristlelike appendage of a plant, esp. on the glumes of grasses. **2.** such appendages collectively, as those forming the beard of wheat, barley, etc. 3. any similar bristle. [ME *awne, agune* < Scand; cf. Icel *ögn* husk, c. Goth *ahana,* OHG *agana, ahana* (> G *Ahne*)] —**awned,** *adj.* —**awn′less,** *adj.*

awn·ing (ô′ning), *n.* 1. a rooflike shelter of canvas or other material extending over a doorway, from the top of a window, over a deck, etc., in order to provide protection, as from the sun. 2. a shelter. [?] —**awn′inged,** *adj.*

a·woke (ə wōk′), *v.* a pt. and pp. of **awake.**

A.W.O.L. (*pronounced as initials or, in Mil. slang,* ā′wôl), away from military duties without permission, but without the intention of deserting. Also, **a.w.o.l.** [*A*(*bsent*) *W*(*ith*)*o*(*ut*) *L*(*eave*)]

a·wry (ə rī′), *adv., adj.* 1. with a turn or twist to one side; askew: *to glance or look awry.* 2. away from the expected or proper direction; amiss; wrong: *Our plans went awry.* [ME *on wry.* See A-[1], WRY]

ax (aks), *n., pl.* **ax·es** (ak′siz), *v.,* **axed, ax·ing.** —*n.* 1. an instrument with a bladed head on a handle or helve, used for hewing, cleaving, chopping, etc. 2. **get the ax,** *Informal.* to be dismissed, expelled, or rejected summarily. 3. **have an ax to grind,** *Informal.* to have a personal or selfish motive. —*v.t.* 4. to shape or trim with an ax. 5. to chop, cut, split, or sever with an ax. 6. *Informal.* to dismiss, restrict, or destroy brutally. Also, **axe.** [ME; OE *æx;* akin to Goth *aquizi,* OHG *acchus* (> G *Axt*), L *ascia* (< **acsiā*), Gk *axī́ne*] —**ax′like′,** *adj.*

Axes
A, Common ax
B, Hatchet
C, Stonemason's ax

ax., axiom.

a·xen·ic (ā zen′ik), *adj.* uncontaminated; germfree.

ax·es[1] (ak′sēz), *n.* pl. of **axis**[1].

ax·es[2] (ak′siz), *n.* pl. of **ax.**

axi-, a word element meaning "axis": *axial.* Also, **axo-;** *esp. before a vowel,* **ax-.** [comb. form repr. L *axi*(*s*) axle, wheel; c. Gk *áxōn,* Skt *ákṣas,* Lith *ašìs,* OE *eax*]

ax·i·al (ak′sē əl), *adj.* 1. of, pertaining to, characterized by, or forming an axis: *an axial relationship.* 2. situated in an axis or on the axis. Also, **ax·ile** (ak′sil, -sīl). —**ax′i·al′i·ty,** *n.*

ax·i·al·ly (ak′sē ə lē), *adv.* in the line of the axis.

ax′ial skel′eton, *Anat.* the skeleton of the head and trunk.

ax·il (ak′sil), *n. Bot.* the angle between the upper side of a leaf or stem and the supporting stem or branch. [< L *axil*(*la*) armpit]

A, Axil

ax·il·la (ak sil′ə), *n., pl.* **ax·il·lae** (ak sil′ē). 1. *Anat.* the armpit. 2. *Ornith.* the corresponding region under the wing of a bird. 3. *Bot.* an axil. [< L]

ax·il·lar (ak′sə lər), *n.* 1. Usually, **axillars.** *Ornith.* a number of the feathers growing from the axilla of a bird. 2. *Biol.* any axillary part.

ax·il·lar·y (ak′se ler′ē), *adj., n., pl.* **-lar·ies.** —*adj.* 1. pertaining to the axilla. 2. *Bot.* pertaining to or growing from the axil. —*n.* 3. Usually, **axillaries.** *Ornith.* axillars.

ax·i·ol·o·gy (ak′sē ol′ə jē), *n.* the branch of philosophy dealing with values, as those of ethics, aesthetics, or religion. [< Gk *áxio*(*s*) worthy, estimable + -LOGY] —**ax·i·o·log·i·cal** (ak′sē ə loj′i kəl), *adj.* —**ax′i·o·log′i·cal·ly,** *adv.* —**ax′i·ol′o·gist,** *n.*

ax·i·om (ak′sē əm), *n.* 1. a self-evident truth. 2. a universally accepted principle or rule. 3. *Logic, Math.* a proposition that is assumed without proof for the sake of studying the consequences that follow from it. [late ME < L *axiōm*(*a*) < Gk: something worthy = *axió*(*ein*) (to) reckon worthy + *-ma* n. suffix]

ax·i·o·mat·ic (ak′sē ə mat′ik), *adj.* 1. pertaining to or of the nature of an axiom; self-evident. 2. aphoristic. Also, **ax′i·o·mat′i·cal.** [< Gk *axiōmatikós* = *axiōmat-* (s. of *axíōma* AXIOM) + *-ikos* -IC] —**ax′i·o·mat′i·cal·ly,** *adv.*

ax·is[1] (ak′sis), *n., pl.* **ax·es** (ak′sēz). 1. the line about which a rotating body turns or may be supposed to turn. 2. a central line bisecting a body, form, or the like, and in relation to which symmetry is determined. 3. *Anat.* **a.** a central or principal structure, about which something turns or is arranged: *the skeletal axis.* **b.** the second cervical vertebra. 4. *Bot.* the longitudinal support on which organs or parts are arranged; the stem and root; the central line of any body. 5. *Analytic Geom.* any line used as a fixed reference in conjunction with one or more other references for determining the position of a point or of a series of points forming a curve or a surface. Cf. **x-axis, y-axis.** 6. *Fine Arts.* an imaginary line, in a given formal structure, about which a form, area, or plane is organized. 7. an alliance of two or more nations to coordinate their foreign and military policies. 8. **the Axis,** (in World War II) Germany, Italy, and Japan, often with Bulgaria, Hungary, and Rumania. 9. a principal line of development, movement, etc. [< L *axis* an axletree, axle, axis. See AXON, AX] —**ax·ised** (ak′sist), *adj.*

ax·is[2] (ak′sis), *n., pl.* **ax·is·es.** a deer, *Axis axis,* of India and Ceylon, having a reddish-brown coat spotted with white. Also, called **ax′is deer′.** [< L *axis* a wild animal of India]

ax·le (ak′səl), *n.* 1. *Mach.* the pin, bar, shaft, or the like, on which or by means of which a wheel or pair of wheels rotates. 2. the spindle at either end of an axletree. 3. an axletree. [ME *axel,* OE *eaxl* shoulder, crossbeam (in *eaxlegespann*); c. OHG *ahsala* shoulder (> G *Achsel*), Icel *öxull,* L *āla* (< **akslā*)] —**ax′led,** *adj.*

ax·le·tree (ak′səl trē′), *n.* a bar, fixed crosswise under an animal-drawn vehicle, with a rounded spindle at each end upon which a wheel rotates. [ME]

ax·man (aks′mən), *n., pl.* **-men.** a person who wields an ax.

Ax′min·ster car′pet (aks′min′stər), a carpet having a stiff, ribbed backing, as of jute, and an even yarn pile that is usually cut. [named after a town in SW England, although orig. manufactured in the U.S.]

axo-, var. of **axi-,** esp. before a consonant.

ax·o·lotl (ak′sə lot′[ə]l), *n.* any larval salamander of the genus *Ambystoma,* found esp. in lakes and ponds of the southwestern U.S. and Mexico, that is capable of breeding in its larval state. [< Nahuatl]

ax·on (ak′son), *n. Anat.* the appendage of the neuron that transmits impulses away from the cell. Also, **ax·one** (ak′sōn). [< NL < Gk *áxōn* an axle, axis; c. L *axis*] —**ax′on·al,** *adj.*

Axolotl, *Ambystoma mexicanus* (Length 6 to 12 in.)

ax·o·no·met·ric (ak′sə nō me′trik, -nə-), *adj. Drafting.* designating a method of projection (**ax′onomet′ric projec′tion**) in which a three-dimensional object is represented by a drawing (**ax′onomet′ric draw′ing**) having all lines drawn to exact scale, resulting in the optical distortion of diagonals and curves. Cf. **cabinet** (def. 17), **isometric** (def. 4), **oblique** (def. 13). See illus. at **isometric.** [< Gk *áxōn* (see AXON) + -o- + -METRIC]

ay[1] (ā), *adv. Literary or Dial.* ever; always. Also, **aye.** [ME *ei, ai* < Scand; cf. Icel *ei,* c. OE *ā* ever]

ay[2] (ā), *interj. Dial.* Ah! Oh!

ay[3] (ī), *adv., n.* aye[1].

A·ya·cu·cho (ä′yä ko͞o′chô), *n.* a city in SW Peru: victory of Bolívar over Spanish troops 1824. 40,000 (est. 1961).

a·yah (ä′yə), *n.* (in India) a native maid or nurse. [< Hindi *āyā* < Pg *aia* female servant < L *avia* grandmother]

a·ya·tol·lah (ä′yə tō′lə), *n.* (among Shiites) a title in the religious hierarchy achieved by scholars who have demonstrated highly advanced knowledge of Islamic law. [< Pers < Ar *āyat* sign or token (of) + ALLAH]

aye[1] (ī), *adv.* 1. yes. —*n.* 2. an affirmative vote or voter. Also, **ay.** [earlier *I,* ME *yie,* alter. of *ye,* OE *gī* YEA]

aye[2] (ā), *adv.* ay[1].

aye-aye (ī′ī′), *n.* a nocturnal lemur, *Daubentonia madagascariensis,* of Madagascar, feeding on insects and fruit, and having rodentlike incisors and long fingers. [< F < Malagasy *aiay,* prob. imit. of its cry]

Aye-aye (Total length 3 ft.; tail 22 in.)

A·ye·sha (ä′ē shä′), *n.* Aisha.

a·yin (ä′yin; *Heb.* ä′yēn), *n.* the 16th letter of the Hebrew alphabet. [< Heb]

Ay·ma·ra (ī′mä rä′), *n., pl.* **-ras,** (*esp. collectively*) **-ra** for 1. 1. a member of an Indian people living in the mountainous regions around Lake Titicaca in Bolivia and Peru. 2. the language of the Aymara people. [< Sp *armará, aymará,* of AmerInd orig.] —**Ay′ma·ran′,** *adj.*

Ay·mé (e mā′), *n.* **Mar·cel** (MAR sel′), born 1902, French novelist and short-story writer.

Ayn·tab (īn tab′), *n.* Aintab.

Ayr (âr), *n.* 1. a seaport in and the county seat of Ayrshire. 46,200 (est. 1965). 2. Ayrshire (def. 2).

Ayr·shire (âr′shēr, -shər), *n.* 1. one of a Scottish breed of hardy dairy cattle having long, curving horns. 2. Also called **Ayr.** a county in SW Scotland. 347,670 (est. 1965); 1132 sq. mi. *Co. seat:* Ayr.

A·yub Khan (ä yo͞ob′ kän′), **Mohammed,** 1907–74, Pakistani political leader: president 1958–69.

A·yur·ve·da (ä′yər vā′də), *n.* the ancient Hindu art of medicine and of prolonging life. [< Skt = *āyur-* life, vital power + *veda* knowledge] —**A′yur·ve′dic,** *adj.*

AZ, Arizona (approved esp. for use with zip code).

az-, var. of **azo-,** esp. before a vowel: *azine.*

a·zal·ea (ə zāl′yə), *n.* any ericaceous plant of a particular group (*Azalea*) of the genus *Rhododendron,* comprising species with variously colored flowers. [< NL < Gk *azaléa,* n. use of fem. of *azaléos* dry; so named as growing in dry soil]

a·zan (ä zän′), *n.* (in Islamic countries) the call to prayer proclaimed five times a day by the muezzin. [< Ar *adhān* invitation. See MUEZZIN]

A·za·ña (ä thä′nyä), *n.* **Ma·nuel** (mä nwel′), (*Manuel Azaña y Diez*), 1880–1940, Spanish statesman: prime minister 1931–33, 1936; president 1936–39.

A·za·zel (ə zā′zəl, az′ə zel′), *n.* 1. the scapegoat released on the Day of Atonement, or its destination, hell. Lev. 16:8, 10, 21. 2. *Islamic Myth.* the jinn who became Shaitan. 3. one of the fallen angels.

a·zed·a·rach (ə zed′ə rak′), *n.* chinaberry (def. 1). [< F *azédarac* << Pers *āzād dirakht* noble tree]

a·ze·o·trope (ə zē′ə trōp′), *n. Physical Chem.* any liquid mixture having constant minimum and maximum boiling points and distilling off without decomposition and in a fixed ratio, as isopropyl alcohol and water. [A-[6] + Gk *zé*(*ein*) (to) boil + -o- + -TROPE] —**a·ze·o·trop·ic** (ā′zē ə trop′ik), *adj.* —**a·ze·ot·ro·py** (ā′zē o′trə pē), **a′ze·ot′ro·pism,** *n.*

A·zer·bai·jan (ä′zər bī jän′, az′ər bī jan′; *Russ.* ä′zer bī jän′), *n.* 1. Official name, **Azerbaijan′ So′viet So′cialist Repub′lic.** a constituent republic of the Soviet Union, in Caucasia. 4,500,000 (est. 1965); ab. 33,000 sq. mi. *Cap.:* Baku. 2. a province in NW Iran. 2,859,132 (1956); ab. 35,000 sq. mi. *Cap.:* Tabriz. Also, **A′zer·bai·dzhan′.**

A·zer·bai·ja·ni (ä′zər bī jä′nē, az′ər bī jan′ē), *n., pl.* **-ja·nis,** (*esp. collectively*) **-ja·ni.** a native or inhabitant of Azerbaijan.

az·ide (az′īd, -id, ā′zīd, ā′zid), *n. Chem.* any compound containing the azido group, as sodium azide, NaN_3. [AZ- + -IDE]

az′i·do group′ (az′i dō′), *Chem.* the univalent group, N_3–, derived from hydrazoic acid. Also called **az′ido·rad′i·cal.** [AZID(E) + -O-]

A·zil·ian (ə zēl′yən, -ē ən, ə zil′-), *adj.* of, pertaining to, or characteristic of a Mesolithic culture of southern France. [named after Mas d'Azil, town in S France, where the culture flourished; see -IAN]

az·i·muth (az′ə məth), *n.* 1. *Astron., Navig.* the arc of the horizon measured clockwise from the south point, in astronomy, or from the north point, in navigation, to the point where a vertical circle through a given heavenly body intersects the horizon. **2.** *Survey., Gunnery.* the angle of horizontal deviation, measured clockwise, of a bearing from a standard direction, as from north or south. [ME *azimut* < MF << Ar *as sumūt* the ways (i.e., directions)] —**az·i·muth·al** (az/ə mut͟h/əl), *adj.* —**az/i·muth/al·ly,** *adv.*

azimuth/al equidis/tant projec/tion, *Cartog.* a projection in which the shortest distance between any point and a central point is a straight line, such a line representing a great circle through the central point.

az·ine (az/ēn, -in), *n.* *Chem.* any of a group of six-membered heterocyclic compounds containing one or more nitrogen atoms in the ring, the number of nitrogen atoms present being indicated by a prefix, as in "diazine."

azo-, **1.** a combining form meaning "containing nitrogen." **2.** a combining form of the azo group, used esp. before a consonant: *azobenzene.* Also, *esp. before a vowel,* **az-.** [< Gk *ázō(os)* without life = *a-* A-[6] + *zō-* ZO-]

az·o·ben·zene (az/ō ben/zēn, -ben zēn/), *n.* *Chem.* an orange-red, water-insoluble powder, $C_6H_5N{=}NC_6H_5$, obtained from nitrobenzene by reduction: used chiefly in the manufacture of dyes and as an insecticide.

az/o dye/ (az/ō), *Chem.* any of a large class of dyes containing one or more azo groups.

A·zof (ä zôf/), *n.* Azov.

az/o group/, *Chem.* the bivalent group, $-N{=}N-$, united to two hydrocarbon groups, as in azobenzene, $C_6H_5{-}N{=}N{-}C_6H_5$. Also called **az/o rad/ical.**

a·zo·ic (ə zō/ik, ā-), *adj.* *Geol.* (formerly) noting or pertaining to the Precambrian era, esp. that part formerly believed to precede the first appearance of life; Archean. Cf. **Eozoic.** [< Gk *ázō(os)* lifeless (see AZO-) + -IC]

az·ole (az/ōl, ə zōl/), *n.* *Chem.* any of a group of five-membered heterocyclic compounds containing one or more nitrogen atoms in the ring, the number of nitrogen atoms present being indicated by a prefix, as in "diazole."

A·zores (ə zōrz/, ə zôrz/, ā/zōrz, ā/zôrz), *n.* a group of islands in the N Atlantic, W of Portugal: politically part of Portugal. 325,000 (est. 1960); 890 sq. mi. —**A·zo·ri·an** (ə-zōr/ē ən, -zôr/-), *adj., n.*

az·ote (az/ōt, ə zōt/), *n.* *Chem.* nitrogen. [< F < Gk *ázōt(os)* ungirt, taken to mean lifeless] —**az·ot·ed** (az/ō-tid, ə zō/tid), *adj.* —**a·zot·ic** (a zot/ik), *adj.*

az·oth (az/ot͟h), *n.* *Alchemy.* **1.** mercury, as the assumed first principle of all metals. **2.** the universal remedy of Paracelsus. [late ME *azot* << Ar *az zā'ūq* the quicksilver]

az·o·tise (az/ə tīz/), *v.t.,* **-tised, -tis·ing.** *Chiefly Brit.* azotize.

az·o·tize (az/ə tīz/), *v.t.,* **-tized, -tiz·ing.** to nitrogenize.

A·zov (ä zôf/), *n.* **Sea of,** a northern arm of the Black Sea in the Soviet Union in Europe. ab. 14,500 sq. mi. Also, **Azof.**

Az·ra·el (az/rē əl, -rā-), *n.* (in Jewish and Islamic angelology) the angel who separates the soul from the body at death.

Az·tec (az/tek), *n.* **1.** a member of a Nahuatl people whose complex empire in central Mexico was conquered by Cortés in 1519. **2.** an extinct dialect of Nahuatl, formerly the language of Aztec civilization, written in a chiefly pictographic script. Cf. **Nahuatl** (def. 2). **3.** the Nahuatl language. —**Az/tec·an,** *adj.*

az·ure (azh/ər, ā/zhər), *adj.* **1.** of a sky-blue color. —*n.* **2.** the blue of a clear or unclouded sky. **3.** *Literary.* a clear, unclouded sky. [ME *asure* < ML*az ura* < Ar *(l)azuwar(d)* < Pers *lazhward* lapis lazuli]

az·ur·ite (azh/ə rīt/), *n.* **1.** a blue mineral, a hydrous copper carbonate, $Cu_3(CO_3)_2(OH)_2$; an ore of copper. **2.** a gem of moderate value cut from this mineral.

A·zu·sa (ə zo͞o/sə), *n.* a city in SW California, near Los Angeles. 25,217 (1970).

az·y·gous (az/ə gəs), *adj.* *Zool., Bot.* not being one of a pair; single. [< Gk *ázygos* = *a-* A-[6] + *zygós* < *zygón* YOKE]

DEVELOPMENT OF MAJUSCULE								
NORTH SEMITIC	GREEK		ETR.	LATIN		MODERN		
						GOTHIC	ITALIC	ROMAN
9	𐌁	B	8	B	B	𝔅	*B*	B

DEVELOPMENT OF MINUSCULE					
ROMAN CURSIVE	ROMAN UNCIAL	CAROL. MIN.	MODERN		
			GOTHIC	ITALIC	ROMAN
∂	B	b	𝔟	*b*	b

The second letter of the English alphabet developed from North Semitic *beth* through Greek *beta* (*β*, B). The capital (B) goes back to North Semitic *beth* and particularly to Greek B, retained in the Latin monumental script. The minuscule (b) derives from cursive *b*, formed by eliminating the upper loop.

B, b (bē), *n., pl.* **B's** or **Bs, b's** or **bs. 1.** the second letter of the English alphabet, a consonant. **2.** any spoken sound represented by the letter *B* or *b*, as in *bid, bubble,* or *rob.* **3.** a written or printed representation of the letter *B* or *b.* **4.** a device, as a printer's type, for reproducing the letter *B* or *b.*

B, *Chess.* bishop.

B, 1. the second in order or in a series. **2.** (*sometimes l.c.*) (in some grading systems) a grade or mark that indicates academic work, a product, etc., that is good but not of the highest quality. **3.** *Music.* **a.** the seventh tone in the scale of C major or the second tone in the relative minor scale, A minor. **b.** a written or printed note representing this tone. **c.** a string, key, or pipe tuned to this tone. **d.** the tonality having B as the tonic note. **4.** a major blood group or type usually enabling a person of this group to donate to persons of group B or AB and to receive blood from persons of group O or B. **5.** a mediocre or poor motion picture. **6.** *Chem.* boron. **7.** *Physics.* See **magnetic induction. 8.** *Elect.* susceptance.

b, 1. *Physics.* bar; bars. **2.** barn; barns.

B., 1. bass. **2.** basso. **3.** bay. **4.** Bible. **5.** bolivar. **6.** boliviano. **7.** book. **8.** born. **9.** British. **10.** brother.

b., 1. *Baseball.* base; baseman. **2.** bass. **3.** basso. **4.** bay. **5.** blend of; blended. **6.** book. **7.** born. **8.** breadth.

B-, *U.S. Mil.* (in designations of aircraft) bomber: *B-26.*

B-1 (bē′wun′), *n.* a U.S. long-range bomber having swept-back wings and traveling at subsonic speeds: introduced for the 1980's.

B-17 (bē′sev′ən tēn′), *n.* See **Flying Fortress.**

B-29 (bē′twen′tē nīn′), *n.* Superfortress.

B-50 (bē′fif′tē), *n.* Superfortress.

B-52 (bē′fif′tē to͞o′), *n.* U.S. eight-jet bomber.

Ba, *Chem.* barium.

B.A., 1. See **Bachelor of Arts.** [< L *Baccalaureus Artium*] **2.** British America.

baa (ba, bä), *v.,* **baaed, baa·ing,** *n.* —*v.i.* **1.** to cry as a sheep; bleat. —*n.* **2.** the bleating cry of a sheep. [imit.]

Ba·al (bā′əl, bāl, bäl), *n., pl.* **Ba·al·im** (bā′ə lim, bā′lim, bä′lim). **1.** the fertility god of the Canaanites. **2.** any of numerous local deities among the ancient Semitic peoples, typifying the generative forces of nature. **3.** (*sometimes l.c.*) a false god. [< Heb *ba'al* lord, owner] —**Ba′al·ish,** *adj.*

Baal·bek (bäl′bek, bā′əl-, bäl′-), *n.* a town in E Lebanon: ruins of ancient city; Temple of the Sun. 16,000. Ancient Greek name, **Heliopolis.**

Ba·al·ism (bā′ə liz′əm, bā′liz əm, bä′-), *n.* **1.** the worship of Baal. **2.** idolatry. —**Ba′al·ist, Ba·al·ite** (bā′ə līt′, bā′-līt, bä′-), *n.* —**Ba′al·is′tic,** *adj.*

Baal Shem-Tov (bäl′ shem′tōv′, shäm′-), (*Israel ben Eliezer*) ("*BeShT*") c1700–60, Ukrainian teacher and religious leader: founder of the Hasidic movement of Judaism in Poland. Also, **Baal Shem-Tob** (bäl′ shem′tōb′, shäm′-).

Baath (bath), *n.* the socialist party of some Arab countries, esp. Syria. —**Baath·ist,** *n.*

Bāb (bäb), *n.* (*the Bab, Ali Muhammad of Shiraz*) 1819–50, Persian religious leader: founder of Bābī. Also, **Bab.** Also called **Bab ed-Din.**

ba·ba (bä′bə; *Fr.* bᴀ bᴀ′), *n., pl.* **-bas** (-bəz; *Fr.* -bᴀ′). a leavened cake, usually made with raisins and soaked in rum or kirsch. [< F < Pol: kind of cake; lit., old woman]

ba·ba au rhum (bä′bə ō rum′; *Fr.* bᴀ bᴀ ō rôm′), *pl.* **ba·bas au rhum** (bä′bəz ō rum′; *Fr.* bᴀ bᴀ ō rôm′). a baba soaked in rum syrup.

Ba·bar (bä′bər), *n.* Baber.

ba·bas·su (bä′bə so͞o′), *n.* a palm, *Orbignya Martiana,* of northeastern Brazil, bearing nuts that yield babassu oil. [< Pg *babaçú* < native Brazilian name]

babassu′ oil′, a yellow oil extracted from babassu nuts, used chiefly in the manufacture of soaps and cosmetics and as a cooking oil.

bab·bitt (bab′it), *n.* **1.** See **Babbitt metal.** —*v.t.* **2.** to line, face, or furnish with Babbitt metal. [short for BABBITT METAL]

Bab·bitt (bab′it), *n.* a self-satisfied person who conforms readily to middle-class attitudes and ideals. [after the character in *Babbitt,* a novel (1922) by Sinclair Lewis] —**Bab′-bitt·ry, Bab′bit·ry,** *n.*

Bab·bitt (bab′it), *n.* **Irving,** 1865–1933, U.S. educator and critic.

Bab′bitt met′al, *Metall.* any of various alloys of tin with smaller amounts of antimony and copper, used as an antifriction lining for bearings. Also, **bab′bitt met′al.** Also called **babbitt.** [after Isaac *Babbitt* (1799–1862), Amer. inventor]

bab·ble (bab′əl), *v.,* **-bled, -bling,** *n.* —*v.i.* **1.** to utter sounds or words imperfectly or indistinctly. **2.** to talk idly, irrationally, or excessively. **3.** to make a continuous, murmuring sound. —*v.t.* **4.** to utter in a foolish, meaningless, or incoherent manner. **5.** to reveal foolishly or thoughtlessly. —*n.* Also called **bab′ble·ment. 6.** inarticulate or imperfect speech. **7.** meaningless or incoherent speech; prattle. **8.** a murmuring sound or a confusion of sounds. [ME *babele(n)*; c. Icel *babbla,* D *babbelen,* G *pappelen*] —**bab′bler,** *n.*

bab·bling (bab′ling), *n.* **1.** foolish or meaningless chatter. **2.** a soft gurgling or murmuring sound. —*adj.* **3.** chattering or prattling aimlessly. **4.** flowing with a babbling sound: *a babbling brook.* [ME] —**bab′bling·ly,** *adv.*

babe (bāb), *n.* **1.** a baby or small child. **2.** an innocent or inexperienced person. **3.** *Slang.* **a.** a girl or woman, esp. an attractive one. **b.** (*often cap.*) a term of endearment or familiar address to a woman. **4. babe in the woods,** an innocent, unsuspecting person: *We're babes in the woods where the stock market is concerned.* [ME; early ME *baban,* prob. orig. nursery word]

Bab ed-Din (bäb′ ed dēn′), Bāb.

Ba·bel (bā′bəl, bab′əl), *n.* **1.** an ancient city in the land of Shinar in which the building of a tower **(Tower of Babel)** intended to reach heaven was begun and the confusion of the language of the people took place. Gen. 11:4–9. **2.** (*often l.c.*) a confused mixture of sounds or voices. **3.** (*often l.c.*) a scene of noise and confusion. [< Heb *Bābel* Babylon, lit., gate of God] —**Ba·bel·ic** (bā bel′ik, ba-), *adj.*

Ba·bel (bab′əl; *Russ.* bä′bel), *n.* **I·saak Em·ma·nu·i·lo·vich** (ī′zək; *Russ.* i säk′ i mä′no͝o ē′lo vich), 1894–1941, Russian author.

Bab el Man·deb (bäb′ el män′deb), a strait between NE Africa and SW Arabia, connecting the Red Sea and the Gulf of Aden. 20 mi. wide.

Ba·ber (bä′bər), *n.* (*Zahir ed-Din Mohammed*) 1483–1530, founder of the Mogul Empire. Also, **Babar, Babur.**

Ba·beuf (bᴀ bœf′), *n.* **Fran·çois No·ël** (fräɴ swᴀ′ nō el′), (*Gracchus Babeuf*), 1760–97, French revolutionary.

Bā·bī (bä′bē), *n.* **1.** Also called **Babism.** a Persian religion, originated in the 19th century, now supplanted by Bahā'ī. **2.** an adherent of Bābī. Also **Ba′bi.**

ba·bies'-breath (bā′bēz breth′), *n.* **1.** a tall herb, *Gypsophila paniculata,* of the pink family, having numerous small, fragrant, white or pink flowers. **2.** any of certain other plants, as the grape hyacinth. Also **baby's-breath.** [so called from its delicate odor and bloom]

bab·i·ru·sa (bab′ə ro͞o′sə, bä′bə-), *n.* an East Indian swine, *Babirussa babyrussa,* the male of which has upper canine teeth growing upward through the roof of the mouth and curving toward the eyes, and lower canine teeth growing upward outside the upper jaw. Also, **bab′i·rous′sa, bab′i·rus′sa.** [< Malay *bābi* hog + *rūsa* deer]

Babirusa
(2½ ft. high at shoulder; length 3½ ft.)

Bab·ism (bä′biz əm), *n.* Bābī (def. 1). [BAB (ED-DIN) + -ISM] —**Bab′ist,** *n., adj.* —**Bab′ite,** *adj.*

ba·boo (bä′bo͞o), *n., pl.* **-boos.** babu.

ba·boon (ba bo͞on′ *or, esp. Brit.,* bə-), *n.* **1.** any of various large, terrestrial monkeys of the genus *Papio* and related genera, of Africa and Arabia, having a doglike muzzle, large cheek pouches, and a short tail. **2.** a coarse or brutish person. [ME *babewyn* gargoyle, late ME: baboon (AL *babewynus*) < MF *babouin* baboon, simpleton] —**ba·boon′ish,** *adj.*

ba·bu (bä′bo͞o), *n.* **1.** a Hindu title of courteous address equivalent to Sir or Mr. **2.** a Hindu gentleman. **3.** a native Indian knowing some English. Also, **baboo.** [< Hindi *bābū* father]

ba·bul (bä bo͞ol′, bä′bo͞ol), *n.* **1.** any of several mimosaceous trees of the genus *Acacia* that yield a gum, esp. *A. arabica,* of India. **2.** the gum, pods, or bark of such a tree. [< Hindi *babūl* < Pers]

Ba·bur (bä′bər), *n.* Baber.

ba·bush·ka (bə bo͝osh′kə, -bo͞osh′-), *n.* a woman's scarf, often triangular, used as a hood with two ends tied under the chin. [< Russ: grandmother = *bab(a)* old woman + *-ushka* dim. suffix]

Ba·bush·kin (bä′bo͝osh kin), *n.* a city in the W RSFSR in the central Soviet Union in Europe. 112,000 (1959).

ba·by (bā′bē), *n., pl.* **-bies,** *adj., v.,* **-bied, -by·ing.** —*n.* **1.** an infant; very young child. **2.** a newborn or very young animal. **3.** the youngest member of a family or group. **4.** an immature or childish person. **5.** *Slang.* **a.** a girl or woman, esp. an attractive one. **b.** (*often cap.*) a term of endearment or familiar address. **6.** *Slang.* a project or object requiring or eliciting a person's special attention or pride. —*adj.* **7.** of or suitable for a baby. **8.** of or like a baby; infantile: *baby face.* **9.** *Informal.* small; comparatively little: *a baby spotlight.* —*v.t.* **10.** to treat like a young child; pamper. **11.** to handle or use with special care; treat gently. [ME] —**ba′by·hood′,** *n.* —**ba′by·ish,** *adj.* —**ba′by·ish·ly,** *adv.* —**Syn. 10.** indulge, spoil, humor, coddle.

ba·by-blue-eyes (bā′bē blo͞o′īz′), *n., pl.* **-eyes.** (*construed as sing. or pl.*) **1.** a plant, *Nemophila insignis,* of the Pacific coast of the U.S., with spotted blue blossoms. **2.** a related plant, *N. phaceloides,* common in Oklahoma. **3.** a related plant, *N. menziesi atomaria,* of the western U.S. [so called from fancied resemblance of its spots to eyes]

ba′by grand′ pian′o, the smallest form of grand piano.

Bab·y·lon (bab′ə lən, -lon′), *n.* **1.** an ancient city of SW Asia, on the Euphrates River: the capital of Babylonia and later of the Chaldean empire. See map at **Chaldea. 2.** any city regarded as a place of excessive luxury and wickedness.

Bab·y·lo·ni·a (bab′ə lō′nē ə), *n.* an ancient empire in SW Asia, in the lower Euphrates valley: flourished 2800–1750 B.C. *Cap.:* Babylon. See map at **Mesopotamia.**

Bab·y·lo·ni·an (bab′ə lō′nē ən), *adj.* **1.** of or pertaining to Babylon or Babylonia. **2.** excessively or sinfully luxurious. —*n.* **3.** an inhabitant of ancient Babylonia. **4.** the dialect of Akkadian spoken in Babylonia. Cf. **Akkadian** (def. 1).

Babylo′nian captiv′ity, 1. the period of the exile of the Jews in Babylonia, 597–538 B.C. **2.** the exile of the popes at Avignon, 1309–77.

ba·by's-breath (bā′bēz breth′), *n.* babies'-breath.

ba·by-sit (bā′bē sit′), *v.i.,* **-sat, -sit·ting.** to take charge of a child or of children while the parents are temporarily away. —**ba′by-sit′ter,** *n.*

ba′by talk′, 1. the speech of children learning to talk, esp. as marked by syntactic distortion and phonetic modifications such as lisping and omitting and substituting sounds. **2.** a style of speech used esp. in addressing children, pets, or sweethearts, in imitation of the voice and pronunciation of young children and characterized by the addition of diminutive endings to words and the omission and substitution of certain sounds.

ba′by tooth′. See **milk tooth.**

bac·ca·lau·re·ate (bak′ə lôr′ē it), *n.* **1.** See **bachelor's degree. 2.** a religious service held for a graduating class. **3.** Also called **baccalau′reate ser′mon.** the sermon delivered at such a religious service. [< ML *baccalaureāt(us)* = *baccalaure(us)* advanced student, BACHELOR (for *baccalārius,* alter. by assoc. with L phrase *bacca laureus* laurel berry) + *-ātus* -ATE[1]]

bac·ca·rat (bä′kə rä′, bak′ə-; bä′kə rä′, bak′ə-; *Fr.* BA-KA RA′), *n.* a gambling game at cards played by a banker and two or more players who bet against him. Also, **bac′ca·ra′.** [var. of *baccara* < F < ?]

bac·cate (bak′āt), *adj. Bot.* **1.** berrylike. **2.** bearing berries. [< L *bāc(a), bacc(a)* berry + -ATE[1]]

Bac·chae (bak′ē), *n.pl. Class. Myth.* **1.** the female attendants or priestesses of Bacchus. **2.** the women who took part in the Bacchanalia. [< L < Gk *Bákchai,* pl. of *Bákchē* maenad]

bac·cha·nal (bä′kə näl′, bak′ə nal′, bak′ə nᵊl), *n.* **1.** a follower of Bacchus. **2.** an occasion of drunken revelry; bacchanalia. —*adj.* **3.** pertaining to Bacchus. [< L *Bacchā-nāl(is)* = *Bacch(us)* + *-ānālis;* see BACCHANALIA]

Bac·cha·na·li·a (bak′ə nā′lē ə, -nāl′yə), *n., pl.* **-li·a, -li·as. 1.** (*sometimes construed as pl.*) a festival in honor of Bacchus. Cf. **Dionysia. 2.** (*l.c.*) a drunken feast. [< L = *Bacch(us)* + *-ān(us)* -AN + *-ālia,* neut. pl. of *-ālis* -AL[1]] —**bac′cha·na′li·an,** *adj.*

bac·chant (bak′ənt), *n., pl.* **bac·chants, bac·chan·tes** (bə-kan′tēz), *adj.* —*n.* **1.** a priest, priestess, or votary of Bacchus. —*adj.* **2.** worshiping Bacchus. [< L *bacchant-* (s. of *bacchāns,* prp. of *bacchārī* to revel)] —**bac·chan·tic** (bə kan′-tik), *adj.*

bac·chan·te (bə kan′tē, bə kant′, bak′ənt), *n.* a female bacchant. Also called **maenad.** [back formation from L *bacchante(s),* fem. pl. of *bacchāns* BACCHANT; var. with silent *-e* < F *bacchante,* fem. of *bacchant* bacchant]

Bac·chic (bak′ik), *adj.* **1.** of, pertaining to, or honoring Bacchus. **2.** (*l.c.*) riotously intoxicated. [< L *Bacchic(us)* < Gk *Bakchikós*]

bac·chi·us (bə kī′əs, ba-), *n., pl.* **-chi·i** (-kī′ī). *Pros.* a foot of three syllables that in quantitative meter consists of one short syllable followed by two long ones and in accentual meter consists of one unstressed syllable followed by two stressed ones. Cf. **antibacchius.** [< L < Gk *Bakcheîos* (*poûs*) (foot) of BACCHUS]

Bac·chus (bak′əs), *n. Class. Myth.* the god of wine; Dionysus. [< L < Gk *Bákchos;* akin to L *bacca* berry. See BAY[4]]

bacci-, a learned borrowing from Latin meaning "berry," used in the formation of compound words: *baccivorous.* [< L, comb. form of *bacca, bāca*]

bac·civ·or·ous (bak siv′ər əs), *adj.* feeding on berries.

bach (bach), *v.i. Informal.* **bach it,** to keep house alone, as a man does whose wife is away. [< BACHELOR, by apocope]

Bach (bäKH), *n.* **1. Jo·hann Se·bas·ti·an** (yō′hän si bas′-chən; *Ger.* yō′hän zā bäs′tē än′), 1685–1750, German composer and organist. **2.** his son, **Carl Philipp E·ma·nu·el** (kärl fil′ip i man′yo͞o əl′; *Ger.* kärl fē′lip ā mä′no͞o el′), 1714–88, German composer.

bach·e·lor (bach′ə lər, bach′lər), *n.* **1.** an unmarried man. **2.** a person who has been awarded a bachelor's degree. **3.** Also called **bachelor-at-arms.** a young knight who followed the banner of another. **4.** a male animal without a mate during breeding season. [ME *bacheler* < OF < VL **baccalār(is)* farm hand; akin to LL *baccalāria* piece of land, orig. pl. of **baccalārium* dairy farm = **baccāl(is)* of cows (*bacca,* var. of L *vacca* cow + *-ālis* -AL[1]) + *-ārium* place] —**bach′e·lor·dom, bach′e·lor·hood′,** *n.* —**bach′e·lor·ism,** *n.*

bach·e·lor-at-arms (bach′ə lər ət ärmz′, bach′lər-), *n., pl.* **bach·e·lors-at-arms.** bachelor (def. 3).

Bach′elor of Arts′, 1. a bachelor's degree in the liberal arts. **2.** a person having this degree. *Abbr.:* A.B., B.A.

Bach′elor of Sci′ence, 1. a bachelor's degree, usually awarded for studies in natural science, pure science, or technology. **2.** a person having this degree. *Abbr.:* B.S., B.Sc., S.B., Sc.B.

bach·e·lor's-but·ton (bach′ə lərz but′ᵊn, bach′lərz-), *n.* any of various plants with round flower heads, esp. the cornflower, or double-flowered varieties of ranunculus.

bach′elor's degree′, a degree awarded by a college or university to a person who has completed his undergraduate studies. Also called **baccalaureate.**

bacill-, a combining form of **bacillus:** *bacillary.*

bac·il·lar·y (bas′ə ler′ē), *adj.* **1.** Also called **ba·cil·li·form** (bə sil′ə fôrm′). of or like a bacillus; rod-shaped. **2.** *Bacteriol.* characterized by bacilli. Also, **ba·cil·lar** (bə sil′ər, bas′ə lər).

ba·cil·lus (bə sil′əs), *n., pl.* **-cil·li** (-sil′ī). **1.** any of several rod-shaped, aerobic bacteria of the genus *Bacillus,* that produce spores. **2.** any rod-shaped or cylindrical bacterium. **3.** any bacterium. See diag. at **bacteria.** [< NL, LL, var. of L *bacillum* (lictor's) wand = *bac(ulum)* walking stick + *-illum* dim. suffix]

bac·i·tra·cin (bas′i trā′sin), *n. Pharm.* an antibiotic polypeptide, used chiefly in the treatment of infections caused by gonococci, and Gram-positive bacteria.

back[1] (bak), *n.* **1.** the rear part of the human body, extending from the neck to the end of the spine. **2.** the part of the body of animals corresponding to the human back. **3.** the side, area, or part of anything that is opposite to or farthest from the front or that forms the rear area or part: *Move to the back of the bus. He put his coat on the back of a chair.* **4.** the whole body, esp. considered as a support or for bearing clothes or burdens: *the clothes on his back.* **5.** the spine or backbone: *to break one's back.* **6.** *Naut., Aeron.* the forward side of a propeller blade (opposed to *face*). **7.** the narrow, bound side, or spine of a book. **8.** *Carpentry.* the upper side of a joist, rafter, or the like. **9.** *Sports.* a player whose regular position is behind the line, forward line, etc., as a fullback or halfback in football. **10. be flat on one's back,** to be helpless, as with illness. **11. behind one's back,** secretly; in one's absence. **12. get one's back up,** to become annoyed. **13. have one's back to the wall,** to be in a difficult or hopeless situation. **14. in back of** or **back of,** *Informal.* behind: *He hid in back of the billboard.* **15. turn one's back on,** to forsake or neglect. —*v.t.* **16.** to support or help, as with personal authority, evidence, or money: *to back a favorite candidate.* **17.** to substantiate (a theory or claim) with evidence or reasoning (often fol. by *up*): *to back up a theory with facts.* **18.** to bet on: *to back a horse in the race.* **19.** to cause to move backward (often fol. by *up*): *to back a car.* **20.** to furnish with a back. **21.** to lie at the back of; form a back or background for: *a beach backed by hills.* **22.** to provide with an accompaniment: *a singer backed by piano and bass.* **23.** *Naut.* **a.** to alter the position of (a sail) so that the wind will strike the forward face. **b.** to brace (yards) in backing a sail. —*v.i.* **24.** to go or move backward (often fol. by *up*). **25.** *Naut.* (of wind) to change direction counterclockwise (opposed to *veer*). **26. back and fill, a.** *Naut.* to trim sails so that the wind strikes them first on the forward and then on the after side, in order to maneuver a ship in a narrow channel. **b.** *U.S. Informal.* to change one's opinion or position; vacillate. **27. back down,** *Informal.* to abandon an argument, opinion, or claim. **28. back off,** to back away from something. **29. back out** or **out of,** *Informal.* to fail to keep an engagement or promise. **30. back water, a.** *Naut.* to reverse the direction of a vessel. **b.** to withdraw an opinion. —*adj.* **31.** situated behind something else or at or in the rear: *the back fence.* **32.** remote from the front or main area, position, or rank. **33.** pertaining to the past: *back files.* **34.** in arrears; overdue: *back pay.* **35.** coming or going back; moving backward: *back current.* **36.** *Navig.* reciprocal (def. 5). **37.** *Phonet.* (of a speech sound) produced with the tongue articulating in the back part of the mouth, as in either of the sounds of *go.* [ME *bak,* OE *bæc;* c. OFris *bek,* OS *bak,* Icel *bak*] —**back′less** *adj.*

—**Syn. 16.** sustain, favor, assist; endorse. **31.** BACK, HIND, POSTERIOR, REAR refer to something situated behind something else. BACK means the opposite of front: *back window.* HIND, and the more formal word POSTERIOR, suggest the rearmost of two or more, often similar objects: *hind legs; posterior lobe.* REAR is used of buildings, conveyances, etc., and in military language it is the opposite of fore: *rear end of a truck; rear echelon.* —**Ant. 1, 31.** front.

—**Usage. 14.** The use of BACK OF instead of IN BACK OF or BEHIND is common in informal English and is rapidly gaining general acceptance in standard English: *He hid back of the billboard.* In formal usage, BEHIND is usually preferred to IN BACK OF: *He hid behind the billboard.*

back[2] (bak), *adv.* **1.** at, to, or toward the rear; backward: *to step back.* **2.** in or into the past: *to look back on one's youth.* **3.** at or toward the original starting point, place, or condition: *to go back to the old neighborhood.* **4.** in direct payment or return: *to pay back a loan.* **5.** in a state of restraint or retention: *to hold back salary.* **6.** so as to register a later time: *to put a clock back.* **7. back and forth,** from side to side; to and fro. [aph. var. of ABACK]

back[3] (bak), *n.* a large tub, vat, or the like, used by dyers, brewers, distillers, etc. [< D *bak* tub, trough < LL *bacc(a)* water container; cf. F *bac* ferryboat, punt]

back·ache (bak′āk′), *n.* a pain esp. in the lumbar region of the back.

back′ bench′, any of the seats occupied by backbenchers.

back·bench·er (bak′ben′chər, -ben′-), *n.* any of the members of a legislature, esp. of the House of Commons of Great Britain, except the party leaders.

back·bend (bak′bend′), *n.* an acrobatic feat in which a person bends backward from a standing position until his hands touch the floor.

back·bite (bak′bīt′), *v.,* **-bit, -bit·ten** or (*Informal*) **-bit, -bit·ing.** —*v.t.* **1.** to attack the character or reputation of (a person who is not present). —*v.i.* **2.** to slander an absent person. [ME] —**back′bit′er,** *n.*

back·board (bak′bōrd′, -bôrd′), *n.* **1.** a board placed at or forming the back of anything. **2.** *Basketball.* a board or other flat surface to which the basket is attached.

back·bone (bak′bōn′), *n.* **1.** *Anat.* the spinal or vertebral column; spine. **2.** strength of character. **3.** something resembling a backbone in appearance, position, or function. **4.** *Bookbinding.* a back or bound edge of a book; spine. **5.** *Naval Archit.* the central fore-and-aft assembly giving longitudinal strength to the bottom of a vessel. [ME *bacbon*] —**back′boned′,** *adj.* —**back′bone′less,** *adj.*

back·break·ing (bak′brā′king), *adj.* demanding great effort, endurance, etc.; exhausting. Also, **back′-break′ing.** —**back′break′er,** *n.*

back′ burn′er, low priority (usually prec. by *on the*): *The matter is now put on the back burner.* —**back′-burn′er,** *adj.*

back·court (bak′kōrt′, -kôrt′), *n.* **1.** *Basketball.* the half of a court in which the basket being defended is located. **2.** *Tennis.* the part of a tennis court between the base line and the line, parallel to the net, that marks the in-bounds limit of a service. Cf. **forecourt** (def. 2).

back·cross (bak′krôs′, -kros′), *Genetics.* —*v.t.* **1.** to cross (a hybrid of the first generation) with either of its parents. —*n.* **2.** an instance of such crossing.

back·drop (bak′drop′), *n.* **1.** *Theat.* the rear curtain of a stage setting. **2.** the setting of an event.

backed (bakt), *adj.* **1.** having a back, setting, or support (often used in combination): *a low-backed sofa; a well-backed candidate.* **2.** (of fabric) having an extra set of threads in the warp or weft for added warmth.

back·er (bak′ər), *n.* **1.** a person who supports or aids a cause, enterprise, etc. **2.** canvas or other material used for backing. —**Syn. 1.** supporter, sponsor, guarantor.

back·field (bak′fēld′), *n.* *Football.* **1.** (*construed as pl.*) the members of the team who, on offense, are stationed behind the linemen and, on defense, behind the linebackers. **2.** their positions considered as a unit. **3.** the area where the backs play.

back·fire (bak′fīər′), *v.*, **-fired, -fir·ing,** *n.* —*v.i.* **1.** (of an internal-combustion engine) to have a loud, premature explosion in the intake manifold. **2.** to burn an area clear in order to check a spreading prairie or forest fire. **3.** (of a plan) to result in consequences that were to be avoided. —*n.* **4.** (in an internal-combustion engine) premature ignition of fuel in the intake manifold, from contact with flame from a cylinder. **5.** a fire started intentionally to check the advance of a forest or prairie fire.

back′ forma′tion, *Linguistics.* **1.** the analogical creation of one word from another word that appears to be a derived or inflected form of the first by dropping the apparent affix or by modification. **2.** a word so formed, as *typewrite* from *typewriter.*

back·gam·mon (bak′gam′ən, bak′gam′-), *n.* a game for two persons played on a board having two parts, with pieces or men moved in accordance with throws of the dice.

back·ground (bak′ground′), *n.* **1.** the ground or parts situated in the rear, as in a scene (opposed to *foreground*). **2.** *Fine Arts.* the part of a painted or carved surface against which represented objects and forms are perceived or depicted. **3.** the social, historical, technical, or other circumstances whose understanding gives meaning to a fact, event, etc.: *the background of the war.* **4.** a person's origin, education, experience, etc., in relation to his present character, status, etc. **5.** a subordinate or unobtrusive accompaniment or impression: *The music was a fine background to dinner.* **6.** *Physics.* the totality of effects that tend to obscure a phenomenon under investigation and above which the phenomenon must be detected. **7. in** or **into the background,** out of sight or notice; unobtrusive. —*adj.* **8.** of, pertaining to, or serving as a background: *background music.*

back′ground mu′sic, **1.** music intended to provide a soothing background, as recorded music played over loudspeaker systems in public places. **2.** music composed to accompany and heighten the mood of a visual production, as a motion picture.

back·hand (bak′hand′), *n.* **1.** a stroke, slap, etc., made with the back of the hand forward. **2.** (in tennis, squash, etc.) a stroke made from the side of the body opposite to that of the hand holding the racket, paddle, etc. **3.** writing that slopes toward the left. —*adj.* **4.** backhanded. **5.** (in tennis, squash, etc.) of, pertaining to, or noting a backhand. Cf. **forehand** (def. 1). —*adv.* **6.** with the back of the hand: *He hit him backhand across the face.* **7.** from across the body; backhanded: *He returned the ball backhand on the first serve.* —*v.t.* **8.** to strike with the back of the hand. **9.** to hit, produce, or accomplish with a backhand. **10.** to catch (a ball or the like) backhanded.

back·hand·ed (bak′han′did), *adj.* **1.** performed with the hand turned so that the back of the hand faces forward. **2.** sloping in a downward direction from left to right: *backhanded writing.* **3.** oblique or ambiguous in meaning: *a backhanded compliment.* —*adv.* **4.** with the hand across the body; backhand: *He caught the ball backhanded.* —**back′hand′ed·ly,** *adv.* —**back′hand′ed·ness,** *n.*

back·ing (bak′ing), *n.* **1.** aid or support of any kind. **2.** supporters or backers collectively. **3.** something that forms a back or is placed at or attached to the back of anything, esp. for support or protection. **4.** *Theat.* a curtain or flat placed behind a window, entrance, or other opening in a stage set to conceal the offstage area. **5.** the musical accompaniment for a soloist.

back·lash (bak′lash′), *n.* **1.** any sudden and forceful recoil or reaction. **2.** the play or lost motion between loosely fitting machine parts. **3.** a strong or violent reaction, as to some social change, often provoked by fear or prejudice. **4.** *Angling.* a snarled line on a reel, usually caused by a faulty cast. —*v.i.* **5.** to make a backlash.

back·light (bak′līt′), *n.*, *v.*, **-light·ed** or **-lit, -light·ing.** —*n.* **1.** the illumination produced by a light behind or at a right angle to an object, person, or scene. —*v.t.* **2.** to illuminate (something) from behind.

back·light·ing (bak′lī′ting), *n.* a controlled technique of lighting, used in photography or the theater, in which a light is placed behind or at right angles to an object, person, or scene to produce such effects as depth, separation of subject and background, etc.

back·log (bak′lôg′, -log′), *n.*, *v.*, **-logged, -log·ging.** —*n.* **1.** a reserve or accumulation, as of stock, work, or business. **2.** a large log at the back of a hearth to keep up a fire. —*v.t.* **3.** to hold in reserve, as for future handling, repair, etc.

back′ mat′ter, *Print.* the parts of a book appearing after the text, as the bibliography and index. Also called **end matter.** Cf. **front matter.**

back′ num′ber, **1.** an out-of-date issue of a magazine or newspaper. **2.** anything out of date.

back′ or′der, *Com.* part of an order to be filled or delivered at some future date.

back·out (bak′out′), *n.* *Rocketry.* a step-by-step reversal or cancellation of launching procedures during a countdown that has been halted.

back·pack (bak′pak′), *n.* **1.** a pack or bundle of supplies to be carried on one's back, often supported on a metal frame strapped to the body. **2.** a trip or outing requiring such a pack. —*v.i.* **3.** to go on an outing, using a backpack: *to backpack through the mountains.* —*v.t.* **4.** to place or carry in a backpack or on one's back. [BACK[1] + PACK[1]] —**back′pack′er,** *n.*

back·ped·al (bak′ped′əl), *v.i.*, **-aled, -al·ing** or (*esp. Brit.*) **-alled, -al·ling.** **1.** to retard the forward motion of a bicycle by pressing backward on the pedal. **2.** to reverse or retreat from an argument, opponent, position, or the like.

back·rest (bak′rest′), *n.* a support used by a person for resting his back.

back′ road′, a little used, often unpaved country road.

back′ seat′, **1.** a seat behind another seat or seats. **2. take a back seat,** *Informal.* to occupy a secondary or inferior position.

back′-seat driv′er (bak′sēt′), *Usually Disparaging.* **1.** an automobile passenger who offers the driver unsolicited advice, esp. from the back seat. **2.** any officious person who offers criticism, unsolicited advice, or the like.

back·sheesh (bak′shēsh), *n.*, *v.t.*, *v.i.* baksheesh. Also, **back′shish.**

back·side (bak′sīd′), *n.* **1.** the rear or back part or view of an object, person, place, etc. **2.** the buttocks.

back·sight (bak′sīt′), *n.* *Survey.* **1.** a sight on a previously occupied instrument station. **2.** (in leveling) the reading on a rod that is held on a point of known elevation, used in computing the elevation of the instrument.

back·slap·ping (bak′slap′ing), *n.* *Informal.* a loud and effusive display of friendliness, cordiality, etc. —**back′slap′per,** *n.*

back·slide (bak′slīd′), *v.*, **-slid, -slid** or **-slid·den, -slid·ing,** *n.* —*v.i.* **1.** to relapse into error or sin. —*n.* **2.** an act or instance of backsliding. —**back′slid′er,** *n.*

back·space (bak′spās′), *v.*, **-spaced, -spac·ing,** *n.* —*v.i.* **1.** to shift the carriage of a typewriter one space backward by depressing a special key. —*n.* **2.** Also called **back′spac′er, back′space key′.** the key on a typewriter used for backspacing.

back·spin (bak′spin′), *n.* the reverse spin imparted to a ball causing it to bounce or roll backward or stop short, as in billiards or table tennis. Also called **underspin.**

back·stage (bak′stāj′), *adv.* **1.** behind the proscenium in a theater, esp. in the wings or dressing rooms. **2.** upstage. —*adj.* **3.** located or occurring backstage. —*n.* **4.** *Theat.* a backstage area.

back′ stairs′, **1.** stairs at the back of a house, as for use by servants. **2.** a means of intrigue.

back·stairs (bak′stârz′), *adj.* indirect; underhand: *backstairs gossip.* Also, **back′stair′.**

back·stay (bak′stā′), *n.* **1.** *Mach.* a supporting or checking piece in a mechanism. **2.** *Naut.* any of various shrouds forming part of a vessel's standing rigging and leading aft from masts above a lower mast to the sides or stern of the vessel in order to reinforce the masts against forward pull.

back·stitch (bak′stich′), *n.* **1.** stitching or a stitch in which the thread is doubled back on the preceding stitch. —*v.t.*, *v.i.* **2.** to sew by backstitch.

back·stop (bak′stop′), *n.* **1.** *Sports.* a wall, wire screen, or the like, serving to prevent a ball from going too far beyond the normal playing area. **2.** *Informal.* a safeguard or reinforcement, as for a mechanism.

back·stretch (bak′strech′), *n.* the straight part of a race track opposite the part leading to the finish line. Cf. **homestretch.**

back·stroke (bak′strōk′), *n.*, *v.*, **-stroked, -strok·ing.** —*n.* **1.** a backhanded stroke. **2.** a blow or stroke in return; recoil. **3.** *Swimming.* a stroke resembling an inverted crawl, executed while on one's back. —*v.i.* **4.** *Swimming.* to swim with a backstroke.

back·swept (bak′swept′), *adj.* **1.** slanting backward or away from the front. **2.** *Aeron. Rare.* sweptback.

back·swing (bak′swing′), *n.* *Sports.* the movement of a bat, racket, or the like, toward the back of a player in preparation for the forward movement with which the ball is struck.

back·sword (bak′sōrd′, -sôrd′), *n.* **1.** a sword with only one sharp edge; broadsword. **2.** (formerly) a cudgel having a basket hilt, used in fencing exhibitions. **3.** a backswordman.

back·sword·man (bak′sōrd′mən, -sôrd′-), *n.*, *pl.* **-men.** a person who uses a backsword. Also, **back·swords·man** (bak′sōrdz′mən, -sôrdz′-).

back′ talk′, an impudent response; impudent or impertinent replies in general.

back-talk (bak′tôk′), *v.i.*, *v.t.* to answer back.

back′ to back′, **1.** having the backs close together or adjoining. **2.** (of similar events) following one immediately after the other; consecutive. —**back′-to-back′,** *adj.*, *adv.*

back·track (bak′trak′), *v.i.* *U.S.* **1.** to return over the same course or route. **2.** to withdraw, as from an undertaking or position.

back·up (bak′up′), *n.* **1.** a person or thing that supports or reinforces another. **2.** an overflow or accumulation due to a stoppage. **3.** an alternate or substitute kept in reserve for an emergency.

back·ward (bak′wərd), *adv.* Also, **back′wards.** **1.** toward the back or rear. **2.** with the back foremost. **3.** in the reverse of the usual or right way: *counting backward from 100.* **4.** toward the past: *to look backward over the past year.* **5.** toward a less advanced state; retrogressively. **6. backward and forward,** *Informal.* thoroughly: *He knew his lesson backward and forward.* Also, **backwards and forwards.** —*adj.* **7.** directed toward the back or past. **8.** reversed; returning: *a backward movement.* **9.** slow to advance, progress, or learn: *a backward student.* **10.** bashful or hesitant. [ME *bakwarde*] —**back′ward·ly,** *adv.* —**back′ward·ness,** *n.*

back·wash (bak′wosh′, -wôsh′), *n.* **1.** *Naut.* water thrown backward by the motion of oars, propellers, paddle wheels, etc. **2.** *Aeron.* the portion of the wash of an aircraft that flows to the rear, usually created by the power plant. **3.** an unexpected, and usually undesirable, subsidiary result or reaction. —*v.t.* **4.** to spray or rock with a backwash.

back·wa·ter (bak′wô′tər, -wot′ər), *n.* **1.** water held or forced back, as by a dam, flood, tide, etc. **2.** a retired or stagnant area or place.

back·woods (bak′wŏŏdz′), *n.pl.* **1.** (*often construed as sing.*) wooded or partially uncleared and unsettled districts. —*adj.* Also, **back′wood′. 2.** of or pertaining to the backwoods. **3.** unsophisticated; uncouth.

back·woods·man (bak′wŏŏdz′mən), *n., pl.* **-men.** a person living in or coming from the backwoods.

Ba·co·lod (bä kō′lôd), *n.* a seaport on N Negros, in the central Philippines. 140,300 (est. 1965).

ba·con (bā′kən), *n.* **1.** the back and sides of the hog, salted and dried or smoked, usually sliced thin and fried for food. **2. bring home the bacon,** *Slang.* **a.** to provide for material needs; earn a living. **b.** to accomplish a task; be successful or victorious. [ME *bacoun* < AF, c. OF *bacon* < Gmc **bakōn-*, weak var. of **baka-* BACK[1]; cf. OD *baken* bacon]

Ba·con (bā′kən), *n.* **1. Francis** (*Baron Verulam, Viscount St. Albans*), 1561–1626, English essayist, philosopher, and statesman. **2. Francis,** born 1910, English painter, born in Ireland. **3. Nathaniel,** 1647–76, American colonist, born in England: leader of a rebellion in Virginia 1676. **4. Roger** ("*The Admirable Doctor*"), 1214?–94?, English philosopher and scientist.

Ba·co·ni·an (bā kō′nē ən), *adj.* **1.** of or pertaining to the philosopher Francis Bacon or his doctrines. —*n.* **2.** an adherent of the philosophy of Francis Bacon. —**Ba·co′ni·an·ism, Ba′co·nism,** *n.*

bac·te·re·mi·a (bak′tə rē′mē ə), *n. Pathol.* the presence of bacteria in the blood.

bacteri-, a learned borrowing from Greek originally meaning "staff," "cane," used with the meaning "bacteria" in the formation of compound words: *bactericide.* Also, **bacterio-;** *esp. before a vowel,* **bacter-.** [< Gk *baktēría* staff, cane]

bac·te·ri·a (bak tēr′ē ə), *n.pl., sing.* **-te·ri·um** (-tēr′ē əm). any of numerous microscopic, spherical, rod-shaped, or spiral organisms of the class *Schizomycetes,* various species of which are concerned in fermentation and putrefaction, the production of disease, the fixing of atmospheric nitrogen, etc.; schizomycete. [< NL < Gk *baktḗria,* pl. of *baktḗrion;* see BACTERIUM] —**bac·te′ri·al,** *adj.* —**bac·te′ri·al·ly,** *adv.*

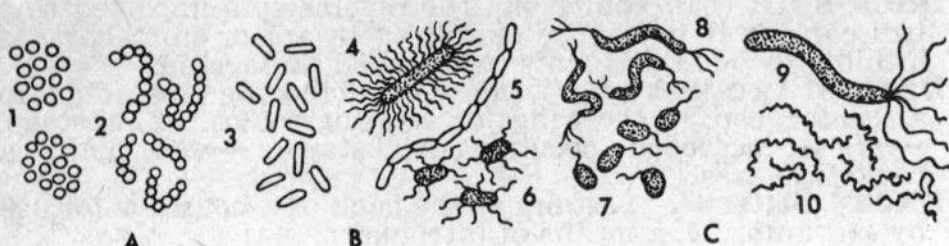

Bacteria (greatly magnified)
A, Cocci (spherical): 1, *Staphylococcus pyogenes aureus;* 2, *Streptococcus pyogenes.* B, Bacilli (rod): 3, *Bacillus sporogenes;* 4, *Bacillus proteus;* 5, *Bacillus subtilis;* 6, *Bacillus typhosus.* C, Spirilla (spiral): 7, *Vibrio cholerae asiaticae;* 8, *Spirillum undulum;* 9, *Theospirillum;* 10, *Spirochaeta*

bac·te·ri·cide (bak tēr′i sīd′), *n.* an agent capable of killing bacteria. —**bac·te′ri·cid′al,** *adj.*

bac·te·rin (bak′tə rin), *n. Immunol.* a vaccine prepared from bacteria.

bacterio-, var. of **bacteri-.**

bacteriol., bacteriology.

bac·te·ri·ol·o·gy (bak tēr′ē ol′ə jē), *n.* the science that deals with bacteria. —**bac·te·ri·o·log·i·cal** (bak tēr′ē ə loj′i kəl), **bac·te′ri·o·log′ic,** *adj.* —**bac·te′ri·o·log′i·cal·ly,** *adv.* —**bac·te′ri·ol′o·gist,** *n.*

bac·te·ri·ol·y·sis (bak tēr′ē ol′i sis), *n.* the disintegration or dissolution of bacteria. —**bac·te·ri·o·lyt·ic** (bak tēr′ē ə lit′ik), *n., adj.*

bac·te·ri·o·phage (bak tēr′ē ə fāj′), *n.* one of a group of viruses that infect specific bacteria, usually causing their disintegration or dissolution. —**bac·te·ri·o·phag·ic** (bak tēr′ē ə faj′ik), **bac·te·ri·oph·a·gous** (bak tēr′ē of′ə gəs), *adj.* —**bac·te·ri·oph·a·gy** (bak tēr′ē of′ə jē), *n.*

bac·te·ri·o·sta·sis (bak tēr′ē ə stā′sis), *n. Bacteriol.* the prevention of the further growth of bacteria. —**bac·te·ri·o·stat·ic** (bak tēr′ē ə stat′ik), *adj.* —**bac·te′ri·o·stat′i·cal·ly,** *adv.*

bac·te·ri·o·stat (bak tēr′ē ə stat′), *n. Bacteriol.* a substance inhibiting the further growth of bacteria.

bac·te·ri·um (bak tēr′ē əm), *n.* sing. of **bacteria.** [< NL < Gk *baktḗrion,* dim. of *baktēría* staff; akin to *bάktron* walking stick, L *baculum, bacillum*]

bac·ter·ize (bak′tə rīz′), *v.t.,* **-ized, -iz·ing.** to change in composition by means of bacteria. —**bac′ter·i·za′tion,** *n.*

bac·ter·oid (bak′tə roid′), *Bacteriol.* —*n.* **1.** any of the rod-shaped or branched bacteria in the root nodules of nitrogen-fixing plants. —*adj.* **2.** Also, **bac′te·roi′dal.** resembling bacteria.

Bac·tra (bak′trə), *n.* ancient name of **Balkh.**

Bac·tri·a (bak′trē ə), *n.* an ancient country in W Asia, between the Oxus River and the Hindu Kush Mountains. *Cap.:* Bactra. —**Bac′tri·an,** *adj., n.*

Bac′trian cam′el, an Asian camel, *Camelus bactrianus,* having two humps on the back.

Bactrian camel
(7 ft. high at top of humps; length about 9 ft.)

ba·cu·li·form (bə kyōō′lə fôrm′, bak′yə-), *adj. Biol.* rod-shaped. [< L *bacul(um)* walking stick, staff + -I- + -FORM]

bac·u·line (bak′yə lin, -līn′), *adj.* pertaining to the rod or its use in punishing: *baculine discipline in the classroom.* [< L *bacul(um)* walking stick, staff + -INE[1]]

bad[1] (bad), *adj.,* **worse, worst,** *n., adv.* —*adj.* **1.** not good in any manner or degree. **2.** lacking or characterized by a lack of moral qualities. **3.** of poor quality, in poor condition, or inadequate. **4.** incorrect or faulty: *a bad guess.* **5.** invalid or false: *a bad insurance claim.* **6.** disobedient, naughty, or misbehaving. **7.** suffering from ill health, pain, or injury. **8.** not in good physical condition: *bad eyes.* **9.** tainted, spoiled, or rotten. **10.** having a detrimental effect, result, or tendency. **11.** causing or characterized by uneasiness, or annoyance. **12.** cross, irritable, or surly: *a bad mood.* **13.** more uncomfortable or dangerous than usual; severe: *a bad attack of asthma.* **14.** regretful, contrite, dejected, or upset: *to feel bad about something.* **15.** disreputable or dishonorable: *to get a bad name.* **16.** displaying a lack of skill, talent, or judgment. **17.** causing distress; unfortunate or unfavorable: *bad news.* **18.** not suitable or appropriate; disadvantageous or dangerous. **19.** adverse; unfavorable: *a bad opinion of someone.* **20.** inclement, as weather. **21.** disagreeable or offensive to the senses. **22.** not in keeping with a standard of behavior or conduct. **23.** vulgar, obscene, or blasphemous: *bad language.* **24.** not properly observing rules or customs of grammar, usage, spelling, etc. **25.** unattractive, esp. because of a lack of pleasing proportions: *She has a bad figure.* **26.** (of the complexion) marred by defects; blemished. **27.** not profitable or worth the price paid: *a bad buy.* **28.** counterfeit; not genuine. **29.** not collectible or payable: *a bad check; a bad debt.* **30. too bad,** unfortunate or disappointing.
—*n.* **31.** that which is bad: *You have to take the bad with the good.* **32.** a bad condition, character, or quality: *from bad to worse.* **33.** (*construed as pl.*) evil persons collectively (usually preceded by *the*): *the bad and the beautiful.* **34. in bad,** *Informal* **a.** in distress. **b.** in disfavor.
—*adv. Informal.* **35.** badly: *He wanted it bad enough to steal it.* **36. badly off,** in poor or distressed condition or circumstances; destitute. Also, **bad off.** Cf. **well-off.** [ME *badde,* back formation from OE *bæddel* hermaphrodite, *bædling* womanish man] —**bad′ness,** *n.*
—**Syn. 2.** depraved, corrupt, base, sinful, criminal, atrocious. BAD, EVIL, ILL, WICKED are closest in meaning in reference to that which is lacking in moral qualities or is actually vicious and reprehensible. BAD is the broadest and simplest term: *a bad man; bad habits.* EVIL applies to that which violates or leads to the violation of moral law: *evil practices.* ILL now appears mainly in certain fixed expressions, with a milder implication than that in EVIL: *ill will; ill-natured.* WICKED implies willful and determined doing of what is very wrong: *a wicked plan.* **3.** inferior, poor, deficient. **9.** putrefied. **17.** adverse, unlucky, unhappy. —**Ant. 1–12, 14–29, 31–33.** good.
—**Usage.** BAD and BADLY are found with almost equal acceptance in spoken English when following *feel,* although *bad* is usually preferred in formal writing: *I feel bad about my mistake. She felt badly about being late.* When preceded by *look, sound, smell,* etc., the usual choice is *bad: It looks bad for our team.*

bad[2] (bad), *v. Archaic.* a pt. of **bid.**

Ba·da·joz (bä′thä hôth′), *n.* a city in SW Spain. 102,499 (1965).

Ba·da·lo·na (bä′thä lô′nä), *n.* a seaport in NE Spain, near Barcelona. 120,014 (1965).

bad′ blood′, unfriendly or hostile relations; enmity.

bad′ con′duct dis′charge, 1. a discharge of a person from military service for an offense less serious than one for which a dishonorable discharge is given. **2.** a certificate of such a discharge.

bade (bad), *v.* a pt. of **bid.**

Ba·den (bäd′ən), *n.* **1.** a former state in SW West Germany, now incorporated in Baden-Württemberg. **2.** Also called **Ba′den-Ba′den.** a city in W Baden-Württemberg, in SW West Germany. 40,200 (1963).

Ba·den-Pow·ell (bād′ən pō′əl, bad′ən pou′əl), *n.* **Robert Stephenson Smyth** (smith, smīth), **1st Baron,** 1857–1941, British general who founded the Boy Scouts in 1908 and, with his sister Lady Agnes, the Girl Guides in 1910.

Ba·den-Würt·tem·berg (bäd′ən VYRT′əm BERK′), *n.* a state in SW West Germany: formed 1951. 8,066,000 (1963); 13,800 sq. mi. *Cap.:* Stuttgart.

badge (baj), *n., v.,* **badged, badg·ing.** —*n.* **1.** a special or distinctive mark, token, or device worn as a sign of membership, authority, etc. **2.** any emblem, token, or distinctive mark. **3.** an identifying symbol, generally of a simple heraldic design, worn by servants, retainers, or employees. —*v.t.* **4.** to furnish or mark with a badge. [ME *bag(g)e* < ?] —**badge′less,** *adj.*

badg·er (baj′ər), *n.* **1.** any of various burrowing, carnivorous mammals of the family *Mustelidae,* as *Taxidea taxus,* of North America, and *Meles meles,* of Europe and Asia. **2.** the fur of this mammal. **3.** *Australian.* **a.** a wombat. **b.** bandicoot (def. 2). **4.** (*cap.*) a native or inhabitant of Wisconsin (the **Badger State**) (used as a nickname). —*v.t.* **5.** to harass persistently. [var. of *badgeard* = BADGE + -ARD, in allusion to white mark or badge on head] —**badg′er·ing·ly,** *adv.* —**badg′er·ly,** *adj.* —**Syn. 5.** vex, bedevil, plague, worry, disturb, bait.

Badger,
Taxidea taxus
(Total length 2½ ft.; tail 6 in.)

Badg′er State′, Wisconsin (used as a nickname).

Bad′ Go′desberg (bät), official name of **Godesberg.**

bad·i·nage (bad′ən äzh′, bad′ən ij), *n., v.,* **-naged, -nag·ing.** —*n.* **1.** light, playful banter or raillery. —*v.t.* **2.** to banter or tease (someone) playfully. [< F = *badin* jester (whence *badiner* to jest) + *-age* -AGE]

Bad′ Lands′, a barren, severely eroded region in SW South Dakota and NW Nebraska.

bad·lands (bad′landz′), *n.* (*construed as pl.*) a barren area in which soft rock strata are eroded into varied, fantastic forms.

bad·ly (bad′lē), *adv.* **worse, worst,** *adj.* —*adv.* **1.** in a defective or incorrect way. **2.** in an unsatisfactory, inadequate, or unskilled manner. **3.** unfavorably: *to speak badly of someone.* **4.** in a wicked, evil, or morally or legally wrong way. **5.** in a naughty, or socially wrong way. **6.** to a great extent or degree: *to want something badly.* **7.** with great dis-

tress, resentment, or emotion. **8. badly off.** See **bad**[1] (def. 36). **—***adj. Informal.* **9.** in ill health; sick: *He felt badly.* **10.** sorry; regretful: *I feel badly about your leaving so soon* **11.** dejected; downcast.
—Usage. In the sense of "very much," the word BADLY is now common in standard English, although many users regard it as informal: *I need help badly. He wants that hat badly.* See also **bad.**

bad·man (bad′man′), *n., pl.* **-men.** a bandit, outlaw, etc., esp. in the early history of the western U.S.

bad·min·ton (bad′min t^{ə}n), *n.* a game played on a rectangular court by two players or two pairs of players equipped with light rackets used to volley a shuttlecock over a high net. [named after *Badminton,* the country seat of the duke of Beaufort in Gloucestershire, England]

bad·mouth (bad′mouth′), *v.t.* to speak unfavorably or critically of.

bad-tem·pered (bad′tem′pərd), *adj.* cross; cranky; surly.

Bae·da (bē′də), *n.* **Saint.** See **Bede, Saint.**

Bae·de·ker (bā′də kər), *n.* any of the series of guidebooks for travelers issued by the German publisher Karl Baedeker, 1801–59, and his successors.

Baeke·land (bāk′land′; *Flem.* bäk′ə länt′), *n.* **Le·o Hen·drik** (lē′ō hen′drik; *Flem.* lā′ō hen′drik), 1863–1944, U.S. chemist, born in Belgium.

Baer (bâr), *n.* **Karl Ernst von** (kärl ûrnst fən), 1792–1876, Estonian zoologist and pioneer embryologist.

Bae·yer (bā′ər; *Ger.* be′yər), *n.* **(Jo·hann Frie·drich Wil·helm) A·dolf von** (yō′hän frē′drik wil′helm ad′olf von, ā′dolf; *Ger.* yō′hän frē′drikh vil′helm ä′dôlf fən), 1835–1917, German chemist: Nobel prize 1905.

Ba·ez (bī ez′, bī′iz), *n.* **Joan,** born 1941, U.S. folk singer.

Baf·fin (baf′in), *n.* **William,** 1584?–1622, an English navigator who explored arctic North America.

Baf′fin Bay′, a part of the Arctic Ocean between W Greenland and E Baffin Island.

Baf′fin Is′land, a Canadian island in the Arctic Ocean, between Greenland and N Canada. ab. 1000 mi. long; 190,000 sq. mi. Also called **Baf′fin Land′.**

baf·fle (baf′əl), *v.,* **-fled, -fling,** *n.* **—***v.t.* **1.** to confuse, bewilder, or perplex. **2.** to frustrate or confound; thwart by creating confusion or bewilderment. **3.** to check or deflect the movement of (sound, light, fluids, etc.). **4.** to equip with a baffle or baffles. **5.** *Obs.* to cheat; trick. **—***n.* **6.** something that balks, checks, or deflects; bafflement or perplexity. **7.** an artificial obstruction for checking or deflecting the flow of gases, sounds, light, etc. [? < Scot *bauchle* to disgrace, treat with contempt = *bauch,* weak, poor, shaky + -LE] **—baf′fle·ment,** *n.* **—baf′fler,** *n.* **—baf′fling,** *adj.* **—baf′fling·ly,** *adv.*

bag (bag), *n., v.,* **bagged, bag·ging.** **—***n.* **1.** a container or receptacle capable of being closed at the mouth. **2.** a suitcase or other such portable receptacle. **3.** a purse or moneybag. **4.** any of various measures of capacity; bagful. **5.** a sac, as in an animal body. **6.** an udder. **7.** *Hunting.* the amount of game taken, esp. by one hunter in one hunting trip or over a specified period. **8.** something hanging in a loose, pouchlike manner, as skin or cloth. **9.** *Baseball.* base[1] (def. 8b). **10.** *Slang.* an unattractive, often slatternly woman. **11.** *Slang.* **a.** a person's avocation, hobby, major interest, or obsession: *Jazz isn't my bag. He's in the opera bag.* **b.** a person's mood or frame of mind: *The boss is in a mean bag today.* **c.** an environment, condition, or situation. **12. bag and baggage,** *Informal.* completely; totally. **13. hold the bag,** *U.S. Informal.* to be forced to bear the entire blame or responsibility. **14. in the bag,** *Slang.* virtually certain; assured. **—***v.i.* **15.** to swell or bulge. **16.** to hang loosely like an empty bag. **—***v.t.* **17.** to put into a bag. **18.** to kill or catch, as in hunting. **19.** to cause to swell or bulge. [ME *bagge* < Scand; cf. Icel *baggi* pack, bundle]

ba·gasse (bə gas′), *n.* **1.** crushed sugar-cane or beet refuse from sugar making. **2.** a kind of paper made from fibers of bagasse. [< F < Sp *bagazo* husks left after pressing of grapes or the like = *bag(a)* refuse (see BAGGAGE) + *-azo* aug. suffix]

bag·a·telle (bag′ə tel′), *n.* **1.** something of little value; a trifle. **2.** a game played on a board having at one end holes into which balls are to be struck with a cue. **3.** pinball. **4.** a short and light musical composition, usually for the piano. [< F < It *bagattella* = *baga* (< L *bāca* berry, fruit) + *-tt-* dim. suffix + *-ella* < L *-illa* dim. suffix]

Bag·dad (bag′dad, bäg däd′), *n.* Baghdad.

Bage·hot (baj′ət), *n.* **Walter,** 1826–77, English economist, political journalist, and critic.

ba·gel (bā′gəl), *n.* a leavened, doughnut-shaped, hard roll. [< Yiddish *beygel,* var. of dial. G *Beugel* < Gmc **baug-* ring]

bag·ful (bag′fo͝ol), *n., pl.* **-fuls.** **1.** the contents of or amount held by a bag. **2.** the quantity required to fill a bag; a considerable amount. [ME]

bag·gage (bag′ij), *n.* **1.** *Chiefly U.S.* trunks, suitcases, etc., used in traveling; luggage. **2.** the portable equipment of an army. **3.** a prostitute. **4.** any immoral, dishonorable, or undignified woman. **5.** *Informal.* a pert, playful young woman or girl. [late ME *bagage* = OF *bag(ues)* bundles, packs (? < Scand; see BAG) + *-age* -AGE]

bag·gage·mas·ter (bag′ij mas′tər), *n.* *U.S.* a person employed, esp. by a railroad, bus company, or steamship line, to take charge of passengers' baggage.

bag·ger (bag′ər), *n.* a person who packs groceries or other items into bags [BAG + -ER[1]]

bag·ging (bag′ing), *n.* woven material for bags.

bag·gy (bag′ē), *adj.,* **-gi·er, -gi·est.** baglike; hanging loosely. **—bag′gi·ly,** *adv.* **—bag′gi·ness,** *n.*

Bagh·dad (bag′dad, bäg däd′), *n.* a city in and the capital of Iraq, in the central part, on the Tigris. 2,800,000. Also, **Bagdad.**

bag′ la′dy, a homeless woman, usually impoverished and elderly, who carries all her possessions with her in shopping bags and lives on the streets and in public places, as railroad stations. Also called **shopping-bag lady.**

bag·man (bag′mən), *n., pl.* **-men.** **1.** *Brit.* a traveling salesman; drummer. **2.** *Slang.* a racketeer assigned by his superiors to collect, carry, or distribute payoff money.

bagn·io (ban′yō, bän′-), *n., pl.* **-ios.** **1.** a brothel. **2.** (esp. in Italy or Turkey) a bath or bathing house. **3.** *Archaic.* a prison for slaves, esp. in the Orient. [< It *bagno* < L *balneum, balineum* < Gk *balaneion* bath]

bag·pipe (bag′pīp′), *n.* a reed instrument consisting of a melody pipe and one or more accompanying drone pipes protruding from a windbag into which the air is blown by the mouth or a bellows. Also, **bag′pipes′.** [late ME *baggepipe*] **—bag′pip′er,** *n.*

ba·guette (ba get′), *n.* *Jewelry.* **1.** a rectangular cut given to a small gem, esp. a diamond. **2.** a gem having this cut. Also, **ba·guet′.** [< F < It *bacchetta* little stick = *bacch(io)* stick (< L *baculus*) + *-etta* -ETTE]

Bagpipe

Ba·gui·o (bag′ē ō′; *Sp.* bä′gyô), *n.* a city on W Luzon, in the N Philippines: summer capital. 100,209 (1975); 4961 ft. high.

bah (bä, ba), *interj.* (used as an exclamation of contempt or annoyance.)

Ba·há'í (bə hī′), *n., pl.* **-há'ís,** *adj.* **—***n.* **1.** Also called **Bahá'í′ Faith′.** a religion founded in Iran in 1863 by Husayn 'Alí, surnamed Bahá'u'lláh, and teaching the essential worth of all religions, the unity of all races, and the equality of the sexes. **2.** an adherent of Bahá'í. **—***adj.* **3.** of or pertaining to Bahá'í or the Bahá'ís. Also, **Ba·ha'i′.** [< Pers < Ar = *bahā'* (*u'llah*) splendor (of God) + *-i* suffix of membership]

Ba·há'ísm (bə hī′iz əm, -hä′-), *n.* Bahá'í. **—Ba·há'′ist,** *n., adj.*

Ba·ha·mas (bə hä′məz, -hā′-), *n.* a group of islands in the British West Indies, SE of Florida: a sovereign member of the British Commonwealth; formerly a colony. 210,000; 4404 sq. mi. *Cap.:* Nassau. Also called **Baha′ma Is′lands.** **—Ba·ha·mi·an** (bə hā′mē ən, -hä′-), *n., adj.*

Ba·ha′sa Indone′sia (bä hä′sə), official name of the Indonesian language.

Ba·há·'u'l·láh (bä hä′o͞ol lä′), *n.* (*Husayn 'Alí*) 1817–92, Persian religious leader: founder of Bahá'í. Also, **Ba·há′'u'l-lah′.**

Ba·ha·wal·pur (bə hä′wəl po͝or′, bä′wəl-), *n.* **1.** a state in E Pakistan. 146,800; 32,443 sq. mi. **2.** a city in and the capital of this state. 133,956.

Ba·hi·a (bä ē′ə, bə-), *n.* **1.** a coastal state of E Brazil. 8,438,900; 216,130 sq. mi. *Cap.:* Salvador. **2.** See **São Salvador.**

Ba·hí·a Blan·ca (bä ē′ä bläng′kä), a seaport in E Argentina. 182,000.

Bah·rain (bə rīn′, -rān′, bä-), *n.* **1.** an independent state in the W Persian Gulf, consisting of a group of islands: formerly a British protectorate. 300,000; 232 sq.; mi. *Cap.:* Manama. **2.** the largest island in this group; oil fields. 265,000; 213 sq. mi. Also, **Bah·rein′.**

baht (bät), *n., pl.* **bahts, baht.** a paper money and monetary unit of Thailand; tical. [< Thai *bāt*]

bai·dar·ka (bī där′kə), *n.* bidarka.

Bai·kal (bī käl′), *n.* **Lake,** a lake in the S Soviet Union in Asia: deepest lake in the world. 13,200 sq. mi.; 5714 ft. deep.

bail[1] (bāl), *Law.* **—***n.* **1.** property given as surety that a person released from custody will return at an appointed time. **2.** the person or persons giving it. **3.** the position or the privilege of being released on bail. **4. go** or **stand bail for,** to provide bail for. **5. jump bail,** to abscond while free on bail. **6. on bail,** released temporarily after providing bail. **—***v.t.* **7.** to provide bail for (a person under arrest) (often fol. by *out*): *Shall I bail him out?* **8.** to release (a person) under bail. **9.** to deliver possession of (goods) for storage, hire, etc., without transfer of ownership. [late ME *bayle* < AF *bail* custody, charge < OF < *baillier* to hand over < L *bāiulāre* to serve as porter < *bāiulus* porter]

bail[2] (bāl), *n.* **1.** the semicircular handle of a kettle or pail. **2.** a hooplike support, as for fabric. Also, **bale.** [late ME *beyl* < Scand; cf. Icel *beyglast* to become bent = *baug(r)* ring + *-*(i)l* n. suffix + *-ast* middle inf. suffix]

bail[3] (bāl), *v.t.* **1.** to dip (water) out of a boat, as with a bucket. **2.** to clear of water by dipping (usually fol. by *out*): *to bail out a boat.* **—***v.i.* **3.** to bail water. **4. bail out, a.** *Informal.* to make a parachute jump from an airplane. **b.** *Slang.* to relieve or assist (a person, company, etc.) in an emergency, esp. a financial crisis. **—***n.* **5.** Also, **bail′er.** a bucket, dipper, or other container used for bailing. Also, **bale** (for defs. 1–3). [late ME *bayle* < MF *baille* a bucket < VL **bāi(u)la;* akin to L *bāiulus* carrier. See BAIL[1]]

bail[4] (bāl), *n.* **1.** *Cricket.* either of the two small bars or sticks laid across the tops of the stumps that form the wicket. **2.** *Chiefly Brit.* a bar, framework, partition, or the like, for confining or separating cows, horses, etc., in a stable. **—***v.t.* **3. bail up,** *Australian.* **a.** to confine a cow for milking, as in a bail. **b.** to force (a person) to surrender or identify himself or to state his business. **c.** to waylay or rob (someone). [ME *baile* < OF < L *bacula,* pl. of *baculum* stick]

bail·a·ble (bā′lə bəl), *adj.* *Law.* **1.** capable of being set free on bail. **2.** admitting of bail: *a bailable offense.*

bail·ee (bā′lē′), *n.* *Law.* a person to whom goods are delivered in bailment.

bai·ley (bā′lē), *n., pl.* **-leys.** **1.** the wall surrounding an outer court of a castle. **2.** the courtyard itself. [var. of BAIL[4]]

Bai′ley bridge′, a temporary bridge formed of prefabricated, interchangeable, steel truss panels bolted together. [named after Sir Donald *Bailey* (b. 1901), British engineer, its designer]

bail·ie (bā′lē), *n.* (in Scotland) a municipal officer or magistrate, corresponding to an English alderman. [ME *baillie* < OF *bailli,* var. of *baillif* BAILIFF]

bail·iff (bā′lif), *n.* **1.** an officer similar to a sheriff or his deputy, employed to execute writs and processes, make arrests, etc. **2.** (in Britain) **a.** a person charged with local administrative authority, or the chief magistrate in certain towns. **b.** an overseer of a landed estate or farm. [ME *baillif* < OF = *bail* custody (see BAIL[1]) + *-if* -IVE]

bail·i·wick (bā′lə wik), *n.* **1.** the district within which a bailie or bailiff has jurisdiction. **2.** a person's area of skill, knowledge, or training. [late ME = *baili-* BAILIE + *wick,* OE *wīc* << L *vīcus* hamlet]

bail·ment (bāl′mənt), *n.* *Law.* **1.** the delivery of personal property returnable to the bailor after being held for some purpose, as for surety of a contract. **2.** bail[1] (defs. 1, 3). [earlier *bailement* < AF, OF *baillement*]

bail·or (bā′lər, bā lôr′), *n.* a person who delivers goods or money in bailment.

bail·out (bāl′out′), *n.* the act of parachuting from an aircraft, esp. to escape a crash, fire, etc. Also, **bail′-out′.**

bails·man (bālz′mən), *n., pl.* **-men.** *Law.* a person who provides bail or surety.

Bai′ly's beads′, *Astron.* spots of light that encircle the moon immediately before and after a total eclipse, caused by the sun's light shining between the mountains on the moon. Cf. **diamond ring effect.** [named after Francis *Baily* (1774–1844), English astronomer who first described them]

Bai·ram (bī räm′, bī′räm), *n.* *Islam.* (in Turkey) the name for two Muslim holidays, a fast day **(Lesser Bairam)** and a time of sacrifice **(Greater Bairam).**

Baird′ Moun′tains (bârd), a mountain range in NW Alaska, forming the west range of the Brooks Range.

bairn (bârn; *Scot.* bārn), *n.* *Scot. and North Eng.* a child; son or daughter. [ME *berne, barn,* OE *bearn;* c. Icel, OHG, OS, Goth *barn,* OFris *bern,* MD *baren;* akin to BEAR[1]] —**bairn′ish, bairn′ly,** *adj.* —**bairn′ish·ness,** *n.*

Ba. Is., Bahama Islands.

bait (bāt), *n.* **1.** food or the like used as a lure in angling, trapping, etc. **2.** anything that entices or lures. —*v.t.* **3.** to prepare (a hook or trap) with bait. **4.** to lure as with bait. **5.** to set dogs upon (an animal) for sport. **6.** to worry or torment. **7.** to tease. **8.** to feed and water (a horse or other animal), esp. during a journey. —*v.i.* *Archaic.* **9.** to stop for food or refreshment during a journey. **10.** (of a horse or other animal) to take food; feed. [ME *baite(n)* < Scand; cf. Icel *beita* to cause to bite (see BATE[3]), *beita* food, akin to BIT[2]] —**bait′er,** *n.* —**Syn. 6.** badger, heckle, pester.

bait′ cast′ing, *Angling.* the act or technique of casting an artificial or natural lure attached to a silk or nylon line wound on a reel having a revolving spool, the rod used being shorter and less flexible than that used in fly casting.

baize (bāz), *n.* **1.** a soft, usually green, woolen fabric resembling felt, used chiefly for the tops of billiard tables. **2.** an article of this fabric or of a fabric resembling it. [earlier *bayes* < F *baies* (n.) < fem. pl. of *bai* (adj.) BAY[5]]

Ba·ja Ca·li·for·nia (bä′hä kä′lē fôr′nyä; *Eng.* bä′hə kal′ə fôr′nyə, -fôr′nē ə), Spanish name of **Lower California.** Also called **Baja.**

Baj·er (bī′ər), *n.* **Fred·rik** (fred′rik; *Dan.* frith′rik), 1837–1922, Danish politician and author.

bake (bāk), *v.,* **baked, bak·ing,** *n.* —*v.t.* **1.** to cook by dry heat in an oven, under coals, or on heated metal or stones. **2.** to harden by heat, as pottery. —*v.i.* **3.** to bake bread, a casserole, etc. **4.** to become baked. —*n.* **5.** *U.S.* a social occasion at which the chief food is baked. [ME *bake(n),* OE *bacan;* c. D *bakken,* G *backen,* Icel *baka;* akin to Gk *phṓgein* to roast]

baked′ Alas′ka, a dessert of ice cream on a cake base, covered with meringue and browned in an oven.

baked′ beans′, beans that have been baked, usually with salt pork, brown sugar or molasses, and other seasonings. Also called **Boston baked beans.**

bake·house (bāk′hous′), *n., pl.* **-hous·es** (-hou′ziz). a building or room to bake in; bakery. [late ME]

Ba·ke·lite (bā′kə līt′, bāk′līt′), *n.* *Trademark.* any of a series of thermosetting plastics prepared by heating phenol or cresol with formaldehyde and ammonia under pressure: used for radio cabinets, molded plastic ware, etc.

bake·meat (bāk′mēt′), *n.* *Obs.* **1.** pastry; pie. **2.** cooked food, esp. a meat pie. Also, **baked′ meat′.** [ME *bake mete,* OE *bacen mete* baked food]

bak·er (bā′kər), *n.* **1.** a person who bakes, esp. one who makes and sells bread, cake, etc. **2.** a small portable oven. [ME *baker(e),* OE *bæcere*]

Bak·er (bā′kər), *n.* **1. Sir Benjamin,** 1840–1907, English engineer. **2. George Pierce,** 1866–1935, U.S. critic, author, and professor of drama and playwriting. **3. Mount,** a mountain in NW Washington, in the Cascade Range: 10,750 ft.

Bak′er Is′land, an island in the Pacific near the equator, belonging to the U.S. 1 sq. mi.

bak′er's doz′en, a group of 13; a dozen plus one: from the former practice of giving 13 items to the dozen.

Bak·ers·field (bā′kərz fēld′), *n.* a city in S California. 69,515 (1970).

bak·er·y (bā′kə rē), *n., pl.* **-er·ies.** a place where baked goods are made or sold. Also called **bake·shop** (bāk′shop′). [BAKER + -Y[3]; now taken as BAKE + -ERY]

Bakh·mut (bäk′mo͝ot), *n.* former name of **Artemovsk.**

bak·ing (bā′king), *n.* **1.** the act of a person or thing that bakes. **2.** the quantity baked at one time; batch. [ME]

bak′ing pow′der, any of various powders used as a substitute for yeast in baking, composed of sodium bicarbonate mixed with an acid substance capable of setting carbon dioxide free when the mixture is moistened, causing the dough to rise.

bak′ing so′da. See **sodium bicarbonate.**

ba·kla·va (bä′klə vä′, bä′klə vä′), *n.* a Middle Eastern pastry made of many layers of paper-thin dough with a filling, usually of honey and ground nuts. Also, **ba·kla·wa** (bä′klə vä′, bä′klə vä′). [< Turk]

bak·sheesh (bak′shēsh), (in India, Turkey, etc.) —*n.* **1.** a tip, present, or gratuity. —*v.t., v.i.* **2.** to give a tip. Also, **bak′shish, backsheesh, backshish.** [< Pers *bakhshīsh* = *bakhshī(dan)* (to) give + *-sh* n. suffix]

Bakst (bäkst), *n.* **Lé·on Ni·ko·la·e·vich** (le ôn′ ni ko lä′yə vich), 1866–1924, Russian painter and designer.

Ba·ku (bä ko͞o′), *n.* a city in and the capital of Azerbaijan, in the SW Soviet Union, on the Caspian Sea. 636,000; with suburbs, 1,060,000 (1965).

Ba·ku·nin (bä ko͞o′nin), *n.* **Mi·kha·il A·le·ksan·dro·vich** (mi кнä ēl′ ä′le ksän′dro vich), 1814–76, Russian anarchist and writer.

bal (bal), *n.* Balmoral (def. 1).

bal., 1. balance. **2.** balancing.

Ba·laam (bā′ləm), *n.* a Mesopotamian diviner who, when commanded to curse the Israelites, blessed them instead, after being rebuked by the ass he rode. Num. 22–23.

Bal·a·kla·va (bal′ə klä′və; *Russ.* bä′lä klä′vä), *n.* a seaport in S Crimea, in the SW Soviet Union, on the Black Sea: scene of English cavalry charge against Russians 1854.

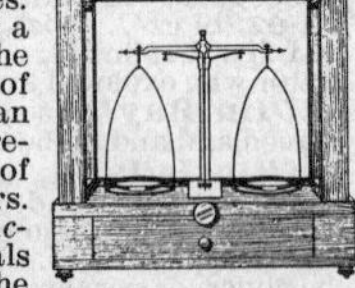
Balalaika

bal·a·lai·ka (bal′ə lī′kə), *n.* a Russian musical instrument having a triangular body, a neck like that of a guitar, and usually three strings tuned in fourths. [< Russ]

bal·ance (bal′əns), *n., v.,* **-anced, -anc·ing.** —*n.* **1.** an instrument for determining weight, esp. by the equilibrium of weights suspended from opposite ends of a bar having a fulcrum at its center. **2.** a state of equilibrium, as among weights or forces. **3.** something that brings about such a state. **4.** a state of stability, as of the body or the emotions. **5.** a state of harmony, as among the elements of an artistic composition. **6.** the act of creating a state of balance. **7.** a state of dominance or authority over others. **8.** *U.S.* the remainder or rest. **9.** *Accounting.* **a.** equality between the totals of the two sides of an account. **b.** the difference between the debit total and the credit total of an account. **c.** an unpaid difference represented by the excess of debits over credits. **10.** an adjustment of accounts. **11.** Also called **balance wheel.** *Horol.* a wheel that oscillates against the tension of a hairspring to regulate the beats of a watch or clock. **12.** (*cap.*) *Astron., Astrol.* the constellation or sign of Libra. **13. hang in the balance.** See **hang** (def. 29). **14. on balance,** everything considered; in general. —*v.t.* **15.** to weigh in a balance. **16.** to estimate the relative weight or importance of. **17.** to serve as a counterpoise to; counterbalance. **18.** to bring to or hold in equilibrium. **19.** to arrange or proportion the parts of harmoniously. **20.** to be equal or proportionate to: *Cash on hand balances expenses.* **21.** to arrange (a slate of candidates) so as to appeal to a majority of voters, esp. to large ethnic or religious groups. **22.** *Accounting.* **a.** to add up the two sides of (an account) and determine the difference. **b.** to make the necessary entries in (an account) so that the sums of the two sides will be equal. **c.** to settle by paying what remains due on an account; equalize or adjust. —*v.i.* **23.** to be in equilibrium; to have an equality or equivalence in weight, parts, etc.: *These scales don't balance.* **24.** *Accounting.* to reckon or adjust accounts. **25.** to waver or hesitate. [ME *balaunce* < AF; c. OF *balance* < VL **balancia,* var. of **bilancia* = L *bilanc-* (s. of *bilanx* = *bi-* BI-[1] + *lanx* scale) + *-ia* -IA] —**bal′ance·a·ble,** *adj.* —**Syn. 4.** poise, composure. **5.** See **symmetry. 8.** See **remainder.** —**Usage. 8.** Although BALANCE in the sense of "remainder" is now generally acceptable in all varieties of usage, there are still some who regard its use in this sense as colloquial: *The balance of the class was absent.*

Balance (def. 1)

bal′ance beam′, 1. a narrow wooden rail set horizontally on upright posts, used by women for feats of balancing, posture, and gymnastic ability. **2.** a gymnastic event in which such apparatus is used.

bal·anced (bal′ənst), *adj.* being in harmonious or proper arrangement or adjustment, proportion, etc.

bal′anced di′et, a diet consisting of the proper quantities and proportions of foods needed to maintain health or growth.

bal′ance of pay′ments, the difference between a nation's total payments to foreign countries and its total receipts from foreign countries.

bal′ance of pow′er, a distribution of forces among nations or branches of government such that no single one is strong enough to dominate all the others.

bal′ance of trade′, the difference between the values of exports and imports of countries: said to be favorable or unfavorable as exports are greater or less than imports.

bal·anc·er (bal′ən sər), *n.* **1.** a person or thing that balances. **2.** *Entomol.* halter[2]. **3.** an acrobat or ropedancer.

bal′ance sheet′, *Accounting.* a statement of the financial position of a business on a specified date.

bal′ance spring′, *Horol.* hairspring.

bal′ance staff′, *Horol.* a pivoted axle or shaft on which the balance is mounted.

bal′ance wheel′, *Horol.* balance (def. 11).

Bal·an·chine (bal′ən chēn′, bal′ən chēn′), *n.* **George,** 1904–83, U.S. choreographer, born in Russia.

bal·as (bal′əs, bā′ləs), *n.* *Mineral.* a rose-red variety of spinel. Also called **bal′as ru′by.** [late ME < ML *balas(ius),* var. of *balascius* < Ar *balakhsh,* back formation from Pers *Badakhshān,* district near Samarkand, where gem is found]

bal·a·ta (bal′ə tə), *n.* **1.** a nonelastic, rubberlike, water-resistant gum that softens in hot water, obtained from the latex of the bully tree, *Mimusops balata:* used in machinery belts, golf balls, etc. **2.** See **bully tree.** [< AmerSp < Carib]

Ba·la·ton (bo′lo tôn′), *n.* a lake in W Hungary: the largest lake in central Europe. ab. 50 mi. long; 230 sq. mi. German, **Plattensee.**

Bal·bo (bäl′bô), *n.* **I·ta·lo** (ē′tä lô), 1896–1940, Italian aviator, general, and statesman.

Bal·bo·a (bal bō′ə; *Sp.* bäl bô′ä), *n.* **1. Vas·co Nú·ñez de** (bäs′kô nōō′nyeth de), 1475?–1517, Spanish adventurer and explorer who discovered the Pacific Ocean in 1513. **2.** a seaport in the Canal Zone at the Pacific terminus of the Panama Canal. 2569 (1970). **3.** (*l.c.*) a silver coin and monetary unit of Panama.

bal·brig·gan (bal brig′ən), *n.* a plain-knit cotton fabric, used esp. in hosiery and underwear. [after *Balbriggan,* Ireland, where first made]

bal·co·ny (bal′kə nē), *n., pl.* **-nies. 1.** a balustraded or railed elevated platform projecting from the wall of a building. **2.** a gallery in a theater. [< It *balcone* = *balc(o)* scaffold (< OHG *balcho* beam; see BALK) + *-one* aug. suffix] —**bal′co·nied,** *adj.*

bald (bôld), *adj.* **1.** lacking hair on the scalp: *a bald head; a bald person.* **2.** destitute of some natural growth or covering: *a bald mountain.* **3.** lacking detail or vividness; plain: *a bald prose style.* **4.** open or forthright; undisguised: *a bald lie.* **5.** *Zool.* having white on the head: *the bald eagle.* —*v.i.* **6.** to become bald. [ME *ball(e)d* = obs. *ball* white spot (cf. Welsh *bàl,* Gk *phaliós* having a white spot) + *-ed* -ED] —**bald′ish,** *adj.* —**bald′ly,** *adv.* —**bald′ness,** *n.*

bal·da·chin (bal′də kin, bôl′-), *n.* **1.** *Textiles.* a silk brocade interwoven with gold or silver threads. **2.** *Archit.* a permanent ornamental canopy, as above a freestanding altar or tomb. **3.** a portable canopy carried in religious processions. Also, **bal·dac·chi·no, bal·da·chi·no** (bal′də kē′nō). [earlier *baldakin* < ML *baldakin(us)* < It *baldacchino* = *Baldacc(o)* Baghdad + *-ino* -INE[1]]

bald′ cy′press, a tree, *Taxodium distichum,* of the southern U.S., yielding a strong, hard wood used in construction, shipbuilding, etc.

Bald eagle (Length 2½ ft.; wingspread to 7½ ft.)

bald′ ea′gle, a large eagle, *Haliaetus leucocephalus,* of the U.S. and Canada, having a white head and tail.

Bal·der (bôl′dər), *n. Scand. Myth.* a god of peace and light, a son of Odin and Frigg.

bal·der·dash (bôl′dər-dash′), *n.* a senseless jumble of words; nonsense; twaddle. [?]

bald·head·ed (bôld′hed′id), *adj.* having a bald head.

bald·pate (bôld′pāt′), *n.* **1.** a baldheaded person. **2.** a brown American widgeon, *Anas americana,* having a gray head with a white crown.

bal·dric (bôl′drik), *n.* a belt, sometimes richly ornamented, worn diagonally from shoulder to hip, supporting a sword, horn, etc. Also, **bal′drick.** [late ME *bawdrick,* appar. special use of man's name *Baldric* (cf. SAM BROWNE BELT); r. ME *baudry* < OF *baudrei* < Frankish *Baldric,* lit., bold king] —**bal′dricked,** *adj.*

Bald·win (bôld′win), *n.* **1. James,** 1924–87, U.S. writer. **2. Stanley** (*1st Earl Baldwin of Bewdley*), 1867–1947, British statesman: prime minister 1923–24, 1924–29, 1935–37. **3.** a variety of red or red-and-yellow winter apple, grown esp. in the northeast U.S. **4.** a town on S Long Island, in SE New York. 34,525 (1970). **5.** a city in W Pennsylvania, near Pittsburgh. 26,729 (1970).

Baldwin I, 1058–1118, king of Jerusalem 1100–18: fought in the first crusade.

Bald′win Park′, a city in SW California, near Los Angeles. 47,285 (1970).

bale[1] (bāl), *n., v.,* **baled, bal·ing.** —*n.* **1.** a large, usually tightly compressed, bundle of something, often secured by wires, hoops, cords, or the like: *a bale of cotton; a bale of hay.* **2.** a group of turtles. —*v.t.* **3.** to make or form into bales. [ME < Flem < OF < Gmc; cf. OHG *ballā* BALL[1]] —**bal′er,** *n.*

bale[2] (bāl), *n. Archaic.* **1.** evil; misfortune. **2.** woe; sorrow. [ME; OE *bealu, balu;* c. Icel *böl,* OHG *balo,* Goth *balw-*]

bale[3] (bāl), *n.* bail[2].

bale[4] (bāl), *v.t., v.i.,* **baled, bal·ing.** bail[3] (defs. 1–3).

Bâle (bäl), *n.* French name of **Basel.**

Bal·e·ar′ic Is′lands (bal′ē ar′ik), a group of islands including Ibiza, Mallorca, and Minorca, and constituting a province of Spain in the W Mediterranean Sea. 436,435 (est. 1960); 1936 sq. mi. *Cap.:* Palma. Spanish, **Ba·le·a·res** (bä′le ä′res).

ba·leen (bə lēn′), *n. Zool.* whalebone (def. 1). [late ME *balene* < L *balēna,* var. of *balaena* whale (c. Gk, *phálaina*); r. ME *balayn* < MF *balaine* whale(bone) < L]

baleen′ whale′. See **whalebone whale.**

bale·fire (bāl′fīər′), *n.* **1.** a large fire in the open air; bonfire. **2.** a signal fire; beacon. **3.** *Obs.* a funeral pyre. [late ME = *bale* (< Scand; cf. Icel *bāl* funeral pyre) + *fire* FIRE; r. OE *bælfȳr*]

bale·ful (bāl′fəl), *adj.* **1.** full of menacing or malign influences; pernicious. **2.** *Obs.* wretched; miserable. [ME; OE *bealofull*] —**bale′ful·ly,** *adv.* —**bale′ful·ness,** *n.*

Bal·four (bal′fŏŏr), *n.* **Arthur James** (*1st Earl of Balfour*), 1848–1930, British statesman and writer.

Bal′four Declara′tion, a statement issued (1917) by the British government favoring the establishment of a Jewish national home in Palestine. [after A. J. BALFOUR]

Ba·li (bä′lē), *n.* an island in Indonesia, E of Java. 1,775,000. (est. 1961); 2147 sq. mi. *Cap.:* Singaraja.

Ba·lik·pa·pan (bä′lik pä′pän), *n.* a seaport on E Borneo, in central Indonesia. 88,534 (1961).

Ba·li·nese (bä′lə nēz′, -nēs′), *adj., n., pl.* **-nese.** —*adj.* **1.** of or pertaining to Bali, its people, or their language. —*n.* **2.** a native or inhabitant of Bali. **3.** the language of Bali, an Indonesian language of the Malayo-Polynesian family. [< D *Balinees* = *Bali* + *-n-* connective + *-ees* -ESE]

Bal·iol (bāl′yəl, bā′lē əl), *n.* **John de,** 1249–1315, king of Scotland 1292–96.

balk (bôk), *v.i.* **1.** to stop, as at an obstacle, and refuse to proceed or to do something specified (usually fol. by *at*): *He balked at making the speech.* **2.** (of a horse, mule, etc.) to stop short and stubbornly refuse to go on. **3.** *Baseball.* to commit a balk. —*v.t.* **4.** to place an obstacle in the way of; hinder; thwart. —*n.* **5.** a check or hindrance; defeat; disappointment. **6.** a strip of land left unplowed. **7.** any heavy timber used for building purposes. **8.** *Baseball.* an illegal motion by a pitcher while one or more runners are on base, as a feigned pitch, a pitch in which there is too long a pause after the windup, etc. **9.** *Billiards.* any of the eight sections lying between the cushions of the table and the balklines. **10.** *Obs.* a miss, slip, or failure. [ME; OE *balc(a)* bank, ridge; c. Icel *balkr* bar, partition, D *balk,* G *Balken* beam. See BALCONY] —**balk′er,** *n.* —**balk′ing·ly,** *adv.* —**Syn. 4.** obstruct, impede, prevent; frustrate.

Bal·kan (bôl′kən), *adj.* **1.** pertaining to the Balkan States or their inhabitants. **2.** pertaining to the Balkan Peninsula. **3.** pertaining to the Balkan Mountains. —*n.* **4. the Balkans,** the Balkan States or the land within their borders. —**Bal′kan·ite′,** *n., adj.*

Bal·kan·ise (bôl′kə nīz′), *v.t.,* **-ised, -is·ing.** *Chiefly Brit.* Balkanize.

Bal·kan·ize (bôl′kə nīz′), *v.t.,* **-ized, -iz·ing.** to divide (a country, territory, etc.) into small, quarrelsome, ineffectual states. —**Bal′kan·ism,** *n.*

Bal′kan Moun′tains, a mountain range extending from W Bulgaria to the Black Sea: highest peak, 7794 ft.

Bal′kan Penin′sula, a peninsula in S Europe, bordered by the Adriatic, Ionian, Aegean, and Black Seas.

Bal′kan States′, the countries in the Balkan Peninsula: Yugoslavia, Rumania, Bulgaria, Albania, Greece, and the European part of Turkey.

Bal′kan War′, 1. Also called **First Balkan War.** a war (1912–13) in which Bulgaria, Serbia, and Greece opposed Turkey. **2.** Also called **Second Balkan War.** a war (1913) between Bulgaria and Serbia, Greece, etc.

Balkh (bälkh), *n.* a town in N Afghanistan: capital of ancient Bactria; center of Zoroastrianism. Also called **Wazirabad.** Ancient, **Bactra.**

Bal·khash (bäl khäsh′), *n.* a salt lake in the SW Soviet Union in Asia, in Kazakstan. ab. 7115 sq. mi.

balk·line (bôk′līn′), *n.* **1.** *Sports.* (in track events) the starting line. **2.** *Billiards.* **a.** a straight line drawn across the table behind which the cue ball is placed in beginning a game. **b.** any of four lines, each near to and parallel with one side of the cushion, that divide the table into a large central panel or section and eight smaller sections or balks lying between these. **c.** a balk lying inside one of these sections. **d.** balk (def. 9).

balk·y (bô′kē), *adj.,* **balk·i·er, balk·i·est.** *U.S.* given to balking; stubborn; obstinate. —**balk′i·ly,** *adv.* —**balk′i·ness,** *n.* —**Syn.** contrary, perverse.

ball[1] (bôl), *n.* **1.** a spherical or approximately spherical body; sphere. **2.** a round or roundish body, of various sizes and materials, either hollow or solid, for use in games, as baseball, football, tennis, or golf. **3.** a game played with a ball, esp. baseball: *The boys are out playing ball.* **4.** *Baseball.* a pitched ball, not swung at by the batter, that does not pass over home plate between the batter's shoulders and knees. Cf. **strike** (def. 65). **5.** *Mil.* **a.** a solid, usually spherical, projectile for a cannon, rifle, pistol, etc., as distinguished from a shell. **b.** projectiles, esp. bullets, collectively. **6.** any part of a thing, esp. of the human body, that is rounded or protuberant. **7.** *Slang* (*usually vulgar*). a testis. **8. balls,** *Slang* (*usually vulgar*). **a.** nonsense (often used as an interjection). **b.** strength, power, or energy. **9.** bolus (def. 1). **10.** *Astron. Rare.* a planetary or celestial body, esp. the earth. **11. carry the ball,** to assume the responsibility; bear the burden: *He always carries the ball in an emergency.* **12. have something or a lot on the ball,** *Slang.* to be capable or efficient; have a talent or gift. **13. keep the ball rolling,** to continue or give renewed vigor to an activity already under way. **14. on the ball,** *Slang.* **a.** alert or vital. **b.** efficient, able, competent: *Her typing is on the ball.* **15. play ball,** to work together; cooperate. **16. start the ball rolling,** to begin; set an activity going. —*v.t.* **17.** to make into a ball or balls. **18.** *Slang* (*usually vulgar*). to have sexual intercourse with. —*v.i.* **19.** to gather or form into a ball or balls. **20.** *Slang* (*usually vulgar*). to have sexual intercourse. **21. ball the jack,** *Slang.* **a.** to act with speed. **b.** to stake everything on one attempt. **22. ball up,** *Slang.* to make or become hopelessly confused; muddle: *Don't ball up the records, file everything neatly.* [ME *bal, balle* < Scand (cf. Icel *böllr,* Sw *bål*); c. G *Ball*] —**ball′er,** *n.*

—**Syn. 1.** BALL, GLOBE, SPHERE, ORB agree in referring to a round or rounded object. BALL may be applied to any round or roundish object or part: *a rubber ball.* GLOBE and SPHERE denote something thought of as either exactly or approximately round: *in the form of a globe; a perfect sphere.* ORB is now found only in elevated or scientific use; it is applied esp. to the eye and to the heavenly bodies: *the orb of the full moon.*

ball[2] (bôl), *n.* **1.** a large, usually lavish party featuring social dancing. **2.** *Slang.* a thoroughly good time: *Have a ball on your vacation.* —*v.i.* **3.** *Slang.* to have a thoroughly good time. [< F *bal* < OF *baller* to dance < LL *ballāre* < Gk *ballízein* to dance = *ball-* throw + *-izein* -IZE]

Ball (bôl), *n.* **John,** died 1381, English priest: one of the leaders of Wat Tyler's peasants' revolt in 1381.

bal·lad (bal′əd), *n.* **1.** a simple narrative poem of popular origin, composed in short stanzas, esp. one of romantic character and adapted for singing. **2.** any light, simple song, esp. one of sentimental or romantic character, having two or more stanzas, all sung to the same melody. [earlier *balade* < MF < OPr *balada* dance, dancing song = *bal(ar)* (to) dance (< LL *ballāre;* see BALL[2]) + *-ada* -ADE[1]]

bal·lade (bə läd′, ba-; *Fr.* BA LAD′), *n., pl.* **-lades** (-lädz′; *Fr.* -LAD′). **1.** a poem consisting commonly of three stanzas having an identical rhyme scheme, followed by an envoy, and having the same last line for each of the stanzas and the envoy. **2.** *Music.* a composition in free style and romantic mood, often for solo piano or for orchestra. [< F, var. of OF *balade* BALLAD]

bal·lad·eer (bal′ə dēr′), *n.* a person who sings ballads.
bal·lad·ry (bal′ə drē), *n.* ballad poetry.
bal′lad stan′za, a stanza often used in ballad poetry, composed of lines of four, three, four, and three stresses, respectively, usually having the rhyme scheme *abcb.*
ball′ and chain′, **1.** a heavy iron ball fastened by a chain to a prisoner's leg. **2.** *Slang.* a man's wife.
ball′-and-sock′et joint′ (bôl′ən-sok′it), a joint between rods, links, pipes, etc., consisting of a ball-like termination on one part held within a concave, spherical socket on the other. Also called **ball joint.**

Ball-and-socket joint

Bal·la·rat (bal′ə rat′, bal′ə rat′), *n.* a city in S Victoria, in SE Australia. 54,880 (1961).
bal·last (bal′əst), *n.* **1.** *Naut.* any heavy material carried in a ship to provide desired draft and stability. **2.** *Aeron.* any heavy material, as sandbags, carried in the car of a balloon for control of altitude and stability. **3.** gravel, broken stone, slag, etc., placed between and under the ties of a railroad to give stability, provide drainage, and distribute loads. —*v.t.* **4.** to furnish with ballast. [< MLG = *bal-* bad (see BALE[2]) + *last* load (see LAST[4]); but cf. ODan, OSw *barlast* = *bar* BARE[1] + *last* load]
ball′ bear′ing, *Mach.* **1.** a bearing consisting of a number of hard balls running in grooves in the surfaces of two concentric rings, one of which is mounted on a rotating or oscillating shaft or the like. **2.** any of the balls so used.
ball′ club′, a team of professional players of a ball game, esp. baseball.
ball′ cock′, a device for regulating the supply of water in a tank, cistern, or the like, consisting essentially of a valve shut or opened by the rise or fall of a hollow floating ball.
bal·le·ri·na (bal′ə rē′nə; *It.* bäl′le RE′nä), *n., pl.* **-nas,** *It.* **-ne** (-ne). **1.** a principal female dancer in a ballet company. Cf. **prima ballerina. 2.** (loosely) any female ballet dancer. [< It, fem. of *ballerino* professional dancer < *ball(are)* (to) dance < LL; see BALL[2]]
bal·let (ba lā′, bal′ā; *Fr.* BA lā′), *n., pl.* **bal·lets** (ba lāz′, bal′āz; *Fr.* BA lā′). **1.** a classical dance form demanding grace and precision and employing conventional steps and gestures set in intricate, flowing patterns. **2.** a theatrical entertainment of such dancing and its accompanying music. **3.** the musical score for such an entertainment. **4.** a company of professional dancers. [< F < It *balletto* = *ball(o)* BALL[2] + *-etto* -ET] —**bal·let·ic** (ba let′ik), *adj.* —**bal·let′i·cal·ly,** *adv.*
bal·let·o·mane (ba let′ə mān′, bə-), *n.* a ballet enthusiast. [back formation from *balletomania;* see BALLET, -O-, -MANIA] —**bal·let′o·ma′ni·a,** *n.*
ballet′ slip′per, **1.** a heelless cloth or leather slipper worn by ballet dancers. **2.** a similar woman's shoe.
bal·lis·ta (bə lis′tə), *n., pl.* **-tae** (-tē). an ancient military engine for throwing stones or other missiles. [< L, prob. < Gk **ballistá(s),* dial. var. of **ballistḗs* = *bállein* (to) throw + *-istēs* -IST]

Ballista

bal·lis·tic (bə lis′tik), *adj.* of or pertaining to ballistics or its laws. [BALLIST(A) + -IC] —**bal·lis′ti·cal·ly,** *adv.*
ballis′tic mis′sile, *Rocketry.* any missile that, after being guided during take-off, travels unpowered in a ballistic trajectory.
bal·lis·tics (bə lis′tiks), *n.* (*usually construed as sing.*) **1.** the science or study of the motion of projectiles. **2.** the art or science of designing projectiles for maximum flight performance. [see BALLISTIC, -ICS] —**bal·lis·ti·cian** (bal′i-stish′ən), *n.*
ballis′tic trajec′tory, the path of a projectile when influenced only by external forces, as gravity and atmospheric friction.
bal·lis·tite (bal′i stīt′), *n.* a smokeless powder consisting of nitroglycerine and cellulose nitrate, used as a solid fuel for rockets. [formerly trademark]
ball′ joint′. See **ball-and-socket joint.**
bal·lo·net (bal′ə net′), *n.* an air or gasbag compartment in a balloon or airship, used to control buoyancy and maintain shape. [< F = *ballon* BALLOON + *-et* -ET]
bal·loon (bə lo͞on′), *n.* **1.** a bag made of a light material, as silk, plastic, etc., filled with a gas lighter than air, designed to rise and float in the atmosphere and often having a car or gondola for carrying passengers or scientific instruments. **2.** an inflatable rubber bag used as a children's plaything. **3.** (in drawings, cartoons, etc.) a balloon-shaped figure enclosing words represented as issuing from the mouth of the speaker. **4.** *Chem. Obs.* a round-bottomed flask. —*v.i.* **5.** to ascend or ride in a balloon. **6.** to swell or puff out like a balloon. **7.** to multiply or increase at a rapid rate. —*adj.* **8.** puffed out like a balloon: *balloon sleeves.* [< It *ballone* = *ball(a)* BALL[1] + *-one* aug. suffix] —**bal·loon′like′,** *adj.*
balloon′ sail′, *Naut.* any light, loose sail, as a jib or spinnaker, used by a yacht in light wind.
balloon′ tire′, a broad tire filled with air at low pressure for cushioning shock or facilitating travel on sand.
bal·lot (bal′ət), *n., v.,* **-lot·ed, -lot·ing.** —*n.* **1.** a sheet of paper or the like on which a voter marks his choice or choices. **2.** the whole number of votes cast or recorded: *There was a large ballot.* **3.** the method of secret voting by means of printed or written ballots or by means of voting machines. **4.** voting in general, or a round of voting: *Our candidate was defeated on the third ballot.* **5.** the list of candidates to be voted on: *He demanded his name be placed on the ballot.* **6.** (formerly) a little ball used in voting. —*v.i.* **7.** to vote by ballot. **8.** to draw lots: *to ballot for places.* —*v.t.* **9.** to vote on by ballot (often fol. by *on* or *for*). [< It *ballott(a)* = *ball(a)* BALL[1] + *-otta* dim. suffix] —**bal′lot·er,** *n.*
bal·lotte·ment (bə lot′mənt), *n. Med.* **1.** a method of diagnosing pregnancy by the rebound of a fetal part displaced from its position by a sudden push of the uterus with the examining finger. **2.** a similar method employed in testing for floating kidney, movable abdominal tumors, etc. [< F: a tossing = *ballotte(r)* (to) toss here and there like a ball (< *ballotte* little ball < It; see BALLOT) + *-ment* -MENT]
ball′ park′, an open or covered tract of land where ball games are played, enclosed by a fence and having stands for spectators. —**ball′-park′,** *adj.*
ball′-peen ham′mer (bôl′pēn′), a hammer having a hemispherical peen **(ball′ peen′)** for beating metal. See illus. at **hammer.**
ball·play·er (bôl′plā′ər), *n.* a person who plays ball professionally, esp. baseball.
ball′-point pen′ (bôl′point′), a fountain pen in which the point is a fine ball bearing. Also, **ball′point′ pen′.** Also called **ball′ pen′, ball′-point′, ball′point′.**
ball·room (bôl′ro͞om′, -ro͝om′), *n.* a large room, as in a hotel, resort, etc., with a polished floor for dancing.
ball′room dance′, any of a variety of social or recreational dances, by couples or by groups.
ball′ valve′, *Mach.* **1.** a valve that controls flow by means of a ball pierced with an opening in one direction and fixed to rotate on a spindle at right angles to the opening. **2.** any valve that checks flow by the seating of a ball.

Ball valve (Checks motion of fluid in direction shown by arrow)

bal·ly·hoo (*n.* bal′ē ho͞o′; *v.* bal′ē ho͞o′, bal′ē ho͞o′), *n., pl.* **-hoos,** *v.,* **-hooed, -hoo·ing.** —*n.* **1.** a clamorous attempt to win customers or advance any cause; blatant advertising or publicity. **2.** clamor or outcry. —*v.t., v.i.* **3.** to advertise or push by ballyhoo. [?]
bal·ly·rag (bal′ē rag′), *v.t.,* **-ragged, -rag·ging.** bullyrag.
balm (bäm), *n.* **1.** any of various oily, fragrant, resinous substances, often of medicinal value, exuding from certain plants, esp. tropical, burseraceous trees of the genus *Commiphora.* **2.** a plant or tree yielding such a substance. **3.** any aromatic or fragrant ointment. **4.** aromatic fragrance; sweet odor: *the balm of orange blossoms.* **5.** any of various aromatic, menthaceous plants, esp. of the genus *Melissa,* as *M. officinalis* **(balm′ mint′, garden balm,** or **lemon balm),** used as a seasoning. **6.** anything that heals, soothes, or mitigates pain: *the balm of friendship.* [ME *basme, ba(u)me* < OF *basme* < L *balsam(um)* BALSAM] —**balm′like′,** *adj.*
bal·ma·caan (bal′mə kän′), *n.* a man's short, full-skirted overcoat, often of rough woolen cloth, having raglan sleeves. [after *Balmacaan* near Inverness, Scotland]
balm′ of Gil′ead, **1.** any of several plants of the genus *Commiphora,* esp. *C. opobalsamum* and *C. meccanensis,* that yield a fragrant oleoresin. **2.** the resin itself, a yellow, green, or brownish-red, turbid, viscid, water-insoluble liquid, used chiefly in perfumery. **3.** a North American poplar, *Populus candicans,* having fragrant buds and foliage.
Bal·mor·al (bal môr′əl, -mor′əl), *n.* **1.** (*l.c.*) Also called **bal.** an ankle-high shoe, laced in front. **2.** a brimless Scottish cap with a flat top that projects all around the head. Cf. **tam-o'-shanter.** [after *Balmoral* Castle in Scotland]
Bal·mung (bäl′mo͝ong), *n.* (in the *Nibelungenlied*) a sword seized from the Nibelungs by Siegfried. Also, **Bal·munc** (bäl′mo͝ongk). Cf. **Gram.**
balm·y (bä′mē), *adj.,* **balm·i·er, balm·i·est.** **1.** mild and refreshing; soft; soothing: *balmy weather.* **2.** having the qualities of balm; aromatic; fragrant. **3.** producing balm: *balmy plants.* **4.** *Slang.* silly, foolish, or eccentric. —**balm′i·ly,** *adv.* —**balm′i·ness,** *n.* —**Syn. 1.** fair, gentle, temperate, clement.
bal·ne·al (bal′nē əl), *adj.* of or pertaining to baths or bathing. [< L *balne(um)* < Gk *balaneion* bathing room, bath + -AL[1]]
bal·ne·ol·o·gy (bal′nē ol′ə jē), *n. Med.* the science dealing with the therapeutic effects of baths and bathing. [*balne-* (see BALNEAL) + -O- + -LOGY] —**bal·ne·o·log·ic** (bal′nē ə loj′ik), **bal′ne·o·log′i·cal,** *adj.*
ba·lo·ney (bə lō′nē), *n.* **1.** *Informal.* bologna. **2.** *Slang.* foolishness; nonsense. Also, **boloney.** [alter. of BOLOGNA (SAUSAGE)]
bal·sa (bôl′sə, bäl′-), *n.* **1.** a bombacaceous tree, *Ochroma Lagopus,* of tropical America, yielding an exceedingly light wood used for life preservers, rafts, toy airplanes, etc. **2.** any life raft. [< Sp: raft]
bal·sam (bôl′səm), *n.* **1.** any of various fragrant exudations from certain trees, esp. burseraceous trees of the genus *Commiphora,* as balm of Gilead. Cf. **balm** (def. 1). **2.** the similar products yielded by the leguminous trees *Myroxylon Pereirae* and *M. Balsamum,* of Central and South America. Cf. **tolu. 3.** oleoresin (def. 1). **4.** any of certain transparent turpentines, as Canada balsam. **5.** a plant or tree yielding a balsam. **6.** See **balsam fir. 7.** any of several balsaminaceous plants of the genus *Impatiens,* as *I. Balsamina,* a common garden annual. **8.** any aromatic ointment for ceremonial or medicinal use. **9.** balm (def. 6). [OE < L *balsam(um)* < Gk *bálsamon.* See BALM] —**bal·sam·ic** (bôl sam′ik, bal-), *adj.*
bal′sam fir′, a North American fir, *Abies balsamea,* that yields Canada balsam.
bal·sam·if·er·ous (bôl′sə mif′ər əs, bal′-), *adj.* yielding balsam.
bal·sa·mi·na·ceous (bôl′sə mə nā′shəs, bal′-), *adj.* belonging to the *Balsaminaceae,* a family of plants with oddly shaped flowers, including many tropical species and also the balsams of the genus *Impatiens.* [< Gk *balsamín(ē)* garden balsam + -ACEOUS]
bal′sam of tolu′, tolu.
bal′sam pop′lar, a poplar, *Populus Tacamahaca,* having broad, heart-shaped leaves, cultivated as a shade tree.

bal′sam spruce′, an evergreen conifer of the genus *Abies.*

Balt., Baltic.

Bal·tha·zar (bal thā′zər, -thaz′ər, bôl-, bäl′thə zär′), *n.* **1.** one of the Magi. **2.** a wine bottle holding 13 quarts. [after *Balthazar* BELSHAZZAR]

Bal·tic (bôl′tik), *adj.* **1.** of, near, or on the Baltic Sea. **2.** of or pertaining to the Baltic States. **3.** of or pertaining to a group of languages, including Lettish, Lithuanian, and Old Prussian, that constitute a branch of the Indo-European family. **—*n.* 4.** the Baltic branch of the Indo-European family of languages.

Bal′tic Sea′, a sea in N Europe, bounded by Sweden, Finland, the Soviet Union, Poland, Germany, and Denmark. ab. 160,000 sq. mi.

Bal′tic States′, the formerly independent republics of Estonia, Latvia, Lithuania, and sometimes Finland.

Bal·ti·more (bôl′tə mōr′, -môr′), *n.* **1. Lord.** See **Calvert, Sir George. 2.** a seaport in N Maryland, on an estuary near the Chesapeake Bay. 905,759 (1970).

Bal·ti·more (bôl′tə mōr′, -môr′), *n.* a black nymphalid butterfly, *Melitaea phaeton,* characterized by orange-red, yellow, and white markings, common in those areas of the northeastern U.S. where turtlehead, the food plant of its larvae, is found. [named after Lord *Baltimore;* see BALTIMORE ORIOLE]

Bal′timore o′riole, an orange and black oriole, *Icterus galbula,* of North America. [so named because black and orange were the colors of Lord Baltimore's livery]

Bal·to-Sla·vic (bôl′tō slä′vik, -slav′ik), *n.* a grouping of Indo-European languages comprising the Baltic and Slavic groups.

Ba·lu·chi (bə lo͞o′chē), *n., pl.* **-chis,** (*esp. collectively*) **-chi.** a member of a nomadic people of Baluchistan. [< Pers]

Ba·lu·chi·stan (bə lo͞o′chi stän′, -stan′), *n.* an arid mountainous region in SW Asia, in SE Iran and NW Pakistan, bordering on the Arabian Sea.

bal·us·ter (bal′ə stər), *n.* **1.** *Archit.* any of a number of closely spaced supports for a railing. **2. balusters,** a balustrade. **3.** any of various tapering or swelling supports, as table legs or spindles. [< F *balustre* < It *balaustro* pillar shaped like calyx tube of pomegranate flower < *balaust(r)a* < L *balaust(ium)* < Gk *balaústion* flower of pomegranate] **—bal′us·tered,** *adj.*

A B
A, Baluster
B, Balustrade

bal·us·trade (bal′ə strād′, bal′ə strād′), *n. Archit.* a railing with supporting balusters. [< F *balustre* BALUSTER + *-ade* -ADE[1]; cf. Sp *balaustrada,* It *balaustrata*] **—bal′us·trad′ed,** *adj.*

Bal·zac (bal′zak, bôl′-; *Fr.* bal zak′), *n.* **Ho·no·ré de** (on′ə rā′ də; *Fr.* ô nô rā′ də), 1799–1850, French novelist.

B.A.M., 1. Bachelor of Applied Mathematics. **2.** Bachelor of Arts in Music.

Ba·ma·ko (bam′ə kō′; *Fr.* ba ma kō′), *n.* a city in and the capital of Mali: inland port on the Niger River. 380,000.

Bam·berg (bäm′berk′), *n.* a city in N Bavaria in S central West Germany. 73,700 (1963).

bam·bi·no (bam bē′nō; *It.* bäm bē′nô), *n., pl.* **-nos,** *It.,* **-ni** (-nē). **1.** a child or baby. **2.** an image of the infant Jesus. [< It = *bamb(o)* childish, simple + *-ino* dim. suffix]

bam·boo (bam bo͞o′), *n., pl.* **-boos. 1.** any of the woody or treelike tropical and semitropical grasses of the genera *Bambusa, Dendrocalamus,* and allied genera. **2.** the hollow, woody stem of such a plant, used as a building material and for making furniture, poles, etc. [sp. var. of earlier *bambu* < Malay; r. *bambus* < D *bamboes* = NL *bambūsa*]

Bamboo

bam′boo cur′tain, the barrier of censorship and secrecy formerly maintained by the People's Republic of China.

bam·boo·zle (bam bo͞o′zəl), *v.t.,* **-zled, -zling.** *Informal.* **1.** to deceive or get the better of (someone) by trickery, flattery, or the like; humbug; hoodwink (often fol. by *into*): *They bamboozled us into joining the club.* **2.** to perplex or mystify. [?] **—bam·boo′zle·ment,** *n.* **—bam·boo′zler,** *n.*

ban[1] (ban), *v.,* **banned, ban·ning,** *n.* **—*v.t.* 1.** to prohibit, forbid, or bar; interdict: *to ban atomic weapons.* **2.** *Archaic.* **a.** to pronounce an ecclesiastical curse upon. **b.** to curse or execrate. **—*n.* 3.** act of prohibiting by law; interdiction. **4.** informal denunciation or prohibition, as by public opinion. **5.** *Law.* **a.** a proclamation. **b.** a public condemnation. **6.** *Eccles.* a formal condemnation; excommunication. **7.** a malediction or curse. [ME *banne* < Scand; cf. Icel *banna* to curse, forbid; c. OE *bannan* to summon, proclaim; akin to L *fārī* to speak, Skt *bhanati* speaks, etc.] **—Syn. 1.** taboo, outlaw, proscribe. **3.** prohibition, proscription, interdict. **3, 4.** taboo. **—Ant. 1.** allow. **3.** permission.

ban[2] (ban), *n.* **1.** a public proclamation or edict. **2. bans,** *Eccles.* banns. **3.** (in the feudal system) **a.** the summoning of the sovereign's vassals for military service. **b.** the body of vassals summoned. [ME; OE *bannan* to summon, proclaim + *gebann* summons, proclamation + OF *ban* summons < Gmc; cf. G *Bann*]

ban[3] (ban), *n. Hist.* the governor or viceroy of certain military districts of Croatia, Hungary, and Slavonia. [< Hung < Pers *bān* lord]

ban[4] (bän), *n., pl.* **ba·ni** (bä′nē). a Rumanian coin, the 100th part of a leu. [< Rumanian]

ba·nal (bə nal′, -näl′, ban′əl, bān′əl), *adj.* devoid of freshness or originality; hackneyed or trite. [< F; OF = *ban* (see BAN[2], def. 3) + *-al* -AL[1]] **—ba·nal·i·ty** (bə nal′i tē, bā-), *n.* **—ba·nal′ly,** *adv.* **—Syn.** See **commonplace.**

ba·nan·a (bə nan′ə), *n.* **1.** a tropical plant of the genus *Musa,* certain species of which are cultivated for their nutritious fruit. **2.** the fruit, esp. that of *M. sapientum,* with yellow or red rind. [< Sp < Pg < WAfr native name]

banan′a oil′, a sweet-smelling liquid ester, $CH_3COOC_5H_{11}$, having a bananalike odor; amyl acetate: used chiefly as a paint solvent and artificial flavor.

banan′a repub′lic, *Sometimes Disparaging.* any of the small countries in the tropics, esp. in the Western Hemisphere, whose economies are largely dependent on fruit exports, tourism, and foreign investors.

banan′a split′, an elaborate confection, typically consisting of a banana sliced lengthwise, on top of which are placed two or more scoops of ice cream, syrup, and a topping of whipped cream, nuts, and a maraschino cherry.

ba·nan·as (bə nan′əs), *adj. Slang.* crazy, mad, or insane (usually used in the phrase *go bananas*).

Ba·na·ras (bə när′is), *n.* Benares.

Ban·at (ban′it, bä′nit), *n.* a fertile low-lying region extending through Hungary, Rumania, and Yugoslavia. [< Serb or Croat *bānat* = *bān* BAN[3] + *-at* suffix akin to -ATE[1]]

Ban·bur·y (ban′ber′ē, -bə rē, bam′-), *n.* a town in N Oxfordshire, in S England. 20,996 (1961).

Ban·croft (ban′krôft, -kroft, bang′-), *n.* **1. George,** 1800–91, U.S. historian and statesman. **2. Hubert Howe,** 1832–1918, U.S. publisher and historian.

band[1] (band), *n.* **1.** a company of persons or, sometimes, animals or things, acting or functioning together; aggregation, party, or troop. **2.** a musical group, usually employing brass, percussion, and often woodwind instruments. **3.** a division of a nomadic tribe; a group of individuals who move and camp together. **4. to beat the band,** energetically; abundantly: *It rained to beat the band.* **—*v.t.* 5.** to unite in a troop, company, or confederacy. **—*v.i.* 6.** to unite or confederate (often fol. by *together*). [late ME *bande* < MF < OPr *banda* < Goth *bandwa* standard; akin to BAND[2], BAND[3], BEND[1], BOND[1]] **—Syn. 1.** gang, group; society, association. See **company.**

band[2] (band), *n.* **1.** a thin, flat strip of some material for binding, confining, trimming, or some other purpose. **2.** a fillet, belt, or strap: *a band for the hair.* **3.** a stripe, as of color or decorative work. **4.** a strip of paper or other material, esp. one serving as a label: *a cigar band.* **5.** a flat collar commonly worn by men and women in the 17th century in western Europe. **6. bands.** See **Geneva bands. 7.** (on a phonograph record) one of two or more sets of grooves in which sound has been recorded, separated from an adjacent set or sets by silent grooves. **8.** *Radio.* a set of frequencies that can be tuned in closely together, as by means of a particular set of condensers. **9.** *Computer Technol.* one or more tracks or channels on a magnetic drum. **10.** *Anat., Zool.* a ribbonlike or cordlike structure encircling, binding, or connecting a part or parts. **—*v.t.* 11.** to mark, decorate, or furnish with a band or bands. [late ME *bande* < MF; OF *bende* < Gmc; cf. OHG *binta* fillet. See BIND, BAND[1], etc.] **—band′er,** *n.*

band[3] (band), *n. Archaic.* **1.** Usually, **bands.** articles for binding the person or the limbs; shackles; manacles; fetters. **2.** an obligation; bond: *the nuptial bands.* [ME < Scand; cf. Icel *band,* OHG *bant*]

band·age (ban′dij), *n., v.,* **-aged, -ag·ing. —*n.* 1.** a strip of cloth or other material used to bind up a wound, sore, sprain, etc. **2.** anything used as a band or ligature. **—*v.t.* 3.** to bind or cover with a bandage. **—*v.i.* 4.** to put a bandage on a wound, sprain, etc. [< MF] **—band′ag·er,** *n.*

Band-Aid (ban′dād′), *n. Trademark.* an adhesive covering with a gauze pad in the center, used for protecting minor abrasions and cuts.

ban·dan·na (ban dan′ə), *n.* **1.** a large, colored handkerchief, typically with white spots or figures on a red or blue background. **2.** any large scarf for the neck or head. Also, **ban·dan′a.** [earlier *bandanno* (second syll. unstressed) < Hindi *bāndhnū* way of dyeing with cloth knotted to keep dye from reaching some parts]

Ban′da Sea′ (bän′dä), a sea between Celebes and New Guinea, S of the Moluccas and N of Timor.

band·box (band′boks′), *n.* a lightweight, usually cylindrical box of pasteboard, thin wood, etc., for holding a hat or other articles of apparel.

ban·deau (ban dō′, ban′dō), *n., pl.* **-deaux** (-dōz′, -dōz). **1.** a headband, esp. one worn about the forehead. **2.** a narrow brassiere. [< F; OF *bandel,* dim. of *bande* BAND[2]]

ban·de·ril·la (ban′də rē′ə, -rēl′yə; *Sp.* bän′de rē′lyä, -yä), *n., pl.* **-ril·las** (-rē′əz, -rēl′yəz; *Sp.* -rē′lyäs, -yäs). a long ornamented dart with barbs used by banderilleros for sticking into the neck or shoulder of the bull. [< Sp = *bander(a)* BANNER + *-illa* dim. suffix < L]

ban·de·ril·le·ro (ban′də rē âr′ō, -rēl yâr′-; *Sp.* bän′de rē lye′rô, -ye′-), *n., pl.* **-ril·le·ros** (-rē âr′ōz, -rēl yâr′-; *Sp.* -rē lye′rôs, -ye′-). a matador's assistant who sticks the banderillas into the bull. [< Sp = *banderill(a)* BANDERILLA + *-ero* -ARY]

ban·de·role (ban′də rōl′), *n.* **1.** a small flag or streamer fastened to a lance, masthead, etc. **2.** a narrow scroll usually bearing an inscription. Also, **ban′de·rol.** [< MF < It *banderuola* = *bandier(a)* BANNER + *-uola* < L *-ola* dim. suffix]

Bandicoot, *Perameles nasuta* (Total length 2 ft.; tail 8 in.)

ban·di·coot (ban′də ko͞ot′), *n.* **1.** any of several large, East Indian rats of the genus *Nesokia.* **2.** any of several insectivorous and herbivorous marsupials of the family *Peramelidae,* of Australia and New Guinea. [< Telugu *pandi-kokku* pig rat]

ban·dit (ban′dit), *n., pl.* **ban·dits, ban·dit·ti** (ban dit′ē). **1.** a robber, esp. a member of a marauding band infesting the mountain districts of southern Europe and the Middle East; brigand. **2.** an outlaw. [earlier *bandetto,* pl. *banditti* < It *banditi* outlaws, pl. of *bandito* proscribed (ptp. of *bandire,* c. ML *bannīre;* see BAN[1]) = *band(o)* decree, BAN[2] + *-ito* < L *-ītus* ptp. suffix]

ban·dit·ry (ban′di trē), *n.* **1.** the activities or practices of bandits. **2.** bandits collectively; banditti.

Ban·djer·ma·sin (ban′jər mä′sin), *n.* Banjermasin. Also **Ban′djar·ma′sin.**

band·lead·er (band′lē′dər), *n.* the leader of a band.
band·mas·ter (band′mas′tər, -mä′stər), *n.* the conductor of a military band, circus band, etc.
Ban·doeng (bän′dŏŏng), *n.* Dutch name of **Bandung.**
ban·do·leer (ban′dᵊlēr′), *n.* a broad belt worn over the shoulder by soldiers and having a number of small loops or pockets, for containing a cartridge or cartridges. Also, **ban′do·lier′.** [earlier *bandollier* < MF *bandoulliere*, fem. of *bandoullier* < Catalan *bandoler* member of a band of men (*bandol* (< Sp *bando* BAND[1]) + *-er* -ER[2])]
ban·do·line (ban′dᵊlēn′, -dᵊlin), *n.* a mucilaginous preparation made from quince seeds and used for smoothing, glossing, or waving the hair. [< F *bandeau* BANDEAU + L *line(re)* (to) anoint, smear]
ban·dore (ban dōr′, -dôr′, ban′dōr, -dôr), *n.* any of various obsolete musical instruments resembling the lute or the guitar. Also called **ban·do·ra** (ban dōr′ə, -dôr′ə), **pandora, pandore.** [earlier *bandurion* < Sp *bandurria* < L *pandūra* < Gk *pandoûra* three-stringed instrument]
band′ saw′, *Mach.* a saw consisting of an endless toothed steel band passing over two wheels.
bands·man (bandz′mən), *n., pl.* **-men.** a musician who plays in a band.
band′ spec′trum, *Physics.* a spectrum consisting of groups of closely spaced lines, usually associated with excited molecules.
band·stand (band′stand′), *n.* a raised platform where the members of a band or orchestra sit while performing.
Ban·dung (bän′dŏŏng), *n.* a city in W Java, in Indonesia. 1,190,000 (est. 1972). Dutch, **Bandoeng.**
band·wag·on (band′wag′ən), *n.* **1.** a wagon, usually large and ornately decorated, for carrying a musical band, as in a circus parade, at the head of a procession. **2. be** or **jump on** or **aboard the bandwagon,** *U.S. Informal.* to support a candidate, cause, movement, etc., that seems assured of success.
band·width (band′width′, -with′), *Radio.* a certain range of frequencies within a band.
ban·dy (ban′dē), *v.,* **-died, -dy·ing,** *adj., n., pl.* **-dies.** —*v.t.* **1.** to throw or strike to and fro or from side to side, as a ball in tennis. **2.** to pass from one to another or back and forth; give and take; trade; exchange: *to bandy blows; to bandy words.* —*adj.* **3.** (of legs) having a bend or crook outward; bowed. —*n.* **4.** an early form of tennis. [? < Sp *bande(ar)* (to) conduct, bandy, orig. help, i.e., serve as member of a band of men]
ban·dy-leg·ged (ban′dē leg′id, -legd′), *adj.* having crooked legs; bowlegged.
bane (bān), *n.* **1.** a person or thing that ruins or spoils: *Gambling was the bane of his existence.* **2.** a deadly poison (often used in combination, as in the names of poisonous plants): *wolfsbane; henbane.* **3.** death, destruction, or ruin. **4.** *Literary.* a thing that causes death or destroys life. [ME; OE *bana* slayer; c. Icel *bani* death, murderer, OHG *bano* death; akin to Goth *banja* wound, Gk *phónos* slaughter]
bane·ber·ry (bān′ber′ē, -bə rē), *n., pl.* **-ries.** **1.** any ranunculaceous plant of the genus *Actaea*, bearing poisonous red or white berries. **2.** the berry of such a plant.
bane·ful (bān′fəl), *adj.* destructive, pernicious, or poisonous: *baneful herbs.* —**bane′ful·ly,** *adv.* —**bane′ful·ness,** *n.*
Banff (bamf), *n.* a resort town in a national reserve (**Banff′ Na′tional Park′,** 2585 sq. mi.) in the Rocky Mountains, in SW Alberta, Canada. 3318 (est. 1964).
bang[1] (bang), *n.* **1.** a loud, sudden, explosive noise, as the discharge of a gun. **2.** a resounding stroke or blow: *an awful bang on the head.* **3.** *Informal.* a sudden movement or show of energy. **4.** *U.S. Slang.* sudden or intense pleasure; thrill or excitement: *to get a big bang out of movies.* **5.** *Slang* (*usually vulgar*). sexual intercourse. —*v.t.* **6.** to strike or beat resoundingly; slam. **7.** *Slang* (*usually vulgar*). to have sexual intercourse with. —*v.i.* **8.** to strike violently or noisily. **9.** to make a loud, sudden, explosive noise. —*adv.* **10.** suddenly and loudly; abruptly or violently: *He fell bang against the wall.* **11.** directly; precisely; right: *He stood bang in the center of the flower bed.* [cf. Icel *banga* to beat, hammer, LG *bangen* to strike, beat]
bang[2] (bang), *n.* **1.** Usually, **bangs.** a fringe of hair combed or brushed forward over the forehead. —*v.t.* **2.** to cut (the hair) so as to form such a fringe. [short for BANGTAIL]
bang[3] (bang), *n.* bhang.
Ban·ga·lore (bang′gə lōr′, -lôr′), *n.* a city in and the capital of Mysore, in S India. 959,803 (est. 1965).
Ban′galore torpe′do, a metal tube filled with explosives and equipped with a firing mechanism, esp. for destroying barbed-wire entanglements, minefields, etc.
Bang·ka (bang′kə; *Du.* bäng′kä), *n.* an island in Indonesia, E of Sumatra: tin mines. 250,452 (est. 1961); 4611 sq. mi. Also, **Banka.**
Bang·kok (bang′kok), *n.* a seaport in and the capital of Thailand, in the S central part, on the Menam River. 4,000,000.
Ban·gla·desh (bang′glə desh′, bäng′-), *n.* a republic, E of India on the Bay of Bengal; a member of the British Commonwealth of Nations. 85,000,000; 54,501 sq. mi. *Cap.:* Dacca. Also, **Ban′gla Desh′.** Formerly (1947–71), **East Pakistan.**
ban·gle (bang′gəl), *n.* a bracelet or anklet in the form of a ring, sometimes without a clasp. [< Hindi *banglī*, var. of *bangrī* glass ring, armlet]
Ban·gor (bang′gôr, -gər), *n.* a seaport in S Maine, on the Penobscot River. 33,168 (1970).
Bang's′ disease′ (bangz), *Vet. Pathol.* an infectious disease of cattle caused by a bacterium, *Brucella abortus*, that infects the genital organs and frequently causes abortions. [named after B. L. F. *Bang* (1848–1932), Danish biologist]
bang·tail (bang′tāl′), *n.* *Slang.* a race horse. [*bang* cut (nasal var. of *bag* cut < ?) + TAIL[1]]
Ban·gui (*Fr.* bäN gē′), *n.* a city in and the capital of the Central African Republic, in the SW part. 350,000.
bang-up (bang′up′), *adj.* excellent; extraordinary.
ba·ni (bä′nē), *n.* pl. of **ban**[4].
ban·ian (ban′yən), *n.* banyan.
ban·ish (ban′ish), *v.t.* **1.** to condemn to exile; expel from or relegate to a country or place by authoritative decree. **2.** to send, drive, or put away: *to banish sorrow.* [ME *banisshe(n)* < MF *baniss-* (long s. of *banir*) = *ban-* (see BAN[1]) + *-iss-* -ISH[2]] —**ban′ish·er,** *n.* —**ban′ish·ment,** *n.*
ban·is·ter (ban′i stər), *n.* **1.** a baluster, esp. a slender one at the edge of a staircase. **2.** Sometimes, **banisters.** the balustrade of a staircase. Also, **bannister.** [var. of BALUSTER]
Ban·jer·ma·sin (bän′jər mä′sin), *n.* a seaport on the S coast of Borneo, in Indonesia. 212,683 (est. 1961). Also, **Bandjermasin.**
ban·jo (ban′jō), *n., pl.* **-jos, -joes.** a musical instrument of the guitar family, having a circular body covered in front with tightly stretched parchment and either four or five strings played with the fingers or a plectrum. [var. of BANDORE] —**ban′jo·ist,** *n.*

Banjo

Ban·jul (bän′jŏŏl), *n.* a port in and the capital of The Gambia. 42,689.
bank[1] (bangk), *n.* **1.** a long pile or heap; mass: *a bank of earth; a bank of clouds.* **2.** a slope or acclivity. **3.** *Phys. Geol.* the slope immediately bordering a stream course along which the water normally runs. **4.** a broad elevation of the sea floor around which the water is relatively shallow: not a hazard to surface navigation. **5.** *Coal Mining.* the surface around the mouth of a shaft. **6.** Also called **cant, superelevation.** the inclination of the bed of a banked road or railroad. **7.** *Aeron.* the lateral inclination of an aircraft, esp. during a turn. **8.** *Billiards, Pool.* the cushion of the table. —*v.t.* **9.** to border with or like a bank; embank: *banking the river with sandbags.* **10.** to form into a bank or heap (usually fol. by *up*): *to bank up snow.* **11.** to slope the bed of (a road or railroad) to compensate for transverse forces, esp. centrifugal forces at curves. **12.** *Aeron.* to tip or incline (an airplane) laterally. **13.** *Billiards, Pool.* **a.** to drive (a ball) to the cushion. **b.** to pocket (the object ball) by driving it against the bank. **14.** to cover up (a fire) with ashes or fuel and close the dampers to make it burn long and slowly. —*v.i.* **15.** to build up in or form banks, as clouds or snow. **16.** *Aeron.* to tip or incline an airplane laterally. [ME *banke* < *Scand;* cf. Icel *bakki* elevation, hill, Sw *backe*] —**Syn. 1.** mound.
bank[2] (bangk), *n.* **1.** an institution for receiving, lending, exchanging, and safeguarding money. **2.** the office or quarters of such an institution. **3.** *Games.* **a.** the stock or fund of pieces from which the players draw. **b.** the fund of the manager or the dealer. **4.** a storage place: *a blood bank.* **5.** a store or reserve. **6.** *Obs.* **a.** a sum of money, esp. a fund for use in business. **b.** a moneychanger's table, counter, or shop. —*v.i.* **7.** to keep money in or have an account with a bank: *Do you bank with the Fifth National?* **8.** to exercise the functions of a bank or banker. —*v.t.* **9.** to deposit in a bank: *to bank one's pay check.* **10. bank on** or **upon,** *Informal.* to count on; depend on: *You can bank on him to help.* [< It *banc(a)* table, counter, moneychanger's table < Gmc; cf. OHG *bank* bench]
bank[3] (bangk), *n.* **1.** an arrangement of objects in a line or in tiers: *a bank of seats; a bank of lights.* **2.** *Music.* a row of keys on an organ. **3.** a bench for rowers in a galley. **4.** a row or tier of oars. **5.** *Print.* **a.** a bench on which sheets are placed as printed. **b.** a table or rack on which type material is stored before being made up in forms. —*v.t.* **6.** to arrange in a bank. [ME *boncke*, OE *-banca* (in *hobanca* bedstead, lit., heel bench) + OF *banc* bench < Gmc; see BANK[2]]
Ban·ka (bang′kə), *n.* Bangka.
bank·a·ble (bang′kə bəl), *adj.* **1.** acceptable by a bank. **2.** having a likelihood of financial success: *a bankable project.*
bank′ accept′ance, a draft endorsed or otherwise formally acknowledged by a bank on which it is drawn. Also called **banker's acceptance.**
bank′ account′, **1.** an account with a bank. **2.** balance standing to the credit of a depositor at a bank. Also called, *Brit.,* **banking account.**
bank′ annu′ities, Sometimes, **bank annuity.** consols.
bank′ bal′ance, **1.** balance standing to the credit of a depositor at a bank. **2.** *Finance.* the balance that a bank has in the clearing house at a given time.
bank′ bill′, **1.** *Chiefly U.S.* a bank note. **2.** Also called **banker's bill.** See **bank draft.**
bank·book (bangk′bŏŏk′), *n.* a book held by a depositor in which a bank enters a record of his account.
bank′ card′, a credit card issued by a commercial bank.
bank′ check′, a check that the depositor of a checking account draws on a bank for payment.
bank′ clerk′, *Brit.* teller (def. 2).
bank′ depos′it, money placed in a bank against which the depositor can withdraw under prescribed conditions.
bank′ dis′count, interest on a loan, deducted in advance from the face value of the note.
bank′ draft′, a draft drawn by one bank on another. Also called **bank′er's draft′.**
bank·er[1] (bang′kər), *n.* **1.** a person employed by a bank, esp. as an executive or other official. **2.** *Games.* the keeper or holder of the bank. [BANK[2] + -ER[2]]
bank·er[2] (bang′kər), *n.* a vessel or fisherman employed in cod fishery on the banks off Newfoundland. [BANK[1] + -ER[1]]
bank·er[3] (bang′kər), *n.* a bench or table used by masons for dressing stones or bricks. [BANK[3] + -ER[1]]
bank′er's accep′tance. See **bank acceptance.**
bank′er's bill′. See **bank draft.**
bank′ hol′iday, **1.** a weekday on which banks are closed by law; legal holiday. **2.** *Brit.* a secular day on which banks are closed, obligations then falling due and being performable on the secular day next following.
bank·ing (bang′king), *n.* **1.** the business carried on by a bank or a banker. **2.** banking as a profession.
bank′ing account′, *Brit.* See **bank account.**
bank′ loan′, an amount of money loaned at interest by a bank to a borrower for a certain period of time.
bank′ night′, *U.S.* an evening when prizes are awarded to members of the audience at a motion-picture theater.

bank′ note′, a promissory note, payable on demand, issued by an authorized bank and intended to circulate as money. Also, **bank′note′.**

bank′ pa′per, **1.** drafts, bills, and acceptances payable by banks. **2.** commercial paper which may be discounted in a bank.

bank′ rate′, the rate of discount fixed by a bank or banks.

bank·roll (bangk′rōl′), *U.S.* —*n.* **1.** money in one's possession; monetary resources. —*v.t.* **2.** *Slang.* to finance: *to bankroll a new housing development.*

bank·rupt (bangk′rupt, -rəpt), *n.* **1.** *Law.* a person who upon his own petition or that of his creditors is adjudged insolvent by a court and whose property is administered for and divided among his creditors under a bankruptcy law. **2.** any insolvent debtor; one unable to satisfy any just claims made upon him. **3.** a person lacking in a particular thing or quality: *a moral bankrupt.* —*adj.* **4.** *Law.* subject to or under legal process because of insolvency; insolvent. **5.** pertaining to bankrupts or bankruptcy. —*v.t.* **6.** to make bankrupt. [< ML *banca rupta* bank broken; r. It *banca rota* and F *banqueroute* in same sense]

bank·rupt·cy (bangk′rupt sē, -rəp sē), *n., pl.* **-cies.** **1.** the state of being or becoming bankrupt. **2.** utter ruin or failure.

Banks (bangks), *n.* **Sir Joseph,** 1734–1820, English naturalist.

bank′ shot′, **1.** *Basketball.* a basket made by rebounding the ball off the backboard. **2.** *Billiards, Pool.* a shot in which the cue ball or object ball is banked.

bank·si·a (bangk′sē ə), *n.* any Australian shrub or tree of the genus *Banksia,* having leathery leaves and dense cylindrical heads of yellow flowers. [< NL; after Sir Joseph BANKS; see -IA]

Bank·side (bangk′sīd′), *n.* a district in London, England, on the S side of the Thames River.

bank′ state′ment, **1.** a monthly statement of account mailed by a bank to each of its depositors recording the banking transactions during a period and usually including canceled checks. **2.** a statement required to be published periodically by a bank showing its financial status, as assets, liabilities, etc.

ban·ner (ban′ər), *n.* **1.** the flag of a country, army, troop, etc. **2.** an ensign or the like bearing some device, motto, or slogan, as one carried in religious processions, political demonstrations, etc. **3.** a flag formerly used as the standard of a sovereign, lord, or knight. **4.** a sign painted on cloth and hung over a street, entrance, etc.: *Banners at the intersection announced the tennis tournament.* **5.** anything regarded or displayed as a symbol of principles. **6.** Also called **ban′ner line′, line, screamer, streamer.** *Journalism.* a headline extending across a newspaper page, usually across the top of the front page. **7.** *Bot.* vexillum (def. 3). —*adj.* **8.** leading or foremost: *a banner year for crops.* [ME *banere* < OF *ban(i)ere* < LL *bann(um)* (var. of *bandum* standard < Goth *bandwa* sign; see BAND[1]) + OF *-iere* < L *-āria* -ARY]

ban·ner·et[1] (ban′ər it, -ə ret′), *n.* **1.** *Hist.* a knight who could bring a company of followers into the field under his own banner. **2.** a rank of knighthood; knight banneret. [ME *baneret* < OF = *baner(e)* BANNER + *-et* < L *-ātus* -ATE[1]]

ban·ner·et[2] (ban′ə ret′), *n.* a small banner. Also, **ban′ner·ette′.** [ME *banerett* < MF *banerete* little banner]

ban·nis·ter (ban′i stər), *n.* banister.

ban·nock (ban′ək), *n.* *Scot. and Brit. Cookery.* a flat cake made of oatmeal, barley meal, etc., usually baked on a griddle. [ME *bannok,* OE *bannuc* morsel; cf. Gael *bannach*]

Ban·nock·burn (ban′ək bûrn′, ban′ək bûrn′), *n.* a village in central Scotland, in Stirling county: site of the defeat (1314) of the English by the Scots under Robert the Bruce.

banns (banz), *n.pl.* *Eccles.* the notice of an intended marriage, given three times in the parish church of each of the betrothed. Also, **bans.** [var. of *bans,* pl. of BAN[2]]

ban·quet (bang′kwit), *n., v.,* **-quet·ed, -quet·ing.** —*n.* **1.** a lavish meal; feast. **2.** a ceremonious public dinner, esp. one honoring a person, benefiting a charity, etc. —*v.t.* **3.** to entertain or regale (a person or oneself) at a banquet. —*v.i.* **4.** to have or attend a banquet; feast. [< F < It *banchetto* = *banc(o)* table (see BANK[2]) + *-etto* -ET; r. *bankett* < It] —**ban′quet·er,** *n.* —**Syn. 1.** See **feast.**

ban·quette (bang ket′), *n.* **1.** an upholstered bench, as along a wall in a restaurant. **2.** *Fort.* a platform or step along the inside of a parapet, for soldiers to stand on when firing. **3.** *Southern U.S.* a sidewalk. [< MF < Pr *banqueta* = *banc* bench (see BANK[3]) + *-eta* -ETTE]

ban·shee (ban′shē, ban shē′), *n.* (in Irish folklore) a spirit in the form of a woman whose appearance or wailing is a sign that a loved one will soon die. Also, **ban′shie.** [< Ir *bean sīdhe* woman of the fairies]

ban·tam (ban′təm), *n.* **1.** (*often cap.*) a chicken of any of several varieties or breeds characterized by very small size. **2.** a small, quarrelsome person. —*adj.* **3.** diminutive or tiny: *bantam editions of the classics.* [after *Bantam,* village in W Java, in S Indonesia]

ban·tam·weight (ban′təm wāt′), *n.* a boxer or other contestant intermediate in weight between a flyweight and a featherweight, esp. a professional boxer weighing up to 118 pounds.

ban·ter (ban′tər), *n.* **1.** an exchange of light, playful, teasing remarks; good-natured raillery. —*v.t.* **2.** to address with banter; chaff. —*v.i.* **3.** to use banter. [?] —**ban′ter·er,** *n.* —**ban′ter·ing·ly,** *adv.* —**Syn. 1.** badinage, joking, jesting. **2.** tease, twit; ridicule, deride, mock.

Ban·ting (ban′ting), *n.* **Sir Frederick Grant,** 1891–1941, Canadian physician: discoverer of insulin; Nobel prize 1923.

bant·ling (bant′ling), *n.* *Disparaging.* a young child; brat. [m. G *Bänkling* illegitimate child = *Bank* BENCH + *-ling* -LING[1]]

Ban·tu (ban′to͞o), *n., pl.* **-tus,** (*esp. collectively*) **-tu,** *adj.* —*n.* **1.** a member of any of several linguistically interrelated Negroid peoples in central and southern Africa. **2.** a grouping of more than 500 languages of central and southern Africa, as Kikuyu, Swahili, and Zulu. —*adj.* **3.** of, pertaining to, or characteristic of Bantu or the Bantu.

ban·yan (ban′yən), *n.* **1.** Also called **ban′yan tree′.** an East Indian fig tree, *Ficus benghalensis,* whose branches send out adventitious roots to the ground, sometimes causing the tree to spread over a wide area. **2.** (in India) **a.** a loose shirt, jacket, or gown. **b.** a Hindu trader or merchant of a particular caste the rules of which forbid eating flesh. Also, **banian.** [< Pg << Gujarati *vāṇiyān,* pl. of *vāṇiyo* man of trading caste < Skt *vaṇij* merchant, orig. applied to a particular tree of this species near which the traders had built a booth]

Banyan, *Ficus benghalensis* (Height 70 to 100 ft.)

ban·zai (bän zī′, bän′-; *Jap.* bän′dzī′), *interj.* **1.** (used by the Japanese as a patriotic shout or cheer addressed to the emperor and wishing him long life.) **2.** (used as a shout, esp. among Japanese combat troops, when attacking.) —*adj.* **3.** reckless; suicidal: *a banzai attack.* [< Jap = *ban* ten thousand + *zai* year]

ba·o·bab (bā′ō bab′, bä′-), *n.* any large, bombacaceous tree of the genus *Adansonia,* esp. *A. digitata,* which is native to tropical Africa, has an exceedingly thick trunk, and bears a gourdlike fruit. [from a language of equatorial Africa]

Bap., Baptist. Also, **Bapt.**

bap., baptized.

bap·tise (bap tīz′, bap′tīz), *v.t., v.i.,* **-tised, -tis·ing.** *Chiefly Brit.* baptize.

bap·tism (bap′tiz əm), *n.* **1.** *Eccles.* a ceremonial immersion in water, or application of water, as an initiatory rite or sacrament of the Christian church. **2.** any similar ceremony or action of initiation, dedication, etc. [< LL *baptisma* < Gk = *bapt(izein)* (to) BAPTIZE + *-isma* -ISM; r. ME *bapteme* < OF] —**bap·tis·mal** (bap tiz′məl), *adj.* —**bap·tis′mal·ly,** *adv.*

baptis′mal name′. See **Christian name** (def. 1).

bap′tism of fire′, **1.** spiritual sanctification as a gift of the Holy Ghost. **2.** the first time a soldier faces battle. **3.** any severe ordeal that tests one's endurance.

Bap·tist (bap′tist), *n.* **1.** a member of a Christian denomination that baptizes believers by immersion and that is usually Calvinistic in doctrine. **2.** (*l.c.*) a person who baptizes. **3. the Baptist.** See **John the Baptist.** —*adj.* **4.** Also, **Bap·tis′tic.** of or pertaining to Baptists or their doctrines or practices. [ME *baptiste* < OF < LL *baptista* < Gk *baptistḗs* = *bapt(izein)* (to) BAPTIZE + *-istēs* -IST]

bap·tis·ter·y (bap′ti stə rē, -ti strē), *n., pl.* **-ter·ies.** **1.** a building or a part of a church in which baptism is administered. **2.** (esp. in Baptist churches) a tank for administering baptism by immersion. [< LL *baptistēri(um)* < Gk *baptistḗrion* bathing-place (see BAPTIST, -ERY); r. late ME *baptizatory* < ML *baptizātōri(um)*]

bap·tist·ry (bap′ti strē), *n., pl.* **-ries.** baptistery.

bap·tize (bap tīz′, bap′tīz), *v.,* **-tized, -tiz·ing.** —*v.t.* **1.** to immerse in water, sprinkle, or pour water on, in the Christian rite of baptism. **2.** to cleanse spiritually; initiate or dedicate by purifying. **3.** to christen. —*v.i.* **4.** to administer baptism: *a sect that does not baptize.* Also, *esp. Brit.,* **baptise.** [ME < LL *baptiz(āre)* < Gk *baptízein* to immerse = *bápt(ein)* (to) bathe + *-izein* -IZE] —**bap·tiz′er,** *n.*

bar (bär), *n., v.,* **barred, bar·ring,** *prep.* —*n.* **1.** a relatively long, evenly shaped piece of some solid substance, as metal or wood, used as a guard or obstruction or for some mechanical purpose: *the bars of a cage.* **2.** an oblong piece of any solid material: *a bar of soap.* **3.** the amount of material in a bar. **4.** an ingot, lump, or wedge of gold or silver. **5.** a long ridge of sand, gravel, or other material near or slightly above the surface of a body of water: often an obstruction to navigation. **6.** anything that obstructs, hinders, or impedes; obstacle: *a bar to important legislation.* **7.** a counter or a place where beverages, esp. liquors, or light meals are served to customers; barroom (sometimes used in combination): *a bar and grill; snack bar.* **8.** (in a home) a counter or similar piece of furniture for serving food or beverages. **9.** the legal profession. **10.** the practicing members of the legal profession. **11.** any tribunal: *the bar of public opinion.* **12.** a band or strip: *a bar of light; a bar of color.* **13.** a railing in a courtroom separating the general public from the part of the room occupied by the judges, jury, attorneys, etc. **14.** *Music.* **a.** the line marking the division between two measures of music. **b.** See **double bar. c.** the unit of music contained between two bar lines; measure. **15.** *Ballet.* a handrail placed along a wall at hip height, used by a dancer to maintain balance during practice. **16.** *Law.* **a.** an objection that nullifies an action. **b.** a stoppage of an alleged right of action. **17.** *Building Trades.* **a.** an iron or steel shape: *I-bar.* **b.** a muntin. **18.** *Mil.* one of a pair of metal or cloth insignia worn by certain commissioned officers. **19.** (in a bridle) the mouthpiece connecting the cheeks. **20.** thread joining across an open space in lace; bride. **21.** *Physics.* **a.** a centimeter-gram-second unit of pressure, equal to 1,000,000 dynes per square centimeter. **b.** (formerly) microbar. *Abbr.:* b **22.** *Heraldry.* a horizontal band, narrower than a fess, that crosses the field of an escutcheon. —*v.t.* **23.** to equip or fasten with a bar or bars: *Bar the door before retiring for the night.* **24.** to shut in or out by or as by bars: *The police barred the exits.* **25.** to block (a way, passage, etc.), as with a barrier; prevent or hinder, as access: *They barred his entrance to the club.* **26.** to exclude or except: *He was barred from membership because of his reputation.* **27.** to mark with bars, stripes, or bands. —*prep.* **28.** except; omitting; but: *bar none.* [ME *barre* < OF < VL *barra rod < ?] —**bar′less,** *adj.* —**bar′ra·ble,** *adj.*

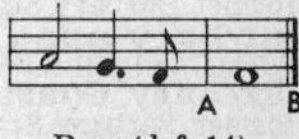

Bars (def. 14) A, Single; B, Double

—Syn. 1. rod, pole. **5.** shoal, reef, bank, sand bar. **6.** deterrent, stop. BAR, BARRIER, BARRICADE mean something put in the way of advance. BAR has the general meaning of hindrance or obstruction: *a bar across the doorway.* BARRIER suggests an impediment to progress, literal or figurative, or a defensive obstruction against attack: *a river barrier.* A BARRICADE is esp. a pile of articles hastily gathered or a rude earthwork for protection in street fighting: *a barricade of wooden boxes.* **7.** saloon, café. **25.** obstruct, barricade.

BAR, See **Browning automatic rifle.**

Bar., *Bible.* Baruch.

bar., **1.** barometer. **2.** barrel. **3.** barrister.

B.Ar., Bachelor of Architecture.

Bar·a (bar′ə), *n.* **The·da** (thē′də), (*Theodosia Goodman*), 1890–1955, U.S. actress.

Bar·ab·bas (bə rab′əs), *n.* a condemned criminal pardoned by Pilate to appease the mob, which demanded that he be freed instead of Jesus. Mark 15:6–11; John 18:40.

barb[1] (bärb), *n.* **1.** a point or pointed part projecting backward from a main point, as of a fishhook, an arrowhead, or the like. **2.** an obviously or openly unpleasant or carping remark. **3.** *Bot., Zool.* a beardlike growth or part. **4.** *Ornith.* one of the processes attached to the rachis of a feather. **5.** one of a breed of domestic pigeons, similar to the carriers or homers, having a short, broad bill. **6.** any of numerous, small, Old World cyprinid fishes of the genera *Barbus* and *Puntius*, often kept in aquariums. **7.** Usually, **barbs.** *Vet. Pathol.* a small protuberance under the tongue in horses and cattle, esp. when inflamed and swollen. **8.** Also, **barbe.** *Clothing.* a linen covering for the throat and breast, worn by nuns. **9.** *Obs.* a beard. **—*v.t.* 10.** to furnish with a barb or barbs. [ME *barbe* < MF << L *barba* beard or beardlike projection] **—barb′less,** *adj.*

barb[2] (bärb), *n.* one of a breed of horses raised originally in Barbary. [< F *barbe*, short for It *barbero* Barbary steed]

barb[3] (bärb), *n. Slang.* barbiturate. [by shortening]

Bar·ba·dos (bär bā′dōz, -dōs, bär′bə dōz′, -dōs′), *n.* an island in the E West Indies constituting an independent republic in the British Commonwealth of Nations: formerly a colony. 245,000; 161 sq. mi. *Cap.:* Bridgetown. **—Bar·ba·di·an** (bär bā′dē ən), *adj., n.*

bar·bar·i·an (bär bâr′ē ən), *n.* **1.** a person in a savage, primitive state; uncivilized person. **2.** a person without culture or education; philistine. **3.** (esp. in ancient and medieval periods) a foreigner. **—*adj.* 4.** uncivilized, crude, or savage. **5.** foreign or alien. [< L *barbari(a)* barbarous country + -AN] **—bar·bar′i·an·ism,** *n.* **—Syn. 3.** alien. **4.** rude, primitive, wild, rough, coarse, ignorant, uncultivated. **—Ant. 4.** cultivated, civilized.

bar·bar·ic (bär bar′ik), *adj.* **1.** not civilized; primitive: *barbaric invaders.* **2.** of, like, or befitting barbarians: *a barbaric empire.* [< L *barbaric(us)* < Gk *barbarikós* = *bárbar(os)* (see BARBAROUS) + *-ikos* -IC]

bar·ba·rise (bär′bə rīz′), *v.t., v.i.,* **-rised, -ris·ing.** *Chiefly Brit.* barbarize.

bar·ba·rism (bär′bə riz′əm), *n.* **1.** a barbarous or uncivilized state or condition. **2.** a barbarous act. **3.** the use of words or linguistic forms felt to be contrary to the established standards. **4.** such a word or form. [< L *barbarismus* < Gk *barbarismós* foreign way of speaking. See BARBAROUS, -ISM]

bar·bar·i·ty (bär bar′i tē), *n., pl.* **-ties. 1.** brutal or inhuman conduct; cruelty. **2.** an act or instance of cruelty or inhumanity. **3.** crudity of style, taste, expression, etc. [< L *barbar(us)* (see BARBAROUS) + -ITY]

bar·ba·rize (bär′bə rīz′), *v.,* **-rized, -riz·ing. —*v.t.* 1.** to make barbarous; brutalize; corrupt: *foreign influences barbarizing the Latin language.* **—*v.i.* 2.** to become barbarous or lapse into barbarism. **3.** to use barbarisms in speaking or writing. Also, *esp. Brit.,* **barbarise.** [partly < Gk *barbarízein* = *bárbar(os)* (see BARBAROUS) + *-izein* -IZE; partly BARBAR(OUS) + -IZE]

Bar·ba·ros·sa (bär′bə ros′ə), *n.* **Frederick.** See **Frederick I** (def. 1).

bar·ba·rous (bär′bər əs), *adj.* **1.** uncivilized, savage, or crude. **2.** savagely cruel or harsh: *barbarous treatment.* **3.** not conforming to classical standards or accepted usage, as language. **4.** foreign; alien. [< L *barbarus* < Gk *bárbaros* non-Greek, foreign, barbarian; akin to Skt *barbara* stammering, non-Aryan] **—bar′ba·rous·ly,** *adv.* **—bar′ba·rous·ness,** *n.* **—Syn. 2.** ferocious, brutal.

Bar·ba·ry (bär′bə rē), *n.* a region in N Africa, extending from W of Egypt to the Atlantic Ocean and including the former Barbary States.

Bar′bary ape′, an ape, *Macaca sylvana,* of northern Africa and Gibraltar.

Bar′bary Coast′, the Mediterranean coastline of the former Barbary States: former pirate refuge.

Bar′bary sheep′, aoudad.

Bar′bary States′, Morocco, Algiers, Tunis, and Tripoli.

bar·bate (bär′bāt), *adj. Zool., Bot.* bearded; tufted or furnished with hairs. [< L *barbāt(us)* = *barb(a)* beard + *-ātus* -ATE[1]]

barbe (bärb), *n.* barb[1] (def. 8).

bar·be·cue (bär′bə kyōō′), *n., v.,* **-cued, -cu·ing. —*n.* 1.** *U.S.* a social entertainment, usually in the open air, at which meats are roasted over an open hearth or pit. **2.** a framework, as a grill or a spit, on which meat or vegetables are cooked before or over an open fire. **3.** pieces of meat or fish roasted over an open fire. **4.** a dressed steer, lamb, or other animal, roasted whole. **—*v.t.* 5.** to broil or roast whole or in large pieces before an open fire, on a spit or grid iron. **6.** to cook (sliced or diced meat or fish) in a highly seasoned sauce. [< Sp *barbacoa* < WInd (? Taino) *barbacoa,* a frame of sticks]

barbed′ wire′, a wire or strand of wires having small pieces of sharply pointed wire twisted around them at short intervals, used chiefly for fencing in livestock. Also called **barbwire.**

bar·bel (bär′bəl), *n.* **1.** a slender, external process on the jaw or other part of the head of certain fishes. **2.** any of various cyprinoid fishes of the genus *Barbus,* esp. *B. barbus,* of Europe. [late ME *barbell* < MF *barbel* (now *barbeau*) < L *barb(us)* bearded fish + *-ellus* dim. suffix]

bar·bell (bär′bel′), *n.* an apparatus used in weight lifting, consisting of a bar with replaceable, disk-shaped weights fastened to the ends.

bar·bel·late (bär′bə lāt′, bär bel′it, -āt), *adj. Bot., Zool.* having short, stiff hairs. [< NL *barbell(a)* (dim. of L *barbula* little beard). See BARBULE, -ATE[1]]

bar·ber (bär′bər), *n.* **1.** a person whose occupation it is to cut and dress the hair of customers, esp. men, and to shave or trim the beard. **—*v.t.* 2.** to trim or dress the hair or beard of. [ME *barbour* < AF; OF *barbeor* = *barb(e)* (< L *barba* beard) + *-eor* -OR[2]]

Bar·ber (bär′bər), *n.* **Samuel,** 1910–81, U.S. composer.

bar′ber pole′, a pole with red and white spiral stripes symbolizing the barber's former sideline of surgery. Also, **bar′ber's pole′.**

bar·ber·ry (bär′ber′ē, -bə rē), *n., pl.* **-ries. 1.** a shrub of the genus *Berberis,* esp. *B. vulgaris.* **2.** its red, elongated, acid fruit. [late ME *barbere* < ML *bar(baris)* (< Ar) + *-bere* for *berie* BERRY]

bar·ber·shop (bär′bər shop′), *n.* **1.** Also, *esp. Brit.,* **bar′ber's shop′.** the place of business of a barber. **—*adj.* 2.** of or pertaining to a barbershop. **3.** specializing in the part singing of popular songs in which four voices move in close, highly chromatic harmony: *a barbershop quartet.*

bar′ber's itch′, *Pathol.* ringworm of the bearded areas of the face and neck, caused by any of certain fungi and characterized by reddish patches.

Bar·ber·ton (bär′bər tən), *n.* a city in NE Ohio. 33,052.

bar·bet (bär′bit), *n.* any of several stocky, tropical birds of the family *Capitonidae,* having a stout bill with bristles at the base. [< F << L *barbāt(us);* see BARBATE]

bar·bette (bär bet′), *n.* **1.** (within a fortification) a platform or mound of earth from which guns may be fired over the parapet instead of through embrasures. **2.** *Navy.* an armored cylinder for protecting the lower part of a turret on a warship. [< F; see BARB[1] (def. 8), -ETTE; so called from the resemblance in shape]

bar·bi·can (bär′bə kən), *n.* an outwork of a fortified place, as a castle. [ME < ML *barbican(a),* var. of *barbacana* < ?. Cf. OF *barbaquenne*]

bar·bi·cel (bär′bi sel′), *n. Ornith.* one of the minute processes fringing the barbules of certain feathers. [< NL *barbicell(a)* = L *barbi-* (comb. form of *barba* beard) + *-cella* dim. suffix]

bar·bi·tal (bär′bi tal′, -tôl′). *n. Pharm.* a barbiturate compound, $CO(NHCO)_2(C_2H_5)_2$, used as a hypnotic. [BARBIT(URIC ACID) + (VERON)AL]

bar·bi·tu·rate (bär bich′ə rāt′, -ər it; bär′bə tyŏŏr′āt, -it), *n. Chem.* any of a group of barbituric acid derivatives, used in medicine as sedatives and hypnotics. [BARBITUR(IC ACID) + -ATE[2]]

bar′bi·tu′ric ac′id (bär′bi tyŏŏr′ik, -tŏŏr′-, bär′-), a slightly water-soluble powder, $CO(NHCO)_2CH_2$, used chiefly in the synthesis of barbiturates. Also called **malonylurea.**

bar·bi·tur·ism (bär bich′ə riz′əm), *n. Med.* chronic poisoning caused by the excessive use of a barbiturate. [BARBITUR(ATE) + -ISM]

Bar′bi·zon School′ (bär′bi zon′), a group of French painters of the mid-19th century whose landscapes and genre paintings depicted peasant life and the quality of natural light on objects. [after *Barbizon,* village near Paris, where the painters gathered]

Bar·bu·da (bär bōō′də), *n.* a member of the W Indies Associated States in the NE Leeward Islands, in the E West Indies; formerly a British colony: a dependency of Antigua. 1,145 (1963); 62 sq. mi.

bar·bule (bär′byōōl), *n.* **1.** a small barb. **2.** one of the small processes fringing the barbs of a feather. [< L *barbul(a)*]

Barbut

Bar·busse (BAR BYS′), *n.* **Hen·ri** (äN RĒ′), 1873?–1935, French journalist and author.

bar·but (bär′bət), *n.* a steel helmet of the 15th century completely enclosing the head and having a T-shaped face slit. [< MF *barbute* < Pr *barbuta,* fem. of *barbut* < LL **barbūt(us),* for L *barbātus* bearded. See BARBATE]

barb·wire (bärb′wīər′), *n.* See **barbed wire.**

Bar·ca (bär′kə), *n.* **1.** an ancient Carthaginian family to which Hamilcar, Hasdrubal, and Hannibal belonged. **2.** Cyrenaica. **—Bar′can,** *adj.*

bar′ car′, a railroad car equipped with a bar that serves beverages, esp. liquors, or refreshments.

bar·ca·role (bär′kə rōl′), *n.* **1.** a boating song of the Venetian gondoliers. **2.** a piece of music composed in the style of such songs. Also, **bar′ca·rolle′.** [< It *barcarola* boatman's song, fem. of *barcarolo* boatman = *barc(a)* BARK[3] + *-ar(i)o* -ER[2] + *-(o)lo* dim. suffix]

Bar·ce·lon·a (bär′sə lō′nə; *Sp.* bär′the lô′nä), *n.* a seaport in NE Spain, on the Mediterranean. 2,000,000.

B.Arch., Bachelor of Architecture.

Bar·clay de Tol·ly (bär klī′ də tô′lyə), **Prince Mi·kha·il** (mi khä ēl′), 1761–1818, Russian field marshal: commander in chief against Napoleon I in 1812.

Bar Coche·ba (bär′ kôkh′bä′). See **Bar Kokba.** Also, **Bar′ Coch′ba.**

bar′ code′, a set of lines of varying width printed on a product and containing encoded information readable by an optical scanner.

bard[1] (bärd), *n.* **1.** one of an ancient Celtic order of poets. **2.** (formerly) a person who composed and recited epic or heroic poems, often accompanying himself on the harp or lyre. **3.** (loosely) any poet. **4. the Bard,** William Shakespeare. [late ME < Celt; cf. Ir, Gael *bard*] **—bard′ic,** *adj.*

bard[2] (bärd), *Armor.* **—*n.* 1.** any of various pieces of defensive armor for a horse. **—*v.t.* 2.** to caparison with bards. [late ME *barde* < MF < OSp *barda* armor for a horse < Ar *barda'ah* packsaddle]

barde (bärd), *n., v.t.* **bard·ed, bard·ing.** bard[2].

Bar·deen (bär dēn′), *n.* **John,** born 1908, U.S. physicist: Nobel prize 1956, 1972.

Bard′ of A′von (bärd), William Shakespeare: so called from his birthplace, Stratford-on-Avon.

bare[1] (bâr), *adj.*, **bar·er, bar·est,** *v.*, **bared, bar·ing.** —*adj.* **1.** without covering or clothing; naked; nude: *bare knees.* **2.** without the usual furnishings, contents, etc.: *bare walls.* **3.** open to view; unconcealed or undisguised: *his bare dislike.* **4.** unadorned, bald, or plain: *the bare facts.* **5.** scarcely or just sufficient; mere: *bare necessities.* —*v.t.* **6.** to remove the clothes or covering from. **7.** to open to view; reveal or divulge: *to bare damaging new facts.* [ME; OE *bær;* c. D *baar,* G *bar,* Icel *berr;* akin to Lith *basas* barefoot] —**bare′ness,** *n.* —**Syn. 1.** undressed. **2.** plain, stark, empty, barren. **5.** simple, sheer. **6.** uncover, strip. **7.** unmask, disclose, expose. —**Ant. 1.** covered.

bare[2] (bâr), *v. Archaic.* pt. of **bear.**

bare·back (bâr′bak′), *adv., adj.* without a saddle on the back of a horse, burro, etc: *to ride bareback; a bareback rider.* Also, **bare′backed′.**

bare′ bones′, the irreducible minimum or the most essential. —**bare′-bones′,** *adj.*

bare·faced (bâr′fāst′), *adj.* **1.** with the face uncovered. **2.** without concealment or disguise; boldly open: *a barefaced approach.* **3.** shameless or impudent; audacious: *a barefaced lie.* —**bare·fac·ed·ly** (bâr′fā′sid lē, -fāst′lē), *adv.* —**bare′fac′ed·ness,** *n.*

bare·foot (bâr′fo͝ot′), *adj., adv.* with the feet bare. Also, **bare′foot′ed.** [ME *barfot,* OE *bærfōt*]

bare·hand·ed (bâr′han′did), *adj., adv.* **1.** with hands uncovered. **2.** without tools, weapons, or other aids.

bare·head·ed (bâr′hed′id), *adj., adv.* with the head uncovered. Also, **bare′head′.** —**bare′head′ed·ness,** *n.*

Ba·reil·ly (bə rā′lē), *n.* a city in central Uttar Pradesh, in N India. 254,400 (1961). Also, **Ba·re′li.**

bare·knuck·le (bâr′nuk′əl), *adj.* **1.** (of a prizefight, prizefighter, etc.) without boxing gloves; using the bare fists. **2.** without conventional niceties; rough-and-tumble. —*adv.* **3.** in a rough-and-tumble manner. Also, **bare′knuck′led.**

bare·leg·ged (bâr′leg′id, -legd′), *adj., adv.* with bare legs.

bare·ly (bâr′lē), *adv.* **1.** only; just; no more than: *She is barely 16.* **2.** without disguise or concealment. **3.** nakedly; scantily. **4.** *Archaic.* merely; only. [ME; OE *bærlīce*] —**Syn. 1.** See **hardly.** —**Usage. 1.** See **hardly.**

Bar·ents (bar′ənts, bär′-; *Du.* bä ʀents′), *n.* **Wil·lem** (wil′əm), died 1597, Dutch navigator and explorer.

Bar′ents Sea′, a part of the Arctic Ocean between NE Europe and the islands of Spitzbergen, Franz Josef Land, and Novaya Zemlya.

bare·sark (bâr′särk), *n.* **1.** *Scand. Legend.* a berserker. —*adv.* **2.** without armor. [var. of BERSERK, as if BARE[1] + SARK]

barf (bärf), *v., n. Slang.* vomit. [?]

bar·fly (bär′flī′), *n., pl.* **-flies.** *U.S. Slang.* a person who frequents barrooms.

bar·gain (bär′gin), *n.* **1.** an agreement settling what each party shall give and take or perform and receive in a transaction. **2.** something acquired by bargaining. **3.** something well worth what is given in exchange, esp. in being cheaper than usual. **4. in** or **into the bargain,** over and above what has been stipulated; moreover; besides: *The new housekeeper proved to be a fine cook in the bargain.* **5. strike a bargain,** to make a bargain; agree to terms. —*v.i.* **6.** to discuss the terms of a bargain; haggle over terms. **7.** to come to an agreement; make a bargain: *We bargained on a three-year term.* —*v.t.* **8.** to arrange by bargain: *to bargain a new wage increase.* **9. bargain for,** to anticipate or take into account: *more than one had bargained for.* **10. bargain on,** to expect or anticipate; count or rely on: *You can't bargain on what he'll do in this situation.* [ME *bargaine* < MF *bargaigne* (n.), *bargaigner* (v.); c. ML *barcāniāre* to trade < ?] —**bar′gain·er,** *n.* —**Syn. 1.** stipulation, arrangement, transaction. See **agreement. 6.** See **trade. 7.** contract.

bar′gain base′ment, a basement area in some department stores where the less expensive merchandise is offered for sale.

barge (bärj), *n., v.,* **barged, barg·ing.** —*n.* **1.** a flat-bottomed vessel, usually without power and intended to be pushed or towed, for transporting freight or passengers. **2.** a vessel of state used in pageants: *elegant barges on the Grand Canal in Venice.* **3.** *Navy.* a boat reserved for a flag officer. —*v.t.* **4.** to carry or transport by barge. —*v.i.* **5.** *Informal.* to move clumsily; bump into things; collide: *to barge through a crowd.* **6. barge in** or **into,** *Informal.* to intrude, interrupt, or interfere, esp. rudely or clumsily: *I hated to barge in without an invitation. He barged into the conversation.* [ME < MF = ML *barga,* ? var. of LL *barca* BARK[3]]

barge·board (bärj′bōrd′, -bôrd′), *n.* a board, often carved, hanging from the projecting end of a sloping roof. Also called **vergeboard.** [?]

barge·man (bärj′mən), *n., pl.* **-men. 1.** one of the crew of a barge. **2.** a person who owns, manages, or captains a barge or barges. Also called, *esp. Brit.,* **bar·gee** (bär jē′).

bar′ graph′, a graph using parallel bars of varying lengths, as to illustrate comparative costs, exports, birth rates, etc.

Bar′ Har′bor, a town on Mount Desert Island, in S Maine: summer resort. 2392 (1970).

Ba·ri (bär′ē), *n.* a seaport in SE Italy, on the Adriatic. 311,268 (1961). Italian, **Ba·ri del·le Pu·glie** (bä′ʀē del′le po͞o′lye).

bar·ic[1] (bar′ik), *adj. Chem.* of or containing barium. [BAR(IUM) + -IC]

bar·ic[2] (bar′ik), *adj.* of or pertaining to weight, esp. that of the atmosphere. [BAR(O)- + -IC]

ba·ril·la (bə ril′ə), *n.* **1.** either of two European saltworts, *Salsola Kali* or *S. Soda,* whose ashes yield an impure carbonate of soda. **2.** the alkali obtained from the ashes of these and certain other maritime plants. [< Sp *barrilla,* dim. of *barra* BAR]

Bar·ing (bâr′ing), *n.* **1. Alexander, 1st Baron Ashburton,** 1774–1848, British financier and statesman. **2. Evelyn, 1st Earl of Cromer,** 1841–1917, British statesman and diplomat.

barit., *Music.* baritone.

bar·ite (bâr′īt, bar′-), *n.* a common mineral, barium sulfate, $BaSO_4$: the principal ore of barium. Also, **barytes.** Also called **heavy spar.** [BAR(IUM) + -ITE[1]]

bar·i·tone (bar′i tōn′), *Music.* —*n.* **1.** a male voice or voice part intermediate between tenor and bass. **2.** a singer with such a voice. **3.** a large, valved brass instrument shaped like a trumpet or coiled in oval form, used esp. in military bands. —*adj.* **4.** of or pertaining to a baritone; having the compass of a baritone. Also, **barytone.** [< It *baritono* low voice < Gk *barýtonos* deep-sounding]

bar′itone clef′, *Music.* an F clef locating F below middle C on the third line of the staff.

bar·i·um (bâr′ē əm, bar′-), *n. Chem.* an active, divalent, metallic element, occurring in combination chiefly as barite or as witherite. *Symbol:* Ba; *at. wt.:* 137.34; *at. no.:* 56; *sp. gr.:* 3.5 at 20°C. [BAR(YTA) + -IUM]

bar′ium sul′fate, *Chem.* a white powder, $BaSO_4$, used chiefly as a pigment in paints and printing inks, and in medicine, because of its radiopacity, for x-ray diagnosis.

bark[1] (bärk), *n.* **1.** the abrupt, harsh, explosive cry of a dog or other animal. **2.** a sharp, explosive noise. **3.** a brusque order, reply, etc. —*v.i.* **4.** to utter an abrupt, explosive cry or a series of such cries, as a dog. **5.** to emit a sharp, explosive noise. **6.** to speak or cry out sharply or gruffly: *a man who barks at his children.* **7.** *Chiefly U.S. Informal.* to attract passers-by to a carnival, side show, or the like, by standing at the entrance and shouting its merits and the price of admission. —*v.t.* **8.** to utter or express with a bark or barks: *The director barked his orders at the actors.* **9. bark up the wrong tree,** *U.S.* to misdirect one's efforts: *If she expects me to get her a job, she's barking up the wrong tree.* [ME *berk(en),* OE *beorcan;* akin to OE *borcian* to bark, Icel *berkja* to bluster, Lith *burgėti* to growl, quarrel] —**bark′less,** *adj.*

bark[2] (bärk), *n.* **1.** *Bot.* the external covering of the woody stems, branches, and roots of plants, as distinct and separable from the wood itself. **2.** *Tanning.* a mixture of oak and hemlock barks. —*v.t.* **3.** to strip the bark from. **4.** to remove a circle of bark from. **5.** to rub off the skin of: *to bark one's shins.* **6.** to cover, enclose, or incrust with or as with bark. **7.** to treat with a bark infusion; tan. [ME < Scand; cf. Icel *börkr,* Dan, Sw *bark*] —**bark′less,** *adj.*

bark[3] (bärk), *n.* **1.** *Naut.* a sailing vessel having three or more masts, square-rigged on all but the aftermost mast, which is fore-and-aft-rigged. **2.** *Literary.* a boat or sailing vessel. Also, **barque.** [late ME *barke* << LL *barca* < ?]

Bark[3]

bark′ bee′tle, any of numerous beetles of the family *Scolytidae* that nest under the bark of trees.

bar·keep·er (bär′kē′pər), *n.* **1.** a person who owns or manages a bar where alcoholic beverages are sold. **2.** a bartender. Also, **bar′keep′.**

bark·en·tine (bär′kən tēn′), *n. Naut.* a sailing vessel having three or more masts, square-rigged on the foremast and fore-and-aft-rigged on the other masts. Also, **bark′an·tine′, barquentine, barquantine.** [BARK[3] + (BRIG)ANTINE]

bark·er[1] (bär′kər), *n.* **1.** an animal or person that barks. **2.** *Chiefly U.S. Informal.* a person who stands before a theater, side show of a carnival, etc., calling out to passers-by to enter. [BARK[1] + -ER[1]]

bark·er[2] (bär′kər), *n.* **1.** a person or thing that removes bark from trees. **2.** a person or thing that prepares bark for tanning. [BARK[2] + -ER[1]]

Bark·ley (bärk′lē), *n.* **Al·ben William** (al′bən), 1877–1956, vice president of the U.S. 1949–53.

Bar Kok·ba (bär′ kôḵ′bä), **Simon,** died A.D. 135, Hebrew leader of insurrection against the Romans 132–135. Also, **Bar Cocheba, Bar Cochba, Bar′ Koch′ba.**

bar·ley (bär′lē), *n.* **1.** a cereal plant of the genus *Hordeum,* whose awned flowers grow in tightly bunched spikes, with three small additional spikes at each node. **2.** the grain of this plant, used as food and in making beer, ale, and whiskey. [ME, OE *bærlīc* (adj.) = *bær-* (var. of *bere* barley; akin to Icel *barr* barley, L *far* spelt) + *-līc* -LY]

bar·ley·corn (bär′lē kôrn′), *n.* **1.** barley or a grain of barley. **2.** a measure equal to 1/3 of an inch.

Bar·ley·corn (bär′lē kôrn′), *n.* **John.** See **John Barleycorn.**

bar′ley sug′ar, a brittle, amber-colored, citrus-flavored candy, usually twisted into strips or molded into a variety of shapes. Also called **bar′ley can′dy.**

bar′ley wa′ter, a decoction of barley, used esp. as a medicament in the treatment of diarrhea in infants.

Bar·low (bär′lō), *n.* **Joel,** 1754–1812, U.S. poet and diplomat.

barm (bärm), *n. Brit. Informal.* yeast formed on malt liquors while fermenting. [ME *berme,* OE *beorma;* c. Fris *berme,* G *Bärme,* Sw *bärme;* akin to FERMENT]

bar·maid (bär′mād′), *n.* a female bartender.

bar·man (bär′mən), *n., pl.* **-men.** bartender.

Bar·me·cid·al (bär′mi sīd′ᵊl), *adj.* giving only the illusion of plenty; illusory: *a Barmecidal feast.*

Bar·me·cide (bär′mi sīd′), *n.* **1.** a Persian of Baghdad who, in a tale in *The Arabian Nights' Entertainments,* gave a beggar a pretended feast with empty dishes. —*adj.* **2.** Barmecidal. [Pers family name, lit., offspring of *Barmek,* with *-ide* -ID[2] for Pers *-ī* < Ar]

Bar·men (bär′mən), *n.* Wuppertal.

bar mitz·vah (bär mits′və; *Heb.* bäʀ′ mēts vä′), (*often caps.*) *Judaism.* **1.** a solemn ceremony held for admitting a Jewish boy as an adult member of the Jewish community and therefore responsible for religious duty, usually at the age of 13 and after having completed a study of Judaism. **2.** the boy participating in this ceremony. Also, **bar mits′-vah.** [< BiblAram *bar* son + Heb *miṣvāh* divine law, commandment]

barm·y (bär′mē), *adj.,* **barm·i·er, barm·i·est.** *Brit.* **1.** *Informal.* containing or resembling barm; frothy. **2.** *Slang.* balmy (def. 4).

barn[1] (bärn), *n.* a large building, as on a farm, for storing hay, grain, etc., and often for housing livestock. [ME *bern,* OE *berern* = *bere* (see BARLEY) + *ern, ærn* house, c. Goth *razn* house]

barn[2] (bärn), *n.* *Physics.* a unit of nuclear cross section, equal to 10^{-24} square centimeter. *Abbr.:* b [special use of BARN[1]; so called because the cross section was found to be surprisingly large]

Bar·na·bas (bär′nə bəs), *n.* the surname of the Cyprian Levite Joseph, a companion of Paul on his first missionary journey. Acts 4:36, 37.

bar·na·cle (bär′nə kəl), *n.* **1.** any marine crustacean of the group *Cirripedia,* usually having a calcareous shell, being either stalked **(goose barnacle)** and found attached to ship bottoms and floating timber, or stalkless **(rock barnacle** or **acorn barnacle)** and found attached to rocks, esp. in the intertidal zone. **2.** a thing or person that clings tenaciously. [dim. of early ME *bernekke* kind of goose, perh. < Celt; so called from a medieval belief that barnacles were a larval form of goose] —**bar′na·cled,** *adj.*

bar·na·cles (bär′nə kəlz), *n.* a pair of hinged branches for pinching the nose of an unruly horse. [ME *bernacle* bit, dim. of *bernac* < OF < ?]

Bar·nard (bär′närd), *n.* **Chris·tiaan N(eeth·ling)** (kris′-tyän nit′liŋ), born 1923, South African surgeon: performed first human-heart transplant 1967.

Bar·na·ul (bäʀ′nä o͞ol′), *n.* a city in the S RSFSR, on the Ob River. 373,000 (est. 1964).

barn′ dance′, **1.** a social gathering typically held in a barn and featuring square dances. **2.** any party featuring country dances, dress, music, etc.

Barns·ley (bärnz′lē), *n.* a city in S Yorkshire, in N England. 74,650 (1961).

barn·storm (bärn′stôrm′), *v.i.* **1.** to tour rural areas giving political campaign speeches, staging theatrical performances, playing exhibition baseball games, or the like. **2.** (of a pilot) to give exhibitions of stunt flying, participate in airplane races, etc., in the course of touring rural areas. —*v.t.* **3.** to tour (rural areas) as a barnstormer. —**barn′storm′er,** *n.*

barn′ swal′low, a common swallow, *Hirundo rustica,* that nests in barns and other similar buildings.

Bar·num (bär′nəm), *n.* **P(hineas) T(aylor),** 1810–91, U.S. showman and circus owner.

barn·yard (bärn′yärd′), *n.* **1.** a yard next to or around a barn, esp. a fenced area for animals. —*adj.* **2.** of, like, or befitting a barnyard. **3.** bawdy; off-color: *barnyard humor.*

baro-, a learned borrowing from Greek meaning "weight," "pressure," used in the formation of compound words: *barograph.* [comb. form of Gk *báros* weight; akin to Skt *guru,* L *gravis,* Goth *kaurus* heavy]

Ba·roc·chio (*It.* bä ʀôk′kyô), *n.* **Gia·co·mo** (jä′kô mô). See **Vignola, Giacomo da.**

Ba·ro·da (bə rō′də), *n.* a city in SE Gujarat state, in W India: former capital of the state of Baroda. 298,400 (1961).

bar·o·gram (bar′ə gram′), *n.* *Meteorol.* a record traced by a barograph.

bar·o·graph (bar′ə graf′, -gräf′), *n.* an automatic recording barometer. Also called **bar·o·met·ro·graph** (bar′ə me′-trə graf′, -gräf′). —**bar·o·graph·ic** (bar′ə graf′ik), *adj.*

Ba·ro·ja (bä ʀô′hä), *n.* **Pí·o** (pē′ô), 1872–1956, Spanish novelist.

ba·rom·e·ter (bə rom′i tər), *n.* **1.** *Meteorol.* any instrument that measures atmospheric pressure. Cf. **aneroid barometer, mercury barometer.** **2.** anything that indicates changes. —**bar·o·met·ric** (bar′ə me′trik), **bar′o-met′ri·cal,** *adj.* —**bar′o·met′ri·cal·ly,** *adv.*

bar′omet′ric pres′sure. See **atmospheric pressure.**

bar·on (bar′ən), *n.* **1.** a member of the lowest grade of nobility. **2.** (in Britain) **a.** a feudal vassal holding his lands under a direct grant from the king. **b.** a direct descendant of such a vassal or his equal in the nobility. **c.** a member of the House of Lords. **3.** *U.S.* an important financier or industrialist, esp. one with great power in a particular area: *an oil baron.* [ME < OF < LL *barōn-* (s. of *barō*) man < Gmc]

bar·on·age (bar′ə nij), *n.* **1.** the entire British peerage, including all dukes, marquesses, earls, viscounts, and barons. **2.** Also, **barony.** the dignity or rank of a baron. [ME *barunage* (see BARON, -AGE); r. ME *barnage* < OF]

bar·on·ess (bar′ə nis), *n.* **1.** the wife of a baron. **2.** a lady holding a baronial title in her own right. [late ME *baronnesse* < MF (see BARON, -ESS); r. ME *barnesse* < OF]

bar·on·et (bar′ə nit, -net′), *n.* a member of a British hereditary order of honor, ranking below the barons and above the knights, designated by *Sir* before the name, and *Baronet,* usually abbreviated *Bart.,* after: *Sir John Smith, Bart.* [late ME] —**bar′o·net′i·cal,** *adj.*

bar·on·et·age (bar′ə nit ij, -net′-), *n.* **1.** baronets collectively. **2.** baronetcy.

bar·on·et·cy (bar′ə nit sē, -net′-), *n., pl.* **-cies.** the rank or dignity of a baronet.

ba·rong (bä rông′, -roŋ′), *n.* a large, broad-bladed knife or cleaver used by the Moros. [appar. Philippine var. of PARANG]

ba·ro·ni·al (bə rō′nē əl), *adj.* **1.** pertaining to a baron, a barony, or to the order of barons. **2.** befitting a baron: *baronial splendor.* [BARONY + -AL[1]]

bar′on of beef′, *Chiefly Brit.* a joint of beef consisting of the two sirloins joined at the backbone; double sirloin.

bar·o·ny (bar′ə nē), *n., pl.* **-nies.** **1.** the domain of a baron. **2.** baronage (def. 2). [ME *baronie* < OF]

ba·roque (bə rōk′; *Fr.* bᴀ rôk′), *n.* **1.** (*often cap.*) the baroque style or period. **2.** anything extravagantly ornamented, esp. something so ornate as to be in bad taste. **3.** an irregularly shaped pearl. —*adj.* **4.** (*often cap.*) of or pertaining to a style of art and architecture prevailing in Europe during the 17th and first half of the 18th centuries that was characterized by elaborate and grotesque forms and ornamentation. **5.** (*sometimes cap.*) of or pertaining to the musical period following the Renaissance, extending roughly from 1600 to 1750. **6.** irregular in shape: *baroque pearls.* [< F < Pg *barroco* rough pearl < ?]

Baroque cupboard c1700

bar·o·scope (bar′ə skōp′), *n.* an instrument showing roughly the variations in atmospheric pressure. —**bar-o·scop·ic** (bar′ə skop′ik), **bar′o·scop′i·cal,** *adj.*

Ba·rot·se·land (bə rot′sə land′), *n.* a province in W Zambia: savannah grasslands. 366,100 (1963); 44,920 sq. mi.

ba·rouche (bə ro͞osh′), *n.* a four-wheeled carriage with a seat outside for the driver, facing seats inside for two couples, and with a calash top for the back seat. [< dial. G *Barutsche* < It *baroccio* < L *birōtus* two-wheeled = *bi-* BI-[2] + *rot(a)* wheel + *-us* adj. suffix]

Barouche

Ba·roz·zi (*It.* bä rôt′tsē), *n.* **Gia·co·mo** (jä′kô mô). See **Vignola, Giacomo da.**

barque (bärk), *n.* bark[3].

bar·quen·tine (bär′kən tēn′), *n.* barkentine. Also, **bar′quan·tine′.**

Bar·qui·si·me·to (bäʀ′kē sē me′tô), *n.* a city in N Venezuela: sugar and railroad center. 235,805 (est. 1965).

barr., barrister.

bar·rack[1] (bar′ək), *n.* Usually, **barracks. 1.** a building or range of buildings for lodging soldiers, esp. in garrison. **2.** any large, plain building in which many people are lodged. —*v.t., v.i.* **3.** to lodge in barracks. [< F *baraque* < Sp or Catalan *barraca* hut < ?]

bar·rack[2] (bar′ək), *Australian, Brit.* —*v.i.* **1.** to shout boisterously for or against a player or team; root. —*v.t.* **2.** to shout for or against. [? back formation from *barracking,* var. of *barrakin* gibberish (Cockney) < ?] —**bar′-rack·er,** *n.*

bar′racks bag′, a cylindrical, heavy cotton bag typically having a drawstring top, as used by military personnel for carrying personal belongings.

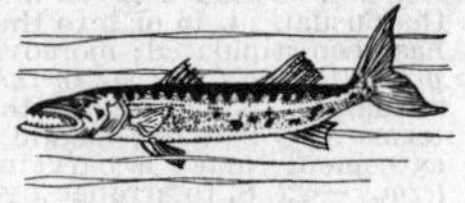

Barracuda, *Sphyraena barracuda* (Length 6 ft.)

bar·ra·cu·da (bar′ə ko͞o′-də), *n., pl.* (*esp. collectively*) **-da,** (*esp. referring to two or more kinds or species*) **-das.** any of several elongated, predaceous, tropical and subtropical marine fishes of the genus *Sphyraena,* certain species of which are used for food. [< AmerSp < ?]

bar·rage (bə räzh′; *esp. Brit.* bar′äzh *for 1, 2, 4;* bär′ij *for 3*), *n., v.,* **-raged, -rag·ing.** —*n.* **1.** *Mil.* a barrier of artillery fire. **2.** an overwhelming quantity: *a barrage of questions.* **3.** *Civ. Eng.* an artificial obstruction in a watercourse to increase the depth of the water, facilitate irrigation, etc. —*v.t.* **4.** to subject to a barrage. [< F; see BAR[1], -AGE]

barrage′ balloon′, a balloon or blimp from which wires or nets are hung for protecting military areas and cities against attacks from low-flying enemy aircraft.

bar·ra·mun·da (bar′ə mun′də), *n., pl.* **-das,** (*esp. collectively*) **-da.** a lungfish, *Neoceratodus forsteri,* of the rivers of Australia. [< native Austral]

bar·ra·mun·di (bar′ə mun′dē), *n., pl.* **-dis, -dies,** (*esp. collectively*) **-di.** barramunda.

bar·ran·ca (bə raŋ′kə; *Sp.* bäʀ räŋ′kä), *n., pl.* **-cas** (-kəz; *Sp.* -käs). a steep-walled ravine, gorge, or gully. [< Sp, var. of *barranco* < ?]

Bar·ran·quil·la (bäʀ′rän kē′yä), *n.* a seaport in N Colombia, on the Magdalena River. 452,140 (est. 1961).

bar·ra·tor (bar′ə tər), *n.* *Law.* a person who commits barratry. Also, **bar′ra·ter, barretor.** [ME *barettour* brawler, fighter = *barete, barate* (< Scand; cf. Icel *barātta* contention, fighting, akin to *berja* to fight) + *-our* -OR[2]]

bar·ra·try (bar′ə trē), *n.* *Law.* **1.** fraud by a master or crew at the expense of the owners of a ship or its cargo. **2.** the offense of frequently exciting and stirring up suits and quarrels. **3.** the purchase or sale of ecclesiastical preferments. Also, **barretry.** [late ME *barratrie* < MF *baraterie* combat, fighting. See BARRATOR, -Y[3]] —**bar′ra·trous,** *adj.* —**bar′ra-trous·ly,** *adv.*

Bar·rault (bᴀ rō′), *n.* **Jean-Louis** (zhäɴ lwē′), born 1910, French actor and director.

barre (bär), *v.t., v.i.,* **barred, barr·ing.** to place a finger across (two or more strings simultaneously) on a guitar, lute, banjo, etc. [alter. of F *barré* ptp. of *barrer* to BAR]

barred (bärd), *adj.* **1.** provided with one or more bars. **2.** closed, protected, or locked against attack or intruders, as with a bolt or bar. **3.** striped; streaked. **4.** *Ornith.* (of feathers) marked with transverse bands of distinctive color.

bar·rel (bar′əl), *n., v.,* **-reled, -rel·ing** or (*esp. Brit.*) **-relled, -rel·ling.** —*n.* **1.** a cylindrical vessel, usually of wood, with slightly bulging sides made of staves hooped together, and with flat, parallel ends. **2.** a standard quantity that such a vessel can hold, as, in the U.S., 31½ gallons of liquid or 105 dry quarts of fruits or vegetables. **3.** any large quantity:

a barrel of fun. **4.** a cylindrical container, case, or part. **5.** *Ordn.* the tube of a gun. **6.** *Horol.* the cylindrical case in a watch or clock within which the mainspring is coiled. **7.** the trunk of a quadruped, esp. of a horse, cow, etc. **8. over a barrel,** in no position to resist a demand. —*v.t.* **9.** to put or pack in a barrel or barrels. —*v.i.* **10.** *Slang.* to travel or drive very fast: *to barrel down a road.* [ME *barell* < OF *baril,* ? = *barre* stave (see BAR¹) + *-il* < L *-īle,* neut. of *-īlis* -ILE]

bar·rel-chest·ed (bar′əl ches′tid), *adj.* having a massive, well-developed chest or thorax.

bar′rel cuff′, a cuff on a sleeve, formed by a band of material, usually fastened by a button. Cf. **French cuff.**

bar·rel·ful (bar′əl fo͝ol′), *n., pl.* **-fuls.** the amount that a barrel can hold; the contents of a filled barrel. [ME]

bar·rel·head (bar′əl hed′), *n.* either of the round, flat sections which form the top and bottom of a barrel. **2. on the barrelhead,** in advance or on demand: *to pay cash on the barrelhead.* [BARREL + HEAD]

bar·rel·house (bar′əl hous′), *n., pl.* **-hous·es** (-hou′ziz) for 1. **1.** *U.S. Slang.* a disreputable drinking place, esp. one in New Orleans in the early part of the 20th century. **2.** a vigorous, unpolished, and loud style of jazz originating in the barrelhouses of New Orleans.

bar′rel or′gan, a musical instrument in which air from a bellows is admitted to a set of pipes by means of pins inserted into a revolving barrel; hand organ.

bar′rel roll′, *Aeron.* a maneuver in which an airplane executes a complete roll by revolving once around an axis parallel to the longitudinal axis of the airplane.

bar′rel vault′, *Archit.* a vault having the form of a very deep arch, as in a tunnel. See illus. at **vault¹.** —**bar′rel-vault′ed,** *adj.*

bar·ren (bar′ən), *adj.* **1.** not producing or incapable of producing offspring: *a barren woman.* **2.** unproductive; unfruitful: *barren land; a barren effort.* **3.** without features of interest; dull: *a barren period in American architecture.* **4.** destitute; bereft; lacking (usually fol. by *of*): *barren of tender feelings.* —*n.* **5.** Usually, **barrens.** level or slightly rolling land, usually with a sandy soil and few trees, and relatively infertile. [ME *barain* < AF; OF *brahain* < ?] —**bar′ren·ly,** *adv.* —**bar′ren·ness,** *n.* —**Syn. 1.** childless, infertile. **2.** ineffectual, ineffective. —**Ant. 1–4.** fertile.

Bar′ren Grounds′, a sparsely inhabited region of tundras in N Canada, esp. in the area W of Hudson Bay. Also called **Bar′ren Lands′.**

Bar·rès (bA res′), *n.* **Mau·rice** (mō rēs′), 1862–1923, French novelist, writer on politics, and politician.

bar·ret (bar′it), *n.* a small cap, akin to the biretta, worn in the Middle Ages by soldiers and ecclesiastics. [< F *barrette* < It *berretta* BIRETTA]

bar·re·tor (bar′i tər), *n.* *Law.* barrator.

bar·re·try (bar′i trē), *n.* *Law.* barratry.

bar·rette (bə ret′), *n.* a clasp for holding a woman's hair. [earlier *barette;* see BAR¹, -ETTE]

bar·ri·cade (bar′ə kād′, bar′ə kād′), *n., v.,* **-cad·ed, -cad·ing.** —*n.* **1.** a hastily constructed defensive barrier. **2.** any barrier that obstructs passage. —*v.t.* **3.** to obstruct or block with or as with a barricade. **4.** to shut in and defend with or as with a barricade. [< F; r. earlier *barricado* < Sp *barricada* = *barric(a)* barrel + *-ada* -ADE¹] —**bar′ri·cad′er,** *n.* —**Syn. 1.** See **bar. 4.** fortify.

Bar·rie (bar′ē), *n.* **Sir James M(atthew),** 1860–1937, Scottish novelist, short-story writer, and playwright.

bar·ri·er (bar′ē ər), *n.* **1.** anything built or serving to bar passage, as a railing or fence. **2.** any natural bar or obstacle: *a mountain barrier.* **3.** anything that restrains or obstructs: *a trade barrier.* **4.** a limit or boundary of any kind: *the barriers of caste.* **5.** (*often cap.*) *Phys. Geog.* the portion of the antarctic ice sheet extending beyond the land. [< MF *barriere* = *barre* BAR¹ + *-iere* < L *-āria* -ARY; r. ME *barrere* < AF < ML *barrera*] —**Syn. 1.** palisade, wall. See **bar.**

bar′rier reef′, *Oceanog.* a reef of coral running roughly parallel to the shore and separated from it by deep water.

Bar′rier Reef′. See **Great Barrier Reef.**

bar·ring (bär′ing), *prep.* excepting; except for: *Barring accidents, I'll be there.*

bar·rio (bäR′Ryô; *Eng.* bar′ē ō′), *n., pl.* **-rios** (-Ryôs; *Eng.* -ē ōz′). **1.** (in Spain and countries colonized by Spain) one of the districts into which a town or city, together with the contiguous rural territory, is divided. **2.** *U.S. Slang.* a slum inhabited predominantly by Puerto Ricans or Mexicans. [< Sp = Ar *barrī* of open country (*barr* outside, open country + *-ī* adj. suffix) + Sp *-o* n. suffix]

bar·ris·ter (bar′i stər), *n.* *Law.* **1.** (in England) a lawyer who is a member of one of the Inns of Court and has the privilege of pleading in the higher courts. Cf. **solicitor** (def. 4). **2.** *U.S. Informal.* a lawyer. [*barri-* (comb. form of BAR¹) + -STER] —**bar·ri·ste·ri·al** (bar′i stēr′ē əl), *adj.*

bar·room (bär′ro͞om′, -ro͝om′), *n.* *U.S.* an establishment or room where alcoholic beverages are served.

bar·row¹ (bar′ō), *n.* **1.** a flat, rectangular frame used for carrying a load, esp. one with projecting shafts at each end for handles; handbarrow. **2.** a wheelbarrow. **3.** *Brit.* a pushcart used by street vendors, esp. by costermongers. [ME *bar(e)we,* OE *bearwe;* akin to BEAR¹]

bar·row² (bar′ō), *n.* **1.** Also called **tumulus.** a burial mound of the prehistoric inhabitants of Great Britain and Scandinavia. **2.** *Chiefly Brit.* a hill (sometimes used in combination): *Whitbarrow.* [ME *berwe;* OE *beorg* hill, mound; c. D, G *Berg,* Icel *bjarg, berg,* Skt *bṛh-* in *bṛhant* high]

bar·row³ (bar′ō), *n.* a castrated male swine. [ME *barow,* OE *bearg;* c. OHG *barug,* Icel *börgr*]

Bar·row (bar′ō), *n.* **1.** Also called **Bar·row-in-Fur·ness** (bar′ō in fûr′nis). a seaport in NW Lancashire, in NW England. 64,824 (1961). **2. Point,** the N tip of Alaska.

Bar·ry (bar′ē), *n.* **1. Sir Charles,** 1795–1860, English architect. **2. Philip,** 1896–1949, U.S. playwright.

Bar·ry·more (bar′ə mōr′, -môr′), *n.* **1. Maurice** (*Herbert Blythe*), 1847–1905, U.S. and English actor, born in India. **2.** his children: **Ethel,** 1879–1959, **John,** 1882–1942, and **Lionel,** 1878–1954, U.S. actors.

bar′ sin′ister, **1.** *Heraldry.* (not in technical use) a bend sinister or a baton. **2.** the proof, condition, or stigma of illegitimate birth in the family line.

bar·stool (bär′sto͞ol′), *n.* a high stool or seat, often used for seating a customer at a bar.

Bart., Baronet.

bar·tend (bär′tend′), *v.i.* to serve or work as a bartender, esp. as an occupation. [back formation from BARTENDER]

bar·tend·er (bär′ten′dər), *n.* *Chiefly U.S.* a person who mixes and serves drinks at a bar.

bar·ter (bär′tər), *v.i.* **1.** to trade by exchange of commodities. —*v.t.* **2.** to exchange in trade, as one commodity for another; trade. **3.** to bargain away unwisely or dishonorably (usually fol. by *away*). —*n.* **4.** the act or practice of bartering. **5.** merchandise for bartering. [late ME, of unexplained orig.; cf. MF *barater* to cheat, exchange < *barate* confusion, trouble, deceit, appar. < Scand; cf. Icel *barātta* trouble, strife] —**bar′ter·er,** *n.* —**Syn. 1, 2.** See **trade.**

Barth (bärth *for 1;* bärt *for 2*), *n.* **1. John Sim·mons** (sim′ənz), born 1930, U.S. novelist. **2. Karl,** 1886–1968, Swiss theologian.

Bar·thol·di (bär thol′dē; *Fr.* bAR tôl dē′), *n.* **Fré·dé·ric Au·guste** (fRā dā RēK′ ō gYst′), 1834–1904, French sculptor who designed the Statue of Liberty.

Bar·thol·o·mew (bär thol′ə myo͞o′), *n.* one of the 12 apostles. Mark 3:18.

Bar·thou (bAR to͞o′), *n.* **(Jean) Louis** (zhäN lwē), 1862–1934, French statesman and author.

bar·ti·zan (bär′ti zən, bär′ti zan′), *n.* *Archit.* a small overhanging turret on a wall or tower. [alter. of *bertisene,* misspelling of *bretising,* var. of *brattising.* See BRATTICE] —**bar′ti·zaned,** *adj.*

Bartizan

Bar·tles·ville (bär′tᵊlz vil′), *n.* a city in NE Oklahoma. 29,683 (1970).

Bart·lett (bärt′lit), *n.* *Hort.* **1.** a large, yellow, juicy variety of pear. **2.** the tree bearing this fruit. Also called **Bart′lett pear′.** [so named by Enoch *Bartlett* of Dorchester, Mass.]

Bart·lett (bärt′lit), *n.* **1. John,** 1820–1905, U.S. publisher and compiler. **2. Josiah,** 1729–95, U.S. physician and statesman. **3. Vernon,** born 1894, English writer.

Bar·tók (bär′tok; *Hung.* bor′tōk), *n.* **Bé·la** (bā′lə; *Hung.* bâ′lo), 1881–1945, Hungarian composer.

Bar·to·lom·me·o (bär tol′ə mā′ō), *n.* **Fra** (frä), (*Baccio della Porta*), 1475–1517, Italian painter.

Bar·ton (bär′tᵊn), *n.* **Clara,** 1821–1912, U.S. philanthropist who organized the American Red Cross in 1881.

Bar·tram (bär′trəm), *n.* **John,** 1699–1777, U.S. botanist.

Bar·uch (bâr′ək *for 1;* bə ro͞ok′ *for 2*), *n.* **1.** the friend of Jeremiah and nominal author of the book of Baruch in the Apocrypha. Jer. 32:12. **2. Bernard Man·nes** (man′əs), 1870–1965, U.S. statesman and financier.

bar·y·on (bar′ē on′), *n.* *Physics.* a nucleon or a hyperon. [< Gk *barý(s)* heavy + -ON¹]

ba·ry·ta (bə rī′tə), *n.* *Chem.* **1.** a poisonous solid, BaO, highly reactive with water, used chiefly as a dehydrating agent and in the manufacture of glass. **2.** the hydrated form of this compound, $Ba(OH)_2{\cdot}8H_2O$, used chiefly in the industrial preparation of beet sugar and for refining animal and vegetable oils. [< NL = *bary-* (< Gk *barýs* heavy) + *-ta* (< Gk *-tēs* n. suffix)] —**ba·ryt·ic** (bə rit′ik), *adj.*

ba·ry·tes (bə rī′tēz), *n.* *Mineral.* barite.

bar·y·tone¹ (bar′i tōn′), *n., adj.* *Music.* baritone.

bar·y·tone² (bar′i tōn′), *Classical Gk. Gram.* —*adj.* **1.** having the last syllable unaccented. —*n.* **2.** a barytone word. [< Gk *barýton(os)* = *barý(s)* heavy, deep (of sound) + *tónos* TONE]

ba·sal (bā′səl, -zəl), *adj.* **1.** of, at, or forming the base of something. **2.** forming a basis; fundamental; basic. **3.** *Physiol.* **a.** indicating a standard low level of activity of an organism as present during total rest. **b.** of an amount required to maintain this level. **4.** *Med.* serving to induce a preliminary or light anesthesia prior to total anesthetization. —**ba′sal·ly,** *adv.*

ba′sal metabol′ic rate′, *Physiol.* the rate of oxygen intake and heat discharge in an organism in a basal state. *Abbr.:* B.M.R.

ba′sal metab′olism, *Physiol.* the energy turnover of the body in a basal state.

ba·salt (bə sôlt′, bas′ôlt, bā′sôlt), *n.* the dark, dense igneous rock of a lava flow or minor intrusion, composed essentially of labradorite and pyroxene and often displaying a columnar structure. [< LL *basalt(es),* alter. of L *basanītes* < Gk *basanī́tēs* (*líthos*) touchstone, prob. of Afr orig.] —**ba·sal′tic, ba·sal·tine** (bə sôl′tin, -tīn), *adj.*

ba·salt·ware (bə sôlt′wâr′, bas′ôlt-, bā′sôlt-), *n.* unglazed stoneware, usually black with a dull gloss, developed by Josiah Wedgwood. Also called **ba·sal·tes** (bə-sôl′tēz).

bas bleu (bä blœ′), *pl.* **bas bleus** (bä blœ′). *French.* a bluestocking.

bas·cule (bas′kyo͞ol), *n.* *Civ. Eng.* a device operating like a balance or seesaw, esp. an arrangement of a movable bridge (**bas′cule bridge′**) by which the rising floor or section is counterbalanced by a weight. [< F *ba(s)cule* = *bas* low (see BASE²) + *cul* rump (see CULET) + *-e* fem. suffix]

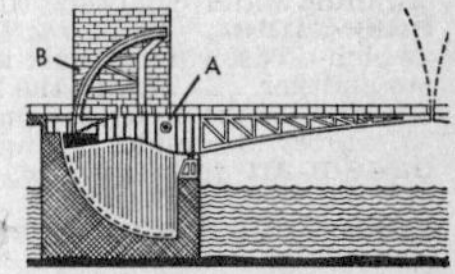

Bascule bridge
A, Pivot about which bridge swings in rising; B, Toothed quadrant engaging with machinery

base¹ (bās), *n., adj., v.,* **based, bas·ing.** —*n.* **1.** the bottom support or part of anything; that on which a thing stands or rests. **2.** a fundamental principle or groundwork; foundation; basis: *the base of needed reforms.* **3.** the bottom layer or coating, as of make-up or paint. **4.** *Archit.* **a.** the distinctively treated portion of a column or pier below the shaft or shafts. **b.** the distinctively treated lowermost portion of any construction, as a monument, exterior wall, etc. **5.**

Bot., Zool. **a.** the part of an organ nearest its point of attachment. **b.** the point of attachment. **6.** the principal element or ingredient of a compound: *face cream with a lard base.* **7.** that from which a commencement, as of action or reckoning, is made; starting point or point of departure. **8.** *Baseball.* **a.** any of the four corners of the diamond, esp. first, second, or third base. Cf. **home plate. b.** a stuffed square sack for marking first, second, or third base. **9.** a starting line or point for a race or game. **10.** a goal line or goal, as in hockey. **11.** *Mil.* **a.** an area or place from which military or naval operations proceed. **b.** a supply installation for a large military force. **12.** *Geom.* the line or surface forming the part of a figure that is most nearly horizontal or on which it is supposed to stand. **13.** a point, line, or surface from which measurements are taken. **14.** *Math.* the number that serves as a starting point for a logarithmic or other numerical system. **15.** *Survey.* See under **triangulation** (def. 1). **16.** *Painting.* **a.** vehicle (def. 7). **b.** Also called **carrier.** inert matter, used in the preparation of lakes, onto which a coloring compound is precipitated. **17.** *Chem.* **a.** a compound that reacts with an acid to form a salt. **b.** the hydroxide of a metal or of an electropositive element or group. **c.** a group or molecule that accepts protons. **d.** a molecule or ion containing an atom with a free pair of electrons that can be donated to an acid. **18.** *Gram.* the part of a complex word, consisting of one or more morphemes, to which derivational or inflectional affixes may be added, as *want* in *unwanted, biolog-* in *biological,* etc. Cf. **root**[1] (def. 11), **stem**[1] (def. 12). **19.** *Heraldry.* the lower part of an escutcheon. **20.** *Jewelry.* pavilion (def. 5). **21. get to first base.** See **first base** (def. 2). **22. in base,** *Heraldry.* in the lower part of an escutcheon. **23. off base, a.** *Baseball.* not touching a base *The pitcher caught him off base.* **b.** *Informal.* badly mistaken **24. on base,** *Baseball.* having reached a base or bases. Also, **on.** —*adj.* **25.** serving as or forming a base.
—*v.t.* **26.** to make or form a base or foundation for. **27.** to establish, as a fact or conclusion (usually fol. by *on* or *upon*): *He based his assumption on the fact that she had no alibi.* **28.** to place or establish on a base or basis; ground; establish: *Our plan is based on a rising economy.* **29.** to station, place, or establish (usually fol. by *at* or *on*): *He is based at Fort Benning.* [ME < MF < L *basis* BASIS]
—Syn. 1. BASE, BASIS, FOUNDATION refer to anything upon which a structure is built and upon which it rests. BASE usually refers to a literal supporting structure: *the base of a statue.* BASIS more often refers to a figurative support: *the basis of a report.* FOUNDATION implies a solid, secure understructure: *the foundation of a skyscraper.*

base[2] (bās), *adj.,* **bas·er, bas·est,** *n.* —*adj.* **1.** morally low; without dignity of sentiment; mean-spirited, selfish, or cowardly. **2.** of little or no value; worthless: *base materials.* **3.** debased or counterfeit, as coinage. Cf. **base metal** (def. 1). **4.** of illegitimate birth. **5.** *Old Eng. Law.* held by tenure less than freehold in return for a service viewed as somewhat demeaning to the tenant. **6.** not classical or refined: *base language.* **7.** *Archaic.* **a.** of humble origin or station. **b.** of small height. **c.** low in place, position, or degree: *base employment.* **8.** *Obs.* deep or grave in sound; bass: *the base tones of a viol.* **9.** *Music. Obs.* bass[1] (def. 4). —*n.* **10.** *Music. Obs.* bass[1] (defs. 1, 2). [late ME *bass, bace* < MF *bas* (masc.), *basse* (fem.) < LL *bass(us), -a, -um* low, short, perh. < Gk *bássōn* deeper] **—base′ly,** *adv.* **—base′ness,** *n.*
—Syn. 1. despicable, contemptible, ignoble. See **mean**[2].

base·ball (bās′bôl′), *n.* **1.** a game of ball played by two nine-man teams on a square formed by lines connecting four bases, all of which must be touched by a base runner in order to score a run. **2.** the ball used in this game, typically a sphere approximately three inches in diameter with a twine-covered center of cork covered by stitched horsehide.

base′ball glove′, a padded leather glove having a pocket in the area over the palm and webbing between the sections for the thumb and forefinger, for use by baseball players in the field. Cf. **mitt** (def. 2).

base·board (bās′bōrd′, -bôrd′), *n.* **1.** Also called **mop-board, skirting.** a board forming the foot of an interior wall. **2.** a board forming the base of anything.

base·born (bās′bôrn′), *adj.* **1.** of humble birth. **2.** born out of wedlock; illegitimate. **3.** having a base character or nature; mean.

base·burn·er (bās′bûr′nər), *n.* *U.S.* a stove or furnace with a self-acting fuel hopper over the fire chamber. Also, **base′ burn′er, base′-burn′er.**

base′ hit′, *Baseball.* a fair ball enabling the batter to reach base safely without the commission of an error in the field or a force-out or fielder's choice on a base runner.

Ba·sel (bä′zəl), *n.* a city in NW Switzerland, on the Rhine River. 213,000 (est. 1970). Also, **Basle.** French, **Bâle.**

base·less (bās′lis), *adj.* having no base in reason or fact.

base′ lev′el, *Phys. Geog.* the lowest level to which running water can erode the land.

base′ line′, **1.** *Baseball.* the area between bases within which a base runner must keep when running from one base to another. **2.** *Tennis.* the line at each end of a tennis court, parallel to the net, that marks the in-bounds limit of play. **3.** *Survey.* See under **triangulation** (def. 1).

base·man (bās′mən), *n., pl.* **-men.** *Baseball.* the first, second, or third baseman.

base·ment (bās′mənt), *n.* **1.** a story of a building, partly or wholly underground. **2.** (in classical architecture) the portion of a building beneath the principal story, treated as a single unit. **3.** the lowermost portion of a structure.

base′ met′al, **1.** any metal other than a precious or noble metal, as copper, lead, zinc, tin, etc. Cf. **precious metal. 2.** the principal metal of an alloy. **3.** the principal metal of a piece underlying a coating of another metal; core.

Ba·sen·ji (bə sen′jē), *n.* one of an African breed of dogs having a chestnut coat, with white points and a curled tail and characterized by the inability to bark. [pl. of Bantu *mosenji, musenji* native]

base′ on balls′, *pl.* **bases on balls.** *Baseball.* the advancing to first base of a batter to whom four balls have been pitched. Also called **walk, pass.**

base′ pay′, pay received for a given work period, as an hour or week, but not including additional pay, as for overtime work.

base′ run′ner, *Baseball.* a player of the team at bat who is on base or is trying to run from one base to another.

ba·ses[1] (bā′sēz), *n.* pl. of **basis.**

bas·es[2] (bā′siz), *n.* pl. of **base**[1].

bash (bash), *Slang.* —*v.t.* **1.** to strike with a crushing or smashing blow. —*n.* **2.** a crushing blow. **3.** *Slang.* a lively party; a wildly good time. [? alter. of *pash,* ME *pas(s)he(n)*; appar. imit.]

Ba·shan (bā′shən), *n.* a region in ancient Palestine, E of the Jordan River.

ba·shaw (bə shô′), *n.* **1.** pasha. **2.** *Informal.* a person who is important, imperious, or self-important. [< Turk *bāshā,* var. of *pāshā* PASHA]

bash·ful (bash′fəl), *adj.* **1.** uncomfortably diffident and easily embarrassed. **2.** indicative of, accompanied by, or proceeding from bashfulness. [(A)BASH + -FUL] **—bash′ful·ly,** *adv.* **—bash′ful·ness,** *n.* **—Syn.** See **shy**[1].

bash·i-ba·zouk (bash′ē bə zōōk′), *n.* one of a class of irregular mounted troops in the Turkish military service. [< Turk *bashi bozuk,* lit., the head (is) turned]

Bash·kir′ Auton′omous So′viet So′cialist Re·pub′lic (bäsh kēr′), an administrative division of the RSFSR, in E Soviet Union in Europe. 3,335,000 (1959); ab. 54,200 sq. mi. *Cap.:* Ufa.

ba·sic (bā′sik), *adj.* **1.** of, pertaining to, or forming a base or basis; fundamental: *a basic principle; the basic ingredient.* **2.** *Chem.* **a.** pertaining to, of the nature of, or containing a base. **b.** not having all of the hydroxyls of the base replaced by the acid group, or having the metal or its equivalent united partly to the acid group and partly to oxygen. **c.** alkaline. **3.** *Metall.* noting, pertaining to, or made by a steelmaking process in which the furnace or converter is lined with a basic or nonsiliceous material. Cf. **acid** (def. 8). **4.** *Geol.* (of a rock) having relatively little silica. —*n.* **5.** something that is basic or fundamental.

BASIC (bā′sik), *n.* a widely adopted programming language that uses English words, punctuation marks, and algebraic notation to facilitate communication between the operator or lay user and the computer. [*b(eginner's) a(ll-purpose) s(ymbolic) i(nstruction) c(ode)*]

ba′sic air′man. See under **airman** (def. 2).

ba·si·cal·ly (bā′sik lē), *adv.* fundamentally.

Ba′sic Eng′lish, a simplified form of English restricted to an 850-word vocabulary and a few simple rules of grammar, intended esp. as an international auxiliary language.

ba·sic·i·ty (bā sis′i tē), *n.* *Chem.* **1.** the state of being a base. **2.** the power of an acid to react with bases, dependent on the number of replaceable hydrogen atoms of the acid.

ba′sic lead′ car′bonate (led), *Chem.* ceruse.

ba′sic magen′ta, fuchsin.

ba′sic ox′ygen proc′ess, an improved high-speed method of steelmaking, in which oxygen of high purity is blown at high velocity through a water-cooled pipe onto the surface of a bath **(ba′sic ox′ygen fur′nace)** containing steel scrap and molten pig iron.

ba′sic train′ing, *Mil.* a period following a person's induction into the armed forces devoted to training in basic military comportment, duties, and combat.

ba·sid·i·o·my·cete (bə sid′ē ō mī sēt′), *n.* a fungus of the class *Basidiomycetes,* characterized by bearing the spores on a basidium, including the smuts, rust, mushrooms, puffballs, etc. [BASIDI(UM) + -o- + *-mycete,* sing. of -MYCETES] **—ba·sid′i·o·my·ce′tous,** *adj.*

ba·sid·i·o·spore (bə sid′ē ō spōr′, -spôr′), *n.* *Bot.* a spore that is borne by a basidium. **—ba·sid·i·os·por·ous** (bə sid′ē os′pər əs, -ē ə spōr′əs, -spôr′-), *adj.*

ba·sid·i·um (bə sid′ē əm), *n., pl.* **-sid·i·a** (-sid′ē ə). *Bot.* a special form of sporophore, characteristic of basidiomycetous fungi, on which the sexual spores are borne, usually at the tips of slender projections. [< NL = BAS(IS) + -IDIUM] **—ba·sid′i·al,** *adj.*

Ba·sie (bā′sē), *n.* **William** ("*Count*"), born 1904, U.S. jazz pianist, bandleader, and composer.

bas·il (baz′əl, bā′zəl), *n.* any of several aromatic, labiate herbs of the genus *Ocimum,* as *O. Basilicum* **(sweet basil)** or *O. minimum* **(bush basil),** the leaves of which are used in cooking. [late ME *basile* < MF < LL *basil(icum)* < Gk *basilikón,* neut. of *basilikós* royal. See BASILIC]

Bas·il (baz′əl, bas′-), *n.* **Saint** ("*the Great*") A.D. 329?–379, bishop of Caesarea in Asia Minor (brother of Saint Gregory of Nyssa). Also, **Basilius.**

bas·i·lar (bas′ə lər), *adj.* **1.** pertaining to or situated at the base, esp. the base of the skull. **2.** basal. Also, **bas·i·lar·y** (bas′ə ler′ē). [< early NL *basilāre,* ML *bassil(e)* pelvis + *-āre,* neut. of *-āris* -AR[1]]

Ba·sil·don (bā′zəl dən), *n.* a town in S Essex, in SE England: designated as a model residential community after World War II. 53,707 (1961).

ba·sil·ic (bə sil′ik), *adj.* **1.** kingly; royal. **2.** Also, **ba·sil·i·can** (bə sil′i kən), **ba·sil′i·cal.** of, pertaining to, or like a basilica. [< L *basilic(us)* < Gk *basilikós* royal = *basil(eús)* king + *-ikos* -IC]

ba·sil·i·ca (bə sil′i kə), *n.* **1.** (in ancient Rome) a large oblong building used as a hall of justice and public meeting place. **2.** an early Christian or medieval church having a nave, two or four aisles, one or more semicircular vaulted apses, and open timber roofs. **3.** one of the seven main churches of Rome or any Roman Catholic church or cathedral accorded the same ceremonial privileges. [< L < Gk *basilikḗ* hall, short for *basilikḗ oikía* royal house. See BASILIC]

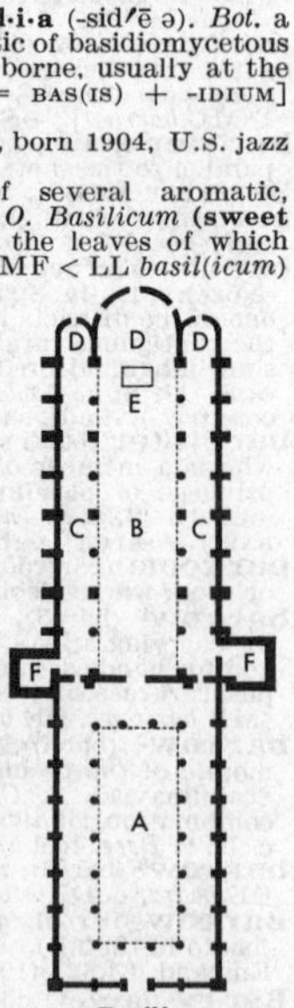

Basilica (Christian)
A, Atrium; B, Nave; C, Aisle; D, Apse; E, High altar; F, Tower

Ba·si·li·ca·ta (bä zē′lē kä′tä), *n.* Italian name of **Lucania.**

basil′ic vein′, *Anat.* a large vein on the inner side of the arm. [< L *vēna basilica* royal vein]

bas·i·lisk (bas′ə lisk, baz′-), *n.* **1.** *Class. Myth.* a creature, variously described as a serpent, lizard, or dragon, said to kill by its breath or look. **2.** any of several tropical American lizards of the genus *Basiliscus,* noted for their ability to run at high speeds on the hind legs: capable of short dashes across the surface of water. [< L *basilisc(us)* < Gk *basilískos* princeling, basilisk = *basil(eús)* king + *-iskos* dim. suffix] —**bas·i·lis·cine** (bas′ə lis′in, -īn, baz′-), **bas′i·lis′can,** *adj.*

Basilisk, *Basiliscus mitratu* (Length 2½ to 3 ft.)

Ba·sil·i·us (bə sil′ē əs, -zil′-), *n.* **Saint.** See **Basil, Saint.**

ba·sin (bā′sən), *n.* **1.** a shallow, usually round container or pan, used chiefly to hold water or other liquid, esp. for washing. **2.** the quantity held by such a container. **3.** a partially sheltered area along a shore where boats may be moored: *a yacht basin.* **4.** *Geol.* an area in which the strata dip from the margins toward a common center. **5.** *Phys. Geog.* **a.** a depression in the earth's surface or ocean floor: *river basin.* **b.** the tract of country drained by a river and its tributaries. [ME *bacin* < OF < LL *bacchīn(on)* = *bacc(a)* water vessel + *-īnum* -INE[1]] —**ba′sined,** *adj.* —**ba′sin·like′,** *adj.*

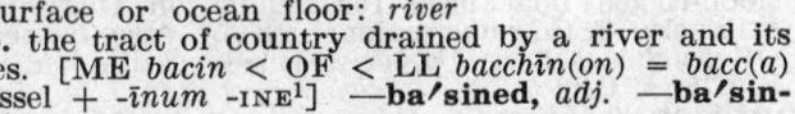

bas·i·net (bas′ə nit, -net′, bas′ə net′), *n.* *Armor.* **1.** a globular or pointed helmet of the 14th century, often provided with a visor or aventail. **2.** a supplementary cap that is worn underneath a helm. [ME *bas(e)net* < MF *bacinet* = *bacin* BASIN + *-et* -ET]

ba·sip·e·tal (bā sip′i tᵊl), *adj.* *Bot.* (of a plant structure) developing toward the base during growth. [BASI(S) + -PETAL]

ba·sis (bā′sis), *n., pl.* **-ses** (-sēz). **1.** the bottom or base of anything. **2.** anything upon which something is based; fundamental. **3.** the principal constituent or ingredient. [< L < Gk *básis;* cf. BASE[1]] —**Syn. 1, 2.** See **base**[1]. **2.** footing. **3.** element; essential.

bask (bask, bäsk), *v.i.* **1.** to lie in or be exposed to a pleasant warmth: *to bask in the sunshine.* **2.** to enjoy something, as favor or praise: *He basked in royal favor.* —*v.t.* **3.** to expose to warmth, heat, etc. (usually used reflexively): *to bask oneself.* [late ME < Scand; cf. Icel *bathask* to bathe oneself = *bath-* BATH[1] + *-ask* reflexive suffix]

Bas·ker·ville (bas′kər vil′), *n.* **1. John,** 1706–75, English typographer and manufacturer of lacquered ware. **2.** a style of type.

bas·ket (bas′kit, bä′skit), *n.* **1.** a container made of straw, rushes, thin strips of wood, string, strands of wire, or the like, woven, sewn, interlaced, or looped together. **2.** the contents or quantity held by such a basket: *How much is a basket of plums?* **3.** an open gondola, as for passengers, suspended beneath a balloon. **4.** *Basketball.* **a.** an open net suspended from a metal rim attached to a backboard and through which the ball must pass in order for a player to score points. **b.** a score, counting two for a field goal and one for a free throw. [ME, perh. north OE *bæstet (by dissimilation) = *bæste (adj.) (c. OE *bæsten* made of BAST) + *-et* n. suffix. Cf. THICKET] —**bas′ket·like′,** *adj.*

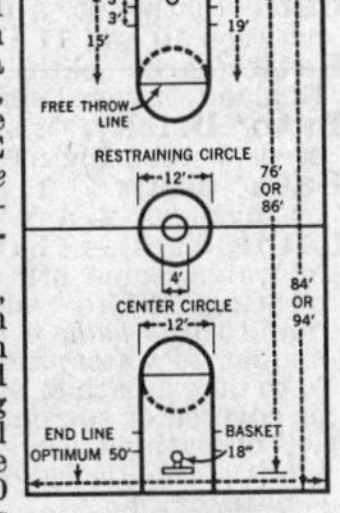

Basketball court

bas·ket·ball (bas′kit bôl′, bä′skit-), *n.* **1.** a game played by two five-man teams or by teams of six, if women, on a rectangular court having a raised basket at each end, points being scored by tossing a large, round ball through the opponent's basket. **2.** the round, inflated ball, approximately 30 inches in circumference, used in this game.

bas′ket chair′, a wicker chair having arms that are a forward continuation of the back.

bas·ket·ful (bas′kit fo͝ol′, bä′skit-), *n., pl.* **-fuls.** a sufficient quantity to fill a basket; the contents of a filled basket.

bas′ket hilt′, the basketlike hilt of a sword, foil, etc., serving to cover and protect the hand. —**bas′ket-hilt′ed,** *adj.*

Bas′ket Mak′er, **1.** an American Indian culture of the southwestern U.S. that immediately preceded the Pueblo culture, and was noted for its basketry, agriculture, use of the bow and arrow, and, in its later stages, the building of semisubterranean houses. **2.** an American Indian belonging to the Basket Maker culture.

bas·ket·ry (bas′ki trē, bä′ski-), *n.* **1.** baskets collectively; basketwork. **2.** the art or process of making baskets or objects woven in the manner of baskets.

bas′ket weave′, a plain weave with two or more yarns woven together, resembling that of a basket.

bas·ket·work (bas′kit wûrk′, bä′skit-), *n.* objects, textiles, etc., made or woven in the manner of a basket.

Bas·kin (bas′kin), *n.* **Leonard,** born 1922, U.S. sculptor and artist.

Basle (bäl), *n.* Basel.

bas mitz·vah (bäs mits′və; *Heb.* bät′ mēts vä′), (*often caps.*) *Judaism.* See **bath mitzvah.**

ba·so·phil (bā′sə fil), *n.* **1.** *Biol.* a basophilic cell, tissue, organism, or substance. **2.** *Anat.* a leukocyte having a bilobate nucleus and basophilic granules in the cytoplasm. —*adj.* **3.** *Biol.* basophilic. Also, **ba·so·phile** (bā′sə fīl′, -fil). [*bas(ic dye)* + -o- + -PHIL]

ba·so·phil·ic (bā′sə fil′ik), *adj.* *Biol.* having an affinity for basic stains. Also, **ba·soph·i·lous** (bā sof′ə ləs).

Ba·sov (bä′səf), *n.* **Ni·ko·lai Gen·ne·di·ye·vich** (nē ko lī′ ge ne dē′yə vich), born 1922, Russian physicist: Nobel prize 1964.

basque (bask), *n.* **1.** a close-fitting bodice, sometimes having an extension that covers the hips. **2.** the extension, or that of a doublet. [< MF, alter. (after BASQUE) of *baste* basting, seam, tuck in a garment < OPr; akin to BASTE[1]]

Basque (bask), *n.* **1.** a member of a people of unknown origin inhabiting the western Pyrenees regions in France and Spain. **2.** their language, not known to be related to any other. —*adj.* **3.** of or pertaining to the Basques or their language.

Basque′ Prov′inces, **1.** a region in N Spain, bordering on the Bay of Biscay. **2.** (loosely) the areas of N Spain and SW France inhabited by Basques.

Bas·ra (bus′rə, bäs′rä), *n.* a port in SE Iraq, N of the Persian Gulf. 175,678 (est. 1963). Also, **Busra, Busrah.**

bas-re·lief (bä′ri lēf′, bas′-; bä′ri lēf′, bas′-), *n.* relief sculpture in which the figures project slightly from the background. Also called **low relief.** See illus. at **relief**[2]. [< F < It *basso rilievo* low RELIEF. See BASE[2]]

bass[1] (bās), *Music.* —*n.* **1.** the lowest male voice or voice part. **2.** a singer with such a voice. **3.** See **double bass.** —*adj.* **4.** of or pertaining to the lowest part in harmonic music; having the compass of a bass. [var. of BASE[2] with *ss* of BASSO] —**bass′ly,** *adv.* —**bass′ness,** *n.* —**bass′y,** *adj.*

bass[2] (bas), *n., pl.* (*esp. collectively*) **bass,** (*esp. referring to two or more kinds or species*), **bass·es.** **1.** any of numerous edible, spiny-finned, freshwater or marine fishes of the families *Serranidae* and *Centrarchidae.* **2.** (originally) the European perch, *Perca fluviatilis.* [assimilated var. of OE *bærs;* c. D *baars,* G *Barsch*]

Largemouth bass, *Micropterus salmoides* (Length to 2½ ft.)

bass[3] (bas), *n.* **1.** the basswood or linden. **2.** *Bot.* bast. [var. of BAST]

bass′ clef′ (bās), *Music.* the symbol placed on the fourth line of a staff to indicate that the fourth line of the staff corresponds to the F next below middle C; F clef. See illus: at **clef.**

bass′ drum′ (bās), a large drum having a cylindrical body and two membrane heads.

bas·set[1] (bas′it), *n.* one of a breed of hounds having short legs, long body and ears, and usually a black, tan, and white coat. Also called **bas′set hound′.** [< F, n. use of *basset* (adj.), of low stature = *bass-* low (see BASE[2]) + *-et* somewhat (see -ET)]

Basset (14 in. high at shoulder)

bas·set[2] (bas′it), *n., v.,* **-set·ed, -set·ing.** *Geol., Mining.* —*n.* **1.** an outcrop, as of the edges of strata. —*v.i.* **2.** to crop out: *strata of limestone which basset along the riverbank.* [appar. < obs. F *basset* low stool < *basset* (adj.). See BASSET[1]]

Basse-Terre (bäs târ′; *Fr.* bas ter′), *n.* a seaport in and the capital of Guadeloupe, in the French West Indies. 15,000 (est. 1960).

Basse·terre (bäs târ′), *n.* a seaport in and the capital of St. Kitts island, in the West Indies. 15,742 (1960).

bass′ fid′dle (bās). See **double bass.**

bass′ horn′ (bās), **1.** tuba. **2.** an obsolete wind instrument related to the tuba.

bas·si·net (bas′ə net′, bas′ə net′), *n.* **1.** a basket with a hood over one end, for use as a baby's cradle. **2.** a style of perambulator resembling this. [< F: pan = *bassin* BASIN + *-et* -ET]

bass·ist (bā′sist), *n.* a player of the double bass.

bas·so (bas′ō, bä′sō; *It.* bäs′sô), *n., pl.* **-sos,** *It.* **-si** (-sē). *Music.* a person who sings bass. [< It < LL *bassus.* See BASE[2]]

bas′so contin′uo, *Music.* continuo.

bas·soon (ba so͞on′, bə-), *n.* a large woodwind instrument of low range, with a doubled tube and a curved metal crook to which a double reed is attached. [< F *basson* < It *basson(e)* = *bass(o)* low (see BASE[2]) + *-one* aug. suffix] —**bas·soon′ist,** *n.*

Bassoon

bas·so pro·fun·do (bas′ō prō fun′dō, bä′sō), *pl.* **bas·si pro·fun·di** (bas′ē prō fun′dē, bä′sē). a singer with a bass voice of the lowest range. [< It *basso profondo,* lit., deep bass]

bas·so-re·lie·vo (bas′ō ri lē′vō), *n., pl.* **-vos.** bas-relief.

bas·so-ri·lie·vo (bäs′sô rē lye′vô), *n., pl.* **bas·si-ri·lie·vi** (bäs′sē rē lye′vē). *Italian.* bas-relief.

bass′ re′flex (bās), a loudspeaker equipped with a baffle having openings designed to improve the reproduction of low-frequency sounds.

bass′ response′ (bās), the response of a loudspeaker or other amplifying device to low-frequency sounds.

bass′ staff′ (bās), *Music.* a staff marked with a bass clef.

Bass′ Strait′ (bas), a strait between Australia and Tasmania. 80–150 mi. wide.

bass′ vi′ol (bās), **1.** See **viola da gamba.** **2.** See **double bass.**

bass·wood (bas′wo͝od′), *n.* **1.** any tree of the genus *Tilia,* esp. *T. americana,* the American linden. **2.** the wood of a linden.

bast (bast), *n.* **1.** *Bot.* phloem. **2.** Also called **bast′ fi′ber.** any of several strong, ligneous fibers, as flax, hemp, ramie, or jute, obtained from phloem tissue and used in the manufacture of woven goods and cordage. [ME; OE *bæst;* c. D, G, Icel *bast*]

bas·tard (bas′tərd), *n.* **1.** a person born of unmarried parents; an illegitimate child. **2.** something irregular, inferior, spurious, or unusual. **3.** *Slang.* a vicious, despicable, or thoroughly disliked person. —*adj.* **4.** illegitimate in birth. **5.** not genuine; spurious. **6.** irregular or intermediate, as in form, grade, or size. **7.** having the appearance of; resembling in some degree: *a bastard Michelangelo; bastard emeralds.* [ME < OF = *bast* bastardy (lit., packsaddle, i.e., makeshift bed in phrase *fils de bast* son of an irregular bed) + *-ard* -ARD. Cf. BANTLING]

bas·tard·ise (bas′tər dīz′), *v.t., v.i.,* **-ised, -is·ing.** *Chiefly Brit.* bastardize. —**bas′tard·i·sa′tion,** *n.*

bas·tard·ize (bas′tər dīz′), *v.,* **-ized, -iz·ing.** —*v.t.* **1.** to declare or prove (someone) to be a bastard. **2.** to lower in condition or worth; debase. —*v.i.* **3.** to become debased. —**bas′tard·i·za′tion,** *n.*

bas·tard·ly (bas′tərd lē), *adj.* **1.** bastard; baseborn. **2.** worthless; of no value. **3.** spurious; counterfeit. **4.** *Slang.* vicious or despicable.

bas′tard ti′tle. See **half title** (def. 1).

bas′tard wing′, *Ornith.* alula.

bas·tar·dy (bas′tər dē), *n.* **1.** the state or condition of being a bastard; illegitimacy. **2.** the act of begetting a bastard. [late ME < AF, OF *bastardie*]

baste[1] (bāst), *v.t.,* **bast·ed, bast·ing.** to sew with long, loose stitches, as in temporarily tacking together pieces of a garment in the early stages of making it. [late ME *bastin* < MF *basti(r)* (to) build, baste < Gmc; cf. OHG *bestan* to mend, patch < *bastian to bring together with bast thread or string = *bast* BAST + *-ian* inf. suffix]

baste[2] (bāst), *v.t.,* **bast·ed, bast·ing.** to moisten (meat or other food) while cooking. [?]

baste[3] (bāst), *v.t.,* **bast·ed, bast·ing. 1.** to beat with a stick; thrash; cudgel. **2.** to denounce or scold vigorously. [var. of *baist* < Scand; cf. Icel *beysta* to beat, thrash]

Bas·tia (bäs′tyä), *n.* a seaport on the NE coast of Corsica: the former capital of Corsica. 50,881 (1962).

bas·tille (ba stēl′; *Fr.* bA stē′yə), *n., pl.* **bas·tilles** (ba-stēlz′; *Fr.* bA stē′yə). **1.** (*cap.*) a fortress and prison in Paris, captured by French Revolutionaries on July 14, 1789. **2.** any prison or jail. **3.** a fortified tower, as of a castle; a small fortress; citadel. Also, **bas·tile** (ba stēl′). [late ME *bastile* < MF = *bast-* build (see BASTE[1]) + L *-īle* n. suffix of place, neut. of *-īlis* -ILE; r. ME *bastel* < OF *bassstel*]

Bastille′ Day′, July 14, a French national holiday commemorating the fall of the Bastille in 1789.

bas·ti·nade (bas′tə nād′), *n., v.t.,* **-nad·ed, -nad·ing.** bastinado.

bas·ti·na·do (bas′tə nā′dō), *n., pl.* **-does,** *v.,* **-doed, -do·ing.** —*n.* **1.** a blow or a beating with a stick, cudgel, etc. **2.** an Oriental mode of punishment, consisting of blows with a stick on the soles of the feet or on the buttocks. **3.** a stick or cudgel. —*v.t.* **4.** to beat with a stick, cane, etc., esp. on the soles of the feet or on the buttocks. [earlier *bastanado* < Sp *bastonada* = *bastón* stick + *-ada* -ADE[1]]

bast·ing (bā′sting), *n.* **1.** sewing with long, loose stitches to hold material in place until the final sewing. **2. bastings,** the stitches taken or the threads used.

bas·tion (bas′chən, -tē ən), *n.* **1.** *Fort.* a projecting portion of a rampart or fortification that forms an irregular pentagon attached at the base to the main work. **2.** a fortified place. [< MF < It *bastion(e)* = *basti(a)* bastion (*basti-* build (see BASTE[1]) + *-a* n. suffix) + *-one* aug. suffix] —**bas·tion·ar·y** (bas′chə ner′ē), *adj.* —**bas′tioned,** *adj.*

Bas·togne (ba stōn′; *Fr.* bA stôn′yə), *n.* a town in SE Belgium: battle December, 1944. 6332 (est. 1964).

Ba·su·to·land (bə so͞o′tō land′), *n.* former name of **Lesotho.**

bat[1] (bat), *n., v.,* **bat·ted, bat·ting.** —*n.* **1.** *Sports.* **a.** the wooden club used in certain games, as baseball and cricket, to strike the ball. **b.** a racket, esp. one used in badminton or table tennis. **c.** a whip used by a jockey. **d.** the act of using a club or racket in a game. **e.** the right or turn to use a club or racket. **2.** a heavy stick, club, or cudgel. **3.** *Informal.* a blow, as with a bat. **4.** a piece of brick or lump of hard clay. **5.** *Brit. Slang.* a pace or rate of speed. **6.** *Slang.* a spree; binge. **7.** batt. **8. at bat,** *Baseball.* **a.** taking one's turn to bat in a game. **b.** a turn at batting officially charged to a batter: *two hits in three at bats.* **9. go to bat for,** *Slang.* to intercede for; vouch for; defend. **10. right off the bat,** at once; without delay. —*v.t.* **11.** to strike or hit with, or as with, a bat or club. **12.** *Baseball.* to have a batting average of; hit: *He batted .325 in spring training.* —*v.i.* **13.** *Sports.* **a.** to strike at the ball with the bat. **b.** to take one's turn as a batter. **14. bat the breeze.** See **breeze**[1] (def. 3). [ME *batte,* OE *batt,* prob. < Celt; cf. Ir, Gael *bat, bata* staff, cudgel; c. Russ *bat* cudgel. See BATE[2]]

bat[2] (bat), *n.* **1.** any nocturnal or crepuscular flying mammal of the order *Chiroptera,* having modified forelimbs that serve as wings and are covered with a membranous skin extending to the hind limbs. **2. blind as a bat,** having very poor vision. **3. have bats in one's belfry,** *Slang.* to have crazy ideas; be very peculiar. [appar. < Scand; cf. dial. Sw *natt-batta,* var. of earlier *natt-bakka* night bat; r. ME *bakke* < Scand; ME *balke* for **blake* < Scand; cf. dial. Sw *natt-blacka*] —**bat′like′,** *adj.*

Bat, *Desmodus rufus* (Length 3½ in.; wingspread 14 in.)

bat[3] (bat), *v.t.,* **bat·ted, bat·ting. 1.** *Informal.* to blink; wink; flutter. **2. not bat an eye,** *Informal.* to show no emotion or surprise; maintain a calm exterior. [var. of BATE[2]]

bat[4] (bät), *n.* **1.** *Anglo-Indian.* a spoken language of India, esp. its slang, idioms, and informal expressions. **2.** *Brit. Slang.* the spoken language of any foreign country, esp. its vernacular. [< Hindi *bāt* speech, word < Skt *vārttā*]

bat., 1. battalion. 2. battery.

Ba·taan (bə tan′, -tän′; *local* bä′tä än′), *n.* a peninsula on W Luzon, in the Philippines. Also, **Ba·taán′.**

Ba·tan·gas (bä täng′gäs), *n.* a seaport on SW Luzon, in the N Philippines. 59,582 (1948).

Ba·ta·vi·a (bə tā′vē ə), *n.* former name of **Djakarta.**

batch (bach), *n.* **1.** a quantity of material or number of things of the same kind made or handled at one time or considered as one group. **2.** the quantity of bread, cookies, dough, or the like, made at one baking. [late ME *bache,* OE *gebæc,* akin to *bacan* to BAKE; c. G *Gebäck* batch]

bate[1] (bāt), *v.,* **bat·ed, bat·ing.** —*v.t.* **1.** to moderate or restrain: *unable to bate our enthusiasm.* **2.** to lessen or diminish; abate. —*v.i.* **3.** to diminish or subside; abate. **4. with bated breath,** with breath drawn in or held because of anticipation or suspense. [ME, aph. var. of ABATE]

bate[2] (bāt), *v.,* **bat·ed, bat·ing,** *n.* —*v.i.* **1.** (of a hawk) to flutter the wings in anger or fear. —*n.* **2.** a state of violent anger or fear in a hawk. [late ME < MF *(se) bat(re)* << L *battuere* to beat; akin to BAT[1]]

bate[3] (bāt), *v.,* **bat·ed, bat·ing,** *n.* —*v.t., v.i.* **1.** *Tanning.* to soak (leather) after liming in an alkaline solution to soften it and remove the lime. —*n.* **2.** the solution used. [var. of *beat* to pare off turf, OE *bǣt(an)* (to) BAIT; c. Sw *beta* to tan, G *beissen* to macerate]

ba·teau (ba tō′; *Fr.* bA tō′), *n., pl.* **-teaux** (-tōz′; *Fr.* -tō′). **1.** a double-ended, flat-bottomed rowboat used on rivers in Canada and the northern United States. **2.** a half-decked, sloop-rigged boat used for fishing on Chesapeake Bay; skipjack. **3.** (in some regions) a scow. Also, **batteau.** [< F; OF *batel* = *bat* (< OE *bāt* BOAT) + *-el* dim. suffix; cf. ML *batellus* < OF]

bat·fish (bat′fish′), *n., pl.* (*esp. collectively*) **-fish,** (*esp. referring to two or more kinds or species*) **-fish·es. 1.** any of the flat-bodied, marine fishes of the family *Ogcocephalidae,* as *Ogcocephalus vespertilio,* common along the southern Atlantic coast of the U.S. **2.** a stingray, *Aetobatis californicus,* found off the coast of California.

bat·fowl (bat′foul′), *v.i.* to catch birds at night by dazzling them with a light and then capturing them in a net. [late ME *batfowlyn.* See BAT[2], FOWL (v.)] —**bat′fowl′er,** *n.*

bath[1] (bath, bäth), *n., pl.* **baths** (bathz, bäthz, baths, bäths), *v.* —*n.* **1.** a washing or immersion of something, esp. the body, in water, steam, etc., as for cleansing or therapy. **2.** a quantity of water or other agent used for this purpose: *running a bath.* **3.** a container for water or other cleansing liquid, as a bathtub. **4.** a bathroom or any room equipped for bathing: *a room and bath.* **5.** an establishment for bathing, as a steam bath or one having therapeutic or recreational facilities. **6.** bathhouse. **7.** Often, **baths.** an elaborate bathing establishment of the ancients: *the baths of Caracalla.* **8.** Usually, **baths.** spa. **9.** a preparation, as an acid solution, in which something is immersed. **10.** a liquid for treatment, cooling, etc. **11.** the container for such a preparation. **12.** a device for controlling the temperature by the use of a surrounding medium, as sand, water, oil, etc. **13.** *Metall.* the depressed hearth of an open-hearth furnace. **14. take a bath,** *Informal.* to suffer a financial loss: *Many investors took a terrible bath in the stock market during 1969.* —*v.t., v.i.* **15.** to wash or soak in a bath. [ME; OE *bæth;* c. G *Bad,* Icel *bath;* akin to G *bähen,* Sw *basa* to warm. See BASK] —**bath′less,** *adj.*

bath[2] (bath), *n.* a Hebrew unit of liquid measure, equal to between 10 and 11 U.S. gallons. [< Heb]

Bath (bath, bäth), *n.* a city in NE Somerset, in SW England: mineral springs. 80,856 (1961).

Bath′ brick′, a brick-shaped mass of fine siliceous sand, used for scouring metal.

Bath′ chair′, **1.** a wheeled and hooded chair, used esp. by invalids. **2.** any wheelchair. Also, **bath′ chair′.**

bathe (bāth), *v.,* **bathed, bath·ing,** *n.* —*v.t.* **1.** to immerse in water, some other liquid, or steam, as for cleaning or treating. **2.** to wet; wash. **3.** to apply water or other liquid to: *to bathe a wound.* **4.** to cover or surround in the manner of water: *a shaft of sunlight bathing the room.* —*v.i.* **5.** to take a bath or sun bath. **6.** to swim for pleasure. **7.** to be covered or surrounded as if with water. —*n.* **8.** *Brit.* the act of bathing, esp. in the sea, a lake, or a river. [ME *bath(i)e(n),* OE *bathian* = *bæth* BATH[1] + *-ian* inf. suffix] —**bath′er,** *n.*

bath·house (bath′hous′, bäth′-), *n., pl.* **-hous·es** (-hou′ziz). **1.** a structure, as at the seaside, containing dressing rooms for bathers. **2.** a building having bathing facilities.

Bath·i·nette (bath′ə net′, bä′thə-), *n.* *Trademark.* a folding bathtub for babies, usually of rubberized cloth.

bath′ing beau′ty, a girl or woman in a bathing suit, esp. an entrant in a beauty contest.

bath′ing cap′, a tight-fitting elastic cap worn esp. by women to keep the hair dry while swimming.

bath·ing-ma·chine (bā′thing mə shēn′), *n.* *Archaic.* a small bathhouse on wheels used by bathers as a dressing room and also, esp. by women, as a means of transportation between the beach and the water.

bath′ing suit′, a garment worn for swimming. Also called **swimsuit.**

bath′ mat′, a mat or washable rug used to stand on when entering or leaving a bath.

bath mitz·vah (bäs mits′və; *Heb.* bät′ mēts vä′), (*often caps.*) *Judaism.* **1.** a ceremony for a girl, chiefly among Reform and Conservative Jews, paralleling the Bar Mitzvah. **2.** the girl participating in this ceremony. Also, **bas mitzvah.** [< Heb: daughter of the law]

batho-, a learned borrowing from Greek meaning "depth," used in the formation of compound words: *bathometer.* Also, **bathy-.** [comb. form of Gk *báthos; bathy-,* s. of *bathýs* deep]

bath·o·lith (bath′ə lith), *n.* *Geol.* a large body of igneous rock bounded by irregular, cross-cutting surfaces or fault planes, believed to have crystallized at a considerable depth below the earth's surface. Also, **bath·o·lite** (bath′ə līt′). —**bath′o·lith′ic, bath·o·lit·ic** (bath′ə lit′ik), *adj.*

ba·thom·e·ter (bə thom′i tər), *n.* *Oceanog.* a device for ascertaining the depth of water.

ba·thos (bā′thos), *n.* **1.** a ludicrous descent from the exalted or lofty to the commonplace; anticlimax. **2.** triteness or triviality in style. **3.** insincere pathos; obvious sentimentality; mawkishness. [< Gk: depth] —**ba·thet·ic** (bə thet′ik), *adj.*

bath·robe (bath′rōb′, bäth′-), *n.* a long, loose, coatlike garment, for wearing before and after a bath, over sleepwear, or as leisure wear at home.

bath·room (bath′ro͞om′, -ro͝om′, bäth′-), *n.* a room containing a bathtub or shower and, typically, a washbowl and toilet.

bath′ salts′, a preparation of flakes or crystals used to soften or give a pleasant scent to a bath.

Bath·she·ba (bath shē′bə, bath′shə-), *n.* the wife of Uriah and later of David: mother of Solomon. II Sam. 11, 12.

bath′ tow′el, a large towel used to dry the body after bathing, usually of heavy, absorbent material.

bath·tub (bath′tub′, bäth′-), *n.* a tub to bathe in, esp. one forming a permanent fixture in a bathroom.

Bath·urst (bath′ərst), *n.* **1.** former name of **Banjul. 2.** a town in E New South Wales, in SE Australia. 18,060.

bathy-, var. of **batho-:** *bathysphere.*

bath·y·al (bath′ē əl), *adj.* of or pertaining to the deeper parts of an ocean, esp. that part between 100 and 1000 fathoms.

bath·y·met·ric (bath′ə me′trik), *adj.* **1.** of or pertaining to the measurement of the depths of oceans, seas, or other large bodies of water. **2.** of or pertaining to the contour of the bed of an ocean, sea, or other large body of water. —**bath′y·met′ri·cal·ly,** *adv.*

ba·thym·e·try (bə thim′i trē), *n.* the measurement of the depths of oceans, seas, or other large bodies of water. —**ba·thym′e·ter,** *n.*

bath·y·scaphe (bath′i skāf′, -skaf′), *n.* *Oceanog.* a small, specially built submarine for deep-sea exploration, usually having a spherical observation chamber under the hull. Also, **bath·y·scaph** (bath′i skaf′), **bath·y·scape** (bath′i skāp′). [BATHY- + *Gk skáphē* light boat, skiff]

bath·y·sphere (bath′i sfēr′), *n.* *Oceanog.* a spherical diving apparatus from which to study deep-sea life.

ba·tik (bə tēk′, bat′ik), *n.* **1.** a technique of hand-dyeing fabrics by using wax as a dye repellent to cover parts of a design not to be dyed. **2.** the fabric so decorated. [< Javanese: painted]

Ba·tis·ta (bä tēs′tä), *n.* **Ful·gen·cio** (fo͞ol hen′syô), (*Fulgencio Batista y Zaldívar*), 1901–73, Cuban military leader: dictator of Cuba 1934–40; president 1940–44, 1952–59.

ba·tiste (bə tēst′, ba-), *n.* a fine, sheer fabric made of any of various fibers. [< F; MF *(toile de) ba(p)tiste,* after *Baptiste* of Cambrai, said to have been first maker]

bat·man (bat′mən), *n., pl.* **-men.** (in the British army) a soldier assigned to an officer as a servant. [short for *bathorse man; bat* < F *bât* packsaddle (see BASTARD)]

ba·ton (ba ton′, bə-, bat′ən), *n.* **1.** a staff, club, or truncheon, esp. one serving as a mark of office or authority. **2.** *Music.* the wand used by a conductor. **3.** *Track.* a hollow cylinder that is passed from one member of a relay team to the member next to compete. **4.** a staff carried and twirled by a drum major or drum majorette. **5.** *Heraldry.* a diminutive of the bend, esp. the bend sinister. [< F *bâton;* OF *baston* < VL **baston-* (s. of **bastō*) stick, club < ?]

Bat·on Rouge (bat′ən ro͞ozh′), the capital of Louisiana, in the SE part: a river port on the Mississippi. 165,963 (1970).

ba·tra·chi·an (bə trā′kē ən), *adj.* **1.** belonging or pertaining to the *Batrachia,* a former group comprising the amphibians, and sometimes restricted to the salientians. —*n.* **2.** an amphibian, esp. a salientian. [< NL *Batrach(ia)* (< Gk *bátrach(os)* frog) + -IAN]

bats (bats), *adj.* *Slang.* batty.

bats·man (bats′mən), *n., pl.* **-men.** a batter, esp. in cricket. —**bats′man·ship′,** *n.*

batt (bat), *n.* a sheet of matted cotton or wool. Also, **bat.** [special use of BAT[1]]

batt., **1.** battalion. **2.** battery.

bat·ta·lia (bə tāl′yə, -täl′-), *n.* *Obs.* **1.** order of battle. **2.** an armed or arrayed body of troops. [< It *battaglia*]

bat·tal·ion (bə tal′yən), *n.* **1.** *Mil.* a ground-force unit composed of a headquarters and two or more companies or similar units. **2.** an army in battle array. **3.** Often, **battalions.** a large number of persons or things; force: *battalions of bureaucrats.* [< F *bataillon* < It *battaglione* large squadron of soldiers = *battagli(a)* BATTLE[1] + *-one* aug. suffix]

bat·teau (ba tō′; *Fr.* BA tō′), *n., pl.* **-teaux** (-tōz′; *Fr.* -tō′). bateau.

bat·ten[1] (bat′ən), *v.i.* **1.** to thrive by feeding; grow fat. **2.** to feed gluttonously, as on a particular thing. **3.** to thrive, prosper, or live in luxury, esp. at the expense of others. —*v.t.* **4.** to cause to thrive by or as by feeding; fatten. [< Scand; cf. Icel *batna* to improve (c. Goth *(ga)batnan*) = *bat(i)* change for the better + *-na* inf. suffix]

bat·ten[2] (bat′ən), *n.* **1.** a small board or strip of wood used for various building purposes, as to cover joints between boards, reinforce certain doors, or supply a foundation for lathing. **2.** *Naut.* **a.** a thin strip of wood inserted in a sail to keep it flat. **b.** a thin, flat length of wood or metal used for various purposes, as to hold the tarpaulin covering a hatch in place. —*v.t.* **3.** to furnish or bolster with battens. **4.** *Naut.* to cover (a hatch) so as to make it watertight, using tarpaulins held in place with battens and wedges (usually fol. by *down*). [var. of BATON] —**bat′ten·er,** *n.*

bat·ter[1] (bat′ər), *v.t.* **1.** to beat persistently or hard; pound repeatedly. **2.** to damage by beating or subjecting to rough usage. —*v.i.* **3.** to deal heavy, repeated blows; pound steadily. [ME *bater(en).* See BAT[1], -ER[6]] —**Syn. 1.** pelt.

bat·ter[2] (bat′ər), *n.* a mixture of flour, milk or water, eggs, etc., beaten together for use in cookery. [late ME *bater,* ME *bater(en)* BATTER[1]]

bat·ter[3] (bat′ər), *n.* a person who bats, or whose turn it is to bat, as in baseball or cricket. [BAT[1] + -ER[1]]

bat·ter[4] (bat′ər), *n.* *Archit.* a backward and upward slope of the face of a wall or the like. [?]

bat′tering ram′, an ancient military device with a heavy horizontal ram for battering down walls, gates, etc.

Bat·ter·sea (bat′ər sē), *n.* a borough of London, in the SW part, on the Thames. 105,758 (1961).

bat·ter·y (bat′ə rē), *n., pl.* **-ter·ies. 1.** *Elect.* **a.** a combination of two or more galvanic cells electrically connected to work together to produce electric energy. **b.** See **galvanic cell. 2.** any group or series of similar or related items, machines, parts, etc., esp. a set of components arranged for a common end: *a battery of tests.* **3.** *Mil.* **a.** a parapet or fortification equipped with artillery. **b.** two or more pieces of artillery used for combined action. **c.** a tactical artillery unit, usually consisting of six guns together with the artillerymen, equipment, etc., required to operate them. **4.** *Navy.* **a.** (on a warship) a group of guns having the same caliber or used for combined action. **b.** the whole armament of a warship. **5.** *Baseball.* a team's pitcher and catcher of a game considered as a unit. **6.** act of battering. **7.** *Law.* an unlawful attack upon another person by beating, wounding, or touching in an offensive manner. **8.** an instrument used in battering. **9.** any imposing group of persons or things acting or directed in unison: *a battery of experts.* [< MF *batterie* = *batt(re)* (to) beat (see BATE[2]) + *-erie* -ERY]

bat·ting (bat′ing), *n.* **1.** act or manner of using a bat in a game of ball. **2.** cotton or wool in batts or sheets, used as filling for quilts or bedcovers.

bat′ting av′erage, *Baseball.* a measure of the batting ability of a player, obtained by dividing his number of base hits by his number of official times at bat and carrying out the result to three decimal places.

bat·tle[1] (bat′əl), *n., v.,* **-tled, -tling.** —*n.* **1.** a hostile encounter or engagement between opposing military forces or armed forces. **2.** a fight or contest, as between two persons or teams. **3.** *Archaic.* a battalion. **4. give** or **do battle,** to enter into conflict; fight. —*v.i.* **5.** to engage in battle or conflict. —*v.t.* **6.** to fight (a person, army, cause, etc.). **7.** to force or accomplish by fighting, struggling, etc.: *He battled his way to the top of his profession.* [ME *bataile* < OF < LL *battālia,* L *battuālia* (neut. pl.) gladiatorial exercises = *battu(ere)* (to) strike (see BATE[2]) + *-ālia* -AL[2]] —**bat′tler,** *n.* —**Syn. 1.** conflict, war. BATTLE, ACTION, SKIRMISH mean a conflict between organized armed forces. A BATTLE is a prolonged and general conflict pursued to a definite decision: *the Battle of the Bulge in World War II.* An ACTION is part of a spirited military operation, offensive or defensive: *The army was involved in a number of brilliant actions during the battle.* A SKIRMISH is a slight engagement, often preparatory to larger movements: *several minor skirmishes between scouting forces.* **6.** contest.

bat·tle[2] (bat′əl), *v.t.,* **-tled, -tling.** *Archaic.* to furnish (a building or wall) with battlements. [ME *bataile(n)* < MF *batailli(er)* (to) provide with *batailles* See BATTLEMENT]

bat·tle-ax (bat′əl aks′), *n., pl.* **-ax·es. 1.** a broadax for use as a weapon of war. **2.** *Slang.* a domineering, sharp-tempered woman, esp. a wife. Also, **bat′tle-axe′.**

Bat′tle Creek′, a city in S Michigan. 38,931 (1970).

bat′tle cruis′er, a warship of maximum speed and firepower, but with lighter armor than a battleship.

bat′tle cry′, **1.** a cry or shout of enthusiasm or encouragement of troops in battle. **2.** the phrase or slogan used in any contest or campaign.

bat·tle·dore (bat′əl dōr′, -dôr′), *n., v.,* **-dored, -dor·ing.** —*n.* **1.** Also called **bat′tledore and shut′tlecock.** a game from which badminton was developed, played in Asia since ancient times **2.** a light racket used in this game. —*v.t., v.i.* **3.** to toss or fly back and forth. [late ME *batyldo(u)re* washing beetle = *batyl* to beat (clothes) in washing (freq. of BAT[1]) + *-dore* dung beetle (BEETLE[1] for BEETLE[2] by way of pun, with allusion to filth on clothes). See DOR[1]]

bat′tle fatigue′, *Psychiatry.* psychoneurosis resulting from combat duty. Also called **combat fatigue.** Cf. **shell shock.**

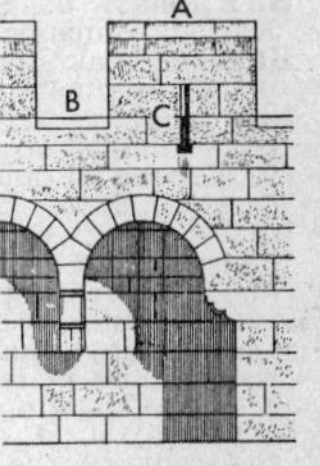

Battlement
A, Merlon; B, Crenel; C, Loophole

bat·tle·field (bat′əl fēld′), *n.* the field or ground on which a battle is fought. Also called **bat·tle·ground** (bat′əl ground′).

bat·tle·front (bat′əl frunt′), *n.* front (def. 5c).

bat′tle jack′et, *U.S.* a waist-length woolen jacket with snugly fitting cuffs and waist, formerly worn as part of the military uniform.

bat′tle line′, the line along which warring troops meet.

bat·tle·ment (bat′əl mənt), *n.* Often, **battlements.** a parapet or cresting consisting of a regular alternation of merlons and crenels; crenelation. [ME *batelment* < MF *bataille* battlement; see -MENT] —**bat·tle·ment·ed** (bat′əl-men′tid), *adj.*

Bat′tle of Brit′ain, (in World War II) the series of aerial combats that took place during the bombardment of England by German aircraft during the autumn of 1940.

bat′tle roy′al, **1.** a fight among more than two combatants. **2.** a violent, exciting, or noisy fight or dispute.

bat·tle-scarred (bat′əl skärd′), *adj.* bearing scars or damages received in battle.

bat·tle·ship (bat′əl ship′), *n.* **1.** any of a class of warships that are the most heavily armored and are equipped with the most powerful armament. **2.** See **ship of the line.**

bat′tle star′, *U.S. Mil.* **1.** a small bronze star worn on a campaign ribbon by members of organizations taking part in specific battles or wartime operations. **2.** a small silver star similarly worn, equivalent to five such bronze stars.

bat′tle sta′tion, *Mil., Navy.* the place or position that one is assigned to for battle.

bat′tle wag′on, *Informal.* a battleship.

bat·tue (ba to͞o′, -tyo͞o′; *Fr.* BA ty′), *n., pl.* **-tues** (-to͞oz′, -tyo͞oz′; *Fr.* -ty′). *Chiefly Brit. Hunting.* **1.** the beating or driving of game from cover toward a stationary hunter. **2.** a hunt or hunting party using this method. [< F, n. use of *battue* beaten (fem. ptp. of *battre* < L *battuere*) < L **battūta* (fem. ptp.)]

bat·ty (bat′ē), *adj.,* **-ti·er, -ti·est.** *Slang.* insane; crazy; silly. [BAT[2] + -Y[1]]

Ba·tu Khan (bä′to͞o kän′), d. 1255, Mongol conqueror: leader of the Golden Horde (grandson of Genghis Khan).

Ba·tum (bä to͞om′), *n.* a seaport in SW Georgia, in the S Soviet Union in Europe, on the Black Sea. 82,000 (1959). Also, **Ba·tu·mi** (bä to͞o′mē).

bat·wing (bat′wing′), *adj.* formed, shaped, etc., in the manner of a bat's wing or wings: *a dress with batwing sleeves.*

bau·ble (bô′bəl), *n.* **1.** a cheap piece of ornament; trinket; gewgaw. **2.** a jester's staff. [< F *beaubel,* lit., pretty-pretty; r. ME *babel* < MF, perh. var. of *beaubel*]

Bau·de·laire (bōd′əlâr′; *Fr.* bōdəlεʀ′), *n.* **Charles Pierre** (sharl pyεʀ), 1821–67, French poet and critic.

Bau·douin I (*Fr.* bō dwaN′), born 1930, king of Belgium since 1951.

bau·drons (bô′drənz), *n.* (*construed as sing.*) *Chiefly Scot.* a cat. [late ME *balderonis;* ? akin to ME *badde* cat]

Bau·haus (bou′hous′), *n.* a school of design established in Weimar in 1919 by Walter Gropius, developing a style characterized chiefly by an emphasis on functional design in architecture and the applied arts. [< G = *Bau-* building + *Haus* house]

Baum (bôm, bäm), *n.* **L(y·man) Frank** (lī′mən), 1856–1919, U.S. playwright and author of children's books.

Bau·mé′ scale′ (bō mā′, bō′mā), a scale for use with a hydrometer, calibrated so that specific gravity may be easily computed. [named after A. *Baumé* (1728–1804), French chemist]

baum′ mar′ten (boum), **1.** the European marten. **2.** the fur of this animal. [< G *Baum(marder)* tree marten + MARTEN]

Bau·ru (bou ro͞o′), *n.* a city in E Brazil. 85,881 (1960).

Bau·tzen (bout′sən), *n.* a city in E East Germany, on the Spree River: scene of defeat of Prussian and Russian armies by Napoleon I, 1813. 42,008 (1955).

baux·ite (bôk′sīt, bō′zīt), *n.* a rock consisting of hydrous aluminum oxide or hydroxides with various impurities: the principal ore of aluminum. [named after (*Les*) *Baux,* near Arles in southern France; see -ITE[1]]

Ba·var·i·a (bə vâr′ē ə), *n.* a state in S West Germany: formerly a kingdom. 9,799,000 (1963); 27,239 sq. mi. *Cap.:* Munich. German, **Bayern.**

Ba·var·i·an (bə vâr′ē ən), *adj.* **1.** of or pertaining to Bavaria, its inhabitants, or their dialect. —*n.* **2.** a native or an inhabitant of Bavaria. **3.** the High German speech of Bavaria and Austria. Cf. **Alemannic** (def. 1).

Bavar′ian cream′, a soufflélike dessert made with custard, gelatin, and whipped cream.

baw·bee (bô bē′, bô′bē), *n.* *Informal.* anything of little value. [orig. a Scottish coin of little value named after A. Orok, 16th-century mint official, laird of Sille*bawby*]

bawd (bôd), *n.* **1.** a woman who maintains a brothel; madam. **2.** a prostitute. **3.** *Archaic.* a procuress. [ME *bawde,* n. use of MF *baude,* fem. of *baud* gay, dissolute < WGmc; cf. OE *bald* BOLD]

baw·dry (bô′drē), *n.* **1.** *Archaic.* lewdness; obscenity; bawdiness. **2.** *Obs.* fornication. [late ME *bawdery.* See BAWD, -ERY]

bawd·y (bô′dē), *adj.,* **bawd·i·er, bawd·i·est,** *n.* —*adj.* **1.** obscene; indecent; coarse. —*n.* **2.** coarse or indecent talk or writing. —**bawd′i·ly,** *adv.* —**bawd′i·ness,** *n.*

bawd·y·house (bô′dē hous′), *n., pl.* **-hous·es** (-hou′ziz). a brothel.

bawl (bôl), *v.t.* **1.** to utter or proclaim by outcry; shout out. —*v.i.* **2.** to cry or wail loudly. **3.** **bawl out,** *U.S. Informal.* to scold vociferously or vigorously. —*n.* **4.** a loud shout; outcry. [late ME < ML *baul(āre)* (to) bark < Gmc; cf. Icel *baula* to low, *baula* cow] —**bawl′er,** *n.*

Bax (baks), *n.* **Sir Arnold Edward Trevor,** 1883–1953, English composer.

Bax·ter (bak′stər), *n.* **Richard,** 1615–91, English Puritan preacher, scholar, and writer.

bay[1] (bā), *n.* **1.** a body of water forming an indentation of the shoreline, larger than a cove but smaller than a gulf. **2.** a recess of land, partly surrounded by hills. [late ME *baye* < MF *baie* < LL *baia*]

bay[2] (bā), *n.* **1.** *Archit.* **a.** any of a number of major vertical divisions of a large interior, wall, etc. **b.** See **bay window** (def. 1). **2.** a compartment set off by walls or bulkheads, as in a barn for storing hay, on a ship for use as a hospital, or on an aircraft for storing bombs. [ME < MF *baee* an opening in a wall, n. use of fem. ptp. of *baer* to stand open, gape < LL *batāre* to stand open, gape (lit., open the mouth)]

bay[3] (bā), *n.* **1.** a deep, prolonged howl, as of a hound on the scent. **2.** the position or situation of an animal or fugitive being forced to turn and resist pursuers because it is no longer possible to escape (usually prec. by *at* or *to*): *a stag at bay.* —*v.i.* **3.** to howl, esp. with a deep, prolonged sound, as a hound on the scent. —*v.t.* **4.** to howl at: *a troubled hound baying the moon.* **5.** to bring to or to hold at bay. [ME, aph. var. of *abay* < OF *abai* barking < *abaier* to bark]

bay[4] (bā), *n.* **1.** Also called **bay tree, sweet bay.** the European laurel, *Laurus nobilis.* **2.** Also called **bayberry.** a West Indian tree, *Pimenta acris,* whose leaves are used in making bay rum. **3.** any of various laurellike trees. **4.** *U.S.* any of several magnolias. **5.** an honorary garland or crown bestowed for victory or excellence. **6. bays,** fame; renown. [ME *bai(e),* OE *beg-* (in *begbēam,* lit., berry tree) + MF *baie* < L *bāca, bacca* berry. See BACCHUS]

bay[5] (bā), *n.* **1.** reddish brown. **2.** a horse or other animal of reddish-brown color. —*adj.* **3.** reddish-brown. [late ME < MF *bai* < L *badius;* cf. OIr *buide* yellow]

Ba·ya·món (bä′yä mōn′), *n.* a city in Puerto Rico, near San Juan. 147,552 (1970).

bay′ ant′ler, the second prong from the base of a stag's antler. [*bay* for earlier *bes, bez,* ME *bes* secondary (< MF < L *bis* BIS)]

Ba·yar (bä yäʀ′), *n.* **Ce·lâl** (je läl′), born 1884, Turkish statesman: president 1950–60.

Ba·yard (bA yAʀ′), *n.* **Pierre Ter·rail** (pyεʀ te ʀA′yə), **Sei·gneur de** (se nyœʀ′ də), ("*the knight without fear and without reproach*"), 1473–1524, heroic French soldier.

bay·ber·ry (bā′ber′ē, -bə rē), *n., pl.* **-ries. 1.** any of certain shrubs or trees of the genus *Myrica,* as *M. carolinensis,* a shrub common on seacoasts, or *M. cerifera.* **2.** the berry of such a plant. **3.** bay[4] (def. 2).

Bay′ Cit′y, a lake port in E Michigan, near the mouth of the Saginaw River. 49,449 (1970).

Bay·ern (bī′əʀn), *n.* German name of **Bavaria.**

Ba·yeux′ tap′estry (bā yo͞o′, bä-; *Fr.* bA yœ′), a horizontal strip of embroidered linen 231 feet long and 20 inches high, depicting the Norman conquest of England and dating from c1100. [after *Bayeux,* Norman town where it is located]

Bayle (bāl), *n.* **Pierre** (pyεʀ), 1647–1706, French philosopher and critic.

bay′ leaf′, the dried leaf of the bay tree, *Pimenta acris,* used in cookery and in making bay rum.

Bay·liss (bā′lis), *n.* **William Maddock** (mad′ək), **Sir,** 1860–1924, English physiologist; codiscoverer of secretin.

bay′ lynx′, bobcat.

bay·o·net (bā′ə nit, -net′, bā′ə net′), *n., v.,* **-net·ed** or **-net·ted, -net·ing** or **-net·ting.** —*n.* **1.** a daggerlike steel weapon for attaching to the muzzle end of a gun and used for stabbing or slashing in hand-to-hand combat. **2.** a pin projecting from the side of an object, as the base of a flashbulb, for securing the object in a socket. —*v.t.* **3.** to kill or wound with a bayonet. [< F *baïonnette,* after BAYONNE in France (where the weapon was first made or used); see -ET]

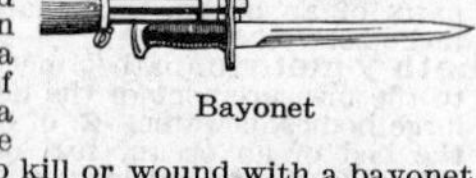
Bayonet

Ba·yonne (bā yōn′ *for 1;* bA yôn′ *for 2*), *n.* **1.** a seaport in NE New Jersey. 72,743 (1970). **2.** a seaport in SW France, near the Bay of Biscay. 41,149 (1962).

bay·ou (bī′o͞o, bī′ō), *n., pl.* **-ous.** *Southern U.S.* an arm, outlet, or tributary of a lake, river, etc.; any stagnant or sluggish creek, marshy lake, or the like. [< LaF < Choctaw *bayuk* small stream]

Bay′ Psalm′ Book′, a translation of the Psalms by John Eliot and others: the first book published (1640) in America.

Bay·reuth (bī′roit; *Ger.* bī roit′), *n.* a city in SE West Germany: annual music festivals. 61,700 (1963).

bay′ rum′, a fragrant liquid used chiefly as an after-shaving lotion, prepared by distilling the leaves of the bayberry, with rum or by mixing oil from the leaves with alcohol.

Bay′ State′, Massachusetts (used as a nickname). —**Bay′ Stat′er.**

Bay·town (bā′toun′), *n.* a city in SE Texas, on Galveston Bay. 43,980 (1970).

bay′ tree′, bay[4] (def. 1).

bay′ win′dow, 1. an alcove of a room, projecting from an outside wall and having its own windows, esp. one having its own foundations. Cf. **bow window, oriel. 2.** *Informal* a large, protruding belly; paunch.

bay·wood (bā′wo͝od′), *n.* a kind of mahogany, found chiefly near the Gulf of Campeche, in Mexico.

ba·zaar (bə zär′), *n.* **1.** a market place or shopping quarter, esp. in the Middle East. **2.** a place in which many kinds of goods are offered for sale. **3.** a sale of miscellaneous articles to benefit some charity, organization, etc. Also, **ba·zar′.** [earlier *bazarro* < It < < Pers *bāzār* market]

ba·zoo·ka (bə zo͞o′kə), *n.* *Mil.* a tube-shaped, portable rocket launcher that fires an armor-piercing rocket. [after musical instrument invented and played by Bob Burns, U.S. comedian, in the late 1930's and 1940's]

BB (bē′bē′), *n.* a size of shot, .18 inch in diameter, for firing from an air rifle (**BB gun**). [? from the letter *b*]

bb., *Baseball.* base on balls; bases on balls.

b.b., bail bond. Also, **B.B.**

B battery, *Electronics.* an electric battery for supplying a constant, positive voltage to the plate of a vacuum tube. Cf. **A battery, C battery.**

B.B.C., British Broadcasting Corporation. Also, **BBC**

bbl., *pl.* **bbls.** barrel.

B.C., 1. before Christ (used in reckoning dates). **2.** British Columbia.

BCD, 1. *Mil.* bad conduct discharge. **2.** *Computer Technology.* binary-coded decimal.

B.C.E., before Common Era.

BCG vaccine, *Immunol.* a vaccine made from weakened strains of tubercle bacilli, used to produce immunity against tuberculosis. [*B(acillus) C(almette)-G(uérin)*]

B complex. See **vitamin B complex.**

B/D, 1. bank draft. **2.** bills discounted. **3.** *Accounting.* brought down.

bd., *pl.* **bds. 1.** board. **2.** bond. **3.** bound. **4.** bundle.

B.D., bills discounted.

bdel·li·um (del′ē əm, -yəm), *n.* **1.** a fragrant gum resin obtained from certain burseraceous plants, as of the genus *Commiphora.* **2.** a plant yielding it. [< L < Gk *bdéllion,* prob. from a Sem word akin to Heb *bedhōlah,* name of a fragrant yellowish transparent gum]

bd. ft., board foot; board feet.

bdl., *pl.* **bdls.** bundle.

be (bē; *unstressed* bē, bi), *v.* and *auxiliary v., pres. sing. 1st pers.* **am,** *2nd* **are** or (*Archaic*) **art,** *3rd* **is,** *pres. pl.* **are;** *past sing. 1st pers.* **was,** *2nd* **were** or (*Archaic*) **wast** or **wert,** *3rd* **was,** *past pl.* **were;** *pres. subj.* **be;** *past subj. sing. 1st pers.* **were,** *2nd* **were** or (*Archaic*) **wert,** *3rd* **were;** *past subj. pl.* **were;** *past part.* **been;** *pres. part.* **be·ing.** —*v.i.* **1.** to exist or live. **2.** to take place; occur: *The wedding was last week.* **3.** to occupy a place or position: *The book is on the table.* **4.** to continue or remain as before: *Let it be.* **5.** to belong; attend; befall: *May good fortune be with you.* **6.** (used as a copula to connect the subject with its predicate adjective, or predicate nominative, in order to describe, identify, or amplify the subject): *Martha is tall.* **7.** (used as a copula to introduce or form interrogative or imperative sentences): *Is that right? Be quiet!* —*auxiliary verb.* **8.** (used with the present participle of another verb to form the progressive tense): *I am waiting.* **9.** (used with the present participle or infinitive of the principal verb to indicate future action): *She is visiting there next week. He is to see me today.* **10.** (used with the past participle of another verb to form the passive voice): *The date was fixed.* **11.** (used in archaic or poetic constructions with some intransitive verbs to form the perfect tense): *He is come. Agamemnon to the wars is gone.* [ME *been,* OE *bēon* = *bēo-* (akin to G *bin* (I) am, L *fuī* I have been, Skt *bhávati* he becomes, is) + *-n* inf. suffix. See AM, IS, ARE[1], WAS, WERE]

Be, *Chem.* beryllium.

be-, a prefix of West Germanic origin, meaning "about," "around," "all over," and hence having an intensive and often disparaging force, much used as an English formative of verbs and their derivatives (*besiege; becloud; bedaub*), and often serving to form transitive verbs from intransitives or from nouns or adjectives (*begrudge; belabor; befriend; belittle*). [ME, OE, unstressed form of *bī* BY]

B/E, bill of exchange. Also, **B.E., b.e.**

beach (bēch), *n.* **1.** an expanse of sand or pebbles along a seashore. **2.** the part of the shore of an ocean, sea, large river, lake, etc., washed by the tide or waves. **3.** the area adjacent to a seashore: *We're vacationing at the beach.* —*v.t., v.i.* **4.** *Naut.* to haul or run onto a beach: *We beached the ship to save her.* [?] —**beach′less,** *adj.* —**Syn. 2.** seashore, strand. See **shore**[1]. **4.** ground.

beach′ ball′, a large, light, buoyant ball, used esp. for games at the seashore, at swimming pools, etc.

beach·boy (bēch′boi′), *n.* a male attendant or instructor at a beach.

beach′ bug′gy, *U.S.* an automobile equipped with oversize tires for traveling on sand beaches.

beach·comb·er (bēch′kō′mər), *n.* **1.** a person who lives by gathering salable articles of jetsam, refuse, etc., from beaches. **2.** a vagrant who lives on the seashore, esp. a white man on a South Pacific island. **3.** a long wave rolling in from the ocean onto the beach.

beach′ flea′, any of various small crustaceans, found on beaches, that jump about like fleas.

Beach flea, *Orchestia agilis* (Length ½ in.)

beach′ grass′, any of several erect, strongly rooted grasses, esp. of the genus *Ammophila,* common on exposed sandy shores and dunes.

beach·head (bēch′hed′), *n.* the area that is the first objective of a military force landing on an enemy shore.

bea·con (bē′kən), *n.* **1.** a guiding or warning signal, such as a light or fire, esp. one in an elevated position. **2.** a tower or hill used for such purposes. **3.** a lighthouse, signal buoy, etc., on a shore or at sea to warn and guide vessels. **4.** See **radio beacon. 5.** a radar device transmitting a pulse from a fixed location for aid in navigation. **6.** a person, act, or thing that warns or guides. —*v.t.* **7.** to serve as a beacon to; warn or guide. **8.** to furnish or mark with beacons. —*v.i.* **9.** to serve or shine as a beacon. [ME *beken,* OE *bēacen* sign, signal; c. OFris *bāken,* OS *bōkan,* OHG *bouhhan*] —**bea′con·less,** *adj.*

Bea·cons·field (bē′kənz fēld′), *n.* **Earl of.** See **Disraeli, Benjamin.**

bead (bēd), *n.* **1.** a small, usually round object of glass, wood, stone, or the like, with a hole through it, often strung with others of its kind in necklaces, rosaries, etc. **2. beads, a.** a necklace of such objects. **b.** a rosary. **3.** any small, globular or cylindrical body, as a drop of liquid, a bubble of gas in a liquid, or the like: *beads of sweat.* **4.** the front sight of a gun. **5.** *Archit., Furniture.* a small molding having a convex circular section; astragal. **6.** *Chem.* a globule of borax or some other flux, supported on a platinum wire, in which a small amount of some substance is heated in a flame as a test for its constituents. **7.** *Metall.* the rounded mass of refined metal obtained by cupellation. **8. count, say,** or **tell one's beads,** to say one's prayers with rosary beads. —*v.t.* **9.** to ornament with beads. **10.** to form beads or a bead on. —*v.i.* **11.** to form beads; form in beads or drops. [ME *bede* prayer, prayer bead, OE *(ge)bed* prayer; akin to BID[1], G *gebet,* etc.] —**bead′like′,** *adj.*

bead′ and reel′, *Archit.* a convex molding having the form of elongated beads alternating with disks placed edge-on, or with spherical beads, or with both. Also, **reel and bead.**

bead·house (bēd′hous′), *n., pl.* **-hous·es** (-hou′ziz). (formerly) an almshouse in which the residents were required to pray for the founder. Also, **bedehouse.**

bead·ing (bē′ding), *n.* **1.** material composed of or adorned with beads. **2.** narrow, lacelike trimming or edging. **3.** narrow openwork trimming through which ribbon may be run. **4.** *Archit., Furniture.* **a.** a bead molding. **b.** the total number of bead moldings in a single design. Also called **beadwork** (for defs. 1, 4).

bea·dle (bēd′əl), *n.* **1.** (in British universities) an official who supervises and leads processions; macebearer. **2.** a parish officer who keeps order during services, waits on the clergyman, etc. [ME *bedel,* dial. (SE) var. of *bidel,* OE *bydel* apparitor, herald (c. G *Büttel*) = *bud-* (weak s. of *bēodan* to command) + *-il* n. suffix]

Bea·dle (bēd′əl), *n.* **George Wells,** born 1903, U.S. biologist and educator: Nobel prize for medicine 1958.

bead′ mold′ing, *Archit.* bead (def. 5).

bead·roll (bēd′rōl′), *n.* **1.** *Rom. Cath. Ch.* a list of persons to be prayed for. **2.** any list or catalogue.

beads·man (bēdz′mən), *n., pl.* **-men.** a person who prays for another as a duty, esp. when paid. Also, **bedesman, bedeman.** [*bead's man* man of prayer; r. ME *bedeman; bede* prayer (see BEAD)]

bead·work (bēd′wûrk′), *n.* beading (defs. 1, 4).

bead·y (bē′dē), *adj.,* **bead·i·er, bead·i·est. 1.** beadlike; small, round, and glittering: *beady eyes.* **2.** covered with or full of beads. —**bead′i·ly,** *adv.* —**bead′i·ness,** *n.*

bea·gle (bē′gəl), *n.* one of a breed of small hounds having long ears, short legs, and a usually black, tan, and white coat. [ME *begle* < ?]

Beagle (15 in. high at shoulder)

beak (bēk), *n.* **1.** the bill of a bird; neb. **2.** any similar horny mouthpart in other animals, such as the turtle, duckbill, etc. **3.** *Slang.* a person's nose. **4.** anything beaklike or ending in a point, as the spout of a pitcher. **5.** *Entomol.* proboscis (def. 3). **6.** *Bot.* a narrowed or prolonged tip. **7.** *Naut.* a metal or metal-sheathed projection from the bow of a warship for ramming enemy vessels; ram. **8.** *Chiefly Brit. Slang.* **a.** a judge; magistrate. **b.** a schoolmaster. [ME *bec* < OF < L *becc(us)* < Gaulish] —**beaked** (bēkt, bē′kid), *adj.* —**beak′less,** *adj.* —**beak′like′,** *adj.* —**beak′y,** *adj.*

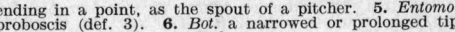

B, Beak (def. 7)

beak·er (bē′kər), *n.* **1.** a large drinking cup or glass with a wide mouth. **2.** the contents of a beaker: *consuming a beaker of gin at one gulp.* **3.** a flat-bottomed, cylindrical vessel, usually with a pouring lip, esp. as used by chemists. [alter. of ME *biker* < Scand; cf. Icel *bikarr;* c. OS *bikeri,* OHG *behhar* (> G *Becher,* D *beker*)]

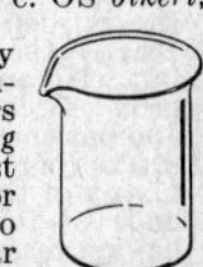

Beaker (def. 3)

beam (bēm), *n.* **1.** any of various relatively long pieces of metal, wood, stone, etc., manufactured or shaped esp. for use as rigid members or parts of structures or machines. **2.** *Building Trades.* a horizontal bearing member, as a joist or lintel. **3.** *Engineering.* a rigid member or structure supported at each end, subject to bending stresses from a direction perpendicular to its length. **4.** *Naut.* **a.** a horizontal structural member, usually transverse, for supporting the decks and flats of a vessel. **b.** the extreme width of a vessel. **c.** the shank of an anchor. **5.** the widest part. **6.** a ray of light: *The sun shed its beams upon the vineyard.* **7.** a group of nearly parallel rays. **8.** *Radio, Aeron.* a signal transmitted along a narrow course, used to guide pilots through darkness, bad weather, etc. **9.** *Mach.* **a.** See **walking beam. b.** (in a loom) a roller or cylinder on which the warp is wound before weaving. **c.** a similar cylinder on which cloth is wound as it is woven. **10.** the crossbar of a balance, from the ends of which the scales or pans are suspended. **11.** the principal stem of the antler of a deer. **12. off the beam, a.** not on the course indicated by a radio beam. **b.** *Slang.* proceeding incorrectly or mistakenly. **13. on the beam, a.** on the course indicated by a radio beam, as an airplane. **b.** *Naut.* at right angles to the keel. **c.** *Slang.* proceeding correctly or exactly. —*v.t.* **14.** to emit in or as in beams or rays. **15.** *Radio.* to transmit (a signal) in a particular direction. —*v.i.* **16.** to emit beams, as of light. **17.** to smile radiantly or happily. [ME *beem,* OE *bēam* tree, post, ray of light; c. D *boom,* G *Baum* tree; akin to Goth *bagms,* Icel *bathmr* tree] —**Syn. 6.** See **gleam. 14.** See **shine.**

beam-ends (bēm′endz′), *n.pl. Naut.* **1.** the ends of the transverse deck beams of a vessel. **2. on her beam-ends,** heeled so far on one side that the deck is practically vertical.

beam·ing (bē′ming), *adj.* radiant; bright; cheerful. —**beam′ing·ly,** *adv.*

beam·ish (bē′mish), *adj. Often Disparaging.* bright, cheerful, and optimistic.

beam·y (bē′mē), *adj.,* **beam·i·er, beam·i·est. 1.** emitting beams of or as of light; radiant. **2.** broad in the beam, as a ship. **3.** *Zool.* having antlers, as a stag. —**beam′i·ly,** *adv.* —**beam′i·ness,** *n.*

bean (bēn), *n.* **1.** the edible nutritious seed of various species of leguminous plants, esp. of the genus *Phaseolus.* **2.** a plant producing such seeds, used as a snap bean, as a shell bean, or as dry beans. **3.** any of various other beanlike seeds or plants, as the coffee bean. **4.** *Slang.* a person's head. **5. beans,** *Informal.* the slightest amount: *He doesn't know beans about navigation.* **6. full of beans,** *Informal.* **a.** energetic; vigorously active; vital: *He is still full of beans at 65.* **b.** erroneous or misinformed. **7. spill the beans,** *Informal.* to disclose a secret, either accidentally or imprudently, thereby ruining a surprise or plan. —*v.t.* **8.** *Informal.* to hit on the head. [ME *bene,* OE *bēan;* c. Icel *baun,* D *boon,* OHG *bona* (G *Bohne*)] —**bean′like′,** *adj.*

bean-bag (bēn′bag′), *n.* a small cloth bag filled with beans, used as a toy.

bean′ ball′, *Baseball Slang.* a ball thrown by a pitcher purposely at or near the head of the batter.

bean′ ca′per, a small tree, *Zygophyllum Fabago,* of the eastern Mediterranean regions, whose flower buds are used as a substitute for capers.

bean′ curd′, tofu.

bean·er·y (bē′nə rē), *n., pl.* **-er·ies.** *Slang.* a cheap, usually inferior, restaurant.

bean·ie (bē′nē), *n.* a skullcap, often brightly colored, worn esp. by children and college freshmen.

bean·pole (bēn′pōl′), *n.* **1.** a tall pole for a bean plant to climb on. **2.** *Informal.* a tall, lanky person.

bean·shoot·er (bēn′sho͞o′tər), *n.* a child's toy, consisting of a small tube through which dried beans are blown. Cf. **peashooter.**

bean′ sprouts′, the sprouts of newly germinated beans used as a vegetable.

bean·stalk (bēn′stôk′), *n.* the stem of a bean plant.

bean′ tree′, any of several trees bearing pods resembling those of a bean, as the catalpa and the carob tree.

bear[1] (bâr), *v.,* **bore** or (*Archaic*) **bare; borne** or **born; bear·ing.** —*v.t.* **1.** to give birth to: *to bear a child.* **2.** to produce by natural growth: *a tree that bears fruit.* **3.** to support or to hold or remain firm under (a load): *The columns bear the weight of the roof.* **4.** to sustain or be capable of: *His claim doesn't bear close examination.* **5.** to press or push against: *The crowd was borne back by the police.* **6.** to manage or conduct (oneself, one's body, one's head, etc.): *to bear oneself erectly; to bear oneself bravely.* **7.** to suffer; endure or tolerate: *He bore the blame. I can't bear your nagging.* **8.** to warrant or be worthy of: *It doesn't bear repeating.* **9.** to carry; bring: *to bear gifts.* **10.** to carry in the mind or heart: *to bear love; to bear malice.* **11.** to transmit or spread (gossip,

tales, etc.). **12.** to render; afford; give: *to bear testimony.* **13.** to have and be entitled to: *to bear title.* **14.** to exhibit; show: *to bear a resemblance.* **15.** to accept or have, as an obligation: *to bear the cost.* **16.** to possess, as a quality, characteristic, etc.; have in or on: *to bear traces; to bear an inscription.* —*v.i.* **17.** to tend in a course or direction; move; go: *to bear west.* **18.** to be located or situated: *The lighthouse bears due north.* **19.** to bring forth young or fruit: *Next year the tree will bear.* **20.** **bear down, a.** to press or weigh down. **b.** to strive harder; intensify one's efforts. **c.** to approach rapidly, as a ship or opponent. **21.** **bear on** or **upon,** to affect, relate to, or have connection with; be relevant: *This information may bear on the case.* **22.** **bear out,** to substantiate; confirm: *The facts bear me out.* **23.** **bear up,** to endure; face hardship bravely. **24.** **bear with,** to be patient; be forbearing. **25.** **bring to bear,** to concentrate on with a specific purpose. [ME *bere(n),* OE *beran;* c. D *baren,* Icel *bera,* Goth *bairan,* G *(ge)bären,* L *fer(re),* Gk *phér(ein),* Skt *bhar(ati)*]
—**Syn. 2.** yield. **3.** uphold, sustain. **5.** thrust, drive, force. **7.** brook, abide. BEAR, STAND, ENDURE refer to supporting the burden of something distressing, irksome, or painful. BEAR is the general word and STAND its colloquial equivalent, but with an implication of stout spirit: *to bear a disappointment well; to stand a loss.* ENDURE implies continued resistance and patience in bearing through a long time: *to endure torture.*

bear[2] (bâr), *n., pl.* **bears,** (*esp. collectively*) **bear,** *adj.* —*n.* **1.** any of the plantigrade, carnivorous or omnivorous mammals of the family *Ursidae,* having massive bodies, coarse heavy fur, relatively short limbs, and almost rudimentary tails. **2.** any of various animals resembling the bear, as the ant bear. **3.** a gruff, clumsy, or rude person. **4.** a person who believes that general business conditions are becoming or will be unfavorable. **5.** one who sells stocks or commodities short in the hope of buying later at a lower price (opposed to *bull*). **6.** *Informal.* one who shows great ability, enthusiasm, interest, etc.: *a bear for physics.* **7.** (*cap.*) *Astron.* either of two constellations, Ursa Major or Ursa Minor. **8.** (*cap.*) Russia. —*adj.* **9.** having to do with or marked by declining prices, as of stocks: *bear market.* [ME *bere,* OE *bera;* c. D *beer,* OHG *bero* (G *Bär*); akin to Lith *beras* brown. See BRUIN] —**bear′like′,** *adj.*

Black bear,
Ursus americanus
(3 ft. high at shoulder;
length 5 ft.)

bear·a·ble (bâr′ə bəl), *adj.* capable of being borne; endurable. —**bear′a·ble·ness,** *n.* —**bear′a·bly,** *adv.*

bear·bait·ing (bâr′bā′ting), *n.* the former practice of setting dogs to fight a captive bear. —**bear′bait′er,** *n.*

bear·ber·ry (bâr′ber′ē, -bə rē), *n., pl.* **-ries. 1.** a trailing evergreen ericaceous shrub, *Arctostaphylos Uvaursi,* bearing small bright-red berries and tonic, astringent leaves. **2.** a related species, *A. alpina,* bearing black berries. **3.** any of certain other plants, as *Ilex decidua,* a holly of the southern U.S. **4.** the cranberry, *Oxycoccus macrocarpus.*

bear·cat (bâr′kat′), *n.* **1.** a panda, *Ailurus fulgens.* **2.** *Informal.* a person who fights or conducts himself with force or fierceness.

beard (bērd), *n.* **1.** the growth of hair on the face of an adult man. **2.** *Zool.* a tuft, growth, or part resembling or suggesting a human beard, as the tuft of long hairs on the lower jaw of a goat. **3.** *Bot.* a tuft or growth of awns or the like, as in wheat, barley, etc. **4.** a barb or catch on an arrow, fishhook, etc. **5.** Also called **neck.** *Print. U.S.* the sloping part of a type which connects the face with the shoulder. —*v.t.* **6.** to seize, pluck, or pull the beard of: *The hoodlums bearded the old man.* **7.** to defy; oppose boldly. [ME *berd,* OE *beard;* c. G *Bart,* D *baard,* OSlav *brada,* Russ *boroda*] —**beard′less,** *adj.* —**beard′less·ness,** *n.* —**beard′-like′,** *adj.*

Beard (bērd), *n.* **1.** **Charles A(ustin),** 1874–1948, U.S. historian. **2.** his wife, **Mary,** 1876–1958, U.S. historian. **3.** **Daniel Carter,** 1850–1941, U.S. artist and naturalist: organized the Boy Scouts of America in 1910.

beard·ed (bēr′did), *adj.* **1.** having a beard. **2.** having a hairlike growth or tuft, as certain wheats. **3.** having a barb, as a fishhook. [ME *beerdid*]

Beards·ley (bērdz′lē), *n.* **Aubrey Vincent,** 1872–98, English illustrator.

bear·er (bâr′ər), *n.* **1.** a person or thing that carries, upholds, or brings. **2.** the person who presents an order for money or goods: *Pay to the bearer.* **3.** a tree or plant that yields fruit or flowers. **4.** the holder of rank or office; incumbent. **5.** (esp. in India) a native boy or man employed as a personal or household servant. [ME *berere*]

bear′ gar′den, 1. (formerly) a place for keeping or exhibiting bears, as for bearbaiting. **2.** a place or scene of tumult.

bear′ grass′, 1. any of several American liliaceous plants of the genus *Yucca,* having grasslike foliage. **2.** any of certain similar liliaceous plants, as the camass.

bear′ hug′, 1. a forcefully tight embrace. **2.** *Wrestling.* a hold in which a contestant locks both arms around his opponent from the front.

bear·ing (bâr′ing), *n.* **1.** the manner in which a person conducts or carries himself, including posture, gestures, etc.: *a man of dignified bearing.* **2.** act, capability, or period of producing or bringing forth: *a tree past bearing.* **3.** a thing that is produced; crop. **4.** act of enduring or capacity to endure. **5.** reference or relation (usually fol. by *on*): *It has some bearing on the problem.* **6.** *Mach.* the support and guide for a rotating, oscillating, or sliding element, as a shaft, pivot, or wheel. **7.** Often, **bearings, a.** direction or relative position: *The pilot radioed his bearings.* **b.** comprehension of one's situation or position. **8.** *Survey.* a horizontal direction expressed in degrees east or west of a true or magnetic north or south direction. **9.** *Heraldry.* any single device on an escutcheon; charge. [ME *beryng*] —**Syn. 1.** carriage, mien, demeanor, behavior, conduct. See **manner. 5.** connection, dependency; application.

bear′ing bronze′, any bronze alloy used for bearings.

bear′ing rein′, checkrein (def. 1).

bear·ish (bâr′ish), *adj.* **1.** like a bear; rough; burly; clumsy; grumpy; bad-mannered; rude. **2.** *Com.* **a.** declining or tending toward a decline in prices. **b.** characterized by unfavorable prospects for the economy or some aspect of it. —**bear′ish·ly,** *adv.* —**bear′ish·ness,** *n.*

Bé·ar·naise (ber nāz′; *Fr.* bā AR nez′), *n.* (*sometimes l.c.*) a sauce of egg yolks, shallots, butter, vinegar, etc. Also called **Béarnaise′ sauce′.** [< F, after *Béarn* district in SW France + *-aise* fem. of *-ais* -ESE]

Bear′ Riv′er, a river in NE Utah, SW Wyoming, and SE Idaho, flowing into the Great Salt Lake. 350 mi. long.

bear's-ear (bârz′ēr′), *n.* auricula.

bear·skin (bâr′skin′), *n.* **1.** the skin or pelt of a bear. **2.** a tall, black fur cap forming part of the dress uniform of a soldier in some armies.

beast (bēst), *n.* **1.** any animal other than man, esp. a large, four-footed mammal. **2.** the crude animal nature common to humans and nonhumans: *Hunger brought out the beast in him.* **3.** a cruel, coarse, beastlike person. **4.** beasts, or animals, collectively. [ME *be(e)ste* < OF *beste* (F *bête*) < L *bestia*] —**Syn. 1.** See **animal.**

beast·ie (bē′stē), *n.* *Chiefly Literary.* a small animal, esp. one toward which affection is felt.

beast·ly (bēst′lē), *adj.,* **-li·er, -li·est,** *adv.* —*adj.* **1.** of or like a beast; bestial. **2.** *Chiefly Brit. Informal.* nasty; unpleasant; disagreeable. —*adv.* **3.** *Brit. Informal.* very; exceedingly: *It's beastly cold out.* [ME *beasteliche,* later *be(e)stly*] —**beast′li·ness,** *n.*

beast′ of bur′den, an animal used for carrying heavy loads or pulling heavy equipment, as a donkey, mule, or ox.

beat (bēt), *v.,* **beat, beat·en** or **beat, beat·ing,** *n., adj.* —*v.t.* **1.** to give a series of blows to; strike repeatedly. **2.** to flutter, flap, or rotate in or against: *a bird beating the air with its wings.* **3.** to sound, as on a drum: *beating a message.* **4.** to stir vigorously: *Beat the egg whites well.* **5.** to break, forge, or make by blows: *to beat swords into plowshares.* **6.** to make (a path) by repeated treading. **7.** to thrash (a person) soundly (often fol. by *up*): *He beat up the ruffian.* **8.** *Music.* to mark (time) by strokes, as with the hand or a metronome. **9.** *Hunting.* to scour (the forest, grass, or brush) in order to rouse game. **10.** to overcome in or as in a contest; defeat. **11.** to be superior to: *Making reservations beats waiting in line.* **12.** *Slang.* to be incomprehensible to; baffle: *It beats me how he got the job.* **13.** *U.S. Slang.* to swindle; cheat (often fol. by *out*): *He beat him out of hundreds of dollars on that deal.*
—*v.i.* **14.** to strike with or as with repeated blows; pound. **15.** to throb or pulsate: *His heart began to beat faster.* **16.** to resound under blows, as a drum. **17.** to achieve victory in a contest; win: *Which team will beat?* **18.** to scour cover for game. **19.** to permit beating: *This cream won't beat.* **20.** **beat around** or **about the bush.** See **bush**[1] (def. 8). **21.** **beat a retreat.** See **retreat** (def. 7). **22.** **beat back,** to force back; compel to withdraw: *to beat back an attacker.* **23.** **beat it,** *Slang.* to leave; go away. **24.** **beat off,** to ward off; repulse. **25.** **beat the rap.** See **rap**[1] (def. 8). **26.** **beat up,** to administer a severe beating to.
—*n.* **27.** a stroke or blow. **28.** the sound made by one or more such blows: *the beat of drums.* **29.** a throb or pulsation: *a pulse of 60 beats per minute.* **30.** the ticking sound made by a clock or watch. **31.** a person's assigned or regular path or habitual round: *a policeman's beat.* **32.** *Music.* **a.** the audible, visual, or mental marking of the metrical divisions of music. **b.** a stroke of the hand, baton, etc., marking time division or accent for music during performance. **33.** *Pros.* the accent stress, or ictus, in a foot or rhythmical unit of poetry. **34.** *Physics.* a pulsation caused by the interference of two oscillations of unequal frequencies. **35.** *Journalism.* **a.** the reporting of a piece of news in advance of a rival or rivals. Cf. **exclusive** (def. 7), **scoop** (def. 7). **b.** the particular news source or activity that a reporter is responsible for covering. **36.** *Informal.* beatnik.
—*adj. Informal.* **37.** exhausted; worn out. **38.** of or characteristic of members of the Beat Generation or beatniks. [ME *bete(n),* OE *bēatan;* c. Icel *bauta,* OHG *bōzzan*] —**beat′a·ble,** *adj.*
—**Syn. 1.** batter, pommel, buffet, flog. BEAT, HIT, POUND, STRIKE, THRASH refer to the giving of a blow or blows. BEAT implies the giving of repeated blows: *to beat a rug.* To HIT is usually to give a single blow, definitely directed: *to hit a ball.* To POUND is to give heavy and repeated blows, often with the fist: *to pound a nail, the table.* To STRIKE is to give one or more forceful blows suddenly or swiftly: *to strike a gong.* To THRASH implies inflicting repeated blows as punishment, to show superior strength, and the like: *to thrash a child.* **10.** conquer, subdue, vanquish. **11.** outdo, surpass. **15.** See **pulsate.**

beat·en (bēt′ən), *adj.* **1.** formed or shaped by blows; hammered: *a tray of beaten brass.* **2.** much trodden; commonly used: *a beaten path.* **3.** defeated; vanquished; thwarted. **4.** (of food) whipped up, pounded, pulverized, or the like: *adding three beaten eggs.* **5.** **off the beaten track** or **path,** novel; uncommon; out of the ordinary. [ME *beten,* OE *bēaten,* ptp. of *bēatan* to BEAT]

beat·er (bē′tər), *n.* **1.** a person or thing that beats. **2.** an implement or device for beating something. **3.** *Hunting.* a person who rouses or drives game from cover.

Beat′ Genera′tion, members of the generation that came of age after World War II, esp. in the late 1950's, and espoused mystical detachment and the relaxation of authority and social inhibitions. Also, **beat′ genera′tion.** [phrase popularized by Jack KEROUAC]

be·a·tif·ic (bē′ə tif′ik), *adj.* **1.** bestowing bliss, blessings, happiness, or the like: *a period of beatific peace.* **2.** blissful; saintly: *a beatific smile.* [< LL *beātific(us)* making happy = *beāt(us)* (ptp. of *beāre:* be- bless + *-āt(us)* -ATE[1]) + *-i-* -I- + *-ficus* -FIC] —**be′a·tif′i·cal·ly,** *adv.*

be·at·i·fi·ca·tion (bē at′ə fə kā′shən), *n.* **1.** act of beatifying. **2.** state of being beatified. **3.** *Rom. Cath. Ch.* the official act of the pope whereby a deceased person is beatified, therefore becoming a proper subject of religious veneration. [< LL *beātificātiōn-* (s. of *beātificātiō*)]

be·at·i·fy (bē at′ə fī′), *v.t.,* **-fied, -fy·ing. 1.** to make blissfully happy. **2.** *Rom. Cath. Ch.* to declare (a deceased person) to be among the blessed in heaven and thus entitled to specific religious honor. [< MF *beatifi(er)* < LL *beātificāre*]

beat·ing (bē′ting), *n.* **1.** the act of a person or thing that beats, as to punish, clean, mix, etc.: *Give the rug a good beating.* **2.** a severe punishing with blows, as of the fists or with a cudgel; thrashing. **3.** a defeat. **4.** pulsation; throbbing: *the beating of her heart.* [ME *betynge*]

be·at·i·tude (bē at′ə to͞od′, -tyo͞od′), *n.* **1.** supreme blessedness; exalted happiness. **2.** (*often cap.*) any of the declarations of blessedness pronounced by Jesus in the Sermon on the Mount. [< L *beātitūdō* perfect happiness = *beāti-* (see BEATIFIC) + *-tūdō* -TUDE]

beat·nik (bēt′nik), *n.* *Informal.* **1.** a member of the Beat Generation. **2.** a person who rejects or avoids conventional behavior, dress, etc. [BEAT (adj.) (as in BEAT GENERATION) + *-nik* Russ n. suffix designating an agent or one concerned with something; cf. CHETNIK]

Be·a·trix (bē′ə triks, bā′-), *n.* (*Beatrix Wilhelmina Armgard*) born 1939, queen of the Netherlands since 1980 (daughter of Juliana).

Beat·tie (bē′tē), *n.* **James,** 1735–1803, Scottish poet.

Beat·ty (bē′tē), *n.* **David** (*1st Earl of the North Sea and of Brooksby*), 1871–1936, British admiral.

beat-up (bēt′up′), *adj.* *Informal.* dilapidated; in poor condition from use: *a beat-up old jalopy.*

beau (bō), *n., pl.* **beaus, beaux** (bōz). **1.** a frequent and attentive male escort for a girl or woman. **2.** a dandy; fop. [ME < F < L *bellus* beautiful] —**beau′ish,** *adj.*

Beau′ Brum′mell (brum′əl), **1.** (*George Bryan Brummell*) 1778–1840, English dandy: set standards of fashion for men. **2.** a man who is excessively concerned with fashionable clothes, manners, etc.; fop; dandy.

Beau′fort scale′ (bō′fərt), **1.** a scale of wind forces, described by name and range of velocity, and classified from force 0 to force 12, or, sometimes, to force 17. **2.** a scale of the states of sea created by winds of these various forces up to and including force 10. [named after Sir Francis *Beaufort* (1774–1857), British admiral who devised it]

BEAUFORT WIND SCALE

Beaufort Force Number	State of Air	Wind Velocity in Knots
0	calm	0–1
1	light airs	1–3
2	slight breeze	4–6
3	gentle breeze	7–10
4	moderate breeze	11–16
5	fresh breeze	17–21
6	strong breeze	22–27
7	moderate gale	28–33
8	fresh gale	34–40
9	strong gale	41–47
10	whole gale	48–55
11	storm	56–65
12	hurricane	above 65

Beau′fort Sea′ (bō′fərt), a part of the Arctic Ocean, NE of Alaska.

beau geste (bō zhest′), *pl.* **beaux gestes** (bō zhest′). *French.* a fine gesture, often only for effect.

Beau·har·nais (bō AR ne′), *n.* **1. Eu·gé·nie Hortense de** (œ zhā nē′ ôR täNs′ də), 1782–1837, queen of Holland: wife of Louis Bonaparte. **2. Jo·sé·phine de** (zhō zā fēn′ də), 1763–1814, empress of France 1804–09: first wife of Napoleon I.

beau′ ide′al, *pl.* **beaus ideal, beaux ideal** for 1; **beau ideals** for 2. **1.** a conception of perfect beauty. **2.** a model of excellence. [< F *beau idéal,* lit., ideal beauty]

Beau·jo·lais (bō′zhə lā′), *n., pl.* **-laises** (-lāz′). a dry, fruity, red Burgundy wine. [after *Beaujolais,* region in France where produced]

Beau·mar·chais (bō MAR she′), *n.* **Pierre Au·gus·tin Ca·ron de** (pyeR ō GY STAN′ KA RôN′ də), 1732–99, French dramatist.

beau monde (bō′ mond′; *Fr.* bō môNd′), the fashionable world; high society. [< F: lit., fine world]

Beau·mont (bō′mont), *n.* **1. Francis,** 1584–1616, English dramatist who collaborated with John Fletcher. **2. William,** 1785–1853, U.S. surgeon. **3.** a city in SE Texas. 117,548.

Beau·re·gard (bō′rə gärd′; *Fr.* bōR GAR′), *n.* **Pierre Gus·tave Tou·tant** (pyeR GY STAV′ to͞o täN′), 1818–93, Confederate general in the U.S. Civil War.

beaut (byo͞ot), *n.* *Informal.* (often ironical) something or someone beautiful, remarkable, or perfect. [by shortening from BEAUTY]

beau·te·ous (byo͞o′tē əs, -tyəs), *adj.* *Chiefly Literary.* beautiful. [late ME] —**beau′te·ous·ly,** *adv.* —**beau′te·ous·ness,** *n.*

beau·ti·cian (byo͞o tish′ən), *n.* a manager or an employee of a beauty parlor.

beau·ti·ful (byo͞o′tə fəl), *adj.* **1.** having beauty; delighting the senses or mind. **2.** excellent of its kind: *a beautiful putt on the seventh hole.* **3.** wonderful; very pleasing or satisfying. —*n.* **4.** a concept or ideal of beauty (usually prec. by *the*). —**beau′ti·ful·ly,** *adv.* —**beau′ti·ful·ness,** *n.* —**Syn. 1.** comely, seemly, attractive. BEAUTIFUL, HANDSOME, LOVELY, PRETTY refer to a pleasing appearance. That which is BEAUTIFUL has perfection of form, color, etc., or noble and spiritual qualities: *a beautiful landscape, girl* (not *man*). HANDSOME often implies stateliness or pleasing proportion and symmetry: *a handsome man; a handsome woman.* That which is LOVELY is beautiful but in a warm and endearing way: *a lovely smile.* PRETTY implies a moderate but noticeable beauty, esp. in that which is small.

beau·ti·fy (byo͞o′tə fī′), *v.t., v.i.,* **-fied, -fy·ing.** to make or become beautiful. —**beau·ti·fi·ca·tion** (byo͞o′tə fə kā′shən), *n.* —**beau′ti·fi′er,** *n.* —**Syn.** adorn, embellish.

beau′tiful peo′ple, wealthy, sophisticated people who set trends, fads, and fashions; the jet set.

beau·ty (byo͞o′tē), *n., pl.* **-ties** for 2–6. **1.** a quality that is present in a thing or person giving intense aesthetic pleasure or deep satisfaction to the senses or the mind. **2.** an attractive, well-formed girl or woman. **3.** a beautiful thing, as a work of art, building, etc. **4.** Often, **beauties.** that which is beautiful in nature or in some natural or artificial environment. **5.** a particular advantage: *One of the beauties of this medicine is the absence of aftereffects.* **6.** a person or thing that excels or is remarkable of its kind: *His black eye was a beauty.* [ME *be(a)ute* < OF *beaute;* r. ME *bealte* < OF, var. of *beltet* < VL **bellitāt-* (s. of **bellitās*) = L *bell(us)* fine + *-itāt-* -ITY] —**Syn. 1.** loveliness, pulchritude.

beau′ty par′lor, *U.S.* an establishment for the hairdressing, manicuring, or other beauty treatment of women. Also called **beau′ty salon′, beau′ty shop′.**

beau′ty spot′, **1.** a tiny patch worn, usually on the face, to set off the fairness of the skin. **2.** a mole or other dark mark on the skin.

Beau·vais (bō vā′; *Fr.* bō ve′), *n.* a city in NW France: 13th century cathedral. 36,533 (1962).

Beau·voir (bōv wär′; *Fr.* bō VWAR′), *n.* **Si·mone de** (sē-môn′ də), 1908–86, French writer.

beaux (bōz; *Fr.* bō), *n.* a pl. of **beau.**

Beaux-Arts (bō zär′; *Fr.* bō ZAR′), *adj.* **1.** noting or pertaining to a style of architecture that prevailed in France in the late 19th century, characterized by the free and eclectic use and adaptation of French architectural features of the 16th–18th centuries, combined to give a massive, elaborate, and often ostentatious effect. —*n.* **2.** (*l.c.*) the fine arts.

bea·ver[1] (bē′vər), *n., pl.* **-vers,** (*esp. collectively*) **-ver** for 1. **1.** an amphibious rodent of the genus *Castor,* having sharp incisors, webbed hind feet, and a flattened tail. **2.** the fur of this animal. **3.** a flat, round hat usually made of beaver fur. **4.** See **top hat.** Cf. **opera hat, silk hat.** **5.** *Informal.* a full beard or a man wearing one. **6.** *Informal.* an exceptionally active or hard-working person. **7.** *Textiles.* a cotton or woolen cloth with a thick nap. **8.** (*cap.*) a native or inhabitant of Oregon (the **Beaver State**) (used as a nickname). [ME *bever,* OE *beofor, befor;* c. G *Biber,* Lith *bebrùs,* L *fiber,* Skt *babhrūs* reddish brown, large ichneumon] —**bea′ver·like′, bea′ver·ish,** *adj.*

Beaver, *Castor canadensis* (Total length 3½ ft.; tail 1 ft.)

bea·ver[2] (bē′vər), *n.* *Armor.* a piece of plate armor for covering the lower part of the face and throat, worn esp. with a helmet or as part of a close helmet. Also, **bevor.** [earlier *bever,* orig. short for *bever hat,* hat made of beaver's fur, but also used, by transfer, in sense of face guard; r. late ME *baviere* < MF, in same sense (OF: bib) = *bave* slaver + *-iere* < L *-āria,* fem. of *-ārius* -ER[2]]

Bea·ver·board (bē′vər bōrd′, -bôrd′), *n.* *Trademark.* a light, stiff sheeting made of wood fiber and used in building, esp. for partitions, temporary structures, etc.

Bea·ver·brook (bē′vər bro͝ok′), *n.* **William Maxwell Aitken, Lord** (*1st Baron*), 1879–1964, English publisher.

bea′ver cloth′, beaver[1] (def. 7).

Bea′ver State′, Oregon (used as a nickname).

be·bee·rine (bə bēr′ēn, -in, beb′ē ə rēn′), *n.* *Pharm.* an alkaloid resembling quinine. [< G *Bebeerin* = *Bebeer-(ubaum)* bebeeru tree + *-in* -INE[2]]

be·bee·ru (bə bēr′o͞o), *n.* greenheart (def. 1). [< Sp *bibirú* < Carib]

Be·bel (bā′bəl), *n.* **Fer·di·nand Au·gust** (fûr′dᵊnand′ ô′gəst; *Ger.* feR′di nänt′ ou′go͞ost), 1840–1913, German socialist and writer.

be·bop (bē′bop′), *n.* *Jazz.* bop[1]. [imit. of staccato beat found in phrasing] —**be′bop′per,** *n.*

be·calm (bi käm′), *v.t.* **1.** to deprive (a sailing vessel) of the wind necessary to move it; subject to a calm: *The schooner was becalmed in the horse latitudes.* **2.** *Archaic.* to calm; soothe; pacify.

be·came (bi kām′), *v.* pt. of **become.**

be·cause (bi kôz′, -koz′, -kuz′), *conj.* **1.** for the reason that; due to the fact that: *The boy was absent because he was ill.* —*adv.* **2.** by reason; on account (usually fol. by *of*): *The game was called because of rain.* [ME *bi cause* BY CAUSE] —**Syn. 1.** BECAUSE, AS, SINCE, FOR, INASMUCH AS agree in implying a reason for an occurrence or action. BECAUSE introduces a direct reason: *I was sleeping because I was tired.* AS and SINCE are so casual as to imply merely circumstances attendant on the main statement: *As* (or *since*) *I was tired, I was sleeping.* The reason, proof, or justification introduced by FOR is like an afterthought or a parenthetical statement: *I was sleeping, for I was tired.* INASMUCH AS implies concession; the main statement is true in view of the circumstances introduced by this conjunction: *Inasmuch as I was tired, it seemed best to sleep.* —**Usage. 1.** See **reason.**

bec·ca·fi·co (bek′ə fē′kō), *n., pl.* **-cos, -coes.** any of several small, European birds, esp. the garden warbler, *Sylvia hortensis,* esteemed as a delicacy. [< It = *becca(re)* (to) peck + *fico* FIG[1]]

bé·cha·mel (bā′shə mel′; *Fr.* bā SHA mel′), *n.* a white sauce, sometimes seasoned with onion and nutmeg. Also called **bé′chamel sauce′.** [named after Louis, Marquis de *Béchamel* (steward of Louis XIV of France), its originator]

be·chance (bi chans′, -chäns′), *v.i., v.t.,* **-chanced, -chancing.** *Archaic.* to befall. [from phrase *by chance*]

Béchar (*Fr.* bā SHAR′), *n.* a city in W Algeria. 148,101. Formerly, **Colomb-Béchar.**

bêche-de-mer (besh′də mâr′), *n., pl.* **bêch·es-de-mer,** (*esp. collectively*) **bêche-de-mer.** a trepang. [< F: lit., spade of (the) sea, alter. of Pg *biche do mar* worm of the sea]

Bech·u·a·na·land (bech′o͞o ä′nə land′, bek′yo͞o-), *n.* former name of **Botswana.**

beck[1] (bek), *n.* **1.** a beckoning gesture. **2. at someone's beck and call,** ready to do someone's bidding; subject to someone's slightest wish. **3.** *Chiefly Scot.* a bow or curtsy of greeting. —*v.t., v.i.* **4.** *Archaic.* beckon. [ME *becke,* short var. of *becne(n)* (to) BECKON]

beck[2] (bek), *n.* *Brit. Dial.* a brook, esp. a swiftly running stream with steep banks. [ME *becc* < Scand; cf. Icel *bekkr;* akin to OE *bece,* D *beek,* G *Bach* brook]

beck·et (bek′it), *n.* *Naut.* **1.** a short length of rope for securing spars, coils of rope, etc., having an eye at one end to hold a thick knot or a toggle at the other. **2.** any of various other devices for securing sails or the like, as a grommet or cleat. [?]

Beck·et (bek′it), *n.* **Saint Thomas à,** 1118?–70, archbishop of Canterbury: murdered because of his opposition to Henry II's policies toward the Church.

beck′et bend′, *Naut.* See **sheet bend.**

Beck·ett (bek′it), *n.* **Samuel,** born 1906, Irish playwright and novelist, living in France.

Beck·ford (bek′fərd), *n.* **William,** 1759–1844, English writer.

Beck·mann (bek′män′), *n.* **Max** (mäks), 1884–1950, German painter.

beck·on (bek′ən), *v.t., v.i.* **1.** to signal, summon, or direct by a gesture of the head or hand. **2.** to lure; entice. —*n.* **3.** a nod, gesture, etc., that beckons, indicates agreement, or the like. [ME *beknen,* OE *gebē(a)cnian* < *bēacen* BEACON] —**beck′on·er,** *n.* —**beck′on·ing·ly,** *adv.*

be·cloud (bi kloud′), *v.t.* **1.** to darken or obscure with clouds. **2.** to make confused.

be·come (bi kum′), *v.,* **be·came, be·come, be·com·ing.** —*v.i.* **1.** to come, change, or grow to be (as specified): *He became tired.* **2.** to come into being. —*v.t.* **3.** to be attractive on; befit in appearance; suit: *That gown becomes you.* **4.** to be suitable or necessary to the dignity, situation, or responsibility of: *conduct that becomes an officer and a gentleman.* **5. become of,** to happen to; be the fate of: *What will become of him?* [ME *becumen,* OE *becuman* to come about, happen; c. D *bekomen,* G *bekommen,* Goth *biqiman*]

be·com·ing (bi kum′ing), *adj.* **1.** tending to suit or to have a pleasing effect or attractive appearance. —*n.* **2.** any process of change. —**be·com′ing·ly,** *adv.* —**be·com′ing·ness,** *n.* —**Syn. 1.** comely; fitting, appropriate, apt, seemly.

Bé·cquer (be′keʀ), *n.* **Gus·ta·vo A·dol·fo** (go͞os tä′vô ä dôl′fô), 1836–70, Spanish poet.

Bec·que·rel (bek′ə rel′; *Fr.* bekə ʀel′), *n.* **1. A·lex·an·dre Ed·mond** (A lek sän′dʀə ed môn′), 1820–91, French physicist (son of Antoine César). **2. An·toine Cé·sar** (än twan′ sā zar′), 1788–1878, French physicist. **3. An·toine Hen·ri** (än twan′ än ʀē′), 1852–1908. French physicist (son of Alexandre Edmond): Nobel prize 1903.

bed (bed), *n., v.,* **bed·ded, bed·ding.** —*n.* **1.** a piece of furniture upon which or within which a person sleeps. **2.** the mattress and bedclothes together with the bedstead of a bed. **3.** the bedstead alone. **4.** the act of or time for sleeping; sleep: *a cup of cocoa and then bed.* **5.** the use of a bed for the night; lodging: *fifteen shillings for bed and breakfast.* **6.** the marital relationship. **7.** any resting place: *making his bed under a tree.* **8.** a piece or area of ground in a garden or lawn in which plants are grown. **9.** the plants in such areas. **10.** the bottom of a lake, river, or other body of water. **11.** an area on the bottom of a body of water abounding in a particular kind of plant or animal life: *an oyster bed.* **12.** a piece or part forming a foundation or base: *sliced tomatoes on a bed of lettuce.* **13.** *Geol.* a layer of rock; stratum. **14.** a foundation surface of earth or rock supporting a track, pavement, or the like: *a gravel bed for the roadway.* **15.** *Building Trades.* **a.** the underside of a stone, brick, slate, tile, etc., laid in position. **b.** the layer of mortar in which a brick, stone, etc., is laid. **16.** *Furniture.* skirt (def. 5b). **17.** the flat surface in a printing press on which the form of type is laid. **18. get up on the wrong side of the bed,** to be irritable or bad-tempered from the start of a day. **19. make a bed,** to fit a bed with sheets and blankets. **20. put to bed, a.** to help (someone) go to bed. **b.** *Printing.* to lock up (forms) in a press in preparation for printing. —*v.t.* **21.** to provide with a bed. **22.** to put to bed. **23.** *Hort.* to plant in or as in a bed. **24.** to place in a bed or layer: *to bed oysters.* **25.** to embed, as in a substance: *bedding the flagstones in concrete.* —*v.i.* **26.** to go to bed. **27.** to have sleeping accommodations: *wanting to bed in the best hotels.* **28.** *Geol.* to form a compact layer or stratum. **29. bed down, a.** to make a bed for (a person, animal, etc.). **b.** to retire to bed. [ME; OE *bedd;* c. D *bed,* Icel *bethr,* Goth *badi,* OHG *betti* (G *Bett*); akin to L *fodere* to dig] —**bed′less,** *adj.* —**bed′like′,** *adj.*

be·dab·ble (bi dab′əl), *v.t.,* **-bled, -bling.** to dabble all over: *His clothes were bedabbled with paint.*

bed′ and board′, **1.** living quarters and meals. **2.** *Law.* obligations of marriage; charge of a household.

be·daub (bi dôb′), *v.t.* **1.** to daub all over; besmear; soil. **2.** to ornament gaudily or excessively.

be·daz·zle (bi daz′əl), *v.t.,* **-zled, -zling. 1.** to dazzle so as to blind or confuse. **2.** to impress forcefully, esp. so as to make oblivious to faults or shortcomings. —**be·daz′zle·ment,** *n.* —**be·daz′zling·ly,** *adv.*

bed′ board′, a hard, thin board, usually of plywood, placed between the mattress and bedspring to give firm support to one's body.

bed·bug (bed′bug′), *n.* **1.** a flat, wingless, bloodsucking hemipterous insect, *Cimex lectularius,* that infests houses and esp. beds. **2.** any of several other bloodsucking bugs of the family *Cimicidae.*

Bedbug, *Cimex lectularius* (Length ⅛ in.)

bed·cham·ber (bed′chām′bər), *n.* bedroom. [ME *bedchaumbre*]

bed′ check′, an inspection, usually at night, to detect the unauthorized absence of persons from a dormitory, barracks, or the like.

bed·clothes (bed′klōz′, -klōthz′), *n.pl.* coverings for a bed, as sheets, blankets, etc.; bedding. Also, **bed·cloth·ing** (bed′klō′thing). [ME]

bed·da·ble (bed′ə bəl), *adj.* **1.** *Slang.* readily willing to have sexual relations: *a beddable young actress.* **2.** suitable for use as a bed.

bed·ding (bed′ing), *n.* **1.** bedclothes. **2.** litter, straw, etc., as a bed for animals. **3.** *Building Trades.* a foundation or bottom layer. **4.** *Geol.* arrangement of rocks in strata. [ME, OE]

Bed·does (bed′ōz), *n.* **Thomas Lov·ell** (luv′əl), 1803–49, English dramatist and poet.

Bede (bēd), *n.* **Saint** ("*the Venerable Bede*"), A.D. 673?–735, English monk, historian, and theologian: wrote earliest history of England. Also, **Baeda.**

be·deck (bi dek′), *v.t.* to deck out; adorn, esp. in a showy or gaudy manner. —**Syn.** array, decorate, ornament.

bede·house (bēd′hous′), *n., pl.* **-hous·es** (-hou′ziz). beadhouse.

bede·man (bēd′mən), *n., pl.* **-men.** beadsman.

bedes·man (bēdz′mən), *n., pl.* **-men.** beadsman.

be·dev·il (bi dev′əl), *v.t.,* **-iled, -il·ing** or (*esp. Brit.*) **-illed, -il·ling. 1.** to torment or harass maliciously or diabolically. **2.** to possess as with a devil; bewitch. —**be·dev′il·ment,** *n.*

be·dew (bi do͞o′, -dyo͞o′), *v.t.* to wet or cover with or as with dew. [ME *bydewe*]

bed·fast (bed′fast′, -fäst′), *adj.* confined to bed.

bed·fel·low (bed′fel′ō), *n.* **1.** a person who shares one's bed. **2.** a collaborator, esp. one who forms a temporary alliance for reasons of expediency: *Politics makes strange bedfellows.* [late ME *bedfelow*]

Bed·ford (bed′fərd), *n.* **1. John of Lancaster, Duke of,** 1389–1435, English regent of France. **2.** a city in and the county seat of Bedfordshire, in central England. 63,317 (1961). **3.** Bedfordshire.

Bed·ford·shire (bed′fərd shēr′, -shər), *n.* a county in central England. 380,704 (1961); 473 sq. mi. *Co. seat:* Bedford. Also called **Bedford, Beds.**

bed·frame (bed′frām′), *n.* the frame of a bed, including the bedrails, headboard, and footboard.

be·dight (bi dīt′), *v.t.,* **-dight, -dight** or **dight·ed, -dight·ing.** *Archaic.* to deck out; array. [late ME]

be·dim (bi dim′), *v.t.,* **-dimmed, -dim·ming.** to make dim.

Bed·i·vere (bed′ə vēr′), *n.* **Sir,** *Arthurian Legend.* the knight who brought the dying King Arthur to the barge in which the three queens bore him to the Isle of Avalon.

be·di·zen (bi dī′zən, -diz′ən), *v.t.* to dress or adorn in a showy, gaudy, or vulgar manner. —**be·di′zen·ment,** *n.*

bed·lam (bed′ləm), *n.* **1.** a scene of wild uproar and confusion. **2.** (*cap.*) popular name for the Hospital of St. Mary of Bethlehem, formerly an insane asylum in SE London, England. **3.** *Obs.* any lunatic asylum or madhouse. [ME *bedlem, bethlem,* after *Bethlehem*]

bed·lam·ite (bed′lə mīt′), *n.* a lunatic.

bed·lamp (bed′lamp′), *n.* a lamp at the side or head of a bed.

bed′ lin′en, sheets and pillowcases.

Bed·ling·ton (bed′ling tən), *n.* **1.** Also called **Bed·ling·ton·shire** (bed′ling tən shēr′, -shər). an urban area in E Northumberland, in N England. 29,373 (1961). **2.** See **Bedlington terrier.**

Bed′lington ter′rier, one of an English breed of terriers having a thick, fleecy, blue or liver coat, groomed to resemble a lamb.

Bedlington terrier (15 in. high at shoulder)

Bed′loe's Is′land (bed′lōz), former name of **Liberty Island.** Also, **Bed′loe Is′land.**

bed′ mold′ing, *Archit.* the molding or group of moldings immediately beneath the corona of a cornice.

bed′ of ros′es, a situation of luxurious ease; a highly agreeable position: *Professional boxing is no bed of roses.*

Bed·ou·in (bed′o͞o in, bed′win), *n., pl.* **-ins,** (*esp. collectively*) **-in,** *adj.* —*n.* **1.** an Arab of the desert, in Asia or Africa; nomadic Arab. **2.** a nomad; wanderer. —*adj.* **3.** of, pertaining to, or characteristic of the Bedouin. Also, **Beduin.** [late ME *Bedoyn* < MF *beduyn* (sing.) < Ar *badawīn,* pl. of *badawīy* desert dweller = *badw* desert + -*īy* suffix of appurtenance] —**Bed′ou·in·ism,** *n.*

bed·pan (bed′pan′), *n.* a shallow toilet pan for use by persons confined to bed.

bed·post (bed′pōst′), *n.* one of the upright supports of a bedstead.

be·drag·gle (bi drag′əl), *v.t.,* **-gled, -gling.** to make limp and soiled, as with rain or dirt.

bed·rail (bed′rāl′), *n.* a board at the side of a bed connecting the footboard and headboard.

bed·rid·den (bed′rid′ən), *adj.* confined to bed. [var. (by confusion with ptp. of RIDE) of *bedrid,* ME *bedrede,* OE *bedreda, -rida* = *bed* BED + *-rida* rider, akin to RIDE]

bed·rock (bed′rok′), *n.* **1.** *Geol.* unbroken solid rock, overlaid in most places by soil or rock fragments. **2.** the bottom layer; lowest level. **3.** any firm foundation or basis.

bed·roll (bed′rōl′), *n.* bedding rolled for portability and used esp. for sleeping out-of-doors.

bed·room (bed′ro͞om′, -ro͝om′), *n.* a room furnished and used for sleeping.

bed′room slip′per, a house slipper, often heelless and backless and with a flexible sole.

Beds (bedz), *n.* Bedfordshire.

bed·side (bed′sīd′), *n.* **1.** the side of a bed, esp. as the place of one attending the sick. —*adj.* **2.** at or for a bedside: *a bedside table.*

bed′side man′ner, the attitude or behavior of a doctor to his patients.

bed·sore (bed′sōr′, -sôr′), *n.* *Pathol.* a sore caused by malnutrition of tissue due to prolonged pressure of the body against bedding, as in a long illness.

bed·spread (bed′spred′), *n.* an outer covering, usually decorative, for a bed.

bed·spring (bed′spring′), *n.* a set of springs for the support of a mattress.

bed·stand (bed′stand′), *n.* a small table next to a bed. Also called **nightstand, night table.**

bed·stead (bed′sted′, -stid), *n.* the framework of a bed supporting the springs and mattress. [late ME *bedstede*]

bed·straw (bed′strô′), *n.* a rubiaceous plant, *Galium verum,* or some allied species, formerly used as straw for stuffing mattresses. [late ME]

bed·tick (bed′tick′), *n.* tick[3].

bed·time (bed′tīm′), *n.* the time at which one goes to bed [ME; see BED, TIME]

bed′time sto′ry, a story told to a child at bedtime.

Bed·u·in (bed′o͞o in, bed′win), *n., pl.* **-ins,** (*esp. collectively*) **-in,** *adj.* Bedouin.

bed·warm·er (bed′wôr′mər), *n.* a long-handled, covered pan containing hot coals, formerly used for warming beds.

bed-wet·ting (bed′wet′ing), *n.* urinating in bed, esp. habitually and involuntarily; enuresis. —**bed′-wet′ter,** *n.*

bee (bē), *n.* **1.** any hymenopterous insect of the superfamily *Apoidea,* including social and solitary species of several families, as the bumblebees, honeybees, etc. **2.** the common honeybee, *Apis mellifera.* **3.** *Chiefly U.S.* a community social gathering in order to perform some task, engage in a contest, etc.: *a sewing bee; a spelling bee.* **4. have a bee in one's bonnet, a.** to be obsessed with one idea. **b.** to have eccentric or fanciful ideas or schemes. [ME; OE *bīo, bēo;* c. D *bij,* OHG *bīa,* Icel *bȳ;* akin to G *Biene*] —**bee′-like′,** *adj.*

Bee, *Apis mellifera*
A, Queen; B, Drone;
C, Worker

Bee·be (bē′bē), *n.* **(Charles) William,** 1877–1962, U.S. naturalist, explorer, and writer.

bee·bread (bē′bred′), *n.* a mixture of pollen and honey stored by bees and fed to their young.

beech (bēch), *n.* **1.** any tree of the genus *Fagus,* of temperate regions, having a smooth gray bark, and bearing small, edible, triangular nuts. **2.** Also called **beech·wood** (bēch′wo͝od′). the wood of such a tree. [ME *beche,* OE *bēce* < Gmc **bōkjōn-;* akin to OE *bōc* beech, BOOK] —**beech′en,** *adj.* —**beech′y,** *adj.*

Bee·cham (bē′chəm), *n.* **Sir Thomas,** 1879–1961, English conductor and impresario.

beech·drops (bēch′drops′), *n,* (*construed as sing. or pl.*) **1.** a low annual plant, *Epifagus virginiana,* without green foliage, parasitic upon the roots of the beech. **2.** the squawroot.

Bee·cher (bē′chər), *n.* **1. Henry Ward,** 1813–87, U.S. preacher and writer. **2. Ly·man** (lī′mən), 1775–1863, U.S. preacher and theologian (father of Henry Ward Beecher and Harriet Beecher Stowe).

beech′ mast′, the edible nuts of the beech, esp. when lying on the ground.

beech·nut (bēch′nut′), *n.* the small, triangular, edible nut of the beech.

bee-eat·er (bē′ē′tər), *n.* any of several colorful, insectivorous birds of the family *Meropidae,* of the Old World tropics, which feed chiefly on bees.

beef (bēf), *n., pl.* **beeves** (bēvz) for 2, **beefs** for 4, *v.* —*n.* **1.** the flesh of a cow, steer, or bull for use as meat. **2.** an adult cow, steer, or bull raised for its meat. **3.** *Informal.* **a.** brawn; muscular strength. **b.** strength; power. **c.** weight, as of a person. **4.** *Slang.* a complaint. —*v.i.* **5.** *Slang.* to complain; grumble. **6. beef up,** *Informal.* to strengthen; add strength, numbers, force, etc., to: *He beefed up his speech with more facts.* [ME < OF *boef* < L *bov-* (s. of *bōs*) ox, cow; akin to cow¹] —**beef′less,** *adj.*

beef′ bouil′lon, a thin beef-flavored broth. Also called, *esp. Brit.,* **beef tea.**

beef·burg·er (bēf′bûr′gər), *n.* a hamburger. [BEEF + (HAM)BURGER]

beef′ cat′tle, cattle raised for meat.

beef·eat·er (bēf′ē′tər), *n.* **1.** a yeoman of the English royal guard or a warder of the Tower of London. **2.** *Slang.* an Englishman.

bee′ fly′, any of numerous dipterous insects of the family *Bombyliidae,* some of which resemble bees.

beef·steak (bēf′stāk′), *n.* a steak of beef for broiling, pan-frying, etc.

beef′ tea′, *Chiefly Brit.* See **beef bouillon.**

beef·y (bē′fē), *adj.,* **beef·i·er, beef·i·est. 1.** of or like beef. **2.** brawny; thickset; heavy. **3.** obese. —**beef′i·ly,** *adv.* —**beef′i·ness,** *n.*

bee′ gum′, *Southern and Western U.S.* **1.** a gum tree, hollowed as by decay, in which bees live or from which hives are made. **2.** a beehive.

bee·hive (bē′hīv′), *n.* **1.** a hive for bees. **2.** a crowded, busy place.

Bee′hive State′, Utah (used as a nickname).

bee·keep·er (bē′kē′pər), *n.* a person who raises bees. —**bee′keep′ing,** *n.*

bee·line (bē′līn′), *n.* a direct course or route: *He made a beeline for the kitchen.*

Be·el·ze·bub (bē el′zə bub′), *n.* **1.** the chief devil; Satan. **2.** a devil. **3.** (in Milton's *Paradise Lost*) one of the fallen angels, second only to Satan.

been (bin), *v.* pp. of **be.**

beep (bēp), *n.* **1.** a short, usually high-pitched, tone used as a signal, warning, or the like. —*v.i.* **2.** to make or emit a beeping sound. —*v.t.* **3.** to sound (a horn, warning signal, etc.): *impatient drivers beeping their horns.* [imit.]

beep·er (bē′pər), *n.* a device that connects into a telephone circuit and transmits a periodic signal to indicate that conversation is being recorded.

bee′ plant′, any plant frequently used by bees as a source of nectar, esp. the figwort.

beer (bēr), *n.* **1.** an alcoholic beverage brewed by fermentation from cereals, usually malted barley, and flavored with hops for a slightly bitter taste. **2.** any of various carbonated or fermented beverages, whether alcoholic or not, made from roots, molasses or sugar, yeast, etc.: *root beer; ginger beer.* [ME *bere,* OE *bēor;* c. D, G *Bier* (Icel *bjórr,* prob. < OE)]

Beer (bēr), *n.* **Thomas,** 1889–1940, U.S. author.

beer′ and skit′tles, *Brit.* amusement; pleasure; fun, with or without beer or other drinks.

Beer·bohm (bēr′bōm), *n.* **Sir Max,** 1872–1956, English essayist, critic, and caricaturist.

beer′ gar′den, an outdoor tavern, usually resembling a garden, where beer and other alcoholic beverages are served.

beer′ hall′, a bar, cabaret, or the like, serving beer and usually offering music, dancing, etc.

beer·house (bēr′hous′), *n., pl.* **-hous·es** (-hou′ziz). *Brit.* an establishment licensed to serve only liquors fermented from malt, as beer, ale, or the like.

Beer·naert (*Fr.* ber nart′; *Eng.* bâr′närt), *n.* **Au·guste Ma·rie Fran·çois** (*Fr.* ō gyst′ ma rē′ fräN swa′), 1829–1912, Belgian statesman: Nobel peace prize 1909.

Beers (bērz), *n.* **Clifford Whit·ting·ham** (hwit′ing əm, wit′-), 1876–1943, U.S. pioneer in mental hygiene.

Beer·she·ba (bēr shē′bə, bēr′shə-; *Heb.* ber she′bä), *n.* a city in Israel: the southernmost city of ancient Palestine. 60,000 (est. 1966).

beer·y (bēr′ē), *adj.,* **beer·i·er, beer·i·est. 1.** of, like, or abounding in beer. **2.** affected by or suggestive of beer: *beery exuberance; a beery breath.* —**beer′i·ness,** *n.*

beest·ings (bē′stingz), *n.* (*construed as sing.*) the first milk or colostrum of a mammal, esp. a cow, after giving birth. [late ME *bestynge,* OE *bȳsting* = *bēost* beestings (c. OHG *biost* > G *Biest*) + *-ing* -ING¹]

bees·wax (bēz′waks′), *n.* wax¹ (def. 1).

bees·wing (bēz′wing′), *n.* a light, flaky deposit found in port and some other old wines.

beet (bēt), *n.* **1.** any of various biennial chenopodiaceous plants of the genus *Beta,* esp. *B. vulgaris,* having a fleshy red or white root. Cf. **sugar beet. 2.** the edible root of such a plant. **3.** the leaves of such a plant, served as a salad or a cooked vegetable. [late ME *bete,* OE *bēte* < L *bēta*]

Bee·tho·ven (bā′tō vən; *Ger.* bāt′hō fən), *n.* **Lud·wig van** (lud′wig van, lo͝od′-; *Ger.* lo͞ot′viKH fän, lo͞od′-), 1770–1827, German composer.

bee·tle¹ (bēt′ᵊl), *n.* **1.** any of numerous insects of the order *Coleoptera,* characterized by hard, horny forewings that cover and protect the membranous flight wings **2.** (loosely) any of various insects resembling this insect, as a cockroach. [ME *bētylle, bityl,* OE *bitela* = *bitel-* biting (*bit-* BITE + *-el* adj. suffix) + *-a* n. suffix]

Beetle¹ (def. 1), *Pantomorus godmani* (Length ⅓ in.)

bee·tle² (bēt′ᵊl), *n., v.,* **-tled, -tling.** —*n.* **1.** a heavy hammering or ramming instrument, usually of wood, used to force down paving stones, compress loose earth, etc. **2.** any of various wooden instruments for beating linen, mashing potatoes, etc. —*v.t.* **3.** to use a beetle on; drive, ram, beat, or crush with a beetle. **4.** to finish (cloth) by means of a beetling machine. [late ME *betel,* OE *bētl, bȳtel* hammer (c. MLG *bētel* chisel) = *bēat-* BEAT + *-il* n. suffix] —**bee′tler,** *n.*

bee·tle³ (bēt′ᵊl), *adj., v.,* **-tled, -tling.** —*adj.* **1.** projecting or overhanging: *beetle brows.* —*v.i.* **2.** to project or overhang: *a cliff that beetles over the sea.* [back formation from BEETLE-BROWED]

bee·tle-browed (bēt′ᵊl broud′), *adj.* **1.** having heavy, projecting eyebrows. **2.** scowling. [ME *bitel-browed*]

bee′ tree′, a hollow tree used by wild bees as a hive, esp. the basswood or American linden.

beet′ sug′ar, sugar from the roots of the sugar beet.

beeves (bēvz), *n.* a pl. of **beef.**

bef., before.

B.E.F., British Expeditionary Force; British Expeditionary Forces.

be·fall (bi fôl′), *v.,* **-fell, -fall·en, -fall·ing.** —*v.i.* **1.** to happen or occur. —*v.t.* **2.** to happen to, esp. by chance or fate. [ME *befall(en),* OE *befeallan.* See BE-, FALL (v.)]

be·fit (bi fit′), *v.t.,* **-fit·ted, -fit·ting.** to be fitting or appropriate for; be suited or becoming to: *His clothes befit the occasion.* [late ME]

be·fit·ting (bi fit′ing), *adj.* fitting or proper. —**be·fit′ting·ly,** *adv.* —**be·fit′ting·ness,** *n.*

be·flag (bi flag′), *v.t.,* **-flagged, -flag·ging.** to cover or deck with flags.

be·fog (bi fog′, -fôg′), *v.t.,* **-fogged, -fog·ging. 1.** to envelop in fog. **2.** to render unclear; confuse by irrelevancies or distractions.

be·fool (bi fo͞ol′), *v.t.* **1.** to deceive or dupe: *innocents befooled by confidence men.* **2.** *Obs.* to treat as a fool. [late ME *befole(n)*]

be·fore (bi fōr′, -fôr′), *adv.* **1.** in front; in advance; ahead: *The king entered with macebearers walking before.* **2.** in time preceding; previously: *If we'd known before, we'd have let you know.* **3.** earlier or sooner: *Begin at noon, not before.* —*prep.* **4.** in front of; ahead of; in advance of: *one's shadow advancing before him.* **5.** previous to; earlier than: *life before the war.* **6.** in the future of; awaiting: *The golden age is before us.* **7.** in precedence of, as in order or rank: *age before beauty.* **8.** in the presence or sight of: *to appear before an audience.* **9.** under the jurisdiction or consideration of: *He was summoned before a magistrate.* **10.** confronted by; in the face of: *Before such wild accusations, he was too stunned to reply.* **11.** in the regard of: *a crime before man and God.* **12.** under the overwhelming influence of: *bending before the storm.* —*conj.* **13.** previously to the time when: *before we go.* [ME *before(n),* OE *beforan* = *be* BY + *foran before* (< *fore* FORE¹) + *-an* adv. suffix] —**Ant. 1, 4.** behind. **2.** afterward. **3.** later.

be·fore·hand (bi fōr′hand′, -fôr′-), *adv., adj.* in advance; ahead of time: *We should have known that beforehand. I hope to be beforehand with my report.* [ME *bifor-hand*]

be·fore·time (bi fōr′tīm′, -fôr′-), *adv. Archaic.* formerly. [ME *bifor time*]

be·foul (bi foul′), *v.t.* to make foul; defile or sully. [ME *bi-foulen*] —**be·foul′er,** *n.* —**be·foul′ment,** *n.*

be·friend (bi frend′), *v.t.* to make friends with, esp. to act as a friend to: *to befriend the poor.*

be·fud·dle (bi fud′ᵊl), *v.t.,* **-dled, -dling. 1.** to make stupidly drunk. **2.** to confuse, as with glib statements: *Stop befuddling the public with campaign promises.* —**be·fud′dler,** *n.* —**be·fud′dle·ment,** *n.*

beg (beg), *v.,* **begged, beg·ging.** —*v.t.* **1.** to ask for as a gift, as charity, or as a favor: *to beg alms; to beg forgiveness.* **2.** to ask to give one something or to do something; implore: *Sit down, I beg you.* **3.** to take for granted without basis or justification: *a statement that begs the very point we're disputing.* **4.** to avoid or evade: *a report that consistently begs the question.* —*v.i.* **5.** to ask alms or charity; live by asking alms. **6.** to ask humbly or earnestly: *begging for help.* **7.** (of a dog) to sit up, as trained, in a posture of entreaty. **8. beg off,** to request release from or excuse oneself from fulfilling (an obligation, promise, etc.): *He begged off driving us to the recital. I'd love to go, but I have to beg off.* [ME *begg(en),* by assimilation, OE **bedcian,* syncopated var. of *bedecian* to beg; cf. Goth *bidagwa* beggar. See BEAD] —**Syn. 2.** entreat, pray, crave, beseech, petition.

beg (bāg; *Eng.* beg), *n. Turkish.* bey.

beg., 1. begin. **2.** beginning.

be·gan (bi gan′), *v.* pt. of **begin.**

be·gat (bi gat′), *v. Archaic.* pt. of **beget.**

be·get (bi get′), *v.t.,* **be·got** or (*Archaic*) **be·gat; be·got·ten** or **be·got; be·get·ting. 1.** (esp. of a male parent) to procreate or generate (offspring). **2.** to cause; produce as an effect: *the belief that power begets power.* [ME *beget(en)*; r. ME *biyete(n),* OE *begetan;* c. Goth *bigitan,* OHG *bigezzan*] —**be·get′ter,** *n.*

beg·gar (beg′ər), *n.* **1.** a person who begs alms, or lives by begging. **2.** a penniless person. **3.** a wretched fellow; rogue. —*v.t.* **4.** to reduce to beggary; impoverish. **5.** to cause to seem poor or inadequate; exhaust the resources of: *The costume beggars description.* [ME *beggare, -ere*] —**beg′gar·hood′,** *n.*

beg·gar·ly (beg′ər lē), *adj.* **1.** like or befitting a beggar. **2.** meanly inadequate: *His salary was a beggarly $2500 a year.* —**beg′gar·li·ness,** *n.*

beg·gar's-tick (beg′ərz tik′), *n.* **1.** one of the prickly awns or achenes of *Bidens frondosa* or similar plants. **2. beggar's-ticks,** (*construed as sing. or pl.*) the plant itself. Also, **beg′gar-tick′.**

beg·gar·weed (beg′ər wēd′), *n.* **1.** any of various tick trefoils, esp. *Desmodium purpureum,* grown for forage in subtropical regions. **2.** *Chiefly Brit.* any weed, as the knotweed, that impoverishes soil.

beg·gar·y (beg′ə rē), *n.* **1.** poverty. **2.** beggars collectively. [late ME *beogerie*]

be·gin (bi gin′), *v.,* **be·gan, be·gun, be·gin·ning.** —*v.i.* **1.** to proceed to perform the first or earliest part of some action; commence or start. **2.** to come into existence; originate: *The custom began during the Civil War.* —*v.t.* **3.** to proceed to perform the first or earliest part of (some action): *Begin the job tomorrow.* **4.** to originate; be the originator of: *Civic leaders began the reform movement.* [ME *beginn(en),* OE *beginnan* = *be-* BE- + *-ginnan* to begin, perh. orig. to open, akin to YAWN] —**be·gin′ner,** *n.*

—**Syn. 3.** BEGIN, COMMENCE, INITIATE, START (when followed by noun or gerund) refer to setting into motion or progress something that continues for some time. BEGIN is the common term: *to begin knitting a sweater.* COMMENCE is a more formal word, often suggesting a more prolonged or elaborate beginning: *to commence proceedings in court.* INITIATE implies an active and often ingenious first act in a new field: *to initiate a new procedure.* START means to make a first move or to set out on a course of action: *to start paving a street.* **4.** inaugurate, initiate. —**Ant. 1.** end.

Be·gin (bā′gin), *n.* **Me·na·hem** (mə nä′ᴋʜəm), born 1913, Israeli statesman, born in Poland: prime minister 1977–83; Nobel peace prize 1978.

be·gin·ning (bi gin′ing), *n.* **1.** act or circumstance of entering upon an action or state. **2.** the point of time or space at which anything begins: *the beginning of the Christian Era.* **3.** Often, **beginnings.** the first part or initial stage of anything: *the beginnings of science.* **4.** origin; source; first cause: *A misunderstanding was the beginning of their quarrel.* [ME *beginnung, -ing*] —**Syn. 1.** initiation, inauguration, inception. **2.** start, onset. —**Ant. 1.** ending. **2.** end.

be·gird (bi gûrd′), *v.t.,* **-girt** or **-gird·ed, -gird·ing.** to gird about; encompass; surround. [ME *begird(en),* OE *begierdan*]

be·gone (bi gôn′, -gon′), *v.i.* to go away; depart (usually used in the imperative). [ME; see BE (impv.), GONE]

be·gon·ia (bi gōn′yə, -gō′nē ə), *n.* any tropical plant of the genus *Begonia,* including species cultivated for the handsome, succulent, often varicolored leaves and waxy flowers. [< NL, named after Michel *Bégon* (1638–1710), French patron of science; see -IA]

be·gor·ra (bi gôr′ə, -gor′ə, bē-), *interj. Irish Eng.* (used as a euphemism for *by God*): *Begorra, it's a fine day.* Also **be·gor′ah, be·gor′rah.**

be·got (bi got′), *v.* pt. and a pp. of **beget.**

be·got·ten (bi got′ᵊn), *v.* a pp. of **beget.**

be·grime (bi grīm′), *v.t.,* **-grimed, -grim·ing.** to make grimy.

be·grudge (bi gruj′), *v.t.,* **-grudged, -grudg·ing. 1.** to envy or resent the pleasure or good fortune of (someone): *She begrudged her friend the award.* **2.** to be reluctant to give, grant, or allow: *She did not begrudge the money spent on her children's education.* [late ME *bigrucche(n)*] —**be·grudg′ing·ly,** *adv.* —**Syn. 1.** See **envy.**

be·guile (bi gīl′), *v.t.,* **-guiled, -guil·ing. 1.** to influence by guile; delude. **2.** to take away from by cheating or deceiving (usually fol. by *of*): *to be beguiled of money.* **3.** to charm or divert: *a multitude of attractions to beguile the tourist.* [ME *bigile(n)*] —**be·guile′ment,** *n.* —**be·guil′er,** *n.* —**Syn. 1.** deceive, cheat. **3.** amuse, entertain.

be·guine (bi gēn′), *n.* **1.** a South American dance in bolero rhythm. **2.** a modern social dance based on the beguine. **3.** music for either of these dances. [< F (West Indies) *béguine* = *béguin* trifling love affair (orig., hood; see BIGGIN[1]) + *-e* fem. n. suffix]

Beg·uine (beg′ēn), *n. Rom. Cath. Ch.* a member of a lay sisterhood, founded in Liège in the 12th century, in which private property is retained and vows may be revoked at any time. [late ME *begyne* < MF *beguine,* fem. of *beguin,* ? < D *beggaert* mendicant monk; see -INE[1]]

be·gum (bē′gəm), *n.* (in India) a high-ranking Muslim lady, often a widow. [< Urdu *begam* << Turkic *bigim* = *big* prince + *-im* fem. suffix]

be·gun (bi gun′), *v.* pp. of **begin.**

be·half (bi haf′, -häf′), *n.* **1. in** or **on behalf of,** as a representative of or a proxy for: *On behalf of my colleagues, I thank you.* **2. in** or **on one's behalf,** in the interest or aid of someone: *He interceded in my behalf.* [ME *behalve* beside, OE *behealfe* (*him*) by (his) side]

Be·han (bē′ən), *n.* **Bren·dan (Francis)** (bren′dən), 1923–64, Irish playwright.

Be·har (bi här′, bə-), *n.* Bihar.

be·have (bi hāv′), *v.,* **-haved, -hav·ing.** —*v.i.* **1.** to act in a particular way; conduct oneself or itself. **2.** to act properly: *Did the child behave?* —*v.t.* **3.** to comport (oneself) properly: *Sit up and behave yourself.* [ME *behave(n)* (orig. in reflexive use: to hold oneself in a certain way). See BE-, HAVE] —**Syn. 1.** perform, acquit oneself, deport oneself.

be·hav·ior (bi hāv′yər), *n.* **1.** manner of behaving or acting. **2.** *Psychol.* **a.** the aggregate of observable responses of an organism to internal and external stimuli. **b.** any activity of an organism taken as the subject matter of psychology. **3.** the action or reaction of any material under given circumstances: *the behavior of tin under heat.* Also, *esp. Brit.,* **be·hav·iour.** [BEHAVE + *-ior* (on model of *havior,* var. of *havor* < MF *(h)avoir* << L *habēre* to have); r. earlier *behavoure, behaver.* See BEHAVE, -OR[1]]

—**Syn. 1.** demeanor, manners. BEHAVIOR, CONDUCT, DEPORTMENT, COMPORTMENT refer to one's actions before or toward others, esp. on a particular occasion. BEHAVIOR refers to actions usually measured by commonly accepted standards: *His behavior at the party was childish.* CONDUCT refers to actions viewed collectively, esp. as measured by an ideal standard: *Conduct is judged according to principles of ethics.* DEPORTMENT is behavior related to a code or to an arbitrary standard: *Deportment is guided by rules of etiquette. The teacher gave Susan a mark of B in deportment.* COMPORTMENT is behavior as viewed from the standpoint of one's management of one's own actions: *His comportment was marked by a quiet assurance.*

be·hav·ior·al (bi hāv′yər əl), *adj.* of or pertaining to human or animal behavior. Also, *esp. Brit.,* **be·hav′iour·al.** —**be·hav′ior·al·ly;** *esp. Brit.,* **be·hav′iour·al·ly,** *adv.*

behav′ioral sci′ence, any of various sciences, as psychology or sociology, concerned with human behavior as manifested individually or in groups.

be·hav·ior·ism (bi hāv′yə riz′əm), *n. Psychol.* the theory or doctrine that regards objective and accessible facts of behavior or activity of man and animals as the only proper subject for psychological study. Also, *esp. Brit.,* **be·hav′iour·ism.** —**be·hav′ior·ist;** *esp. Brit.,* **be·hav′iour·ist,** *n., adj.* —**be·hav′ior·is′tic;** *esp. Brit.,* **be·hav′iour·is′tic,** *adj.* —**be·hav′ior·is′ti·cal·ly;** *esp. Brit.,* **be·hav′iour·is′ti·cal·ly,** *adv.*

be·head (bi hed′), *v.t.* to cut off the head of; kill or execute by decapitation. [ME *behe(f)d(en), beheved(en),* EO *beheafdian*]

be·held (bi held′), *v.* pt. and pp. of **behold.**

be·he·moth (bi hē′məth, bē′ə-), *n.* **1.** an animal, perhaps the hippopotamus, mentioned in Job 40:15–24. **2.** *U.S. Informal.* any monstrous or grotesque creature or thing. [< Heb *b'hēmōth* (expressing dignity, greatness), pl. of *b'hēmāh* beast; r. ME *bemoth*]

be·hest (bi hest′), *n.* **1.** a command or directive. **2.** an earnest or urgent request. [ME, OE *behǣs* promise]

be·hind (bi hīnd′), *prep.* **1.** at or toward the rear of or in back of: *Look behind the sofa.* **2.** later than; after: *behind schedule.* **3.** in the state of making less progress than: *to fall behind one's competitors.* **4.** on the farther side of; beyond: *behind the mountain range.* **5.** supporting; promoting: *Who's behind this program?* **6.** hidden or unrevealed by: *Malice lay behind her smile.* —*adv.* **7.** at or toward the rear: *to lag behind.* **8.** in a place, state, or stage already passed. **9.** in arrears; behindhand: *to be behind in one's rent.* **10.** slow, as a watch or clock. **11.** as a cause or often latent feature of: *Behind their harassment lay the traditional fear of foreigners.* **12.** *Archaic.* in reserve; to come: *Greater support is yet behind.* —*adj.* **13.** following: *the man behind.* —*n.* **14.** *Slang.* the buttocks. [ME *behinde(n),* OE *behindan*]

—**Syn. 1, 2.** BEHIND, AFTER both refer to a position following something else. BEHIND applies primarily to position in space, and suggests that one person or thing is at the back of another; it may also refer to (a fixed) time: *He stood behind the chair. The train is behind schedule.* AFTER applies primarily to time; when it denotes position in space, it is not used with precision, and refers usually to bodies in motion: *Rest after a hard day's work. They entered the room, one after another.*

—**Usage.** See **back**[1].

be·hind·hand (bi hīnd′hand′), *adv., adj.* **1.** late or tardy. **2.** behind in progress; backward: *She was never behindhand in following artistic fads.* **3.** in debt or arrears.

Be·his·tun (bā′hi sto͞on′), *n.* a ruined town in W Iran: site of a cliff which bears on its face a cuneiform inscription in Old Persian, Elamite, and Babylonian that provided a key for the decipherment of cuneiform in other languages. Also, **Bisitun, Bisutun.**

Beh·men (bā′mən), *n.* **Ja·kob** (yä′kəb). See **Böhme.**

be·hold (bi hōld′), *v.,* **be·held, be·hold·ing,** *interj.* —*v.t.* **1.** to observe; look at; see. —*interj.* **2.** look; see: *And, behold, three sentries of the King did appear.* [ME *behold(en),* OE *behaldan* to keep] —**be·hold′er,** *n.* —**Syn. 1.** view; watch.

be·hold·en (bi hōl′dᵊn), *adj.* obligated or indebted: *a man beholden to no one.* [ME < *beholden,* old ptp. of BEHOLD]

be·hoof (bi ho͞of′), *n., pl.* **-hooves** (-ho͞ovz′). use, advantage, or benefit. [ME *behove,* OE *behōf* profit, need; c. D *behoef,* G *Behuf*]

be·hoove (bi ho͞ov′), *v.,* **-hooved, -hoov·ing.** (chiefly in impersonal use) —*v.t.* **1.** to be necessary or proper for, as for moral or ethical considerations; be incumbent on: *It behooves the court to weigh evidence impartially.* **2.** to be worthwhile to, as for personal profit or advantage: *It would behoove you to be nicer to her because she could do a lot for you.* —*v.i.* **3.** *Archaic.* to be needful, proper, or due: *a quality that behooves in a scholar.* [ME *behove(n),* OE *behōfian* to need = *behōf* BEHOOF + *-ian* inf. suffix]

be·hove (bi hōv′), *v.t., v.i.,* **-hoved, -hov·ing.** *Brit.* behoove.

Beh·ring (bā′ring), *n.* **1. E·mil von** (ā′mēl fən), 1854–1917, German physician and bacteriologist: Nobel prize in medicine 1901. **2. Vi·tus** (vē′to͞os). See **Bering, Vitus.**

Behr·man (bâr′mən), *n.* **S(amuel) N(athan),** 1893–1973, U.S. playwright and author.

Bei·der·becke (bī′dər bek′), *n.* **Leon Bismarck** ("*Bix*"), 1903–31, U.S. jazz cornetist and composer.

beige (bāzh), *n.* **1.** light grayish brown. **—***adj.* **2.** of the color beige. [< F < ?]

Bei·jing (bā′jing′), *n.* Pinyin spelling of **Peking.**

be·ing (bē′ing), *n.* **1.** the fact of existing; existence as opposed to nonexistence. **2.** conscious, mortal existence; life. **3.** substance or nature: *of such a being as to arouse fear.* **4.** something that exists: *inanimate beings.* **5.** a living thing: *strange, exotic beings that live in the depths of the sea.* **6.** a human being; person. **7.** (*cap.*) God. **8.** *Philos.* **a.** that which has actuality either materially or in idea. **b.** absolute existence in a complete or perfect state, lacking no essential characteristic; essence [ME]
—Usage. The expressions BEING AS and BEING THAT (*Being as it's midnight, let's go home*) are not generally accepted in standard English as substitutes for SINCE, AS, or BECAUSE (*Since it's midnight, let's go home*).

Bei·ra (bā′rə), *n.* a seaport in E central Mozambique. 115,000.

Bei·rut (bā ro͞ot′, bā′ro͞ot), *n.* a seaport in and the capital of Lebanon. 702,000. Also, **Beyrouth.**

be·jew·el (bi jo͞o′əl), *v.t.*, **-eled, -el·ing** or (*esp. Brit.*) **-elled, -el·ling.** to adorn with or as with jewels.

bel (bel), *n.* *Physics.* a unit of power ratio, equal to 10 decibels. [named after A. G. BELL]

Bel (bāl, bel), *n.* a deity of the Babylonians and Assyrians, god of the earth. [< L *Bēl(us)* < Gk *Bêlos* BAAL]

Bel., **1.** Belgian. **2.** Belgic. **3.** Belgium.

be·la·bor (bi lā′bər), *v.t.* **1.** to discuss, work at, or worry about for an unreasonable amount of time: *He kept belaboring the point long after we had agreed.* **2.** to scorn or ridicule persistently. **3.** *Literary.* to beat vigorously. Also, *Brit.*, **be·la′bour.**

Be·las·co (bi las′kō), *n.* **David,** 1854–1931, U.S. playwright, actor, and producer.

be·lat·ed (bi lā′tid), *adj.* **1.** coming or being after the customary, useful, or expected time: *belated birthday greetings.* **2.** delayed or detained. [archaic *belate* to delay (BE- + LATE) + -ED[2]] **—be·lat′ed·ly,** *adv.* **—be·lat′ed·ness,** *n.*

Be·la·ún·de (be′lä o͞on′de), *n.* **Fer·nan·do** (fer nän′dô), (*Fernando Belaúnde Terry*), born 1913, Peruvian architect and statesman: president 1963–68.

be·lay (bi lā′), *v.*, **-layed, -lay·ing.** **—***v.t.* **1.** *Naut.* to fasten (a rope) by winding around a pin or cleat. **2.** *Mountain Climbing.* **a.** to secure (a person) at one end of a rope. **b.** to secure (a rope) to a person or object offering stable support. **3.** *Naut.* (used chiefly in the imperative) to cease an action; stop. **—***v.i.* **4.** to belay a rope. [ME *beleg-ge(n),* OE *belecgan*]

belay′ing pin′, *Naut.* a short, round bar of metal or wood, inserted in a fife rail or pin rail, to which a rope is belayed.

Belaying pins

bel can·to (bel′ kan′tō; *It.* bel kän′tô), *Music.* a smooth, cantabile style of singing. [< It: lit., fine singing]

belch (belch), *v.i.* **1.** to eject gas spasmodically and noisily from the stomach through the mouth; eruct. **2.** to emit contents violently, as a gun, geyser, or volcano. **3.** to issue spasmodically; gush forth. **—***v.t.* **4.** to eject (gas or the like) spasmodically or violently; give forth. **—***n.* **5.** an instance of belching; eructation. **6.** a violent emission of flame, smoke, etc. [ME *belche(n),* OE *bealcan;* c. D *balken* to bray]

bel·dam (bel′dəm), *n.* **1.** an old woman, esp. an ugly one; hag. **2.** *Obs.* grandmother. Also, **bel·dame** (bel′dəm, -dām′). [late ME = *bel-* grand- (< MF *bel, belle* fine; see BEAU, BELLE) + *dam* mother (see DAM[2])]

be·lea·guer (bi lē′gər), *v.t.* **1.** to surround with an army. **2.** to surround with annoyances or troubles. [BE- + LEAGUER[1]] **—be·lea′guer·er,** *n.*

Be·lém (bə lem′; *Port.* be leNm′), *n.* a seaport in N Brazil on the Pará River. 565,097. Also called **Pará.**

bel·em·nite (bel′əm nīt′), *n.* *Paleontol.* a conical fossil, several inches long, consisting of the internal calcareous rod of an extinct animal allied to the cuttlefish; a thunderstone. [< Gk *bélemn(on)* a dart + -ITE[1]]

bel-es·prit (bel es prē′), *n.*, *pl.* **beaux-es·prits** (bō zes prē′). *French.* a person of great wit or intellect.

Bel·fast (bel′fast, -fäst, bel fast′, -fäst′), *n.* a seaport in and capital of Northern Ireland, on the E coast. 374,300.

Bel·fort (bā fôr′, bel-), *n.* a fortress city in E France: siege 1870–71; battle 1944. 57,317.

bel·fry (bel′frē), *n., pl.* **-fries.** **1.** a bell tower, either attached to a building or standing apart. **2.** the part of a steeple or other structure in which a bell is hung. **3.** a frame of timberwork for sustaining a bell. [late ME *belfray,* appar. b. earlier *berfray* (< MF < Gmc) + ML *belfredus,* dissimilated var. of *berefredus* < Gmc; cf. MHG *ber(c)frit* = *berc* defense, protection, refuge (c. OE *gebeorg;* see HARBOR) + *frit* peace, (place of) safety (c. OE *frith*)]

Belg., **1.** Belgian. **2.** Belgium.

Bel·gae (bel′jē), *n.* (*construed as pl.*) an ancient people, chiefly of Celtic origin, that lived in northern Gaul.

Bel·gian (bel′jən, -jē ən), *n.* **1.** a native or an inhabitant of Belgium. **2.** one of a breed of large, strong, draft horses, raised originally in Belgium. **—***adj.* **3.** of or pertaining to Belgium.

Bel′gian Con′go, a former name of **Zaïre** (def. 1).

Bel′gian hare′, one of a breed of domestic rabbits.

Bel′gian sheep′dog, one of a breed of dogs raised originally in Belgium for herding sheep.

Bel·gic (bel′jik), *adj.* **1.** of or pertaining to the Belgae. **2.** Belgian. [< L *belgic(us)*]

Bel·gium (bel′jəm, -jē əm), *n.* a kingdom in W Europe, bordering the North Sea, N of France. 9,813,152; 11,779 sq. mi. *Cap.:* Brussels. French, **Bel·gique** (bel zhēk′). Flemish, **Bel·gi·ë** (bel′кнē ə).

Bel·go·rod-Dnes·trov·ski (byel′go rôd′dnye strôf′ski), *n.* a seaport in SE Moldavia, in the SW Soviet Union in Europe, on the Black Sea. 37,000. Rumanian, **Cetatea Albă.** Formerly, **Akkerman.**

Bel·grade (bel grād′, bel′grād), *n.* a city in and the capital of Yugoslavia, in the E part, on the Danube River. 1,209,360. Serbian, **Beograd.**

Bel·gra·vi·a (bel grā′vē ə), *n.* **1.** a formerly fashionable district in London, England, adjoining Hyde Park. **2.** *Brit.* a newly rich, upper middle class. **—Bel·gra′vi·an,** *n., adj.*

Be·li·al (bē′lē əl, bēl′yəl), *n.* *Theol.* the spirit of evil personified; the devil; Satan. [< Heb = *b'lī* negative + *ya'al* use, profit]

be·lie (bi lī′), *v.t.*, **-lied, -ly·ing.** **1.** to show to be false; contradict: *His trembling hands belied his calm voice.* **2.** to misrepresent: *The newspaper belied the facts.* **3.** *Archaic.* to lie about; slander. [ME *belye(n),* OE *belēogan*] **—be·li′er,** *n.*

be·lief (bi lēf′), *n.* **1.** something believed; an opinion or conviction. **2.** confidence in the truth or existence of something not immediately susceptible to rigorous proof: *a statement unworthy of belief.* **3.** confidence, faith, or trust: *a child's belief in his parents.* **4.** a religious tenet or tenets: *the Christian belief.* [earlier *bile(e)ve* (n. use of v.); r. ME *bileave* = *bi-* BE- + *leave,* OE *(ge)lēafa*]
—Syn. 1. view, tenet, persuasion. **2.** assurance. BELIEF, CONVICTION refer to acceptance of or confidence in an alleged fact or body of facts as true or right without positive knowledge or proof. BELIEF is such acceptance in general: *belief in astrology.* CONVICTION is settled, profound, or earnest belief that something is right: *a conviction that a decision is just.* **4.** doctrine, dogma.

be·lieve (bi lēv′), *v.*, **-lieved, -liev·ing.** **—***v.i.* **1.** to have confidence in the truth or the reliability of something without absolute proof. **—***v.t.* **2.** to have confidence or faith in the truth of (a positive assertion, story, etc.). **3.** to have confidence in the statement or assertion of (a person). **4.** to be more or less confident; suppose (usually fol. by a noun clause): *I believe that he has left town.* **5. believe in, a.** to be persuaded of the truth or existence of: *to believe in Zoroastrianism; to believe in ghosts.* **b.** to have faith in the reliability, honesty, benevolence, etc., of: *I can help you only if you believe in me.* [ME *bileve(n)* = *bi-* BE- + *leven,* OE (Anglian) *(ge)lēfan;* c. D *gelooven,* G *glauben,* Goth *galaubjan*] **—be·liev′a·bil′i·ty,** *n.* **—be·liev′a·ble,** *adj.* **—be·liev′a·bly,** *adv.* **—be·liev′er,** *n.*

be·like (bi līk′), *adv.* *Archaic.* perhaps; probably.

Bel·i·sar·i·us (bel′i sâr′ē əs), *n.* A.D. 505?–565, general of the Eastern Roman Empire.

Be·li·tong (be lē′tong), *n.* Billiton. Also, **Be·li·toeng, Be·li·tung** (be lē′to͝ong).

be·lit·tle (bi lit′ᵊl), *v.t.*, **-tled, -tling.** to regard, consider, or portray (something) as less impressive or important than it apparently is; depreciate; disparage. **—be·lit′tle·ment,** *n.* **—be·lit′tler,** *n.* **—Syn.** minimize, decry.

be·live (bi līv′), *adv.* *Scot.* before long; soon. [ME *bi live* BY LIFE, i.e., with liveliness]

Be·lize (be lēz′), *n.* **1.** a republic in N Central America: formerly a British colony; independent since 1981; member of the British Commonwealth of Nations. 151,607; 8867 sq. mi. *Cap.:* Belmopan. Formerly **British Honduras.** **2.** a port in and the largest city in Belize. 45,000.

bell[1] (bel), *n.* **1.** a hollow instrument of cast metal, typically cup-shaped, suspended from the vertex and rung by the strokes of a clapper, hammer, or the like. **2.** the stroke or sound of such an instrument. **3.** anything in the form of a bell. **4.** the large end of a funnel, or the end of a pipe, tube, or any musical wind instrument, when its edge is turned out and enlarged. **5.** *Naut.* **a.** any of the half-hour units of nautical time rung on the bell of a ship. **b.** each individual ring of the bell, counted with others to reckon the time. **6.** *Zool.* umbrella (def. 2). **7. ring a bell,** to strike a response; remind one of something: *His name rings a bell.* **8. saved by the bell, a.** (of a boxer) saved from a knockout by the ringing of a gong signaling the end of a round. **b.** (of any person) spared from anticipated trouble by some extraneous event. **9. with bells on,** *Informal.* eagerly; ready to enjoy oneself: *I'll come to your party with bells on.* **—***v.t.* **10.** to cause to swell or expand into a bulbous shape like a bell (often fol. by *out*). **11.** to put a bell on: *The cat was belled to warn the birds.* **—***v.i.* **12.** to take or have the form of a bell. [ME, OE *belle;* c. D *bel*] **—bell′-like′,** *adj.*

bell[2] (bel), *v.i., v.t.* **1.** to bellow like a deer in rutting time. **2.** *Obs.* to bellow; roar. **—***n.* **3.** the cry of a rutting deer. [ME *bell(en),* OE *bellan* to roar; c. OHG *bellan* (G *bellen* to bark), Icel *belja.* See BELLOW]

Bell (bel), *n.* **1. Ac·ton** (ak′tən). See **Brontë, Anne.** **2. Alexander Graham,** 1847–1922, U.S. scientist, born in Scotland: inventor of the telephone. **3. (Arthur) Clive (Howard),** 1881–1964, English critic of literature and art. **4. Cur·rer** (kûr′ər). See **Brontë, Charlotte.** **5. Ellis.** See **Brontë, Emily.**

bel·la·don·na (bel′ə don′ə), *n.* **1.** Also called **deadly nightshade.** a poisonous, solanaceous herb, *Atropa Belladonna,* having purplish-red flowers and black berries. **2.** *Pharm.* a drug from the leaves and root of this plant, containing atropine and related alkaloids: used to check secretions and spasms and as a cardiac and respiratory stimulant. [< It *bella donna,* lit., fair lady (from its supposed use by women to dilate the pupils of the eyes and to create an artificial pallor)]

bel′ladon′na lil′y, amaryllis (def. 1).

Bel·la·my (bel′ə mē), *n.* **Edward,** 1850–98, U.S. author.

Bel·lay (be lā′), *n.* **Jo·a·chim du** (zhô A kēm′ dʏ), c1525–60. French poet, member of the Pléiade.

bell·bird (bel′bûrd′), *n.* any of several birds whose song is bell-like, esp. certain South American cotingas of the genus *Procnias.*

bell-bot·tom (bel′bot′əm), *adj.* **1.** Also, **bell′-bot′tomed.** (of trousers) wide and flaring at the bottoms of the legs. **—***n.* **2. bell-bottoms,** (*construed as pl.*) bell-bottom trousers.

bell·boy (bel′boi′), *n.* *U.S.* a man who is employed to carry luggage, run errands, etc., at a hotel, club, etc. Also called **bellhop.**

bell′ bu′oy, *Naut.* a buoy having a bell that is rung by the motion of the buoy.
bell′ cap′tain, a hotel employee who supervises the work of bellboys.
belle (bel), *n.* a woman or girl admired for her beauty and charm, esp. the most beautiful among a number of rivals: *the belle of the ball.* [< F; OF *bele* < L *bella,* fem. of *bellus* fine, good-looking. See BEAU]
Bel′leau Wood′ (bel′ō; *Fr.* be lō′), a forest in N France, NW of Château-Thierry: U.S. Marine battle, 1918.
Belle′ Isle′, Strait of, a strait between Newfoundland island and Labrador, Canada. 10–15 mi. wide.
Bel·ler·o·phon (bə ler′ə fon′), *n. Class. Myth.* a Corinthian hero who, mounted on Pegasus, killed the Chimera.
belles-let·tres (*Fr.* bel le′tʀᵊ), *n.pl.* literature regarded as a fine art, esp. as having a purely aesthetic function. [< F: lit., fine letters] **—bel·let·rist** (bel le′trist), *n.* **—bel·let·ris·tic** (bel′li tris′tik), *adj.* **—Syn.** See **literature.**
Belle·ville (bel′vil), *n.* **1.** a city in SW Illinois. 41,699 (1970). **2.** a city in NE New Jersey. 34,772 (1970).
Belle·vue (bel′vyo͞o), *n.* a city in W Washington, E of Seattle. 61,102 (1970).
bell·flow·er (bel′flou′ər), *n.* a campanula.
Bell·flow·er (bel′flou′ər), *n.* a city in SW California, near Los Angeles. 51,454 (1970).
Bell′ Gar′dens, a city in SW California, near Los Angeles. 29,308 (1970).
bell′ glass′. See **bell jar.**
bell·hop (bel′hop′), *n. U.S.* bellboy.
bel·li·cose (bel′ə kōs′), *adj.* inclined or eager to fight; pugnacious. [< L *bellicōs(us)* = *bellic(us)* (*belli-,* s. of *bellum* war + *-icus* -IC) + *-ōsus* -OSE¹] **—bel′li·cose′ly,** *adv.* **—bel·li·cos·i·ty** (bel′ə kos′i tē), **bel′li·cose′ness,** *n.*
bel·lig·er·ence (bə lij′ər əns), *n.* **1.** a warlike nature. **2.** act of carrying on war; warfare.
bel·lig·er·en·cy (bə lij′ər ən sē), *n.* position or status as a belligerent; state of being actually engaged in war.
bel·lig·er·ent (bə lij′ər ənt), *adj.* **1.** warlike; given to waging war. **2.** of warlike character; aggressively hostile: *a belligerent tone.* **3.** waging war; engaged in war: *a peace treaty between belligerent powers.* **4.** pertaining to war or to those engaged in war: *belligerent rights.* **—*n.* 5.** a state or nation at war. **6.** a member of the military forces of such a state. [< L *belliger* waging war (*belli-,* comb. form of *bellum* war + *-ger-,* root of *gerere* to conduct) + -ENT] **—bel·lig′er·ent·ly,** *adv*
Bel·ling·ham (bel′ing ham′), *n.* a seaport in NW Washington. 39,375 (1970).
Bel·li·ni (bə lē′nē; *It.* bel lē′nē), *n.* **1. Gen·ti·le** (jen tē′le), 1427?–1507, Venetian painter (son of Jacopo): teacher of Giorgione and Titian. **2. Gio·van·ni** (jô vän′nē), 1430?–1516, Venetian painter (son of Jacopo). **3. Ja·co·po** (yä′kô pô), 1400?–70, Venetian painter. **4. Vin·cen·zo** (vēn chen′dzô), 1801?–35, Italian composer of opera.
bell′ jar′, a bell-shaped glass vessel or cover for protecting delicate instruments, bric-a-brac, or the like, or for holding gases, a vacuum, etc., in chemical experiments. Also called **bell glass.**
bell·man (bel′mən), *n., pl.* **-men.** a person who carries or rings a bell, esp. a town crier or watchman.
bell′ met′al, an alloy of about 80 percent copper and 20 percent tin, used esp. for bells.
Bel·loc (bel′ək, -ok), *n.* **Hi·laire** (hi lâr′), 1870–1953, English essayist, poet, and satirist; born in France.
Bel·lo·na (bə lō′nə), *n.* the ancient Roman goddess of war, the wife or sister of Mars.
bel·low (bel′ō), *v.i.* **1.** to emit a hollow, loud, animal cry, as a bull or cow. **2.** to roar or bawl: *bellowing with rage.* **—*v.t.* 3.** to utter in a loud deep voice: *He bellowed his answer across the room.* **—*n.* 4.** act or sound of bellowing. [ME *belwe(n),* OE *bylgan* to roar; akin to BELL²] **—bel′low·er,** *n.* **—Syn. 2.** See **cry.**
Bel·low (bel′ō), *n.* **Saul,** born 1915, U.S. novelist, born in Canada: Nobel prize 1976.
bel·lows (bel′ōz, -əs), *n.* (*construed as sing. or pl.*) **1.** an instrument or machine for producing a strong current of air, as for a draft for a fire or sounding a musical instrument, consisting essentially of an air chamber that can be expanded to draw in air through a valve and contracted to expel the air through a tube or tubes. **2.** anything resembling or suggesting a bellows in form, as the collapsible part of a camera or enlarger. **3.** the lungs. [ME *belwes* (pl.), OE *belg,* short for *blǣst belg* blast bag. See BELLY] **—bel′lows·like′,** *adj.*
Bel·lows (bel′ōz), *n.* **George Wesley,** 1882–1925, U.S. painter and lithographer.
bell′ pep′per. See **sweet pepper.**
bell·pull (bel′po͝ol′), *n.* a handle, cord, or strip of cloth pulled to ring a doorbell, servant's bell, etc.
Bell′ pur′chase, a tackle consisting of two standing single blocks, two running single blocks, a fall, and a runner. Also, **Bell's′ pur′chase.** See diag. at **tackle.**
bells (belz), *n. Informal.* bell-bottom trousers.
bell·weth·er (bel′weth′ər), *n.* **1.** a wether or other male sheep that leads the flock, usually bearing a bell. **2.** a person or thing that takes the lead: *Paris remains the bellwether of the fashion industry.*
bell·wort (bel′wûrt′), *n.* **1.** any campanulaceous plant. **2.** a liliaceous plant of the genus *Uvularia,* having a bell-shaped, yellow flower.
bel·ly (bel′ē), *n., pl.* **-lies,** *v.,* **-lied, -ly·ing. —*n.* 1.** the front or under part of a vertebrate body from the breastbone to the pelvis, containing the abdominal viscera; the abdomen. **2.** the stomach with its adjuncts. **3.** appetite or capacity for food; gluttony. **4.** the womb. **5.** the inside or interior of anything. **6.** a protuberant or bulging surface of anything: *the belly of a flask.* **7.** *Anat.* the fleshy part of a muscle. **8.** the front, inner, or under surface or part, as distinguished from the back. **—*v.t., v.i.* 9.** to swell out. [ME *bely,* OE *belig, belg* bag, skin; c. G *Balg,* Goth *balg(s),* Icel *belgr,* MIr *bolg* sack]
bel·ly·ache (bel′ē āk′), *n., v.,* **-ached, -ach·ing. —*n.* 1.** *Informal.* a stomach ache. **—*v.i.* 2.** *Slang.* to complain or grumble. **—bel′ly·ach′er,** *n.*
bel·ly·band (bel′ē band′), *n.* **1.** a band worn about the belly, as of a harnessed horse. **2.** *Naut.* a thickness of canvas sewn to a sail as a reinforcement for the reef points.
bel·ly·but·ton (bel′ē but′ᵊn), *n. Informal.* the navel. Also, **bel′ly but′ton.**
bel′ly dance′, an Oriental solo dance, performed by a woman, emphasizing exaggerated movements of the abdominal muscles. **—bel′ly danc′er.**
bel′ly flop′, a dive in which the abdomen bears the brunt of the impact with the water. Also, **bel′ly flop′per.** Also called **bel′ly whop′, bel′ly whop′per, bel′ly bust′er.**
bel·ly·ful (bel′ē fo͝ol′), *n., pl.* **-fuls.** *Slang.* all that one can tolerate.
bel·ly-land (bel′ē land′), *v.i. Aeron.* (of an aircraft) to land directly on the fuselage, without using the landing gear. **—bel′ly-land′ing,** *n.*
bel′ly laugh′, *Informal.* a deep, loud, hearty laugh.
Bel·mont (bel′mont), *n.* a town in E Massachusetts near Boston. 28,285 (1970).
Bel·mo·pan (bel mō pan′), *n.* a city in and the capital of Belize, in the N central part. 4000.
Be·lo Ho·ri·zon·te (be′lo͝o ô ʀē zôɴ′ti), a city in SE Brazil. 1,106,722.
Be·loit (bə loit′), *n.* a city in S Wisconsin. 35,729 (1970).
be·long (bi lông′, -long′), *v.i.* **1.** to be a member, adherent, inhabitant, etc. (usually fol. by *to*): *He belongs to the tennis club.* **2.** to have the proper qualifications to be a member of a group: *You don't belong in this club.* **3.** to be proper or due; be properly or appropriately placed, situated, etc.: *This belongs on the shelf.* **4. belong to, a.** to be the property of: *The book belongs to him.* **b.** to be a part, adjunct, or function of: *That lid belongs to this jar.* [ME *belong(en)* = *be-* BE- + *longen* to belong, v. use of *long* (adj.) belonging, OE *gelang* ALONG¹]
be·long·ing (bi lông′ing, -long′-), *n.* **1.** something that belongs. **2. belongings,** possessions; effects.
Be·lo·rus·sia (byel′ə rush′ə, bel′ə-), *n.* Byelorussia. **—Be′lo·rus′sian,** *adj., n.*
Be·los·tok (bye lə stôk′), *n.* Białystok.
be·lov·ed (bi luv′id, -luvd′), *adj.* **1.** greatly loved; dear to the heart. **—*n.* 2.** a person who is greatly loved. [ME, ptp. of *beluven*]
Be·lo·vo (be′lo vo), *n.* a city in the SW RSFSR, in the S Soviet Union in Asia. 112,000.
be·low (bi lō′), *adv.* **1.** in or toward a lower place. **2.** on, in, or toward a lower level, floor, or deck. **3.** on earth: *the fate of creatures here below.* **4.** in hell or the infernal regions. **5.** at a later point on a page or in a text: *See the statistics below.* Cf. **above** (def. 5). **6.** in a lower rank, grade, or number: *He was demoted to the class below.* **—*prep.* 7.** lower down than: *below the knee.* **8.** lower in rank, degree, amount, rate, etc., than: *below cost; below freezing.* **9.** too low or undignified to be worthy of; beneath: *an action below one's notice.* [ME *biloogh*e = *bi-* by (see BE-) + *looghe* LOW¹]
—Syn. 7. BELOW, UNDER, BENEATH indicate position in some way lower than something else. BELOW implies being in a lower plane: *below the horizon, the water line.* UNDER implies being lower in a perpendicular line: *The plaything is under a chair.* BENEATH may have a meaning similar to BELOW, but more usually denotes being under so as to be covered, overhung, or overtopped: *the pool beneath the falls.*
Bel Pa·e·se (bel′ pä ā′zē; *It.* bel′ pä e′ze), *Trademark.* a semisoft, mild Italian cheese.
Bel·sen (bel′zən), *n.* locality in NE West Germany: site of Nazi concentration camp during World War II.
Bel·shaz·zar (bel shaz′ər), *n.* the last king of Babylon and a son of Nebuchadnezzar. Dan 5. [< Heb < Babylonian *Bēl-sharra-uzur* may Bel guard the king]
belt (belt), *n.* **1.** a band of flexible material, as leather, for encircling the waist. **2.** any encircling or transverse band, strip, or stripe. **3.** an elongated area or region having distinctive properties or characteristics: *a belt of cotton plantations.* **4.** *Mach.* an endless flexible band passing about two or more pulleys, used to transmit motion from one pulley to the other or others or to convey materials and objects. **5.** *Slang.* a hard blow or hit, as with the fist. **6.** *Mil.* **a.** a cloth strip with loops or a series of metal links with grips, for holding cartridges fed into an automatic gun. **b.** a band of leather or webbing, worn around the waist and used as a support for weapons, ammunition, etc. **7.** beltway. **8.** *Slang.* a shot of liquor, usually taken in one swallow. **9. below the belt,** contrary to rules or to principles of fairness: *criticism that hit below the belt.* **10. under one's belt,** *Informal.* **a.** in one's stomach, as food and drink. **b.** considered as a matter of past experience: *He has two years of sea duty under his belt.* **—*v.t.* 11.** to gird or furnish with a belt. **12.** to surround or mark as if with a belt, band, or stripe. **13.** to fasten on (a sword, gun, etc.) by means of a belt. **14.** to beat with a belt, strap, etc. **15.** *Slang.* to give a hard blow to; hit. **16.** *Informal.* to sing (a song) in a loud or forceful manner. [ME, OE < L *balte(us)*]
—Syn. 3. BELT and ZONE agree in their original meaning of a girdle or band. BELT is more used in popular or journalistic writing: *the corn or wheat belt.* ZONE tends to be used in technical language: *the Torrid Zone; a parcel-post zone.* **11.** girdle, encircle. **14.** flog, lash.
belt·ed (bel′tid), *adj.* **1.** having or made with a belt: *a belted dress.* **2.** girded with or wearing a belt, sash, or the like, esp. as a mark of distinction: *the belted lords and emissaries.* **3.** marked with a band of color: *a belted cow.*
belt′ed-bi′as tire′, a motor-vehicle tire with the same construction as a bias-ply tire but with a belt of steel or synthetic material added under the tread. Also called **bias-belted tire.** Cf. **radial-ply tire.**
belt′ high′way, beltway.
belt·ing (bel′ting), *n.* **1.** material for belts. **2.** belts collectively. **3.** a beating or thrashing.
belt·line (belt′līn′), *n.* the waistline.
belt′way (belt′wā′), *n.* a highway around the edges of an urban area. Also called **belt, belt highway.**
be·lu·ga (bə lo͞o′gə), *n.* **1.** a white sturgeon, *Acipenser huso,* found in the Black and Caspian Seas, valued as a source of caviar and isinglass. **2.** Also called **white whale.** a cetacean, *Delphinapterus leucas,* of northern seas, that has a rounded head and is white when adult. [< Russ *byeluga* (def. 1), *byelukha* (def. 2); both akin to *byelyi* white]
bel·ve·dere (bel′vi dēr′, bel′vi dēr′; *for 2 also It.* bel′-

ve de′re), *n.* **1.** a building designed and situated to look out upon a pleasing view. **2.** (*cap.*) a palace in Vatican City, Rome, used as an art gallery. [< It: fine view = *bel(lo)* beautiful (< L *bellus*) + *vedere* view (n. use of inf. < L *vidēre* to see)]

Bel·zon·i (bel tsô′nē), *n.* **Gio·van·ni Bat·tis·ta** (jô vän′nē bät tē′stä), 1778–1823, Italian explorer and Egyptologist.

be·ma (bē′mə), *n., pl.* **-ma·ta** (-mə tə), **-mas. 1.** *Eastern Ch.* the enclosed space surrounding the altar; sanctuary. **2.** bimah. [< LL < Gk *bêma* step, platform]

Be·mel·mans (bē′məl mənz, bem′əl-), *n.* **Lud·wig** (lud′wig, lo͝od′-), 1898–1962, U.S. author, illustrator, and painter; born in Austria.

be·mire (bi mīər′), *v.t.,* **-mired, -mir·ing. 1.** to soil with mire. **2.** to sink (an object or person) in mire: *The muddy road bemired the wagon.*

be·moan (bi mōn′), *v.t.* **1.** to moan over; bewail or lament: *to bemoan one's fate.* **2.** to express pity for. **—*v.i.* 3.** to lament; mourn. [BE- + MOAN; ME *bimene(n),* OE *bimǣnan*]

be·muse (bi myo͞oz′), *v.t.,* **-mused, -mus·ing.** to bewilder, confuse, or muddle (someone).

be·mused (bi myo͞ozd′), *adj.* **1.** confused; muddled; stupefied. **2.** lost in thought; preoccupied. **—be·mus·ed·ly** (bi myo͞o′zid lē), *adv.*

ben[1] (ben), *Scot.* **—*n.* 1.** the inner or back room of a two-room cottage, esp. when used as a combined parlor and bedroom. **—*adv., prep.* 2.** within; inside. **—*adj.* 3.** inside; inner. [late ME, north var. of *bin,* ME *binne,* OE *binna(n)*]

ben[2] (ben), *n.* **1.** a tree, *Moringa oleifera,* of Arabia, India, and elsewhere, bearing a winged seed that yields an oil used in extracting flower perfumes, lubricating delicate machinery, etc. **2.** the seed of such a tree. [< Ar *bān*]

ben[3] (ben), *n.* (*often cap.*) *Scot., Irish.* a mountain peak; a high hill. [< Gael *beann* peak]

ben[4] (ben), *n.* (*often cap.*) son of (used esp. in Hebrew and N African Arabic names): *Moses ben Maimon.*

Ben·a·dryl (ben′ə dril), *n. Pharm., Trademark.* diphenhydramine.

be·name (bi nām′), *v.t.,* **-named; -named, -nempt,** or **-nempt·ed; -nam·ing.** *Obs.* to name; call by name. [ME; see BE-, NAME; r. OE *benemnan*]; akin to G *benennen*]

Be·nar·es (be när′is, -ēz), *n.* a city in SE Uttar Pradesh, in NE India, on the Ganges River: Hindu holy city. 582,915. Also called **Banaras, Varanasi.**

Be·na·ven·te y Mar·ti·nez (be′nä ven′te ē mär tē′neth), **Ja·cin·to** (hä then′tô), 1866–1954, Spanish dramatist: Nobel prize 1922.

Ben Bel·la (ben bel′lä, bel′ə), **Mohammed,** born 1916, Algerian revolutionary leader and statesman: premier 1962–1965; president 1963–65.

bench (bench), *n.* **1.** a long seat for several persons. **2.** a seat occupied by an official or officials, esp. judges. **3.** the office and dignity of a judge, of judges as a group, or of various other officials. **4.** *Sports.* **a.** the seat on which players of a team sit during a game while not in action. **b.** the players usually used as substitutes on a team. **5.** workbench. **6.** *Phys. Geog.* a shelflike area of rock with steep slopes above and below. **7.** *Mining.* a step or working elevation in a mine. **—*v.t.* 8.** to furnish with benches. **9.** to seat on a bench or on the bench: *an election that benched him in the district court.* **10.** to place in exhibition: *to bench a dog.* **11.** *Sports.* to remove from a game or keep from participating in a game. [ME, OE *benc;* c. D, G *Bank* BANK[3]]

Bench·ley (bench′lē), *n.* **Robert (Charles),** 1889–1945, U.S. humorist.

bench-made (bench′mād′), *adj.* custom-made.

bench′ mark′, *Survey.* a marked point of known or assumed elevation.

bench′ press′, 1. a weightlifting exercise in which one lies supine on a bench and with both hands pushes a weight upward from chest level to arm's length and then lowers it back to chest level: usually repeated in sets. **2.** one complete repetition of this exercise. **3.** this exercise as an event in weightlifting competition.

bench-press (bench′pres′), *v.t., v.i.* to lift (a weight) in performing a bench press: *A champion weightlifter can bench-press more than 400 pounds.*

bench′ show′, a dog show in which the animals of each breed are judged and awarded prizes on the basis of meeting certain standards established for that breed.

bench′ war′rant, *Law.* a warrant issued or ordered by a judge or court for the apprehension of an offender.

bend[1] (bend), *v.,* **bent** or (*Archaic*) **bend·ed; bend·ing,** *n.* **—*v.t.* 1.** to force (an object, esp. a long or thin one) from a straight form into a curved or angular one, or from a curved or angular form into some different form: *to bend an iron rod into a hoop; to bend a crooked thing straight.* **2.** to cause to submit: *to bend someone to one's will.* **3.** to turn in a particular direction: *to bend one's steps homeward.* **4.** to incline mentally (usually fol. by *to* or *toward*): *bending his thoughts back toward his childhood.* **5.** to pull back the string of (a bow or the like) in preparation for shooting. **6.** *Naut.* to fasten. **7.** *Archaic.* to strain or brace tensely (often fol. by *up*). **—*v.i.* 8.** to become curved, crooked, or bent. **9.** to assume a bent posture; stoop (often fol. by *over*): *to bend over and pick up something.* **10.** to bow in submission or reverence; yield; submit. **11.** to turn or incline in a particular direction; be directed: *The road bent toward the south.* **12.** to direct one's energies: *We bent to our work as the bell sounded.* **13. bend over backward** or **backwards,** to exert oneself to the utmost; make a serious effort. **—*n.* 14.** the act of bending. **15.** the state of being bent. **16.** a bent thing or part; curve or crook: *a bend in the road.* **17.** *Naut.* any of various loops or knots for joining the ends of two ropes or the like, or for joining the end of a rope or the like to some other object. **18. bends, a.** *Naut.* thick planking immediately below the waterways of a wooden vessel. **b.** *Naut.* the wales of a vessel. **c.** See **caisson disease. d.** aeroembolism (usually prec. by *the*). **19. round the bend,** *Brit. Slang.* insane; crazy. [ME *bend(en),* OE *bendan* to bind, bend (a bow); c. Icel *benda* to bend] **—bend′a·ble,** *adj.* **—Syn. 1.** crook, flex, bow. **9.** BEND, BOW, STOOP imply taking a bent posture. BEND and BOW are used of the head and upper body; STOOP is used of the body only.

bend[2] (bend), *n.* **1.** *Heraldry.* a diagonal band extending from the dexter chief of an escutcheon to the sinister base. Cf. **bend sinister. 2.** *Tanning.* half of a trimmed butt or hide. [ME: coalescence of OE *bend* band (see BEND[1]) and MF *bende* BAND[2]]

Ben′ Day′ proc′ess (ben′ dā′), *Photoengraving.* a technique for producing shading, texture, or tone in line drawings and photographs with a fine screen or a pattern of dots. Also, **Ben′day′ proc′ess.** [named after *Ben(jamin) Day* (1838–1916), American printer]

bend′ dex′ter, *Heraldry.* the ordinary bend, extending from the dexter chief to the sinister base.

bend·ed (ben′did), *v. Archaic.* pp. of **bend.**

bend·er (ben′dər), *n.* **1.** a person or thing that bends, as a pair of pliers. **2.** *U.S. Slang.* a drinking spree. [BEND[1] + -ER[1]]

Ben·di·go (ben′də gō′), *n.* a city in central Victoria in SE Australia: gold mining. 32,650.

bend′ sin′ister, *n. Heraldry.* a diagonal band extending from the sinister chief of an escutcheon to the dexter base: a supposed mark of bastardy.

Bend sinister

bend·wise (bend′wīz′), *adj. Heraldry.* in the direction or manner of a bend. Also, **bend·ways** (bend′wāz′).

bend·y (ben′dē), *adj. Heraldry.* divided bendwise into areas of equal width, usually having two alternating tinctures: *bendy of six, argent and gules.* [ME]

bene-, an element occurring in loan words from Latin where it meant "well": *benediction.* [comb. form of *bene* (adv.) well]

be·neath (bi nēth′, -nēth′), *adv.* **1.** below; in or to a lower place, position, state, or the like. **2.** underneath: *heaven above and the earth beneath.* **—*prep.* 3.** below; under: *beneath the same roof.* **4.** further down than; underneath; lower in place than: *The first drawer beneath the top one.* **5.** inferior in position, rank, power, etc.: *A captain is beneath a major.* **6.** unworthy of; below the level or dignity of: *beneath contempt.* [ME *benethe,* OE *beneothan* = *be-* BE- + *neothan* below, akin to OHG *nidana,* Icel *nithan.* See NETHER] **—Syn. 3.** See **below. —Ant. 1.** above.

ben·e·dic·i·te (ben′i dis′i tē), *interj.* (*sometimes cap.*) *Obs.* bless you! [< L, impv. 2nd person pl. of *benedīcere* (*bene* BENE- + *dīcere* to speak)]

ben·e·dict (ben′i dikt), *n.* **1.** a newly married man, esp. one who has long been a bachelor. **2.** a married man. Also, **ben·e·dick** (ben′i dik). [var. of *Benedick,* bachelor character in Shakespeare's comedy *Much Ado About Nothing* (1598?)]

Ben·e·dict (ben′i dikt), *n.* **1. Ruth (Fulton),** 1887–1948, U.S. writer and anthropologist. **2. Saint,** A.D. 480?–543?, Italian monk: founded Benedictine order.

Benedict I, died A.D. 579, pope 575–579.

Benedict II, Saint, died A.D. 685, pope 684–685.

Benedict III, died A.D. 858, pope 855–858.

Benedict IV, died A.D. 903, pope 900–903.

Benedict V, died A.D. 966, pope 964.

Benedict VI, died A.D. 974, pope 973–974.

Benedict VII, died A.D. 983, pope 974–983.

Benedict VIII, died 1024, pope 1012–24.

Benedict IX, died 1056?, pope 1032–44; 1045; 1047–48.

Benedict XI, (*Niccolò Boccasini*) 1240–1304, Italian ecclesiastic: pope 1303–04.

Benedict XII, (*Jacques Fournier*) died 1342, French ecclesiastic: pope 1334–42.

Benedict XIII, (*Pietro Francesco Orsini*) 1649–1730, Italian ecclesiastic: pope 1724–30.

Benedict XIV, (*Prospero Lambertini*) 1675–1758, Italian pope 1740–58, scholar and patron of the arts.

Benedict XV, (*Giacomo della Chiesa*) 1854–1922, Italian ecclesiastic: pope 1914–22.

Ben·e·dic·tine (ben′i dik′tin, -tēn, -tīn *for 1;* ben′i dik′tēn *for 2, 3*), *n.* **1.** *Rom. Cath. Ch.* **a.** a member of an order of monks founded at Monte Cassino by St. Benedict about A.D. 530. **b.** a member of any congregation of nuns following the rule of St. Benedict. **2.** a French liqueur originally made by Benedictine monks. **—*adj.* 3.** of or pertaining to St. Benedict or the Benedictines.

ben·e·dic·tion (ben′i dik′shən), *n. Eccles.* **1.** the invocation of a blessing, esp. the short blessing pronounced by an officiating minister at the close of a religious service. **2.** (*usually cap.*) Also called **Benedic′tion of the Bless′ed Sac′rament.** *Rom. Cath. Ch.* a service consisting of prayers, at least one prescribed hymn, censing of the congregation and the Host, and a blessing of the congregation. [late ME < L *benedictiōn-* (s. of *benedictiō*). See BENEDICTUS, -ION] **—ben·e·dic·to·ry** (ben′i dik′tə rē), *adj.*

Ben·e·dic·tus (ben′i dik′təs), *n. Eccles.* **1.** the short canticle or hymn beginning in Latin *Benedictus qui venit in nomine Domini* (Blessed is He that cometh in the name of the Lord). **2.** the canticle or hymn beginning in Latin *Benedictus Dominus Deus Israel* (Blessed be the Lord God of Israel). **3.** a musical setting of either of these canticles. [< L: blessed (ptp. of *benedīcere* to commend, bless). See BENE-, DICTUM]

ben·e·fac·tion (ben′ə fak′shən, ben′ə fak′-), *n.* **1.** act of conferring a benefit; the doing of good. **2.** the benefit conferred; charitable donation. [< LL *benefactiōn-* (s. of *benefactiō*) = *bene* BENE- + *fact(us)* done (see FACT) + *-iōn-* -ION]

ben·e·fac·tor (ben′ə fak′tər, ben′ə fak′-), *n.* **1.** a person who confers a benefit; kindly helper. **2.** a person who makes a bequest or endowment, as to an institution. Also, *referring to a woman,* **ben·e·fac·tress** (ben′ə fak′tris, ben′ə fak′-) [< LL = *benefact-* (see BENEFACTION) + *-or* -OR[2]]

be·nef·ic (bə nef′ik), *adj.* doing or promoting good; beneficent: *a benefic truce.* [< L *benefic(us).* See BENE-, -FIC]

ben·e·fice (ben′ə fis), *n., v.,* **-ficed, -fic·ing. —*n.* 1.** a position or post granted to an ecclesiastic that guarantees a fixed amount of property or income. 2. the revenue itself. —*v.t.* 3. to invest with a benefice or ecclesiastical living. [ME < MF < L *benefic(ium)* = *benefic(us)* BENEFIC + *-ium* n. suffix]

be·nef·i·cence (bə nef′i səns), *n.* 1. the doing of good; active goodness or kindness; charity. 2. a beneficent act or gift; benefaction. [< L *beneficentia.* See BENEFIC, -ENCE]

be·nef·i·cent (bə nef′i sənt), *adj.* doing good or causing good to be done; conferring benefits; kindly in action or purpose. [BENEFIC(ENCE) + -ENT] —**be·nef′i·cent·ly,** *adv.*

ben·e·fi·cial (ben′ə fish′əl), *adj.* 1. conferring benefit; advantageous or helpful: *the beneficial effect of sunshine.* 2. *Law.* a. helpful in the meeting of needs: *a beneficial association.* b. receiving or entitling a person to receive for personal use, enjoyment, or benefit: *a beneficial owner.* [< LL *beneficiāl(is)* = L *benefici(um)* kindness (see BENEFICE) + *-ālis* -AL[1]] —**ben′e·fi′cial·ly,** *adv.* —**ben′e·fi′cial·ness,** *n.* —**Syn. 1.** salutary, wholesome. —**Ant. 1.** harmful.

ben·e·fi·ci·ar·y (ben′ə fish′ē er′ē, -fish′ə rē), *n., pl.* **-ar·ies.** 1. a person who receives benefits, profits, or advantages. 2. a person designated as the recipient of funds or other property under a will, trust, insurance policy, etc. 3. *Eccles.* the holder of a benefice. [< L *beneficiāri(us)*]

ben·e·fit (ben′ə fit), *n., v.,* **-fit·ed** or **-fit·ted, -fit·ing** or **-fit·ting.** —*n.* 1. anything that is advantageous or for the good of a person or thing: *He explained the benefits of owning stock.* 2. a theatrical performance or other public entertainment to raise money for a charitable organization or cause. 3. a payment or other assistance given by an insurance company, mutual benefit society, or public agency. —*v.t.* 4. to do good to; be of service to: *a health program to benefit all mankind.* —*v.i.* 5. to derive benefit or advantage; profit: *someone who has never benefited from experience.* [late ME *benefytt, -fett* (see BENE-); r. ME *b(i)enfet, -fait* < AF *benfet,* MF *bienfait* < L *benefact(um)* good deed; see FACT] —**Syn. 1.** favor, service. See **advantage.**

ben′efit of cler′gy, 1. the rites or sanctions of a church. 2. the privilege formerly claimed by church authorities that clerics be tried by ecclesiastical rather than secular courts.

Ben·e·lux (ben′ᵊluks′), *n.* 1. a customs union comprising Belgium, the Netherlands, and Luxembourg, begun January 1, 1948. 2. Belgium, the Netherlands, and Luxembourg considered together.

be·nempt (bi nempt′), *v. Obs.* a pp. of **bename.** Also, **be·nempt′ed.**

Be·neš (ben′esh), *n.* **Ed·u·ard** (e′do͝o ärt′), 1884–1948, Czech patriot and statesman: president, 1935–38; 1945–48.

Be·nét (bi nā′), *n.* 1. **Stephen Vincent,** 1898–1943, U.S. poet and novelist. 2. his brother, **William Rose,** 1886–1950, U.S. poet and critic.

Be·ne·ven·to (ben′ə ven′tō; *It.* be′ne ven′tô), *n.* a city in N Campania, in S Italy. 62,131.

be·nev·o·lence (bə nev′ə ləns), *n.* 1. desire to do good to others; good will or charitableness. 2. an act of kindness; charitable gift. 3. *Eng. Hist.* a forced contribution to the sovereign. [ME < L *benevolentia.* See BENEVOLENT, -IA, -ENCE] —**Ant. 1.** malevolence.

be·nev·o·lent (bə nev′ə lənt), *adj.* 1. desiring to do good to others: *gifts from several benevolent alumni.* 2. intended for benefits rather than profit: *a benevolent institution.* 3. characterized by good will: *a benevolent attitude.* [< L *benevolent-* (s. of *benevolēns*) kindhearted = *bene-* BENE- + *vol-* wish (akin to WILL[1]) + *-ent-* -ENT] —**be·nev′o·lent·ly,** *adv.* —**Syn. 1.** generous, benign, charitable. —**Ant.** cruel.

Beng., 1. Bengal. 2. Bengali.

Ben·gal (ben gôl′, beng-; ben′gəl, beng′-), *n.* 1. a former province in NE India: now divided between India and Bangladesh. Cf. **East Bengal, West Bengal.** 2. **Bay of,** a part of the Indian Ocean between India and Burma.

Ben·ga·lese (ben′gə lēz′, -lēs′, beng′-), *adj., n., pl.* **-lese.** —*adj.* 1. of or pertaining to Bengal. —*n.* 2. a native or inhabitant of Bengal.

Ben·ga·li (ben gô′lē, -gä′-, beng-), *n.* 1. a native or an inhabitant of Bengal. 2. the modern language of Bengal, a language of the Indic subbranch of Indo-European. —*adj.* 3. of or pertaining to Bengal, its inhabitants, or their language.

ben·ga·line (beng′gə lēn′, beng′gə lēn′), *n.* a poplinlike fabric having a crosswise corded effect, woven with coarse yarn in the filling direction. [< F; see BENGAL, -INE[2]]

Ben′gal light′, a vivid, sustained, blue light used in signaling, fireworks, etc.

Ben·gha·zi (ben gä′zē), *n.* a seaport in and a capital of Libya, in the N part. 325,000. Also, **Ben·ga′si.**

Ben-Gu·rion (ben go͞o RYôN′; *Eng.* ben go͝or′ē ən), *n.* **David,** 1886–1973, Israeli statesman, born in Poland: prime minister of Israel 1948–53; 1955–63.

Be·ni (be′nē), *n.* a river flowing NE from W Bolivia to the Madeira River. ab. 600 mi. long.

be·night·ed (bi nī′tid), *adj.* 1. intellectually or morally ignorant; unenlightened. 2. overtaken by darkness of night. [*benight* (BE- + NIGHT) + -ED[2]] —**be·night′ed·ness,** *n.*

be·nign (bi nīn′), *adj.* 1. having a kindly disposition; gracious. 2. showing or caused by gentleness or kindness: *a benign smile.* 3. favorable or propitious: *benign omens.* 4. (of weather) salubrious; pleasant. 5. *Pathol.* not malignant: *a benign tumor.* [ME *benigne* < MF < L *benigna,* fem. of *benignus* kindly < *benigenus, lit., born good. See BENE-, GENUS] —**be·nign′ly,** *adv.* —**Syn. 1, 2.** kindly, humane.

be·nig·nant (bi nig′nənt), *adj.* 1. kind, esp. to inferiors; gracious: *a benignant sovereign.* 2. exerting a good influence; beneficial. 3. *Pathol.* benign. [BENIGN + -ANT, modeled on *malignant*] —**be·nig·nan·cy** (bi nig′nən sē), *n.* —**be·nig′nant·ly,** *adv.* —**Syn. 1.** benevolent, benign.

be·nig·ni·ty (bi nig′ni tē), *n., pl.* **-ties.** 1. the quality of being benign; kindness. 2. *Archaic.* a good deed or favor. [ME *benignite* < MF < L *benignitāt-* (s. of *benignitās*)]

Be·ni Ha·san (ben′ē hä′sän), a village in central Egypt, on the Nile, N of Asyut: ancient cliff tombs.

Be·nin (be nēn′), *n.* 1. a republic in W Africa: formerly part of French West Africa; independent since 1960. 3,197,000; 44,290 sq. mi. *Cap.:* Porto Novo. Formerly, **Dahomey.** 2. a former native kingdom in W Africa: now incorporated into Nigeria. 3. a river in S Nigeria, flowing into the Bight of Benin. 4. **Bight of,** a bay in the W part of the Gulf of Guinea, off the W coast of Africa.

Benin′ Cit′y, a city in S Nigeria. 53,753 (1960).

ben·i·son (ben′i zən, -sən), *n. Archaic.* benediction. [ME < MF *beneison* < L *benedictiōn-* BENEDICTION]

Ben·ja·min (ben′jə mən), *n.* 1. the younger son of Jacob and Rachel, and the brother of Joseph. Gen. 35:18. 2. one of the 12 tribes of ancient Israel, traditionally descended from him. 3. **Judah Philip,** 1811–84, Confederate statesman.

ben·ja·min-bush (ben′jə mən bo͝osh′), *n.* spicebush.

Ben·ja·min-Con·stant (baN zhA maN′kôN stäN′), *n.* **Jean Jo·seph** (zhäN zhō zef′). See **Constant.**

Ben Lo·mond (ben lō′mənd), a mountain in central Scotland, on the E shore of Loch Lomond. 3192 ft.

Benn (ben), *n.* **Gott·fried** (gôt′frēd), 1886–1956, German physician, critic, poet, and essayist.

ben·ne (ben′ē), *n.* sesame (defs. 1, 2). [< Malay *bene* < ?]

ben·net (ben′it), *n.* either of two American avens, *Geum virginianum,* or *G. canadense.* [ME (*herbe*) *beneit* < OF (*herbe*) *beneite,* trans. of L (*herba*) *benedicta* blessed (herb)]

Ben·nett (ben′it), *n.* 1. **(Enoch) Arnold,** 1867–1931, English novelist. 2. **Floyd,** 1890–1928, U.S. aviator. 3. **James Gordon,** 1795–1872, U.S. journalist.

Ben Ne·vis (ben nē′vis, nev′is), a mountain in NW Scotland, in the Grampians. 4406 ft.

Ben·ning·ton (ben′ing tən), *n.* a town in SW Vermont: defeat of British by the Green Mountain Boys 1777. 7950 (1970).

ben·ny (ben′ē), *n., pl.* **-nies.** *Slang.* 1. Benzedrine, esp. in tablet form. 2. any amphetamine tablet. [by alter. and shortening of BENZEDRINE; see -Y[2]]

Be·noît de Sainte-Maure (bə nwä də saNt môR′), fl. 12th century, French trouvère.

Be·no·ni (bə nō′nī), *n.* a city in NE South Africa, near Johannesburg: gold mines. 167,000.

bent[1] (bent), *adj.* 1. curved or crooked: *a bent bow; a bent stick.* 2. determined, set, or resolved (usually fol. by *on*): *to be bent on buying a new car.* —*n.* 3. a direction taken by one's interests; inclination, leaning, or bias: *a bent for painting.* 4. *Civ. Eng.* a transverse frame of a bridge or a building, designed to support either vertical or horizontal loads. 5. *Archaic.* curvature. [ptp. of BEND[1]] —**Syn. 1.** bowed, flexed. 2. fixed. 3. propensity, penchant, partiality.

bent[2] (bent), *n.* 1. See **bent grass.** 2. a stalk of bent grass. 3. *Scot., North. Eng.* (formerly) any stiff grass or sedge. [ME; OE *bionot-, beonot-;* c. OHG *binuz* (cf. G *Binse*) rush]

bent′ grass′, any grass of the genus *Agrostis,* esp. redtop.

Ben·tham (ben′thəm, -təm), *n.* **Jeremy,** 1748–1832, English jurist and philosopher. —**Ben·tham·ic** (ben tham′ik, -tam′-), *adj.* —**Ben′tham·ism,** *n.* —**Ben·tham·ite** (ben′ thə mīt′, -tə-), *n.*

ben·thos (ben′thos), *n.* the aggregate of organisms living on or at the bottom of a body of water. [< Gk *bénthos* depth (of the sea); akin to BATHOS, BATHY-] —**ben′thic, ben′thal, ben·thon·ic** (ben thon′ik), *adj.*

Ben·tinck (ben′tingk), *n.* **William Henry Cavendish, Duke of Portland,** 1738–1809, British statesman.

Bent·ley (bent′lē), *n.* 1. **Eric (Russell),** born 1916, U.S. critic, editor, and translator; born in England. 2. **Richard,** 1662–1742, English scholar and critic.

Ben·ton (ben′tᵊn), *n.* 1. **Thomas Hart** ("*Old Bullion*"), 1782–1858, U.S. political leader. 2. his grandnephew, **Thomas Hart,** 1889–1975, U.S. painter and lithographer.

ben·ton·ite (ben′tᵊnīt′), *n. Mineral.* a clay formed by the decomposition of volcanic ash, having the ability to absorb large quantities of water and to expand to several times its normal volume. [named after Fort *Benton,* Montana; see -ITE[1]]

bent·wood (bent′wo͝od′), *n.* 1. wood steamed and bent for use in furniture. —*adj.* 2. noting or pertaining to furniture made principally of pieces of wood of circular or oval section, steamed, bent, and screwed together.

Be·nue (bā′nwā), *n.* a river in W Africa, flowing W from Cameroon to the Niger River in Nigeria. 870 mi. long.

be·numb (bi num′), *v.t.* 1. to make numb; deprive of sensation: *benumbed by cold.* 2. to render inactive; stupefy. [back formation from ME *benomen,* ptp. of *benimen* to take away, OE *beniman;* c. D *benemen,* G *benehmen,* Goth *biniman*] —**be·numbed·ness** (bi numd′nis, -num′id-), *n.*

benz-, var. of **benzo-** before a vowel: *benzal.*

benz·al·de·hyde (ben zal′də hīd′), *n. Chem.* a volatile oil, C_6H_5CHO, having a bitter, almondlike odor; artificial oil of bitter almond: used chiefly in the synthesis of dyes, perfumes, and flavors, and as a solvent.

ben′zal group′, *Chem.* the bivalent group, $C_6H_5CH–$, derived from benzaldehyde. Also called **ben′zal rad′ical.** —**ben·zal** (ben′zal), *adj.*

ben·zal·ko′ni·um chlo′ride (ben′zal kō′nē əm), *Chem.* a mixture of ammonium chloride derivatives having the structure, $[C_6H_5CH_2N(CH_3)_2R]Cl$, where R is a mixture of radicals ranging from $C_8H_{17}–$ to $C_{18}H_{37}–$: used chiefly as an antiseptic and a disinfectant. [BENZ- + ALK(YL) + (AMM)ONIUM]

Ben·ze·drine (ben′zi drēn′, -drin), *n. Pharm., Trademark.* amphetamine.

ben·zene (ben′zēn, ben zēn′), *n. Chem.* a volatile, flammable liquid, C_6H_6, obtained chiefly from coal tar: used in the manufacture of chemicals, dyes, and as a solvent. Also called **benzol.**

H
HC CH
HC CH
C
H
1 2 3 4 5 6
X Y Z

Benzene ring
(Kekulé's formula)
X, Graphic representation;
Y, Positions numbered for replacement of one or more hydrogen atoms, leading to benzene derivatives; Z, Used when cyclohexane is not indicated. Double bonds are assumed.

ben′zene hex·a·chlo′·ride (hek′sə klôr′īd, -klōr′-), *Chem.* a poisonous solid, $C_6H_6Cl_6$, used chiefly as an insecticide.

ben′zene ring′, *Chem.* the graphic representation of the structure of benzene as a hexagon with a carbon atom at each of its points.

ben·ze·noid (ben′zə noid′), *adj. Chem.* of an unsaturated organic compound related to benzene and used in the synthesis of dyes, medicines, and plastics.

ben·zi·dine (ben′zi dēn′, -din), *n.* *Chem.* a grayish compound, $NH_2(C_6H_4)_2NH_2$, used chiefly in the synthesis of certain azo dyes.

ben·zine (ben′zēn, ben zēn′), *n.* a liquid mixture of various hydrocarbons, used in cleaning, dyeing, etc. Also, **ben·zin** (ben′zin).

benzo-, a combining form indicating benzene, benzoic acid, or the presence of one or more phenyl groups in a substance: *benzocaine.* Also, *esp. before a vowel,* **benz-.** [comb. form of BENZOIN[1]]

ben·zo·ate (ben′zō āt′, -it), *n.* *Chem.* a salt or ester of benzoic acid.

ben′zoate of so′da, *Chem.* See **sodium benzoate.**

ben·zo·caine (ben′zō kān′), *n.* *Pharm.* a powder, $H_2N\,C_6H_4COOC_2H_5$, used as a local anesthetic. [BENZO- + (CO)CAINE]

ben·zo·ic (ben zō′ik), *adj.* *Chem.* of or derived from benzoin or benzoic acid.

benzo′ic ac′id, *Chem., Pharm.* a powder, C_6H_5COOH, used chiefly as a preservative, in the synthesis of dyes, and as a germicide.

ben·zo·in[1] (ben′zō in, -zoin, ben zō′in), *n.* **1.** a reddish-brown, aromatic resin having a vanillalike odor, used in the manufacture of perfume and cosmetics and as an expectorant and an antiseptic. **2.** any lauraceous plant of the genus *Lindera* (*Benzoin*), which includes the spicebush and other aromatic plants. [earlier *benjoin* < MF < Pg *beijoim* + Sp *benjuí* (c. It *benzoi*) < Ar (*lu*)*bān jāwī* frankincense of Java]

ben·zo·in[2] (ben′zō in, -zoin, ben zō′in), *n.* *Chem.* a powder, $C_6H_5CHOHCOC_6H_5$, used in organic synthesis. [BENZO- + -IN[2]]

ben·zol (ben′zōl, -zôl, -zol), *n.* **1.** *Chem.* benzene. **2.** an impure form of this, used for industrial purposes.

ben·zo·phe·none (ben′zō fi nōn′), *n.* *Chem.* a ketone, $C_6H_5COC_6H_5$, used in organic synthesis.

ben·zo·py·rene (ben′zō pī′rēn), *n.* a carcinogenic hydrocarbon, $C_{20}H_{12}$, found in coal tar, cigarette smoke, and auto exhaust. [BENZO + PYRENE[2]]

ben′zoyl group′, *Chem.* the univalent group, C_6H_5CO-. Also called **ben′zoyl rad′ical.** —**ben·zo·yl** (ben′zō il), *adj.*

ben′zoyl perox′ide, *Chem.* a crystalline solid, $(C_6H_5CO)_2O_2$, used chiefly as a bleaching agent and a catalyst in polymerization reactions.

Ben-Zvi (ben tsvē′), *n.* **Itz·hak** (yits′hok), 1884?–1963, Israeli statesman, born in Russia: president of Israel 1952–63.

ben′zyl al′cohol, *Chem.* a colorless liquid, $C_6H_5CH_2OH$, several of whose esters are used in flavorings and perfumes.

ben′zyl group′, *Chem.* the univalent group, $C_6H_5CH_2-$. Also called **ben′zyl rad′ical.** —**ben·zyl** (ben′zil), *adj.* —**ben·zyl′ic,** *adj.*

Be·o·grad (be′ô gräd), *n.* Serbian name of **Belgrade.**

Be·o·wulf (bā′ə wo͝olf′), *n.* an English alliterative epic poem of the early 8th century A.D.

be·queath (bi kwēth′, -kwēth′), *v.t.* **1.** *Law.* to dispose of (property, esp. personal property) by will. **2.** to hand down; pass on. **3.** *Obs.* to commit; entrust. [ME *bequethe(n),* OE *becwethan* = *be-* BE- + *cwethan* to say, c. OHG *quedan,* Goth *qithan*] —**be·queath·al** (bi kwē′thəl, -thəl), **be·queath′ment,** *n.*

be·quest (bi kwest′), *n.* *Law.* **1.** a disposition by will of property, esp. personal property. **2.** that which is so disposed; legacy. [ME *biqueste* = *bi-* BE- + *-queste* (*-ques-* (OE *-cwiss-;* akin to BEQUEATH) + *-te,* var. of -TH[1])]

Bé·ran·ger (bā räN zhā′), *n.* **Pierre Jean de** (pyeʀ zhäN də), 1780–1857, French poet.

be·rate (bi rāt′), *v.t.,* **-rat·ed, -rat·ing.** to scold or rebuke. —**Syn.** abuse, vilify, vituperate, objurgate.

Ber·ber (bûr′bər), *n.* **1.** a member of a group of North African tribes living in Barbary and the Sahara. **2.** a subfamily of Afro-Asiatic, consisting of the languages of the Berbers, including Tuareg and Kabyle. —*adj.* **3.** of or pertaining to the Berbers or their languages.

Ber·ber·a (bûr′bər ə), *n.* a seaport in the Somali Republic, on the Gulf of Aden. 65,000.

ber·ber·i·da·ceous (bûr′bər i dā′shəs), *adj.* belonging to the *Berberidaceae,* a family of plants including the barberry, May apple, blue cohosh, etc. [< ML *berberid-* (s. of *berberis*) BARBERRY + -ACEOUS]

ber·ceuse (*Fr.* beʀ sœz′), *n., pl.* **-ceuses** (*Fr.* -sœz′). *Music.* a cradlesong; lullaby. [< F = *berc(er)* (to) rock + *-euse,* fem. suffix of agency]

Berch·tes·ga·den (beʀᴋʜ′təs gäd′ən), *n.* a town in the Bavarian Alps in SE Bavaria, in SE West Germany: site of the fortified mountain chalet of Adolf Hitler. 39,800.

be·reave (bi rēv′), *v.t.,* **-reaved** or **-reft, -reav·ing. 1.** to deprive ruthlessly or by force (usually fol. by *of*): *The war bereaved them of their home.* **2.** to deprive, esp. by death (usually fol. by *of*): *Illness bereaved them of their mother.* **3.** *Obs.* to take away by violence. [ME *bereve(n),* OE *berēafian;* c. D *berooven,* G *berauben,* Goth *biraubōn.* See BE-, REAVE[1]] —**be·reave′ment,** *n.*

be·reft (bi reft′), *v.* **1.** a pt. and pp. of **bereave.** —*adj.* **2.** deprived: *They are bereft of their senses.*

Ber·e·ni′ce's Hair′ (ber′ə nī′sēz), *Astron.* the constellation Coma Berenices.

Ber·en·son (ber′ən sən), *n.* **Bernard** or **Bernhard,** 1865–1959, U.S. art critic, born in Lithuania.

Ber·es·ford (ber′iz fərd, -is-), *n.* **Lord Charles William de la Poer** (po͝or), 1846–1919, English admiral, explorer, and author.

be·ret (bə rā′, ber′ā; *Fr.* be ʀe′), *n., pl.* **be·rets** (bə rāz′, ber′āz; *Fr.* be ʀe′). a soft, visorless cap with a close-fitting headband and a wide, round top often with a tab at its center. [< F *béret* < dial. *berret(o).* See BIRETTA]

Be·re·zi·na (*Pol.* be′ʀe zē′nä; *Russ.* be′ʀe zi nä′), *n.* a river in the W Soviet Union in Europe, flowing SE into the Dnieper River: crossed by Napoleon 1812. 350 mi. long.

Be·rez·ni·ki (bi ʀez′ni ki), *n.* a city in the RSFSR, in the E Soviet Union, near the Ural Mountains. 120,000 (est. 1962).

berg (bûrg), *n.* *Oceanog.* iceberg. [by shortening]

Berg (berg; *Ger.* beʀk), *n.* **Al·ban** (äl bän′, äl′bän), 1885–1935, Austrian composer.

Ber·ga·ma (ber gä′mə, bər-, bûr′gə mə), *n.* a town in W Turkey in Asia. 24,113 (1965). Ancient, **Pergamum.**

Ber·ga·mo (beʀ′gä mō), *n.* a city in central Lombardy, in N Italy. 113,512 (1961).

ber·ga·mot (bûr′gə mot′), *n.* **1.** a small citrus tree, *Citrus Bergamia,* having fruit whose rind yields a fragrant essential oil. **2.** the oil or essence itself. **3.** any of various plants of the mint family, as *Monarda fistulosa,* yielding an oil resembling essence of bergamot. [< F *bergamote,* variety of pear, hence sweet lemon < It *bergamotta* < Turkic **beg-armutu* lord-pear, akin to Turk *bey* BEY + *armudu* pear]

Ber·gen (bûr′gən; *Norw.* beʀ′gən), *n.* a city in SW Norway, on the Atlantic Ocean. 117,290 (est. 1960).

Ber·gen·field (bûr′gən fēld′), *n.* a city in NE New Jersey. 29,000 (1970).

Ber·ge·rac (beʀ zhə ʀak′), *n.* **Sa·vi·nien Cy·ra·no de** (sa vē nyaN′ sē ʀa nō′ də), 1619–55, French soldier, swordsman, and writer: hero of play by Rostand.

Ber·gi·us (beʀ′gē o͝os′), *n.* **Frie·drich** (fʀē′dʀiᴋʜ), 1884–1949, German chemist: Nobel prize 1931.

Berg·son (bûrg′sən, berg′-; *Fr.* beʀg sôN′), *n.* **Hen·ri** (äN ʀē′), 1859–1941, French philosopher and writer: Nobel prize for literature 1927. —**Berg·so·ni·an** (bûrg sō′nē ən, berg-), *adj., n.* —**Berg·son·ism** (bûrg′sə niz′əm, berg′-), *n.*

Be·ri·a (ber′ē ə), *n.* **La·vren·ti Pa·vlo·vich** (lä vʀen′ti pä vlô′vich), 1899–1953, Soviet official: executed for treason.

be·rib·boned (bi rib′ənd), *adj.* adorned with ribbons. [*beribbon* (BE- + RIBBON) + -ED[2]]

ber·i·ber·i (ber′ē ber′ē), *n.* *Pathol.* a disease of the peripheral nerves caused by a deficiency of vitamin B_1, characterized by pain in and paralysis of the extremities, and severe emaciation or swelling of the body. [< Singhalese redupl. of *beri* weakness] —**ber′i·ber′ic,** *adj.*

Ber·ing (bēr′ing, ber′-, bâr′-; *Dan.* bā′ʀing), *n.* **Vi·tus** (vē′to͝os), 1680–1741, Danish navigator: explorer of the N Pacific. Also, **Behring.**

Ber′ing Sea′, a part of the N Pacific, N of the Aleutian Islands. 878,000 sq. mi.

Ber′ing Strait′, a strait between Alaska and the Soviet Union in Asia, connecting the Bering Sea and the Arctic Ocean. 36 mi. wide.

Ber′ing time′. See under **standard time.**

Ber. Is., Bermuda Islands.

Be·rith (bə ʀēt′; *Eng.* bris), *n.* *Hebrew.* the Jewish rite of circumcising a male child eight days after his birth. Also, **Be·rit′, Brith, Brit.** [lit., covenant]

Berke·ley (bûrk′lē; *for 1, 2 also Brit.* bärk′lē), *n.* **1. George,** 1685?–1753, Irish bishop and philosopher. **2. Sir William,** 1610–77, British colonial governor of Virginia 1642–76. **3.** a city in W California, on San Francisco Bay. 116,716 (1970).

ber·ke·li·um (bər kē′lē əm), *n.* *Chem.* a synthetic, radioactive, metallic element. *Symbol:* Bk; *at. no.:* 97. [named after BERKELEY, California, where it was discovered; see -IUM]

Berk·shire (bûrk′shēr, -shər; *Brit.* bärk′shēr, -shər), *n.* **1.** Also called **Berks** (bûrks; *Brit.* bärks). a county in S England. 503,357 (1961); 725 sq. mi. *Co. seat:* Reading. **2.** one of an English breed of black hogs, having white markings on the feet, face, and tail.

Berk′shire Hills′ (bûrk′shēr, -shər), a range of low mountains in W Massachusetts: resort region. Highest peak, Mt. Greylock, 3505 ft. Also called **Berk′shires.**

ber·lin (bər lin′, bûr′lin), *n.* a large, four-wheeled, closed carriage hung between two perches and having two interior seats. Also, **ber·line** (bər lin′; *Fr.* beʀ lēn′). [< F *berline;* after BERLIN, Germany, where it was first made]

Berlin

Ber·lin (bər lin′ *for 1, 2;* bûr′lin *for 3; for 2 also Ger.* beʀ lēn′), *n.* **1. Irving,** born 1888, U.S. songwriter. **2.** a city in E East Germany and former capital of Germany: now divided into a western zone **(West Berlin),** tied with West Germany, 1,984,800; and an eastern zone **(East Berlin),** the capital of East Germany, 1,098,200.

Berlin′ Wall′, a long, guarded wall erected in Berlin by East Germany in 1961 to prevent passage to and from West Germany.

Ber·li·oz (ber′lē ōz′; *Fr.* beʀ lyôz′), *n.* **Louis Hec·tor** (lwē ek tôʀ′), 1803–69, French composer.

berm (bûrm), *n.* **1.** an edge or shoulder running alongside a road, canal, etc. **2.** Also, **berme.** *Fort.* a horizontal surface between the exterior slope of a rampart and the moat. **3.** any level strip of ground at the summit or sides, or along the base, of a slope. [< D (> F *berme*); akin to BRIM]

Ber·me·jo (beʀ me′hō), *n.* a river in N Argentina, flowing SE to the Paraguay River. 1000 mi. long.

Ber·mu·da (bər myo͞o′də), *n.* a group of islands in the Atlantic, 580 miles E of North Carolina: a British colony. 56,056 (1960); 19 sq. mi. *Cap.:* Hamilton. Also, **Ber·mu′das.** —**Ber·mu′dan, Ber·mu·di·an** (bər myo͞o′dē ən), *adj., n.*

Bermu′da grass′, a perennial, creeping grass, *Cynodon Dactylon,* of southern Europe, grown in the southern U.S. and Bermuda for lawns and pastures.

Bermu′da on′ion, any of several mild varieties of onion, grown in parts of the southern U.S. and in Bermuda.

Bermu′da shorts′, close-fitting shorts or short pants extending almost to the knee, worn by men and women for informal dress. Also called **Bermu′das.**

Bermu′da Tri′angle, the triangular area in the Atlantic Ocean bounded by lines drawn between Bermuda, Puerto Rico, and a point west of Florida, in which a number of ships and aircraft are alleged to have disappeared mysteriously esp. since 1945.

Bern (bûrn; *also Ger.* beʀn), *n.* a city in and the capital of Switzerland, in the W part. 149,800. Also, **Berne.**

Ber·na·dette (bûr′nə det′; *Fr.* beʀ na det′), *n.* **Saint** (*Marie Bernarde Soubirous* or *Soubiroux*), 1844–79, French nun. Also called **Bernadette′ of Lourdes′.**

Ber·na·dotte (bûr′nə dot′; *Fr.* beʀ na dôt′), *n.* **Jean Bap·tiste Jules** (zhäɴ ba tēst′ zhyl), 1764–1844, French marshal under Napoleon: as Charles XIV, king of Sweden and Norway 1818–44.

Ber·na·nos (beʀ na nôs′), *n.* **Georges** (zhôʀzh), 1888–1948, French novelist and pamphleteer.

Ber·nard (beʀ naʀ′), *n.* **Claude** (klōd), 1813–78, French physiologist.

Ber·nar·din de Saint-Pierre (beʀ naʀ daɴ′ də saɴ-pyeʀ′), **Jacques Hen·ri** (zhäk äɴ rē′), 1737–1814, French writer.

Ber·nard·ine (bûr′nər din, -dēn′), *adj.* **1.** of or pertaining to St. Bernard of Clairvaux or to the Cistercians. —*n.* **2.** a Cistercian. [< ML *Bernardīn(us)*; see -INE[1]]

Ber·nard of Clair·vaux (bûr närd′ əv klâr vō′), **Saint** ("*the Mellifluous Doctor*"), 1090–1153, French monk, preacher, and mystical writer.

Berne (bûrn; *also Fr.* beʀn), *n.* Bern.

Ber′nese Alps′ (bûr′nēz, -nēs, bûr nēz′, -nēs′), a mountain range in SW Switzerland, part of the Alps: highest peak, 14,026 ft.

Bern·har·di (beʀn här′dē), *n.* **Frie·drich A. J. von** (frē′dʀiKH fən), 1849–1930, German general.

Bern·hardt (bûrn′härt; *Fr.* beʀ naʀ′), *n.* **Sar·ah** (sâr′ə, sar′ə; *Fr.* sa ʀa′), (*Rosine Bernard*), 1845–1923, French actress.

Ber·ni·na (bər nē′nə; *It.* beʀ nē′nä), *n.* a mountain in SE Switzerland, in the Rhaetian Alps. 13,295 ft.

Berni′na Pass′, a pass traversing Bernina Mountain, between SE Switzerland and N Italy. 7640 ft. high.

Ber·ni·ni (bər nē′nē; *It.* beʀ nē′nē), *n.* **Gio·van·ni Lo·ren·zo** (jē′ə vä′nē lə ren′zō; *It.* jô vän′nē lô ʀen′dzô), 1598–1680, Italian sculptor, architect, and painter.

Ber·noul·li (bər nōō′lē; *Ger.* beʀ nōō′lē; *Fr.* beʀ nōō yē′), *n.* **1. Dan·iel** (dan′yəl; *Ger.* dä′nē el′; *Fr.* da nyel′), 1700–1782, Swiss physicist and mathematician, born in the Netherlands (son of Johann Bernoulli). **2. Ja·kob** (*Ger.* yä′kôp) or **Jacques** (*Fr.* zhäk), 1654–1705, Swiss mathematician and physicist. **3. Jo·hann** (*Ger.* yō′hän) or **Jean** (*Fr.* zhäɴ), 1667–1748, Swiss mathematician (brother of Jakob Bernoulli). Also, **Ber·nouil′li.** —**Ber·noul′li·an, Ber·nouil′li·an,** *adj.*

Bernoul′li effect′, *Hydraulics.* the decrease in pressure as the velocity of a fluid increases. [named after Jakob BERNOULLI]

Bernoul′li's the′orem. See **law of averages** (def. 1). [named after Daniel BERNOULLI]

Bern·stein (bûrn′stīn, -stēn), *n.* **Leonard,** born 1918, U.S. conductor, composer, and pianist.

Bern·storff (beʀn′shtôʀf), *n.* **Count Jo·hann-Hein·rich** (yō′hän hīn′ʀiKH), 1862–1939, German diplomat.

ber·ried (ber′ēd), *adj.* **1.** covered with or yielding berries. **2.** (of lobsters, crayfish, etc.) bearing or containing eggs.

ber·ry (ber′ē), *n., pl.* **-ries,** *v.,* **-ried, -ry·ing.** —*n.* **1.** any small, usually stoneless, juicy fruit, irrespective of botanical structure, as the gooseberry, strawberry, hackberry, etc. **2.** a dry seed or kernel, as of wheat. **3.** *Bot.* a simple fruit having a pulpy pericarp in which the seeds are embedded, as the grape, gooseberry, currant, tomato, etc. **4.** one of the eggs of a lobster, crayfish, etc. —*v.i.* **5.** to bear or produce berries. **6.** to gather or pick berries. [ME *berie,* OE; c. OHG *beri* (G *Beere*), Icel *ber;* akin to D *besie,* Goth *-basi*] —**ber′ry·less,** *adj.* —**ber′ry·like′,** *adj.*

Ber·ry (ber′ē; *Fr.* be ʀē′), *n.* a former province in central France. Also, **Ber′ri.**

Ber·ry·man (ber′ē mən), *n.* **John,** 1914–72, U.S. poet and critic.

ber·seem (bər sēm′), *n.* a clover, *Trifolium alexandrinum,* of Egypt and Syria, grown for forage in the southwestern U.S. [< Ar *barsīm* < Coptic *bersīm*]

ber·serk (bər sûrk′, -zûrk′), *adj.* **1.** violently and destructively enraged; frenzied. —*adv.* **2.** into a frenzied, violent rage. —*n.* **3.** a berserker. [see BERSERKER]

ber·serk·er (bər sûr′kər, -zûr′-), *n.* *Scand. Legend.* any ancient Norse warrior of great strength and courage who fought with frenzied rage in battle; baresark. [< Icel *berserkr* = *ber-* meaning and orig. uncert. + *serkr* SARK]

berth (bûrth), *n.* **1.** a shelflike sleeping space for one person, as on a ship, railroad car, etc. **2.** *Naut.* **a.** the cabin of a ship's officer. **b.** the distance maintained between a vessel and the shore, another vessel, or any object. **c.** the space allotted to a vessel at anchor or at a wharf. **d.** the position or rank of a ship's officer. **3.** a job; position. **4. give a wide berth to,** to shun; remain discreetly away from. —*v.t.* **5.** *Naut.* to allot to (a vessel) a certain space at which to moor. —*v.i.* **6.** *Naut.* to come into a dock or anchorage. [? BEAR[1] + -TH[1]]

ber·tha (bûr′thə), *n.* a collar or trimming, as of lace, worn about the shoulders by women, as over a low-necked waist or dress. [named after *Bertha* (d. A.D. 783), wife of Pepin the Short, famed for her modesty]

Ber′tillon sys′tem (bûr′tᵊlon′; *Fr.* beʀ tē yôɴ′), a system of identifying persons, esp. criminals, by a record of individual physical measurements and peculiarities. [named after A. *Bertillon* (1853–1914), French anthropologist]

Ber·to (beʀ′tô), *n.* **Giu·sep·pe** (jōō zep′pe), born 1914, Italian novelist.

Ber·wick (ber′ik), *n.* **1.** Also called **Ber·wick·shire** (ber′ik shēr′, -shər). a county in SE Scotland. 22,044 (est. 1964); 457 sq. mi. *Co. seat:* Duns. **2.** Berwick-upon-Tweed.

Ber·wick-up·on-Tweed (ber′ik ə pon′twēd′), *n.* a town in N Northumberland, in N England, on the North Sea at the mouth of the Tweed. 12,166 (1961). Also called **Berwick.**

Ber·wyn (bûr′win), *n.* a city in NE Illinois, near Chicago. 52,502 (1970).

ber·yl (ber′əl), *n.* a usually green mineral, beryllium aluminum silicate, $Be_3Al_2Si_6O_{18}$, occurring in both opaque and transparent varieties, the latter variety including the gems emerald and aquamarine: the principal ore of beryllium. [ME *beril* < ML *bērill(us),* L *bēryllus* < Gk *bḗryllos*] —**ber·yl·ine** (ber′ə lin, -līn′), *adj.*

be·ryl·li·um (bi ril′ē əm), *n.* *Chem.* a steel-gray, bivalent, hard, light, metallic element: used chiefly in copper alloys for better fatigue endurance in springs and in contacts. *Symbol:* Be; *at. wt.:* 9.0122; *at. no.:* 4; *sp. gr.:* 1.8 at 20°C. Also called **glucinum, glucinium.** [< L *bēryll(us)* BERYL + -IUM]

Ber·ze·li·us (bər zē′lē əs; *Swed.* beʀ sā′lē ōōs′), *n.* **Jöns Ja·kob** (yœns yä′kôp), **Baron,** 1779–1848, Swedish chemist.

Bes (bes), *n.* *Egyptian Religion.* the patron deity of music, dancing, and children, represented as a hairy dwarf having a tail and wearing a lion's skin.

Be·san·çon (bə zäɴ sôɴ′), *n.* a city in E France: Roman ruins. 101,729 (1962).

Bes·ant (bez′ənt), *n.* **Annie (Wood),** 1847–1933, English theosophist.

be·seech (bi sēch′), *v.,* **-sought** or, often, **-seeched, -seech·ing.** —*v.t.* **1.** to implore urgently. **2.** to beg eagerly for. —*v.i.* **3.** to make urgent appeal. [ME *biseche(n),* OE *besēcan.* See BE-, SEEK] —**be·seech′er,** *n.* —**be·seech′ing·ly,** *adv.* —**be·seech′ing·ness,** *n.* —**Syn. 1.** pray, supplicate. **1, 2.** entreat.

be·seem (bi sēm′), *v.t.* *Archaic.* **1.** to be fit for or worthy of; become. —*v.i.* **2.** to be suitable or fitting. [ME *bisem(en)*]

be·set (bi set′), *v.t.,* **-set, -set·ting. 1.** to attack on all sides; assail; harass: *to be beset by difficulties.* **2.** to surround; hem in. **3.** to set or place upon; bestud: *beset with jewels.* [ME *besett(en),* OE *besettan*] —**be·set′ment,** *n.* —**be·set′ter,** *n.*

be·set·ting (bi set′ing), *adj.* constantly assailing or obsessing: *a besetting sin.*

be·shrew (bi shrōō′), *v.t.* *Archaic.* to curse; invoke evil upon. [ME *beshrew(en).* See BE-, SHREW[1]]

be·side (bi sīd′), *prep.* **1.** by or at the side of; near: *Sit down beside me.* **2.** compared with: *Beside him other writers seem amateurish.* **3.** apart from; not connected with: *His comment was beside the point.* **4.** besides (def. 4). **5. beside oneself,** almost out of one's senses from a strong emotion: *He was beside himself with rage.* —*adv.* **6.** along the side of something. **7.** *Rare.* besides (def. 2). [ME, OE *be sīdan* by side] —**Usage.** BESIDE, BESIDES may both be used as prepositions, although with different meanings. BESIDE is almost exclusively used as a preposition meaning by the side of: *beside the house, the stream.* BESIDES is used as a preposition meaning in addition to or over and above: *Besides these honors he received a sum of money.*

be·sides (bi sīdz′), *adv.* **1.** moreover; furthermore: *Besides, I promised her we would come.* **2.** in addition: *There are three elm trees and two maples besides.* **3.** otherwise; else: *They had a roof over their heads but not much besides.* —*prep.* **4.** over and above; in addition to: *Besides a mother he has a sister to support.* **5.** other than; except: *There's no one here besides Bill and me.*
—**Syn. 1.** further. BESIDES, MOREOVER both indicate something additional to what has already been stated. BESIDES often suggests that the addition is in the nature of an afterthought: *The bill cannot be paid as yet; besides, the work is not completed.* MOREOVER is more formal and implies that the addition is something particular, emphatic, or important: *I did not like the house; moreover, it was too high-priced.* —**Usage.** See **beside.**

be·siege (bi sēj′), *v.t.,* **-sieged, -sieg·ing. 1.** to lay siege to. **2.** to surround or beset with requests, work, annoyances, or the like: *Vacationers besieged the travel office.* [ME *bysege(n)*] —**be·siege′ment,** *n.* —**be·sieg′er,** *n.* —**be·sieg′ing·ly,** *adv.*

be·smear (bi smēr′), *v.t.* **1.** to smear all over; bedaub. **2.** to sully; defile; soil: *to besmear someone's reputation.* [ME *bismer(en),* OE *besmerian*]

be·smirch (bi smûrch′), *v.t.* **1.** to soil; tarnish; discolor. **2.** to detract from the honor or luster of: *to besmirch someone's good name.*

be·som (bē′zəm), *n.* **1.** a broom, esp. one of brush or twigs. **2.** broom (def. 2). [ME *besem,* OE *bes(e)ma;* c. D *bezem,* G *Besen*]

be·sot (bi sot′), *v.t.,* **-sot·ted, -sot·ting.** to stupefy or make foolish, as with drink or emotion. —**be·sot′ted·ly,** *adv.* —**be·sot′ted·ness,** *n.* —**be·sot′ting·ly,** *adv.*

be·sought (bi sôt′), *v.* pt. and pp. of **beseech.**

be·span·gle (bi spang′gəl), *v.t.,* **-gled, -gling.** to cover or adorn with, or as with, spangles.

be·spat·ter (bi spat′ər), *v.t.* **1.** to soil by spattering; splash with water, dirt, etc. **2.** to slander.

be·speak (bi spēk′), *v.t.,* **-spoke** or (*Archaic*) **-spake** (-spāk′); **-spo·ken** or **-spoke; -speak·ing. 1.** to ask for or reserve in advance: *to bespeak the reader's patience.* **2.** *Poetic.* to speak to; address. **3.** to show; indicate: *This bespeaks a kindly heart.* **4.** *Obs.* to foretell; forebode. [ME *bespek(en),* OE *besprecan*]

be·spec·ta·cled (bi spek′tə kəld), *adj.* wearing eyeglasses.

be·spoke (bi spōk′), *v.* **1.** a pt. and pp. of **bespeak.** —*adj.* **2.** *Brit.* **a.** (of clothes) made to individual order; custom-made. **b.** making or selling such clothes: *a bespoke tailor.* **3.** spoken for; engaged to be married.

be·spo·ken (bi spō′kən), *v.* **1.** a pp. of **bespeak.** —*adj.* **2.** bespoke.

be·spread (bi spred′), *v.t.,* **-spread, -spread·ing.** to spread over (a surface); cover (usually fol. by *with*): *to bespread a table with fine linens.* [ME *bespred(en)*]

be·sprin·kle (bi spring′kəl), *v.t.,* **-kled, -kling.** to sprinkle (something) all over, as with water, flour, seasoning, etc.

Bes·sa·ra·bi·a (bes′ə rā′bē ə), *n.* a region in Moldavia, in the SW Soviet Union in Europe, on the W shore of the Black Sea, formerly in Rumania. —**Bes′sa·ra′bi·an,** *adj., n.*

Bes·sel (bes′əl), *n.* **Frie·drich Wil·helm** (frē′drik wil′helm; *Ger.* frē′dʀiKH vil′helm), 1784–1846, German astronomer.

Bes·se·mer (bes′ə mər), *n.* **1. Sir Henry,** 1813–98, English engineer: inventor of the Bessemer process. **2.** a city in central Alabama. 33,663 (1970).

Bes′semer convert′er, the refractory-lined metal container in which steel is produced by the Bessemer process.

Bes′semer proc′ess, *Metall.* a process of producing steel (**Bes′semer steel′**), in which impurities are removed by forcing a blast of air through molten iron.

best (best), *adj., superl. of* **good** *with* **better** *as compar.* **1.** of the highest quality, excellence, or standing: *the best work; the best students.* **2.** most advantageous, suitable, or desirable: *the best way.* **3.** largest; most: *the best part of a day.* —*adv., superl. of* **well** *with* **better** *as compar.* **4.** most excellently or suitably; with most advantage or success: *a hairdo that best shows her beauty.* **5.** in or to the highest degree; most fully (usually used in combination): *best-suited; best-known; best-loved.* **6. as best one can,** in the most suitable or most successful way possible under the circumstances: *We tried to smooth over the difficulties as best we could.* **7. had best,** ought to: *You had best phone your mother before you go.* —*n.* **8.** that which is best, as a part, state, circumstance, etc.: *You haven't heard the best. The best of us can make mistakes.* **9.** a person's finest clothing: *It's important that you wear your best.* **10.** a person's most agreeable emotional state, highest degree of competence, or the like (often prec. by *at*): *After a good night's sleep, he was at his best.* **11.** the highest quality (often prec. by *at*): *cabinet, making at its best.* **12.** the best effort that a person, group, or thing can make: *Their best fell far short of excellence.* **13.** a person's best wishes or kindest regards: *Please give my best to your father.* **14. at best,** under the most favorable circumstances: *You may expect to be treated civilly, at best.* **15. get or have the best of, a.** to gain the advantage over. **b.** to defeat; subdue: *His arthritis gets the best of him from time to time.* **16. make the best of,** to manage as well as one can under unfavorable or adverse circumstances. —*v.t.* **17.** to defeat; get the better of; beat: *He easily bested his opponent in hand-to-hand combat.* [ME *beste,* OE *betst, best;* c. D *best,* OHG *bezzist* (G *best*), Icel *bezt,* Goth *batists.* See BETTER[1], -EST[1]]

be·stead (bi sted′), *v.,* **-stead·ed, -stead·ed** or **-stead, -stead·ing,** *adj.* —*v.t. Archaic.* **1.** to help; assist; avail. —*adj.* **2.** placed or situated, often unfavorably or in difficulty. [(v.) BE- + STEAD; (adj.) ME *bestedd* = *be-* BE- + *stedd,* var. of *stadd* placed < Scand; cf. Icel *staddr,* ptp. of *stethja* to place < *stathr* place]

bes·tial (bes′chəl, best′yəl *or, often,* bēs′chəl), *adj.* **1.** of, pertaining to, or having the form of a beast. **2.** brutal; inhuman; without reason or intelligence: *bestial treatment of prisoners.* **3.** carnal; debased. [late ME < LL *bēstiāl(is)* = L *bēsti(a)* BEAST + *-ālis* -AL[1]] —**bes′tial·ly,** *adv.*

bes·tial·ise (bes′chə līz′, best′yə- *or, often,* bēs′chə līz′), *v.t.,* **-ised, -is·ing.** *Chiefly Brit.* bestialize.

bes·ti·al·i·ty (bes′chē al′i tē, -tē al′- *or, often,* bēs′chē-al′i tē), *n., pl.* **-ties. 1.** brutish or beastly character or behavior; beastliness. **2.** indulgence in beastlike appetites, instincts, impulses, etc. **3.** sexual relations between a human and an animal. [late ME *bestialite* < ML *bēstiālitāt-* (s. of *bēstiālitās*)]

bes·tial·ize (bes′chə līz′, best′yə- *or, often,* bēs′chə līz′), *v.t.,* **-ized, -iz·ing.** to make bestial or beastlike: *War bestializes its participants.* Also, *esp. Brit.,* **bestialise.**

bes·ti·ar·y (bes′chē er′ē, -tē- *or, often,* bēs′chē er′ē), *n., pl.* **-ar·ies.** a collection of moralized descriptions of actual or mythical animals. [< ML *bēstiāri(um),* neut. of L *bēstiārius.* See BEAST, -ARY] —**bes·ti·a·rist** (bes′chē ər ist, -tē ər-, -chər- *or, often,* bēs′chē ər ist, -chər-), *n.*

be·stir (bi stûr′), *v.t.,* **-stirred, -stir·ring.** to stir up; rouse to action (often used reflexively): *She bestirred herself at the first light of morning.* [ME *bestire(n),* OE *bestyrian* to heap up]

best′ man′, the chief attendant of the bridegroom at a wedding.

be·stow (bi stō′), *v.t.* **1.** to present as a gift or prize; give or confer (usually fol. by *on* or *upon*): *The trophy was bestowed upon the winner.* **2.** to put to some use; apply. **3.** *Archaic.* **a.** to house; provide quarters for. **b.** to put; stow; deposit; store. [ME *bestowe(n)*] —**be·stow′al, be·stow′ment,** *n.* —**Syn. 1.** grant, vouchsafe.

be·strad·dle (bi strad′əl), *v.t.,* **-dled, -dling.** to bestride.

be·strew (bi strōō′), *v.t.,* **-strewed, -strewed** or **-strewn, -strew·ing. 1.** to strew or cover (a surface). **2.** to strew or scatter about. **3.** to lie scattered over. [ME *bistrewe(n),* OE *bestrēowian*]

be·stride (bi strīd′), *v.t.,* **-strode** or **-strid, -strid·den** or **-strid, -strid·ing. 1.** to get or be astride of; spread the legs on both sides of. **2.** to step over or across with long strides. **3.** to stand or tower over; dominate. [ME *bestride(n),* OE *bestrīdan*]

best′ sell′er, a book or other product that is among those having the largest sales during a given period. Also, **best′sell′er.** —**best′-sell′ing,** *adj.*

be·stud (bi stud′), *v.t.,* **-stud·ded, -stud·ding.** to set with or as with studs distributed over a surface; dot: *an evening sky bestudded with stars.*

bet (bet), *v.,* **bet** or **bet·ted, bet·ting,** *n.* —*v.t.* **1.** to pledge (something) as a forfeit if one's forecast of a future event is wrong, usually in return for a similar pledge by another if the forecast is right. —*v.i.* **2.** to make a wager: *Do you want to bet?* **3. you bet!** *Informal.* of course! surely!: *You bet I'd like to be there!* —*n.* **4.** a pledge made in betting: *Where do we place our bets?* **5.** that which is pledged: *a two-dollar bet.* **6.** a person, thing, event, etc., considered as something to bet on: *That horse looks like a good bet.* **7.** an act or instance of betting. **8.** an alternative: *Your best bet is to sell your stocks now.* [? special use of *bet* better, in phrase *the bet* the advantage, i.e., the odds]

bet., between.

be·ta (bā′tə, bē′-), *n.* **1.** the second letter of the Greek alphabet (B, β). **2.** (*cap.*) *Astron.* the second brightest star of a constellation. **3.** *Chem.* **a.** one of the possible positions of an atom or group in a compound. **b.** one of two or more isomeric compounds. **4.** See **beta particle.** [< L < Gk *bêta* < Sem; cf. Heb *bēth* BETH]

be·ta·caine (bā′tə kān′, bē′-), *n. Pharm.* eucaine. [BETA + (EU)CAINE]

be′ta decay′, *Physics.* a radioactive process in which a beta particle is emitted from the nucleus of an atom, raising the atomic number of the atom by one if the particle is negatively charged, lowering it by one if positively charged.

be·take (bi tāk′), *v.t.,* **-took, -tak·en, -tak·ing. 1.** to cause to go (usually used reflexively): *She betook herself to town.* **2.** *Archaic.* to resort or have recourse (usually used reflexively). [ME *bitake(n)*]

be·ta-naph·thol (bā′tə naf′thōl, -thôl, -thol, -nap′-, bē′tə-), *n. Chem.* naphthol (def. 2).

be·ta-naph·thyl·a·mine (bā′tə naf′thə lə mēn′, -nap′-, bē′-), *n. Chem.* a white to reddish toxic solid, $C_{10}H_7NH_2$, used chiefly in the manufacture of azo dyes.

Bet·an·court (bet′ən kōōr′, -kôr′; *Sp.* bet′än kōōrt′), *n.* **Ró·mu·lo** (rom′yə lō′; *Sp.* rô′mōō lô′), 1908–81, Venezuelan political leader: president of Venezuela 1945–48; 1959–63.

be′ta par′ticle, *Physics.* a charged particle equivalent to an electron if negative or a positron if positive, emitted from a nucleus in radioactive decay or fission.

be′ta ray′, *Physics.* a stream of beta particles.

be·ta·tron (bā′tə tron′, bē′-), *n. Physics.* an accelerator in which electrons are accelerated to high energies by an electric field produced by a changing magnetic field. [BETA (see BETA PARTICLE) + -TRON]

be·tel (bēt′əl), *n.* an East Indian pepper plant, *Piper Betle.* Also called **be′tel pep′per.** [< Pg *betele,* var. of *vitele* < Tamil *vettilei*]

Be·tel·geuse (bēt′əl jōōz′, bet′əl jœz′), *n. Astron.* a first-magnitude red giant star in the constellation Orion. Also, **Be′tel·geux′.** [< F < Ar *bīt al jauzā′* shoulder of the giant (i.e., of Orion)]

be′tel nut′, the areca nut, the seed of the betel palm, chewed with dried betel leaves and lime by East Indians as a stimulant.

be′tel palm′, a tall, graceful, Asiatic palm, *Areca Catechu,* that bears the areca nut or betel nut, so named because the nuts are chewed with betel leaves.

bête noire (bet nwar′; *Eng.* bāt′ nwär′), *pl.* **bêtes noires** (bet nwar′; *Eng.* bāt′ nwärz′). *French.* something or someone that a person dislikes or dreads; bugbear. [lit., black beast]

beth (bās; *Heb.* bet), *n.* the second letter of the Hebrew alphabet. [< Heb *bēth* house, from an earlier form of the letter; see BETA]

Beth·a·ny (beth′ə nē), *n.* a village in W Jordan, near Jerusalem, at the foot of the Mount of Olives: Biblical home of Lazarus. John 11:1.

Be·the (bā′tə), *n.* **Hans Al·brecht** (hanz ôl′brekt, häns; *Ger.* häns äl′brekht), born 1906, U.S. physicist, born in Alsace-Lorraine: Nobel prize 1967.

beth·el (beth′əl), *n.* **1.** a sacred area or sanctuary. Gen. 28:19. **2.** a church or hostel for sailors. **3.** *Brit.* a dissenters' chapel or meeting house. [< Heb *bēth 'ēl* house of God]

Beth·el (beth′əl; *for 1 also* beth′el, beth′el′), *n.* **1.** a village in NW Jordan, near Jerusalem: dream of Jacob, Gen. 28:19. **2.** a city in W Pennsylvania, near Pittsburgh. 34,791 (1970).

Be·thes·da (bə thez′də), *n.* **1.** a pool in Biblical Jerusalem, believed to have healing powers. John 5:2–4. **2.** a city in central Maryland; residential suburb of Washington, D.C. 71,621 (1970). **3.** (*l.c.*) a chapel.

be·think (bi thingk′), *v.,* **-thought, -think·ing.** —*v.t.* (usually used reflexively) **1.** to cause (oneself) to consider: *He bethought himself a moment.* **2.** to cause (oneself) to recall or remember: *She bethought herself of happier days.* [ME *bethenk(en),* OE *bethencan.* See BE-, THINK[1]]

Beth·le·hem (beth′lē əm, -li hem′), *n.* **1.** a town in NW Jordan, near Jerusalem; occupied by Israel since 1967: birthplace of Jesus and David. 15,000. **2.** a city in E Pennsylvania. 72,686 (1970).

Beth·mann-Holl·weg (bāt′män hôl′vāk), *n.* **Theo·bald von** (tā′ō bält′ fən), 1856–1921, German statesman: chancellor 1909–17.

Beth′nal Green′ (beth′nəl), a borough of London, England, N of the Thames. 47,018 (1961).

be·thought (bi thôt′), *v.* pt. and pp. of **bethink.**

Beth·sa·i·da (beth sā′i də), *n.* an ancient town in N Israel, near the N shore of the Sea of Galilee.

be·tide (bi tīd′), *v.,* **-tid·ed, -tid·ing.** —*v.t.* **1.** to happen to; befall; come to: *Woe betide the villain!* —*v.i.* **2.** to come to pass. [ME *betide(n).* See BE-, TIDE[2]]

be·times (bi tīmz′), *adv.* **1.** early; in good time: *I awoke betimes.* **2.** *Archaic.* within a short time; soon: *The debt will be repaid betimes.* [ME *bitimes* = *bitime* (< phrase *bi time* by time) + *-s* -s[1]]

bê·tise (be tēz′), *n.* **1.** lack of understanding, perception, or the like; stupidity. **2.** a stupid, foolish, or inconsequential act or remark. [< F: lit., foolishness = *bête* foolish (< *bête* BEAST) + *-ise* -ICE]

Bet·je·man (bech′ə mən), *n.* **Sir John,** 1906–84, English poet: poet laureate 1972–84.

be·to·ken (bi tō′kən), *v.t.* **1.** to give evidence of; indicate: *a kiss that betokens one's affection.* **2.** to portend; foreshadow: *a thunderclap that betokens foul weather.* [ME *bitocnen, bitacnen*]

bet·o·ny (bet′ənē), *n., pl.* **-nies. 1.** a plant, *Stachys* (formerly *Betonica*) *officinalis,* of the mint family, formerly used in medicine and dyeing. **2.** any of various similar plants, esp. of the genus *Pedicularis.* [late ME, appar. short for OE *betonice* < L *betonica,* var. of *vettonica* (*herba*) Vettonic (herb) = *Vetton(es)* an Iberian tribe + *-ica,* fem. of *-icus* -IC; r. ME *beteine,* c. OF *betoine* < VL **betonia*]

be·took (bi tōōk′), *v.* pt. of **betake.**

be·tray (bi trā′), *v.t.* **1.** to deliver or expose to an enemy by treachery or disloyalty. **2.** to be unfaithful in guarding or maintaining: *to betray a trust.* **3.** to disappoint the hopes or expectations of; be unfaithful in fulfilling: *to betray one's talent.* **4.** to show or exhibit; reveal; disclose: *an unfeeling remark that betrays his lack of concern.* **5.** to deceive; mislead: *a woman betrayed by social ambitions into irreparable folly.* **6.** to seduce and desert (a woman). [ME *bitrai* = *bi-* BE- + *trai* < OF *trai(r)* < L *trādere* to betray. See TRAITOR] —**be·tray′al,** *n.* —**be·tray′er,** *n.* —**Syn. 4.** display, manifest.

be·troth (bi trōth′, -trôth′), *v.t.* **1.** to arrange for the marriage of; affiance (usually used in passive constructions): *The couple was betrothed with the approval of both families.* **2.** *Archaic.* to promise to marry: *He betrothed a maiden of the neighboring village.* [ME *betrouthe,* var. of *betreuthe* = *be-* BE- + *treuthe* TRUTH; see TROTH]

be·troth·al (bi trō′thəl, -trô′thəl), *n.* act or fact of being betrothed; engagement. Also, **be·troth′ment.**

be·trothed (bi trōthd′, -trôtht′), *adj.* **1.** engaged to be married: *She is betrothed to that young lieutenant.* —*n.* **2.** the person to whom one is engaged.
bet·ta (bet′ə), *n.* any of several brightly colored labyrinth fishes of the genus *Betta,* found in southeastern Asia. [< NL < ?]
bet·ted (bet′id), *v.* a pt. and pp. of **bet.**
bet·ter[1] (bet′ər), *adj., compar. of* **good** *with* **best** *as superl.* **1.** of superior quality or excellence: *a better coat.* **2.** morally superior; more virtuous: *He's no better than a thief!* **3.** of superior value, use, fitness, desirability, acceptableness, etc.: *a better time for action.* **4.** larger; greater: *the better part of a lifetime.* **5.** improved in health; healthier: *Is your mother better?* —*adv., compar. of* **well** *with* **best** *as superl.* **6.** in a more excellent way or manner: *to behave better.* **7.** to a greater degree; more completely or thoroughly: *I probably know him better than anyone else.* **8.** more: *I walked better than a mile to town.* **9. better off, a.** in better circumstances. **b.** more fortunate; happier. **10. go (someone) one better,** to exceed another's effort; be superior to. **11. had better,** would be wiser or more reasonable to; ought to: *We had better stay indoors today.* **12. think better of,** to reconsider and decide more favorably or wisely: *She was tempted to make a sarcastic retort, but thought better of it.* —*v.t.* **13.** to make better; improve; increase the good qualities of. **14.** to improve upon; surpass; exceed: *We have bettered last year's production record.* **15. better oneself,** to improve one's social standing, financial position, or education. —*n.* **16.** that which has greater excellence: *the better of two choices.* **17.** Usually, **betters.** those superior to one in wisdom, social position, etc. **18. for the better,** in a way that is an improvement: *His health changed for the better.* **19. get the better of, a.** to get an advantage over. **b.** to prevail against. [ME *bettre,* OE *betera;* c. OHG *bezziro* (G *besser*), Goth *batiza* = *bat-* (akin to BOOT[2]) + *-iza* comp. suffix] —**Syn. 13.** amend; advance, promote. See **improve.**
bet·ter[2] (bet′ər), *n.* bettor.
Bet′ter Busi′ness Bu′reau, (in the U.S. and Canada) any of a nationwide system of local organizations, supported by businessmen, whose function is to receive and investigate customer complaints of dishonest business practices.
bet′ter half′, *Informal.* a person's spouse, esp. a wife.
bet·ter·ment (bet′ər mənt), *n.* **1.** the act or process of bettering something; improvement. **2.** that which is made or becomes better; an improvement. **3.** *Law.* an improvement of property other than by mere repairs.
Bet·ter·ton (bet′ər tən), *n.* **Thomas,** 1635?–1710, English actor and dramatist.
bet′ting shop′, *Brit.* a licensed bookmaking establishment that takes bets on sporting events, esp. on horse races; the shop or office of a legalized bookmaker.
bet·tor (bet′ər), *n.* a person who bets. Also, **better.**
bet·u·la·ceous (bech′o͝o lā′shəs), *adj.* belonging to the *Betulaceae,* a family of trees and shrubs including the birch, alder, etc. [< L *betul(a)* birch + -ACEOUS]
be·tween (bi twēn′), *prep.* **1.** in, linking, or connecting the space separating (two points, objects, etc.): *between New York and Chicago.* **2.** intermediate to in time, quantity, or degree: *between 12 and 1 o'clock; between pink and red.* **3.** by the common action, involvement, participation, or sharing of: *war between nations; We'll split the profits between us.* **4.** distinguishing one from the other in comparison: *the difference between good and bad.* **5.** *Heraldry.* in the midst of, so as to make a symmetrical composition. **6. between ourselves,** confidentially; in trust. Also, **between you and me, between you, me, and the post (lamppost, gatepost, etc.).** —*adv.* **7.** in the intervening space or time; in an intermediate position or relation: *two windows with a door between; visits that were far between.* **8. in between,** situated between two points, things, etc.: *a yard in between two houses.* [ME *betwene,* OE *betwēonan, betwēonum* = *be-* BE- + *twēon-* (c. Goth *tweihn(ai)* two each) + *-um* dat. pl. suffix] —**be·tween′ness,** *n.* —**Syn.** See **among.**
—**Usage.** BETWEEN YOU AND I, occasionally heard in the usage of educated persons, is not the commonly accepted form. Since the pronouns are objects of the preposition BETWEEN, the usual form is *between you and me.* See also **among.**
be·tween·brain (bi twēn′brān′), *n.* the diencephalon.
be·tween·times (bi twēn′tīmz′), *adv.* between periods of work, activity, etc.
be·twixt (bi twikst′), *prep., adv.* **1.** *Archaic.* between. **2. betwixt and between,** neither the one nor the other; in a middle position. [ME *betwix,* OE *betwix, betweox* = *be-* BE- + *tweox,* c. OHG *zwisk(i)* two each; akin to G *zwischen* between (prep.)]
Beu·lah (byo͞o′lə), *n.* a name applied to the land of Israel or Jerusalem, possibly as denoting their future prosperity. Isa. 62:4. Cf. **Hephzibah** (def. 2). [< Heb: married woman]
beurre noir (bûr′ nwär′; *Fr.* bœr NWAR′), a sauce of darkly browned butter, sometimes flavored with herbs, vinegar, etc. [< F: lit., black butter]
Beu·then (boit′ən), *n.* German name of **Bytom.**
BeV (bev), *Physics.* billion electron-volts. Also, **Bev, bev**
Bev·an (bev′ən), *n.* **A·neu·rin** (ə nī′rən), 1897–1960, British political leader: Minister of Health 1945–50.
bev·a·tron (bev′ə tron′), *n.* *Physics.* an accelerator in which the energies of protons are raised to several billion electron-volts. [BEV + *-a-* connective + -TRON]
bev·el (bev′əl), *n., v.,* **-eled, -el·ing** or (*esp. Brit.*) **-elled, -el·ling,** *adj.* —*n.* **1.** the slant or slope of a line or surface when not at right angles with another. **2.** See **bevel square. 3.** an adjustable instrument for drawing angles or adjusting the surface of work to a particular inclination. **4.** *Print.* beard (def. 5). **5.** bezel (def. 1). —*v.t., v.i.* **6.** to cut or slant at a bevel: *to bevel an edge to prevent splintering.* —*adj.* **7.** Also, **beveled;** *esp. Brit.,* **bevelled.** oblique; sloping; slanted. [< MF **bevel* (> F *béveau*) < ?] —**bev′el·er;** *esp. Brit.,* **bev′el·ler,** *n.*
bev′el gear′, *Mach.* a gear having teeth cut into a conical surface, usually meshing with a similar gear that is set at right angles to it. Cf. **hypoid gear.**

Bevel gears

bev′el joint′, *Carpentry.* a miter joint, esp. one in which two pieces meet at other than a right angle.

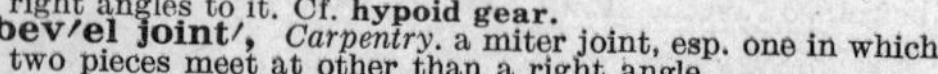

bev′el square′, an adjustable tool used by woodworkers for laying out angles and for testing the accuracy of surfaces worked to a slope.

Bevel square

bev·er·age (bev′ər ij, bev′rij), *n.* any liquid for drinking, esp. other than water. [ME < MF *bevrage* = *bevr* (< L *bibere* to drink; see BIB) + *-age* -AGE]
Bev·er·idge (bev′ər ij, bev′rij), *n.* **1. Albert Jeremiah,** 1862–1927, U.S. Senator and historian. **2. Sir William Henry,** 1879–1963, English economist.
Bev·er·ly (bev′ər lē), *n.* a city in NE Massachusetts. 38,348 (1970).
Bev′erly Hills′, a city in SW California, near Los Angeles. 33,416 (1970).
bev·or (bē′vər), *n.* *Armor.* beaver[2].
bev·y (bev′ē), *n., pl.* **bev·ies. 1.** a flock of birds, esp. larks or quail. **2.** a group, esp. of girls or women. **3.** a group of roebucks. [late ME *bevey* < ?] —**Syn. 1.** covey, flight.
be·wail (bi wāl′), *v.t.* **1.** to express deep sorrow for; lament. —*v.i.* **2.** to express grief. —**be·wail′ing·ly,** *adv.* —**be·wail′ment,** *n.* —**Syn. 1.** bemoan, mourn.
be·ware (bi wâr′), *v.,* **-wared, -war·ing.** —*v.t.* **1.** to be wary, cautious, or careful of. —*v.i.* **2.** to be wary, cautious, or careful: *Beware of the dog.* [from phrase of warning *be ware*]
be·whisk·ered (bi hwis′kərd, -wis′-), *adj.* having whiskers; bearded.
be·wil·der (bi wil′dər), *v.t.* to confuse or puzzle completely; perplex. [BE- + WILDER[1]] —**be·wil′der·ing·ly,** *adv.* —**be·wil′der·ment,** *n.* —**Syn.** mystify, nonplus, confound.
be·witch (bi wich′), *v.t.* **1.** to affect by witchcraft or magic; cast a spell over. **2.** to enchant; charm; fascinate. [ME *biwicche(n)*] —**be·witch′er,** *n.* —**be·witch′er·y,** *n.* —**be·witch′ing·ly,** *adv.* —**be·witch′ing·ness,** *n.* —**be·witch′ment,** *n.* —**Syn. 2.** captivate, enrapture.
be·wray (bi rā′), *v.t.* *Obs.* to betray. [ME *bewraie(n)* = *be-* BE- + *wraien,* OE *wrēgan* to accuse, c. OHG *ruogen* (G *rügen*), Goth *wrohjan*] —**be·wray′er,** *n.*
bey (bā), *n., pl.* **beys. 1.** a provincial governor in the Ottoman Empire. **2.** (formerly) a title of respect for Turkish dignitaries. **3.** (formerly) the title of the native ruler of Tunis or Tunisia. Turkish, **beg.** [< Turk: lord, prince]
Beyle (bāl), *n.* **Ma·rie Hen·ri** (MA RĒ′ ÄN RĒ′). See **Stendhal.**
bey·lic (bā′lik), *n.* the power or jurisdiction of a bey. Also, **bey′lik.** [< Turk = *bey* BEY + *-lik* -Y[3]]
Bey·og·lu (bā′ə lo͞o′; *Turk.* bā′ôKH lo͞o′), *n.* Pera.
be·yond (bē ond′, bi yond′), *prep.* **1.** on or to the farther side of: *Beyond those trees you'll find his house.* **2.** farther on than; more distant than: *beyond the horizon.* **3.** outside the understanding, limits, or reach of; in excess of: *beyond human comprehension; beyond endurance.* **4.** superior to; surpassing; above: *wise beyond all others.* —*adv.* **5.** farther on or away: *as far as the house and beyond.* —*n.* **6. the beyond, a.** that which is at a great distance. **b.** Also, **the great beyond.** the life after the present one. [ME *beyonde(n),* OE *begeondan*]
Bey·routh (bā′ro͞ot, bā ro͞ot′), *n.* Beirut.
bez·ant (bez′ənt, bi zant′), *n.* the gold solidus of the Byzantine Empire. Also, **bezzant.** [ME *besant* < OF < L *byzant(ius)* (*nummus*) Byzantine (coin)]
bez·el (bez′əl), *n.* **1.** the diagonal face at the end or edge of a chisel or other cutting-tool blade; the beveled edge of a cutting tool. **2.** *Jewelry.* **a.** that part of a ring, bracelet, etc., to which gems are attached. **b.** crown (def. 20). **3.** the grooved ring or rim holding a gem or watch crystal in its setting. [akin to F *biseau* bevel, chamfer. See BEVEL]
Bé·ziers (bā zyā′), *n.* a city in S France, SW of Montpellier. 75,541 (1962).
be·zique (bə zēk′), *n.* *Cards.* a game resembling pinochle, played with 64 cards. [alter. of F *bésigue* < ?]
be·zoar (bē′zōr, -zôr), *n.* **1.** a calculus or concretion found in the stomach or intestines of certain animals, esp. ruminants, formerly reputed to be an effective remedy for poison. **2.** *Obs.* a counterpoison or antidote. [late ME *bezear* < ML *bezahar* < Ar *bā(di)zahr* < Pers *bādzahr,* var. of *pād-zahr* counterpoison; *-o-* < NL]
bez·zant (bez′ənt, bi zant′), *n.* bezant.
b.f., *Printing.* boldface. Also, **bf**
B/F, *Accounting.* brought forward.
B.F.A., Bachelor of Fine Arts.
bg., bag.
B-girl (bē′gûrl′), *n.* a woman employed by a bar, nightclub, etc., to act as a companion to male customers and induce them to buy expensive drinks. [prob. B(AR)[1] + GIRL]
Bhad·gaon (bud′goun), *n.* a city in central Nepal, near Katmandu. ab. 100,000. Also, **Bhatgaon.**
Bha·ga·vad-Gi·ta (bug′ə vəd gē′tä), *n.* *Hinduism.* a portion of the Mahabharata, having the form of a dialogue between the hero Arjuna and his charioteer, the avatar Krishna, in which a doctrine combining Brahmanical and other elements is evolved. [< Skt: Song of the Blessed One]
bhak·ta (buk′tə), *n.* a person who practices bhakti. [< Skt: devoted]
bhak·ti (buk′tē), *n.* *Hinduism.* **1.** selfless devotion as a means of reaching Brahman. Cf. **jnana, karma** (def. 1). **2.** (*cap.*) a popular religious movement centered around the personal worship of gods, esp. Vishnu and Shiva. Cf. **Saiva, Vaishnava.** [< Skt: share, portion, devotion]
bhang (bang), *n.* **1.** the Indian hemp plant. **2.** a preparation of its leaves and tops used in India as an intoxicant and narcotic. Also, **bang.** [< Hindi *bhāng* < Skt *bhangā* hemp]
Bha·rat (bu′RUT), *n.* Hindi name of **India.**
Bhat·gaon (bud′goun), *n.* Bhadgaon.
Bhau·na·gar (bou nug′ər), *n.* a seaport in S Gujarat, in W India. 176,000 (1961). Also, **Bhav·na·gar** (bäv nug′ər).
Bha·ve (bä′vā), *n.* **Vi·no·ba** (vē nō′bə), born 1895, Indian religious leader and land reformer.
bhees·ty (bē′stē), *n., pl.* **-ties.** (in India) water carrier. Also, **bhees′tie.** [< Urdu *bhīstī* < Pers *bihishtī* = *bihisht* paradise + *-ī* suffix of membership]
Bho·pal (bō päl′), *n.* **1.** a former state in central India: now part of Madhya Pradesh. **2.** a city in and the capital of Madhya Pradesh, in central India. 185,400 (1961).

B horizon, *Geol.* the subsoil in a soil profile. Cf. **A horizon, C horizon.**

bhut (bo͞ot), *n.* See **dust devil.** Also, **bhoot** (bo͞ot). [< Hindi < Skt *bhūta* = *bhū* BE + *-ta* verbal suffix]

Bhu·tan (bo͞o tän′), *n.* a kingdom in the Himalayas, NE of India: foreign affairs guided by India. 1,100,000; ab. 19,300 sq. mi. *Cap.:* Thimbu.

Bhu·tan·ese (bo͞ot′ᵊnēz′, -ᵊnēs′), *n., pl.* **-ese,** *adj.* —*n.* **1.** a native or inhabitant of Bhutan. **2.** the Tibetan language as spoken in Bhutan. —*adj.* **3.** of, pertaining to, or characteristic of Bhutan, its inhabitants, or their language.

Bhut·to (bo͞o′tō), *n.* **Zul·fi·kar A·li** (zo͝ol′fē kär′ ä lē′), 1928–79, Pakistani political leader: president 1971–73; prime minister 1973–77.

Bi, *Chem.* bismuth.

bi-¹, a learned borrowing from Latin meaning "twice," "two," used in the formation of compound words: *bifacial.* Cf. **bin-.** [< L, comb. form of *bis* TWICE]

bi-², var. of **bio-,** esp. before a vowel: *biopsy.*

B.I., British India.

bi·a·ce·tyl (bī′ə sēt′ᵊl, -set′-, bī as′i tᵊl), *n. Chem.* a yellow liquid, $CH_3COCOCH_3$, used chiefly to augment the flavor of vinegar, coffee, and other foods. Also, **diacetyl.**

Bi·a·fra (bē ä′frə), *n.* **1.** a former secessionist state (1967–70) in SE Nigeria, in W Africa. 12,348,646 (1963); 29,484 sq. mi. *Cap.:* Enugu. **2. Bight of,** a wide bay in the E part of the Gulf of Guinea, off the W coast of Africa. —**Bi·a′fran,** *adj., n.*

Bi·ak (bē yäk′), *n.* an island N of West Irian, in Indonesia. 948 sq. mi. Also, **Wiak.**

Bia·lik (byä′lik), *n.* **Cha·im Nach·man** (ḵʜī ēm′ näḵʜ-män′; *Eng.* ḵʜī′im näḵʜ′mən), 1873–1934, Hebrew poet, born in Russia.

bi·a·ly (bē ä′lē), *n., pl.* **-lys.** a small, flattish, onion-flavored roll made of white flour. [after BIAŁYSTOK]

Bia·ły·stok (byä′wi stôk; *Eng.* bē ä′lē stok), *n.* a city in E Poland. 130,000 (est. 1963). Also, **Belostok.** Russian, **Byelostok.**

Bian·co (byäng′kô), *n.* **Mon·te** (môn′te), Italian name of **Mont Blanc.**

bi·an·gu·lar (bī ang′gyə lər), *adj.* having two angles.

bi·an·nu·al (bī an′yo͞o əl), *adj.* **1.** occurring twice a year; semiannual: *a biannual meeting.* **2.** (loosely) occurring every two years; biennial. —**bi·an′nu·al·ly,** *adv.*

Biar·ritz (bē′ə rits′; *Fr.* byA Rēts′), *n.* a city in SW France, on the Bay of Biscay: resort. 25,514 (1962).

bi·as (bī′əs), *n., adj., adv., v.,* **bi·ased, bi·as·ing** or (*esp. Brit.*) **bi·assed, bi·as·sing.** —*n.* **1.** an oblique or diagonal line of direction, esp. across a woven fabric. **2.** a tendency or inclination of outlook; a subjective point of view. **3.** *Statistics.* a systematic distortion of a statistic as a result of sampling procedure. **4.** *Electronics.* a steady voltage inserted in series with an element of an electronic device, as of a vacuum tube or transistor. **5. on the bias, a.** in the diagonal direction of the cloth. **b.** out of line; slanting. —*adj.* **6.** cut, set, folded, etc., diagonally. —*adv.* **7.** in a diagonal manner; obliquely; slantingly. —*v.t.* **8.** to cause prejudice in (a person); influence, esp. unfairly: *a tearful plea designed to bias the jury.* [< MF *biais* oblique < OPr, prob. << Gk *epikársios* oblique = *epi-* EPI- + *-karsios* oblique] —**bi′ased·ly;** *esp. Brit.,* **bi′assed·ly,** *adv.* —**bi′as·ness,** *n.*
—**Syn. 2.** predisposition, preconception, predilection, partiality, proclivity; bent, leaning. BIAS, PREJUDICE mean a strong inclination of the mind or a preconceived opinion about something or someone. A BIAS may be favorable or unfavorable: *bias in favor of or against an idea.* PREJUDICE implies a preformed judgment even more unreasoning than BIAS, and usually implies an unfavorable opinion: *prejudice against a race.* **8.** predispose, bend. —**Ant. 2.** impartiality.

bi′as-belt′ed tire′. See **belted-bias tire.**

bi′as-ply′ tire′, a motor-vehicle tire in which the rayon, nylon, polyester or steel plies are put in alternate directions on the bias. Cf. **belted-bias tire, radial-ply tire.**

bi·au·ric·u·late (bī′ô rik′yə lit, -lāt′), *adj. Biol.* having two auricles or earlike parts. Also, **bi′au·ric′u·lar.**

bi·ax·i·al (bī ak′sē əl), *adj.* **1.** having two axes. **2.** (of a crystal) having two optical axes along which double refraction does not occur. —**bi·ax′i·al′i·ty,** *n.* —**bi·ax′i·al·ly,** *adv.*

bib (bib), *n., v.,* **bibbed, bib·bing.** —*n.* **1.** a cloth for tying under the chin of a child to protect its clothing while the child is eating or being fed. **2.** the upper part of an apron. —*v.t., v.i.* **3.** *Archaic.* to tipple; drink. [ME *bibb(en)* < L *bibe(re)* (to) drink] —**bib′less,** *adj.* —**bib′like′,** *adj.*

Bib., **1.** Bible. **2.** Biblical.

bib′ and tuck′er, *Informal.* clothes: *to dress in one's best bib and tucker.*

bi·ba·sic (bī bā′sik), *adj. Chem.* dibasic.

bibb (bib), *n.* **1.** *Naut.* any of several brackets or timbers bolted to the hounds of a mast to give additional support to the trestletrees. **2.** bibcock. [alter. of BIB]

bib·ber (bib′ər), *n.* a steady drinker; tippler (usually used in combination): *winebibber.*

bib·cock (bib′kok′), *n. Plumbing.* a faucet having a nozzle that is bent downward. Also called **bibb.**

bi·be·lot (bib′lō; *Fr.* bēbᵊ lō′), *n., pl.* **-lots** (-lōz; *Fr.* -lō′). a small object of curiosity, beauty, or rarity. [< F = *bibel-* (? alter. of *belbel;* see BAUBLE) + *-ot* n. suffix]

bibl., **1.** biblical. **2.** bibliographical. **3.** bibliography.

Bibl., **1.** Biblical. **2.** bibliographical.

Bi·ble (bī′bəl), *n.* **1.** the collection of sacred writings of the Christian religion, comprising the Old and New Testaments. **2.** the collection of sacred writings of the Jewish religion, comprising the Old Testament only. **3.** (*often l.c.*) the sacred writings of any religion. **4.** (*l.c.*) a book, reference work, etc., accepted as final authority. [ME, OE *bibli-* (var. of *biblio-*) in *biblithēca* < LL *bibliotheca* Bible. See BIBLIOTHECA]

Bi′ble Belt′, an area of the U.S., chiefly in the South, noted for religious fundamentalism.

Bi′ble pa′per, a very thin, strong, opaque rag paper often used for Bibles, prayer books, dictionaries, and the like. Also called **India paper.**

Bib·li·cal (bib′li kəl), *adj.* (*sometimes l.c.*) **1.** of or in the Bible: *a Biblical name.* **2.** in accord with the Bible. [< ML *biblic(us)* (see BIBLE, -IC) + -AL¹] —**Bib′li·cal·ly,** *adv.*

Bib′lical Lat′in, the form of Latin used in the translation of the Bible and which became current in western Europe at the beginning of the Middle Ages.

Bib·li·cist (bib′li sist), *n.* **1.** a Biblical scholar. **2.** a person who interprets the Bible literally. [< ML *biblic(us)* (see BIBLICAL) + -IST] —**Bib′li·cis′tic,** *adj.*

biblio-, a prefix occurring in loan words from Greek (*bibliography*); on this model, used in the formation of compound words with the meaning "book" (*bibliophile*), and sometimes with the meaning "Bible" (*bibliolatry*), on the model of *idolatry*). [< L < Gk, comb. form of *biblíon* book, var. of *byblíon* = *býbl(os)* book, paper (*Býblos* city in Phoenicia noted for export trade in paper) + *-ion* dim. suffix]

bibliog., **1.** bibliographer. **2.** bibliography.

bib·li·og·ra·pher (bib′lē og′rə fər), *n.* an expert in bibliography. [< Gk *bibliográph(os)* writer of books (see BIBLIO-, -GRAPH) + -ER¹]

bib·li·og·ra·phy (bib′lē og′rə fē), *n., pl.* **-phies. 1.** a list of readings on a particular subject. **2.** a list of works by a particular author. **3.** a list of source materials that are used or consulted in the preparation of a work or that are referred to in the text. **4.** the science that deals with the history of books, their physical description, printing, publication, editions, etc. [< Gk *bibliographía*] —**bib·li·o·graph·ic** (bib′lē ə graf′ik), **bib′li·o·graph′i·cal,** *adj.* —**bib′li·o·graph′i·cal·ly,** *adv.*

bib·li·ol·a·try (bib′lē ol′ə trē), *n.* **1.** excessive reverence for the Bible as literally interpreted. **2.** extravagant devotion to or dependence upon books. —**bib′li·ol′a·ter, bib′li·ol′a·trist,** *n.* —**bib′li·ol′a·trous,** *adj.*

bib·li·o·man·cy (bib′lē ō man′sē), *n.* divination by means of a book, esp. the Bible, opened at random to some verse or passage, which is then interpreted.

bib·li·o·ma·ni·a (bib′lē ō mā′nē ə, -mān′yə), *n.* excessive fondness for acquiring and possessing books. [BIBLIO- + -MANIA; r. *bibliomanie* < F] —**bib·li·o·ma·ni·ac** (bib′lē ō-mā′nē ak′), *n.* —**bib·li·o·ma·ni·a·cal** (bib′lē ō mə nī′ə kəl), *adj.*

bib·li·op·e·gy (bib′lē op′ə jē), *n.* the art of binding books. [BIBLIO- + Gk *pēg-* (s. of *pēgnýnai* to fasten) + -Y³] —**bib·li·o·peg·ic** (bib′lē ə pej′ik, -pē′jik), *adj.* —**bib′li·op′e·gist,** *n.* —**bib′li·op′e·gis′tic, bib′li·op′e·gis′ti·cal,** *adj.*

bib·li·o·phile (bib′lē ə fīl′, -fil), *n.* a person who loves or collects books, esp. as examples of fine or unusual printing, binding, or the like. Also, **bib·li·oph·i·list** (bib′lē of′ə list). —**bib′li·oph′i·lism, bib′li·oph′i·ly,** *n.* —**bib′li·oph′i·lis′tic, bib·li·o·phil·ic** (bib′lē ō fil′ik), *adj.*

bib·li·o·pole (bib′lē ə pōl′), *n.* a bookseller, esp. a dealer in rare or secondhand books. Also, **bib·li·op·o·list** (bib′lē-op′ə list). [< L *bibliopōl(a)* < Gk *bibliopṓlēs* = *biblio-* BIBLIO- + *pōl-* (s. of *pōleîsthai* to sell) + *-ēs* agentive suffix] —**bib·li·o·pol·ic** (bib′lē ə pol′ik), **bib′li·o·pol′i·cal, bib′-li·o·po′lar,** *adj.* —**bib′li·o·pol′i·cal·ly,** *adv.* —**bib·li·op·o·lism** (bib′lē op′ə liz′əm), **bib′li·op′o·ly,** *n.*

bib·li·o·the·ca (bib′lē ə thē′kə), *n., pl.* **-cas, -cae** (-kē). **1.** a collection of books; library. **2.** a list of books, esp. a bookseller's catalog. [< L: library, collection of books (ML: Bible; cf. OE *biblioth̄ece* Bible) < Gk *biblioth̄ékē.* See BIBLIO-, THECA] —**bib′li·o·the′cal,** *adj.*

bib·li·ot·ics (bib′lē ot′iks), *n.* (*construed as sing. or pl.*) the analysis of handwriting and documents, esp. for authentication of authorship. [BIBLIO- + *-t-* (connective) + -ICS] —**bib′li·ot′ic,** *adj.* —**bib·li·o·tist** (bib′lē ə tist), *n.*

Bib·list (bib′list, bī′blist), *n.* Biblicist. —**Bib′lism,** *n.*

bib·u·lous (bib′yə ləs), *adj.* **1.** addicted to alcoholic drinking. **2.** absorbent; spongy. [< L *bibulus* = *bib(ere)* (to) drink (c. Skt *pībati* he drinks) + *-ulus* -ULOUS] —**bib′-u·lous·ly,** *adv.* —**bib′u·lous·ness, bib·u·los·i·ty** (bib′yə-los′i tē), *n.*

bi·cam·er·al (bī kam′ər əl), *adj. Govt.* having two branches, chambers, or houses, as a legislative body. [BI-¹ + L *camer(a)* CHAMBER + -AL¹] —**bi·cam′er·al·ism,** *n.* —**bi·cam′er·al·ist,** *n.*

bi·carb (bī′kärb′), *n. Informal.* See **sodium bicarbonate.**

bi·car·bo·nate (bī kär′bə nit, -nāt′), *n. Chem.* a salt of carbonic acid, containing the HCO_3^{-1} group; an acid carbonate, as sodium bicarbonate, $NaHCO_3$.

bicar′bonate of so′da. See **sodium bicarbonate.**

bice (bīs), *n.* blue or green, as prepared from carbonates of copper. [ME *bis* dark gray < MF; c. with Pr *bis,* It *bigio*]

bi·cen·te·nar·y (bī sen′tᵊner′ē, bī′sen ten′ə rē), *adj., n., pl.* **-nar·ies.** *Chiefly Brit.* bicentennial.

bi·cen·ten·ni·al (bī′sen ten′ē əl), *adj.* **1.** pertaining to or in honor of a 200th anniversary. **2.** consisting of or lasting 200 years. **3.** occurring every 200 years. —*n.* **4.** a 200th anniversary: *The town will have its bicentennial next year.* —**bi′cen·ten′ni·al·ly,** *adv.*

bi·ceph·a·lous (bī sef′ə ləs), *adj. Bot., Zool.* having two heads.

bi·ceps (bī′seps), *n., pl.* **-ceps·es** (-sep siz), **-ceps.** *Anat.* **1.** a muscle on the front of the arm, the action of which bends the elbow. **2.** the hamstring muscle on the back of the thigh, the action of which assists in bending the knee and extending the leg at the hip. [< L = *bi-* BI-¹ + *-ceps* (s., *-cipit-*), comb. form of *caput* head]

bi·chlo·ride (bī klôr′īd, -id, -klōr′-), *n. Chem.* **1.** a compound in which two atoms of chlorine are combined with another element or group. **2.** See **mercuric chloride.**

bichlo′ride of mer′cury. See **mercuric chloride.**

bi·chro·mate (bī krō′māt), *n. Chem.* **1.** dichromate. **2.** See **potassium dichromate.**

bi·cip·i·tal (bī sip′i tᵊl), *adj.* **1.** having two heads; two-headed. **2.** *Anat.* pertaining to the biceps. [< L *bicipit-* (s. of *biceps*) + -AL¹]

bick·er (bik′ər), *v.i.* **1.** to engage in petulant or peevish argument; wrangle. **2.** to flow or run rapidly; move quickly. **3.** to quiver; flicker; glitter. —*n.* **4.** an angry dispute; quarrel; contention. [ME *biker(en)* < ?] —**bick′er·er,** *n.*

bick·er·ing (bik′ər ing), *n.* peevish or ill-natured quarreling, disputing, etc. [ME]

bi·col·or (bī′kul′ər), *adj.* having two colors. Also, **bi′col′ored;** *esp. Brit.,* **bi′col′our, bi′col′oured.** [< L]
bi·con·cave (bī kon′kāv, bī′kon kāv′), *adj.* concave on both sides, as a lens. —**bi·con·cav·i·ty** (bī′kᵊn kav′i tē), *n.*
bi·con·vex (bī kon′veks, bī′kon veks′), *adj.* convex on both sides, as a lens.
bi·corn (bī′kôrn), *adj.* shaped like a crescent. Also, **bi·cor·nate** (bī kôr′nit, -nāt), **bi·cor·nu·ate** (bī kôr′no͞o it, -āt′, -nyo͞o-), **bi·cor′nu·ous.** [< L *bicorn(is)* = *bi-* BI-[1] + *corn(u)* horn + *-is* adj. suffix]
bi·cor·po·ral (bī kôr′pər əl), *adj.* having two bodies, main divisions, symbols, etc. Also, **bi·cor·po·re·al** (bī′kôr pôr′ē əl, -pôr′-). [< L *bicorpor* (*bi-* BI-[1] + *corpor-,* s. of *corpus* body) + -AL[1]]
bi·cron (bī′kron, bik′ron), *n. Physics.* one billionth of a meter. [BI(LLION) + *-cron,* as in *micron*]
bi·cul·tur·al·ism (bī kul′chər ə liz′əm), *n.* the presence of two different cultures in the same country. —**bi·cul′tur·al,** *adj.*
bi·cus·pid (bī kus′pid), *adj.* **1.** Also, **bi·cus′pi·date′.** having or terminating in two cusps or points, as certain teeth. —*n.* **2.** premolar (def. 4).
bicus′pid valve′. See **mitral valve.**
bi·cy·cle (bī′si kəl, -sik′əl), *n., v.,* **-cled, -cling.** —*n.* **1.** a vehicle with two wheels in tandem, typically propelled by pedals and having handlebars for steering and a saddlelike seat. —*v.i.* **2.** to ride a bicycle. [< F] —**bi′cy·clist, bi′cy·cler,** *n.*
bi′cycle race′, *Sports.* cycling (def. 2). Also called **bi′cycle rac′ing.**
bi·cy·clic (bī sī′klik, -sik′lik), *adj.* **1.** consisting of or having two cycles or circles. **2.** *Bot.* in two whorls, as the stamens of a flower. Also, **bi·cy′cli·cal.**
bid[1] (bid), *v.,* **bade** or **bad** for 1, 2, 5, 6, 8 or **bid** for 3, 4, 7; **bid·den** or **bid** for 1, 2, 5, 6, 8 or **bid** for 3, 4, 7; **bid·ding;** *n.* —*v.t.* **1.** to command; order; direct: *Bid them depart.* **2.** to say as a greeting, farewell, benediction, or wish: *I bid you adieu.* **3.** *Com.* to make an offer of (a price at an auction or as terms in a competition) to secure a contract: *They bid $25,000 and got the contract.* **4.** *Cards.* to enter a bid of a given quantity or suit. **5.** to summon by invitation; invite. —*v.i.* **6.** to command; order; direct: *I will do as you bid.* **7.** to make an offer to purchase at a price: *She bid frantically for the old chair.* **8. bid fair.** See **fair[1]** (def. 19). —*n.* **9.** act or instance of bidding: *My bid was rejected in favor of his.* **10.** *Cards.* **a.** an offer to make a specified number of points or to take a specified number of tricks. **b.** the amount of such an offer. **c.** the turn of a person to bid. **11.** *Informal.* an invitation: *a bid to join the club.* **12.** an attempt to attain some goal or purpose: *a bid for election.* [ME *bidd(en),* OE *biddan* to beg, ask, pray, require, demand; c. G *bitten,* Icel *bithja,* Goth *bidjan*] —**bid′der,** *n.* —**Syn. 3.** offer, proffer.
bid[2] (bid), *v. Archaic.* pp. of **bide.**
b.i.d., (in prescriptions) twice a day. [< L *bis in diē*]
bi·dar·ka (bī där′kə), *n.* the sealskin boat of the Alaskan Eskimo. Also, **bi·dar·kee** (bī där′kē), **baidarka.** [< Russ *baidarka* (*baidar(a)* coracle + *-ka* dim. suffix)]
Bi·dault (bē dō′), *n.* **Georges** (zhôrzh), 1899–1983, French statesman.
bid·da·ble (bid′ə bəl), *adj.* **1.** willing to do what is asked; obedient; docile. **2.** *Cards.* adequate to bid upon. —**bid′da·bil′i·ty, bid′da·ble·ness,** *n.* —**bid′da·bly,** *adv.*
bid·den (bid′ᵊn), *v.* a pp. of **bid.**
bid·ding (bid′ing), *n.* **1.** command; summons; invitation: *I went there at his bidding.* **2.** a bid. **3.** bids collectively, or a period during which bids are made or received: *The bidding began furiously.* **4. at someone's bidding,** subordinate to one; performing one's orders: *He seemed to have the whole world at his bidding.* **5. do someone's bidding,** to submit to one's orders; perform services for one.
Bid·dle (bid′ᵊl), *n.* **1. Francis,** 1886–1968, U.S. attorney general, 1941–45. **2. John,** 1615–62, English theologian: founder of English Unitarianism. **3. Nicholas,** 1786–1844, U.S. financier.
bid·dy[1] (bid′ē), *n., pl.* **-dies.** a chicken; fowl. [?]
bid·dy[2] (bid′ē), *n., pl.* **-dies.** a fussbudget, esp. a fussy old woman. [special use of *Biddy,* girl's given name]
bide (bīd), *v.,* **bid·ed** or **bode; bid·ed** or (*Archaic*) **bid; bid·ing.** —*v.t.* **1.** *Archaic.* to endure; bear. **2.** *Obs.* to encounter. —*v.i.* **3.** *Archaic.* to dwell; abide; wait; remain; continue. **4. bide one's time,** to wait for a favorable opportunity. [ME *bide(n),* OE *bīdan;* c. OHG *bītan,* Icel *bītha,* Goth *beidan*] —**bid′er,** *n.*
bi·den·tate (bī den′tāt), *adj. Biol.* having two teeth or toothlike parts or processes. [< L *bident-* (s. of *bidēns* = *bi-* BI-[1] + *dēns* tooth) + -ATE[1]]
bi·det (bē dā′, bi det′), *n.* **1.** a low, basinlike bath, used esp. in France, for bathing one's private parts. **2.** a small saddle horse. [< MF: pony; akin to OF *bider* to trot]
Bie·der·mei·er (bē′dər mī′ər), *adj.* noting or pertaining to a style of furnishings common in German-speaking areas in the early and middle 19th century, generally existing as a simplification of the French Empire style usually executed in fruitwood with much use of matched veneers, with accents of ebony inlay or black paint, and often displaying architectural motifs. [after Gottlieb *Biedermeier,* imaginary unsophisticated author of poems actually composed by various writers and published in German magazine *Fliegende Blätter*]

Biedermeier cabinet

Biel (bēl), *n.* **Lake.** See **Bienne, Lake of.**
Bie·le·feld (bē′lə felt′), *n.* a city in N West Germany. 172,800 (1963).
Bienne (*Fr.* byen), *n.* **Lake of,** a lake in NW Switzerland: traces of prehistoric lake dwellings. 16 sq. mi. Also called **Lake Biel.** German, **Bie·ler·see** (bē′lər zā′).
bi·en·ni·al (bī en′ē əl), *adj.* **1.** happening every two years: *biennial games.* **2.** lasting or enduring for two years: *a biennial cycle.* **3.** *Bot.* completing the normal term of life in two years, flowering and fruiting the second year, as beets or winter wheat. —*n.* **4.** any event occurring once in two years. **5.** *Bot.* a biennial plant. Also, **biyearly** (for defs. 1, 2). [BIENNI(UM) + -AL[1]] —**bi·en′ni·al·ly,** *adv.*
bi·en·ni·um (bī en′ē əm), *n., pl.* **-en·ni·ums, -en·ni·a** (-en′ē ə). a period of two years. [< L = *bi-* BI-[1] + *enn-* (var. s. of *annus* year) + *-ium* n. suffix]
Bien·ville (byaN vēl′), *n.* **Jean Bap·tiste Le Moyne** (zhäN bA tēst′ lə mwAN′), **Sieur de** (syœr də), 1680–1768, French governor of Louisiana: founder of New Orleans.
bier (bēr), *n.* a frame or stand on which a corpse or the coffin containing it is laid before burial. [ME *bere,* OE *bēr, bær;* c. OHG *bāra* (G *Bahre*); akin to BEAR[1]]
Bierce (bērs), *n.* **Ambrose (Gwin·nett)** (gwi net′), 1842–1914?, U.S. journalist and short-story writer.
bi·fa·cial (bī fā′shəl), *adj.* **1.** having two faces or fronts. **2.** having the opposite surfaces alike. **3.** *Bot.* having the opposite surfaces unlike, as a leaf.
biff (bif), *n. U.S. Slang.* a blow; punch. [? imit.]
bi·fid (bī′fid), *adj.* separated or cleft into two equal parts or lobes. [< L *bifid(us)* = *bi-* BI-[1] + *fid-* (var. s. of *findere* to split; akin to BITE) + *-us* adj. suffix] —**bi·fid′i·ty,** *n.* —**bi′fid·ly,** *adv.*
bi·fi·lar (bī fī′lər), *adj.* furnished or fitted with two filaments or threads. [BI-[1] + L *fīl(um)* (see FILE[1]) + -AR[1]] —**bi·fi′lar·ly,** *adv.*
bi·flag·el·late (bī flaj′ə lāt′, -lit), *adj. Zool.* having two whiplike appendages.
bi·fo·cal (bī fō′kəl, bī′fō-), *adj.* **1.** *Chiefly Optics.* having two foci. **2.** (of an eyeglass lens) having two portions, one for near and one for far vision. —*n.* **3. bifocals,** eyeglasses with bifocal lenses.
bi·fold (bī′fōld), *adj.* that can be folded into two parts.
bi·fo·li·ate (bī fō′lē it, -āt′), *adj.* having two leaves.
bi·fo·li·o·late (bī fō′lē ə lāt′, -lit), *adj. Bot.* having two leaflets.
bi·form (bī′fôrm′), *adj.* having or combining two forms, as a centaur, mermaid, etc. Also, **bi′formed′.** [< L *biform(is)* = *bi-* BI-[1] + *form(a)* FORM + *-is* adj. suffix] —**bi·for′mi·ty,** *n.*
Bif·rost (biv′rost), *n. Scand. Myth.* the rainbow bridge of the gods from Asgard to earth. [< Icel *Bifröst* = *bif-* (root of *bifa,* c. OE *bifian* to shake) + *röst,* c. OHG *rasta* stretch of road]
bi·fur·cate (*v., adj.* bī′fər kāt′, bī fûr′kāt; *adj. also* bī′fər kit, bī fûr′-), *v.,* **-cat·ed, -cat·ing,** *adj.* —*v.t., v.i.* **1.** to divide or fork into two branches. —*adj.* **2.** divided into two branches. [< ML *bifurcāt(us)* (ptp. of *bifurcāre*). See BI-[1], FORK, -ATE[1]] —**bi·fur·cate·ly** (bī′fər kāt′lē; bī fûr′kāt lē, -kit-), *adv.* —**bi′fur·ca′tion,** *n.*
big (big), *adj.,* **big·ger, big·gest,** *adv.* —*adj.* **1.** large, as in size, height, width, amount, etc. **2.** important; of major concern, influence, standing, etc.: *a big problem; the big man of his town.* **3.** boastful; pretentious; haughty: *a big talker.* **4.** magnanimous; generous; kindly: *He certainly has a big heart.* **5.** loud; orotund: *a big voice.* **6.** near the full term of pregnancy (usually fol. by *with*): *big with child.* **7.** outstanding for a specified quality: *He's a big liar.* **8.** *Obs.* very strong; powerful. —*adv.* **9.** *Informal.* boastfully; pretentiously: *to talk big.* [ME *big(ge)* < ?] —**big′gish,** *adj.* —**big′ly,** *adv.* —**big′ness,** *n.* —**Syn. 1.** huge, immense; extensive. See **great. 2.** consequential. **3.** arrogant.
big·a·mist (big′ə mist), *n.* a person who commits bigamy. —**big′a·mis′tic,** *adj.* —**big′a·mis′ti·cal·ly,** *adv.*
big·a·mous (big′ə məs), *adj.* **1.** having two wives or husbands at the same time; guilty of bigamy. **2.** involving bigamy. [< LL *bigamus* = *bi-* BI-[1] + Gk *-gamos* -GAMOUS] —**big′a·mous·ly,** *adv.*
big·a·my (big′ə mē), *n., pl.* **-mies.** *Law.* the crime of marrying while one has a legal wife or husband still living. Cf. **monogamy** (def. 1), **polygamy** (def. 1). [ME *bigamie* < ML *bigamia* = LL *bigam(us)* BIGAMOUS + L *-ia* -Y[3]]
Big′ Ap′ple, the, *Slang.* **1.** New York City. **2.** any large city.
Big·ar·reau (big′ə rō′, big′ə rō′), *n.* a large, heart-shaped variety of sweet cherry, having firm flesh. [< F = *bigarr(é)* variegated + *-eau* n. suffix (earlier *-el* < L *-ellus*)]
big′ bang′ the′ory, *Astron.* the theory that the universe was created from the explosion of a mass of hydrogen atoms, is still expanding as a result of this force, and will eventually contract back into one mass which will then explode and begin the cycle over again, the complete cycle to take 80 billion years. Cf. **steady state theory.**
Big′ Ben′, the bell in the clock tower of the Houses of Parliament in London, England.
Big′ Bend′ Na′tional Park′, a national park in W Texas on the Rio Grande. 1080 sq. mi.
Big′ Ber′tha, a large German cannon of World War I.
Big′ Board′, *Informal.* the New York Stock Exchange.
big′ broth′er, **1.** an elder brother. **2.** (*sometimes caps.*) a man who sponsors or assists a boy in need of help, guidance, or the like, as an orphan, juvenile delinquent, etc. **3.** (*usually caps.*) the head of a totalitarian regime.
big′ busi′ness, large and influential business, commercial, and financial firms considered collectively.
Big′ Di′omede. See under **Diomede Islands.**
Big′ Dip′per, *Astron.* dipper (def. 3a).
big·eye (big′ī′), *n., pl.* (*esp. collectively*) **-eye,** (*esp. referring to two or more kinds or species*) **-eyes.** any of several silver and red fishes of the family *Priacanthidae,* found in the warm waters of the Pacific Ocean and in the West Indies, having a short, flattened body and large eyes.
Big′ Five′, **1.** the United States, Great Britain, France, Italy, and Japan after World War I. **2.** (after World War II) the United States, Great Britain, the Soviet Union, China, and France.
big′ game′, **1.** large or ferocious wild animals hunted for sport, as deer, bear, tigers, or the like. **2.** *Angling.* large game fish, as marlin.
big·gie (big′ē), *n. Slang.* **1.** See **big shot. 2.** something large, important, or very successful.
big·gin (big′in), *n.* **1.** a close-fitting cap worn esp. by children. **2.** *Brit. Archaic.* a nightcap. [< MF *beguin* kind of hood or cap, orig. one worn by a BEGUINE]
Biggs (bigz), *n.* **E(dward George) Pow·er** (pou′ər), 1906–77, English organist, in the U.S.
big′ gun′, *Slang.* an influential or important person.

big·head (big′hed′), *n.* *Vet. Pathol.* an inflammatory swelling of the tissues of the head of sheep, caused by the anaerobic bacillus, *Clostridium novyi.* —**big′head′ed,** *adj.*

big·heart·ed (big′här′tid), *adj.* generous; kind. —**big′-heart′ed·ly,** *adv.*

big·horn (big′hôrn′), *n., pl.* **-horns,** (*esp. collectively*) **-horn.** a wild sheep, *Ovis canadensis,* of the Rocky Mountains, with large, curving horns. Also called **Rocky Mountain sheep.**

Bighorn
(3½ ft. high at shoulder; horns to 3½ ft.; length to 5½ ft.)

Big·horn (big′hôrn′), *n.* a river flowing from Wyoming to the Yellowstone River in S Montana. 336 mi. long.

Big′horn′ Moun′tains, a mountain range in N Wyoming, part of the Rocky Mountains. Highest peak, Cloud Peak, 13,165 ft. Also called **the Big′horns′.**

big′ house′, *U.S. Slang.* a penitentiary (prec. by *the*).

bight (bīt), *n.* **1.** the middle, loop, or bent part of a rope, as distinguished from the ends. **2.** an indentation or curve in the shore of a sea or river. **3.** a body of water bounded by such an indentation or curve, as a bay or gulf or a bend in a river. —*v.t.* **4.** to fasten with a bight of rope. [ME *byght,* OE *byht* bend, bay; c. D *bocht,* G *Bucht;* akin to BOW[1]]

big′ league′, *Sports Informal.* See **major league.** —**big′-lea′guer,** *n.*

big-league (big′lēg′), *adj.* among the foremost or largest of its kind; major: *the big-league oil companies.*

big′ lie′, a false statement of outrageous magnitude employed as a propaganda measure.

big·mouth (big′mouth′), *n., pl.* **-mouths** (-mouthz′, -mouths′) for 1; (*esp. collectively*) **-mouth,** (*esp. referring to two or more kinds or species*) **-mouths** for 2. **1.** *Slang.* a loud, talkative person, esp. one who lacks discretion. **2.** any of several fishes having an unusually large mouth.

Big′ Mud′dy Riv′er, a river in SW Illinois, flowing SW into the Mississippi, ab. 120 mi. long.

big·no·ni·a (big nō′nē ə), *n.* any chiefly tropical American climbing shrub of the genus *Bignonia,* cultivated for its showy, trumpet-shaped flowers. [< NL, after Abbé *Bignon* (librarian of Louis XIV of France); see -IA]

big·no·ni·a·ceous (big nō′nē ā′shəs), *adj.* belonging or pertaining to the *Bignoniaceae,* a family of plants including trumpet creeper, catalpa, etc.

big·ot (big′ət), *n.* a person who is utterly intolerant of any creed, belief, or race that is not his own. [< MF (OF: derogatory name applied by the French to the Normans) ? < OE *bī God* by God] —**Syn.** dogmatist, zealot, fanatic.

big·ot·ed (big′ə tid), *adj.* utterly intolerant of any creed, belief, or race that differs from one's own. —**big′ot·ed·ly,** *adv.* —**Syn.** See **intolerant.**

big·ot·ry (big′ə trē), *n., pl.* **-ries.** **1.** stubborn and complete intolerance of any creed, belief, or opinion that differs from one's own. **2.** actions, beliefs, prejudices, etc., of a bigot. [BIGOT + -RY, formation parallel to F *bigoterie*]

big′ shot′, *Slang.* an important or influential person.

Big′ Spring′, a city in W Texas. 28,735 (1970).

big-tick·et (big′tik′it), *adj.* costing a great deal; expensive: *Color TV is still a big-ticket item.*

big′ time′, **1.** *Slang.* the top level or rank in any profession or occupation. **2.** *Slang.* a very good time. **3.** *Theat.* (in vaudeville) any highly successful circuit of theaters that presents only two performances daily. —**big′-time′,** *adj.* —**big′-tim′er,** *n.*

big′ toe′, the innermost and largest digit of the foot.

big′ top′, **1.** the main tent of a circus. **2.** a circus.

big′ tree′, a large coniferous tree, *Sequoiadendron giganteum* (formerly *Sequoia gigantea*), of California, often reaching 300 feet in height. Cf. **sequoia.**

big·wig (big′wig′), *n.* *Informal.* an important person, esp. an official: *senators and other political bigwigs.* [rhyming compound from phrase *big wig,* i.e., person important enough to wear such a wig] —**big′wigged′,** *adj.* —**big·wig·ged·ness** (big′wig′id nis), *n.*

Bi·har (bē här′), *n.* **1.** a state in NE India. 46,455,610 (1961); 67,164 sq. mi. *Cap.:* Patna. **2.** a city in central Bihar. 78,600 (1961). Also, **Behar.**

Bihar′ and Oris′sa, a former province of NE India: now divided into the states of Bihar and Orissa.

Bi·ha·ri (bē här′ē), *n.* the Indic language of Bihar.

Bi·isk (bē′isk), *n.* Bisk.

bi·jou (bē′zhōō, bē zhōō′), *n., pl.* **-joux** (-zhōōz, -zhōōz′). **1.** a jewel. **2.** something delicate and exquisitely wrought. [< F < Breton *bizou,* earlier *besou* jeweled ring; c. Cornish *bisou* finger ring < *bis* finger]

bi·jou·te·rie (bē zhōō′tə rē), *n.* jewelry. [< F = *bijou* BIJOU + *-t-* (connective) + *-erie* -ERY]

bi·ju·gate (bī′jŏŏ gāt′, bī jōō′gāt, -git), *adj.* *Bot.* (of leaves) having two pairs of leaflets or pinnae. Also, **bi·ju·gous** (bī′jŏŏ gəs, bī jōō′gəs).

bike (bīk), *n., v.,* **biked, bik·ing.** *Informal.* —*n.* **1.** a bicycle. **2.** a motorcycle. **3.** a motorbike. —*v.i.* **4.** to ride a bike. [*bi(cy)c(le)*] —**bik′er,** *n.*

bike·way (bīk′wā′), *n.* a road or path built or reserved for bicycle traffic.

bi·ki·ni (bi kē′nē), *n.* a very brief two-piece bathing suit for women. [named after BIKINI]

Bi·ki·ni (bi kē′nē), *n.* an atoll in the N Pacific, in the Marshall Islands: atomic bomb tests 1946. 3 sq. mi.

bi·la·bi·al (bī lā′bē əl), *Phonet.* —*adj.* **1.** produced with the lips close together or touching, as the consonants *p, b,* and *m.* —*n.* **2.** a bilabial speech sound.

bi·la·bi·ate (bī lā′bē āt′, -it), *adj.* *Bot.* two-lipped, as a corolla.

bil·an·der (bil′ən dər, bī′lən-), *n.* *Naut.* a small merchant vessel with two masts, used on canals and along the coast of Holland. [< D *bijlander* = *bij* BY + *land* LAND + *-er* -ER[1]]

bi·lat·er·al (bī lat′ər əl), *adj.* **1.** *Bot., Zool.* pertaining to the right and left sides of a structure, plane, etc. **2.** pertaining to or affecting two or both sides, factions, parties, or the like: *a bilateral agreement.* **3.** located on opposite sides of an axis; two-sided, esp. when of equal size, value, etc. **4.** *Chiefly Law.* (of a contract) binding the parties to reciprocal obligations. **5.** through both parents equally: *bilateral affiliation.* Cf. **unilateral** (def. 6). —**bi·lat′er·al·ism, bi·lat′er·al·ness,** *n.* —**bi·lat′er·al·ly,** *adv.*

Bil·ba·o (bēl bä′ō), *n.* a seaport in N Spain, near the Bay of Biscay. 317,639 (est. 1963).

bil·ber·ry (bil′ber′ē, -bə rē), *n., pl.* **-ries.** the fruit of several shrubby species of the genus *Vaccinium.* [obs. *bil* (< Scand; cf. Dan *bölle* bilberry) + BERRY]

bil·bo[1] (bil′bō), *n., pl.* **-boes.** Usually, **bilboes.** a long iron bar or bolt with sliding shackles and a lock, formerly used to confine the feet of prisoners. [earlier *bilbow* < ?]

bil·bo[2] (bil′bō), *n., pl.* **-boes.** *Archaic.* a finely tempered sword. [short for *Bilboa blade* sword made in *Bilboa* (var. of BILBAO)]

bile (bīl), *n.* **1.** *Physiol.* a bitter, alkaline, yellow or greenish liquid, secreted by the liver, that aids in absorption and digestion, esp. of fats. **2.** ill temper; peevishness. [< F < L *bīl(is)*]

bi·lec·tion (bī lek′shən), *n.* *Archit., Furniture.* bolection.

bile·stone (bīl′stōn′), *n.* *Pathol.* a gallstone.

bilge (bilj), *n., v.,* **bilged, bilg·ing.** —*n.* **1.** *Naut.* **a.** either of the rounded areas that form the transition between the bottom and the sides on the exterior of a hull. **b.** Also, **bilges.** (in a hull with a double bottom) an enclosed area between frames at each side of the floors, where seepage collects. **c.** Also called **bilge water.** seepage accumulated in a bilge. **2.** *Slang.* See **bilge water** (def. 2). **3.** the widest circumference or belly of a cask. —*v.i.* **4.** *Naut.* to leak in the bilge. —*v.t.* **5.** *Naut.* to damage the lower part of (a hull) so as to open it to the sea. [perh. var. of BULGE]

bilge′ keel′, *Naut.* either of two keellike projections extending lengthwise along a ship's bilge, one on each side, to retard rolling. Also called **bilge′ piece′.**

bilge′ wa′ter, **1.** *Naut.* bilge (def. 1c). **2.** *Slang.* nonsense; rubbish.

bilg·y (bil′jē), *adj.,* **bilg·i·er, bilg·i·est.** *Naut.* smelling like bilge water.

bil·har·zi·a·sis (bil′här zī′ə sis), *n.* *Pathol.* schistosomiasis. Also, **bil·har·zi·o·sis** (bil här′zē ō′sis). [named after Theodor *Bilharz* (d. 1862), German physician; see -IASIS]

bil·i·ar·y (bil′ē er′ē), *adj.* **1.** *Physiol.* **a.** of bile. **b.** conveying bile: *a biliary duct.* **2.** *Archaic.* bilious. [< NL *biliāri(s)*]

bi·lin·e·ar (bī lin′ē ər), *adj.* *Math.* **1.** of, pertaining to, or having reference to two lines: *bilinear coordinates.* **2.** of the first degree in each of two variables, as an equation.

bi·lin·gual (bī ling′gwəl), *adj.* **1.** able to speak two languages with nearly equal facility. **2.** spoken or written in two languages. [< L *bilingu(is)* (*bi-* BI-[1] + *lingu-,* s. of *lingua* tongue + *-is* adj. suffix) + -AL[1]] —**bi·lin′gual·ism, bi·lin·gual·i·ty** (bī′ling gwal′i tē), *n.* —**bi·lin′gual·ly,** *adv.*

bil·ious (bil′yəs), *adj.* **1.** *Physiol., Pathol.* pertaining to bile or to an excess secretion of bile. **2.** *Pathol.* suffering from, caused by, or attended by trouble with the bile or liver. **3.** peevish or irritable. **4.** extremely unpleasant or distasteful: *bright, bilious green.* [< L *bīliōs(us)*] —**bil′ious·ly,** *adv.* —**bil′ious·ness,** *n.*

bi·lit·er·al (bī lit′ər əl), *adj.* using or consisting of two letters. —**bi·lit′er·al·ism,** *n.*

-bility, a suffix used to form nouns from adjectives with stems ending in **-ble:** *nobility; credibility.* Also, **-ability, -ibility.** [ME *-bilite* < MF < L *-bilitāt-* (s. of *-bilitās*)]

bilk (bilk), *v.t.* **1.** to evade payment of; defraud; cheat: *He bilked his creditors.* **2.** to frustrate: *a career bilked by poor health.* **3.** to escape from; elude: *to bilk one's pursuers.* —*n.* **4.** a cheat; swindler. **5.** *Obs.* a trick. [?] —**bilk′er,** *n.*

bill[1] (bil), *n.* **1.** a statement of money owed for goods or services supplied. **2.** See **bill of exchange.** **3.** a piece of paper money worth a specified amount: *a ten-dollar bill.* **4.** *Govt.* a form or draft of a proposed statute presented to a legislature. **5.** a written or printed public notice or advertisement: *Post no bills.* **6.** a written paper containing a statement of particulars: *a bill of expenditures.* **7.** *Law.* a written statement, usually of complaint, presented to a court. **8.** playbill. **9.** entertainment scheduled; program: *a good bill at the movies.* **10.** *Obs.* **a.** a promissory note. **b.** a written and sealed document. **c.** a written, formal petition. **11. fill the bill,** *Informal.* to fulfill all requirements: *This meal really fills the bill.* —*v.t.* **12.** to enter (charges) in a bill; make a bill or list of: *to bill goods.* **13.** to charge for by bill; send a bill to. **14.** to advertise by bill or public notice. **15.** to schedule on a program: *The new play is billed in two weeks.* [ME *bille* < AL *billa* for LL *bulla* BULL[2]] —**bill′a·ble,** *adj.* —**bill′er,** *n.* —**Syn. 1.** reckoning, invoice, statement. **5.** handbill, notice, poster, placard, circular.

bill[2] (bil), *n.* **1.** the parts of a bird's jaws that are covered with a horny or leathery sheath; beak. —*v.i.* **2.** to join bills or beaks, as doves. **3. bill and coo,** to whisper endearments, as lovers. [ME *bile, bille,* OE *bile* beak, trunk; akin to BILL[3]]

bill[3] (bil), *n.* **1.** a medieval shafted weapon having at its head a hooklike cutting blade with a beak at the back. **2.** Also called **billhook.** a sharp, hooked instrument used for pruning, cutting, etc. **3.** Also called **pea.** *Naut.* the extremity of a fluke of an anchor. [ME *bil,* OE *bill* sword; c. OHG *bil* pickax]

Bill[3] (def. 2)

bil·la·bong (bil′ə bong′), *n.* *Australian.* **1.** a branch of a river flowing away from the main stream but leading to no other body of water. **2.** a creek bed holding water only in the rainy season. [< native Austral *billa* water, river, stream + *bong* dead]

bill·board (bil′bōrd′, -bôrd′), *n.* a board, usually outdoors, on which large advertisements or notices are posted.

Bil·le·ri·ca (bil′ri kə), *n.* a city in NE Massachusetts. 31,648 (1970).

bil·let[1] (bil′it), *n., v.,* **-let·ed, -let·ing.** —*n.* **1.** lodging for soldiers in nonmilitary buildings. **2.** *Mil.* an official order directing a person to provide such lodging. **3.** a bunk, berth, or the like, assigned to a seaman. **4.** a job or appointment. **5.** *Obs.* a written note, short letter, or the like. —*v.t.* **6.** *Mil.* to assign lodging to (a soldier). **7.** to provide lodging for; quarter. —*v.i.* **8.** to obtain lodging; stay. [late ME *bylet, billett* < AL *billetta* = *bill(a)* BILL[1] + *-etta* dim. suffix] —**bil′let·er,** *n.*

bil·let[2] (bil′it), *n.* **1.** a small chunk of wood, esp. one cut for fuel. **2.** *Metalworking.* a narrow, generally square bar of steel, esp. one rolled or forged from an ingot; a narrow bloom. **3.** *Archit.* any of a series of closely spaced cylindrical objects used as ornaments. **4.** a strap that passes through a buckle, as to connect the ends of a girth. **5.** a pocket or loop for securing the end of a strap that has been buckled. [late ME *bylet, bel(l)et* < MF *billette* = *bille* log, tree trunk]

bil·let-doux (bil′ē do͞o′, bil′ā-; *Fr.* bē yā do͞o′), *n., pl.* **bil·lets-doux** (bil′ē do͞oz′, bil′ā-; *Fr.* bē yā do͞o′). a love letter. [< F: lit., sweet little letter. See BILLET[1], DOUCE]

bill·fish (bil′fish′), *n., pl.* (*esp. collectively*) **-fish,** (*esp. referring to two or more kinds or species*) **-fish·es.** any of various fishes having a long, sharp bill or snout, as a gar, needlefish, or saury.

bill·fold (bil′fōld′), *n.* *U.S.* a folding leather case for carrying paper money; wallet. Also called, *esp. Brit.,* **notecase.**

bill·head (bil′hed′), *n.* a printed form, usually giving one's name and address, on which a statement of money due is rendered.

bill·hook (bil′ho͝ok′), *n.* bill[3] (def. 2).

bil·liard (bil′yərd), *adj.* **1.** of or used in billiards. —*n.* **2.** *U.S. Informal.* carom (def. 1). [< F *billard* cue = *bille* stick (see BILLET[2]) + *-ard* -ARD]

bil·liards (bil′yərdz), *n.* (*construed as sing.*) any of several games played with hard balls of ivory or of a similar material that are driven with a cue on a cloth-covered table enclosed by a cushioned rim, esp. a game played with a cue ball and two object balls on a table without pockets. Cf. **pool**[2] (def. 7). —**bil′liard·ist,** *n.*

bill·ing (bil′ing), *n.* **1.** the relative position in which a performer or act is listed on handbills, posters, etc. **2.** advertising or publicity: *the advance billing for a play.* **3.** the amount of business done by a firm, esp. an advertising agency, within a specified period of time.

Bil·lings (bil′ingz), *n.* **1. Josh** (josh) (pen name of *Henry Wheeler Shaw*), 1818–85, U.S. humorist. **2.** a city in S Montana. 61,581 (1970).

bil·lings·gate (bil′ingz gāt′ *or, esp. Brit.,* -git), *n.* coarsely or vulgarly abusive language. [orig. the kind of speech often heard at *Billingsgate,* a London fishmarket at the *gate* named after a certain *Billing*]

bil·lion (bil′yən), *n., pl.* **-lions,** (*as after a numeral*) **-lion,** *adj.* —*n.* **1.** *U.S.* a thousand millions. **2.** *Brit.* a million millions. —*adj.* **3.** equal in number to a billion. [< F; see BI-[1], MILLION] —**bil′lionth,** *adj., n.*

bil·lion·aire (bil′yə nâr′), *n.* a person who has assets worth a billion or more dollars, francs, pounds, or the like. [BILLION + *-aire,* modeled after *millionaire*]

Bil·li·ton (bē′lē ton′, bē lē′ton), *n.* an island in Indonesia, between Borneo and Sumatra. ab. 73,500; 1866 sq. mi. Also, **Belitong, Belitoeng, Belitung.**

bill′ of attain′der, *Hist.* an act of legislature finding a person guilty of treason or felony.

bill′ of exchange′, a written authorization or order to pay a specified sum to a specified person, used chiefly in transacting foreign business.

bill′ of fare′, a list of foods that are served; menu.

bill′ of goods′, **1.** a quantity of salable items, as merchandise. **2.** *U.S. Slang.* a misrepresented, fraudulent, or defective article. **3. sell (someone) a bill of goods,** to defraud or deceive (another person): *He sold me a bill of goods about those big jobs he'd had.*

bill′ of health′, **1.** a certificate, carried by a ship, attesting to the prevailing state of health in a port from which it has come. **2. clean bill of health,** *Informal.* an attestation of fitness or qualification: *The investigating committee gave him a clean bill of health.*

bill′ of lad′ing, a receipt given by a carrier for goods accepted for transportation. *Abbr.:* b.l., B.L., b/l, B/L

bill′ of partic′ulars, *Law.* **1.** a formal statement prepared by a plaintiff or a defendant itemizing his claim or counterclaim in a suit. **2.** an itemized statement prepared by the prosecution and informing the accused of the charges in a criminal case.

Bill′ of Rights′, **1.** (*l.c.*) a formal statement of the fundamental rights of the people of a nation. **2.** such a statement incorporated in the Constitution of the United States as Amendments 1–10, and in all state constitutions. **3.** an English statute of 1689 confirming the rights and liberties of the subjects and settling the succession on William III and Mary II.

bill′ of sale′, a document transferring title in personal property from seller to buyer. *Abbr.:* b.s., B.S., b/s, B/S

bil·lon (bil′ən), *n.* **1.** an alloy used in coinage, consisting of gold or silver with a larger amount of base metal. **2.** an alloy of silver with copper or the like, used for coins of small denomination. [< F: debased metal, orig. ingot = MF *bille* log (see BILLET[2]) + *-on* n. suffix]

bil·low (bil′ō), *n.* **1.** a great wave or surge of the sea. **2.** any surging mass: *billows of smoke.* —*v.i.* **3.** to rise, swell out, puff up, or roll in or like billows; surge: *flags billowing in the breeze.* —*v.t.* **4.** to cause to rise, surge, swell, or the like. [< Scand; cf. Icel *bylgja* a wave, c. MLG *bulge;* akin to OE *gebylgan* to anger, provoke]

bil·low·y (bil′ō ē), *adj.,* **-low·i·er, -low·i·est.** characterized by or full of billows; surging: *a rough, billowy sea.* —**bil′low·i·ness,** *n.*

bill·post·er (bil′pō′stər), *n.* a person who posts bills and advertisements. Also called **bill·stick·er** (bil′stik′ər). —**bill′post′ing, bill′stick′ing,** *n.*

bil·ly[1] (bil′ē), *n.; pl.* **-lies.** **1.** Also called **bil′ly club′.** *Informal.* a policeman's club or baton. **2.** a heavy wooden stick for use as a weapon; cudgel. [BILL[3] + -Y[2]]

bil·ly[2] (bil′ē), *n., pl.* **-lies.** *Australian.* any container in which water may be carried and boiled over a campfire. Also called **bil·ly·can** (bil′ē kan′). [shortened form of BILLYCAN = *billy* (< native Austral *billa* water, river; see BILLABONG) + CAN[2]]

bil·ly·cock (bil′ē kok′), *n.* *Chiefly Brit.* **1.** a round, low-crowned, soft felt hat. **2.** a derby hat. Also called **bil′lycock hat′.** [alter. of *bullycocked* (*hat*). See BULLY[1], COCKED]

bil′ly goat′, a male goat.

Bil′ly the Kid′, (*William H. Bonney*) 1859–81, U.S. outlaw.

bi·lo·bate (bī lō′bāt), *adj.* consisting of or divided into two lobes. Also, **bi·lo′bat·ed, bi·lobed** (bī′lōbd′).

bi·lo·ca·tion (bī′lō kā′shən), *n.* the state of being or the ability to be in two places at the same time.

bi·loc·u·lar (bī lok′yə lər), *adj.* *Biol.* divided into two chambers or cells, or containing two cells internally. Also, **bi·loc·u·late** (bī lok′yə lit, -lāt′). [BI-[1] + L *locul(us)* (*loc(us)* place + *-ulus* -ULE) + -AR[1]]

Bi·lox·i (bi luk′sē, -lok′-), *n.* a city in SE Mississippi, on the Gulf of Mexico. 48,486 (1970).

bil·tong (bil′tông′), *n.* (in South Africa) strips of dried lean meat. [< SAfrD = *bil* rump + *tong* TONGUE]

bi·mah (bē′mə, bim′ə), *n.* a platform in a synagogue holding the reading table used in chanting or reading the designated portions of the Torah and the Prophets on the days prescribed. Also, **bema, bi′ma.** Also called **almemar.** [< Heb < Gk *bêma* BEMA]

bim·a·nous (bim′ə nəs, bī mā′-), *adj.* *Zool.* having two hands, as primates. [< NL *biman(a)* (*animalia*) two-handed (animals) (*bi-* BI-[1] + *-mana* < L *manus* hand) + -OUS]

bi·man·u·al (bī man′yo͞o əl), *adj.* involving or requiring the use of both hands. —**bi·man′u·al·ly,** *adv.*

bi·men·sal (bī men′səl), *adj.* *Obs.* occurring once in two months; bimonthly.

bi·mes·ter (bī mes′tər, bī′mes-), *n.* a two-month period. [< L *bimēstr(is)* = *bi-* BI-[1] + *mē(n)s-* (s. of *mēnsis*) month + *-tris* adj. suffix]

bi·mes·tri·al (bī mes′trē əl), *adj.* **1.** occurring every two months; bimonthly. **2.** lasting two months. [< L *bimestri(s)* BIMESTER + -AL[1]]

bi·me·tal·lic (bī′mə tal′ik), *adj.* **1.** made or consisting of two metals. **2.** pertaining to bimetallism. [< F *bimétallique*]

bi·met·al·lism (bī met′əliz′əm), *n.* **1.** the use of two metals, ordinarily gold and silver, at a fixed relative value, as a monetary standard. **2.** the doctrine or policies supporting such a standard. —**bi·met′al·list,** *n.* —**bi·met′al·lis′tic,** *adj.*

bi·meth·yl (bī meth′əl), *n.* *Chem.* ethane.

Bim′i·ni Is′lands (bim′ə nē), a group of islands in the W Bahamas: resort center; supposed site of the Fountain of Youth for which Ponce de León searched. 1652 (1963); 9 sq. mi. Also called **Bim′i·nis.**

bi·mod·al (bī mōd′əl), *adj.* *Statistics.* (of a distribution) having two modes. —**bi′mo·dal′i·ty,** *n.*

bi·mo·lec·u·lar (bī′mə lek′yə lər), *adj.* *Chem.* having or involving two molecules. —**bi′mo·lec′u·lar·ly,** *adv.*

bi·month·ly (bī munth′lē), *adj., n., pl.* **-lies,** *adv.* —*adj.* **1.** occurring every two months. **2.** (loosely) occurring twice a month; semimonthly. —*n.* **3.** a bimonthly publication. —*adv.* **4.** every two months: *The magazine is published bimonthly.* **5.** (loosely) twice a month; semimonthly. —**Usage.** Since it is not always clear which meaning of BIMONTHLY is intended—"twice a month" or "every two months"—the use of SEMIMONTHLY for "twice a month" is preferable because it is unambiguous. Since there is no single, unambiguous term for "every two months," this phrase itself is the least confusing to use.

bi·mo·tored (bī mō′tərd), *adj.* *Aeron.* having two engines.

bin (bin), *n., v.,* **binned, bin·ning.** —*n.* **1.** a box or enclosed place for storing grain, coal, or the like. —*v.t.* **2.** to store in a bin. [ME *binne,* OE *binn(e)* crib, perh. < Celt]

bin-, a learned borrowing from Latin meaning "two," "two at a time," used in the formation of compound words: *binary; binocular.* Cf. **bi-**[1]. [comb. form of L *bīnī* two by two]

bi·nal (bīn′əl), *adj.* double. [< NL *bīnāl(is)* double]

bi·na·ry (bī′nə rē, -ne-), *adj., n., pl.* **-ries.** —*adj.* **1.** consisting of, indicating, or involving two. **2.** of or pertaining to a system of numerical notation to the base 2, in which each place of a number, expressed as 0 or 1, corresponds to a power of 2. **3.** of or pertaining to the digits or numbers used in binary notation. **4.** *Math.* **a.** of or pertaining to a binary system. **b.** (of an operation) assigning a third quantity to two given quantities, as in the addition of two numbers. **5.** *Chem.* noting a compound containing only two elements or groups. **6.** *Metall.* (of an alloy) having two principal constituents. —*n.* **7.** a whole composed of two. **8.** *Astron.* See **binary star.** **9.** Also called **bi′nary num′ber.** a number of a binary system. [< LL *bīnāri(us)*]

bi′nary cell′, *Computer Technol.* an electronic element that can assume either of two stable states and is capable of storing a binary digit.

bi′nary code′, *Computer Technol.* a system of representing letters, numbers, or other characters, using binary notation.

bi′nary fis′sion, *Biol.* fission into two organisms approximately equal in size.

bi′nary star′, *Astron.* a system of two stars that revolve around their common center of gravity.

bi′nary sys′tem, **1.** a system involving only two elements, as 0 and 1 or yes and no. **2.** a system of counting or measurement whose units are powers of two. Cf. **binary** (def. 2). Also called **dyadic system.**

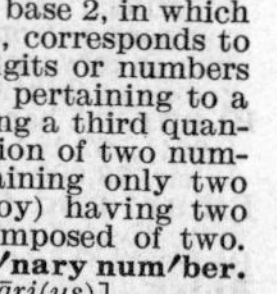

bi·nate (bī′nāt), *adj.* *Bot.* double; produced or borne in pairs. [< NL *bīnāt(us),* appar. abstracted from LL *combīnātus* yoked together. See BIN-, -ATE[1]] —**bi′nate·ly,** *adv.*

Binate leaf

bin·au·ral (bī nôr′əl, bin ôr′əl), *adj.* of, with, or for both ears: *a binaural stethoscope.*

binau′ral broad′casting, a system of radio broadcasting in which the signal picked up by a microphone in one part of a studio is broadcast via FM and that picked up by a second microphone is broadcast via AM: FM and AM receivers similarly separated then provide a stereophonic effect for the listener.

bind (bīnd), *v.*, **bound, bind·ing,** *n.* —*v.t.* **1.** to fasten or secure with a band or bond. **2.** to encircle with a band or ligature: *She bound her hair with a ribbon.* **3.** to swathe or bandage (often fol. by *up*): *to bind up one's wounds.* **4.** to fasten around; fix in place by girding: *They bound his hands behind him.* **5.** to tie into bundles, sheaves, or the like. **6.** to cause to cohere: *Ice bound the soil.* **7.** to unite by any legal or moral tie: *to be bound by the ties of matrimony.* **8.** to hold to a particular state, place, employment, etc.: *Business kept him bound to the city.* **9.** to place under obligation or compulsion (usually used passively): *We are bound by good sense to obey the laws.* **10.** *Law.* to put under legal obligation, as to keep the peace or appear as a witness (often fol. by *over*): *This action binds them to keep the peace. He was bound over to the grand jury.* **11.** to make compulsory or obligatory: *to bind the order with a deposit.* **12.** to indenture as an apprentice (often fol. by *out*). **13.** (of clothing) to chafe or restrict (the wearer). **14.** *Pathol.* to hinder or restrain (the bowels) from their natural operations; constipate. **15.** to fasten or secure within a cover, as a book. **16.** to cover the edge of, as for protection or ornament. **17.** *Falconry.* (of a hawk) to grasp prey firmly in flight. —*v.i.* **18.** to become compact or solid; cohere. **19.** to be obligatory. **20.** to chafe or restrict, as poorly fitting garments: *This jacket binds through the shoulders.* **21.** to stick fast, as a drill in a hole. **22. bind off,** *Textiles.* to loop (one stitch) over another in making an edge on knitted fabric. —*n.* **23.** the act or process of binding. **24.** the state or an instance of being bound. **25.** something that binds. **26.** *Music.* a tie, slur, or brace. [ME *bind(en)*, OE *bindan;* c. OHG *bintan*, Icel *binda*, Goth *bindan*, Skt *bandh(ati)*] —**bind′a·ble,** *adj.* —**Syn. 1.** attach, tie. **9.** oblige, obligate.

bind·er (bīn′dər), *n.* **1.** a person or thing that binds. **2.** a detachable cover for loose papers. **3.** a bookbinder. **4.** *Agric.* **a.** an attachment to a harvester or reaper for binding the cut grain. **b.** a machine that cuts and binds grain. **5.** *Insurance.* an agreement by which property or liability coverage is granted pending issuance of a policy. **6.** *U.S.* **a.** a preliminary agreement for the purchase of real estate. **b.** the deposit paid in connection with such an agreement. **7.** *Metall.* a material for holding crushed ore dust together while it is being sintered. **8.** *Painting.* a vehicle in which pigment is suspended. **9.** *Building Trades.* a substance for holding loose material together.

bind·er·y (bīn′də rē, -drē), *n., pl.* **-er·ies.** a place where books are bound.

bind·ing (bīn′diṉg), *n.* **1.** act of fastening, securing, uniting, or the like. **2.** anything that binds. **3.** the covering within which the leaves of a book are bound. **4.** a strip of material for edging a tablecloth, rug, etc. —*adj.* **5.** obligatory. —**bind′ing·ly,** *adv.* —**bind′ing·ness,** *n.*

bind′ing en′ergy, *Physics.* **1.** the energy required to decompose a molecule, atom, or nucleus into its constituent particles. **2.** the energy required to separate a single particle or group of particles from a molecule, atom, or nucleus. Cf. **mass defect.**

bin·dle (bin′dᵊl), *n.* *Slang.* a bundle, usually of bedding, carried by a hobo. [special use of Scot *bindle* binding rope < ME *bindel*, OE *bindele* bandage]

bin′dle stiff′, *Slang.* a hobo.

bind·weed (bīnd′wēd′), *n.* any of various twining or vinelike plants, esp. certain species of the genus *Convolvulus.*

bine (bīn), *n.* **1.** a twining plant stem, as of the hop. **2.** any bindweed. **3.** woodbine (defs. 1, 2). [var. of BIND]

Bi·net′-Si′mon scale′ (bi nā′sī′mən; *Fr.* bē ne′sē-môɴ′), *Psychol.* a system for determining the relative development of the intelligence, esp. of children, according to tests graded with reference to the ability of the normal child. Also called **Binet′-Si′mon test′, Binet′ scale′, Binet′ test′.** Cf. **Stanford-Binet test.**

Bing (biṉg), *n.* **1.** a variety of sweet cherry having a dark red fruit. **2.** the fruit itself. Also called **Bing′ cher′ry.** [?]

binge (binj), *n.* *Informal.* a period of excessive indulgence, as in eating, drinking, etc.; spree. [dial. (Lincolnshire) *binge* to soak < ?]

Bing·en (biṉg′ən), *n.* a town in W West Germany, on the Rhine River: whirlpool; tourist center. 20,500 (1963).

Bing·ham (biṉg′əm), *n.* **George Caleb,** 1811–79, U.S. painter.

Bing·ham·ton (biṉg′əm tən), *n.* a city in S New York, on the Susquehanna River. 64,123 (1970).

bin·go (biṉg′gō), *n.* (*sometimes cap.*) a game similar to lotto, played usually by a large number of persons in competition for prizes. [orig. uncert.]

Binh Dinh (bin′yᵊ din′yᵊ, bin′din′), a city in E South Vietnam. ab. 147,000. Also, **Binh′dinh′.**

bin·na·cle (bin′ə kəl), *n.* *Naut.* a stand or case for supporting or housing a ship's compass. [BIN + (*bitt*)*acle* (late ME *bitakille*) < Pg *bitácula* < L *habitācul(um)* lodge = *habitā-* (see INHABIT) + *-culum* -CULE]

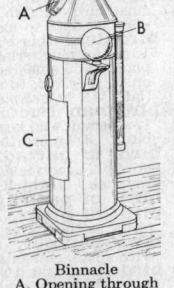

A
B
C

Binnacle
A, Opening through which compass is read; B, Quadrantal corrector; C, Magnet chamber

bin·o·cle (bin′ə kəl), *n.* binocular. [< F < NL *bīnocul(us)* = *bīn-* BIN- + L *oculus* eye]

bin·oc·u·lar (bə nok′yə lər, bī-), *adj.* **1.** involving two eyes: *binocular vision.* —*n.* **2.** Usually, **binoculars.** an optical device for use with both eyes, consisting of two small telescopes fitted together side by side. —**bin·oc′u·lar′i·ty,** *n.* —**bin·oc′u·lar·ly,** *adv.*

bi·no·mi·al (bī nō′mē əl), *n.* **1.** *Algebra.* an expression that is a sum or difference of two terms, as $3x + 2y$ and $x^2 - 4x$. **2.** *Zool., Bot.* a taxonomic name consisting of a generic and specific term. —*adj.* **3.** *Algebra.* consisting of or pertaining to two terms or a binomial. **4.** *Zool., Bot.* consisting of or characterized by binomials. [< ML *binōmi(us)* having two names (r. L *binōminis*) + -AL[1]. See BI-[1], NOMINAL] —**bi·no′mi·al·ism,** *n.* —**bi·no′mi·al·ly,** *adv.*

bino′mial distribu′tion, *Statistics.* a distribution giving the probability of obtaining a specified number of successes in a finite set of independent trials in which the probability of a success remains the same from trial to trial.

bino′mial no′menclature, *Zool., Bot.* a system of nomenclature in which each organism is given a name that consists of a generic and specific term.

bino′mial the′orem, *Math.* the theorem giving the expansion of a binomial raised to a given power expressed as

$$(x+y)^n = x^n + nx^{n-1}y + \frac{n(n-1)}{1\cdot 2}x^{n-2}y^2 + \frac{n(n-1)(n-2)}{1\cdot 2\cdot 3}x^{n-3}y^3 + \ldots + y^n.$$

bio-, a prefix meaning "life" occurring in loan words from Greek (*biography*); on this model, used in the formation of compound words (*bioluminescence*). Also, *esp. before a vowel,* **bi-.** [comb. form of Gk *bíos* life; akin to L *vīvus* living, Skt *jīvás.* See QUICK]

bi·o·as·say (*n.* bī′ō ə sā′, -as′ā; *v.* bī′ō ə sā′), *n., v.,* **-sayed, -say·ing.** —*n.* **1.** determination of the biological activity or potency of a substance, as a vitamin or hormone, by testing its effect on the growth of an organism. —*v.t.* **2.** to subject to a bioassay.

bi·o·as·tro·nau·tics (bī′ō as′trə nô′tiks), *n.* (*construed as sing.*) the science dealing with the effects of space travel upon life.

bi·o·cat·a·lyst (bī′ō kat′ᵊlist), *n.* *Biochem.* an agent, as an enzyme, element, etc., that acts as a biochemical catalyst.

bi·o·chem·is·try (bī′ō kem′i strē), *n.* the science dealing with the chemistry of living matter. —**bi·o·chem·i·cal** (bī′ō kem′i kəl), *adj., n.* —**bi′o·chem′ic,** *adj.* —**bi′o·chem′i·cal·ly,** *adv.* —**bi′o·chem′ist,** *n.*

bi·o·cli·mat·ic (bī′ō klī mat′ik), *adj.* of or pertaining to the effects of climate on living organisms.

bi·o·de·grad·a·ble (bī′ō di grā′də bəl), *adj.* capable of decaying and being absorbed by the environment, as paper and kitchen scraps, and as opposed to aluminum cans and many plastics which do not decay but remain garbage permanently. [BIO- + DEGRADE + ABLE] —**bi′o·de·grad′a·bil′i·ty,** *n.*

bi·o·dy·nam·ics (bī′ō dī nam′iks, -di-), *n.* (*construed as sing.*) the branch of biology dealing with energy or the activity of living organisms (opposed to *biostatics*). —**bi′o·dy·nam′ic, bi′o·dy·nam′i·cal,** *adj.*

bi·o·e·col·o·gy (bī′ō i kol′ə jē), *n.* the study of the interrelations between plants and animals and their environment. —**bi·o·ec·o·log·ic** (bī′ō ek′ə loj′ik), **bi′o·ec′o·log′i·cal,** *adj.* —**bi′o·ec′o·log′i·cal·ly,** *adv.* —**bi′o·e·col′o·gist,** *n.*

bi·o·en·gi·neer·ing (bī′ō en′jə nēr′ing), *n.* the application of engineering principles and techniques to problems in medicine and biology, such as the design and production of artificial limbs and organs. [BIO- + ENGINEERING]

bi·o·feed·back (bī′ō fēd′bak′), *n.* a method of learning to control one's bodily and mental functions with the aid of a visual or auditory display of one's own brain waves, blood pressure, muscle tension, etc.

biog., **1.** biographer. **2.** biographical. **3.** biography.

bi·o·gen (bī′ə jən), *n.* *Biol., Biochem.* a hypothetical protein molecule assumed to be basic to fundamental biological processes.

bi·o·gen·e·sis (bī′ō jen′i sis), *n.* the production of living organisms from other living organisms. Also, **bi·og·e·ny** (bī oj′ə nē). —**bi·o·ge·net·ic** (bī′ō jə net′ik), **bi′o·ge·net′i·cal, bi·og·e·nous** (bī oj′ə nəs), *adj.* —**bi′o·ge·net′i·cal·ly,** *adv.*

bi·o·gen·ic (bī′ō jen′ik), *adj.* **1.** resulting from the activity of living organisms, as fermentation. **2.** necessary for the life process.

bi·o·ge·og·ra·phy (bī′ō jē og′rə fē), *n.* *Ecol.* the study of the geographical distribution of living things. —**bi·o·ge·o·graph·ic** (bī′ō jē′ə graf′ik), **bi′o·ge′o·graph′i·cal,** *adj.* —**bi′o·ge′o·graph′i·cal·ly,** *adv.*

bi·og·ra·pher (bī og′rə fər, bē-), *n.* a writer of biography.

bi·o·graph·i·cal (bī′ə graf′i kəl), *adj.* **1.** of or pertaining to a person's life: *He's gathering biographical data for his book on Milton.* **2.** pertaining to biography: *a biographical dictionary.* Also, **bi′o·graph′ic.** —**bi′o·graph′i·cal·ly,** *adv.*

bi·og·ra·phy (bī og′rə fē, bē-), *n., pl.* **-phies.** **1.** a written account of another person's life. **2.** an account in biographical form of an organization, society, theater, animal, etc. **3.** such writings collectively. **4.** the writing of biography as an occupation or field of endeavor. [< Gk *biographía*]

biol., **1.** biological. **2.** biology.

bi·o·log·i·cal (bī′ə loj′i kəl), *adj.* Also, **bi′o·log′ic.** **1.** pertaining to biology. **2.** of or pertaining to the products and operations of applied biology: *a biological preparation.* —*n.* **3.** *Pharm.* a biochemical product, as a serum, vaccine, etc., used in the diagnosis, prevention, or treatment of disease. —**bi′o·log′i·cal·ly,** *adv.*

biolog′ical clock′, the innate system in people, animals, organisms, etc., that causes regular cycles of function or behavior, esp on a daily basis.

biolog′ical war′fare, warfare using bacteria, viruses, toxins, etc., to disable or kill man, to kill domestic animals, or to destroy food crops.

bi·ol·o·gism (bī ol′ə jiz′əm), *n.* any of various doctrines formulated on the principles of or according to the methods of biological science.

bi·ol·o·gist (bī ol′ə jist), *n.* a specialist in biology.

bi·ol·o·gy (bī ol′ə jē), *n.* **1.** the science of life or living matter in all its forms and phenomena, esp. with reference to origin, growth, reproduction, structure, etc. **2.** the plant and animal life of a region: *the biology of Pennsylvania.* **3.** the biological phenomena characteristic of an organism or a group of organisms: *the biology of a worm.* [< G *Biologie*]

bi·o·lu·mi·nes·cence (bī′ō lo͞o′mə nes′əns), *n.* the production of light by living organisms. —**bi′o·lu′mi·nes′cent,** *adj.*

bi·ol·y·sis (bī ol′i sis), *n.* *Biol.* dissolution of a living organism; death. [< NL] —**bi·o·lyt·ic** (bī′ə lit′ik), *adj.*

bi·o·mag·net·ism (bī′ō mag′ni tiz′əm), *n.* See **animal magnetism.** —**bi·o·mag·net·ic** (bī′ō mag net′ik), *adj.*

bi·o·mass (bī′ō mas′), *n.* *Ecol.* that part of a given habitat consisting of living matter, as per unit area or per unit volume of habitat.
bi·o·met·rics (bī′ə me′triks), *n.* (*construed as sing.*) **1.** *Biol.* the application of mathematical-statistical theory to biology. **2.** biometry (def. 1). —**bi′o·met′ric, bi′o·met′ri·cal,** *adj.* —**bi′o·met′ri·cal·ly,** *adv.*
bi·om·e·try (bī om′i trē), *n.* **1.** the calculation of the probable duration of human life. **2.** biometrics (def. 1).
Bi·on (bī′on), *n.* fl. c100 B.C., Greek pastoral poet.
bi·on·ic (bī on′ik), *adj.* **1.** utilizing electronic devices and mechanical parts to assist humans in performing extremely difficult or intricate tasks, as by supplementing or duplicating parts of the body: *The scientist used a bionic arm to examine the radioactive material.* **2.** *Informal.* having superhuman strength, or capacity.
bi·on·ics (bī on′iks), *n.* (*construed as sing.*) the study of how man and animals perform certain tasks and solve certain problems, and of the application of the findings to the design of computers and other electronic equipment. [BI- + (ELEC-TR)ON + -ICS]
bi·o·nom·ics (bī′ə nom′iks), *n.* (*construed as sing.*) ecology (def. 1). [BIONOM(Y) + -ICS] —**bi′o·nom′ic, bi′o·nom′i·cal,** *adj.* —**bi′o·nom′i·cal·ly,** *adv.* —**bi·on·o·mist** (bī on′ə mist), *n.*
bi·on·omy (bī on′ə mē), *n.* ecology.
bi·o·phys·ics (bī′ō fiz′iks), *n.* (*construed as sing.*) the branch of biology dealing with the study of biological structures and processes by means of the methods of physics. —**bi′o·phys′i·cal,** *adj.* —**bi′o·phys′i·cal·ly,** *adv.* —**bi·o·phys·i·cist** (bī′ō fiz′i sist), *n.*
bi·op·sy (bī′op sē), *n., pl.* **-sies.** *Med.* the excision for diagnostic study of a piece of tissue from a living body. [BI-[2] + *-opsy* < Gk *-opsia*] —**bi·op·tic** (bī op′tik), *adj.*
bi·o·rhythm (bī′ō rith′əm), *n.* an innate rhythm in certain biological processes of organisms that in humans can be charted in long-term (22- to 28-day) cycles of physical, emotional, and intellectual behavior.
bi·o·sci·ence (bī′ō sī′əns), *n.* any science that deals with the biological aspects of living organisms, esp. in outer space.
bi·o·scope (bī′ə skōp′), *n.* an early form of motion-picture projector, used about 1900.
bi·o·sen·sor (bī′ō sen′sər), *n.* a sensor designed to detect and transmit information about living organisms.
bi·o·sphere (bī′ə sfēr′), *n.* the part of the earth's crust, waters, and atmosphere where living organisms can subsist.
bi·o·stat·ics (bī′ō stat′iks), *n.* (*construed as sing.*) the branch of biology dealing with the structure of organisms in relation to their functions (opposed to *biodynamics*). —**bi′o·stat′ic, bi′o·stat′i·cal,** *adj.*
bi·o·syn·the·sis (bī′ō sin′thi sis), *n.* *Biochem.* the formation, by synthesis or degradation, of chemical compounds by a living organism. —**bi·o·syn·thet·ic** (bī′ō sin thet′ik), *adj.* —**bi′o·syn·thet′i·cal·ly,** *adv.*
bi·o·ta (bī ō′tə), *n.* *Ecol.* the animal and plant life of a region or period. [< NL < Gk *biotḗ* life]
bi·o·tech·nol·o·gy (bī′ō tek nol′ə jē), *n.* the study of the relationship between humans and machines, esp. in terms of physiological, psychological, and technological requirements. Cf. **psychotechnology.** —**bi·o·tech·no·log·i·cal** (bī′ō tek′nəloj′i kəl), *adj.* —**bi′o·tech′no·log′i·cal·ly,** *adv.*
bi·ot·ic (bī ot′ik), *adj.* pertaining to life. Also, **bi·ot′i·cal.** [< Gk *biōtik(ós)* of, pertaining to life]
biot′ic poten′tial, the capacity of a population of animals or plants to increase in numbers under optimum environmental conditions.
bi·o·tin (bī′ə tin), *n.* *Biochem.* a growth vitamin, $C_{10}H_{16}O_3N_2S$, of the vitamin-B complex; vitamin H. [*biot-* (< Gk *biotḗ* life) + -IN[2]]
bi·o·tite (bī′ə tīt′), *n.* a common mineral of the mica group, an important constituent of igneous rocks. [named after J. B. *Biot* (1774–1862), French mineralogist and mathematician; see -ITE[1]] —**bi·o·tit·ic** (bī′ə tit′ik), *adj.*
bi·o·type (bī′ə tīp′), *n.* *Biol.* a group of organisms having the same hereditary characteristics. —**bi′o·typ·ol′o·gy,** *n.* —**bi·o·typ·ic** (bī′ə tip′ik), *adj.*
bi·pa·ri·e·tal (bī′pə rī′i tᵊl), *adj.* *Anat.* of or pertaining to both parietal bones.
bip·a·rous (bip′ər əs), *adj.* **1.** *Zool.* bringing forth offspring in pairs. **2.** *Bot.* bearing two branches or axes.
bi·par·ti·san (bī pär′ti zən), *adj.* representing, characterized by, or including members from two parties or factions: *a bipartisan Congressional committee.* —**bi·par′ti·san·ism,** *n.* —**bi·par′ti·san·ship′,** *n.*
bi·par·tite (bī pär′tīt), *adj.* **1.** divided into or consisting of two parts. **2.** *Law.* being in two corresponding parts: *a bipartite contract.* **3.** shared by two; joint: *a bipartite pact.* **4.** *Bot.* divided into two parts nearly to the base, as a leaf. [< L *bipartīt(us)* divided into two parts] —**bi·par′tite·ly,** *adv.* —**bi·par·ti·tion** (bī′pär tish′ən), *n.*
bi·par·ty (bī′pär′tē), *adj.* of two distinct political parties, business groups, etc.: *biparty support of a bill in Congress.*
bi·ped (bī′ped), *Zool.* —*n.* **1.** a two-footed animal. —*adj.* **2.** having two feet. [< L *biped-* (s. of *bipēs*) two-footed]
bi·pe·dal (bī′ped′ᵊl, bip′i dᵊl), *adj.* biped.
bi·pet·al·ous (bī pet′ᵊləs), *adj.* *Bot.* having two petals.
bi·phen·yl (bī fen′ᵊl, -fēn′-), *n.* *Chem.* a crystalline powder $C_6H_5C_6H_5$, composed of two phenyl groups, from which benzidine dyes are derived. Also called **diphenyl.**
bi·pin·nate (bī pin′āt), *adj.* *Bot.* pinnate, as a leaf, with pinnate divisions. [< NL *bipinnāt(us)*] —**bi·pin′nate·ly,** *adv.*

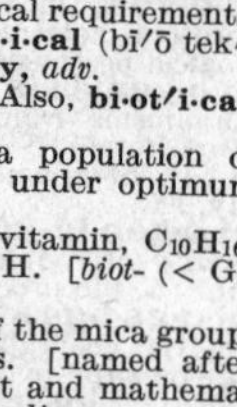

Bipinnate leaf

bi·plane (bī′plān′), *n.* an airplane with two sets of wings, one above and usually slightly forward of the other.
bi·pod (bī′pod), *n.* a two-legged support.
bi·po·lar (bī pō′lər), *adj.* **1.** having two poles, as the earth. **2.** pertaining to or found at both poles. —**bi·po·lar·i·ty** (bī′pō lar′i tē), *n.*
bi·pro·pel·lant (bī′prə pel′ənt), *n.* *Rocketry.* a missile or rocket propellant, composed of fuel and oxidizer, the components of which are kept in separate compartments prior to combustion.
bi·quad·rate (bī kwod′rāt, -rit), *n.* *Math.* the fourth power.
bi·quad·rat·ic (bī′kwo drat′ik), *adj.* **1.** *Math.* involving the fourth, but no higher, power of the unknown or variable. —*n.* **2.** quartic (def. 2). **3.** biquadrate.
bi·quar·ter·ly (bī kwôr′tər lē), *adj.* occurring twice in each quarter of a year.
bi·ra·cial (bī rā′shəl), *adj.* representing, characterized by, or including members from two separate races, esp. white and black: *a biracial committee on neighborhood problems.* —**bi·ra′cial·ism,** *n.*
bi·ra·di·al (bī rā′dē əl), *adj.* having both bilateral and radial symmetry, as ctenophores.
bi·ra·mous (bī rā′məs), *adj.* consisting of or divided into two branches. Also, **bi·ra·mose** (bī rā′mōs, bī′rə mōs′).
birch (bûrch), *n.* **1.** any tree or shrub of the genus *Betula,* comprising species with a smooth, laminated outer bark and close-grained wood. **2.** the wood itself. **3.** a birch rod, or a bundle of birch twigs, used as a whip. —*adj.* **4.** birchen. —*v.t.* **5.** to beat with or as with a birch. [ME *birche*]
birch′ beer′, a carbonated or fermented drink containing an extract from the bark of the birch tree. Cf. **root beer.**
birch·en (bûr′chən), *adj.* **1.** of or pertaining to birch. **2.** made or consisting of birch: *birchen furniture.* [late ME]
bird (bûrd), *n.* **1.** any warm-blooded vertebrate of the class *Aves,* having a body covered with feathers and forelimbs modified into wings. **2.** *Sports.* **a.** a game bird. **b.** See **clay pigeon. c.** a shuttlecock. **3.** *Slang.* a person, esp. one having some peculiarity: *He's a queer bird.* **4.** *Informal.* an airplane, guided missile, or spacecraft. **5.** *Chiefly Brit. Slang.* a girl. **6.** *Archaic.* the young of any fowl. **7. birds of a feather,** people with interests, opinions, or backgrounds in common: *Birds of a feather flock together.* **8. eat like a bird,** to eat sparingly. **9. for the birds,** *Slang.* contemptible or ridiculous: *Their opinions on art are for the birds.* **10. give (someone) the bird,** *Slang.* to disapprove of; scoff at; ridicule: *He was trying to be serious, but we all gave him the bird.* —*v.i.* **11.** to catch or shoot birds. **12.** to observe birds in their natural habitats. [ME *byrd, bryd,* OE *brid(d)* young bird, chick < ?] —**bird′like′,** *adj.*

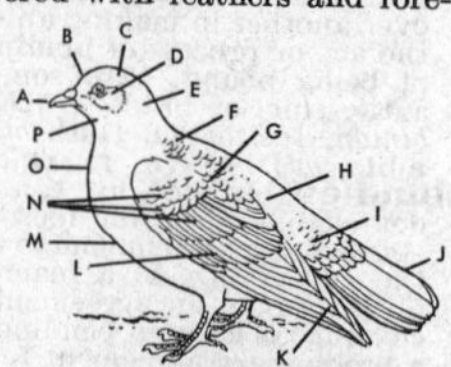

Bird (pigeon)
A, Bill; B, Forehead; C, Crown; D, Ear opening covered by feathers; E, Nape; F, Back; G, Scapulars; H, Rump; I, Upper tail coverts; J, Tail; K, Primary feathers; L, Secondary feathers; M, Abdomen; N, Coverts; O, Breast; P, Throat

bird·bath (bûrd′bath′, -bäth′), *n., pl.* **-baths** (-baṯhz′, -bäṯhz′, -baths, -bäths). a basin or tublike garden ornament for birds to drink from or bathe in.
bird·brain (bûrd′brān′), *n.* *Slang.* a dolt or scatterbrain. —**bird′brained′,** *adj.*
bird·cage (bûrd′kāj′), *n.* a small, usually portable, cage for confining pet birds. [ME]
bird′ call′, **1.** a sound made by a bird. **2.** a sound imitating that of a bird. **3.** a device for making such a sound.
bird′ dog′, one of any of various breeds of dogs trained to hunt or retrieve birds.
bird·er (bûr′dər), *n.* **1.** a person who hunts or raises birds. **2.** See **bird watcher.**
bird-foot (bûrd′fo͝ot′), *n., pl.* **-foots.** bird's-foot.
bird′ grass′, **1.** a grass, *Poa trivialis,* grown in temperate regions of North America largely for lawns and turf. **2.** the knotgrass, *Polygonum aviculare.*
bird·house (bûrd′hous′), *n., pl.* **-hous·es** (-hou′ziz). **1.** a box, usually fashioned to resemble a house, for birds to live in. **2.** an aviary.
bird·ie (bûr′dē), *n., v.,* **bird·ied, bird·ie·ing.** —*n.* **1.** a small bird. **2.** *Golf.* a score of one stroke under par on a hole. —*v.t.* **3.** *Golf.* to make a birdie on (a hole).
bird·lime (bûrd′līm′), *n., v.,* **-limed, -lim·ing.** —*n.* **1.** a sticky material prepared from holly, mistletoe, or other plants, and smeared on twigs to catch small birds that light on it. —*v.t.* **2.** to smear or catch with or as with birdlime. [late ME *brydelyme*]
bird·man (bûrd′man′, -mən), *n., pl.* **-men** (-men′, -mən). **1.** a person who keeps or tends birds. **2.** a person who hunts birds. **3.** an ornithologist. **4.** *Informal.* aviator.
bird′ of par′adise, any of several passerine birds of the family *Paradisaeidae,* of New Guinea and adjacent islands, the males of which have ornate, colorful plumage.
bird′ of pas′sage, a bird that migrates seasonally.
bird′ of prey′, any of numerous predacious, flesh-eating birds, as the eagles, hawks, vultures, etc.
bird′ pep′per, a variety of pepper, *Capsicum frutescens,* with small, elongated berries.
bird·seed (bûrd′sēd′), *n.* a small seed, esp. that of a grass, *Phalaris canariensis,* or mixture of small seeds, used as food for birds.
bird's-eye (bûrdz′ī′), *adj., n., pl.* **-eyes.** —*adj.* **1.** seen from above, as by a bird in flight; panoramic: *a bird's-eye view of the city.* **2.** lacking in details; hasty, superficial, or general: *a bird's-eye view of ancient history.* **3.** having spots or markings resembling birds' eyes: *bird's-eye tweed.* —*n.* **4.** any of various plants having small, round, bright-colored flowers, as a primrose, *Primula farinosa,* or the germander speedwell, *Veronica Chamaedrys.* **5.** *Textiles.* **a.** a woven, allover pattern on fabrics, having diamond shapes resembling the eye of a bird. **b.** a fabric having this pattern.
bird's′-eye ma′ple, a cut of sugar-maple wood used esp. for veneers, having a wavy grain with many dark, circular markings.
bird's-foot (bûrdz′fo͝ot′), *n., pl.* **-foots. 1.** any of various plants whose leaves, flowers, or pods resemble or suggest the foot or claw of a bird, esp. leguminous plants of the genus *Ornithopus,* which have clawlike pods. **2.** any similar plant, esp. bird's-foot trefoil. Also, **bird-foot.**
bird's′-foot tre′foil, a fabaceous plant, *Lotus corniculatus,* the legumes of which spread like a crow's foot.

bird's'-foot vi'olet, *Bot.* a violet, *Viola pedata,* having large, light-blue or whitish flowers with yellow centers: the state flower of Wisconsin.

bird' shot', small-sized shot used for shooting birds.

bird-watch (bûrd'woch'), *v.i.* to note and study the appearance, activities, etc., of wild birds.

bird' watch'er, a person who bird-watches.

bi·re·frin·gence (bī'ri frin'jəns), *n.* See **double refraction.** —**bi're·frin'gent,** *adj.*

bi·reme (bī'rēm), *n.* a galley having two banks or tiers of oars. [< L *birēm(is)* two-oared, having two banks of oars = *bi-* BI-[1] + *rēm(us)* oar + *-is* adj. suffix]

bi·ret·ta (bə ret'ə), *n.* *Rom. Cath. Ch.* a stiff square cap with three or four upright projecting pieces, worn by the clergy. [< It *berretta* < OPr *berret* < ML *birrett(um)* cap = LL *birr(us)* hooded cape + *-ettum* -ET]

Biretta

Birk·beck (bûrk'bek), *n.* **George,** 1776–1841, English physician and educator.

Bir·ken·head (bûr'kən hed', bûr'kən hed'), *n.* a seaport in NW Cheshire, in W England, on the Mersey River. 141,683 (1961).

birl (bûrl), *v.t.* **1.** *Lumbering.* to rotate (a floating log) rapidly by treading upon it. —*v.i.* **2.** *Lumbering.* to rotate a floating log rapidly by treading on it. **3.** *Brit.* **a.** to rotate rapidly; spin. **b.** *Informal.* to spend money freely. **c.** *Informal.* to gamble. [? special use of dial. *birle* to pour a drink, carouse (ME *birlen,* OE *byrelian* < *byrele* butler; akin to BEAR[1]), by assoc. with words of like sound, as WHIRL]

birl·ing (bûr'ling), *n.* a competitive game played by two lumberjacks, in which the winner keeps his balance longer as he stands on a floating log and rotates it with his feet. [ME *birlynge*]

Bir·ming·ham (bûr'ming əm *for 1;* bûr'ming ham' *for 2, 3*), *n.* **1.** a city in NW Warwickshire, in central England. 1,105,651 (1961). **2.** a city in central Alabama. 300,910 (1970). **3.** a city in SE Michigan, near Detroit. 26,170 (1970).

Bi·ro·bi·zhan (bir'ō bi jän'), *n.* **1.** Official name, **Jewish Autonomous Region.** an administrative division of the RSFSR, in E Siberia, in the SE Soviet Union in Asia. 198,000; 14,085 sq. mi. **2.** a city in and the capital of this division, on the Amur River. 62,000. Also, **Bi'ro·bi·jan', Bi'ro·bi·dzhan'.**

birr (bûr), *n.* **1.** force, energy, or vigor. **2.** emphasis in statement, speech, etc. **3.** a whirring sound. —*v.i.* **4.** to move with or make a whirring sound. [ME *bire, bur,* OE *byre* strong wind; c. Icel *byrr* favorable wind; akin to BEAR[1]]

birse (bûrs; *Scot.* birs), *n.* *Scot.* **1.** a bristle. **2.** a short hair of the beard or body. **3.** anger; rage. [OE *byrst;* c. OHG *borst, burst,* Icel *burst*]

birth (bûrth), *n.* **1.** fact or act of being born: *the day of his birth.* **2.** act of bearing offspring; childbirth. **3.** lineage, extraction, or descent: *of Grecian birth.* **4.** high or noble lineage. **5.** supposedly natural heritage: *a musician by birth.* **6.** any coming into existence; origin: *the birth of jazz.* **7.** *Archaic.* a thing that is born. **8. give birth to, a.** to bear as an offspring. **b.** to originate. [ME *byrth(e)* < Scand; cf. ON *byrth,* c. OE *gebyrd,* OHG *(gi)burt,* Goth *(ga)baurth(s)*] —**Syn. 3.** parentage, ancestry, blood, race.

birth' certif'icate, an official form recording the birth of a baby, noting name, sex, date, place, parents' names, and the like.

birth' control', regulation of the number of one's children through the restriction of ovulation or conception. —**birth'-control',** *adj.*

birth'-control' pill', an oral contraceptive for women that inhibits ovulation, fertilization, or implantation of a fertilized ovum, causing temporary infertility.

birth·day (bûrth'dā'), *n.* **1.** the anniversary of a person's birth or of the date of origin of something. **2.** the day of a person's birth or the date marking the origin of something. [ME]

birth'day suit', *Informal.* bare skin; nakedness.

birth·mark (bûrth'märk'), *n.* a mark or blemish on a person's skin at birth.

birth·place (bûrth'plās'), *n.* place of birth or origin.

birth' rate', the proportion of the number of births in a place in a given time to the total population, usually expressed as a quantity per 1000 of population.

birth·right (bûrth'rīt'), *n.* any right or privilege to which a person is entitled by birth.

birth·root (bûrth'ro͞ot', -ro͝ot'), *n.* **1.** a trillium, *Trillium erectum,* the roots of which are used in medicine. **2.** any of certain other species of trillium.

birth·stone (bûrth'stōn'), *n.* a precious or semiprecious stone traditionally considered appropriate for wear by persons born within a particular month or sign of the zodiac and believed to be lucky.

birth·wort (bûrth'wûrt'), *n.* **1.** a plant, *Aristolochia Clematitis,* native to Europe, reputed to facilitate childbirth. **2.** any of certain other species of the same genus. **3.** the birthroot.

bis (bis), *adv.* **1.** twice. **2.** a second time. —*interj.* **3.** encore (def. 1). [< It < L; OL *duis* TWICE]

Bi·sa·yan (bē sä'yən), *n., pl.* **-yans,** (*esp. collectively*) **-yan.** Visayan.

Bi·sa·yas (bē sä'yäs), *n.pl.* Spanish name of the **Visayan Islands.**

Bis·cay (bis'kā, -kē), *n.* **Bay of,** a bay of the Atlantic between W France and N Spain.

Bis'cayne Bay' (bis'kān, bis kān'), an inlet of the Atlantic Ocean, on the SE coast of Florida, separating the cities of Miami and Miami Beach.

bis·cuit (bis'kit), *n.* **1.** *U.S.* a kind of bread in small, soft cakes, raised with baking powder or soda. **2.** *Brit.* **a.** a cookie. **b.** a cracker. **3.** Also called **bisque.** *Ceram.* unglazed earthenware or porcelain after firing. [ME *bysquyte* < MF *biscuit* (ML *biscoctus*), var. of *bescuit* seamen's bread, lit., twice cooked = *bes* BIS + *cuit,* ptp. of *cuire* < L *coquere* to COOK]

bis'cuit torto'ni, an individual portion of tortoni, frozen and served in a small cup, often topped with minced almonds.

bise (bēz), *n.* a dry, cold north or northeast wind in SE France, Switzerland, and adjoining regions. Also, **bize.** [ME < OF < Gmc, cf. OHG *bīsa* north wind]

bi·sect (bī sekt', bī'sekt), *v.t.* **1.** to cut or divide into two approximately equal parts. **2.** *Geom.* to cut or divide into two equal parts, as an angle. **3.** to intersect or cross: *The railroad bridge bisects the highway.* —*v.i.* **4.** to split into two, as a road; fork or divide. —**bi·sec'tion,** *n.* —**bi·sec'tion·al,** *adj.* —**bi·sec'tion·al·ly,** *adv.*

bi·sec·tor (bī sek'tər, bī'sek-), *n.* *Geom.* a line or plane that bisects an angle or line segment.

bi·sec·trix (bī sek'triks), *n., pl.* **bi·sec·tri·ces** (bī'sek trī'sēz). **1.** *Crystall.* an imaginary line bisecting either the acute angle or the obtuse angle of the optic axes of a biaxial crystal. **2.** *Geom.* a bisector. [BISEC(TOR) + -TRIX]

bi·ser·rate (bī ser'āt, -it), *adj.* *Bot.* notched like a saw, with the teeth also notched.

bi·sex·u·al (bī sek'sho͞o əl), *adj.* **1.** *Biol.* **a.** of both sexes. **b.** combining male and female organs in one individual; hermaphroditic. **2.** *Psychiatry.* sexually responsive to both sexes. —*n.* **3.** *Biol.* a hermaphrodite. **4.** *Psychiatry.* a person sexually responsive to both sexes. —**bi·sex'u·al·ism, bi'sex·u·al'i·ty,** *n.* —**bi·sex'u·al·ly,** *adv.*

bish·op (bish'əp), *n., v.,* **-oped, -op·ing.** —*n.* **1.** a prelate who oversees a number of local churches or a diocese, being in the Orthodox, Roman Catholic, Anglican, and other churches a member of the highest order in the priesthood. **2.** a spiritual supervisor, overseer, or the like. **3.** *Chess.* one of two pieces of the same color that may be moved any unobstructed distance diagonally. —*v.t.* **4.** to appoint to the office of bishop. [ME, OE *bisc(e)op* < VL **(e)biscop(us),* for LL *episcopus* < Gk *epískopos* overseer = *epi-* EPI- + *skopós* watcher]

Bish·op (bish'əp), *n.* **1. Elizabeth,** 1911–79, U.S. poet. **2. John Peale,** 1892–1944, U.S. poet and essayist.

bish·op·ric (bish'əp rik), *n.* the see, diocese, or office of a bishop. [ME *bisshoprike,* OE *biscoprīce* = *biscop* BISHOP + *rīce* realm; see RICH]

bish·op's-cap (bish'əps kap'), *n.* miterwort (def. 1).

Bi·si·tun (bē'si to͞on'), *n.* Behistun.

bisk (bisk), *n.* bisque[1].

Bisk (bēsk), *n.* a city in the S RSFSR, in the S Soviet Union in Asia, near the Ob River. 214,000. Also, **Biisk, Biysk.**

Bis·kra (bis'krä), *n.* a town and oasis in NE Algeria, in the Sahara. 52,511 (1954).

Bis·marck (biz'märk; *for 1 also Ger.* bis'märk), *n.* **1. Ot·to von** (ot'ō von; *Ger.* ô'tō fən), 1815–98, German statesman: first chancellor of modern German Empire 1871–90. **2.** a city in and the capital of N Dakota, in the central part. 34,703 (1970).

Bis'marck Archipel'ago, a group of islands in the SW Pacific NE of New Guinea, including the Admiralty Islands, New Britain, New Ireland, and adjacent islands: under Australian administration. ab. 23,000 sq. mi.

Bis'marck her'ring, salted fillet and roe of herring, pickled in vinegar, white wine, and spices, served cold as an hors d'oeuvre.

bis·muth (biz'məth), *n.* *Chem.* a metallic element used in the manufacture of fusible alloys and in medicine. *Symbol:* Bi; *at. no.:* 83; *at. wt.:* 208.980. [earlier *bismut(um)* < NL *bisemūtum,* Latinized form of G *Wissmuth* (now *Wismut*) < ?] —**bis'muth·al,** *adj.*

bis·mu·thic (biz myo͞o'thik, -muth'ik), *adj.* *Chem.* of or containing bismuth, esp. in the pentavalent state.

bis·muth·in·ite (biz muth'ə nīt', biz'mə thə-), *n.* a mineral, bismuth sulfide, Bi_2S_3, an ore of bismuth. Also called **bis'muth glance'.** [BISMUTH + -INE[2] + -ITE[1]]

bis·muth·ous (biz'mə thəs), *adj.* *Chem.* containing trivalent bismuth.

bis'muth oxychlo'ride, *Chem.* a water-insoluble powder, BiOCl, used chiefly in the manufacture of pigments, face powders, and artificial pearls.

Bison, *Bison bison* (7 ft. high at shoulder; total length to 12 ft.; tail 1½ ft.)

bi·son (bī'sən, -zən), *n., pl.* **-son.** **1.** a North American, oxlike ruminant, *Bison bison,* having a large head and high, humped shoulders. **2.** Also called **wisent.** a related animal, *Bison bonasus,* of Europe, larger and less shaggy than the American bison. [ME *bisontes* (pl.) < L (nom. sing. *bison*) < Gmc; cf. OHG *wisunt,* OE *wesend,* Icel *visundr*]

bisque[1] (bisk), *n.* **1.** a heavy cream soup of puréed shellfish, game, or vegetables. **2.** ice cream made with powdered macaroons or nuts. Also, **bisk.** [< F]

bisque[2] (bisk), *n.* *Sports.* a point, extra turn, or the like, as in court tennis or croquet. [< F]

bisque[3] (bisk), *n.* biscuit (def. 3). [short for BISCUIT]

Bis·sau (bi sou'), *n.* a seaport in and the capital of Guinea-Bissau, in the W part. 75,000. Also, **Bis·são** (bē soun').

bis·sex·tile (bī seks'til, bi-), *adj.* **1.** containing or noting the extra day of leap year. —*n.* **2.** See **leap year.** [< LL *bi(s)sextil(is)* (*annus*) leap year = *bissext(us)* BISSEXTUS + *-ilis* -ILE]

bis·sex·tus (bī seks'təs, bi-), *n.* February twenty-ninth: the extra day added to the Julian calendar every fourth year (except for centenary years not evenly divisible by 400) to compensate for the approximately six hours a year by which the common year of 365 days falls short of the solar year. [< LL *bissextus* (*diēs*) intercalary (day); see BIS, SEXT; so called because the 6th day before the Calends of March (Feb. 24th) appeared twice every leap year]

bis·tort (bis′tôrt), *n.* **1.** Also called **snakeweed.** a European perennial herb, *Polygonum Bistorta,* having a twisted root, which is sometimes used as an astringent. **2.** any of several related plants, as *P. virginianum* (**Virgin′ia bis′tort**) and *P. viviparum* (**al′pine bis′tort**). [< ML *bistort(a)* twice twisted. See BIS, TORT]

bis·tre (bis′tər), *n.* **1.** a brown pigment extracted from the soot of wood, much used in pen and wash drawings. **2.** a yellowish to dark-brown color. Also, **bis′ter.** [< F] —**bis′tred, bis′tered,** *adj.*

bis·tro (bis′trō; *Fr.* bē strō′), *n., pl.* **bis·tros** (bis′trōz; *Fr.* bē strō′). *Informal.* **1.** a small, unpretentious tavern or café. **2.** a small night club or restaurant. [< F]

bi·sul·cate (bī sul′kāt), *adj.* **1.** with two grooves. **2.** cloven-hoofed. [< L *bisulc(us)* two-furrowed, cloven (see BI-[1], SULCUS) + -ATE[1]]

bi·sul·fate (bī sul′fāt), *n. Chem.* a salt of sulfuric acid, containing the HSO_4^- group; an acid sulfate; a hydrogen sulfate, as sodium bisulfate, $NaHSO_4$. Also, **bi·sul′phate.**

bi·sul·fide (bī sul′fīd, -fid), *n. Chem.* a disulfide. Also, **bi·sul′phide.**

bi·sul·fite (bī sul′fīt), *n. Chem.* a salt of sulfurous acid, containing the HSO_3^- group; an acid sulfite; a hydrogen sulfite, as sodium bisulfite, $NaHSO_3$. Also, **bi·sul′phite.**

Bi·su·tun (bē′sə to͞on′), *n.* Behistun.

bi·sym·met·ri·cal (bī′si me′tri kəl), *adj. Bot.* having two planes of symmetry at right angles to each other. Also, **bi′sym·met′ric.** —**bi′sym·met′ri·cal·ly,** *adv.* —**bi·sym·me·try** (bī sim′i trē), *n.*

bit[1] (bit), *n., v.,* **bit·ted, bit·ting.** —*n.* **1.** the mouthpiece of a bridle. **2.** something that curbs or restrains. **3.** *Mach.* **a.** a removable drilling or boring tool for use in a brace, drill press, or the like. **b.** a removable boring head used on certain kinds of drills, as a rock drill. **c.** a device for drilling oil wells or the like. **4.** the cutting part of an ax or hatchet. **5.** the wide portion at the end of an ordinary key that moves the bolt. **6. take the bit in** or **between one's teeth,** to cast off control; rebel: *He took the bit in his teeth and acted against his parents' wishes.* —*v.t.* **7.** to put a bit in the mouth of (a horse). **8.** to curb or restrain with or as with a bit. **9.** to grind a bit on (a key). [ME *bite,* OE: action of biting; c. G *Biss,* Icel *bit;* akin to BITE]

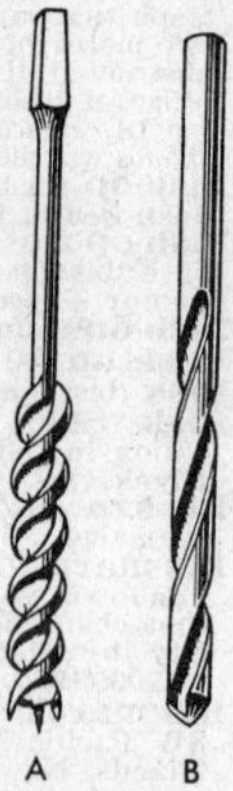

A B

Bits[1] (def. 3a)
A, Auger bit;
B, Straight shank drill bit

bit[2] (bit), *n.* **1.** a small piece or quantity of anything. **2.** a short time: *Wait a bit.* **3.** *U.S. Slang.* **a.** an amount equivalent to 12½ cents (used only in even multiples): *two bits.* **b.** an act, performance, or routine: *She's doing the Camille bit.* **4.** Also called **bit part.** a very small role, as in a play or motion picture. Cf. **walk-on. 5.** any small coin. **6.** a Spanish or Mexican silver real worth 12½ cents, formerly current in parts of the U.S. **7. bit by bit,** by degrees; gradually. **8. do one's bit,** *Informal.* to contribute one's share to an effort. [ME *bite,* OE *bita* bit, morsel; c. G *Bissen,* Icel *biti;* akin to BITE] —**Syn. 1.** particle, mite; piece; jot, fragment.

bit[3] (bit), *n.* a single, basic unit of information, used in connection with computers and communication theory. [B(INARY + DIG)IT]

bit[4] (bit), *v.* pt. and a pp. of **bite.**

bi·tar·trate (bī tär′trāt), *n. Chem.* a tartrate in which only one of the two acidic hydrogen atoms of tartaric acid is replaced by a metal or positive group; an acid tartrate; a hydrogen tartrate, as sodium bitartrate, $NaHC_4H_4O_6$.

bitch (bich), *n.* **1.** a female dog. **2.** a female of canines generally. **3.** *Slang.* **a.** a malicious, unpleasant, selfish woman. **b.** a lewd woman. **4.** *Slang.* **a.** a complaint. **b.** anything difficult or unpleasant. —*v.i.* **5.** *Slang.* to complain or gripe: *He bitched about the slow service.* [ME *bicche,* OE *bicce;* c. Icel *bikkja*]

bitch·y (bich′ē), *adj.,* **bitch·i·er, bitch·i·est.** *Slang.* pertaining to or characteristic of a bitch; spiteful; malicious. —**bitch′i·ness,** *n.*

bite (bīt), *v.,* **bit, bit·ten** or **bit, bit·ing,** *n.* —*v.t.* **1.** to cut, wound, or tear with the teeth. **2.** to grip or hold with the teeth: *Stop biting your thumb!* **3.** to sting, as an insect. **4.** to cause to smart or sting: *An icy wind bit our faces.* **5.** to sever with the teeth (often fol. by *off*). **6.** to sink one's teeth into; start to eat: *He bit the apple hungrily.* **7.** to eat into or corrode, as an acid does. **8.** to cut or pierce with or as with a weapon: *The sword bit him fatally.* **9.** *Etching.* to etch with acid (a copper or other surface) in such parts as are left bare of a protective coating. **10.** to take firm hold or act effectively on: *We need a clamp to bite the wood while the glue dries.* **11.** *Slang.* **a.** to take advantage of; cheat or deceive (sometimes used passively): *I got bitten in a mail-order swindle.* **b.** to annoy or upset; anger: *What's biting you, sorehead?* **12.** *Archaic.* to make a decided impression on; affect. —*v.i.* **13.** to press the teeth into something; attack with the jaws, bill, sting, etc.; snap: *Does your parrot bite?* **14.** *Angling.* (of fish) to take bait: *The fish aren't biting today.* **15.** to accept an offer or suggestion, esp. one intended to trick or deceive: *I knew it was a trick, but I bit anyway.* **16.** to admit defeat in guessing: *I'll bite, who is it?* **17.** to act effectively; grip; hold: *This wood is so dry the screws don't bite.* **18. bite someone's head off,** to respond with anger or impatience to someone's question or comment. **19. bite the dust.** See **dust** (def. 14). **20. bite the hand that feeds one,** to repay kindness with malice or injury. —*n.* **21.** act of biting. **22.** a wound made by a bite or sting. **23.** a cutting, stinging, or nipping effect: *the bite of an icy wind.* **24.** sharpness; incisiveness; effectiveness: *The bite of his story is spoiled by his slovenly style.* **25.** a piece bitten off. **26.** *Slang.* an exacted portion: *the government's weekly bite of my paycheck.* **27.** a morsel of food: *not a bite to eat.* **28.** a small meal: *Let's grab a bite before the theater.* **29.** *Mach.* **a.** the catch or hold that one object or one part of a mechanical apparatus has on another. **b.** a surface brought into contact to obtain a hold or grip, as in a lathe, chuck, or similar device. **30.** the roughness of the surface of a file. **31.** the occlusion of one's teeth: *The dentist said I had a good bite.* **32. put the bite on,** *Slang.* to solicit or attempt to borrow or extort money from. [ME *bite(n),* OE *bītan;* c. OHG *bīzan* (G *beissen*), Goth *beitan,* Icel *bīta;* akin to L *findere* to split] —**bit′a·ble, bite′a·ble,** *adj.* —**Syn. 1.** gnaw, nip. **25.** mouthful, morsel. **28.** snack.

bit·er (bī′tər), *n.* **1.** a person or thing that bites. **2.** an animal that bites or snaps at people habitually. **3.** *Obs.* a cheat; swindler; fraud. [ME]

bit′ gauge′, *Carpentry.* a device for stopping a bit when it has reached the desired depth. Also called **bit′ stop′.**

Bi·thyn·i·a (bi thin′ē ə), *n.* an ancient country in NW Asia Minor. —**Bi·thyn′i·an,** *adj., n.*

bit·ing (bī′ting), *adj.* **1.** nipping; smarting; keen: *biting cold; a biting sensation on the tongue.* **2.** cutting or sarcastic: *a biting remark; a biting essay on politics.* [ME *bitynge*] —**bit′ing·ly,** *adv.* —**bit′ing·ness,** *n.* —**Syn. 2.** incisive, trenchant; caustic, mordant.

bit′ing midge′, punkie.

bit′ part′, bit[2] (def. 4).

bit·stock (bit′stok′), *n. Mach.* the handle by which a boring bit is rotated; brace.

bitt (bit), *Naut.* —*n.* **1.** a strong post of wood or iron projecting, usually in pairs, above the deck of a ship, used for securing cables, lines for towing, etc. **2.** bollard (def. 1). —*v.t.* **3.** to wrap (a cable) around a bitt or bitts to secure it. [var. of BIT[1]]

bit·te (bit′ə), *interj. German.* **1.** please. **2.** I beg your pardon. **3.** you're welcome; don't mention it. [short for *ich bitte* I beg]

bit·ten (bit′ən), *v.* a pp. of **bite.**

bit·ter (bit′ər), *adj.* **1.** having a harsh, acrid taste. **2.** producing one of the four basic taste sensations; not sour, sweet, or salt. **3.** hard to admit or accept: *a bitter lesson.* **4.** hard to bear; grievous: *a bitter sorrow.* **5.** piercing or stinging: *a bitter chill.* **6.** characterized by intense hostility: *bitter hatred.* **7.** sarcastic or cutting: *bitter words.* —*n.* **8.** that which is bitter; bitterness. —*v.t.* **9.** to make bitter: *Herbs were used to bitter the wine.* —*adv.* **10.** extremely; very: *a bitter cold night.* [ME, OE *biter;* c. G *bitter,* Icel *bitr,* Goth *baitr(s);* akin to BITE] —**bit′ter·ish,** *adj.* —**bit′ter·ly,** *adv.* —**bit′ter·ness,** *n.* —**Syn. 1.** acrid, biting. **4.** painful. **5.** biting, nipping. **6.** fierce, relentless. **7.** caustic, sardonic.

bit·ter end (bit′ər end′ *for 1;* bit′ər end′ *for 2*), **1.** the conclusion of a difficult or unpleasant situation; the last or furthest extremity: *It was a dull movie, but we stayed to the bitter end.* **2.** *Naut.* **a.** the inboard end of an anchor chain or cable, secured in the chain locker of a vessel. **b.** the end of any chain or cable.

Bit′ter Lakes′, two lakes in the NE United Arab Republic, forming part of the Suez Canal.

bit·tern[1] (bit′ərn), *n.* **1.** any of several tawny brown herons that inhabit reedy marshes, as *Botaurus lentiginosus* of North America and *B. stellaris,* of Europe. **2.** any of several small herons of the genus *Ixobrychus,* as *I. exilis,* of temperate and tropical North and South America. [earlier *bittorn* = ME *bitor* (var. of *botor* < MF *butor*) + *-n* < ?]

Bittern,
Botaurus lentiginosus
(Length 2½ ft.; wingspread 3 ft.)

bit·tern[2] (bit′ərn), *n. Chem.* a bitter solution remaining in saltmaking after the salt has crystallized out of sea water or brine, used as a commercial source of bromides, iodides, and certain other salts. [var. of *bittering*]

bit′ter or′ange. See under **orange** (def. 2).

bit′ter prin′ciple, *Chem.* any of several hundred natural, chemically unclassified compounds, usually of vegetable origin, having a bitter taste.

bit·ter·root (bit′ər ro͞ot′, -ro͝ot′), *n.* a portulacaceous plant, *Lewisia rediviva,* having fleshy roots and handsome pink flowers: the state flower of Montana.

Bit′terroot Range′, a mountain range on the boundary between Idaho and Montana: highest peak, ab. 10,000 ft. Also, **Bit′ter Root′ Range′.**

bit·ters (bit′ərz), *n.* (*construed as pl.*) **1.** a liquid, often an alcoholic liquor, in which bitter herbs or roots have steeped, used as a flavoring, esp. in mixed drinks, or as a tonic. **2.** *Brit.* a very dry ale having a strong taste of hops. **3.** *Pharm.* **a.** a liquid, usually alcoholic, impregnated with a bitter medicine, as gentian, quassia, etc., used as a stomachic, tonic, or the like. **b.** bitter medicinal substances in general, as quinine, gentian, etc.

bit·ter·sweet (*n.* bit′ər swēt′; *adj.* bit′ər swēt′), *n.* **1.** a climbing or trailing solanaceous plant, *Solanum Dulcamara,* having scarlet berries. **2.** any climbing plant of the genus *Celastrus,* bearing orange capsules opening to expose red-coated seeds, esp. *Celastrus scandens.* **3.** pleasure mingled with pain or regret. —*adj.* **4.** both bitter and sweet to the taste: *bittersweet chocolate.* **5.** both pleasant and painful: *a bittersweet memory.*

bit·ter·weed (bit′ər wēd′), *n.* **1.** a plant containing a bitter principle, as the ragweed. **2.** any sneezeweed of the genus *Helenium,* esp. *H. tenuifolium.*

bit′ter wood′, *Pharm.* quassia (def. 2).

bit·ting (bit′ing), *n.* one of the indentations on the bit of a key.

bi·tu·men (bī to͞o′mən, -tyo͞o′-, bi-, bich′o͞o-), *n.* **1.** any of various natural substances, as asphalt, maltha, gilsonite, etc., consisting mainly of hydrocarbons. **2.** (formerly) an asphalt of Asia Minor used as cement and mortar. [late ME *bithumen* < L *bitūmen*] —**bi·tu·mi·noid** (bī to͞o′mə noid′, -tyo͞o′-, bi-), *adj.*

bi·tu·mi·nise (bī to͞o′mə nīz′, -tyo͞o′-, bi-), *v.t.,* **-nised, -nis·ing.** *Chiefly Brit.* bituminize. —**bi·tu′mi·ni·sa′tion,** *n.*

bi·tu·mi·nize (bī to͞o′mə nīz′, -tyo͞o′-, bi-), *v.t.,* **-nized, -niz·ing.** to convert into or treat with bitumen. [< L *bitūmin-* (s. of *bitūmen*) + -IZE] —**bi·tu′mi·ni·za′tion,** *n.*

bi·tu·mi·nous (bī to͞o′mə nəs, -tyo͞o′-, bi-), *adj.* resembling or containing bitumen: *bituminous shale.* [< L *bitūminōs(us)* = *bitūmin-* (s. of *bitūmen*) + *-ōsus* -OUS]

bitu′minous coal′, a mineral coal that contains volatile hydrocarbons and tarry matter, and burns with a yellow, smoky flame; soft coal. Cf. **anthracite.**

bi·va·lent (bī vā′lənt, biv′ə-), *adj.* **1.** *Chem.* **a.** having a valence of two. **b.** having two valences, as aluminum with valences of two and three. **2.** *Genetics.* pertaining to associations of two similar or identical chromosomes. **—***n.* **3.** *Genetics.* a pair of bivalent chromosomes. **—bi·va·lence** (bī vā′ləns, biv′ə-), **bi·va′len·cy,** *n.*

bi·valve (bī′valv′), *n.* **1.** *Zool.* a mollusk having two shells hinged together, as the oyster, clam, or mussel; a lamellibranch. **—***adj.* **2.** Also, **bi′valved′.** *Bot.* having two valves, as a seedcase. **3.** *Zool.* having two shells, usually united by a hinge.

bi·vi·nyl (bī vī′nil, -vīn′əl, -vin′il, -vin′əl), *n.* butadiene.

biv·ou·ac (biv′o͞o ak′, biv′wak), *n., v.,* **-acked, -ack·ing.** **—***n.* **1.** a military encampment made with tents or improvised shelters, usually without shelter or protection from enemy fire. **—***v.i.* **2.** to rest or assemble in such an area. [< F < dial. G *Biwache* night watch (lit. by-watch)]

bi·week·ly (bī wēk′lē), *adj., n., pl.* **-lies,** *adv.* **—***adj.* **1.** occurring every two weeks. **2.** (loosely) occurring twice a week; semiweekly. **—***n.* **3.** a periodical issued every other week. **—***adv.* **4.** every two weeks: *Our club meets biweekly.* **5.** (loosely) twice a week.
—Usage. Since it is not always clear which meaning of BIWEEKLY is intended—"twice a week" or "every two weeks"—the use of SEMIWEEKLY for "twice a week" is preferable because it is unambiguous. Since there is no single, unambiguous term for "every two weeks," this phrase itself is the least confusing to use.

bi·year·ly (bī yēr′lē), *adj.* **1.** biennial (defs. 1, 2). **—***adv.* **2.** biennially; biannually. **3.** (loosely) twice yearly.

Bi·ysk (bē′isk), *n.* Bisk.

bi·zarre (bi zär′), *adj.* markedly unusual, esp. whimsically strange or odd: *bizarre clothing; bizarre behavior.* [< F < It *bizzarro* lively, capricious, eccentric < ?] **—bi·zarre′ly,** *adv.* **—bi·zarre′ness,** *n.*

bize (bēz), *n.* bise.

Bi·zer·te (bi zûr′tə; *Fr.* bē zert′), *n.* a seaport in N Tunisia. 44,681 (1956). Also, **Bi·zer·ta** (bi zûr′tə; *Sp.* bēther′tä, -ser′-). Ancient, **Hippo Zarytus.**

Bi·zet (bē zā′), *n.* **Georges** (zhôrzh), (*Alexandre César Léopold*), 1838–75, French composer, esp. of opera.

bi·zone (bī′zōn′), *n.* two combined zones. [short for *bizonal territory.*] **—bi·zon′al,** *adj.*

Bjoer·ling (byœr′ling), *n.* **Jus·si** (yo͝os′ē), 1911–60, Swedish tenor. Also, **Björ′ling.**

Björn·son (byûrn′sən; *Norw.* byœrn′so͝on), *n.* **Björnstjer·ne** (byœrn′styer′nə), 1832–1910, Norwegian poet, novelist, and playwright: Nobel prize 1903.

Bk, *Chem.* berkelium.

bk., **1.** bank. **2.** book.

bkcy., *Law.* bankruptcy.

bkg., banking.

bkpr., bookkeeper.

bks., **1.** banks. **2.** barracks. **3.** books.

bl., **1.** bale; bales. **2.** barrel; barrels. **3.** black. **4.** block. **5.** blue.

b/l, See **bill of lading.** Also, **B/L**

B.L., **1.** Bachelor of Laws. **2.** Bachelor of Letters. **3.** See **bill of lading.**

b.l., See **bill of lading.**

blab (blab), *v.,* **blabbed, blab·bing,** *n.* **—***v.t.* **1.** to reveal indiscreetly and thoughtlessly: *She blabbed my confidences to everyone.* **—***v.i.* **2.** to talk or chatter indiscreetly and thoughtlessly. **—***n.* **3.** idle, indiscreet chattering. **4.** a blabbermouth. [ME *blabbe* (n.), perh. back formation from *blaberen* to blabber; c. Icel *blabbra,* G *plappern*] **—blab′ber,** *n.*

blab·ber·mouth (blab′ər mouth′), *n., pl.* **-mouths** (-mouthz′, -mouths′). a person who talks too much, esp. indiscreetly.

black (blak), *adj.* **1.** lacking hue and brightness; absorbing light without reflecting any of the rays composing it, as the type on this page. **2.** wearing black or dark clothing, armor, etc.: *the black prince.* **3.** (*sometimes cap.*) of, pertaining to, or belonging to an ethnic group characterized by dark skin pigmentation; Negro. **4.** soiled or stained with dirt: *That shirt was black within an hour.* **5.** characterized by absence of light; involved or enveloped in darkness: *a black night.* **6.** gloomy, pessimistic, or dismal: *a black outlook.* **7.** boding ill; sullen or hostile: *black words.* **8.** harmful; inexcusable: *a black lie.* **9.** without any moral light or goodness; evil or wicked: *a black heart.* **10.** marked by ruin or desolation, as would be indicated in black on a map: *black areas of drought.* **11.** indicating censure, disgrace, etc.: *a black mark on one's record.* **12.** (of coffee) without milk or cream. **13. black or white,** completely either one way or another. **—***n.* **14.** the color at the extreme end of grays, opposite to white, absorbing all light incident upon it. Cf. **white** (def. 18). **15.** (*often cap.*) a member of a dark-skinned people; Negro. **16.** black clothing: *He wore black at the funeral.* **17.** *Chess, Checkers.* the dark-colored pieces or squares. **18.** black pigment. **19.** a black horse. Cf. **brown** (def. 2). **20. in the black,** operating at a profit or being out of debt. **—***v.t.* **21.** to make black; put black on; blacken. **22.** to polish (shoes, boots, etc.) with blacking. **—***v.i.* **23.** to become black; take on a black color; blacken. **24. black out, a.** *Mil.* to obscure by concealing all light in defense against air raids. **b.** to lose consciousness. **c.** *Theat.* to extinguish all of the stage lights. **d.** to make or become inoperable: *to black out radio broadcasts.* [ME *blak,* OE *blæc;* c. OHG *blah-;* akin to Icel *blakkr* black, *blek* ink] **—black′ish,** *adj.* **—black′ish·ly,** *adv.* **—black′ish·ness,** *n.* **—black′ness,** *n.* **—Syn. 1.** dusky; sooty, inky; swarthy; sable, ebony. **4.** dirty, dingy. **6.** sad, depressing, somber. **7.** disastrous, calamitous. **9.** sinful. **—Ant. 1.** white. **4.** clean. **5.** bright. **6.** hopeful, cheerful.

Black (blak), *n.* **1. Hugo Lafayette,** 1886–1971, U.S. political official and jurist: associate justice of the U.S. Supreme Court 1937–71. **2. Joseph,** 1728–99, Scottish physician and chemist.

black·a·moor (blak′ə mo͝or′), *n.* *Offensive.* **1.** a Negro. **2.** any dark-skinned person. [unexplained var. of *black Moor*]

black-and-blue (blak′ən blo͞o′), *adj.* discolored, as by bruising; exhibiting ecchymosis.

Black′ and Tan′, **1.** Usually, **Black and Tans.** an armed force sent by the British government to Ireland (1920) to suppress revolutionary activity. **2.** a member of this force.

black-and-tan (blak′ən tan′), *adj.* **1.** (of a dog) of a black color with tan markings above the eyes and on the muzzle, chest, legs, feet, and breech. **2.** *Slang.* frequented by or catering to both Negroes and whites.

black′ and white′, **1.** print or writing: *I want to see the answer in black and white.* **2.** a monochromatic picture done with black and white only.

black-and-white (blak′ən hwīt′, -wīt′), *adj.* **1.** displaying only black and white tones; without color, as a picture, chart, etc. **2.** of, pertaining to, or constituting an absolute two-valued system, as of logic, morality, etc.: *To those who think in black-and-white terms, a person must be either entirely good or entirely bad.*

black′ art′, witchcraft or magic.

black-a-vised (blak′ə vīst′, -vīzd′), *adj.* dark-complexioned. Also, **black-a-viced** (blak′ə vīst′). [Scot *black-aviced* = *black a vice* (one) black of face (BLACK + A[3] + obs. *vice* < MF *vis;* see VISAGE) + -ED[3]]

black·ball (blak′bôl′), *v.t.* **1.** to vote against (a candidate, applicant, etc.) **2.** to ostracize (a person or group). **3.** to revoke the membership or entrance privilege of: *After the scandal, he was blackballed from the club.* **—***n.* **4.** a negative vote, esp. in deciding on an applicant or candidate. **5.** a black ball placed in a ballot box signifying a negative vote.

black′ bass′ (bas), any fresh-water, American game fish of the genus *Micropterus.*

black′ bear′, a North American bear, *Ursus americanus,* having a brown face and dense black fur. See illus. at **bear**[2].

Black·beard (blak′bērd′), *n.* See **Teach, Edward.**

black′-bel·lied plov′er (blak′bel′ēd), a large plover, *Squatarola squatarola,* of both the New and Old Worlds, having black underparts when in nuptial plumage.

black belt (blak′ belt′ *for 1, 3;* blak′ belt′ *for 2*), **1.** a narrow belt of dark-colored, calcareous soils in central Alabama and Mississippi highly adapted to agriculture, esp. the growing of cotton. **2.** *Judo.* **a.** a black waistband, worn with a judo costume, conferred by a judo association upon a player to indicate that he is of the highest rank. **b.** a player entitled to wear such a waistband, or the rank indicated by it. Cf. **brown belt, white belt. 3.** (*usually caps.*) **a.** the predominantly Negro section of a city. **b.** a predominantly Negro region in the southeastern U.S.

black·ber·ry (blak′ber′ē, -bə rē), *n., pl.* **-ries. 1.** the fruit, black or very dark purple when ripe, of certain species of the genus *Rubus.* **2.** the plant itself. [ME *blakeberie,* OE *blaceberie*]

black′ bile′, *Old Physiol.* a humor causing gloominess.

black′ bind′weed, **1.** a twining Old World vine, *Tamus communis,* bearing red berries. **2.** a climbing European herb, *Polygonum Convolvulus,* found in America as a tenacious weed.

black·bird (blak′bûrd′), *n.* **1.** a common European thrush, *Turdus merula,* the male of which is black with a yellow bill. **2.** any of several American birds of the family *Icteridae,* having black plumage. **3.** any of several other unrelated birds having black plumage. **4.** (formerly) a person, esp. a Kanaka, who was kidnaped and sold abroad, usually in Australia, as a slave. **—***v.t.* **5.** to kidnap (a person), as for selling as a slave. **—***v.i.* **6.** to engage in blackbirding. [late ME *blacke bride*]

black·bird·er (blak′bûr′dər), *n.* (formerly) a person or ship illegally engaged in the slave trade, esp. in the Pacific.

black·board (blak′bōrd′, -bôrd′), *n.* a sheet of smooth, hard material, esp. dark slate, for writing or drawing on with chalk.

black′ bod′y, *Physics.* a hypothetical body that absorbs without reflection all of the electromagnetic radiation incident on its surface.

black′ book′, a book of names of people liable to censure or punishment.

black′ bot′tom, a lively American dance, popular in the late 1920's, marked by emphatic, sinuous movements of the hips.

black·boy (blak′boi′), *n.* the grass tree.

black′ bread′, a coarse-grained dark bread, often sour and made from whole-grain rye flour.

black′ buck′, a blackish-brown antelope, *Antilope cervicapra,* of India.

Black buck (2½ ft. high at shoulder; horns 2 ft.; length 4 ft.)

Black·burn (blak′bərn), *n.* **1.** a city in central Lancashire, in NW England. 106,114 (1961). **2. Mount,** a mountain in SE Alaska, in the Wrangel Mountains. 16,140 ft.

black′ but′ter. See **beurre noir.**

Black′ Can′yon, a canyon of the Colorado River between Arizona and Nevada: site of Boulder Dam.

black·cap (blak′kap′), *n.* **1.** any of several birds having the top of the head black, as the chickadee and certain warblers, esp. the Old World blackcap, *Sylvia atricapilla.* **2.** *U.S.* the black raspberry plant or fruit.

black′ cher′ry, **1.** a North American cherry, *Prunus serotina,* bearing a black, sour, edible fruit. **2.** the tree itself. **3.** the hard, reddish-brown wood of this tree, used for making furniture.

black·cock (blak′kok′), *n.* the male of the black grouse. [late ME]

Black′ Code′, *U.S.* any code of law limiting the rights of Negroes, esp. as passed in some Southern states after the Civil War.

black′ co′hosh. See under **cohosh.**

black′ crap′pie. See under **crappie.**

black·damp (blak′damp′), *n.* *Mining.* chokedamp.

Black′ Death′, a form of bubonic plague that spread over Europe in the 14th century and is estimated to have killed a quarter of the population.

black′ dia′mond, **1.** carbonado[2]. **2. black diamonds,** anthracite or bituminous coal.

black′ disease′, *Vet. Pathol.* an acute, usually fatal disease of sheep caused by general intoxication from *Clostridium novyi*, an anaerobic organism that multiplies in the liver in areas damaged by the common liver fluke.
black·en (blak′ən), *v.t.* **1.** to make black; darken. **2.** to speak evil of (a person's character, reputation, etc.); defame. —*v.i.* **3.** to grow or become black. [ME] —**black′en·er,** *n.*
Black′ Eng′lish, a complex dialect of American English characterized by certain distinctive pronunciations, intonations, vocabulary items, and syntactic constructions, used by some North American blacks.
black′ eye′, **1.** a discoloration of the skin around the eye, resulting from a blow, bruise, etc. **2.** *Informal.* a mark of shame, dishonor, etc.
black′-eyed pea′ (blak′īd′), cowpea.
black′-eyed Su′san, any of a number of plants having flowers with a dark center against a lighter, usually yellow, background, esp. the composite herb, *Rudbeckia hirta.*
black·face (blak′fās′), *n.* **1.** *Theat.* **a.** an entertainer, esp. one in a minstrel show, made up to resemble a black. **b.** the make-up, as burnt cork, used in this role. **2.** *Print.* boldface.
black·fel·low (blak′fel′ō), *n.* an Australian aborigine.
black·fin (blak′fin′), *n.* a cisco, *Coregonus nigripinnis*, found in the Great Lakes. Also called **black′fin cis′co.**
black·fish (blak′fish′), *n., pl.* (*esp. collectively*) **-fish,** (*esp. referring to two or more kinds or species*) **-fish·es. 1.** See **black whale. 2.** any of various dark-colored fishes, as the tautog, *Tautoga onitis*, or the sea bass, *Centropristes striatus.*
black′ flag′. See **Jolly Roger.**
black′ fly′, any of the minute, black gnats of the dipterous family *Simuliidae*, having aquatic larvae. Also called **buffalo gnat.**
Black·foot (blak′fo͝ot′), *n., pl.* **-feet,** (*esp. collectively*) **-foot. 1.** a member of a North American tribe of Indians of Algonquian stock. **2.** the Algonquian language of the Blackfeet. [trans. of Blackfoot *Siksika*]
black′-foot·ed fer′ret (blak′fo͝ot′id), a weasel, *Mustela nigripes*, having a yellowish-brown body with the legs and tip of the tail black.

Black-footed ferret (Total length 2 ft.; tail 6 in.)

Black′ For′est, a wooded mountain region in SW West Germany. Highest peak, Feldberg, 4905 ft. German, **Schwarzwald.**
Black′ Fri′ar, a Dominican friar: so called from the distinctive black mantle worn by the order.
Black′ Fri′day, any Friday on which a misfortune occurs: *Friday, September 24, the day the financial panic of 1869 began, has since been known as Black Friday.*
black′ gold′, petroleum.
black′ grouse′, a large grouse, *Lyrurus tetrix*, of Europe and western Asia, the male of which is black, the female, mottled gray and brown.
black·guard (blag′ärd, -ərd), *n.* **1.** a low, contemptible person; scoundrel. **2.** *Obs.* **a.** a body of kitchen menials. **b.** servants of an army. **c.** camp followers. —*v.t.* **3.** to revile in scurrilous language. —*v.i.* **4.** to behave like a blackguard. —*adj.* **5.** *Obs.* scurrilous; abusive. [BLACK + GUARD, earlier meaning a body of retainers either dressed in black or criminal in character; orig. sense obscure] —**black′guard·ism,** *n.* —**black·guard·ly** (blag′ərd lē), *adj., adv.*
black′ gum′, any of several trees of the genus *Nyssa*, esp. *N. sylvatica*, of E North America. Cf. **tupelo.**
Black′ Hand′, a secret criminal society organized in Italy. —**Black′hand′er,** *n.*
black′ haw′, **1.** Also called **stag bush.** a North American shrub or small tree of the honeysuckle family, *Viburnum prunifolium*, having white flowers and black drupes. **2.** the sheepberry, *Viburnum Lentago.*
Black′ Hawk′, 1767–1838, American Indian chief of the Sac tribe: leader in the Black Hawk War 1831–32.
black·head (blak′hed′), *n.* **1.** a small, black-tipped, fatty mass in a skin follicle, esp. of the face; comedo. **2.** *Dial.* any of several birds having a black head, as the scaup duck, *Aythya marila.* **3.** *Vet. Pathol.* a malignant, infectious, protozoan disease of domestic fowl and many wild birds.
black·heart (blak′härt′), *n.* **1.** *Plant Pathol.* a disease of plants, as of potatoes and various trees, in which internal tissues blacken. **2.** *Hort.* a heart cherry having a dark skin.
black-heart·ed (blak′här′tid), *adj.* malevolent. —**black′heart′ed·ly,** *adv.* —**black′heart′ed·ness,** *n.*
Black′ Hills′, a group of mountains in W South Dakota and NE Wyoming. Harney Peak, 7242 ft.
black′ hole′, a region or object in space in which the gravitational pull is so great that even light cannot escape: one possible cause is the collapse of a star.
Black′ Hole′, a small prison cell in Fort William, Calcutta, in which, in 1756, Indians are said to have imprisoned 146 Europeans, only 23 of whom were alive the following morning. Also called **Black′ Hole′ of Cal·cut′ta.**
black′ hore′hound, a fetid European weed, *Ballota nigra*, having purple flowers.
black·ing (blak′ing), *n.* any preparation for producing a black coating or finish, as on shoes, stoves, etc.
black·jack (blak′jak′), *n.* **1.** a short, leather-covered club, consisting of a heavy head on a flexible handle, used as a weapon. **2.** a large drinking cup or jug for beer, ale, etc., originally made of leather coated externally with tar. **3.** a small oak, *Quercus marilandica*, of the eastern U.S., having a nearly black bark and a wood of little value except for fuel. **4.** *Mineral.* a dark, iron-rich sphalerite. **5.** *Cards.* **a.** twenty-one, esp. a variety of twenty-one in which a player can become dealer. **b.** Also called **natural.** (in twenty-one) an ace together with a ten or a face card as the first two cards dealt. —*v.t.* **6.** to strike or beat with a blackjack. **7.** to compel by threat. [rhyming compound]

Leather blackjacks (17th century)

black′ knot′, *Plant Pathol.* a disease, esp. of plums and cherries, characterized by black, knotlike overgrowths on the branches, twigs, etc., caused by a fungus, *Dibotryon morbosa.*
black′ lead′ (led), graphite; plumbago.
black·leg (blak′leg′), *n.* **1.** *Vet. Pathol.* an infectious, generally fatal disease of cattle and sheep, caused by the soil bacterium *Clostridium chauvoei* and characterized by painful, gaseous swellings in the muscles, usually of the upper parts of the legs. **2.** *Plant Pathol.* **a.** a disease of cabbage and other cruciferous plants, characterized by dry, black lesions on the base of the stem, caused by a fungus, *Phoma lingam.* **b.** a disease of potatoes, characterized by wet, black lesions on the base of the stem, caused by a bacterium, *Erwinia atroseptica.* **3.** a swindler, esp. in racing or gambling. **4.** *Brit. Informal.* a strikebreaker; scab.
black′ let′ter, *Print.* a heavy-faced type in a style like that of early European handlettering and earliest printed books. Also called **text.** —**black′-let′ter,** *adj.*

This is a sample of black letter

black′ light′, invisible infrared or ultraviolet light.
black·list (blak′list′), *n.* **1.** a list of persons or organizations under suspicion, disfavor, censure, or the like. —*v.t.* **2.** to put (a person) on a blacklist.
black·ly (blak′lē), *adv.* **1.** darkly; gloomily. **2.** wickedly or angrily.
black′ mag′ic, witchcraft; sorcery.
black·mail (blak′māl′), *n.* **1.** any payment extorted by intimidation, as by threats of injurious revelations or accusations. **2.** the extortion or attempted extortion of such payment. **3.** a tribute formerly exacted in the north of England and in Scotland by bandit chiefs for protection from pillage. —*v.t.* **4.** to extort money from (a person) by the use of threats. **5.** to force or coerce into a particular action, statement, etc. [BLACK + *mail*, sp. var. of north ME *mal(e)* tribute, rent, OE *māl* agreement < Scand] —**black′mail′er,** *n.*
Black′ Ma·ri′a (mə rī′ə), *Informal.* See **patrol wagon.**
black′ mark′, a detrimental trait, fact, or facet.
black′ mar′ket, a market consisting of the illicit buying and selling of goods in violation of legal price controls, rationing, etc.
black-mar·ket (blak′mär′kit), *v.i.* **1.** to sell in the black market. —*v.t.* **2.** to sell (something) in the black market.
black′ mar·ke·teer′ (mär′ki tēr′), a person who sells articles in the black market. Also, **black′ mar′ket·er** (mär′ki tər).
Black′ Mass′, **1.** a blasphemous ceremony mocking the Christian Mass, esp. one by an alleged worshiper of the devil. **2.** a Requiem Mass. Also, **black′ mass′.**
black′ mea′sles, *Pathol.* a severe form of measles characterized by dark, hemorrhagic eruptions.
black′ mold′. See **bread mold.**
Black′ Monk′, a Benedictine monk: so called from the black habit worn by the order. Also, **black′ monk′.** [ME]
Black′ Moun′tains, a mountain range in W North Carolina, part of the Appalachian Mountains.
Black·mun (blak′mən), *n.* **Harry A(ndrew),** born 1908, U.S. jurist: associate justice of the U.S. Supreme Court since 1970.
Black·mur (blak′mər), *n.* **R(ichard) P(almer),** 1904–1965, U.S. critic and poet.
Black′ Mus′lim, a member of an organization of blacks, esp. black Americans advocating the religious and ethical teachings of Islam and complete separation of races.
black′ mus′tard. See under **mustard** (def 2).
black·ness (blak′nis), *n.* quality or state of being black. [ME]
black′ night′shade, a common weed, *Solanum nigrum*, having white flowers and black edible berries.
black·out (blak′out′), *n.* **1.** the extinguishing or concealment of all lights throughout a city or area, as from a power failure or to reduce visibility in an air raid. **2.** complete stoppage of operations within a communications medium, resulting from a strike, power failure, or the like: *a newspaper blackout.* **3.** unconsciousness. **4.** *Theat.* **a.** the extinguishing of all stage lights for a special effect or to indicate the end of a skit or scene. **b.** a skit ending in a blackout.
Black′ Pan′ther, a member of a militant black organization **(Black′ Pan′ther par′ty)** formed to protect black communities and to work for reforms favoring blacks.
black′ pep′per, a hot, sharp condiment prepared from the dried berries of a tropical vine, *Piper nigrum.*
black·poll (blak′pōl′), *n.* a North American warbler, *Dendroica striata*, the adult male of which has the top of the head black. Also called **black′poll war′bler.**
Black·pool (blak′po͞ol′), *n.* a seaport in W Lancashire, in NW England: resort. 147,000.
Black′ Pope′, *Disparaging and Offensive.* the head of the Jesuit order: so called from the power he once possessed and from the black habit worn by the order.
black′ pow′der, an explosive powder consisting of saltpeter, sulfur, and charcoal, used chiefly in old guns fired for sport, in fireworks, and for charges in practice bombs.
black′ pow′er, the political and economic power of black Americans as a group, esp. such power used for achieving racial equality.
Black′ Prince′. See **Edward** (def. 1).
black′ pud′ding. See **blood sausage.**
black′ race′, (loosely) Negroid peoples.
black′ rat′, an Old World rat, *Rattus rattus*, now common in the southern U.S., having a black or brown body with grayish or white underparts.
Black′ Rod′, **1.** (in England) an official of the Order of the Garter and chief ceremonial usher of the House of Lords: so called from the rod he carries. **2.** a similar official in British colonial and Commonwealth legislatures.
black′ rot′, *Plant Pathol.* any of several diseases of fruits and vegetables, characterized by black discoloration and decay of affected parts, caused by fungi, as *Guignardia bidwellii*, or bacteria, as *Xanthomonas campestris.*
Black′ Rus′sian, a cocktail of coffee liqueur and vodka.
Black′ Sea′, a sea between Europe and Asia, bordered by the Soviet Union, Turkey, Rumania, and Bulgaria. 164,000 sq. mi. Also called **Euxine Sea.** Ancient, **Pontus Euxinus.**

black′ sheep′, 1. a sheep with black fleece. 2. a person who causes shame or embarrassment because of his deviation from the accepted standards of his group.

Black′ Shirt′, *Europ. Hist.* a member of a fascist organization, esp. the Italian fascist militia.

black·smith (blak′smith′), *n.* 1. a person who makes horseshoes and shoes horses. 2. a person who forges objects of iron. [late ME]

black·snake (blak′snāk′), *n.* 1. a blackish racer, *Coluber constrictor*, of the eastern U.S., that grows to a length of five to six feet. 2. any of various other snakes of a black or very dark color. 3. a heavy, tapering, flexible whip of braided cowhide or the like. Also, **black′ snake′.**

black′ spruce′, a spruce, *Picea mariana*, of North America, having bluish-green needles.

Black·stone (blak′stōn′, -stən), *n.* **Sir William,** 1723–80, English jurist and writer on law.

black′strap molas′ses (blak′strap′), molasses remaining after maximum extraction of sugar from the raw product.

Black′ Stream′. See **Japan Current.**

black·tail (blak′tāl′), *n.* an animal, esp. a deer, having a black tail.

black′ tea′, a tea that has been allowed to wither and ferment in the air before being subjected to a heating process.

black·thorn (blak′thôrn′), *n.* 1. Also called **sloe.** a much-branched, thorny, Old World shrub, *Prunus spinosa*, having white flowers and small plumlike fruits. 2. a cane or walking stick made of the wood of this shrub. 3. a shrub or tree of the genus *Crataegus*, as *C. tomentosa*. [ME *blak thorn*]

black′ tie′, 1. a black bow tie, worn with a dinner jacket. 2. semiformal evening wear for men (distinguished from *white tie*).

black-tie (blak′tī′), *adj.* (of a social occasion) requiring that guests wear semiformal attire, esp. that men wear black bow ties with dinner jackets.

black·top (blak′top′), *n.* 1. a bituminous substance, usually asphalt, for paving roads, parking lots, playgrounds, etc. 2. a road covered with such a substance.

black′ vel′vet, a cocktail of stout and champagne.

Black′ Vol′ta, a river in W Africa, in Ghana: the upper branch of the Volta River. ab. 500 mi. long.

black′ vom′it, *Pathol.* 1. a dark-colored substance, consisting chiefly of altered blood, vomited in some cases of yellow fever, usually presaging a fatal issue of the disease. 2. any disease characterized by such vomiting.

Black′wall hitch′ (blak′wôl′), a hitch made with a rope over a hook so that it holds fast when pulled. See illus. at **knot.** [after *Blackwall*, a London shipyard]

black′ wal′nut, 1. a tree, *Juglans nigra*, of North America, that yields a valuable wood. 2. the nut of this tree.

Black′ Watch′, a famous regiment of Scottish infantry in the British army: so called because of the dark colors in their tartan.

black′wa·ter fe′ver (blak′wô′tər, -wot′ər), *Pathol.* a form of malaria in which the urine is dark red or black.

Black·well (blak′wəl, -wel′), *n.* **Henry Brown,** 1825?–1909, U.S. editor, abolitionist, and suffragist, born in England (husband of Lucy Stone).

black′ whale′, any of several black, dolphinlike cetaceans of the genus *Globicephalus*. Also called **blackfish.**

black′ wid′ow, a small, jet-black, venomous spider, *Latrodectus mactans*, widely distributed in the U.S., having an hourglass-shaped red mark on the underside of its abdomen.

Black·wood (blak′wo͝od′), *n.* **William,** 1776–1834, English publisher.

blad·der (blad′ər), *n.* 1. *Anat., Zool.* **a.** a membranous sac or organ serving as a receptacle for a fluid or gas. **b.** See **urinary bladder.** 2. *Pathol.* a vesicle, blister, cyst, etc., filled with fluid or air. 3. *Bot.* an air-filled sac or float, as in certain seaweeds. 4. something resembling a bladder, as the inflatable lining of a football, basketball, etc. 5. an air-filled sac used for hitting someone over the head in low comedy or the like. [ME; OE *blǣddre, blǣdre* bladder, blister, pimple; c. Icel *blāthra*, Flem *bladder*, G *Blatter;* akin to BLOW²] —**blad′der·less,** *adj.* —**blad′der·like′,** *adj.*

blad′der cam′pion, a plant, *Silene latifolia* (*Silene inflata*), having an inflated calyx.

blad′der ket′mi·a (ket′mē ə), a cultivated annual plant, *Hibiscus Trionum*, having a bladdery calyx. [*ketmia* < NL]

blad·der·nose (blad′ər nōz′), *n.* a large seal, *Cystophora cristata*, the male of which has a large, distensible, hoodlike sac on the head. Also called **hooded seal.**

blad·der·nut (blad′ər nut′), *n.* 1. the bladderlike fruit capsule of any shrub, or small tree, of the genus *Staphylea*, as *S. trifolia*, of the eastern U.S. 2. the shrub itself.

blad′der worm′, *Zool.* the bladderlike, encysted larva of a tapeworm; a cysticercus, coenurus, or hydatid.

blad·der·wort (blad′ər wûrt′), *n.* any of various herbs of the genus *Utricularia*, including aquatic, terrestrial, and epiphytic forms throughout the world.

blade (blād), *n.* 1. the flat cutting part of a sword, knife, etc. 2. a sword, rapier, or the like. 3. the leaf of a plant, esp. of a grass or cereal. 4. *Bot.* the broad part of a leaf, as distinguished from the stalk or petiole. 5. the long, narrow part of an ice skate that comes into contact with the ice; runner. 6. a thin, flat part of something, as of an oar or a bone. 7. a dashing, swaggering, or jaunty young man. 8. the scapula or shoulder blade. 9. *Phonet.* the foremost and most readily flexible portion of the tongue, including the tip, upper and lower surfaces, and edges. [ME; OE *blæd;* c. D *blad*, Icel *blath*, G *Blatt;* akin to BLOW³] —**blade′less,** *adj.* —**blade′like′,** *adj.*

blae (blā, blē), *adj.* *Scot. and North Eng.* livid; bluish-black; blue-gray. [ME *bla* (north) < Scand; cf. Icel *blā* blackish blue; c. G *blau*, whence F *bleu* BLUE]

Bla·go·vesh·chensk (blä′go vesh′chensk), *n.* a city in the SE Soviet Union in Asia, on the Amur River. 108,000 (est. 1964).

blah (blä), *U.S. Slang.* —*n.* 1. nonsense; rubbish. —*adj.* 2. insipid; dull; uninteresting. [imit.]

blain (blān), *n.* *Pathol.* an inflammatory swelling or sore. [ME *bleine*, OE *blegen(e)*. See CHILBLAIN]

Blaine (blān), *n.* **James Gil·les·pie** (gi les′pē), 1830–93, U.S. statesman.

Blair′ House′ (blâr), the guest house of the President of the United States, near the White House.

Blake (blāk), *n.* 1. **Robert,** 1599–1657, British admiral. 2. **William,** 1757–1827, English poet, engraver, and painter.

blam·a·ble (blā′mə bəl), *adj.* deserving blame; censurable. Also, **blameable.** [ME] —**blam′a·ble·ness,** *n.* —**blam′a·bly,** *adv.*

blame (blām), *v.*, **blamed, blam·ing,** *n.* —*v.t.* 1. to place the responsibility for (a fault, error, etc.) on a person. 2. to find fault with; censure. 3. *U.S. Slang and Dial.* (used as a humorous imperative or optative): *Blame my hide if I go!* 4. **to blame,** at fault; blamable: *I am to blame for his lateness.* —*n.* 5. act of attributing fault; censure; reproof. 6. responsibility for anything deserving of censure. [ME *blame(n)* < OF *blasme(r)* << LL *blasphēmāre* to BLASPHEME] —**blam′er,** *n.*

—**Syn. 1, 2.** reproach, reprove, reprehend. BLAME, CENSURE, CONDEMN imply finding fault with someone or something. To BLAME is to hold accountable for, and disapprove because of, some error, mistake, omission, or the like: *Who is to blame for the disaster?* The verb CENSURE differs from the noun in connoting scolding or rebuking even more than adverse criticism: *to censure one for extravagance.* To CONDEMN is to express an adverse (esp. legal) judgment, without recourse: *to condemn conduct, a building, a man to death.* 5. condemnation, stricture, reproach. 6. guilt, culpability, fault, sin, defect. —**Ant. 2.** praise.

—**Usage.** Some speakers avoid BLAME ON as informal (*He blamed it on me*), preferring PUT THE BLAME ON (*He put the blame on me*), BLAME alone (*He blamed me*), or BLAME FOR (*He blamed me for it*).

blame·a·ble (blā′mə bəl), *adj.* blamable. —**blame′a·ble·ness,** *n.* —**blame′a·bly,** *adv.*

blamed (blāmd), *U.S. Slang and Dial.* —*adj.* 1. confounded: *The blamed car won't start.* —*adv.* 2. confoundedly; excessively.

blame·ful (blām′fəl), *adj.* 1. deserving blame; blameworthy: *blameful neglect.* 2. *Archaic.* imputing blame; accusing. [ME] —**blame′ful·ly,** *adv.* —**blame′ful·ness,** *n.*

blame·less (blām′lis), *adj.* free from blame; guiltless: *a blameless child.* [ME] —**blame′less·ly,** *adv.* —**blame′less·ness,** *n.* —**Syn.** irreproachable. See **innocent.** —**Ant.** guilty.

blame·wor·thy (blām′wûr′thē), *adj.* deserving blame; blameful. [ME] —**blame′wor′thi·ness,** *n.*

Blanc (bläɴ), *n.* **Mont.** See **Mont Blanc.**

Blan′ca Peak′ (blaŋ′kə), a mountain in S Colorado: highest peak in the Sangre de Cristo Range. 14,390 ft.

blanc fixe (blaŋk′ fēks′; *Fr.* bläɴ fēks′), barium sulfate used as a white pigment in paints. [< F: lit., fixed white]

blanch (blanch, blänch), *v.t.* 1. to whiten by removing color; bleach. 2. *Hort.* to whiten or prevent from becoming green (the stems or leaves of plants, as celery, lettuce, etc.) by excluding light. 3. *Cookery.* **a.** to scald briefly to facilitate removal of skins or to separate the grains or strands, as of rice. **b.** to scald or parboil (meat or vegetables) so as to whiten, remove the odor, prepare for cooking by other means, etc. 4. *Metall.* to give a white luster to (metals), as by means of acids. 5. to make pale, as with sickness or fear: *The long illness had blanched her cheeks.* —*v.i.* 6. to become white; turn pale: *The very thought of going made her blanch.* [ME *bla(u)nche* < MF *blanch(ir)* (to) whiten < *blanc, blanche* white; see BLANK] —**blanch′er,** *n.* —**Syn. 1.** See **whiten.**

blanc·mange (blə mänj′, -mänzh′), *n.* a white, sweet pudding made with milk and cornstarch or almond milk and gelatin and flavored with vanilla or rum. [apocopated var. of ME *blancmanger* < MF, lit., white eating. See BLANK, MANGER]

bland (bland), *adj.* 1. pleasantly gentle or agreeable: *a bland manner in company.* 2. soothing or balmy, as air. 3. nonirritating, as foods or medicines: *a bland diet.* 4. nonstimulating, as medicines: *a bland cough syrup.* 5. lacking in interest, liveliness, individuality, etc. 6. unemotional, indifferent, or casual: *his bland acknowledgment of guilt.* [< L *bland(us)* of a smooth tongue, pleasant, soothing] —**bland′ly,** *adv.* —**bland′ness,** *n.* —**Syn. 1.** affable, mild, amiable. **2, 3.** soft, mild. —**Ant. 2.** harsh. **3.** irritating.

blan·dish (blan′dish), *v.t.* 1. to coax or influence by gentle flattery; cajole. —*v.i.* 2. to use flattery or cajolery. [ME *blandisshe* < MF *blandiss-*, long s. of *blandir* < L *blandīr(ī)* (to) soothe, flatter] —**blan′dish·er,** *n.* —**blan′dish·ing·ly,** *adv.*

blan·dish·ment (blan′dish mənt), *n.* Often, **blandishments.** something, as an action or speech, that tends to flatter or coax: *Her blandishments won't change my mind.*

blank (blaŋk), *adj.* 1. (of paper or other writing surfaces) having no marks; not written or printed on. 2. not completed or filled in, as a printed form: *a blank check.* 3. unrelieved or unbroken by ornament, opening, decoration, etc.: *a blank wall.* 4. lacking some usual or completing feature: *a blank piece of film.* 5. void of interest, variety, results, etc. 6. showing no attention, interest, or emotion: *a blank face.* 7. complete; utter; unmitigated: *a blank denial.* 8. *Archaic.* white; pale; colorless. —*n.* 9. a place where something is lacking: *a blank in one's memory.* 10. (on a printed form) a space to be filled in: *Write your name in the blank.* 11. a printed form containing such spaces: *Have you filled out one of these application blanks?* 12. a blank cartridge. 13. a dash put in place of an omitted letter, series of letters, etc., to avoid writing a word considered profane or obscene. 14. *Mach.* a piece of metal ready to be drawn, pressed, or machined into a finished object. 15. *Archery.* the bull's-eye. 16. **draw a blank,** *Informal.* to fail to remember or recognize. —*v.t.* 17. to cross out or delete, esp. in order to invalidate or void (usually fol. by *out*): *to blank out an entry.* 18. *Informal.* to keep (an opponent) from scoring in a game. 19. *Mach.* to stamp or punch out of flat stock, as with a die. [ME < MF *blanc* < Gmc; cf. OE *blanca* white horse, OHG *blanch* bright, white] —**blank′ness,** *n.* —**Syn. 1–4.** See **empty. 7.** absolute, unqualified. **9.** void, vacancy.

blank′ car′tridge, *Ordn.* a cartridge containing powder only, without a bullet.

blank′ check′, **1.** a bank check bearing a signature but no stated amount. **2.** *Informal.* unrestricted authority; complete freedom of action, decision, or the like.

blan·ket (blang′kit), *n.* **1.** a large, typically rectangular piece of soft fabric, often with bound edges, used as a bed covering for warmth. **2.** a similar piece of fabric used as a covering for a horse, dog, etc. **3.** the chief garment worn by some American Indians. **4.** any extended covering or layer: *a blanket of snow.* —*v.t.* **5.** to cover with or as with a blanket: *wild flowers blanketing the hillside.* **6.** to obscure or obstruct; interfere with; overpower (usually fol. by *out*): *An electrical storm blanketed out the radio program.* **7.** *Naut.* (of a vessel) to take wind from the sails of (another vessel) by passing closely to windward of it. —*adj.* **8.** covering or intended to cover all members or aspects of a large group or class of things, conditions, situations, etc.: *a blanket indictment.* [ME < OF = *blanc* white (see BLANK) + *-et* -ET]

blan·ket-flow·er (blang′kit flou′ər), *n.* any composite herb of the genus *Gaillardia,* having showy heads of yellow or purple flowers.

blan′ket stitch′, a basic sewing stitch with widely spaced, interlocking loops, used esp. as a decorative finish for edges, etc.

blank·e·ty-blank (blang′ki tē blangk′), *adj., adv. Informal* (used as a euphemism) damned. [after the former practice of leaving blank spaces to represent profanity]

blank·ly (blangk′lē), *adv.* **1.** without expression or understanding: *She stared blankly at her inquisitors.* **2.** totally; fully; in every respect: *He blankly denied having said it.*

blank′ verse′, unrhymed verse, esp. the unrhymed iambic pentameter in verse.

Blan·tyre (blan tīər′), *n.* a city in S Malawi. 30,000 (est. 1956).

blare (blâr), *v.,* **blared, blar·ing,** *n.* —*v.i.* **1.** to emit a loud raucous sound: *The trumpets blared as the procession got under way.* —*v.t.* **2.** to sound loudly; proclaim noisily: *The radio blared the awful news.* —*n.* **3.** a loud raucous noise: *the blare of the phonograph.* **4.** glaring intensity of light or color. [late ME *blere(n)*; akin to MD *blaren,* MLG *blarren,* MHG *blerren* (G *plärren*)]

blar·ney (blär′nē), *n., v.,* **-neyed, -ney·ing.** —*n.* **1.** flattering or wheedling talk; cajolery. —*v.t., v.i.* **2.** to ply or beguile with blarney; use blarney; wheedle. [after the hamlet *Blarney,* in Ireland; see BLARNEY STONE]

Blar′ney stone′, a stone in Blarney Castle near Cork, Ireland, said to impart skill in flattery to those who kiss it.

Blas·co I·bá·ñez (blä′skô ē vä′nyeth), **Vi·cen·te** (bē then′te), 1867–1928, Spanish novelist, journalist, and politician.

bla·sé (blä zā′, blä′zā; *Fr.* blȧ zā′), *adj.* indifferent to or bored with life or any particular activity, entertainment, etc.; unimpressed, as or as if from an excess of worldly pleasures. [< F, ptp. of *blaser* to cloy, sicken from surfeit, perh. < D *blasen* to blow]

blas·pheme (blas fēm′, blas′fēm), *v.,* **-phemed, -phem·ing.** —*v.t.* **1.** to speak impiously or irreverently of (God or sacred things). **2.** to speak evil of; slander. —*v.i.* **3.** to speak irreverently of God or sacred things; utter impieties. [ME < eccl. L *blasphēm(āre)* < Gk *blasphēmeîn* to speak profanely < *blásphēm(os)* BLASPHEMOUS] —**blas·phem′er,** *n.* —**Syn. 1, 3.** See **curse.**

blas·phe·mous (blas′fə məs), *adj.* uttering, containing, or exhibiting blasphemy; irreverent; profane. [< eccl. L *blasphēmus* < Gk *blásphēmos* defaming, speaking evil = *blá(p)s(is)* harm, evil (akin to *bláptein* to harm) + *-phēmos* speaking (*phēm(e)* speech + *-os* adj. suffix)] —**blas′phe·mous·ly,** *adv.* —**blas′phe·mous·ness,** *n.*

blas·phe·my (blas′fə mē), *n., pl.* **-mies. 1.** impious or irreverent utterance or action concerning God or sacred things. **2.** *Theol.* the crime of assuming to oneself the rights or qualities of God. [ME *blasphemie* < eccl. L *blasphēmia* < Gk *blásphēm(os)* BLASPHEMOUS + *-ia* -Y³] —**Syn. 1.** profanity, cursing; sacrilege.

blast (blast, bläst), *n.* **1.** a sudden and violent gust of wind: *Wintry blasts chilled us to the marrow.* **2.** the blowing of a trumpet, whistle, etc.: *a blast of the siren.* **3.** a loud, sudden sound or noise: *The radio let out an awful blast.* **4.** a forcible stream of air, as from a bellows. **5.** *Mach.* **a.** air forced into a furnace by a blower to increase the rate of combustion. **b.** a jet of steam directed up a smokestack, as of a steam locomotive, to increase draft. **c.** a draft thus increased. **6.** *Slang.* a party, esp. a wild, abandoned one. **7.** *Mining, Civ. Eng.* a charge of dynamite or other explosive used at one firing. **8.** the act of exploding; explosion. **9.** a shock wave in areas within the radius of an explosion, due to changes in atmospheric pressure. **10. at full blast,** *Informal.* at maximum capacity; at or with full volume or speed: *The factory is going at full blast.* Also, **full blast.** —*v.t.* **11.** to make a loud noise on (a trumpet, automobile horn, etc.); blow: *He blasted his horn irritably at every car in his way.* **12.** to cause to shrivel or wither; blight. **13.** to affect with any pernicious influence; ruin; destroy: *Failure in the exam blasted his hopes for college.* **14.** to make, form, open up, break up, etc., by blasting: *to blast a tunnel through a mountain.* **15.** (euphemistically) to curse; damn (usually fol. by *it* or an object): *Blast it, there's the phone again! Blast the time, we've got to finish this work!* **16.** *Informal.* to censure or criticize vigorously; denounce. —*v.i.* **17.** to produce a loud, blaring sound: *His voice blasted until the microphone was turned down.* **18. blast off,** (of a rocket) to leave a launch pad under self-propulsion. [ME; OE *blǣst* a blowing; akin to Icel *blāstr,* OHG *blāst* (< OHG *blās(an)*; c. Goth *(uf)blēsan,* Icel *blāsa*). See BLOW²] —**blast′er,** *n.* —**blast′y,** *adj.* —**Syn. 1.** See **wind¹. 2.** blare, screech.

-blast, var. of **blasto-** as final element of a compound word: *ectoblast.*

blast·ed (blas′tid, blä′stid), *adj.* **1.** withered; shriveled; blighted; ruined. **2.** (used as a euphemism) damned.

blas·te·ma (bla stē′mə), *n., pl.* **-mas, -ma·ta** (-mə tə). *Embryol.* an aggregation of cells in a young embryo, capable of differentiation into primordia and organs. [< NL < Gk = *blastē-* (long s. of *blastéein* to sprout) + *-ma* n. suffix] —**blas·te′mal, blas·te·mat·ic** (blas′tə mat′ik), **blas·tem·ic** (bla stem′ik), *adj.*

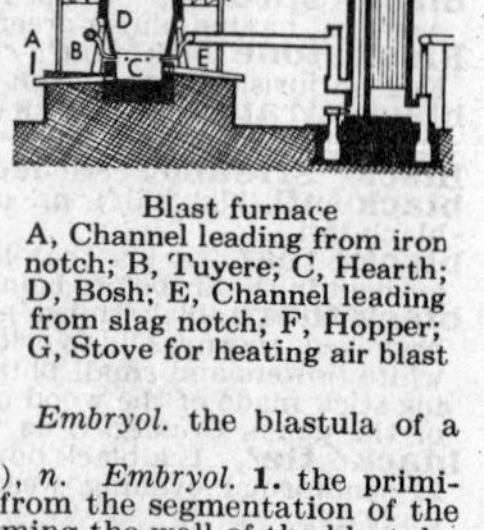

Blast furnace
A, Channel leading from iron notch; B, Tuyere; C, Hearth; D, Bosh; E, Channel leading from slag notch; F, Hopper; G, Stove for heating air blast

blast′ fur′nace, a large vertical furnace for smelting iron from ore.

blast′ing pow′der, a form of gunpowder made with sodium nitrate instead of saltpeter, used chiefly for blasting rock, ore, etc.

blasto-, a learned borrowing from Greek meaning "embryo," used in the formation of compound words: *blastosphere.* Also, **-blast.** [comb. form of Gk *blastós* a bud, sprout]

blas·to·coel (blas′tə sēl′), *n. Embryol.* the cavity of a blastula, arising in the course of cleavage. Also, **blas′to·coele′.** Also called **segmentation cavity.** —**blas′to·coel′ic,** *adj.*

blas·to·cyst (blas′tə sist), *n. Embryol.* the blastula of a mammalian embryo.

blas·to·derm (blas′tə dûrm′), *n. Embryol.* **1.** the primitive layer of cells that results from the segmentation of the ovum. **2.** the layer of cells forming the wall of the blastula, and in most vertebrates enclosing a cavity or a yolk mass. —**blas′to·der′mic, blas′to·der·mat′ic,** *adj.*

blas·to·disk (blas′tə disk′), *n. Embryol.* the small disk of protoplasm, containing the egg nucleus, that appears on the surface of the yolk mass in the very heavily yolked eggs, as of birds and reptiles. Also, **blas′to·disc′.**

blast-off (blast′ôf′, -of′, bläst′-), *n. Rocketry.* the launching of a rocket or guided missile.

blas·to·gen·e·sis (blas′tə jen′i sis), *n. Biol.* **1.** reproduction by gemmation or budding. **2.** the theory of the transmission of hereditary characters by germ plasm. **3.** the formation of the blastula of an embryo.

blas·to·ma (bla stō′mə), *n., pl.* **-mas, -ma·ta** (-mə tə). *Pathol.* a tumor originating from undifferentiated embryonic cells and having little or no connective tissue.

blas·to·mere (blas′tə mēr′), *n. Embryol.* any cell produced during cleavage. —**blas·to·mer·ic** (blas′tə mer′ik), *adj.*

blas·to·my·cete (blas′tə mī′sēt, -mī sēt′), *n.* a yeastlike pathogenic fungus of the genus *Blastomyces.*

blas·to·pore (blas′tə pōr′, -pôr′), *n. Embryol.* the opening of an archenteron. [BLASTO- + *-pore* passage; see PORE²] —**blas·to·por·ic** (blas′tə pōr′ik, -por′-), **blas·to·po·ral** (blas′tə pōr′əl, -pôr′-), *adj.*

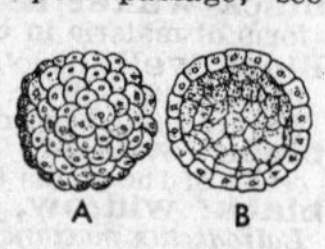

Blastula
A, Exterior view
B, Cross section

blas·to·sphere (blas′tə sfēr′), *n. Embryol.* **1.** a blastula. **2.** a blastocyst.

blas·tu·la (blas′cho͝o lə), *n., pl.* **-las, -lae** (-lē′). *Embryol.* the early developmental stage of a metazoan, following the morula stage and consisting of a single, spherical layer of cells that encloses a hollow, central cavity. [< NL; see BLASTO-, -ULE] —**blas′tu·lar,** *adj.*

blat (blat), *v.,* **blat·ted, blat·ting.** —*v.i.* **1.** to cry out, as a calf or sheep; bleat. —*v.t.* **2.** *Informal.* to utter loudly and indiscreetly; blurt. [back formation from *blattant,* var. of BLATANT]

bla·tant (blāt′ənt), *adj.* **1.** obtrusive; brazenly obvious: *a blatant error.* **2.** offensively noisy or loud; clamorous. **3.** tastelessly conspicuous: *the blatant colors of her dress.* **4.** *Literary.* bleating: *blatant herds.* [coined by Edmund Spenser; cf. L *blatīre* to babble, prate; *blaterāre* to talk foolishly, babble] —**bla′tan·cy,** *n.* —**bla′tant·ly,** *adv.*

blath·er (blath′ər), *n.* **1.** foolish talk, esp. in great quantity. —*v.i., v.t.* **2.** to speak foolishly; babble. Also, **blether.** [ME < Scand; cf. Icel *blathra* to chatter]

blath·er·skite (blath′ər skīt′), *n.* **1.** a person given to voluble, empty talk. **2.** nonsense; blather. [BLATHER + *skite* SKATE³]

blau·bok (blou′bok′), *n., pl.* **-boks,** (*esp. collectively*) **-bok.** an extinct bluish antelope, *Hippotragus leucophaeus,* of southern Africa, whose horns curved up and back toward the head. [< D *blauwbok* blue buck]

Blau·e Rei·ter (blou′ə rī′tər), *German.* (*sometimes l.c.*) a group of artists active in Germany, esp. in or near Munich, during the early 20th century whose works were characterized by the use of Fauve color and distorted forms. Also called **Blue Rider.** [lit., blue riders]

Bla·vat·sky (blə vat′skē), *n.* **Madame** (*Elena Petrovna Blavatskaya, née Hahn*), 1831–91, Russian theosophist.

blaze¹ (blāz), *n., v.,* **blazed, blaz·ing.** —*n.* **1.** a bright flame or fire. **2.** a bright, hot gleam or glow: *the blaze of day.* **3.** a sparkling brightness: *a blaze of jewels.* **4.** a sudden, intense outburst, as of fire, passion, fury, etc.: *a blaze of glory.* —*v.i.* **5.** to burn brightly. **6.** to shine like flame: *Their faces blazed with enthusiasm.* **7.** to burn with intense feeling or passion (sometimes fol. by *up*): *He blazed up at the insult.* **8.** to shoot firearms or a firearm steadily or continuously (usually fol. by *away*): *The contestants blazed away at the clay pigeons.* [ME, OE *blase* torch, flame; c. MHG *blas* torch] —**blaz′ing·ly,** *adv.* —**Syn. 1.** See **flame.**

blaze² (blāz), *n., v.,* **blazed, blaz·ing.** —*n.* **1.** a spot or mark made on a tree, as by notching or by chipping away a piece of the bark, to indicate a boundary or a path in a forest. **2.** a white area down the center of the face of a horse, cow, etc. —*v.t.* **3.** to mark with blazes: *to blaze a trail.* **4.** to lead in forming or finding (a new method, course, etc.): *His research in rocketry blazed the way for space travel.* [akin to Icel *blesi,* D *bles,* G *Blässe* white mark on a beast's face, and to G *blass* pale]

blaze³ (blāz), *v.t.,* **blazed, blaz·ing. 1.** to make known; proclaim; publish: *Headlines blazed the shocking news.* **2.** *Obs.* to blow, as from a trumpet. [ME *blase(n)* < MD; c. Icel *blāsa* to blow]

blaz·er (blā′zər), *n.* **1.** *Informal.* that which blazes or shines brightly. **2.** a solid-color sports jacket, often with metal buttons and a school or club insignia on the breast pocket.

blaz′ing star′, any of certain plants with showy flower clusters, as the liliaceous herb *Aletris farinosa* or the composite perennial *Liatris squarrosa.*

bla·zon (blā′zən), *v.t.* **1.** to set forth conspicuously or publicly; display; proclaim. **2.** to describe in heraldic terminology. **3.** to depict (heraldic arms or the like) in proper form and color. —*n.* **4.** an escutcheon; coat of arms. **5.** the heraldic description of armorial bearings. [ME *blaso(u)n* < MF *blason* buckler] —**bla′zon·er,** *n.* —**bla′zon·ment,** *n.*

bla·zon·ry (blā′zən rē), *n.* **1.** brilliant decoration or display. **2.** *Heraldry.* **a.** the act or technique of describing coats of arms. **b.** a coat of arms. **c.** coats of arms collectively.

bldg., building.

-ble, var. of **-able** (*soluble*), occurring first in words of Latin origin that came into English through French, later in words taken directly from Latin. Also, *esp. after a consonant stem,* **-ible.** [ME < OF < L *-bilis, -bile* adj. suffix]

bleach (blēch), *v.t.* **1.** to make whiter or lighter in color; remove the color from. —*v.i.* **2.** to become whiter or lighter in color. —*n.* **3.** a bleaching agent. **4.** act of bleaching. **5.** the degree of paleness achieved in bleaching. [ME *bleche(n),* OE *blǣcean* (< *blāc* pale); c. Icel *bleikja,* MHG *bleichen*] —**bleach′a·bil′i·ty,** *n.* —**bleach′a·ble,** *adj.* —**Syn. 1.** See **whiten.**

bleach·er (blē′chər), *n.* **1.** a person or thing that bleaches. **2.** a container, as a vat or tank, used in bleaching. **3.** Usually, **bleachers.** a typically roofless section of inexpensive and unreserved seats in tiers, esp. at an open-air athletic stadium.

bleach′ing pow′der, *Chem.* a white powder having the odor of gaseous chlorine and regarded, when dry, as a mixed calcium hypochloritechloride, Ca(OCl)Cl: used as a commercial bleach and in laundering. Also called **chloride of lime.**

bleak[1] (blēk), *adj.* **1.** bare, desolate, and windswept: *a bleak plain.* **2.** cold and piercing; raw: *a bleak wind.* **3.** offering no or little hope or encouragement; depressing: *a bleak prospect.* [ME *bleke* pale, b. variants *bleche* (OE *blǣc*) and *blake* (OE *blāc*); both c. Icel *bleikr,* G *bleich;* akin to BLEACH] —**bleak′ish,** *adj.* —**bleak′ly,** *adv.* —**bleak′ness,** *n.*

bleak[2] (blēk), *n.* a European fresh-water fish, *Alburnus alburnus,* having scales with a silvery pigment that is used in the production of artificial pearls. [late ME *bleke,* n. use of BLEAK[1]]

blear (blēr), *v.t.* **1.** to make (the eyes or sight) dim, as with tears or inflammation. —*adj.* **2.** (of the eyes) dim from a watery discharge. [ME *bleri, blere* (v.), *blere* (adj.) < ?] —**blear·ed·ness** (blēr′id nis), *n.*

blear-eyed (blēr′īd′), *adj.* **1.** having blear eyes. **2.** dull of perception; short-sighted. Also, **blear′y-eyed′.** —**blear′-eyed′ness, blear′y-eyed′ness,** *n.*

blear·y (blēr′ē), *adj.,* **blear·i·er, blear·i·est. 1.** (of the eyes or sight) blurred or dimmed, as from sleep or weariness. **2.** indistinct; unclear: *a bleary view.* **3.** fatigued; worn-out. [ME *blery*] —**blear′i·ly,** *adv.* —**blear′i·ness,** *n.*

bleat (blēt), *n.* **1.** the cry of a sheep, goat, or calf. **2.** any similar sound: *the bleat of distant horns.* —*v.i.* **3.** to utter a bleat. —*v.t.* **4.** to give forth with or as with a bleat. **5.** to babble; prate. [ME *blete(n),* OE *blǣtan;* c. D *blaten,* OHG *blāzen;* akin to L *flēre* to weep] —**bleat′er,** *n.* —**bleat′ing·ly,** *adv.*

Bled (bled), *n.* a village in NW Yugoslavia: mountain resort. 2500 (est. 1962).

bleed (blēd), *v.,* **bled** (bled), **bleed·ing,** *n., adj.* —*v.i.* **1.** to lose blood from the vascular system, either internally or externally through a natural orifice or break in the skin. **2.** (of blood) to flow out. **3.** (of a plant) to exude sap, resin, etc., from a wound. **4.** (of dye or paint) to run or become diffused: *All the colors bled when the dress was washed.* **5.** to feel pity, sorrow, or anguish: *My heart bleeds for you.* **6.** *Print.* (of printed matter) to run off the edges of a page as by design. —*v.t.* **7.** to cause to lose blood, esp. surgically. **8.** to lose or emit (blood or sap). **9.** to drain or draw sap, water, electricity, etc., from (something): *to bleed a pipeline of excess air.* **10.** *Print.* to design, size, or print (an illustration or ornamentation) to run off the page or sheet. —*n.* *Print.* **11.** a sheet or page margin trimmed so as to remove part of the text or illustration. **12.** a part thus trimmed off. —*adj.* **13.** *Print.* characterized by bleeding: *a bleed page.* [ME *blede(n),* OE *blēdan* < *blōd* BLOOD]

bleed·er (blē′dər), *n.* a person predisposed to bleeding, as a hemophiliac or prizefighter easily cut by a blow.

bleed·ing (blē′ding), *n.* **1.** act, fact, or process of losing blood or having blood flow. **2.** act or process of drawing blood from a person, esp. surgically; bloodletting. **3.** *Print.* the extension of color beyond an edge or border, esp. so as to combine with a contiguous color or to affect an adjacent area. —*adj.* **4.** sending forth blood: *a bleeding sore.* **5.** *Brit. Slang.* bloody (def. 5). [ME]

bleed′ing heart′, **1.** any of various plants of the genus *Dicentra,* esp. *D. spectabilis,* a common garden plant having racemes of red, heart-shaped flowers. **2.** *Disparaging.* a person who makes an ostentatious or excessive display of pity or concern for others.

blem·ish (blem′ish), *v.t.* **1.** to destroy or diminish the perfection of. —*n.* **2.** a defect or flaw; disfigurement; stain. **3.** a pimple or blackhead. [ME *blemysh* < MF *blemiss-,* long s. of *ble(s)mir* to make livid, perh. < Gmc; see BLAZE[2]] —**blem′ish·er,** *n.* —**Syn. 1.** injure, mar, impair. **2.** blot. See **defect.** —**Ant. 1.** purify, repair.

blench[1] (blench), *v.i.* to shrink; flinch; quail. [ME *blenche(n),* OE *blencan;* c. Icel *blekkja,* MHG *blenken*] —**blench′er,** *n.* —**blench′ing·ly,** *adv.*

blench[2] (blench), *v.t., v.i.* to make or become pale or white; blanch. [var. of BLANCH[1]]

blend (blend), *v.,* **blend·ed** or **blent, blend·ing,** *n.* —*v.t.* **1.** to mix smoothly and inseparably together: *to blend the ingredients in a recipe.* **2.** to prepare by such mixture: *This tea is blended by mixing camomile with pekoe.* —*v.i.* **3.** to mix or intermingle smoothly and inseparably. **4.** to fit or relate harmoniously: *The red sofa did not blend with the purple wall.* **5.** to have no perceptible separation: *Sea and sky seemed to blend.* —*n.* **6.** act or manner of blending: *tea of our own blend.* **7.** a mixture or kind produced by blending: *a mild blend of pipe tobacco.* **8.** *Linguistics.* a word made by putting together parts of other words, as *dandle,* made from *dance* and *handle.* [ME *blend(en),* OE *blendan* to mix, akin to *blandan* to mix; c. Icel *blanda,* OHG *blantan* to mix] —**Syn. 1, 3.** commingle, combine, unite. **6.** combination, amalgamation. —**Ant. 1.** separate.

blende (blend), *n.* **1.** sphalerite; zinc sulfide. **2.** any of certain other sulfides. [< G; MHG *blende(n)* (to) make blind, deceive; so called because often deceptively like galena]

blend′ed whis′key, a blend of two or more whiskeys or of whiskey and neutral spirits that contains at least 20 percent of 100-proof straight whiskey by volume after blending.

blend·er (blen′dər), *n.* **1.** a person or thing that blends. **2.** a kitchen appliance with propellerlike blades for puréeing foods, grinding coffee, mixing beverages, etc. **3.** a kitchen appliance having several parallel wires bent in a semicircle and secured by a handle, used esp. for mixing pastry.

Blen·heim (blen′əm), *n.* a village in S West Germany, on the Danube: victory of the Duke of Marlborough over the French 1704. German, **Blindheim.**

blen·ny (blen′ē), *n., pl.* **-nies.** any of several fishes of the genus *Blennius* and related genera having an elongated tapering body and small pelvic fins inserted before the pectoral fins. [< L *blenni(us)* a kind of fish < Gk *blénnos* slime, mucus; so called from its slimy coating]

blent (blent), *v.* a pt. and pp. of **blend.**

blephar-, a learned borrowing from Greek meaning "eyelid," used in the formation of compound words: *blepharitis.* [< Gk *blephar-,* comb. form of *blépharon*]

bleph·a·ri·tis (blef′ə rī′tis), *n.* *Pathol.* inflammation of the eyelids. —**bleph·a·rit·ic** (blef′ə rit′ik), *adj.*

Blé·riot (blā ʀyô′), *n.* **Louis** (lwē), 1872–1936, French aviator, pioneer aeronautical engineer, and inventor.

bles·bok (bles′bok′), *n., pl.* **-boks,** (*esp. collectively*) **-bok.** a large antelope, *Damaliscus albifrons,* of southern Africa, having a blaze on the face. [< SAfrD = D *bles* BLAZE[2] + *bok* BUCK[1]]

bless (bles), *v.t.,* **blessed** or **blest, bless·ing. 1.** to consecrate or sanctify by a religious rite. **2.** to request of God the bestowal of divine favor on: *Bless this house.* **3.** to bestow good of any kind upon: *a nation blessed with peace.* **4.** to extol as holy; glorify: *Bless the name of the Lord.* **5.** to protect or guard from evil (usually used interjectionally): *Bless you!* **6.** to condemn or curse: *I'll be blessed if I can see your reasoning.* **7.** to make the sign of the cross over or upon. [ME *bless(en),* OE *blētsian, blēdsian* to consecrate, orig. with blood < earlier **blōdisōian* = *blōd* blood + *-isō-* derivational suffix + *-ian* v. suffix] —**bless′er,** *n.* —**bless′ing·ly,** *adv.*

bless·ed (bles′id *for 1, 2, 4, 5, 7;* blest *for 1, 3, 4, 6*), *adj.* Also, **blest. 1.** consecrated; sacred; holy; sanctified. **2.** worthy of adoration, reverence, or worship. **3.** divinely or supremely favored; fortunate: *to be blessed with a healthy body.* **4.** blissfully happy or contented. **5.** *Rom. Cath. Ch.* beatified. **6.** (used as a euphemism) damned: *I'm blessed if I know.* —*n.* **7. the blessed,** *Rom. Cath. Ch.* the aggregate of deceased persons who have received beatification. [ME] —**bless′ed·ly,** *adv.* —**bless′ed·ness,** *n.*

Bless′ed Sac′rament, *Eccles.* the consecrated Host.

bless·ing (bles′ing), *n.* **1.** the act or words of a person who blesses. **2.** a special favor, mercy, or benefit: *the blessings of liberty.* **3.** a favor or gift bestowed by God. **4.** the invocation of God's favor upon a person: *The son was denied his father's blessing.* **5.** praise, devotion, or worship, esp. grace said before a meal. **6.** approval: *a proposed law having the blessing of the governor.* [ME *blessinge, -unge,* OE *bletsung, bledsung*]

blest (blest), *v.* **1.** a pt. and pp. of **bless.** —*adj.* **2.** blessed.

bleth·er (bleth′ər), *n., v.i., v.t.* blather.

blew (blo͞o), *v.* pt. of **blow**[2].

Bli·da (blē′dä), *n.* a city in N Algeria. 93,000 (1960).

Bligh (blī), *n.* **William,** 1754–1817, British naval officer: captain of H.M.S. *Bounty,* the crew of which mutinied 1789.

blight (blīt), *n.* **1.** *Plant Pathol.* **a.** the rapid and extensive discoloration, wilting, and death of plant tissues. **b.** a disease so characterized. **2.** any cause of impairment, destruction, ruin, or frustration. —*v.t.* **3.** to cause to wither or decay; blast: *Frost blighted the crops.* **4.** to destroy; ruin; frustrate: *Illness blighted his hopes.* —*v.i.* **5.** to suffer blight. [?] —**blight′ing·ly,** *adj.*

blight·er (blī′tər), *n.* *Brit. Slang.* **1.** a contemptible, worthless man; rascal. **2.** a fellow; guy; bloke.

blight·y (blī′tē), *n., pl.* **blight·ies.** *Brit. Slang.* **1.** (*often cap.*) England as one's native land or home: *We're sailing for old Blighty tomorrow.* **2.** a wound or furlough permitting a soldier to be sent back to England from the front during World War I. [< Hindi *bilāyatī* the country (i.e., Gt. Britain), var. of *wilāyatī* < Ar *wilāyat*]

bli·mey (blī′mē), *interj.* *Brit. Slang.* (used to express surprise or amazement): *Blimey, it's old Bates himself!* Also, **bli′my.** [contr. of *blind me*]

blimp (blimp), *n.* **1.** a small, nonrigid airship or dirigible, used chiefly for observation. **2.** *Informal.* any dirigible. [? from phrase *Type B-limp* a kind of nonrigid dirigible]

blind (blīnd), *adj.* **1.** unable to see; lacking the sense of sight. **2.** unwilling or unable to understand: *He was blind to all arguments.* **3.** not characterized or determined by reason or control: *blind chance.* **4.** characterized by a lack of consciousness or awareness: *a blind stupor.* **5.** *Slang.* drunk. **6.** hidden from immediate view, esp. from oncoming motorists: *a blind corner.* **7.** of concealed or undisclosed identity; sponsored anonymously: *a blind ad signed only with a box number.* **8.** having no outlets; closed at one end: *a blind alley.* **9.** *Archit.* (of an archway, arcade, etc.)

having no windows, passageways, or the like. **10.** done without seeing; using instruments alone: *blind flying.* **11.** made without some prior knowledge: *a blind purchase.* **12.** of, pertaining to, or for blind persons. —*v.t.* **13.** to make blind permanently, temporarily, or momentarily: *We were blinded by the bright lights.* **14.** to make obscure or dark. **15.** to deprive of discernment, reason, or judgment: *Resentment blinds his good sense.* **16.** to outshine; eclipse: *a radiance that doth blind the sun.* —*n.* **17.** something that obstructs vision or keeps out light, as a window shade or a blinker for a horse. **18.** a lightly built structure, often of brush or other growth, esp. one in which hunters conceal themselves. **19.** an activity, organization, or the like, for concealing or masking action or purpose; subterfuge: *The store was just a blind for their gambling operation.* **20.** a decoy. **21.** (*construed as pl.*) persons who lack the sense of sight (usually prec. by *the*). —*adv.* **22.** without the ability to see; blindly: *They were driving blind through the snowstorm.* **23.** (of the operation of an aircraft) by instruments alone. **24.** without guidance or forethought: *They were working blind.* [OE *blind;* c. Goth *blind(s),* Icel *blindr,* G, D *blind,* Lith *blę̃ndzas* blind] —**blind′ness,** *n.* —**Syn. 1.** sightless. **3.** irrational, thoughtless, unreasoning. **6.** concealed. **19.** ruse, stratagem. —**Ant. 1.** seeing. **3.** rational.

blind′ al′ley, **1.** a road, alley, etc., that is open at only one end. **2.** a position or situation offering no hope of progress or improvement.

blind′ date′, *Informal.* **1.** a prearranged date between a man and a woman who have never before met. **2.** either of the participants.

blind·er (blīn′dər), *n.* a blinker for a horse.

blind·fish (blīnd′fish′), *n., pl.* **-fish·es,** (*esp. collectively*) **-fish.** a cavefish.

blind·fold (blīnd′fōld′), *v.t.* **1.** to cover the eyes of with a cloth, bandage, or the like, to keep from seeing. **2.** to impair the awareness or clear thinking of: *Don't let their hospitality blindfold you to the true purpose of your visit.* —*n.* **3.** a cloth or bandage put before the eyes to prevent seeing. —*adj.* **4.** with the eyes covered: *a blindfold test.* [BLIND + FOLD[1]; r. *blindfell,* lit., a blind fall < OE *blindfellian* to strike blind. See BLIND, FELL[2]]

blind′ gut′, the cecum.

Blind·heim (blint′hīm′), *n.* German name of **Blenheim.**

blind·ly (blīnd′lē), *adv.* **1.** in a blind manner: *We felt our way blindly through the black tunnel.* **2.** without understanding, reservation, or objection: *They followed their leaders blindly.* **3.** without continuation: *The passage ended blindly 50 feet away.*

blind·man's buff (blīnd′manz′ buf′), a game in which a blindfolded player tries to catch and identify one of the others. Also called **blind′man's bluff′.**

blind′ spot′, **1.** *Anat.* a small area on the retina where the optic nerve leaves the eye and which is insensitive to light. **2.** an area or subject about which one is uninformed, prejudiced, or undiscerning. **3.** *Radio.* an area in which signals are weak and their reception poor. **4.** any part of an auditorium, arena, or the like, in which one is unable to see or hear satisfactorily.

blind′ stag′gers, *Vet. Pathol.* stagger (def. 10).

blind-stamp (blīnd′stamp′), *v.t.* to emboss or impress (letters, a design, or the like) by a die without ink or foil.

blind′ ti′ger, *U.S. Slang.* an illegal liquor saloon, esp. during Prohibition. Also called **blind′ pig′.**

blind·worm (blīnd′wûrm′), *n.* a limbless European lizard, *Anguis fragilis,* related to the glass lizards: so called because its eyes are very small.

blink (bliŋk), *v.i.* **1.** to open and close the eye quickly, esp. involuntarily; wink rapidly and usually repeatedly. **2.** to look with winking or half-shut eyes: *I blinked at the harsh morning light.* **3.** to look evasively or with indifference; ignore (often fol. by *at*): *a person who blinks at responsibility.* **4.** to shine unsteadily, dimly, or intermittently; twinkle: *The light blinked in the distance.* —*v.t.* **5.** to open and close (the eye) rapidly and repeatedly; wink. **6.** to remove (tears, a foreign body, etc.) from the eyes by blinking. **7.** to cause (something) to blink: *We blinked the light.* —*n.* **8.** act of blinking. **9.** *Chiefly Scot.* a glance or glimpse. **10.** a gleam; glimmer: *There was not a blink of light anywhere.* **11. on the blink,** *Slang.* not in proper working order; in need of repair. [ME *blink(en),* var. of *blenken* to BLENCH[1]; c. D, G *blinken*] —**Syn. 1.** See **wink**[1]. **8.** wink, twinkle.

blink·er (bliŋ′kər), *n.* **1.** a person or thing that blinks. **2.** a device for flashing light signals. **3.** a light that flashes intermittently, esp. a traffic light. **4.** either of two leather flaps on a bridle, to prevent a horse from seeing sideways; a blinder. **5. blinkers,** goggles (def. 1).

blink·ing (bliŋ′kiŋ), *adj.* **1.** that blinks. **2.** (used as a euphemism) damned. —**blink′ing·ly,** *adv.*

blintze (blints), *n.* *Jewish Cookery.* a thin pancake folded around a filling, as of cheese or fruit. Also, **blintz** (blints). [< Yiddish *blintse* < Russ *blinets,* dim. of *blin* pancake]

blip (blip), *n., v.,* **blipped, blip·ping.** —*n.* **1.** a spot of light on a radar screen indicating the position of an object. **2.** a quick, sharp sound. **3.** *Television.* an instant interruption of the audio by blipping. **4.** a brief unimportant interruption. —*v.i.* **5.** to make a blip or blips. —*v.t.* **6.** to activate by flipping a switch. **7.** *Television.* to erase (an unwanted word, passage, sound, etc.) from a tape. [?]

bliss (blis), *n.* **1.** supreme happiness. **2.** *Theol.* the joy of heaven. **3.** heaven; paradise. **4.** *Archaic.* a cause of great joy. [ME *blisse,* OE *bliss, bliths* = *blīthe* BLITHE + *-s* suffix, c. L *-itia* -ICE] —**bliss′less,** *adj.* —**Syn. 1.** See **happiness.** —**Ant. 1.** misery.

bliss·ful (blis′fəl), *adj.* full of, abounding in, enjoying, or conferring bliss. [ME; r. OE *blissig*] —**bliss′ful·ly,** *adv.* —**bliss′ful·ness,** *n.*

blis·ter (blis′tər), *n.* **1.** a thin vesicle on the skin, containing watery matter or serum, caused by a burn or other injury. **2.** any similar swelling, as an air bubble in a coat of paint. **3.** *Mil.* a transparent bulge or dome on the fuselage of an airplane, usually for mounting a gun. —*v.t.* **4.** to raise a blister or blisters on. **5.** to criticize, rebuke, or punish severely. —*v.i.* **6.** to rise in blisters; become blistered. [ME *blister, blester* < Scand; cf. Icel *blǣstri,* dat. of *blāstr* swelling. See BLAST, BLOW[2]] —**blis′ter·ing·ly,** *adv.* —**blis′ter·y,** *adj.*

blis′ter bee′tle, any of various beetles of the family *Meloidae,* many of which produce a secretion capable of blistering the skin.

blis′ter cop′per, *Metall.* a matte of 96–99 percent copper, having a blistered surface after smelting.

blis′ter rust′, *Plant Pathol.* a disease, esp. of white pines, characterized by cankers and by blisters on the stems, caused by a fungus of the genus *Cronartium.*

blithe (blīth, blīth), *adj.* **1.** joyous, merry, or gay in disposition. **2.** without thought or regard; heedless: *a blithe indifference to anyone's feelings.* [ME, OE; c. Icel *blīthr,* OHG *blīdi,* Goth *bleith(s)*] —**blithe′ful,** *adj.* —**blithe′ful·ly,** *adv.* —**blithe′ly,** *adv.* —**blithe′ness,** *n.* —**Syn. 1.** happy, light-hearted, joyful. —**Ant. 1.** joyless.

blith·er·ing (blith′ər iŋ), *adj.* talking nonsensically: *a blithering idiot.* [*blither,* var. of BLATHER + -ING[2]]

blithe·some (blīth′səm, blīth′-), *adj.* light-hearted; merry; cheerful: *a blithesome nature.* —**blithe′some·ly,** *adv.* —**blithe′some·ness,** *n.*

blitz (blits), *n.* **1.** *Mil.* **a.** an overwhelming all-out attack, esp. a swift ground attack using armored units and air support. **b.** an intensive aerial bombing. **2.** any swift attack. —*v.t.* **3.** to attack with a blitz. [short for BLITZKRIEG]

blitz·krieg (blits′krēg′), *n., v.t.* blitz. [< G: lit., lightning war]

Blitz·stein (blits′stīn), *n.* **Marc,** 1905–64, U.S. composer.

bliz·zard (bliz′ərd), *n.* **1.** a heavy and prolonged snowstorm covering a wide area. **2.** a violent windstorm with dry, driving snow and intense cold. [var. of dial. *blizzer* blaze, flash, blinding flash of lightning; sense widened from lightning to storm; akin to OE *blysa, blyse* torch, *blysian* to burn] —**bliz′zard·y, bliz′zard·ly,** *adj.*

blk., **1.** black. **2.** block. **3.** bulk.

bloat (blōt), *v.t.* **1.** to expand or distend, as with air or water; cause to swell. **2.** to puff up; make vain or conceited: *The promotion has bloated his ego to an alarming degree.* **3.** to cure (fish) as bloaters. —*v.i.* **4.** to become swollen; be puffed out or dilated. —*n.* **5.** *Vet. Pathol.* (in cattle, sheep, and horses) a distention of the rumen or paunch or of the large colon by gases of fermentation, caused by eating ravenously of green forage, esp. legumes. **6.** a person or thing that is bloated. **7.** bloater (defs. 1 and 2). [*bloat* (adj.), ME *blout* soft, puffy < Scand; cf. Icel *blaut(r)* soft]

bloat·er (blō′tər), *n.* **1.** a herring cured by being salted and briefly smoked and dried. **2.** a mackerel similarly cured. **3.** a fresh-water cisco, *Coregonus hoyi,* found in the Great Lakes. [*bloat* (adj.) + -ER[1]]

blob (blob), *n., v.,* **blobbed, blob·bing.** —*n.* **1.** a small lump, drop, splotch, or daub. **2.** an indistinct or indefinite object, esp. a large one: *There was a blob off to the left that could have been the house.* **3.** a globule of liquid; bubble. —*v.t.* **4.** to mark or splotch with blobs. [? imit.]

bloc (blok), *n.* a group of people, as voters or legislators, or a coalition of factions, political parties, or interest groups, that works or votes for or against specific bills, proposals, or ideas: *the farm bloc.* [< F; see BLOCK]

Bloch (blok; *Ger.* blôkh), *n.* **Ernest,** 1880–1959, Swiss composer, in the U.S. after 1916.

block (blok), *n.* **1.** a solid mass of wood, stone, etc., usually with one or more flat or approximately flat faces. **2.** a hollow masonry building unit of cement, terra cotta, etc.: *a wall made of concrete blocks.* **3.** one of a set of regularly shaped pieces of wood, plastic, or the like, for use as a child's toy in building. **4.** a mold or piece on which something is shaped or kept in shape: *a hat block.* **5.** a piece of wood used in making woodcuts or wood engravings. **6.** *Print.* the base on which a plate is mounted to make it type-high. **7.** a stump or wooden structure on which a condemned person is beheaded. **8.** a platform from which an auctioneer sells. **9.** *Mach.* a part enclosing one or more freely rotating, grooved pulleys, about which ropes or chains pass to form a hoisting or hauling tackle. **10.** an obstacle or obstruction; hindrance. **11.** the state or condition of being obstructed; blockage: *The traffic block lasted several hours.* **12.** *Pathol.* an obstruction, as of a nerve. **13.** *Sports.* a hindering of an opponent's actions. **14.** a quantity, portion, or section taken as a unit or dealt with at one time: *a large block of theater tickets.* **15.** a small section of a city, town, etc., enclosed by neighboring and intersecting streets or the length of one side of such a section: *She lives on my block. We walked two blocks over.* **16.** *Chiefly Brit.* a large building divided into separate apartments, offices, shops, etc. **17.** a large number of bonds or shares of stock sold together as a unit. **18.** *Computer Technol.* **a.** (on a flow chart) a symbol representing an operation, device, or instruction in a computer program. **b.** a section of storage locations in a computer allocated to a particular set of instructions or data. **c.** a group of consecutive machine words organized as a unit and guiding a particular computer operation, esp. with reference to input and output. **19.** *Railroads.* any of the short lengths into which a track is divided for signaling purposes. **20.** *Philately.* a group of four or more unseparated stamps, not in a strip. **21.** *Psychiatry.* a sudden stoppage of speech or thought, usually caused by emotional tension. **22.** (in Canada) a wild or remote area of land that has not yet been surveyed. **23. have a block,** to be chronically unable to perform a particular mental operation: *He has a block when it comes to math.* —*v.t.* **24.** to fit with blocks; mount on a block. **25.** to shape or prepare on or with a block: *to block a hat; to block a sweater.* **26.** to obstruct (someone or something) by placing obstacles in the way (sometimes fol. by *up*): *to block one's exit; to block up a passage.* **27.** *Pathol., Physiol.* to stop the passage of impulses in (a nerve). **28.** *Sports.* to hinder or bar the actions or movements of (an opposing player), esp. legitimately. **29.** *Metalworking.* to give (a forging) a rough form before finishing. —*v.i.* **30.**

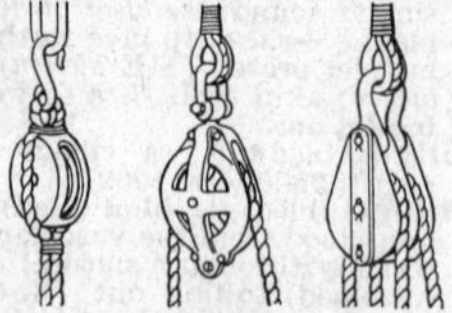

Blocks (def. 9) with single and double sheaves

to act so as to obstruct an opponent, as in football, boxing, and baseball. **31.** *Psychiatry.* to suffer a block. **32. block in** or **out,** to sketch or outline roughly or generally, without details. [ME *blok* log or stump < MD (directly or < MF *bloc* in same sense); perh. akin to BALK] **—Syn. 10.** impediment, blockade, stoppage, jam. **25.** mold, form. **26.** close.

Block (blok), *n.* **Herbert Lawrence** ("*Herblock*"), born 1909, U.S. cartoonist.

block·ade (blo kād′), *n., v.,* **-ad·ed, -ad·ing.** **—*n.* 1.** *Navy, Mil.* the isolating of a place, esp. a port, harbor, or part of a coast, by hostile ships or troops by preventing entrance or exit. **2.** any obstruction of passage or progress. **—*v.t.* 3.** to subject to a blockade. **—block·ad′er,** *n.*

block·ade-run·ner (blo kād′run′ər), *n.* a ship that or person who attempts to pass through a blockade. **—block·ade′-run′ning,** *n.*

block·age (blok′ij), *n.* **1.** act of blocking. **2.** state of being blocked; an obstructed condition or situation.

block′ and tack′le, the ropes or chains and blocks used in a hoisting tackle.

block·bust·er (blok′bus′tər), *n.* **1.** *Informal.* a 4–8 ton aerial bomb for large-scale demolition. **2.** something or someone that is forcefully or overwhelmingly impressive, effective, or influential. **3.** a person who practices blockbusting.

block·bust·ing (blok′bus′ting), *adj.* **1.** forcefully or overwhelmingly impressive or effective. **—*n.* 2.** the buying, selling, or renting to a black person of a home in a block inhabited exclusively by white people. **3.** the practice of exploiting racial prejudice and the fear of general decline in a neighborhood's real-estate values to induce home owners to sell their property at a low price, as upon the entrance into the neighborhood of a single black family.

block′ front′, the frontage of an entire block, esp. in a city or town.

block′ grant′, a consolidated grant of federal funds, formerly allocated for specific programs, which a state or local government may use at its discretion for such generalized programs as education or urban development.

block·head (blok′hed′), *n.* a stupid, doltish person; dunce. **—block′head′ed,** *adj.* **—block′head′ed·ly,** *adv.* **—block′head′ed·ness,** *n.* **—block′head′ism,** *n.*

block·house (blok′hous′), *n., pl.* **-hous·es** (hou′ziz). **1.** *Mil.* a fortified structure with ports or loopholes through which defenders may direct gunfire. **2.** (formerly) a building, usually of hewn timber and with a projecting upper story, having loopholes for musketry. **3.** a house built of squared logs. **4.** *Rocketry.* a structure for housing and protecting personnel and electronic controls before and during launching operations. [< MD or Flem *blochuus*]

block·ish (blok′ish), *adj.* like a block; dull; stupid. **—block′ish·ly,** *adv.* **—block′ish·ness,** *n.*

Block′ Is′land, an island off the coast of and a part of Rhode Island, at the E entrance to Long Island Sound.

block′ la′va, *Geol.* lava in the form of rough blocks.

block′ let′ter, **1.** *Print.* a sans-serif typeface or letter, usually compressed and having tight curves. **2.** a simple, squared off hand-printed capital letter.

This is a sample of block letter

block′ par′ty, a public, neighborhood festival or carnival, usually held in a closed-off city street.

block′ plane′, *Carpentry.* a small plane for cutting across grain.

block′ print′, *Fine Arts.* a design printed by means of one or more blocks of wood or metal.

block′ sig′nal, a fixed railroad signal governing the movements of trains entering and using a given section of track. **—block′ sig′naling.**

block′ tin′, pure tin.

block·y (blok′ē), *adj.* **block·i·er, block·i·est.** **1.** heavily built; stocky. **2.** marked by patches of unequally distributed light and shade, as in a photograph.

Bloem·fon·tein (blo͞om′fon tān′), *n.* a city in and the capital of the Orange Free State, in the central Republic of South Africa. 182,000.

Blois (blwa), *n.* a city in central France, on the Loire River: historic castle. 51,950.

Blok (blôk), *n.* **A·lex·an·der A·lex·an·dro·vich** (ä′leksän′dər ä′le ksän′dro vich), 1880–1921, Russian poet.

bloke (blōk), *n.* *Chiefly Brit. Slang.* man; fellow; guy. [?]

blond (blond) *adj.* **1.** (of hair, fur, the human skin, etc.) light-colored. **2.** (of a person) having light-colored hair and skin. **3.** (of furniture wood) light in tone. **—*n.* 4.** a blond person. Also, *esp. referring to a woman,* **blonde.** [ME *blounde* light brown < MF *blonde,* fem. of *blond*] **—blond′ness, blonde′ness,** *n.* **—blond′ish,** *adj.*

blood (blud), *n.* **1.** the fluid that circulates in the principal vascular system of man and other vertebrates. **2.** the vital principle; life: *The excitement had got into the very blood of the nation.* **3.** a fresh source of energy, vitality, or vigor, as personnel: *It's time we got some new blood in this company.* **4.** bloodshed; slaughter; murder: *to avenge the blood of his father.* **5.** the juice or sap of a plant. **6.** temperament; state of mind: *a person of hot blood.* **7.** man's corporeal or physical nature: *the frailty of men's blood.* **8.** *Chiefly Brit.* a high-spirited dandy; an adventuresome youth. **9.** physical and cultural extraction: *It was a trait that seemed to be in the blood.* **10.** royal extraction: *a prince of the blood.* **11.** descent from a common ancestor; ancestry; lineage: *related by blood.* **12.** *Stockbreeding.* recorded and respected ancestry; purebred breeding. **13. have someone's blood on one's head** or **hands,** to be to blame for someone's affliction or death. **14. in cold blood,** deliberately; ruthlessly. **15. make one's blood boil,** to inspire resentment, anger, or indignation. **16. make one's blood run cold,** to fill with terror. **—*v.t.* 17.** *Hunting.* to give (hounds) a first sight or taste of blood. Cf. **flesh** (def. 14). **18.** *Brit.* (in fox hunting) to perform the ceremony of blooding on (someone). **19.** *Obs.* to stain with blood. [ME *blo(o)d,* OE *blōd;* c. OHG *bluot* (G *Blut*)]

blood′ bank′, a place where blood or blood plasma is collected, processed, stored, and distributed.

blood′ bath′, the ruthless slaughter of great numbers of people; massacre.

blood′ broth′er, **1.** a person's brother by birth. **2.** a male person bound to another by ties of great friendship. **3.** a male bound to another male by a specific ritual, usually the commingling of blood.

blood′ cell′, the cellular elements of blood, as erythrocytes or leukocytes. Also called **blood′ cor′puscle.**

blood′ count′, the number of red and white corpuscles and platelets in a specific volume of blood.

blood·cur·dling (blud′kûrd′ling), *adj.* terrifyingly horrible.

blood·ed (blud′id), *adj.* **1.** having blood (usually used in combination: *warm-blooded animals.* **2.** (of horses, cattle, etc.) derived from ancestors of good blood; pedigreed. [ME]

blood·fin (blud′fin′), *n.* a South American characin fish, *Aphyocharax rubropinnis,* having a silvery body and blood-red fins, often kept in aquariums.

blood′ group′, one of several classes into which human blood can be separated according to its agglutinogens. Also called **blood type.**

blood·guilt·y (blud′gil′tē), *adj.* guilty of murder or bloodshed. [BLOOD(SHED) + GUILTY] **—blood′guilt′i·ness,** *n.*

blood·hound (blud′hound′), *n.* one of a breed of medium- to large-sized dogs, usually having a black-and-tan coat, very long ears, loose skin, and an acute sense of smell: used chiefly for following human scents. [ME *blodhound*]

Bloodhound (26 in. high at shoulder)

blood·ing (blud′ing), *n.* *Fox Hunting.* (chiefly in Britain) an informal initiation ceremony in which the face of a novice is smeared with the blood of the first fox he has seen killed.

blood·less (blud′lis), *adj.* **1.** without blood. **2.** pale: *a bloodless face* **3.** free from bloodshed: *a bloodless victory.* **4.** spiritless; without vigor, zest, or energy: *a dull, bloodless young man.* [ME *blodles,* OE *blōdlēas*] **—blood′less·ly,** *adv.* **—blood′less·ness,** *n.*

blood·let·ting (blud′let′ing), *n.* act or practice of letting blood by opening a vein; phlebotomy. [ME *blod letunge*] **—blood′let′ter,** *n.*

blood·line (blud′līn′), *n.* (usually of animals) the line of descent; pedigree; strain.

blood·mo·bile (blud′mə bēl′), *n.* a small truck with medical equipment for receiving blood donations to be used for blood transfusions.

blood′ mon′ey, **1.** a fee paid to a hired murderer. **2.** compensation paid to the survivors of a slain man. **3.** money paid to an informer, esp. when the criminal's arrest is followed by his execution.

blood′ plas′ma, the liquid portion of human blood.

blood′ plate′let, one of numerous, minute, protoplasmic bodies in mammalian blood that aid in coagulation.

blood′ poi′soning, *Pathol.* a condition of the blood caused by presence of toxic matter or microorganisms, characterized by chills, sweating, fever, and prostration; toxemia; septicemia; pyemia.

blood′ pres′sure, *Physiol.* the pressure of the blood against the inner walls of the blood vessels.

blood′ rel′ative, a person related to one by birth. Also, **blood′ re·la′tion.**

blood·root (blud′ro͞ot′, -ro͝ot′), *n.* **1.** a North American papaveraceous plant, *Sanguinaria canadensis,* having a red root and root sap. **2.** an Old World, rosaceous plant, *Potentilla tormentilla,* having a reddish root.

blood′ sau′sage, a dark sausage containing diced pork fat, pork blood, chopped onion, etc. Also called **black pudding, blood′ pud′ding.**

blood′ se′rum, serum (def 1).

blood·shed (blud′shed′), *n.* **1.** destruction of life, as in war, murder, etc.; slaughter. **2.** the shedding of blood by injury, wound, etc. Also, **blood′shed′ding.**

blood·shot (blud′shot′), *adj.* (of the eyes) exhibiting dilated blood vessels. [apocopated var. of *blood-shotten.* See BLOOD, SHOTTEN]

blood′ spav′in, *Vet. Pathol.* See under **spavin** (def. 1).

blood′ sport′, any sport involving killing or the shedding of blood, as bullfighting, hunting, etc.

blood·stain (blud′stān′), *n.* a spot or stain made by blood. [back formation from BLOODSTAINED]

blood·stained (blud′stānd′), *adj.* **1.** stained with blood. **2.** guilty of bloodshed.

blood·stone (blud′stōn′), *n.* a greenish variety of chalcedony with small bloodlike spots of red jasper scattered through it. Also called **heliotrope.**

blood·stream (blud′strēm′), *n.* the blood flowing through a circulatory system. [ME]

blood·suck·er (blud′suk′ər), *n.* **1.** any animal that sucks blood, esp. a leech. **2.** an extortioner or usurer. **3.** sponger (def. 1). **—blood′suck′ing,** *adj.*

blood′ sug′ar, **1.** glucose in the blood. **2.** the quantity or percentage of glucose in the blood.

blood′ test′, a test of a sample of blood to determine blood group, presence of infection, parentage, etc.

blood·thirst·y (blud′thûr′stē), *adj.* **1.** eager to shed blood; murderous. **2.** enjoying or encouraging bloodshed or violence, esp. as a spectator or clamorous partisan. **—blood′thirst′i·ly,** *adv.* **—blood′thirst′i·ness,** *n.*

blood′ transfu′sion, the injection of blood from one person or animal into the bloodstream of another.

blood′ type′. See **blood group.**

blood′ ves′sel, any of the vessels, as arteries, veins, or capillaries, through which the blood circulates.

blood·worm (blud′wûrm′), *n.* any of several red or red-blooded annelid worms, esp. various earthworms used for bait.

blood·wort (blud′wûrt′), *n.* **1.** any plant of the *Haemodoracene* having red roots, esp. the redroot, *Gyrotheca tinctoria,* of North America. **2.** any of various plants having red roots, leaves, etc., as the dock or the rattlesnake weed. **3.** bloodroot. [ME *blodwurt*]

blood·y (blud′ē), *adj.,* **blood·i·er, blood·i·est,** *v.,* **blood·ied, blood·y·ing,** *adv.* **—*adj.* 1.** stained with blood or bleeding:

a bloody handkerchief. **2.** characterized by bloodshed: *bloody battle.* **3.** inclined to bloodshed; bloodthirsty. **4.** of, pertaining to, or resembling blood; containing or composed of blood. **5.** *Brit. Slang.* damned; extraordinary. **—v.t. 6.** to stain or smear with blood. **—adv. 7.** *Brit. Slang.* damned or damnably; very; exceedingly. [ME *blody,* OE *blōdig*] **—blood′i·ly,** *adv.* **—blood′i·ness,** *n.*

Blood′y Mar′y, 1. a mixed drink made principally with vodka and tomato juice. **2.** See **Mary I.**

bloom[1] (blo͞om), *n.* **1.** the flower of a plant. **2.** flowers collectively: *the bloom of the cherry tree.* **3.** state of having the buds open: *The gardens are all in bloom.* **4.** a flourishing, healthy condition; the time or period of greatest beauty, artistry, etc.: *the bloom of youth.* **5.** a glow or flush on the cheek indicative of youth and health. **6.** *Bot.* a whitish powdery deposit or coating, as on the surface of certain fruits and leaves: *the bloom of the grape.* **7.** any similar surface coating or appearance. **8.** any of certain minerals occurring as powdery coatings on other materials. **9.** Also called **chill.** a clouded or dull area on a varnished or lacquered surface. **—v.i. 10.** to produce or yield blossoms. **11.** to flourish: *a recurrent fad that blooms from time to time.* **12.** to be in or achieve a state of healthful beauty and vigor. **—v.t. 13.** to cause to yield blossoms. **14.** to make bloom or cause to flourish: *a happiness that blooms the cheek.* **15.** to cause a cloudy area on (something shiny); dampen; chill: *Their breath bloomed the frosty pane.* [ME *blom, blome* < Scand; c. Goth *blōma* lily, G *Blume* flower] **—bloom′less,** *adj.*

bloom[2] (blo͞om), *n.* *Metalworking.* **1.** a piece of steel, square or slightly oblong in section, reduced from an ingot to dimensions suitable for further rolling. **2.** a large lump of iron and slag produced in a puddling furnace or bloomery and hammered into wrought iron. [OE *blōma* lump of metal]

bloom·er[1] (blo͞o′mər), *n.* **1. bloomers, a.** (formerly) a woman's athletic costume of loose trousers gathered at the knee. **b.** a woman's undergarment of similar, but less bulky, design. **2.** a costume for women consisting of a short skirt and loose trousers gathered and buttoning at the ankle. [named after Amelia Jenks *Bloomer* (1818–94), American advocate of the costume]

bloom·er[2] (blo͞o′mər), *n.* **1.** a plant that blooms. **2.** a person, esp. a youth, who develops skills, abilities, interests, etc., commensurate with his capacities. [BLOOM[1] + -ER[1]]

bloom·er·y (blo͞o′mə rē), *n., pl.* **-er·ies.** a hearth for smelting iron in blooms of pasty consistency by means of charcoal.

Bloom·field (blo͞om′fēld′), *n.* **1. Leonard,** 1887–1949, U.S. linguist and educator. **2.** a city in NE New Jersey. 52,029 (1970).

bloom·ing (blo͞o′ming), *adj.* **1.** in bloom; flowering; blossoming. **2.** glowing, as with youthful vigor and freshness: *blooming cheeks.* **3.** flourishing; prospering: *a blooming business.* **4.** *Informal.* damned (euphemism for *bloody*). **—bloom′ing·ly,** *adv.* **—bloom′ing·ness,** *n.*

Bloom·ing·ton (blo͞o′ming tən), *n.* **1.** a city in SE Minnesota. 81,970 (1970). **2.** a city in central Illinois. 39,992 (1970). **3.** a city in S Indiana. 43,262 (1970).

Blooms·bur·y (blo͞omz′bə rē, -brē), *n.* a district in London, N of the Thames and Charing Cross, considered an artistic and intellectual center, esp. in the early 20th century.

bloom·y (blo͞o′mē), *adj.,* **bloom·i·er, bloom·i·est. 1.** covered with blossoms; in full flower. **2.** *Bot.* having a bloom, as fruit.

bloop·er (blo͞o′pər), *n.* **1.** *Slang.* a blunder, as one spoken over radio or TV. **2.** *Baseball.* a fly ball that carries just beyond the infield. [*bloop* (imit. of an electronic signal) + -ER[1]]

blos·som (blos′əm), *n.* *Bot.* **1.** the flower of a plant, esp. of one producing an edible fruit. **2.** the state of flowering: *The apple tree is in blossom.* **—v.i. 3.** *Bot.* to produce or yield blossoms. **4.** to flourish; develop (often fol. by *into* or *out*): *a tunesmith who blossomed out into an important composer.* [ME *blossem,* OE *blōs(t)m(a)* flower] **—blos′som·er,** *n.* **—blos′som·less,** *adj.* **—blos′som·y,** *adj.*

blot[1] (blot), *n., v.,* **blot·ted, blot·ting.** **—n. 1.** a spot or stain, esp. of ink on paper. **2.** a blemish on one's character or reputation. **3.** *Archaic.* an erasure or obliteration, as in a writing. **—v.t. 4.** to spot, stain, soil, or the like. **5.** to darken; make dim; obscure or eclipse (usually fol. by *out*): *We watched as the moon blotted the sun.* **6.** to dry or remove something moist from, as with absorbent paper: *to blot the wet pane.* **—v.i. 7.** to make a blot; spread ink, dye, etc., in a stain. **8.** to become blotted or stained. **9. blot out, a.** to make indistinguishable: *to blot out a name from the record.* **b.** to wipe out completely; destroy: *Whole cities were blotted out by bombs.* [ME *blot(te);* akin to Icel *blettur* blot, spot, stain] **—blot′less,** *adj.* **—blot′ting·ly,** *adv.* **—blot′ty,** *adj.*

blot[2] (blot), *n.* **1.** *Backgammon.* an exposed piece liable to be taken or forfeited. **2.** *Archaic.* an exposed or weak point, as in an argument or course of action. [< LG *blat,* akin to *bloot* bare, exposed, unprotected; c. D *bloot,* G *bloss* bare]

blotch (bloch), *n.* **1.** a large, irregular spot or blot. **2.** *Plant Pathol.* **a.** a diseased, discolored spot or area on a plant. **b.** a disease so characterized, usually accompanied by cankers and lesions. **3.** a skin eruption; blemish. **—v.t. 4.** to mark with blotches; blot, spot, or blur. [BL(OT[1] + B)OTCH[2]]

blotch·y (bloch′ē), *adj.,* **blotch·i·er, blotch·i·est. 1.** having blotches: *a blotchy complexion.* **2.** resembling a blotch.

blot·ter (blot′ər), *n.* **1.** a piece of blotting paper used to absorb excess ink, to protect a desk top, etc. **2.** a book in which transactions or events, as sales, arrests, etc., are recorded as they occur: *a police blotter.*

blot′ting pa′per, a soft, absorbent, unsized paper, used esp. to dry the ink on a piece of writing.

blot·to (blot′ō), *adj.* *Slang.* so drunk as to be unconscious. [BLOT[1] (v.) + -o < ?]

blouse (blous, blouz), *n., v.,* **bloused, blous·ing.** **—n. 1.** a garment for women and children, covering the body from the neck or shoulders to the waistline, with or without a collar and sleeves; waist. **2.** (formerly) a single-breasted, semifitted jacket worn as part of the service uniform of the U.S. Army. **3.** a loose outer garment, reaching to the hip or sometimes below the knee, and often belted, as worn by French and Russian peasants. **—v.i. 4.** to puff out in a drooping fullness. **—v.t. 5.** to dispose the material of a garment in loose folds. [< F]

blous·y[1] (blou′zē), *adj.,* **blous·i·er, blous·i·est.** blowzy. **—blous′i·ly,** *adv.*

blous·y[2] (blou′sē, -zē), *adj.,* **blous·i·er, blous·i·est.** of or resembling a blouse. [BLOUSE + -Y[1]]

blow[1] (blō), *n.* **1.** a sudden, hard stroke with a hand, fist, or weapon: *a blow to the head.* **2.** a sudden shock, calamity, reversal, etc.: *His wife's death was a terrible blow to him.* **3.** a sudden attack or drastic action: *The invaders struck a blow to the south.* **4. come to blows,** to begin to fight, esp. to engage in physical combat: *They came to blows over the referee's ruling.* [late ME *blaw* (n.), north var. of later *blowe*]
—Syn. 1. thwack, rap, slap, cuff, box, knock. **1, 2.** BLOW, STROKE, HIT, SLAP refer to a sudden or forceful impact. BLOW emphasizes the violence of impact or the adversity of fortune: *a blow from a hammer; a blow to one's hopes.* STROKE emphasizes movement as well as impact and usually connotes speed, suddenness, good fortune, or unexpected pain: *the stroke of a piston; a stroke of luck, of lightning; a paralytic stroke.* HIT, in its current uses, emphasizes the successful result of a literal or figurative blow, impact, or impression: *a two-base hit; to make a hit with someone; a smash hit.* SLAP, a blow with the open hand or with something flat, emphasizes the instrument with which the blow is delivered and, often, the resulting sound; figuratively, it connotes an unfriendly or sarcastic statement, action, or attitude: *Her coldness was like a slap in the face; the slap of a beaver's tail on the water.*

blow[2] (blō), *v.,* **blew, blown, blow·ing,** *n.* **—v.i. 1.** (of the wind or air) to move swiftly or forcefully. **2.** to move along, carried by or as by the wind: *Dust seemed to blow through every crack in the house.* **3.** to produce or emit a current of air, as with the mouth, a bellows, etc.: *Blow on your hands to warm them.* **4.** *Music.* (of a horn, trumpet, etc.) to give out sound. **5.** to sound shrilly; whistle: *The siren blew at noon.* **6.** (of horses) to breathe hard or quickly; pant. **7.** *Zool.* (of a whale) to spout. **8.** (of a fuse, light bulb, vacuum tube, tire, etc.) to burst, stop functioning, or be destroyed by exploding, overloading, etc.: *A fuse blew just as we sat down to dinner.* **9.** *Slang.* to leave; depart: *Let's blow.* **—v.t. 10.** to drive by means of a current of air: *A breeze blew the smoke from the fire right into the house.* **11.** to drive a current of air upon. **12.** to clear or empty by forcing air through: *Blow your nose.* **13.** to shape (glass, smoke, etc.) with a current of air: *to blow smoke rings.* **14.** to cause to sound, by or as by a current of air: *Blow your horn at the next crossing.* **15.** to cause to explode (often fol. by *up*): *A mine blew the ship to bits.* **16.** to burst, burn out, or destroy by exploding, overloading, etc. (often fol. by *out*): *to blow a tire.* **17.** to put (a horse) out of breath by fatigue. **18.** *U.S. Slang.* **a.** to squander; spend quickly: *He blew a fortune on racing cars.* **b.** to depart from: *to blow town.* **c.** to botch; bungle: *With one stupid mistake he'll blow the whole project.* **19. blow hot and cold,** to favor something at first and reject it later on; waver; vacillate. **20. blow in,** *U.S. Slang.* to arrive at a place: *My uncle just blew in from Sacramento.* **21. blow one's lines,** *Theat.* to forget or make an error in a speaking part. **22. blow one's stack.** See **stack** (def. 10). **23. blow one's top.** See **top**[1] (def. 15). **24. blow over,** to pass away; subside: *His anger soon blew over.* **25. blow the** (or **one's**) **mind,** *Slang.* **a.** to change one's perceptions, awareness, etc., esp. through the use of drugs or narcotics. **b.** to give or receive intense pleasure or stimulation. **26. blow up, a.** to cause to explode or to destroy or demolish by explosion: *to blow up a bridge.* **b.** to exaggerate; enlarge: *He blew up his own role in his account of the battle.* **c.** *Informal.* to lose one's temper: *When he heard she was going to quit school, he simply blew up.* **d.** to fill with air; inflate: *to blow up a tire.* **e.** *Photog.* to make an enlarged reproduction of. **—n. 27.** a blast of air or wind. **28.** a violent windstorm, gale, hurricane, or the like. **29.** act of producing a blast of air, as in playing a wind instrument: *a few discordant blows by the bugler.* [ME *blow(en)* (v.), OE *blāwan;* c. L *flā(re)* (to) blow]

blow[3] (blō), *v.,* **blew, blown, blow·ing,** *n.* *Archaic.* **—v.i., v.t. 1.** to blossom or cause to blossom. **—n. 2.** a yield or display of blossoms. **3.** state of blossoming; a flowering: *a honeysuckle in full blow.* [ME *blow(en)* (v.), OE *blōwan;* akin to G *blühen* to bloom, L *flōs* flower]

blow-by (blō′bī′), *n., pl.* **-bies.** *Auto.* **1.** leakage of the air-fuel mixture or of combustion gases between a piston and the cylinder wall into the crankcase of an automobile. **2.** a device, fitted to a crankcase, for conducting such gases back to the cylinders for combustion.

blow-by-blow (blō′bi′blō′), *adj.* (of an oral or written account) precisely detailed; action by action.

blow-dry (blō′drī′), *v.,* **-dried, -dry·ing,** *n.* **—v.t. 1.** to dry or style (shampooed or wet hair) with a blow-dryer. **—n. 2.** the act or an instance of blow-drying: *How much does the beauty parlor charge for a wash, cut, and blow-dry?* **—blow-dried,** *adj.*

blow-dry·er (blō′drī′ər), *n.* a small, usually hand-held electrical appliance that dries hair by emitting a stream of warm air.

blow·er (blō′ər), *n.* **1.** a person or thing that blows. **2.** a machine for supplying air at a moderate pressure, as to supply forced drafts, supercharge and scavenge diesel engines, etc. **3.** *Brit. Slang.* a telephone.

blow·fish (blō′fish′), *n., pl.* (*esp. collectively*) **-fish,** (*esp. referring to two or more kinds or species*) **-fishes.** puffer (def. 2).

blow·fly (blō′flī′), *n., pl.* **-flies.** any of numerous dipterous insects of the family *Calliphoridae* that deposit their eggs or larvae on carrion, excrement, etc., or in wounds of living animals.

blow·gun (blō′gun′), *n.* a pipe or tube through which missiles are blown by the breath. Also called **blowpipe, blowtube.**

blow-hard (blō′härd′), *n.* *Slang.* an exceptionally boastful or talkative person.

blow·hole (blō′hōl′), *n.* **1.** an air or gas vent, esp. one to carry off fumes from a tunnel, underground passage, etc. **2.** a nostril or spiracle at the top of the head in whales and other cetaceans, through which they breathe. **3.** a hole in the ice to which whales or seals come to breathe. **4.** *Metall.* a defect in a casting or ingot caused by the escape of gas.

blown (blōn), *adj.* **1.** inflated; swollen. **2.** out of breath; exhausted: *The horses were blown by the violent exercise.*

blow·off (blō′ôf′, -of′), *n.* a current of escaping surplus steam, water, etc.: *The safety valve released a violent blowoff from the furnace.*

blow·out (blō′out′), *n.* **1.** a sudden bursting or rupture of an automobile tire. **2.** a sudden, violent, or uncontrollable escape of air, steam, oil, water, or the like. **3.** *Elect.* the melting of a fuse under excessive load. **4.** *Aeron.* flameout. **5.** *Slang.* a big, usually lavish party or entertainment.

blow·pipe (blō′pīp′), *n.* **1.** a tube through which a stream of air or gas is forced into a flame to concentrate and increase its heating action. **2.** *Glass Blowing.* a long metal pipe used to gather and blow the molten glass into hollowware. **3.** blowgun. **4.** *Med.* an instrument used to observe or clean a cavity.

blowsed (blouzd), *adj.* blowzy.

blows·y (blou′zē), *adj.*, **blows·i·er, blows·i·est.** blowzy. —**blows′i·ly,** *adv.*

blow·torch (blō′tôrch′), *n.* a small portable apparatus that gives an extremely hot gasoline flame intensified by air under pressure, used esp. in metalworking.

Blowtorch

blow·tube (blō′to͞ob′, -tyo͞ob′), *n.* blowgun.

blow·up (blō′up′), *n.* **1.** an explosion. **2.** a violent argument, outburst of temper, or the like, esp. one resulting in estrangement. **3.** Also, **blow′-up′.** *Photog.* an enlargement.

blow·y (blō′ē), *adj.*, **blow·i·er, blow·i·est. 1.** windy: *a chill, blowy day.* **2.** easily blown about: *flimsy, blowy curtain material.* —**blow′i·ness,** *n.*

blowz·y (blou′zē), *adj.*, **blowz·i·er, blowz·i·est. 1.** having a coarse, ruddy complexion. **2.** disheveled; unkempt: *blowzy hair.* Also, **blowsy, blowzed** (blouzd), **blowsed, blousy.** [obs. *blowze* wench (< ?) + -Y[1]] —**blowz′i·ly,** *adv.*

bls., 1. bales. **2.** barrels.

B.L.S., Bachelor of Library Science.

blub·ber (blub′ər), *n.* **1.** *Zool.* the fat found between the skin and muscle of whales and other cetaceans, from which oil is made. **2.** the act of weeping noisily and without restraint. —*v.i.* **3.** to weep noisily and without restraint (usually used contemptuously): *Don't blubber—tell me what's wrong.* —*v.t.* **4.** to say, esp. incoherently, while weeping. —*adj.* **5.** fatty; swollen; puffed out (often used in combination): *thick, blubber lips; blubber-faced.* [late ME *bluber* bubble, bubbling water, entrails, whale oil; appar. imit.] —**blub′ber·er,** *n.* —**blub′ber·ing·ly,** *adv.*

blub·ber·y (blub′ə rē), *adj.* **1.** abounding in blubber, as a cetacean; resembling blubber. **2.** fat; swollen.

blu·cher (blo͞o′kər, -chər), *n.* **1.** a strong, leather half boot. **2.** a shoe with the vamp continued up beneath the top, which laps over it from the sides. [named after Field Marshal von BLÜCHER]

Blü·cher (blo͞o′kər, -chər; *Ger.* blʏ′ᴋʜəʀ), *n.* **Geb·hart Le·be·recht von** (gep′härt lā′bə ʀeᴋʜt′ fən), 1742–1819, Prussian field marshal.

bludg·eon (bluj′ən), *n.* **1.** a short, heavy club with one end weighted or thicker and heavier than the other. —*v.t.* **2.** to strike or fell with a bludgeon. **3.** to force (someone) into something; coerce; bully: *The boss finally bludgeoned him into accepting responsibility.* [?] —**bludg′eon·er, bludg·eon·eer** (bluj′ə nēr′), *n.*

blue (blo͞o), *n., adj.*, **blu·er, blu·est,** *v.*, **blued, blu·ing** or **blue·ing.** —*n.* **1.** the pure color of a clear sky; azure; the hue between green and violet in the spectrum. **2.** bluing. **3.** something having a blue color: *Place the blue next to the red.* **4.** a person who wears blue or is a member of a group characterized by some blue symbol: *Tomorrow the blues will play the reds.* **5.** a member of the Union army in the American Civil War. Cf. **gray** (def. 9). **6.** bluestocking. **7. out of the blue,** suddenly and unexpectedly. **8. the blue, a.** the sky. **b.** the sea. **c.** the unknown: *to vanish into the blue.* —*adj.* **9.** of the color blue. **10.** (of the skin) discolored by cold, contusion, fear, or vascular collapse. **11.** depressed in spirits; dejected; melancholy: *She was blue about not being invited to the dance.* **12.** *Informal.* indecent; risqué: *blue jokes; blue movies.* **13. blue in the face,** exhausted or speechless, as from excessive anger, physical strain, etc. —*v.t.* **14.** to make blue; dye a blue color. **15.** to tinge with bluing. [ME *blewe,* OE *blǣwe(n),* contr. of *blǣhǣwe(n)* = *blǣ* dark blue (see BLAE) + *hǣwe,* light blue, gray + *-en* -EN[2]] —**blue′ly,** *adv.* —**blue′ness,** *n.* —**blu′ish, blue′ish,** *adj.* —**blu′ish·ness,** *n.* —**Syn. 11.** despondent, morose, downcast.

blue′ alert′, (in military or civilian defense) an alert following the first, or yellow, alert, in which air attack seems probable.

blue′ bab′y, *Pathol.* an infant born with cyanosis resulting from a congenital heart or lung defect.

Blue·beard (blo͞o′bērd′), *n.* (in folklore) a nickname of the Chevalier Raoul, whose seventh wife found the murdered bodies of the other six in a room forbidden to her.

blue·bell (blo͞o′bel′), *n.* **1.** any of various plants with blue, bell-shaped flowers, as the harebell, a liliaceous plant, *Scilla nonscripta,* of the Old World. **2.** the lungwort, *Mertensia virginica,* of the U.S.

blue·ber·ry (blo͞o′ber′ē, -bə rē), *n., pl.* **-ries. 1.** the edible, usually bluish berry of various ericaceous shrubs of the genus *Vaccinium.* **2.** any of these shrubs.

blue·bill (blo͞o′bil′), *n.* *U.S. Dial.* the scaup duck.

blue·bird (blo͞o′bûrd′), *n.* any of several small North American songbirds of the genus *Sialia,* having predominantly blue plumage.

Bluebird,
Sialia sialis
(Length 7 in.)

blue′ blood′, 1. an aristocrat, noble, or member of a socially prominent family. **2.** aristocratic, noble, or socially prominent lineage or relatives. [trans. of Sp *sangre azul.* See SANGUINE, AZURE] —**blue′-blood′ed,** *adj.*

blue·bon·net (blo͞o′bon′it), *n.* **1.** the cornflower, *Centaurea cyanus.* **2.** a blue-flowered lupine, esp. *Lupinus subcarnosus;* the state flower of Texas. **3.** a broad, flat bonnet of blue wool, formerly much worn in Scotland. **4.** a Scottish soldier who wore such a bonnet. **5.** any Scot. Also called **blue-cap** (blo͞o′kap′).

blue′ book′, 1. *Informal.* a register or directory of socially prominent persons. **2.** *U.S.* a blank booklet used in taking college examinations, usually with a blue paper cover. **3.** a government publication bound in a blue cover. Also, **blue′book′.**

blue·bot·tle (blo͞o′bot′əl), *n.* **1.** cornflower (def. 1). **2.** any of various other plants having blue flowers, esp. of the genera *Campanula* and *Scilla.*

blue′bottle fly′, any of several iridescent blue blowflies, esp. those of the genus *Calliphora,* some of which are parasitic on domestic animals.

blue′ cheese′, a rich, blue-veined cheese, similar to Roquefort, made from cow's milk.

blue′ chip′, 1. *Chiefly Poker.* a blue-colored chip of high value. **2.** a relatively high-priced common-stock issue of a leading company that pays regular dividends. —**blue-chip** (blo͞o′chip′), *adj.*

blue·coat (blo͞o′kōt′), *n.* **1.** a person who wears a blue coat or uniform, as a policeman. **2.** *U.S.* a soldier in the Union army during the Civil War.

blue′ co′hosh. See under **cohosh.**

blue-col·lar (blo͞o′kol′ər), *adj.* of or pertaining to factory workers or manual labor. Cf. **white-collar.**

blue′ cop′peras, *Chem.* See **blue vitriol.**

blue′ crab′, an edible crab, *Callinectes sapidus,* having a dark green body and bluish legs, found along the Atlantic and Gulf coasts of North America.

blue′ dev′ils, 1. low spirits; depression. **2.** See **delirium tremens.**

blue′-eyed grass′ (blo͞o′īd′), any of numerous iridaceous plants of the genus *Sisyrinchium,* having grasslike leaves and small, usually blue flowers.

blue′fin tu′na (blo͞o′fin′), a large tuna, *Thunnus thynnus,* common in temperate seas, used, canned, as food. See illus. at **tuna.**

blue·fish (blo͞o′fish′), *n., pl.* (*esp. collectively*) **-fish,** (*esp. referring to two or more kinds or species*) **-fish·es. 1.** a predaceous, marine, bluish or greenish food fish, *Pomatomus saltatrix,* found along the Atlantic coast of North and South America. **2.** any of various fishes, usually of a bluish color.

blue′ flag′, any North American plant of the genus *Iris,* esp. *I. prismatica,* or *I. versicolor:* the state flower of Tennessee.

blue′ fox′, 1. a bluish-gray winter color phase of the arctic fox. **2.** the arctic fox in summer pelage. **3.** the blue fur of this animal. **4.** any white fox fur dyed blue.

blue′ gas′, *Chem.* See **water gas.**

blue·gill (blo͞o′gil′), *n.* a fresh-water sunfish, *Lepomis macrochirus,* found in the Mississippi River valley, used for food.

blue′ goose′, a bluish-gray wild goose, *Chen caerulescens,* of North America.

blue′ gra′ma. See under **grama grass.**

blue·grass (blo͞o′gras′, -gräs′), *n.* **1.** any grass of the genus *Poa,* as the Kentucky bluegrass, *P. pratensis.* **2.** country music that is polyphonic in character and is played on unamplified stringed instruments.

Blue′grass Re′gion, a region in central Kentucky, famous for its horse farms and fields of bluegrass.

Blue′grass State′, Kentucky (used as a nickname).

blue′-green al′ga (blo͞o′grēn′), any unicellular or filamentous alga of the class *Myxophyceae* (*Cyanophycaea*), usually bluish green owing to the presence of blue pigments in addition to the chlorophyll.

blue′ grouse′, *U.S. Dial.* any of several mottled, slaty gray, North American grouses of the genus *Dendragapus,* esp. the dusky grouse.

blue′ gum′, eucalyptus.

blue·ing (blo͞o′ing), *n.* *Chem.* bluing.

blue·jack (blo͞o′jak′), *n.* a small oak, *Quercus cinerea* or *brevifolia,* of the southern U.S. [BLUE + JACK[1], modeled after BLACKJACK; so called from the bluish look of the leaves]

blue·jack·et (blo͞o′jak′it), *n.* a sailor, esp. an enlisted man in the navy.

blue′ jay′, a common, crested jay, *Cyanocitta cristata,* of eastern North America, having a bright blue back and a gray breast.

blue′ jeans′, blue denim trousers having reinforced pockets and seams, worn originally as work pants but now also as leisure attire. Cf. **Levis.**

blue′ laws′, *U.S.* puritanical laws, originating in colonial New England, that forbid certain practices, esp. drinking or working on Sunday, dancing, etc.

blue′ line′, *Ice Hockey.* either of two lines of the color blue that are parallel to and equidistant from the goal lines and divide the rink into three zones of equal size.

blue′ mold′, 1. Also called **green mold.** any fungus of the genus *Penicillium,* that forms a bluish-green, furry coating on foodstuffs inoculated by its spores. **2.** *Plant Pathol.* a disease of plants, characterized by necrosis of leaves or fruit and the growth of bluish or grayish mold on affected parts, caused by any of several fungi, as of the genus *Penicillium* or *Peronospora tabicina.*

blue′ moon′, *Informal.* a very long time: *I haven't seen him in a blue moon.*

Blue′ Moun′tains, a range of low mountains in NE Oregon and SE Washington.

Blue′ Nile′, a river in E Africa, flowing NNW from Lake Tana in Ethiopia into the Nile at Khartoum: a tributary of the Nile. ab. 950 mi. long. Cf. **Nile.**

blue·nose (blo͞o′nōz′), *n.* a puritanical person; prude.

blue′ note′, *Jazz.* a flatted note, esp. the third or the seventh degree of the scale, recurring frequently in blues and jazz as a characteristic feature.

blue-pen·cil (blo͞o′pen′səl), *v.t.*, **-ciled, -cil·ing** or (*esp. Brit.*) **-cilled, -cil·ling.** to edit or delete with or as with a blue pencil.

blue′ pe′ter, *Naut.* a blue flag with a white square in the center, flown at the head of the foremast of a vessel about to leave port.

blue′ pike′, a variety of the walleye, *Strizostedion vitreum glaucum*, found in the Great Lakes. Also called **blue′ pick′erel, blue′ pike′perch.**

blue′ plate′, 1. a plate, usually decorated with a blue willow pattern, divided by ridges into sections for holding apart several kinds of food. 2. a main course, as of meat and vegetables, listed as a single item on a menu.

blue′ point′, a Siamese cat having a light-colored body and darker, bluish-gray points.

blue·point (blo͞o′point′), *n.* a small oyster, esp. one from the oyster beds near Blue Point, Long Island.

blue·print (blo͞o′print′), *n.* 1. a process of photographic printing, used chiefly in copying architectural and mechanical drawings, that produces a white line on a blue background. 2. a print made by this process. 3. a detailed outline or plan: *a blueprint for the new sales campaign.* —*v.t.* 4. to make a blueprint of.

blue′ rac′er, a bluish racer, *Coluber constrictor flaviventris*, found from Ohio to Texas, a subspecies of the blacksnake.

blue′ rib′bon, 1. the highest award or distinction, as the first prize in a contest. 2. a blue ribbon worn as a badge of honor, esp. by members of the Order of the Garter of the British knighthood. —**blue-rib·bon** (blo͞o′rib′ən), *adj.*

blue′-ribbon ju′ry, a jury composed of persons on a high educational and economic level.

Blue′ Rid′er. See **Blaue Reiter.**

Blue′ Ridge′, a mountain range extending SW from N Virginia to N Georgia: part of the Appalachian Mountains. Also called **Blue′ Ridge′ Moun′tains.**

blues[1] (blo͞oz), *n.* 1. (*construed as pl.*) despondency; melancholy: *This rainy spell is giving me the blues.* 2. (*often construed as sing.*) *Jazz.* a. a song of American Negro origin that is marked by frequent minor intervals and takes the basic form of a 12-bar chorus consisting of a 3-line stanza with the second line repeating the first. b. the genre constituting such songs. [BLUE (DEVIL)S]

blues[2] (blo͞oz), *n.*, (*construed as pl.*) 1. any of several blue uniforms worn by members of the U.S. Navy, Army, or Air Force. 2. a U.S. Army uniform for formal wear. 3. a U.S. Air Force dress uniform.

blue-sky (blo͞o′skī′), *adj.* 1. having dubious value; not sound. 2. fanciful or impractical: *blue-sky ideas.* [so called from the lack of clouds in the sky, i.e., lack of substance]

blue′-sky′ law′, *U.S.* a law regulating the sale of securities, esp. one designed to prevent the promotion of fraudulent stocks.

blue′ stel′lar ob′ject, *Astron.* any of a class of blue celestial objects, at one time thought to be stars, that do not emit appreciable radio waves. *Abbr.:* BSO

blue·stem (blo͞o′stem′), *n.* any of several prairie grasses of the genus *Andropogon*, having bluish leaf sheaths, now grown in the western U.S. for forage.

blue·stock·ing (blo͞o′stok′ing), *n.* a woman with considerable scholarly, literary, or intellectual ability or interest. [so called from the informal dress, esp. the blue wool stockings, worn by some female members of 18th-century literary clubs in England]

blue′ stone′, *Chem.* See **blue vitriol.**

blue·stone (blo͞o′stōn′), *n.* a bluish, argillaceous sandstone used for building purposes, flagging, etc.

blue′ streak′, *Informal.* 1. something moving very fast. 2. something continuous or interminable: *to talk a blue streak.*

blu·et (blo͞o′it), *n.* 1. any of various plants having blue flowers, as the cornflower. 2. Often, **bluets.** Also called **innocence, innocents, Quaker-ladies.** any of various species of *Houstonia*, esp. *H. caerulea.* [late ME *blewet, blewed*, var. of ME *bloweth, blowed(e)* (see BLUE, BLAE); suffix perh. OE *-et*, as in THICKET]

blue′ vit′riol, *Chem.* a salt, $CuSO_4 \cdot 5H_2O$, occurring in large transparent, deep-blue triclinic crystals, appearing in its anhydrous state as a white powder: used chiefly as a mordant, insecticide, fungicide, and in engraving. Also called **blue copperas, blue stone, copper sulfate, cupric sulfate.**

blue·weed (blo͞o′wēd′), *n.* a bristly, boraginaceous weed, *Echium vulgare*, having showy blue flowers, a native of Europe naturalized in the U.S.

blue′ whale′, sulphur-bottom.

blue′-winged teal′ (blo͞o′wingd′), a small pond and river duck, *Anas discors*, of North America, having grayish-blue patches on the wings.

blue·wood (blo͞o′wo͝od′), *n.* a rhamnaceous shrub or small tree, *Condalia obovata*, of western Texas and northern Mexico, often forming dense chaparral.

bluff[1] (bluf), *adj.* 1. good-naturedly abrupt or frank; heartily outspoken: *a big, bluff, generous man.* 2. presenting a nearly perpendicular front, as on a coastline. 3. *Naut.* (of the bow of a vessel) having a full, blunt form. —*n.* 4. a cliff, headland, or hill with a broad, steep face. 5. *Chiefly Canadian.* a copse. [perh. < MLG *blaff* smooth, even, or < MD *blaf* broad, flat (now obs.)] —**bluff′ly,** *adv.* —**bluff′ness,** *n.* —**Syn.** 1. open, honest; rough. See **blunt.** 2. steep, precipitous. —**Ant.** 1. subtle.

bluff[2] (bluf), *v.t.* 1. to mislead by feigning confidence; deceive. 2. *Poker.* to bet heavily on a weak hand in order to mislead an opposing player. —*v.i.* 3. to mislead someone by acting boldly. —*n.* 4. act, instance, or practice of bluffing. 5. a person who bluffs; bluffer. [perh. < LG *bluff(en)* (to) bluster, frighten; akin to MD *bluffen* to make a trick at cards] —**bluff′er,** *n.*

blu·ing (blo͞o′ing), *n.* *Chem.* a substance, as indigo, used to whiten clothes or give them a bluish tinge. Also, **blueing.**

Blum (blo͞om), *n.* **Lé·on** (lē′on; *Fr.* lā ōN′), 1872–1950, French statesman: premier of France 1936–37; 1938; 1946–47.

blun·der (blun′dər), *n.* 1. a gross, stupid, or careless mistake. —*v.i.* 2. to move or act blindly, stupidly, or without direction or steady guidance: *Without my glasses I blundered into the wrong room.* 3. to make a gross or stupid mistake, esp. through carelessness or mental confusion. —*v.t.* 4. to bungle; botch. 5. to utter thoughtlessly; blurt out. [ME *blunder(en), blondre(n)* < Scand; cf. dial. Norw *blundra* to behave as if blind, akin to Icel *blunda* to keep the eyes shut. See BLIND] —**blun′der·er,** *n.* —**blun′der·ful,** *adj.* —**blun′der·ing·ly,** *adv.* —**Syn.** 1. error.

blun·der·buss (blun′dər bus′), *n.* a short musket of wide bore with expanded muzzle to scatter shot, bullets, or slugs at close range. [< D *donderbus* (*donder* thunder + *bus* gun) with BLUNDER r. *donder.* See HARQUEBUS]

blunt (blunt), *adj.* 1. having a thick or dull edge or point; not sharp. 2. abrupt in address or manner: *a blunt question.* 3. slow in perception or understanding; insensitive or obtuse. —*v.t.* 4. to make blunt. 5. to weaken or impair the force or keenness of: *Wine first excites, then blunts the imagination.* [ME; perh. akin to BLIND] —**blunt′ly,** *adv.* —**blunt′ness,** *n.* —**Syn.** 2. short, gruff, rough, rude, difficult, uncivil, impolite. BLUNT, BLUFF, BRUSQUE, CURT characterize manners and speech. BLUNT suggests lack of polish and of regard for the feelings of others: *blunt and tactless.* BLUFF implies an unintentional roughness together with so much good-natured heartiness that others rarely take offense: *a bluff sea captain.* BRUSQUE connotes sharpness and abruptness of speech or manner: *a brusque denial.* CURT applies esp. to disconcertingly concise language: *a curt reply.* 3. thick, stolid. 4. dull.

blur (blûr), *v.*, **blurred, blur·ring,** *n.* —*v.t.* 1. to obscure, make indistinct, or sully (something) as by smearing, staining, or partially covering. 2. to dim the perception or susceptibility of; make dull or insensible: *The blow on the head blurred his senses.* —*v.i.* 3. to become indistinct: *Everything blurred as he ran.* 4. to make blurs. —*n.* 5. a smudge or smear that obscures: *a blur of smoke.* 6. a blurred condition or thing: *The ship was just a blur in the fog.* [? akin to BLEAR] —**blur·red·ly** (blûr′id lē, blûrd′-), *adv.* —**blur′red·ness,** *n.* —**blur′ry,** *adj.*

blurb (blûrb), *n.* a brief advertisement, as on a book jacket. [coined by F. G. Burgess (1866–1951), American humorist]

blurt (blûrt), *v.t.* 1. to utter suddenly, inadvertently or indiscreetly (usually fol. by *out*): *He blurted out the secret.* —*n.* 2. an abrupt utterance. [appar. imit.]

blush (blush), *v.i.* 1. to redden, esp. in the face, from modesty, shame, or embarrassment. 2. to feel shame or embarrassment (usually fol. by *at* or *for*): *Your bad behavior makes me blush for your mother.* 3. to become a pink or rosy color. —*v.t.* 4. to make red; flush. 5. to make known by a blush: *She could not help blushing the truth.* —*n.* 6. a reddening, as of the face in modesty, shame, or embarrassment. 7. rosy or pinkish tinge. 8. **at first blush,** without previous knowledge; at first glance. [ME *blusche(n)* (v.), OE *blyscan* to redden; akin to OE *blysa*, Icel *blys*, MLG *blus* torch, *bloschen* to blaze] —**blush′er,** *n.* —**blush′ful,** *adj.* —**blush′ful·ly,** *adv.* —**blush′ful·ness,** *n.* —**blush′ing·ly,** *adv.*

blus·ter (blus′tər), *v.i.* 1. to blow gustily, as wind. 2. to be loud, noisy, or swaggering, esp. to utter loud, empty menaces or protests. —*v.t.* 3. to force or accomplish by blustering. —*n.* 4. boisterous noise and violence. 5. noisy, empty menaces or protests; inflated talk. [perh. < LG *bluster(n)*, *blüstern* to blow violently; cf. Icel *blāstr* blowing, hissing] —**blus′ter·er,** *n.* —**blus′ter·ing·ly,** *adv.* —**blus′ter·ous·ly,** *adv.* —**blus′ter·y, blus′ter·ous,** *adj.*

blvd., boulevard.

-bly, var. of **-ably:** *solubly.* Also, **-ibly.** [-B(LE) + -LY]

BM, *Informal.* bowel movement.

B.M., 1. Bachelor of Medicine. 2. Bachelor of Music. 3. British Museum.

B.M.E., 1. Bachelor of Mechanical Engineering. 2. Bachelor of Mining Engineering.

B.M.Ed., Bachelor of Music Education.

B.M.O.C., big man on campus.

B.M.R., See **basal metabolic rate.**

B.Mus., Bachelor of Music.

B.M.V., Blessed Mary the Virgin. [< L *Beāta Maria Virgō*]

Bn., 1. Baron. 2. Battalion.

bn., battalion.

B'nai B'rith (bə nā′ brith′), an international Jewish organization seeking to promote the social, educational, and cultural betterment of Jews and of the general public. [< Heb *bĕnē bĕrīth* sons of the covenant]

B.O., 1. *Informal.* body odor. 2. *Theat.* box office.

b.o., 1. back order. 2. bad order. 3. box office. 4. branch office. 5. broker's order. 6. buyer's option.

bo·a (bō′ə), *n.*, *pl.* **bo·as.** 1. any of several nonvenomous, chiefly tropical constrictors of the family *Boidae*, having vestigial hind limbs at the base of the tail. 2. a stole of feathers, fur, silk, or the like. [< NL < L: water adder]

Boa constrictor, *Constrictor constrictor* (Length 10 ft.)

Bo·ab·dil (bō′äb dil; *Sp.* bô′äb dēl′), *n.* (*abu-Abdallah*) ("*El Chico*") died 1533?, last Moorish king of Granada 1482–83, 1486–92.

bo′a constric′tor, 1. a boa, *Constrictor constrictor*, of tropical America, noted for its size and ability to crush its prey in its coils. 2. any large snake of the boa family, such as the python or anaconda.

Bo·ad·i·ce·a (bō′ad i sē′ə), *n.* died A.D. 62, queen of the Iceni: leader of an unsuccessful revolt against the Romans in Britain. Also, **Boudicca.**

Bo·a·ner·ges (bō′ə nûr′jēz), *n.* 1. a surname given by Jesus to James and John. Mark 3:17. 2. (*construed as sing.*) a vociferous preacher or orator. [< LL < Gk << Heb *bĕnē regesh* sons of thunder]

boar (bōr, bôr), *n.* 1. the uncastrated male of swine. 2. See **wild boar.** [ME *boor*, OE *bār*; c. D *beer*, G *Bär*]

board (bōrd, bôrd), *n.* 1. a piece of timber sawed thin, and of considerable length and breadth compared with the thickness. 2. a sheet of wood, cardboard, paper, or the like, with or without markings, for some special use (sometimes used in combination): *a cutting board; a checkerboard.* 3. **boards, a.** *Theat.* the stage: *The play will go on the boards next week.* b. the wooden fence surrounding the playing area of an ice-hockey rink. 4. stiff cardboard or other material covered with paper, cloth, or the like, to form the covers for a book. 5. *Building Trades.* composition material made in large sheets, as plasterboard, corkboard, etc. 6. a table, esp. to serve food on. 7. daily meals, esp. as provided for pay: *room and board.* 8. an official group of persons who direct or supervise some activity: *a board of directors.* 9. *Naut.* a. the side of a ship. b. one leg, or tack, of the course of a ship beating to windward. 10. a flat surface, as a wall or an object of rectangular shape, on which something is posted: *a bulletin board.* **11.** *Informal.* a switchboard. **12.** *Obs.* the edge, border, or side of anything. **13. across the board, a.** *Racing.* betting on a horse or dog to win, place, and show. **b.** applying to all or everything equally or proportionately: *to cut the budget across the board.* **14. go by the board,** to be destroyed, neglected, or forgotten. **15. on board, a.** on or in a ship, train, or other vehicle. **b.** *Baseball Slang.* on base. Also, **aboard.** —*v.t.* **16.** to cover or close with or as with boards (often fol. by *up* or *over*): *to board up a house.* **17.** to furnish with meals, or with meals and lodging, esp. for pay. **18.** to go on board of or enter (a ship, train, etc.). **19.** *Obs.* to approach; accost. —*v.i.* **20.** to take one's meals, or be supplied with food and lodging, at a fixed price: *Several of us board at the same rooming house.* [ME, OE *bord* board, table, shield; c. D *boord* board, *bord* plate, G *Bort,* Icel *borth,* Goth *-baurd*] —**board′a·ble,** *adj.*

board′ and bat′ten, *Carpentry.* a siding consisting of wide boards or of sheets of plywood set vertically with butt joints covered by battens. See illus. at **siding.**

board·er (bōr′dər, bôr′-), *n.* a person, esp. a lodger, who is supplied with regular meals.

board′ foot′, a unit equal to the cubic contents of a piece one foot square and one inch thick, used in measuring logs and lumber.

board·ing (bōr′ding, bôr′-), *n.* **1.** wooden boards collectively. **2.** a surface of boards, as in a fence or a floor. **3.** act of a person who boards a ship, train, airplane, or the like.

board·ing·house (bōr′ding hous′, bôr′-), *n., pl.* **-hous·es** (-hou′ziz). a house at which board, or board and lodging, may be obtained for payment, esp. on a weekly or monthly basis. Also, **board′ing house′.**

board′ing ramp′, ramp (def. 5a).

board′ing school′, a school at which board and lodging are furnished for the pupils (distinguished from *day school*).

Board·man (bōrd′man, bôrd′-), *n.* a town in NE Ohio, S of Youngstown. 30,852 (1970).

board′ meas′ure, *Building Trades.* a system of cubic measure in which the unit is the board foot.

board′ of educa′tion, *U.S.* an appointive or elective body that directs and administers chiefly the primary and secondary public schools in a town, city, county, or state.

board′ of elec′tions, *U.S. Politics.* a bipartisan board appointed usually by local authorities and charged with control of elections and voting procedure.

board′ of es′timate, *U.S.* a special organ of a municipal government, as of New York, charged with approving the city's budget and fiscal matters.

board′ of health′, a government department concerned with public health.

board′ of trade′, **1.** a businessmen's association. **2.** Also, **Board′ of Trade′.** (in England) the national ministry responsible for commerce and industry.

board′ rule′, a measuring device having scales for finding the cubic contents of a board without calculation.

board·walk (bōrd′wôk′, bôrd′-), *n.* *U.S.* a promenade made of wooden boards, usually at a commercial beach.

boar·fish (bōr′fish′, bôr′-), *n., pl.* (*esp. collectively*) **-fish,** (*esp. referring to two or more kinds or species*) **-fish·es.** any fish having a projecting snout, esp. a small, spiny-rayed, European fish, *Capros aper.*

boar·ish (bōr′ish, bôr′-), *adj.* swinish; sensual; cruel. —**boar′ish·ly,** *adv.* —**boar′ish·ness,** *n.*

boart (bôrt), *n.* bort.

Bo·as (bō′az), *n.* **Franz** (fränts), 1858–1942, U.S. ethnologist, born in Germany.

boast[1] (bōst), *v.i.* **1.** to speak with exaggeration and pride, esp. about oneself or someone or something connected with oneself. —*v.t.* **2.** to speak of with excessive pride or vanity. **3.** to be proud in the possession of: *The town boasts a new school.* —*n.* **4.** the act or an instance of boasting. **5.** a thing boasted of: *Talent is his boast.* [ME *bost* (n.), *bosten* (v.) < ?] —**boast′er,** *n.* —**boast′ing·ly,** *adv.*

boast[2] (bōst), *v.t.* to dress or shape (stone) roughly. [?]

boast·ful (bōst′fəl), *adj.* given to or characterized by boasting. [ME *bostful*] —**boast′ful·ly,** *adv.* —**boast′ful·ness,** *n.*

boat (bōt), *n.* **1.** a vessel for transport by water, constructed to provide buoyancy by excluding water and shaped to give stability and permit propulsion. **2.** a small ship, generally for specialized use: *a fishing boat.* **3.** a small vessel carried for use by a large one, as a lifeboat: *The ship lowered the boats.* **4.** a serving dish resembling a boat: *a gravy boat.* **5. in the same boat,** in the same circumstances; faced with the same problems: *The new recruits were all in the same boat.* **6. miss the boat,** *Slang.* **a.** to fail to take advantage of an opportunity. **b.** to miss the point of, or fail to grasp, something. —*v.i.* **7.** to go in a boat: *We boated down the Thames.* —*v.t.* **8.** to transport in a boat. **9.** to remove (an oar) from the water and place it athwartships. [ME *boot,* OE *bāt;* c. Icel *beit*] —**boat′a·ble,** *adj.*

boat·el (bō tel′), *n.* *U.S.* a waterside hotel with dock space for persons who travel by private boat. [BOAT + (HOT)EL]

boat·er (bō′tər), *n.* **1.** a person who boats, esp. for pleasure. **2.** a stiff straw hat with a shallow, flat-topped crown, ribbon band, and straight brim.

boat′ hook′, a hook mounted at the end of a pole, used to pull or push boats toward or away from a landing, to pick up a mooring, etc.

boat·house (bōt′hous′), *n., pl.* **-hous·es** (-hou′ziz). a building or shed, usually built partly over water, for sheltering a boat or boats.

boat·ing (bō′ting), *n.* **1.** the use of boats, esp. for pleasure. —*adj.* **2.** of or pertaining to boats or their use: *a boating fan.*

boat·load (bōt′lōd′), *n.* the cargo that a boat carries.

boat·man (bōt′mən), *n., pl.* **-men. 1.** a person skilled in the use of small craft. **2.** a person who sells, rents, or works on boats. —**boat′man·ship′,** *n.*

boat′ nail′, a nail with a convex head and a chisel point.

boat′ peo′ple, *Informal.* Indochinese refugees (primarily ethnic Chinese) fleeing esp. from Vietnam in large numbers in the late 1970's, many by small, overcrowded, unseaworthy boats.

boats·man (bōts′mən), *n., pl.* **-men.** boatman.

boat·swain (bō′sən; *spelling pron.* bōt′swān′), *n.* a warrant officer on a warship, or a petty officer on a merchant vessel, in charge of rigging, anchors, cables, etc. Also, **bo's'n, bosun.** [late ME *bote-swayn*]

boat′swain's chair′, a wooden plank seat attached to ropes for suspending over the side of a ship, building, or the like, for inspecting, cleaning, painting, etc.

boat′swain's pipe′, a high-pitched whistle used by a boatswain for giving signals. Also called **boat′swain's call′.**

boat′ train′, a train scheduled to carry passengers to or from a certain dock to connect with a ship.

boat·wright (bōt′rīt′), *n.* a man who builds wooden boats.

boat·yard (bōt′yärd′), *n.* a yard or waterside location at which boats are built, maintained, or stored. Cf. **shipyard.**

Bo·az (bō′az), *n.* husband of Ruth. Ruth 2–4.

bob[1] (bob), *n., v.,* **bobbed, bob·bing.** —*n.* **1.** a short, jerky motion: *a bob of the head.* —*v.t.* **2.** to move quickly down and up: *to bob the head.* —*v.i.* **3.** to make a jerky motion with the head or body. **4.** to move about with jerky motions: *The cork bobbed on the waves.* [ME *bob(ben)* (v.) to move like a bob in the wind. See BOB[2]]

bob[2] (bob), *n., v.,* **bobbed, bob·bing.** —*n.* **1.** a style of short haircut for women and children. **2.** a horse's docked tail. **3.** a small, dangling or terminal object, as the weight on a pendulum or a plumb line. **4.** *Angling.* **a.** a float for a fishing line. **b.** a knot of worms, rags, etc., on a string. **5.** a bobsled or bob skate. —*v.t.* **6.** to cut short: *They bobbed their hair to be in style.* —*v.i.* **7.** to try to snatch floating or dangling objects with the teeth: *to bob for apples.* **8.** *Angling.* to fish with a bob. [ME *bobbe* (n.) spray, cluster, bunch (of leaves, flowers, fruit, etc.) < ?]

bob[3] (bob), *n., v.,* **bobbed, bob·bing.** —*n.* **1.** a tap; light blow. **2.** a polishing wheel of leather, felt, or the like. —*v.t.* **3.** to tap; strike lightly. [ME *bob(ben)* (v.) (to) strike, beat, perh. imit. See BOP[2]]

bob[4] (bob), *n., pl.* **bob.** *Brit. Informal.* a shilling. [perh. from given name *Bob* (Robert)]

Bo·ba·di·lla (bô′vä thē′lyä, -thē′yä), *n.* **Fran·cis·co de** (frän thēs′kô the, -sēs′-), died 1502, Spanish colonial governor in the West Indies: sent Columbus back to Spain in chains.

bob·ber (bob′ər), *n.* **1.** a person or thing that bobs. **2.** a fishing bob.

bob·bin (bob′in), *n.* a reel, cylinder, or spool upon which yarn or thread is wound, as used in spinning, machine sewing, lacemaking, etc. [< MF *bobine* hank of thread, perh. BOB[2] + MF *-ine* -INE[2]]

bob·bi·net (bob′ə net′), *n.* a net of hexagonal mesh, made on a lace machine. [BOBBIN + NET[1]]

bob′bin lace′, lace made by hand with bobbins of thread, the thread being twisted around pins stuck into a pattern placed on a pillow or pad. Also called **pillow lace.**

bob·ble (bob′əl), *n., v.,* **-bled, -bling.** —*n.* **1.** a repeated, jerky movement; bob. **2.** *Sports.* a momentary fumbling of a baseball. **3.** *U.S. Informal.* an error; mistake. —*v.t.* **4.** *Sports.* to fumble (a ball) momentarily. [BOB[1] + -LE]

bob·by (bob′ē), *n., pl.* **-bies.** *Brit. Informal.* a policeman. [special use of *Bobby,* for Sir *Robert* PEEL, who set up the Metropolitan Police system of London in 1828]

bob′by pin′, a flat, springlike metal hairpin having the prongs held close together by tension. [BOB[2] + -Y[2]]

bob·by·socks (bob′ē soks′), *n.pl.* *Informal.* anklets, esp. as worn by teen-age girls. [*bobby* (for *bobbed,* altered by assoc. with BOBBY PIN) + SOCKS[1]]

bob·by·sox·er (bob′ē sok′sər), *n.* *Informal.* an adolescent girl, esp. during the 1940's, following youthful fads and fashions. Also, **bob′by sox′er.**

bob·cat (bob′kat′), *n., pl.* **-cats,** (*esp. collectively*) **-cat.** an American wildcat, *Lynx rufus,* having a brownish coat with black spots. Also called **bay lynx.** [BOB(TAIL) + CAT]

Bobolink
(Length 7 in.)

Bo·bo-Diou·las·so (bō′bō dyōō las′ō), *n.* a city in W Upper Volta. ab. 45,000.

bob·o·link (bob′ə lingk′), *n.* a common North American passerine songbird, *Dolichonyx oryzivorus.* [short for *Bob o' Lincoln,* the bird's call as heard by speakers of English]

bob′ skate′, an ice skate with two parallel blades. [BOB(SLED) + SKATE[1]]

bob·sled (bob′sled′), *n., v.,* **-sled·ded, -sled·ding.** —*n.* **1.** a sled having two pairs of runners, a brake, and a steering wheel or other steering mechanism. **2.** a sled formed of two short sleds in tandem. —*v.i.* **3.** to ride on a bobsled. —**bob′sled′der,** *n.*

bob·stay (bob′stā′), *n.* *Naut.* a rope, chain, or rod from the outer end of the bowsprit to the cutwater.

bob·tail (bob′tāl′), *n.* **1.** a short or docked tail. **2.** an animal with such a tail. —*adj.* **3.** docked; cut short. —*v.t.* **4.** to cut short the tail of; dock.

bob·white (bob′hwīt′, -wīt′), *n.* a common North American quail, *Colinus virginianus,* having mottled reddish-brown, black, and white plumage. See illus. at **quail**[1]. [from its cry, as heard by speakers of English]

bo·cac·cio (bō kä′chō), *n., pl.* **-cios.** a large, brown, big-mouthed rockfish, *Sebastodes paucispinis,* found in California. [< It *boccaccio* ugly mouth = *bocc(a)* mouth (< L *bucca*) + *-accio* pejorative suffix]

Bo′ca Raton′ (bō′kə rə ton′), *n.* a city in SE Florida. 28,506 (1970).

Boc·cac·ci·o (bō kä′chē ō′, -chō, bə-; *It.* bôk kät′chō), *n.* **Gio·van·ni** (jē′ə vä′nē; *It.* jō vän′nē), 1313–75, Italian writer and poet.

Boc·che·ri·ni (bok′ə rē′nē; *It.* bôk′ke rē′nē), *n.* **Lu·i·gi** (lōō ē′jē), 1743–1805, Italian composer and cellist.

boc·cie (boch′ē), *n.* an Italian variety of lawn bowling, played in a small court. Also, **boc·ci** (boch′ē; *It.* bôt′chē), **boc·ce** (boch′ē; *It.* bôt′che), **boc·cia** (boch′ə; *It.* bôt′chä). [< It *bocce* bowls, pl. of *boccia* ball]

Boche (bosh, bôsh), *n. Disparaging.* a German, esp. a German soldier in World War I. Also, **boche.** [< F, aph. var. of *Alboche* German = *Al(lemand)* German + *(ca)boche* blockhead, head of a nail]

Bo·chum (bō′KHōōm), *n.* a city in central North Rhine-Westphalia, in W West Germany. 361,000 (1963).

bock′ beer′ (bok), a heavy, dark beer brewed in the fall for consumption the following spring. Also called **bock.** [< G *Bockbier*, lit., buck beer, nickname of *Eimbecker Bier* beer of Eimbeck (now Einbeck) in Lower Saxony, Germany]

bode[1] (bōd), *v.t.*, **bod·ed, bod·ing. 1.** to be an omen of; portend. **2.** *Archaic.* to predict. [ME *bode*, OE *bodian* to announce, foretell (c. Icel *botha*) < *boda* messenger, c. G *Bote*, Icel *bothi*] —**bode′ment,** *n.*

bode[2] (bōd), *v.* a pt. of **bide.**

bo·de·ga (bô the′gä; *Eng.* bō dā′gə), *n., pl.* **-gas** (-gäs; *Eng.* -gəz). *Spanish.* **1.** (esp. among Spanish-speaking Americans) a grocery store. **2.** a warehouse, esp. for wine.

Bo·den·heim (bōd′ᵊn hīm′), *n.* **Max·well,** (maks′wəl, -wel′), 1892–1954, U.S. poet and novelist.

Bo·den See (bōd′ᵊn zā′), German name of Lake Constance. Also, **Bo′den·see′.**

Bo·dhi·dhar·ma (bō′di dur′mə), *n.* died A.D. c530, Indian Buddhist philosopher and missionary: founder of Ch'an Buddhism in China, which was later called Zen Buddhism in Japan.

Bo·dhi·satt·va (bō′di sat′wa), *n. Buddhism.* a person who has attained enlightenment, but who postpones Nirvana in order to help others to attain enlightenment. Cf. **Arhat.** [< Skt = *bodhi* illumination + *sattva* existence; see SOOTH]

bod·ice (bod′is), *n.* **1.** a woman's cross-laced outer garment covering the waist and bust, common in peasant dress. **2.** the part of a woman's dress covering the body between the neck or shoulders and the waist. Cf. **waist** (def. 4). **3.** *Obs.* stays or a corset. [earlier *bodies*, pl. of BODY (def. 14)]

Bodice[1] (def. 1)

bod·i·less (bod′ē lis), *adj.* lacking a body or a material form. [ME *bodiles*] —**bod′i·less·ness,** *n.*

bod·i·ly (bod′ᵊlē), *adj.* **1.** of or pertaining to the body —*adv.* **2.** as a physical entity; as a complete physical unit: *The tornado picked him up bodily and threw him against the wall.* [ME *bodylich*] —**Syn. 1.** See **physical.**

bod·ing (bō′ding), *n.* **1.** a foreboding; omen. —*adj.* **2.** foreboding; ominous. —**bod′ing·ly,** *adv.*

bod·kin (bod′kin), *n.* **1.** a small, pointed instrument for making holes in cloth, leather, etc. **2.** a long, slender hairpin. **3.** a blunt, needlelike instrument for drawing tape, cord, etc., through a loop, hem, or the like. **4.** *Obs.* a small dagger; stiletto. [ME *badeken, bo(i)dekyn* < ?]

Bod·lei·an (bod lē′ən, bod′lē-), *n.* **1.** the library of Oxford University, in Oxford, England: major collection of manuscripts and English books. —*adj.* **2.** of or pertaining to this library. [named after Sir Thomas *Bodley* (1545–1613), English diplomat and scholar who founded it; see -IAN]

Bo·do·ni (bə dō′nē; *for 1 also It.* bô dô′nē), *n.* **1. Giam·bat·tis·ta** (jäm′bät tēs′tä), 1740–1813, Italian painter and printer. **2.** *Print.* a style of type based on a design by G. Bodoni.

bod·y (bod′ē), *n., pl.* **bod·ies,** *v.,* **bod·ied, bod·y·ing.** —*n.* **1.** the physical structure and material substance of an animal or plant, living or dead. **2.** a corpse; carcass. **3.** the main or central mass of a thing, as the hull of a ship, fuselage of a plane, or chassis of a car. **4.** *Zool., Anat.* the physical structure of man or an animal not including the head, limbs, and tail; trunk. **5.** *Print.* the shank of a type, supporting the face. **6.** *Geom.* a three-dimensional figure; a solid. **7.** *Physics.* a mass, esp. one considered as a totality. **8.** the major portion of an army, population, etc.: *The body of the American people favors the president's policy.* **9.** the principal part of a discourse, minus introduction, conclusion, etc. **10.** *Informal.* a person: *She's a quiet sort of body.* **11.** a collective group of people or an artificial person: *student body; corporate body.* **12.** a separate physical entity, mass, or quantity, esp. as distinguished from other masses or quantities: *a heavenly body.* **13.** richness; substance: *This wine has good body.* **14.** the part of a dress that covers the trunk. **15.** *Ceram.* the basic material of which a ceramic article is made. —*v.t.* **16.** to represent in bodily form (usually fol. by *forth*). [ME; OE *bodig*; akin to OHG *botah*]
—**Syn. 1, 2.** BODY, CARCASS, CORPSE, CADAVER agree in referring to a physical organism, usually human or animal. BODY refers to the material organism of an individual man or animal, either living or dead: *the muscles in a horse's body; the body of a victim (man or animal).* CARCASS refers only to the dead body of an animal, unless applied humorously or contemptuously to the human body: *a sheep's carcass; Save your carcass.* CORPSE refers only to the dead body of a human being: *preparing a corpse for burial.* CADAVER refers to a dead body, usually of a human, particularly one used for scientific study: *dissection of cadavers in anatomy classes.*

bod′y cav′ity, *Zool., Anat.* the space or cavity in the body of man or animals containing the viscera.

bod·y-cen·tered (bod′ē sen′tərd), *adj. Crystall.* (of a crystal structure) having lattice points at the centers of the unit cells. Cf. **face-centered.**

bod′y check′, *Ice Hockey.* an obstructing or impeding with the body of the movement or progress of an opponent. Cf. **check** (def. 40).

bod·y·check (bod′ē chek′), *v.t., v.i. Ice Hockey.* to block with a body check.

bod′y cor′porate, *Law.* a corporation.

bod·y·guard (bod′ē gärd′), *n.* **1.** a person employed to guard an individual, as a high official, from bodily harm. **2.** a retinue; escort.

bod′y lan′guage, kinesics.

bod′y louse′. See under **louse** (def. 1).

Bod′y of Christ′, 1. the community of believers of which Christ is the head. I Cor. 12:27. **2.** the consecrated bread of the Eucharist.

bod′y plan′, *Naval Archit.* a diagrammatic elevation of a hull, consisting of an end view of the bow on one side of the center line and an end view of the stern on the other side. Cf. **half-breadth plan, sheer plan.**

bod′y pol′itic, *Political Science.* a people as forming a political unit under an organized government.

bod′y shirt′, a close-fitting shirt having a shape and seams that follow the contours of the body.

bod′y slam′, *Wrestling.* a throw in which an opponent is lifted and hurled to the mat on his back.

bod′y snatch′ing, the act of robbing a grave to obtain a subject for dissection. —**bod′y snatch′er.**

bod′y stock′ing, a woman's close-fitting, one-piece sheer garment covering the feet, legs, trunk, and arms.

bod′y type′, *Print.* type used in the main text of printed matter, generally less than 14 points. Cf. **display type.**

Bo·ece (bō ēs′), *n.* Boethius.

Boeh·me (*Ger.* bœ′mə), *n.* **Ja·kob** (*Ger.* yä′kōp). See **Böhme, Jakob.**

Boehm·ite (bā′mīt, bō′-), *n.* a mineral, hydrous aluminum oxide, AlO(OH), a major component of bauxite. [< G *Böhmit*, named after J. *Böhm*, 20th-century German scientist; see -ITE[1]]

Boe·o·tia (bē ō′shə), *n.* a district in ancient Greece, NW of Athens. *Cap.:* Thebes. See map at **Attica.**

Boe·o·tian (bē ō′shən), *adj.* **1.** of or pertaining to Boeotia or its inhabitants. **2.** dull; obtuse; without cultural refinement. —*n.* **3.** a native or inhabitant of Boeotia. **4.** a dull, obtuse person.

Boer (bōr, bôr; *Du.* bōōr), *n.* **1.** a South African of Dutch extraction. —*adj.* **2.** of or pertaining to the Boers. [< D: peasant, countryman. See BOOR]

Boer′ War′, a war in South Africa between Great Britain and the Dutch colonists of the Transvaal and Orange Free State, 1899–1902.

Bo·e·thi·us (bō ē′thē əs), *n.* **A·ni·ci·us Man·li·us Sev·e·ri·nus** (ə nish′ē əs man′lē əs sev′ə rī′nəs), A.D. 475?–525?, Roman philosopher and statesman. Also, **Bo·e·tius** (bō ē′shəs). Also called **Boece.** —**Bo·e′thi·an,** *adj.*

BOF, basic oxygen furnace: See under **basic oxygen process.**

bof·fo (bof′ō), *adj. Slang.* highly effective or successful.

Bo′fors gun′ (bō′fôrz, -fôrs), **1.** a 40-millimeter automatic gun used chiefly as an antiaircraft weapon. **2.** two such guns mounted and fired together as one unit. [named after *Bofors*, Sweden, where first made]

bog (bog, bôg), *n., v.,* **bogged, bog·ging.** —*n.* **1.** wet, spongy ground, with soil composed mainly of decayed vegetable matter. **2.** an area or stretch of such ground. —*v.t., v.i.* **3.** to sink in or as in a bog (often fol. by *down*): *We were bogged down with a lot of work.* [< Ir or Gael *bog(ach)* soft ground = *bog* soft + *-ach* n. suffix] —**bog′gi·ness,** *n.* —**bog′gish, bog′gy,** *adj.*

Bo·gan (bō′gən), *n.* **Louise,** 1897–1970, U.S. poet.

bog′ as′phodel, either of two liliaceous plants, *Narthecium ossifragum*, of Europe, and *N. americanum*, of the U.S., growing in boggy places.

bo·gey (bō′gē), *n., pl.* **-geys,** *v.,* **-geyed, -gey·ing.** —*n.* **1.** bogy. **2.** *Golf.* **a.** a score of one stroke over par on a hole. **b.** par (def. 4). **3.** *Australian.* a swim. —*v.t.* **4.** *Golf.* to make a bogey on (a hole). [sp. var. of BOGY]

bo·gey·man (bō′gē man′, bōō′-, bōōg′ē-), *n., pl.* **-men.** boogeyman.

bog·gle[1] (bog′əl), *v.,* **-gled, -gling.** —*v.i.* **1.** to take alarm; start with fright. **2.** to hesitate in doubt or fear; shrink: *The mind boggles at such arrogance.* **3.** to be awkward; bungle. —*v.t.* **4.** to astound; shock; overwhelm: *The distance of the stars boggles the imagination.* [? < BOGGLE[2]] —**bog′gler,** *n.* —**bog′gling·ly,** *adv.*

bog·gle[2] (bog′əl), *n.* bogle.

bo·gie (bō′gē), *n.* **1.** bogy. **2.** *Auto.* (on a truck) a rear wheel assembly composed of four wheels on two driving axles. **3.** *Chiefly Brit.* a swivel truck under a locomotive or railroad car. **4.** *Brit. Informal.* any low, strong, four-wheeled cart or truck. [?]

bo·gle (bō′gəl, bog′əl), *n.* a bogy; specter. [*bog* (var. of BUG[2] bugbear) + -LE]

bog′ oak′, oak or other wood preserved in peat bogs.

Bo·gor (bō′gôr), *n.* a city on W Java, in Indonesia. 195,882. Former Dutch name, **Buitenzorg.**

Bo·go·tá (bō′gə tä′; *Sp.* bô′gô tä′), *n.* a city in and the capital of Colombia. 2,855,065.

bog′ spav′in, *Vet. Pathol.* See under **spavin** (def. 1).

bog·trot·ter (bog′trot′ər, bôg′-), *n.* **1.** a person who lives among bogs. **2.** *Disparaging.* a rural Irishman.

bo·gus (bō′gəs), *adj.* counterfeit; spurious; sham. [orig. an apparatus for coining false money; ? akin to BOGIE]

bo·gy (bō′gē), *n., pl.* **-gies. 1.** a hobgoblin; evil spirit. **2.** anything that haunts, frightens, or harasses. **3.** *Mil. Slang.* an unidentified or an enemy aircraft. Also, **bogey, bogie.** [*bog* var. of BUG[2] + -Y[2]]

Bo·he·mi·a (bō hē′mē ə, -hēm′yə), *n.* **1.** Czech, **Čechy.** a region in W Czechoslovakia: formerly in Austria; a part of Bohemia-Moravia 1939–45. 6,072,744 (est. 1963); 20,101 sq. mi. **2.** a district inhabited by, or the world of, persons living an unconventional life, typically artists and writers.

Bo·he·mi·a-Mo·ra·vi·a (bō hē′mē ə mō rā′vē ə, -mô-, bō hēm′yə-), *n.* a former German protectorate including Bohemia and Moravia, 1939–45.

Bo·he·mi·an (bō hē′mē ən, -hēm′yən), *n.* **1.** a native or inhabitant of Bohemia. **2.** (*often l.c.*) a person, typically one with artistic or intellectual aspirations, who lives an unconventional life. **3.** a gypsy. **4.** *Archaic.* the Czech language. —*adj.* **5.** of or pertaining to Bohemia, its people, or their language. **6.** (*often l.c.*) pertaining to or characteristic of a bohemian. **7.** living a wandering or vagabond life, as a gypsy. —**Bo·he′mi·an·ism,** *n.*

Bohe′mian Breth′ren, a Christian denomination formed in Bohemia in 1467 from various Hussite groups, reorganized in 1722 as the Moravian Church.

Böh·me (bœ′mə), *n.* **Ja·kob** (yä′kōp), 1575–1624, German theosophist and mystic. Also, **Behmen, Boehme, Böhm** (bœm).

Bo·hol (bô hôl′), *n.* an island in the central Philippines. 680,870 (est. 1960); 1492 sq. mi.

Bohr (bōr, bôr), *n.* **Niels Hen·rik Dav·id** (nēls hen′rek dav′id), 1885–1962, Danish atomic physicist: Nobel prize 1922.

Bohr′ the′ory, *Physics.* a theory of atomic structure hypothesizing that electrons revolve in individual orbits around a nucleus, that the possible energy states in which the atom may appear are quantized, and that radiation is emitted when the atom moves from one energy state to a lower energy state. [named after N. BOHR]

bo·hunk (bō′hungk′), *n. Disparaging.* an unskilled or semiskilled foreign-born laborer, esp. from east central or southeastern Europe. Cf. **hunky.** [Bo(HEMIAN) + HUN-G(ARIAN), with devoicing of the *-g-*]

Bo·iar·do (boi är′dō; *It.* bô yäʀ′dô), *n.* **Mat·te·o Ma·ri·a** (mä tā′ō mə rē′ə; *It.* mät te′ô mä ʀē′ä), 1434–94, Italian poet. Also, **Bojardo.**

boil[1] (boil), *v.i.* **1.** to change from a liquid to a gaseous state, typically as a result of heat, producing bubbles of gas that rise to the surface of the liquid. **2.** to reach or be brought to the boiling point: *When the water boils, add the meat.* **3.** to move or toss about like boiling water. **4.** to be intensely angry: *She was boiling when he arrived late.* **5.** to contain, or be contained in, a liquid that boils: *The kettle is boiling. The vegetables are boiling.* —*v.t.* **6.** to cause to boil or to bring to the boiling point. **7.** to cook (something) in boiling water: *to boil eggs.* **8.** to separate (sugar, salt, etc.) from a solution containing it by boiling off the liquid. **9. boil down, a.** to reduce the quantity of something by boiling off some of its liquid. **b.** to shorten; abridge. **c.** to point; indicate, esp. as a final judgment or analysis: *It all boils down to a clear case of murder.* **10. boil off,** *Textiles.* **a.** to degum (silk). **b.** to remove (the size and impurities) from a fabric by subjecting it to a hot scouring solution. **11. boil over, a.** to overflow while or as while boiling; burst forth; erupt. **b.** to be unable to repress excitement, anger, etc. —*n.* **12.** the act or state of boiling. [ME *boill(en)* < OF *boill(ir)* < L *bullīre* = *bull(a)* bubble + *-īre* inf. suffix] —**boil′a·ble,** *adj.* —**boil′ing·ly,** *adv.*

—**Syn. 3.** foam, churn, froth. **4.** rage. BOIL, SEETHE, SIMMER, STEW are used figuratively to refer to agitated states of emotion. To BOIL suggests the state of being very hot with anger or rage: *Her behavior made him boil.* To SEETHE is to be deeply stirred, violently agitated, or greatly excited: *a mind seething with conflicting ideas.* To SIMMER means to be on the point of bursting out or boiling over: *to simmer with curiosity, with anger.* To STEW is informal for to worry, to be in a restless state of anxiety and excitement: *to stew about* (or *over*) *one's troubles.*

boil[2] (boil), *n. Pathol.* a painful, suppurating, inflammatory sore forming a central core, caused by microbic infection. Also called **furuncle.** [ME *bile, bule,* OE *bȳle;* c. G *Beule* boil, hump, akin to Icel *beyla* hump, swelling]

Boi·leau-Des·pré·aux (bwa lō′dā pʀā ō′), *n.* **Ni·co·las** (nē kô lä′), 1636–1711, French critic and poet.

boiled′ din′ner, a meal of meat and vegetables, as of corned beef, cabbage, and potatoes, prepared by boiling. Also called **New England boiled dinner.**

boiled′ dress′ing, a cooked dressing thickened with egg yolks and often containing mustard, served with various kinds of salads.

boiled′ shirt′, *Slang.* a man's formal or semiformal dress shirt with a starched front.

boil·er (boi′lər), *n.* **1.** a closed vessel or arrangement of vessels and tubes, together with a furnace or other heat source, in which steam is generated. **2.** a vessel, as a kettle, for boiling or heating. **3.** *Brit.* a large tub in which laundry is boiled or sterilized. **4.** a tank in which water is heated and stored, as for supplying hot water.

boil·er·mak·er (boi′lər mā′kər), *n.* **1.** a person who makes and repairs boilers or other heavy metal items. **2.** whiskey with beer as a chaser. —**boi′ler·mak′ing,** *n.*

boil′er plate′, 1. plating of iron or steel for making the shells of boilers, covering the hulls of ships, etc. **2.** *Journalism.* syndicated copy in the form of stereotype plates. **3.** the detailed standard wording of a contract, warranty, etc. **4.** a thin layer of powdery snow on a base of hard-packed snow. Also, **boil·er·plate** (boil′ər plāt′).

boil′er suit′, *Brit.* coveralls.

boil′ing point′, *Physical Chem.* the temperature at which a liquid boils, being the temperature at which its vapor pressure is equal to the pressure of the atmosphere on it, equal to 212°F or 100°C for water at sea level.

boil-off (boil′ôf′, -of′), *n. Rocketry Slang.* any vapor loss from the oxidizer or fuel in a rocket during countdown.

bois brû·lé (*Fr.* bwä bʀʏ lā′), *pl.* **bois brû·lés** (bwä bʀʏ lā′). *Canadian.* an offspring or descendant of an Indian and a white Canadian, esp. a French-Canadian. [< F: lit., burnt wood]

Bois de Bou·logne (bwä′ də bo͞o lōn′; *Fr.* bwä də bo͞o lôn′yə), a park in Paris, France. 2095 acres.

bois de vache (bwä′ də vash′), (esp. in the 18th and 19th centuries) dried buffalo dung, used as fuel. [< CanF: cow's wood]

Boi·se (boi′zē, -sē), *n.* a city in and the capital of Idaho, in the SW part: built on the site of an army post on the Oregon Trail. 74,990 (1970). Also called **Boi′se Cit′y.**

Bois-le-Duc (bwä lə dʏk′), *n.* French name of **'s Hertogenbosch.**

bois·ter·ous (boi′stər əs, -strəs), *adj.* **1.** rough and noisy; noisily jolly or rowdy; clamorous. **2.** (of weather, wind, etc.) stormy. **3.** *Obs.* rough and massive. [late ME *boistre(ou)s,* var. of ME *boistous* crude, strong, fierce, gross; by some said to be < MF *boisteux* lame] —**bois′ter·ous·ly,** *adv.* —**bois′ter·ous·ness,** *n.* —**Syn. 1.** obstreperous, roistering, loud. **1, 2.** turbulent, wild. —**Ant. 1, 2.** calm, serene.

boite (bwat), *n., pl.* **boites** (bwat). *French.* a night club; cabaret. Also called **boîte de nuit** (bwat də nwē′).

Boi·to (bō′ē tō′; *It.* boi′tô), *n.* **Ar·ri·go** (ə rē′gō; *It.* är ʀē′gô), 1842–1918, Italian opera composer and poet.

Bo·jar·do (boi är′dō; *It.* bô yär′dô), *n.* **Mat·te·o Ma·ri·a** (mä tā′ō mə rē′ə; *It.* mät te′ô mä ʀē′ä). See **Boiardo, Matteo Maria.**

Bok (bok), *n.* **Edward William,** 1863–1930, U.S. editor and writer, born in the Netherlands.

Bo·kha·ra (bō kär′ə; *Russ.* bo͝o ḵʜä′ʀä), *n.* Bukhara. —**Bo·kha′ran,** *adj.*

Bok·mål (bo͝ok′môl′), *n.* one of the two official norms for writing Norwegian, being the one derived from the Danish writing of urban Norwegians. Also called **Riksmål.** Cf. **Nynorsk.** [< Norw: book language]

Bo·ko Gun·to (bô′kô go͞on′tô), Japanese name of the **Pescadores.** Also called **Bo·ko·to** (bô′kô tô′).

Bol., Bolivia.

bol., (in prescriptions) bolus.

bo·la (bō′lə), *n., pl.* **-las** (-ləz). a weapon consisting of two or more heavy balls secured to the ends of one or more strong cords, hurled by the Indians and gauchos of southern South America to entangle the legs of cattle and other animals. Also, **bolas.** [< Sp: ball < L *bulla* bubble, ball; see BOIL[1]]

Bo·lan′ Pass′ (bō län′), a mountain pass in W Pakistan. ab. 60 mi. long.

bo·las (bō′ləs), *n., pl.* **bo·las** (bō′ləz), **bo·las·es** (bō′lə siz). (*construed as sing.*) bola.

bold (bōld), *adj.* **1.** courageous and daring: *a bold hero; bold adventure.* **2.** not hesitating to breach the rules of propriety; forward; immodest. **3.** imaginative; beyond the usual limits of conventional thought or action: *Einstein was a bold mathematician.* **4.** conspicuous to the eye; flashy; showy: *a bold pattern.* **5.** steep; abrupt: *a bold promontory.* **6.** *Print.* typeset in boldface. **7.** *Obs.* trusting; assured. **8. make bold,** to venture; dare: *I made bold to offer my suggestion.* [ME *bald, bold,* OE *b(e)ald;* c. OS, OHG *bald,* D *boud* bold, OIcel *ballr* dire] —**bold′ly,** *adv.* —**bold′ness,** *n.*

—**Syn. 1.** fearless, brave, valiant, intrepid, dauntless. **2.** BOLD, BRAZEN, FORWARD, PRESUMPTUOUS may refer to manners in a derogatory sense. BOLD suggests impudence, shamelessness, and immodesty (esp. in women): *a bold stare.* BRAZEN suggests the same, together with a defiant manner: *a brazen hussy.* FORWARD implies making oneself unduly prominent or bringing oneself to notice with too much assurance. PRESUMPTUOUS implies overconfidence, effrontery, taking too much for granted. —**Ant. 2.** modest.

bold·face (bōld′fās′), *Print.* —*n.* **1.** type that has thick, heavy lines, used for emphasis, headings, etc. —*adj.* **2.** typeset in boldface. Cf. **lightface.**

This is a sample of boldface

bold-faced (bōld′fāst′), *adj.* **1.** impudent; brazen; full of gall. **2.** *Print.* (of type) having thick, heavy lines. —**bold-fac·ed·ly** (bōld′fā′sid lē, -fāst′-), *adv.* —**bold′-fac′ed·ness,** *n.*

bole[1] (bōl), *n. Bot.* the stem or trunk of a tree. [ME < Scand; cf. Icel *bolr* trunk (of a tree), torso, c. G *Bohle* thick plank; see BULWARK]

bole[2] (bōl), *n.* any of a variety of soft, unctuous clays of various colors, used as pigments. Also, **bolus.** [ME *bol* < LL *bōl(us)* lump; see BOLUS]

bo·lec·tion (bō lek′shən), *n. Archit., Furniture.* a raised molding, esp. one having flat edges and a raised center, for framing a panel, doorway, fireplace, etc. Also, **bilection.** [?] —**bo·lec′tioned,** *adj.*

bo·le·ro (bə lâr′ō, bō-; *Sp.* bô le′ʀô), *n., pl.* **-le·ros** (-lâr′-ōz; *Sp.* -le′ʀôs). **1.** a lively Spanish dance in triple meter. **2.** the music for this dance. **3.** a waist-length jacket, worn open in front. [< Sp]

bo·le′tic ac′id (bō lē′tik), *Chem.* See **fumaric acid.** [BOLET(US) + -IC]

bo·le·tus (bō lē′təs), *n., pl.* **-tus·es, -ti** (-tī). any mushroomlike fungus of the genus *Boletus,* having an easily separable layer of tubes on the underside of the cap or pileus. [< L < Gk *bōlítēs* a kind of mushroom, perh. = *bôl(os)* (see BOLUS) + *-ítēs* -ITE[1]]

Bol·eyn (bo͝ol′in, bo͝o lin′), *n.* **Anne,** 1507–36, second wife of Henry VIII of England: mother of Queen Elizabeth I.

bo·lide (bō′līd, -lid), *n. Astron.* a large, brilliant meteor, esp. one that explodes; fireball. [< F < Gk *bolid-* (s. of *bolís*) missile]

Bol·ing·broke (bol′ing bro͝ok′; *older* bo͝ol′-), *n.* **1.** See **Henry IV** (def. 2). **2. Henry St. John** (sin′jən), **1st Viscount,** 1678–1751, British statesman, writer, and orator.

bol·i·var (bol′ə vər; *Sp.* bô lē′vär), *n., pl.* **bol·i·vars,** *Sp.* **bo·li·va·res** (bô′lē vä′ʀes). a silver coin and monetary unit of Venezuela, equal to 100 centimos. *Abbr.:* B. [< AmerSp, after Simón BOLÍVAR]

Bol·í·var (bol′ə vər; *Sp.* bô lē′vär), *n.* **Si·món** (sī′mən; *Sp.* sē mōn′), ("*El Libertador*"), 1783–1830, South American statesman and revolutionary leader.

Bo·liv·i·a (bō liv′ē ə, bə-; *Sp.* bô lē′vyä), *n.* a republic in W South America. 5,633,800; 404,388 sq. mi. *Caps.:* La Paz and Sucre. —**Bo·liv′i·an,** *adj., n.*

bo·li·vi·a·no (bō liv′ē ä′nō, bə-; *Sp.* bô′lē vyä′nô), *n., pl.* **-nos** (-nōz; *Sp.* -nôs). the former paper money and monetary unit of Bolivia, equal to 100 centavos. *Abbr.:* B. [< Sp; see BOLIVIA, -AN]

boll (bōl), *n. Bot.* a rounded seed vessel or pod of a plant, as of flax or cotton. [earlier sp. of BOWL[1]]

bol·lard (bol′ərd), *n. Naut.* **1.** a thick, low post, usually of iron or steel, mounted on a wharf or the like, to which mooring lines from vessels are attached. **2.** a small post to which lines are attached. **3.** *Brit.* one of a series of protective posts bordering a road. **4.** bitt (def. 1). [? BOLE[1] + -ARD]

bol·lix (bol′iks), *v.t. Informal.* to bungle (often fol. by *up*). Also, **bol′lox.** [ME *ballokes* (pl.), OE *beallucas* testicles]

boll′ wee′vil, a snout beetle, *Anthonomus grandis,* that attacks the bolls of cotton.

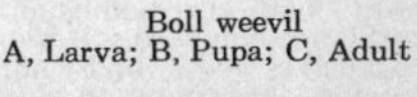

Boll weevil
A, Larva; B, Pupa; C, Adult

boll·worm (bōl′wûrm′), *n.* **1.** See **pink bollworm. 2.** See **corn earworm.**

bo·lo (bō′lō), *n., pl.* **-los.** a large, heavy, single-edged military knife or machete for hacking through bush. [< Philippine Sp < native dial.]

bo·lo·gna (bə lō′nē, -nə, -lōn′yə), *n.* a large seasoned sausage made of finely ground beef and pork that has been cooked and smoked. Also called **bolo′gna sau′sage.** [after BOLOGNA, Italy]

Bo·lo·gna (bə lōn′yə; *It.* bô lô′nyä), *n.* **1. Gio·van·ni da** (jē/ə vä′nē; *It.* jô vän′nē), (*Jean de Boulogne, Giambologna*), c1525–1608, Italian sculptor, born in France. **2.** a city in N Italy. 441,143 (1961).

Bo·lo·gnese (bō′lə nēz′, -nēs′, -lən yēz′, -yēs′), *adj., n., pl.* **-gnese.** —*adj.* **1.** of or pertaining to Bologna or its inhabitants. —*n.* **2.** a native or inhabitant of Bologna.

bo·lo·graph (bō′lə graf′, -gräf′), *n. Physics.* (formerly) the record produced by a bolometer. [< Gk *bol(ē)* ray + -o- + -GRAPH] —**bo·lo·graph·ic** (bō′lə graf′ik), *adj.* —**bo′lo·graph′i·cal·ly,** *adv.* —**bo·log·ra·phy** (bə log′rə fē), *n.*

bo·lom·e·ter (bō lom′i tər, bə-), *n. Physics.* a device for measuring minute amounts of radiant energy by means of changes in the resistance of an electric conductor caused by changes in its temperature. [< Gk *bol(ē)* ray + -o- + -METER] —**bo·lo·met·ric** (bō′lə me′trik), *adj.* —**bo′lo·met′ri·cal·ly,** *adv.*

bo·lo·ney (bə lō′nē), *n.* baloney.

Bol·she·vik (bōl′shə vik, bol′-; *Russ.* bôl′shə vēk′), *n., pl.* **-viks, -vik·i** (-vik′ē, -vē′kē; *Russ.* -vi kē′). **1.** (in Russia) **a.** a member of the more radical majority of the Social Democratic party, 1903–17. **b.** (since 1918) a member of the Russian Communist party. **2.** (loosely) a member of any communist party. **3.** *Derogatory.* an extreme political radical; revolutionary or anarchist. Also, **bol′she·vik.** [back formation from Russ *Bolsheviki* (pl.) = *bolshe* greater (i.e., majority, position held by this group in Social Democratic party in 1903), comp. of *bolshoi* big + *-vik* n. suffix + *-i* pl. suffix] —**Bol′she·vism, bol′she·vism, Bol′she·vik·ism, bol′she·vik·ism,** *n.* —**Bol′she·vist, bol′she·vist,** *n.* —**Bol′she·vis′tic, bol′she·vis′tic,** *adj.* —**Bol′she·vis′ti·cal·ly, bol′she·vis′ti·cal·ly,** *adv.*

bol·ster (bōl′stər), *n.* **1.** a long, often cylindrical cushion or pillow for a bed, sofa, etc. **2.** something resembling this in form or in use. **3.** any pillow, cushion, or pad. **4.** *Carpentry.* a horizontal timber on a post for lessening the free span of a beam. —*v.t.* **5.** to support as with a pillow or cushion. **6.** to add to, support, or uphold (a theory, quality, belief, etc.) (sometimes fol by *up*): *They bolstered their morale by singing.* [ME *bolstre,* OE *bolster;* c. Icel *bolstr,* D *bolster,* G *Polster*] —**bol′ster·er,** *n.*

bolt[1] (bōlt), *n.* **1.** a movable bar or rod that slides into a socket to fasten a door, gate, etc. **2.** the part of a lock that is shot from and drawn back into the case, as by the action of the key. **3.** any of several types of strong fastening rods, pins, or screws, usually threaded to receive a nut. **4.** a sudden dash, run, flight, or escape. **5.** a sudden desertion from a political party, social movement, etc. **6.** a length of woven goods, esp. as it comes on a roll from the loom. **7.** a roll of wallpaper. **8.** a rod, bar, or plate that closes the breech of a breechloading rifle, esp. a sliding rod or bar that shoves a cartridge into the firing chamber as it closes the breech. **9.** a jet of water, molten glass, etc. **10.** an arrow, esp. a short, heavy one for a crossbow. **11.** thunderbolt. **12. bolt from the blue,** a sudden and entirely unforeseen event; a complete surprise. —*v.t.* **13.** to fasten with or as with a bolt or bolts. **14.** to discontinue support of or participation in; break with: *to bolt a political party.* **15.** to shoot or discharge (a missile), as from a crossbow or catapult. **16.** to utter hastily; say impulsively; blurt out. **17.** to swallow (one's food or drink) hurriedly; eat without chewing: *He bolted his breakfast.* **18.** to make (cloth, wallpaper, etc.) into bolts. —*v.i.* **19.** to make a sudden, swift dash, run, flight, or escape; spring away suddenly: *The rabbit bolted into its burrow.* **20.** *U.S.* to break away, as from one's political party. **21.** to eat hurriedly or without chewing. —*adv.* **22.** suddenly. **23. bolt upright,** stiffly upright; rigidly straight. [ME, OE; c. D *bout,* G *Bolz*] —**bolt′er,** *n.*

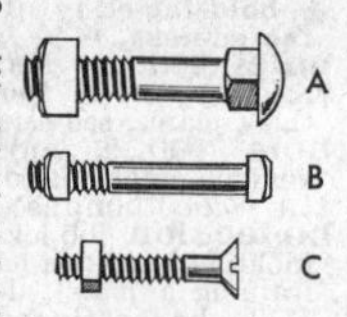

Bolts (def. 3)
A, Carriage bolt
B, Machine bolt
C, Stove bolt

bolt[2] (bōlt), *v.t.* **1.** to sift through a cloth or sieve. **2.** to examine or search into, as if by sifting. [ME *bult(en)* < OF *bul(e)ter,* metathetic var. of *buteler < Gmc; cf. MHG *biuteln* to sift < *biutel,* OHG *būtil* bag, whence G *Beutel* bolting bag] —**bolt′er,** *n.*

bolt-ac·tion (bōlt′ak′shən), *adj.* (of a rifle) equipped with a manually operated sliding bolt.

Bol·ton (bōl′tᵊn), *n.* a city in S Lancashire, in NW England. 160,887 (1961).

bol·to·ni·a (bōl tō′nē ə), *n.* any asterlike, perennial herb of the genus *Boltonia,* of the U.S. [< NL; named after James *Bolton,* 18th-century English botanist; see -IA]

bolt·rope (bōlt′rōp′), *n. Naut.* a rope or the cordage sewn on the edges of a sail to strengthen it. Also, **bolt′ rope′.**

Boltz·mann (bōlts′män′; *Eng.* bōlts′mən), *n.* **Lud·wig** (lo͝od′vɪkн, lo͞ot′-), 1844–1906, Austrian physicist.

bo·lus (bō′ləs), *n., pl.* **-lus·es. 1.** *Pharm., Vet. Med.* a round mass of medicine, larger than an ordinary pill. *Abbr.:* bol. **2.** a soft, roundish mass or lump, esp. of chewed food. **3.** bole[2]. [< LL < Gk *bôlos* clod, lump; see BOLE[2]]

Bol·za·no (bôl tsä′nô), *n.* a city in NE Italy. 88,980 (1961). German, **Bozen.**

Bo·ma (bō′mə), *n.* a city in W Zaïre, on the Congo River. 31,598 (est. 1958).

bomb (bom), *n.* **1.** *Mil.* a projectile exploded by means of a fuze, by impact, or otherwise, now generally designed to be dropped from an aircraft. **2.** any similar missile or explosive device used as a weapon, to disperse crowds, etc.: *a smoke bomb; a time bomb.* **3.** *Geol.* a rough spherical or ellipsoidal mass of lava, ejected from a volcano and hardened while falling. **4.** See **aerosol bomb. 5.** *Slang.* an absolute failure; fiasco. **6. the bomb,** nuclear weapons collectively. —*v.t.* **7.** to hurl bombs at or drop bombs upon, as from an airplane; bombard. **8.** to explode by means of a bomb or explosive. —*v.i.* **9.** to hurl, drop, or explode a bomb or bombs. **10.** *Slang.* to be or make a complete failure; flop: *His last play bombed on Broadway.* [earlier *bom(b)e* < Sp *bomba (de fuego)* ball (of fire), akin to *bombo* drum < L *bomb(us)* a booming sound < Gk *bómbos*]

bom·ba·ca·ceous (bom′bə kā′shəs), *adj.* belonging to the *Bombacaceae,* a family of woody plants including the silk-cotton trees and the baobab. [< NL *Bombācāce(ae)* = ML *bombāc-* (s. of *bombāx* cotton, L *bombȳx* silk < Gk) + *-āceae* -ACEAE + -OUS]

bom·bard (*v.* bom bärd′; *n.* bom′bärd), *v.t.* **1.** to attack or batter with artillery fire. **2.** to assail vigorously: *to bombard someone with questions.* **3.** *Physics.* to direct high energy particles or radiations against: *to bombard a nucleus.* —*n.* **4.** the earliest kind of cannon, originally throwing stone balls. [ME < ML *bombard(a)* stone-throwing engine = L *bomb(us)* booming noise (see BOMB) + *-arda* -ARD] —**bom·bard′er,** *n.* —**bom·bard′ment,** *n.*

bom·bar·dier (bom′bər dēr′), *n.* **1.** *Mil.* the member of a bomber crew who operates the bombsight and bomb-release mechanism. **2.** *Hist.* artilleryman. [< MF]

bom·bast (bom′bast), *n.* **1.** pretentious words; speech too pompous for an occasion. **2.** *Obs.* cotton or other material used to stuff garments; padding. —*adj.* **3.** *Obs.* bombastic. [earlier *bombace* < MF < ML *bombāce(m),* acc. of *bombāx* cotton; see BOMBACACEOUS]

bom·bas·tic (bom bas′tik), *adj.* (of speech, writing, etc.) high-sounding; high-flown; inflated; pretentious. Also, **bom·bas′ti·cal.** —**bom·bas′ti·cal·ly,** *adv.*

Bom·bay (bom bā′), *n.* **1.** a seaport in and the capital of Maharashtra, in W India, on the Arabian Sea. 4,537,926 (est. 1964). **2.** a former state in W India: divided in 1960 into the Gujarat and Maharashtra states.

bom·ba·zine (bom′bə zēn′, bom′bə zēn′), *n.* a twill fabric constructed of a silk or rayon warp and worsted filling, often dyed black for mourning wear. Also, **bom′ba·sine′, bom′ba·zeen′.** [earlier *bombasin* < MF < ML *bombasin(um),* var. of LL *bombȳcinum,* n. use of neut. of *bombȳcinus* silken = L *bombȳc-* (s. of *bombȳx* silk, silkworm < Gk) + *-inus* -INE[1]]

bomb′ bay′, *Aeron., Mil.* (in the fuselage of a bomber) the compartment in which bombs are carried and from which they are dropped.

bombe (bom, bomb; *Fr.* bôɴb), *n., pl.* **bombes** (bomz, bombz; *Fr.* bôɴb). a round or melon-shaped frozen mold made from a combination of ice creams, mousses, or ices. [< F: lit., BOMB, i.e., ball, from its shape]

bom·bé (bom bā′; *Fr.* bôɴ-bā′), *adj. Furniture.* curving or swelling outward. Cf. **swell front.** [< F: lit., rounded like a bomb = *bombe* BOMB + *-é* adj. suffix < L *-ātus* -ATE[1]]

Bombé desk
(Massachusetts, 1765)

bomb·er (bom′ər), *n. Mil.* an airplane equipped to carry and drop bombs.

bomb·load (bom′lōd′), *n.* the total load of bombs carried by an airplane, usually expressed in terms of their total weight.

bomb·proof (bom′pro͞of′), *adj.* **1.** able to withstand the impact of bombs. —*n.* **2.** a bombproof structure.

bomb′ run′, *Mil.* the part of a bombing mission between the sighting of the target and the release of the bombs. Also, **bomb′ing run′.**

bomb·shell (bom′shel′), *n.* **1.** a bomb. **2.** something or someone that has a sudden and sensational effect.

bomb′ shel′ter, a room, area, or small building reinforced against the effects of bombs, used as a shelter during an air raid. Cf. **air-raid shelter.**

bomb·sight (bom′sīt′), *n. Mil.* (in an aircraft) an instrument for aiming bombs at a target.

Bo·mu (bō′mo͞o), *n.* a river in central Africa, forming part of the boundary between Zaïre and the Central African Republic, flowing N and W into the Uele River to form the Ubangi River. ab. 450 mi. long. Also called **Mbomu.**

Bon (bon), *n.* **Cape,** a cape on the NE coast of Tunisia: surrender of the German forces in Africa, May 12, 1943. Also called **Ras Addar.**

Bon (bôn), *n.* an annual festival of the Japanese Buddhists, welcoming ancestral spirits to household altars. [< Jap]

bo·na·ci (bō′nə sē′), *n., pl.* (*esp. collectively*) **-ci,** (*esp. referring to two or more kinds or species*) **-cis.** any of several edible serranid fishes, as *Mycteroperca bonaci.* [< Sp *bonasí* a fish]

bo·na fide (bō′nə fīd′, bon′ə; bō′nə fī′dē), **1.** genuine; real. **2.** in good faith; without fraud. [< L] —**bo·na-fide** (bō′nə fīd′, bon′ə-), *adj.*

Bon·aire (bô nâr′), *n.* an island in the E Netherlands Antilles, in the S West Indies. 5614 (1960); 112 sq. mi.

bon a·mi (bôɴ ɴᴀ mē′), *pl.* **bons a·mis** (bôɴ zᴀ mē′). *French.* **1.** a good friend. **2.** a lover.

bo·nan·za (bə nan′zə, bō-), *n. U.S.* **1.** a rich mass of ore, as found in mining. **2.** a source of great and sudden wealth or luck: *The investment proved to be a bonanza.* [< Sp: lit., smooth sea (hence, good luck, rich vein of ore) < nasalized var. of ML *bonacia* = L *bon(us)* good + *(mal)acia* calm sea < Gk *malachía* softness (*malach(ós)* soft + *-ia* -IA)]

Bo·na·parte (bō′nə pärt′; *Fr.* bô ɴᴀ ᴘᴀʀᴛ′), *n.* **1. Jé·rôme** (jə rōm′; *Fr.* zhā ʀōm′), 1784–1860, king of Westphalia 1807 (brother of Napoleon I). **2. Jo·seph** (jō′zəf; *Fr.* zhô zef′), 1768–1844, king of Naples 1806–08; king of Spain 1808–13 (brother of Napoleon I). **3. Lou·is** (lo͞o′ē; *Fr.* lwē; *Du.* lo͞o ē′), 1778–1846, king of Holland 1806–10 (brother of Napoleon I). **4. Lou·is Na·po·lé·on** (lo͞o′ē nə-pō′lē ən; *Fr.* lwē ɴᴀ pô lā ôɴ′). See **Napoleon III. 5. Lu·cien** (lo͞o′shən; *Fr.* lʏ syaɴ′), 1775–1840, Prince of Cannino (brother of Napoleon I). **6. Napoléon.** See **Napoleon I. 7. Napoléon.** See **Napoleon II.** Italian, **Buonaparte.** —**Bo′na·part′ist,** *adj., n.* —**Bo′na·part′ism,** *n.*

bon ap·pé·tit (bô ɴᴀ pā tē′), *French.* (I wish you) a hearty appetite.

Bon·a·ven·ture (bon′ə ven′chər), *n.* **Saint** ("*the Seraphic Doctor*"), 1221–74, Italian scholastic theologian. Also, **Bon·a·ven·tu·ra** (bon′ə ven cho͞or′ə; *It.* bô′nä ven to͞o′rä).

bon·bon (bon′bon′; *Fr.* bôɴ bôɴ′), *n., pl.* **-bons** (-bonz′; *Fr.* -bôɴ′). a small, fondant-coated candy, typically having a filling of fruit jam. [< F: lit., good-good; a repetitive compound, orig. nursery word]

bon·bon·nière (bôN bô nyeʀ′), *n., pl.* **-nières** (-nyeʀ′). **1.** a confectioner's store. **2.** (*italics*) *French.* a box or dish for candies. [< F: lit., candy-holder]

bond[1] (bond), *n.* **1.** something that binds, fastens, or confines. **2.** a cord or rope for tying something. **3.** something that binds a person or persons to a certain behavior: *the bond of matrimony.* **4.** something, as an agreement, that unites individuals or peoples; covenant: *the bond between nations.* **5.** binding security; firm assurance: *My word is my bond.* **6.** a sealed instrument under which a person, corporation, or government guarantees to pay a stated sum of money on or before a specified day. **7.** *Law.* a written promise of a surety or the amount assured. Cf. **bail**[1]. **8.** *Govt.* the state of dutiable goods stored under a bond in charge of the government: *goods in bond.* **9.** Also called **bonded whiskey.** *U.S.* a whiskey that has been aged at least four years in a bonded warehouse before bottling. **10.** *Finance.* a certificate of ownership of a specified portion of a debt due to be paid by a government or corporation to an individual holder and usually bearing a fixed rate of interest. **11.** *Insurance.* **a.** a surety agreement. **b.** the money deposited, or the promissory arrangement entered into, under any such agreement. **12.** a substance that causes particles to adhere; binder. **13.** adhesion between two substances or objects. **14.** *Chem.* the attraction between atoms in a molecule. **15.** See **bond paper. 16.** *Masonry.* **a.** any of various arrangements of bricks, stones, etc., having a regular pattern and intended to increase the strength or enhance the appearance of a construction. **b.** the overlap of bricks, stones, etc., in a construction so as to increase its strength. **17.** *Obs.* bondsman[1]. —*v.t.* **18.** to put (goods, an employee, etc.) on or under bond. **19.** to connect or bind. **20.** *Finance.* to place a bonded debt on or secure a debt by bonds. **21.** to join (two materials). **22.** *Masonry.* to lay (bricks, stones, etc.) so as to produce a strong construction. —*v.i.* **23.** to hold together or cohere, as bricks in a wall or particles in a mass. [ME; var. of BAND[3]] —**bond′er,** *n.*

—**Syn. 1.** chains, fetters. **3.** BOND, LINK, TIE agree in referring to a force or influence that unites people. BOND, however, usually emphasizes the strong and enduring quality of affection, whereas TIE may refer more esp. to duty, obligation, or responsibility: *bonds of memory; Blessed be the tie that binds; family ties.* A LINK is a definite connection, though a slighter one; it may indicate affection or merely some traceable influence or desultory communication: *a close link between friends.*

bond[2] (bond), *adj. Obs.* in serfdom or slavery. [ME *bond(e),* OE *bōnda* < Scand; cf. Icel *bōndi* HUSBAND(MAN), contr. of **bōunde,* var. of *būande,* c. OE *būend* dweller = *bū(an)* (to) dwell (see BOOR) + *-end* n. suffix, as in *fiend, friend*]

Bond (bond), *n.* **Car·rie** (kar′ē) (née **Jacobs**) (jā′kəbz), 1862–1946, U.S. songwriter and author.

bond·age (bon′dij), *n.* **1.** slavery or involuntary servitude; serfdom. **2.** the state of being bound by or subjected to external control. **3.** *Early Eng. Law.* personal subjection to the control of a superior; villeinage. [ME < AL *bondag(ium)*] —**Syn. 1.** captivity. See **slavery. 2.** thralldom, captivity.

bond·ed (bon′did), *adj.* **1.** secured by or consisting of bonds: *bonded debt.* **2.** placed in bond: *bonded goods.*

bond′ed ware′house, a warehouse for goods held in bond by the government.

bond′ed whis′key, bond[1] (def. 9).

bond·hold·er (bond′hōl′dər), *n.* a holder of a bond or bonds issued by a government or corporation. —**bond′hold′ing,** *adj., n.*

bond·maid (bond′mād′), *n.* **1.** a female slave. **2.** a female bound to service without wages.

bond·man (bond′mən), *n., pl.* **-men. 1.** a male slave. **2.** a male bound to service without wages. [ME *bonde man*]

bond′ pa′per, a durable paper of high quality, used esp. for stationery. Also called **bond.**

bond′ serv′ant, 1. a person who serves in bondage; slave. **2.** a person bound to service without wages. Also, **bond′-serv′ant.**

bonds·man[1] (bondz′mən), *n., pl.* **-men.** *Law.* a person who is bound or who by bond becomes surety for another. [*bond's man* man of the bond, i.e., its signer; see BOND[1], MAN[1]]

bonds·man[2] (bondz′mən), *n., pl.* **-men.** bondman. [ME *bondesman.* See BOND[2], MAN[1]]

bond·stone (bond′stōn′), *n.* a stone, as a perpend, for bonding facing masonry to a masonry backing.

bonds·wom·an[1] (bondz′wo͝om′ən), *n., pl.* **-wom·en.** *Law.* a woman who is bound or who by bond becomes surety for another. [*bond's woman* woman of the bond, i.e., its signer]

bonds·wom·an[2] (bondz′wo͝om′ən), *n., pl.* **-wom·en.** bondwoman. [BOND[2] + WOMAN]

bond·wom·an (bond′wo͝om′ən), *n., pl.* **-wom·en. 1.** a female slave. **2.** a woman bound to service without wages. [ME *bonde womman.* See BOND[2], WOMAN]

bone (bōn), *n., v.,* **boned, bon·ing.** —*n.* **1.** *Anat., Zool.* **a.** one of the structures composing the skeleton of a vertebrate. **b.** the hard connective tissue forming the skeleton of most vertebrates. **2.** such a structure from an edible animal, usually with meat adhering to it, used as an article of food: *a ham bone.* **3.** any of various similarly hard or structural animal substances, as ivory, whalebone, etc. **4. bones, a.** the skeleton. **b.** one's body: *Let me rest my weary bones for a minute.* **c.** *Games Slang.* dice. **d.** a simple rhythm instrument consisting of two bars or short strips of bone, ivory, wood, or the like, held between the fingers of one hand and clacked together. **5.** a flat strip of whalebone or other material for stiffening corsets, petticoats, etc.; stay. **6.** *Games Slang.* a domino. **7. feel in one's bones,** to think or feel intuitively: *She felt in her bones that it was going to be a momentous day.* **8. have a bone to pick with someone,** to have cause to disagree or argue with someone. **9. make no bones about,** to deal with in a direct manner; act or speak openly concerning: *She made no bones about her distaste for the subject.* —*v.t.* **10.** to remove the bones from: *to bone a turkey.* **11.** to put whalebone or another stiffener into (clothing). —*v.i.* **12.** *Slang.* to study intensely; cram (often fol. by *up*): *She's boning up for her finals.* [ME *boon,* OE *bān;* c. D *been* bone, leg, Icel *bein* bone, G *Bein* leg] —**bone′less,** *adj.*

Bône (bōn), *n.* former name of **Annaba.**

bone′ ash′, the remains of bones calcined in the air, used as a fertilizer and in the making of bone china. Also called **bone′ earth′.**

bone·black (bōn′blak′), *n.* a black, carbonaceous substance obtained by calcining bones in closed vessels, used as a black pigment, a decolorizing agent, etc. Also, **bone′ black′.**

bone′ chi′na, a fine, naturally white china made with bone ash.

boned (bōnd), *adj.* **1.** having a specified kind of bones or bony structure (often used in combination): *small-boned.* **2.** cooked or served with the bones removed: *boned chicken.* **3.** braced or supported with stays, as a corset. **4.** fertilized with bone meal: *boned land.*

bone-dry (bōn′drī′), *adj. Informal.* very dry or thirsty.

bone·fish (bōn′fish′), *n., pl.* **-fish·es,** (*esp. collectively*) **-fish.** a marine game fish, *Albula vulpes,* found in shallow tropical waters, having a skeleton composed of numerous small, fine bones.

bone·head (bōn′hed′), *n.* a stupid, obstinate person; blockhead. —**bone′head′ed,** *adj.*

bone′ meal′, *Agric.* bones ground to a coarse powder, used as fertilizer or feed.

bone′ of conten′tion, the subject or focal point of a dispute.

bone′ oil′, a fetid, tarry liquid obtained in the dry distillation of bone.

bon·er[1] (bō′nər), *n.* a person or thing that bones.

bon·er[2] (bō′nər), *n. Slang.* a foolish and obvious blunder. [BONE(HEAD) + -ER[1]]

Boneset, *Eupatorium perfoliatum* (Height 3 to 6 ft.)

bone·set (bōn′set′), *n.* any plant of the genus *Eupatorium,* esp. *E. perfoliatum,* of North America. Also called **thoroughwort.** [BONE + SET, so named (by hyperbole) because it is supposed to have healing properties]

bone′ spav′in, *Vet. Pathol.* See under **spavin** (def. 1).

bon·fire (bon′fīər′), *n.* a large fire in the open air, for warmth, entertainment, as a signal, or the like. [late ME *bone fire,* i.e., a fire with bones for fuel]

Bongo (4 ft. high at shoulder)

bon·go[1] (boŋ′gō, bôŋ′-), *n., pl.* **-gos,** (*esp. collectively*) **-go.** a reddish-brown antelope, *Taurotragus eurycerus,* of the forests of tropical Africa, having white stripes and large, spirally twisted horns. [< an African language]

bon·go[2] (boŋ′gō, bôŋ′-), *n., pl.* **-gos, -goes.** one of a pair of small tuned drums played by beating with the fingers. Also called **bon′go drum′.** [< AmerSp *bongó*]

Bon·heur (bo nûr′; *Fr.* bô nœʀ′), *n.* **Ro·sa** (rō′zə; *Fr.* ʀô zȧ′), (*Maria Rosalie Bonheur*), 1822–99, French painter.

bon·ho·mie (bon′ə mē′; *Fr.* bô nô mē′), *n.* friendliness; geniality. [< F = *bonhomme* good-natured man (see BOON[2], HOMO) + *-ie* -Y[3]]

Bon·i·face (bon′ə fās′), *n.* **Saint** (*Wynfrith*), A.D. 680?–755?, English monk who became a missionary in Germany.

Boniface I, Saint, died A.D. 422, pope 418–422.

Boniface II, pope A.D. 530–532.

Boniface III, pope A.D. 607.

Boniface IV, Saint, pope A.D. 608–615.

Boniface V, died A.D. 625, pope 619–625.

Boniface VI, pope A.D. 896.

Boniface VII, antipope A.D. 974, 984–985.

Boniface VIII, (*Benedetto Caetani*) c1235–1303, Italian ecclesiastic: pope 1294–1303.

Boniface IX, (*Pietro Tomacelli*) died 1404, Italian ecclesiastic: pope 1389–1404.

Bo′nin Is′lands (bō′nin), a group of islands in the N Pacific, SE of and belonging to Japan: under U.S. administration 1945–68. 40 sq. mi. Japanese, **Ogasawara Jima.**

bo·ni·to (bə nē′tō), *n., pl.* (*esp. collectively*) **-to,** (*esp. referring to two or more kinds or species*) **-tos. 1.** any mackerellike fish of the genus *Sarda,* as *S. sarda,* found in the Atlantic Ocean. **2.** any of several related species, as the skipjack, *Katsuwonus pelamis.* [< Sp < Ar *bainīth*]

bon·jour (bôN zho͞or′), *interj. French.* good day; hello.

bon mar·ché (bôN mar shā′), *pl.* **bons mar·chés** (bôN mar shā′). *French.* a bargain. [lit., good market]

bon mot (bon′ mō′; *Fr.* bôN mō′), *pl.* **bons mots** (bon′ mōz′; *Fr.* bôN mō′), an especially fitting word or expression; clever saying; witticism. [< F: lit., good word; see BOON[2], MOTTO]

Bonn (bon; *Ger.* bôn), *n.* a city in and the capital of West Germany, on the Rhine River. 283,500.

Bon·nard (bô naʀ′), *n.* **Pierre** (pyeʀ), 1867–1947, French painter.

bonne a·mie (bô na mē′), *pl.* **bonnes a·mies** (bôn za mē′). *French.* **1.** a good (female) friend. **2.** a (female) lover.

bonne nuit (bôn nwē′), *French.* good night.

bon·net (bon′it), *n.* **1.** an outdoor head covering, usually having a wide brim and tying under the chin, formerly much worn by women but now worn principally by children or as part of a nun's habit. **2.** *Chiefly Scot.* a man's or boy's large-crowned, visorless cap. **3.** a bonnetlike headdress: *an Indian war bonnet.* **4.** any of various hoods, covers, or protective devices. **5.** a cowl, hood, or wind cap for a fireplace or chimney, to stabilize the draft. **6.** the part of a valve casing through which the stem passes and that forms a guide and seal for the stem. **7.** *Brit.* an automobile hood. **8.** *Naut.* a supplementary piece of canvas laced to the foot of a fore-and-aft sail, esp. a jib, in light winds. —*v.t.* **9.** to put a bonnet on. [late ME *bonet* < MF; akin to LL *abonnis* kind of cap < ?]

bon·net rouge (bô ne ʀo͞ozh′), *pl.* **bon·nets rouges** (bô ne ʀo͞ozh′). *French.* **1.** a red liberty cap, worn by extremists at the time of the French Revolution. **2.** an extremist or radical.

Bon·ne·ville (bon′ə vil′), *n.* **Lake,** a prehistoric lake in Utah, E Nevada, and S Idaho: Great Salt Lake is its remnant. 350 mi. long.

Bon′neville flats′ (flats), an area of salt flats in the W part of Great Salt Lake Desert, in NW Utah: automobile speed tests. Also called **Bon′neville Salt′ flats′.**

bon·ny (bon′ē), *adj.*, **-ni·er, -ni·est,** *adv.* —*adj.* **1.** *Chiefly Scot.* pleasing to the eye; handsome; pretty. **2.** *Brit. Dial.* **a.** (of people) healthy, sweet, and lively. **b.** (of places) placid; tranquil. **c.** pleasing; agreeable; good. —*adv.* **3.** *Brit. Dial.* pleasingly; agreeably; very well. Also, **bon′nie.** [ME *bonie* < OF *bon* good + *-ie* -Y[1], perh. by analogy with *jolie* JOLLY] —**bon′ni·ly,** *adv.* —**bon′ni·ness,** *n.*

bon·ny·clab·ber (bon′ē klab′ər), *n.* sour, thick milk. [< Ir *bainne clabair*, lit., milk of the clapper (i.e., of the churn lid or dasher)]

bon·sai (bōn′sī, bon′-), *n.*, *pl.* **-sai.** **1.** a potted tree or shrub that has been dwarfed by any of certain methods, as by pruning the roots and pinching and wiring the shoots and branches to produce a desired shape or effect. **2.** the art or hobby of developing and growing such a plant or plants. [< Jap]

bon·soir (bôɴ swar′), *interj.* *French.* good evening; good night.

bon·spiel (bon′spēl, -spəl), *n.* *Curling.* a match or tournament. [?]

bon·te·bok (bon′tē bok′), *n.*, *pl.* **-boks,** (*esp. collectively*) **-bok.** a nearly extinct, purplish-red antelope, *Damaliscus pygarus*, of southern Africa, having a white face and rump. [< SAfrD = *bont* piebald (< ML *punctus* dotted; see POINT) + *bok* BUCK[1]]

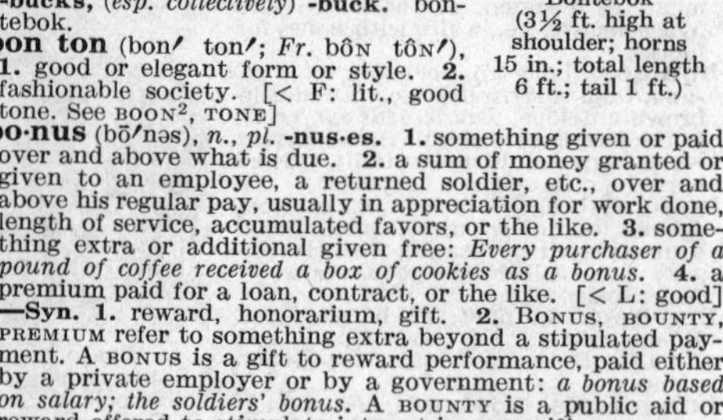

Bontebok (3½ ft. high at shoulder; horns 15 in.; total length 6 ft.; tail 1 ft.)

bon·te·buck (bon′tē buk′), *n.*, *pl.* **-bucks,** (*esp. collectively*) **-buck.** bontebok.

bon ton (bon′ ton′; *Fr.* bôɴ tôɴ′), **1.** good or elegant form or style. **2.** fashionable society. [< F: lit., good tone. See BOON[2], TONE]

bo·nus (bō′nəs), *n.*, *pl.* **-nus·es.** **1.** something given or paid over and above what is due. **2.** a sum of money granted or given to an employee, a returned soldier, etc., over and above his regular pay, usually in appreciation for work done, length of service, accumulated favors, or the like. **3.** something extra or additional given free: *Every purchaser of a pound of coffee received a box of cookies as a bonus.* **4.** a premium paid for a loan, contract, or the like. [< L: good] —**Syn. 1.** reward, honorarium, gift. **2.** BONUS, BOUNTY, PREMIUM refer to something extra beyond a stipulated payment. A BONUS is a gift to reward performance, paid either by a private employer or by a government: *a bonus based on salary; the soldiers' bonus.* A BOUNTY is a public aid or reward offered to stimulate interest in a specific purpose or undertaking and to encourage performance: *a bounty for killing wolves.* A PREMIUM is usually something additional given as an inducement to buy, produce, or the like: *a premium received with a magazine subscription.*

bon vi·vant (bôɴ vē väɴ′), *pl.* **bons vi·vants** (bôɴ vē väɴ′). *French.* **1.** a person who lives luxuriously and enjoys good food and drink. **2.** a jovial companion.

bon vo·yage (bon′ voi äzh′; *Fr.* bôɴ vwa yazh′), (have a) pleasant trip. [< F: lit., good journey. See BOON[2], VOYAGE]

bon·y (bō′nē), *adj.*, **bon·i·er, bon·i·est.** **1.** of or like bone. **2.** full of bones. **3.** having prominent bones; big-boned. —**bon′i·ness,** *n.*

bon′y fish′, any fish of the class *Osteichthyes*, characterized by a skeleton composed of bone in addition to cartilage, gill covers, and an air bladder.

bonze (bonz), *n.* a Buddhist monk, esp. of Japan or China. [appar. back formation from *bonzes* < NL *bonzī* (pl. of *bonzus*) < Jap *bonso* < Chin characters *fan seng*]

bon·zer (bon′zər), *adj.* *Australian.* **1.** very big. **2.** remarkable; wonderful. [?]

boo[1] (bo͞o), *interj.*, *n.*, *pl.* **boos,** *v.*, **booed, boo·ing.** —*interj.* **1.** (used as an exclamation of contempt, disapproval, etc., usually shouted by an audience at a performer or speaker.) **2.** (used as an exclamation to frighten or startle an individual.) —*n.* **3.** an exclamation of contempt or disapproval: *a loud boo from the bleachers.* —*v.i.* **4.** to cry "boo." —*v.t.* **5.** to cry "boo" at; show disapproval of by booing. [imit.]

boo[2] (bo͞o), *n.* *Slang.* marijuana.

boob (bo͞ob), *n.* **1.** *U.S. Slang.* a fool or dunce. **2.** *Slang.* (*usually vulgar*). a female breast. [back formation from BOOBY]

boob·oi·sie (bo͞o′bwä zē′), *n.* *Facetious.* a class of the general public composed of uneducated, uncultured persons. [BOOB + (BOURGE)OISIE]

boo-boo (bo͞o′bo͞o′), *n.*, *pl.* **-boos.** *Slang.* **1.** a silly mistake; blunder. **2.** a minor injury. [baby talk ?, based on *boohoo*]

boob′ tube′, *Slang.* **1.** television. **2.** a television set.

boo·by (bo͞o′bē), *n.*, *pl.* **-bies.** **1.** a stupid person; dunce. **2.** the worst student, player, etc., of a group. **3.** any of several tropical sea birds of the genus *Sula*, related to the gannets. [earlier *pooby*, appar. b. *poop* to befool (now obs.) and BABY; def. 3, perh. by assoc. with Sp *bobo* < L *balbus* stuttering]

boo′by hatch′, **1.** *Naut.* a small companion secured over a deck opening. **2.** *U.S. Slang.* an insane asylum.

boo′by prize′, a prize given in good-natured ridicule to the worst player in a game or contest.

boo′by trap′, **1.** a hidden bomb or mine so placed that it will be set off by an unsuspecting person through such means as moving an apparently harmless object. **2.** any trap set for a person.

boo·by-trap (bo͞o′bē trap′), *v.t.*, **-trapped, -trap·ping.** to set with a booby trap; attach a booby trap to or in.

boo·dle (bo͞od′əl), *n.* *U.S. Slang.* **1.** the lot, pack, or crowd: *Send the whole boodle back to the factory.* **2.** a bribe or other illicit payment. **3.** stolen goods; loot; booty. [< D *boedel* stock, lot]

boo·gey·man (bo͝og′ē man′, bo͞o′gē-), *n.*, *pl.* **-men.** a hobgoblin supposed to carry off naughty children. Also, **bogeyman, boo·ger·man** (bo͝og′ər man′, bo͞o′gər-), **boo·gie·man** (bo͝og′ē man′, bo͞o′gē-). [var. of *bogyman*]

boog·ie-woog·ie (bo͝og′ē wo͝og′ē, bo͞o′gē wo͞o′gē), *n.* *Jazz.* a form of instrumental blues, esp. for piano, using melodic variations over a constantly repeated bass figure. Also called **boog′ie.** [rhyming compound based on *boogie* (? BUGG(ER) + -IE)]

boo·hoo (bo͞o′ho͞o′), *v.*, **-hooed, -hoo·ing,** *n.*, *pl.* **-hoos.** —*v.i.* **1.** to weep noisily; blubber. —*n.* **2.** the sound of noisy weeping. [rhyming compound based on BOO]

book (bo͝ok), *n.* **1.** a written or printed literary composition, esp. on consecutive sheets of paper bound together in a volume. **2.** a number of sheets of blank or ruled paper bound together for writing, recording commercial transactions, etc. **3.** a division of a literary work. **4. the Book,** the Bible. **5.** the text or libretto of an opera, musical play, etc. **6. books.** See **book of account.** **7.** *Cards.* the number of basic tricks or cards that must be taken before any trick or card counts in the score. **8.** a set of tickets, checks, stamps, matches, etc., bound together. **9. by the book,** according to the correct form; in the usual manner. **10. close the books,** to balance accounts at the end of an accounting period; settle accounts. **11. in one's book,** in one's judgment or opinion. **12. like a book,** completely; thoroughly: *He knew the area like a book.* **13. make book,** to accept or place the bets of others, as on horse races, esp. as a business. **14. one for the book,** a noteworthy incident; something extraordinary. **15. the book,** the telephone book: *I've looked him up, but he's not in the book.* **16. throw the book at,** *Slang.* **a.** to sentence (an offender, lawbreaker, etc.) to the maximum penalties for all charges against him. **b.** to punish or chide severely. —*v.t.* **17.** to enter in a book or list; record or register. **18.** to engage (a place, passage, etc.) beforehand. **19.** to register or list (a person) for a place, passage, appointment, etc. **20.** to reserve or make a reservation for (a hotel room, theater tickets, or the like). **21.** to engage (a person or company) for a performance or performances. **22.** to enter an official charge against (an arrested suspect) on a police register. **23.** to act as a bookmaker for (a bettor, bet, or sum of money). —*v.i.* **24.** to engage a place, services, etc. —*adj.* **25.** of or pertaining to a book or books: *The book department was downstairs.* **26.** derived from or based chiefly on books or their contents: *a book knowledge of sailing.* **27.** shown by a book of account: *The firm's book profit was $53,680.* [ME, OE *bōc*; c. D *boek*, Icel *bōk*, G *Buch*; akin to Goth *boka* letter (of the alphabet), OE *bēce* BEECH]

book·bind·er (bo͝ok′bīn′dər), *n.* a person whose business or work is the binding of books. [ME]

book·bind·er·y (bo͝ok′bīn′də rē), *n.*, *pl.* **-er·ies.** an establishment for binding books.

book·bind·ing (bo͝ok′bīn′ding), *n.* the process or art of binding books.

book·case (bo͝ok′kās′), *n.* a set of shelves for books.

book′ club′, a club that lends or sells books to its members, usually at a discount. Also called, *esp. Brit.*, **book society.**

book′ end′, a support, usually one of a pair, placed at the end of a row of books to hold them upright. Also, **book′end′.**

book·ie (bo͝ok′ē), *n.* *Informal.* bookmaker (def. 2).

book·ing (bo͝ok′ing), *n.* a contract, engagement, or scheduled performance of a professional entertainer.

book·ish (bo͝ok′ish), *adj.* **1.** given or devoted to reading or study. **2.** more acquainted with books than with real life. **3.** of or pertaining to books; literary. —**book′ish·ly,** *adv.* —**book′ish·ness,** *n.*

book′ jack′et, a detachable paper cover, usually colored and illustrated, for protecting a book.

book·keep·er (bo͝ok′kē′pər), *n.* a person who keeps account books, as for a business.

book·keep·ing (bo͝ok′kē′ping), *n.* the work or skill of keeping account books or systematic records of money transactions (distinguished from *accounting*).

book′ learn′ing, **1.** knowledge gained by reading books, esp. as distinguished from that obtained through observation and experience. **2.** formal education. —**book-learn·ed** (bo͝ok′lûr′nid, -lûrnd′), *adj.*

book·let (bo͝ok′lit), *n.* a little book, esp. one with a paper cover; pamphlet.

book′ louse′, any of several minute insects of the order *Corrodentia*, often found living among books or papers.

book·mak·er (bo͝ok′mā′kər), *n.* **1.** a maker of books. **2.** a person who makes a business of accepting the bets of others on the outcome of sports contests, esp. of horse races. [ME *bokmakere*] —**book′mak′ing,** *n.*, *adj.*

book·man (bo͝ok′mən, -man′), *n.*, *pl.* **-men** (-mən, -men′). **1.** a studious or learned man; scholar. **2.** a person whose occupation is selling or publishing books. [ME *bokeman*]

book·mark (bo͝ok′märk′), *n.* a ribbon or the like placed between the pages of a book to mark a place.

book′match′, a match in or from a matchbook.

book·mo·bile (bo͝ok′mə bēl′), *n.* *U.S.* an automobile, small truck, or trailer constructed to serve as a traveling library. [BOOK + (AUTO)MOBILE]

book′ of account′, **1.** any journal or ledger, with supporting vouchers, included in a system of accounts. **2. books of account,** the original records and books used in recording business transactions.

Book′ of Books′, the Bible.

Book′ of Com′mon Prayer′, the service book of the Church of England, essentially adopted by the Anglican communion.

book′ of hours′, a book containing the prescribed order of prayers, readings from the Scripture, and rites for the canonical hours. Also, **Book′ of Hours′.**

Book′ of Mor′mon, a sacred book of the Mormon

Church, believed by Mormons to be an abridgment by a prophet **(Mormon)** of a record of certain ancient peoples in America, written on golden plates, and discovered and translated (1827–30) by Joseph Smith.

book·plate (bŏŏk′plāt′), *n.* a label bearing the owner's name and often a design, coat of arms, or the like, for pasting on the front end paper of a book.

book·rack (bŏŏk′rak′), *n.* **1.** Also called **book′rest′, book′stand′.** a support for an open book. **2.** a rack for holding books.

book′ review′, **1.** a critical description, evaluation, or analysis of a book. **2.** a section or page of a newspaper or magazine devoted to such descriptions and evaluations of newly published books. —**book′ review′er.** —**book′ review′ing.**

book·sel·ler (bŏŏk′sel′ər), *n.* a person whose occupation or business is selling books.

book·shelf (bŏŏk′shelf′), *n., pl.* **-shelves.** a shelf for holding books, esp. one of the shelves in a bookcase.

book′ soci′ety, *Chiefly Brit.* See **book club.**

book·stall (bŏŏk′stôl′), *n.* **1.** a stall at which books are sold, usually secondhand. **2.** *Brit.* a newsstand.

book·store (bŏŏk′stōr′, -stôr′), *n.* a store where books are sold. Also called **book·shop** (bŏŏk′shop′).

book′ val′ue, the value of a business, property, etc., as stated in a book of accounts (distinguished from *market value*).

book·worm (bŏŏk′wûrm′), *n.* **1.** a person devoted to reading or studying. **2.** any of various insects that feed on books, esp. the book louse.

Boole (bōōl), *n.* **George,** 1815–64, English mathematician and logician.

Bool′e·an al′gebra (bōō′lē ən), *Logic.* a deductive logical system, usually applied to classes, in which, under the operations of intersection and symmetric difference, classes are treated as algebraic quantities. [named after G. BOOLE; see -AN]

boom[1] (bōōm), *v.i.* **1.** to make a deep, prolonged, resonant sound. **2.** to move with a resounding rush. **3.** to progress, grow, or flourish vigorously, as a business, a city, etc. —*v.t.* **4.** to give forth with a booming sound (often fol. by *out*): *The clock boomed out nine.* **5.** to boost or campaign vigorously for (a cause, candidate, new product, etc.): *His followers are booming George for mayor.* —*n.* **6.** a deep, prolonged, resonant sound. **7.** a roaring, rumbling, or reverberation, as of waves or distant guns. **8.** a buzzing, humming, or droning, as of a bee or beetle. **9.** a rapid increase in price, development, sales, or the like. **10.** a period of rapid economic growth. **11.** a rise in popularity, as of a political candidate, or efforts to promote such popularity. —*adj.* **12.** *U.S.* caused by or characteristic of a boom: *boom prices.* [late ME *bombon, bummyn* to buzz; c. D *bommen,* G *bummen,* orig. imit.]

boom[2] (bōōm), *n.* **1.** *Naut.* any of various more or less horizontal spars or poles for extending the feet of sails, handling cargo, etc. **2.** a chain, cable, etc., serving to obstruct navigation, confine floating timber, or the like. **3.** the area thus shut off. **4.** *Mach.* a spar or beam projecting from the mast of a derrick for supporting or guiding the weights to be lifted. **5.** chord[1] (def. 4). **6.** (on motion-picture and television stages) a spar or beam on a mobile crane for holding or manipulating a microphone or camera. **7. lower the boom on (someone),** *Slang.* to censure or punish; force (someone) to stop doing something that is annoying, unethical, insincere, or the like. —*v.t.* **8.** to extend or position, as a sail (usually fol. by *out* or *off*). **9.** to manipulate (an object) by or as by means of a crane or derrick. [< D: tree, pole, BEAM]

boom·er·ang (bōō′mə rang′), *n.* **1.** a bent or curved throwing club of tough wood, used by the Australian aborigines, one form of which can be thrown so as to return to the thrower. **2.** a scheme, plan, argument, etc., that recoils upon the user. —*v.i.* **3.** to come back or return, as a boomerang. **4.** (of a scheme, plan, etc.) to cause unexpected harm to the originator. [< native language of New South Wales, Australia]

Boomerangs

Boom′er State′, Oklahoma (used as a nickname).

boom·kin (bōōm′kin), *n.* *Naut.* bumpkin[2]. [< Flem *boomken.* See BOOM[2], -KIN]

boom·let (bōōm′lit), *n.* a small boom or increase in prosperity, development, popularity, etc.

boom′ town′, a town that has grown rapidly as a result of sudden prosperity. Also, **boom′town′.**

boon[1] (bōōn), *n.* **1.** a benefit enjoyed; a thing to be thankful for; blessing. **2.** *Archaic.* that which is asked; a favor sought. [ME *bone* < Scand; cf. Icel *bōn* prayer; c. OE *bēn*]

boon[2] (bōōn), *adj.* **1.** jolly; jovial; convivial: *boon companion.* **2.** *Literary.* kindly; gracious; bounteous. [ME *bone* < MF < L *bon(us)* good]

boon·docks (bōōn′doks′), *n.* (*construed as pl.*) *Slang.* **1.** a backwoods or marsh (usually prec. by *the*). **2.** a remote rural area (usually prec. by *the*). [< Tagalog *bundok* mountain + (*the stick*)*s;* see STICK[1]]

boon·dog·gle (bōōn′dog′əl), *n., v.,* **-gled, -gling.** *U.S.* —*n.* **1.** a cord of plaited leather worn around the neck by Boy Scouts. **2.** *Informal.* work of little or no practical value done merely to keep or look busy. —*v.i.* **3.** *Informal.* to do work of little or no practical value merely to keep or look busy. [said to have been coined by R. H. Link, American scoutmaster, as name for def. 1] —**boon′dog′gler,** *n.*

Boone (bōōn), *n.* **Daniel,** 1734–1820, American pioneer, mainly in Kentucky.

boor (bŏŏr), *n.* **1.** a clownish, rude, or unmannerly person. **2.** a rustic or yokel. **3.** an illiterate, dull, or insensitive peasant. [< D *boer* or LG *būr;* c. G *Bauer* peasant, countryman; see BOND[2]]

boor·ish (bŏŏr′ish), *adj.* of or like a boor; rude. —**boor′ish·ly,** *adv.* —**boor′ish·ness,** *n.*

boost (bōōst), *U.S.* —*v.t.* **1.** to lift or raise by pushing from behind or below. **2.** to advance or aid by speaking well of; promote: *He always boosts his home town.* **3.** to increase or raise: *to boost prices.* —*n.* **4.** an upward shove or raise; lift. **5.** an increase or rise: *a boost in food prices.* **6.** an act, remark, or the like, that helps one's progress, morale, efforts, etc. [? Scot dial. *boose* (var. of *pouss* PUSH) + (HOI)ST]

boost·er (bōō′stər), *n.* *U.S.* **1.** a person or thing that boosts, esp. an energetic and enthusiastic supporter. **2.** *Elect.* a device connected in series with a current for increasing or decreasing the nominal circuit voltage. **3.** *Rocketry.* the first stage of a multistage rocket, used as the principal source of thrust in takeoff and early flight. **4.** *Med.* Also called **boost′er dose′, boost′er shot′.** a dose of an immunizing substance given to maintain or renew the effect of a previous one. **5.** *Pharm.* a chemical compound, medicinal substance, or the like, that serves as a synergist. **6.** a radio-frequency amplifier for connecting between a radio or television antenna and the receiving set to intensify the received signal. **7.** an auxiliary pump, used in a pipeline or other system, to add to or maintain a prevailing amount of pressure or vacuum.

boot[1] (bōōt), *n.* **1.** a covering of leather, rubber, or the like, for the foot and all or part of the leg. **2.** *Brit.* **a.** any shoe or outer foot-covering reaching above the ankle. **b.** a rubber overshoe. **3.** any sheathlike protective covering: *a boot for a weak automobile tire.* **4.** a protective covering for the foot and part of the leg of a horse. **5.** a protecting apron or cover for the driver's seat of a vehicle. **6.** *U.S. Navy, Marines.* a recruit. **7.** the receptacle or place into which the top of a convertible car fits when lowered. **8.** a cloth covering for this receptacle or place. **9.** *Brit.* a compartment or receptacle for baggage in or on a vehicle; an automobile trunk. **10.** a kick. **11.** *Slang.* a dismissal; discharge: *They gave him the boot for coming in late.* **12.** an instrument of torture, fitting over the leg and foot and tightened by means of screws. **13. bet your boots,** to be sure of; be certain: *You can bet your boots I'll be there!* **14. die with one's boots on, a.** to die while actively engaged in one's work, profession, etc. **b.** to die fighting. **15. lick someone's boots,** to be subservient to; flatter. —*v.t.* **16.** *Slang.* to kick; drive by kicking: *The boy booted a tin can down the street.* **17.** to put boots on; equip or provide with boots. [ME *bote* < MF]

boot[2] (bōōt), *n.* **1.** *Archaic.* something given into the bargain. **2.** *Obs.* **a.** advantage. **b.** remedy; relief; help. **3. to boot,** into the bargain; besides. —*v.i.* **4.** *Archaic.* to be of profit, advantage, or avail: *It boots not to complain.* [ME *bote,* OE *bōt* advantage; c. D *boete,* G *Busse,* Icel *bōt,* Goth *bota.* See BET, BETTER[1]]

boot[3] (bōōt), *n.* *Archaic.* booty, spoil, or plunder. [special use of BOOT[2] by assoc. with BOOTY]

boot·black (bōōt′blak′), *n.* a person whose occupation is shining shoes, boots, etc.

boot′ camp′, *U.S. Navy, Marines.* a camp for training recruits.

boot·ed (bōō′tid), *adj.* **1.** equipped with boots. **2.** *Ornith.* (of the tarsus of certain birds) covered with a continuous horny, bootlike sheath.

boot·ee (bōō tē′ *or, esp. for 1,* bōō′tē), *n.* **1.** a baby's socklike shoe, usually knitted or crocheted. **2.** any boot having a short leg. [BOOT[1] + *-ee* dim. suffix]

boot·er·y (bōō′tə rē), *n., pl.* **-er·ies.** a store selling boots, shoes, etc.

Bo·ö·tes (bō ō′tēz), *n., gen.* **-tis** (-tis). *Astron.* the Herdsman, a northern constellation containing the bright star Arcturus. [< L < Gk: lit., ox-driver; see BOSS[3]]

booth (bōōth, bōōth), *n., pl.* **booths** (bōōthz, bōōths). **1.** a stall or light structure for the sale of goods or for display purposes, as at a market or fair. **2.** a small compartment or boxlike room for a specific use by one occupant: *a telephone booth; voting booth.* **3.** a partly enclosed compartment or partitioned area, as in a restaurant, music store, etc. **4.** a temporary structure of any material, as boughs, canvas, boards, etc., used esp. for shelter; shed. [ME *bōthe* < Scand; c. Icel *būth,* G *Bude,* Pol *buda*]

Booth (bōōth; *Brit.* bōōth), *n.* **1. Bal·ling·ton** (bal′ing tən), 1859–1940, founder of the Volunteers of America 1896 (son of William Booth). **2. Edwin (Thomas),** 1833–93, U.S. actor (brother of John Wilkes Booth). **3. Evangeline Co·ry** (kōr′ē, kôr′ē), 1865?–1950, general of the Salvation Army 1934–39 (daughter of William Booth). **4. John Wilkes,** 1838–65, U.S. actor: assassin of Abraham Lincoln (brother of Edwin Booth). **5. Ju·ni·us Brutus** (jōō′nē əs), 1796–1852, English actor (father of Edwin and John Booth). **6. William** ("*General Booth*"), 1829–1912, English religious leader: founder of the Salvation Army 1865. **7. William Bramwell** (bram′wel′, -wəl), 1856–1929, general of the Salvation Army (son of William Booth).

Boo·thi·a (bōō′thē ə), *n.* **1.** a peninsula in N Canada: the northernmost part of the mainland of North America; former location of the north magnetic pole. **2. Gulf of,** a gulf between this peninsula and Baffin Island.

boot′ hill′, *Western U.S.* a cemetery of a frontier settlement, esp. one in which gunfighters were buried.

boot′ hook′, one of a pair of J-shaped metal hooks fixed to a handle, for drawing on a boot by inserting it through a bootstrap.

boot·jack (bōōt′jak′), *n.* a yokelike device for catching the heel of a boot, as a riding boot, to aid in removing it.

boot·lace (bōōt′lās′), *n.* **1.** a long, strong lace used to fasten a boot. **2.** *Brit.* a shoelace.

Boo·tle (bōōt′əl), *n.* a city in SW Lancashire, in NW England, on the Mersey estuary. 82,829 (1961).

boot·leg (bōōt′leg′), *n., v.,* **-legged, -leg·ging,** *adj.* *U.S.* —*n.* **1.** alcoholic liquor unlawfully made, sold, or transported, without registration or payment of taxes. —*v.t.* **2.** to deal in (liquor or other goods) unlawfully. —*v.i.* **3.** to make, transport, or sell something illegally, esp. liquor. —*adj.* **4.** made, sold, or transported unlawfully. **5.** illegal or clandestine. **6.** of or pertaining to bootlegging. [BOOT[1] + LEG; secondary senses arose from practice of hiding a liquor bottle in the leg of one's boot] —**boot′leg′ger,** *n.*

boot·less (bōōt′lis), *adj.* offering no advantage; unavailing. [ME *bot(e)les,* OE *bōtlēas* unpardonable] —**boot′less·ly,** *adv.* —**boot′less·ness,** *n.*

boot·lick (bo͞ot′lik′), *Informal.* —*v.t.* **1.** to seek the favor or good will of (someone) in a servile, degrading way; toady to. —*v.i.* **2.** to be a toady. —**boot′lick′er,** *n.*

boots (bo͞ots), *n., pl.* **boots.** *Brit.* a bootblack, esp. at a hotel.

boots′ and sad′dles, *U.S. Army.* (formerly) a cavalry bugle call for mounted drill or formation.

boot·strap (bo͞ot′strap′), *n.* **1.** a loop of leather or cloth sewn at the top rear, or sometimes on each side, of a boot to facilitate pulling it on. **2. pull oneself up by one's (own) bootstraps,** to succeed on one's own.

boo·ty (bo͞o′tē), *n., pl.* **-ties. 1.** loot or plunder seized in war or by robbery. **2.** any prize or gain. [late ME *botye,* var. of *buty* < MLG *bute* booty (orig. a sharing of the spoils), c. Icel *bȳti* exchange, barter; *oo* < BOOT[2]]

booze (bo͞oz), *n., v.,* **boozed, booz·ing.** *Informal.* —*n.* **1.** any alcoholic beverage; whiskey. —*v.t., v.i.* **2.** to drink excessively. [var. of BOUSE[2]] —**booz′er,** *n.*

bop[1] (bop), *n.* a form of modern jazz marked by chromatic and dissonant harmony, complex rhythms, and obscured melodic line. [(BE)BOP]

bop[2] (bop), *v.,* **bopped, bop·ping,** *n. Slang.* —*v.t.* **1.** to strike, as with the fist, a stick, etc. —*n.* **2.** a blow. [var. of BOB[3]]

bor-, var. of **boro-,** esp. before a vowel: *borate.*

bor., borough.

Bo·ra Bo·ra (bôr′ə bôr′ə; bôr′ə bôr′ə), an island in the Society Islands, in the S Pacific, NW of Tahiti. ab. 1400; 15 sq. mi.

bo·rac·ic (bə ras′ik, bō-, bô-), *adj. Chem.* boric. [*borac-* (s. of BORAX) + -IC]

bo·ra·cite (bōr′ə sīt′, bôr′-), *n.* a strongly pyroelectric mineral, a borate and chloride of magnesium, $Mg_6Cl_2B_{14}O_{26}$. [*borac-* (s. of BORAX) + -ITE[1]]

bor·age (bûr′ij, bôr′-, bor′-), *n.* **1.** a plant, *Borago officinalis,* native of southern Europe, having hairy leaves and stems, used medicinally and in salads. **2.** any of various allied or similar plants of the family *Boraginaceae.* [ME *burage* < MF *bourage* < VL **burrāgō* = LL *burra* hair stuffing + *-gō* n. suffix]

bo·rag·i·na·ceous (bə raj′ə nā′shəs, bō-, bô-), *adj.* belonging to the *Boraginaceae,* or borage family of plants, including borage, bugloss, heliotrope, forget-me-not, etc. [< NL *Borāgināc(ae)* = *Borāgin-,* s. of *Borāgō* genus name (see BORAGE) + *-āceae* -ACEAE + -OUS]

Bo·rah (bōr′ə, bôr′ə), *n.* **William Edgar,** 1865–1940, U.S. senator from Idaho 1906–40.

Bo·rås (bo͞o RÔS′), *n.* a city in S Sweden, near Göteborg. 68,900 (1965).

bo·rate (bōr′āt, -it, bôr′-), *n.* **1.** *Chem.* a salt or ester of boric acid. **2.** a salt or ester of any acid containing boron.

bo·rax[1] (bōr′aks, -əks, bôr′-), *n., pl.* **bo·rax·es, bo·ra·ces** (bōr′ə sēz′, bôr′-). a white substance, $Na_2B_4O_7 \cdot 10H_2O$, occurring naturally or obtained from naturally occurring borates; tincal: used as a flux, cleansing agent, in the manufacture of glass, porcelain, and enamel, and in tanning. [< ML < Ar *būraq* < Pers *būrah;* r. ME *boras* < MF < ML *borax*]

bo·rax[2] (bōr′aks, -əks, bôr′-), *Slang.* —*n.* **1.** cheap, showy, poorly made merchandise. —*adj.* **2.** of or pertaining to such merchandise.

Bor·deaux (bôR dō′), *n.* **1.** a seaport in SW France, on the Garonne River. 254,122 (1962). **2.** any of various wines produced in the region surrounding Bordeaux, esp. claret.

Bordeaux′ mix′ture, *Hort.* a fungicide consisting of a mixture of copper sulfate, lime, and water. [free trans. of F *bouillie bordelaise.* See BOIL[1], BORDELAISE]

bor·del (bôr′dəl), *n. Archaic.* a brothel. [ME < AF, OF = *borde* wooden hut (< Gmc; akin to BOARD) + *-el* < L *-ell(us)* dim. suffix]

Bor·de·laise (bôr′dəlāz′; *Fr.* bôR də lez′), *n.* a brown sauce flavored with red wine and shallots. Also called **Bordelaise′ sauce′.** [< F, fem. of *bordelais* of Bordeaux = *Bordel-* Bordeaux + *-ais* -ESE]

bor·del·lo (bôr del′ō), *n., pl.* **-los.** a brothel. [< It; see BORDEL]

Bor·den (bôr′dən), *n.* **Sir Robert Laird** (lârd), 1854–1937, Canadian statesman: prime minister 1911–20.

bor·der (bôr′dər), *n.* **1.** the part or edge of a surface or area that forms its outer boundary. **2.** the line that separates one country, state, province, etc., from another; frontier line. **3.** the district or region that lies along the boundary line of another. **4. the border,** *U.S.* the border between the U.S. and Mexico, esp. along the Rio Grande. **5.** brink or verge: *on the border of insanity.* **6.** an ornamental strip or design around the edge of a printed page, a drawing, etc. **7.** an ornamental design or piece of ornamental trimming around the edge of a fabric, rug, garment, article of furniture, etc. **8.** *Hort.* a long, narrow bed planted with flowers, shrubs, or trees. —*v.t.* **9.** to make a border about; adorn with a border. **10.** to form a border or boundary to. **11.** to lie on the border of; adjoin. **12. border on** or **upon,** to approach closely in character; verge on: *The situation borders on tragedy.* [ME *bordure* < AF, OF = *bord(er)* (to) border (*bord* ship's side, edge < Gmc; see BOARD) + *-ure* -URE] —**Syn. 1.** rim, periphery. See **edge.**

bor·der·land (bôr′dər land′), *n.* **1.** land forming a border or frontier. **2.** an uncertain, intermediate district, space, or condition.

bor′der line′, boundary line; frontier.

bor·der·line (bôr′dər līn′), *adj.* **1.** on or near a border or boundary. **2.** not quite meeting accepted, expected, or average standards; not quite fitting into any one category: *His work is improving, but he's still a borderline case.*

Bor′der States′, *U.S. Hist.* the slave states bordering the free states of the North and inclined to compromise rather than secede from the Union, comprising Delaware, Maryland, Kentucky, and Missouri, and sometimes extended to include West Virginia and Tennessee.

Bor′der ter′rier, one of a British breed of small terriers having a dense, wiry coat.

bor·dure (bôr′jər), *n. Heraldry.* the area adjacent to the outer edges of an escutcheon, esp. when distinctively treated. [ME; see BORDER]

bore[1] (bōr, bôr), *v.,* **bored, bor·ing,** *n.* —*v.t.* **1.** to pierce (a solid substance) with some rotary cutting instrument. **2.** to make (a hole) with such an instrument. **3.** to make (a tunnel, mine, well, passage, etc.) by hollowing out, cutting through, or removing a core of material: *to bore a tunnel through the Alps.* **4.** *Mach.* to enlarge (a hole) to a precise diameter with a single-edged cutting tool within the hole, by rotating either the tool or the work. **5.** to force or make (a passage); to force (an opening), as through a crowd, by persistent forward thrusting (usually fol. by *through* or *into*). —*v.i.* **6.** to make a hole in a solid substance with a rotary cutting instrument. **7.** *Mach.* to enlarge a hole to a precise diameter. —*n.* **8.** a hole made or enlarged by boring. **9.** the inside diameter of a hole, tube, gun barrel, etc. [ME *bore(n),* OE *borian;* c. D *boren,* G *bohren,* Icel *bora,* L *for(āre)*] —**Syn. 1.** perforate, drill. **9.** caliber.

bore[2] (bōr, bôr), *v.,* **bored, bor·ing,** *n.* —*v.t.* **1.** to weary by dullness, tedious repetition, unwelcome attentions, etc. —*n.* **2.** a dull, tiresome, or uncongenial person. **3.** a cause of ennui or petty annoyance: *The play was a bore.* [? < BORE[1]] —**Syn. 1.** fatigue, tire, annoy. —**Ant. 1.** amuse.

bore[3] (bōr, bôr), *n.* an abrupt rise of tidal water moving rapidly inland from the mouth of an estuary. [ME *bare* < Scand; cf. Icel *bāra* wave]

bore[4] (bōr, bôr), *v.* pt. of **bear**[1].

bo·re·al (bōr′ē əl, bôr′-), *adj.* **1.** of or pertaining to the north wind. **2.** of or pertaining to the north. [late ME *boriall* < LL *boreāl(is)* northern = L *bore(ās)* BOREAS + *-ālis* -AL[1]]

Bo·re·as (bōr′ē əs, bôr′-), *n.* the ancient Greek personification of the north wind.

bore·dom (bōr′dəm, bôr′-), *n.* the state or an instance of being bored; tedium; ennui.

Bo·rel (bô rel′, bə-; *Fr.* bô REL′), *n.* **Fé·lix É·douard É·mile** (fā lēks′ ā dwAR′ ā mēl′), 1871–1956, French mathematician.

bor·er (bōr′ər, bôr′-), *n.* **1.** a person or thing that bores or pierces. **2.** *Mach.* a tool used for boring; auger. **3.** *Entomol.* any of several insects that bore into trees, fruits, etc., esp. a beetle that bores into the woody part of plants. **4.** *Zool.* any of various mollusks, worms, etc., that bore into wood, stone, etc.

Bor·ger·hout (*Flemish.* bôR′KHəR hout′), *n.* a city in N Belgium, near Antwerp. 50,527 (est. 1964).

Bor·ghe·se (bôR ge′ze), *n.* a member of a noble Italian family, important in Italian politics and society from the 16th to the early 19th century.

Bor·gia (bôr′jə, -jä; *It.* bôR′jä), *n.* **1. Ce·sa·re** (che′zä-Re), 1476?–1507, Italian cardinal, military leader, and politician. **2. Lu·cre·zia** (lo͞o krē′zhə; *It.* lo͞o kRe′tsyä), (*Duchess of Ferrara*), 1480–1519, sister and political pawn of Cesare Borgia: patroness of the arts. **3.** their father, **Ro·dri·go** (Rô dRē′gô). See **Alexander VI.**

Bor·glum (bôr′gləm), *n.* **John Gut·zon** (gut′sən), 1867–1941, U.S. sculptor.

bo·ric (bōr′ik, bôr′-), *adj. Chem.* of or containing boron.

bo′ric ac′id, 1. Also called **orthoboric acid.** *Chem., Pharm.* an acid, H_3BO_3, used chiefly in the manufacture of ceramics and glass and as a mild antiseptic. **2.** *Chem.* any of a group of acids containing boron.

bo·ride (bōr′īd, bôr′-), *n. Chem.* a compound consisting of two elements of which boron is the more electronegative.

bor·ing[1] (bōr′ing, bôr′-), *n. Mach.* **1.** the act or process of making or enlarging a hole. **2.** the hole so made. **3.** a cylindrical sample of earth strata obtained by boring a vertical hole. **4. borings,** the chips, fragments, or dust produced in boring. [BORE[1] + -ING[1]]

bor·ing[2] (bōr′ing, bôr′-), *adj.* dull; tedious; annoyingly repetitious. [BORE[2] + -ING[2]]

Boris III (bo RIS′, bô′ris), 1894–1943, king of Bulgaria 1918–43.

born (bôrn), *adj.* **1.** brought forth by birth. **2.** possessing from birth the quality, circumstances, or character stated: *a born musician; a born fool.* **3.** native to the locale stated: *a German-born scientist.* **4. born yesterday,** naïve; inexperienced: *He tried to short-change me, but I wasn't born yesterday.* [ME; OE *boren* (ptp. of *beran* to BEAR[1]) = *bor-* ptp. s. + *-en* -EN[3]]

Born (bôrn), *n.* **Max,** 1882–1970, German physicist: Nobel prize 1954.

born-a·gain (bôrn′ə gen′), *adj. U.S. Informal.* **1.** recommitted to religious faith through an intensely personal experience of salvation through acceptance of Christ: *a born-again Christian.* **2.** enthusiastically committed: *a born-again jogger.*

borne (bōrn, bôrn), *v.* a pp. of **bear**[1].

Bor·ne·o (bôr′nē ō′), *n.* an island in the Malay Archipelago, including Sabah and Sarawak (formerly British), Brunei, and Kalimantan (formerly Dutch). ab. 4,600,000; ab. 290,000 sq. mi. —**Bor′ne·an,** *adj., n.*

bor·ne·ol (bôr′nē ōl′, -ôl′, -ol′), *n. Chem.* a solid terpene alcohol, $C_{10}H_{17}OH$, used in the form of its esters in the manufacture of synthetic camphor and in perfumery. Also called **Bor′neo cam′phor, bor′nyl al′cohol** (bôr′nəl, -nil). [BORNE(O) + -OL[1]]

Born·holm (bôRN′hôlm′; *Eng.* bôrn′hōm, -hōlm), *n.* a Danish island in the Baltic Sea, S of Sweden. 48,217 (1960); 227 sq. mi.

born·ite (bôr′nīt), *n.* a common mineral copper iron sulfide, Cu_5FeS_4: an important ore of copper; peacock ore. [named after I. von *Born* (1742–91), Austrian mineralogist; see -ITE[1]]

boro-, a combining form of **boron,** used esp. before a consonant: *borohydride.* Also, *esp. before a vowel,* **bor-.**

Bo·ro·din (bôr′ə dēn′; *Russ.* bo Ro dēn′), *n.* **A·le·ksan·dr Por·fir·e·vich** (ä′le ksän′dRə poR fiR ye′vich), 1834–87, Russian composer and chemist.

Bo·ro·di·no (bo Ro dē nô′), *n.* a village in the W Soviet Union, 70 mi. W of Moscow: Napoleon's victory here made possible the capture of Moscow, 1812.

bo·ro·hy·dride (bōr′ə hī′drīd, -drid, bôr′-), *n. Chem.* any of the class of compounds containing the group BH_4-, used chiefly as reducing agents.

bo·ron (bōr′on, bôr′-), *n. Chem.* a nonmetallic element occurring naturally only in combination, as in borax, boric acid, etc. *Symbol:* B; *at. wt.:* 10.811; *at. no.:* 5. [BOR(AX) + (CARB)ON] —**bo·ron·ic** (bō ron′ik, bô-, bə-), *adj.*

bo′ron car′bide, *Chem.* an extremely hard solid, B_4C, used chiefly as a moderator in nuclear reactors, as an abrasive, and as a refractory.

bo·ro·sil·i·cate (bōr′ə sil′ə kit, -kāt′, bôr′-), *n.* *Chem.* a salt of boric and silicic acids.

bo′ro·si·lic′ic ac′id (bōr′ō si lis′ik, bôr′-, bōr′-, bôr′-), *Chem.* any of several hypothetical acids which form borosilicates.

bor·ough (bûr′ō, bur′ō), *n.* **1.** *U.S.* (in certain states) an incorporated municipality smaller than a city. **2.** one of the five administrative divisions of New York City. **3.** *Brit.* **a.** an urban community incorporated by royal charter, similar to an incorporated city or municipality in the U.S. **b.** a town, area, or constituency represented by a member of Parliament. **c.** (formerly) a fortified town organized as and having some of the powers of an independent country. [ME *burgh* town, OE *burg* fortified town; c. Icel *borg*, G *Burg* castle, Goth *baurgs* city]

bor·ough-Eng·lish (bûr′ō iṉg′glish, -lish, bur′-), *n.* (formerly, in some English boroughs) a custom by which the youngest son or youngest heir inherited the entire estate.

Bor·ro·mi·ni (bôr′ō mē′nē; *It.* bôr′rô mē′nē), *n.* **Fran·ces·co** (frän ches′kō; *It.* frän ches′kô), 1599–1667, Italian architect and sculptor.

bor·row (bor′ō, bôr′ō), *v.t.* **1.** to take or obtain (something) with the promise to return it or its equivalent. **2.** to appropriate or introduce from another source: *to borrow a word from French.* **3.** *Arith.* (in subtraction) to take from one denomination and add to the next lower. —*v.i.* **4.** to borrow something: *Don't borrow unless you expect to repay.* **5.** *Naut.* **a.** to sail close to the wind; luff. **b.** to sail close to the shore. **6. borrow trouble,** to worry prematurely or unnecessarily; be pessimistic. [ME *borow(en)*, OE *borgian* to borrow, lend < *borg* a pledge; akin to D *borg* a pledge, *borgen* to charge, give credit, G *Borg* credit, *borg(en)* (to) take on credit] —**bor′row·er,** *n.*

Bor·row (bor′ō, bôr′ō), *n.* **George,** 1803–81, English traveler, writer, and student of languages, esp. Romany.

bor·row·ing (bor′ō iṉg, bôr′-), *n.* **1.** the act of a person who borrows. **2.** the process by which something is borrowed. **3.** the result of such an act or process; something that is borrowed, as a word or phrase taken from a foreign language.

Bors (bôrs), *n.* **Sir,** *Arthurian Romance.* **1.** Also called **Sir Bors de Gan·is** (də gan′is). a knight of the Round Table, nephew of Lancelot. **2.** a natural son of King Arthur.

borscht (bôrsht), *n.* soup containing beets and usually cabbage, served hot or chilled, often with sour cream. Also, **borsch** (bôrsh), **borsht.** [< Russ *borshtsh*]

borscht′ belt′, the hotels of the Jewish resort area in the Catskill Mountains. Also called **borscht′ cir′cuit.** [so called from its being associated with Jewish cuisine]

bor·stal (bôr′stəl), *n.* (in England) a school for delinquent boys that provides therapy and vocational training. [named after *Borstal,* village in Kent]

bort (bôrt), *n.* a quantity of low-quality diamonds and small fragments, valuable only in crushed or powdered form. Also, **boart, bortz** (bôrts). [appar. metathetic var. of **brot* (OE *gebrot* fragment); akin to ME *brotel* brittle, Icel *brot* fragment, etc.] —**bort′y,** *adj.*

bor·zoi (bôr′zoi), *n., pl.* **-zois.** one of a breed of tall, slender dogs having long, silky hair, raised originally in Russia for hunting wolves. Also called **Russian wolfhound.** [< Russ: lit., swift]

Borzoi (2½ ft. high at shoulder)

Bo·san·quet (bō′zən ket′, -kit), *n.* **Bernard,** 1848–1923, English philosopher and writer.

Bosc (bosk), *n.* **1.** a large, greenish-yellow variety of pear. **2.** the tree bearing this fruit.

bos·cage (bos′kij), *n.* a mass of trees or shrubs; wood, grove, or thicket. Also, **boskage.** [late ME *boskage* < MF *boscage.* See BOSK, -AGE]

Bosch (bosh, bôsh; *for 2 also Du.* bôs), *n.* **1. Carl,** 1874–1940, German chemist: Nobel prize 1933. **2. Hie·ro·ny·mus** (hē rô′ni mœs), (*Hieronymus van Akeen*), 1450?–1516, Dutch painter.

bosch·bok (bosh′bok′), *n., pl.* **-boks,** (*esp. collectively*) **-bok.** bushbuck.

bosch·vark (bosh′värk′), *n.* See **bush pig.** [< SAfrD = *bosch* wood, BUSH[1] + *vark* pig; see AARDVARK]

Bose (bōs), *n.* **Sir Ja·ga·dis Chan·dre** (jə gə dēs′ chun′drə), 1858–1937, Indian physicist and plant physiologist.

bosh[1] (bosh), *n.* *Informal.* nonsense; absurd or foolish talk. [< Turk *boş* empty, useless]

bosh[2] (bosh), *n.* *Metall.* the section of a blast furnace between the hearth and the stack, having the form of a frustum of an inverted cone. [prob. < G; akin to G *böschen* to slope, *Böschung* slope, scarp]

bosk (bosk), *n.* *Archaic.* a small wood or thicket, esp. of bushes. [ME *boske,* var. of *busk(e)* < Scand; cf. Icel *buskr* (now obs.), Dan *busk* BUSH[1]]

bos·kage (bos′kij), *n.* boscage.

bos·ker (bos′kər), *adj.* *Australian Slang.* excellent; very good. [?]

bos·ket (bos′kit), *n.* a grove or thicket. Also, **bosquet.** [earlier *bosquet* < F < It *boschetto* = *bosc(o)* wood (see BUSH[1]) + *-etto* -ET]

bosk·y (bos′kē), *adj.,* **bosk·i·er, bosk·i·est. 1.** woody; covered with bushes. **2.** shady. —**bosk′i·ness,** *n.*

bo's'n (bō′sən), *n.* boatswain.

Bos·ni·a (boz′nē ə), *n.* a former Turkish province in S Europe: formerly occupied by Austria; now part of Bosnia and Herzegovina. —**Bos′ni·an,** *adj., n.*

Bos′nia and Herzegovi′na, a constituent republic of Yugoslavia, in the W part. 3,347,000 (est. 1960); 19,909 sq. mi. *Cap.:* Sarajevo.

bos·om (bo͝oz′əm, bo͞o′zəm), *n.* **1.** the breast or chest of a human being. **2.** the part of a garment that covers the breast. **3.** the breast, conceived of as the center of thought or emotion. **4.** the breasts of a woman. **5.** something likened to the human breast: *the bosom of the earth.* **6.** any warm, comfortable, familiar place: *the bosom of the family.* —*adj.* **7.** of, pertaining to, or worn on or over the bosom. **8.** intimate or confidential: *a bosom friend.* —*v.t.* **9.** to take to the bosom; embrace; cherish. **10.** to hide from view; conceal. [ME; OE *bōs(u)m;* c. D *boesem,* G *Busen*] —**Syn. 3.** heart, affection. **8.** close.

bos·omed (bo͝oz′əmd, bo͞o′zəmd), *adj.* having a specified type of bosom (usually used in combination): *a full-bosomed garment.*

bos·om·y (bo͝oz′ə mē, bo͞o′zə-), *adj.* (of a woman) having a large or prominent bosom.

Bos·po·rus (bos′pər əs), *n.* a strait connecting the Black Sea and the Sea of Marmara. 18 mi. long. Also, **Bos·pho·rus** (bos′fər əs). —**Bos′po·ran, Bos·po·ran·ic** (bos′pə ran′ik), **Bos·po·ri·an** (bo spōr′ē ən, -spôr′-), *adj.*

bos·quet (bos′kit), *n.* bosket.

boss[1] (bôs, bos), *n.* **1.** a person who employs or superintends others; foreman or manager. **2.** *U.S.* a politician who controls his party organization, as in a particular district. **3.** *Informal.* a person who exercises authority, dominates, etc.: *His wife's the boss in his family.* —*v.t.* **4.** to be master of or over; direct; control. —*v.i.* **5.** to be boss. **6.** to be too domineering and authoritative. —*adj.* **7.** chief; master. **8.** *Slang.* first-rate. [< D *baas* master, foreman]

boss[2] (bôs, bos), *n.* **1.** *Bot., Zool.* a protuberance or roundish excrescence on the body or on some organ of an animal or plant. **2.** *Geol.* a knoblike mass of rock, esp. an outcrop of igneous or metamorphic rock. **3.** an ornamental protuberance of metal, ivory etc.; stud. **4.** *Archit.* an ornamental, knoblike projection, as a carved keystone at the intersection of ogives. **5.** *Archit.* a stone roughly formed and set in place for later carving. —*v.t.* **6.** to ornament with bosses. **7.** to emboss. [ME *boce* < OF; c. It *bozza* metal projecting part; see BOTCH[2]]

boss[3] (bos, bôs), *n.* *U.S.* a name for a cow. [var. of dial. *buss* young calf; perh. << L *bōs* ox, cow (see BOVINE)]

bos·sa no·va (bos′ə nō′və), jazz-influenced music of Brazilian origin, rhythmically related to the samba. [< Pg: lit., new voice]

Bos·sier′ Cit′y (bo sēr′), a city in NW Louisiana. 41,595 (1970).

boss·ism (bô′siz əm, bos′iz-), *n.* control by bosses, esp. political bosses.

Bos·suet (bô swe′), *n.* **Jacques Bé·ni·gne** (zhäk bā nēn′yə), 1627–1704, French bishop, writer, and orator.

boss·y[1] (bô′sē, bos′ē), *adj.* **boss·i·er, boss·i·est.** *Informal.* domineering; given to acting like a boss. [BOSS[1] + -Y[1]] —**boss′i·ness,** *n.*

boss·y[2] (bô′sē, bos′ē), *adj.* **boss·i·er, boss·i·est.** studded with bosses. [BOSS[2] + -Y[1]]

bos·sy[3] (bos′ē, bô′sē), *n., pl.* **-sies.** *U.S.* a familiar name for a cow or calf. [BOSS[3] + -Y[2]]

Bos·ton (bô′stən, bos′tən), *n.* a seaport in and the capital of Massachusetts, in the E part. 641,071 (1970).

Bos′ton bag′, *U.S.* **1.** (formerly) a two-handled bag for carrying books, papers, etc. **2.** See **club bag.**

Bos′ton baked′ beans′. See **baked beans.**

Bos′ton brown′ bread′, a dark-brown steamed bread made of corn meal and rye meal, or graham or wheat flour, sweetened with molasses.

Bos′ton bull′. See **Boston terrier.**

Bos′ton cream′ pie′, a two-layer cake with a thick filling of cream or custard between the layers, often having a chocolate icing on top.

Bos·to·ni·an (bô stō′nē ən, bo stō′-), *adj.* **1.** of, pertaining to, or typical of Boston, Mass., or its residents: *a Bostonian childhood.* —*n.* **2.** a native or inhabitant of Boston, Mass.

Bos′ton i′vy, a woody, Oriental, climbing vine, *Parthenocissus tricuspidata,* grown in the U.S. as a wall covering. Also called **Japanese ivy.**

Bos′ton Mas′sacre, *Amer. Hist.* a riot (March 5, 1770) of Boston colonists against British troops quartered in the city, in which the troops fired on the mob and killed several persons.

Bos′ton rock′er, a wooden American rocking chair having a solid, curved seat, a spindle back, narrow rockers, and usually having gilt designs stenciled on the headpiece.

Bos′ton Tea′ Par′ty, *Amer. Hist.* a raid on three British ships in Boston Harbor (December 16, 1773) by Boston colonists, disguised as Indians, who threw the contents of several hundred chests of tea into the harbor in protest against British taxes on tea and the monopoly granted the East India Company.

Boston terrier (14 in. high at shoulder)

Bos′ton ter′rier, one of an American breed of small, pug-faced, short-haired dogs having erect ears, a short tail, and a brindled or black coat with white markings. Also called **Boston bull.**

bo·sun (bō′sən), *n.* boatswain.

Bos·well (boz′wel′, -wəl), *n.* **1. James,** 1740–95, Scottish author: biographer of Samuel Johnson. **2.** any devoted or thorough biographer of a specific person. —**Bos·well·i·an** (boz wel′ē ən), *adj.*

Bos′worth Field′ (boz′wərth), a battlefield in central England, near Leicester, where Richard III was defeated and slain by the future Henry VII (the first Tudor ruler of England) in 1485.

bot (bot), *n.* the larva of a botfly. Also, **bott.** [?]

bot., 1. botanical. **2.** botanist. **3.** botany.

bo·tan·i·cal (bə tan′i kəl), *adj.* **1.** Also, **bo·tan′ic.** of, pertaining to, made from, or containing plants: *botanical survey; botanical drugs.* —*n.* **2.** *Pharm.* a drug made from part of a plant, as from roots, leaves, bark, etc. [earlier *botanic* (< ML *botanic(us)* < Gk *botanikós* of plants = *botán(ē)* herb + *-ikos* -IC) + -AL[1]] —**bo·tan′i·cal·ly,** *adv.*

botan′ical gar′den, a garden for the exhibition and scientific study of collected growing plants.

bot·a·nist (bot′ᵊnist), *n.* a person skilled in botany. [earlier *botan(ism)* botany (< Gk *botanism(ós)* = *botán(ē)* plant + *-ismos* -ISM) + -IST]

bot·a·nize (bot′ᵊnīz′), *v.*, **-nized, -niz·ing.** —*v.i.* **1.** to study plants or plant life. **2.** to collect plants for scientific study. —*v.t.* **3.** to explore botanically; study the plant life of. Also, *esp. Brit.,* **botanise.** [< NL *botaniz(āre)* < Gk *botaníz(ein)* (to) gather plants. See BOTANIST, -IZE] —**bot′a·niz′er,** *n.*

bot·a·ny (bot′ᵊnē, bot′nē), *n., pl.* **-nies. 1.** the science of plants; the branch of biology that deals with plant life. **2.** the plant life of a region. **3.** the biology of a plant or plant group. [earlier *botan(ic)* (see BOTANICAL) + -Y[3]]

Bot′any Bay′, a bay on the SE coast of Australia, near Sydney.

botch[1] (boch), *v.t.* **1.** to spoil by poor work; bungle. **2.** to do or say in a bungling manner. —*n.* **3.** a clumsy or poor piece of work; bungle. **4.** a disorderly or confused combination; jumble; hodgepodge. [ME *bocche(n)* < ?] —**botch′er,** *n.*

botch[2] (boch), *n. Archaic.* a swelling on the skin; boil. [ME *bocche* < OF *boche,* dial. var. of *boce* BOSS[2]]

botch·y (boch′ē), *adj.,* **botch·i·er, botch·i·est.** poorly made or done; bungled. —**botch′i·ly,** *adv.* —**botch′i·ness,** *n.*

bot·fly (bot′flī′), *n., pl.* **-flies.** any of several dipterous insects of the families *Oestridae* and *Gasterophilidae,* the larvae of which are parasitic in animals or man.

both (bōth), *adj.* **1.** one and the other; two together: *Both girls were beautiful.* —*pron.* **2.** the one as well as the other: *Both of us were going to the party.* —*conj.* **3.** alike; equally: *He is both ready and willing.* [ME *bōthe, bāthe* < Scand (cf. Icel *bāthir* both; c. G *beide*); r. ME *bo, ba,* OE *bā;* c. Goth *bai;* akin to L *(am)bō,* Gk *(ám)phō*]

Bo·tha (bō′tə), *n.* **1. Lou·is** (lo͞o ē′), 1862–1919, South African general and statesman. **2. Pie·ter Willem** (pē′tər), born 1916, South African political leader; state president since 1984.

both·er (bot͟h′ər), *v.t.* **1.** to give trouble to; annoy or pester. **2.** to bewilder or confuse. —*v.i.* **3.** to take the trouble; trouble or inconvenience oneself: *He has no time to bother with trifles.* —*n.* **4.** something or someone troublesome, burdensome, or annoying: *Doing the laundry can be a terrible bother.* **5.** effort, work, or worry: *Gardening takes more bother than it's worth.* **6.** a worried or perplexed state: *Don't get into such a bother about small matters.* —*interj.* **7.** *Chiefly Brit.* (used to express mild irritation.) [? Anglo Ir var. of POTHER] —**Syn. 1.** harass, vex, irritate; molest, disturb. BOTHER, ANNOY, PLAGUE, TEASE imply persistent interference with one's comfort or peace of mind. BOTHER suggests causing trouble or weariness or repeatedly interrupting one in the midst of pressing duties. TO ANNOY is to vex or irritate by bothering. PLAGUE is a strong word, connoting unremitting annoyance and harassment. TO TEASE is to pester, as by long-continued whining and begging. —**Ant. 1.** solace.

both·er·a·tion (bot͟h′ə rā′shən), *interj.* **1.** (used as an exclamation of vexation or annoyance.) —*n.* **2.** the act of bothering. **3.** the state of being bothered.

both·er·some (bot͟h′ər səm), *adj.* troublesome.

Both·ni·a (both′nē ə), *n.* **Gulf of,** an arm of the Baltic Sea, extending N between Sweden and Finland. ab. 400 mi. long.

Both·well (both′wel′, -wəl, bot͟h′-) *n.* **James Hep·burn** (hep′bûrn *or, esp. Brit.,* heb′ərn), **Earl of,** 1536?–78, third husband of Mary, Queen of Scots.

bot·o·née (bot′ᵊnā′, bot′ᵊ nā′), *adj. Heraldry.* (of a cross) having arms terminating in the form of a trefoil: *cross botonée.* See illus. at **cross.** [< MF: covered with buds = *boton* bud, BUTTON + *-ée;* see -EE]

bo′ tree′ (bō), the pipal, or sacred fig tree, *Ficus religiosa,* of India, under which the founder of Buddhism is reputed to have attained the enlightenment that constituted him the Buddha. [*bo* < Singhalese *bogaha* = *bo* (< Pali *bodhi* < Skt; see BODHISATTVA) + *gaha* tree]

bot·ry·oi·dal (bo′trē oid′ᵊl), *adj.* having the form of a bunch of grapes. Also, **bot′ry·oid′, botryose.** [< Gk *botryoeid(ḗs)* shaped like a bunch of grapes (*bótry(s)* bunch of grapes + *-oeidēs* -OID) + -AL[1]]

bot·ry·ose (bo′trē ōs′), *adj.* **1.** botryoidal. **2.** racemose. [< Gk *bótry(s)* bunch of grapes + -OSE[1]]

bots (bots), *n.* (*construed as pl.*) *Vet. Pathol.* a disease caused by the attachment of the larvae of botflies to the stomach of a horse. [pl. of BOT]

Bot·sa·res (*Gk.* bô′tsä rēs), *n.* **Mar·kos** (*Gk.* mär′kôs). See **Bozzaris, Marco**

Bot·swa·na (bot swä′nä), *n.* a republic in S Africa: formerly a British protectorate; gained independence 1966; member of the Commonwealth of Nations. 514,378 (1964); 275,000 sq. mi. *Cap.:* Gaborone. Formerly, **Bechuanaland.**

bott (bot), *n.* bot.

Bött·ger (bœt′gər), *n.* **Jo·hann Frie·drich** (yō′hän frē′driкн), 1682–1719, German chemist.

Bot·ti·cel·li (bot′i chel′ē; *It.* bôt′tē chel′lē), *n.* **San·dro** (*It.* sän′drô), (*Alessandro di Mariano dei Filipepi*), 1444?–1510, Italian painter. —**Bot′ti·cel′li·an,** *adj.*

bot·tle (bot′ᵊl), *n., v.,* **-tled, -tling.** —*n.* **1.** a portable container for holding liquids, characteristically having a neck and mouth and made of glass. **2.** the contents or capacity of such a container: *a bottle of wine.* **3.** bottled cow's milk and milk formulas given to infants, as opposed to mother's milk: *raised on the bottle.* **4. hit the bottle,** *Slang.* to drink to excess often or habitually. —*v.t.* **5.** to put into or seal in a bottle: *to bottle grape juice.* **6.** *Brit.* to can or put up fruit or vegetables. **7. bottle up, a.** to repress or restrain: *He kept all of his anger bottled up inside him.* **b.** to enclose or entrap: *Traffic was bottled up in the tunnel.* [ME *botel* < MF, var. of *bo(u)teille* < ML *butticula* = LL *butti(s)* BUTT[4] + *-cula* -CULE] —**bot′tler,** *n.*

bot′tle ba′by, an infant fed by bottle from birth, as distinguished from one who is breast-fed.

bot′tle club′, a club serving drinks to members who have reserved or purchased their own bottles of liquor.

bot′tled gas′, 1. gas stored in portable cylinders under pressure. **2.** See **liquefied petroleum gas.** Also, **bot′tle gas′.**

bot′tled in bond′, *U.S.* (of a straight whiskey or brandy) bottled at 100 proof after aging at least four years and being stored untaxed under government supervision until removed by the manufacturer for market.

bot′tle gourd′. See under **gourd** (def. 1).

bot′tle green′, a deep green. —**bot′tle-green′,** *adj.*

bot·tle·neck (bot′ᵊl nek′), *n.* **1.** a narrow entrance or passageway. **2.** a place or a stage in a process at which progress is impeded. —*v.t.* **3.** to hamper or confine by or as by a bottleneck. —*v.i.* **4.** to become like a bottleneck; be hindered by or as by a bottleneck.

bot·tle·nose (bot′ᵊl nōz′), *n.* any of various cetaceans having a bottle-shaped nose, as a bottle-nosed dolphin. —**bot′tle-nosed′,** *adj.*

bot′tle-nosed dol′phin, any of several dolphins of the genus *Tursiops,* common in warm seas, having a bottle-shaped nose. Also, **bot′tlenose dol′phin.** See illus. at **dolphin.**

bot′tle par′ty, a party to which guests bring their own liquor.

bot′tle tree′, any of several trees, species of the genus *Sterculia* (*Firmiana*), native to warmer regions, as *S. rupestris* **(narrow-leaved bottle tree)** and *S. trichosiphon* **(broad-leaved bottle tree).**

bot·tom (bot′əm), *n.* **1.** the lowest or deepest part of anything, as distinguished from the top. **2.** the under or lower side; underside: *the bottom of a flatiron.* **3.** the ground under any body of water: *the bottom of the sea.* **4.** Also called **bottom land.** Usually, **bottoms.** *Phys. Geog.* low alluvial land next to a river. **5.** *Naut.* **a.** the part of a hull that is immersed at all times. **b.** a cargo vessel. **6.** the seat of a chair. **7.** the buttocks; rump. **8.** the fundamental part; basic aspect. **9. bottoms,** (*construed as pl.*) the trousers of a pair of pajamas. **10.** the working part of a plow, comprising the plowshare, landside, and moldboard. **11.** the cause or origin: *Try getting to the bottom of the problem.* **12.** *Chiefly Brit.* **a.** the inmost part or inner end of a recess, bay, lane, etc. **b.** the most remote section of a garden or field. **13.** *Baseball.* **a.** the second half of an inning. **b.** players low in the batting order, esp. the last three. **14.** lowest limit, esp. of dignity, status, or rank; nadir. **15. at bottom,** in reality; fundamentally. Also, **at the bottom. 16. at the bottom of,** really causing; responsible for. **17. bottoms up!** *Informal.* drink up! —*v.t.* **18.** to furnish with a bottom. **19.** to base or found (usually fol. by *on* or *upon*). **20.** to discover the full meaning of (something); fathom. —*v.i.* **21.** to be based; rest. **22.** to strike against or reach the bottom. —*adj.* **23.** of or pertaining to the bottom or a bottom. **24.** located on or at the bottom: *I want the bottom book in the stack.* **25.** lowest: *bottom prices.* **26.** fundamental: *the bottom cause.* **27. bet one's bottom dollar, a.** to wager the last of one's money or resources. **b.** to be positive or assured. [ME *botme,* OE *botm;* akin to Icel *botn,* D *bodem,* G *Boden,* L *fundus,* Gk *pythmḗn,* Skt *budhná*] —**Syn. 1.** base, foot. **8, 11.** foundation, groundwork. **26.** basic.

bot′tom land′, bottom (def. 4).

bot·tom·less (bot′əm lis), *adj.* **1.** lacking a bottom. **2.** immeasurably deep. **3.** unfathomable; mysterious. **4.** unlimited; without bounds: *a bottomless supply of money.* [ME *botomles*] —**bot′tom·less·ly,** *adv.* —**bot′tom·less·ness,** *n.*

bot′tom line′, *Informal.* **1.** the final figure, showing profit or loss, in a financial statement. **2.** the ultimate result or consideration.

bot·tom·most (bot′əm mōst′ *or, esp. Brit,* -məst), *adj.* **1.** of, pertaining to, or situated at the bottom. **2.** (of one of a series) farthest down; lowest. **3.** bottom.

bot′tom round′, a cut of beef taken from outside the round, which is below the rump and above the upper leg. Cf. **top round.**

bot·tom·ry (bot′əm rē), *n., pl.* **-ries.** *Marine Law.* a contract by which the owner of a ship borrows money to make a voyage, pledging the ship as security. [modeled on D *bodemerij* = *bodem* BOTTOM + *-erij* -RY]

Bot·trop (bôt′rôp), *n.* a city in W West Germany, in the Ruhr region. 112,200 (1963).

bot·u·lin (boch′ə lin), *n.* the toxin formed by botulinus and causing botulism. [BOTULIN(US)]

bot·u·li·nus (boch′ə lī′nəs), *n., pl.* **-nus·es.** the bacterium, *Clostridium botulinum,* that forms botulin. [< NL = L *botul(us)* a sausage + *-inus* -INE[2]]

bot·u·lism (boch′ə liz′əm), *n. Pathol.* a disease of the nervous system caused by botulin developed in spoiled foods eaten by animals and man. [< L *botul(us)* a sausage + -ISM]

Bot·vin·nik (bôt′vē nik), *n.* **Mi·kha·il** (mi кнä ēl′), born 1911, Russian chess master.

Boua·ké (bwä kā′, bwä′kā), *n.* a city in central Ivory Coast. 100,000 (est. 1964).

Bou·cher (bo͞o shā′), *n.* **Fran·çois** (frän swa′), 1703–70, French painter.

Bou·ci·cault (bo͞o′sē kôlt′, -kō′), *n.* **Di·on** (dī′on, -ən), 1822–90, Irish playwright and actor, in the U.S. after 1853.

bou·clé (bo͞o klā′), *n.* **1.** yarn with loops producing a rough, nubby appearance on woven or knitted fabrics. **2.** a fabric made of this yarn. Also, **bou·cle′.** [< F: lit., curled; see BUCKLE]

Bou·dic·ca (bo͞o dik′ə), *n.* Boadicea.

bou·doir (bo͞o′dwär, -dwôr), *n.* a lady's bedroom or private sitting room. [< F: lit., a sulking place = *boud(er)* to sulk + *-oir* -ORY[2]]

bouf·fant (bo͞o fänt′; *Fr.* bo͞o fäɴ′), *adj.* **1.** puffed out; full: *a bouffant skirt.* —*n.* **2.** a woman's coiffure in which the hair hangs straight from the top of the head and puffs out over the ears and neck to frame the face. [< F: lit., swelling = *bouff(er)* to swell + *-ant* -ANT]

bouffe (bo͞of), *n. Music.* See **opéra bouffe.** [< F < It *buffo* (fem. *buffa*) comic; see BUFFOON]

bou·gain·vil·lae·a (bo͞o′gən vil′ē ə, -vil′yə), *n.* any South American, nyctaginaceous shrub of the genus *Bougainvillaea,* having small flowers, cultivated for ornament. [< NL, named after L. A. de BOUGAINVILLE]

Bou·gain·ville (bo͞o gaɴ vēl′ *for 1;* bo͞o′gən vil′, *Fr.* bo͞o gaɴ vēl′ *for 2*), *n.* **1. Louis An·toine de** (lwē äɴ-twan′ də), 1729–1811, French navigator. **2.** the largest of the Solomon Islands, in the W Pacific Ocean. 56,768 (est. 1961). 4080 sq. mi.

bough (bou), *n.* a branch of a tree, esp. one of the larger or main branches. [ME *bogh*, OE *bōg*, *bōh* shoulder, bough; c. Icel *bōgr*, D *boeg*, G *Bug*, Gk *pêchys*, Skt *bāhu*] **—Syn.** See **branch.**

bough·pot (bou′pot′; *dial.* bo͞o′pot′), *n.* a large vase or pot for cut flowers or small branches. Also, **bowpot.**

bought (bôt), *v.* pt. and pp. of **buy.**

bought·en (bôt′ən), *adj. Chiefly Northern U.S. Dial.* bought or purchased, esp. as opposed to homemade.

bou·gie (bo͞o′jē, -zhē, bo͞o zhē′), *n.* **1.** *Med.* **a.** a slender, flexible instrument for introduction into passages of the body for dilating or opening, medicating, etc. **b.** a suppository. **2.** a wax candle. [< F, after *Bougie*, town in Algeria, center of the wax trade]

Bou·gue·reau (bo͞og*ə* rō′), *n.* **A·dolphe Wil·liam** (A dôlf′ vēl yAm′), 1825–1905, French painter.

bouil·la·baisse (bo͞ol′yə bās′, bo͞ol′yə bās′; *Fr.* bo͞o yA bes′), *n.* a soup or stew containing several kinds of fish and shellfish. [< F < Pr *bouiabaisso*, lit., boil (it, then let it simmer) down. See BOIL[1], ABASE]

bouil·lon (bo͝ol′yon, -yən; *Fr.* bo͞o yôN′), *n.* a clear, seasoned broth, flavored with beef, chicken, etc. [< F = *bouill(ir)* (to) BOIL[1] + *-on* n. suffix]

bouil′lon cube′, a small cube of dehydrated beef, chicken, or vegetable stock.

Bou·lan·ger (bo͞o län zhā′), *n.* **1. Georges Er·nest Jean Ma·rie** (zhôrzh er nest′ zhäN mA rē′), 1837–91, French general and politician. **2. Na·dia (Ju·liette)** (nA dyA′ zhy-lyet′), 1887–1979, French musician and teacher.

boul·der (bōl′dər), *n.* a detached and rounded or worn rock, esp. a large one. Also, **bowlder.** [short for *boulder stone;* ME *bulderston* < Scand; cf. dial. Sw *bullersten* big stone (in a stream) = *buller* rumbling noise + *sten* STONE]

Boul·der (bōl′dər), *n.* a city in N Colorado. 66,870 (1970).

Boul′der Can′yon, a canyon of the Colorado River between Arizona and Nevada, above Boulder Dam.

Boul′der Dam′, a dam on the Colorado River, between SE Nevada and NW Arizona: one of the highest dams in the world. 726 ft. high; 1244 ft. long. Official name, **Hoover Dam.**

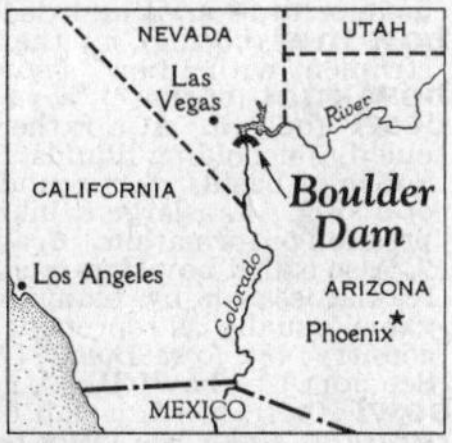

boule[1] (bo͞ol), *n.* a cylindrical lump of material for synthetic gems. [< F: lit., a ball; see BOWL[2]]

boule[2] (bo͞ol), *n.* (*often cap.*) *Furniture.* buhl. Also, **boulle.** Also called **boule·work** (bo͞ol′wûrk′).

Bou·le (bo͞o′lē), *n.* **1.** the legislative assembly of modern Greece. **2.** (*sometimes l.c.*) a state legislative, advisory, or administrative council in ancient Greece. [< Gk: a council, body of chosen ones]

boul·e·vard (bo͝ol′ə värd′, bo͞o′lə-), *n.* a broad avenue in a city, often landscaped or lined with trees. [< F < MD *boliverc;* see BULWARK] **—Syn.** See **street.**

bou·le·var·dier (bo͝ol′ə vär dēr′, bo͞o′lə-; *Fr.* bo͞ol*ə* vAR-dyā′), *n., pl.* **-diers** (-dērz′; *Fr.* -dyā′). (in Paris) a person who frequents the most fashionable places. [< F]

bou·le·ver·se·ment (bo͞ol*ə* veRs mäN′), *n. French.* an overturning; upsetting; confusion; turmoil.

Bou·logne (bo͝o lōn′, -loin′, bə-; *Fr.* bo͞o lôn′y*ə*), *n.* a seaport in France, on the English Channel. 50,036 (1962). Also called **Bou·logne-sur-Mer** (bo͞o lôn′y*ə* syR meR′).

Bou·logne Bil·lan·court (bo͞o lôn′y*ə* bē yäN ko͞oR′), a suburb of Paris, in N France. 107,074 (1962). Also called **Bou·logne-sur-Seine** (bo͞o lôn′y*ə* syR sen′).

Boul·war·ism (bo͞ol′wə riz′əm), *n.* a method of labor negotiation in which management makes a generous initial offer that is open to little or no modification. [after L.R. *Boulware* (b. 1895), American business executive]

bounce (bouns), *v.,* **bounced, bounc·ing,** *n.* **—***v.i.* **1.** (of an object) to strike a surface and spring back or rebound: *The ball bounced off the wall.* **2.** to move or walk in a lively, exuberant, or energetic manner. **3.** *Informal.* (of a check or the like) to fail to be honored by the bank against which it was drawn, due to lack of sufficient funds. **—***v.t.* **4.** to cause to strike and rebound: *to bounce a ball; to bounce a child on one's knee.* **5.** *Slang.* to eject, expel, or dismiss summarily or forcibly. **6. bounce back,** to recover quickly, as from a blow, defeat, shock, etc. **—***n.* **7.** a bound or rebound. **8.** a sudden spring or leap. **9.** ability to rebound; resilience. **10.** vitality; energy; liveliness. **11.** *Slang.* the fact of being dismissed or rejected. [ME *bunci(n)*, *bounse*, var. of *bunkin*, appar. c. D *bonken* to thump, belabor, *bonzen* to knock, bump] **—bounce′a·ble,** *adj.*

bounc·er (boun′sər), *n.* **1.** a person or thing that bounces. **2.** *Slang.* a man employed at a bar, nightclub, etc., to eject disorderly persons.

bounc·ing (boun′sing), *adj.* stout, strong, or vigorous: *a bouncing baby boy.*

boun·cy (boun′sē), *adj.,* **-ci·er, -ci·est. 1.** resilient; animated; lively. **2.** tending to bounce, as a tennis ball.

bound[1] (bound), *adj.* **1.** tied; in bonds: *a bound prisoner.* **2.** made fast as if by a band or bond. **3.** secured within a cover, as a book. **4.** under a legal or moral obligation. **5.** destined; sure; certain (usually fol. by an infinitive): *It is bound to happen. He is bound to go.* **6.** *Pathol.* constipated; costive. **7.** held with another element, substance, or material in chemical or physical union. **8. bound up in** or **with, a.** inseparably connected with. **b.** devoted or attached to. [ptp. of BIND] **—bound′ness,** *n.*

bound[2] (bound), *v.i.* **1.** to move by leaps. **2.** to rebound; bounce. **—***n.* **3.** a leap onward or upward; jump. **4.** a rebound; bounce. [< MF *bond* a leap, *bond(ir)* (to) leap, orig. resound << VL **bombitīre* for **bombitāre* to buzz, whiz = L *bomb(us)* (see BOMB) + *-it-* intensive suffix + *-āre* inf. suffix] **—bound′ing·ly,** *adv.* **—Syn. 1.** See **skip**[1].

bound[3] (bound), *n.* **1.** Usually, **bounds.** limits or boundaries: *within the bounds of reason.* **2.** something that limits, confines, or restrains. **3. bounds, a.** territories on or near a boundary. **b.** land within boundary lines. **4.** *Math.* a number greater than or equal to, or less than or equal to, all the numbers in a given set. **5. out of bounds, a.** beyond prescribed limits or restricted area. **b.** forbidden; prohibited. **—***v.t.* **6.** to limit by or as by bounds. **7.** to form the boundary or limit of. **8.** to name the boundaries of. **—***v.i.* **9.** to abut or border. [ME *bounde* < AF; OF *bonde*, var. of *bodne* < ML *bodina*] **—bound′a·ble,** *adj.* **—Syn. 1.** border, confine. **7.** demarcate, circumscribe.

bound[4] (bound), *adj.* **1.** going or intending to go; on the way to; destined (usually fol. by *for*): *The train is bound for Denver.* **2.** *Archaic.* prepared; ready. [ME *b(o)un* ready < Scand; cf. Icel *būinn*, ptp. of *būa* to get ready]

-bound[1], a combining form of **bound**[1]: *snowbound.*

-bound[2], a combining form of **bound**[4]: *eastbound.*

bound·a·ry (boun′də rē, -drē), *n., pl.* **-ries. 1.** something that indicates bounds or limits; a limiting or bounding line. **2.** *Math.* the collection of all points of a given set having the property that every neighborhood of each point contains points in the set and in the complement of the set.

bound′ary lay′er, *Physics.* the portion of a fluid flowing past a body that is in the immediate vicinity of the body and that has a reduced flow due to the forces of adhesion and viscosity.

bound′ary line′. See **partition line.**

bound·en (boun′dən), *adj.* **1.** obliged; under obligation. **2.** obligatory; compulsory: *one's bounden duty.* [var. of BOUND[1]]

bound·er (boun′dər), *n. Chiefly Brit. Slang.* an obtrusive, ill-bred person. [BOUND[2] + -ER[1]]

bound′ form′, a linguistic form that never occurs by itself but always as part of some larger construction, as *-ed* in *seated.* Cf. **free form** (def. 1).

bound·less (bound′lis), *adj.* without bounds; unlimited; immense. **—bound′less·ly,** *adv.* **—bound′less·ness,** *n.*

boun·te·ous (boun′tē əs), *adj.* **1.** giving or disposed to give freely; generous; liberal. **2.** freely bestowed; plentiful; abundant. [late ME *bounte* BOUNTY + -OUS; r. ME *bountevous* < MF *bontive* (*bonte* BOUNTY + *-ive*, fem. of *-if* -IVE) + -OUS] **—boun′te·ous·ly,** *adv.* **—boun′te·ous·ness,** *n.*

boun·ti·ful (boun′tə fəl), *adj.* **1.** liberal in bestowing gifts, favors, or bounties; munificent; generous. **2.** abundant; ample: *a bountiful supply.* **—boun′ti·ful·ly,** *adv.* **—boun′ti·ful·ness,** *n.* **—Syn. 2.** See **plentiful.**

Boun·ti·ful (boun′tə fəl), *n.* a city in N Utah, near Salt Lake City. 27,956 (1970).

boun·ty (boun′tē), *n., pl.* **-ties. 1.** generosity in giving. **2.** a generous gift. **3.** a premium or reward, esp. one offered by a government. [ME *b(o)unte* < MF *bonte*, OF *bontet* < L *bonitāt-* (s. of *bonitās*) goodness. See BOON[2], -ITY] **—boun′ty·less,** *adj.* **—Syn. 1.** munificence, liberality, charity, beneficence. **2.** present, benefaction. **3.** See **bonus.**

boun′ty hun′ter, a person who hunts criminals, wild animals, etc., for the reward or bounty offered for capturing or killing them.

bou·quet (bō kā′, bo͞o- *for 1, 2;* bo͞o kā′ *or, occas.,* bō- *for 3*), *n.* **1.** a bunch of flowers; nosegay. **2.** a compliment. **3.** the characteristic aroma of wines, liqueurs, etc. [< F: bunch, orig. thicket, grove; OF *bosquet* = *bosc* wood (< Gmc; see BOSK, BUSH[1]) + *-et* -ET]

Bour·bon (bo͝or′bən; *Fr.* bo͞oR bôN′ *for 1–3;* bûr′bən *for 4, occas. for 3*), *n.* **1.** a member of a French royal family that ruled in France 1589–1792, Spain 1700–1931, and Naples 1735–1806, 1815–60. **2. Charles** (shARl), ("*Constable de Bourbon*"), 1490–1527, French general. **3.** a person who is extremely conservative or reactionary. **4.** (*l.c.*) Also called **bour′bon whis′key.** a straight whiskey distilled from a mash having 51 percent or more corn.

Bour·bon·ism (bo͝or′bə niz′əm; *occas.* bûr′-), *n.* **1.** adherence to the social and political practices of the Bourbons. **2.** extreme conservatism, esp. in politics.

Bour·bon·nais (bo͞oR bô nā′), *n.* a region and former province in central France. See map at **Burgundy.**

bour′bon rose′, a hybrid rose, *Rosa borboniana*, cultivated in many horticultural varieties.

bour·don (bo͝or′dən, bōr′-, bôr′-), *n. Music.* **1.** the drone pipe of a bagpipe. **2.** a pipe-organ stop of a soft quality, usually an octave below standard pitch. [ME < MF; see BURDEN[2]]

bourg (bo͝org; *Fr.* bo͞oR), *n., pl.* **bourgs** (bo͝orgz; *Fr.* bo͞oR). **1.** a town. **2.** a French market town. [late ME < MF << LL *burg(us)* < Gmc; see BOROUGH]

bour·geois[1] (bo͝or zhwä′, bo͝or′zhwä; *Fr.* bo͞oR zhwA′), *n., pl.* **-geois,** *adj.* **—***n.* **1.** a member of the middle class. **2.** a shopkeeper, merchant, or businessman. **3.** a person whose values and beliefs are petty and materialistic. **—***adj.* **4.** belonging to, characteristic of, or consisting of the middle class. **5.** lacking in refinement or culture; philistine: *bourgeois taste.* **6.** dominated or characterized by materialistic pursuits or concerns. [< F; OF *borgeis* BURGESS]

bour·geois[2] (bər jois′), *n. Print.* a size of type approximately 9-point, between brevier and long primer. [? from a printer so named]

Bour·geois (bo͝or zhwä′, bo͝or′zhwä; *Fr.* bo͞oR zhwA′), *n.* **Lé·on Vic·tor Au·guste** (lā ôN′ vēk tôR′ ō gyst′), 1851–1925, French statesman: Nobel peace prize 1920.

bour·geoise (bo͝or′zhwäz, bo͝or zhwäz′; *Fr.* bo͞oR zhwAz′), *n., pl.* **-geois·es** (-zhwä ziz, -zhwä′-; *Fr.* -zhwAz′). a female bourgeois. [< F; fem. of BOURGEOIS[1]]

bour·geoi·sie (bo͝or′zhwä zē′; *Fr.* bo͞oR zhwA zē′), *n.* **1.** the bourgeois class. **2.** (in Marxist theory) the class opposed to the proletariat. [< F; see BOURGEOIS[1], -Y[3]]

bour·geon (bûr′jən), *n., v.i., v.t.* burgeon.

Bourges (bo͞oRzh), *n.* a city in central France: cathedral. 63,479 (1962).

Bour·get (bo͝or zhā′; *Fr.* bo͞oR zhe′), *n.* **Paul** (pôl), 1852–1935, French novelist and critic.

Bour·gogne (bo͞oR gôn′y*ə*), *n.* French name of **Burgundy.**

Bour·gui·ba (bo͝or gē′bə), *n.* **Ha·bib ben A·li** (hä′bēb ben ä′lē), born 1903, leader in Tunisian independence movements: president of Tunisia since 1957.

Bourke-White (bûrk′hwīt′, -wīt′), *n.* **Margaret,** 1906–71, U.S. photographer.

bourn (bōrn, bôrn, bo͝orn), *n.* **1.** a bound; limit. **2.** destination; goal. **3.** realm; domain. [earlier *borne* < MF; OF *bodne,* etc., BOUND[3]] —**bourn′less,** *adj.*

Bourne·mouth (bo͝orn′məth, bōrn′-, bôrn′-), *n.* a city in SW Hampshire in S England: seashore resort. 153,965 (1961).

bour·rée (bo͝o rā′; *Fr.* bo͞o RĀ′), *n., pl.* **-rées** (-rāz′; *Fr.* -RĀ′). **1.** an old French and Spanish dance, somewhat like a gavotte. **2.** the music for it. [< F]

Bourse (bo͝ors), *n.* a stock exchange, esp. that of Paris, France. [< F: lit., purse; see BURSA]

bouse[1] (bous, bouz), *v.t.,* **boused, bous·ing.** *Naut.* to haul with tackle. Also, **bowse.** [?]

bouse[2] (bo͞oz, bouz), *n., v.t., v.i.,* **boused, bous·ing.** *Archaic.* booze. Also, **bowse.** [ME *bous* strong drink < MD *buse* drinking vessel]

bou·stro·phe·don (bo͞o′strə fēd′ən, bou′-), *n.* an ancient method of writing in which the lines run alternately from right to left and from left to right. [< Gk: lit., like ox-turning (in plowing) = *bou-* (s. of *boûs* ox) + *-strophē-* (see STROPHE) + *-don* adv. suffix]

bout (bout), *n.* **1.** a contest, as of boxing. **2.** a turn at work or any action. **3.** the act of going and returning across a field, as in mowing or reaping. **4.** period; session; spell: *a bout of illness.* [var. of obs. *bought* bend, turn < *bow* BOW[1]]

bou·tique (bo͞o tēk′), *n.* a small shop, esp. one that sells fashionable clothes and accessories for women. [< F << Gk *apothḗkē;* see APOTHECARY]

bou·ton·niere (bo͞ot′ənēr′, -ənyâr′), *n.* a flower or small bouquet worn, usually by a man, in the buttonhole of a lapel. [< F: buttonhole = *bouton* BUTTON + *-ière* suffix of appurtenance; see -ARIOUS]

bou·ton·nière (bo͞o tô nyeR′), *n., pl.* **-nières** (-nyeR′). *French.* boutonniere.

bou·zou·ki (bə zo͞o′kē), *n.* a long-necked, fretted lute of modern Greece. Also, **buzuki.** [< Gk < Turk *buzurk* large]

bo·vid (bō′vid), *adj. Zool.* of or pertaining to the *Bovidae,* or ox family. [< NL *Bovid(ae)* = L *bov-* (s. of *bōs* ox) + *-idae* -ID[2]]

bo·vine (bō′vīn, -vin, -vēn), *adj.* **1.** of the ox family, *Bovidae.* **2.** oxlike; cowlike. **3.** stolid; dull. —*n.* **4.** a bovine animal. [< LL *bovīn(us)* of, pertaining to oxen or cows = L *bov-* (s. of *bōs* ox) + *-īnus* -INE[1]] —**bo′vine·ly,** *adv.* —**bo·vin·i·ty** (bō vin′i tē), *n.*

bow[1] (bou), *v.i.* **1.** to bend the knee or body or incline the head, as in submission, salutation, or acknowledgment. **2.** to yield; submit: *to bow to the inevitable.* **3.** to bend or curve downward. —*v.t.* **4.** to bend or incline (the knee, body, or head). **5.** to cause to submit; subdue; crush. **6.** to cause to stoop, bend, or incline. **7.** to express by bowing. **8.** to usher (someone) with a bow (usually fol. by *in, out,* etc.): *We were bowed in by the footman.* **9. bow and scrape,** to be excessively polite or deferential. **10. bow out,** to resign a position or withdraw from a competition: *He bowed out after two terms as governor.* —*n.* **11.** an inclination of the head or body, as in submission, salutation, or acknowledgment. **12. make one's bow,** to appear publicly for the first time, as a performer, politician, etc. **13. take a bow,** to step forward or stand up in order to receive recognition, applause, etc. [ME *bow(en)* (v.), OE *būgan;* c. D *buigen;* akin to G *biegen,* Goth *biugan,* Icel *buga,* etc.] —**bowed′-ness,** *n.* —**bow′ing·ly,** *adv.* —**Syn. 1.** See **bend**[1].

bow[2] (bō), *n.* **1.** a flexible strip of wood or other material, bent by a string stretched between its ends, esp. for propelling arrows. **2.** a bend or curve. **3.** Also called **bowknot.** a readily loosened knot for joining the ends of two cords or ribbons, having two projecting loops. **4.** a loop or gathering of ribbon, paper, or the like, used as an ornament on packages, clothing, etc. **5.** a long rod with horsehairs stretched from one end to the other, used for playing on a musical instrument of the violin or viol families. **6.** a single stroke of such a device. **7.** something curved or arc-shaped. **8.** a saddlebow. **9.** an archer; bowman: *He is the best bow in the county.* **10.** temple[2] (def. 3). **11.** a U-shaped piece for placing under an animal's neck to hold a yoke. **12.** a rainbow. —*adj.* **13.** curved; bent like a bow: *bow legs.* —*v.t., v.i.* **14.** to bend into the form of a bow; curve. **15.** *Music.* to perform by means of a bow upon a stringed instrument. [ME *bowe* (n.), OE *boga;* c. D *boog,* G *Bogen,* Icel *bogi;* akin to BOW[1]] —**bowed′ness,** *n.* —**bow′less,** *adj.* —**bow′like′,** *adj.*

bow[3] (bou), *n.* **1.** *Naut., Aeron.* **a.** the forward end of a vessel or airship. **b.** either side of this forward end, esp. with reference to the direction of a distant object: *a mooring two points off the port bow.* **2. bows,** *Naut.* the exterior of the forward end of a vessel. **3.** the foremost oar in rowing a boat. **4.** Also called **bowman, bow oar.** the person who pulls that oar. —*adj.* **5.** of or pertaining to the bow of a ship. [< LG *boog* (n.) or D *boeg* or Dan *bov;* see BOUGH]

Bow′ bells′ (bō), the bells of Bow Church, in the East End district of London.

bow′ com′pass (bō), any of several types of compasses having the legs joined by a bow-shaped piece.

Bow·ditch (bou′dich′), *n.* **Nathaniel,** 1773–1838, U.S. mathematician, astronomer, and navigator.

bowd·ler·ise (boud′lə rīz′), *v.t.,* **-ised, -is·ing.** *Chiefly Brit.* bowdlerize. —**bowd′ler·i·sa′tion,** *n.*

bowd·ler·ize (bōd′lə rīz′, boud′-), *v.t.,* **-ized, -iz·ing.** to expurgate (a play, novel, etc.) in a prudish manner. [after Thomas *Bowdler* (1754–1825), English editor of an expurgated edition of Shakespeare] —**bowd′ler·ism,** *n.* —**bowd′-ler·i·za′tion,** *n.*

bow·el (bou′əl, boul), *n., v.,* **-eled, -el·ing** or (*esp. Brit.*) **-elled, -el·ling.** —*n.* **1.** *Anat.* **a.** Usually, **bowels.** the intestine. **b.** a part of the intestine. **2. bowels, a.** the inward or interior parts: *the bowels of the earth.* **b.** *Archaic.* feelings of pity or compassion. —*v.t.* **3.** to disembowel. [ME *b(o)uel* < OF < L *botell(us)* little sausage = *bot(ulus)* sausage + *-ellus* dim. suffix] —**bow′el·less,** *adj.*

bow′el move′ment, 1. the evacuation of the bowels; defecation. **2.** excrement from the bowels; feces.

Bow·en (bō′ən), *n.* **1. Catherine (Sho·ber) Drink·er** (sho͞o′bər dring′kər), 1897–1973, U.S. biographer and essayist. **2. Elizabeth (Dorothea Cole)** 1899–1973, Anglo-Irish novelist and short-story writer.

bow·er[1] (bou′ər), *n.* **1.** a leafy shelter or recess; arbor. **2.** a rustic dwelling; cottage. **3.** a lady's boudoir in a medieval castle. —*v.t.* **4.** to enclose in or as in a bower; embower. [ME *bour,* OE *būr* chamber; c. Icel *būr* pantry, G *Bauer* birdcage; see BOOR] —**bow′er·like′,** *adj.*

bow·er[2] (bou′ər), *n.* an anchor carried at a ship's bow. Also called **bow′er an′chor.** [BOW[3] + -ER[1]]

bow·er[3] (bou′ər), *n.* a person or thing that bows or bends. [BOW[1] + -ER[1]]

bow·er·bird (bou′ər bûrd′), *n.* any of several oscine birds of the family *Ptilonorhynchidae,* of Australia, New Guinea, and adjacent islands, the males of which build bowerlike structures to attract the females.

bow·er·y (bou′ə rē, bou′rē), *n., pl.* **-er·ies. 1.** (among the Dutch settlers of New York) a farm or country seat. **2. the Bowery,** a street and area in New York City, noted for its cheap hotels and saloons. [< D *bouwerij* farm = *bouw* agriculture + *-erij* -ERY]

bow·fin (bō′fin′), *n.* a carnivorous ganoid fish, *Amia calva,* found in sluggish fresh waters of eastern North America.

bow′ front′ (bō), *Furniture.* See **swell front.**

bow·head (bō′hed′), *n.* a whalebone whale, *Balaena mysticetus,* of northern seas, having an enormous head and mouth.

Bow·ie (bō′ē, bo͞o′ē *for 1;* bo͞o′ē *for 2*), *n.* **1. James,** 1799–1836, U.S. soldier and pioneer. **2.** a town in S Maryland, NE of Washington, D.C. 35,028 (1970).

bow′ie knife′ (bō′ē, bo͞o′ē), a heavy sheath knife having a long, single-edged, pointed blade. [named after James BOWIE]

Bowie knife

Bow′ie State′, Arkansas (used as a nickname).

bow·ing[1] (bou′ing), *n.* the act of a person who bows, as in salutation, acknowledgment, etc. [BOW[1] + -ING[1]]

bow·ing[2] (bō′ing), *n.* the act or art of playing a stringed instrument with a bow. [BOW[2] + -ING[1]]

bow·knot (bō′not′), *n.* bow[2] (def. 3).

bowl[1] (bōl), *n.* **1.** a rather deep, round dish or basin, used chiefly for holding liquids, food, etc. **2.** the contents of such a dish or basin. **3.** a rounded, cuplike, hollow part: *the bowl of a sink.* **4.** a large drinking cup. **5.** any bowl-shaped depression or formation. **6.** an oval, amphitheaterlike stadium. **7.** Also called **bowl′ game′.** a football game played after the regular season by teams selected by the sponsors of the game, usually as representing the best from a region of the country: *the Rose Bowl.* [ME *bolle,* OE *bolla;* c. Icel *bolli.* See BOLL] —**bowl′like′,** *adj.*

bowl[2] (bōl), *n.* **1.** a ball used in bowling. **2. bowls,** (*construed as sing.*) See **lawn bowling. 3.** a cast or delivery of the ball in bowling or lawn bowling. —*v.i.* **4.** to play at bowling or bowls. **5.** to roll a bowl or ball. **6.** to move along smoothly and rapidly. **7.** *Cricket.* to deliver the ball to be played by the batsman. —*v.t.* **8.** to roll or trundle, as a ball, hoop, etc. **9.** to perform or attain in bowling: *He bowls a good game.* **10.** to knock or strike, as by the ball in bowling. **11.** to carry or convey, as in a wheeled vehicle. **12.** *Cricket.* to eliminate (a batsman) by bowling (usually fol. by *out*): *He was bowled out for a duck.* **13. bowl over,** *Informal.* to surprise greatly. [late ME *bowle,* var. of *boule* < MF << L *bulla* bubble, hence, round object]

bowl·der (bōl′dər), *n.* boulder.

bow·leg (bō′leg′), *n. Pathol.* **1.** outward curvature of the legs causing a separation of the knees when the ankles are close or in contact. **2.** a leg so curved. —**bow·leg·ged** (bō′leg′id, bō′legd′), *adj.* —**bow·leg·ged·ness** (bō′leg′-id nis), *n.*

bowl·er[1] (bō′lər), *n.* **1.** a person who bowls, esp. a participant in a bowling game. **2.** *Cricket.* the player who throws the ball to be played by the batsman. [BOWL[2] + -ER[1]]

bowl·er[2] (bō′lər), *n. Chiefly Brit.* derby (def. 4). [BOWL[1] + -ER[1]]

bow′ line′ (bou), *Naval Archit.* any of a set of lines on the hull plans of a vessel, formed by the intersection of the forebody of the hull with vertical longitudinal planes at certain distances.

bow·line (bō′lin, -līn′), *n.* **1.** Also called **bow′line knot′.** a knot used to make a nonslipping loop on the end of a rope. See illus. at **knot. 2.** *Naut.* a rope made fast to the weather leech of a square sail, for keeping the sail as flat as possible when close-hauled. **3. on a bowline,** *Naut.* sailing close-hauled. [ME *bouline* = *bou-* (? *boue* BOW[2]) + *line* LINE[1]]

bowl·ing (bō′ling), *n.* **1.** any of several games in which players roll balls toward standing objects or a mark, esp. a game in which a heavy ball is rolled along a wooden alley to knock down wooden pins at the far end. Cf. **boccie, candlepin** (def. 2), **duckpin** (def. 2), **lawn bowling, ninepin** (def. 2), **tenpin** (def. 2). **2.** the game of bowls. **3.** the act or an instance of playing or participating in any such game.

Bowling (Arrangement of pins in tenpins)

bowl′ing al′ley, a long, narrow wooden lane or alley, for the game of tenpins.

bowl′ing green′, a level, closely mowed green for lawn bowling.

Bowl′ing Green′, a city in S Kentucky. 36,253 (1970).

bow·man[1] (bō′mən), *n., pl.* **-men.** an archer. [BOW[2] + MAN[1]]

bow·man[2] (bou′mən), *n., pl.* **-men.** *Naut.* bow[3] (def. 4). [BOW[3] + MAN[1]]

bow′ oar′ (bou), bow[3] (def. 4).

bow′ pen′ (bō), *Geom.* a bow compass that has a pen at the end of one leg.

bow·pot (bou′pot′; *dial.* bo͞o′pot′), *n.* boughpot.

bowse[1] (bous, bouz), *v.t.,* **bowsed, bows·ing.** bouse[1].

bowse[2] (bo͞oz, bouz), *n., v.t., v.i.,* **bowsed, bows·ing.** *Archaic.* booze.

bow·shot (bō′shot′), *n.* the distance a bow sends an arrow.

bow·sprit (bou′sprit, bō′-), *n. Naut.* a spar projecting from the upper end of the bow of a sailing vessel, for holding the tacks of various jibs or stays and often supporting a jib boom. [ME *bouspret* < MLG *bōchspret* (c. D *boegsprit*) = *bōch* BOW[3] + *spret* pole (c. OE *sprēot*)]

bow·string (bō′string′), *n.*, *v.*, **-stringed** or **-strung, -string·ing.** —*n.* **1.** the string of an archer's bow. **2.** a string, typically of horsehair, for the bow of an instrument of the violin and viol families. —*v.t.* **3.** to strangle with a bowstring or any string or band.

bow′string hemp′, any of various fibrous plants of the genus *Sansevieria*, of Asia and Africa, cultivated in the U.S. for ornament.

bow′ tie′ (bō), **1.** a small necktie tied in a bow. **2.** a sweet roll having a shape similar to that of a bow tie.

bow′ win′dow (bō), a rounded bay window. —**bow′-win′dowed,** *adj.*

bow·wow (bou′wou′, -wou′), *n.* **1.** the bark of a dog. **2.** an imitation of this. **3.** *Chiefly Baby Talk.* a dog. [rhyming compound; imit.]

bow·yer (bō′yər), *n.* a person who makes or sells archers' bows. [BOW[2] + *-yer*, var. of -ER[1] after *w*]

box[1] (boks), *n.* **1.** a container or receptacle, often rectangular and having a lid or removable cover. **2.** the quantity contained in a box. **3.** a compartment for the accommodation of a small number of people, as in a theater. **4.** a small enclosure or area in a courtroom for witnesses or the jury. **5.** a small shelter: *a sentry's box.* **6.** *Brit.* **a.** a small house, cabin, or cottage, as for use while hunting: *a shooting box.* **b.** a telephone booth. **7.** the driver's seat on a coach. **8.** the section of a wagon in which passengers or parcels are carried. **9.** part of a page of a periodical set off by lines, a border, or a white space. **10.** any enclosing, protective case or housing, sometimes including its contents. **11.** *Baseball.* any of various spaces on a baseball diamond marking the playing positions of the pitcher, catcher, batter, or coaches. **12.** *Slang* (*usually vulgar*). the vagina. —*v.t.* **13.** to put into a box. **14.** to enclose or confine as in a box (often fol. by *in* or *up*). **15.** to furnish with a box. **16.** to form into a box or the shape of a box. **17.** to block so as to keep from passing or achieving better position (often fol. by *in*). **18.** *Agric.* to make a hole or cut in (a tree) for sap to collect. **19. box the compass,** *Naut.* to recite all of the points of the compass in clockwise order. [OE, special use of BOX[3]; akin to D *bus*, G *Büchse* < LL *buxis* < Gk *pyxís*] —**box′like′,** *adj.*

box[2] (boks), *n.* **1.** a blow, as with the hand or fist. —*v.t.* **2.** to strike with the hand or fist, esp. on the ear. **3.** to fight against (someone) in a boxing match. —*v.i.* **4.** to fight in a boxing match; spar. [ME: a buffet < ?]

box[3] (boks), *n.* **1.** an evergreen shrub or small tree of the genus *Buxus*, esp. *B. sempervirens*, used for ornamental borders, hedges, etc., and yielding a hard, durable wood. **2.** the wood itself. Cf. **boxwood. 3.** any of various other shrubs or trees, esp. species of eucalyptus. [OE < L *bux(us)* box-tree, boxwood < Gk *pýxos*]

box·ber·ry (boks′ber′ē, -bə rē), *n.*, *pl.* **-ries. 1.** the checkerberry. **2.** the partridgeberry.

box′ calf′, a chrome-tanned calfskin with square markings produced by graining.

box′ cam′era, a simple, boxlike camera, without bellows, sometimes allowing for adjustment of lens opening but usually not of shutter speed.

box·car (boks′kär′), *n.* **1.** *Railroads.* a completely enclosed freight car. **2. boxcars,** a pair of sixes on the first throw of the dice in the game of craps.

box′ coat′, an outer coat with an unfitted back.

box′ el′der, a North American maple, *Acer Negundo*, cultivated as a shade tree, yielding a light, soft wood used in making furniture, woodenware, etc.

box·er (bok′sər), *n.* **1.** a prize fighter; pugilist. **2.** one of a German breed of medium-sized, stocky, short-haired, pug-faced dogs having a brindled or tan coat, sometimes with white markings.

Box·er (bok′sər), *n.* a member of a Chinese secret society that carried on an unsuccessful uprising in 1900 (**Box′er Rebel′lion**), principally against foreigners. [rough rendering of Chin *I Ho Ch'üan* virtuous harmony fist, a perversion of true name of group, with *ch'üan* fist, for orig. *t'uan* society]

box·fish (boks′fish′), *n.*, *pl.* **-fish·es,** (*esp. collectively*) **-fish.** trunkfish.

box·ful (boks′fəl), *n.*, *pl.* **-fuls.** the amount that a box can hold.

box·haul (boks′hôl′), *v.t.* *Naut.* to put (a square-rigged sailing vessel) on a new tack by bracing the head yards aback and backing the vessel onto the new heading.

box·ing[1] (bok′sing), *n.* **1.** the material used to make boxes or castings. **2.** a boxlike enclosure; casing. **3.** the act or an instance of putting into or furnishing with a box. [BOX[1] + -ING[1]]

box·ing[2] (bok′sing), *n.* the act, technique, or profession of fighting with the fists. [BOX[2] + -ING[1]]

Box′ing Day′, (in Britain) the first weekday after Christmas, when Christmas gifts or boxes are given to employees, postmen, etc.

box′ing glove′, one of a pair of heavily padded leather mittens worn by boxers.

box′ lunch′, a light meal packed in a small paper box, as for easy serving at a picnic, rally, or the like.

box′ of′fice, 1. the office of a theater, stadium, or the like, at which tickets are sold. **2.** *Theat.* **a.** receipts from a play or other entertainment. **b.** entertainment popular enough to attract paying audiences and make a profit. —**box′-of′fice,** *adj.*

box′ pleat′, a double pleat, with the material folded under at each side. Also called **box′ plait′.**

box′ room′, *Brit.* a storage room, esp. one for trunks, suitcases, etc.

box′ score′, *Sports.* a record of the play of a game, esp. a baseball or basketball game.

box′ seat′, a seat in a box at the theater, opera, etc.

box′ set′, *Theat.* a stage set representing the interior of a room. Also called, *esp. Brit.*, **box′ scene′.**

box′ so′cial, a gathering, usually to raise funds, at which individually contributed box lunches or dinners are auctioned off, the highest bidder in each case often having the privilege of sharing the contents with the preparer.

box′ spring′, an upholstered bedspring composed of a number of helical springs, each in a cylindrical cloth pocket.

box′ stall′, a room-sized stall, usually square, for a horse or other large animal.

box·thorn (boks′thôrn′), *n.* See **matrimony vine.**

box′ tur′tle, any of several terrestrial turtles of the genus *Terrapene*, of North America, having a hinged shell that can be tightly shut to enclose and protect the body. Also called **box′ tor′toise.** See illus. at **turtle.**

box·wood (boks′wo͝od′), *n.* **1.** the hard, fine-grained, compact wood of the box shrub or tree, used for wood engravers' blocks, musical instruments, etc. **2.** the tree or shrub itself. Cf. **box**[3] (defs. 1, 2).

box′ wrench′, a wrench having ends that surround the nut or head of a bolt. See illus. at **wrench.**

boy (boi), *n.* **1.** a male child, from birth to full growth, esp. one less than 18 years of age. **2.** a young man who lacks maturity, judgment, etc. **3.** *Informal.* a grown man, esp. when referred to familiarly: *He liked to play poker with the boys.* **4. boys,** *U.S.* military personnel, esp. combat soldiers: *The boys overseas will have a bleak Christmas.* **5.** a servant, waiter, or the like. **6.** *Naut.* an apprentice seaman or fisherman. —*interj.* **7.** (used as an exclamation of wonder, contempt, etc.) [ME *boy(e)*, prob. after OE *Bōia* man's name; c. Fris *boi* young man; akin to OE *bōfa*, Icel *bōfi*, OHG *Buobo* man's name (> G *Bube* knave, dial. boy, lad)]

bo·yar (bō yär′, boi′ər), *n.* *Russ. Hist.* a nobleman below the rank of prince in Russia, esp. before Peter the Great. Also, **bo·yard** (bō yärd′, boi′ərd). [earlier *boiaren* < Russ *boiarin* lord] —**bo·yar′ism, bo·yard′ism,** *n.*

boy·cott (boi′kot), *v.t.* **1.** to combine in abstaining from, or preventing dealings with (a person or organization) as a means of coercion. **2.** to abstain from buying or using. —*n.* **3.** the act or practice of boycotting. [after C. C. *Boycott* (1832–97), British army officer, first victim] —**boy′cott·er,** *n.*

boy·friend (boi′frend′), *n.* *Informal.* a frequent or favorite male companion; beau.

boy·hood (boi′ho͝od), *n.* **1.** the state or period of being a boy. **2.** boys collectively.

boy·ish (boi′ish), *adj.* of, like, or befitting a boy. —**boy′ish·ly,** *adv.* —**boy′ish·ness,** *n.*

boy·la (boi′lə), *n.* *Australian.* a witch doctor; sorcerer. [< Austral name]

Boyle (boil), *n.* **1. Kay,** born 1903, U.S. writer. **2. Robert,** 1627–91, English chemist and physicist.

Boyle's′ law′, *Thermodynamics.* the principle that, for relatively low pressures, the pressure of an ideal gas kept at constant temperature varies inversely with the volume of the gas. Cf. **Gay-Lussac's law.** [named after R. BOYLE]

Boyne (boin), *n.* a river in E Ireland: William III defeated James II near here 1690. 70 mi. long.

boy·o (boi′ō), *n.*, *pl.* **boy·os.** *Irish Eng., Australian Informal.* boy; lad. Also, **boy′-o.** [BOY + *-o* associative suffix]

boy′ scout′, a member of an organization of boys (**Boy′ Scouts′**), having as its purpose the development of character and self-reliance.

boy·sen·ber·ry (boi′zən ber′ē), *n.*, *pl.* **-ries.** a blackberrylike fruit with a flavor similar to that of raspberries, developed by crossing various plants of the genus *Rubus.* [named after R. *Boysen*, 20th-century American botanist who bred it]

Boz (boz), *n.* See **Dickens, Charles.**

Boz·ca·a·da (*Turk.* bôz′jä ä dä′), *n.* Tenedos.

Bo·zen (bō′tsən), *n.* German name of **Bolzano.**

bo·zo (bō′zō), *n.*, *pl.* **-zos.** *Slang.* a fellow, esp. a big, strong, stupid fellow. [rhyming compound based on *bo*, var. sp. of BEAU]

Boz·za·ris (bō zar′is, -zär′-), *n.* **Mar·co** (mär′kō), 1788?–1823, Greek patriot. Also, **Botsares.**

bp., 1. baptized. **2.** birthplace. **3.** bishop.

B/P, *Com.* bills payable.

B.P., *Com.* bills payable.

b.p., 1. below proof. **2.** *Com.* bills payable. **3.** *Physics, Chem.* boiling point.

bpi, bits per inch.

B.P.O.E., Benevolent and Protective Order of Elks.

bps, bits per second.

Br, *Chem.* bromine.

Br., 1. Britain. **2.** British.

br., 1. branch. **2.** brig. **3.** bronze. **4.** brother.

b.r., *Com.* bills receivable. Also, **B.R., B/R**

bra (brä), *n.* brassiere. [by shortening]

Bra·bant (brə bant′, brä′bənt; *Du.* brä′bänt; *Fr.* BRA-BÄN′), *n.* a former duchy in W Europe: now divided between the Netherlands and Belgium. See map at **Agincourt.** —**Bra·bant·ine** (brə ban′tin, -tīn), *adj.*

brab·ble (brab′əl), *v.*, **-bled, -bling,** *n.* *Obs.* —*v.i.* **1.** to argue stubbornly about trifles; wrangle. —*n.* **2.** noisy, quarrelsome chatter. [< D *brabbelen* to quarrel, jabber] —**brab′ble·ment,** *n.* —**brab′bler,** *n.*

brace (brās), *n.*, *v.*, **braced, brac·ing.** —*n.* **1.** something that holds parts together or in place, as a clasp or clamp. **2.** anything that imparts rigidity or steadiness, as to a framework. **3.** *Mach.* a device for holding and turning a bit. **4.** *Naut.* (on a square-rigged ship) a rope by which a yard is swung about and secured horizontally. **5.** Often, **braces.** *Dentistry.* an appliance for straightening irregularly arranged teeth. **6.** *Med.* an appliance for supporting a weak joint or joints. **7. braces,** *Chiefly Brit.* suspender (def. 1). **8.** a pair; couple: *a brace of grouse.* **9.** *Printing.* **a.** one of two characters { or } used to enclose words or lines to be considered together. **b.** bracket (def. 5). **10.** *Music.* connected staves. **11.** a protective band covering the wrist or lower part of the arm, esp. a bracer. —*v.t.* **12.** to furnish, fasten, or strengthen with or as with a brace. **13.** to steady (oneself), as against a shock. **14.** to make tight; increase the tension of. **15.** to act as a stimulant to. **16.** *Naut.* to swing or turn around (the yards of a ship) by means of the braces. **17. brace up,** *Informal.* to summon up one's courage; become resolute. [(n.) ME < MF: ell < L *brāchia,* pl. of *brāchium,* var. of *bracchium* < Gk *brachī́ōn* arm; (v.) ME < MF *brac(ier)* < *brace* (n.)] **—Syn. 1.** vise. **2.** stay, prop, strut. **8.** See **pair. 12.** support, fortify, prop. **14.** tauten, tense. **15.** fortify.

brace′ and bit′, a boring tool consisting of an auger rotated by a brace.

Brace and bit

brace·let (brās′lit), *n.* **1.** an ornamental band or circlet for the wrist or arm. **2. bracelets,** *Slang.* a pair of handcuffs. [late ME < MF; OF *bracel* (< L *brāchiāle,* n. use of neut. of *brāchiālis* BRACHIAL) + *-et* -ET] **—brace′let·ed,** *adj.*

brac·er[1] (brā′sər), *n.* **1.** a person or thing that braces, binds, or makes firm. **2.** *Informal.* a stimulating drink, esp. one of liquor. [BRACE + -ER[1]]

brac·er[2] (brā′sər), *n. Archery.* a guard or band worn over the wrist of the bow hand to protect it from the snap of the bowstring. [ME < AF; OF *braceure* = *brace* arm (see BRACE (n.)) + *-ure* -URE]

bra·ce·ro (brə sâr′ō; *Sp.* brä se′rô), *n., pl.* **-ce·ros** (-sâr′ōz; *Sp.* -se′rôs). a Mexican laborer admitted legally into the U.S. for a short period to perform seasonal, usually agricultural, labor. [< Sp: laborer, lit., one who uses his arms. See BRACE, -ER[2]]

brach (brach, brak), *n. Obs.* a hound bitch. [late ME *brach(e),* back formation from *braches* < MF; OF *brachez,* pl. of *brachet* = *brac-* (< Gmc; cf. OHG *bracco* hound that hunts by scent) + *-et* -ET]

brachi-, var. of **brachio-** before a vowel.

bra·chi·al (brā′kē əl, brak′ē-), *Anat., Zool.* **—***adj.* **1.** belonging to the arm, foreleg, wing, pectoral fin, or other forelimb of a vertebrate. **2.** belonging to the upper part of such a member, from the shoulder to the elbow. **3.** armlike, as an appendage. **—***n.* **4.** a brachial part or structure. [< L *brāchiāl(is)* of, belonging to the arm]

bra·chi·al·gi·a (brā′kē al′jē ə, -jə, brak′ē-), *n. Pathol.* pain in the nerves of the upper arm.

bra·chi·ate (*adj.* brā′kē it, -āt′, brak′ē-; *v.* brā′kē āt′, brak′ē-), *adj., v.,* **-at·ed, -at·ing. —***adj.* **1.** *Bot.* having widely spreading branches in alternate pairs. **—***v.i.* **2.** to progress by means of brachiation. [< L *brāchiāt(us)* with branches like arms]

bra·chi·a·tion (brā′kē ā′shən, brak′ē-), *n. Zool.* locomotion accomplished by swinging by the arms from one hold to another.

brachio-, a learned borrowing from Greek meaning "arm," used in the formation of compound words: *brachiopod.* Also, *esp. before a vowel,* **brachi-.** [comb. form repr. L *brāchium* and Gk *brachī́ōn*]

bra·chi·o·pod (brā′kē ə pod′, brak′ē-), *n.* **1.** any mollusklike, marine animal of the phylum *Brachiopoda,* having a dorsal and ventral shell; a lamp shell. **—***adj.* **2.** Also, **brach·i·op·o·dous** (brak′ē op′ə dəs). belonging or pertaining to the *Brachiopoda.*

bra·chi·um (brā′kē əm, brak′ē-), *n., pl.* **bra·chi·a** (brā′kē ə, brak′ē ə). **1.** *Anat.* the part of the arm from the shoulder to the elbow. **2.** the corresponding part of any limb, as in the wing of a bird. **3.** an armlike part or process. [< NL, L, var. of *bracchium* the arm < Gk *brachī́ōn*]

brachy-, a learned borrowing from Greek meaning "short," used in the formation of compound words: *brachycephalic.* [< Gk, comb. form of *brachýs;* akin to L *brevis*]

brach·y·car·di·a (brak′i kär′dē ə), *n. Pathol.* bradycardia. [BRACHY- + Gk *kardía* heart]

brach·y·ce·phal·ic (brak′ē sə fal′ik), *adj. Cephalom.* shortheaded; having a breadth of head at least four-fifths as great as the length from front to back. Also, **brach·y·ceph·a·lous** (brak′ē sef′ə ləs). Cf. **dolichocephalic** (def. 1). **—brach·y·ceph·a·ly** (brak′ē sef′ə lē), **brach′y·ceph′a·lism,** *n.*

bra·chyc·er·ous (brə kis′ər əs), *adj.* having very short antennae, as certain insects. [BRACHY- + Gk *kér(as)* a horn + -OUS]

brach·y·cra·nic (brak′ē krā′nik), *adj. Craniom.* shortheaded; having a breadth of skull at least four-fifths as great as the length from front to back.

bra·chyl·o·gy (brə kil′ə jē), *n., pl.* **-gies.** brevity of diction; concise or abridged form of expression. [< Gk *brachylogía* brevity in speech]

bra·chyp·ter·ous (brə kip′tər əs), *adj. Zool., Ornith.* having short wings.

brach·y·sto·ma·tous (brak′ē stom′ə təs, -stō′mə-), *adj.* having a short proboscis, as certain insects.

brach·y·ur·an (brak′ē yŏŏr′ən), *adj.* **1.** belonging or pertaining to the suborder *Brachyura,* comprising the true crabs. **—***n.* **2.** a brachyuran crustacean. [< NL *Brachyur(a)* (see BRACHY-, UR-[2]) + -AN]

brac·ing (brā′sing), *adj.* **1.** strengthening; invigorating. **2.** of, pertaining to, or serving as a brace. **—***n.* **3.** a brace. **4.** braces collectively. **5.** material, as timber, used for braces. **—brac′ing·ly,** *adv.* **—brac′ing·ness,** *n.*

brack·en (brak′ən), *n. Brit.* **1.** a large fern or brake, esp. *Pteridium aquilinum.* **2.** a cluster or thicket of such ferns. [ME *braken* < Scand; cf. Sw *bräken* fern]

brack·et (brak′it), *n.* **1.** a support projecting from a wall or the like to hold or bear the weight of a shelf, part of a cornice, etc. **2.** a shelf or shelves so supported. **3.** any member for reinforcing the angle between two members or surfaces. **4.** a projecting fixture for gas or electricity. **5.** one of two marks [or] used in writing or printing to enclose parenthetical matter, interpolations, etc. **6.** *Math.* **a. brackets,** parentheses indicating that the enclosed quantity is to be treated as a unit. **b.** (loosely) vinculum (def. 2). **7.** a class or grouping, esp. a grouping of taxpayers based on the amount of their income: *the low-income bracket.* **8.** *Gunnery.* range or elevation producing both shorts and overs on a target. **—***v.t.* **9.** to furnish with or support by a bracket or brackets. **10.** to place within brackets. **11.** to associate, mention, or class together: *The problems were bracketed into groups.* **12.** *Gunnery.* to place (shots) both over and short of a target. [late ME *braket* kind of nail, prob. < ML *braca* (var. of *broca* projecting part); see -ET]

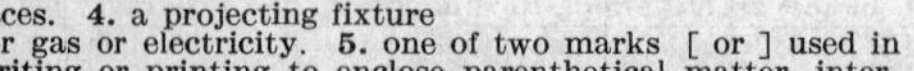
Brackets
(Beneath wooden cornice)

brack′eted blen′ny, gunnel[1].

brack·et·ing (brak′i ting), *n.* a series of brackets.

brack·ish (brak′ish), *adj.* **1.** having a salty or briny flavor. **2.** distasteful; unpleasant. [< D *brak* salty (c. MLG *brach*) + -ISH[1]] **—brack′ish·ness,** *n.*

bract (brakt), *n. Bot.* a specialized leaf or leaflike part, usually situated at the base of a flower or inflorescence. [earlier *bracte(a)* < L: a thin plate of metal (sp. var. of *brattea*)] **—brac·te·al** (brak′tē əl), *adj.* **—bract′ed,** *adj.* **—bract′less,** *adj.*

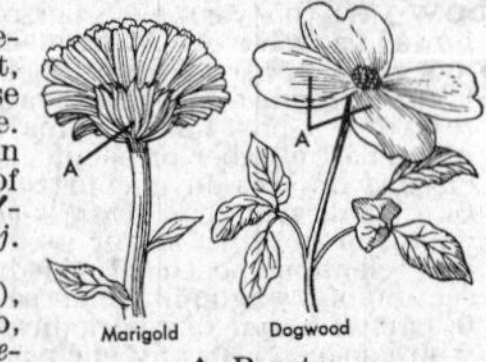

A, Bracts

brac·te·ate (brak′tē it, -āt′), *adj. Bot.* having bracts. Also, **brac′te·ose′.** [< L *bracteāt(us)* covered with gold leaf, gilded. See BRACT, -ATE[1]]

brac·te·o·late (brak′tē ə lit, -lāt′), *adj. Bot.* having a bracteole or bracteoles. [< NL *bracteolāt(us)*]

brac·te·ole (brak′tē ōl′), *n. Bot.* a small or secondary bract, as on a pedicel. Also, **bract·let** (brakt′lit). [< NL *bracteola* = L *bracte(a)* a thin plate of metal, gold leaf + *-ola* dim. suffix]

brad (brad), *n.* **1.** a slender wire nail having either a small, deep head or a projection to one side of the head end. See illus. at **nail. —***v.t.* **2.** to fasten with brads. [late ME *brad,* var. of ME, OE *brod* < Scand; cf. Icel *broddr,* c. OE *brord* spike]

brad·awl (brad′ôl′), *n. Carpentry.* an awl for making small holes in wood for brads. See illus. at **awl.**

Brad·bur·y (brad′bə rē), *n.* **Ray (Douglas),** born 1920, U.S. science-fiction writer.

Brad·dock (brad′ək), *n.* **1. Edward,** 1695–1755, British general in America. **2.** a city in SW Pennsylvania, near Pittsburgh: the site of General Braddock's defeat by the French and Indians 1755. 8,682 (1970).

Brad·ford (brad′fərd), *n.* **1. Gamaliel,** 1863–1932, U.S. biographer and novelist. **2. Roark** (rōrk, rôrk), 1896–1948, U.S. writer. **3. William,** 1590–1657, Pilgrim settler: second governor of Plymouth Colony 1621–56. **4.** a city in SW Yorkshire, in N England. 460,600.

Brad·ley (brad′lē), *n.* **1. Francis Herbert,** 1846–1924, English philosopher. **2. Omar (Nelson),** 1893–1981, U.S. general: Chief of Staff 1948–49; chairman of the Joint Chiefs of Staff 1949–53.

bra·doon (brə do͞on′), *n.* bridoon.

Brad·street (brad′strēt′), *n.* **1. Anne (Dudley),** 1612?–72, American poet. **2.** her husband, **Simon,** 1603–97, governor of the Massachusetts colony 1679–86, 1689–92.

Bra·dy (brā′dē), *n.* **Mathew B.,** 1823?–96, U.S. photographer.

brady-, a learned borrowing from Greek meaning "slow," used in the formation of compound words: *bradykinetic.* [< Gk, comb. form of *bradýs* slow, heavy]

brad·y·car·di·a (brad′i kär′dē ə), *n. Med.* a slow heartbeat rate. [BRADY- + Gk *kardía* heart] **—brad′y·car′dic,** *adj.*

brad·y·ki·net·ic (brad′i ki net′ik, -kī-), *adj.* characterized by slowness in motion. **—brad·y·ki·ne·sia** (brad′i-ki nē′zhə, -kī-), **brad′y·ki·ne′sis,** *n.*

brae (brā, brē; *Scot.* brā, brē), *n. Scot. and North Eng.* a slope; declivity; hillside. [ME *brā* < Scand; cf. Icel *brā* eyelash, c. OE *brǣw* eyebrow, eyelid, OHG *brāwa* (G *Braue*)]

brag (brag), *v.,* **bragged, brag·ging,** *n., adj.* **—***v.i.* **1.** to speak boastfully. **—***v.t.* **2.** to declare or maintain boastfully. **—***n.* **3.** a boast or vaunt. **4.** a thing to boast of. **5.** a boaster. **6.** an old English card game similar to poker. **—***adj.* **7.** *Archaic.* unusually fine; first-rate. [ME *brag* (n.), *braggen* (v.) < Scand; cf. Icel *bragga sig* to hearten oneself, dress up] **—brag′ger,** *n.* **—brag′ging·ly,** *adv.* **—brag′gy,** *adj.*

Bra·ga (brä′gə), *n.* a city in N Portugal: an ecclesiastical center. 48,735.

Bragg (brag), *n.* **1. Brax·ton** (brak′stən), 1817–76, Confederate general in the Civil War. **2. Sir William Henry,** 1862–1942, English physicist: Nobel prize 1915. **3.** his son, **Sir William Lawrence,** 1890–1971, English physicist: Nobel prize 1915.

brag·ga·do·ci·o (brag′ə dō′shē ō′), *n., pl.* **-os. 1.** empty boasting; brag. **2.** a boasting person; braggart. [after *Braggadocchio,* boastful character in Spenser's *Faerie Queene,* appar. BRAG + -ADE[1] + It *-occhio* aug. suffix]

brag·gart (brag′ərt), *n.* **1.** a person given to bragging. **—***adj.* **2.** bragging; boastful. **—brag′gart·ly,** *adv.*

Bra·gi (brä′gē), *n. Scand. Myth.* the god of poetry and music, a son and the principal counselor of Odin, and the husband of Idun. Also, **Bra·ge** (brä′gə).

Brahe (brä, brä′hē; *Dan.* brä′e), *n.* **Ty·cho** (tē′kō; *Dan.* ty′kō), 1546–1601, Danish astronomer.

Brah·ma (brä′mə, brā′-), *n.* one of a breed of large Asian chickens, having feathered legs and small wings and tail. [short for *Brahmaputra fowl,* so called because brought to England from a town on that river]

Brah·ma (brä′mə, brā′-), *n.* a Brahman bull, steer, or cow. [alter. of BRAHMAN]

Brah·ma (brä′mə), *n. Hinduism.* **1.** Brahman (def. 2). **2.** (in later Hinduism) "the Creator," the first member of the Trimurti, with Vishnu the Preserver and Shiva the Destroyer. [< Skt *brahmā* masc. nom. (see def. 2), *brahma* neut. nom. (see def. 1) of *brahman* worship]

Brah·ma·jna·na (brä′mə jə nyä′nə, -gə nyä′-, -jnyä′-, -gnyä′-), *n. Hinduism.* jnana. [< Skt]

Brah·man (brä′mən), *n., pl.* **-mans.** *Hinduism.* **1.** Also, **Brahmin.** a member of the highest, or priestly, caste among the Hindus. Cf. **Kshatriya, Sudra, Vaisya. 2.** Also, **Brahma.** the impersonal supreme being, the primal source and ultimate goal of all beings, with which Atman, when enlightened, knows itself to be identical. [< Skt *brāhmaṇa* < *brahman* worship] —**Brah·man·ic** (brä man′ik), **Brah·man′i·cal,** *adj.*

Brah·man (brä′mən), *n.* any of several breeds of Indian cattle, esp. a grayish, heat-resistant American breed raised chiefly in the Gulf states. [special use of BRAHMAN priest]

Brah·ma·na (brä′mə nə), *n.* *Hinduism.* one of a class of prose pieces dealing with Vedic rituals and sacrifices. Cf. **Veda.** [< Skt *brāhmaṇa*]

Brah·man·ism (brä′mə niz′əm), *n.* **1.** the religious and social system of the Brahmans and orthodox Hindus, characterized by the caste system and diversified pantheism. **2.** the Hinduism of the Vedas, Brahmanas, and Upanishads. Also, **Brah′min·ism.** —**Brah′man·ist, Brah′min·ist,** *n.*

Brah·ma·pu·tra (brä′mə po͞o′trə), *n.* a river in S Asia, flowing from SW Tibet through NE India and joining the Ganges River in central Bangladesh. ab. 1700 mi.

Brah·min (brä′min), *n., pl.* **-min, -mins. 1.** *Hinduism.* Brahman (def. 1). **2.** a person of great culture and intellect, esp. a member of a New England family that is considered aristocratic. **3.** a person who is intellectually or socially aloof. [var. of BRAHMAN] —**Brah·min·ic** (brä min′ik), **Brah·min′i·cal,** *adj.*

Brahms (brämz; *Ger.* bʀäms), *n.* **Jo·han·nes** (yō hä′nəs), 1833–97, German composer. —**Brahms′i·an,** *adj.*

braid (brād), *v.t.* **1.** to weave together strips or strands of; plait: *to braid hair.* **2.** to form by such weaving: *to braid a rope.* **3.** to bind or confine (the hair) with a band, ribbon, etc. **4.** to trim with braid, as a garment. —*n.* **5.** a braided length or plait, esp. of hair. **6.** a hair style formed by interweaving three or more strands of hair. **7.** a narrow, ropelike band of plaited or woven strands of silk, cotton, etc., used as trimming. **8.** a band, ribbon, etc., for binding or confining the hair. [ME *braide(n), breide(n)* (v.), OE *bregdan* to move quickly, move to and fro, weave; c. Icel *bregtha,* D *breien*] —**braid′er,** *n.*

braid·ing (brā′ding), *n.* **1.** braids collectively. **2.** braided work. [late ME *breydyng*]

brail (brāl), *Naut.* —*n.* **1.** any of several horizontal lines fastened to the after leech of a fore-and-aft sail or lateen sail, for gathering the sail in to a mast, yard, or gaff. —*v.t.* **2.** to gather or haul in (a sail) by means of brails (usually fol. by *up*). [late ME, var. of *brayell* < AF *braiel;* OF < ML *brācāle* breech belt, n. use of neut. of *brācālis* = L *brāc(a)* BREECH + *-ālis* -AL[1]]

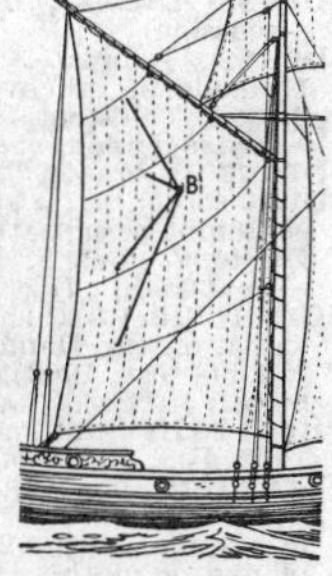

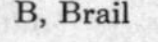
B, Brail

Bră·i·la (brə ē′lä), *n.* a port in E Rumania, on the Danube River. 121,-628 (est. 1964).

Braille (brāl), *n., v.,* **Brailled, Braill·ing.** —*n.* **1. Louis** (lo͞o′is, lo͞o′ē; *Fr.* lwē), 1809–52, French teacher of the blind. **2.** a system of lettering, devised by L. Braille for use by the blind, in which each character is a combination of raised dots that are read by touch. —*v.t.* **3.** to write in Braille characters. Also, **braille** (for defs. 2, 3).

brain (brān), *n.* **1.** *Anat., Zool.* the part of the central nervous system enclosed in the cranium of man and other vertebrates, consisting of a soft, convoluted mass of gray and white matter and serving to control and coordinate the mental and physical actions. **2.** *Zool.* (in many invertebrates) a part of the nervous system more or less corresponding to the brain of vertebrates. **3.** Sometimes, **brains.** (*construed as pl.*) intelligence. **4.** the brain as the center of thought or understanding; the mind or intellect. **5. brains,** *Slang.* a member of a group who is regarded as its intellectual leader. **6.** *Informal.* a very intelligent person. **7. beat one's brains out,** *Slang.* to exhaust one's mental resources, as in dealing with a task or problem. **8. have something on the brain,** to have an obsession; be occupied with. —*v.t.* **9.** to hit or club (someone) on the head; dash out the brains of. [ME; OE *bræg(e)n, bregen;* c. LG *brägen,* D *brein*] —**brain′like′,** *adj.* —**Syn. 3.** sense; capacity. See **mind.**

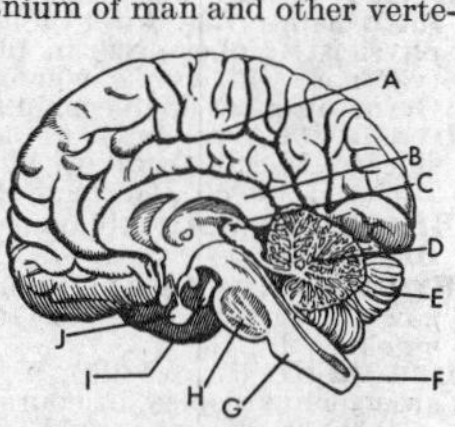

Human brain (cross section) A, Cerebrum; B, Corpus callosum; C, Pineal body; D, Vermis; E, Cerebellum; F, Spinal cord; G, Medulla oblongata; H, Pons; I, Oculomotor nerve; J, Pituitary gland

brain·child (brān′chīld′), *n., pl.* **-chil·dren.** *Informal.* a product of one's creative work or thought. Also, **brain′ child′, brain′-child′.**

brain′ death′, complete cessation of brain function as evidenced by absence of brain-wave activity on an electroencephalogram: sometimes used as a legal definition of death. —**brain-dead** (brān′ded′), *adj.*

brain′ drain′, the loss of trained professional personnel to a competing company or to a foreign country, esp. to a more highly technologically developed country.

brain′ fe′ver. See **cerebrospinal meningitis.**

brain·less (brān′lis), *adj.* witless or stupid. [late ME *braynles*] —**brain′less·ly,** *adv.* —**brain′less·ness,** *n.*

brain·pan (brān′pan′), *n.* the skull or cranium. [ME *brayn panne,* OE *brægenpanne*]

brain·sick (brān′sik′), *adj.* crazy; mad. [ME *brain-seke,* OE *brægensēoc*] —**brain′sick′ly,** *adv.* —**brain′sick′ness,** *n.*

brain·storm (brān′stôrm′), *n.* **1.** *Informal.* **a.** a sudden impulse, idea, etc. **b.** a fit of mental confusion. **2.** brainstorming. —*adj.* **3.** of or pertaining to brainstorming. —*v.i.* **4.** to conduct or practice brainstorming. —*v.t.* **5.** to subject (a problem) to brainstorming. —**brain′storm′er,** *n.*

brain·storm·ing (brān′stôr′ming), *n.* a conference technique of solving specific problems, developing new ideas, etc., by unrestrained participation in discussion.

brain·teas·er (brān′tē′zər), *n.* a very difficult or complicated puzzle or problem, as in mathematics, requiring great ingenuity and patience for its solution.

Brain·tree (brān′trē′), *n.* a town in E Massachusetts, near Boston. 35,050 (1970).

brain′ trust′, a group of experts from various fields who serve a government, corporation, etc., as unofficial consultants on matters of policy and strategy. —**brain′ trust′er.**

brain·wash (brān′wosh′, -wôsh′), *v.t.* **1.** to subject (someone) to brainwashing. —*n.* **2.** the process of brainwashing. **3.** a subjection to brainwashing. Also, **brain′-wash′.** [back formation from BRAINWASHING] —**brain′wash′er,** *n.*

brain·wash·ing (brān′wosh′ing, -wô′shing), *n.* **1.** a method for systematically changing attitudes or altering beliefs, esp. through the use of torture, drugs, or psychological-stress techniques. **2.** any method of controlled systematic indoctrination. **3.** an instance of treatment by such a method. Also, **brain′-wash′ing.**

brain′ wave′, 1. Usually, **brain waves.** *Med.* electrical potentials or impulses given off by brain tissue. Cf. **electroencephalogram. 2.** *Informal.* a sudden idea or thought.

brain·work (brān′wûrk′), *n.* mental effort.

brain·y (brā′nē), *adj.,* **brain·i·er, brain·i·est.** *Informal.* intelligent; intellectual. —**brain′i·ness,** *n.*

braise (brāz), *v.t.,* **braised, brais·ing.** to cook (meat or vegetables) by sautéeing in fat and then cooking slowly in very little liquid. [< F *braise(r)* < *braise* live coals < Gmc; akin to Sw *brasa* pyre, fire > *brasa* to roast, c. Dan *brase*]

brake[1] (brāk), *n., v.,* **braked, brak·ing.** —*n.* **1.** a device for slowing or stopping a vehicle or other moving mechanism. **2.** anything that has a slowing or stopping effect. **3.** *Obs.* an instrument of torture. —*v.t.* **4.** to slow or stop by or as if by a brake. **5.** to furnish with brakes. —*v.i.* **6.** to use or run a brake. **7.** to stop or slow upon being braked. [late ME < MD, MLG; akin to BREAK] —**brake′less,** *adj.*

brake[2] (brāk), *n.* a place overgrown with bushes, shrubs, brambles, or cane; thicket. [late ME (in phrase *brake of fern* thicket of fern) < MLG *brake* thicket]

brake[3] (brāk), *n.* any large or coarse fern, esp. *Pteridium aquilinum* or some allied species. [ME *brake,* var. of BRACKEN]

brake[4] (brāk), *v.* *Archaic.* a pt. of **break.**

brake′ band′, a flexible strap, usually of steel, lined with a friction-producing material and tightened against a brake drum to produce a braking action.

brake′ drum′, a narrow metal cylinder, fixed to a rotating shaft or wheel, against which brake shoes or brake bands act.

brake′ lin′ing, the material, usually containing asbestos, used as the friction-producing element of a brake.

brake·man (brāk′mən), *n., pl.* **-men.** a trainman who assists the conductor in the operation of a train.

brake′ shoe′, a rigid plate, usually of steel in the shape of an arc of a cylinder, coated on the outside of its curved surface with a friction-producing material and tightened against the inside of a brake drum to produce a braking action.

Brak·pan (brak′pan′), *n.* a city in the E Republic of South Africa, near Johannesburg. 78,778 (1960).

Bra·man·te (brə män′tā; *It.* bʀä män′te), *n.* **Do·na·to d'A·gno·lo** (dô nä′tô dä′nyô lô), 1444–1514, Italian architect and painter.

bram·ble (bram′bəl), *n., v.,* **-bled, -bling.** —*n.* **1.** any rosaceous plant of the genus *Rubus.* **2.** *Brit. Dial.* the common blackberry, *R. fruticosus.* **3.** any prickly shrub, as the dog rose. —*v.i.* **4.** *Brit. Dial.* to look for and gather wild blackberries. [ME; OE *bræmbel,* var. of *brǣmel* = *brǣm-* (c. D *braam* BROOM) + *-el* -LE]

bram·bly (bram′blē), *adj.,* **-bli·er, -bli·est.** having or resembling brambles.

bran (bran), *n., v.,* **branned, bran·ning.** —*n.* **1.** the partly ground husk of wheat or other grain, separated from flour meal by bolting. **2.** a by-product of grain processing, used as feed. —*v.t.* **3.** to soak or boil in water mixed with bran. [ME < OF, var. of *bren* < ?] —**bran′ner,** *n.*

Bran (bran), *n.* *Welsh Legend.* a king of Britain, whose head was buried at London as a magical defense against invasion.

branch (branch, bränch), *n.* **1.** *Bot.* a division or subdivision of the stem or axis of a tree, shrub, or other plant. **2.** a limb, offshoot, or ramification of any main stem: *the branches of a deer's antlers.* **3.** any member or part of a body or system; a section or subdivision: *the various branches of learning.* **4.** a local operating division of an organization. **5.** a line of family descent stemming from a particular ancestor; a division of a family. **6.** a tributary stream. **7.** *Linguistics.* (in the classification of related languages within a family) a category of a lower order than a subfamily and of a higher order than a subbranch or a group. Cf. **group** (def. 4a). **8.** *Computer Technol.* a point in a computer program where the computer selects one of two or more subroutines, according to the conditions of the program. **9.** See **branch water.** —*v.i.* **10.** to put forth branches; spread in branches. **11.** to diverge, as a branch from a tree trunk. —*v.t.* **12.** to divide, as into branches. **13.** to adorn with needlework or decorate with embroidery. **14. branch out,** to expand or extend, as business activities or pursuits. [ME *branch(e)* < OF *branche* < LL *branca* paw] —**branch′less,** *adj.* —**Syn. 1.** offshoot, shoot. BRANCH, BOUGH, LIMB refer to divisions of a tree. BRANCH is general, meaning either a large or a small division. BOUGH refers only to the larger branches: *a bough loaded with apples.* A LIMB is a large primary division of a tree trunk or of a bough: *to climb out on a limb.* **11.** ramify.

branched′ chain′, *Chem.* an open chain of atoms, usually carbon, with one or more side chains attached to it. Cf. **straight chain.**

branchi-, var. of **branchio-** before a vowel: *branchiate.*

bran·chi·a (braŋ′kē ə), *n., pl.* **-chi·ae** (-kē ē′). *Zool.* a gill. [< Gk: gills, pl. of *bránchion* fin] —**bran′chi·al,** *adj.*

bran·chi·ate (braŋ′kē it, -āt′), *adj. Zool.* having gills.

branchio-, a learned borrowing from Greek meaning "gills," used in the formation of compound words: *branchiopod.* Also, *esp. before a vowel,* **branchi-.** [comb. form repr. Gk *bránchia* BRANCHIA]

bran·chi·o·pod (braŋ′kē ə pod′), *n.* **1.** any crustacean of the subclass *Branchiopoda,* having gills on the feet. —*adj.* **2.** Also, **bran·chi·op·o·dous** (braŋ′kē op′ə dəs). belonging or pertaining to the *Branchiopoda.*

branch′ wa′ter, water in or from a branch, creek, stream, etc. Also called **branch.**

Bran·cu·si (bräŋ ko͞o′zē; *Rum.* bʀäŋ ko͞osh′), *n.* **Constan·tin** (kon′stən tin; *Rum.* kôn′stän tēn′), 1876–1957, Rumanian sculptor.

brand (brand), *n.* **1.** kind, grade, or make, as indicated by a stamp, trademark, or the like. **2.** a mark made by burning or otherwise, to indicate kind, grade, make, ownership, etc. **3.** any mark of infamy; stigma. **4.** an iron for branding. **5.** a burning or partly burned piece of wood. **6.** *Archaic.* a sword. —*v.t.* **7.** to mark with a brand. **8.** to mark with infamy; stigmatize. [ME, OE: burning, a burning piece of wood, torch, sword; c. D *brand,* G *Brand,* Icel *brandr;* akin to BURN[1]] —**brand′er,** *n.* —**brand′less,** *adj.*

Bran·deis (bran′dīs), *n.* **Louis Dem·bitz** (dem′bits), 1856–1941, U.S. lawyer and writer: associate justice of the U.S. Supreme Court 1916–39.

Bran·den·burg (bran′dən bûrg′; *Ger.* bʀän′dən bo͝oʀk′), *n.* **1.** a former province in E Germany. **2.** a city in central East Germany: former capital of Brandenburg province. 87,700 (est. 1959). —**Bran′den·burg′er,** *n.*

Bran·des (bʀän′dəs), *n.* **Ge·org Mor·ris** (gē ôʀg′ mō′ʀis), (*Georg Morris Cohen*), 1842–1927, Danish historian and literary critic.

bran·died (bran′dēd), *adj.* flavored, soaked in, or treated with brandy.

bran·dish (bran′dish), *v.t.* **1.** to shake or wave, as a weapon; flourish. —*n.* **2.** a wave or flourish, as of a weapon. [ME *bra(u)ndisshe(n)* < MF *brandiss-* (long s. of *brandir* < *brand* sword < Gmc)] —**bran′dish·er,** *n.*

brand·ling (brand′liŋ), *n.* a small, reddish-brown earthworm, *Ersenia foetida,* having yellow markings.

brand-new (brand′no͞o′, -nyo͞o′, bran′-), *adj.* entirely new. Also, **bran-new.** —**brand′-new′ness,** *n.*

Bran·don (bran′dən), *n.* a city in SW Manitoba, in S central Canada. 28,166 (1961).

Brandt (brant; *Ger.* bʀänt), *n.* **Wil·ly** (wil′ē; *Ger.* vil′ē), born 1913, West German political leader: chancellor 1969–74; Nobel peace prize 1971.

bran·dy (bran′dē), *n., pl.* **-dies,** *v.,* **-died, -dy·ing.** —*n.* **1.** a spirit distilled from the fermented juice of grapes, apples, peaches, plums, etc. —*v.t.* **2.** to mix, flavor, or preserve with brandy. [short for *brandywine* < D *brandewijn* burnt (i.e., distilled) wine]

Bran·dy·wine (bran′dē wīn′), *n.* a creek in SE Pennsylvania and N Delaware: British defeat of the Americans 1777.

branks (braŋks), *n.* (*construed as pl.*) a device to restrain the tongue, formerly used to punish a shrew or scold. [?]

bran-new (bran′no͞o′, -nyo͞o′), *adj.* brand-new.

bran·ni·gan (bran′ə gən), *n.* **1.** a carouse. **2.** a squabble; brawl. [prob. from proper name]

bran·ny (bran′ē), *adj.,* **-ni·er, -ni·est.** of, containing, or like bran.

Bran·stock (brän′stok′), *n.* (in the *Volsunga Saga*) an oak tree in the house of Volsung into which Odin, disguised as a traveler, thrusts the sword Gram, which only Sigmund can withdraw.

brant (brant), *n., pl.* **brants,** (*esp. collectively*), **brant.** any of several species of small, dark-colored geese of the genus *Branta,* esp. *B. bernicla,* breeding in high northern latitudes and migrating south in the autumn. Also called **brant′ goose′;** *Brit.,* **brent, brent goose.** [short for *brantgoose, brentgoose;* akin to Icel *brandgās,* G *Brandgans*]

Brant (brant), *n.* **Joseph** (native name, *Thayendanegea*), 1742–1807, Mohawk Indian chief who fought on the side of the British in the American Revolution.

Brant·ford (brant′fərd), *n.* a city in S Ontario, in SE Canada, near Lake Erie. 55,201 (1961).

Bran·ting (bran′tiŋ, brän′-), *n.* **Karl Hjal·mar** (kärl yäl′mär), 1860–1925, Swedish statesman: prime minister 1920, 1921–23, 1924–25: Nobel peace prize 1921.

Braque (bräk; *Fr.* bʀak), *n.* **Georges** (jôrj; *Fr.* zhôʀzh), 1882–1963, French painter.

brash (brash), *adj.* Also, **brashy. 1.** hasty; rash; impetuous. **2.** impertinent; impudent; tactless. **3.** (used esp. of wood) brittle. —*n.* **4.** a pile or stack of loose fragments or debris, as of rocks, clippings of hedges, etc. **5.** *Pathol.* heartburn (def. 1). **6.** any sudden, minor sickness or indisposition, esp. of the digestive tract. [(adj.) in sense of brittle < n.; in sense of hasty, by confusion with RASH[1]; (n.) late ME *brass(c)he* a slap, crash, perh. b. *brok(e)* (OE *broc* breach, fragment, sickness; akin to BREAK) and *dasch* smashing blow; see DASH[1]] —**brash′ly,** *adv.* —**brash′ness,** *n.*

brash·y (brash′ē), *adj.,* **brash·i·er, brash·i·est.** brash. —**brash′i·ness,** *n.*

bra·sier (brā′zhər), *n.* brazier.

bra·sil (brə sēl′, -sil′), *n.* brazil.

Bra·sil (*Port.* bʀä zēl′; *Sp.* bʀä sēl′), *n.* Portuguese and Spanish name of **Brazil.**

bra·sil·e·in (brə zil′ē in), *n. Chem.* brazilein.

Bra·síl·ia (bʀä zēl′yə), *n.* a city in and the capital of Brazil, on the central plateau. 540,000 (est. 1972).

bras·i·lin (braz′ə lin), *n. Chem.* brazilin.

Bra·şov (bʀä shôv′), *n.* a city in central Rumania. 137,231 (est. 1964). Hungarian, **Brassó.** German, **Kronstadt.** Formerly, **Stalin.**

brass (bras, bräs), *n.* **1.** any of various metal alloys consisting mainly of copper and zinc. **2.** an article made of such an alloy. **3.** *Mach.* a partial lining of soft metal for a bearing. **4.** *Music.* **a.** an instrument of the trumpet or horn family. **b.** such instruments collectively. **5.** *Brit.* **a.** a memorial tablet or plaque incised with an effigy, coat of arms, or the like. **b.** *Slang.* money. **6.** *Furniture.* any piece of ornamental or functional hardware. **7.** *U.S. Slang.* **a.** high-ranking military officers. **b.** any very important officials. **8.** *Informal.* excessive assurance; impudence; effrontery. —*adj.* **9.** of or pertaining to brass. [ME *bras,* OE *bræs;* c. OFris *bres* copper, MLG *bras* metal] —**brass′ish,** *adj.*

brass·age (bras′ij, brä′sij), *n.* a charge to cover the costs of coining money. [< F = *brass(er)* (to) stir (OF *bracier*) + *-age* -AGE]

bras·sard (bras′ärd), *n.* **1.** a badge worn around the upper arm. **2.** Also, **bras·sart** (bras′ärt). a piece of plate armor for protecting the arm. [< F = *bras* arm (see BRACE) + *-ard* -ARD]

brass′ band′, *Music.* a band made up principally of brass wind instruments.

brass·bound (bras′bound′, bräs′-), *adj.* **1.** having a frame or reinforcements strengthened or made rigid by brass, bronze, etc. **2.** rigid; unyielding; inflexible: *brassbound regulations.* **3.** impudent; brazen: *brassbound presumption.*

brass′ hat′, *Slang.* a high-ranking military officer.

bras·si·ca·ceous (bras′ə kā′shəs), *adj.* belonging to the family *Brassicaceae* (or *Cruciferae*), including the common cabbage, watercress, etc. [< NL *Brassicace(ae)* = *brassica* < L: cabbage + *-aceae* -ACEAE; see -OUS]

brass·ie (bras′ē, brä′sē), *n. Golf.* a club with a wooden head and a brass-plated face, for hitting long, low drives. Also, **brassy.**

bras·siere (brə zēr′), *n.* a woman's undergarment for supporting the breasts. Also, **bras·sière′.** Also called **bra.** [< F *brassière* = *bras* arm + *-ière* < L *-āria* -ER[2]]

brass′ knuck′les, a band of metal with four finger holes that fits over the root knuckles of the hand, used for increasing the effect of a blow from the fist.

Bras·só (bʀosh′shô), *n.* Hungarian name of **Braşov.**

brass′ tacks′, *Informal.* the essentials of a subject under discussion.

brass·y[1] (bras′ē, brä′sē), *adj.,* **brass·i·er, brass·i·est. 1.** made of or covered with brass. **2.** resembling brass. **3.** noisy or ostentatious. [BRASS + -Y[1]] —**brass′i·ly,** *adv.* —**brass′i·ness,** *n.*

brass·y[2] (bras′ē, brä′sē), *n., pl.* **brass·ies.** *Golf.* brassie.

brat (brat), *n.* a spoiled or impolite child (usually used in contempt or irritation). [perh. transferred use of *brat* rag, OE *bratt* cloak < Celt; cf. Ir *brat* outer garment, cloth] —**brat′tish,** *adj.*

Bra·ti·sla·va (bʀä′tyi slä′vä), *n.* a city in S Czechoslovakia, on the Danube River: a former capital of Hungary. 259,508 (est. 1963). Hungarian, **Pozsony.** German, **Pressburg.**

Brat·tain (brat′ᵊn), *n.* **Walter Hou·ser** (hou′zər), born 1902, U.S. physicist: Nobel prize 1956.

brat·tice (brat′is), *n., v.,* **-ticed, -tic·ing.** —*n.* **1.** a partition or lining, as of planks or cloth, forming an air passage in a mine. —*v.t.* **2.** to provide with a brattice; line with planks or cloth. [ME *bretax, bretask, bretice,* etc. < ML *bretescia, bratascia* < OE *brettisc* BRITISH]

brat·tle (brat′ᵊl), *n., v.,* **-tled, -tling.** —*n.* **1.** a clattering noise. —*v.i.* **2.** to scamper noisily. [imit; see RATTLE[1]]

brat·ty (brat′ē), *adj.,* **-ti·er, -ti·est.** characteristic of or resembling a brat; brattish.

Brau·haus (bʀou′hous′), *n., pl.* **-häu·ser** (-hoi′zəʀ). *German.* a tavern or brewery.

Braun (broun; *Ger.* bʀoun), *n.* **1. Karl Fer·di·nand** (kärl fûr′dᵊnand; *Ger.* käʀl feʀ′dē nänt), 1850–1918, German physicist: Nobel prize in physics 1909. **2. Wern·her von** (vär′nər von, vûr′-, wûr′-; *Ger.* veʀ′nəʀ fən), 1912–77, German rocket engineer, in the U.S. after 1945.

braun·ite (brou′nīt), *n.* a mineral, manganese oxide and silicate, Mn_7SiO_{12}: an ore of manganese. [named after A. E. *Braun* (1809–56), German official; see -ITE[1]]

Braun·schweig (bʀoun′shvīk′), *n.* German name of **Brunswick.**

Braun·schwei·ger (broun′shwī′gər; *Ger.* bʀoun′shvī′gəʀ), *n.* (*sometimes l.c.*) a spiced liver sausage, usually smoked. [< G]

bra·va·do (brə vä′dō), *n., pl.* **-does, -dos.** a pretentious, swaggering display of courage. [< Sp *bravada* (now *bravata* < It). See BRAVE, -ADE[1]] —**Syn.** bluster, braggadocio. See **courage.**

brave (brāv), *adj.,* **brav·er, brav·est,** *n., v.,* **braved, braving.** —*adj.* **1.** possessing or exhibiting courage or courageous endurance. **2.** making a fine appearance. **3.** *Archaic.* excellent; fine; admirable. —*n.* **4.** a brave person. **5.** a warrior, esp. among North American Indian tribes. —*v.t.* **6.** to meet or face courageously. **7.** to defy; challenge; dare. **8.** *Obs.* to make splendid. —*v.i.* **9.** *Obs.* to boast; brag. [late ME < MF < It *bravo,* perh. < VL **brabus* for L *barbarus* BARBAROUS] —**brave′ly,** *adv.* —**brave′ness,** *n.* —**Syn. 1.** bold, intrepid, daring, dauntless, heroic. BRAVE, COURAGEOUS, VALIANT, FEARLESS, GALLANT refer to confident bearing in the face of difficulties or dangers. BRAVE is the most comprehensive: it is especially used of that confident fortitude or daring that actively faces and endures anything threatening. COURAGEOUS implies a higher or nobler kind of bravery, esp. as resulting from an inborn quality of mind or spirit that faces or endures perils or difficulties without fear and even with enthusiasm. VALIANT implies a correspondence between an inner courageousness and external deeds, particularly of physical strength or endurance. FEARLESS implies unflinching spirit and coolness in the face of danger. GALLANT implies chivalrous, impetuous, dashing, or showy bravery. —**Ant. 1.** cowardly.

brav·er·y (brā′və rē, brāv′rē), *n., pl.* **-er·ies. 1.** brave spirit or conduct; courage; valor. **2.** showiness; splendor; magnificence. [prob. < It *braveria* = *brav(are)* (to) BRAVE + *-eria* -ERY] —**Syn. 1.** intrepidity, fearlessness, boldness, daring, heroism. See **courage.** —**Ant. 1.** cowardice.

bra·vis·si·mo (brä vis′ə mō′; *It.* bʀä vēs′sē mô), *interj.* excellently done! splendid! [< It, superl. of BRAVO]

bra·vo (brä′vō, brä vō′), *interj., n., pl.* **-vos** for 2, 3, **-voes** for 3, *v.,* **-voed, -vo·ing.** —*interj.* **1.** well done! good! —*n.* **2.**

a shout of "bravo!" **3.** a hired bandit or assassin. **4.** a word used in communications to represent the letter *B.* —*v.t.* **5.** to shout "bravo!" in approbation of (something). —*v.i.* **6.** to shout "bravo!" [< It; see BRAVE]

bra·vu·ra (brə vyŏŏr′ə; *It.* brä vōō′rä), *n., pl.* **-ras,** *It.* **-re** (-re). **1.** *Music.* a florid passage or piece requiring great skill and spirit in the performer. **2.** a display of daring; brilliant performance. [< It: spirit, dash. See BRAVE, -URE]

braw (brô, brä; *Scot.* brô, brä), *adj.* *Scot. and North Eng.* **1.** fine or fine-looking; excellent. **2.** dressed in a splendid or gaudy fashion. [var. of BRAVE] —**braw′ly, braw′lie,** *adv.*

brawl (brôl), *n.* **1.** a noisy quarrel, squabble, or fight. **2.** a bubbling or roaring noise; a clamor. —*v.i.* **3.** to quarrel angrily and noisily; wrangle. **4.** to flow noisily, as turbulent water. [ME *bral(l), brawl* bully, var. of *broll* brat, wretch contr. of *brothel.* See BROTHEL] —**brawl′er,** *n.* —**Syn. 1.** wrangle, row, altercation. See **disorder. 3.** squabble, fight.

brawn (brôn), *n.* **1.** well-developed muscles. **2.** muscular strength. **3.** a boar's or swine's flesh, esp. when boiled and pickled. [ME *brawne* < OF *braon* slice of flesh (Pr *bradon*) < Gmc; cf. G *Braten* joint of meat, akin to OE *brǣd* flesh]

brawn·y (brô′nē), *adj.* **brawn·i·er, brawn·i·est.** muscular; strong. —**brawn′i·ly,** *adv.* —**brawn′i·ness,** *n.*

bray[1] (brā), *n.* **1.** a harsh, breathy cry, as of a donkey. **2.** any similar loud, harsh sound. —*v.i.* **3.** to utter a loud and harsh cry, as a donkey. **4.** to make a loud, harsh, disagreeable sound. —*v.t.* **5.** to utter with a loud, harsh sound, like a donkey. [ME *braye(n)* < OF *braire* to cry out (c. ML *bragire* to neigh) < Celt; cf. OIr *braigim* I break wind]

bray[2] (brā), *v.t.* **1.** to pound or crush fine, as in a mortar. **2.** *Print.* to thin (ink) on a slate before placing it on the ink plate of a press. [ME *braye(n)* < AF, OF *breier* < Gmc; see BREAK]

bray·er (brā′ər), *n.* *Print.* a small roller for inking type by hand.

Braz., 1. Brazil. **2.** Brazilian.

bra·za (brä′thä, -sä), *n., pl.* **-zas** (-thäs, -säs). a unit of length in some Spanish-speaking countries, representing the reach of outspread arms, officially 5.48 U.S. feet in Spain, and 5.68 U.S. feet in Argentina. [< Sp < L *brāchia* the two arms (neut. pl.), taken as fem. sing.; see BRACHIUM]

braze[1] (brāz), *v.t.,* **brazed, braz·ing. 1.** to make of brass. **2.** to cover or ornament with or as with brass. [ME *brase(n),* OE *brǣsian;* see BRASS]

braze[2] (brāz), *v.t.,* **brazed, braz·ing.** *Metall.* to unite (metal objects), usually over a hearth, by soldering with materials, as of copper or zinc, that have a high melting point. [< F *brase(r)* (to) solder (MF), burn (OF) < Gmc; cf. Sw *brasa,* Dan *brase* to roast; see BRAISE] —**braz′er,** *n.*

bra·zen (brā′zən), *adj.* **1.** made of brass. **2.** like brass, as in color or strength. **3.** shameless or impudent. —*v.t.* **4.** to make brazen or bold. **5. brazen out** or **through,** to face (a challenge or rebuke) boldly or shamelessly. [ME *brasen* (adj.), OE *brǣsen* of BRASS] —**bra′zen·ly,** *adv.* —**bra′zen·ness,** *n.* —**Syn. 2, 3.** brassy. **3.** insolent, defiant. See **bold.** —**Ant. 3.** shy.

bra·zen-faced (brā′zən fāst′), *adj.* openly shameless; impudent. —**bra·zen-fac·ed·ly** (brā′zən fā′sid lē, -fāst′-), *adv.*

bra·zier[1] (brā′zhər), *n.* a person who makes articles of brass. Also, **brasier.** [ME *brasier* = OE *brǣsi(an)* (to) work in brass + *-er* -ER[1]]

bra·zier[2] (brā′zhər), *n.* **1.** a metal receptacle for holding live coals, as for heating a room. **2.** a container for live coals covered by a grill, used esp. for cooking meat. Also, **brasier.** [earlier *brasier* < F. See BRAISE, -ER[2]]

bra·zil (brə zil′), *n.* **1.** a dyewood from various tropical American trees of the genus *Caesalpinia,* esp. *C. echinata,* and allied genera, yielding reds and purples. **2.** the red dye extracted from it. **3.** a hard, East Indian dyewood yielding a red color, from the tree *Caesalpinia sappan.* Also, **brasil.** Also called **brazilwood.** [ME *brasile* < ML < It < Sp *brasil* < *brasa* live coal (the wood being red in color) < Gmc; see BRAISE]

Bra·zil (brə zil′), *n.* a republic in South America. 123,000,000; 3,286,170 sq. mi. *Cap.:* Brasília. Portuguese and Spanish, **Brasil.** Official name, **United States of Brazil.** —**Bra·zil·ian** (brə zil′ yən), *adj., n.*

bra·zil·e·in (brə zil′ē in), *n.* *Chem.* a red solid, $C_{16}H_{12}O_5$, used chiefly as a dye for wood and textiles. Also, **brasilein.** [BRAZIL(IN) + *-ein,* var. of -IN[2]]

bra·zil·ian·ite (brə zil′yə nīt′), *n.* a mineral, sodium aluminum phosphate, $Na_2Al_6P_4O_{16}(OH)_8$, used as a gem [BRAZILIAN (after the place of origin) + -ITE[1]]

Brazil′ian rhat′any. See under **rhatany** (def. 1).

braz·i·lin (braz′ə lin, brə zil′in), *n.* *Chem.* a yellow solid, $C_{16}H_{14}O_5$, used as a dye and an indicator. Also, **brasilin.**

Brazil′ nut′, the triangular edible seed of the tree *Bertholletia excelsa* and related species, of South America.

bra·zil·wood (brə zil′wŏŏd′), *n.* brazil.

Bra·zos (brä′zōs; *locally* braz′əs, brā′zəs), *n.* a river flowing SE from N Texas to the Gulf of Mexico. 870 mi. long.

Braz·za·ville (braz′ə vil′; *Fr.* bra za vēl′), *n.* a port in and the capital of the People's Republic of the Congo, in the S part, on the Congo River: former capital of French Equatorial Africa. 290,000.

breach (brēch), *n.* **1.** the act or a result of breaking; break or rupture. **2.** a gap made in a wall, fortification, line of soldiers, etc. **3.** an infraction or violation, as of a law, trust or promise. **4.** a severance of friendly relations. **5.** the leap of a whale above the surface of the water. **6.** *Archaic.* the breaking of waves or the dashing of surf. **7.** *Obs.* wound[1]. —*v.t.* **8.** to make a breach or opening in. **9.** to break (a law, promise, etc.). —*v.i.* **10.** (of a whale) to leap above the surface of the water. [ME *breche,* OE *bræc* breaking; see BREAK] —**breach′er,** *n.* —**Syn. 1.** fracture. **2.** crack, rent, opening. **4.** alienation, split, rift; dissension, dispute.

breach′ of prom′ise, *Law.* a violation of one's promise, esp. of one to marry a specific person.

bread (bred), *n.* **1.** a food made of baked dough or batter. **2.** such a food as a symbol of one's livelihood; sustenance. **3.** *Slang.* money. **4. break bread,** to eat a meal, esp. in companionable association with others. **5. know which side one's bread is buttered on,** to be aware of what is to one's advantage. —*v.t.* **6.** *Cookery.* to cover or coat with bread crumbs or meal. [ME *breed,* OE *brēad* fragment, morsel, bread; c. G *Brot*] —**bread′less,** *adj.*

bread′ and but′ter, 1. bread spread with butter. **2.** *Informal.* a source of livelihood; sustenance.

bread-and-but·ter (bred′ən but′ər), *adj.* **1.** providing the basic means of self-support, as a job. **2.** practical; realistic. **3.** expressing thanks for hospitality, as a letter.

bread·bas·ket (bred′bas′kit, -bä′skit), *n.* **1.** a basket for bread or rolls. **2.** an agricultural area that provides large amounts of grain. **3.** *Slang.* a person's stomach. or midsection

bread·board (bred′bōrd′, -bôrd′), *n.* **1.** a slab of wood on which dough is kneaded and bread is sliced. **2.** *Elect.* an experimental assembly of electronic and electric components for a proposed circuit for testing and evaluating their arrangement.

bread·fruit (bred′frōōt′), *n., pl.* **-fruits,** (*esp. collectively*) **-fruit. 1.** a large, round, starchy fruit borne by a moraceous tree, *Artocarpus communis* (*A. altilis*), native to the Pacific islands, used, baked or roasted, for food. **2.** the tree bearing this fruit.

Breadfruit (Diameter of fruit, 5 in.)

bread′ mold′, any fungus of the family *Mucoraceae,* esp. *Rhizopus nigricans,* that forms a black, furry coating on foodstuffs. Also called **black mold.**

bread·nut (bred′nut′), *n.* the round, yellow or brown fruit of a tropical tree, *Brosimum Alicastrum,* used, roasted or boiled, as a substitute for bread in the West Indies.

bread·root (bred′rōōt′, -rŏŏt′), *n.* the edible root of *Psoralea esculenta,* a fabaceous plant of central North America.

bread·stuff (bred′stuf′), *n.* **1.** grain, flour, or meal for making bread. **2. breadstuffs,** bread or rolls.

breadth (bredth, bretth), *n.* **1.** the measure of the side-to-side dimension of a plane or solid figure. **2.** a piece of something of definite or full width or as measured by its width: *a breadth of cloth.* **3.** freedom from narrowness, as of viewpoint or interests. **4.** size in general; extent. **5.** *Art.* a general effect involving subordination of details or nonessentials. [earlier *bredeth* = *brede* breadth (ME, OE *brǣdu: brǣd-,* mutated var. of *brād* BROAD + *-u* n. suffix) + -TH[1]; akin to G *Breite,* Goth *braidei*] —**breadth′less,** *adj.*

breadth·ways (bredth′wāz′, bretth′-), *adv.* in the direction of the breadth. Also, **breadth·wise** (bredth′wīz′, bretth′-).

bread·win·ner (bred′win′ər), *n.* a person who earns a livelihood for himself and those dependent upon him. —**bread′win′ning,** *n.*

break (brāk), *v.,* **broke** or (*Archaic*) **brake, bro·ken** or (*Archaic*) **broke; break·ing;** *n.* —*v.t.* **1.** to injure so as to crack or divide. **2.** to injure so as to render useless. **3.** to twist or wrench away from something (often fol. by *off*). **4.** to burst or pierce, as a blister or the skin. **5.** to interrupt (a continuous action). **6.** to terminate (a continuous action) (sometimes fol. by *off*): *to break off negotiations.* **7.** to divide into component elements or parts. **8.** to end or impair the otherwise complete or perfect condition of. **9.** to fracture a bone in. **10.** to reveal or make public at a certain time, as news. **11.** to tame or train to obedience, as an animal. **12.** to train away from a habit (often fol. by *of*). **13.** to overcome emotionally or master. **14.** to find the truth or meaning of (something doubtful or puzzling): *to break a code.* **15.** to bankrupt. **16.** to reduce in rank. **17.** to weaken the direct impact of. **18.** to outdo or surpass: *to break the record for the high jump.* **19.** to escape from, esp. by force: *to break jail.* **20.** to overwhelm (the heart) with grief or compassion. **21.** to violate or disregard: *to break the law; to break training.* **22.** *Law.* **a.** to force one's way into (a dwelling, store, etc.). **b.** to contest (a will) successfully by judicial action. **23.** *Pool.* to cause (racked billiard balls) to scatter by striking with the cue ball. **24.** *Naut.* to unfurl (a flag) suddenly by an easily released knot after hoisting it secured in a furled position. **25.** to open the breech or action of (a shotgun, rifle, or revolver), as by snapping open the hinge between the barrel and the butt. —*v.i.* **26.** to become cracked or divided through injury. **27.** to become useless through injury. **28.** to become detached or separated (usually fol. by *away* or *off*). **29.** to be discontinued or interrupted (often fol. by *off*). **30.** to subdivide itself (usually fol. by *into*). **31.** to burst. **32.** to intrude or force oneself or itself (usually fol. by *in, in upon, into,* or *through*). **33.** to emit a sound, an expression of feeling, etc. (usually fol. by *into*). **34.** (of a sound, expression of feeling, etc.) to be emitted suddenly. **35.** (of a natural phenomenon, illness, event, etc.) to happen or manifest itself suddenly. **36.** to appear, as a light or the dawn. **37.** to become public, as news. **38.** to make a sudden dash. **39.** to escape (usually fol. by *away*). **40.** to fail, as one's health, resistance, or spirit. **41.** to cease to resist coercion or adversity. **42.** to subside, as a spell of weather. **43.** (of the heart) to be overwhelmed by grief or compassion. **44.** (of the voice) to change pitch suddenly or unpleasantly. **45.** (of value or prices) to drop sharply and considerably. **46.** *Music.* **a.** to change or go from one register to another, as a musical instrument or the voice. **b.** to change or be interrupted, as a voice or tone. **47.** (of a horse in a harness race) to fail to keep to a trot or pace, as by starting to gallop. **48.** *Linguistics.* to undergo breaking. **49.** *Billiards, Pool.* to make a break; take the first turn in a game. **50.** *Boxing.* to step back or separate from a clinch. **51. break camp,** to pack up equipment and resume a journey or march. **52. break down, a.** to become ineffective. **b.** to abandon resistance or self-control. **c.** to cease to function. **d.** *Elect.* (of an insulator) to fail, as when subjected to excessively high voltage, permitting a current to pass. **e.** to decompose. **f.** to analyze. **g.** to classify. **53. break even,** to finish a business transaction, series of games, etc., with no loss or gain in money or prestige. **54. break ground,** to begin construction, esp. of a building. **55. break in, a.** to enter enclosed property by force or cunning. **b.** to train: *The boss is breaking in a new*

assistant. **c.** to begin to wear or use: *to break in a new pair of shoes.* **56. break into, a.** to enter (a profession or activity). **b.** to enter by force or cunning. **57. break out, a.** to begin abruptly; arise: *An epidemic broke out.* **b.** *Pathol.* (of certain diseases) to appear in eruptions. **c.** (of a person) to manifest a skin eruption. **d.** to take out of storage for use. **e.** to escape, as from confinement. **58. break up, a.** to separate; scatter. **b.** to put an end to; discontinue. **c.** to dissolve. **d.** to disrupt; upset. **e.** (of a personal relationship) to come to an end. **f.** to end a personal relationship. **g.** to be or cause to be overcome with laughter. **59. break with,** to sever relations with; separate from. —*n.* **60.** the act of breaking or an instance of being broken. **61.** a crack or opening made by breaking: *a break in the plaster.* **62.** the act or an instance of severing relations with a person, thing, tradition, etc. **63.** an interruption in a continuous action. **64.** a brief respite or rest. **65.** a sudden dash, as in making an escape. **66.** *Informal.* **a.** a stroke of luck. **b.** a chance to improve one's lot, esp. one unlooked for or undeserved. **67.** an abrupt change of direction, pitch, etc. **68.** *Pros.* a pause or caesura. **69.** *Jazz.* a solo passage, usually of from 2 to 12 bars, during which the rest of the instruments are silent. **70.** *Music.* the point in the scale where the quality of voice of one register changes to that of another. **71.** a sharp and considerable drop in prices. **72.** *Elect.* an opening or discontinuity in a circuit. **73.** *Print.* **a.** one or more blank lines between two paragraphs. **b. breaks.** See **suspension points. 74.** the place, after a letter, where a word is or may be divided at the end of a line. **75.** *Billiards, Pool.* a series of successful strokes; run. **76.** *Pool.* the opening play, in which the cue ball is shot to scatter the other balls. **77.** *Sports.* a change in direction of a pitched or bowled ball. **78.** *Horse Racing, Track.* the start of a race. **79.** (in harness racing) the act or an instance of a horse's changing from a trot or pace into a gallop or other step. **80.** *Bowling.* a failure to knock down all 10 pins after bowling twice. **81.** *Boxing.* the act or an instance of stepping back or separating from a clinch. **82.** *Naut.* the place at which a superstructure, deckhouse, or the like, rises from the main deck of a vessel. [ME *breke(n)* (v.), OE *brecan;* c. D *breken,* G *brechen,* Goth *brikan;* akin to L *frangere;* see FRAGILE] —**break′a·ble,** *adj.* —**break′a·ble·ness,** *n.*
—**Syn. 1.** fracture, splinter, shiver. BREAK, CRUSH, SHATTER, SMASH mean to reduce to parts, violently or by force. BREAK means to divide by means of a blow, a collision, a pull, or the like. To CRUSH is to subject to (usually heavy or violent) pressure so as to press out of shape or reduce to shapelessness or to small particles. To SHATTER is to break in such a way as to cause the pieces to fly in many directions. To SMASH is to break noisily and suddenly into many pieces. **5.** disrupt.

break·age (brā′kij), *n.* **1.** the act of breaking. **2.** the state of being broken. **3.** the amount or value of things broken: *What was the breakage in that shipment?* **4.** *Com.* an allowance for articles broken, as in transit.

break′bone fe′ver (brāk′bōn′), *Pathol.* dengue. [BREAK + BONE, so called because it makes the bones ache as if breaking at the joints]

break′ danc′ing, a style of dancing often performed to rap music and marked typically by intricate footwork, pantomime, spinning headstands, and tumbling. —**break′ danc′er.**

break·down (brāk′doun′), *n.* **1.** a breaking down, as of a machine or of physical or mental capacities; collapse. **2.** *Chem.* **a.** decomposition. **b.** analysis. **3.** a division into categories; classification.

break·er[1] (brā′kər), *n.* **1.** a person or thing that breaks. **2.** a wave that breaks into foam. **3.** *Textiles.* a machine that separates the fiber from foreign matter prior to carding. **4.** Also called **prairie breaker.** a plow with a long, low moldboard for turning virgin land. [ME] —**Syn. 2.** See **wave.**

break·er[2] (brā′kər), *n.* *Naut.* a small water cask. [said to be alter. of Sp *bareca,* var. of *barrica* small keg]

break-e·ven (brāk′ē′vən), *adj.* having income exactly equal to expenditure or costs, thus showing neither profit nor loss.

break·fast (brek′fəst), *n.* **1.** the first meal of the day; morning meal. **2.** the food eaten at this meal. —*v.i.* **3.** to eat breakfast. [late ME *brekfast*] —**break′fast·er,** *n.*

break′fast food′, a cold or hot cereal eaten chiefly for breakfast.

break·front (brāk′frunt′), *adj.* **1.** (of a cabinet, bookcase, etc.) having a central section extending forward from those at either side. —*n.* **2.** a cabinet or the like having such a front. Also, **break′-front′.**

break-in (brāk′in′), *n.* **1.** an illegal entry into a home, car, office, or the like. **2.** initial stage of operation or use.

break·ing (brā′king), *n.* the change of a pure vowel to a diphthong in certain environments, as, in Old English, the change of a vowel to a diphthong under the influence of a following consonant or combination of consonants, as the change of *-a-* to *-ea-* and of *-e-* to *-eo-* before preconsonantal *r* or *l* and before *h,* as in *earm* "arm" developed from *arm,* and *eorthe* "earth" from *erthe.* [trans. of G *Brechung*]

break′ing and en′tering, *Crim. Law.* forcible entry into the home or office of another.

break·neck (brāk′nek′), *adj.* (of speed) dangerously excessive.

break′ of day′, dawn; daybreak.

break·out (brāk′out′), *n.* **1.** an escape, often by force, as from a prison or mental institution. **2.** an appearance, as of a disease, that is sudden and often widespread.

break·point (brāk′point′), *n.* a convenient point at which to make a change, interruption, or the like.

break·through (brāk′thro͞o′), *n.* **1.** *Mil.* a movement or advance through and beyond an enemy's defensive system into the unorganized areas in the rear. **2.** a significant development or action in scientific knowledge, diplomacy, etc., that removes a barrier to progress.

break·up (brāk′up′), *n.* **1.** disintegration; disruption; dispersal. **2.** (in Alaska and Canada) the melting and loosening of ice in rivers and harbors during the early spring. **3.** a separation, as between friends or a married couple.

break·wa·ter (brāk′wô′tər, -wot′ər), *n.* a barrier that breaks the force of waves, as before a harbor.

bream[1] (brēm), *n., pl.* (*esp. collectively*) **bream,** (*esp. referring to two or more kinds or species*) **breams. 1.** any of various fresh-water cyprinoid fishes of the genus *Abramis,* as *A. brama,* of Europe, with a compressed, deep body. **2.** any of various related and similar fishes. **3.** any of several porgies, as the sea bream, *Archosargus rhomboidalis.* **4.** any of several fresh-water sunfishes of the genus *Lepomis.* [ME *breme* < MF; OF *bresme* < Gmc; cf. OHG *brahsema,* D *brasem*]

bream[2] (brēm), *v.t.* *Naut.* to clean (a ship's bottom) by applying burning furze, reeds, etc., to soften the pitch and loosen adherent matter. [< MD *brem(e)* furze]

breast (brest), *n.* **1.** *Anat., Zool.* the outer front part of the thorax, or the front part of the body from the neck to abdomen; chest. **2.** *Zool.* the corresponding part in lower animals. **3.** *Anat., Zool.* either of two projecting, milk-secreting organs on the front of the thorax of a woman or certain female mammals. **4.** either of two flat organs on the front of the thorax of a man, usually having no anatomical function. **5.** the part of a garment that covers the chest. **6.** the bosom conceived of as the center of thought and feeling. **7.** a projection from a wall, as part of a chimney. **8.** *Mining.* the face or heading at which the work is going on. **9. make a clean breast of,** to confess. —*v.t.* **10.** to meet or oppose with the breast; confront. **11.** to contend with or advance against. **12.** to climb or climb over (a mountain, obstacle, etc.). **13.** to come alongside or abreast of. [ME *brest,* OE *brēost;* c. Icel *brjōst;* akin to G *Brust,* Goth *brusts,* D *borst*] —**breast′less,** *adj.*

breast-beat·ing (brest′bē′ting), *n.* **1.** a display of highly vocal and self-conscious emotionalism, remorse, or the like. —*adj.* **2.** characterized by or involving breast-beating. —**breast′-beat′er,** *n.*

breast·bone (brest′bōn′), *n.* the sternum. [ME *brustbon,* OE *breostban*]

breast-feed (brest′fēd′), *v.t.,* **-fed, -feed·ing.** to nurse (a baby) at the breast; suckle.

breast·pin (brest′pin′), *n.* a pin worn on the breast or at the throat; brooch.

breast·plate (brest′plāt′), *n.* **1.** a piece of plate armor for the front of the torso. **2.** the part of the harness that runs across the chest of a saddle horse. **3.** *Judaism.* a vestment ornamented with 12 precious stones, representing the 12 tribes of Israel, and worn on the chest by the high priest. Ex. 28:15–28. [ME *brestplate*]

breast·stroke (brest′strōk′), *n.* *Swimming.* a stroke made in the prone position in which both hands move simultaneously forward, outward, and rearward from in front of the chest while the legs move in a frog kick.

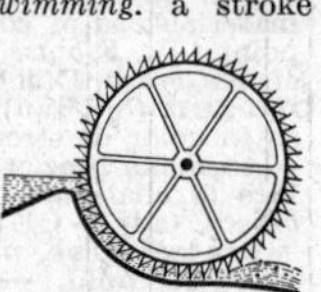
Breast wheel

breast′ wheel′, a water wheel onto which the propelling water is fed at the height of a horizontal axle.

breast·work (brest′wûrk′), *n.* *Fort.* a hastily constructed defensive work, usually breast high.

breath (breth), *n.* **1.** *Physiol.* the air inhaled and exhaled in respiration. **2.** respiration, esp. as necessary to life. **3.** life; vitality. **4.** the ability to breathe easily and normally. **5.** a pause or respite to recover one's breathing. **6.** a single inhalation or respiration. **7.** the brief time required for a single respiration; an instant. **8.** the slightest suggestion; whisper: *not a breath of scandal.* **9.** a light current of air. **10.** *Phonet.* **a.** the air drawn into or expelled from the lungs to provide the generative source for most speech sounds. **b.** the audible expiration generating voiceless speech sounds, as *p, k, sh,* etc. **11.** moisture emitted in respiration. **12.** an odorous exhalation, or the air impregnated by it. **13.** *Obs.* odor; vapor. **14. below** or **under one's breath,** in a low voice or whisper; sotto voce. **15. in the same breath,** at once; immediately. **16. save one's breath,** to avoid futile discussion. **17. take away one's breath,** to make one as if breathless with astonishment. Also, **take one's breath away.** [ME *breth, breeth,* OE *brǣth* smell, exhalation; akin to G *Brodem* vapor]

Breath·a·lyz·er (breth′ə lī′zər), *n.* *Trademark.* an instrument consisting of a small bag or tube filled with chemically treated crystals, into which a sample of a motorist's breath is taken as a test for intoxication.

breathe (brēth), *v.,* **breathed** (brēthd), **breath·ing.** —*v.i.* **1.** to inhale and exhale air, oxygen, or the like, in respiration. **2.** to pause, as to rest or recover one's breath. **3.** (in speech) to control the outgoing breath in producing voice and speech sounds. **4.** to stir gently, as a breeze. **5.** to live; exist. **6.** to exhale an odor. —*v.t.* **7.** to inhale and exhale in respiration. **8.** to exhale. **9.** to whisper. **10.** to inject as if by breathing; infuse: *She breathed life into the party.* **11.** to allow (a horse or other animal) to rest or recover breath. **12. breathe freely,** to have relief from anxiety or tension. Also, **breathe easily, breathe easy. 13. breathe one's last,** to die. [ME *brethe(n)*] —**breath′a·ble,** *adj.*

breathed (bretht, brēthd), *adj.* *Phonet.* **1.** not phonated; voiceless. **2.** utilizing the breath exclusively in the production of a speech sound. [ME *brethed*]

breath·er (brē′thər), *n.* **1.** a pause, as for breath. **2.** a person who breathes, as in a particular way. **3.** a vent in a container or covering. **4.** a device for providing air from the atmosphere to submerged or otherwise sealed-off persons, combustion engines, etc. [ME *brethere*]

breath·ing (brē′thing), *n.* **1.** the act of a person or thing that breathes. **2.** a single breath, or the time for this. **3.** a pause, as for breath. **4.** utterance or words. **5.** aspiration or longing. **6.** a gentle stirring, as of a breeze. **7.** *Class. Gk. Gram.* **a.** the manner of articulating the beginning of a word written with an initial vowel sign, with or without aspiration before the vowel. **b.** one of the two symbols used to indicate this. Cf. **rough breathing, smooth breathing.** [ME *brethynge*] —**breath′ing·ly,** *adv.*

breath′ing space′, 1. Also called **breath′ing spell′.** an opportunity to rest or think. **2.** sufficient space in which to move, work, etc.

breath·less (breth′lis), *adj.* **1.** deprived of breath. **2.** with the breath held, as in suspense. **3.** causing suspension of breath, as from excitement. **4.** dead; lifeless. **5.** motionless; still, as air. [ME *brethles*] —**breath′less·ly,** *adv.* —**breath′less·ness,** *n.*

breath-tak·ing (breth′tā′king), *adj.* causing extreme pleasure, awe, or excitement. Also, **breath′tak′ing.**

breath·y (breth′ē), *adj.*, **breath·i·er, breath·i·est.** (of the voice) characterized by excessive emission of breath. —**breath′i·ness,** *n.*

brec·ci·a (brech′ē ə, bresh′-), *n.* rock composed of angular fragments of older rocks melded together. [< It < Gmc; cf. OHG *brecha* breaking] —**brec′ci·al,** *adj.*

brec·ci·ate (brech′ē āt′, bresh′-), *v.t.*, **-at·ed, -at·ing.** to form as breccia. —**brec′ci·a′tion,** *n.*

Brecht (brekt; *Ger.* brekht), *n.* **Ber·tolt** (ber′tōlt), 1898–1956, German dramatist and poet.

Breck·in·ridge (brek′ən rij′), *n.* **John Cabell,** 1821–75, vice president of the U.S. 1857–61: Confederate general in the American Civil War.

Breck·nock·shire (brek′nək shēr′, -shər), *n.* a county in S Wales. 55,544 (1961). 733 sq. mi. *Co. seat:* Brecon. Also called **Breck′nock, Brec·on** (brek′ən).

bred (bred), *v.* pt. and pp. of **breed.**

Bre·da (brā dä′), *n.* a city in the S Netherlands. 113,193 (1962).

brede (brēd), *n. Archaic.* a braid.

bree (brē), *n. Scot. and North Eng.* broo. [late ME *bre*, alter. of earlier *brī*, OE *brīg*, var. of *brīw* pottage; c. D *brij*, G *Brei*]

breech (*n.* brēch; *v.* brēch, brich), *n.* **1.** the lower, rear part of the trunk of the body; buttocks. **2.** the hinder or lower part of anything. **3.** *Ordn.* the rear part of the bore of a gun, esp. the opening and associated mechanism that permits insertion of a projectile. **4.** *Mach.* the bottom of a block or pulley. —*v.t.* **5.** *Ordn.* to fit or furnish (a gun) with a breech. **6.** to clothe with breeches. [ME *breeche*, OE *brēc*, pl. of *brōc*, c. Icel *brōk*, OHG *bruoh*, L *brācae* trousers; see BROGUE[2]]

breech·block (brēch′blok′), *n. Ordn.* a movable piece of metal for closing the breech in certain firearms. Also, **breech′-block′.**

breech·cloth (brēch′klôth′, -kloth′), *n., pl.* **-cloths** (-klôthz′, -klothz′, -klôths′, -kloths′). a cloth worn about the breech and loins; loincloth. Also, **breech-clout** (brēch′klout′).

breech′ deliv′ery, *Obstet.* the delivery of an infant with the feet or breech appearing first.

breech·es (brich′iz), *n.* (*construed as pl.*) **1.** Also called **knee breeches.** men's or boys' knee-length trousers. **2.** See **riding breeches. 3.** *Informal.* trousers. [pl. of BREECH]

breech′es bu′oy, *Naut.* a rescue device consisting of a life buoy from which is suspended a canvas sling, similar in form to a pair of breeches, in which shipwrecked or disabled persons are hauled from a vessel by means of a rope.

Breeches buoy

breech·ing (brich′ing, brē′ching), *n.* **1.** the part of a harness that passes around the haunches of a horse. **2.** *Navy.* (formerly) a strong rope fastened to a ship's side for securing a gun or checking its recoil.

breech·load·er (brēch′lō′dər), *n. Ordn.* a firearm, as a rifle, loaded at the breech.

breech·load·ing (brēch′lō′ding), *adj. Ordn.* loaded at the breech.

breed (brēd), *v.*, **bred, breed·ing,** *n.* —*v.t.* **1.** to produce (offspring). **2.** to cause to be born. **3.** *Hort.* to improve by controlled pollination and selection. **4.** to raise for use, as a plant or animal. **5.** to engender or give rise to. **6.** to be a fertile or native area for. **7.** to develop by environment and education. **8.** to render (an animal) pregnant. —*v.i.* **9.** to produce offspring. **10.** to be engendered or produced. **11.** to procure the birth of young, as in raising stock. **12.** to be pregnant. —*n.* **13.** *Genetics.* a relatively homogenous group of animals within a species, developed and maintained by man. **14.** race; lineage; strain. **15.** sort; kind; group. **16.** *Offensive.* half-breed (def. 2). [ME *brede(n)* (v.), OE *brēdan* to nourish (c. OHG *bruotan*, G *brüten*)] —**breed′a·ble,** *adj.* —**Syn. 1, 2.** beget, bear, produce, generate. **7.** raise, nurture. **14.** family, pedigree, line, stock.

breed·er (brē′dər), *n.* **1.** a person or thing that produces offspring or reproduces. **2.** a person who breeds animals or plants. **3.** Also called **breed′er reac′tor.** *Physics.* a nuclear reactor in which a fissionable element is produced by bombarding a nonfissionable element with neutrons from a radioactive element.

breed·ing (brē′ding), *n.* **1.** the act of a person or thing that breeds. **2.** the improvement of livestock by selective mating and hybridization. **3.** *Hort.* the production of new forms by selection, crossing, and hybridizing. **4.** training; nurture. **5.** manners, esp. good manners. **6.** *Physics.* the production of fissionable material by the nuclear fission of a second material, in a process in which more fissionable material is produced than consumed. Cf. **conversion** (def. 12). [ME]

Breed's′ Hill′ (brēdz), a hill adjoining Bunker Hill, where the Battle of Bunker Hill was actually fought.

breeze[1] (brēz), *n., v.*, **breezed, breez·ing.** —*n.* **1.** a light wind or current of air. **2.** *Informal.* an easy task. **3. bat** or **shoot the breeze,** *Slang.* **a.** to converse aimlessly. **b.** to talk nonsense or exaggerate. —*v.i.* **4.** (of the wind) to blow a breeze (usually used impersonally with *it* as subject): *It breezed from the west all day.* **5.** to move in a carefree or jaunty manner. **6.** *Informal.* to progress quickly and easily (often fol. by *along, into,* or *through*): *The car breezed along the highway. He breezed through the work in an hour.* [earlier *brize* < OSp *briza*, Sp *brisa*, name of a Central and South American trade wind] —**breeze′less,** *adj.* —**breeze′-like′,** *adj.* —**Syn. 1.** See **wind**[1].

breeze[2] (brēz), *n. Brit.* **1.** a pile of cinders; bed of ashes. **2.** dust from coal, coke, or charcoal. **3.** a pile of small particles of or siftings from coal, coke, or charcoal. [var. of dial. *brays* < F *braise* live coals, cinders; see BRAZE[2]]

breeze·way (brēz′wā′), *n.* a porch or roofed passageway with open sides, for connecting two buildings, as a house and a garage.

breez·y (brē′zē), *adj.*, **breez·i·er, breez·i·est. 1.** abounding in breezes; windy. **2.** fresh; sprightly. —**breez′i·ly,** *adv.* —**breez′i·ness,** *n.*

Bre·genz (brā′gents), *n.* a city in W Austria, on the Lake of Constance. 78,729 (1961).

breg·ma (breg′mə), *n., pl.* **-ma·ta** (-mə tə). *Anat.* the junction point of the sagittal and coronal sutures of the skull. [< Gk: front of the head] —**breg·mat·ic** (breg-mat′ik), **breg·mate** (breg′māt), *adj.*

Brem·en (brem′ən; *Ger.* brā′mən), *n.* a port in N West Germany, on the Weser River: formerly a member of the Hanseatic League. 577,900 (1963).

Brem·er·ha·ven (brem′ər hā′vən; *Ger.* brā′mər hä′fən), *n.* a seaport in N West Germany, at the mouth of the Weser River. 143,200 (1963). Formerly, **Wesermünde.**

Brem·er·ton (brem′ər tən, -tən), *n.* a city in W Washington, on Puget Sound: navy yard. 35,307 (1970).

brems·strah·lung (brem′shträ′lo͝ong), *n. Physics.* x-rays produced in the collision of an electron with an atomic nucleus. [< G = *Brems(e)* brake + *Strahlung* radiation]

Bren′ gun′ (bren), a .303-caliber, gas-operated, air-cooled, clip-fed submachine gun. Also, **bren′ gun′.** Also called **Bren, bren.** [named after *Br(no)*, Moravia + *En(field)*, England, towns of manufacture]

Bren·nan (bren′ən), *n.* **Wil·liam J(oseph), Jr.,** born 1906, U.S. jurist: associate justice of the U.S. Supreme Court since 1956.

Bren′ner Pass′ (bren′ər), a mountain pass in the Alps, on the border between Italy and Austria. 4494 ft. high.

brent (brent), *n. Brit.* brant. Also called **brent′ goose′.**

Bren·ta·no (bren tä′nō), *n.* **Franz** (fränz; *Ger.* fränts), 1838–1917, German philosopher and psychologist.

Brent·wood (brent′wo͝od′), *n.* a town on central Long Island, in SE New York. 28,327 (1970).

br'er (brûr, brâr; *Sou. dial.* bûr), *n. Chiefly Southern U.S.* brother.

Bre·scia (bre′shä), *n.* a city in central Lombardy, in N Italy. 174,116 (1961). —**Bre·scian** (bresh′ən), *adj.*

Bres·lau (brez′lou; *Ger.* bres′lou), *n.* a city on the Oder River in SW Poland: formerly in Germany. 509,400 (est. 1968). Polish, **Wrocław.**

Brest (brest), *n.* **1.** a seaport in the W extremity of France. 172,176. **2.** Formerly, **Brest Litovsk.** a city in SW Byelorussia, on the Bug River: formerly in Poland; German-Russian peace treaty 1918. 167,000.

Brest Li·tovsk (brest′ li tôfsk′), former name (until 1921) of **Brest.** Polish, **Brześć nad Bugiem.**

Bre·tagne (brə tän′yə), *n.* French name of **Brittany.**

breth·ren (breth′rin), *n.pl.* **1.** fellow members. **2.** *Archaic.* brothers.

Bret·on (bret′ən; *Fr.* brə tôn′), *n.* **1.** a native or inhabitant of Brittany. **2.** Also called **Armorican, Armoric.** the Celtic language of Brittany. —*adj.* **3.** pertaining to Brittany, the Bretons, or their language. [< F; see BRITON]

Bre·ton (brə tôn′), *n.* **An·dré** (än drā′), 1896–1966, French poet, essayist, and critic.

Breu·er (broi′ər), *n.* **1. Jo·sef** (yō′zef), 1842–1925, Austrian neurologist; pioneer in psychoanalytic techniques. **2. Mar·cel La·jos** (mär sel′ lô′yōsh), 1902–81, Hungarian architect, in the U.S. after 1937.

Breu·ghel (broi′gəl, bro͞o′-; *Flemish.* brœ′gəl), *n.* **Pie·ter** (pē′tər; *Flemish.* pē′tər), ("*Peasant Breughel*"), c1525–69, Flemish genre and landscape painter. Also, **Breu′gel, Brueghel, Bruegel.**

brev., 1. brevet. **2.** brevier.

breve (brēv, brev), *n.* **1.** a mark (˘) over a vowel to show that it is short, as ŭ in (kŭt) *cut.* **2.** *Law.* an initial writ. **3.** *Music.* the longest modern note, equivalent to two semibreves or whole notes. See illus. at **note. 4.** *Prosody.* a mark (˘) over a syllable to show that it is not stressed. [ME < ML, L *breve*, neut. of *brevis* short; see BRIEF]

bre·vet (brə vet′ *or, esp. Brit.,* brev′it), *n., v.*, **-vet·ted, -vet·ting** or **-vet·ed, -vet·ing.** —*n.* **1.** a commission promoting a military officer to a higher rank without increase of pay and with limited exercise of the rank. —*v.t.* **2.** to promote by brevet. [ME < AF; OF *brievet.* See BRIEF, -ET]

brevi-, a learned borrowing from Latin meaning "short," used in the formation of compound words. [< L, comb. form of *brevis;* akin to Gk *brachýs*]

bre·vi·ar·y (brē′vē er′ē, brev′ē-), *n., pl.* **-ar·ies.** *Rom. Cath. Ch.* a book containing all daily hymns, prayers, lessons, etc., necessary to enable a cleric to recite the daily Divine Office. [< L *breviāri(um)* an abridgment]

bre·vier (brə vēr′), *n. Print.* a size of type approximately 8-point, between minion and bourgeois. [< G: lit., BREVIARY; so called from use in printing breviaries]

brev·i·ty (brev′i tē), *n.* **1.** shortness of time or duration; briefness. **2.** expression of much in few words; conciseness. [earlier *brevitie* < L *brevitāt-* (s. of *brevitās*) shortness]

brew (bro͞o), *v.t.* **1.** to make (beer, ale, etc.) by steeping, boiling, and fermenting malt and hops. **2.** to make or prepare a beverage, as tea, by steeping, soaking, etc. **3.** to concoct in an improvised manner or of strange ingredients. **4.** to contrive or bring about: *to brew mischief.* —*v.i.* **5.** to make beer, ale, etc. **6.** to be in the course of preparation, as a beverage. **7.** to gather or form, esp. in an ominous manner: *Trouble was brewing.* —*n.* **8.** a quantity brewed at one time. **9.** a particular variety of beer, ale, etc. **10.** a beverage made by cooking or steeping a solid in water, esp.

tea or coffee. **11.** any bizarre or improvised concoction. **12.** *Informal.* a glass or bottle of beer or ale. [ME *brew(en),* OE *brēowan;* akin to D *brouwen,* G *brauen,* Icel *brugga*] —**brew′er,** *n.*

brew·age (brōō′ij), *n.* a fermented liquor brewed from malt. [BREW + -AGE; modeled on *beverage*]

brew′er's yeast′, a yeast, as of the genus *Saccharomyces,* suitable for use as a ferment in the manufacture of wine and beer.

brew·er·y (brōō′ə rē, brŏŏr′ē), *n., pl.* **-er·ies.** a building or establishment for brewing malt liquors. [BREW + -ERY; r. *brewhouse*]

brew·house (brōō′hous′), *n., pl.* **-hous·es** (-hou′ziz). brewery. [ME]

brew·ing (brōō′ing), *n.* **1.** the activity or trade of a brewer. **2.** the process of making malt liquors, as beer or ale. **3.** a quantity or batch brewed in a single process or at one time. [ME]

brew·is (brōō′is), *n.* *Dial.* **1.** broth. **2.** bread soaked in broth, gravy, etc. [earlier *brewz, brewes,* appar. b. Scot *bree* (late ME *bro(o)*) broth + *browes,* ME *broys* < OF *broez* (nom.), *broet* (acc.) = *bro* (< OHG *brod* BROTH) + *-et* -ET]

Brew·ster (brōō′stər), *n.* **William,** 1560?–1644, Pilgrim settler: leader of the colonists at Plymouth.

Brezh·nev (brezh′nef; *Russ.* brezh′nyef), *n.* **Le·o·nid Il·yich** (le o nēt′ il yēch′), 1906–82, Russian engineer and politician: general secretary of the Soviet Communist party 1964–82; president of the Soviet Union 1977–82.

Bri·an Bo·ru (brī′ən bô rō′, -rōō′, brēn′), A.D. 926–1014, king of Ireland 1002–14. Also, **Bri·an Bo·ramha, Bri·an Bo·raimhe, Bri·an Bo·roimhe, Bri·an Bo·rumha** (*all pronounced* brī′ən bô rō′, -rōō′, brēn′).

Bri·and (brē änd′; *Fr.* brē äN′), *n.* **A·ri·stide** (A rē stēd′), 1862–1932, French statesman: minister of France 11 times; Nobel peace prize 1926.

bri·ar (brī′ər), *n.* brier. —**bri′ar·y,** *adj.*

Bri·ar·e·us (brī âr′ē əs), *n.* *Class. Myth.* one of the three Hecatonchires. Also called **Aegaeon.** —**Bri·ar′e·an,** *adj.*

bri·ar·root (brī′ər rōōt′, -rŏŏt′), *n.* brierroot.

bri·ar·wood (brī′ər wŏŏd′), *n.* brierwood.

bribe (brīb), *n., v.,* **bribed, brib·ing.** —*n.* **1.** anything promised or given as illicit payment. **2.** anything given or serving to persuade or induce. —*v.t.* **3.** to give or promise a bribe to. **4.** to influence or corrupt by a bribe. [ME < MF *bribe* alms, *briber* to beg] —**brib′a·ble, bribe′a·ble,** *adj.* —**brib′er,** *n.*

brib·er·y (brī′bə rē), *n., pl.* **-er·ies.** the act or practice of giving or accepting a bribe. [ME *briberie* theft < MF: begging]

bric-a-brac (brik′ə brak′), *n.* miscellaneous small articles of antiquarian, decorative, or other interest. Also, **bric′-à-brac′.** [< F, a gradational formation based on *bric* piece; see BRICK, BREAK]

brick (brik), *n.* **1.** a rectangular block of clay hardened by drying in the sun or burning in a kiln, and used for building, paving, etc. **2.** such blocks collectively. **3.** the material of which such blocks are made. **4.** any block or bar suggesting a builder's brick in size or shape. **5.** *Informal.* a good or generous person. —*v.t.* **6.** to pave, line, wall, fill, or build with brick. —*adj.* **7.** made of, constructed with, or resembling bricks. [late ME *brike* < MD *bricke;* akin to BREAK]

Brick (brik), *n.* a township in E New Jersey. 35,057 (1970).

brick·bat (brik′bat′), *n.* **1.** a piece of broken brick, esp. one used as a missile. **2.** any rocklike missile. **3.** *Informal.* an unkind remark; caustic criticism. [BRICK + BAT[1]; an alliterative compound]

brick·kiln (brik′kil′, -kiln′), *n.* a kiln or furnace in which bricks are baked or burned.

brick·lay·ing (brik′lā′ing), *n.* the process or occupation of laying bricks in construction. —**brick′lay′er,** *n.*

brick·le (brik′əl), *adj.* *Dial.* easily broken; brittle. [late ME *bryckell,* OE *-brycel* tending to break = *bryc-* (mutated ptp. s. of *brecan* to BREAK) + *-el* adj. suffix] —**brick′le·ness,** *n.*

brick·work (brik′wûrk′), *n.* brick construction, as contrasted with that using other materials.

brick·yard (brik′yärd′), *n.* a place where bricks are made, stored, or sold.

bri·cole (bri kōl′, brik′əl), *n.* **1.** *Billiards.* a shot in which the cue ball strikes a cushion after touching the object ball and before hitting the carom ball. **2.** an indirect action or unexpected stroke. [< MF < ML *bricola* catapult; perh. akin to BRICK]

brid·al (brīd′əl), *adj.* **1.** of or pertaining to a bride or a wedding. —*n.* **2.** a wedding. **3.** *Archaic.* a wedding feast. [ME *bridale,* OE *brȳdealu* BRIDE[1] ALE, i.e., wedding feast; adj. sense influenced by confusion of second element (ALE) with -AL[1]] —**brid′al·ly,** *adv.*

Brid·al·veil (brīd′əl vāl′), *n.* a waterfall in Yosemite National Park, California. 620 ft. high. Also called **Brid′alveil Fall′.**

brid′al wreath′, any of several rosaceous shrubs of the genus *Spiraea,* esp. *S. prunifolia,* having sprays of small white flowers.

bride[1] (brīd), *n.* a newly married woman or a woman about to be married. [ME; OE *brȳd;* c. D *bruid,* G *Braut,* Icel *brūthr,* Goth *brūths*]

bride[2] (brīd), *n.* a thread or threads for joining ornamental details in embroidery or lacemaking. Also called **tie.** [< F: bonnet string (ME *bride* bridle < OF did not survive into E) < Gmc; see BRIDLE]

Bride (brīd), *n.* **Saint.** See **Brigid, Saint.**

bride·groom (brīd′grōōm′, -grŏŏm′), *n.* a newly married man or a man about to be married. [BRIDE[1] + GROOM; r. ME *bridegome,* OE *brȳdguma* = *brȳd* bride + *guma* man, c. L *homo*]

brides·maid (brīdz′mād′), *n.* a young woman who attends the bride at the wedding ceremony.

bride·well (brīd′wel′, -wəl), *n.* *Brit.* a house of correction for the confinement of vagrants and disorderly persons: so called from a former prison in London at St. Bride's Well.

bridge[1] (brij), *n., v.,* **bridged, bridg·ing.** —*n.* **1.** a structure spanning and permitting passage over a river, chasm, road, or the like. **2.** a connection or transition between two adjacent elements, conditions, or the like. **3.** *Naut.* a raised structure or platform, esp. that from which a power vessel is navigated, often including a pilothouse. **4.** *Anat.* the ridge or upper line of the nose. **5.** *Dentistry.* an artificial replacement for a missing tooth or teeth, supported by natural teeth or roots adjacent to the space. **6.** *Music.* a thin, fixed wedge raising the strings of a musical instrument above the sounding board. **7.** a transitional passage connecting major sections of a musical composition. **8.** *Ophthalm.* the part of a pair of eyeglasses that joins the two lenses and rests on the bridge or sides of the nose. **9.** *Elect.* an electrical circuit or instrument for measuring resistance, capacitance, inductance, or impedance. Cf. **Wheatstone bridge. 10.** *Railroads.* a gantry over a track or tracks for supporting waterspouts, signals, etc. **11.** *Billiards, Pool.* **a.** the arch formed by the hand and fingers to support and guide the striking end of a cue. **b.** a notched piece of wood with a long handle, used to support the cue when the hand cannot do so comfortably. **12.** *Theat.* a gallery or platform that can be raised or lowered over a stage for painting scenery, arranging lights, etc. **13.** *Chem.* a valence bond illustrating the connection of two parts of a molecule. **14.** any arch or rooflike figure formed by acrobats, dancers, etc., as by joining and raising hands. **15. burn one's bridges (behind one),** to eliminate all possibilities of retreat; make one's decision irrevocable. —*v.t.* **16.** to make a bridge or passage over; span. **17.** to make (a way) by a bridge. [ME *brigge,* OE *brycg;* c. D *brug,* G *Brücke;* akin to Icel *bryggja* pier] —**bridge′a·ble,** *adj.*

bridge[2] (brij), *n.* *Cards.* a game derived from whist in which one partnership of two players attempts to fulfill a certain declaration against an opposing partnership. Cf. **auction bridge, contract** (def. 6). [appar. alter. of earlier *biritch* < ?]

bridge·head (brij′hed′), *n.* **1.** a position held or to be gained on the enemy side of a river, defile, or other obstacle, to cover the crossing of friendly troops. **2.** a defensive work covering or protecting the end of a bridge toward the enemy.

bridge′ house′, *Naut.* a deckhouse including a bridge or bridges for navigation.

bridge′ lamp′, a floor lamp, esp. one having the light source on a hinged, horizontally adjustable arm.

Bridge′ of Sighs′, a bridge in Venice across which prisoners were formerly led for trial in the ducal palace.

Bridge·port (brij′pōrt′, -pôrt′), *n.* a seaport in SW Connecticut, on Long Island Sound. 156,542 (1970).

Bridg·es (brij′iz), *n.* **1. Harry (Alfred Bryant Ren·ton)** (ren′tən), born 1900, U.S. labor leader, born in Australia. **2. Robert (Seymour),** 1844–1930, English poet and essayist: poet laureate 1913–30.

Bridg·et (brij′it), *n.* **Saint.** See **Brigid, Saint.**

bridge′ ta′ble, a square table with folding legs, for card games.

Bridge·town (brij′toun′), *n.* a seaport on and the capital of Barbados. 8,789.

bridge·work (brij′wûrk′), *n.* **1.** *Dentistry.* **a.** a dental bridge or dental bridges collectively. **b.** any of several different types of dental bridges. **2.** the process or occupation of bridge building.

bridg·ing (brij′ing), *n.* *Building Trades.* a brace or an arrangement of braces fixed between floor or roof joists to keep them in place.

Bridg·man (brij′mən), *n.* **Percy Williams,** 1882–1961, U.S. physicist: Nobel prize 1946.

bri·dle (brīd′əl), *n., v.,* **-dled, -dling.** —*n.* **1.** part of the harness of a horse, consisting usually of a headstall, bit, and reins. **2.** anything that restrains or curbs. **3.** *Mach.* a link, flange, or other attachment for limiting the movement of any part of a machine. **4.** *Naut.* a rope or chain for lifting or towing, secured at both ends, and itself held or lifted by a rope or chain secured at its center. **5.** a raising up of the head, as in disdain. —*v.t.* **6.** to put a bridle on. **7.** to control as with a bridle; restrain; curb. —*v.i.* **8.** to draw up the head and draw in the chin, as in disdain or resentment. [ME *bridel,* OE *brīdel* < *brigdels* = *brigd-* (var. s. of *bregdan* to BRAID) + *-els* n. suffix; akin to D *breidel,* OHG *brittel*] —**bri′dle·less,** *adj.* —**bri′dler,** *n.* —**Syn. 2, 7.** check, control. **8.** bristle.

bri′dle path′, a wide path for riding horses.

bri·dle·wise (brīd′əl wīz′), *adj.* (of a horse) obedient to a touch of the reins on the neck, without pressure of the bit on the mouth.

bri·doon (bri dōōn′), *n.* a snaffle when used with a curb on a full bridle. Also, **bradoon.** [< F *bridon* = *bride* bridle (see BRIDE[2]) + *-on* n. suffix]

Brie (brē), *n.* a white, soft cheese, ripened with bacterial action, originating in Brie, France.

Brie (brē), *n.* a region in NE France between the Seine and the Marne.

brief (brēf), *adj.* **1.** of short duration. **2.** using few words; concise; succinct. **3.** abrupt or curt. —*n.* **4.** a short and concise statement or written item; synopsis; summary. **5.** an outline, in a form determined by set rules, of the information and possible arguments on one side of a controversy. **6.** *Law.* **a.** a memorandum of points of fact or of law for use in conducting a case. **b.** a written argument submitted to a court. **c.** (in England) the material relevant to a case, delivered by a solicitor to the barrister who tries the case. **7. briefs,** close-fitting, legless underpants. **8.** briefing. **9.** *Rom. Cath. Ch.* a papal letter less formal than a bull. **10.** *Obs.* a letter. **11. hold a brief for,** to support or defend by argument; endorse. **12. in brief,** in a few words; in short. —*v.t.* **13.** to make an abstract or summary of. **14.** to instruct by a brief or briefing. **15.** *Law.* to retain as advocate in a suit. [ME *bref* < OF < L *brev(is)* short; see BREVE] —**brief′ly,** *adv.* —**brief′ness,** *n.* —**Syn. 1.** short-lived, fleeting, transitory, ephemeral. See **short. 2.** terse, compact, pithy. **4.** précis, abstract. See **summary. 13.** summarize, epitomize, digest. —**Ant. 1.** long.

brief·case (brēf′kās′), *n.* a flat, rectangular leather case for carrying documents, books, manuscripts, etc.

brief·ing (brē′fing), *n.* **1.** *Mil.* a short, factual oral summary of the details of a current or projected military opera-

tion given to the participants or observers. **2.** any set of concise instructions or a summary of events.
brief′ of ti′tle. See **abstract of title.**
bri·er[1] (brī′ər), *n.* **1.** a prickly plant or shrub, esp. the sweetbrier or a greenbrier. **2.** a tangled mass of prickly plants. **3.** a thorny stem or twig. Also, **briar.** [ME *brer,* OE *brǣr, brēr;* akin to BRAMBLE] —**bri′er·y,** *adj.*
bri·er[2] (brī′ər), *n.* **1.** the white heath, *Erica arborea,* of France and Corsica, the woody root of which is used for making tobacco pipes. **2.** a pipe made of this woody root. Also, **briar.** [earlier *bruyer* < F *bruyère* < LL *brūcus* heather (< Celt); see -ER[2]]
bri·er·root (brī′ər ro͞ot′, -ro͝ot′), *n.* **1.** the root wood of the brier. **2.** certain other woods from which tobacco pipes are made. **3.** a pipe made of brierroot. Also, **briarroot.**
bri·er·wood (brī′ər wo͝od′), *n.* brierroot. Also, **briarwood.**
brig (brig), *n.* **1.** *Naut.* **a.** a two-masted vessel square-rigged on both masts. **b.** the compartment of a ship where prisoners are confined. **2.** *U.S.* a place of confinement or detention, esp. in the U.S. Navy or Marines. [short for BRIGANTINE]

Brig

Brig., 1. brigade. **2.** brigadier.
bri·gade (bri gād′), *n., v.,* **-gad·ed, -gad·ing.** —*n.* **1.** a military unit consisting of several regiments, squadrons, groups, or battalions. **2.** a large body of troops. **3.** a group of individuals organized for a particular purpose. **4.** See **bucket brigade.** —*v.t.* **5.** to form into a brigade. **6.** to group together. [< MF < OIt *brigata* troop, band = *brig(are)* (to) fight (see BRIGAND) + *-ata* -ADE[1]]
brig·a·dier (brig′ə dēr′), *n.* **1.** *Brit. Army.* a rank between colonel and major general. **2.** *U.S. Army Informal.* a brigadier general. **3.** *Hist.* a noncommissioned rank in the Napoleonic armies. [short for BRIGADIER GENERAL] —**brig′a·dier′ship,** *n.*
brig′adier gen′eral, *pl.* **brigadier generals.** *U.S. Army.* an officer or the rank between colonel and major general. [< F; see BRIGADE, -IER]
brig·and (brig′ənd), *n.* a bandit, esp. one of a gang of robbers in mountain or forest regions. [var. of ME *briga(u)nt* < MF *brigand* < OIt *brigante,* lit., fighting-man = *brig(are)* (to) fight (< *briga* quarreling < ?) + *-ante* -ANT] —**brig′and·age, brig′and·ism,** *n.* —**brig′and·ish,** *adj.* —**brig′and·ish·ly,** *adv.*
brig·an·dine (brig′ən dēn′, -dīn′), *n.* *Armor.* a flexible body armor of overlapping steel plates with an exterior covering of linen, velvet, leather, etc. [late ME *brigandyn* < MF *brigandine.* See BRIGAND, -INE[2]]
brig·an·tine (brig′ən tēn′, -tīn′), *n.* *Naut.* **1.** a two-masted sailing vessel, square-rigged on the foremast and having a fore-and-aft mainsail with square upper sails. **2.** See **hermaphrodite brig.** [< ML *brigantin(us)* or OIt *brigantino,* orig., fighting-ship (see BRIGAND, -INE[2]); r. *brigandyn* < MF *brigandin*]
Briggs (brigz), *n.* **Henry,** 1561–1630, English mathematician. —**Briggs′i·an,** *adj.*
bright (brīt), *adj.* **1.** radiating or reflecting much light; luminous; shining. **2.** filled with light. **3.** vivid or brilliant. **4.** clear or translucent, as liquid. **5.** radiant or splendid: *the bright pageantry of court.* **6.** illustrious or glorious, as an era. **7.** quick-witted or intelligent. **8.** showing quick wit or intelligence. **9.** animated, lively, cheerful. **10.** favorable or auspicious: *bright prospects.* **11.** having a glossy, glazed, or polished finish. —*n.* **12. brights, a.** the automobile or truck headlights used for driving (opposed to *parking lights* and *signal lights*). **b.** the brighter level of intensity of these lights. **13.** light-hued tobacco. **14.** an artist's paintbrush having short, square-edged bristles. **15.** *Archaic.* brightness; splendor. —*adv.* **16.** in a bright manner; brightly. [ME; OE *briht, beorht;* c. Goth *bairht(s),* OS, OHG *beraht,* Icel *bjartr;* akin to L *flagrāre* to blaze (see FLAGRANT)] —**bright′ish,** *adj.* —**bright′ly,** *adv.*
—**Syn. 1.** refulgent, effulgent, lustrous, lucent, beaming, lambent. BRIGHT, BRILLIANT, RADIANT, SHINING refer to that which gives forth, is filled with, or reflects light. BRIGHT suggests the general idea: *bright flare, stars, mirror.* BRILLIANT implies a strong, unusual, or sparkling brightness, often changeful or varied and too strong to be agreeable: *brilliant sunlight.* RADIANT implies the pouring forth of steady rays of light, esp. as are agreeable to the eyes: *a radiant moon.* SHINING implies giving forth or reflecting a strong or steady light: *shining eyes.* **7, 8.** keen, discerning. **10.** promising, encouraging. —**Ant. 1.** dull, dim.
Bright (brīt), *n.* **John,** 1811–89, British statesman and economist.
bright·en (brīt′ən), *v.i., v.t.* to become or make bright or brighter. [ME *brightne(n)*] —**bright′en·er,** *n.*
bright·ness (brīt′nis), *n.* **1.** the quality of being bright. **2.** *Optics.* the luminance of a body, apart from its hue or saturation: pure white has the maximum brightness, and pure black the minimum brightness. [ME *brihtnes,* OE *beorhtnes*]
Bright·on (brīt′ən), *n.* **1.** a city in S Sussex, in SE England: seashore resort. 162,650 (est. 1964). **2.** a city near Melbourne in S Victoria, in SE Australia. 41,302 (1961).
Bright's′ disease′, *Pathol.* a disease characterized by albuminuria and heightened blood pressure. [named after Richard *Bright* (1789–1858), English physician]
bright·work (brīt′wûrk′), *n.* **1.** polished metal parts, as on a ship or automobile. **2.** *Naut.* all plain or varnished woodwork that is kept scoured on a vessel.
Brig·id (brij′id, brē′id), *n.* **Saint.** A.D. 453–523, Irish abbess: a patron saint of Ireland. Also, **Bride, Bridget, Brig·it** (brij′it).
brill (bril), *n., pl.* **brills,** (*esp. collectively*) **brill.** a European flatfish, *Scophthalmus rhombus,* closely related to the turbot. [?]
Bril·lat-Sa·va·rin (brē ya′sa va raN′), *n.* **An·thelme** (äN telm′), 1755–1826, French jurist, writer, and gastronome.
bril·liance (bril′yəns), *n.* **1.** great brightness; splendor; luster. **2.** excellence or distinction, esp. in talent or mental ability. [BRILLI(ANT) + -ANCE] —**Syn. 1.** radiance. **2.** preeminence, renown; genius. —**Ant. 1, 2.** dullness.
bril·lian·cy (bril′yən sē), *n., pl.* **-cies** for 1. **1.** an instance of brilliance. **2.** brilliance.
bril·liant (bril′yənt), *adj.* **1.** shining brightly; sparkling; glittering; lustrous. **2.** distinguished; illustrious. **3.** having or showing great intelligence or talent. —*n.* **4.** *Jewelry.* a gem, esp. a diamond, having any of several varieties of the brilliant cut. **5.** *Print.* a size of type about 3½-point. [< F *brillant* shining (prp. of *briller* < It *brillare* to glitter) = *brill-* (? akin to BERYL) + *-ant* -ANT] —**bril′liant·ly,** *adv.* —**bril′liant·ness,** *n.* —**Syn. 1.** See **bright.**
bril′liant cut′, *Jewelry.* a cut intended to enhance the brilliance of a gem with the least sacrifice of weight, characterized by a form resembling two pyramids set base to base, truncated so as to give a broad table and a very small culet, and having from 18 to 104 facets, 58 being typical. —**bril′liant-cut′,** *adj.*
bril·lian·tine (bril′yən tēn′), *n.* **1.** a preparation used to make the hair manageable and lustrous. **2.** a dress fabric resembling alpaca. [< F *brillantine.* See BRILLIANT, -INE[2]] —**bril′lian·tined′,** *adj.*
brim (brim), *n., v.,* **brimmed, brim·ming.** —*n.* **1.** the upper edge of anything hollow; rim; brink. **2.** a projecting edge: *the brim of a hat.* **3.** *Archaic.* edge or margin. —*v.i.* **4.** to be full to the brim. —*v.t.* **5.** to fill to the brim. [ME *brimme* shore, OE *brymm* sea, surf, hence seaside; akin to Icel *brim* surf, breakers, OE *bremman* to roar, rage] —**brim′less,** *adj.* —**brim′ming·ly,** *adv.*
brim·ful (brim′fo͝ol′), *adj.* full to the brim. Also, **brim′full′.** —**brim′ful′ly,** *adv.*
brim·mer (brim′ər), *n.* a cup, glass, or bowl full to the brim.
brim·stone (brim′stōn′), *n.* **1.** sulfur. **2.** a virago; shrew. [ME *brinston,* etc., late OE *brynstān.* See BURN[1], STONE] —**brim′ston′y,** *adj.*
Brin·di·si (brēn′dē zē), *n.* an Adriatic seaport in SE Apulia, in SE Italy: important Roman city and naval station. 70,084 (1961). Ancient, **Brundisium.**
brin·dle (brin′dəl), *n.* **1.** a brindled coloring. **2.** a brindled animal. —*adj.* **3.** brindled. [back formation from BRINDLED]
brin·dled (brin′dəld), *adj.* gray or tawny with darker streaks or spots. Also, **brin·ded** (brin′did). [var. of *brin(ded)* variegated (lit., branded, burnt); r. late ME *brended,* var. of *branded.* See BRAND, -LE, -ED[3]]
brine (brīn), *n., v.,* **brined, brin·ing.** —*n.* **1.** water saturated or strongly impregnated with salt. **2.** a salt and water solution for pickling. **3.** the sea or ocean. **4.** the water of the sea. **5.** *Chem.* any saline solution. —*v.t.* **6.** to treat with or steep in brine. [ME; OE *brȳne;* c. D *brijn*] —**brine′less,** *adj.* —**brin′er,** *n.* —**brin′ish,** *adj.* —**brin′ish·ness,** *n.*
Bri·nell′ machine′ (bri nel′), *Metall.* an instrument for determining the hardness (**Brinell′ hard′ness**) of metal by forcing a hard ball into the material being tested. Also called **Brinell′ test′er.** [named after J. A. *Brinell* (1849–1925), Swedish engineer]
Brinell′ num′ber, *Metall.* a numerical expression of Brinell hardness. Also called **Brinell′ hard′ness num′ber.**
bring (briŋ), *v.t.,* **brought, bring·ing. 1.** to cause to come to the speaker or to accompany the speaker to another person or place. **2.** to cause to come to or toward oneself, as by attracting the attention. **3.** to cause to happen to one. **4.** to cause to come to mind: *The memory brought sadness.* **5.** to cause to occur, or come into a particular position or state. **6.** to persuade, convince, or compel: *He couldn't bring himself to do it.* **7.** to sell for; fetch: *to bring a good price.* **8.** *Law.* to commence: *to bring an action for damages.* **9. bring about,** to accomplish; cause. **10. bring around** or **round, a.** to convince of an opinion; persuade. **b.** to restore to consciousness, as after a faint. **11. bring down, a.** to cause to fall, as with a shot, blow, etc. **b.** to lessen; reduce, esp. in price. **c.** *Slang.* to put in low spirits; depress: *The bad news brought him down.* **12. bring forth, a.** to produce. **b.** to present for consideration. **13. bring forward, a.** to bring to view; show. **b.** to present for consideration. **14. bring in,** to yield, as profits or income. **15. bring off,** to accomplish or achieve. **16. bring on, a.** to cause to happen or exist. **b.** to introduce; cause to appear. **17. bring out, a.** to expose; reveal. **b.** to make noticeable or conspicuous in a contrast. **c.** to publish, as a book, play, etc. **d.** to introduce formally into society. **18. bring to, a.** to bring back to consciousness; revive. **b.** *Naut.* to head (a

vessel) close to or into the wind. **19. bring up, a.** to care for during childhood; rear. **b.** to introduce to notice or consideration. **c.** to vomit. **d.** to stop or cause to stop, esp. abruptly. [ME *bringen,* OE *bringan;* c. D *brengen,* G *bringen,* Goth *briggan*] —**bring′er,** *n.*
—**Syn. 1.** transport; lead, guide. BRING, TAKE, FETCH imply conveying or conducting in relation to the place where the speaker is. To BRING is simply so to convey or conduct: *Bring it to me. I'm permitted to bring my dog here with me.* It is the opposite of TAKE, which means to convey or conduct away from the place where the speaker is: *Bring it back here. Take it back there.* FETCH means to go, get, and bring back: *Fetch me that bottle, please.* —**Ant. 1.** take.

bring·ing-up (bring′ing up′), *n.* childhood training or care; upbringing.

brink (bringk), *n.* **1.** the edge or margin of a steep place or of land bordering water. **2.** any extreme edge. **3.** the extreme point beyond which an event, usually bad, is inevitable. [ME *brink* < Scand or LG; cf. Dan *brink* brink, MLG *brink* edge, hillside, c. Icel *brekka* slope, hill] —**brink′less,** *adj.*

brinks·man·ship (bringks′mən ship′), *n.* the technique of maneuvering a dangerous situation to the limits of tolerance or safety in order to secure the greatest advantage. Also, **brink·man·ship** (bringk′mən ship′).

brin·y[1] (brī′nē), *adj.,* **brin·i·er, brin·i·est.** of or like brine; salty: *a briny taste.* [BRINE + -Y[1]] —**brin′i·ness,** *n.*

brin·y[2] (brī′nē), *n. Informal.* the ocean. [BRINE + -Y[2]]

bri·oche (brē′ōsh, -osh; *Fr.* brē ôsh′), *n., pl.* **-och·es** (-ō shiz, -osh iz; *Fr.* -ôsh′). a light, sweet bun or roll made with eggs, yeast, and butter. [< F, MF (Norman dial) = *bri(er)* (to) knead (< Gmc; see BREAK) + *-oche* n. suffix]

bri·o·lette (brē′ə let′; *Fr.* brē ô let′), *n., pl.* **-lettes** (-lets′; *Fr.* -let′). any pear-shaped gem having its entire surface cut with triangular facets. [< F, var. of *brillolette,* itself alter. (by assoc. with *brillant* diamond) of *brignolette,* lit., little dried plum (facetious coinage) = *brignole* (after *Brignoles* in Provence, where the plums are dried) + *-ette* -ETTE]

bri·o·ny (brī′ə nē), *n., pl.* **-nies.** bryony.

bri·quet (bri ket′), *n., v.t.,* **-quet·ted, -quet·ting.** briquette.

bri·quette (bri ket′), *n., v.,* **-quet·ted, -quet·ting.** —*n.* **1.** a small brick of compressed coal dust or charcoal used for fuel, esp. in barbecuing. **2.** a molded block of any material. —*v.t.* **3.** to mold into briquettes. [< F; see BRICK, -ETTE]

bri·sance (bri zäns′; *Fr.* brē zäns′), *n.* the shattering power of high explosives. [< F = *bris(er)* (to) break (< Celt; akin to Ir *brisim* I break) + *-ance* -ANCE] —**bri·sant** (bri zänt′; *Fr.* brē zän′), *adj.*

Bris·bane (briz′bān, -bən), *n.* a seaport in and the capital of Queensland, in E Australia. 958,800.

Bri·se·is (brī sē′is), *n.* (in the *Iliad*) a beautiful woman captured by Achilles: cause of his quarrel with Agamemnon.

brisk (brisk), *adj.* **1.** quick and active; lively. **2.** sharp and stimulating. **3.** (of liquors) effervescing vigorously: *brisk cider.* —*v.t., v.i.* **4.** to make or become brisk; liven (often fol. by *up*). [< Welsh *brysg;* c. Ir *briosc* crisp, quick, akin to *brisim* I break; see BRISANCE] —**brisk′ly,** *adv.* —**brisk′ness,** *n.* —**Syn. 1.** spry, energetic, alert, spirited. —**Ant. 1.** languid.

bris·ket (bris′kit), *n.* the breast of an animal, or the part of the breast lying next to the ribs. [ME *brusket* < Scand; cf. Icel *brjōskit* the gristle = *brjōsk* cartilage + *-it* the]

bris·ling (bris′ling), *n.* the sprat. [< Norw; akin to obs. Dan *bretling,* G *Brätling, Breitling*]

bris·tle (bris′əl), *n., v.,* **-tled, -tling.** —*n.* **1.** a short, stiff hair of an animal, as a hog. **2.** something made of or suggesting such a hair. —*v.i.* **3.** to stand or rise stiffly, like bristles. **4.** to erect the bristles, as an irritated animal (often fol. by *up*). **5.** to become rigid with anger or irritation. **6.** to be thickly set or filled with something suggestive of bristles. —*v.t.* **7.** to erect like bristles: *The rooster bristled his crest.* **8.** to furnish with a bristle or bristles. **9.** to make bristly. [ME *bristel* = *brist* (OE *byrst* bristle, c. G *Borste,* Icel *burst,* etc.) + *-el* dim. suffix] —**bris′tle·less,** *adj.* —**bris′tle·like′,** *adj.* —**bris′tli·ness,** *n.* —**bris′tly,** *adj.*

bris·tle·tail (bris′əl tāl′), *n.* any of various wingless insects of the order *Thysanura,* having long, bristlelike, caudal appendages.

Bris·tol (bris′tᵊl), *n.* **1.** a seaport in S Gloucestershire, in SW England, on the Avon River near its confluence with the Severn estuary. 420,100. **2.** a city in central Connecticut. 55,487 (1970).

Bris′tol board′, a fine, smooth pasteboard, sometimes glazed.

Bris′tol Chan′nel, an inlet of the Atlantic, between S Wales and SW England, extending to the mouth of the Severn estuary. ab. 85 mi. long.

Bris′tol fash′ion, *Naut.* in a tidy, seamanlike manner. [after BRISTOL, England]

brit (brit), *n.* **1.** the group of small marine animals forming the food of whalebone whales. **2.** the young of herring and sprat. [< Cornish; akin to Welsh *brith* speckled]

Brit (brit), *n. Informal.* a British person (sometimes used derogatively).

Brit (bə rēt′; *Eng.* bris), *n. Hebrew.* Berith.

Brit., 1. Britain. **2.** British.

Brit·ain (brit′ᵊn), *n.* **1.** See **Great Britain. 2.** Britannia (def. 1).

Bri·tan·ni·a (bri tan′ē ə, -tan′yə), *n.* **1.** the ancient Roman name of the island of Great Britain, esp. the S part where the early Roman provinces were. **2.** the British Empire. **3.** *Chiefly Literary.* **a.** Great Britain. **b.** the United Kingdom of Great Britain and Ireland. **4.** the figure of a seated woman with trident and helmet used as a symbolic representation of Great Britain and the British Empire. **5.** See **Britannia metal.**

Britan′nia met′al, a white alloy of tin, antimony, and copper, sometimes with small amounts of zinc, lead, and bismuth, used for tableware and as an antifriction material.

Bri·tan·nic (bri tan′ik), *adj.* **1.** of Britain; British. **2.** Brythonic. [< L *Britannic(us).* See BRITANNIA, -IC]

britch·es (brich′iz), *n.pl. Informal.* breeches.

Brith (bə rēt′; *Eng.* bris), *n. Hebrew.* Berith.

Brit·i·cism (brit′i siz′əm), *n.* a word, idiom, or phrase characteristic of or restricted to British English. Also, **Britishism.** [*Britic-* (alter. of BRITISH) + -ISM]

Brit·ish (brit′ish), *adj.* **1.** of or pertaining to Great Britain, the British Commonwealth, or its inhabitants. —*n.* **2.** people native to or inhabiting Great Britain or the British Commonwealth, taken collectively. **3.** See **British English. 4.** the Celtic language of the ancient Britons. [ME *Brittische,* OE *Bryttisc* = *Brytt(as)* Britons + *-isc* -ISH[1]] —**Brit′ish·ly,** *adv.* —**Brit′ish·ness,** *n.*

Brit′ish Amer′ica. See **British North America.**

Brit′ish Antarc′tic Ter′ritory, a British colony in the S Atlantic, comprising the South Shetland Islands, the South Orkney Islands, and Graham Land: formerly dependencies of the Falkland Islands.

Brit′ish Cameroons′, Cameroons (def. 2).

Brit′ish Colum′bia, a province in W Canada on the Pacific coast. 2,406,212; 366,255 sq. mi. *Cap.:* Victoria. —**Brit′ish Colum′bian.**

Brit′ish Com′monwealth of Na′tions, a group of nations and dependent territories united by a common allegiance to the British crown, including the nations of the United Kingdom of Great Britain and Northern Ireland, Australia, The Bahamas, Bangladesh, Barbados, Botswana, Canada, Cyprus, Fiji, The Gambia, Ghana, Guyana, India, Jamaica, Kenya, Lesotho, Malawi, Malaysia, Malta, Mauritius, New Zealand, Nigeria, Sierra Leone, Singapore, Sri Lanka, Swaziland, Tanzania, Tonga, Trinidad and Tobago, Uganda, Western Samoa, and Zambia, and their colonies, protectorates, and trusteeships. Also called **Brit′ish Com′monwealth, the Commonwealth.** Official name, **Commonwealth of Nations.**

Brit′ish East′ Af′rica, a comprehensive term for the former British territories of Kenya, Uganda, and Tanzania.

Brit′ish Em′pire, a former collective term for the territories under the control of the British crown.

Brit′ish Eng′lish, the English language as spoken and written in Great Britain. Also called **British.**

Brit·ish·er (brit′i shər), *n.* a native or inhabitant of Great Britain, esp. of England.

Brit′ish gal′lon, *Chiefly Brit.* See **Imperial gallon.**

Brit′ish Gui′na, former name of **Guyana.**

Brit′ish gum′, dextrin.

Brit′ish Hondu′ras, former name of **Belize.** —**Brit′ish Hondu′ran.**

Brit′ish In′dia, a part of India, comprising 17 provinces, that prior to 1947 was subject to British law: now divided among India, Pakistan, and Bangladesh.

Brit′ish In′dian O′cean Ter′ritory, a British colony in the Indian Ocean, comprising some islands of the Seychelles and the Chagos Archipelago. 1384 (est. 1965); ab. 120 sq. mi.

Brit′ish Isles′, a group of islands in W Europe: Great Britain, Ireland, the Isle of Man, and adjacent small islands. 53,978,538; 120,592 sq. mi.

Brit·ish·ism (brit′i shiz′əm), *n.* **1.** Briticism. **2.** any custom or manner characteristic of the British people.

Brit′ish Malay′a, the former British possessions on the Malay Peninsula and the Malay Archipelago: now part of the federation of Malaysia.

Brit′ish New′ Guin′ea, former name of the Territory of Papua.

Brit′ish North′ Amer′ica, 1. Canada. **2.** all parts of the British Commonwealth in or near North America.

Brit′ish North′ Bor′neo, former name of **Sabah.**

Brit′ish Soma′liland, a former British protectorate in E Africa, on the Gulf of Aden: now the N province of the Somali Republic. Former official name, **Somaliland Protectorate.** Cf. **Somali Republic.**

Brit′ish ther′mal u′nit, the amount of heat required to raise the temperature of one pound of water one degree F. *Abbr.:* Btu, BTU, B.t.u., B.T.U.

Brit′ish Vir′gin Is′lands, a British colony comprising several small islands in the West Indies, E of Puerto Rico. 10,500; 59 sq. mi. *Cap.:* Road Town.

Brit′ish West′ Af′rica, a former comprehensive term for Cameroons, The Gambia, the Gold Coast, Nigeria, Sierra Leone, and Togo.

Brit′ish West′ In′dies, the members of the British Commonwealth in the Caribbean, including the Bahamas, Barbados, Jamaica, Trinidad and Tobago, and the islands of the Leeward and Windward groups. ab. 12,500 sq. mi. Cf. **West Indies** (def. 2).

Brit·on (brit′ᵊn), *n.* **1.** a native or inhabitant of Great Britain or the British Commonwealth, esp. of England. **2.** one of the Celtic people formerly occupying the southern part of the island of Britain. [< ML *Britōn-* (s. of *Britō*); r. ME *Breton* < OF < LL *Britton(es)* Britons]

brits·ka (brits′kə), *n.* an open carriage with a calash top. Also, **britzka, britzska.** [< G *Britzka,* var. of *Britschka* < Pol *bryczka,* dim. of *bryka* cart, wagon]

Brit·ta·ny (brit′ᵊnē), *n.* a region in NW France, on a peninsula between the English Channel and the Bay of Biscay: a former duchy and province. French, **Bretagne.**

Brit′tany span′iel, one of a French breed of large spaniels developed as a game pointer.

Brit·ten (brit′ᵊn), *n.* **(Edward) Benjamin,** 1913–76, English composer.

brit·tle (brit′ᵊl), *adj.* **1.** breaking readily with a comparatively smooth fracture, as glass. **2.** (of a person) inflexible, not adaptable. —*n.* **3.** a brittle candy. [ME *britel* = *brit-* (akin to OE *brytsen* fragment) + *-el* adj. suffix] —**brit′tle·ness,** *n.* —**Syn. 1.** fragile. See **frail**[1].

britz·ka (brits′kə; *Pol.* brich′kä), *n.* britska. Also, **britzs′ka.**

Brix′ scale′, a graduated scale, used on a hydrometer, that indicates the weight of sugar per volume of solution at a given temperature. [named after A. F. W. *Brix,* 19th-century German inventor]

Br·no (bər′nô; *Eng.* bûr′nō), *n.* a city in central Czechoslovakia: former capital of Moravia. 359,540. German, **Brünn.**

bro., *pl.* **bros.** brother. Also, **Bro.**

broach (brōch), *n.* **1.** *Mach.* an elongated, tapered, tool for shaping and enlarging holes. **2.** a spit for roasting meat. **3.** a gimlet for tapping casks. **4.** Also called **broach′ spire′.** an octagonal spire rising directly from a tower without any intervening feature. —*v.t.* **5.** to enlarge and finish with a broach. **6.** to mention or suggest for the first time: *to broach a subject.* **7.** to draw (beer, liquor, etc.) as by tapping. **8.** to tap or pierce. —*v.i.* **9.** *Naut.* (of a sailing vessel) to veer to windward, esp. so as to be broadside to the wind (usually fol. by *to*). **10.** to break the surface of water, as a fish or a submarine. [ME *broche* < MF < VL **brocca* spike, horn, tap of a cask, etc. (ML *broca*), n. use of fem. of L adj. *brocc(h)us* projecting (said of teeth)] —**broach′er,** *n.*

broad (brôd), *adj.* **1.** of great breadth. **2.** measured from side to side: *The desk was three feet broad.* **3.** of great area: *a broad expanse.* **4.** widely diffused; open; full: *broad daylight.* **5.** not limited; of extensive range or scope. **6.** liberal; tolerant. **7.** main or general: *the broad outlines of a subject.* **8.** plain or clear: *a broad hint.* **9.** bold; plain-spoken. **10.** indelicate: *a broad joke.* **11.** (of conversation) rough; countrified. **12.** unconfined; free; unrestrained: *broad mirth.* **13.** (of pronunciation) strongly dialectal. —*adv.* **14.** fully: *He was broad awake.* —*n.* **15.** the broad part of anything. **16.** *Slang.* **a.** a woman. **b.** a promiscuous woman. [ME *brood,* OE *brād;* c. D *breed,* G *breit,* Icel *breithr,* Goth *braiths*] —**broad′ish,** *adj.* —**broad′ly,** *adv.* —**Syn. 1.** See **wide. 3.** extensive, ample, vast. **6.** open. **10.** gross. —**Ant. 1.** narrow.

Broad arrow (def. 1)

broad *a*, the *a*-sound (ä) when used in place of the more common *a*-sound (a) in such words as *half, can't,* or *laugh.*

broad′ ar′row, 1. a mark in the shape of a broad arrowhead, placed upon British government property. **2.** *Archery.* an arrow having an expanded head.

broad·ax (brôd′aks′), *n., pl.* **-ax·es** (-ak′siz). an ax for hewing timber. Also, **broad′axe′.** [ME *brodax,* OE *brādæx*]

broad·band (brôd′band′), *adj.* *Radio, Electronics.* of, pertaining to, or responsive to a continuous, wide range of frequencies.

broad′ bean′, a variety of edible bean, *Vicia Faba.* Also called **fava bean.**

broad·cast (brôd′kast′, -käst′), *v.,* **-cast** or **-cast·ed, -cast·ing,** *n., adj., adv.* —*v.t.* **1.** to transmit over radio or television. **2.** to speak, perform, sponsor, or present on a radio or television program. **3.** to cast or scatter over an area, as seed. **4.** to spread widely, as news. —*v.i.* **5.** to transmit programs or signals from a radio or television station. **6.** to scatter or disseminate something widely. —*n.* **7.** that which is broadcast. **8.** a single radio or television program. **9.** a method of sowing by scattering seed. —*adj.* **10.** transmitted from a radio or television station. **11.** of or pertaining to broadcasting. **12.** cast or widely scattered over an area. **13.** widely spread or disseminated. —*adv.* **14.** so as to be cast abroad over an area: *seed sown broadcast.* [BROAD (adv.) + CAST (ptp.)] —**broad′cast′er,** *n.*

Broad′ Church′, pertaining or belonging to a party in the Anglican Church emphasizing a liberal interpretation of ritual and such conditions of membership as will promote wide Christian inclusiveness. Cf. **High Church, Low Church.** —**Broad′-Church′,** *adj.* —**Broad′ Church′-man.**

broad·cloth (brôd′klôth′, -kloth′), *n.* *Textiles.* **1.** any fabric woven on a wide loom. **2.** a woolen or worsted dress-goods fabric constructed in a plain or twill weave, having a compact texture and lustrous finish. **3.** a closely woven dress-goods fabric of cotton, rayon, silk, or a mixture of these fibers, having a soft, mercerized finish and resembling poplin. [ME *brode clothe*]

broad·en (brôd′ᵊn), *v.i., v.t.* to become or make broad.

broad′ gauge′, *Railroads.* See under **gauge** (def. 11). Also, *esp. in technical use,* **broad′ gage′.** —**broad′-gauge′, broad′-gage′,** *adj.* —**broad′-gauged′, broad′-gaged′,** *adj.*

broad′ hatch′et, a hatchet with a broad cutting edge. Also called **hand ax.**

broad′ jump′, *Track.* a jump for distance, either from a standing position **(standing broad jump)** or with a running start **(running broad jump).** Also called, *esp. Brit.,* **long jump.** —**broad′ jump′er.**

broad·leaf (brôd′lēf′), *n., pl.* **-leaves.** any of several cigar tobaccos having broad leaves.

broad′-leaved bot′tle tree′ (brôd′lēvd′). See under **bottle tree.**

broad′-leaved ma′ple, a maple, *Acer macrophyllum,* of western North America, characterized by dark green, leathery leaves that are sometimes one foot or more in width.

broad·loom (brôd′lo͞om′), *adj.* **1.** of or pertaining to rugs or carpets woven on a wide loom. —*n.* **2.** See **broadloom carpet.**

broad′loom car′pet, any seamless carpet woven on a wide loom, esp. one wider than 54 inches.

broad-mind·ed (brôd′mīn′did), *adj.* free from prejudice or bigotry; liberal; tolerant. —**broad′-mind′ed·ly,** *adv.* —**broad′-mind′ed·ness,** *n.*

Broads (brôdz), *n.* (*construed as pl.*) **The,** a low-lying, marshy region in E England, in Norfolk and Suffolk.

broad′ seal′, the official seal of a country or state.

broad·side (brôd′sīd′), *n., adv., v.,* **-sid·ed, -sid·ing.** —*n.* **1.** *Naut.* the whole side of a ship above the water line, from the bow to the quarter. **2.** *Navy.* **a.** all the guns on one side of a warship. **b.** their simultaneous discharge. **3.** any strong or comprehensive attack, as by criticism. **4.** Also called **broad·sheet** (brôd′shēt′). a sheet of paper printed on one side only, as for distribution or posting. **5.** any broad surface or side, as of a house. **6.** Also called **broad′side bal′lad.** (in 16th- and 17th-century England) a song on a topical subject, printed on broadsides, and sold. —*adv.* **7.** with the broader side toward a given point or object: *The truck hit the fence broadside.* —*v.i.* **8.** to proceed or go broadside. **9.** to fire a broadside or broadsides.

broad-spec·trum (brôd′spek′trəm), *adj.* *Pharm.* noting an antibiotic effective against a wide range of organisms.

broad·sword (brôd′sôrd′, -sōrd′), *n.* a sword having a straight, broad, flat blade, usually with a basket hilt. [ME *brood swerd,* OE *brād sweord*]

broad·tail (brôd′tāl′), *n.* the wavy, moirélike fur or pelt of a young or stillborn karakul lamb. Cf. **caracul** (def. 1), **Persian lamb** (def. 2).

Broad·way (brôd′wā′), *n.* **1.** a major avenue in New York City. **2.** the theater district located on or near this avenue, esp. as the center of the professional or commercial theater in the U.S. —*adj.* **3.** of, pertaining to, or characteristic of the commercial theater, esp. on Broadway. —**Broad′way·ite′,** *n.*

broad·wife (brôd′wīf′), *n., pl.* **-wives.** *U.S. Hist.* a female slave whose husband was owned by another master. [BROAD (adv.: far) + WIFE]

Brob·ding·nag·i·an (brob′ding nag′ē ən), *adj.* of huge size; gigantic. [after *Brobdingnag,* a land of gigantic inhabitants in Jonathan Swift's 1726 satire, *Gulliver's Travels*]

bro·cade (brō kād′), *n., v.,* **-cad·ed, -cad·ing.** —*n.* **1.** fabric woven with a raised overall pattern. —*v.t.* **2.** to weave with a design. [earlier *brocado* < Sp: lit., studded = *broc(a)* stud (see BROACH) + *-ado* -ADE[1]]

Bro′ca's ar′ea, *Anat.* a cerebral area, usually in the left inferior frontal gyrus, associated with the movements necessary for speech production. Also called **Bro′ca's gy′rus, Bro′ca's convolu′tion.** [named after P. BROCA]

broc·a·tel (brok′ə tel′), *n.* **1.** a brocade with a design in high relief. **2.** an ornamental marble with variegated coloring. Also **broc′a·telle′.** [< late MF < It *broccatell(o)* = *broccat(o)* (see BROCADE) + *-ello* dim. suffix]

broc·co·li (brok′ə lē), *n.* **1.** a plant of the mustard family, *Brassica oleracea botrytis,* resembling the cauliflower. **2.** a form of this plant without a head, the green florets and the stalk of which are a common vegetable. [< It, pl. of *broccolo* = *brocc(o)* sprout (see BROACH) + *-olo* dim. suffix]

bro·ché (brō shā′; *Fr.* brô shā′), *adj.* brocaded. [<F, ptp. of *brocher* to emboss (linen), weave (cloth) with a figure]

bro·chette (brō shet′; *Fr.* brô shet′), *n., pl.* **-chettes** (-shets′; *Fr.* -shet′). **1.** a skewer for use in cookery. **2. en brochette** (en, on; *Fr.* äN), on a skewer. [late ME < MF; OF *brochete.* See BROACH, -ETTE]

bro·chure (brō sho͝or′), *n.* a pamphlet. [< F < *broch(er)* (to) stitch (a book). See BROACH, -URE]

Brock·en (brok′ən), *n.* a mountain in E West Germany and W East Germany: the highest peak in the Harz Mountains. 3745 ft.

brock·et (brok′it), *n.* **1.** any of several small, red, South American deer of the genus *Mazama,* having short, unbranched antlers. **2.** the male red deer in the second year, with the first growth of straight horns. [late ME *broket* < AF *broquet* = *broque* horn (ML *broca;* see BROACH) + *-et* -ET]

Brock·ton (brok′tən), *n.* a city in E Massachusetts. 89,040 (1970).

bro·gan (brō′gən), *n.* a coarse, stout shoe, esp. an ankle-high work shoe. Cf. **brogue**[2]. [< Gael: pair of shoes; see BROGUE[2]]

Bro·glie (brô′yə; *Eng.* brō glē′), *n.* **1. A·chille Charles Lé·once Vic·tor de** (A shēl′ sharl lā ôNs′ vēk tôr′ də), 1785–1870, French statesman. **2.** his grandson **Louis Victor de** (lwē vēk tôr′ də), born 1892, French physicist: Nobel prize 1929. Also called **de Broglie.**

brogue[1] (brōg), *n.* a regional or dialectal pronunciation, esp. an Irish accent in the pronunciation of English. [? special use of BROGUE[2]] —**bro′guer·y,** *n.* —**bro′guish,** *adj.*

brogue[2] (brōg), *n.* a durable, oxford shoe, often having decorative perforations. [< Ir *brōg* shoe, OIr *brōce;* c. L *brācae* trousers < Gaulish; see BREECHES]

broi·der (broi′dər), *v.t.* *Archaic.* to embroider. [var. of *browder,* ME *broide(n), browde(n)* (ptp., taken as inf. of BRAID[1]) + -ER[6]] —**broi′der·er,** *n.* —**broi′der·y,** *n.*

broil[1] (broil), *v.t.* **1.** to cook by direct heat, as on a gridiron or in a broiler. **2.** to make very hot. —*v.i.* **3.** to be subjected to great heat. **4.** to burn with impatience, annoyance, etc. —*n.* **5.** the act of broiling. **6.** the state of being broiled. **7.** something broiled: *He ordered a beef broil and salad.* [ME *broille, bruyle* < MF *bruill(ir)* (to) broil, burn, perh. < Gmc] —**broil′ing·ly,** *adv.*

broil[2] (broil), *n.* **1.** a quarrel or brawl. —*v.i.* **2.** to quarrel; brawl. [late ME *broyle* to bring into confusion < MF *brouill(er)* (to) mix, OF *brooillier* < Gmc] —**broil′ing·ly,** *adv.*

broil·er (broi′lər), *n.* **1.** any device for broiling meat or fish; a grate, pan, or compartment in a stove for broiling. **2.** a young chicken suitable for broiling.

broke (brōk), *v.* **1.** a pt. of **break. 2.** *Nonstandard.* a pp. of **break. 3.** *Archaic.* a pp. of **break.** —*adj.* **4.** *Informal.* without money; penniless; bankrupt.

bro·ken (brō′kən), *v.* **1.** a pp. of **break.** —*adj.* **2.** reduced to fragments; fragmented. **3.** ruptured; torn; fractured. **4.** changing direction abruptly: *The fox ran in a broken line.* **5.** fragmentary or incomplete: *a broken ton.* **6.** infringed or violated: *A broken promise.* **7.** interrupted, disrupted, or disconnected. **8.** weakened in strength, spirit, etc.: *broken health.* **9.** tamed, trained, or reduced to submission: *broken to the saddle.* **10.** imperfectly spoken, as language: *He speaks broken English.* **11.** rough or irregular in surface: *broken country.* **12.** disunited or divided: *a broken family.* —**bro′ken·ly,** *adv.* —**bro′ken·ness,** *n.*

bro·ken-down (brō′kən doun′), *adj.* **1.** shattered or collapsed with use or age. **2.** out of working order.

bro′ken heart′, complete despair or disillusionment; devastating sorrow, esp. from disappointment in love.

bro·ken-heart·ed (brō′kən här′tid), *adj.* burdened with great sorrow, grief, or disappointment. —**bro′ken-heart′ed·ly,** *adv.* —**bro′ken-heart′ed·ness,** *n.*

Bro′ken Hill′, a city in W New South Wales, in SE Australia: mining center. 31,267 (1961).

bro′ken wind′ (wind), *Vet. Pathol.* heave (def. 23). —**bro′ken-wind′ed,** *adj.*

bro·ker (brō′kər), *n.* an agent who buys or sells for a principal on a commission basis. [ME *broco(u)r* << OF *brokeor* (north) < VL **broccātor* tapster. See BROACH, -OR[2]] —**bro′ker·ship′,** *n.*

bro·ker·age (brō′kər ij), *n.* **1.** the business of a broker. **2.** the commission of a broker.

brol·ly (brol′ē), *n., pl.* **-lies.** *Brit. Slang.* an umbrella. [(UM)BRELL(A) + -Y[2]]

brom-, a combining form of **bromine,** used esp. before a vowel: *bromate.*

bro·mal (brō′mal), *n. Pharm.* an oily, colorless liquid, CBr_3CHO, used in medicine chiefly as an anodyne and hypnotic.

bro·mate (brō′māt), *n., v.,* **-mat·ed, -mat·ing.** *Chem.* **—***n.* **1.** a salt of bromic acid. **—***v.t.* **2.** to treat with bromine; brominate.

Brom·berg (brom′bûrg; *Ger.* brôm′berkh), *n.* German name of **Bydgoszcz.**

brome′ grass′ (brōm), any of numerous grasses of the genus *Bromus,* esp. *B. inermis,* a perennial used for hay and pasture. Also called **brome.** [< NL *Brom(us)* (< Gk *brômos* oats)]

bro·me·li·a·ceous (brō mē′lē ā′shəs), *adj.* belonging to the *Bromeliaceae,* a family of herbaceous, chiefly tropical, American plants, including the pineapple, the Spanish moss, and many ornamentals. [< NL *Bromeli(a)* type genus of family (named after O. *Bromelius* (1639–1705), Swedish botanist) + -ACEOUS]

bro·mic (brō′mik), *adj. Chem.* containing pentavalent bromine.

bro′mic ac′id, *Chem.* an acid, $HBrO_3$, stable only in very dilute solutions, used chiefly as an oxidizing agent.

bro·mide (brō′mīd, -mid), *n.* **1.** *Chem.* **a.** a salt of hydrobromic acid consisting of two elements of which one is bromine, as sodium bromide, NaBr. **b.** a compound containing bromine, as methyl bromide. **2.** *Informal.* **a.** a platitude. **b.** a boring person. [BROM- + -IDE; in def. 2 from use of some bromides as sedatives]

bro′mide pa′per, *Photog.* a fast printing paper coated with an emulsion of silver bromide.

bro·min·ate (brō′mə nāt′), *v.t.,* **-at·ed, -at·ing.** *Chem.* to treat or combine with bromine; bromate. —**bro′mi·na′tion,** *n.*

bro·mine (brō′mēn, -min), *n. Chem.* a halogen element that is a dark-reddish, fuming, toxic liquid, used chiefly in the manufacture of antiknock compounds, pharmaceuticals, and dyes. *Symbol:* Br; *at. wt.:* 79.909; *at. no.:* 35; *sp. gr.* (*liquid*): 3.119 at 20°C. [< F *brome* bromine (< Gk *brômos* stench) + -INE[2]]

bro·mism (brō′miz əm), *n. Pathol.* a condition due to excessive use of bromides, characterized by skin eruptions. Also, **bro·min·ism** (brō′mə niz′əm).

bronc (brongk), *n.* bronco.

bronch-, var. of **broncho-** before a vowel.

bron·chi (brong′kī), *n. Anat.* pl. of **bronchus.**

bron·chi·a (brong′kē ə), *n. Anat.* (*construed as pl.*) the ramifications or branches of the bronchi. [< LL < Gk, pl. of *brônchion* = *brônch(os)* windpipe + *-ion* dim. suffix]

bron·chi·al (brong′kē əl), *adj. Anat.* pertaining to the bronchia or bronchi. —**bron′chi·al·ly,** *adv.*

bron′chial pneumo′nia, *Pathol.* bronchopneumonia.

bron′chial tube′, a bronchus or any of its ramifications or branches.

bron·chi·ole (brong′kē ōl′), *n. Anat.* a small branch of a bronchus. [< NL *bronchiol(um),* dim. of BRONCHIA] —**bron·chi·o·lar** (brong′kē ō′lər, brong kī′ə-), *adj.*

bron·chi·tis (brong kī′tis), *n. Pathol.* inflammation of the membrane lining of the bronchial tubes. [< NL] —**bron·chit·ic** (brong kit′ik), *adj.*

bron·cho (brong′kō), *n., pl.* **-chos.** bronco.

broncho-, a combining form of **bronchus:** *bronchopneumonia.*

bron·cho·cele (brong′kə sēl′), *n. Pathol.* dilatation of a bronchus. [< Gk *bronchokḗlē*]

bron·cho·pneu·mo·nia (brong′kō no͞o mōn′yə, -mō′nē ə, -nyo͞o-, -nə mōn′-), *n. Pathol.* inflammation of the bronchia and lungs; a form of pneumonia. Also called **bronchial pneumonia.** —**bron·cho·pneu·mon·ic** (brong′kō no͞o-mon′ik, -nyo͞o-), *adj.*

bron·chor·rha·gi·a (brong′kə rā′jē ə), *n. Pathol. Obs.* hemorrhage from the bronchial tubes.

bron·cho·scope (brong′kə skōp′), *n. Med.* a tubular instrument for examining bronchi and for removing foreign bodies from them. —**bron·cho·scop·ic** (brong′kə skop′ik), *adj.* —**bron′cho·scop′i·cal·ly,** *adv.* —**bron·chos·co·pist** (brong kos′kə pist), *n.* —**bron·chos′co·py,** *n.*

bron·chus (brong′kəs), *n., pl.* **-chi** (-kī). *Anat.* either of the two main branches of the trachea. [< NL < Gk *brónchos* windpipe]

bron·co (brong′kō), *n., pl.* **-cos.** **1.** a range pony or mustang of the western U.S., esp. one that is not broken. **2.** *Canadian Slang.* a Britisher, esp. a recent British immigrant. Also, **broncho.** [< MexSp, short for Sp *potro bronco* colt untamed (in MexSp: wild horse, half-tamed horse); appar. nasalized var. of L *broccus* projecting, hence rough; see BROACH]

bron·co·bust·er (brong′kō bus′tər), *n.* a person who breaks broncos to the saddle.

Bron·të (bron′tē), *n.* **1.** **Anne** (*Acton Bell*), 1820–49, English novelist. **2.** her sister, **Charlotte** (*Currer Bell*), 1816–1855, English novelist. **3.** her sister, **Emily Jane** (*Ellis Bell*), 1818–48, English novelist.

bron·to·saur (bron′tə sôr′), *n.* an amphibious, herbivorous dinosaur of the genus *Brontosaurus,* from the Jurassic period of North America. [*bronto-* (comb. form of Gk *brontḗ* thunder) + -SAUR]

Brontosaur (Length 65 to 77 ft.)

Bronx (brongks), *n.* **the,** a borough of New York City, NE of Manhattan. 1,471,701 (1970); 43.4 sq. mi. —**Bronx′ite,** *n.*

Bronx′ cheer′, *U.S.* a vulgar spluttering noise made with the tongue protruding from the lips to show contempt or disgust. Also called **raspberry.** Cf. **bird** (def. 9).

bronze (bronz), *n., v.,* **bronzed, bronz·ing.** **—***n.* **1.** *Metall.* **a.** any of various alloys consisting essentially of copper and tin, the tin content not exceeding 11 percent. **b.** any of various other alloys having a large copper content. **2.** a metallic brownish color. **3.** a work of art, as a statue, made of bronze. **4.** *Numis.* a coin made of bronze. **—***v.t.* **5.** to give the appearance or color of bronze to. **6.** to make brown, as by exposure to the sun. [earlier *bronzo* < It, prob. back formation from *bronzino* (adj.) < L (*aes*) *Brundusīnum* (brass) of Brindisi] —**bronz′y, bronze′like′,** *adj.*

Bronze′ Age′, **1.** a period in the history of mankind, following the Stone Age and preceding the Iron Age, during which bronze weapons and implements were used. **2.** (*l.c.*) *Class. Myth.* the third of the four ages of man, marked by war and violence.

Bron·zi·no (brôn dzē′nô), *n.* **A·gno·lo (di Co·si·mo di Ma·ria·no)** (ä′nyô lô dē kô′zē mô dē mä ryä′nô), 1502–1572, Italian painter.

broo (bro͞o; *Scot.* brœ, bry), *n. Scot. and North Eng.* any clear, palatable liquid, as broth, juice, or water. Also, **bree.** [late ME *bro(o),* perh. c. G *Brühe* broth, gravy, juice, Crimean Goth *broe* bread]

brooch (brōch, bro͞och), *n.* a clasp or ornament having a pin at the back for fastening to the clothing. [sp. var. of BROACH]

brood (bro͞od), *n.* **1.** a number of young produced or hatched at one time. **2.** a breed, species, group, or kind. **—***v.t.* **3.** to sit upon (eggs) to hatch, as a bird. **4.** (of a bird) to warm, protect, or cover (young) with the wings or body. **5.** to think persistently or moodily about: *He brooded the problem.* **—***v.i.* **6.** to sit upon eggs to be hatched, as a bird. **7.** to dwell on a subject with morbid persistence (usually fol. by *on* or *over*). **8.** to be in a morbid state of mind or indulge a melancholy disposition. **—***adj.* **9.** kept for breeding purposes: *brood hens.* [ME; OE *brōd;* c. D *broed,* G *Brut.* See BREED] —**brood′less,** *adj.*

—Syn. 1. BROOD, LITTER refer to young creatures. BROOD is esp. applied to the young of fowls and birds hatched from eggs at one time and raised under their mother's care: *a brood of young turkeys.* LITTER is applied to a group of young animals brought forth at a birth: *a litter of kittens.*

brood·er (bro͞o′dər), *n.* **1.** a device or structure for the artificial rearing of young chickens or other birds. **2.** a person or thing that broods.

brood·mare (bro͞od′mâr′), *n.* a mare used for breeding.

brood·y (bro͞o′dē), *adj.,* **brood·i·er, brood·i·est.** **1.** moody; gloomy. **2.** inclined to brood or sit on eggs: *a broody hen.* —**brood′i·ness,** *n.*

brook[1] (bro͝ok), *n.* a small, natural stream of fresh water. [ME; OE *brōc* stream; c. D *broek,* G *Bruch* marsh] —**brook′less,** *adj.* —**brook′like′,** *adj.*

brook[2] (bro͝ok), *v.t.* to bear; suffer; tolerate: *I will brook no interference.* [ME *brouke(n),* OE *brūcan;* c. D *bruiken,* G *brauchen;* akin to Goth *brukjan,* L *fru(ī)* enjoy] —**brook′a·ble,** *adj.*

Brooke (bro͝ok), *n.* **Rupert,** 1887–1915, English poet.

Brook′ Farm′, a farm in West Roxbury, Massachusetts, where a communistic community was established from 1841 to 1847.

Brook·field (bro͝ok′fēld′), *n.* a city in SE Wisconsin, near Milwaukee. 32,140 (1970).

brook·let (bro͝ok′lit), *n.* a small brook.

Brook·line (bro͝ok′līn′), *n.* a town in E Massachusetts, near Boston. 58,689 (1970).

Brook·lyn (bro͝ok′lin), *n.* a borough of New York City, on W Long Island. 2,602,012 (1970); 76.4 sq. mi. —**Brook·lyn·ite** (bro͝ok′lə nīt′), *n.*

Brook′lyn Cen′ter, a city in SE Minnesota, near Minneapolis. 35,173 (1970).

Brook′lyn Park′, a city in SE Minnesota, near Minneapolis. 26,230 (1970).

Brook′ Park′, a city in N Ohio, near Cleveland. 30,774 (1970).

Brooks (bro͝oks), *n.* **1. Phillips,** 1835–93, U.S. Protestant Episcopal bishop and pulpit orator. **2. Van Wyck,** 1886–1963, U.S. author and critic.

Brooks′ Range′, a mountain range in N Alaska, forming a watershed between the Yukon River and the Arctic Ocean: highest peak, 9239 ft.

brook′ trout′, a trout, *Salvelinus fontinalis,* of eastern North America. Also called **speckled trout.** See **trout.**

brook·weed (bro͝ok′wēd′), *n.* either of two Old World primulaceous plants having small white flowers, *Samolus Valerandi* or *S. floribundus.*

broom (bro͞om, bro͝om), *n.* **1.** an implement for sweeping, consisting of a brush of straw or similar material bound to a long handle. **2.** any of the shrubby fabaceous plants of the genus *Cytisus,* esp. *C. scoparius,* common in Western Europe, having long, slender branches with yellow flowers. **—***v.t.* **3.** to sweep. **4.** to splinter or fray mechanically. [ME *brome,* OE *brōm;* c. D *braam* bramble, G *Bram* broom, *Brombeere* blackberry]

broom·corn (bro͞om′kôrn′, bro͝om′-), *n.* any of several varieties of sorghum having a long, stiff-branched panicle used in brooms.

broom·rape (bro͞om′rāp′, bro͝om′-), *n.* any of various parasitic plants, esp. of the genus *Orobanche,* living on the roots of broom and other plants. [half trans., half adoption of ML *rāpum genistae* tuber of the broom plant]

broom·stick (bro͞om′stik′, bro͝om′-), *n.* the long sticklike handle of a broom.

bros., brothers. Also, **Bros.**

brose (brōz), *n. Scot.* a dish made by stirring boiling liquid into oatmeal or other meal. [ME *broys,* etc. < OF *broez;* see BREWIS] —**bros′y,** *adj.*

broth (brôth, broth), *n.* **1.** thin soup of concentrated meat or fish stock. **2.** water that has been boiled with meat, fish, vegetables, or barley. [ME, OE; c. Icel *broth,* OHG *brod;* akin to BREW] —**broth′y,** *adj.*

broth·el (broth′əl, broth′-, brô′thəl, -thəl), *n.* a house of prostitution; bordello. [short for *brothel-house* whorehouse; ME *brothel* harlot, orig. worthless person = *broth-* (ptp. s. of *brethen,* OE *brēothan* to decay, degenerate) + *-el* n. suffix]

broth·er (bruth′ər *or, for* 8, bruth′ûr′), *n., pl.* **brothers,** (*Archaic*) **brethren,** *interj.* **—***n.* **1.** a male offspring having both parents in common with another offspring; a male sibling. **2.** Also called **half brother.** a male offspring having only one parent in common with another offspring. **3.** stepbrother. **4.** a male numbered among the same kinship group, nationality, profession, etc., as another; a fellow member, fellow countryman, fellow-man, etc.: *He is a fraternity brother of mine.* **5.** *Eccles.* **a.** (*often cap.*) a male lay member of a religious organization that has a priesthood. **b.** a man who devotes himself to the duties of a religious order without taking holy orders, or while preparing for holy orders. **6. brothers,** human beings generally, esp. when regarded as deserving sympathy or respect. **7.** *Slang.* (used in direct address) fellow; buddy. **—***interj.* **8.** *Slang.* (used to express disappointment, disgust, or surprise.) [ME; OE *brōthor;* c. G *Bruder,* Icel *brōthir,* Goth *brothar,* Skt *bhrātr,* Gk *phrā́tēr,* L *frāter*] **—broth′er·less,** *adj.* **—broth′er·like′,** *adj.*

broth·er·hood (bruth′ər ho͝od′), *n.* **1.** the condition or quality of being a brother or brothers. **2.** the quality of being brotherly; fellowship. **3.** a fraternal or trade organization. **4.** all those engaged in a particular trade, profession, pursuit, etc. **5.** the belief that all men should act brotherly toward one another, regardless of differences in race, creed, nationality, etc. [ME *brithirhod* (see BROTHER, -HOOD); r. early ME *brotherhede;* see -HEAD]

broth·er-in-law (bruth′ər in lô′), *n., pl.* **broth·ers-in-law. 1.** the brother of one's husband or wife. **2.** the husband of one's sister. **3.** (loosely) the husband of one's wife's or husband's sister. [ME]

Broth′er Jon′athan, *Brit. Archaic.* **1.** the government of the United States. **2.** the typical American.

broth·er·ly (bruth′ər lē), *adj.* **1.** of, like, or befitting a brother or brothers, as in being affectionate or loyal. **—***adv.* **2.** *Archaic.* as a brother. [ME; OE *brōthorlīc*] **—broth′er·li·ness,** *n.*

brough·am (bro͞o′əm, bro͞om, brō′əm), *n.* **1.** a four-wheeled, boxlike, closed carriage for two or four persons, having the driver's perch outside. **2.** *Auto. Obs.* **a.** a limousine having an open driver's compartment. **b.** an early type of automobile resembling a coupé, often powered by an electric motor. [named after Lord *Brougham* (1778–1868), English statesman]

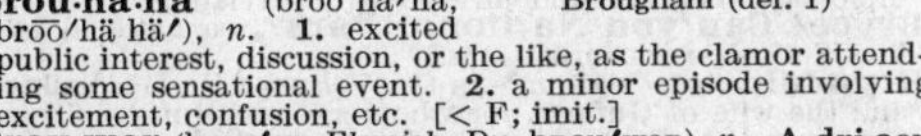
Brougham (def. 1)

brought (brôt), *v.* pt. and pp. of **bring.**

brou·ha·ha (bro͞o hä′hä, bro͞o′hä hä′), *n.* **1.** excited public interest, discussion, or the like, as the clamor attending some sensational event. **2.** a minor episode involving excitement, confusion, etc. [< F; imit.]

Brou·wer (brou′ər; *Flemish, Du.* BROU′WƏR), *n.* **A·dri·aen** (ä′drē än′), 1606?–38, Flemish painter.

brow (brou), *n.* **1.** *Anat.* the ridge over the eye; eyebrow. **2.** the hair growing on that ridge; eyebrow. **3.** the forehead. **4.** a person's countenance or mien. **5.** the edge of a steep place: *the brow of a hill.* [ME *browe,* OE *brū;* akin to Icel *brūn,* Skt *bhrūs*] **—brow′less,** *adj.*

brow′ ant′ler, the first prong from the base of a stag's antler.

brow·beat (brou′bēt′), *v.t.,* **-beat, -beat·en, -beat·ing.** to intimidate by overbearing looks or words; bully. **—brow′beat′er,** *n.*

brown (broun), *n.* **1.** a dark shade with a yellowish or reddish hue. **2.** a black horse with brown points. **3.** *Brit. Slang.* any copper coin. **—***adj.* **4.** of the color brown. **5.** having skin, fur, hair, or feathers of that color. **6.** sunburned or tanned. **7. do it up brown,** *Slang.* to do thoroughly, excellently, or perfectly. **—***v.t., v.i.* **8.** to make or become brown. **9.** to fry, sauté, or scorch slightly in cooking. [ME; OE *brūn;* c. D *bruin,* G *braun,* Icel *brūnn;* akin to Lith *brunas* brown] **—brown′ish, brown′y,** *adj.* **—brown′ness,** *n.*

Brown (broun), *n.* **1. Charles Brock·den** (brok′dən), 1771–1810, U.S. novelist. **2. John** ("*Old Brown of Osawatomie*"), 1800–59, U.S. abolitionist: leader of the attack at Harpers Ferry where he was captured, tried for treason, and hanged.

brown′ al′ga, an alga of the class *Phaeophyceae,* usually brown owing to the presence of brown pigments in addition to the chlorophyll.

brown-bag (broun′bag′), *v.,* **-bagged, -bag·ging,** *adj.* **—***v.t.* **1.** to bring (one's own liquor) to a restaurant or club, as when it has no liquor license. **2.** to bring (one's lunch) to work, usually in a small brown paper bag. **—***adj.* **3.** brought to work, usually in a small brown paper bag: *a brown-bag lunch.* **—brown′-bag′ger,** *n.* **—brown′-bag′ging,** *adj., n.*

brown′ bear′, **1.** a variety of the American black bear, having a brownish coat. **2.** a European bear, *Ursus arctos,* having a brownish coat.

brown′ belt′, *Judo.* **1.** a brown waistband worn with a judo costume, conferred by a judo association upon a player to indicate that he is of intermediate rank. **2.** a player entitled to wear such a belt or the rank indicated by it. Cf. **black belt** (def. 2), **white belt.**

brown′ bet′ty, a baked pudding made of apples or other fruit, bread crumbs, sugar, butter, spice, etc.

brown′ bread′, **1.** any bread made of flour darker in color than the bolted wheat flour, esp. graham or whole wheat bread. **2.** See **Boston brown bread.**

brown′ but′ter. See **beurre noir.**

brown′ coal′, lignite.

Browne (broun), *n.* **1. Charles Far·rer** (far′ər), ("*Artemus Ward*"), 1834–67, U.S. humorist. **2. Sir Thomas,** 1605–82, English physician and author.

brown′ hack′le, *Angling.* an artificial fly having a peacock herl body, golden tag and tail, and brown hackle.

brown′ hem′atite, *Mineral.* limonite.

Brown′i·an move′ment (brou′nē ən), the irregular motion of small particles suspended in a liquid or a gas, caused by the bombardment of the particles by molecules of the medium. Also called **Brown′ian mo′tion.** [named after Robert *Brown* (1773–1858), Scottish botanist, who first observed it in 1827]

brown·ie (brou′nē), *n.* **1.** (in folklore) a little brown fairy or goblin, esp. one who helps secretly in household work. **2.** *U.S.* a small, chewy, chocolate cake, usually containing nuts. **3.** (*cap.*) a member of the junior division (ages 8–11) of the Girl Scouts or the Girl Guides. **—Syn. 1.** See **fairy.**

Brown′ie point′, a credit toward advancement or good standing, esp. when gained by servility, opportunism, or the like. [from the point system used by Brownies for advancement]

Brown·ing (brou′ning), *n.* **1. Elizabeth Bar·rett** (bar′it), 1806–61, English poet. **2. John Moses,** 1885–1926, U.S. designer of firearms. **3. Robert,** 1812–89, English poet (husband of Elizabeth Barrett Browning).

Brown′ing automat′ic ri′fle, an air-cooled, fully automatic rifle capable of firing 200 to 350 rounds per minute. *Abbr.:* BAR [named after J. M. BROWNING]

brown-nose (broun′nōz′), *v.,* **-nosed, -nos·ing,** *n. Slang.* **—***v.i.* **1.** to curry favor; to behave obsequiously. **—***v.t.* **2.** to seek favors from (a person) in an obsequious manner. **—***n.* **3.** a toady; obsequious sycophant. [figurative reference to kissing the buttocks of the person whose favor is sought]

brown·out (broun′out′), *n.* **1.** the elimination of some or reduction of all electric lights of a city, esp. as a precaution in time of war. **2.** any curtailment of electric power, as by a severe storm. [BROWN + OUT, modeled on *blackout*]

brown′ rat′. See **Norway rat.**

brown′ rice′, unpolished rice that retains the bran layers and germs.

Brown′ Shirt′, **1.** a member of the Nazi political militia; storm trooper. **2.** Also, **brown′ shirt′.** any fascist.

brown·stone (broun′stōn′), *n. U.S.* **1.** a reddish-brown sandstone, used extensively as a building material. **2.** Also called **brown′stone front′.** a building, esp. a row house, fronted with this stone.

brown′ stud′y, deep, serious absorption in thought: *Lost in a brown study, she was oblivious to the noise.*

brown′ sug′ar, unrefined or partially refined sugar.

Browns·ville (brounz′vil), *n.* a seaport in S Texas, near the mouth of the Rio Grande. 52,522 (1970).

Brown′ Swiss′, one of a breed of brownish dairy cattle raised originally in Switzerland.

brown′-tail moth′ (broun′tāl′), a white moth, *Nygmia phaerrhoea,* having a brown tuft at the end of the abdomen, the larvae of which feed on the foliage of shade and fruit trees. Also called **brown′tail′.**

brown′ trout′, a common trout, *Salmo trutta fario,* found in streams of northern Europe.

browse (brouz), *v.,* **browsed, brows·ing,** *n.* **—***v.t.* **1.** (of cattle, deer, etc.) to eat; nibble at; eat from. **2.** (of cattle, deer, etc.) to graze; feed on; pasture on. **3.** to look through or over casually: *He's browsing the shelves for something to read.* **—***v.i.* **4.** (of cattle, deer, etc.) to graze. **5.** to look through or over something in a casual, unhurried manner, as goods displayed for sale in a booth or store. **—***n.* **6.** tender shoots or twigs of shrubs and trees as food for cattle, deer, etc. **7.** the act or an instance of browsing. [late ME *browse(n)* < ?] **—brows′er,** *n.*

Broz (brōz), *n.* **Jo·sip** (yō′sip). See **Tito, Marshal.**

Br. Som., British Somaliland.

B.R.T., Brotherhood of Railroad Trainmen.

Bruce (bro͞os), *n.* **1. Robert.** See **Robert I** (def. 1). **2. Stanley Melbourne** (*1st Viscount Bruce of Melbourne*), 1883–1967, Australian statesman: prime minister 1923–29.

bru·cel·lo·sis (bro͞o′sə lō′sis), *n. Pathol.* infection with bacteria of the *Brucella* group, frequently causing abortions in animals and remittent fever in man. Also called **undulant fever, Malta fever, Mediterranean fever.** [< NL *Brucella* (named after Sir David *Bruce* (1855–1931), Australian physician; L *-ella* fem. dim. suffix) + -OSIS]

Bruch (bro͝okh), *n.* **Max** (mäks), 1838–1920, German composer and conductor.

bru·cine (bro͞o′sēn, -sin), *n. Chem.* a very poisonous alkaloid, $C_{23}H_{26}N_2O_4$, resembling strychnine in its pharmacological action: used chiefly in the denaturation of alcohol. [named after J. *Bruce* (1730–94), Scottish explorer; see -INE[2]]

Bruck·ner (bruk′nər; *Ger.* BRO͝OK′NƏR), *n.* **An·ton** (an′tən, -ton, -tōn; *Ger.* än′tōn), 1824–96, Austrian composer.

Brue·ghel (broi′gəl, bro͞o′-; *Flemish* BRŒ′gəl), *n.* Breughel. Also, **Brue′gel.**

Bru·ges (bro͞o′jiz, bro͞ozh; *Fr.* BRYZH), *n.* a city in NW Belgium: connected by canal with its seaport, Zeebrugge. 52,448 (est. 1964). Flemish, **Brug·ge** (BRŒKH′ə).

bru·in (bro͞o′in), *n.* a bear. [late ME *bruyn* < MD: lit., the brown one, name of bear in fable of Reynard the Fox]

bruise (bro͞oz), *v.,* **bruised, bruis·ing,** *n.* **—***v.t.* **1.** to injure by striking or pressing without breaking the skin, causing a subcutaneous hemorrhage. **2.** to offend or hurt superficially, as with an insult or unkind remark: *to bruise a person's feelings.* **3.** to crush (drugs or food) by beating or pounding. **—***v.i.* **4.** to develop or bear a discolored spot on the skin as the result of a blow, fall, etc. **5.** to be readily susceptible to offense, as of one's feelings. **—***n.* **6.** a discolored spot on the skin due to bruising; contusion. [ME *bro(o)sen, bres(s)en, bris(s)en, bruisen,* OE *brȳsan, brēsan,* coalescing with MF *bruisier* to shatter < Celt; cf. Ir *brūigim* I bruise, mash]

bruis·er (bro͞o′zər), *n. Informal.* a strong, tough person.

bruit (bro͞ot), *v.t.* **1.** to voice abroad; rumor (used chiefly in the passive): *The report was bruited through the village.* **—***n.* **2.** *Med.* any generally abnormal sound or murmur heard on auscultation. **3.** *Archaic.* rumor; report. [late ME < ML *brūgīt(us)* a roar, rumble = *brūg-* (< ?) + *-ītus* -ITE[2]]

Bru·maire (BRY MER′), *n.* (in the French Revolutionary calendar) the second month of the year, extending from October 22 to November 20. [< F = *brume* BRUME + *-aire* -ARY]

bru·mal (bro͞o′məl), *adj.* wintry. [< L *brūmāl(is)* of, pertaining to winter. See BRUME, -AL[1]]

brume (bro͞om), *n.* mist; fog. [< F: fog < Pr *bruma* < L: winter, orig. winter solstice, contr. of **brevima* (*diēs*) shortest (day)] **—bru·mous** (bro͞o′məs), *adj.*

brum·ma·gem (brum′ə jəm), *adj.* **1.** showy but inferior and worthless. **—***n.* **2.** a showy but inferior and worthless thing. [an old local var. of BIRMINGHAM, England, by metathesis in first syllable and dissimilative loss of second nasal]

Brum·mell (brum′əl), *n.* See **Beau Brummell.**

brunch (brunch), *n.* **1.** a late-morning meal that serves both as breakfast and lunch. **—***v.i.* **2.** to eat brunch. [BR(EAKFAST + L)UNCH]

Brun·dis·i·um (brun diz′ē əm), *n.* ancient name of **Brindisi.**

Bru·nei (bro͞o nī′), *n.* **1.** a sultanate under British protection on the NW coast of Borneo. 83,869 (1960); 2220 sq. mi. **2.** a seaport in and the capital of this British sultanate. 9702 (1960).

Bru·nel (brōō nel′), *n.* **1. Is·am·bard Kingdom** (iz′əm-bärd′), 1806–59, English civil engineer and naval architect. **2.** his father, **Sir Marc Isambard,** 1769–1849, English civil engineer, born in France: chief engineer of New York City 1793–99.

Bru·nel·les·chi (brōōn′ᵊles′kē; *It.* brōō′nel les′kē), *n.* **Fi·lip·po** (fi lip′ō; *It.* fē lĕp′pô), 1377?–1446, Italian architect. Also, **Bru·nel·les·co** (brōōn′ᵊles′kō; *It.* brōō′nel-les′kô).

bru·net (brōō net′), *adj.* **1.** (esp. of a male) brunette. —*n.* **2.** a person, usually a male, with dark hair, eyes, and skin. [< F = *brun* BROWN + *-et* -ET] —**bru·net′ness,** *n.*

bru·nette (brōō net′), *adj.* **1.** (of skin, eyes, or hair) dark; brown. **2.** (esp. of a female) having dark hair, eyes, or skin. —*n.* **3.** a person, esp. a female, with dark hair, eyes, and skin. [< F; fem. of BRUNET] —**bru·nette′ness,** *n.*

Brun·hild (brŏŏn′hilt, -hild), *n.* (in the *Nibelungenlied*) a queen of Isenland and the bride of Gunther, won for him by Siegfried: corresponds to Brynhild in Scandinavian legends. Also, **Brun·hil·de** (brŏŏn hil′də), **Brünn·hil·de** (brŏŏn hil′-də; *Ger.* bryn hil′də).

Brünn (bryn), *n.* German name of **Brno.**

Bru·no (brōō′nō; *for 1 also It.* brōō′nô), *n.* **1. Gior·da·no** (jôr dä′nô), 1548?–1600, Italian philosopher. **2. Saint,** c1030–1101, German ecclesiastical writer: founder of the Carthusian order.

Bruns·wick (brunz′wik), *n.* **1.** a former state of Germany: now part of Lower Saxony in E West Germany. **2.** a city in Lower Saxony, in E West Germany. 241,300 (1963). German, **Braunschweig.**

Bruns′wick stew′, a stew usually consisting of rabbit or squirrel meat, onions, and other vegetables.

brunt (brunt), *n.* **1.** the main shock, force, or impact, as of an attack or blow. **2.** *Obs.* a violent attack; assault. [ME; perh. orig. sexual assault, akin to Icel *brundr,* G *Brunft* heat, ruttish state, OE *brunetha* heat, itching; c. OHG *bronado*]

Bru·sa (*Turk.* brōō′sä), *n.* Bursa.

brush[1] (brush), *n.* **1.** an implement consisting of bristles, hair, or the like, set in or attached to a handle, used for painting, cleaning, polishing, grooming, etc. **2.** the act or an instance of brushing. **3.** the bushy tail of an animal, esp. a fox. **4.** a slight encounter: *a brush with the law.* **5.** *Elect.* **a.** a conductor serving to maintain electric contact between the stationary and moving parts of a machine, generator, or other apparatus. **b.** See **brush discharge. 6.** any feathery or hairy tuft or tassel, as on the tip of a kernel of grain, worn as an ornament on a man's hat, etc. —*v.t.* **7.** to paint, clean, polish, groom, etc., with a brush. **8.** to touch lightly in passing: *His lips brushed her ear.* **9.** to remove by brushing or by lightly passing over: *He brushed a speck of lint from his coat.* —*v.i.* **10.** to brush one's teeth: *Brush after each meal.* **11.** to brush one's hair. **12.** to move or skim with a slight contact. **13.** to push someone or something. **14. brush aside,** to disregard; ignore. **15. brush off,** *U.S. Slang.* to rebuff; send away. **16. brush up on,** to review or resume (studies, a skill, etc.). [ME *brusshe* < MF *broisse,* OF *broce* < VL **brustia* < Gmc; cf. MHG *büriste* brush, OE *bryst* BRISTLE] —**brush′a·ble,** *adj.* —**brush′er,** *n.* —**brush′less,** *adj.* —**brush′like′, brush′y,** *adj.* —**Syn. 4.** engagement, action, skirmish.

brush[2] (brush), *n.* **1.** a dense growth of bushes, shrubs, etc.; scrub; thicket. **2.** a pile or covering of lopped or broken branches; brushwood. **3.** land or an area covered with thickly growing bushes and low trees. **4.** *U.S.* backwoods; a sparsely settled wooded region. [late ME *brusshe;* see BRUSH[1]] —**brush′i·ness,** *n.* —**brush′less,** *adj.* —**brush′-less·ness,** *n.* —**brush′y,** *adj.*

brush′ dis′charge, *Elect.* a type of corona discharge that takes place between two electrodes at atmospheric pressure, characterized by long, branched, luminous streamers of ionized particles.

brush′ fire′, a fire in an area of bushes, shrubs, or brush, as distinct from a forest fire.

brush′-foot·ed but′terfly (brush′fŏŏt′id), any of several butterflies of the family *Nymphalidae,* including the fritillaries, mourning cloaks, anglewings, commas, etc., characterized by reduced, nonfunctional forelegs.

brush-off (brush′ôf′, -of′), *n.* *U.S. Slang.* an abrupt dismissal or rebuff.

brush·up (brush′up′), *n.* the act or process of reviewing something for the purpose of renewing one's memory or skill.

brush·wood (brush′wŏŏd′), *n.* **1.** branches that have been cut or broken off a tree or shrub. **2.** brush[2] (def. 1).

brush·work (brush′wûrk′), *n.* **1.** the use of a brush as a tool, as in painting. **2.** *Fine Arts.* the surface quality of a painting as affected by the brush. **3.** work for which a brush is used, as painting.

brusque (brusk; *esp. Brit.* brŏŏsk), *adj.* abrupt in manner; blunt; rough. [< MF < It *brusco* sour, rough, unripe] —**brusque′ly,** *adv.* —**brusque′ness,** *n.* —**Syn.** unceremonious, short, curt. See **blunt.**

brus·que·rie (brus′kə rē; *esp. Brit.* brŏŏs′kə rē; *Fr.* brys-kə rē′), *n.* brusqueness. [< F; see BRUSQUE, -ERY]

Brus·sels (brus′əlz), *n.* a city in and the capital of Belgium, in the central part. 1,050,787. Flemish, **Brus·sel** (brys′əl); French, **Bruxelles.**

Brus′sels car′pet, a carpet made with three-ply or four-ply worsted yarn drawn up in uncut loops to form a pattern over the entire surface, or made of worsted or woolen yarns on which a pattern is printed **(tapestry Brussels).**

Brus′sels grif′fon, one of a Belgian breed of toy dogs having a thick, wiry, reddish-brown coat.

Brus′sels lace′, any fine handmade lace with a floral pattern.

Brus·sels sprout (brus′əl sprout′), **1.** a plant, *Brassica oleracea gemmifera,* having small, cabbagelike, edible heads or sprouts along the stalk. **2.** Usually, **Brussels sprouts.** the heads or sprouts of this plant used as a table vegetable.

brut (brōōt; *Fr.* bryt), *adj.* (of wine, esp. champagne) very dry. [< F: raw; see BRUTE[2]]

bru·tal (brōōt′ᵊl), *adj.* **1.** savage; cruel; inhuman. **2.** crude; coarse; harsh. **3.** irrational; unreasoning. **4.** of or pertaining to lower animals. [late ME < ML *brūtāl(is).* See BRUTE[1], -AL[1]] —**bru′tal·ly,** *adv.* —**Syn. 1.** brutish. See **cruel. 2.** gross, rude, rough, uncivil. **4.** beastlike, beastly, animal.

bru·tal·ise (brōōt′ᵊlīz′), *v.t., v.i.,* **-ised, -is·ing.** *Chiefly Brit.* brutalize. —**bru′tal·i·sa′tion,** *n.*

bru·tal·i·ty (brōō tal′i tē), *n., pl.* **-ties. 1.** the quality of being brutal. **2.** a brutal act or practice.

bru·tal·ize (brōōt′ᵊlīz′), *v.t., v.i.,* **-ized, -iz·ing. 1.** to make or become brutal. **2.** to treat with brutality. Also, *esp. Brit.,* **brutalise.** —**bru′tal·i·za′tion,** *n.*

brute[1] (brōōt), *n.* **1.** a nonhuman creature; beast. **2.** a brutal, insensitive, or crude person. **3.** the animal qualities, desires, etc., of man. —*adj.* **4.** animal; not human. **5.** not characterized by intelligence or reason; irrational. **6.** characteristic of animals. **7.** savage; cruel. **8.** carnal; sensual. [late ME < L *brūt(us)* heavy, stupid, irrational] —**brute′-like′,** *adj.* —**brute′ly,** *adv.* —**brute′ness,** *n.* —**Syn. 1.** See **animal.**

brute[2] (brōōt), *v.t.,* **brut·ed, brut·ing.** to shape (a diamond) by rubbing it with another diamond or a diamond chip. [back formation from *bruting* a rough hewing (of a diamond), half-adoption, half-trans. of F *brutage,* lit., a roughing = *brut* rough, raw (see BRUT) + *-age* -AGE]

bru·ti·fy (brōō′tə fī′), *v.t., v.i.,* **-fied, -fy·ing.** to brutalize. —**brut′i·fi·ca′tion,** *n.*

brut·ish (brōō′tish), *adj.* **1.** brutal; cruel. **2.** gross; carnal; bestial. **3.** uncivilized; animallike. —**brut′ish·ly,** *adv.* —**brut′ish·ness,** *n.*

Bru·tus (brōō′təs), *n.* **Marcus Jun·ius** (jōōn′yəs), 85?–42 B.C., Roman provincial administrator: one of the assassins of Julius Caesar.

Brux·elles (bry sel′, bryk sel′), *n.* French name of **Brussels.**

Bry·an (brī′ən), *n.* **1. William Jen·nings** (jen′ingz), 1860–1925, U.S. political leader. **2.** a city in E Texas. 33,719 (1970).

Bry·ansk (brē änsk′; *Russ.* bryänsk), *n.* a city in the W RSFSR, in the W Soviet Union in Europe, SW of Moscow. 259,000 (est. 1964).

Bry·ant (brī′ənt), *n.* **William Cullen,** 1794–1878, U.S. poet and journalist.

Bryce (brīs), *n.* **James, 1st Viscount,** 1838–1922, British diplomat, historian, and jurist; born in Ireland.

Bryce′ Can′yon Na′tional Park′, a national park in SW Utah: rock formations.

Bryn·hild (brin′hild), *n.* (in the *Volsunga Saga*) a Valkyrie and the wife of Gunnar, for whom she was won by Sigurd: corresponds to Brunhild in the *Nibelungenlied.*

bry·ol·o·gy (brī ol′ə jē), *n.* the branch of botany dealing with bryophytes. [< Gk *brýo(n)* moss + -LOGY] —**bry·o·log·i·cal** (brī′ə loj′i kəl), *adj.* —**bry·ol′o·gist,** *n.*

bry·o·ny (brī′ə nē), *n., pl.* **-nies.** any Old World, cucurbitaceous vine or climbing plant of the genus *Bryonia,* yielding an acrid juice used as a purgative or emetic. Also, **briony.** [OE *bryōnia* < L < Gk: a wild vine]

bry·o·phyte (brī′ə fīt′), *n.* *Bot.* any of the *Bryophyta,* a primary division or group of plants comprising the true mosses and liverworts. [< NL *Bryophyta* = Gk *brýo(n)* moss + *phytá* pl. of *phytón* -PHYTE] —**bry·o·phyt·ic** (brī′ə-fit′ik), *adj.*

Bry·o·zo·a (brī′ə zō′ə), *n.* the phylum comprising the bryozoans. [< NL < Gk *bryō-* (s. of *brýon*) + *-zoa* -ZOA]

bry·o·zo·an (brī′ə zō′ən), *adj.* **1.** belonging or pertaining to the *Bryozoa.* —*n.* **2.** any sessile, marine or fresh-water animal of the phylum *Bryozoa,* forming branching, encrusting, or gelatinous colonies of many small polyps, each having a circular or horseshoe-shaped ridge bearing ciliated tentacles.

Bryth·on (brith′ən), *n.* **1.** a member of the Brythonic-speaking Celts. **2.** a Briton. [< Welsh; see BRITON]

Bry·thon·ic (bri thon′ik), *adj.* **1.** of or belonging to P-Celtic. —*n.* **2.** P-Celtic, esp. that part either spoken in Britain, as Welsh and Cornish, or descended from the P-Celtic speech of Britain, as Breton. Also, **Britannic.**

Brześć nad Bu·giem (bzheshch′ näd bŏŏ′gyem), Polish name of **Brest Litovsk.**

B/S, See **bill of sale.**

b/s, 1. bags. **2.** bales, **3.** See **bill of sale.**

B.S., 1. See **Bachelor of Science. 2.** See **bill of sale. 3.** Also, **b.s.** *Slang.* bullshit.

b.s., 1. balance sheet. **2.** See **bill of sale.**

B.S.A., Boy Scouts of America.

B.Sc., See **Bachelor of Science.**

B.S.C.P., Brotherhood of Sleeping Car Porters.

bsh., bushel; bushels.

bskt., basket.

Bs/L, bills of lading.

BSO, See **blue stellar object.**

Bt., Baronet.

B.Th., Bachelor of Theology. Also, **B.T.**

btl., bottle.

btry., battery.

Btu, *Physics.* See **British thermal unit.** Also, **BTU, B.t.u., B.T.U.**

bu., 1. bureau. **2.** bushel; bushels.

bub (bub), *n.* *Chiefly U.S. Slang.* (used in direct address) brother; boy; buddy. [perh. < G *Bub,* short for *Bube* boy]

bu·bal (byōō′bəl), *n.* a hartebeest, *Alcelaphus boselaphus,* of N Africa. Also, **bu·ba·lis** (byōō′bə lis). [ME < L *būbal-(us)* < Gk *boúbalos* a kind of gazelle or buffalo]

bub·ble (bub′əl), *n., v.,* **-bled, -bling.** —*n.* **1.** a nearly spherical body of gas contained in a liquid. **2.** a small globule of gas in a thin liquid envelope. **3.** a globule of gas, or a globular vacuum, contained in a solid. **4.** anything that lacks firmness, substance, or permanence; delusion. **5.** an inflated speculation, esp. if fraudulent: *the Florida real-estate bubble.* **6.** the act or sound of bubbling. **7.** a usually transparent hemispherical canopy or shelter. —*v.i.* **8.** to form, produce, or release bubbles. **9.** to flow or spout with a gurgling noise. **10.** to boil: *The tea bubbled in the pot.* **11.** to act or exist in a lively, sparkling manner; exude cheer: *The play bubbled with songs and dances.* **12.** to seethe or stir, as with excitement: *His mind bubbles with plans and schemes.* —*v.t.* **13.** to cause to bubble; make bubbles in. **14. bubble**

over, to be overflowing with good spirits or liveliness. [ME *bobel* (n.); c. MD *bobbel*, MLG *bubbele*, Sw *bubbla*] **—bub′ble·less,** *adj.* **—bub′ble·like′,** *adj.* **—bub′bling·ly,** *adv.*

bub′ble and squeak′, *Brit.* a dish of meat and cabbage cooked together, sometimes with potatoes added.

bub′ble bath′, 1. a crystal, powder, or liquid preparation that foams in, scents, and softens bath water. 2. a bath with such a preparation added to the water.

bub′ble cham′ber, *Physics.* an apparatus consisting of a chamber containing a superheated transparent liquid that, by boiling and producing bubbles in the path of an ionizing particle, indicates the path of the particle. Cf. **cloud chamber.**

bub′ble gum′, a variety of chewing gum that can be blown into large bubbles through the lips.

bub·bler (bub′lər), *n.* 1. a drinking fountain which spouts water directly into the mouth. 2. *Chem.* any device for bubbling gas through a liquid.

bub·bly (bub′lē), *adj.*, **-bli·er, -bli·est,** *n.* **—***adj.* 1. full of, producing, or characterized by bubbles. **—***n.* 2. *Chiefly Brit. Slang.* champagne (def. 1).

Bub·er (bo͞o′bər), *n.* **Martin,** 1878–1965, Jewish philosopher, theologian, and scholar of Hasidism: born in Austria, in Israel from 1938.

bu·bo (byo͞o′bō), *n., pl.* **-boes.** *Pathol.* an inflammatory swelling of a lymphatic gland, esp. in the groin or armpit. [< LL < Gk *boubṓn*, lit., groin] **—bu′boed,** *adj.*

bu·bon·ic (byo͞o bon′ik, bo͞o-), *adj.* *Pathol.* 1. of or pertaining to a bubo. 2. accompanied by or affected with buboes. [< LL *būbōn-* (s. of *būbō*) BUBO + -IC]

bubon′ic plague′, *Pathol.* a form of plague characterized by buboes. Cf. **plague** (def. 2).

Bu·ca·ra·man·ga (bo͞o kä′rä mäng′gä), *n.* a city in N Colombia. 208,640 (est. 1961).

bucc-, a learned borrowing from Latin meaning "cheek," "mouth," used in the formation of compound words: *buccal.* [comb. form repr. L *bucca*]

buc·cal (buk′əl), *adj.* *Anat.* 1. of or pertaining to the cheek. 2. pertaining to the sides of the mouth or to the mouth; oral. **—buc′cal·ly,** *adv.*

buc·ca·neer (buk′ə nēr′), *n.* a pirate, esp. one of those who raided Spanish colonies and ships along the American coast in the second half of the 17th century. [< F *boucanier*, lit., barbecuer = *boucan* barbecue (< Tupi, var. of *mukém*) + *-ier* -EER] **—buc′ca·neer′ish,** *adj.*

buc·ci·na·tor (buk′sə nā′tər), *n.* *Anat.* a thin, flat muscle lining the cheek, acting as a contractor and compressor. [< L: trumpeter = *buccinā(tus)* trumpeted (ptp. of *buccināre* < *buccina* horn; see -ATE[1]) + *-or* -OR[2]] **—buc·ci·na·to·ry** (buk′sə nə tōr′ē, -tôr′ē, buk′sə nā′tə rē), *adj.*

bu·cen·taur (byo͞o sen′tôr), *n.* the state barge of Venice, from which the doge and other officials performed the ceremonial marriage of the state with the Adriatic, by dropping a ring into the sea on Ascension Day. [alter. of It *bucintoro, bucentauro*, prob. contr. of *ippocentauro* < L *hippocentaurus* < Gk *hippokéntauros;* see HIPPO-, CENTAUR; so called from its figurehead]

Bu·ceph·a·lus (byo͞o sef′ə ləs), *n.* the horse used by Alexander the Great on most of his military campaigns.

Buch·an (buk′ən; *Scot.* bukʜ′ən), *n.* **John, 1st Baron Tweedsmuir,** 1875–1940, Scottish novelist and historian: governor general of Canada 1935–40.

Bu·chan·an (byo͞o kan′ən, bə-), *n.* **James,** 1791–1868, 15th president of the U.S. 1857–61.

Bu·cha·rest (bo͞o′kə rest′, byo͞o′-), *n.* a city in and the capital of Rumania, in the S part. 1,588,592. Rumanian, **București.**

Buch·en·wald (bo͝ok′ən wôld′; *Ger.* bo͞oʜ′ən vält′), *n.* site of a former Nazi concentration camp in SW East Germany, near Weimar.

Buch·man (bo͝ok′mən, buk′-), *n.* **Frank N(athan) D(aniel),** 1879–1961, U.S. religious leader: founder of Moral Re-Armament. **—Buch′man·ism,** *n.* **—Buch′man·ite′,** *n.*

buck[1] (buk), *n.* 1. the male of the deer, antelope, rabbit, hare, sheep, or goat. 2. the male of certain other animals, as the shad. 3. an impetuous or spirited man or youth. 4. *Often Disparaging.* a male American Indian or Negro. 5. *U.S. Slang.* a dollar. 6. any of various heavy frames, racks, or jigs used to support materials or partially assembled items during manufacture. 7. **pass the buck,** *U.S. Informal.* to shift responsibility or blame to another person; evade responsibility: *Never one to admit error, he passed the buck on to his subordinates.* [ME *bukke*, OE *bucca* he goat, *bucc* male deer; c. D *bok*, G *Bock*, Icel *bukkr;* in def. 7, *buck* (short for *buckhorn knife*) used in poker to keep track of the deal]

buck[2] (buk), *v.i.* 1. (of a saddle or pack animal) to leap with arched back and come down with head low and forelegs stiff, in order to dislodge a rider or pack. 2. *U.S. Informal.* to resist obstinately; object strongly: *The mayor bucked at the school board's suggestion.* 3. *U.S. Informal.* (of a vehicle) to move by jerks and bounces. **—***v.t.* 4. to throw or attempt to throw (a rider) by bucking. 5. to force a way through or against (an obstacle): *The plane bucked a strong head wind.* 6. *U.S.* to strike with the head; butt. 7. *U.S. Informal.* to resist obstinately; object strongly to. 8. *Football.* (of a ball-carrier) to charge into (the opponent's line). 9. to gamble, play, or take a risk against: *to buck the odds.* 10. to carry, load, or lift, esp. heavy or bulky objects. 11. **buck for,** *Slang.* to strive for an advantage: *to buck for a raise.* 12. **buck up,** *Informal.* to make or become more cheerful, vigorous, etc. **—***n.* 13. the act of bucking. **—***adj.* 14. *Mil. Slang.* of the lowest of several ranks involving the same principal designation: *buck private; buck sergeant.* [special use of BUCK[1]; in def. 6, alter. of BUTT[3]]

buck[3] (buk), *n.* 1. a sawhorse. 2. a doorframe of wood or metal. **—***v.t.* 3. to split or saw (logs, felled trees, etc.). [short for SAWBUCK]

Buck (buk), *n.* **Pearl (Sy·den·strick·er)** (sīd′ən strik′ər), 1892–1973, U.S. novelist: Nobel prize 1938.

buck·a·roo (buk′ə ro͞o′, buk′ə ro͞o′), *n., pl.* **-roos.** *Western U.S.* a cowboy. [alter. of Sp *vaquero* = *vac(a)* cow (< L *vacca*) + *-ero* -ER]

buck′ bean′, a plant, *Menyanthes trifoliata,* having white or pink flowers, growing in bogs. [earlier *buckes beanes,* for MFlem *bocx boonen,* lit., goat's beans]

buck·board (buk′bōrd′, -bôrd′), *n.* a light, four-wheeled carriage in which a long elastic board or lattice frame is used in place of body and springs. [obs. *buck* body, holder (see BUCKET) + BOARD]

Buckboard

bucked (bukt), *adj.* *Brit. Slang.* 1. tired; exhausted. 2. happy; elated. [BUCK[2] + -ED[2]]

buck·een (bu kēn′), *n.* *Chiefly Irish Eng.* a poor young man who attempts to copy the habits and dress of the wealthy. [BUCK[1] + *-een* < Ir *-īn* dim. suffix]

buck·er (buk′ər), *n.* 1. a horse that bucks. 2. a person employed to carry, shovel, lift, or load, as coal, farm produce, etc.

buck·et (buk′it), *n., v.,* **-et·ed, -et·ing.** **—***n.* 1. a vessel, usually cylindrical, with a flat bottom and a semicircular bail, for collecting, carrying, or holding water, sand, fruit, etc. 2. anything resembling or suggesting this. 3. a scoop, as on a power shovel or conveyor. 4. a vane or blade of a water wheel, paddle wheel, water turbine, or the like. 5. a bucketful: *a bucket of sand.* 6. **drop in the bucket,** a small or inadequate amount. 7. **kick the bucket,** *Slang.* to die. **—***v.t.* 8. to lift, carry, or handle in a bucket (often fol. by *up* or *out*). 9. *Chiefly Brit.* to ride (a horse) fast and without concern for tiring it. [ME *buket* < AF < OE *bucc* (var. of *būc* vessel, belly, c. G *Bauch*) + OF *-et* -ET]

buck′et brigade′, a line of persons formed to extinguish a fire by passing on buckets of water from a distant source.

buck·et·ful (buk′it fo͝ol′), *n., pl.* **-fuls.** the amount that a bucket can hold.

buck′et seat′, an individual seat with a rounded back, as in some cars, airplanes, etc.

buck′et shop′, *Finance.* (formerly) a fraudulent brokerage house that speculates on its own account against its customers' interests, failing to execute certain orders so that customers' losses are the establishment's gain.

buck·eye (buk′ī′), *n., pl.* **-eyes,** *adj.* **—***n.* 1. any of various trees or shrubs of the genus *Aesculus,* allied to the true horse chestnut, as *A. glabra* **(Ohio buckeye),** the state tree of Ohio. 2. (*cap.*) a native or inhabitant of Ohio (the **Buckeye State**) (used as a nickname). 3. a poorly designed, ostentatious advertisement. **—***adj.* 4. gaudy and cheap looking, as a painting, advertisement, etc. [BUCK[1] stag + EYE, orig. used to designate def. 1, in allusion to the looks of the seed]

Buck′eye State′, Ohio (used as a nickname).

buck′ fe′ver, nervous excitement of an inexperienced hunter upon the approach of game.

Buck·ing·ham (buk′ing əm, -ham′), *n.* 1. **George Villiers, 1st Duke of,** 1592–1628, English courtier, politician, and military leader: lord high admiral 1617. 2. his son, **George Villiers, 2nd Duke of,** 1628–87, English courtier and author. 3. Buckinghamshire.

Buck′ingham Pal′ace, a residence of the British sovereigns since 1837, in London, England: built 1703.

Buck·ing·ham·shire (buk′ing əm shēr′, -shər), *n.* a county in S England. 486,183 (1961); 749 sq. mi. *Co. seat:* Aylesbury. Also called **Buckingham, Bucks.**

buck·ish (buk′ish), *adj.* impetuous; dashing. [BUCK[1] + -ISH[1]] **—buck′ish·ly,** *adv.* **—buck′ish·ness,** *n.*

buck·le (buk′əl), *n., v.,* **-led, -ling.** **—***n.* 1. a device for fastening two loose ends, as of a belt or strap, usually attached to one end and grasping a hole in the other by a prong or tongue. 2. an ornament resembling such a device. 3. a bend, bulge, or kink, as in a board or saw blade. **—***v.t.* 4. to fasten with a buckle or buckles. 5. to prepare (oneself) for action; apply (oneself) vigorously to something. 6. to bend, warp, or cause to give way suddenly, as with heat or pressure. **—***v.i.* 7. to be closed or fastened with a buckle: *His boot wouldn't buckle.* 8. to prepare oneself or apply oneself (often fol. by *down*). 9. to bend, warp, bulge, or collapse: *The bridge buckled in the storm.* 10. to yield, surrender, or give way to another (often fol. by *under*). [ME *bocle* < MF < L *buccula* beaver (of a helmet), boss (of a shield) = *bucc(a)* cheek + *-ula* -ULE] **—buck′le·less,** *adj.*

Buck·le (buk′əl), *n.* **Henry Thomas,** 1821–62, English historian.

buck·ler (buk′lər), *n.* 1. a round shield with a grip for holding and sometimes with straps through which the arm is passed. 2. any means of defense; protection. **—***v.t.* 3. to be a buckler or shield to; support; defend. [ME *bokeler* < MF *bocler* = *bocle* BOSS[2] + *-er* -ER[2]]

Buck·ner (buk′nər), *n.* **Simon Bol·i·var** (bol′ə vər), 1823–1914, U.S. Confederate general and politician.

buck·o (buk′ō), *n., pl.* **-oes.** 1. *Chiefly Irish Eng.* young fellow; chap; young companion. 2. *Brit. Slang.* a manly, swaggering sailor. 3. a bully. [alter. of BUCK[1]]

buck·ra (buk′rə), *n.* *Chiefly Southern U.S.* a white man. [< Calabar *mbakara* master]

buck·ram (buk′rəm), *n., v.,* **-ramed, -ram·ing.** **—***n.* 1. a stiff cotton fabric for interlinings, book bindings, etc. **—***v.t.* 2. to strengthen with buckram. 3. *Archaic.* to give a false appearance of importance, value, or strength to. [early ME *bukeram* < MHG *buckeram* or OIt *bucherame,* said to be named after BUKHARA, once noted for textiles]

Bucksaw

buck·saw (buk′sô′), *n.* a two-handed saw consisting of a blade set across an upright frame, for cutting wood on a sawbuck.

buck·shot (buk′shot′), *n.* a large size of lead shot used for hunting game.

buck·skin (buk′skin′), *n.* 1. the skin of a buck or deer. 2. a strong, soft, yellowish or grayish leather, now usually made from sheepskins. 3. **buckskins,** breeches or shoes made of buckskin. 4. a stiff, firm, starched cotton cloth. 5. a sturdy wool fabric, in satin weave and with a smooth finish, used for outer garments. 6. a horse the color of buckskin. —*adj.* 7. having the color of buckskin; yellowish or grayish. 8. made of buckskin.

buck′ slip′, a piece of paper attached to and showing the routing and handling of an interoffice memo, file, or the like. Also called **buck′ sheet′.**

buck·thorn (buk′thôrn′), *n.* 1. any of several, sometimes thorny trees or shrubs of the genus *Rhamnus,* esp. *R. cathartica,* whose berries were formerly used in medicine as a purgative, and *R. frangula,* the bark of which is used in medicine. 2. a sapotaceous tree or shrub of the genus *Bumelia,* esp. *B. lycioides,* a tree common in the southern and part of the central U.S. [BUCK[1] + THORN, rendering NL *cervi spina*]

buck·tooth (buk′to͞oth′), *n., pl.* **-teeth** (-tēth′). a projecting tooth, esp. an upper front tooth. —**buck′toothed′,** *adj.*

buck·wheat (buk′hwēt′, -wēt′), *n.* 1. a herbaceous plant, esp. *Fagopyrum esculentum,* cultivated for its triangular seeds, which are used as a feed for animals or made into a flour for human consumption. 2. the seeds of this plant. 3. Also, **buck′wheat flour′.** the flour made from these seeds. [obs. *buck* (OE *bōc* BEECH) + WHEAT; cf. D *boekweit,* G *Buchweizen;* so called because its seeds resemble beechnuts]

buck′wheat cake′, a pancake made with buckwheat.

bu·col·ic (byo͞o kol′ik), *adj.* Also, **bu·col′i·cal.** 1. of or pertaining to shepherds; pastoral. 2. of, pertaining to, or suggesting an idyllic rural life. —*n.* 3. a pastoral poem. 4. *Archaic.* a farmer; shepherd; rustic. [< L *būcolic(us)* < Gk *boukolikós* rustic = *boukól(os)* herdsman (*bou-,* s. of *boûs* ox + *-kol(os)* keeper) + *-ikos* -IC] —**bu·col′i·cal·ly,** *adv.*

Bu·co·vi·na (bo͞o′kə vē′nə; *Rum.* bo͝o kô vē′nä), *n.* a region in E central Europe, formerly a district in N Rumania: northern part ceded to Russia 1947. 4031 sq. mi. Also, **Bukovina.**

Bu·cu·rești (bo͝o ko͝o resht′), *n.* Rumanian name of **Bucharest.**

bud[1] (bud), *n., v.,* **bud·ded, bud·ding.** —*n.* 1. *Bot.* **a.** a small axillary or terminal protuberance on a plant, containing rudimentary foliage **(leaf bud),** the rudimentary inflorescence **(flower bud),** or both **(mixed bud).** **b.** an undeveloped or rudimentary stem or branch of a plant. 2. *Zool.* (in certain animals of low organization) a prominence that develops into a new individual; gemma. 3. *Anat.* any small rounded part, as a tactile bud or a gustatory bud. 4. an immature or undeveloped person or thing. 5. **nip in the bud,** to stop something in the beginning of its development. —*v.i.* 6. to put forth or produce buds, as a plant. 7. to begin to grow and develop. —*v.t.* 8. to cause to bud. 9. *Hort.* to graft by inserting a single bud into the stock. [ME *budde* bud, spray, pod; akin to G (*Hage*)*butte* hip, Icel *budda* purse, dial. Sw *bodd* head, D *buidel* bag, purse, MLG *buddich* swollen] —**bud′der,** *n.* —**bud′less,** *adj.* —**bud′like′,** *adj.*

Leaf buds of the elm

bud[2] (bud), *n. Informal.* 1. pal or chum. 2. a familiar and often condescending term of address to a man or boy. [back formation from BUDDY]

Bu·da·pest (bo͞o′də pest′, bo͞o′də pest′; *Hung.* bo͞o′dô-pesht′), *n.* a city in and the capital of Hungary, in the central part, on the Danube River. 2,070,966.

Buddha

Bud·dha (bo͝od′ə, bo͞o′də), *n.* 1. Also called **Butsu, Gautama, Gautama Buddha.** (*Prince Siddhāttha* or *Siddhartha*) 566?–c480 B.C., Indian religious leader: founder of Buddhism. 2. (*sometimes l.c.*) *Buddhism.* a person who has attained full prajna, or enlightenment; Arhat. 3. a representation of Buddha. [< Skt: awakened = *budh-* notice, understand + *-ta* ptp. suffix]

Buddh Ga·ya (bo͝od′ gə-yä′), a village in central Bihar, in NE India: site of tree under which Siddhartha became the Buddha.

Bud·dhism (bo͝od′iz əm, bo͞o′diz-), *n.* a religion, originated in India by Buddha (Gautama) and later spreading to China, Burma, Japan, Tibet, and parts of southeast Asia, holding that suffering is caused by desire and that the way to end this suffering is through an enlightenment that enables one to halt the endless sequence of births and deaths to which one is otherwise subject. —**Bud′dhist,** *n., adj.* —**Bud·dhis′tic,** *adj.*

bud·dy (bud′ē), *n., pl.* **-dies.** *U.S. Informal.* 1. comrade or chum. 2. a familiar and often condescending term of address to a man or boy. [perh. childish var. of BROTHER]

bud′dy sys′tem, 1. (in recreational swimming) the practice of pairing swimmers, each being responsible for the other's safety. 2. any arrangement whereby two or more persons, teams, etc., may aid or assist each other.

budge[1] (buj), *v.,* **budged, budg·ing.** (usually used negatively) —*v.i.* 1. to move slightly; begin to move. 2. to change one's opinion or stated position: *Once her father had said "no," he wouldn't budge.* —*v.t.* 3. to cause to move; begin to move. 4. to cause to reconsider or change an opinion or stated position. [< MF *boug(er)* (to) stir < VL **bullicāre* to bubble, freq. of L *bullīre* to BOIL[1]] —**budg′er,** *n.*

budge[2] (buj), *n.* 1. a fur made from lambskin with the wool dressed outward. —*adj.* 2. *Obs.* pompous; solemn. [ME *bugee,* perh. akin to BUDGET]

budg·er·i·gar (buj′ə rē gär′), *n.* an Australian parakeet, *Melopsittacus undulatus,* having greenish plumage with black and yellow markings, bred as a pet. Also, **budg·er·ee·gah, budg·er·y·gah** (buj′ə rē gä′). See illus. at **parakeet.** [< native Austral]

budg·et (buj′it), *n., v.,* **-et·ed, -et·ing.** —*n.* 1. an estimate, often itemized, of expected income and expense. 2. a plan of operations based on such an estimate. 3. an itemized allotment of funds for a given period. 4. the total sum of money set aside or needed for a specific purpose: *a vacation budget of $300.* 5. a limited stock or supply of something: *His budget of good will was running out.* 6. *Obs.* a small bag; pouch. —*v.t.* 7. to plan allotment of (funds, time, etc.). 8. to deal with (specific funds) in a budget. [late ME *bowgett* < MF *bougette* = *bouge* bag (< L *bulga*) + *-ette* -ETTE] —**budg·et·ar·y** (buj′i ter′ē), *adj.* —**budg′et·er,** *n.*

bud·ge·teer (buj′i tēr′), *n.* a person, esp. a government or business official, who prepares the budget.

budg·ie (buj′ē), *n. Informal.* budgerigar.

bud′ scale′, scale[1] (def. 3a).

Bud·weis (*Ger.* bo͞ot′vīs), *n.* a city in SW Czechoslovakia, on the Moldau River. 67,944 (1963). Czech, **České Budějovice.**

Bue′na Park′ (bwā′nə), a city in SW California. 63,646 (1970).

bue·nas no·ches (bwe′näs nô′ches), *Spanish.* good night.

Bue·na·ven·tu·ra (bwā′nə ven to͝or′ə, -tyo͝or′ə; *Sp.* bwe′nä ven to͞o′rä), *n.* a seaport in W Colombia. 110,660 (est. 1964).

Bue·na Vis·ta (bwe′nä vēs′tä), *n.* a village in NE Mexico, near Saltillo: American victory in battle (1847) during the Mexican War.

bue·no (bwe′nô), *interj. Spanish.* good; all right.

Bue·nos Ai·res (bwā′nəs īər′iz, bō′nəs âr′ēz; *Sp.* bwe′nôs ī′res), a seaport in and the capital of Argentina, in the E part, on the Río de la Plata. 8,925,000.

bue·nos dí·as (bwe′nôs dē′äs), *Spanish.* good morning; good day.

buff[1] (buf), *n.* 1. a thick, light-yellow leather with a napped surface, originally, and properly made of buffalo skin but later also of other skins. 2. a buff stick or buff wheel. 3. a thick, short coat of buff leather, worn esp. by soldiers in 17th-century England and by American colonists. 4. yellowish-brown; medium or dark tan. 5. *Informal.* the bare skin. 6. *Informal.* a devotee or well-informed student of some hobby, activity, or subject. —*adj.* 7. made of buff leather. —*v.t.* 8. to clean or polish with a buff stick, buff wheel, or buffer. [earlier *buffe* wild ox, back formation from *buffle* < F < LL *būfalus;* see BUFFALO] —**buff′a·bil′i·ty,** *n.* —**buff′a·ble,** *adj.* —**Syn.** 8. burnish, shine.

buff[2] (buf), *v.t.* to reduce the force of; act as a buffer. [late ME *buffe,* back formation from BUFFET[1]]

buf·fa·lo (buf′ə lō′), *n., pl.* **-loes, -los,** (*esp. collectively*) **-lo,** *v.,* **-loed, -lo·ing.** —*n.* 1. any of several large wild oxen of the family *Bovidae.* Cf. **bison, water buffalo.** 2. See **buffalo robe.** —*v.t. U.S. Informal.* 3. to baffle; confuse; mystify. 4. to impress or intimidate by a display of power, importance, etc.: *He didn't let the older boys buffalo him.* [earlier *buffalo* < It < LL *būfalus,* var. of L *būbalus* BUBAL]

Buf·fa·lo (buf′ə lō′), *n.* a port in W New York, on Lake Erie. 462,768 (1970).

buf′falo ber′ry, either of two North American, shrubs, *Shepherdia argentea,* or *S. canadensis,* belonging to the genus *Elaeagnus,* bearing an edible, yellow or red berry. Also called **buf′falo bush′.**

Buf′falo Bill′. See **Cody, William Frederick.**

buf·fa·lo·fish (buf′ə lō′fish′), *n., pl.* (*esp. collectively*) **-fish,** (*esp. referring to two or more kinds or species*) **-fish·es.** any of several large, carplike, North American, fresh-water fishes of the genus *Ictiobus,* of the sucker family.

buf′falo gnat′. See **black fly.**

buf′falo grass′, 1. a short grass, *Buchloë dactyloides,* prevalent on the dry plains east of the Rocky Mountains. 2. any of several short, tufted grasses that do not form continuous sod.

Buf′falo In′dian. See **Plains Indian.**

buf′falo robe′, the prepared skin of an American bison, with the hair left on, used as a lap robe.

buff·er[1] (buf′ər), *n.* 1. an apparatus at the end of a railroad car, railroad track, etc., for absorbing shock during coupling, collision stops, etc. 2. any device, material, or apparatus used as a shield, cushion, or bumper, esp. on machinery. 3. any intermediate or intervening shield or device reducing the danger of interaction between two machines, chemicals, electronic components, etc. 4. See **buffer state.** 5. any person or thing that shields another or protects against danger, loss, despair, or annoyance. 6. *Computer Technol.* an intermediate memory unit for temporarily holding computer data until the proper unit is ready to receive the data, as when the receiving unit has an operating speed lower than that of the unit feeding the data to it. 7. *Chem.* **a.** any substance or mixture of compounds that, added to a solution, is capable of neutralizing both acids and bases without appreciably changing the original acidity or alkalinity of the solution. **b.** Also called **buff′er solu′tion.** a solution containing such a substance. —*v.t.* 8. *Chem.* to treat with a buffer. 9. to cushion, shield, or protect. 10. to lessen the adverse effect of; ease: *to buffer pain.* [BUFF[2] + -ER[1]]

buff·er[2] (buf′ər), *n.* 1. a device for polishing or buffing. 2. a worker who uses such a device. [BUFF[1] + -ER[1]]

buff′er state′, a small neutral state lying between potentially hostile larger powers.

buf·fet[1] (buf′it), *n., v.,* **-fet·ed, -fet·ing.** —*n.* 1. a blow, as with the hand or fist. 2. a violent shock or concussion. —*v.t.* 3. to strike, as with the hand or fist. 4. to strike against or push repeatedly: *The wind buffeted the house.* 5. to contend against; battle. —*v.i.* 6. to struggle with blows of hand or fist. 7. to force one's way by a fight, struggle, etc. [ME < OF *buffe* a blow + *-et* -ET] —**buf′fet·er,** *n.*

buf·fet[2] (bə fā′, bo͞o-; *Brit.* buf′it; *Fr.* bʏ fe′), *n., pl.* **buffets** (bə fāz′, bo͞o-; *Brit.* buf′its; *Fr.* bʏ fe′), *adj.* —*n.* 1. a sideboard or cabinet for holding china, table linen, etc. 2. a counter, bar, or the like, for lunch or refreshments. 3. a restaurant containing such a counter or bar. 4. a meal laid out on a table or sideboard so that guests may serve themselves and eat in small, informal groups rather than sitting at a dining table. —*adj.* **5.** consisting of food, refreshments, etc., laid out on tables or buffets from which guests or customers serve themselves: *buffet supper.* [< F < ?]

buff′ing wheel′. See **buff wheel.**

buf·fle·head (buf′əl hed′), *n.* a small North American duck, *Bucephala albeola,* the male of which has bushy head plumage. [*buffle* (see BUFF¹) + HEAD] —**buf′fle·head′ed,** *adj.*

buf·fo (bo͞o′fō; *It.* bo͞of′fô), *n., pl.* **-fi** (-fē), **-fos.** *Music.* **1.** (in opera) a comedy part, usually bass. **2.** a male opera singer who specializes in comic roles. [< It: ridiculous (adj.), buffoon (n.), akin to *buffa* a jest (orig. a puff of air), *buffare* to puff, blow]

Buf·fon (bʏ fôɴ′), *n.* **Georges Louis Le·clerc** (zhôrzh lwē lə klɛʀ′), **Comte de,** 1707–88, French naturalist.

buf·foon (bə fo͞on′), *n.* **1.** a person who amuses others by tricks, jokes, odd gestures and postures, etc. **2.** a person given to coarse joking. [earlier *buffon* < F < It *buffone* = *buff(o)* BUFFO + *-one* aug. suffix] —**buf·foon·er·y** (bə fo͞o′nə rē), **buf·foon′ism,** *n.* —**buf·foon′ish,** *adj.* —**buf·foon′ish·ness,** *n.*

buff′ stick′, a small stick covered with leather or the like, used in polishing.

buff′ wheel′, a wheel for buffing, consisting of a number of leather or canvas disks. Also called **buffing wheel.**

buf′fy coat′ (buf′ē), *Biochem.* a yellowish-white layer of leukocytes that, upon centrifugation of blood, covers the erythrocytes. [BUFF¹ + -Y¹]

bug¹ (bug), *n., v.,* **bugged, bug·ging.** —*n.* **1.** Also called **true bug.** a hemipterous insect. **2.** (not used scientifically) any insect or insectlike invertebrate. **3.** *Chiefly Brit.* a bedbug. **4.** *Informal.* any microorganism, esp. a virus: *He was laid up for a week by an intestinal bug.* **5.** *U.S. Informal.* a defect or imperfection, as in a mechanical device or a new airplane: *The test flight was to discover the bugs in the new plane.* **6.** *Slang.* **a.** a person who has a great enthusiasm for something; fan or hobbyist. **b.** a craze or obsession: *the sports-car bug.* **7.** *Slang.* a hidden microphone. **8.** an asterisk. **9.** *Horse Racing.* the five-pound weight allowance that can be claimed by an apprentice jockey. **10.** any of various fishing plugs resembling an insect. —*v.t. U.S. Slang.* **11.** to install a secret listening device in (a room, building, etc.) or on (a telephone or other device). **12.** *Slang.* to bother; annoy; pester. [earlier *bugge* beetle, appar. alter. of ME *budde* (as in *maggot, maddock*), OE *buddha* beetle]

bug² (bug), *n. Obs.* a bogy; hobgoblin. [ME *bugge* scarecrow, demon, perh. < Welsh *bwg* ghost]

Bug (bug; *Pol.* bo͝og, bo͝ok; *Russ.* bo͝ok), *n.* **1.** a river in E central Europe, forming part of the boundary between E Poland and the W Soviet Union, flowing NW to the Vistula River. 450 mi. long. **2.** a river in the SW Soviet Union in Europe, flowing from the SW Ukraine to the Dnieper estuary. ab. 530 mi. long.

bug·a·boo (bug′ə bo͞o′), *n., pl.* **-boos.** bugbear (def. 1). [earlier *buggybow.* See BOGY, BOO]

bug·bane (bug′bān′), *n.* any of several tall, erect, ranunculaceous herbs of the genus *Cimicifuga,* as *C. americana,* of the eastern U.S., having clusters of white flowers supposedly repellent to insects.

bug·bear (bug′bâr′), *n.* **1.** a source of fears, often groundless. **2.** *Folklore Obs.* a goblin that eats naughty children. [BUG² + BEAR²] —**bug′bear′ish,** *adj.*

bug-eyed (bug′īd′), *adj. Slang.* with bulging eyes, as from surprise; astonished.

bug·ger (bug′ər), *n.* **1.** a sodomite. **2.** a fellow, lad, or child, often used affectionately: *a cute little bugger.* —*v.t.* **3.** to commit sodomy on. —*v.i.* **4. bugger off,** *Brit. Slang.* Beat it! Scram! [ME *bougre,* var. of *bolgre* < LL *Bulgar(us)* heretic, lit., Bulgarian]

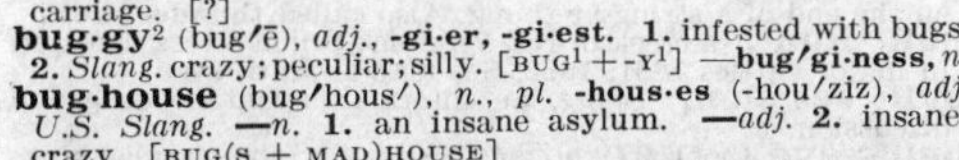

Buggy

bug·ger·y (bug′ə rē), *n.* sodomy.

bug·gy¹ (bug′ē), *n., pl.* **-gies.** **1.** *U.S.* a light, four-wheeled carriage with a single seat and a transverse spring. **2.** *Brit.* a light, two-wheeled, open carriage. [?]

bug·gy² (bug′ē), *adj.,* **-gi·er, -gi·est.** **1.** infested with bugs. **2.** *Slang.* crazy; peculiar; silly. [BUG¹ + -Y¹] —**bug′gi·ness,** *n.*

bug·house (bug′hous′), *n., pl.* **-hous·es** (-hou′ziz), *adj. U.S. Slang.* —*n.* **1.** an insane asylum. —*adj.* **2.** insane; crazy. [BUG(S + MAD)HOUSE]

bug-juice (bug′jo͞os′), *n. Slang.* **1.** an alcoholic beverage, esp. one of inferior quality. **2.** any unusual drink.

bu·gle¹ (byo͞o′gəl), *n., v.,* **-gled, -gling.** —*n.* **1.** a brass wind instrument resembling a cornet and sometimes having keys or valves. —*v.i.* **2.** to sound a bugle. **3.** (of bull elks) to utter a rutting call. —*v.t.* **4.** to call by or with a bugle: *to bugle reveille.* [ME *bugle* (*horn*) instrument made of an ox horn (< OF < L *būcul(us)* bullock, young ox = *bū-* var. s. of *bōs* ox + *-culus* -CLE] —**bu′gler,** *n.*

Bugle

bu·gle² (byo͞o′gəl), *n.* any menthaceous plant of the genus *Ajuga,* esp. *A. reptans,* a low, blue-flowered herb. [ME < OF < LL *bugul(a)* a kind of plant]

bu·gle³ (byo͞o′gəl), *n.* a tubular glass bead for ornamenting women's clothing. [?]

bu·gle·weed (byo͞o′gəl wēd′), *n.* **1.** a menthaceous plant of the genus *Lycopus,* esp. *L. virginicus,* reputed to have medicinal properties. **2.** See **wild indigo. 3.** bugle². [BUGLE² + WEED¹]

bu·gloss (byo͞o′glos, -glôs), *n.* any of various Old World, boraginaceous herbs, as *Anchusa officinalis,* having rough leaves, used in medicine, and *Lycopsis arvensis,* a bristly, blue-flowered herb. [late ME *buglossa* < L = *bū-* ox (see BUGLE¹) + *glōssa* tongue (< Gk); alter. of Gk *boúglōssos*]

bugs (bugz), *adj. Slang.* crazy; insane. [*bug* maniac, mania, perhaps < *bug* adj. (now dial.) self-important, pompous, appar. var. of BIG¹]

bug·seed (bug′sēd′), *n.* an annual, chenopodiaceous herb, *Corispermum hyssopifolium,* of northern temperate regions; so called from the flat, oval shape of its seeds.

buhl (bo͞ol), *n.* (*often cap.*) elaborate inlaid work of woods, metals, tortoise shell, ivory, etc. Also, **boule, boulle.** Also called **buhl·work** (bo͞ol′wûrk′), **boulework.** [from Germanized form of F *boulle* or *boule,* named after A. C. *Boulle* or *Boule* (1642–1732), French cabinetmaker]

buhr (bûr), *n.* **1.** burr¹ (def. 4). **2.** burr³. **3.** burstone.

buhr·stone (bûr′stōn′), *n.* burstone.

build (bild), *v.,* **built** or (*Archaic*) **build·ed; build·ing;** *n.* —*v.t.* **1.** to construct by assembling and joining parts or materials. **2.** to establish, increase, or strengthen (often fol. by *up*): *to build a business; to build up one's hopes.* **3.** to mold, form, or create: *to build boys into men.* —*v.i.* **4.** to engage in the art, practice, or business of building. **5.** to form or construct a plan, system of thought, etc. (usually fol. by *on* or *upon*): *He built on the philosophies of the past.* **6.** to increase or develop toward a maximum, as of intensity, tempo, magnitude, etc. (often fol. by *up*): *The plot builds steadily toward a climax.* **7. build up, a.** to increase or strengthen: *to build up a bank account.* **b.** to prepare in stages. **c.** to develop into an urban area. **d.** *Slang.* to praise or flatter (someone). —*n.* **8.** the manner or form of construction, structure, physique, etc.: *He had a strong build.* **9.** *Slang.* a good figure or physique: *The new secretary has some build!* [ME *bilde(n),* OE *byldan* < *bold,* var. of *botl* dwelling, house] —**build′a·ble,** *adj.* —**build′er,** *n.*

build·ing (bil′diŋ), *n.* **1.** a relatively permanent, essentially boxlike construction having a roof and used for any of a wide variety of activities, as living, entertaining, or manufacturing. **2.** anything built or constructed. **3.** the act, business, or practice of constructing houses, office buildings, etc. [ME *byldinge*] —**build′ing·less,** *adj.*

build′ing and loan′ associa′tion. See **savings and loan association.**

build′ing trades′, the trades, as carpentry, masonry, or plastering, that are primarily concerned with the construction and finishing of buildings.

build-up (bild′up′), *n.* **1.** building up; increase in amount or number. **2.** a process of growth; strengthening; development: *the build-up of heavy industry.* **3.** a publicity, public-relations, or advertising campaign. **4.** a process of preparation making possible an ultimate objective: *a lengthy build-up to an offer to buy the property for next to nothing.* **5.** encouragement; a psychological lift. Also, **build′up′.**

built (bilt), *v.* **1.** pt. and pp. of **build.** —*adj.* **2.** *Naut.* noting any member or part of a vessel assembled from pieces rather than formed as a solid or a single piece: *built frame; built spar.* **3.** *Slang.* having a good figure or physique: *She sure is built!*

built-in (bilt′in′), *adj.* **1.** built as an integral, permanent part of a larger construction: *a built-in bookcase.* **2.** existing as an integral; inherent: *a built-in contempt for daydreaming.*

Bui·ten·zorg (boit′ən zôʀkh′, bœit′-), *n.* the former Dutch name of **Bogor.**

Bu·jum·bu·ra (bo͞o′zho͞om bo͝o′rä), *n.* a port in and the capital of Burundi, in the W part, on Lake Tanganyika. 70,000 (est. 1965). Formerly, **Usumbura.**

Bu·ka·vu (bo͞o kä′vo͞o), *n.* a city in the E Republic of the Congo. 33,268 (est. 1958). Formerly, **Costermansville.**

Bu·kha·ra (bo͝o kär′ə; *Russ.* bo͝o кнä′ʀä), *n.* **1.** a former state in SW Asia: now incorporated into Uzbekistan, in the SW Soviet Union in Asia. **2.** a city in SE Uzbekistan, in the SW Soviet Union in Asia. 69,000 (1959). Also, **Bokhara.**

Bu·kha·rin (bo͞o кнä′ʀin), *n.* **Ni·ko·lai I·va·no·vich** (ni ko lī′ i vä′no vich), 1888–1938, Russian editor, writer, and Communist leader.

Bu·ko·vi·na (bo͞o′kə vē′nə; *Rum.* bo͝o kô vē′nä), *n.* Bucovina.

Bul (bo͞ol), *n. Chiefly Biblical.* a month equivalent to Heshvan of the modern Jewish calendar. I Kings 6:38.

bul., bulletin.

Bu·la·wa·yo (bo͞o′lə wä′yō), *n.* a city in SW Rhodesia: mining center. 214,400 with suburbs (est. 1964).

bulb (bulb), *n.* **1.** *Bot.* **a.** a usually subterranean bud having fleshy leaves, the stem of which is reduced to a flat disk, rooting from the under side, as in the onion, lily, etc. **b.** a plant growing from such a bud. **2.** any round, enlarged part, esp. at the end of a cylindrical object: *the bulb of a thermometer.* **3.** *Elect.* **a.** the glass housing, in which partial vacuum has been established, that contains the filament of an incandescent electric lamp. **b.** an incandescent electric lamp. **4.** See **medulla oblongata. 5.** a cylindrical or spherical prominence at the forefoot of certain vessels to improve hull characteristics. [< L *bulb(us)* < Gk *bolbós* onion]

bulb·ar (bul′bər, -bär), *adj.* of or pertaining to a bulb, esp. to the medulla oblongata.

bulb·if·er·ous (bul bif′ər əs), *adj. Bot.* producing bulbs. [< NL *bulbifer* (see BULB, -I-, -FER) + -OUS]

bul·bil (bul′bil), *n. Bot.* **1.** a little bulb. **2.** a small, aerial bulb growing in the axils of leaves, as in the tiger lily, or replacing flower buds, as in the common onion. Also, **bul·bel** (bul′bəl, -bel). [< NL *bulbill(us)* = L *bulb(us)* BULB + *-illus* dim. suffix]

bulb·ous (bul′bəs), *adj.* **1.** bulb-shaped; bulging. **2.** having or growing from bulbs. Also, **bul·ba·ceous** (bul bā′shəs). [< L *bulbōs(us)*] —**bul′bous·ly,** *adv.*

bul·bul (bo͝ol′bo͝ol), *n.* **1.** a songbird often mentioned in Persian poetry, regarded as being a nightingale. **2.** any of several oscine birds of the family *Pycnonotidae,* of the Old World tropics. [< Pers]

Bul·finch (bo͝ol′finch′), *n.* **1. Charles,** 1763–1844, U.S. architect. **2.** his son, **Thomas,** 1796–1867, U.S. author and mythologist.

Bulg, Bulgarian (def. 2).

Bulg., **1.** Bulgaria. **2.** Bulgarian.

Bul·ga·nin (bo͝ol gä′nin), *n.* **Ni·ko·lai A·le·ksan·dro·vich** (ni ko lī′ ä′le ksän′dʀo vich), 1895–1975, Soviet political leader: premier 1955–58.

Bul·gar (bul′gər, bo͝ol′gär), *n.* Bulgarian (def. 1). [< LL *Bulgar(us)*]

Bul·gar·i·a (bul gâr′ē ə, bo͝ol-), *n.* a republic in SE Europe. 8,880,000; 42,800 sq. mi. *Cap.:* Sofia.

Bul·gar·i·an (bul gâr′ē ən, bo͝ol-), *n.* **1.** Also, **Bulgar.** a native or inhabitant of Bulgaria. **2.** a Slavic language, the language of Bulgaria. *Abbr.:* Bulg, Bulg. —*adj.* **3.** of or pertaining to Bulgaria, its people, or their language.

bulge (bulj), *n., v.,* **bulged, bulg·ing.** —*n.* **1.** a rounded projection, bend, or protruding part. **2.** any sudden increase, as of numbers, sales, prices, etc.: *a bulge in profits.* —*v.i.* **3.** to swell or bend outward. **4.** to be filled to capacity: *The box bulged with cookies.* —*v.t.* **5.** to make protuberant. [ME: bag, hump < OF < L *bulga* bag < Celt; cf. Ir *bolg* bag] —**bulg′i·ness,** *n.* —**bulg′ing·ly,** *adv.* —**bulg′y,** *adj.*

Bulge (bulj), *n.* **Battle of the,** the final major German counteroffensive in World War II: begun December 16, 1944, thrusting into Allied territory in N and E Belgium, and repulsed January 1945.

bul·gur (bo͝ol′gûr, bo͝ol′gər), *n.* a highly nutritious form of wheat that has been parboiled, cracked, and dried.

-bulia, *Chiefly Psychiatry.* a learned borrowing from Greek meaning "will," used in the formation of compound words: *abulia.* [< NL < Gk *-boulia* = *boul(ē)* will + *-ia* -IA]

bu·lim·a·rex·i·a (byo͞o lim′ə rek′sē ə), *n.* bulimia, esp. affecting young women, characterized by compulsive overeating followed by self-induced vomiting, consumption of laxatives, fasting, or other action to avert weight gain. [BULIM(I)A + (ANO)REXIA] —**bu·lim′a·rex′ic,** *adj., n.*

bu·lim·i·a (byo͞o lim′ē ə), *n.* *Pathol.* an abnormally voracious appetite. [< NL < Gk *boulīmía* extreme hunger = *bou-* intensive prefix (< *bou-*, s. of *boûs* ox) + *līm(ós)* hunger + *-ia* -IA] —**bu·lim′ic, bu·lim·i·ac** (byo͞o lim′ē ak′), *adj.*

bulk (bulk), *n.* **1.** magnitude in three dimensions: *a ship of great bulk.* **2.** the greater part; the main mass or body: *The bulk of the debt was paid.* **3.** loose goods or cargo, not in packages, boxes, bags, etc. **4.** food that forms a fibrous residue in digestion, allaying hunger and promoting normal elimination. **5.** (of paper, cardboard, etc.) thickness, esp. in relation to weight. **6. in bulk, a.** unpackaged: *oranges shipped in freight cars in bulk.* **b.** in large quantities. —*v.i.* **7.** to increase in size; expand. **8.** to be of or give the appearance of great weight, size, or importance; loom: *The problem bulks large in his mind.* **9.** (of paper, cardboard, etc.) to be of a specific thickness, esp. in relation to weight. —*v.t.* **10.** to cause to swell, grow, or increase in weight or thickness. [ME *bolke* heap, cargo, hold < Scand; cf. Icel *búlki* cargo, ship's hold] —**Syn. 1.** See **size**[1].

bulk·head (bulk′hed′), *n.* **1.** *Naut.* any of various wall-like constructions inside a vessel for forming watertight compartments, strengthening the structure, etc. **2.** *Civ. Eng.* **a.** a partition built in a subterranean passage to prevent the passage of air, water, or mud. **b.** a retaining structure used for shore protection and in harbor works. **3.** *Building Trades.* **a.** a horizontal or inclined outside door over a cellar stairway. **b.** a boxlike structure, as on a roof, covering a stairwell or other opening. —**bulk′head′ed,** *adj.*

bulk′ mail′, a category of mail established for mailing large numbers of identical printed items to individual addressees at less than first-class rates.

bulk·y (bul′kē), *adj.,* **bulk·i·er, bulk·i·est.** of relatively great and cumbersome bulk or size. —**bulk′i·ly,** *adv.* —**bulk′i·ness,** *n.* —**Syn.** massive, unwieldy. —**Ant.** small.

bull[1] (bo͝ol), *n.* **1.** the male of a bovine animal, esp. of the genus *Bos,* with sexual organs intact and capable of reproduction. **2.** the male of certain other animals: *an elephant bull.* **3.** a large, solidly built person. **4.** a person who believes that general business conditions are or will be favorable. **5.** a person who buys, speculates, or operates in stocks or commodities to profit from or cause a rise in prices (opposed to *bear*). **6.** (*cap.*) *Astron., Astrol.* the constellation or sign of Taurus. **7.** a bulldog. **8.** *Slang.* a policeman. **9. take the bull by the horns,** to attack a problem fearlessly. —*adj.* **10.** male. **11.** of, pertaining to, or resembling a bull, as in strength. **12.** having to do with or marked by rising prices, as of stocks: *bull market.* [ME *bule,* OE *bula;* akin to Icel *boli*] —**bull′-like′,** *adj.*

bull[2] (bo͝ol), *n.* **1.** a bulla or seal. **2.** *Rom. Cath. Ch.* a formal papal document having a bulla attached. [ME *bulle* < ML *bulla* seal, sealed document]

bull[3] (bo͝ol), *n.* *Slang.* **1.** exaggerations; lies; nonsense. **2. shoot the bull, a.** to talk aimlessly. **b.** to brag or exaggerate. [< ML *bulla* play, game, jest (whence also Icel *bull* nonsense)]

Bull (bo͝ol), *n.* **John.** See **John Bull.**

bull., bulletin.

bul·la (bo͝ol′ə, bul′ə), *n., pl.* **bul·lae** (bo͝ol′ē, bul′ē). **1.** a seal attached to an official document, as a papal bull. **2.** an ancient Roman pendant, consisting of a rounded box containing an amulet. **3.** *Pathol.* a large vesicle. **4.** *Zool.* a bubblelike prominence of a bone, as that of the tympanic bone in the skull of certain mammals. [<ML < L: bubble, also stud, boss, knob, official decoration]

bull·bait·ing (bo͝ol′bā′ting), *n.* the sport of setting dogs upon a bull in an arena.

bull·dog (bo͝ol′dôg′, -dog′), *n., adj., v.,* **-dogged, -dog·ging.** —*n.* **1.** one of an English breed of medium-sized, short-haired, muscular dogs with prominent, undershot jaws, usually having a white and tan or brindled coat, raised originally for bullbaiting. **2.** a short-barreled revolver of large caliber. —*adj.* **3.** like or characteristic of a bulldog or of a bulldog's jaws: *bulldog obstinacy.* —*v.t.* **4.** *Western U.S.* to throw (a calf, steer, etc.) to the ground by seizing the horns and twisting the head. —**bull′dog′ged·ness** *n.*

Bulldog
(13 in. high at shoulder)

bull′dog edi′tion, *U.S.* the earliest daily edition of a newspaper.

bull·doze (bo͝ol′dōz′), *v.t.,* **-dozed, -doz·ing.** **1.** to coerce or intimidate, as with threats. **2.** to clear, level, or reshape the contours of (land) by or as by using a bulldozer: *to bulldoze a building site.* **3.** to clear away by or as by using a bulldozer: *to bulldoze trees from a building site.* [BULL[1] + *doze,* Louisiana var. (French pronunciation) of DOSE, taken as v.]

bull·doz·er (bo͝ol′dō′zər), *n.* a large powerful tractor having a vertical blade at the front end for moving earth, tree stumps, rocks, etc.

Bulldozer

bul·let (bo͝ol′it), *n., v.,* **-let·ed, -let·ing.** —*n.* **1.** a small metal projectile, part of a cartridge, for firing from small arms. See diag. under **cartridge. 2.** a cartridge. **3.** a small ball. **4.** *Print.* a heavy dot for calling attention to particular sections of text. **5. bite the bullet,** to force oneself to perform a painful, difficult task or to endure an unpleasant situation: *We'll just have to bite the bullet and pay higher taxes.* —*v.i.* **6.** to move swiftly. [< MF *boullette* = *boulle* ball (see BOWL[2]) + *-ette* -ETTE] —**bul′let·less,** *adj.*

bul·le·tin (bo͝ol′i tən, -tin), *n.* **1.** a brief account or statement, as of the most recent news or important events, issued for the information of the public. **2.** a pamphlet or monograph as one cataloguing the courses taught at a college or university. **3.** a periodical publication, as of a learned society. [< F < It *bullettino* = *bullett(a)* (*bulla* BULL[2] + *-etta* -ETTE) + *-ino* -INE[2]]

bul·let·proof (bo͝ol′it pro͞of′), *adj.* **1.** capable of resisting the impact of a bullet. —*v.t.* **2.** to make (something) bulletproof.

bull′ fid′dle, *Informal.* See **double bass.**

bull·fight (bo͝ol′fīt′), *n.* a traditional Spanish and Latin American spectacle in which a special breed of fighting bull is tested and tired by banderilleros and mounted picadors, then fought and killed in a prescribed way by a matador using only a cape and sword. —**bull′fight′ing,** *n.*

bull·fight·er (bo͝ol′fī′tər), *n.* a person who participates in a bullfight, esp. a matador.

bull·finch (bo͝ol′finch′), *n.* **1.** a European, fringilline bird, *Pyrrhula pyrrhula,* often kept as a pet, the male of which has a black, white, and bluish-gray back and a rosy breast. **2.** any of several related or similar birds. [BULL[1] (? bull-necked) + FINCH]

bull·frog (bo͝ol′frog′, -frôg′), *n.* a large frog, esp. the North American *Rana catesbeiana,* having a deep voice. [BULL[1] + FROG[1]; so called from its size and voice]

bull·head (bo͝ol′hed′), *n.* **1.** any of several North American, fresh-water catfishes of the genus *Ictalurus,* having a rounded or truncate caudal fin. **2.** any of several other fishes, as the fresh-water sculpins of the genus *Cottus,* esp. the species having a hornlike spine on each side of the head.

bull·head·ed (bo͝ol′hed′id), *adj.* obstinate; blunderingly stubborn. —**bull′head′ed·ly,** *adv.* —**bull′head′ed·ness,** *n.*

bull′ horn′, a high-powered, electrical loudspeaker or an electrical megaphone. Also, **bull′horn′.**

bul·lion (bo͝ol′yən), *n.* **1.** gold or silver considered in mass rather than in value. **2.** gold or silver in the form of bars or ingots. **3.** Also called **bul′lion fringe′.** a thick trimming of gold or silver thread. [ME: melted mass of gold or silver < AL *bulliōn-* lit., a boiling = *bull(īre)* (to) bubble, BOIL[1] + *-iōn-* -ION] —**bul′lion·less,** *adj.*

bull·ish (bo͝ol′ish), *adj.* **1.** like a bull. **2.** obstinate or stupid. **3.** *Com.* **a.** rising or tending toward a rise in prices. **b.** characterized by favorable prospects for the economy.

bull-mas·tiff (bo͝ol′mas′tif, -mä′stif), *n.* one of an English breed of dogs having a short, fawn or brindled coat, produced by crossing the bulldog and the mastiff.

Bull′ Moose′, a member of the Progressive party under the leadership of Theodore Roosevelt.

bull-necked (bo͝ol′nekt′), *adj.* having a thick neck. Also, **bull′necked′.**

bull·ock (bo͝ol′ək), *n.* **1.** a castrated bull; steer. **2.** a young bull. [ME *bullok,* OE *bulluc*]

bull′ pen′, **1.** *U.S. Informal.* a large cell for the temporary detention of prisoners. **2.** *Baseball.* a place where relief pitchers warm up during a game.

bull·pout (bo͝ol′pout′), *n.* See **horned pout.** [BULL(HEAD) + POUT[2]]

bull·ring (bo͝ol′ring′), *n.* a bullfight arena.

bull-roar·er (bo͝ol′rōr′ər, -rôr′-), *n.* a wooden slat that produces a roaring sound when whirled around one's head on the end of a string or thong. Also called **thunderstick.**

Bull′ Run′, a creek in NE Virginia: Union forces defeated in major battles 1861, 1862. See map at **Antietam.**

bull′ ses′sion, *Slang.* an informal, spontaneous group discussion.

bull's-eye (bo͝olz′ī′), *n., pl.* **-eyes. 1.** the circular spot, usually black or outlined in black, at the center of a target. **2.** the center or central area of an actual target, as of a town in a bombing raid. **3.** a missile that strikes the center of a target. **4.** an instance of hitting the center of a target. **5.** *Informal.* any precise or notably effective statement or act. **6.** a small circular opening, window, or piece of glass in a wall, roof, ship's deck, etc., to admit light. **7.** *Naut.* an oval or circular wooden block having a groove around it and a hole in the center, through which to reeve a rope.

bull·shit (bo͝ol′shit′), *Slang* (*vulgar*). —*n.* **1.** nonsense, lies, or exaggeration. —*interj.* **2.** (used to express disagreement, disapproval, or the like.) [BULL[1] + SHIT]

bull·snake (bo͝ol′snāk′), *n.* any of several large, North American constrictors of the genus *Pituophis,* as the gopher snake and pine snake, that feed chiefly upon small rodents. Also, **bull′ snake′.**

bull·ter·ri·er (bo͝ol′ter′ē ər), *n.* one of an English breed of medium-sized, short-haired dogs having a white, brindled, or tan and white coat, produced by crossing the bulldog and the terrier. [BULL(DOG) + TERRIER[1]]

Bullterrier,
white variety
(18 in. high at shoulder)

bull′ tongue′, a plow having a vertical moldboard, used in cultivating cotton.

bull·whip (bo͝ol′hwip′, -wip′), *n.* a rawhide whip having a short handle and a long, plaited lash. Also, **bull′-whip′.** Also called **bull-whack** (bo͝ol′hwak′, -wak′). [so called from its size; see BULL[1], WHIP]

bul·ly[1] (bo͝ol′ē), *n., pl.* **-lies,** *v.,* **-lied, -ly·ing,** *adj., interj.* —*n.* **1.** a blustering, quarrelsome, overbearing person who habitually badgers and intimidates smaller or weaker people. **2.** *Archaic.* a man hired to do violence. **3.** *Obs.* a pimp; procurer. **4.** *Obs.* a good friend; good fellow. **5.** *Obs.* a sweetheart; darling. —*v.t.* **6.** to intimidate; domineer. —*v.i.* **7.** to be loudly arrogant and overbearing. —*adj.* **8.** *Informal.* fine; excellent; very good. **9.** dashing; jovial; high-spirited. —*interj.* **10.** *Informal.* **a.** good! well done! **b.** hurrah!: *Bully for you!* [< D *boele* (later *boel*) lover]

bul·ly[2] (bo͝ol′ē), *n.* See **bully beef.** [< F *bouilli,* short for *boeuf bouilli* boiled meat]

bul′ly beef′, canned or pickled beef.

bul·ly·rag (bo͝ol′ē rag′), *v.t.,* **-ragged, -rag·ging.** to bully; harass; abuse; tease: *to bullyrag fraternity plebs.* Also, **bally-rag.** [earlier *ballarag* < ?] —**bul′ly·rag′ger,** *n.*

bul′ly tree′, any of various tropical American, sapotaceous trees, as *Manilkara bidentata,* of Guiana, which yields the gum balata. [*bully,* alter. of BALATA]

Bü·low (bʏ′lō), *n.* **Prince Bern·hard von** (bern′härt fən), 1849–1929, chancellor of Germany 1900–09.

bul·rush (bo͝ol′rush′), *n.* **1.** (in Biblical use) the papyrus, *Cyperus Papyrus.* **2.** any of various rushes of the genera *Scirpus, Juncus,* or *Typha.* [late ME *bulrish* papyrus, prob. BULL[1] + *rish* RUSH[2]]

bul·wark (bo͝ol′wərk, bul′-), *n.* **1.** *Fort.* a wall of earth or other material built for defense; rampart. **2.** any protection against external danger, injury, or annoyance: *The new dam was a bulwark against floods.* **3.** any person or thing giving strong support or encouragement in time of need, danger, or doubt: *During the crisis, religion was his bulwark.* **4.** Usually, **bulwarks.** (on a ship) a solid structure extending above the level of a weather or main deck for the protection of persons or objects on deck. —*v.t.* **5.** to fortify, protect, or secure with or as with a bulwark. [ME *bulwerk,* prob. < MD, MLG *bolwerk* = *bol(l)e* BOLE[1] + *werk* WORK]

Bul·wer (bo͝ol′wər), *n.* **Sir Henry** (*William Henry Lytton Earle Bulwer; Baron Dalling and Bulwer*), 1801–72, British diplomat and author.

Bul·wer-Lyt·ton (bo͝ol′wər lit′ən), *n.* **1st Baron.** See **Lytton, Edward George.**

bum (bum), *n., v.,* **bummed, bum·ming,** *adj.* —*n. Informal.* **1.** a shiftless or dissolute person, esp. a tramp or hobo. **2.** *Chiefly Brit.* the buttocks; rump. —*v.t.* **3.** *Informal.* to get for nothing; borrow without expectation of returning: *He's always bumming cigarettes.* —*adj. Slang.* **4.** of poor, wretched, or miserable quality; bad. **5.** false; misleading: *a bum steer.* [ME *bom* anus < ?]

bum·ber·shoot (bum′bər sho͞ot′), *n. Informal.* an umbrella. [*bumber* < *umbr(ella)* + *-shoot* < *-chute* as in *parachute*]

bum·ble[1] (bum′bəl), *v.,* **-bled, -bling,** *n.* —*v.i.* **1.** to bungle or blunder; muddle: *He bumbled through college.* **2.** to stumble. **3.** to mumble. —*v.t.* **4.** to do clumsily; botch. —*n.* **5.** a blunder. [? b. BUNGLE and STUMBLE] —**bum′bler,** *n.*

bum·ble[2] (bum′bəl), *v.i.,* **-bled, -bling.** to make a buzzing, humming sound, as a bee. [ME *bomblen,* freq. of *bomben* to boom, buzz; imit.]

bum·ble·bee (bum′bəl bē′), *n.* any of several large, hairy social bees of the family *Apidae.*

bum·ble·foot (bum′bəl fo͝ot′), *n. Vet. Pathol.* a swelling, sometimes purulent, of the soft underside of the foot in fowl.

bum·boat (bum′bōt′), *n. Naut.* a boat used in peddling provisions and small wares among vessels in port or off shore. [BUM + BOAT, alliterative compound]

bum·kin (bum′kin), *n. Naut.* bumpkin[2].

bum·mer (bum′ər), *n. Slang.* **1.** one who bums. **2.** an unpleasant instance of taking narcotic drugs, as one accompanied by hallucinations or followed by bad physical aftereffects. **3.** an unpleasant experience of any kind. [BUM + -ER[1]]

bump (bump), *v.t.* **1.** to come more or less violently in contact with; collide with; strike. **2.** to cause to strike or collide: *The boy bumped the stick against every fence post.* **3.** to dislodge or displace by the force of collision: *The cat bumped the vase off the shelf.* **4.** *Poker Slang.* raise (def. 18). **5.** to dismiss from a job, vote down, or reject. **6.** to force upward; raise. —*v.i.* **7.** to come in contact or collide with (often fol. by *against* or *into*): *She bumped into me.* **8.** to bounce along; proceed in a series of jolts: *The old car bumped down the road.* **9.** to dance by thrusting the pelvis forward abruptly, in a provocative manner. Cf. **grind** (def. 12). **10. bump into,** *Informal.* to meet by chance. **11. bump off,** *Slang.* to kill, esp. to murder. —*n.* **12.** the act or an instance of bumping; collision; blow. **13.** the shock of a blow or collision. **14.** a swelling or contusion from a blow. **15.** a small area raised above the level of the surrounding surface; protuberance. **16.** *Aeron.* a rapidly rising current of air that gives an airplane a severe upward thrust. **17.** a dance movement in which the pelvis is abruptly thrust forward, in a provocative manner. Cf. **grind** (def. 17). [imit.] —**bump′ing·ly,** *adv.*

bump·er (bum′pər), *n.* **1.** a person or thing that bumps. **2.** a horizontal metal guard for protecting the front or rear of an automobile, truck, etc. **3.** any protective rim, guard, pad, or disk for absorbing shock and preventing damage from bumping, as a rubber-tipped doorstop, an old tire on the side of a boat, etc. **4.** a cup or glass filled to the brim, esp. when drunk as a toast. —*adj.* **5.** unusually abundant: *bumper crops.* —*v.t.* **6.** to fill to the brim. **7.** to drink a bumper as a toast to. —*v.i.* **8.** to drink toasts.

bump′er guard′, either of two vertical crosspieces attached to a bumper of a motor vehicle to prevent it from locking bumpers with another vehicle.

bump·kin[1] (bump′kin), *n.* an awkward, clumsy yokel. [< MD *bommekijn* little barrel] —**bump′kin·ish, bump′kin·ly,** *adj.*

bump·kin[2] (bump′kin), *n. Naut.* a beam or spar projecting outward from the hull of a vessel, for extending a sail, securing blocks, etc. Also, **bumkin, boomkin.** [< D *boomken* little tree. See BEAM, -KIN]

bump·tious (bump′shəs), *adj.* offensively self-assertive: *He's a bumptious young upstart.* [BUMP + (FRAC)TIOUS] —**bump′tious·ly,** *adv.* —**bump′tious·ness,** *n.*

bump·y (bum′pē), *adj.,* **bump·i·er, bump·i·est.** **1.** of uneven surface: *a bumpy road.* **2.** full of jolts: *a bumpy ride.* —**bump′i·ly,** *adv.* —**bump′i·ness,** *n.*

bum's′ rush′, *Slang.* **1.** forcible ejection from a place. **2.** any rude or abrupt dismissal: *He gave the job seekers the bum's rush.*

bun (bun), *n.* **1.** any of variously shaped bread rolls, either plain or leavened and slightly sweetened, sometimes containing spices, dried currants, citron, etc. **2.** hair gathered into a round coil or knot at the nape of the neck or on top of the head. Also, **bunn.** [ME *bunne* < ?]

Bu·na (bo͞o′nə, byo͞o′-), *n. Trademark.* a synthetic rubber made by copolymerizing butadiene with acrylonitrile, styrene, or other materials.

bunch (bunch), *n.* **1.** a connected group; cluster: *a bunch of grapes.* **2.** *Informal.* a group of people or things: *a bunch of papers; a fine bunch of students.* **3.** a knob; lump; protuberance. —*v.t.* **4.** to group together; make a bunch of. —*v.i.* **5.** to gather into a cluster; gather together. [ME *bunche,* perh. var. of **bunge* < Flem *bondje* bundle = *bond* (see BUNDLE) + *-je* dim. suffix]

bunch·ber·ry (bunch′ber′ē, -bə rē), *n., pl.* **-ries.** a dwarf cornel, *Cornus canadensis,* bearing dense clusters of bright-red berries.

Bunche (bunch), *n.* **Ralph (Johnson),** 1904–71, U.S. diplomat: at the United Nations 1946–71; Nobel peace prize 1950.

bunch·flow·er (bunch′flou′ər), *n.* **1.** a liliaceous plant, *Melanthium virginicum,* of the U.S., having grasslike leaves and a panicle of small greenish flowers. **2.** any other plant of the same genus.

bunch′ grass′, any of various grasses in different regions of the U.S., growing in distinct clumps.

bunch·y (bun′chē), *adj.,* **bunch·i·er, bunch·i·est.** **1.** having bunches. **2.** bulging or protuberant. [ME] —**bunch′i·ly,** *adv.* —**bunch′i·ness,** *n.*

bun·co (bung′kō), *n., pl.* **-cos,** *v.,* **-coed, -co·ing.** *U.S. Informal.* —*n.* **1.** a swindle or misrepresentation. —*v.t.* **2.** to victimize by a bunco. Also, **bunko.** [prob. < Sp or It *banca* or *banco* bank, name of a card game]

bun·combe (bung′kəm), *n.* bunkum.

Bund (bo͝ond; *Ger.* bo͝ont), *n., pl.* **Bün·de** (bo͝on′də; *Ger.* bʏn′də). **1.** a short form of "German-American Volksbund," a pro-Nazi organization in the U.S. during the 1930's and 1940's. **2.** an alliance or league. [< G: association, league] —**Bund′ist,** *n.*

Bun·des·rat (bo͝on′dəs rät′; *Ger.* bo͝on′dəs rät′), *n.* the upper house of the Federal Republic of Germany. Also, **Bun·des·rath** (bo͝on′dəs rät′). [< G: federal council = *Bund* federation + *-es* genitive ending + *Rat* council]

Bun·des·tag (bo͝on′dəs täg′; *Ger.* bo͝on′dəs täk′), *n.* the lower house of the Federal Republic of Germany. [< G: federal assembly = *Bund* federation + *-es* genitive ending + *-tag* < *tagen* to meet, assemble; see DIET[2]]

bun·dle (bun′dəl), *n., v.,* **-dled, -dling.** —*n.* **1.** several objects or a quantity of material gathered or bound together. **2.** an item, group, or quantity wrapped for carrying; package. **3.** a number of things, thoughts, etc., considered together: *He presented a bundle of ideas to the committee.* **4.** *Bot.* an aggregation of strands of specialized conductive and mechanical tissues. **5.** *Anat., Zool.* an aggregation of fibers, as of nerves or muscles. **6.** *Slang.* a great deal of money. —*v.t.* **7.** to tie together or wrap in a bundle. **8.** to send away hurriedly or unceremoniously (usually fol. by *off, out,* etc.): *They bundled her off to the country.* **9.** to offer or supply (related products or services) in a single transaction at one all-inclusive price. —*v.i.* **10.** to leave hurriedly or unceremoniously (usually fol. by *off, out,* etc.). **11.** (esp. of sweethearts in early New England) to sleep or lie in the same bed while fully clothed. **12. bundle up,** to dress warmly or snugly. [ME *bundel* < MD *bundel, bondel* (c. G *Bündel*); akin to OE *bindele* bandage] —**bun′dler,** *n.*

bung (bung), *n.* **1.** a stopper for the opening of a cask. **2.** a bunghole. —*v.t.* **3.** to close with or as with a bung; cork; plug (often fol. by *up*). **4.** to beat; bruise; maul (often fol. by *up*). [ME *bunge* < MD *bonghe* stopper]

bun·ga·low (bung′gə lō′), *n.* **1.** a cottage. **2.** (in India) a one-storied thatched or tiled house, usually surrounded by a veranda. [< Hindi *banglā,* lit., of Bengal]

bung·hole (bung′hōl′), *n.* a hole or orifice for filling or tapping a cask.

bun·gle (bung′gəl), *v.,* **-gled, -gling,** *n.* —*v.t.* **1.** to do something clumsily and awkwardly; botch. —*v.i.* **2.** to do something awkwardly and clumsily. —*n.* **3.** something that has been done clumsily or inadequately. [? < Scand; cf. dial. Sw *bangla* to work ineffectively] —**bun′gler,** *n.* —**bun′gling·ly,** *adv.*

Bu·nin (bo͞o′nin), *n.* **I·van A·lek·se·e·vich** (i vän′ ä′le kse′yə vich), 1870–1953, Russian poet and novelist.

bun·ion (bun′yən), *n. Pathol.* a swelling on the foot caused by the inflammation of a synovial bursa, esp. of the great toe. [perh. < older It *bugnone* blain = *bugn(a)* projection + *-one* aug. suffix]

bunk[1] (bungk), *n.* **1.** a built-in platform bed, as on a ship. **2.** *Informal.* any bed. —*v.i.* **3.** *Informal.* to occupy a bunk; sleep, esp. in rough quarters. [back formation from BUNKER]

bunk[2] (bungk), *n. U.S. Slang.* humbug; nonsense. [short for BUNKUM]

bunk′ bed′, a piece of furniture containing two platformlike single beds, one above the other.

bunk·er (bung′kər), *n.* **1.** a large bin or receptacle; a fixed chest or box: *a coal bunker.* **2.** *Golf.* any obstacle, as a sand trap or mound of dirt, constituting a hazard. **3.** a fortification set mostly below the surface of the ground, fitted with openings through which to fire, and having overhead protection provided by logs and earth or by reinforced concrete. —*v.t.* **4.** *Golf.* to hit (a ball) into a bunker. **5.** *Naut.* to provide fuel for (a vessel). [earlier *bonkar* (Scot) box, chest, serving also as a seat < ?]

Bunk′er Hill′, a hill in Charlestown, Massachusetts: the first major battle of the American Revolution, known as the Battle of Bunker Hill, was fought on adjoining Breed's Hill on June 17, 1775.

bunk·house (bungk′hous′), *n.*, *pl.* **-hous·es** (-hou′ziz). a rough building used for sleeping quarters, as for construction crews or ranch hands.
bun·ko (bung′kō), *n.*, *pl.* **-kos**, *v.*, **-koed, -ko·ing.** *U.S. Informal.* bunco.
bun·kum (bung′kəm), *n.* **1.** insincere speechmaking by a politician intended merely top lease local constituents. **2.** insincere talk; claptrap; humbug. Also, **buncombe.** [after speech in 16th Congress, 1819–21, by F. Walker, who said he was bound to speak for *Buncombe* (N.C. county in district he represented)]
bunn (bun), *n.* bun.
bun·ny (bun′ē), *n.*, *pl.* **-nies.** *Informal.* a rabbit, esp. a young one. [dial. *bun* (tail of a) hare or rabbit, in Scot: buttocks (< Gael *bun* bottom) + -Y[2]]

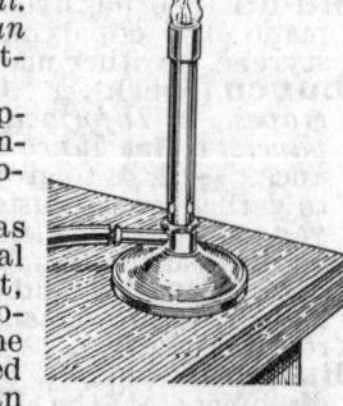
Bunsen burner

bun′ny hug′, a ballroom dance popular in the U.S. in the early 20th century and characterized by a syncopated rhythm.
Bun′sen burn′er (bun′sən), a gas burner, commonly used in chemical laboratories, with which a very hot, practically nonluminous flame is obtained by allowing air to enter at the base and mix with the gas. [named after R. W. *Bunsen* (1811–99), German chemist]
bunt[1] (bunt), *v.t.* **1.** (of a goat or calf) to push with the horns or head; butt. **2.** *Baseball.* to bat (a pitched ball) very gently so that it does not roll far into the infield. —*v.i.* **3.** to push (something) with the horns or head. **4.** *Baseball.* to bunt a ball. —*n.* **5.** a push with the head or horns; butt. **6.** *Baseball.* **a.** the act of bunting. **b.** a bunted ball. [nasalized var. of BUTT[2]]
bunt[2] (bunt), *n.* **1.** *Naut.* the middle part of a square sail. **2.** the bagging part of a fishing net or bagging middle area of various cloth objects. [?]
bunt[3] (bunt), *n.* *Plant Pathol.* a smut disease of wheat in which the kernels are replaced by the black, foul-smelling spores of fungi of the genus *Tilletia.* Also called **stinking smut.** [?] —**bunt′ed,** *adj.*
bun·ting[1] (bun′ting), *n.* **1.** a coarse open fabric of worsted. **2.** patriotic and festive decorations made from such cloth, or from paper, usually in the form of draperies, wide streamers, etc., esp. in the colors of the national flag. **3.** flags, esp. a vessel's flags, collectively. [? orig. cloth for sifting, ME *bont(en)* (to) sift + -ING[1]]
bun·ting[2] (bun′ting), *n.* any of several small, fringilline birds of the genera *Emberiza, Passerina,* or *Plectrophenax.* [ME < ?]
bun·ting[3] (bun′ting), *n.* a hooded sleeping garment for infants, usually made of blanket cloth. Also called **sleeper.** [special use of BUNTING[1]]
bunt·line (bunt′lin, -līn′), *n.* *Naut.* one of the ropes attached to the foot of a square sail to haul it up for furling.
Bun·yan (bun′yən), *n.* **1. John,** 1628–88, English preacher and writer. **2. Paul.** See **Paul Bunyan.**
buo·na not·te (bwô′nä nôt′te), *Italian.* good night.
Buo·na·par·te (*It.* bwô′nä pär′te), *n.* Bonaparte.
Buo·nar·ro·ti (*It.* bwô′när rô′tē), *n.* **Michelangelo,** Michelangelo.
buo·na se·ra (bwô′nä se′rä), *Italian.* good evening.
buon gior·no (bwôn jôr′nô), *Italian.* good morning; good day.
bu·oy (bo͞o′ē, boi), *n.* *Naut.* **1.** a distinctively shaped and marked float, anchored to mark a channel, anchorage, navigational hazard, etc., or to provide a mooring place. **2.** a life buoy. —*v.t.* **3.** to keep from sinking; keep afloat (often fol. by *up*): *The life jacket buoyed her up until help arrived.* **4.** *Naut.* to mark with a buoy or buoys. **5.** to sustain or encourage (often fol. by *up*): *Her courage was buoyed up by the doctor's calmness.* —*v.i.* **6.** to float; rise by reason of lightness. [late ME *boye* a float < MF **boie, boue(e)* < Gmc, akin to BEACON]

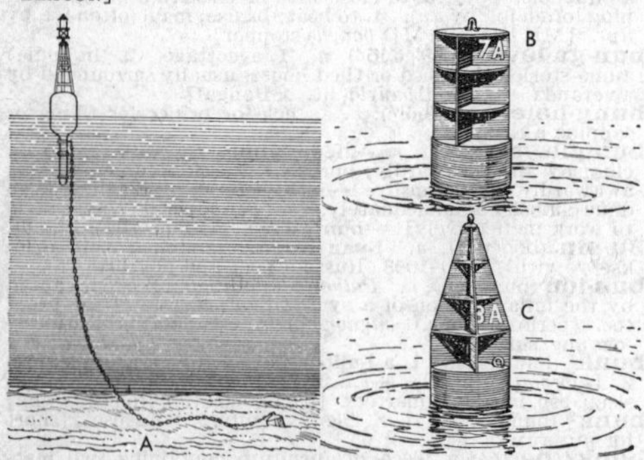

Buoys
A, Light buoy; B, Can buoy; C, Nun buoy

bu·oy·age (bo͞o′ē ij, boi′ij), *n.* *Naut.* **1.** a system or group of buoys. **2.** the provision of buoys. **3.** a fee for the use of a mooring buoy.
buoy·an·cy (boi′ən sē, bo͞o′yən sē), *n.* **1.** the tendency to float or rise in a fluid. **2.** the tendency of supporting a body so that it floats; upward pressure exerted by the fluid in which an object is immersed. **3.** elasticity of spirit; cheerfulness. [BUOY(ANT) + -ANCY]
buoy·ant (boi′ənt, bo͞o′yənt), *adj.* **1.** tending to float or rise in a fluid. **2.** capable of keeping an object afloat, as a liquid. **3.** cheerful. **4.** cheering or invigorating. —**buoy′ant·ly,** *adv.*
buoy′ant force′, *Physics.* See under **Archimedes' principle.** Also called **buoy′ancy force′.**
bur (bûr), *n., v.,* **burred, bur·ring.** —*n.* **1.** *Bot.* the rough, prickly case around the seeds of certain plants, as of the chestnut and burdock. **2.** any bur-bearing plant. **3.** *Mach.* burr[1] (defs. 1, 4). **4.** *Dentistry.* burr[1] (def. 2). **5.** *Surg.* burr[1] (def. 3). —*v.t.* **6.** to extract or remove burs from. **7.** burr[1]. [ME *burre* < Scand; cf. Dan *burre* bur]
Bur., Burma.
bur., bureau.
Bur·bage (bûr′bij), *n.* **Richard,** 1567?–1619, English actor: associate of Shakespeare.
Bur·bank (bûr′bangk′), *n.* **1. Luther,** 1849–1926, U.S. horticulturist and plant breeder. **2.** a city in SW California. 88,871 (1970).
Bur·ber·ry (bûr′bə rē, -ber′ē), *n.*, *pl.* **-ries.** a light raincoat made of a waterproof, mercerized cotton fabric. [after *Burberrys,* a trademark]
bur·ble (bûr′bəl), *v.*, **-bled, -bling,** *n.* —*v.i.* **1.** to make a bubbling sound. **2.** to speak with such a sound. —*n.* **3.** a bubbling or gentle flow. **4.** *Aeron.* the breakdown of smooth airflow around a wing at a high angle of attack. [ME; perh. var. of BUBBLE] —**bur′bler,** *n.* —**bur′bly,** *adv.*
bur·bot (bûr′bət), *n.*, *pl.* **-bots,** (*esp. collectively*) **-bot.** a fresh-water gadid fish, *Lota lota,* having an elongated body and a barbel on the chin. [ME < MF *bourbotte,* var. of *bourbete* < *bourbeter* to wallow in mud = *bourbe* mud + *-t-* freq. suffix + *-er* inf. ending]
Burch·field (bûrch′fēld′), *n.* **Charles Ephraim,** 1893–1967, U.S. painter.
Burck·hardt (bûrk′härt; *Ger.* bo͝ork′härt′), *n.* **Ja·kob** (yä′kôp), 1818–97, Swiss historian.
bur·den[1] (bûr′dən), *n.* **1.** that which is carried; load. **2.** that which is borne with difficulty: *the burden of leadership.* **3.** *Naut.* the carrying capacity of a ship: *a ship of a hundred-ton burden.* **4.** *Mining.* the earth or rock to be moved by a charge of explosives. **5.** *Accounting.* overhead (def. 6). —*v.t.* **6.** to load heavily. **7.** to load oppressively; trouble. [ME, var. of *burthen,* OE *byrthen;* akin to G *Bürde,* Goth *baurthei;* see BEAR[1]] —**bur′den·er,** *n.* —**bur′den·less,** *adj.* —**Syn. 1.** See **load. 2.** weight, encumbrance.
bur·den[2] (bûr′dən), *n.* **1.** something often repeated or much dwelt upon; principal idea. **2.** *Music.* the refrain or recurring chorus of a song. [ME *bordoun* < MF *bourdon* droning sound, instrument making such a sound, etc., orig. imit.]
bur·dened (bûr′dənd), *adj.* *Navig.* (of a vessel) required to yield to a vessel having the right of way. Cf. **privileged** (def. 5).
bur′den of proof′, *Chiefly Law.* the obligation to offer evidence that the court or jury could reasonably believe, in support of a contention, failing which the case will be lost.
bur·den·some (bûr′dən səm), *adj.* **1.** oppressively heavy. **2.** distressing; troublesome. —**bur′den·some·ly,** *adv.*
bur·dock (bûr′dok), *n.* a composite plant of the genus *Arctium,* esp. *A. lappa,* a coarse, broad-leaved weed bearing prickly heads of burs. [BUR + DOCK[4]]
bu·reau (byo͝or′ō), *n.*, *pl.* **bu·reaus, bu·reaux** (byo͝or′ōz). **1.** a chest of drawers, often with a mirror at the top. **2.** *Chiefly Brit.* a desk or writing table with drawers for papers. **3.** a division of a government department. **4.** an agency or office for collecting or distributing news or information, coordinating the work of related businesses, etc.: *a travel bureau.* [< F: desk, office, orig., kind of cloth (used to cover desks, etc.), OF *burel* = *bur-* (< LL *burra* rough cloth) + *-el* n. suffix]
bu·reauc·ra·cy (byo͝o rok′rə sē), *n.*, *pl.* **-cies.** **1.** government characterized by a rigid hierarchy of bureaus, administrators, and petty officials. **2.** a body of officials and administrators. **3.** administration characterized by excessive red tape and routine. [BUREAU + -CRACY, modeled on F *bureaucratie*]
bu·reau·crat (byo͝or′ə krat′), *n.* **1.** an official of a bureaucracy. **2.** an official who works by fixed routine without exercising intelligent judgment. [< F *bureaucrate*] —**bu′reau·crat′ic,** *adj.* —**bu′reau·crat′i·cal·ly,** *adv.* —**bu·reau·crat·ism** (byo͝or′ə krat iz′əm, byo͝o rok′rə-tiz′əm), *n.*
bu·rette (byo͝o ret′), *n.* *Chem.* a graduated glass tube, commonly having a stopcock at the bottom, used for measuring or measuring out small quantities of liquid. Also, **bu·ret′.** [< F: cruet, MF, var. of *buirette* = *buire* ewer (var. of *buie* < Gmc; cf. OE *būc* pitcher) + *-ette* -ETTE]

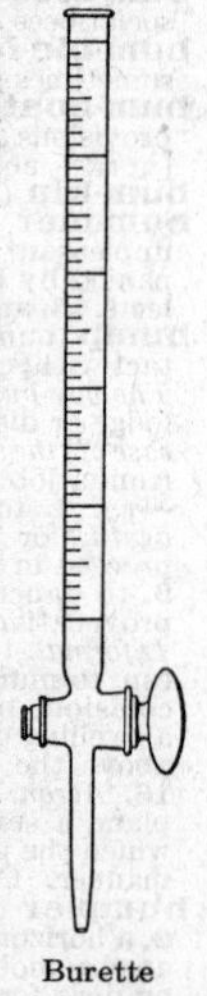
Burette

burg (bûrg), *n.* **1.** *Informal.* a city or town. **2.** *Hist.* a fortified town. [var. of BURGH]
burg·age (bûr′gij), *n.* *Law.* **1.** (in England) a tenure whereby burgesses or townsmen hold lands or tenements of the king or other lord, usually for a fixed money rent. **2.** (in Scotland) tenure directly from the crown of property in royal burghs in return for the service of watching and warding. [ME *borgage* < ML *burgāg(i-um)* = *burg(us)* burgh, borough + *-āgium* -AGE]
Bur·gas (bo͝or gäs′), *n.* a seaport in E Bulgaria, on the Black Sea. 106,284 (1964).
bur·gee (bûr′jē), *n.* a triangular or swallow-tail-shaped identification flag, esp. as flown by yachts. [perh. < F (dial.) *bourgeais* shipowner, akin to BOURGEOIS[1]]
Bur·gen·land (*Ger.* bo͝or′gən länt′), *n.* a province in E Austria, bordering Hungary. 271,001 (1961); 1530 sq. mi. *Cap.:* Eisenstadt.
bur·geon (bûr′jən), *n.* **1.** a bud; sprout. —*v.i.* **2.** to begin to grow, as a bud; to put forth buds, shoots, etc., as a plant (often fol. by *out, forth*). **3.** to grow or develop suddenly: *The town burgeoned into a city.* —*v.t.* **4.** to put forth as buds. Also, **bourgeon.** [ME *burjon* bud < OF < ?]
burg·er (bûr′gər), *n.* **1.** *Informal.* a hamburger. **2.** (in compounds) a patty or small cake of food, as specified, usually ground or chopped, grilled, and served on a bun: *turkey-burger.* [abstracted from HAMBURGER by false analysis as HAM[1] + *burger*]
Bur·ger (bûr′gər), *n.* **Warren Earl,** born 1907, U.S. jurist: Chief Justice of the U.S. Supreme Court 1969–1986.
bur·gess (bûr′jis), *n.* **1.** an inhabitant, esp. a citizen or freeman, of an English borough. **2.** *Hist.* a representative of

a borough, corporate town, or university in the British Parliament. **3.** *Amer. Hist.* a representative in the colonial legislature of Virginia or Maryland. [ME *burgeis* < OF = *burg* city (< Gmc) + *-eis* -ESE]

Bur·gess (bûr′jis), *n.* **(Frank) Ge·lett** (jə let′), 1866–1951, U.S. illustrator and humorist.

burgh (bûrg; *Scot.* bur′ō, bur′ə), *n.* (in Scotland) an incorporated town having some degree of political independence. [var. of BOROUGH] —**burgh·al** (bûr′gəl), *adj.*

burgh·er (bûr′gər), *n.* an inhabitant of a town or city, esp. a conservative, well-to-do member of the middle class; citizen. [< MD < MHG *burger* = *burg* BOROUGH + *-er* -ER[1]] —**burgh′er·ship′**, *n.*

Burgh·ley (bûr′lē), *n.* **1st Baron.** See **Cecil, William.**

bur·glar (bûr′glər), *n.* a person who commits burglary. [< AF *burgler* < AL *burglātor*, appar. = *burgl-* (< OE *burghal* as in *burghal-penny*) + *-ātor* -OR[2]; OE *burghal* = *burg* BOROUGH + *hal* HALL]

bur·glar·ize (bûr′glə rīz′), *v.*, **-ized, -iz·ing.** —*v.t.* **1.** to break into and steal from (a place): *Thieves burglarized the warehouse.* —*v.i.* **2.** to commit burglary.

bur·gla·ry (bûr′glə rē), *n., pl.* **-ries.** *Crim. Law.* the felony of breaking into and entering the building of another with intent to commit a felony. [< AF *burglarie* < AL *burglaria*, alter. (with *-l-* of *burglātor*) of *burgaria*, var. of *burgeria* = *burger-* BURGHER + *-ia* -IA] —**bur·glar·i·ous** (bər glâr′ē əs), *adj.* —**bur·glar′i·ous·ly,** *adv.*

bur·gle (bûr′gəl), *v.t., v.i.,* **-gled, -gling.** *Informal.* to burglarize. [back formation from BURGLAR]

bur·go·mas·ter (bûr′gə mas′tər, -mä′stər), *n.* the chief magistrate of a municipal town of Holland, Flanders, Germany, or Austria. [< D *burgemeester* = *burg* BOROUGH + *meester* MASTER; akin to G *Bürgermeister* mayor]

bur·go·net (bûr′gə net′), *n.* *Armor.* an open helmet, usually having a peak and hinged cheek pieces. [< ME *burgon* of Burgundy (< MF *Bourgogne* Burgundy) + -ET, modeled on MF *bourguignotte*]

bur·goo (bûr′goo, bûr goo′), *n.* **1.** a thick oatmeal gruel, esp. as eaten by seamen. **2.** *U.S. Dial.* a highly seasoned, thick soup or stew, usually made of chicken, small game, and vegetables. [?]

Bur·gos (boor′gôs), *n.* a city in N Spain: Gothic cathedral. 89,864 (est. 1960).

Bur·goyne (bər goin′), *n.* **John,** 1722–92, British general and dramatist: surrendered at Saratoga in the American Revolutionary War.

Bur·gun·dy (bûr′gən dē), *n., pl.* **-dies** for 2, 3. **1.** French, **Bourgogne.** a region in central France: a former kingdom, duchy, and province. **2.** (*often l.c.*) any of the various red or white table wines produced in this region, or a similar red wine made elsewhere. **3.** a reddish-purple color. [< ML *Burgundi(a)* = L *Burgundi(ōnes)*, Latinized form of Germanic tribal name + *-a* territorial suffix]

bur·i·al (ber′ē əl), *n.* **1.** the act or ceremony of burying. **2.** the place of burying. [BURY + -AL[2]; r. ME *buriel*, back formation from OE *byrgels* burial place = *byrg(an)* (to) BURY + *-els* n. suffix]

Bur·iat′ Auton′omous So′viet So′cialist Repub′lic (boor yät′, boor′ē ät′). See **Buryat Autonomous Soviet Socialist Republic.**

bur·i·er (ber′ē ər), *n.* a person or thing that buries.

bu·rin (byoor′in), *n.* **1.** a steel tool with an oblique point and rounded handle for carving stone and engraving metal. **2.** a prehistoric chisellike flint tool. [< F < It *burino* (now *bulino*) graving tool = *bur-* (? < Gmc; see BORE[1]) + *-ino* -INE[2]]

Burin (def. 1)

burke (bûrk), *v.t.,* **burked, burk·ing.** **1.** to murder by suffocation, so as to leave no marks of violence. **2.** to suppress or get rid of quietly or indirectly. [after W. *Burke*, hanged in 1829 in Edinburgh for murders of this kind] —**burk′er, burk·ite** (bûr′kīt), *n.*

Burke (bûrk), *n.* **1. Edmund,** 1729–97, Irish statesman, orator, and writer. **2. Kenneth Du·va** (doo vā′), born 1897, U.S. literary critic.

Bur·ki·na Fa·so (bər kē′nə fä′sō), a republic in W Africa: formerly a French territory. 6,774,000; 106,111 sq. mi. *Cap.:* Ouagadougou. Formerly, **Upper Volta.**

burl (bûrl), *n.* **1.** a knot or lump in wool, thread, or cloth. **2.** a dome-shaped growth on the trunk of a tree, sliced to make veneer. —*v.t.* **3.** to remove burls from (cloth) in finishing. [late ME *burle* << OF; akin to ML *burla* bunch, sheaf, LL *burra* tuft of wool] —**burl′er,** *n.*

bur·lap (bûr′lap), *n.* a plain-woven, coarse fabric of jute, hemp, or the like; gunny. [earlier *borelap* = *bore(l)* coarse cloth (see BUREAU) + LAP[1]]

Bur·leigh (bûr′lē), *n.* **1st Baron.** See **Cecil, William.**

bur·lesque (bər lesk′), *n., adj., v.,* **-lesqued, -les·quing.** —*n.* **1.** an artistic composition that, for the sake of laughter, vulgarizes lofty material or treats ordinary material with mock dignity. **2.** any ludicrous parody or grotesque caricature. **3.** Also, **bur·lesk′.** *Theat. U.S.* a stage show featuring slapstick humor and striptease acts. —*adj.* **4.** involving ludicrous or mocking treatment of a solemn subject. **5.** of or pertaining to stage-show burlesque. —*v.t.* **6.** to make ridiculous by mocking representation. [< F < It *burlesco* = *burl(a)* jest + *-esco-* ESQUE] —**bur·les′quer,** *n.*
—**Syn. 1.** satire, lampoon, farce. BURLESQUE, CARICATURE, PARODY, TRAVESTY refer to the literary or dramatic forms that imitate serious works or subjects to achieve a humorous or satiric purpose. The characteristic device of BURLESQUE is mockery of both high and low through association with their opposites: *a burlesque of high and low life.* CARICATURE, usually associated with visual arts or with visual effects in literary works, implies exaggeration of characteristic details: *The caricature emphasized his nose.* PARODY achieves its humor through application of the manner or technique, usually of a well-known writer, to unaccustomed subjects: *a parody of Swift.* TRAVESTY implies a grotesque form of burlesque: *characters so changed as to produce a travesty.*

bur·ley (bûr′lē), *n., pl.* **-leys.** (*often cap.*) an American tobacco grown esp. in Kentucky and southern Ohio. [appar. from proper name]

Bur·lin·game (bûr′lin gām′, -liŋ gām′), *n.* a city in W California, S of San Francisco. 27,320 (1970).

Bur·ling·ton (bûr′liŋ tən), *n.* **1.** a city in NW Vermont, on Lake Champlain. 38,633 (1970). **2.** a city in N North Carolina. 35,930 (1970). **3.** a city in SE Iowa, on the Mississippi River. 32,366 (1970).

bur·ly (bûr′lē), *adj.,* **-li·er, -li·est.** **1.** great in bodily size; stout; sturdy. **2.** bluff; brusque. [ME *borli, burli*, OE *borlīce* excellent(ly) = *bor(a)* ruler (lit., highborn one; see BEAR[1]) + *-līce* -LY] —**bur′li·ly,** *adv.* —**bur′li·ness,** *n.*

Bur·ma (bûr′mə), *n.* an independent republic in SE Asia: traditionally divided into the coastal region W of Thailand **(Lower Burma),** the inland area **(Upper Burma),** and the Shan State. 24,229,000 (est. 1964); 261,789 sq. mi. *Cap.:* Rangoon. Official name, **Union of Burma.** Cf. **Shan State.**

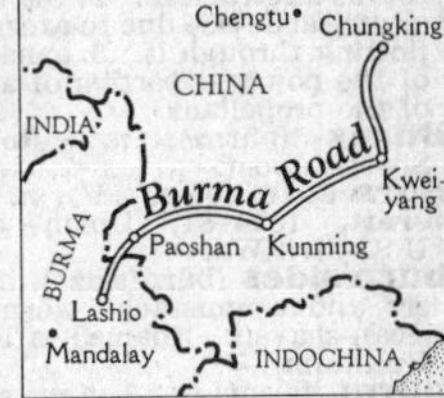

bur′ mar′igold, any of various composite herbs of the genus *Bidens*, esp. those having conspicuous yellow flowers.

Bur′ma Road′, a road extending from Lashio, Burma to Chungking, China: used during World War II to supply Allied military forces in China.

Bur·mese (bər mēz′, -mēs′), *n., pl.* **-mese,** *adj.* —*n.* **1.** a native or inhabitant of Burma. **2.** the principal language of Burma, a Sino-Tibetan language. —*adj.* **3.** of or pertaining to Burma, its people, or their language. Also, **Bur·man** (bûr′mən) (for defs. 1, 3).

burn[1] (bûrn), *v.,* **burned** or **burnt, burn·ing,** *n.* —*v.i.* **1.** to undergo rapid combustion or consume fuel in such a way as to give off heat, gases, and usually, light; be on fire. **2.** (of a fireplace, furnace, etc.) to contain a fire. **3.** to feel heat or pain from or as from a fire: *His face burned in the wind.* **4.** to give off light or glow brightly: *The lights burned all night.* **5.** to give off heat or be hot. **6.** to cause to smart or sting: *The whiskey burned in his throat.* **7.** to feel extreme anger: *When she said I was rude, I really burned.* **8.** to feel strong emotion or passion: *to burn with desire.* **9.** *Chem.* **a.** to undergo combustion, either fast or slow; oxidize. **b.** to undergo fission or fusion. **10.** to become charred or overcooked. **11.** to receive a sunburn: *She burns easily and has to stay in the shade.* **12.** to be damned. **13.** *Slang.* to be executed in an electric chair. —*v.t.* **14.** to cause to undergo combustion or be consumed partly or wholly by fire. **15.** to use as fuel or as a source of light: *He burns coal to heat his house.* **16.** to cause to feel the sensation of heat. **17.** to overcook, char, or scald: *She burned the roast again.* **18.** (of the sun or a sun lamp) to redden (a person's skin). **19.** to injure with or as with fire: *Look out, you'll burn yourself!* **20.** to subject to fire or treat with heat as a process of manufacturing. **21.** to produce with or as with fire: *He burned the image of a horse into the wood panel.* **22.** to cause sharp pain or a stinging sensation: *The iodine burned his wound.* **23.** *Informal.* to suffer heavy financial losses or be badly disillusioned. **24.** *Chem.* to cause to undergo combustion; oxidize. **25.** to damage or mar by friction. **26. burn down,** to burn to the ground. **27. burn in,** *Photog.* (in printing) to expose (one part of an image) to more light by masking the other parts. **28. burn out, a.** (of an electrical device) to cease to operate because of a broken circuit. **b.** to deprive of a place to live, work, etc., by reason of fire. **29. burn up, a.** to burn completely; be consumed in fire. **b.** to incite to anger. **c.** to become angry. —*n.* **30.** a burned place or area. **31.** *Pathol.* an injury caused by heat, abnormal cold, chemicals, poison gas, electricity, or lightning, and characterized by reddening **(first-degree burn),** blistering **(second-degree burn),** or charring **(third-degree burn).** **32.** the process or an instance of burning. [ME *bernen, brennen*, OE *beornan* (v.i., c. Goth, OHG *brinnan*) and OE *bærnan* (v.t., c. Goth *brannjan*, OHG *brennen*)] —**burn′a·ble,** *adj.* —**Syn. 1.** flame. **3.** tingle, glow. **14.** char, incinerate.

burn[2] (bûrn; *Scot.* burn), *n.* *Scot. and North Eng.* a brook or rivulet. [ME *burne, bourne*, OE *burna, brunna* brook; c. Goth *brunna*, D *born, bron*, G *Brunnen*, Icel *brunnr* spring]

Burne-Jones (bûrn′jōnz′), *n.* **Sir Edward Co·ley** (kō′lē), 1833–98, English painter and designer.

burn·er (bûr′nər), *n.* **1.** a person or thing that burns. **2.** the part of a gas or electric fixture or appliance, as a stove or oven, from which flame or heat issues. [ME *brenner*]

bur·net (bûr′nit), *n.* a rosaceous plant of the genus *Sanguisorba*, esp. *S. minor*, an erect herb having leaves that are used for salads. [ME < MF *burnete*, var. of *brunete* (see BRUNET); so called from its hue]

Bur·nett (bər net′), *n.* **Frances Hodg·son** (hoj′sən), 1849–1924, U.S. novelist, born in England.

Bur·ney (bûr′nē), *n.* **Fanny** or **Frances** (*Madame D'Arblay*), 1752–1840, English novelist and diarist.

burn·ing (bûr′niŋ), *adj.* **1.** aflame; on fire. **2.** very hot; simmering: *The soup was burning.* **3.** very bright; glowing: *She wore a burning red bathing suit.* **4.** affecting with or as with fire, a burn, or heat: *He had a burning sensation in his throat.* **5.** intense; passionate: *a burning desire.* **6.** urgent or crucial: *a burning question.* —*n.* **7.** the state, process, sensation, or effect of being on fire, burned, or subjected to intense heat. **8.** the baking of ceramic products to develop hardness and other properties. **9.** the heating or the calcining of certain ores and rocks as a preliminary stage in various industrial processes. [ME *brenning* (n., adj.), OE *byrnendum* (adj.)] —**burn′ing·ly,** *adv.*

burn·ing-bush (bûr′ning bo͝osh′), *n.* **1.** any of various plants, esp. the wahoo, *Euonymus atropurpureus.* **2.** dittany (def. 3). Also, **burn′ing bush′.**

burn′ing glass′, a lens used to produce heat or ignite substances by focusing the sun's rays.

bur·nish (bûr′nish), *v.t.* **1.** to polish (a surface) by friction. **2.** to make smooth and bright. —*n.* **3.** gloss; brightness; luster: *the burnish of brass andirons.* [ME *burnissh* < MF *bruniss-* (long s. of *brunir* to brown, polish) = *brun-* BROWN + *-iss-* -ISH[2]] —**bur′nish·a·ble,** *adj.* —**bur′nish·er,** *n.* —**bur′nish·ment,** *n.*

Burn·ley (bûrn′lē), *n.* a city in E Lancashire, in NW England. 80,588 (1961).

bur·noose (bər no͞os′, bûr′no͞os), *n.* a hooded mantle or cloak, as that worn by Arabs. Also, **bur·nous′.** [< F *burnous* < Ar *burnus*] —**bur·noosed′, bur·noused′,** *adj.*

Burnoose

burn·out (bûrn′out′), *n.* **1.** a fire that is totally destructive. **2.** the breakdown of an electrical device due to excessive heat created by the current flowing through it. **3.** exhaustion. **4.** *Rocketry.* termination of the powered portion of a rocket's flight upon exhaustion of the propellant.

Burns (bûrnz), *n.* **Robert.** 1759–96, Scottish poet.

Burn·side (bûrn′sīd′), *n.* **Ambrose Everett,** 1824–81, Union general in the U.S. Civil War.

burn·sides (bûrn′sīdz′), *n.pl.* full whiskers and a mustache worn with the chin clean-shaven. [named after Gen. A. E. BURNSIDE]

Burnsides

burnt (bûrnt), *v.* **1.** a pt. and pp. of **burn.** —*adj.* **2.** *Fine Arts.* **a.** of earth pigments that have been calcined and changed to a deeper and warmer color: *burnt umber.* **b.** of or pertaining to colors having a deeper or grayer hue than usual: *burnt orange.*

burnt′ of′fering, an offering burnt upon an altar in sacrifice to a deity.

burnt′ sien′na. See under **sienna** (def. 1).

burp (bûrp), *Informal.* —*n.* **1.** a belch; eructation. —*v.i.* **2.** to belch; eruct. —*v.t.* **3.** to cause (a baby) to belch by patting or rubbing its back, esp. to relieve flatulence after feeding. [imit.]

burp′ gun′, *Mil.* See **machine pistol.**

burr[1] (bûr), *n.* **1.** a small, hand-held, power-driven milling cutter, used by machinists, die makers, etc., for deepening, widening, or undercutting small recesses. **2.** *Dentistry.* a similar tool shaped into a shank and a head for removing decayed material from teeth and preparing cavities for filling. **3.** *Surg.* a similar tool used for the excavation of bone. **4.** Also, **buhr.** a protruding, ragged metal edge raised on a surface in drilling, shearing, etc. **5.** a rough or irregular protuberance on any object. —*v.t.* **6.** to form a rough point or edge on. Also, **bur.** [var. of BUR]

burr[2] (bûr), *n.* **1.** a guttural pronunciation of the *r*-sound, as in certain Northern English dialects. **2.** any pronunciation popularly considered rough or nonurban. **3.** a whirring noise or sound. —*v.i.* **4.** to speak with a burr. **5.** to speak roughly or inarticulately. **6.** to make a whirring noise or sound. —*v.t.* **7.** to pronounce (words, sounds, etc.) with a burr. [appar. both imit. and assoc., the sound being thought of as rough like a bur]

burr[3] (bûr), *n.* **1.** burstone. **2.** a mass of harder siliceous rock in soft rock. Also, **buhr.** [ME *burre,* prob. so called from its prickliness]

Burr (bûr), *n.* **Aaron,** 1756–1836, vice president of the U.S. 1801–05.

bur′ reed′, any plant of the genus *Sparganium,* having ribbonlike leaves and bearing burlike heads of fruit.

bur·ro (bûr′ō, bo͝or′ō, bur′ō), *n., pl.* **-ros. 1.** a small donkey used as a pack animal in the southwestern U.S. and Mexico **2.** any donkey. [< Sp < Pg, back formation from *burrico* ass < VL **burriccus* for LL *burrīcus* pony]

Bur·roughs (bûr′ōz, bur′-), *n.* **1. Edgar Rice,** 1875–1950, U.S. writer: creator of a series of jungle stories whose hero is *Tarzan.* **2. John,** 1837–1921, U.S. naturalist and essayist. **3. William,** born 1914, U.S. writer.

bur·row (bûr′ō, bur′ō), *n.* **1.** a hole or tunnel in the ground made by a small animal for habitation and refuge. **2.** any place of retreat; shelter or refuge. —*v.i.* **3.** to make a hole or passage in, into, or under something. **4.** to lodge or hide in a burrow. —*v.t.* **5.** to put a burrow or burrows into (a hill, mountainside, etc.). **6.** to make by or as by burrowing: *We burrowed a path through the crowd.* [ME *borow,* earlier *burh,* appar. gradational var. of late ME *beri* burrow, var. of earlier *berg* refuge, OE *gebeorg* < *beorgan* to protect; akin to OE *burgen* grave, i.e., place of protection for body; see BURY] —**bur′row·er,** *n.*

bur′rowing owl′, a long-legged, terrestrial owl, *Speotyto cunicularia,* of North and South America, that digs its nesting burrow in open prairie land.

burr·stone (bûr′stōn′), *n.* burstone.

bur·sa (bûr′sə), *n., pl.* **-sae** (-sē), **-sas. 1.** *Anat., Zool.* a pouch, sac, or vesicle, esp. a sac containing synovia, to facilitate motion, as between a tendon and a bone. **2.** (in the Middle Ages) a dormitory of a university. [< NL, ML: a bag, pouch, purse < Gk *býrsa* a skin, hide] —**bur·sate** (bûr′sāt), *adj.*

Bur·sa (bo͝or′sä), *n.* a city in NW Turkey in Asia: a former Ottoman capital. 275,917 (est. 1970). Also, **Brusa.**

bur·sar (bûr′sər, -sär), *n.* **1.** a treasurer or business officer, esp. of a college or university. **2.** (in the Middle Ages) a university student. **3.** *Chiefly Scot.* a student attending a university on a scholarship. [< ML *bursār(ius)* a purse-keeper, treasurer (see BURSA, -AR[2]); r. late ME *bouser,* var. of *bourser* < AF; OF *borsier*]

bur·sar·i·al (bər sâr′ē əl), *adj.* of, pertaining to, or paid to or by a bursar or a bursary.

bur·sa·ry (bûr′sə rē), *n., pl.* **-ries. 1.** *Eccles.* the treasury of a monastery. **2.** *Brit.* a college scholarship. [< ML *bursāria* treasurer's room < *bursārius* a treasurer]

burse (bûrs), *n.* **1.** a pouch or case for some special purpose. **2.** *Eccles.* a case or receptacle for a corporal. [ME < AF < ML *bursa* purse; see BURSA]

bur·seed (bûr′sēd′), *n.* a stickseed, *Lappula echinata.*

bur·ser·a·ceous (bûr′sə rā′shəs), *adj.* belonging to the family *Burseraceae,* comprising shrubs or trees of warm, often arid, countries, having compound leaves. [< NL *Burserace(ae)* = *Bursera* type genus, named after J. *Burser* (1593–1649), German botanist + *-aceae* -ACEAE; see -OUS]

bur·si·form (bûr′sə fôrm′), *adj. Anat., Zool.* pouch-shaped; saccate. [< NL *bursiform(is).* See BURSA, -I-, -FORM]

bur·si·tis (bər sī′tis), *n. Pathol.* inflammation of a bursa. [< NL]

burst (bûrst), *v.,* **burst, burst·ing,** *n.* —*v.i.* **1.** to break, break open, or fly apart with sudden violence: *The vase burst when the bullet hit it.* **2.** to issue forth suddenly and forcibly, as from confinement or through an obstacle: *He burst through the doorway.* **3.** to give sudden expression to or as to emotion: *She burst into tears.* **4.** to be extremely full, as if ready to break open: *The house was bursting with people.* **5.** to become visible, audible, evident, etc., suddenly and completely: *The sun burst through the clouds.* —*v.t.* **6.** to cause to break or break open suddenly and violently. **7.** to cause or suffer the rupture of (the appendix, a blood vessel, etc.). —*n.* **8.** the act or an instance of bursting. **9.** a sudden display of intense activity, energy, or effort: *a burst of speed.* **10.** a sudden expression of emotion: *a burst of affection.* **11.** a sudden and violent issuing forth: *a burst of steam.* **12.** *Mil.* **a.** the explosion of a projectile: *an air burst.* **b.** a group of shots fired by one pull on the trigger of an automatic weapon. **13.** the result of bursting; breach; gap. [ME *berste(n), burste(n),* OE *berstan* (past pl. *burston*), c. OHG *brestan* (G *bersten*), Icel *bresta;* akin to BREAK]

burst·er (bûr′stər), *n.* **1.** *Australian.* buster (def. 5). **2.** a person or thing that bursts.

bur·stone (bûr′stōn′), *n.* **1.** *Geol.* any of various siliceous rocks used for millstones. **2.** a millstone of such material. Also, **buhrstone, burrstone.** Also called **buhr, burr.** [BURR[3] + STONE]

bur·then (bûr′thən), *n., v.t. Archaic.* burden[1].

bur·ton (bûr′tən), *n.* **1.** *Naut.* any of various small tackles for use on shipboard. **2.** See **Spanish burton.** [?]

Bur·ton (bûr′tən), *n.* **1. Sir Richard Francis,** 1821–90, English explorer and writer. **2. Robert** (pen name: *Democritus Junior*), 1577–1640. English clergyman and author.

Bur·ton-on-Trent (bûr′tən on trent′), *n.* a city in E Staffordshire, in central England. 50,766 (1961).

Bu·run·di (bə run′dē, bo͝o ro͞on′dē), *n.* a republic in central Africa, E of the Democratic Republic of the Congo: formerly the S part of the Belgian trust territory of Ruanda-Urundi; gained independence 1962. 3,500,000 (est. 1970); 10,747 sq. mi. *Cap.:* Bujumbura. Formerly, **Urundi.**

bur·weed (bûr′wēd′), *n.* any of various plants bearing a burlike fruit, as the cocklebur or burdock.

bur·y (ber′ē), *v.t.,* **bur·ied, bur·y·ing. 1.** to put in the ground and cover with earth: *The pirates buried the chest on the island.* **2.** to put (a corpse) in the ground or a vault, or into the sea, often with ceremony. **3.** to plunge in deeply; cause to sink in: *to bury an arrow in a target.* **4.** to cover in order to conceal from sight. **5.** to immerse, or totally involve (oneself): *He buried himself in his work.* **6.** to put out of one's mind: *to bury an insult.* **7. bury one's head in the sand,** to avoid reality; ignore the facts of a situation. [ME *berie(n), burye(n),* OE *byrgan* to bury, conceal; akin to OE *beorgan* to hide, protect, preserve; c. D, G *bergen,* Goth *bairgan,* Icel *bjarga*] —**Syn. 2.** inter, entomb, inhume. **4.** hide, secrete. —**Ant. 2.** disinter, exhume. **4.** uncover.

Bur·yat′ Auton′omous So′viet So′cialist Repub′lic (bo͝or yät′, bo͝or′ē ät′), an administrative division of the RSFSR, in the SE Soviet Union in Asia. 671,000 (1959); ab. 127,000 sq. mi. *Cap.:* Ulan Ude. Also, **Buriat Autonomous Soviet Socialist Republic.**

bur′ying bee′tle, any of various carrion beetles that bury the carcasses of small animals, esp. rodents, in which their eggs have been deposited.

Bur·y St. Ed·munds (ber′ē sānt ed′məndz), a city in W Suffolk, in E England: medieval shrine. 21,144 (1961).

bus (bus), *n., pl.* **bus·es, bus·ses,** *v.,* **bused** or **bussed, bus·ing** or **bus·sing.** —*n.* **1.** a large motor vehicle with a long body equipped with seats or benches for passengers, usually operating as part of a scheduled service line; omnibus. **2.** a similar horse-drawn vehicle. **3.** *Informal.* a passenger automobile or airplane. **4.** *Elect.* a rigid conductor in an electric circuit, used to connect three or more circuits. —*v.t.* **5.** to convey or transport by bus. **6.** to transport (pupils) to more distant schools, esp. as a compulsory-integration measure. —*v.i.* **7.** to travel on or by means of a bus. [short for OMNIBUS] —**bus′ing, bus′sing,** *n., adj.*

bus., **1.** business. **2.** bushel; bushels.

bus·boy (bus′boi′), *n.* a boy or man employed in a public dining room to reset tables, clear dishes, and help waiters. Also, **bus′ boy′.**

bus·by (buz′bē), *n., pl.* **-bies. 1.** a tall fur hat with a baglike ornament hanging from the top over the right side. **2.** the tall bearskin hat worn by certain British guardsmen. [from proper name]

Busby (def. 1)

bush[1] (bo͝osh), *n.* **1.** a low plant having many branches arising from or near the ground. **2.** *Bot.* a small cluster of shrubs appearing as a single plant. **3.** something resembling or suggesting this, as a thick, shaggy head of hair. **4.** the tail of a fox; brush. **5.** a large uncleared area thickly covered with mixed plant growth, trees, etc., as a jungle. **6.** a large, sparsely populated area most of which is uncleared, as areas of Australia. **7.** (formerly) a free branch hung as a sign before a tavern or vintner's shop. **8. beat around** or **about the bush,** to avoid coming to the point. —*v.i.* **9.** to be or become bushy; branch or spread like a bush. —*v.t.* **10.** to cover, protect, or mark with a bush or bushes. [ME *busshe,* OE *busc* (in place-names); c. D *bos* wood, G *Busch,* Icel *buskr* bush] —**bush′less,** *adj.* —**bush′like′,** *adj.*

bush[2] (bo͝osh), *Chiefly Brit.* —*n.* **1.** a lining of metal or the like let into an orifice to guard against wearing by friction, erosion, etc. **2.** a bushing. —*v.t.* **3.** to furnish with a bush; line with metal. [earlier *busche* < MD *busse* bushing, box]

Bush (bo͝osh), *n.* **1. George (Herbert Walker), born 1924, 41st president of the U.S. since 1989. 2. Van·ne·var** (və nē′vär, -vər), **1890–1974, U.S. electrical engineer: educational administrator.**

bush., bushel; bushels.

bush′ bas′il. See under **basil.**

bush·buck (bo͝osh′buk′), *n., pl.* **-bucks,** (*esp. collectively*) **-buck.** an African antelope, *Tragelaphus scriptus,* found in wooded and bushy regions, having a reddish body streaked with white. Also, **boschbok.** [trans. of SAfrD *boschbok*]

bushed (bo͝osht), *adj.* **1.** overgrown with bushes. **2.** *Informal.* exhausted; tired out.

bush·el[1] (bo͝osh′əl), *n.* **1.** a unit of dry measure containing 4 pecks, equivalent in the U.S. (and formerly in England) to 2150.42 cubic inches (**Winchester bushel),** and in Great Britain to 2219.36 cubic inches (**imperial bushel). 2.** a container of this capacity. **3.** a unit of weight equal to the weight of a bushel of a given commodity. **4.** *Informal.* a large amount. [ME *bu(i)sshel* < MF *boissel* = *boisse* unit of measure (< Celt; cf. Ir *bos* pl. of *bas* hand, handbreadth) + *-el* n. suffix]

bush·el[2] (bo͝osh′əl), *v.t.,* **-eled, -el·ing** or (*esp. Brit.*) **-elled, -el·ling.** to alter or repair (a garment). [< G *bosseln* to patch < F *bosseler* to emboss] —**bush′el·er;** *esp. Brit.,* **bush′el·ler,** *n.*

bush·el·bas·ket (bo͝osh′əl bas′kət, -bä′skit), *n.* a round basket capable of holding one bushel.

bush·el·ful (bo͝osh′əl fo͝ol′), *n., pl.* **-fuls.** an amount equal to the capacity of a bushel.

bush·er (bo͝osh′ər), *n.* *Baseball Slang.* See **bush leaguer** (def. 1). [BUSH(LEAGUE) + -ER[1]]

bush·ham·mer (bo͝osh′ham′ər), *n.* a hammer for dressing stone, having one or two square faces composed of a number of pyramidal points. Also, **bush′ ham′mer.** [< G *Bosshammer* = obs. *boss(en)* (to) BEAT + *hammer* HAMMER]

Bu·shi·do (bo͞o′shē dō′), *n.* (in feudal Japan) the code of the samurai, stressing unquestioning loyalty and obedience, and valuing honor above life. [< Jap = *bushi* (*bu* military + *shi* man) + *dō* code]

bush·ing (bo͝osh′ing), *n.* **1.** *Elect.* a lining for a hole, intended to insulate and/or protect from abrasion one or more conductors that pass through it. **2.** *Mach.* **a.** a replaceable thin tube or sleeve, usually of bronze, mounted in a case or housing as a bearing. **b.** a replaceable hardened steel tube used as a guide for various tools or parts, as a drill or valve rod.

Bu·shire (bo͞o shēr′), *n.* a seaport in SW Iran, on the Persian Gulf. 27,317.

bush′ league′, *Baseball Slang.* See **minor league.**

bush′ lea′guer, **1.** Also called **busher.** *Baseball Slang.* **a.** a player in a minor league. **b.** an incompetent player, as one who plays as if he belonged in a minor league. **2.** *U.S. Slang.* a person who performs in an inferior manner.

bush·man (bo͝osh′mən), *n., pl.* **-men. 1.** a woodsman. **2.** *Australian.* a pioneer; dweller in the bush. **3.** (*cap.*) *Anthropol.* a member of a nomadic, racially distinct people of southern Africa, typically of short stature, having brown skin and peppercorn hair. **4.** (*cap.*) any of more than a dozen related Khoisan languages spoken by the Bushmen of southern Africa. [BUSH[1] + MAN[1], modeled on SAfrD *boschjesman,* lit., man of the bush]

bush·mas·ter (bo͝osh′mas′tər, -mä′stər), *n.* a pit viper, *Lachesis muta,* of tropical America: grows to 12 feet long.

bush′ pig′, a wild swine, *Potamochaerus porcus,* of southern and eastern Africa, having white facial markings. Also called **boschvark.**

bush·rang·er (bo͝osh′rān′jər), *n.* **1.** a person who lives in the bush or woods. **2.** *Australian.* a bandit living in the bush. —**bush′rang′ing,** *n.*

bush′ tit′, any of several North American titmice of the genus *Psaltriparus,* that construct pendent nests.

bush·whack (bo͝osh′hwak′, -wak′), *U.S.* —*v.i.* **1.** to make one's way through woods by cutting at undergrowth, branches, etc. —*v.t.* **2.** to fight as a bushwhacker; ambush. [back formation from BUSHWHACKER]

bush·whack·er (bo͝osh′hwak′ər, -wak′ər), *n.* **1.** *U.S. Hist.* a Confederate guerrilla. **2.** any guerrilla. —**bush′-whack′ing,** *n.*

bush·y (bo͝osh′ē), *adj.,* **bush·i·er, bush·i·est. 1.** resembling a bush. **2.** full of or overgrown with bushes. [ME *busshi*] —**bush′i·ly,** *adv.* —**bush′i·ness,** *n.*

busi·ness (biz′nis), *n.* **1.** an occupation, profession, or trade: *His business is poultry farming.* **2.** *Econ.* the purchase and sale of goods in an attempt to make a profit. **3.** *Com.* a person, partnership, or corporation engaged in commerce, manufacturing, or a service; profit-seeking enterprise or concern. **4.** volume of trade; patronage: *Most of the store's business comes from women.* **5.** a building or locale where commercial work is carried on, as a factory, store, or office; place of work: *His business is on the corner of Broadway and Elm Street.* **6.** that with which one is principally and seriously concerned: *Words are a writer's business.* **7.** a person's rightful concern; legitimate field of inquiry: *I don't think my plans are your business.* **8.** affair; situation: *She was exasperated by the whole business.* **9.** a task or duty; chore: *It's your business to wash the dishes now.* **10.** Also called **stage business.** *Theat.* a movement or gesture, used by an actor to give atmosphere to a scene or to help portray a character. **11. mean business,** *Informal.* to propose to take action; be serious in intent. —*adj.* **12.** of, noting, or pertaining to business or its organization or procedures. [ME; OE *bisignes.* See BUSY, -NESS] —**Syn. 1.** calling, vocation, employment. See **occupation. 2.** commerce, trade. **3.** company, firm.

busi′ness card′, a card on which is printed, typically, a businessman's name, title, firm, business address, and telephone number.

bus′iness col′lege, *U.S.* a school offering instruction in the clerical aspects of business, as typing, bookkeeping, etc.

busi′ness cy′cle, a recurrent fluctuation in the total business activity of a country.

busi·ness·like (biz′nis līk′), *adj.* **1.** conforming to, attending to, or characteristic of business. **2.** efficient, practical, or serious.

busi′ness machine′, a machine for expediting clerical work, as a tabulator or adding machine.

busi·ness·man (biz′nis man′), *n., pl.* **-men.** a man who engages in business or commerce.

busi·ness·wom·an (biz′nis wo͝om′-ən), *n., pl.* **-wom·en.** a woman who engages in business or commerce.

bus·kin (bus′kin), *n.* **1.** a thick-soled, laced boot or half boot. **2.** Also called **cothurnus.** the high, thick-soled shoe worn by ancient Greek and Roman actors. **3.** tragic drama; tragedy. **4.** the art of acting, esp. tragic acting. Cf. **sock**[1] (def. 3). [perh. < earlier *bursakin < It *borzacchino,* with loss of *r* before *s* (as in *cuss* < *curse, bass* < *barse,* etc.)]

Buskins (def. 1)

bus·man (bus′mən), *n., pl.* **-men.** an operator of a bus.

bus′man's hol′iday, *Informal.* a vacation or day off from work spent in an activity closely resembling one's work, as a bus driver driving his car.

Bus·ra (bus′rə), *n.* Basra. Also, **Bus′rah.**

buss (bus), *n., v.t., v.i.* *Informal.* kiss. [? b. obs. *bass* kiss and obs. *cuss* KISS, r. ME, OE *coss*]

bust[1] (bust), *n.* **1.** *Fine Arts.* a representation, esp. in sculpture, of the head and shoulders of a human subject. **2.** the chest or breast, esp. a woman's bosom. [< F *buste* < It *busto* < ML *bustum* torso, perh. orig. tree trunk, log]

bust[2] (bust), *Informal.* —*v.i.* **1.** to burst. **2.** to go bankrupt. **3.** to collapse from the strain of making a supreme effort: *Pike's Peak or bust.* —*v.t.* **4.** to burst. **5.** to bankrupt; ruin financially. **6.** to demote in military rank or grade. **7.** to tame or break: *to bust a bronco.* **8.** *Slang.* to arrest: *I was busted on a narcotics charge.* **9.** to hit. **10. bust up,** to break up; separate: *Sam and his wife busted up a year ago.* —*n.* **11.** a failure. **12.** a hit; sock; punch. **13.** a spree or binge. **14.** a sudden decline in the economic conditions of a country, marked by an extreme drop in stock-market prices, business activity, and employment; depression. **15.** *Slang.* an arrest. —*adj.* **16.** bankrupt; broke. [dial. or vulgar var. of BURST]

bus·tard (bus′tərd), *n.* any of several large, cursorial, chiefly terrestrial birds of the family *Otididae,* of the Old World and Australia, that are related to the cranes. [late ME, appar. b. MF *bistarde* (OIt *bistarda*) and MF *oustarde,* both < L *avis tarda* slow bird]

bust·er (bus′tər), *n.* **1.** *U.S. Informal.* a person who breaks up something: *crime busters.* **2.** *Slang.* something that is very big or unusual for its kind. **3.** *Slang.* **a.** a loud, uproarious reveler. **b.** a frolic; spree. **4.** (*cap.*) *Informal.* (used as a familiar term of address to a man or boy who is an object of the speaker's annoyance or anger). **5.** Also, **burster.** Also called **southerly buster, southerly burster.** *Australian.* a violent, cold, southerly wind.

bus·tle[1] (bus′əl), *v.i.,* **-tled, -tling,** *n.* —*v.i.* **1.** to move or act with a great show of energy (often fol. by *about*): *She bustles about cooking breakfast.* **2.** to abound or teem with something (often fol. by *with*): *The office bustled with people.* —*n.* **3.** activity with great show of energy; commotion. [ME *bustelen* to hurry aimlessly along, perh. akin to Icel *busla* to splash about, bustle] —**bus′tling·ly,** *adv.*

bus·tle[2] (bus′əl), *n.* **1.** fullness around or below the waist of a dress, as added by a peplum, bows, ruffles, etc. **2.** a pad or framework formerly worn by women to expand the back of a skirt. [?]

bus·y (biz′ē), *adj.,* **bus·i·er, bus·i·est,** *v.,* **bus·ied, bus·y·ing.** —*adj.* **1.** actively and attentively engaged in work or a pastime. **2.** not at leisure; otherwise engaged: *He was too busy to see visitors.* **3.** full of or characterized by activity: *a busy life.* **4.** (of a telephone line) engaged and therefore not immediately available for use. **5.** officious or meddlesome. **6.** ornate; cluttered with small unharmonious details; fussy: *a busy design.* —*v.t.* **7.** to keep occupied. [ME *busi, bisi,* OE *bysig, bisig;* c. MLG, MD *besich,* D *bezig*] —**bus′i·ly,** *adv.*

—**Syn. 1.** assiduous, hard-working. BUSY, DILIGENT, INDUSTRIOUS imply active or earnest effort to accomplish something, or a habitual attitude of such earnestness. BUSY means actively employed, temporarily or habitually: *a busy official.* DILIGENT suggests earnest and constant effort or application, and usually connotes fondness for, or enjoyment of, what one is doing: *a diligent student.* INDUSTRIOUS often implies a habitual characteristic of steady and zealous application, often with a definite goal: *an industrious clerk working for promotion.* **2.** occupied. —**Ant. 1.** indolent. **2.** unoccupied.

bus·y·bod·y (biz′ē bod′ē), *n., pl.* **-bod·ies.** a person who meddles in the affairs of others.

bus·y·ness (biz′ē nis), *n.* **1.** the quality or condition of being busy. **2.** lively but meaningless activity.

bus′y sig′nal, (in a dial telephone) a rapid succession of buzzing tones, indicating that the line dialed is busy.

but[1] (but; *unstressed* bət), *conj.* **1.** on the contrary; yet: *My brother went, but I did not.* **2.** except; save: *She was so overcome with grief she could do nothing but weep.* **3.** unless; if not; except that (fol. by a clause, often with *that* expressed): *Nothing would do but that I should come in.* **4.** without the circumstance that: *It never rains but it pours.* **5.** otherwise

than: *There is no hope but by prayer.* **6.** that (used esp. after *doubt, deny,* etc., with a negative): *I don't doubt but he will do it.* **7.** that not (used after a negative or question): *The children never played with anyone but a quarrel followed.* **8.** who or which not: *No leader ever existed but he was an optimist.* **9.** (used as an intensifier to introduce an exclamatory expression): *But she's beautiful!* —*prep.* **10.** with the exception of: *No one replied but me.* —*adv.* **11.** only; just: *There is but one God.* **12. but for,** except for: *But for the excessive humidity, it might have been a pleasant day.* —*n.* **13.** buts. [ME *bute(n),* OE *būtan* < phrase *be ūtan* on the outside, without = *be* BY + *ūt* OUT + *-an* adv. suffix]
—**Syn. 1.** BUT, HOWEVER, NEVERTHELESS, STILL, YET are words implying opposition (with a possible concession). BUT marks an opposition or contrast, though in a casual way: *We are going, but we shall return.* HOWEVER indicates a less marked opposition, but displays a second consideration to be compared with the first: *We are going; however* ("*notice this also*"), *we shall return.* NEVERTHELESS implies a concession, something which should not be forgotten in making a summing up: *We are going; nevertheless* ("*do not forget that*"), *we shall return.* STILL implies that in spite of a preceding concession, something must be considered as possible or even inevitable: *We have to go on foot; still* ("*it is probable and possible that*"), *we'll get there.* YET implies that in spite of a preceding concession, there is still a chance for a different outcome: *We are going; yet* ("*in spite of all, some day*"), *we shall return.* **2.** See **except**[1].
—**Usage.** Many users of English regard BUT WHAT as informal (*I have no doubt but what he'll protest*), preferring BUT THAT (*I have no doubt but that he'll protest*) or THAT alone (*I have no doubt that he'll protest*).

but[2] (but), *n. Scot.* **1.** the outer or front room of a house. **2.** the kitchen of a two-room cottage. [n. use of *but* (adv.) outside, hence outer room; see BUT[1]]

bu·ta·caine (byo͞o′tə kān′), *n. Pharm.* a compound, $H_2NC_6H_4COO(CH_2)_3N(C_4H_9)_2$, used in the form of its sulfate as a local anesthetic for mucous membranes, esp. the cornea. [BUTA(NE) + CO)CAINE]

bu·ta·di·ene (byo͞o′tə dī′ēn, -dī ēn′), *n. Chem.* a flammable gas, $H_2C{-}CHHC{-}CH_2$: used chiefly in the manufacture of rubber and paint, and in organic synthesis. Also called **vinylethylene, bivinyl.** [BUTA(NE) + DI-[1] + -ENE]

bu·tane (byo͞o′tān, byo͞o tān′), *n. Chem.* a colorless, flammable gas, C_4H_{10}, used chiefly in the manufacture of rubber and fuel. [BUT(YL) + -ANE]

bu·ta·nol (byo͞ot′ᵊnōl′, -ᵊnôl′, -ᵊnol′), *n. Chem.* See **butyl alcohol.**

butch (bo͝och), *n. Slang.* the partner in a Lesbian relationship who assumes the dominant role.

butch·er (bo͝och′ər), *n.* **1.** a retail or wholesale dealer in meat. **2.** a person who slaughters or dresses animals, fish, or poultry, for food or market. **3.** a person guilty of brutal murder. **4.** a vendor who hawks newspapers, candy, beverages, etc., as on a train, at a stadium, etc. —*v.t.* **5.** to slaughter or dress (animals, fish, or poultry) for market. **6.** to kill indiscriminately or brutally. **7.** to bungle or botch: *to butcher a job.* [ME *bocher* < AF; OF *bo(u)chier* = *bo(u)c* he-goat (< Gmc; see BUCK[1]) + *-ier* -ER[2]] —**butch′er·er,** *n.*

butch·er·bird (bo͝och′ər bûrd′), *n.* any of various shrikes of the genus *Lanius* that impale their prey upon thorns.

butch·er's-broom (bo͝och′ərz bro͞om′, -bro͝om′), *n.* a shrubby, liliaceous evergreen, *Ruscus aculeatus,* of England: used for making brooms.

butch′er's saw′, a type of hacksaw used esp. by butchers for cutting through meat and bones. See illus. at **saw.**

butch·er·y (bo͝och′ə rē), *n., pl.* **-er·ies. 1.** a slaughterhouse. **2.** the trade or business of a butcher. **3.** brutal or wanton slaughter. [ME *bocherie* < MF *boucherie*]

bu·tene (byo͞o′tēn), *n. Chem.* butylene. [BUT(YL) + -ENE]

but·ler (but′lər), *n.* **1.** the chief male servant of a household. **2.** a male servant having charge of the wines and liquors. [ME *buteler* < AF *butuiller,* OF *bouteillier* = *bouteille* BOTTLE + *-ier* -ER[2]]

But·ler (but′lər), *n.* **1. Benjamin Franklin,** 1818–93, U.S. politician and a Union general in the Civil War. **2. Joseph,** 1692–1752, English bishop, theologian, and author. **3. Nicholas Murray,** 1862–1947, U.S. educator: president of Columbia University 1902–45; Nobel peace prize 1931. **4. Pierce,** 1866–1939, U.S. jurist: associate justice of the U.S. Supreme Court 1923–39. **5. Samuel,** 1612–80, English poet. **6. Samuel,** 1835–1902, English novelist, essayist, and satirist. **7. Smed·ley Dar·ling·ton** (smed′lē där′ling tən), 1881–1940, U.S. Marine Corps general.

buts (buts), *n.pl.* restrictions or objections: *Do as I tell you, no buts about it.*

But·su (bo͝ot′so͝o), *n.* Buddha (def. 1). [< Jap: BUDDHA]

butt[1] (but), *n.* **1.** the end or extremity of anything, esp. the thicker, larger, or blunt end considered as a support or handle, as of a log, fishing rod, pistol, etc.: *a pork butt; rifle butt.* **2.** an end that is not used or consumed; remnant: *a cigar butt.* **3.** *Slang.* the buttocks. **4.** *Slang.* a cigarette. [ME *bott* (thick) end, buttock, OE *butt* tree stump (in place names); akin to Sw *but* stump, Dan *but* stubby]

butt[2] (but), *n.* **1.** a person or thing that is an object of sarcasm, contempt, etc. **2.** (on a rifle range) **a.** a wall of earth located behind the targets to stop bullets. **b. butts,** a wall behind which men can safely lower, score, and raise targets. —*v.i.* **3.** to be adjacent; abut. —*v.t.* **4.** to position or fasten an end (of something). **5.** to place or join the ends (of two things) together; set end-to-end. [ME < MF *but* target, goal < Gmc; see BUTT[1]]

butt[3] (but), *v.t.* **1.** to strike or push (something) with the head or horns. —*v.i.* **2.** to strike or push with the head or horns. **3.** to project. **4. butt in,** *Slang.* to intrude in the affairs or conversation of others. —*n.* **5.** a push or blow with the head or horns. [ME *butte(n)* < OF *bo(u)ter* to thrust, strike < Gmc; see BEAT]

butt[4] (but), *n.* **1.** a large cask or barrel, esp. for wine, beer, or ale. **2.** any of various units of capacity, most generally considered equal to two hogsheads. [ME *bote* < MF < OPr *bota* < LL *butta, buttis,* akin to LG *bōut(t)is,* Gk *bytínē, pytínē;* all of non-IE origin]

but·tals (but′ᵊlz), *n.pl. Law.* abuttal (def. 1b).

butte (byo͞ot), *n. Western U.S., Canadian.* an isolated hill or mountain, usually having a flat top, rising abruptly above the surrounding land. [< F: hillock; MF *bute* mound for target < *but* BUTT[2]]

Butte (byo͞ot), *n.* a city in SW Montana: mining center. 23,368 (1970).

but·ter (but′ər), *n.* **1.** the fatty portion of milk, separating as a soft whitish or yellowish solid when milk or cream is agitated or churned and used for cooking, as a spread for bread, etc. **2.** any of various other soft spreads for bread: *apple butter; peanut butter.* **3.** any of various substances of butterlike consistency, as various metallic chlorides, and certain vegetable oils solid at room temperature. —*v.t.* **4.** to put butter on or in; spread or grease with butter. **5.** to apply a liquified bonding material to (a piece or area), as mortar to a course of bricks. **6. butter up,** *Informal.* to flatter (someone) in order to gain a favor. [ME; OE *butere* < L *būtyr(um)* < Gk *boútyron*]

but·ter-and-eggs (but′ər ən egz′), *n., pl.* **but·ter-and-eggs.** (*construed as sing. or pl.*) any of certain plants whose flowers are of two shades of yellow, as the toadflax, *Linaria vulgaris.*

but·ter·ball (but′ər bôl′), *n.* **1.** *U.S. Dial.* the bufflehead. **2.** *Informal.* a chubby person.

but′ter bean′, a variety of small-seeded lima bean, *Phaseolus lunatus,* grown in the southern U.S.

but·ter·bur (but′ər bûr′), *n.* an Old World, perennial, composite herb, *Petasites vulgaris,* having large woolly leaves.

but·ter·cup (but′ər kup′), *n.* any of numerous plants of the genus *Ranunculus,* having red, white, or esp. yellow flowers; crowfoot. [from the color and shape of the flower]

but·ter·fat (but′ər fat′), *n.* butter; milk fat; a mixture of glycerides, mainly butyrin, olein, and palmitin.

but·ter·fin·gers (but′ər fing′gərz), *n., pl.* **-gers.** (*construed as sing.*) a person who is likely to drop things, as an inept fielder in baseball, a pass receiver in football, or any clumsy person. —**but′ter·fin′gered,** *adj.*

but·ter·fish (but′ər fish′), *n., pl.* (*esp. collectively*) **-fish·es,** (*esp. referring to two or more kinds or species*) **-fish.** a small, flattened, marine food fish, *Poronotus triacanthus,* found off the Atlantic coast of the U.S.

but·ter·fly (but′ər flī′), *n., pl.* **-flies,** *adj.* —*n.* **1.** any of numerous diurnal insects of the order *Lepidoptera,* characterized by clubbed antennae, a slender body and large, broad, often conspicuously marked wings. **2.** a person who flits aimlessly from one interest or group to another: *a social butterfly.* **3.** a racing breaststroke in which the swimmer brings both arms forward out of the water. —*adj.* **4.** *Cookery.* split open and spread apart to resemble a butterfly: *butterfly shrimp.* [ME *boterflye,* OE *buttorflēoge*]

but′terfly fish′, 1. any tropical marine fish of the family *Chaetodontidae,* having large, broad fins or brilliant coloration, or both. **2.** See **flying gurnard. 3.** a blenny, *Blennius ocellaris,* of Europe.

but′terfly net′, a conical net of fine mesh held open by a round rim to which a long handle is attached, used for collecting butterflies and other insects.

but′terfly ta′ble, a small occasional table, usually having a round or oval top and drop leaves.

but′terfly valve′, 1. a clack valve having two flaps with a common hinge. **2.** a valve that swings about a central axis across its face.

but′terfly weed′, 1. either of two North American milkweeds, *Asclepias tuberosa* or *A. decumbens,* having orange-colored flowers. **2.** an erect North American herb, *Gaura coccinea,* having wandlike spikes of red flowers.

but·ter·milk (but′ər milk′), *n.* **1.** the acidulous liquid remaining after the butter has been separated from milk or cream. **2.** a similar liquid made from skim milk with the aid of a bacterial culture.

but·ter·nut (but′ər nut′), *n.* **1.** the edible oily nut of an American tree, *Juglans cinerea,* of the walnut family. **2.** the tree itself. **3.** the light brown wood of this tree, used for making furniture. **4.** See **souari nut.**

but′ter of ar′senic. See **arsenic trichloride.**

but·ter·scotch (but′ər skoch′), *n.* **1.** a hard, brittle taffy made with butter, brown sugar, etc. **2.** a flavor as for puddings, frostings, ice cream, etc., produced by combining brown sugar, vanilla extract, and butter with other ingredients. —*adj.* **3.** having the flavor of butterscotch. [perh. orig. made in Scotland]

but·ter·weed (but′ər wēd′), *n.* **1.** any wild plant having conspicuously yellow flowers or leaves. **2.** the horseweed. **3.** a ragwort or groundsel, *Senecio glabellus.*

but·ter·wort (but′ər wûrt′), *n.* any small herb of the genus *Pinguicula,* having leaves that secrete a viscid substance in which small insects are caught.

but·ter·y[1] (but′ə rē), *adj.* like, containing, or spread with butter. [ME *buttry.* See BUTTER, -Y[1]]

but·ter·y[2] (but′ə rē, bu′trē), *n., pl.* **-ter·ies. 1.** a room or rooms in which the wines, liquors, and provisions of a household are kept; larder. **2.** a room in colleges, esp. at Oxford and Cambridge Universities, from which certain articles of food and drink are dispensed to the students. [ME *boterie* < AF < AL *buteria* = *but(t)a* BUTT[4] + *-eria* -ERY]

butt′ hinge′, a hinge for a door or the like, secured to the butting surfaces rather than to the adjacent sides of the door and its frame. Cf. **flap** (def. 15). See illus. at **hinge.**

butt′ joint′, *Building Trades.* a joint formed by two pieces of wood or metal united end to end without overlapping.

but·tock (but′ək), *n.* Usually, **buttocks. 1.** (in humans) either of the two fleshy protuberances forming the lower and back part of the trunk. **2.** (in animals) the rump. [ME *buttok,* OE *buttuc* = *butt* (see BUTT[1]) + *-uc* -OCK]

but·ton (but′ᵊn), *n.* **1.** a small disk, knob, or the like, for attaching to an article, as of clothing, serving as a fastening when passed through a buttonhole or loop. **2.** anything resembling a button, esp. in being small and round, as any of various candies, ornaments, tags, identification badges, reflectors, markers, etc. **3.** *Bot.* a bud or other protuberant part of a plant. **4.** a young or undeveloped mushroom. **5.** a small knob or disk pressed to operate an electric circuit. **6.** Also called **turn button.** a fastener for a door, window, etc., having two arms and rotating on a pivot attached to the frame. **7.** *Metall.* (in assaying) a small globule or lump of metal at the bottom of a crucible after fusion. **8.** *Fencing.* the protective knob fixed to the point of a foil. **9.** *Boxing Slang.* the point of the chin. **10.** the hard bonelike structure at the end of the rattles of a rattlesnake. **11.** *Horol.* crown (def. 18). —*v.t.* **12.** to fasten with a button or buttons: *He quickly buttoned his jacket.* **13.** to insert (a button) in a buttonhole or loop: *He buttoned the top button of his shirt.* —*v.i.* **14.** to be capable of being buttoned: *This coat buttons, but that one zips.* [ME *boto(u)n* < MF *boton* = *bot-* (s. of *boter* to BUTT[3]) + *-on* n. suffix] —**but′ton·er,** *n.* —**but′-ton·less,** *adj.*

but·ton·bush (but′ᵊn bo͝osh′), *n.* a North American shrub, *Cephalanthus occidentalis,* having globular flowers.

but·ton·hole (but′ᵊn hōl′), *n., v.,* **-holed, -hol·ing.** —*n.* **1.** the hole, slit, or loop through which a button is passed and by which it is secured. **2.** *Chiefly Brit.* a boutonniere. —*v.t.* **3.** to sew with a buttonhole stitch. **4.** to make buttonholes in. **5.** to hold by or as by the buttonhole, as to detain (someone) in conversation: *The reporter tried to buttonhole the mayor for a statement on the bond issue.* —**but′ton·hol′er,** *n.*

but′tonhole stitch′, *Sewing.* a looped stitch used to strengthen the edge of material and keep it from raveling, as around a buttonhole.

but·ton·hook (but′ᵊn ho͝ok′), *n.* a small, usually metal hook for pulling buttons through buttonholes, as on gloves, shoes, riding breeches, etc.

but·ton·mold (but′ᵊn mōld′), *n.* a small disk or knob of wood, metal, etc., to be covered with fabric to form an ornamental button.

but′ton quail′, any of several birds of the family *Turnicidae,* of warmer parts of the Old World, resembling but not related to the true quail.

but·tons (but′ᵊnz), *n.* (*construed as sing.*) *Chiefly Brit.* a bellboy or page. [so called from the many buttons of his uniform]

but′ton snake′root, 1. any composite herb of the genus *Liatris,* having racemose or spicate heads of handsome rose-purple flowers. **2.** an eryngo, *Eryngium yuccifolium,* of the southeastern U.S., having blue or whitish flowers.

but′ton tree′, 1. a tropical tree or shrub, *Conocarpus erecta,* yielding heavy, hard, compact wood and bearing buttonlike fruits. **2.** buttonwood (def. 1).

but·ton·wood (but′ᵊn wo͝od′), *n.* **1.** Also called **button tree.** a tall, North American plane tree, *Platanus occidentalis,* bearing small, pendulous fruit and yielding a useful timber. **2.** See **button tree** (def. 1).

butt′ plate′, a protective plate on the butt end of a gunstock, usually of metal.

but·tress (bu′tris), *n.* **1.** any external prop or support built to steady a structure by opposing its outward thrusts, esp. a projecting support built into or against the outside of a masonry wall. **2.** any prop or support. **3.** a thing shaped like a buttress, as a tree trunk with a widening base. —*v.t.* **4.** to support by a buttress; prop up. **5.** to give encouragement or support to (a person, plan, etc.). [ME *butres* << OF *boterez,* nom. sing. of *boteret* (acc.) = *boter-* abutment (? < Gmc; see BUTT[3]) + *-et* -ET]

A, Buttress
B, Flying buttress

butt′ shaft′, a blunt or barbless arrow.

butt·stock (but′stok′), *n.* the part of the stock located behind the breech mechanism of a firearm.

butt′ weld′, a butt joint made by welding.

bu·tyl (byo͞o′til, byo͞ot′ᵊl), *adj.* *Chem.* containing a butyl group. [BUT(YRIC) + -YL]

Bu·tyl (byo͞o′til, byo͞ot′ᵊl), *n.* *Trademark.* a synthetic rubber, particularly useful for inner tubes of automobile tires because of its leakproof qualities.

bu′tyl al′cohol, *Chem.* any of four isomeric alcohols having the formula C_4H_9OH, used as solvents and in organic synthesis.

bu·tyl·ene (byo͞ot′ᵊlēn′), *n.* *Chem.* any of three isomeric, gaseous hydrocarbons of the alkene series having the formula C_4H_8. Also, **butene.**

bu′tyl group′, *Chem.* any of four univalent, isomeric groups having the formula C_4H_9–. Also called **bu′tyl rad′-ical.**

bu·tyr·a·ceous (byo͞o′tə rā′shəs), *adj.* of the nature of, resembling, or containing butter. [< L *būtyr(um)* BUTTER + -ACEOUS]

bu·tyr·al·de·hyde (byo͞o′tə ral′də hīd′), *n.* *Chem.* a flammable liquid, $CH_3(CH_2)_2CHO$, used chiefly as an intermediate in the manufacture of resins and rubber cement. [BUTYR(IC) + ALDEHYDE]

bu·tyr·ate (byo͞o′tə rāt′), *n.* *Chem.* a salt or ester of butyric acid. [BUTYR(IC) + -ATE[2]]

bu·tyr·ic (byo͞o tir′ik), *adj.* *Chem.* pertaining to or derived from butyric acid. [< L *būtyr(um)* BUTTER + -IC]

butyr′ic a′cid, *Chem.* either of two isomeric acids having the formula C_3H_7COOH, whose esters are used as flavorings.

bu·tyr·in (byo͞o′tər in), *n.* *Chem.* a colorless, liquid ester present in butter, formed from glycerin and butyric acid. [BUTYR(IC + GLYCER)IN]

bux·om (buk′səm), *adj.* **1.** (of a woman) full-bosomed. **2.** (of a woman) healthy, plump, cheerful, and lively. [ME, earlier *buhsum* pliant, OE *būh* (impv. of *būgan* to BOW[1]) + *-sum* -SOME[1]] —**bux′om·ly,** *adv.* —**bux′om·ness,** *n.*

Bux·te·hu·de (bo͝oks′tə ho͞o′də), *n.* **Die·trich** (dē′trikh), 1637–1707, Danish organist and composer, in Germany after 1668.

buy (bī), *v.,* **bought, buy·ing,** *n.* —*v.t.* **1.** to acquire the possession of, or the right to, by paying or promising to pay an equivalent, esp. in money; purchase. **2.** to acquire by any kind of recompense: *to buy favor with flattery.* **3.** to hire or obtain the services of: *The Yankees bought a new center fielder.* **4.** to bribe: *Most public officials cannot be bought.* **5.** to be the monetary or purchasing equivalent of: *Ten dollars will buy a lot of meat and beans.* **6.** *Chiefly Theol.* to redeem; ransom. **7.** *Slang.* to accept or believe: *I don't buy that explanation.* —*v.i.* **8.** to be or become a purchaser. **9. buy it,** *Brit. Slang.* to be killed, esp. in military action: *He bought it at Dunkirk.* **10. buy off,** to get rid of by payment; bribe. **11. buy out,** to secure all of (an owner or partner's) share or interest in an enterprise: *He bought out an established pharmacist.* **12. buy up,** to buy as much as one can of (something): *She bought up the last of the strawberries.* —*n.* **13.** the act or an instance of buying. **14.** something bought; a purchase. **15.** *U.S. Informal.* a bargain: *The couch was a real buy.* [ME *by(en),* var. of *byggen, buggen,* OE *bycgan;* c. OS *buggjan,* Goth *bugjan* to buy, Icel *byggja* to lend, rent]
—**Syn. 1.** BUY, PURCHASE imply obtaining or acquiring property or goods for a price. BUY is the common and informal word, applying to any such transaction: *to buy a house, vegetables at the market.* PURCHASE is more formal and may connote buying on a larger scale, in a finer store, and the like: *to purchase a year's supplies.* —**Ant. 1.** sell.

buy·er (bī′ər), *n.* **1.** a person who buys; purchaser. **2.** a purchasing agent, as for a retail store. [ME *beger, bier*]

buy′ers' mar′ket, a market in which goods and services are plentiful and prices relatively low. Cf. **sellers' market.**

buzz (buz), *n.* **1.** a low, vibrating, humming sound, as of bees, machinery, or people talking. **2.** a rumor or report. **3.** *Informal.* a telephone call. —*v.i.* **4.** to make a low, vibrating, humming sound. **5.** to speak or whisper with such a sound. **6.** to make a humming noise, as in talking. **7.** *Chiefly Brit. Slang.* to go; leave (usually fol. by *off* or *along*). —*v.t.* **8.** to make a buzzing sound with: *The fly buzzed its wings.* **9.** to tell or spread (a rumor, gossip, etc.) secretively. **10.** to signal or summon with a buzzer. **11.** *Informal.* to telephone (someone). **12.** *Aeron.* to fly a plane very low over: *to buzz a field.* [imit.]

buz·zard (buz′ərd), *n.* **1.** any of several broad-winged, soaring hawks of the genus *Buteo* and allied genera, esp. *B. buteo,* of Europe. **2.** any of several New World vultures of the family *Cathartidae,* esp. the turkey vulture. **3.** *Slang.* a contemptible or cantankerous man (often prec. by *old*). [ME *busard* < OF, var. of *buisard* = *buis(on)* buzzard (< L *būteōn-,* s. of *būteō* kind of hawk) + *-ard* -ARD]

Buz′zards Bay′, an inlet of the Atlantic, in SE Massachusetts. 30 mi. long.

buzz′ bomb′. See **robot bomb.**

buzz·er (buz′ər), *n.* **1.** a person or thing that buzzes. **2.** an electric signaling apparatus producing a buzzing sound.

buzz′ saw′, a power-operated circular saw.

buzz·word (buz′wûrd′), *n.* a word or phrase, sometimes sounding technical, that is a popular cliché of a particular group or field.

B.V., 1. Blessed Virgin. [< L *Beāta Virgō*] **2.** farewell. [< L *bene valē*]

B.V.D., *Trademark.* a suit of men's underwear. Also, **BVD's**

B.V.M., Blessed Virgin Mary. [< L *Beāta Virgō Marīa*]

bvt., 1. brevet. **2.** brevetted.

bwa·na (bwä′nə), *n.* (in Africa) master; boss: applied by natives to a European. [< Swahili < Ar *abūna* our father]

B.W.I., British West Indies.

bx., *pl.* **bxs.** box.

by (bī), *prep., adv., adj., n., pl.* **byes.** —*prep.* **1.** near to or next to: *a home by a lake.* **2.** over the surface of, through the medium of, along, or using as a route: *He came by the highway. She arrived by air.* **3.** on, as a means of conveyance: *They arrived by ship.* **4.** to and beyond the vicinity of; past: *He went by the church.* **5.** within the extent or period of, during: *by day; by night.* **6.** not later than; at or before: *I usually finish work by five o'clock.* **7.** to the extent or amount of: *larger by a great deal; taller by three inches.* **8.** according to; from the opinion, evidence, or authority of: *By his own account he was in Chicago at the time.* **9.** in conformity with: *This is a bad movie by any standards.* **10.** with (something) at stake; on: *to swear by all that is sacred.* **11.** through the agency or authority of: *The document was distributed by a local group.* **12.** from the hand, mind, invention, or creativity of: *Read a poem by Keats. The phonograph was invented by Edison.* **13.** in consequence or on the basis of: *We met by chance.* **14.** accompanied with or in the atmosphere of: *Lovers walk by moonlight.* **15.** on behalf of: *He did well by his children.* **16.** after; in serial order: *piece by piece; little by little.* **17.** taken with (a certain number of) times or (of a shape longer than wide) the other dimension: *Multiply 18 by 57. The room was 10 feet by 12 feet.* **18.** using as a divisor: *Divide 99 by 33.* **19.** according to or involving as a unit of measure: *Apples are sold by the bushel. I'm paid by the week.* **20.** begot or born of: *Eve had two sons by Adam. My brother has one child by his first wife.* **21.** (of quadrupeds) having as a sire: *Equipoise II by Equipoise.* **22.** (on a compass) one point toward the east, west, north, or south of: *He sailed NE by N from Pago Pago.* **23.** into, at, or to: *Drop by my office this afternoon.* —*adv.* **24.** near; at hand: *The school is close by.* **25.** to and beyond a point near something; past: *The car drove by.* **26.** aside; away: *Put your work by for the moment.* **27.** over; past: *in times gone by.* **28. by and by,** before long; presently. **29. by and large,** in general; on the whole. —*adj.* Also, **bye. 30.** situated to one side: *They came down a by passage.* **31.** secondary or incidental. —*n.* **32.** bye. **33. by the by.** See **bye** (def. 5). [ME; OE *bī;* c. D *bij,* OHG *bī* (G *bei*), Goth *bi.* See BE-]
—**Syn. 11.** BY, THROUGH, WITH indicate agency or means of getting something done or accomplished. BY is regularly used to denote the agent (person or force) in passive constructions: *It is done by many; destroyed by fire.* It also indicates means: *Send it by airmail.* WITH denotes the instrument (usually consciously) employed by an agent: *He cut it with the scissors.* THROUGH designates particularly immediate agency or instrumentality or reason or motive: *through outside aid; to yield through fear; wounded through carelessness.*

by-, a combining form of **by:** *by-product; bystander; byway.* Also, **bye-.**

by-and-by (bī′ən bī′), *n.* the future; hereafter: *in the sweet by-and-by.* [ME *bi and bi* one by one, at once. See BY]

Byb·los (bib′ləs), *n.* an ancient Phoenician seaport near the modern city of Beirut, Lebanon.

by-blow (bī′blō′), *n.* **1.** an incidental or accidental blow. **2.** an illegitimate child.

Byd·goszcz (bid′gôshch), *n.* a city in N Poland. 246,000 (est. 1963). German, **Bromberg.**

bye (bī), *n.* Also, **by. 1.** *Sports.* the position of a player or team not paired with a competitor in an early round and thus automatically advanced to play in the next round, as in a tournament: *The top three seeded players received byes in the first round.* **2.** *Golf.* the holes of a stipulated course still unplayed after the match is finished. **3.** *Cricket.* a run made on a ball not struck by the batsman. **4.** something subsidiary, secondary, or out of the way. **5. by the bye,** by the way; incidentally. Also, **by the by.** —*adj.* **6.** by. [var. sp. of BY in its n. use]

bye-, var. of **by-:** *bye-election.*

bye-bye (bī′bī′), *interj.* *Informal.* good-by. [redupl. based on *good-by*]

bye·law (bī′lô′), *n.* bylaw.

by-e·lec·tion (bī′i lek′shən), *n.* *Brit.* a special election not held at the time of a general election, to fill a vacancy in Parliament. Also, **bye′-e·lec′tion.**

Bye·lo·rus·sia (byel′ō rush′ə, bel′ō-), *n.* **1.** Also called **White Russian Soviet Socialist Republic.** Official name, **Byelorus′sian So′viet So′cialist Repub′lic.** a constituent republic of the Soviet Union, in the W part. 9,468,000; 80,154 sq. mi. *Cap.:* Minsk. **2.** a region in the W part of former czarist Russia. Also, **Belorussia.** Also called **White Russia.**

Bye·lo·rus·sian (byel′ō rush′ən, bel′ō-), *n.* a dialect of Russian, spoken by the population of the Byelorussian S.S.R. and using an alphabet slightly different from the Russian alphabet. Also, **Belorussian.**

Bye·lo·stok (bye′lo stôk′, be′-), *n.* Russian name of **Białystok.**

by·gone (bī′gôn′, -gon′), *adj.* **1.** past; gone by; out of date: *memories of bygone days.* —*n.* **2. bygones,** that which is past. **3. let bygones be bygones,** to decide to forget past disagreements; become reconciled. [late ME (north) *bygane* GONE BY]

by·law (bī′lô′), *n.* **1.** a standing rule governing the regulation of a corporation's or society's internal affairs. **2.** a subsidiary law. **3.** *Brit.* an ordinance of a municipality or community. Also, **byelaw.** [BY- + LAW[1]; r. ME *bilawe* = *by* town (< Scand; cf. Dan *by*) + *lawe* law]

by-line (bī′līn′), *n.* *Journalism.* a printed line accompanying a news story, article, or the like, giving the author's name. —**by′lin′er,** *n.*

by-name (bī′nām′), *n.* **1.** a secondary name; cognomen; surname. **2.** a nickname. Also, **by′name′.** [ME]

Byng (bing), *n.* **Julian Hed·worth George** (hed′wərth), (*Viscount Byng of Vimy*), 1862–1935, English general: governor general of Canada 1921–26.

by-pass (bī′pas′, -päs′), *n., v.,* **-passed** or (*Rare*) **-past; -passed** or **-past; -pass·ing.** —*n.* **1.** a road enabling motorists to avoid a city or other heavy traffic points or to drive around an obstruction. **2.** a secondary pipe or other channel connected with a main passage, as for conducting a liquid or gas around a fixture, pipe, or appliance. **3.** *Elect.* shunt (def. 8). —*v.t.* **4.** to avoid (an obstruction, city, etc.) by following a by-pass. **5.** to cause (fluid or gas) to follow a secondary pipe or by-pass. **6.** to neglect to consult or to ignore the opinion or decision of (one's superior, a critic, or the like): *He by-passed the boss and took his grievance to the owner.* Also, **by′pass′.** [appar. back formation from *by-passage*]

by-past (bī′past′, -päst′), *adj.* **1.** bygone; past. —*v.* **2.** a pp. of **by-pass. 3.** *Rare.* a pt. of **by-pass.** [late ME: passed by]

by-path (bī′path′, -päth′), *n., pl.* **-paths** (-pathz′, -päthz′, -paths′, -päths′). a secondary or indirect path or road. Also, **by′path′.** [ME *bi path*]

by-play (bī′plā′), *n.* an action or speech carried on to the side while the main action proceeds, esp. on the stage. Also, **by′play′.**

by-prod·uct (bī′prod′əkt), *n.* a secondary or incidental product, as in a process of manufacture.

Byrd (bûrd), *n.* **1. Richard E(velyn),** 1888–1957, rear admiral in the U.S. Navy: polar explorer. **2. William,** c1540–1623, English composer and organist.

Byrd′ Land′ a part of Antarctica, SE of the Ross Sea: discovered and explored by Adm. Richard E. Byrd. Formerly, **Marie Byrd Land.**

byre (bīər), *n.* *Brit.* a cow barn or shed. [ME, OE: barn, shed < *būr* hut. See BOWER[1]]

Byrnes (bûrnz), *n.* **James Francis,** 1879–1972, U.S. statesman and jurist: Secretary of State 1945–47.

byr·nie (bûr′nē), *n.* *Armor.* a defensive shirt, usually of mail; hauberk. [ME *byrny,* Scot var. of *brynie, brinie* < Scand; cf. Icel *brynja,* c. OE *byrne* coat of mail, OHG *brunnia*]

by-road (bī′rōd′), *n.* a secondary road. Also, **by′road′.**

By·ron (bī′rən), *n.* **George Gordon, Lord** (*6th Baron Byron*), 1788–1824, English poet.

By·ron·ic (bī ron′ik), *adj.* **1.** of or pertaining to Lord Byron. **2.** possessing the characteristics of Byron or his poetry, esp. melancholy, melodramatic energy, etc.

bys·sus (bis′əs), *n., pl.* **bys·sus·es, bys·si** (bis′ī). **1.** *Zool.* a collection of silky filaments by which certain mollusks attach themselves to rocks. **2.** an ancient cloth, thought to be of linen, cotton, or silk. [< L < Gk *býssos* a fine cotton or linen < Heb *būtz* or some kindred Sem word]

by·stand·er (bī′stan′dər), *n.* a person present but not involved; chance spectator.

by-street (bī′strēt′), *n.* a side street or a private or obscure street; byway. Also, **by′street′.**

by-talk (bī′tôk′), *n.* incidental conversation; small talk.

byte (bīt), *n.* *Computer Technol.* a unit of information for processing in certain kinds of electronic computers, equal to one character or eight bits. [arbitrary coinage]

By·tom (bi′tôm), *n.* a city in S Poland: formerly in Germany. 190,000 (est. 1963). German, **Beuthen.**

by·way (bī′wā′), *n.* **1.** a secluded, private, or obscure road. **2.** a subsidiary or obscure field of research, endeavor, etc. [ME *bywey*]

by·word (bī′wûrd′), *n.* **1.** a word or phrase associated with some person, group, idea, etc.; a characteristic expression, as *hail-fellow well met.* **2.** a common saying; proverb. **3.** an object of general reproach, derision, scorn, etc. **4.** an epithet, often of scorn. [ME *bi worde,* OE *biwyrde*] —**Syn. 1.** slogan, motto. **2.** maxim, aphorism, adage.

by-work (bī′wûrk′), *n.* work done during intervals of leisure.

by-your-leave (bī′yər lēv′), *n.* an apology for not having sought permission.

Byz., Byzantine.

Byz·an·tine (biz′ən tēn′, -tīn′, bi zan′tin), *adj.* **1.** of or pertaining to Byzantium or the Byzantine Empire. **2.** noting or pertaining to the architecture of the Byzantine Empire and to architecture influenced by it: characterized by masonry construction, round arches, and low domes on pendentives. **3.** *Fine Arts.* designating the style of the fine arts of the Byzantine Empire and its provinces, characterized chiefly by a highly formal structure and the use of rich color. **4.** complex or intricate. —*n.* **5.** a native or inhabitant of Byzantium.

Byz′antine Church′. See **Orthodox Church** (def. 1).

Byz′antine Em′pire, the Eastern Roman Empire, esp. from A.D. 476–1453. *Cap.:* Constantinople. Cf. **Western Roman Empire.**

By·zan·ti·um (bi zan′shē əm, -tē əm), *n.* an ancient Greek city on the Bosporus and the Sea of Marmara. Cf. **Constantinople, Istanbul.**

Bz., benzene.

DEVELOPMENT OF MAJUSCULE								
NORTH SEMITIC	GREEK		ETR.	LATIN		MODERN		
						GOTHIC	ITALIC	ROMAN
7	1	Γ	⌉	(	C	𝕮	*C*	C

DEVELOPMENT OF MINUSCULE					
ROMAN CURSIVE	ROMAN UNCIAL	CAROL. MIN.	MODERN		
			GOTHIC	ITALIC	ROMAN
<	C	c	𝔠	*c*	c

The third letter of the English alphabet developed from North Semitic *ghimel* and Greek *gamma* through the Etruscans, in whose language there was no meaningful distinction between the *g*-sound and the *k*-sound, and who used C for both. In Latin, C, pronounced like English K, was used mainly before A and O, and retained this sound when introduced into Britain. The capital and minuscule, which assumed their present form in Latin, were originally angular and faced to the left, as in North Semitic *ghimel* and early Greek *gamma* (⅂).

C, c (sē), *n., pl.* **C's** or **Cs, c's** or **cs. 1.** the third letter of the English alphabet, a consonant. **2.** any spoken sound represented by the letter *C* or *c*, as in *cat, race,* or *circle.* **3.** something having the shape of a C. **4.** a written or printed representation of the letter *C* or *c*. **5.** a device, as a printer's type, for reproducing the letter *C* or *c*.

C, 1. Calorie. **2.** Celsius. **3.** centigrade. **4.** coulomb.

C, 1. the third in order or in a series. **2.** (*sometimes l.c.*) (in some grading systems) a grade or mark indicating fair or average quality. **3.** *Music.* **a.** the first tone, or keynote, in the scale of C major or the third tone in the relative minor scale, A minor. **b.** a written or printed note representing this tone. **c.** a string, key, or pipe tuned to this tone. **d.** the tonality having C as the tonic note. **e.** a symbol indicating quadruple time and appearing after the clef sign on a musical staff. **4.** (*sometimes l.c.*) the Roman numeral for 100. Cf. **Roman numerals. 5.** *Chem.* carbon. **6.** *Elect.* capacitance.

c, 1. calorie. **2.** *Optics.* candle; candles. **3.** (with a year) about: *c1775.* [< L *circā, circiter, circum*] **4.** *Physics, Chem.* curie; curies. **5.** *Computer Technol.* cycle; cycles.

c, *Optics, Physics.* the velocity of light in a vacuum: approximately 186,282 miles per second or 299,793 kilometers per second.

C., 1. calorie. **2.** Cape. **3.** Catholic. **4.** Celsius. **5.** Celtic. **6.** Centigrade. **7.** College. **8.** Conservative.

c., 1. calorie. **2.** *Optics.* candle; candles. **3.** carat. **4.** (in stationery and clerical work) carbon. **5.** carton. **6.** case. **7.** *Baseball.* catcher. **8.** cathode. **9.** cent; cents. **10.** *Football.* center. **11.** centigrade. **12.** centime. **13.** centimeter. **14.** century. **15.** chairman. **16.** chapter. **17.** chief. **18.** child. **19.** church. **20.** (with a year) about: *c.1775.* [< L *circā, circiter, circum*] **21.** cirrus. **22.** city. **23.** cloudy. **24.** cognate. **25.** gallon. [< L *congius*] **26.** copper. **27.** copy. **28.** Also, ©. copyright. **29.** corps. **30.** cubic. **31.** *Computer Technol.* cycle; cycles.

CA, 1. California (approved esp. for use with zip code). **2.** chronological age.

Ca, *Chem.* calcium.

ca' (kä, kô), *v.t., v.i. Scot.* to call, as to call an animal toward one; urge or drive forward by calling. [var. of CALL]

ca., 1. cathode. **2.** centiare. **3.** Also, **ca** (with a year) about: *ca. 1872.* [< L *circā*]

C/A, 1. capital account. **2.** cash account. **3.** credit account. **4.** current account.

C.A., 1. Central America. **2.** chartered accountant. **3.** Coast Artillery.

CAA, Civil Aeronautics Administration. Also, **C.A.A.**

Caa·ba (kä′bə), *n.* Kaaba.

cab[1] (kab), *n.* **1.** a taxicab. **2.** any of various horse-drawn vehicles, as the hansom or brougham, esp. one for public hire. **3.** the covered or enclosed part of a locomotive, truck, crane, etc., where the operator sits. [short for CABRIOLET]

cab[2] (kab), *n.* an ancient Hebrew measure equal to about two quarts. Also, **kab.** [< Heb *qabh*]

CAB, Civil Aeronautics Board. Also, **C.A.B.**

ca·bal (kə bal′), *n., v.,* **-balled, -bal·ling.** —*n.* **1.** a small group of plotters, esp. against a government. **2.** the plottings of such a group. **3.** a clique. —*v.i.* **4.** to form a cabal; conspire or plot. [earlier *cabbal* < ML *cabbal(a).* See CABALA]

cab·a·la (kab′ə lə, kə bä′-), *n.* **1.** a system of esoteric theosophy and theurgy developed by rabbis from about the 7th to 18th centuries, reaching its peak about the 12th and 13th centuries, and based on a mystical method of interpreting the Scriptures to penetrate sacred mysteries and foretell the future. **2.** any occult or secret doctrine or science. Also, **cabbala, kabala, kabbala.** [< ML *cab(b)ala* < Heb *qabbālāh* tradition, lit., something received, i.e., handed down] —**cab′a·lism,** *n.* —**cab′a·list,** *n.* —**cab′a·lis′tic, cab′a·lis′ti·cal,** *adj.* —**cab′a·lis′ti·cal·ly,** *adv.*

ca·bal·le·ro (kab′əl yâr′ō, kab′ə lâr′ō; *Sp.* kä′vä lye′rō), *n., pl.* **ca·bal·le·ros** (kab′əl yâr′ōz, kab′ə lâr′ōz; *Sp.* kä′vä lye′rōs). **1.** a Spanish gentleman. **2.** *Southwestern U.S.* **a.** a horseman. **b.** a lady's escort. [< Sp < LL *caballār(ius)* groom; see CAVALIER]

ca·ban·a (kə ban′ə, -ban′yə, bä′nə, -bän′yə), *n.* **1.** a cabin or cottage. **2.** a small cabin or tentlike structure for use as a bathhouse. Also, **ca·ba·ña** (kä bä′nyä). [< Sp; see CABIN]

Ca·ba·na·tuan (kä′vä nä twän′), *n.* a city on S Luzon, in the N Philippines. 54,668 (1960).

cab·a·ret (kab′ə rā′), *n.* **1.** a large restaurant providing food, drink, music, a dance floor, and floor show. **2.** *Brit.* a floor show. [< F: taproom; orig. disputed]

cab·bage[1] (kab′ij), *n., v.,* **-baged, -bag·ing.** —*n.* **1.** any of several cultivated varieties of a cruciferous plant, *Brassica oleracea capitata,* having a short stem and leaves formed into a compact, edible head. **2.** *Slang.* money, esp. paper money. —*v.i.* **3.** (of a plant) to form a head like that of a cabbage. [ME *caboche* < dial. OF (north): head << L *caput* head]

cab·bage[2] (kab′ij), *n., v.,* **-baged, -bag·ing.** *Brit. Archaic.* —*n.* **1.** something stolen, esp. portions of cloth by a tailor in making a garment. —*v.t., v.i.* **2.** to steal or pilfer. [earlier *carbage* shred, piece of cloth, appar. var. of GARBAGE wheat straw chopped small (obs. sense)]

cab′bage but′terfly, any of several white or chiefly white butterflies of the family *Pieridae,* as *Pieris rapae,* the larvae of which feed on the leaves of cabbages and other cruciferous plants.

cab′bage palm′, any of several palms, as *Sabal Palmetto,* having terminal leaf buds that are eaten like cabbage.

cab′bage palmet′to, a cabbage palm, *Sabal Palmetto,* of the southeastern U.S.: the state tree of Florida and South Carolina.

cab·bage·worm (kab′ij wûrm′), *n.* a caterpillar that feeds on cabbages.

cab·ba·la (kab′ə lə, kə bä′-), *n.* cabala. —**cab′ba·lism,** *n.* —**cab′ba·list,** *n.* —**cab′ba·lis′tic, cab′ba·lis′ti·cal,** *adj.* —**cab′ba·lis′ti·cal·ly,** *adv.*

cab·by (kab′ē), *n., pl.* **-bies.** *Informal.* a cabdriver. Also, **cab′bie.**

cab·driv·er (kab′drī′vər), *n.* a driver of a taxicab or of a horse-drawn carriage.

Cab·ell (kab′əl), *n.* **James Branch** (branch), 1879–1958, U.S. novelist, essayist, and critic.

ca·ber (kā′bər), *n. Scot.* a pole or beam, esp. one thrown as a trial of strength. [< Gael *cabar* pole]

Ca·be·za de Va·ca (kä ve′thä the vä′kä, -ve′sä), **Ál·var Nú·ñez** (äl′vär noo′nyeth, -nyes), c1490–1557?, Spanish explorer in the Americas.

ca·bil·do (kä vēl′thô; *Eng.* kə bil′dō), *n., pl.* **-dos** (-thôs; *Eng.* -dōz). *Spanish.* **1.** the chapter house of a cathedral. **2.** a town council. **3.** See **town hall.**

Ca·bi·mas (kä vē′mäs), *n.* a city in N Venezuela. 117,734 (est. 1965).

cab·in (kab′in), *n.* **1.** a small house or cottage, usually of simple design and construction. **2.** an enclosed space for more or less temporary occupancy, as the passenger space in a cable car. **3.** an apartment or room in a ship. **4.** See **cabin class. 5.** *Aeron.* the enclosed space for the pilot, passengers, or cargo in an air or space vehicle. —*v.i.* **6.** to live in a cabin. —*v.t.* **7.** to confine. [ME *cabane* < MF < OPr *caban(a)* < LL *capanna*] —**Syn. 1.** See **cottage.**

cab′in boy′, a boy employed to wait on the officers and passengers in a merchant vessel.

cab′in class′, the class of accommodations on a passenger ship less costly and luxurious than first class but more so than tourist class. Cf. **second class** (def. 1). —**cab′in-class′,** *adj., adv.*

cab′in cruis′er, a power-driven pleasure boat having a cabin equipped for living aboard.

Ca·bin·da (kə bēn′də), *n.* **1.** a Portuguese territory and exclave of Angola, on the W coast of Africa. 50,233 (est. 1950); 2807 sq. mi. **2.** a seaport in and the capital of this territory, N of the mouth of the Congo River. 1554 (1950).

cab·i·net (kab′ə nit), *n.* **1.** (*often cap.*) a council advising a sovereign, president, etc. **2.** a piece of furniture with shelves, drawers, etc., for holding or displaying objects. **3.** a large piece of furniture containing a radio or television set and often a record player or a place for phonograph records. **4.** an upright box or movable closet for storage. **5.** a wall cupboard for storage. **6.** a small case with compartments for valuables. **7.** a small chamber or booth for a special use, as a shower stall. **8.** a room set aside specifically for the exhibition of small works of art or objets d'art. **9.** *Archaic.* a small, private room. **10.** *Obs.* a small cabin. —*adj.* **11.** of or pertaining to a political cabinet. **12.** pertaining to a private room. **13.** private, confidential, or secret. **14.** of suitable value, beauty, or size for a private room, small case, etc.: *a cabinet edition of Milton.* **15.** of, pertaining to, or used by a cabinetmaker or in cabinetmaking. **16.** noting a high-quality bottled wine from Germany. **17.** *Drafting.* designating a method of projection (**cab′inet projec′tion**) in which a three-dimensional object is represented by a drawing (**cab′inet draw′ing**) having all vertical and horizontal lines drawn to exact scale, with oblique lines reduced to about half scale so as to offset the appearance of distortion. Cf. **axonometric, isometric** (def. 4), **oblique** (def. 10). See illus. at **isometric.** [< MF < ONF *cabin(e)* gaming house (< ?) + *-et* -ET; in def. 10, CABIN + -ET]

cab·i·net·mak·er (kab′ə nit mā′kər), *n.* a person who makes fine furniture, esp. cabinets, chests, etc.

cab·i·net·mak·ing (kab′ə nit mā′king), *n.* the occupation or craft of a cabinetmaker.

cab·i·net·work (kab′ə nit wûrk′), *n.* **1.** fine woodwork, as cabinets or chests. **2.** cabinetmaking.

ca·ble (kā′bəl), *n., v.,* **-bled, -bling.** —*n.* **1.** a heavy, strong rope. **2.** *Naut.* **a.** a rope or chain for mooring a vessel at anchor. **b.** See **cable's length. 3.** *Elect.* an insulated electrical conductor, often in strands, or a combination of electrical conductors insulated from one another. **4.** cablegram. **5.** cable-stitch. **6.** See **cable TV.** —*v.t.* **7.** to send (a message) by underwater cable. **8.** to send a cablegram to. **9.** to fasten with a cable. —*v.i.* **10.** to send a message by submarine cable. —*adj.* **11.** of or pertaining to cable TV: *a cable station; cable subscribers.* [ME; OE **cæbl* (var. of *cæfl*) < LL *cap(u)lum* halter = L *cap(istrum)* halter (< OE *cæbester*) + *-ulum* -ULE]

ca′ble car′, an enclosed vehicle used on a cable railway. Also, **ca′ble-car′.**

ca·ble·gram (kā′bəl gram′), *n.* a telegram sent by underwater cable. Also called **cable.** [CABLE + (TELE)GRAM]

ca·ble-laid (kā′bəl lād′), *adj. Ropemaking.* noting a rope formed of three plain-laid ropes twisted together in a left-handed direction.

ca′ble rail′way, a railway on which the cars are pulled by a moving cable under the roadway.

ca′ble's length′, a nautical unit of length: 720 feet in the U.S. Navy; 608 feet in the British Navy.

ca·ble-stitch (kā′bəl stich′), *n.* **1.** a series of stitches used in knitting to produce the effect of a cable or rope. **2.** the pattern produced by such stitches.

ca·blet (kā′blit), *n.* a small cable, esp. a cable-laid rope under 10 inches in circumference.

ca′ble TV′, **1.** a system for offering television programs on channels other than those regularly available over the air, by coaxial cable to paying subscribers. **2.** See **CATV** (def. 1). Also called **ca′ble tel′evi′sion.**

cab·man (kab′mən), *n., pl.* **-men.** cabdriver.

ca·bob (kə bob′), *n.* kabob.

cab·o·chon (kab′ə shon′; *Fr.* KA bô shôN′), *n., pl.* **-chons** (-shonz′; *Fr.* -shôN′), *adv.* —*n.* **1.** a precious stone of convex hemispherical or oval form, highly polished but not cut into facets. —*adv.* **2.** in the form of a cabochon: *a turquoise cut cabochon.* [< MF = *caboche* head + *-on* aug. suffix]

ca·boo·dle (kə bo͞od′əl), *n.* **1.** *Informal.* the lot, pack, or crowd: *I have no use for the whole caboodle.* **2. kit and caboodle.** See **kit**[1] (def. 5). [*ca-* (< ?) + BOODLE]

ca·boose (kə bo͞os′), *n.* **1.** *Railroads.* a car for the use of the crew of a freight train, esp. when attached to the rear of the train. **2.** *Brit.* a kitchen on the deck of a ship; galley. [< MLG *kabūse* < ?]

Cab·ot (kab′ət), *n.* **1. John** (*Giovanni Caboto*), c1450–98?, Italian navigator in the service of England: discoverer of the North American mainland 1497. **2.** his son, **Sebastian,** 1474?–1557, English navigator and explorer.

cab·o·tage (kab′ə tij; *Fr.* KA bô TAZH′), *n.* **1.** navigation or trade along the coast. **2.** *Aeron.* the legal restriction to domestic carriers of air transport between points within a country's borders. [< F < *caboter* to sail coastwise < *cabo* (now obs.) < Sp *cabo* headland, CAPE[2]; see -AGE]

Ca·bral (kə brôl′), *n.* **Pe·dro Al·va·res** (pe′dro͞o ôl′və rash), c1460–c1520, Portuguese navigator.

ca·bril·la (kə bril′ə), *n.* any of several sea basses, esp. *Epinephelus analogus,* found in the tropical part of the eastern Pacific Ocean. [< Sp: prawn = *cabr(a)* she-goat (< L *capra*) + *-illa* dim. suffix]

Ca·bri·ni (kə brē′nē; *It.* kä brē′nē), *n.* **Saint Frances Xavier** (*Mother Cabrini*), 1850–1917, American nun, born in Italy: founder of the Missionary Sisters of the Sacred Heart of Jesus.

Cabriole

cab·ri·ole (kab′rē ōl′; *Fr.* KA brē ôl′), *n., pl.* **-oles** (-ōlz′; *Fr.* -ôl′). *Furniture.* a tapering leg curving outward at the top and inward farther down so as to end in a round pad often resembling an animal's paw: used esp. in the early 18th century. [< F: orig. caper; so called because modeled on leg of a capering animal; see CAPRIOLE]

cab·ri·o·let (kab′rē ə lā′), *n.* **1.** a light, two-wheeled, one-horse carriage with a folding top, capable of seating two persons. **2.** *Auto. Obs.* an automobile resembling a coupé but with a folding top; a convertible coupé. [< F: lit., little caper; so called from its light movement]

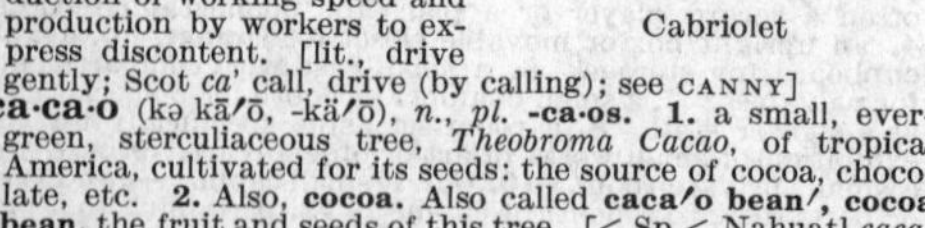
Cabriolet

ca′can·ny (kä kan′ē, kô-), *n. Brit. Slang.* a deliberate reduction of working speed and production by workers to express discontent. [lit., drive gently; Scot *ca′* call, drive (by calling); see CANNY]

ca·ca·o (kə kā′ō, -kä′ō), *n., pl.* **-ca·os.** **1.** a small, evergreen, sterculiaceous tree, *Theobroma Cacao,* of tropical America, cultivated for its seeds: the source of cocoa, chocolate, etc. **2.** Also, **cocoa.** Also called **caca′o bean′, cocoa bean.** the fruit and seeds of this tree. [< Sp < Nahuatl *cacahuatl* cacao seeds]

caca′o but′ter. See **cocoa butter.**

cac·cia·to·re (kä′chə tôr′ē, -tôr′ē), *adj. Italian Cookery.* prepared with tomatoes, mushrooms, herbs, and other seasonings. Also, **cac·cia·to·ra** (kä′chə tôr′ə, -tôr′ə). [< It: lit., hunter = *cacciat(o)* (ptp. of *cacciare* to hunt; see CATCH, -ATE[1]) + *-ore* -OR[2]]

cach·a·lot (kash′ə lot′, -lō′), *n.* See **sperm whale.** [< F]

cache (kash), *n., v.,* **cached, cach·ing.** —*n.* **1.** a hiding place, esp. one in the ground, for provisions, treasures, etc. **2.** anything hidden or stored. —*v.t.* **3.** to put in a cache; conceal; hide. [< F < *cacher* to hide, press < VL **coacticāre* to stow away, orig. to pack together = L *coact(us)* collected (ptp. of *cōgere*) + *-icā-* formative v. suffix + *-re* inf. ending]

cache·pot (kash′pot′, -pō′), *n.* an ornamental container, usually of china or tole, for holding and concealing a flowerpot. [< F: lit., hide pot]

ca·chet (ka shā′, kash′ā; *Fr.* KA she′), *n., pl.* **ca·chets** (ka shāz′, kash′āz; *Fr.* KA she′). **1.** an official seal, as on a letter or document. **2.** a distinguishing mark or feature: *Courtesy is the cachet of good breeding.* **3.** a sign or expression of approval, esp. from someone of great prestige. **4.** prestige; high standing. **5.** *Philately.* a slogan, design, etc., stamped or printed on an envelope or folded letter. [< MF: lit., something compressed to a small size]

ca·chex·i·a (kə kek′sē ə), *n. Pathol.* general ill health, with emaciation, due to a chronic disease, as cancer. Also, **ca·chex·y** (kə kek′sē) [< LL < Gk = *kak(ós)* bad + *héx(is)* condition (*éch(ein)* (to) have + *-sis* -SIS) + *-ia* -IA] —**ca·chec·tic** (kə kek′tik), **ca·chec′ti·cal, ca·chex′ic,** *adj.*

cach·in·nate (kak′ə nāt′), *v.i.,* **-nat·ed, -nat·ing.** to laugh loudly or immoderately. [< L *cachinnāt(us)* laughed aloud, laughed immoderately (ptp. of *cachinnāre*) —**cach′-in·na′tion,** *n.*

ca·chou (kə sho͞o′, ka-), *n.* **1.** catechu. **2.** lozenge to sweeten the breath. [< F < Pg *cachu* < Malay; see CATECHU]

ca·cique (kə sēk′), *n.* **1.** a chief of an Indian clan or tribe in Mexico and the West Indies. **2.** a local political boss in Spain and Spanish America. **3.** any of several oscine birds of the family *Icteridae,* of the American tropics, that construct long, pendent nests. [< Sp < Taino (Hispaniola), prob. < Arawak]

cack·le (kak′əl), *v.,* **-led, -ling,** *n.* —*v.i.* **1.** to utter the shrill, broken sound or cry of a hen. **2.** to laugh in a shrill, broken manner. **3.** to chatter noisily; prattle. —*v.t.* **4.** to utter with cackles: *to cackle one's disapproval.* —*n.* **5.** the act or sound of cackling. [ME *cakel(en);* c. D *kakelen,* LG *kakeln,* Sw *kackla*] —**cack′ler,** *n.*

caco-, an element meaning "bad," occurring in loan words from Greek (*cacodemon*) and on this model, used in the formation of compound words (*cacogenics*). [< Gk *kakó(s)*]

cac·o·de·mon (kak′ə dē′mən), *n.* an evil spirit; devil or demon. Also, **cac′o·dae′mon.** [< Gk *kakodaímōn* having an evil genius, ill-fated] —**cac·o·de·mon·ic, cac·o·dae·mon·ic** (kak′ə di mon′ik), *adj.*

cac·o·dyl (kak′ə dil), *Chem.* —*adj.* **1.** containing the cacodyl group. —*n.* **2.** a poisonous liquid $(CH_3)_2As–As(CH_3)_2$, that has a vile, garliclike odor and undergoes spontaneous combustion in dry air. [< Gk *kakṓd(es)* ill-smelling (*kak(o)* CACO- + *-od-* smell + *-ēs* adj. suffix) + -YL]

cac′odyl group′, *Chem.* the univalent group, $(CH_3)_2As–$. Also called **cac′odyl rad′ical.**

cac·o·ë·thes (kak′ō ē′thēz), *n.* an irresistible urge; mania. [< L < Gk *kakoḗthes,* neut. (used as n.) of *kakoḗthēs* malignant, lit., of bad character. See CACO-, ETHOS]

cac·o·gen·ics (kak′ə jen′iks), *n.* (*construed as sing.*) dysgenics. [CACO- + (EU)GENICS] —**cac′o·gen′ic,** *adj.*

ca·cog·ra·phy (kə kog′rə fē), *n.* **1.** bad handwriting; poor penmanship. Cf. **calligraphy** (def 1). **2.** incorrect spelling. Cf. **orthography** (def. 1). —**ca·cog′ra·pher,** *n.* —**cac·o·graph·ic** (kak′ə graf′ik), **cac′o·graph′i·cal,** *adj.*

Cacomistle (Total length 2½ ft.; tail 1½ ft.)

cac·o·mis·tle (kak′ə mis′əl), *n.* a carnivorous animal, *Bassariscus astutus,* of Mexico and the southwestern U.S., related to the raccoon. Also, **cac·o·mix·le** (kak′ə mis′əl, -mik′səl). Also called **ringtail.** [< MexSp < Nahuatl *tlacomiztli* = *tlaco* half + *miztli* cougar]

ca·coph·o·nous (kə kof′ə nəs), *adj.* having a harsh or discordant sound. Also, **cac·o·phon·ic** (kak′ə fon′ik). [< Gk *kakóphōnos.* See CACO-, -PHONE, -OUS] —**ca·coph′o·nous·ly, cac′o·phon′i·cal·ly,** *adv.*

ca·coph·o·ny (kə kof′ə nē), *n., pl.* **-nies.** **1.** harsh, discordant sound; dissonance. **2.** a discordant and meaningless mixture of different sounds. **3.** *Music.* the frequent use of discords of complex relationship. [< NL *cacophonia* < Gk *kakophōnía*]

cac·ta·ceous (kak tā′shəs), *adj.* belonging to the *Cactaceae,* or cactus family. [< NL *Cactace(ae)* (see CACTUS, -ACEAE) + -OUS]

cac·tus (kak′təs), *n., pl.* **-tus·es, -ti** (-tī). any of various fleshy-stemmed plants of the family *Cactaceae,* usually leafless and spiny, often producing showy flowers, chiefly native to the hot, dry regions of America. [< L < Gk *káktos* cardoon] —**cac′toid,** *adj.*

ca·cu·mi·nal (kə kyo͞o′mə nəl), *Phonet.* —*adj.* **1.** pronounced with the tip of the tongue curled back so as to touch the roof of the mouth above the gums; retroflex; cerebral. —*n.* **2.** a cacuminal sound. [< L *cacūmin-* (s. of *cacūmen*) top, tip + -AL[1]]

Cactus (Saguaro), *Carnegiea gigantea* (Height to 50 ft.)

cad (kad), *n.* a man who behaves crudely or irresponsibly toward women. [short for CADDIE (def. 2)]

CAD (kad), *n.* computer-aided design.

ca·das·tral (kə das′trəl), *adj.* **1.** *Survey.* (of a map or survey) showing or including boundaries, property lines, etc. **2.** of or pertaining to a cadastre. [< F]

ca·das·tre (kə das′tər), *n.* an official register of the ownership, extent, and value of real property, used as a basis of taxation. Also, **ca·das′ter.** [< F < Pr *cadastr(o)* < It *catastro,* earlier *catastico* (Venetian) < LGk *katástich(on)* register < phrase *katà stíchon* by line. See CATA-, STICH]

ca·dav·er (kə dav′ər), *n.* a dead body, esp. a human body used for dissection; corpse. [< L *cadāver* dead body, corpse, akin to *cadere* to fall, perish] —**ca·dav′er·ic,** *adj.* —**Syn.** See **body.**

ca·dav·er·ine (kə dav′ə rēn′), *n. Biochem.* a toxic ptomaine, $NH_2(CH_2)_5$, having an offensive odor, formed by the action of bacilli on protein: used in polymerization and biological research.

ca·dav·er·ous (kə dav′ər əs), *adj.* **1.** of or like a corpse. **2.** pale, wan, or ghastly. **3.** haggard and thin. [< L *cadāverōs(us)*] —**ca·dav′er·ous·ly,** *adv.* —**ca·dav′er·ous·ness,** *n.*

CAD/CAM (kad′kam′), *n.* computer-aided design and computer-aided manufacturing.

cad·dice[1] (kad′is, kä′dis), *n.* caddis[1].

cad·dice[2] (kad′is), *n.* caddisworm.

cad·die (kad′ē), *n.*, *v.*, **-died, -dy·ing.** —*n.* **1.** *Golf.* a person hired to carry a player's clubs, find the ball, etc. **2.** a person who runs errands, does odd jobs, etc. —*v.i.* **3.** to work as a caddie. Also, **caddy.** [earlier *cadee*, var. of *cadet* < F; see CADET]

cad·dis[1] (kad′is, kä′dis), *n.* a kind of woolen yarn or braid. Also, **caddice.** [< MF *cadis* < OPr *cadis, cadiz*, perh. so called because imported from Cádiz, Spain; r. ME *cadas* < MF, of obscure orig.]

cad·dis[2] (kad′is), *n.* caddisworm. [by shortening]

cad·dis·fly (kad′is flī′), *n.*, *pl.* **-flies.** any of numerous insects of the order *Trichoptera*, having two pairs of membranous, often hairy wings. Also, **cad′dice·fly′.** Cf. **caddisworm.** [see CADDISWORM, FLY[2]]

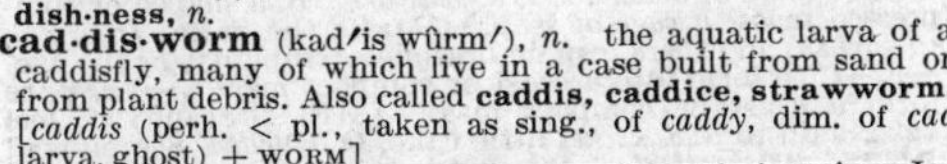

A, Caddisfly
B, Caddisfly larva in case formed of small stones;
C, Larva in case formed of grass roots

cad·dish (kad′ish), *adj.* of or like a cad; ungentlemanly. —**cad′dish·ly,** *adv.* —**cad′dish·ness,** *n.*

cad·dis·worm (kad′is wûrm′), *n.* the aquatic larva of a caddisfly, many of which live in a case built from sand or from plant debris. Also called **caddis, caddice, strawworm.** [*caddis* (perh. < pl., taken as sing., of *caddy*, dim. of *cad* larva, ghost) + WORM]

Cad·do·an (kad′ō ən), *n.* a family of North American Indian languages spoken in the upper Missouri valley in N Dakota, in the Platte valley in Nebraska and SW Arkansas, and in neighboring parts of Oklahoma, Texas, and Louisiana. [*Caddo* group of American Indian tribes + -AN]

cad·dy[1] (kad′ē), *n.*, *pl.* **-dies.** *Chiefly Brit.* **1.** a small box, can, or chest for holding or organizing small items: *pencil caddy.* **2.** See **tea caddy.** [var. of CATTY[2]]

cad·dy[2] (kad′ē), *n.*, *pl.* **-dies,** *v.i.*, **-died, -dy·ing.** caddie.

cade[1] (kād), *n.* a juniper, *Juniperus Oxycedrus*, of the Mediterranean area, whose wood yields an oily liquid **(oil of cade),** used in treating skin diseases. [< MF < OPr; akin to LL *catanus*]

cade[2] (kād), *adj.* (of the young of animals) abandoned by the mother and raised by humans. [late ME < ?]

-cade, a formal element derived from the analysis of *cavalcade*, used with the meaning "procession" in the formation of compound words: *motorcade.*

ca·delle (kə del′), *n.* a small, blackish beetle, *Tenebroides mauritanicus*, that feeds, as both larva and adult, on stored grain and on other insects. [< F < Pr *cadell(o)* < L *catell(us), catell(a)* puppy = *cat(ulus)* young of an animal + *-ellus, -ella* dim. suffix]

ca·dence (kād′ᵊns), *n.*, *v.*, **-denced, -denc·ing.** —*n.* Also, **cadency. 1.** rhythmic flow of a sequence of sounds or words: *the cadence of language.* **2.** a rhythmic pattern that is nonmetrically structured in free verse. **3.** the beat, rate, or measure of any rhythmic movement. **4.** the flow or rhythm of events, esp. the pattern in which something is experienced: *the frenetic cadence of modern life.* **5.** a slight falling in pitch of the voice in speaking, as at the end of a declarative sentence. **6.** the general modulation of the voice. **7.** *Music.* a sequence of notes or chords indicating the momentary or complete end of a composition, section, phrase, etc. —*v.t.* **8.** to make rhythmical. [ME < MF < It *cadenz(a)*, lit., a falling; see CADENZA] —**ca·den·tial** (kā den′shəl), *adj.*

ca·den·cy (kād′ᵊn sē), *n.*, *pl.* **-cies. 1.** cadence. **2.** *Heraldry.* the relationship to one another and to their common ancestor of the various members and branches of a family, as indicated by the introduction of cadency marks into their various coats of arms. [CAD(ENCE) + -ENCY]

ca′dency mark′, *Heraldry.* a charge or minor heraldic difference introduced into the arms of a family to show that it is related by blood to the main branch of the family, which bears the arms as originally granted. Also, **ca′dence mark′.**

ca·dent (kād′ᵊnt), *adj.* **1.** having cadence. **2.** *Archaic.* falling. [< L *cadent-*, (s. of *cadēns* falling, prp. of *cadere*) = *cad-* fall + *-ent-* -ENT]

ca·den·za (kə den′zə), *n.* *Music.* an elaborate flourish or showy passage introduced near the end of an aria or in a movement of a concerto. [< It < VL **cadentia* a falling = L *cad(ere)* to fall + *-entia* -ENCY]

ca·det (kə det′), *n.* **1.** a student in a national service academy, a private military school, or on a training ship. **2.** a young man in training for service as a commissioned officer in the U.S. Army, Air Force, or Coast Guard. Cf. **midshipman** (def. 1). **3.** a trainee in a business or profession. **4.** a younger son or brother. **5.** the youngest son. **6.** (formerly) a gentleman, usually a younger son, who entered the army to prepare for a commission. [< F < Gascon *capdet* little chief = *capd* (< L *capit-* head) + *-et* -ET] —**ca·det′ship′,** *n.*

cadge (kaj), *v.*, **cadged, cadg·ing.** —*v.t.* **1.** to obtain by imposing on another's generosity or friendship. **2.** to borrow without intent to repay. **3.** *Brit.* to beg or obtain by begging. —*v.i.* **4.** to ask, expect, or encourage another person to pay for or provide one's drinks, meals, etc. [ME *cagge(n)* (to) tie, perh. orig. said of hawks; see CAGE] —**cadg′er,** *n.*

cadg·y (kaj′ē), *adj.* *Scot.* (of animals) in rut. [?]

ca·di (kä′dē, kā′-), *n.*, *pl.* **-dis.** a judge, in a Muslim community, whose decisions are based on Islamic religious law. Also, **kadi.** [< Ar *qāḍī* judge]

Cad·il·lac (kad′ᵊlak′; *Fr.* kȧ dē yȧk′), *n.* **An·toine de la Mothe** (äɴ twȧn′ də lȧ môt′), 1657?–1730, French colonial governor in North America: founder of Detroit.

Cá·diz (kā′diz, kə diz′; *Sp.* kä′thēth), *n.* a seaport in SW Spain, on a bay of the Atlantic **(Gulf′ of Cá′diz).** 122,568 (est. 1963).

Cad·me·an (kad mē′ən), *adj.* of or pertaining to Cadmus. [< L *Cadmē(us)* (< Gk *Kadmeîos* of CADMUS) + -AN]

Cadme′an vic′tory, a victory disastrously costly to the victor.

cad·mi·um (kad′mē əm), *n.* *Chem.* a white, ductile divalent metallic element, used in plating and in making alloys. *Symbol:* Cd; *at. wt.:* 112.41; *at. no.:* 48; *sp. gr.:* 8.6 at 20° C. [< NL = L *cadm(īa)* calamine (orig. *Cadmēa terra* < Gk *Kadmeía gê*, earth of Cadmus) + -IUM]

cad′mium sul′fide, *Chem.* a light yellow or orange, water-insoluble powder, CdS, used chiefly as a pigment.

cad′mium yel′low, a pigment used in painting, consisting of cadmium sulfide and characterized by its strong yellow color and permanence.

Cad·mus (kad′məs), *n.* *Class. Myth.* a Phoenician prince who introduced writing to the Greeks and founded Thebes with the five warriors remaining from those sprung from the dragon's teeth he had planted. Cf. **Sparti.**

Ca·dor·na (kə dôr′nə; *It.* kä dôʀ′nä), *n.* **Count Lu·i·gi** (lo͞o ē′jē), 1850–1928, Italian general: chief of staff 1914–17.

ca·dre (kä′drə; *Mil. usually* kad′rē), *n.* **1.** *Mil.* the key group of officers and enlisted men necessary to establish and train a new military unit. **2.** a group of experienced persons for organizing or expanding a business, political party, etc.: *Cadres of construction engineers were sent to underdeveloped countries.* **3.** a member of a cadre. **4.** a framework or outline. [< F: frame < It *quadr(o)* < L *quadr(um)* a square]

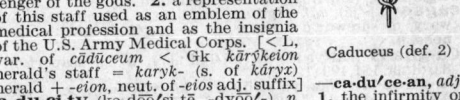

ca·du·ce·us (kə do͞o′sē əs, dyo͞o′-), *n.*, *pl.* **-ce·i** (-sē ī′). **1.** *Class. Myth.* the staff carried by Mercury as messenger of the gods. **2.** a representation of this staff used as an emblem of the medical profession and as the insignia of the U.S. Army Medical Corps. [< L, var. of *cādūceum* < Gk *kārȳkeion* herald's staff = *karyk-* (s. of *kāryx*) herald + *-eion*, neut. of *-eios* adj. suffix] —**ca·du′ce·an,** *adj.*

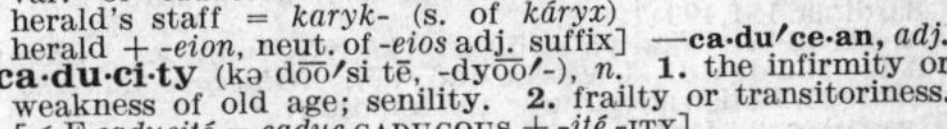
Caduceus (def. 2)

ca·du·ci·ty (kə do͞o′si tē, -dyo͞o′-), *n.* **1.** the infirmity or weakness of old age; senility. **2.** frailty or transitoriness. [< F *caducité* = *caduc* CADUCOUS + *-ité* -ITY]

ca·du·cous (kə do͞o′kəs, -dyo͞o′-), *adj.* **1.** *Bot.* **a.** tending to fall. **b.** dropping off very early, as leaves; deciduous. **2.** *Zool.* subject to shedding. **3.** transitory. [< L *cadūcus* destined to fall, perishable = *cad(ere)* (to) fall + *-ūcus* adj. suffix]

cae·cil·i·an (sē sil′ē ən), *n.* any wormlike, almost blind, tropical amphibian of the order *Apoda*, certain of which have small scales embedded in the skin. [< L *caecili(a)* a kind of lizard + -AN]

cae·cum (sē′kəm), *n.*, *pl.* **-ca** (-kə). cecum. —**cae′cal,** *adj.* —**cae′cal·ly,** *adv.*

Cæd·mon (kad′mən), *n.*, fl. A.D. c670, Anglo-Saxon religious poet.

Cae·li·an (sē′lē ən), *n.* one of the seven hills on which ancient Rome was built.

Caen (kän; *Fr.* käɴ), *n.* a city in NW France, SW of Le Havre. 95,238 (1962).

Caer·le·on (kär lē′ən), *n.* a town in S Monmouthshire, in SE Wales: site of ancient Roman fortress, a supposed seat of King Arthur's court. 4184 (1961).

Caer·nar·von (kär när′vən), *n.* **1.** a seaport in and the county seat of Caernarvonshire, in NW Wales, on Menai Strait: 13th-century castle of Edward II. 9225 (1961). **2.** Caernarvonshire. Also, **Carnarvon.**

Caer·nar·von·shire (kär när′vən shēr′, -shər), *n.* a county in NW Wales. 121,194 (1961); 569 sq. mi. *Co. seat:* Caernarvon. Also, **Carnarvonshire.** Also called **Caernarvon, Carnarvon.**

caes·al·pin·i·a·ceous (sez′al pin′ē ā′shəs, ses′-), *adj.* belonging to the *Caesalpiniaceae*, a family of leguminous plants including the honey locust, royal poinciana, Kentucky coffee tree, etc. [< NL *Caesalpini(a)* name of the genus (named after Andrea *Caesalpino* (1519–1603), Italian botanist; see -IA) + -ACEOUS]

Cae·sar (sē′zər), *n.* **1.** a title of the Roman emperors from Augustus to Hadrian. **2.** any emperor. **3.** a tyrant or dictator. **4.** any temporal ruler, in contrast with God; the civil authority. Matt. 22:21. **5. Ga·ius** (gā′əs) (or **Ca·ius**) (kā′əs) **Julius,** c100–44 B.C., Roman general, statesman, and historian.

Caes·a·re·a (ses′ə rē′ə, sez′-), *n.* **1.** an ancient seaport in NW Israel: Roman capital of Palestine. **2.** ancient name of **Kayseri.**

Cae·sar·e·an (si zâr′ē ən), *adj.* **1.** pertaining to Caesar or the Caesars: *a Caesarean conquest.* —*n.* **2.** (*sometimes l.c.*) See **Caesarean section.** Also, **Cae·sar′i·an, Cesarean, Cesarian.**

Caesar′ean sec′tion, a method of delivery by operation, in which a fetus is taken from the uterus by cutting through the walls of the abdomen and uterus. Also, **caesar′ean sec′tion.** [so called because CAESAR was supposedly born this way; but cf. ML *sectio caesaria*]

Cae·sar·ism (sē′zə riz′əm), *n.* absolute government; imperialism. —**Cae′sar·ist,** *n.*

cae·si·um (sē′zē əm), *n.* *Chem.* cesium.

caes·pi·tose (ses′pi tōs′), *adj.* cespitose.

cae·su·ra (si zho͝or′ə, -zo͝or′ə, siz yo͝or′ə), *n.*, *pl.* **cae·su·ras, cae·su·rae** (si zho͝or′ē, -zo͝or′ē, siz yo͝or′ē). **1.** *Pros.* a break, esp. a sense pause, usually near the middle of a verse, and marked in scansion by a double vertical line, as in *know then thyself ‖ presume not God to scan.* **2.** *Class. Pros.* a division made by the ending of a word within a foot, or sometimes at the end of a foot, esp. in certain recognized places near the middle of a verse. Also, **cesura.** [< L = *caes(us)* cut (ptp. of *caedere*) (*caed-* cut + *-tus* ptp. suffix) + *-ūra* -URE] —**cae·su′ral,** *adj.*

Ca·e·ta·no (kä e tä′nô), *n.* **Mar·ce·lo** (mär se′lô), born 1906, Portuguese premier 1968–74.

ca·fé (ka fā′, kə-; *Fr.* kȧ fā′), *n.*, *pl.* **-fés** (-fāz′; *Fr.* -fā′). **1.** a restaurant, usually small and unpretentious. **2.** a barroom, cabaret, or night club. **3.** coffee. Also, **ca·fe′.** [< F: lit., COFFEE]

ca·fé au lait (kaf′ā ō lā′, ka fā′; *Fr.* kȧ fā′ ō le′), **1.**

hot coffee poured in equal portions with scalded milk. **2.** light brown. [< F: lit., coffee with milk]

café noir (kA fā′ nwAR′), *French.* black coffee. Also called **ca·fé na·ture** (kA fā′ nA tYR′).

ca′fé soci′ety, the group of socialites regularly frequenting fashionable night clubs, resorts, etc.

caf·e·te·ri·a (kaf′i tēr′ē ə), *n. U.S.* a restaurant in which the patrons wait on themselves, carrying their food to their tables from counters where it is displayed and served. [< AmerSp *cafetería* coffee shop]

caf·feine (ka fēn′, kaf′ēn, kaf′ē in), *n. Chem., Pharm.* a bitter alkaloid, $C_8H_{10}N_4O_2$, usually obtained from coffee or tea: used chiefly as a stimulant and diuretic. [< F *caféine* = *café* COFFEE + *-ine* -INE[2]] **—caf·fein·ic** (ka fē′nik, kaf′ē-in′ik), *adj.*

caf·tan (kaf′tən, käf tän′), *n.* (in the Near East) a long coatlike garment tied at the waist with a sash. Also, **kaftan.** [< Russ *kaftan* < Turk < Pers *qaftān*]

cage (kāj), *n., v.,* **caged, cag·ing.** **—***n.* **1.** a boxlike receptacle or enclosure having wires, bars, or the like, for confining and displaying birds or animals. **2.** anything that confines or imprisons; prison. **3.** any enclosure like a cage in structure, as for a cashier, an elevator in a mine, etc. **4.** any skeleton framework. **5.** *Ordn.* a steel framework for supporting guns. **6.** *Baseball.* a movable backstop for use mainly in batting practice. **7.** the goal in hockey. **—***v.t.* **8.** to put or confine in or as in a cage. [ME < OF < L *cavea* birdcage = *cav(us)* hollow + *-ea,* fem. of *-eus* adj. suffix]

Cage (kāj), *n.* **John,** born 1912, U.S. composer.

cage·ling (kāj′ling), *n.* a caged bird.

cage·y (kā′jē), *adj.* **cag·i·er, cag·i·est.** *Informal.* cautious, wary, or shrewd: *a cagey reply.* **—cag′i·ly,** *adv.* **—cag′i·ness,** *n.*

Ca·glia·ri (käl′yə rē; *It.* kä′lyä RE′), *n.* a seaport in S Sardinia. 181,499 (1961).

Ca·glios·tro (kal yō′strō; *It.* kä lyôs′tRō), *n.* **Count A·les·san·dro di** (ä′les sän′dRō dē), (*Giuseppe Balsamo*), 1743–95, Italian adventurer and impostor.

Ca·guas (kä′gwäs), *n.* a city in E central Puerto Rico. 63,215 (1970).

ca·hier (ka yā′, kä-; *Fr.* kA yā′), *n., pl.* **-hiers** (-yāz′; *Fr.* -yā′). **1.** *Bookbinding.* a number of sheets of paper or leaves of a book placed together, as for binding. **2.** a report of proceedings, esp. of a legislative body. **3.** (*italics.*) *French.* a notebook, exercise book, or journal. [< F; MF *quaer* gathering (of sheets of a book); see QUIRE]

ca·hoot (kə ho͞ot′), *n. U.S. Slang.* **1. go cahoots,** to share equally; become partners: *They went cahoots in the establishment of the store.* Also, **go in cahoot with, go in cahoots. 2. in cahoot or cahoots, a.** in partnership; in league. **b.** in conspiracy: *in cahoots with the enemy.* [perh. < F *cahute* cabin, hut, b. *cabane* CABIN + *hutte* HUT]

CAI, computer-assisted instruction.

Cai·a·phas (kā′ə fəs, kī′-), *n.* a high priest of the Jews from sometime before A.D. 37 who presided at the Sanhedrin that condemned Jesus to death.

Cai′cos Is′lands (kī′kōs). See **Turks and Caicos Islands.**

ca·id (kä ēth′, kīth), *n.* **1.** (in North Africa) a Muslim tribal chief, judge, or senior official. **2.** a Berber chieftain. **3.** an alcaide. Also, **qaid.** [< Sp *caíd* < Ar *qā'id.* See ALCAIDE]

cai·man (kā′mən), *n., pl.* **-mans.** any of several tropical American crocodilians of the genus *Caiman* and allied genera, related to the alligators. Also, **cayman.** [< Sp *caimán* < Carib]

Cain (kān), *n.* **1.** the first son of Adam and Eve, who murdered his brother Abel. Gen. 4. **2. raise Cain,** *Slang.* to behave in a boisterous manner; cause a disturbance.

Cain·gang (kīn′gang′), *n., pl.* **-gangs,** (*esp. collectively*) **-gang. 1.** a member of an Indian people of southern Brazil. **2.** a family of languages spoken by the Caingang. Also, **Kaingang.**

ca·ïque (kä ēk′), *n.* **1.** a long, narrow rowboat used on the Bosporus. **2.** a single-masted sailing vessel used on the eastern Mediterranean Sea, having a sprit mainsail, a square topsail, and two or more other sails. Also, **ca·ique′.** [< F < It *caicc(o)* < Turk *kayık;* r. *caik* < Turk *kayık*]

caird (kârd; *Scot.* kārd), *n. Scot.* **1.** a traveling tinker, esp. a gypsy. **2.** a wandering tramp or vagrant. [< Gael *ceard* tinker; akin to L *cerdo* workman, Gk *kerdō* cunning one]

Caird (kârd), *n.* **Edward,** 1835–1908, Scottish philosopher and theologian.

cairn (kârn), *n.* a heap of stones set up as a landmark, monument, tombstone, etc. Also, **carn.** [ME (north) *carn* < Gael: pile of stones; perh. akin to HORN] **—cairn′y,** *adj.*

cairn·gorm (kârn′gôrm′), *n. Mineral.* See **smoky quartz.** Also called **Cairn′gorm stone′.** [after *Cairngorm,* name of Scottish mountain, its source]

Cairns (kârnz), *n.* a seaport in NE Australia. 25,204 (1961).

cairn′ ter′rier, one of a Scottish breed of small, short-legged terriers having a rough coat. [said to be so called because they frequent areas abounding in cairns]

Cai·ro (kī′rō *for 1;* kâr′ō *for 2*), *n.* **1.** a city in and the capital of the Arab Republic of Egypt, in the N part on the E bank of the Nile. 5,517,000. **2.** a city in S Illinois at the confluence of the Mississippi and Ohio rivers. 6277 (1970).

cais·son (kā′sən, -son), *n.* **1.** a structure used in underwater work, consisting of an airtight chamber, open at the bottom and containing air under sufficient pressure to exclude the water. **2.** *Naut.* **a.** a float for raising a sunken vessel. **b.** a watertight structure built against a damaged area of a hull to render the hull watertight; cofferdam. **3.** a two-wheeled ammunition wagon, esp. for the artillery. **4.** (formerly) a wooden chest containing bombs or explosives, used as a mine. [< F = *caisse* box (see CASE[2]) + *-on* aug. suffix]

cais′son disease′, *Pathol.* a condition marked by paralysis, pain, etc., developed in coming from an atmosphere of high pressure, as in a caisson, to air of ordinary pressure, and caused by the formation in the blood of bubbles of nitrogen released from solution; bends.

Caith·ness (kāth′nes, kāth nes′), *n.* a county in NE Scotland. 27,345 (1961); 686 sq. mi. *Co. seat:* Wick.

cai·tiff (kā′tif), *Archaic.* **—***n.* **1.** a base, despicable person. **—***adj.* **2.** base or despicable. [ME *caitif* < AF < L *captīv(us)* CAPTIVE]

Ca·ius (kā′əs), *n.* **1.** Also, **Gaius. Saint,** died A.D. 296, pope 283–296. **2.** Gaius (def. 1).

ca·jole (kə jōl′), *v.t., v.i.,* **-joled, -jol·ing.** to persuade by flattery or promises; wheedle. [< F *cajol(er),* lit., to chatter like a jaybird, appar. = **cajole* birdcage (< LL *caveol(a)* = L *cave(a)* CAGE + *-ola* dim. suffix) + *-er* inf. suffix] **—ca·jole′ment,** *n.* **—ca·jol′er,** *n.* **—ca·jol′ing·ly,** *adv.*

ca·jol·er·y (kə jō′lə rē), *n., pl.* **-er·ies.** persuasion by flattery or promises; wheedling; coaxing. [< F *cajolerie*]

Ca·jun (kā′jən), *n.* **1.** *Dial.* Acadian. **2.** the French dialect of the Acadians. [aph. var. of ACADIAN; cf. *Injun* for INDIAN]

caj·u·put (kaj′ə pət, -po͝ot′), *n.* **1.** an Australian, myrtaceous tree or shrub, *Melaleuca Leucadendron,* having lanceolate, aromatic leaves. **2.** *Pharm.* a green, odorous oil distilled from the leaves of this tree, used for skin conditions, toothaches, and various intestinal disorders. [< Malay *kaju-puteh* = *kaju* (sp. var. of *kayu*) wood + *puteh* white]

cake (kāk), *n., v.,* **caked, cak·ing. —***n.* **1.** a sweet, baked, breadlike food, made with or without shortening and usually containing flour, sugar, baking powder or soda, eggs, and liquid flavoring. **2.** a flat, thin mass of bread, esp. unleavened bread. **3.** a pancake or griddlecake. **4.** a shaped or molded mass of other food: *a fish cake.* **5.** a shaped or compressed mass: *a cake of soap.* **6. take the cake,** *Informal.* to surpass all others, esp. in brashness, stupidity, or the like. **—***v.t.* **7.** to form into a crust or compact mass. **—***v.i.* **8.** to form a crust or compact mass. [ME < Scand; cf. Icel *kaka;* akin to ME *kechel* little cake, G *Kuchen.* See COOKY]

cakes′ and ale′, the good things of life; material pleasures; enjoyment.

cake·walk (kāk′wôk′), *n.* **1.** a promenade or march, of American Negro origin, in which the couples performing the most intricate or eccentric steps receive cakes as prizes. **2.** a dance based on this promenade. **—***v.i.* **3.** to walk or dance in or as in a cakewalk. **—cake′walk′er,** *n.*

Cal., **1.** California. **2.** *Physics.* calorie (def. 1a).

cal., **1.** caliber. **2.** *Physics.* calorie (def. 1b).

Cal·a·bar (kal′ə bär′, kal′ə bär′), *n.* **1.** a river in SE Nigeria. ab. 70 mi. long. **2.** a seaport near the mouth of this river. 46,705 (1953).

Cal′abar bean′, the violently poisonous seed of a fabaceous African climbing plant, *Physostigma venenosum,* the active principle of which is physostigmine. [named after CALABAR, Nigeria]

cal·a·bash (kal′ə bash′), *n.* **1.** any of various gourds, esp. the fruit of the bottle gourd, *Lagenaria Siceraria.* **2.** any of the plants bearing them. **3.** the fruit of a bignoniaceous tree, *Crescentia Cujete,* of tropical America. **4.** Also called **cal′abash tree′.** the tree itself. **5.** the dried, hollow shell of the fruit of the calabash, used as a container. **6.** *U.S.* a gourd used as a rattle, drum, etc., esp. by Indians. [< MF *calabasse* < Sp *calabaz(a)* < Catalan *carabaça* < Ar *qar'ah yābisah* gourd (that is) dry]

cal·a·boose (kal′ə bo͞os′, kal′ə bo͞os′), *n. Informal.* jail; lockup. [< Creole F, alter. of Sp *calabozo* dungeon < ?]

Ca·la·bri·a (kə lā′brē ə; *It.* kä lä′bRyä), *n.* **1.** a region in S Italy. 2,045,215 (1961); 5828 sq. mi. *Cap.:* Reggio Calabria. **2.** an ancient district at the extreme SE part of the Italian peninsula. **—Ca·la′bri·an,** *n., adj.*

ca·la·di·um (kə lā′dē əm), *n.* any araceous plant of the genus *Caladium,* mostly herbs of the American tropics, cultivated for their variegated, colorful leaves. [< NL < Malay *kaladi* araceous plant + -IUM]

Cal·ais (kal′ā, kal′is; *Fr.* kA le′), *n.* a seaport in N France, on the Strait of Dover: the French port nearest England. 70,707 (1962).

cal·a·man·co (kal′ə mang′kō), *n.* a glossy woolen fabric checkered or brocaded in the warp so that the pattern shows on one side only, much used in the 18th century. [alter. of AmerSp *calamaco,* perh. < Araucan *kelü* red + *mákuñ* poncho]

cal·a·man·der (kal′ə man′dər), *n.* the hard wood of a tree, *Diospyros quaesita,* of Ceylon and India, used for cabinetwork. [metathetic var. of COROMANDEL]

cal·a·mar·y (kal′ə mer′ē, -mə rē), *n., pl.* **-mar·ies.** a squid, esp. of the genus *Loligo.* Also, **cal·a·mar** (kal′ə mär′). [< L *calamāri(us)* pertaining to a writing reed. See CALAMUS, -ARY]

cal·a·mine (kal′ə mīn′, -min), *n.* **1.** a powder consisting of zinc oxide and about 0.5 percent ferric oxide, used in skin ointments, lotions, etc. **2.** *Mineral.* hemimorphite. **3.** *Chiefly Brit.* smithsonite (def. 1). [< ML *calamīn(a),* unexplained alter. of L *cadmia* CADMIUM]

cal·a·mint (kal′ə mint), *n.* any labiate plant of the genus *Satureja,* esp. *S. Calaminthe* or *S. Nepeta.* [m. (by assoc. with MINT[2]) ME *calament* < ML *calament(um),* L *calaminth(a)* < Gk *kalaminthē*]

cal·a·mite (kal′ə mīt′), *n.* a Paleozoic fossil plant. [< NL *Calamīte(s)* name of the genus < Gk *kalamítēs* reedlike. See CALAMUS, -ITE[1]] **—cal·a·mi·te·an** (kal′ə mī′tē ən), *adj.* **—ca·lam·i·toid** (kə lam′i toid′), *adj.*

ca·lam·i·tous (kə lam′i təs), *adj.* causing or involving calamity; disastrous: *a calamitous defeat.* **—ca·lam′i·tous·ly,** *adv.* **—ca·lam′i·tous·ness,** *n.*

ca·lam·i·ty (kə lam′i tē), *n., pl.* **-ties. 1.** grievous affliction; adversity; misery. **2.** a great misfortune; disaster. [late ME *calamite* < MF < L *calamitāt-* (s. of *calamitās*), perh. akin to *incolumitās* safety] **—Syn. 1.** hardship. **2.** catastrophe, mishap. See **disaster.**

Calam′ity Jane′, (*Martha Jane Canary Burke*) 1852?–1903, U.S. frontier markswoman.

cal·a·mon·din (kal′ə mun′dən), *n.* **1.** a small citrus tree, *Citrus mitis,* of the Philippines. **2.** the small, tart mandarinlike fruit of this tree. Also called **cal′amondin or′ange.** [< Tagalog *kalamunding*]

cal·a·mus (kal′ə məs), *n., pl.* **-mi** (-mī′). **1.** the sweet flag, *Acorus Calamus.* **2.** its aromatic root. **3.** any palm of the genus *Calamus,* yielding rattan, canes, etc. **4.** the hollow base of a feather; quill. [< L < Gk *kálamos* reed, stalk]

Ca·la·pan (kä′lä pän′), *n.* a seaport on NE Mindoro, in the central Philippines. 33,060 (1960).

ca·lash (kə lash′), *n.* **1.** Also, **calèche.** a light, two-wheeled, horse-drawn carriage having inside seats for two passengers, an outside seat for the driver, and, usually, a folding top. **2.** a folding top of a carriage. **3.** a bonnet resembling the top of a calash, worn by women in the 18th century. [< F *calèche* < G *Kalesche* < Czech *kolesa* carriage, lit., something with wheels; see WHEEL]

Calash

cal·a·ver·ite (kal′ə vâr′īt), *n.* a silver-white mineral, gold telluride, $AuTe_2$, containing a little silver: an ore of gold. [*Calaver(as)*, county in California where first found; see -ITE[1]]

calc-, **1.** a combining form of **calcareous:** *calc-tufa.* **2.** var. of **calci-** before a vowel: *calcic; calcium.* [< G *Kalk* lime < L *calc-* (s. of *calx*) lime(stone); see CALX, CHALK]

cal·ca·ne·um (kal kā′nē əm), *n., pl.* **-ne·a** (-nē ə). calcaneus. [short for L *(os) calcāneum* (bone) of the heel = *calc-* (s. of *calx*) *heel* + *-āneum,* neut. of *-āneus;* see -AN, -EOUS]

cal·ca·ne·us (kal kā′nē əs), *n., pl.* **-ne·i** (-nē ī′). **1.** the largest tarsal bone in man, forming the prominence of the heel. **2.** the corresponding bone in other vertebrates. [< LL: heel, n. use of *calcāneus* of the heel. See CALCANEUM] —**cal·ca′ne·al, cal·ca′ne·an,** *adj.*

cal·car (kal′kär), *n., pl.* **cal·car·i·a** (kal-kâr′ē ə). *Biol.* a spur or spurlike process. [< L: spur = *calc-* (s. of *calx*) heel + *-ar* -AR[2]]

cal·ca·rate (kal′kə rāt′), *adj.* *Biol.* having a calcar or calcaria; spurred. Also, **cal′ca·rat′ed.**

Calcarate foot

cal·car·e·ous (kal kâr′ē əs), *adj.* of, containing, or like calcium carbonate; chalky: *calcareous earth.* [var. of *calcarious* < L *calcārius* of lime; see CALX, -ARIOUS] —**cal·car′e·ous·ly,** *adv.* —**cal·car′e·ous·ness,** *n.*

cal·ce·i·form (kal′sē ə fôrm′, kal sē′-), *adj.* *Bot.* calceolate. [< L *calce(us)* shoe, half-boot + -I- + -FORM]

cal·ce·o·lar·i·a (kal′sē ə lâr′ē ə), *n.* any plant of the genus *Calceolaria,* often cultivated for its slipperlike flowers. [< L *calceol(us)* small shoe (*calce(us)* shoe + *-olus* dim. suffix) + -ARIA]

cal·ce·o·late (kal′sē ə lāt′), *adj.* *Bot.* having the form of a shoe or slipper, as the labellum of certain orchids. [< L *calceol(us)* a small shoe (*calce(us)* a shoe + *-olus* dim. suffix) + -ATE[1]]

cal·ces (kal′sēz), *n.* a pl. of **calx.**

Cal·chas (kal′kəs), *n.* *Class. Myth.* the chief soothsayer of the Greeks in the Trojan War.

calci-, a combining form of **calcium,** used with the meaning "calcium salt" or "calcite" in the formation of compound words: *calciferous.* Also, *esp. before a vowel,* **calc-.** [< L *calc-* (s. of *calx* lime; see CHALK) + -I-]

cal·cic (kal′sik), *adj.* pertaining to or containing lime or calcium.

cal·cif·er·ol (kal sif′ə rōl′, -rôl′, -rol′), *n.* *Biochem.* an unsaturated alcohol, $C_{28}H_{43}OH$, occurring in milk, fish-liver oils, etc., and used as a dietary supplement, and in the prevention and treatment of rickets. Also called **vitamin D_2.** [CALCIF(EROUS + ERGOST)EROL]

cal·cif·er·ous (kal sif′ər əs), *adj.* *Chem.* **1.** forming salts of calcium, esp. calcium carbonate. **2.** containing calcium carbonate.

cal·cif·ic (kal sif′ik), *adj.* *Zool., Anat.* making or converting into salt of lime or chalk.

cal·ci·fi·ca·tion (kal′sə fə kā′shən), *n.* **1.** a changing into lime. **2.** *Physiol.* the deposition of lime or insoluble salts of calcium and magnesium, as in a tissue. **3.** *Anat., Geol.* a calcified formation. **4.** a soil process in which the surface soil is supplied with calcium in such a way that the soil colloids are always close to saturation. **5.** the act of calcifying. **6.** the state of being calcified.

cal·ci·fy (kal′sə fī′), *v.t., v.i.,* **-fied, -fy·ing.** **1.** *Physiol.* to make or become calcareous or bony; harden by the deposit of calcium salts. **2.** to make or become rigid or inflexible, as in an intellectual or political position.

cal·ci·mine (kal′sə mīn′, -min), *n., v.,* **-mined, -min·ing.** —*n.* **1.** a white or tinted wash for walls, ceilings, etc. —*v.t.* **2.** to wash or cover with calcimine. Also, **kalsomine.** [CALCI- + (KALSO)MINE]

cal·cine (kal′sīn, -sin), *v.t., v.i.,* **-cined, -cin·ing.** **1.** to convert or be converted into calx by heat. **2.** to burn to a friable substance; roast. **3.** to oxidize by heating. **4.** to frit. [ME < ML *calcināre* to heat, orig. used by alchemists] —**cal·ci·na·tion** (kal′sə nā′shən), *n.* —**cal·cin·a·to·ry** (kal sin′ə tōr′ē, -tôr′ē, kal′sin ə-), *adj., n.*

cal·cite (kal′sīt), *n.* one of the commonest minerals, calcium carbonate, $CaCO_3$, occurring in crystalline forms and a major constituent of limestone, marble, and chalk. —**cal·cit·ic** (kal sit′ik), *adj.*

cal·ci·um (kal′sē əm), *n.* *Chem.* a silver-white divalent metal, occurring combined in limestone, chalk, gypsum, etc. *Symbol:* Ca; *at. wt.:* 40.08; *at. no.:* 20; *sp. gr.:* 1.52 at 20°C.

cal′cium car′bide, *Chem.* a powder, CaC_2, usually derived from coke or anthracite: used chiefly for the generation of acetylene, which it yields upon decomposing in water. Also called **carbide.**

cal′cium car′bonate, *Chem.* a powder, $CaCO_3$, occurring in nature in various forms, as calcite, chalk, and limestone: used chiefly in dentifrices, polishes, and in the manufacture of lime and cement.

cal′cium chlo′ride, *Chem.* a deliquescent solid, $CaCl_2$, usually derived from calcium carbonate: used chiefly as a drying agent and for preventing dust.

cal′cium cyan′amide, *Chem.* a powder, CaNCN, used chiefly as a fertilizer, as an herbicide, and in the synthesis of nitrogen compounds; cyanamide.

cal′cium cyc′la·mate (sik′lə māt′, sī′klə-), *Chem.* a powder, $(C_6H_{11}NHSO_3)_2Ca \cdot 2H_2O$, used chiefly as a sweetening agent in soft drinks. Cf. **soldium cyclamate.**

cal′cium hydrox′ide, *Chem.* See **slaked lime.** Also called **cal′cium hy′drate.**

cal′cium light′, a brilliant white light produced by heating lime to incandescence in an oxyhydrogen or other hot flame; limelight. Also called **oxycalcium light.**

cal′cium ni′trate, *Chem.* a solid, $Ca(NO_3)_2$, used chiefly in the manufacture of fertilizers, matches, and explosives. Also called **Norwegian saltpeter.**

cal′cium ox′ide, *Chem.* lime[1] (def. 1).

cal′cium phos′phate, *Chem.* any of several phosphates of calcium occurring naturally in some rocks and in animal bones.

cal′cium pro′pionate, *Chem.* a powder, $Ca(CH_3CH_2COO)_2$, used in bakery products to inhibit the growth of fungi.

calc-sin·ter (kalk′sin′tər), *n.* *Mineral.* travertine. [< G *Kalksinter.* See CALC-, SINTER]

calc-tu·fa (kalk′tōō′fə), *n.* tufa (def. 1). Also, **calc-tuff** (kalk′tuf′).

cal·cu·la·ble (kal′kyə lə bəl), *adj.* **1.** determinable by calculation or computation. **2.** reliable or trustworthy. [< L *calculā(re)* (to) reckon + -BLE] —**cal′cu·la·bil′i·ty,** *n.* —**cal′cu·la·bly,** *adv.*

cal·cu·late (kal′kyə lāt′), *v.,* **-lat·ed, -lat·ing.** —*v.t.* **1.** to ascertain by mathematical methods; compute. **2.** to determine by reasoning, common sense, or practical experience; estimate. **3.** to make suitable or fit for a purpose; adapt (usually used passively and with an infinitive): *a remark calculated to inspire confidence.* **4.** *Chiefly Northern U.S.* **a.** to think; guess. **b.** to intend; plan. —*v.i.* **5.** to make a computation; form an estimate. **6.** to count or rely (usually fol. by *on* or *upon*). [< L *calculāt(us)* reckoned (ptp. of *calculāre*) = *calcul(us)* pebble (see CALCULUS) + *-ātus* -ATE[1]] —**Syn. 1.** count, figure, cast, estimate, weigh.

cal·cu·lat·ed (kal′kyə lā′tid), *adj.* **1.** arrived at by mathematical calculation. **2.** carefully thought out or planned. —**cal′cu·lat′ed·ly,** *adv.*

cal·cu·lat·ing (kal′kyə lā′ting), *adj.* **1.** capable of performing calculations. **2.** shrewd or cautious. **3.** selfishly scheming. —**cal′cu·lat′ing·ly,** *adv.*

cal′culating machine′, calculator (def. 2).

cal·cu·la·tion (kal′kyə lā′shən), *n.* **1.** the act or process of calculating; computation. **2.** the result or product of calculating: *His calculations agree with ours.* **3.** an estimate based on the various facts in a case; forecast. **4.** forethought; prior or careful planning. **5.** scheming selfishness. [< L *calculātiōn-* (s. of *calculātiō* reckoning)] —**cal·cu·la·tive** (kal′kyə lā′tiv, -lə tiv), *adj.* —**Syn. 1.** figuring, reckoning.

cal·cu·la·tor (kal′kyə lā′tər), *n.* **1.** a person who calculates or computes. **2.** Also called **calculating machine.** a machine that performs mathematical operations. **3.** a person who operates such a machine. **4.** a set of tables that facilitates calculation. [< L]

cal·cu·lous (kal′kyə ləs), *adj.* *Pathol.* characterized by the presence of calculus or stone. [< L *calculōs(us)* = *calcul(us)* small stone (see CALCULUS) + *-ōsus* -OUS]

cal·cu·lus (kal′kyə ləs), *n., pl.* **-li** (-lī′), **-lus·es.** **1.** *Math.* a method of calculation, esp. one of several highly systematic methods of treating problems by a special system of algebraic notations, as differential or integral calculus. **2.** *Pathol.* a stone, or concretion, found in the gall bladder, kidneys, or other parts of the body. [< L: pebble, small stone (used in reckoning) = *calc-* (s. of *calx* stone) + *-ulus* -ULE]

Cal·cut·ta (kal kut′ə), *n.* a seaport in and the capital of West Bengal state, in E India, on the Hooghly River: former capital of British India. 3,003,556 (est. 1964).

Cal·der (kôl′dər), *n.* **Alexander,** 1898–1976, U.S. sculptor: originator of mobiles.

cal·de·ra (kal der′ə; *Sp.* käl de′rä), *n., pl.* **-de·ras** (-der′əz; *Sp.* -de′räs). a large, basinlike depression resulting from the explosion or collapse of the center of a volcano. [< Sp *Caldera,* name of a crater on Canary Islands, lit., CAULDRON]

Cal·de·rón de la Bar·ca (kol′dər ən del′ə bär′kə; *Sp.* käl′de rôn′ de lä bär′kä), **Pe·dro** (pā′drō, ped′ro; *Sp.* pe′thrō), 1600–81, Spanish dramatist and poet.

cal·dron (kôl′drən), *n.* cauldron.

Cald·well (kôld′wel, -wəl), *n.* **Erskine,** 1903–87, U.S. novelist.

Ca·leb (kā′ləb), *n.* a Hebrew leader, sent as a spy into Canaan. Num. 13:6.

ca·lèche (ka lesh′), *n., pl.* **-lèches** (-lesh′). calash (def. 1).

Cal·e·do·ni·a (kal′i dō′nē ə), *n.* *Chiefly Literary.* Scotland. —**Cal′e·do′ni·an,** *n., adj.*

Caledo′nian Canal′, a canal in N Scotland, extending NE from the Atlantic to the North Sea. 60½ mi. long.

cal·e·fa·cient (kal′ə fā′shənt), *adj.* providing heat or warmth. [< L *calefacient-* (s. of *calefaciēns,* prp. of *calefacere* to make warm) = *cale-* warm (s. of *calēre* to be warm) + *-facient-* -FACIENT] —**cal·e·fac·tion** (kal′ə fak′shən), *n.*

cal·e·fac·to·ry (kal′ə fak′tə rē), *adj., n., pl.* **-ries.** —*adj.* **1.** serving to heat. —*n.* **2.** a parlor or sitting room in a monastery. [< L *calefactōri(us)* having a warming or heating power = *calefact(us)* made warm or hot, heated (ptp. of *calefacere* to make warm) + *-ōrius* -ORY[1]]

cal·en·dar (kal′ən dər), *n.* **1.** any of various systems of reckoning the beginning, length, and divisions of the year: *the Aztec calendar.* Cf. **Gregorian calendar, Jewish calendar, Julian calendar.** **2.** a tabular arrangement of the days, weeks, and months in a year. **3.** a list or register, esp. one arranged chronologically, of appointments, work to be done, or matters to be considered, as of the cases to be tried in a court or of bills to be considered by a legislature. —*v.t.* **4.** to enter in a calendar; register. [< L *calendār(ium)* account book = *Calend(ae)* CALENDS (when debts were due) + *-ārium* -AR[2]; r. ME *calender* < AF] —**ca·len·dri·cal** (kə len′dri kəl), **ca·len′dric,** *adj.*

cal′endar day′, the period from one midnight to the following midnight.

cal′endar year′. See under **year** (def. 1).

cal·en·der (kal′ən dər), *n.* **1.** a machine in which cloth, paper, or the like, is smoothed, glazed, etc., by pressing between revolving cylinders. —*v.t.* **2.** to press in a calender. [< ML *calendr(a)*, alter. of L *cylindrus* CYLINDER] —**cal′en·der·er,** *n.*

cal·ends (kal′əndz), *n.* (*usually construed as pl.*) the first day of the month in the ancient Roman calendar. Also, **kalends.** Cf. **ides.** [ME *kalendes* < L *kalendae* = *cal-* (base of *calāre* to proclaim) + *-end-* formative suffix + *-ae* pl. ending; r. OE *calend* beginning of a month < L]

ca·len·du·la (kə len′jə lə), *n.* **1.** any asteraceous plant of the genus *Calendula,* esp. *C. officinalis,* a common marigold. **2.** the dried florets of this plant, used in medicine for healing wounds. [< ML = L *calend(ae)* CALENDS + *-ula* -ULE]

cal·en·ture (kal′ən chər, -choor′), *n.* *Pathol.* a violent fever with delirium, affecting persons in the tropics. [earlier *calentura* < Sp: fever = *calent(ar)* (to) heat (< L *calent-,* s. of *calēns,* prp. of *calēre* to be hot) + *-ura* -URE]

ca·les·cent (kə les′ənt), *adj.* growing warm; increasing in heat. [< L *calescent-* (s. of *calescēns* becoming warm, prp. of *calescere*) = *cal-* (base of *calēre* to be warm) + *-escent-* -ESCENT] —**ca·les′cence,** *n.*

calf[1] (kaf, käf), *n., pl.* **calves** (kavz, kävz). **1.** the young of the domestic cow or of other bovine animals. **2.** the young of certain other mammals, as the elephant, seal, or whale. **3.** calfskin leather. **4.** *Informal.* an awkward, silly boy or man. **5.** a mass of ice detached from a glacier, iceberg, or floe. [ME; OE *cealf, calf;* c. OS *kalf,* Icel *kalfr,* OHG *kalb*]

calf[2] (kaf, käf), *n., pl.* **calves** (kavz, kävz). the fleshy part of the back of the human leg below the knee. [ME < Scand; cf. Icel *kalfi;* akin to CALF[1]]

calf's-foot jel′ly (kavz′foot′, kävz′-; kafs′foot′, käfs′-), jelly made from the stock of boiled calves' feet and flavoring.

calf·skin (kaf′skin′, käf′-), *n.* **1.** the skin or hide of a calf. **2.** leather made from this skin.

Cal·ga·ry (kal′gə rē), *n.* a city in S Alberta, in SW Canada. 249,641 (1961).

Cal·houn (kal hōōn′, kəl-), *n.* **John Caldwell,** 1782–1850, vice president of the U.S. 1825–32.

Ca·li (kä′lē), *n.* a city in SW Colombia. 639,900 (est. 1961).

Cal·i·ban (kal′ə ban′), *n.* an ugly, beastlike person. [after *Caliban,* in Shakespeare's comedy *The Tempest* (1611)]

cal·i·ber (kal′ə bər), *n.* **1.** the diameter of something of circular section, esp. that of the inside of a tube. **2.** *Ordn.* the diameter of the bore of a gun taken as a unit of measurement. **3.** degree of competence, merit, or importance: *a mathematician of high caliber; the high moral caliber of the era.* Also, *esp. Brit.,* **cal′i·bre.** [var. of *calibre* < MF < early It *calibro,* ? alter. of Ar *qālib* mold, last < Gk *kalópous* shoemaker's last = *kálo(n)* wood + *poús* foot] —**cal′i·bered;** *esp. Brit.,* **cal′i·bred,** *adj.*

cal·i·brate (kal′ə brāt′), *v.t.,* **-brat·ed, -brat·ing. 1.** to determine, check, or rectify the graduation of (any instrument giving quantitative measurements). **2.** to divide or mark with gradations, graduations, or other indexes of degree, quantity, etc., as on a thermometer or measuring cup. **3.** to determine the correct range for (an artillery gun, mortar, etc.) by observing where the fired projectile hits. —**cal′i·bra′tion,** *n.* —**cal′i·bra′tor, cal′i·brat′er,** *n.*

cal·i·ces (kal′i sēz′), *n.* pl. of **calix.**

ca·li·che (kə lē′chē), *n.* *Geol.* **1.** a surface deposit consisting of sand or clay impregnated with crystalline salts, such as sodium nitrate or sodium chloride. **2.** a zone of calcium or mixed carbonates in soils of semiarid regions. [< Sp: flake of lime = *cal* lime (< L *calc-;* see CHALK) + *-iche* n. suffix]

cal·i·co (kal′ə kō′), *n., pl.* **-coes, -cos,** *adj.* —*n.* **1.** a plain-woven cotton cloth printed with a figured pattern. **2.** *Brit.* plain white cotton cloth. **3.** *Obs.* a figured cotton cloth imported from India. —*adj.* **4.** made of calico. **5.** resembling printed calico; spotted. [short for *Calico cloth,* var. of *Calicut cloth,* named after city in India that orig. exported it]

cal′ico bass′ (bas), the black crappie. See under **crappie.**

cal′ico bush′, the mountain laurel, *Kalmia latifolia.*

cal′ico cat′, a domestic cat, esp. a female one, of variegated black, yellow, and white coloring. Also called **tortoise-shell cat.**

Cal·i·cut (kal′ə kut′), *n.* a city in W Kerala, in SW India. 192,500 (1961). Malayalam, **Kozhikode.**

cal·if (kal′if, kā′lif, kä lif′), *n.* caliph.

Calif., California.

cal·if·ate (kal′ə fāt′, -fit, kā′lə-), *n.* caliphate.

Cal·i·for·nia (kal′ə fôr′nyə, -fôr′nē ə), *n.* **1.** a state in the W United States, on the Pacific coast. 19,953,134 (1970); 158,693 sq. mi. *Cap.:* Sacramento. *Abbr.:* Calif., Cal., CA **2. Gulf of,** an arm of the Pacific, extending NW between the coast of W Mexico and the peninsula of Lower California. ab. 750 mi. long; 62,600 sq. mi. —**Cal′i·for′nian,** *adj., n.*

Cal′ifor′nia lau′rel, a lauraceous tree, *Umbellularia californica,* of the western coast of the U.S., having aromatic leaves and umbels of yellowish-green flowers.

Califor′nia live′ oak′, an evergreen oak, *Quercus agrifolia,* of the western coast of the U.S., having leathery leaves.

Califor′nia nut′meg, an evergreen tree, *Torreya californica,* of California, having a gray-brown bark and small, purple-streaked, light-green, egg-shaped fruit.

Cal′ifor′nia pop′py, a papaveraceous herb, *Eschscholtzia californica,* having showy, orange-yellow flowers: the state flower of California.

Califor′nia priv′et, a privet, *Ligustrum ovalifolium,* indigenous to Japan, widely used for hedges in the U.S.

Califor′nia rose′, a climbing plant, *Convolvulus japonicus,* of eastern Asia, having pink flowers two inches wide.

Cal′ifor′nia rose′bay. See **pink rhododendron.**

Cal′ifor′nia sea′ li′on. See under **sea lion.**

cal·i·for·ni·um (kal′ə fôr′nē əm), *n.* *Chem.* a synthetic, radioactive, metallic element. *Symbol:* Cf; *at no.:* 98. [named after the University of *California,* where it was discovered]

ca·lig·i·nous (kə lij′ə nəs), *adj.* *Archaic.* misty or dim; dark. [< L *cālīginōs(us)* misty = *cālīgin-* (s. of *cālīgō*) mist + *-ōsus* -OUS]

Ca·lig·u·la (kə lig′yə lə), *n.* (*Gaius Caesar*), A.D. 12–41, Roman emperor 37–41.

cal·i·pash (kal′ə pash′, kal′ə pash′), *n.* the part of a turtle next to the upper shield, a greenish gelatinous substance, considered a delicacy. Also, **callipash.** Cf. **calipee.** [?]

cal·i·pee (kal′ə pē′, kal′ə pē′), *n.* the part of a turtle next to the lower shield, a yellowish gelatinous substance, considered a delicacy. Cf. **calipash.** [?]

cal·i·per (kal′ə pər), *n.* **1.** Usually, **calipers.** an instrument for measuring thicknesses and internal or external diameters inaccessible to a scale, consisting usually of a pair of pivoted legs adjustable at any distance. **2.** any of various calibrated instruments for measuring thicknesses or distances between surfaces, usually having a screwed or sliding adjustable piece. **3.** thickness or three-dimensional depth. —*v.t.* **4.** to measure with calipers. Also, **calliper.** [var. of CALIBER]

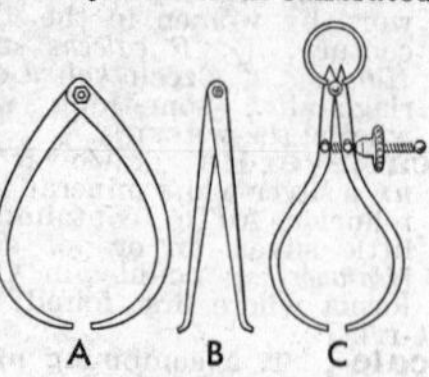

Calipers
A, Calipers for measuring external dimensions; B, For internal dimensions; C, Spring-adjusting calipers

ca·liph (kal′if, kā′lif, kä-lēf′), *n.* *Islam.* **1.** a spiritual leader of Islam, claiming succession from Muhammad. **2.** the former Muslim rulers of Baghdad (until 1258), and of the Ottoman Empire (from 1571 until 1924). Also, **calif, kalif, khalif.** [ME *caliphe,* etc. < MF < Ar *khalīf(a)* successor (of Muhammad) < *khalafa* succeed]

cal·iph·ate (kal′ə fāt′, -fit, kā′lə-), *n.* the rank, jurisdiction, or government of a caliph. Also, **califate, kalifate, khalifate.** [< ML *calīphāt(us)*]

cal·i·sa·ya (kal′i sā′yə), *n.* the medicinal bark of the tree *Cinchona Calisaya.* [< *Calisaya,* name of the Bolivian Indian who told the whites about its medicinal values]

cal·is·then·ics (kal′is then′iks), *n.* **1.** (*construed as sing.*) the practice or art of performing gymnastic exercises for health, strength, and grace. **2.** any such exercises. Also, **callisthenics.** [*cali-* (var. of CALLI-) + Gk *sthén(os)* strength + -ICS] —**cal′is·then′ic, cal′is·then′i·cal,** *adj.*

ca·lix (kā′liks, kal′iks), *n., pl.* **cal·i·ces** (kal′i sēz′). *Rom. Cath. Ch.* chalice (def. 2a). [< L]

Ca·lix·tus I (kə lik′stəs), **Saint,** A.D. c160–222, Italian ecclesiastic: pope 218–222.

Calixtus II, died 1124, French ecclesiastic: pope 1119–24.

Calixtus III, (*Alfonso de Borja* or *Alfonso Borgia*) 1378–1458, Spanish ecclesiastic: pope 1455–58.

calk[1] (kôk), *v.t.* caulk.

calk[2] (kôk), *n.* **1.** Also, **cal·kin** (kô′kin, kal′-). a projection on a horseshoe to prevent slipping on ice, pavement, etc. **2.** Also, **calker.** a similar device on the heel or sole of a shoe. —*v.t.* **3.** to provide with calks. **4.** to injure with a calk. [appar. < L *calc-* (s. of *calx*) spur, heel; cf. OE *calsrond* shod]

calk·er[1] (kô′kər), *n.* caulker.

calk·er[2] (kô′kər), *n.* calk[2] (def. 2). [CALK[2] + -ER[1]]

call (kôl), *v.t.* **1.** to cry out in a loud voice: *to call someone's name.* **2.** to ask or invite to come: *Will you call the family to dinner?* **3.** to read over (a roll or a list) in a loud voice. **4.** to attract (someone's attention) to something: *She tried not to call attention to herself.* **5.** to rouse from sleep, as by a call: *Call me at eight o'clock.* **6.** to telephone to: *Call me when you arrive.* **7.** to command or request to come; summon: *to call a dog; to call a cab.* **8.** to announce authoritatively; proclaim; order: *to call a halt.* **9.** to order into effect: *The union leader called a strike.* **10.** to summon to an office, duty, etc.: *His country called him to the colors.* **11.** to summon by or as by divine command. **12.** to cause to come; bring: *to call to mind; to call into existence.* **13.** to convoke or convene, as a meeting or assembly: *to call Congress into session.* **14.** to bring under consideration or discussion: *The judge called the case.* **15.** to attract or lure (birds or animals) by imitating the characteristic sounds of. **16.** *Informal.* **a.** to require (someone) to furnish evidence for a statement, fulfill a promise, etc.: *They called him on his story.* **b.** to criticize adversely; censure: *She called him on his vulgar language.* **17.** *Sports.* (of an official) **a.** to pronounce a judgment on (a shot, pitch, batter, etc.): *The umpire called the pitch a strike.* **b.** to put an end to (a contest) because of inclement weather, darkness, or the like: *to call the game because of rain.* **18.** to demand payment of (a loan). **19.** to demand presentation of (bonds) for redemption. **20.** to give a name to: *The boys call him Tex.* **21.** to designate as something specified: *He called me a liar.* **22.** to think of as something specified; consider: *I call that a mean remark.* **23.** *Cards.* **a.** to demand (a card). **b.** to demand of (a player) that he show his hand. **c.** *Poker.* to equal (a bet) or equal the bet made by (the preceding bettor) in a round. **d.** *Bridge.* to signal one's partner for a lead of (a certain card or suit). **24.** *Informal.* to forecast correctly. —*v.i.* **25.** to speak loudly, as to attract attention; shout. **26.** to make a short visit. **27.** to telephone a person: *He promised to call at noon.* **28.** *Cards.* **a.** to demand a card. **b.** to demand a showing of hands. **c.** *Poker.* to equal a bet. **d.** *Bridge.* to bid or pass. **29.** (of a bird or animal) to utter a characteristic cry. **30. call away,** to cause to leave or go; summon. **31. call back,** to summon or bring back; recall. **32. call down,** to request or pray for; invoke: *to call down the wrath of God.* **33. call for, a.** to go or come to get; pick up; fetch. **b.** to request or summon. **c.** to require, demand, or need: *The occasion calls for a cool head.* **34. call forth,** to summon into action; bring into existence. **35. call in, a.** to call for payment; collect. **b.** to withdraw from circulation: *to call in gold certificates.* **c.** to call upon for consultation; ask for help: *Two specialists were called in to assist in the operation.* **36. call off, a.** to distract; take away: *Please call off your dog.* **b.** *Informal.* to cancel: *The picnic was called off because of rain.* **37. call on** or **upon, a.** to require; appeal to: *They called on him to represent them.* **b.** to visit for a short time: *to call on friends.* **38. call out, a.** to speak in a loud voice; shout. **b.** to summon into service: *Call out the militia!* **39. call up, a.** to evoke. **b.** to communicate with by telephone. **c.** to summon for action or service: *to call up the reserves.* —*n.* **40.** a cry or shout. **41.** the cry of a bird or other animal. **42.** an instrument for imitating this cry and attracting or luring the animal. **43.** a summons or signal sounded by a bugle, bell, etc. **44.** *Fox Hunting.* any of several cries, or sounds made on a horn by the huntsman to encourage the hounds. **45.** a short visit: *to make a call on someone.* **46.** a summons, invitation, or bidding. **47.** *Theat.* a notice of rehearsal posted by the stage manager. **48.** a mystic experience of divine appointment to a vocation or service: *He had a call to become a minister.* **49.** the fascination or appeal of a given place, vocation, etc.: *the call of the sea.* **50.** a request or invitation to become pastor of a church, a professor in a university, etc. **51.** a need or occasion: *He had no call to say such things.* **52.** a demand or claim: *to make a call on a person's time.* **53.** a calling of a roll; roll call. **54.** the act or an instance of telephoning. **55.** *Cards.* **a.** a demand for a card or a showing of hands. **b.** *Poker.* an equaling of the preceding bet. **c.** *Bridge.* a bid or pass. **56.** *Sports.* a judgment or decision by an official. **57.** *Finance.* a contract that permits the holder to exercise an option to buy a certain amount of stock or a commodity at a set price within a given time. Cf. **put** (def. 43). **58.** a demand for payment of an obligation. **59. on call, a.** payable or subject to return without advance notice. **b.** (of a soldier, nurse, etc.) immediately available for duty. **60. within call,** within distance or range of being spoken to or summoned. [ME *call(en),* OE **callian* (Anglian dial.) < *-calla* herald; c. OE *ceallian* (WS dial.) to shout, MD *kallen* to talk, OHG *kallōn* to shout, Icel *kalla* to call out] —**Syn. 2, 7, 10.** CALL, INVITE, SUMMON imply requesting the presence or attendance of someone at a particular place. CALL is the general word: *to call a meeting.* To INVITE is to ask someone courteously to come as a guest, a participant, etc., leaving him free to refuse: *to invite guests to a concert; to invite them to contribute to a fund.* SUMMON implies sending for someone, using authority or formality in requesting his presence, and (theoretically) not leaving him free to refuse: *to summon a witness, members of a committee,* etc.

cal·la (kal′ə), *n.* **1.** any plant of the genus *Zantedeschia* (or *Richardia*), native to Africa, esp. *Z. aethiopicum* (**cal′la lil′y**), having a large white spathe enclosing a yellow spadix. **2.** an araceous plant, *Calla palustris,* of cold marshes of Europe and North America, having heart-shaped leaves. [< NL perh. special use of L *calla* a plant]

call·a·ble (kô′lə bəl), *adj.* **1.** capable of being called. **2.** subject to redemption prior to maturity, as a bond. **3.** subject to payment on demand, as a call loan.

Cal·la·ghan (kal′ə han′), *n.* **(Leonard) James,** born 1912, British statesman: prime minister 1976–79.

cal·lant (kä′lənt), *n. Scot. and North Eng.* a lad; boy. Also, **cal·lan** (kä′lən). [< D *kalant* fellow < ONF *caland* customer]

Ca·lla·o (kä yä′ō), *n.* a seaport in W Peru, near Lima. 161,286 (1961).

Cal·las (kal′əs), *n.* **Maria,** 1923–77, U.S. soprano.

call·back (kôl′bak′), *n.* recall (def. 10). [CALL + BACK[2]]

call′ box′, 1. an outdoor telephone or signal box for calling the police or fire department. **2.** *Brit.* a telephone booth.

call·boy (kôl′boi′), *n.* **1.** a boy or man who summons actors in time to go on stage. **2.** a bellboy.

call·er[1] (kô′lər), *n.* **1.** a person or thing that calls. **2.** a person who makes a short visit. [CALL + -ER[1]] —**Syn. 2.** See **visitor.**

cal·ler[2] (kal′ər, kä′lər), *adj. Scot. and North Eng.* (of fruit, fish, vegetables, etc.) fresh; recently picked or caught. [ME, north. var. of *calver* fresh, alive (said of fish) < ?]

Ca·lles (kä′yes), *n.* **Plu·tar·co E·lí·as** (plōō tär′kō e lē′äs), 1877–1945, Mexican general and statesman.

call′ girl′, a prostitute with whom an appointment can be arranged by telephone.

calli-, an element meaning "beautiful," occurring in loan words from Greek (*calligraphy*) and on this model used in forming compound words (*callisthenics*). [< Gk *kalli-* comb. form of *kállos* beauty, akin to *kalós* beautiful, fair]

cal·lig·ra·phy (kə lig′rə fē), *n.* **1.** beautiful handwriting; fine penmanship. **2.** handwriting or penmanship. **3.** fancy penmanship, esp. highly decorative handwriting, as with a great many flourishes. **4.** the art of writing beautifully: *He studied calligraphy when he was a young man.* [< Gk *kalligraphía* beautiful writing] —**cal·lig′ra·pher, cal·lig′ra·phist,** *n.* —**cal·li·graph·ic** (kal′ə graf′ik), **cal′li·graph′i·cal,** *adj.* —**cal′li·graph′i·cal·ly,** *adv.*

Cal·lim·a·chus (kə lim′ə kəs), *n.* c310–c240 B.C., Greek poet, grammarian, and critic.

call-in (kôl′in′), *Radio and Television.* —*n.* **1.** a telephone conversation, intended for broadcasting, between a host and a listener or viewer. —*adj.* **2.** of, pertaining to, or showing such a conversation or conversations: *a call-in program.*

call·ing (kô′ling), *n.* **1.** the act of a person or thing that calls. **2.** vocation, profession, or trade: *What is your calling?* **3.** a call or summons: *He had a calling to join the church.* **4.** a strong impulse or inclination: *He did it in response to an inner calling.* **5.** a convocation: *the calling of Congress.*

call′ing card′, *U.S.* a small card with the name and often the address of a person or couple, for presenting when making a visit, for enclosing in a present, etc. Also called **card;** *esp. Brit.,* **visiting card.**

cal·li·o·pe (kə lī′ə pē; *for 1 also* kal′ē ōp′), *n.* **1.** a musical instrument consisting of a set of harsh-sounding steam whistles that are activated by a keyboard. **2.** (*cap.*) *Class. Myth.* the Muse of heroic poetry. [< L < Gk *Kalliópē* = *kalli-* CALLI- + *op-* (s. of *óps*) voice + *-ē* fem. ending]

cal·li·op·sis (kal′ē op′sis), *n.* a coreopsis.

cal·li·pash (kal′ə pash′, kal′ə pash′), *n.* calipash.

cal·li·per (kal′ə pər), *n., v.t.* caliper. —**cal′li·per·er,** *n.*

cal·li·pyg·i·an (kal′ə pij′ē ən), *adj.* having well-shaped buttocks. Also, **cal·li·py·gous** (kal′ə pī′gəs). [< Gk *kallipýg(os)* with beautiful buttocks (referring to a statue of Aphrodite) = *kalli-* CALLI- + *pyg(ē)* rump + *-os* adj. suffix + -IAN]

cal·lis·then·ics (kal′is then′iks), *n.* calisthenics. —**cal′lis·then′ic,** *adj.*

Cal·lis·to (kə lis′tō), *n.* **1.** *Class. Myth.* a nymph attendant on Artemis, punished for a love affair with Zeus by being changed into a bear and slain by Artemis. **2.** *Astron.* one of the 12 satellites of Jupiter: about 3200 miles in diameter and the largest known satellite in the solar system.

call′ let′ters, *Radio and Television.* the identifying letters or letters and numbers of a broadcasting station.

call′ loan′, a loan repayable on demand. Cf. **time loan.**

call′ num′ber, *Library Science.* a number, frequently accompanied by a classification symbol and an author's designation, indicating the specific location of a book.

cal·los·i·ty (kə los′i tē), *n., pl.* **-ties. 1.** a callous condition. **2.** *Bot.* a hardened or thickened part of a plant. **3.** *Pathol.* callus (def. 1). [< LL *callōsitās.* See CALLOUS, -ITY]

cal·lous (kal′əs), *adj.* **1.** made hard; hardened. **2.** insensitive; indifferent; unsympathetic: *a callous person; a callous attitude.* **3.** having a callus; indurated, as parts of the skin exposed to friction. —*v.t., v.i.* **4.** to make or become hard or callous [< L *callōs(us)* hard-skinned, with a hard skin = *call(um)* hard, thick skin + *-ōsus* -OUS] —**cal′lous·ly,** *adv.* —**cal′lous·ness,** *n.* —**Syn. 1.** hard. **2.** inured. See **hard.** —**Ant. 1.** soft. **2.** sensitive.

cal·low (kal′ō), *adj.* **1.** immature or inexperienced: *a callow young man.* **2.** *Rare.* (of a young bird) featherless; unfledged. [ME, OE *calu* bald; c. D *kaal,* G *kahl* bald, OSlav *golŭ* bare] —**cal′low·ness,** *n.*

call′ rate′, interest charge on call loans.

call′ slip′, a printed form used by a library patron to request the use of a particular book.

call′ to quar′ters, *U.S. Army.* a bugle call summoning soldiers to their quarters.

call-up (kôl′up′), *n.* **1.** an order to report for active military service. **2.** the number of men drafted during a specific period of time.

cal·lus (kal′əs), *n., pl.* **-lus·es,** *v.,* **-lused, -lus·ing.** —*n.* **1.** *Pathol., Physiol.* **a.** a hardened or thickened part of the skin. **b.** a new growth of osseous matter uniting the ends of a fractured bone. **2.** *Bot.* protective tissue that forms over the wounds of plants. —*v.i.* **3.** to form a callus. —*v.t.* **4.** to produce a callus or calluses on. [< L, var. of *callum* hard, thick skin; see CALLOUS]

calm (käm), *adj.* **1.** without rough motion; still or nearly still: *a calm sea.* **2.** not windy: *a calm day.* **3.** free from excitement or passion; tranquil: *a calm face; a calm manner.* —*n.* **4.** freedom from motion or disturbance; stillness. **5.** absence of wind on the Beaufort scale. **6.** freedom from agitation, excitement, etc.; tranquillity; serenity. —*v.t.* **7.** to make calm. —*v.i.* **8.** to become calm (usually fol. by *down*): *to calm down after an argument.* [ME *calme* < MF < early It *calm(a),* alter. of LL *cauma* heat < Gk *kaûma* burning heat] —**calm′ly,** *adv.* —**calm′ness,** *n.* —**Syn. 1.** quiet, motionless. **3.** placid, peaceful, serene. **7.** still, quiet, tranquilize; allay, soothe. —**Ant. 2.** tempestuous. **3.** agitated.

cal·ma·tive (kal′mə tiv, kä′mə-), *Med.* —*adj.* **1.** having a sedative effect. —*n.* **2.** a calmative agent.

cal·o·mel (kal′ə mel′, -məl), *n. Pharm.* a white, tasteless powder, Hg_2Cl_2, used chiefly as a purgative and fungicide. Also called **mercurous chloride.** [? < NL **calomel(as)* < Gk *kaló(s)* fair + *mélas* black]

calori-, a combining form meaning "heat," used in the formation of compound words: *calorimeter.* [< L, comb. form repr. *calor*]

ca·lor·ic (kə lôr′ik, -lor′-), *adj.* **1.** *Physiol.* of or pertaining to calories: *the caloric content of food.* **2.** of or pertaining to heat. —*n.* **3.** heat. **4.** *Old Physics.* a hypothetical fluid whose presence in matter determined its thermal state. [< F *calorique*] —**cal·o·ric·i·ty** (kal′ə ris′i tē), *n.*

cal·o·rie (kal′ə rē), *n.* **1.** *Physics.* **a.** (*often cap.*) Also called **kilocalorie.** a quantity of heat equal to 1000 gram calories. *Abbr.:* Cal. **b.** Also called **gram calorie, small calorie.** (formerly) the amount of heat necessary to raise the temperature of one gram of water from 14.5°C to 15.5°C when the water is at atmospheric pressure. *Abbr.:* cal. **2.** *Physiol.* **a.** a unit equal to the kilocalorie, used to express the heat output of an organism and the fuel or energy value of food. **b.** a quantity of food capable of producing such a unit of energy. Also, **calory.** [< F = CALOR(I)- + *-ie* -Y[3]]

cal·o·rif·ic (kal′ə rif′ik), *adj.* pertaining to conversion into heat. [< L *calōrific(us)* causing warmth, warming. See CALORI-, -FIC] —**cal′o·rif′i·cal·ly,** *adv.*

cal·o·rim·e·ter (kal′ə rim′i tər), *n. Physics.* an apparatus for measuring quantities of heat. —**cal·o·ri·met·ric** (kal′ər ə me′trik, kə lôr′-, -lor′-), **cal′o·ri·met′ri·cal,** *adj.* —**cal′o·ri·met′ri·cal·ly,** *adv.* —**cal′o·rim′e·try,** *n.*

cal·o·ry (kal′ə rē), *n., pl.* **-ries.** calorie.

ca·lotte (kə lot′), *n.* **1.** zucchetto. **2.** skullcap (def. 1). [< MF < It *calott(a)* < Gk *kalýptra* a cover, with loss of *r* by dissimilation; see CALYPTRA]

cal·o·yer (kal′ə yər, kə loi′ər), *n.* a monk of the Eastern Church. [< MF *caloyer* < ModGk *kalógeros* venerable = *kaló(s)* beautiful + *-geros* old]

cal·pac (kal′pak), *n.* a large black cap of sheepskin or other heavy material, worn by Armenians, Turks, etc. Also, **cal′pack.** [< Turk *kalpak*]

Cal·pe (kal′pē), *n.* ancient name of the Rock of Gibraltar.

Cal·pur·ni·a (kal pûr′nē ə), *n.* fl. 1st century B.C., third wife of Julius Caesar 59–44. Cf. **Cornelia** (def. 2), **Pompeia.**

Cal·ta·nis·set·ta (kal′tə ni set′ə; *It.* käl′tä nēs set′tä), *n.* a city in central Sicily: cathedral; Norman monastery. 63,011 (1959).

Caltrop (def. 2)

cal·trop (kal′trəp), *n.* **1.** *Bot.* **a.** any of various plants having spiny heads or fruit, esp. of the genera *Tribulus* and *Kallstroemia.* **b.** an Old World plant, *Tribulus terrestris.* **c.** See **water chestnut. 2.** *Mil.* an iron ball with four projecting spikes so disposed that when the ball is on the ground one of them always points upward, for obstructing cavalry, armored vehicles, etc. Also, **cal·throp** (kal′thrəp), **cal′trap.** [ME *calketrappe,* OE *calca(trippe)* + *(colte)træppe* = *calce-* (< L *calci-,* s. of *calx* spur, heel) + *træppe* TRAP[1]]

cal·u·met (kal′yə met′, kal′yə met′), *n.* a long, ornamented tobacco pipe used by North American Indians on ceremonial occasions, esp. in token of peace. Also called **peace pipe.** [< F < VL **calum(us)* reed, pipe (unexplained var. of L *calamus;* see CALAMUS) + F *-et* -ET]

Calumet

Cal′u·met Cit′y (kal′yə mit), a city in NE Illinois, near Chicago. 33,107 (1970).

ca·lum·ni·ate (kə lum′nē āt′), *v.t.,* **-at·ed, -at·ing.** to make false and malicious statements about; slander. [< L *calumniāt(us)* accused falsely, tricked (ptp. of *calumniārī*). See CALUMNY, -ATE[1]] —**ca·lum′ni·a′tor,** *n.*

ca·lum·ni·a·tion (kə lum′nē ā′shən), *n.* **1.** the act of calumniating; slander. **2.** a calumny. [< LL *calumniātiōn-* (s. of *calumniātiō*)]

ca·lum·ni·ous (kə lum′nē əs), *adj.* of, involving, or using calumny; slanderous; defamatory. Also, **ca·lum·ni·a·to·ry** (kə lum′nē ə tōr′ē, -tôr′ē). [< L *calumniōs(us)* full of tricks or artifices] —**ca·lum′ni·ous·ly,** *adv.*

cal·um·ny (kal′əm nē), *n., pl.* **-nies.** **1.** a false and malicious statement designed to injure the reputation of someone or something. **2.** slander; defamation. [< L *calumni(a)* = *calv(ī)* (to) deceive + *-mnia* (*-mn-* formative suffix + *-ia* -Y[3])]

cal·u·tron (kal′yə tron′), *n.* *Physics.* a device for separating isotopes by atomic mass, operating in a manner similar to that of a mass spectrograph. [*Cal(ifornia) U(niversity)* + -TRON]

Cal·va·dos (kal′və dōs′, -dos′, kal′və dōs′, -dos′), *n.* (*sometimes l.c.*) a dry apple brandy made from apple cider in Normandy.

cal·var·i·a (kal vâr′ē ə), *n.* the dome of the skull. [< L = *calv(a)* hairless scalp (n. use of fem. of *calvus* bald) + *-āria* -ARY]

Cal·va·ry (kal′və rē), *n., pl.* **-ries** for 2. **1.** Golgotha, the place where Jesus was crucified. Luke 23:33. **2.** (*often l.c.*) anything representing the Crucifixion. [< LL *Calvāri(a)* Calvary, L *calvāria* a skull, used to translate Gk *kranīon* CRANIUM, itself a trans. of the Aramaic name; see GOLGOTHA]

Cal′vary cross′. See **cross of Calvary.**

calve (kav, käv), *v.,* **calved, calv·ing.** —*v.i.* **1.** to give birth to a calf. **2.** (of a glacier, an iceberg, etc.) to break up or splinter so as to produce a detached piece. —*v.t.* **3.** to give birth to (a calf). **4.** (of a glacier, an iceberg, etc.) to break off or detach (a piece): *The iceberg calved a floe.* [ME *calve(n),* OE **calfian* (Anglian) < *calf* CALF[1]; c. OE *cealfian* (WS)]

Cal·vé (KAL vā′), *n.* **Em·ma** (em′ə; *Fr.* em MA′), (*Emma de Roquer Gaspari*), 1863?–1942, French operatic soprano.

Cal·vert (kal′vərt), *n.* **1. Sir George** (*1st Baron Baltimore*), c1580–1632, British statesman: founder of the colony of Maryland. **2.** his son, **Leonard,** 1606–47, first colonial governor of Maryland 1634–47.

calves (kavz, kävz), *n.* pl. of **calf.**

Cal·vin (kal′vin), *n.* **John** (*Jean Chauvin* or *Caulvin*), 1509–64, French theologian and reformer in Switzerland: leader in the Protestant Reformation.

Cal·vin·ism (kal′və niz′əm), *n.* *Theol.* **1.** the doctrines and teachings of John Calvin or his followers, emphasizing predestination, the sovereignty of God, the supreme authority of the Scriptures, and the irresistibility of grace. Cf. **Arminianism.** **2.** adherence to these doctrines. —**Cal′vin·ist,** *n., adj.* —**Cal′vin·is′tic,** *adj.*

calx (kalks), *n., pl.* **calx·es, cal·ces** (kal′sēz). the oxide or ash remaining after calcination of metals, minerals, etc. [< L: lime; r. late ME *cals,* appar. back formation < L *calcis,* etc., obl. cases of *calx*]

cal·y·ces (kal′i sēz′, kā′li-), *n.* a pl. of **calyx.**

cal·y·cine (kal′i sin, -sīn′), *adj.* pertaining to or resembling a calyx. Also, **ca·lyc·i·nal** (kə lis′ə nəl). [< L *calyc-* (s. of *calyx*) + -INE[1]]

cal·y·cle (kal′i kəl), *n.* *Bot.* a set of bracts resembling an outer calyx. [var. of CALYCULUS]

ca·lyc·u·lus (kə lik′yə ləs), *n., pl.* **-li** (-lī′). *Zool.* a structure shaped like a cup. [< L = *calyc-* (s. of *calyx*) + *-ulus* -ULE]

Cal·y·don (kal′i don′), *n.* an ancient city in W Greece, in Aetolia. —**Cal·y·do·ni·an** (kal′i dō′nē ən, -dōn′yən), *adj.*

Calydo′nian hunt′, *Class. Myth.* the pursuit by Meleager, Atalanta, and others of a savage boar **(Calydo′nian boar′)** sent by Artemis to lay waste to Calydon.

Ca·lyp·so (kə lip′sō), *n., pl.* **-sos.** **1.** (in the *Odyssey*) a nymph who detained Odysseus on Ogygia for seven years. **2.** (*l.c.*) a topical ballad of West Indian Negro origin.

ca·lyp·tra (kə lip′trə), *n.* *Bot.* **1.** a hoodlike part covering moss capsules or connected with the organs of fructification in flowering plants. **2.** a root cap. [< NL < Gk *kalýptra* veil, covering = *kalýpt(ein)* (to) veil, cover + *-ra* n. suffix] —**ca·lyp·trate** (kə-lip′trāt), *adj.*

ca·lyx (kā′liks, kal′iks), *n., pl.* **ca·lyx·es, cal·y·ces** (kal′i sēz′, kā′li-). **1.** *Bot.* the outermost group of floral parts, usually green; the sepals. **2.** *Anat., Zool.* a cuplike part. [< L < Gk *kályx* husk, covering, akin to *kalýptein* to veil, cover] —**cal·y·cate** (kal′i kāt′), *adj.*

Calyxes
A, Gamosepalous calyx;
B, Bilabiate calyx

cam (kam), *n.* *Mach.* an irregularly shaped disk or cylinder that imparts a rocking motion to any contiguous part. [< D or LG *kam, kamm.* See COMB[1]]

Cam (kam), *n.* a river in E England flowing NE by Cambridge, into the Ouse River. 40 mi. long. Also called **Granta.**

CAM (kam), *n.* computer-aided manufacturing; computer-aided manufacture.

Ca·ma·güey (kam′ə gwā′; *Sp.* kä′mä gwā′), *n.* a city in central Cuba. 162,400 (est. 1962).

ca·ma·ra·de·rie (kä′mə rä′də rē), *n.* comradeship; good-fellowship. [< F; see COMRADE, -ERY]

cam·a·ril·la (kam′ə ril′ə; *Sp.* kä′mä RĒ′lyä, -yä), *n., pl.* **-ril·las** (-ril′əz; *Sp.* -RĒ′lyäs, -yäs). a group of advisers; cabal; clique. [< Sp = *camar(a)* room (see CAMERA) + *-illa* dim. suffix]

cam·as (kam′as), *n.* **1.** any of several liliaceous plants of the genus *Camassia,* esp. *C. quamash,* of western North America, having sweet, edible bulbs. **2.** See **death camas.** Also, **cam′ass.** [< Chinook Jargon *kamass* < Nootka *chamas* sweet]

Camb., Cambridge.

cam·ber (kam′bər), *v.t., v.i.* **1.** to arch slightly; bend or curve upward in the middle. —*n.* **2.** a slight arching, upward curve, or convexity, as of the deck of a ship. **3.** a slightly arching piece of timber. **4.** *Aeron.* the rise of the curve of an airfoil, usually expressed as the ratio of the rise to the length of the chord of the airfoil. [< MF (north) *cambre* bent < L *camur* hooked, curved]

Cam·ber·well (kam′bər wel′, -wəl), *n.* a residential borough of S London, England. 174,697 (1961).

cam·bist (kam′bist), *n.* *Finance.* a dealer in bills of exchange. [< F *cambiste* < It *cambist(a)* = *cambi(o)* change, exchange + *-ista* -IST] —**cam′bist·ry,** *n.*

cam·bi·um (kam′bē əm), *n., pl.* **-bi·ums, -bi·a** (-bē ə). *Bot.* a layer of delicate meristematic tissue between the inner bark or phloem and the wood or xylem, that produces all secondary growth in plants and is responsible for the annual rings of wood. [< LL: an exchange, barter; akin to L *cambiāre* to exchange] —**cam′bi·al,** *adj.*

Cam·bo·di·a (kam bō′dē ə), *n.* a republic in SE Asia: formerly part of French Indochina. 8,110,000; 69,866 sq. mi. *Cap.:* Phnom Penh. French, **Cam·bodge** (kän bôj′). Official name (since 1976), **Democratic Kampuchea.**

Cam·bo·di·an (kam bō′dē ən), *adj.* **1.** of, pertaining to, or characteristic of Cambodia, its people, or its culture. —*n.* **2.** a native or inhabitant of Cambodia. **3.** Khmer (def. 2).

cam·bo·gi·a (kam bō′jē ə), *n.* gamboge (def. 1).

Cam·brai (käN bRe′), *n.* a city in N France: battles 1917, 1918. 35,373 (1962).

Cam·bri·a (kam′brē ə), *n.* medieval name of **Wales.**

Cam·bri·an (kam′brē ən), *adj.* **1.** *Geol.* noting or pertaining to a period of the Paleozoic era, occurring 500–600 million years ago and characterized by the presence of algae and marine invertebrates. See table at **era.** **2.** of or pertaining to Cambria; Welsh. —*n.* **3.** *Geol.* the Cambrian period or system. **4.** a native of Cambria; Welshman.

cam·bric (kām′brik), *n.* a thin, plain cotton or linen fabric of fine close weave, usually white. [earlier *cameryk* < *Kameryk,* Flemish name of CAMBRAI]

cam′bric tea′, a mixture of hot water and milk, with sugar and, sometimes, a little tea.

Cam·bridge (kām′brij), *n.* **1.** a city in and the county seat of Cambridgeshire, in E England: famous university founded in 12th century. 95,358 (1961). **2.** a city in E Massachusetts, near Boston. 100,361 (1970).

Cam·bridge·shire (kām′brij shēr′, -shər), *n.* a county in E England. 189,913 (1961); 492 sq. mi. *Co. seat:* Cambridge. Also called **Cambridge.**

Cam·by·ses (kam bī′sēz), *n.* died 522 B.C., king of Persia 529–522 (son of Cyrus the Great).

cam·cord·er (kam′kôr′dər), *n.* a lightweight hand-held television camera with a built-in VCR. [CAM(ERA) + (RE)CORDER]

Cam·den (kam′dən), *n.* a port in SW New Jersey, on the Delaware River opposite Philadelphia. 102,551 (1970).

came[1] (kām), *v.* pt. of **come.**

came[2] (kām), *n.* a slender, grooved bar of lead for holding together the pieces of glass in windows of latticework or stained glass. [appar. special use of *came* ridge. See KAME]

cam·el (kam′əl), *n.* **1.** either of two large, humped, ruminant quadrupeds of the genus *Camelus,* of the Old World. Cf. **Bactrian camel, dromedary.** **2.** *Naut.* a float for increasing the buoyancy of a heavily loaded vessel. [ME, OE < L *camēl(us)* < Gk *kámēlos* < Sem, as Heb *gāmāl*]

cam·el·eer (kam′ə lēr′), *n.* a camel driver.

cam·el·hair (kam′əl hâr′), *n.* **1.** See **camel's hair.** —*adj.* **2.** camel's-hair.

ca·mel·lia (kə mēl′yə, -mē′lē ə), *n.* a woody plant, *Camellia* (or *Thea*) *japonica,* native to Asia, having glossy evergreen leaves and white, pink, red, or variegated waxy, roselike flowers. [named after G. J. *Camellus* (1661–1706), Jesuit missionary, who brought it to Europe; see -IA]

ca·mel·o·pard (kə mel′ə pärd′), *n.* *Obs.* a giraffe. [ME < ML *camēlopard(us),* L *camēlopard(ālis)* < Gk *kamēlopárdalis* giraffe. See CAMEL, PARD]

Ca·mel·o·par·da·lis (kə mel′ə pär′dəlis, kam′ə lō-), *n., gen.* **-lis.** *Astron.* the Giraffe, a northern constellation between Ursa Major and Perseus.

Cam·e·lot (kam′ə lot′), *n.* the legendary site of King Arthur's palace and court, possibly near Exeter, England.

cam′el's hair′, **1.** the hair of a camel or of a substitute, as the tail hair of a squirrel. **2.** cloth made of this hair, sometimes mixed with wool, usually tan in color. Also, **camelhair.** —**cam′el's-hair′,** *adj.*

Cam·em·bert (kam′əm bâr′; *Fr.* KA mäN beR′), *n.* a mellow, soft cheese, with a creamy center. [after *Camembert,* village in Normandy where it was first marketed]

cam·e·o (kam′ē ō′), *n., pl.* **cam·e·os,** *adj.* **1.** a technique of engraving upon a gem or other stone, as onyx, in such a way that an underlying stone of one color is exposed as a background for a low-relief design of another color. **2.** a gem or other stone so engraved. **3.** Also called **cam′eo role′.** *Motion Pictures, Television.* a minor, distinct part played by a prominent actor or actress, confined to a single dramatic scene. [< It *cam(m)eo:* cf. ML *cam(m)aeus*]

cam′eo ware′, jasper (def. 2).

cam·er·a (kam′ər ə, kam′rə), *n., pl.* **-er·as** for 1, 2, **-er·ae** (-ə rē′) for 3. **1.** a boxlike device for holding a film or plate sensitive to light, having an aperture controlled by a shutter that, when opened, admits light enabling an object to be focused, usually by means of a lens, on the film or plate, thereby producing a photographic image. **2.** *Television.* the device in which the picture to be transmitted is formed before it is changed into electric impulses. **3.** a judge's private office. **4. in camera,** privately. [< L *camera* vaulted room, vault < Gk *kamára* vault; see CHAMBER]

cam·er·al (kam′ər əl), *adj.* of or pertaining to a judicial or legislative chamber or the privacy of such a chamber. [< ML *camerāl(is)* < *camer(a)* treasury, governmental chamber]

cam·er·a·list (kam′ər ə list), *n.* any of the mercantilist economists or public servants in Europe in the 17th and 18th centuries who held that the economic power of a nation can be enhanced by increasing its monetary wealth. [< G *Kameralist* < NL *cameralist(a)*] —**cam′er·a·lism,** *n.*

cam′era lu′ci·da (lo͞o′si də), *Optics.* an optical instrument, often attached to the eyepiece of a microscope, by which the image of an external object is projected on a sheet of paper or the like for tracing. [< NL: clear chamber]

cam·er·a·man (kam′ər ə man′, -mən, kam′rə-), *n., pl.* **-men** (-men′, -mən). a man who operates a camera, esp. a motion-picture camera.

cam′era ob·scu′ra (ob skyŏŏr′ə), a darkened, boxlike device in which images of external objects are received through an aperture to be projected on a surface arranged to receive them. [< NL: dark chamber]

cam·er·len·go (kam′ər leng′gō), *n., pl.* **-gos.** *Rom. Cath. Ch.* the cardinal who is the treasurer of the Holy See and who presides over the conclave that elects the pope. [< It *camerlingo* < Gmc; akin to OHG *chamarlinc* CHAMBERLAIN]

Cam·e·roon (kam′ə rōōn′), *n.* **1.** Also, **Cameroun.** Official name, **Unit′ed Repub′lic of Cameroon′.** an independent republic in W Africa: formed 1960 by the French trusteeship of Cameroun; Southern Cameroons incorporated as a self-governing province 1961. 6,600,000; 183,350 sq. mi. *Cap.:* Yaoundé. **2.** an active volcano in W Cameroon: highest peak on the coast of W Africa. 13,350 ft.

Cam·e·roons (kam′ə rōōnz′), *n.* (*construed as sing.*) **1.** German, **Kamerun.** a region in W Africa: a German protectorate 1884–1919; divided in 1919 into British and French mandates. **2.** Also called **British Cameroons.** the NW part of this region: a British mandate 1919–46 and trusteeship 1946–61; by a 1961 plebiscite the S part **(Southern Cameroons)** joined the Federal Republic of Cameroon and the N part **(Northern Cameroons)** joined Nigeria.

Came·roun (KAM RŌŌN′), *n.* **1.** Cameroon (def. 1). **2.** Also called **French Cameroons.** a former French mandate (1919–46) and trusteeship (1946–60) in W Africa: independence 1960; now part of the United Republic of Cameroon.

cam·i·on (kam′ē ən; *Fr.* KA MYÔN′), *n., pl.* **cam·i·ons** (kam′ē ənz; *Fr.* KA MYÔN′). **1.** a strongly built cart or wagon for transporting heavy loads. **2.** a truck, esp. one for transporting military supplies. [< F < ?]

cam·i·sa·do (kam′i sā′dō, -sä′-), *n., pl.* **-dos.** *Archaic.* a military attack made at night. Also, **cam·i·sade** (kam′i sād′, -säd′). [< Sp *camisada* (now obs.) = *camis(a)* shirt + *-ada* -ADE[1]]

ca·mise (kə mēz′, -mēs′), *n.* a lightweight, loose-fitting shirt or smock with long sleeves. [< Ar *qamīṣ* < LL *camīs(a)*, var. of *camīsia* shirt; see CHEMISE]

cam·i·sole (kam′i sōl′), *n.* **1.** a short garment worn underneath a sheer bodice to conceal the underwear. **2.** a woman's dressing jacket. [< F < Pr *camisol(a)* < LL *camis(a)* shirt (see CHEMISE) + *-ola* -ULE]

cam·let (kam′lit), *n.* **1.** a durable, waterproof cloth, esp. for outerwear. **2.** apparel made of this material. **3.** a rich fabric of medieval Asia, believed to have been made of camel's hair or angora wool. [late ME *camelot* < MF < Ar *khamlat* kind of plush fabric, akin to *khaml* nap, pile]

Cam·o·ëns (kam′ō ens′), *n.* **Lu·is Vaz de** (lōō ēsh′ väzh də), 1524?–80, Portuguese poet. Portuguese, **Ca·mões** (kə MOINSH′).

cam·o·mile (kam′ə mīl′), *n.* **1.** any asteraceous plant of the genus *Anthemis*, esp. *A. nobilis*, of Europe, having strongly scented foliage and flowers that are used in medicine. **2.** any of various allied plants, as *Matricaria Chamomilla*. Also, **chamomile.** [ME *camemille* < ML *c(h)amomill(a)* (sing.) < L *chamaemēla* (pl.) < Gk *chamaímēla* earth apples = *chamaí* on the ground + *mêla*, pl. of *mêlon* apple]

Ca·mor·ra (kə môr′ə, -mor′ə; *It.* kä MÔR′RÄ), *n.* a secret society of Naples, Italy: disbanded in 1911. [< It < Sp: dispute, quarrel]—**Ca·mor′rism,** *n.*—**Ca·mor′rist,** *n.*

cam·ou·flage (kam′ə fläzh′), *n., v.,* **-flaged, -flag·ing.** —*n.* **1.** *Mil.* the act, art, means, or result of disguising things to deceive an enemy, as by painted patterns or screens of foliage. **2.** disguise or deception. —*v.t.* **3.** to disguise, hide, or deceive by means of camouflage. [< F = *camoufl(er)* (to) disguise (It *camuffare* to disguise + F *moufler* to cover up) + *-age* -AGE] —**cam′ou·flag′er,** *n.*

camp[1] (kamp), *n.* **1.** a place where an army or other body of persons is lodged in tents or other temporary means of shelter. **2.** such tents or shelters collectively. **3.** the persons so sheltered. **4.** the act of camping out. **5.** any temporary structure, as a tent or cabin, used on an outing or vacation. **6.** a body of troops, workers, etc., camping and moving together. **7.** army life. **8.** a group of persons favoring the same ideals, doctrines, etc. **9.** any position in which ideals, doctrines, etc., are strongly entrenched. **10.** a recreation area in the country, equipped with extensive facilities for sports. **11.** See **day camp.** **12.** See **summer camp.** —*v.i.* **13.** to establish or pitch a camp. **14.** to live temporarily in or as in a camp (often fol. by *out*): *The boys will camp out for a week.* **15.** *Informal.* to become ensconced: *to camp in a friend's apartment.* **16.** *Informal.* to take up a position stubbornly: *They camped in front of the president's office.* —*v.t.* **17.** to put or station (troops) in a camp; shelter. [OE: battle(field), field < L *camp(us)* field]

camp[2] (kamp), *n.* **1.** a pretentious gesture, style, or form, esp. when amusing or when consciously contrived. **2.** a person or his works displaying such pretentiousness. —*v.i.* **3.** to act in an amusingly pretentious way. —*v.t.* **4.** to perform or imbue (something) with such pretentiousness. **5. camp it up,** *Slang.* **a.** to make an ostentatious or affected display. **b.** to flaunt homosexuality. —*adj.* **6.** campy. [? dial. *camp* impetuous, uncouth person (see KEMP[1]); hence, slightly objectionable, effeminate, homosexual]

Camp (kamp), *n.* **Walter Chaun·cey** (chôn′sē, chän′-), 1859–1925, U.S. football coach: developed rules and traditions of American football.

Cam·pa·gna (kam pän′yə, kəm-; *It.* käm pä′nyä), *n., pl.* **-pa·gne** (-pän′yā; *It.* -pä′nye) for 2. **1.** a low plain surrounding the city of Rome, Italy. **2.** (*l.c.*) any flat open plain; champaign. [< It; see CAMPAIGN]

cam·paign (kam pān′), *n.* **1.** *Mil.* **a.** military operations for a specific objective. **b.** *Obs.* the military operations of an army in the field for one season. **2.** any systematic course of aggressive activities for some special purpose: *a sales campaign.* **3.** the competition by rival political candidates and organizations for public office. —*v.i.* **4.** to serve in or go on a campaign. —*v.t.* **5.** to race (a boat, car, horse, etc.) in a series of competitions. [< F *campagne* < It *campagn(a)* < LL *campānia* level district = *camp(us)* field + *-ānia* regional suffix] —**cam·paign′er,** *n.*

campaign′ but′ton, a disk-shaped pin worn by a supporter of a political candidate, usually bearing the name of the candidate and sometimes containing a slogan or the candidate's picture.

campaign′ rib′bon, a distinctively colored ribbon, either on a small, narrow bar or in the form of a strip, representing a military campaign participated in by the wearer.

Campanile

Cam·pa·nia (kam pā′nē ə; *It.* käm pä′nyä), *n.* a region in SW Italy. 4,756,094 (1961); 5214 sq. mi. *Cap.:* Naples. —**Cam·pa′ni·an,** *adj., n.*

cam·pa·ni·le (kam′pə nē′lē; *It.* käm′pä nē′le), *n., pl.* **-ni·les, -ni·li** (-nē′lē). a bell tower, esp. one somewhat detached from the body of a church. [< It = *campan(a)* bell + *-ile* locative suffix]

cam·pa·nol·o·gy (kam′pə nol′ə jē), *n.* **1.** the study of bells. **2.** the principles, science, or art of making bells, bell ringing, etc. [< NL *campānologia* = LL *campān(a)* bell + *-o-* -o- + *-logia* -LOGY] —**cam′pa·nol′o·gist,** *n.*

cam·pan·u·la (kam pan′yə lə), *n.* any plant of the genus *Campanula*, as the harebell or the Canterbury bell; bellflower. [< NL = LL *campān(a)* bell + L *-ula* -ULE]

cam·pan·u·la·ceous (kam pan′yə lā′shəs), *adj.* belonging to the *Campanulaceae*, or campanula family of plants. [< NL *Campanulace(ae)* (see CAMPANULA, -ACEAE) + -OUS]

cam·pan·u·late (kam pan′yə lit, -lāt′), *adj.* bell-shaped, as a corolla. [< NL *campanulāt(us)*]

camp′ bed′, a lightweight, folding bed.

Camp·bell (kam′bəl, kam′əl), *n.* **1. Alexander,** 1788–1866, U.S. religious leader, born in Ireland: cofounder with his father, Thomas, of the Disciples of Christ Church. **2. Colin** (*Baron Clyde*), 1792–1863, Scottish general. **3. Mrs. Patrick** (*Beatrice Stella Tanner*), 1865–1940, English actress. **4. Thomas,** 1763–1854, Irish religious leader, in the U.S. after 1807: cofounder with his son, Alexander, of the Disciples of Christ Church. **5. Thomas,** 1777–1844, Scottish poet and editor.

Camp·bell-Ban·ner·man (kam′bəl ban′ər mən, kam′-əl-), *n.* **Sir Henry,** 1836–1908, British statesman, born in Ireland: prime minister 1905–08.

Camp·bell·ite (kam′bə līt′, kam′ə-), *n.* *Sometimes Derogatory.* a member of the Disciples of Christ.

camp′ chair′, a lightweight folding chair.

camp·craft (kamp′kraft′, -kräft′), *n.* the methods or techniques of outdoor camping.

Cam·pe·che (käm pe′che), *n.* **1.** a state in SE Mexico, on the peninsula of Yucatán. 158,219 (1960); 19,672 sq. mi. **2.** a seaport in and the capital of this state. 43,874 (1960). **3. Gulf of,** the SW part of the Gulf of Mexico.

camp·er (kam′pər), *n.* **1.** a person who camps out for recreation, esp. in the wilderness. **2.** a person who attends a summer camp or day camp. **3.** a station wagon with enclosed sides or a pickup truck with a roomlike addition over the cab and truck bed, outfitted as temporary living quarters for use in camping or extended motor excursions.

cam·pes·tral (kam pes′trəl), *adj.* of or pertaining to fields or open country. [< L *campestr-* (s. of *campester* flat = *camp(us)* field + *-ester* adj. suffix) + -AL[1]]

camp·fire (kamp′fīər′), *n.* **1.** an outdoor fire for warmth or cooking, as at a camp. **2.** a reunion of soldiers, scouts, etc.

camp′fire girl′, a member of an organization **(Camp Fire Girls, Inc.)** for girls aged 7–18.

camp′ fol′lower, a civilian not officially connected with a military unit, esp. a prostitute, who follows an army or settles near an army camp.

camp·ground (kamp′ground′), *n.* a place for a camp or for a camp meeting.

cam·phene (kam′fēn, kam fēn′), *n.* *Chem.* a colorless, crystalline, water-insoluble substance, $C_{10}H_{16}$, occurring in turpentine and other oils: used chiefly in the manufacture of synthetic camphor. [< NL *camph(ora)* CAMPHOR + -ENE]

cam·phor (kam′fər), *n.* *Chem., Pharm.* **1.** a whitish, terpene ketone, $C_{10}H_{16}O$, used chiefly in the manufacture of celluloid and as a counterirritant. **2.** any of various similar substances. [< NL, ML *camphor(a)* < Ar *kāfūr* < Malay *kāpūr;* r. ME *caumfre* < AF] —**cam·phor·ic** (kam fôr′ik, -for′-), *adj.*

cam·pho·rate (kam′fə rāt′), *v.t.,* **-rat·ed, -rat·ing.** to impregnate with camphor. [< ML *camphorāt(us)*, ptp.]

cam′phorated oil′, *Pharm.* a solution of one part camphor oil in four parts cottonseed oil, used as a counterirritant.

cam′phor ball′, a small ball of naphthalene, camphor, etc., used as a moth repellent.

cam′phor ice′, a cosmetic preparation composed of camphor, spermaceti, white beeswax, and a vegetable oil: used chiefly in the treatment of mild skin eruptions.

cam′phor tree′, **1.** a lauraceous tree, *Cinnamomum Camphora*, of Japan, Taiwan, China, etc., yielding camphor. **2.** any of various similar trees, as *Dryobalanops aromatica*, of Borneo, SE Asia, etc., yielding borneol.

Cam·pi·na Gran·de (käɴ pē′nə gräɴ′də), a city in NE Brazil. 126,274 (est. 1960).

Cam·pi·nas (kam pē′nəs; *Port.* käɴ pē′nəs), *n.* a city in SE Brazil, NNW of São Paulo. 184,529 (1960).

cam·pi·on (kam′pē ən), *n.* any of several caryophyllaceous plants of the genera *Lychnis* and *Silene*. [special use of *campion*, old var. (< AF) of CHAMPION]

Cam·pi·on (kam′pē ən), *n.* **Thomas,** 1567–1620, English songwriter and poet.

Camp′ Le·jeune′ Cen′tral (lə jōōn′), a town in SE North Carolina. 34,549 (1970).

camp′ meet′ing, a religious gathering, usually lasting for some days, held in a tent or in the open air.

cam·po (kam′pō, käm′-), *n., pl.* **-pos.** (in South America) an extensive, level, grassy plain. [< Sp < L *camp(us)* field]

Cam·po·bel·lo (kam′pō bel′ō, -pə-), *n.* an island in SE Canada, in New Brunswick province. 1137 (1961).

cam·pong (käm′pông, -pong, käm pông′, -pong′), *n.* kampong.

camp·o·ree (kam′pə rē′), *n.* a small camp gathering of Boy Scouts, usually from a region or district (distinguished from *jamboree*). [CAMP[1] + (JAMB)OREE]

Cam·pos (känm′po͞os), *n.* a city in E Brazil, near Rio de Janeiro. 131,974 (1960).

camp·site (kamp′sīt′), *n.* a place used or suitable for camping.

camp·stool (kamp′sto͞ol′), *n.* a lightweight folding seat.

cam·pus (kam′pəs), *n., pl.* **-pus·es.** *U.S.* **1.** the grounds of a college or other school. **2.** a college or university. [< L: flat place, field, plain]

camp·y (kam′pē), *adj.*, **camp·i·er, camp·i·est.** *Slang.* **1.** amusingly outlandish, affected, or theatrical: *He had a campy British accent.* **2.** conspicuously displaying homosexual gestures, speech mannerisms, etc.

cam·shaft (kam′shaft′, -shäft′), *n.* a shaft bearing integral cams.

Ca·mus (KA MY′), *n.* **Al·bert** (AL BER′), 1913–60, French existentialist novelist, short-story writer, playwright, and essayist: Nobel prize 1957.

can[1] (kan; *unstressed* kən), *auxiliary v.* and *v., pres. sing. 1st pers.* **can,** *2nd* **can** or (*Archaic*) **canst,** *3rd* **can,** *pres. pl.* **can;** *past sing. 1st pers.* **could,** *2nd* **could** or (*Archaic*) **couldst,** *3rd* **could,** *past pl.* **could.** *For auxiliary v.: imperative, infinitive, and participles lacking. For v.* (*Obs.*): *imperative* **can;** *infinitive* **can;** *past part.* **could;** *pres. part.* **cun·ning.** —*auxiliary verb.* **1.** to be able to; have the ability, power, or skill to: *She can solve the problem easily, I'm sure.* **2.** to know how to: *He can play chess, although he's not particularly good at it.* **3.** to have the power or means to: *A dictator can impose his will on the people.* **4.** to have the right or qualifications to: *He can change the script.* **5.** may; have permission to: *Can I speak to you a moment?* —*v.t., v.i.* **6.** *Obs.* to know. [ME, OE, pres. ind. sing. 1st, 3rd pers. of *cunnan* to know, know how; c. G, Icel, Goth *kann;* see KEN, KNOW]
—**Syn. 1–5.** CAN denotes power or ability to do something: *The child can talk.* MAY refers to probability, possibility, or permission: *Our son may* (possibility or probability) *play football Saturday if the doctor says he may* (permission). The two words are often confused in asking or granting permission; MAY is the preferred usage. On the other hand, CANNOT is often used in nonformal situations to deny permission: *May I go? Yes, you may go* (or, *You may not* or *cannot go*). CANNOT is also used to express either extreme negation of ability or probability: *I cannot work such long hours.*
—**Usage.** CAN BUT, CANNOT BUT are formal expressions suggesting that there is no possible alternative to doing a certain thing. CAN BUT is equivalent to informal CAN ONLY: *We can but do our best* (1. and *must* make the attempt; or 2. and no more than that should be expected of us). CANNOT BUT (do) is equivalent to informal CAN'T HELP (doing): *We cannot but protest against injustice* (we are under moral obligation to do so). CANNOT HELP BUT is common in familiar use but frowned upon by some careful speakers and writers.

can[2] (kan), *n., v.*, **canned, can·ning.** —*n.* **1.** a container for food, milk, etc., usually of sheet iron coated with tin or other metal. **2.** a receptacle for garbage, ashes, etc. **3.** a bucket, pail, or other container for holding or carrying liquids. **4.** a drinking cup; tankard. **5.** *Slang.* toilet; bathroom. **6.** *Slang.* jail. **7.** *Slang.* the buttocks. **8.** *Mil. Slang.* a depth charge. **9. in the can,** (of a commercial film) ready for distribution or exhibition. —*v.t.* **10.** to preserve by sealing in a can, jar, etc. **11.** *Slang.* to dismiss; fire. **12.** *Slang.* to stop (saying, doing, or making something): *Can that noise!* [ME, OE *canne*, c. G *Kanne*, Icel *kanna*, all perh. < WGmc; cf. LL *canna* small vessel < L, c. Gk *kánna* CANE] —**can′ner,** *n.*

Can., 1. Canada. **2.** Canadian.

can., 1. canon. **2.** canto.

Ca·na (kā′nə), *n.* an ancient town in N Israel, in Galilee: scene of Jesus' first miracle. John 2:1,11.

Ca·naan (kā′nən), *n.* **1.** the ancient region lying between the Jordan, the Dead Sea, and the Mediterranean: the land promised by God to Abraham. Gen. 12:5–10. **2.** Biblical name of **Palestine. 3.** any land of promise. **4.** a descendant of Ham, the son of Noah. Gen. 10. [< LL *Chanaan* < Gk < Heb *Kena'an*]

Ca·naan·ite (kā′nə nīt′), *n.* **1.** a member of a Semitic people that inhabited parts of ancient Palestine and were conquered by the Israelites. **2.** a group of Semitic languages, including Hebrew and Phoenician, spoken chiefly in ancient Palestine and Syria. —*adj.* **3.** of, pertaining to, or characteristic of Canaan, the Canaanites, or the group of Semitic languages known as Canaanite.

Canad., Canadian.

Can·a·da (kan′ə də), *n.* a nation in N North America: a member of the British Commonwealth of Nations. 23,110,000; 3,690,410 sq. mi. *Cap.:* Ottawa.

Can′ada bal′sam, a clear, viscous liquid that solidifies on exposure to air: obtained from the balsam fir, *Abies balsamea*, and used chiefly for mounting objects on microscope slides and in the manufacture of lacquers.

Can′ada blue′grass, a European, perennial grass, *Poa compressa*, naturalized in North America.

Can′ada goose′, a common wild goose, *Branta canadensis*, of North America. See illus. at **goose.**

Can′ada jay′, a gray jay, *Perisoreus canadensis*, of northern North America, noted for its boldness in stealing food from houses, traps, camps, etc.

Can′ada lynx′. See under **lynx** (def. 1).

Can′ada this′tle, an Old World herb, *Cirsium arvense*, having small purple or white flower heads, now a troublesome weed in North America.

Ca·na·di·an (kə nā′dē ən), *adj.* **1.** of or pertaining to Canada or its people. —*n.* **2.** a native or inhabitant of Canada.

Cana′dian ba′con, bacon taken from a boned strip of pork loin.

Cana′dian French′, French spoken as a native language in Canada, esp. in Quebec province, by descendants of the settlers of New France. *Abbr.:* CanF

Ca·na·di·an·ism (kə nā′dē ə niz′əm), *n.* a custom, trait, English usage, or thing peculiar to Canada or its citizens.

Cana′dian Riv′er, a river flowing E from the Rocky Mountains in NE New Mexico to the Arkansas River in E Oklahoma. 906 mi. long.

Cana′dian whis′key, rye[1] (def. 3).

ca·naille (kə nāl′; *Fr.* KA NA′yᵊ), *n.* riffraff; the rabble. [< F < It *canaglia* pack of dogs = *can(e)* dog (< L *canis*) + *-aglia* collective suffix]

can·a·kin (kan′ə kin), *n.* cannikin.

ca·nal[1] (kə nal′), *n., v.*, **-nalled** or **-naled, -nal·ling** or **-nal·ing.** —*n.* **1.** an artificial waterway for navigation, irrigation, etc. **2.** a tubular passage or cavity for food, air, etc., esp. in an animal or plant; duct. **3.** *Obs.* a channel or watercourse. —*v.t.* **4.** canalize (def. 1). [late ME: waterpipe < L *canāl(i)s*, perh. = *can(na)* reed, pipe (see CANE) + *-ālis* -AL[1]]

ca·nal[2] (kə nal′), *n.* *Astron.* one of the long, narrow, lines seen on the planet Mars by telescope. [< It *canal(e)* channel < L *canāl(is);* see CANAL[1]]

Ca·na·let·to (kan′ᵊlet′ō; *It.* kä′nä let′tô), *n.* **An·to·nio** (än tô′nyô), (*Canale*), 1697–1768, Italian painter.

can·a·lic·u·lus (kan′ᵊlik′yə ləs), *n., pl.* **-li** (-lī′). *Anat., Zool.* a small canal or tubular passage, as in bone. [< L = *canāli(s)* CANAL[1] + *-culus* -CULE] —**can′a·lic′u·lar, can·a·lic·u·late** (kan′ᵊlik′yə lit, -yə lāt′), **can′a·lic′u·lat′ed,** *adj.*

ca·nal·ise (kə nal′īz, kan′ᵊlīz′), *v.t.*, **-ised, -is·ing.** *Chiefly Brit.* canalize. —**ca·nal′i·sa′tion,** *n.*

ca·nal·ize (kə nal′īz, kan′ᵊlīz′), *v.t.*, **-ized, -iz·ing. 1.** to make a canal or canals through. **2.** to convert into a canal. **3.** channelize —**ca·nal′i·za′tion,** *n.*

ca·nal·ler (kə nal′ər), *n.* a freight boat built for use on canals.

canal′ ray′, *Physics.* a stream of positive ions traveling from a metallic anode to the cathode in a gas-discharge tube. Also called **positive ray.**

Canal′ Zone′, a zone in central Panama, crossing the Isthmus of Panama on both sides of the Panama Canal: leased to and governed by the U.S.; ab. 10 mi. wide; excludes the cities of Panama and Colón. 44,198 (1970); 553 sq. mi. *Abbr.:* C.Z., CZ

can·a·pé (kan′ə pē, -pā′; *Fr.* KA NA pā′), *n., pl.* **-pés** (-pēz, -pāz′; *Fr.* -pā′). a thin piece of bread, toast, etc., spread or topped with cheese, caviar, anchovies, or other appetizing foods. [< F: lit., a covering or netting, orig. for a bed (see CANOPY), by extension for a piece of bread]

Ca·na·ra (kə när′ə, kä′nər ə), *n.* Kanara.

ca·nard (kə närd′; *Fr.* KA NAR′), *n., pl.* **-nards** (-närdz′; *Fr.* -NAR′). a false story, report, or rumor, usually derogatory; hoax. [< F: lit., duck; OF *quanart* drake, orig. cackler = *can(er)* (to) cackle + *-art* -ART]

Ca·na·rese (kä′nə rēz′, -rēs′), *adj., n., pl.* **-rese.** Kanarese.

ca·nar·y (kə nâr′ē), *n., pl.* **-nar·ies. 1.** a finch, *Serinus canarius*, native to the Canary Islands and often kept as a pet, in the wild state greenish with brown streaks above and yellow below, and in the domesticated state usually bright or pale yellow. **2.** Also called **canary yellow.** a light, clear yellow. **3.** a sweet white wine of the Canary Islands, resembling sherry. **4.** *Slang.* an informer. Cf. **stool pigeon** (def. 2). [< Sp (*Gran*) *Canaria* (Grand) Canary < L *Canāria* (*insula*) Dog (Island) = *can(is)* dog + *-āria*, fem. of *-ārius* -ARY]

canar′y grass′, any of various grasses of the genus *Phalaris*, as *P. canariensis*, native to the Canary Islands, bearing a seed used as food for cage birds, or *P. arundinacea*, used throughout the Northern Hemisphere as fodder.

Canar′y Is′lands, a group of mountainous islands in the Atlantic Ocean, near the NW coast of Africa: comprising two provinces of Spain. 918,060 (est. 1960); 2894 sq. mi. Also called **Ca·nar′ies.** —**Ca·nar′i·an,** *adj., n.*

canar′y seed′, birdseed.

canar′y yel′low, canary (def. 2).

ca·nas·ta (kə nas′tə), *n.* *Cards.* a variety of rummy in which the main object is to meld sets of seven or more cards. [< Sp: lit., basket, appar. var. of *canastro* < Gk *kánastron* wicker basket]

Ca·nav·er·al (kə nav′ər əl), *n.* **Cape,** a cape on an island in E Florida: site of John F. Kennedy Space Center. Formerly (1963–73), **Cape Kennedy.**

Can·ber·ra (kan′ber ə, -bər ə), *n.* a city in and the capital of Australia, in the SE part, in the Australian Capital Territory. 210,600 with suburbs.

can′ bu′oy, a cylindrical, unlighted buoy, painted black and given an odd number. Cf. **nun buoy.** See illus. at **buoy.**

canc., 1. cancel. **2.** cancellation.

can·can (kan′kan′; *Fr.* kän kän′), *n., pl.* **-cans** (-kanz′; *Fr.* -kän′). an exhibition dance marked by high kicking. [< F, repetitive compound (based on *can*) said to be nursery var. of *canard* duck]

can·cel (kan′səl), *v.*, **-celed, -cel·ing** or (*esp. Brit.*) **-celled, -cel·ling,** *n.* —*v.t.* **1.** to make void; revoke; annul. **2.** to mark or perforate (a postage stamp, admission ticket, etc.) to render it invalid for reuse. **3.** to neutralize; counterbalance; compensate for. **4.** *Accounting.* **a.** to close (an account) by crediting or paying all outstanding charges. **b.** to eliminate or offset (a debit, credit, etc.) with an entry for an equal amount on the opposite side of a ledger, as when a payment is received on a debt (often fol. by *out*). **5.** *Math.* to eliminate by striking out a factor common to both the denominator and numerator of a fraction, equivalent terms on opposite sides of an equation, etc. **6.** to cross out (words, letters, etc.) by drawing a line or lines through the item. **7.** *Print.* to omit. —*v.i.* **8.** to counterbalance or compensate for one another; become neutralized or equivalent (often fol. by *out*). —*n.* **9.** the act of canceling. **10.** *Print., Bookbinding.* **a.** an omission. **b.** the replacement for an

omitted part. [late ME *cancelle* < ML *cancell(āre)* (to) cross out, L: to make like a lattice < *cancellī* grating, pl. of *cancellus* = *canc(rī)* grating (var. of *carcer* prison) + *-ellus* dim. suffix] —**can′cel·er;** *esp. Brit.,* **can′cel·ler,** *n.*
—**Syn. 1.** countermand, rescind. **2, 6.** CANCEL, DELETE, ERASE, OBLITERATE indicate that something is no longer to be considered usable or in force. To CANCEL is to cross something out by stamping a mark over it, drawing lines through it, or the like: *to cancel a stamp, a word.* To DELETE is to cross something out from written matter or from matter to be printed, often in accordance with a printer's or proofreader's symbol indicating the material is to be omitted: *to delete part of a line.* To ERASE is to remove by scraping or rubbing: *to erase a capital letter.* To OBLITERATE is to blot out entirely, so as to remove all sign or trace of: *to obliterate a record, an inscription.*

can·cel·late (kan′sə lāt′, -lit), *adj.* **1.** *Anat.* of spongy or porous structure, as bone. **2.** reticulate. Also, **can·cel·lat·ed** (kan′sə lā′tid). [< L *cancell(ātus).* See CANCEL, -ATE[1]]

can·cel·la·tion (kan′sə lā′shən), *n.* **1.** act of canceling. **2.** the marks or perforations made in canceling. **3.** something canceled, esp. a reservation for a hotel room, airplane ticket, or the like, allowing someone else to obtain the accommodation. [< L *cancellātiōn-* (s. of *cancellātiō*)]

can·cer (kan′sər), *n., gen.* **Can·cri** (kang′krē) for 3. **1.** *Pathol.* a malignant and invasive growth or tumor, esp. one originating in epithelium, tending to recur after excision and to metastasize to other sites. **2.** any evil condition or thing that spreads destructively; blight. **3.** (*cap.*) *Astron.* the Crab, a zodiacal constellation between Gemini and Leo. **4.** (*cap.*) *Astrol.* the fourth sign of the zodiac. See diag. at **zodiac. 5.** (*cap.*) **tropic of.** See under **tropic** (def. 1a). [ME < L: lit., crab; akin to Gk *karkínos,* Skt *karkata* crab; see CANKER] —**can′cer·ous,** *adj.* —**can′cer·ous·ly,** *adv.*

can·cer·ate (kan′sə rāt′), *v.i.,* **-at·ed, -at·ing.** to become cancerous; develop into cancer. [< L *cancerāt(us)* cancerous] —**can′cer·a′tion, can·cer·i·za·tion** (kan′sər i zā′shən *or, esp. Brit.,* -sə rī-), *n.*

can·croid (kang′kroid), *adj.* **1.** *Pathol.* resembling a cancer, as certain tumors. **2.** *Zool.* resembling a crab. —*n.* **3.** *Pathol.* a form of cancer of the skin. [< L *cancr-* (s. of *cancer*) CANCER + -OID]

can·de·la (kan dē′lə), *n.* *Optics.* a unit of luminous intensity, equal to 1/60 of the luminous intensity of a square centimeter of a black body heated to the temperature of the solidification of platinum (1773.5°C): adopted in 1948 as the international standard of luminous intensity. *Abbr.:* cd Also called **candle.** [< L: candle]

can·de·la·bra (kan′dᵊlä′brə, -dᵊlā′-), *n., pl.* **-bras** for 2. **1.** a pl. of **candelabrum. 2.** a candelabrum.

can·de·la·brum (kan′dᵊlä′brəm, -dᵊlā′-), *n., pl.* **-bra** (-brə). **-brums.** an ornamental branched holder for more than one candle. [< L: candlestick = *candēl(a)* CANDLE + *-ābrum* neut. suffix]

Candelabrum

can·dent (kan′dənt), *adj.* glowing with heat; at a white heat. [< L *candent-* (s. of *candēns,* prp. of *candēre* to be shining white) = *cand-* bright (see CANDID) + *-ent-* -ENT]

can·des·cent (kan des′ənt), *adj.* glowing; incandescent. [< L *candescent-* (s. of *candescēns,* prp. of *candescere* to become bright) = *cand-* bright (see CANDID) + *-escent-* -ESCENT] —**can·des′cence,** *n.* —**can·des′cent·ly,** *adv.*

C. & F., cost and freight (included in the price quoted). Also, **c. & f., c & f, C & F, C and F**

Can·di·a (kan′dē ə), *n.* **1.** Greek, **Herakleion.** a seaport in N Crete. 77,506. **2.** Crete (def. 1).

can·did (kan′did), *adj.* **1.** frank; outspoken; open and sincere: *a candid reply.* **2.** without reservation, disguise, or subterfuge; straightforward: *a candid opinion.* **3.** informal; unposed: *a candid photo.* **4.** honest; impartial: *a candid mind.* **5.** *Archaic.* white. **6.** *Archaic.* clear; pure. —*n.* **7.** an unposed photograph. [< L *candid(us)* shining white = *cand(ēre)* (to) be shining white + *-idus* -ID[4]] —**can′did·ly,** *adv.* —**can′did·ness,** *n.* —**Syn. 1.** See **frank.**

can·di·date (kan′di dāt′, -dit), *n.* **1.** a person who seeks an office, honor, etc. **2.** a person selected by others as a contestant for an office, honor, etc. [< L *candidāt(us)* clothed in white (adj.), candidate for office (n.: because he wore a white toga). See CANDID, -ATE[1]] —**can′di·da·cy** (kan′di də sē); *Brit.,* **can·di·da·ture** (kan′di də chər), **can′di·date·ship′,** *n.*

can′did cam′era, a small, handy camera, esp. one having a fast lens for unposed or informal pictures.

can·died (kan′dēd), *adj.* **1.** impregnated or incrusted with or as with sugar: *candied ginger.* **2.** prepared by cooking in sugar or syrup: *candied yams.* **3.** honeyed or sweet; flattering.

Can·di·ot (kan′dē ot′), *adj.* **1.** of or pertaining to Candia or Crete; Cretan. —*n.* **2.** a Cretan. Also, **Can·di·ote** (kan′dē ōt′).

can·dle (kan′dᵊl), *n., v.,* **-dled, -dling.** —*n.* **1.** a long, usually slender piece of tallow, wax, etc., with an embedded wick, burned to give light. **2.** something like this in appearance or use. **3.** *Optics.* candela. **4. not hold a candle to,** to compare unfavorably with. —*v.t.* **5.** to examine (eggs) for freshness by holding them up to a bright light. [ME, OE *candel* < L *candēl(a)* = *candē(re)* (to) shine + *-la* fem. suffix; see CANDID] —**can′dler,** *n.*

can·dle·ber·ry (kan′dᵊl ber′ē), *n., pl.* **-ries. 1.** a wax myrtle of the genus *Myrica.* **2.** its berry. **3.** the candlenut.

can·dle·fish (kan′dᵊl fish′), *n., pl.* (*esp. collectively*) **-fish,** (*esp. referring to two or more kinds or species*) **-fish·es. 1.** a small, edible, oily, smeltlike fish, *Thaleichthys pacificus,* of the North Pacific that can be dried and burned as a candle. **2.** sablefish. Also called **eulachon.**

can·dle·light (kan′dᵊl līt′), *n.* **1.** the light of a candle. **2.** a dim artificial light. **3.** twilight; dusk. [ME *candel-liht,* OE *candel-lēoht*]

Can·dle·mas (kan′dᵊl məs, -mas′), *n.* a religious festival, February 2, in honor of the presentation of the infant Jesus in the temple and the purification of the Virgin Mary: candles are blessed on this day. Also, called **Can′dlemas Day′.** [ME, OE]

can·dle·nut (kan′dᵊl nut′), *n.* **1.** the oily fruit or nut of a euphorbiaceous tree, *Aleurites moluccana,* of the South Sea Islands, Southeast Asia, etc., used as candles by the natives. **2.** the tree itself.

can·dle·pin (kan′dᵊl pin′), *n.* **1.** a bowling pin that is almost cylindrical, used in a game resembling tenpins. **2. candlepins,** (*construed as sing.*) the game played with these pins.

can·dle·pow·er (kan′dᵊl pou′ər), *n.* *Optics.* **1.** candela. **2.** luminous intensity, as of light, or illuminating capacity, as of a lamp, measured in candelas.

can·dle·stick (kan′dᵊl stik′), *n.* a holder having a socket or a spike for a candle. [ME, OE]

can·dle·wick (kan′dᵊl wik′), *n.* **1.** the wick of a candle. —*adj.* **2.** (of a fabric, usually unbleached muslin) having small, short bunches of wicking tufted to form a design.

can·dle·wood (kan′dᵊl wo͝od′), *n.* **1.** any resinous wood used for torches or as a substitute for candles. **2.** any of various trees or shrubs yielding such wood.

can·dor (kan′dər), *n.* **1.** the state or quality of being frank, open, and sincere in speech or expression; candidness. **2.** freedom from bias; fairness; impartiality: *to consider an issue with candor.* **3.** *Obs.* kindliness. **4.** *Obs.* purity. Also, *esp. Brit.,* **can′dour.** [< L: sincerity, lit., luster; see CANDID, -OR[1]]

can·dy (kan′dē), *n., pl.* **-dies,** *v.,* **-died, -dy·ing.** —*n.* **1.** any of a variety of confections made with sugar, syrup, etc., combined with other ingredients. **2.** a single piece of such a confection. —*v.t.* **3.** to cook in sugar or syrup, as sweet potatoes or carrots. **4.** to cook in heavy syrup until transparent, as fruit, fruit peel, or ginger. **5.** to reduce (sugar, syrup, etc.) to a crystalline form, usually by boiling down. **6.** to cover with sugar or sugarlike crystals. **7.** to make sweet, palatable, or agreeable. —*v.i.* **8.** to become covered with sugar. **9.** to crystallize. [short for *sugar candy,* ME *sugre candy* candied sugar < MF *sucre candi; candy* << Ar *qandī* of sugar = *qand* sugar (< Pers; perh. orig. piece of sugar cane; if so, akin to Skt *khaṇḍa* piece) + *-ī* suffix]

can·dy·tuft (kan′dē tuft′), *n.* a brassicaceous plant of the genus *Iberis,* esp. *I. umbellata,* a cultivated annual with tufted flowers, originally from the island of Crete. [*Candy* (var. of CANDIA) + TUFT]

cane (kān), *n., v.,* **caned, can·ing.** —*n.* **1.** a short staff, often having a curved handle, used as a support in walking; walking stick. **2.** a long, hollow or pithy, jointed woody stem, as that of bamboo, rattan, sugar cane, certain palms, etc. **3.** a plant having such a stem. **4.** split rattan, used for chair seats, wickerwork, etc. **5.** any of several tall, bamboolike grasses, esp. of the genus *Arundinaria.* **6.** the stem of the raspberry or blackberry. **7.** See **sugar cane. 8.** any rod used for flogging. **9.** a slender cylinder or rod, as of sealing wax, glass, etc. —*v.t.* **10.** to flog with a cane. **11.** to furnish or make with cane: *to cane chairs.* [ME < MF < L *cann(a)* < Gk *kánna* < Sem.; cf. Ar *qanāh,* Heb *qāneh* reed]

Ca·ne·a (kə nē′ə), *n.* a seaport on and the capital of Crete, on the W part. 40,564. Greek, **Khania.**

cane·brake (kān′brāk′), *n.* a thicket of canes.

ca·nel·la (kə nel′ə), *n.* the cinnamonlike bark of a West Indian tree, *Canella winterana,* used as a condiment and in medicine. [< ML: cinnamon = L *cann(a)* CANE + *ella* dim. suffix]

cane′ sug′ar, sugar obtained from sugar cane, identical with that obtained from the sugar beet.

Ca·net·ti (kə net′ē), *n.* **Elias,** born 1905 in Bulgaria; novelist, essayist, and playwright (writing in German); in England since 1939: Nobel prize 1981.

CanF, Canadian French.

can·field (kan′fēld′), *n.* *Cards.* a form of solitaire often used as a gambling game. [named after R. A. *Canfield* (1855–1914), its inventor]

cangue (kang), *n.* (formerly in China) a wooden framework fastened about the neck of an offender as a portable pillory. [F sp. of *cang* < Pg *cang(o),* var. of *canga* yoke < ?]

ca·nic′o·la fe′ver (kə nik′ə lə), *Pathol.* an acute febrile disease of man and dogs, characterized by inflammation of the stomach and intestines and by jaundice: caused by a spirochete, *Leptospira canicola.* [< NL *canicola* dog-dweller = L *cani(s)* dog + *-cola* dweller; see -COLOUS]

Ca·nic·u·la (kə nik′yə lə), *n.* *Astron. Rare.* Sirius; the Dog Star. [< L: lit., little dog; see CANINE, -CULE]

ca·nic·u·lar (kə nik′yə lər), *adj.* *Astron.* pertaining to the rising of the Dog Star or to the star itself; Sothic. [< L *canīculār(is)* of Sirius]

can·i·kin (kan′ə kin), *n.* cannikin.

ca·nine (kā′nīn, kə nīn′), *adj.* **1.** of or like a dog; pertaining to or characteristic of dogs. **2.** *Anat., Zool.* of or pertaining to the four pointed teeth, esp. prominent in dogs, situated one on each side of each jaw, next to the incisors. —*n.* **3.** any animal of the *Canidae,* or dog family, including the wolves, jackals, hyenas, coyotes, and foxes. **4.** a dog. **5.** a canine tooth; cuspid. [< L *canīn(us)* = *can(is)* dog + *-īnus* -INE[1]] —**ca·nin·i·ty** (kā nin′i tē), *n.*

Ca·nis Ma·jor (kā′nis mā′jər), *gen.* **Ca·nis Ma·jo·ris** (kā′nis mə jôr′is, -jōr′-). *Astron.* the Great Dog, a southern constellation containing Sirius, the Dog Star, the brightest of the stars. [< L: greater dog]

Ca·nis Mi·nor (kā′nis mī′nər), *gen.* **Ca·nis Mi·no·ris** (kā′nis mī nōr′is, -nôr′-). *Astron.* the Little or Lesser Dog, a small southern constellation west of Orion and south of Gemini, containing the bright star Procyon. [< L: lesser dog]

can·is·ter (kan′i stər), *n.* **1.** a small box, usually of metal, for holding tea, coffee, etc. **2.** Also called **can′ister shot′.** See **case shot. 3.** the part of a gas mask containing the neutralizing substances through which poisoned air is filtered. [< L *canistr(um)* wicker basket < Gk *kánastron* = *kánn(a)* reed (see CANE) + *-astron* neut. suffix]

can·ker (kaŋg′kər), *n.* **1.** *Pathol.* a gangrenous or ulcerous sore, esp. in the mouth. **2.** *Vet. Pathol.* a disease affecting horses' feet, usually the soles, characterized by a foul-smelling exudate. **3.** *Plant Pathol.* a defined area of diseased tissue, esp. in woody stems. **4.** anything that corrodes, corrupts, destroys, or irritates. **5.** *Dial.* See **dog rose.** —*v.t.* **6.** to infect with canker. **7.** to corrupt; destroy slowly. —*v.i.* **8.** to become infected with or as with canker. [ME; OE *cancer* < L *cancer* crab, gangrene] —**can′ker·ous,** *adj.*

can′ker sore′, *Pathol.* an ulceration of the mucous membrane of the mouth.

can·ker·worm (kaŋg′kər wûrm′), *n.* the larva of any of several geometrid moths, which destroys fruit and shade trees. See illus. at **geometrid.**

can·na (kan′ə), *n.* any tropical plant of the genus *Canna*, of the family *Cannaceae* having large leaves and showy flowers. [< NL, L: reed; see CANE]

can·na·bin (kan′ə bin), *n.* a poisonous resin extracted from Indian hemp. [< L *cannab(is)* hemp + -IN²]

can·na·bis (kan′ə bis), *n.* hashish; the dried pistillate parts of Indian hemp, *Cannabis sativa.* [< L: hemp < Gk *kánnabis*; see HEMP] —**can′na·bic,** *adj.*

Can·nae (kan′ē), *n.* an ancient town in SE Italy: Hannibal defeated the Romans here 216 B.C.

Can·na·nore (kan′ə nōr′, -nôr′), *n.* a port in SW India, on the Arabian Sea. 46,100 (1961). Also, **Kananur.**

canned (kand), *adj.* **1.** preserved in a can or jar: *canned peaches.* **2.** *Slang.* **a.** recorded or taped: *canned music.* **b.** prepared in advance for repeated use: *a canned program.*

can′nel coal′ (kan′ᵊl), an oily, compact coal, burning readily and brightly. Also called **can′nel.** [dial. *cannel* CANDLE]

can·ner·y (kan′ə rē), *n., pl.* **-ner·ies.** a place where foodstuffs are canned.

Cannes (kan, kanz; *Fr.* KAN), *n.* a city in SE France, on the Mediterranean Sea: resort. 59,173 (1962).

can·ni·bal (kan′ə bəl), *n.* **1.** a person who eats human flesh. **2.** any animal that eats its own kind. —*adj.* **3.** cannibalistic. [< Sp *Caníbal*, var. of *Caribal* = *Canib-*, *Carib-* (< Arawak) + *-al* -AL¹; the Caribs of the West Indies were thought to eat human flesh] —**can′ni·bal·ism,** *n.*

can·ni·bal·is·tic (kan′ə bə lis′tik), *adj.* of, pertaining to, or characteristic of a cannibal or cannibals; man-eating. —**can′ni·bal·is′ti·cal·ly,** *adv.*

can·ni·bal·ize (kan′ə bə līz′), *v.t., v.i.,* **-ized, -iz·ing.** **1.** to subject to or practice cannibalism. **2.** *Chiefly Mil.* to take from one thing, as a part from a machine, and add it to another. —**can′ni·bal·i·za′tion,** *n.*

can·ni·kin (kan′ə kin), *n.* **1.** a small can or drinking cup. **2.** a small wooden bucket. Also, **canakin, canikin.** [< MD *cannekin* little can = *canne* CAN² + *-kin* -KIN]

Can·ning (kan′iŋg), *n.* **1. Charles John, 1st Earl,** 1812–62, British statesman: governor general of India 1856–62. **2.** his father, **George,** 1770–1827, British statesman: prime minister 1827. **3. Sir Stratford.** See **Stratford de Radcliffe, 1st Viscount.**

Can·niz·za·ro (kän′nēd dsär′rô), *n.* **Sta·nis·la·o** (stä′nēz lä′ô), 1826–1910, Italian chemist.

can·non (kan′ən), *n., pl.* **-nons,** (*esp. collectively*) **-non,** *v.* —*n.* **1.** a mounted gun for firing heavy projectiles; a gun, howitzer, or mortar. **2.** a round bit for a horse. **3.** (on a bell) the metal loop by which a bell is hung. **4.** the part of the leg in which the cannon bone is situated. **5.** *Brit.* a carom in billiards. —*v.i.* **6.** to discharge cannon. **7.** *Brit.* to make a carom in billiards. [earlier *canon* < MF < It *cannon(e)* = *cann(a)* tube (< L; see CANE) + *-one* aug. suffix]

Can·non (kan′ən), *n.* **Joseph Gur·ney** (gûr′nē), ("*Uncle Joe*"), 1836–1926, U.S. politician and legislator.

can·non·ade (kan′ə nād′), *n., v.,* **-ad·ed, -ad·ing.** —*n.* **1.** a continued discharge of cannon, esp. during an attack. —*v.t., v.i.* **2.** to attack with or discharge cannon. [< F *canonnade* < It *cannonat(a)* = *cannon(e)* CANNON + *-ata* -ADE¹]

can·non·ball (kan′ən bôl′), *n.* Also, **can′non ball′.** **1.** a missile, usually round and made of iron or steel, designed to be fired from a cannon. **2.** *Tennis.* a served ball that travels with great speed and describes little or no arc in flight. **3.** an express train. —*v.i.* **4.** to move like a cannonball, with great rapidity or force.

can′non bone′, *Zool.* the greatly developed middle metacarpal or metatarsal bone of hoofed quadruped mammals, extending from the hock to the fetlock. [CANNON in obs. sense, tube]

can·non·eer (kan′ə nēr′), *n.* an artilleryman. [< MF *canonnier*] —**can′non·eer′ing,** *n.*

can′non fod′der, soldiers, regarded as the cheapest material consumed in war.

can·non·ry (kan′ən rē), *n., pl.* **-ries.** **1.** a discharge of artillery. **2.** artillery (def. 1).

can·not (kan′ot, ka not′, kə-), *v.* a form of **can not.**

can·nu·la (kan′yə lə), *n., pl.* **-las, -lae** (-lē′). *Surg.* a tube for insertion into the body, used to draw off fluid or to introduce medication. Also, **canula.** [< NL, L: small reed = *cann(a)* CANE + *-ula* -ULE] —**can′nu·la′tion,** *n.*

can·nu·lar (kan′yə lər), *adj.* tubular.

can·ny (kan′ē), *adj.,* **-ni·er, -ni·est.** **1.** careful; cautious; prudent. **2.** astute; shrewd; knowing; sagacious. **3.** *Scot.* **a.** frugal; thrifty. **b.** safe to deal with, invest in, or work at (usually used with a negative). **c.** gentle; careful; steady. **d.** snug; cozy; comfortable. **e.** pleasing; attractive; pretty. **f.** *Archaic.* having supernatural or occult powers. [CAN¹ + -Y¹] —**can′ni·ness,** *n.* —**can′ni·ly,** *adv.*

ca·noe (kə no͞o′), *n., v.,* **-noed, -noe·ing.** —*n.* **1.** any of various slender, open boats propelled by paddles or sails and formed of light framework covered with bark, skins, canvas, aluminum, etc., or formed from a dug-out or burned-out log or logs. —*v.i.* **2.** to paddle a canoe. **3.** to go in a canoe. —*v.t.* **4.** to transport or carry by canoe. [< F < Sp *canoa* < Arawak; r. *canoa* < Sp] —**ca·noe′ist,** *n.*

ca·noe·wood (kə no͞o′wo͝od′), *n.* See **tulip tree.**

can·on¹ (kan′ən), *n.* **1.** an ecclesiastical rule or law enacted by a council or other competent authority and, in the Roman Catholic Church, approved by the pope. **2.** the body of ecclesiastical law. **3.** a body of rules, principles, or standards accepted as axiomatic and universally binding, as in a field of study or art. **4.** a standard; criterion. **5.** the books of the Bible recognized as holy by any Christian church. **6.** any officially recognized set of sacred books. **7.** *Literature.* the works of an author that have been accepted as authentic. Cf. **apocrypha** (def. 3). **8.** *Liturgy.* that part of the Mass between the Sanctus and the Communion. **9.** *Music.* consistent, note-for-note imitation of one melodic line by another, in which the second line starts after the first. **10.** *Print.* a 48-point type. [ME, OE < L < Gk *kanṓn* measuring rod, rule, akin to *kánna* CANE]

can·on² (kan′ən), *n.* **1.** a clergyman who is a member of the chapter of a cathedral or a collegiate church. **2.** *Rom. Cath. Ch.* one of the members **(canons regular)** of certain religious orders. [back formation from OE *canōnic* (one) under rule < ML *canōnic(us)*, L: of or under rule < Gk *kanōnikós.* See CANON¹, -IC]

ca·ñon (kan′yən), *n.* canyon.

can·on·ess (kan′ə nis), *n.* a member of a Christian community of women living under a rule but not under a vow.

ca·non·i·cal (kə non′i kəl), *adj.* Also, **ca·non′ic.** **1.** pertaining to, established by, or conforming to a canon or canons. **2.** included in the canon of the Bible. **3.** authorized; recognized; accepted. **4.** *Math.* (of an equation, coordinate, etc.) in simplest or standard form. —*n.* **5. canonicals,** garments prescribed by canon law for clergy when officiating. [late ME < ML *canōnicāl(is)*] —**ca·non′i·cal·ly,** *adv.* —**can·on·ic·i·ty** (kan′ə nis′i tē), *n.*

canon′ical hour′, **1.** *Eccles.* any of certain periods of the day set apart for prayer and devotion: these are matins (with lauds), prime, tierce, sext, nones, vespers, and complin. **2.** *Brit.* any hour between 8 A.M. and 3 P.M. during which marriage may be legally performed in parish churches.

can·on·ise (kan′ə nīz′), *v.t.,* **-ised, -is·ing.** *Chiefly Brit.* canonize. —**can′on·i·sa′tion,** *n.* —**can′on·is′er,** *n.*

can·on·ist (kan′ə nist), *n.* an expert in canon law. —**can′on·is′tic, can′on·is′ti·cal,** *adj.*

can·on·ize (kan′ə nīz′), *v.t.,* **-ized, -iz·ing.** **1.** *Eccles.* to declare to be a saint. **2.** to glorify. **3.** to make canonical; place or include within a canon, esp. of scriptural works. **4.** to consider or treat as sacrosanct or holy. **5.** to sanction or approve authoritatively, esp. ecclesiastically. **6.** *Archaic.* to deify. Also, *esp. Brit.,* **canonise.** —**can′on·i·za′tion,** *n.* —**can′on·iz′er,** *n.*

can′on law′, the body of codified ecclesiastical law, esp. of the Roman Catholic Church as promulgated in ecclesiastical councils and by the pope.

can·on·ry (kan′ən rē), *n., pl.* **-ries.** the office or benefice of a canon.

can′ons reg′ular. See under **canon²** (def. 2).

Ca·no′pic jar′ (kə nō′pik), a jar used in ancient Egypt to hold the entrails of an embalmed body. Also called **Cano′pic vase′.** [< L *Canōpicus* of Canopus]

Ca·no·pus (kə nō′pəs), *n.* **1.** *Astron.* a first-magnitude star in the constellation Carina: the second brightest star in the heavens. **2.** an ancient seacoast city in Lower Egypt, 15 miles east of Alexandria.

can·o·py (kan′ə pē), *n., pl.* **-pies,** *v.,* **-pied, -py·ing.** —*n.* **1.** a covering, usually of fabric, supported on poles or suspended above a bed, throne, etc. **2.** an overhanging projection or covering as one stretching from a doorway to the curb. **3.** the sky. **4.** the part of a parachute that opens up and catches the air. **5.** the transparent cover over the cockpit of an airplane. —*v.t.* **6.** to cover with or as with a canopy. [ME *canope* < ML *canōpē(um)*, var. of L *cōnōpēum* mosquito net < Gk *kōnōpeîon* bed with net to keep gnats off = *kṓnōp(s)* gnat + *-eion*, neut. of *-eios* adj. suffix]

ca·no·rous (kə nōr′əs, -nôr′-), *adj.* melodious; musical. [< L *canōrus* = *canōr-* (s. of *canor* song = *can(ere)* (to) sing + *-or* -OR¹) + *-us* -OUS] —**ca·no′rous·ly,** *adv.* —**ca·no′rous·ness,** *n.*

Ca·nos·sa (kə nos′ə; *It.* kä nôs′sä), *n.* a ruined castle in N Italy: scene of the penance of Emperor Henry IV of the Holy Roman Empire before Pope Gregory VII in 1077.

Ca·no·va (kə nō′və; *It.* kä nô′vä), *n.* **An·to·nio** (än tô′nyô), 1757–1822, Italian sculptor.

Can·so (kan′sō), *n.* **Cape,** a cape in SE Canada, the NE extremity of Nova Scotia.

canst (kanst), *v.* *Archaic or Literary.* 2nd pers. sing. pres. of **can.**

cant¹ (kant), *n.* **1.** insincere statements, esp. pious or sanctimonious platitudes. **2.** the special language or jargon spoken by a particular class, profession, etc. **3.** singsong speech. —*v.i.* **4.** to pretend goodness or piety, esp. by speaking sanctimoniously. **5.** to beg in a singsong tone. [< L base *cant*, in *cantus* song, *canticus* singsong, etc., whence OE *cantere* singer, *cantic* song; see CHANT]

cant² (kant), *n.* **1.** a salient angle. **2.** a sudden movement that tilts or overturns a thing. **3.** a slanting or tilted position. **4.** an oblique line or surface, as one formed by cutting off the corner of a square or cube. **5.** an oblique or slanting face of anything. **6.** bank¹ (def. 6). **7.** a sudden pitch or toss. —*v.t.* **8.** to bevel; form an oblique surface upon. **9.** to put in an oblique position; tilt; tip. **10.** to throw with a sudden jerk. —*v.i.* **11.** to assume or have an inclined position; tilt; turn; slant. [ME: corner, angle, niche, perh. OE *cant(el)* buttress, support < L *cant(h)us* tire of a wheel, corner of the eye < Gk *kanthós* felloe, corner of the eye] —**cant′ic,** *adj.*

cant³ (känt), *adj.* *Brit. Dial.* hearty; merry. [< LG *kant* merry, bold]

can't (kant, känt), contraction of *cannot.*

Cant., **1.** Canterbury. **2.** Canticles.

Cantab., Cantabrigian.

can·ta·bi·le (kän tä′bi lā′, -bē-, kən-; *It.* kän tä′bē le′), *Music.* —*adj.* **1.** songlike and flowing in style. —*n.* **2.** a cantabile style, passage, or piece. [< It < LL *cantābil(is)* worth singing = L *cantā(re)* (to) sing (see CANT¹) + *-bilis* -BLE]

Can·ta·brig·i·an (kan′tə brij′ē ən), *adj.* **1.** of Cambridge, England, or Cambridge University. **2.** of Cambridge, Massachusetts, or Harvard University. —*n.* **3.** a native or inhabitant of Cambridge. **4.** a student at or graduate of Cambridge University or Harvard University. [< ML *Cantabrigi(a)* Cambridge + -AN]

can·ta·lev·er (kan′tᵊlev′ər, -tᵊlē′vər), *n.* cantilever. Also, **can·ta·li·ver** (kan′tᵊlē′vər).

can·ta·loupe (kan′tᵊlōp′), *n.* **1.** a variety of melon, *Cucumis Melo cantalupensis,* having a hard, scaly, or warty rind, grown chiefly in Europe. **2.** any of several muskmelons resembling the cantaloupe. Also, **can′ta·loup′.** [< F, after *Cantelupo,* former papal estate near Rome where the cultivation of this Armenian melon was begun in Europe]

can·tan·ker·ous (kan tang′kər əs), *adj.* quarrelsome, grouchy, and contentious; peevish; ill-natured; irritable: *a cantankerous old maid.* [perh. var. of earlier **contenkerous;* see CONTENTIOUS, RANCOROUS] —**can·tan′ker·ous·ly,** *adv.* —**can·tan′ker·ous·ness,** *n.*

can·ta·ta (kən tä′tə), *n. Music.* a choral composition, either sacred and resembling a short oratorio, or secular, as a drama set to music but not to be acted. [< It = *cant(are)* (to) sing (see CHANT) + *-ata* -ADE[1]]

can·ta·tri·ce (*It.* kän′tä trē′che; *Fr.* kän ta trēs′), *n., pl. It.* **-tri·ci** (trē′chē), *Fr.* **-trices** (-trēs′). *Italian, French.* a professional female singer.

can·teen (kan tēn′), *n.* **1.** *U.S.* a small container used by soldiers and others for carrying water or other liquids. **2.** *U.S. Army.* (formerly) a post exchange. **3.** a place where free entertainment is provided for enlisted men, usually in a town or city near a military installation. **4.** a box or chest for cutlery and other table utensils. [< F *cantine* < It *cantin(a)* cellar = *cant(o)* corner (< L; see CANT[2]) + *-ina* -INE[1]]

can·ter (kan′tər), *n.* **1.** an easy gallop. —*v.t., v.i.* **2.** to go or ride at a canter. [short for *Canterbury* to ride at a pace like that of Canterbury pilgrims]

Can·ter·bur·y (kan′tər ber′ē, -bə rē, -brē), *n.* **1.** a city in E Kent, in SE England: cathedral; early ecclesiastical center of England. 30,376 (1961). **2.** a municipality in E New South Wales, in SE Australia: a part of Sydney. 113,820 (1961). —**Can·ter·bu·ri·an** (kan′tər byŏŏr′ē ən), *adj.*

Can′terbury bell′, a plant, *Campanula media,* cultivated for its showy violet-blue, pink, or white flowers.

Can′terbury Tales′, The, an uncompleted sequence of tales by Chaucer, for the most part written after 1387.

can·thar·i·des (kan thar′i dēz′), *n. pl., sing.* **can·thar·is** (kan thar′is). **1.** See **Spanish fly** (def. 1). **2.** cantharis. See **Spanish fly** (def. 2). [ME < L, pl. of *cantharis* < Gk *kantharis* blister fly]

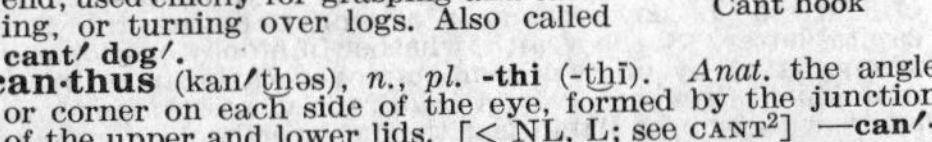

Cant hook

cant′ hook′ (kant), a wooden lever with a movable iron hook near the lower end, used chiefly for grasping and canting, or turning over logs. Also called **cant′ dog′.**

can·thus (kan′thəs), *n., pl.* **-thi** (-thī). *Anat.* the angle or corner on each side of the eye, formed by the junction of the upper and lower lids. [< NL, L; see CANT[2]] —**can′-thal,** *adj.*

can·ti·cle (kan′ti kəl), *n.* **1.** a nonmetrical, liturgical hymn, esp. one from the Bible. **2.** a song, poem, or hymn, esp. in praise. [< L *canticul(um)* = *cantic(um)* song (*cant(us),* ptp. of *canere* to sing, + *-icum* neut. of *-icus* -IC) + *-ulum* -ULE]

A B

Canthus
A, Inner canthus
B, Outer canthus

Can′ticle of Can′ticles, *Douay Bible.* See **Song of Solomon, The.**

Can·ti·gny (käN tē nyē′), *n.* a village in N France, S of Amiens: first major battle of U.S. forces in World War I, May 1918.

can·ti·lev·er (kan′tᵊlev′ər, -tᵊlē′vər), *n.* **1.** any rigid structural member projecting from a vertical support, esp. one in which the projection is great with relation to the depth, so that the upper part is in tension and the lower part in compression. **2.** *Building Trades, Civ. Eng.* any rigid construction extending horizontally well beyond its vertical support, used as a structural element of a bridge, building foundation, etc. **3.** *Aeron.* a form of wing construction in which no external bracing is used. **4.** *Archit.* a bracket, low in proportion to its extent, for supporting a balcony, cornice, etc. —*v.i.* **5.** to project in the manner of a cantilever. —*v.t.* **6.** to construct in the manner of a cantilever. Also, **cantalever, cantaliver.** [? CANT[2] + -I- + LEVER]

can·til·late (kan′tᵊlāt′), *v.t.,* **-lat·ed, -lat·ing.** to chant (a liturgical text) in plainsong style; intone. [< LL *cantillāt(us)* sung low, hummed (ptp. of *cantillāre*) = *cant-* sing (see CANT[1]) + *-ill-* dim. suffix + *-ātus* -ATE[1]] —**can′-til·la′tion,** *n.*

can·ti·na (kan tē′nə; *Sp.* kän tē′nä), *n., pl.* **-nas** (-nəz; *Sp.* -näs). *Southwestern U.S.* a saloon. [< Sp < It; see CANTEEN]

cant′ing arms′, *Heraldry.* a coat of arms whose blazon contains a punning reference to the family name of the owner, as a heart within a padlock for Lockhart.

can·tle (kan′tᵊl), *n.* **1.** the hind part of a saddle, usually curved upward. **2.** a corner; piece; portion: *a cantle of land.* [ME *cantel* < ML *cantell(us)* = L *cant(us)* (see CANT[2]) + *-ellus* dim. suffix]

can·to (kan′tō), *n., pl.* **-tos.** one of the main or larger divisions of a long poem. [< It < L *cant(us)* song, n. use of *cantus* sung (ptp. of *canere*) = *can-* sing + *-tus* ptp. suffix]

can·ton (kan′tᵊn, -ton, kan ton′ *for 1–6;* kan ton′, -tōn′ or, *esp. Brit.,* -tōōn′ *for 7*), *n.* **1.** a small territorial district, esp. one of the states of the Swiss confederation. **2.** (in a department of France) a division of an arrondissement. **3.** *Heraldry.* a square area in the dexter chief, or right-hand corner, of an escutcheon, often distinctively treated: a diminutive of the dexter chief quarter. **4.** *Obs.* a division, part, or portion of anything. —*v.t.* **5.** to divide into parts or portions. **6.** to divide into cantons or territorial districts. **7.** to allot quarters to (soldiers, troops, etc.). [< MF < It *canton(e)* = *cant(o)* corner (see CANT[2]) + *-one* aug. suffix] —**can′ton·al,** *adj.*

Can·ton (kan ton′, kan′ton *for 1;* kan′tᵊn *for 2*), *n.* **1.** Chinese, **Kuangchou, Kwangchow.** a seaport in and the capital of Kwangtung province, in SE China, on the Chu-Kiang River. 1,840,000 (est. 1957). **2.** a city in NE Ohio. 110,053 (1970).

Can′ton crepe′, a thin, light, silk or rayon crepe with a finely wrinkled surface. [after CANTON, China]

Can·ton·ese (kan′tᵊnēz′, -tᵊnēs′), *n., pl.* **-ese,** *adj.* —*n.* **1.** a Chinese language spoken in Canton, the surrounding area of southern China, and Hong Kong. **2.** a native or inhabitant of Canton, China. —*adj.* **3.** pertaining to Canton, China, or to its inhabitants or their language.

Can′ton flan′nel, a plain-weave or twill-weave cotton fabric, napped only on the face. Also called **cotton flannel.** [after CANTON, China]

can·ton·ment (kan ton′mənt, -tōn′-; *esp. Brit.* kan tōōn′-mənt), *n.* **1.** a camp, usually of large size, where men are trained for military service. **2.** military quarters. **3.** the winter quarters of an army. [< F *cantonnement* = *cantonne(r)* (to) quarter troops (see CANTON) + *-ment* -MENT]

Can·ton′ Riv′er (kan ton′, kan′ton), Chu-Kiang.

can·tor (kan′tər, -tôr), *n.* **1.** *Eccles.* a precentor. **2.** *Judaism.* the religious official of a synagogue who sings or chants the prayers designed to be performed as solos. Cf. **rabbi** (def. 1). [< L = *cant(us)* sung (ptp. of *canere;* see CANTO) + *-or* -OR[2]]

Can·tor (kan′tər; *also Ger.* kän′tôR), *n.* **Ge·org** (gā′ôRk), 1845–1918, German mathematician, born in Russia.

can·trip (kän′tRip), *n. Chiefly Scot.* **1.** a spell. **2.** mischief; trick. Also, **can·trap, can·traip** (kän′tRip). [appar. dissimilated var. of OE *calcatrippe;* see CALTROP]

can·tus (kan′təs), *n., pl.* **-tus. 1.** a melody, esp. for the soprano part, in polyphonic compositions. **2.** See **cantus firmus** (def. 2). [< L; see CANTO]

can·tus fir·mus (kan′təs fûr′məs), **1.** *Eccles.* the ancient traditional vocal music of the Christian church, having its form set and its use prescribed by ecclesiastical authority. **2.** *Music.* (in polyphonic compositions) a fixed melody to which other melodic parts are added. [< ML: lit., firm song]

Ca·nuck (kə nuk′), *n. Offensive.* a Canadian, esp. a French Canadian. [CAN(ADA) + *-uck* < ?]

ca·nu·la (kan′yə lə), *n., pl.* **-las, -lae** (-lē′). *Surg.* cannula.

Ca·nute (kə nōōt′, -nyōōt′), *n.* A.D. 994?–1035, Danish king of England, 1017–35; of Denmark, 1018–35; and of Norway, 1028–35. Also, **Cnut, Knut.**

can·vas (kan′vəs), *n.* **1.** a closely woven, heavy cloth of hemp, flax, or cotton, used for tents, sails, etc. **2.** a piece of this or similar material on which an oil painting is made. **3.** an oil painting on canvas. **4.** a tent, or tents collectively. **5.** sailcloth. **6.** sails collectively. **7.** any fabric of a coarse loose weave used as a foundation for embroidery stitches, interlining, etc. **8. under canvas, a.** *Naut.* with set sails. **b.** *Mil.* in tents; in the field: *to sleep under canvas.* [ME *canevas* < ONF < VL **cannabaceus* = L *cannab(is)* HEMP + *-aceus* -ACEOUS]

can·vas·back (kan′vəs bak′), *n., pl.* **-backs,** (*esp. collectively*) **-back.** a North American wild duck, *Aythya valisineria,* the male of which has a whitish back and a reddish-brown head and neck. [after the canvaslike color of its back]

can·vass (kan′vəs), *v.t.* **1.** to solicit votes, sales, opinions, etc., from (a district, group of people, etc.). **2.** to investigate by inquiry; discuss; debate. **3.** *Obs.* to criticize severely. —*v.i.* **4.** to solicit votes, opinions, etc. —*n.* **5.** a soliciting of votes, sales, etc. **6.** a campaign for election to government office. **7.** examination; close inspection; scrutiny. [var. of CANVAS (n.); orig. meaning of v.: to toss (a person) in a canvas sheet] —**can′vass·er,** *n.*

can·yon (kan′yən), *n.* a deep valley with steep sides, often with a stream flowing through it. Also, **cañon.** [< Sp *cañón* a long tube, a hollow = *cañ(a)* tube (< L *canna* CANE) + *-on* aug. suffix]

can·zo·ne (kän tsô′ne), *n., pl.* **-zo·ni** (-tsô′nē). a variety of lyric poetry in the Italian style, of Provençal origin, that closely resembles the madrigal. [< It < L *cantiōn-* (s. of *cantiō*) song = *cant(us)* sung (see CANTO) + *-iōn-* -ION]

can·zo·net (kan′zə net′), *n.* a short song, esp. a light and gay one. [< It *canzonett(a).* See CANZONE, -ET]

caou·tchouc (kou′chŏŏk, kou chŏŏk′), *n.* **1.** rubber[1] (def. 1). **2.** pure rubber. [< F < Sp *cauchuc* (now obs.) < Quechua]

cap[1] (kap), *n., v.,* **capped, cap·ping.** —*n.* **1.** a covering for the head, made of soft, usually close-fitting material, and having a small visor. **2.** a covering of lace or the like for a woman's head. **3.** a headdress denoting rank, occupation, or the like: *a nurse's cap.* **4.** a mortarboard. **5.** anything resembling a covering for the head in shape, use, or position: *a cap on a bottle.* **6.** *Bot.* the pileus of a mushroom. **7.** a percussion cap. **8.** a noisemaking device for toy pistols, made of a small quantity of explosive wrapped in paper. **9.** *Archit.* a capital. **10. cap in hand,** humbly; in supplication. **11. set one's cap for,** to attempt to catch as a husband. —*v.t.* **12.** to provide or cover with or as with a cap. **13.** to complete. **14.** to surpass with something better: *to cap one joke with another.* **15.** to serve as a cap, covering, or top to; overlie. [ME *cappe,* OE *cæppe* < LL *capp(a)* hooded cloak, cap; perh. akin to L *caput* head] —**cap′less,** *adj.* —**cap′per,** *n.*

cap[2] (kap), *n., v.,* **capped, cap·ping.** —*n.* **1.** a capital letter. **2.** Usually, **caps.** upper case. —*v.t.* **3.** to write or print in capital letters; capitalize. [by shortening]

CAP, Civil Air Patrol. Also, **C.A.P.**

cap., 1. capital. **2.** capitalize. **3.** capitalized. **4.** capital letter. **5.** chapter. [< L *capitulum, caput*] **6.** foolscap.

ca·pa·bil·i·ty (kā′pə bil′i tē), *n., pl.* **-ties. 1.** the quality of being capable; capacity; ability. **2.** the ability to undergo or be affected by a given treatment or action: *the capability of glass in resisting heat.* **3.** Usually, **capabilities.** qualities, abilities, etc., that can be used or developed: *Though dilapidated, the house has great capabilities.* [< LL *capābili(s)* CAPABLE + -TY[2]]

Ca·pa·blan·ca (kap′ə blang′kə; *Sp.* kä′pä vläng′kä), *n.* **Jo·sé Ra·oul** (hô se′ rä ōōl′), 1888–1942, Cuban chess master.

ca·pa·ble (kā′pə bəl), *adj.* **1.** having intelligence and ability; competent: *a capable instructor.* **2. capable of, a.** having the ability, skill, or experience for: *a man capable of judging art.* **b.** susceptible of: *a situation capable of improvement.* **c.** having the personality or character or being in the mood for: *capable of murder.* [< LL *capābil(is)* roomy, appar. = *capā(x)* roomy + *-bilis* -BLE; see CAPACITY] —**ca′pa·ble·ness,** *n.* —**ca′pa·bly,** *adv.* —**Syn. 1.** skillful, accomplished. See **able.**

ca·pa·cious (kə pā′shəs), *adj.* capable of holding a great quantity; very large. [CAPACI(TY) + -OUS] —**ca·pa′cious·ly,** *adv.* —**ca·pa′cious·ness,** *n.* —**Syn.** spacious, roomy.

ca·pac·i·tance (kə pas′i tᵊns), *n.* *Elect.* **1.** the ratio of the charge on either of a pair of conductors of a capacitor to the potential difference between the conductors. **2.** the property of being able to collect a charge of electricity. *Symbol:* C [CAPACIT(Y) + -ANCE] —**ca·pac′i·tive,** *adj.* —**ca·pac′i·tive·ly,** *adv.*

ca·pac·i·tate (kə pas′i tāt′), *v.t.,* **-tat·ed, -tat·ing.** to enable. [CAPACIT(Y) + -ATE[1]] —**ca·pac′i·ta′tion,** *n.*

capac′itive react′ance, *Elect.* the opposition of capacitance to alternating current, equal to the reciprocal of the product of the angular frequency of the current times the capacitance. *Symbol:* X_C Cf. **inductive reactance.**

ca·pac·i·tor (kə pas′i tər), *n.* *Elect.* a device for accumulating and holding a charge of electricity, consisting of two conductors separated by a dielectric and having equal, opposite charges. Also called **condenser.** [CAPACIT(Y) + -OR[2]]

ca·pac·i·ty (kə pas′i tē), *n., pl.* **-ties,** *adj.* —*n.* **1.** the ability to receive or contain: *This hotel has a large capacity.* **2.** cubic contents; volume; the amount that can be contained: *The gas tank has a capacity of 20 gallons.* **3.** power of receiving impressions, knowledge, etc.; mental ability: *the capacity to learn calculus.* **4.** actual or potential ability to do something: *He has no capacity for hard work. The capacity of the oil well was 150 barrels a day.* **5.** position; function; relation: *He served in the capacity of legal adviser.* **6.** legal qualification. **7.** *Elect.* **a.** capacitance. **b.** maximum possible output. —*adj.* **8.** holding or packed to fullest capacity: *a capacity audience.* [late ME *capacite* < MF < L *capācitāt-* (s. of *capācitās*) = *capāci-* (s. of *capāx*) roomy (*cap(ere)* (to) hold + *-āci-* adj. suffix) + *-tāt-* -TY[2]] —**Syn. 4.** aptitude, capability.

cap′ and gown′, a mortarboard and gown worn as academic costume.

Ca·pa·ne·us (kə pā′nē əs, kap′ə nōōs′, -nyōōs′), *n.* *Class. Myth.* one of the Seven against Thebes, who was destroyed by Zeus for blasphemy.

cap-a-pie (kap′ə pē′), *adv.* from head to foot. Also, **cap′-à-pie′.** [< MF *de cap a pe* from head to foot < OPr < L *dē capite ad pedem*]

ca·par·i·son (kə par′i sən), *n.* **1.** a decorative covering for the tack or harness of a horse; trappings. **2.** rich and sumptuous clothing or equipment. —*v.t.* **3.** to cover with a caparison. **4.** to dress richly. [< MF *caparasson* (F *caparaçon*) < OSp *caparazōn*, akin to *capa* CAPE[1]]

cape[1] (kāp), *n.* **1.** a sleeveless garment fastened at the neck and falling loosely from the shoulders. **2.** the capa of a bullfighter. [ME (north); OE *-cāp* (see COPE[2]), reinforced by Sp *capa* < LL *cappa* hooded cloak, COPE[2]] —**caped,** *adj.*

cape[2] (kāp), *n.* **1.** a piece of land jutting into a large body of water. **2. the Cape.** See **Cape of Good Hope. 3.** capeskin. —*adj.* **4.** (*cap.*) of the Cape of Good Hope or South Africa. [ME *cap* < MF < OPr < L *cap(ut)* head]

Cape′ Bret′on (brit′ᵊn, bret′ᵊn), an island forming the NE part of Nova Scotia, in SE Canada. 169,865 (1961); 3970 sq. mi. Also called **Cape′ Bret′on Is′land.**

Cape′ buf′falo, a large black buffalo, *Syncerus caffer,* of southern Africa, having horns that meet at the base forming a helmetlike structure over the forehead.

Cape′ Cod′, 1. a sandy peninsula in SE Massachusetts between Cape Cod Bay and the Atlantic Ocean. **2.** a style of cottage developed mainly on Cape Cod, Massachusetts, in the 18th and early 19th centuries, typically a one-story wooden cottage covered by a gable roof having a rise equal to the span.

Cape′ Cod′ Bay′, a part of Massachusetts Bay, enclosed by the Cape Cod peninsula.

Cape′ Col′ony, former name of **Cape of Good Hope.**

Cape′ Dutch′, Afrikaans.

Cape′ Gi·rar′deau (jə rär′dō), a city in SE Missouri, on the Mississippi River. 31,282 (1970).

Cape′ Horn′, a headland on a small island at the S extremity of South America: belongs to Chile.

Ča·pek (chä′pek), *n.* **Ka·rel** (kar′əl, kär′-; *Czech.* kä′rel), 1890–1938, Czech playwright and novelist.

cap·e·lin (kap′ə lin), *n.* either of two small fishes of the smelt family, *Mallotus villosus,* found off the coast of North America, or *M. catervarius,* found in the North Pacific. [< MF *capelan* < OPr: codfish, lit., CHAPLAIN]

Cape′ May′, a town in S New Jersey. 4392 (1970).

Cape′ of Good′ Hope′, 1. a cape in S Africa, in the SW Republic of South Africa. **2.** Also called **Cape′ Prov′ince.** Formerly, **Cape Colony.** a province in the Republic of South Africa. 5,308,839 (1960); 277,169 sq. mi. *Cap.:* Cape Town.

ca·per[1] (kā′pər), *v.i.* **1.** to leap or skip about in a sprightly manner; prance; gambol. —*n.* **2.** a playful leap or skip. **3.** a frivolous, carefree episode or activity. **4.** *Slang.* a criminal or illegal act, as a robbery. [fig. use of L *caper* he-goat (c. OE *hæfer,* Icel *hafr*); for the meaning, cf. DOG] —**ca′per·er,** *n.* —**ca′per·ing·ly,** *adv.*

ca·per[2] (kā′pər), *n.* **1.** a shrub, *Capparis spinosa,* of Mediterranean regions. **2.** its flower bud, which is pickled and used for garnish or seasoning. [back formation from *capers* (taken for pl.), ME *caperes* < L *capparis* < Gk *kápparis*]

cap·er·cail·lie (kap′ər kāl′yē), *n.* a large grouse, *Tetrao urogallus,* of Eurasian forests. Also, **cap·er·cail·zie** (kap′ər kāl′yē, -kāl′zē). [< ScotGael *capullcoille* (by dissimilation), lit., horse of the woods; cf. ME *capel* horse, Icel *kapall* nag, akin to L *caballus* horse]

Ca·per·na·um (kə pûr′nā əm, -nē-), *n.* ancient site in N Israel, on the Sea of Galilee: a center of Jesus' ministry.

cape·skin (kāp′skin′), *n.* a light, pliable leather made from lambskin or sheepskin and used esp. for gloves. [CAPE[2] + SKIN; orig. from goatskin from the Cape of Good Hope]

Ca·pet (kā′pit, kap′it; *Fr.* KA pe′), *n.* **Hugh** or *Fr.* **Hugues** (YG), A.D. 938?–996, king of France 987–996.

Ca·pe·tian (kə pē′shən), *adj.* **1.** of or pertaining to the French dynasty that ruled France A.D. 987–1328 in the direct line, and in collateral branches, as the Valois and Bourbons, until 1848 (except 1795–1814). —*n.* **2.** a member of this dynasty. [Hugh CAPET + -IAN, modeled on F *capétien*]

Cape′ Town′, a seaport in and the legislative capital of the Republic of South Africa, in the SW part: also capital of Cape of Good Hope province. 1,108,000. Also, **Cape′town′.** Afrikaans, **Kaapstad.** —**Cape·to·ni·an** (kāp tō′nē ən), *n.*

Cape′ Verde′ (vûrd), a republic consisting of a group of islands in the Atlantic, W of Senegal: formerly an overseas territory of Portugal; independent since 1975. 360,000; 1557 sq. mi. *Cap.:* Praia.

Cape′ York′ Penin′sula, a peninsula in NE Australia, in N Queensland, between the Gulf of Carpentaria and the Coral Sea.

cap·ful (kap′fōōl′), *n., pl* **-fuls.** the amount that a cap will hold.

cap′ gun′. See **cap pistol.**

Cap-Ha·i·tien (*Fr.* KAP A ē syaN′, -tyaN′), *n.* a seaport in N Haiti. 30,000 (est. 1960).

ca·pi·as (kā′pē əs, kap′ē-), *n.* *Law.* a writ commanding an officer to take a specified person into custody. [late ME < L: lit., you are to take, subj. 2nd sing. of *capere*]

cap·il·la·ceous (kap′ə lā′shəs), *adj.* capillary. [< L *capillāceus* hairy = *capill(us)* hair + *-āceus* -ACEOUS]

cap·il·lar·i·ty (kap′ə lar′i tē), *n.* **1.** the state of being capillary. **2.** Also called **cap′illary ac′tion.** *Physics.* a manifestation of surface tension by which the portion of the surface of a liquid coming in contact with a solid is elevated or depressed, depending on the adhesive or cohesive properties of the liquid. [CAPILLARY + -TY[2]]

cap·il·lar·y (kap′ə ler′ē), *n., pl.* **-lar·ies,** *adj.* —*n.* **1.** *Anat.* one of the minute blood vessels between the terminations of the arteries and the beginnings of the veins. —*adj.* **2.** pertaining to or occurring in or as in a tube of fine bore. **3.** *Physics.* **a.** pertaining to capillarity. **b.** of or pertaining to the apparent attraction or repulsion between a liquid and a solid, observed in capillarity. **4.** *Bot.* resembling hair in the manner of growth or shape. **5.** *Anat.* pertaining to or occurring in a capillary or capillaries. [< L *capillāri(s)* of, pertaining to the hair = *capill(us)* hair + *-āris* -ARY]

ca·pi·ta (kap′i tə), *n.* pl. of **caput.**

cap·i·tal (kap′i tᵊl), *n.* **1.** the city or town that is the official seat of government in a county, state, etc. **2.** a capital letter. **3.** the wealth, whether in money or property, accumulated by or owned or employed in business by an individual, firm, etc. **4.** *Accounting.* **a.** assets remaining after deduction of liabilities; the net worth of a business. **b.** the ownership interest in a business. **5.** capitalists as a group or class. —*adj.* **6.** pertaining to capital: *capital stock.* **7.** principal; highly important. **8.** chief, esp. as being the official seat of government of a country, state, etc. **9.** excellent or first-rate: *a capital fellow.* **10.** (of an alphabetic letter) of a form different from and higher than its corresponding lower-case letter, and occurring as the initial letter of a proper name, of the first word of a sentence, etc., as A, B, Q, R. **11.** involving the loss of life. **12.** punishable by death: *a capital crime.* [ME < L *capitāl(is)* of the head (*capit-*, s. of *caput* head + *-ālis* -AL[1]) + ML *capitāle* wealth, n. use of neut. of *capitālis* (adj.)] —**cap′i·tal·ness,** *n.* —**Syn. 3, 4.** principal, investment, assets. **7.** prime, first.

cap·i·tal[2] (kap′i tᵊl), *n.* *Archit.* the uppermost portion of a column, pillar, or shaft supporting the entablature. [ME *capitale* head (n. use of neut. of L adj.) for L *capitellum* = *capit-* (s. of *caput*) head + *-ellum* dim. suffix]

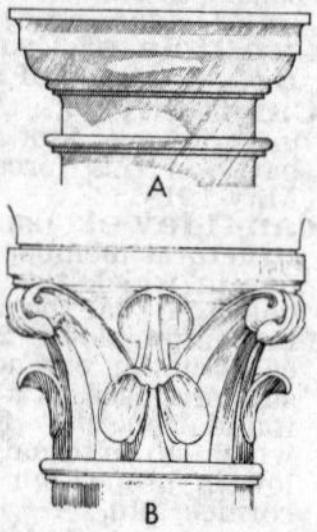

A

B

Capitals[2]
A, Tuscan
B, Gothic

cap′ital account′, 1. a business account stating the owner's or shareholder's interest in the assets. **2. capital accounts,** *Accounting.* accounts showing the net worth in a business enterprise, as assets minus liabilities.

cap′ital as′set. See **fixed asset.**

cap′ital expen′diture, *Accounting.* an addition to the value of fixed assets, as by the purchase of a new building.

cap′ital gain′, profit from the sale of assets, such as bonds, real estate, etc.

cap′ital goods′, *Econ.* machines and tools used in the production of other goods (contrasted with *consumer goods*).

cap·i·tal-in·ten·sive (kap′i tᵊl in ten′siv), *adj.* requiring or using a very large amount of capital relative to labor needs. Cf. **labor-intensive.**

cap′ital invest′ment, (in a business) the total funds invested in an enterprise.

cap·i·tal·ise (kap′i tᵊlīz′, kə pit′ᵊlīz′), *v.t.,* **-ised, -is·ing.** *Chiefly Brit.* capitalize. —**cap′i·tal·is′a·ble,** *adj.*

cap·i·tal·ism (kap′i tᵊliz′əm; *Brit. also* kə pit′ᵊliz′əm), *n.* an economic system in which investment in and ownership of the means of production, distribution, and exchange of wealth is made and maintained chiefly by private individuals or corporations.

cap·i·tal·ist (kap′i tᵊlist; *Brit. also* kə pit′ᵊlist), *n.* a person who has capital, esp. extensive capital, invested in business enterprises.

cap·i·tal·is·tic (kap′i tᵊlis′tik; *Brit. also* kə pit′ᵊlis′tik), *adj.* pertaining to capital or capitalists; founded on or believing in capitalism. —**cap′i·tal·is′ti·cal·ly,** *adv.*

cap·i·tal·i·za·tion (kap′i tᵊli zā′shən; *Brit. also* kə pit′ᵊlī zā′shən), *n.* **1.** the act of capitalizing. **2.** the authorized or outstanding stocks and bonds of a corporation. **3.** *Accounting.* **a.** the total investment of the owner or owners in a business enterprise. **b.** the total corporate liability. **c.** the total arrived at after addition of liabilities. Also, *esp. Brit.,* **cap′i·tal·i·sa′tion.**

cap·i·tal·ize (kap′i tᵊlīz′; *Brit.* also kə pit′ᵊlīz′), *v.t.* **-ized, -iz·ing.** **1.** to write or print in capital letters or with an initial capital. **2.** to authorize a certain amount of stocks and bonds in the corporate charter: *to capitalize a corporation.* **3.** *Accounting.* to set up (expenditures) as business assets in the books of account instead of treating as expense. **4.** to supply with capital. **5.** to estimate the value of (a stock or an enterprise). **6.** to take advantage of; turn to one's advantage (often fol. by *on*). Also, *esp. Brit.,* **capitalise.** —**cap′i·tal·iz′a·ble,** *adj.* —**cap′i·tal·iz′er,** *n.*

cap′ital lev′y, a tax based on capital, as distinguished from a tax on income.

cap·i·tal·ly (kap′i tᵊlē), *adv.* excellently; very well.

cap′ital pun′ishment, punishment by death for a crime; death penalty.

cap′ital ship′, one of a class of the largest warships; a battleship, battle cruiser, or aircraft carrier.

cap′ital stock′, **1.** the total stock authorized or issued by a corporation. **2.** the book value of the outstanding shares of a corporation.

cap·i·tate (kap′i tāt′), *adj.* **1.** *Bot.* having a globular head; collected in a head. **2.** *Biol.* having an enlarged, headlike termination. [< L *capitāt(us)* headed = *capit-* (s. of *caput*) head + *-ātus* -ATE[1]]

cap·i·ta·tion (kap′i tā′shən), *n.* **1.** a poll tax. **2.** a uniform fee or payment for each person. [< LL *capitātiōn-* (s. of *capitātiō*) = L *capit-* (s. of *caput*) head + *-ātiōn-* -ATION] —**cap′i·ta′tive,** *adj.*

Cap·i·tol (kap′i tᵊl), *n.* **1.** the building in Washington, D.C., in which the U.S. Congress holds its sessions. **2.** (*often l.c.*) a building occupied by a state legislature; statehouse. **3.** the ancient temple of Jupiter on the Capitoline. **4.** the Capitoline. [< L *capitōl(ium)* temple of Jupiter on Capitoline hill, Rome = *capit-* (s. of *caput*) head + *-ōlium* < ?; r. ME *capitolie* < ONF]

Cap·i·to·line (kap′i tᵊlīn′), *adj.* **1.** of or pertaining to the Capitoline or to the ancient temple of Jupiter on this hill. —*n.* **2.** one of the seven hills on which ancient Rome was built. [< L *Capitōlīn(us)*]

ca·pit·u·lar (kə pich′ə lər), *adj.* **1.** *Bot.* capitate. **2.** of or pertaining to an ecclesiastical chapter: *a capitular cathedral.* [< ML *capitulār(is)* = *capitul(um)* chapter (lit., small head; see CAPITULUM) + *-āris* -AR[1]] —**ca·pit′u·lar·ly,** *adv.*

ca·pit·u·lar·y (kə pich′ə ler′ē), *adj., n., pl.* **-lar·ies.** —*adj.* **1.** pertaining to an ecclesiastical chapter. —*n.* **2.** a member of an ecclesiastical chapter. [< ML *capitulāri(us)*]

ca·pit·u·late (kə pich′ə lāt′), *v.i.,* **-lat·ed, -lat·ing.** to surrender unconditionally or on stipulated terms. [< ML *capitulāt(us)* drawn up in sections (ptp. of *capitulāre*) = *capitul(um)* section (lit., small head; see CAPITULUM) + *-ātus* -ATE[1]] —**ca·pit′u·lant,** *n.* —**ca·pit′u·la′tor,** *n.*

ca·pit·u·la·tion (kə pich′ə lā′shən), *n.* **1.** the act of capitulating. **2.** the document containing the terms of a surrender. **3.** a list of the headings or main divisions of a subject; summary. [< ML *capitulātiōn-* (s. of *capitulātiō*)] —**ca·pit·u·la·to·ry** (kə pich′ə lə tôr′ē, -tōr′ē), *adj.*

ca·pit·u·lum (kə pich′ə ləm), *n., pl.* **-la** (-lə). **1.** *Bot.* a close head of sessile flowers; a flower head. **2.** *Anat.* the head of a bone. [< L = *capit-* (s. of *caput*) head + *-ulum,* neut. of *-ulus* -ULE]

cap·let (kap′lit), *n.* *Pharm.* a tablet that is coated to facilitate swallowing.

ca·po (kā′pō), *n., pl.* **-pos.** **1.** any of various devices for a guitar, lute, banjo, etc., which when clamped or screwed down across the strings at a given fret will raise each string a corresponding number of half tones. **2.** the nut of a guitar, lute, banjo, etc. [< It *capotasto* = *capo* head, top (L *caput*) + *tasto* touch, key < *tastare* to touch << L *taxāre,* freq. of *tangere*]

ca·pon (kā′pon, -pən), *n.* a rooster castrated to improve its flesh for use as food. [ME; OE *capun* < L *capōn-* (s. of *capō*) castrated cock; akin to Gk *kóptein* to cut, OSlav *skopiti* to castrate]

cap·o·ral (kap′ər əl, kap′ə ral′), *n.* a kind of tobacco. [short for F *tabāc du caporal* tobacco of the CORPORAL]

Cap·o·ret·to (kap′ə ret′ō; *It.* kä′pô ret′tô), *n.* Italian name of **Kobarid.**

ca·pote (kə pōt′; *Fr.* KA pôt′), *n., pl.* **-potes** (-pōts′; *Fr.* -pôt′). **1.** a long cloak with a hood. **2.** an adjustable top or hood of a vehicle, as a buggy. [< F = *cape* (< Sp *capa* CAPE[1]) + *-ote* fem. of *-ot* dim. suffix]

Ca·po·te (kə pō′tē), *n.* **Truman,** 1924–84, U.S. novelist, short-story writer, and playwright.

Cap·pa·do·cia (kap′ə dō′shə), *n.* an ancient country in E Asia Minor: it became a Roman province in A.D. 17. —**Cap′pa·do′cian,** *adj., n.*

cap·pa·ri·da·ceous (kap′ə ri dā′shəs), *adj.* belonging to the *Capparidaceae,* or caper family of plants. [< NL *Capparidace(ae)* (*Capp(aris)* genus name (see CAPER[2]) + *-id-* -ID[2] + *-aceae* -ACEAE) + -OUS]

cap′ pis′tol, a toy gun using caps.

cap·puc·ci·no (kap′o͝o chē′nō, kä′po͝o-; *It.* käp′po͞ot chē′nô), *n.* a hot beverage consisting of espresso coffee and steamed milk, often served with powdered cinnamon and topped with whipped cream. [< It; see CAPUCHIN]

cap·re·o·late (kap′rē ə lāt′, kə prē′-), *adj.* *Anat.* resembling tendrils. [< L *capreol(ī)* props (pl. of *capreolus* roebuck; see CAPRIOLE) + -ATE[1]]

Ca·pri (kä′prē, kap′rē, kə prē′), *n.* an island in W Italy, in the Bay of Naples: grottoes. 5½ sq. mi.

capri-, an element meaning "goat," occurring in loan words from Latin (*capricious*) and used in the formation of compound words. [< L, comb. form of *caper* a goat; see CAPER[1]]

ca·pric·ci·o (kə prē′chē ō′; *It.* kä pRet′chô), *n., pl.* **-ci·os,** *It.* **-ci** (-chē). **1.** a caper; prank. **2.** a caprice. **3.** *Music.* a composition in a free, irregular style. [< It, earlier *caporiccio,* lit., shiver, chill = *capo* head (< L *caput*) + *riccio* frizzled < L *ēricius* hedgehog]

ca·pric·ci·o·so (kə prē′chē ō′sō; *It.* kä′pRet chô′sô), *adj.* *Music.* capricious; fantastic in style. [< It]

ca·price (kə prēs′), *n.* **1.** a sudden, unpredictable change, as of one's mind, the weather, etc. **2.** a tendency to change one's mind without motive; whimsicality; capriciousness. **3.** *Music.* capriccio (def. 3). [< F < It; see CAPRICCIO]

ca·pri·cious (kə prish′əs, -prē′shəs), *adj.* **1.** subject to, led by, or indicative of caprice or whim; erratic. **2.** *Obs.* fanciful or witty. [< It *capriccioso* = *capricci(o)* CAPRICE + *-oso* -OUS] —**ca·pri′cious·ly,** *adv.* —**ca·pri′cious·ness,** *n.*

Cap·ri·corn (kap′rə kôrn′), *n.* **1.** *Astron.* the Goat, a zodiacal constellation between Sagittarius and Aquarius. **2.** *Astrol.* the 10th sign of the zodiac. See diag. at **zodiac.** **3.** **tropic of.** See under **tropic** (def. 1a). Also, **Capricornus** (for defs. 1, 2). [ME *Capricorne* < L *Capricorn(us)* (trans. of Gk *aigókerōs* goat-horned) = *capri-* CAPRI- + *corn(ū)* HORN + *-us* adj. suffix]

Cap·ri·cor·nus (kap′rə kôr′nəs), *n., gen.* **-ni** (-nī). Capricorn (defs. 1, 2). [< L]

cap·ri·fi·ca·tion (kap′rə fə kā′shən), *n.* the pollination of figs by fig wasps attracted by the caprifig fruit hung in the branches of the trees. [< L *caprificātiōn-* (s. of *caprificātiō*) = *caprificāt(us)* pollinated from the wild fig tree (ptp. of *caprificāre;* see CAPRIFIG) + *-iōn-* -ION] —**cap′ri·fi·ca′tor,** *n.*

cap·ri·fig (kap′rə fig′), *n.* a fig, *Ficus carica sylvestris,* bearing an inedible fruit used in caprification. [< L *caprific(us)* the wild fig tree, lit., the goat-fig = *capri-* CAPRI- + *ficus* FIG[1]]

cap·ri·fo·li·a·ceous (kap′rə fō′lē ā′shəs), *adj.* belonging to the *Caprifoliaceae,* plants including the honeysuckle, elder, etc. [< NL *caprifoliāce(ae)* honeysuckle family (*caprifoli(um)* honeysuckle (genus) < ML = L *capri-* CAPRI- + *folium* leaf + NL *-acea* -ACEAE) + -OUS]

cap·ri·ole (kap′rē ōl′), *n., v.,* **-oled, -ol·ing.** —*n.* **1.** a caper or leap. **2.** *Dressage.* a movement in which the horse jumps up with its forelegs well drawn in and kicks out with its hind legs. —*v.i.* **3.** to execute a capriole. [< MF < OIt *capriol(a),* var. of *capriolo* roebuck < L *capreol(us)* = *capre(us)* roe (*caper* he goat (see CAPER[1]) + *-eus* adj. suffix) + *-olus* dim.]

ca·pro′ic ac′id (kə prō′ik), *Chem.* a liquid, $CH_3(CH_2)_4COOH$, having a limburger-cheeselike odor, used in the manufacture of flavoring agents. [CAPR(I)- + *-oic* (-O- + -IC)]

caps., capital letters. [< L *capsula*]

cap·sa·i·cin (kap sā′i sin), *n.* *Chem.* a bitter compound, $C_{18}H_{27}NO_3$, present in capsicum. [earlier *capsicine* = CAPSIC(UM) + -INE[2]; refashioned with *capsa* (< L: box) for *caps-* and -IN[2] for -INE[2]]

cap·si·cum (kap′sə kəm), *n.* **1.** any solanaceous plant of the genus *Capsicum,* as *C. frutescens,* the common pepper of the garden, occurring in many varieties that range from mild to hot, having pungent seeds enclosed in a podded or bell-shaped pericarp. **2.** the fruit of these plants, or some preparation of it, used as a condiment. [< NL = L *caps(a)* CASE[2] + *-icum,* neut. of *-icus* -IC]

cap·size (kap′sīz, kap sīz′), *v.,* **-sized, -siz·ing.** —*v.i., v.t.* to overturn: *The boat capsized. They capsized the boat.* [?] —**cap′siz·a·ble,** *adj.*

Capstan

cap·stan (kap′stən), *n.* any of various windlasses, rotated in a horizontal plane by hand or by machinery, for winding in ropes, cables, etc. [ME < OPr *cabestan,* var. of *cabestran* << L *capistrant-* (s. of *capistrāns*) prp. of *capistrāre* to fasten with a halter < *capistrum* halter < ?]

cap·stone (kap′stōn′), *n.* a finishing stone of a structure.

cap·su·late (kap′sə lāt′), *adj.* enclosed or encapsulated. Also, **cap′su·lat′ed.** [< NL *capsulāt(us)*] —**cap′su·la′tion,** *n.*

cap·sule (kap′səl), *n., v.,* **-suled, -sul·ing,** *adj.* —*n.* **1.** *Pharm.* a gelatinous case enclosing a dose of medicine. **2.** *Bot.* **a.** a dry dehiscent fruit, composed of two or more carpels. **b.** the sporangium of various cryptogamic plants. **3.** *Anat., Zool.* **a.** a membranous sac or integument. **b.** either of two strata of white matter in the cerebrum. **4.** a small case, envelope, or covering. **5.** *Aeron., Rocketry.* **a.** a small, sealed and pressurized cabin in which a man or animal may ride in flight above the earth's atmosphere. **b.** a similar cabin in a military aircraft that can be ejected from the aircraft in an emergency. —*v.t.* **6.** to furnish with or enclose in or as in a capsule; encapsulate. **7.** to summarize. —*adj.* **8.** small and compact or brief and summarized. [< L *capsul(a)* = *caps(a)* box + *-ula* -ULE] —**cap′su·lar,** *adj.*

Capsules (after dehiscence) A, Asphodel; B, Prickly poppy; C, Violet

Capt., Captain.

cap·tain (kap′tən, -tin), *n.* **1.** a person in authority over others; chief; leader. **2.** an officer ranking in most armies above a first lieutenant and below a major. **3.** an officer in the U.S. Navy ranking above a commander and below a rear admiral. **4.** a military leader. **5.** an officer in the police department, ranking above a lieutenant and usually below an inspector. **6.** the pilot of an airplane. **7.** headwaiter. **8.** the master of a merchant vessel. **9.** *Sports.* the field leader of a team. —*v.t.* **10.** to lead or command as a captain. [ME *capitain* < MF *capitaine* < LL *capitān(eus)* chief = *capit-* (s. of *caput*) head + *-ānus* -AN + *-eus* -EOUS] —**cap′tain·cy, cap′tain·ship′,** *n.*

cap·tion (kap′shən), *n.* **1.** a heading or title, as of a chapter, article, or page. **2.** *Print.* a legend for a picture or illustration, esp. in a magazine. **3.** *Law.* the heading of a legal document stating the time, place, etc., of execution or performance. —*v.t.* **4.** to supply a caption or captions for; entitle. [ME *capcio(u)n* seizure < L *captiōn-* (s. of *captiō*) = *capt(us)* taken (see CAPTOR) + *-iōn-* -ION]

cap·tious (kap′shəs), *adj.* **1.** exaggerating trivial faults or defects; faultfinding. **2.** apt or designed to ensnare or perplex: *captious questions.* [ME *capcious* < L *captiōs(us)* sophistical = *capti(ō)* a taking, hence, sophism (see CAPTION) + *-ōsus* -OUS] —**cap′tious·ly,** *adv.* —**cap′tious·ness,** *n.*

cap·ti·vate (kap′tə vāt′), *v.t.,* **-vat·ed, -vat·ing.** **1.** to enthrall charm, as by beauty or excellence; enchant. **2.**

Obs. to capture; subjugate. [< LL *captivāt(us)* taken captive (ptp. of *captivāre*) = L *captīv(us)* CAPTIVE + *-ātus* -ATE[1]] —**cap′ti·vat′ing·ly,** *adv.* —**cap′ti·va′tion,** *n.* —**cap′ti·va′tive,** *adj.* —**cap′ti·va′tor,** *n.* —**Syn. 1.** fascinate, bewitch. —**Ant. 1.** repel.

cap·tive (kap′tiv), *n.* **1.** a prisoner. **2.** a person who is captivated or dominated: *He is the captive of his own fears.* —*adj.* **3.** made or held prisoner, esp. in war: *captive troops.* **4.** kept in confinement or restraint: *captive animals.* **5.** enslaved by love, beauty, etc.; captivated. [ME < L *captīv(us)* = *capt(us)* taken (see CAPTOR) + *-īvus* -IVE]

cap′tive au′dience, people who have entered into a situation for a particular purpose, as on a bus or at a restaurant, and are involuntarily subjected to advertisements, recorded music, or the like, from which they cannot escape.

cap·tiv·i·ty (kap tiv′i tē), *n., pl* **-ties. 1.** the state or period of being captive. **2.** (*cap.*) *Bible.* the abduction of Israelite hostages by the Babylonian king Nebuchadnezzar. [ME *captivite* < L *captīvitās*] —**Syn. 1.** bondage, servitude; imprisonment, incarceration.

cap·tor (kap′tər), *n.* a person who takes a prisoner or captures a thing. [< L = *capt(us)* taken (ptp. of *capere*) (*cap-* take + *-tus* ptp. suffix) + *-or* -OR[2]]

cap·ture (kap′chər), *v.,* **-tured, -tur·ing,** *n.* —*v.t.* **1.** to take by force or stratagem; take prisoner; seize. **2.** *Physics.* (of an atomic or nuclear system) to acquire (an additional particle). —*n.* **3.** the act or process of capturing. **4.** the thing or person captured. [< MF < L *captūr(a)* = *capt(us)* taken (see CAPTOR) + *-ūra* -URE] —**cap′tur·a·ble,** *adj.* —**cap′tur·er,** *n.* —**Syn. 1.** catch, arrest, apprehend. **3.** seizure, arrest, apprehension. —**Ant. 1, 3.** release.

Cap·u·a (kap′yo͞o ə; *It.* kä′pwä), *n.* a town in NW Campania, in S Italy, N of Naples. 18,305 (1961). —**Cap′u·an,** *adj.*

ca·puche (kə po͞osh′, -po͞och′), *n.* a hood or cowl, esp. the long, pointed cowl of the Capuchins. [< MF < It *cappucci(o)* = *capp(a)* cloak (see CAP[1]) + *-uccio* aug. suffix] —**ca·puched′,** *adj.*

cap·u·chin (kap′yo͝o chin, -shin), *n.* **1.** a Central and South American monkey, *Cebus capucinus,* having a prehensile tail and hair on the head resembling a cowl. **2.** any monkey of the genus *Cebus.* **3.** a hooded cloak for women. **4.** (*cap.*) *Rom. Cath. Ch.* a friar belonging to the branch of the Franciscan order that observes vows of poverty and austerity. Cf. **Friar Minor.** [< MF < It *cappuccin(o)* = *cappucc(io)* CAPUCHE + *-ino* -INE[1]]

Capuchin, *Cebus capucinus* (Total length 2½ ft.; tail 17 in.)

ca·put (kā′pət, kap′ət), *n., pl.* **ca·pi·ta** (kap′i tə). *Anat.* any head or headlike expansion on a structure, as on a bone. [< L: head]

cap·y·ba·ra (kap′ə bär′ə), *n.* a South American rodent, *Hydrochoerus capybara,* living along the banks of rivers and lakes, having no tail and partly webbed feet: the largest living rodent. [< NL < Pg *capibara* < Tupi]

Capybara (About 2 ft. high at shoulder; length 3 to 4 ft.)

car (kär), *n.* **1.** an automobile. **2.** a vehicle running on rails, as a streetcar. **3.** *Brit. Dial.* any wheeled vehicle, as a farm cart, wagon, etc. **4.** the part of an elevator, balloon, or the like, that carries the passengers, freight, etc. **5.** *Literary.* a chariot, as of war or triumph. [ME *carre* < AF < LL *carr(a)* (fem. sing.), L *carra,* neut. pl. of *carrum,* var. of *carrus* < Celt.; cf. OIr *carr* wheeled vehicle] —**car′less,** *adj.*

ca·ra·ba·o (kär′ə bä′ō), *n., pl.* **-ba·os.** (in the Philippines) the water buffalo. [< Philippine Sp << Malay *karbau*]

car·a·bi·neer (kar′ə bə nēr′), *n.* carbineer. Also, **car′a·bi·nier′.**

ca·ra·bi·nie·re (kä′rä bē nye′re; *Eng.* kar′ə bin yâr′ē), *n., pl.* **-bi·nie·ri** (-bē nye′rē; *Eng.* -bin yâr′ē). *Italian.* **1.** a policeman. **2.** carbineer.

Car·a·cal·la (kar′ə kal′ə), *n.* (*Marcus Aurelius Antoninus Bassianus*) A.D. 188–217, Roman emperor 211–217.

ca·ra·ca·ra (kär′ə kär′ə), *n.* any of certain long-legged hawks of the southern U.S. and Central and South America that feed on carrion. [< Sp or Pg < Tupi; imit. of its cry]

Ca·ra·cas (kə rä′kəs; *Sp.* kä rä′käs), *n.* a city in and the capital of Venezuela, in the N part. 1,035,499.

car·a·cole (kar′ə kōl′), *n., v.,* **-coled, -col·ing.** —*n.* **1.** a half turn executed by a horseman in riding. —*v.i.* **2.** to execute caracoles; wheel. [< F < Sp *caracol* snail, spiral shell or stair, turning movement (of a horse)] —**car′a·col′er,** *n.*

Ca·rac·ta·cus (kə rak′tə kəs), *n.* fl. A.D. c50, British chieftain: opposed the Romans. Also, **Ca·rad·oc** (kə rad′ək).

car·a·cul (kar′ə kəl), *n.* **1.** the skin of karakul lamb, dressed as a fur. **2.** karakul (def. 1). [after *Kara Kul* Black Lake, in Uzbek Republic, USSR, home of the breed]

ca·rafe (kə raf′, -räf′), *n.* a bottle, usually of glass, for holding water or other beverages. [< F < It *caraff(a)* < Sp *garrafa* < Ar *gharrāfah* dipper, drinking vessel]

car·a·mel (kar′ə məl, -mel′; *Midwest often* kär′məl), *n.* **1.** a liquid made by cooking sugar until it changes color, used for coloring and flavoring food. **2.** a kind of candy, commonly in small blocks, made from sugar, butter, milk, etc. [< F < Sp or Pg *caramel(o)* < LL *calamellus* little reed (by dissimilation) = *calam(us)* reed (see CALAMUS) + *-ellus* dim. suffix; meaning changed by assoc. with ML *cannamella, canna mellis,* etc., sugar cane = L *canna* CANE + *mel* honey (gen. *mellis*)]

car·a·mel·ise (kar′ə mə līz′), *v.t., v.i.,* **-ised, -is·ing.** *Chiefly Brit.* caramelize. —**car′a·mel·i·sa′tion,** *n.*

car·a·mel·ize (kar′ə mə līz′; *Midwest often* kär′mə līz′), *v.t., v.i.,* **-ized, -iz·ing.** to convert or be converted into caramel. —**car′a·mel·i·za′tion,** *n.*

ca·ran·gid (kə ran′jid), *n.* **1.** any of numerous fishes of the family *Carangidae,* comprising the jacks, scads, pompanos, and cavallas. —*adj.* **2.** belonging or pertaining to the family *Carangidae.* [< NL *Carangid(ae)* = *Carang-* (s. of *Caranx*) name of the genus + *-idae* -ID[2]]

ca·ran·goid (kə rang′goid), *adj.* **1.** resembling a fish of the family *Carangidae;* carangid. —*n.* **2.** a carangoid fish. [< NL *Carang-* (s. of *Caranx*) genus name, pseudo-Gk + -OID]

car·a·pace (kar′ə pās′), *n.* a shield, test, or shell covering some or all of the dorsal part of an animal. [< F < Sp *carapach(o)* < ?] —**car′a·paced′,** *adj.* —**car·a·pa·cial** (kar′ə-pā′shəl), *adj.*

car·at (kar′ət), *n.* a unit of weight in gemstones, 200 milligrams (about 3 grains of troy or avoirdupois weight). *Abbr.:* c., ct. [< ML *carrat(us)* (used by alchemists) < Ar *qīrāt* weight of 4 grains < Gk *kerátion* carob bean, weight of 3⅓ grains, lit., little horn = *kerat-* (s. of *kéras*) horn + *-ion* dim.]

Ca·ra·vag·gio (kar′ə vä′jō; *It.* kä′rä väd′jô), *n.* **Mi·chel·an·ge·lo Me·ri·si da** (mī′kəl an′jə lō′ mə rē′zē dä, mik′əl-; *It.* mē′kel än′je lô me rē′zē dä), c1565–1609?, Italian painter.

car·a·van (kar′ə van′), *n.* **1.** a group of travelers, as merchants or pilgrims, banded together for safety in journeying through deserts, hostile territory, etc. **2.** any group traveling in or as if in a caravan and using a specific mode of transportation, as pack animals or motor vehicles: *a camel caravan.* **3.** a large covered vehicle; van. **4.** *Brit.* a house on wheels; trailer. [earlier *carovan* < It *carovan(a)* < Pers *kārwān*]

car·a·van·sa·ry (kar′ə van′sə rē), *n., pl.* **-ries. 1.** (in the Near East) an inn, usually with a large courtyard, for the overnight accommodation of caravans. **2.** any large inn or hotel. Also, **car·a·van·se·rai** (kar′ə van′sə rī′, -rā′). [< Pers *kārwānsarāī* = *kārwān* CARAVAN + *sarāī* mansion, inn] —**car·a·van·se·ri·al** (kar′ə van sēr′ē əl), *adj.*

car·a·vel (kar′ə vel′), *n.* a small Spanish or Portuguese sailing vessel of the 15th–16th centuries, usually lateen-rigged on two or three masts. Also, **carvel.** [< Pg *caravel(a)* = *carav(o)* kind of ship (< LL *carabus* < Gk *kárabos* skiff, horned beetle) + *-ela* dim. suffix]

Caravel

car·a·way (kar′ə wā′), *n.* **1.** an umbelliferous herb, *Carum Carvi.* **2.** Also called **car′away seed′.** the aromatic seedlike fruit of this plant used in cooking and medicine. [ME *car(a)wai,* var. of *carwy* < ML *carui* < Ar *karawyā* < Gk *kár(on)* caraway]

carb (kärb), *n.* *Informal.* a carburetor. [by shortening]

carb-, var. of **carbo-** before a vowel: *carbazole.*

car·ba·mate (kär′bə māt′, kär bam′āt), *n.* *Chem.* a salt or ester of carbamic acid. [CARBAM(IC) + -ATE[2]]

car·bam·ic (kär bam′ik), *adj.* *Chem.* of or derived from carbamic acid. [CARB- + AM(IDE) + -IC]

carbam′ic ac′id, *Chem.* a hypothetical compound, NH_2COOH, known only in the form of its salts, as ammonium carbamate, or its esters, as urethan.

car·barn (kär′bärn′), *n.* a garage for streetcars or buses.

car·ba·zole (kär′bə zōl′), *n.* *Chem.* a white compound, $(C_6H_4)_2NH$, used chiefly in the manufacture of dyes.

car·bide (kär′bīd, -bid), *n.* *Chem.* **1.** a compound of carbon with a more electropositive element or group. **2.** See **calcium carbide. 3.** a very hard mixture of sintered carbides of various metals, esp. tungsten carbide, used for cutting edges and for dies.

car·bine (kär′bīn, -bēn), *n.* a short rifle (or, formerly, musket) carried by combat soldiers and noncommissioned officers who are not equipped with rifles. [earlier *carabine* < MF: small harquebus, weapon borne by a *carabin* carabineer, ? aph. var. of ONF *escarrabin* corpse bearer (in epidemics) << L *scarabacus* SCARAB]

car·bi·neer (kär′bə nēr′), *n.* (formerly) a soldier armed with a carbine. Also, **carabineer, carabinier.** [earlier *carabineer* = *carabine* CARBINE + -EER]

car·bi·nol (kär′bə nōl′, -nôl′, -nol′), *n.* *Chem.* **1.** See **methyl alcohol. 2.** an alcohol derived from methyl alcohol. [< G *Karbinol* = *Karbin* methyl (*karb-* CARB- + *-in* -IN[2]) + *-ol* -OL[1]]

carbo-, a combining form of **carbon:** *carbohydrate.*

car·bo·hy·drate (kär′bō hī′drāt, -bə-), *n.* any of a class of organic compounds that are polyhydroxy aldehydes or polyhydroxy ketones, or change to such substances on simple chemical transformations, as hydrolysis, oxidation, or reduction, and that form the supporting tissues of plants and are important food for animals and man.

car·bo·lat·ed (kär′bə lā′tid), *adj.* containing carbolic acid. [CARBOL(IC) + -ATE[2] + -ED[2]]

car·bol′ic ac′id, (kär bol′ik), *Chem.* phenol (def. 1). [*carbol* (CARB- + -OL[2]) + -IC]

car·bon (kär′bən), *n.* **1.** *Chem.* an element that forms organic compounds in combination with hydrogen, oxygen, etc., and that occurs in a pure state as the diamond and as graphite, and in an impure state as charcoal. *Symbol:* C; *at. wt.:* 12.011; *at. no.:* 6; *sp. gr.:* (of diamond) 3.51 at 20°C; (of graphite) 2.26 at 20°C. **2.** *Elect.* **a.** the carbon rod through which current is conducted between the electrode holder and the arc in carbon arc lighting or welding. **b.** the rod or plate, composed in part of carbon, used in batteries. **3.** a sheet of carbon paper. **4.** See **carbon copy.** [< F *carbone,* coinage based on L *carbōn-* (s. of *carbō*) charcoal]

carbon 12, *Chem.* the isotopic carbon atom that comprises 99 percent of naturally occurring carbon and is used as the standard for atomic weight by representing a unit of 12.00000. Also, **car·bon-12** (kär′bən twelv′).

carbon 13, *Chem.* the stable isotope of carbon having an atomic mass number 13, used as a tracer. Also, **carbon-13** (kär′bən thûr tēn′).

carbon 14, *Chem.* radiocarbon (def. 1). Also, **carbon-14** (kär′bən fôr tēn′, -fôr-).

car·bon-14 dat·ing. See **radiocarbon dating.**

car·bo·na·ceous (kär′bə nā′shəs), *adj.* of, like, or containing carbon.

car·bo·na·do[1] (kär′bə nā′dō), *n., pl.* **-does, -dos,** *v.,* **-doed, -do·ing.** —*n.* **1.** a piece of meat, fish, etc., scored and broiled.

—*v.t.* **2.** to score and broil. **3.** *Archaic.* to slash; hack. [< Sp *carbonada* = *carbón* charcoal + *-ada* -ADE]

car·bo·na·do² (kär′bə nā′dō), *n., pl.* **-dos, -does.** a massive, black variety of diamond, found chiefly near São Salvador, Brazil, and formerly used for drilling and other cutting purposes. [< Pg: carbonate]

car·bon·a·ta·tion (kär′bə nə tā′shən), *n. Chem.* saturation or reaction with carbon dioxide.

car·bon·ate (*n.* kär′bə nāt′, -nit; *v.* kär′bə nāt′), *n., v.,* **-at·ed, -at·ing.** —*n.* **1.** *Chem.* a salt or ester of carbonic acid. —*v.t.* **2.** to charge or impregnate with carbon dioxide. [< NL *carbōnāt(um)* something carbonated] —**car′bon·a′tor,** *n.*

car·bon·a·tion (kär′bə nā′shən), *n.* **1.** saturation with carbon dioxide, as in making soda water. **2.** reaction with carbon dioxide to remove lime, as in sugar refining. **3.** carbonization.

car′bon bisul′fide, *Chem.* See **carbon disulfide.**

car′bon black′, any of various finely divided forms of amorphous carbon used in pigments, in the manufacture of rubber products, and as clarifying or filtering agents.

car′bon cop′y, **1.** a duplicate of anything written or typed, made by using carbon paper. *Abbr.:* cc, CC **2.** a near or exact duplicate: *Mary is a carbon copy of her mother.*

car′bon cy′cle, *Astrophysics.* a series of nuclear transformations taking place in the interiors of stars by means of which hydrogen is eventually converted to helium with the release of large amounts of energy.

car′bon dat′ing. See **radiocarbon dating.**

car′bon diox′ide, *Chem.* an incombustible gas, CO_2, present in the atmosphere and formed during respiration: used extensively in industry as dry ice and in carbonated beverages, fire extinguishers, etc. Also called **carbonic-acid gas, carbonic anhydride.**

car′bon disul′fide, *Chem.* a poisonous, flammable liquid, CS_2, used chiefly in the manufacture of cellophane, viscose rayon, and pesticides and as a solvent for fats, resins, and rubber. Also called **carbon bisulfide.**

car·bon·ic (kär bon′ik), *adj. Chem.* containing tetravalent carbon, as carbonic acid, H_2CO_3.

carbon′ic ac′id, the acid, H_2CO_3, formed when carbon dioxide dissolves in water.

car·bon′ic-ac′id gas′ (kär bon′ik as′id). See **carbon dioxide.** Also called **carbon′ic anhy′dride.**

Car·bon·if·er·ous (kär′bə nif′ər əs), *Geol.* —*adj.* **1.** noting or pertaining to a period of the Paleozoic era, including the Pennsylvanian, Mississippian, and formerly the Permian periods as epochs: from 270 million to 350 million years ago. **2.** (*l.c.*) producing coal. —*n.* **3.** the Carboniferous period or system. See table at **era.** [< L *carbōn-* (s. of *carbō*) coal + -I- + -FEROUS]

car·bon·ise (kär′bə nīz′), *v.t.,* **-ised, -is·ing.** *Chiefly Brit.* carbonize. —**car′bon·i·sa′tion,** *n.* —**car′bon·is′a·ble,** *adj.* —**car′bon·is′er,** *n.*

car·bon·i·za·tion (kär′bə ni zā′shən *or, esp. Brit.,* -nī-), *n.* **1.** formation of carbon from organic matter. **2.** coal distillation, as in coke ovens.

car·bon·ize (kär′bə nīz′), *v.t.,* **-ized, -iz·ing. 1.** to char, forming carbon. **2.** to coat, treat, or enrich with carbon. Also, *esp. Brit.,* **carbonise.** —**car′bon·iz′a·ble,** *adj.* —**car′bon·iz′er,** *n.*

car′bon monox′ide, *Chem.* an odorless, poisonous, flammable gas, CO, produced when carbon burns with insufficient air.

car·bon·ous (kär′bə nəs), *adj.* of, containing, or derived from carbon.

car′bon pa′per, **1.** paper faced with a preparation of carbon or other material, used between two sheets of plain paper to reproduce on the lower sheet that which is written on the upper. **2.** a special photographic paper.

car′bon steel′, steel owing its properties principally to its carbon content; ordinary, unalloyed steel.

car′bon tet·ra·chlo′ride, (te′trə klōr′īd, -id, -klôr′-), *Chem., Pharm.* a nonflammable, vaporous, toxic liquid, CCl_4, used as a fire extinguisher, cleaning fluid, solvent, etc.

car·bon·yl (kär′bə nil), *Chem.* —*adj.* **1.** containing the carbonyl group. —*n.* **2.** a compound containing metal combined with carbon monoxide, as nickel carbonyl, $Ni(CO)_4$.

car′bonyl chlo′ride, *Chem.* phosgene.

car′bonyl group′, *Chem.* the bivalent group, C–O. Also called **car′bonyl rad′ical.**

Car·bo·run·dum (kär′bə run′dəm), *n. Trademark.* any of various abrasives or refractories of silicon carbide, fused alumina, and other materials.

car·box·yl (kär bok′sil), *adj. Chem.* containing the carboxyl group. [CARB- + OX(YGEN) + -YL] —**car′box·yl′ic,** *adj.*

car·box·yl·ase (kär bok′sə lās′), *n. Biochem.* decarboxylase.

car·box·yl·ate (kär bok′sə lāt′), *v.,* **-at·ed, -at·ing,** *n. Chem.* —*v.t.* **1.** to introduce the carboxyl group into (an organic compound). —*n.* **2.** a salt or ester of a carboxylic acid.

car·box·yl·a·tion (kär bok′sə lā′shən), *n. Chem.* the process of carboxylating.

carbox′yl group′, *Chem.* the univalent group, –COOH, present in and characteristic of organic acids. Also called **carbox′yl rad′ical.**

car·boy (kär′boi), *n.* a large glass bottle protected by basketwork or a wooden box, used esp. for holding corrosive liquids. [< Pers *qarāba(h)* < Ar *qarrābah* big jug] —**car′boyed,** *adj.*

car·bun·cle (kär′bung kəl), *n.* **1.** *Pathol.* a painful, circumscribed inflammation of the subcutaneous tissue, resulting in suppuration and sloughing, somewhat like a boil, but more serious in its effects. **2.** a garnet cut in a convex, rounded form without facets. [ME < L *carbuncul(us)* red object (stone or tumor), orig. live coal = *carbōn-* (s. of *carbō*) burning or burnt wood + *-culus* -CULE] —**car′bun·cled,** *adj.* —**car·bun·cu·lar** (kär bung′kyə lər), *adj.*

car·bu·ret (kär′bə rāt′, -byə-, -byə ret′), *v.t.,* **-ret·ed, -ret·ing** or (*esp. Brit.*) **-ret·ted, -ret·ting.** to combine or mix with carbon or hydrocarbons. [CARB- + -URET]

car·bu·re·tion (kär′bə rā′shən, -byə-, -byə resh′ən), *n.* (in an internal-combustion engine) the process of producing a mixture of air and fuel in the correct proportion for engine combustion.

car·bu·re·tor (kär′bə rā′tər, -byə-), *n.* a device for mixing vaporized fuel with air to produce a combustible or explosive mixture, as for an internal-combustion engine. Also, *esp. Brit.,* **car·bu·ret·tor** (kär′byə ret′ər).

car·bu·rise (kär′bə rīz′, -byə-), *v.t.,* **-rised, -ris·ing.** *Chiefly Brit.* carburize. —**car′bu·ri·sa′tion,** *n.* —**car′bu·ris′er,** *n.*

car·bu·rize (kär′bə rīz′, -byə-), *v.t.,* **-rized, -riz·ing. 1.** to cause to unite with carbon. **2.** to carburet. [CARBUR(ET) + -IZE] —**car′bu·ri·za′tion,** *n.* —**car′bu·riz′er,** *n.*

car·ca·jou (kär′kə jōō′, -zhōō′), *n.* wolverine (def. 1). [< CanF < Algonquian *karkaju*]

car·ca·net (kär′kə net′, -nit), *n.* **1.** *Archaic.* a jeweled collar or necklace. **2.** *Obs.* an ornamental circlet for the hair. [*carcan* choker < MF = *carc-* throat (< Gmc) + *-an* ring (< L *ānus*) + -ET] —**car′ca·net′ed, car′ca·net′ted,** *adj.*

car·cass (kär′kəs), *n.* **1.** the body of a slaughtered animal after removal of the offal. **2.** the dead body of an animal. **3.** *Disparaging.* the body of a human being, living or dead. **4.** the framework or skeleton of a structure, as of a house, ship, or automobile tire. Also, **car′case.** [< MF *carcasse* < It *carcass(a)* < ?; r. ME *carkeis, -ois* < AF, answering to ML *carcosium* < ?] —**car′cass·less,** *adj.* —**Syn. 2.** See **body.**

Car·cas·sonne (KAR KA sôn′), *n.* a city in S France: medieval fortifications. 43,709 (1962).

Car·chem·ish (kär′kə mish, kär kē′-), *n.* an ancient city in S Turkey, on the upper Euphrates: capital of the Hittite empire. Also, **Charchemish.**

car·cin·o·gen (kär sin′ə jən), *n. Pathol.* a substance that tends to produce a cancer. [*carcino-* (comb. form of Gk *karkínos* crab, cancer) + -GEN] —**car·cin·o·gen·ic** (kär′sə nō jen′ik), *adj.* —**car·ci·no·ge·nic·i·ty** (kär′sə nō jə nis′i tē), *n.*

car·ci·no·ma (kär′sə nō′mə), *n., pl.* **-mas, -ma·ta** (-mə tə). *Pathol.* a malignant and invasive tumor that spreads by metastasis and often recurs after excision; cancer. [< L < Gk *karkínōma* = *karkín(os)* crab, cancer + *-ōma* -OMA] —**car′ci·no′ma·toid′,** *adj.*

car′ coat′, a hip-length overcoat for informal wear.

card¹ (kärd), *n.* **1.** a piece of stiff paper or thin pasteboard, usually rectangular, for various uses, as to write information on, printed as a means of identifying the holder, etc.: *a 3″ x 5″ card; a membership card.* **2.** one of a set of small cardboards with spots, figures, etc., used in playing various games. **3.** **cards,** (*usually construed as sing.*) **a.** a game played with such a set. **b.** the playing of such a game: *to win at cards.* **4.** something useful, comparable to a high card held in a game: *If negotiation fails, we still have another card to play.* **5.** Also called **greeting card.** a piece of paper or thin cardboard, usually small and rectangular, printed with a message of holiday greeting, congratulations, good wishes, or other sentiment, often with an illustration or decorations, for mailing to a friend or relative on an appropriate occasion. **6.** See **post card. 7.** See **calling card. 8.** a program of the events at races, boxing matches, etc. **9.** the circular piece of paper, cardboard, etc., on which the 32 points indicating direction are marked on a compass. **10.** *Informal.* a person who is amusing or facetious. **11. in** or **on the cards,** impending; likely; probable. **12. play one's cards,** to execute one's plans. **13. put one's cards on the table,** to be completely straightforward and open; conceal nothing. —*v.t.* **14.** to provide with a card. **15.** to fasten on a card. **16.** to write, list, etc., on cards. [ME *carde,* unexplained var. of CARTE²]

card² (kärd), *n.* **1.** Also called **carding machine.** a machine for combing and paralleling fibers of cotton, flax, wool, etc., prior to spinning in order to remove short, undesirable fibers and produce a sliver. **2.** a similar implement for raising the nap on cloth. —*v.t.* **3.** to dress (wool or the like) with a card. [ME *carde* < MF: lit., teasel head < LL *card(us)* thistle, var. of L *carduus*] —**card′er,** *n.*

Card., Cardinal.

car·da·mom (kär′də məm), *n.* **1.** the aromatic seed capsule of various zingiberaceous plants of the genera *Amomum* and *Elettaria,* native to tropical Asia, used as a spice or condiment and in medicine. **2.** any of these plants. Also, **car·da·mon** (kär′də mən), **car′da·mum.** [< L *cardamōm(um)* < Gk *kardámōmon* = *kárd(amon)* cress + *ámōmon* a spice plant]

card·board (kärd′bōrd′, -bôrd′), *n.* a thin, stiff pasteboard, used for signs, boxes, etc.

card-car·ry·ing (kärd′kar′ē ing), *adj.* admittedly belonging to a group or party.

card′ cat′alog, a file of cards in alphabetical sequence listing the items in a library collection, each card typically identifying a single item by author, title, or subject.

Cár·de·nas (kär′the näs′), *n.* **1. Lá·za·ro** (lä′sä RŌ′), 1895–1970, Mexican general and political reformer: president 1934–40. **2.** a seaport in NW Cuba. 43,750 (1953).

card′ field′, field (def. 16b).

cardi-, var. of **cardio-** before a vowel: *cardialgia.*

car·di·ac (kär′dē ak′), *adj.* **1.** pertaining to the heart. **2.** pertaining to the esophageal portion of the stomach. —*n.* **3.** a person suffering from a heart disease: *A cardiac often requires a special diet.* [< medical L *cardiac(us)* < Gk *kardiakós* = *kardí(a)* heart + *-akos* -AC]

car·di·al·gi·a (kär′dē al′jē ə, -jə), *n. Pathol.* **1.** heartburn (def. 1). **2.** pain in the region of the heart.

Car·diff (kär′dif), *n.* a seaport in and the county seat of Glamorganshire, in SE Wales. 256,270 (1961).

car·di·gan (kär′də gən), *n.* a knitted jacket or sweater, collarless and open in front. Also called **car′digan jack′et, car′digan sweat′er.** [named after J. T. Brudnell, 7th Earl of *Cardigan* (1797–1868), British cavalryman of Crimean War fame]

Car·di·gan (kär′də gən), *n.* Cardiganshire.

Car′digan Bay′, an inlet of St. George's Channel, on the W coast of Wales.

Car·di·gan·shire (kär′də gən shēr′, -shər), *n.* a county in W Wales. 53,564 (1961); 692 sq. mi. *Co. seat:* Cardigan. Also called **Cardigan.**

car·di·nal (kär′dᵊnᵊl), *n.* **1.** *Rom. Cath. Ch.* a high ecclesiastic appointed to the College of Cardinals by the pope, and ranking next to him. **2.** a crested grosbeak, *Richmondena cardinalis,* of North America, the male of which is bright red. **3.** a deep, rich red. **4.** See **cardinal number.** —*adj.* **5.** of prime or fundamental importance: *a cardinal rule of behavior.* **6.** of the color cardinal. [ME < L *cardināl(is)* = *cardin-* (s. of *cardō*) hinge, hence, something on which other things hinge + *-ālis* -AL[1]] —**car′di·nal·ly,** *adv.* —**car′di·nal·ship′,** *n.*

Cardinal, *Richmondena cardinalis* (Length 9½ in.)

car·di·nal·ate (kär′dᵊnᵊlāt′), *n. Rom. Cath. Ch.* **1.** the body of cardinals. **2.** the office, rank, or dignity of a cardinal.

car′dinal flow′er, a North American plant, *Lobelia cardinalis,* with showy red flowers.

car′dinal num′ber, any of the numbers that express amount, as *one, two, three,* etc. (distinguished from *ordinal number*). Also called **car′dinal nu′meral.**

car′dinal points′, the four chief directions of the compass; the north, south, east, and west points.

car′dinal vir′tues, *Ancient Philos.* justice, prudence, temperance, and fortitude.

card·ing (kär′diŋ), *n.* the process in which fibers, as cotton, worsted, or wool, are manipulated into sliver form prior to spinning.

card′ing machine′, card[2] (defs. 1, 2).

cardio-, a learned borrowing from Greek meaning "heart," used in forming compound words: *cardiogram.* Also, *esp. before a vowel,* **cardi-.** [< Gk *kardio-,* comb. form of *kardía*]

car·di·o·gram (kär′dē ə gram′), *n.* electrocardiogram.

car·di·o·graph (kär′dē ə graf′, -gräf′), *n.* electrocardiograph. —**car·di·o·graph·ic** (kär′dē ə graf′ik), *adj.* —**car·di·og·ra·phy** (kär′dē og′rə fē), *n.*

car·di·oid (kär′dē oid′), *n. Math.* a somewhat heart-shaped curve, being the path of a point on a circle that rolls externally, without slipping, on another equal circle. Equation: $r = a\,(1-\cos A)$. [< Gk *kardioeid(ḗs)* heart-shaped]

car·di·ol·o·gy (kär′dē ol′ə jē), *n.* the study of the heart and its functions in health and disease. —**car·di·o·log·ic** (kär′dē ə loj′ik), **car′di·o·log′i·cal,** *adj.* —**car′di·ol′o·gist,** *n.*

car·di·o·pul·mo·nar·y (kär′dē ō pul′mə ner′ē, -pŏŏl-′), *adj.* of, pertaining to, or affecting the heart and lungs: *cardiopulmonary resuscitation.* [CARDIO- + PULMONARY]

car·di·o·vas·cu·lar (kär′dē ō vas′kyə lər), *adj. Anat.* of, pertaining to, or affecting the heart and blood vessels.

car·di·tis (kär dī′tis), *n. Pathol.* inflammation of the pericardium, myocardium, or endocardium, separately or in combination. [< NL; see CARDI-, -ITIS] —**car·dit·ic** (kär dit′ik), *adj.*

car·doon (kär do͞on′), *n.* a perennial plant, *Cynara Cardunculus,* of Mediterranean regions, the leaves and leafstalks of which are blanched and eaten like celery. [< MF *cardon* < It *cardon(e)* = *card(o)* thistle (< L *cardu(u)s*) + *-one* aug. suffix]

Car·do·zo (kär dō′zō), *n.* **Benjamin Nathan,** 1870–1938, associate justice of the U.S. Supreme Court 1932–38.

card·sharp (kärd′shärp′), *n.* a person, esp. a professional gambler, who cheats at card games. Also, **card′sharp′er.** —**card′sharp′ing,** *n.*

car·du·a·ceous (kär′jo͞o ā′shəs), *adj.* belonging to the *Carduaceae* or thistle family of plants, usually regarded as part of the *Compositae,* comprising the goldenrods, asters, boltonias, fleabanes, etc. [< NL *Carduāce(ae)* (L *cardu-,* s. of *carduus* thistle + *-āceae* -ACEAE) + -OUS]

Car·duc·ci (kär do͞ot′chē), *n.* **Gio·suè** (jô swe′), ("*Enotrio Romano*"), 1835–1907, Italian poet and critic.

care (kâr), *n., v.,* **cared, car·ing.** —*n.* **1.** worry; anxiety; concern: *Care had aged him.* **2.** a cause or object of concern, worry, anxiety, distress, etc.: *Her child is her major care.* **3.** serious attention; solicitude; caution: *He devotes great care to his work.* **4.** protection; charge or temporary keeping: *He's under the care of a doctor. Address my mail in care of the American Embassy.* **5.** *Obs.* grief; suffering; sorrow. **6. take care,** be alert; be careful: *Take care that you don't fall on the ice!* Also, **have a care. 7. take care of, a.** to watch over; be responsible for: *to take care of an invalid.* **b.** to act on; deal with; attend to: *to take care of paying a bill.* —*v.i.* **8.** to be concerned or solicitous. **9.** to make provision or look out (usually fol. by *for*): *Will you care for the children while I am away?* **10.** to have an inclination, liking, fondness, or affection (usually fol. by *for*): *She doesn't care for desserts.* **11.** to wish or be inclined (often fol. by an infinitive): *Would you care to dance?* [(n.) ME; OE *car(u)* anxiety; c. Goth *kara,* OHG *chara* lament; akin to L *garrire* to chatter; (v.) ME *care(n),* OE *c(e)arian* to worry < n.] —**car′er,** *n.* —**Syn. 1.** solicitude, trouble. See **concern.**

CARE (kâr), *n.* a private organization for the collection of funds, goods, etc., for the needy in foreign countries. Also, **Care.** [*C(ooperative for) A(merican) R(elief) E(verywhere)*]

ca·reen (kə rēn′), *v.t.* **1.** to cause (a vessel) to lie over on its side, as on a beach, in order to repair, clean, or otherwise work on its bottom; heave down. **2.** to clean or repair (a vessel lying on its side). **3.** to cause (a vessel) to heel over or list, as by the the force of a beam wind. —*v.i.* **4.** (of a vessel) to heel over or list. **5.** (of a vehicle) to lean, sway, or tip to one side while in motion: *The car careened around the corner.* **6.** career (def. 7). **7.** to careen a vessel. —*n.* **8.** a careening. [< MF *carine* < L *carīn(a)* keel, nutshell; akin to Gk *káryon* nut] —**ca·reen′er,** *n.*

ca·reer (kə rēr′), *n.* **1.** progress or general course of action of a person through life, or through some phase of life, as in some profession or undertaking, some moral or intellectual action, etc.: *His career as a soldier ended with the armistice.* **2.** an occupation or profession followed as one's lifework: *He sought a career as a lawyer.* **3.** success in a profession, occupation, etc. **4.** a course, esp. a swift one. **5.** speed, esp. full speed: *The horse stumbled in full career.* **6.** *Obs.* a charge at full speed. —*v.i.* **7.** to run or move rapidly along; go at full speed. —*adj.* **8.** having or following a career: *a career girl.* [< MF *carriere* < LL *carrāria (via)* vehicular (road) = L *carr(us)* wagon (see CAR) + *-āria,* fem. of *-ārius* -ARY]

ca·reer·ism (kə rēr′iz əm), *n.* devotion to a successful career, often at the expense of one's personal life, ethics, etc. —**ca·reer′ist,** *n.*

care·free (kâr′frē′), *adj.* without anxiety or worry. —**care′free′ness,** *n.*

care·ful (kâr′fəl), *adj.* **1.** cautious in one's actions. **2.** taking pains in one's work; exact; thorough: *a careful typist.* **3.** (of things) done or performed with accuracy or caution: *careful research.* **4.** solicitously mindful (usually fol. by *of, about,* or *in*): *careful of the rights of others.* **5.** *Archaic.* **a.** troubled. **b.** attended with anxiety. [ME; OE *carful*] —**care′ful·ly,** *adv.* —**care′ful·ness,** *n.* —**Syn. 1.** watchful, chary, circumspect, cautious, wary. **2.** painstaking, meticulous. **3.** conscientious. **4.** thoughtful, concerned, solicitous, attentive. —**Ant. 1–4.** careless.

care·less (kâr′lis), *adj.* **1.** not paying enough attention to what one does: *a careless typist.* **2.** not exact or thorough: *careless work.* **3.** done or said heedlessly or negligently; unconsidered: *a careless remark.* **4.** not caring or troubling; having no care or concern; unconcerned (usually fol. by *of, about,* or *in*): *careless of the rights of others.* **5.** artless; unstudied. **6.** *Archaic.* free from anxiety. [ME; OE *carlēas*] —**care′less·ly,** *adv.* —**care′less·ness,** *n.* —**Syn. 1.** inattentive, unwary, reckless. **2.** inaccurate, negligent. **3.** unthoughtful, unmindful. **4.** thoughtless; inconsiderate. —**Ant. 1–4.** careful.

ca·ress (kə res′), *n.* **1.** an act or gesture expressing affection, as a gentle stroking or a kiss or embrace. —*v.t.* **2.** to touch or stroke gently with or as with affection: *The breeze caressed the trees.* **3.** to treat with favor, kindness, etc. [< F *caresse* < It *carezz(a)* < VL *caritia = L *cār(us)* dear + *-itia* n. suffix (cf. *-ess,* as in *largess,* etc.)] —**ca·ress′er,** *n.* —**ca·ress′ing·ly,** *adv.* —**ca·ress′ive,** *adj.* —**ca·ress′ive·ly,** *adv.*

car·et (kar′it), *n.* a mark (∧) made in written or printed matter to show the place where something is to be inserted. [< L *caret* (there) is lacking or wanting, 3rd pers. sing. pres. ind. of *carēre* to be without]

care·tak·er (kâr′tā′kər), *n.* **1.** a person who is in charge of the maintenance of a building, estate, etc.; superintendent. **2.** *Brit.* a janitor. —**care′tak′ing,** *n.*

Ca·rew (kə ro͞o′; *sometimes* kâr′o͞o), *n.* **Thomas,** 1598?–1639?, English poet.

care·worn (kâr′wōrn′, -wôrn′), *adj.* showing signs of care or worry; haggard.

car·fare (kär′fâr′), *n.* the amount charged for a ride on a streetcar, bus, etc.

car·go (kär′gō), *n., pl.* **-goes, -gos. 1.** the lading or freight of a ship, airplane, etc. **2.** load. [< Sp: a load < *cargar* to load < LL *carricāre;* see CHARGE] —**Syn. 2.** burden.

car·hop (kär′hop′), *n.* a waiter or waitress at a drive-in restaurant.

Car·i·a (kâr′ē ə), *n.* an ancient district in SW Asia Minor. —**Car′i·an,** *adj., n.*

Car·ib (kar′ib), *n., pl.* **-ibs,** (*esp. collectively*) **-ib. 1.** a member of an Indian people of NE South America. **2.** the language of the Caribs. [< Sp *Carib(e)* < Arawak *Carib*]

Car·ib·be·an (kar′ə bē′ən, kə rib′ē-), *adj.* **1.** pertaining to the Caribs, the Lesser Antilles, or the Caribbean Sea. —*n.* **2.** a Carib. **3.** See **Caribbean Sea.**

Car′ibbe′an Sea′, a part of the Atlantic Ocean bounded by Central America, the West Indies, and South America. ab. 750,000 sq. mi.; greatest known depth 22,788 ft. Also called **Caribbean.**

ca·ri·be (kə rē′bē; *Sp.* kä rē′ve), *n., pl.* **-bes** (-bēz; *Sp.* -ves). piranha. [< Sp: cannibal, CARIB]

Car·i·bees (kar′ə bēz′), *n.* the Lesser Antilles. See under **Antilles.**

Car′i·boo Moun′tains (kar′ə bo͞o′), a mountain range in SW Canada, in E central British Columbia, part of the Rocky Mountains: highest peak, ab. 11,750 ft.

car·i·bou (kar′ə bo͞o′), *n., pl.* **-bous,** (*esp. collectively*) **-bou.** any of several large, North American deer of the genus *Rangifer,* related to the reindeer of the Old World. [< CanF < Algonquian *khalibu,* lit., pawer, scratcher]

Caribou, *Rangifer caribou* (About 4 ft. high at shoulder; length 6 ft.)

car·i·ca·ture (kar′ə kə chər, -cho͝or′), *n., v.,* **-tured, -turing.** —*n.* **1.** a picture, description, etc., ludicrously exaggerating the peculiarities or defects of persons or things. **2.** the art or process of producing such pictures, descriptions, etc. **3.** any imitation or copy so inferior as to be ludicrous. —*v.t.* **4.** to make a caricature of; represent in caricature. [earlier *caricatura* < It = *caricat(o)* loaded, i.e., distorted (ptp. of *caricare;* see CHARGE) + *-ura* -URE] —**car′i·ca·tur·a·ble,** *adj.* —**car′i·ca·tur·ist,** *n.* —**Syn. 1.** cartoon. See **burlesque. 3.** travesty.

car·ies (kâr′ēz, -ē ēz′), *n., pl.* **-ies.** decay, as of bone or teeth, or of plant tissue. [< L: decay; akin to Gk *Kḗr* goddess of death]

car·il·lon (kar′ə lon′, -lən *or, esp. Brit.,* kə ril′yən; *Fr.* KA RĒ YÔN′), *n., pl.* **car·il·lons** (kar′ə lonz′, -lənz *or, esp. Brit.,* kə ril′yənz; *Fr.* KA RĒ YÔN′). **1.** a set of stationary bells hung in a tower and sounded by manual or pedal action, or by machinery. **2.** a melody played on such bells. [< F: set of bells, orig. four; of disputed orig. but based on L *quattuor* four]

car·il·lon·neur (kar′ə lə nûr′ *or, esp. Brit.,* kə ril′yə nər; *Fr.* KA RĒ YÔ NŒR′), *n., pl.* **car·il·lon·neurs** (kar′ə lə nûrz′ *or, esp. Brit.,* kə ril′yə nərz; *Fr.* KA RĒ YÔ NŒR′). a person who plays a carillon. [< F]

ca·ri·na (kə rī′nə, -rē′-), *n., pl.* **-nas, -nae** (-nē). *Bot., Zool.* a keellike part or ridge. [< L: keel] —**ca·ri′nal,** *adj.*

Ca·ri·na (kə rī′nə), *n., gen.* **-nae** (-nē). *Astron.* the Keel, a southern constellation, containing the bright star Canopus: one of the constellations into which Argo is divided.

car·i·nate (kar′ə nāt′), *adj. Bot., Zool.* formed with a carina; keellike. Also, **car′i·nat′ed.**

Ca·rin·thi·a (kə rin′thē ə), *n.* a province in S Austria. 493,972 (1961); 3681 sq. mi. *Cap.:* Klagenfurt. —**Ca·rin′thi·an,** *adj.*

car·i·o·ca (kar′ē ō′kə), *n.* a modification of the samba.

Car·i·o·ca (kar′ē ō′kə; *Port.* kä′RĒ ô′kə), *n.* a native of Rio de Janeiro. [< Brazilian Pg < Tupi = *cari* white + *oca* house]

car·i·ole (kar′ē ōl′), *n.* **1.** a small, open, two-wheeled carriage. **2.** a covered cart. Also, **carriole.** [< F *carriole* < OPr *carriol(a)* = *carri* carriage (see CARRY) + *-ola* -ULE]

car·i·ous (kâr′ē əs), *adj.* having caries, as teeth; decayed. [< L *cariōs(us)* decayed, rotten] —**car·i·os·i·ty** (kâr′ē os′i tē), **car′i·ous·ness,** *n.*

cark (kärk), *n.* **1.** care or worry. —*v.t., v.i.* **2.** *Archaic.* to worry. [ME *cark(en)* (to) be anxious, OE *(be)carcian,* appar. = *car-* (base of *caru* CARE) + *k-* suffix]

carl (kärl), *n.* *Archaic.* a churl. Also, **carle.** [ME, OE < Scand; cf. Icel *karl* man; c. OHG *karl;* akin to CHURL] —**carl′ish,** *adj.* —**carl′ish·ness,** *n.*

car·ling (kär′ling), *n.* *Naut.* a short fore-and-aft beam framing a hatchway, mast hole, or other deck opening to support the inner ends of the partial deck beams in way of the opening. [< F *carlingue* < Scand; cf. Icel *kerling* keelson, lit., old woman = *kerl* (mutated var. of *karl* man; see CARL) + *-ing* -ING[1]]

Car·lisle (kär līl′, kär′līl), *n.* a city in and the county seat of Cumberland, in NW England. 71,112 (1961).

Car·list (kär′list), *n.* a supporter of the claims of Don Carlos of Spain or of his successors to the Spanish throne. —**Car′lism,** *n.*

car·load (kär′lōd′), *n.* *Chiefly U.S.* **1.** the amount carried by a car, esp. a freight car. **2.** the legal minimum weight entitling a railroad shipper to a reduced rate **(car′load rate′).**

car′load lot′, a standard carload shipment of freight that measures up to the legal minimum weight.

Car·los (kär′ləs, -lōs; *Sp.* kär′lôs), *n.* **Don** (don; *Sp.* dôn), (*Carlos María Isidro de Borbón*), 1788–1855, pretender to the Spanish throne.

Car·lo·ta (kär lô′tä), *n.* 1840–1927, wife of Maximilian: empress of Mexico 1864–67 (daughter of Leopold I of Belgium). English, **Charlotte.**

Car·lo·vin·gi·an (kär′lə vin′jē ən), *adj., n.* Carolingian.

Car·low (kär′lō), *n.* a county in Leinster, in the SE Republic of Ireland. 33,342 (1961); 346 sq. mi. *Co. seat:* Carlow.

Carls·bad (kärlz′bad), *n.* a city in W Czechoslovakia: hot springs. 43,819 (1963). German, **Karlsbad.** Czech, **Karlovy Vary.**

Carls′bad Cav′erns, a series of limestone caverns, near Carlsbad, New Mexico; now part of a national park **(Carls′bad Cav′erns Na′tional Park′).** 71 sq. mi.

Car·lyle (kär līl′), *n.* **Thomas,** 1795–1881, Scottish essayist and historian.

car·ma·gnole (kär′mən yōl′; *Fr.* KAR MA nyôl′), *n., pl.* **-ma·gnoles** (-mən yōlz′; *Fr.* -MA nyôl′). **1.** a dance and song popular during the French Revolution. **2.** the common costume of the French revolutionists, consisting chiefly of a loose jacket with wide lapels and metal buttons, black pantaloons, and a red liberty cap. [< F < provincial *carmagnola* ceremonial jacket worn by peasants of Dauphiné and Savoy, named after *Carmagnola,* town in Piedmont, Italy]

Car·man (kär′mən), *n.* **(William) Bliss,** 1861–1929, Canadian poet and journalist in the U.S.

Car·mar·then (kär mär′thən), *n.* **1.** a seaport in and the county seat of Carmarthenshire, in S Wales. 12,121 (1961). **2.** Carmarthenshire.

Car·mar·then·shire (kär mär′thən shēr′, -shər), *n.* a county in S Wales. 167,736 (1961); 919 sq. mi. *Co. seat:* Carmarthen. Also called **Carmarthen.**

Car·mel (kär mel′), *n.* **1. Mount,** a mountain in NW Israel, near the Mediterranean coast. Highest point, 1818 ft. ab. 14 mi. long. **2.** Carmel-by-the-Sea.

Car·mel-by-the-Sea (kär mel′ bī thə sē′), *n.* a town in W California. 4525 (1970).

Car·mel·ite (kär′mə līt′), *n.* **1.** a mendicant friar belonging to a religious order founded at Mt. Carmel in the 12th century. **2.** a nun belonging to this order. —*adj.* **3.** of or pertaining to Carmelites or their order. [late ME < ML *Carmelīt(a)*]

Car·mi·chael (kär′mī kəl), *n.* **1. Hoa·gy** (hō′gē) (*Hoagland Howard*), 1899–1981, U.S. songwriter and musician. **2. Stoke·ly** (stōk′lē), born 1941, U.S. civil-rights leader, born in Trinidad: chairman of the Student Nonviolent Coordinating Committee 1966–67. **3.** a town in central California, near Sacramento. 37,625 (1970).

car·min·a·tive (kär min′ə tiv, kär′mə nā′tiv), *n.* **1.** a drug causing expulsion of gas from the stomach or bowel. —*adj.* **2.** expelling gas from the body; relieving flatulence. [< L *carmināt(us)* carded (ptp. of *carmināre* = *carmin-* (s. of *carmen*) CARD[2] + *-ātus* -ATE[1]) + -IVE]

car·mine (kär′min, -mīn), *n.* **1.** a crimson or purplish red. **2.** a crimson pigment obtained from cochineal. [< ML *carmīn(us),* syncopated var. of *carmesīnus* = *carmes-* (< Ar *qirmiz* KERMES) + *-īnus* -INE[1]]

carn (kärn), *n.* cairn.

Car·nac (kär′nak; *Fr.* KAR NAK′), *n.* a commune in NW France, SE of Lorient: megalithic monuments. 3641 (1962).

car·nage (kär′nij), *n.* **1.** the slaughter of many people, as in battle. **2.** *Archaic.* dead bodies, as of soldiers. [< MF < It *carnagg(io)* < ML *carnātic(um)* payment or offering in meat = L *carn-* (s. of *caro*) flesh + *-āticum* -AGE]

car·nal (kär′nᵊl), *adj.* **1.** not spiritual; merely human; temporal; worldly. **2.** pertaining to or characterized by the flesh or the body, its passions and appetites; sensual: *carnal pleasures.* [ME < L *carnāl(is)* = *carn-* (s. of *caro*) flesh + *-ālis* -AL[1]] —**car·nal′i·ty,** *n.* —**car′nal·ly,** *adv.* —**Syn. 1.** earthly, natural. **2.** fleshly, bodily, animal, lustful.

car′nal knowl′edge, *Chiefly Law.* sexual intercourse.

car·nall·ite (kär′nᵊlīt′), *n.* a hydrous mineral, $KCl \cdot MgCl_2 \cdot 6H_2O$, used chiefly as a source of potassium. [named after R. von *Carnall* (1804–74), German mining official; see -ITE[1]]

Car·nap (kär′nap), *n.* **Rudolf P.,** 1891–1970, U.S. philosopher, born in Germany.

Car·nar·von (kär när′vən), *n.* **1.** Caernarvon. **2.** Also called **Car·nar′von·shire′.** Caernarvonshire.

car·nas·si·al (kär nas′ē əl), *Zool.* —*adj.* **1.** (of teeth) adapted for shearing flesh. —*n.* **2.** a carnassial tooth, esp. the last upper premolar or the first lower molar tooth of certain carnivores. [< F *carnassi(er)* flesh-eating < Prov, earlier form of *carnassie* (< *carnasso* meat in plenty (< L *carn-* (s. of *caro*) flesh + *-acea* (fem.) -ACEOUS) + *-ie(r)* < L *-ārius* -ARY) + -AL[1]]

Car·nat·ic (kär nat′ik), *n.* a historically important region on the SE coast of India: now in Madras state.

car·na·tion (kär nā′shən), *n.* **1.** any of numerous cultivated varieties of clove pink, *Dianthus Caryophyllus,* having fragrant flowers of various colors: the state flower of Ohio. **2.** pink; light red. [< LL *carnātiōn-* (s. of *carnātiō*) fleshiness, hence flesh color = L *carn-* (s. of *caro*) flesh + *-ātiōn-* -ATION]

car·nau·ba (kär nou′bə), *n.* **1.** See **wax palm** (def. 2). **2.** a wax derived from the young leaves of this tree, used as a polish and in phonograph records. [< Brazilian Pg]

Car·ne·gie (kär nā′gē, kär′nə-), *n.* **Andrew,** 1835–1919, U.S. steel manufacturer and philanthropist, born in Scotland.

car·nel·ian (kär nēl′yən), *n.* a red or reddish variety of chalcedony, used in jewelry. Also, **cornelian.** [var. (with *a* of CARNATION) of *cornelian,* ME *cornel(ine)* (< MF, prob. = OF *cornele* cornel cherry + *-ine* -INE[1], they being alike in color) + -IAN]

car·ney (kär′nē), *n.* carny. Also, **car′nie.**

Car·ni·o·la (kär′nē ō′lə, kärn yō′-), *n.* a former duchy and crown land of Austria: now in NW Yugoslavia. —**Car′ni·o′lan,** *adj.*

car·ni·val (kär′nə vəl), *n.* **1.** a traveling amusement show, typically having side shows, a Ferris wheel, merry-go-rounds, shooting galleries, etc. **2.** any merrymaking, revelry, or festival, as a program of sports, entertainment, etc.: *a winter sports carnival.* **3.** the season of merrymaking immediately preceding Lent. [< It *carneval(e),* OIt *carnelevare* taking meat away = *carne* flesh (< L *carn(e)-,* s. of *caro*) + *levare* < L: lit., to lift] —**car′ni·val·esque′, car′ni·val·like′,** *adj.*

Car·niv·o·ra (kär niv′ər ə), *n.* the order comprising the carnivores. [< NL, (neut. pl.); see CARNIVOROUS]

car·ni·vore (kär′nə vōr′, -vôr′), *n.* **1.** any chiefly flesh-eating mammal of the order *Carnivora,* comprising the dogs, cats, bears, seals, weasels, etc. **2.** an insectivorous plant. [back formation from NL *Carnivora* or CARNIVOROUS] —**car·niv·o·ral** (kär niv′ər əl), *adj.*

car·niv·o·rous (kär niv′ər əs), *adj.* flesh-eating. [< L *carnivorus* = *carni-* (comb. form of *caro* flesh) + *-vorus* -VOROUS] —**car·niv′o·rism,** *n.* —**car·niv′o·rous·ly,** *adv.* —**car·niv′o·rous·ness,** *n.*

Car·not (kär nō′; *Fr.* KAR nō′), *n.* **1. La·zare Ni·co·las Mar·gue·rite** (LA ZAR′ nē kô lä′ MAR gə RĒT′), 1753–1823, French general and statesman. **2. (Ma·rie Fran·çois) Sa·di** (mə rē′ fran swä′ sad′ē; *Fr.* MA RĒ′ FRÄN SWA′ SA dē′), 1837–94, French statesman: president of the Republic 1887–94. **3. Ni·co·las Lé·o·nard Sa·di** (nik′ə ləs len′ərd sad′ē; *Fr.* nē kô lä′ lā ô NAR′ SA dē′), 1796–1832, French physicist: pioneer in the field of thermodynamics.

car·no·tite (kär′nə tīt′), *n.* a mineral, a yellow, earthy, hydrous vanadate of potassium and uranium: an ore of uranium. [named after A. *Carnot* (d. 1920), French mining official; see -ITE[1]]

car·ny (kär′nē), *n., pl.* **-nies.** *Informal.* **1.** a person employed by a carnival. **2.** carnival (def. 1). Also, **carney, carnie.** [CARN(IVAL) + -Y[2]]

car·ob (kar′əb), *n.* the edible fruit of a caesalpiniaceous tree, *Ceratonia Siliqua,* of the Mediterranean regions, a long, dry pod containing hard seeds in a sweet pulp. [< MF *carobe* < ML *carrūb(ium)* < Ar *al kharrūbah* bean pods, carobs]

ca·roche (kə rōch′, -rōsh′), *n.* (in the 17th century) a luxurious or stately coach or carriage. [< MF < It *carrocc(io)* = *carr(o)* wheeled conveyance (see CAR) + *-occio* aug. suffix]

car·ol (kar′əl), *n., v.,* **-oled, -ol·ing** or (*esp. Brit.*) **-olled, -ol·ling.** —*n.* **1.** a song, esp. of joy. **2.** a Christmas song or hymn. **3.** *Obs.* a kind of circular dance. —*v.i.* **4.** to sing in a lively, joyous manner; warble. —*v.t.* **5.** to sing joyously. **6.** to praise or celebrate in song. [ME *carole* ring, circle (of stones), enclosed place for study (see CARREL), ring dance with song (hence, song) < OF, appar. < L *coroll(a)* circlet (*cor(ōna)* CROWN + *-olla* dim. suffix) + Gk *choraúlēs* piper for choral dance = *chor(ós)* chorus + *aul(ós)* pipe + *-ēs* agent suffix] —**car′ol·er,** *esp. Brit.,* **car′ol·ler,** *n.*

Carol., Carolingian.

Car′ol Cit′y (kar′əl), a town in SE Florida, near Miami. 27,361 (1970).

Car·o·le·an (kar′ə lē′ən), *adj.* Caroline. [< ML *Carolae(us)* (*Carol(us)* Charles + *-aeus* adj. suffix) + -AN]

Car·o·li·na (kar′ə lī′nə), *n.* **1.** a former English colony on the Atlantic coast of North America: officially divided into North Carolina and South Carolina in 1729. **2.** North Carolina or South Carolina. **3. the Car′o·li′nas.** North Carolina and South Carolina. **4.** a city in NE Puerto Rico. 94,271 (1970).

Car′oli′na jes′samine, a vine, *Gelsemium sempervirens,* having fragrant, yellow flowers: the state flower of South Carolina. Also, **Car′oli′na jas′mine.**

Car·o·line (kar′ə līn′, -lin), *adj.* of or pertaining to Charles, esp. Charles I and Charles II of England or their times. Also, **Carolean, Carolinian.** [< ML *Carolīn(us)* = *Carol(us)* Charles + *-īnus* -INE[1]]

Car′oline Is′lands, a group of over 500 islands in the Pacific, E of the Philippines: under U.S. administration. 58,412 (1970); 525 sq. mi.

Car·o·lin·gi·an (kar′ə lin′jē ən), *adj.* **1.** of or pertaining to the Frankish dynasty that reigned in France A.D. 751–987 and in Germany until A.D. 911. —*n.* **2.** a member of the Carolingian dynasty. *Abbr.:* Carol. Also, **Carlovingian, Carolinian.** [< F *Carolingien* < ML *Caroling(ī)* (pl.) family of Charles (*Carol(us)* Charles + *-ing-* offspring (< Gmc) + *-ī* pl. ending) + F *-ien* -IAN]

Car·o·lin·i·an (kar′ə lin′ē ən), *adj.* **1.** of or pertaining to North Carolina or South Carolina or both. —*n.* **2.** a native or inhabitant of North Carolina or of South Carolina.

Car·o·lin·i·an (kar′ə lin′ē ən), *adj.* **1.** Carolingian. **2.** Caroline. —*n.* **3.** Carolingian. [< ML *Carolīn(us)* CAROLINE + -IAN]

car·om (kar′əm) *n.* **1.** *Billiards, Pool.* a shot in which the cue ball hits two balls in succession. **2.** any strike and rebound. —*v.i.* **3.** to make a carom. **4.** to strike and rebound. Also, **carrom.** [back formation from *carambole* (taken as *carom ball* by folk etym.) < F < Sp *carambol(a)*, special use of fruit name < Marathi *karambal*]

car·o·tene (kar′ə tēn′), *n. Chem.* any of three isomeric red hydrocarbons, $C_{40}H_{56}$, found in many plants, esp. carrots, and transformed to vitamin A in the liver. Also, **carotin.** [< L *carōt(a)* CARROT + -ENE]

ca·rot·e·noid (kə rot′ᵊnoid′), *Biochem.* —*n.* **1.** any of a group of red and yellow pigments, chemically similar to carotene, contained in animal fat and some plants. —*adj.* **2.** similar to carotene. **3.** pertaining to carotenoids. Also, **ca·rot′i·noid′.**

ca·rot·id (kə rot′id), *Anat.* —*n.* **1.** Also called **carot′id ar′tery.** either of the two large arteries, one on each side of the head, that carry blood to the head. —*adj.* **2.** pertaining to a carotid artery. [< Gk *karōtíd(es)* neck arteries = *karōt(ikós)* soporific (*kár(os)* stupor + *-ōtikos* -OTIC) + *-ides* -ID[3]; so called by Galen, who found that their compression causes stupor] —**ca·rot′id·al,** *adj.*

car·o·tin (kar′ə tin), *n.* carotene.

ca·rous·al (kə rou′zəl), *n.* a noisy or drunken feast; jovial revelry.

ca·rouse (kə rouz′), *n., v.,* **-roused, -rous·ing.** —*n.* **1.** carousal. —*v.i.* **2.** to engage in a drunken revel. **3.** to drink deeply and frequently. [var. of *garouse* < G *gar aus (trinken)* (drink) fully out, i.e., drain the cup; cf. MF *carous* < dial. G *gar ūs*] —**ca·rous′er,** *n.* —**ca·rous′ing·ly,** *adv.*

car·ou·sel (kar′ə sel′, -zel′; kar′ə sel′, -zel′), *n.* carrousel.

carp[1] (kärp), *v.i.* to find fault; cavil; complain unreasonably. [ME *carp(en)* (to) speak, prate < Scand; cf. Icel *karpa* to brag, wrangle] —**carp′er,** *n.*

carp[2] (kärp), *n., pl. (esp. collectively)* **carp,** *(esp. referring to two or more kinds or species)* **carps. 1.** a large, fresh-water food fish, *Cyprinus carpio.* **2.** any of various other fishes of the family *Cyprinidae.* [ME *carpe* < MF < MD or MLG *karpe;* c. OHG *karpfo*]

-carp, var. of **carpo-**[1] as final element in a compound word: *endocarp.*

carp., carpentry.

Car·pac·cio (kär pät′chô), *n.* **Vit·to·re** (vēt tô′re), c1450–1525, Italian painter.

car·pal (kär′pəl), *Anat.* —*adj.* **1.** pertaining to the carpus: *the carpal joint.* —*n.* **2.** carpale. [< NL *carpāl(is)*]

car·pa·le (kär pā′lē), *n., pl.* **-li·a** (-lē ə). *Anat.* any of the bones of the wrist. [< NL, neut. of *carpālis* CARPAL]

car′ park′, *Chiefly Brit.* a parking lot.

Car·pa′thi·an Moun′tains (kär pā′thē ən), a mountain range in central Europe, extending from N Czechoslovakia to central Rumania. Highest peak, Gerlachovka, 8737 ft. Also called **Car·pa′thi·ans.**

Car·pa·tho-U·kraine (kär pā′thō yōō krān′), *n.* a region in the E Ukraine, in the SW Soviet Union: ceded by Czechoslovakia in 1945. Cf. **Ruthenia.**

car·pe di·em (kär′pe dē′em; *Eng.* kär′pē dī′em), *Latin.* seize the day; enjoy the present, as opposed to placing all hope in the future.

car·pel (kär′pəl), *n. Bot.* a simple pistil, or a single member of a compound pistil, regarded as a modified leaf. [< NL *carpell(um)* = Gk *karp(ós)* fruit + L *-ellum* dim. suffix] —**car·pel·lar·y** (kär′pə ler′ē), *adj.*

A B

Carpels
A, Flower with simple pistils
B, Tricarpellary fruit

Car·pen·tar·i·a (kär′pən târ′ē ə), *n.* **Gulf of,** a gulf on the coast of N Australia. ab. 480 mi. long; ab. 300 mi. wide.

car·pen·ter (kär′pən tər), *n.* **1.** a person who builds or repairs wooden structures. —*v.i.* **2.** to do carpenter's work. [ME < AF < LL *carpentār(ius)* wainwright = *carpent(um)* two-wheeled carriage + *-ārius* -ER[2]]

Car·pen·ter (kär′pən tər), *n.* **John Alden,** 1876–1951, U.S. composer.

car′penter ant′, a black or brown ant of the genus *Camponotus* that nests in the wood of decaying or dead trees in which it bores tunnels for depositing its eggs.

car′penter bee′, any of several solitary bees of the family *Xylocopidae* that nest in solid wood, boring tunnels in which to deposit their eggs.

car·pen·try (kär′pən trē), *n.* **1.** the trade of a carpenter. **2.** the work produced by a carpenter. Also, **car·pen·ter·ing** (kär′pən tər ing). [ME *carpentrie* < ONF < L *carpentāria (fabrica)* carriage maker's workshop]

car·pet (kär′pit), *n.* **1.** a heavy fabric for covering floors. Cf. **rug** (def. 1). **2.** a covering of this material. **3.** any covering like a carpet: *a carpet of grass.* **4. on the carpet,** before an authority for a reprimand. —*v.t.* **5.** to cover or furnish with or as with a carpet. [ME *carpete* < ML, LL *carpet(a)* kind of wool fabric, lit., (wool) divided, i.e., carded = L *carpe(re)* (to) pluck, separate + *-ta* fem. of *-tus* ptp. suffix]

car·pet·bag (kär′pit bag′), *n., v.,* **-bagged, -bag·ging.** —*n.* **1.** a bag for traveling, esp. one made of carpeting. —*v.i.* **2.** to act as a carpetbagger.

car·pet·bag·ger (kär′pit bag′ər), *n.* **1.** any person, esp. a politician, who takes up residence in a place in order to seek special advantages for himself. **2.** *U.S. Hist.* a Northerner who went to the South seeking private gain during the Reconstruction period. [CARPETBAG + -ER[1]; so called because he came South carrying his belongings in a carpetbag]

car′pet bee′tle, any of several small beetles of the family *Dermestidae,* the larvae of which are household pests, feeding on woolen fabrics. Also called **car′pet bug′.**

car·pet·ing (kär′pi ting), *n.* **1.** material for carpets. **2.** carpets in general.

car′pet sweep′er, an implement for removing dirt, lint, etc., from rugs and carpets, consisting of a metal case enclosing one or more brushes that are rotated by wheeling it by the attached handle.

car′pet tack′, a flat-headed, sharply pointed nail, used esp. to tack down carpets.

car·pet·weed (kär′pit wēd′), *n.* a North American prostrate weed, *Mollugo verticillata.* [so called because procumbent]

car·pi (kär′pī), *n.* pl. of **carpus.**

-carpic, a combination of **-carp** and **-ic** used in the formation of adjectives from stems in **-carp:** *endocarpic.*

carp·ing (kär′ping), *adj.* characterized by fussy or petulant faultfinding; querulous or ill-natured: *carping criticism.* —**carp′ing·ly,** *adv.*

carpo-[1], a learned borrowing from Greek meaning "fruit," used in the formation of compound words: *carpophore.* Also, **-carp.** [< Gk *karpo-*, comb. form of *karpós* fruit]

carpo-[2], a learned borrowing from Greek meaning "wrist," used in the formation of compound words. [< Gk *karpo-*, comb. form of *karpós* wrist]

car·po·go·ni·um (kär′pə gō′nē əm), *n., pl* **-ni·a** (nē ə). *Bot.* the one-celled female sex organ of the red algae that, when fertilized, gives rise to the carpospores. —**car′po·go′ni·al,** *adj.*

car·pol·o·gy (kär pol′ə jē), *n.* the branch of botany dealing with fruits. —**car·po·log·i·cal** (kär′pə loj′i kəl), *adj.* —**car′po·log′i·cal·ly,** *adv.* —**car·pol′o·gist,** *n.*

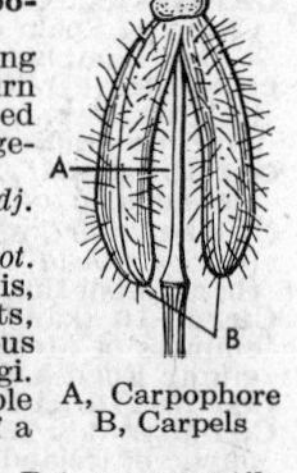

A, Carpophore
B, Carpels

car′ pool′, **1.** an arrangement among automobile owners by which each in turn drives the others to and from a designated place. **2.** those included in such an arrangement.

car·poph·a·gous (kär pof′ə gəs), *adj.* that eats fruit.

car·po·phore (kär′pə fōr′, -fôr′), *n. Bot.* **1.** a slender prolongation of the floral axis, bearing the carpels of some compound fruits, as in the geranium and in many umbelliferous plants. **2.** the fruit body of the higher fungi.

car·port (kär′pōrt′, -pôrt′), *n.* a simple shed or a roof projecting from the side of a building for sheltering an automobile.

car·po·spore (kär′pə spōr′, -spôr′), *n. Bot.* a nonmotile spore of the red algae. —**car·po·spor·ic** (kär′pə spôr′ik, -spor′-), *adj.*

-carpous, a combination of **-carp** and **-ous** used in the formation of adjectives from stems in **-carp:** *apocarpous.*

carp·suck·er (kärp′suk′ər), *n.* any of several fresh-water suckers of the genus *Carpiodes,* as the quillback and the river carpsucker.

car·pus (kär′pəs), *n., pl.* **-pi** (-pī). *Anat.* **1.** the part of the upper extremity between the hand and the forearm; wrist. **2.** the wrist bones collectively. [< NL < Gk *karpós* wrist]

Car·rac·ci (kə rä′chē; *It.* käR rät′chē), *n.* **1. A·go·sti·no** (ä′gô stē′nô), 1557–1602, and his brother, **An·ni·ba·le** (än-nē′bä le), 1560–1609, Italian painters. **2.** their cousin, **Lu·do·vi·co** (lōō′dô vē′kô), 1555–1619, Italian painter.

car·rack (kar′ək), *n.* a merchant vessel used esp. by Mediterranean countries in the 15th and 16th centuries; galleon. [ME *carrake* < MF *carraque* < OSp *carrac(a),* back formation from Ar *qarāqīr* (pl. of *qurqūr* ship of burden), the *-īr* being taken as pl. ending]

car·ra·geen (kar′ə gēn′), *n.* See **Irish moss.** Also, **car′ra·gheen′.** [named after *Carrageen* in SE Ireland]

Car·ran·za (kə ran′zə; *Sp.* käR Rän′sä), *n.* **Ve·nus·tia·no** (be′nōōs tyä′nô), 1859–1920, Mexican revolutionary and political leader: president 1915–20.

Car·ra·ra (kə rär′ə; *It.* käR Rä′Rä), *n.* a city in NW Tuscany, in NW Italy: marble quarries. 64,962 (1961).

car·re·four (kar′ə fōōr′, kar′ə fōōr′), *n.* **1.** a crossroads. **2.** a public square, as a plaza or marketplace. [< F; MF *quarrefour* < LL *quadrifurc(um),* neut. of *quadrifurc(us)* with four forks = *quadri-* QUADRI- + *furc(us), furc(a)* FORK + *-us* adj. suffix]

car·rel (kar′əl), *n.* a small recess in a library stack, for individual study. Also, **car′rell.** [var. of CAROL, enclosure]

Car·rel (kə rel′, kar′əl; *Fr.* KA Rel′), *n.* **A·lex·is** (ə lek′sis; *Fr.* A lek sē′), 1873–1944, French surgeon and biologist, in U.S. 1905–39: Nobel prize 1912.

car·riage (kar′ij; *also for 6* kar′ē ij), *n.* **1.** a wheeled vehicle for conveying persons, esp. one drawn by horses. **2.** *Brit.* a railway passenger coach. **3.** a wheeled support, as for a cannon. **4.** a movable part, as of a machine, designed for carrying another part: *the carriage of a typewriter.* **5.** manner of carrying the head and body; bearing. **6.** *Chiefly Brit.* **a.** the act of transporting; conveyance: *the expenses of carriage.* **b.** the price or cost of transportation. **7.** *Archaic.* management or administration. [ME *cariage* < ONF *cari(er)* (to) CARRY + *-age* -AGE] —**Syn. 1.** cart, car, wagon.

car′riage bolt′, a round-headed bolt for timber, threaded along part of its shank, inserted into holes already drilled. See illus. at **bolt.**

car′riage trade′, wealthy patrons, esp. of a store.

car′rick bend′ (kar′ik), a knot or bend for joining the ends of two ropes. See illus. at **knot.** [? ME *carryk,* var. of *carrake* CARRACK]

car′rick bitt′, *Naut.* either of a pair of heavy wooden uprights supporting the barrel of a windlass.

car·ri·er (kar′ē ər), *n.* **1.** a person or thing that carries. **2.** a mail carrier; mailman. **3.** a newsboy who delivers newspapers, magazines, etc., on a particular route. **4.** See **aircraft carrier. 5.** a metallic or wooden frame attached to a vehicle for carrying skis, luggage, etc. **6.** See **common carrier. 7.** *Mach.* a mechanism by which something is carried or moved. **8.** *Immunol.* an individual harboring specific pathogenic organisms who, though often immune to the agent harbored, may transmit the disease to others. **9.** *Chem.* a catalytic agent that brings about a transfer of an element or group of atoms from one compound to another. **10.** *Physical Chem.* a usually inactive substance that acts as a vehicle for an active substance. **11.** Also called **car′rier wave′.** *Radio.* the wave whose amplitude, frequency, or phase is to be varied or modulated to transmit a signal. **12.** See **carrier pigeon. 13.** base[1] (def. 16b). [ME]

car′rier pig′eon, 1. one of a breed of domestic pigeons having a large wattle around the base of the beak. 2. a homing pigeon.

car·ri·ole (kar′ē ōl′), *n.* cariole.

car·ri·on (kar′ē ən), *n.* **1.** dead and putrefying flesh. —*adj.* **2.** feeding on carrion. **3.** of or like carrion. [ME *carion,* var. of *caronye* < ONF *caronie* < VL **caronia* = L *carun-* (see CARUNCLE) + *-ia* -Y[3]]

Car·roll (kar′əl), *n.* **1. Charles,** 1737–1832, American patriot and legislator. **2. Lewis** (pen name of *Charles Lutwidge Dodgson*), 1832–98, English mathematician and writer of children's books.

car·rom (kar′əm), *n., v.i.* carom.

car·ron·ade (kar′ə nād′), *n.* a short piece of muzzle-loading ordnance, formerly in use, esp. in ships. [named after *Carron,* Scotland, where first cast; see -ADE[1]]

car′ron oil′ (kar′ən), *Pharm.* a liniment containing limewater and linseed oil, used chiefly for burns. Also called **lime liniment.** [named after *Carron,* Scotland, where it was used for treatment of ironworks laborers]

car·rot (kar′ət), *n.* **1.** an umbelliferous plant of the genus *Daucus,* esp. *D. carota,* in its wild form a widespread weed, and in cultivation valued for its edible orange root. **2.** the root. [< MF *carotte* < L *carōt(a)* < Gk *karōtón,* perh. < *karō-,* comb. form of *kárē* head + *-ton* neut. n. suffix]

car·rou·sel (kar′ə sel′, -zel′; kar′ə sel′, -zel′), *n.* **1.** *U.S.* merry-go-round (def. 1). **2.** a large, rotating conveyor, used esp. at an airport to deliver passengers' baggage. **3.** *Hist.* a tournament in which horsemen executed various formations. Also, **carousel.** [< F: kind of tournament < It *carosell(o)* kind of ball game, var. of dial. (Neapolitan) *carusello* clay ball, lit., little head = *carus(o)* shorn head (akin to Gk *kartós* shorn) + *-ello* < L *-ellus* dim. suffix]

car·ry (kar′ē), *v.,* **-ried, -ry·ing,** *n., pl.* **-ries.** —*v.t.* **1.** to move while supporting; convey; transport. **2.** to wear, hold, or have around one: *He carries his change in his coat pocket.* **3.** to contain or be capable of containing; hold: *The suitcase will carry enough clothes for a week.* **4.** to serve as an agency or medium for the transmission of: *The wind carried the sound.* **5.** to be pregnant with. **6.** to put forward or transfer: *to carry a case to a higher court.* **7.** to bear the weight, burden, etc., of: *These piers once carried an arch.* **8.** to take (a leading or guiding part), as in singing; bear or sustain (a part or melody). **9.** to hold (the body, head, etc.) in a certain manner: *She carries her head high.* **10.** to behave or comport (oneself): *She carries herself with decorum.* **11.** to take the initiative in (a contest). **12.** to secure the adoption of (a motion or bill). **13.** to get a plurality or majority of votes in (a district). **14.** to extend or continue in a given direction or to a certain point: *to carry the war into enemy territory.* **15.** to bring, transmit, or communicate, as news, a message, etc. **16.** to lead or influence by emotional or intellectual appeal. **17.** to bear the major burden of (a group, performance, etc.) by superior skill: *The star carried the play.* **18.** to lead or impel; conduct: *This pipe carries water.* **19.** to have as an attribute, property, consequence, etc.: *Violation carries a severe penalty.* **20.** to support or give validity to (a related claim, argument, etc.): *One decision carries another.* **21.** *Com.* **a.** to keep on hand or in stock. **b.** to keep on one's account books. **22.** to bear as a crop: *This land will not carry corn.* **23.** to support: *This money will carry us for about a week.* **24.** *Golf.* to advance beyond or go by (an object or expanse) with one stroke. **25.** *Hunting.* to retain and pursue (a scent). **26.** (in addition) to transfer (a number) from one denomination to the succeeding one. **27.** to have as a maximum working pressure.
—*v.i.* **28.** to act as a bearer or conductor. **29.** to have or exert propelling force: *The rifle carries almost a mile.* **30.** to be transmitted, propelled, or sustained: *My voice carries farther than his.* **31. carry a tune,** to sing accurately or on key. **32. carry away,** to influence greatly or unreasonably; excite; transport: *The spectators were carried away by fear.* **33. carry back,** *Accounting.* to apply (an unused credit or operating loss) to the net income of a prior period in order to reduce the tax for that period. **34. carry forward, a.** to make progress with. **b.** *Bookkeeping.* to transfer (an amount) to the next page, column, or book. **c.** *Accounting.* See **carry** (def. 38d.) **35. carry off, a.** to win (a prize, honor, etc.). **b.** to deal with successfully. **c.** to cause the death of. **36. carry on, a.** to manage; conduct. **b.** *Informal.* to behave in an agitated, foolish, or indiscreet manner. **c.** to continue without stopping; persevere. **37. carry out, a.** to put into operation; execute: *He hasn't the funds to carry out his design.* **b.** to bring to an end; accomplish; complete. **38. carry over, a.** to hold until a later time; postpone. **b.** to be left; remain. **c.** *Bookkeeping.* to transfer (an amount) to the next page, column, or book. **d.** Also, **carry forward.** *Accounting.* to apply (an unused credit or operating loss) to the net income of a succeeding period in order to reduce the tax for that period. **e.** to extend from one activity or time to another: *He does not carry over his business ethics into his personal relationships.* **39. carry (something) too far,** to exceed the limits of good taste, credibility, etc., in; go to excess with. **40. carry through, a.** to accomplish or complete. **b.** to support or help through a difficult situation. **c.** to continue or persist: *a theme that carried through all his writing.*
—*n.* **41.** range, as of a gun. **42.** *Sports.* the distance a batted, kicked, or stroked ball travels. **43.** *U.S.* land that separates navigable waters and over which a canoe or boat must be carried; a portage. **44.** a carrying. [ME *cari(en)* < ONF *carie(r)* < LL *carricāre,* appar. var. of **carrucāre* < L *carruca* four-wheeled vehicle < Celt; see CAR[1]]
—**Syn. 1.** CARRY, CONVEY, TRANSPORT, TRANSMIT imply taking or sending something from one place to another. CARRY means to take by means of the hands, of a vehicle, etc.: *to carry a book.* CONVEY is a more formal word, suggesting a means but not any particular method of taking; it is also used figuratively: *to convey wheat to market; to convey one's sympathies.* TRANSPORT means to carry or convey goods, now usually by vehicle or vessel: *to transport milk to customers.* TRANSMIT implies sending or transferring messages or hereditary tendencies: *to transmit a telegram.*

car·ry·all[1] (kar′ē ôl′), *n.* **1.** a light, four-wheeled, covered carriage having seats for four persons, usually drawn by one horse. **2.** a passenger automobile or bus having two facing benches running the length of the body. [folk-etym. alter. of CARIOLE]

car·ry·all[2] (kar′ē ôl′), *n.* a large basket, bag, etc.

car′rying charge′, **1.** a charge made for paying for goods by installments. **2.** cost incurred while an asset is unproductive.

car·ry·ing-on (kar′ē ing on′, -ôn′), *n., pl.* **car·ry·ings-on.** *Informal.* excited, foolish, or improper behavior.

car·ry-on (kar′ē on′, -ôn′), *adj.* **1.** suitable for being kept with an airplane passenger during flight. —*n.* **2.** a piece of carry-on luggage. **3.** *Brit. Informal.* carrying-on.

car·ry-out (kar′ē out′), *n., adj.* takeout. Also, **car′ry·out′.**

car·ry-o·ver (kar′ē ō′vər), *n.* **1.** the act of carrying over. **2.** that which is carried over, as to a later time, account, etc.

car·sick (kär′sik′), *adj.* ill with carsickness.

car·sick·ness (kär′sik′nis), *n.* a feeling of nausea resulting from the motion of the car in which one is traveling.

Car·son (kär′sən), *n.* **1. Christopher** ("*Kit*"), 1809–68, U.S. frontiersman and scout. **2. Rachel (Louise),** 1907–1964, U.S. marine biologist and author. **3.** a city in SW California, S of Los Angeles. 71,150 (1970).

Car′son Cit′y, a town in and the capital of Nevada, in the W part. 15,468 (1970).

Car·stensz (kär′stənz), *n.* **Mount,** a mountain in W central West Irian, the highest in New Guinea. 16,404 ft.

cart (kärt), *n.* **1.** a heavy two-wheeled vehicle drawn by mules, oxen, or the like, used for the conveyance of heavy goods. **2.** a light two-wheeled vehicle with springs, drawn by a horse or pony. **3.** any small vehicle moved by hand. **4.** *Obs.* a chariot. **5. put the cart before the horse,** to do or place things in improper order; be illogical. —*v.t.* **6.** to convey in or as in a cart. —*v.i.* **7.** to drive a cart. [ME *cart(e),* OE *cræt* (by metathesis); c. Icel *kartr*] —**cart′er,** *n.*

cart·age (kär′tij), *n.* the act or cost of carting. [ME]

Car·ta·ge·na (kär′tə jē′nə; *Sp.* kär′tä he′nä), *n.* **1.** a seaport in SE Spain. 118,049 (est. 1955). **2.** a seaport in N Colombia. 197,590 (est. 1964).

carte (kärt; *Fr.* KART), *n., pl.* **cartes** (kärts; *Fr.* KART). **1.** (*italics*) *French.* menu; bill of fare. Cf. **à la carte. 2.** *Scot.* a playing card. **3.** *Obs.* a map or chart. [ME, OE: writing paper, document, letter < L *charta* < Gk *chártēs* leaf of paper]

Carte (kärt), *n.* **Richard D'Oy·ly.** See **D'Oyly Carte.**

carte blanche (kärt′ blänch′, blänch′; *Fr.* KART bläNsh′), *pl.* **cartes blanches** (kärts′ blänch′, blänch′; *Fr.* KART bläNsh′). **1.** a blank sheet of paper that is signed and given by the signer to another person to write in what he pleases. **2.** unconditional authority; full discretionary power. [< F: lit., blank document]

carte de vi·site (KART də vē zēt′), *pl.* **cartes de visite** (KART də vē zēt′). *French.* See **calling card.**

car·tel (kär tel′, kär′tᵊl), *n.* **1.** an international combine formed to regulate prices and output in some field of business. **2.** a written agreement between belligerents, esp. for the exchange of prisoners. **3.** (*often cap.*) (in French or Belgian politics) a group acting as a unit toward a common goal. **4.** a written challenge to a duel. [< MF < It *cartell(o)* letter of defiance, poster, dim. of *carta* paper; see CARTE] —**Syn. 1.** monopoly, merger, combination.

Car·ter (kär′tər), *n.* **1. Howard,** 1873–1939, English Egyptologist. **2. Jim·my** (jim′ē) **(James Earl, Jr.),** born 1924, 39th president of the U.S. 1977–81.

Car·ter·et (kär′tər it), *n.* **John, Earl Granville,** 1690–1763, British statesman and orator.

Car·te·sian (kär tē′zhən), *adj.* **1.** of or pertaining to Descartes, or to his mathematical methods or philosophy. —*n.* **2.** a person who advocates the philosophy of Descartes. [< NL *Cartesiān(us)* = *Cartesi(us)* (Latinization of Descartes) + *-ānus* -AN] —**Car·te′sian·ism,** *n.*

Carte′sian coor′dinates, *Math.* a system of coordinates for locating a point on a plane by its distance from each of two perpendicular intersecting lines, or in space by its distance from each of three mutually perpendicular planes intersecting at a point.

Car·thage (kär′thij), *n.* an ancient city-state in N Africa, near modern Tunis: founded by the Phoenicians in the 9th century B.C.; destroyed in 146 B.C. by the Romans. —**Car·tha·gin·i·an** (kär′thə jin′ē ən), *adj., n.*

Car·thu·sian (kär thōō′zhən), *Rom. Cath. Ch.* —*n.* **1.** a member of an austere monastic order founded by St. Bruno in 1086 near Grenoble, France. —*adj.* **2.** of or pertaining to the Carthusians. [< ML *Cartusiān(us)* by metathesis for *Catursiānus,* sing. of *Catursiānī* (*montēs*) district where order was founded]

Car·tier (KAR tyā′), *n.* **Jacques** (zhäk), 1491–1557, French navigator and explorer of Canada: discovered the St. Lawrence River.

Car·tier-Bres·son (KAR tyā bre sôN′), *n.* **Hen·ri** (äN-RĒ′), born 1908, French photographer.

car·ti·lage (kär′tᵊlij, kärt′lij), *n.* *Anat., Zool.* **1.** a firm, elastic, flexible type of connective tissue; gristle. **2.** a part or structure composed of cartilage. [< L *cartilāg(ō)* gristle]

car′tilage bone′, a bone that develops from cartilage.

car·ti·lag·i·nous (kär′tə laj′ə nəs), *adj.* **1.** of or resembling cartilage. **2.** *Zool.* having the skeleton composed mostly of cartilage, as sharks and rays. [< L *cartilāginōs(us)* = *cartilāgin-* (s. of *cartilāgō*) CARTILAGE + *-ōsus* -OUS]

cart·load (kärt′lōd′), *n.* the amount a cart can hold.

car·to·gram (kär′tə gram′), *n.* a diagrammatic presentation in highly abstracted or simplified form, commonly of statistical data, on a map base or distorted map base. [< F *cartogramme.* See CARTE, -O-, -GRAM[1]]

car·tog·ra·phy (kär tog′rə fē), *n.* the production of maps, including construction of projections, design, compilation, drafting, and reproduction. Also, **chartography.** [< L *c(h)art(a)* CARTE + -o- + -GRAPHY] —**car·tog′ra·pher,** *n.* —**car·to·graph·ic** (kär′tə graf′ik), **car′to·graph′i·cal,** *adj.* —**car′to·graph′i·cal·ly,** *adv.*

car·ton (kär′tᵊn), *n.* **1.** a large cardboard box. **2.** the contents of a carton. **3.** a small disk within the bull's-eye of a target. **4.** a shot that strikes this disk. [< F < It *carton(e)* pasteboard; see CARTOON]

car·toon (kär to͞on′), *n.* **1.** a sketch or drawing, usually humorous, as in a newspaper, symbolizing, satirizing, or caricaturing some action, subject, or person of popular interest. **2.** *Fine Arts.* a full-scale design for a picture, ornamental motif, pattern, or the like, to be transferred to a fresco, tapestry, etc. **3.** See **comic strip. 4.** See **animated cartoon.** —*v.t.* **5.** to represent by a cartoon. [< It *carton(e)* pasteboard, stout paper, a drawing on such paper = *cart(a)* paper (see CARTE) + *-one* aug. suffix] —**car·toon′ist,** *n.*

car·touche (kär to͞osh′), *n.* **1.** *Archit.* a rounded, convex surface, usually surrounded with carved ornamental scrollwork, for receiving a painted or low-relief decoration, as an escutcheon. **2.** an oval or oblong figure, as on ancient Egyptian monuments, enclosing characters that represent the name of a sovereign. **3.** the case containing the inflammable materials in certain fireworks. **4.** cartridge (def. 1). **5.** a box for cartridges. Also, **car·touch′.** [< MF < It *cartocc(io)* = *cart(a)* paper (see CARTE) + *-occio* aug. suffix]

car·tridge (kär′trij), *n.* **1.** Also called **cartouche.** a cylindrical case of pasteboard, metal, or the like, for holding a complete charge of powder, and often also the bullet or the shot for a rifle, machine gun, or other small arm. **2.** a case containing any explosive charge, as for blasting. **3.** any small container for powder, liquid, or gas, made for ready insertion into some device or mechanism: *an ink cartridge for a pen.* **4.** Also called **cassette, magazine.** *Photog.* a lightproof metal or plastic container for a roll of film, for rapid loading without the necessity of threading the film. **5.** *Radio.* pickup (def. 6). **6.** a flat, compact container measuring 4 x 5¼ inches and enclosing an endless loop of audio tape ¼ inch wide: playable simply by slipping into a slot in a player. [earlier *cartage,* alter. of CARTOUCHE]

Cartridge
A, Metallic case of copper or brass; B, Bullet; R, Primer; F, Fulminate; P, Powder

car′tridge clip′, a metal frame for holding cartridges for a magazine rifle or automatic pistol. Also called **clip.**

car·tu·lar·y (kär′cho͝o ler′ē), *n., pl.* **-lar·ies.** chartulary.

cart·wheel (kärt′hwēl′, -wēl′), *n.* **1.** the wheel of a cart. **2.** a handspring done to the side. **3.** *Slang.* any large, round coin, esp. a U.S. silver dollar. [ME]

Cart·wright (kärt′rīt) *n.* **Edmund,** 1743–1822, English clergyman: inventor of the power-driven loom.

car·un·cle (kar′uŋ kəl, kə ruŋ′-), *n.* **1.** *Bot.* a protuberance at or surrounding the hilum of a seed. **2.** *Zool.* a fleshy excrescence, as on the head of a bird; a fowl's comb. **3.** *Anat.* a small, fleshy growth. [earlier *caruncula* < L = *carun-* (var. of *carn-,* s. of *carō* flesh) + *-cula* -CULE] —**ca·run·cu·lar** (kə ruŋ′kyə lər), **ca·run′cu·lous,** *adj.*

ca·run·cu·late (kə ruŋ′kyə lit, -lāt′), *adj.* having a caruncle. Also, **ca·run′cu·lat′ed.** [< NL *carunculāt(us)*]

Ca·ru·so (kə ro͞o′sō; *It.* kä ro͞o′zô), *n.* **En·ri·co** (en rē′kō; *It.* en rē′kô), 1873–1921, Italian operatic tenor.

carve (kärv), *v.,* **carved, carv·ing.** —*v.t.* **1.** to cut (a solid material) so as to form something: *to carve stone for a statue.* **2.** to form from a solid material by cutting: *to carve a statue out of stone.* **3.** to make or create for oneself (often fol. by *out*): *He carved out a career in business.* **4.** to cut into slices or pieces, as meat. —*v.i.* **5.** to form figures, designs, etc., by cutting. **6.** to cut meat. [ME *kerve(n),* OE *ceorfan* to cut; c. MLG *kerven,* G *kerben,* Gk *gráph(ein)* (to) mark, write] —**carv′er,** *n.*

car·vel (kär′vəl), *n.* caravel. [late ME *carvile* < D *karveel* CARAVEL]

car·vel-built (kär′vəl bilt′), *adj. Shipbuilding.* noting a hull whose shell is formed of planking **(car′vel plank′ing)** or plating laid close on the frames so as to present a smooth exterior.

carv·en (kär′vən), *adj. Literary.* carved. [CARVE + -EN[3]; r. ME *corven,* OE *corfen* (ptp.)]

Car·ver (kär′vər), *n.* **1. George Washington,** 1864?–1943, U.S. botanist and chemist. **2. John,** 1575?–1621, Pilgrim leader: first governor of Plymouth Colony 1620–21.

carv·ing (kär′viŋ), *n.* **1.** act of fashioning or producing by cutting. **2.** carved work; a carved design. [ME]

Car·y (kâr′ē, kar′ē), *n.* **1. (Arthur) Joyce (Lu·nel)** (lo͞on′əl), 1888–1957, English novelist. **2. Henry Francis,** 1772–1844, British writer and translator.

car·y·at·id (kar′ē at′id), *n., pl.* **-ids, -i·des** (-i dēz′). *Archit.* a sculptured female figure used as a column. Cf. **atlas** (def. 8). [back formation from L *Caryātides* (pl.) < Gk *Karyátides* columns shaped like women, lit., women of *Karýai* Laconia] —**car′y·at′i·dal, car·y·at·ic** (kar′ē at′ik), **car·y·at·i·de·an** (kar′ē at′i dē′ən), **car·y·a·tid·ic** (kar′ē ə tid′ik), *adj.*

Caryatids

caryo-, var. of **karyo-.**

car·y·o·phyl·la·ceous (kar′ē ō fə lā′shəs), *adj.* **1.** belonging to the *Caryophyllaceae* or pink family of plants. **2.** resembling the pink. [< NL *Caryophyllāce(ae)* (*caryophyll(us)* the genus < Gk *karyóphyll(on)* clove tree; see CARYO-, -PHYLL, -ACEAE) + -OUS]

car·y·op·sis (kar′ē op′sis), *n., pl.* **-ses** (-sēz), **-si·des** (-si dēz′). *Bot.* a one-celled, one-seeded, dry indehiscent fruit with the pericarp adherent to the seed coat, as in wheat: the typical fruit of all grasses and grains.

ca·sa·ba (kə sä′bə), *n.* a winter muskmelon, having a yellow rind and sweet, juicy flesh. Also, **cassaba.** [named after *Kassaba* (now Turgutlu), town near Izmir (Smyrna) in Turkey, that exported it]

Ca·sa·blan·ca (kä′sä bläŋ′kä, kas′ə blaŋ′kə), *n.* a seaport in NW Morocco. 1,550,000 (est. 1972).

Ca·sa·de·sus (kä′sə dā′səs; *Fr.* KA SADᵊ SYS′), *n.* **Ro·bert** (rob′ərt; *Fr.* RÔ BER′), 1899–1972, French pianist and composer, in the U.S.

Ca·sa Gran·de (kä′sä grän′dā, -dē, -sə-), a national monument in S Arizona, near the Gila River: ruins of a prehistoric culture.

Ca·sals (kə salz′, -sälz′, kä sälz′; *Sp.* kä säls′), *n.* **Pa·blo** (pä′blō; *Sp.* pä′vlô), 1876–1973, Spanish cellist, conductor, and composer; in France after 1936; in Puerto Rico after 1956.

Cas·a·no·va (kaz′ə nō′və, kas′-; *It.* kä′sä nô′vä), *n.* **1. Gio·van·ni Ja·co·po** (jô vän′nē yä′kô pô), 1725–98, Italian amorous adventurer and writer. **2.** a man known for his amorous adventures; rake; Don Juan.

Ca·sau·bon (kə sô′bən; *Fr.* KA ZŌ BÔN′), *n.* **I·saac** (ī′zək; *Fr.* Ē ZAK′), 1559–1614, French classical scholar.

Cas·bah (kaz′bə, -bä, käz′-), *n.* Kasbah.

cas·cade (kas kād′), *n., v.,* **-cad·ed, -cad·ing.** —*n.* **1.** a waterfall descending over a steep, rocky surface. **2.** a series of shallow waterfalls, either natural or artificial. **3.** an arrangement of a lightweight fabric in folds falling one over another. **4.** *Chem.* a series of vessels, from each of which a liquid successively overflows to the next, thus presenting a large absorbing surface, as to a gas. **5.** *Elect.* an arrangement of component devices, as electrolytic cells, each of which feeds into the next in succession. —*v.i.* **6.** to fall in or like a cascade. [< F < It *cascat(a)* = *casc(are)* (to) fall (< VL **cāsicāre* = *cas(us)* fallen (see CASE[1]) + *-icā-* formative v. suffix + *-re* inf. ending) + *-ata* -ADE[1]]

Cascade′ Range′, a mountain range extending from N California to W Canada. Highest peak, Mt. Rainier, 14,408 ft. Also called **the Cascades.**

cas·car·a (kas kâr′ə), *n.* **1.** Also called **cascar′a buck′thorn.** a buckthorn, *Rhamnus Purshiana,* of the Pacific coast of the U.S., yielding cascara sagrada. **2.** See **cascara sagrada.** [< Sp *cáscara* bark, perh. akin to *cascar* to crack << VL **quassicāre* = L *quass(āre)* (to) shatter (see QUASH) + *-icā-* formative v. suffix + *-re* inf. ending]

cascar′a sa·gra′da (sə grā′də, -grä′-, -grad′ə), the bark of the cascara, used as a cathartic or laxative. [< Sp: lit., sacred bark]

cas·ca·ril·la (kas′kə ril′ə), *n.* **1.** Also called **cascaril′la bark′.** the bitter aromatic bark of a West Indian, euphorbiaceous shrub, *Croton Eluteria,* used as a tonic. **2.** the shrub itself. [< Sp, dim. of *cáscara* bark]

Cas′co Bay′ (kas′kō), a bay in SW Maine.

case[1] (kās), *n.* **1.** an instance of the occurrence, existence, etc., of something: *This is a case of poor judgment.* **2.** the actual state of things: *That is not the case.* **3.** situation, condition, or plight: *a sad case.* **4.** a person or thing whose plight or situation calls for attention: *This family is a hardship case.* **5.** a state of things requiring discussion, decision, or investigation: *The police studied the murder case.* **6.** a statement of facts, reasons, etc., used to support an argument: *a strong case against the proposed law.* **7.** an instance of disease, injury, etc. **8.** a medical or surgical patient. **9.** *Law.* **a.** a suit or action at law; cause. **b.** a set of facts giving rise to a legal claim, or to a defense to a legal claim. **10.** *Gram.* a category in the inflection of nouns, pronouns, and adjectives, noting the syntactic relation of these words to other words in the sentence, indicated by the form or position of the words. **11. in any case,** regardless of circumstances; anyhow. **12. in case,** if it should happen that; if: *In case I'm late, start without me.* **13. in case of,** in the event of. **14. in no case,** under no condition; never. [ME *cas,* OE *cas(us)* case (grammatical term) + OF *cas* event, etc.; both < L *cāsus*]
—**Syn. 1.** CASE, INSTANCE, EXAMPLE, ILLUSTRATION suggest the existence or occurrence of a particular thing representative of its type. CASE and INSTANCE are closely allied in meaning, as are EXAMPLE and ILLUSTRATION. CASE is a general word, meaning a fact, occurrence, or situation typical of a class: *a case of assault and battery.* An INSTANCE is a concrete factual case that is adduced to explain a general idea: *an instance of a brawl in which an assault occurred.* An EXAMPLE is one typical case, from many similar ones, used to make clear or explain the working of a principle (what may be expected of any others of the group): *This boy is an example of the effect of strict discipline.* An ILLUSTRATION exemplifies a theory or principle similarly, except that the choice may be purely hypothetical: *The work of Seeing Eye dogs is an illustration of what is thought to be intelligence in animals.* **2.** circumstance.

case[2] (kās), *n., v.,* **cased, cas·ing.** —*n.* **1.** a container for receiving and enclosing something, as for carrying, safekeeping, etc.: *a jewel case.* **2.** a sheath or outer covering. **3.** a box with its contents: *a case of ginger ale.* **4.** the amount contained in a box or other container. **5.** a pair or couple; brace. **6.** a surrounding frame or framework, as of a door. **7.** *Bookbinding.* a completed book cover. **8.** *Print.* a tray divided into compartments for holding types and usually arranged in a set of two, the upper **(upper case)** for capital letters and auxiliary types, the lower **(lower case)** for small letters and auxiliary types. **9.** *Metall.* the hard outer part of a piece of casehardened steel. —*v.t.* **10.** to put or enclose in a case. **11.** *U.S. Slang.* to examine or survey (a house, bank, etc.) in planning a crime. [ME *cas* < ONF *casse* < L *capsa* (book)case = *caps-* (old fut. s. of *capere* to take) + *-a* fem. n. suffix]

ca·se·ate (kā′sē āt′), *v.i.,* **-at·ed, -at·ing.** *Pathol.* to undergo cheeselike degeneration; become like cheese in consistency and appearance. [< L *cāse(us)* CHEESE + -ATE[1]]

ca·se·a·tion (kā′sē ā′shən), *n.* **1.** *Pathol.* transformation into a soft cheeselike mass, as of tissue in tuberculosis. **2.** *Biochem.* the formation of cheese from casein during the coagulation of milk.

case·book (kās′bo͝ok′), *n.* **1.** (esp. in medicine) a book in which detailed records of a case are kept, as in psychology, medicine, or the like. **2.** a law textbook giving the records of cases in some field of law.
case·bound (kās′bound′), *adj. Bookbinding.* **1.** bound in hard covers. **2.** bound by gluing sewn sheets into a separately made cover.
ca·se·fy (kā′sə fī′), *v.t., v.i.*, **-fied, -fy·ing.** to make or become like cheese. [< L *cāse(us)* CHEESE + -FY]
case·hard·en (kās′här′dᵊn), *v.t.* **1.** *Metall.* to harden the outside of (an alloy having an iron base) by carburizing and heat treatment. **2.** to harden in spirit so as to render insensible to external impressions or influences.
case′ his′tory, (in medicine, social work, etc.) a record of information about an individual, family, etc.
ca·sein (kā′sēn, -sē in, kā sēn′), *n.* **1.** *Biochem.* a protein precipitated from milk, as by rennet, and forming the basis of cheese and certain plastics. **2.** *Fine Arts.* **a.** an emulsion made from a solution of this precipitated protein, water, and ammonia carbonate. **b.** a paint in which this emulsion is used as a binder. [< L *cāse(us)* CHEESE + -IN²]
case′ law′, law established by judicial decisions in particular cases.
case·load (kās′lōd′), *n.* the number of cases handled by a court, social worker, etc., either at any given time or over a stated period. Also, **case′ load′.**
case·mate (kās′māt′), *n.* **1.** an armored enclosure for guns in a warship. **2.** a vault or chamber, esp. in a rampart, with embrasures for artillery. [< MF < OIt *casamatt(a)* < Gk *chásmata* embrasures, pl. of *chásma* CHASM]
case·ment (kās′mənt), *n.* **1.** a window sash opening on hinges that are generally attached to the upright side of its frame. **2.** Also called **case′ment win′dow.** a window with such a sash or sashes. **3.** a casing or covering.
Case·ment (kās′mənt), *n.* **Sir Roger (David),** 1864–1916, Irish patriot: hanged by the British for treason.
ca·se·ous (kā′sē əs), *adj.* of or like cheese. [< L *cāse(us)* CHEESE + -OUS]
case′ shot′, a projectile encasing a quantity of balls, metal fragments, etc., to be fired from a cannon. Also called **canister, canister shot.**
case′ stud′y, **1.** the gathering and organization of all relevant material to enable analysis and explication of individual units, as of a person or family. **2.** See **case history.**
case·work (kās′wûrk′), *n. Sociol.* a close study of psychological and sociological factors in the history of an individual or family in unfavorable circumstances, with a view to improving conditions. —**case′work′er,** *n.*
case·worm (kās′wûrm′), *n.* a caddisworm or other insect larva that constructs a case around its body.
cash¹ (kash), *n.* **1.** money in the form of coin or of negotiable paper, esp. that of a government. **2.** money or an equivalent, as a check, paid at the time of making a purchase. —*v.t.* **3.** to give or obtain cash for (a check, money order, etc.). **4. cash in, a.** *U.S.* to turn in and get cash for (one's chips), as in a gambling casino. **b.** *U.S. Slang.* to end or withdraw from a business agreement; convert one's assets into cash. **5. cash in on,** *U.S. Informal.* to profit from; turn to one's advantage. [appar. back formation from CASHIER¹]
cash² (kash), *n., pl.* **cash.** (formerly) any of several low-denomination coins of China, India, and the East Indies. [< Pg *caixa* < Tamil *kācu* copper coin < Skt *karṣa* a weight (of precious metal)]
cash-and-car·ry (kash′ən kar′ē), *adj.* sold or operated on a basis of no credit and no delivery service.
ca·shaw (kə shô′), *n.* cushaw.
cash·book (kash′bo͝ok′), *n.* a book in which to record money received and paid out.
cash·box (kash′boks′), *n.* a container for money, esp. one with separate compartments for coins and bills.
cash′ dis′count, **1.** a term of sale by which the purchaser deducts a percentage from the bill if he pays within a stipulated period. **2.** the amount deducted.
cash·ew (kash′o͞o, kə sho͞o′), *n.* **1.** an anacardiaceous tree, *Anacardium occidentale*, native to tropical America, whose bark yields a medicinal gum. **2.** Also called **cash′ew nut′.** the small, kidney-shaped, edible nut of this tree. [< Pg *cajú*, aph. var. of *acajú* < Tupi]
cash′ flow′, the sum of the after-tax profit of a business plus depreciation and other noncash charges: used as an indication of internal funds available for stock dividends, purchase of buildings and equipment, etc.
cash·ier¹ (ka shēr′), *n.* **1.** an employee, as in a market, restaurant, etc., who collects payments for purchases, gives change, etc. **2.** an executive who has charge of monetary transactions, as in a bank. **3.** an employee of a business establishment who keeps a record of financial transactions. [< MD *kassier* custodian of a money box < MF *cassier* = *casse* money box (< early It *cassa;* see CASE²) + *-ier* -IER]
cash·ier² (ka shēr′), *v.t.* **1.** to dismiss from a position of command or trust, esp. with disgrace. **2.** to discard; reject. [< MD *kasser(en)* < MF *casser* to break, discharge, annul < L *quassāre* to shatter; see QUASH]
cashier's′ check′, a check drawn by a bank on its own funds and signed by its cashier.
cash-in (kash′in′), *n.* redemption, as of savings bonds or mutual-fund shares.
cash·mere (kazh′mēr, kash′-), *n.* **1.** the fine, downy wool at the roots of the hair of Kashmir goats of India. **2.** a yarn made from this wool. **3.** a wool or cashmere fabric. Also, **kashmir.** [after CASHMERE]
Cash·mere (kash mēr′), *n.* Kashmir.
cash′ on deliv′ery. See **C.O.D.**
cash′ reg′ister, a business machine that indicates to customers the amounts of individual sales, records and totals receipts, and has a money drawer from which to make change.
cas·i·mire (kas′ə mēr′), *n.* cassimere. Also, **cas′i·mere′.**
cas·ing (kā′sing), *n.* **1.** a case or covering. **2.** material for a case or covering. **3.** the framework around a door or window. **4.** *U.S.* the outermost covering of an automobile tire. **5.** any frame or framework. **6.** an iron pipe or tubing, esp. as used in oil and gas wells. **7.** a layer of glass that has been fused to an underlying layer. **8.** the intestinal membrane of sheep, cattle, or hogs, or a synthetic facsimile, for encasing sausages, salamis, etc.
ca·si·no (kə sē′nō), *n., pl.* **-nos** for 1–3. **1.** a building or large room used for meetings, dancing, etc. **2.** such a place used for gambling. **3.** (in Italy) a small country house or lodge. **4.** Also, **cassino.** *Cards.* a game in which cards that are face up on the table are taken with eligible cards in the hand. [< It = *cas(a)* house + *-ino* dim. suffix]
cask (kask, käsk), *n.* **1.** a container resembling a barrel but larger and stronger. **2.** the quantity such a container holds: *The wine cost 32 guineas a cask.* —*v.t.* **3.** to place or store in a cask. [back formation from CASKET]
cas·ket (kas′kit, kä′skit), *n.* **1.** *Chiefly U.S.* a coffin. **2.** a small chest or box, as for jewels. —*v.t.* **3.** to put or enclose in a casket. [late ME < ?]
Cas·lon (kaz′lən), *n. Print.* an old-style type modeled after the types designed by William Caslon (1692–1766), the English type founder.
Cas·par (kas′pər), *n.* one of the three magi.
Cas·per (kas′pər), *n.* a city in central Wyoming. 39,361 (1970).
Cas′pi·an Sea′ (kas′pē ən), a salt lake between SE Europe and Asia: the largest inland body of water in the world. ab. 169,000 sq. mi.; 85 ft. below sea level.
casque (kask), *n.* **1.** an open, conical helmet with a nose guard. **2.** *Zool.* a process or formation on the head, resembling a helmet. [< MF < Sp *casc(o)* helmet, head, earthen pot; akin to CASCARA]
Cass (kas), *n.* **Lewis,** 1782–1866, U.S. statesman.
cas·sa·ba (kə sä′bə), *n.* casaba.
Cas·san·dra (kə san′drə), *n.* **1.** *Class. Myth.* a daughter of Priam and Hecuba, a prophetess cursed by Apollo so that her prophecies, though true, were fated never to be believed. **2.** a person who prophesies doom or disaster.
Cas·satt (kə sat′), *n.* **Mary,** 1845–1926, U.S. painter.
cas·sa·va (kə sä′və), *n.* **1.** any of several tropical euphorbiaceous plants of the genus *Manihot*, cultivated for their tuberous roots, which yield important food products. **2.** a nutritious starch from the roots, the source of tapioca. [< Sp *cazabe* cassava bread or meal < Taino *caçábi*]
Cas′se·grain′i·an tel′escope (kas′ə grā′nē ən, kas′-), *Astron.* a reflecting telescope in which the light, passing through a central opening in the primary mirror, is brought into focus a short distance behind it by a secondary mirror.
Cas·sel (kas′əl; *Ger.* käs′əl), *n.* Kassel.
cas·se·role (kas′ə rōl′), *n.* **1.** a baking dish of glass, pottery, etc., usually with a cover. **2.** food cooked in such a dish. **3.** a small dish with a handle, used in chemical laboratories. **4.** *Chiefly Brit.* a stewpan. [< F: ladlelike pan = *casse* ladle (< OPr *cass(a)* < LL *cattia* < Gk *kyáthia*, neut. pl. (taken as fem. sing.) of *kyáthion* = *kýath(os)* cup + *-ion* dim. suffix) + *-(e)role* dim. suffix]
cas·sette (ka set′, kə-), *n.* **1.** a compact case measuring 2½ x 4 inches and enclosing a length of audio tape, ¹/₇ inch wide, that runs between two reels: recordable or playable simply by pushing into a holder in a recorder or player. **2.** a similar compact case of larger size enclosing a length of wider tape for video recording or reproduction. **3.** *Photog.* cartridge (def. 4). [< F = *casse* box (see CASE²) + *-ette* -ETTE]
cas·sia (kash′ə, kas′ē ə), *n.* **1.** Also called **cas′sia bark′.** a variety of cinnamon derived from the cassia-bark tree. **2.** any of the caesalpiniaceous herbs, shrubs, and trees of the genus *Cassia*, as *C. Fistula*, an ornamental tropical tree having long pods whose pulp is a mild laxative, and *C. acutifolia* and *C. angustifolia*, which yield senna. **3.** Also called **cas′sia pods′.** the pods of *C. Fistula.* **4.** Also called **cas′sia pulp′.** the pulp of these pods. [ME *cas(s)ia*, OE < L < Gk *kas(s)ía* < Sem; cf. Heb *qeṣī ʿāh*]
cas′sia-bark tree′ (kash′ə bärk′, kas′ē ə-), a lauraceous tree, *Cinnamomum Cassia*, of eastern Asia.
cas·si·mere (kas′ə mēr′), *n.* a twill-weave, worsted suiting fabric, often with a striped pattern. Also, **casimere, casimire.** [var. of CASHMERE]
cas·si·no (kə sē′nō), *n.* casino (def. 4).
Cas·si·no (kə sē′nō; *It.* käs sē′nô), *n.* a town in central Italy, NW of Naples: site of Monte Cassino. 21,105 (1961).
Cas·si·o·do·rus (kas′ē ə dōr′əs, -dôr′-), *n.* **Fla·vi·us Mag·nus Au·re·li·us** (flā′vē əs mag′nəs ô rē′lē əs, ô rēl′yes), died A.D. 575, Roman statesman and writer.
Cas·si·o·pe·ia (kas′ē ə pē′ə), *n., gen.* **-pe·iae** (-pē′ē) for 1. **1.** *Astron.* a northern constellation between Cepheus and Perseus. **2.** *Class. Myth.* the wife of Cepheus and mother of Andromeda. —**Cas′si·o·pe′ian,** *adj.*
cas·sis (ka sēs′), *n.* a liqueur made from black currants. [< F]
cas·sit·er·ite (kə sit′ə rīt′), *n.* a common mineral, tin dioxide, SnO_2; tinstone: the principal ore of tin. [< Gk *kassíter(os)* tin + -ITE¹]
Cas·sius Lon·gi·nus (kash′əs lon jī′nəs), **Ga·ius** (gā′əs), died 42 B.C., Roman general: leader of the conspiracy against Julius Caesar.
cas·sock (kas′ək), *n.* a long, close-fitting garment worn by clergymen or laymen participating in church services. [< MF *casaque* < early It *casacc(a)* long coat, perh. = *cas(a)* house + *-acca* n. suffix; for sense, cf. HOUSING² and see CHASUBLE]

Cassowary, *Casuarius casuarius* (Height 5 ft.)

cas·so·war·y (kas′ə wer′ē), *n., pl.* **-war·ies.** any of several large, flightless, ratite birds of the genus *Casuarius*, of Australia, New Guinea, and adjacent islands, characterized by a bony casque on the front of the head. [< Malay *kasuāri*]
cast (kast, käst), *v.,* **cast, cast·ing,** *n., adj.* —*v.t.* **1.** to throw or hurl; fling. **2.** to direct (the eye, glance, etc.), esp. in a cursory manner: *She cast her eyes down the page.* **3.**

to cause to fall upon something or in a certain direction; send forth: *to cast a soft light; to cast doubts.* **4.** to draw (lots), as in telling fortunes. **5.** *Angling.* **a.** to throw out (a fishing line, a net, bait, etc.). **b.** to fish in (a stream, an area, etc.): *He has often cast this brook.* **6.** to throw down or bring to the ground. **7.** to part with; lose: *The horse cast a shoe.* **8.** to shed or drop (hair, fruit, etc.): *The snake cast its skin.* **9.** (of an animal) to bring forth (young), esp. abortively. **10.** to send off (a swarm), as bees do. **11.** to set aside; reject; dismiss: *He cast the problem from his mind.* **12.** to throw up (earth, sod, etc.), as with a shovel. **13.** to deposit or give (a ballot or vote). **14.** to bestow; confer: *to cast blessings upon someone.* **15.** to form or arrange: *He cast his remarks to fit the occasion.* **16.** *Theat.* **a.** to select actors for (a play or the like). **b.** to assign a role to (an actor). **c.** to assign an actor to (a role). **17.** to form (an object) by pouring metal, plaster, etc., in a fluid state into a mold and letting it harden. **18.** to form (metal, plaster, etc.) by this process. **19.** to compute, as a column of figures. **20.** to calculate (a horoscope); forecast. **21.** *Naut.* to turn the head of (a vessel), esp. away from the wind in getting under way. **22.** *Archaic.* to contrive, devise, or plan. —*v.i.* **23.** to throw. **24.** to receive form in a mold. **25.** to calculate or add. **26.** to conjecture; forecast. **27.** (of hounds) to search an area for scent. **28.** to warp, as timber. **29.** *Naut.* (of a vessel) to turn, esp. to get the head away from the wind; tack. **30.** to select the actors for a play, motion picture, or the like. **31.** *Obs.* to consider. **32. cast about,** to look. **33. cast off, a.** to let go or let loose, as a vessel from a mooring. **b.** *Print.* to determine the quantity of type or space that a given amount of text will occupy when set. **c.** *Textiles.* to make (the final stitches) in completing a knitted fabric. **34. cast on,** *Textiles.* to set (yarn) on a needle in order to form the initial stitches in knitting. **35. cast up, a.** to add up; compute. **b.** to vomit; eject. —*n.* **36.** act of casting or throwing. **37.** that which is thrown. **38.** the distance a thing may be thrown. **39.** *Games.* **a.** a throw of dice. **b.** the number rolled. **40.** *Angling.* act of throwing a line or net onto the water. **41.** *Hunting.* a searching of an area for a scent by hounds. **42.** fortune or lot. **43.** the form in which something is made or written. **44.** *Theat.* the performers in a play or the like. **45.** *Metall.* **a.** act of casting or founding. **b.** the quantity of metal cast at one time. **46.** something formed from a material poured into a mold; casting. **47.** an impression or mold. **48.** *Med.* a rigid surgical dressing, usually made of plaster of Paris. **49.** outward form; appearance. **50.** sort; kind; style. **51.** tendency; inclination. **52.** a permanent twist or turn: *to have a cast in one's eye.* **53.** a warp. **54.** a slight tinge of some color; hue; shade. **55.** computation; calculation. **56.** a conjecture or forecast. **57.** *Pathol.* effused plastic matter produced in the hollow parts of various diseased organs. —*adj.* **58.** (of an animal, esp. a horse) lying in such a position that it is unable to return to its feet without assistance. [ME *cast(en)* < Scand; cf. Icel *hasta* to throw] —**Syn. 1.** See **throw.**

Castanets

Cas·ta·li·a (ka stā′lē ə), *n.* a spring on Mount Parnassus in Greece, sacred to Apollo and the Muses and regarded as a source of inspiration. —**Cas·ta′li·an,** *adj.*

cas·ta·net (kas′tə net′), *n.* either of a pair of concave pieces of wood held in the palm of the hand and clicked together, usually to accompany dancing. [< Sp *castañet(a)* = *castañ(a)* chestnut (< L *castanea*) + *-eta* dim. suffix; see -ET, -ETTE]

cast·a·way (kast′ə wā′, käst′-), *n.* **1.** a shipwrecked person. **2.** an outcast. —*adj.* **3.** cast adrift. **4.** thrown away.

caste (kast, käst), *n.* **1.** *Sociol.* **a.** a hereditary social group limited to persons of the same rank, occupation, etc., and having distinctive mores. **b.** any rigid system of social distinctions. **2.** *Hinduism.* any of the four social divisions, the Brahman, Kshatriya, Vaisya, and Sudra, into which Hindu society is rigidly divided. **3.** any class or group of society sharing common cultural features. **4.** social position conferred upon one by a caste system: *to lose caste.* **5.** *Entomol.* one of the distinct forms among polymorphous social insects, performing a specialized function in the colony, as a queen bee, worker bee, etc. —*adj.* **6.** of, pertaining to, or characterized by caste: *a caste system.* [< Pg *cast(a)* race, breed, n. use of *casta,* fem. of *casto* < L *cast(us)* pure, CHASTE]

Cas·tel Gan·dol·fo (kä stel′ gän dôl′fô), a village in Italy, 15 mi. SE of Rome: summer palace of the pope.

cas·tel·lan (kas′tᵊlən, ka stel′ən), *n.* the governor of a castle. [< L *castellān(us)* holder of a fort (orig. member of the garrison), n. use of adj. = *castell(um)* CASTLE + *-ānus* -AN; r. ME *castelain* < ONF]

cas·tel·la·ny (kas′tᵊlā′nē), *n., pl.* **-nies. 1.** the rank, office, or jurisdiction of a castellan. **2.** the land belonging to a castle.

cas·tel·lat·ed (kas′tᵊlā′tid), *adj.* **1.** *Archit.* built like a castle, esp. with turrets and battlements. **2.** having many castles. [< ML *castellāt(us)* (see CASTLE, -ATE[1]) + -ED[2]] —**cas′tel·la′tion,** *n.*

Cas·tel·lón de la Pla·na (käs′te lyôn′ de lä plä′nä), a seaport in E Spain. 93,968.

cast·er (kas′tər, kä′stər), *n.* **1.** a person or thing that casts. **2.** a small wheel on a swivel, set under a piece of furniture, a machine, etc., to facilitate moving it. **3.** a bottle or cruet for holding a condiment. **4.** a stand containing such bottles. **5.** a container for sugar, pepper, etc., having a perforated top. Also, **castor** (for defs. 2–5). [ME]

cas·ti·gate (kas′tə gāt′), *v.t.,* **-gat·ed, -gat·ing.** to punish in order to correct; criticize severely. [< L *castīgāt(us)* chastened, lit., driven to be faultless (ptp. of *castīgāre*) = *cast(us)* pure, CHASTE + *-īg-,* var. s. of *agere* to drive, incite + *-ātus* -ATE[1]] —**cas′ti·ga′tion,** *n.* —**cas′ti·ga′tor,** *n.* —**Syn.** discipline, chastise, reprove.

Cas·ti·glio·ne (kä′stē lyô′ne), *n.* **Bal·das·sa·re** (bäl′däs sä′re), 1478–1529, Italian diplomat and author.

Cas·tile (ka stēl′), *n.* **1.** Spanish, **Cas·ti·lla** (käs tē′lyä), a former kingdom comprising most of Spain. **2.** Also called **Castile′ soap′.** a variety of mild soap, made from olive oil and sodium hydroxide. **3.** any hard soap made from fats and oils, often partly from olive oil.

Cas·til·ian (ka stil′yən), *n.* **1.** the dialect of Spanish spoken in Castile. **2.** the accepted standard form of the Spanish language as spoken in Spain, based on this dialect. **3.** a native or inhabitant of Castile. —*adj.* **4.** of or pertaining to Castile.

Cas·ti·lla la Nue·va (käs tē′lyä lä nwe′vä), Spanish name of **New Castile.**

Casti′lla la Vie′ja (lä bye′hä), Spanish name of **Old Castile.**

cast·ing (kas′ting, kä′sting), *n.* **1.** the act or process of one who or that which casts. **2.** that which is cast; any article which has been cast in a mold. **3.** the act or process of choosing actors for a theatrical production, etc. **4.** the act or skill of throwing a fishing line out over the water by means of a rod and reel.

cast′ing vote′, the deciding vote of the presiding officer of a deliberative body, made when the other votes are equally divided.

cast′ i′ron, an alloy of iron, carbon, and other elements, cast as a soft and strong, or as a hard and brittle iron.

cast-i·ron (kast′ī′ərn, käst′-), *adj.* **1.** made of cast iron. **2.** rigid or unyielding: *a cast-iron rule.* **3.** strong; hardy: *a cast-iron stomach.*

cas·tle (kas′əl, kä′səl), *n., v.,* **-tled, -tling.** —*n.* **1.** a fortified residence, as of a prince or noble in feudal times. **2.** the chief part of the fortifications of a medieval city. **3.** a strongly fortified, permanently garrisoned stronghold. **4.** a large and stately residence, esp. one that imitates the forms of a medieval fortified residence of a noble. **5.** *Chess.* the rook. —*v.t.* **6.** to place or enclose in or as in a castle. **7.** *Chess.* to move (the king) in castling. —*v.i. Chess.* **8.** to move the king two squares horizontally and bring the appropriate rook to the first square the king has passed over. **9.** (of the king) to be moved in this manner. [ME, OE *castel* < L *castell(um)* stronghold (in LL, also village) = *cast(rum)* fortress + *-ellum* dim. suffix] —**Syn. 4.** palace.

cas′tle in the air′, a fanciful scheme; daydream. Also called **cas′tle in Spain′.**

Cas·tle·reagh (kas′əl rā′, kä′səl-), *n.* **Robert Stewart, Viscount** (*2nd Marquess of Londonderry*), 1769–1822, British statesman.

cast·off (kast′ôf′, -of′, käst′-), *adj.* **1.** thrown away; rejected; discarded. —*n.* **2.** a person or thing that has been cast off. **3.** *Print.* the estimate by a compositor of how many pages copy will occupy when set in type. [adj., n. use of v. phrase *cast off*]

cas·tor[1] (kas′tər, kä′stər), *n.* **1.** a brownish, unctuous substance with a pungent odor, secreted by glands in the groin of the beaver, used in medicine and perfumery. **2.** a hat made of beaver or rabbit fur. **3.** a beaver. [< L < Gk *kástōr* beaver]

cas·tor[2] (kas′tər, kä′stər), *n.* caster (defs. 2–5).

Cas·tor (kas′tər, kä′stər), *n. Astron.* the more northerly of the two bright stars in the constellation Gemini.

Cas′tor and Pol′lux, *Class. Myth.* twin sons of Leda and brothers of Helen, famous for their fraternal affection and regarded as the protectors of persons at sea.

cas′tor bean′, 1. the seed of the castor-oil plant. **2.** See **castor-oil plant.** —**cas′tor-bean′,** *adj.*

cas′tor oil′, a colorless to pale yellow, viscid liquid obtained from the castor bean: used as a lubricant, cathartic, etc. [*castor* (? var. sp. of CASTER) perh. so called because of its purgative effect]

cas′tor-oil′ plant′ (kas′tər oil′, kä′stər-), a tall euphorbiaceous plant, *Ricinus communis,* originally native to India, bearing a seed that yields castor oil.

cas·trate (kas′trāt), *v.t.,* **-trat·ed, -trat·ing. 1.** to remove the testes of; emasculate. **2.** to remove the ovaries of. **3.** to deprive (a book, text, etc.) of effect or import by deleting certain parts; expurgate. [< L *castrāt(us)* gelded (ptp. of *castrāre*)] —**cas·tra′tion,** *n.* —**cas′tra·tor,** *n.*

castra′tion com′plex, *Psychoanal.* an unconscious fear of losing the genital organs.

Cas·tries (ka strē′, kas′trēz), *n.* a seaport on and the capital of St. Lucia, in the NW part. 45,000.

Cas·tro (kas′trō; *Sp.* käs′trō), *n.* **Fi·del** (fi del′; *Sp.* fē thel′), (*Fidel Castro Ruz*), born 1927, Cuban revolutionary: prime minister since 1959.

Cas·tro·ism (kas′trō iz′əm), *n.* the political, social, and revolutionary theories and policies advocated by Fidel Castro.

Ca·strop-Rau·xel (*Ger.* kä′strôp rouk′səl), *n.* a city in central North Rhine-Westphalia, in W West Germany. 81,900. Also, **Kastrop-Rauxel.**

Cas′tro Val′ley (kas′trō), a town in W California, near San Francisco Bay. 44,760 (1970).

cas·u·al (kazh′o͞o əl), *adj.* **1.** happening by chance: *a casual meeting.* **2.** without definite or serious intention; offhand: *a casual remark.* **3.** seeming or tending to be indifferent; apathetic: *a casual, nonchalant air.* **4.** (of clothes) appropriate for wearing at home; informal. **5.** occasional; random; irregular: *a casual visitor.* **6.** *Obs.* uncertain. —*n.* **7.** a worker employed only irregularly. **8.** a soldier temporarily at a station or other place of duty, and usually en route to another station. [ME < L *cāsuāl(is)* = *cāsu(s)* CASE[1] + *-ālis* -AL[1]] —**cas′u·al·ly,** *adv.* —**cas′u·al·ness,** *n.*

cas·u·al·ty (kazh′o͞o əl tē), *n., pl.* **-ties. 1.** *Mil.* **a.** a member of the armed forces lost to his unit through death, wounds, sickness, capture, or because his whereabouts or condition cannot be determined. **b. casualties,** loss in numerical strength through any cause. **2.** a person who is injured or killed in an accident. **3.** a severe accident, esp. one involving death. **4.** any person, group, thing, etc., that is harmed or destroyed as a result of some act or event: *Their house was a casualty of the new road through town.* [CASUAL + -TY[2]; r. ME *casuelte*]

cas·u·ist (kazh′o͞o ist), *n.* **1.** a person who studies and resolves moral problems arising in specific situations. **2.** an oversubtle or disingenuous reasoner. [< Sp *casuist(a)* < L *cāsu(s)* CASE[1] + *-ista* -IST]

cas·u·is·tic (kazh′o͞o is′tik), *adj.* **1.** pertaining to casuists or casuistry. **2.** oversubtle; intellectually dishonest; sophistical. Also, **cas′u·is′ti·cal.** —**cas′u·is′ti·cal·ly,** *adv.*

cas·u·ist·ry (kazh′o͞o i strē), *n., pl.* **-ries. 1.** application of general ethical principles to particular cases of conscience or conduct. **2.** fallacious or dishonest application of such principles.

ca·sus bel·li (kä′so͞os bel′lē; *Eng.* kā′səs bel′ī), *pl.* **ca·sus bel·li** (kä′so͞os bel′lē; *Eng.* kā′səs bel′ī). *Latin.* an event or political occurrence that brings about a declaration of war.

cat (kat), *n., v.,* **cat·ted, cat·ting.** —*n.* **1.** a domesticated carnivore, *Felis domestica* or *F. catus,* bred in a number of varieties. **2.** the fur of this animal. **3.** any of several carnivores of the family *Felidae,* as the lion, tiger, leopard, jaguar, etc. **4.** *Informal.* a woman given to spiteful or malicious gossip. **5.** *Slang.* **a.** any person; guy. **b.** a devotee of jazz. **6.** a cat-o'-nine-tails. **7.** a catboat. **8.** a catfish. **9.** *Naut.* a tackle used in hoisting an anchor to the cathead. **10. let the cat out of the bag,** to divulge a secret. —*v.t.* **11.** to flog with a cat-o'-nine-tails. **12.** *Naut.* to hoist (an anchor) and secure it to a cathead. [ME *cat, catte,* OE *catt* (masc.), *catte* (fem.); c. Icel *köttr;* perh. < Celt, whence also LL *cattus, catta;* << ?] —**cat′like′,** *adj.*

cat., **1.** catalog; catalogue. **2.** catechism.

cata-, a prefix meaning "down," "against," "back," "according to," "through," "entirely," and "mis-," occurring orig. in loan words from Greek (*cataclysm; catalog; catalepsy*) and on this model used in the formation of other compound words (*catadromous*). Also, **cat-, cath-, kat-, kata-, kath-.** [< Gk *kata-,* comb. form of *katá* down, through, against, according to, toward, during]

ca·tab·a·sis (kə tab′ə sis), *n., pl.* **-ses** (-sēz′). katabasis. —**cat·a·bat·ic** (kat′ə bat′ik), *adj.*

ca·tab·o·lism (kə tab′ə liz′əm), *n. Biol., Physiol.* destructive metabolism; the breaking down in living organisms of more complex substances into simpler ones (opposed to *anabolism*). Also, **katabolism.** [< Gk *katabol(ḗ)* a throwing down (*kata-* CATA- + *bolḗ* a throw; cf. *katabállein* to throw down) + -ISM] —**cat·a·bol·ic** (kat′ə bol′ik), *adj.* —**cat′a·bol′i·cal·ly,** *adv.*

ca·tab·o·lite (kə tab′ə līt′), *n. Biol., Physiol.* a product of catabolic action. [CATABOL(ISM) + -ITE[1]]

cat·a·caus·tic (kat′ə kô′stik), *adj. Math., Optics.* noting a caustic surface or curve formed by the reflection of light.

cat·a·chre·sis (kat′ə krē′sis), *n.* **1.** misuse or strained use of words. **2.** the employment of a word under a false form derived through folk etymology: *causeway* and *crawfish* or *crayfish* have their forms by catachresis. [< L < Gk: a misuse (akin to *katachrêsthai* to misuse) = *kata-* CATA- + *chrêsis* use (*chrê(sthai)* (to) use, need + *-sis* -SIS)] —**cat·a·chres·tic** (kat′ə kres′tik), **cat′a·chres′ti·cal,** *adj.* —**cat′a·chres′ti·cal·ly,** *adv.*

cat·a·cli·nal (kat′ə klīn′^{ə}l), *adj. Geol.* descending in the same direction as the dip of the underlying rock strata. Cf. **anaclinal.** [< Gk *kataklin(ḗs)* sloping (*kataklín(ein)* (to) slope down = *kata-* CATA- + *klínein* to slope, + *-ēs* adj. suffix) + -AL[1]]

cat·a·clysm (kat′ə kliz′əm), *n.* **1.** any violent upheaval, esp. one of a social or political nature. **2.** *Phys. Geog.* a sudden and violent physical action producing changes in the earth's surface. **3.** a flood; deluge. [< LL *cataclysm(os)* (Vulgate) < Gk *kataklysmós* flood (akin to *kataklýzein* to flood) = *kata-* CATA- + *klysmós* a washing (*klý̄z(ein)* (to) wash + *-mos* n. suffix)] —**cat′a·clys′mic, cat′a·clys′mal,** *adj.* —**cat′a·clys′mi·cal·ly,** *adv.* —**Syn. 1.** See **disaster.**

cat·a·comb (kat′ə kōm′), *n.* **1.** Usually, **catacombs.** an underground cemetery, esp. one consisting of tunnels and rooms with recesses for tombs. **2. the Catacombs,** the subterranean burial chambers of the early Christians in and near Rome, Italy. [ME *catacombe,* OE *catacumbe* < LL *catacumbās* (acc. pl.) < Gk **katakýmbās* = *kata-* CATA- + *kýmbās,* acc. pl. of *kýmbē* hollow, cup]

ca·tad·ro·mous (kə tad′rə məs), *adj.* (of fish) migrating down a river to the sea to spawn (opposed to *anadromous*).

cat·a·falque (kat′ə falk′, -fôk′, -fôlk′), *n.* a raised structure on which the body of a deceased person lies in state. [< F < It *catafalc(o)* < LL **catafalic(um)* scaffolding = *cata-* CATA- + *fal(a)* wooden siege tower + *-icum,* neut. of *-icus* -IC]

Cat·a·lan (kat′^{ə}lan′, -^{ə}lən, kat′^{ə}lan′), *adj.* **1.** pertaining to Catalonia, its inhabitants, or their language. —*n.* **2.** a native or inhabitant of Catalonia. **3.** a Romance language spoken in Catalonia, closely related to Provençal. [late ME < Sp]

cat·a·lase (kat′^{ə}lās′), *n. Biochem.* an enzyme that decomposes hydrogen peroxide into oxygen and water. [CATAL(YSIS) + -ASE]

cat·a·lec·tic (kat′^{ə}lek′tik), *Pros.* —*adj.* **1.** (of a line of verse) lacking part of the last foot. —*n.* **2.** a catalectic line of verse. Cf. **acatalectic, hypercatalectic.** [< LL *catalēctic(us)* < Gk *katalēktikós* incomplete = *katalēk-,* var. s. of *katalḗgein* leave off (*kata-* CATA- + *lḗgein* end) + *-tikos* -TIC]

cat·a·lep·sy (kat′^{ə}lep′sē), *n. Pathol., Psychiatry.* a physical condition characterized by suspension of sensation, muscular rigidity, and often by loss of contact with environment. [< ML *catalēpsia,* var. of LL *catalēpsis* < Gk *katálēpsis* seizure (akin to *katalambánein* to hold down) = *kata-* CATA- + *lêpsis* a grasping (*lēp-,* var. s. of *lambánein* to grasp, + *-sis* -SIS); r. ME *cathalempsia* < ML] —**cat′a·lep′tic,** *adj., n.*

cat·a·lex·is (kat′^{ə}lek′sis), *n., pl.* **-a·lex·es** (-^{ə}lek′sēs). the omission of one or more syllables in the final foot of a line of verse; truncation of the end of a line of verse. [<< Gk *katálēxis* termination = *katalḗg(ein)* leave off + *-sis* -SIS]

Cat·a·li′na Is′land (kat′^{ə}lē′nə). See **Santa Catalina.** Also called **Cat′ali′na.**

cat·a·log (kat′^{ə}lôg′, -^{ə}log′), *n.* **1.** *Library Science.* a systematic list of the contents of a library. Cf. **union catalog. 2.** a list, usually in alphabetical order, with brief notes on the names, articles, etc., listed. **3.** a book, leaflet, or file containing such a list or record. —*v.t.* **4.** to enter in a catalog; make a catalog of. [late ME *cataloge* < LL *catalog(us)* < Gk *katálogos* a register (akin to *katalégein* to count up) = *kata-* CATA- + *-logos* reckoning] —**cat′a·log′er, cat′a·log′ist,** *n.* —**Syn. 1.** roster, register, record. See **list**[1].

cat·a·logue (kat′^{ə}lôg′, -^{ə}log′), *n., v.,* **-logued, -logu·ing.** catalog. —**cat′a·logu′er, cat′a·logu′ist,** *n.*

Cat·a·lo·ni·a (kat′^{ə}lō′nē ə, -nyə), *n.* a region in NE Spain: formerly a province. —**Cat′a·lo′ni·an,** *adj.*

ca·tal·pa (kə tal′pə), *n.* any bignoniaceous tree of the genus *Catalpa,* of America and Asia, as *C. speciosa,* of U.S., having large cordate leaves and bell-shaped white flowers. [< NL; adaptation of Creek *kutuhlpa* winged head]

ca·tal·y·sis (kə tal′i sis), *n., pl.* **-ses** (-sēz′). **1.** *Chem.* the causing or accelerating of a chemical change by the addition of a substance that is not permanently affected by the reaction. **2.** an action between two or more persons or forces, initiated by an agent that remains unaffected by the action. [< NL < Gk *katálysis* dissolution = *katalý̄(ein)* (to) dissolve (*kata-* CATA- + *lýein* to loosen) + *-sis* -SIS] —**cat·a·lyt·ic** (kat′^{ə}lit′ik), *adj., n.*

cat·a·lyst (kat′^{ə}list), *n.* **1.** *Chem.* a substance that causes catalysis. **2.** that which causes activity between two or more persons or forces without itself being affected.

cat′alyt′ic convert′er, an antipollution device containing a chemical catalyst that reduces the volume of undesirable substances, such as carbon monoxide, unburned hydrocarbons, and oxides of nitrogen from automotive exhaust.

cat·a·lyze (kat′^{ə}līz′), *v.t.,* **-lyzed, -lyz·ing.** *Chem.* to act upon by catalysis. [CATALY(SIS + -I)ZE] —**cat′a·lyz′er,** *n.*

cat·a·ma·ran (kat′ə mə ran′), *n. Naut.* **1.** a float or sailing raft formed of a number of logs tied side by side some distance apart. **2.** a vessel, usually propelled by sail, formed of two hulls or floats held side by side by a frame above them. Cf. **trimaran.** [< Tamil *kaṭṭa-maram* tied wood]

cat·a·me·ni·a (kat′ə mē′nē ə, -nyə), *n.* (*construed as sing. or pl.*) *Physiol.* menses. [< NL < Gk *katamḗnia,* neut. pl. of Gk *katamḗni(os)* monthly = *kata-* CATA- + *mḗn* month + *-ios* -IOUS] —**cat′a·me′ni·al,** *adj.*

cat·a·mite (kat′ə mīt′), *n.* a boy kept for pederastic purposes. [< L *Catamīt(us)* < Gk *Ganymḗdēs* GANYMEDE]

cat·a·mount (kat′ə mount′), *n.* **1.** a wild animal of the cat family. **2.** *U.S.* **a.** the cougar. **b.** the lynx.

cat·a·moun·tain (kat′ə moun′t^{ə}n, -tin), *n.* a wild animal of the cat family, as the European wildcat, the leopard, or the panther. Also, **cat-o'-mountain.** [var. of *cat o' mountain,* ME *cat of (the) mountaine*]

Ca·ta·nia (kä tä′nyä), *n.* a seaport in E Sicily. 361,466 (1961).

Ca·ta·ño (kä tän′yō), *n.* a city in NE Puerto Rico. 26,459 (1970).

Ca·tan·za·ro (kä′tän dzä′RÔ), *n.* a city in S Italy. 74,352 (1961).

cat·a·pho·re·sis (kat′ə fə rē′sis), *n.* **1.** *Med.* the causing of medicinal substances to pass through or into living tissues in the direction of flow of a positive electric current. **2.** *Physical Chem.* electrophoresis. [< NL = *cata-* CATA- + Gk *phórēsis* a being borne = *phorē-* (var. s. of *pherein* to bear) + *-sis* -SIS)] —**cat·a·pho·ret·ic** (kat′ə fə ret′ik), *adj.*

cat·a·pla·sia (kat′ə plā′zhə, -zhē ə, -zē ə), *n. Biol.* degeneration of a cell or tissue. Also, **kataplasia.** —**cat·a·plas·tic** (kat′ə plas′tik), *adj.*

cat·a·plasm (kat′ə plaz′əm), *n. Med.* poultice. [< L *cataplasm(a)* < Gk *katáplasma*]

cat·a·pult (kat′ə pult′, -po͝olt′), *n.* **1.** an ancient military engine for hurling stones, arrows, etc. **2.** a device for launching an airplane from the deck of a ship. **3.** *Brit.* a slingshot. —*v.t.* **4.** to hurl (a missile), as from a catapult, slingshot, etc. [< L *catapult(a)* < Gk *katapéltēs* = *kata-* CATA- + *péltēs* hurler, akin to *pállein* to hurl]

cat·a·ract (kat′ə rakt′), *n.* **1.** a large waterfall. **2.** a downpour, rush, or deluge. **3.** *Ophthalm.* **a.** an abnormality of the eye, characterized by opacity of the lens. **b.** the opaque area. [ME *cataracte* < L *catar(r)act(a)* < Gk *katarrákt(ēs)* waterfall, floodgate, portcullis, (n.), down-rushing (adj.), akin to *katarássein* to dash down (*kat-* CATA- + *arássein* to smite)]

ca·tarrh (kə tär′), *n. Pathol.* inflammation of a mucous membrane, esp. of the respiratory tract, accompanied by excessive secretions. [< medical L *catarrh(us)* < Gk *katárrous,* lit., a flowing down = *katarr(eîn)* (to) flow down (*kata-* CATA- + *rhein* to flow) + *-ous,* var. of *-oos* adj. suffix] —**ca·tarrh′al, ca·tarrh′ous,** *adj.*

ca·tas·ta·sis (kə tas′tə sis), *n., pl.* **-ses** (-sēz′). the part of a drama, preceding the catastrophe, in which the action is at its height; the climax of a play. Cf. **catastrophe** (def. 4), **epitasis, protasis** (def. 2). [< Gk *katástasis* stability, akin to *kathistánai* to make stand, settle]

ca·tas·tro·phe (kə tas′trə fē), *n.* **1.** a sudden and widespread disaster: *the catastrophe of war.* **2.** a disastrous finish or conclusion. **3.** any misfortune, mishap, or failure; fiasco. **4.** (in a drama) the point following the climax and introducing the close or conclusion; dénouement. Cf. **catastasis, epitasis, protasis** (def. 2). **5.** a sudden, violent disturbance, esp. of a part of the earth's surface; cataclysm. [< Gk *katastrophḗ* an overturning, akin to *katastréphein* to overturn] —**cat·a·stroph·ic** (kat′ə strof′ik), *adj.* —**cat′a·stroph′i·cal·ly,** *adv.* —**Syn. 1, 2.** See **disaster.**

cat·a·to·ni·a (kat′ə tō′nē ə), *n. Psychiatry.* a pathological syndrome, esp. of schizophrenia, characterized by muscular rigidity and mental stupor, sometimes alternating with great excitement and confusion. Also, **katatonia.** [< NL < Gk **katatónia* = *kata-* CATA- + *-tonia* (*tón(os)* TONE + *-ia* -Y[3])] —**cat·a·ton·ic** (kat′ə ton′ik), *adj., n.*

Ca·taw·ba (kə tô′bə), *n.* **1.** a Siouan language of North and South Carolina. **2.** the portion of the Wateree River in North Carolina. Cf. **Wateree. 3.** *Hort.* a red grape of the eastern U.S. **4.** a dry white wine made from this grape. [< Choctaw *Kataba,* dial. var. of *Katapa,* lit., (people) apart]

cat·bird (kat′bûrd′), *n.* a slate-colored North American songbird, *Dumetella carolinensis,* allied to the mockingbird, having a call resembling the mewing of a cat.

cat·boat (kat′bōt′), *n.* a boat having one mast set well forward and one large sail.

Catboat

cat′ bri′er, any of various species of smilax, as the greenbrier, *Smilax rotundifolia.* [so called because it scratches]

cat′ bur′glar, a burglar who breaks into houses through upstairs windows; second-story man.

cat·call (kat′kôl′), *n.* **1.** a cry like that of a cat, made by the human voice and used for expressing disapproval. —*v.i.* **2.** to sound catcalls. —*v.t.* **3.** to express disapproval of by catcalls. —**cat′call′er,** *n.*

catch (kach), *v.,* **caught, catch·ing,** *n., adj.* —*v.t.* **1.** to capture, as in a trap or after pursuit. **2.** to deceive: *to be caught by sugary words.* **3.** to get aboard (a train, boat, etc.). **4.** to see or attend: *to catch a show.* **5.** to come upon suddenly, as in some action: *I caught him doing it.* **6.** to strike; hit: *The blow caught him on the head.* **7.** to intercept and hold (something thrown, falling, etc.): *to catch a ball; a barrel to catch rain.* **8.** to check or restrain suddenly (often used reflexively): *She caught her breath in surprise.* **9.** to receive, incur, or contract: *to catch cold.* **10.** to join in: *I caught the spirit of the occasion.* **11.** to lay hold of; grasp; clasp: *He caught her arm.* **12.** to grip, hook, or entangle: *The closing door caught his arm.* **13.** to allow (something) to become gripped, hooked, snagged, or entangled: *He caught his coat on a nail.* **14.** to fasten with or as with a catch: *to catch the clasp on a necklace.* **15.** to attract or arrest: *His speech caught our attention.* **16.** to captivate or charm: *She was caught by his smile and good nature.* **17.** to grasp with the intellect; comprehend: *She failed to catch his meaning.* **18.** to hear clearly.
—*v.i.* **19.** to become gripped, hooked, or entangled: *Her foot caught in the hole.* **20.** to take hold: *The door lock catches.* **21.** to overtake someone or something moving (usually fol. by *up, up with,* or *up to*). **22.** *Baseball.* to play as catcher: *He catches for the Yankees.* **23.** to become lighted; take fire; ignite. **24. catch it,** *Informal.* to receive a reprimand or punishment. **25. catch on,** *Informal.* **a.** to become popular. **b.** to grasp mentally; understand. **26. catch up, a.** to lift or snatch suddenly. **b.** to bring or get up to date (often fol. by *on* or *with*): *to catch up on one's reading.* **c.** to come up to or overtake (something or someone) (usually fol. by *with*): *Let's hurry and catch up with them.* **d.** to become involved or entangled with: *We were caught up in the excitement.* **e.** to point out to (a person) minor errors, untruths, etc. (usually fol. by *on*): *We caught the teacher up on a number of factual details.*
—*n.* **27.** act of catching. **28.** anything that catches, esp. a device for checking motion, as a latch on a door. **29.** a slight, momentary break or crack in the voice. **30.** that which is caught, as a quantity of fish. **31.** a person or thing worth getting, esp. a person regarded as a desirable matrimonial prospect. **32.** any tricky or concealed drawback: *It seems so easy that there must be a catch somewhere.* **33.** a fragment: *catches of a song.* **34.** a game in which a ball is thrown from one person to another: *to play catch.* **35.** *Sports.* the catching and holding of a batted or thrown ball before it touches the ground.
—*adj.* **36.** catchy (def. 2). [ME *cacche(n)* (to) chase, capture < ONF *cachie(r)* < VL **captiāre* (r. L *captāre* to hunt, seize) = *capt(us)* taken, ptp. of *capere* (*cap-* take + *-tus* ptp. suffix) + *-iā-* v. suffix + *-re* inf. ending] —**catch′a·ble,** *adj.*
—**Syn. 1.** apprehend, arrest. **11.** CATCH, CLUTCH, GRASP, SEIZE imply taking hold suddenly of something. To CATCH may be to reach after and get: *He caught my hand.* To CLUTCH is to take firm hold of (often out of fear or nervousness), and retain: *The child clutched his mother's hand.* To GRASP also suggests both getting and keeping hold of, with a connotation of eagerness and alertness, rather than fear (literally or figuratively): *to grasp someone's hand in welcome; to grasp an idea.* To SEIZE implies the use of force or energy in taking hold of suddenly (literally or figuratively): *to seize a criminal; to seize an opportunity.* **16.** enchant, fascinate, win. **27.** capture, apprehension, arrest. **28.** ratchet, bolt. —**Ant. 1, 11, 27.** release.

catch·all (kach′ôl′), *n.* a receptacle for odds and ends.

catch-as-catch-can (kach′əz kach′kan′), *n.* **1.** a style of wrestling in which the contestants are permitted to trip, tackle, and use holds below the waist. —*adj.* **2.** seizing or taking advantage of any opportunity that comes to hand; using any method that can be applied or that will work, esp. without prior planning or thought: *He was leading a catch-as-catch-can life, working as an itinerant handyman.* —*adv.* **3.** in any way at all; without specific plan or order.

catch′ ba′sin, a receptacle designed to retain matter that might clog a sewer.

catch′ crop′, a fast-growing crop planted as a substitute for a crop that has failed or at a time when the ground would ordinarily lie fallow. —**catch′ crop′ping.**

catch·er (kach′ər), *n.* **1.** a person or thing that catches. **2.** *Baseball.* the player stationed behind home plate whose chief duty is to catch pitches and foul tips. [ME]

catch·fly (kach′flī′), *n., pl.* **-flies.** any of various plants, esp. of the genus *Silene,* that secrete a viscid fluid in which small insects are sometimes caught.

catch·ing (kach′ing), *adj.* **1.** contagious or infectious: *a catching disease; an enthusiasm that was catching.* **2.** attractive; fascinating. [late ME]

catch·ment (kach′mənt), *n.* **1.** act of catching water. **2.** something for catching water, as a reservoir or basin. **3.** the water caught in such a catchment.

catch′ment ba′sin, *Phys. Geog. Brit.* a drainage area, esp. of a reservoir or river. Also called **catch′ment ar′ea.**

catch·pen·ny (kach′pen′ē), *adj., n., pl.* **-nies.** —*adj.* **1.** made to sell readily at a low price. —*n.* **2.** anything of little value or use.

catch′ phrase′, a phrase that attracts attention. Also, **catch′phrase′.**

catch·pole (kach′pōl′), *n.* (formerly) a petty government officer who arrests persons for debt. Also, **catch′poll′.** [ME *cacchepol,* OE *cæcepol* < ML *cacepoll(us)* tax-gatherer, lit., chase-fowl = *cace-* (< ONF; see CATCH) + *pollus* < L *pullus* chick; see PULLET]

Catch-22 (kach′twen′tē to͞o′), *n. Informal.* a frustrating situation in which one is trapped between bureaucratic regulations that appear to contradict each other. [from the novel *Catch-22* (1961) by J. Heller, b. 1923, U.S. author]

catch·up (kach′əp, kech′-), *n.* ketchup.

catch·weight (kach′wāt′), *n. Sports.* the chance or optional weight of a contestant, as contrasted with a weight fixed by agreement or rule.

catch·word (kach′wûrd′), *n.* **1.** a word or phrase repeated so often that it becomes a slogan. **2.** Also called **guide word.** a word at the top of a page in a reference book to indicate the first or last article on that page. **3.** (formerly in bookbinding) the first word of a page inserted at the foot of the preceding page as an aid to the binder.

catch·y (kach′ē), *adj.,* **catch·i·er, catch·i·est. 1.** pleasing and easily remembered: *a catchy tune.* **2.** tricky; deceptive: *a catchy question.* **3.** occurring in snatches; fitful: *a catchy wind.* —**catch′i·ness,** *n.*

cat′ distem′per, *Vet. Pathol.* distemper[1] (def. 1c).

cate (kāt), *n.* Usually, **cates.** *Archaic.* a choice food delicacy; dainty. [back formation from late ME *cates,* aph. var. of ME *acates* things bought, pl. of *acat* buying]

cat·e·chet·i·cal (kat′ə ket′i kəl), *adj.* pertaining to teaching by question and answer. Also, **cat′e·chet′ic.** [< late ML *catēchētic(us)* (< Gk *katēchētikós* = *katēchē-* (var. s. of *katēchein* to teach by word of mouth) + *-tikos* -TIC) + -AL[1]] —**cat′e·chet′i·cal·ly,** *adv.*

cat·e·chin (kat′ə chin, -kin), *n. Chem.* an amorphous, yellow compound, $C_{15}H_{14}O_6$, used chiefly in tanning and dyeing. [CATECH(U) + -IN[2]]

cat·e·chise (kat′ə kīz′), *v.t.,* **-chised, -chis·ing.** *Chiefly Brit.* catechize. —**cat′e·chis′er,** *n.*

cat·e·chism (kat′ə kiz′əm), *n.* **1.** *Eccles.* an elementary book containing a summary of the principles of a Christian religion, in the form of questions and answers. **2.** a series of formal questions and answers used as a test. **3.** catechetical instruction. [< LL *catēchism(us)* book of questions and answers, appar. = *catēch(izāre)* (to) CATECHIZE + *-ismus* -ISM] —**cat′e·chis′mal,** *adj.*

cat·e·chist (kat′ə kist), *n.* **1.** a person who catechizes. **2.** *Eccles.* a person who instructs catechumens. [< LL *catēchist(a)* < Gk *katēchistḗs* = *katēch(eîn)* (to) teach by word of mouth, orig. to din down, i.e., to get results by shouting (*kat-* CATA- + *ēchein* to sound) + *-istēs* -IST] —**cat′e·chis′tic, cat′e·chis′ti·cal,** *adj.* —**cat′e·chis′ti·cal·ly,** *adv.*

cat·e·chize (kat′ə kīz′), *v.t.,* **-chized, -chiz·ing. 1.** to instruct or teach by use of the catechism. **2.** to question closely or excessively. Also, *esp. Brit.,* **catechise.** [< LL *catēchiz(āre)* < Gk *katēchíz(ein)* (to) make (someone) learn by teaching (him) orally = *katēch(ein)* (to) teach orally (see CATECHIST) + *-izein* -IZE] —**cat′e·chiz′er,** *n.*

cat·e·chol (kat′ə chōl′, -chôl′, -kōl′, -kôl′), *n. Chem.* a white crystalline derivative of benzene, HOC_6H_4OH, the ortho isomer, used chiefly in photography and for dyeing; pyrocatechol. [CATECH(U) + -OL[1]]

cat·e·chu (kat′ə cho͞o′, -kyo͞o′), *n.* any of several astringent substances obtained from various tropical plants, esp. from the wood of two East Indian acacias, *Acacia Catechu* and *A. Suma:* used in medicine, dyeing, tanning, etc. Also called **cachou, cashoo, cutch.** [< NL < Malay *kachu*]

cat·e·chu·men (kat′ə kyo͞o′mən), *n.* **1.** *Eccles.* a person undergoing instruction in the rudiments of Christianity; neophyte. **2.** a person being taught the elementary principles of any subject. [< LL *catēchūmen(us)* < Gk *katēchoúmenos* (one who is) being taught by word of mouth = *katēch(eîn)* (to) teach orally (see CATECHIST) + *-oumenos* prp. suffix; r. ME *cathecumyn* < MF *cathecumine* < LL, as above] —**cat′e·chu′me·nal, cat·e·chu·men·i·cal** (kat′ə-kyo͞o men′i kəl), *adj.* —**cat′e·chu′men·ism,** *n.*

cat·e·gor·i·cal (kat′ə gôr′i kəl, -gor′-), *adj.* **1.** absolute; unqualified and unconditional: *a categorical denial.* **2.** of, pertaining to, or in a category. Also, **cat′e·gor′ic.** [< LL *catēgoric(us)* (< Gk *katēgorikós;* see CATEGORY, -IC) + -AL[1]] —**cat′e·gor′i·cal·ly,** *adv.* —**Syn. 1.** positive, flat.

categor′ical imper′ative, *Ethics.* the rule of Immanuel Kant that one's action should be capable of serving as the basis of a universal law.

cat·e·go·rise (kat′ə gə rīz′), *v.t.,* **-rised, -ris·ing.** *Chiefly Brit.* categorize. —**cat′e·go·ri·sa′tion,** *n.*

cat·e·go·rize (kat′ə gə rīz′), *v.t.,* **-rized, -riz·ing. 1.** to arrange in categories or classes; classify. **2.** to describe by labeling or giving a name to; characterize. —**cat·e·go·rist** (kat′ə gôr′ist, -gōr′-), *n.* —**cat′e·go·ri·za′tion,** *n.*

cat·e·go·ry (kat′ə gôr′ē, -gōr′ē), *n., pl.* **-ries. 1.** a classificatory division in a system; class; group. **2.** *Philos.* any classification of terms that is basic and not susceptible of further analysis. [< LL *catēgoria* < Gk *katēgoría* accusation (also, kind of predication) = *katēgor(os)* accuser, affirmer (*katēgor(eîn)* (to) accuse, affirm, lit., speak publicly against = *kat(a)-* CATA- + *agorein* to speak before the AGORA + *-os* n. suffix) + *-ia* -Y[3]]

ca·te·na (kə tē′nə), *n., pl.* **-nae** (-nē). a chain or connected series, esp. of extracts from the writings of the fathers of the church. [< L: a chain]

cat·e·nar·y (kat′ᵊner′ē; *esp. Brit.* kə tē′nə rē), *n., pl.* **-nar·ies,** *adj.* —*n.* **1.** *Math.* the curve assumed approximately by a heavy uniform cord or chain hanging freely from two points not in the same vertical line. Equation: $y = k \cosh\left(\frac{x}{k}\right)$. **2.** (in electric railroads) the cable, running above the track, from which the trolley wire is suspended. —*adj.* **3.** of, pertaining to, or resembling a catenary. **4.** of or pertaining to a chain or linked series. [< L *catēnāri(us)* relating to a chain]

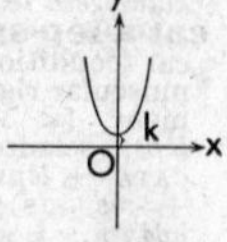

Catenary
k, Distance from the vertex to the origin at O

cat·e·nate (kat′ᵊnāt′), *v.t.*, **-nat·ed, -nat·ing.** to link together; form into a connected series: *catenated cells.* [< L *catēnāt(us)* chained] —**cat′e·na′tion,** *n.*

cat·e·noid (kat′ᵊnoid′), *n. Geom.* the surface generated by rotating a catenary about its axis of symmetry. [< L *catēn(a)* a chain + -OID]

ca·ter (kā′tər), *v.i.* **1.** to provide food, service, etc.: *to cater for a banquet.* **2.** to supply something desired or demanded (usually fol. by *to* or *for*): *to cater to popular demand.* —*v.t.* **3.** to provide food and service for: *to cater a party.* [v. use of obs. *cater*, ME *catour*, aph. var. of *acatour* buyer < AF = *acat(er)* (to) buy (see CATE) + *-our* -OR[2]] —**ca′ter·ing·ly,** *adv.*

cat·er·cor·nered (kat′ə kôr′nərd, kat′ē-, kat′ər-), *adj.* **1.** diagonal. —*adv.* **2.** diagonally. Also, **cat′er·cor′ner, catty-cornered, catty-corner, kitty-cornered, kitty-corner.** [dial. *cater* (adv.) diagonally (< obs. *cater* four < MF *quatre* < L *quattuor*)]

ca·ter-cous·in (kā′tər kuz′ən), *n.* **1.** an intimate friend. **2.** *Obs.* a cousin. [obs. *cater* purveyor, provider (see CATER)]

ca·ter·er (kā′tər ər), *n.* **1.** a person whose business is to provide whatever food, supplies, and service are needed at a social gathering. **2.** a person who caters.

cat·er·pil·lar (kat′ə pil′ər, kat′ər-), *n.* **1.** the wormlike larva of a butterfly or a moth. **2.** (*cap.*) *Trademark.* a tractor having the driving wheels moving inside endless tracks situated on the sides, for use on rough or soft ground. **3.** any device, as a tank or power shovel, moving on such endless tracks. [late ME *catyrpel* = *catyr* tomcat (< MD *cater*) + *pel*, north var. of *pil* skin, rind (akin to OE *pilian* to PEEL[1]); cf. ONF *catepelose* = *cate* cat + *pelose* < L *pilōs(us)* hairy]

cat·er·waul (kat′ər wôl′), *v.i.* **1.** to cry as cats in rutting time; howl or screech. **2.** to quarrel like cats. —*n.* Also, **cat′er·waul′ing. 3.** the cry of a cat in rutting time. **4.** any discordant or screeching cry. [ME *cater(wawen)* = *cater* tomcat (< MD) + *wawen* to howl, OE *wāwan* to blow, said of the wind) + *waul,* var. of WAIL] —**cat′er·waul′er,** *n.*

Catfish, *Ictalurus punctatus* (Length to 4 ft.)

cat·fish (kat′fish′), *n., pl.* (*esp. collectively*) **-fish,** (*esp. referring to two or more kinds or species*) **-fish·es.** any of numerous fishes of the order or suborder *Nematognathi* (or *Siluroidei*), characterized by barbels around the mouth and the absence of scales. [perh. so called from its barbels]

cat·gut (kat′gut′), *n.* a strong cord made by twisting the dried intestines of animals, as sheep. [? CAT[1] + GUT]

cath-, var. of **cata-** before an aspirate: *cathode.*

Cath., 1. (*often l.c.*) cathedral. **2.** Catholic.

ca·thar·sis (kə thär′sis), *n.* **1.** *Med.* purgation. **2.** *Aesthetics.* the purging of an audience's emotions through a work of art. **3.** *Psychiatry.* psychotherapy that encourages or permits the discharge of pent-up, socially unacceptable emotions. Also, **katharsis.** [< NL < Gk *kátharsis* a cleansing = *kathar-* (var. s. of *kathaírein* to cleanse < *katharós* pure) + *-sis* -SIS]

ca·thar·tic (kə thär′tik), *adj.* **1.** Also, **ca·thar′ti·cal.** evacuating the bowels; purgative. **2.** of or pertaining to catharsis. —*n.* **3.** a purgative. [< LL *cathartic(us)* < Gk *kathartikós* fit for cleansing] —**ca·thar′ti·cal·ly,** *adv.* —**ca·thar′ti·cal·ness,** *n.* —**Syn. 3.** laxative, physic.

Ca·thay (ka thā′), *n. Literary.* China. [< ML *Cat(h)aya* < Turkic dial., as Tatar *Kïtai*]

cat·head (kat′hed′), *n. Naut.* a projecting timber or metal beam to which an anchor is hoisted and secured.

ca·the·dra (kə thē′drə, kath′ə-), *n., pl.* **-drae** (-drē, -drē′). **1.** the seat or throne of a bishop. **2.** an official chair, as of a professor in a university. [< L < Gk *kathédra* CHAIR]

ca·the·dral (kə thē′drəl), *n.* **1.** the principal church of a diocese, containing the bishop's throne. **2.** (in nonepiscopal denominations) any of various important churches. —*adj.* **3.** of or pertaining to a cathedral. **4.** authoritative. [ME < LL *cathedrāl(is)* (*ecclesia*) a cathedral (church)] —**ca·the′dral·like′,** *adj.*

Cath·er (kath′ər *or, often,* kath′-), *n.* **Wil·la (Si·bert)** (wil′ə sē′bərt), 1876–1947, U.S. novelist.

Cath·er·ine I (kath′ər in, kath′rin), (*Marfa Skavronskaya*) 1684?–1727, Lithuanian wife of Peter the Great: empress of Russia 1725–27.

Catherine II, (*Sophia Augusta of Anhalt-Zerbst*) ("*Catherine the Great*") 1729–96, wife of Peter III: empress of Russia 1762–96.

Ca·the·rine de Mé·di·cis (kaᴛᵊ ʀēn′ də mā dē sēs′), (*Caterina de' Medici*) 1518–89, queen of Henry II of France (mother of Francis II, Charles IX, and Henry III). Also, **Cath·er·ine de' Med·i·ci** (kath′rin də med′i chē, mā′di-, dā, kath′ər in), **Cath′erine de Med′ici.**

Cath′erine How′ard, 1520?–42, fifth queen of Henry VIII of England.

Cath′erine of Ar′a·gon (ar′ə gən, -gon′), 1485–1536, first queen of Henry VIII of England (mother of Mary I of England).

Cath′erine of Sie′na (sye′nä), **Saint,** 1347–80, Italian ascetic and mystic.

Cath′erine Parr′ (pär), 1512–48, sixth queen of Henry VIII of England.

cath′erine wheel′, pinwheel (def. 2).

cath·e·ter (kath′i tər), *n. Med.* a hollow tube employed to drain fluids from body cavities or to distend body passages. [< LL < Gk *kathetḗr* kind of tube, lit., something sent or let down = *kathe-* (var. s. of *kathiénai* = *kat-* CATA- + *hiénai* to send, let go) + *-tēr* instrumental suffix]

cath·e·ter·ise (kath′i tə rīz′), *v.t.*, **-ised, -is·ing.** *Chiefly Brit.* catheterize. —**cath′e·ter·i·sa′tion,** *n.*

cath·e·ter·ize (kath′i tə rīz′), *v.t.*, **-ized, -iz·ing.** to introduce a catheter into. —**cath′e·ter·i·za′tion,** *n.*

ca·thex·is (kə thek′sis), *n., pl.* **-thex·es** (-thek′sēz). *Psychoanal.* **1.** the investment of emotional significance in an activity, object, or idea. **2.** the charge of psychic energy so invested. [< NL < Gk *káthexis* a keeping = *kathech-* (var. s. of *katéchein* to keep, hold on to = *kat(h)-* CATH- + *échein* to have, hold) + *-sis* -SIS; answering to G *Besetzung* a taking possession of (Freud's term)] —**ca·thec·tic** (kə thek′tik), *adj.*

cath′ode (kath′ōd), *n.* **1.** the electrode or terminal by which current leaves an electrolytic cell, voltaic cell, battery, etc. **2.** the positive terminal of a voltaic cell or battery. **3.** the negative terminal, electrode, or element of an electron tube or electrolytic cell. Also, **kathode.** [< Gk *káthod(os)* a way down = *kat-* CATA- + *hodós* way] —**ca·thod·ic** (ka thod′ik, -thō′dik, kə-), *adj.* —**ca·thod′i·cal·ly,** *adv.*

cath′ode ray′, a flow of electrons emanating from a cathode in a vacuum tube.

cath′ode-ray tube′ (kath′ōd rā′), *Electronics.* a vacuum tube generating a focused beam of electrons that can be deflected by electric fields, magnetic fields, or both. The terminus of the beam is visible as a spot or line of luminescence caused by its impinging on a sensitized screen at one end of the tube.

cath·o·lic (kath′ə lik, kath′lik), *adj.* **1.** pertaining to the whole Christian body or church. **2.** universal in extent; encompassing all; wide-ranging: *He has catholic tastes and interests.* [< L *catholic(us)* < Gk *katholikós* general = *kathól(ou)* universally (contr. of phrase *katà hólou* according to the whole; see CATA-, HOLO-) + *-ikos* -IC] —**ca·thol·i·cal·ly, ca·thol·ic·ly** (kə thol′ik lē), *adv.*

Cath·o·lic (kath′ə lik, kath′lik), *adj.* **1.** of or pertaining to the Roman Catholic Church. **2.** noting or pertaining to the conception of the Church as the body representing the ancient undivided Christian witness, comprising all the orthodox churches that have kept the apostolic succession of bishops. —*n.* **3.** a member of a Catholic church, esp. of the Roman Catholic Church. [ME; see CATHOLIC]

Cath′olic Church′. See **Roman Catholic Church.**

ca·thol·i·cise (kə thol′i sīz′), *v.t., v.i.*, **-cised, -cis·ing.** *Chiefly Brit.* catholicize. —**ca·thol′i·ci·sa′tion,** *n.* —**ca·thol′i·cis′er,** *n.*

Ca·thol·i·cism (kə thol′i siz′əm), *n.* **1.** the faith, system, and practice of the Catholic Church, esp. the Roman Catholic Church. **2.** (*l.c.*) broad-mindedness; catholicity.

cath·o·lic·i·ty (kath′ə lis′i tē), *n.* **1.** the quality of being catholic; universality; broad-mindedness. **2.** (*cap.*) the Roman Catholic Church, or its doctrines and usages.

ca·thol·i·cize (kə thol′i sīz′), *v.t., v.i.*, **-cized, -ciz·ing. 1.** to make or become catholic; universalize. **2.** (*cap.*) to make or become Catholic, esp. Roman Catholic. Also, *esp. Brit.*, **catholicise.** —**ca·thol′i·ci·za′tion,** *n.* —**ca·thol′i·ciz′er,** *n.*

ca·thol·i·con (kə thol′i kən), *n.* a universal remedy; panacea. [late ME < ML < Gk *katholikón* cure-all, neut. of *katholikós* CATHOLIC]

cat·house (kat′hous′), *n., pl.* **-hous·es** (hou′ziz). *Slang.* a brothel. [CAT (in obs. sense of prostitute) + HOUSE]

Cat·i·line (kat′ᵊlīn′), *n.* (*Lucius Sergius Catilina*) 108?–62 B.C., Roman politician and conspirator. —**Cat·i·li·nar·i·an** (kat′ᵊlə nâr′ē ən), *adj., n.*

cat·i·on (kat′ī′ən, -on), *n. Physical Chem.* **1.** a positively charged ion that is attracted to the cathode in electrolysis. **2.** any positively charged atom or group of atoms (opposed to *anion*). Also, **kation.** [< Gk *katión*, neut. of *katión*, going down (prp. of *katiénai*) = *kat-* CAT- + *-i-* go + *-on*, neut. of prp. suffix] —**cat·i·on·ic** (kat′ī on′ik), *adj.*

cat·kin (kat′kin), *n. Bot.* an ament, as of the willow or birch. [< D *katteken* little cat (now obs.). See CAT[1], -KIN] —**cat·kin·ate** (kat′ki nāt′), *adj.*

Cat·lin (kat′lin), *n.* **George,** 1796–1872, U.S. painter.

cat·ling (kat′ling), *n.* **1.** a surgical knife. **2.** *Archaic.* a little cat; kitten.

cat′ nap′, *U.S.* a short, light nap or doze.

cat·nap (kat′nap′), *v.i.*, **-napped, -nap·ping.** *U.S.* to doze or sleep lightly.

cat·nip (kat′nip), *n.* a plant, *Nepeta Cataria*, of the mint family, having strongly scented leaves of which cats are fond. Also called **cat·mint** (kat′mint′). [CAT[1] + *nip*, var. of ME *nep* catnip, apocopated var. of OE *nepte* < ML *nept(a)*, var. of L *nepeta*]

Ca·to (kā′tō), *n.* **1. Marcus Por·ci·us** (pôr′shē əs, -shəs), ("*the Elder*" or "*the Censor*"), 234–149 B.C., Roman statesman, soldier, and writer. **2.** his great-grandson, **Marcus Porcius** ("*the Younger*"), 95–46 B.C., Roman statesman, soldier, and Stoic philosopher.

cat-o'-moun·tain (kat′ə moun′tᵊn, -tin), *n.* catamountain.

cat-o'-nine-tails (kat′ə nīn′tālz′), *n., pl.* **-tails.** a whip, usually having nine knotted lines or cords fastened to a handle, used for flogging. Also called **cat.** [so called in allusion to a cat's scratches]

Ca·tons·ville (kāt′ᵊnz vil′), *n.* a town in central Maryland, near Baltimore. 54,812 (1970).

ca·top·trics (kə top′triks), *n.* (*construed as sing.*) the branch of optics dealing with the formation of images by mirrors. [< Gk *katoptrik(ós)* = *kátoptr(on)* mirror (*kat-* CAT- + *op-* see + *-tron* -TRON) + *-ikos* -IC; see -ICS] —**ca·top′tric, ca·top′tri·cal,** *adj.* —**ca·top′tri·cal·ly,** *adv.*

CAT′ scan′ner, a specialized X-ray instrument that displays computerized cross-sectional images from within the body. Also, **CT scanner.** [C(OMPUTERIZED) A(XIAL) T(OMOGRAPHY) SCANNER]

cat's′ cra′dle, a children's game in which two players alternately stretch a looped string over their fingers in such a way as to produce different designs.

cat's-eye (kats′ī′), *n., pl.* **-eyes.** a gem having a chatoyant luster, esp. chrysoberyl.

Cats′kill Moun′tains (kat′skil), a range of low mountains in E New York. Highest peak, Slide Mountain, 4204 ft. Also called **Cats′kills.**

cat's-paw (kats′pô′), *n.* **1.** a person used by another; tool. **2.** *Naut.* **a.** a hitch made in the bight of a rope to hold the hook of a tackle. **b.** a light breeze that ruffles the surface of water over a small area. Also, **cats′paw′.**

cat·sup (kat′səp, kech′əp, kach′-), *n.* ketchup.

cat's′ whisk′er, **1.** *Radio.* a stiff wire forming one contact in a crystal detector. **2.** *Electronics.* any wire for making contact with a semiconductor.

Catt (kat), *n.* **Carrie Chapman,** nee **Lane** (lān), 1859–1947, U.S. leader in women's suffrage movements.

cat·tail (kat′tāl′), *n.* **1.** Also called **reed mace.** a tall, reedlike, marsh plant, *Typha latifolia,* having flowers in long, dense, cylindrical spikes. **2.** any of several other plants of the same genus. **3.** *Bot.* an ament or catkin. [late ME *cattestail*]

Cattails, *Typha latifolia*

cat·ta·lo (kat′əlō′), *n., pl.* **-loes, -los.** a hybrid produced by mating the American buffalo with domestic cattle. [CATT(LE) + (BUFF)ALO]

Cat·te·gat (kat′ə gat′), *n.* Kattegat.

Cat·tell (kə tel′), *n.* **James Mc·Keen** (mə kēn′), 1860–1944, U.S. psychologist, educator, and editor.

cat·tish (kat′ish), *adj.* catty. **—cat′tish·ly,** *adv.* **—cat′tish·ness,** *n.*

cat·tle (kat′əl), *n.* (*construed as pl.*) bovine animals, esp. domesticated members of the genus *Bos,* as cows and steers. [ME *catel* < ONF: (personal) property < ML *cap(i)tāle* wealth; see CAPITAL[1]] **—cat′tle·less,** *adj.*

cat·tle·man (kat′əl mən, -man′), *n., pl.* **-men** (-mən, -men′). a man engaged in the tending or breeding of cattle, as a rancher or farmer.

cat′tle plague′, *Vet. Pathol.* rinderpest.

catt·ley·a (kat′lē ə, kat lē′ə, -lā′ə), *n.* any of several tropical American orchids of the genus *Cattleya.* [named after William *Cattley* (d. 1832), English botany enthusiast]

cat·ty[1] (kat′ē), *adj.,* **-ti·er, -ti·est.** **1.** catlike; feline. **2.** quietly or slyly malicious; spiteful: *a catty gossip.* **—cat′ti·ly,** *adv.* **—cat′ti·ness,** *n.*

cat·ty[2] (kat′ē), *n., pl.* **-ties.** (in China and Southeast Asia) a weight equal to about 1⅓ pounds avdp. [< Malay *kati*]

cat·ty-cor·nered (kat′ē kôr′nərd), *adj., adv.* cater-cornered. Also, **cat′ty-cor′ner.**

Ca·tul·lus (kə tul′əs), *n.* **Ga·ius Va·le·ri·us** (gā′əs və lēr′ē əs), 84?–54? B.C., Roman poet. **—Ca·tul·li·an** (kə tul′ē ən), *adj.*

CATV, **1.** a system for receiving television broadcasts at an elevated antenna and relaying them by cable to paying subscribers who cannot receive satisfactory, if any, signals directly because of distance or obstruction. **2.** See **cable TV** (def. 1). [C(OMMUNITY) A(NTENNA) TV]

cat·walk (kat′wôk′), *n.* any narrow walkway, esp. one high above a surrounding area, used to provide access or allow movement, as by workers.

Cau·ca (kou′kä), *n.* a river in W Colombia. 600 mi. long.

Cau·ca·sia (kô kā′zhə, -shə), *n.* a region in the Soviet Union between the Black and Caspian seas: divided by the Caucasus Mountains into Ciscaucasia in Europe and Transcaucasia in Asia. Also, **Caucasus.**

Cau·ca·sian (kô kā′zhən, -shən, -kazh′ən, -kash′-), *adj.* Also, **Cau·cas·ic** (kô kas′ik). **1.** Caucasoid. **2.** of or pertaining to the Caucasus mountain range. **—***n.* **3.** a person having Caucasoid characteristics. **4.** a native of Caucasia. [< L *Caucasi(us)* + -AN]

Cau·ca·soid (kô′kə soid′), *n.* **1.** a member of a racial group, or its descendants, originally inhabiting Europe and parts of North Africa, western Asia, and India: complexion varies from fair to very dark; hair texture ranges from kinky to straight; the lips tend to be thin, the nose straight, and the iris either light or dark in hue. **—***adj.* **2.** of or belonging to this subspecies; Caucasian. [CAUCAS(IAN) + -OID]

Cau·ca·sus (kô′kə səs), *n.* **1.** Also called **Cau′casus Moun′tains.** a mountain range in Caucasia, in the SW Soviet Union between the Black and Caspian seas: divides the Soviet Union in Europe from the Soviet Union in Asia. Highest peak, Mt. Elbrus, 18,481 ft. **2.** Caucasia.

cau·cus (kô′kəs), *n., pl.* **-cus·es,** *v.* **—***n.* **1.** *U.S.* a meeting of the local members of a political party to nominate candidates, determine policy, etc. **—***v.i.* **2.** to hold or meet in a caucus. [prob. < Algonquian; akin to *caucauasu* adviser]

cau·dad (kô′dad), *adv.* *Anat., Zool.* toward the tail or posterior end of the body (opposed to *cephalad*). [< L *caud(a)* tail + *ad* to, toward]

cau·dal (kôd′əl), *adj.* **1.** *Anat., Zool.* of, at, or near the tail or the posterior end of the body. **2.** *Zool.* taillike: *caudal appendages.* [< NL *caudāl(is)* = L *caud(a)* tail + *-ālis* -AL[1]] **—cau′dal·ly,** *adv.*

cau′dal fin′, the terminal vertical fin of a fish.

cau·date (kô′dāt), *adj.* *Zool.* having a tail or taillike appendage. Also, **cau′dat·ed.** [< NL *caudāt(us)* = L *caud(a)* tail + *-ātus* -ATE[1]] **—cau·da′tion,** *n.*

cau·dex (kô′deks), *n., pl.* **-di·ces** (-di sēz′), **-dex·es.** *Bot.* **1.** the axis of a plant, including both stem and root. **2.** a stem bearing the remains or scars of petioles. **3.** the woody or thickened persistent base of a herbaceous perennial. [< L: tree trunk]

cau·dil·lo (kô dēl′yō, -dē′ō; *Sp.* kou t͟hē′lyô, -t͟hē′yô), *n., pl.* **-dil·los** (-dēl′yōz, -dē′ōz; *Sp.* -t͟hē′lyôs, -t͟hē′yôs). (in Spanish-speaking countries) the head of the state; leader. [< Sp < LL *capitellu(m)* = L *capit-* (s. of *caput*) head + *-ellum* dim. suffix]

Cau′dine Forks′ (kô′dīn), two mountain passes in S Italy, in the Apennines near Benevento.

cau·dle (kôd′əl), *n.* a warm beverage, esp. for the sick, usually of wine or ale mixed with eggs, bread, sugar, spices, etc. [ME *caudel* < ONF < ML *caldell(um)* = L *calid(um)* warmed watered wine (n. use of neut. of *calidus* warm) + *-ellum* dim. suffix]

caught (kôt), *v.* pt. and pp. of **catch.**

caul (kôl), *n.* a part of the amnion sometimes covering the head of a child at birth. [ME *calle* < MF *cale,* prob. back formation from *calotte* kind of cap; see CALOTTE]

caul-, var. of **caulo-** before a vowel: *caulescent.*

cauld (kôld, käld, kôd), *adj., n.* *Scot.* cold.

caul·dron (kôl′drən), *n.* a large kettle or boiler. Also, **caldron.** [late ME, m. (by assoc. with L *caldus* warm) of ME *cauderon* < AF = *caudere* (< LL *caldāria,* n. use of fem. of *caldārius* of warming = *cal(i)d(us)* warm (*cal(ēre)* (to) be warm + *-idus* -ID[4]) + *-arius* -ARY) + *-on* n. suffix]

cau·les·cent (kô les′ənt), *adj.* *Bot.* having an obvious stem rising above the ground.

cauli-, var. of **caulo-.**

cau·li·cle (kô′li kəl), *n.* *Bot.* a small or rudimentary stem. [< L *caulicul(us).* See CAULI-, -CULE]

cau·li·flow·er (kô′lə flou′ər, -lē-, kol′ə-, kol′ē-), *n.* **1.** a cultivated cruciferous plant, *Brassica oleracea botrytis,* whose inflorescence forms a compact, fleshy head, used as a vegetable. [< L *cauli(s)* COLE + FLOWER; r. *coleflorie* < It *ca(v)olfiore* = *cavol* cole + *fiore* < L *flōri-* (s. of *flōs*) flower]

cau′liflower ear′, an ear that has been deformed by repeated injury and a thickening of scar tissue.

cau·line (kô′lin, -līn), *adj.* *Bot.* of or pertaining to a stem, esp. pertaining to or arising from the upper part of a stem. [CAUL- + -INE[1]]

caulk (kôk), *v.t.* **1.** to fill or close (a seam, joint, etc.) to make watertight, airtight, etc., as in a boat. **2.** to make (a vessel, tank, window, etc.) watertight or airtight by filling the seams with some material. **3.** to drive the edges of (plating) together to prevent leakage. Also, **calk.** [late ME *caulke* < L *calc(āre)* (to) tramp = *calc-* (s. of *calx*) heel + ME *cauken* < OF *cauque(r)* (to) tread < L, as above]

caulk·er (kô′kər), *n.* **1.** a person who caulks the seams of boats or the like. **2.** a caulking tool or device. Also, **calker.**

caulo-, a combining form meaning "stalk," "stem." Also, **caul-, cauli-.** [< L *caul(is)* stalk, stem + -o-]

caus., causative.

caus·al (kô′zəl), *adj.* **1.** of, constituting, or implying a cause: *a causal force.* **2.** *Gram.* expressing a cause, as a conjunction. [< L *causāl(is)*] **—caus′al·ly,** *adv.*

cau·sal·i·ty (kô zal′i tē), *n., pl.* **-ties.** **1.** the relation of cause and effect. **2.** causal quality or agency.

cau·sa·tion (kô zā′shən), *n.* **1.** the action of causing or producing. **2.** the relation of cause to effect. **3.** anything that produces an effect; cause. [< ML *causātiōn-* (s. of *causātiō*) = *causāt(us)* caused (ptp. of *causāre;* see CAUSE, -ATE[1]) + *-iōn-* -ION] **—cau·sa′tion·al,** *adj.*

caus·a·tive (kô′zə tiv), *adj.* **1.** acting as a cause; producing (often fol. by *of*): *a causative agency; an event causative of war.* **2.** *Gram.* noting causation. The causative form of *to fall* is *to fell.* **—***n.* **3.** *Gram.* a word, esp. a verb, noting causation, as *made* in *He made me eat the apple.* [ME < L *causātīv(us)*] **—caus′a·tive·ly,** *adv.* **—caus′a·tive·ness,** *n.*

cause (kôz), *n., v.,* **caused, caus·ing.** **—***n.* **1.** a person or thing that acts, happens, or exists in such a way that some specific thing happens as a result; the producer of an effect: *You have been the cause of much anxiety. What was the cause of the accident?* **2.** the reason or motive for some human action: *This news was a cause for rejoicing.* **3.** good or sufficient reason: *to complain without cause; to be dismissed for cause.* **4.** *Law.* **a.** a ground of legal action. **b.** a case for judicial decision. **5.** any subject of discussion or debate. **6.** the ideal or goal, or the set of these, to which a person or group is dedicated: *the Socialist cause; the cause of better housing.* **7.** the general welfare of a person or group, seen as the subject of concern either to themselves or to others: *liberal support for the cause of the American Negro.* **8.** *Philos.* **a.** the end or purpose for which a thing is done or produced. **b.** *Aristotelianism.* any of the things necessary for the movement or the coming into being of a thing. **9. make common cause with,** to unite with in a joint effort; work together with for the same end. **—***v.t.* **10.** to be the cause of; bring about. [ME < L *caus(a)* reason, sake, case] **—caus′a·bil′i·ty,** *n.* **—caus′a·ble,** *adj.* **—cause′less,** *adj.* **—caus′er,** *n.*
—Syn. 1. CAUSE, OCCASION refer to the starting of effects into motion. A CAUSE is an agency, perhaps acting through a long time, or a long-standing situation, that produces an effect: *The cause of the quarrel between the two men was jealousy.* An OCCASION is an event that provides an opportunity for the effect to become evident, or perhaps promotes its becoming evident: *The occasion was the fact that one man's wages were increased.* **3.** See **reason.** **10.** effect, make.

'cause (kôz, kuz, *unstressed* kəz), *conj., adv.* *Informal.* because. [aph. var.]

cause-and-effect (kôz′ənd i fekt′), *adj.* noting a relationship between actions or events such that one or more are the result of the other or others.

cause cé·lè·bre (kôz′ sə leb′rə, -leb′; *Fr.* kōz sā leb′rə), *pl.* **causes cé·lè·bres** (kôz′ sə leb′rəz, -lebz′, kô′ziz sə-leb′rə, -leb′; *Fr.* kōz sā leb′rə). any controversy that attracts great public attention. [< F: lit., famous case]

cau·se·rie (kō′zə rē′, kô′-; *Fr.* kōzə rē′), *n., pl.* **-ries** (-rēz′; *Fr.* -rē′). **1.** a talk or chat. **2.** a short, informal essay, article, etc. [< F = *caus(er)* (to) chat (< L *causārī* to plead at law < *causa* case) + *-erie* -ERY]

cause·way (kôz′wā′), *n.* **1.** a raised road or path, as across low or wet ground. **2.** a highway. **—***v.t.* **3.** to provide with or make a causeway. [ME *cauce* < AF < ONF *caucie,* var. of *cauciee* < LL (*via*) *calciāta* (road) paved with limestone = L *calci-* (s. of *calx*) limestone + *-āta,* fem. of *-ātus* -ATE[1]; see WAY]

caus·tic (kô′stik), *adj.* **1.** severely critical or sarcastic: *a caustic remark.* **2.** capable of burning, corroding, or destroying living tissue. **—***n.* **3.** a caustic substance. [< L *caustic(us)* < Gk *kaustikós* burning, caustic = *kaust(ós)* burnt (*kaus-* (ptp. s. of *kaíein* to burn) + *-tos* ptp. suffix) + *-ikos* -IC] **—caus′ti·cal,** *adj.* **—caus′ti·cal·ly, caus′tic·ly,** *adv.* **—caus·tic·i·ty** (kô stis′i tē), **caus′tic·ness,** *n.*

caus′tic pot′ash. See **potassium hydroxide.**

caus′tic so′da. See **sodium hydroxide.**

cau·ter·ise (kô′tə rīz′), *v.t.,* **-ised, -is·ing.** *Chiefly Brit.* cauterize. **—cau′ter·i·sa′tion,** *n.*

cau·ter·ize (kô′tə rīz′), *v.t.,* **-ized, -iz·ing.** to burn with a hot iron, fire, or a caustic, esp. for curative purposes. [< LL *cautērīz(āre)* (to) brand = *cautēr-* (< Gk *kautḗr* branding iron = *kau-,* var. s. of *kaíein* to burn, + *-tēr* instrumental suffix) + *-īzāre* -IZE] **—cau′ter·i·za′tion,** *n.*

cau·ter·y (kô′tə rē), *n., pl.* **-ter·ies.** **1.** something, as a caustic substance or a hot iron, used to destroy tissue. **2.** the process of cauterizing tissue. [< L *cautēri(um)* < Gk *kautḗrion* = *kautḗr* branding iron (see CAUTERIZE) + *-ion* dim. suffix]

cau·tion (kô′shən), *n.* **1.** alertness and prudence in a hazardous situation; care; wariness. **2.** a warning against danger or evil; anything serving as a warning. **3.** *Informal.* someone or something that astonishes or causes mild apprehension: *She's a caution.* —*v.t.* **4.** to give warning to; advise or urge to take heed. —*v.i.* **5.** to warn or advise. [ME *caucion* < L *cautiōn-* (s. of *cautiō*) a taking care = *caut(us)* guarded against, ptp. of *cavēre* (*cau-* take care + *-tus* ptp. suffix) + *-iōn-* -ION] —**cau′tion·er,** *n.* —**Syn. 1.** circumspection, discretion, heed. **2.** admonition, advice, counsel. **4.** counsel, forewarn. See **warn.** —**Ant. 1.** carelessness.

cau·tion·ar·y (kô′shə ner′ē), *adj.* of the nature of or containing a warning.

cau·tious (kô′shəs), *adj.* manifesting or characterized by caution: *a cautious man.* [CAUTI(ON) + -OUS] —**cau′tious·ly,** *adv.* —**cau′tious·ness,** *n.* —**Syn.** prudent, guarded.

Cau·ver·y (kô′və rē), *n.* a river in S India, flowing SE from the Western Ghats in Mysore state through Madras state to the Bay of Bengal: sacred to the Hindus. 475 mi. long. Also, **Kaveri.**

Cav., cavalry.

cav., **1.** cavalier. **2.** cavalry.

Ca·va·fy (kä vä′fē), *n.* **Constantine,** 1868–1933, Greek poet in Egypt. Also, **Kavaphis.**

cav·al·cade (kav′əl kād′, kav′əl kād′), *n.* **1.** a procession, esp. of persons riding on horses or in horsedrawn vehicles. **2.** a pageant or pageantlike sequence: *a cavalcade of movie stars.* [< MF < early It *cavalcat(a)* horseback raid = *cavalc(are)* (to) ride (< LL *caballicāre* = *caball(us)* horse (see CAVALIER) + *-icā-* v. suffix + *-re* inf. ending) + *-ata* -ADE[1]]

cav·a·le·ro (kav′ə lâr′ō, -əl yâr′ō), *n., pl.* **-ros.** **1.** a cavalier. **2.** a caballero.

cav·a·lier (kav′ə lēr′, kav′ə lēr′), *n.* **1.** a horseman, esp. a mounted soldier; knight. **2.** a person having the manner or bearing of a courtier. **3.** a man who escorts a woman; beau. **4.** (*cap.*) an adherent of Charles I of England, esp. a courtier or soldier. —*adj.* **5.** haughty, disdainful, or supercilious: *an arrogant and cavalier attitude toward others.* **6.** offhand or unceremonious. **7.** (*cap.*) of or pertaining to the Cavaliers. —*v.i.* **8.** to behave in a cavalier manner. [< MF: horseman, knight << OPr < LL *caballāri(us)* groom = L *caball(us)* nag (< Gk *kabállēs,* perh. < Galatian Celt) + *-ārius* -ARY] —**cav′a·lier′ism,** *n.* —**cav′a·lier′ness,** *n.*

cav·a·lier·ly (kav′ə lēr′lē, kav′ə lēr′-), *adv.* **1.** in an arrogant or disdainful manner. —*adj.* **2.** haughty; arrogant.

Cav′alier po′ets, a group of English lyric poets at the court of Charles I, including Herrick, Carew, Lovelace, and Suckling.

cav·al·ry (kav′əl rē), *n., pl.* **-ries.** **1.** *Mil.* **a.** the part of a military force composed of troops that serve on horseback. **b.** mounted soldiers collectively. **c.** the motorized, armored units of a military force organized for maximum mobility. **2.** horsemen, horses, etc., collectively. [syncopated var. of *cavallery* < It *cavalleria* = *cavall(o)* horse (see CAVALIER) + *-eria* -ERY]

cav·al·ry·man (kav′əl rē mən, -man′), *n., pl.* **-men** (-mən, -men′). a member of the cavalry.

Cav·an (kav′ən), *n.* a county in Ulster, in the N Republic of Ireland. 56,594 (1961); 730 sq. mi.

cav·a·ti·na (kav′ə tē′nə; *It.* kä′vä tē′nä), *n., pl.* **-ne** (-nā; *It.* -ne). *Music.* a simple song or melody; air. [< It = *cavat(a)* song (lit., something drawn out, n. use of fem. ptp. of *cavare* < L: to hollow out; see CAVE, -ATE[1]) + *-ina* -INE[1]]

cave (kāv), *n., v.,* **caved, cav·ing.** —*n.* **1.** a hollow in the earth, esp. one opening more or less horizontally into a hill, mountain, etc. **2.** a storage cellar, esp. for wine. **3.** *Eng. Pol.* a secession, or a faction of seceders, from a political party. —*v.t.* **4.** to hollow out. **5.** **cave in, a.** to fall in; collapse. **b.** to cause to fall in or collapse. **c.** *Informal.* to yield; submit; surrender. [ME < OF < LL *cav(a)* (fem. sing.), L *cava,* neut. pl. of *cavum* hole, n. use of neut. o *cavus* (adj.) hollow] —**cave′like′,** *adj.*

ca·ve·at (kā′vē at′), *n.* **1.** *Law.* a legal notice to a court or public officer to suspend a certain proceeding until the notifier is given a hearing. **2.** any warning or caution. [< L: let him beware, 3rd pers. sing. pres. subj. of *cavēre* to take care; see CAUTION]

ca·ve·at emp·tor (kā′vē at′ emp′tôr; *Lat.* kä′we ät′ emp′tōr). the principle that the seller cannot be held responsible for the quality of his product unless guaranteed in a warranty. [< L: lit., let the buyer beware]

ca·ve·a·tor (kā′vē ā′tər), *n.* a person who files or enters a caveat.

ca·ve ca·nem (kä′we kä′nem; *Eng.* kā′vē kā′nem), *Latin.* beware of the dog.

cave′ dwell′er, a person whose home is a cave, esp. a prehistoric man.

cave·fish (kāv′fish′), *n., pl.* (*esp. collectively*) **-fish,** (*esp. referring to two or more kinds or species*) **-fish·es.** any of several fishes that live in cave waters, as species of the genus *Amblyopsis,* having no body pigment and rudimentary, functionless eyes.

cave-in (kāv′in′), *n.* a collapse, as of anything hollow: *the worst cave-in in the history of mining.*

Cav·ell (kav′əl), *n.* **Edith Louisa,** 1865–1915, English nurse: executed by the Germans in World War I.

cave′ man′, **1.** a cave dweller, esp. of the Stone Age. **2.** *Informal.* a rough, brutal man.

cav·en·dish (kav′ən dish), *n.* tobacco that has been softened, sweetened, and pressed into cakes. [presumably named after maker or handler]

Cav·en·dish (kav′ən dish), *n.* **1. Henry,** 1731–1810, English chemist and physicist. **2. William, 4th Duke of Devonshire,** 1720–64, British statesman: prime minister 1756–57.

cav·ern (kav′ərn), *n.* a cave, esp. one that is large and mostly underground. [ME *caverne* < L *cavern(a)* = *cav(us)* hollow + *-erna,* as in *cisterna* CISTERN]

cav·ern·ous (kav′ər nəs), *adj.* **1.** containing caverns. **2.** deep-set: *cavernous eyes.* **3.** hollow and deep-sounding: *a cavernous voice.* **4.** full of small cavities; porous. **5.** being, resembling, or suggestive of a cavern. [late ME < L *cavernōs(us)*] —**cav′ern·ous·ly,** *adv.*

ca·vet·to (kə vet′ō; *It.* kä vet′tô), *n., pl.* **-ti** (-tē), **-tos.** *Archit.* a concave molding the outline of which is a quarter circle. See illus. at **molding.** [< It = *cav(o)* (< L *cavus* or *cavum* hollow place; see CAVE) + *-etto* -ET]

cav·i·ar (kav′ē är′, kav′ē är′), *n.* the roe of sturgeon, esp. the beluga, usually served as an appetizer. Also, **cav′i·are′.** [appar. back formation from *caviarie* (taken, perh. rightly, as *caviar* + pl. ending, L or It *-i*) < ?; cf. It *caviaro,* Turk *khavyar*]

ca·vie (kā′vē), *n.* *Scot.* a hen coop; a cage for fowls. [< D or Flem *kavie* (now obs.) << L *cavea* birdcage, cavity = *cav(us)* hollow + *-ea* n. suffix, fem. of *-eus* -EOUS]

cav·il (kav′əl), *v.,* **-iled, -il·ing** or (*esp. Brit.*) **-illed, -il·ling,** *n.* —*v.i.* **1.** to raise irritating and trivial objections; find fault unnecessarily (usually fol. by *at* or *about*). —*v.t.* **2.** to oppose by inconsequential, frivolous, or sham objections. —*n.* **3.** a trivial and annoying objection. **4.** the raising of such objections. [< L *cavill(ārī)* (to) jeer, scoff, quibble = *cavill(a)* scoffing + *-ā-* thematic vowel + *-rī* inf. ending] —**cav′il·er;** *esp. Brit.,* **cav′il·ler,** *n.* —**cav′il·ing·ly;** *esp. Brit.,* **cav′il·ling·ly,** *adv.* —**Syn. 1.** carp, complain. criticize.

cav·i·ta·tion (kav′i tā′shən), *n.* the rapid formation and collapse of vapor pockets in a flowing liquid in regions of very low pressure. [CAVIT(Y) + -ATION]

Ca·vi·te (kə vē′tē, -tā; *Sp.* kä vē′te), *n.* a seaport on S Luzon, in the N Philippines, on Manila Bay: naval base. 64,700 (est. 1965).

cav·i·ty (kav′i tē), *n., pl.* **-ties.** **1.** any hollow place: *a cavity in the earth.* **2.** *Anat.* a hollow space within the body, an organ, a bone, etc. **3.** *Dentistry.* a hollow place in a tooth structure, commonly caused by decay. [< MF *cavite* < LL *cavit(ās)* hollowness = L *cav(us)* hollow + *-itās* -ITY] —**cav′i·tied,** *adj.*

ca·vort (kə vôrt′), *v.i.* to caper about [earlier *cavault,* perh. CUR(VET) + VAULT[2]] —**ca·vort′er,** *n.*

Ca·vour (kä vōōr′), *n.* **Ca·mil·lo Ben·so di** (kä mēl′lô ben′sô dē), 1810–61, Italian statesman: leader in the unification of Italy.

CAVU, *Aeron.* ceiling and visibility unlimited. Also, **cavu.**

ca·vy (kā′vē), *n., pl.* **-vies.** any of several short-tailed or tailless South American rodents of the family *Caviidae,* as the guinea pig, capybara, or agouti. [< NL *Cavi(a)* name of the genus < Carib *cabiai*]

caw (kô), *n.* **1.** the cry of the crow, raven, etc. —*v.i.* **2.** to utter this cry or a similar sound. [imit.]

Cawn·pore (kôn′pōr′, -pôr′), *n.* a city in S Uttar Pradesh, in NE India on the Ganges River. 895,106 (1961). Also, **Cawn·pur** (kôn′pŏŏr′). Indian, **Kanpur.**

Ca·xi·as do Sul (kä shē′əs dŏŏ sōōl′), a city in S Brazil. 69,269 (1960).

Cax·ton (kak′stən), *n.* **1. William,** 1422?–91, English printer, translator, and author: established first printing press in England 1476. **2.** *Bibliog.* any one of the books printed by Caxton, all of which are in black letter. **3.** *Print.* a kind of type imitating Caxton's black letter. —**Cax·to·ni·an** (kak stō′nē ən), *adj.*

cay (kā, kē), *n.* a small low island; key. [< Sp *cay(o)*; see KEY[2]]

cay·enne (kī en′, kā-), *n.* a hot condiment composed of the ground pods and seeds of the pepper *Capsicum frutescens longum.* Also called **cayenne′ pep′per.** [short for *cayenne pepper,* formerly *cayan* < Tupi *kyinha,* but long assoc. with CAYENNE] —**cay·enned′,** *adj.*

Cay·enne (kī en′, kā-), *n.* a seaport in and the capital of French Guiana. 18,635 (1961).

Cayes (kā; *Fr.* KA′y^{ə}), *n.* **Les.** See **Les Cayes.**

Cay·ley (kā′lē), *n.* **Arthur,** 1821–95, English mathematician. —**Cay′ley·an,** *adj.*

cay·man (kā′mən), *n., pl.* **-mans.** caiman.

Cay·man′ Is′lands (kī män′), three islands in the West Indies, NW of Jamaica: dependencies of Jamaica. 8803 (est. 1960); 104 sq. mi.

Ca·yu·ga (kā yōō′gə, kī-), *n., pl.* **-gas,** (*esp. collectively*) **-ga.** a member of a tribe of North American Indians, the smallest tribe of the Iroquois Confederacy.

Cayu′ga Lake′, a lake in central New York: one of the Finger Lakes. 40 mi. long.

cay·use (kī yōōs′, kī′ōōs), *n.* *Western U.S.* an Indian pony. [named after the *Cayuse* American Indian tribe, now living in Oregon]

CB, **1.** See **citizens band** **2.** *Mil.* construction battalion.

Cb, *Chem.* columbium.

C.B., *Brit.* Companion of the Bath.

C battery, *Electronics.* an electric battery for supplying a constant voltage bias to a control electrode of a vacuum tube. Cf. **A battery, B battery.**

CBC, Canadian Broadcasting Corporation.

C.B.E., Commander of the Order of the British Empire.

CC, See **carbon copy** (def. 1).

cc, **1.** See **carbon copy** (def. 1). **2.** cubic centimeter.

cc., **1.** chapters. **2.** cubic centimeter. Also, **c.c.**

C.C., **1.** cashier's check. **2.** company commander. Also, **c.c.**

C.C.A., **1.** Chief Clerk of the Admiralty. **2.** Circuit Court of Appeals. **3.** County Court of Appeals.

CCC, Civilian Conservation Corps.

C clef, *Music.* a movable clef that, according to its position, locates middle C on a specific line of the staff.

Cd, *Chem.* cadmium.

cd, candela; candelas.

cd., cord; cords. Also, **cd**

C/D, certificate of deposit.

CD, **1.** certificate of deposit. **2.** Civil Defense. **3.** compact disk. Also, **C.D.**

c.d., cash discount.

Cdr., Commander. Also, **CDR**

Ce, *Chem.* cerium.

C Clefs

-ce, a multiplicative suffix occurring in *once, twice, thrice.* [ME, OE *-es* adv. suffix, orig. gen. sing. ending; see -s[1]]

C.E., **1.** Civil Engineer. **2.** See **Christian Era.**

CEA, Council of Economic Advisers.

Ce·a·rá (*Port.* se/ä rä/), *n.* Fortaleza.

cease (sēs), *v.*, **ceased, ceas·ing,** *n.* —*v.i.* **1.** to stop; discontinue. **2.** to come to an end: *At last the war has ceased.* **3.** *Obs.* to pass away; die out. —*v.t.* **4.** to put a stop or end to; discontinue. —*n.* **5.** cessation. [ME *ces(s)e(n)* < OF *cesse(r)* < L *cessāre* to leave off = *cess(us)* withdrawn, gone (ptp. of *cēdere;* see CEDE) + *-āre* inf. ending] —**Syn. 2.** terminate, end. —**Ant. 1.** begin.

cease-fire (sēs/fīər/), *n.* **1.** a cessation of hostilities; truce. **2.** *Mil.* an order issued for a cease-fire.

cease·less (sēs/lis), *adj.* without stop or pause; unending; incessant. —**cease/less·ly,** *adv.* —**cease/less·ness,** *n.*

Ce·bú (*Sp.* se bo͞o/), *n.* **1.** an island in the central Philippines. 1,586,000 (est. 1965); 1703 sq. mi. **2.** a seaport on this island. 296,000 (est. 1965).

Če·chy (che/KHi), *n.* Czech name of **Bohemia.**

Cec·il (ses/əl), *n.* **1.** (**Edgar Al·ger·non**) **Robert** (al/jər nən) (*1st Viscount Cecil of Chelwood*), 1864–1958, British statesman: Nobel peace prize 1937. **2. William** (*1st Baron Burghley* or *Burleigh*), 1520–98, British statesman: adviser to Elizabeth I.

Ce·cil·ia (si sēl/yə), *n.* **Saint,** died A.D. 230?, Roman martyr: patron saint of music.

Ce·cro/pi·a moth/ (si krō/pē ə), (*sometimes l.c.*) a large, North American silkworm moth, *Hyalophora cecropia.* Also called **Ce·cro/pi·a.** [< NL *Cecropia* name of the genus < L: fem. of *Cecropius* pertaining to CECROPS]

Ce·crops (sē/krops), *n.* *Class. Myth.* the founder and first king of Attica, portrayed as half man, half dragon.

ce·cum (sē/kəm), *n., pl.* **-ca** (-kə). *Anat., Zool.* a cul-de-sac, esp. that in which the large intestine begins. Also, **caecum.** [short for L *intestinum caecum* blind gut] —**ce/cal,** *adj.*

ce·dar (sē/dər), *n.* **1.** any of several Old World, coniferous trees of the genus *Cedrus,* as the cedar of Lebanon, *C. Libani.* **2.** any of various junipers, as the red cedar, *Juniperus virginiana.* **3.** any of various other coniferous trees. Cf. **white cedar. 4.** any of several meliaceous trees of the genus *Cedrela,* as the Spanish cedar. **5.** the wood of any of these trees. [ME *cedir,* etc., OE *ceder* < L *cedr(us)* < Gk *kédros;* r. ME *cedre* < OF < L, as above]

ce/dar chest/, a chest made of cedar for storing fur coats, woolen clothing, etc., esp. to prevent insect damage.

Ce/dar Falls/, a city in central Iowa. 29,597 (1970).

ce·darn (sē/dərn), *adj.* *Literary.* of cedar trees. [CEDAR + -(E)N[2]]

ce/dar of Leb/anon, a cedar, *Cedrus Libani,* of Asia Minor, having wide, spreading branches.

Ce/dar Rap/ids, a city in E Iowa. 110,642 (1970).

ce/dar wax/wing, a North American waxwing, *Bombycilla cedorum,* having yellowish-brown plumage. Also called **ce/dar bird/.**

cede (sēd), *v.t.,* **ced·ed, ced·ing.** to yield or formally resign and surrender to another; make over, as by treaty. [< L *cēde(re)* (to) go, yield] —**ced/er,** *n.* —**Syn.** relinquish, abandon; grant, transfer, convey. —**Ant.** retain.

ce·dil·la (si dil/ə), *n.* a mark (̧) placed under a consonant letter, as under *c* in French, Portuguese, and formerly in Spanish, to indicate that it is pronounced (s), or under *c* and *s* in Turkish to indicate that they are pronounced, respectively, (ch) and (sh). [< Sp, var. sp. of *zedilla* little *z* = *zed(a)* ZED + *-illa* dim. suffix; mark so called from its orig. form]

ced·u·la (sej/ə lə), *n.* **1.** (in Spanish-speaking countries) any of various orders, certificates, or the like. **2.** (in the Philippines) **a.** a personal registration tax certificate. **b.** the tax itself. Also, **cé·du·la** (sej/ə lə; *Sp.* the/tho͞o lä/, se/-). [< Sp; see SCHEDULE]

cei·ba (sā/bə *or, for 2,* sī/-; *Sp.* thā/vä, sā/-), *n., pl.* **-bas** (-bəz; *Sp.* -väs). **1.** the silk-cotton tree, *Ceiba pentandra.* **2.** silk cotton; kapok. [< Sp < Taino *ceyba*]

ceil (sēl), *v.t.* to overlay (the interior upper surface of a building or room) with wood or plaster so as to provide with a ceiling. [ME *cele(n)* (to) drape, screen, line, perh. << L *caelāre* to engrave or L *caelum* heaven, vault (of the sky)]

ceil·er (sē/lər), *n.* *U.S. Shipbuilding.* a carpenter who applies ceiling to the frames of a wooden vessel.

ceil·ing (sē/ling), *n.* **1.** the overhead interior lining of a room. **2.** a lining applied for structural reasons to a framework. **3.** the top limit, as on the production of goods. **4.** *Aeron.* **a.** the maximum altitude from which the earth can be seen on a particular day. **b.** the maximum altitude to which a particular aircraft can rise under specified conditions. **5.** *Meteorol.* the height of the lowest layer of clouds or other obscuring phenomena in the atmosphere. **6.** the interior surfacing attached to the frames of a wooden vessel. **7.** the act or work of one who ceils. —**ceil/inged,** *adj.*

ceil·om·e·ter (sē lom/i tər, si-), *n.* *Meteorol.* an automatic device for measuring and recording the height of clouds by triangulation. [CEIL(ING) + -O- + -METER]

cel·a·don (sel/ə don/, -dən), *n.* any of several Chinese porcelains having a translucent, pale green glaze. [after *Céladon,* name of a character in *L'Astrée,* a tale by H. d'Urfé (1568–1625), French writer]

Ce·lae·no (sə lē/nō), *n.* *Class. Myth.* **1.** one of the Pleiades. **2.** (in the *Aeneid*) one of the Harpies.

cel·an·dine (sel/ən dīn/), *n.* **1.** a papaveraceous plant, *Chelidonium majus,* having yellow flowers. **2.** a ranunculaceous plant, *Ranunculus Ficaria,* having yellow flowers. [late ME *selandyne,* nasalized var. of ME *celydon* < L *chelidon(ia),* n. use of fem. of *chelidonius* < Gk *chelidónios* = *chelidoni-* (s. of *chelidṓn*) the swallow + *-os* adj. suffix]

-cele[1], a learned borrowing from Greek meaning "tumor," used in the formation of compound words: *variocele.* [comb. form repr. Gk *kḗlē* a tumor; akin to OE *hēala* hydrocele]

-cele[2], var. of **-coele:** *blastocele.*

ce·leb (sə leb/), *n.* *Slang.* a celebrity. [by shortening]

Cel·e·bes (sel/ə bēz/; *Du.* se lā/bes), *n.* an island in E Indonesia. 6,571,000 with adjacent islands (est. 1961); 72,986 sq. mi. Indonesian, **Sulawesi.** —**Cel·e·be·sian** (sel/ə bē/zhən), *adj.*

cel·e·brant (sel/ə brənt), *n.* **1.** the officiating priest in the celebration of the Eucharist. **2.** a participant in a public religious rite. **3.** a participant in any celebration. **4.** a person who praises or extols a person or thing. [< L *celebrant-* (s. of *celebrāns* solemnizing, prp. of *celebrāre*) = *celebr-* (see CELEBRATE) + *-ant-* -ANT]

cel·e·brate (sel/ə brāt/), *v.,* **-brat·ed, -brat·ing.** —*v.t.* **1.** to observe (a day) or commemorate (an event) with ceremonies or festivities. **2.** to make known publicly; proclaim. **3.** to praise widely or to present to widespread and favorable public notice, as through newspapers, novels, etc. **4.** to perform with appropriate rites and ceremonies; solemnize. —*v.i.* **5.** to observe a day or commemorate an event with ceremonies or festivities. **6.** to perform a religious ceremony. [< L *celebrāt(us)* solemnized, celebrated, honored (ptp. of *celebrāre*) = *celebr-* (s. of *celeber*) often repeated, famous + *-ātus* -ATE[1]] —**cel/e·bra/tive,** *adj.* —**cel/e·bra/tor,** *n.* —**Syn. 1.** commemorate, honor, solemnize. **3.** laud, glorify.

cel·e·brat·ed (sel/ə brā/tid), *adj.* famous; renowned; well-known. —**cel/e·brat/ed·ness,** *n.* —**Syn.** See **famous.**

cel·e·bra·tion (sel/ə brā/shən), *n.* **1.** the act of celebrating. **2.** that which is done to celebrate anything. [< L *celebrātiōn-* (s. of *celebrātiō*) big assembly]

ce·leb·ri·ty (sə leb/ri tē), *n., pl.* **-ties** for 1. **1.** a famous or well-known person. **2.** fame; renown. [< L *celebritās* multitude, fame, festal celebration = *celebr-* (s. of *celeber*) often repeated, famous + *-itās* -ITY]

ce·ler·i·ac (sə ler/ē ak/, -lēr-/), *n.* a variety of celery, *Apium graveolens rapaceum,* having a large, edible, turniplike root. [CELERY + -AC]

ce·ler·i·ty (sə ler/i tē), *n.* swiftness; speed. [ME *celerite* < MF < L *celeritāt-* (s. of *celeritās*) = *celer* swift + *-itāt-* -ITY] —**Syn.** alacrity, dispatch. See **speed.**

cel·er·y (sel/ə rē), *n.* a plant, *Apium graveolens,* of the parsley family. [< F *céleri* < It *seleri,* pl. of *selero* << Gk *sélin(on)* parsley]

ce·les·ta (sə les/tə), *n.* *Music.* a keyboard instrument consisting principally of a set of graduated steel plates struck with hammers. [< F *célest(a),* pseudo-Italian alter. of *céleste,* lit., heavenly]

Celesta

ce·les·tial (sə les/chəl), *adj.* **1.** pertaining to the spiritual heaven; heavenly; divine: *celestial bliss.* **2.** pertaining to the sky or visible heaven. **3.** (*cap.*) of or pertaining to the former Chinese Empire or the Chinese people. —*n.* **4.** an inhabitant of heaven. **5.** (*cap.*) a citizen of the Celestial Empire. [ME < ML *cēlestiāl(is)* = L *caelesti(s)* heavenly (*cael(um)* heaven, sky + *-estis* adj. suffix) + *-ālis* -AL[1]] —**ce·les/tial·ly,** *adv.*

Celes/tial Em/pire, the former Chinese Empire.

celes/tial equa/tor, *Astron., Navig.* the great circle of the celestial sphere, lying in the same plane as the earth's equator. Also called **equator, equinoctial, equinoctial line.**

celes/tial globe/. See under **globe** (def. 3).

celes/tial guid/ance, *Rocketry.* a guidance system in a missile or spacecraft that automatically takes periodic fixes on celestial bodies.

celes/tial hori/zon, *Astron.* See under **horizon** (def. 2b).

celes/tial lat/itude, *Astron.* the angular distance of a point on the celestial sphere from the ecliptic.

celes/tial lon/gitude, *Astron.* the angular distance eastward of a celestial point from the great circle perpendicular to the ecliptic at the vernal equinox, measured through 360° eastward parallel to the ecliptic.

celes/tial mechan/ics, the branch of astronomy that deals with the application of the laws of dynamics and gravitation to the motions of heavenly bodies.

celes/tial naviga/tion, navigation by observing the position of heavenly bodies. Also called **astronavigation, celo-navigation.**

celes/tial pole/, *Astron.* each of the two points in which the extended axis of the earth cuts the celestial sphere and around which the stars seem to revolve. Also called **pole.**

celes/tial sphere/, the imaginary, infinite, spherical shell formed by the sky.

Cel·es·tine I (sel/i stīn/; si les/tin, -tīn), **Saint,** died A.D. 432, Italian ecclesiastic: pope 422–432.

Celestine II, (*Guido di Castello*), fl. 12th century, Italian ecclesiastic: pope 1143–44.

Celestine III, (*Giacinto Bobone*), died 1198, Italian ecclesiastic: pope 1191–98.

Celestine IV, (*Godfrey Castiglione*), died 1241, Italian ecclesiastic: pope 1241.

Celestine V, **Saint** (*Pietro di Murrone* or *Morone*), 1215–96, Italian ascetic: pope 1294.

cel·es·tite (sel/i stīt/), *n.* a mineral, strontium sulfate, $SrSO_4$, the principal ore of strontium. Also, **cel·es·tine** (sel/i stin, -stīn/). [*celest(ine)* celestite (< G *Zölestin* < L *coelest(is),* var. of *caelestis* CELESTIAL + G *-in* -IN[2]) + -ITE[1]]

celi-, var. of **coeli-:** *celiac.*

ce·li·ac (sē/lē ak/), *adj.* *Anat.* of, pertaining to, or located in the cavity of the abdomen. Also, **coeliac.** [< L *coeliac(us)* < Gk *koiliakós* of the belly]

ce/liac disease/, *Pathol.* a chronic, nutritional disturbance in young children, characterized by marked abdominal distention, malnutrition, difficulty in digesting fat, and diarrhea.

cel·i·ba·cy (sel/ə bə sē; *esp. Brit.* sə lib/ə sē), *n.* **1.** state of being unmarried. **2.** abstention by vow from marriage: *the celibacy of priests.* **3.** abstention from sexual relations. [< L *caelibā(tus)* celibacy (see CELIBATE) + -CY]

cel·i·bate (sel/ə bit, -bāt/), *n.* **1.** a person who remains unmarried, esp. for religious reasons. **2.** a person who abstains from sexual relations. —*adj.* **3.** not married. **4.** pertaining to sexual abstention or a religious vow not to marry. [< L *caelib-* (s. of *caelebs* single) + -ATE[1]]

Cé·line (sā lēn/), *n.* **Louis-Fer·di·nand** (lwē fer dē näN/), (*Louis F. Destouches*), 1894–1961, French novelist.

celio-, var. of **coelio-.**

cell (sel), *n.* **1.** a small room, as in a convent or prison. **2.** any of various small compartments or bounded areas forming part of a whole. **3.** a small group acting as a unit within a larger organization: *a local cell of the Communist party.* **4.**

Biol. a usually microscopic plant or animal structure containing nuclear and cytoplasmic material enclosed by a semipermeable membrane and, in plants, a cell wall; the structural unit of plant and animal life. **5.** *Entomol.* one of the areas into which the wing of an insect is divided by the veins. **6.** *Bot.* the pollen sac of an anther. **7.** *Elect.* a device that generates electricity, usually consisting of two different conducting substances placed in an electrolyte. **8.** *Physical Chem.* a device for producing electrolysis, consisting essentially of the electrolyte, its container, and the electrodes

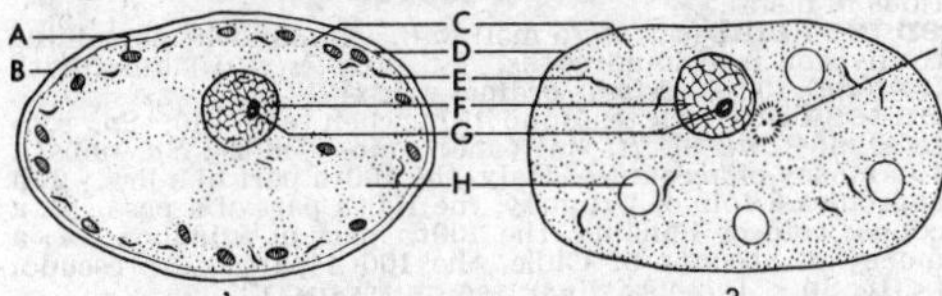

Cells (def. 4); 1, Plant cell; 2, Animal cell; A, Plastid; B, Cell wall; C, Cytoplasm; D, Cell membrane; E, Mitochondrion; F, Nucleus; G, Nucleolus; H, Vacuole; I, Centrosome

(electrolytic cell). **9.** *Eccles.* a monastery or nunnery that is part of a larger religious house. [ME *celle* < ML *cell(a)* monastic cell, L: room; see CELLA] —**cell′-like′,** *adj.*

cel·la (sel′ə), *n., pl.* **cel·lae** (sel′ē). *Archit.* (in a classical temple) the enclosed area containing a statue of a deity. Also called **naos.** [< L: storeroom, shrine, akin to *cēlāre* to hide]

cel·lar (sel′ər), *n.* **1.** a room, or set of rooms, wholly or partly underground and usually beneath a building. **2.** an underground room or story. **3.** See **wine cellar. 4.** *Sports.* the lowest position among a group ranked in order of games won. —*v.t.* **5.** to place or store in a cellar. [< L *cellār(ium)* pantry, n. use of neut. of *cellārius* pertaining to a storeroom; see CELLA, -ARY; r. ME *celer* < AF < L, as above]

cel·lar·age (sel′ər ij), *n.* cellar space.

cel·lar·er (sel′ər ər), *n.* the steward of a monastery. [< LL *cellārār(ius)* = L *cellār(ium)* CELLAR + *-ārius* -ER[2]; r. ME *celerer* < AF < LL, as above]

cel·lar·et (sel′ə ret′), *n.* a cabinet or stand for wine bottles. Also, **cel′lar·ette′.**

cell·block (sel′blok′), *n.* a unit of a prison consisting of a number of cells.

Cel·li·ni (chə lē′nē; *It.* chel lē′nē), *n.* **Ben·ve·nu·to** (ben′və no͞o′tō; *It.* ben′ve no͞o′tô), 1500–71, Italian sculptor, metalsmith, and writer.

cel·list (chel′ist), *n.* a person who plays the cello. Also, **′cel′list.** Also called **violoncellist.**

cell′ mem′brane, *Biol.* the semipermeable membrane enclosing the protoplasmic material of a cell.

cel·lo (chel′ō), *n., pl.* **-los.** the third largest member of the violin family. Also, **′cel′lo.** Also called **violoncello.** [short for VIOLONCELLO]

Cello

cel·loi·din (sə loi′din), *n.* *Microscopy.* a concentrated form of pyroxylin used to embed tissues for cutting and microscopic examination. [CELL(ULOSE) + -OID + -IN[2]]

cel·lo·phane (sel′ə fān′), *n.* **1.** a transparent, paperlike product of viscose. —*adj.* **2.** of, made of, or resembling cellophane. [CELL(UL)O(SE) + -PHANE, formerly a trademark]

cel·lu·lar (sel′yə lər), *adj.* pertaining to or characterized by cellules or cells, esp. minute compartments or cavities. [< NL *cellulār(is)*] —**cel·lu·lar·i·ty** (sel′yə lar′i tē), *n.* —**cel′lu·lar·ly,** *adv.*

cel·lule (sel′yo͞ol), *n.* a minute cell. [< L *cellul(a)* small room. See CELL, -ULE]

cel·lu·li·tis (sel′yə lī′tis), *n.* *Pathol.* inflammation of cellular tissue. [< NL = *cellul(a)* (see CELLULE) + *-itis* -ITIS]

Cel·lu·loid (sel′yə loid′), *n.* *Trademark.* a substance consisting essentially of soluble guncotton and camphor, used for motion-picture and x-ray films, fountain pens, etc.

cel·lu·lose (sel′yə lōs′), *n.* *Biochem.* an inert carbohydrate, $(C_6H_{10}O_5)_n$, the chief constituent of the cell walls of plants, wood, cotton, hemp, paper, etc. [< NL *cellul(a)* live cell (see CELLULE) + -OSE[2]] —**cel·lu·lo·sic** (sel′yə lō′sik), *adj., n.* —**cel·lu·los·i·ty** (sel′yə los′i tē), *n.*

cel′lulose ac′etate, *Chem.* any of a group of acetic esters of cellulose, used to make yarns, textiles, etc.

cel′lulose ni′trate, *Chem.* any of a group of nitric esters of cellulose, used for lacquers and explosives. Also called **nitrocellulose.**

cel·lu·lous (sel′yə ləs), *adj.* full or consisting of cells. [< NL *cellulōs(us).* See CELLULE, -OUS]

cell′ wall′, *Biol.* the cellulose layer around a plant cell.

ce·lom (sē′ləm), *n.* coelom.

ce·lo-nav·i·ga·tion (sē′lō nav′ə gā′shən, sel′ō-), *n.* See **celestial navigation.** [CEL(ESTIAL) + -O- + NAVIGATION]

Cels., Celsius (centigrade).

Cel·si·us (sel′sē əs, -shē-; *for 1 also Swed.* sel′sē o͞os′), *n.* **1. An·ders** (än′dəsh), 1701–44, Swedish astronomer: devised centigrade scale of temperature. —*adj.* **2.** centigrade (def. 2).

celt (selt), *n.* *Archaeol.* a prehistoric ax of stone or metal. [< LL **celt(is)* chisel (found only in the abl. case *celte*)]

Celt (selt, kelt), *n.* a member of an Indo-European people now represented chiefly by the Irish, Gaels, Welsh, and Bretons. Also, **kelt.**

Celt, Celtic (def. 1).

Celt., Celtic.

Celt·ic (sel′tik, kel′-), *n.* **1.** a branch of the Indo-European family of languages including esp. Irish, Scots Gaelic, Welsh, and Breton, which survive now in Ireland, the Scottish Highlands, Wales, and Brittany. *Abbr.:* Celt, Celt. —*adj.* **2.** of the Celts or their language. —**Cel′ti·cal·ly,** *adv.*

Celt′ic cross′, a cross like a Latin cross with a ring intersecting each segment of the shaft and a crossbar at a point equidistant from their junction. See illus. at **cross.**

Celt·i·cism (sel′ti siz′əm, kel′-), *n.* a Celtic custom or usage. —**Celt′i·cist, Celt′ist,** *n.*

Celto-, a combining form of **Celt** or **Celtic.**

cem·ba·lo (chem′bə lō′), *n., pl.* **-li** (-lē′), **-los.** *Music.* harpsichord. [< It *(clavi)cembalo* < L *cymbalum* CYMBAL] —**cem′ba·list,** *n.*

ce·ment (si ment′), *n.* **1.** any of various sticky substances that harden upon drying, used as adhesives. **2.** any of various calcined mixtures of clay and limestone, usually combined with an aggregate to form concrete, that are used as building material. **3.** anything that binds or unites. **4.** *Dentistry.* a hardening, adhesive, plastic substance, used in the repair of teeth. —*v.t.* **5.** to unite by or as by cement. **6.** to coat or cover with cement. —*v.i.* **7.** to become cemented; join together or unite; cohere. [< L *cēment(um),* var. of *caementum* (sing. of *caementa* unprocessed cuttings from the quarry, i.e., rough stone and chips), var. of **caedimentum* = *caedi-* (s. of *caedere* to cut) + *-mentum* -MENT; r. ME *cyment* < OF *ciment*] —**ce·ment′er,** *n.*

ce·men·ta·tion (sē′mən tā′shən, -men-, sem′ən-), *n.* **1.** act, process, or result of cementing. **2.** *Metall.* the heating of two substances in contact in order to effect some change in one of them, esp., the formation of steel by heating iron in powdered charcoal.

ce·ment·ite (si men′tīt), *n.* *Metall.* a carbide, Fe_3C, found as a constituent of steel and cast iron, sometimes having part of its iron replaced by other metals, as manganese.

ce·men·tum (si men′təm), *n.* *Dentistry.* the bonelike tissue that forms the outer surface of the root of the tooth. [< L, var. of *caementum* rough stone]

cem·e·ter·y (sem′i ter′ē), *n., pl.* **-ter·ies.** an area set apart for or containing graves or tombs, esp. one that is not a churchyard; a graveyard. [< LL *coemētēri(um)* < Gk *koimētērion* a sleeping place = *koimē-* (var. s. of *koimân* to put to sleep) + *-tērion* suffix of locality] —**cem·e·te·ri·al** (sem′i tēr′ē əl), *adj.*

cen., **1.** central. **2.** century.

cen·a·cle (sen′ə kəl), *n.* the room where the Last Supper took place. [< F *cénacle* < LL *cēnacul(um),* dim. of L *cēna* dinner, meal]

Cen·ci (chen′chē), *n.* **Be·a·tri·ce** (be′ä trē′che), 1577–1599, Italian parricide whose life is the subject of various novels and poems.

-cene, var. of **ceno-**[1] as final element of a compound word: *Pleistocene.*

ceno-[1], a learned borrowing from Greek meaning "new," "recent," used in the formation of compound words: *cenogenesis.* [comb. form repr. Gk *kainós*]

ceno-[2], a learned borrowing from Greek meaning "common," used in the formation of compound words: *cenobite.* Also, **coeno-.** [< Gk *koino-,* comb. form of *koinós*]

ce·no·bite (sē′nə bīt′, sen′ə-), *n.* a member of a religious order living in a convent or community. Also, **coenobite.** [< LL *coenobīt(a)* = *coenob-* (< Gk *koinóbios* (adj.) conventual, living together = *koino-* CENO-[2] + *bi-* BI-[2] + *-os* adj. suffix) + *-īta* -ITE[1]] —**ce·no·bit·ic** (sē′nə bit′ik, sen′ə-), **ce′no·bit′i·cal,** *adj.*

ce·no·gen·e·sis (sē′nə jen′i sis, sen′ə-), *n.* *Biol.* development of an individual that does not repeat the phylogeny of its race, stock, or group (opposed to *palingenesis*). —**ce·no·ge·net·ic** (sē′nə jə net′ik, sen′ə-), *adj.* —**ce′no·ge·net′i·cal·ly,** *adv.*

cen·o·taph (sen′ə taf′, -täf′), *n.* a monument erected in memory of a deceased person whose body is buried elsewhere. [< L *cenotaph(ium)* < Gk *kenotáphion* = *kenó(s)* empty + *-taphion* (*táph(os)* tomb + *-ion* dim. suffix)] —**ceno·taph·ic** (sen′ə taf′ik), *adj.*

Ce·no·zo·ic (sē′nə zō′ik, sen′ə-), *Geol.* —*adj.* **1.** noting or pertaining to the present era, beginning 70,000,000 years ago and characterized by the appearance of mammals. —*n.* **2.** the Cenozoic era or group of systems. [CENO-[1] + ZO(O)- + -IC]

cense (sens), *v.t.,* **censed, cens·ing.** to perfume with incense. [aph. var. of INCENSE[1]]

cen·ser (sen′sər), *n.* a container in which incense is burned. [ME < AF, aph. var. of *ensenser* < ML *incensār(ium).* See INCENSE[1], -ER[1]]

Censer

cen·sor (sen′sər), *n.* **1.** an official who examines books, plays, etc., for the purpose of suppressing parts deemed objectionable on moral, political, military, or other grounds. **2.** any person who supervises the manners or morality of others. **3.** an adverse critic; faultfinder. **4.** (in the ancient Roman republic) one of two officials who kept the census, awarded public contracts, and supervised manners and morals. —*v.t.* **5.** to examine and act upon as a censor. **6.** to delete (a word or passage of text) in one's capacity as a censor. [< L = *cēns(ēre)* (to) assess, estimate, value, rate + *-or* -OR[2]] —**cen′sor·a·ble,** *adj.* —**cen·so·ri·al** (sen sōr′ē əl, -sôr′-), *adj.*

cen·so·ri·ous (sen sōr′ē əs, -sôr′-), *adj.* severely critical; faultfinding. [< L *censōrius* of a censor, hence rigid, severe = *censōr-* (s. of *censor*) CENSOR + *-ius* -IOUS] —**cen·so′ri·ous·ly,** *adv.* —**cen·so′ri·ous·ness,** *n.*

cen·sor·ship (sen′sər ship′), *n.* **1.** act of censoring. **2.** the office or power of a censor.

cen·sur·a·ble (sen′shər ə bəl), *adj.* deserving censure. —**cen′sur·a·ble·ness,** *n.* —**cen′sur·a·bly,** *adv.*

cen·sure (sen′shər), *n., v.,* **-sured, -sur·ing.** —*n.* **1.** strong or vehement expression of disapproval. —*v.t.* **2.** to criticize or reproach in a harsh or vehement manner. —*v.i.* **3.** to give censure, adverse criticism, or blame. [< L *censūr(a)* censor's office, hence judgment = *cens(or)* CENSOR + *-ūra* -URE] —**cen′sur·er,** *n.* —**Syn. 1.** condemnation, rebuke, reprimand. See **abuse. 2.** rebuke, reprimand. See **blame.** —**Ant. 1–3.** praise.

cen·sus (sen′səs), *n., pl.* **-sus·es.** **1.** an official enumeration of the population, with details as to age, sex, occupation, etc. **2.** (in ancient Rome) the registration of citizens and their property. [< L: a listing and property assessment of the citizens, n. use of *census*, ptp. of *cēnsēre* to assess]

cent (sent), *n.* **1.** a bronze coin of the U.S., the 100th part of a U.S. dollar. **2.** the 100th part of the monetary units of various other nations, as Australia, Canada, Ceylon, Hong Kong, the Netherlands, New Zealand, and South Africa. **3.** sen[3]. [< L *cent(ēsimus)* hundredth (by shortening) = *cent(um)* 100 + *-ēsimus* ordinal suffix]

Centaur

cent-, var. of **centi-** before a vowel: *centare.*

cent., **1.** centigrade. **2.** central. **3.** centum. **4.** century.

cen·tal (sen′tᵊl), *n. Chiefly Brit.* a hundredweight of 100 pounds. [< L *cent(um* 100 + QUINT)AL]

cen·tare (sen′târ; *Fr.* säɴ tar′), *n., pl.* **-tares** (-târz; *Fr.* -tar′). centiare.

cen·taur (sen′tôr), *n.* **1.** *Class. Myth.* one of a race of creatures having the head, trunk, and arms of a man, and the body and legs of a horse. **2.** (*cap.*) *Astron.* the constellation Centaurus. [OE < L *centaur(us)* < Gk *kéntauros*]

Cen·tau·rus (sen tôr′əs), *n., gen.* **-tau·ri** (-tôr′ī). *Astron.* the Centaur, a southern constellation between Lupus and Vela. [< L]

cen·tau·ry (sen′tô rē), *n., pl.* **-ries.** **1.** either of two Old World, gentianaceous herbs, *Chlora perfoliata* or *Centaurium umbellatum* (*Erythraea Centaurium*), having medicinal properties. **2.** any plant of the genus *Centaurium* (*Erythraea*). **3.** any of certain other plants, as those of the gentianaceous genus *Sabatia* (**Amer′ican cen′taury**). [OE *centaurie* < ML *centauria*, appar. < Gk *kentaúria*, neut. pl. (taken in ML as fem. sing.) of *kentaúrion*, n. use of neut. of *kentaúrios* (adj.) = *kéntaur(os)* CENTAUR + *-ios* adj. suffix]

cen·ta·vo (sen tä′vō; *Sp.* sen tä′vô), *n., pl.* **-vos** (-vōz; *Sp.* -vôs). the 100th part of the monetary units of various Spanish American nations. [< Sp: the 100th part = *cent-* 100 (see CENT) + *-avo* < L *-āvum*; see OCTAVO]

cen·te·nar·i·an (sen′tᵊnâr′ē ən), *adj.* **1.** pertaining to or having lived 100 years. —*n.* **2.** a person who has reached the age of 100. [< L *centēnāri(us)* + -AN]

cen·te·nar·y (sen′tᵊner′ē; *esp. Brit.* sen ten′ə rē, -tē′nə rē), *adj., n., pl.* **-nar·ies.** —*adj.* **1.** of or pertaining to a period of 100 years. **2.** recurring once in every 100 years: *a centenary celebration.* —*n.* **3.** a centennial. **4.** a period of 100 years; century. [< L *centēnāri(us)* (adj.) = *centēn(ī)* a hundred each (*cent(um)* 100 + *-ēnī* distributive suffix) + *-ārius* -ARY]

cen·ten·ni·al (sen ten′ē əl), *adj.* **1.** pertaining to a 100th anniversary. **2.** lasting 100 years. **3.** 100 years old. —*n.* **4.** a 100th anniversary; centenary. [< L *cent-* 100 (see CENT) + *-ennial* pertaining to a period of years (from BIENNIAL)]

Centen′nial State′, Colorado (used as a nickname).

cen·ter (sen′tər), *n.* **1.** *Geom.* the middle point, as the point within a circle or sphere equally distant from all points of the circumference or surface. **2.** a point, pivot, axis, etc., around which anything rotates or revolves. **3.** the source of an influence, action, force, etc.: *the center of a problem.* **4.** a point, place, person, etc., upon which interest, emotion, etc., focuses: *She was the center of attraction at the party.* **5.** a principal point, place, or object: *a shipping center.* **6.** a person, thing, group, etc., occupying the middle position, esp. a body of troops. **7.** the core or middle of anything: *hard candies with fruit centers.* **8.** (*usually cap.*) *Govt.* **a.** the part of a legislative assembly, holding political views intermediate between those of the Right and Left. **b.** the members of such a part of an assembly who often sit in the center of the chamber. **c.** the position of persons who hold moderate political views. **d.** politically moderate persons, taken collectively. **9.** *Football.* a lineman who occupies a position in the middle of the line and who puts the ball into play by passing it between his legs to a back. **10.** *Basketball.* a player who primarily plays in the center of the forecourt or backcourt. **11.** *Ice Hockey.* a player who participates in a faceoff at the beginning of play. **12.** *Baseball.* See **center field.** **13.** *Physiol.* a cluster of nerve cells governing a specific organic process: *the vasomotor center.* **14.** *Math.* the mean position of a figure or system. **15.** *Mach.* a tapered rod, mounted in the headstock spindle (**live center**) or the tailstock spindle (**dead center**) of a lathe, upon which the work to be turned is placed. —*v.t.* **16.** to place in or on a center. **17.** to collect around a center; focus: *He centered his novel on the Civil War.* **18.** to determine or mark the center of. **19.** to adjust, shape, or modify (an object, part, etc.) so that its axis or the like is in a central or normal position. —*v.i.* **20.** to be at or come to a center. **21. center around** or **about,** *Informal.* to be focused on or at: *The topic today centers about the crisis in the Far East.* Also, *esp. Brit.,* **centre.** [var. of ME *centre* < L *centr(um)* < Gk *kéntron* needle, spur, pivoting point in drawing a circle = *kent(eîn)* (to) sting + *-ron* n. suffix] —**Syn. 1.** See **middle.**

cen′ter bit′, *Carpentry.* a bit having a sharp, projecting point for fixing it at the center of the hole to be drilled.

cen·ter·board (sen′tər bōrd′, -bôrd′), *n. Naut.* a pivoted fin keel able to be swung upward and aft within a watertight trunk when not in use. Also, *esp. Brit.,* **centreboard.**

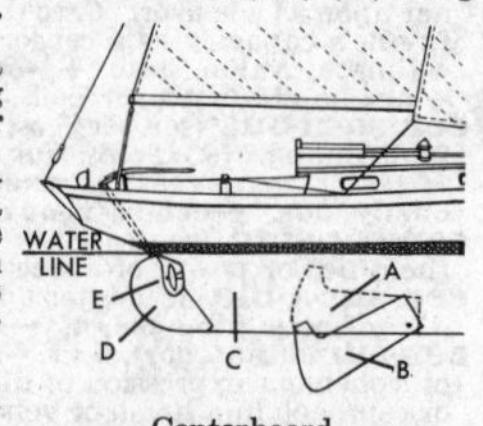

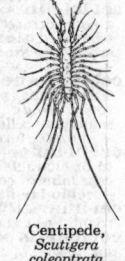

Centerboard
(A, Raised; B, Lowered)
C, Keel; D, Rudder;
E, Propeller

cen′ter field′, *Baseball.* the area of the outfield between right field and left field.

cen′ter field′er, *Baseball.* the player whose position is center field.

cen·ter-fire (sen′tər fīᵊr′), *adj.* **1.** (of a cartridge) having the primer in the center of the base. **2.** (of firearms) designed for the use of such cartridges.

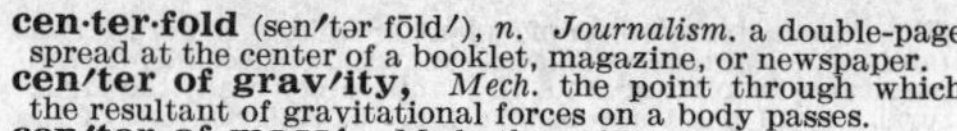

cen·ter·fold (sen′tər fōld′), *n. Journalism.* a double-page spread at the center of a booklet, magazine, or newspaper.

cen′ter of grav′ity, *Mech.* the point through which the resultant of gravitational forces on a body passes.

cen′ter of mass′, *Mech.* the point at which the entire mass of a body may be considered concentrated.

cen·ter·piece (sen′tər pēs′), *n.* an ornamental object used in a central position, esp. on the center of a dining room table. Also, *esp. Brit.,* **centrepiece.**

cen′ter punch′, a punch for making shallow indentations in metal.

cen·tes·i·mal (sen tes′ə məl), *adj.* hundredth; pertaining to division into hundredths. [< L *centēsim(us)* hundredth (*cent(um)* 100 + *-ēsimus* ordinal suffix) + -AL[1]]

cen·tes·i·mo (sen tes′ə mō′; *It.* chen te′zē mô; *Sp.* sente′sē mô′), *n., pl. It.* **-mi** (-mē), **-mos** (-mōz′; *Sp.* -môs′). **1.** a money of account of Italy, the 100th part of a lira. **2.** a cupronickel coin of Uruguay, the 100th part of a peso. **3.** a copper coin of Panama, the 100th part of a balboa. **4.** a money of account of Chile, the 100th part of an escudo. [< It, Sp < L *centēsim(us)*; see CENTESIMAL]

cen·te·sis (sen tē′sis), *n., pl.* **-ses** (-sēz). *Surg.* a puncture or perforation.

centi-, a learned borrowing from Latin usually meaning "hundredth" but sometimes "hundred," used in the formation of compound words: *centiliter; centimeter; centipede.* Also, *esp. before a vowel,* **cent-.** [< L, comb. form of *centum*]

cen·ti·are (sen′tē âr′; *Fr.* säɴ tyar′), *n., pl.* **-ti·ares** (-tē-ârz′; *Fr.* -tyar′). a square meter. Also, **centare.** [< F; see CENTI-, ARE[2]]

cen·ti·grade (sen′tə grād′), *adj.* **1.** divided into 100 degrees, as a scale. **2.** (*cap.*) pertaining to or noting a temperature scale (**Cen′tigrade scale′**) in which 0° represents the ice point and 100° the steam point; Celsius. Celsius is now the preferred term in technical use. *Abbr.:* C [< F]

cen·ti·gram (sen′tə gram′), *n.* one hundredth of a gram. Also, *esp. Brit.,* **cen′ti·gramme′.** [< F *centigramme*]

cen·ti·li·ter (sen′tᵊlē′tər), *n.* one hundredth of a liter. Also, *esp. Brit.,* **cen′ti·li′tre.** [< F *centilitre*]

cen·til·lion (sen til′yən), *n., pl.* **-lions,** (*as after a numeral*) **-lion,** *adj.* —*n.* **1.** a cardinal number represented in the U.S. and France by one followed by 303 zeros, and, in Great Britain and Germany, by one followed by 600 zeros. —*adj.* **2.** amounting to one centillion in number. [< L *cent(um)* 100 + *-illion* (as in *million, billion,* etc.)]

cen·time (sän′tēm; *Fr.* säɴ tēm′), *n., pl.* **-times** (-tēmz′; *Fr.* -tēm′). **1.** the 100th part of the francs of various nations and territories, as Belgium, France, Liechtenstein, Luxembourg, Martinique, Senegal, Switzerland, and Tahiti. **2.** a money of account of Haiti, the 100th part of a gourde. [< F; OF *centiesme* < L *centēsim(um)*, acc. of *centēsimus* hundredth; see CENT]

cen·ti·me·ter (sen′tə mē′tər), *n.* one hundredth of a meter, equivalent to .3937 inch. *Abbr.:* cm, cm. Also, *esp. Brit.,* **cen′ti·me′tre.** [< F *centimètre*]

cen·ti·me·ter-gram-sec·ond (sen′tə-mē′tər gram′sek′ənd), *adj.* of or pertaining to the system of units in which the centimeter, gram, and second are the principal units of length, mass, and time. *Abbr.:* cgs, c.g.s. Also, *esp. Brit.,* **cen′ti·me′tre-gramme′-sec′ond.**

cen·ti·mo (sen′tə mō′; *Sp.* then′tē mô′, sen′-), *n., pl.* **-mos** (-mōz′; *Sp.* -môs′). the 100th part of the monetary units of various countries, as Costa Rica, Paraguay, Spain, and Venezuela. [< Sp < F *centime*]

cen·ti·pede (sen′tə pēd′), *n.* any of numerous predaceous, chiefly nocturnal arthropods of the class *Chilopoda*, having an elongated, flattened body composed of from 15 to 173 segments, each with a pair of legs, the first pair of which is modified into poison fangs. [< L *centiped(a)*]

Centipede, *Scutigera coleoptrata* (Body length about 1 in.)

cent·ner (sent′nər), *n.* **1.** (in several European countries) a unit of weight of 50 kilograms, equivalent to 110.23 pounds avoirdupois. **2.** a unit of 100 kilograms. [< LG; cf. G *Zentner*, OHG *centenari* < L *centēnārius* of a hundred; see CENTENARY]

cen·to (sen′tō), *n., pl.* **-tos.** **1.** a piece of writing, esp. a poem, composed wholly of quotations from the works of other authors. **2.** anything having incongruous parts. [< L; akin to CENTER]

centr-, var. of **centri-** before a vowel: *centroid.*

cen·tra (sen′trə), *n.* a pl. of **centrum.**

cen·tral (sen′trəl), *adj.* **1.** of or forming the center. **2.** in, at, or near the center: *a central position.* **3.** constituting that from which other related things proceed or upon which they depend: *a central agency.* **4.** principal; chief; dominant: *the central character in a novel.* **5.** *Anat., Zool.* **a.** of or pertaining to the central nervous system. **b.** of or pertaining to the centrum of a vertebra. **6.** *Phonet.* (of a speech sound) produced with the tongue articulating neither expressly forward nor in the back part of the mouth, as any of the sounds of *lull.* **7.** *Physics.* (of a force) directed to or from a fixed point. —*n.* **8.** the office of a telephone system, in which connections are made between different lines. **9.** *Obsolesc.* a telephone operator. [< L *centrāl(is)*] —**cen′tral·ly,** *adv.*

Cen′tral Af′rican Federa′tion. See **Rhodesia and Nyasaland, Federation of.**

Cen′tral Af′rican Repub′lic, a republic in central Africa: a member of the French Community. 2,100,000; 241,000 sq. mi. *Cap.:* Bangui. Formerly, **Ubangi-Shari.**

Cen′tral Amer′ica, continental North America, S of Mexico, usually considered to comprise Guatemala, Belize, El Salvador, Honduras, Nicaragua, Costa Rica, and Panama. 18,600,000; 227,933 sq. mi. —**Cen′tral Amer′ican.**

cen′tral an′gle, *Geom.* an angle formed at the center of a circle by two radii.

cen′tral cit′y, a city at the core or center of a metropolitan area, as distinguished from its suburbs or the entire metropolitan area. Cf. **inner city.**

Cen′tral In′dia, a former political agency in central

India uniting various native states and subordinate agencies: now incorporated into Madhya Pradesh. Also called **Cen′tral In′dia A′gency.**

Cen′tral Intel′ligence A′gency. See **CIA.**

cen·tral·i·sa·tion (sen′trə li zā′shən *or, esp. Brit.*, -lī-), *n.* *Chiefly Brit.* centralization.

cen·tral·ise (sen′trə līz′), *v.t.*, **-ised, -is·ing.** *Chiefly Brit.* centralize. —**cen′tral·is′er,** *n.*

Cen′tral I′slip (ī′slip), a town on central Long Island, in SE New York. 36,391 (1970).

cen·tral·ism (sen′trə liz′əm), *n.* a centralizing system; centralization. —**cen′tral·ist,** *n., adj.* —**cen·tral·is·tic** (sen′trə lis′tik), *adj.*

cen·tral·i·ty (sen tral′i tē), *n., pl.* **-ties.** a central position or state: *the centrality of the sun.*

cen·tral·i·za·tion (sen′trə li zā′shən *or, esp. Brit.*, -lī-), *n.* **1.** the act or fact of centralizing. **2.** the state or fact of being centralized. **3.** the concentration of power in a central group or institution. Also, *esp. Brit.*, **centralisation.**

cen·tral·ize (sen′trə līz′), *v.*, **-ized, -iz·ing.** —*v.t.* **1.** to draw to or gather about a center or central point. **2.** to bring under one control, esp. in government. —*v.i.* **3.** to come together at or to form a center. Also, *esp. Brit.*, **centralise.** —**cen′tral·iz′er,** *n.*

cen′tral nerv′ous sys′tem, the part of the nervous system comprising the brain and spinal cord.

Cen′tral Pow′ers, (in World War I) Germany and Austria-Hungary, often with their allies Turkey and Bulgaria.

cen′tral proc′essing u′nit, mainframe.

Cen′tral Prov′inces and Be·rar′ (bā rär′), a former province in central India: became the state of Madhya Pradesh 1950.

Cen′tral time′. See under **standard time.**

cen·tre (sen′tər), *n., v.*, **-tred, -tring.** *Chiefly Brit.* center.

cen·tre·board (sen′tər bōrd′, -bôrd′), *n.* *Naut. Chiefly Brit.* centerboard.

cen·tre·piece (sen′tər pēs′), *n.* *Chiefly Brit.* centerpiece.

centri-, a combining form of **center:** *centrifuge.* Also, **centr-, centro-.** [< NL, comb. form of *centrum* CENTER]

cen·tric (sen′trik), *adj.* **1.** pertaining to or situated at the center; central. **2.** *Anat., Physiol.* pertaining to or originating at a nerve center. Also, **cen′tri·cal.** [< Gk *kentrik(ós)* = *kéntr(on)* CENTER + *-ikos* -IC] —**cen′tri·cal·ly,** *adv.* —**cen·tric·i·ty** (sen tris′i tē), *n.*

cen·trif·u·gal (sen trif′yə gəl, -ə gəl), *adj.* **1.** moving or directed outward away from a center or axis (opposed to *centripetal*). **2.** pertaining to or operated by centrifugal force: *a centrifugal pump.* **3.** *Physiol.* efferent. —*n.* **4.** *Mach.* **a.** a machine for separating different materials by centrifugal force; centrifuge. **b.** a rotating, perforated drum holding the materials to be separated in such a machine. [< NL *centrifug(us)* center-fleeing (*centri-* CENTRI- + *-fugus* = L *fug(ere)* (to) flee + *-us* -OUS) + -AL[1]] —**cen·trif′u·gal·ly,** *adv.*

centrif′ugal force′, the inertial force repelling a particle or body away from the axis around which it rotates or away from the center of curvature of a curved path along which it is moving.

cen·tri·fuge (sen′trə fyōōj′), *n., v.*, **-fuged, -fug·ing.** —*n.* **1.** an apparatus that rotates at high speed and by centrifugal force separates substances of different densities. —*v.t.* **2.** to subject to the action of a centrifuge. [< F, n. use of *centrifuge* (adj.) < NL *centrifug(us)*; see CENTRIFUGAL] —**cen·trif·u·ga·tion** (sen trif′yə gā′shən, -trif′ə-), *n.*

cen·tring (sen′tring), *n.* *Chiefly Brit.* centering.

cen·tri·ole (sen′trē ōl′), *n.* *Biol.* a minute body within the centrosome. [CENTRI- + *-ole* < L *-ol(us)* dim. suffix]

cen·trip·e·tal (sen trip′i t[ə]l), *adj.* **1.** moving or directed inward toward a center or axis (opposed to *centrifugal*). **2.** pertaining to or operated by centripetal force. **3.** *Physiol.* afferent. [< NL *centripet(us)* center-seeking (*centri-* CENTRI- + *-petus* = L *pet(ere)* (to) seek + *-us* -OUS) + -AL[1]] **cen·trip′e·tal·ly,** *adv.*

centrip′etal force′, a force attracting a particle or body toward the axis around which it rotates or toward the center of curvature of a curved path along which it is moving.

cen·trist (sen′trist), *n.* (*sometimes cap.*) a member of a political party of the center. [< F *centriste*]

centro-, var. of **centri-:** *centrosphere.*

cen·troid (sen′troid), *n.* **1.** *Mech.* the point that may be considered as the center of a one- or two-dimensional figure. Cf. **center of mass. 2.** *Geom.* the point where the medians of a triangle intersect. —**cen·troi′dal,** *adj.*

cen·tro·mere (sen′trə mēr′), *n.* *Biol.* (in a chromosome) the specialized region to which a spindle fiber is attached. —**cen·tro·mer·ic** (sen′trə mer′ik, -mēr′-), *adj.*

cen·tro·some (sen′trə sōm′), *n.* *Biol.* a minute, protoplasmic body, regarded as the active center of cell division in mitosis. —**cen·tro·som·ic** (sen′trə som′ik), *adj.*

cen·tro·sphere (sen′trə sfēr′), *n.* **1.** *Biol.* the protoplasm around a centrosome; the central portion of an aster, containing the centrosome. **2.** *Geol.* the central or interior portion of the earth.

cen·trum (sen′trəm), *n., pl.* **-trums, -tra** (-trə). **1.** a center. **2.** *Anat., Zool.* the body of a vertebra. [< L]

cen·tum (sen′təm), *n.* one hundred. [< L; see HUNDRED]

cen·tu·ple (sen′tə pəl, -tyə-, sen tōō′pəl, -tyōō′-), *adj., v.*, **-pled, -pling.** —*adj.* **1.** a hundred times as great; hundredfold. —*v.t.* **2.** to increase 100 times. [< MF < LL *centupl(us)* = L *centu(m)* 100 + *-plus* -FOLD]

cen·tu·ri·al (sen tŏŏr′ē əl, -tyŏŏr′-), *adj.* pertaining to a century. [< L *centuriāl(is).* See CENTURY, -AL[1]]

cen·tu·ried (sen′chə rēd), *adj.* **1.** existing for an indefinite number of centuries. **2.** very old.

cen·tu·ri·on (sen tŏŏr′ē ən, -tyŏŏr′-), *n.* (in the ancient Roman army) the commander of a century. [ME < L *centuriōn-* (s. of *centuriō*) = *centur(ia)* CENTURY + *-iōn-* -ION]

cen·tu·ry (sen′chə rē), *n., pl.* **-ries. 1.** a period of 100 years. **2.** one of the successive periods of 100 years reckoned forward or backward from a recognized chronological epoch, esp. from the assumed date of the birth of Jesus. **3.** any group or collection of 100. **4.** (in the ancient Roman army) a company, consisting of approximately 100 men. **5.** one of the voting divisions of the ancient Roman people, each division having one vote. **6.** (*cap.*) *Print.* a style of type. [< L *centuria* unit made up of 100 parts, esp. company of soldiers = *cent(um)* 100 + *-uria* unexplained suffix]

cen′tury plant′, a Mexican agave, *Agave americana,* erroneously believed to flower only once every century.

Century plant, *Agave americana* (Height 20 to 30 ft.)

ceorl (che′ôrl), *n.* *Obs.* churl (def. 4). [OE]

cephal-, var. of **cephalo-** before a vowel: *cephalitis.*

ceph·a·lad (sef′ə lad′), *adv.* *Anat., Zool.* toward the head (opposed to *caudad*). [CEPHAL- + L *ad* to, toward]

ce·phal·ic (sə fal′ik), *adj.* **1.** of or pertaining to the head. **2.** situated or directed toward the head. [< L *cephalic(us)* < Gk *kephalikós*]

-cephalic, var. of **cephalo-,** as final element of adjectives: *brachycephalic.* [< Gk *-kephal(os)* -CEPHALOUS + -IC]

cephal′ic in′dex, *Cephalom.* the ratio of the greatest breadth of a head to its greatest length from front to back, multiplied by 100.

ceph·a·lin (sef′ə lin), *n.* any of several phosphatides, similar to the lecithins: found in animal tissue.

ceph·a·li·tis (sef′ə lī′tis), *n.* *Pathol.* encephalitis.

ceph·a·li·za·tion (sef′ə li zā′shən), *n.* *Zool.* a tendency in the development of animals to localization of important organs or parts in or near the head.

cephalo-, a learned borrowing from Greek meaning "head," used in the formation of compound words: *cephalometry.* Also, **cephal-, -cephalic, -cephalous, -cephaly.** [< Gk *kephalo-*, comb. form of *kephalḗ* head; akin to GABLE]

ceph·a·lo·chor·date (sef′ə lō kôr′dāt), *adj.* **1.** belonging or pertaining to the *Cephalochordata.* —*n.* **2.** any chordate animal of the subphylum *Cephalochordata,* having fishlike characters but lacking a spinal column, comprising the lancelets.

cephalom., cephalometry.

ceph·a·lom·e·try (sef′ə lom′i trē), *n.* the science of measuring the dimensions of the human head. —**ceph′a·lom′e·ter,** *n.* —**ceph·a·lo·met·ric** (sef′ə lō me′trik), *adj.*

Ceph·a·lo·ni·a (sef′ə lō′nē ə, -lōn′yə), *n.* the largest of the Ionian Islands, off the W coast of Greece. 46,314 (1961); 287 sq. mi. Greek, **Kephallenia.**

ceph·a·lo·pod (sef′ə lə pod′), *n.* **1.** any mollusk of the class *Cephalopoda,* having tentacles attached to the head, including the cuttlefish, squid, octopus, etc. —*adj.* **2.** Also, **ceph′a·lo·pod′ic, ceph·a·lop·o·dous** (sef′ə lop′ə dəs). belonging or pertaining to the *Cephalopoda.*

ceph·a·lo·tho·rax (sef′ə lō thôr′aks, -thōr′-), *n., pl.* **-tho·rax·es, -tho·ra·ces** (-thōr′ə sēz′, -thôr′-). *Zool.* the anterior part of the body in certain arachnids and crustaceans, consisting of the coalesced head and thorax. —**ceph·a·lo·tho·rac·ic** (sef′ə lō thə ras′ik), *adj.*

ceph·a·lous (sef′ə ləs), *adj.* having a head.

-cephalous, var. of **cephalo-,** as final element of adjectives: *brachycephalous.* [< Gk *-kephalos* = *kephal(ḗ)* head + *-os* -OUS]

-cephaly, var. of **cephalo-,** as final element of compound words: *dolichocephaly.*

Ce′pheid var′iable, *Astron.* a variable star in which changes in brightness are due to alternate contractions and expansions in volume. Also, **ce′pheid var′iable.**

Ce·phe·us (sē′fē əs, -fyōōs), *n., gen.* **-phe·i** (-fē ī′) for 1. **1.** *Astron.* a northern circumpolar constellation between Cassiopeia and Draco. **2.** *Class. Myth.* an Ethiopian king, the husband of Cassiopeia and father of Andromeda. —**Ce·phe·id** (sē′fē id), *adj.*

cer-, var. of **cero-** before a vowel: *ceraceous.*

ce·ra·ceous (sə rā′shəs), *adj.* waxlike; waxy.

Ce·ram (sē ram′; *Port.* se RÄN′; *Du.* sā′räm), *n.* an island of the Moluccas in Indonesia, W of New Guinea. 7191 sq. mi. Also called **Serang.**

ce·ram·al (sə ram′əl), *n.* cermet. [CERAM(IC) + AL(LOY)]

ce·ram·ic (sə ram′ik), *adj.* **1.** of or pertaining to products made from clay and similar materials, as pottery, brick, etc. —*n.* **2.** ceramic material. [earlier *keramic* < Gk *keramik(ós)* = *kéram(os)* potters' clay + *-ikos* -IC]

ce·ram·ics (sə ram′iks), *n.* **1.** (*construed as sing.*) the art and technology of making objects of clay and similar materials treated by firing. **2.** (*construed as pl.*) articles of earthenware, porcelain, etc. [see CERAMIC, -ICS] —**cer·a·mist** (ser′ə mist, sə ram′ist), **ce·ram′i·cist,** *n.*

ce·rar·gy·rite (sə rär′jə rīt′), *n.* a very soft mineral, silver chloride, AgCl: an ore of silver; horn silver. [< Gk *kér(as)* horn + *árgyr(os)* silver + -ITE[1]; cf. F *kérargyre*]

cerat-, a learned borrowing from Greek meaning "horn," used in the formation of compound words: *ceratodus.* [< Gk *kerat-*, comb. form of *kéras*; c. L *cornu,* HORN]

ce·rate (sēr′āt), *n.* **1.** *Pharm.* an unctuous, often medicated, preparation for external application, consisting of lard or oil mixed with wax, rosin, or the like. —*adj.* **2.** *Ornith.* having a cere. [< L *cērāt(um),* neut. of *cērātus* waxed (ptp. of *cērāre*). See CER-, -ATE[1]]

ce·rat·ed (sēr′ā tid), *adj.* **1.** covered with wax. **2.** *Ornith.* cerate (def. 2). [< L *cērāt(us)* waxed + -ED[2]]

cer·a·tin (ser′ə tin), *n.* keratin.

ce·rat·o·dus (sə rat′ə dəs, ser′ə tō′dəs), *n., pl.* **-dus·es.** a lungfish of either of two genera, *Ceratodus* or *Neoceratodus,* having hornlike ridges on the teeth. Cf. **barramunda.** [< NL]

cer·a·toid (ser′ə toid′), *adj.* hornlike; horny. [< Gk *kerātoeid(ḗs)*]

Cer·ber·us (sûr′bər əs), *n.* *Class. Myth.* a dog, usually shown with three heads, that guarded the entrance of the infernal regions. —**Cer·be·re·an** (sər bēr′ē ən), *adj.*

cer·car·i·a (sər kâr′ē ə), *n., pl.* **-car·i·ae** (-kâr′ē ē′). *Zool.* the disk-shaped larva of flukes of the class *Trematoda,* having a taillike appendage. [< NL = *cerc-* (< Gk *kérkos* tail) + *-āria* -ARIA] —**cer·car′i·al,** *adj.*

cere¹ (sēr), *n.* *Ornith.* a fleshy, membranous covering of the base of the upper mandible of a bird, esp. a bird of prey or a parrot, through which the nostrils open. [late ME *sere,* sp. var. of **cere* < ML, L *cēra,* lit., wax]

cere² (sēr), *v.t.,* **cered, cer·ing.** *Archaic.* to wrap in or as in a cerecloth, esp. a corpse. [ME *cere(n)* < L *cērā(re)* (to) wax = *cēr(a)* wax + *-āre* inf. ending]

ce·re·al (sēr′ē əl), *n.* **1.** any gramineous plant yielding an edible farinaceous grain, as wheat, rye, oats, rice, or corn. **2.** the grain itself. **3.** some edible preparation of it, esp. a breakfast food. —*adj.* **4.** of or pertaining to grain or the plants producing it. [< L *Cereāl(is)* of, pertaining to CERES; see -AL¹]

cer·e·bel·lum (ser′ə bel′əm), *n., pl.* **-bel·lums, -bel·la** (-bel′ə). *Anat., Zool.* a large portion of the brain, serving to coordinate voluntary movements and balance in man. [< L = *cereb(rum)* brain + *-ellum* dim. suffix] —**cer′e·bel′lar,** *adj.*

cerebr-, var. of **cerebro-** before a vowel: *cerebral.*

cer·e·bral (ser′ə brəl, sə rē′-), *adj.* **1.** *Anat., Zool.* of or pertaining to the cerebrum or the brain. **2.** characterized by the use of the intellect rather than intuition or instinct. **3.** *Phonet.* retroflex (def. 2). —*n.* **4.** *Phonet.* a cerebral sound. [< NL *cerebrāl(is)*] —**cer′e·bral·ly,** *adv.*

cer′ebral pal′sy, *Pathol.* a form of paralysis caused by a prenatal brain defect or by brain injury during birth, characterized by involuntary motions and difficulty in control of the voluntary muscles.

cer·e·brate (ser′ə brāt′), *v.i., v.t.,* **-brat·ed, -brat·ing.** to use the mind; think or think about. [back formation from *cerebration*] —**cer′e·bra′tion,** *n.*

cerebro-, a combining form of **cerebrum:** *cerebrospinal.* Also, *esp. before a vowel,* **cerebr-.**

cer·e·bro·side (ser′ə brə sīd′), *n.* *Biochem.* any of the class of glycolipids, found in brain tissue and the medullary sheaths of nerves, that, upon hydrolysis, yield sphingosine, galactose, or other sugars, and a fatty acid. [CEREBR- + -OSE² + -IDE]

cer·e·bro·spi·nal (ser′ə brō spīn′ᵊl, sə rē′brō-), *adj.* *Anat., Physiol.* **1.** pertaining to or affecting the brain and the spinal cord. **2.** of or pertaining to the central nervous system.

cerebrospi′nal meningi′tis, *Pathol.* an acute inflammation of the meninges of the brain and spinal cord, accompanied by fever. Also called **brain fever, cer′ebrospi′nal fe′ver.**

cer·e·brum (ser′ə brəm, sə rē′-), *n., pl.* **-brums, -bra** (-brə). *Anat., Zool.* **1.** the anterior and largest part of the brain, serving to control voluntary movements and coordinate mental actions. **2.** the forebrain and the midbrain. [< L: brain] —**cer′e·broid′,** *adj.* —**cer·e·bric** (ser′ə brik, sə reb′rik, -rē′brik), *adj.*

cere·cloth (sēr′klôth′, -kloth′), *n., pl.* **-cloths** (-klôthz′, -klothz′, -klôths′, -kloths′). **1.** cloth coated or impregnated with wax so as to be waterproof, used for wrapping the dead, for bandages, etc. **2.** a piece of such cloth. [earlier *cered cloth;* see CERE²]

cere·ment (sēr′mənt), *n.* Usually, **cerements. 1.** a cerecloth used for wrapping the dead. **2.** any graveclothes.

cer·e·mo·ni·al (ser′ə mō′nē əl), *adj.* **1.** of, pertaining to, or characterized by ceremony or ceremonies; formal; ritual: *a ceremonial occasion.* **2.** used in or in connection with ceremonies: *ceremonial robes.* —*n.* **3.** a system of rites or formalities prescribed for a particular occasion. **4.** formal behavior appropriate to a certain occasion: *the ceremonial of a state banquet.* [ME < ML *cēremōniāl(is),* LL *caerimōniālis*] —**cer′e·mo′ni·al·ism,** *n.* —**cer′e·mo′ni·al·ist,** *n.* —**cer′e·mo′ni·al·ly,** *adv.* —**Syn. 1.** solemn, conventional, ceremonious. **3.** ritual, liturgy. —**Ant. 1.** informal.

cer·e·mo·ni·ous (ser′ə mō′nē əs), *adj.* **1.** carefully observant of ceremony; formally or elaborately polite. **2.** pertaining to, marked by, or consisting of ceremony; formal: *a ceremonious reception.* [CEREMONY + -OUS; cf. MF *cerimonieux* < LL *caerimōniōs(us)*] —**cer′e·mo′ni·ous·ly,** *adv.* —**cer′e·mo′ni·ous·ness,** *n.* —**Syn. 1.** ceremonial, conventional, punctilious, courteous.

cer·e·mo·ny (ser′ə mō′nē), *n., pl.* **-nies. 1.** the formalities observed on some solemn occasion. **2.** a formal observance or solemn rite: *a marriage ceremony.* **3.** any formal act or observance, esp. a meaningless one: *His low bow was mere ceremony.* **4.** a gesture or act of politeness. **5.** strict adherence to conventional forms; formality: *to leave a room without ceremony.* **6. stand on ceremony,** to behave in a formal or ceremonious manner: *There is no need to stand on ceremony with us.* [ME *ceremonie* < ML *cēremōni(a),* L *caerimōnia* sacred rite; r. ME *cerymonye* < MF *cerimonie* < L, as above] —**Syn. 1, 2.** CEREMONY, RITE, RITUAL refer to set observances and acts traditional in religious services or on public occasions. CEREMONY applies to more or less formal dignified acts on religious or public occasions: *a marriage ceremony; an inaugural ceremony.* A RITE is an established, prescribed, or customary form of religious or other solemn practice: *the rite of baptism.* RITUAL refers to the form of conducting worship or to a code of ceremonies in general: *Masonic rituals.*

Ce·ren·kov (chə reng′kôf, -kəf, -ren′-; *Russ.* che ʀen′kof), *n.* **Pa·vel A.** (pä′vel), born 1904, Russian physicist: Nobel prize 1958. Also, **Cherenkov.**

Ceren′kov radia′tion, *Physics.* radiation produced by a particle passing through a medium at a speed greater than that of light through the medium. [named after P. A. CERENKOV]

Ce·res (sēr′ēz), *n.* **1.** an ancient Italian goddess of agriculture under whose name the Romans adopted the worship of the Greek goddess Demeter. **2.** *Astron.* the first asteroid to be discovered, being the largest and one of the brightest.

ce·re·us (sēr′ē əs), *n., pl.* **-us·es.** any cactaceous plant of the genus *Cereus,* of tropical America and the western U.S. [< NL, L *cēreus* wax candle, n. use of *cēreus* waxen = *cēr(a)* wax + *-eus* -EOUS]

ce·ri·a (sēr′ē ə), *n.* *Chem.* a heavy powder, CeO_2, used chiefly in ceramics, glass polishing, and decolorizing. Also called **cerium dioxide, cerium oxide, ce′ric ox′ide.** [CERI(UM) + *-a* chemical suffix denoting oxide]

ce·ric (sēr′ik, ser′-), *adj.* *Chem.* containing cerium, esp. in the tetravalent state. [CER(IUM) + -IC]

Ce·ri·go (*It.* che′ʀē gô), *n.* a Greek island in the Mediterranean, S of Peloponnesus: a temple of Aphrodite located here in antiquity. 6297 (1951); 108 sq. mi. Also called **Cythera.** Greek, **Kythera.**

ce·rise (sə rēs′, -rēz′), *adj., n.* moderate to deep red. [< F; see CHERRY]

ce·ri·um (sēr′ē əm), *n.* *Chem.* a steel-gray, ductile metallic element of the rare-earth group found only in combination. *Symbol:* Ce; *at. wt.:* 140.12; *at. no.:* 58. [CER(ES) + -IUM]

ce′rium diox′ide, *Chem.* ceria. Also called **ce′rium ox′ide.**

ce′rium met′al, *Chem.* any of a subgroup of rare-earth metals of which the terbium and yttrium metals comprise the other two subgroups. Cf. **rare-earth element.**

cer·met (sûr′met), *n.* a durable, heat-resistant alloy formed by compacting and sintering a metal and a ceramic substance. Also called **ceramal.** [CER(AMIC) + MET(AL)]

Cer·nă·uţi (cher nə ōōts′), *n.* a city in the SW Ukraine, in the SW Soviet Union: formerly in Rumania. 154,000 (est. 1964). German, **Czernowitz.** Russian, **Chernovtsy.**

cer·nu·ous (sûrn′yōō əs, sûr′nōō-), *adj.* *Bot.* drooping or nodding, as a flower. [< L *cernuus* falling forward, face down]

ce·ro (sēr′ō), *n., pl.* (*esp. collectively*) **-ro,** (*esp. referring to two or more kinds or species*) **-ros. 1.** a large, mackerellike game fish, *Scomberomorus regalis,* found in tropical America. **2.** any of various related fishes. [alter. of SIERRA]

cero-, a learned borrowing from Greek meaning "wax," used in the formation of compound words: *cerotype.* Also, *esp. before a vowel,* **cer-.** [< Gk *kēro-,* comb. form of *kērós* wax]

ce·ro·plas·tic (sēr′ə plas′tik, ser′ə-), *adj.* **1.** pertaining to modeling in wax. **2.** modeled in wax. [< Gk *kēroplastik(ós)*] —**ce′ro·plas′tics,** *n.*

cerot′ic ac′id (si rot′ik, -rō′tik), *Chem.* a white wax, $CH_3(CH_2)_{24}COOH$, usually obtained from beeswax or carnauba wax.

ce·ro·type (sēr′ə tīp′, ser′-), *n.* a process of engraving in which the design or the like is cut on a wax-coated metal plate from which a printing surface is subsequently produced by stereotyping or by electrotyping.

ce·rous (sēr′əs), *adj.* *Chem.* containing trivalent cerium. [CER(IUM) + -OUS]

Cer·ro de Pas·co (seʀ′ʀô the päs′kô), a town in central Peru: silver-mining district. 27,656 (est. 1957); 14,280 ft. above sea level.

Cer·ro Gor·do (seʀ′ʀô gôʀ′dô), a mountain pass in E Mexico between Veracruz and Jalapa: defeat of Mexican troops by U.S. troops 1847.

cert., **1.** certificate. **2.** certified. **3.** certify.

cer·tain (sûr′tᵊn), *adj.* **1.** free from doubt or reservation; confident. **2.** destined; sure (usually fol. by an infinitive): *He is certain to be there.* **3.** inevitable; bound to happen: *They realized then that war was certain.* **4.** established as true or sure; unquestionable: *It is certain that he tried.* **5.** fixed; agreed upon: *on a certain day; for a certain amount.* **6.** definite or particular, but not named or specified: *a certain person; a certain charm.* **7.** that may be depended on; trustworthy: *His aim was certain.* **8.** some though not much: *a certain reluctance.* **9.** *Obs.* steadfast. **10. for certain,** without a doubt; surely: *to know for certain.* [ME < OF < L *cert(us)* sure, settled (*cer-,* base of *cernere* to decide + *-tus* ptp. suffix) + *-ānus* -AN] —**Syn. 1.** convinced, satisfied. See **sure. 4.** indubitable, incontestable, irrefutable. **5.** determined.

cer·tain·ly (sûr′tᵊn lē), *adv.* **1.** without doubt; assuredly: *I'll certainly be there.* **2.** yes, of course: *Certainly, take the keys.* **3.** surely; to be sure: *She certainly is stupid.* [ME]

cer·tain·ty (sûr′tᵊn tē), *n., pl.* **-ties. 1.** the state of being certain. **2.** something certain; an assured fact. [ME *certeinte* < AF = *certein* CERTAIN + *-te* -TY²] —**Syn. 1.** certitude, assurance. **2.** truth.

cer·tes (sûr′tēz), *adv.* *Archaic.* certainly; in truth. [ME < OF < phrase *a certes* < L **ā certīs,* lit., from sure (things). See A-⁴, CERTAIN]

certif., **1.** certificate. **2.** certificated.

cer·ti·fi·a·ble (sûr′tə fī′ə bəl), *adj.* **1.** capable of being certified. **2.** *Brit.* **a.** committable to a mental institution. **b.** *Sometimes facetious.* fit or ready for an insane asylum. **c.** uncontrollable: *a certifiable desire.*

cer·tif·i·cate (*n.* sər tif′ə kit; *v.* sər tif′ə kāt′), *n., v.,* **-cat·ed, -cat·ing.** —*n.* **1.** a document serving as evidence or as written testimony, as of status, qualifications, privileges, the truth of something, etc. **2.** a document attesting to the completion of an educational course. **3.** *Law.* a legally executed statement of a public official that is by law made evidence of the truth of the facts stated. **4.** a form of paper money supported by gold **(gold certificate)** or silver **(silver certificate)** on deposit in the U.S. Treasury. —*v.t.* **5.** to attest by a certificate. **6.** to furnish with or authorize by a certificate. [late ME *certificat* < ML *certificāt(um),* n. use of neut. of *certificātus* certified (ptp. of *certificāre*) = *certific-* (see CERTIFY) + *-ātus* -ATE¹] —**cer·tif·i·ca·to·ry** (sər-tif′ə kə tôr′ē, -tōr′ē), *adj.*

cer·ti·fi·ca·tion (sûr′tə fə kā′shən, sər tif′ə-), *n.* **1.** act of certifying. **2.** state of being certified. **3.** a certified statement. [late ME *certificacio(u)n* < ML *certificātiōn-* (s. of *certificātiō*)]

cer·ti·fied (sûr′tə fīd′), *adj.* **1.** having or proved by a certificate: *a certified representative.* **2.** guaranteed; reliably endorsed: *a certified check.* **3.** *Brit.* **a.** legally declared insane. **b.** committed to a mental institution.

cer′tified mail′, uninsured first-class mail requiring proof of delivery.

cer′tified pub′lic account′ant, *U.S.* a person holding an official certificate as an accountant, having fulfilled all the legal requirements. *Abbr.:* C.P.A.

cer·ti·fy (sûr′tə fī′), *v.,* **-fied, -fy·ing.** —*v.t.* **1.** to attest as certain; give reliable information of; confirm: *to certify the truth of a claim.* **2.** to testify to or vouch for in writing. **3.** to assure or inform with certainty. **4.** to guarantee; endorse reliably: *to certify a document with an official seal.* **5.** to guarantee in writing on (the face of a check) that the account drawn against has sufficient funds to pay it. **—*v.i.* 6.** to give assurance; testify; vouch for the validity or authenticity of something. [ME *certifie(n)* < MF *certifie(r)* < LL *certificāre* = L *certi-* (comb. form of *certus* decided; see CERTAIN) + *-ficāre* -FY] **—cer′ti·fi′er,** *n.*

cer·ti·o·ra·ri (sûr′shē ə râr′ī), *n. Law.* a writ issuing from a superior court calling up the record of a proceeding in an inferior court for review. [< L: to be informed, certified; lit., made surer (pass. inf. of *certiōrāre* to inform) = *certiōr-* (s. of *certior* surer, comp. of *certus* sure; see CERTAIN) + *-ārī* pass. inf. ending; the writ is so called because v. form occurred in the Latin original]

cer·ti·tude (sûr′ti to͞od′, -tyo͞od′), *n.* freedom from doubt; certainty; confidence. [ME < LL *certitūd(ō)* = L *certi-* (comb. form of *certus* sure; see CERTAIN) + *-tūdō* -TUDE] **—Syn.** assurance, conviction, belief.

ce·ru·le·an (sə ro͞o′lē ən), *adj., n.* deep blue; sky blue; azure. [< L *caerule(us)* dark blue, azure (akin to *caelum* sky) + -AN]

ce·ru·men (si ro͞o′mən), *n.* a yellowish, waxlike secretion from certain glands in the external auditory canal. Also called **earwax.** [< NL = L *cēr(a)* wax + *(alb)umen* ALBUMEN] **—ce·ru′mi·nous,** *adj.*

ce·ruse (sēr′o͞os, si ro͞os′), *n. Chem.* a poisonous powder, $(PbCO_3)_2 \cdot Pb(OH)_2$, used chiefly in paints and in putty; white lead. Also called **basic lead carbonate.** [ME < L *cēruss(a)* = *cēr(a)* wax + *-ussa* < ?]

ce·rus·site (sēr′ə sīt′, si rus′īt), *n.* a mineral, lead carbonate, $PbCO_3$: an important ore of lead. [< L *cēruss(a)* CERUSE + -ITE[1]]

Cer·van·tes (sər van′tēz; *Sp.* therr vän′tes), *n.* **Mi·guel de** (mi gel′ dā; *Sp.* mē gel′ de), (*Miguel de Cervantes Saavedra*), 1547–1616, Spanish novelist.

cer·ve·lat (sûr′və lat′, -lä′, ser′-), *n.* a dry, smoked sausage made of beef or pork, fat, and seasonings. [< F (obs.); see SAVELOY]

Cer·ve·ra y To·pe·te (ther ve′rä ē tô pe′te), **Pas·cual** (päs kwäl′), 1839–1909, Spanish admiral.

cervic-, a combining form of **cervix:** *cervicitis.* [< L *cervīc-*, s. of *cervīx*]

cer·vi·cal (sûr′vi kəl), *adj. Anat.* of or pertaining to the cervix or neck.

cer·vi·ces (sər vī′sēz, sûr′vi sēz′), *n.* a pl. of **cervix.**

cer·vi·ci·tis (sûr′vi sī′tis), *n. Pathol.* inflammation of the cervix.

cer·vine (sûr′vīn, -vin), *adj.* **1.** deerlike. **2.** of deer or the deer family. [< L *cervīn(us)* of, pertaining to a deer = *cerv(us)* deer + *-īnus* -INE[1]]

cer·vix (sûr′viks), *n., pl.* **cer·vix·es, cer·vi·ces** (sər vī′sēz, sûr′vi sēz′). *Anat.* **1.** the neck. **2.** any necklike part, esp. the constricted lower end of the uterus. [< L]

Cer′y·ne′an stag′ (ser′ə nē′ən, ser′-), *Class. Myth.* a stag living in Arcadia, captured by Hercules as one of his labors. [named after Mt. *Ceryneia*, between Arcadia and Achaea]

Ce·sar·e·an (si zâr′ē ən), *adj., n.* Caesarean. Also, **Ce·sar′i·an.**

Ce·se·na (che ze′nä), *n.* a city in E Italy. 79,954 (1961).

ce·si·um (sē′zē əm), *n. Chem.* a rare, highly reactive, soft, metallic element of the alkali metal group, used chiefly in photoelectric cells. *Symbol:* Cs; *at. wt.:* 132.905; *at. no.:* 55; *sp. gr.:* 1.9 at 20°C; melts at 28.5°C. Also, **caesium.** [< NL, special use of L *caesium*, neut. of *caesius* bluish gray]

Čes·ké Bu·dě·jo·vi·ce (ches′ke bo͝o′dye yô vi tse), Czech name of **Budweis.**

ces·pi·tose (ses′pi tōs′), *adj. Bot.* matted together; growing in dense tufts. Also, **caespitose.** [< NL *cespitōs(us)* = L *cespit-* (s. of *cespes*, var. of *caespes* turf) + *-ōsus* -OSE[1]]

cess[1] (ses), *Brit.* **—*n.* 1.** a tax, assessment, or lien. **—*v.t.* 2.** to tax or assess. [aph. var. of obs. *assess* assessment, n. use of ASSESS (v.)]

cess[2] (ses), *n. Irish Eng. Informal.* luck: *Bad cess to them!* [? aph. var. of SUCCESS]

ces·sa·tion (se sā′shən), *n.* a temporary or complete ceasing; discontinuance: *a cessation of hostilities.* [ME *cessacio(u)n* < L *cessātiōn-* (s. of *cessātiō*) delay, inactivity, stoppage = *cessāt(us)* delayed, stopped, ptp. of *cessāre* (*cess(us)* yielded, ceded (*ced-* CEDE + *-tus* ptp. suffix) + *-ātus* -ATE[1]) + *-iōn-* -ION]

ces·sion (sesh′ən), *n.* **1.** the act of ceding, as by treaty. **2.** that which is ceded, as territory. [ME < L *cessiōn-* (s. of *cessiō*) a giving up = *cess(us)* yielded, ptp. of *cēdere* (*ced-* perf. s. + *-tus* ptp. suffix) + *-iōn-* -ION]

ces·sion·ar·y (sesh′ə ner′ē), *n., pl.* **-ar·ies.** *Law.* an assignee or grantee. [< ML *cessiōnāri(us)*]

cess·pool (ses′po͞ol′), *n.* **1.** a cistern, well, or pit for retaining the sediment of a drain or for receiving the sewage from the sinks, toilets, etc., of a house. **2.** any filthy receptacle or place. [*cess* (< It *cess(o)* privy < L *rēcessus* RECESS, place of retirement) + POOL[1]]

c'est la vie (se LA vē′), *French.* such is life; that's life.

ces·tode (ses′tōd), *n.* **1.** a parasitic platyhelminth or flatworm of the class *Cestoda*, which comprises the tapeworms. **—*adj.* 2.** belonging or pertaining to the *Cestoda.* [< NL *cestōd(ēs).* See CESTUS[1], -ODE[1]]

ces·toid (ses′toid), *adj.* **1.** *Zool.* (of worms) ribbonlike. **—*n.* 2.** cestode. [< NL *cestoīd(ēs).* See CESTUS[1], -OID]

ces·tus[1] (ses′təs), *n., pl.* **-ti** (-tī). **1.** a girdle or belt, esp. as worn by women of ancient Greece. **2.** *Class. Myth.* the girdle of Venus, decorated with every object that could arouse amorous desire. Also, *esp. Brit.*, **ces′tos.** [< L < Gk *kestós* a girdle, lit., (something) stitched = *kes-* (var. s. of *kentein* to stitch) + *-tos* v. suffix]

ces·tus[2] (ses′təs), *n., pl.* **-tus·es.** *Rom. Antiq.* a hand covering made of leather strips and often loaded with metal, worn by boxers. [< L, var. of *caestus*, perh. = *caes(us)* struck, ptp. of *caedere* (*caed-* strike + *-tus* ptp. suffix) + *-tus* ptp. suffix]

ce·su·ra (sə zho͝or′ə, -zo͝or′ə, siz yo͝or′ə), *n., pl.* **ce·su·ras, ce·su·rae** (sə zho͝or′ē, -zo͝or′ē, siz yo͝or′ē). caesura.

cet-, a learned borrowing from Latin meaning "whale," used in the formation of compound words: *cetacean.* Also, *esp. before a consonant,* **ceto-.** [comb. form repr. L *cētus* < Gk *kētos* whale]

ce·ta·cean (si tā′shən), *adj.* **1.** belonging to the *Cetacea*, an order of aquatic, chiefly marine mammals, including the whales, dolphins, porpoises, etc. **—*n.* 2.** a cetacean mammal. [< NL *Cētāce(a)* (see CET-, -ACEA) + -AN]

ce·tane (sē′tān), *n. Chem.* a colorless, liquid hydrocarbon of the alkane series, $C_{16}H_{34}$, used as a solvent and in cetane number determinations.

ce′tane num′ber, *Chem.* a measure of the ignition quality of a diesel engine fuel by comparison with various mixtures in which alpha methylnaphthaline is given a standard value of 0 and cetane is given a standard value of 100.

Ce·ta·tea Al·bă (che tä′tyä äl′bə), Rumanian name of **Belgorod-Dnestrovski.**

Ce·ti·nje (tse′ti nye), *n.* a city in S Yugoslavia: former capital of Montenegro. 22,032.

ceto-, var. of **cet-** before a consonant: *cetology.*

ce·tol·o·gy (sē tol′ə jē), *n.* the branch of zoology dealing with whales. **—ce·to·log·i·cal** (sēt′ᵊloj′i kəl), *adj.* **—ce·tol′o·gist,** *n.*

Ce·tus (sē′təs), *n., gen.* **Ce·ti** (sē′tī). *Astron.* the Whale, a constellation lying above the equator. [< L; see CET-]

Ceu·ta (syo͞o′tə; *Sp.* the′o͞o tä, se′-), *n.* a seaport and enclave of Spain in N Morocco, on the Strait of Gibraltar. 76,098 (1965).

Cé·vennes (sā ven′), *n.* (*construed as pl.*) a mountain range in S France. Highest peak, Mt. Mézenc, 5753 ft.

Cey·lon (si lon′), *n.* **1.** an island in the Indian Ocean, S of India. 25,332 sq. mi. Formerly, **Serendib. 2.** former name of **Sri Lanka.**

Cey·lo·nese (sē′lə nēz′, -nēs′), *adj., n., pl.* **-nese. —*adj.* 1.** of or pertaining to Ceylon, its people, or their language. **—*n.* 2.** a native or inhabitant of Ceylon.

Ceylon′ moss′, a seaweed, *Gracilaria lichenoides*, of Ceylon and the East Indies.

Ce·yx (sē′iks), *n. Class. Myth.* the husband of Alcyone.

Cé·zanne (si zan′; *Fr.* sā ZAN′), *n.* **Paul** (pôl), 1839–1906, French painter.

Cf, *Chem.* californium.

cf., **1.** *Bookbinding.* calf. **2.** *Baseball.* center fielder. **3.** (in scholarly writing) compare (def. 3). [< L *confer*]

c/f, *Bookkeeping.* carried forward.

C.F., cost and freight. Also, **c.f.**

C.F.I., cost, freight, and insurance. Also, **c.f.i.**

cfm., cubic feet per minute. Also, **c.f.m.**

cfs., cubic feet per second. Also, **c.f.s.**

CG, Commanding General.

cg., centigram; centigrams.

C.G., **1.** center of gravity. **2.** Coast Guard. **3.** Commanding General. **4.** Consul General.

c.g., **1.** center of gravity. **2.** Commanding General. **3.** Consul General.

cgm., centigram.

cgs, centimeter-gram-second. Also, **c.g.s., CGS**

ch, *Survey., Civ. Eng.* chain; chains.

Ch., **1.** Chaldean. **2.** Chaldee. **3.** chapter. **4.** Château. **5.** *Chess.* check. **6.** China. **7.** Chinese. **8.** church.

ch., **1.** chapter. **2.** *Chess.* check. **3.** church.

c.h., **1.** clearing house. **2.** courthouse. **3.** custom house.

chab·a·zite (kab′ə zīt′), *n.* a zeolite mineral, essentially a hydrated sodium calcium aluminum silicate, occurring usually in red to colorless rhombohedral crystals. [*chabaz(ie)* (< F *chabasie* < LGk *chabázios*, misspelling of *chalázios* hailstonelike (stone) = *chálaz(a)* hail, hailstone + *-ios* adj. suffix) + -ITE[1]; cf. G *Chabasit*]

Chab·lis (shab′lē, shä blē′; *Fr.* SHA blē′), *n.* a dry, white Burgundy table wine. [after *Chablis*, town in Burgundy, France, where orig. made]

cha-cha (chä′chä′), *n., pl.* **-chas,** *v.,* **-chaed, -cha·ing. —*n.* 1.** a Latin-American dance similar to the mambo. **—*v.i.* 2.** to dance the cha-cha. Also, **cha′-cha′-cha′.** [< AmerSp (Cuban) *cha-cha-cha*, prob. imit. of the musical accompaniment]

chac·ma (chak′mə), *n.* a large, brownish-gray baboon, *Papio comatus*, of southern Africa. [< Hottentot]

Chacma (About 2 ft. high at shoulder; total length 4 ft.; tail 1½ ft.)

Cha·co (chä′kô), *n.* a part of the Gran Chaco region in central South America, in Bolivia, Paraguay, and Argentina. ab. 100,000 sq. mi.

cha·conne (sha kôn′, -kon′, shä-; *Fr.* SHA kôn′), *n., pl.* **-connes** (-kônz′, -konz′; *Fr.* -kôn′). **1.** an ancient dance in moderate triple meter. **2.** a musical form based on the continuous variation of a series of chords or of a ground bass. [< F < Sp *chacona*]

Chad (chad), *n.* **1. Lake,** a lake in N central Africa, lying between the Republic of Chad, Niger, Nigeria, and Cameroon. 4000 to 10,000 sq. mi. (seasonal variation). **2. Republic of,** a republic in W central Africa, E of Lake Chad: a member of the French Community; formerly part of French Equatorial Africa. 4,100,000; 501,000 sq. mi. *Cap.:* N'Djamena. French, **Tchad.**

Chad·wick (chad′wik), *n.* **James,** 1891–1974, English physicist: discoverer of the neutron; Nobel prize 1935.

chae·ta (kē′tə), *n., pl.* **-tae** (-tē). *Zool.* a bristle or seta, esp. of a chaetopod. [< NL < Gk *chaítē* long hair]

chaeto-, a learned borrowing from Greek meaning "hair," used in the formation of compound words: *chaetopod.* [comb. form repr. Gk *chaítē*; see CHAETA]

chae·tog·nath (kē′tog nath′, -təg-), *n.* **1.** any animal of the group *Chaetognatha*, comprising the arrowworms. **—*adj.* 2.** Also, **chae·tog·na·than** (kē tog′nə thən), **chae·tog′na·thous.** belonging or pertaining to the *Chaetognatha.* [CHAETO- + Gk *gnáth(os)* jaw]

chae·to·pod (kē′tə pod′), *n.* any annelid of the class or group *Chaetopoda*, having the body composed of segments with muscular processes bearing setae.

chafe (chāf), *v.*, **chafed, chaf·ing,** *n.* —*v.t.* **1.** to warm by rubbing: *to chafe cold hands.* **2.** to wear or abrade by rubbing: *He chafed his shoes on the rocks.* **3.** to make sore by rubbing: *His collar chafed his neck.* **4.** to irritate or annoy. **5.** *Obs.* to heat; make warm. —*v.i.* **6.** to rub; press with friction: *The horse chafed against his stall.* **7.** to become worn or sore from rubbing. **8.** to be irritated or annoyed: *He chafed at her constant interruptions.* —*n.* **9.** irritation; annoyance. **10.** heat, wear, or soreness caused by rubbing. [ME *chaufe(n)* (to) heat, rub, chafe < MF *chaufe(r)* < VL *calfāre, var. of L *cal(e)facere* = *cale-* (s. of *calēre* to be hot) + *facere* to make]

chaf·er (chā′fər), *n.* *Chiefly Brit.* any scarabaeid beetle. [ME *cheaffer, chaver,* OE *ceofor;* akin to G *Käfer*]

chaff[1] (chaf, chäf), *n.* **1.** the husks of grains and grasses that are usually separated during threshing. **2.** straw cut up for fodder. **3.** worthless matter; refuse; rubbish. **4.** the membranous, usually dry, brittle bracts of the flowers of certain plants. [ME *chaf,* OE *ceaf;* c. MLG, D *kaf*]

chaff[2] (chaf, chäf), *v.t., v.i.* **1.** to mock, tease, or jest in a good-natured way; banter. —*n.* **2.** good-natured ridicule or teasing; raillery. [perh. from CHAFF[1]]

chaf·fer[1] (chaf′ər), *n.* **1.** bargaining; haggling. —*v.i.* **2.** to bargain or haggle: *to chaffer over a price.* **3.** to bandy words; chatter. —*v.t.* **4.** to bandy (words). **5.** *Obs.* to trade or deal in; barter. [ME *chaffare* < *chapfare* trading journey = OE *cēap* trade (see CHEAP) + *faru* journey; see FARE] —**chaff′er·er,** *n.*

chaf·fer[2] (chaf′ər), *n.* a person who chaffs or banters. [CHAFF[2] + -ER[1]]

chaf·finch (chaf′inch), *n.* a common finch, *Fringilla coelebs,* of the Old World, often kept as a pet. [ME *chaffynch,* OE *ceaffinc*]

chaf′ing dish′ (chā′fing), a metal dish with a lamp or heating appliance beneath it, for cooking or keeping food hot. [ME *chafing* warming]

Cha·gall (shä gäl′), *n.* **Marc,** 1887–1985, Russian painter in France.

Cha′gas′ disease′ (shä′gəs), *Pathol.* trypanosomiasis, caused by the trypanosome *T. cruzi,* occurring chiefly in tropical America and characterized by irregular fever, palpable lymph nodes, and often heart damage. [named after C. *Chagas* (1879–1934), Brazilian physician, who described it]

Cha′gos Archipel′ago (chä′gōs), a group of islands in the British Indian Ocean Territory. ab. 75 sq. mi.

Cha·gres (chä′gres), *n.* a river in Panama, flowing through Gatun Lake into the Caribbean Sea.

cha·grin (shə grin′), *n., v.,* **-grined** or **-grinned, -grin·ing** or **-grin·ning.** —*n.* **1.** a feeling of vexation, marked by disappointment or humiliation. —*v.t.* **2.** to vex by disappointment or humiliation. **3.** *Obs.* shagreen (def. 1). [< F < ?] —**Syn. 1.** See **shame.**

Cha·har (chä′här′), *n.* a former province of Inner Mongolia in NE China: divided among adjacent provinces 1952. 107,698 sq. mi.

Chai·kov·ski (*Russ.* chī kôf′skē), *n.* **Pëtr Il·ich** (pyô′tər il yēch′). See **Tchaikovsky, Peter Ilyich.**

chain (chān), *n.* **1.** a series of metal rings passing through one another, used either for hauling, supporting, or confining, or as an ornament. **2.** something that binds or restrains; bond: *the chain of timidity.* **3. chains, a.** bonds or fetters. **b.** bondage; servitude: *to live one's life in chains.* **c.** *Naut.* (in a sailing vessel) the area outboard at the foot of the shrouds of a mast. **4.** a series of things connected or following in succession: *a chain of events.* **5.** a range of mountains. **6.** a number of similar establishments under one ownership. **7.** *Chem.* two or more atoms of the same element, usually carbon, attached as in a chain. Cf. **ring**[1] (def. 16). **8.** *Survey., Civ. Eng.* **a.** a distance-measuring device consisting of a chain of 100 links of equal length, having a total length either of 66 feet **(Gunter's chain** or **surveyor's chain)** or of 100 feet **(engineer's chain). b.** a unit of length equal to either of these. *Abbr.:* ch —*v.t.* **9.** to fasten or secure with a chain: *to chain a dog to a post.* **10.** to confine or restrain; fetter as with a chain: *His work chained him to his desk.* **11.** to make (a chain stitch or series of chain stitches) in crocheting. [ME *chayne* < OF *chaeine* < L *catēn(a)* fetter] —**Syn. 4.** sequence.

chain′ gang′, *Chiefly U.S.* a group of convicts chained together, esp. when working outside.

chain′ let′ter, a letter sent to a number of persons, each of whom makes and sends copies to a number of other persons who do likewise: often used as a method of spreading a message or raising money. Also called **pyramid letter.**

chain′ light′ning, *U.S.* lightning that seems to move very quickly in wavy or zigzag lines.

chain′ mail′, *Armor.* mail[2] (def. 1).

chain′ reac′tion, 1. *Physics.* a self-sustaining reaction in which the fission of nuclei produces particles that cause the fission of other nuclei. **2.** *Chem.* a reaction that results in a product necessary for the continuance of the reaction. **3.** any series of events in which each event in turn is the result of the one preceding and the cause of the one following. —**chain-re·act·ing** (chān′rē ak′ting, -ak′-), *adj.*

chain′ reac′tor, reactor (def. 4).

chain′ saw′, a power saw, usually portable, having teeth set on an endless chain.

chain′ shot′, *Ordn.* a shot consisting of two balls or half balls connected by a short chain.

chains·man (chānz′mən), *n., pl.* **-men.** *Naut.* a person who stands in the chains to take soundings; leadsman.

chain′ smok′er, a person who smokes cigarettes or cigars continually. Also, **chain-smok·er** (chān′ smō′kər).

chain′ stitch′, a looped stitch resembling links in a chain.

chain′ store′, one of a group of retail stores under the same ownership.

chain′ wale′, *Naut.* channel[2]. Also, **chain-wale** (chān′-wāl′, chan′əl).

chair (châr), *n.* **1.** a seat, esp. for one person, usually having four legs for support and a rest for the back and often having rests for the arms. **2.** a seat of office or authority. **3.** a position of authority, as of a judge, professor, etc. **4.** the person occupying a seat of office, esp. the chairman of a meeting: *The speaker addressed the chair.* **5.** See **electric chair. 6.** See **sedan chair. 7. take the chair,** to preside at a meeting; act as chairman. —*v.t.* **8.** to place or seat in a chair. **9.** to install in office or authority. **10.** to preside over; act as chairman of: *to chair a committee.* [ME *chaiere* < OF < L *cathedr(a);* see CATHEDRA]

chair′ car′, *Railroads.* **1.** a day coach having two adjustable seats on each side of a central aisle. **2.** (not in technical use) See **parlor car.**

chair·man (châr′mən), *n., pl.* **-men,** *v.* **-maned** or **-manned, -man·ing** or **-man·ning.** —*n.* **1.** the presiding officer of a meeting, committee, board, etc. **2.** someone employed to carry or wheel a person in a chair. —*v.t.* **3.** to act as or be chairman of (a meeting, committee, etc.).

chair·man·ship (châr′mən ship′), *n.* the office or rank of chairman.

chair·per·son (châr′pûr′sən), *n.* a person who presides over a meeting, committee, etc.: used by some to replace, or in preference to, the title of "chairwoman."

chair·wom·an (châr′wŏŏm′ən), *n., pl.* **-wom·en.** a woman who presides over a meeting, committee, etc.

chaise (shāz), *n.* **1.** a light, open carriage, usually with a hood, esp. a one-horse, two-wheeled carriage for two persons; shay. **2.** See **post chaise. 3.** a chaise longue, esp. a light one used out of doors. **4.** Also called **chaise d'or** (shāz dôr′). *Numis.* a 14th-century gold coin of France. [< F. var. of *chaire* CHAIR]

Chaise (def. 1)

chaise longue (shāz′ lông′, chāz′; *Fr.* shez lôɴɢ′), *pl.* **chaise longues,** *Fr.* **chaises longues** (shez lôɴɢ′). a couch or day bed in the form of a reclining chair with the seat lengthened to make a complete leg rest. Also, **chaise lounge** (shāz′ lounj′, chāz′). [< F: long chair]

Chal., 1. Chaldaic. **2.** Chaldean. **3.** Chaldee.

cha·la·za (kə lā′zə), *n., pl.* **-zas, -zae** (-zē). **1.** *Zool.* one of the two albuminous twisted cords that fasten an egg yolk to the shell membrane. **2.** *Bot.* the point of an ovule or seed where the integuments are united to the nucellus. [< NL < Gk: hail, lump] —**cha·la′zal,** *adj.*

Chal·ce·don (kal′si don′, kal sēd′ən), *n.* an ancient city in NW Asia Minor, on the Bosporus: ecumenical council A.D. 451. —**Chal·ce·do·ni·an** (kal′si dō′nē ən), *adj., n.*

chal·ced·o·ny (kal sed′ənē, kal′sə dō′nē), *n., pl.* **-nies.** a microcrystalline, translucent variety of quartz, often milky or grayish. [ME *calcedonie* < LL *chalcēdoni(us)* = *chalcēdōn-* (< Gk *chalkēdṓn* chalcedony, identified by Saint Jerome with *Chalcedon,* the city) + *-ius* -IOUS]

chal′cid fly′ (kal′sid), any of numerous small, hymenopterous insects of the family *Chalcididae,* often having bright metallic coloration, the larvae of which are parasitic on other insects. Also called **chal′cid.** [< Gk *chalk(ós)* copper, brass (with allusion to the metallic coloration) + -ID[2]]

Chal·cid·i·ce (kal sid′i sē), *n.* a peninsula in NE Greece. Greek, **Khalkidike.**

Chal·cis (kal′sis; *Gr.* ᴋʜäl kēs′), *n.* a city on Euboea, in SE Greece: important commercial center from ancient times. 24,745 (1961). Also, **Khalkis.**

chalco-, a learned borrowing from Greek meaning "copper," used in the formation of compound words: *Chalcolithic.* [< Gk *chalko-,* comb. form of *chalkós* copper]

chal·co·cite (kal′kə sīt′), *n.* a common mineral, cuprous sulfide, Cu_2S: an important ore of copper. [irreg. CHALCO- + (ANTHRA)CITE]

chal·cog·ra·phy (kal kog′rə fē), *n.* the art of engraving on copper or brass. —**chal·cog′ra·pher, chal·cog′ra·phist,** *n.* —**chal·co·graph·ic** (kal′kə graf′ik), **chal′co·graph′i·cal,** *adj.*

chal·co·lite (kal′kə līt′), *n.* *Mineral.* torbernite.

Chal·co·lith·ic (kal′kə lith′ik), *adj.* of, pertaining to, or characteristic of the Copper Age; Aeneolithic.

chal·co·py·rite (kal′kə pī′rīt, -pēr′īt), *n.* a very common mineral, copper iron sulfide, $CuFeS_2$, occurring in brass-yellow crystals or masses: the most important ore of copper; copper pyrites.

Chald., 1. Chaldaic. **2.** Chaldean. **3.** Chaldee.

Chal·de·a (kal dē′ə), *n.* an ancient region in the lower Tigris and Euphrates valley.

Chal·de·an (kal dē′ən), *n.* **1.** one of an ancient Semitic people that formed the dominant element in Babylonia. **2.** an astrologer or soothsayer. Dan. 1:4; 2:2. —*adj.* **3.** of or belonging to ancient Chaldea. **4.** pertaining to astrology, occult learning, etc. Also, **Chal·da·ic** (kal dā′ik). [< L *Chaldae(us)* (< Gk *Chaldaîos* Chaldaea, an astrologer) + -AN]

chal·dron (chôl′drən), *n.* an English dry measure for coal, coke, lime, and the like, varying in different localities from 32 to 36 or more bushels. [earlier *chaudron* < MF *chauderon* CAULDRON]

cha·let (sha lā′, shal′ā; *Fr.* shä le′), *n., pl.* **cha·lets** (sha-lāz′, shal′āz; *Fr.* shä le′). **1.** a herdsman's hut in the Swiss mountains. **2.** a kind of farmhouse, low and with wide eaves, common in Alpine regions. **3.** a cottage, villa, ski lodge, or the like, built in this style. [< F, SwissF = *cal(a) shelter (c. OPr *cala* COVE[1]) + *-et* -ET]

Chalet (def. 3)

Cha·lia·pin (shä lyä′pin), *n.* **Fë·dor I·va·no·vich** (fyô′dər i vä′no vich), 1873–1938, Russian operatic bass.

chal·ice (chal′is), *n.* **1.** *Literary.* a drinking cup. **2.** *Eccles.* a cup for the wine of the Eucharist. **3.** a cuplike blossom. [ME < MF < L *calici-*

(s. of *calix*) cup; r. ME *caliz, calc,* OE *calic* < L *calici-,* as above] —**chal·iced** (chal′ist), *adj.*

chalk (chôk), *n.* **1.** a soft, white, powdery limestone consisting chiefly of fossil shells of foraminifers. **2.** a prepared piece of chalk or chalklike substance for marking; a blackboard crayon. **3.** a mark made with chalk. **4.** a score, tally, or record of credit. —*v.t.* **5.** to mark with chalk. **6.** to rub over or whiten with chalk. **7.** to treat with chalk: *to chalk a billiard cue.* **8.** to make pale; blanch: *Terror chalked her face.* —*v.i.* **9.** (of paint) to powder from weathering. **10. chalk up, a.** to score or earn: *They chalked up two runs in the first inning.* **b.** to charge or ascribe to: *His poor performance was chalked up to lack of practice.* —*adj.* **11.** of, made of, or drawn with chalk. [ME *chalke,* OE *cealc* < L *calc-* (s. of *calx*) lime]

chalk·board (chôk′bōrd′, -bôrd′), *n.* a blackboard. [CHALK + BOARD]

chalk·stone (chôk′stōn′), *n. Pathol.* a chalklike concretion in the tissues or small joints of a person with gout. [ME: limestone]

chalk·y (chô′kē), *adj.,* **chalk·i·er, chalk·i·est. 1.** of or like chalk. **2.** of a chalklike consistency: *chalky soil.* [late ME]

chal·lah (KHä′lə, hä′-; *Heb.* KHä lä′), *n., pl.* **chal·lahs,** *Heb.* **chal·loth** (KHä lôt′). *Jewish Cookery.* a loaf of bread leavened with yeast and containing eggs: often braided and glazed with egg before baking, prepared esp. for the Jewish Sabbath. Also, **hallah.** [< Heb *ḥallāh*]

chal·lenge (chal′inj), *n., v.,* **-lenged, -leng·ing.** —*n.* **1.** a call or summons to engage in any contest, as of skill, strength, etc. **2.** something that by its nature or character serves as a call to battle, contest, etc.: *Exploring outer space is a challenge to mankind.* **3.** a call to fight, as a battle, a duel, etc. **4.** a demand to explain or justify: *a challenge to the treasurer to itemize expenditures.* **5.** *Mil.* the demand of a sentry for identification or a countersign. **6.** *Law.* a formal objection to the qualifications of a juror. **7.** *U.S.* the assertion that a vote is invalid or that a voter is not legally qualified. **8.** a difficulty in a job or undertaking that is stimulating to one engaged in it. **9.** *Hunting.* the crying of a hound on finding a scent. —*v.t.* **10.** to summon to a contest of skill, strength, etc. **11.** to demand as something due or rightful. **12.** to take exception to; call in question: *to challenge the wisdom of a procedure.* **13.** *Mil.* to halt and demand identification of. **14.** *Law.* to take formal exception to (a juror or jury). **15.** to arouse or stimulate: *a matter that challenges attention.* **16.** *U.S.* **a.** to assert that (a vote) is invalid. **b.** to assert that (a voter) is not qualified to vote. **17.** *Archaic.* to lay claim to. —*v.i.* **18.** to make or issue a challenge. **19.** *Hunting.* (of hounds) to cry or give tongue on picking up the scent. [ME *chalenge* < OF, var. of *chalonge* < L *calumnia* CALUMNY]

chal·leng·er (chal′in jər), *n.* **1.** a person or thing that challenges. **2.** *Boxing.* a boxer who fights a champion for his title. [ME]

chal·leng·ing (chal′in jing), *adj.* **1.** stimulating and thought-provoking: *a challenging idea.* **2.** provocative; intriguing: *a challenging smile.* **3.** offering a challenge; testing one's ability, endurance, etc.: *a challenging game.*

chal·lis (shal′ē), *n.* a soft fabric of plain weave in wool, cotton, or rayon, either in a solid color or, more often, a small print. Also, **chal′lie, chal′ly.** [? after *Challis,* a surname]

chal·one (kal′ōn), *n. Physiol.* an endocrine secretion that depresses or inhibits physiological activity. [< Gk *chalôn* slackening, loosening, relaxing (prp. of *chalân*) = *chal-* slack + *-ōn* prp. suffix]

Châ·lons (shA lôN′), *n.* **1.** Also called **Châ·lons-sur-Marne** (shA lôN′syr MARN′). a city in NE France: defeat of Attila A.D. 451. 45,348 (1962). **2.** Also called **Châ·lons-sur-Saône** (shA lôN′syr sōn′). a city in E France, on the Saône River. 45,993 (1962).

cha·lutz (KHä lo͞ots′; *Eng.* KHä lo͞ots′, hä-), *n., pl.* **-lu·tzim** (-lo͞o tsēm′; *Eng.* -lo͞ot′sim). *Hebrew.* halutz.

cha·lyb·e·ate (kə lib′ē it, -āt′), *adj.* **1.** containing or impregnated with salts of iron, as a mineral spring, medicine, etc. —*n.* **2.** a chalybeate water, medicine, or the like. [< NL *chalybeāt(us)* = L *chalybē(ius)* of steel (< Gk *chalybēïs* = *chalybē-,* var. s. of *chálүps* iron, ironworker, member of the Chalybes, a tribe of Asia Minor noted for their blacksmiths + *-is* adj. suffix) + *-ātus* -ATE[1]]

cham (kam), *n. Archaic.* khan[1].

cham·ber (chām′bər), *n.* **1.** a room, usually private, in a house or apartment, esp. a bedroom: *She retired to her chamber.* **2.** a room in a palace or official residence. **3.** the meeting hall of a legislative or other assembly. **4. chambers, a.** a place where a judge hears matters not requiring action in open court. **b.** (in England) the quarters or rooms that lawyers use to consult with their clients, esp. in the Inns of Court. **5.** a legislative, judicial, or other like body: *the upper chamber of a legislature.* **6.** a compartment or enclosed space; cavity: *a chamber of the heart.* **7.** (in a canal or the like) the space between any two gates of a lock. **8.** a receptacle for one or more cartridges in a firearm, or for a shell in a gun or other cannon. **9.** (in a gun) the part of the barrel that receives the charge. —*v.t.* **10.** to put or enclose in, or as in, a chamber. **11.** to provide with a chamber. [ME *chambre* < OF < L *camer(a),* var. of *camara* vaulted room, vault < Gk *kamára* vault]

cham′bered nau′tilus, nautilus (def. 1).

cham·ber·lain (chām′bər lin), *n.* **1.** an official charged with the management of a sovereign's or nobleman's living quarters. **2.** an official who receives rents and revenues, as of a municipal corporation; treasurer. **3.** the high steward or factor of a nobleman. **4.** a high official of a royal court. [ME < OF, var. of *chamberlenc* < Frankish **kamerling* = *kamer* (< L *camera* room; see CHAMBER) + *-ling* -LING[1]]

Cham·ber·lain (chām′bər lin), *n.* **1. (Arthur) Neville,** 1869–1940, British statesman: prime minister 1937–40. **2. Joseph,** 1836–1914, British statesman (father of Sir Austen and Neville Chamberlain). **3. Sir (Joseph) Austen,** 1863–1937, British statesman: Nobel peace prize 1925.

cham·ber·maid (chām′bər mād′), *n.* a maid who cleans and straightens bedrooms.

cham′ber mu′sic, music for a small number of solo instruments.

cham′ber of com′merce, an association of businessmen to protect and promote the commercial interests in a community.

cham′ber pot′, a vessel for urine, used in bedrooms.

Chameleon (def. 1), *Chamaeleon chamaeleon* (Length 8 in.)

Cham·bé·ry (shäN bā RĀ′), *n.* a city in SE France. 47,447 (1962).

cham·bray (sham′brā), *n.* a fine cloth of cotton, silk, or linen, commonly of plain weave with a colored warp and white weft. [var. of CAMBRIC]

cha·me·le·on (kə mē′lē ən, -mēl′yən), *n.* **1.** any of numerous Old World agamid lizards of the family *Chamaeleontidae,* characterized by the ability to change the color of their skin, very slow locomotion, and a projectile tongue. **2.** any of several American lizards capable of changing the color of the skin, esp. *Anolis carolinensis* **(American chameleon),** of the southeastern U.S. **3.** an inconstant person. [var. of *chamaeleon* < L < Gk *chamailéōn* = *chamaí* on the ground, dwarf + *léōn* LION; r. ME *camelion* < MF < L, as above]

cham·fer (cham′fər), *n.* an oblique face formed at a corner of a board, post, etc.; bevel. [back formation from *chamfering* < MF *chamfrein* (taken as *chamfer* + -ING[1]) var. of *chanfraint* beveled edge, orig. ptp. of *chanfraindre* to bevel = *chant* edge (< L *canthus;* see CANT[2]) + *fraindre* to break < L *frangere;* see FRANGIBLE] —**cham′fer·er,** *n.*

cham·my (sham′ē), *n., pl.* **-mies,** *v.t.,* **-mied, -my·ing.** chamois (defs. 2–6).

Chamois (About 2½ ft. high at shoulder; horns to 10 in.; length 4 ft.)

cham·ois (sham′ē; *Fr.* shA mwä′), *n., pl.* **cham·ois, cham·oix** (sham′ēz; *Fr.* shA mwä′), *v.,* **cham·oised** (sham′ēd), **cham·ois·ing** (sham′ē ing). —*n.* **1.** an agile, goatlike antelope, *Rupicapra rupicapra,* of high mountains of Europe and southwestern Russia. **2.** a soft, pliable leather from any of various skins dressed with oil. **3.** a piece of this leather. **4.** a cotton cloth finished to simulate this leather. —*v.t.* **5.** to dress (a pelt) in order to produce a chamois. **6.** to rub or buff with a chamois. Also, **chammy, shammy, shamoy** (for defs. 2–6). [< MF < LL *camox* < ?; cf. G *Gemse* < OHG *gamiza* in same sense]

cham·o·mile (kam′ə mīl′, -mēl′), *n.* camomile.

Cha·mo·nix (sham′ə nē; *Fr.* shA mô nē′), *n.* a mountain valley in E France, N of Mont Blanc. Also, **Chamouni.**

Cha·mou·ni (*Fr.* shA mo͞o nē′), *n.* Chamonix.

champ[1] (champ), *v.t.* **1.** to bite upon or grind, esp. impatiently. **2.** to crush with the teeth and chew vigorously or noisily; munch. —*v.i.* **3.** to make vigorous chewing or biting movements with the jaws and teeth. **4. champ at the bit,** to betray impatience, as to begin some action. —*n.* **5.** the act of champing. [perh. nasalized var. of CHAP[1]; see CHOP[1]] —**champ′er,** *n.* —**champ′y,** *adj.*

champ[2] (champ), *n. Informal.* a champion. [by shortening]

cham·pac (cham′pak, chum′puk), *n.* an East Indian tree, *Michelia Champaca,* of the magnolia family, with fragrant golden flowers and a handsome wood used for making images, furniture, etc. Also, **cham′pak.** [< Hindi *campak* < Skt *campaka*]

cham·pagne (sham pān′), *n.* **1.** the sparkling, dry, white table wine from the region of Champagne. **2.** a similar sparkling wine produced elsewhere.

Cham·pagne (sham pān′; *Fr.* shäN PAN′yᵊ), *n.* a region and former province in NE France. See map at **Burgundy.**

cham·paign (sham pān′), *n.* **1.** level, open country; plain. **2.** *Obs.* a battlefield. —*adj.* **3.** level and open: *champaign fields.* [ME *champai(g)ne* < MF *champa(i)gne* < LL *campānia;* see CAMPAIGN]

Cham·paign (sham pān′), *n.* a city in E Illinois. 56,532 (1970).

cham·per·ty (cham′pər tē), *n. Law.* a sharing in the proceeds of litigation by a person who promotes it or carries it on, illegal in many jurisdictions. [ME *champartie* = *champart* (< MF: share of the produce, lit., of the field = *champ* field (see CAMP[1]) + *part* share; see PART) + *-ie* -Y[3]] —**cham′per·tous,** *adj.*

cham·pi·gnon (sham pin′yən *or, esp. Brit.,* cham-; *Fr.* shäN pē nyôN′), *n., pl.* **-pi·gnons** (-pin′yənz; *Fr.* -pē nyôN′). mushroom (defs. 2, 3). [< MF, appar. << VL **campīn(us)* of the field (see CAMP[1], -INE[1]) + L *-iōn-* -ION]

cham·pi·on (cham′pē ən), *n.* **1.** a person who has defeated all opponents in a competition or series of competitions and thus holds first place. **2.** anything that takes first place in competition. **3.** an animal that has won a specified number of points in officially recognized shows. **4.** a person who fights for or defends any person or cause. **5.** a fighter or warrior. —*v.t.* **6.** to act as champion of; defend; support. **7.** *Obs.* to defy. —*adj.* **8.** first among all contestants or competitors. [ME < OF < LL *campiōn-* (s. of *campiō*) < WGmc **kampiōn-* = *kamp-* battle (< L *camp(us)* field, battlefield) + *-iōn-* n. suffix (< L); cf. OE *cempa* warrior, etc.] —**Syn. 1.** winner, victor. **4.** defender, protector, vindicator. **6.** maintain, fight for, advocate.

cham·pi·on·ship (cham′pē ən ship′), *n.* **1.** the distinction or condition of being a champion: *to win a championship.* **2.** advocacy or defense: *championship of the underdog.* **3. championships,** competitions to determine a champion: *the tennis championships.*

Cham·plain (sham plān′; *for 1 also Fr.* shäN plaN′), *n.* **1. Sa·mu·el de** (sam′yo͞o əl də; *Fr.* sA mY el′ də), 1567–1635, French explorer in the Americas: founder of Quebec; 1st colonial governor 1633–35. **2. Lake,** a lake between New York and Vermont. 125 mi. long; ab. 600 sq. mi.

Cham·pol·lion (shäN pô lyôN′), *n.* **Jean Fran·çois** (zhäN fräN swA′), 1790–1832, French Egyptologist: deciphered the Rosetta Stone.

Champs É·ly·sées (shäN zā lē zā′), a boulevard in Paris, France: cafés, shops, theaters; a tourist center.

Ch'an (chän), *n. Chinese.* Zen (def. 1).

chance (chans, chäns), *n., v.,* **chanced, chanc·ing,** *adj.* —*n.* **1.** the unpredictable and unwilled element in an occurrence. **2.** luck or fortune: *a game of chance.* **3.** a possibility or probability of anything happening: *a fifty-percent chance of success.* **4.** an opportunity: *Now is your chance.* **5.** *Baseball.* an opportunity to field the ball and make a put-out or assist. **6.** a risk or hazard: *Take a chance.* **7. chances,** probability: *The chances are that the train hasn't left yet.* **8.** *Archaic.* an unfortunate event; mishap. **9. by chance,** without plan or intent; accidentally. **10. on the chance,** in the mild hope or against the possibility. **11. on the off chance,** in the very slight hope or against the very slight possibility. —*v.i.* **12.** to happen or occur by chance: *It chanced that our arrivals coincided.* —*v.t.* **13.** *Informal.* to take the chances or risks of; risk (often fol. by impersonal *it*): *I'll have to chance it, whatever the outcome.* **14. chance on** or **upon,** to come upon by chance. —*adj.* **15.** occurring by chance: *a chance encounter.* [ME < OF, var. of *cheance* < VL **cadentia* a befalling, happening; see CADENZA] —**chance′ful,** *adj.* —**Syn. 2.** accident, fortuity. **3.** contingency. **4.** opening. **12.** befall. See **happen. 15.** casual, accidental, fortuitous. —**Ant. 1.** necessity.

chan·cel (chan′səl, chän′-), *n.* the space about the altar of a church, usually enclosed, for the clergy and other officials. [ME < MF < LL *cancell(us)* lattice, railing, or screen before the altar of a church, L *cancell(ī)* (pl.) lattice, railing, grating; see CANCEL] —**chan′celed, chan′celled,** *adj.*

chan·cel·ler·y (chan′sə lə rē, -slə rē, chän′-), *n., pl.* **-ler·ies. 1.** the position of a chancellor. **2.** the office or department of a chancellor. **3.** the office attached to an embassy or consulate. **4.** a building or room occupied by a chancellor's department. [ME *chancellerie* < AF; see CHANCELLOR, -Y[3]]

chan·cel·lor (chan′sə lər, -slər, chän′-), *n.* **1.** the chief minister of state, as in West Germany. **2.** a secretary, as to a king or nobleman or of an embassy. **3.** the chief administrative officer in certain American universities. **4.** *Brit.* the honorary, nonresident, titular head of a university. Cf. **vice chancellor. 5.** *U.S.* the judge of a court of chancery. [ME *chanceler* < AF < LL *cancellār(ius)* doorkeeper, lit., man at the barrier (see CHANCEL, -ER[2]); r. ME, OE *canceler* << LL, as above] —**chan′cel·lor·ship′,** *n.*

Chan′cellor of the Excheq′uer, the minister of finance in the British government.

Chan·cel·lors·ville (chan′sə lərz vil′, -slərz-, chän′-), *n.* a village in NE Virginia: site of a Confederate victory 1863.

chance-med·ley (chans′med′lē, chäns′-), *n. Law.* a sudden quarrel, with violence. [< AF *chance medlee*]

chan·cer·y (chan′sə rē, chän′-), *n., pl.* **-cer·ies. 1.** the office or department of a chancellor; chancellery. **2.** an office of public records, esp. those of the Lord Chancellor in England. **3.** (in England) the Lord Chancellor's court, now a division of the High Court of Justice. **4.** *Law.* **a.** Also called **court of chancery.** a court having jurisdiction in equity. **b.** equity (defs. 3a, b). **5.** *Rom. Cath. Ch.* a department of the Curia Romana now having the responsibility for issuing bulls to establish new dioceses, benefices, etc. **6. in chancery, a.** *Law.* in litigation in a court of chancery. **b.** in a helpless or embarrassing position. [ME *chancerie,* var. of *chancelrie,* syncopated var. of *chancellerie* CHANCELLERY]

chan·cre (shang′kər), *n. Pathol.* the initial lesion of syphilis, commonly a more or less distinct ulcer or sore with a hard base. [< MF << L *cancr-* (s. of *cancer* CANCER)] —**chan′crous,** *adj.*

chan·croid (shang′kroid), *n. Pathol.* an infectious venereal ulcer with a soft base. Also called **soft chancre.** —**chan·croi′dal,** *adj.*

chanc·y (chan′sē, chän′-), *adj.,* **chanc·i·er, chanc·i·est. 1.** uncertain; risky. **2.** *Chiefly Scot.* lucky.

chan·de·lier (shan′dᵊlēr′), *n.* a light fixture suspended from a ceiling. [< F: lit., something that holds candles; see CHANDLER]

chan·delle (shan del′; *Fr.* shäN del′), *n., pl.* **-delles** (-delz′; *Fr.* -del′). *Aeron.* an abrupt climbing turn in which an aircraft almost stalls while using its momentum to gain a higher rate of climb. [< F: lit., CANDLE]

Chan·der·na·gor (chun′dər nə gōr′, -gôr′), *n.* a port in S West Bengal, in E India, on the Hooghly River: a former French dependency. 67,100 (1961). Also, **Chan·dar·na·gar** (chun′dər nug′ər).

Chan·di·garh (chun′di gur′), *n.* a city in and the capital of Punjab, in N India. 89,300 (1961).

chan·dler (chand′lər, chänd′-), *n.* **1.** a dealer or trader in supplies, provisions, trinkets, etc. **2.** a person who makes or sells candles. [ME *chandeler* candlestick, maker or seller of candles < AF, OF *chandelier,* lit., someone or something connected with candles = *chandelle* CANDLE + *-ier* -IER]

chan·dler·y (chand′lə rē, chänd′-), *n., pl.* **-dler·ies. 1.** a storeroom for candles. **2.** the warehouse, wares, or business of a chandler.

Chan·dra·gup·ta (chun′drə go͝op′tə), *n.* (*Chandragupta Maurya*) died 286? B.C., king of northern India 322?–298: founder of the Maurya empire. Greek, **Sandrocottus, Sandrakottos.**

Cha·nel (shə nel′; *Fr.* shA nel′), *n.* **Ga·bri·elle** (gA brē el′), (*"Coco"*), 1882–1971, French fashion designer.

chan·fron (chan′frən), *n.* a piece of plate armor for defending a horse's head. [late ME *shamfron* < MF *chanfrain* < ?]

Chang·chun (chäng′cho͞on′), *n.* a city in and the capital of Kirin, in NE China: former capital of Manchuria. 975,000 (est. 1957). Also called **Hsinking.**

change (chānj), *v.,* **changed, chang·ing,** *n.* —*v.t.* **1.** to make different the form, nature, content, future course, etc., of (something). **2.** to transform or convert (usually fol. by *into*): *The witch changed the prince into a toad.* **3.** to substitute another or others for; exchange for something else, usually of the same kind. **4.** to give and take reciprocally; interchange. **5.** to give or get money in smaller denominations in exchange for: *to change a five-dollar bill.* **6.** to give or get different money in exchange for: *to change dollars into francs.* **7.** to remove and replace the covering or coverings of: *to change a bed; to change a baby.* —*v.i.* **8.** to become different. **9.** to become altered or modified. **10.** to become transformed or converted (usually fol. by *into*). **11.** to pass gradually (fol. by *to* or *into*): *Summer changed to autumn.* **12.** to make a change or an exchange. **13.** to change trains or other conveyances: *We can change to an express.* **14.** to change one's clothes: *She changed into a dinner dress.* **15.** (of the moon) to pass from one phase to another. **16.** (of the voice) to become deeper in tone; come to have a lower register. **17. change hands.** See **hand** (def. 31). —*n.* **18.** the act or fact of changing. **19.** the fact of being changed. **20.** a transformation or modification; alteration. **21.** a variation or deviation: *a change in the daily routine.* **22.** the substitution of one thing for another. **23.** variety or novelty: *Let's try a new restaurant for a change.* **24.** the passing from one place, state, form, or phase to another: *a change of seasons.* **25.** the supplanting of one thing by another. **26.** anything that is or may be substituted for another. **27.** a fresh set of clothing. **28.** money given in exchange for an equivalent of higher denomination. **29.** a balance of money that is returned when the sum tendered in payment is larger than the sum due. **30.** coins, collectively, as distinguished from paper money or bills. **31.** Also, **'change.** *Brit.* exchange (def. 9). **32.** any of the various sequences in which a peal of bells may be rung. **33.** *Obs.* changefulness; caprice. **34. ring the changes,** to vary the manner of performing an action or of discussing a subject; repeat with variations. [ME *change(n)* < OF *change(r)* < LL *cambiāre,* L *cambīre* to exchange] —**Syn. 1.** transmute, transform; vary, mutate; amend, modify. **3.** replace, trade. **4.** trade. **6.** convert. **9.** vary, mutate, amend. **18, 19.** transmutation, mutation, conversion, vicissitude. **22.** exchange. **25, 26.** replacement. —**Ant. 9.** remain. **18, 19.** permanence.

change·a·ble (chān′jə bəl), *adj.* **1.** liable to change or to be changed; variable. **2.** of changing color or appearance: *changeable silk.* [ME] —**change′a·bil′i·ty, change′a·ble·ness,** *n.* —**change′a·bly,** *adv.*

change·ful (chānj′fəl), *adj.* changing; variable; inconstant. —**change′ful·ly,** *adv.* —**change′ful·ness,** *n.*

change·less (chānj′lis), *adj.* unchanging; constant; steadfast. —**change′less·ly,** *adv.* —**change′less·ness,** *n.*

change·ling (chānj′ling), *n.* **1.** a child surreptitiously or unintentionally substituted for another. **2.** *Archaic.* **a.** a disloyal person. **b.** an imbecile.

change′ of life′, menopause.

change′ of ven′ue, *Law.* the removal of a trial to another jurisdiction, as another district or county.

change·o·ver (chānj′ō′vər), *n.* a conversion or complete change from one thing, condition, or system to another, as in equipment, personnel, methods, etc.

change′ ring′ing, the art of ringing a series of bells of different tones according to any of various orderly sequences.

Chang Hsueh-liang (jäng′ shYe′lyäng′), born 1898, Chinese Nationalist general against the Japanese.

Chang·sha (chäng′shä′), *n.* a city in and the capital of Hunan province, in SE China. 703,000 (est. 1957).

Chang·teh (chäng′du′), *n.* a city in N Hunan, in E China. ab. 300,000.

Chang Tso-lin (jäng′ tsō′lin′), 1873–1928, Chinese general: military ruler of Manchuria 1918–28.

chan·nel[1] (chan′ᵊl), *n., v.,* **-neled, -nel·ing** or (*esp. Brit.*) **-nelled, -nel·ling.** —*n.* **1.** the bed of a stream or waterway. **2.** *Archit.* **a.** a flute in a column, esp. one having no fillet between it and other flutes. **b.** any of the prominent vertical grooves in a triglyph. **3.** the deeper part of a waterway. **4.** a wide strait, as between a continent and an island. **5.** *Naut.* a navigable route between two bodies of water. **6.** a means of access: *He considers the Senate a channel to the White House.* **7.** a course or direction. **8.** a route through which anything passes or progresses: *channels of trade.* **9. channels,** the specific, prescribed, or official course or means of communication. **10.** a frequency band wide enough for one-way communication. **11.** *Computer Technol.* a circuit in a computer for the flow of information. **12.** a tubular passage for liquids or fluids. **13.** a groove or furrow. **14.** *Building Trades.* **a.** any structural member having the form of three sides of a rectangle. **b.** a number of such members: *channel in 100-foot lengths.* **c.** See **channel iron.** —*v.t.* **15.** to convey through or as through a channel: *He channeled the information to us.* **16.** to direct: *to channel one's interests.* **17.** to excavate as a channel: *The river channeled its course through the valley.* **18.** to form a channel in; groove. —*v.i.* **19.** to become marked by a channel or channels. [ME *chanel* < OF < L *canāl(is)* waterpipe; see CANAL[1]] —**chan′nel·er;** *esp. Brit.,* **chan′nel·ler,** *n.*

chan·nel[2] (chan′ᵊl), *n. Naut.* a horizontal timber or ledge built outboard from the side of a sailing vessel to spread shrouds and backstays at their feet. Also called **chain wale, chain-wale.** [var. of CHAIN WALE]

chan′nel i′ron, a rolled steel or iron shape having a U-like cross section. Also called **chan′nel bar′.** See illus. at **shape.**

Chan′nel Is′lands, a British island group in the English Channel, near the coast of France, consisting of Alderney, Guernsey, Jersey, and smaller islands. 104,398 (1961); 75 sq. mi.

chan·nel·ize (chan′ᵊlīz′), *v.t., v.i.,* **-ized, -iz·ing.** to channel —**chan′nel·i·za′tion,** *n.*

Chan·ning (chan′ing), *n.* **1. Edward,** 1856–1931, U.S. historian. **2. William El·ler·y** (el′ə rē), 1780–1842, U.S. Unitarian clergyman and writer.

chan·son (shan′sən; *Fr.* shäN sôN′), *n., pl.* **-sons** (-sənz; *Fr.* -sôN′). any of several types of song with French lyrics. [< F < L *cantiōn-* (s. of *cantiō*) song; see CANZONE]

chan·son de geste (shäN sôN də zhest′), *pl.* **chan·sons de geste** (shäN sôN də zhest′). (in medieval French literature) an epic poem written in assonant verse and based on historical or legendary events or figures. [< F: lit., song of deeds; see CHANSON, GEST[1]]

chant (chant, chänt), *n.* **1.** a song; singing. **2.** a short, simple melody, esp. one characterized by single notes to which an indefinite number of syllables are intoned, used in singing the psalms, canticles, etc., in the church service. **3.** a monotonous song. **4.** a monotonous intonation of the voice in speaking. —*v.t.* **5.** to sing. **6.** to celebrate in song. **7.** to sing to a chant, or in the manner of a chant, esp. in the church service. —*v.i.* **8.** to sing. **9.** to sing a chant. [ME *chant(en)* < MF *chante(r)* < L *cantāre*, freq. of *canere* to sing] —**chant′ing·ly,** *adv.*

chant·er (chan′tər, chän′-), *n.* **1.** a person who chants; singer. **2.** a chorister; precentor. **3.** the chief singer or priest of a chantry. **4.** the pipe of a bagpipe provided with finger holes for playing the melody. [CHANT + -ER[1]; r. ME *chantour* < AF, var. of OF *chanteor* < L *cantātōr-* (s. of *cantātor*) singer; see -OR[2]] —**chant′er·ship′,** *n.*

chan·te·relle (shan′tə rel′, chan′-), *n.* a mushroom, *Cantharellus cibarius*, a favorite edible species in France. [< F < NL *cantharell(a)* = L *canthar(us)* tankard (< Gk *kántharos*) + *-ella* dim. suffix]

chan·teuse (shan to͞os′; *Fr.* shäN tœz′), *n., pl.* **-teuses** (-to͞o′siz; *Fr.* -tœz′). a female singer, esp. a woman who sings in nightclubs and cabarets. [< F, fem. of *chanteur*, OF *chanteor;* see CHANTER]

chant·ey (shan′tē, chan′-), *n., pl.* **-eys.** a sailors' song, esp. one sung in rhythm to work. Also, **chanty, shantey, shanty.** [alter. of F *chanter* to sing; see CHANT]

chan·ti·cleer (chan′tə klēr′), *n.* a rooster. Also, **chan·te·cler** (chan′tə klâr′). [ME *Chauntecler* < OF *Chantecler*, n. use of v. phrase *chante cler* sing clear. See CHANT, CLEAR]

Chan·til·ly (shan til′ē; *Fr.* shäN tē yē′), *n.* **1.** a town in N France, N of Paris: lace manufacture. 8324 (1962). **2.** (*sometimes l.c.*) Also called **Chantil′ly lace′.** a delicate silk or linen bobbin lace, widely used for bridal gowns and evening gowns. —*adj.* **3.** (of food) prepared or served with whipped cream: *strawberries Chantilly.*

chan·try (chan′trē, chän′-), *n., pl.* **-tries.** *Eccles.* **1.** an endowment for the singing or saying of Mass for the souls of the founders or of persons named by them. **2.** a chapel or the like so endowed. **3.** a chapel attached to a church, used for minor services. [ME *chanterie* < MF; see CHANT, -ERY]

chant·y (shan′tē, chan′tē), *n., pl.* **chant·ies.** chantey.

Cha·nu·kah (KHä′nə kə, -no͝o kä′, hä′-; *Heb.* KHä no͝o kä′), *n. Judaism.* Hanukkah.

Cha·ny (chä′nē, *Russ.* chä′ni), *n.* **Lake,** a salt lake in SW Siberia, in the W Soviet Union in Asia. ab. 1300 sq. mi.

Chao K'uang-yin (jou′ kwäng′yin′), 927–976 A.D., Chinese emperor 960–976: founder of the Sung dynasty. Also called **Kao Tsu.**

Chao Phra·ya (chou′ PRä yä′), Menam.

cha·os (kā′os), *n.* **1.** a state of utter confusion or disorder. **2.** any confused, disorderly mass: *a chaos of meaningless phrases.* **3.** the infinity of space or formless matter supposed to have preceded the existence of the ordered universe. **4.** (*cap.*) a personification of this in any of several ancient Greek myths. **5.** *Obs.* a chasm or abyss. [ME < L < Gk]

cha·ot·ic (kā ot′ik), *adj.* wholly confused or disordered: *a chaotic mind; a chaotic mass of books and papers.* [CHAO(S) + -TIC] —**cha·ot′i·cal·ly,** *adv.* —**Ant.** orderly, systematic.

chap[1] (chap), *v.,* **chapped, chap·ping,** *n.* —*v.t.* **1.** (of cold or exposure) to crack, roughen, and redden (the skin). —*v.i.* **2.** to become chapped. —*n.* **3.** a fissure or crack, esp. in the skin. [ME *chapp(en)*; c. D *kappen* to cut; akin to CHIP[1]]

chap[2] (chap), *n. Informal.* a fellow; man or boy. [short for CHAPMAN]

chap[3] (chop, chap), *n.* chop[3]. [? special use of CHAP[1]]

chap., **1.** Chaplain. **2.** chapter. Also, **Chap.**

cha·pa·ra·jos (shap′ə rā′ōs; *Sp.* chä′pä Rä′hôs), *n.pl.* (in Mexico) chaps. Also, **cha·pa·re·jos** (shap′ə rā′ōs; *Sp.* chä′pä Re′hôs). [< MexSp, var. of *chaparejos* = *chapa(rral)* CHAPARRAL + *aparejos*, pl. of *aparejo* gear; akin to APPAREL]

chap·ar·ral (chap′ə ral′), *n. Southwestern U.S.* **1.** a close growth of low, evergreen oaks. **2.** any dense thicket. [< Sp = *chaparr(o)* evergreen oak (< Basque *tshapar*) + *-al* collective suffix]

chaparral′ bird′, roadrunner. Also called **chaparral′ cock′.**

chap·book (chap′bo͝ok′), *n.* a small book or pamphlet of popular tales, ballads, etc., formerly hawked about by chapmen. [*chap* (as in CHAPMAN) + BOOK]

chape (chāp), *n.* the lowermost terminal mount of a scabbard. [ME < MF: (metal) covering < LL *cap(p)a*. See CAP[1], CAPE[1]] —**chape′less,** *adj.*

cha·peau (sha pō′; *Fr.* shA pō′), *n., pl.* **-peaux** (-pōz′; *Fr.* -pō′), **-peaus.** **1.** a hat. **2.** *Heraldry.* **a.** a representation of a low-crowned hat with a turned-up brim, usually of a different tincture, used either as a charge or as part of a crest. **b.** a cap depicted within a representation of a crown or coronet. [< F; OF *chapel* wreath, hat < LL *cappell(us)* hood, hat = *capp(a)* (see CAP[1]) + *-ellus* dim. suffix]

chap·el (chap′əl), *n.* **1.** a private or subordinate place of prayer or worship; oratory. **2.** a separately dedicated part of a church, or a small independent churchlike edifice, devoted to special services. **3.** a room or building for worship in an institution, palace, etc. **4.** (in Great Britain) a place of worship for members of various dissenting Protestant churches, as Baptists or Methodists. **5.** a separate place of public worship dependent on the church of a parish. **6.** a choir or orchestra of a chapel, court, etc. **7.** a print shop or printing house. **8.** the body of printers belonging to a printing house. —*adj.* **9.** (in England) belonging to any of various dissenting Protestant sects, as the Baptists or Methodists. [ME *chapele* < OF < LL *cappell(a)* hooded cloak = *capp(a)* (see CAP[1]) + *-ella* dim. suffix; first applied to the sanctuary where the cloak of St. Martin (4th-century bishop of Tours) was kept as a relic]

Chap′el Hill′, a city in North Carolina. 25,537 (1970)

chap·er·on (shap′ə rōn′), *n.* **1.** a person, usually a married or elderly woman, who, for reasons of propriety, accompanies a young unmarried woman or attends a party of young unmarried men and women. —*v.t.* **2.** to attend or accompany as chaperon. [< F: hood, protection, protector = *chaper-* (? var. of *chapel* CHAPEAU, with *r* for *l* as in CHAPTER) + *-on* dim. suffix] —**chap·er·on·age** (shap′ə rō′nij), *n.* —**Syn. 1, 2.** escort.

chap·er·one (shap′ə rōn′), *n., v.t.,* **-oned, -on·ing.** chaperon.

chap·fall·en (chop′fô′lən, chap′-), *adj.* dispirited; chagrined; dejected. Also, **chopfallen.**

chap·lain (chap′lin), *n.* **1.** an ecclesiastic attached to the chapel of a royal court, college, etc., or to a military unit. **2.** a person who says the prayer, invocation, etc., for an organization or at an assembly or gathering. [ME *chapelain* < MF < LL *cappellān(us)* custodian of St. Martin's cloak (see CHAPEL, -AN); r. OE *capellan* < LL] —**chap′lain·cy, chap′lain·ship′, chap′lain·ry,** *n.*

chap·let (chap′lit), *n.* **1.** a wreath or garland for the head. **2.** a string of beads. **3.** *Rom. Cath. Ch.* a string of beads, one third the length of a rosary, for counting prayers. [ME *chapelet* wreath < OF; see CHAPEAU, -ET] —**chap′let·ed,** *adj.*

Chap·lin (chap′lin), *n.* **Sir Charles Spencer** (*Charlie*), 1889–1977, English motion-picture actor, mime, producer, and director; in U.S. 1910–52.

chap·man (chap′mən), *n., pl.* **-men.** **1.** *Brit.* a hawker or peddler. **2.** *Archaic.* a merchant. [ME; OE *cēapman* (*cēap* buying and selling + *man* MAN[1]); c. D *koopman*, G *Kaufmann;* see CHEAP] —**chap′man·ship′,** *n.*

Chap·man (chap′mən), *n.* **1. George,** 1559–1634, English poet, dramatist, and translator. **2. John.** See **Appleseed.**

chaps (chaps, shaps), *n.pl. Western U.S.* strong, trouserlike leggings of leather, often widely flared, worn esp. by cowboys. Also called **chaparajos, chaparejos.** [short for CHAPARAJOS]

Chap Stick (chap′stik′), *n. Trademark.* a small stick of medicated petrolatum, wax, etc., used as a salve for chapped lips, cold sores, etc.

chap·ter (chap′tər), *n.* **1.** a main division of a book, treatise, or the like, usually bearing a number or title. **2.** an important portion or division of anything. **3.** a branch, usually restricted to a given locality, of a society, organization, fraternity, etc. **4.** *Eccles.* **a.** an assembly of the monks in a monastery, of those in a province, or of the entire order. **b.** a general assembly of the canons of a church. **c.** the body of such monks or canons collectively. **5.** any general assembly. **6.** *Liturgy.* a short Scriptural quotation read at various parts of the office. —*v.t.* **7.** to divide into or arrange in chapters. [ME *chapiter*, var. of *chapitre* < OF < L *capitul(um)* little head (*capit-*, s. of *caput* head + *-ulum* -ULE); in LL, also section of a book; in ML, section read at a meeting, hence, the meeting, esp. one of canons, hence, a body of canons] —**chap′ter·al,** *adj.*

chap′ter house′, **1.** *Eccles.* a building attached to a cathedral or monastery, used as a meeting place for the chapter. **2.** a building used as a meeting place by a chapter of a society, fraternity, etc. [ME *chapitelhus*]

chap′ter ring′, a ringlike band on the dial of a clock that bears the numerals or other symbols of the hours.

Cha·pul·te·pec (chə pul′tə pek′; *Sp.* chä po͞ol′te pek′), *n.* a large park in Mexico City: includes a castle-fortress captured by U.S. forces (1847) in the Mexican War.

char[1] (chär), *v.,* **charred, char·ring,** *n.* —*v.t.* **1.** to burn or reduce to charcoal. **2.** to burn slightly; scorch. —*v.i.* **3.** to become charred. —*n.* **4.** a charred material or surface. **5.** charcoal. **6.** a superior fuel, a by-product of converting coal into gaseous or liquid fuel. [appar. abstraction of *char-* of CHARCOAL]

char[2] (chär), *n., pl.* (*esp. collectively*) **char,** (*esp. referring to two or more kinds or species*) **chars.** any trout of the genus *Salvelinus* (or *Christovomer*), esp. *S. alpinus*, found in Europe. Also, **charr.** [perh. OE **ceorr(a)*, lit., turner < *ceorran* to turn, it being thought of as swimming to and fro time and again; see CHAR[3]]

char[3] (chär), *n. Chiefly Brit.* **1.** a charwoman. **2.** a task, esp. a household chore. [ME *cherre*, OE *cerr, cierr* turn, time, occasion, affair < *cierran* to turn]

char[4] (chär), *n. Brit. Slang.* tea. [< AInd < Hindi *cā* TEA]

char., **1.** character. **2.** charter.

char-à-banc (shar′ə bang′, -bangk′; *Fr.* shA RA bäN′), *n., pl.* **-bancs** (-bangz′, -bangks′; *Fr.* -bäN′). *Brit.* a sightseeing bus with open sides. Also, **char′a·banc′.** [back formation from F *char-à-bancs*, lit., car with benches, the *-s* being taken as pl. ending of word as a whole]

char·a·cin (kar′ə sin), *n.* any fresh-water fish of the family *Characinidae*, found in Africa and Central and South America. [< NL *Characin(idae)* = *characin(us)* the genus (*charac-* (< Gk *charak-*, s. of *chárax* a sea fish) + *-inus* -IN[1]) + *-idae* -IDAE]

char·ac·ter (kar′ik tər), *n.* **1.** the aggregate of features and traits that form the individual nature of some person or thing. **2.** one such feature or trait; characteristic. **3.** moral or ethical quality. **4.** qualities of honesty, courage, or the like; integrity: *It takes character to talk up to a bully like that.* **5.** reputation. **6.** good repute. **7.** an account of the qualities or peculiarities of a person or thing. **8.** a formal statement from an employer concerning the qualities and habits of a former servant or employee; reference. **9.** status or capacity. **10.** a person, esp. with reference to behavior or personality: *a suspicious character; a weak character.* **11.** *Informal.* an odd or eccentric person. **12.** a person represented in a drama, story, etc. **13.** *Literature.* (esp. in 17th- and 18th-century England) a formal character sketch or descriptive analysis of a particular human virtue or vice as represented in a person or type. **14.** a part or role, as in a play, motion picture, or the like. **15.** *Genetics.* any trait, function, structure, or substance of an organism resulting from the effect of one or more genes as modified by the environment. **16.** a significant visual mark or symbol. **17.** a symbol as used in a writing system, as a letter of the alphabet. **18.** the symbols of a writing system collectively. **19.** *Computer Technol.* **a.** any

symbol, as a number or letter that represents information and, when encoded, is usable by a machine. **b.** a pattern of ones and zeros representing the relationship of positive and negative pulses in a computer. **20.** a style of writing or printing. **21. in** or **out of character,** in or out of harmony with one's nature or disposition. —*adj.* **22.** *Theat.* representing or portraying a marked or distinctive personality type: *character actor.* —*v.t. Archaic.* **23.** to portray; describe. **24.** to engrave; inscribe. [< L < Gk *charaktḗr* graving tool, its mark = *charak-* (var. s. of *charássein* to engrave) + *-tēr* instrumental suffix; r. ME *caractere* < MF < L, as above] —**char′ac·ter·ful,** *adj.* —**char′ac·ter·less,** *adj.*
—**Syn. 1.** Character, individuality, personality refer to the sum of the characteristics possessed by a person. Character refers esp. to moral qualities, ethical standards, principles, and the like: *a man of sterling character.* Individuality refers to the distinctive qualities that make one recognizable as a person differentiated from others: *a man of strong individuality.* Personality refers particularly to the combination of outer and inner characteristics that determine the impression that a person makes upon others: *a man of pleasing personality.* **5.** name, repute. See **reputation. 16.** sign, figure, emblem.

char·ac·ter·i·sa·tion (kar′ik tər i zā′shən, -tri zā′- *or, esp. Brit.,* -tə rī-), *n. Chiefly Brit.* characterization.

char·ac·ter·ise (kar′ik tə rīz′), *v.t.,* **-ised, -is·ing.** *Chiefly Brit.* characterize. —**char′ac·ter·is′a·ble,** *adj.* —**char′ac·ter·is′er,** *n.*

char·ac·ter·is·tic (kar′ik tə ris′tik), *adj.* **1.** Also, **char′ac·ter·is′ti·cal.** pertaining to, constituting, or indicating the character or peculiar quality of a person or thing; typical; distinctive. —*n.* **2.** a distinguishing feature or quality. **3.** *Math.* **a.** the integral part of a common logarithm. Cf. **mantissa. b.** the exponent of 10 in a number expressed in scientific notation. [< Gk *charaktēristik(ós)*] —**char′ac·ter·is′ti·cal·ly,** *adv.* —**Syn. 1.** special, peculiar. **2.** attribute, property, trait. See **feature.**

char·ac·ter·i·za·tion (kar′ik tər i zā′shən, -tri zā′- *or, esp. Brit.,* -tə rī-), *n.* **1.** portrayal; description: *The actor's characterization of a politician was received with enthusiasm.* **2.** act of characterizing. **3.** the creation and convincing representation of fictitious characters. Also, *esp. Brit.,* **characterisation.** [< ML *charactērizāt(us)* marked (ptp. of *charactērizāre* to characterize; see -ate[1]) + L *-iōn-* -ion]

char·ac·ter·ize (kar′ik tə rīz′), *v.t.,* **-ized, -iz·ing. 1.** to mark or distinguish as a characteristic; be a characteristic of. **2.** to describe the character or individual quality of. **3.** to attribute character to: *to characterize someone as a coward.* Also, *esp. Brit.,* **characterise.** [< ML *charactēriz(āre)* < Gk *charaktērízein*] —**char′ac·ter·iz′a·ble,** *adj.* —**char′ac·ter·iz′er,** *n.*

char·ac·ter·ol·o·gy (kar′ik tər ol′ə jē), *n.* the study of the nature and development of personal character. —**char′ac·ter·o·log′i·cal,** *adj.* —**char′ac·ter·o·log′i·cal′ly,** *adv.*

char′acter sketch′, a short essay in prose or verse describing a person.

char′acter wit′ness, a person who testifies as to the moral character and reputation of a litigant in a court of law or other legal proceeding.

char·ac·ter·y (kar′ik tə rē, -trē), *n.* characters or symbols collectively.

cha·rades (shə rādz′; *esp. Brit.* shə rädz′), *n.* (*construed as sing.*) a parlor game in which players act out in pantomime a word or phrase, often syllable by syllable, that their own team must guess. [< F *charade* < Pr *charrad(o)* entertainment = *charr(a)* (to) chat, chatter + *-ado* -ade[1]]

char·broil (chär′broil′), *v.t., v.i.* to broil (food) over a charcoal fire. Also, **char-broil.** [char(coal) + broil[1]]

Char·che·mish (kär′kə mish, kär kē′-), *n.* Carchemish.

char·coal (chär′kōl′), *n.* **1.** the carbonaceous material obtained by heating wood or other organic substances in the absence of air. **2.** a drawing pencil of charcoal. **3.** a drawing made with charcoal. —*v.t.* **4.** to blacken, write, or draw with charcoal. [ME *charcole,* perh. orig. live coal = OE **cear-* red (< Celt; cf. Gael *cear* blood, *ceara* red) + *col* live coal]

char′coal bur′ner, 1. a person employed in the manufacture of charcoal. **2.** a device burning charcoal, as a brazier or stove.

Char·cot (shar kō′), *n.* **Jean Mar·tin** (zhän mar taN′), 1825–93, French neuropathologist.

chard (chärd), *n.* a variety of beet, *Beta vulgaris Cicla,* having large leafstalks and midribs that are used as a vegetable **(Swiss chard).** [appar. < F *chard(on)* thistle; see cardoon]

Char·din (shar daN′), *n.* **Jean Bap·tiste Si·mé·on** (zhäN ba tēst′ sē mā ôN′), 1699–1779, French painter.

Char·don·net (shär′dᵊnā′; *Fr.* shar dô ne′), *n.* **Hilaire Ber·ni·gaud** (ē ler′ ber nē gō′), **Comte de,** 1839–1924, French chemist and inventor.

charge (chärj), *v.,* **charged, charg·ing,** *n.* —*v.t.* **1.** to fill or furnish (a thing) with the quantity, as of powder or fuel, that it is fitted to receive: *to charge a musket.* **2.** to supply with a quantity of electricity or electrical energy: *to charge a storage battery.* **3.** to suffuse, as with emotion: *The air was charged with excitement.* **4.** *Physics.* to change the net amount of positive or negative electricity of (a particle, body, or system). **5.** to fill (air, water, etc.) with other matter in a state of diffusion or solution: *The air was charged with pollen.* **6.** *Metall.* to insert (materials) into a furnace, converter, etc. **7.** to load or burden (the mind, heart, etc.). **8.** to lay a command or injunction upon. **9.** to instruct authoritatively, as a judge does a jury. **10.** to impute; ascribe the responsibility for: *He charged the accident to his own carelessness.* **11.** to accuse formally or explicitly (usually fol. by *with*): *They charged him with theft.* **12.** to hold liable for payment. **13.** to list or record as a debt. **14.** to impose or ask as a price: *That store charged $12 for these gloves.* **15.** (of a purchaser) to defer payment for (a purchase) until a bill is rendered by the creditor. **16.** to attack by rushing violently against. **17.** *Heraldry.* to place charges on (an escutcheon).
—*v.i.* **18.** to make an onset; rush, as to an attack. **19.** to place the price of a thing to one's debit. **20.** to require payment: *to charge for a service.* **21.** to make a debit. **22.** (of dogs) to lie down at command. **23. charge off,** to write off as an expense or loss.
—*n.* **24.** the quantity of anything that an apparatus is fitted to hold at one time. **25.** a quantity of explosive to be set off at one time. **26.** a duty or responsibility laid upon or entrusted to one. **27.** care, custody, or superintendence. **28.** anything or anybody committed to one's care or management. **29.** *Eccles.* a parish or congregation committed to the spiritual care of a pastor. **30.** a command or injunction; exhortation. **31.** an accusation: *He was arrested on a charge of theft.* **32.** *Law.* an address by a judge to a jury at the close of a trial, instructing them as to the legal points involved in the case. **33.** expense or cost. **34.** a fee or price charged. **35.** a pecuniary burden, encumbrance, tax, or lien; cost; expense; liability. **36.** an entry in an account of something due. **37.** an assault or attack, as of soldiers. **38.** a signal by bugle, drum, etc., for a military charge. **39.** *Elect.* **a.** Also called **electric charge.** the quantity of electricity or electric energy in or upon an object or substance, noting an excess or deficiency of electrons. **b.** the process of charging a storage battery. **40.** *Heraldry.* any distinctive mark upon an escutcheon, as an ordinary or device, not considered as belonging to the field; bearing. **41.** *Rocketry.* grains of a solid propellant, usually including an inhibitor. **42.** a load or burden. **43.** *Slang.* kick (def. 26a). **44. in charge, a.** in command; having supervisory power. **b.** *Brit.* under arrest; in or into the custody of the police. [ME *charge(n)* < OF *charg(i)e(r)* < LL *carricāre* to load a wagon = *carr(us)* wagon (see car) + *-icā-* v. suffix + *-re* inf. ending] —**charge′a·ble,** *adj.* —**charge′a·ble·ness, charge′a·bil′i·ty,** *n.* —**charge′a·bly,** *adv.*
—**Syn. 8.** enjoin, exhort, bid, order. **11.** indict, arraign, impeach. **16.** assault. **26.** commission, trust. **27.** management. **31.** indictment. **34.** See **price. 37.** onslaught.

charge′ account′, an account, esp. in retailing, that permits a customer to buy merchandise for which he is billed at a later date.

charge′ card′, a credit card.

char·gé d'af·faires (shär zhā′ də fâr′, shär′zhā; *Fr.* shar zha da fer′), *pl.* **char·gés d'af·faires** (shär zhāz′ də fâr′, shär′zhāz; *Fr.* shar zha da fer′). *Govt.* **1.** Official name, **chargé′ d'affaires′ ad in′terim.** an official placed in charge of diplomatic business during the temporary absence of the ambassador or minister. **2.** an envoy to a state to which a diplomat of higher standing is not sent. Also called **char·gé′.** [< F: one in charge of things]

charg·er[1] (chär′jər), *n.* **1.** a person or thing that charges. **2.** (formerly) a horse suitable to be ridden in battle. **3.** an apparatus to charge storage batteries. [charge + -er[1]]

charg·er[2] (chär′jər), *n. Archaic.* a platter. [ME *chargeour,* lit., load bearer. See charge, -or[2]]

Cha·ri (*Fr.* sha rē′), *n.* Shari.

char·i·ly (châr′ə lē), *adv.* **1.** carefully; warily. **2.** sparingly; frugally. —**Syn. 1.** cautiously. —**Ant. 1.** boldly.

char·i·ness (châr′ē nis), *n.* **1.** the state or quality of being chary. **2.** *Obs.* scrupulous integrity.

Char′ing Cross′ (char′ing), a district in central London, England.

char·i·ot (char′ē ət), *n.* **1.** (in ancient Egypt, Greece, Rome, etc.) a light two-wheeled vehicle, usually drawn by two horses and driven from a standing position. **2.** a light, four-wheeled pleasure carriage. **3.** any rather stately carriage. **4.** *Informal.* an automobile. —*v.t.* **5.** to convey in a chariot. —*v.t.* **6.** to ride in or drive a chariot. [ME < MF, OF = *char* car + *-iot* dim. suffix]

Chariot (def. 1)

char·i·ot·eer (char′ē ə tēr′), *n.* **1.** a chariot driver. **2.** (*cap.*) *Astron.* the constellation Auriga. [chariot + -eer; r. ME *charietere* < MF *charetier* = OF *charete* (*char* car + *-ete* -ette) + *-ier* -eer]

cha·ris·ma (kə riz′mə), *n., pl.* **-ma·ta** (-mə tə) for 1, 3. **1.** *Theol.* a divinely conferred gift or power. **2.** the special quality that gives an individual influence or authority over large numbers of people. **3.** the special virtue of an office, position, etc., that confers or is thought to confer on the person holding it an unusual ability for leadership, worthiness of veneration, or the like. Also, **char·ism** (kar′iz əm). [< eccl. L < Gk = *char-* (root of *cháris* favor and *charízesthai* to favor) + *-isma* -ism] —**char′is·mat′ic,** *adj.*

char·i·ta·ble (char′i tə bəl), *adj.* **1.** generous in gifts to aid the poor. **2.** kindly or lenient in judging people, acts, etc. **3.** pertaining to or concerned with charity: *a charitable institution.* [ME < OF] —**char′i·ta·ble·ness,** *n.* —**char′i·ta·bly,** *adv.* —**Syn. 1.** beneficent, bountiful, benevolent. **2.** considerate, mild. —**Ant. 1.** selfish. **2.** severe, intolerant.

char·i·ty (char′i tē), *n., pl.* **-ties. 1.** charitable actions considered collectively, as almsgiving, or the performance of other benevolent actions for the needy with no expectation of material reward. **2.** something given to a person or persons in need; alms. **3.** a charitable act or work. **4.** a charitable fund, foundation, or institution. **5.** benevolent feeling, esp. toward those in need or in disfavor. **6.** Christian love; agape. I Cor. 13. [ME *charite* < OF < L *cāritāt-* (s. of *cāritās*) = *cār(us)* dear + *-itāt-* -ity] —**Syn. 5.** consideration, humanity, benignity. —**Ant. 5.** malevolence.

cha·riv·a·ri (shə riv′ə rē′, shiv′ə rē′, shä′rə vä′rē), *n. pl.* **-ris,** *v.t.,* **-ried, -ri·ing.** shivaree. [< F << LL *caribari(a)* headache < Gk *karēbaría* = *kárē* head + *-baria* heaviness (*bar(ýs)* heavy + *-ia* -ia)]

char·kha (chär′kə), *n.* (in India and East Indies) a cotton gin or spinning wheel. Also, **char′ka.** [< Urdu < Pers]

char·la·dy (chär′lā′dē), *n., pl.* **-dies.** *Brit.* a charwoman.

char·la·tan (shär′lə tᵊn), *n.* a person who pretends to knowledge or skill; quack. [< MF < It *ciarlatan(o)* = *ciarla(tore)* chatterer (< *ciarlare* to chatter) + *(cerre)tano* hawker, quack, lit., native of *Cerreto,* a village in Umbria, central Italy] —**char′la·tan·is′tic,** *adj.* —**char′la·tan·ism,** *n.* —**Syn.** imposter, mountebank, fraud.

char·la·tan·ry (shär′lə tən rē), *n., pl.* **-ries.** charlatanism.

Char·le·magne (shär′lə män′; *Fr.* shar lə man′yə), *n.* (“*Charles the Great*”) A.D. 742–814, king of the Franks 768–814; as Charles I, emperor of the Holy Roman Empire 800–814.

Charles (chärlz), *n.* **1.** (*Prince of Edinburgh and of Wales*) born 1948, heir apparent to the throne of Great Britain (son of Elizabeth II). **2. Cape,** a cape in E Virginia, N of the entrance to the Chesapeake Bay. **3.** a river in E Massachusetts, flowing between Boston and Cambridge into the Atlantic. 47 mi. long.

Charles I (chärlz; *Fr.* sharl), **1.** Charlemagne. **2.** (“*the Bald*”) A.D. 823–877, king of France 840–877; as Charles II, emperor of the Holy Roman Empire 875–877. **3.** 1600–49, king of England, Ireland, and Scotland 1625–49 (son of James I). **4.** 1500–58, king of Spain 1516–56; as Charles V, emperor of the Holy Roman Empire 1519–56. **5.** 1887–1922, emperor of Austria 1916–18; as Charles IV, king of Hungary 1916–18.

Charles II, **1.** See **Charles I** (def. 2). **2.** 1630–85, king of England, Ireland, and Scotland 1660–85 (son of Charles I). **3.** (“*Charles the Fat*”) A.D. 809–888, king of France 884–887; as Charles III, emperor of the Holy Roman Empire 881–887.

Charles III, **1.** See **Charles II** (def. 3). **2.** See **Charles VI** (def. 2).

Charles IV, **1.**(“*Charles the Fair*”) 1294–1328, king of France 1322–28. **2.** See **Charles I** (def. 5).

Charles V, **1.** (“*Charles the Wise*”) 1337–81, king of France 1364–80. **2.** See **Charles I** (def. 4).

Charles VI, **1.** (“*Charles the Mad*” or “*Charles the Well-beloved*”) 1368–1422, king of France 1380–1422. **2.** 1685–1740, emperor of the Holy Roman Empire 1711–40; as Charles III, king of Hungary 1711–40.

Charles VII, (“*Charles the Victorious*”) 1403–61, king of France 1422–61 (son of Charles VI).

Charles VIII, 1470–98, King of France 1483–98.

Charles IX, 1550–74, king of France 1560–74.

Charles X, 1757–1836, king of France 1824–30.

Charles XII, 1682–1718, king of Sweden 1697–1718.

Charles XIV. See **Bernadotte, Jean Baptiste Jules.**

Charles XVI, (*Carl Gustaf*) born 1946, king of Sweden since 1973 (grandson of Gustavus VI).

Charles′ Ed′ward Stu′art. See **Stuart, Charles.**

Charles′ Lou′is, (*Karl Ludwig Johann*) 1771–1847, archduke of Austria.

Charles′ Mar·tel′ (mär tel′; *Fr.* mar tel′), A.D. 690?–741, ruler of the Franks 714–741 (grandfather of Charlemagne).

Charles′′s law′ (chärl′ziz), *Thermodynamics.* See **Gay-Lussac's law.** [named after J. A. C. *Charles* (1746–1823), French physicist, who stated it]

Charles′′s Wain′ (wān′), *Brit.* dipper (def. 3). [OE *Carles wægn* Carl's wagon (Carl for Charlemagne); see WAIN]

Charles′ the Great′, Charlemagne.

Charles·ton (chärlz′tən, chärl′stən), *n.* **1.** a city in and the capital of West Virginia, in the W part. 71,505 (1970). **2.** a seaport in SE South Carolina. 66,945 (1970).

Charles·ton (chärlz′tən, chärl′stən), *n.* a vigorous, rhythmic ballroom dance popular in the 1920's. [named after CHARLESTON, South Carolina]

Charles·town (chärlz′toun′), *n.* a former city in E Massachusetts: since 1874 a part of Boston; navy yard; battle of Bunker Hill June 17, 1775.

char′ley horse′ (chär′lē), a painful, involuntary contraction of an arm or leg muscle resulting from excessive muscular strain or a blow. [orig. baseball slang]

Char·lie (chär′lē), *n.* a word used in communications to represent the letter C.

char·lock (chär′lək), *n.* the wild mustard, *Brassica arvensis,* often troublesome as a weed in grainfields. [ME *cherlok,* OE *cerlic* < ?]

char·lotte (shär′lət), *n.* a dessert commonly made by lining a mold with cake and filling it with fruit, whipped cream, and custard. [< F, special use of woman's name]

Char·lotte (shär′lət), *n.* **1. Grand Duchess** (*Aldegonde Elise Marie Wilhelmine*), born 1896, sovereign of Luxembourg 1919–64. **2.** a city in S North Carolina. 241,178 (1970).

Char·lot·te A·ma·li·e (shär lot′ə ä mä′lē ə), a seaport in and the capital of the Virgin Islands of the United States, on St. Thomas. 12,220 (1970). Formerly, **St. Thomas.**

char′lotte russe′ (rōōs), a dessert made by lining a mold with sponge cake or ladyfingers and filling it with Bavarian cream. [< F: lit., Russian charlotte]

Char·lottes·ville (shär′ləts vil′), *n.* a city in central Virginia. 38,880 (1970).

Char·lotte·town (shär′lət toun′), *n.* a seaport on and the capital of Prince Edward Island, in SE Canada. 17,063.

charm (chärm), *n.* **1.** a power of pleasing or attracting, as through personality or beauty. **2.** a trait or feature imparting this power. **3. charms,** attractiveness. **4.** a trinket to be worn on a chain, bracelet, etc. **5.** something worn for its supposed magical effect; amulet. **6.** any action supposed to have magical power. **7.** the chanting or recitation of a magic verse or formula. **8.** a verse or formula credited with magical power. **9.** *Physics.* a hypothetical quality of an elementary nuclear particle thought to be a fourth quark (**charmed quark**). —*v.t.* **10.** to delight or please greatly by beauty, attractiveness, etc.; enchant. **11.** to act upon (someone or something) with or as with a compelling or magical force: *to charm a bird from a tree.* **12.** to endow with or protect by supernatural powers: *His life seemed to be charmed.* **13.** to gain or influence through personal charm: *He's used to charming his way out of the trouble he causes.* —*v.i.* **14.** to be fascinating or pleasing. **15.** to use charms. **16.** to act as a charm. [ME *charme* < OF < L *carm(en)* song, magical formula, var. of **canmen* (by assimilation) = *can(ere)* (to) sing + *-men* n. suffix] —**charm·ed·ly** (chär′mid-lē), *adv.* —**charm′er,** *n.* —**Syn. 1.** attractiveness, allurement. **4.** bauble. **5.** talisman. **6.** enchantment, spell, sorcery. **8.** spell. **11.** fascinate, entrance, enrapture. —**Ant. 1.** repulsion. **10.** revolt, repel.

charmed′ quark′. See under **charm** (def. 9).

char·meuse (shär mōōz′; *Fr.* shar mœz′), *n.* a soft, flexible satin. [formerly trademark]

charm·ing (chär′ming), *adj.* pleasing; delightful. [ME] —**charm′ing·ly,** *adv.*

char·nel (chär′nᵊl), *n.* **1.** a repository for dead bodies. —*adj.* **2.** of, like, or fit for a charnel; sepulchral. [ME < MF < LL *carnāl(e),* n. use of neut. of *carnālis* CARNAL]

char′nel house′, a house or place in which the bodies or bones of the dead are deposited.

Char·on (kâr′ən, kar′-), *n.* *Class. Myth.* the ferryman who conveyed the souls of the dead across the Styx. —**Cha·ro·ni·an** (kə rō′nē ən), **Cha·ron·ic** (kə ron′ik), *adj.*

Char·pen·tier (shar pän tyā′), *n.* **1. Gus·tave** (gy-stav′), 1860–1956, French composer. **2. Marc An·toine** (mark än twan′), 1634–1704, French composer.

char·qui (chär′kē), *n.* jerky². [< Sp < Quechuan *ch'arki* dried meat] —**char·quid** (chär′kid), *adj.*

charr (chär), *n., pl.* **charrs,** (*esp. collectively*) **charr,** (*esp. referring to two or more kinds or species*) **charrs.** char².

char·ro (chär′ō; *Sp.* chär′rô), *n., pl.* **char·ros** (chär′ōz; *Sp.* chär′rôs). (in Mexico) a cowboy. [< MexSp, Sp: coarse, flashy < Basque *txar* poor, weak]

chart (chärt), *n.* **1.** a sheet exhibiting information in tabular form. **2.** a graphic representation, as by curves, of a dependent variable, as temperature, price, etc.; graph. **3.** any of various other graphic representations. **4.** a map, esp. a hydrographic or marine map. **5.** an outline map showing special conditions or facts: *a weather chart.* —*v.t.* **6.** to make a chart of. **7.** to plan: *to chart a course of action.* [< MF *charte* < L *c(h)arta* sheet of paper, document < Gk *chártēs* papyrus leaf, sheet of paper] —**chart′a·ble,** *adj.* —**chart′less,** *adj.* —**Syn. 3.** See **map.**

char·ter (chär′tər), *n.* **1.** a document, issued by a sovereign or state, outlining the conditions under which a corporation, colony, city, or other corporate body is organized. **2.** (*often cap.*) a document defining the formal organization of a corporate body; constitution: *the Charter of the United Nations.* **3.** authorization from a central or parent organization to establish a new branch, chapter, etc. **4.** a special privilege or immunity. —*v.t.* **5.** to establish by charter: *to charter a bank.* **6.** to lease or hire: *The company will charter six buses for the picnic.* **7.** to give special favor or privilege to. —*adj.* **8.** done or held in accordance with a charter: *a charter school.* [ME *chartre* < OF < L *chartul(a)* little paper (by assimilation). See CHART, -ULE] —**char′ter·er,** *n.* —**Syn. 6.** See **hire.**

char′ter col′ony, *Amer. Hist.* a colony, as Virginia, Massachusetts, Connecticut, or Rhode Island, chartered to an individual, trading company, etc., by the British crown. Cf. **royal colony** (def. 2).

Char·ter·house (chär′tər hous′), *n., pl.* **-hous·es** (-hou′-ziz). a Carthusian monastery. [< AF *chartrouse* (taken as CHARTER + HOUSE), after *Chatrousse,* village in Dauphiné near which the order was founded; see CARTHUSIAN, whence the first *r* of the AF word]

char′ter mem′ber, an original member of a club, organization, etc.

Chart·ism (chär′tiz əm), *n.* the principles of a group of English political and social reformers, 1838–48. —**Chart′-ist,** *n., adj.* [obs. *chart* CHARTER + -ISM]

char·tist (chär′tist), *n.* **1.** a specialist in the stock market who studies and draws charts of trading actions. **2.** a cartographer.

char·tog·ra·phy (kär tog′rə fe), *n.* cartography. —**char·tog′ra·pher,** *n.* —**char·to·graph·ic** (kär′tə graf′ik), **char′to·graph′i·cal,** *adj.* —**char′to·graph′i·cal·ly,** *adv.*

Char·tres (shar′trə, shärt; *Fr.* shar′trᵊ), *n.* a city in N France, SW of Paris: cathedral. 41,251.

char·treuse (shär trōōz′; *Fr.* shar trœz′), *n.* **1.** (*sometimes cap.*) green or yellow aromatic liqueur. **2.** a clear, light green with a yellowish tinge. [< F, after La Grande *Chartreuse,* Carthusian monastery near Grenoble, where the liqueur is made]

char·tu·lar·y (kär′chə ler′ē), *n., pl.* **-lar·ies. 1.** a register of charters, deeds, etc. **2.** an archivist. Also, **cartulary.** [< ML *chartulāri(um)* = L *chartul(a)* CHARTER + *-ārium* -ARY]

char·wom·an (chär′wŏŏm′ən), *n., pl.* **-wom·en.** a woman hired to do general cleaning, esp. in a house or office.

char·y (chär′ē), *adj.,* **char·i·er, char·i·est. 1.** careful; wary. **2.** shy; timid. **3.** fastidious; choosy. **4.** sparing (often fol. by *of*): *chary of his praise.* [ME; OE *cearig* sorrowful (*c(e)ar(u)* CARE + *-ig* -Y¹); c. OS *karag,* OHG *karag* (G *karg* scanty, paltry)] —**Syn. 1.** cautious, circumspect.

Cha·ryb·dis (kə rib′dis), *n.* **1.** Modern, **Galofalo, Garofalo.** a whirlpool in the Strait of Messina off the NE coast of Sicily. **2.** *Class. Myth.* a daughter of Gaea and Poseidon, a monster mentioned in Homer and later identified with the whirlpool Charybdis. Cf. **Scylla** (def. 2). —**Cha·ryb′-di·an,** *adj.*

chase¹ (chās), *v.,* **chased, chas·ing,** *n.* —*v.t.* **1.** to pursue in order to seize, overtake, etc. **2.** to pursue with intent to capture or kill, as game; hunt. **3.** to follow or devote one's attention to with the hope of attracting, winning, gaining, etc. **4.** to drive by pursuing: *She chased him out of the room.* **5.** to drive by any means: *Her look of contempt chased her would-be suitor away.* —*v.i.* **6.** to follow in pursuit: *to chase after someone.* —*n.* **7.** the act of chasing; pursuit. **8.** an object of pursuit; something chased. **9.** *Chiefly Brit.* a private game preserve. **10.** a steeplechase. **11. give chase,** to pursue. **12. the chase,** the sport or occupation of hunting. [ME *chace(n)* < MF *chasse(r)* (to) hunt, OF *chacier* < VL **captiāre;* see CATCH] —**chase′a·ble,** *adj.*

chase[2] (chās), *n.* **1.** a rectangular iron frame in which composed type is secured or locked for printing or plate-making. **2.** a groove, furrow, or trench. **3.** *Ordn.* **a.** the part of a gun in front of the trunnions. **b.** the part containing the bore. [< MF *chas* < LL *capsus* (masc.), *capsum* (neut.) fully or partly enclosed space, var. of *capsa* CASE[2]; def. 1 < MF *chasse* box, case < L *capsa*]

chase[3] (chās), *v.t.* **chased, chas·ing.** to ornament (metal) by engraving or embossing. [aph. var. of ENCHASE]

Chase (chās), *n.* **1. Sal·mon P(ortland)** (sal′mən), 1808–1873, U.S. statesman: Chief Justice of the U.S. 1864–73. **2. Samuel,** 1741–1811, U.S. jurist and leader in the American Revolution: associate justice of the U.S. Supreme Court 1796–1811.

chas·er (chā′sər), *n.* **1.** a person or thing that chases. **2.** *U.S. Informal.* a drink of water, beer, or other mild beverage taken after a drink of liquor. **3.** a hunter. [ME]

Cha·sid (hä′sid; *Heb.* ᴋʜä sēd′), *n., pl.* **Cha·sid·im** (hä′si-dim, hä sid′im; *Heb.* ᴋʜä sē dēm′). *Judaism.* Hasid. —**Cha·sid·ic** (hä sid′ik, hə-), *adj.* —**Cha′sid·ism,** *n.*

chas·ing (chā′sing), *n.* a design chased on metal.

chasm (kaz′əm), *n.* **1.** a yawning fissure or deep cleft in the earth's surface; gorge. **2.** a breach in a structure. **3.** a marked interruption of continuity; gap: *a chasm in time.* **4.** a breach in relations, as a divergence of opinions. [apocopated var. of *chasma* < L < Gk = *cha-* (root of *chaínein* to gape; see YAWN) + *-(a)sma* resultative suffix] —**chas′mal, chas′mic,** *adj.* —**chasmed,** *adj.* —**chasm′y,** *adj.*

chas·sé (sha sā′; *or, esp. in square dancing,* sa shā′), *n., v.,* **chas·séd, chas·sé·ing.** *Dance.* —*n.* **1.** a gliding step in which one foot is kept in advance of the other. —*v.i.* **2.** to execute a chassé. [< F: lit., chased, followed, ptp. of *chasser* to CHASE[1]]

chasse·pot (shas′pō; *Fr.* shas pō′), *n., pl.* **-pots** (-pōz; *Fr.* -pō′). a breechloading rifle, closed with a sliding bolt, introduced into the French army after the war between Austria and Prussia in 1866. [named after A. A. *Chassepot* (1833–1905), French mechanic, its inventor]

chas·seur (sha sûr′; *Fr.* sha sœr′), *n., pl.* **-seurs** (-sûrz′; *Fr.* -sœr′). **1.** (in the French army) a member of a troop equipped and trained for rapid movement. **2.** a uniformed attendant. **3.** a hunter. [< F: lit., chaser; see CHASE[1]]

chas·sis (shas′ē, -is, chas′ē), *n., pl.* **chas·sis** (shas′ēz, chas′-). **1.** *Auto.* the frame, wheels, and machinery of a motor vehicle, on which the body is supported. **2.** *Ordn.* the frame or railway on which a gun carriage moves backward and forward. **3.** the main landing gear of an aircraft. **4.** *Radio and Television.* the collection of various sections of a receiving set mounted on a foundation. **5.** a construction forming the sides, top, and bottom of a cabinet, showcase, or the like. [< F *châssis* frame; akin to CHASE[2]]

chaste (chāst), *adj.,* **chast·er, chast·est. 1.** not having engaged in unlawful sexual intercourse; virtuous. **2.** free from obscenity; decent: *chaste conversation.* **3.** undefiled or stainless: *chaste, white snow.* **4.** pure in style; subdued; simple. **5.** *Obs.* not married. [ME < OF < L *cast(us)* clean, pure, chaste] —**chaste′ly,** *adv.* —**chaste′ness,** *n.*

chas·ten (chā′sən), *v.t.* **1.** to inflict suffering upon for purposes of moral improvement; chastise. **2.** to restrain; subdue: *Age has chastened his violent temper.* **3.** to make chaste in style. [CHASTE + -EN[1]; r. *chaste* (v.), ME *chast(ien)* < OF *chastie(r)* < L *castigāre;* see CASTIGATE] —**chas′ten·er,** *n.* —**chas′ten·ing·ly,** *adv.* —**chas′ten·ment,** *n.*

chas·tise (chas tīz′, chas′tīz), *v.t.,* **-tised, -tis·ing. 1.** to discipline. **2.** *Archaic.* to restrain; chasten. [ME *chastise(n)* = *chasti(en)* (to) CHASTEN + *-se(n)* < ?] —**chas·tis′a·ble,** *adj.* —**chas·tise·ment** (chas′tiz mənt, chas tīz′-), *n.* —**chas·tis′er,** *n.*

chas·ti·ty (chas′ti tē), *n.* **1.** the state or quality of being chaste. **2.** virginity. [ME *chastite,* var. of *chastete* < OF < L *castitāt-* (s. of *castitās*) = *cast(us)* CHASTE + *-itāt-* -ITY]

chas′tity belt′, a beltlike device, worn by women esp. in the Middle Ages, designed to prevent sexual intercourse.

chas·u·ble (chaz′yə bəl, -ə bəl, chas′-), *n.* *Eccles.* a sleeveless outer vestment worn by the celebrant at Mass. [< F < LL *casubla,* unexplained var. of L *casula* little house (dim. of *casa* house); r. ME *chesible* < OF]

A, Chasuble
B, Maniple

chat (chat), *v.,* **chat·ted, chat·ting,** *n.* —*v.i.* **1.** to converse in a familiar or informal manner. —*n.* **2.** informal conversation. **3.** any of several small, Old World thrushes, esp. of the genus *Saxicola,* having a chattering cry. [short for CHATTER] —**chat′ting·ly,** *adv.*

châ·teau (sha tō′; *Fr.* shä tō′), *n., pl.* **-teaus, -teaux** (-tōz′; *Fr.* -tō′). **1.** a castle in a French-speaking country. **2.** a stately residence imitating a distinctively French castle. **3.** a European country estate, esp. in France. **4.** a vineyard estate in the Bordeaux wine region of France. [< F << L *castell(um)* CASTLE]

Châ·teau·bri·and (shä tō brē äɴ′), *n.* **1. Fran·çois Re·né** (fräɴ swa′ rə nā′), **Vicomte de,** 1768–1848, French author and statesman. **2.** (*sometimes l.c.*) a thick slice of broiled tenderloin, served with a sauce.

Châ·teau·roux (shä tō rōō′), *n.* a city in central France. 46,772 (1962).

Châ·teau-Thier·ry (sha tō′tē′ə rē; *Fr.* shä tō tye rē′), *n.* a town in N France, on the Marne River: scene of heavy fighting 1918. 10,619 (1962).

château′ wine′, wine made at a vineyard estate in the Bordeaux region of France.

chat·e·lain (shat′ᵊlān′; *Fr.* shätᵊ laɴ′), *n., pl.* **chat·e·lains** (shat′ᵊlānz′; *Fr.* shätᵊ laɴ′). a castellan. [< MF < L *castellān(us)* CASTELLAN]

chat·e·laine (shat′ᵊlān′; *Fr.* shätᵊ len′), *n., pl.* **chat·e·laines** (shat′ᵊlānz′; *Fr.* shätᵊ len′). **1.** the mistress of a castle or of an elegant or fashionable household. **2.** a hook-like clasp for suspending keys, trinkets, etc., worn at the waist by women. **3.** a woman's lapel ornament. [< F, fem. of CHATELAIN]

Chat·ham (chat′əm), *n.* **1. 1st Earl of.** See **Pitt, William, 1st Earl of Chatham. 2.** a city in N Kent in SE England. 48,989 (1961).

Chat′ham Is′lands, a group of islands in the S Pacific, E of and belonging to New Zealand. 372 sq. mi.

cha·toy·ant (shə toi′ənt), *adj.* **1.** changing in luster or color: *chatoyant silk.* **2.** *Jewelry.* reflecting a single streak of light when cut in a cabochon. [< F, special use of prp. of *chatoyer* to change luster like a cat's eye = *chat* CAT + *-oy-* v. suffix + *-ant* -ANT] —**cha·toy′an·cy,** *n.*

Chat·ta·hoo·chee (chat′ə hōō′chē), *n.* a river flowing S from N Georgia along part of the boundary between Alabama and Georgia into the Apalachicola River. ab. 418 mi. long.

Chat·ta·noo·ga (chat′ᵊnōō′gə), *n.* a city in SE Tennessee, on the Tennessee River: Civil War battles 1863. 119,082 (1970).

chat·tel (chat′ᵊl), *n.* **1.** a movable article of property. **2.** any article of tangible property other than land, buildings, and other things annexed to land. **3.** a slave. [ME *chatel* < OF. See CATTLE] —**Syn. 1.** See **property.**

chat′tel mort′gage, *U.S.* a mortgage on movable property.

chat·ter (chat′ər), *v.i.* **1.** to talk rapidly and to little purpose; jabber. **2.** to utter a succession of quick, inarticulate, speechlike sounds, as certain animals and birds. **3.** to make a rapid clicking noise by striking together. **4.** *Mach.* (of a cutting tool or piece of metal) to vibrate during cutting so as to produce surface flaws on the work. —*v.t.* **5.** to utter rapidly or idly. **6.** to cause to chatter. —*n.* **7.** idle or foolish talk. **8.** the act or sound of chattering. [ME *chater(en);* imit.] —**chat′ter·ing·ly,** *adv.* —**chat′ter·y,** *adj.*

chat·ter·box (chat′ər boks′), *n.* an excessively talkative person. [i.e., one whose voice box is full of chatter]

chat·ter·er (chat′ər ər), *n.* **1.** a person who chatters; chatterbox. **2.** any of several passerine birds having a chattering cry.

chat′ter mark′, any of a series of irregular gouges made on rock surfaces by the slipping of rock fragments held in the lower portion of a glacier.

Chat·ter·ton (chat′ər tən), *n.* **Thomas,** 1752–70, English poet. —**Chat·ter·to·ni·an** (chat′ər tō′nē ən), *adj., n.*

chat·ty (chat′ē), *adj.,* **-ti·er, -ti·est.** given to or full of chat or familiar talk; conversational: *a chatty letter; a chatty person.* —**chat′ti·ly,** *adv.* —**chat′ti·ness,** *n.*

Chau·cer (chô′sər), *n.* **Geoffrey,** 1340?–1400, English poet. —**Chau·ce·ri·an** (chô sēr′ē ən), *adj., n.*

chauf·feur (shō′fər, shō fûr′), *n.* **1.** a person employed to drive another's automobile. —*v.t., v.i.* **2.** to drive or work as a chauffeur: *He chauffeured my car for years. He chauffeurs for me.* [< F = *chauff(er)* (to) heat (see CHAFE) + *-eur* -OR[2]]

chaul·moo·gra (chôl mōō′grə), *n.* an East Indian tree, of the genus *Taraktogenos* (or *Hydnocarpus*), the seeds of which yield an oil **(chaulmoo′gra oil′)** formerly used in treating leprosy and skin diseases. [< Bengali *cāulmugrā* kind of tree]

chaunt (chônt, chänt), *n., v.t., v.i.* *Obs.* chant. —**chaunt′er,** *n.*

chausses (shōs), *n.* (*construed as pl.*) medieval armor of mail for the legs and feet. [late ME *chauces* < MF, pl. of *chauce* << L *calce(us)* shoe]

chaus·sure (shō syr′), *n., pl.* **-sures** (-syr′). *French.* **1.** footwear. **2.** any foot covering, as a shoe or boot.

Chau·tau·qua (shə tô′kwə, chə-), *n.* **1. Lake,** a lake in SW New York. 18 mi. long. **2.** a village on this lake: summer educational center. **3.** the annual summer meeting of this center, providing public lectures, concerts, etc. **4.** (*often l.c.*) any similar assembly. —*adj.* **5.** of or pertaining to a system of summer education flourishing in the late 19th and early 20th centuries, originating at Chautauqua. **6.** (*often l.c.*) pertaining to a chautauqua: *a chautauqua program.*

Chau·temps (shō täɴ′), *n.* **Ca·mille** (ka mē′yᵊ), 1885–1963, French politician: premier 1930, 1933–34, 1937–38.

chau·vin·ism ((shō′və niz′əm), *n.* **1.** zealous and belligerent patriotism. **2.** prejudiced devotion to any attitude or cause: *male chauvinism.* [< F *chauvinisme* = *chauvin* jingo (after N. *Chauvin,* a soldier in Napoleon's army noted for loud-mouthed patriotism) + *-isme* -ISM] —**chau′vin·ist,** *n.* —**chau′vin·is′tic,** *adj.* —**chau′vin·is′ti·cal·ly,** *adv.*

Cha·vannes (sha van′), *n.* **Pu·vis de** (py vē′ də). See **Puvis de Chavannes, Pierre.**

Cha·vez (chä′vez; *Sp.* chä′ves), *n.* **Car·los** (kär′lōs; *Sp.* kär′lôs), 1899–1978, Mexican composer and conductor.

chaw (chô), *v.t., v.i., n.* *Dial.* chew. —**chaw′er,** *n.*

cha·zan (ᴋʜä zän′; *Eng.* ᴋʜä′zən, hä′-), *n. pl.* **cha·za·nim** (ᴋʜä zä nēm′; *Eng.* ᴋʜä zô′nim, hä-), *Eng.* **cha·zans.** *Hebrew.* hazan.

Ch.E., Chemical Engineer.

cheap (chēp), *adj.* **1.** of a relatively low price; inexpensive. **2.** costing little labor or trouble: *Words are cheap.* **3.** charging low prices: *a very cheap store.* **4.** of little account; of small value; mean; shoddy: *cheap workmanship.* **5.** vulgar, common, or immoral: *cheap conduct.* **6.** embarrassed; sheepish: *He felt cheap about his mistake.* **7.** (of money) obtainable at a low rate of interest. **8.** of decreased value or purchasing power, as currency depreciated due to inflation. **9.** stingy; miserly. —*adv.* **10.** at a low price; at small cost: *He is willing to sell cheap.* [ME *cheep* (short for phrases, as *good cheep* cheap, lit., good bargain), OE *cēap* bargain, market, trade; c. G *Kauf,* Icel *kaup,* etc.; all < L *caupō* innkeeper, tradesman; see CHAPMAN] —**cheap′ly,** *adv.* —**cheap′ness,** *n.*

—**Syn. 1, 4.** CHEAP, INEXPENSIVE agree in their suggestion of low cost. CHEAP now often suggests shoddiness, inferiority, showy imitation, complete unworthiness, and the like: *a cheap kind of fur.* INEXPENSIVE emphasizes lowness of price and suggests that the value is fully equal to the cost: *an inexpensive dress.* It is often used as an evasion for the more pejorative CHEAP. **4.** low, poor. **5.** inferior, base. —**Ant. 1.** costly, dear, expensive.

cheap·en (chē′pən), *v.t.* **1.** to make cheap or cheaper. **2.** to belittle; bring into contempt: *Constant swearing cheapened him.* **3.** to decrease the quality or beauty of; make inferior or vulgar. **4.** *Archaic.* to bargain for. —*v.i.* **5.** to become cheap or cheaper. [CHEAP + -EN[1]; r. ME *chepe(n)* (to) price, bargain, OE *cēapian* to bargain, trade, buy; c. Icel *kaupa*, Goth *kaupōn*, G *kaufen*]

Cheap·side (chēp′sīd′), *n.* a district and thoroughfare in London, England.

cheap·skate (chēp′skāt′), *n. Slang.* a stingy person.

cheat (chēt), *n.* **1.** a person who cheats or defrauds. **2.** a fraud; swindle. **3.** *Law.* the fraudulent obtaining of another's property. **4.** an impostor. **5.** Also called **chess.** an annual, weedy grass, *Bromus secalinus.* —*v.t.* **6.** to defraud; swindle. **7.** to deceive; influence by fraud. **8.** to elude; deprive of something expected. —*v.i.* **9.** to practice fraud or deceit. **10.** to violate rules or regulations. **11.** *Slang.* to be sexually unfaithful (often fol. by *on*): *He was cheating on his wife.* [ME *chet* (n.) (aph. for *achet*, var. of *eschet* ESCHEAT), *chete(n)* (to) escheat < *chet* (n.)] —**cheat′er,** *n.* —**cheat′ing·ly,** *adv.*
—**Syn. 1.** swindler, trickster, charlatan, fraud, mountebank. **2.** imposture, artifice, trick, hoax. **6.** dupe, gull, con; hoax. CHEAT, DECEIVE, TRICK, VICTIMIZE refer to the use of fraud or artifice deliberately to hoodwink someone or to obtain an unfair advantage over him. CHEAT implies conducting matters fraudulently, esp. for profit to oneself: *to cheat at cards.* DECEIVE suggests deliberately misleading or deluding, to produce misunderstanding or to prevent someone from knowing the truth: *to deceive one's parents.* To TRICK is to deceive by a stratagem, often of a petty, crafty, or dishonorable kind: *to trick someone into signing a note.* To VICTIMIZE is to make a victim of; the emotional connotation makes the cheating, deception, or trickery seem particularly dastardly: *to victimize a blind man.*

Che·bo·ksa·ry (chi bo ksä′Ri), *n.* a port in and the capital of the Chuvash Autonomous Soviet Socialist Republic, in the W RSFSR, in the central Soviet Union in Europe, on the Volga. 163,000 (est. 1965).

che·cha·ko (chē chä′kō), *n., pl.* **-kos.** cheechako.

check (chek), *v.t.* **1.** to stop or arrest the motion of suddenly or forcibly. **2.** to restrain. **3.** to cause a reduction, as in rate or intensity. **4.** to investigate or verify as to correctness. **5.** to make an inquiry into, search through, etc.: *We checked the files.* **6.** to inspect or test the performance, condition, safety, etc., of (something). **7.** to mark (something) so as to indicate examination, correctness, preference, etc. (often fol. by *off*): *Please check the correct answer.* **8.** to leave in temporary custody: *Check your umbrellas at the door.* **9.** to accept for temporary custody. **10.** *U.S.* **a.** to send to a destination under the privilege of a passage ticket: *We checked two trunks through to Portland.* **b.** to accept for conveyance, and to convey, under the privilege of a passage ticket: *Check this trunk to Portland.* **11.** to mark with or in a pattern of squares: *to check fabric.* **12.** *Agric.* to plant in checkrows. **13.** *Chess.* to place (an opponent's king) under direct attack. **14.** *Ice Hockey.* to obstruct or impede the movement or progress of (an opponent).
—*v.i.* **15.** to prove or turn out to be right; correspond accurately. **16.** *U.S.* to make an inquiry, investigation, etc., as for verification (often fol. by *up, into,* etc.). **17.** to make an abrupt stop; pause. **18.** *Chess.* to make a move that puts the opponent's king under direct attack. **19.** to crack or split, esp. in small checks or squares. **20.** *Poker.* to decline to initiate the betting in a betting round, usually to force another player to make the first bet rather than raise it. **21.** *Hunting.* (of hounds) to stop, esp. because the scent has been lost. **22.** *Falconry.* (of a hawk) to forsake the proper prey and follow baser game (fol. by *at*). **23. check in,** to register, as at a hotel. **24. check on** or **up on,** to investigate, scrutinize, or inspect something or someone. **25. check out, a.** *U.S.* to leave and pay for one's quarters at a hotel. **b.** *Slang.* to die. **c.** to verify or become verified. **d.** to fulfill requirements, as by passing a test. **26. check the helm,** *Naut.* to alter the helm of a turning vessel to keep the bow from swinging too far or too rapidly.
—*n.* **27.** a person who or thing that stops, limits, slows, or restrains. **28.** a sudden arrest or stoppage; repulse; rebuff. **29.** a control, test, or inspection that ascertains performance or prevents error. **30.** a criterion, standard, or means to insure against error, fraud, etc. Cf. **checks and balances. 31.** an inquiry, search, or examination. **32.** See **check mark. 33.** Also, *Brit.,* **cheque.** *Banking.* a written order, usually on a standard printed form, directing a bank to pay money. **34.** a slip or ticket showing the amount owed, esp. a bill for food or beverages consumed. **35.** a ticket or token identifying the owner of an article left in the temporary custody of another, a person who is to be served next, etc. **36.** a pattern formed of squares. **37.** one of the squares in such a pattern. **38.** a fabric having a check pattern. **39.** *Chess.* the exposure of the king to direct attack: *The king was in check.* **40.** *Ice Hockey.* any of several maneuvers designed to obstruct or impede the forward progress of an opponent. Cf. **body check. 41.** a counter used in card games, as the chip in poker. **42.** a small crack. **43.** *Hunting.* the losing of the scent by a dog or pack. **44. in check,** under restraint: *He held his anger in check.*
—*adj.* **45.** serving to check, control, verify, etc.: *a check system.* **46.** ornamented with a checkered pattern; checkered: *a check border.*
—*interj.* **47.** *Chess.* (used as a call to warn one's opponent that his king is exposed to direct attack, having just one move in which to escape or parry.) [ME *chek* (at chess), etc. < OF *eschec* (by aphesis), var. of *eschac* < Ar *shāh* check (at chess) < Pers: lit., king (an exclamation: i.e., look to your king); see SHAH] —**check′a·ble,** *adj.* —**check′less,** *adj.*
—**Syn. 1.** See **stop. 2.** hinder, hamper, obstruct, curtail; bridle, hobble. CHECK, CURB, REPRESS, RESTRAIN refer to putting a control on movement, progress, action, etc. CHECK implies restraining suddenly, halting or causing to halt. CURB implies the use of a means such as a chain or wall to guide or control or to force to stay within definite limits: *to curb a horse.* REPRESS, formerly meaning to suppress, now implies preventing the action or development that might naturally be expected: *to repress evidence of excitement.* RESTRAIN implies the use of force to put under control, or chiefly, to hold back: *to restrain a person from violent acts.* **6.** examine. **15.** agree. **27.** obstacle, obstruction, impediment; bar, barrier. **34.** receipt, tab, counterfoil. **35.** coupon, tag, stub. —**Ant. 1.** advance.

check·book (chek′bo͝ok′), *n.* a book containing blank checks or orders on a bank.

checked (chekt), *adj.* **1.** having a pattern of squares; checkered: *a checked shirt.* **2.** *Phonet.* (of a vowel) situated in a closed syllable (opposed to *free*).

check·er[1] (chek′ər), *n.* **1.** a small, usually red or black disk of plastic or wood, used in playing checkers. **2. checkers.** Also called, *Brit.,* **draughts.** (*construed as sing.*) a game played by two persons, each with 12 playing pieces, on a checkerboard. **3.** a checkered pattern. **4.** one of the squares of a checkered pattern. **5.** *Bot.* **a.** See **service tree** (def. 1). **b.** the fruit of this tree. —*v.t.* **6.** to mark like a checkerboard. **7.** to diversify in color; variegate. **8.** to diversify in character; subject to alternations. Also, *Brit.,* **chequer.** [ME *checker* chessboard < AF *escheker* (by aphesis) = *eschec* CHECK + *-er* -ER[2]]

check·er[2] (chek′ər), *n.* **1.** a person or thing that checks. **2.** a person who checks coats, baggage, etc. **3.** a cashier in a supermarket, cafeteria, or the like. [CHECK + -ER[1]]

check·er·ber·ry (chek′ər ber′ē), *n., pl.* **-ries. 1.** the red fruit of the American wintergreen, *Gaultheria procumbens.* **2.** the plant itself. **3.** the partridgeberry. [perh. so named from its appearance]

check·er·board (chek′ər bōrd′, -bôrd′), *n.* **1.** Also called, *Brit.,* **draughtboard.** a board marked off into sixty-four squares of two alternating colors, arranged in eight vertical and eight horizontal rows, on which checkers or chess is played. —*v.t.* **2.** to arrange in or mark with a checkerboard pattern. Also, *Brit.,* **chequerboard.**

check·ered (chek′ərd), *adj.* **1.** marked by wide or frequent alternations; diversified: *a checkered career.* **2.** marked with squares: *a checkered fabric.* **3.** diversified in color; alternately light and shadowed: *the checkered shade beneath trees.* Also, *Brit.,* **chequered.**

check′er tree′. See **service tree** (def. 1).

check·hook (chek′ho͝ok′), *n.* a hook on the saddle of a harness, for holding the end of the checkrein. [CHECK(REIN) + HOOK]

check-in (chek′in′), *n.* the act or fact of checking in.

check′ing account′, *U.S.* a bank deposit against which checks can be drawn. Cf. **savings account.**

check′ line′, a checkrein.

check′ list′, *U.S.* items listed together for convenience of comparison or other checking purposes.

check′ mark′, a mark, often indicated by (√), to indicate that an item has been considered, acted upon, or approved. Also called **check.**

check·mate (chek′māt′), *n., v.,* **-mat·ed, -mat·ing.** —*n.* **1.** Also called **mate.** *Chess.* **a.** the act or an instance of maneuvering the opponent's king into a check from which it cannot escape, thus bringing the game to a victorious conclusion. **b.** the position of the pieces when a king is checkmated. **2.** a complete check; defeat. —*v.t.* **3.** *Chess.* to maneuver (an opponent's king) into a check from which it cannot escape; mate. **4.** to check completely; defeat. [ME *chek mat(e)* < MF *escec mat* < Ar *shāh māt* < Pers: lit., the king (is) dead]

check·off (chek′ôf′, -of′), *n.* collection of union dues by employers through deduction from wages.

check-out (chek′out′), *n.* **1.** the procedure of vacating a hotel room. **2.** the time before which a hotel room must be vacated if another day's charge is not to be made. **3.** an examination of fitness for performance. **4.** the itemization and collection of amounts due for purchases, as in a supermarket.

check·point (chek′point′), *n.* a place, as at a border, where vehicles or travelers are stopped for inspection.

check·rein (chek′rān′), *n.* **1.** a short rein passing from the bit to the saddle of a harness, to prevent the horse from lowering its head. Cf. **overcheck. 2.** a short rein joining the bit of one of a span of horses to the driving rein of the other.

check·room (chek′ro͞om′, -ro͝om′), *n.* a room where hats, coats, parcels, etc., may be checked.

check·row (chek′rō′), *Agric.* —*n.* **1.** one of a number of rows of trees or plants, esp. corn, in which the distance between adjacent trees or plants is equal to that between adjacent rows. —*v.t.* **2.** to plant in checkrows.

checks′ and bal′ances, limits imposed on all branches of a government by vesting in each branch the right to amend or void those acts of another that fall within its purview.

check·up (chek′up′), *n.* **1.** an examination for purposes of verification as to accuracy, for comparison, etc. **2.** a comprehensive physical examination: *He went to the doctor for a checkup.*

check′ valve′, a valve permitting liquids or gases to flow in one direction only.

Ched·dar (ched′ər), *n.* a hard, smooth-textured cheese. Also called **Ched′dar cheese′.** [after *Cheddar,* village in Somersetshire, England, where it was first made]

chedd·ite (ched′īt, shed′-), *n. Chem.* an explosive composed of a chlorate or perchlorate mixed with a fatty substance, as castor oil. [named after *Chedde,* town in Savoy where it was first made; see -ITE[1]]

che·der (KHe′deR; *Eng.* KHā′dər, hā′-), *n., pl.* **cha·da·rim** (KHä dä Rēm′), *Eng.* **che·ders.** *Hebrew.* heder.

Che.E., Chemical Engineer.

chee·cha·ko (chē chä′kō), *n., pl.* **-kos.** *Informal.* (in the Pacific Northwest) a tenderfoot; greenhorn; newcomer. Also, **chechako, chee·cha′co.** [< Chinook jargon *chee chalico* < Chinook *t'shi* new + Nootka *chako* to come]

cheek (chēk), *n.* **1.** either side of the face below the eye and above the jaw. **2.** the side wall of the mouth between the upper and lower jaws. **3.** something resembling the side of the human face in form or position, as either of two parts forming corresponding sides of various objects. **4.** *Mach.* either of the sides of a pulley or block. **5.** *Informal.* impudence or effrontery. **6.** *Slang.* a buttock. **7. cheek by jowl,** in close intimacy; side by side. **8. with one's tongue in one's cheek.** See **tongue** (def. 22). [ME *cheke,* OE *cē(a)ce;* akin to D *kaak,* MLG *kake*] —**cheek′less,** *adj.*

cheek·bone (chēk′bōn′), *n.* See **zygomatic bone.** [ME *chekbon,* OE *ceacban*]

cheek·piece (chēk′pēs′), *n.* **1.** either of two vertical bars of a bit, one on each end of the mouthpiece. **2.** See **cheek strap.**

cheek′ pouch′, a bag in the cheek of certain animals, as squirrels, for carrying food.

cheek′ strap′, (of a bridle) one of two straps passing over the cheeks of a horse and connecting the crown piece with the bit or noseband. Also called **cheekpiece.**

Cheek·to·wa·ga (chēk′tə wä′gə), *n.* a town in NW New York, near Buffalo. 113,844 (1970).

cheek·y (chē′kē), *adj.,* **cheek·i·er, cheek·i·est.** *Informal.* impudent; insolent. —**cheek′i·ly,** *adv.* —**cheek′i·ness,** *n.*

cheep (chēp), *v.i.* **1.** to chirp; peep. —*v.t.* **2.** to express by cheeps. —*n.* **3.** a chirp. [imit.] —**cheep′er,** *n.*

cheer (chēr), *n.* **1.** a shout of encouragement, approval, congratulation, etc. **2.** a traditional shout used by spectators to encourage or show enthusiasm for an athletic team, contestant, etc., as *rah! rah! rah!* **3.** anything that gives joy or gladness; encouragement; comfort: *He spoke words of cheer.* **4.** a state of feeling or spirits. **5.** gladness, gaiety, or animation. **6.** food; provisions: *The tables were overflowing with good cheer.* **7.** *Archaic.* facial expression. **8. be of good cheer,** be cheerful or hopeful; cheer up; take heart. **9. with good cheer,** cheerfully; willingly. —*interj.* **10. cheers,** *Chiefly Brit.* (used as a salutation or toast.) —*v.t.* **11.** to salute with shouts of approval, triumph, etc. **12.** to restore cheerfulness or hope to; inspire with cheer (often fol. by *up*): *The good news cheered her up.* **13.** to encourage or incite. —*v.i.* **14.** to utter cheers of approval, encouragement, triumph, etc. **15.** to become more cheerful (often fol. by *up*). **16.** *Obs.* to be in a particular state of mind or spirits. [ME *chere* face < OF < LL *cara* face, head < Gk *kára* head] —**cheer′er,** *n.* —**cheer′ing·ly,** *adv.*
—**Syn. 3.** solace. **5.** joy, mirth, glee, merriment. **11.** applaud. **12.** CHEER, GLADDEN mean to make happy or lively. To CHEER is to comfort, to restore hope and cheerfulness to (now often CHEER UP, when thoroughness, a definite time, or a particular point in the action is referred to): *He went to cheer a sick friend. She soon cheered him up.* (Similar to "eat up," "hurry up.") To GLADDEN does not imply a state of sadness to begin with, but suggests bringing pleasure or happiness to someone: *to gladden someone's heart with good news.* **12.** exhilarate, animate. **13.** inspirit. —**Ant. 12.** discourage, depress.

cheer·ful (chēr′fəl), *adj.* **1.** full of cheer; in good spirits. **2.** promoting, inducing, or expressing cheer; pleasant; bright: *cheerful surroundings.* **3.** hearty or ungrudging: *cheerful giving.* [late ME *cherfull*] —**cheer′ful·ly,** *adv.* —**cheer′ful·ness,** *n.* —**Syn. 1.** cheery, gay, blithe, joyful, joyous, happy, jolly. **3.** generous. —**Ant. 1.** miserable. **3.** grudging.

cheer·i·o (chēr′ē ō′, chēr′ē ō′), *interj.* *Chiefly Brit.* **1.** good-by; good-by and good luck. **2.** (used as a toast to one's drinking companions.) [CHEERY + exclamatory O]

cheer·lead·er (chēr′lē′dər), *n.* a person who leads spectators in traditional or formal cheering, esp. at a pep rally or athletic contest.

cheer·lead·ing (chēr′lē′ding), *n.* the action or skill of a cheerleader.

cheer·less (chēr′lis), *adj.* without cheer; joyless; gloomy: *drab and cheerless surroundings.* —**cheer′less·ly,** *adv.* —**cheer′less·ness,** *n.*

cheer·y (chēr′ē), *adj.,* **cheer·i·er, cheer·i·est. 1.** in good spirits; blithe; gay. **2.** promoting cheer; enlivening. —**cheer′i·ly,** *adv.* —**cheer′i·ness,** *n.*

cheese[1] (chēz), *n.* **1.** the curd of milk separated from the whey and prepared in many ways as a food. **2.** a definite mass of this substance, often in the shape of a wheel or cylinder. **3.** something of similar shape or consistency, as a mass of pomace in cider-making. [ME *chese,* OE *cēse* (c. OS *kāsi,* G *Käse*) < L *cāse(us)*]

cheese[2] (chēz), *v.t.,* **cheesed, chees·ing.** *Slang.* **1.** to stop; desist. **2. cheese it, a.** look out! **b.** flee! run away! [? alter. of CEASE]

cheese[3] (chēz), *n.* *Slang.* a person or thing that is splendid or important: *He's the big cheese in this outfit.* [? < Urdu *chīz* thing < Pers]

cheese·burg·er (chēz′bûr′gər), *n.* a hamburger cooked with a slice of cheese on top of it. [CHEESE[1] + (HAM)BURGER]

cheese·cake (chēz′kāk′), *n.* **1.** Also, **cheese′ cake′.** a rich, custardlike cake prepared with cottage cheese or cream cheese. **2.** *Slang.* photographs featuring the legs and body of an attractive woman: *magazines full of cheesecake.*

cheese·cloth (chēz′klôth′, -kloth′), *n.* a coarse, lightweight cotton fabric of open texture. [so called because first used to wrap cheese]

cheese·par·ing (chēz′pâr′ing), *adj.* **1.** meanly economical; parsimonious. —*n.* **2.** something of little or no value. **3.** niggardly economy. —**cheese′par′er,** *n.*

chees·y (chē′zē), *adj.,* **chees·i·er, chees·i·est. 1.** of or like cheese. **2.** *Slang.* of substandard quality. —**chees′i·ly,** *adv.* —**chees′i·ness,** *n.*

Cheetah
(2½ ft. high at shoulder; total length 7½ ft.; tail 2½ ft.)

chee·tah (chē′tə), *n.* a cat, *Acinonyx jubatus,* of southwestern Asia and Africa, resembling a leopard but having certain doglike characteristics, often trained for hunting. Also, **chetah.** [< Hindi *cītā,* appar. shortened < Skt *citrakāya* = *citra* mottled + *kāya* body]

chef (shef), *n.* a cook, esp. a male head cook. [< F; see CHIEF]

chef-d'oeu·vre (*Fr.* she dœ′vrᵊ), *n., pl.* **chefs-d'oeu·vre** (*Fr.* she dœ′vrᵊ). a masterpiece, esp. in art, literature, or music. [< F]

Che·foo (chē′fōō′), *n.* a seaport in NE Shantung, in E China. 116,000 (1953). Also called **Yentai.**

Chei·ron (kī′ron), *n.* *Class. Myth.* Chiron.

Che·ju (che′jōō′), *n.* an island S of and belonging to South Korea. 326,405 (est. 1965); 718 sq. mi. Also called **Quelpart.** Japanese, **Saishuto, Saishu.**

Che·ka (che′kä), *n.* the special commission in the U.S.S.R. (1917–22) charged with preventing counterrevolutionary activities: replaced by G.P.U. Cf. **G.P.U., MVD, NKVD.** [< Russ = *che* + *ka,* names of initial letters of *Chrezvychainaya Kommissiya* Special Commission] —**Che′kist,** *n.*

Che·khov (chek′ôf, -of; *Russ.* che′khof), *n.* **An·ton Pa·vlo·vich** (än tôn′ pä vlô′vich), 1860–1904, Russian short-story writer and dramatist. —**Che·khov·i·an** (chek′ô fē ən, -of ē-, che kô′fē-, -kof′ē-, -kō′vē-), *adj.*

Che·kiang (che′kyang′; *Chin.* ju′gyäng′), *n.* a province in E China, on the East China Sea. 25,280,000 (est. 1957); 39,768 sq. mi. *Cap.:* Hangchow.

che·la[1] (kē′lə), *n., pl.* **-lae** (-lē). the pincerlike organ or claw terminating certain limbs of crustaceans and arachnids. [< NL < Gk *chēlḗ* claw]

che·la[2] (chā′lä), *n.* (in India) a disciple of a religious teacher. [< Hindi *celā* < Skt *ceṭa* slave] —**che′la·ship′,** *n.*

che·late (kē′lāt), *adj., n., v.,* **-lat·ed, -lat·ing.** —*adj.* **1.** *Zool.* having a chela or chelae. **2.** *Chem.* **a.** of or noting a heterocyclic compound having a central metallic ion attached by covalent bonds to two or more nonmetallic atoms in the same molecule. **b.** of or noting a compound having a cyclic structure resulting from the formation of one or more hydrogen bonds in the same molecule. —*n.* **3.** *Chem.* a chelate compound. —*v.i.* *Chem.* **4.** (of a heterocyclic compound) to combine with a metallic ion to form a chelate. **5.** (of a compound) to form a ring by one or more hydrogen bonds.

che·lic·er·a (kə lis′ər ə), *n., pl.* **-er·ae** (-ə rē′). one member of the first pair of usually pincerlike appendages of spiders and other arachnids. [< NL < Gk *chēl(ḗ)* CHELA[1] + -I- + Gk *kér(as)* horn + L *-a* fem. n. ending] —**che·lic′er·al,** *adj.* —**che·lic·er·ate** (kə lis′ə rāt′), *adj.*

Chel·le·an (shel′ē ən), *adj.* Abbevillian. [< F *chelléen,* after *Chelles,* France, where Paleolithic tools were unearthed]

Chelms·ford (chemz′fərd, chelmz′-), *n.* a city in NE Massachusetts. 31,432 (1970).

che·loid (kē′loid), *n.* *Pathol.* keloid.

che·lo·ni·an (ki lō′nē ən), *adj.* **1.** belonging or pertaining to the order *Chelonia,* comprising the turtles. —*n.* **2.** a turtle. [< NL *Chelōni(a)* (*chelōn-* (< Gk *chelṓnē* tortoise) + *-ia* -IA) + -AN]

Chel·sea (chel′sē), *n.* **1.** a borough in SW London, England: many residences of artists and writers. 47,085 (1961). **2.** a city in E Massachusetts, near Boston. 30,625 (1970).

Chel·ten·ham (chelt′nəm *for 1, 3;* chel′tᵊn ham′ *for 2*), *n.* **1.** a city in N Gloucestershire, in W England: resort. 71,968 (1961). **2.** a township in SE Pennsylvania, near Philadelphia. 40,238 (1970). **3.** *Print.* a style of type.

Chel·ya·binsk (chel yä′binsk), *n.* a city in the S RSFSR, in the SW Soviet Union in Asia, near the Ural Mountains. 803,000 (1965).

Chel·yus·kin (chel yōōs′kin), *n.* **Cape,** a cape in the N Soviet Union in Asia: the northernmost point of Asia.

chem-, an element derived from the analysis of *chemical, chemistry,* used with elements of Greek origin in the formation of compound words: *chemurgy.* Also, *esp. before a consonant,* **chemo-.** [<< Gk *chēmeía* alloying of metals. See ALCHEMY]

chem., **1.** chemical. **2.** chemist. **3.** chemistry.

Chem.E., Chemical Engineer.

chem·ic (kem′ik), *adj.* **1.** of or pertaining to alchemy; alchemic. **2.** of or pertaining to chemistry; chemical. [< Gk *chēm(ía)* alchemy + -IC; r. *chimic* < ML *(al)chimic(us)*; see ALCHEMY]

chem·i·cal (kem′i kəl), *n.* **1.** a substance produced by or used in a chemical process. —*adj.* **2.** of, used in, produced by, or concerned with chemistry or chemicals. [CHEMIC + -AL[1]; r. *chimical* chemic] —**chem′i·cal·ly,** *adv.*

chem′ical engineer′ing, the science or profession of applying chemistry to industrial processes. —**chem′ical engineer′.**

Chem′ical Mace′, **1.** *Trademark.* an aerosol container for spraying Mace. **2.** Mace.

chem′ical war′fare, warfare with asphyxiating, poisonous, corrosive, or debilitating gases, oil flames, etc.

chem·i·lum·i·nes·cence (kem′ə lōō′mə nes′əns), *n.* (in chemical reactions) the production of light at low temperatures. —**chem′i·lu′mi·nes′cent,** *adj.*

che·min de fer (shə man′ də fâr′; *Fr.* shə maNᵊ fer′), *Cards.* a variation of baccarat. [< F: railroad; so called from the speed of the game]

che·mise (shə mēz′), *n.* **1.** a woman's loose-fitting, shirt-like undergarment. **2.** a shiftlike dress with an unfitted waistline. [ME < OF: shirt < LL *camis(ia),* prob. < Celt; r. ME *kemes,* OE *cemes* < LL *camisia*]

chem·i·sette (shem′i zet′), *n.* (in the late Victorian era) a woman's garment, esp. of lace, worn over a low-cut or open bodice. [< F; see CHEMISE, -ETTE]

chem·ism (kem′iz əm), *n.* chemical action. [CHEM- + -ISM, modeled on F *chimisme*]

chem·i·sorp·tion (kem′i sôrp′shən, -zôrp′-), *n.* *Chem.* adsorption involving a chemical linkage between the adsorbant and the adsorbate. [CHEM- + -I- + (AD)SORPTION]

chem·ist (kem′ist), *n.* **1.** a person versed in chemistry or professionally engaged in chemical operations. **2.** *Brit.* a pharmacist; druggist. **3.** *Obs.* alchemist. [< Gk *chēm(ía)* alchemy + -IST; r. *chymist* < ML *(al)chimist(a)*]

chem·is·try (kem′i strē), *n., pl.* **-tries. 1.** the science that deals with or investigates the composition, properties, and transformations of substances and various elementary forms of matter. Cf. **organic chemistry, inorganic chemistry, element** (def. 6). **2.** a group of chemical properties, reactions, phenomena, etc.: *the chemistry of carbon.* [CHEMIST + -RY; r. *chymist, chimist* + -RY]

Chem·nitz (kem′nits), *n.* former name of **Karl-Marx-Stadt.**

chemo-, var. of **chem-,** esp. before a consonant, in imitation of forms of Greek origin: *chemosynthesis; chemotherapy.*

chem·o·re·cep·tor (kem′ō ri sep′tər, kē′mō-), *n.* *Physiol.* a receptor stimulated by chemical means.

chem·o·sphere (kem′ə sfēr′, kē′mə-), *n.* the region of the atmosphere characterized by chemical, esp. photochemical, activity.

chem·o·sur·ger·y (kem′ō sûr′jə rē, kē′mō-), *n. Surg.* the use of chemical means to obtain a result usually achieved by surgical means, as the removal or destruction of tissue. [CHEMO- + SURGERY]

chem·o·syn·the·sis (kem′ə sin′thi sis, kē′mə-), *n. Biol., Biochem.* (of an organism) the synthesis of organic compounds with energy derived from chemical reactions. —**chem·o·syn·thet·ic** (kem′ō sin thet′ik, kē′mō-), *adj.* —**chem′o·syn·thet′i·cal·ly,** *adv.*

chem·o·tax·is (kem′ə tak′sis, kē′mə-), *n. Biol.* oriented movement toward or away from a chemical substance. —**chem·o·tac·tic** (kem′ə tak′tik, kē′mə-), *adj.* —**chem′o·tac′ti·cal·ly,** *adv.*

chem·o·ther·a·peu·tics (kem′ō ther′ə pyōō′tiks, kē′mō-), *n.* (*construed as sing.*) chemotherapy. —**chem′o·ther′a·peu′tic,** *adj.*

chem·o·ther·a·py (kem′ə ther′ə pē, kē′mə-), *n. Med.* the treatment of disease by means of chemicals that have a specific toxic effect upon the disease-producing microorganisms or that selectively destroy neoplastic tissue. —**chem′o·ther′a·pist,** *n.*

che·mot·ro·pism (ki mo′trə piz′əm), *n. Biol.* oriented growth or movement in response to a chemical stimulus. —**chem·o·trop·ic** (kem′ə trop′ik, kē′mə-), *adj.* —**chem′o·trop′i·cal·ly,** *adv.*

Che·mul·po (*Kor.* che′mōōl pô′), *n.* Inchon.

chem·ur·gy (kem′ûr jē), *n.* a division of applied chemistry concerned with the industrial use of organic substances, esp. from farm produce, as soybeans, peanuts, etc. —**chem·ur′gic, chem·ur′gi·cal,** *adj.*

Che·nab (chi nab′), *n.* a river in S Asia, flowing SW from N India to the Sutlej River in E Pakistan. ab. 675 mi.

Cheng·teh (chung′du′), *n.* a city in NE Hopeh, in NE China: former summer residence of the Manchu emperors. 92,900 (est. 1957). Also called **Jehol.**

Cheng·tu (chung′dōō′), *n.* a city in and the capital of Szechwan, in central China. 1,107,000 (est. 1957).

Ché·nier (shā nyā′), *n.* **An·dré Ma·rie de** (äN drā′ ma-rē′ də), 1762–94, French poet.

che·nille (shə nēl′), *n.* **1.** a velvety cord of silk or worsted, for embroidery, fringes, etc. **2.** fabric made with a fringed silken thread used as the weft in combination with wool or cotton. **3.** any fabric with a protruding pile. **4.** a deep-pile, durable, woolen carpeting with chenille weft. [< F: fuzzy cord, lit., hairy caterpillar < L *canicul(a)* little dog]

Chen·nault (shə nôlt′), *n.* **Claire Lee** (klâr), 1890–1958, U.S. Air Force general.

che·no·pod (kē′nə pod′, ken′ə-), *n.* any plant of the genus *Chenopodium* or the family *Chenopodiaceae.* [< Gk *chḗno-* (comb. form of *chḗn* goose) + -POD]

che·no·po·di·a·ceous (kē′nə pō′dē ā′shəs, ken′ə-), *adj.* belonging to the *Chenopodiaceae,* or goosefoot family of plants, including the beet, mangelwurzel, spinach, orach, and many species peculiar to saline, alkaline, or desert regions. [< NL *Chenopodiāce(ae)* (*chēnopodi-* CHENOPOD + *-āceae* -ACEAE) + -OUS]

cheong·sam (jông′säm′), *n.* a form-fitting, knee-length Chinese dress, esp. as worn in Hong Kong, usually having short sleeves and a mandarin collar and often slit to the thighs at the sides. [< Chin (Cantonese), Mandarin *ch'ang shan* long jacket]

Che·ops (kē′ops), *n.* king of Egypt c2650–c2630 B.C.: builder of the great pyramid at Giza (brother of Khafre). Also called **Khufu.**

cheque (chek), *n. Brit.* check (def. 33).

cheq·uer (chek′ər), *n. Brit.* checker[1].

cheq·uer·board (chek′ər bōrd′, -bôrd′), *n. Brit.* checkerboard; draughtboard.

cheq·uered (chek′ərd), *adj. Brit.* checkered.

Cher (shâr; *Fr.* sher), *n.* a river in central France, flowing NW to the Loire River. 220 mi. long.

Cher·bourg (shâr′bōōrg; *Fr.* sher bōōr′), *n.* a seaport in NW France. 40,018 (1962).

cher·chez la femme (sher shā′ la fam′), *French.* look for the woman: advice offered facetiously in any situation, esp. one of doubt or mystery.

Cher·e·mis (cher′ə mis′, -mēs′, cher′ə mis′, -mēs′), *n.* a Uralic language spoken in scattered communities 300–800 miles E of Moscow. Also, **Cher′e·miss′.**

Che·rem·kho·vo (che′rem khô′vo), *n.* a city in the SE RSFSR, in the S Soviet Union in Asia, on the Trans-Siberian Railroad, near Lake Baikal. 113,000 (est. 1965).

Che·ren·kov (chə reng′kôf, -kəf, -ren′-; *Russ.* che ren′-kof), *n.* **Pa·vel A.** (pä′vəl). See **Cerenkov, Pavel A.**

ché·rie (shā rē′), *n., pl.* **-ries** (-rē′). *French.* (in addressing or referring to a woman) dear; sweetheart.

cher·ish (cher′ish), *v.t.* **1.** to hold dear: *to cherish one's native land.* **2.** to care for tenderly; nurture: *to cherish a child.* **3.** to cling fondly or inveterately to (hopes, ideas, etc.): *cherishing no resentment.* [ME *cherissh(en)* < MF *cheriss-* (long s. of *cherir*) = *cher* dear (< L *cārus*) + *-iss-* -ISH[2]] —**cher′ish·a·ble,** *adj.* —**cher′ish·er,** *n.* —**cher′ish·ing·ly,** *adv.*

—**Syn. 1.** CHERISH, FOSTER, HARBOR imply giving affection, care, or shelter to something. CHERISH suggests regarding or treating something as an object of affection or as valuable: *to cherish a memory or a friendship.* FOSTER implies sustaining and nourishing something with care, esp. in order to promote, increase or strengthen it: *to foster a hope; to foster enmity.* HARBOR suggests giving shelter to or entertaining something undesirable, esp. evil thoughts or intentions: *to harbor malice or a grudge.* **2.** nurse, nourish, sustain. **3.** treasure. —**Ant. 2.** neglect. **3.** relinquish.

Cher·no·byl (chər nō′bəl; *Russ.* cher nô′bil), *n.* a city in the Ukraine in the SW Soviet Union in Europe, 80 mi. NW of Kiev: nuclear-plant accident 1986.

Cher·nov·tsy (cher nôf′tsi), *n.* Russian name of **Cernăuţi.**

cher·no·zem (cher′no zem′), *n.* tschernosem.

Cher·o·kee (cher′ə kē′, cher′ə kē′), *n., pl.* **-kees,** (*esp. collectively*) **-kee** for 1. **1.** a member of a tribe of North American Indians whose present center is Oklahoma. **2.** the Iroquoian language of the Cherokee, written since 1822 in a syllabic script.

Cher′okee rose′, a smooth-stemmed white rose, *Rosa laevigata,* of Chinese origin, cultivated in the Southern U.S.: the state flower of Georgia.

che·root (shə rōōt′), *n.* a cigar having open, untapered ends. [< Tamil *curuṭṭu* roll (of tobacco)]

cher′ries ju′bilee, a dessert of vanilla ice cream topped with black cherries and served flambé with brandy or kirschwasser.

cher·ry (cher′ē), *n., pl.* **-ries. 1.** the fruit of any of various trees of the genus *Prunus,* consisting of a pulpy, globular drupe enclosing a one-seeded smooth stone. **2.** the tree itself. **3.** its wood. **4.** any of various fruits or plants resembling the cherry. **5.** bright red; cerise. **6.** *Slang* (*vulgar*). the hymen or the state of virginity. [late ME *chery,* var. of *chirie,* back formation from OE *ciris-* (taken for pl.) << VL **ceresium* for **cerasium,* (L *cerasum*) < Gk *kerásion* cherry]

cher′ry bomb′, a red, globe-shaped, highly explosive firecracker.

Cher′ry Hill′, a township in W New Jersey. 64,395 (1970). Formerly, **Delaware.**

cher′ry pick′er, any of several types of crane for lifting in a generally vertical direction, characterized chiefly by a long, curved boom.

cher·ry·stone (cher′ē stōn′), *n.* the quahog, *Venus mercenaria,* when larger than a littleneck. [ME *cheriston*]

cher·so·nese (kûr′sə nēz′, nēs′), *n.* a peninsula. [< L *chersonēs(us)* < Gk *chersónēsos* = *chérs(os)* dry + *nēsos* island]

chert (chûrt), *n.* a compact rock consisting essentially of microcrystalline quartz. [?] —**chert′y,** *adj.*

cher·ub (cher′əb), *n., pl.* **cher·ubs** for 3; **cher·u·bim** (cher′ə bim, -yōō bim) for 1, 2. **1.** a celestial being. Gen 3:24; Ezek. 1,10. **2.** *Theol.* a member of the second order of angels, often represented as a winged child. **3.** an innocent person, esp. a child [ME < L < Gk *cheroúb* < Heb *kərūbh;* r. ME *cherub(in),* OE *c(h)erubin, cerubim* < L *cherūbim* < Gk < Heb *kərūbhīm* (pl.)] —**che·ru·bic** (chə rōō′bik), **che·ru′bi·cal,** *adj.* —**che·ru′bi·cal·ly,** *adv.*

Che·ru·bi·ni (ker′ōō bē′nē; *It.* ke′rōō bē′nē), *n.* **Ma·ri·a Lu·i·gi Car·lo Ze·no·bio Sal·va·to·re** (mä rē′ä lōō ē′jē kär′lô dze nô′byô säl′vä tô′re), 1760–1842, Italian composer, esp. of opera; in France after 1788.

cher·vil (chûr′vil), *n.* **1.** a herbaceous plant, *Anthriscus Cerefolium,* of the parsley family, having aromatic leaves used to flavor soups, salads, etc. **2.** any of various plants of the same genus or allied genera. [ME *chervelle,* OE *cerfelle* < L *caerephyll(a),* pl. of *caerephyllum* < Gk *chairéphyllon* = *chaîre* hail (greeting) + *phýllon* leaf]

cher·vo·nets (cher vô′nits, -nets), *n., pl.* **-von·tsi** (-vônt′-sē). a former gold coin and monetary unit of the U.S.S.R., equal to 10 rubles. Also, **tchervonetz.** [< Russ *chervon(yi)* (< Pol *czerwony* red, golden) + *-ets* n. suffix]

Ches·a·peake (ches′ə pēk′), *n.* a city in SE Virginia, W of Norfolk. 89,850 (1970).

Ches′apeake Bay′, an inlet of the Atlantic, in Maryland and Virginia. 200 mi. long; 4–40 mi. wide.

Chesh·ire (chesh′ər, -ēr), *n.* **1.** a county in NW England. 1,367,860 (1961); 1015 sq. mi. *Co. seat:* Chester. **2.** Also called **Chesh′ire cheese′.** a hard cheese, yellowish, orange, or white in color, made of cow's milk and similar to cheddar cheese. **3. to grin like a Cheshire cat,** to smile or grin inscrutably: after the constantly grinning cat in the children's story *Alice's Adventures in Wonderland* (1865) by Lewis Carroll. Also called **Chester** (for defs. 1, 2).

Chesh·van (khesh′vən, hesh′-; *Heb.* khesh vän′), *n.* Heshvan.

chess[1] (ches), *n.* a game played by two persons, each with sixteen chessmen, on a chessboard. [ME < OF *esches,* pl. of *eschec* CHECK]

chess[2] (ches), *n.* cheat (def. 5). [?]

chess·board (ches′bōrd′, -bôrd′), *n.* the board, identical with a checkerboard, used for playing chess.

chess·man (ches′man′, -mən), *n., pl.* **-men** (-men′, -mən). one of the pieces used in chess. [earlier *chesse meyne* = *chesse* CHESS[1] + *meyne* household (man, men by folk etym.) < MF *mesniee* < L *mansiōn-* (s. of *mansiō*); see MANSION]

chest (chest), *n.* **1.** the trunk of the body from the neck to the abdomen; thorax. **2.** a box, usually a large, strong one with a lid, for storage, safekeeping of valuables, etc.: *a jewelry chest.* **3.** the place where the funds of a public institution or charitable organization are kept; treasury; coffer. **4.** the funds themselves. **5.** a box in which to pack any of certain goods, as tea, for transit. **6.** the quantity contained in such a box: *a chest of spices.* **7.** See **chest of drawers. 8. get something off one's chest,** *Informal.* to reveal to someone something that is oppressing one's mind or conscience. [ME; OE *cest, cist* < L *cist(a)* < Gk *kístē* box]

Ches·ter (ches′tər), *n.* **1.** a city in SE Pennsylvania. 56,331 (1970). **2.** a city in and the county seat of Cheshire, in NW England: only English city with the Roman walls still intact. 59,283 (1961). **3.** Cheshire (defs. 1, 2).

ches·ter·bed (ches′tər bed′), *n. Chiefly Canadian.* a sofa that opens into a bed. [CHESTER(FIELD) + BED]

ches·ter·field (ches′tər fēld′), *n.* **1.** (*sometimes cap.*) a single- or double-breasted topcoat or overcoat with a narrow velvet collar. **2.** a large overstuffed sofa or divan with a back and upholstered arms. **3.** *Chiefly Canadian.* any large sofa or couch. [after a 19th-c. Earl of *Chesterfield*]

Ches·ter·field (ches′tər fēld′), *n.* **Philip Dor·mer Stan·hope** (dôr′mər stan′əp), **4th Earl of,** 1694–1773, British statesman and author. —**Ches′ter·field′i·an,** *adj.*

Ches·ter·ton (ches′tər tən), *n.* **G(ilbert) K(eith),** 1874–1936, English essayist, critic, and novelist.

Ches′ter White′, one of an American breed of white hogs, having drooping ears. [named after *Chester,* county in Pennsylvania where first bred]

chest·nut (ches′nut′, -nət), *n.* **1.** the edible nut of trees of the genus *Castanea,* of the beech family. **2.** any of these trees. **3.** the wood of these trees. **4.** any of various fruits or trees resembling the chestnut, as the horse chestnut. **5.** dark reddish brown. **6.** *Informal.* an old or stale joke, anecdote, etc. **7.** the callosity on the inner side of the leg of a horse. **8.** a reddish-brown horse having the mane and tail of the same color. Cf. **bay**⁵. **9.** a horse of a solid, dark-brown color. **10. pull someone's chestnuts out of the fire,** to rescue someone from a difficulty by remedying it oneself. [earlier *chesten nut,* ME *chesten,* OE *cysten* chestnut tree (< L *castanea* < Gk *kastanéa*) + NUT]

Chestnut (def. 1), *Castanea dentata* A, Closed bur; B, Nuts

chest′nut blight′, *Plant Pathol.* a disease of chestnuts, esp. the American chestnut, characterized by bark lesions that girdle and eventually kill the tree, caused by a fungus, *Endothia parasitica.*

chest′ of drawers′, *Furniture.* a piece of furniture consisting of a set of drawers in a frame set on short legs, or feet, for holding clothing, household linens, etc.

chest·y (ches′tē), *adj.,* **chest·i·er, chest·i·est.** *Informal.* having a well-developed chest or bosom. —**chest′i·ness,** *n.*

che·tah (chē′tə), *n.* cheetah.

cheth (ḵhes, hes; *Heb.* ḵhet), *n.* heth.

Che·tu·mal (che′to͞o mäl′), *n.* a city in and the capital of the territory of Quintana Roo, in SE Mexico. 12,855 (1960).

che·val-de-frise (shə val′də frēz′), *n., pl.* **che·vaux-de-frise** (shə vō′də frēz′). Usually, **chevaux-de-frise.** a portable obstacle, usually a sawhorse, covered with spikes or barbed wire, for military use, as in closing a passage. [< F; lit., horse of Frisia, so called because it was first used by Frisians]

che·val′ glass′ (shə val′), a full-length mirror mounted in a frame so that it can be tilted. [< F *cheval* horse, supporting framework (see CHEVALIER)]

chev·a·lier (shev′ə lēr′, shə val′yā, -väl′-), *n.* **1.** a member of certain orders of honor or merit: *a chevalier of the Legion of Honor.* **2.** *Fr. Hist.* the lowest rank of the nobility. **3.** a chivalrous man. **4.** *Archaic.* a knight. [< MF; r. late ME *chivaler* < AF. See CAVALIER]

Chev·i·ot (chev′ē ət, chē′vē-; *commonly* shev′ē ət *for 2*), *n.* **1.** one of a British breed of sheep, noted for its heavy fleece of medium length. **2.** (*l.c.*) a woolen fabric in a coarse twill weave, for coats, suits, etc. [after the Cheviot Hills]

Chev′iot Hills′, a range of hills on the boundary between England and Scotland: highest point, 2676 ft.

chev·ron (shev′rən), *n.* **1.** a badge consisting of stripes meeting at an angle, worn on the sleeve by noncommissioned officers, policemen, etc., as an indication of rank, service, or the like. **2.** *Heraldry.* an ordinary in the form of an inverted V. [< F: rafter, chevron < VL *caprōn- (s. of *caprō) = *capri-* goat + *-ōn-* n. suffix]

Chevrons A, U.S. Army Sergeant; B, U.S. Air Force Staff Sergeant; C, U.S. Navy Petty Officer Second Class

chev·ro·tain (shev′rə tān′, -tin), *n.* any very small, deerlike ruminant of the family *Tragulidae,* of Africa, tropical Asia, the Malay Peninsula, etc. Also called **mouse deer.** [< F = *chevrot* kid (*chèvre* goat + *-ot* dim. suffix) + *-ain* -AN]

chev·y (chev′ē), *v.,* **chev·ied, chev·y·ing,** *n., pl.* **chev·ies.** *Brit.* —*v.t.* **1.** to harass; nag; torment. —*v.i.* **2.** to race; scamper. —*n.* **3.** a hunting cry. **4.** a hunt, chase, or pursuit. **5.** the game of prisoner's base. Also, **chivvy, chivy.** [perh. short for *Chevy Chase,* 15th-century English ballad]

Chev′y Chase′ (chev′ē), a town in Maryland. 16,244 (1970).

chew (cho͞o), *v.t.* **1.** to crush or grind with the teeth; masticate. **2.** to crush, damage, injure, etc., as if by chewing (often fol. by *up*): *The faulty lawn mower chewed up the grass.* **3.** to meditate on; consider deliberately (often fol. by *over*): *He chewed the problem over in his mind.* —*v.i.* **4.** to perform the act of crushing. **5.** *Informal.* to chew tobacco. **6.** to meditate. **7. chew out,** *Slang.* to scold harshly. **8. chew the fat** or **rag,** *Slang.* to have a chat. —*n.* **9.** the act or an instance of chewing. **10.** a mouthful or portion for chewing, esp. of tobacco. [ME *chew(en),* OE *ceowan;* c. OHG *kiuwan* (G *kauen*)] —**chew′a·ble,** *adj.* —**chew′er,** *n.*

chew′ing gum′ (cho͞o′ing), a preparation for chewing, usually made of sweetened and flavored chicle.

che·wink (chi wingk′), *n.* a towhee, *Pipilo erythrophthalmus,* of eastern North America. [imit. of its call]

chew·y (cho͞o′ē), *adj.,* **chew·i·er, chew·i·est.** (of food) not easily chewed, as because of toughness or stickiness. —**chew′i·ness,** *n.*

Chey·enne (shī en′, -an′), *n., pl.* **-ennes,** (*esp. collectively*) **-enne** for 1. **1.** a member of an American Indian people of the western plains, living in Montana and Oklahoma. **2.** an Algonquian language, the language of the Cheyenne Indians. **3.** a city in and the capital of Wyoming, in the S part. 40,914 (1970).

Cheyenne′ Riv′er, a river flowing NE from E Wyoming to the Missouri River in South Dakota. ab. 500 mi. long.

Chey·ne (chā′nē, chān), *n.* **Thomas Kel·ly** (kel′ē), 1841–1915, English clergyman and Biblical scholar.

chez (shā), *prep. French.* at or in the home of; with.

chg., 1. change. **2.** charge.

chi (kī), *n., pl.* **chis.** the 22nd letter of the Greek alphabet (X, χ). [< Gk]

Chiang Kai-shek (jyäng′ kī′shek′, chang′), (*Chiang Chung-cheng*) 1886?–1975, Chinese army officer and political leader: president of Nationalist China 1950–75. Also, **Chiang Chieh-shih** (jyäng′ jye′shœ′).

Chi·an·ti (kē än′tē, -an′-; *It.* kyän′tē), *n.* a dry, red, Italian table wine. [after the *Chianti* Mountains in Tuscany]

Chi·a·pas (chē ä′päs), *n.* a state in S Mexico. 1,215,475 (1960); 28,732 sq. mi. *Cap.:* Tuxtla Gutierrez.

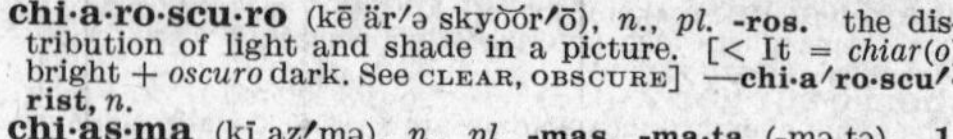

chi·a·ro·scu·ro (kē är′ə skyo͝or′ō), *n., pl.* **-ros.** the distribution of light and shade in a picture. [< It = *chiar(o)* bright + *oscuro* dark. See CLEAR, OBSCURE] —**chi·a′ro·scu′rist,** *n.*

chi·as·ma (kī az′mə), *n., pl.* **-mas, -ma·ta** (-mə tə). **1.** *Genetics.* an exchange of segments between two of the four chromatids of paired chromosomes during late prophase and metaphase. **2.** *Anat.* a crossing or decussation, esp. that of the optic nerves at the base of the brain. Also, **chi·asm** (kī′az əm). [< Gk: crosspiece of wood, cross-bandage = *chi* CHI + *-asma* n. suffix] —**chi·as′mal, chi·as′mic,** *adj.*

chi·as·ma·typ·y (kī az′mə tī′pē), *n. Genetics.* the process of chiasma formation that is the basis for crossing over. Cf. **crossing over.** [CHIASMA + -TYPE + -Y³] —**chi·as′ma·type′,** *adj., n.*

chi·as·mus (kī az′məs), *n., pl.* **-mi** (-mī). *Rhet.* a reversal in the order of words in one of two otherwise parallel phrases, as in "He went to the country, to the town went she." [< Gk *chiasmós* = *chi* CHI + *-asmos* masc. n. suffix, akin to *-asma;* see CHIASMA] —**chi·as·tic** (kī as′tik), *adj.*

chiaus (chous, choush), *n., pl.* **chiaus·es.** (in Turkey) a messenger, emissary, etc. [< Turk *çavus* < Pers *chāwush*]

Chia·yi (jyä′ē′), *n.* a city on W Taiwan. 191,074 (est. 1962).

Chi·ba (chē′bä′), *n.* a city on SE Honshu, in central Japan, near Tokyo. 291,000 (est. 1963).

Chib·cha (chib′chə), *n., pl.* **-chas,** (*esp. collectively*) **-cha.** a member of a now extinct tribe of Amerindians of advanced culture, who lived on a high plateau of Bogotá, Colombia.

Chib·chan (chib′chən), *n.* a family of languages indigenous to Colombia, Central America, and Ecuador.

chi·bouk (chi bo͝ok′, -bo͞ok′), *n.* a Turkish tobacco pipe with a stiff stem sometimes four or five feet long. Also, **chi·bouque′.** [< Turk *çibuk,* var. of *çubuk* pipe]

chic (shēk, shik), *adj.* **1.** attractive and fashionable in style; stylish: *a chic hat.* —*n.* **2.** style and elegance, esp. in dress: *Paris clothes have such chic.* **3.** stylishness; fashionableness: *She admired the chic of the first-nighters.* [< F < G *Schick* skill; or, short for CHICANE] —**chic′ly,** *adv.*

Chi·ca·go (shi kä′gō, -kô′-), *n.* a city in NE Illinois, on Lake Michigan: second largest city in the U.S. 3,369,359 (1970). —**Chica′go·an,** *n.*

Chica′go Heights′, a city in NE Illinois, S of Chicago. 40,900 (1970).

chi·ca·lo·te (chē′kä lô′te), *n.* any of several prickly, papaveraceous plants of arid tropical and subtropical America, as *Argemone mexicana.* [< Sp < Nahuatl *chicalotl*]

chi·cane (shi kān′), *n., v.,* **-caned, -can·ing.** —*n.* **1.** deception; chicanery. —*v.i.* **2.** to use chicanery. —*v.t.* **3.** to trick by chicanery. **4.** to quibble over; cavil at. [< F *chicane* (n.), *chican(er)* (v.)] —**chi·can′er,** *n.*

chi·can·er·y (shi kā′nə rē), *n., pl.* **-er·ies. 1.** trickery or deception by the use of cunning or clever devices. **2.** a quibble or subterfuge used to trick, deceive, or evade. [< F *chicanerie*] —**Syn. 1.** fraud, knavery.

Chi·ca·no (chi ka′nō, -kä′nō), *n., pl.* **-nos. 1.** an American born of Mexican parents. **2.** a Mexican worker residing in the U.S. —*adj.* **3.** of or pertaining to Mexican-Americans. [MexSp, by shortening and alter. of *Mexicano* Mexican]

chic·co·ry (chik′ə rē), *n., pl.* **-ries.** chicory.

Chi·chén It·zá (chē chen′ ēt sä′, ēt′sə), the ruins of an ancient Mayan city, in central Yucatan state, Mexico.

chi·chi (shē′shē′), *adj.* showily elegant, sophisticated, or stylish. [< F]

Chi·chi·har (*Chin.* chē′chē′här′), *n.* Tsitsihar. Also, **Chi′chi′haerh′.**

chick (chik), *n.* **1.** a young chicken or other bird. **2.** a child. **3.** *Slang.* a girl or young woman. [ME *chike,* var. of *chiken* CHICKEN]

Chickadee, *Parus atricapillus* (Length 5¼ in.)

chick·a·dee (chik′ə dē′), *n.* any of several North American titmice of the genus *Parus* (*Penthestes*), having the throat and top of the head black. [imit.]

Chick·a·mau·ga (chik′ə-mô′gə), *n.* a creek in NW Georgia: scene of a Confederate victory 1863.

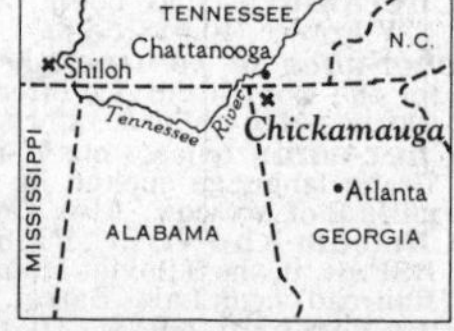
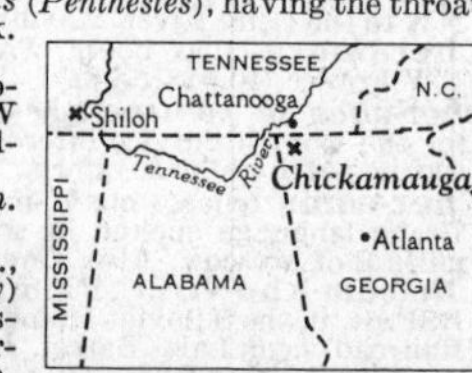

chick·a·ree (chik′ə rē′), *n.* See **red squirrel.** [imit.]

Chick·a·saw (chik′ə sô′), *n., pl.* **-saws,** (*esp. collectively*) **-saw.** a member of a Muskhogean tribe of North American Indians now in Oklahoma.

chick·en (chik′ən, -in), *n.* **1.** a gallinaceous bird, the domestic fowl, descended from the jungle fowl, *Gallus gallus.* **2.** the young of this bird when less than a year old. **3.** the flesh of the chicken, esp. of the young bird, used as food. **4.** *Informal.* a young or inexperienced person, esp. a young girl. **5. count one's chickens before they are hatched,** to rely on an event or factor that is still uncertain. —*adj.* **6.** (of food) containing, made from, or flavored by chicken. **7.** *Slang.* cowardly. —*v.i.* **8. chicken out,** *Slang.* to refrain from doing something because of fear or cowardice. [ME *chiken,* OE *cicen;* akin to D *kieken, kuiken,* LG *küken*]

chick′en colo′nel, *U.S. Mil. Slang.* a full colonel, as distinguished from a lieutenant colonel.

chick′en feed′, *U.S. Slang.* an insignificant sum of money.

chick′en hawk′, (not used scientifically) any of various hawks that sometimes prey or are said to prey on poultry.

chick·en-heart·ed (chik′ən här′tid, chik′in-), *adj. Informal.* timid; cowardly. —**chick′en-heart′ed·ly,** *adv.*

chick·en-liv·ered (chik′ən liv′ərd, chik′in-), *adj. Informal.* timid; cowardly.

chick′en pox′, *Pathol.* a mild, contagious, eruptive children's disease. Also called **varicella, water pox.**

chick′en snake′. See **rat snake.**

chick′en wire′, a light, wire netting having a large, hexagonal mesh, used esp. in building fences or barriers.

chick·pea (chik′pē′), *n.* **1.** a leguminous plant, *Cicer arietinum,* bearing edible pealike seeds, used for food esp. in southern Europe and Latin America. **2.** its seed. Also called garbanzo. [alter. of *chic-pea* = late ME *chiche* (< MF << L *cicer* chickpea) + PEA]

chick·weed (chik′wēd′), *n.* **1.** any of various caryophyllaceous plants of the genus *Stellaria,* as *S. media,* a common Old World weed whose leaves and seeds are relished by birds. **2.** any of various allied plants. [ME *chiken wede*]

Chi·cla·yo (chē klä′yô), *n.* a city in NW Peru. 127,040 (est. 1966).

chic·le (chik′əl), *n.* a gumlike substance obtained from the latex of certain tropical American trees, as the sapodilla, used chiefly in the manufacture of chewing gum. Also called **chic′le gum′.** [< Sp < Nahuatl *chictli*]

chi·co (chē′kō), *n., pl.* **-cos.** greasewood (def. 1). [short for CHICALOTE]

Chic·o·pee (chik′ə pē′), n. a city in SW Massachusetts, on the Connecticut River. 66,676 (1970).

chic·o·ry (chik′ə rē), *n., pl.* **-ries.** **1.** a perennial plant, *Chicorium intybus,* having bright-blue flowers, cultivated as a salad plant and for its root, which is used roasted and ground as a substitute or additive for coffee. **2.** the root of this plant. **3.** *Brit.* endive (def. 1). Also, **chiccory.** [< MF *chicoree;* r. late ME *cicoree* < MF < L *cichorēa* (pl. of *cichorēum*) < Gk *kichṓreia* endive, succory]

chide (chīd), *v.,* **chid·ed** or **chid, chid·ed** or **chid** or **chid·den, chid·ing.** —*v.i.* **1.** to scold; find fault. —*v.t.* **2.** to harass, nag, impel, or the like by chiding: *She chided him into apologizing.* **3.** to express disapproval of. [ME *chide(n),* OE *cīdan*] —**chid′er,** *n.*

chief (chēf), *n.* **1.** the head or leader of an organized body of men; the person highest in authority. **2.** the head or ruler of a clan or tribe: *Indian chief.* **3.** *Slang.* boss or leader: *We'll have to talk to the chief about this.* **4.** (*cap.*) *U.S. Army.* a title of some advisers to the Chief of Staff, who do not, in most instances, command the troop units of their arms or services: *Chief of Engineers; Chief Signal Officer.* **5.** *Heraldry.* **a.** the upper area of an escutcheon. **b.** an ordinary occupying this area. **6. in chief, a.** in the chief position; highest in rank: *editor in chief; commander in chief.* **b.** *Heraldry.* in the upper part of an escutcheon. —*adj.* **7.** highest in rank or authority: *the chief priest; the chief administrator.* **8.** most important; principal: *his chief merit; the chief difficulty.* [ME < OF < VL **cap(um),* alter. of L *caput* HEAD] —**Syn. 8.** foremost, essential, leading, prime.

Chief′ Exec′utive, *U.S.* **1.** the President of the United States. **2.** (*l.c.*) the governor of a state. **3.** (*l.c.*) the head of a government.

chief′ jus′tice, **1.** *Law.* the presiding judge of a court having several members. **2.** (*caps.*) Official title, **Chief′ Jus′tice of the Unit′ed States′.** the presiding judge of the U.S. Supreme Court. —**chief′ jus′tice·ship′.**

chief·ly (chēf′lē), *adv.* **1.** principally; essentially. **2.** mainly; mostly: *He went along chiefly for the ride.* [ME]

chief′ mas′ter ser′geant, *U.S. Air Force.* a noncommissioned officer of the top grade, ranking above a senior master sergeant.

chief′ mate′, *Naut.* See **first mate.** Also called **chief′ of′ficer.**

Chief′ of Staff′, *U.S.* **1.** the senior officer of the Army or Air Force, a member of the Joint Chiefs of Staff, responsible to the Secretary of his service branch. **2.** (*l.c.*) the senior or principal staff officer in a brigade or division or higher unit in the Army or Marine Corps, in a numbered unit in the Air Force, or in a unit in the Navy commanded by a rear admiral or his superior. **3.** (*l.c.*) the senior officer in command of a general staff, esp. that of the military forces.

chief′ of state′, the titular head of a nation.

chief′ pet′ty of′ficer, *U.S. Navy and Coast Guard.* a noncommissioned rank above petty officer first class and below senior petty officer. *Abbr.:* CPO, C.P.O.

chief·tain (chēf′tən, -tin), *n.* **1.** a leader of a group, band, etc.: *the robbers' chieftain.* **2.** the chief of a clan or a tribe. [ME *cheftayne,* var. of *chevetaine* < OF < LL *capitān(e)us* CAPTAIN] —**chief′tain·cy, chief′tain·ship′,** *n.*

chief′ war′rant of′ficer, *U.S. Mil.* a warrant officer ranking immediately below a second lieutenant or ensign.

chield (chēld), *n.* *Scot.* a young man; fellow. Also, **chiel** (chēl). [var. of CHILD]

Ch'ien Lung (chyen′ lo͝ong′), (*Kao Tsung*) 1711–99, Chinese emperor of the Ch'ing dynasty 1736–96. Also, **Kien Lung.**

chiff·chaff (chif′chaf′, -chäf′), *n.* a common, gray, Old World warbler, *Phylloscopus collybita.* [gradational compound; imit.]

chif·fon (shi fon′, shif′on), *n.* **1.** a sheer fabric of silk, nylon, or rayon in plain weave. **2.** any bit of feminine finery, as of ribbon or lace. —*adj.* **3.** (of women's dresses, scarves, etc.) resembling or made of chiffon. **4.** (in cooking) having a light, frothy texture, as certain pies and cakes containing beaten egg whites. [< F = *chiffe* rag + *-on* n. suffix]

Chiffonier

chif·fo·nier (shif′ə nēr′), *n.* a high chest of drawers or bureau, often having a mirror on top. Also, **chif′fon·nier′.** [< F *chiffonnier*]

chif·fo·robe (shif′ə rōb′), *n.* a piece of furniture having both drawers and space for hanging clothes. [CHIFFO(NIER + WARD)ROBE]

chig·e·tai (chig′i tī′), *n.* a Mongolian wild ass, *Equus hemionus hemionus,* related to the onager. Also, **dziggetai.** [< Mongolian *tchikhitei,* lit., with long ears. < *tchikhi* ear]

chig·ger (chig′ər), *n.* **1.** the six-legged larva of a mite of the family *Trombiculidae,* parasitic on man and other vertebrates, sucking blood and causing severe itching, and acting as a vector of scrub typhus and other infectious diseases. **2.** chigoe. Also, **jigger.** [var. of CHIGOE]

Chigger, *Eutrombicula alfreddugesi* (Length 1/16 in.)

chi·gnon (shēn′yon, shēn yun′; *Fr.* shē nyôN′), *n., pl.* **chi·gnons** (shēn′yonz, shēn yunz′; *Fr.* shē nyôN′). a large, smooth twist, roll, or knot of hair, worn by a woman at the nape of the neck or the back of the head. [< F: nape, roll of hair at nape = MF *ch(aignon)* (var. of *chainon* link = *chaine* CHAIN + *-on* n. suffix) + *(t)ignon* twist of hair (*tigne* (< L *tinea* worm) + *-on* n. suffix)] —**chi·gnoned′,** *adj.*

chig·oe (chig′ō), *n.* a flea, *Tunga penetrans,* of tropical America, Africa, and other warm regions, the impregnated female of which imbeds itself in the skin, esp. of the feet and legs of both man and animals and becomes greatly distended with eggs. Also called **chig′oe flea′, chigger, sand flea.** [< Carib]

Chih·li (chē′lē; *Chin.* ju′lē′), *n.* **1.** former name of **Hopeh. 2. Gulf of,** former name of **Pohai.**

Chi·hua·hua (chi wä′wä, -wə), *n.* **1.** a state in N Mexico. 1,374,358 (est. 1963); 94,831 sq. mi. **2.** the capital of this state. 198,461 (est. 1965). **3.** one of a Mexican or Aztec breed of very small dogs having either short or long hair.

chil·blain (chil′blān′), *n.* Usually, **chilblains.** *Pathol.* an inflammation of the hands and feet caused by exposure to cold and moisture. [CHILL + BLAIN] —**chil′blained′,** *adj.*

child (chīld), *n., pl.* **chil·dren. 1.** a boy or girl. **2.** a son or daughter. **3.** a baby or infant. **4.** a childish person: *He's such a child about money.* **5.** a descendant: *a child of an ancient breed.* **6.** any person or thing regarded as the product or result of particular agencies, influences, etc.: *a child of poverty.* **7.** *Brit. Dial. Archaic.* a female infant. **8.** *Archaic.* childe. **9. with child,** pregnant. [ME *child,* OE *cild;* akin to Goth *kilthai* womb] —**child′less,** *adj.* —**child′less·ness,** *n.*

Child (chīld), *n.* **Francis James,** 1825–96, American philologist: authority on the English and Scottish ballad.

child·bear·ing (chīld′bâr′ing), *n.* **1.** the act of producing or bringing forth children. —*adj.* **2.** capable of, suitable for, or relating to the bearing of a child or of children: *the childbearing years.* [ME]

child·bed (chīld′bed′), *n.* the condition of a woman giving birth to a child; parturition. [ME]

child′bed fe′ver, *Pathol.* See **puerperal fever.**

child·birth (chīld′bûrth′), *n.* the act or an instance of bringing forth a child; parturition: *a difficult childbirth.*

childe (chīld), *n.* *Archaic.* a youth of noble birth. [var. of CHILD]

Chil·der·mas (chil′dər məs), *n.* See **Holy Innocents' Day.** [ME *chyldermasse* = OE *cildra* (gen. pl. of *cild* CHILD) + *mæsse* MASS]

child·hood (chīld′ho͝od), *n.* **1.** the state or period of being a child. **2.** the early stage in the existence of something. [ME *childhode,* OE *cildhād*]

child·ish (chīl′dish), *adj.* **1.** of, like, or befitting a child. **2.** puerile; weak; silly: *childish fears.* [ME *childisch,* OE *cildisc*] —**child′ish·ly,** *adv.* —**child′ish·ness,** *n.*
—**Syn.** CHILDISH, INFANTILE, CHILDLIKE refer to characteristics or qualities of childhood. The ending *-ish* often has unfavorable connotations; CHILDISH therefore refers to characteristics that are undesirable and unpleasant: *childish selfishness, outbursts of temper.* INFANTILE, originally a general word, now often carries an even stronger idea of disapproval or scorn than does CHILDISH: *infantile reasoning, behavior.* The ending *-like* has pleasing or neutral connotations; CHILDLIKE therefore refers to the characteristics that are desirable and admirable: *childlike innocence.* —**Ant.** mature, adult.

child′ la′bor, the employment in gainful occupations of children below a minimum age determined by law or custom.

child·like (chīld′līk′), *adj.* like a child, as in innocence, frankness, etc.; befitting a child: *childlike candor.* —**child′like′ness,** *n.* —**Syn.** young, ingenuous, guileless, innocent. See **childish.** —**Ant.** sophisticated, adult.

child·proof (chīld′pro͞of′), *adj.* **1.** resistant to being opened, tampered with, or operated by a young child: *a childproof medicine bottle cap.* **2.** made free of hazard for a young child: *a childproof home.* **3.** made safe from damage by children: *an elegant and childproof living room.* —*v.t.* **4.** to make childproof.

chil·dren (chil′drən, -drin), *n.* pl. of **child.**

Chil′dren of God′, a highly disciplined, fundamentalist Christian sect whose converts, mostly young, live in a commune.

chil′dren of Is′rael, the Hebrews; Jews.

Chil′dren's Crusade′, the ill-fated crusade (1212) to recover Jerusalem from the Saracens, undertaken by thousands of French and German children.

child's′ play′, something very easily done.

chil·e (chil′ē), *n.* chili.

Chil·e (chil′ē; *Sp.* chē′le), *n.* a republic in SW South America, on the Pacific Coast. 10,800,000; 286,396 sq. mi. *Cap.:* Santiago. —**Chil′e·an,** *adj., n.*

chil·e con car·ne (chil′ē kon kär′nē; *Sp.* chē′le kôn kär′ne). See **chili con carne.**

Chil′e saltpe′ter, the naturally occurring form of sodium nitrate, $NaNO_3$, used as a fertilizer and in the manufacture of sulfuric and nitric acids and of potassium nitrate.

chil·i (chil′ē), *n., pl.* **chil·ies. 1.** the pod of any species of capsicum, esp. *Capsicum frutescens.* **2.** *U.S.* See **chili con carne.** Also, **chile, chilli.** [< Sp *chile* < Nahuatl *chilli*]

chil·i·ad (kil′ē ad′), *n.* **1.** a group of 1000. **2.** a period of 1000 years. [< LL *chīliad-* (s. of *chīlias*) < Gk = *chīli(oi)* 1000 + *-ad-* -AD[1]] —**chil′i·ad′al, chil′i·ad′ic,** *adj.*

chil·i·arch (kil′ē ärk′), *n.* the commander of 1000 men. [< L *chīliarch(ēs)* (or *chīliarch(us)*) < Gk *chīliárch(ēs)* (or *chīliárch(os)* = *chīli(oi)* 1000 + *-archēs* (or *-archos*) -ARCH] —**chil′i·arch′y,** *n.*

chil·i·asm (kil′ē az′əm), *n.* *Theol.* the doctrine of Christ's expected return to reign on earth for 1000 years; millennialism. [< Gk *chīliasm(ós)* = *chīli(oi)* 1000 + *-asmos,* var. of *-ismos* -ISM] —**chil·i·ast** (kil′ē ast′), *n.* —**chil′i·as′tic,** *adj.*

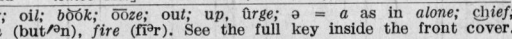

chil·i con car·ne (chil′ē kon kär′nē; *Sp.* chē′lē kôn kär′ne), a Mexican dish of meat, beans, onion, chopped pepper, etc. Also, **chile con carne.** Also called **chile, chili, chilli.** [< Sp *chile con carne* chili with meat]
chil′i pow′der, a powdered mixture of dried chilies, cumin, oregano, garlic, etc., used as a seasoning.
chil′i sauce′, a sauce made of tomatoes simmered with chili peppers and spices.
Chil′koot Pass′ (chil′ko͞ot), a mountain pass on the boundary between SE Alaska and British Columbia, Canada, in the Coast Range. ab. 3500 ft. high.
chill (chil), *n.* **1.** coldness, esp. when moderate but penetrating: *the chill of evening.* **2.** a sensation of cold, usually with shivering. **3.** sudden coldness of the body, as during the cold stage of an ague: *fevers and chills.* **4.** a depressing influence or sensation: *His entrance cast a chill over everyone in the room.* **5.** bloom[1] (def. 9). **—*adj.* 6.** cold; tending to cause shivering; chilly: *a chill wind.* **7.** shivering with or affected by cold; chilly: *I feel chill.* **8.** depressing or discouraging: *chill prospects.* **9.** unduly formal; unfriendly; chilly: *a chill reception.* **—*v.i.* 10.** to become cold: *The earth chills when the sun sets.* **11.** to be seized with or shiver from a chill. **12.** *Foundry.* (of a casting) to become hard on the surface by being subjected to a cooling process. **—*v.t.* 13.** to affect with cold; make chilly: *The rain has chilled me to the bone.* **14.** to make cool: *to chill a dessert.* **15.** to depress; discourage: *The news chilled his hopes.* **16.** bloom[1] (def. 15). **17.** to cause a sensation of fear in. [ME *chile,* OE *ci(e)le, cele* coolness] **—chill′ing·ly,** *adv.* **—chill′ness,** *n.* **—Syn. 6.** See **cold.**
Chi·llán (chē yän′), *n.* a city in central Chile: earthquakes 1835, 1939. 102,210.
chil·ler (chil′ər), *n.* **1.** a device for cooling or refrigerating. **2.** *Informal.* a frightening story of murder; melodrama.
chill′ fac′tor. See **wind chill.**
chil·li (chil′ē), *n., pl.* **-lies.** chili.
Chil·lum (chil′əm), *n.* a town in central Maryland, near Washington, D.C. 35,656 (1970).
chill·y (chil′ē), *adj.,* **-i·er, -i·est,** *adv.* **—*adj.* 1.** mildly cold or producing a sensation of cold; causing shivering. **2.** feeling cold; sensitive to cold; chill: *Her hands were chilly.* **3.** without warmth of feeling; cool: *a chilly reply.* **—*adv.* 4.** Also, **chil′li·ly.** in a chill manner: *The wind blew chilly.* **—chil′li·ness,** *n.* **—Syn. 1.** See **cold.**
Chi·lo·é′ Is′land (chil′ō ā′; *Sp.* chē′lô e′), an island off the SW coast of Chile. 4700 sq. mi.
chi·lo·pod (kī′lə pod′), *n.* any arthropod of the class *Chilopoda,* comprising the centipedes. [< NL *Chilopoda* = *chilo-* comb. form repr. Gk *cheîlos* lip + *-poda* -POD; so named from their having the first pair of legs modified into poison claws] **—chi·lop·o·dous** (kī lop′ə dəs), *adj.*
Chil·pan·cin·go (chēl′pän sēng′gō), *n.* a city in and the capital of Guerrero, in SW Mexico. 56,904.
Chi·lung (chē′lo͝ong′), *n.* Keelung.
chi·mae·ra (ki mēr′ə, kī-), *n.* **1.** any fish of the family *Chimaeridae,* the male of which has a spiny clasping organ over the mouth. **2.** chimera. [< L < Gk *chímaira,* fem. of *chímaros* goat]
chimb (chīm), *n.* chime[2].
Chim·bo·ra·zo (chim′bə rä′zō, -rā′-; *Sp.* chēm′bô rä′sô), *n.* a volcano in central Ecuador, in the Andes. 20,702 ft.
chime[1] (chīm), *n., v.,* **chimed, chim·ing.** **—*n.* 1.** an apparatus for striking a bell or bells so as to produce a musical sound, as one used as a doorbell. **2.** Often, **chimes. a.** a set of bells or of slabs of metal, stone, wood, etc., producing musical tones when struck. **b.** a musical instrument consisting of such a set, esp. a glockenspiel. **3.** harmonious sound in general; music; melody. **4.** harmonious relation; accord. **—*v.i.* 5.** to sound harmoniously or in chimes, as a set of bells: *The tower bells chime every hour.* **6.** to produce a musical sound by striking a bell, gong, etc.; ring chimes. **7.** to speak in cadence or singsong. **8.** to harmonize; agree: *The scenery chimed perfectly with the eerie mood of the play.* **—*v.t.* 9.** to give forth (music, sound, etc.), as a bell or bells. **10.** to strike (a bell, set of bells, etc.) so as to produce musical sound. **11.** to put, bring, indicate, announce, etc., by chiming: *The bells chimed the hour.* **12.** to utter or repeat in cadence or singsong. **13. chime in, a.** to break suddenly and unwelcomely into a conversation, esp. to express agreement. **b.** to harmonize, as in singing. [ME *chymbe belle,* var. of **chimbel* (by false analysis), OE *cimbal* CYMBAL] **—chim′er,** *n.*
chime[2] (chīm), *n.* the edge or brim of a cask, barrel, or the like, formed by the ends of the staves projecting beyond the head or bottom. Also, **chimb, chine.** [ME *chimb(e),* OE *cimb-;* c. MLG, MD *kimme* edge]
chi·me·ra (ki mēr′ə, kī-), *n., pl.* **-ras. 1.** (*often cap.*) a mythological fire-breathing monster, commonly represented with a lion's head, a goat's body, and a serpent's tail. **2.** any similarly grotesque monster having disparate parts, esp. as depicted in decorative art. **3.** a horrible or unreal creature of the imagination; a vain or idle fancy. **4.** *Genetics.* an organism composed of two or more genetically distinct tissues, as an organism that is partly male and partly female, or an artificially produced individual having tissues of several species. Also, **chimaera.** [var. of CHIMAERA]
chi·mere (chi mēr′, shi-), *n.* a loose, sleeveless, upper robe, as of a bishop. Also, **chim·er** (chim′ər, shim′-). [ME *chemer, chymere* < AL *chimēra,* special use of CHIMERA]
chi·mer·i·cal (ki mer′i kəl, -mēr′-, kī-), *adj.* unreal, imaginary, or wildly fanciful. Also, **chi·mer′ic.** [CHIMER(A) + -ICAL] **—chi·mer′i·cal·ly,** *adv.* **—chi·mer′i·cal·ness,** *n.*
Chim·kent (chim kent′), *n.* a city in S Kazakstan, in the SW Soviet Union in Asia. 303,000.
chim·ney (chim′nē), *n., pl.* **-neys. 1.** a structure, usually vertical, containing a passage or flue by which the smoke, gases, etc., of a fire or furnace are carried off and by means of which a draft is created. **2.** the part of such a structure that rises above a roof. **3.** the smokestack or funnel of a locomotive, steamship, etc. **4.** a tube, usually of glass, surrounding the flame of a lamp to promote combustion and keep the flame steady. **5.** *Dial.* fireplace. [ME *chimenai* < MF *cheminee* < L *(camera) camīnāta* (room) having a fireplace = *camīn(us)* (< Gk *káminos* furnace) + *-āta* -ATE[1]]
chim′ney cor′ner, 1. the corner or side of a fireplace. **2.** a place near the fire. **3.** fireside; hearth.
chim′ney piece′, 1. *Chiefly Brit.* mantelpiece. **2.** *Obs.* a decoration over a fireplace.
chim′ney pot′, *Chiefly Brit.* an earthenware or metal pipe or deflector, often cylindrical, fitted on the top of a chimney to increase draft and reduce or disperse smoke.
chim′ney swal′low, 1. *Brit.* See **barn swallow. 2.** *U.S.* See **chimney swift.**
chim′ney sweep′, a person whose business it is to clean out chimneys. Also, **chim′ney sweep′er.**
chim′ney swift′, an American swift, *Chaetura pelagica,* that often builds its nest in an unused chimney.
chimp (chimp), *n. Informal.* chimpanzee. [by shortening]
chim·pan·zee (chim′pan zē′, chim pan′zē), *n.* a highly intelligent anthropoid ape, *Pan troglodytes,* of equatorial Africa, smaller, larger-eared, and more arboreal than the gorilla. [< Bantu (northern Angola)]

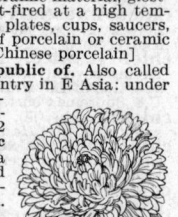

Chimpanzee
(Height 4 ft.)

Chi·mu (chē mo͞o′), *n., pl.* **-mus,** (*esp. collectively*) **-mu,** *adj.* **—*n.* 1.** a member of an extinct Amerindian people who inhabited the northern coast of Peru and had a highly developed urban culture until their conquest by the Incas. **2.** the language of this people. **—*adj.* 3.** of, pertaining to, or characteristic of the Chimu, their language, or their culture.
chin (chin), *n., v.,* **chinned, chin·ning.** **—*n.* 1.** the lower extremity of the face, below the mouth. **2.** the prominence of the lower jaw. **3. keep your chin up,** cheer up; don't give up hope. Also, **chin up! 4. take it on the chin,** *Slang.* **a.** to suffer defeat; fail completely. **b.** to endure suffering or punishment. **—*v.t.* 5.** *Gymnastics.* **a.** to bring one's chin up to (a horizontal bar, from which one is hanging by the hands), by bending the elbows. **b.** to raise (oneself) to this position by this means. **6.** *Informal.* to raise or bring up to the chin, as a violin. **7.** *Archaic.* to talk to; chatter with. **—*v.i.* 8.** *Gymnastics.* to chin oneself. **9.** *Slang.* to talk; chatter. [ME; OE *cin(n);* c. D *kin,* G *Kinn* chin, Icel *kinn,* Goth *kinnus* cheek, L *gena,* Gk *génu(s)* chin, jaw, Skt *hanus* jaw]
Chin, Chinese (def. 2).
Chin., 1. China. 2. Chinese.
chi·na (chī′nə), *n.* **1.** a translucent ceramic material, glost-fired at a low temperature and biscuit-fired at a high temperature. **2.** any porcelain ware. **3.** plates, cups, saucers, etc., collectively. **4.** figurines made of porcelain or ceramic material, collectively. [< Pers *chīnī* Chinese porcelain]
Chi·na (chī′nə), *n.* **1. People's Republic of.** Also called **Communist China, Red China.** a country in E Asia: under communist control since 1949. 930,000,000 including 13,000,000 in Inner Mongolia and 1,400,000 in Tibet; 3,691,502 sq. mi. *Cap.:* Peking. **2. Republic of.** Also called **Nationalist China.** a republic consisting chiefly of the island of Taiwan off the SE coast of mainland China. 16,100,000; 13,885 sq. mi. *Cap.:* Taipei.
Chi′na as′ter, an asterlike plant, *Callistephus chinensis,* cultivated in numerous varieties having white, yellow, blue, red, or purple flowers.

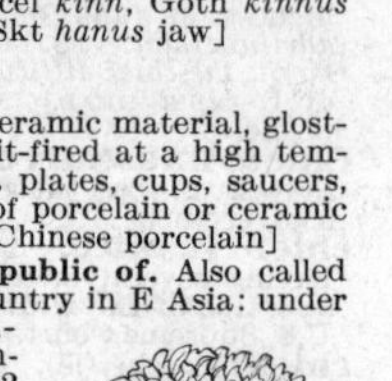
China aster,
Callistephus chinensis

chi′na bark′ (kī′nə, kē′nə), cinchona (def. 1).
chi·na·ber·ry (chī′nə ber′ē), *n., pl.* **-ries. 1.** a tree, *Melia Azedarach,* native to Asia but widely planted elsewhere for its ornamental yellow fruits. **2.** a soapberry, *Sapindus marginatus,* of Mexico, the West Indies, and the southern U.S. Also called **chi′naberry tree′, China tree.**
Chi·na·man (chī′nə mən), *n., pl.* **-men.** *Usually Offensive.* a native or inhabitant of China; a Chinese.
Chi′na Sea′, the East China Sea and the South China Sea, taken together.
Chi′na Syn′drome, a theoretical nuclear-reactor disaster in which an uncontrollable melting core burns through the earth to the other side of the globe.
Chi·na·town (chī′nə toun′), *n.* the Chinese quarter of a city.
Chi′na tree′, chinaberry.
chi·na·ware (chī′nə wâr′), *n.* dishes, ornaments, etc., made of china. [CHINA + WARE[1]; r. *Cheney ware* = Pers *chīnī* CHINA + WARE[1]]
chin·ca·pin (ching′kə pin), *n.* chinquapin.
chinch (chinch), *n.* **1.** See **chinch bug. 2.** (loosely) a bedbug. [< Sp *chinche* < L *cīmic-* (s. of *cīmex*) bug]
chinch′ bug′, a small lygaeid bug, *Blissus leucopterus,* that feeds on corn, wheat, and other grains.
chin·chil·la (chin chil′ə), *n.* **1.** a small, South American rodent, *Chinchilla laniger,* having a soft, silvery gray fur. **2.** the fur of this animal. **3.** something, as a coat, jacket, etc., made of chinchilla fur. **4.** a thick, napped, woolen fabric for coats, esp. children's coats. [< Sp, perh. = *chinche* CHINCH + *-illa* < L *-illa* dim. suffix]

Chinchilla,
Chinchilla laniger
(Total length to 20 in.; tail to 6 in.)

chin-chin (chin′chin′), *n.* **1.** polite and ceremonious speech. **2.** light conversation; chitchat. [< Chin (Peking dial.) *ch'ing-ch'ing* please-please]
chinch·y (chin′chē), *adj.,* **chinch·i·er, chinch·i·est.** *Chiefly Midland and Southern U.S.* stingy; cheap. Also **chintzy.** [ME *chinche* (n. and adj.) < OF *chinche, chiche* < VL **cicc(us),* L *cicc(um)* a bagatelle; see -Y[1]]
chin·cough (chin′kôf′, -kof′), *n. Pathol.* See **whooping cough.** [*chink* violent gasp (OE *cinc-* as in *cincung* boisterous laughter) + COUGH]
Chin·dwin (chin′dwin′), *n.* a river in N Burma, flowing S to the Irrawaddy River. 550 mi. long.
chine[1] (chīn), *n.* **1.** the backbone or spine, esp. of an animal. **2.** the whole or a piece of the backbone of an animal

with adjoining parts, cut for cooking. **3.** a ridge or crest, as of land. **4.** *Naut.* an angular intersection of the sides and bottom of a vessel. [ME *eschine* < OF *eschine* < Gmc]

chine[2] (chīn), *n.* chime[2].

Chi·nese (chī nēz′, -nēs′), *n., pl.* **-nese,** *adj.* **—***n.* **1.** the standard language of China, based on the speech of Peking; Mandarin. **2.** a group of languages of the Sino-Tibetan family, including standard Chinese and most of the other languages of China. *Abbr.:* Chin, Chin. **3.** any of the Chinese languages, which vary among themselves to the point of mutual unintelligibility. **4.** a native or descendant of a native of China. **—***adj.* **5.** of or pertaining to China, its inhabitants, or one of their languages.

Chi′nese cab′bage, a lettucelike plant, *Brassica pekinensis,* of China, having an elongated, compact head of light green leaves. Also called **pe-tsai.**

Chi′nese cal′endar, the former calendar of China, in which the year consisted of 12 lunar months.

Chi′nese check′ers, a board game for two to six players in which marbles resting in holes are moved to the opposite side by jumping intervening pieces or moving to adjacent holes that are unoccupied.

Chi′nese Chip′pendale, (esp. in furniture) an English rococo style using Chinese or quasi-Chinese motifs.

Chinese Chippendale stand

Chi′nese Em′pire, China under the rule of various imperial dynasties until replaced by a republic in 1912.

Chi′nese lan′tern, a collapsible lantern of thin, colored paper, often used for decorative lighting. Also called **Japanese lantern.**

Chi′nese puz′zle, anything very complicated or perplexing.

Chi′nese red′, vermilion; orange red.

Chi′nese-res′taurant syn′drome, physical distress (headache, sweating, etc.) believed to be caused by the monosodium glutamate often used in Chinese food.

Chinese′ Revolu′tion, the revolution in China in 1911, resulting in the overthrow of the Manchu dynasty and the establishment of a republic in 1912.

Chi′nese Turk′estan. See under **Turkestan.**

Chi′nese Wall′. See **Great Wall of China.**

Chi′nese wax′, a water-insoluble substance obtained from the wax secreted by certain insects, esp. a Chinese scale (*Ericerus pela*): used chiefly in the manufacture of polishes, sizes, and candles. Also called **Chi′nese tree′ wax′, insect wax.**

Chi′nese white′, a white pigment made from barium sulfate.

Chi′nese wood′ oil′. See **tung oil.**

Ch'ing (ching), *n.* See under **Manchu** (def. 1). Also called **Ta Ch'ing.**

Ching·hai (ching′hī′), *n.* a province in W China. 2,050,000 (est. 1957); 269,187 sq. mi. *Cap.:* Sining. Also, **Tsinghai.** Also called **Koko Nor.**

chink[1] (chingk), *n.* **1.** a crack, cleft, or fissure: *a chink in a wall.* **2.** a narrow opening: *a chink between two buildings.* **—***v.t.* **3.** to fill up chinks in. [dial. *chine* ravine (ME; OE *cinu* crevice, fissure; c. MD *kene*) + *-k* suffix (see -OCK)]

chink[2] (chingk), *v.t., v.i.* **1.** to make or cause to make a short, sharp, ringing sound, as of coins or glasses striking together. **—***n.* **2.** a chinking sound: *the chink of ice in a glass.* [imit.]

Chink (chingk), *n. Offensive.* a Chinese. [alter., perh. after dial. *chink,* var. of KINK, with reference to the slant of the eye]

chin·ka·pin (ching′kə pin), *n.* chinquapin.

Chin·kiang (chin′kyang′), *n.* a port in S Kiangsu, in E China, on the Yangtze River, 179,000 (est. 1950).

chi·no (chē′nō), *n., pl.* **-nos** for 2. **1.** a tough, twilled cotton cloth used for uniforms, sports clothes, etc. **2.** Usually, **chinos.** a pair of trousers or slacks made of this material. [? special use of CHINO-, with reference to yellowish color of cloth]

Chino-, a combining form of **Chinese:** *Chino-Tibetan.*

chi·noi·se·rie (shēn woz′ə rē′, -woz′ə rē), *n.* (*sometimes cap.*) **1.** an 18th-century European style of decoration in which supposedly Chinese motifs were extensively used. **2.** an object decorated in this style. [< F = *chinois* CHINESE + *-erie* -ERY]

chin·o·line (kin′ᵊlēn′, -ᵊlin, chin′-), *n. Chem.* quinoline. Also, **chin·o·leine** (kin′ᵊlēn′, chin′-).

Chi·nook (shi no͝ok′, -no͞ok′, chi-), *n., pl.* **-nooks,** (*esp. collectively*) **-nook. 1.** a member of a formerly numerous North American Indian people originally inhabiting the northern shore of the mouth of the Columbia River and the adjacent territory. **2.** either of the two languages of the Chinook Indians. **3.** (*l.c.*) a warm, dry wind that blows at intervals down the eastern slopes of the Rocky Mountains. **4.** (*l.c.*) a warm, moist, southwest wind on the coast of Oregon (**wet chinook**) and Washington. **5.** (*l.c.*) See **chinook salmon.**

Chi·nook·an (shi no͝ok′ən, -no͞o′kən, chi-), *n.* **1.** a language family comprising only Lower Chinook and Upper Chinook. **—***adj.* **2.** of the Chinooks or Chinookan.

Chinook′ Jar′gon, a jargon based on one of the Chinook languages, now extinct but once widely used as a lingua franca along the NW coast of North America, esp. in the regions along the Columbia River.

chinook′ salm′on, a large salmon, *Oncorhynchus tshawytscha,* found in the northern Pacific Ocean. Also called **king salmon, quinnat salmon.** See illus. at **salmon.**

chin·qua·pin (ching′kə pin), *n.* **1.** a shrubby chestnut, *Castanea pumila,* of the U.S., bearing small edible nuts. **2.** an evergreen, fagaceous tree, *Castanopsis chrysophylla,* of the Pacific coast, bearing inedible nuts. **3.** the nut of either of these trees. Also, **chincapin, chinkapin.** [dissimilated var. of *chincomen,* of Algonquian orig.; cf. Delaware *chinkwa* big, *min* fruit, seed]

chin′ strap′, **1.** a strap attached to a hat for passing under the chin of the wearer. **2.** a strap to support the chin in cosmetic facial treatment. **3.** a strap on a bridle or halter that joins the throatlatch and noseband.

chintz (chints), *n.* **1.** a printed cotton fabric, used esp. for draperies. **2.** a painted or stained calico from India. [earlier *chints,* pl. of *chint* < Hindi]

chintz·y (chint′sē), *adj.,* **chintz·i·er, chintz·i·est. 1.** decorated with chintz. **2.** *Informal.* cheap or gaudy. **3.** chinchy.

chin-up (chin′up′), *n.* the act or an instance of chinning a horizontal bar, rod, or the like.

Chi·os (kī′os, -ōs, kē′-; *Gk.* кнē′ôs), *n.* **1.** a Greek island in the Aegean, near the W coast of Turkey. 62,223 (1961); 322 sq. mi. **2.** a seaport on and the capital of this island. 24,053 (1961). Greek, **Khios.** —**Chi·an** (kī′ən), *adj., n.*

chip[1] (chip), *n., v.,* **chipped, chip·ping. —***n.* **1.** a small piece, as of wood, separated by chopping, cutting, or breaking. **2.** a very thin slice or small piece of food, candy, etc.: *chocolate chips.* **3. chips,** *Chiefly Brit.* See **French fried potatoes. 4.** a mark or flaw made by the breaking off or gouging out of a small piece: *This glass has a chip.* **5.** any of the small round disks, usually of plastic or ivory, used as tokens for money in certain gambling games, as roulette, poker etc.; counter. **6.** *Electronics.* a tiny square piece of thin semiconducting material on which an integrated circuit is formed or to be formed. **7.** *Informal.* a small cut or uncut piece of a diamond or crystal. **8.** anything trivial or worthless. **9.** something dried up or without flavor. **10.** a piece of dried dung. **11.** wood, straw, etc., in thin strips for weaving into hats, baskets, etc. **12.** *Golf.* See **chip shot. 13. chip off the old block,** a person who resembles his parent in appearance or behavior. **14. chip on one's shoulder,** a disposition to quarrel; a grievance. **15. in the chips,** *Slang.* wealthy; rich. **16. when the chips are down,** in a crucial situation. **—***v.t.* **17.** to hew or cut with an ax, chisel, or the like. **18.** to cut, break off, or gouge out (bits or fragments): *He chipped a few pieces of ice from the large block.* **19.** to break off a fragment of: *to chip the edge of a saucer.* **20.** to shape or produce by cutting or flaking away pieces: *to chip a figure out of wood.* **21.** *Brit. Slang.* to jeer or criticize severely; deride; taunt. **—***v.i.* **22.** to break off in small pieces. **23.** *Golf.* to make a chip shot. **24. chip in,** *Informal.* **a.** to contribute money, as to a fund; participate. **b.** to butt in. [(n.) ME; OE *cipp* log, i.e., piece cut off; (v.) ME *chipp(en),* OE *-cippian* (in *forcippian* to cut off); akin to MLG, MD *kippen* to chip eggs]

chip[2] (chip), *v.,* **chipped, chip·ping,** *n.* **—***v.i.* **1.** to utter a short chirping or squeaking sound; cheep. **—***n.* **2.** a short chirping or squeaking sound. [var. of CHEEP]

chip·board (chip′bōrd′, -bôrd′), *n.* **1.** a low grade of cardboard, used as a backing for pads of paper, a stiffener for photographs in mailing, etc. **2.** a thin, stiff sheet material made from wastepaper.

chip·munk (chip′mungk), *n.* any of several small, striped, terrestrial squirrels of the genera *Tamias,* of North America, and *Eutamia,* of Asia and North America, esp. *T. striatus,* of eastern North America. [assimilated var. of *chitmunk* < Algonquian; akin to Ojibwa *atchitamon* squirrel, lit., head first, with reference to its way of coming down a tree trunk]

Chipmunk,
Tamias striatus
(Total length 10 in.; tail 4 in.)

chipped′ beef′, *U.S.* very thin slices or shavings of dried, smoked beef.

Chip·pen·dale (chip′ən dāl′), *n.* **1. Thomas,** 1718?–79, English cabinetmaker and furniture designer. **—***adj.* **2.** of or in the style of Thomas Chippendale.

chip·per[1] (chip′ər), *adj. Chiefly U.S. Informal.* lively; cheerful. [var. of dial. *kipper* frisky < ?]

chip·per[2] (chip′ər), *v.i.* **1.** to chirp or twitter. **2.** to chatter or babble. [CHIP[2] + -ER[6]]

chip·per[3] (chip′ər), *n.* a person or thing that chips or cuts. [CHIP[1] + -ER[1]]

Chip·pe·wa (chip′ə wä′, -wā′, -wə), *n., pl.* **-was,** (*esp. collectively*) **-wa.** Ojibwa.

Chip·pe·way (chip′ə wā′), *n., pl.* **-ways,** (*esp. collectively*) **-way.** Chippewa.

chip′ping spar′row, a small, North American sparrow, *Spizella passerina,* commonly found in urban areas.

chip·py[1] (chip′ē), *n., pl.* **-pies.** *Informal.* **1.** a prostitute. **2.** a promiscuous or a flirtatious woman. Also, **chip′pie.** [short for *chipping sparrow*]

chip·py[2] (chip′ē), *n.* a chipmunk. [CHIP(MUNK) + -Y[2]]

chip′ shot′, *Golf.* a shot that is purposely hit fairly high into the air and is meant to roll upon landing, used in approaching the green.

Chi·ri·co (kē′rē kō), *n.* **Gior·gio de** (jôr′jô de), 1888–1978, Italian painter.

chirk (chûrk), *U.S. Informal.* **—***v.i.* **1.** to make a shrill, chirping noise. **—***v.t.* **2.** to cheer (usually fol. by *up*). **—***adj.* **3.** cheerful. [ME *chirk(en)* (v.), OE *circian* to roar]

chirm (chûrm), *v.i.* **1.** to chirp, as a bird; sing; warble. **—***n.* **2.** the chirping of birds. [ME; OE *cierm* noise]

chi·ro (chē′rō), *n., pl.* **-ros.** the ladyfish, *Elops saurus.* [?]

chiro-, a learned borrowing from Greek meaning "hand," used in the formation of compound words: *chiromancy; chiropter.* [comb. form of Gk *cheir* hand]

chi·rog·ra·phy (kī rog′rə fē), *n.* handwriting; penmanship. —**chi·rog′ra·pher,** *n.* —**chi·ro·graph·ic** (kī′rə graf′ik), **chi′ro·graph′i·cal,** *adj.*

chi·ro·man·cy (kī′rə man′sē), *n.* the art of divination by analyzing the appearance of the hand; palmistry. —**chi′ro·man′cer,** *n.* —**chi′ro·man′tic, chi′ro·man′ti·cal,** *adj.*

Chi·ron (kī′ron), *n. Class. Myth.* a wise and beneficent centaur, teacher of Achilles and Asclepius. Also, **Cheiron.**

chi·rop·o·dist (kī rop′ə dist, ki-, shə-), *n.* a person whose occupation is the practice of chiropody.

chi·rop·o·dy (kī rop′ə dē, ki-, shə-), *n.* podiatry.
chi·ro·prac·tic (kī′rə prak′tik), *n.* a therapeutic system based upon the premise that disease is caused by interference with nerve function, the method being to restore normal condition by adjusting the segments of the spinal column. [CHIRO- + *-practic* < Gk *praktik(ós)*; see PRACTICAL]
chi·ro·prac·tor (kī′rə prak′tər), *n.* a person whose occupation is the practice of chiropractic.
chi·rop·ter (kī rop′tər), *n.* any mammal of the order *Chiroptera*, comprising the bats.
chi·rop·ter·an (kī rop′tər ən), *n.* **1.** chiropter. —*adj.* **2.** of or pertaining to a chiropter.
chirp (chûrp), *v.i.* **1.** to make a short, sharp sound, as small birds and certain insects. **2.** to make any similar sound: *The children chirped with amusement.* —*v.t.* **3.** to sound or utter in a chirping manner. —*n.* **4.** a chirping sound. [? var. of CHIRK] —**chirp′er,** *n.* —**chirp′ing·ly,** *adv.*
chirp·y (chûr′pē), *adj.,* **chirp·i·er, chirp·i·est.** *Informal.* cheerful; lively; gay. —**chirp′i·ly,** *adv.* —**chirp′i·ness,** *n.*
chirr (chûr), *v.i.* **1.** to make a shrill, trilling sound, as a grasshopper. **2.** to make a similar sound. —*n.* **3.** the sound of chirring. Also, **churr.** [alter. of CHIRP]
chir·rup (chēr′əp, chûr′-), *v.,* **-ruped, -rup·ing,** *n.* —*v.i.* **1.** to chirp. **2.** to make a similar sound, as to a horse. —*v.t.* **3.** to utter with chirps. **4.** to make a chirping sound to. —*n.* **5.** the act or sound of chirruping. [var. of CHIRP]
chi·rur·geon (kī rûr′jən), *n.* *Archaic.* a surgeon. [< L *chīrūr(gus)* (< Gk *cheirourgós* hand worker, surgeon; see CHIRO-, DEMIURGE) + (SUR)GEON; r. ME *cirurgian* < OF *cirurgien* surgeon]
chi·rur·ger·y (kī rûr′jə rē), *n.* *Archaic.* surgery. [CHIRURG(EON) + -ERY; r. late ME *sirurgerie* < MF *cirurgerie* < L *chīrūrg(ia)* (< Gk *cheirourgía;* see CHIRURGEON, -IA) + OF *-erie* -ERY] —**chi·rur′gic, chi·rur′gi·cal,** *adj.*
chis·el (chiz′əl), *n., v.,* **-eled, -el·ing** or (*esp. Brit.*), **-elled, -el·ling.** —*n.* **1.** a wedgelike tool with a cutting edge at the end of the blade, often made of steel, used for cutting or shaping wood, stone, etc. —*v.t.* **2.** to cut or form with a chisel. **3.** *U.S. Slang.* **a.** to cheat or swindle (someone). **b.** to get (something) by cheating or trickery. —*v.i.* **4.** to work with a chisel. [late ME < AF, var. of OF *cisel* < LL **cīsell(us)*, dim. of **cīsus,* akin to L *caesus,* ptp. of *caedere* to cut]

A B C
Chisels
A, Wood chisel; B, Bricklayer's chisel; C, Cold chisel

chis·eled (chiz′əld), *adj.* **1.** cut, shaped, etc., with a chisel. **2.** formed as with a chisel; clear-cut: *She has finely chiseled features.* Also, *esp. Brit.,* **chis′elled.**
chis·el·er (chiz′ə lər, chiz′lər), *n.* **1.** *U.S. Slang.* a person who cheats, swindles, or uses unethical practices. **2.** a person who uses a chisel. Also, *esp. Brit.,* **chis′el·ler.**
Chi·shi·ma (chē′shē mä′), *n.* Japanese name of the **Kurile Islands.**
Chis′holm Trail′ (chiz′əm), a cattle trail leading N from San Antonio, Texas, to Abilene, Kansas: used for about 20 years after the Civil War. [named after Jesse *Chisholm* (1806–68), American scout]
Chi·şi·nă·u (kē′shē nœ′o͞o), *n.* Rumanian name of **Kishinev.**
chi-square (kī′skwâr′), *n.* *Statistics.* a quantity equal to the summation over all variables of the quotient of the square of the difference between the observed and expected values divided by the expected value of the variable.
chi′-square test′, *Statistics.* a test devised by Karl Pearson for determining the mathematical fit of a frequency curve to an observed frequency distribution. Also, **chi′-squared test′.**
chit[1] (chit), *n.* **1.** a voucher of money owed for food, drink, etc. **2.** *U.S. Mil.* any official or semiofficial receipt, voucher, or similar document. [short for *chitty* < Hindi *chiṭṭī*]
chit[2] (chit), *n.* a child or young person, esp. a pert girl. [late ME; perh. akin to KITTEN or KID[1]]
Chi·ta (chi tä′), *n.* a city in the SE RSFSR, in the Soviet Union in Asia. 198,000 (est. 1964).
chi·tar·ro·ne (kē′tə rō′nā; *It.* kē′tär rô′ne), *n., pl.* **-ni** (-nē). a bass lute having two pegboxes, one above the other. [< It = *chitarr(a)* (< Gk *kithára* lyre) + *-one* aug. suffix]
chit·chat (chit′chat′), *n., v.,* **-chat·ted, -chat·ting.** —*n.* **1.** light conversation; small talk. **2.** idle talk; gossip. —*v.i.* **3.** to indulge in chitchat; gossip. [gradative compound based on CHAT] —**chit′chat′ty,** *adj.*
chi·tin (kī′tin), *n.* a characteristic, horny, organic component of the cuticula of arthropods. [< F *chitine* < Gk *chit(ṓn)* CHITON + F *-ine* -IN[2]] —**chi′tin·ous,** *adj.* —**chi′tin·oid′,** *adj.*
chit·ling (chit′lin, -ling), *n.* Usually, **chitlings.** chitterling. Also, **chit·lin** (chit′lin).
chi·ton (kīt′ən, kī′ton), *n.* **1.** *Gk. Antiq.* a gown or tunic, usually worn next to the skin. **2.** Also called **sea cradle.** a mollusk of the class *Amphineura,* having a mantle covered with calcareous plates, found adhering to rocks. [< Gk *chitṓn* tunic < Sem, cf. Heb *kuttōneth* tunic]
Chit·ta·gong (chit′ə gong′), *n.* a port in SE East Bengal, in E Pakistan, near the Bay of Bengal. 363,000 (est. 1961).
chit·ter (chit′ər), *v.i.* **1.** to twitter. **2.** *Brit. Dial.* to shiver. [ME *che(a)ter(en), chiter(en),* var. of *chateren* to CHATTER]
chit·ter·ling (chit′ər ling, chit′lin), *n.* Usually, **chitterlings.** a part of the small intestine of swine, usually served fried or in a sauce. Also, **chitling, chitlin.** [ME *cheterling;* akin to G *Kutteln* in same sense]
chiv·al·ric (shiv′əl rik, shi val′rik), *adj.* **1.** pertaining to chivalry. **2.** chivalrous (def. 1).
chiv·al·rous (shiv′əl rəs), *adj.* **1.** having the qualities of chivalry, as courage, courtesy, and loyalty. **2.** considerate and courteous to women; gallant. **3.** chivalric (def. 1). [ME *chevalrous* < MF *chevalerous* = *chevalier* CHEVALIER + *-ous* -OUS] —**chiv′al·rous·ly,** *adv.* —**chiv′al·rous·ness,** *n.*
chiv·al·ry (shiv′əl rē), *n., pl.* **-ries** for 5. **1.** the combination of qualities ideally expected of a knight, including courage, generosity, and courtesy. **2.** the medieval institution and principles of knighthood. **3.** knights or other chivalrous persons as a group. **4.** courtesy or gallantry toward women. **5.** *Archaic.* a chivalrous act. **6.** *Obs.* the position or rank of a knight. [ME *chivalrie* < AF, c. OF *chevalerie* = *chevalier* CHEVALIER + *-ie* -Y[3]]
chiv·a·ree (shiv′ə rē′, shiv′ə rē′), *n., v.t.,* **-reed, -ree·ing.** shivaree. Also, **chiv′a·ri′.**
chive (chīv), *n.* a small bulbous plant, *Allium Schoenoprasum,* related to the leek and onion, having long, slender leaves that are used as a seasoning in cookery. [late ME *chyve* < AF *chive,* OF *cive* << L *caepa* onion]
chiv·vy (chiv′ē), *v.t., v.i.,* **-vied, -vy·ing,** *n., pl.* **-vies.** *Brit.* chevy.
chiv·y (chiv′ē), *v.t., v.i.* **chiv·ied, chiv·y·ing,** *n., pl.* **chivies.** *Brit.* chevy.
Chka·lov (chkä′lof), *n.* a city in the E Soviet Union in Europe, on the Ural River. 300,000 (est. 1964). Also called **Orenburg.**
chlam·y·date (klam′i dāt′), *adj.* *Zool.* having a mantle or pallium, as a mollusk. [< L *chlamydāt(us)* = *chlamyd-* (s. of *chlamys*) CHLAMYS + *-ātus* -ATE[1]]
chla·myd·e·ous (klə mid′ē əs), *adj.* *Bot.* pertaining to or having a floral envelope. [< Gk *chlamyd-* (s. of *chlamýs*) CHLAMYS + -EOUS]
chla·mys (klā′mis, klam′is), *n., pl.* **chla·mys·es** (klā′mi siz, klam′i-), **chlam·y·des** (klam′i dēz′). *Gk. Antiq.* a short, fine woolen mantle worn by men. [< L < Gk *chlamýs* type of cloak or mantle]

Chlamys

Chlod·wig (klōt′viKH), *n.* German name of **Clovis I.**
chlor-[1], a learned borrowing from Greek meaning "green," used in the formation of compound words: *chlorine.* Also, *esp. before a consonant,* **chloro-.** [comb. form of Gk *chlōrós* light green, greenish yellow]
chlor-[2], a combining form of **chlorine:** *chloric.* Also, *esp. before a consonant,* **chloro-.**
chlo·ral (klōr′əl, klôr′-), *n.* **1.** *Chem.* an oily liquid, CCl_3CHO, that combines with water to form chloral hydrate. **2.** Also called **chlo′ral hy′drate.** *Pharm.* a white, crystalline solid, $CCl_3CH(OH)_2$, used as a hypnotic.
chlo·ra·mine (klōr′ə mēn′, klôr′-, klō ram′ēn, klô-), *n.* *Chem.* **1.** a liquid, NH_2Cl, with a pungent odor, derived from ammonia. **2.** any of a class of compounds obtained by replacing a hydrogen atom of an $=NH$ or $-NH_2$ group with chlorine.
chlo·ram·phen·i·col (klōr′am fen′ə kōl′, -kôl′, -kol′, klôr′-), *n.* *Pharm.* an antibiotic, $C_{11}H_{12}Cl_2N_2O_5$, obtained from cultures of *Streptomyces venezuelae* or synthesized: used chiefly in the treatment of infections caused by certain bacteria, rickettsiae, and viruses. [CHLOR-[2] + AM(IDO)- + PHEN- + NI(TR)- + (GLY)COL]
chlo·rate (klōr′āt, -it, klôr′-), *n.* *Chem.* a salt of chloric acid.
chlor·dane (klōr′dān, klôr′-), *n.* *Chem.* a toxic liquid, $C_{10}H_6Cl_8$, used as an insecticide. Also, **chlor·dan** (klōr′dan, klôr′-). [CHLOR-[2] + *(in)dane* an oily, cyclic hydrocarbon = IND- + -ANE]
chlo·rel·la (klə rel′ə), *n.* any fresh-water, unicellular green alga of the genus *Chlorella.* [CHLOR-[1] + L *-ella* dim. suffix] —**chlo·rel·la·ceous** (klōr′ə lā′shəs, klôr′-), *adj.*
chlo·ric (klōr′ik, klôr′-), *adj.* *Chem.* of or containing chlorine in the pentavalent state.
chlo′ric ac′id, *Chem.* a hypothetical acid, $HClO_3$, known only in solution or in the form of its salts.
chlo·ride (klōr′īd, -id, klôr′-), *n.* *Chem.* **1.** a salt of hydrochloric acid consisting of two elements, one of which is chlorine, as sodium chloride, NaCl. **2.** a compound containing chlorine, as methyl chloride, CH_3Cl.
chlo′ride of lime′. See **bleaching powder.** Also called **chlo′rinated lime′.**
chlo·rin·ate (klōr′ə nāt′, klôr′-), *v.t.,* **-at·ed, -at·ing.** **1.** *Chem.* to combine or treat with chlorine. **2.** to disinfect (water) by means of chlorine. **3.** *Metall.* to treat (a gold ore) with chlorine gas in order that the gold may be removed as a soluble chloride. —**chlo′rin·a′tion,** *n.* —**chlo′rin·a′tor,** *n.*
chlo·rine (klōr′ēn, -in, klôr′-), *n.* *Chem.* a halogen element, a greenish-yellow, incombustible, poisonous gas that is highly irritating to the respiratory organs, obtained chiefly by electrolysis of sodium chloride brine: used for water purification, in the making of bleaching powder, and in the manufacture of chemicals. *Symbol:* Cl; *at. wt.:* 35.453; *at. no.:* 17. —**chlo·rin·i·ty** (klō rin′i tē, klô-), *n.* —**chlo·rin·ous** (klōr′ə nəs, klôr′-), *adj.*
chlo·rite[1] (klōr′īt, klôr′-), *n.* a group of minerals, hydrous silicates of aluminum, ferrous iron, and magnesium, occurring in green platelike crystals or scales. [CHLOR-[1] + -ITE[1]] —**chlo·rit·ic** (klō rit′ik, klô-), *adj.*
chlo·rite[2] (klōr′īt, klôr′-), *n.* *Chem.* a salt of chlorous acid, as potassium chlorite, $KClO_2$. [CHLOR-[2] + -ITE[1]]
chloro-[1], var. of **chlor-**[1] before a consonant: *chlorophyll.*
chloro-[2], var. of **chlor-**[2] before a consonant: *chloroform.*
chlo·ro·ac·e·to·phe·none (klōr′ō as′i tō fə nōn′, -ə sē′tō-, klôr′-), *n.* *Chem.* a poisonous solid, $C_6H_5COCH_2Cl$, used in solution as a tear gas.
chlo·ro·form (klōr′ə fôrm′, klôr′-), *n.* **1.** *Chem., Pharm.* a colorless, volatile, nonflammable, slightly water-soluble liquid, $CHCl_3$, used chiefly in medicine as an anesthetic and as a solvent. —*v.t.* **2.** to administer chloroform to. [CHLORO-[2] + FORM(YL)] —**chlo′ro·for′mic,** *adj.*
chlo·ro·hy·drin (klōr′ə hī′drin, klôr′-), *n.* *Chem.* any of a class of organic compounds containing a chlorine atom and a hydroxyl group, usually on adjacent carbon atoms.
chlo·ro·hy·dro·qui·none (klōr′ə hī′drō kwi nōn′, klôr′-), *n.* *Chem.* a white to light tan, crystalline, water-soluble solid, $C_6H_3Cl(OH)_2$, used chiefly in organic synthesis and as a developer in photography.
Chlo·ro·my·ce·tin (klōr′ō mī sēt′ən, klôr′-), *n.* *Pharm., Trademark.* chloramphenicol.
chlo·ro·phe·no·thane (klōr′ə fē′nə thān′, klôr′-), *n.* See **DDT.** [CHLORO-[2] + PHENO- + (E)THANE]
chlo·ro·phyll (klōr′ə fil, klôr′-), *n.* *Bot., Biochem.* the green coloring matter of leaves and plants, essential to the

production of carbohydrates by photosynthesis, and occurring in a bluish-black form, $C_{55}H_{72}MgN_4O_5$ **(chlorophyll a),** and a dark-green form, $C_{55}H_{70}MgN_4O_6$ **(chlorophyll b),** used as a dye for cosmetics, oils, etc., and as a deodorant. Also, **chlo′ro·phyl.** —**chlo′ro·phyl′loid,** *adj.*

chlo·ro·phyl·lous (klōr′ə fil′əs, klôr′-), *adj.* of or containing chlorophyll. Also, **chlo·ro·phyl·lose** (klōr′ə fil′ōs, klôr′-).

chlo·ro·pic·rin (klōr′ə pik′rin, -pī′krin, klôr′-), *n. Chem., Mil.* a poisonous liquid, CCl_3NO_2, that causes lachrymation and headache: used as an insecticide, a fungicide, in organic synthesis, and in chemical warfare. Also, **chlorpicrin.** Also called **nitrochloroform.** [CHLORO-[2] + PICR(IC ACID) + -IN[2]]

chlo·ro·plast (klōr′ə plast′, klôr′-), *n. Bot.* a plastid containing chlorophyll. —**chlo′ro·plas′tic,** *adj.*

chlo·ro·prene (klōr′ə prēn′, klôr′-), *n. Chem.* a colorless liquid, $H_2C{=}CClCH{=}CH_2$, that polymerizes to neoprene. [CHLORO-[2] + (ISO)PRENE]

chlo·ro·sis (klō rō′sis, klô-), *n.* **1.** an abnormally yellow color of plant tissues, resulting from partial failure to develop chlorophyll, caused by a nutrient deficiency or the activities of a pathogen. **2.** Also called **greensickness.** *Pathol.* a benign type of iron-deficiency anemia in adolescent girls, marked by a pale yellow-green complexion. [CHLOR-[1] + -OSIS] —**chlo·rot·ic** (klō rot′ik, klô-), *adj.*

chlo·rous (klōr′əs, klôr′-), *adj. Chem.* containing trivalent chlorine.

chlor·phe·nir·a·mine (klōr′fə nir′ə mēn′, klôr′-), *n. Pharm.* an antihistaminic compound, $C_{20}H_{23}ClN_2O_4$, used chiefly in the form of its maleate in treating the symptoms of allergies. [CHLOR-[2] + PHEN- + (P)YR- + -AMINE]

chlor·pic·rin (klōr pik′rin, klôr-), *n. Chem.* chloropicrin.

chlor·prom·a·zine (klōr prom′ə zēn′, klôr-), *n.* a powder, $C_{17}H_{19}ClN_2S$, used in the form of its hydrochloride chiefly to inhibit nausea and vomiting and as a sedative in the treatment of certain mental disorders. [CHLOR-[2] + PRO(PYL + A)M(INE) + AZINE]

chlor·tet·ra·cy·cline (klōr te′trə sī′klin, klôr-), *n. Pharm.* an antibiotic powder, $C_{22}H_{23}N_2O_8Cl$, biosynthesized by *Streptomyces aureofaciens,* used in the treatment of infections.

chm., 1. chairman. **2.** checkmate.

chmn., chairman.

cho·a·no·cyte (kō′ə nə sīt′, kō an′ə sīt′), *n. Zool.* one of the flagellated cells lining the inner cavity of a sponge, having a collar of protoplasm encircling the base of the flagellum. Also called **collar cell.** [< Gk *choán(ē)* funnel + -O- + -CYTE] —**cho′a·no·cyt′al,** *adj.*

Choate (chōt), *n.* **1. Joseph Hodges,** 1832–1917, U.S. lawyer and diplomat. **2. Rufus,** 1799–1859, U.S. lawyer, orator, and statesman.

chock (chok), *n.* **1.** a wedge or block of wood, metal, or the like, for filling in a space, holding an object steady, preventing motion, etc. **2.** *Naut.* **a.** any of various heavy metal fittings that serve as fairleads. **b.** a shaped support or cradle for a ship's boat, barrel, etc. —*v.t.* **3.** to furnish with or secure by a chock or chocks. **4.** *Naut.* to place (a boat) upon chocks. —*adv.* **5.** as close or tight as possible. [?]

Chock (def. 2a)

chock-a-block (chok′ə blok′), *adv.* **1.** *Naut.* with the blocks drawn close together, as when a tackle is hauled to the utmost; ablock. **2.** in a jammed or crowded condition.

chock-full (chok′fŏŏl′), *adj.* full to the utmost; crammed. Also, **chuck-full, choke-full.** [late ME *chokke-fulle* = *chokke* (< ?) + *fulle* FULL[1]]

choc·o·late (chô′kə lit, chok′ə-, chôk′lit, chok′-), *n.* **1.** a preparation of the seeds of cacao, often sweetened and flavored. **2.** a beverage made by combining such a preparation with milk or water. **3.** a candy made from such a preparation, often in combination with milk. **4.** a syrup or sauce having a chocolate flavor. **5.** a small, individually made piece of candy consisting of or coated with chocolate. **6.** dark brown. —*adj.* **7.** made, flavored, or covered with chocolate. **8.** having the color of chocolate. [< F *chocolat* < Sp *chocolate* < Nahuatl *chocolatl*] —**choc′o·lat·y,** *adj.*

Choc·taw (chok′tô), *n., pl.* **-taws,** (*esp. collectively*) **-taw. 1.** a member of a large Muskhogean tribe of North American Indians living in Oklahoma. **2.** the language of the Choctaw and Chickasaw Indians.

choice (chois), *n., adj.,* **choic·er, choic·est.** —*n.* **1.** the act or an instance of choosing; selection. **2.** the right or opportunity to choose. **3.** a person or thing that is chosen. **4.** a person or thing that may be chosen. **5.** an alternative. **6.** a variety of persons or things from which one may choose. **7.** *U.S.* (in the grading of beef) **a.** a grade of beef between prime and good. **b.** a cut of beef of this grade. —*adj.* **8.** worthy of being chosen; excellent; superior. **9.** carefully selected. **10.** *U.S.* (in the grading of beef) rated between prime and good. [ME *chois* < OF < *choisir* to perceive, choose < Gmc; see CHOOSE] —**choice′less,** *adj.* —**choice′ly,** *adv.* —**choice′ness,** *n.*

—**Syn. 2.** CHOICE, ALTERNATIVE, OPTION all suggest the power of choosing between things. CHOICE implies the opportunity to choose. ALTERNATIVE suggests that a person has a choice between only two possibilities. It is often used with a negative to mean that there is no second possibility: *to have no alternative.* OPTION emphasizes free right or privilege of choosing: *to exercise one's option.* **8.** See **fine**[1].

choir (kwīᵊr), *n.* **1.** an organized group of singers, as for a church. **2.** any group of musicians or musical instruments: *string choir.* **3.** *Archit.* **a.** the part of a church occupied by the singers. **b.** (in a cruciform church) the part of the chancel reserved for the choir. **4.** (in medieval angelology) one of the orders of angels. —*v.t., v.i.* **5.** to sing or sound in chorus. [ME *quer* < OF *cuer* < L *chor(us)* CHORUS; r. OE *chor* choir < L] —**choir′like′,** *adj.*

choir·boy (kwīᵊr′boi′), *n.* a boy who sings in a choir.

choir·girl (kwīᵊr′gûrl′), *n.* a girl who sings in a choir.

choir′ loft′, a raised gallery for a choir.

choir·mas·ter (kwīᵊr′mas′tər, -mä′stər), *n.* the leader or director of a choir.

Choi·seul (*Fr.* shwA zœl′), *n.* an island E of New Guinea; one of the British Solomon Islands. 1500 sq. mi.

choke (chōk), *v.,* **choked, chok·ing,** *n.* —*v.t.* **1.** to stop or hinder the breathing of, as by obstructing, squeezing, or irritating the windpipe. **2.** to clog or obstruct, as a pipe or passage. **3.** to arrest the growth or activity of by force (often fol. by *off*): *to choke off discussion.* **4.** to swallow in spite of choking (usually fol. by *down*): *to choke down a plate of spinach.* **5.** to suppress, as an emotion or its expression (often fol. by *back* or *down*): *She choked back her tears.* **6.** to enrich the fuel mixture of (an internal-combustion engine) by diminishing the air supply to the carburetor. —*v.i.* **7.** to suffer from or as from strangling or suffocating. **8.** to become obstructed, clogged, or otherwise stopped. **9. choke up,** *Informal.* to become speechless, as from emotion, tension, or stress. —*n.* **10.** the act or sound of choking. **11.** *Mach.* any mechanism that, by blocking a passage, regulates the flow of air, gas, etc. **12.** *Elect.* See **choke coil.** [ME *choke(n), cheken,* var. of *achoken, acheken,* OE *āc̄eōcian* to suffocate; akin to Icel *kōk* gullet] —**choke′a·ble,** *adj.*

choke·ber·ry (chōk′ber′ē, -bə rē), *n., pl.* **-ries. 1.** the berrylike fruit of any North American, rosaceous shrub of the genus *Aronia.* **2.** the plant bearing this fruit.

choke·bore (chōk′bōr′, -bôr′), *n.* **1.** (in a shotgun) a bore that narrows toward the muzzle to prevent shot from scattering too widely. **2.** a shotgun with such a bore.

choke·cher·ry (chōk′cher′ē), *n., pl.* **-ries. 1.** any of several cherries, esp. *Prunus virginiana,* of North America, that bear an astringent fruit. **2.** the fruit itself.

choke′ coil′, *Elect.* a coil of large inductance that gives relatively large impedance to alternating current. Also called **choke.**

choke′ col′lar, a strong, nooselike collar for restraining powerful dogs.

choke·damp (chōk′damp′), *n. Mining.* mine atmosphere so low in oxygen and high in carbon dioxide as to cause choking. Also called **blackdamp.**

choke-full (chōk′fŏŏl′), *adj.* chock-full.

chok·er (chō′kər), *n.* **1.** a person or thing that chokes. **2.** *Informal.* **a.** a necklace that fits snugly around the neck. **b.** a neckcloth or high collar.

chok·ey (chō′kē), *adj.,* **chok·i·er, chok·i·est.** choky.

chok·ing (chō′king), *adj.* **1.** (of the voice) husky and strained, esp. because of emotion. **2.** causing a feeling of being choked. —**chok′ing·ly,** *adv.*

chok·y (chō′kē), *adj.,* **chok·i·er, chok·i·est.** tending to choke or suffocate one. Also, **chokey.**

chol-, var. of **chole-** before a vowel: *choline.*

chole-, a learned borrowing from Greek meaning "bile," "gall," used in the formation of compound words: *cholesterol.* Also, *esp. before a vowel,* **chol-.** [comb. form of Gk *cholḗ* bile]

cho·le·cal·cif·er·ol (kō′lə kal sif′ə rōl′, -rôl′, -rol′, -käl-), *n.* See **vitamin D_3.** [CHOLE- + CALCI- + -FER + -OL[1]]

chol·e·cys·tec·to·my (kol′i si stek′tə mē, kō′li-), *n., pl.* **-mies.** *Surg.* removal of the gall bladder.

cho·le·cys·ti·tis (kol′i si stī′tis, kō′li-), *n. Pathol.* inflammation of the gall bladder.

chol·er (kol′ər), *n.* **1.** irascibility; anger; irritability. **2.** *Old Physiol.* See **yellow bile. 3.** *Obs.* biliousness. [ME *coler(a)* < ML; L *cholera* < Gk *cholérā* CHOLERA]

chol·er·a (kol′ər ə), *n.* **1.** Also called **Asian cholera.** *Pathol.* an acute, infectious, often fatal disease, endemic in India and China, and occasionally epidemic elsewhere, characterized by profuse diarrhea, vomiting, cramps, dehydration, etc. **2.** *Vet. Pathol.* any of several diseases characterized by depression, sleepiness, lack of appetite, and diarrhea. Cf. **fowl cholera, hog cholera.** [< L < Gk *cholérā* name of several intestinal diseases] —**chol·e·ra·ic** (kol′ə rā′ik), *adj.*

chol·er·ic (kol′ər ik, kə ler′ik), *adj.* **1.** irascible; characterized by anger: *a choleric disposition.* **2.** *Obs.* **a.** bilious. **b.** causing biliousness. [ME *colerik* < ML *coleric(us)* bilious, L *cholericus* < Gk *cholerikos.* See CHOLERA, -IC] —**chol′er·i·cal·ly, chol′er·ic·ly,** *adv.* —**chol′er·ic·ness,** *n.*

cho·les·ter·ol (kə les′tə rōl′, -rôl′, -rol′), *n.* **1.** *Biochem.* a sterol, $C_{27}H_{45}OH$, occurring in all animal fats and oils, bile, gallstones, nerve tissue, blood, etc. **2.** the commercial form of this compound, used chiefly as an emulsifying agent in cosmetics and pharmaceuticals, and in the synthesis of vitamin D. Also, **cho·les·ter·in** (kə les′tər in).

cho′lic ac′id (kō′lik, kol′ik), *Biochem.* a hydroxy acid, $C_{24}H_{40}O_5$, related to the sex hormones and cholesterol. [< Gk *cholik(ós)* bilious. See CHOLE-, -IC]

cho·line (kō′lēn, kol′ēn, -in), *n.* **1.** *Biochem.* one of the B-complex vitamins, $C_5H_{15}NO_2$, found in lecithin. **2.** the commercial form of this compound, used as a feed supplement, esp. for poultry, and in medicine.

cho·lin·es·ter·ase (kō′lə nes′tə rās′, kol′ə-), *n. Biochem.* an enzyme, found esp. in the heart, brain, and blood, that hydrolyzes acetylcholine to acetic acid and choline.

chol·la (chōl′yä, -yə; *Sp.* chō′yä), *n., pl.* **chol·las** (chōl′yäz, -yəz; *Sp.* chō′yäs). any of several spiny treelike cacti of the genus *Opuntia,* esp. *O. fulgida* of the southwestern U.S. and Mexico; prickly pear. [< MexSp < Sp: head, perh. < OF (dial.) *cholle* ball < Gmc; see KEEL[1]]

Cho·lon (chə lun′; *Fr.* shô lôN′), *n.* a city in S South Vietnam: merged with Saigon to form an urban complex 1932. 1,336,000 with Saigon (est. 1963).

Cho·lu·la (chô lōō′lä), *n.* a town in S Mexico, SE of Mexico City: ancient Aztec ruins. 12,833 (1960).

chomp (chomp), *v.t., v.i. Dial.* chump[2].

chondr-, var. of **chondrio-** before a vowel.

chondrio-, a learned borrowing from Greek meaning "cartilage," used in the formation of compound words: *chondriosome.* Also, **chondr-.** [< Gk *chondrío(n),* dim. of *chóndros* cartilage]

chon·dri·o·some (kon′drē ō sōm′), *n. Biol.* mitochondrion. [CHONDRIO- + -SOME[3]] —**chon′dri·o·so′mal,** *adj.*

chon·drite (kon′drīt), *n. Mineral.* a stony meteorite containing chondrules. —**chon·drit·ic** (kon drit′ik), *adj.*

chon·dro·ma (kon drō′mə), *n., pl.* **-mas, -ma·ta** (-mə tə). *Pathol.* a cartilaginous tumor or growth. —**chon·dro′ma·tous,** *adj.*
chon·drule (kon′dro͞ol), *n.* *Mineral.* a small round mass of olivine or pyroxene found in stony meteorites.
Chong·jin (chœng′jin′), *n.* a seaport in W North Korea. 200,000 (est. 1963). Japanese, **Seishin.**
Chon·ju (chœn′jo͞o′), *n.* a city in SW South Korea. 188,216 (1960).
choose (cho͞oz), *v.,* **chose; cho·sen** or (*Obs.*) **chose; choos·ing.** —*v.t.* **1.** to select from or in preference to another or other things or persons: *She chose Sunday for her departure.* **2.** to prefer or decide (to do something): *He chose to run for election.* —*v.i.* **3.** to make a choice. **4.** to be inclined: *You may stay here if you choose.* **5. cannot choose but,** cannot do otherwise than; is or are obliged to: *He cannot choose but hear.* **6. choose up,** *Informal.* to select players or assemble teams for a contest or game. [ME *chose(n), chēse(n),* OE *cēosan;* c. Goth *kiusan,* OHG *kiosan* (G *kiesen*); akin to Gk *geú(omai)* (to) enjoy, L *gus(tāre)* (to) taste] —**choos′a·ble,** *adj.* —**choos′er,** *n.* —**choos′ing·ly,** *adv.*
—**Syn. 1.** CHOOSE, SELECT, PICK, ELECT, PREFER indicate a decision that one or more possibilities are to be regarded more highly than others. CHOOSE suggests a decision on one of a number of possibilities because of its apparent superiority: *to choose a course of action.* SELECT suggests a choice made for fitness: *to select the proper golf club.* PICK, an informal word, suggests a selection on personal grounds: *to pick a winner.* The formal word ELECT suggests a kind of official action: *to elect a chairman.* PREFER, also formal, emphasizes the desire or liking for one thing more than for another or others: *to prefer coffee to tea.* —**Ant. 1.** reject.
choos·ey (cho͞o′zē), *adj.,* **choos·i·er, choos·i·est.** *Informal.* choosy.
choos·y (cho͞o′zē), *adj.,* **choos·i·er, choos·i·est.** *Informal.* hard to please; particular; fastidious, esp. in making a choice.
chop[1] (chop), *v.,* **chopped, chop·ping,** *n.* —*v.t.* **1.** to cut or sever with a quick, heavy blow or a series of blows (often fol. by *down, off,* etc.): *to chop down a tree.* **2.** to make or prepare for use by so cutting: *to chop kindling.* **3.** to cut in pieces; mince (often fol. by *up*): *to chop up an onion.* **4.** (in tennis, cricket, etc.) to hit (a ball) with a short downward stroke that imparts backspin. —*v.i.* **5.** to make a quick, heavy stroke or a series of strokes, as with an ax. **6.** *Boxing.* to throw or deliver a short blow, esp. a downward one while in a clinch. **7.** (in tennis, cricket, etc.) to employ or deliver a short downward stroke that imparts backspin to the ball. —*n.* **8.** the act or an instance of chopping. **9.** a cutting blow. **10.** *Boxing.* a short blow, esp. a downward one, executed while in a clinch. **11.** a piece chopped off. **12.** an individual cut, thick slice, or portion of lamb, pork, etc., usually containing a rib. **13.** a short, irregular, broken motion of waves. **14.** (in tennis, cricket, etc.) a short downward stroke that imparts backspin to the ball. [var. of CHAP[1]] —**Syn. 1.** See **cut.**
chop[2] (chop), *v.,* **chopped, chop·ping.** —*v.i.* **1.** to turn, shift, or change suddenly, as the wind. **2.** *Obs.* to bandy words; argue. —*v.t.* **3. chop logic,** to make unnecessary distinctions in reasoning. [var. of obs. *chap* barter, ME *chap(ien),* OE *cēapian* (< *cēap* sale, trade; see CHEAP)]
chop[3] (chop), *n.* **1.** Usually, **chops.** the jaw. **2. chops,** the oral cavity; mouth. **3. lick one's chops,** *Slang.* to await with pleasure; anticipate; relish. Also, **chap.** [? special use of CHOP[1]]
chop[4] (chop), *n.* **1.** (in India, China, etc.) **a.** an official stamp or seal, or a permit or clearance. **b.** a design stamped on goods to indicate their special identity. **2.** *Anglo-Indian Informal.* quality, class, or grade: *first chop.* [< Hindi *chāp* impression, stamp]
chop′ chop′, (in pidgin English) quickly! right away! [repetitive based on pidgin English *chop* quick]
chop·fall·en (chop′fô′lən), *adj.* chapfallen.
chop·house (chop′hous′), *n., pl.* **-hous·es** (-hou′ziz). a restaurant specializing in chops, steaks, and the like.
Cho·pin (shō′pan; *Fr.* shô paN′), *n.* **Fré·dé·ric Fran·çois** (fred′ə rik fran swä′, fred′rik; *Fr.* frā dā rēk′ frāN swa′), 1810–49, Polish composer and pianist, in France after 1831.
cho·pine (chō pēn′, chop′in), *n.* (formerly) a shoe having a thick sole of cork or other material suggesting a short stilt. [< Sp *chapín* = *chap(a)* (< MF *chape* CHAPE) + *-ín* -IN[1]]
chop·log·ic (chop′loj′ik), *n.* **1.** sophistic or overly complicated argumentation. —*adj.* **2.** Also, **chop′log′i·cal.** exhibiting or indulging in choplogic.
chop·per (chop′ər), *n.* **1.** a person or thing that chops. **2.** a short ax with a large blade, used for cutting up meat. **3.** *Informal.* a helicopter.
chop·ping (chop′ing), *adj.* *Brit. Informal.* large and strong; hardy.
chop′ping block′, a thick block of wood on which meat, vegetables, etc., are placed for cutting, trimming, chopping, and the like.
chop·py (chop′ē), *adj.,* **-pi·er, -pi·est. 1.** (of the sea, a lake, etc.) forming short, irregular, broken waves. **2.** (of the wind) shifting or changing suddenly or irregularly; variable. **3.** uneven in style or quality or characterized by poorly related parts. —**chop′pi·ly,** *adv.* —**chop′pi·ness,** *n.*
chop·stick (chop′stik′), *n.* one of a pair of thin sticks used as eating utensils by certain Oriental peoples. [pidgin English *chop* quick + STICK[1]]
chop′ su′ey (chop′so͞o′ē), *U.S.* a Chinese-style dish of meat, onions, bean sprouts, green peppers, mushrooms, etc., often served with rice and soy sauce. Also, **chop′ soo′y.** [< Chin (Cantonese dial.) *shap sui* mixed bits]
cho·ra·gus (kə rā′gəs, kō-, kô-), *n., pl.* **-gi** (-jī), **-gus·es. 1.** (in ancient Greece) the leader of a dramatic chorus. **2.** any conductor of an entertainment or festival. Also, **choregus.** [< L < Gk *chorāgós,* dial. var. of *chorēgós* = *chor(ós)* CHORUS + *-ēgos,* comb. form of *ágein* to lead] —**cho·rag·ic** (kə raj′ik, -rā′jik), *adj.*
cho·ral (*adj.* kôr′əl, kôr′-; *n.* kə ral′, kō-, kô-, kôr′əl, kôr′-), *adj.* **1.** of a chorus or a choir. **2.** sung by, adapted for, or containing a chorus or a choir. —*n.* **3.** chorale. [< ML *chorāl(is)*] —**cho′ral·ly,** *adv.*
cho·rale (kə ral′, -räl′, kō-, kô-; kôr′əl, kôr′-), *n.* **1.** a hymn, either played or sung, esp. a Lutheran hymn that is sung in unison or in parts. **2.** a choral group. [< G *Choral,* short for *Choralgesang,* trans. of L *cantus chorālis;* see CHORAL]
chord[1] (kôrd), *n.* **1.** *Geom.* the line segment between two points on a given curve. **2.** *Engineering, Building Trades.* a principal longitudinal member of a truss, usually one of a pair connected by a web of compression and tension members. **3.** a feeling or emotion: *His story struck a chord of pity in the listeners.* **4.** *Aeron.* a straight line joining the trailing and leading edges of an airfoil section. **5.** *Anat.* cord (def. 6). [< L *chord(a)* < Gk *chordḗ* gut, string; r. CORD in senses given] —**chord′ed,** *adj.*

C
A B

Chords (Geometrical) AB, AC, chords subtending arcs ACB, AC

chord[2] (kôrd), *n.* *Music.* a combination of three or more different tones sounded simultaneously. [earlier *cord,* short for ACCORD; *ch-* of CHORD[1]] —**chord′al,** *adj.*
chor·da·mes·o·derm (kôr′də mez′ə dûrm′, -mes′-, -mē′zə-, -sə-), *n.* *Embryol.* the part of the blastoderm of a young embryo that forms the notochord and related structures. [< NL *chorda* (see CHORD[1]) + MESODERM] —**chor′da·mes′o·der′mal, chor′da·mes′o·der′mic,** *adj.*
Chor·da·ta (kôr dā′tə, -dä′-), *n.* *Zool.* the phylum comprising the chordates. [< NL]
chor·date (kôr′dāt), *Zool.* —*adj.* **1.** belonging or pertaining to the phylum *Chordata,* comprising the true vertebrates and those animals having a notochord, as the lancelets and tunicates. —*n.* **2.** a chordate animal. [< NL *Chordata* = *chord(a)* (see CHORD[1]) + *-ata* -ATE[1]]
chore (chôr, chōr), *n.* **1.** a small or odd job, esp. around a house or farm. **2.** a hard or unpleasant task. [ME *churre,* OE *cyrr,* var. of *cierr, cerr* CHAR[3]]
cho·re·a (kə rē′ə, kō-, kô-), *n.* *Pathol.* **1.** any of several diseases of the nervous system characterized by jerky, involuntary movements, chiefly of the face and extremities. **2.** Also called **St. Vitus's dance.** such a disease occurring chiefly in children. **3.** *Vet. Pathol.* a disease of the central nervous system caused by bacterial or organic degeneration, most common in dogs following canine distemper, characterized by irregular, jerky, involuntary muscular movements. [< Gk *choreía* a dance = *chor(ós)* CHORUS + *-eia* -Y[3]] —**cho·re′al, cho·re′ic, cho·re·at·ic** (kôr′ē at′ik, kôr′-), *adj.* —**cho·re·oid** (kôr′ē oid′, kôr′-), *adj.*
cho·re·gus (kə rē′gəs, kō-, kô-), *n., pl.* **-gi** (-jī), **-gus·es.** choragus.
cho·re·o·graph (kôr′ē ə graf′, -gräf′, kôr′-), *v.t.* *Dance.* to provide the choreography for: *to choreograph a musical comedy.* [back formation from CHOREOGRAPHY]
cho·re·og·ra·pher (kôr′ē og′rə fər, kôr′-), *n.* a person who composes and arranges dances, esp. ballets, for the stage. Also, *esp. Brit.,* **cho·reg·ra·pher** (kə reg′rə fər). [CHOREOGRAPH(Y) + -ER[1]]
cho·re·og·ra·phy (kôr′ē og′rə fē, kôr′-), *n.* **1.** the art of composing ballets and other dances for the stage, esp. planning and arranging the movements of dancers. **2.** the technique of representing the various movements in dancing by a system of notation. **3.** the art of dancing. Also, *esp. Brit.,* **cho·reg·ra·phy** (kə reg′rə fē). [< Gk *chore-* (s. of *choreía* a dance; see CHOREA) + -O- + -GRAPHY] —**cho·re·o·graph·ic** (kôr′ē ə graf′ik, kôr′-); *esp. Brit.,* **cho·re·graph·ic** (kôr′ə graf′ik, kôr′-), *adj.* —**cho′re·o·graph′i·cal·ly;** *esp. Brit.,* **cho′re·graph′i·cal·ly,** *adv.*
chori-, var. of **chorio-.**
cho·ri·amb (kôr′ē amb′, kôr′-), *n.* *Pros.* a foot of four syllables, two short between two long or two unstressed between two stressed. [short for CHORIAMBUS] —**cho′ri·am′bic,** *adj.*
cho·ri·am·bus (kôr′ē am′bəs, kôr′-), *n., pl.* **-bi** (-bī), **-bus·es.** choriamb. [< LL < Gk *choríambos* = *chor(eîos)* trochaic + *íambos* IAMB]
cho·ric (kôr′ik, kôr′-), *adj.* of, pertaining to, or written for a chorus. [< LL *choric(us)* < Gk *chorikós* = *chor(ós)* CHORUS + *-ikos* -IC]
cho·rine (kôr′in, kôr′ēn), *n.* *Slang.* a chorus girl. [CHOR(US) + -INE[2]]
chorio-, a learned borrowing from Greek meaning "chorion," "choroid," used in the formation of compound words: *chorioallantois.* Also, **chori-.** [comb. form repr. Gk *chórion*]
cho·ri·o·al·lan·to·is (kôr′ē ō ə lan′tō is, -tois, kôr′-), *n.* *Embryol., Zool.* a vascular, extraembryonic membrane of birds, reptiles, and certain mammals, formed by the fusion of the wall of the chorion with the wall of the allantois. Also called **cho′rioallanto′ic mem′brane.** —**cho·ri·o·al·lan·to·ic** (kôr′ē ō al′ən tō′ik, kôr′-), *adj.*
cho·ri·on (kôr′ē on′, kôr′-), *n.* *Embryol.* the outermost of the extraembryonic membranes of land vertebrates, contributing to the formation of the placenta in the placental mammals. [< NL < Gk *chórion*] —**cho′ri·on′ic, cho′ri·al,** *adj.*
chor·is·ter (kôr′i stər, kor′-), *n.* **1.** a singer in a choir. **2.** a male singer in a church choir; choirboy. [< ML *chorist(a)* singer in a choir + -ER[1]; r. ME *queristre* < AF = *quer* CHOIR + *-istre* -IST]
C horizon, *Geol.* the layer in a soil profile below the B horizon and immediately above the bedrock, consisting chiefly of weathered, partially decomposed rock. Cf. **A horizon, B horizon.**
cho·rog·ra·phy (kə rog′rə fē, kō-, kô-), *n.* *Geog.* a systematic, detailed description and analysis of a region or regions. [< L *chōrographia* < Gk *chōrographía* = *chōro(s)* ground, place, space + *-graphia* -GRAPHY] —**cho·rog′ra·pher,** *n.* —**cho·ro·graph·ic** (kôr′ə graf′ik, kôr′-), **cho′ro·graph′i·cal,** *adj.* —**cho′ro·graph′i·cal·ly,** *adv.*
cho·roid (kôr′oid, kôr′-), *Anat.* —*adj.* **1.** like the chorion; membranous. —*n.* **2.** See **choroid coat.** [< Gk *choroeid(ḗs)* false reading for *chorioeidḗs*]
cho′roid coat′, *Anat.* a delicate, highly vascular layer of the eye that is continuous with the iris and lies between the sclera and the retina. Also called **choroid, cho′roid mem′brane.**

chor·tle (chôr′tᵊl), *v.*, **-tled, -tling,** *n.* —*v.t., v.i.* **1.** to chuckle or utter with glee. —*n.* **2.** a gleeful chuckle. [b. CHUCKLE and SNORT; coined by Lewis Carroll in *Through the Looking Glass* (1871)] —**chor′tler,** *n.*

cho·rus (kōr′əs, kôr′-), *n., pl.* **-rus·es,** *v.*, **-rused, -rus·ing.** —*n.* **1.** *Music.* **a.** a musical composition, in unison or in parts, to be sung by a large group, often as part of an opera, oratorio, musical comedy, etc. **b.** a group performing such a composition. **c.** (in an opera, musical comedy, etc.) a company of singers, dancers, or both. **d.** a part of a song, as the refrain (distinguished from *verse*). **2.** simultaneous utterance in singing, speaking, shouting, etc.; unison. **3.** the sounds so uttered. **4.** (in ancient Greek drama) **a.** an ode or series of odes commenting on the main action of the drama and sung by a group of actors. **b.** the group of actors that performed the chorus. **5.** *Theat.* **a.** a single actor commenting on the main action of a play, as in Elizabethan drama. **b.** the part of a play performed by such an individual. —*v.t., v.i.* **6.** to sing or speak in chorus. [< L < Gk *chorós* a dance, band of dancers and singers]

cho′rus boy′, a male singer or dancer of the chorus of a musical comedy, vaudeville show, etc.

cho′rus girl′, a female member of the chorus of a musical comedy, vaudeville show, etc.

Cho·rzów (KHô′zhōōf), *n.* a city in S Poland. 152,000 (est. 1963). German, **Königshütte.** Formerly, **Królewska Huta.**

chose[1] (chōz), *v.* **1.** pt. of **choose. 2.** *Obs.* pp. of **choose.**

chose[2] (shōz), *n.* *Law.* a thing; an article of personal property. [< F < L *causa* case, thing]

cho·sen (chō′zən), *v.* **1.** a pp. of **choose.** —*adj.* **2.** selected from a number; preferred. **3.** *Theol.* elect (def. 9).

Cho·sen (chō′sen′), *n.* Japanese name of **Korea.**

cho′sen peo′ple, the Israelites. Ex. 19.

Chou (jō), *n.* a dynasty in China, 1122?–256? B.C., marked by the founding of important philosophical schools, esp. those of Confucius and Lao-tse.

Chou En-lai (jō′ en′lī′), 1898–1976, Chinese Communist leader: premier 1949–76.

chough (chuf), *n.* any of several crowlike, Old World birds, esp. *Pyrrhocorax pyrrhocorax,* of Europe. [ME *choghe;* akin to OE *cēo,* D *kauw,* Dan *kaa*]

chouse (chous), *v.t.*, **choused, chous·ing.** *Archaic.* to swindle; cheat; dupe (often fol. by *of* or *out of*): *to be choused out of a week's pay.* [< Turk *çavuş* messenger] —**chous′er,** *n.*

chow[1] (chou), *n.* *U.S. Slang.* food. [short for CHOW-CHOW]

chow[2] (chou), *n.* (*often cap.*) See **chow chow.** [short form]

chow chow (chou′ chou′), (*often cap.*) one of a Chinese breed of medium-sized dogs having a thick black, blue, red, or cream coat and a black tongue. [< Chin (dial.); akin to Cantonese *kaú* dog]

Chow chow
(20 in. high at shoulder)

chow-chow (chou′chou′), *n.* **1.** a Chinese mixed fruit preserve. **2.** (in China, India, etc.) any mixed food, food in general, or a meal. **3.** a relish or mixed pickles in mustard. [pidgin English]

chow·der (chou′dər), *n.* *U.S.* a thick soup or stew, typically made of clams or fish and various vegetables. [< F *chaudière* pot, kettle < LL *caldāria* CAULDRON]

chow mein (chou′ mān′), a dish of mushrooms, celery, and other vegetables, topped with shrimp, shredded chicken, etc., and served with fried noodles. [< Chin: fried dough]

Chr., Christian.

Chres·tien de Troyes (KRā tyan′ də TRWä′), c1140–c1190, French poet. Also, **Chré·tien′ de Troyes′.**

chres·tom·a·thy (kres tom′ə thē), *n., pl.* **-thies.** a collection of selected literary passages, often by one author and esp. from a foreign language. [< NL *chrestomathia* < Gk *chrēstomátheia* = *chrēstó(s)* useful (*chrēs-,* s. of *chrêsthai* to use + *-tos* v. adj. suffix) + *math-* (var. s. of *manthánein* to learn) + *-eia* -Y³] —**chres·to·math·ic** (kres′tə math′ik), *adj.*

chrism (kriz′əm), *n.* *Eccles.* **1.** a consecrated oil, used by certain churches in various rites, as in baptism. **2.** a sacramental anointing. Also, **chrisom.** [learned respelling of ME *crisme,* OE *crisma* < L *chrisma* < Gk *chrîsma* unguent, unction] —**chris′mal,** *adj.*

chris·om (kriz′əm), *n.* *Eccles.* **1.** chrism. **2.** *Obs.* a white cloth or robe formerly put on a child at baptism, and if the child died soon after, at burial. [var. of CHRISM]

Christ (krīst), *n.* **1.** Jesus of Nazareth, held by Christians to be the fulfillment of prophecies in the Old Testament regarding the eventual coming of a Messiah. **2.** the Messiah prophesied in the Old Testament (used chiefly in versions of the New Testament). **3.** *Obs.* someone anointed as a ruler. [learned respelling of ME, OE *Crīst* < L *Chrīst(us)* < Gk *christós* anointed, trans. of Heb *māshīah* anointed, Messiah] —**Christ′like′,** *adj.* —**Christ′li·ness,** *n.* —**Christ′ly,** *adj.*

Christ·church (krīst′chûrch′), *n.* a city on E South Island, in New Zealand. 151,671 (1961).

christ·cross (kris′krôs′, -kros′), *n.* the figure or mark of a cross. [late ME *Crist cross*]

christ·cross-row (kris′krôs′rō′, -kros′-), *n.* *Archaic.* the alphabet. Also, **criss′cross-row′.**

chris·ten (kris′ən), *v.t.* **1.** baptize. **2.** to give a name to at baptism. **3.** to give a name to, as a ship at its launching. **4.** *Informal.* to use for the first time. [ME *cristen(en),* OE *cristnian* < *cristen* CHRISTIAN] —**chris′ten·er,** *n.*

Chris·ten·dom (kris′ən dəm), *n.* **1.** Christians collectively. **2.** the Christian world. **3.** *Obs.* Christianity. [ME; OE *cristendōm*]

chris·ten·ing (kris′ə ning, kris′ning), *n.* **1.** the ceremony of baptism. **2.** a public ceremony in which a new ship is formally named and launched. **3.** the act or an instance of naming or dedicating something. [ME]

Christ·hood (krīst′hŏŏd), *n.* the condition of being the Christ. [late ME]

Chris·tian (kris′chən), *adj.* **1.** of, pertaining to, or derived from Jesus Christ or His teachings. **2.** of, pertaining to, or adhering to the religion based on the teachings of Jesus Christ. **3.** of or pertaining to Christians. **4.** exhibiting a spirit proper to a follower of Jesus Christ, as in having a loving regard for other persons. —*n.* **5.** a person who believes in Jesus Christ; an adherent of Christianity. **6.** a person who exemplifies in his life the teachings of Christ. [< L *Chrīstiān(us)* < Gk *Chrīstiānós* = *Christ(ós)* CHRIST + *-iānos* < L *-iānus* -IAN; r. ME *cristen,* OE < L, as above] —**Chris′tian·ly,** *adj., adv.*

Christian IX, 1818–1906, king of Denmark 1863–1906.

Christian X, 1870–1947, king of Denmark 1912–47.

Chris′tian E′ra, the period, in Christian countries, since the assumed year of Jesus' birth. Also called **Common Era.**

Chris·tia·ni·a (kris tyä′nē ä; *also for 2* kris′chē an′ē ə, -tē-), *n.* **1.** former name of **Oslo. 2.** Also called **Christie, Christy.** *Skiing.* any of several turns for changing direction in descent, or for decreasing speed or stopping, esp. a turn in which the body is swung around with the skis kept parallel.

Chris·tian·ise (kris′chə nīz′), *v.t.*, **-ised, -is·ing.** *Chiefly Brit.* Christianize. —**Chris′tian·i·sa′tion,** *n.* —**Chris′tian·is′er,** *n.*

Chris·ti·an·i·ty (kris′chē an′i tē), *n., pl.* **-ties. 1.** the Christian religion, including the Catholic, Protestant, and Eastern Orthodox churches. **2.** Christian beliefs or practices; Christian quality or character. **3.** the state of being a Christian. **4.** Christendom. [ME *cristianite* < L *chrīstiānitāt-* (s. of *chrīstiānitās*) = *chrīstiān-* CHRISTIAN + *-itāt-* -ITY; r. ME *cristiente* < MF < L, as above]

Chris·tian·ize (kris′chə nīz′), *v.t.*, **-ized, -iz·ing. 1.** to make Christian. **2.** to imbue with Christian principles. Also, *esp. Brit.,* **Christianise.** —**Chris′tian·i·za′tion,** *n.* —**Chris′tian·iz′er,** *n.*

Chris′tian name′, 1. Also called **baptismal name.** the name given one at baptism. **2.** a person's given name.

Chris·tian·sand (kris′chən sand′; *Norw.* KRis′tyän sän′), *n.* former name of **Kristiansand.**

Chris′tian Sci′ence, a religion based on the Scriptures, teaching the treatment of disease by mental and spiritual means, founded about 1866 by Mary Baker Eddy.

Chris·tie (kris′tē), *n.* *Skiing.* Christiania (def. 2). [by shortening]

Chris·tie (kris′tē), *n.* **Agatha,** 1891–1976, English novelist of detective fiction.

Chris·ti·na (kri stē′nə), *n.* 1626–89, queen of Sweden 1632–54 (daughter of Gustavus Adolphus).

Christ·less (krīst′lis), *adj.* **1.** without Christ or the religion or spirit of Christ; nonchristian. **2.** unchristian.

Christ·mas (kris′məs), *n.* **1.** the annual festival of the Christian church commemorating the birth of Jesus: celebrated by most Christians on December 25. **2.** December 25, now generally observed as a legal holiday and an occasion for exchanging gifts or greetings. **3.** Christmastide. [ME *cristmasse;* OE *Cristes mæsse* MASS of CHRIST]

Christ′mas card′, a printed and often decorated card for mailing at Christmas to express good wishes.

Christ′mas Eve′, the evening preceding Christmas.

Christ′mas Is′land, 1. one of the Gilbert and Ellice Islands, in the central Pacific: largest atoll in the Pacific; U.S. test center for nuclear warheads. 300 (1964). ab. 222 sq. mi. **2.** an Australian island in the Indian Ocean, S of Java. 3333 (1965). 62 sq. mi.

Christ′mas pud′ding, *Brit.* See **plum pudding.**

Christ·mas·tide (kris′məs tīd′), *n.* **1.** the season of Christmas. **2.** the period from Christmas Eve to Epiphany.

Christ′mas tree′, an evergreen tree decorated at Christmas with ornaments and lights.

Christo-, a combining form of **Christ:** *Christology.* [< Gk *Christó(s)*]

Chris·tol·o·gy (kri stol′ə jē), *n., pl.* **-gies** for 2. **1.** the branch of theology dealing with the nature, person, and deeds of Jesus Christ. **2.** an interpretation of the nature, person, and deeds of Christ. —**Chris·to·log·i·cal** (kris′tᵊloj′i kəl), *adj.* —**Chris·tol′o·gist,** *n.*

Chris·tophe (KRē stôf′), *n.* **Hen·ry** (äN Rē′), ("*Henri I*"), 1767–1820, revolutionary general: king of Haiti 1811–20. Also, **Cristophe.**

Chris·to·pher (kris′tə fər), *n.* **Saint,** died A.D. c250, Christian martyr: patron saint of travelers.

Christ's-thorn (krīsts′thôrn′), *n.* any of certain Old World thorny shrubs or small trees supposed to have been used for Christ's crown of thorns, as the shrub, *Paliurus Spina-Christi,* or the jujube, *Zizyphus Jujuba.* [trans. of L *spīna Chrīstī*]

Chris·ty (kris′tē), *n., pl.* **-ties.** *Skiing.* Christiania (def. 2). [by shortening]

Chris·ty (kris′tē), *n.* **Howard Chan·dler** (chand′lər, chänd′-), 1873–1952, U.S. illustrator and painter.

-chroic, adjectival word element indicating color (of skin, plants, etc.). Also, **-chroous.** [< Gk *chrōik(ós)* colored = *chrṓ(s)* skin (color) + *-ikos* -IC]

chrom-, 1. a learned borrowing from Greek meaning "color," "colored," "pigmented," used in the formation of compound words: *chromomere; chromite.* **2.** *Chem.* **a.** a word element referring to chromium: *bichromate.* **b.** a combining form used to distinguish a colored compound from its colorless form. Also, **-chrome;** *esp. before a consonant,* **chromo-.** [def. 1, for Gk *chrôma* color; def. 2, for CHROMIUM]

chro·ma (krō′mə), *n.* **1.** the purity of a color, or its freedom from white or gray. **2.** intensity of distinctive hue; saturation of a color. [< Gk *chrôma* color]

chromat-, var. of **chromato-** before a vowel: *chromatid.*

chro·mate (krō′māt), *n.* *Chem.* a salt of chromic acid, as potassium chromate, K_2CrO_4.

chro·mat·ic (krō mat′ik, krə-), *adj.* **1.** pertaining to color or colors. **2.** *Music.* **a.** involving a modification of the normal scale by the use of accidentals. **b.** progressing by semitones, esp. to a tone having the same letter name, as C to C sharp. [< Gk *chrōmatik(ós)*] —**chro·mat′i·cal·ly,** *adv.*

chromat′ic aberra′tion, *Optics.* the variation of either the focal length or the magnification of a lens with different wavelengths of light.

chro·mat·i·cism (krō mat′i siz′əm, krə-), *n. Music.* **1.** the use of chromatic tones. **2.** a style in which chromatic tones predominate.

chro·ma·tic·i·ty (krō′mə tis′i tē), *n. Optics.* the quality of a color as determined by its dominant wavelength and its purity.

chro·mat·ics (krō mat′iks, krə-), *n.* (*construed as sing.*) the science of colors. Also called **chromatology.** —**chro·ma·tist** (krō′mə tist), *n.*

chromat′ic scale′, *Music.* a scale progressing entirely by semitones.

chro·ma·tid (krō′mə tid), *n. Genetics.* one of two identical chromosomal strands into which a chromosome splits before cell division.

chro·ma·tin (krō′mə tin), *n. Biol.* the readily stainable substance of a cell nucleus, consisting of DNA, RNA, and various proteins, that forms chromosomes during cell division. —**chro′ma·tin′ic,** *adj.* —**chro′ma·toid′,** *adj.*

chromato-, a learned borrowing from Greek meaning "color," "colored," used in the formation of compound words in this sense and in the specialized sense of "chromatin": *chromatophore; chromatolysis.* Also, *esp. before a vowel,* **chromat-.** [< Gk *chromat-,* s. of *chrôma* color + -o-]

chro·ma·to·gram (krō′mə tə gram′, krō mat′ə-, krə-), *n. Chem.* the column or paper strip on which some or all of the constituents of a mixture have been adsorbed in chromatographic analysis.

chro·ma·tog·ra·phy (krō′mə tog′rə fē), *n. Chem.* the separation of mixtures into their constituents by preferential adsorption by a solid, as a column of silica or a strip of filter paper. —**chro·ma·to·graph·ic** (krō′mə tə graf′ik, krō-mat′ō-, krə-), *adj.* —**chro′ma·to·graph′i·cal·ly,** *adv.*

chro·ma·tol·o·gy (krō′mə tol′ə jē), *n.* chromatics.

chro·ma·tol·y·sis (krō′mə tol′i sis), *n. Biol., Pathol.* the dissolution and disintegration of chromatin. —**chro·ma·to·lyt·ic** (krō′mə tᵊlit′ik, krō mat′ᵊlit′-, krə-), *adj.*

chro·ma·to·phore (krō′mə tə fōr′, -fôr′, krō mat′ə-, krə-), *n.* **1.** *Zool.* a cell containing pigment, esp. one that through contraction and expansion produces a temporary color, as in cuttlefishes. **2.** *Bot.* one of the colored plastids in plant cells. —**chro·ma·to·phor·ic** (krō′mə tə fôr′ik, -for′ik, krō mat′ə-, krə-), **chro·ma·toph·or·ous** (krō′mə-tof′ər əs), *adj.*

chrome (krōm), *n., v.,* **chromed, chrom·ing.** —*n.* **1.** chromium, esp. as a source of various pigments, as chrome yellow and chrome green. **2.** *Informal.* chromium-plated or other bright metallic trim, as on an automobile. —*v.t.* **3.** to plate or treat with a compound of chromium. [< F < Gk *chrôm(a)* color]

-chrome, var. of **chrom-** as the final element of a compound word: *ferrochrome.*

chrome′ al′um, *Chem.* **1.** a green powder, $CrNH_4(SO_4)_2 \cdot 12H_2O$, used chiefly as a mordant in dyeing. **2.** a violet powder, $CrK(SO_4)_2 \cdot 12H_2O$, used chiefly as a mordant in dyeing.

chrome′ green′, the permanent green color made from chrome yellow and Prussian blue.

chrome′ red′, a bright-red pigment consisting of the basic chromate of lead.

chrome′ steel′, any of various steels containing chromium.

chrome′ yel′low, any of several yellow pigments composed chiefly of chromates of lead, barium, or zinc.

chro·mic (krō′mik), *adj. Chem.* of or containing chromium in the trivalent state, as chromic hydroxide, $Cr(OH)_3$.

chro′mic ac′id, *Chem.* a hypothetical acid, H_2CrO_4, known only in solution or in the form of its salts.

chro·mi·nance (krō′mə nəns), *n. Optics.* the difference in color quality between a color and a reference color that has an equal brightness and a specified chromaticity. [CHROM- + (LUM)INANCE]

chro·mite (krō′mīt), *n.* **1.** *Chem.* a salt of chromium in the bivalent state. **2.** a mineral, ferrous chromate, $Fe_3Cr_2O_3$, the principal ore of chromium.

chro·mi·um (krō′mē əm), *n. Chem.* a lustrous, metallic element used in alloy steels for hardness and corrosion resistance, as in stainless steel, and for plating: its salts are used as pigments and mordants. *Symbol:* Cr; *at. wt.:* 51.996; *at. no.:* 24; *sp. gr.:* 7.1.

chro·mo (krō′mō), *n., pl.* **-mos.** chromolithograph. [by shortening]

chromo-, var. of **chrom-** before a consonant: *chromophore.*

chro·mo·gen (krō′mə jən), *n.* **1.** *Chem.* **a.** any substance found in organic fluids that forms colored compounds when oxidized. **b.** a colored compound that can be converted into a dye. **2.** a chromogenic bacterium.

chro·mo·gen·ic (krō′mə jen′ik), *adj.* **1.** producing color. **2.** *Chem.* pertaining to chromogen or a chromogen. **3.** (of bacteria) producing some characteristic color or pigment that is useful as a means of identification.

chro·mo·lith·o·graph (krō′mə lith′ə graf′, -gräf′), *n.* a picture produced by chromolithography. Also called **chromo.**

chro·mo·li·thog·ra·phy (krō′mō li thog′rə fē), *n.* the process of lithographing in colors. —**chro′mo·li·thog′ra·pher,** *n.* —**chro·mo·lith·o·graph·ic** (krō′mō lith′ə graf′ik), *adj.*

chro·mo·mere (krō′mə mēr′), *n.* **1.** *Genetics.* one of the beadlike granules arranged in a linear series in a chromonema. **2.** *Anat.* the central, granular part of a blood platelet.

chro·mo·ne·ma (krō′mə nē′mə), *n., pl.* **-ma·ta** (-mə tə). *Genetics.* a chromosome thread that is relatively uncoiled at early prophase, but assumes a spiral form at metaphase. [CHROMO- + Gk *nêma* thread]

chro·mo·phore (krō′mə fōr′, -fôr′), *n. Chem.* any chemical group that produces color in a compound, as the azo group –N=N–. —**chro·mo·phor·ic** (krō′mə fôr′ik, -for′ik), *adj.*

chro·mo·plasm (krō′mə plaz′əm), *n. Biol.* chromatin. —**chro′mo·plas′mic,** *adj.*

chro·mo·plast (krō′mə plast′), *n. Bot.* a plastid, or specialized mass of protoplasm, containing coloring matter other than chlorophyll.

chro·mo·some (krō′mə sōm′), *n. Genetics.* any of several threadlike bodies, consisting of chromatin, that are found in a cell nucleus, and carry the genes in a linear order. [CHROMO- + -SOME³; so called because chromosomes take on color when a cell is stained] —**chro′mo·so′mal,** *adj.* —**chro′mo·so′mal·ly,** *adv.*

chro′mosome num′ber, *Genetics.* the characteristic number of chromosomes in each plant or animal species.

chro·mo·sphere (krō′mə sfēr′), *n. Astron.* **1.** a scarlet, gaseous envelope surrounding the sun outside the photosphere. **2.** a gaseous envelope surrounding a star. —**chro·mo·spher·ic** (krō′mə sfer′ik), *adj.*

chro·mous (krō′məs), *adj. Chem.* containing chromium in the divalent state, as chromous carbonate, $CrCO_3$.

chro·myl (krō′məl), *adj. Chem.* containing chromium in the hexavalent state, as chromyl chloride, CrO_2Cl_2.

chron-, var. of **chrono-** before a vowel: *chronaxie; chronon.*

Chron., *Bible.* Chronicles.

chron., **1.** chronological. **2.** chronology.

chro·nax·ie (krō′nak sē), *n. Physiol.* the minimum time that a current of twice the threshold strength must flow in order to excite a tissue. Also, **chro′nax·y.** [< F = *chron-* CHRON- + *-axie* < Gk *axíā* worth, value]

chron·ic (kron′ik), *adj.* **1.** inveterate; constant; habitual: *a chronic smoker.* **2.** continuing a long time or recurring frequently: *a chronic state of civil war.* **3.** having long had a disease, habit, weakness, or the like: *a chronic invalid.* **4.** (of disease) having long duration (opposed to *acute*). Also, **chron′i·cal.** [< L *chronic(us)* < Gk *chronikós* = *chrón(os)* time + *-ikos* -IC] —**chron′i·cal·ly,** *adv.* —**chro·nic·i·ty** (kro nis′i tē), *n.* —**Syn. 1.** confirmed, hardened.

chron·i·cle (kron′i kəl), *n., v.,* **-cled, -cling.** —*n.* **1.** a chronological record of events; a history. —*v.t.* **2.** to record in or as in a chronicle. [ME *cronicle* < AF < *cronic-* (= OF *cronique* < ML *cronica* (sing.) < L *chronica* (pl.) < Gk *chroniká* annals, chronology; see CHRONIC) + *-le* -ULE] —**chron′i·cler,** *n.*

Chron·i·cles (kron′i kəlz), *n.* (*construed as sing.*) either of two books of the Old Testament, I Chronicles or II Chronicles.

chrono-, a learned borrowing from Greek meaning "time," used in the formation of compound words: *chronometer.* Also, *esp. before a vowel,* **chron-.** [< Gk, comb. form of *chrónos*]

chron·o·gram (kron′ə gram′), *n.* **1.** an inscription in which certain letters, as Roman numerals, are to be read as numbers giving a date. **2.** a record made by a chronograph. —**chron·o·gram·mat·ic** (kron′ō grə mat′ik), **chron′o·gram·mat′i·cal,** *adj.*

chron·o·graph (kron′ə graf′, -gräf′, krō′nə-), *n.* **1.** a timepiece fitted with a recording device for marking the exact instant of an occurrence. **2.** a timepiece capable of measuring extremely brief intervals of time accurately. —**chro·nog·ra·pher** (kro nog′rə fər), *n.* —**chron·o·graph·ic** (kron′ə graf′ik), *adj.* —**chron′o·graph′i·cal·ly,** *adv.*

chron·o·log·i·cal (kron′ᵊloj′i kəl), *adj.* **1.** arranged with earlier things or events preceding later ones: *chronological order.* **2.** pertaining to or in accordance with chronology. Also, **chron′o·log′ic.** —**chron′o·log′i·cal·ly,** *adv.*

chro·nol·o·gist (krə nol′ə jist), *n.* a person skilled in chronology. Also, **chro·nol′o·ger.**

chro·nol·o·gy (krə nol′ə jē), *n., pl.* **-gies.** **1.** an order of events from earliest to latest, or a particular statement of this order. **2.** the science of arranging time in periods and ascertaining the dates and historical order of past events. **3.** a reference work in the field of history organized according to the dates of past events.

chro·nom·e·ter (krə nom′i tər), *n.* a highly accurate timepiece. —**chron·o·met·ric** (kron′ə me′trik), **chron′o·met′ri·cal,** *adj.* —**chron′o·met′ri·cal·ly,** *adv.*

chro·nom·e·try (krə nom′i trē), *n.* **1.** the method or technique of measuring time accurately. **2.** measurement of time by periods or divisions.

chro·non (krō′non), *n.* a hypothetical unit of time, taken as a ratio between the diameter of the electron and the velocity of light, equivalent to approximately 10^{-24} second.

chron·o·scope (kron′ə skōp′, krō′nə-), *n.* an instrument for measuring accurately very brief intervals of time. —**chron·o·scop·ic** (kron′ə skop′ik), *adj.* —**chron′o·scop′i·cal·ly,** *adv.* —**chro·nos·co·py** (krə nos′kə pē), *n.*

-chroous, -chroic. [comb. form repr. Gk *chrós*; see -OUS]

chrys-, var. of **chryso-** before a vowel: *chryselephantine.*

chrys·a·lid (kris′ə lid), *Entomol.* —*n.* **1.** a chrysalis. —*adj.* **2.** of a chrysalis. [< Gk *chrysalid-,* var. s. of *chrysallís* CHRYSALIS]

chrys·a·lis (kris′ə lis), *n., pl.* **chrys·a·lis·es, chry·sal·i·des** (kri sal′i dēz′). the hard-shelled pupa of a moth or butterfly; an obtect pupa. [< L *chrȳsallis* < Gk *chrȳsallís* = *chrȳs-* CHRYS- + *-allis* suffix prob. with dim. value]

Chrysalis of swallowtail butterfly

chry·san·the·mum (kri san′thə məm), *n.* **1.** any of the perennial asteraceous plants of the genus *Chrysanthemum,* as *C. leucanthemum,* the oxeye daisy. **2.** any of many cultivated varieties of the plant *C. morifolium,* a native of China, and of other species of *Chrysanthemum,* notable for the diversity of color and size of their autumnal flowers. **3.** the flower of any such plant. [< L < Gk *chrȳsánthemon* = *chrȳs-* CHRYS- + *ánthemon* flower, akin to *ánthos*; see ANTHOLOGY]

chrys·a·ro·bin (kris′ə rō′bin), *n. Pharm.* a mixture of principles obtained from Goa powder, used in the treatment of psoriasis and other skin conditions. [CHRYS- + (AR)AROB(A) + -IN²]

Chry·se·is (krī sē′is), *n.* (in the *Iliad*) the beautiful daughter of a priest of Apollo, captured and given to Agamemnon.

chrys·el·e·phan·tine (kris′el ə fan′tin, -tīn), *adj.* made of or overlaid with gold and ivory, as certain objects made in ancient Greece. [< Gk *chrȳselephántin(os)* = *chrȳs-* CHRYS- + *elephántinos* (*elephant-,* s. of *eléphās* ELEPHANT, ivory + *-inos* -INE¹)]

chryso-, a learned borrowing from Greek meaning "gold," used in the formation of compound words: *chrysolite.* Also, *esp. before a vowel,* **chrys-.** [comb. form of Gk *chrȳsós*]
chrys·o·ber·yl (kris′ə ber′əl), *n.* a green or yellow mineral, beryllium aluminate, $BeAl_2O_4$, sometimes used as a gem. Also called **cymophane.** [< L *chrysoberyll(us)* < Gk *chrȳsobḗryllos*]
chrys·o·lite (kris′ə līt′), *n. Mineral.* olivine. [< L *chrȳsolith(us)* < Gk *chrȳsólithos*] —**chrys·o·lit·ic** (kris′ə-lit′ik), *adj.*
chrys·o·prase (kris′ə prāz′), *n. Mineral.* a green variety of chalcedony, sometimes used as a gem. [< L *chrȳsopras(us)* < Gk *chrȳsóprasos* = *chrȳso-* CHRYSO- + *prás(on)* leek + *-os* adj. suffix]
Chrys·os·tom (kris′ə stəm, kri sos′təm), *n.* **Saint John,** A.D. 347?–407, ecumenical patriarch of Constantinople.
chrys·o·tile (kris′ə til), *n. Mineral.* a fibrous variety of serpentine; asbestos. [CHRYSO- + Gk *tíl(os)* something plucked]
chs., chapters.
chtho·ni·an (thō′nē ən), *adj. Class. Myth.* of or pertaining to the deities, spirits, and other beings dwelling under the earth. Also, **chtho·nic** (thon′ik). [< Gk *chthóni(os)* (*chthṓn* earth + *-ios* adj. suffix) + -AN]
Chtho·ni·us (thō′nē əs), *n. Class. Myth.* one of the Sparti.
Chuan·chow (chwän′jō′), *n.* former name of **Tsinkiang.**
Chuang-tzu (jwäng′dzu′), *n.* (*Chuang Chow*) fl. 4th century B.C., Chinese mystic and philosopher. Also, **Chwang-tse.**
chub (chub), *n., pl.* (*esp. collectively*) **chub,** (*esp. referring to two or more kinds or species*) **chubs. 1.** a common, freshwater fish, *Leuciscus cephalus,* found in Europe, having a thick, fusiform body. **2.** any of various related fishes. **3.** any of several unrelated American fishes, esp. the tautog and whitefishes of the genus *Coregonus,* found in the Great Lakes. [late ME *chubbe* < ?]
chu·bas·co (cho͞o bä′skō), *n., pl.* **-cos.** a violent thundersquall on the Pacific Coast of Central America. [< Sp < Pg *chuvasco* = *chuv(a)* rain (< L *pluvia,* fem of *pluvius* rainy) + *-asco* intensive suffix]
chub·by (chub′ē), *adj.,* **-bi·er, -bi·est.** round and plump: *a chubby child; a chubby face.* [CHUB + -Y[1], ? from the thick shape of the chub] —**chub′bi·ly,** *adv.* —**chub′bi·ness,** *n.*
chuck[1] (chuk), *v.t.* **1.** to pat or tap lightly, as under the chin. **2.** to toss; throw with a quick motion, usually a short distance. **3.** *Informal.* to eject (a person) from a public place; throw out. **4.** *Informal.* to resign from; relinquish; give up: *He's chucked his job.* —*n.* **5.** a light pat or tap, as under the chin. [?]
chuck[2] (chuk), *n.* **1.** the cut of beef between the neck and the shoulder blade. **2.** a block or log used as a chock. **3.** *Mach.* **a.** a device for centering and clamping work in a lathe or other machine tool. **b.** a device for holding a drill bit. [var. of CHOCK. See CHUNK]

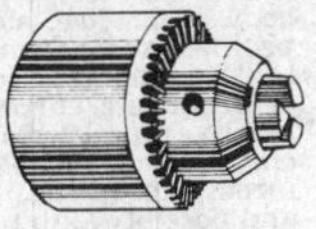
Chuck[2] (def. 3b)

chuck[3] (chuk), *v.t., v.i.* **1.** to cluck. —*n.* **2.** a clucking sound. **3.** *Archaic.* (used as a term of endearment): *my love, my chuck.* [ME *chuk* < ?]
chuck[4] (chuk), *n. Western U.S. Slang.* food; provisions. [special use of CHUCK[2]]
chuck[5] (chuk), *n. U.S. Informal.* woodchuck. [by shortening]
chuck-a-luck (chuk′ə luk′), *n.* a game played with three dice at which the players bet that a certain number will come up on one die, that the three dice will total a certain number, etc. Also, **chuck-luck** (chuk′luk′).
chuck-full (chuk′fo͝ol′), *adj.* chock-full.
chuck·hole (chuk′hōl′), *n.* a hole or depression in a road or street.
chuck·le (chuk′əl), *v.,* **chuck·led, chuck·ling,** *n.* —*v.i.* **1.** to laugh softly or to oneself. **2.** to cluck, as a fowl. —*n.* **3.** a soft, amused laugh. —**chuck′ler,** *n.* —**chuck′ling·ly,** *adv.*
chuck·le·head (chuk′əl hed′), *n. Slang.* a stupid person; blockhead. [*chuckle* clumsy (CHUCK[2] + -LE) + HEAD] —**chuck′le·head′ed,** *adj.*
chuck′ wag′on, *Western U.S.* a wagon carrying cooking facilities and food for serving men working outdoors, as at a ranch or lumber camp.
chuck·wal·la (chuk′wä′lə), *n.* an iguanid lizard, *Sauromelus ohesus,* of arid parts of the southwestern U.S. and Mexico, that feeds on desert plants. [< MexSp *chacahuala,* of native (Shoshonean) orig.]
chuck-will's-wid·ow (chuk′wilz wid′ō), *n.* a goatsucker, *Caprimulgus carolinensis,* of southern U.S. [fanciful imit. of its twitter]
Chud·sko·ye O·ze·ro (cho͞ot′sko ye ô′ze ro), Russian name of **Peipus.**
chuff[1] (chuf), *n.* **1.** a rustic. **2.** a boor; churl. **3.** a miserly fellow. [late ME *chuffe* < ?]
chuff[2] (chuf, cho͝of), *adj. Brit. Dial.* **1.** chubby; fat. **2.** proud; elated; swollen with pride. [adj. use of obs. *chuff* muzzle, fat cheek]
chuff[3] (chuf), *n.* **1.** a sound of or like the exhaust of a steam engine. —*v.i.* **2.** to emit or proceed with chuffs: *The train chuffed along.* [imit.]
chug (chug), *n., v.,* **chugged, chug·ging.** —*n.* **1.** a short, dull, explosive sound: *the chug of an engine.* —*v.i.* **2.** to make this sound. **3.** to move with this sound. [imit.]
chu·kar (chu kär′), *n.* a partridge, *Alectoris chukar,* of Asia and the Near East, introduced into North America as a game bird. Also called **chukar′ par′tridge.** [< Hindi *cakor* < Skt *cakor(a),* prob. of imit. orig.]
Chuk′chi Sea′ (cho͝ok′chē), a part of the Arctic Ocean, N of the Bering Strait. Russian, **Chukotskoe More.**
Chu-Kiang (jo͞o′gyäng′), *n.* a river in SE China, in S Kwangtung, flowing E and S from Canton and forming an estuary near Hong Kong. ab. 110 mi. long. Also called **Canton River, Pearl River.**
chuk′ka boot′ (chuk′ə), an ankle-high shoe, laced through two pairs of eyelets, often made of suede. Also called **chuk′ka.** [so called from its resemblance to a polo boot. See CHUKKER]
chuk·ker (chuk′ər), *n. Polo.* one of the periods of play. Also, **chuk′kar.** [< Hindi *chakkar* < Skt *cakra* WHEEL]
Chu·kot·sko·e Mo·re (cho͞o kôt′sko ye mô′re), Russian name of the **Chukchi Sea.**
Chu·la Vis·ta (cho͞o′lə vis′tə), a city in SW California, near San Diego. 67,901 (1970).
chum[1] (chum), *n., v.,* **chummed, chum·ming.** —*n.* **1.** an intimate friend or companion: *boyhood chums.* **2.** a roommate, as at college. —*v.i.* **3.** to associate closely. **4.** to share a room or rooms with another, esp. in a dormitory at a college or prep school. [?]
chum[2] (chum), *n., v.,* **chummed, chum·ming.** —*n.* **1.** cut or ground bait dumped into the water to attract fish. —*v.i.* **2.** to fish by dumping chum into the water. —*v.t.* **3.** to dump chum into (the water) to attract fish. **4.** to bait (fish) with chum. [?]
chum·my (chum′ē), *adj.,* **-mi·er, -mi·est.** *Informal.* friendly; intimate. —**chum′mi·ly,** *adv.* —**chum′mi·ness,** *n.*
chump[1] (chump), *n.* **1.** *Informal.* a blockhead or dolt. **2.** a short, thick piece of wood. **3.** the thick, blunt end of anything. **4.** *Slang.* the head. [? b. CHUNK and LUMP]
chump[2] (chump), *v.t., v.i.* to munch. Also, **chomp.** [var. of CHAMP[1]]
Chun Doo Hwan (jœn′ dō′ hwän′), born 1931, South Korean political leader: president since 1980.
Chung·king (cho͝ong′king′), *n.* a city in SW China, on the Yangtze: capital of China 1937–46. 2,400,000.
chunk (chungk), *n.* **1.** a thick mass or lump of anything. **2.** a strong and stoutly built horse or other animal. **3.** a substantial amount of something. [nasalized var. of CHUCK[2]]
chunk·y (chung′kē), *adj.,* **chunk·i·er, chunk·i·est. 1.** thick or stout; thick-set; stocky. **2.** in a chunk or chunks. —**chunk′i·ly,** *adv.* —**chunk′i·ness,** *n.*
church (chûrch), *n.* **1.** a building for public Christian worship. **2.** an occasion of such worship: *to be late for church.* **3.** (*sometimes cap.*) the whole number of Christian believers or of their organized bodies. **4.** (*sometimes cap.*) any major division of this body; a Christian denomination. **5.** an organized congregation forming part of such a division. **6.** the Christian faith: *a return of intellectuals to the church.* **7.** organized religion as a political or social factor. **8.** the profession of an ecclesiastic: *to enter the church after college.* —*v.t.* **9.** to conduct or bring to church, esp. for special services. **10.** *Chiefly Midland U.S.* to subject to church discipline. **11.** to perform a church service of thanksgiving for (a woman after childbirth). [ME *chir(i)che;* OE *cir(i)ce* << Gk *kȳri(a)kón* (*dôma*) the Lord's (house) = *kȳri(os)* master (*kŷr(os)* power + *-ios* adj. suffix) + *-akos,* var. of *-ikos* -IC; akin to D *kerk,* G *Kirche,* Icel *kirkja*]
church·go·er (chûrch′gō′ər), *n.* **1.** a person who goes to church, esp. habitually. **2.** *Chiefly Brit.* a member of the Established Church, in contrast to a Nonconformist. —**church′go′ing,** *n., adj.*
Church·ill (chûr′chil, -chəl), *n.* **1. John, 1st Duke of Marlborough** ("*Corporal John*"), 1650–1722, British military commander. **2. Lord Randolph (Henry Spencer),** 1849–95, British statesman (father of Winston L. S. Churchill). **3. Winston,** 1871–1947, U.S. novelist. **4. Sir Winston (Leonard Spencer),** 1874–1965, British statesman and author: prime minister 1940–45, 1951–55; Nobel prize for literature 1953. **5.** a river in Canada, flowing NE from E Saskatchewan through Manitoba to Hudson Bay. ab. 1000 mi. long. **6.** a seaport and railway terminus on Hudson Bay at the mouth of this river. 3932 (1961).
church·less (chûrch′lis), *adj.* **1.** without a church. **2.** not belonging to or attending any church.
church·ly (chûrch′lē), *adj.* of or appropriate for the church or a church; ecclesiastical: *churchly vestments.* [OE *ciriclīc*] —**church′li·ness,** *n.*
church·man (chûrch′mən), *n., pl.* **-men. 1.** a clergyman. **2.** a church member. **3.** *Brit.* a member of the Established Church. —**church′man·ly,** *adj.* —**church′man·ship′,** *n.*
Church′ of Christ′, Sci′entist, the official name of the Christian Science Church.
Church′ of Eng′land, the established church in England, Catholic in faith and order, but incorporating many principles of the Protestant Reformation and independent of the papacy.
Church′ of Je′sus Christ′ of Lat′ter-day Saints′, the official name of the Mormon Church.
Church′ of Rome′. See **Roman Catholic Church.**
Church′ of the Breth′ren, the official name of the church of the Dunkers.
Church′ Slav′ic, a liturgical language used in Eastern Orthodox churches in Slavic countries since the 11th or 12th century, representing a development of Old Church Slavonic through contact with the national Slavic languages.
church′ text′, *Print.* See **Old English** (def. 2).
church·ward·en (chûrch′wôr′dᵊn), *n.* **1.** *Anglican Ch.* a lay officer who looks after the secular affairs of the church, and who, in England, is the legal representative of the parish. **2.** *Episc. Ch.* a lay church officer in charge of the temporal management of the parish. **3.** a long-stemmed clay pipe for smoking. [late ME *chirche wardeyn*]
church·wom·an (chûrch′wo͝om′ən), *n., pl.* **-wom·en.** a female member of a church, esp. of an Anglican church.
church·yard (chûrch′yärd′), *n.* the ground adjoining a church, often used as a graveyard. [ME *chirche yeard*]
churl (chûrl), *n.* **1.** a peasant; rustic. **2.** a rude, boorish, or surly person. **3.** a niggard or miser. **4.** *Eng. Hist.* a freeman of the lowest rank. [ME *cherl,* OE *ceorl* man, freeman; c. D *kerel,* G *Kerl;* akin to CARL, Gk *gérōn* old man]
churl·ish (chûr′lish), *adj.* **1.** peasantlike: *The churlish life in olden times was a difficult one.* **2.** boorish, rude, or surly. **3.** niggardly; sordid. **4.** difficult to work or deal with, as soil. [ME *cherlish,* OE *ceorlisc*] —**churl′ish·ly,** *adv.* —**churl′ish·ness,** *n.*
churn (chûrn), *n.* **1.** a vessel or machine in which cream or milk is agitated to make butter. **2.** any similar machine for mixing beverages. **3.** *Brit.* a large milk can. —*v.t.* **4.**

to stir or agitate in order to make into butter: *to churn cream.* **5.** to make (butter) by the agitation of cream. **6.** to shake or agitate with violent or continued motion: *The storm churned the sea.* **7.** (of a stockbroker) to trade (a customer's securities) excessively in order to earn more in commissions. —*v.i.* **8.** to operate a churn. **9.** to move or shake in agitation. [ME *cyrn(a)* (n.), OE *cyr(i)n;* c. MLG *kerne,* Icel *kjarni, kirna*] —**churn′er,** *n.*

churn·ing (chûr′ning), *n.* **1.** the act of a person or thing that churns. **2.** the butter made at any one time. [late ME *chyrnynge*]

churr (chûr), *v.i., n.* chirr.

chur·ri·gue·resque (cho͝or′ē gə resk′), *adj.* noting or pertaining to the baroque architecture of Spain and its colonies in the late 17th and early 18th centuries, characterized by fantastic and lavish detailing. Also, **chur·ri·gue·res·co** (cho͝or rē′ge res′kō). [< F < Sp *churrigueresc(o),* after José *Churriguera* (1650–1725), architect + *-esco* -ESQUE]

chute[1] (sho͞ot), *n., v.,* **chut·ed, chut·ing.** —*n.* **1.** an inclined channel, trough, or shaft for conveying water, grain, coal, etc. **2.** a waterfall or steep descent, as in a river. —*v.t.* **3.** to move or deposit by a chute. —*v.i.* **4.** to descend by a chute. [< F; OF *cheue* (< VL **caduta*) + *cheoite* (< VL **cadecta*), fem. ptps. of *cheoir* < L *cadere* to fall; in some senses, var. spelling of SHOOT]

chute[2] (sho͞ot), *n.* a steep slope, as for tobogganing. [Frenchified spelling of *shoot, shute,* ME *shote* steep slope]

chute[3] (sho͞ot), *n., v.,* **chut·ed, chut·ing.** —*n.* **1.** a parachute. —*v.i.* **2.** to descend from the air by a parachute. —*v.t.* **3.** to drop from an aircraft by parachute: *Supplies were chuted to the snowbound troops.* [by shortening] —**chut′ist,** *n.*

chut·ney (chut′nē), *n.* a sweet and sour sauce or relish of East Indian origin compounded of fruits, herbs, etc., with spices and other seasoning. [< Hindi *caṭnī*]

chutz·pa (KHo͝ot′spə), *n. Slang.* unmitigated effrontery or impudence. Also, **chutz′pah.** [< Yiddish]

Chu′vash Auton′omous So′viet So′cialist Repub′lic (cho͞o′väsh), an administrative division of the RSFSR, in the central Soviet Union in Europe. 1,098,000 (1959); 6909 sq. mi. *Cap.:* Cheboksary.

Chwang-tse (jwäng′dzu′), *n.* Chuang-tzu.

chyle (kīl), *n.* a milky fluid containing emulsified fat and other products of digestion, formed from the chyme in the small intestine and conveyed by the lacteals and the thoracic duct to the veins. [< LL *chȳl(us)* < Gk *chȳlós* juice, akin to *chein* to pour, L *fundere* to pour] —**chy·la·ceous** (kī lā′shəs), **chy′lous,** *adj.*

chyme (kīm), *n.* the semifluid mass into which food is converted by gastric secretion and which passes from the stomach into the small intestine. [< L *chȳm(us)* < Gk *chȳmós* juice, akin to *chȳlós* CHYLE] —**chy′mous,** *adj.*

chym·is·try (kim′i strē), *n. Archaic.* chemistry. —**chym′ic,** *adj.* —**chym′ist,** *n.*

chy·mo·tryp·sin (kī′mō trip′sin), *n. Biochem.* a proteolytic enzyme, found in pancreatic juice, that catalyzes the hydrolysis of proteins into short polypeptides and free amino acids. [CHYME + -O- + TRYPSIN]

Ci, *Physics, Chem.* curie; curies.

CIA, Central Intelligence Agency: the U.S. federal agency that coordinates governmental intelligence activities.

Cía., Company. [< Sp *Compañía*]

Cia·no (chä′nō; *It.* chä′nô), *n.* **Count Ga·le·az·zo** (gä′le ät′tsô), (*Ciano di Cortellazzo*) 1903–44, Italian Fascist leader: minister of foreign affairs 1936–1943.

cia·o (chä′ô; *Eng.* chou), *interj. Italian Informal.* hi; so long; see you later.

Cib·ber (sib′ər), *n.* **Col·ley** (kol′ē), 1671–1757, English actor and dramatist: poet laureate 1730–57.

ci·bo·ri·um (si bōr′ē əm, -bôr′-), *n., pl.* **-bo·ri·a** (-bōr′ē ə, -bôr′-). **1.** a permanent canopy over an altar; baldachin. **2.** a vessel for holding the consecrated bread or sacred wafers for the Eucharist. [< L: drinking cup < Gk *kibṓrion* Egyptian lotus, the seed vessel of which the cup resembles]

Ciborium

C.I.C., **1.** Commander in Chief. **2.** Counterintelligence Corps.

ci·ca·da (si kā′də, -kä′-), *n., pl.* **-das, -dae** (-dē). any large homopterous insect of the family *Cicadidae,* the male of which produces a shrill sound by means of vibrating membranes on the underside of the abdomen. [< L]

ci·ca·la (si kä′lə; *It.* chē kä′lä), *n., pl.* **-las,** *It.* **-le** (-le). cicada. [< It < L *cicāda* CICADA]

Cicada, *Magicicada septendecim* (Length about 1 in.)

cic·a·trise (sik′ə trīz′), *v.t., v.i.,* **-trised, -tris·ing.** *Chiefly Brit.* cicatrize. —**cic′a·tri′sant,** *adj.* —**cic′a·tri·sa′tion,** *n.* —**cic′a·tris′er,** *n.*

cic·a·trix (sik′ə triks, si kā′triks), *n., pl.* **cic·a·tri·ces** (sik′ə trī′sēz). **1.** *Med.* new tissue that forms over a wound and later contracts into a scar; scar. **2.** *Bot.* a scar left by a fallen leaf, seed, etc. Also, **cic·a·trice** (sik′ə tris). [< L: scar] —**cic·a·tri·cial** (sik′ə trish′əl), *adj.* —**ci·cat·ri·cose** (si ka′trə kōs′, sik′ə-), *adj.*

cic·a·trize (sik′ə trīz′), *v.,* **-trized, -triz·ing.** —*v.t.* **1.** to heal by inducing the formation of a cicatrix. —*v.i.* **2.** to become healed by the formation of a cicatrix. Also, *esp. Brit.,* **cicatrise.** [< ML *cicātrīz(āre).* See CICATRIX, -IZE] —**cic′a·tri′zant,** *adj.* —**cic′a·tri·za′tion,** *n.* —**cic′a·triz′er,** *n.*

cic·e·ly (sis′ə lē), *n., pl.* **-lies.** a plant, *Myrrhis odorata,* of the parsley family, having a fragrant aroma and sometimes used as a potherb. [< L *seseli* < Gk *séselis, séseli* hartwort, alter. through influence of proper name *Cicely*]

Cic·e·ro (sis′ə rō′), *n.* **1.** **Marcus Tul·li·us** (tul′ē əs), ("*Tully*"), 106–43 B.C., Roman statesman, orator, and writer. **2.** a town in NE Illinois, near Chicago. 67,058 (1970).

cic·e·ro·ne (sis′ə rō′nē, chich′ə-; *It.* chē′che RÔ′ne), *n., pl.* **-nes,** *It.* **-ni** (-nē). a person who shows and explains the antiquities, curiosities, history, etc., of a place; guide. [< It < L *Cicerōne(m),* acc. of *Cicerō* CICERO, the guide being thought of as having the knowledge and eloquence of Cicero]

Cic·e·ro·ni·an (sis′ə rō′nē ən), *adj.* **1.** of or pertaining to Cicero, his writings, or his rhetorical style: *the Ciceronian orations.* —*n.* **2.** a person who specializes in the study of the works of Cicero or who admires or imitates his style. [< L *Cicerōniān(us)* = *Cicerōn-* (s. of *Cicerō*) + *-iānus* -IAN] —**Cic·e·ron·i·cal·ly** (sis′ə ron′ik lē), *adv.*

cich·lid (sik′lid), *n.* **1.** any of the *Cichlidae,* a family of spiny-rayed, fresh-water fishes of South America, Africa, and southern Asia, superficially resembling the American sunfishes: often kept in home aquariums. —*adj.* **2.** belonging or pertaining to the family *Cichlidae.* [< Gk *kích(lē)* thrush, wrasse + -ID[2]]

ci·cho·ri·a·ceous (si kōr′ē ā′shəs, -kôr′-), *adj.* belonging to the *Cichoriaceae,* or chicory family of composite plants, as the dandelion, lettuce, and salsify. [< L *cichori(um)* (< Gk *kichṓrion* CHICORY) + -ACEOUS]

ci·cis·be·o (chē′chēz be′ô; *Eng.* si sis′bē ō′), *n., pl.* **-be·i** (-be′ē; *Eng.* -bē ē′). *Italian.* (esp. during the 18th century) an escort or lover of a married woman.

Cid (sid; *Sp.* thēd), *n.* **The,** ("*El Cid Campeador*") (*Rodrigo Díaz de Bivar*), c1040–99, Spanish soldier: hero of the wars against the Moors.

-cide, a learned borrowing from Latin meaning "killer," "act of killing," used in the formation of compound words: *homicide.* [late ME < L *-cīda* cutter, killer, *-cidium* act of killing = *-cīd-* (comb. form of *caedere* to cut, kill) + *-a* agent suffix, *-ium* suffix of action or result]

ci·der (sī′dər), *n.* the expressed juice of apples used for drinking, either before fermentation **(sweet cider)** or after fermentation **(hard cider),** or for making applejack, vinegar, etc. Also, *Brit.,* **cyder.** [late ME *sidre* < MF; OF *si(s)dre* < LL *sīcera* strong drink < Septuagint Gk *síkera* < Heb *shēkār* (Levit. X, 9); r. ME *sithere* < OF *sidre*]

ci′der press′, a press for crushing apples for cider.

ci-de·vant (sēdə vän′), *adj. French.* former; retired, esp. in reference to an officeholder. [lit., heretofore]

Cie., company. Also, **cie.** [< F *Compagnie*]

Cien·fue·gos (syen fwe′gôs), *n.* a seaport in S Cuba. 99,530 (1960).

C.I.F., cost, insurance, and freight (included in the price quoted). Also, **CIF, c.i.f.**

ci·gar (si gär′), *n.* a cured cylindrical roll of tobacco leaves for smoking. [< Sp *cigarr(o)*]

cig·a·rette (sig′ə ret′, sig′ə ret′), *n.* a narrow, short roll of finely cut, cured tobacco for smoking, usually wrapped in thin white paper. Also, **cig′a·ret′.** [< F = *cigare* CIGAR + *-ette* -ETTE]

cig·a·ril·lo (sig′ə ril′ō), *n., pl.* **-los.** a small, thin cigar. [< Sp, dim. of *cigarro* CIGAR]

cil·i·a (sil′ē ə), *n.pl., sing.* **cil·i·um** (sil′ē əm). **1.** the eyelashes. **2.** *Zool.* short, hairlike processes on the surface of protozoans or of metazoan cells, which by their motion accomplish locomotion or produce a current. **3.** *Bot.* minute, hairlike processes. [< L, pl. of *cilium* eyelid, eyelash, possibly a back formation from *supercilium* eyebrow, and possibly akin to *cēlāre* to CONCEAL]

Cilia of a flower

cil·i·ar·y (sil′ē er′ē), *adj.* **1.** noting or pertaining to various anatomical structures in or about the eye. **2.** pertaining to cilia.

cil′iary bod′y, *Anat.* the part of the tunic of the eye consisting chiefly of the ciliary muscle and the ciliary processes.

cil′iary mus′cle, *Anat.* the smooth muscle in the ciliary body that affects the accommodation of the eye.

cil′iary proc′ess, one of the folds on the ciliary body, connected with the suspensory ligament of the crystalline lens.

cil·i·ate (sil′ē it, -āt′), *n.* **1.** any protozoan of the class *Ciliata,* having cilia on part or all of the body. —*adj.* **2.** Also, **cil·i·at·ed** (sil′ē ā′tid). *Bot., Zool.* having cilia. **3.** belonging or pertaining to the *Ciliata.* [< NL *ciliāt(us)*] —**cil′i·ate·ly,** *adv.* —**cil′i·a′tion,** *n.*

cil·ice (sil′is), *n.* haircloth. [< MF; r. OE *cilic* < L *cilic(ium)* < Gk *kilíkion,* neut. of *kilíkios* Cilician, so called because first made of Cilician goathair]

Ci·li·cia (si lish′ə), *n.* an ancient country in SE Asia Minor: later a Roman province. —**Ci·li′cian,** *adj., n.*

Cili′cian Gates′, a mountain pass in SE Asia Minor, connecting Cappadocia and Cilicia. Turkish, **Gülek Bogaz.**

cil·i·o·late (sil′ē ə lit, -lāt′), *adj.* furnished with minute cilia. [< NL *ciliol(um)* (*cili(um)* (see CILIA) + *-olum,* var. of *-ulum* -ULE) + -ATE[1]]

cil·i·um (sil′ē əm), *n.* sing. of **cilia.**

Ci·ma·bu·e (chē′mä bo͞o′e), *n.* **Gio·van·ni** (jô vän′nē), (*Cenni di Pepo*), c1240–1302?, Italian painter and mosaicist.

Cim·ar·ron (sim′ə ron′, -rōn′, -ər ən; sim′ə rōn′), *n.* a river flowing E from NE New Mexico to the Arkansas River in Oklahoma. 600 mi. long.

Cim·bri (sim′brī, -brē, kim′-), *n.pl.* a Germanic or Celtic people who invaded Gaul and northern Italy, and were destroyed by the Romans in 101 B.C. —**Cim′bri·an,** *adj., n.* —**Cim′bric,** *adj.*

ci·mex (sī′meks), *n., pl.* **cim·i·ces** (sim′i sēz′). a bedbug of the genus *Cimex.* [< L: a bug]

Cim·me·ri·an (si mēr′ē ən), *adj.* **1.** *Class. Myth.* of, pertaining to, or suggestive of a western people believed to dwell in perpetual darkness. **2.** very dark; gloomy.

Ci·mon (sī′mən), *n.* 507–449 B.C., Athenian military leader and statesman (son of Miltiades).

C. in C., Commander in Chief. Also, **C-in-C.**

cinch (sinch), *n.* **1.** a strong girth for securing a pack or saddle. **2.** *Informal.* a tight grip. **3.** *Slang.* **a.** something sure or easy: *This problem is a cinch.* **b.** a person or thing certain to fulfill an expectation: *He's a cinch to win the contest.* —*v.t.* **4.** to gird with a cinch; gird or bind firmly. **5.** *Slang.* to make sure of; guarantee: *Hard work cinched his success.* [< Sp *cinch(a)* < L *cingula* girth = *cing(ere)* (to) gird + *-ula* -ULE]

cin·cho·na (sin kō′nə), *n.* **1.** any of several rubiaceous trees or shrubs of the genus *Cinchona,* as *C. Calisaya,* native to the Andes, cultivated there and in Java and India for their bark, which yields quinine and other alkaloids. **2.** Also called **Peruvian bark.** the medicinal bark of such trees or shrubs. [< NL, named after Countess of *Chinchón* (1576–1639), wife of a Spanish viceroy of Peru; the bark cured her of a fever] —**cin·chon·ic** (sin kon′ik), *adj.*

cin·cho·nine (sin′kə nēn′, -nin), *n. Pharm.* a crystalline alkaloid, $C_{19}H_{22}ON_2$, obtained from cinchona bark: used chiefly as a quinine substitute.

cin·cho·nise (sin′kə nīz′), *v.t.*, **-nised, -nis·ing.** *Chiefly Brit.* cinchonize. —**cin′cho·ni·sa′tion,** *n.*

cin·chon·ism (sin′kə niz′əm), *n. Pathol.* poisoning by any of the cinchona alkaloids, characterized by headache, deafness, and ringing in the ears.

cin·cho·nize (sin′kə nīz′), *v.t.*, **-nized, -niz·ing.** to treat with cinchona or quinine. Also, *esp. Brit.*, **cinchonise.** —**cin′cho·ni·za′tion,** *n.*

Cin·cin·nat·i (sin′sə nat′ē), *n.* a city in SW Ohio, on the Ohio River. 452,524 (1970).

Cin·cin·na·tus (sin′sə nā′təs), *n.* **Lucius Quinc·ti·us** (kwin͡gk′tē əs), 519?–439? B.C., Roman general and statesman: dictator 458, 439.

cinc·ture (sin͡gk′c͟hər), *n.*, *v.*, **-tured, -tur·ing.** —*n.* **1.** *Archaic, Literary.* a belt or girdle. **2.** something that surrounds or encompasses as a girdle does; a surrounding border. **3.** the act of girding or encompassing. —*v.t.* **4.** to gird, as with a cincture; encircle. [< L *cinctūr(a)* = *cinct(us)* (*cinc-*, var. s. of *cingere* to gird + *-tus* ptp. suffix) + *-ūra* -URE]

cin·der (sin′dər), *n.* **1.** a burned-out or partially burned piece of coal, wood, etc. **2. cinders, a.** any residue of combustion; ashes. **b.** *Geol.* coarse scoriae thrown out of volcanoes. **3.** a live, flameless coal; ember. **4.** *Metall.* a mixture of ashes and slag. —*v.t.* **5.** *Archaic.* to reduce to cinders. [ME *synder*, OE *sinder* slag; c. G *Sinter*, Icel *sindr; c-* (for *s-*) < F *cendre* ashes] —**cin′der·y, cin′der·ous,** *adj.* —**cin′der·like′,** *adj.*

cin′der block′, a concrete building block made with a cinder aggregate.

Cin·der·el·la (sin′də rel′ə), *n.* **1.** a heroine of a fairy tale who is oppressed by a malevolent stepmother but achieves happiness through the intervention of a fairy godmother. **2.** any girl who achieves happiness or sudden success after a period of wretchedness.

cin′der track′, a race track covered with small cinders.

cine-, a combining form of **cinema.**

cin·e·ma (sin′ə mə), *n.* **1.** *Chiefly Brit.* See **motion picture. 2. the cinema,** motion pictures collectively, as an art form. **3.** *Chiefly Brit.* a motion-picture theater. [short for CINEMATOGRAPH] —**cin·e·mat·ic** (sin′ə mat′ik), *adj.* —**cin′e·mat′i·cal·ly,** *adv.*

cin·e·ma·theque (sin′ə mə tek′), *n.* a motion-picture theater, sometimes associated with an archive, showing experimentally or historically important films. Also, **cin·é·ma·thèque.** [< F *cinémathèque*]

cin·e·mat·o·graph (sin′ə mat′ə graf′, -gräf′), *n. Chiefly Brit.* **1.** a motion-picture projector. **2.** a motion-picture camera. Also, **kinematograph.** [< F *cinématographe* = *cinémat-* (< Gk *kīnēmat-*, s. of *kī́nēma* motion) + *-o-* -O- + *-graphe* -GRAPH] —**cin·e·ma·tog·ra·pher** (sin′ə mə tog′rə fər), *n.* —**cin·e·mat·o·graph·ic** (sin′ə mat′ə graf′ik), *adj.* —**cin′e·mat′o·graph′i·cal·ly,** *adv.* —**cin′e·ma·tog′ra·phy,** *n.*

ci·né·ma vé·ri·té (sē nā mä′ vā rē tā′), *French.* a technique of filmmaking in which life and people are recorded as they actually are, without script or rehearsal, with a minimum of editing and with synchronous sound.

cin·e·ole (sin′ē ōl), *n. Chem., Pharm.* a colorless, slightly water-soluble, liquid terpene ether, $C_{10}H_{18}O$, having a camphorlike odor and pungent, spicy, cooling taste, found in eucalyptus, cajuput, and other essential oils: used in flavoring, perfumery, and in medicine chiefly as an expectorant. Also, **cin·e·ol** (sin′ē ōl′, -ôl′, -ol′). [alter. of NL *oleum cinae* = *oleum* OIL + gen. sing. of *cina* wormseed]

Cin·e·ram·a (sin′ə ram′ə, -rä′mə), *n. Trademark.* a motion-picture process designed to produce a realistic effect by using three cameras, set at different angles, to photograph separate, overlapping images that are projected on a large, concave screen in conjunction with stereophonic sound.

cin·e·rar·i·a (sin′ə râr′ē ə), *n.* any of several horticultural varieties of an asteraceous herb, *Senecio cruentus*, of the Canary Islands, having heart-shaped leaves and clusters of flowers with white, blue, purple, red, or variegated rays. [< NL, fem. of L *cinerārius* ashen = *ciner-* (s. of *cinis* ashes) + *-ārius* -ARY; from ash-colored down on leaves]

cin·e·rar·i·um (sin′ə râr′ē əm), *n.*, *pl.* **-rar·i·a** (-râr′ē ə). a place for depositing the ashes of the dead after cremation. [< L, neut. of *cinerārius*; see CINERARIA, -ARIUM] —**cin·e·rar·y** (sin′ə rer′ē), *adj.*

cin·er·a·tor (sin′ə rā′tər), *n.* an incinerator. [< L *cinerāt(us)* (ptp. of *cinerāre*) = *ciner-* (s. of *cinis*; see CINERARIA) + *-ātus* -ATE[1] + -OR[2]] —**cin′e·ra′tion,** *n.*

ci·ne·re·ous (si nēr′ē əs), *adj.* **1.** in the state of ashes: *cinereous bodies.* **2.** resembling ashes. **3.** ashen; ash-colored; grayish. Also, **cin·er·i·tious** (sin′ə ris͟h′əs). [< L *cinereus* = *ciner-* (s. of *cinis*) ashes + *-eus* -EOUS]

Cin·ga·lese (sin͡g′gə lēz′, -lēs′), *adj.*, *n.*, *pl.* **-lese.** Singhalese.

cin·gu·lum (sin͡g′gyə ləm), *n.*, *pl.* **-la** (-lə). **1.** *Anat., Zool.* a belt, zone, or girdlelike part. **2.** *Anat.* a band of association fibers in the cerebrum. [< L: girdle, zone = *cing-* (s. of *cingere* to gird; see CINCTURE) + *-ulum* -ULE] —**cin·gu·late** (sin͡g′gyə lit, -lāt′), *adj.*

cin·na·bar (sin′ə bär′), *n.* **1.** a mineral, mercuric sulfide, occurring in red crystals or masses: the principal ore of mercury. **2.** red mercuric sulfide, used as a pigment. **3.** bright red; vermilion. [< L *cinnabar(is)* < Gk *kinnábari* < ?; r. ME *cynoper* < ML] —**cin·na·bar·ine** (sin′ə bə rēn′, -bär′in, -bär′īn, -ēn), *adj.*

cin·nam·ic (si nam′ik, sin′ə mik), *adj.* of or obtained from cinnamon. [CINNAM(ON) + -IC]

cinnam′ic ac′id, *Chem.* a powder, $C_6H_5CH{=}CHCOOH$, usually obtained from cinnamon or synthesized: used chiefly in the manufacture of perfumes and medicines.

cin·na·mon (sin′ə mən), *n.* **1.** the aromatic inner bark of any of several lauraceous trees of the genus *Cinnamonum*, of the East Indies, used as a spice. **2.** a tree yielding such bark. **3.** cassia (def. 1). **4.** a yellowish or reddish brown. [< L < Gk *kínnamon* < Sem, as Heb *qinnāmōn*; r. late ME *cinamome* < MF < L *cinnamōm(um)* < Gk *kinnámōmon*]

cin′namon bear′, a cinnamon-colored variety of the black bear of North America.

cin′namon stone′, a light, brown grossularite garnet. Also called **essonite, hessonite.**

cin·quain (sin͡g kān′, sin͡g′kān), *n.* a stanza of five lines. [< F < LL *cinque* (see CINQUE) + F *-ain* collective suffix]

cinque (sin͡gk), *n.* the five at dice, cards, etc. [ME *cink* < OF *cinq* < LL *cinque*, L *quinque* five]

cin·que·cen·tist (c͟hin͡g′kwi c͟hen′tist), *n.* an Italian writer or artist of the 16th century. [< It *cinquecentist(a)*]

cin·que·cen·to (c͟hin͡g′kwi c͟hen′tō), *n.* (*often cap.*) the 16th century, esp. with reference to Italian art or literature. [< It, short for *milcinquecento* 1500, used for period A.D. 1500–1599]

cinque·foil (sin͡gk′foil′), *n.* **1.** any of several rosaceous plants of the genus *Potentilla*, having five-lobed leaves. **2.** *Archit.* a panellike ornament consisting of five lobes, divided by cusps, radiating from a common center. [ME *sink foil* < MF *cincfoille* < L *quinque folia* five leaves, trans. of Gk *pentáphyllon*]

Cinquefoil (def. 2)

Cinque′ Ports′, (formerly) an association of five maritime towns in SE England, consisting of Hastings, Romney, Hythe, Dover, and Sandwich, formed in 1278 to assist in the naval defense of England. [ME *cink pors* < OF *cink porz*]

C.I.O., See **Congress of Industrial Organizations.** Also, **CIO**

ci·on (sī′ən), *n.* scion (def. 2).

-cion, var. of **-tion**: *suspicion.* [< L = *-c-* final in v. stem + *-iōn-* -ION]

Ci·pan·go (si pan͡g′gō), *n. Archaic.* Japan.

ci·pher (sī′fər), *n.* **1.** zero. **2.** any Arabic numeral. **3.** a person or thing of no influence or importance; nonentity. **4.** a secret method of writing by coded symbols. Cf. **cryptography. 5.** a coded message. **6.** the key to a secret method of writing. **7.** a combination of letters, as the initials of a name; monogram. —*v.i.* **8.** to use figures or numerals arithmetically. —*v.t.* **9.** to calculate numerically; figure. **10.** to write in cipher. Also, *esp. Brit.*, **cypher.** [late ME *siphre* < ML *ciphr(a)* < Ar *çifr* empty, zero]

cip·o·lin (sip′ə lin), *n.* an impure variety of marble with alternate white and greenish zones and a layered structure. [< F < It *cipollin(o)* = *cipoll(a)* onion (< LL *cēpulla* = L *cēp(a)* onion + *-ulla* dim. suffix) + *-ino* -INE[1]]

cir., about: *cir. 1800.* [< L *circā, circiter, circum*]

circ., **1.** about: *circ. 1800.* [< L *circā, circiter, circum*] **2.** circuit. **3.** circulation. **4.** circumference.

cir·ca (sûr′kə), *prep.*, *adv.* about: used esp. in approximate dates. *Abbr.*: c, c., ca, ca., cir., circ. [< L: around, about]

cir·ca·di·an (sûr′kə dē′ən), *adj.* noting or pertaining to rhythmic biological cycles recurring at approximately 24-hour intervals. [< L *circa* about + *di(em)* day + -AN]

Cir·cas·sia (sər kas͟h′ə, -ē ə), *n.* a region in the S Soviet Union in Europe, bordering on the Black Sea.

Cir·cas·sian (sər kas͟h′ən, -ē ən), *n.* **1.** Also called **Adyghe.** a native or inhabitant of Circassia. **2.** the North Caucasian language of the Circassians. —*adj.* **3.** of or pertaining to Circassia, its inhabitants, or their language.

Cir·ce (sûr′sē), *n. Class. Myth.* the enchantress represented by Homer as turning the companions of Odysseus into swine by means of a magic drink. —**Cir·ce·an** (sər sē′ən), *adj.*

Circinate fronds

cir·ci·nate (sûr′sə nāt′), *adj.* **1.** made round; ring-shaped. **2.** *Bot.* rolled up on the axis at the apex, as a leaf. [< L *circināt(us)* (ptp. of *circināre*) = *circin(us)* pair of compasses (akin to CIRCUS) + *-ātus* -ATE[1]] —**cir′ci·nate′ly,** *adv.*

cir·cle (sûr′kəl), *n.*, *v.*, **-cled, -cling.** —*n.* **1.** a closed plane curve of which all points are at an equal distance from the center. **2.** the portion of a plane bounded by such a curve. **3.** any circular object, formation, or arrangement: *a circle of dancers.* **4.** a ring, circlet, or crown. **5.** a section of seats in a theater: *dress circle.* **6.** the area within which something or someone exerts influence; realm; sphere. **7.** a series ending where it began, esp. when perpetually repeated; cycle: *the circle of the year.* **8.** *Logic.* an argument ostensibly proving a conclusion but actually assuming the conclusion as a premise; vicious circle. **9.** a number of persons bound by a common tie; coterie: *She told no one outside the family circle.* **10.** *Geog.* a parallel of latitude. **11.** *Astron. Rare.* the orbit of a heavenly body. **12.** a sphere or orb: *the circle of the earth.* —*v.t.* **13.** to enclose in a circle; surround; encircle: *Circle the correct answer.* **14.** to move or revolve around: *He circled the house cautiously.* **15.** to by-pass; evade: *The ship carefully circled the iceberg.* —*v.i.* **16.** to move in a circle or circuit. [< L *circul(us)* = *circ(us)* + *-ulus* -ULE; r. ME *cercle* < OF; r. OE *circul* < L] —**cir′cler,** *n.*

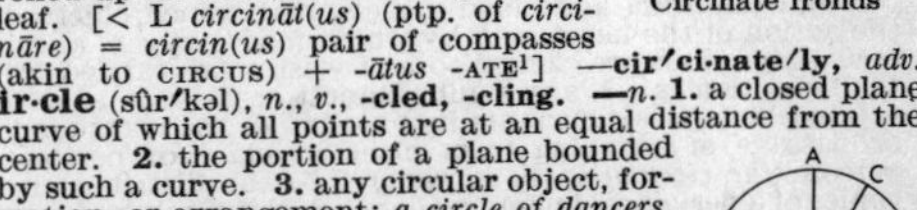

Circle
AD, Diameter;
AB,BC,BD,
Radii

cir·clet (sûr′klit), *n.* **1.** a small circle. **2.** a ring. **3.** a ring-shaped ornament, esp. for the head. [r. late ME *serclett* < MF]

cir·cuit (sûr′kit), *n.* **1.** act of going or moving around. **2.** a circular journey; round. **3.** a roundabout journey or course. **4.** a periodical journey around an accustomed territory to perform certain duties, as by judges, ministers, or salesmen. **5.** the persons making such a journey. **6.** the route followed or district covered. **7.** the line bounding any area or object. **8.** the distance around an area or object. **9.** a number of theaters, night clubs, etc., controlled by one owner or manager or visited in turn by the same entertainers. **10.** *Elect.* **a.** the complete path of an electric current, including the source of the current, intervening resistors, capacitors, etc. **b.** any well-defined segment of a complete circuit. **11.** a league or association: *He played baseball for the Texas circuit.* —*v.t.* **12.** to move around; make the circuit of. —*v.i.* **13.** to go or move in a circuit. [late ME < L *circuit(us),* var. of *circumitus* = *circ(um)* (see CIRCUM-) + *-itus* (ptp. of *īre* to go)] —**cir′cuit·al,** *adj.* —**Syn. 2.** tour, revolution, orbit. **7.** perimeter, periphery, boundary. **9.** chain.

cir′cuit break′er, *Elect.* a device for interrupting an electric circuit when the current becomes excessive.

cir′cuit court′, **1.** a court holding sessions at various intervals in different sections of a judicial district. **2.** (*caps.*) (in the U.S.) the court of general jurisdiction in some states.

cir′cuit judge′, a judge of a circuit court.

cir·cu·i·tous (sər kyo͞o′i təs), *adj.* roundabout; not direct: *a circuitous argument.* [< ML *circuitōs(us).* See CIRCUIT, -OUS] —**cir·cu′i·tous·ly,** *adv.* —**cir·cu′i·tous·ness,** *n.*

cir′cuit rid′er, (formerly) a minister who rode from place to place to preach along a circuit.

cir·cuit·ry (sûr′ki trē), *n.* **1.** electric or electronic circuits collectively, as in a device. **2.** the components of such circuits, collectively. **3.** the science of designing such circuits.

cir·cu·i·ty (sər kyo͞o′i tē), *n.* circuitous quality or roundabout character.

cir·cu·lar (sûr′kyə lər), *adj.* **1.** of or pertaining to a circle. **2.** having the form of a circle; round. **3.** moving in or forming a circle or a circuit. **4.** moving or occurring in a cycle or round: *the circular succession of the seasons.* **5.** circuitous; indirect. **6.** (of a letter, memorandum, etc.) addressed to a number of persons or intended for general circulation. —*n.* **7.** a letter, advertisement, or statement for general circulation. [< LL *circulār(is).* See CIRCLE, -AR[1]] —**cir·cu·lar·i·ty** (sûr′kyə lar′i tē), **cir′cu·lar·ness,** *n.* —**cir′cu·lar·ly,** *adv.*

cir′cular func′tion, *Math.* See **trigonometric function.**

cir·cu·lar·ise (sûr′kyə lə rīz′), *v.t.,* **-ised, -is·ing.** *Chiefly Brit.* circularize. —**cir′cu·lar·i·sa′tion,** *n.* —**cir′cu·lar·is′er,** *n.*

cir·cu·lar·ize (sûr′kyə lə rīz′), *v.t.,* **-ized, -iz·ing. 1.** to send circulars to. **2.** to circulate (a letter, memorandum, etc.). **3.** to make circular. —**cir′cu·lar·i·za′tion,** *n.* —**cir′cu·lar·iz′er,** *n.*

cir′cular meas′ure, a measurement system for circles: 1 circle = 360 degrees; 1 degree = 60 minutes; 1 minute = 60 seconds.

cir′cular saw′, **1.** a power saw having a disk-shaped blade, usually with a toothed edge. **2.** the blade of such a saw. See illus. at **saw**[1].

cir′cular tri′angle, a triangle that has arcs of circles as sides.

cir·cu·late (sûr′kyə lāt′), *v.,* **-lat·ed, -lat·ing.** —*v.i.* **1.** to move in a circle or circuit; move or pass through a circuit back to the starting point, as the blood in the body. **2.** to pass from place to place, from person to person, etc.: *She circulated among her guests.* **3.** to be distributed or sold, esp. over a wide area. —*v.t.* **4.** to cause to pass from place to place, person to person, etc.; disseminate or distribute: *to circulate a rumor.* [< L *circulāt(us)* (ptp. of *circulārī* to gather round one, LL *circulāre* to encircle) = *circul(us)* CIRCLE + *-ātus* -ATE[1]] —**cir·cu·la·tive** (sûr′kyə lā′tiv, -lə tiv), *adj.* —**cir′cu·la′tor,** *n.* —**cir·cu·la·to·ry** (sûr′kyə lə tōr′ē, -tôr′ē), *adj.*

cir′culating dec′imal, a decimal in which a series of digits is repeated ad infinitum, as 0.147232323 . . . . Also called **recurring decimal, repeating decimal.**

cir′culating li′brary, **1.** a library whose books circulate among its members or subscribers. **2.** See **lending library.**

cir′culating me′dium, any coin or note passing as a medium of exchange.

cir·cu·la·tion (sûr′kyə lā′shən), *n.* **1.** the act or an instance of circulating. **2.** the continuous movement of blood through the heart and blood vessels, maintained chiefly by the action of the heart, and by which food, oxygen, and internal secretions are carried to and wastes are carried from the body tissues. **3.** any similar circuit or passage, as of the sap in plants or air currents in a room. **4.** the transmission or passage of anything from place to place or person to person: *the circulation of a rumor.* **5.** the distribution of copies of a periodical among readers. **6.** the number of copies of each issue of a newspaper, magazine, etc., distributed. **7.** coins, notes, bills, etc., in use as money; currency. **8. in circulation,** participating actively in social or business life. [< L *circulātiōn-* (s. of *circulātiō*)]

cir′culatory sys′tem, *Anat., Zool.* the system of organs and tissues, including the heart, blood, blood vessels, lymph, lymphatic vessels, and lymph glands, involved in circulating blood and lymph through the body.

circum-, an element occurring in loan words from Latin (*circumstance*) and used, with the meaning "around," "about," in the formation of compound words (*circumpolar*). [< L, prefix akin to CIRCUS, CIRCA]

cir·cum·am·bi·ent (sûr′kəm am′bē ənt), *adj.* surrounding or encompassing. [< LL *circumambient-* (s. of *circumambiēns*)] —**cir′cum·am′bi·ence, cir′cum·am′bi·en·cy,** *n.*

cir·cum·am·bu·late (sûr′kəm am′byə lāt′), *v.t., v.i.,* **-lat·ed, -lat·ing.** to walk or go about or around. [< LL *circumambulāt(us)* (ptp. of *circumambulāre*)] —**cir′cum·am′bu·la′tion,** *n.* —**cir′cum·am′bu·la′tor,** *n.* —**cir·cum·am·bu·la·to·ry** (sûr′kəm am′byə lə tōr′ē, -tôr′ē), *adj.*

cir·cum·cise (sûr′kəm sīz′), *v.t.,* **-cised, -cis·ing. 1.** to remove the prepuce of (a male), esp. as a religious rite. **2.** to remove the clitoris, prepuce, or labia of (a female). **3.** to purify spiritually. [ME *circumcise(n)* < L *circumcīs(us)* (ptp. of *circumcīdere* to cut around) = *circum-* CIRCUM- + *-cīsus* (*cīd-* cut + *-tus* ptp. suffix)]

cir·cum·ci·sion (sûr′kəm sizh′ən), *n.* **1.** act or rite of circumcising. **2.** spiritual purification. **3.** (*cap.*) a church festival in honor of the circumcision of Jesus, observed on January 1. [ME < LL *circumcīsiōn-* (s. of *circumcīsiō*)]

cir·cum·fer·ence (sər kum′fər əns, -frəns), *n.* **1.** the outer boundary, esp. of a circular area; perimeter. **2.** the length of such a boundary. [late ME < LL *circumferentia* = *circum-* CIRCUM- + *fer-* (s. of *ferre* to carry) + *-entia* -ENCE] —**Syn. 1.** periphery, circuit.

cir·cum·fer·en·tial (sər kum′fə ren′shəl), *adj.* **1.** of, at, or near the circumference; surrounding; lying along the outskirts. **2.** circuitous or indirect.

cir·cum·flex (sûr′kəm fleks′), *adj.* **1.** (in some languages) consisting of, indicated by, or bearing the mark ^, ⌢, or ~, placed over a vowel to indicate nasalization, length, pitch, stress, etc. **2.** pronounced as indicated by such a mark. **3.** bending or winding around. —*n.* **4.** a circumflex mark or accent. —*v.t.* **5.** to bend around. [< L *circumflex(us)* = *circum-* CIRCUM- + *flexus,* ptp. of *flectere* to bend; see FLEX]

cir·cum·flu·ent (sər kum′flo͞o ənt), *adj.* flowing around; encompassing. [< L *circumfluent-* (s. of *circumfluēns,* prp. of *circumfluere* to flow around)] —**cir·cum′flu·ence,** *n.*

cir·cum·flu·ous (sər kum′flo͞o əs), *adj.* **1.** circumfluent. **2.** surrounded by water. [< L *circumfluus* = *circum-* CIRCUM- + *flu-* (s. of *fluere* to flow) + *-us* -OUS]

cir·cum·fuse (sûr′kəm fyo͞oz′), *v.t.,* **-fused, -fus·ing. 1.** to pour around; diffuse. **2.** to surround as with a fluid; suffuse. [< L *circumfūs(us)* (ptp. of *circumfundere* to pour around)] —**cir′cum·fu′sion,** *n.*

cir·cum·gy·ra·tion (sûr′kəm jī rā′shən), *n.* a revolution or circular movement. [< LL *circumgȳrātiōn-* (s. of *circumgȳrātiō*)]

cir·cum·ja·cent (sûr′kəm jā′sənt), *adj.* lying around; surrounding: *the circumjacent parishes.* [< L *circumjacent-* (s. of *circumjacēns,* prp. of *circumjacēre* to lie around) = *circum-* CIRCUM- + *jac-* lie + *-ent-* -ENT]

cir·cum·lo·cu·tion (sûr′kəm lō kyo͞o′shən), *n.* **1.** a roundabout or indirect way of speaking; the use of superfluous words. **2.** a roundabout expression. [< L *circumlocūtiōn-* (s. of *circumlocūtiō*). See CIRCUM-, LOCUTION] —**cir·cum·loc·u·to·ry** (sûr′kəm lok′yə tōr′ē, -tôr′ē), *adj.*

cir·cum·lu·nar (sûr′kəm lo͞o′nər), *adj.* rotating about or surrounding the moon.

cir·cum·nav·i·gate (sûr′kəm nav′ə gāt′), *v.t.,* **-gat·ed, -gat·ing.** to sail around; make the circuit of by navigation. [< L *circumnāvigāt(us)* (ptp. of *circumnāvigāre*] —**cir·cum·nav·i·ga·ble** (sûr′kəm nav′ə gə bəl), *adj.* —**cir′cum·nav′i·ga′tion,** *n.* —**cir′cum·nav′i·ga′tor,** *n.*

cir·cum·po·lar (sûr′kəm pō′lər), *adj.* around or near one of the poles of the earth or of the heavens.

cir·cum·ro·tate (sûr′kəm rō′tāt), *v.i.,* **-tat·ed, -tat·ing.** to rotate like a wheel. [< L *circumrotāt(us)* (ptp. of *circumrotāre*)] —**cir′cum·ro·ta′tion,** *n.* —**cir·cum·ro·ta·to·ry** (sûr′kəm rō′tə tōr′ē, -tôr′ē), *adj.*

cir·cum·scis·sile (sûr′kəm sis′il), *adj. Bot.* opening along a transverse circular line, as a seed vessel.

Circumscissile pod of plantain, genus *Plantago*

cir·cum·scribe (sûr′kəm skrīb′, sûr′kəm skrīb′), *v.t.,* **-scribed, -scrib·ing. 1.** to draw a line around; encircle; surround. **2.** to limit or confine the scope of; restrict. **3.** to mark off; define; delimit. **4.** *Geom.* **a.** to draw (a figure) around another figure so as to touch as many points as possible. **b.** (of a figure) to enclose (another figure) in this manner. [< L *circumscrīb(ere)* = *circum-* CIRCUM- + *scrībere* to write] —**cir′cum·scrib′a·ble,** *adj.* —**Syn. 1.** circle. **2.** restrain, check, hamper.

cir·cum·scrip·tion (sûr′kəm skrip′shən), *n.* **1.** act of circumscribing. **2.** circumscribed state; limitation. **3.** anything that surrounds or encloses; boundary; restriction. **4.** periphery; outline. **5.** a circumscribed area. **6.** a circular inscription on a coin, seal, etc. **7.** *Archaic.* limitation of a meaning; definition. [< L *circumscrīptiōn-* (s. of *circumscriptiō*) = *circumscrīpt(us)* (ptp. of *circumscrībere* to CIRCUMSCRIBE) + *-iōn-* -ION] —**cir′cum·scrip′tive,** *adj.* —**cir′cum·scrip′tive·ly,** *adv.*

cir·cum·so·lar (sûr′kəm sō′lər), *adj.* around the sun: *the earth's circumsolar course.*

cir·cum·spect (sûr′kəm spekt′), *adj.* watchful and discreet; cautious; prudent: *circumspect behavior.* [< L *circumspect(us)* (ptp. of *circumspicere* to look around) = *circum-* CIRCUM- + *spec(ere)* (to) look + *-tus* ptp. suffix] —**cir′cum·spect′ly,** *adv.* —**cir′cum·spect′ness,** *n.* —**Syn.** careful, guarded. —**Ant.** careless, indiscreet.

cir·cum·spec·tion (sûr′kəm spek′shən), *n.* circumspect observation or action; caution; prudence. [< L *circumspectiōn-* (s. of *circumspectiō*)]

cir·cum·stance (sûr′kəm stans′ *or, esp. Brit.,* -stəns), *n., v.,* **-stanced, -stanc·ing.** —*n.* **1.** a condition or attribute that accompanies, determines, or modifies a fact or event; a modifying or influencing factor. **2.** Usually, **circumstances.** the existing conditions or state of affairs surrounding and affecting an agent: *Circumstances permitting, we sail on Monday.* **3.** an unessential accompaniment; minor detail. **4. circumstances,** the condition or state of a person with respect to material welfare: *a family in reduced circumstances.* **5.** an incident or occurrence: *His arrival was a fortunate circumstance.* **6.** detailed or circuitous narration. **7.** ceremonious accompaniment or display: *pomp and circumstance.* **8. under no circumstances,** regardless of events or conditions; never: *Under no circumstances should you see them again.* **9. under the circumstances,** because of the conditions; as the case stands: *Under the circumstances, we are suspending operations.* Also, **in the circumstances.** —*v.t.* **10.** to place in particular circumstances or relations. **11.** *Obs.* **a.** to furnish with details. **b.** to control or guide by circumstances. [ME < L *circumstantia* (*circumstant-,* s. of *circumstāns,* prp. of *circumstāre* to stand round) = *circum-* CIRCUM- + *stā-* stand + *-nt-* prp. suffix + *-ia* n. suffix]

cir·cum·stanced (sûr′kəm stanst′ *or, esp. Brit.,* -stənst), *v.* **1.** pt. and pp. of **circumstance.** —*adj.* **2.** being in a particular condition, esp. with respect to income and material welfare: *They were far better circumstanced than we were.*

cir·cum·stan·tial (sûr′kəm stan′shəl), *adj.* **1.** of, pertaining to, or derived from circumstances: *a circumstantial result.* **2.** unessential; secondary; incidental. **3.** giving circumstances or details; detailed; particular. **4.** pertaining to conditions of material welfare. [< L *circumstanti(a)* CIRCUMSTANCE + -AL[1]] —**cir′cum·stan′tial·ly,** *adv.*

cir′cumstan′tial ev′idence, proof of facts offered as evidence from which other facts are to be inferred (contrasted with *direct evidence*).

cir·cum·stan·ti·al·i·ty (sûr′kəm stan′shē al′i tē), *n., pl.* **-ties** for 2. **1.** quality of being circumstantial; minuteness or fullness of detail. **2.** a circumstance; a particular detail.

cir·cum·stan·ti·ate (sûr′kəm stan′shē āt′), *v.t.,* **-at·ed, -at·ing. 1.** to set forth or support with circumstances or particulars. **2.** to describe fully or minutely. [< L *circumstanti(a)* CIRCUMSTANCE + -ATE[1]] —**cir′cum·stan′ti·a′tion,** *n.*

cir·cum·val·late (*adj.* sûr′kəm val′āt, -it; *v.* sûr′kəm val′āt), *adj., v.,* **-lat·ed, -lat·ing.** —*adj.* **1.** surrounded by or as by a rampart. —*v.t.* **2.** to surround with or as with a rampart. [< L *circumvallāt(us)* (ptp. of *circumvallāre*) = *circum-* CIRCUM- + *vall(um)* rampart, wall + *-ātus* -ATE[1]] —**cir·cum·val·la·tion** (sûr′kəm va lā′shən), *n.*

cir·cum·vent (sûr′kəm vent′, sûr′kəm vent′), *v.t.* **1.** to surround or encompass, as by stratagem; entrap. **2.** to go around or by-pass: *to circumvent the lake.* **3.** to avoid by artfulness; outwit. [< L *circumvent(us)* (ptp. of *circumvenīre* to come around, surround, oppress, defraud) = *circum-* CIRCUM- + *ven(īre)* (to) come + *-tus* ptp. suffix] —**cir′cum·vent′er, cir′cum·ven′tor,** *n.* —**cir′cum·ven′tion,** *n.* —**cir′cum·ven′tive,** *adj.* —**Syn. 1.** encircle; ensnare.

cir·cum·vo·lu·tion (sûr′kəm və lo͞o′shən), *n.* **1.** the act of rolling or turning around. **2.** a single complete turn or cycle. **3.** a winding or folding about something. **4.** a fold so wound: *the circumvolution of a snail shell.* **5.** a winding in a sinuous course; sinuosity. **6.** a roundabout course or procedure: *The speaker's circumvolutions bored the audience.* [< ML *circumvolūtiōn-* (s. of *circumvolūtiō*) = L *circumvolūt(us)* (ptp. of *circumvolvere* to CIRCUMVOLVE) + *-iōn* -ION]

cir·cum·volve (sûr′kəm volv′), *v.t., v.i.,* **-volved, -volv·ing.** to revolve or wind about. [< L *circumvolv(ere)* = *circum-* CIRCUM- + *volvere* to roll]

cir·cus (sûr′kəs), *n., pl.* **-cus·es. 1.** a large public entertainment featuring performing animals, clowns, feats of skill and daring, pageantry, etc. **2.** the physical equipment, personnel, etc., necessary for its presentation. **3.** the performance itself. **4.** a circular arena, surrounded by tiers of seats and often covered by a tent, used for such shows. Cf. **big top. 5.** (in ancient Rome) **a.** a large, oblong, roofless enclosure, surrounded by tiers of seats, for chariot races, public games, etc. **b.** an entertainment given in this arena. **6.** anything resembling the Roman circus, or arena, as a natural amphitheater. **7.** *Brit.* an open circle or plaza where several streets converge: *Piccadilly Circus.* **8.** uproar; a display of rowdy sport. **9.** *Obs.* a circlet or ring. [< L: ring, circle]

Cir′cus Max′i·mus (mak′sə məs), the great ancient Roman circus between the Palatine and Aventine hills.

Cir·e·na·i·ca (sir′ə nā′ə kə, sī′rə-; *It.* chē re nä′ē kä), *n.* Cyrenaica.

cirque (sûrk), *n.* **1.** a circular space, esp. a natural amphitheater, as in mountains. **2.** *Literary.* a circle or ring. **3.** a circus. [< F < L *circ(us)* circle < Gk *kírkos* ring]

cir·rate (sir′āt), *adj.* *Bot., Zool.* having tendrils or filaments. [< L *cirrāt(us)* = *cirr(us)* a curl + *-ātus* -ATE[1]]

cir·rho·sis (si rō′sis), *n.* *Pathol.* a disease of the liver characterized by increase of connective tissue and alteration in gross and microscopic make-up. [< Gk *kirrh(ós)* orange-tawny + -OSIS] —**cir·rhosed′,** *adj.* —**cir·rhot·ic** (si rot′ik), *adj.*

cirri-, var. of **cirro-.**

cir·ri·ped (sir′ə ped′), *n.* **1.** any crustacean of the subclass *Cirripedia,* chiefly comprising the barnacles, typically free-swimming in the larval stage and attached or parasitic in the adult stage, with slender, bristly appendages for gathering food. —*adj.* **2.** belonging or pertaining to the *Cirripedia.*

cirro-, a combining form of **cirrus:** *cirrostratus.* Also, **cirri-.**

cir·ro·cu·mu·lus (sir′ō kyo͞o′myə ləs), *n., pl.* **-lus.** *Meteorol.* a cloud of a class characterized by thin, white, granular patches, of high altitude, about 20,000–40,000 feet.

cir·rose (sir′ōs, si rōs′), *adj.* *Bot., Zool.* **1.** having a cirrus or cirri. **2.** resembling cirri. Also, **cir·rous** (sir′əs). [< NL *cirrōs(us).* See CIRRO-, -OSE[1]]

cir·ro·stra·tus (sir′ō strā′təs, -strat′əs), *n., pl.* **-tus.** *Meteorol.* a cloud of a class characterized by a composition of ice crystals and often by the production of halo phenomena and appearing as a whitish and usually fibrous veil, of high altitude, about 20,000–40,000 feet.

cir·rus (sir′əs), *n., pl.* **cir·ri** (sir′ī) for 1, 2, **cir·rus** for 3. **1.** *Bot.* a tendril. **2.** *Zool.* a filament or slender appendage serving as a barbel, tentacle, foot, arm, etc. **3.** *Meteorol.* a cloud of a class characterized by thin white filaments or narrow bands and a composition of ice crystals: of high altitude, about 20,000–40,000 feet. [< L: a curl, tuft, plant filament like a tuft of hair]

cir·soid (sûr′soid), *adj.* *Pathol.* varixlike; varicose. [< Gk *kirsoeid(ḗs)* = *kirs(ós)* enlargement of a vein + *-oeidēs* -OID]

cis-, 1. an element occurring in loan words from Latin meaning "on the near side of" (*cisalpine*) and, on this model, used in the formation of compound words (*cisatlantic*). **2.** *Chem.* a specialization of this denoting a geometric isomer having a pair of identical atoms or groups attached on the same side of two atoms linked by a double bond. Cf. **trans-** (def. 2). [< L; akin to HERE]

cis·al·pine (sis al′pīn, -pin), *adj.* on this, the Roman or south, side of the Alps. [< L *Cisalpin(us)* = *cis-* CIS- + *Alpinus* ALPINE]

Cisal′pine Gaul′. See under **Gaul** (def. 1).

cis·at·lan·tic (sis′ət lan′tik), *adj.* on this, the speaker's or writer's, side of the Atlantic.

Cis·cau·ca·sia (sis′kô kā′zhə, -shə), *n.* the part of Caucasia north of the Caucasus Mountains.

cis·co (sis′kō), *n., pl.* **-coes, -cos.** any of several whitefishes of the genus *Coregonus,* of the Great Lakes and eastern North America. [< CanF *cisco(ette),* alter. of Ojibwa *pemitewiskawet,* lit., that which has oily flesh]

cis·lu·nar (sis lo͞o′nər), *adj.* *Astron.* lying between the earth and the orbit of the moon.

cis·mon·tane (sis mon′tān), *adj.* on this, the speaker's or writer's, side of the mountains, esp. the Alps. [< L *cismontān(us)*]

cis·pa·dane (sis′pə dān′, sis pā′dān), *adj.* on this, the Roman or south, side of the Po River. [CIS- + LL *Padān(us)* = L *Pad(us)* the Po + *-ānus* -AN]

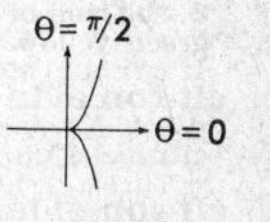

cis·soid (sis′oid), *Geom.* —*n.* **1.** a curve having a cusp at the origin and a point of inflection at infinity. —*adj.* **2.** *Rare.* included between the concave sides of two intersecting curves (opposed to *sistroid*): *a cissoid angle.* [< Gk *kissoeid(ḗs)* = *kiss(ós)* ivy + *-oeid(ēs)* -OID]

$\theta = \pi/2$ $\theta = 0$

Cissoid (def. 1)

cis·ta·ceous (si stā′shəs), *adj.* belonging to the *Cistaceae,* or rockrose family of plants. [< Gk *kíst(os),* var. of *kísthos* rockrose + -ACEOUS]

Cis·ter·cian (si stûr′shən), *n.* **1.** a member of an order of monks and nuns founded in 1098 in France, under Benedictine rule. —*adj.* **2.** of or pertaining to the Cistercians. [< ML *Cisterciān(us)* < L *Cisterci(um)* (now *Cîteaux,* where the order was founded) + *-ānus* -AN]

cis·tern (sis′tərn), *n.* **1.** a reservoir or tank for storing water or other liquid. **2.** *Anat.* a reservoir or receptacle of some natural fluid of the body. [ME *cistern(e)* < L *cistern(a)* = *cist(a)* (see CIST) + *-erna* n. suffix]

cis′tern barom′eter, a mercury barometer having the lower mercury surface of greater area than the upper. Cf. **mercury barometer.**

cit., 1. citation. **2.** cited. **3.** citizen. **4.** citrate.

cit·a·del (sit′ə dᵊl, -ə del′), *n.* **1.** a fortress for commanding or defending a city. **2.** any strongly fortified place. **3.** (formerly) a heavily armored structure on a warship, for protecting the engines, magazines, etc. [< MF *citadelle* < OIt *cittadell(a)* = *cittad(e)* CITY + *-ella* dim. suffix]

ci·ta·tion (sī tā′shən), *n.* **1.** the act of citing or quoting. **2.** the quoting of a passage, book, author, etc.; a reference to an authority or a precedent. **3.** a passage cited; quotation. **4.** mention or enumeration. **5.** a call or summons, esp. to appear in court. **6.** a document containing such a summons. **7.** *Mil.* mention of a soldier or a unit in orders, usually for gallantry: *Presidential citation.* **8.** any award or commendation, as for outstanding service, devotion to duty, etc., esp. a formal letter or statement recounting a person's achievements. [ME *citacio(u)n* < L *citātiōn-* (s. of *citātiō*) = *citāt(us)* (ptp. of *citāre;* see CITE[1]) + *-iōn-* -ION] —**ci·ta·to·ry** (sī′tə tôr′ē, -tōr′ē), *adj.*

cite[1] (sīt), *v.t.,* **cit·ed, cit·ing. 1.** to quote (a passage, book, author, etc.), esp. as an authority. **2.** to mention in support or proof; refer to as an example: *He cited many instances of abuse of power.* **3.** to summon to appear in court. **4.** to call to mind; recall: *citing my gratitude to him.* **5.** *Mil.* to mention (a soldier, unit, etc.) in orders, as for gallantry. **6.** to commend, as for outstanding service, devotion to duty, etc. **7.** to summon or call; rouse to action. [late ME < eccl. L *cit(āre)* (to) summon before a church court; in L, to hurry < *cit(us)* quick] —**cit′a·ble, cite′a·ble,** *adj.* —**cit′er,** *n.*

cite[2] (sīt), *n.* *Informal.* citation (def. 3). [by shortening]

cith·a·ra (sith′ər ə), *n.* kithara.

cith·er (sith′ər), *n.* cittern. Also, **cith·ern** (sith′ərn). [< L *cithar(a)* < Gk *kithára*]

cit·ied (sit′ēd), *adj.* **1.** occupied by a city or cities. **2.** formed into or like a city.

cit·i·fied (sit′i fīd′), *adj.* *Sometimes Disparaging.* having city habits, fashions, etc.

cit·i·fy (sit′i fī′), *v.t.,* **-fied, -fy·ing.** to cause to conform to city habits, fashions, etc. —**cit′i·fi·ca′tion,** *n.*

cit·i·zen (sit′i zən, -sən), *n.* **1.** a native or naturalized member of a state or nation who owes allegiance to its government and is entitled to its protection (distinguished from *alien*). **2.** an inhabitant of a city or town, esp. one entitled to its privileges or franchises. **3.** an inhabitant or denizen: *The deer is a citizen of our woods.* **4.** a civilian, as distinguished from a soldier, police officer, etc. Also, *referring to a woman,* **cit·i·zen·ess** (sit′i zə nis, -sə-). [ME *citisein* < AF *citesein,* OF *citeain* (with hiatus-filling *-s-*) = *cite* CITY + *-ain* -AN] —**cit′i·zen·ly,** *adj.*

cit·i·zen·ry (sit′i zən rē, -sən-), *n., pl.* **-ries.** citizens collectively.

cit′izens band′, federally designated frequencies for short-distance two-way radio communication between licensed individuals with mobile or base stations. *Abbr.:* CB

cit·i·zen·ship (sit′i zən ship′, -sən-), *n.* **1.** the state of being vested with the rights, privileges, and duties of a citizen. **2.** the character of an individual viewed as a member of society: *an award for good citizenship.*

cit′izenship pa′per, Usually, **citizenship papers.** *U.S.* **1.** a certificate of citizenship, as one issued to an American citizen born abroad. **2.** (loosely) a certificate of naturalization conferring citizenship on a resident alien.

Ci·tlal·te·petl (sē′tläl tā′petᵊl), *n.* Orizaba (def. 1).

ci·toy·en (sē twa yaN′), *n., pl.* **-toy·ens** (-twa yaN′). *French.* citizen.

cit·ral (si′trəl), *n.* *Chem.* an aldehyde, $(CH_3)_2C{=}CH(CH_2)_2C(CH_3){=}CHCHO$, with a strong lemonlike odor, used chiefly in perfumery, flavoring, and the synthesis of vitamin A. [CITR(US) + -AL[3]]

cit·rate (si′trāt, sī′-), *n.* *Chem.* a salt or ester of citric acid. [CITR(IC ACID) + -ATE[2]]

cit·ric (si′trik), *adj.* *Chem.* of or derived from citric acid. [CITR(US) + -IC]

cit′ric ac′id (si′trik), *Chem.* a powder, $HOOCCH_2(OH)C(COOH)CH_2COOH \cdot H_2O$, having a sour taste, an intermediate in the metabolism of carbohydrates occurring in many fruits, esp. limes and lemons: used as a flavoring.

cit·ri·cul·ture (si′trə kul′chər), *n.* the cultivation of citrus fruits. —**cit′ri·cul′tur·ist,** *n.*

cit·rin (si′trin), *n.* *Biochem.* See **vitamin P.** [CITR(US) + -IN[2]]

cit·rine (si′trēn, -trīn, -trin), *adj.* **1.** pale-yellow; lemon-colored. —*n.* **2.** a translucent, yellow variety of quartz resembling topaz. Also called **false topaz, topaz quartz.** [CITR(US) + -INE[1]]

cit·ron (si′trən), *n.* **1.** a pale yellow fruit, larger than the lemon, borne by the tree *Citrus medica.* **2.** the tree itself. **3.** the rind of the fruit, candied and preserved. **4.** a grayish-green yellow. —*adj.* **5.** having the color citron. [< MF < It *citron(e)* < L *citr(us)* + It *-one* aug. suffix]

cit·ron·el·la (si′trə nel′ə), *n.* **1.** a fragrant grass, *Cymbopogon Nardus,* of southern Asia, cultivated as the source of citronella oil. **2.** See **citronella oil.** [< NL < F *citronelle* = *citron* CITRON + *-elle* dim. suffix]

cit·ron·el·lal (si′trə nel′al), *n.* *Chem.* a mixture of isometric aldehydes having the formula $C_9H_{17}CHO$, with a strong lemonlike odor, occurring in many essential oils: used chiefly as a flavoring agent and in the manufacture of perfume. [CITRONELL(A) + -AL[3]]

citronel′la oil′, a pungent oil, distilled from citronella, used in the manufacture of liniment, perfume, and soap, and as an insect repellant. Also called **citronella.**

cit′ron wood′, **1.** the wood of the citron. **2.** the wood of the sandarac.

cit·rus (si′trəs), *n., pl.* **-rus·es.** **1.** any rutaceous tree or shrub of the genus *Citrus,* which includes the citron, lemon, lime, orange, grapefruit, etc. —*adj.* **2.** Also, **cit′rous.** of or pertaining to such trees or shrubs. [< L: citrus tree, citron tree]

Cit·tà del Va·ti·ca·no (chēt tä′ del vä′tē kä′nô), Italian name of **Vatican City.**

cit·tern (sit′ərn), *n.* an old musical instrument related to the guitar, having a flat, pear-shaped soundbox and wire strings. Also, **cither, cithern, gittern.** [b. CITHER and GITTERN]

Cittern

cit·y (sit′ē), *n., pl.* **cit·ies.** **1.** a large or important town. **2.** an incorporated municipality, usually governed by a mayor. **3.** the inhabitants of a city collectively: *The entire city is mourning his death.* **4.** *Canadian.* a municipality of high rank, usually based on population. **5.** *Brit.* a borough, usually the seat of a bishop. **6. the City,** the commercial and financial area of London, England. **7.** city-state. [ME *cite* < OF *cite(t)* < L *cīvitāt-* (s. of *cīvitās*) citizenry, town = *cīvi(s)* citizen + *-tāt-* -TY[2]] —**Syn. 1.** See **community.**

cit·y-bred (sit′ē bred′), *adj.* reared in a city, esp. in a major metropolitan area.

cit′y desk′, a newspaper department responsible for editing local news.

cit′y ed′itor, **1.** a newspaper editor in charge of local news and assignments to reporters. **2.** *Brit.* a newspaper or magazine editor in charge of the financial and commercial news.

cit′y fa′ther, one of the officials and prominent citizens of a city.

cit′y hall′, (*often caps.*) the administration building of a city government.

cit′y man′ager, a person appointed by a city council to manage a city.

Cit′y of God′, the New Jerusalem; heaven.

cit′y plan′ning, the activity or profession of determining the future physical arrangement and condition of a community. —**cit′y plan′ner.**

cit′y room′, **1.** the room in which local news is handled for a newspaper, radio station, etc. **2.** the editorial staff of this room.

cit·y·scape (sit′ē skāp′), *n.* a view of a city, esp. a large urban center: *the cityscape of New York from the bay.* [CITY + *-scape,* as in *landscape*]

cit′y slick′er, *Informal.* slicker[1] (def. 2).

cit·y-state (sit′ē stāt′), *n.* a sovereign state consisting of an autonomous city with its dependencies.

cit·y·ward (sit′ē wərd), *adv.* to, toward, or in the direction of the city. Also, **cit′y·wards.** [ME]

Ciu·dad Bo·lí·var (syo͞o thäth′ bô lē′vär), a port in E Venezuela, on the Orinoco River. 40,111 (est. 1955).

Ciu·dad Juá·rez (syo͞o thäth′ hwä′res), a city in N Mexico, across the Rio Grande from El Paso, Texas. 385,082 (est. 1965).

Ciu·dad Tru·jil·lo (syo͞o-thäth′ tro͞o hē′yô), former name (1936–61) of **Santo Domingo.**

Ciu·dad Vic·to·ria (syo͞o-thäth′ bēk tô′ryä), a city in and the capital of Tamaulipas, in NE Mexico. 50,797 (1960).

Civet, *Civettictis civetta* (Total length 4 ft.; tail 1½ ft.)

civ., **1.** civil. **2.** civilian.

civ·et (siv′it), *n.* **1.** any catlike, carnivorous mammal of the subfamily *Viverrinae* that secretes a yellowish, unctuous substance with a strong musklike odor. **2.** this substance, used in perfumery. **3.** any of various animals related or similar to the civet, as the palm civet. Also called **civ′et cat′** (for defs. 1, 3). [< MF *civette* < It *zibett(o)* < Ar *zubād* civet perfume]

civ·ic (siv′ik), *adj.* **1.** of or pertaining to a city; municipal: *civic problems.* **2.** of or pertaining to citizenship; civil: *civic duties.* **3.** of citizens: *civic pride.* [< L *cīvic(us)* = *cīv(is)* citizen + *-icus* -IC] —**civ′i·cal·ly,** *adv.*

civ·ic-mind·ed (siv′ik mīn′did), *adj.* concerned with the well-being of the community. —**civ′ic-mind′ed·ly,** *adv.* —**civ′ic-mind′ed·ness,** *n.*

civ·ics (siv′iks), *n.* (*construed as sing.*) the science of civic affairs. [see CIVIC, -ICS]

civ·ies (siv′ēz), *n.pl.* *U.S. Informal.* civilian clothes, as distinguished from a military uniform. Also, **civvies.** [short for *civilian clothes*]

civ·il (siv′əl), *adj.* **1.** of or pertaining to citizens: *civil life; civil society.* **2.** of the commonwealth or state: *civil affairs.* **3.** of the ordinary life and affairs of citizens, as distinguished from military and ecclesiastical life and affairs. **4.** befitting a citizen: *a civil duty.* **5.** of social order or organized government; civilized. **6.** adhering to the norms of politeness and courtesy: *a civil reply.* **7.** (of divisions of time) legally recognized in the ordinary affairs of life: *the civil year.* **8.** *Law.* **a.** of or in agreement with Roman civil law. **b.** pertaining to the private rights of individuals and to legal proceedings connected with these. [< L *cīvīl(is)* = *cīv(is)* citizen + *-īlis* -IL] —**civ′il·ness,** *n.*
—**Syn. 6.** respectful, deferential, gracious, complaisant, suave, affable, urbane, courtly. CIVIL, AFFABLE, COURTEOUS, POLITE all imply avoidance of rudeness toward others. CIVIL suggests a minimum of observance of social requirements. AFFABLE suggests ease of approach, often with a touch of condescension. COURTEOUS implies positive, dignified, sincere, and thoughtful consideration for others. POLITE implies habitual courtesy, arising from a consciousness of one's training and the demands of good manners. —**Ant. 6.** boorish, churlish.

civ′il day′, *Astron.* day (def. 3c).

civ′il death′, *Law.* loss or deprivation of civil rights, sometimes consequent of conviction of some grave crime.

civ′il defense′, plans or activities organized by civilians for the protection of population and property in times of such emergencies as war, floods, etc.

civ′il disobe′dience, the refusal to obey certain governmental laws or demands for the purpose of influencing legislation or government policy, characterized by such nonviolent techniques as boycotting, picketing, and nonpayment of taxes.

civ′il engineer′, a person trained to design, build, and maintain public works, as roads, bridges, canals, dams, harbors, etc.

civ′il engineer′ing, the work or profession of a civil engineer.

ci·vil·ian (si vil′yən), *n.* **1.** a person engaged in civil pursuits, as distinguished from a soldier, sailor, etc. **2.** a person versed in or studying Roman or civil law. —*adj.* **3.** of, pertaining to, formed by, or administered by a civilian or civilians. [late ME < L (*jūs*) *cīvīl(e)* civil (law) + -IAN]

civ·i·li·sa·tion (siv′ə li zā′shən *or, esp. Brit.,* -lī-), *n.* *Chiefly Brit.* civilization.

civ·i·lise (siv′ə līz′), *v.t.,* **-lised, -lis·ing.** *Chiefly Brit.* civilize. —**civ′i·lis′a·ble,** *adj.* —**civ′i·lis′er,** *n.*

civ·i·lised (siv′ə līzd′), *adj.* *Chiefly Brit.* civilized.

ci·vil·i·ty (si vil′i tē), *n., pl.* **-ties.** **1.** courtesy; politeness. **2.** a polite attention or expression: *an exchange of civilities.* **3.** *Archaic.* civilization; culture; good breeding. [late ME *civilite* < MF < L *cīvīlitāt-* (s. of *cīvīlitās*) courtesy]

civ·i·li·za·tion (siv′ə li zā′shən *or, esp. Brit.* -lī-), *n.* **1.** an advanced state of human society, in which a high level of culture, science, industry, and government has been reached. **2.** those people or nations that have reached such a state. **3.** the type of culture of a specific place, time, or group: *Greek civilization.* **4.** the act of civilizing or process of becoming civilized. **5.** cultural and intellectual refinement. **6.** cities or populated areas in general, as opposed to unpopulated or wilderness areas. **7.** modern comforts and conveniences, as made possible by science and technology. Also, *esp. Brit.,* **civilisation.**

civ·i·lize (siv′ə līz′), *v.t.,* **-lized, -liz·ing.** to make civil; bring out of a primitive or uneducated state; elevate in social and private life; enlighten; refine. Also, *esp. Brit.,* **civilise.** —**civ′i·liz′a·ble,** *adj.* —**civ′i·liz′er,** *n.*

civ·i·lized (siv′ə līzd′), *adj.* **1.** having an advanced culture, society, etc. **2.** polite; well-bred; refined. **3.** of or pertaining to civilized people. Also, *esp. Brit.,* **civilised.**

civ′il law′, **1.** the body of laws of a state or nation regulating ordinary private matters, as distinct from laws regulating criminal, political, or military matters. **2.** *Rom. Hist.* the body of law proper to the city or state of Rome, as distinct from that common to all nations. **3.** the system of law derived from Roman law, as distinct from common law and canon or ecclesiastical law. —**civ′il-law′,** *adj.*

civ′il lib′erty, the liberty of an individual to exercise those rights guaranteed by the laws of a country.

civ·il·ly (siv′ə lē), *adv.* **1.** in accordance with civil law. **2.** politely; courteously.

civ′il mar′riage, a marriage performed by a government official rather than a clergyman.

civ′il rights′, (*often caps.*) **1.** the rights to personal liberty established by the 13th and 14th Amendments to the U.S. Constitution and certain Congressional Acts. **2.** the rights to full legal, economic, and social equality extended to Negroes.

civil-rights (siv′əl rīts′), *adj.* **1.** of or pertaining to civil rights: *a civil-rights law.* **2.** for or promoting the cause of civil rights: *a civil-rights worker.*

civ′il serv′ant, *Chiefly Brit.* a civil-service employee.

civ′il serv′ice, **1.** those branches of public service concerned with all governmental functions outside the armed services. **2.** the body of persons employed in these branches. **3.** a system or method of appointing government employees on the basis of competitive examinations, rather than by political patronage. —**civ′il-serv′ice,** *adj.*

civ′il war′, **1.** a war between political factions or regions within the same country. **2.** (*caps.*) *U.S.* the war between the North and the South, 1861–65. Cf. **Spanish Civil War.**

civ·ism (siv′iz əm), *n.* good citizenship. [< F *civisme* < L *cīv(is)* citizen + F *-isme* -ISM]

civ·vies (siv′ēz), *n.pl.* civies.

CJ, Chief Justice.

ck., **1.** cask. **2.** check.

ckw., clockwise.

Cl, *Chem.* chlorine.

cl, centiliter; centiliters.

C/L, **1.** carload. **2.** carload lot. **3.** cash letter.

cl., **1.** carload. **2.** centiliter; centiliters. **3.** claim. **4.** class. **5.** classification. **6.** clause. **7.** clearance. **8.** clerk. **9.** cloth.

c.l., **1.** carload. **2.** carload lot. **3.** centerline. **4.** civil law.

clab·ber (klab′ər), *n.* **1.** bonnyclabber. —*v.i.* **2.** (of milk) to become thick in souring. [< Ir *clabar* short for *bainne clabair* BONNYCLABBER]

cla·chan (klä′ᴋʜən, klä′-), *n.* *Scot., Irish.* a small village. [< ScotGael = *clach* stone + *-an* dim. suffix]

clack (klak), *v.i.* **1.** to make a quick, sharp sound, or a succession of such sounds, as by striking or cracking. **2.** to talk rapidly and continually, or with sharpness and abruptness; chatter. **3.** to cluck or cackle. —*v.t.* **4.** to utter by clacking. **5.** to cause to clack. —*n.* **6.** a clacking sound. **7.** something that clacks, as a rattle. **8.** rapid, continual talk; chatter. [ME *clack(en)*; imit.] —**clack′er,** *n.*

Clack·man·nan (klak man′ən), *n.* a county in central Scotland. 41,391 (1961); 55 sq. mi. *Co. seat:* Clackmannan. Also called **Clack·man·nan·shire** (klak man′ən shēr′, -shər).

clack′ valve′, a valve having a hinged flap permitting flow only in the direction in which the flap opens.

Clac·to·ni·an (klak tō′nē ən), *adj.* of, pertaining to, or characteristic of a Lower Paleolithic culture in which tools were made from stone flakes. [after *Clacton-on-Sea,* English town where the tools were first unearthed; see -IAN]

clad[1] (klad), *v.* a pt. and pp. of **clothe.** [ME *cladd(e),* OE *clāthod(e)* clothed. See CLOTHE]

clad[2] (klad), *v.t.,* **clad, clad·ding.** to bond a metal to (another metal), esp. to provide with a protective coat. [special use of CLAD[1]]

clad-, var. of **clado-** before a vowel.

clad·ding (klad′ing), *n.* **1.** the act or process of bonding one metal to another, usually to protect the inner metal from corrosion. **2.** metal bonded to an inner core of another metal.

clado-, a learned borrowing from Greek meaning "branch," used in the formation of compound words: *cladophyll.* Also, *esp. before a vowel,* **clad-.** [comb. form of Gk *kládos*]

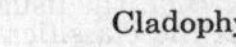
Cladophyll

clad·o·phyll (klad′ə fil), *n.* *Bot.* a leaflike flattened branch. Also called **clad·ode**(klad′ōd).

claim (klām), *v.t.* **1.** to demand by or as by virtue of a right; demand as a right or as due: *to claim an estate by inheritance.* **2.** to assert and demand the recognition of (a right, title, possession, etc.); assert one's right to: *to claim payment.* **3.** to assert or maintain as a fact: *She claimed that he was telling the truth.* **4.** to require as due or fitting: *to claim respect.* —*n.* **5.** a demand for something as due; an assertion of a right or an alleged right: *He made unreasonable claims on the doctor's time.* **6.** an assertion of something as a fact: *He made no claims to originality.* **7.** a right to claim or demand; a just title to something: *His claim to the heavyweight title is disputed.* **8.** something that is claimed, esp. a piece of public land for which formal request is made for mining or other purposes. **9.** a payment demanded in accordance with an insurance policy, a workmen's compensation law, etc.: *We filed a claim for compensation from the company.* **10. lay claim to,** to declare oneself entitled to: *I have never laid claim to being an expert in this field.* [ME *claim(en)* < MF *claime(r)* < L *clāmāre* to cry out. See CLAMANT] —**claim′a·ble,** *adj.* —**claim′er,** *n.* —**Syn. 1.** See **demand. 5.** request, requisition, call.

claim·ant (klā′mənt), *n.* a person who makes a claim.

claim′ing race′, *Horse Racing.* a race in which any horse entered can be purchased at a fixed price by anyone who has made a bid or claim before the start of the race. Cf. **selling race.**

claim-jump·er (klām′jum′pər), *n.* a person who seizes another's claim of land. —**claim′-jump′ing,** *n.*

Clair (klâr; *Fr.* klᴇʀ), *n.* **Re·né** (ʀə nā′), 1898–1981, French motion-picture director and writer.

clair·voy·ance (klâr voi′əns), *n.* **1.** the alleged supernatural power of seeing objects or actions removed from natural viewing. **2.** quick, intuitive knowledge of things and people; sagacity. [< F = *clairvoy(ant)* CLAIRVOYANT + *-ance* -ANCE] —**Syn. 2.** intuition, discernment, vision.

clair·voy·ant (klâr voi′ənt), *adj.* **1.** having the alleged supernatural power of seeing objects or actions beyond the range of natural vision. **2.** of, by, or pertaining to clairvoyance. —*n.* **3.** a clairvoyant person. [< F = *clair* CLEAR + *voyant* seeing (*voi(r)* (to) see (< L *vidēre*) + *-ant* -ANT)] —**clair·voy′ant·ly,** *adv.*

Clam, genus *Anodonta*

clam (klam), *n., v.,* **clammed, clam·ming.** —*n.* **1.** any of various bivalve mollusks, esp. certain edible species as the quahog and the softshell clam. **2.** *U.S. Informal.* a secretive or silent person. —*v.i.* **3.** to gather or dig clams. **4. clam up,** *Slang.* to restrain oneself from talking; withhold information. [short for *clamshell,* i.e., bivalve with a shell that clamps; ME, OE *clamm* fetter, grasp; c. G *Klamm* fetter; akin to CLAMP[1]]

cla·mant (klā′mənt), *adj.* **1.** clamorous; noisy. **2.** compelling or pressing; urgent. [< L *clāmant-* (s. of *clāmāns,* prp. of *clāmāre* to cry out) = *clām-* (see CLAIM) + *-ant-* -ANT] —**cla′mant·ly,** *adv.*

clam·a·to·ri·al (klam′ə tōr′ē əl, -tôr′-), *adj.* of or pertaining to the *Clamatores,* a large group of passerine birds with little power of song, as the flycatchers. [< NL *clāmātōr(es),* pl. of L *clāmātor* bawler = *clāmāt(us)* (ptp. of *clāmāre* to cry out) + *-or* -OR[2] + -IAL]

clam·bake (klam′bāk′), *n.* **1.** a seashore picnic at which clams and other foods are baked, usually on hot stones under seaweed. **2.** *Informal.* any social gathering, esp. a very noisy one.

clam·ber (klam′bər, -ər), *v.t., v.i.* **1.** to climb, using both feet and hands; climb with effort or difficulty. —*n.* **2.** the act or an instance of clambering. [late ME *clambre* = *clamb-* (akin to CLIMB) + *-re* -ER[6]] —**clam′ber·er,** *n.*

clam·jam·fry (klam jam′frē, kläm jäm′-), *n.* *Scot. and North Eng.* **1.** the rabble; the mass of undistinguished people. **2.** insincere or impertinent talk. Also, **clam·jam′phrie.** [?]

clam·my (klam′ē), *adj.,* **-mi·er, -mi·est. 1.** covered with a cold, sticky moisture; cold and damp: *clammy hands.* **2.** sickly; morbid: *a clammy feeling.* [perh. < Flem *klammig;* akin to OE *clām* mud, clay; c. MD *klēm*] —**clam′mi·ly,** *adv.* —**clam′mi·ness,** *n.*

clam·or[1] (klam′ər), *n.* **1.** a persistent uproar, as from a crowd of people. **2.** a vehement expression of desire or dissatisfaction: *The clamor of the dissenting members broke up the meeting.* **3.** popular outcry: *The senators could not ignore the clamor against higher taxation.* **4.** any loud and continued noise: *the clamor of traffic.* —*v.i.* **5.** to make a clamor; raise an outcry. —*v.t.* **6.** to drive, force, influence, etc., by clamoring: *The newspapers clamored him out of office.* **7.** to utter noisily: *They clamored their demands at the meeting.* **8.** *Obs.* to disturb with clamor. Also, *esp. Brit.,* **clam′our.** [ME *clamor* < L = *clām-* (see CLAIM) + *-or* -OR[1]; r. ME *clamour* < MF < L *clāmōr-* (s. of *clāmor*)] —**Syn. 4.** See **noise.**

clam·or[2] (klam′ər), *v.t.* *Obs.* to silence. [? sp. var. of *clammer,* obs. var. of CLAMBER in sense to clutch, hence reduce to silence]

clam·or·ous (klam′ər əs), *adj.* **1.** full of clamor; vociferous; noisy. **2.** vigorous in demands or complaints. —**clam′or·ous·ly,** *adv.* —**clam′or·ous·ness,** *n.*

clamp[1] (klamp), *n.* **1.** a device for strengthening or supporting objects or fastening them together. **2.** an appliance with opposite parts that may be brought closer together to hold or compress something. **3.** one of a pair of movable pieces, made of lead or other soft material, for covering the jaws of a vise and enabling it to grasp without bruising. —*v.t.* **4.** to fasten with or fix in a clamp. **5. clamp down,** *Informal.* to impose or increase controls; become more strict: *The government is clamping down on tax dodgers.* [late ME (n.) < MD *clampe* clamp, cleat; c. MLG *klampe*]

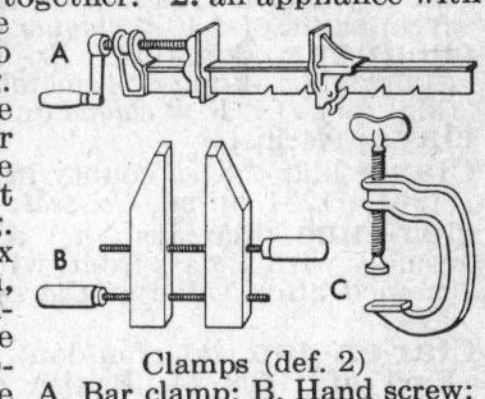

Clamps (def. 2)
A, Bar clamp; B, Hand screw; C, C Clamp

clamp[2] (klamp), *v.i.* to walk or tread in a heavy, clumsy, or halting manner; clump. [imit.; akin to CLUMP]

clamp·down (klamp′doun′), *n.* crackdown.

clamp·er (klam′pər, kläm′-), *n.* a spiked metal plate worn on the sole of a shoe to prevent slipping on ice.

clamp′ truck′, a vehicle having movable parallel arms for clasping and carrying large objects.

clam·shell (klam′shel′), *n.* **1.** the shell of a clam. **2.** a dredging bucket opening at the bottom, consisting of two similar pieces hinged together at the top.

clam·worm (klam′wûrm′), *n.* any of several burrowing polychaete worms of the genus *Nereis,* used as bait for fishing.

clan (klan), *n.* **1.** a group of families or households, as among the Scottish Highlanders, the heads of which claim descent from a common ancestor. **2.** a group of people of common descent; family. **3.** a group of people, as a clique, set, or society, united by some common trait or interest. **4.** *Anthropol.* the principal kinship unit of tribal organization based on unilateral descent; sib. [< ScotGael *clann* < OIr *cland* offspring < L *planta* scion, PLANT]

clan·des·tine (klan des′tin), *adj.* done in secrecy or concealment, esp. for purposes of subversion or deception; private or surreptitious: *clandestine meetings.* [< L *clandestīn(us)* = *clam* secretly + *-des-* (< *diēs* day) + *-tīnus* adj. suffix; see VESPERTINE] —**clan·des′tine·ly,** *adv.* —**clan·des′tine·ness,** *n.* —**Syn.** hidden, underhand, confidential. —**Ant.** open.

clang (klang), *v.i.* **1.** to give out a loud, resonant sound, as that produced by a large bell or two heavy pieces of metal striking together. **2.** to move with such sounds: *The fire engine clanged down the street.* —*v.t.* **3.** to cause to resound or ring loudly. —*n.* **4.** a clanging sound. [< L *clang(ere)* (to) resound, clang]

clang·or (klang′ər, klang′gər), *n.* **1.** a loud, resonant sound; clang. **2.** clamorous noise. —*v.i.* **3.** to make a clangor; clang. Also, *esp. Brit.,* **clang′our.** [< L: loud sound, noise = *clang(ere)* (to) CLANG + *-or* -OR[1]] —**clang′or·ous,** *adj.* —**clang′or·ous·ly,** *adv.*

clank (klangk), *n.* **1.** a sharp, hard, nonresonant sound, like that produced by two pieces of metal striking, one against the other: *the clank of chains.* —*v.i.* **2.** to make such a sound. **3.** to move with such sounds: *The old jalopy clanked up the hill.* —*v.t.* **4.** to cause to make a sharp sound, as metal in collision. [< D *klank* clinking sound] —**clank′ing·ly,** *adv.*

clan·nish (klan′ish), *adj.* **1.** of, pertaining to, or characteristic of a clan. **2.** inclined to associate exclusively with the members of one's own group; cliquish. **3.** imbued with or influenced by the sentiments, prejudices, or the like, of a clan. —**clan′nish·ly,** *adv.* —**clan′nish·ness,** *n.*

clans·man (klanz′mən), *n., pl.* **-men.** a member of a clan. —**clans′man·ship′,** *n.*

clans·wom·an (klanz′wo͝om′ən), *n., pl.* **-wom·en** (-wim′-ən). a female clansman.

clap[1] (klap), *v.,* **clapped** or (*Archaic*) **clapt; clap·ping;** *n.* —*v.t.* **1.** to strike (an object) against something quickly and forcefully, producing an abrupt, sharp sound. **2.** to strike the palms of (one's hands) against one another resoundingly, and usually repeatedly, esp. to express approval. **3.** to strike (someone) amicably with a light, open-handed slap, as in greeting, encouragement, or the like: *He clapped his friend on the back.* **4.** to bring together forcefully (facing surfaces of the same object): *She clapped the book shut.* **5.** to applaud (a performance, speech, speaker, etc.) by clapping the hands. **6.** (of a bird) to flap or beat (the wings). **7.** to put or place quickly or forcefully. —*v.i.* **8.** to make an abrupt, sharp sound, as of flat surfaces striking against one another: *The shutters clapped in the wind.* **9.** to move or strike with such a sound: *She clapped across the room in her slippers.* **10.** to clap the hands, as to express approval; applaud. **11. clap eyes on.** See **eye** (def. 20). **12. clap hold of,** *Naut.* to take hold of. **13. clap on,** *Naut.* **a.** to attach. **b.** to set (additional sails). —*n.* **14.** the act or an instance of clapping. **15.** the abrupt, sharp sound produced by clapping. **16.** a resounding blow; slap. **17.** a loud and abrupt or explosive noise, as of thunder. **18.** a sudden stroke, blow, or act. **19.** *Obs.* a sudden mishap. [ME *clapp(en),* OE *clæppan;* c. MLG *kleppen*]

clap[2] (klap), *n.* *Slang.* gonorrhea (often prec. by *the*). [akin to MF *clapoir* bubo, *clapier* brothel, OPr *clapier* warren]

clap·board (klab′ərd, klap′bōrd′, -bôrd′), *n.* **1.** a long, thin board, thicker along one edge than along the other, used in covering the outer walls of buildings, being laid horizontally, the thick edge of each board overlapping the thin edge of the board below it. See illus. at **siding.** —*adj.* **2.** of or made of clapboard. —*v.t.* **3.** to cover with clapboards. [< MD *klap(holt)* (*klap(pen)* (to) clap + *holt* wood; (see CLAP[1], defs. 4, 7) + BOARD]

clap·per (klap′ər), *n.* **1.** a person or thing that claps or produces a sharp, clapping sound. **2.** the tongue of a bell.

clap·per claw (klap′ər klô′), *v.t.* *Archaic.* **1.** to claw or scratch with the hand and nails. **2.** to revile.

clapt (klapt), *v.* *Archaic.* pt. or pp. of **clap.**

clap·trap (klap′trap′), *n.* **1.** pretentious but insincere language. **2.** any artifice or expedient for winning applause or impressing the public.

claque (klak), *n.* **1.** a group of persons hired to applaud an act or performer, as in a theater or night club. **2.** a group of sycophants. [< F < *claquer* to clap]

cla·queur (kla kûr′; *Fr.* klA kœr′), *n., pl.* **-queurs** (-kûrz′; *Fr.* -kœr′). a member of a claque. Also, **claqu·er** (klak′ər). [< F = *claque* CLAQUE + *-eur* -ER[1]]

clar., clarinet.

Clare (klâr), *n.* a county in W Republic of Ireland. 73,702 (1961); 1231 sq. mi. *Co. seat:* Ennis.

clar·ence (klar′əns), *n.* a closed, four-wheeled carriage, usually with a glass front, with seats inside for four persons. [named after Duke of *Clarence* (1765–1837), later William IV]

Clar·en·don (klar′ən dən), *n.* **1. Edward Hyde, 1st Earl of,** 1609–74, British statesman and historian. **2. Council of,** the ecumenical council (1164) occasioned by the opposition of Thomas à Becket to Henry II. **3.** (*l.c.*) *Print.* a condensed form of printing type, like roman in outline but with thicker serifs.

Clare′ of Assi′si, Saint, 1194–1253, Italian nun: founder of the Franciscan order of nuns. Also, **Clar′a of Assi′si.**

clar·et (klar′it), *n.* **1.** a dry, red table wine, esp. that produced in the Bordeaux region of France. **2.** Also called **clar′et red′.** a deep purplish red. [late ME < MF (*vin*) *claret* clearish (wine) = *clar-* CLEAR + *-et* adj. suffix]

clar′et cup′, an iced beverage made of claret and carbonated water with lemon juice, brandy or other spirits, fruits, sugar, etc.

clar·i·fy (klar′ə fī′), *v.,* **-fied, -fy·ing.** —*v.t.* **1.** to make (an idea, statement, etc.) clear or intelligible; to free from ambiguity. **2.** to remove impurities from: *to clarify butter.* **3.** to free (the mind, intelligence, etc.) from confusion; revive. —*v.i.* **4.** to become clear, pure, or intelligible: *He was certain that the political situation would eventually clarify.* [late ME < MF *clarifi(er)* < LL *clārificāre* = L *clār(us)* clear + *-ificāre* -IFY] —**clar′i·fi·ca′tion,** *n.* —**clar′i·fi′er,** *n.*

Clarinet

clar·i·net (klar′ə net′), *n.* a woodwind instrument in the form of a cylindrical tube with a single reed attached to its mouthpiece. Also, **clar·i·o·net** (klar′ē ə net′). [< F *clarinette* = OF *clarin* clarion + *-ette* -ETTE] —**clar′i·net′ist, clar′i·net′tist,** *n.*

clar·i·on (klar′ē ən), *adj.* **1.** clear and shrill. —*n.* **2.** an ancient trumpet with a curved shape. **3.** the sound of this instrument. **4.** any similar sound. [ME < ML *clāriōn-* (s. of *clāriō*) trumpet = *clār-* CLEAR + *-iōn-* -ION]

clar·i·ty (klar′i tē), *n.* **1.** the state or quality of being clear or transparent to the eye; clearness: *the clarity of pure water.* **2.** clearness or lucidity as to perception or understanding; freedom from ambiguity: *a difficult proposition presented with such clarity that everyone understood.* [ME *clarite* < L *clāritās* (see CLEAR, -ITY); r. ME *clarte* < MF]

Clark (klärk), *n.* **1. Champ** (champ), (*James Beauchamp*), 1850–1921, U.S. political leader: Speaker of the House 1911–1919. **2. George Rogers,** 1752–1818, U.S. soldier and explorer. **3. Mark Wayne,** 1896–1984, U.S. general. **4. Thomas Campbell** (*Tom*), 1899–1977, associate justice of the U.S. Supreme Court, 1949–67. **5. William,** 1770–1838, U.S. soldier and explorer (brother of George R. Clark): on expedition with Meriwether Lewis 1804–06.

clark·i·a (klär′kē ə), *n.* any onagraceous herb of the genus *Clarkia,* of the western U.S., having narrow leaves and ornamental rose or purple flowers. [named after William CLARK; see -IA]

Clarks·burg (klärks′bûrg), *n.* a city in N West Virginia, on the Monongahela River. 24,864 (1970).

Clarks·ville (klärks′vil), *n.* a city in N Tennessee. 31,719 (1970).

clar·o (klär′ō), *adj., n., pl.* **clar·os.** —*adj.* **1.** (of cigars) light-colored and, usually, mild. —*n.* **2.** such a cigar. [< Sp: CLEAR]

clar·y (klâr′ē), *n., pl.* **clar·ies.** any of several plants of the genus *Salvia,* esp. *S. Sclarea,* grown as ornamentals. [late ME (*s*)*clar(re)y(e),* OE *slarege* < ML *sclareia*]

-clase, a combining form used in names of minerals to indicate a particular type of cleavage: *euclase.* [< F < Gk *klásis* a breaking]

clash (klash), *v.i.* **1.** to make a loud, harsh noise: *The gears of the old car clashed and grated.* **2.** to collide, esp. noisily: *The cymbals clashed.* **3.** to conflict; disagree. **4.** (of juxtaposed colors) to be offensive to the eye. **5.** to engage in a physical conflict or contest (often fol. by *with*): *The Yankees clash with the White Sox next Sunday. The armies clashed in battle.* —*v.t.* **6.** to strike with a resounding or violent collision. **7.** to produce (sound) by or as by collision: *The tower bell clashed its mournful note.* —*n.* **8.** a loud, harsh noise, as of a collision. **9.** a conflict; opposition, esp. of views or interests. **10.** a battle, fight, or skirmish. [b. CLAP[1] and DASH[1]] —**clash′er,** *n.* —**clash′ing·ly,** *adv.* —**Syn. 1.** clang, crash. **9.** disagreement, dispute. —**Ant. 9.** agreement, cooperation.

-clasis, a learned borrowing from Greek meaning "a breaking," used in the formation of compound words: *thromboclasis.* [< NL < Gk *klásis*]

clasp (klasp, kläsp), *n., v.,* **clasped** or (*Archaic*) **claspt; clasp·ing.** —*n.* **1.** a device, usually of metal, for fastening together two or more things or parts of the same thing: *a clasp on a necklace.* **2.** a firm grasp or embrace. **3.** cluster (def. 3). —*v.t.* **4.** to fasten with or as with a clasp. **5.** to furnish with a clasp. **6.** to seize, grasp, or grip with the hand: *He clasped the club in his right hand.* **7.** to hold in a tight embrace; hug. [ME < ?] —**clasp′er,** *n.* —**Syn. 1.** brooch, pin, clip, hook, catch. **2.** hug. **4.** clip, hook, catch.

clasp′ knife′, a large pocketknife having a blade or blades that can be folded into the handle.

claspt (klaspt, kläspt), *v.* *Archaic.* pt. or pp. of **clasp.**

class (klas, kläs), *n.* **1.** a number of persons or things regarded as forming a group by reason of common attributes, characteristics, qualities, or traits; kind; sort. **2.** any division of persons or things according to rank or grade: *Do you know anything about second-class hotels in France?* **3.** *U.S.* a number of pupils in a school, or of students in a college, pursuing the same studies, ranked together, or graduated in the same year: *He got his degree from Ohio State, class of '59.* **4.** a group of students meeting regularly to study a subject under the guidance of a teacher. **5.** the period during which a group of students meets for instruction. **6.** *Sociol.* a social stratum sharing basic economic, political, or cultural characteristics, and having the same social position: *Mexico has a growing middle class.* **7.** the system of dividing society; caste. **8.** social rank, esp. high rank. **9.** the members of a given group in society, regarded as a single entity. **10.** *Slang.* elegance of dress and behavior: *His girl friend has real class.* **11.** any of several grades of accommodations available on ships, airplanes, and the like: *We bought tickets for first class.* **12.** *Biol.* the usual major subdivision of a phylum or division in the classification of plants and animals, usually consisting of several orders. **13.** *Gram.* See **form class. 14. in a class by itself** or **oneself,** having no peer; unequaled: *As a cook she was in a class by herself.* **15. the classes,** the higher ranks of society, as distinguished from the masses. —*v.t.* **16.** to place or arrange in a class; classify: *to class justice with wisdom.* —*v.i.* **17.** to take or have a place in a particular class: *those who class as believers.* [earlier *classis,* pl. *classes* < L: class, division, fleet, army; sing. class back formation from pl.] —**class′a·ble,** *adj.* —**class′er,** *n.*

class., **1.** classic. **2.** classical. **3.** classification. **4.** classified.

class′ ac′tion, a legal proceeding against a single party filed on behalf of all people having a common complaint. —**class′-ac′tion,** *adj.*

class′ con′sciousness, awareness of one's social or economic rank in society. —**class-con·scious** (klas′kon′shəs, kläs′-), *adj.*

class′ day′, (*sometimes cap.*) a day prior to commencement set aside for a celebration by the graduating class in American colleges and schools.

clas·sic (klas′ik), *adj.* **1.** of the first or highest class or rank. *a classic piece of work.* **2.** serving as a standard, model, or guide: *a classic method.* **3.** of or pertaining to Greek and Roman antiquity, esp. with reference to literature and art. **4.** modeled upon or imitating the style or thought of ancient Greece and Rome. **5.** of or adhering to an established set of artistic or scientific standards or methods: *a classic example of mid-Victorian architecture.* **6.** basic; fundamental. **7.** of enduring interest, quality, or style: *a classic design.* **8.** of literary or historical renown: *the classic haunts of famous writers.* **9.** traditional or typical: *a classic comedy routine.* **10.** definitive: *the classic reference work on ornithology.* —*n.* **11.** an author or a literary production of the first rank, esp. in Greek or Latin. **12. the classics,** the literature of ancient Greece and Rome. **13.** an artist or artistic production considered a standard. **14.** a work that is considered definitive in its field. **15.** something noteworthy of its kind and worth remembering: *His reply was a classic.* **16.** *Archaic.* a classicist. Also **classical** (for defs. 1–5, 8, 10). [< L *classic(us)* belonging to a class, belonging to the first or highest class = *class(is)* CLASS + *-icus* -IC]

clas·si·cal (klas′i kəl), *adj.* **1.** of, pertaining to, or characteristic of Greek and Roman antiquity: *The classical period.* **2.** (*cap.*) pertaining to or designating the style of the fine arts, esp. painting and sculpture, developed in Greece during the 5th and 4th centuries B.C. Cf. **archaic** (def. 3), **Hellenistic** (def. 5). **3.** *Archit.* noting or pertaining to the architectures of ancient Greece and Rome, to any of several styles of architecture closely imitating these, or to architectural details or motifs adapted from them. **4.** conforming to ancient Greek and Roman models in literature or art, or to later systems modeled upon them. **5.** pertaining to or versed in the ancient classics: *a classical scholar.* **6.** marked by classicism: *classical simplicity.* **7.** of or pertaining to a style of literature and art characterized by conformity to established treatments, taste, or critical standards, and by attention to form with the general effect of regularity, simplicity, balance, proportion, and controlled emotion (contrasted with *romantic*). **8.** *Music.* **a.** of, pertaining to, or constituting the formally and artistically more sophisticated and enduring types of music, as distinguished from popular and folk music and jazz. Classical music includes symphonies, operas, sonatas, song cycles, and lieder. **b.** of, pertaining to, characterized by, or adhering to the well-ordered, chiefly homophonic musical style of the latter half of the 18th and early 19th centuries. **9.** relating to or teaching academic branches of knowledge, as the humanities, general sciences, etc. (as distinguished from technical subjects). **10.** (of a given field of knowledge) accepted as standard and authoritative, as distinguished from novel or experimental: *classical physics.* —**clas′si·cal′i·ty, clas′si·cal·ness,** *n.* —**clas′si·cal·ly,** *adv.*

clas′sical econom′ics, a system of economic thought developed by Adam Smith, Jeremy Bentham, Thomas Malthus, and David Ricardo, advocating minimum governmental intervention, free enterprise, and free trade, considering labor the source of wealth and dealing with problems concerning overpopulation. —**clas′sical econ′omist.**

clas′sical mechan′ics, *Physics.* the branch of mechanics based on Newton's laws of motion and applicable to systems that are so large that Planck's constant can be regarded as negligibly small (distinguished from *quantum mechanics*).

clas·si·cise (klas′i sīz′), *v.t., v.i.,* **-cised, -cis·ing.** *Chiefly Brit.* classicize.

clas·si·cism (klas′i siz′əm), *n.* **1.** the principles of classic literature and art. **2.** adherence to such principles. **3.** the classical style in literature and art, or adherence to its principles (contrasted with *romanticism*). Cf. **classical** (def. 7). **4.** classical scholarship or learning. Also, **clas·si·cal·ism** (klas′i kə liz′əm).

clas·si·cist (klas′i sist), *n.* **1.** a person who advocates study of the classics. **2.** an adherent of classicism in literature or art (contrasted with *romanticist*). **3.** an authority on the classics; a classical scholar. Also, **clas·si·cal·ist** (klas′i kə list). —**clas′si·cis′tic,** *adj.*

clas·si·cize (klas′i sīz′), *v.,* **-cized, -ciz·ing.** —*v.t.* **1.** to make classic. —*v.i.* **2.** to conform to the classic style. Also, *esp. Brit.,* **classicise.**

clas·si·fi·ca·tion (klas′ə fə kā′shən), *n.* **1.** the act of classifying. **2.** the result of classifying or being classified. **3.** one of the groups or classes into which things may be or have been classified. **4.** *Biol.* the assignment of plants and animals to groups within a system of categories distinguished by structure, origin, etc. The usual series of categories is *phylum* (in zoology) or *division* (in botany), *class, order, family, genus, species,* and *variety.* **5.** *U.S. Govt., Mil.* the category, as *restricted, confidential, secret,* or *top secret,* to which information, a document, etc., is assigned, based on the degree of protection considered necessary to safeguard it from unauthorized use. **6.** *Library Science.* any of various systems for arranging books and other materials, esp. according to subject or format. [< L *classi(s)* CLASS + -FICATION] —**clas·si·fi·ca·to·ry** (klə sif′ə kə tôr′ē, -tôr′ē, klas′ə fə- *or, esp. Brit.,* klas′ə fə kā′tə rē), *adj.* —**clas′si·fi·ca′tion·al,** *adj.*

clas·si·fied (klas′ə fīd′), *adj.* **1.** arranged or distributed according to class. **2.** *U.S. Govt., Mil.* (of information, a document, etc.) assigned to a classification that limits its use to authorized persons. Cf. **classification** (def. 5). **3.** containing classified ads: *the classified section of a newspaper.* —*n.* **4.** See **classified ad.**

clas′sified ad′ a brief advertisement, as in a newspaper or magazine, typically one column wide, that offers or requests jobs, houses, etc. Also called **classified, clas′sified adver′tise′ment, want ad.**

clas·si·fi·er (klas′ə fī′ər), *n.* **1.** a person or thing that classifies. **2.** *Chem.* a device for separating solids of different characteristics by controlled rates of settling.

clas·si·fy (klas′ə fī′), *v.t.,* **-fied, -fy·ing. 1.** to arrange or organize by classes; order according to class. **2.** *U.S. Govt., Mil.* **a.** to assign a classification to (information, a document, etc.). **b.** to limit the availability of (information, a document, etc.) to authorized persons. **c.** to designate the availability of for military service: *He was classified 1-A in the draft.* [< L *classi(s)* CLASS + -FY] —**clas′si·fi′a·ble,** *adj.*

clas·sis (klas′is), *n., pl.* **clas·ses** (klas′ēz). (in certain Reformed churches) **1.** the organization of pastors and elders that governs a group of local churches; a presbytery. **2.** the group of churches governed by such an organization. [< L: class]

class·less (klas′lis, kläs′-), *adj.* **1.** of or pertaining to a society in which there are no economic or social distinctions. **2.** (of an individual) not in a social class or group.

class·mate (klas′māt′, kläs′-), *n.* a member of the same class at a school or college.

class′ mean′ing, *Gram.* the meaning of a form class, common to all members of the class, as in the meaning of number common to plural and singular nouns and verbs.

class′ num′ber, *Library Science.* a classification number on a book indicating its location on the shelves.

class·room (klas′rōōm′, -rŏŏm′, kläs′-), *n.* a room in a school or college in which classes meet.

class′ strug′gle, (in Marxist thought) the struggle for political and economic power carried on between capitalists and workers.

class·work (klas′wûrk′, kläs′-), *n.* **1.** the written or oral work done in a classroom by a student (distinguished from *homework*). **2.** work done in a classroom by teacher and students jointly.

class·y (klas′ē), *adj.,* **class·i·er, class·i·est.** *Slang.* elegant; stylish. —**class′i·ly,** *adv.* —**class′i·ness,** *n.*

clas·tic (klas′tik), *adj. Geol.* noting or pertaining to rock or rocks composed of fragments or particles of older rocks or previously existing solid matter; fragmental. [< Gk *klastó(s)* broken in pieces (*klas-* var. s. of *klân* to break + *-tos* verbal adj. suffix) + -IC]

clath·rate (klath′rāt), *adj. Biol.* resembling a lattice; divided or marked like latticework. [< L *clāthrāt(us)* (ptp. of *clāthrāre* to furnish with lattice) < Doric Gk *klaithr(on)* a bar + L *-ātus* -ATE[1]]

clat·ter (klat′ər), *v.i.* **1.** to make a loud, rattling sound, as that produced by hard objects striking rapidly one against the other: *The shutters clattered in the wind.* **2.** to move rapidly with such a sound: *The iron-wheeled cart clattered down the street.* **3.** to talk fast and noisily; chatter. —*v.t.* **4.** to cause to clatter: *The maid clattered the pots and pans in the sink.* —*n.* **5.** a rattling noise or series of rattling noises: *The stagecoach made a terrible clatter on the wooden bridge.* **6.** noisy disturbance; din; racket. **7.** idle talk; gossip. [ME *claterin,* OE *clatr-* (in *clatrunge*); c. D *klateren* to rattle] —**clat′ter·er,** *n.* —**clat′ter·ing·ly,** *adv.* —**clat′ter·y,** *adj.*

Clau·del (klō del′), *n.* **Paul (Louis Charles)** (pôl lwē shARl), 1868–1955, French diplomat, poet, and dramatist.

clau·di·ca·tion (klô′də kā′shən), *n.* a limp. [< L *claudicātiōn-* (s. of *claudicātiō*) = *claudic(āre)* (to) limp (*claud(us)* lame + *-ic-* intensive suffix) + *-ātiōn-* -ATION]

Clau·di·us I (klô′dē əs), 10 B.C.–A.D. 54, Roman emperor A.D. 41–54.

Claudius II, ("*Gothicus*") A.D. 214–270, Roman emperor 268–270.

clause (klôz), *n.* **1.** *Gram.* a syntactic construction containing a subject and predicate and forming part of a sentence or constituting a whole simple sentence. **2.** part of a written composition, as a distinct provision of a law or treaty. [ME *claus(e)* < ML *clausa,* back formation from L *clausula* a closing, conclusion = *claus(us)* (ptp. of *claudere* to close) + *-ula* -ULE] —**claus′al,** *adj.*

Clau·se·witz (klou′zə vits), *n.* **Karl von** (käRl fən), 1780–1831, German military officer and author of books on military science.

Clau·si·us (klou′zē əs), *n.* **Ru·dolf Jul·ius E·man·u·el** (rōō′dolf jōōl′yəs i man′yōō əl; *Ger.* Rōō′dôlf yōō′lē ŏŏs′ ā mä′nōō el′), 1822–88, German mathematical physicist: pioneer in the field of thermodynamics.

claus·tral (klô′strəl), *adj.* cloistral; cloisterlike. [< LL *claustrāl(is)* = *claustr(um)* bolt, barrier (*claus-* perf. s. of *claudere* to shut + *-trum* n. suffix of instrument) + *-ālis* -AL[1]]

claus·tro·pho·bi·a (klô′strə fō′bē ə), *n. Psychiatry.* an abnormal fear of enclosed or narrow places. [*claustro-* (< L, comb. form of *claustrum;* see CLAUSTRAL) + -PHOBIA] —**claus′tro·phobe′,** *n.* —**claus·tro·pho·bic** (klô′strə fō′bik, -fob′ik), *adj.*

cla·vate (klā′vāt), *adj.* club-shaped; claviform. [< NL *clāvāt(us)* = L *clāv(a)* club + *-ātus* -ATE[1]] —**cla′vate·ly,** *adv.*

clave (klāv), *v. Archaic.* pt. of **cleave.**

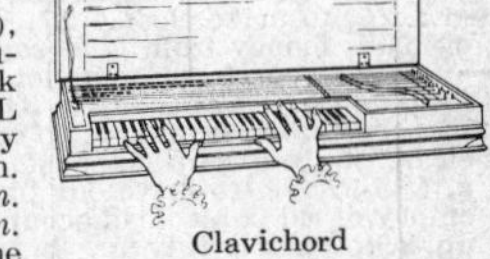

Clavichord

clav·i·chord (klav′ə kôrd′), *n.* an early keyboard instrument whose strings are struck by metal blades. [< ML *clāvichord(ium)* = L *clāvi(s)* key + *chord(a)* CHORD[2] + *-ium* n. suffix] —**clav′i·chord′ist,** *n.*

clav·i·cle (klav′ə kəl), *n. Anat., Zool.* **1.** a bone of the pectoral arch. **2.** (in man) either of two slender bones, each articulating with the sternum and a scapula and forming the anterior part of a shoulder; collarbone. [< ML *clāvicula* collarbone, in L: tendril, doorbolt, little key = *clāvi(s)* key + *-cula* -CULE] —**cla·vic·u·lar** (klə vik′yə lər), *adj.* —**cla·vic·u·late** (klə vik′yə lāt′), *adj.*

clav·i·corn (klav′ə kôrn′), *adj.* **1.** having club-shaped antennae, as many beetles of the group *Clavicornia.* **2.** belonging or pertaining to the group *Clavicornia.* —*n.* **3.** a clavicorn beetle. [< NL *clāvicorn(is)* = L *clāv(a)* club + *-i-* -I- + *-cornis,* comb. form of *cornū* horn]

cla·vier[1] (klə vēr′, klav′ē ər, klā′vē-), *n.* the keyboard of a musical instrument. [< F: keyboard, OF: keyholder = L *clāvi(s)* key + *-ārius* -ARY]

cla·vier[2] (klə vēr′), *n.* any musical instrument having a keyboard, esp. a stringed keyboard instrument. [< G *Klavier* < F *clavier* keyboard; see CLAVIER[1]] —**cla·vier′ist,** *n.*

clav·i·form (klav′ə fôrm′), *adj.* club-shaped; clavate. [< L *clāv(a)* club + -I- + -FORM]

claw (klô), *n.* **1.** a sharp, usually curved, nail on the foot of an animal. **2.** a similar curved process at the end of the leg of an insect. **3.** the pincerlike extremity of specific limbs of certain arthropods: *lobster claws.* **4.** any part or thing resembling a claw, as the cleft end of the head of a hammer. —*v.t.* **5.** to tear, scratch, seize, pull, etc., with or as with claws: *The kitten clawed my sweater to shreds.* **6.** to make by or as by scratching, digging, etc., with hands or claws: *to claw a hole in the earth.* —*v.i.* **7.** to scratch, tear, or dig with or as with claws: *The cat clawed and hissed in fear.* **8.** *Scot.* to scratch gently, as to relieve itching. [(n.) ME; OE *clawu,* c. OHG *chlō(a),* akin to D *klauw,* G *Klaue;* (v.) ME *claw(en),* OE *claw(i)an* < *clawu* (n.); akin to D *klauwen,* G *klauen*] —**claw′er,** *n.* —**claw′less,** *adj.*

claw′ ham′mer, **1.** a hammer having a head with one end curved and cleft for pulling out nails. **2.** *Informal.* a dress coat.

claw′ hatch′et, a carpenter's hatchet having a claw at its back for pulling out nails.

clay (klā), *n.* **1.** a natural earthy material that is plastic when wet, consisting essentially of hydrated silicates of aluminum: used for making bricks, pottery, etc. **2.** earth; mud. **3.** earth, esp. regarded as the material from which the human body was formed. **4.** the human body, esp. as distinguished from the soul; the flesh. —*v.t.* **5.** to treat or mix with clay; cover, daub, or fill with clay. [ME; OE *clǣg;* c. D, G *Klei;* akin to GLUE] —**clay′ey, clay′ish, clay′like′,** *adj.* —**clay′i·ness,** *n.*

Clay (klā), *n.* **Henry,** 1777–1852, U.S. statesman.

clay·more (klā′mōr′, -môr′), *n.* **1.** a two-handed sword with a double-edged blade, used by Scottish Highlanders in the 16th century. **2.** (loosely) a Scottish broadsword with a basket hilt. [< ScotGael *claidheamh mōr* great sword]

clay′more mine′, *Mil.* a type of antipersonnel mine designed to produce a direction-guided fan-shaped pattern of fragments.

clay·pan (klā′pan′), *n. Australian.* a shallow, normally dry depression in the ground that holds water after a heavy rain.

clay′ pig′eon, **1.** *Trapshooting.* a disk of baked clay or other material hurled into the air from a trap as a target. **2.** *Slang.* a person in a situation where he can be taken advantage of by others.

clay′ stone′, *Obs.* **1.** a deeply decomposed igneous rock. **2.** argillite.

Clay·ton (klāt′ᵊn), *n.* a city in E Missouri, near St. Louis. 16,222 (1970).

Clay′ton Antitrust′ Act′ (klāt′ᵊn), an act of Congress in 1914 supplementing the Sherman Antitrust Act and establishing the FTC. [named after Henry La Mar *Clayton* (1857–1929), American legislator and jurist]

clay·to·ni·a (klā tō′nē ə), *n.* any of the low, succulent, portulacaceous herbs of the genus *Claytonia.* [named after Dr. John *Clayton* (1693–1773), Virginia botanist; see -IA]

-cle, var. of **-cule:** *cubicle.* [< L *-culus, -cula, -culum;* in some words < F *-cle*]

clean (klēn), *adj.* **1.** free from dirt; unsoiled; unstained. **2.** free from foreign or extraneous matter. **3.** *Physics.* **a.** (of a nuclear weapon) producing little or no radioactive fallout. **b.** not radioactive. **4.** free from defect or blemish: *a clean* *diamond.* **5.** unadulterated; pure. **6.** having few or no corrections; easily readable: *The printer submitted clean proofs.* **7.** free from encumbrances or obstructions: *a clean harbor.* **8.** characterized by a fresh, wholesome quality. **9.** free from roughness or irregularity: *a clean cut with a razor.* **10.** free from defilement; upright; honorable: *He leads a clean life.* **11.** habitually free of dirt: *Cats are considered clean animals.* **12.** fair: *a clean fighter.* **13.** *Chiefly Biblical.* having no physical or moral blemish or carrying no taboo so as to make ceremonially impure according to the dietary laws. **14.** neatly or evenly made or proportioned; shapely; trim: *She has a clean profile.* **15.** not ornate; gracefully simple: *a clean literary style; the clean lines of the church steeple.* **16.** *Slang.* not using narcotics. **17.** dexterously performed; adroit: *a clean serve in tennis; a clean jump.* **18.** made without any unanticipated difficulty or interference: *The bank robbers made a clean getaway.* **19.** complete; thorough; unqualified: *a clean break with tradition.* **20.** *Slang.* innocent. **21.** unobjectionable in language or concept: *a clean show for the whole family.* **22.** *Slang.* having no concealed weapons. —*adv.* **23.** in a clean manner; cleanly. **24.** wholly; completely; quite: *The sharp carving knife sliced clean through the roast.* **25. come clean,** *Slang.* to tell the truth, esp. to admit guilt. —*v.t.* **26.** to make clean. **27.** *Slang.* to take away or win all of one's money from: *The cards were marked; I got cleaned.* —*v.i.* **28.** to perform or undergo a process of cleaning: *This kind of fabric cleans easily. Detergents clean better than most soaps.* **29. clean out, a.** to empty in order to straighten or clean. **b.** to use up; exhaust: *He had cleaned out his savings.* **c.** *U.S. Slang.* to drive out by force. **d.** *U.S. Informal.* to empty or rid (a place) of occupants, contents, etc. **30. clean up, a.** to wash or tidy up. **b.** to rid of undesirable elements or features: *They cleaned up the local bars.* **c.** to put an end to; finish: *to clean up yesterday's chores.* **d.** *U.S. Informal.* to make a large profit: *They cleaned up in the stock market.* [ME *clene,* OE *clǣne* pure, clear; c. OHG *kleini* (G *klein* small)] —**clean′a·ble,** *adj.* —**clean′ness,** *n.*

—**Syn. 1.** neat, immaculate. **4.** unblemished, flawless. **6.** legible. **10.** chaste, virtuous. **24.** entirely, thoroughly. **26.** scour, scrub, sweep, brush, wipe, mop, dust, wash, purify, clear; decontaminate. CLEAN, CLEANSE refer to removing dirt or impurities. To CLEAN is the general word with no implication of method or means: *to clean windows, a kitchen, streets.* CLEANSE is esp. used of thorough cleaning by chemical or other technical process; figuratively it applies to moral or spiritual purification: *to cleanse parts of machinery, one's soul of guilt.* —**Ant. 1.** dirty. **3b.** contaminated.

clean-cut (klēn′kut′), *adj.* **1.** having a distinct, regular shape. **2.** clearly outlined. **3.** firmly established; unmistakable. **4.** neat and wholesome.

clean′ en′ergy, energy, such as electricity and atomic power, which does not pollute the atmosphere when used, as opposed to coal, gasoline, etc., which do.

clean·er (klē′nər), *n.* **1.** a person or thing that cleans. **2.** an apparatus or preparation for cleaning. **3.** the owner or operator of a dry-cleaning establishment. **4.** Usually, **cleaners.** a dry-cleaning establishment. **5. take to the cleaners,** *Slang.* to cause to lose one's money or property.

clean-hand·ed (klēn′han′did), *adj.* free from wrongdoing; guiltless. —**clean′hand′ed·ness,** *n.*

clean′ hands′, *Informal.* honesty; innocence; guiltlessness: *The verdict in the bribery investigation proved that he had clean hands.*

clean-limbed (klēn′limd′), *adj.* having slender, well-proportioned arms and legs: *a clean-limbed athlete.*

clean·ly (*adj.* klen′lē; *adv.* klēn′lē), *adj.,* **-li·er, -li·est,** *adv.* —*adj.* **1.** personally neat; careful to keep or make clean; habitually clean: *The cat is by nature a cleanly animal.* **2.** *Obs.* cleansing; making clean. —*adv.* **3.** in a clean manner. [ME *clenlich(e),* OE *clǣnlīc*] —**clean·li·ness** (klen′lē nis), *n.*

cleanse (klenz), *v.,* **cleansed, cleans·ing.** —*v.t.* **1.** to make clean. **2.** to remove by or as by cleaning: *to cleanse sin from the soul.* —*v.i.* **3.** to become clean. [ME *clense(n),* OE *clǣnsian* = *clǣne* CLEAN + *-si* v. suffix + *-an* inf. suffix] —**cleans′a·ble,** *adj.* —**Syn. 1.** See **clean.**

cleans·er (klen′zər), *n.* **1.** a liquid or powdered preparation for cleansing, esp. for scouring porcelain. **2.** a person or thing that cleanses.

clean-shav·en (klēn′shā′vən), *adj.* (of men) having the beard and mustache shaved off.

cleans′ing tis′sue, a piece of absorbent paper, used esp. to remove cosmetics or as a disposable handkerchief.

Cle·an·thes (klē an′thēz), *n.* c300–232? B.C., Greek Stoic philosopher.

clean·up (klēn′up′), *n.* the act or process of cleaning up.

clear (klēr), *adj.* **1.** free from darkness, obscurity, or cloudiness: *a clear day.* **2.** bright; shining: *a clear flame.* **3.** transparent; pellucid: *good, clear water.* **4.** of a pure, even color: *a clear yellow.* **5.** without discoloration, defect, or blemish: *a clear complexion.* **6.** easily seen; sharply defined: *a clear outline.* **7.** distinctly perceptible to the ear; easily heard: *a clear sound.* **8.** free from hoarse, harsh, or rasping qualities: *a clear voice.* **9.** easily understood; without ambiguity: *clear, concise answers.* **10.** entirely comprehensible; completely understood: *The ultimate causes of war may never be clear.* **11.** distinct; evident; plain: *a clear case of misbehavior.* **12.** free from confusion, uncertainty, or doubt: *clear thinking.* **13.** perceiving or discerning distinctly: *a clear mind.* **14.** free from blame or guilt. **15.** serene; calm; untroubled: *a clear brow.* **16.** free from obstructions or obstacles; open: *a clear view; a clear road.* **17.** free from contact or entanglement: *He kept clear of her after the argument.* **18.** (of tree trunks or timber) free from branches, knots, etc.: *The trunk was clear for 20 feet above the ground.* **19.** freed or emptied of contents, cargo, etc. **20.** without limitation or qualification; absolute: *a clear victory.* **21.** free from obligation, liability, or debt: *Municipal bonds return as much as 4 percent, clear of taxes.* **22.** without deduction or diminution: *a clear $1000 after taxes.* —*adv.* **23.** in a clear or distinct manner; clearly. **24.** entirely; completely: *to run clear off the road.* —*v.t.* **25.** to make clear, transparent, or pellucid; free from cloudiness or impurities. **26.** to make free of confusion, doubt, or uncertainty. **27.** to make understandable or lucid; free from ambiguity or obscurity. **28.** to remove people or objects from (usually fol. by *of*): *to clear a courtroom of photographers.* **29.** to remove (people or objects) (usually fol. by *from*): *to clear the photographers from the courtroom.* **30.** to make (a path, road, etc.) by removing any obstruction. **31.** to remove trees, buildings, etc., from (land), as for farming or construction. **32.** to relieve (the throat) of phlegm or other obstruction, as by hawking. **33.** to make a rasping noise in (the throat), as to express disapproval or to attract attention. **34.** to free from suspicion, accusation, defamation, etc. **35.** to pass by or over without contact or entanglement: *The ship cleared the reef.* **36.** to pass through or away from. **37.** to pass (checks or other commercial paper) through a clearing house. **38.** (of mail, telephone calls, etc.) to process, handle, reroute, etc.: *The dispatcher clears hundreds of items each day.* **39.** to gain as clear profit: *to clear $1000 in a transaction.* **40.** to free (a ship, cargo, etc.) from legal detention at a port by satisfying customs and other requirements. **41.** to receive authorization before taking action on: *You must clear your plan with headquarters.* **42.** to give clearance to; authorize: *The chairman must clear our speeches before the meeting.* **43.** *Govt., Mil.* to authorize (a person, agency, etc.) to use classified information, documents, etc. —*v.i.* **44.** to become clear. **45.** to exchange checks and bills, and settle balances, as in a clearing house. **46.** (of a ship) **a.** to comply with customs and other requirements legally imposed on entering or leaving a port (often fol. by *in* or *out*). **b.** to leave port after having complied with such requirements. **47.** (of a commodity for sale) to sell out; become bought out: *Wheat cleared rapidly.* **48.** to pass an authority for review, approval, etc. **49. clear away** or **off, a.** to leave; escape: *We were warned to clear off before the floods came.* **b.** to disappear; vanish: *When the smoke cleared away, we saw that the house was in ruins.* **50. clear out, a.** to remove the contents of: *Clear out the closet.* **b.** to remove; take away: *Clear out your clothes from the closet.* **c.** to go away, esp. quickly or abruptly. **d.** *Informal.* to drive or force out: *The police cleared out the pickets by force.* **51. clear up, a.** to make clear; explain; solve. **b.** to put in order; tidy up. **c.** to become better or brighter, as weather. —*n.* **52.** a clear or unobstructed space. **53. in the clear,** absolved of blame or guilt; free. [ME *clere* < OF *cler* < L *clār(us)* clear] —**clear′a·ble,** *adj.* —**clear′er,** *n.*

—**Syn. 1.** fair, cloudless, sunny. **3.** translucent, limpid. **9.** intelligible, comprehensible, lucid, plain. **11.** obvious, manifest, apparent. **12.** positive, definite, assured. **16.** unimpeded, unobstructed. **17.** unhampered, unencumbered. **25.** clarify, purify, refine. **34.** exonerate, absolve, vindicate. —**Ant. 1.** cloudy, dark. **9, 11.** obscure. **12.** uncertain.

clear·ance (klēr′əns), *n.* **1.** the act of clearing. **2.** the amount of clear space between two things, as between a road and a bridge overhead. **3.** a clearing. **4.** Also called **clear′ance sale′.** the disposal of merchandise at reduced prices to make room for new goods. **5.** *Banking.* an exchange of checks and other commercial paper drawn on members of a clearing house. **6.** the clearing of a ship at a port. **7.** Also called **clear′ance pa′pers.** the official papers certifying this. **8.** *Govt., Mil.* a formal authorization permitting access to classified information, documents, etc.

Cle·ar·chus (klē är′kəs), *n.* died 401 B.C., Spartan general.

clear-cut (klēr′kut′), *adj.* **1.** formed with clearly defined outlines. **2.** completely evident; definite. —**Syn. 1.** crisp.

clear-eyed (klēr′īd′), *adj.* **1.** having clear, bright eyes. **2.** mentally acute or perceptive; discerning; realistic.

clear·head·ed (klēr′hed′id), *adj.* having or showing an alert, wide-awake mind. —**clear′head′ed·ly,** *adv.* —**clear′head′ed·ness,** *n.*

clear·ing (klēr′ing), *n.* **1.** act of a person or thing that clears. **2.** a tract of land, as in a forest, that contains no trees or bushes. **3.** the reciprocal exchange between banks of checks and drafts, and the settlement of the differences. **4. clearings,** the total of claims settled at a clearing house. [ME *clering*]

clear′ing house′, an institution where mutual claims and accounts are settled, as between banks.

clear·ly (klēr′lē), *adv.* **1.** in a clear manner. **2.** without equivocation; decidedly. [ME *clerli*]

—**Syn. 1.** plainly, understandably. CLEARLY, DEFINITELY, DISTINCTLY, EVIDENTLY, imply the way in which something is plainly understood or understandable. CLEARLY suggests without doubt or obscurity: *expressed clearly.* DEFINITELY means explicitly; with precision: *definitely phrased.* DISTINCTLY means without blurring or confusion: *distinctly enunciated.* EVIDENTLY means patently, unquestionably: *evidently an error.*

clear·ness (klēr′nis), *n.* the state or quality of being clear; distinctness; plainness. [ME *clernes*]

clear-sight·ed (klēr′sī′tid), *adj.* **1.** having clear eyesight. **2.** having or marked by keen perception or sound judgment: —**clear′-sight′ed·ly,** *adv.* —**clear′-sight′ed·ness,** *n.*

clear·sto·ry (klēr′stôr′ē, -stôr′ē), *n., pl.* **-ries.** clerestory. —**clear′sto′ried,** *adj.*

Clear·wa·ter (klēr′wô′tər, -wot′ər), *n.* a city in W Florida. 52,074 (1970).

clear·wing (klēr′wing′), *n.* a moth having wings for the most part devoid of scales and transparent, esp. any of the family *Aegeriidae,* many species of which are injurious to plants. Also, called **clear′wing moth′.**

cleat (klēt), *n.* **1.** a wedge-shaped block fastened to a surface to serve as a check or support. **2.** an object of wood or metal having one or two projecting horns to which ropes may be belayed or made fast, found esp. on board vessels, as fixed to a deck or stanchion. **3.** a length of wood or the like fixed to a surface, as a ramp, to give a firm foothold or to maintain an object in place. **4.** a strip of wood, metal, etc., fastened across a surface, as of a plank or series of adjacent planks, for strength or support. **5.** an iron plate fastened to the sole or heel of a shoe, to protect it against wear. **6.** a rectangular or conical projection, usually of hard rubber, built or screwed into the sole of a shoe to provide greater traction. **7.** a shoe fitted with such projections. **8.** calk[2] (def.

Cleat (def. 2)

1). —*v.t.* **9.** to supply or strengthen with cleats; fasten to or with a cleat. [ME *clete* wedge, OE *clēot;* c. OHG *klōz* lump, ball, D *kloot;* akin to CLOT]

cleav·a·ble (klē′və bəl), *adj.* capable of being cleft or split. —**cleav′a·bil′i·ty,** *n.*

cleav·age (klē′vij), *n.* **1.** the act of cleaving or splitting. **2.** the state of being cleft. **3.** *Biol.* the total or partial division of the egg into smaller cells or blastomeres. **4.** the tendency to break in certain definite directions, as in crystals, minerals, and certain rocks. **5.** *Chem.* the breaking down of a molecule or compound into simpler structures. **6.** the area between a woman's breasts, esp. when revealed by a low-cut neckline. **7.** critical division in opinion, beliefs, interests, etc., as one leading to opposition between two groups.

cleave[1] (klēv), *v.i.,* **cleaved** or (*Archaic*) **clave; cleaved; cleav·ing. 1.** to adhere closely; stick; cling (usually fol. by *to*). **2.** to remain faithful (usually fol. by *to*): *to cleave to one's principles in spite of persecution.* [ME *cleve(n),* OE *cleofian;* c. OHG *klebēn* (G *kleben*)] —**cleav′ing·ly,** *adv.*

cleave[2] (klēv), *v.,* **cleft** or **cleaved** or **clove, cleft** or **cleaved** or **clo·ven, cleav·ing.** —*v.t.* **1.** to split or divide by or as by a cutting blow, esp. along a natural line of division, as the grain of wood. **2.** to make by or as by cutting: *to cleave a path through the wilderness.* **3.** to cut off; sever: *to cleave a branch from a tree.* —*v.i.* **4.** to part or split, esp. along a natural line of division. **5.** to penetrate or advance by or as by cutting (usually fol. by *through*): *to cleave through the water.* [ME *cleve(n),* OE *clēofan;* c. OHG *klioban* (G *klieben*), Icel *kljūfa;* akin to Gk *glýphein* to carve, L *glūbere* to peel]

cleav·er (klē′vər), *n.* **1.** a person or thing that cleaves. **2.** a heavy knife or long-bladed hatchet, esp. one used by butchers. [late ME *clevere*]

cleav·ers (klē′vərz), *n., pl.* **cleav·ers. 1.** a rubiaceous plant, *Galium Aparine,* having short, hooked bristles by which it adheres to clothing, fur, etc. **2.** any of certain related species. Also, **clivers.** [late ME *clivre* = OE *clife* burdock + *-ere* -ER[1]]

cleek (klēk), *n.* **1.** *Scot. and North Eng.* any large hook, esp. a hook fixed to an inside wall of a house to hold clothing, pots, or food. **2.** *Golf.* a club with an iron head, a narrow face, and little slope, used for shots from a poor lie on the fairway and sometimes for putting. [late ME (Scot) *cleke* hook < *cleke* to take hold of, var. of *cleche,* akin to CLUTCH[1]]

A B C

Clefs
A, Treble clef (G clef); B, Bass clef (F clef); C, Alto clef (C clef)

clef (klef), *n.* *Music.* a symbol placed upon a staff to indicate the names and pitches of the notes corresponding to its lines and spaces. Cf. **bass clef, C clef, treble clef.** [< MF < L *clāvis* key]

cleft[1] (kleft), *n.* **1.** a space or opening made by cleavage; split. **2.** *Vet. Pathol.* a crack on the bend of the pastern of a horse. [ME *clift,* OE *(ge)clyft* split, crack; c. G, Icel *Hluft;* akin to CLEAVE[2]] —**Syn. 1.** fissure, crevice, crack, rift, chasm, crevasse.

cleft[2] (kleft), *v.* **1.** a pt. and pp. of **cleave**[2]. —*adj.* **2.** cloven; split; divided. **3.** (of a plant leaf, corolla, lobe, etc.) having divisions formed by incisions or narrow sinuses that extend at least halfway to the midrib or the base.

cleft′ pal′ate, a congenital defect in which a longitudinal fissure exists in the roof of the mouth.

Cleis·the·nes (klīs′thə nēz′), *n.* active c515–c495 B.C., Athenian statesman. Also, **Clisthenes.**

cleisto-, a learned borrowing from Greek meaning "closed," "capable of being closed," used in the formation of compound words: *cleistogamy.* [comb. form repr. Gk *kleistós*]

cleis·tog·a·my (klī stog′ə mē), *n.* *Bot.* the condition of having small, inconspicuous flowers, in addition to fully developed ones, that do not open but are pollinated from their own anthers, as in the case of the pansy. —**cleis·tog′a·mous,** *adj.*

clem·a·tis (klem′ə tis), *n.* **1.** any of the flowering vines or erect ranunculaceous shrubs of the genus *Clematis,* as *C. virginiana,* the virgin's-bower of the U.S. **2.** any species of the allied genera *Atragene* or *Viorna.* [< L < Gk *klēmatis* name of several climbing plants]

Cle·men·ceau (klem′ən sō′; *Fr.* kle mäɴ sō′), *n.* **Georges Eu·gène Ben·ja·min** (jôrj yo͞o jēn′ ben′jə min, yo͞o′jēn; *Fr.* zhôrzh œ zhen′ baɴ zhä maɴ′), 1841–1929, French statesman, journalist, and editor: premier 1906–09, 1917–20.

clem·en·cy (klem′ən sē), *n., pl.* **-cies. 1.** the tendency or willingness to show forbearance, compassion, or forgiveness in judging or punishing; leniency; mercy. **2.** an act or deed of mercy or leniency. **3.** (of the weather) mildness or temperateness. [< L *clēmentia*] —**Syn. 1.** mercifulness. —**Ant. 1.** harshness.

Clem·ens (klem′ənz), *n.* **Samuel Lang·horne** (laŋ′hôrn, -ərn). See **Twain, Mark.**

clem·ent (klem′ənt), *adj.* **1.** mild or merciful in disposition or character; lenient; compassionate. **2.** (of the weather) mild or temperate; pleasant. [late ME < L *clēment-,* s. of *clēmēns* gentle, merciful] —**clem′ent·ly,** *adv.*

Clem·ent I (klem′ənt), **Saint** (*Clemnet of Rome*), A.D. c30–c100, first of the Apostolic Fathers: pope 88?–97?.

Clement II, (*Suidger*) died 1047, pope 1046–47.

Clement III, (*Paolo Scolari*) died 1191, Italian ecclesiastic: pope 1187–91.

Clement IV, (*Guy Foulques*) died 1268, French ecclesiastic: pope 1265–68.

Clement V, (*Bertrand de Got*) 1264–1314, French ecclesiastic: pope 1305–14.

Clement VI, (*Pierre Roger*) 1291–1352, French ecclesiastic: pope 1342–52.

Clement VII, (*Giulio de' Medici*) 1478–1534, Italian ecclesiastic: pope 1523–34 (nephew of Lorenzo de' Medici).

Clement VIII, (*Ippolito Aldobrandini*) 1536–1605, Italian ecclesiastic: pope 1592–1605.

Clement IX, (*Giulio Rospigliosi*) 1600–69, Italian ecclesiastic: pope 1667–69.

Clement X, (*Emilio Altieri*) 1590–1676, Italian ecclesiastic: pope 1670–76.

Clement XI, (*Giovanni Francesco Albani*) 1649–1721, Italian ecclesiastic: pope 1700–21.

Clement XII, (*Lorenzo Corsini*) 1652–1740, Italian ecclesiastic: pope 1730–40.

Clement XIII, (*Carlo della Torre Rezzonico*) 1693–1769, Italian ecclesiastic: pope 1758–69.

Clement XIV, (*Giovanni Vincenzo Antonio Ganganelli* or *Lorenzo Ganganelli*) 1705–74, Italian ecclesiastic: pope 1769–1774.

Cle·men·ti (klə men′tē; *It.* kle men′tē), *n.* **Mu·zio** (mo͞o′tsyô), 1752–1832, Italian pianist and composer in England.

Clem′ent of Alexan′dria, A.D. c150–c215, Greek Christian theologian and writer.

clench (klench), *v.t.* **1.** to close (the hands, teeth, etc.) tightly. **2.** to grasp firmly; grip. **3.** clinch (defs. 1–3). —*n.* **4.** the act or an instance of clenching. **5.** something that clenches or holds fast. **6.** clinch (defs. 8, 9). [ME *clenche(n),* OE *(be)clencan* to hold fast]

cle·o·me (klē ō′mē), *n.* any of the numerous herbaceous or shrubby plants of the genus *Cleome,* mostly natives of tropical regions, and often bearing showy flowers. [< NL, LL, name of some plant]

Cle·om·e·nes III (klē om′ə nēz′), died c220 B.C., king of Sparta c235–c220.

Cle·on (klē′on), *n.* died 442 B.C., Athenian general and political opponent of Pericles.

Cle·o·pat·ra (klē′ə pa′trə, -pä′-, -pā′-), *n.* 69–30 B.C., queen of Egypt 51–49, 48–30; last of the Ptolemys.

clepe (klēp), *v.t.,* **cleped** or **clept** (also **y·cleped** or **y·clept**), **clep·ing.** *Archaic.* to call; name (now chiefly in the pp. as *ycleped* or *yclept*). [ME *clep(en),* OE *cleopian,* var. of *clipian;* akin to MLG *kleperen* to rattle]

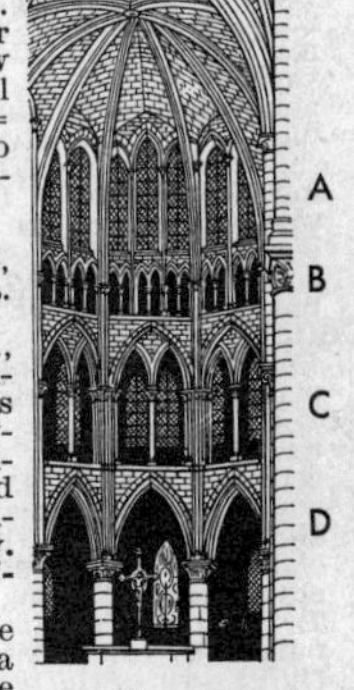

A, Clerestory of early Gothic cathedral; B, Triforium; C, Gallery; D, Ambulatory arcade

clep·sy·dra (klep′si drə), *n., pl.* **-dras, -drae** (-drē′). a device for measuring time by the regulated flow of water or mercury through a small aperture. [< L < Gk *klepsýdrā* = *kleps-* (var. of *klept-,* s. of *kléptein* to steal) + *hydr-* HYDR-[1] + *-ā* fem. n. suffix]

clept (klept), *v.* a pt. of **clepe.**

clep·to·ma·ni·a (klep′tə mā′nē ə, -mān′yə), *n.* *Psychol.* kleptomania. —**clep′to·ma′ni·ac′,** *n.*

clere·sto·ry (klēr′stôr′ē, -stōr′ē), *n., pl.* **-ries. 1.** *Archit.* a portion of an interior rising above adjacent rooftops and having windows admitting daylight to the interior. **2.** a raised construction, as on the roof of a railroad car, having windows or slits for admitting light or air. Also, **clearstory.** [late ME; see CLEAR, STORY[2]] —**clere′sto′ried,** *adj.*

cler·gy (klûr′jē), *n., pl.* **-gies.** the group or body of ordained persons in a religion, as distinguished from the laity. [ME *clergie* < OF = *clerg-* (var. of *clerc-* CLERK) + *-ie* -Y[3]] —**cler′gy·like′,** *adj.*

cler·gy·man (klûr′jē mən), *n., pl.* **-men.** a member of the clergy.

cler·ic (kler′ik), *n.* **1.** a member of the clergy. **2.** a member of a clerical party. —*adj.* **3.** pertaining to the clergy; clerical. [< LL *clēric(us)* priest < Gk *klērikós* = *klēr(os)* lot, allotment + *-ikos* -IC]

cler·i·cal (kler′i kəl), *adj.* **1.** of, pertaining to, appropriate for, or assigned to a clerk or clerks: *a clerical job.* **2.** of, pertaining to, or characteristic of the clergy or a clergyman. **3.** advocating clericalism. —*n.* **4.** a cleric. **5. clericals,** *Informal.* clerical garments. **6.** a clericalist. [< LL *clēricālis*] —**cler′i·cal·ly,** *adv.*

cler′ical col′lar, a stiff, narrow, bandlike white collar fastened at the back of the neck, worn by certain clerics. Also called **Roman collar.**

cler·i·cal·ism (kler′i kə liz′əm), *n.* **1.** clerical principles. **2.** clerical power or influence in government, politics, etc. (distinguished from *laicism*). **3.** support of such power or influence. —**cler′i·cal·ist,** *n.*

cler·i·hew (kler′i hyo͞o′), *n.* *Pros.* a light verse form, usually consisting of two couplets, with lines of uneven length and irregular meter, the first line usually containing the name of a well-known person. [named after E. *Clerihew* Bentley (1875–1956), English writer, its inventor]

cler·i·sy (kler′i sē), *n.* learned men as a class; literati; intelligentsia. [< G *Klerisei* clergy < ML *clēricia* = *clēric(us)* CLERIC + *-ia* -IA]

clerk (klûrk; *Brit.* klärk), *n.* **1.** a person employed, as in an office, to keep records, accounts, files, handle correspondence, or the like. **2.** *U.S.* a salesclerk. **3.** a person who keeps the records and performs the routine business of a court, legislature, board, etc. **4.** cleric. **5.** *Archaic.* **a.** a person who is able to read and write. **b.** a scholar. —*v.i.* **6.** to act or serve as a clerk. [ME, OE *clerc,* var. of *cleric* < eccl. L *clēric(us)* CLERIC] —**clerk′ish,** *adj.* —**clerk′ship,** *n.*

clerk·ly (klûrk′lē; *Brit.* klärk′lē), *adj.,* **-li·er, -li·est,** *adv.* —*adj.* **1.** of, pertaining to, or characteristic of a clerk or clerks. **2.** *Archaic.* scholarly. —*adv.* **3.** in the manner of a clerk. —**clerk′li·ness,** *n.*

Cler·mont-Fer·rand (kler môɴ′fe räɴ′), *n.* a city in central France. 134,263 (1963).

cleve·ite (klē′vīt, klā′və īt′), *n.* *Mineral.* a variety of uraninite containing up to 10 percent of rare earth oxides. [named after R. T. *Cleve* (1840–1905), Swedish chemist; see -ITE[1]]

Cleve·land (klēv′lənd), *n.* **1. (Stephen) Gro·ver** (grō′vər), 1837–1908, 22nd and 24th president of the U.S. 1885–89, 1893–97. **2.** a port in NE Ohio, on Lake Erie. 750,879 (1970).

Cleve′land Heights′, a city in NE Ohio, near Cleveland. 60,767 (1970).

clev·er (klev′ər), *adj.* **1.** mentally bright; having quick intelligence; able. **2.** superficially skillful, witty, or original in character or construction; facile. **3.** adroit with the hands or body; dexterous or nimble. **4.** showing inventiveness or originality; ingenious. **5.** *Dial.* suitable; convenient; satisfactory. [ME *cliver*, akin to OE *clifer* claw, *clife* burdock. See CLEAVERS] —**clev′er·ly,** *adv.* —**clev′er·ness,** *n.* —**Syn. 1.** quick-witted; smart, gifted; apt, expert. **3.** skillful, agile, handy. —**Ant. 1.** stupid.

clev·is (klev′is), *n.* a U-shaped yoke at the end of a chain or rod, between the ends of which a lever, hook, etc., can be pinned or bolted. [akin to CLEAVE²]

C, Clevis

clew (klo͞o), *n.* **1.** a ball or skein of thread, yarn, etc. **2.** *Chiefly Brit.* clue (def. 1). **3.** Usually, **clews.** the rigging for a hammock. **4.** *Naut.* either lower corner of a square sail or the after lower corner of a fore-and-aft sail. —*v.t.* **5.** to coil into a ball. **6.** *Chiefly Brit.* clue (def. 3). **7.** *Naut.* to haul or secure (a sail) by the clews. [ME *clewe*, OE *cleowen, cliewen* = *cliew-* (c. OHG *kliu* ball) + *-en* -EN⁵; akin to D *kluwen*]

clew′ line′, *Naut.* a rope or tackle for raising the clews of square sails and certain fore-and-aft sails.

cli·ché (klē shā′, kli-), *n.* **1.** a trite, stereotyped expression that has lost originality and impact by long overuse, as *strong as an ox.* **2.** (in art, literature, drama, etc.) a trite or hackneyed plot, character development, use of form, musical expression, etc. **3.** *Print. Brit.* **a.** a stereotype or electrotype plate. **b.** a reproduction made in a like manner. —*adj.* **4.** trite; hackneyed; stereotyped; commonplace. [< F, ptp. of *clicher* to stereotype] —**Syn. 1.** platitude, bromide.

Cli·chy (klē shē′), *n.* an industrial suburb of Paris, France, on the Seine. 56,495 (1962).

click (klik), *n.* **1.** a slight, sharp sound: *the click of a latch.* **2.** a small device for preventing backward movement of a mechanism, as a detent or pawl. **3.** *Phonet.* any one of a variety of ingressive, usually implosive speech sounds, phonemic in some languages, produced by suction occlusion and plosive or affricative release. —*v.i.* **4.** to emit or make a slight, sharp sound, or series of such sounds, as by the cocking of a pistol. **5.** *Informal.* **a.** to succeed; make a hit. **b.** to fit together; function well together: *Their personalities don't really click.* —*v.t.* **6.** to cause to click. **7.** to strike together with a click: *He clicked his heels and saluted.* [? imit., but perh. < D *klick* (n.), *klikken* (v.)] —**click′er,** *n.*

click′ bee′tle, any of numerous beetles of the family *Elateridae*, that can spring up with a clicking sound when placed on their backs. Also called **snapping beetle.**

cli·ent (klī′ənt), *n.* **1.** a person who commits his legal interests to a lawyer's management. **2.** a person who is receiving the benefits, services, etc., of a social welfare agency, a government bureau, etc. **3.** a customer. **4.** (in ancient Rome) a plebeian who lived under the patronage of a patrician. **5.** anyone under the patronage of another; dependent. —*adj.* **6.** being a regular customer: *a client company.* **7.** economically and militarily dependent upon a major nation: *a client state.* [late ME < L *client-*, s. of *cliēns*, var. of *cluēns*, prp. of *cluēre* to hear; see -ENT] —**cli·en·tal** (klī en′tᵊl, klī′ən tᵊl), *adj.* —**cli′ent·less,** *adj.*

cli·en·tele (klī′ən tel′), *n.* **1.** the clients (as of a lawyer or businessman) or the customers (as of a shop) considered collectively: *a wealthy clientele.* **2.** dependents or followers. [< L *clientēla* = *client-* (see CLIENT) + *-ēla* collective n. suffix]

cliff (klif), *n.* the high steep face of a rocky mass overlooking a lower area; precipice. [ME, OE *clif*; c. D, LG, Icel *klif*]

cliff′ dwell′er, 1. (*usually cap.*) a member of a prehistoric people of the southwestern U.S., who built houses in caves or on ledges of cliffs. **2.** a person who lives in an apartment house, esp. in a large city. —**cliff′ dwell′ing.**

cliff-hang·er (klif′hang′ər), *n.* **1.** a melodramatic adventure serial in which each installment ends in suspense. **2.** an event or contest whose outcome is suspensefully uncertain. Also, **cliff′hang′er.** —**cliff′-hang′ing, cliff′hang′ing,** *adj.*

cliff′ swal′low, a colonial North American bird, *Petrochelidon pyrrhonota*, which attaches its bottle-shaped nests of mud to cliffs and walls.

cliff·y (klif′ē), *adj.*, **cliff·i·er, cliff·i·est.** abounding in or formed by cliffs.

Clif·ton (klif′tən), *n.* a city in NE New Jersey. 82,437 (1970).

cli·mac·ter·ic (klī mak′tər ik, klī′mak ter′ik), *n.* **1.** *Physiol.* the period of decreasing reproductive capacity in men and women, culminating, in women, in menopause. **2.** any critical period. **3.** a year in which important changes in health, fortune, etc., are held by some theories to occur, as one's sixty-third year **(grand climacteric).** —*adj.* **4.** Also, **cli·mac·ter·i·cal** (klī′mak ter′i kəl). pertaining to a critical period; crucial. [< L *clīmactēric(us)* < Gk *klīmaktērikós* = *klīmaktḗr* rung of a ladder, critical point in life (*klimak-*, s. of *klimax* (see CLIMAX) + *-tēr* n. suffix) + *-ikos* -IC] —**cli′mac·ter′i·cal·ly,** *adv.*

cli·mac·tic (klī mak′tik), *adj.* pertaining to or coming to a climax. Also, **cli·mac′ti·cal.** [from CLIMAX, on model of pairs like *syntax, syntactic*] —**cli·mac′ti·cal·ly,** *adv.*

climat-, var. of **climato-** before a vowel: *climatic.*

cli·mate (klī′mit), *n.* **1.** the composite or generally prevailing weather conditions of a region, as temperature, barometric pressure, humidity, precipitation, sunshine, cloudiness, and winds, throughout the year, averaged over a series of years. **2.** a region or area characterized by its prevailing weather. **3.** the prevailing attitudes, standards, or environmental conditions of a group, period, or place: *a climate of political unrest.* [late ME *climat* < L *climāt-* (s. of *clima*) < Gk *klimat-*, s. of *klima* slope = *kli-* (akin to *klīnein* to slope, lean) + *-ma* n. suffix] —**cli·mat·ic** (klī mat′ik), **cli·mat′i·cal, cli′mat·al,** *adj.* —**cli·mat′i·cal·ly,** *adv.*

climato-, a combining form of **climate:** *climatology.* Also, *esp. before a vowel,* **climat-.**

cli·ma·tol·o·gy (klī′mə tol′ə jē), *n.* the science that deals with climates or climatic conditions. —**cli·ma·to·log·ic** (klī′mə tᵊloj′ik), **cli′ma·to·log′i·cal,** *adj.* —**cli′ma·to·log′i·cal·ly,** *adv.* —**cli′ma·tol′o·gist,** *n.*

cli·max (klī′maks), *n.* **1.** the highest or most intense point in the development or resolution of something; culmination: *His career reached its climax when he was elected president.* **2.** a decisive point in the plot of a dramatic or literary work. **3.** *Rhet.* **a.** a figure consisting of a series of related ideas so arranged that each surpasses the preceding in force or intensity. **b.** the last term or member of this figure. **4.** an orgasm. **5.** *Ecol.* any stage in the ecological evolution of a plant and animal community, that is stable and self-perpetuating. —*v.t., v.i.* **6.** to bring to or reach a climax. [< LL < Gk *klīmax* ladder, akin to *klīnein* to lean] —**Syn. 1.** summit, zenith, acme, apex.

climb (klīm), *v.*, **climbed** or (*Archaic*) **clomb; climbed** or (*Archaic*) **clomb; climb·ing;** *n.* —*v.i.* **1.** to ascend; move upward or toward the top of something. **2.** to slope upward. **3.** to ascend by twining or by means of tendrils, adhesive tissues, etc., as a plant: *The ivy climbed to the roof.* **4.** to proceed or move by using the hands and feet; crawl: *to climb around on the roof.* **5.** to ascend in prominence, fortune, etc. —*v.t.* **6.** to ascend, go up, or get to the top of, esp. by the use of the hands and feet. **7. climb down, a.** to descend, esp. by using both the hands and feet. **b.** *Informal.* to retreat, as from an indefensible opinion or position. —*n.* **8.** a climbing; an ascent by climbing: *It was a long climb to the top.* **9.** a place to be climbed: *That peak is quite a climb.* [ME *climbe(n)*, OE *climban*; c. D, G *klimmen*; akin to CLAMBER] —**climb′a·ble,** *adj.*

—**Syn. 6.** CLIMB, ASCEND, MOUNT, SCALE imply a moving upward. To CLIMB is to make one's way upward with effort: *to climb a mountain.* ASCEND, in its literal meaning (to go up), is general, but it now usually suggests a gradual or stately movement, with or without effort, often to a considerable degree of altitude: *to ascend the Hudson River; to ascend the Himalayas.* MOUNT may be interchangeable with ASCEND, but also suggests climbing on top of or astride of: *to mount a platform, a horse.* SCALE, a more literary word, implies difficult or hazardous climbing up or over something: *to scale a summit.* —**Ant. 1, 6.** descend. **8.** descent.

climb·er (klī′mər), *n.* **1.** a person or thing that climbs. **2.** See **social climber. 3.** a climbing plant. **4.** a device to assist in climbing, as a climbing iron or a spiked metal plate fastened to a shoe. [late ME]

climb′ing i′rons, one of a pair of spiked iron frames for strapping to the shoe, leg, or knee, to help in climbing trees, telephone poles, etc.

clime (klīm), *n.* *Literary.* **1.** a tract or region of the earth. **2.** climate. [< L *clima*; see CLIMATE]

clinch (klinch), *v.t.* **1.** to secure (a nail, screw, etc.) in position by beating down the protruding point. **2.** to fasten (objects) together by nails, screws, etc., secured in this manner. **3.** to settle (a matter) decisively: *The salesman clinched the deal and went out to celebrate.* —*v.i.* **4.** *Boxing.* to engage in a clinch. **5.** *Slang.* to embrace and kiss passionately. **6.** (of a clinched nail, screw, etc.) to hold fast; be secure. —*n.* **7.** the act of clinching. **8.** *Boxing.* a holding about the opponent's arms or body, by one or both boxers, to prevent or hinder punching. **9.** the bent part of a clinched nail, screw, etc. **10.** *Slang.* a passionate embrace and kiss. **11.** *Obs.* a pun. Also, **clench** (for defs. 1–3, 8, 9). [later var. of CLENCH]

clinch·er (klin′chər), *n.* **1.** a person or thing that clinches. **2.** a nail, screw, etc., for clinching. **3.** a statement, argument, fact, situation, or the like, that is decisive or conclusive.

cline (klīn), *n.* **1.** *Biol.* the gradual change in certain characteristics exhibited by members of a series of adjacent populations of organisms of the same species. **2.** *Anthropol.* a gradient of the frequency with which a biological characteristic occurs in one area and not in another. [< Gk *klīn(ein)* to LEAN¹] —**clin′al,** *adj.* —**clin′al·ly,** *adv.*

cling¹ (kling), *v.i.*, **clung, cling·ing. 1.** to adhere closely; stick to. **2.** to hold tight, as by grasping or embracing; cleave: *The children clung to each other in the dark.* **3.** to be or remain close. **4.** to remain attached, as to an idea, hope, memory, etc. **5.** *Obs.* to cohere. [ME *cling(en)*, OE *clingan* to stick together, shrink, wither; akin to CLENCH] —**cling′er,** *n.* —**cling′ing·ly,** *adv.* —**cling′i·ness, cling′ing·ness,** *n.*

cling² (kling), *v.*, **clinged, cling·ing,** *n.* —*v.t., v.i.* **1.** to make, or cause to make, a high-pitched, ringing sound. —*n.* **2.** such a sound, as of a small bell. [? alter. of CLINK¹; imit.]

cling′ing vine′, *Informal.* a woman who behaves in a dependent manner in her relationships with men.

Cling′mans Dome′ (kling′mənz), a mountain on the border between North Carolina and Tennessee: the highest peak in the Great Smoky Mountains. 6642 ft.

cling·stone (kling′stōn′), *adj.* **1.** having a stone to which the pulp adheres closely, as certain peaches. —*n.* **2.** a clingstone peach.

cling·y (kling′ē), *adj.*, **cling·i·er, cling·i·est.** apt to cling; adhesive or tenacious: *wet and clingy dirt.*

clin·ic (klin′ik), *n.* **1.** a place, as in connection with a medical school or a hospital, for the treatment of nonresident patients. **2.** such a place where treatment is given at reduced cost or without charge. **3.** an infirmary. **4.** a group of physicians working in cooperation and sharing the same offices and facilities. **5.** a class of medical students assembled for instruction in the diagnosis and treatment of patients. **6.** the place for such instruction. **7.** any class or group convening for instruction, advice, remedial work, etc., in a special field: *a marriage clinic; a speech clinic.* —*adj.* **8.** of a clinic; clinical. [< L *clīnic(us)* < Gk *klīnikós* pertaining to a (sick)bed = *klī́n(ē)* bed + *-ikos* -IC]

clin·i·cal (klin′i kəl), *adj.* **1.** pertaining to a clinic. **2.** pertaining to or used in a sickroom. **3.** concerned with or based on actual observation and treatment of disease in patients rather than artificial experimentation or theory. **4.** dispassionately analytic; unemotionally critical. **5.** *Eccles.* (of a sacrament) administered on a deathbed or sickbed. —**clin′i·cal·ly,** *adv.*

clin′ical psychol′ogy, the branch of psychology dealing with the diagnosis and treatment of personality and behavioral disorders. —**clin′ical psychol′ogist.**

clin′ical thermom′eter, a small thermometer used to determine the body temperature.

cli·ni·cian (kli nish′ən), *n.* a physician who studies diseases at the bedside, or is skilled in clinical methods.

clink[1] (klingk), *v.t., v.i.* **1.** to make, or cause to make, a light, sharp, ringing sound: *The coins clinked together.* **2.** *Rare.* to rhyme or jingle. —*n.* **3.** a clinking sound. **4.** *Metall.* a small crack in a steel ingot resulting from uneven expanding or contracting. [ME *clink(en)* (v.), perh. < MD *clinken*]
clink[2] (klingk), *n. Slang.* a jail. [after *Clink*, name of prison in Southwark, London, perh. < D *klink* doorlatch]
clink·er[1] (kling′kər), *n.* **1.** a partially vitrified mass, as of ash. **2.** a hard paving brick. [< D *klinker* kind of brick]
clink·er[2] (kling′kər), *n.* a person or thing that clinks. [CLINK[1] + -ER[1]]
clink·er[3] (kling′kər), *n. Slang.* **1.** any mistake or error. **2.** that which is a failure; a product of inferior quality. [special use of CLINKER[2]]
clink·er-built (kling′kər bilt′), *adj.* faced or surfaced with boards, plates, etc., each course of which overlaps the one below. [*clinker* (var. of CLINCHER) + BUILT]
clink·stone (klingk′stōn′), *n. Petrog.* any of several varieties of phonolite that give out a ringing sound when struck. [CLINK[1] + STONE, modeled on G *Klingstein*]
clino-, a learned borrowing from Latin meaning "slope," used in the formation of compound words: *clinometer.* [< L *clin(āre)* (c. Gk *klīnein* to cause to lean, Skt *śrayati* he causes to lean) + -O-]
cli·nom·e·ter (klī nom′i tər, kli-), *n.* an instrument for determining angles of inclination or slope. —**cli·nom′e·try,** *n.*
cli·no·met·ric (klī′nə me′trik), *adj.* **1.** (of crystals) having oblique angles between one or all axes. **2.** pertaining to or determined by a clinometer. Also, **cli′no·met′ri·cal.**
clin·quant (kling′kənt), *adj.* **1.** glittering, esp. with tinsel; decked with garish finery. —*n.* **2.** imitation gold leaf; tinsel. **3.** *Obs.* tinsel; false glitter. [< MF: clinking, prp. of *clinquer* (< D *klinken* to clink); see -ANT]
Clin·ton (klin′tᵊn), *n.* **1. De Witt** (də wit′), 1769–1828, U.S. political leader and statesman: governor of New York 1817–21, 1825–28 (son of James Clinton). **2. George,** 1739–1812, governor of New York 1777–95, 1801–04: vice-president of the U.S. 1805–12. **3. Sir Henry,** 1738?–95, commander in chief of the British forces in the American Revolutionary War. **4. James,** 1733–1812, American general in the Revolutionary War (brother of George Clinton). **5.** a city in E Iowa, on the Mississippi River. 34,719 (1970).
clin·to·ni·a (klin tō′nē ə), *n.* any liliaceous plant of the genus *Clintonia*, comprising stemless, perennial herbs with broad, ribbed, basal leaves, and white or greenish-yellow flowers. [named after De Witt CLINTON; see -IA]
Cli·o (klī′ō), *n. Class. Myth.* the Muse of history. [< L < Gk *Kleiṓ* = *klei-* (s. of *kléein* to make famous, celebrate) + *-ō* suffix used for women's names]
clip[1] (klip), *v.*, **clipped, clipped** or **clipt, clip·ping,** *n.* —*v.t.* **1.** to cut, or cut off or out, as with shears. **2.** to trim by cutting. **3.** to cut or trim the hair or fleece of; shear: *to clip a poodle.* **4.** to pare the edge of (a coin). Cf. **sweat** (def. 19). **5.** to cut short; curtail. **6.** to pronounce rapidly, with precise articulation and with omission of certain sounds, as of unstressed vowels. **7.** *Informal.* to hit with a quick, sharp blow: *He clipped him on the jaw and knocked him down.* **8.** *Slang.* to take or get money from by dishonest means; swindle; rook. —*v.i.* **9.** to clip or cut something. **10.** to cut articles or pictures from a newspaper, magazine, etc. **11.** to move swiftly. **12.** *Archaic.* to fly rapidly. —*n.* **13.** the act of clipping. **14.** anything clipped off, esp. the wool shorn at a single shearing of sheep. **15. clips,** an instrument for clipping; shears. **16.** *Informal.* a quick, sharp blow or punch: *a clip on the nose.* **17.** *Informal.* rate; pace: *at a rapid clip.* [ME *clippe(n)* < Scand; cf. Icel *klippa* to cut] —**clip′pa·ble,** *adj.*
clip[2] (klip), *n., v.*, **clipped, clip·ping.** —*n.* **1.** a device that grips and holds tightly. **2.** See **paper clip. 3.** a flange on the upper surface of a horseshoe. **4.** See **cartridge clip. 5.** an article of jewelry or other decoration, clipped onto clothing, shoes, hats, etc. **6.** *Archaic.* an embrace. —*v.t., v.i.* **7.** to grip tightly; fasten with or as with a clip. **8.** to encircle. **9.** *Football.* to block by illegally throwing the body across a player's legs from behind. [ME *clippe(n)*, OE *clyppan* to embrace, surround; c. OFris *kleppa*]
clip·board (klip′bōrd′, -bôrd′), *n.* a board with a heavy spring clip at one end for holding paper, a writing pad, or the like, and serving as a portable writing surface.
clip-fed (klip′fed′), *adj.* (of a rifle) loading from a cartridge clip into the magazine.
clip′ joint′, *Slang.* a night club, bar, restaurant, or the like, that makes a practice of overcharging or cheating customers.
clip-on (klip′on′), *adj.* **1.** designed to be clipped on easily, as a bow tie, sunglasses, or the like. —*n.* **2.** a clip-on device, ornament, or the like.

Clipper (def. 5)

clip·per (klip′ər), *n.* **1.** a person or thing that clips or cuts. **2.** Often, **clippers.** a cutting tool, esp. shears: *hedge clippers.* **3.** Usually, **clippers.** a mechanical or electric tool for cutting hair, fingernails. or the like. **4.** a person or thing that moves along swiftly. **5.** a sailing vessel built and rigged for speed, esp. a type of three-masted ship built in the U.S. c1845–70. [ME]
clip·ping (klip′ing), *n.* **1.** the act of a person or thing that clips. **2.** a piece clipped off or out, as from a newspaper or magazine. —*adj.* **3.** serving or tending to clip. [ME (adj.), late ME (n.)] —**clip′ping·ly,** *adv.*
clip·sheet (klip′shēt′), *n.* a sheet of paper printed on one side for convenience in cutting and reprinting, containing news items, features, etc., and distributed by public-relations firms, publishers, and the like.
clipt (klipt), *v.* a pp. of **clip**[1].
clique (klēk, klik), *n., v.*, **cliqued, cli·quing.** —*n.* **1.** a small, exclusive group of people; coterie; set. —*v.i.* **2.** *Informal.* to form or associate in a clique. [< F, perh. alter. of *claque* (see CLAQUE) but MF has *clique* clicking sound] —**cli′quey, cli′quy,** *adj.* —**Syn. 1.** circle, crowd. See **ring**[1].
cli·quish (klē′kish, klik′ish), *adj.* **1.** of, pertaining to, or characteristic of a clique. **2.** tending to divide into cliques: *a cliquish neighborhood.* **3.** associating exclusively with the members of one's own clique; clannish. —**cli′quish·ly,** *adv.* —**cli′quish·ness,** *n.*
Clis·the·nes (klis′thə nēz′), *n.* Cleisthenes.
clit·o·ris (klit′ər is, klī′tər is), *n. Anat.* the erectile organ of the vulva, homologous to the penis of the male. [< Gk *kleitorís*, akin to *kleíein* to shut] —**clit′o·ral, clit·o·rid·e·an** (klit′ə rid′ē ən), *adj.*
Clive (klīv), *n.* **Robert** (*Baron Clive of Plassey*), 1725–74, British general and statesman in India.
cliv·ers (kliv′ərz), *n., pl.* **cliv·ers.** cleavers.
clo·a·ca (klō ā′kə), *n., pl.* **-cae** (-sē). **1.** a sewer, esp. an ancient sewer. **2.** a privy. **3.** *Zool.* **a.** the common cavity into which the intestinal, urinary, and generative canals open in birds, reptiles, amphibians, many fishes, and certain mammals. **b.** a similar cavity in invertebrates. [< L: sewer, drain; prob. akin to Gk *klýzein* to wash, wash away] —**clo·a′cal,** *adj.*
cloak (klōk), *n.* **1.** a loose outer garment. **2.** that which covers or conceals; disguise; pretext: *He conducts his affairs under a cloak of secrecy.* —*v.t.* **3.** to cover with or as with a cloak. **4.** to conceal: *The mission was cloaked in mystery.* [ME *cloke* (< OF) < ML *cloca*, var. of *clocca* (bell-shaped) cape, orig. bell; see CLOCK[1]] —**cloak′less,** *adj.*
cloak-and-dag·ger (klōk′ən dag′ər), *adj.* pertaining to or characteristic of intrigue or espionage.
cloak·room (klōk′rōōm′, -rŏŏm′), *n.* **1.** a room in which outer garments may be left temporarily, as in a club, restaurant, etc. **2.** *Brit.* a baggage room, as at a railway station.
clob·ber (klob′ər), *v.t. Slang.* **1.** to batter severely; strike heavily. **2.** to defeat decisively; drub; trounce. [?]
cloche (klōsh, klôsh), *n.* a bell-shaped, close-fitting hat for women. [< F: bell jar < ML *clocca.* See CLOAK]
clock[1] (klok), **1.** any of various instruments for measuring and recording time, esp. by mechanical means, usually with hands to indicate the hour and minute. **2. around the clock, a.** during all 24 hours; ceaselessly. **b.** without stopping for rest; tirelessly. —*v.t.* **3.** to time, test, or determine by means of a clock or watch: *The race horse was clocked at two minutes thirty seconds.* —*v.i.* **4. clock in** or **out,** to begin or end work, esp. by punching a time clock. [ME *clok(ke)* < MD *clocke* instrument for measuring time; akin to OHG *glocka* (G *Glocke*), OE *clucge*, OIr *clocc* bell. See CLOAK] —**clock′like′,** *adj.*
clock[2] (klok), *n.* **1.** a short embroidered or woven ornament on each side or on the outer side of a stocking. —*v.t.* **2.** to embroider with such an ornament. [?]
clock·er (klok′ər), *n.* **1.** a person who times race horses during workouts. **2.** an official who times a race.
clock′ watch′, a watch that strikes the hours. Cf. **repeater** (def. 3).
clock·wise (klok′wīz′), *adv.* **1.** in the direction of the rotation of the hands of a clock as viewed from the front; circularly to the right from a point taken as the top. —*adj.* **2.** directed clockwise: *a clockwise movement.*
clock·work (klok′wûrk′), *n.* **1.** the mechanism of a clock. **2.** any mechanism similar to that of a clock. **3. like clockwork,** with perfect regularity or precision.
clod (klod), *n.* **1.** a lump or mass, esp. of earth or clay. **2.** earth; soil. **3.** a stupid person; blockhead; dolt. [late ME *clodde*, OE *clodd-* (in *clodhamer* fieldfare)] —**clod′dy,** *adj.* —**clod′dish,** *adj.* —**clod′dish·ly,** *adv.* —**clod′dish·ness,** *n.*
clod·hop·per (klod′hop′ər), *n.* **1.** a clumsy boor; rustic; bumpkin. **2. clodhoppers,** strong, heavy shoes.
clod·poll (klod′pōl′), *n.* a stupid person; blockhead. Also, **clod′pole′.** Also called **clod·pate** (klod′pāt′).
clog (klog, klôg), *v.*, **clogged, clog·ging,** *n.* —*v.t.* **1.** to hinder or obstruct with thick or sticky matter; choke up. **2.** to encumber; hamper; hinder. **3.** to crowd excessively; overfill. —*v.i.* **4.** to become clogged, encumbered, or choked up. **5.** to stick; stick together. **6.** to do a clog dance. —*n.* **7.** anything that impedes motion or action; encumbrance; hindrance. **8.** a shoe with a thick sole of wood or cork. [late ME *clog(ge)* short log or block of wood < ?] —**clog′gi·ness,** *n.* —**clog′gy,** *adj.* —**Syn. 2.** impede, trammel, fetter.
clog′ dance′, a dance in which clogs, or heavy shoes, are worn for hammering out a lively rhythm. —**clog′ danc′er.** —**clog′ danc′ing.**
cloi·son·né (kloi′zə nā′; *Fr.* klwa zô nā′), *n.* enamelwork in which colored areas are separated by thin, metal bands. [< F = *cloison* partition (< VL **clausiōn-* (s. of **clausiō*) = L *claus(us)* (see CLAUSE, CLOSE) + *-iōn-* -ION) + F *-é* < L *-ātus* -ATE[1]]
clois·ter (kloi′stər), *n.* **1.** a place of religious seclusion, as a monastery or convent. **2.** any quiet, secluded place. **3.** life in a monastery or convent. **4.** *Archit.* **a.** a covered walk, esp. in a religious institution, having an open arcade or colonnade, usually opening onto a courtyard. **b.** a courtyard, esp. in a religious institution, bordered with such walks. —*v.t.* **5.** to confine in a monastery or convent. **6.** to confine in retirement; seclude. [ME *cloistre* < OF = *cloi(son)* partition (see CLOISONNÉ) + *(clo)stre* < L *claustrum* barrier (ML: enclosed place) = *claus(us)* (see CLOSE) + *-trum* n. suffix]

clois·tered (kloi′stərd), *adj.* **1.** secluded from the world; sheltered: *a cloistered life.* **2.** having a cloister or cloisters.
clois·tral (kloi′strəl), *adj.* **1.** of, pertaining to, or living in a cloister. **2.** cloisterlike.
clomb (klōm), *v.* *Archaic or Dial.* pt. and pp. of **climb.**
clomp (klomp), *v.i.* clump (def. 5).
clone (klōn), *n., v.,* **cloned, clon·ing.** *Biol.* —*n.* **1.** Also, **clon** (klon, klōn). a group of organisms derived from a single individual by various types of asexual reproduction. —*v.i., v.t.* **2.** to grow or cause to grow as or into a clone. —**clon·al** (klon′əl), *adj.* —**clon′al·ly,** *adv.* [< Gk *klṓn* a slip, twig]
clon·ic (klon′ik, klō′nik), *adj.* *Pathol.* of or relating to clonus. —**clo·nic·i·ty** (klo nis′i tē, klō-), *n.* —**clo′nism,** *n.*
clon′ic spasm′, *Med.* See under **spasm** (def. 1).
clo·nus (klō′nəs), *n., pl.* **-nus·es.** *Pathol.* a rapid succession of flexions and extensions of a group of muscles. [< NL < Gk *klónos* turmoil]
Cloots (klōts), *n.* **Jean Bap·tiste du Val-de-Grâce** (zhäɴ bᴀ tēst′ dʏ vᴀl də gʀäs′), **Baron de** ("*Anacharsis Cloots*"), 1755–94, Prussian leader in French Revolution.
clop (klop), *n., v.,* **clopped, clop·ping.** —*n.* **1.** a sound made by or as if by a horse's hoof. —*v.i.* **2.** to make or walk with such a sound. [imit.]
close (*v.* klōz; *adj.* klōs *for 24–48, 51,* klōz *for 49,50; adv.* klōs; *n.* klōz *for 56, 57, 60, 62,* klōs *for 58, 59, 61*), *v.,* **closed, clos·ing,** *adj.,* **clos·er, clos·est,** *adv., n.* —*v.t.* **1.** to put (something) in a position to obstruct an entrance, opening, etc.; shut. **2.** to stop or obstruct (a gap, entrance, aperture, etc.): *to close a hole in a wall with plaster.* **3.** to block or hinder passage across; prevent access to: *to close a border to tourists.* **4.** to stop or obstruct the entrances, apertures, or gaps in. **5.** (of the mind) to make imperceptive or inaccessible: *to close one's mind to another's arguments.* **6.** to bring together the parts of; join; unite (often fol. by *up*): *Close up those ranks!* **7.** to bring to an end. **8.** to conclude successfully by arranging the final details of: *to close a sale on a car.* **9.** to stop rendering the customary services of: *to close a store for the night.* **10.** to force to suspend an illegal or unhealthy practice by revoking the license of. **11.** *Naut.* to come close to. **12.** *Archaic.* to enclose; cover in. —*v.i.* **13.** to become closed; shut: *The door closed with a bang.* **14.** to come together; unite: *Her lips closed firmly.* **15.** to come close: *His pursuers closed rapidly.* **16.** to grapple; engage in close encounter (often fol. by *with*): *We closed with the invaders shortly before sundown.* **17.** to come to an end; terminate. **18.** to cease to offer the customary activities or services: *The school closed for the summer.* **19.** (of a theatrical production) to cease to be performed: *The play closed yesterday.* **20.** *Stock Exchange.* (of a stock, a group of stocks, etc.) to be or to be priced as specified at the end of a trading day or other trading period. **21. close down, a.** to terminate the operation of; discontinue. **b.** to attempt to control or eliminate. **22. close in on** or **upon, a.** to approach so as to capture, attack, arrest, etc. **b.** to surround or envelop so as to entrap. **23. close out, a.** to reduce the price of (merchandise) for quick sale. **b.** to liquidate or dispose of finally and completely. —*adj.* **24.** having the parts or elements near to one another: *a close formation of battleships.* **25.** compact; dense: *a close weave.* **26.** being in or having proximity in space or time. **27.** marked by similarity in degree, action, feeling, etc.: *This dark pink is close to red.* **28.** near or near together in kind or relationship: *a close relative.* **29.** intimate; confidential: *a close friend.* **30.** based on a strong, uniting feeling of respect, honor, or love: *a close friendship.* **31.** fitting tightly: *a close, clinging sweater.* **32.** (of a haircut or shave, the mowing of a lawn, etc.) so executed that the hair, grass, or the like, is left flush with the surface or very short. **33.** not deviating from the subject under consideration. **34.** strict; searching; minute. **35.** not deviating from a model or original. **36.** nearly even or equal: *a close contest.* **37.** shut; shut tight; not open: *a close hatch.* **38.** shut in; enclosed. **39.** completely enclosing or surrounding: *a close siege.* **40.** without opening; with all openings covered or closed. **41.** confined; narrow: *close quarters.* **42.** lacking fresh or freely circulating air: *a hot, close room.* **43.** heavy; oppressive: *a spell of close, sultry weather.* **44.** narrowly confined, as a prisoner. **45.** practicing secrecy; secretive; reticent. **46.** parsimonious; stingy. **47.** scarce, as money. **48.** not open to public or general admission, competition, etc. **49.** *Hunting, Angling.* closed (def. 5). **50.** *Phonet.* (of a vowel) articulated with a relatively small opening between the tongue and the roof of the mouth. Cf. **high** (def. 23), **open** (def. 26a). **51.** *Rare.* viscous; not volatile. —*adv.* **52.** in a close manner; closely. **53.** near; close by. **54. close to the wind,** *Naut.* in a direction nearly opposite to that from which the wind is coming. **55. close up,** *Naut.* fully raised; at the top of the halyard. —*n.* **56.** the act of closing. **57.** the end or conclusion: *at the close of day; the close of the speech.* **58.** an enclosed place, or enclosure, esp. one beside a cathedral. **59.** any piece of land held as private property. **60.** *Music.* cadence (def. 7). **61.** *Brit. Dial.* **a.** a narrow entry or alley terminating in a dead end. **b.** a courtyard enclosed except for one narrow entrance. **62.** *Obs.* a close encounter; grapple. [(v.) ME *close(n)* < OF *clos-* (< L *claus-* perf. s. of *claudere* to shut); r. OE *(be)clysan* < *clūse* enclosure < LL *clūsa;* (adj.) ME *clos* < MF < L *clausus* (ptp. of *claudere*); (adv.) ME *clos* < adj.] —**clos·a·ble, close·a·ble** (klō′zə bəl), *adj.* —**close·ly** (klōs′lē), *adv.* —**close·ness** (klōs′nis), *n.* —**clos·er** (klō′zər), *n.*
—**Syn. 2.** Close, shut mean to cause something not to be open. Close suggests blocking an opening or vacant place: *to close a breach in a wall.* It also connotes more force or more refinement than shut. The word shut refers esp. to blocking or barring openings intended for literal or figurative entering and leaving: *to shut a door, mouth, gate, etc.* **7.** complete, end, conclude, terminate, finish. **26.** immediate, proximate, nearby. **34.** intent, concentrated. **56.** See **end**[1].
close-at-hand (klōs′ət hand′), *adj.* nearby or imminent.
close-by (klōs′bī′), *adj.* nearby; adjacent; neighboring.
close′ call′ (klōs), *U.S. Informal.* a narrow escape from danger, failure, or the like.
closed (klōzd), *adj.* **1.** having or forming a boundary or barrier: *He was blocked by a closed door.* **2.** brought to a close; concluded. **3.** not public; restricted; exclusive. **4.** *Phonet.* (of a syllable) ending with a consonant or a consonant cluster, as *has, hasp.* Cf. **open** (def. 26b). **5.** *Hunting, Angling.* restricted as to the kind of game or fish that may legally be taken and as to where or when it may be taken: *a closed season on deer.* **6.** *Math.* **a.** (of a set and a mathematical operation defined on the set) such that performing the operation on elements of the set results in elements of the set, as multiplication in the set of integers. **b.** (of a curve) not having endpoints; enclosing an area. **c.** (of a function or operator) having as its graph a closed set. [ME]
closed-cap·tioned (klōzd′kap′shənd), *adj.* (of a television program) broadcast with captions that are visible only with the use of a decoder.
closed′ chain′, *Chem.* three or more atoms linked together to form a ring or cycle and represented accordingly by its structural formula. Cf. **open chain.**
closed′ cir′cuit, *Elect.* a circuit without interruption, providing a continuous path through which a current can flow. —**closed′-cir′cuit,** *adj.*
closed′-cir′cuit tel′evision, a system of televising by means of cable to a designated number of viewing sets.
closed′ corpora′tion, an incorporated business whose stock is owned by a small group.
closed′ cou′plet, a couplet that concludes with an end-stopped line. Cf. **open couplet.**
closed′-end invest′ment com′pany (klōzd′end′), an investment company that issues its shares in large blocks at infrequent intervals and is not obligated to redeem or repurchase them. Cf. **open-end investment company.**
closed′ frac′ture. See **simple fracture.**
closed′ pri′mary, a direct primary in which only persons meeting tests of party membership may vote.
closed′ shop′, a shop in which union membership is a condition of employment.
close·fist·ed (klōs′fis′tid), *adj.* stingy; miserly. —**close′-fist′ed·ness,** *n.*
close-fit·ting (klōs′fit′ing), *adj.* (of a garment) fitting closely or snugly to the body.
close′ har′mony (klōs), *Music.* harmony in which the voices, excluding the bass, occur within an octave or, sometimes, within the interval of a tenth.
close-hauled (klōs′hôld′), *adj., adv.* *Naut.* as close to the wind as a vessel will sail, with sails as flat as possible.
close-knit (klōs′nit′), *adj.* tightly connected or organized.
close-lipped (klōs′lipt′), *adj.* not talking or telling much.
close-mouthed (klōs′mouthd′, -moutht′), *adj.* reticent; uncommunicative.
close′-or′der drill′ (klōs′ôr′dər), *U.S. Army.* practice in formation marching and other movements, in the carrying of arms during formal marching, and in the formal handling of arms for ceremonies and guard.
close·out (klōz′out′), *n.* **1.** a sale on all goods in liquidating a business. **2.** a sale on goods of a type that will no longer be carried by a store.
close′ quar′ters (klōs), **1.** a small, cramped place or position. **2.** direct and close contact in a fight.
close′ shave′ (klōs), *U.S. Informal.* See **close call.**
clos·et (kloz′it), *n.* **1.** a small room or enclosed recess for storing clothing. **2.** a cabinet, enclosed recess, or small room for storing food, utensils, etc. **3.** a small private room, esp. one used for prayer or meditation. **4.** See **water closet.** —*adj.* **5.** private; secluded. **6.** suited for use or enjoyment in privacy: *closet reflections.* **7.** engaged in private study or speculation; speculative; impractical: *a closet thinker with no practical experience.* —*v.t.* **8.** to shut up in a private room for a conference, interview, etc. [ME < MF = *clos* close (n.) + *-et* -et]
clos′et dra′ma, drama appropriate for reading rather than for acting.
clos′et queen′, *Slang.* a person who conceals his homosexual nature and activity.
close-up (klōs′up′), *n.* **1.** *Photog.* a picture taken at close range or with a long focal-length lens, on a relatively large scale. **2.** *Motion Pictures, Television.* a camera shot taken at a very short distance from the subject, to permit a close and detailed view of an object or action. Cf. **long shot** (def. 3). **3.** an intimate view or presentation of anything.
clos′ing costs′, various charges (for title insurance, property survey, etc.) paid by the buyer and seller of real property when the sale is executed. Also called **clos′ing fees′.**
clos·trid·i·um (klo strid′ē əm), *n., pl.* **clos·trid·i·a** (klo-strid′ē ə). *Bacteriol.* any of several rod-shaped, spore-forming, anaerobic bacteria of the genus *Clostridium,* found in soil and in the intestinal tract of man and animals. [< Gk *klōstr-,* var. s. of *klōstḗr* spindle (*klōs-,* var. s. of *klṓthein* to spin) + *-tēr* suffix making n. of agent or instrument) + -idium] —**clos·trid′i·al, clos·trid′i·an,** *adj.*
clo·sure (klō′zhər), *n., v.,* **-sured, -sur·ing.** —*n.* **1.** the act or state of closing. **2.** the state of being closed. **3.** a bringing to an end; conclusion. **4.** something that closes. **5.** *Parl. Proc.* a cloture. **6.** *Obs.* that which encloses or shuts in; enclosure. —*v.t., v.i.* **7.** *Parl. Proc.* to cloture. [ME < MF < L *clausūra.* See close, -ure]
clot (klot), *n., v.,* **clot·ted, clot·ting.** —*n.* **1.** a mass or lump. **2.** a semisolid mass of coagulated blood. **3.** a small compact group of individuals; cluster. —*v.i.* **4.** to form into clots; coagulate. —*v.t.* **5.** to cause to clot. **6.** to cover with clots. **7.** to cause to become blocked or obscured. [ME; OE *clott* lump; c. MD *klotte,* G *Klotz* block, log] —**clot′ty,** *adj.*
cloth (klôth, kloth), *n., pl.* **cloths** (klôthz, klothz, klôths, kloths). **1.** a fabric formed by weaving, felting, etc., used for garments, upholstery, and many other items. **2.** a piece of such a fabric for a particular purpose: *an altar cloth.* **3.** the particular attire of any profession, esp. that of the clergy. **4. the cloth,** the profession of clergymen; ministry. [ME *cloth, clath* cloth, garment, OE *clāth;* c. D *kleed,* G *Kleid*]
clothe (klōth), *v.t.,* **clothed** or **clad, cloth·ing. 1.** to dress; attire. **2.** to provide with clothing. **3.** to cover with or as with clothing. [ME *clothe(n),* OE *clāthian* < *clāth* cloth]
clothes (klōz, klōthz), *n.pl.* garments for the body; articles of dress; wearing apparel. [ME; OE *clāthas,* pl. of *clāth* cloth] —**Syn.** clothing, attire, garb; habiliments.

clothes·horse (klōz′hôrs′, klōthz′-), *n.* **1.** a person, esp. a woman, whose chief interest and pleasure is dressing fashionably. **2.** a frame on which to hang wet laundry for drying.

clothes·line (klōz′līn′, klōthz′-), *n.* a strong, thin rope, cord, wire, etc., usually stretched between two poles or posts, on or from which clean laundry is hung to dry.

clothes′ moth′, any of several small moths of the family *Tineidae,* the larvae of which feed on wool, fur, etc.

Clothes moth, *Tinea pellionella* A, Adult; B, Larva

clothes·pin (klōz′pin′, klōthz′-), *n.* a device, such as a forked piece of wood or plastic, for fastening articles to a clothesline. Also, *Brit.,* **clothes-peg** (klōz′peg′, klōthz′-).

clothes·press (klōz′pres′, klōthz′-), *n.* a receptacle for clothes, as a chest of drawers, a wardrobe, or a closet.

clothes′ tree′, an upright pole with hooks near the top for hanging coats, hats, etc.

cloth·ier (klōth′yər, -ē ər), *n.* **1.** a retailer of clothing, esp. for men. **2.** a person who makes or sells cloth. [CLOTH + *-ier,* var. of -ER[1]; r. ME *clother*]

cloth·ing (klō′thing), *n.* **1.** garments collectively; clothes; raiment; apparel. **2.** a covering. [ME]

Clo·tho (klō′thō), *n. Class. Myth.* the Fate who spins the thread of life. Cf. **Atropos, Lachesis.** [< L < Gk *Klōtho,* lit., the Spinner = *klṓth(ein)* (to) spin + -ō suffix used in making names of women]

cloth′ yard′, a unit of measure for cloth, now the equivalent of the standard yard; 36 inches; 3 feet.

clo·ture (klō′chər), *n., v.,* **-tured, -tur·ing.** *U.S. Parl. Proc.* —*n.* **1.** a method of closing debate and causing an immediate vote to be taken. —*v.t., v.i.* **2.** to close (a debate) by cloture. [< F *clôture,* MF *closture* < VL **clōstūra,* alter. of L *clōstra, claustra,* pl. of *claustrum* barrier. See CLOISTER]

cloud (kloud), *n.* **1.** a visible collection of particles of water or ice suspended in the air, usually at a considerable elevation above the earth's surface. **2.** any similar mass, esp. of smoke or dust. **3.** a dim or obscure area in something otherwise clear or transparent. **4.** a patch or spot differing in color from the surrounding surface. **5.** anything that obscures or darkens something or causes gloom, disgrace, etc. **6.** a great number of insects, birds, etc., flying together: *a cloud of locusts.* **7. in the clouds, a.** in a condition of absent-mindedness; lost in reverie. **b.** impractical. **8. on a cloud,** *Slang.* exceedingly happy; in high spirits. **9. under a cloud,** in disgrace; under suspicion: *After the fight he left town under a cloud.* —*v.t.* **10.** to overspread or cover with or as with a cloud or clouds. **11.** to overshadow; obscure; darken: *The hardships of war cloud his childhood memories.* **12.** to make gloomy. **13.** (of distress, anxiety, etc.) to reveal itself in (a part of one's face): *Worry clouded his brow.* **14.** to make obscure or indistinct; confuse. **15.** to place under suspicion, disgrace, etc. —*v.i.* **16.** to grow cloudy; become clouded. **17.** (of a part of one's face) to reveal one's distress, anxiety, etc.: *His brow clouded with anger.* [ME; OE *clūd* rock, hill; prob. akin to CLOD] —**cloud′less,** *adj.* —**cloud′like′,** *adj.* —**Syn. 1.** CLOUD, FOG, HAZE, MIST differ somewhat in their figurative uses. CLOUD connotes esp. daydreaming: *His mind is in the clouds.* FOG and HAZE connote esp. bewilderment or confusion: *to go around in a fog* (*haze*). MIST has an emotional connotation: *a mist in one's eyes.* **6.** swarm, horde, multitude, throng, host.

cloud·ber·ry (kloud′ber′ē, -bə rē), *n., pl.* **-ries. 1.** the orange-yellow edible fruit of a raspberry, *Rubus Chamaemorus,* of the Northern Hemisphere. **2.** the plant itself.

cloud·burst (kloud′bûrst′), *n.* a sudden and very heavy rainfall.

cloud′ cham′ber, *Physics.* a chamber containing a supersaturated mixture of gas and vapor, the vapor condensing around ions created by the passage of a charged particle, thereby revealing the path of the particle. Also called **Wilson cloud chamber.** Cf. **bubble chamber.**

cloud·land (kloud′land′), *n.* a region of unreality, imagination, etc.; dreamland.

cloud·let (kloud′lit), *n.* a small cloud.

cloud′ nine′, *Informal.* a state of perfect happiness or bliss: *The newlyweds seemed to be on cloud nine.*

cloud′ rack′, rack[4] (def. 1).

cloud·y (klou′dē), *adj.,* **cloud·i·er, cloud·i·est. 1.** full of or overcast by clouds: *a cloudy sky.* **2.** having little or no sunshine: *a cloudy day.* **3.** of, like, or pertaining to a cloud or clouds. **4.** having cloudlike markings: *cloudy marble.* **5.** not clear or transparent. **6.** obscure; indistinct. **7.** darkened by gloom, trouble, etc. **8.** under suspicion, disgrace, etc. [ME *cloudi,* OE *clūdig* rocky, hilly] —**cloud′i·ly,** *adv.* —**cloud′i·ness,** *n.* —**Syn. 1, 2.** murky, shadowy, gloomy. **5.** murky, turbid, muddy. **6.** dim, blurred.

Clou·et (klōō e′), *n.* **1. Fran·çois** (fräN swA′), c1510–72, French painter. **2.** his father, **Jean** (zhäN), c1485–1545, French painter.

clough (kluf, klou), *n. Brit. Dial.* a narrow valley; ravine; glen. [ME *clough, cloge;* c. OHG *klāh-*]

Clough (kluf), *n.* **Arthur Hugh,** 1819–61, English poet.

clout (klout), *n.* **1.** *Informal.* a blow, esp. with the hand; cuff. **2.** *Baseball Slang.* a long hit. **3.** *Informal.* the influential effect of an idea, news story, personality, etc.: *His peace plan has a good deal of clout.* **4.** *Archery.* **a.** the mark or target shot at. **b.** a shot that hits the mark. **5.** *Archaic.* **a.** a patch or piece of cloth or other material used to mend something. **b.** any worthless piece of cloth; rag. —*v.t.* **6.** *Informal.* to strike, esp. with the hand; cuff. **7.** *Dial.* **a.** to bandage. **b.** to patch; mend. [ME; OE *clūt* piece of cloth or metal; c. MLG *klūt(e),* Icel *klūt(r)*] —**clout′er,** *n.*

clove[1] (klōv), *n.* **1.** the dried flower bud of a tropical myrtaceous tree, *Eugenia aromatica,* used whole or ground as a spice. **2.** the tree. [ME *clow(e),* short for *clow-gilofre* clove-gillyflower < F *clou de gilofre; clou,* lit., nail < L *clāvus*]

clove[2] (klōv), *n. Bot.* one of the small bulbs formed in the axils of the scales of a mother bulb, as in garlic. [ME; OE *clufu* bulb (c. MD *clōve,* D *kloof*); akin to CLEAVE[2]]

clove[3] (klōv), *v.* a pt. of **cleave**[2].

clove′ hitch′, a knot or hitch for fastening a rope to a spar or larger rope, consisting of two half hitches made in opposite directions, the two parts of the rope emerging also in opposite directions. See illus. at **knot.** [CLOVE[3] + HITCH]

clo·ven (klō′vən), *v.* **1.** a pp. of **cleave**[2]. —*adj.* **2.** cleft; split; divided: *the cloven hoof of a goat.*

clo′ven hoof′, the figurative indication of Satan or evil temptation. Also called **clo′ven foot′.**

clo·ven-hoofed (klō′vən ho͝oft′, -ho͞oft′), *adj.* **1.** having split hoofs, once assumed to represent the halves of a single undivided hoof, as in cattle. **2.** devilish; satanic. Also, **clo′ven-foot′ed.**

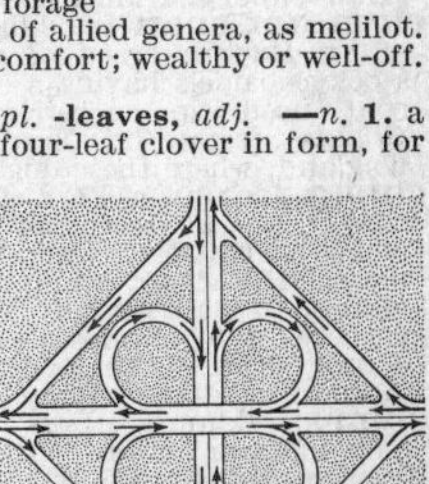
White clover, *Trifolium repens*

clove′ pink′, a pink, *Dianthus Caryophyllus,* having a spicy scent resembling that of cloves. Cf. **carnation** (def. 1).

clo·ver (klō′vər), *n., pl.* **-vers,** (*esp. collectively*) **-ver. 1.** any of various fabaceous herbs of the genus *Trifolium,* having trifoliolate leaves and dense flower heads, many species of which, as *T. pratense,* are cultivated as forage plants. **2.** any of various plants of allied genera, as melilot. **3. in clover,** enjoying luxury or comfort; wealthy or well-off. [ME *clovere,* OE *clāfre*]

clo·ver·leaf (klō′vər lēf′), *n., pl.* **-leaves,** *adj.* —*n.* **1.** a road arrangement, resembling a four-leaf clover in form, for permitting easy traffic movement between two intersecting high-speed highways. —*adj.* **2.** shaped like or resembling a leaf of clover.

Cloverleaf (def. 1)

Clo·vis (klō′vis), *n.* a city in E New Mexico. 28,495 (1970).

Clo·vis I (klō′vis; *Fr.* klô-vēs′), A.D. c465–511, king of the Franks 481–511. German, **Chlodwig.**

clowd·er (klou′dər), *n.* a group or collection of cats. [alter. of CLUTTER]

clown (kloun), *n.* **1.** a comic performer, esp. in a circus, who wears an outlandish costume and extravagant make-up and entertains by pantomime, juggling, tumbling, etc. **2.** a prankster or practical joker. **3.** a coarse, ill-bred person; boor. —*v.i.* **4.** to act like a clown. [akin to Icel *klunni* boor, Dan (dial.) *klunds*] —**clown′ish,** *adj.* —**clown′ish·ly,** *adv.* —**clown′ish·ness,** *n.*

clown·er·y (klou′nə rē), *n., pl.* **-er·ies** for 2. **1.** clownish behavior. **2.** an instance of this.

cloy (kloi), *v.t.* **1.** to weary by excess, as of food, sweetness, or pleasure; surfeit; satiate. —*v.i.* **2.** to become uninteresting or distasteful through overabundance: *A diet of candy soon cloys.* [aph. var. of ME *acloye(n)* < MF *enclo(y)er* < ML *inclāvāre* to nail in = *in-* IN-[2] + *clāv(us)* nail + *-āre* inf. suffix] —**cloy·ed·ness** (kloi′id nis), *n.* —**cloy′ing·ly,** *adv.* —**cloy′ing·ness,** *n.*

CLU, Civil Liberties Union.

club (klub), *n., v.,* **clubbed, club·bing,** *adj.* —*n.* **1.** a heavy stick, usually thicker at one end than at the other, suitable for use as a weapon; cudgel. **2.** *Sports.* **a.** a stick or bat used to drive a ball in various games, as golf. **b.** See **Indian club. 3.** a group of persons organized for a social, literary, athletic, political, or other purpose. **4.** the building or rooms occupied by such a group. **5.** an organization that offers its subscribers certain benefits, in return for regular purchases or payments: *a book club.* **6.** a night club or cabaret. **7.** a black trefoil-shaped figure on a playing card. **8.** a card bearing such figures. **9. clubs,** (*construed as sing. or pl.*) the suit so marked: *Clubs is trump. Clubs are trump.* **10.** *Naut.* a short spar attached to the end of a gaff to allow the clew of a gaff topsail to extend beyond the peak of the gaff. —*v.t.* **11.** to beat with or as with a club. **12.** to gather or form into a clublike mass. **13.** to unite; combine; join together. **14.** to contribute toward a joint expense (often fol. by *up* or *together*): *They clubbed their dollars together to buy the present.* **15.** to defray by proportional shares. —*v.i.* **16.** to combine or join together, as for a common purpose. **17.** to gather into a mass. **18.** to contribute to a common fund. **19.** *Naut.* to drift in a current with an anchor, usually rigged with a spring, dragging or dangling to reduce speed. —*adj.* **20.** of or pertaining to a club. **21.** consisting of a combination of foods offered at the price set on the menu: *a club luncheon.* [ME *clubbe* < Scand; cf. Icel *klubba* cudgel; akin to CLUMP] —**Syn. 3, 5.** association, society. **11.** bludgeon, cudgel.

club·ba·ble (klub′ə bəl), *adj.* fit to be a member of a social club. Also, **club′a·ble.** —**club′ba·bil′i·ty, club′a·bil′i·ty,** *n.*

club′ bag′, *U.S.* a soft, usually leather, two-handled bag suitable for use in traveling or for general utility.

club·by (klub′ē), *adj.,* **-bi·er, -bi·est. 1.** characteristic of a club. **2.** socially exclusive; cliquish. **3.** inclined to join clubs. —**club′bi·ly,** *adv.*

club′ car′, *U.S.* a railroad passenger car equipped with easy chairs, card tables, a buffet, etc. Also called **lounge car.**

club′ chair′, a heavily upholstered chair having solid sides and a low back.

club·foot (klub′fo͝ot′), *n., pl.* **-feet** for 1. **1.** a deformed or distorted foot. **2.** the condition of having such a foot; talipes. —**club′foot′ed,** *adj.*

club·house (klub′hous′), *n., pl.* **-hous·es** (-hou′ziz). a building or room occupied by a club.

club·man (klub′mən, -man′), *n., pl.* **-men** (-mən, -men′). a man who belongs to a club, esp. a fashionable club, and is active in club life.

club′ moss′, any plant of the genus *Lycopodium.*

club′ sand′wich, *U.S.* a sandwich having two layers of sliced meat, lettuce, tomato, etc., between three slices of bread; double-decker.
club′ so′da. See **soda water** (def. 1).
club′ steak′, a beefsteak cut from the rib end of the short loin.
club·wom·an (klub′wo͝om′ən), *n., pl.* **-wom·en.** a woman who engages in club activities, esp. one prominent in social or civic organizations.
cluck[1] (kluk), *v.i.* **1.** to utter the cry of a hen brooding or calling her chicks. **2.** to make a similar sound to express concern, approval, etc. **—***v.t.* **3.** to call or utter by clucking. **—***n.* **4.** the sound uttered by a hen when brooding or calling her chicks. **5.** any similar sound. [var. of *clock* (now dial. and Scot), ME *clokk(en),* OE *cloccian* to cluck]
cluck[2] (kluk), *n. Slang.* a dull-witted person; dolt. [special use of CLUCK[1]]
clue (klo͞o), *n., v.,* **clued, clu·ing.** **—***n.* **1.** anything that serves to guide or direct in the solution of a problem, mystery, etc. **2.** clew (defs. 1, 3, 4). **—***v.t.* **3.** *Informal.* to direct or point out to by a clue. **4.** clew (defs. 5, 7). **5. clue in,** *Slang.* to tell (someone) the facts. [var. of CLEW]
Cluj (klo͞ozh), *n.* a city in NW Rumania. 167,011 (est. 1964). German, **Klausenberg.** Hungarian, **Kolozsvár.**
clum′ber span′iel (klum′bər), one of an English breed of short-legged, stocky spaniels having a chiefly white coat, used esp. as retrievers. [after *Clumber,* estate in Nottinghamshire, England, where these dogs were bred]

Clumber spaniel (1½ ft. high at shoulder)

clump (klump), *n.* **1.** a close group or cluster, esp. of trees or other plants. **2.** *Immunol.* a cluster of agglutinated bacteria, erythrocytes, etc. **3.** a lump or mass. **4.** a heavy, thumping step, sound, etc. **—***v.i.* **5.** Also, **clomp.** to walk heavily and clumsily. **6.** to gather or be gathered into clumps. **—***v.t.* **7.** to gather or form into a clump; mass. [akin to D *klompe* lump, mass, OE *clympre* lump of metal] **—clump′y, clump′ish, clump′like′,** *adj.*
clum·sy (klum′zē), *adj.,* **-si·er, -si·est.** **1.** awkward in movement or action; without skill or grace. **2.** awkwardly done or made; unwieldy; ill-contrived. [obs. *clums* benumbed with cold + -Y[1]; akin to ME *clumsen* to be stiff with cold, Sw (Skåne) *klumsig* benumbed, awkward, *klums* numbskull, Icel *klumsa* afflicted with lockjaw, etc.] **—clum′si·ly,** *adv.* **—clum′si·ness,** *n.* **—Syn. 1.** ungraceful, ungainly, lumbering. **2.** inexpert, bungling, inept. **—Ant. 2.** adroit.
clung (klung), *v.* pt. and pp. of **cling.**
Clu·ny (klo͞o′nē; *Fr.* kly nē′), *n.* a town in E France, N of Lyons: ruins of a Benedictine abbey. 4412 (1962).
clu·pe·id (klo͞o′pē id), *n.* **1.** any of the *Clupeidae,* a family of chiefly marine, teleostean fishes, including the herrings, sardines, menhaden, and shad. **—***adj.* **2.** belonging or pertaining to the family *Clupeidae.* [< L *clupe(a)* a type of small river fish + -ID[2]]
clu·pe·oid (klo͞o′pē oid′), *adj.* **1.** resembling a fish of the family *Clupeidae;* clupeid. **—***n.* **2.** a clupeoid fish. [< L *clupe(a)* (see CLUPEID) + -OID]
clus·ter (klus′tər), *n.* **1.** a number of things of the same kind, growing or held together; bunch. **2.** a group of things or persons close together. **3.** *U.S. Army.* a small metal design placed on a ribbon representing an awarded medal to indicate that the same medal has been awarded again. **4.** *Phonet.* a succession of two or more contiguous consonants in an utterance, as the *str-* cluster of *strap.* **—***v.t.* **5.** to gather into a cluster or clusters. **6.** to furnish or cover with clusters. **—***v.i.* **7.** to form a cluster or clusters. [ME; OE *cluster, clyster* bunch; c. LG *kluster*] **—clus′ter·ing·ly,** *adv.* **—clus′ter·y,** *adj.*
clutch[1] (kluch), *v.t.* **1.** to seize with or as with the hands or claws; snatch. **2.** to grip or hold tightly or firmly. **—***v.i.* **3.** to try to seize or grasp (usually fol. by *at*): *She clutched at the fleeing child.* **4.** to operate the clutch in a vehicle. **—***n.* **5.** the hand, claw, etc., when grasping. **6.** Usually, **clutches.** power of disposal or control: *She fell into the clutches of the enemy.* **7.** the act of clutching; snatch or grasp. **8.** a tight grip or hold. **9.** a device for gripping something. **10.** *Mach.* **a.** a mechanism for readily engaging or disengaging a shaft with or from another shaft or rotating part. Cf. **coupling** (def. 2a). **b.** a control for operating this mechanism. **—***adj.* **11.** (of a handbag or purse) without a strap or handle; small and of a shape that may be grasped by the hand. [ME *clucche(n), clicche(n),* OE *clyccan* to clench] **—clutch′ing·ly,** *adv.* **—clutch′y,** *adj.* **—Syn. 1.** See **catch.**
clutch[2] (kluch), *n.* **1.** a hatch of eggs; the number of eggs produced or incubated at one time. **2.** a brood of chickens. **3.** a number of similar individuals: *a clutch of chorus girls.* **—***v.t.* **4.** to hatch (chickens). [var. of dial. *cletch;* akin to Scot *cleck* to hatch < Scand; cf. Icel *klekja*]
clut·ter (klut′ər), *v.t.* **1.** to fill or litter with things in a disorderly manner: *Newspapers cluttered the living room.* **—***v.i.* **2.** *Dial.* to run in disorder; move with bustle and confusion. **3.** *Dial.* to make a clatter. **—***n.* **4.** a disorderly heap or assemblage; litter. **5.** a state or condition of confusion; disorderly mess. **6.** confused noise; clatter. [var. of obs. *clotter.* See CLOT, -ER[6]]
Clyde (klīd), *n.* **1.** a river in S Scotland, flowing NW into the Firth of Clyde. 106 mi. long. **2. Firth of,** an inlet of the Atlantic, in SW Scotland. 64 mi. long.
Clyde·bank (klīd′baŋgk′), *n.* a city in SW Scotland, on the Clyde River. 49,654 (1961).
Clydes·dale (klīdz′dāl′), *n.* one of a Scottish breed of strong, hardy draft horses having a feathering of long hairs along the backs of the legs. [after *Clydesdale,* Scotland]
clyp·e·ate (klip′ē āt′), *adj. Biol.* shaped like a round shield or buckler. Also, **clyp·e·i·form** (klip′ē ə fôrm′). [< L *clypeāt(us).* See CLYPEUS, -ATE[1]]
clyp·e·us (klip′ē əs), *n., pl.* **clyp·e·i** (klip′ē ī′). the area of the facial wall of an insect's head between the labrum and the frons, usually separated from the latter by a groove. [< NL, special use of var. of L *clipeus* round shield] **—clyp′e·al,** *adj.*
clys·ter (klis′tər), *n. Med.* an enema. [late ME < medical L < Gk *klystḗr* = *klys-* (var. s. of *klȳ́zein* to rinse out) + *-tēr* n. suffix]
Cly·tem·nes·tra (klī′təm nes′trə), *n. Class. Myth.* the daughter of Tyndareus and Leda, the wife of Agamemnon, and the mother of Orestes, Electra, and Iphigenia. She killed Agamemnon and was herself killed, along with her lover, Aegisthus, by Orestes. Also, **Cly′taem·nes′tra.**
Cm, *Chem.* curium.
cm, centimeter; centimeters. Also, **cm.**
Cmdr., Commander.
cml., commercial.
C/N, **1.** circular note. **2.** credit note.
Cni·dus (nī′dəs), *n.* an ancient city in SW Asia Minor.
CNO, Chief of Naval Operations.
Cnos·sus (nos′əs, knos′-), *n.* Knossos. **—Cnos′si·an,** *adj.*
CNS, central nervous system. Also, **cns**
Cnut (kə no͞ot′, -nyo͞ot′), *n.* Canute.
CO, **1.** Colorado (approved esp. for use with zip code). **2.** Commanding Officer.
Co, *Chem.* cobalt.
co-, **1.** var. of **com-** before a vowel, *h,* and *gn*: *coadjutor; cohabit; cognate.* **2.** *Math., Astron.* a prefix meaning "complement of": *cosine; codeclination.* [< L]
C/O, cash order.
C/o, **1.** care of. **2.** *Bookkeeping.* carried over.
c/o, **1.** care of. **2.** *Bookkeeping.* carried over. **3.** cash order.
Co., **1.** Company. **2.** County. Also, **co.**
C.O., **1.** cash order. **2.** Commanding Officer. **3.** conscientious objector.
c.o., **1.** care of. **2.** carried over.
co·ac·er·vate (*n.* kō as′ər vit, -vāt′, kō′ə sûr′vit; *v.* kō as′ər vāt′, kō′ə sûr′vāt), *n., v.,* **-vat·ed, -vat·ing.** **—***n.* **1.** *Physical Chem.* a reversible aggregation of liquid particles in an emulsion. **—***v.t., v.i.* **2.** to make or become a coacervate. [< L *coacervāt(us)* (ptp. of *coacervāre*) = *co-* co- + *acerv(us)* heap + *-ātus* -ATE[1]] **—co·ac′er·va′tion,** *n.*
coach (kōch), *n.* **1.** a large, horse-drawn, four-wheeled carriage, usually enclosed. **2.** a public motor coach. **3.** *Railroads U.S.* the least expensive class of passenger accommodation, as distinguished from a parlor car, a sleeping car, etc. **4.** Also called **air coach.** *U.S.* a class of airline travel less expensive and providing less luxurious accommodations than first class. **5.** a person who trains an athlete or a team of athletes: *a football coach.* **6.** *Baseball.* a member of the team at bat who is stationed near first or third base to advise base runners and batters. **7.** a private tutor who prepares a student for an examination. **8.** a person who instructs an actor or singer. **9.** *U.S.* a type of inexpensive automobile with a boxlike, usually two-door, body manufactured in the 1920's. **—***v.t.* **10.** to give instruction or advice to in the capacity of a coach. **—***v.i.* **11.** to act as a coach. **12.** to study with or be instructed by a coach. **—***adv.* **13.** by coach or in coach-class accommodations: *We flew coach from Denver to New York.* [earlier *coche(e)* < MF *coche* < G *Kotsche, Kutsche* < Hung *kocsi,* short for *kocsi szekér* cart of Kocs, place in Hungary; senses referring to tutoring and instruction, orig. student slang, from the conception of the tutor as one who carries the student through examinations] **—coach′er,** *n.*
coach-and-four (kōch′ən fōr′, -fôr′), *n.* a coach together with the four horses by which it is drawn.
coach′ box′, the seat for the driver of a coach or carriage.
coach′ dog′, Dalmatian (def. 3).
coach·man (kōch′mən), *n., pl.* **-men.** a man employed to drive a coach or carriage. **—coach′man·ship′,** *n.*
coach′ screw′. See **lag screw.**
coach·work (kōch′wûrk′), *n.* the craftsmanship involved in the production of an automobile body.
co·act (kō akt′), *v.t., v.i.* to do or act together. **—co·ac′tive,** *adj.* **—co·ac′tive·ly,** *adv.* **—co·ac·tiv′i·ty,** *n.*
co·ac·tion[1] (kō ak′shən), *n.* force or compulsion, either in restraining or in impelling. [< L *coāctiōn-* (s. of *coāctiō*) = *coāct(us)* (ptp. of *cōgere;* see COGENT, CO-, ACT) + *-iōn-* -ION]
co·ac·tion[2] (kō ak′shən), *n.* **1.** joint action. **2.** *Ecol.* any interaction among organisms within a community.
co·ad·ju·tant (kō aj′ə tənt), *adj.* **1.** helping reciprocally; cooperating. **—***n.* **2.** an assistant; aide.
co·ad·ju·tor (kō aj′ə tər, kō′ə jo͞o′tər), *n.* **1.** an assistant. **2.** a bishop who assists another bishop and has the right of succession. [< L = *co-* co- + *adjūtor* helper (see ADJUTANT, -OR[2]); r. late ME *coadjutour* < AF < L]
co·ad·u·nate (kō aj′ə nit, -nāt′), *adj. Zool., Bot.* united by growth. [< LL *coadūnāt(us)* (ptp. of *coadūnāre*) = *co-* co- + *ad-* AD- + *ūn(us)* one + *-ātus* -ATE[1]] **—co·ad′u·na′tion,** *n.*
co·ag·u·lant (kō ag′yə lənt), *n.* a substance that produces or aids coagulation. Also called **co·ag·u·la·tor** (kō ag′yə lā′tər). [< L *coāgulant-* (s. of *coāgulāns,* prp. of *coāgulāre*). See COAGULUM, -ANT]
co·ag·u·lase (kō ag′yə lās′), *n. Biochem.* any of several enzymes, esp. one secreted by certain staphylococci, that cause coagulation of blood or blood plasma. [COAGUL(ATE) + -ASE]
co·ag·u·late (*v.* kō ag′yə lāt′; *adj.* kō ag′yə lit, -lāt′), *v.,* **-lat·ed, -lat·ing,** *adj.* **—***v.t., v.i.* **1.** to change from a fluid into a thickened mass; curdle; congeal. **—***adj.* **2.** *Obs.* coagulated. [< L *coāgulāt(us)* (ptp. of *coāgulāre*). See COAGULUM, -ATE[1]] **—co·ag·u·la·bil·i·ty** (kō ag′yə lə bil′i tē), *n.* **—co·ag′u·la·ble,** *adj.* **—co·ag′u·la′tion,** *n.* **—co·ag·u·la·to·ry** (kō ag′yə lə tōr′ē, -tôr′ē); *Archaic.* **co·ag·u·la·tive** (kō ag′yə lā′tiv, -lə tiv), *adj.*
co·ag·u·lum (kō ag′yə ləm), *n., pl.* **-la** (-lə). any coagulated mass; precipitate; clump; clot. [< L: that which binds together or coagulates, rennet = *coāg-* (*co-* co- + *āg-* impel; see AGENT) + *-ulum* n. suffix denoting means or instrument]
Co·a·hui·la (kô′ä wē′lä), *n.* a state in N Mexico. 896,509 (1960); 58,067 sq. mi. *Cap.:* Saltillo.
coal (kōl), *n.* **1.** a black or dark-brown combustible mineral substance consisting of carbonized vegetable matter, used as a fuel. Cf. **anthracite, bituminous coal, lignite.** **2.** a piece of glowing, charred, or burned wood or other combustible substance. **3.** charcoal (def. 1). **4. rake, haul,** or

drag over the coals, to reprimand or scold severely. —*v.t.* **5.** to burn to coal or charcoal. **6.** to provide with coal. —*v.i.* **7.** to take in coal for fuel. [ME *cole,* OE *col;* c. D *kool,* G *Kohle,* Icel *kol*] —**coal′less,** *adj.*

co·a·la (kō ä′lə), *n.* koala.

coal·er (kō′lər), *n.* a railroad, ship, etc., used mainly to haul or supply coal.

co·a·lesce (kō′ə les′), *v.,* **-lesced, -lesc·ing.** —*v.i.* **1.** to grow together or into one body. **2.** to unite so as to form one mass, community, etc.; blend; fuse; join. —*v.t.* **3.** to cause to unite in one body or mass. [< L *coalēsc(re)* = *co-* CO- + *al-* (s. of *alere* to nourish, make grow) + *-ēscere* -ESCE] —**co′a·les′cence,** *n.* —**co′a·les′cent,** *adj.* —**Syn. 1, 2.** unite, combine. **2.** amalgamate.

coal′ field′, an area containing coal deposits.

coal·fish (kōl′fish′), *n., pl.* **-fish·es,** (*esp. collectively*) **-fish. 1.** a sablefish. **2.** the pollack, *Pollachius virens.*

coal′ gas′, 1. the gas formed by burning coal. **2.** a gas used for illuminating and heating, produced by distilling bituminous coal and consisting chiefly of hydrogen, methane, and carbon monoxide.

coal′ing sta′tion, a place at which coal is supplied to ships, locomotives, etc.

co·a·li·tion (kō′ə lish′ən), *n.* **1.** union into one body or mass; fusion. **2.** an alliance, esp. a temporary one between persons, factions, etc. [< L *coalitiōn-* (s. of *coalitiō*) = *coalit(us),* ptp. of *coalēscere* (*co-* CO- + *ali-,* ptp. s. of *alere* to feed + *-tus* ptp. suffix) + *-iōn-* -ION; see COALESCE] —**co′a·li′tion·al,** *adj.* —**co′a·li′tion·ist, co′a·li′tion·er,** *n.* —**Syn. 2.** partnership; league.

coal′ meas′ures, *Geol.* **1.** coal-bearing strata. **2.** (*caps.*) a portion of the Carboniferous system, characterized by coal deposits.

coal′ oil′, *Chiefly Dial.* **1.** petroleum obtained by the destructive distillation of bituminous coal. **2.** kerosene.

Coal·sack (kōl′sak′), *n. Astron.* either of two large dark spaces in the Milky Way, one **(Southern Coalsack)** located in the southern skies near the Southern Cross, the other **(Northern Coalsack)** located in the northern skies in the constellation Cygnus.

coal′ scut′tle, a metal bucket, usually with a lip, for holding and carrying coal.

coal′ tar′, a thick, black, viscid liquid formed during the distillation of coal that, upon further distillation, yields benzene, anthracene, phenol, and other compounds from which are derived a large number of dyes, drugs, and other synthetic compounds, and that yields a final residuum **(coal′-tar pitch′)** used chiefly in making pavements. —**coal-tar** (kōl′tär′), *adj.*

C, Coaming

coam·ing (kō′ming), *n.* a raised border around an opening in a deck, roof, or floor, designed to prevent water from running below. [earlier *coming,* appar. = COMB[1] (in sense of crest) + -ING[1]]

co·ap·ta·tion (kō′ap tā′shən), *n.* a joining or adjustment of parts to one another: *the coaptation of a broken bone.* [< LL *coaptātiōn-* (s. of *coaptātiō*) = *coaptāt(us)* fitted together, ptp. of *coaptāre* (*co-* CO- + *aptātus,* ptp. of *aptāre;* see APT, -ATE[1]) + *-iōn-* -ION]

co·arc·tate (kō ärk′tāt, -tit), *adj.* (of a pupa) having the body enclosed in a hardened shell or puparium. [< L *coarctāt(us),* var. of *coartātus* (ptp. of *coartāre*) pressed together = *co-* CO- + *art(us)* tight + *-ātus* -ATE[1]] —**co′arc·ta′tion,** *n.*

Coarctate pupa of fly, *Hylemya cilicrura*

coarse (kōrs, kôrs), *adj.,* **coars·er, coars·est. 1.** of inferior or faulty quality; common; base. **2.** composed of relatively large parts or particles: *coarse sand.* **3.** lacking in fineness or delicacy of texture, structure, etc.: *coarse fabric.* **4.** harsh; grating. **5.** lacking delicacy, taste, or refinement. **6.** vulgar or obscene: *coarse language.* **7.** (of metals) unrefined. [earlier *cowarce* (see COW[1], ARSE), *co(u)rs;* appar. adj. use of abusive vulgarism] —**coarse′ly,** *adv.* —**coarse′ness,** *n.* —**Syn. 3.** rough. **5.** crude, rude; gross, crass. **6.** indecent, ribald. —**Ant. 5.** refined, sensitive.

coarse-grained (kōrs′grānd′, kôrs′-), *adj.* **1.** having a coarse texture or grain. **2.** indelicate; crude; gross. —**coarse′-grained′ness,** *n.*

coars·en (kōr′sən, kôr′-), *v.t., v.i.* to make or become coarse.

coast (kōst) *n.* **1.** the land or region next to the sea; seashore. **2.** a hill or slope down which a person may slide on a sled. **3.** a slide or ride down a hill or slope, as on a sled. **4.** *Obs.* the boundary or border of a country. **5. the Coast,** *Informal.* (in the U.S.) the West Coast. —*v.i.* **6.** *U.S.* to slide on a sled down a snowy or icy hillside or incline. **7.** to sail along, or call at the various ports of a coast. **8.** to continue to move or advance after effort has ceased; keep going on acquired momentum: *We cut off the car engine and coasted for a while.* **9.** to advance or proceed with little or no effort, esp. owing to one's present or former assets, as wealth, position, or social connections: *The actor coasted to stardom on his good looks.* **10.** *Obs.* to proceed in a roundabout way. —*v.t.* **11.** to cause to move along under acquired momentum. **12.** to proceed along or near the coast of. **13.** *Obs.* to keep alongside of (a person moving). **14.** *Obs.* to go by the side or border of. [late ME *cost(e)* < MF < L *costa* rib, side, wall] —**Syn. 1.** strand, seaside. See **shore**[1].

coast·al (kōs′tᵊl), *adj.* of, relating to, bordering on, or located near a coast. —**coast′al·ly,** *adv.*

coast′ artil′lery, 1. artillery used for defending coastal areas. **2.** a military unit manning such artillery.

coast·er (kō′stər), *n.* **1.** a person or thing that coasts. **2.** a small dish, tray, or mat, esp. for placing under a glass to protect a table from moisture. **3.** a ship engaged in coastwise trade. **4.** a sled for coasting. **5.** *U.S.* See **roller coaster.**

coast′er brake′, a brake on freewheeling bicycles, operated by back pressure on the pedals.

Coast′ Guard′, 1. *U.S.* a military service under the Department of Transportation that in peacetime enforces maritime laws, saves lives and property at sea, and operates aids to navigation, and that in wartime may be placed under the Department of the Navy to augment the Navy. **2.** (*l.c.*) any similar organization for aiding navigation, preventing smuggling, etc. **3.** (*l.c.*) Also called **coastguardsman.** a member of any such organization.

coast·guards·man (kōst′gärdz′mən), *n., pl.* **-men.** See **Coast Guard** (def. 3).

coast·land (kōst′land′), *n.* land along a coast; seacoast.

coast·line (kōst′līn′), *n.* **1.** the outline or contour of a coast; shoreline. **2.** the land and water lying adjacent to a shoreline.

Coast′ Range′, a series of mountain ranges along the Pacific coast of North America, extending from Lower California to SE Alaska. Also called **Coast′ Moun′tains.**

coast·ward (kōst′wərd), *adv.* **1.** Also, **coast′wards.** toward the coast: *to row coastward.* —*adj.* **2.** directed toward the coast: *a coastward migration.*

coast·ways (kōst′wāz′), *adv., adj. Archaic.* coastwise.

coast·wise (kōst′wīz′), *adv.* **1.** along the coast. —*adj.* **2.** following the coast.

coat (kōt), *n.* **1.** an outer garment with sleeves, covering at least the upper part of the body. **2.** a natural integument or covering, as the hair, fur, or wool of an animal, the bark of a tree, or the skin of a fruit. **3.** a layer of anything that covers a surface. **4.** See **coat of arms. 5.** *Archaic.* a petticoat or skirt. **6.** *Obs.* a garment indicating profession, class, etc. —*v.t.* **7.** to cover or provide with a coat. **8.** to cover with a layer or coating. **9.** to cover (something) as a layer or coating: *The paint coated the wall.* [ME *cote* < OF < Gmc; cf. G *Kotze,* OS *cott* woolen coat]

Coat·bridge (kōt′brij′), *n.* a city in central Scotland, near Glasgow. 53,946 (1961).

coat·ed (kō′tid), *adj.* **1.** having a coat. **2.** (of paper) having a highly polished coating applied to provide a smooth surface for printing. **3.** (of a fabric) having a coating to make it impervious to moisture.

Coates (kōts), *n.* **1. Eric,** 1886–1957, English violist, composer, and songwriter. **2. Joseph Gordon,** 1878–1943, New Zealand statesman: prime minister 1925–28.

coat′ hang′er, hanger (def. 1).

Coati, *Nasua narica* (1 ft. high at shoulder; total length 4 ft.; tail to 2½ ft.)

co·a·ti (kō ä′tē), *n., pl.* **-tis.** any tropical American carnivore of the genus *Nasua,* related to the raccoon, having an elongated body, long, ringed tail, and a slender, flexible snout. Also called **co·a·ti-mon·di, co·a·ti-mun·di** (kō ä′tē mun′dē). [< Pg < Tupi]

coat·ing (kō′ting), *n.* **1.** a layer of any substance spread over a surface. **2.** fabric for making coats.

coat′ of arms′, 1. a surcoat or tabard embroidered with heraldic devices, worn by medieval knights over their armor. **2.** a heraldic achievement of arms. [parallel to F *cotte d'armes*]

coat′ of mail′, a long defensive garment made of interlinked metal rings; hauberk; byrnie. [parallel to F *cotte de mailles*]

coat·room (kōt′ro͞om′, -ro͝om′), *n.* cloakroom (def. 1).

coat·tail (kōt′tāl′), *n.* **1.** the back of the skirt on a man's coat or jacket. **2.** one of the two back parts of the skirt of a tail coat or cutaway. **3. on someone's coattails,** aided by association with another person: *The senator rode into office on the president's coattails.* **4. on the coattails of,** immediately after: *His decline in popularity followed on the coattails of the scandal.*

Coat of arms A, Crest; B, Torse; C, Helmet; D, Mantling; E, Escutcheon; F, Scroll; G, Motto

co·au·thor (kō ô′thər, kō′ô′-), *n.* **1.** one of two or more joint authors, as of a book. —*v.t.* **2.** to write in joint authorship with another.

coax[1] (kōks), *v.t.* **1.** to attempt to influence by gentle persuasion, flattery, etc.; cajole. **2.** to obtain by coaxing. **3.** to manipulate to a desired end by adroit handling or persistent effort: *He coaxed the large chair through the door.* **4.** *Obs.* **a.** to fondle. **b.** to fool; deceive. —*v.i.* **5.** to use gentle persuasion, flattery, etc. [v. use of *cokes* fool (now obs.), perh. var. of COX(COMB)] —**coax′er,** *n.* —**coax′ing·ly,** *adv.* —**Syn. 1.** wheedle, beguile.

co·ax[2] (kō aks′, kō′aks), *n. Elect.* See **coaxial cable.** [by shortening]

co·ax·i·al (kō ak′sē əl), *adj.* **1.** Also, **co·ax·al** (kō ak′səl). having a common axis or coincident axes. **2.** (of a loud-speaker) having two or more cones with their centers mounted on the same axis. **3.** *Geom.* **a.** (of a set of circles) having the property that each pair of circles has the same radical axis. **b.** (of planes) intersecting in a straight line.

coax′ial ca′ble, *Elect.* an insulated conducting tube through which a central, insulated conductor runs, used for transmitting high-frequency telephone, telegraph, or television signals. Also called **coax.**

cob (kob), *n.* **1.** *U.S.* a corncob. **2.** a male swan. **3.** a short-legged, thick-set horse, often having a high gait and frequently used for driving. **4.** *Brit.* a mixture of clay and straw, used as a building material. **5.** *Brit. Dial.* **a.** a man of importance; leader. **b.** a rounded mass, lump, or heap. [late ME *cob(be)* < Scand; cf. Icel *kubbi* log, lump]

co·balt (kō′bôlt), *n. Chem.* a silver-white metallic element, occurring in compounds that provide blue coloring substances. *Symbol:* Co; *at. wt.:* 58.933; *at. no.:* 27; *sp. gr.:* 8.9 at 20°C. [< G *Kobalt,* var. of *Kobold* goblin]

cobalt 60, *Chem.* the radioactive isotope of cobalt, having a mass number of 60 and a halflife of 5.2 years.

co′balt bloom′, erythrite (def. 1).

co′balt blue′, 1. any of a number of pigments containing an oxide of cobalt. 2. a deep blue to a strong greenish blue.
co′balt green′, 1. a yellowish-green color. 2. a green pigment consisting mainly of oxides of cobalt and zinc.
co·bal·tic (kō bôl′tik), *adj. Chem.* of or containing cobalt, esp. in the trivalent state.
co·bal·tite (kō bôl′tīt, kō′bôl tīt′), *n.* a mineral, cobalt arsenic sulfide, CoAsS, an ore of cobalt. Also, **co·balt·ine** (kō′bôl tēn′, -tin).
co·bal·tous (kō bôl′təs), *adj. Chem.* containing bivalent cobalt.
Cobb (kob), *n.* **1. Irvin S(hrewsbury),** 1876–1944, U.S. humorist and writer. **2. Ty(rus Raymond)** (tī′rəs), (“*the Georgia Peach*”), 1886–1961, U.S. baseball player.
cob·ber (kob′ər), *n. Australian.* (of men) a close friend; partner. [? < Yiddish (< Heb) *chaber* friend]
Cob·bett (kob′it), *n.* **William** (pen name: *Peter Porcupine*), 1763–1835, English political essayist and journalist.
cob·ble[1] (kob′əl), *n., v.,* **-bled, -bling.** —*n.* **1.** a cobblestone. **2. cobbles.** Also called **cob′ coal′.** coal in lumps larger than a pebble and smaller than a boulder. —*v.t.* **3.** to pave with cobblestones. [? COB + -LE]
cob·ble[2] (kob′əl), *v.t.,* **-bled, -bling. 1.** to mend (shoes, boots, etc.); patch. **2.** to put together roughly or clumsily. [? back formation from COBBLER]
cob·bler (kob′lər), *n.* **1.** a person who mends shoes. **2.** *U.S.* a deep-dish fruit pie with a rich biscuit crust, usually covering only the top. **3.** an iced drink made of wine or liquor, fruits, sugar, etc. **4.** *Archaic.* a clumsy workman. [ME *cobelere* = *cobel* (< ?) + *-ere* -ER[1]]
cob·ble·stone (kob′əl stōn′), *n.* a naturally rounded stone for use in paving. [late ME *cobylstone*]
Cob·den (kob′dən), *n.* **Richard,** 1804–65, English manufacturer, merchant, economist, and statesman.
co·bel·lig·er·ent (kō′bə lij′ər ənt), *n.* a nation that cooperates with another in carrying on war.
Cóbh (kōv), *n.* a seaport in S Republic of Ireland: port for Cork. 5266 (1961). Formerly, **Queenstown.**
Cob·ham (kob′əm), *n.* **Sir John.** See **Oldcastle, Sir John.**
co·bi·a (kō′bē ə), *n.* a large, fusiform fish, *Rachycentron canadum,* found off the eastern coast of temperate and tropical America, in the East Indies, and in Japan. [?]
co·ble (kō′bəl, kob′əl), *n. Scot. and North Eng.* a small, flat-bottomed fishing boat with one mast. [ME (Scot), OE (north) *cuople* (dat. sing.) small boat]
Co·blenz (kō′blents), *n.* a city in W West Germany. 101,200 (1963). Also, **Koblenz.**
cob·nut (kob′nut′), *n.* **1.** the nut of certain cultivated varieties of hazel, *Corylus Avellana grandis.* **2.** a tree bearing such nuts. [late ME *cobylle nutt*]
COBOL (kō′bôl, -bôl′), *n. Computer Technol.* a programming language for writing programs to process large quantities of uniformly related data items: the syntax is English-like and there is a large vocabulary of reserved English words. [*co*(*mmon*) *b*(*usiness*) *o*(*riented*) *l*(*anguage*)]
co·bra (kō′brə), *n.* **1.** any of several highly venomous, Old World snakes of the genus *Naja,* characterized by the ability to flatten the neck into a hoodlike form when disturbed. **2.** any of several similar, related African snakes, as the ringhals. **3.** leather made from the skin of a cobra. [short for Pg *cobra de capello* hooded snake; *cobra* < L *colubra* snake]

Cobra, *Naja naja* (Length to 6 ft.)

Co·burg (kō′bûrg; *Ger.* kō′bo͝ork), *n.* a city in N Bavaria, in E West Germany. 43,100 (1963).
cob·web (kob′web′), *n., v.,* **-webbed, -web·bing.** —*n.* **1.** a web spun by a spider to entrap its prey. **2.** a single thread spun by a spider. **3.** something resembling a cobweb; anything finespun, flimsy, or insubstantial. **4.** a network of plot or intrigue. **5. cobwebs,** confusion, indistinctness, or lack of order: *a mind full of cobwebs.* —*v.t.* **6.** to cover with or as with cobwebs. **7.** to confuse or muddle. [ME *coppeweb,* OE *-coppe* spider (in *ātorcoppe*); c. MD *koppe;* see WEB]
cob·web·by (kob′web′ē), *adj.* **1.** full of cobwebs. **2.** having the form, texture, or quality of cobwebs.
co·ca (kō′kə), *n.* **1.** either of two shrubs, *Erythroxylon Coca* or *E. truxillense,* native to the Andes. **2.** their dried leaves, which are chewed for their stimulant properties and yield cocaine and other alkaloids. [< Sp < Quechuan *kuka*]
co·caine (kō kān′, kō′kān; *tech. often* kō′kə ēn′), *n. Pharm.* a narcotic, bitter, crystalline alkaloid, $C_{17}H_{21}NO_4$, obtained from coca leaves: used as a surface anesthetic. [COCA + -INE[1]]
co·cain·ise (kō kā′nīz, kō′kə nīz′), *v.t.,* **-ised, -is·ing.** *Chiefly Brit.* cocainize. —**co·cain′i·sa′tion,** *n.*
co·cain·ism (kō kā′niz əm, kō′kə niz′əm), *n. Pathol.* an abnormal condition caused by excessive or habitual use of cocaine.
co·cain·ize (kō kā′nīz, kō′kə nīz′), *v.t.,* **-ized, -iz·ing.** to treat with or affect by cocaine. Also, *esp. Brit.,* **cocainise.** —**co·cain′i·za′tion,** *n.*
coc·ci (kok′sī), *n.* pl. of **coccus.**
coc·cid (kok′sid), *n.* any homopterous insect of the superfamily *Coccoidea,* including the scale insects. [< NL *Coccid(ae).* See COCCUS, -ID[2]]
coc·cid·i·oi·do·my·co·sis (kok sid′ē oi′dō mī kō′sis), *n. Pathol.* a disease chiefly of the lungs and skin, caused by infection with the organism *Coccidioides immitis,* characterized by the production of excessive sputum and the development of nodules. [< NL *Coccidioid(es)* name of the genus + -o- + MYCOSIS]
coc·cid·i·o·sis (kok sid′ē ō′sis), *n. Vet. Pathol.* any of a series of specific infectious diseases caused by epithelial protozoan parasites, usually affecting the intestines. [< NL *coccidi(a),* pl. of *coccidium* (*cocc(us)* COCCUS + *-idium* -IDIUM) + -OSIS]
coc·coid (kok′oid), *adj.* **1.** Also, **coc·coi′dal.** resembling a coccus; globular. —*n.* **2.** a coccoid cell or organism.
coc·cus (kok′əs), *n., pl.* **-ci** (-sī). **1.** *Bacteriol.* a spherical bacterium. See diag. at **bacteria. 2.** *Bot.* one of the carpels of a schizocarp. [< NL < Gk *kókkos* grain, seed, berry] —**coc′cal, coc·cic** (kok′sik), *adj.* —**coc′cous,** *adj.*
coc·cyx (kok′siks), *n., pl.* **coc·cy·ges** (kok sī′jēz, kok′si-jēz′). **1.** a small triangular bone forming the lower extremity of the spinal column in man. **2.** a corresponding part in animals. [< NL < Gk *kókkyx* cuckoo, from its resemblance to a cuckoo's beak] —**coc·cyg·e·al** (kok sij′ē əl), *adj.*
Co·cha·bam·ba (kô′chä bäm′bä), *n.* a city in central Bolivia. 95,000 (est. 1965); 8394 ft. above sea level.
co·chair·man (kō châr′mən), *n., pl.* **-men.** one of two or more joint chairmen.
co·chin (kō′chin, koch′in), *n.* one of an Asian breed of chickens, resembling the Brahma but slightly smaller. [short for *Cochin-China fowl*]
Co·chin-Chi·na (kō′chin chī′nə, koch′in-), *n.* a former state in S French Indochina: now part of South Vietnam. French, **Co·chin·chine** (kô shan shēn′).
coch·i·neal (koch′ə nēl′, koch′ə nēl′), *n.* a red dye prepared from the dried bodies of the females of a scale insect, *Dactylopius coccus.* [< Sp *cochinilla* < L *coccin(eus)* scarlet-colored (< *coccum* scarlet dye, orig. berry (see COCCUS) + *-eus* adj. suffix) + Sp *-illa* (< L *-illa* dim. suffix)]
Co·chise (kō chēs′, -chēz′), *n.* c1815–74, a chief of the Apaches.
coch·le·a (kok′lē ə), *n., pl.* **coch·le·ae** (kok′lē ē′, -lē ī′), **coch·le·as.** *Anat.* a spiral-shaped cavity forming a division of the internal ear in man and in most other mammals. [< L < Gk *kochliás* snail (with spiral shell), screw, prob. akin to *kónchē* CONCH] —**coch′le·ar,** *adj.*
coch·le·ate (kok′lē it, -āt′), *adj.* shaped like a snail shell; spiral. Also, **coch′le·at′ed.** [< L *cochleāt(us)* spiral]
cock[1] (kok), *n.* **1.** a rooster. **2.** the male of any bird, esp. of the gallinaceous kind. **3.** a weathercock. **4.** a leader; chief person; ruling spirit. **5.** a hand-operated valve or faucet. **6.** (in a firearm) **a.** the part of the lock that, by its fall or action, causes the discharge; hammer. **b.** the position into which this cock, or hammer, is brought by being drawn partly or completely back, preparatory to firing. **7.** *Slang* (*usually vulgar*). penis. **8.** *Archaic.* the time of the crowing of the cock; early in the morning; cockcrow. —*v.t.* **9.** to pull back and set the cock, or hammer, of (a firearm) preparatory to firing. —*v.i.* **10.** to cock the firing mechanism of a firearm. [ME *cock,* OE *cocc;* c. Icel *kokkr;* orig. imit.] —**cock′like′,** *adj.*
cock[2] (kok), *v.t.* **1.** to set or turn up or to one side, often in an assertive, jaunty, or significant manner: *to cock one's head while listening.* —*v.i.* **2.** to stand or stick up conspicuously. **3.** *Dial.* to strut; swagger; put on airs of importance. —*n.* **4.** the act of turning the head, a hat, etc., up or to one side in a jaunty or significant way. **5.** the position of anything thus placed. [prob. special use of COCK[1]]
cock[3] (kok), *n.* **1.** a conical pile of hay, dung, etc. —*v.t.* **2.** to pile (hay, dung, etc.) in cocks. [late ME; c. G (dial.) *Kocke* heap of hay or dung, Norw *kok* heap, lump]
cock·ade (ko kād′), *n.* a rosette, knot of ribbon, etc., usually worn on the hat as part of a uniform, esp. as an indication of rank, office, or the like. [alter. of *cocarde* < F = *coc* COCK[2] + *-arde* -ARD] —**cock·ad′ed,** *adj.*
cock-a-doo·dle-doo (kok′ə do͞od′əl do͞o′), *n., pl.* **-doos,** *v.,* **-dooed, -doo·ing.** —*n.* **1.** the loud crow of a cock. —*v.i.* **2.** to crow. [fanciful imit.]
cock-a-hoop (kok′ə ho͞op′, -ho͝op′, kok′ə ho͞op′, -ho͝op′), *adj.* **1.** in a state of unrestrained joy or exultation. **2.** askew; out of kilter. [?]
Cock·aigne (ko kān′), *n.* a fabled land of luxury and idleness. Also, **Cockayne.** [ME *cokaygn(e)* < MF (*trouver*) *Cocaigne* (find) an idler's paradise, perh. orig. land of cookies < MD *kokenje* = *koken* (see COOKIE) + *-je* dim. suffix]
cock-a-leek·ie (kok′ə lē′kē), *n. Scot. Cookery.* chicken broth, flavored with chopped leeks and sometimes oatmeal. [var. of *cockie-leekie.* See COCK[1], -IE, LEEK]
cock·a·lo·rum (kok′ə lōr′əm, -lôr′-), *n. Informal.* a self-important, pretentious little man. [< Flem *cockeloeren* to crow (now obs.), whimsically altered to make it rhyme with L gen. pl. *-ōrum,* in words like QUORUM. See COCK[1]]
cock·a·ma·mie (kok′ə mā′mē), *adj.* **1.** *Slang.* ridiculous, pointless, or nonsensical. —*n.* **2.** decalcomania. [alter. of DECALCOMANIA]
cock′-and-bull′ sto′ry (kok′ən bo͝ol′), an absurd, improbable story presented as the truth. [prob. with orig. reference to some fable in which a cock and bull figure]
cock·a·teel (kok′ə tēl′), *n.* a small, crested, long-tailed Australian parrot, *Nymphicus hollandicus,* often kept as a pet. Also, **cock′a·tiel′.** [alter. of D *kaketielje* itself alter. of Pg *cacatilha* = *cacat(ua)* COCKATOO + *-ilha* < L *-illa* dim. suffix]
cock·a·too (kok′ə to͞o′ kok′ə to͞o′), *n., pl.* **-toos.** any of numerous crested parrots of the genera *Cacatua, Callocephalon, Calyptorhynchus,* etc., of the Australasian region, having chiefly white plumage tinged with yellow, pink, or red. [< D *kaketoe* < Malay *kakatua*]

Cockatoo, *Cacatua galerita* (Length 1½ ft.)

cock·a·trice (kok′ə tris), *n.* **1.** a legendary monster with a deadly glance, supposedly hatched by a serpent from the egg of a cock, and commonly shown with the body of a serpent and the head, tail, and wings of a cock. Cf. **basilisk** (def. 1). **2.** a venomous serpent. Isa. 11:8. [late ME *cocatrice* < MF *cocatris* < ML *caucātrīces* (pl.), L **calcātrix* (see -TRIX), fem. of **calcātor* tracker = *calcāt(us),* ptp. of *calcāre* to tread, make tracks (*calc-* heel + *-ātus* -ATE[1]) + *-or* -OR[2]; rendering Gk *ichneúmon* ICHNEUMON]
Cock·ayne (ko kān′), *n.* Cockaigne.
cock·bill (kok′bil′), *v.t. Naut.* to raise one end of (a yard) so that it is at a steep angle, as to permit unloading a vessel or to show that a ship's company is in mourning. [aph. var. of *acockbill;* see ACOCK, BILL[3]]
cock·boat (kok′bōt′), *n.* a small boat, esp. one used as a tender. Also, **cockleboat.** Also called **cockleshell.**

cock·chaf·er (kok′chā′fər), *n.* any of certain scarabaeid beetles, esp. the European species, *Melolontha melolontha,* that is very destructive to forest trees. [COCK[1] (with reference to its size) + CHAFER]
cock·crow (kok′krō′), *n.* the time at which a cock characteristically crows; daybreak; dawn. Also called **cock′-crow′ing.**
cocked′ hat′, **1.** a man's wide-brimmed hat, turned up on two or three sides toward a peaked crown. Cf. **tricorne.** **2. knock into a cocked hat,** *Slang.* to destroy completely; render unachievable.

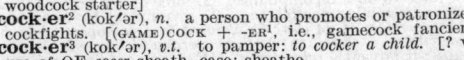

Cocked hat

cock·er[1] (kok′ər), *n.* See **cocker spaniel.** [(WOOD)COCK + -ER[1], i.e., woodcock starter]
cock·er[2] (kok′ər), *n.* a person who promotes or patronizes cockfights. [(GAME)COCK + -ER[1], i.e., gamecock fancier]
cock·er[3] (kok′ər), *v.t.* to pamper: *to cocker a child.* [? v. use of OE *cocer* sheath, case: sheathe, encase, hence protect, thus cherish too much]
cock·er·el (kok′ər əl, kok′rəl), *n.* a young domestic cock. [late ME *cokerelle.* See COCK[1], -REL]
cock′er span′iel, one of a breed of small spaniels having a flat or slightly waved, soft, dense coat of any of several colors.

Cocker spaniel (15 in. high at shoulder)

cock·eye (kok′ī′), *n., pl.* **-eyes.** an eye that squints or is affected with strabismus.
cock·eyed (kok′īd′), *adj.* **1.** cross-eyed. **2.** having a squinting eye. **3.** *Slang.* **a.** twisted or slanted to one side. **b.** foolish; absurd. **c.** completely wrong.
cock·fight (kok′fīt′), *n.* a fight between gamecocks, usually fitted with spurs. —**cock′fight′ing,** *n., adj.*
cock·horse (kok′hôrs′), *n.* a child's rocking horse or hobby-horse. [orig. father's leg, on which child rides astride, from COCK[1] in sense projection + HORSE]
cock·le (kok′əl), *n., v.,* **-led, -ling.** —*n.* **1.** any bivalve mollusk of the genus *Cardium,* having somewhat heart-shaped, radially ribbed valves, esp. *C. edule,* the common edible species of Europe. **2.** any of various allied or similar mollusks. **3.** cockleshell (def. 1). **4.** a wrinkle; pucker: *a cockle in fabric.* **5.** a light, shallow boat. **6. cockles of one's heart,** the depths of one's emotions or feelings: *The happy family scene warmed the cockles of his heart.* —*v.i.* **7.** to contract into wrinkles; pucker. **8.** to rise in short, irregular waves; ripple. —*v.t.* **9.** to cause to wrinkle, pucker, or ripple. [late ME *cokel,* ME *cock* (OE *-cocc,* n. *sǣ-cocc* cockle < VL **coccus* for L *concha* CONCH) + *-el* dim. suffix; r. late ME *cokille* < MF < VL **cocchīlia,* L *conchylia,* pl. of *conchylium* < Gk *konchýlion* = *konchýl(e)* mussel + *-ion* dim.]
cock·le·boat (kok′əl bōt′), *n.* cockboat.
cock·le·bur (kok′əl bûr′), *n.* **1.** any composite plant of the genus *Zanthium,* comprising coarse weeds with spiny burs. **2.** the burdock, *Arctium Lappa.*
cock·le·shell (kok′əl shel′), *n.* **1.** a shell of the cockle or of some other mollusk, as the scallop. **2.** *Naut.* **a.** cockboat. **b.** any light or frail vessel. [late ME *cokille shell*]
cock·ney (kok′nē), *n., pl.* **-neys,** *adj.* (*sometimes cap.*) —*n.* **1.** a native of the East End district of London, England. **2.** the pronunciation or dialect of cockneys. —*adj.* **3.** of or pertaining to cockneys or their dialect. [ME *cokeney* foolish person, lit., cock's egg (i.e., malformed egg) = *coken,* gen. pl. of *cok* COCK[1] + *ey,* OE *æg,* c. G *Ei,* Icel *egg* EGG[1]] —**cock′ney·ish,** *adj.* —**cock′ney·ism,** *n.*
cock·ney·fy (kok′ni fī′), *v.t.,* **-fied, -fy·ing.** to give a cockney character to. —**cock′ney·fi·ca′tion,** *n.*
cock-of-the-rock (kok′əv thə rok′), *n., pl.* **cocks-of-the-rock.** a brilliant orange-red bird of the genus *Rupicola,* of northern South America, having an erect crest that conceals the bill.
cock′ of the walk′, the leader in a group, esp. one with a conceited, domineering manner.
cock·pit (kok′pit′), *n.* **1.** a separate area in some airplanes containing seats for the pilot and copilot, all necessary flying controls, the instrument panel, etc. **2.** a sunken, open area, generally in the after part of a small vessel, as a yacht, providing space for the helmsman, part or all of the crew, or guests. **3.** the enclosed space in racing cars and some sports cars, usually open at the top, containing a seat for the driver and often a seat for a passenger. **4.** (formerly) a space below the water line in a warship, occupied by the quarters of the junior officers and used as a dressing station for the wounded. **5.** a pit or enclosed place for cockfights.
cock·roach (kok′rōch′), *n.* any of numerous orthopterous insects of the family *Blattidae,* characterized by a flattened body, rapid movements, and nocturnal habits and including several common household pests. [< Sp *cucaracha* < *cuca* butterfly larva, insect, perh. < Indian language]

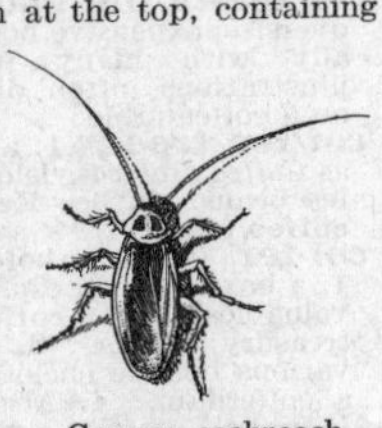

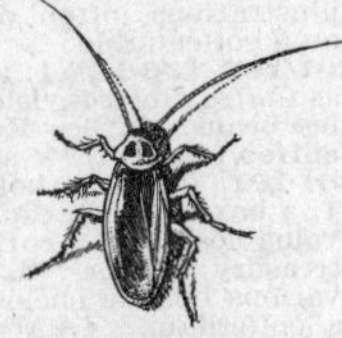
German cockroach, *Blatta germanica* (Length ½ in.)

cocks·comb (koks′kōm′), *n.* **1.** an amaranthaceous garden plant, *Celosia cristata,* with flowers, commonly crimson or purple, in a broad spike somewhat resembling the comb of a cock. **2.** any of several other species of the genus *Celosia.* **3.** coxcomb (def. 1).
cock·shut (kok′shut′), *n.* *Brit. Dial.* the close of the day;
cock·shy (kok′shī′), *n., pl.* **-shies.** *Brit.* the act or sport of throwing missiles at a target.
cock·suck·er (kok′suk′ər), *n.* *Slang* (*usually vulgar*). a person who performs fellatio.
cock·sure (kok′shŏŏr′), *adj.* **1.** perfectly sure or certain; completely confident. **2.** too certain; overconfident. **3.** *Obs.* perfectly secure or safe. —**cock′sure′ly,** *adv.* —**cock′sure′ness,** *n.* —**Ant. 1.** doubtful. **2.** cautious.
cock·swain (kok′sən; *spelling pron.* kok′swān′), *n.* coxwain.
cock·tail[1] (kok′tāl′), *n.* **1.** a chilled, mixed drink of liquor and juice or other flavorings. **2.** an appetizer of seafood, mixed fruits, juice, etc. —*v.i.* **3.** to drink cocktails, esp. at a cocktail party. —*adj.* **4.** (of women's clothing) styled for semiformal wear: *a cocktail dress.* [?]
cock·tail[2] (kok′tāl′), *n.* **1.** a horse with a docked tail. **2.** a horse that is not a thoroughbred. **3.** a person of little breeding who passes for a gentleman. [COCK[2] + TAIL[1]]
cock′tail ta′ble. See **coffee table.**
cock·up (kok′up′), *n.* an upward turn or curl at the top of something.
cock·y (kok′ē), *adj.,* **cock·i·er, cock·i·est.** arrogantly self-assertive; conceited. —**cock′i·ly,** *adv.* —**cock′i·ness,** *n.*
co·co (kō′kō), *n., pl.* **-cos. 1.** See **coconut palm. 2.** coconut (def. 1). [< Pg: grimace; the three holes at the nut's base give it this appearance]
co·coa[1] (kō′kō) *n.* **1.** the roasted, husked, and ground seeds of the cacao, *Theobroma Cacao,* from which much of the fat has been removed. **2.** cacao (def. 2). **3.** a beverage made from cocoa powder. **4.** brown; reddish brown. [earlier *cocao, cacoa,* var. of CACAO]
co·coa[2] (kō′kō), *n.* coco. [misspelling of COCO, by confusion with COCOA[1]]
co′coa bean′, cacao (def. 2).
co′coa but′ter, a fatty substance obtained from cacao seeds, used in making soaps, cosmetics, etc. Also, **cacao butter.**
co·co·mat (kō′kō mat′), *n.* **1.** matting made of the fiber from the outer husk of the coconut. **2.** a mat, esp. a door mat, made from this.
co·con·scious·ness (kō kon′shəs nis), *n.* *Psychol.* a system of mental processes dissociated from the main stream of consciousness and sometimes capable of influencing it, as by causing slips of the tongue. —**co·con′scious,** *adj.* —**co·con′scious·ly,** *adv.*
co·co·nut (kō′kə nut′, -nət), *n.* **1.** the large, hard-shelled seed of the coconut palm, lined with a white edible meat and containing a milky liquid (**co′conut milk′**). **2.** the meat of the coconut, often shredded and used as a dessert topping. **3.** See **coconut palm.** Also, **co′coa·nut′.**
co′conut oil′, a white, semisolid fat or nearly colorless fatty oil extracted from coconuts, used chiefly in cooking and in soaps, cosmetics, and candles.
co′conut palm′, a tall, tropical palm, *Cocos nucifera,* bearing a large, edible fruit. Also called **co′conut tree′, co′co palm′, coco.**
co·coon (kə ko͞on′), *n.* **1.** the silky envelope spun by the larvae of many insects, as silkworms, that serves as a covering while they are in the pupal stage. **2.** any of various similar protective coverings, as the silky case in which certain spiders enclose their eggs. **3.** a protective covering sprayed over machinery, large guns on board ships, etc., to provide an airtight seal and prevent rust during long periods of storage. [< F *cocon* < Pr *coucoun* egg-shell = *coco* shell (< L *coccum;* see COCHINEAL) + F *-on* dim. suffix]
Co′cos Is′lands (kō′kōs), an Australian group of 27 coral islands in the Indian Ocean, SW of Java. 675 (1965); 5½ sq. mi. Also called **Keeling Islands.**
co·cotte (kō kot′, kə-; *Fr.* kō kôt′), *n., pl.* **-cottes** (-kots′; *Fr.* -kôt′). a prostitute. [< F: hen = *coq* COCK[1] + *-otte* fem. suffix]
Coc·teau (kok tō′; *Fr.* kôk tō′), *n.* **Jean** (zhäN), 1889–1963, French writer, dramatist, film maker, and painter.
Co·cy·tus (kō sī′təs), *n.* *Class. Myth.* a river of Hades connected with the Acheron. [< L < Gk *kōkytós* wailing = *kōký(ein)* (to) wail + *-tos* n. suffix]
cod[1] (kod), *n., pl.* (*esp. collectively*) **cod,** (*esp. referring to two or more kinds or species*) **cods. 1.** any of several food fishes of the family *Gadidae,* esp. *Gadus callarias,* found in the colder waters of the North Atlantic. **2.** a closely related fish, *Gadus macrocephalus,* found in the North Pacific. **3.** any of several unrelated fishes, as rockfishes of the genus *Sebastodes.* [ME < ?]

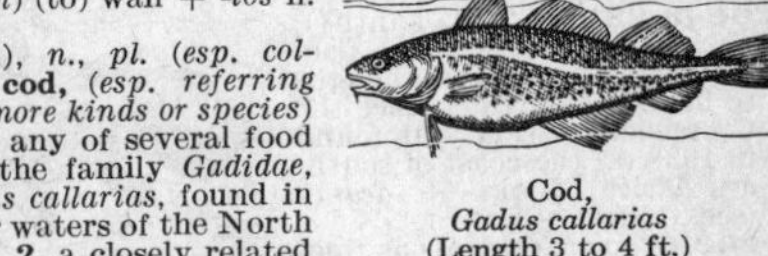
Cod, *Gadus callarias* (Length 3 to 4 ft.)

cod[2] (kod), *n.* **1.** a bag or sack. **2.** *Slang* (*usually vulgar*). **a.** penis. **b.** scrotum. **3.** *Dial.* a pod. [ME; OE *codd*]
Cod (kod), *n.* **Cape.** See **Cape Cod.**
COD., codex. Also, **cod.**
C.O.D., *Com.* cash, or collect, on delivery (payment to be made when delivered to the purchaser). Also, **c.o.d.**
co·da (kō′də), *n.* *Music.* a more or less independent passage concluding a composition. [< It < L *cauda* tail]
cod·dle (kod′əl), *v.t.,* **-dled, -dling. 1.** to treat tenderly or indulgently; pamper: *to coddle children when they're sick.* **2.** to cook in water just below the boiling point. [var. of *caudle,* v. use of CAUDLE] —**cod′dler,** *n.*
code (kōd), *n., v.,* **cod·ed, cod·ing.** —*n.* **1.** a system for communication by telegraph, heliograph, etc., using long and short sounds, light flashes, colored flags, or the like, to symbolize letters, words, or phrases: *Morse code.* **2.** a system used for brevity or secrecy of communication, in which arbitrarily chosen words, letters, or symbols are assigned definite meanings. **3.** a word, letter, number, or other symbol used in a code system to represent or identify something: *The code on the label shows the date of manufacture.* **4.** any systematic collection of the existing laws of a country, or of laws relating to a particular subject: *the civil code of France.* **5.** any system or collection of rules and regulations: *a gentleman's code of behavior.* —*v.t.* **6.** to translate (a message) into a code; encode. **7.** to put or arrange in a code; encode: *to code information.* [ME < F < L *cōdex* CODEX] —**cod′er,** *n.*
co·dec·li·na·tion (kō′dek lə nā′shən), *n.* *Astron.* the

complement of declination; the angular distance along a great circle from the celestial pole.

co·de·fend·ant (kō′di fen′dənt), *n.* a joint defendant.

co·deine (kō′dēn), *n. Pharm.* an alkaloid, $C_{18}H_{21}NO_3H_2O$, obtained from opium: used chiefly as an analgesic, a sedative or hypnotic, and to inhibit coughing. Also, **co·de·ia** (kō dē′ə), **co·de·i·na** (kō′dē ē′nə). [< Gk *kṓde(ia)* head, poppy-head + -INE²]

Code Na·po·lé·on (kôd NA pô lā ôN′), the civil code of France, enacted in 1804.

Code′ of Hammura′bi, a Babylonian legal code of the 18th century B.C. or earlier, instituted by Hammurabi and dealing with criminal and civil matters.

co·dex (kō′deks), *n., pl.* **co·dices** (kō′di sēz′, kod′i-). **1.** a manuscript volume, usually of an ancient classic or the Scriptures. **2.** *Archaic.* a code; book of statutes. [< L: tree trunk, block of wood, writing tablet, book]

cod·fish (kod′fish′), *n., pl.* (*esp. collectively*) **-fish,** (*esp. referring to two or more kinds or species*) **-fish·es.** cod¹.

codg·er (koj′ər), *n.* **1.** *Informal.* an odd or eccentric man, esp. one who is old. **2.** *Brit. Dial.* a mean, miserly person. [? var. of *cadger;* see CADGE]

co·di·ces (kō′di sēz′, kod′i-), *n.* pl. of **codex.**

cod·i·cil (kod′i səl), *n.* **1.** *Law.* a supplement to a will, containing an addition, modification, etc. **2.** any similar supplement; appendix. [< LL *cōdicill(us)* (in L, commonly in pl. only) = L *cōdic-* (s. of *cōdex*) CODEX + *-illus* dim. suffix] —**cod·i·cil·la·ry** (kod′i sil′ə rē), *adj.*

cod·i·fi·ca·tion (kod′ə fə kā′shən, kō′də-), *n.* the act, process, or result of arranging in a systematic form or code.

cod·i·fy (kod′ə fī′, kō′də-), *v.t.,* **-fied, -fy·ing. 1.** to reduce (laws, rules, etc.) to a code. **2.** to classify or arrange in a systematic collection. —**cod′i·fi′er,** *n.*

co·dis·cov·er·er (kō′dis kuv′ər ər), *n.* one of two or more discoverers.

cod·ling¹ (kod′ling), *n.* **1.** *Brit.* any of several varieties of elongated apples, used for cooking. **2.** an unripe, half-grown apple. Also, **cod·lin** (kod′lin). [ME *querdling* = *querd* (< ?) + *-ling* -LING¹]

cod·ling² (kod′ling), *n.* the young of the cod. [ME]

cod′ling moth′, a small, olethreutid moth, *Carpocapsa pomonella,* the larvae of which feed on the pulp of apples and other fruits.

cod′-liv·er oil′ (kod′liv′ər), a pale-yellow, fixed oil, extracted from the liver of the common cod or of allied species, used chiefly as a source of vitamins A and D.

cod·piece (kod′pēs′), *n.* (in the 15th and 16th centuries) a flap or cover for the crotch in men's hose or breeches.

Co·dy (kō′dē), *n.* **William Frederick** ("*Buffalo Bill*"), 1846–1917, U.S. Army scout and showman.

co·ed (kō′ed′, -ed′), *U.S. Informal.* —*n.* **1.** a female student, esp. in a college or university. —*adj.* **2.** of, pertaining to, or characteristic of a coed. **3.** coeducational. Also, **co′-ed′.** [short for *coeducational (student)*]

co·ed·i·tor (kō ed′i tər), *n.* a person who cooperates or collaborates as editor with another.

co·ed·u·ca·tion (kō′ej o͝o kā′shən, -ed yo͞o-), *n.* the education of both sexes at the same institution and in the same classes. —**co′ed·u·ca′tion·al,** *adj.* —**co′ed·u·ca′tion·al·ly,** *adv.*

co·ef·fi·cient (kō′ə fish′ənt), *n.* **1.** *Math.* a number or quantity placed generally before and multiplying another quantity, as *3* in the expression *3x.* **2.** *Physics.* a number that is constant for a given substance, body, or process under certain specified conditions, serving as a measure of one of its properties: *coefficient of friction.* —*adj.* **3.** acting in consort. [< NL *coefficient-* (s. of *coefficiēns*)]

coel-, a learned borrowing from Greek meaning "cavity," used in the formation of compound words: *coelenteron.* Also, **-cele, -coele.** [comb. form repr. Gk *koîlos* hollow]

coe·la·canth (sē′lə kanth′), *n.* a crossopterygian fish, *Latimeria chalumnae,* thought to have been extinct since the Cretaceous period, but found in 1938 off the coast of southern Africa. [COEL- + *-acanth* (see ACANTHO-)]

Coelacanth
(Length 5 to 6 ft.)

-coele, var. of **coel-** as final element of a compound word: *blastocoele.* Also, **-cele, -coel.**

coe·len·ter·ate (si len′tə-rāt′, -tər it), *n.* **1.** any invertebrate animal of the phylum *Coelenterata,* having a single internal cavity serving for digestion, excretion, and other functions and having tentacles on the oral end, including the hydras, jellyfishes, sea anemones, corals, etc. —*adj.* **2.** belonging or pertaining to the *Coelenterata.* [COELENTER(ON) + -ATE¹]

coe·len·ter·on (si len′tə ron′), *n., pl.* **-ter·a** (-tər ə). *Zool.* the body cavity of a coelenterate.

coe·li·ac (sē′lē ak′), *adj.* celiac.

coe·lom (sē′ləm), *n. Zool.* the body cavity of higher metazoans, between the body wall and intestine, lined with a mesodermal epithelium. Also, **coe·lome** (sē′lōm), **celom.** [< Gk *koílōma* cavity = *koîl(os)* hollow + *-ōma* n. suffix denoting result]

coe·lo·mate (sē′lə māt′, si lō′mit), *adj.* **1.** having a coelom. —*n.* **2.** a coelomate animal.

coe·nes·the·sia (sē′nis thē′zhə, -zhē ə, -zē ə, sen′is-), *n. Psychol.* the aggregate of impressions arising from organic sensations that forms the basis of a person's awareness of body or bodily state, as the feeling of health, vigor, or lethargy. [COEN(O)- + ESTHESIA]

coeno-, var. of **ceno-**²: *coenocyte.*

coe·no·bite (sē′nə bīt′, sen′ə-), *n.* cenobite. —**coe·no·bit·ic** (sē′nə bit′ik, sen′ə-), **coe′no·bit′i·cal,** *adj.*

coe·no·cyte (sē′nə sīt′, sen′ə-), *n. Biol.* an organism made up of a multinucleate, continuous mass of protoplasm enclosed by one cell wall, as some algae and fungi.

coe·nu·rus (si no͝or′əs, -nyo͝or′-), *n., pl.* **-nu·ri** (-no͝or′ī, -nyo͝or′ī). *Zool.* the larva of a tapeworm of the genus *Multiceps,* consisting of a hollow, fluid-filled, bladderlike structure in which a number of heads or scoleces form. [< NL; see COENO-, URO-²]

co·en·zyme (kō en′zīm), *n. Biochem.* a biocatalyst required by certain enzymes to produce their reactions.

co·e·qual (kō ē′kwəl), *adj.* **1.** equal in rank, ability, etc. —*n.* **2.** a person or thing coequal with another. —**co·e·qual·i·ty** (kō′i kwol′i tē), **co·e′qual·ness,** *n.* —**co·e′qual·ly,** *adv.*

co·erce (kō ûrs′), *v.t.,* **-erced, -erc·ing. 1.** to compel by force, intimidation, etc., esp. without regard for individual desire or volition: *They coerced him into signing the document.* **2.** to bring about by using force or other forms of compulsion. **3.** to dominate or control, esp. by exploiting fear, anxiety, etc. [< L *coercē(re)* (to) hold in, restrain = *co-* co- + *-ercēre,* var. of *arcēre* to keep in, keep away, akin to *arca* ARK] —**co·erc′er,** *n.* —**co·er′ci·ble,** *adj.*

co·er·cion (kō ûr′shən), *n.* **1.** the act of coercing; exercise of force to obtain compliance. **2.** force or the power to use force in gaining compliance. **3.** government by force. [< ML *coerciōn-* (s. of *coerciō*), L *coerctiōn-,* syncopated var. of *coercitiōn-* = *coercit(us)* (ptp. of *coercēre* to COERCE) + *-iōn-* -ION; r. late ME *cohercion* < MF] —**co·er′cion·ar·y,** *adj.* —**co·er′cion·ist,** *n.*

co·er·cive (kō ûr′siv), *adj.* serving or tending to coerce. —**co·er′cive·ly,** *adv.* —**co·er′cive·ness,** *n.*

co·es·sen·tial (kō′i sen′shəl), *adj.* united in essence; having the same essence or nature.

co·e·ta·ne·ous (kō′i tā′nē əs), *adj.* of the same age or duration. [< L *coaetāneus* = *co-* co- + *aet(ās)* age + *-āneus* compound adj. suffix; see -AN, -EOUS] —**co′e·ta′ne·ous·ly,** *adv.* —**co′e·ta′ne·ous·ness,** *n.*

co·e·ter·nal (kō′i tûr′nəl), *adj.* equally eternal; existing with another eternally. [CO- + ETERNAL, prob. influenced by LL *coaeternus* = *co-* co- + *aet(ās)* age + *-ernus* adj. suffix] —**co′e·ter′nal·ly,** *adv.*

co·e·ter·ni·ty (kō′i tûr′ni tē), *n.* coexistence in eternity with another eternal being.

Coeur de Li·on (kûr′ dəlē′ən; *Fr.* kœr də lyôN′), an epithet of Richard I, meaning "lionhearted."

co·e·val (kō ē′vəl), *adj.* **1.** of the same or of equal age, date, or duration; contemporary. —*n.* **2.** a contemporary. [< LL *coaev(us)* (*co-* co- + *aev(um)* age + *-us* adj. suffix) + -AL¹] —**co·e·val·i·ty** (kō′i val′i tē), *n.* —**co·e′val·ly,** *adv.*

co·ex·ist (kō′ig zist′), *v.i.* **1.** to exist together or at the same time. **2.** to exist together peacefully. —**co′ex·ist′ent,** *adj.*

co·ex·ist·ence (kō′ig zis′təns), *n.* **1.** the act or state of coexisting. **2.** a policy of living peacefully with other nations, religions, etc., despite fundamental disagreements.

co·ex·tend (kō′ik stend′), *v.t., v.i.* to extend equally through the same space or duration. —**co·ex·ten·sion** (kō′ik sten′shən), *n.*

co·ex·ten·sive (kō′ik sten′siv), *adj.* equal or coincident in space, time, or scope. —**co′ex·ten′sive·ly,** *adv.*

cof·fee (kô′fē, kof′ē), *n.* **1.** a beverage consisting of a decoction or infusion of the roasted ground or crushed seeds (**cof′fee beans′**) of the two-seeded fruit (**cof′fee ber′ry**) of *Coffea arabica* and other species of *Coffea.* **2.** the seeds or berries of coffee plants. **3.** the coffee tree or shrub. **4.** dark brown. [< It *caffè* < Turk *kahve* < Ar *qahwah*]

cof′fee break′, a short intermission from work for coffee or other refreshments.

cof·fee·cake (kô′fē kāk′, kof′ē-), *n.* a sweetened cake or bread, usually containing nuts and raisins.

cof·fee·house (kô′fē hous′, kof′ē-), *n., pl.* **-hous·es** (-hou′ziz). a café specializing in serving different kinds of coffee, often with pastries or snacks.

cof′fee klatsch′ (klach, kläch), a social gathering for informal conversation at which coffee is served. Also, **cof′fee klatch′, kaffee klatsch.** [< G *Kaffeeklatsch* = *Kaffee* coffee + *Klatsch* noise (e.g., of conversation)]

cof′fee mill′, a small mill for grinding coffee beans.

cof′fee nut′, 1. the fruit of the Kentucky coffee tree. **2.** the tree bearing this fruit.

cof·fee·pot (kô′fē pot′, kof′ē-), *n.* a utensil, usually with a handle and spout, for brewing and serving coffee.

cof′fee shop′, a small restaurant where refreshments and light meals are served.

cof′fee spoon′, a small spoon used with demitasse cups.

cof′fee ta′ble, a low table, usually placed in front of a sofa, for holding ashtrays, glasses, cups, plates, etc. Also called **cocktail table.**

cof′fee-ta′ble book′, an oversize, expensive book, usually with many full-color illustrations, often displayed on a coffee table.

cof′fee tree′, 1. any tree, as *Coffea arabica,* yielding coffee beans. **2.** See **Kentucky coffee tree.**

Coffers of a ceiling (def. 4)

cof·fer (kô′fər, kof′ər), *n.* **1.** a box or chest, esp. one for valuables. **2. coffers,** a treasury; funds. **3.** any of various boxlike enclosures, as a cofferdam. **4.** Also called **lacunar.** *Archit.* one of a number of sunken panels, usually square or octagonal, in a vault, ceiling, or soffit. —*v.t.* **5.** to deposit or lay up in or as in a coffer or chest. **6.** to ornament with coffers; design or construct coffers for (a vault, ceiling, or soffit). [ME *cofre* < OF << L *cophinus* basket; see COFFIN]

cof·fer·dam (kô′fər dam′, kof′ər-), *n.* a watertight enclosure placed or constructed in waterlogged soil or under water and pumped dry to allow construction or repairs.

cof·fin (kô′fin, kof′in), *n.* **1.** the box or case in which a corpse is placed for burial. **2.** the part of a horse's foot containing the coffin bone. —*v.t.* **3.** to put in a coffin. [ME *cofin* < MF < L *cophin(us)* < Gk *kóphinos* a kind of basket]

cof′fin bone′, the terminal phalanx in the foot of the horse and allied animals, enclosed in the hoof.

cof′fin nail′, *Slang.* a cigarette.

cof·fle (kof′əl), *n.* a train of men, esp. slaves, or of beasts fastened together. [< Ar *qāfilah* caravan]

cof·fret (kô′frit, kof′rit), *n.* a small coffer. [late ME < MF. See COFFER, -ET]

C. of S., Chief of Staff.

co·func·tion (kō′fuŋk′shən), *n.* *Trig.* the function of the complement of a given angle or arc: *cosθ is the cofunction of sinθ.*

cog[1] (kog, kôg), *n.* **1.** (not in technical use) a gear tooth, formerly esp. one of hardwood or metal, fitted into a slot in a gearwheel of less durable material. **2.** a cogwheel. **3.** *Informal.* a minor person in a large organization, movement, etc. [ME *cogge* < Scand; cf. Sw *kugge,* akin to CUDGEL]

cog[2] (kog, kôg), *v.*, **cogged, cog·ging,** *n.* —*v.t.* **1.** to manipulate or load (dice) unfairly. —*n.* **2.** *Obs.* a deception, trick, etc., esp. at dice. [?]

cog[3] (kog, kôg), *n.*, *v.*, **cogged, cog·ging.** *Carpentry.* —*n.* **1.** (in a cogged joint) the tongue in one timber, fitting into a corresponding slot in another. —*v.t., v.i.* **2.** to join with a cog. [special use of COG[1]; r. *cock* in same sense, special use of COCK[1] (in sense of projection)]

cog., cognate.

co·gen·cy (kō′jən sē), *n.* the quality or state of being cogent. [COG(ENT) + -ENCY]

co·gent (kō′jənt), *adj.* **1.** convincing or believable by virtue of forcible, clear, or incisive presentation. **2.** to the point; relevant. [< L *cōgent-* (s. of *cōgēns,* prp. of *cōgere* to drive together, collect, compel) = *cōg-* (*co-* co- + *ag-*, root of *agere* to drive) + *-ent-* -ENT] —**co′gent·ly,** *adv.*

cog·i·ta·ble (koj′i tə bəl), *adj.* able to be considered. [< L *cōgitābil(is)* = *cōgitā(re)* (see COGITATE) + *-bilis* -BLE]

cog·i·tate (koj′i tāt′), *v.*, **-tat·ed, -tat·ing.** —*v.i.* **1.** to think hard; ponder; meditate. —*v.t.* **2.** to think about; devise. [< L *cōgitāt(us)* (ptp. of *cōgitāre* = *co-* co- + *agitāre;* see AGITATE] —**cog′i·tat′ing·ly,** *adv.* —**cog′i·ta′tor,** *n.*

cog·i·ta·tion (koj′i tā′shən), *n.* **1.** meditation; contemplation. **2.** the faculty of thinking. **3.** a thought; scheme or plan. [< L *cōgitātiōn-* (s. of *cōgitātiō*) = *cōgitāt(us)* (see COGITATE) + *-iōn-* -ION; r. ME *cogitaciun* < OF < L]

cog·i·ta·tive (koj′i tā′tiv), *adj.* **1.** meditating; contemplating. **2.** given to meditation; thoughtful. [< ML *cōgitātīv(us)* = *cōgitāt(us)* (see COGITATE) + *-īvus* -IVE] —**cog′i·ta′tive·ly,** *adv.* —**cog′i·ta′tive·ness,** *n.*

co·gi·to, er·go sum (kō′gi tō′ er′gō so͝om′; *Eng.* koj′i-tō′ ûr′gō sum′), *Latin.* I think, therefore I am (stated by Descartes as the first certitude in resolving universal doubt).

co·gnac (kōn′yak, kon′-; *Fr.* kô nyak′), *n.* **1.** (*often cap.*) brandy distilled in a legally delimited area in W central France. **2.** (loosely) any French brandy. [< F, after *Cognac* a town in the area]

cog·nate (kog′nāt), *adj.* **1.** related by birth; of the same parentage, descent, etc. **2.** *Linguistics.* descended or borrowed from the same earlier form: *cognate languages; cognate words.* **3.** allied or similar in nature or quality. —*n.* **4.** a person or thing cognate with another. **5.** a cognate word. English *cold* is a cognate of German *kalt.* [< L *cognāt(us)* = *co-* co- + *gnātus* (ptp. of *gnāscī,* var. of *nāscī* to be born)]

cog′nate ob′ject, a substantive functioning as the object of a verb, esp. when both object and verb are derived from the same base. *Speech* in *Speak the speech* is a cognate object.

cog·na·tion (kog nā′shən), *n.* cognate relationship. [< L *cognātiōn-* (s. of *cognātiō*) kinship]

cog·ni·sa·ble (kog′ni zə bəl, kon′i-, kog nī′-), *adj.* *Chiefly Brit.* cognizable. —**cog′ni·sa·bly,** *adv.*

cog·ni·sance (kog′ni zəns, kon′i-), *n.* *Chiefly Brit.* cognizance.

cog·ni·sant (kog′ni zənt, kon′i-), *adj.* *Chiefly Brit.* cognizant.

cog·nise (kog′nīz), *v.t.*, **-nised, -nis·ing.** *Chiefly Brit.* cognize.

cog·ni·tion (kog nish′ən), *n.* **1.** the act or process of knowing; perception. **2.** something known or perceived. **3.** *Obs.* knowledge. [< L *cognitiōn-* (s. of *cognitiō*) = *cognit(us),* ptp. of *cognōscere* (*co-* co- + *gni-*, var. s. of *gnōscere, nōscere,* to learn (see KNOW[1]) + *-tus* ptp. suffix) + *-iōn-* -ION] —**cog·ni′tion·al,** *adj.* —**cog·ni·tive** (kog′ni tiv), *adj.*

cog·ni·za·ble (kog′ni zə bəl, kon′i-, kog nī′-), *adj.* **1.** capable of being perceived or known. **2.** *Law.* being within the jurisdiction of a court. Also, *esp. Brit.,* **cognisable.** —**cog′ni·za·bly,** *adv.*

cog·ni·zance (kog′ni zəns, kon′i-), *n.* **1.** recognition; notice; acknowledgment: *The guests took no cognizance of her rudeness.* **2.** *Law.* **a.** judicial notice as taken by a court in dealing with a cause. **b.** the right of taking jurisdiction, as possessed by a court. **3.** the range or scope of knowledge, observation, etc.: *Such understanding is beyond his cognizance.* **4.** *Heraldry.* a device by which a person, his servants, or his property can be recognized; badge. Also, *esp. Brit.,* **cognisance.** [ME *conisa(u)nce* < MF *con(o)is(s)ance* = *conois(tre)* (to) know (< L *cognōscere;* see COGNITION) + *-ance* -ANCE; *-g-* < L]

cog·ni·zant (kog′ni zənt, kon′i-), *adj.* having cognizance; aware (usually fol. by *of*): *He was cognizant of the difficulty.* Also, *esp. Brit.,* **cognisant.** —**Syn.** See **conscious.**

cog·nize (kog′nīz), *v.t.*, **-nized, -niz·ing.** to perceive; become conscious of; know. Also, *esp. Brit.,* **cognise.** [back formation from COGNIZANCE]

cog·no·men (kog nō′mən), *n.*, *pl.* **-no·mens, -nom·i·na** (-nom′ə nə). **1.** a surname. **2.** any name, esp. a nickname. **3.** the third and commonly the last name of a citizen of ancient Rome, indicating his house or family, as "Caesar" in "Gaius Julius Caesar." [< L = *co-* co- + *nōmen* name, with *-g-* after model of *nōscī: cognōscī;* see COGNIZANCE] —**cog·nom·i·nal** (kog nom′ə nᵊl, -nō′mə-), *adj.* —**cog·nom′i·nal·ly,** *adv.*

co·gno·scen·ti (kon′yə shen′tē, kog′nə-), *n.pl., sing.* **-te** (-tē). those who have superior knowledge and understanding of a particular field, esp. in the fine arts, literature, and the world of fashion. Also, **conoscenti.** [< It, Latinized var. of *conoscente* (prp. of *conoscere* to know) < L; see COGNITION, -ENT]

cog·nos·ci·ble (kog nos′ə bəl), *adj.* capable of being known. [< LL *cognōscibil(is)* = *cognōsc(ere)* (see COGNIZANCE) + *-ibilis* -IBLE] —**cog·nos′ci·bil′i·ty,** *n.*

cog·no·vit (kog nō′vit), *n.* *Law.* an acknowledgment by a defendant in a civil case that the plaintiff's cause or a part of it is just, made chiefly to save the expense of litigation. [< L: perf. 3rd pers. sing. of *cognōscere* to recognize; see COGNIZANCE]

co·gon (kō gōn′), *n.* a tall, coarse grass, *Imperata cylindrica,* of the tropics and subtropics, furnishing a material for thatching. [< Sp < Tagalog *kugon*]

cog′ rail′way, a railway having locomotives with a cogged center driving wheel engaging with a cogged rail, to provide sufficient traction for climbing steep grades. Also called **rack railway.**

cog·wheel (kog′hwēl′, -wēl′), *n.* (not in technical use) a gearwheel, formerly esp. one having teeth of hardwood or metal inserted into slots. [late ME]

Cogwheels

co·hab·it (kō hab′it), *v.i.* **1.** to live together as man and wife, usually without legal or religious sanction. **2.** *Archaic.* to dwell or reside in company or in the same place. [< LL *cohabit(āre)* = *co-* co- + *habitāre* to have possession, abide, freq. of *habēre*] —**co·hab′it·ant,** *n.* —**co·hab′i·ta′tion,** *n.*

Co·han (kō han′, kō′han), *n.* **George M(ichael),** 1878–1942, U.S. entertainer, songwriter, and playwright.

co·heir (kō âr′), *n.* a joint heir. Also, *referring to a woman,* **co·heir·ess** (kō âr′is). —**co·heir′ship,** *n.*

Co·hen (kō′ən), *n.* **Oc·tav·us Roy** (ok tav′əs), 1891–1959, U.S. short-story writer and novelist.

co·here (kō hēr′), *v.i.*, **-hered, -her·ing.** **1.** to stick together; hold fast, as parts of the same mass. **2.** *Physics.* (of two or more similar substances) to be united within a body by the action of molecular forces. **3.** to be naturally or logically connected. **4.** to agree; be congruous. [< L *cohaer(ēre)* = *co-* co- + *haerēre* to stick, cling] —**Syn. 1.** See **stick**[2].

co·her·ence (kō hēr′əns), *n.* **1.** the act or state of cohering; cohesion. **2.** natural or logical connection. **3.** congruity; consistency. Also, **co·her′en·cy.** [COHER(ENT) + -ENCE] —**Syn. 1, 2.** COHERENCE, COHESION imply a sticking together. COHERENCE is more often applied figuratively, relating to the order and consistency of thought or of statements: *the coherence of an argument; the coherence of a report.* COHESION usually applies to the literal sticking together of material things: *the cohesion of wood and glue in plywood.*

co·her·ent (kō hēr′ənt), *adj.* **1.** cohering; sticking together: *a coherent mass of sticky candies.* **2.** having a natural or due agreement of parts; connected: *a coherent design.* **3.** consistent; logical: *a coherent argument.* [< ML *cohērent-,* var. of L *cohaerent-* (s. of *cohaerēns*), prp. of *cohaerēre*] —**co·her′ent·ly,** *adv.*

coher′ent light′, *Optics.* light in which the electromagnetic waves maintain a fixed phase relationship.

co·he·sion (kō hē′zhən), *n.* **1.** the act or state of cohering or uniting. **2.** *Physics.* the molecular force between particles within a body or substance that acts to unite them. Cf. **adhesion** (def. 4). **3.** *Bot.* the congenital union of one part with another. [var. of *cohaesion* < L *cohaes-* (var. s. of *cohaerēre* to COHERE) + *-iōn-* -ION] —**Syn. 1.** See **coherence.**

co·he·sive (kō hē′siv), *adj.* **1.** characterized by or causing cohesion: *a cohesive agent.* **2.** cohering; tending to cohere: *a cohesive organization.* **3.** *Physics.* of or pertaining to the molecular force within a body or substance acting to unite its parts. —**co·he′sive·ly,** *adv.* —**co·he′sive·ness,** *n.*

Cohn (kōn), *n.* **Fer·di·nand Ju·li·us** (fûr′dᵊnand′ jo͞ol′yəs; *Ger.* fer′di nänt′ yo͞o′lē o͝os′), 1828–98, German botanist and bacteriologist.

co·hort (kō′hôrt), *n.* **1.** a companion or associate. **2.** a group or company: *She has a cohort of admirers.* **3.** one of the ten divisions in an ancient Roman legion, numbering from 300 to 600 men. **4.** any group of warriors. [< L *cohort-* (s. of *cohors*) yard, military unit = *co-* co- + *-hort-* (akin to *hortus* garden); r. late ME *cohorte* < MF]

co·hosh (kō′hosh, kō hosh′), *n.* either of two perennial herbs of the Eastern U.S., the ranunculaceous *Cimicifuga racemosa* **(black cohosh),** or the berberidaceous *Caulophyllum thalictroides* **(blue cohosh),** both used medicinally. [< Algonquian (Mass.): rough]

co·hune (kō ho͞on′), *n.* a pinnate-leaved palm, *Orbignya Cohune,* native to Central America, bearing large nuts whose meat yields an oil resembling that of the coconut. Also called **cohune′ palm′.** [< AmerSp < some native Central American dial.]

coif (koif *for 1–5, 7;* kwäf *for 6, 8*), *n.* **1.** a hood-shaped cap, worn beneath a veil by nuns. **2.** any of various hoodlike caps, worn by men or women. **3.** (formerly) a cap similar to a skullcap, worn by a sergeant at law. **4.** *Armor.* a covering for the head and neck, made of leather, padded cloth, or mail. **5.** *Brit.* the rank or position of a sergeant at law. **6.** *Informal.* coiffure (def. 1). —*v.t.* **7.** to cover or dress with or as with a coif. **8.** to dress (the hair) by arranging or styling. [ME *coyf(e)* < OF *coiffe* < LL *cofea, cuphia* < OHG **kupfia* cap; akin to COP[2]]

coiffe (kwäf), *n.*, *v.t.*, **coiffed, coif·fing.** coif (defs. 6, 8).

coif·feur (kwa fœr′), *n.*, *pl.* **-feurs** (-fœr′). *French.* a male hairdresser.

coif·fure (kwä fyo͝or′; *Fr.* kwa fyr′), *n.*, *pl.* **-fures** (-fyo͝orz′; *Fr.* -fyr′), *v.*, **-fured** (-fyo͝ord′), **-fur·ing** (-fyo͝or′iŋ). —*n.* **1.** a style of arranging or combing the hair. **2.** a head covering; headdress. —*v.t.* **3.** to provide with or arrange in a coiffure. [< F = *coiff(er)* (to) dress the hair (see COIF) + *-ure* -URE]

coif·fur·ist (kwä fyo͝or′ist), *n.* a person who arranges hair styles, esp. for women.

coign (koin), *n.*, *v.t.* quoin.

coigne (koin), *n.*, *v.t.*, **coigned, coign·ing.** quoin.

coign′ of van′tage, a favorable position for observation or action.

coil[1] (koil), *v.t.* **1.** to wind into regularly spaced rings one above the other or one around the other: *to coil a wire around a pencil; He coiled the rope on the deck.* **2.** to gather (rope, wire, etc.) into loops: *She coiled the clothesline and hung it on the hook.* **—v.i. 3.** to form rings, spirals, etc.; wind: *The snake coiled, ready to strike.* **4.** to move in or follow a winding course: *The river coiled through the valley.* **—n. 5.** a connected series of spirals or rings into which a rope or the like is wound. **6.** a single such ring. **7.** an arrangement of pipes, coiled or in a series, as in a radiator. **8.** *Elect.* **a.** a conductor, as a copper wire, wound up in a spiral or other form. **b.** a device composed essentially of such a conductor. **9.** *Philately.* **a.** a stamp issued in a roll, usually of 500 stamps, and usually perforated vertically or horizontally only. **b.** a roll of such stamps. **10.** See **IUD.** [? var. of CULL[1]]

coil[2] (koil), *n.* **1.** a noisy disturbance; tumult. **2.** trouble; bustle; ado. [?]

coil′ spring′, any spring of wire coiled helically, having a cylindrical or conical outline. See illus. at **spring.**

Co·im·ba·tore (kō im′bä tōr′, -tôr′), *n.* a city in W Madras, in SW India. 405,592.

Coim·bra (kwēnm′bʀə), *n.* a city in central Portugal: ancient university. 55,985.

coin (koin), *n.* **1.** a piece of metal stamped and issued by the authority of the government for use as money. **2.** a number of such pieces. **—v.t. 3.** to make (money) by stamping metal: *The mint is coining pennies.* **4.** to convert (metal) into money: *The mint coins copper into pennies.* **5.** to make; invent; fabricate: *to coin words.* **—v.i. 6.** *Brit. Informal.* to counterfeit, esp. to make counterfeit money. [ME *coyn(e), coygne* < MF *coin, cuigne* wedge, corner, die < L *cuneus* wedge] **—coin′er,** *n.*

COIN (koin), *n., adj.* counterinsurgency. [*co(unter)in(surgency)*]

coin·age (koi′nij), *n.* **1.** the act, process, or right of making coins. **2.** the categories, types, or quantity of coins issued by a nation. **3.** coins collectively. **4.** anything made, invented, or fabricated, esp. a word or phrase. [late ME *coy(g)nage* < MF *coignaige*]

coin′ box′, a locked receptacle for holding the coins deposited in a pay telephone or other coin-operated machine.

co·in·cide (kō′in sīd′), *v.i.,* **-cid·ed, -cid·ing. 1.** to come to occupy the same place in space, the same point or period in time, or the same relative position: *The centers of concentric circles coincide. Our vacations coincided this year.* **2.** to correspond exactly, as in nature, character, etc.: *His vocation coincides with his avocation.* **3.** to agree or concur, as in thought, opinion, etc.: *Their views coincide.* [< ML *coincide(re)* = L *co-* co- + *incidere* to befall; see INCIDENT]

co·in·ci·dence (kō in′si dəns), *n.* **1.** the condition or fact of coinciding. **2.** an instance of this. **3.** an event or two or more events at one time happening apparently by mere chance. [COINCID(ENT) + -ENCE]

co·in·ci·dent (kō in′si dənt), *adj.* **1.** coinciding; occupying the same place or position. **2.** happening at the same time. **3.** exactly corresponding. **4.** in exact agreement (usually fol. by *with*). [< ML *coincident-* (s. of *coincidēns*) prp. of *coincidere* to COINCIDE; see -ENT] **—Syn. 2.** simultaneous, synchronous, contemporary.

co·in·ci·den·tal (kō in′si den′tᵊl), *adj.* showing or involving coincidence: *a coincidental meeting.* **—co·in′ci·den′tal·ly, co·in·ci·dent·ly** (kō in′si dᵊnt lē), *adv.*

co·in·her·it·ance (kō′in her′i tᵊns), *n.* joint inheritance.

coin′ of the realm′, *Usually Facetious.* See **legal tender.**

co·in·stan·ta·ne·ous (kō′in stən tā′nē əs), *adj.* occurring or existing at the same instant; simultaneous. **—co′in·stan·ta′ne·ous·ly,** *adv.*

co·in·sur·ance (kō′in shŏŏr′əns), *n.* **1.** insurance underwritten jointly with another or others. **2.** a form of property insurance in which an insurer assumes liability only for that proportion of a loss which the amount of insurance bears to a specified percentage of the value of the property.

co·in·sure (kō′in shŏŏr′), *v.t., v.i.,* **-sured, -sur·ing. 1.** to insure jointly with another or others. **2.** to insure on the basis of coinsurance. **—co′in·sur′er,** *n.*

co·in·ven·tor (kō′in ven′tər), *n.* one of two or more joint inventors.

coir (koir), *n.* the fiber of the coconut husk, used in making rope, matting, etc. [< Malayalam *kāyar* cord; r. *cairo* < Pg < Tamil *kayiru* rope]

cois·trel (koi′strəl), *n.* *Archaic.* **1.** a groom in charge of a knight's horses. **2.** a scoundrel; knave. [ME *quystron, custrun, custrell,* appar. b. MF *quistron* (< LL *cocistrōn-,* s. of *cocistrō* taverner) and *coustillier* esquire (lit., dagger man) < *coustille* dagger]

co·i·tion (kō ish′ən), *n.* coitus. [< L *coitiōn-* (s. of *coitiō*) a coming together (*co-* co- + *-itus,* ptp. of *īre* to go = *i-* v. stem + *-tus* ptp. suffix) + *-iōn-* -ION]

co·i·tus (kō′i təs), *n.* the act of sexual intercourse, esp. between human beings. [< L: a coming together, uniting; see COITION] **—co′i·tal,** *adj.*

coke[1] (kōk), *n., v.,* **coked, cok·ing.** *Chem.* **—n. 1.** the solid product resulting from the destructive distillation of coal in an oven or closed chamber or by imperfect combustion, consisting principally of carbon: used chiefly as a fuel and in metallurgy to reduce metallic oxides to metals. **—v.t., v.i. 2.** to convert into or become coke. [var. of *colk* core, ME *colke* = OE *col* COAL + *-(o)ca* -OCK]

coke[2] (kōk), *n.* *Slang.* cocaine. [short for COCAINE]

Coke (kŏŏk), *n.* **Sir Edward,** 1552–1634, English jurist and writer on law.

col (kol; *Fr.* kôl), *n., pl.* **cols** (kolz; *Fr.* kôl). **1.** *Phys. Geog.* a pass or depression in a mountain range or ridge. **2.** *Meteorol.* the region of relatively low pressure between two anticyclones. [< F < L *coll(um)* neck]

col-[1], var. of **com-** before *l*: *collateral.*

col-[2], var. of **colo-** before a vowel: *colectomy.*

Col., **1.** Colombia. **2.** Colonel. **3.** Colorado. **4.** Colossians.

col., **1.** (in prescriptions) strain. [< L *colā*] **2.** collected. **3.** collector. **4.** college. **5.** colonial. **6.** colony. **7.** color. **8.** colored. **9.** column.

co·la[1] (kō′lə), *n.* a carbonated soft drink having a syrup base made from the dried leaves of the coca plant and the seeds of kola nuts, together with sweeteners and other flavorings. Also, **kola.** [var. of KOLA]

co·la[2] (kō′lə), *n.* a pl. of **colon.**

COLA (kō′lə), *n.* cost of living adjustment: an escalator clause, esp. in union contracts, that grants automatic wage increases to cover the rising cost of living due to inflation. [*C(ost) o(f) L(iving) A(djustment)*]

col·an·der (kul′ən dər, kol′-), *n.* a metal or plastic container with a perforated bottom, for draining and straining foods. Also, **cullender.** [late ME *colyndore,* < ML *cōlātōrium* = *cōlāt(us),* ptp. of *cōlāre* to strain (L *cōl(um)* strainer + *-ātus* -ATE[1]) + *-ōrium* -ORY[2]]

co′la nut′. See **kola nut.**

co·lat·i·tude (kō lat′i tōōd′, -tyōōd′), *n.* *Astron., Navig.* the complement of the latitude; the difference between a given latitude and 90°.

Col·bert (kôl beʀ′), *n.* **Jean Bap·tiste** (zhäɴ bᴀ tēst′), 1619–83, French statesman and finance minister under Louis XIV.

col·can·non (kəl kan′ən, kôl′kan-), *n.* an Irish dish made of cabbage, kale or other greens, and potatoes boiled and mashed together. [< Ir *cāl ceannann* white-head cabbage]

Col·ches·ter (kōl′ches′tər; *Brit.* kōl′chi stər), *n.* a city in NE Essex, in E England. 76,145.

col·chi·cine (kol′chi sēn′, -sin, kol′ki-), *n.* *Pharm.* an alkaloid, $C_{22}H_{25}NO_6$, the active principle of colchicum. [COLCHIC(UM) + -INE[2]]

col·chi·cum (kol′chə kəm, kol′kə-), *n.* **1.** any Old World liliaceous plant of the genus *Colchicum,* esp. *C. autumnale,* a crocuslike plant. **2.** the dried seeds or corms of this plant. **3.** *Pharm.* a medicine or drug prepared from them, used in treating gout. [< L < Gk *kolchikón* meadow saffron]

Col·chis (kol′kis), *n.* an ancient country in Asia, S of the Caucasus and bordering on the Black Sea: the land of the Golden Fleece and of Medea in Greek mythology.

col·co·thar (kol′kə thər), *n.* *Chem.* the brownish-red oxide of iron which remains after heating ferrous sulfate: used chiefly as a pigment, in theatrical rouge, and as a polishing agent. Also called **jewelers' rouge.** [< ML < OSp *colcotar,* SpAr *qulquṭār,* perh. < Gk *chálkanthos*]

cold (kōld), *adj.* **1.** having a temperature lower than the normal temperature of the body: *cold hands.* **2.** having a relatively low temperature; having little or no warmth: *cold water; a cold day.* **3.** feeling an uncomfortable lack of warmth; chilled: *The skaters were cold.* **4.** lacking the warmth of life; dead. **5.** *Informal.* unconscious because of a severe blow, shock, etc. **6.** lacking in passion, emotion, enthusiasm, ardor, etc.: *cold reason.* **7.** not affectionate, cordial, or friendly; unresponsive: *a cold reply.* **8.** depressing; dispiriting: *the cold atmosphere of a hospital waiting room.* **9.** faint; weak: *The dogs lost the cold scent.* **10.** (in children's games) distant from the object of search or the correct answer. **11.** *Art.* **a.** having cool colors, esp. muted tones tending toward grayish blue. **b.** being a cool color. **12. in cold blood.** See **blood** (def. 14). **—n. 13.** the relative absence of heat: *Everyone suffered from the intense cold.* **14.** the sensation produced by loss of heat from the body: *He felt the cold of the steel against his cheek.* **15.** Also called **common cold.** a respiratory viral infection characterized by catarrh, sneezing, sore throat, coughing, etc. **—adv. 16.** with complete certainty; absolutely: *He learned his lesson cold.* **17.** without preparation or prior notice: *She had to play the lead role cold.* **18.** in an abrupt unceremonious manner: *He quit the job cold.* **19.** *Metalworking.* at a temperature below that at which recrystallization can occur (sometimes used in combination): *The wire was drawn cold; to cold-hammer an iron bar.* [ME; OE *cald, ceald;* c. Goth *kald(s),* Icel *kald(r),* G *kalt,* D *koud;* akin to L *gel-* in *gelidus* GELID] **—cold′ly,** *adv.* **—cold′ness,** *n.*

—Syn. 2. frigid, frozen, freezing. COLD, CHILL, CHILLING, CHILLY, COOL refer to various degrees of absence of heat. COLD refers to temperature possibly so low as to cause suffering: *cold water.* CHILL suggests a penetrating cold which causes shivering and numbness: *There was a chill wind blowing.* CHILLING carries a connotation of destructive frost: *a chilling wind.* CHILLY is a weaker word, though it also connotes shivering and discomfort: *a chilly room.* COOL means merely somewhat cold, not warm: *cool and comfortable.* All have figurative uses. **6.** indifferent, uninvolved, cool, unconcerned, imperturbable. **7.** unsympathetic, unfeeling, heartless; reserved; unfriendly, hostile. **—Ant. 2.** hot. **6.** warm, emotional. **10.** warm.

Cold (kōld), *n.* **Sea of.** See **Mare Frigoris.**

cold-blood·ed (kōld′blud′id), *adj.* **1.** designating or pertaining to animals, as fishes and reptiles, whose blood temperature ranges from the freezing point upward, in accordance with the temperature of the surrounding medium; poikilothermal. **2.** without emotion or feeling; dispassionate; cruel: *a cold-blooded murder.* **3.** sensitive to cold. **—cold′-blood′ed·ly,** *adv.* **—cold′-blood′ed·ness,** *n.*

cold′ chis′el, a steel chisel used on cold metal. See illus. at **chisel.**

cold′ cream′, a cosmetic, typically of oily and heavy consistency, used to soothe and cleanse the skin.

cold′ cuts′, various meats and sometimes cheeses, sliced and served cold.

cold-draw (kōld′drô′), *v.t.,* **-drew, -drawn, -draw·ing.** *Metalworking.* to draw (wire, tubing, etc.) without preheating the metal.

cold′ feet′, *Informal.* a lack of courage or confidence; uncertainty or fear.

cold′ fish′, a person who is very reserved or aloof in manner or lacking in normal cordiality, sympathy, or the like.

cold′ frame′, a bottomless, boxlike, usually glass-covered structure and the bed of earth that it covers, used to protect plants.

cold′ front′, the zone separating two air masses, of which the cooler, denser mass is advancing and replacing the warmer.

Cold′ Har′bor, a locality in Virginia, NE of Richmond: Civil War battle in 1864.

cold-heart·ed (kōld′här′tid), *adj.* lacking sympathy or feeling; indifferent; unkind. **—cold′-heart′ed·ly,** *adj.* **—cold′-heart′ed·ness,** *n.*

cold′ light′, light emitted by a source that is not incandescent, as from a firefly.

cold′ pack′, a cold towel, ice bag, etc., for applying to the body to reduce swelling, relieve pain, etc.

cold′ rub′ber, *Chem.* a synthetic rubber made at a relatively low temperature (about 40°F).

cold′ shoul′der, a show of deliberate indifference.

cold′ snap′, a sudden onset of a relatively brief period of cold weather. Also called **cold′ spell′.**

cold′ sore′, a vesicular eruption on the face, often accompanying a cold or a febrile condition.

cold′ steel′, a weapon made of steel, esp. a sword, bayonet, etc.

cold′ stor′age, the storage of food, furs, etc., in any artificially cooled place.

Cold′stream Guards′, a guard regiment of the English royal household: formed in Scotland, 1659–60. Also called **Cold·stream·ers** (kōld′strē′mərz). [after *Coldstream,* a town in SE Scotland]

cold′ sweat′, a chill accompanied by perspiration, caused by fear, nervousness, or the like.

cold′ tur′key, *Slang.* **1.** the sudden and complete withholding of narcotics from an addict, as to effect a cure. **2.** without preparation; impromptu. —**cold-tur·key** (kōld′tûr′kē), *adj.*

cold′ type′, printing that does not involve the casting of type, as from type set photographically or by varityping.

cold′ war′, intense economic, political, military, and ideological rivalry between nations just short of military conflict.

cold′ wave′, **1.** *Meteorol.* a rapid and considerable fall in temperature. **2.** a permanent wave in the hair set by special solutions without the aid of any heating machine.

cole (kōl), *n.* any of various plants of the genus *Brassica,* esp. the rape. [ME *col(e),* OE *cāl, cāw(e)l* < L *caulis* stalk, cabbage; c. Gk *kaulós* stalk]

co·lec·to·my (kə lek′tə mē), *n., pl.* **-mies.** *Surg.* the removal of all or part of the colon or large intestine.

cole·man·ite (kōl′mə nīt′), *n.* a mineral, hydrous calcium borate, $Ca_2B_6O_{11}\cdot 5H_2O$. [named in 1884 after W.T. *Coleman* of San Francisco, in whose mine it was found]

Co·le·op·ter·a (kō′lē op′tər ə, kol′ē-), *n.* the order comprising the beetles. [< NL < Gk *koleóptera,* neut. pl. of *koleópter(os)* sheath-winged = *koleó(n)* sheath + *-pteros* -PTEROUS]

co·le·op·ter·an (kō′lē op′tər ən, kol′ē-), *adj.* **1.** belonging or pertaining to the order *Coleoptera.* —*n.* **2.** a beetle.

co·le·op·ter·on (kō′lē op′tə ron′, kol′ē-), *n., pl.* **-ter·a** (-tər ə). a coleopterous insect; beetle. [< NL < Gk *koleópteron* = *koleó(n)* sheath, scabbard + *pterón* feather, wing]

co·le·op·ter·ous (kō′lē op′tər əs, kol′ē-), *adj.* belonging or pertaining to the order *Coleoptera,* comprising the beetles.

co·le·op·tile (kō′lē op′til, kol′ē-), *n.* *Bot.* (in grasses) the first leaf above the ground, forming a sheath around the stem tip. [< NL *coleoptil(um)* < Gk *koleó(n)* sheath, scabbard + *ptílon* soft feathers, down]

Coleopteron
A, Head; B, Thorax; C, Abdomen; D, Elytron; E, Wing; F, Antenna

co·le·o·rhi·za (kō′lē ə rī′zə, kol′ē-), *n., pl.* **-zae** (-zē). *Bot.* the sheath which envelops the radicle in certain plants, penetrated by the root in germination. [< NL < Gk *koleó(n)* sheath, scabbard + *rhíza* root]

Cole·ridge (kōl′rij), *n.* **Samuel Taylor,** 1772–1834, English poet and critic.

cole·slaw (kōl′slô′), *n.* a salad of finely sliced or chopped raw cabbage. [alter. of D *koolsla* = *kool* cabbage, COLE + *sla,* contr. of *salade* salad]

Col·et (kol′it), *n.* **John,** 1467?–1519, English educator and clergyman.

Co·lette (kō let′, ko-; *Fr.* kô let′), *n.* (*Sidonie Gabrielle Claudine Colette*) 1873–1954, French novelist.

co·le·us (kō′lē əs), *n., pl.* **-us·es.** any of several menthaceous plants of the genus *Coleus,* of tropical Asia and Africa, certain species of which are cultivated for their colored foliage and blue flowers. [< NL < Gk *koleós,* var. of *koleón* sheath, scabbard]

cole·wort (kōl′wûrt′), *n.* any plant of the genus *Brassica,* esp. kale and rape. [ME]

Col·fax (kōl′faks), *n.* **Schuy·ler** (skī′lər), 1823–85, U.S. political leader: vice president of the U.S. 1869–73.

col·ic (kol′ik), *n.* *Pathol., Vet. Pathol.* paroxysmal pain in the abdomen or bowels. [late ME *colike* < L *colica* (*passiō*) (suffering) of the colon < Gk *kolikós.* See COLON², -IC] —**col·ick·y** (kol′ə kē), *adj.*

col·ic·root (kol′ik ro͞ot′, -ro͝ot′), *n.* **1.** either of two North American liliaceous herbs, *Aletris farinosa* or *A. aurea,* having small yellow or white flowers in a spikelike raceme and a root reputed to relieve colic. **2.** any of certain other plants reputed to relieve colic.

col·ic·weed (kol′ik wēd′), *n.* **1.** See **squirrel corn. 2.** the Dutchman's-breeches. **3.** any of several plants of the genus *Carydalis,* esp. *C. flavula,* of the eastern U.S.

col′i·form bacil′lus (kol′ə fôrm′, kō′lə-), *Bacteriol.* any of several bacilli, esp. of the genera *Escherichia* or *Aerobacter,* found as commensals in the large intestine of man and animals, the presence of which in water indicates fecal pollution. [< L *cōl(um)* sieve, strainer + -I- + -FORM]

Co·li·gny (kô lē nyē′), *n.* **Gas·pard de** (GA SPAR′ də), 1519–72, French admiral and Huguenot leader. Also, **Co·li·gni′.**

Co·li·ma (kô lē′mä), *n.* **1.** a state in SW Mexico, on the Pacific Coast. 157,339 (1960); 2010 sq. mi. **2.** a city in and the capital of this state, in the E part. 41,007 (1960). **3.** a volcano NW of this city, in Jalisco state.

col·in (kol′in), *n.* any of several American quails, esp. the bobwhite. [< Sp *colín,* misprint for Nahuatl *çolin*]

col·i·se·um (kol′i sē′əm), *n.* an amphitheater, stadium, large theater, or other building for public meetings, sports, exhibitions, etc. Also, **colosseum.** [< ML *Colisseum;* var. of COLOSSEUM]

co·li·tis (kə lī′tis, kō-), *n.* *Pathol.* inflammation of the colon. —**co·lit·ic** (kō lit′ik), *adj.*

coll., **1.** collect. **2.** collection. **3.** collective. **4.** collector. **5.** college. **6.** collegiate. **7.** colloquial.

collab., **1.** collaboration. **2.** collaborator.

col·lab·o·rate (kə lab′ə rāt′), *v.i.,* **-rat·ed, -rat·ing. 1.** to work with another or others, esp. as a coauthor. **2.** to cooperate, usually willingly, with an enemy nation, esp. with an enemy occupying one's country. [< LL *collabōrāt(us)* (ptp. of *collabōrāre*) = *col-* COL-¹ + *labor* work + *-ātus* -ATE¹] —**col·lab′o·ra′tor,** *n.*

col·lab·o·ra·tion (kə lab′ə rā′shən), *n.* **1.** the act or process of collaborating. **2.** a product resulting from collaboration: *The book was a collaboration of three authors.* [< F < LL *collabōrāt(us)* (see COLLABORATE) + F *-ion* -ION]

col·lab·o·ra·tion·ist (kə lab′ə rā′shə nist), *n.* a person who collaborates with an enemy.

col·lab·o·ra·tive (kə lab′ə rā′tiv, -ər ə tiv), *adj.* characterized or accomplished by collaboration: *collaborative methods; a collaborative report.* —**col·lab′o·ra′tive·ly,** *adv.*

col·lage (kə läzh′, kō-; *Fr.* kô lAzh′), *n., pl.* **-lages** (-lä′zhiz; *Fr.* -lAzh′) for 2. **1.** a technique of composing a work of art by pasting on a single surface various materials not normally associated with one another, as newspaper clippings, theater tickets, fragments of an envelope, etc. **2.** a work of art produced by this technique. Cf. **assemblage** (def. 4). [< F = *colle* paste, glue (< Gk *kólla*) + *-age* -AGE] —**col·lag′ist,** *n.*

col·la·gen (kol′ə jən), *n.* *Biochem.* the protein that yields gelatin on boiling, contained in connective tissue and bones. [< Gk *kólla* glue + -GEN]

col·lapse (kə laps′), *v.,* **-lapsed, -laps·ing,** *n.* —*v.i.* **1.** to fall or cave in; crumble suddenly: *The roof collapsed.* **2.** to be made so that parts can be folded, placed, etc., together: *This bridge table collapses.* **3.** to break down; fail: *Despite their efforts the project collapsed.* **4.** to fall unconscious from a stroke, heart attack, disease, or exhaustion. **5.** to lose self-control or presence of mind. —*v.t.* **6.** to cause to collapse: *He collapsed the table easily.* —*n.* **7.** a falling in or together: *Three miners were trapped by the collapse of the tunnel roof.* **8.** a sudden, complete failure; breakdown. [< L *collāps(us)* (ptp. of *collābī* to fall, fall in ruins) = *col-* COL-¹ + *lāp-,* var. s. of *lābī* to fall + *-sus,* var. of *-tus* ptp. ending] —**col·laps′i·ble, col·laps′a·ble,** *adj.* —**col·laps′i·bil′i·ty,** *n.*

col·lar (kol′ər), *n.* **1.** anything worn or placed around the neck: *a collar of flowers.* **2.** the part of a shirt, coat, etc., around or near the neck, usually folded over. **3.** a leather or metal band or a chain, fastened around the neck of an animal, used esp. as a means of restraint or identification. **4.** the part of the harness that fits across the withers and over the shoulders of a draft animal. **5.** an ornamental necklace worn as insignia of an order of knighthood. **6.** *Zool.* any of various collarlike markings or structures around the neck; torque. **7.** *Metall.* a raised area of metal for reinforcing a weld. **8.** *Mach.* a short ring formed on or fastened over a rod or shaft as a locating or holding part. **9.** the upper rim of a vertical mine shaft. **10. hot under the collar,** *Slang.* angry; excited; upset. —*v.t.* **11.** to put a collar on; furnish with a collar: *They finally succeeded in collaring the unwilling dog.* **12.** to seize by the collar or neck. **13.** to detain (someone anxious to leave) in conversation: *The reporters collared him for an hour.* **14.** *Informal.* to lay hold of, seize, or take prisoner. [< L *collār(e)* neckband = *coll(um)* neck + *-āre* -AR²; r. ME *coler* < AF < L]

col·lar·bone (kol′ər bōn′), *n.* the clavicle.

col′lar but′ton, a button or stud for fastening a detachable collar to the neckband of a shirt or for fastening together the ends of a neckband.

col′lar cell′, choanocyte.

col·lard (kol′ərd), *n.* a variety of kale, *Brassica oleracea acephala,* grown in the southern U.S. [var. of COLEWORT, with assimilation of *-wort* to -ARD]

col′lared pec′cary. See under **peccary.**

collat., collateral.

col·late (ko lāt′, kə-, kol′āt, kō′lāt), *v.t.,* **-lat·ed, -lat·ing. 1.** to compare (texts, statements, etc.) in order to note points of agreement or disagreement. **2.** to collect or arrange (the sheets of a book, pages of a manuscript, etc.) in proper order. **3.** to check or verify the number and order of (the sheets of a book, pages of a manuscript, etc.). **4.** *Eccles.* to present by collation, as to a benefice. [< L *collāt(us)* (ptp. of *conferre* to bring together) = *col-* COL-¹ + *lā-* (var. s. of *ferre*) + *-tus* ptp. ending]

col·lat·er·al (kə lat′ər əl), *adj.* **1.** situated at the side: *a collateral wing of a house.* **2.** situated or running side by side; parallel: *collateral mountain ridges.* **3.** accompanying; auxiliary: *He received a scholarship and collateral aid.* **4.** additional; confirming: *collateral evidence.* **5.** secured by collateral: *a collateral loan.* **6.** aside from the main subject, course, etc.; secondary; indirect: *These accomplishments are merely collateral to his primary goal.* **7.** descended from the same stock, but in a different line; not lineal: *A cousin is a collateral relative.* **8.** pertaining to those so descended. —*n.* **9.** security pledged for the payment of a loan: *He gave the bank his stocks and bonds as collateral for the money he borrowed.* **10.** a collateral kinsman. [< ML *collaterāl(is).* See COL-¹, LATERAL] —**col·lat′er·al·ly,** *adv.*

col·la·tion (ko lā′shən, kə-, kō-), *n.* **1.** the act of collating. **2.** *Bibliog.* the verification of the number and order of the leaves and signatures of a volume. **3.** *Eccles.* the presentation of a clergyman to a benefice. **4.** a light meal that may be permitted on days of general fast. **5.** any light meal. **6.** (in a monastery) the practice of reading and conversing on the lives of the saints or the Scriptures at the close of the day. [ME *collacion,* etc. < ML *collāciōn-, collātiōn-* (s. of *collātiō*) = L *collāt(us)* (see COLLATE) + *-iōn-* -ION]

col·la·tive (ko lā′tiv, kō-, kol′ā-), *adj.* marked by collation. [< L *collātīv(us)*. See COLLATE, -IVE]

col·la·tor (ko lā′tər, kō-, kol′ā-), *n.* a person or thing that collates, as a machine that collects and sometimes binds printed leaves for a book. [< L]

col·league (kol′ēg), *n.* an associate in an office, profession, work, or the like: *his colleagues in the English Department.* [< MF *collegue* < L *collēga* = *col-* COL-[1] + *lēg-*, perf. s. of *legere* to choose + *-a* n. suffix]

col·lect[1] (kə lekt′), *v.t.* **1.** to gather together; assemble: *The professor collected the students' exams.* **2.** to accumulate; make a collection of: *to collect stamps.* **3.** to receive or compel payment of: *to collect a bill.* **4.** to regain control of (oneself or one's thoughts, faculties, composure, or the like). **5.** to call for and take with one: *They collected their mail.* **6.** *Archaic.* to infer. **—***v.i.* **7.** to gather together; assemble: *The students collected in the assembly hall.* **8.** to accumulate: *Rain water collected in the drainpipe.* **9.** to receive payment (often fol. by *on*): *He collected on the damage to his house.* **10.** to gather or bring together books, stamps, coins, etc., usually as a hobby: *He's been collecting for years.* **—***adj., adv.* **11.** *U.S.* requiring payment by the recipient: *a collect telephone call; a telegram sent collect.* [< L *collēct(us)* (ptp. of *colligere* to collect) = *col-* COL-[1] + *lēc-* (ptp. s. of *legere* to gather) + *-tus* ptp. suffix] **—Syn. 1.** See **gather.**

col·lect[2] (kol′ekt), *n.* any of certain brief prayers used in Western churches before the epistle in the communion service. [ME *collecte*, OE *collecta* < ML, short for *ōrātiō ad collēctam* prayer at collection (see COLLECT[1]), r. *collēctiō* summary (prayer)]

col·lect·a·ble (kə lek′tə bəl), *adj.* **1.** capable of being collected. **—***n.* **2.** an object suitable for a collection, originally a work of fine art or an antique, now including also any of a wide variety of items such as bottles, commemorative plates, and memorabilia. Also, **col·lect′i·ble.** [COLLECT + -ABLE]

col·lec·ta·ne·a (kol′ek tā′nē ə), *n.pl.* collected passages, esp. as arranged in a miscellany or anthology. [< L, neut. pl. of *collectāneus* gathered together = *collect(us)* (ptp. of *colligere*; see COLLECT[1]) + *-āneus* adj. suffix]

col·lect·ed (kə lek′tid), *adj.* **1.** having control of one's faculties; self-possessed: *He remained collected during the emergency.* **2.** brought or placed together; forming an aggregation from various sources: *the collected essays of Thoreau.* **—col·lect′ed·ly,** *adv.* **—col·lect′ed·ness,** *n.*

col·lec·tion (kə lek′shən), *n.* **1.** the act of collecting. **2.** something that is collected, as a group of objects or an amount of material accumulated in one location, esp. for some purpose or as a result of some process: *a stamp collection; a collection of new books in the library.* **3.** a sum of money collected, esp. for charity or church use. [< L *collēctiōn-* (s. of *collēctiō*)] **—Syn. 2.** accumulation, hoard.

col·lec·tive (kə lek′tiv), *adj.* **1.** formed by collection. **2.** forming a whole; combined: *the collective assets of a corporation.* **3.** of or characteristic of a group of individuals taken together: *the collective wishes of the membership.* **4.** (of a fruit) formed by the coalescence of the pistils of several flowers, as the mulberry or the pineapple. **5.** organized according to the principles of collectivism: *a collective farm.* **—***n.* **6.** See **collective noun. 7.** a collective body; aggregate. **8.** *Govt.* a unit of organization or the organization in a collectivist system. [< L *collēctīv(us)* = *collēct(us)* (see COLLECT[1]) + *-īvus* -IVE] **—col·lec′tive·ly,** *adv.*

collec′tive bar′gaining, negotiation between a union and an employer for determining wages, hours, rules, and working conditions.

collec′tive farm′, (esp. in the Soviet Union) a farm or a number of farms organized as a unit, worked by a community under the supervision of the state.

collec′tive noun′, *Gram.* a noun, as *herd, jury,* or *clergy,* that appears singular in formal shape but denotes a group of persons or objects.

collec′tive secu′rity, a policy or principle in international relations, designed to preserve world peace, according to which countries collectively guarantee the security of individual countries, as by sanctions or multilateral alliances against an agressor.

collec′tive uncon′scious, (in Jungian psychology) racially inherited psychic material present in the individual unconscious.

col·lec·tiv·ism (kə lek′tə viz′əm), *n.* the political principle of centralized social and economic control, esp. of all means of production. **—col·lec′tiv·ist,** *n., adj.* **—col·lec′tiv·is′tic,** *adj.*

col·lec·tiv·i·ty (kol′ek tiv′i tē), *n., pl.* **-ties. 1.** collective character. **2.** a collective whole. **3.** the people collectively.

col·lec·ti·vize (kə lek′tə vīz′), *v.t.,* **-vized, -viz·ing.** to organize (a people, industry, etc.) under collectivism. **—col·lec′ti·vi·za′tion,** *n.*

collect′ on deliv′ery. See **C.O.D.**

col·lec·tor (kə lek′tər), *n.* **1.** a person or thing that collects. **2.** a person employed to collect debts, duties, taxes, etc. **3.** a person who collects books, paintings, stamps, shells, etc., esp. as a hobby. **4.** *Electronics.* an electrode in a transistor or vacuum tube for collecting electrons, ions, or holes. [late ME < ML; see COLLECT[1], -OR[2]] **—col·lec′tor·ship′,** *n.*

col·leen (kol′ēn, ko lēn′), *n.* **1.** *Irish. Eng.* a young girl. **2.** *U.S.* a young Irish girl. [< Ir *cailīn* = *caile* countrywoman + *-īn* dim. suffix]

col·lege (kol′ij), *n.* **1.** an institution of higher learning primarily providing a general or liberal-arts education. Cf. **university. 2.** a constituent unit of a university, furnishing courses of instruction in a particular field of study. **3.** an institution for vocational, technical, or professional instruction: *a barber college.* **4.** an endowed, self-governing association of scholars incorporated within a university as at Oxford and Cambridge universities in England. **5.** the building or buildings occupied by an institution of higher education. **6.** the administrators, faculty, and students of a college. **7.** (in Britain and Canada) a private secondary school. **8.** an organized association of persons having certain powers and rights, and performing certain duties or engaged in a particular pursuit: *the electoral college.* **9.** a company; assemblage. **10.** a body of clergy living on a foundation. **—***adj.* **11.** collegiate. [late ME < MF < L *collēg(ium)* = *collēg(a)* COLLEAGUE + *-ium* -Y[3]]

col′lege boards′, (*sometimes caps.*) a standard set of examinations required by many colleges for admission.

Col′lege of Arms′. See **Herald's College.**

Col′lege of Car′dinals, the chief ecclesiastical body of the Roman Catholic Church, electing and advising the pope and comprising all of the cardinals of the church. Official name, **Sacred College of Cardinals.**

Col′lege Park′, a city in central Maryland. 26,156 (1970).

col·leg·er (kol′i jər), *n.* (at Eton College, England) a student supported by funds provided by the college.

col·le·gi·al (kə lē′jē əl, -jəl), *adj.* **1.** collegiate. **2.** characterized by the collective responsibility shared by each of the colleagues, esp. in a church. **—col·le′gi·al′i·ty,** *n.*

col·le·gian (kə lē′jən, -jē ən), *n.* **1.** a student in or a graduate of a college. **2.** a member of a college. [late ME < ML *collēgiān(us)*. See COLLEGE, -AN]

col·le·giate (kə lē′jit, -jē it), *adj.* **1.** of or pertaining to a college: *collegiate life.* **2.** of, characteristic of, or intended for college students: *collegiate clothes.* **3.** of the nature of or constituted as a college. Also, **collegial.** [< LL *collēgiāt(us)*. See COLLEGE, -ATE[1]]

colle′giate church′, **1.** a church that is endowed for a chapter of canons, but which has no bishop's see. **2.** *Informal.* a chapel connected with a college. **3.** a church or group of churches under the general management of one consistory or session.

colle′giate in′stitute, (in Canada) an academic high school under the supervision of a provincial government.

col·len·chy·ma (kə leng′kə mə), *n.* *Bot.* a layer of modified parenchyma consisting of cells which are thickened at the angles and usually elongated. [< NL < Gk *kóll(a)* glue + *énchyma* (*en-* EN-[2] + *chy-*, s. of *chein* to pour + *-ma* n. suffix denoting result of action)] **—col·len·chym·a·tous** (kol′ən kim′ə təs), *adj.*

col·let (kol′it), *n., v.,* **-let·ed, -let·ing. —***n.* **1.** a collar or enclosing band. **2.** the enclosing rim within which a jewel is set. **3.** a slotted cylindrical clamp inserted tightly into the tapered interior of a sleeve or chuck on a lathe to hold a cylindrical piece of work. **—***v.t.* **4.** to set (a gem or other stone) in a collet. [< F = *col* neck (< L *collum*) + *-et* -ET]

col·lide (kə līd′), *v.i.,* **-lid·ed, -lid·ing. 1.** to strike one another with a forceful impact; come into violent contact; crash. **2.** to clash, conflict, or disagree. [< L *collīde(re)* to strike together = *col-* COL-[1] + *-līdere*, var. of *laedere* to strike]

Collie (2 ft. high at shoulder)

col·lie (kol′ē), *n.* one of a breed of dogs having a usually long, black, tan, and white or sable and white coat, raised originally in Scotland for herding sheep. [ME *Colle* dog's name (OE *col* COAL + *-la* suffix used in personal names); see -IE]

col·lier (kol′yər), *n.* *Chiefly Brit.* **1.** a ship for carrying coal. **2.** a coal miner. **3.** *Obs.* a seller of coal. [ME *koliere* = *col-* COAL + *-iere*, var. of *-ere* -ER[1]]

Col·lier (kol′yər), *n.* **Jeremy,** 1650–1726, English clergyman and author.

col·lier·y (kol′yə rē), *n., pl.* **-lier·ies.** *Chiefly Brit.* a coal mine, including all buildings and equipment.

col·li·gate (kol′ə gāt′), *v.t.,* **-gat·ed, -gat·ing. 1.** to bind or fasten together. **2.** *Logic.* to bind (facts) together by a general description or by a hypothesis which applies to them all. [< L *colligāt(us)* (ptp. of *colligāre*) = *col-* COL-[1] + *ligā-* (s. of *ligāre* to bind) + *-tus* ptp. ending] **—col′li·ga′tion,** *n.* **—col′li·ga′tive,** *adj.*

col·li·mate (kol′ə māt′), *v.t.,* **-mat·ed, -mat·ing. 1.** to bring into line; make parallel. **2.** to adjust accurately the line of sight of, as of a telescope. [< L *collimāt(us)*, var. reading for *collineāt(us)* (ptp. of *collineāre* to direct in a straight line) = *col-* COL-[1] + *linea* line + *-tus* ptp. ending] **—col′li·ma′tion,** *n.*

col·li·ma·tor (kol′ə mā′tər), *n.* **1.** *Optics.* a fixed telescope for use in collimating other instruments. **2.** an optical system that transmits parallel rays of light, as the receiving lens or telescope of a spectroscope. **3.** *Physics.* a device for producing a beam of particles with parallel paths.

col·lin·e·ar (kə lin′ē ər, kō-), *adj.* lying in the same straight line.

col·lins (kol′inz), *n.* (*often cap.*) a tall drink made with gin, whiskey, rum, or vodka, lemon or lime juice, soda water, and sugar. [after the proper name *Collins*]

Col·lins (kol′inz), *n.* **1. Michael,** 1890–1922, Irish revolutionist and patriot. **2. William,** 1721–59, English poet. **3. (William) Wil·kie** (wil′kē), 1824–89, English novelist.

col·lin·si·a (kə lin′sē ə, -zē ə), *n.* any of the scrophulariaceous herbs of the genus *Collinsia.* [named after Zaccheus *Collins* (1764–1831), American botanist; see -IA]

col·li·sion (kə lizh′ən), *n.* **1.** the act of colliding; crash: *the collision of two airplanes.* **2.** a clash or conflict. **3.** *Physics.* the meeting of particles or of bodies in which each exerts a force upon the other, causing the exchange of energy or momentum. [late ME < LL *collīsiōn-* (s. of *collīsiō*) = *collīs(us)* (ptp. of *collīdere* to COLLIDE) + *-iōn-* -ION]

col·lo·cate (kol′ə kāt′), *v.t.,* **-cat·ed, -cat·ing. 1.** to set or place together. **2.** to arrange in proper order: *to collocate events.* [< L *collocāt(us)* (ptp. of *collocāre*) = *col-* COL-[1] + *loc(us)* place + *-ātus* -ATE[1]]

col·lo·ca·tion (kol′ə kā′shən), *n.* **1.** act of collocating. **2.** state or manner of being collocated. **3.** arrangement, esp. of words in a sentence. [< L *collocātiōn-* (s. of *collocātiō*)]

Col·lo·di (kə lō′dē; *It.* kôl lô′dē), *n.* **Carlo** (kär′lō; *It.* kär′lô), (pen name of *Carlo Lorenzini*), 1826–90, Italian writer.

col·lo·di·on (kə lō′dē ən), *n.* *Chem.* a viscous solution of pyroxylin in ether and alcohol: used in the manufacture of photographic film, in engraving and lithography, and for cementing dressings and sealing wounds. [alter. of NL *collōdium* < Gk *kollṓd(ēs)* glutinous (*kóll(a)* glue + *-ōdēs* -ODE[1]) + *-ium* n. suffix]

col·logue (kə lōg′), *v.i.,* **-logued, -lo·guing.** *Dial.* to confer secretly; conspire. [? b. COLLUDE and DIALOGUE]

col·loid (kol′oid), *n.* **1.** *Physical Chem.* **a.** a colloidal system, esp. one in which a finely divided solid is suspended in a liquid: such colloids range in character from sols to gels. **b.** a colloidal suspension. **c.** a substance that when dissolved in a liquid will not diffuse readily through vegetable or animal membranes. **2.** *Med.* a homogeneous, gelatinous substance occurring in some diseased states. **—***adj.* **3.** *Physical Chem.* colloidal. [< Gk *kóll(a)* glue + -OID]

col·loi·dal (kə loid′ᵊl), *adj.* *Physical Chem.* **1.** pertaining to or of the nature of a colloid. **2.** having very finely divided particles only 1 to about 500 millimicrons in diameter: *colloidal gold.* —**col·loi·dal·i·ty** (kol′oi dal′i tē), *n.*

colloi′dal sys′tem, *Physical Chem.* a mixture of a solid, liquid, or gas in a solid, liquid, or gas that does not separate on standing, as a solid solution, gel, colloidal suspension, emulsion, foam, smoke, or fog.

col·lop (kol′əp), *n.* *Brit. Dial.* **1.** a small slice or portion of meat, esp. a small rasher of bacon. **2.** a small portion or piece of anything. **3.** a fold of flesh on the body. [ME *colopes* (pl.) (> Sw *kalops*) < ?]

colloq., **1.** colloquial. **2.** colloquialism. **3.** colloquially.

col·lo·qui·al (kə lō′kwē əl), *adj.* **1.** characteristic of or appropriate to ordinary or familiar conversation rather than formal speech or writing. In standard American English, *He hasn't got any* is colloquial, while *He has none* is formal. **2.** conversational. [COLLOQUY + -AL[1]] —**col·lo′qui·al·ly,** *adv.* —**co·lo′qui·al·ness,** *n.*

—Syn. 1, 2. COLLOQUIAL, CONVERSATIONAL, INFORMAL refer to types of speech or to usages not on a formal level. COLLOQUIAL is often mistakenly used with a connotation of disapproval, as if it meant "vulgar" or "bad" or "incorrect" usage, whereas it is merely a familiar style used in speaking rather than in writing. CONVERSATIONAL refers to a style used in the oral exchange of ideas, opinions, etc.: *an easy, conversational style.* INFORMAL means without formality, without strict attention to set forms, unceremonious: *an informal manner of speaking;* it describes the ordinary everyday language of cultivated speakers. **—Ant. 1, 2.** formal.

col·lo·qui·al·ism (kə lō′kwē ə liz′əm), *n.* **1.** a colloquial word or expression. **2.** colloquial style or usage.

col·lo·qui·um (kə lō′kwē əm), *n., pl.* **-qui·ums, -qui·a** (-kwē ə). an informal conference or group discussion. [< L = *colloqu(ī)* (*col-* COL-[1] + *loquī* to speak) + *-ium* abstract n. suffix]

col·lo·quy (kol′ə kwē), *n., pl.* **-quies. 1.** a conversational exchange; dialogue. **2.** a conference. [< L *colloqui(um)*] —**col′lo·quist,** *n.*

col·lo·type (kol′ə tīp′), *n.* **1.** any photomechanical process of printing from a plate coated with gelatin. **2.** the plate. **3.** a print made from it. [< Gk *kóll(a)* glue + -o- + -TYPE] —**col·lo·typ·ic** (kol′ə tip′ik), *adj.*

col·lude (kə lo͞od′), *v.i.,* **-lud·ed, -lud·ing. 1.** to act together through a secret understanding. **2.** to conspire. [< L *collūde(re)* (to) play together = *col-* COL-[1] + *lūdere*]

col·lu·sion (kə lo͞o′zhən), *n.* **1.** a secret agreement for fraudulent or treacherous purposes; conspiracy. **2.** *Law.* a secret understanding between two or more persons prejudicial to another, or a secret understanding to appear as adversaries though in agreement: *collusion of husband and wife to obtain a divorce.* [< L *collūsiōn-* (s. of *collūsiō*) = *collūs(us)* (ptp. of *collūdere* to COLLUDE) + *-iōn-* -ION]

col·lu·sive (kə lo͞o′siv), *adj.* involving collusion; fraudulently contrived. [COLLUS(ION) + -IVE] —**col·lu′sive·ly,** *adv.* —**col·lu′sive·ness,** *n.*

col·ly (kol′ē), *v.,* **-lied, -ly·ing,** *n.* *Brit. Dial.* **—***v.t.* **1.** to blacken as with coal dust; begrime. **—***n.* **2.** grime; soot. [var. of *collow* (v.), ME *colwen* < OE *col* COAL; see -Y[1]]

col·lyr·i·um (kə lēr′ē əm), *n., pl.* **-lyr·i·a** (-lēr′ē ə), **-lyr·i·ums.** eyewash (def. 1). [< L < Gk *kollýrion* eye salve]

Col·mar (*Fr.* kôl MAR′; *Ger.* kôl′mär), *n.* a city in NE France. 54,264 (1962).

Cöln (kœln), *n.* former German name of **Cologne.**

colo-, a combining form of **colon**[2]: *colostomy.* Also, *esp. before a vowel,* **col-.**

Colo., Colorado.

col·o·cynth (kol′ə sinth), *n.* **1.** a cucurbitaceous plant, *Citrullus Colocynthis,* of the warmer parts of Asia, the Mediterranean region, etc., bearing a fruit with a bitter pulp. **2.** *Pharm.* the drug derived from the pulp of the unripe but full-grown fruit of this plant, used chiefly as a purgative. [< L *colocynth(is)* < Gk *kolokynthís,* var. of *kolókyntha* bitter gourd, bitter cucumber]

co·log (kō′lôg, -log), *n.* cologarithm.

co·log·a·rithm (kō lô′gə rith′əm, -rith′əm, -log′ə-), *n.* *Math.* the logarithm of the reciprocal of a number, often used in expressing the logarithm of a fraction: log 7/25 = log 7 + colog 25. *Symbol:* colog

co·logne (kə lōn′), *n.* a perfumed toilet water; eau de Cologne. Also called **Cologne′ wa′ter.** [short for *Cologne water,* made in COLOGNE since 1709]

Co·logne (kə lōn′), *n.* a city in W West Germany. 832,400 (1963). German, **Köln,** (formerly) **Cöln.**

Co·lomb-Bé·char (kô lôɴ′bā SHAR′), *n.* former name of **Béchar.**

Co·lombes (kô lôɴb′), *n.* a city in N France, NW of Paris. 77,090 (1962).

Co·lom·bi·a (kə lum′bē ə; *Sp.* kô lôm′byä), *n.* a republic in NW South America. 24,500,000; 439,828 sq. mi. *Cap.:* Bogotá. —**Co·lom′bi·an,** *adj., n.*

Co·lom·bo (kə lum′bō), *n.* a seaport in and the capital of Sri Lanka, on the W coast. 870,000.

co·lon[1] (kō′lən), *n., pl.* **-lons** for 1, **-la** (-lə) for 2. **1.** the sign (:) used to mark a major division in a sentence, to indicate that what follows is an elaboration, summation, implication, etc., of what precedes, or to separate groups of numbers referring to different things, as hours from minutes in *5:30,* or as the members of a proportion in *1 : 2 :: 3 : 6.* **2.** *Class. Pros.* one of the members or sections of a rhythmical period, consisting of a sequence of from two to six feet united under a principal ictus or beat. [< L < Gk *kôlon* limb, member, clause]

co·lon[2] (kō′lən), *n., pl.* **-lons, -la** (-lə). *Anat.* the part of the large intestine extending from the cecum to the rectum. [< L < Gk *kólon* large intestine]

co·lon[3] (kō lōn′; *Sp.* kô lôn′), *n., pl.* **-lons,** *Sp.* **-lo·nes** (-lô′-nes). **1.** the paper monetary unit of El Salvador, equal to 100 centavos. **2.** a cupronickel or steel coin and monetary unit of Costa Rica, equal to 100 centimos. [< AmerSp, after *Colón* Columbus]

co·lon[4] (kō′lon, kə lon′), *n.* a colonial farmer or plantation owner, esp. in Algeria. [< F < L *colōn(us)* colonist]

Co·lón (kō lon′; *Sp.* kô lôn′), *n.* a seaport in Panama at the Atlantic end of the Panama Canal. 72,889 (1960).

colo·nel (kûr′nᵊl), *n.* an officer in the U.S. Army, Air Force, or Marine Corps ranking between lieutenant colonel and brigadier general: corresponding to a captain in the U.S. Navy. [< MF < It *colon(n)ello* = *colonn(a)* COLUMN + *-ello* < L *-ellus* dim. suffix; r. (in writing) *coronel* < MF, metathetic var. of *colonel*]

colo·nel·cy (kûr′nᵊl sē), *n.* the rank, position, or status of a colonel. Also called **colo′nel·ship′.**

co·lo·ni·al (kə lō′nē əl), *adj.* **1.** of, concerning, or pertaining to a colony or colonies: *the colonial policies of France.* **2.** pertaining to the 13 British colonies that became the United States of America. **3.** *Ecol.* forming a colony. **4.** (*cap.*) *Archit., Furniture.* noting or pertaining to the styles of architecture, ornament, and furnishings of the British colonies in America in the 17th and 18th centuries. **—***n.* **5.** an inhabitant of a colony. —**co·lo′ni·al·ly,** *adv.*

co·lo·ni·al·ise (kə lō′nē ə līz′), *v.t.,* **-ised, -is·ing.** *Chiefly Brit.* colonialize. —**co·lo·ni·al·i·sa·tion** (kə lō′nē ə li zā′-shən *or, esp. Brit.,* -lī-), *n.*

co·lo·ni·al·ism (kə lō′nē ə liz′əm), *n.* **1.** the policy of a nation seeking to extend its authority over other territories. **2.** control by a nation over a dependent territory. —**co·lo′-ni·al·ist,** *n., adj.*

co·lo·ni·al·ize (kə lō′nē ə līz′), *v.t.,* **-ized, -iz·ing.** to make colonial. Also, *esp. Brit.,* **colonialise.** —**co·lo·ni·al·i·za·tion** (kə lō′nē ə li zā′shən *or, esp. Brit.,* -lī-), *n.*

co·lon·ic (kō lon′ik, kə-), *adj.* *Anat.* of or pertaining to the colon.

col·o·nise (kol′ə nīz′), *v.t.,* **-nised, -nis·ing.** *Chiefly Brit.* colonize. —**col′o·nis′a·ble,** *adj.* —**col′o·ni·sa′tion,** *n.* —**col′o·nis′er,** *n.*

col·o·nist (kol′ə nist), *n.* **1.** an inhabitant of a colony. **2.** a member of a colonizing expedition.

col·o·nize (kol′ə nīz′), *v.,* **-nized, -niz·ing. —***v.t.* **1.** to plant or establish a colony in; settle: *to colonize the New World.* **2.** to form a colony of: *to colonize laborers in a mining region.* **—***v.i.* **3.** to form a colony: *They went out to Australia to colonize.* **4.** to settle in a colony. Also, *esp. Brit.,* **colonise.** —**col′o·niz′a·ble,** *adj.* —**col′o·ni·za′tion,** *n.* —**col′o·niz′er,** *n.*

col·on·nade (kol′ə nād′), *n.* **1.** *Archit.* a series of regularly spaced columns supporting an entablature and usually one side of a roof. **2.** a series of trees planted in a long row, as on each side of a driveway or road. [< F = *colonne* COLUMN + *-ade* -ADE[1], modeled on It *colonnato* = *colonn(a)* column + *-ato* -ATE[1]]

col·o·ny (kol′ə nē), *n., pl.* **-nies. 1.** a group of people who form in a new land a settlement subject to a parent state. **2.** the country or district settled or colonized: *Many nations are former European colonies.* **3.** any people or territory separated from but subject to a ruling power. **4. the Colonies,** those British colonies that formed the original 13 states of the United States: New Hampshire, Massachusetts, Rhode Island, Connecticut, New York, New Jersey, Pennsylvania, Delaware, Maryland, Virginia, North Carolina, South Carolina, and Georgia. **5.** a number of people coming from the same country or speaking the same language residing in a foreign country or city, or a particular section of it: *the American colony in Paris.* **6.** any group of individuals having similar interests, occupations, etc., usually living in a particular locality. **7.** the district, quarter, or dwellings inhabited by any such number or group: *They live in an artists' colony.* **8.** an aggregation of bacteria growing together as the descendants of a single cell. **9.** *Ecol.* a group of animals or plants of the same kind living together in close association. [late ME *colonie* < L *colōnia*]

col·o·phon (kol′ə fon′, -fən), *n.* **1.** a publisher's distinctive emblem. **2.** an inscription at the end of a book or manuscript, used esp. in the 15th and 16th centuries, giving the title or subject of the work, its author, the name of the printer or publisher, and the date and place of publication. [< L < Gk *kolophṓn* summit, finishing touch]

Col·o·phon (kol′ə fon′), *n.* an ancient city in Asia Minor: one of the 12 Ionian cities; largely depopulated in 286 B.C. —**Col·o·pho·ni·an** (kol′ə fō′nē ən), *adj.*

col·o·pho·ny (kol′ə fō′nē, kə lof′ə nē), *n.* rosin. [< L *Colophōnia* (*rēsina*) (resin) of Colophon < Gk *Kolophōnía,* fem. of *Kolophṓnios* = *Kolophṓn* Colophon + *-ios* adj. suffix; see -Y[3]]

col·or (kul′ər), *n.* **1.** the quality of an object or substance with respect to light reflected by it, usually determined visually by measurement of hue, saturation, and brightness of the reflected light; saturation or chroma; hue. **2.** the natural appearance of the skin, esp. of the face: *She has a good color.* **3.** a ruddy complexion: *The sun had given color to the sailor's face.* **4.** a blush: *His remarks brought the color to her face.* **5.** racial complexion other than white, esp. Negro. **6.** vivid or distinctive quality: *The color of his writing excites me.* **7.** a detail or details in description, customs, speech, habits, or the like: *a novel of 19th-century London with much local color; His injured state lent color to his accusation of mistreatment.* **8.** something that is used for coloring; pigment; tint. **9.** *Painting.* the general effect of all the hues entering into the composition of a picture. **10. colors, a.** any distinctive color or pattern of colors, esp. of a badge, ribbon, uniform, or the like, worn or displayed as a symbol of membership in or sponsorship by a school, organization, etc. **b.** a flag, ensign, etc., particularly the national flag. **c.** attitude; characteristics; personality: *to reveal one's true colors.* **11.** *Phonet.* timbre. **12.** *Chiefly Law.* an apparent or prima facie right or ground: *to hold possession* *under color of title.* **13.** *U.S.* a trace or particle of valuable mineral, esp. gold, as shown by washing auriferous gravel. **14.** *Heraldry.* a tincture other than a fur or metal, usually including gules, azure, vert, sable, and purpure. **15. call to the colors,** to summon for service in the armed forces. —*v.t.* **16.** to give or apply color to; tinge; paint; dye. **17.** to cause to appear different from the reality: *to color one's account of an incident.* **18.** to give a special character or distinguishing quality to: *His personal feelings color his writing.* —*v.i.* **19.** to take on or change color. **20.** to flush or blush. Also, *esp. Brit.,* **colour.** [ME *col(o)ur* < AF (F *couleur*) < L *colōr-* (s. of *color*) hue] —**col′or·er,** *n.*

col·or·a·ble (kul′ər ə bəl), *adj.* **1.** capable of being colored. **2.** specious; plausible. **3.** pretended; deceptive. Also, *esp. Brit.,* **colourable.** [late ME] —**col′or·a·bly,** *adv.*

col·o·rad·o (kol′ə rad′ō, -rä′dō), *adj.* (of cigars) of medium color and strength. [< Sp < L *colōrātus* colored. See COLOR, -ATE[1]]

Col·o·rad·o (kol′ə rad′ō, -rä′dō), *n.* **1.** a state in the W United States. 2,207,259 (1970); 104,247 sq. mi. *Cap.:* Denver. *Abbr.:* Col., Colo., CO **2.** a river flowing SW from N Colorado through Utah and Arizona into the Gulf of California: Grand Canyon; Boulder Dam. 1450 mi. long. **3.** a river flowing SE from W Texas to the Gulf of Mexico. 840 mi. long. —**Col′o·rad′an, Col′o·rad′o·an,** *adj., n.*

Col′orad′o Des′ert, an arid region in SE California, W of the Colorado River. ab. 2500 sq. mi.

Colorad′o Plateau′, a plateau in the SW United States, in N Arizona, NW New Mexico, S Utah, and SW Colorado: location of the Grand Canyon.

Col′orad′o Springs′, a city in central Colorado: resort; U.S. Air Force Academy. 135,060 (1970).

col·or·ant (kul′ər ənt), *n.* a pigment or dye. [< F, prp. of *colorer* < L *colōrāre* to COLOR; see -ANT]

col·or·a·tion (kul′ə rā′shən), *n.* coloring; appearance as to color: *the striking coloration of tropical birds.*

col·o·ra·tu·ra (kul′ər ə to͝or′ə, -tyo͝or′ə, kol′-, kōl′-), *n.* **1.** runs, trills, and other florid decorations in vocal music. **2.** music marked by this. **3.** a lyric soprano of high range who specializes in such music. —*adj.* **4.** of, pertaining to, or characteristic of coloratura or a coloratura soprano. [< It < LL: lit., coloring. See COLOR, -ATE[1], -URE]

col′or bar′. See **color line.**

col·or·bear·er (kul′ər bâr′ər), *n.* a person who carries the colors or standard, esp. of a military body.

col·or-blind (kul′ər blīnd′), *adj.* pertaining to or affected with color blindness.

col′or blind′ness, defective color perception, independent of the capacity for distinguishing light, shade, and form.

col·or·cast (kul′ər kast′, -käst′), *n., v.,* **-cast, -cast·ing.** —*n.* **1.** a television program broadcast in color. —*v.t., v.i.* **2.** to televise in color.

col·or-code (kul′ər kōd′), *v.t.,* **-cod·ed, -cod·ing.** to classify by different colors for various types, categories, etc.: *They color-coded the tickets to know which were bought at the box office.*

col·ored (kul′ərd), *adj.* **1.** having color. **2.** (*often cap.*) belonging wholly or in part to a race other than the white, esp. to the Negro race. **3.** pertaining to the Negro race. **4.** specious or deceptive. **5.** influenced or biased. **6.** *Bot.* of some hue other than green. Also, *esp. Brit.,* **coloured.** [ME]

col·or·fast (kul′ər fast′, -fäst′), *adj.* maintaining or capable of maintaining its exact color shade despite the effects of cleaning, weather, sunlight, etc.: *colorfast textile.* —**col′or·fast′ness,** *n.*

col′or fil′ter, *Photog.* a screen of dyed gelatin or glass for controlling or modifying the reproduction of the colors of the subject as photographed. Cf. **filter** (def. 4).

col·or·ful (kul′ər fəl), *adj.* **1.** abounding in color. **2.** richly picturesque: *a colorful historical period.* Also, *esp. Brit.,* **colourful.** —**col′or·ful·ly,** *adv.* —**col′or·ful·ness,** *n.*

col′or guard′, a guard unit serving as a guard of honor for the colors, as of a military regiment.

col·or·if·ic (kul′ə rif′ik), *adj.* **1.** producing or imparting color. **2.** pertaining to color.

col·or·im·e·ter (kul′ə rim′i tər), *n.* a device that analyzes color by measuring it in terms of a standard color, a scale of colors, or certain primary colors. —**col·or·i·met·ric** (kul′ər ə me′trik), *adj.* —**col′or·i·met′ri·cal·ly,** *adv.*

col·or·ing (kul′ər ing), *n.* **1.** act or method of applying color. **2.** appearance as to color: *healthy coloring.* **3.** aspect or tone: *the ethical coloring of the story.* **4.** specious appearance; show. **5.** a substance used to color something: *food coloring.* Also, *esp. Brit.,* **colouring.** [late ME]

col′oring book′, a book of outline drawings for coloring in crayons or watercolors.

col·or·ist (kul′ər ist), *n.* **1.** a person who uses color, esp. a painter who emphasizes color relationships in his pictures. **2.** a person who colors photographs. **3.** a hairdresser who is skilled in coloring or tinting women's hair. Also, *esp. Brit.,* **colourist.** —**col′or·is′tic,** *adj.*

col·or·ize (kul′ə rīz′), *v.t.,* **-ized, -iz·ing.** to cause to appear in color: *to colorize old black-and-white movies.* —**col′or·i·za′tion,** *n.*

col·or-key (kul′ər kē′), *v.t.,* **-keyed, -key·ing.** color-code.

col·or·less (kul′ər lis), *adj.* **1.** without color. **2.** pallid; dull in color: *a colorless complexion.* **3.** lacking vividness or distinctive character; dull; insipid: *a colorless description.* [ME] —**col′or·less·ly,** *adv.* —**col′or·less·ness,** *n.*

col′or line′, social or political distinction based on differences of skin pigmentation, as between white and colored people. Also called **color bar.**

col′or phase′, 1. a genetically controlled variation in the normal color of the skin or pelt of an animal. **2.** an animal exhibiting such variation. **3.** one of two or more color types assumed by an animal, varying with age or season.

col′or wheel′. See under **complementary color** (def. 1a).

Co·los·sae (kə los′ē), *n.* an ancient city in SW Phrygia.

co·los·sal (kə los′əl), *adj.* **1.** gigantic; huge; vast. **2.** of or resembling a colossus. —**co·los′sal·ly,** *adv.* —**Syn. 1.** See **gigantic.**

Col·os·se·um (kol′ə sē′əm), *n.* **1.** an ancient amphitheater in Rome, begun A.D. c70 by Vespasian. **2.** (*l.c.*) coliseum. [< L, neut. of *colossēus* gigantic, alter. of Gk *kolossiaîos* = *koloss(ós)* COLOSSUS + *-iaios* adj. suffix]

Co·los·sian (kə losh′ən), *n.* **1.** a native or inhabitant of Colossae, Phrygia. **2.** one of the Christians of Colossae, to whom Paul addressed one of his Epistles. —*adj.* **3.** of or pertaining to Colossae or its inhabitants. [< L *Coloss(ae)* (< Gk *Kolossai*) + -IAN]

Co·los·sians (kə losh′ənz), *n.* (*construed as sing.*) a book of the New Testament, written by Paul.

co·los·sus (kə los′əs), *n., pl.* **-los·si** (-los′ī), **-los·sus·es. 1.** (*cap.*) the legendary bronze statue of Helios at Rhodes. Cf. **Seven Wonders of the World. 2.** any statue of gigantic size. **3.** anything colossal, gigantic, or very powerful. [< L < Gk *kolossós* gigantic statue]

co·los·to·my (kə los′tə mē), *n., pl.* **-mies.** *Surg.* incision of a temporary or permanent artificial opening into the colon to effect an artificial anus.

co·los·trum (kə los′trəm), *n.* the milk secreted for a few days after childbirth. [< L, var. of *colostra* beestings]

co·lot·o·my (kə lot′ə mē), *n., pl.* **-mies.** *Surg.* incision or opening of the colon.

col·our (kul′ər), *n., v.t., v.i.* *Chiefly Brit.* color. —**col′our·a′tion,** *n.* —**col′our·er,** *n.* —**col′our·ful,** *adj.* —**col′our·ful·ly,** *adv.* —**col′our·ful·ness,** *n.* —**col′our·ing,** *n.* —**col′our·ist,** *n.* —**col′our·is′tic,** *adj.* —**col′our·less,** *adj.* —**col′our·less·ly,** *adv.* —**col′our·less·ness,** *n.*

col·our·a·ble (kul′ər ə bəl), *adj.* *Chiefly Brit.* colorable. —**col′our·a·bil′i·ty, col′our·a·ble·ness,** *n.* —**col′our·a·bly,** *adv.*

-colous, a learned borrowing from Latin meaning "inhabiting," used in the formation of compound words: *nidicolous.* [< L *-col(a)*, comb. form repr. *colere* to inhabit + -OUS]

col·por·tage (kol′pōr′tij, -pôr′-; *Fr.* kôl pôr tazh′), *n.* the work of a colporteur. [< F = *colport(er)* (to) hawk (lit., carry on the neck; see COL, PORT[5]) + *-age* -AGE]

col·por·teur (kol′pōr′tər, -pôr′-; *Fr.* kôl pôr tœr′), *n., pl.* **-teurs** (-tərz; *Fr.* -tœr′). **1.** a peddler of books. **2.** a person employed to travel about distributing Bibles, religious tracts, etc., gratuitously or at a low price. [< F = *colport(er)* (see COLPORTAGE) + *-eur* -OR[2]]

colt (kōlt), *n.* **1.** a young male animal of the horse family. **2.** a male horse of not more than four years of age. **3.** a young or inexperienced person. [ME; OE *colt*]

Colt (kōlt), *n.* *Trademark.* a revolver.

Colt (kōlt), *n.* **Samuel,** 1814–62, U.S. inventor of the revolver.

col·ter (kōl′tər), *n.* a sharp blade or wheel attached to the beam of a plow, used to cut the ground in advance of the plowshare. Also, **coulter.** [ME, OE *culter* < L: plowshare]

colt·ish (kōl′tish), *adj.* **1.** not trained or disciplined; unruly; wild. **2.** playful; frolicsome. **3.** of, pertaining to, or resembling a colt. —**colt′ish·ly,** *adv.* —**colt′ish·ness,** *n.*

colts·foot (kōlts′fo͝ot′), *n., pl.* **-foots.** a composite perennial, *Tussilago Farfara,* widespread as a weed: formerly used in medicine. [so called from the shape of the leaves]

col·u·brid (kol′ə brid, -yə-), *n.* **1.** any of numerous cosmopolitan snakes of the family *Colubridae,* including fossorial, arboreal, terrestrial, and aquatic species that comprise about two-thirds of all living snakes. —*adj.* **2.** belonging or pertaining to the *Colubridae.* [< NL *Colubrid(ae)* = *Colubr-* (s. of *Coluber* name of genus, L *coluber* snake) + *-idae* -ID[2]]

col·u·brine (kol′ə brīn′, -brin, -yə-), *adj.* **1.** of or resembling a snake; snakelike. **2.** belonging to the subfamily *Colubrinae,* comprising the typical colubrid snakes. [< L *colubrīn(us)* = *colubr-* (s. of *coluber*) snake + *-īnus* -INE[1]]

co·lu·go (kə lo͞o′gō), *n., pl.* **-gos.** See **flying lemur.** [< Malayan native name]

Col·um (kol′əm), *n.* **Pa·draic** (pô′drik), 1881-1972, Irish poet and dramatist, in the U.S. after 1914.

Co·lum·ba (kə lum′bə), *n.* **Saint,** A.D. 521–597, Irish missionary in Scotland.

col·um·bar·i·um (kol′əm bâr′ē əm), *n., pl.* **-bar·i·a** (-bâr′ē ə). **1.** a sepulchral vault or other structure with recesses in the walls to receive the ashes of the dead. **2.** columbary. [< L = *columb(a)* dove + *-ārium* -ARY]

col·um·bar·y (kol′əm ber′ē), *n., pl.* **-bar·ies.** a dovecote. [see COLUMBARIUM]

Co·lum·bi·a (kə lum′bē ə), *n.* **1.** a river in SW Canada and the NW United States, flowing S and W from SE British Columbia through Washington along the boundary between Washington and Oregon and into the Pacific. 1214 mi. long. **2.** a city in and the capital of South Carolina, in the central part. 113,542 (1970). **3.** a city in central Missouri. 58,804 (1970). **4.** *Literary.* the United States of America.

Co·lum·bi·an (kə lum′bē ən), *adj.* **1.** pertaining to America or the United States. **2.** pertaining to Christopher Columbus. —*n.* **3.** *Print.* a 16-point type of a size between English and great primer. [COLUMB(IA) or COLUMB(US) + -IAN]

col·um·bine[1] (kol′əm bīn′), *n.* any of several ranunculaceous plants of the genus *Aquilegia,* as *A. caerula,* having bluish-purple flowers: the state flower of Colorado. [ME < ML *columbīn(a)* (*herba*) dovelike (plant), fem. of L *columbīnus* (see COLUMBINE[2]); the inverted flower looks like a group of doves]

col·um·bine[2] (kol′əm bīn′, -bin), *adj.* **1.** of or like a dove. **2.** dove-colored. [ME < L *columbīn(us)* = *columb(a)* dove + *-īnus* -INE[1]]

Col·um·bine (kol′əm bīn′), *n.* a female character in comedy, esp. commedia dell'arte and pantomime: sweetheart of Harlequin.

co·lum·bite (kə lum′bīt), *n.* a black, crystalline mineral, $FeNb_2O_6$, often containing manganese and tantalum: the principal ore of niobium. [COLUMB(IUM) + -ITE[1]]

co·lum·bi·um (kə lum′bē əm), *n.* *Chem.* (formerly) niobium. *Symbol:* Cb [COLUMB(IA) (def. 5) + -IUM]

Co·lum·bus (kə lum′bəs), *n.* **1. Christopher** (Sp. *Cristóbal Colón;* It. *Cristoforo Colombo*), 1446?–1506, Italian navigator in Spanish service: discoverer of America 1492. **2.** a city in and the capital of Ohio, in the central part. 540,025 (1970). **3.** a city in W Georgia. 155,028 (1970). **4.** a city in E Mississippi. 25,795 (1970). **5.** a city in central Indiana. 26,457 (1970).

Colum′bus Day′, a day, October 12, observed as a holiday in various states of the U.S. in honor of the discovery of the New World by Columbus and his landing in the West Indies on October 12, 1492.

col·u·mel·la (kol′yə mel′ə), *n., pl.* **-mel·lae** (-mel′ē). *Anat., Zool., Bot.* a small columnlike part; axis. [< L: small column = *colum-* (var. of *column-*, s. of *columna* COLUMN) + *-ella* dim. suffix] —**col′u·mel′lar,** *adj.* —**col·u·mel·late** (kol′yə mel′it, -āt), *adj.*

col·umn (kol′əm), *n.* **1.** *Archit.* **a.** a rigid, relatively slender, upright support, composed of relatively few pieces. **b.** a decorative pillar, most often composed of stone and typically having a cylindrical or polygonal shaft with a capital and usually a base. **2.** any columnlike object, mass, or formation: *a column of smoke.* **3.** a vertical arrangement on a page of horizontal lines of type, usually justified: *There are two columns on this page.* **4.** a vertical row or list. **5.** a regular article or feature in a newspaper or magazine. **6.** a formation of ships in single file. **7.** a long, narrow formation of troops in which there are more members in line in the direction of movement than at right angles to the direction (distinguished from *line*). [late ME *columne* < L *columna* = *colum(e)n* peak + *-a* fem. ending; akin to (EX)CEL; r. late ME *colompne* < MF] —**col·umned** (kol′əmd), **col·um·nat·ed** (kol′əm nā′tid), *adj.* —**Syn. 1.** COLUMN, PILLAR refer to upright supports in architectural structures. PILLAR is the general word: *the pillars supporting the roof.* A COLUMN is a particular kind of pillar, esp. one with an identifiable shaft, base, and capital: *columns of the Corinthian order.*

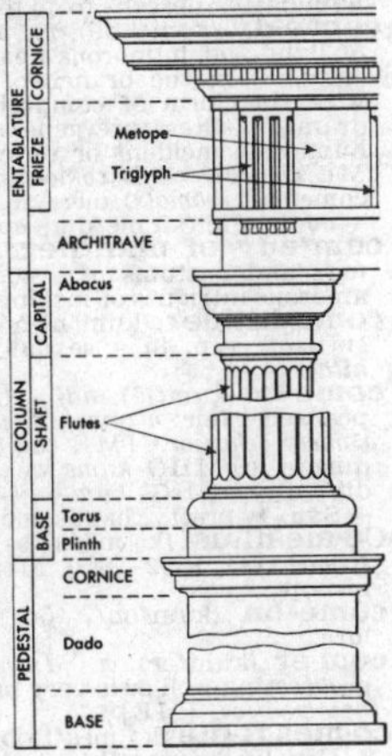

Column, Roman Doric order

co·lum·nar (kə lum′nər), *adj.* **1.** shaped like a column. **2.** characterized by columns: *columnar architecture.* **3.** Also, **co·lum′nal.** printed, arranged, etc., in columns. [< LL *columnār(is)*]

co·lum·ni·a·tion (kə lum′nē ā′shən), *n.* *Archit.* **1.** the employment of columns. **2.** the system of columns in a structure. [abstracted from (INTER)COLUMNIATION]

col·umn·ist (kol′əm nist, -ə mist), *n.* the writer or editor of a journalistic column.

co·lure (kə lo͝or′, kō-, kō′lo͝or), *n.* *Astron.* either of two great circles of the celestial sphere intersecting each other at the poles, one passing through both equinoxes and the other through both solstices. [< LL *colūr(us)* < Gk *kólour(os)* dock-tailed = *kól(os)* docked + *our(á)* tail + *-os* adj. suffix]

col·za (kol′zə), *n.* rape[2]. [< F < D *koolzaad* = *kool* COLE + *zaad* SEED]

col′za oil′. See **rape oil.**

com-, a prefix meaning "with," "together," "in association," and (with intensive force) "completely," occurring in loan words from Latin (*commit*): used in the formation of compound words before *b, p, m: combine; compare; commingle.* Also, **co-, con-, col-, cor-.** [< L, var. of prep. *cum* with]

Com., 1. Commander. **2.** Commission. **3.** Commissioner. **4.** Commodore.

com., 1. comedy. **2.** commerce. **3.** common. **4.** commonly. **5.** committee.

co·ma[1] (kō′mə), *n., pl.* **-mas.** a state of prolonged unconsciousness due to disease, injury, poison, etc.; stupor. [< Gk *kôma* deep sleep]

co·ma[2] (kō′mə), *n., pl.* **-mae** (-mē). **1.** *Astron.* the nebulous envelope around the nucleus of a comet. **2.** *Optics.* a monochromatic aberration of a lens or other optical system in which the image from a point source cannot be brought into focus, the image of a point having the shape of a comet. **3.** *Bot.* **a.** a tuft of silky hairs at the end of a seed. **b.** the leafy crown of a tree; cluster of leaves at the end of a stem. **c.** a terminal cluster of bracts, as in the pineapple. [< L: hair < Gk *kómē*]

Coma[2] (def. 3a) on seed of milkweed, *Asclepias syriaca*

Co·ma Ber·e·ni·ces (kō′mə ber′ə nī′sēz), *gen.* **Co·mae Ber·e·ni·ces** (kō′mē ber′ə nī′sēz). *Astron.* Berenice's Hair, a northern constellation situated north of Virgo and between Boötes and Leo. [< L]

co·mak·er (kō mā′kər, kō′mā′kər), *n.* *Finance.* a person who formally undertakes to discharge the duties of the maker of an instrument, esp. a promissory note, in the event of the maker's default.

Co·man·che (kō man′chē, kə-), *n., pl.* **-ches,** (*esp. collectively*) **-che** for 1. **1.** a member of a Shoshonean tribe, formerly ranging from Wyoming to Texas, now in Oklahoma. **2.** their speech, a dialect of Shoshone. [< MexSp < Shoshone]

Co·man·che·an (kō man′chē ən, kə), *Geol.* —*adj.* **1.** pertaining to an epoch or series of rocks in parts of North America comprising the early portion of the Cretaceous period or system. —*n.* **2.** an epoch or series of early Cretaceous rocks typically represented in the Gulf of Mexico region.

co·man·dan·te (kom′ən dan′tē; *Sp., It.* kō′män dän′te), *n., pl.* **-tes** (-tēz; *Sp.* -tes), *It.* **-ti** (-tē). commandant. [< Sp, It]

co·mate[1] (kō māt′), *n.* a companion. [co- + MATE[1]]

co·mate[2] (kō′māt), *adj.* **1.** *Bot.* having a coma. **2.** hairy; tufted. [< L *comāt(us)*]

com·a·tose (kom′ə tōs′, kō′mə-), *adj.* **1.** affected with or characterized by coma: *The patient was comatose after the stroke.* **2.** lacking alertness or energy; lethargic. [< Gk *komat-* (s. of *kôma* COMA[1]) + -OSE[1]] —**com′a·tose′ly,** *adv.*

co·mat·u·lid (kə mach′ə lid), *n.* a free-swimming, stalkless crinoid; a feather star. [< NL *Comatulid(ae)* = *Comatul(a)* genus name (see COMATE[2]) + *-idae* -IDAE]

comb[1] (kōm), *n.* **1.** a toothed strip of bone, metal, plastic, etc., for arranging the hair or holding it in place. **2.** a currycomb. **3.** any comblike instrument, object, or formation. **4.** a machine for separating choice cotton or worsted fibers from noil. **5.** the fleshy, more or less serrated excrescence or growth on the head of certain gallinaceous birds, esp. the domestic fowl. **6.** something resembling or suggesting this, as the crest of a wave. **7.** a honeycomb, or any similar group of cells. —*v.t.* **8.** to arrange or adorn (the hair) with or as with a comb. **9.** to remove (anything undesirable) with or as with a comb: *to comb burs from one's hair.* **10.** to search everywhere in: *to comb the files.* **11.** to separate (wool fibers) with a comb. —*v.i.* **12.** to roll over or break at the crest, as a wave. [ME; OE *comb, camb;* c. OHG *kamb* (G *Kamm*), Icel *kambr,* Gk *gómphos* pin, peg, *gomphíos* molar tooth; see CAM]

comb[2] (ko͞om, kōm), *n.* combe.

comb., combining.

com·bat (*v.* kəm bat′, kom′bat, kum′-; *n.* kom′bat, kum′-), *v.,* **-bat·ed, -bat·ing** or (*esp. Brit.*) **-bat·ted, -bat·ting,** *n.* —*v.t.* **1.** to fight or contend against; oppose vigorously. —*v.i.* **2.** to fight; contend: *to combat with crippling diseases.* —*n.* **3.** a controversy, or fight between two ideals, men, etc. **4.** *Mil.* active fighting between enemy forces. [< MF *combatt(re)* < VL **combattere* = L *com-* COM- + *battuere* to strike, beat] —**Syn. 1, 2.** struggle, contest. **3.** contention, battle. See **fight.**

com·bat·ant (kəm bat′ənt, kom′bə tənt, kum′-), *n.* **1.** a person or group that fights. —*adj.* **2.** combating; fighting: *the combatant armies.* **3.** disposed to combat. [late ME *combataunt* < MF *combatant.* See COMBAT, -ANT]

com′bat boot′, a heavy leather shoe having a buckled extension above the ankle and a sole and heel of hard rubber.

com′bat fatigue′. See **battle fatigue.**

Com′bat In′fantryman Badge′, a U.S. military badge awarded to an infantryman in recognition of satisfactory performance of duty in ground combat.

com·bat·ive (kəm bat′iv, kom′bə tiv, kum′-), *adj.* ready or inclined to fight; pugnacious. —**com·bat′ive·ly,** *adv.* —**com·bat′ive·ness,** *n.*

combe (ko͞om, kōm), *n.* *Brit.* a narrow valley or deep hollow, esp. one enclosed on all but one side. Also, **comb, coomb, coombe.** [OE *cumb* valley < Celt; cf. Gaulish *cumba,* Welsh *cwm* valley]

combed′ yarn′, cotton or worsted yarn of fibers laid parallel, superior in smoothness to carded yarn.

comb·er (kō′mər), *n.* **1.** a person or thing that combs. **2.** a long, curling wave.

com·bi·na·tion (kom′bə nā′shən), *n.* **1.** the act of combining. **2.** the state of being combined. **3.** a number of things combined: *a combination of ideas.* **4.** something formed by combining: *A chord is a combination of notes.* **5.** an alliance of persons or parties. **6.** the set or series of numbers or letters used in setting the mechanism of a combination lock. **7.** the parts of the mechanism operated by this. **8.** *Math.* **a.** the arrangement of a number of individuals into various groups, as *a, b,* and *c* into *ab, ac,* and *bc.* **b.** a group thus formed. [< LL *combīnātiōn-* (s. of *combīnātiō*) = *combīnāt(us)* combined (see COMBINE, -ATE[1]) + *-iōn-* -ION] —**com′bi·na′tion·al,** *adj.* —**Syn. 1.** association, union, coalescence. **3.** mixture, amalgamation, amalgam. COMBINATION, COMPOSITE, COMPOUND all mean a union of individual parts. COMBINATION implies a grouping that is close but that may easily be dissolved. A COMPOSITE is a stronger union, in which the parts have become subordinate to a unity. COMPOUND implies a more or less complete merging of individual parts into an organic whole. **5.** association, federation, coalition; bloc.

combina′tion last′, a shoe last that has a narrower heel or instep than the standard last.

combina′tion lock′, a lock opened by turning one or more dials a given number of times through a particular set of positions in a prescribed order and direction.

com·bi·na·tive (kom′bə nā′tiv, kəm bī′nə-), *adj.* **1.** tending or serving to combine. **2.** of, pertaining to, or resulting from combination.

com·bi·na·to·ri·al (kəm bī′nə tôr′ē əl, -tōr′-), *adj.* *Math.* of or pertaining to combination, or the modes, properties, etc., of combinations. Also, **com·bi′na·to′ry.**

combinato′rial anal′ysis, *Math.* the branch of mathematics that deals with permutations and combinations, esp. used in statistics and probability.

com·bine (*v.* kəm bīn′; *n.* kom′bīn), *v.,* **-bined, -bin·ing,** *n.* —*v.t.* **1.** to bring or join into a close union or whole; unite; associate; coalesce: *She combined the ingredients to make the dough.* —*v.i.* **2.** to unite; coalesce: *The clay combined with the water to form a milky suspension.* **3.** to unite for a common purpose; join forces: *After the two armies had combined, they proved invincible.* **4.** to enter into chemical union. —*n.* **5.** a combination. **6.** *U.S. Informal.* a combination of persons or groups for the furtherance of their political, commercial, or other interests. **7.** a machine for cutting and threshing grain in the field. [late ME *combynyn* < LL *combīnāre* = *com-* COM- + *bīn-* (s. of *bīnī* two by two) + *-ā-* v. suffix + *-re* inf. ending] —**com·bin′a·bil′i·ty,** *n.* —**com·bin′a·ble,** *adj.* —**com·bin′er,** *n.* —**Syn. 1.** compound, amalgamate. **6.** merger, alignment, bloc. —**Ant. 1, 2.** separate.

comb·ings (kō′mingz), *n.pl.* hairs removed with a comb or a brush.

combin′ing form′, *Gram.* a linguistic form used only in compound words, never independently, as *hemato-* in *hematology.*

combin′ing weight′, *Chem.* the atomic weight of an atom or radical divided by its valence.

comb′ jel′ly (kōm), ctenophore.

com·bo (kom′bō), *n., pl.* **-bos.** **1.** a small jazz or dance band. **2.** *Informal.* **a.** a group of things combined. **b.** something formed by combining. [alter. and shortening of COMBINATION]

com·bus·ti·ble (kəm bus′tə bəl), *adj.* **1.** capable of catching fire and burning; inflammable; flammable. **2.** easily excited. —*n.* **3.** a combustible substance. [< LL *combūstibil(is)* < L *combūst(us)* burnt up (ptp. of *combūrere* = *com-* COM- + *-b-* < *ambūrere* to char) + *-ibilis* -IBLE] —**com·bus′ti·bil′i·ty,** *n.* —**com·bus′ti·bly,** *adv.*

com·bus·tion (kəm bus′chən, -bush′-), *n.* **1.** the act or process of burning. **2.** *Chem.* **a.** rapid oxidation accompanied by heat and, usually, light. **b.** chemical combination attended by heat and light. **c.** slow oxidation not accompanied by high temperature and light. [< LL *combūstiōn-* (s. of *combūstiō*). See COMBUSTIBLE, -ION] —**com·bus′tive,** *adj.*

com·bus·tor (kəm bus′tər), *n.* *Aeron.* the apparatus in a ramjet or other jet engine for initiating and sustaining combustion. [COMBUST(ION) + -OR[2]]

comdg., commanding.

Comdr., Commander. Also, **comdr.**

Comdt., Commandant. Also, **comdt.**

come (kum), *v.,* **came, come, com·ing.** —*v.i.* **1.** to move toward a particular person or place; approach. **2.** to arrive by movement or in course of progress: *The train is coming now.* **3.** to approach or arrive in time, in succession, etc.: *Christmas comes once a year.* **4.** to move into view; appear: *The light comes and goes.* **5.** to extend; reach: *The dress comes to her knees.* **6.** to take place; occur; happen: *Success comes to those who strive.* **7.** to occur at a certain point, position, etc.: *Three comes after two.* **8.** to be available, produced, offered, etc.: *Toothpaste comes in a tube.* **9.** to occur to the mind: *The idea just came to me.* **10.** to befall: *They promised no harm would come to us.* **11.** to issue; emanate. **12.** to arrive or appear as a result: *This comes of carelessness.* **13.** to enter or be brought into a specified state or condition: *to come into popular use.* **14.** to do or manage; fare: *He is coming along well with his work.* **15.** to enter into being or existence; be born: *The baby came at dawn.* **16.** to have been a resident or to be a native of (usually fol. by *from*): *She comes from Florida.* **17.** to become: *His shoes came untied.* **18.** *Slang.* to have an orgasm. **19.** (used in the imperative to call attention, express remonstrance, etc.): *Come, that will do!* —*v.t.* **20.** *Chiefly Brit.* to do; perform; accomplish. **21. come about, a.** to come to pass; happen. **b.** *Naut.* to tack. **22. come across, a.** to find or meet, esp. by chance. **b.** *Slang.* to make good one's promise; do what is expected of one. **c.** to be understandable or convincing: *The moral of this story doesn't come across.* **23. come around** or **round, a.** to change one's opinion, decision, etc., esp. so as to agree with another's. **b.** to recover consciousness; revive. **c.** to cease being angry, hurt, etc. **d.** to visit. **24. come back, a.** to return, esp. to a person's memory: *It all comes back to me now.* **b.** *Informal.* to return to a former position or state which a person has lost. **25. come between,** to estrange; separate. **26. come by,** to obtain; acquire: *How did he ever come by so much money?* **27. come down with,** to become afflicted with (an illness). **28. come forward,** to offer one's services; volunteer. **29. come in, a.** to enter. **b.** to come into use or fashion. **c.** to finish in a race or any competition, as specified: *My horse came in third.* **30. come in for,** to receive; get; be subjected to: *This article will come in for a great deal of criticism.* **31. come into, a.** to acquire; get. **b.** to inherit: *He came into a large fortune.* **32. come off, a.** to happen; occur. **b.** to reach the end; acquit oneself: *to come off with honors.* **c.** to be given or completed; occur; result. **33. come off it,** *Slang.* to stop being pretentious. **34. come on, a.** Also, **come upon.** to meet or find unexpectedly. **b.** to appear on stage; make one's entrance. **c.** *Informal.* (used chiefly in the imperative) to hurry; begin: *Come on, before it rains!* **d.** *Informal.* (as an entreaty or attempt at persuasion) please: *Come on, go with us to the movies.* **e.** *Slang.* to make an impression; have an effect: *She comes on a bit too strong for my taste.* **f.** used as an expression of impatience, disbelief, or the like: *Aw, come on! You can't expect me to swallow that story!* **35. come out, a.** to be published; appear. **b.** to become known; be revealed. **c.** to make a debut in society, the theater, etc. **d.** to end; terminate; emerge: *The fight came out badly.* **36. come out with, a.** to speak, esp. to confess or reveal something. **b.** to make available to the public; bring out. **37. come over,** to happen to; affect: *What's come over him?* **38. come round, a.** See **come** (def. 23). **b.** *Naut.* (of a sailing vessel) to head toward the wind; come to. **39. come through,** *U.S. Slang.* **a.** to finish successfully. **b.** to do as expected or hoped; perform. **40. come to, a.** to recover consciousness. **b.** to amount to; total. **c.** *Naut.* to take the way off a vessel, as by bringing her head into the wind, anchoring, etc. **41. come to pass,** to happen; occur. **42. come under,** to fit into a category or classification. **43. come up, a.** to be referred to; arise: *The subject kept coming up in conversation.* **b.** *Brit.* to come into residence at a school or university. **c.** to be presented for action or discussion: *The farm bill comes up for a vote next Monday.* **44. come up to, a.** to approach; near: *He came up to us in the street.* **b.** to compare with as to quantity, excellence, etc.; equal: *This piece of work does not come up to your usual standard.* **45. come up with, a.** to reach; approach: *I came up with them as they were rounding the corner.* **b.** to produce; supply. **c.** to present; propose: *We weren't able to come up with any new suggestions.* [ME *come(n),* OE *cuman;* c. D *komen,* G *kommen,* Goth *qiman,* Icel *koma,* L *ven(īre),* Gk *baín(ein),* Skt *gám(ati)* goes] —**Syn. 2.** See **arrive.** —**Ant. 2.** leave, depart.

come·back (kum′bak′), *n.* **1.** *Informal.* a return to a former rank, popularity, position, prosperity, etc. **2.** *Slang.* a clever or effective retort.

co·me·di·an (kə mē′dē ən), *n.* **1.** a professional entertainer who amuses by telling jokes, acting out comical situations, engaging in repartee, etc. **2.** an actor in comedy.

Co·mé·die Fran·çaise (kô mā dē frän sez′), the French national theater, founded in Paris in 1680, famous for its repertoire of classical French drama.

co·me·di·enne (kə mē′dē en′, -mā′-), *n.* **1.** a woman who is a professional comic entertainer. **2.** an actress in comedy. [< F *comédienne* = *comédie* COMEDY + *-enne,* fem. of *-en* -AN]

com·e·do (kom′i dō′), *n., pl.* **com·e·dos, com·e·do·nes** (kom′i dō′nēz). *Med.* a thickened secretion plugging a duct of the skin, esp. of a sebaceous gland; blackhead. [< NL, L: glutton = *com-* COM- + *ed-* EAT + *-ō* aug. n. suffix]

come·down (kum′doun′), *n.* *Informal.* an unexpected or humiliating descent from dignity, importance, or prosperity.

com·e·dy (kom′i dē), *n., pl.* **-dies. 1.** a play, movie, etc., of light and humorous character with a happy or cheerful ending. **2.** the branch of the drama that concerns itself with this form of composition. **3.** the comic element of drama, of literature generally, or of life. **4.** any comic or humorous incident or series of incidents. [ME *comedye* < ML *cōmēdia* = L *cōmoedia* < Gk *kōmōidía* = *kōmōid(ós)* comedian (*kômo(s)* merrymaking + *aoidós* singer) + *-ia* -Y[3]] —**co·me·dic** (kə mē′dik, -med′ik), **co·me′di·cal,** *adj.*

com′edy of man′ners, a comedy satirizing the manners and customs of a social class, esp. dealing with the amorous intrigues of fashionable society.

come-hith·er (kum′hith′ər, kə mith′-), *adj.* inviting or enticing, esp. in a sexually provocative manner: *a come-hither look.*

come·ly (kum′lē), *adj.,* **-li·er, -li·est. 1.** pleasing in appearance; fair: *a comely face.* **2.** proper; seemly; becoming: *comely behavior.* [ME *cumli,* OE *cȳmlīc* lovely = *cȳme* exquisite (c. MHG *kūme* weak, tender; akin to G *kaum* with difficulty, OHG *kūmo*) + *-līc* -LY] —**come′li·ness,** *n.* —**Syn. 1.** pretty, handsome, personable.

Co·me·ni·us (kə mē′nē əs), *n.* **John Amos** (*Jan Amos Komensky*), 1592–1670, Moravian educational reformer and bishop.

come-on (kum′on′, -ôn′), *n.* *U.S. Slang.* inducement; lure.

com·er (kum′ər), *n.* *Informal.* a person or thing that is progressing well or is very promising: *He looks like a comer in state politics.* [ME]

co·mes·ti·ble (kə mes′tə bəl), *adj.* **1.** edible; eatable. —*n.* **2.** Usually, **comestibles.** edibles; articles of food. [late ME <LL *comēstibil(is)* = L *comēst(us),* ptp. of *comēsse* to eat up (*com-* COM- + *-ēs-, -ēss-* (*ēd-* perf. s. + *-t-* ptp. suffix) + *-tus* ptp. suffix, added a second time) + *-ibilis* -IBLE; see EAT]

com·et (kom′it), *n.* *Astron.* a celestial body moving about the sun, usually in a highly eccentric orbit, consisting of a central mass surrounded by a misty envelope, that may form a tail that streams away from the sun. [< L *comēt(ēs),* *comēt(a)* < Gk *komḗt(ēs)* long-haired = *kómē* hair of the head + *-tēs* n. suffix denoting agent] —**com·et·ar·y** (kom′i ter′ē), **co·met·ic** (kə met′ik) *adj.*

com·eth (kum′ith), *v.* *Archaic.* 3rd pers. sing. pres. indic. of **come.**

come·up·pance (kum′up′əns), *n.* *U.S. Informal.* a deserved rebuke or reprimand.

com·fit (kum′fit, kom′-), *n.* a dry sweetmeat containing a nut or piece of fruit. [ME *confit* < MF < L *confectum* something prepared. See CONFECT]

com·fort (kum′fərt), *v.t.* **1.** to soothe or console; cheer, as someone grieved. **2.** to make physically comfortable. **3.** *Obs.* to aid; encourage. —*n.* **4.** relief in affliction; consolation; solace: *Her presence was a comfort to him.* **5.** a person or thing that gives consolation: *She was a great comfort to him.* **6.** a cause or matter of relief or satisfaction. **7.** a state of ease and satisfaction of bodily wants, with freedom from pain and anxiety: *He is a man who enjoys his comfort.* **8.** *Chiefly Midland and Southern U.S.* comforter (def. 3). **9.** *Obs.* strengthening aid; assistance. [ME *comfortie(n),* var. of *confortie(n), conforte(n)* < OF *conforter* < LL *confortāre* to strengthen = *con-* CON- + *fort(is)* strong + *-āre* inf. suffix] —**com′fort·ing·ly,** *adv.* —**Syn. 1.** calm, solace, gladden. **7.** See **ease.**

com·fort·a·ble (kumf′tə bəl, kum′fər tə bəl), *adj.* **1.** (of clothing, furniture, etc.) allowing physical comfort, easy support, or ease: *a comfortable chair.* **2.** being in a state of physical or mental comfort; contented and undisturbed; at ease: *I don't feel comfortable in the same room with her.* **3.** (of a person, situation, etc.) producing mental comfort or ease; easy to associate with. **4.** adequate; sufficient: *a comfortable salary.* —*n.* **5.** *Chiefly Northern U.S.* comforter (def. 3). [late ME < AF *confortable*] —**com′fort·a·bly,** *adv.*

com·fort·er (kum′fər tər), *n.* **1.** a person or thing that comforts. **2.** a long, woolen scarf, usually knitted. **3.** *U.S.* a thick, quilted bedcover. **4.** *Brit.* pacifier (def. 2). [ME *confortour* < AF, OF *conforteor* << L **confortātōr-*]

com·fort·ing (kum′fər ting), *adj.* affording comfort. —**com′fort·ing·ly,** *adv.*

com′fort sta′tion, *U.S.* a place with toilet and lavatory facilities for public use.

com·frey (kum′frē), *n., pl.* **-freys.** any boraginaceous plant of the genus *Symphytum,* of Europe and Asia, as *S. officinale,* formerly used as a vulnerary. [ME *cumfirie* < ML *cumfiria,* appar. alter. of L *conferva* CONFERVA]

com·fy (kum′fē), *adj.,* **-fi·er, -fi·est.** *Informal.* comfortable. [by shortening and alter.]

com·ic (kom′ik), *adj.* **1.** of, pertaining to, or characterized by comedy. **2.** acting in or writing comedies: *a comic actor.* **3.** of, pertaining to, or characteristic of comedy: *a comic sense.* —*n.* **4.** a comic actor or comedian. **5.** *Informal.* **a.** See **comic book. b. comics,** comic strips. [< L *cōmic(us)* < Gk *kōmikós* = *kôm(os)* a revel + *-ikos* -IC]

com·i·cal (kom′i kəl), *adj.* **1.** producing laughter; amusing; funny. **2.** *Obs.* pertaining to or of the nature of comedy. —**com′i·cal′i·ty,** *n.* —**com′i·cal·ly,** *adv.* —**Syn. 1.** See **amusing.**

com′ic book′, a booklet of comic strips. Also called **comic.**

com′ic op′era, a diverting opera with spoken dialogue and a happy ending. —**com′ic-op′era,** *adj.*

com′ic relief′, 1. an amusing scene, incident, character, or speech introduced into serious or tragic elements, as in a play, in order to provide temporary relief from tension or to intensify the dramatic action. **2.** relief from tension caused by the introduction of a comic element.

com′ic strip′, a sequence of drawings relating a comic incident, an adventure or mystery story, etc.

Com. in Chf., Commander in Chief.

Co·mines (kô mēn′), *n.* **Phi·lippe de** (fē lēp′ də), 1445?–1511?, French historian and diplomat. Also, **Commines.**

Com·in·form (kom′in fôrm′), *n.* an organization (1947–56) established by the Communist parties of nine European countries for mutual advice and coordinated activity. [*Com(munist) Inform(ation Bureau)*]

com·ing (kum′ing), *n.* **1.** arrival; advent: *His coming here was a mistake.* —*adj.* **2.** that comes next or soon; approaching: *the coming year.* [ME]

Com·in·tern (kom′in tûrn′, kom′in tûrn′), *n.* See **Third International.** Also, **Komintern.** [*Com(munist) Inter-n(ational)*]

co·mi·ti·a (kə mish′ē ə), *n.* *Rom. Antiq.* an assembly of the people convened to pass on laws, nominate magistrates, etc. [< L, pl. of *comitium* assembly = *com-* COM- + *it(us),* ptp. of *īre* to go (*i-* perf. s. + *-tus* ptp. suffix) + *-ium* n. suffix] —**co·mi·tial** (kə mish′əl), *adj.*

com·i·ty (kom′i tē), *n., pl.* **-ties. 1.** mutual courtesy; civility. **2.** *Internat. Law.* courtesy between nations, as in respect shown by one country for the laws and institutions of another. [< L *cōmitās* = *cōm(is)* affable + *-itās* -ITY]

comm., 1. commander. **2.** commerce. **3.** commission. **4.** committee. **5.** commonwealth.

com·ma (kom′ə), *n.* **1.** the sign (,), a mark of punctuation used for indicating a division in a sentence (as by an interpolated word, phrase, or clause), to separate items in a list, to mark off thousands in numerals, or to separate types or levels of information in bibliographic and other data. **2.** *Class. Pros.* **a.** a fragment or smaller section of a colon. **b.** the part of dactylic hexameter beginning or ending with the caesura. **c.** the caesura itself. [<LL: mark of punctuation, L: division of a period < Gk *kómma* = *kop-* (var. s. of *kóptein* to strike, chop) + *-ma* n. suffix denoting result of action]

com′ma bacil′lus, a curved, rod-shaped bacterium, *Vibrio comma,* causing Asiatic cholera.

com′ma fault′, *Gram.* the use of a comma, rather than a semicolon, colon, or period, to separate related main clauses not joined by a conjunction.

Com·ma·ger (kom′ə jər), *n.* **Henry Steele,** born 1902, U.S. historian, author, and teacher.

com·mand (kə mand′, -mänd′), *v.t.* **1.** to direct with authority; order. **2.** to require with authority; demand: *He commanded silence.* **3.** to have control over; be master of: *The Pharaoh commanded 10,000 slaves.* **4.** to deserve and receive (respect, sympathy, attention, etc.). **5.** to dominate by reason of location; overlook: *The hill commands the sea.* **6.** to have authority over and responsibility for (a military installation). —*v.i.* **7.** to issue an order or orders. **8.** to be in charge; have authority. **9.** to occupy a dominating position; look down upon or over a body of water, region, etc. —*n.* **10.** the act of commanding or ordering. **11.** an order given by a person in authority. **12.** *Mil.* **a.** an order to troops at close-order drill: *The command was "Right shoulder arms!"* **b.** (*cap.*) a principal component of the U.S. Air Force: *Strategic Air Command.* **c.** a body of troops or a station, ship, etc., under a commander. **13.** the possession or exercise of controlling authority: *a lieutenant in command of a platoon.* **14.** control or mastery: *He has a command of French, Russian, and German.* **15.** *Brit.* a royal invitation. **16.** power of dominating a region by reason of location; extent of view or outlook: *the command of the valley from the hill.* **17.** *Computer Technol.* a character, symbol, or item of information for instructing a computer to perform a specific task. —*adj.* **18.** pertaining to or resulting from a command. [ME *coma(u)nd(en)* < MF *commande(r)* < ML *commandāre* = L *com-* COM- + *mandāre* to entrust, order; see MANDATE] —**Syn. 1.** charge, instruct. See **direct. 3.** govern, manage, lead. See **rule. 4.** exact, compel, require. **10.** direction, bidding, charge. —**Ant. 1, 7.** obey.

com·man·dant (kom′ən dant′, -dänt′), *n.* **1.** the commanding officer of a place, group, etc. **2.** the title of the senior officer and head of the U.S. Marine Corps. **3.** *U.S. Army.* a title generally given to the heads of military schools. [< F, n. use of prp. of *commander* to COMMAND; see -ANT]

com·man·deer (kom′ən dēr′), *v.t.* **1.** to order or force a civilian into fighting or working for a military unit. **2.** to seize (private property) for military or other public use. **3.** to seize arbitrarily. [< SAfrD *kommandeer* < F *commander* to COMMAND]

com·mand·er (kə man′dər, -män′-), *n.* **1.** a person who commands. **2.** a person who exercises authority; leader; chief officer. **3.** the commissioned officer in command of a military unit. **4.** *U.S. Navy.* an officer ranking below a captain and above a lieutenant commander. **5.** a police officer in charge of a precinct or other unit. **6.** the chief officer of a medieval order of knights. [ME < OF *comandere* < *comand-* COMMAND + *-ere* < L *-ātor* -ATOR] —**com·mand′er·ship′,** *n.*

command′er in chief′, *pl.* **commanders in chief. 1.** Also, **Comman′der in Chief′.** the supreme commander of the armed forces of a nation or, sometimes, of several allied nations. **2.** an officer in command of a particular portion of an armed force who has been given this title by specific authorization. **3.** the president of the U.S. considered as the supreme commander of the armed forces.

com·mand·er·y (kə man′də rē, -män′-), *n., pl.* **-er·ies. 1.** the office or rank of a commander. **2.** the district of a commander, esp. of a medieval order of knights. **3.** a local branch or lodge of certain secret or fraternal orders.

com·mand·ing (kə man′ding, -män′-), *adj.* **1.** having the air, tone, etc., of command; imposing; authoritative: *a commanding voice.* **2.** being in command. **3.** dominating by position or location, usually elevation; overlooking. **4.** of, pertaining to, or afforded by such a location: *a commanding view of the river.* [ME] —**com·mand′ing·ly,** *adv.*

command′ing of′ficer, *U.S. Army.* a commander of any rank from second lieutenant to colonel.

com·mand·ment (kə mand′mənt, -mänd′-), *n.* **1.** a command or mandate. **2.** any of the Ten Commandments. **3.** the act or power of commanding. [ME *com(m)and(e)ment* < OF *com(m)andement*]

com·man·do (kə man′dō, -män′-), *n., pl.* **-dos, -does. 1.** a specially trained military unit used for surprise, destructive raids, esp. as used by the allies in World War II. **2.** *Chiefly U.S.* a member of such a unit. **3.** (in South Africa) an armed force raised for service against marauders. [< SAfrD *kommando* a unit of militia < D *commando* command < Sp *comando* = *comand-* COMMAND + *-o* n. ending]

command′ perform′ance, a performance of a play, opera, ballet, or the like, given at the request of a sovereign.

command′ post′, *U.S. Army.* the headquarters of the commander of a military unit.

com·meas·ure (kə mezh′ər), *v.t.,* **-ured, -ur·ing.** to equal in measure; be coextensive with. —**com·meas′ur·a·ble,** *adj.*

com·me·dia dell'ar·te (kə mā′dē ə del är′tē; *It.* kôm-me′dyä del lär′te), *pl.* **com·me·di·a dell'ar·tes, com·me-di·as dell'ar·te,** *It.* **com·me·die dell'ar·te** (kôm me′dye del lär′te). Italian popular comedy, developed during the 16th–18th centuries, in which masked entertainers improvised from a plot outline based on themes associated with stock characters and situations. [< It: lit., comedy of art]

comme il faut (kô mēl fō′; *Eng.* kum′ ēl fō′), *French.* as it should be; proper; fitting. [< F]

com·mem·o·rate (kə mem′ə rāt′), *v.t.,* **-rat·ed, -rat·ing. 1.** to serve as a memento or reminder of. **2.** to honor the memory of by some observance or celebration. **3.** to make honorable mention of. [< L *commemorāt(us)* (ptp. of *commemorāre*) = *com-* COM- + *memor* mindful + *-ātus* -ATE[1]] —**com·mem′o·ra′tor,** *n.*

com·mem·o·ra·tion (kə mem′ə rā′shən), *n.* **1.** the act of commemorating. **2.** a service, celebration, etc., in memory of some person or event. **3.** a memorial. [< L *commemorātiōn-* (s. of *commemorātiō*)] —**com·mem′o·ra′tion·al,** *adj.*

com·mem·o·ra·tive (kə mem′ə rā′tiv, -ər ə tiv), *adj.* **1.** serving to commemorate. **2.** (of a coin, medal, or postage stamp) issued to commemorate a historical event or to honor the memory of a personage. —*n.* **3.** anything that commemorates. —**com·mem′o·ra′tive·ly,** *adv.*

com·mem·o·ra·to·ry (kə mem′ər ə tôr′ē, -tôr′ē), *adj.* commemorative (def. 1).

com·mence (kə mens′), *v.i., v.t.,* **-menced, -menc·ing.** to begin; start. [ME *comenci, comence* < MF *comenc(er)* < VL **cominitiāre* = L *com-* COM- + *initiāre* to begin; see INITIATE] —**com·menc′er,** *n.* —**Syn.** See **begin.** —**Ant.** finish, end.

com·mence·ment (kə mens′mənt), *n.* **1.** the act or an instance of commencing; beginning. **2.** (in schools, universities, colleges, etc.) the ceremony of conferring degrees or granting diplomas at the end of the academic year. **3.** the day on which this ceremony takes place. [ME < OF]

com·mend (kə mend′), *v.t.* **1.** to present or mention as worthy of confidence, notice, kindness, etc.; recommend. **2.** to entrust; give in charge; deliver with confidence: *I commend my child to your care.* **3.** to cite or name with approval or special praise: *to commend a soldier for bravery.* **4.** *Archaic.* to recommend (a person) to the kind remembrance of another. [ME *commend(e)* < L *commend(āre)* = *com-* COM- + *-mendāre,* comb. form of *mandāre;* see MANDATE] —**com·mend′a·ble,** *adj.* —**com·mend′a·ble·ness,** *n.* —**com·mend′a·bly,** *adv.* —**Syn. 1.** praise, laud, extol.

com·men·dam (kə men′dam), *n.* *Eccles.* **1.** the tenure of a benefice to be held until the appointment of a regular incumbent. **2.** a benefice so held. [< ML, short for (*dare*) *in commendam* (to give) in trust; *commendam,* acc. sing. of *commenda,* back formation from L *commendāre* to COMMEND]

com·men·da·tion (kom′ən dā′shən), *n.* **1.** the act of commending; recommendation; praise: *to earn commendation for a job well done.* **2.** something that commends. **3.** **commendations,** *Archaic.* complimentary greeting. [ME *commendacioun* < eccl. L *commendātiōn-* (s. of *commendātiō*) a commending to God < L] —**Syn. 1.** approval, approbation, applause. **2.** eulogy, encomium, panegyric. —**Ant. 1, 2.** condemnation.

com·mend·a·to·ry (kə men′də tôr′ē, -tôr′ē), *adj.* **1.** serving to commend; approving; praising. **2.** holding a benefice in commendam. [< LL *commendātōri(us)* = *commendāt(us)* (ptp. of *commendāre* to COMMEND; see -ATE[1]) + *-ōrius* -ORY[1]]

com·men·sal (kə men′səl), *adj.* **1.** eating together at the same table. **2.** (of an animal or plant) living with, on, or in another, without injury to either. **3.** *Sociol.* (of a person or group) not competing while residing in the same area as another individual or group having different values or customs. —*n.* **4.** a companion at table. **5.** a commensal animal or plant. [late ME < ML *commensāl(is).* See COM-, MENSAL[2]] —**com·men′sal·ism,** *n.* —**com·men·sal·i·ty** (kom′en sal′i tē), *n.* —**com·men′sal·ly,** *adv.*

com·men·su·ra·ble (kə men′sər ə bəl, -shər ə-), *adj.* **1.** having a common measure or divisor. **2.** suitable in measure; proportionate. [< LL *commēnsūrābil(is)* = L *com-* COM- + *mēnsūrābilis* = *mēnsūrā(re)* (see COMMENSURATE) + *-bilis* -BLE] —**com·men′su·ra·bil′i·ty,** *n.* —**com·men′su·ra·bly,** *adv.*

com·men·su·rate (kə men′sər it, -shər-), *adj.* **1.** having the same measure; of equal extent or duration. **2.** corresponding in amount, magnitude, or degree. **3.** proportionate; adequate. **4.** having a common measure; commensurable. [< LL *commēnsūrāt(us)* = L *com-* COM- + *mēnsūrātus* (ptp. of *mēnsūrāre*); see MEASURE, -ATE[1]] —**com·men′su·rate·ly,** *adv.* —**com·men·su·ra·tion** (kə men′sə rā′shən, -shə-), *n.*

com·ment (kom′ent), *n.* **1.** a note in explanation, expansion, or criticism of a passage in a book, article, or the like; annotation. **2.** explanatory or critical matter added to a text. **3.** a remark, observation, or criticism. —*v.i.* **4.** to write explanatory or critical notes upon a text. **5.** to make remarks. —*v.t.* **6.** to make comments or remarks on; furnish with comments. [late ME *coment* < L *comment(um)* invention, contrivance, comment, n. use of neut. of *commentus* (ptp. of *comminīscī* to devise) = *com-* COM- + *men-* (s. of *mēns, mentis* MIND) + *-tus* ptp. ending] —**com′ment·er,** *n.* —**Syn. 3.** See **remark. 4.** annotate, elucidate.

com·men·tar·y (kom′ən ter′ē), *n., pl.* **-tar·ies. 1.** a series of comments, explanations, or annotations. **2.** an explanatory essay or treatise. **3.** anything serving to illustrate a point; comment. **4.** Usually, **commentaries.** records of facts or events. [< L *commentāri(um)* notebook, n. use of neut. of *commentāri(us)*. See COMMENT, -ARY] —**com·men·tar·i·al** (kom′ən târ′ē əl), *adj.*

com·men·ta·tor (kom′ən tā′tər), *n.* **1.** a person who makes commentaries. **2.** a person who discusses news, sports events, weather, or the like, as on radio or television. [late ME < LL = *commentāt(us)* (ptp. of *commentārī* to study, discuss, write upon; see COMMENT, -ATE[1]) + *-or* -OR[2]]

com·merce (kom′ərs), *n.* **1.** an interchange of goods or commodities, esp. on a large scale; trade; business. **2.** social relations, esp. the exchange of views, attitudes, etc. **3.** sexual intercourse. **4.** intellectual or spiritual interchange; communion. [< MF < L *commerc(ium)* = *commerc(ārī)* (to) trade together (*com-* COM- + *mercārī* < *merc-*, s. of *merx* goods) + *-ium* n. suffix] —**Syn. 1.** See **trade.**

com·mer·cial (kə mûr′shəl), *adj.* **1.** of, pertaining to, or characteristic of commerce. **2.** engaged in commerce. **3.** prepared, done, or acting with emphasis on salability, profit, or success: *a commercial product; His attitude toward the theater is very commercial.* **4.** (of an airplane, airline, or flight) **a.** engaged in transporting passengers or cargo for profit. **b.** civilian and public, as distinguished from military or private. **5.** not entirely or chemically pure: *commercial soda.* **6.** catering especially to traveling salesmen by offering reduced rates, space for exhibiting products, etc.: *a commercial hotel.* —*n.* **7.** *Radio and Television.* an announcement advertising or promoting a product. **8.** *Brit. Informal.* a traveling salesman. —**com·mer′cial·ly,** *adv.*

commer′cial art′, graphic art created specifically for commercial uses, esp. for advertising, magazines or books, or the like. Cf. **fine art.** —**com·mer′cial art′ist.**

com·mer·cial·ise (kə mûr′shə līz′), *v.t.*, **-ised, -is·ing.** *Chiefly Brit.* commercialize. —**com·mer′cial·i·sa′tion,** *n.*

com·mer·cial·ism (kə mûr′shə liz′əm), *n.* **1.** the principles, practices, and spirit of commerce. **2.** a commercial attitude in noncommercial affairs; inappropriate or excessive emphasis on profit, success, or immediate results. **3.** a commercial custom or expression. —**com·mer′cial·ist,** *n.* —**com·mer′cial·is′tic,** *adj.*

com·mer·cial·ize (kə mûr′shə līz′), *v.t.*, **-ized, -iz·ing. 1.** to make commercial in character, methods, or spirit. **2.** to emphasize the profitable aspects of. **3.** to offer for sale; make available as a commodity. Also, *esp. Brit.*, **commercialise.** —**com·mer′cial·i·za′tion,** *n.*

commer′cial pa′per, negotiable paper, as drafts, bills of exchange, etc., given in the course of business.

commer′cial trav′eler. See **traveling salesman.**

com·mie (kom′ē), *n., adj.* (*often cap.*) *Informal.* communist. Also, **commy.** [by shortening and alter.]

com·mi·na·tion (kom′ə nā′shən), *n.* a denunciation or threat of punishment, esp. of sinners. [< L *comminātiōn-* (s. of *comminātiō*) = *comminat(us)*, ptp. of *comminārī* (*com-* COM- + *min(ae)* threats + *-ātus* -ATE[1]) + *-iōn-* -ION] —**com·min·a·to·ry** (kə min′ə tôr′ē, -tōr′ē, kom′in ə-), *adj.*

Com·mines (*Fr.* kô mēn′), *n.* **Phi·lippe de** (fē lēp′ də). See **Comines, Philippe de.**

com·min·gle (kə ming′gəl), *v.t., v.i.*, **-gled, -gling.** to mix or mingle together; combine.

com·mi·nute (kom′ə no͞ot′, -nyo͞ot′), *v.*, **-nut·ed, -nut·ing,** *adj.* —*v.t.* **1.** to pulverize; triturate. —*adj.* **2.** comminuted; divided into small parts. **3.** powdered; pulverized. [< L *comminūt(us)*, ptp. of *comminuere* = *com-* COM- + *minuere* to lessen, akin to *minor* MINOR] —**com′mi·nu′tion,** *n.*

com′minuted frac′ture, a fracture of a bone in which the separated parts are splintered or fragmented. See illus. at **fracture.**

com·mis·er·ate (kə miz′ə rāt′), *v.*, **-at·ed, -at·ing.** —*v.t.* **1.** to feel or express sorrow or sympathy for; pity. —*v.i.* **2.** to sympathize; condole (usually fol. by *with*): *They commiserated with him over the loss of his job.* [< L *commiserāt(us)* (ptp. of *commiserārī*) = *com-* COM- + *miser* pitiable + *-ātus* -ATE[1]] —**com·mis′er·a′tion,** *n.* —**com·mis′er·a′tive,** *adj.*

com·mis·sar (kom′i sär′, kom′i sär′), *n.* **1.** (formerly) the head of a major governmental division in the U.S.S.R. **2.** an official in any communist government whose duties include political indoctrination, detection of political deviation, etc. [< Russ *Kommissar* < G < ML *commissār(ius)* COMMISSARY]

com·mis·sar·i·at (kom′i sâr′ē ət), *n.* **1.** (formerly) a major governmental division in the U.S.S.R. **2.** the organized method or manner by which food, equipment, transport, etc., are delivered to armies. **3.** the department of an army charged with supplying provisions. **4.** (in some European countries) police headquarters. [< NL *commissāriāt(us)*]

com·mis·sar·y (kom′i ser′ē), *n., pl.* **-sar·ies. 1.** *U.S.* a store that sells food and supplies, esp. in a military post, mining camp, or lumber camp. **2.** *U.S.* a dining room or cafeteria, as one in a motion-picture studio, factory, or college. **3.** a person to whom some responsibility or role is delegated by a superior power; deputy. **4.** *Eccles.* an officer delegated by a bishop to represent him. **5.** commissar. **6.** (in France) a police official, usually just below the police chief and mayor. [late ME *commissarie* < ML *commissāri(us)* = L *commiss(us)* (ptp. of *committere* to COMMIT) + *-ārius* -ARY]

com·mis·sion (kə mish′ən), *n.* **1.** the act of committing or giving in charge. **2.** an authoritative order, charge, or direction. **3.** authority granted for a particular action or function. **4.** a document granting such authority. **5.** a document conferring authority issued by the president of the U.S. to officers in the Army, Navy, and other military services. **6.** the power thus granted. **7.** the position or rank of an officer in any of the armed forces. **8.** a group of persons authoritatively charged with particular functions: *a parks commission.* **9.** the condition of being placed under special authoritative responsibility or charge. **10.** a task or matter committed to a person's charge: *a commission to design a building.* **11.** the act of committing or perpetrating a crime, error, etc.: *The commission of a misdemeanor is punishable by law.* **12.** something that is committed. **13.** authority to act as agent for another or others in commercial transactions. **14.** a sum or percentage allowed to an agent, salesman, etc., for his services. **15. in commission, a.** in service. **b.** in operating order. **c.** Also, **into commission.** *Navy.* (of a ship) manned and in condition for or ordered to active service. **16. out of commission, a.** not in service. **b.** not in operating order. —*v.t.* **17.** to give a commission to: *to commission a graduate of a military academy.* **18.** to authorize; send on a mission. **19.** to order (a warship, freighter, etc.) to active duty. **20.** to give a commission or order for: *to commission a painting.* [ME < L *commissiōn-* (s. of *commissiō*) a committing. See COM-, MISSION, COMMIT]

com·mis·sion·aire (kə mish′ə nâr′), *n.* *Brit.* a person who performs minor services, as a doorman, porter, etc. [< F *commissionnaire* = *commission* COMMISSION + *-aire* -ER[2]]

commis′sioned of′ficer, a military officer holding rank by commission (including, in the U.S., second lieutenants, ensigns, and all higher ranks).

com·mis·sion·er (kə mish′ə nər), *n.* **1.** a person commissioned to act officially; a member of a commission. **2.** a government official or representative in charge of a department or district: *a police commissioner.* **3.** an official chosen by an athletic league or association to exercise broad administrative or judicial authority: *the baseball commissioner.* [late ME *comyscioner*]

commis′sion house′, a brokerage firm that buys and sells securities on commission for its clients.

commis′sion mer′chant, an agent who receives goods for sale on a commission basis or who buys on this basis and has the goods delivered to a principal.

commis′sion plan′, a system of municipal government in which all legislative and executive powers are in the hands of a commission.

Commissure (def. 2) AB, Line of the commissural faces of the two carpels

com·mis·sure (kom′i sho͝or′), *n.* **1.** a joint; seam; suture. **2.** *Bot.* the joint or face by which one carpel coheres with another. **3.** *Anat., Zool.* a connecting band, as of nerve tissue. [late ME < L *commissūr(a)* = *com-miss-* (see COMMISSARY) + *-ūra* -URE] —**com·mis·su·ral** (kə mish′ər əl, kom′i sho͝or′əl, -so͝or′-), *adj.*

com·mit (kə mit′), *v.t.*, **-mit·ted, -mit·ting. 1.** to give in trust or charge; consign. **2.** to consign for preservation: *to commit to memory.* **3.** to consign to custody: *to commit a delinquent to a reformatory.* **4.** to pledge or devote (oneself) to a position on an issue or question. **5.** to place in a mental institution or hospital by or as if by legal authority. **6.** to bind or obligate, as by pledge or assurance; pledge. **7.** to entrust, esp. for safekeeping; commend: *to commit one's soul to God.* **8.** to deliver for treatment, disposal, etc.: *to commit a manuscript to the flames.* **9.** to do; perform; perpetrate: *to commit a crime.* **10.** *Parl. Proc.* to refer (a bill or the like) to a committee for consideration. [ME *committe* < L *committ(re)* = *com-* COM- + *mittere* to send, give over] —**com·mit′ta·ble,** *adj.*

com·mit·ment (kə mit′mənt), *n.* **1.** the act of committing. **2.** the state of being committed. **3.** *Parl. Proc.* the act of referring or entrusting to a committee for consideration. **4.** consignment, as to prison. **5.** confinement to a mental institution or hospital. **6.** an order issued for such confinement. **7.** *Law.* a written order of a court directing that someone be confined in prison; mittimus. **8.** perpetration or commission, as of a crime. **9.** the act of committing, pledging, or engaging oneself. **10.** a pledge or promise; obligation: *We have made a commitment to pay our bills on time.* **11.** engagement; involvement: *They have a sincere commitment to religion.* Also, **committal** (for defs. 1, 3–11).

com·mit·tal (kə mit′əl), *n.* an act or instance of committing, as to an institution, a cause, the grave, etc.; commitment.

com·mit·tee (kə mit′ē), *n.* **1.** a person or group of persons elected or appointed to perform some service or function, as to investigate, report on, or act upon a particular matter. **2.** *Law.* a person to whom the care of a person or his estate is committed. [late ME < AF = *committ* (< E; see COMMIT) + *-ee* -EE]

com·mit·tee·man (kə mit′ē mən, -man′), *n., pl.* **-men** (-mən, -men′). **1.** a member of a committee. **2.** the leader of a political ward or precinct.

commit′tee of the whole′, the entire membership of a legislative body, sitting in a deliberative rather than in a legislative capacity, for informal debate on special business.

com·mit·tee·wom·an (kə mit′ē wo͝om′ən), *n., pl.* **-wom·en.** a female member of a committee.

com·mix (kə miks′), *v.t., v.i.* to mix together; blend. [back formation from earlier *commixt* < L *commixt(us)* (ptp. of *commiscēre*) = *com-* COM- + *mix-* (var. s. of *miscēre* to mix) + *-tus* ptp. ending]

com·mix·ture (kə miks′chər), *n.* **1.** the act or process of commixing. **2.** the condition of being commixed; mixture. [< L *commixtūr(a)* = *commixt(us)* (see COMMIX) + *-ūra* -URE]

com·mode (kə mōd′), *n.* **1.** a low cabinet, often highly ornamented, containing shelves behind doors or drawers. **2.** a stand or cupboard containing a chamber pot or washbasin. **3.** toilet (def. 1). **4.** an elaborate headdress consisting chiefly of a high framework decorated with lace, ribbons, etc., worn by women in the 17th and 18th centuries. [< F < L *commod(us)* convenient = *com-* COM- + *modus* MODE[1]]

Commode (def. 1)

com·mo·di·ous (kə mō′dē əs), *adj.* **1.** spacious and convenient; roomy. **2.** ample or adequate for the purpose. [late ME < ML *commodiōs(us)* = L *commodi(tās)* convenience (see COMMODITY) + *-ōsus* -OUS] —**com·mo′di·ous·ly,** *adv.* —**com·mo′di·ous·ness,** *n.*

com·mod·i·ty (kə mod′i tē), *n., pl.* **-ties. 1.** something of use, advantage, or value. **2.** an article of trade or commerce, esp. a product as distinguished from a service. **3.**

Obs. a quantity of goods. [late ME *commodite* < MF < L *commoditāt-* (s. of *commoditās*). See COMMODE, -ITY]

commod′ity exchange′, an exchange for the buying and selling of commodities (such as butter, coffee, sugar, and grains) for future delivery.

com·mo·dore (kom′ə dōr′, -dôr′), *n.* **1.** *U.S. Navy.* (not used in peacetime) a grade of flag officer next in rank below a rear admiral. **2.** *Brit. Navy.* an officer in temporary command of a squadron, sometimes over a captain on the same ship. **3.** (in the U.S. Navy and Merchant Marine) the senior captain when two or more ships are cruising in company or the officer in command of a convoy. **4.** the senior captain of a line of merchant vessels. **5.** the president or head of a yacht club or boat club. [var. of *commandore* = COMMAND + *-ore*, unexplained var. of -OR[2]]

Com·mo·dus (kom′ə dəs), *n.* **Lucius Ae·li·us Aurelius** (ē′lē əs), A.D. 161–192, Roman emperor 180–192; son and successor of Marcus Aurelius.

com·mon (kom′ən), *adj.* **1.** belonging equally to or shared alike by two or more or all in question: *common property; common interests.* **2.** pertaining or belonging equally to an entire community, nation, or culture; public: *a common language.* **3.** joint; united: *a common defense.* **4.** widely and unfavorably known; notorious: *a common thief.* **5.** widespread; general: *common knowledge.* **6.** of frequent occurrence; usual; familiar: *a common mistake.* **7.** hackneyed; trite. **8.** of mediocre or inferior quality; mean; low: *a rough-textured suit of the most common fabric.* **9.** coarse or vulgar: *common manners.* **10.** having no rank, station, distinction, etc.; ordinary: *a common soldier.* **11.** *Anat.* forming or formed by two or more parts or branches: *the common carotid arteries.* **12.** *Pros.* (of a syllable) able to be considered as either long or short. **13.** *Gram.* **a.** not belonging to an inflectional paradigm; fulfilling different functions which in some languages require different inflected forms: *English nouns are in the common case whether used as subject or object.* **b.** constituting a gender comprising nouns that were formerly masculine or feminine: *Swedish nouns are either common or neuter.* **c.** noting a word that may refer to either a male or a female. **14.** *Math.* bearing a similar relation to two or more entities. **—*n.*** **15.** Often, **commons.** a tract of land owned or used jointly by the members of a community, usually a pasture or a park. **16.** *Law.* the right or liberty, in common with other persons, to take profit from the land or waters of another. **17. commons, a.** the commonalty; the nonruling class. **b.** the body of people not of noble birth or not ennobled, as represented in England by the House of Commons. **c.** (*cap.*) the representatives of this body. **d.** (*cap.*) the House of Commons. **e.** a large dining room, esp. at a university or college. **f.** *Brit.* food provided in such a dining room. **g.** food or provisions for any group. **18.** (*sometimes cap.*) *Eccles.* **a.** an office or form of service used on a festival of a particular kind. **b.** the ordinary of the Mass, esp. those parts sung by the choir. **19.** *Obs.* **a.** the community or public. **b.** the common people. **20. in common,** in joint possession or use; shared equally. [ME *comun* < OF < L *commūn(is)* = *com-* COM- + *mūnis* serviceable, obliging, akin to MEAN[2]] **—com′mon·ness,** *n.*
—Syn. 5. universal, prevalent, popular. See **general. 6.** customary, everyday. **10.** COMMON, VULGAR, ORDINARY refer, often with derogatory connotations of cheapness or inferiority, to what is usual or most often experienced. COMMON applies to what is accustomed, usually experienced, or inferior, to the opposite of what is exclusive or aristocratic: *She is a common person.* VULGAR properly means belonging to the people, or characteristic of common people; it connotes low taste, coarseness, or ill breeding: *the vulgar view of things; vulgar in manners and speech.* ORDINARY means what is to be expected in the usual order of things; or only average, or below average: *That is a high price for something of such ordinary quality.* **—Ant. 1.** individual, private, personal. **6.** unusual, strange.

com·mon·a·ble (kom′ə nə bəl), *adj.* **1.** held jointly; for general use; public: *commonable lands.* **2.** allowed to be pastured on common land: *commonable cattle.*

com·mon·age (kom′ə nij), *n.* **1.** the joint use of anything, esp. a pasture. **2.** the right to such use. **3.** the state of being held in common. **4.** something that is so held, as land. **5.** the commonalty.

com·mon·al·ty (kom′ə n^{ə}l tē), *n., pl.* **-ties. 1.** Also **com·mon·al·i·ty** (kom′ə nal′i tē). the ordinary or common people. **2.** an incorporated body or its members. [late ME < MF *comunalte* (see COMMUNAL, -TY); r. ME *communaute* < OF]

com′mon car′rier, an individual or company, as a railroad or steamship line, engaged in transporting passengers or cargo or both for payment. Also called **carrier.**

com′mon cold′, cold (def. 15).

com′mon coun′cil, the local legislative body of a municipal government.

com′mon denom′inator, 1. *Math.* a number that is a multiple of all the denominators of a set of fractions. **2.** a trait, characteristic, belief, or the like, common to or shared by all members of a group.

com′mon divi′sor, *Math.* a number that is a submultiple of all the numbers of a given set. Also called **com′mon fac′tor.**

com·mon·er (kom′ə nər), *n.* **1.** a member of the commonalty. **2.** *Brit.* **a.** a person without a title of nobility. **b.** a member of the House of Commons. **c.** (at Oxford and some other universities) a student who pays for his commons and other expenses and is not supported by any scholarship or foundation. **3.** a person who has a joint right in common land. [ME *cominer*]

Com′mon E′ra. See **Christian Era.**

com′mon frac′tion, *Arith.* a fraction represented as a numerator above and a denominator below a horizontal or diagonal line. Cf. **decimal fraction.**

com′mon law′, 1. the system of law originating in England, as distinct from the civil or Roman law and the canon or ecclesiastical law. **2.** the unwritten law, esp. of England, based on custom or court decision, as distinct from statute law. **3.** the general law administered through the system of courts, as distinct from equity, admiralty, etc. [ME *commune lawe*]

com·mon-law (kom′ən lô′), *adj.* of, pertaining to, or established by common law.

com′mon-law mar′riage, a marriage without a civil or ecclesiastical marriage ceremony, generally resulting from a couple's living together as man and wife for a specified time.

com′mon log′arithm, *Math.* a logarithm having 10 as the base. Cf. **natural logarithm.**

com·mon·ly (kom′ən lē), *adv.* **1.** in a common manner. **2.** usually; generally; ordinarily. [ME *communelich*]

com′mon man′, a man who is not distinguished by birth, station, education, or the like; the average man.

Com′mon Mar′ket, 1. Official name, **European Economic Community.** an economic association established in 1958, originally composed of Belgium, France, Italy, Luxembourg, the Netherlands, and West Germany, created chiefly to abolish barriers to free trade among member nations and to adopt common import duties on goods from other countries. **2.** (*sometimes l.c.*) any economic association of nations created for a similar purpose.

com′mon meas′ure, 1. See **common time. 2.** Also called **hymnal stanza.** *Pros.* a ballad stanza of four iambic lines and strict rhymes, often used in hymns, rhyming *abcb* or *abab.*

com′mon mul′tiple, *Math.* a number that is a multiple of all the numbers of a given set.

com′mon noun′, *Gram.* a noun that denotes a class or any member of a class of entities and not an individual, as *man, city, horse.* Cf. **proper noun.**

com′mon peo′ple, those people who do not belong to the aristocracy or who lack social distinction; the masses.

com·mon·place (kom′ən plās′), *adj.* **1.** ordinary; undistinguished or uninteresting. **2.** platitudinous or dull. **—*n.*** **3.** a well-known, customary, or obvious remark; a trite or uninteresting saying. **4.** anything common, ordinary, or uninteresting. **5.** *Archaic.* a place or passage in a book or writing noted as important for reference or quotation. [trans. of L *locus commūnis*, itself trans. of Gk *koinòs tópos*] **—com′mon·place′ness,** *n.*
—Syn. 2. COMMONPLACE, BANAL, HACKNEYED, STEREOTYPED, TRITE describe words, remarks, and styles of expression that are lifeless and uninteresting. COMMONPLACE characterizes thought that is dull, ordinary, and platitudinous: *commonplace and boring.* Something is BANAL that seems inane, insipid, and pointless: *a heavy-handed and banal affirmation of the obvious.* HACKNEYED characterizes that which seems stale and worn out through overuse: *a hackneyed comparison.* STEREOTYPED emphasizes the fact that situations felt to be similar invariably call for the same thought in exactly the same form and the same words: *so stereotyped as to seem automatic.* TRITE describes that which was originally striking and apt, but which has become so well known and been so commonly used that all interest has been worn out of it: *true but trite.* **3.** cliché, platitude.

com′monplace book′, a book in which noteworthy quotations, poems, comments, etc., are written.

com′mon pleas′, 1. any of various courts of civil jurisdiction in several U.S. states. **2.** the chief common-law court of civil jurisdiction in England, now merged in the King's Bench Division of the High Court.

com′mon pray′er, 1. prayer for reciting by a group of worshipers. **2.** (*caps.*) See **Book of Common Prayer.**

com′mon prop′erty, 1. property belonging to all members of a community. **2.** someone or something regarded as belonging to the public in general: *The personal lives of celebrities become common property.* **3.** information that is commonly known; common knowledge.

com′mon room′, *Chiefly Brit.* (in institutions, esp. schools and colleges) a room or lounge for informal use by all.

com′mon school′, *U.S.* a public school.

com′mon sense′, sound practical judgment that is independent of specialized knowledge, training, or the like; normal native intelligence. [trans. of L *sensus commūnis*, itself trans. of Gk *koinḕ aísthēsis*] **—com′mon·sen′si·cal, com′mon·sen′si·ble,** *adj.*

com′mon snipe′. See under **snipe** (def. 1).

com′mon stock′, stock that ordinarily has no preference in the matter of dividends or assets and represents the residual ownership of a corporate business.

com′mon time′, *Music.* a meter consisting usually of four quarter notes, or their equivalent, to the measure; 4/4 time. Also called **four-four time.**

com·mon·weal (kom′ən wēl′), *n.* **1.** the common welfare; the public good. **2.** *Archaic.* the body politic; a commonwealth. [ME *comen wele*]

com·mon·wealth (kom′ən welth′), *n.* **1.** (*cap.*) a group of sovereign states and their dependencies associated by their own choice and linked with common objectives and interests. **2. the Commonwealth.** See **British Commonwealth of Nations. 3.** (*cap.*) a federation of former colonies, esp. as a dominion of the British Commonwealth: *the Commonwealth of Australia.* **4.** (*cap.*) a self-governing territory associated with the U.S.: official designation of Puerto Rico. **5.** (*cap.*) *Eng. Hist.* the English government from the abolition of the monarchy in 1649 until the establishment of the Protectorate in 1653, sometimes extended to include the restoration of Charles II in 1660. **6.** (*cap.*) the official designation (rather than "State") of Kentucky, Massachusetts, Pennsylvania, and Virginia. **7.** any group of persons united by some common interest. **8.** the people of a nation or state; the body politic. **9.** a state in which the supreme power is held by the people. **10.** *Obs.* the public welfare. [late ME *commen wealthe*]

Com′monwealth Day′, May 24, the anniversary of Queen Victoria's birth, observed in some countries of the British Commonwealth of Nations. Formerly, **Empire Day.**

Com′monwealth of Na′tions. See **British Commonwealth of Nations.**

com′mon year′, an ordinary year of 365 days; a year having no intercalary period. Cf. **leap year.**

com·mo·tion (kə mō′shən), *n.* **1.** violent or tumultuous motion; agitation; noisy disturbance. **2.** political or social disturbance or upheaval. [< L *commōtiōn-* (s. of *commōtiō*) = *commōt(us)* (ptp. of *commovēre* to COMMOVE) + *-iōn-* -ION] —**Syn. 1.** disorder, turmoil, tumult, riot. See **ado.**

com·move (kə mo͞ov′), *v.t.*, **-moved, -mov·ing.** to move violently; agitate; excite. [< L *commov(ēre)* (see COM-, MOVE); r. ME *commoeve* < MF]

com·mu·nal (kə myo͞on′əl, kom′yə nəl), *adj.* **1.** pertaining to a commune or a community. **2.** of, by, or belonging to the people of a community: *communal land.* [< F < ML *commūnāl(is)*] —**com·mu·nal·i·ty** (kom′yo͞o nal′i tē), *n.* —**com·mu′nal·ly,** *adv.*

com·mu·nal·ise (kə myo͞on′əlīz′, kom′yə nəlīz′), *v.t.*, **-ised, -is·ing.** *Chiefly Brit.* communalize. —**com·mu′nal·i·sa′tion,** *n.* —**com·mu′nal·is′er,** *n.*

com·mu·nal·ism (kə myo͞on′əliz′əm, kom′yə nəliz′-), *n.* **1.** a theory or system of government whereby each commune is virtually an independent state. **2.** the principles or practices of communal ownership. **3.** strong allegiance to one's own ethnic group rather than to society as a whole. —**com·mu′nal·ist,** *n.* —**com·mu′nal·is′tic,** *adj.*

com·mu·nal·ize (kə myo͞on′əlīz′, kom′yə nəlīz′), *v.t.*, **-ized, -iz·ing.** to make communal; make (land, a business, etc.) the property of the community. Also, *esp. Brit.*, **communalise.** —**com·mu′nal·i·za′tion,** *n.* —**com·mu′nal·iz′er,** *n.*

commu′nal mar′riage. See **group marriage.**

Com·mu·nard (kom′yə närd′, kom′yə närd′), *n.* **1.** (*often l.c.*) *Fr. Hist.* a member or supporter of the Commune of 1871. Cf. **commune**[3] (def. 7b). **2.** (*l.c.*) a person who lives in a commune. [< F; see COMMUNE[3], -ARD]

com·mune[1] (*v.* kə myo͞on′; *n.* kom′yo͞on), *v.*, **-muned, -mun·ing,** *n.* —*v.i.* **1.** to converse or talk together intimately. —*n.* **2.** interchange of ideas or sentiments. [ME < MF *comun(er)* (to) share < *comun* COMMON]

com·mune[2] (kə myo͞on′), *v.i.*, **-muned, -mun·ing.** to partake of the Eucharist. [back formation from COMMUNION]

com·mune[3] (kom′yo͞on), *n.* **1.** the smallest administrative division in France, Italy, Switzerland, etc., governed by a mayor assisted by a municipal council. **2.** any community organized for local interests, and subordinate to the state. **3.** the government or citizens of a commune. **4.** a close-knit community of people who share common interests. **5.** a place for group living and sharing of work and income by people seeking radical personal changes. **6.** See **people's commune. 7. the Commune.** Also called **Com′mune of Par′is, Paris Commune. a.** a revolutionary committee that took control of the government of Paris, 1789–1794. **b.** a socialistic government of Paris from March 18 to May 27, 1871. [< F < ML *commūn(a)* (fem.), alter. of L *commūne* community, state, orig. neut. of *commūnis* COMMON]

com·mu·ni·ca·ble (kə myo͞o′nə kə bəl), *adj.* **1.** capable of being easily communicated or transmitted: *a communicable disease.* **2.** talkative. [< LL *commūnicābil(is)* = *commūnicā(re)* + *-bilis* -BLE] —**com·mu′ni·ca·bil′i·ty, com·mu′ni·ca·ble·ness,** *n.* —**com·mu′ni·ca·bly,** *adv.*

com·mu·ni·cant (kə myo͞o′nə kənt), *n.* **1.** a member of a church entitled to partake of the Eucharist. **2.** a person who communicates. —*adj.* **3.** communicating; imparting. [< L *commūnicant-* (s. of *commūnicāns*) = *communic(āre)* (to) share with (see COMMUNICATE) + *-ant-* -ANT]

com·mu·ni·cate (kə myo͞o′nə kāt′), *v.*, **-cat·ed, -cat·ing.** —*v.t.* **1.** to impart knowledge of; make known. **2.** to give to another; impart; transmit. **3.** to administer the Eucharist to. **4.** *Archaic.* to share in or partake of. —*v.i.* **5.** to give or interchange thoughts, information, or the like, by writing, speaking, etc.: *They communicate with each other every day.* **6.** to express one's true thoughts, feelings, and moods easily. **7.** to have or form a connecting passage. **8.** to partake of the Eucharist. **9.** *Obs.* to take part or participate. [< L *commūnicāt(us)* (ptp. of *commūnicāre* to impart, make common) = *commūn(is)* common + *-ic(us)* -IC + *-ātus* -ATE[1]] —**com·mu′ni·ca′tor,** *n.* —**Syn. 1.** divulge, announce, disclose.

com·mu·ni·ca·tion (kə myo͞o′nə kā′shən), *n.* **1.** the act or process of communicating. **2.** the imparting or interchange of thoughts, opinions, or information by speech, writing, etc. **3.** something imparted, interchanged, or transmitted. **4.** a document or message imparting information, opinion, etc. **5.** a passage or means of passage between places. **6. communications, a.** the means of sending messages, orders, etc., including telephone, telegraph, radio, and couriers. **b.** routes and transportation for moving troops and supplies from a base to an area of operations. [< L *commūnicātiōn-* (s. of *commūnicātiō*) = *commūnicāt(us)* (see COMMUNICATE) + *-iōn-* -ION; r. ME *comynycacioun* < AF]

com·mu·ni·ca·tive (kə myo͞o′nə kā′tiv, -kə tiv), *adj.* **1.** inclined to communicate. **2.** of or pertaining to communication. [< ML *commūnicātīv(us)*] —**com·mu′ni·ca′tive·ly,** *adv.* —**com·mu′ni·ca′tive·ness,** *n.*

com·mu·ni·ca·to·ry (kə myo͞o′nə kə tōr′ē, -tôr′ē), *adj.* inclined to communicate; communicative. [< ML *commūnicātōri(us)*]

com·mun·ion (kə myo͞on′yən), *n.* **1.** the act of sharing, or holding in common; participation. **2.** the state of things so held. **3.** association or fellowship. **4.** interchange or sharing of thoughts or emotions; intimate communication: *communion with nature.* **5.** a group of persons having a common religious faith; a religious denomination: *Anglican communion.* **6.** (*often cap.*) Also called **Holy Communion.** *Eccles.* **a.** the act of receiving the Eucharistic elements. **b.** the elements of the Eucharist. **c.** the celebration of the Eucharist. **d.** the antiphon sung at a Eucharistic service. [late ME < L *commūniōn-* (s. of *commūniō*) a sharing]

com·mun·ion·ist (kə myo͞on′yə nist), *n.* *Eccles.* a person with a particular view or interpretation of communion, as specified.

commun′ion ta′ble, *Eccles.* the table used in the celebration of communion, or the Lord's Supper; the Lord's table.

com·mu·ni·qué (kə myo͞o′nə kā′, kə myo͞o′nə kā′), *n.* an official bulletin or communication, usually to the press or public. [< F: lit., communicated, ptp. of *communiquer* to communicate]

com·mu·nise (kom′yə nīz′), *v.t.*, **-nised, -nis·ing.** *Chiefly Brit.* communize. —**com′mu·ni·sa′tion,** *n.*

com·mun·ism (kom′yə niz′əm), *n.* **1.** a theory or system of social organization based on the holding of all property in common, actual ownership being ascribed to the community as a whole or to the state. **2.** (*sometimes cap.*) a system of social organization in which all economic and social activity is controlled by a totalitarian state dominated by a single and self-perpetuating political party. **3.** (*cap.*) the principles and practices of the Communist party. **4.** communalism. [< L *commūn(is)* COMMON + -ISM]

com·mun·ist (kom′yə nist), *n.* **1.** an advocate of communism. **2.** (*cap.*) a member of the Communist party or movement. **3.** (*usually cap.*) a Communard. **4.** *U.S.* (loosely) a person who is regarded as supporting politically leftist or subversive causes. —*adj.* **5.** pertaining to communists or communism. **6.** (*cap.*) of or pertaining to the Communist party or to Communism. [< L *commūn(is)* COMMON + -IST] —**com′mu·nis′tic,** *adj.* —**com′mu·nis′ti·cal·ly,** *adv.*

Com′munist Interna′tional. See **Third International.**

Com′munist Manifes′to, a pamphlet (1848) by Karl Marx and Friedrich Engels: first statement of the principles of modern communism.

Com′munist par′ty, a political party advocating the principles of communism, esp. as developed by Marx and Lenin.

com·mu·ni·tar·i·an (kə myo͞o′ni târ′ē ən), *n.* a member or advocate of a communist community.

com·mu·ni·ty (kə myo͞o′ni tē), *n., pl.* **-ties. 1.** a social group of any size whose members reside in a specific locality, share government, and have a common cultural and historical heritage. **2.** a social, religious, occupational, or other group sharing common characteristics or interests (usually prec. by *the*): *the business community; the community of scholars.* **3.** *Ecol.* the plant and animal populations occupying a given area. **4.** joint possession, enjoyment, liability, etc.: *community of property.* **5.** similar character; agreement: *community of interests.* **6. the community,** the public; society. [< L *commūnitāt-* (s. of *commūnitās*) (see COMMON, -TY[2]); r. ME *comunete* < MF]
—**Syn. 1.** COMMUNITY, HAMLET, VILLAGE, TOWN, CITY are terms for groups of people living in somewhat close association, and usually under common rules. COMMUNITY is a general term, and TOWN is often loosely applied. A commonly accepted set of connotations envisages HAMLET as a small group, VILLAGE as a somewhat larger one, TOWN still larger, and CITY as very large. Size is, however, not the true basis of differentiation, but properly sets off only HAMLET. Incorporation, or the absence of it, and the type of government properly determine the classification of the others. **5.** similarity, likeness.

commu′nity cen′ter, (in the U.S. and Canada) a building in which members of a community may gather for social, educational, or cultural activities.

commu′nity chest′, (in the U.S. and Canada) a fund for local welfare activities collected by voluntary contributions.

commu′nity prop′erty, *U.S. Law.* (in some states) property acquired by a husband, wife, or both together, that is considered by law to be jointly owned and equally shared.

com·mu·nize (kom′yə nīz′), *v.t.*, **-nized, -niz·ing. 1.** to make (land, a house, etc.) the property of the community; transfer from individual to community ownership. **2.** to make communistic. **3.** (*often cap.*) to impose Communist principles or systems of government on (a country or people). Also, *esp. Brit.*, **communise.** [back formation from *communization* = L *commūn(is)* COMMON + -IZATION] —**com′mu·ni·za′tion,** *n.*

com·mu·tate (kom′yə tāt′), *v.t.*, **-tat·ed, -tat·ing.** *Elect.* **1.** to reverse the direction of (a current or currents), as by a commutator. **2.** to convert (alternating current) into direct current by use of a commutator. [back formation from COMMUTATION]

com·mu·ta·tion (kom′yə tā′shən), *n.* **1.** the act of substituting one thing for another; substitution; exchange. **2.** the substitution of one kind of payment for another. **3.** regular travel over some distance between home and work, as from a suburb into a city and back. **4.** the changing of a prison sentence or other penalty to another less severe. **5.** *Elect.* the act or process of commutating. [< L *commūtātiōn-* (s. of *commūtātiō*) change. See COMMUTE, -ATION]

com·mu·ta·tive (kə myo͞o′tə tiv, kom′yə tā′tiv), *adj.* **1.** of or pertaining to commutation, exchange, substitution, or interchange. **2.** *Math.* **a.** (of a binary operation) having the property that one term operating on a second is equal to the second operating on the first, as $a \times b = b \times a$. **b.** having reference to this property. [< ML *commūtātīv(us)* = L *commūtāt(us)* (ptp. of *commūtāre;* see COMMUTE, -ATE[1]) + *-īvus* -IVE]

commu′tative law′, *Logic.* a law asserting that the order in which certain logical operations are performed is indifferent.

com·mu·ta·tor (kom′yə tā′tər), *n.* *Elect.* **1.** a device for reversing the direction of a current. **2.** (in a DC motor or generator) a cylindrical ring or disk assembly of conducting members, individually insulated in a supporting structure with an exposed surface for contact with current-collecting brushes and mounted on the armature shaft, for changing the frequency or direction of the current in the armature windings.

com·mute (kə myo͞ot′), *v.*, **-mut·ed, -mut·ing.** —*v.t.* **1.** to exchange for another or for something else. **2.** to change: *to commute iron into silver.* **3.** to change (one kind of payment) into or for another, as by substitution. **4.** to change (a prison sentence or other penalty) to a less severe one. —*v.i.* **5.** to make substitution. **6.** to serve as a substitute. **7.** to make a collective payment, esp. of a reduced amount, as an equivalent for a number of payments. **8.** to travel regularly over some distance between one's home and office, esp. between the suburbs and the city or between one city and another. [< L *commūt(āre)* = *com-* COM- + *mūtāre* to change] —**com·mut′a·ble,** *adj.* —**com·mut′er,** *n.*

com·my (kom′ē), *n., pl.* **-mies,** *adj.* (*often cap.*) *Informal.* commie.

Com·ne·nus (kom nē′nəs), *n.* a dynasty of Byzantine

emperors that ruled at Constantinople, 1057?–1185, and at Trebizond in Asia Minor, 1204–1461?.

Co·mo (kō′mō; *It.* kô′mô), *n.* **1. Lake,** a lake in N Italy, in Lombardy. 35 mi. long; 56 sq. mi. **2.** a city at the SW end of this lake. 97,169.

Com·o·rin (kom′ər in), *n.* **Cape,** a cape on the S tip of India, extending into the Indian Ocean.

Com′o·ro Is′lands (kom′ə rō′), a group of islands in the Indian Ocean between N Madagascar and E Africa: formerly an overseas territory of France. ab. 800 sq. mi.

Com·o·ros (kom′ə rōz′), *n.* a republic, established 1975, comprising three of the Comoro Islands. 344,000; 719 sq. mi. *Cap.:* Moroni.

comp (komp), *n. Informal.* composition (def. 16).

comp., **1.** comparative. **2.** compare. **3.** compensation. **4.** compilation. **5.** compiled. **6.** composition. **7.** compound.

com·pact[1] (*adj., v.* kəm pakt′; *n.* kom′pakt), *adj.* **1.** joined or packed together; closely and firmly united; dense; solid: *compact soil.* **2.** arranged within a relatively small space: *a compact shopping center; a compact kitchen.* **3.** of a size smaller than an intermediate automobile but larger than a subcompact automobile: *a compact car.* **4.** solidly or firmly built: *the compact body of a lightweight wrestler.* **5.** expressed concisely; pithy; terse. **—***v.t.* **6.** to join or pack closely together; consolidate; condense. **7.** to make firm or stable. **8.** to form or make by close union or conjunction; compose. **—***n.* **9.** a small case containing a mirror, face powder, a puff, and, sometimes, rouge. **10.** a compact automobile. [late ME < L *compact(us)* (ptp. of *compingere*) = *com-* COM- + *pāc-* ptp. s. + *-tus* ptp. ending; akin to PACT, COMPACT[2]] **—com·pact′ed·ly,** *adv.* **—com·pact′ed·ness,** *n.* **—com·pact′i·ble,** *adj.* **—com·pac′tion,** *n.* **—com·pact′ly,** *adv.* **—com·pact′ness,** *n.* **—Syn. 5.** concise, succinct.

com·pact[2] (kom′pakt), *n.* a formal agreement; contract. [< L *compact(um),* n. use of neut. of *compactus* (ptp. of *compacīscī* to make an agreement) = *com-* COM- + *pac-* (s. of *pacīscī* to bargain; akin to PACT, COMPACT[1]) + *-tus* ptp. ending] **—Syn.** treaty, pact, entente. See **agreement.**

com′pact disk′, a grooveless disk on which a program, data, music, etc., is digitally encoded for a laser beam to scan, decode, and transmit. *Abbr.:* CD

com·pac·tor (kəm pak′tər), *n.* a kitchen appliance or other machine for grinding and compressing refuse, esp. to facilitate disposal.

com·pan·ion[1] (kəm pan′yən), *n.* **1.** a person who frequently associates with another or others; comrade: *my son and his two companions.* **2.** a person employed to accompany, assist, and live with another in the capacity of a helpful friend. **3.** a mate or match for something: *White wine is the usual companion of fish.* **4.** a handbook or guide to a specific subject. **5.** a member of the lowest rank in an order of knighthood or of a grade in an order. **6.** Also called **companion star.** *Astron.* the fainter of the two stars that constitute a double star. Cf. **primary** (def. 14b). **7.** *Obs.* a fellow. **—***v.t.* **8.** to be a companion to; accompany. [< LL *companiōn-* (s. of *compāniō*) messmate = *com-* COM- + *pān(is)* bread + *-iōn-* -ION; r. ME *compainoun* < AF = OF *compaignon*] **—Syn. 1.** friend, partner, mate. See **acquaintance.**

com·pan·ion[2] (kəm pan′yən), *n. Naut.* **1.** a covering or hood over the top of a companionway. **2.** a companionway. [alter. of D *kampanje* quarterdeck < F phrase *chambre de la compagne* pantry of a medieval galley]

com·pan·ion·a·ble (kəm pan′yə nə bəl), *adj.* possessing the qualities of a good companion; congenial. **—com·pan′ion·a·ble·ness,** *n.* **—com·pan′ion·a·bly,** *adv.*

com·pan·ion·ate (kəm pan′yə nit), *adj.* **1.** of, by, or like companions. **2.** tastefully harmonious.

compan′ionate mar′riage, a form of marriage permitting the divorce of a childless couple by mutual consent.

com·pan·ion·ship (kəm pan′yən ship′), *n.* association as companions; fellowship.

compan′ion star′, *Astron.* companion[1] (def. 6).

com·pan·ion·way (kəm pan′yən wā′), *n. Naut.* **1.** a stair or ladder within the hull of a vessel. **2.** the space occupied by this stair or ladder.

com·pa·ny (kum′pə nē), *n., pl.* **-nies,** *v.,* **-nied, -ny·ing.** **—***n.* **1.** a number of individuals assembled or associated together. **2.** an assemblage of persons for social purposes. **3.** companionship or fellowship: *They invited two people along for company.* **4.** a guest or guests: *We're having company for the weekend.* **5.** society, taken collectively. **6.** a number of persons united or incorporated for joint action, esp. for business: *a company of actors.* **7.** (*cap.*) the member or members of a firm not specifically named in the firm's title (often used in the abbreviation *Co.*): *George Higgins and Company.* **8.** a medieval trade guild. **9.** *Mil.* **a.** a subdivision of a regiment, battle group, or battalion. **b.** any relatively small group of soldiers. **c.** *U.S. Army.* a basic unit with both tactical and administrative functions. **10.** a ship's crew, including the officers. **11.** a unit of firemen, including their special apparatus. **12. keep company, a.** to associate with; be a friend of. **b.** *Informal.* to go together, as in courtship: *My sister has been keeping company with a young lawyer.* **13. part company, a.** to cease association or friendship with: *We parted company after the argument.* **b.** to take a different or opposite view; differ: *He parted company with his father on politics.* **c.** to separate: *We parted company at the airport.* **—***v.i.* **14.** *Archaic.* to associate. **—***v.t.* **15.** *Archaic.* to accompany. [ME, var. of *compaignie* < OF: companionship = *compain* (< LL *compāniō;* see COMPANION[1]) + *-ie* -Y[3]] **—Syn. 1.** group, assemblage, body. COMPANY, BAND, PARTY, TROOP refer to a group of people formally or informally associated. COMPANY is the general word and means any group of people: *a company of motorists.* BAND, used esp. of a band of musicians, suggests a relatively small group pursuing the same purpose or sharing a common fate: *a concert by a band; a band of survivors.* PARTY, except when used of a political group, usually implies an indefinite and temporary assemblage, as for some common pursuit: *a spelunking party.* TROOP, used specifically of a body of cavalry, usually implies a number of individuals organized as a unit: *a troop of boy scouts.*

com′pany un′ion, *U.S.* **1.** a labor union dominated by management rather than controlled by the membership. **2.** a union confined to employees of one business or corporation.

compar., comparative.

com·pa·ra·ble (kom′pər ə bəl), *adj.* **1.** capable of being compared; having sufficient features in common with something else to afford comparison. **2.** worthy of comparison: *shops comparable to the finest in Paris.* **3.** usable or suitable for comparison. [late ME < L *comparābil(is)*] **—com′pa·ra·bil′i·ty, com′pa·ra·ble·ness,** *n.* **—com′pa·ra·bly,** *adv.*

com·par·a·tive (kəm par′ə tiv), *adj.* **1.** of or pertaining to comparison. **2.** proceeding by, founded on, or using comparison as a method of study: *comparative anatomy; comparative literature.* **3.** estimated by comparison; not positive or absolute; relative: *a comparative newcomer in politics.* **4.** *Gram.* being, noting, or pertaining to the intermediate degree of the comparison of adjectives and adverbs, as *surer* and *more beautiful,* the comparative forms of *sure* and *beautiful,* and adverbs, as *faster* and *more carefully,* the comparative forms of *fast* and *carefully.* Cf. **positive** (def. 18), **superlative** (def. 3). **—***n. Gram.* **5.** the comparative degree. **6.** a form in the comparative. [< L *comparātīv(us)* = *comparāt(us)* (ptp. of *comparāre;* see COMPARE, -ATE[1]) + *-īvus* -IVE] **—com·par′a·tive·ly,** *adv.*

compar′ative linguis′tics, the study of the correspondences between languages that have a common origin. **—compar′ative lin′guist.**

com·pa·ra·tor (kom′pə rā′tər), *n.* any of various instruments for making comparisons, as of lengths or distances, tints of colors, etc. [< LL *comparātor* a comparer. See COMPARE, -ATE[1], -OR[2]]

com·pare (kəm pâr′), *v.,* **-pared, -par·ing,** *n.* **—***v.t.* **1.** to examine (two or more things, ideas, people, etc.) for the purpose of noting similarities and differences: *to compare two pieces of cloth.* **2.** to consider or describe as similar; liken. **3.** *Gram.* to form or display the degrees of comparison of (an adjective or adverb). **—***v.i.* **4.** to bear comparison; be held equal: *Dekker's plays cannot compare with Shakespeare's.* **5.** to differ in quality or accomplishment as specified: *His work compares poorly with yours.* **6. compare notes.** See **note** (def. 16). **—***n.* **7.** comparison: *Her beauty is beyond compare.* [late ME < L *compar(āre)* (to) match together = *compār* a perfect match (see COM-, PAR) + *-āre* inf. ending; r. ME *comper* < OF *comperer*] **—com·par′er,** *n.*

—Syn. 1, 2. COMPARE, CONTRAST agree in placing together two or more things and examining them to discover characteristics, qualities, etc. To COMPARE means to examine in order to discover like or unlike characteristics. We compare things of the same class *with* each other; things of unlike classes *to* each other: *to compare one story with another, a man to a mountain.* To CONTRAST is to examine with an eye to differences, or to place together so that the differences are striking. We contrast one thing *with* another: *to contrast living conditions in peace and in war.*

com·par·i·son (kəm par′i sən), *n.* **1.** the act of comparing. **2.** the state of being compared. **3.** a likening; illustration by similitude; comparative estimate or statement. **4.** capability of being compared or likened. **5.** *Gram.* the inflection or modification of an adverb or adjective that indicates the degree of superiority or inferiority in quality, quantity, or intensity, as *mild, milder, mildest, less mild, least mild.* [ME *comparesoun* < OF *comparaison* < L *comparātiōn-* (s. of *comparātiō*). See COMPARE, -ATION]

com·part (kəm pärt′), *v.t.* to separate or mark out in parts; subdivide. [< LL *compart(īre)* (to) divide up]

com·part·ment (kəm pärt′mənt), *n.* **1.** a part or space marked or partitioned off. **2.** a separate room, section, etc.: *a sleeping compartment on a train; a watertight compartment in a ship.* **3.** *Railroads U.S.* a private bedroom with toilet facilities. **4.** a separate aspect, function, or the like. **5.** *Heraldry.* a decorative base, as a grassy mound, on which the supporters of an escutcheon stand or rest. **—***v.t.* **6.** to divide into compartments. [< MF *compartiment* < It *compartimento*] **—com·part·men·tal** (kəm pärt men′tᵊl, kom′pärt-), *adj.* **—com·part·men′tal·ly,** *adv.* **—Syn. 1.** division.

com·part·men·tal·ize (kəm pärt men′tᵊlīz′, kom′pärt-), *v.t.,* **-ized, -iz·ing.** to divide into categories or compartments. **—com·part·men′tal·i·za′tion,** *n.*

com·pass (kum′pəs), *n.* **1.** an instrument for determining directions, as by means of a freely rotating magnetized needle that indicates magnetic north. **2.** the enclosing line or limits of any area; perimeter: *within the compass of 10 square blocks.* **3.** space within limits; area; extent; range; scope: *the broad compass of the novel.* **4.** Also called **range.** the total range of tones of a voice or of a musical instrument. **5.** due or proper limits: *within the compass of propriety.* **6.** a passing round; circuit: *the compass of a year.* **7.** Often, **compasses.** an instrument for drawing or describing circles, measuring distances, etc., consisting generally of two movable, rigid legs hinged to each other at one end. **8.** *Obs.* a circle. **—***adj.* **9.** curved; forming a curve or arc: *compass roof.* **—***v.t.* **10.** to go or move round; make the circuit of. **11.** to surround or encircle. **12.** to attain or achieve; accomplish. **13.** to contrive, plot, or scheme. **14.** to make curved or circular. **15.** to comprehend; grasp mentally. [(v.) ME *compass(en)* < OF *compasser* to measure < VL **compāssāre* < **compāss(us)* equal step (L *com-* COM- + *pāssus* PACE[1]); (n.) ME *compas* < OF < the v.] **—com′pass·a·ble,** *adj.* **—Syn. 3.** See **range.**

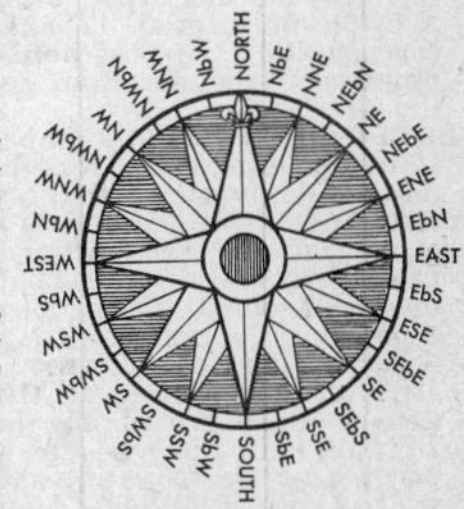

Compass card

com′pass card′, *Navig.* a circular card with magnets attached to its underside, the face divided on its rim into points of the compass, and floating or suspended from a pivot within the bowl of a compass so as to rotate freely.

com′pass course′, *Naut.* a course whose bearing is relative to the meridian as given by the navigator's compass, no compensation being made for variation or deviation. Cf. **magnetic course, true course.**

com·pas·sion (kəm pash′ən), *n.* a feeling of deep sympathy and sorrow for another's suffering or misfortune, accompanied by a desire to alleviate the pain or remove its cause. [ME < LL *compassiōn-* (s. of *compassiō*)] —**Syn.** commiseration, tenderness, heart, clemency. —**Ant.** mercilessness, indifference.

com·pas·sion·ate (*adj.* kəm pash′ə nit; *v.* kəm pash′ənāt′), *adj.*, *v.*, **-at·ed, -at·ing.** —*adj.* **1.** having or showing compassion. **2.** *Obs.* pitiable. —*v.t.* **3.** to have compassion for; pity. —**com·pas′sion·ate·ly,** *adv.* —**com·pas′sion·ate·ness,** *n.* —**Syn. 1.** pitying, sympathetic, tender, merciful.

com′pass plant′, any of various plants, esp. *Silphium laciniatum*, whose leaves tend to lie in a plane at right angles to the strongest light, hence usually north and south.

com′pass rose′, 1. *Navig.* a circle divided into 32 points or 360 degrees numbered clockwise from true or magnetic north, printed on a chart or the like as a means of determining the course of a vessel or aircraft. **2.** a similar design, often ornamented, used on maps to indicate the points of the compass.

com·pat·i·ble (kəm pat′ə bəl), *adj.* **1.** capable of existing together in harmony. **2.** able to exist together with something else (often fol. by *with*): *Prejudice is not compatible with true religion.* **3.** consistent; congruous (often fol. by *with*): *His claims are not compatible with the facts.* **4.** *Television.* noting a system in which color broadcasts can be received on ordinary sets in black and white. [late ME < ML *compatibil(is)* < LL *compatī* (L *com-* COM- + *patī* to suffer); see -BLE] —**com·pat′i·bil′i·ty, com·pat′i·ble·ness,** *n.* —**com·pat′i·bly,** *adv.*

com·pa·tri·ot (kəm pā′trē ət *or, esp. Brit.,* -pa′-), *n.* **1.** a native or inhabitant of a person's own country; fellow countryman or countrywoman. —*adj.* **2.** of the same country. [< LL *compatriōt(a)*] —**com·pa·tri·ot·ic** (kəm pā′trē ot′ik *or, esp. Brit.,* -pa′-), *adj.* —**com·pa′tri·ot·ism,** *n.*

com·peer (kəm pēr′, kom′pēr), *n.* **1.** an equal in rank, ability, accomplishment, etc.; peer; colleague. **2.** close friend; comrade. —*v.t.* **3.** *Archaic.* to be the equal of; match. [late ME *comper* < MF]

com·pel (kəm pel′), *v.*, **-pelled, -pel·ling.** —*v.t.* **1.** to force or drive, esp. to a course of action: *His flouting of rules compels us to dismiss him.* **2.** to secure or bring about by force. **3.** to force to submit; subdue. **4.** *Archaic.* to drive together; unite by force; herd. —*v.i.* **5.** to use force. **6.** to have a powerful and irresistible effect, influence, etc. [ME *compelle* < L *compelle(re)* (to) crowd, force = *com-* COM- + *pellere* to push, drive] —**com·pel′la·ble,** *adj.* —**com·pel′la·bly,** *adv.* —**com·pel′ler,** *n.* —**Syn. 1.** constrain, oblige, coerce.

com·pel·la·tion (kom′pə lā′shən), *n.* **1.** the act of addressing a person. **2.** manner or form of address or designation; appellation. [< L *compellātiōn-* (s. of *compellātiō*) an accosting, a rebuke. See COM-, APPELLATION]

com·pel·ling (kəm pel′ing), *adj.* **1.** tending to compel; driving: *compelling reasons.* **2.** having a powerful and irresistible effect: *a compelling drama.* —**com·pel′ling·ly,** *adv.*

com·pen·di·ous (kəm pen′dē əs), *adj.* of or like a compendium; concise: *a compendious history of the world.* [late ME < L *compendiōs(us).* See COMPENDIUM, -OSE[1]] —**com·pen′di·ous·ly,** *adv.* —**com·pen′di·ous·ness,** *n.* —**Syn.** summary, comprehensive, succinct, packed.

com·pen·di·um (kəm pen′dē əm), *n., pl.* **-di·ums, -di·a** (-dē ə). **1.** a brief treatment or account of a subject, esp. an extensive subject: *a compendium of modern medicine.* **2.** a summary, epitome, or abridgment. **3.** a full list or inventory. Also, **com·pend** (kom′pend). [< L: a shortening (orig. a careful weighing) = *com-* COM- + *pend-* (s. of *pendere* to cause to hang down, weigh) + *-ium* n. suffix] —**Syn. 1.** survey.

com·pen·sa·ble (kəm pen′sə bəl), *adj.* eligible for or subject to compensation. [COMPENS(ATE) + -ABLE]

com·pen·sate (kom′pən sāt′), *v.*, **-sat·ed, -sat·ing.** —*v.t.* **1.** to counterbalance; offset; be equivalent to. **2.** to recompense for something: *They gave him 10 dollars to compensate him for his trouble.* **3.** *Mech.* to counterbalance (a force or the like). —*v.i.* **4.** to provide an equivalent; make amends (usually fol. by *for*): *His occasional courtesies did not compensate for his general rudeness.* **5.** to develop psychological mechanisms of compensation. [< L *compēnsāt(us)* (ptp. of *compēnsāre* to counterbalance; orig., weigh together). See COM-, PENSIVE, -ATE[1]] —**com′pen·sa′tor,** *n.* —**Syn. 1.** counterpoise, countervail. **2.** remunerate, reward, pay. **4.** atone.

com·pen·sa·tion (kom′pən sā′shən), *n.* **1.** the act of compensating. **2.** something given or received as an equivalent for services, debt, loss, injury, suffering, lack, etc.; indemnity: *The insurance company paid him $2,000 as compensation for the loss of his car.* **3.** *Biol.* the offsetting of any defect by the exceptional development or action of another structure or organ. **4.** a psychological mechanism by which an individual attempts to compensate for some real or imagined deficiency of personality or behavior by developing or stressing another aspect of his personality or by substituting a different form of behavior. [< L *compēnsātiōn-* (s. of *compēnsātiō*)] —**com′pen·sa′tion·al,** *adj.* —**Syn. 2.** recompense, remuneration, payment, amends, reparation; indemnification.

com·pen·sa·to·ry (kəm pen′sə tōr′ē, -tôr′ē), *adj.* serving to compensate, as for loss, lack, injury, etc. Also, **com·pen·sa·tive** (kom′pən sā′tiv, kəm pen′sə-).

com·pete (kəm pēt′), *v.i.*, **-pet·ed, -pet·ing.** to strive to outdo another for acknowledgment, a prize, supremacy, profit, etc.; engage in a contest; vie. [< L *compete(re)* (to) meet, coincide, be fitting, be capable, LL: strive together (for something) = *com-* COM- + *petere* to seek]

—**Syn.** struggle. COMPETE, CONTEND, CONTEST mean to strive to outdo or excel: they may apply to individuals or groups. COMPETE implies having a sense of rivalry and of striving to do one's best as well as to outdo another: *to compete for a prize.* CONTEND suggests opposition or disputing as well as rivalry: *to contend with an opponent, against obstacles.* CONTEST suggests struggling to gain or hold something, as well as contending or disputing: *to contest a position or ground (in battle); to contest a decision.*

com·pe·tence (kom′pi təns), *n.* **1.** the quality of being competent; adequacy. **2.** sufficiency; a sufficient quantity. **3.** an income sufficient to furnish the necessities and modest comforts of life. **4.** *Law.* the quality or state of being legally competent; legal capacity or qualification based on the meeting of certain minimum requirements of age, soundness of mind, citizenship, or the like. [COMPET(ENT) + -ENCE]

com·pe·ten·cy (kom′pi tən sē), *n., pl.* **-cies.** competence. [< L *competentia* agreement. See COMPETENT, -CY]

com·pe·tent (kom′pi tənt), *adj.* **1.** having suitable or sufficient skill, knowledge, experience, etc., for some purpose; properly qualified. **2.** adequate but not exceptional. **3.** *Law.* having legal capacity or qualification. [late ME < L *competent-* (s. of *competēns*, prp. of *competere* to meet, agree). See COMPETE, -ENT] —**com′pe·tent·ly,** *adv.* —**Syn. 1.** fit, qualified, capable. See **able.**

com·pe·ti·tion (kom′pi tish′ən), *n.* **1.** the act of competing; struggle or rivalry. **2.** a contest for some prize, honor, or advantage: *Both girls entered the competition.* **3.** the rivalry offered by a competitor. **4.** *U.S. Informal.* a competitor or competitors: *What is your competition offering?* **5.** *Ecol.* the struggle among organisms for food, space, and other requirements for existence. [< LL *competītiōn-* (s. of *competītiō*) = *competīt(us)* (see COMPETITOR) + *-iōn-* -ION] —**Syn. 1.** emulation. **2.** struggle.

com·pet·i·tive (kəm pet′i tiv), *adj.* **1.** of, pertaining to, involving, or decided by competition: *competitive sports; a competitive examination.* **2.** able to compete, as in quality, price, etc. **3.** having a strong desire to compete or to succeed. Also, **com·pet·i·to·ry** (kəm pet′i tōr′ē, -tôr′ē). [< L *competīt(us)* (see COMPETITOR) + -IVE] —**com·pet′i·tive·ly,** *adv.* —**com·pet′i·tive·ness,** *n.*

com·pet·i·tor (kəm pet′i tər), *n.* a person, team, company, etc., that competes; rival. [< L = *competīt(us)*, ptp. of *competere* to COMPETE (*com-* COM- + *petī-* ptp. s. + *-tus* ptp. suffix) + *-or* -OR[2]] —**Syn.** See **opponent.**

Com·piègne (kôN pyen′yə), *n.* a city in N France, on the Oise River: nearby were signed the armistices between the Allies and Germany 1918 and between Germany and France 1940. 28,415 (1962).

com·pi·la·tion (kom′pə lā′shən), *n.* **1.** the act of compiling. **2.** something compiled, as a book. [< L *compīlātiōn-* (s. of *compīlātiō*)]

com·pile (kəm pīl′), *v.t.*, **-piled, -pil·ing. 1.** to put together (documents, selections, etc.) in one book or work. **2.** to make (a book, writing, or the like) of materials from various sources: *to compile an anthology of poems.* **3.** to gather together: *to compile data.* **4.** *Computer Technol.* to translate (a pseudo-code) into another pseudo-code or into machine language; assemble. [late ME < L *compīl(āre)* (to) cram together hastily = *com-* COM- + *pīlāre* < ?]

com·pil·er (kəm pī′lər), *n.* **1.** a person who compiles. **2.** Also called **compil′ing routine′.** *Computer Technol.* a programming routine enabling a computer to translate a program expressed in a pseudo-code into machine language or another pseudo-code for later translation. [ME *compilour* < AF; OF *compileor* < L *compīlātōr-*]

com·pla·cen·cy (kəm plā′sən sē), *n.* **1.** a feeling of quiet pleasure or security, often while unaware of some potential danger, defect, or the like; self-satisfaction or smug satisfaction with an existing situation, condition, etc. **2.** *Archaic.* friendly civility. Also, **com·pla·cence** (kəm plā′səns). [< ML *complacentia.* See COMPLACENT, -CY]

com·pla·cent (kəm plā′sənt), *adj.* **1.** pleased, esp. with oneself or one's merits, advantages, situation, etc., often without awareness of some potential danger, defect, or the like; self-satisfied: *She stopped being so complacent after she was demoted.* **2.** pleasant; agreeable. Cf. **complaisant.** [< L *complacent-* (s. of *complacēns*, prp. of *complacēre* to please greatly). See COM-, PLEASE, -ENT] —**com·pla′cent·ly,** *adv.*

com·plain (kəm plān′), *v.i.* **1.** to express dissatisfaction, pain, censure, grief, or the like; find fault. **2.** to make a formal accusation: *The ambassador complained about the student demonstrations.* [ME *complei(g)ne(n)* < MF *complaign-*, s. of *complaindre* < VL **complangere* = L *com-* COM- + *plangere* to lament; see PLAINT] —**com·plain′er,** *n.* —**com·plain′ing·ly,** *adv.*

—**Syn. 1.** COMPLAIN, GRUMBLE, GROWL, WHINE are terms for expressing dissatisfaction or discomfort. To COMPLAIN is to protest against or lament a condition or cause of wrong: *to complain about high prices.* To GRUMBLE is to utter surly, ill-natured complaints half to oneself: *to grumble about the service.* GROWL may express more anger than GRUMBLE: *to growl ungraciously in reply to a question.* To WHINE is to complain or beg in a mean-spirited, objectionable way, using a nasal tone; whining often connotes persistence in begging or complaining: *to whine like a coward, like a spoiled child.* —**Ant. 1.** rejoice.

com·plain·ant (kəm plā′nənt), *n.* a person, group, or company that makes a complaint, as in a legal action. [late ME < MF *complaignant* (prp. of *complaindre*)]

com·plaint (kəm plānt′), *n.* **1.** an expression of discontent, pain, censure, grief, or the like: *a complaint about rising taxes.* **2.** a cause of discontent, pain, censure, grief, or the like: *She suffered from a vast collection of real and imagined complaints.* **3.** *U.S. Law.* the first pleading of the plaintiff in a civil action, stating his cause of action. [ME < MF *complainte* < L *com-* COM- + *plancta* PLAINT]

com·plai·sance (kəm plā′səns, -zəns, kom′plə zans′), *n.* **1.** the quality of being complaisant. **2.** a complaisant act. [< F; see COMPLAISANT, -ANCE]

com·plai·sant (kəm plā′sənt, -zənt, kom′plə zant′), *adj.* inclined or disposed to please; obliging; agreeable. Cf. **complacent.** [< F (prp. of *complaire*) < L *complacent-* (s. of *complacēns*, prp. of *complacēre* to please highly). See COM-, PLEASE, -ANT] —**com·plai′sant·ly,** *adv.*

com·plect·ed (kəm plek′tid), *adj.* *U.S.* complexioned. [*complect-* (irreg. var. s. of COMPLEXION) + -ED[3]]

com·ple·ment (*n.* kom′plə mənt; *v.* kom′plə ment′), *n.* **1.** something that completes or makes perfect: *A good cigar is a complement to a good meal.* **2.** the quantity or amount that completes anything. **3.** either of two parts or things constituting a whole; counterpart. **4.** full quantity or amount; complete allowance. **5.** the full number of officers and crew required to man a ship. **6.** *Gram.* a word or words

used to complete a grammatical construction, esp. in the predicate, as an object, as *ball* in *He caught the ball,* predicate adjective, as *large* in *The house is large,* or predicate noun, as *John* in *His name is John.* **7.** *Geom.* the quantity by which an angle or an arc falls short of 90°, or a quarter of a circle. Cf. **supplement** (def. 4). **8.** *Music.* the interval that completes an octave when added to a given interval. **9.** *Immunol.* a thermolabile substance in blood serum and plasma that in combination with antibodies destroys bacteria, foreign cells, and other antigens. **10.** See **complementary color.** —*v.t.* **11.** to complete; form a complement to. **12.** *Obs.* to compliment. —*v.i.* **13.** *Obs.* to compliment. [ME < L *complēment(um)* that which completes = *complē(re)* (to) fill up (see COMPLETE) + *-mentum* -MENT]
—**Syn. 11.** COMPLEMENT, SUPPLEMENT both mean to make an addition or additions to something. To COMPLEMENT is to provide something felt to be lacking or needed; it is often applied to putting together two things, each of which supplies what is lacking in the other, to make a complete whole: *Two statements from different points of view may complement each other.* To SUPPLEMENT is merely to add to; no definite lack or deficiency is implied nor is there an idea of a definite relationship between parts: *Some additional remarks may supplement either statement or both.*

com·ple·men·tal (kom′plə men′tᵊl), *adj.* **1.** complementary; completing. **2.** *Obs.* **a.** accomplished. **b.** ceremonious. **c.** complimentary.

com·ple·men·ta·ry (kom′plə men′tə rē, -trē), *adj., n., pl.* **-ries.** —*adj.* **1.** forming a complement; completing. **2.** complementing each other. —*n.* **3.** See **complementary color.**

com′plemen′tary an′gle, *Math.* either of two angles that added together produce an angle of 90°. Cf. **supplementary angle.**

Complementary angles (Angle BCD, complement of angle ACB; arc BD, complement of arc AB)

com′plemen′tary col′or, **1.** *Art.* **a.** one of a pair of primary or secondary colors opposed to the other member of the pair on a schematic chart or scale **(color wheel),** as green opposed to red, orange opposed to blue, or violet opposed to yellow. **b.** the relationship of these pairs of colors perceived as completing or enhancing each other. **2.** See **secondary color.**

com·plete (kəm plēt′), *adj., v.,* **-plet·ed, -plet·ing.** —*adj.* **1.** having all its parts or elements; whole; entire: *a complete set of dishes.* **2.** finished; concluded: *a complete month; a complete orbit.* **3.** having all the required or customary characteristics, skills, or the like; consummate: *a complete gentleman.* **4.** thorough; entire; unmodified: *a complete victory.* **5.** *Gram.* having all modifying or complementary elements included: *The complete subject of "The dappled pony gazed over the fence" is "The dappled pony."* **6.** Also, **completed.** *Football.* (of a forward pass) caught by a receiver. **7.** *Archaic.* (of persons) accomplished; skilled; expert. —*v.t.* **8.** to make whole, entire, or perfect: *I need three more words to complete the puzzle.* **9.** to bring to an end; finish: *Has he completed his new novel yet?* **10.** *Football.* to execute (a forward pass) successfully. [ME < L *complēt(us)* (ptp. of *complēre* to fill up, fulfill) = *com-* COM- + *plē-* fill + *-tus* ptp. suffix] —**com·plete′ly,** *adv.* —**com·plete′ness,** *n.*
—**Syn. 1.** unbroken, unimpaired, undivided. **3.** developed. **1–3.** COMPLETE, ENTIRE, INTACT, PERFECT imply that there is no lack or defect, nor has any part been removed. COMPLETE implies that a certain unit has all its parts, fully developed or perfected, and may apply to a process or purpose carried to fulfillment: *a complete explanation.* ENTIRE means whole, having unbroken unity: *an entire book.* INTACT implies retaining completeness and original condition: *a package delivered intact.* PERFECT emphasizes not only completeness but also high quality and absence of defects or blemishes: *a perfect diamond.* **8.** accomplish, consummate. **9.** conclude, terminate. —**Ant. 1.** partial.

com·ple·tion (kəm plē′shən), *n.* **1.** the act of completing. **2.** the state of being completed. **3.** conclusion; fulfillment: *His last novel represented the completion of his literary achievement.* **4.** *Football.* a forward pass that has been completed. [< L *complētiōn-* (s. of *complētiō*)]

com·plex (*adj.* kəm pleks′, kom′pleks; *n.* kom′pleks), *adj.* **1.** composed of interconnected parts; compound; composite: *a complex highway system.* **2.** characterized by a very complicated or involved arrangement of parts, units, etc.: *a complex machine.* **3.** so complicated or intricate as to be hard to understand or deal with: *a complex problem.* **4.** *Gram.* **a.** (of a word) consisting of two parts, at least one of which is a bound form, as *childish,* which consists of the word *child* and the bound form *-ish.* **b.** See **complex sentence. 5.** *Math.* pertaining to a complex number. —*n.* **6.** an intricate or complicated association or assemblage of related things, parts, units, etc. **7.** *Psychol.* a system of interrelated, emotion-charged ideas, feelings, memories, and impulses that is usually repressed and that gives rise to abnormal or pathological behavior. **8.** a fixed idea; an obsessive notion. [(adj.) < L *complex(us)* ptp. of *complectī* to embrace, enfold = *com-* COM- + *plect(ere)* (to) fold, braid + *-ī* pass. inf. ending; (n.) < L *complex(us)* an embrace = *complex(us)* (ptp. s. of *complectī*) + *-us* 4th decl. n. suffix] —**Syn. 2, 3.** involved, perplexing. **3.** knotty, tangled, labyrinthine. **6.** network, web, tangle, labyrinth. —**Ant. 2, 3.** simple.

com′plex frac′tion, *Math.* a fraction in which the numerator or the denominator or both contain one or more fractions. Also called **compound fraction.**

com·plex·ion (kəm plek′shən), *n.* **1.** the natural color and appearance of a person's skin, esp. of the face: *a clear, smooth, rosy complexion.* **2.** appearance, aspect, or character: *Her departure put a different complexion on the situation.* **3.** viewpoint, attitude, or conviction. **4.** *Old Physiol.* constitution or nature of body and mind, regarded as the result of certain combined qualities. **5.** *Obs.* nature; disposition; temperament. [ME < medical L *complexiōn-* (s. of *complexiō*) bodily make-up, shape, etc., orig., combination] —**com·plex′ion·al,** *adj.*

com·plex·ioned (kəm plek′shənd), *adj.* having a specified complexion (usually used in combination): *a light-complexioned person.* [late ME]

com·plex·i·ty (kəm plek′si tē), *n., pl.* **-ties** for 2. **1.** the state or quality of being complex; intricacy: *the complexity of urban life.* **2.** something complex: *the endless complexities of our foreign policy.*

com′plex num′ber, *Math.* a mathematical expression $(a + bi)$ in which a and b are real numbers and i is defined as $\sqrt{-1}$

com′plex plane′, *Math.* a plane the points of which are complex numbers.

com′plex sen′tence, a sentence containing one or more dependent clauses in addition to the main clause, as *When the bell rings* (dependent clause), *walk out* (main clause).

com′plex var′iable, *Math.* a variable to which complex numbers may be assigned as values.

com·pli·ance (kəm plī′əns), *n.* **1.** the act of conforming, acquiescing, or yielding. **2.** a tendency to yield readily to others, esp. in a weak and subservient way. **3.** conformity or accordance: *in compliance with your orders.* **4.** cooperation or obedience. **5.** *Physics.* **a.** the strain of an elastic body expressed as a function of the force producing the strain. **b.** a coefficient expressing the responsiveness of a mechanical system to a periodic force.

com·pli·an·cy (kəm plī′ən sē), *n., pl.* **-cies.** compliance (defs. 1, 2, 4).

com·pli·ant (kəm plī′ənt), *adj.* complying; obeying, obliging, or yielding, esp. in a submissive way: *a man with a compliant nature.* —**com·pli′ant·ly,** *adv.*

com·pli·ca·cy (kom′plə kə sē), *n., pl.* **-cies.** **1.** the state of being complicated; complicatedness. **2.** a complication: *the numerous complicacies of travel in Albania.* [COMPLIC(ATE) + -ACY, modeled on such pairs as *confederacy, confederate*]

com·pli·cate (*v.* kom′plə kāt′; *adj.* kom′plə kit), *v.,* **-cat·ed, -cat·ing,** *adj.* —*v.t.* **1.** to make complex, intricate, involved, or difficult. —*adj.* **2.** complex or involved. **3.** *Bot.* folded upon itself: *a complicate embryo.* **4.** *Entomol.* folded longitudinally one or more times, as the wings of certain insects. [< L *complicāt(us)* (ptp. of *complicāre* to fold together) = *com-* COM- + *plic-* (s. of *plicāre* to fold, akin to *plec-*; see COMPLEX) + *-ātus* -ATE[1]]

com·pli·cat·ed (kom′plə kā′tid), *adj.* **1.** composed of elaborately interconnected parts; complex: *a laboratory of complicated apparatus.* **2.** consisting of many parts not easily separable; difficult to analyze, understand, explain, etc.: *a complicated problem.* —**com′pli·cat′ed·ly,** *adv.* —**com′pli·cat′ed·ness,** *n.* —**Syn. 2.** involved, tangled, knotty.

com·pli·ca·tion (kom′plə kā′shən), *n.* **1.** the act of complicating. **2.** a complicated or involved state or condition. **3.** a complex combination of elements or things. **4.** an element that introduces, usually unexpectedly, some difficulty, problem, or change. **5.** *Pathol.* a concurrent disease or a fortuitous condition that aggravates the original disease. [< LL *complicātiōn-* (s. of *complicātiō*)]

com·plice (kom′plis), *n.* *Archaic.* an accomplice or associate. [late ME < MF < LL *complic(e)-,* obl. s. of *complex* confederate (formation modeled on *simplex*) = *com-* COM- + *-plex* -FOLD]

com·plic·i·ty (kəm plis′i tē), *n., pl.* **-ties.** the state of being an accomplice; partnership or involvement in wrongdoing: *He was accused of complicity in the crime.*

com·pli·ment (*n.* kom′plə mənt; *v.* kom′plə ment′), *n.* **1.** an expression of praise, commendation, or admiration. **2.** a formal act or expression of civility, respect, or regard: *The mayor paid her the compliment of escorting her.* **3. compliments,** a courteous greeting; good wishes; regards: *He sends you his compliments.* **4.** *Archaic.* a gift; present. —*v.t.* **5.** to pay a compliment to. **6.** to show kindness or regard for by a gift or other favor. **7.** to congratulate or felicitate. —*v.i.* **8.** to pay compliments. [< F < It *compliment(o)* < Sp *cumplimiento* = *cumpli-* (see COMPLY) + *-miento* -MENT; r. COMPLEMENT in same sense] —**Syn. 1.** praise, tribute, eulogy. **5.** commend, praise, honor. —**Ant. 1.** disparagement.

com·pli·men·ta·ry (kom′plə men′tə rē, -trē), *adj.* **1.** of the nature of, conveying, or expressing a compliment, often one that is politely flattering: *complimentary reviews of his novel; a complimentary remark.* **2.** free: *a complimentary ticket.* —**com′pli·men′ta·ri·ly,** *adv.*

com·plin (kom′plin), *n.* *Eccles.* the last of the seven canonical hours, or the service for it. Also, **com·pline** (kom′plin, -plīn). [ME *comp(e)lin* = *compli, cump(e)lie* (< OF *complie, cumplie* < L *complēta* (*hōra*) COMPLETE (hour) + *-in* (of MATIN)]

com·plot (*n.* kom′plot′; *v.* kəm plot′), *n., v.,* **-plot·ted, -plot·ting.** —*n.* **1.** a joint plot; conspiracy. —*v.t., v.i.* **2.** to plot together; conspire. [< MF < ?] —**com·plot′ter,** *n.*

com·ply (kəm plī′), *v.i.,* **-plied, -ply·ing.** **1.** to act in accordance with wishes, requests, demands, requirements, conditions, etc. (sometimes fol. by *with*): *to comply with regulations; They asked him to leave and he complied.* **2.** *Obs.* to be courteous or conciliatory. [< It *compli(re)* < Sp. *cumplir* (see COMPLIMENT) to fulfill, accomplish < L *complēre* = *com-* COM- + *plē-* fill + *-re* inf. suffix] —**com·pli′er,** *n.* —**Syn. 1.** acquiesce, yield, conform, obey. —**Ant. 1.** refuse, resist.

com·po·nent (kəm pō′nənt), *adj.* **1.** being or serving as an element (in something larger); composing; constituent: *the component parts.* —*n.* **2.** a component part; constituent: *hi-fi components.* **3.** *Physics.* the projection of a vector quantity, as force, velocity, or the like, along an axis. **4.** *Physical Chem.* one of the set of the minimum number of chemical constituents by which every phase of a given system can be described. **5.** *Math.* a coordinate of a vector. [< L *compōnent-* (s. of *compōnēns,* prp. of *compōnere* to put together) = *com-* COM- + *pōn(ere)* (to) put + *-ent-* -ENT] —**com·po·nen·tial** (kom′pə nen′shəl), **com′po·nen′tal,** *adj.* —**Syn. 2.** See **element.**

com·po·ny (kəm pō′nē), *adj.* *Heraldry.* composed of a single row of squares, metal and color alternating; gobony. Also, **com·po·né** (kəm pō′nē; *Fr.* kôN pô nā′). [< MF *compone,* nasalized var. of *copone* = *copon* COUPON + *-e* -EE]

com·port (kəm pôrt′, -pōrt′), *v.t.* **1.** to bear or conduct (oneself); behave: *He comported himself with dignity.* —*v.i.* **2.** to be in agreement, harmony, or conformity (usually fol. by *with*): *His statement does not comport with the facts.* —*n.* **3.** *Obs.* comportment. [< MF *comport(er)* < L *comportāre* to transport, support = *com-* COM- + *portāre* to PORT[5]]

com·port·ment (kəm pōrt′mənt, -pôrt′-), *n.* bearing; demeanor. [< MF *comportement*] —**Syn.** See **behavior.**

com·pose (kəm pōz′), *v.*, **-posed, -pos·ing.** —*v.t.* **1.** to make or form by combining things, parts, or elements: *He composed his speech from research notes.* **2.** to be or constitute a part or element of: *a rich sauce composed of many ingredients.* **3.** to make up or form the basis of. **4.** to put in proper form or order: *to compose laws into a coherent system.* **5.** *Art.* to organize the parts or elements of (a painting or the like). **6.** to create (a literary, musical, or choreographic work). **7.** to end or settle (a quarrel, dispute, etc.). **8.** to bring (the body, mind, or emotions) to a condition of repose, calmness, etc.; calm; quiet. **9.** *Print.* **a.** to set (type). **b.** to set type for (an article, book, etc.). —*v.i.* **10.** to engage in composition, esp. musical composition. **11.** to enter into composition; fall into an arrangement: *He photographs any scene that composes well.* [late ME < MF *compose(r)*]

com·posed (kəm pōzd′), *adj.*, calm, tranquil, or serene. —**com·pos·ed·ly** (kəm pō′zid lē), *adv.* —**com·pos′ed·ness,** *n.*

com·pos·er (kəm pō′zər), *n.* **1.** a person or thing that composes. **2.** a person who writes music.

compos′ing stick′, *Print.* a portable, adjustable tray, usually of metal, in which a compositor places type as he gathers it.

Composing stick

com·pos·ite (kəm poz′it; *Brit.* kom′pə zit), *adj.* **1.** made up of disparate or separate parts or elements. **2.** *Bot.* belonging to the *Compositae,* a family of plants, including the daisy, dandelion, and aster, in which the florets are borne in a close head surrounded by a common involucre of bracts. **3.** (*cap.*) *Archit.* noting or pertaining to one of the five classical orders, popular esp. since the beginning of the Renaissance but invented by the ancient Romans, in which the Roman Ionic and Corinthian orders are combined. Cf. **Corinthian** (def. 4), **Doric** (def. 2), **Ionic** (def. 1), **Tuscan** (def. 2). See illus. at **order.** **4.** *Math.* of or pertaining to a composite number. —*n.* **5.** something composite; a compound. **6.** *Bot.* a composite plant. **7.** a picture, photograph, or the like, that combines several separate pictures. [< L *composit(us)* (ptp. of *compōnere* to put together) = *com-* COM- + *positus* placed; see POSIT] —**com·pos′ite·ly,** *adv.* —**com·pos′ite·ness,** *n.* —**Syn. 5.** mixture, blend, amalgamation; association. See **combination.**

compos′ite num′ber, *Math.* a multiple of at least two other numbers, none of which is equal to 1.

compos′ite school′, (in Canada) a secondary school that offers courses in academic, commercial, and industrial subjects. Also called **comprehensive school.**

com·po·si·tion (kom′pə zish′ən), *n.* **1.** the act of combining parts or elements to form a whole. **2.** the resulting state or product. **3.** manner of being composed; structure: *This painting has an orderly composition.* **4.** make-up or constitution. **5.** an aggregate material formed from two or more substances. **6.** *Fine Arts.* the organization of the parts of a work to achieve a unified whole. **7.** the art of putting words and sentences together in accordance with the rules of grammar and rhetoric. **8.** the act or process of producing a literary work. **9.** a short essay written as a school exercise. **10.** the art of composing music. **11.** a piece of music. **12.** *Gram.* the formation of compounds: *the composition of "bootblack" consists of "boot" and "black."* **13.** a settlement by mutual agreement. **14.** an agreement or compromise, esp. one by which a creditor accepts partial payment from a debtor. **15.** a sum of money so paid. **16.** the setting up of type for printing. [< L *compositiōn-* (s. of *compositiō*) = *composit(us)* (see COMPOSITE) + *-iōn-* -ION; r. ME *composicioun* < AF] —**com′po·si′tion·al,** *adj.*

com·pos·i·tor (kəm poz′i tər), *n.* a person who sets up type and cuts for printing. [< L; see COMPOSITE, -OR[2]]

com·pos men·tis (kōm′pōs men′tis; *Eng.* kom′pəs men′tis), *Latin.* sane; mentally sound. [lit., being in full possession of one's mind]

com·post (kom′pōst), *n.* **1.** a mixture of various decaying organic substances, as dead leaves, manure, etc., for fertilizing land. **2.** a composition or compound. [late ME < MF < L *compos(i)t(um),* n. use of neut. of *compositus* COMPOSITE]

com·po·sure (kəm pō′zhər), *n.* serene state of mind; calmness or tranquillity. —**Syn.** serenity, coolness, equanimity, self-possession. —**Ant.** agitation.

com·po·ta·tion (kom′pə tā′shən), *n.* the act or an instance of drinking or tippling together. [< L *compōtātiōn-* (s. of *compōtātiō,* trans. of Gk *sympósion* symposium)]

com·pote (kom′pōt; *Fr.* kôɴ pôt′), *n., pl.* **-potes** (-pōts; *Fr.* -pôt′). **1.** fruit stewed or cooked in a syrup, usually served as a dessert. **2.** a dish, usually of glass, china, or silver, having a base, stem, and often a lid, used for serving fruit, nuts, candy, etc. [< F; MF *composte* < L *composita,* fem. of *compositus* COMPOSITE]

com·pound[1] (*adj.* kom′pound, kom pound′; *n.* kom′pound; *v.* kəm pound′), *adj.* **1.** composed of two or more parts, elements, or ingredients. **2.** having or involving two or more actions or functions. **3.** *Gram.* **a.** of or pertaining to a compound sentence or compound-complex sentence. **b.** (of a word) consisting of two or more parts that are bases, or that include a base and a noninflectional affix (*return, follower*), a base and a combining form (*biochemistry*), two combining forms (*ethnography*), or a combining form and a noninflectional affix (*aviary, dentoid*). **4.** *Zool.* (of an animal) composed of a number of distinct individuals connected to form a united whole or colony. **5.** *Music.* of or pertaining to compound time. **6.** *Mach.* noting an engine or turbine expanding the same steam or the like in two successive chambers to do work at two ranges of pressure. —*n.* **7.** something formed by compounding or combining parts, elements, etc. **8.** *Chem.* a substance composed of two or more elements chemically united in a fixed proportion, as water (H_2O), each molecule of which contains two atoms of hydrogen and one atom of oxygen. Cf. **element** (def. 6), **mixture** (def. 3). **9.** a word composed of two or more parts that are also bases, as *house-top, many-sided, playact,* or *upon.* —*v.t.* **10.** to put together into a whole; combine: *to compound various well-known drugs to form a new medicine.* **11.** to make or form by combining parts, elements, etc.: *to compound a new medicine from drugs.* **12.** to make up or constitute. **13.** to settle or adjust by agreement. **14.** *Law.* to agree, for a consideration, not to prosecute or punish a wrongdoer. **15.** to pay (interest) on the accrued interest as well as the principal: *My bank compounds interest quarterly.* **16.** to increase or add to: *The misery of his loneliness was now compounded by his poverty.* **17.** *Elect.* to connect a portion of the field turns of (a direct-current dynamo) in series with the armature circuit. —*v.i.* **18.** to make a bargain; come to terms; compromise. **19.** to settle a debt, claim, etc., by compromise. [(adj.) ME *compouned,* ptp. of *compounen;* now used also as v., r. ME *compoune(n)* < MF *compon-* (s. of *compondre*) < L *compōnere* = *com-* COM- + *pōnere* to put] —**com·pound′a·ble,** *adj.* —**com·pound′er,** *n.* —**Syn. 7.** See **combination.**

com·pound[2] (kom′pound), *n.* **1.** an enclosure containing living quarters, medical facilities, or the like, esp. for Europeans in the Far East. **2.** any fenced area or enclosure, as for prisoners of war. [folk-etym. alter., by assoc. with COMPOUND[1], of Malay *kampong* cluster of buildings]

com′pound-com′plex sen′tence (kom′pound kom′pleks), a compound sentence having one or more dependent clauses, as *The wind blew* (independent clause) *and the rain fell* (independent clause) *as he arrived* (dependent clause).

Compound E, cortisone.

com′pound eye′, an arthropod eye subdivided into many individual light-receptive elements, each including a lens, a transmitting apparatus, and retinal cells.

Compound F, hydrocortisone.

com′pound flow′er, the flower head of a composite plant.

com′pound frac′tion, *Math.* See **complex fraction.**

com′pound frac′ture, a fracture in which the broken bone is exposed through a wound in the skin. Also called **open fracture.**

com′pound in′terest, interest paid on both the principal and accrued interest.

com′pound leaf′, a leaf composed of a number of leaflets on a common stalk.

Compound leaf

com′pound mi′croscope, a microscope consisting of an objective lens with a short focal length and an eyepiece with a longer focal length, mounted in the same tube.

com′pound num′ber, a quantity expressed in more than one denomination or unit, as one foot six inches.

com′pound sen′tence, a sentence containing two or more coordinate independent clauses, usually joined by one or more conjunctions, but no dependent clause, as *The lightning flashed* (independent clause) *and* (conjunction) *the rain fell* (independent clause).

com′pound time′, *Music.* a meter, as $^6/_8$, in which the beats are grouped in threes.

com·pra·dor (kom′prə dôr′), *n.* (formerly in China) a native agent or factotum, as of a foreign business house. Also, **com·pra·dore** (kom′prə dōr′, -dôr′). [< Pg: buyer = *com-* COM- + *prad-* < L *parāt(us)* provision (see PREPARATION) + *-or* -OR[2]]

com·pre·hend (kom′pri hend′), *v.t.* **1.** to understand the nature or meaning of; grasp with the mind; perceive. **2.** to take in or embrace; include; comprise. [ME *comprehende(n)* < L *comprehende(re)* = *com-* COM- + *prehendere* to grasp; see PREHENSILE] —**Syn. 1.** See **know. 2.** See **include.**

com·pre·hen·si·ble (kom′pri hen′sə bəl), *adj.* capable of being comprehended, or understood; intelligible. Also, **com·pre·hend·i·ble** (kom′pri hen′də bəl). [< L *comprehensibil(is).* See COMPREHENSION, -IBLE] —**com′pre·hen′si·bil′i·ty, com′pre·hen′si·ble·ness,** *n.* —**com′pre·hen′si·bly,** *adv.*

com·pre·hen·sion (kom′pri hen′shən), *n.* **1.** the act or process of comprehending. **2.** the state of being comprehended. **3.** inclusion. **4.** comprehensiveness. **5.** perception or understanding: *His comprehension of physics is amazing.* **6.** capacity of the mind to perceive and understand; power to grasp ideas; ability to know. **7.** *Logic.* the connotation of a term. [< L *comprehensiōn-* (s. of *comprehensiō*) = *comprehens(us)* (ptp. of *comprehendere* to COMPREHEND) + *-iōn-* -ION]

com·pre·hen·sive (kom′pri hen′siv), *adj.* **1.** of large scope; inclusive: *a comprehensive study of world affairs.* **2.** comprehending mentally; having an extensive mental range or grasp. **3.** *Insurance.* covering or providing broad protection against loss. —*n.* **4.** Often, **comprehensives.** Also called **comprehen′sive examina′tion.** an examination of extensive coverage given to measure a student's proficiency in his major field of study. [< LL *comprehensīv(us).* See COMPREHENSION, -IVE] —**com′pre·hen′sive·ly,** *adv.* —**com′pre·hen′sive·ness,** *n.* —**Syn. 1.** broad, extensive.

comprehen′sive school′. See **composite school.**

com·press (*v.* kəm pres′; *n.* kom′pres), *v.t.* **1.** to press together; force into less space. **2.** to cause to become a solid mass: *to compress cotton into bales.* —*n.* **3.** *Med.* a soft cloth pad held in place by a bandage and used to provide pressure or to supply moisture, cold, heat, or medication. **4.** an apparatus for compressing. [late ME < LL *compress(āre),* freq. of L *comprimere* to squeeze together] —**com·press′i·bil′i·ty,** *n.* —**com·press′i·ble,** *adj.* —**com·press′i·bly,** *adv.* —**Syn. 1.** condense, squeeze, constrict. See **contract.** —**Ant. 1.** expand, spread.

com·pressed (kəm prest′), *adj.* **1.** pressed into less space; condensed: *compressed gases.* **2.** pressed together. **3.** flattened by or as by pressure: *compressed wallboard.* **4.** *Bot.* flattened laterally or along the length. **5.** *Zool.* narrow from side to side, and therefore of greater height than width. [ME] —**com·press·ed·ly** (kəm pres′id lē, -prest′lē), *adv.*

compressed′ air′, air compressed, esp. by mechanical

means, to a pressure higher than the surrounding atmospheric pressure.

com·pres·sion (kəm presh′ən), *n.* **1.** the act of compressing. **2.** the state of being compressed. **3.** the result of being compressed. **4.** (in internal-combustion engines) the reduction in volume and increase of pressure of the air or combustible mixture in the cylinder prior to ignition. Also, **com·pres·sure** (kəm presh′ər) (for defs. 1, 2). [< L *compressiōn-* (s. of *compressiō*)] —**com·pres′sion·al,** *adj.*

com·pres·sive (kəm pres′iv), *adj.* compressing; tending to compress. —**com·pres′sive·ly,** *adv.*

com·pres·sor (kəm pres′ər), *n.* **1.** a person or thing that compresses. **2.** *Anat.* a muscle that compresses some part of the body. **3.** *Surg.* an instrument for compressing a part of the body. **4.** a pump or other machine for reducing the volume and increasing the pressure of gases in order to condense the gases, drive pneumatically powered machinery, etc. [< L *compress(us)* (see COMPRESS) + -OR[2]]

com·prise (kəm prīz′), *v.t.,* **-prised, -pris·ing.** **1.** to include or contain: *The Soviet Union comprises several socialist republics.* **2.** *Informal.* to consist of; be composed of: *The advisory board comprises six members.* **3.** *Informal.* to form or constitute: *His speech comprised the evening's program.* [late ME < MF *compris* (ptp. of *comprendre*) < L *comprehensus;* see COMPREHENSION] —**Syn. 1.** See **include.**

com·prize (kəm prīz′), *v.t.,* **-prized, -priz·ing.** comprise.

com·pro·mise (kom′prə mīz′), *n., v.,* **-mised, -mis·ing.** —*n.* **1.** a settlement of differences by mutual concessions. **2.** the result of such a settlement. **3.** something intermediate between different things. **4.** an endangering, esp. of reputation; exposure to danger, suspicion, etc.: *a compromise of one's integrity.* —*v.t.* **5.** to settle by a compromise. **6.** to make liable to danger, suspicion, scandal, etc.; endanger the reputation of. **7.** to involve or affect unfavorably: *Being seen with him compromised my reputation.* **8.** *Obs.* **a.** to bind by bargain or agreement. **b.** to bring to terms. —*v.i.* **9.** to make a compromise. **10.** to make a dishonorable or shameful concession: *Don't compromise with your principles.* [late ME < MF *compromis* < L *comprōmiss(um).* See COM-, PROMISE] —**com′pro·mis′er,** *n.* —**com′pro·mis′ing·ly,** *adv.*

compt (kount), *v.t., v.i., n. Archaic.* count[1].

compte ren·du (kôɴt räɴ dy′), *pl.* **comptes ren·dus** (kôɴt räɴ dy′). *French.* a report, account, review, or record, as of a transaction, a book, the proceedings of a meeting, etc. [lit., account rendered]

Comp·ton (komp′tən), *n.* **1. Arthur Hol·ly** (hol′ē), 1892–1962, U.S. physicist: Nobel prize 1927. **2.** his brother, **Karl Taylor,** 1887–1954, U.S. physicist. **3.** a city in SW California. 78,611 (1970).

comp·trol·ler (kən trō′lər), *n.* controller (def. 1). [var. sp. by confusion with COMPT] —**comp·trol′ler·ship′,** *n.*

com·pul·sion (kəm pul′shən), *n.* **1.** the act of compelling; constraint; coercion. **2.** the state or condition of being compelled. **3.** *Psychol.* a strong, usually irresistible impulse to perform an act that is contrary to the will of the subject. [late ME < LL *compulsiōn-* (s. of *compulsiō*) = L *compuls(us),* ptp. of *compellere* to COMPEL (*com-* COM- + *pul-* v. s. + *-sus* ptp. suffix) + *-iōn-* -ION]

com·pul·sive (kəm pul′siv), *adj.* **1.** compelling; compulsory. **2.** *Psychol.* **a.** pertaining to, characterized by, or involving compulsion: *a compulsive desire to cry.* **b.** governed by an obsessive need to achieve some desired ideal of behavior, as to conform, be scrupulous, etc.: *the compulsive personality.* —*n.* **3.** *Psychol.* a person whose behavior is governed by a compulsion. [obs. *compulse* (< L *compuls(us);* see COMPULSION) + -IVE] —**com·pul′sive·ly,** *adv.* —**com·pul′sive·ness,** *n.*

com·pul·so·ry (kəm pul′sə rē), *adj.* **1.** using compulsion; compelling or constraining. **2.** mandatory; obligatory: *compulsory education.* [< ML *compulsōri(us)* = L *compuls(us)* (see COMPULSION) + *-ōrius* -ORY[1]] —**com·pul′so·ri·ly,** *adv.* —**com·pul′so·ri·ness,** *n.* —**Ant.** voluntary.

com·punc·tion (kəm pungk′shən), *n.* **1.** remorse for wrongdoing; contrition. **2.** any uneasiness or hesitation about the rightness of an action. [< eccl. L *compunctiōn-* (s. of *compunctiō*) = L *compūnct(us),* ptp. of *compungere* to prick severely (*com-* COM- + *pūnctus;* see POINT) + *-iōn-* -ION; r. late ME *compunccioun* < AF] —**com·punc′tious,** *adj.* —**com·punc′tious·ly,** *adv.*

com·pur·ga·tion (kom′pər gā′shən), *n.* (in early common law) an acquittal based on the sworn endorsement of a defendant's friends or neighbors. [< LL *compurgātiōn-* (s. of *compurgātiō*) = L *compurgāt(us)* (ptp. of *compurgāre;* see COM-, PURGE) + *-iōn-* -ION]

com·pur·ga·tor (kom′pər gā′tər), *n.* a person who vouches for the innocence of another. [< ML; see COMPURGATION, -OR[2]]

com·pu·ta·tion (kom′pyə tā′shən), *n.* **1.** an act or method of computing; calculation. **2.** a result of computing. **3.** the amount computed. [late ME < L *computātiōn-* (s. of *computātiō*) = *computāt(us)* (ptp. of *computāre;* see COMPUTE) + *-iōn-* -ION] —**com′pu·ta′tion·al,** *adj.*

com·pute (kəm pyo͞ot′), *v.,* **-put·ed, -put·ing,** *n.* —*v.t.* **1.** to determine by calculation; reckon; calculate. —*v.i.* **2.** to reckon; calculate. —*n.* **3.** computation. [< L *comput(āre)* = *com-* COM- + *putāre* to think; see PUTATIVE] —**com·put′a·bil′i·ty,** *n.* —**com·put′a·ble,** *adj.* —**Syn. 1.** estimate, count, figure.

com·put·er (kəm pyo͞o′tər), *n.* **1.** a person or thing that computes. **2.** a mechanical or electronic apparatus capable of carrying out repetitious and highly complex mathematical operations at high speeds. Cf. **analog computer, digital computer.**

com·pu·ter·ese (kəm pyo͞o′tə rēz′), *n.* the jargon or special vocabulary used in the computer field.

com·pu·ter·ize (kəm pyo͞o′tə rīz′), *v.t.* **-ized, -iz·ing.** to control, perform, or store (information or a system or operation) by or in an electronic computer or computers. —**com·pu′ter·i·za′tion,** *n.*

com·pu·ter·ized (kəm pyo͞o′tə rīzd′), *adj.* utilizing or concerned with electronic computers or their use.

compu′ter lan′guage, **1.** See **machine language. 2.** any of the artificial languages, such as programming language, devised for communicating data, questions, instructions, etc., to a computer.

Comr., Commissioner.

com·rade (kom′rad *or, esp. Brit.,* -rid, kum′rid), *n.* **1.** a person who shares closely in the activities, occupation, or interests of another; intimate companion, associate, or friend. **2.** a fellow member of a fraternal group, political party, etc. **3.** a member of the Communist party or someone with strongly leftist views. [< MF *camarade* < Sp *camarada* group of soldiers billeted together = *cámar(a)* room (< L; see CAMERA) + *-ada* < L *-āta,* fem. of *-ātus* -ATE[1]] —**com′rade·ship′,** *n.* —**Syn. 1.** crony, fellow, mate.

Com·stock (kum′stok, kom′-), *n.* **Anthony,** 1844–1915, U.S. crusader against vice.

com·stock·er·y (kum′stok′ə rē, kom′-), *n.* overzealous moral censorship of the fine arts and literature. [after Anthony COMSTOCK; see -ERY]

Com′stock Lode′, the most valuable deposit of silver ore ever recorded, discovered in 1859 near Virginia City, Nevada. Also called **Com′stock Sil′ver Lode′.** [named after Henry T. P. *Comstock* (1820–1870), U.S. prospector]

comte (kôɴt), *n., pl.* **comtes** (kôɴt). *French.* count[2].

Comte (kônt; *Fr.* kôɴt), *n.* **(I·si·dore) Au·guste (Ma·rie Fran·çois)** (ē zē dôr′ ō gyst′ mȧ rē′ fräɴ swȧ′), 1798–1857, French philosopher: founder of positivism. —**Com·ti·an** (kom′tē ən, kôn′-), *adj.*

Co·mus (kō′məs), *n.* an ancient Roman god of drinking and revelry, represented as a winged young man dressed in white. [< Gk *kômos* a revel]

Com. Ver., Common Version (of the Bible).

con[1] (kon), *adv.* **1.** in opposition; against. —*n.* **2.** the argument, position, arguer, or voter against something. Cf. **pro**[1]. [short for L *contrā* in opposition, against]

con[2] (kon), *v.t.,* **conned, con·ning. 1.** to learn; study; peruse or examine carefully. **2.** commit to memory. [var. of CAN[1] to become acquainted with, learn to know]

con[3] (kon), *v.,* **conned, con·ning,** *n. Naut.* —*v.t.* **1.** to direct the steering of (a ship). —*n.* **2.** the station of the person who cons. **3.** the act of conning. Also, **conn.** [earlier *cond,* apocopated var. of ME *condie, condue* < MF *cond(u)ire* < L *condūcere* to CONDUCT]

con[4] (kon), *adj., v.,* **conned, con·ning.** —*adj.* **1.** *Informal.* involving abuse of confidence: *a con trick.* —*v.t.* **2.** *Slang.* to swindle; trick. **3.** *Slang.* to persuade by deception, cajolery, etc. [CON(FIDENCE)]

con[5] (kon), *n. Slang.* a convict.

con-, var. of **com-** before a consonant (except *b, h, l, p, r, w*) and, by assimilation, before *n: convene; condone; connection.* [< L]

Con., **1.** Conformist. **2.** Consul.

con., **1.** concerto. **2.** connection. **3.** consolidated. **4.** consul. **5.** continued. **6.** against. [< L *contrā*]

Co·na·kry (*Fr.* kô nȧ krē′), *n.* a seaport in and the capital of Guinea, in NW Africa. 525,671 with suburbs. Also, **Konakri.**

con a·mo·re (*It.* kôn ä mô′re *for 1;* kon ə mōr′ē, -mōr′ā, -môr′ē, -môr′ā, kōn *for 2*). **1.** (*italics.*) *Italian.* with love, tender enthusiasm, or zeal. **2.** tenderly and lovingly (used as a musical direction).

Co·nant (kō′nənt), *n.* **James Bryant,** 1893–1978, U.S. educator: president of Harvard University 1933–53.

co·na·tion (kō nā′shən), *n. Psychol.* the aspect of mental life having to do with striving, including desire and volition. [< L *cōnātiōn-* (s. of *cōnātiō*) an effort = *cōnāt(us)* (ptp. of *cōnārī* to try) + *-iōn-* -ION]

con·a·tive (kon′ə tiv, kō′nə-), *adj.* **1.** *Psychol.* pertaining to or of the nature of conation. **2.** *Gram.* expressing endeavor or effort: *a conative verb.*

co·na·tus (kō nā′təs), *n., pl.* **-tus. 1.** an effort or striving. **2.** a force or tendency simulating a human effort. [< L: exertion, n. use of *cōnātus* (ptp.); see CONATION]

con bri·o (kon brē′ō, kōn; *It.* kôn brē′ô), with vigor; vivaciously (used as a musical direction). [< It]

conc., **1.** concentrate. **2.** concentrated. **3.** concentration. **4.** concerning.

con·cat·e·nate (kon kat′ᵊnāt′), *v.,* **-nat·ed, -nat·ing,** *adj.* —*v.t.* **1.** to link together; unite in a series or chain. —*adj.* **2.** linked together, as in a chain. [< LL *concatēnāt(us)* (ptp. of *concatēnāre*) = *con-* CON- + L *catēn(a)* CHAIN + *-ātus* -ATE[1]] —**con·cat′e·na′tion,** *n.*

A, Concave or plano-concave lens; B, Concavo-concave lens; C, Concavo-convex lens

con·cave (*adj., v.* kon kāv′, kon′kāv; *n.* kon′kāv), *adj., n., v.,* **-caved, -cav·ing.** —*adj.* **1.** curved like a segment of the interior of a circle or hollow sphere; hollow and curved. Cf. **convex** (def. 1). **2.** *Geom.* (of a polygon) having at least one interior angle greater than 180°. **3.** *Obs.* hollow. —*n.* **4.** a concave surface, part, line, etc. —*v.t.* **5.** to make concave. [< L *concav(us).* See CON-, CAVE] —**con·cave′ly,** *adv.* —**con·cave′ness,** *n.*

con·cav·i·ty (kon kav′i tē), *n., pl.* **-ties. 1.** the state or quality of being concave. **2.** a concave surface or thing; a hollow; cavity. [late ME *concavite* < LL *concavitāt-* (s. of *concavitās*). See CON-, CAVE, -ITY]

con·ca·vo-con·cave (kon kā′vō kon kāv′), *adj.* concave on both sides. [< L *concav(us)* + -o- + CONCAVE]

con·ca·vo-con·vex (kon kā′vō kon veks′), *adj.* **1.** concave on one side and convex on the other. **2.** *Optics.* pertaining to or noting a lens in which the concave face has a greater degree of curvature than the convex face. Cf. **convexo-concave.** [< L *concav(us)* + -o- + CONVEX]

con·ceal (kən sēl′), *v.t.* **1.** to hide; withdraw or remove from observation; cover or keep from sight. **2.** to keep secret; to prevent or avoid disclosing or divulging: *He concealed the true source of the gold.* [late ME *consele, concele* < AF *conceler* (r) < L *concēlāre* = *con-* CON- + *cēlāre* to hide; see OCCULT] —**con·ceal′a·ble,** *adj.* —**con·ceal′ed·ly,** *adv.* —**con·ceal′ed·ness,** *n.* —**con·ceal′er,** *n.* —**Syn. 1.** See **hide**[1].

con·ceal·ment (kən sēl′mənt), *n.* **1.** the act of concealing. **2.** the state of being concealed. **3.** a means or place of hiding. [ME *concelement* < AF]

con·cede (kən sēd′), *v.*, **-ced·ed, -ced·ing.** —*v.t.* **1.** to acknowledge as true, just, or proper; admit. **2.** to acknowledge (an opponent's victory, score, etc.) before it is officially established: *to concede an election before all the votes are counted.* **3.** to grant as a right or privilege; yield. —*v.i.* **4.** to make concession; yield. [< L *concēde(re)* = *con-* CON- + *cēdere* to withdraw, yield, CEDE] —**con·ced′er,** *n.* —**Syn. 1.** yield, grant. —**Ant. 1.** deny. **3.** refuse.

con·ceit (kən sēt′), *n.* **1.** an exaggerated estimate of one's own ability, importance, wit, etc. **2.** something that is conceived in the mind; a thought; idea: *He jotted down the conceits of his idle hours.* **3.** imagination or fancy. **4.** a fancy or whim; fanciful notion. **5.** an elaborate, fanciful metaphor, esp. of a strained or far-fetched nature. **6.** a fancy, purely decorative article. **7.** *Archaic.* **a.** favorable opinion; esteem. **b.** personal opinion or estimation. **8.** *Obs.* the faculty of conceiving; apprehension. —*v.t.* **9.** *Archaic.* to take a fancy to; have a good opinion of. **10.** *Obs.* **a.** to imagine. **b.** to conceive; apprehend. [ME *conceyte, conceipt* < CONCEIVE + L *conceptum* CONCEPT] —**Syn. 1.** self-esteem, vanity, egotism. See **pride.** —**Ant. 1.** humility.

con·ceit·ed (kən sē′tid), *adj.* **1.** having an exaggerated opinion of one's own abilities, importance, etc. **2.** *Archaic.* **a.** having an opinion. **b.** fanciful; whimsical. **3.** *Obs.* intelligent; clever. —**con·ceit′ed·ly,** *adv.* —**con·ceit′ed·ness,** *n.* —**Syn. 1.** vain, proud, egotistical, self-important, smug.

con·ceiv·a·ble (kən sē′və bəl), *adj.* capable of being conceived; imaginable. —**con·ceiv′a·bil′i·ty, con·ceiv′a·ble·ness,** *n.* —**con·ceiv′a·bly,** *adv.*

con·ceive (kən sēv′), *v.*, **-ceived, -ceiv·ing.** —*v.t.* **1.** to form (a notion, opinion, purpose, etc.): *He conceived the project while on vacation.* **2.** to form a notion or idea of; imagine. **3.** to hold as an opinion; think; believe. **4.** to experience or form (a feeling): *to conceive a great love for music.* **5.** to express, as in words. **6.** to beget. **7.** to become pregnant with. **8.** to begin, originate, or found (something) in a particular way (usually used in the passive): *a new nation conceived in liberty.* **9.** *Archaic.* to understand; comprehend. —*v.i.* **10.** to form an idea; think (usually fol. by *of*). **11.** to become pregnant. [ME < OF *conceiv(re)* < L *concipere* to take fully, take in = *con-* CON- + *-cipere*, comb. form of *capere* to take] —**con·ceiv′er,** *n.* —**Syn. 2, 8.** See **imagine.**

con·cent (kən sent′), *n.* *Obs.* concord; harmony. [< L *concent(us)* harmony, n. use of *concentus* harmonized (ptp. of *concinere*) = *con-* CON- + *cen-* (var. s. of *-cinere*, comb. form of *canere* to sing) + *-tus* ptp. ending]

con·cen·ter (kon sen′tər), *v.t.*, *v.i.* to bring or converge to a common center; concentrate. Also, *esp. Brit.*, **concentre.** [< MF *concentr(er)*]

con·cen·trate (kon′sən trāt′), *v.*, **-trat·ed, -trat·ing,** *n.* —*v.t.* **1.** to bring or draw to a common center or point of union; focus: *to concentrate one's attention on a problem; to concentrate the rays of the sun with a lens.* **2.** to put or bring into a single place, group, etc.: *The nation's population had been concentrated in a few cities.* **3.** to intensify; make denser, stronger, etc.: *to concentrate fruit juice.* **4.** *Mining.* to separate (metal or ore) from rock, sand, etc., so as to improve the quality of the valuable portion. —*v.i.* **5.** to come to or toward a common center; converge; collect. **6.** to bring all efforts, faculties, activities, etc., to bear on one thing or activity (often fol. by *on* or *upon*): *to concentrate on solving a problem.* **7.** to become more intense, stronger, or purer. —*n.* **8.** a concentrated form of something; a product of concentration: *Frozen orange juice is a concentrate.* [back formation from CONCENTRATION] —**con·cen·tra·tive** (kon′sən trā′tiv, kən-sen′trə-), *adj.* —**con′cen·tra′tor,** *n.* —**Syn. 1.** See **contract.** —**Ant. 1.** disperse. **5.** diverge.

con·cen·trat·ed (kon′sən trā′tid), *adj.* **1.** applied with all one's attention, energy, etc.: *their concentrated efforts to win the election.* **2.** clustered or gathered together closely. **3.** treated to remove what is inessential: *concentrated orange juice.*

con·cen·tra·tion (kon′sən trā′shən), *n.* **1.** the act of concentrating. **2.** the state of being concentrated. **3.** something concentrated: *a concentration of stars.* **4.** exclusive attention to one object; close mental application: *He focused his concentration on the swinging pendulum.* **5.** *Mil.* **a.** the assembling of military forces in a particular area in preparation for further operations. **b.** a specified intensity and duration of artillery fire placed on a small area. **6.** the focusing of a student's academic program on advanced study in a specific subject or field. **7.** *Chem.* (in a solution) a measure of the amount of dissolved substance contained per unit of volume. **8.** *Cards.* a game for two or more players in which the pack is spread out face down on the table and each player in turn exposes two cards at a time and replaces them face down if they do not constitute a pair, the object being to take the most pairs by remembering the location of the cards previously exposed. [CON- + L *centr(um)* CENTER + -ATION]

concentra′tion camp′, a guarded compound for the detention or imprisonment of aliens, political opponents, etc., esp. any of the camps established by the Nazis in World War II for the confinement, persecution, and mass execution of prisoners.

con·cen·tre (kon sen′tər), *v.t.*, *v.i.*, **-tred, -tring.** *Chiefly Brit.* concenter.

con·cen·tric (kən sen′trik), *adj.* having a common center, as circles or spheres. Also, **con·cen′tri·cal.** [ME *consentrik* < ML *concentric(us)*] —**con·cen′tri·cal·ly,** *adv.* —**con·cen·tric·i·ty** (kon′sən tris′i tē), *n.*

Con·cep·ción (kôn′sep syôn′), *n.* a city in central Chile, near the mouth of the Bío-Bío River. 167,946 (est. 1963).

con·cept (kon′sept), *n.* **1.** a general notion or idea; conception. **2.** an idea of something formed by mentally combining all its characteristics or particulars; a construct. [< L *concept(um)* something conceived, orig. neut. of *conceptus* (ptp. of *concipere*) = *con-* CON- + *cep-* (var. s. of *-cipere*, comb. form of *capere* to seize) + *-tus* ptp. ending]

con·cep·ta·cle (kən sep′tə kəl), *n.* *Biol.* an organ or cavity enclosing reproductive bodies. [< L *conceptāculum* = *concept(us)* conceived (see CONCEPT) + *āculum;* see RECEPTACLE] —**con·cep·tac·u·lar** (kon′sep tak′yə lər), *adj.*

con·cep·tion (kən sep′shən), *n.* **1.** the act of conceiving. **2.** the state of being conceived. **3.** fertilization; inception of pregnancy. **4.** origination or beginning. **5.** something that is conceived: *That machine is the conception of a genius.* **6.** the act or power of forming notions, ideas, or concepts. **7.** a notion, idea, or concept. **8.** a design or plan. [ME *concepcion* < eccl. L *conceptiōn-* (s. of *conceptiō*). See CONCEPT, -ION] —**con·cep′tion·al,** *adj.* —**con·cep′tive,** *adj.* —**Syn. 6.** See **idea.**

con·cep·tu·al (kən sep′cho͞o əl), *adj.* pertaining to concepts or to the forming of concepts. [< ML *conceptuāl(is).* See CONCEPT, -AL¹] —**con·cep′tu·al·ly,** *adv.*

con·cep·tu·al·ise (kən sep′cho͞o ə līz′), *v.t.*, *v.i.*, **-ised, -is·ing.** *Chiefly Brit.* conceptualize.

con·cep·tu·al·ism (kən sep′cho͞o ə liz′əm), *n.* *Philos.* any of several doctrines existing as a compromise between realism and nominalism and regarding universals as concepts. Cf. **nominalism, realism** (def. 5a). —**con·cep′tu·al·ist,** *n.* —**con·cep′tu·al·is′tic,** *adj.*

con·cep·tu·al·ize (kən sep′cho͞o ə līz′), *v.*, **-ized, -iz·ing.** —*v.t.* **1.** to form into a concept; make a concept of. —*v.i.* **2.** to form a concept; think in concepts.

con·cern (kən sûrn′), *v.t.* **1.** to relate to; be connected with; be of interest or importance to; affect: *The water shortage concerns us all.* **2.** to interest, engage, or involve (used reflexively or in the passive, often fol. by *with* or *in*): *He concerns himself with trivialities.* **3.** to trouble, worry, or disquiet: *I am concerned about his health.* —*n.* **4.** something that relates or pertains to a person; business; affair. **5.** a matter that engages a person's attention, interest, or care, or that affects his welfare or happiness. **6.** worry, solicitude, or anxiety: *to show concern for someone in trouble.* **7.** important relation or bearing: *This news is of concern to the issue under consideration.* **8.** a commercial or manufacturing company or establishment: *the headquarters of an insurance concern.* [late ME *conserne* to distinguish < LL *concern(ere)* < L *con-* CON- + *cernere* to separate, sift]
—**Syn. 1.** touch, involve. **3.** disturb. **5.** burden, responsibility. CONCERN, CARE, WORRY connote an uneasy and burdened state of mind. CONCERN implies an anxious sense of interest in, or responsibility for, something: *concern over a friend's misfortune.* CARE suggests a heaviness of spirit caused by dread, or by the constant pressure of burdensome demands: *Poverty weighs a person down with care.* WORRY is an active state of agitated uneasiness and restless apprehension: *He was distracted by worry over the stock market.* **8.** firm, house. —**Ant. 6.** indifference.

con·cerned (kən sûrnd′), *adj.* **1.** interested or participating: *all concerned citizens.* **2.** troubled or anxious: *a concerned look.* —**con·cern·ed·ly** (kən sûr′nid lē′), *adv.* —**con·cern′ed·ness,** *n.*

con·cern·ing (kən sûr′ning), *prep.* relating to; regarding; about: *a discussion concerning foreign aid.* [late ME]

con·cern·ment (kən sûrn′mənt), *n.* *Archaic.* **1.** importance or moment: *a matter of concernment to all voters.* **2.** relation or bearing. **3.** anxiety or solicitude. **4.** a thing in which a person is involved or interested. **5.** interest; participation; involvement.

con·cert (*n.*, *adj.* kon′sûrt, -sərt; *v.* kən sûrt′), *n.* **1.** a public musical performance in which several singers or players, or both, participate. **2.** recital. **3.** agreement of two or more individuals in a design or plan; combined action; accord or harmony. **4. in concert,** together; jointly: *The thief and the insured acted in concert.* —*adj.* **5.** designed or intended for concerts: *concert hall.* **6.** performed at concerts: *concert music.* **7.** performing or capable of performing at concerts: *a concert pianist.* —*v.t.* **8.** to contrive or arrange by agreement: *They were able to concert their differences.* **9.** to plan or devise. —*v.i.* **10.** to plan or act together. [(v.) < F *concert(er)* < It *concertare* < LL: to decide together (in L: to contend) = L *con-* CON- + *certāre* to decide by debate or warfare < *certus* settled, certain; (n.) < F < It *concerto*]

con·cert·ed (kən sûr′tid), *adj.* **1.** contrived or arranged by agreement; planned or devised together. **2.** done or performed together or in cooperation. **3.** *Music.* arranged in parts for several voices or instruments. —**con·cert′ed·ly,** *adv.*

con·cer·ti·na (kon′sər tē′nə), *n.* a small musical instrument somewhat resembling an accordion but having buttonlike keys, hexagonal bellows and ends, and more limited range. [CONCERT + *-ina* fem. of L *-īnus* -INE¹]

Concertina

con·cer·ti·no (kon′chər tē′nō; *It.* kôn′cher tē′nô), *n.*, *pl.* **-ni** (-nē). *Music.* **1.** a short concerto. **2.** the group of solo instruments in a concerto grosso. [< It = *concert(o)* (see CONCERTO) + *-ino* dim. suffix]

con·cert·ise (kon′sər tīz′), *v.i.*, **-ised, -is·ing.** *Chiefly Brit.* concertize.

con·cert·ize (kon′sər tīz′), *v.i.*, **-ized, -iz·ing.** to give concerts or recitals professionally, esp. while on tour.

con·cert·mas·ter (kon′sərt mas′tər, -mä′stər), *n.* the leader of the first violins in a symphony orchestra, usually the assistant to the conductor. [< G *Konzertmeister*]

con·cer·to (kən cher′tō; *It.* kôn cher′tô), *n.*, *pl.* **-tos,** *It.* **-ti** (-tē). *Music.* a composition for one or more instruments with orchestral accompaniment. [< It: CONCERT]

con·cer·to gros·so (kən cher′tō grō′sō; *It.* kôn cher′tô grôs′sô), *pl.* **con·cer·ti gros·si** (kən cher′tē grō′sē; *It.* kôn cher′tē grôs′sē), **con·cer·to gros·sos.** a musical composition for a group of solists, as a string quartet, and orchestral accompaniment. [< It: lit., big concert; see GROSS]

con′cert pitch′, *Music.* the pitch used in tuning instruments for concert performance; philharmonic pitch or international pitch.

con·ces·sion (kən sesh′ən), *n.* **1.** the act of conceding or yielding, as a right, a point in an argument, etc. **2.** the thing or point yielded. **3.** something conceded by a government or a controlling authority, as a grant of land, a privilege, or a franchise. **4.** *U.S.* a space or privilege within certain premises for a subsidiary business or service: *the checkroom concession at a restaurant.* [< L *concessiōn-* (s. of *concessiō*) = *concess-(us)*, (ptp. of *concēdere* to CONCEDE) + *-iōn-* -ION]

con·ces·sion·aire (kən sesh′ə nâr′), *n.* **1.** a person who holds a concession, grant, etc. **2.** *U.S.* a person or company to whom a concession has been granted to operate a subsidiary business or service. Also, **con·ces·sion·er** (kən sesh′ə nər). [< F *concessionnaire* CONCESSIONARY]

con·ces·sion·ar·y (kən sesh′ə ner′ē), *adj., n., pl.* **-ar·ies.** —*adj.* **1.** pertaining to concession; of the nature of a concession: *concessionary agreements.* —*n.* **2.** a concessionaire.

con·ces·sive (kən ses′iv), *adj.* **1.** tending or serving to concede. **2.** *Gram.* expressing concession, as the English conjunction *though.* [< LL *concessīv(us).* See CONCESSION, -IVE]

conch (kongk, konch), *n., pl.* **conchs** (kongks), **con·ches** (kon′chiz). **1.** the spiral shell of a gastropod, often used as a horn. **2.** any of various marine gastropods. **3.** the fabled shell trumpet of the Tritons. [ME < L *concha* < Gk *konchē* mussel, shell]

Conch (def. 2), *Strombus alatus* (Length 3 to 4 in.)

con·cha (kong′kə), *n., pl.* **-chae** (-kē). *Anat.* **1.** a shell-like structure, esp. the external ear. **2.** any turbinate bone, esp. in the nose. [< L: CONCH] —**con′chal,** *adj.*

con·chif·er·ous (kong kif′ər əs), *adj.* having a shell.

con·chi·o·lin (kong kī′ə lin), *n. Biochem.* an albuminoid, $C_{30}H_{48}O_{11}N_9$, that serves to form a matrix in the shells of mollusks. [CONCH + -I- + *-ol* (< L *-olus* dim. suffix) + -IN[2]]

Con·cho·bar (kong′kō wər, kon′ə hōōr′, kon′ōōr), *n. Irish Legend.* a king of Ulster, the uncle of Cuchulainn and the abductor of Deirdre.

con·choid (kong′koid), *n. Geom.* a plane curve such that if a straight line is drawn from a certain fixed point, called the pole of the curve, to the curve, the part of the line intersected between the curve and its asymptote is always equal to a fixed distance. Equation: $r = b \pm a \sec \theta$. [< Gk *konchoeid(ēs).* See CONCH, -OID]

Conchoid

con·choi·dal (kong koid′əl), *adj. Mineral.* noting a shell-like fracture form produced on certain minerals by a blow.

con·chol·o·gy (kong kol′ə jē), *n.* the branch of zoology dealing with the shells of mollusks. —**con·cho·log·i·cal** (kong′kə loj′i kəl), *adj.* —**con·chol′o·gist,** *n.*

con·cierge (kon′sē ârzh′; *Fr.* kôn syerzh′), *n., pl.* **-cierges** (-sē âr′zhiz; *Fr.* -syerzh′). (esp. in France) a person who has charge of the entrance of a building; a janitor or doorkeeper. [< F; OF *cumserges* < L *con-* CON- + *serviēns,* prp. of *servīre* to SERVE]

con·cil·i·ar (kən sil′ē ər), *adj.* of, pertaining to, or issued by an ecclesiastical council. [< L *concili(um)* COUNCIL + -AR[1]] —**con·cil′i·ar·ly,** *adv.*

con·cil·i·ate (kən sil′ē āt′), *v.t.,* **-at·ed, -at·ing. 1.** to overcome the distrust or hostility of; placate; win over. **2.** to win or gain (regard or favor). **3.** to make compatible; reconcile. [< L *conciliāt(us)* (ptp. of *conciliāre* to bring together, unite). See COUNCIL, -ATE[1]] —**con·cil′i·a′tion,** *n.*

con·cil·i·a·tor (kən sil′ē ā′tər), *n.* **1.** a person who conciliates. **2.** arbitrator. [< L *conciliātor*]

con·cil·i·a·to·ry (kən sil′ē ə tōr′ē, -tôr′ē), *adj.* tending to conciliate: *a conciliatory manner.* Also, **con·cil·i·a·tive** (kən sil′ē ā′tiv, -ə tiv, -sil′yə-). —**con·cil′i·a·to′ri·ly,** *adv.* —**con·cil′i·a·to′ri·ness,** *n.*

con·cin·ni·ty (kən sin′i tē), *n., pl.* **-ties.** *Rhet.* **1.** a close harmony of tone as well as logic among the elements of a discourse. **2.** an instance of this harmony. [< L *concinnitās* < *concinn(us)* well put together (*con-* CON- + *cinnus* a mixed drink) + *-itās* -ITY] —**con·cin′nous,** *adj.*

con·cise (kən sīs′), *adj.* expressing or covering much in few words; succinct; terse. [< L *concīs(us)* cut short (ptp. of *concīdere*) = *con-* CON- + *-cīd-* (comb. s. of *caedere* to cut) + *-tus* ptp. ending] —**con·cise′ly,** *adv.* —**Syn.** pithy, compendious, laconic.

con·cise·ness (kən sīs′nis), *n.* the quality of being concise.

con·ci·sion (kən sizh′ən), *n.* **1.** concise quality; brevity; terseness. **2.** *Obs.* a cutting up or off; mutilation. [< L *concīsiōn-* (s. of *concīsiō*). See CONCISE, -ION]

con·clave (kon′klāv, kong′-), *n.* **1.** a private or secret meeting. **2.** the place in which the cardinals of the Roman Catholic Church meet in private for the election of a pope. **3.** the assembly or meeting of the cardinals for the election of a pope. **4.** the College of Cardinals. [late ME < ML, L, repr. (*camera*) *cum clāve* (room) with key. See CON-, CLEF]

con·clude (kən klōōd′), *v.,* **-clud·ed, -clud·ing.** —*v.t.* **1.** to bring to an end; finish or terminate. **2.** to say in conclusion. **3.** to bring to a decision or settlement: *to conclude a treaty.* **4.** to determine by reasoning; deduce or infer. **5.** to decide, determine, or resolve. **6.** *Obs.* **a.** to shut up or enclose. **b.** to restrict or confine. —*v.i.* **7.** to come to an end; finish. **8.** to arrive at an opinion or judgment; decide. [ME < L *conclūde(re)* (to) close, to end an argument = *con-* CON- + *-clūdere,* var. of *claudere* to close] —**con·clud′er,** *n.*

con·clu·sion (kən klōō′zhən), *n.* **1.** the end or close; final part. **2.** the last main division of a discourse, usually containing a summation and a statement of opinion or decisions reached. **3.** a result, issue, or outcome. **4.** final settlement or arrangement. **5.** final decision: *The judge has reached his conclusion.* **6.** a reasoned deduction or inference. **7.** *Logic.* a proposition derived by deduction or inference from the premises of an argument. **8.** *Law.* the end of a pleading or conveyance. **9.** *Gram.* apodosis. [ME < L *conclūsiōn-* (s. of *conclūsiō*) = *conclūs(us)* closed (ptp. of *conclūdere* to CONCLUDE) + *-iōn-* -ION] —**Syn. 1.** termination. See **end.**

con·clu·sive (kən klōō′siv), *adj.* **1.** serving to settle or decide a question; decisive: *conclusive evidence.* **2.** tending to terminate; closing. [< LL *conclūsīv(us)* = L *conclūs(us)* (ptp of *conclūdere* to CONCLUDE) + *-īvus* -IVE] —**con·clu′sive·ly,** *adv.* —**con·clu′sive·ness,** *n.* —**Syn. 1.** definitive.

con·coct (kon kokt′, kən-), *v.t.* **1.** to prepare or make by combining ingredients, as in cookery: *to concoct a meal from leftovers.* **2.** to devise or contrive: *to concoct an excuse.* [< L *concoct(us)* (ptp. of *concoquere* to cook together) = *con-* CON- + *coc-,* s. of *coquere* to boil, cook (akin to Gk *péptein;* see PEPSIN, PEPTIC) + *-tus* ptp. ending]

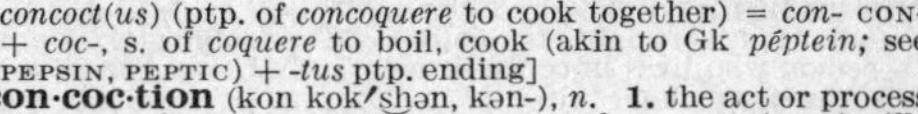

con·coc·tion (kon kok′shən, kən-), *n.* **1.** the act or process of concocting. **2.** something concocted: *a concoction of milk, egg, and lemon.* [< L *concoctiōn-* (s. of *concoctiō*) digestion]

con·com·i·tance (kən kom′i təns), *n.* **1.** the quality or relation of being concomitant. **2.** concomitant (def. 2). [< ML *concomitantia.* See CONCOMITANT, -ANCE]

con·com·i·tant (kon kom′i tᵊnt, kən-), *adj.* **1.** existing or occurring with something else, often in a lesser way; accompanying; concurrent: *an event and its concomitant circumstances.* —*n.* **2.** a concomitant quality, circumstance, or thing. [< L *concomitant-* (s. of *concomitāns,* prp. of *concomitārī*) = *con-* CON- + *comit-* (s. of *comes* companion = *com-* COM- + *e-* (var. of *i-,* s. of *ire* to go) + *-s* nom. sing. ending) + *-ant-* -ANT] —**con·com′i·tant·ly,** *adv.*

con·cord (kon′kôrd, kong′-), *n.* **1.** agreement between persons; accord. **2.** agreement between things; mutual fitness; harmony. **3.** *Gram.* agreement (def. 6). **4.** peace or amity. **5.** a treaty, compact, or covenant. **6.** *Music.* a stable combination of tones; a chord requiring no resolution. [ME *concorde* < OF < L *concord(ia)* = *concord-* (s. of *concors*) harmonious (*con-* CON- + *cord-,* s. of *cors* heart) + *-ia* -IA]

Con·cord (kong′kərd), *n.* **1.** a city in E Massachusetts, NW of Boston: second battle of the Revolution fought here April 19, 1775. 6148 (1970). **2.** a city in and the capital of New Hampshire, in the S part. 30,022 (1970). **3.** a city in W California, near San Francisco. 85,164 (1970).

con·cord·ance (kon kôr′dᵊns, kən-), *n.* **1.** agreement, concord, or harmony. **2.** an alphabetical index of the principal words of a book, as of the Bible, with a reference to the passage in which each occurs and usually some part of the context. **3.** an alphabetical index of subjects or topics. [late ME *concordaunce* < AF = MF *concordance* < ML *concordantia.* See CONCORD, -ANCE]

con·cord·ant (kon kôr′dᵊnt, kən-), *adj.* agreeing; harmonious. [late ME *concordaunt* < AF; MF *concordant.* See CONCORD, -ANT] —**con·cord′ant·ly,** *adv.*

con·cor·dat (kon kôr′dat), *n.* **1.** an official agreement or compact. **2.** an agreement between the pope and a secular government regarding ecclesiastical matters. [< F; r. *concordate* < ML *concordāt(um)* < L, neut. of *concordātus,* ptp. of *concordāre* to be agreed. See CONCORD, -ATE[1]] —**con·cor·da·to·ry** (kon kôr′də tōr′ē, -tôr′ē), *adj.*

Con·corde (kong′kôrd, kon kôrd′, kong-), *n. Trademark.* a supersonic, passenger-carrying airplane designed, manufactured, and operated as a joint British-French venture. [< F: concord, harmony]

Con′cord grape′ (kong′kərd, kon′kôrd), **1.** a large, dark-blue grape grown for table use. **2.** the vine bearing this fruit, grown in the eastern U.S.

con·course (kon′kōrs, -kôrs, kong′-), *n.* **1.** an assemblage; gathering; throng. **2.** a driveway or promenade, esp. in a park. **3.** a boulevard or other broad thoroughfare. **4.** a large open space for accommodating crowds, as in a railroad station. **5.** an area or grounds for racing, athletic sports, etc. **6.** a coming together; confluence: *a concourse of events.* [late ME *concours* < MF; r. ME *concurs* < L *concurs(us)* assembly, n. use of ptp. of *concurrere* to run together]

con·cres·cence (kon kres′əns), *n.* **1.** a growing together, as of parts, cells, etc.; coalescence. **2.** *Embryol.* the moving and growing together of the lips of the blastopore to form the body of the embryo. [< L *concrēscentia* = *concrēscent-* (s. of *concrēscēns,* prp. of *concrēscere*) + *-ia* -IA; see -ENCE]

con·crete (kon′krēt, kong′-, kon krēt′ *for 1-10, 13;* kon-krēt′ *for 11, 12*), *adj., n., v.,* **-cret·ed, -cret·ing.** —*adj.* **1.** constituting an actual thing or instance; real: *a concrete proof of his sincerity.* **2.** pertaining to realities or actual instances; particular (opposed to *general*): *concrete ideas.* **3.** representing or applied to an actual substance or thing, as contrasted to an abstract quality. **4.** made of concrete. **5.** formed by coalescence of separate particles into a mass; solid. —*n.* **6.** a concrete idea or term; a word or notion having an actual or existent thing or instance as its referent. **7.** a mass formed by coalescence or concretion of particles of matter. **8.** a stonelike building material, made by mixing cement and various aggregates, as sand or gravel, with water and allowing the mixture to harden. Cf. **reinforced concrete. 9.** any of various other artificial building or paving materials, as those containing tar. —*v.t.* **10.** to treat or lay with concrete. **11.** to form into a mass by coalescence of particles; render solid. **12.** to concretize (something). —*v.i.* **13.** to coalesce into a mass; become solid; harden. **14.** to use or apply concrete. [< L *concrēt(us)* (ptp. of *concrēscere* to grow together) = *con-* CON- + *crē-* (s. of *crēscere* to grow, increase) + *-tus* ptp. ending] —**con·crete′ly,** *adv.* —**con·crete′ness,** *n.* —**con·cre′tive,** *adj.* —**con·cre′tive·ly,** *adv.* —**Ant. 1, 2.** abstract.

con′crete mu′sic. See **musique concrète.**

con′crete noun′, *Gram.* a noun that denotes something material and nonabstract. Cf. **abstract noun.**

con′crete num′ber, *Arith.* a number that relates to a particular object or thing.

con′crete po′etry, poetry in which effects are created by the physical arrangement of words in patterns or forms rather than by the use of traditional language structure.

con·cre·tion (kon krē′shən, kən-), *n.* **1.** the act or process of concretizing or becoming substantial. **2.** a solid mass formed by or as by coalescence or cohesion. **3.** anything that is made real, tangible, or particular. **4.** *Pathol.* a solid or calcified mass in the body formed by a disease process. **5.** *Geol.* a rounded mass of mineral matter occurring in sandstone, clay, etc., often in concentric layers about a nucleus. [< L *concrētiōn-* (s. of *concrētiō*). See CONCRETE, -ION]

con·cre·tion·ar·y (kon krē′shə ner′ē), *adj.* formed by concretion; consisting of concreted matter or masses.

con·cret·ism (kon′krēt′izəm), *n.* the theory or practice of concrete poetry. —**con′cret′ist,** *n.*

con·cre·tize (kon′kri tīz′, kong′-; kon krē′tīz, kən-), *v.t.,* **-tized, -tiz·ing.** to make concrete, real, or particular; give tangible or definite form to. —**con·cret′i·za′tion,** *n.*

con·cu·bi·nage (kon kyōō′bə nij), *n.* **1.** cohabitation without legal marriage. **2.** the state of being a concubine.

con·cu·bi·nar·y (kon kyo͞o′bə ner′ē), *adj., n., pl.* **-nar·ies.** —*adj.* **1.** of, pertaining to, or living in concubinage. —*n.* **2.** a person who lives in concubinage. [< ML *concubīnāri(us)*]

con·cu·bine (koŋ′kyə bīn′, kon′-), *n.* **1.** a woman who cohabits with a man to whom she is not married. **2.** (among polygamous peoples) a secondary wife. [ME < L *concubīn(a)* = *concub-* (var. s. of *concumbere* to lie together; see CON-, INCUMBENT) + *-ina* fem. suffix]

con·cu·pis·cence (kon kyo͞o′pi səns), *n.* **1.** ardent, usually sensuous longing. **2.** sexual desire; lust. [ME < eccl. L *concupiscentia.* See CONCUPISCENT, -ENCE]

con·cu·pis·cent (kon kyo͞o′pi sənt), *adj.* **1.** lustful or sensual. **2.** eagerly desirous. [< L *concupiscent-* (s. of *concupiscēns,* prp. of *concupiscere* to desire greatly) = *con-* CON- + *cup-* (s. of *cupere* to desire) + *-iscent-,* var. of *-ēscent-* -ESCENT]

con·cur (kən kûr′), *v.i.,* **-curred, -cur·ring. 1.** to accord in opinion; agree. **2.** to cooperate; work together; combine: *Members of both parties concurred in urging passage of the bill.* **3.** to coincide; occur simultaneously: *His graduation day concurred with his birthday.* **4.** *Obs.* to run or come together; converge. [late ME < L *concurr(ere)* (to) run together, meet (LL: to agree with) = *con-* CON- + *currere* to run] —**con·cur′ring·ly,** *adv.* —**Syn. 1.** See **agree.**

con·cur·rence (kən kûr′əns, -kur′-), *n.* **1.** the act of concurring. **2.** accordance in opinion; agreement. **3.** cooperation, as of agents or causes; combined action or effort. **4.** simultaneous occurrence; coincidence: *The concurrence of several unusual events produced a good news story.* **5.** *Geom.* a point that is in three or more lines simultaneously. **6.** *Law.* a power equally held or a claim shared equally. Also, **con·cur′ren·cy** (for defs. 1–4). [< ML *concurrentia*]

con·cur·rent (kən kûr′ənt, -kur′-), *adj.* **1.** occurring or existing at the same time or side by side. **2.** acting in conjunction. **3.** having equal authority or jurisdiction. **4.** accordant or agreeing. **5.** tending to or intersecting at the same point: *four concurrent lines.* —*n.* **6.** something joint or contributory. **7.** *Archaic.* a rival or competitor. [< L *concurrent-* (s. of *concurrēns,* prp. of *concurrere* to CONCUR); see CON-, CURRENT; r. late ME *concurrant* < MF] —**con·cur′rent·ly,** *adv.*

concur′rent resolu′tion, a resolution adopted by both branches of a legislative assembly that does not require the signature of the chief executive.

con·cus·sion (kən kush′ən), *n.* **1.** the act of shaking or shocking, as by a blow. **2.** shock caused by the impact of a collision, blow, etc. **3.** *Pathol.* jarring of the brain, spinal cord, etc., from a blow, fall, or the like. [late ME < L *concussiōn-* (s. of *concussiō*) a shaking = *concuss(us),* ptp. of *concutere* (*con-* CON- + *cut-,* var. of *quat-,* s. of *quatere* to shake + *-tus* ptp. ending) + *-iōn-* -ION] —**con·cus′sion·al, con·cus·sant** (kən kus′ənt), *adj.* —**con·cus′sive,** *adj.*

cond., 1. condenser. **2.** conditional. **3.** conductor.

Con·dé (kôN dā′), *n.* **Louis II de Bour·bon** (lwē, də bo͞or-bôN′), **Prince de** (*Duc d'Enghien*) ("*the Great Condé*"), 1621–86, French general.

con·demn (kən dem′), *v.t.* **1.** to pronounce adverse judgment on; express strong disapproval of. **2.** to give grounds or reason for convicting or for censure: *His very looks condemn him.* **3.** to pronounce guilty or sentence to punishment: *to condemn a murderer to life imprisonment.* **4.** to judge or pronounce to be unfit for use or service: *The old ship was condemned and sold for scrap.* **5.** to declare incurable. **6.** to force into a specific state or activity: *His amiability condemns him to being a constant listener to others' troubles.* **7.** *Law U.S.* to acquire ownership of for a public purpose, under the right of eminent domain: *The city condemned the property.* [ME *condempn(en)* < OF *condem(p)ne(r)* < L *condem(p)nāre.* See CON-, DAMN] —**con·dem·na·ble** (kən dem′nə bəl), *adj.* —**con·dem′na·bly,** *adv.* —**con·demn′ing·ly,** *adv.* —**Syn. 1.** See **blame.**

con·dem·na·tion (kon′dem nā′shən, -dəm-), *n.* **1.** the act of condemning. **2.** the state of being condemned. **3.** strong censure; disapprobation; reproof. **4.** a cause or reason for condemning. **5.** *Law U.S.* the seizure, as of property, for public use. [late ME *condempnacioun* < LL *condemnātiōn-* (s. of *condemnātiō*)] —**con·dem·na·to·ry** (kən dem′nə-tôr′ē, -tōr′ē), *adj.*

con·den·sate (kən den′sāt), *n.* something formed by condensation, as a liquid reduced from a gas or vapor. [< L *condēnsāt(us)* (ptp. of *condēnsāre* to CONDENSE); see -ATE[1]]

con·den·sa·tion (kon′den sā′shən, -dən-), *n.* **1.** the act of condensing. **2.** the state of being condensed. **3.** a condensed form, as of a book or statement; abridgment. **4.** a condensed mass. **5.** the act or process of reducing a gas or vapor to a liquid or solid form. **6.** *Chem.* a reaction between two or more organic molecules leading to the formation of a larger molecule and the elimination of a simple molecule such as water or alcohol. **7.** *Psychoanal.* the representation of two or more ideas, memories, or impulses by one word or image, as in a person's humor, accidental slips, and dreams. [< LL *condēnsātiōn-* (s. of *condēnsātiō*)] —**con′den·sa′tion·al,** *adj.* —**con′den·sa′tive,** *adj.*

condensa′tion trail′, contrail.

con·dense (kən dens′), *v.,* **-densed, -dens·ing.** —*v.t.* **1.** to make more dense or compact; reduce the volume or extent of. **2.** to shorten; make concise, as a book; abridge. **3.** to reduce to another and denser form, as a gas or vapor to a liquid or solid state. —*v.i.* **4.** to become denser or more compact. **5.** to become liquid or solid, as a gas or vapor. [ME *condense(n)* < MF *condense(r)* < L *condēnsāre* = *con-* CON- + *dēnsāre* (*dēns(us)* DENSE + *-āre* inf. ending)] —**con·den′sa·bil′i·ty, con·den′si·bil′i·ty,** *n.* —**con·den′sa·ble, con·den′si·ble,** *adj.* —**Syn. 1.** compress, concentrate, consolidate. **2.** digest, epitomize, abstract, abbreviate. See **contract.**

condensed′ milk′, whole milk reduced by evaporation to a thick consistency, with sugar added.

con·dens·er (kən den′sər), *n.* **1.** a person or thing that condenses. **2.** any device for reducing gases or vapors to liquid or solid form. **3.** *Optics.* a lens or combination of lenses that gathers and concentrates light in a specified direction. **4.** *Elect.* capacitor.

con·de·scend (kon′di send′), *v.i.* **1.** to waive superiority voluntarily and assume equality with an inferior. **2.** to stoop or deign to do something: *He condescended to accompany her.* **3.** to behave as if one is conscious of descending from a superior position, rank, or dignity. **4.** *Obs.* **a.** to yield. **b.** to assent. [ME *condescende* < LL *condēscende(re)* (see CON-, DESCEND); r. ME *condescendre* < MF] —**con′de·scend′er, con′de·scend′ent,** *n.*

con·de·scend·ing (kon′di sen′diŋ), *adj.* showing or implying a gracious or patronizing descent from dignity or superiority. —**con′de·scend′ing·ly,** *adv.*

con·de·scen·sion (kon′di sen′shən), *n.* **1.** an act or instance of condescending. **2.** voluntary assumption of equality with an inferior person. **3.** patronizing or condescending behavior. Also, **con·de·scend·ence** (kon′di sen′dəns). [< LL *condēscensiōn-* (s. of *condēscensiō*)] —**con·de·scen·sive** (kon′di sen′siv), *adj.* —**con′de·scen′sive·ly,** *adv.*

con·dign (kən dīn′), *adj.* (chiefly of punishment) well-deserved; fitting. [late ME *condigne* < MF < L *condign(us)* = *con-* CON- + *dignus* worthy] —**con·dign′ly,** *adv.*

Con·dil·lac (kôN dē yak′), *n.* **É·tienne Bon·not de** (ā-tyen′ bô nō′ də), 1715–80, French philosopher.

con·di·ment (kon′də mənt), *n.* something used to give additional flavor to food, as a mustard or spice. [late ME < MF < L *condīment(um)* spice = *condī(re)* (to) season + *-mentum* -MENT] —**con·di·men·tal** (kon′də men′tᵊl), *adj.*

con·di·tion (kən dish′ən), *n.* **1.** a particular mode of being of a person or thing; situation with respect to circumstances; existing state or case. **2.** state of health: *to be in grave condition.* **3.** social position: *in a lowly condition.* **4.** a restricting, limiting, or modifying circumstance: *It can happen only under certain conditions.* **5.** a circumstance indispensable to some result; prerequisite: *conditions of acceptance.* **6.** something demanded as an essential part of an agreement; provision; stipulation: *He accepted on one condition.* **7.** an abnormal state of part of the body; disorder: *a heart condition; a skin condition.* **8.** *Law.* **a.** a stipulation in an agreement that provides for a change consequent on the occurrence of a future event. **b.** the event itself. **9.** *U.S.* a requirement imposed on a college student who fails a course, permitting credit to be established by later performance. **10.** *Gram.* protasis. **11.** *Logic.* the antecedent of a conditional proposition. **12. on** or **upon condition that,** provided that; if. —*v.t.* **13.** to put in a fit or proper state. **14.** to accustom or inure: *conditioned to the cold.* **15.** to air-condition. **16.** to form or be a condition of; determine, limit, or restrict as a condition: *Her attitude will condition her success in the job.* **17.** *U.S.* **a.** to impose a condition on (a student). **b.** to receive a conditional grade in a course. **18.** to test (a commodity) to ascertain its condition. **19.** to make (something) a condition; stipulate. **20.** *Psychol.* to establish a conditioned response in (a subject). —*v.i.* **21.** to make conditions. [< L *conditiōn-,* earlier *condiciōn-* (s. of *condiciō*) arrangement = *con-* CON- + *dic-* say + *-iōn-* -ION; r. ME *condicioun* < AF] —**Syn. 1.** See **state. 6.** requirement, proviso.

con·di·tion·al (kən dish′ə nᵊl), *adj.* **1.** imposing, containing, or depending on a condition or conditions; not absolute: *conditional acceptance.* **2.** *Gram.* (of a sentence, clause, mood, or word) involving or expressing a condition, as by the first clause in the sentence *If it rains, he won't go.* **3.** *Logic.* **a.** (of a proposition) asserting that the existence or occurrence of one thing or event depends on the existence or occurrence of another thing or event; hypothetical. **b.** (of a syllogism) containing at least one conditional proposition as a premise. —*n.* **4.** *Gram.* (in certain languages) a mood, tense, or other category used in expressing conditions, often corresponding to an English verb preceded by *if.* Spanish *comería* "he would eat" is in the conditional. [< LL *condiciōnāl(is)* (see CONDITION, -AL[1]); r. ME *condicionel* < MF] —**con·di′tion·al′i·ty,** *n.* —**con·di′tion·al·ly,** *adv.* —**Syn. 1.** contingent.

con·di·tioned (kən dish′ənd), *adj.* **1.** existing under or subject to conditions. **2.** characterized by a predictable or consistent pattern of behavior or thought as a result of having been subjected to certain circumstances or conditions. **3.** *Psychol.* proceeding from or dependent on conditioning; learned; acquired: *conditioned behavior patterns.* Cf. **unconditioned** (def. 2). **4.** made suitable for a given purpose. **5.** accustomed; inured. **6.** air-conditioned. [late ME]

condi′tioned response′, *Psychol.* a response that becomes associated with a previously unrelated stimulus through repeated presentation of the stimulus to a subject at the same or almost the same time with a stimulus normally yielding the response. Also called **condi′tioned re′flex.**

con·di·tion·er (kən dish′ə nər), *n.* **1.** a person or thing that conditions. **2.** something added to another substance to increase its usability, as a water softener.

con·do (kon′dō), *n., pl.* **-dos.** *Informal.* condominium (defs. 2, 3).

con·dole (kən dōl′), *v.,* **-doled, -dol·ing.** —*v.i.* **1.** to express sympathy with a person who is in sorrow, grief, or pain. —*v.t.* **2.** *Obs.* to grieve with. [< LL *condol(ēre)* = *con-* CON- + *dolēre* to feel pain; akin to DOLOR] —**con·do·la·to·ry** (kən dō′lə tôr′ē, -tōr′ē), *adj.* —**con·dol′er,** *n.* —**con·dol′ing·ly,** *adv.*

con·do·lence (kən dō′ləns), *n.* expression of sympathy with a person who is suffering sorrow, misfortune, or grief. Also, **con·dole′ment.**

con do·lo·re (kon′ dᵊlôr′ā, dᵊlōr′ā, kōn′; *It.* kôn dô-lô′re), sorrowfully (used as a direction in music). [< It: lit., with sadness; see DOLOR]

con·dom (kon′dəm, kun′-), *n.* a thin sheath, usually of rubber, worn over the penis during sexual intercourse to prevent conception or venereal infection. Also called **prophylactic.** [named after an 18th-century English physician, said to have devised it]

con·do·min·i·um (kon′də min′ē əm), *n., pl.* **-ums. 1.** joint or concurrent dominion. **2.** an apartment house or complex in which the dwelling units are individually owned, each owner receiving a recordable deed enabling him to sell, mortgage, exchange, etc., his unit independent of the owners of the others in the building. **3.** a unit in such a building. **4.** *Internat. Law.* joint sovereignty over a territory by several states. [< NL; see CON-, DOMINION, -IUM]

con·do·na·tion (kon′dō nā′shən,) *n.* the act of condoning; the overlooking or implied forgiving of an offense. [< NL *condōnātiōn-* (s. of *condōnātiō*), L: a giving away = *condōnāt(us)* (ptp. of *condonare* to CONDONE) + *-iōn-* -ION]

con·done (kən dōn′), *v.t.*, **-doned, -don·ing.** **1.** to pardon, forgive, or overlook (something illegal, objectionable, or the like). **2.** to cause the condonation of. [< L *condōn(āre)* (to) grant, remit = *con-* CON- + *dōnare* to give; see DONATE] —**con·don′a·ble,** *adj.* —**con·don′er,** *n.*

con·dor (kon′dər), *n.* either of two large, New World vultures of the family *Cathartidae, Gymnogyps californianus* or *Vultur gryphus:* the largest flying birds in the Western Hemisphere. [< Sp < Quechuan *kuntur*]

Condor, *Gymnogyps californianus* (Length 4 ft.; wingspread 10 ft.)

Con·dor·cet (kôɴ dôʀ se′), *n.* **Ma·rie Jean An·toine Ni·co·las Ca·ri·tat** (MA ʀē′ zhäɴ äɴ twAn′ nē kô lä′ KA ʀē tA′), **Marquis de,** 1743–94, French mathematician and philosopher.

con·dot·tie·re (kôn′də tyâr′ā; *It.* kôn′dôt tye′ʀe), *n., pl.* **-tie·ri** (-tyâr′ē; *It.* -tye′ʀē). **1.** a leader of a private band of mercenaries in Italy, esp. in the 14th and 15th centuries. **2.** a mercenary; soldier of fortune. [< It = *condott(o)* (< L *conductus* hireling soldier, lit., led; see CONDUCT) + *-iere* -IER]

con·duce (kən do͞os′, -dyo͞os′), *v.i.*, **-duced, -duc·ing.** to lead or contribute to a result (usually fol. by *to* or *toward*). [< L *condūce(re)* (to) lead, bring together = *con-* CON- + *dūcere* to lead, akin to *dux* (see DUKE) and to TOW[1], TUG] —**con·duc′i·ble,** *adj.* —**con·duc′i·ble·ness, con·duce′a·bil′i·ty,** *n.* —**con·duc′i·bly,** *adv.* —**con·duc′ing·ly,** *adv.*

con·du·cive (kən do͞o′siv, -dyo͞o′-), *adj.* contributive; helpful (usually fol. by *to*): *Good eating is conducive to good health.* —**con·du′cive·ness,** *n.*

con·duct (*n.* kon′dukt; *v.* kən dukt′), *n.* **1.** personal behavior; way of acting; deportment. **2.** direction or management; execution: *the conduct of a business.* **3.** the act of conducting; guidance; escort. **4.** *Obs.* a guide; an escort. —*v.t.* **5.** to behave or manage (oneself): *He conducted himself well.* **6.** to direct in action or course; manage; carry on: *to conduct a meeting.* **7.** to direct, as an orchestra. **8.** to lead or guide; escort. **9.** to serve as a channel or medium for (heat, electricity, sound, etc.): *Copper conducts electricity.* —*v.i.* **10.** to lead. **11.** to act as conductor, esp. of a musical group. [< LL *conduct(us)* escort, n. use of L *conductus* (ptp. of *condūcere* to CONDUCE) = *con-* CON- + *duc-* lead + *-tus* ptp. suffix; r. ME *conduyt(e)* < OF; see CONDUIT] —**con·duct′i·ble,** *adj.* —**con·duct′i·bil′i·ty,** *n.* —**Syn. 1.** comportment, bearing, manners. See **behavior. 2.** guidance, administration. **8.** See **guide.**

con·duct·ance (kən duk′təns), *n.* *Elect.* the ability of a conductor to transmit current; the reciprocal of the resistance. *Symbol:* G

con·duc·tion (kən duk′shən), *n.* **1.** the act of conducting, as of water through a pipe. **2.** *Physics.* **a.** the transfer of heat between two parts of a stationary system, caused by a temperature difference between the parts. **b.** conductivity. **3.** *Physiol.* the carrying of an impulse by a nerve or other tissue. [< L *conductiōn-* (s. of *conductiō*) a bringing together, a hiring] —**con·duc′tion·al,** *adj.*

con·duc·tive (kən duk′tiv), *adj.* having the property or capability of conducting. —**con·duc′tive·ly,** *adv.*

con·duc·tiv·i·ty (kon′duk tiv′i tē), *n., pl.* **-ties. 1.** *Physics.* the property or power of conducting heat, electricity, or sound. **2.** *Elect.* the ability of a given substance to conduct electric current; the reciprocal of resistance. *Symbol:* σ

con·duc·tor (kən duk′tər), *n.* **1.** a person who conducts; a leader, guide, director, or manager. **2.** a railroad employee in charge of a train and train crew. **3.** the driver or collector of fares on a bus, streetcar, or other public conveyance. **4.** a person who directs an orchestra or chorus. **5.** something that conducts. **6.** a substance or device that readily conducts heat, electricity, sound, etc. **7.** See **lightning rod.** [< L (see CONDUCT, -OR[2]); r. late ME *cond(u)itour* < AF, MF *conduiteur*] —**con·duc·to·ri·al** (kon′duk tōr′ē əl, -tôr′-), *adj.* —**con·duc′tor·less,** *adj.* —**con·duc′tor·ship′,** *n.*

con·duc·tress (kən duk′tris), *n.* a female conductor.

con·duit (kon′dwit, -do͞o it, -dyo͞o it, -dit), *n.* **1.** a pipe or natural channel for conveying water or other fluid. **2.** *Elect.* a pipe or tube for protecting electric wires. **3.** *Archaic.* a fountain. [ME < OF = ML *conductus* pipe channel, special use of L *conductus* (ptp.) led; see CONDUCT]

con·du·pli·cate (kon do͞o′plə kit, -dyo͞o′-), *adj.* *Bot.* (of a leaf in the bud) folded lengthwise with the upper face of the blade within. [< L *conduplicāt(us)* (ptp. of *conduplicāre* to double)] —**con·du′pli·ca′tion,** *n.*

con·dyle (kon′dīl, -dəl), *n.* *Anat.* a rounded protuberance on a bone, serving to form an articulation with another bone. [var. of *condyl* < L *condyl(us)* knuckle < Gk *kóndylos*] —**con′dy·lar,** *adj.*

con·dy·loid (kon′dəloid′), *adj.* of or like a condyle.

con·dy·lo·ma (kon′dəlō′mə), *n., pl.* **-mas, -ma·ta** (-mə tə). *Pathol.* a wartlike excrescence on the skin, usually in the region of the anus or genitals. [< NL < Gk *kondýlōma.* See CONDYLE, -OMA]

cone (kōn), *n., v.,* **coned, con·ing.** —*n.* **1.** *Geom.* a solid whose surface is generated by a line passing through a fixed point and a fixed plane curve not containing the point, consisting of two equal sections joined at a vertex. **2.** *Bot.* **a.** the more or less conical multiple fruit of the pine, fir, etc., consisting of imbricated or valvate scales bearing naked ovules or seeds; a strobile. **b.** a similar fruit, as in cycads, club mosses, etc. **3.** anything shaped like a cone: *sawdust piled up in a great cone.* **4.** *Anat.* one of the cone-shaped cells in the retina of the eye, sensitive to color and intensity of light. Cf. **rod** (def. 15). —*v.t.* **5.** to shape like a cone or the segment of a cone. [< L *cōn(us)* < Gk *kônos* pine cone, cone-shaped figure]

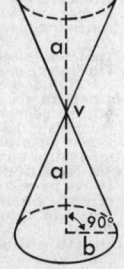

Cone (Right circular) a = Axis (altitude); b = Base; v = Vertex

cone·flow·er (kōn′flou′ər), *n.* **1.** any of several composite herbs of the genus *Rudbeckia,* having flowers usually with yellow rays and a brown or black disk. **2.** any of various allied plants.

Con·el·rad (kon′əl rad′), *n.* *U.S.* an arrangement of the civil-defense system whereby the usual radio and television broadcasts cease in the event of an air attack to prevent enemy planes or missiles from homing on radio frequencies, and brief emergency instructions are broadcast to the public over one or two special frequencies. [*con(trol of) el(ectromagnetic) rad(iation)*]

cone·nose (kōn′nōz′), *n.* any of several bloodsucking assassin bugs of the genus *Triatoma,* some of which inflict a painful bite and serve as vectors of Chagas' disease.

Con′es·to′ga wag′on (kon′i stō′gə, kon′-), a large, heavy, broad-wheeled covered wagon, used esp. in North America during the early westward migration. Also called **Con′es·to′ga.** [named after *Conestoga,* Pa., where it was first made]

co·ney (kō′nē, kun′ē), *n., pl.* **-neys. 1.** a serranid fish, *Cephalopholis fulva,* of the tropical Atlantic. **2.** cony.

Co′ney Is′land (kō′nē), a beach along the oceanfront in New York City, S of Brooklyn: seashore resort and amusement center. 5 mi. long.

conf., 1. compare. [< L *confer*] **2.** conference.

con·fab (kon′fab), *n., v.,* **-fabbed, -fab·bing.** *Informal.* —*n.* **1.** a confabulation. —*v.i.* **2.** to confabulate. [short form]

con·fab·u·late (kən fab′yə lāt′), *v.i.,* **-lat·ed, -lat·ing.** to converse informally; chat. [< L *confābulāt(us)* (ptp. of *confābulārī* to talk together). See CON-, FABLE, -ATE[1]] —**con·fab′u·la′tor,** *n.*

con·fab·u·la·tion (kən fab′yə lā′shən), *n.* **1.** the act of confabulating; conversation; discussion. **2.** *Psychiatry.* replacement of a gap in memory by a falsification that the subject accepts as correct. [ME < LL *confabulātiōn-* (s. of *confābulātiō*) conversation] —**con·fab·u·la·to·ry** (kən fab′yə lə tōr′ē, -tôr′ē), *adj.*

con·fect (*v.* kən fekt′; *n.* kon′fekt), *v.t.* **1.** to make up, compound, or prepare from ingredients or materials. **2.** to make into a preserve or confection. —*n.* **3.** a confection. [< L *confect(us)* (ptp. of *conficere* to produce, effect) = *con-* CON- + *fec-* (ptp. s. of *-ficere,* comb. form of *facere* to make) + *-tus* ptp. suffix]

con·fec·tion (kən fek′shən), *n.* **1.** the process of compounding, preparing, or making something. **2.** a sweet preparation of fruit or the like, as a preserve or candy. **3.** a piece of candy; bonbon. [ME < L *confectiōn-* (s. of *confectiō*) completion]

con·fec·tion·ar·y (kən fek′shə ner′ē), *n., pl.* **-ar·ies,** *adj.* —*n.* **1.** a place where confections are kept or made. **2.** a candy; sweetmeat. —*adj.* **3.** of or pertaining to confections or their production. [< ML *confectiōnāri(us)*]

con·fec·tion·er (kən fek′shə nər), *n.* a person who makes or sells candies and, sometimes, ice cream, cakes, etc.

confec′tioners' sug′ar, an extra-fine variety of powdered sugar, used in confections, etc.

con·fec·tion·er·y (kən fek′shə ner′ē), *n., pl.* **-er·ies. 1.** confections or sweetmeats collectively. **2.** the work or business of a confectioner. **3.** confectionary (def. 1).

con·fed·er·a·cy (kən fed′ər ə sē, -fed′rə sē), *n., pl.* **-cies. 1.** a union of persons, parties, states, etc., for some purpose; alliance. **2.** a combination of persons for unlawful purposes; conspiracy. **3. the Confederacy.** See **Confederate States of America.** [ME *confederacie,* alter. of LL *confoederātiō* CONFEDERATION; see -ACY]

con·fed·er·ate (*adj., n.* kən fed′ər it, -fed′rit; *v.* kən fed′ə rāt′), *adj., n., v.,* **-at·ed, -at·ing.** —*adj.* **1.** united in a league, alliance, or conspiracy. **2.** (*cap.*) of or pertaining to the Confederate States of America. —*n.* **3.** a person, group, nation, etc., united with others in a confederacy; ally. **4.** an accomplice, esp. in a mischievous or criminal act. **5.** (*cap.*) *U.S. Hist.* an adherent of the Confederate States of America. —*v.t., v.i.* **6.** to unite in a league, alliance, or a conspiracy. [ME *confederat* < LL *confoederāt(us)* (ptp. of *confoederāre* to unite in a league) = *con-* CON- + *foeder-* (s. of *foedus*) treaty + *-ātus* -ATE[1]]

Confed′erate States′ of Amer′ica, the group of 11 Southern states that seceded from the United States in 1860–61. Also called **the Confederacy.**

con·fed·er·a·tion (kən fed′ə rā′shən), *n.* **1.** the act of confederating. **2.** the state of being confederated. **3.** a league or alliance. **4.** a group of states more or less permanently united. **5. the Confederation,** the union of the 13 original states under the Articles of Confederation 1781–1789. [late ME < LL *confoederātiōn-* (s. of *confoederātiō*) an agreement] —**con·fed′er·a′tion·ism,** *n.* —**con·fed′er·a′tion·ist, con·fed·er·al·ist** (kən fed′ər ə list), *n.* —**con·fed·er·a·tive** (kən fed′ə rā′tiv, -ər ə tiv), *adj.* —**Syn. 3.** coalition, federation. See **alliance.**

con·fer (kən fûr′), *v.,* **-ferred, -fer·ring.** —*v.t.* **1.** to bestow upon as a gift, favor, honor, etc.: *to confer a degree on a graduate.* **2.** *Obs.* to compare. —*v.i.* **3.** to consult together; compare opinions; carry on a discussion or deliberation. [< L *confer(re)* (to) bring together, compare, consult with = *con-* CON- + *ferre* to bring] —**con·fer′ment, con·fer′ral,** *n.* —**con·fer′ra·ble,** *adj.* —**con·fer′rer,** *n.* —**Syn. 1.** See **give.**

con·fer·ee (kon′fə rē′), *n.* **1.** a person on whom something is conferred. **2.** *U.S.* a person, group, etc., that takes part in a conference. Also, **con′fer·ree′.**

con·fer·ence (kon′fər əns, -frəns), *n.* **1.** a meeting for consultation or discussion. **2.** *Govt.* a meeting, as of various committees, to settle disagreements between two legislative groups. **3.** *Eccles.* an official assembly of clergy or of clergy and laymen, customary in many Christian denominations. **4.** an association of athletic teams; league. [< ML *con-*

ferentia. See CONFER, -ENCE] —**con·fer·en·tial** (kon′fə ren′shəl), *adj.* —**Syn. 1.** interview, parley, colloquy.

con·fer·va (kon fûr′və), *n., pl.* **-vae** (-vē), **-vas.** any simple filamentous green alga. [< L: a certain water plant supposed to heal wounds, akin to *confervēre* to grow together, heal] —**con·fer′val, con·fer′vous,** *adj.* —**con·fer′va·like′,** *adj.* —**con·fer·void** (kon fûr′void), *adj., n.*

con·fess (kən fes′), *v.t.* **1.** to acknowledge or avow; reveal: *She confessed her secret.* **2.** to own or admit as true: *I must confess that I haven't read it.* **3.** to declare (one's sins), esp. to God or a priest in order to obtain absolution. **4.** (of a priest) to hear the confession of (a person). **5.** to acknowledge one's belief in; declare adherence to. **6.** *Archaic.* to reveal by circumstances. —*v.i.* **7.** to make confession; plead guilty; own (usually fol. by *to*). **8.** to make confession of sins, esp. to a priest. [ME *confess(en)* < MF *confesse(r)* < LL *confessāre* = L *confess(us)*, ptp. of *confitērī* (CON- + *fet-*, var. of *fat-* admit + *-tus* ptp. suffix) + *-āre* inf. suffix] —**con·fess′a·ble,** *adj.* —**con·fess′ing·ly,** *adv.* —**Syn. 1.** See **acknowledge. 2.** grant, concede.

con·fess·ed·ly (kən fes′id lē), *adv.* by confession or acknowledgment; admittedly.

con·fes·sion (kən fesh′ən), *n.* **1.** acknowledgment; avowal; admission. **2.** acknowledgment of sin, esp. to a priest to obtain absolution. **3.** something that is confessed. **4.** Also called **confes′sion of faith′.** a formal profession of religious belief and acceptance of church doctrines. **5.** the tomb of a martyr or confessor or the altar or shrine connected with it. [< L *confessiōn-* (s. of *confessiō*) (see CONFESS, -ION); r. ME *confessioun* < AF]

con·fes·sion·al (kən fesh′ə nəl), *adj.* **1.** of, pertaining to, or characteristic of confession. —*n.* **2.** the place set apart for the hearing of confessions by a priest. [< ML *confessiōnāle*, neut. of *confessiōnālis* (adj.)]

con·fes·sion·ar·y (kən fesh′ə ner′ē), *adj.* of or pertaining to confession, esp. auricular confession of sins. [< ML *confessiōnāri(us)*]

con·fes·sor (kən fes′ər), *n.* **1.** a person who confesses. **2.** a priest authorized to hear confessions. **3.** a person who confesses and adheres to the Christian religion in spite of persecution. **4. the Confessor.** See **Edward the Confessor.** Also, **con·fess′er.** [ME, OE (in pl: *confessores*) < LL]

con·fet·ti (kən fet′ē *for 1; It.* kōn fet′tē *for 2*), *n.pl., sing.* **-fet·to** (*It.* -fet′tô) for 2. **1.** (*construed as sing.*) small bits of colored paper for throwing to enhance the gaiety of a festive event, as at a parade, wedding, etc. **2.** confections; bonbons. [< It, pl. of *confetto* COMFIT]

con·fi·dant (kon′fi dant′, -dänt′, kon′fi dant′, -dänt′), *n.* a person to whom secrets are confided. [< F *confident* < It *confidente*, n. use of adj.; see CONFIDENT]

con·fi·dante (kon′fi dant′, -dänt′, kon′fi dant′, -dänt′), *n.* a female confidant. [< F *confidente*]

con·fide (kən fīd′), *v.,* **-fid·ed, -fid·ing.** —*v.i.* **1.** to have full trust; have faith. **2.** to impart secrets trustfully; discuss intimate problems (usually fol. by *in*): *She confides in no one.* —*v.t.* **3.** to tell in assurance of secrecy. **4.** to entrust; commit to the charge, knowledge, or good faith of another. [< L *confīde(re)* = *con-* CON- + *fīdere* to trust, akin to *foedus;* see CONFEDERATE] —**con·fid′er,** *n.*

con·fi·dence (kon′fi dəns), *n.* **1.** full trust; belief in the reliability of a person or thing. **2.** (esp. in European politics) the wish to retain an incumbent government in office, as shown by a vote of support. **3.** self-reliance, assurance, or boldness: *He acted immediately with admirable and justifiable confidence.* **4.** certitude; assurance. **5.** a confidential communication: *to exchange confidences.* **6.** *Archaic.* ground of trust. **7. in confidence,** as a secret or private matter, not to be divulged or communicated to others: *I told him in confidence.* [late ME < L *confīdenti(a)*] —**Syn. 1.** faith, reliance, dependence. See **trust. 3.** courage, intrepidity. CONFIDENCE, ASSURANCE both imply a faith in oneself. CONFIDENCE may imply trust in oneself or arrogant self-conceit. ASSURANCE implies even more sureness of oneself; this may be shown as undisturbed calm or as offensive boastfulness or headstrong conduct. —**Ant. 1.** mistrust.

con′fidence game′, any swindle technique in which the swindler, gaining the confidence of the victim, robs him by cheating at cards, appropriating funds entrusted for investment, or the like. Also called, *Brit.,* **con′fidence trick′;** *Informal,* **con game.**

con′fidence man′, a person who practices a confidence game; swindler. Also called, *Informal,* **con man.**

con·fi·dent (kon′fi dənt), *adj.* **1.** having strong belief or full assurance; sure. **2.** sure of oneself; bold: *a confident speaker.* **3.** excessively bold; presumptuous. **4.** *Obs.* trustful or confiding. —*n.* **5.** a confidant. [< L *confīdent-* (s. of *confīdēns*), prp. of *confīdere*] —**con′fi·dent·ly,** *adv.* —**Syn. 1.** certain, positive. See **sure.** —**Ant. 1.** modest.

con·fi·den·tial (kon′fi den′shəl), *adj.* **1.** imparted in confidence; secret: *a confidential remark.* **2.** indicating confidence or intimacy; imparting private matters: *a confidential tone of voice.* **3.** having another's confidence; entrusted with secrets or private affairs: *a confidential secretary.* **4.** *U.S. Govt., Mil.* (of information, a document, etc.) bearing the classification *confidential,* above *restricted* and below *secret.* [< L *confīdenti(a)* CONFIDENCE + -AL[1]] —**con′fi·den′ti·al′i·ty, con′fi·den′tial·ness,** *n.* —**con′fi·den′tial·ly,** *adv.* —**Syn. 1.** restricted, private. **2.** intimate, familiar. **3.** trusted, trustworthy, private. See **familiar.**

con·fid·ing (kən fī′ding), *adj.* trustful; credulous or unsuspicious. —**con·fid′ing·ly,** *adv.*

con·fig·u·ra·tion (kən fig′yə rā′shən), *n.* **1.** the relative disposition of the parts or elements of a thing. **2.** external form, as resulting from this; conformation. **3.** *Astron.* **a.** the relative position or aspect of heavenly bodies. **b.** a group of stars. **4.** *Physics, Chem.* the relative position in space of the atoms in a molecule. [< LL *configūrātiōn-* (s. of *configūrātiō*) = L *configūrāt(us)* shaped like its model, ptp. of *configūrāre* (see CON-, FIGURE, -ATE[1]) + *-iōn-* -ION] —**con·fig′u·ra′tion·al, con·fig·u·ra·tive** (kən fig′yər ə tiv, -yə rā′tiv), *adj.* —**con·fig′u·ra′tion·al·ly,** *adv.*

con·fig·u·ra·tion·ism (kən fig′yə rā′shə niz′əm), *n.* See **Gestalt psychology.** —**con·fig′u·ra′tion·ist,** *n.*

con·fine (kən fīn′ *for 1, 2, 4, 5b;* kon′fīn *for 3, 5a*), *v.,* **-fined, -fin·ing,** *n.* —*v.t.* **1.** to enclose within bounds; limit or restrict: *She confined her remarks to the subject at hand.* **2.** to shut or keep in; prevent from leaving a place because of imprisonment, illness, etc. —*n.* **3.** Usually, **confines.** a boundary or bound; border. **4.** *Archaic.* confinement. **5.** *Obs.* **a.** Often, **confines.** region; territory. **b.** a place of confinement; prison. [< ML *confīn(āre)* (to) border, bound = L *confīn(is)* bordering (see CON-, FINE[2]) + *-āre* inf. suffix] —**con·fin′a·ble, con·fine′a·ble,** *adj.* —**con·fine′less,** *adj.* —**con·fin′er,** *n.* —**Syn. 1.** circumscribe. —**Ant. 1, 2.** free.

con·fined (kən fīnd′), *adj.* **1.** enclosed; restricted; kept in. **2.** being in childbirth; being in parturition. —**con·fin·ed·ly** (kən fī′nid lē, -fīnd′lē), *adv.* —**con·fin′ed·ness,** *n.*

con·fine·ment (kən fīn′mənt), *n.* **1.** the act of confining. **2.** the state of being confined. **3.** the lying-in of a woman in childbed; childbirth. **4.** *Mil.* imprisonment while awaiting trial or as a punishment (distinguished from *arrest*).

con·firm (kən fûrm′), *v.t.* **1.** to establish the validity of; corroborate; verify: *This report confirms my suspicions.* **2.** to make valid or binding by some formal or legal act; sanction; ratify: *to confirm an agreement.* **3.** to make firm or more firm; strenghten: *His support confirmed my determination to run for mayor.* **4.** *Eccles.* to administer the rite of confirmation to. [< L *confirm(āre)* (see CON-, FIRM[1]); r. ME *confermen* < OF] —**con·firm′a·ble,** *adj.* —**con·firm′er;** *Law,* **con·fir·mor** (kon′fər môr′, kən fûr′mər), *n.* —**con·firm′ing·ly,** *adv.* —**Syn. 1.** prove, substantiate, authenticate, validate. **2.** fix. —**Ant. 1.** disprove. **2.** invalidate. **3.** shake.

con·fir·ma·tion (kon′fər mā′shən), *n.* **1.** the act of confirming. **2.** the state of being confirmed. **3.** something that confirms; corroboration; proof. **4.** a rite administered to a baptized person by which he is admitted to full communion with the church. **5.** a solemn ceremony among Reform and certain Conservative Jews to admit formally as adult members of the Jewish community Jewish boys and girls 14 to 16 years of age who have successfully completed a prescribed period or course of study in Judaism. [ME < L *confirmātiōn-* (s. of *confirmātiō*)]

con·firm·a·to·ry (kən fûr′mə tôr′ē, -tōr′ē), *adj.* serving to confirm; corroborative. Also, **con·firm′a·tive.** [< ML *confirmātōri(us)* = L *confirmāt(us)* (ptp. of *confirmāre* to CONFIRM) + *-ōrius* -ORY[1]]

con·firmed (kən fûrmd′), *adj.* **1.** made certain as to truth, accuracy, validity, etc. **2.** settled; ratified. **3.** firmly established in a habit or condition; inveterate: *a confirmed bachelor.* [ME *confermyd*] —**con·firm·ed·ly** (kən fur′mid lē), *adv.* —**con·firm·ed·ness** (kən fûr′mid nis, -fûrmd′-), *n.*

con·fis·ca·ble (kən fis′kə bəl, kon′fi skə bəl), *adj.* liable to be confiscated. [< L *confiscā(re)* (see CONFISCATE) + -BLE]

con·fis·cate (kon′fi skāt′, kən fis′kāt), *v.,* **-cat·ed, -cat·ing,** *adj.* —*v.t.* **1.** to seize as forfeited to the public domain; appropriate, by way of penalty, for public use. **2.** to seize by authority; appropriate summarily. —*adj.* **3.** seized. [< L *confiscāt(us)* (ptp. of *confiscāre* to seize for the public treasury) = *con-* CON- + *fisc(us)* basket, moneybag, public treasury + *-ātus* -ATE[1]] —**con′fis·ca′tion,** *n.* —**con′fis·ca′tor,** *n.*

con·fis·ca·to·ry (kən fis′kə tôr′ē, -tōr′ē), *adj.* characterized by, effecting, or resulting in confiscation.

Con·fit·e·or (kən fit′ē ôr′), *n.* *Rom. Cath. Ch.* the prayer in the form of a general confession said esp. at the beginning of the Mass. [after first word of Latin prayer: I confess]

con·fi·ture (kon′fi choor′), *n.* a confection; a preserve, as of fruit. [ME < MF]

con·fla·grant (kən flā′grənt), *adj.* blazing; burning; on fire. [< L *conflagrant-* (s. of *conflagrāns*), prp. of *conflagrāre.* See CONFLAGRATION, -ANT]

con·fla·gra·tion (kon′flə grā′shən), *n.* a large and destructive fire. [< L *conflagrātiōn-* (s. of *conflagrātiō*) = *conflagrāt(us)* burned up, ptp. of *conflagrāre* (*con-* CON- + *flagr-* (akin to *fulgur* lightning, *flamma* FLAME, Gk *phlóx,* see PHLOX) + *-ātus* -ATE[1]) + *-iōn-* -ION] —**con′fla·gra′tive,** *adj.* —**Syn.** See **flame.**

con·fla·tion (kən flā′shən), *n.* *Bibliog.* **1.** the combination of two variant texts into a new one. **2.** the text resulting from such a combination. [< L *conflātiōn-* (s. of *conflātiō*) a fusing together = *conflāt(us),* ptp. of *conflāre* (*con-* CON- + *flā-* (akin to BLOW[2]) + *-tus* ptp. suffix) + *-iōn-* -ION] —**conflate** (kən flāt′), *adj.*

con·flict (*v.* kən flikt′; *n.* kon′flikt), *v.i.* **1.** to come into collision or disagreement; be at variance or in opposition; clash. **2.** to contend; do battle. —*n.* **3.** a battle or struggle; strife. **4.** controversy; quarrel. **5.** antagonism or opposition between interests or principles: *a conflict of ideas.* **6.** a striking together; collision. **7.** incompatibility or interference, as of events or activities: *I have a conflict between French and music theory classes at that hour.* [< L *conflict(us)* a striking together, n. use of ptp. of *confligere* = *con-* CON- + *flic-* (var. s. of *flīgere* to strike) + *-tus* ptp. suffix] —**con·flict′ing·ly,** *adv.* —**con·flic′tion,** *n.* —**con·flic′tive, con·flic′to·ry,** *adj.* —**Syn. 1.** collide, oppose. **3.** encounter. See **fight. 5.** contention, variance. —**Ant. 4.** accord.

con′flict of in′terest, 1. the situation of a public office holder whose private financial interests might benefit from his official actions or political influence. **2.** the situation of a person who finds that one of his activities, interests, etc., can be forwarded only at the expense of another of them.

con·flu·ence (kon′floo əns), *n.* **1.** a flowing together of two or more streams. **2.** their place of junction. **3.** the body of water so formed. **4.** a coming together; concourse. **5.** a crowd or throng; assemblage. Also called **con·flux** (kon′fluks). [< LL *confluentia.* See CONFLUENT, -ENCE]

con·flu·ent (kon′floo ənt), *adj.* **1.** flowing together; blending into one: *confluent rivers.* **2.** *Pathol.* **a.** running together. **b.** characterized by confluent efflorescences. —*n.* **3.** a confluent stream. **4.** tributary. [< L *confluent-* (s. of *confluēns,* prp. of *confluere*) = *con-* CON- + *flu-* (s. of *fluere* to flow) + *-ent-* -ENT; see FLUENT, FLUID]

con·fo·cal (kon fō′kəl), *adj.* *Math.* having the same focus or foci.

con·form (kən fôrm′), *v.i.* **1.** to act in accord or harmony with a standard or norm; comply. **2.** to be or become similar in form or character. **3.** to comply with the usages of an established church, esp. the Church of England. —*v.t.* **4.** to make similar in form or character. **5.** to bring into correspondence or harmony. **—*adj.*** **6.** *Archaic.* conformable. [ME *confo(u)rme(n)* < MF *conforme(r)* < L *conformāre* to shape] **—con·form′er,** *n.* **—con·form′ing·ly,** *adv.* **—Syn. 1.** yield, consent. **2.** correspond, agree, tally. **5.** adapt, adjust, accommodate. **—Ant. 1, 3.** dissent. **2.** differ.

con·form·a·ble (kən fôr′mə bəl), *adj.* **1.** corresponding in form or character; similar. **2.** compliant; acquiescent; submissive. **3.** *Geol.* (of strata or beds) having the same dip and strike as a result of successive depositions uninterrupted by crustal movement. **—con·form′a·bil′i·ty, con·form′a·ble·ness,** *n.* **—con·form′a·bly,** *adv.*

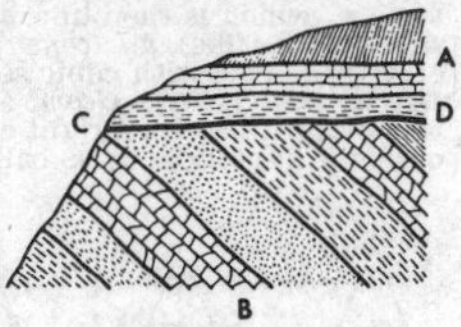

Conformable and unconformable strata; A and B, two sets of unconformable strata; CD, line of junction of A and B

con·for·mal (kən fôr′məl), *adj.* of, pertaining to, or noting a map or transformation in which angles and scale are preserved. [< LL *confōrmāl(is)* of the same shape]

con·form·ance (kən fôr′məns), *n.* the act of conforming; conformity.

con·for·ma·tion (kon′fôr mā′shən), *n.* **1.** manner of formation; structure; form. **2.** symmetrical disposition or arrangement of parts. **3.** the act of conforming; adaptation; adjustment. **4.** the state of being conformed. [< L *confōrmātiōn-* (s. of *confōrmātiō*) = *confōrmāt(us)* made, ptp. of *confōrmāre* (see CON-, FORM) + *-iōn-* -ION]

con·form·ism (kən fôr′miz əm), *n.* the policy, practice, or attitude of conforming.

con·form·ist (kən fôr′mist), *n.* **1.** a person who conforms to a particular usage or practice of a group, society, etc. **2.** (*often cap.*) a person who conforms to the usages of an established church, esp. the Church of England. **—*adj.*** **3.** of or characterized by conforming.

con·form·i·ty (kən fôr′mi tē), *n., pl.* **-ties. 1.** correspondence in form or character; agreement, congruity, or accordance. **2.** compliance or acquiescence. **3.** (*often cap.*) compliance with the usages of an established church, esp. the Church of England. [late ME *conformite* < MF < LL *conformitāt-* (s. of *conformitās*)]

con·found (kon found′, kən-; *for 6 usually* kon′found′), *v.t.* **1.** to perplex or amaze; confuse. **2.** to throw into confusion or disorder. **3.** to contradict or refute: *to confound their arguments.* **4.** to treat or regard erroneously as identical; associate by mistake: *truth confounded with error.* **5.** to mingle so that the elements cannot be distinguished or separated. **6.** to damn (used in mild imprecations): *Confound it!* **7.** *Archaic.* to put to shame; abash. **8.** *Archaic.* **a.** to defeat or overthrow. **b.** to bring to ruin or naught. **9.** *Obs.* to spend uselessly; waste. [ME *conf(o)und(e)* < AF *confound(re)* < L *confundere* to mix. See CON-, FOUND[3]] **—con·found′a·ble,** *adj.* **—con·found′er,** *n.* **—con·found′ing·ly,** *adv.*

con·found·ed (kon foun′did, kən-), *adj.* damned (used euphemistically): *That is a confounded lie.* [ME] **—con·found′ed·ly,** *adv.* **—con·found′ed·ness,** *n.*

con·fra·ter·ni·ty (kon′frə tûr′ni tē), *n., pl.* **-ties. 1.** a lay brotherhood devoted to some religious or charitable service. **2.** a society or body of men united for some purpose or in some profession. [late ME *confraternite* < ML *confrāternitās* = *confrāter* (*con-* CON- + *frāter* brother, fellow member) + (*frater*)*nitās* FRATERNITY] **—con′fra·ter′nal,** *adj.*

con·frere (kon′frâr), *n.* a fellow member of a fraternity, profession, etc.; colleague. [late ME < MF < ML *confrāter* colleague = L *con-* CON- + *frāter* brother]

con·front (kən frunt′), *v.t.* **1.** to stand or come in front of; face. **2.** to face in hostility or defiance; oppose. **3.** to present for acknowledgment, contradiction, etc.; set face to face: *They confronted him with evidence of his crime.* **4.** to bring together for examination or comparison. [< ML *confront(ārī)*] **—con·fron·ta·tion** (kon′frən tā′shən), **con·front′ment,** *n.* **—con·front′er,** *n.*

Con·fu·cian·ism (kən fyōō′shə niz′əm), *n.* the system of ethics, education, and statesmanship taught by Confucius and his disciples, stressing love for humanity, ancestor worship, reverence for parents, and harmony in thought and conduct. **—Con·fu′cian·ist,** *n., adj.*

Con·fu·cius (kən fyōō′shəs), *n.* (*K'ung Ch'iu*) 5th–6th century B.C., Chinese philosopher and teacher. Chinese, **K'ung Fu-tzŭ. —Con·fu′cian,** *n., adj.*

con·fuse (kən fyōōz′), *v.t.,* **-fused, -fus·ing. 1.** to make unclear or indistinct: *The great volume of the evidence tended to confuse the issue.* **2.** to combine without order; jumble; disorder: *Try not to confuse the papers on his desk.* **3.** to fail to distinguish between; associate by mistake; confound: *to confuse dates.* **4.** to perplex or bewilder. **5.** to disconcert or abash: *His candor confused her.* **6.** *Obs.* to bring to ruin or naught. [back formation from *confused* < L *confūs(us)* mixed up (ptp. of *confundere* to CONFOUND) = *con-* CON- + *-fūsus* (see FUSE[2]) + -ED[2]] **—con·fus′a·bil′i·ty,** *n.* **—con·fus′a·ble,** *adj.* **—con·fus′a·bly,** *adv.* **—con·fus·ed·ly** (kən fyōō′zid lē, -fyōōzd′-), *adv.* **—con·fus′ed·ness,** *n.* **—con·fus′ing·ly,** *adv.* **—Syn. 2.** disarray, disarrange, disturb. **4.** mystify. **5.** mortify, shame. **—Ant. 1.** enlighten.

con·fu·sion (kən fyōō′zhən), *n.* **1.** the act of confusing. **2.** the state of being confused. **3.** disorder; upheaval; chaos. **4.** lack of clearness or distinctness. **5.** embarrassment or abashment: *She kissed him suddenly, and he blushed in confusion.* **6.** perplexity; bewilderment. **7.** *Archaic.* defeat, overthrow, or ruin. [ME < L *confūsiōn-* (s. of *confūsiō*)] **—con·fu′sion·al,** *adj.* **—Syn. 2.** distraction. **3.** turmoil, jumble, mess, disarray. **5.** shame, mortification.

con·fu·ta·tion (kon′fyōō tā′shən), *n.* **1.** the act of confuting. **2.** something that confutes. [< L *confūtātiōn-* (s. of *confūtātiō*) = *confūtāt(us)* silenced (ptp.; see CONFUTE, -ATE[1]) + *-iōn-* -ION] **—con·fut·a·tive** (kən fyōō′tə tiv), *adj.*

con·fute (kən fyōōt′), *v.t.,* **-fut·ed, -fut·ing. 1.** to prove to be false or invalid; disprove. **2.** to prove (a person) to be wrong by argument or proof: *to confute one's opponent.* **3.** *Obs.* to bring to naught; confound. [< L *confūt(āre)* (to) repress, put to silence, refute = *con-* CON- + *-fūtāre,* perh. akin to FUTILE] **—con·fut′a·ble,** *adj.* **—con·fut′er,** *n.*

Cong., 1. Congregational. **2.** Congregationalist. **3.** Congress. **4.** Congressional.

cong., gallon. [< L *congius*]

con·ga (koNG′gə), *n., pl.* **-gas,** *v.,* **-gaed, -ga·ing. —*n.*** **1.** a Cuban dance performed by a group following a leader in a single line. **—*v.i.*** **2.** to dance a conga. [< AmerSp, fem. of *Congo* CONGO]

con′ game′, *Informal.* See **confidence game.**

Con·ga·ree (koNG′gə rē), *n.* a river flowing E in central South Carolina, joining with the Watteree River to form the Santee River. ab. 60 mi. long.

con·gé (kon′zhā, -jā; *Fr.* kôN zhā′), *n., pl.* **-gés** (-zhāz, -jāz; *Fr.* -zhā′). **1.** leave-taking; farewell. **2.** permission to depart. **3.** dismissal. **4.** a bow or obeisance. Also, **congee.** [< F; see CONGEE]

con·geal (kən jēl′), *v.t., v.i.* **1.** to change from a soft or fluid state to a rigid or solid state, as by cooling or freezing. **2.** to curdle; coagulate, as a fluid. **3.** to make or become fixed, as sentiments, principles, etc. [ME *congele(n)* < L *congelā(re)* = *con-* CON- + *gelāre* to freeze; see GELID] **—con·geal′a·bil′i·ty, con·geal′a·ble·ness,** *n.* **—con·geal′a·ble,** *adj.* **—con·geal·ed·ness** (kən jē′lid nis), *n.* **—con·geal′er,** *n.* **—con·geal′ment,** *n.* **—con·ge·la·tion** (kon′jə lā′shən), *n.*

con·gee (kon′jē), *n., v.,* **-geed, -gee·ing. —*n.*** **1.** congé. **—*v.i.*** *Obs.* **2.** to take one's leave. **3.** to bow ceremoniously. [late ME *congie* < MF < L *commeāt(us)* furlough = *com-* COM- + *meātus* motion, passage < ptp. of *meāre* to pass]

con·ge·ner (kon′jə nər), *n.* **1.** one of the same kind or class. **2.** a plant or animal belonging to the same genus as another. [< L = *con-* CON- + *gener-* (s. of *genus*); see GENUS, GENERAL] **—con·ge·ner·ic** (kon′jə ner′ik), **con·gen·er·ous** (kən jen′ər əs), *adj.*

con·gen·ial (kən jēn′yəl), *adj.* **1.** suited or adapted in disposition; compatible. **2.** agreeable or pleasing in nature or character: *congenial surroundings.* [< L *con-* CON- + *geni(us)* GENIUS + -AL[1]] **—con·ge·ni·al·i·ty** (kən jē′nē al′i tē), **con·gen′ial·ness,** *n.* **—con·gen′ial·ly,** *adv.* **—Syn. 1.** friendly; genial. **2.** pleasant; harmonious. **—Ant.** disagreeable.

con·gen·i·tal (kən jen′i tᵊl), *adj.* existing at or from one's birth: *a congenital defect.* [< L *congenit(us)* connate (*con-* CON- + *geni-,* ptp. s. of *gignere* to give birth + *-tus* ptp. suffix) + -AL[1]] **—con·gen′i·tal·ly,** *adv.* **—con·gen′i·tal·ness,** *n.* **—Syn.** innate, inborn, hereditary, inherited.

con·ger (koNG′gər), *n.* **1.** a large, marine eel, *Conger conger,* sometimes reaching a length of 10 feet, used for food. **2.** any other eel of the family *Congridae.* Also called **con′ger eel′.** [ME *kunger, congre* < OF *congre* < L *conger* < Gk *góngros* sea eel, gnarl, protuberance; akin to COCK[3]]

con·ge·ries (kon jēr′ēz), *n.* (*construed as sing. or pl.*) an aggregation of objects or ideas; assemblage: *a congeries o tiny boxes.* [< L: a heap = *conger-* (s. of *congerere* to collect, heap up = *con-* CON- + *gerere* to bear, carry) + *-iēs* n. suffix]

con·gest (kən jest′), *v.t.* **1.** to fill to excess; overcrowd or overburden. **2.** *Pathol.* to cause an unnatural accumulation of blood in the vessels of (an organ or part). **3.** *Obs.* to heap together. **—*v.i.*** **4.** to become congested. [< L *congest(us),* ptp. of *congerere;* see CONGERIES] **—con·gest′i·ble,** *adj.* **—con·ges′tion,** *n.* **—con·ges′tive,** *adj.*

con·gi·us (kon′jē əs), *n., pl.* **-gi·i** (-jē ī′). an ancient Roman unit of liquid measure equal to about 0.8 U.S. gallon. [< L < Gk *kónch(ē),* with *-ius* suffix]

con·glo·bate (kon glō′bāt, koNG′glō bāt′), *adj., v.,* **-bat·ed, -bat·ing. —*adj.*** **1.** formed into a ball. **—*v.t., v.i.*** **2.** to collect or form into a ball or rounded mass. [< L *conglobāt(us),* ptp. of *conglobāre*] **—con·glo′bate·ly,** *adv.* **—con′glo·ba′tion,** *n.*

con·globe (kon glōb′), *v.t., v.i.,* **-globed, -glob·ing.** to conglobate. [< L *conglob(āre)*]

con·glom·er·ate (*n., adj.* kən glom′ər it; *v.* kən glom′ə rāt′), *n., adj., v.,* **-at·ed, -at·ing. —*n.*** **1.** anything composed of heterogeneous materials or elements. **2.** Also called **pudding stone.** *Geol.* a rock consisting of pebbles or the like cemented together; consolidated gravel. **3.** a company consisting of a number of subsidiary companies or divisions in a variety of unrelated industries, usually as a result of merger or acquisition. **—*adj.*** **4.** consisting of parts gathered into a mass; clustered. **5.** *Geol.* of the nature of a conglomerate. **6.** noting or pertaining to a corporate conglomerate or conglomerates. **—*v.t.*** **7.** to bring together into a cohering mass. **—*v.i.*** **8.** to collect or cluster together. [< L *conglomerāt(us)* (ptp. of *conglomerāre*) = *con-* CON- + *glomer-* (s. of *glomus*) ball of yarn + *-ātus* -ATE[1]] **—con·glom·er·at·ic** (kən glom′ə rat′ik), **con·glom·er·it·ic** (kən glom′ə rit′ik), *adj.*

con·glom·er·a·tion (kən glom′ə rā′shən), *n.* **1.** the act of conglomerating. **2.** the state of being conglomerated. **3.** a cohering mass; cluster. **4.** a heterogeneous combination: *a conglomeration of ideas.* [< LL *conglomerātiōn-* (s. of *conglomerātiō*)] **—Syn. 3, 4.** aggregate, aggregation.

con·glom·er·a·tor (kən glom′ə rā′tər), *n.* a person who forms or heads a corporate conglomerate. Also, **con·glom·er·a·teur** (kən glom′ə rə tûr′).

con·glu·ti·nate (kən glōōt′ᵊnāt′), *v.,* **-nat·ed, -nat·ing,** *adj.* **—*v.t., v.i.*** **1.** to join or become joined with or as if with glue. **—*adj.*** **2.** glued together; adhering. [< L *conglūtināt(us)* (ptp. of *conglūtināre*) = *con-* CON- + *glūtin-* (var. s. of *glūten*) glue + *-ātus* -ATE[1]] **—con·glu′ti·na′tion,** *n.* **—con·glu′ti·na′tive,** *adj.*

con·go (koNG′gō), *n.* congou.

Con·go (koNG′gō), *n.* **1. Democratic Republic of the,** a former name of **Zaïre** (def. 1). **2. People's Republic of the.** Formerly, **French Congo, Middle Congo.** a republic in central Africa, W of Zaïre: formerly an overseas territory in French Equatorial Africa; now an independent member of the French Community. 1,300,020; 132,046 sq. mi. *Cap.:* Brazzaville. **3.** former name of the Zaïre River.

Con·go·lese (koNG′gə lēz′, -lēs′), *adj., n., pl.* **-lese. —*adj.*** **1.** of or pertaining to either of the Congo republics, its inhabitants, or their language. **—*n.*** **2.** an inhabitant or native of either of the Congo republics. [< F *congolais,* irreg. formation; see -ESE]

con′go snake′, any of several eel-shaped salamanders, as the siren. Also called **con′go eel′.**

con·gou (koŋ′go͞o), *n.* a black tea from China. Also, **congo.** [perh. < dial. Chin *kong-hu* for Mandarin *kung-fu* work, with reference to care involved in growing and processing it]

con·grat·u·late (kən grach′ə lāt′), *v.t.,* **-lat·ed, -lat·ing.** **1.** to express one's pleasure and joy to (a person), as on a happy occasion. **2.** *Obs.* **a.** to express sympathetic joy or satisfaction at (an event). **b.** to salute. [< L *congrātulāt(us)* (ptp. of *congrātulārī*) = *con-* CON- + *grātul-* (*grāt-,* s. of *grātus* pleasing + *-ul-* adj. suffix) + *-ātus* -ATE[1]] —**con·grat′u·la′tor,** *n.* —**con·grat·u·la·to·ry** (kən grach′ə lə tōr′ē, -tôr′ē), *adj.*

con·grat·u·la·tion (kən grach′ə lā′shən), *n.* **1.** the act of congratulating. —*interj.* **2. congratulations!** (used to express joy or satisfaction in the success or good fortune of another.) [< LL *congrātulātiōn-* (s. of *congrātulātiō*)]

con·gre·gate (*v.* koŋ′grə gāt′; *adj.* koŋ′grə git, -gāt′), *v.,* **-gat·ed, -gat·ing,** *adj.* —*v.i., v.t.* **1.** to come or bring together in a body; assemble; collect. —*adj.* **2.** collected; assembled. **3.** formed by collecting; collective. [< L *congregāt(us)* (ptp. of *congregāre* to flock together) = *con-* CON- + *greg-* (s. of *grex*) flock + *-ātus* -ATE[1]] —**con′gre·ga′tive,** *adj.* —**con′gre·ga′tive·ness,** *n.* —**con′gre·ga′tor, con′gre·gant,** *n.*

con·gre·ga·tion (koŋ′grə gā′shən), *n.* **1.** the act of congregating. **2.** a congregated body; assemblage. **3.** an assembly of persons brought together for common religious worship. **4.** an organization formed for providing church activities; a local church society. **5.** the people of Israel. Ex. 12:3,6; Lev. 4:13. **6.** *New Testament.* the Christian church in general. **7.** *Rom. Cath. Ch.* **a.** a committee of cardinals or other ecclesiastics. **b.** a community of men or women, either with or without vows, observing a common rule. [ME *congregacio(u)n* < L *congregātiōn-* (s. of *congregātiō*)]

con·gre·ga·tion·al (koŋ′grə gā′shə nᵊl), *adj.* **1.** of or pertaining to a congregation. **2.** pertaining or adhering to congregationalism. —**con′gre·ga′tion·al·ly,** *adv.*

con·gre·ga·tion·al·ism (koŋ′grə gā′shə nᵊliz′əm), *n.* a form of church government in which each local religious society is independent and self-governing. —**con′gre·ga′tion·al·ist,** *n., adj.*

con·gress (*n.* koŋ′gris; *v.* kən gres′), *n.* **1.** *Govt.* **a.** (*cap.*) the national legislative body of the U.S., consisting of the Senate and the House of Representatives. **b.** (*cap.*) this body as it exists for a period of two years during which it has the same membership: *the 90th Congress.* **c.** (*cap.*) a session of this body. **2.** the national legislative body of a nation, esp. of a republic. **3.** a formal meeting of representatives, as envoys of independent states, for the discussion and solution of some matter. **4.** the act of coming together; an encounter. **5.** familiar relations; dealings; intercourse. **6.** coitus; sexual intercourse. —*v.i.* **7.** to assemble together; meet together in congress. [< L *congress(us)* a coming together, n. use of ptp. of *congredī* = *con-* CON- + *gred-* (var. s. of *gradī* to step; see GRADE) + *-tus* ptp. ending] —**con·gres·sion·al** (kən gresh′ə nᵊl), *adj.* —**con·gres′sion·al·ist,** *n.* —**con·gres′sion·al·ly,** *adv.* —**Syn. 3.** conference, council, convention.

con′gress boot′, *U.S.* a high shoe with elastic inserts in the sides.

Congres′sional dis′trict, *U.S. Govt.* a division of a state, electing one member to the national House of Representatives. Cf. **assembly district, senatorial district.**

Congres′sional Med′al of Hon′or. See **Medal of Honor.**

Congres′sional Rec′ord, the record of the proceedings of the U.S. Congress, with a transcript of the discussion, published daily by the government while Congress is in session.

con·gress·man (koŋ′gris mən), *n., pl.* **-men.** (*often cap.*) a male member of the U.S. Congress, esp. of the House of Representatives.

con·gress·man-at-large (koŋ′gris mən ət lärj′), *n., pl.* **con·gress·men-at-large** (koŋ′gris mən ət lärj′). a U.S. congressman who is elected from a state as a whole and not from a district.

Con′gress of Indus′trial Organiza′tions, a federation of affiliated industrial labor unions, founded 1935 within the American Federation of Labor but independent of it 1938–55. *Abbr.:* C.I.O., CIO

Con′gress of Vien′na, an international conference (1814–15) held at Vienna after Napoleon's banishment to Elba, aimed at territorial resettlement and restoration to power of the crowned heads of Europe.

con·gress·wom·an (koŋ′gris wo͝om′ən), *n., pl.* **-wom·en.** (*often cap.*) a female member of the U.S. Congress, esp. of the House of Representatives.

Con·greve (kon′grēv, koŋ′-), *n.* **1. William,** 1670–1729, English dramatist. **2. Sir William,** 1772–1828, English engineer and inventor.

con·gru·ence (koŋ′gro͞o əns), *n.* **1.** the quality or state of agreeing or corresponding. **2.** *Math.* a relation between two numbers indicating that the numbers give the same remainder when divided by some given number. [ME < L *congruentia.* See CONGRUENT, -ENCE]

con·gru·en·cy (koŋ′gro͞o ən sē), *n., pl.* **-cies.** congruence. [ME < L *congruentia.* See CONGRUENT, -CY]

con·gru·ent (koŋ′gro͞o ənt), *adj.* **1.** agreeing; accordant; congruous. **2.** of or pertaining to a mathematical congruence. **3.** *Geom.* coinciding at all points when superimposed: *congruent triangles.* [< L *congruent-* (s. of *congruēns,* prp. of *congruere* to go or come together, agree) = *con-* CON- + *gru-* move + *-ent-* -ENT] —**con′gru·ent·ly,** *adv.*

con·gru·i·ty (kən gro͞o′i tē, kon-), *n., pl.* **-ties.** **1.** the state or quality of being congruous; agreement; harmony; appropriateness. **2.** the state or quality of being geometrically congruent. **3.** a point of agreement. [late ME *congruite* < MF < LL *congruitāt-* (s. of *congruitās*). See CONGRUOUS, -ITY]

con·gru·ous (koŋ′gro͞o əs), *adj.* **1.** exhibiting harmony of parts. **2.** appropriate or fitting. [< L *congruus* = *con-* CON- + *gru-* (see CONGRUENT) + *-us* -OUS] —**con′gru·ous·ly,** *adv.* —**con′gru·ous·ness,** *n.*

con·ic (kon′ik), *adj.* **1.** Also, **con′i·cal.** having the form of, resembling, or pertaining to a cone. —*n.* **2.** *Geom.* See **conic section.** [< Gk *kōnik(ós)*] —**con′i·cal·ly,** *adv.* —**co·nic·i·ty** (kō nis′i tē), **con′i·cal·ness,** *n.*

con′ic projec′tion, *Cartog.* a map projection based on the concept of projecting the earth's surface on a conical surface, which is then unrolled to a plane surface.

con·ics (kon′iks), *n.* (*construed as sing.*) the branch of geometry that deals with conic sections.

con′ic sec′tion, *Geom.* a curve formed by the intersection of a plane with a right circular cone; an ellipse, a parabola, or a hyperbola. Also called **conic.**

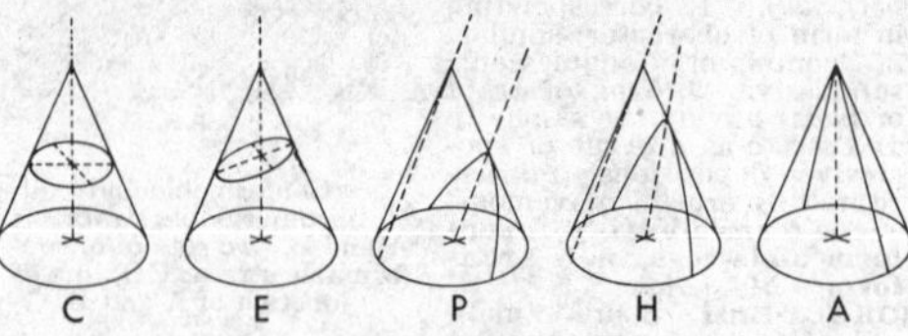

Conic sections
The two principal forms are E, ellipse, and H, hyperbola; P, parabola, is an intermediate case; C, circle, is an ellipse perpendicular to the axis of the cone; A, angle, is a hyperbola whose axis coincides with that of the cone

con′ic sec′tions, the branch of geometry that deals with the ellipse, the parabola, and the hyperbola.

co·nid·i·o·phore (kō nid′ē ə fōr′, -fôr′, kə-), *n.* *Bot.* (in fungi) a special stalk or branch of mycelium, bearing conidia. [CONIDI(UM) + -O- + -PHORE] —**co·nid·i·oph·o·rous** (kō nid′ē of′ər əs, kə-), *adj.*

co·nid·i·um (kō nid′ē əm, kə-), *n., pl.* **-nid·i·a** (-nid′ē ə). *Bot.* (in fungi) an asexual spore formed by abstriction at the top of a hyphal branch. [< Gk *kón(is)* dust + -IDIUM] —**co·nid′i·al, co·nid′i·an,** *adj.*

co·ni·fer (kō′nə fər, kon′ə-), *n.* **1.** any of numerous, cone-bearing evergreen trees or shrubs of the gymnospermous order or group *Coniferales* or *Coniferae,* including the pine, fir, and spruce. **2.** a plant producing naked seeds in cones, or single naked seeds as in yews, but with pollen always borne in cones. [< L; see CONE, -I-, -FER]

co·nif·er·ous (kō nif′ər əs, kə-), *adj.* *Bot.* belonging or pertaining to the conifers. Cf. **conifer** (def. 1).

co·ni·ine (kō′nē ēn′, -in, -nēn), *n.* a highly poisonous alkaloid, $C_8H_{17}N$, the active principle of the poison hemlock. Also, **co·nin** (kō′nin), **co·nine** (kō′nēn, -nin). [CONI(UM) + -INE[2]]

co·ni·ol·o·gy (kō′nē ol′ə jē), *n.* koniology.

co·ni·um (kō′nē əm), *n.* the poison hemlock, *Conium maculatum.* [< LL < Gk *kṓneion*]

conj., 1. conjugation. **2.** conjunction. **3.** conjunctive.

con·jec·tur·al (kən jek′chər əl), *adj.* **1.** of the nature of or involving conjecture; problematical. **2.** given to making conjectures. [< L *conjectūrāl(is)*] —**con·jec′tur·al·ly,** *adv.*

con·jec·ture (kən jek′chər), *n., v.,* **-tured, -tur·ing.** —*n.* **1.** the formation of an opinion without sufficient evidence for proof. **2.** the opinion so formed. **3.** *Obs.* the interpretation of signs or omens. —*v.t.* **4.** to conclude or suppose from evidence insufficient to ensure reliability. —*v.i.* **5.** to form conjectures. [< L *conjectūr(a)* (an opinion based on) a putting together of facts = *con-* CON- + *jec-* (var. s. of *jacere* to throw) + *-t(us)* ptp. suffix + *-ūra* -URE] —**con·jec′tur·a·ble,** *adj.* —**con·jec′tur·a·bly,** *adv.* —**con·jec′tur·er,** *n.* —**Syn. 2.** supposition, theory, hypothesis. **4.** surmise, suppose, presume. See **guess.**

con·join (kən join′), *v.t., v.i.* to join together; unite; combine; associate. [ME *conjoigne(n)* < MF *conjoign-* (s. of *conjoindre*) < L *conjung(ere)*] —**con·join·ed·ly** (kən joi′nid lē, -joind′lē), *adv.* —**con·join′er,** *n.* —**Ant.** disjoin.

con·joint (kən joint′), *adj.* joined together; united; combined; associated. [ME < MF < L *conjunct(us)* (ptp. of *conjungere*)] —**con·joint′ly,** *adv.* —**con·joint′ness,** *n.*

con·ju·gal (kon′jə gəl), *adj.* **1.** of, pertaining to, or characteristic of marriage. **2.** pertaining to the relation of husband and wife. [< L *conjugāl(is)* = *con-* CON- + *jug(um)* YOKE[1] + *-ālis* -AL[1]] —**con′ju·gal′i·ty,** *n.* —**con′ju·gal·ly,** *adv.* —**Syn. 1.** matrimonial, nuptial, connubial. **2.** marital.

con·ju·gate (*v.* kon′jə gāt′; *adj., n.* kon′jə git, -gāt′), *v.,* **-gat·ed, -gat·ing,** *adj., n.* —*v.t.* **1.** *Gram.* to give all or some subsets of the inflected forms of (a verb) in a fixed order: *One conjugates the present-tense verb "be" as I am, you are, he is, we are, you are, they are.* **2.** *Obs.* to join, esp. in marriage. —*v.i.* **3.** *Biol.* to unite; undergo conjugation. **4.** *Gram.* to be characterized by conjugation. —*adj.* **5.** joined together, esp. in a pair or pairs; coupled. **6.** *Bot.* (of a pinnate leaf) having only one pair of leaflets. **7.** *Gram.* (of words) having a common derivation. **8.** *Math.* (of two points, lines, etc.) so related as to be interchangeable in the enunciation of certain properties. **9.** *Chem.* **a.** of or noting two or more liquids in equilibrium with one another. **b.** (of an acid and a base) related by the loss or gain of a proton. **c.** Also, **con′ju·gat′ed.** (of an organic compound) containing two or more double bonds, each separated from the other by a single bond. —*n.* **10.** one of a group of conjugate words. **11.** *Math.* either of two conjugate points, lines, etc. [< L *conjugāt(us)* (ptp. of *conjugāre* to yoke together) = *con-* CON- + *jug(um)* YOKE[1] + *-ātus* -ATE[1]] —**con·ju·ga·ble** (kon′jo͝o gə bəl), *adj.* —**con′ju·ga·bly,** *adv.* —**con′ju·ga′tive,** *adj.* —**con′ju·ga′tor,** *n.*

con·ju·ga·tion (kon′jə gā′shən), *n.* **1.** *Gram.* **a.** the inflection of verbs. **b.** the whole set of inflected forms of a verb: *The conjugation of the Latin verb* amo *begins* amō, amas, amat. **c.** a class of verbs having similar sets of inflected forms: *the Latin second conjugation.* **2.** an act of joining. **3.** the state of being joined together; union; conjunction. **4.** *Biol.* **a.** the sexual process in protozoans, involving the exchange of nuclear material through a temporary area of fusion. **b.** the temporary union or fusion of two cells or organisms, as in certain lower plants. [< LL *conjugātiōn-* (s. of *conjugātiō*)] —**con′ju·ga′tion·al,** *adj.* —**con′ju·ga′tion·al·ly,** *adv.*

con·junct (kən juŋkt′, kon′juŋkt), *adj.* **1.** conjoined; bound in close association. **2.** formed by conjunction. **3.**

Music. progressing melodically by intervals of a second. [< L *conjunct(us)* joined, connected (ptp. of *conjungere*) = *con-* CON- + *junc-* (var. s. of *jungere* to JOIN) + *-tus* ptp. suffix] —**con·junct′ly,** *adv.*

con·junc·tion (kən jungk′shən), *n.* **1.** the act of conjoining; combination. **2.** the state of being conjoined; union; association. **3.** a combination of events or circumstances. **4.** *Gram.* any member of a small class of words functioning as connectors between words, phrases, clauses, or sentences, as *and, because, but, however.* Cf. **coordinating conjunction, subordinating conjunction.** **5.** *Astron.* **a.** the coincidence of two or more heavenly bodies at the same celestial longitude. **b.** the state of two or more such coinciding heavenly bodies. **6.** *Logic.* **a.** a propositional statement that is true if and only if both its components are true. **b.** a connective symbol, as •, usually read as "and." [ME *conjunccio(u)n* < L *conjunctiōn-* (s. of *conjunctiō*)] —**con·junc′tion·al,** *adj.* —**con·junc′tion·al·ly,** *adv.*

con·junc·ti·va (kon′jungk tī′və), *n., pl.* **-vas, -vae** (-vē). *Anat.* the mucous membrane that lines the inner surface of the eyelids. [short for NL *membrāna conjunctīva* conjunctive membrane; see CONJUNCTIVE] —**con′junc·ti′val,** *adj.*

con·junc·tive (kən jungk′tiv), *adj.* **1.** connective. **2.** linked; joint: *a conjunctive action.* **3.** *Gram.* **a.** (of a mode) subjunctive. **b.** (of a pronoun) conjunct. **c.** of the nature of a conjunction. —*n.* **4.** *Gram.* conjunction. [< LL *conjunctīv(us)*] —**con·junc′tive·ly,** *adv.*

con·junc·ti·vi·tis (kən jungk′tə vī′tis), *n.* *Ophthalm.* inflammation of the conjunctiva.

con·junc·ture (kən jungk′chər), *n.* **1.** a combination of circumstances or a particular state of affairs. **2.** a critical state of affairs; crisis. **3.** conjunction; joining; meeting. —**con·junc′tur·al,** *adj.*

con·jur·a·tion (kon′jŏŏ rā′shən), *n.* **1.** the act of calling on or invoking by a sacred name. **2.** an incantation; magical spell or charm. **3.** the practice of legerdemain. **4.** *Archaic.* supplication; solemn entreaty. [ME *conjuracio(u)n* < L *conjūrātiōn-* (s. of *conjūrātiō*) = *conjūrāt(us),* ptp. of *conjūrāre* to swear together, (*con-* CON- + *jūr-* (s. of *jūs*) right, justice, duty + *-ātus* -ATE^1) + *-iōn-* -ION]

con·jure (kon′jər *or, esp. Brit.,* kun′- *for 1–4, 7, 8;* kən jŏŏr′ *for 5, 6, 9*), *v.,* **-jured, -jur·ing.** —*v.t.* **1.** to call upon or command (a devil or spirit) by invocation or spell. **2.** to affect or influence by or as if by invocation or spell. **3.** to effect or produce by or as by magic: *to conjure a miracle.* **4.** to raise up, bring to mind, or recall by or as if by magic (usually fol. by *up*): *to conjure up the happy past.* **5.** to appeal to solemnly or earnestly: *I conjure you to hear my plea.* **6.** *Obs.* to charge solemnly. —*v.i.* **7.** to call upon or command a devil or spirit by invocation or spell. **8.** to practice magic or legerdemain. **9.** *Obs.* to conspire. [ME *conjure(n)* < OF *conjure(r)* < L *conjūrāre* = *con-* CON- + *jūrāre* to swear]

con·jur·er (kon′jər ər *or, esp. Brit.,* kun′- *for 1, 2;* kən jŏŏr′ər *for 3*), *n.* **1.** a person who conjures spirits or practices magic; sorcerer. **2.** a person who practices legerdemain; magician; juggler. **3.** a person who solemnly charges or entreats. Also, **con′ju·ror.** [ME]

conk (kongk, kôngk), *v.t.* *Slang.* to hit or strike on the head. [? alter. of CONCH]

conk′ out′, *Slang.* **1.** to break or fail, as a machine, engine, etc. **2.** to slow down or stop; lose energy. **3.** to lose consciousness; faint. **4.** to die. [*conk,* of imit. orig.]

con′ man′, *Informal.* See **confidence man.**

conn (kon), *v.t., n.* con^3.

Conn., Connecticut.

con·nate (kon′āt), *adj.* **1.** existing in a person or thing from birth or origin; inborn; congenital. **2.** associated in birth or origin. **3.** allied or agreeing in nature; cognate. **4.** *Biol.* congenitally or firmly united into one body. [< L *connāt(us)* (ptp. of *connāscī* to be born at the same time with) = L *con-* CON- + *nā-* (short s. of *nāscī*) + *-tus* ptp. suffix] —**con′nate·ly,** *adv.* —**con′nate·ness,** *n.* —**con·na·tion** (kə nā′shən), *n.*

con·nat·u·ral (kə nach′ər əl, -nach′rəl), *adj.* **1.** belonging to a person or thing by nature or from birth or origin; inborn. **2.** of the same or a similar nature. [< ML *connātūrāl(is)*] —**con·nat′u·ral·ly,** *adv.* —**con·nat′u·ral·ness,** *n.*

Con·naught (kon′ôt), *n.* a province in the NW Republic of Ireland. 419,465 (1961); 6611 sq. mi. Irish, **Con·nacht** (kon′əkнt, -ət).

con·nect (kə nekt′), *v.t.* **1.** to bind or fasten together; join or unite; link: *to connect the two cities by a bridge.* **2.** to establish communication between; put in communication (often fol. by *with*): *The telephone operator connected us.* **3.** to associate, attach, or place in relationship: *to connect oneself with a group.* **4.** to associate mentally or emotionally: *She connects all telegrams with bad news.* —*v.i.* **5.** to become connected; join or unite. **6.** (of trains, buses, etc.) to run so as to make connections (often fol. by *with*). **7.** *Slang.* to make direct contact for the illegal sale or purchase of narcotics. [< L *connect(ere)* = *con-* CON- + *nectere* to tie; see NEXUS] —**con·nect′ed·ly,** *adv.* —**con·nect′ed·ness,** *n.* —**con·nect′i·ble, con·nect′a·ble,** *adj.* —**con·nec′tor, con·nect′er,** *n.* —**Syn. 1.** See **join.** —**Ant. 1.** divide. **3.** dissociate

Con·nect·i·cut (kə net′ə kət), *n.* **1.** a state in the NE United States. 3,032,217 (1970); 5009 sq. mi. *Cap.:* Hartford. *Abbr.:* Conn., Ct., CT **2.** a river flowing S from N New Hampshire along the boundary between New Hampshire and Vermont and then through Massachusetts and Connecticut into Long Island Sound. 407 mi. long.

connec′ting rod′, *Mach.* a rod or link for transmitting motion and force between a rotating and a reciprocating part, as between a piston and a crankshaft.

con·nec·tion (kə nek′shən), *n.* **1.** the act of connecting. **2.** the state of being connected. **3.** anything that connects; link; bond. **4.** association; relationship: *the connection between crime and poverty.* **5.** a circle of friends or associates or a member of such a circle. **6.** association with something observed, imagined, discussed, etc. **7.** contextual relation; context, as of a word. **8.** Often, **connections.** the meeting of trains, planes, etc., for transfer of passengers. **9.** a relative, esp. by marriage or distant blood relationship. **10.** a group of persons connected as by political or religious ties. **11.** Usually, **connections.** associates, relations, or friends, esp. representing or having some influence or power. **12.** a channel of communication. **13.** sexual intercourse. Also, *Brit.,* **connexion.** [var. sp. of *connexion* < L *connexiōn-* (s. of *connexiō*) = *connex(us)* (ptp. of *connectere* to CONNECT) + *-iōn-* -ION] —**con·nec′tion·al,** *adj.* —**Syn. 1.** junction, conjunction, union. **3.** tie, coupling, yoke. **5.** affiliation, alliance, combination. **9.** relation, kinsman.

con·nec·tive (kə nek′tiv), *adj.* **1.** serving or tending to connect. —*n.* **2.** something that connects. **3.** *Gram.* a word used to connect words, phrases, clauses, and sentences, as a conjunction. **4.** *Bot.* the tissue joining the two cells of the anther. —**con·nec′tive·ly,** *adv.* —**con·nec·tiv·i·ty** (kon′ek tiv′i tē), *n.*

connec′tive tis′sue, *Anat.* a tissue, usually of mesoblastic origin, that connects, supports, or surrounds other tissues, organs, etc., and occurs in various forms throughout the body.

con·nex·ion (kə nek′shən), *n.* *Brit.* connection. —**con·nex′ion·al,** *adj.*

conn′ing tow′er (kon′ing), **1.** the low observation tower of a submarine, constituting the main entrance to the interior. **2.** the low, armored pilothouse of a warship.

con·nip·tion (kə nip′shən), *n.* Often, **conniptions.** *Informal.* a fit of hysteria, anger, or the like. [?]

con·niv·ance (kə nī′vəns), *n.* **1.** the act of conniving. **2.** *Law.* tacit encouragement or assent to wrongdoing by another. Also, **con·niv′ence.** [earlier *connivence* < L *conniventia*] —**con·niv′ant, con·niv′ent,** *adj.* —**con·niv′ant·ly, con·niv′ent·ly,** *adv.*

con·nive (kə nīv′), *v.i.,* **-nived, -niv·ing.** **1.** to avoid noticing something that one is expected to oppose or condemn; give aid to wrongdoing by forbearing to act or speak (usually fol. by *at*): *The policeman connived at traffic violations.* **2.** to be indulgent toward something others oppose or criticize (usually fol. by *at*): *to connive at childlike exaggerations.* **3.** to cooperate secretly; conspire (often fol. by *with*): *They connived with army chiefs to take over the government.* [< L *connīv(ēre)* (to) blink, wink at = *con-* CON- + *-nīvēre,* akin to *nictāre* to blink] —**con·niv′er,** *n.* —**con·niv′ing·ly** *adv.*

con·niv·ent (kə nī′vənt), *adj.* *Bot., Zool.* converging, as petals. [< L *connīvent-* (s. of *connīvēns,* prp. of *connīvēre*). See CONNIVE, -ENT]

con·nois·seur (kon′ə sûr′, -sŏŏr′), *n.* a person who is especially competent to pass critical judgments in an art, esp. one of the fine arts, or in matters of taste. [< F; OF *conoiseor* < L *cognōscitōr-* (s. of *cognōscitor*) knower. See COGNOSCIBLE, -OR^2] —**con′nois·seur′ship,** *n.*

con·no·ta·tion (kon′ə tā′shən), *n.* **1.** an act or instance of connoting. **2.** the associated or secondary meaning of a word or expression; implication: *A possible connotation of "home" is "a place of warmth, comfort, and affection."* Cf. **denotation** (def. 1). **3.** *Logic.* the set of attributes constituting the meaning of a term; comprehension; intension. [< ML *connotātiōn-* (s. of *connotātiō*) = *connotāt(us)* (ptp. of *connotāre;* see CONNOTE, -ATE^1) + *-iōn-* -ION] —**con·no·ta·tive** (kon′ə tā′tiv, kə nō′tə-), **con·no′tive,** *adj.* —**con′no·ta′tive·ly, con·no′tive·ly,** *adv.*

con·note (kə nōt′), *v.t.,* **-not·ed, -not·ing.** **1.** to signify or suggest (certain meanings, ideas, etc.) in addition to the explicit or primary meaning: *The word "fireplace" often connotes hospitality, warm comfort, etc.* **2.** to involve as a condition or accompaniment: *Injury connotes pain.* —*v.i.* **3.** to have significance only by association, as with another word: *Adjectives can only connote, nouns can denote.* [< ML *connot(āre)*]

con·nu·bi·al (kə nōō′bē əl, -nyōō′-), *adj.* of marriage; matrimonial; conjugal. [< L *cōnūbiāl(is)* = *cōnūbi(um)* (*cō-* co- + *nūb(āre)* (to) marry + *-ium* n. suffix) + *-ālis* -AL^1] —**con·nu′bi·al′i·ty,** *n.* —**con·nu′bi·al·ly,** *adv.*

co·no·dont (kō′nə dont′, kon′ə-), *n.* a small tooth-shaped fossil, the remains of an unidentified animal of the Paleozoic era. [< Gk *kôn(os)* CONE + *odont-,* s. of *odoús* or *odṓn* tooth]

co·noid (kō′noid), *adj.* **1.** Also, **co·noi′dal.** cone-shaped. —*n.* **2.** a geometrical solid formed by the revolution of a conic section about one of its axes. [< Gk *kōnoeid(ḗs).* See CONE, -OID] —**co·noi′dal·ly,** *adv.*

Co·non (kō′non), *n.* died A.D. 687, pope 686–687.

co·no·scen·ti (kō′nə shen′tē, kon′ə-; *It.* kô′nô shen′tē), *n.pl., sing.* **-te** (-tē; *It.* -te). cognoscenti.

con·quer (kong′kər), *v.t.* **1.** to acquire by force of arms; win in war: *to conquer a country.* **2.** to overcome by force: *to conquer an enemy.* **3.** to gain or obtain by effort. **4.** to overcome by mental or moral power; surmount. —*v.i.* **5.** to be victorious: *Despite their differences, their love will conquer.* [ME *conquer(en)* < OF *conquer(re)* < VL **conquērere* to acquire (alter. of L *conquīrere* to seek out). See CON-, QUERY] —**con′quer·a·ble,** *adj.* —**con′quer·a·ble·ness,** *n.* —**con′quer·ing·ly,** *adv.* —**Syn. 2.** vanquish, subjugate. See **defeat.**

con·quer·or (kong′kər ər), *n.* a person who conquers; victor. [ME *conquerour* < AF; OF *conquereor* = *conquer-* CONQUER + *-eor* -OR^2]

con·quest (kon′kwest, kong′-), *n.* **1.** the act of conquering. **2.** the state of being conquered. **3.** the winning of favor or affection. **4.** a person whose favor or affection has been won: *He's another one of her conquests.* **5.** anything acquired by conquering, as a nation, a territory, spoils, etc. **6. the Conquest.** See **Norman Conquest.** [ME *conqueste* < MF < VL **conquēsta* (alter. of L *conquīsīta,* fem. ptp. of *conquīrere*)] —**Syn. 1.** subjugation, overthrow, defeat. See **victory.**

con·quis·ta·dor (kon kwis′tə dôr′; *Sp.* kông kēs′tä thôr′), *n., pl.* **-dors,** *Sp.* **-do·res** (-thô′res). one of the 16th-century Spanish conquerors in the Americas. [< Sp = *conquistad(o)* (ptp. of *conquistar* to conquer; see CONQUEST, -ADE^1) + *-or* -OR^2]

Con·rad (kon′rad), *n.* **Joseph** (*Teodor Jozef Konrad Korzeniowski*), 1857–1924, English novelist and short-story writer, born in Poland.

Cons., **1.** Constable. **2.** Constitution. **3.** Consul.

cons., **1.** consecrated. **2.** consolidated. **3.** consonant. **4.** constable. **5.** constitution. **6.** constitutional. **7.** consul.

con·san·guin·e·ous (kon′saŋ gwin′ē əs), *adj.* having the same ancestry or descent; related by blood. Also, **con·san·guine** (kon saŋ′gwin). [< L *consanguineus.* See CON-, SANGUINE, -EOUS] —**con′san·guin′e·ous·ly,** *adv.*

con·san·guin·i·ty (kon′saŋ gwin′i tē), *n.* **1.** relationship by blood; kinship. **2.** close relationship or connection. [late ME *consanguinite* < L *consanguinitās.* See CONSANGUINEOUS, -ITY]

con·science (kon′shəns), *n.* **1.** the sense of what is right or wrong in one's conduct or motives, impelling one toward right action. **2.** the ethical and moral principles that control or inhibit the actions or thoughts of an individual. **3.** conscientiousness. **4.** *Obs.* consciousness; self-knowledge. **5.** *Obs.* strict and reverential observance. **6. have something on one's conscience,** to feel guilty about something. **7. in all conscience, a.** in all reason and fairness. **b.** certainly; most assuredly; without doubt. Also, **in conscience.** [ME < OF < L *conscientia* knowledge, awareness, conscience] —**con′science·less,** *adj.* —**con′science·less·ly,** *adv.* —**con′science·less·ness,** *n.*

con′science clause′, an article in a law that exempts persons whose conscientious or religious scruples forbid their compliance.

con·science-strick·en (kon′shəns strik′ən), *adj.* troubled by the idea of having acted wrongfully.

con·sci·en·tious (kon′shē en′shəs, kon′sē-), *adj.* **1.** controlled by or done according to conscience; scrupulous. **2.** meticulous; careful. [< ML *conscientiōs(us).* See CONSCIENCE, -OUS] —**con′sci·en′tious·ly,** *adv.* —**con′sci·en′tious·ness,** *n.* —**Syn. 1.** honest. **2.** particular, painstaking; thorough.

conscien′tious objec′tor, a person who refuses to perform military service for his country for moral or religious reasons.

con·scion·a·ble (kon′shə nə bəl), *adj.* being in conformity with one's conscience; just. [*conscion-* (back formation from *conscions,* var. of CONSCIENCE, the final *-s* taken for pl. sign) + -ABLE] —**con′scion·a·ble·ness,** *n.* —**con′scion·a·bly,** *adv.*

con·scious (kon′shəs), *adj.* **1.** aware of one's own existence, thoughts, surroundings, etc. **2.** fully aware of or sensitive to something (often fol. by *of*): *conscious of one's own faults.* **3.** having the mental faculties fully active: *He was conscious during the operation.* **4.** known to oneself; felt: *conscious guilt.* **5.** aware of what one is doing: *a conscious liar.* **6.** self-conscious. **7.** deliberate; intentional: *a conscious insult.* **8.** *Obs.* inwardly sensible of wrongdoing. —*n.* **9. the conscious,** *Psychoanal.* the part of the mind comprising psychic material of which the individual is aware. [< L *conscius* sharing knowledge with = *con-* CON- + *sci-* (s. of *scīre* to know; see SCIENCE) + *-us* -OUS] —**con′scious·ly,** *adv.*
—**Syn. 2.** knowing, percipient. CONSCIOUS, AWARE, COGNIZANT refer to an individual sense of recognition of something within or without oneself. CONSCIOUS implies to be awake or awakened to an inner realization of a fact, a truth, a condition, etc.: *to be conscious of an extreme weariness; to be conscious of one's inadequacy.* AWARE lays the emphasis on sense perceptions insofar as they are the object of conscious recognition: *He was aware of the odor of tobacco.* COGNIZANT lays the emphasis on an outer recognition more on the level of reason and knowledge than on the sensory level alone: *He was cognizant of their drawbacks, their advantages, our plans.*

con·scious·ness (kon′shəs nis), *n.* **1.** the state of being conscious; awareness. **2.** the thoughts and feelings, collectively, of an individual or of an aggregate of people. **3.** full activity of the mind and senses. **4.** awareness of something for what it is: *consciousness of wrongdoing.*

con·script (*v.* kən skript′; *n., adj.* kon′skript), *v.t.* **1.** to draft for military service. —*n.* **2.** a recruit obtained by conscription. —*adj.* **3.** enrolled or formed by conscription; drafted. [< L *conscrīpt(us)* (ptp. of *conscrībere* to write together, list, enroll; see SCRIBE[1]) = *con-* CON- + *scrīp-* (perf. s. of *scrībere*) + *-tus* ptp. suffix]

con′script fa′thers, **1.** the senators of ancient Rome. **2.** any legislators.

con·scrip·tion (kən skrip′shən), *n.* compulsory enrollment for military service; draft. [< LL *conscrīptiōn-* (s. of *conscrīptiō*) a levying of troops (L: a drawing up in writing)] —**con·scrip′tion·al,** *adj.* —**con·scrip′tion·ist,** *n.*

con·se·crate (kon′sə krāt′), *v.,* **-crat·ed, -crat·ing,** *adj.* —*v.t.* **1.** to make or declare sacred; dedicate to the service of the Deity. **2.** to devote or dedicate to some purpose: *a life consecrated to science.* **3.** to make (something) an object of honor or veneration; hallow. —*adj.* **4.** *Archaic.* consecrated; sacred. [< L *consecrāt(us)* (ptp. of *consecrāre*) = *con-* CON- + *secr-* (var. s. of *sacer*) sacred, holy + *-ātus* -ATE[1]] —**con′se·crat′ed·ness,** *n.* —**con′se·crat′or, con′se·crat′er,** *n.* —**con·se·cra·to·ry** (kon′sə krə tôr′ē, -tōr′ē), **con′se·cra′·tive,** *adj.* —**Syn. 3.** sanctify. —**Ant. 1.** desecrate.

con·se·cra·tion (kon′sə krā′shən), *n.* the act of consecrating; dedication to the service and worship of God. [ME *consecracio(u)n* < L *consecrātiōn-* (s. of *consecrātiō*)]

con·se·cu·tion (kon′sə kyōō′shən), *n.* **1.** succession; sequence. **2.** logical sequence; chain of reasoning. [< L *consecūtiōn-* (s. of *consecūtiō*) = *con-* CON- + *secūt(us),* ptp. of *sequī* to follow + *-iōn-* -ION]

con·sec·u·tive (kən sek′yə tiv), *adj.* **1.** following one another in uninterrupted order; successive. **2.** marked by logical sequence. **3.** *Gram.* expressing consequence or result: *a consecutive clause.* [CONSECUT(ION) + -IVE] —**con·sec′u·tive·ly,** *adv.* —**con·sec′u·tive·ness,** *n.* —**Syn. 1.** continuous.

con·sen·su·al (kən sen′shōō əl), *adj.* **1.** formed or existing merely by consent. **2.** *Physiol.* (of an action) involuntarily correlative with a voluntary action. [CONSENSU(S) + -AL[1]] —**con·sen′su·al·ly,** *adv.*

con·sen·sus (kən sen′səs), *n., pl.* **-sus·es.** **1.** general agreement or concord; harmony. **2.** majority of opinion. [< L, n. use of ptp. of *consentīre* = *con-* CON- + *sent-* (s. of *sentīre* to think, hold an opinion) + *-tus* ptp. suffix]
—**Usage.** CONSENSUS OF OPINION is felt by many grammarians and teachers to be a redundancy, but it is so only if CONSENSUS is taken in sense of "majority of opinion," rather than its equally valid—and, according to available evidence, earlier—sense of "accord or general agreement."

con·sent (kən sent′), *v.i.* **1.** to permit, approve, or agree; comply or yield (often fol. by *to* or an infinitive): *He consented to the proposal. She consented to go.* **2.** *Obs.* to agree in sentiment, opinion, etc.; be in harmony. —*n.* **3.** permission or approval of what is done or proposed by another; agreement; compliance; acquiescence. **4.** agreement in sentiment, opinion, a course of action, etc.: *By common consent he was appointed official delegate.* **5.** *Archaic.* accord; concord; harmony. [ME *consent(en)* < OF *consent(ir)* < L *consentīre.* See CON-, SCENT] —**con·sent′er,** *n.* —**Syn. 1.** See **agree.**

con·sen·ta·ne·ous (kon′sen tā′nē əs), *adj.* **1.** agreeing; accordant. **2.** done by common consent; unanimous. [< L *consentāneus* = *consent-* (s. of *consentīre* to CONSENT) + *-āneus* (*-ān(us)* -AN + *-eus* -EOUS)] —**con′sen·ta′ne·ous·ly,** *adv.* —**con·sen·ta·ne·i·ty** (kən sen′tə nē′i tē), **con′sen·ta′·ne·ous·ness,** *n.*

con·se·quence (kon′sə kwens′, -kwəns), *n.* **1.** something that is the effect or result of an earlier occurrence. **2.** the conclusion reached by a line of reasoning; inference. **3.** importance or significance: *a matter of no consequence.* **4.** importance in rank or position; distinction: *a man of consequence.* **5. in consequence,** consequently; as a result; hence. [late ME < L *consequentia.* See CONSEQUENT, -ENCE] —**Syn. 1.** outcome, upshot, sequel. See **effect. 3.** See **importance.** —**Ant. 1.** cause.

con·se·quent (kon′sə kwent′, -kwənt), *adj.* **1.** following as an effect or result; resulting (often fol. by *on, upon,* or *to*): *a rise in production cost and a consequent fall in price; a fall in price consequent to a rise in production.* **2.** following as a logical conclusion. —*n.* **3.** anything that follows upon something else. **4.** *Logic.* the second member of a conditional proposition, as *"he was a great general"* in *"If Caesar conquered Gaul, he was a great general."* **5.** *Math.* the second term of a ratio. [< L *consequent-* (s. of *consequēns,* prp. of *consequī* to follow closely)]

con·se·quen·tial (kon′sə kwen′shəl), *adj.* **1.** following as an effect, result, or outcome; resultant; consequent. **2.** following as a logical conclusion or inference. **3.** of consequence or importance. **4.** self-important; pompous. [< L *consequenti(a)* CONSEQUENCE + -AL[1]] —**con′se·quen′ti·al′·i·ty, con′se·quen′tial·ness,** *n.* —**con′se·quen′tial·ly,** *adv.*

con·se·quent·ly (kon′sə kwent′lē, -kwənt-), *adv.* as a result, effect, or outcome; therefore. [late ME] —**Syn.** See **therefore.**

con·serv·a·ble (kən sûr′və bəl), *adj.* capable of being conserved. [< LL *conservābil(is)*]

con·serv·an·cy (kən sûr′vən sē), *n., pl.* **-cies.** **1.** *Brit.* a commission regulating navigation, fisheries, etc. **2.** conservation of natural resources. [< ML *conservantia* (see CONSERVE, -ANCY); r. *conservacy* < ML *conservātia;* see -ACY] —**con·serv′ant,** *adj.*

con·ser·va·tion (kon′sər vā′shən), *n.* **1.** the act of conserving; preservation from loss, injury, decay, or waste. **2.** the official protection of rivers, forests, and other natural resources. [< L *conservātiōn-* (s. of *conservātiō*) = *conservāt(us)* (ptp. of *conservāre;* see CONSERVE, -ATE[1]) + *-iōn-* -ION] —**con′ser·va′tion·al,** *adj.*

con·ser·va·tion·ist (kon′sər vā′shə nist), *n.* a person who advocates or promotes conservation, esp. of the natural resources of a country.

conserva′tion of en′ergy, *Physics.* the principle that the amount of energy in a closed system is constant, irrespective of changes in form. Also called **law of conservation of energy.**

conserva′tion of mass′, *Physics.* the principle that the mass in a closed system is constant irrespective of changes in form. Also called **conserva′tion of mat′ter, law of conservation of mass.**

con·serv·a·tism (kən sûr′və tiz′əm), *n.* **1.** the disposition to preserve what is established and to resist change. **2.** the principles and practices of political conservatives. [CONSERVAT(IVE) + -ISM]

con·serv·a·tive (kən sûr′və tiv), *adj.* **1.** disposed to preserve existing conditions, institutions, etc., and to resist change. **2.** cautious; moderate: *a conservative estimate.* **3.** traditional in style or manner; avoiding showiness: *a suit of conservative cut.* **4.** (*cap.*) of or pertaining to the Conservative party. **5.** of or pertaining to political conservatism. **6.** having the power or tendency to conserve; preservative. **7.** of or pertaining to Conservative Judaism or Conservative Jews. —*n.* **8.** a person who is conservative in principles, actions, habits, etc. **9.** a member of a conservative political party. **10.** a preservative. [< LL *conservātīv(us)* (see CONSERVATION, -IVE); r. ME *conservatif* < MF] —**con·serv′a·tive·ly,** *adv.* —**con·serv′a·tive·ness,** *n.*

Conserv′ative Jew′, a Jew who adheres to most principles and practices of traditional Judaism but accepts some adaptation to contemporary conditions. Cf. **Orthodox Jew, Reform Jew.**

Conserv′ative Ju′daism, Judaism as observed by Conservative Jews.

Conserv′ative par′ty, a political party in Great Britain founded about 1832 as successor to the Tory party.

con·ser·va·tor (kon′sər vā′tər, kən sûr′və-), *n.* a guardian; custodian: *the conservator of prints at the museum.* [< L; see CONSERVATION, -OR[2]]

con·serv·a·to·ry (kən sûr′və tôr′ē, -tōr′ē), *n., pl.* **-ries,** *adj.* —*n.* **1.** a greenhouse. **2.** a school of music. **3.** *Obs.* a place where things are preserved. —*adj.* **4.** serving or adapted to conserve; preservative. [< L *conservāt(us)* (see CONSERVATION) + -ORY[2]]

con·serve (*v.* kən sûrv′; *n.* kon′sûrv, kən sûrv′), *v.,* **-served, -serv·ing,** *n.* —*v.t.* **1.** to keep from loss, decay, waste, or injury; preserve: *Conserve your strength for the race.* **2.** to preserve (fruit). —*n.* **3.** Often, **conserves.** preserves prepared from mixed fruits. [(v.) ME < L *conserv(āre)* (to) preserve = *con-* CON- + *servāre* to watch over, akin to OE *searu* armor; (n.) ME < MF < LL **conserv(a)* < L *conservāre,* as above] —**con·serv′er,** *n.*

con·sid·er (kən sid′ər), *v.t.* **1.** to think carefully about, esp. in order to make a decision; contemplate; reflect on. **2.** to regard, think, believe, or suppose. **3.** to bear in mind; make allowance for. **4.** to pay attention to; regard: *He considered the man for some time before speaking to him.* **5.** to regard with respect; esteem. **6.** *Archaic.* to view attentively;

scrutinize. **7.** *Obs.* to recompense or remunerate. **—*v.i.*** **8.** to think or view deliberately or carefully. [ME *consid(e)re* < L *consīderāre* to examine = *con-* CON- + *sīder-* (s. of *sīdus*) star group, sky + *-āre* inf. suffix] **—con·sid′er·er,** *n.* **—Syn. 1.** ponder, deliberate, weigh. See **study.**

con·sid·er·a·ble (kən sid′ər ə bəl), *adj.* **1.** rather large or great, as in size, distance, extent, etc. **2.** worthy of respect. **—*n.*** **3.** *U.S. Informal.* much; not a little. [late ME < ML *consīderābil(is)*] **—con·sid′er·a·bly,** *adv.*

con·sid·er·ate (kən sid′ər it), *adj.* **1.** having regard for another's feelings, circumstances, etc. **2.** carefully considered; deliberate. **3.** *Archaic.* marked by consideration or reflection; deliberate; prudent. [< L *consīderāt(us)*, ptp. of *consīderāre* to CONSIDER] **—con·sid′er·ate·ly,** *adv.* **—con·sid′er·ate·ness,** *n.* **—Syn. 1.** kind, concerned. See **thoughtful.**

con·sid·er·a·tion (kən sid′ə rā′shən), *n.* **1.** the act of considering; careful thought; meditation; deliberation. **2.** something that should be kept in mind in making a decision, evaluating facts, etc.: *The judge said the prisoner's age was an important consideration.* **3.** a thought or reflection. **4.** a payment; compensation. **5.** *Law.* something that suffices to make an informal promise legally binding, usually some value given in exchange for the promise. **6.** thoughtful or sympathetic concern; thoughtfulness for others. **7.** importance or consequence. **8.** estimation; esteem. [< L *consīderātiōn-* (s. of *consīderātiō*)] **—Syn. 1.** contemplation, rumination; attention. **4.** remuneration, fee. **6.** kindness, kindliness. **7.** weight, significance, moment.

con·sid·ered (kən sid′ərd), *adj.* **1.** thought about or decided upon with care: *a considered opinion.* **2.** regarded with esteem: *a highly considered person.*

con·sid·er·ing (kən sid′ər ing), *prep.* **1.** taking into account; in view of. **—*adv.*** **2.** *Informal.* with all things considered (used only after the statement it modifies): *He looks well, considering.* **—*conj.*** **3.** taking into consideration that: *Considering they are newcomers, they've adjusted very well.* [ME]

con·sign (kən sīn′), *v.t.* **1.** to hand over or deliver formally; commit (often fol. by *to*). **2.** to transfer to another's custody or charge; entrust. **3.** to set apart or aside; relegate. **4.** *Com.* **a.** to ship, as by common carrier, esp. for sale or custody. **b.** to address for such shipment. **—*v.i.*** **5.** to agree or assent. **6.** *Obs.* to yield or submit. [appar. < ML *consign(āre)* (to) mark with sign of cross, L: to mark with a seal. See CON-, SIGN] **—con·sign′a·ble,** *adj.* **—con·sig·na·tion** (kon′sig nā′shən), *n.*

con·sign·ee (kon′sī nē′, -si-, kən sī-), *n.* the person or party to whom something is consigned.

con·sign·ment (kən sīn′mənt), *n.* **1.** the act of consigning. **2.** something that is consigned, esp. property sent to an agent for sale, storage, or shipment. **3. on consignment,** (of goods) sent to an agent for sale, with title held by the consignor until a sale is made.

con·sign·or (kən sī′nər, kon′sī nôr′), *n.* a person or company that consigns goods, merchandise, etc. Also, **con·sign·er** (kən sī′nər).

con·sist (kən sist′), *v.i.* **1.** to be made up or composed (usually fol. by *of*). **2.** to inhere, exist, lie, etc. (usually fol. by *in*): *Her charm does not consist only in her beauty.* **3.** to be compatible, consistent, or harmonious (usually fol. by *with*). **4.** *Archaic.* to exist together. [< L *consist(ere)* (to) stand together, stand firm = *con-* CON- + *sistere*, redup. v. akin to *stāre* to STAND]

—Usage. 1, 2. CONSIST OF, CONSIST IN are often confused. With CONSIST OF, parts, materials, or ingredients are spoken of: *Bread consists of flour, yeast, etc.* With CONSIST IN, something resembling a definition is given: *Cooperation consists in helping one another and in sharing losses or gains.*

con·sist·en·cy (kən sis′tən sē), *n., pl.* **-cies. 1.** the condition of cohering or holding together and retaining form. **2.** degree of density, firmness, viscosity, etc.: *The liquid has the consistency of cream.* **3.** steadfast adherence to the same principles, course, form, etc.: *There is consistency in his pattern of behavior.* **4.** agreement among the parts of a complex thing: *consistency of colors throughout the house.* Also, **con·sist′ence.** [CONSIST(ENT) + -ENCY]

con·sist·ent (kən sis′tənt), *adj.* **1.** not self-contradictory. **2.** constantly adhering to the same principles, course, form, etc. **3.** holding firmly together; cohering. **4.** *Archaic.* fixed, firm; solid. [< L *consistent-* (s. of *consistēns*, prp. of *consistere*)] **—con·sist′ent·ly,** *adv.* **—Syn. 1.** congruous, consonant.

con·sis·to·ry (kən sis′tə rē), *n., pl.* **-ries. 1.** any of various assemblies, councils, or tribunals. **2.** the place where such a body meets. **3.** the meeting of any such body. **4.** *Rom. Cath. Ch.* a solemn assembly of the whole body of cardinals, summoned and presided over by the pope. **5.** *Ch. of Eng.* a diocesan court presided over by the bishop, the bishop's chancellor, or the commissary. **6.** (in certain Reformed churches) the governing board of a local church or congregation. **7.** *Obs.* a council chamber. [ME *consistorie* < LL *consistōri(um)*] **—con·sis·to·ri·al** (kon′si stōr′ē əl, -stôr′-), **con′sis·to′ri·an,** *adj.*

con·so·ci·ate (*adj., n.* kən sō′shē it, -āt′; *v.* kən sō′shē āt′), *adj., n., v.i.,* **-at·ed, -at·ing.** associate. [< L *consociāt(us)* (ptp. of *consociāre*) = *con-* CON- + *soci(us)* fellow, partner + *-ātus* -ATE[1]] **—con·so·ci·a·tion** (kən sō′sē ā′shən, -shē-), *n.*

consol., consolidated.

con·so·la·tion (kon′sə lā′shən), *n.* **1.** the act of consoling; comfort; solace. **2.** the state of being consoled. **3.** a person or thing that consoles: *His religious faith was a consolation during his troubles.* [ME *consolacion* < L *consōlātiōn-* (s. of *consōlātiō*) = *consōlāt(us)*, ptp. of *consōlārī* (see CONSOLE[1]) + *-iōn-* -ION] **—con·sol·a·to·ry** (kən sol′ə tōr′ē, -tôr′ē), *adj.* **—con·sol′i·to′ri·ly,** *adv.* **—con·sol′i·to′ri·ness,** *n.*

consola′tion prize′, a prize, usually of minor value, given to the loser or runner-up in a contest.

con·sole[1] (kən sōl′), *v.t.,* **-soled, -sol·ing.** to attempt to lessen the grief, sorrow, or disappointment of; give solace or comfort; cheer up. [< L *consōl(ārī)* = *con-* CON- + *sōlārī* to soothe; perh. akin to OE *sæl* happiness (see SILLY)] **—con·sol′a·ble,** *adj.* **—con·sol′er,** *n.* **—con·sol′ing·ly,** *adj.*

con·sole[2] (kon′sōl), *n.* **1.** a desklike structure containing the keyboards, pedals, etc., by means of which an organ is played. **2.** a radio, phonograph, or television cabinet that stands on the floor. **3.** See **console table. 4.** *Archit.* an ornamental corbel or bracket, esp. one high in relation to its projections. **5.** the control unit of an electrical or electronic system. [< F < ?]

Console[2] (def. 1)

con′sole ta′ble (kon′sōl), **1.** a table supported by consoles or brackets fixed to a wall. **2.** a table, often with bracketlike legs, designed to fit against a wall.

con·sol·i·date (kən sol′i dāt′), *v.,* **-dat·ed, -dat·ing. —*v.t.*** **1.** to bring together (separate parts) into a single whole; unite; combine. **2.** to make firm or secure; strengthen: *to consolidate gains.* **—*v.i.*** **3.** to unite or combine. **4.** to become firm. [< L *consolidāt(us)* (ptp. of *consolidāre*). See CON-, SOLID, -ATE[1]] **—con·sol′i·da′tor,** *n.*

con·sol·i·da·tion (kən sol′i dā′shən), *n.* **1.** an act or instance of consolidating. **2.** the state of being consolidated. **3.** something consolidated. **4.** *Law.* **a.** a statutory combination of two or more corporations. **b.** the union of two or more claims or actions at law for trial or appeal. [< LL *consolidātiōn-* (s. of *consolidātiō*)] **—con·sol′i·da′tive,** *adj.*

con·sols (kon′solz, kən solz′), *n.pl.* the funded government securities of Great Britain. Also called **bank annuities.** [short for *consolidated annuities*]

con·sol·ute (kon′sə lo͞ot′), *adj.* *Chem.* (of two liquids) mutually soluble in all proportions. [< LL *consolūt(us)* dissolved together]

con·som·mé (kon′sə mā′, kon′sə mā′; *Fr.* kôn sô mā′), *n.* a clear soup made by boiling meat, bones, and, sometimes, vegetables; broth. [< F, n. use of ptp. of *consommer* to finish < L *consummāt(us)* CONSUMMATE]

con·so·nance (kon′sə nəns), *n.* **1.** accord or agreement. **2.** correspondence of sounds; harmony of sounds. **3.** *Music.* a simultaneous combination of tones conventionally accepted as being in a state of repose. Cf. **dissonance** (def. 2). See illus. at **resolution. 4.** *Pros.* **a.** the correspondence of consonants, esp. those at the end of a word, in a passage of prose or verse. Cf. **alliteration** (def. 1). **b.** the use of the repetition of consonants or consonant patterns as a rhyming device. Also, **con′so·nan·cy.** [late ME < L *consonantia* concord]

con·so·nant (kon′sə nənt), *n.* **1.** *Phonet.* (in English articulation) a speech sound produced by occluding (*p, b; t, d; k, g*), diverting (*m, n, ng*), or obstructing (*f, v; s, z,* etc.) the flow of air from the lungs (opposed to *vowel*). **2.** a letter that represents a consonant sound. **—*adj.*** **3.** in agreement; agreeable; consistent (usually fol. by *to* or *with*): *behavior consonant with his character.* **4.** corresponding or harmonious in sound. **5.** *Music.* constituting a consonance. **6.** consonantal. [late ME *consona(u)nt* < L *consonant-* (s. of *consonāns*, prp. of *consonāre* to sound with or together)] **—con′so·nant·ly,** *adv.* **—Ant. 5.** dissonant.

con·so·nan·tal (kon′sə nan′tᵊl), *adj.* of, characteristic of, or marked by a consonant. Also, **con′so·nan′tic.** **—con′so·nan′tal·ly,** *adv.*

con·sort (*n.* kon′sôrt; *v.* kən sôrt′), *n.* **1.** a husband or wife; spouse. **2.** the spouse of a royal person. **3.** one vessel or ship accompanying another. **4.** *Music.* **a.** a group of instrumentalists and singers. **b.** a group of instruments of the same family: *a consort of viols.* **5.** *Obs.* **a.** a companion or partner. **b.** company or association. **c.** accord or agreement. **d.** harmony of sounds. **—*v.i.*** **6.** to associate; keep company: *to consort with known criminals.* **7.** to agree or harmonize. **—*v.t.*** **8.** to associate, join, or unite. **9.** *Obs.* to accompany. [late ME < MF < L *consort-* (s. of *consors*) sharer, orig. sharing (adj.)] **—con·sort′a·ble,** *adj.* **—con·sort′er,** *n.* **—con·sor′tion,** *n.*

con·sor·ti·um (kən sôr′shē əm), *n., pl.* **-ti·a** (-shē ə). **1.** a combination of financial institutions for effecting some financial operation requiring large resources of capital. **2.** any association, partnership, or union. [< L: partnership = *consort-* CONSORT + *-ium* n. suffix] **—con·sor′ti·al,** *adj.*

con·spe·cif·ic (kon′spi sif′ik), *adj.* *Bot., Zool.* belonging to the same species. [*conspeci(es)* (see CON-, SPECIES) + -FIC]

con·spec·tus (kən spek′təs), *n., pl.* **-tus·es. 1.** a general or comprehensive view; survey. **2.** a digest; summary; résumé. [< L: survey n. use of ptp. of *conspicere* = *con-* CON- + *spec-* (s. of *specere* to look) + *-tus* ptp. ending] **—Syn. 2.** compendium, brief, abstract.

con·spic·u·ous (kən spik′yo͞o əs), *adj.* **1.** easily seen or noticed; readily observable. **2.** attracting special attention, as by outstanding qualities, eccentricities, etc. [< L *conspicuus* visible, conspicuous = *con-* CON- + *spicu-* (var. s. of *spicere, specere;* see CONSPECTUS) + *-us* -OUS] **—con·spic′u·ous·ly,** *adv.* **—con·spic′u·ous·ness, con·spi·cu·i·ty** (kon′spi kyo͞o′i tē), *n.* **—Syn. 1.** manifest, noticeable, clear, marked. **2.** prominent, striking, noteworthy.

con·spir·a·cy (kən spir′ə sē), *n., pl.* **-cies. 1.** the act of conspiring. **2.** an evil, unlawful, treacherous, or surreptitious plan formulated in secret by two or more persons; plot. **3.** a combination of persons for a secret, unlawful, or evil purpose. **4.** *Law.* an agreement by two or more persons to commit a crime, fraud, or other wrongful act. **5.** any concurrence in action; combination in bringing about a given result. [ME *conspiracie* (see CONSPIRE, -ACY); r. ME *conspiracioun* < AF; MF *conspiration* < L] **—con·spir′a·tive,** *adj.* **—con·spir·a·to·ri·al** (kən spir′ə tōr′ē əl, -tôr′-), **con·spir·a·to·ry** (kən spir′ə tōr′ē, -tôr′ē), *adj.* **—con·spir′a·to′ri·al·ly,** *adv.*

con·spire (kən spīᵊr′), *v.,* **-spired, -spir·ing. —*v.i.*** **1.** to agree together, esp. secretly, to do something wrong, evil, or illegal. **2.** to act or work together toward the same result or goal. —*v.t.* 3. to plot (something wrong, evil, or illegal). [ME < L *conspīr(āre)* (to) plot (lit., breathe) together = *con-* CON- + *spīrāre* to breathe; see SPIRANT, SPIRIT] —**con·spir·a·tor** (kən spir′ə tər), **con·spir′er;** *referring to a woman,* **con·spir′a·tress,** *n.* —**con·spir′ing·ly,** *adv.* —**Syn. 1.** complot, intrigue. See **plot**[1]. **2.** combine, concur, cooperate.

Const., 1. constable. 2. constitution.

con·sta·ble (kon′stə bəl *or, esp. Brit.,* kun′-), *n.* **1.** any of various officers of the peace, as one who executes the processes of a justice of the peace. **2.** *Chiefly Brit.* a policeman. **3.** a military officer of high rank in medieval monarchies. **4.** the keeper or governor of a royal fortress or castle. [ME *conestable* < OF < LL *comes stabulī* COUNT[2] of the STABLE[1]] —**con′sta·ble·ship′,** *n.*

Con·sta·ble (kun′stə bəl, kon′-), *n.* **John,** 1776–1837, English painter.

con·stab·u·lar·y[1] (kən stab′yə ler′ē), *n., pl.* **-lar·ies. 1.** the body of constables of a district or locality. **2.** a body of officers of the peace organized on a military basis. [< ML *constabulāri(a),* fem. of *constabulārius* CONSTABULARY[2]]

con·stab·u·lar·y[2] (kən stab′yə ler′ē), *adj.* pertaining to constables or their duties. Also, **con·stab·u·lar** (kən stab′yə lər). [< ML *constabulāri(us)* = *comes stabul(ī)* CONSTABLE + *-ārius* -ARY]

Con·stance (kon′stəns), *n.* **1. Lake.** German, **Boden See.** a lake in W Europe, bounded by Germany, Austria, and Switzerland. 46 mi. long; 207 sq. mi. **2.** German, **Konstanz.** a city in S West Germany, on this lake: important church council 1414–18. 55,100 (1963).

con·stan·cy (kon′stən sē), *n.* **1.** the quality of being unchanging or unwavering, as in purpose, love, loyalty, etc.; firmness of mind; faithfulness. **2.** uniformity or regularity, as in qualities, conditions, etc.; stability. [< L *constantia*] —**Syn. 1.** resolution; steadfastness, fidelity. **2.** dependability. —**Ant. 1.** irresolution; infidelity. **2.** fickleness.

con·stant (kon′stənt), *adj.* **1.** not changing or varying; uniform. **2.** continuing without pause or letup; unceasing: *constant noise.* **3.** regularly recurrent; continual; persistent: *constant interruption.* **4.** faithful; unswerving in love, devotion, etc. **5.** steadfast; resolute. —*n.* **6.** something that does not or cannot change or vary. [ME < L *constant-* (s. of *constāns,* prp. of *constāre* to stand firm) = *con-* CON- + *stā-* stand + *-nt-* prp. suffix] —**con′stant·ly,** *adv.* —**Syn. 1.** unchanging, immutable, permanent. **2.** perpetual, unremitting, uninterrupted. **3.** incessant, ceaseless. See **continual. 4.** loyal, stanch, true. See **faithful. 5.** unwavering, unswerving, unshaken. —**Ant. 1.** changeable. **5.** wavering.

Con·stant (kôN stäN′), *n.* **Jean Jo·seph Ben·ja·min** (zhäN zhô zef′ baN zhA maN′), 1845–1902, French painter.

Con·stan·ţa (kôn stän′tsä), *n.* a seaport in SE Rumania, on the Black Sea. 198,429.

con·stant·an (kon′stən tan′), *n.* an alloy containing 60 percent copper and 40 percent nickel, used for electrical resistance heating and thermocouples. [CONSTANT + -AN]

Con·stant de Re·becque (kôN stäN′ də rə bek′), **Hen·ri Ben·ja·min** (äN rē′ baN zhA maN′), (*Benjamin Constant*), 1767–1830, French author and statesman, born in Switzerland.

Con·stan·tine (kon′stən tēn′ *or, for 1,* -tīn′; *for 2, also Fr.* kôN staN tēn′), *n.* **1.** died A.D. 715, pope 708–715. **2.** a city in NE Algeria. 1,682,000.

Con·stan·tine I (kon′stən tēn′, -tīn′), **1.** (*Flavius Valerius Aurelius Constantinus*) ("*the Great*") A.D. 288?–337, Roman emperor 324–337. **2.** 1868–1923, king of Greece 1913–17, 1920–22. —**Con·stan·tin·i·an** (kon′stən tin′ē ən), *adj.*

Constantine II, born 1940, king of Greece 1964–67.

Con·stan·ti·no·ple (kon′stan tᵊnō′pəl), *n.* former name of **Istanbul.** See map at **Byzantine Empire.**

con·stel·late (kon′stə lāt′), *v.i., v.t.,* **-lat·ed, -lat·ing.** to cluster together, as stars in a constellation. [< LL *constellāt-(us)* star-studded = L *con-* CON- + *stell(a)* star + *-ātus* -ATE[1]]

con·stel·la·tion (kon′stə lā′shən), *n.* **1.** *Astron.* **a.** any of various configurations of stars to which names have been given. **b.** the section of the heavens occupied by such a configuration. **2.** *Astrol.* **a.** the grouping or relative position of the stars as supposed to influence events, esp. at a person's birth. **b.** *Obs.* character as presumed to be determined by the stars. [ME *constellacioun* < LL *constellātiōn-* (s. of *constellātiō*)] —**con·stel·la·to·ry** (kən stel′ə tōr′ē, -tôr′ē), *adj.*

con·ster·nate (kon′stər nāt′), *v.t.,* **-nat·ed, -nat·ing.** to dismay, confuse, or terrify. [< L *consternāt(us)* (ptp. of *consternāre* to alarm, dismay) = *con-* CON- + *sternā-* make to shy or dodge, startle + *-tus* ptp. suffix; akin to STRATUM]

con·ster·na·tion (kon′stər nā′shən), *n.* a sudden, alarming amazement or dread that results in utter confusion; dismay. [< L *consternātiōn-* (s. of *consternātiō*)] —**Syn.** bewilderment, alarm, fear, panic, horror. —**Ant.** composure, equanimity.

con·sti·pate (kon′stə pāt′), *v.t.,* **-pat·ed, -pat·ing.** to cause constipation in; make costive. [late ME (ptp.) < L *constīpāt(us)* (ptp. of *constīpāre*) = *con-* CON- + *stīpā-* (s. of *stīpāre* to crowd, press) + *-tus* ptp. suffix]

con·sti·pa·tion (kon′stə pā′shən), *n.* a condition of the bowels in which the feces are dry and hardened and evacuation is difficult and infrequent. [late ME *constipacioun* < LL *constīpātiōn-* (s. of *constīpātiō*)]

con·stit·u·en·cy (kən stich′o͞o ən sē), *n., pl.* **-cies. 1.** the residents or voters of a district represented by an elective officer. **2.** the district itself. [CONSTITU(ENT) + -ENCY]

con·stit·u·ent (kən stich′o͞o ənt), *adj.* **1.** serving to compose or make up a thing; component: *the constituent parts of a motor.* **2.** having power to frame or alter a political constitution or fundamental law, as distinguished from lawmaking power: *a constituent assembly.* —*n.* **3.** a constituent element, material, etc.; component. **4.** a person who authorizes another to act for him, as a voter in a Congressional district. **5.** *Gram.* an element considered as part of a construction. [< L *constituent-* (s. of *constituēns,* prp. of *constituere* to set up, found, constitute) = *con-* CON- + *-stitu-* (var. s. of *status* STATUS) + *-ent-* -ENT] —**con·stit′u·ent·ly,** *adv.* —**Syn. 3.** See **element.**

con·sti·tute (kon′sti to͞ot′, -tyo͞ot′), *v.t.,* **-tut·ed, -tut·ing. 1.** to compose; form: *mortar constituted of lime and sand.* **2.** to appoint to an office or function. **3.** to set up or establish (laws, an institution, etc.). **4.** to give legal form to (an assembly, court, etc.). **5.** to create or be tantamount to: *The heavy rain constituted a hazard to the crops.* [late ME < L *constitūt(us)* (ptp. of *constituere;* see CONSTITUENT) = *con-* CON- + *-stitūtum,* comb. form of *statūtum,* ptp. of *statuere* to set up; see STATUTE] —**con′sti·tut′er, con′sti·tu′tor,** *n.*

con·sti·tu·tion (kon′sti to͞o′shən, -tyo͞o′-), *n.* **1.** the way in which a thing is composed or made up; composition. **2.** the physical character of the body as to strength, health, etc.: *Plenty of exercise has given him a strong constitution.* **3.** character or condition of mind; disposition; temperament. **4.** the act or process of constituting; establishment. **5.** the state of being constituted; formation. **6.** any established arrangement or custom. **7.** (*cap.*) See **Constitution of the United States. 8.** the system of fundamental principles according to which a nation, state, corporation, or the like, is governed. **9.** the document embodying these principles. [ME *constitucion* < L *constitūtiōn-* (s. of *constitūtiō*)]

Constitution, The, an American 44-gun frigate, famous for its exploits in the War of 1812: popularly, "Old Ironsides."

con·sti·tu·tion·al (kon′sti to͞o′shə nᵊl, -tyo͞o′-), *adj.* **1.** belonging to or inherent in the character or make-up of a person's body or mind. **2.** beneficial to one's health. **3.** pertaining to the composition of a thing; essential. **4.** of or pertaining to the constitution of a state, organization, etc. **5.** subject to or provided by such a constitution: *constitutional guarantees of freedom of speech.* —*n.* **6.** a walk or other exercise taken for the benefit of one's health. —**con′sti·tu′tion·al·ly,** *adv.*

Constitu′tional Conven′tion, the convention in Philadelphia (1787) of representatives from each of the Colonies except Rhode Island, at which the Constitution of the United States was framed.

con·sti·tu·tion·al·ism (kon′sti to͞o′shə nᵊliz′əm, -tyo͞o′-), *n.* **1.** the principles of constitutional government. **2.** constitutional rule or authority; adherence to constitutional principles. —**con′sti·tu′tion·al·ist,** *n.*

con·sti·tu·tion·al·i·ty (kon′sti to͞o′shə nal′i tē, -tyo͞o′-), *n.* **1.** the quality of being constitutional. **2.** accordance with the constitution of a country, state, etc.

constitu′tional mon′archy. See **limited monarchy.** —**constitu′tional mon′arch.**

Constitu′tion of the Unit′ed States′, the fundamental law of the U.S., framed in 1787 by the Constitutional Convention, and carried into effect March 4, 1789.

Con′stitu′tion State′, Connecticut (used as a nickname).

con·sti·tu·tive (kon′sti to͞o′tiv, -tyo͞o′-), *adj.* **1.** constituent; making a thing what it is; essential. **2.** having power to establish or enact. —**con′sti·tu′tive·ly,** *adv.*

constr., 1. construction. 2. construed.

con·strain (kən strān′), *v.t.* **1.** to force, compel, or oblige; bring about by compulsion. **2.** to confine forcibly, as by bonds. **3.** to repress or restrain. [ME *constrei(g)ne* < MF *constrei(g)n-* (s. of *constreindre*) < L *constringere*] —**con·strain′a·ble,** *adj.* —**con·strain′er,** *n.* —**con·strain′ing·ly,** *adv.* —**Syn. 1.** coerce. **2.** bind, confine.

con·strained (kən strānd′), *adj.* **1.** forced, compelled, or obliged. **2.** stiff or unnatural; uneasy or embarrassed: *a constrained smile.*

con·straint (kən strānt′), *n.* **1.** confinement or restriction. **2.** repression of natural feelings and impulses. **3.** embarrassment. **4.** something that constrains. **5.** the act of constraining. **6.** the condition of being constrained. [ME *constreinte* < MF = *constrein-* (see CONSTRAIN) + *-te* fem. suffix]

con·strict (kən strikt′), *v.t.* **1.** to draw or press in; cause to contract or shrink; compress. **2.** to slow or stop the natural course or development of. [< L *constrict(us)* (ptp. of *constringere* to draw together, tie up) = *con-* CON- + *stric-* (ptp. s. of *stringere* to tie; see STRICT) + *-tus* ptp. suffix] —**con·stric′tive,** *adj.* —**con·stric′tive·ly,** *adv.* —**Syn. 1.** cramp, squeeze, tighten. —**Ant. 1.** expand.

con·stric·tion (kən strik′shən), *n.* **1.** the act of constricting. **2.** the state of being constricted; tightness or inward pressure. **3.** a constricted part. **4.** something that constricts. [< LL *constrictiōn-* (s. of *constrictiō*)]

con·stric·tor (kən strik′tər), *n.* **1.** any snake that kills its prey by coiling tightly around it, causing suffocation. **2.** *Anat.* a muscle that constricts a hollow part of the body, as the pharynx. **3.** a person or thing that constricts. [< NL]

con·stringe (kən strinj′), *v.t.,* **-stringed, -string·ing.** to constrict; compress; cause to contract. [< L *constringe(re)* (to) draw tight, tie up = *con-* CON- + *stringere* to tie] —**con·strin′gent,** *adj.* —**con·strin′gen·cy,** *n.*

con·struct (*v.* kən strukt′; *n.* kon′strukt), *v.t.* **1.** to form by putting together parts; build; devise. **2.** *Geom.* to draw (a figure) fulfilling certain given conditions. —*n.* **3.** something constructed. **4.** a complex image or idea formed from a number of simpler images or ideas. [< L *construct(us)* (ptp. of *construere* to CONSTRUE) = *con-* CON- + *struc-* (ptp. s. of *struere* to build) + *-tus* ptp. suffix] —**con·struct′i·ble,** *adj.* —**con·struc′tor, con·struct′er,** *n.* —**Syn. 1.** erect, form. See **make.**

con·struc·tion (kən struk′shən), *n.* **1.** the act or art of constructing. **2.** the way in which a thing is constructed; structure: *a building of ingenious construction.* **3.** something that is constructed; a structure. **4.** *Gram.* **a.** the arrangement of two or more forms in a grammatical unit. **b.** a word or phrase consisting of two or more forms arranged in a particular way. **c.** a group of words or morphemes. **5.** explanation or interpretation, as of a law, a text, an action, etc. [ME < L *constructiōn-* (s. of *constructiō*) a putting together, building] —**con·struc′tion·al,** *adj.* —**con·struc′tion·al·ly,** *adv.*

con·struc·tion·ist (kən struk′shə nist), *n.* a person who construes or interprets, esp. laws or the like, in a specific manner: *a broad constructionist.* —**con·struc′tion·ism,** *n.*

con·struc·tive (kən struk′tiv), *adj.* **1.** helping to improve (opposed to *destructive*): *constructive criticism.* **2.** of, pertaining to, or of the nature of construction; structural. **3.** deduced by inference or interpretation; inferential: *constructive permission.* [< ML *constructīv(us)*] —**con·struc′tive·ly,** *adv.* —**con·struc′tive·ness,** *n.*

con·strue (*v.* kən stro͞o′ *or, esp. Brit.,* kon′stro͞o; *n.* kon′stro͞o), *v.,* **-strued, -stru·ing,** *n.* —*v.t.* **1.** to show the meaning or intention of; explain; interpret; invest with a particular interpretation. **2.** to deduce by inference or interpretation; infer. **3.** to translate, esp. literally. **4.** to analyze the syntax of: *to construe a sentence.* **5.** to arrange or combine (words, phrases, etc.) syntactically. —*v.i.* **6.** to admit of grammatical analysis or interpretation. —*n.* **7.** the act of construing. **8.** something that is construed. [ME *construe(n)* < L *construere*] (to) put together, build = *con-* CON- + *struere* to pile up, arrange, akin to *sternere* to spread; see STRATUM] —**con·stru′a·ble,** *adj.* —**con·stru′er,** *n.*

con·sub·stan·tial (kon′səb stan′shəl), *adj.* of one and the same substance, essence, or nature. [late ME < LL *consubstantiāl(is)*] —**con′sub·stan′ti·al′i·ty,** *n.*

con·sub·stan·ti·ate (kon′səb stan′shē āt′), *v.,* **-at·ed, -at·ing.** —*v.i.* **1.** to profess the doctrine of consubstantiation. **2.** to become united in one common substance or nature. —*v.t.* **3.** to unite in one common substance or nature. [< NL *consubstantiāt(us)* (ptp. of *consubstantiāre*)]

con·sub·stan·ti·a·tion (kon′səb stan′shē ā′shən), *n.* *Theol.* the doctrine that the substance of the body and blood of Christ coexist in and with the substance of bread and wine of the Eucharist. [< NL *consubstantiātiōn-* (s. of *consubstantiātiō*) = *con-* CON- + *(trans)substantiātiōn-* TRANSUBSTANTIATION]

con·sue·tude (kon′swi to͞od′, -tyo͞od′), *n.* custom, esp. as having legal force. [ME < L *consuētūd(ō)* = *con-* CON- + *suē-* (short s. of *suēscere* to become accustomed, akin to refl. pron. adj. *suus* one's own) + *-tūdō* -TUDE] —**con·sue·tu·di·nar·y** (kon′swi to͞od′^{ə}ner′ē, -tyo͞od′-), *adj.*

con·sul (kon′səl), *n.* **1.** a foreign-service officer stationed abroad to promote trade, protect the rights of his fellow citizens, issue visas to aliens, etc. **2.** either of the two chief magistrates of the ancient Roman republic. **3.** *Fr. Hist.* one of the three supreme magistrates of the First Republic during the period 1799–1804. [ME < L; akin to *consulere* to CONSULT] —**con′su·lar,** *adj.* —**con′sul·ship′,** *n.*

con′sular a′gent, a consular officer of the lowest rank.

con·su·late (kon′sə lit), *n.* **1.** the premises officially occupied by a consul. **2.** the position, work, authority, or term of service of a consul. **3.** (*often cap.*) a government by consuls. [< L *consulāt(us)*]

con′sulate gen′eral, *pl.* **consulates general.** the office or establishment of a consul general.

con′sul gen′eral, *pl.* **consuls general.** a consular officer of the highest rank.

con·sult (*v.* kən sult′; *n.* kon′sult, kən sult′), *v.t.* **1.** to seek advice or information from; ask guidance from. **2.** to refer to for information. **3.** to consider (a person's interest, convenience, etc.) in making plans. **4.** *Obs.* to meditate, plan, or contrive. —*v.i.* **5.** to consider or deliberate; take counsel; confer (usually fol. by *with*): *He consulted with his doctor.* —*n.* **6.** *Archaic.* a consultation. [< L *consult(āre)* (to) deliberate, consult = *consul(ere)* in same sense (*con-* CON- + *-sul-* to summon) + *-t-* freq. suffix + *-āre* inf. suffix] —**con·sult′a·ble,** *adj.* —**con·sult′er,** *n.*

con·sult·ant (kən sul′t^{ə}nt), *n.* **1.** a person who consults someone or something. **2.** a person who gives professional or expert advice. [< L *consultant-* (s. of *consultāns,* prp. of *consultāre*)]

con·sul·ta·tion (kon′səl tā′shən), *n.* **1.** the act of consulting; conference. **2.** a meeting for deliberation, discussion, or decision. [< L *consultātiōn-* (s. of *consultātiō*) = *consultāt(us)* (ptp. of *consultāre;* see CONSULT, -ATE[1]) + *-iōn-* -ION]

con·sult·a·tive (kən sul′tə tiv), *adj.* of or pertaining to consultation; advisory. Also, **con·sul·ta·to·ry** (kən sul′tə-tôr′ē, -tōr′ē), **con·sul′tive.** [CONSULTAT(ION) + -IVE] —**con·sult′a·tive·ly,** *adv.*

con·sult·ing (kən sul′ting), *adj.* employed in giving professional advice, either to the public or to those practicing the profession: *a consulting physician.*

con·sume (kən so͞om′), *v.,* **-sumed, -sum·ing.** —*v.t.* **1.** to destroy or expend by use; use up. **2.** to eat or drink up; devour. **3.** to destroy, as by decomposition or burning: *Fire consumed the forest.* **4.** to spend (money, time, etc.) wastefully. **5.** to absorb; engross: *She was consumed with curiosity.* —*v.i.* **6.** to undergo destruction; waste away. [ME < L *consūm(ere)* = *con-* CON- + *sūmere* to take up (*sub-* SUB- + *emere* to take, get)] —**con·sum′a·ble,** *adj.* —**Syn. 1.** exhaust, expend. **4.** squander, dissipate.

con·sum·ed·ly (kən so͞o′mid lē), *adv.* excessively; extremely: *a consumedly decent thing to do.*

con·sum·er (kən so͞o′mər), *n.* **1.** a person or thing that consumes. **2.** *Econ.* a person who uses a commodity or service.

consum′er goods′, *Econ.* goods that are ready for consumption in satisfaction of human wants, as clothing, food, etc., and are not utilized in any further production (contrasted with *capital goods*).

con·sum·er·ism (kən so͞o′mər iz′əm), *n.* a modern movement for the protection of the consumer against useless, inferior, or dangerous products, misleading advertising, unfair pricing, etc.

con·sum·mate (*v.* kon′sə māt′; *adj.* kən sum′it, kon′sə-mit), *v.,* **-mat·ed, -mat·ing,** *adj.* —*v.t.* **1.** to bring to completion or perfection. **2.** to complete (a marriage) by sexual intercourse. —*adj.* **3.** complete or perfect; superb: *a consummate master of the violin.* [late ME (adj.) < L *consummāt(us)* (ptp. of *consummāre* to complete, bring to perfection). See CON-, SUM, -ATE[1]] —**con·sum′mate·ly,** *adv.* —**con′sum·ma′tion,** *n.* —**con′sum·ma′tive, con·sum·ma·to·ry** (kən sum′ə tôr′ē, -tōr′ē), *adj.* —**con′sum·ma′tor,** *n.* —**Syn. 1.** complete, perfect, accomplish. **3.** finished, supreme. —**Ant. 3.** imperfect, unfinished.

con·sump·tion (kən sump′shən), *n.* **1.** the act of consuming, as by use, decay, or destruction. **2.** an amount consumed. **3.** *Econ.* the using up of goods and services having an exchangeable value. **4.** *Pathol.* **a.** a wasting disease, esp. tuberculosis of the lungs. **b.** progressive wasting of the body. [ME *consumpcyon* < L *consumptiōn-* (s. of *consumptiō*) a consuming, wasting = *consumpt(us),* ptp. of *consūmere* to CONSUME (*con-* CON- + *sump-* (var. s. of *sūmere* to take up, spend) + *-tus* ptp. suffix) + *-iōn-* -ION]

con·sump·tive (kən sump′tiv), *adj.* **1.** tending to consume; destructive; wasteful. **2.** pertaining to consumption by use. **3.** *Pathol.* pertaining to or affected by consumption. —*n.* **4.** a person who suffers from consumption. [CONSUMPT(ION) + -IVE] —**con·sump′tive·ly,** *adv.* —**con·sump′tive·ness,** *n.*

Cont., Continental.

cont., **1.** containing. **2.** contents. **3.** continent. **4.** continental. **5.** continue. **6.** continued. **7.** contra. **8.** contract.

con·tact (kon′takt), *n.* **1.** the act or state of touching; a touching or meeting, as of two things, people, etc. **2.** immediate proximity or association. **3.** an acquaintance or relative through whom one can gain access to information, favors, or the like. **4.** *Elect.* a junction of electric conductors, usually metal, that controls current flow, often completing or interrupting a circuit. **5.** a condition in which two or more individuals or groups are placed in communication with each other. —*v.t.* **6.** to put or bring into contact. **7.** to communicate with (a person): *We'll contact you by telephone.* —*v.i.* **8.** to enter into or be in contact. [< L *contact(us)* a touching (n. use of ptp. of *contingere*) = *con-* CON- + *tac-* (var. of *tag-,* var. s. of *tangere, -tingere* to touch) + *-tus* ptp. suffix] —**con·tac·tu·al** (kon tak′cho͞o əl), *adj.* —**con·tac′tu·al·ly,** *adv.*

con′tact lens′, one of a pair of small, inconspicuous lenses of plastic placed over the cornea to aid defective vision.

con·tac·tor (kon′tak tər, kən tak′tər), *n.* *Elect.* a mechanically operated switch for continuously establishing and interrupting an electric power circuit.

con′tact print′, *Photog.* a print made by placing a negative directly upon sensitized paper and exposing to light.

con·ta·gion (kən tā′jən), *n.* **1.** the communication of disease by direct or indirect contact. **2.** a disease so communicated. **3.** the medium by which a contagious disease is transmitted. **4.** harmful or undesirable contact or influence. **5.** the ready transmission or spread as of an idea, attitude, emotion, etc., from person to person. [ME < L *contāgiōn-* (s. of *contāgiō*) contact, infection = *con-* CON- + *tāg-* (var. s. of *tangere* to touch) + *-iōn-* -ION] —**con·ta′gioned,** *adj.*

con·ta·gious (kən tā′jəs), *adj.* **1.** capable of being transmitted, as from one person to another, by contact with an infected person or object: *contagious diseases.* **2.** carrying or spreading a contagious disease. **3.** tending to spread from person to person: *contagious laughter.* [ME < LL *contāgiōs(us)*] —**con·ta′gious·ly,** *adv.* —**con·ta′gious·ness, con·ta·gi·os·i·ty** (kən tā′jē os′i tē), *n.*
—**Syn. 1.** catching. **3.** CONTAGIOUS, INFECTIOUS have scientific uses in which they are precisely defined; but in popular use in referring to disease, the words are often confused. In popular figurative use, in which both have favorable connotations, they are differentiated to some extent. CONTAGIOUS emphasizes the rapidity with which the contagion spreads: *Contagious laughter ran through the hall.* INFECTIOUS suggests the pleasantly irresistible quality of the source of contagion: *His infectious humor stimulated applause.*

con·ta·gium (kən tā′jəm, -jē əm), *n., pl.* **-gia** (-jə, -jē ə). *Pathol.* the causative agent of a contagious or infectious disease, as a virus. [< L = *contāg-* (see CONTAGION) + *-ium* n. suffix]

con·tain (kən tān′), *v.t.* **1.** to hold or include within a volume or area. **2.** to be capable of holding; have capacity for. **3.** to have as contents or constituent parts; comprise; include. **4.** to keep under proper control; restrain: *He could not contain his amusement.* **5.** to prevent or restrict the success of or damage by (an enemy, competitor, disaster, or the like). **6.** *Math.* (of a number) to be a multiple of; be divisible by, without a remainder: *Ten contains five.* [ME *conte(y)ne* < OF *conteni(r)* < L *continēre* = *con-* CON- + *tenēre* to hold] —**con·tain′a·ble,** *adj.*
—**Syn. 1.** CONTAIN, HOLD, ACCOMMODATE express the idea that something is so designed that something else can exist or be placed within it. CONTAIN refers to what is actually within a given container. HOLD emphasizes the idea of causing to remain in position, or keeping within bounds; it refers also to the greatest amount or number that can be kept within a given container. ACCOMMODATE means to contain comfortably or conveniently, or to meet the needs of a certain number. A passenger plane which ACCOMMODATES fifty passengers may be able to HOLD sixty, but at a given time may CONTAIN only thirty. **3.** embody, embrace.

con·tain·er (kən tā′nər), *n.* anything that contains or can contain something, as a carton, box, crate, can, etc.

con·tain·ment (kən tān′mənt), *n.* **1.** the act or condition of containing. **2.** the act or policy of restricting the territorial growth or ideological influence of a hostile nation.

con·tam·i·nant (kən tam′ə nənt), *n.* something that contaminates. [< L *contāminant-* (s. of *contāmināns*), prp. of *contāmināre.* See CONTAMINATE, -ANT]

con·tam·i·nate (*v.* kən tam′ə nāt′; *adj.* kən tam′ə nit, -nāt′), *v.,* **-nat·ed, -nat·ing,** *adj.* —*v.t.* **1.** to render impure or unsuitable by contact or mixture with something unclean, bad, etc. **2.** to render harmful or unusable by adding radioactive material to: *to contaminate a laboratory.* —*adj.* **3.** *Archaic.* contaminated. [< L *contāmināt(us)* (ptp. of *contāmināre*) = *con-* CON- + *tāmin-* (? for **tagmin-,* s. of **tagmen* a touch, akin to *tangere* to touch; see CONTAGION) + *-ātus* -ATE[1]] —**con·tam′i·na·ble,** *adj.* —**con·tam′i·na′tive,** *adj.* —**con·tam′i·na′tor,** *n.* —**con·tam′i·nous,** *adj.* —**Syn. 1.** pollute, befoul, sully, poison, corrupt.

con·tam·i·na·tion (kən tam′ə nā′shən), *n.* **1.** the act of contaminating. **2.** the state of being contaminated. **3.** something that contaminates. [< LL *contāminātiōn-* (s. of *contāminātiō*)]

contd., continued.

con·té (kôn tā′, kon′tē; *Fr.* kôN tā′), *n., pl.* **-tés** (-tāz′, -tēz; *Fr.* -tā′). a hard crayon of graphite and clay, usually made in black, red, or brown colors. Also called **conté′ cray′on.** [named after N. J. *Conté,* 18th-century French chemist, who invented it]

con·temn (kən tem′), *v.t.* to treat or regard with disdain, scorn, or contempt. [late ME *contempne* < L *contem(p)nā(re)* to despise, scorn = *con-* CON- + *temnere* to slight] —**con·temn·er** (kən tem′ər, -tem′nər), **con·tem·nor** (kən tem′nər), *n.* —**con·tem·ni·ble** (kən tem′nə bəl), *adj.* —**con·tem′ni·bly,** *adv.* —**con·temn′ing·ly,** *adv.* —**Syn.** scorn, disdain.

contemp., contemporary.

con·tem·pla·ble (kən tem′plə bəl), *adj.* capable of being contemplated. [< LL *contemplābil(is)* = L *contemplā(re),* *contemplārī* (see CONTEMPLATE) + *-bilis* -BLE]

con·tem·plate (kon′təm plāt′, kən tem′plāt), *v.*, **-plat·ed, -plat·ing.** —*v.t.* **1.** to look at or view with continued attention; observe thoughtfully. **2.** to consider thoroughly; think fully or deeply about. **3.** to have as a purpose; plan or expect: *to contemplate buying a new car.* —*v.i.* **4.** to think studiously; meditate; consider deliberately. [< L *contemplāt(us),* ptp. of *contemplāre, contemplārī* to survey, observe = *con-* CON- + *templ(um)* space in heavens marked off for augural observation (possibly akin to Gk *témnein* to cut; see -TOMY) + *-ātus* -ATE[1]] —**con′tem·plat′ing·ly,** *adv.* —**con′tem·pla′tor,** *n.* —**Syn. 1.** regard, survey. **2.** study, ponder.

con·tem·pla·tion (kon′təm plā′shən), *n.* **1.** the act of contemplating; thoughtful observation. **2.** full or deep consideration; reflection: *religious contemplation.* **3.** purpose or intention. **4.** prospect or expectation. [< L *contemplātiōn-* (s. of *contemplātiō*); see CONTEMPLATE, -ION; r. ME *contemplaci(o)un* < AF]

con·tem·pla·tive (kən tem′plə tiv, kon′təm plā′-), *adj.* **1.** given to or characterized by contemplation. —*n.* **2.** a person inclined or devoted to contemplation, as a monk. [< L *contemplātīv(us)* (see CONTEMPLATE, -IVE); r. ME *contemplatif* < MF] —**con·tem′pla·tive·ly,** *adv.* —**con·tem′pla·tive·ness,** *n.* —**Syn. 1.** reflective, meditative.

con·tem·po·ra·ne·ous (kən tem′pə rā′nē əs), *adj.* contemporary. [< L *contemporāneus* = *con-* CON- + *tempor-* (s. of *tempus* time) + *-āneus* (-*ān(us)* -AN + *-eus* -EOUS)] —**con·tem·po·ra·ne·i·ty** (kən tem′pər ə nē′i tē), **con·tem′po·ra′ne·ous·ness,** *n.* —**con·tem′po·ra′ne·ous·ly,** *adv.* —**Syn.** simultaneous, concurrent.

con·tem·po·rar·y (kən tem′pə rer′ē), *adj., n., pl.* **-rar·ies.** —*adj.* **1.** existing, occurring, or living at the same time; belonging to the same time. **2.** of the same age or date: *a Georgian table with a contemporary wig stand.* **3.** of the present time: *a lecture on the contemporary novel.* —*n.* **4.** a person or thing belonging to the same time or period with another or others. **5.** a person of the same age as another. [< LL *contempor-* (s. of *contempor(āre)* (to) be at the same time = *con-* CON- + *tempor-* (s. of *tempus*) time) + -ARY] —**con·tem′po·rar′i·ly,** *adv.* —**con·tem′po·rar′i·ness,** *n.* —**Syn. 1.** coeval, coexistent; concurrent, simultaneous.

con·tempt (kən tempt′), *n.* **1.** the feeling with which a person regards anything considered mean, vile, or worthless; disdain; scorn. **2.** the state of being despised; dishonor; disgrace. **3.** *Law.* willful disobedience to or open disrespect for the rules or orders of a court or legislative body. [< L *contempt(us)* a slighting, n. use of ptp. of *contemnere* to CONTEMN] —**Syn. 1.** contumely. CONTEMPT, DISDAIN, SCORN imply strong feelings of disapproval combined with disgust or derision. CONTEMPT is disapproval tinged with disgust for what seems mean, base, or worthless: *to feel contempt for a weakling.* DISDAIN is a feeling that something is beneath the level of one's own dignity or is unworthy of one's notice or acceptance: *disdain for crooked dealing.* SCORN denotes derisive, open, or undisguised contempt, as for a thing thought unworthy of considerate treatment: *He showed only scorn for those who had not been as ambitious as himself.* —**Ant. 1.** respect.

con·tempt·i·ble (kən temp′tə bəl), *adj.* **1.** deserving of or held in contempt; despicable. **2.** *Obs.* contemptuous. [< LL *contemptibil(is)*] —**con·tempt′i·bil′i·ty, con·tempt′i·ble·ness,** *n.* —**con·tempt′i·bly,** *adv.* —**Syn. 1.** mean, abject, low, base. —**Ant. 1.** admirable.

con·temp·tu·ous (kən temp′cho͞o əs), *adj.* manifesting or expressing contempt or disdain; scornful. [< L *contemptu(s)* CONTEMPT + -OUS] —**con·temp′tu·ous·ly,** *adv.* —**con·temp′tu·ous·ness,** *n.* —**Syn.** disdainful, insolent, arrogant. —**Ant.** respectful.

con·tend (kən tend′), *v.i.* **1.** to struggle in opposition. **2.** to strive in rivalry: *to contend for first prize.* **3.** to strive in debate; dispute earnestly: *to contend against falsehood.* —*v.t.* **4.** to assert or maintain earnestly. [< L *contend(ere)* (to) stretch vigorously, strive = *con-* CON- + *tendere* to stretch; see TEND[1]] —**con·tend′ing·ly,** *adv.* —**Syn. 1.** grapple, battle, fight. **2.** See **compete. 4.** claim.

con·tent[1] (kon′tent; *rarely* kən tent′), *n.* **1.** Usually, **contents. a.** something that is contained: *the contents of a box.* **b.** the subjects, topics, chapters, etc., covered in a book or document. **2.** something that is to be expressed through some medium, as speech, writing, or any of various arts. **3.** significance; meaning. **4.** *Philos., Logic.* the sum of the attributes or notions comprised in a given conception; the substance or matter of cognition. **5.** power of containing; holding capacity: *The bowl's content is three quarts.* **6.** volume, area, or extent; size. **7.** the amount contained. [< L *content(um),* n. use of neut. of ptp. of *continēre* = *con-* CON- + *ten-* hold + *-tus* ptp. suffix]

con·tent[2] (kən tent′), *adj.* **1.** satisfied with what a person is or has; not wanting more or anything else. **2.** *Brit.* agreeing; assenting. **3.** *Archaic.* willing. —*v.t.* **4.** to make content; satisfy. —*n.* **5.** contentment. [late ME < MF < L *content(us)* satisfied, special use of ptp. of *continēre;* see CONTENT[1]] —**con·tent′ly,** *adv.* —**Syn. 4.** appease, gratify. See **satisfy.**

con·tent·ed (kən ten′tid), *adj.* satisfied, as with what one has or with something mentioned; content. —**con·tent′ed·ly,** *adv.*

con·ten·tion (kən ten′shən), *n.* **1.** a struggling together in opposition; strife. **2.** a striving in rivalry; competition; contest. **3.** strife in debate; dispute; controversy. **4.** a point contended for or affirmed in controversy. [ME < L *contentiōn-* (s. of *contentiō*) = *content(us),* ptp. of *contendere* to CONTEND (*con-* CON- + *tentus,* alter. of *tensus;* see TENSE[1]) + *-iōn-* -ION] —**con·ten′tion·al,** *adj.* —**Syn. 1.** struggle, conflict, combat. **3.** disagreement, dissension, debate, wrangle. —**Ant. 3.** agreement.

con·ten·tious (kən ten′shəs), *adj.* **1.** tending to argument or strife; quarrelsome: *a contentious crew.* **2.** causing, involving, or characterized by argument or controversy: *contentious issues.* [late ME *contenciose* < L *contentiōs(us)* = *contenti(ō)* CONTENTION + *-ōsus* -OUS] —**con·ten′tious·ly,** *adv.* —**con·ten′tious·ness,** *n.* —**Syn. 1.** competitive.

con·tent·ment (kən tent′mənt), *n.* **1.** the state of being contented; satisfaction; ease of mind. **2.** *Archaic.* the act of making contentedly satisfied. [late ME *contentement* < MF] —**Syn. 1.** See **happiness.**

con·ter·mi·nous (kən tûr′mə nəs), *adj.* **1.** having a common boundary; bordering; contiguous. **2.** meeting at the ends; without an intervening gap: *In our calendar system, the close of one year is conterminous with the beginning of the next.* **3.** having the same boundaries or limits; coextensive. Also, **con·ter′mi·nal, coterminous.** [< L *conterminus*] —**con·ter′mi·nous·ly,** *adv.* —**con·ter′mi·nous·ness,** *n.*

con·test (*n.* kon′test; *v.* kən test′), *n.* **1.** a struggle for victory or superiority. **2.** a race, conflict, or other competition between rivals, as for a prize. **3.** strife in argument; dispute; controversy. —*v.t.* **4.** to struggle or fight for, as in battle. **5.** to argue against; dispute. **6.** to call in question: *They contested his right to speak.* **7.** to contend for in rivalry. —*v.i.* **8.** to dispute; contend; compete. [< legal L *contest(ārī)* (to) call to witness (in a lawsuit) = *con-* CON- + *testārī* to testify < *testis* witness] —**con·test′a·ble,** *adj.* —**con·test′a·ble·ness,** *n.* —**con·test′a·bly,** *adv.* —**con·test′er,** *n.* —**con·test′ing·ly,** *adv.* —**Syn. 1.** battle, encounter. See **fight. 2.** match, tournament, tourney, game. **3.** debate, argument, altercation. **4.** See **compete. 5.** controvert, oppose. **6.** challenge. **7.** strive, compete, vie.

con·test·ant (kən tes′tənt), *n.* **1.** a person who takes part in a contest or competition. **2.** a person who contests the results of an election. [< F]

con·tes·ta·tion (kon′te stā′shən), *n.* **1.** the act of contesting; controversy; dispute. **2.** an assertion contended for. [< L *contestātiōn-* (s. of *contestātiō*)]

con·text (kon′tekst), *n.* **1.** the parts of a written or spoken statement that precede or follow a specific word or passage, usually influencing its meaning or effect. **2.** the set of circumstances or facts that surround a particular event, situation, etc. [late ME < L *context(us)* a joining together, n. use of ptp. of *contexere* = *con-* CON- + *tex-* (s. of *texere* to plait, interweave) + *-tus* ptp. ending]

con·tex·tu·al (kən teks′cho͞o əl), *adj.* of, pertaining to, or depending on the context. [< L *contextu(s)* + -AL[1]] —**con·tex′tu·al·ly,** *adv.*

con·tex·ture (kən teks′chər), *n.* **1.** the arrangement and union of the constituent parts of anything; constitution; structure. **2.** an interwoven structure; fabric. **3.** the act of weaving together. **4.** the process or manner of being ′oven together. [< F] —**con·tex′tur·al,** *adj.* —**con·textured,** *adj.*

contg., containing.

con·ti·gu·i·ty (kon′tə gyo͞o′i tē), *n., pl.* **-ties. 1.** the state of being contiguous; contact or proximity. **2.** a series of things in continuous connection; a continuous mass or extent. [< LL *contiguitās.* See CONTIGUOUS, -ITY]

con·tig·u·ous (kən tig′yo͞o əs), *adj.* **1.** touching; in contact. **2.** in close proximity without actually touching; near. [< L *contiguus* bordering upon = *con-* CON- + *tig-* (perf. s. of *-tingere,* comb. form of *tangere* to touch) + *-uus* -OUS] —**con·tig′u·ous·ly,** *adv.* —**con·tig′u·ous·ness,** *n.* —**Syn. 1.** bordering, adjoining, abutting. **2.** adjacent.

contin., continued.

con·ti·nence (kon′tᵊnəns), *n.* self-restraint, esp. in regard to sexual passion or activity; temperance; moderation. Also, **con′ti·nen·cy.** [ME < L *continentia.* See CONTINENT, -ENCE]

con·ti·nent (kon′tᵊnənt), *n.* **1.** one of the main land masses of the globe, usually reckoned as seven in number (Europe, Asia, Africa, North America, South America, Australia, and Antarctica). **2.** the mainland, as distinguished from islands or peninsulas. **3. the Continent,** the mainland of Europe, as distinguished from the British Isles. **4.** a continuous tract or extent, as of land. **5.** *Archaic.* something that serves as a container or boundary. —*adj.* **6.** exercising or characterized by restraint in relation to the desires or passions and esp. to sexual desires. **7.** *Obs.* restraining or restrictive. **8.** *Obs.* continuous; forming an uninterrupted tract, as land. [ME < L *continent-* (s. of *continēns,* prp. of *continēre* to CONTAIN) = *con-* CON- + *tin-,* var. s. of *ten(ēre)* (to) hold + *-ent-* -ENT] —**con′ti·nent·ly,** *adv.*

con·ti·nen·tal (kon′tᵊnen′tᵊl), *adj.* **1.** of or of the nature of a continent. **2.** (*usually cap.*) of or pertaining to the mainland of Europe, to Europeans, or to European customs and attitudes. **3.** (*cap.*) of or pertaining to the 13 American colonies of the Revolutionary period. **4.** of or pertaining to the continent of North America. —*n.* **5.** (*cap.*) a soldier of the Continental army in the American Revolution. **6.** a piece of paper currency issued by the Continental Congress. **7.** an inhabitant of a continent. **8.** (*usually cap.*) an inhabitant of the mainland of Europe. —**con′ti·nen′tal·ly,** *adv.*

con′tinen′tal code′. See **international Morse code.**

Con′tinen′tal Con′gress, *Amer. Hist.* one of two continental assemblies that first met from September 5 to October 26, 1774, and afterward met from 1775 to 1789, during which period the Declaration of Independence and the Articles of Confederation were adopted.

continen′tal divide′, 1. a divide separating river systems which flow to opposite sides of a continent. **2.** (*caps.*) (in North America) the summits of the Rocky Mountains, separating streams flowing toward the Gulf of California and the Pacific from those flowing toward the Gulf of Mexico, Hudson Bay, and the Arctic Ocean.

con′tinen′tal drift′, the hypothetical tendency or ability of continents to drift on the earth's surface because of the weakness of the suboceanic crust.

con′tinen′tal shelf′, *Phys. Geog.* the part of a continent that is submerged in relatively shallow sea.

con′tinen′tal slope′, *Phys. Geog.* a steep slope separating a continental shelf and a deep ocean basin.

con·tin·gence (kən tin′jəns), *n.* contact or tangency. [CONTING(ENT) + -ENCE]

con·tin·gen·cy (kən tin′jən sē), *n., pl.* **-cies. 1.** dependence on chance or on the fulfillment of a condition. **2.** an uncertain event; chance; possibility: *He was prepared for every contingency.* **3.** something incidental. [CONTING(ENT) + -ENCY]

con·tin·gent (kən tin′jənt), *adj.* **1.** dependent for existence, occurrence, character, etc., on something not yet certain; conditional (often fol. by *on* or *upon*): *Our plans are contingent on the weather.* **2.** happening by chance or without known cause; fortuitous; accidental. **3.** *Logic.* (of a proposition) neither logically necessary nor logically impossible. —*n.* **4.** a quota of troops furnished. **5.** any one of the representative groups composing an assemblage. **6.** something contingent; contingency. [late ME < L *contingent-* (s. of *contingēns*, prp. of *contingere*) = *con-* CON- + *ting-*, var. s. of *tang(ere)* (to) touch + *-ent-* -ENT] —**con·tin′gent·ly,** *adv.*

contin′gent fee, a fee, generally based on a percentage of the sum recovered, paid to a lawyer conducting a suit, esp. a suit for damages, if the suit is successful.

con·tin·u·al (kən tin′yo͞o əl), *adj.* **1.** happening without interruption or cessation; continuous in time. **2.** of regular or frequent recurrence; often repeated; very frequent. [< ML *continuāl(is)* (see CONTINUOUS, -AL[1]); r. ME *continuel* < MF] —**con·tin′u·al′i·ty, con·tin′u·al·ness,** *n.*

—**Syn. 1.** unceasing, ceaseless, incessant, uninterrupted, unending. **1, 2.** CONTINUAL, CONSTANT, CONTINUOUS all refer to a succession of occurrences. CONTINUAL implies that successive recurrences are very close together, with only small breaks between them, or none at all: *continual misunderstanding between nations.* CONSTANT implies always recurring in the same way, under uniform conditions, with similar results, and the like: *constant repetition of the same mistakes.* CONTINUOUS emphasizes the idea that the succession is unbroken: *the continuous life of the universe.*

con·tin·u·al·ly (kən tin′yo͞o ə lē), *adv.* **1.** without cessation or intermission; unceasingly. **2.** at regular or frequent intervals; habitually. [ME *continuelli, continueliche*]

con·tin·u·ance (kən tin′yo͞o əns), *n.* **1.** an act or instance of continuing; continuation: *a continuance of war.* **2.** a remaining in the same place, condition, etc. **3.** sequel. **4.** *Law.* adjournment of a step in a proceeding to a future day. [ME < MF]

con·tin·u·ant (kən tin′yo͞o ənt), *n.* *Phonet.* a consonant, as *f* or *s*, that may be prolonged without change of quality. Cf. **stop** (def. 36a). [< L *continuant-* (s. of *continuāns*), prp. of *continuāre* to CONTINUE; see -ANT]

con·tin·u·a·tion (kən tin′yo͞o ā′shən), *n.* **1.** the act or state of continuing. **2.** the state of being continued. **3.** extension or carrying on to a further point: *to request the continuation of a loan.* **4.** that which continues some preceding thing by being of the same kind or having a similar content: *Today's weather will be a continuation of yesterday's.* **5.** *Library Science.* a publication issued more or less regularly over an indefinite period. [ME *continuacio(u)n* < L *continuātiōn-* (s. of *continuātiō*)]

continua′tion school′, a school providing extension courses for people who have left school in the elementary grades in order to go to work.

con·tin·u·a·tive (kən tin′yo͞o ā′tiv, -ə tiv), *adj.* **1.** tending or serving to continue; causing continuation or prolongation. **2.** expressing continuance of thought. **3.** *Gram.* expressing a following event. In *They arrested a suspect, who gave his name as John Doe,* the second clause is continuative. **4.** *Gram.* (of a verbal form or aspect) expressing continuation of an action. —*n.* **5.** something continuative. [< LL *continuātīv(us)* connecting, copulative] —**con·tin′u·a′tive·ly,** *adv.* —**con·tin′u·a′tive·ness,** *n.*

con·tin·u·a·tor (kən tin′yo͞o ā′tər), *n.* a person or thing that continues.

con·tin·ue (kən tin′yo͞o), *v.,* **-ued, -u·ing.** —*v.i.* **1.** to go on or keep on, as in some course or action; extend. **2.** to go on after suspension or interruption: *The program continued after an intermission.* **3.** to last or endure: *The famine continued for two months.* **4.** to remain in a place; abide; stay. **5.** to remain in a particular state or capacity. —*v.t.* **6.** to go on with or persist in: *to continue an action.* **7.** to extend from one point to another in space; prolong. **8.** to carry on from the point of suspension or interruption. **9.** to say in continuation. **10.** to cause to last or endure; maintain or retain, as in a position. **11.** to carry over, postpone, or adjourn; keep pending, as a legal proceeding. [ME *continue(n)* < L *continuā(re)* to make all one < *continuus* CONTINUOUS] —**con·tin′u·a·ble,** *adj.* —**con·tin′ued·ly,** *adv.* —**con·tin′ued·ness,** *n.* —**con·tin′u·er,** *n.* —**con·tin′u·ing·ly,** *adv.*

—**Syn. 3.** CONTINUE, ENDURE, PERSIST, PERSEVERE, LAST, REMAIN imply existing uninterruptedly for an appreciable length of time. CONTINUE implies duration or existence without break or interruption: *The rain continued two days.* ENDURE, used of people or things, implies persistent continuance against influences that tend to weaken, undermine, or destroy: *The family endured years of poverty.* PERSIST and PERSEVERE, used principally of people, both imply firm and steadfast continuance in the face of opposition. PERSIST suggests human opposition: *He persisted after he had been warned;* and PERSEVERE suggests opposition from any source, often an impersonal one: *He persevered despite fatigue, heat and cold.* LAST often applies to that which holds out to a desired end, fresh, unimpaired, or unexhausted, sometimes under conditions that tend to produce the opposite effect; *They had provisions enough to last all winter.* REMAIN is esp. applied to what continues without change in its essential state; *He remained a bachelor.* —**Ant. 1.** cease.

contin′ued frac′tion, *Math.* a fraction whose numerator contains an integer and whose denominator contains an integer and a fraction whose numerator contains an integer and whose denominator contains an integer and a fraction, and so on.

contin′ued propor′tion, *Math.* an ordered set of numbers such that the ratio between any two successive terms is the same, as 1:3:9:27:81.

con·ti·nu·i·ty (kon′tᵊnōō′i tē, -nyo͞o′-, kon′tᵊno͞o′-, -tᵊnyo͞o′-), *n., pl.* **-ties** for 3, 4. **1.** the state or quality of being continuous. **2.** a continuous or connected whole. **3.** a motion-picture scenario giving the complete action, scenes, etc., in detail and in the order in which they are to be shown on the screen. **4.** the spoken part of a nondramatic radio program. [late ME *continuite* < MF < L *continuitāt-* (s. of *continuitās*)]

con·tin·u·o (kən tin′yo͞o ō′), *n., pl.* **-tin·u·os.** *Music.* a keyboard accompanying part serving to provide or fill out the harmonic texture. [< It: lit., continuous]

con·tin·u·ous (kən tin′yo͞o əs), *adj.* **1.** being in immediate connection or relation: *a continuous pattern of dots.* **2.** uninterrupted in time; without cessation: *continuous coughing during the concert.* [< L *continuus* holding together = *continu-* (perf. s. of *continēre* = *con-* CON- + *-tinēre*, var. of *tenēre* to hold) + *-us* -OUS] —**con·tin′u·ous·ly,** *adv.* —**con·tin′u·ous·ness,** *n.* —**Syn. 2.** See **continual.**

con·tin·u·um (kən tin′yo͞o əm), *n., pl.* **-tin·u·a** (-tin′yo͞o ə). **1.** a continuous extent, series, or whole. **2.** *Math.* **a.** a set of elements such that between any two of them there is a third element. **b.** the set of all real numbers. [< L, neut. of *continuus* CONTINUOUS]

con·to (kon′tō; *Port.* kôn′to͞o), *n., pl.* **-tos** (-tōz; *in Portugal* -to͞osh; *in Brazil* -to͞os). **1.** a money of account in Portugal equal to 1000 escudos. **2.** a former money of account in Portugal and Brazil equal to 1000 milreis. [< Pg < LL *computus* reckoning < L *computāre* to COMPUTE; see COUNT[1]]

con·tort (kən tôrt′), *v.t.* to twist; bend out of shape; distort. [< L *contort(us)* twisted together, ptp. of *contorquēre*]

con·tort·ed (kən tôr′tid), *adj.* **1.** twisted in a violent manner; distorted. **2.** twisted back on itself; convoluted. —**con·tort′ed·ly,** *adv.* —**con·tort′ed·ness,** *n.*

con·tor·tion (kən tôr′shən), *n.* **1.** the act or process of contorting. **2.** the state of being contorted. **3.** a contorted position. **4.** something contorted or twisted, as in position, meaning, etc. [< L *contortiōn-* (s. of *contortiō*) a whirling around] —**con·tor′tion·al,** *adj.* —**con·tor′tioned,** *adj.*

con·tor·tion·ist (kən tôr′shə nist), *n.* **1.** a person who performs gymnastic feats involving contorted postures. **2.** a person who practices contortion: *a verbal contortionist.* —**con·tor′tion·is′tic,** *adj.*

con·tor·tive (kən tôr′tiv), *adj.* characterized by, tending toward, or causing contortions or twisting. —**con·tor′tive·ly,** *adv.*

con·tour (kon′to͝or), *n.* **1.** the outline of a figure or body; the edge of a shape. **2.** See **contour line.** —*v.t.* **3.** to mark with contour lines. **4.** to make or form the contour or outline of. **5.** to build (a road, railroad track, etc.) in conformity with the contour of the land. —*adj.* **6.** of or used in a system of plowing, cultivating, sowing, etc., along the contour lines of the land in order to prevent erosion. [< F = *con-* CON- + *tour* a turn (see TOUR), modeled on It *contorno* < *contornare* to outline; see TURN] —**Syn. 1.** configuration.

con′tour feath′er, *Ornith.* one of the feathers that form the surface plumage of a bird.

con′tour line′, (on a map) a line joining points of equal elevation on a surface.

con′tour map′, a map on which irregularities of land surface are shown by contour lines.

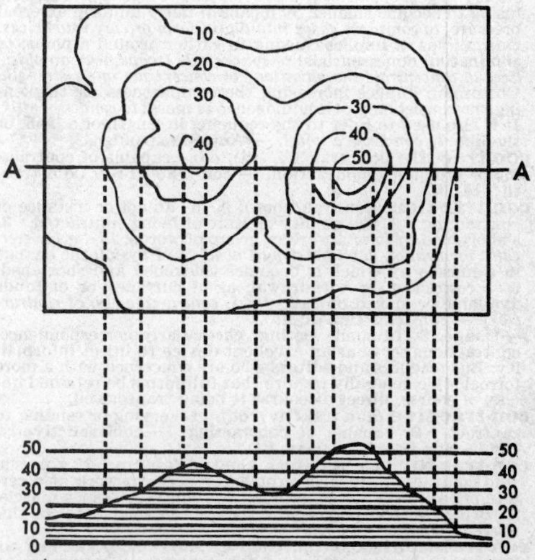

Contour map showing profile through A-A

con′tour sheet′, a bed sheet designed to fit closely over a mattress, often having elastic material to hold down the corners.

contr., **1.** contract. **2.** contracted. **3.** contraction. **4.** contralto. **5.** contrasted. **6.** control. **7.** controller.

con·tra[1] (kon′trə), *prep.* **1.** against; in opposition or contrast to. —*adv.* **2.** contrariwise; on or to the contrary. [ME < L *contrā*]

con·tra[2] (kon′trə; *Sp.* kôn′trä), *n., pl.* **-tras** (-trəz; *Sp.* -träs). (*often cap.*) a member of a counterrevolutionary guerrilla group in Nicaragua. [< AmerSp, shortening of *contrarrevolucionario* COUNTERREVOLUTIONARY]

contra-, **1.** a learned borrowing from Latin meaning "against," "opposite," "opposing," used in the formation of compound words: *contradistinction.* **2.** *Music.* a prefix meaning "pitched an octave below the common instrument": *contrabassoon.* [< L, comb. form of adv. and prep. *contrā*]

con·tra·band (kon′trə band′), *n.* **1.** anything prohibited by law from being imported or exported. **2.** goods imported or exported illegally. **3.** illegal or prohibited trade; smuggling. **—*adj.*** **4.** prohibited from export or import. [earlier *contrabanda* < Sp < It *contrabando* (now *contrabbando*) = *contra-* CONTRA- + ML *bandum,* var. of *bannum* BAN[2]]

con·tra·band·ist (kon′trə ban′dist), *n.* a smuggler. [< Sp *contrabandist(a)*]

con·tra·bass (kon′trə bās′), *Music.* **—*n.*** **1.** (in any family of instruments) the member below the bass. **—*adj.*** **2.** of, pertaining to, or characteristic of such instruments. [< It *contrabass(o)* (now *contrabbasso*)] **—con·tra·bass·ist** (kon′trə bā′sist, -bas′ist), *n.*

con·tra·bas·soon (kon′trə ba so͞on′, -bə-), *n.* a bassoon larger in size and an octave lower in pitch than the ordinary bassoon; a double bassoon. [CONTRA- + BASSOON] **—con′tra·bas·soon′ist,** *n.*

con·tra·cep·tion (kon′trə sep′shən), *n.* the prevention of conception or impregnation; birth control.

con·tra·cep·tive (kon′trə sep′tiv), *adj.* **1.** tending or serving to prevent conception or impregnation. **2.** pertaining to contraception. **—*n.*** **3.** a contraceptive device or drug. [CONTRA- + (CON)CEPTIVE]

con·tra·clock·wise (kon′trə klok′wīz′), *adj., adv.* counterclockwise.

con·tract (*n. and usually for v. 13* kon′trakt; *otherwise v.* kən trakt′), *n.* **1.** an agreement between two or more parties for the doing or not doing of something specified. **2.** an agreement enforceable by law. **3.** the written form of such an agreement. **4.** the division of law dealing with contracts. **5.** the formal agreement of marriage; betrothal. **6.** Also called **con′tract bridge′.** a variety of bridge in which the side that wins the bid can earn toward game only that number of tricks named in the contract, additional points being credited above the line. Cf. **auction bridge. 7.** (in auction or contract bridge) **a.** a commitment by the declarer and his partner to take six tricks plus the number specified by the final bid made. **b.** the final bid itself. **c.** the number of tricks so specified, plus six. **—*v.t.*** **8.** to draw together or into smaller compass; draw the parts of together: *to contract a muscle.* **9.** to wrinkle: *to contract the brows.* **10.** to shorten (a word, phrase, etc.) by combining or omitting some of its elements: *Contracting "do not" yields "don't."* **11.** to get or acquire, as by exposure to something contagious: *to contract a disease.* **12.** to incur, as a liability or obligation: *to contract a debt.* **13.** to settle or establish by agreement: *to contract an alliance.* **14.** to enter into (friendship, acquaintance, etc.). **15.** to betroth. **—*v.i.*** **16.** to become smaller; shrink. **17.** to enter into an agreement or contract: *to contract for snow removal.* [ME < L *contract(us)* transaction, hence, agreement, n. use of *contractus* drawn together (ptp. of *contrahere*). See CON-, TRACT[1]] **—con·tract′i·ble,** *adj.* **—con·tract′i·bil′i·ty, con·tract′i·ble·ness,** *n.* **—con·tract′i·bly,** *adv.*

—Syn. 1. See **agreement. 8.** reduce, shorten, lessen, narrow. CONTRACT, COMPRESS, CONCENTRATE, CONDENSE imply retaining original content but reducing the amount of space occupied. CONTRACT means to cause to draw more closely together: *to contract a muscle.* COMPRESS suggests fusing to become smaller by means of fairly uniform external pressure: *to compress gases into liquid form or clay into bricks.* CONCENTRATE implies causing to gather around a point, or eliminating nonessentials: *to concentrate troops near an objective; to concentrate the attention; to concentrate one's strength.* CONDENSE implies increasing the compactness, or thickening the consistency of a homogeneous mass: *to condense milk.* It is also used to refer to the reducing in length of a book or the like: *to condense a novel.* **—Ant. 8.** expand.

con·trac·tile (kən trak′təl, -til), *adj.* capable of contracting or producing contraction. **—con·trac·til·i·ty** (kon′trak til′i tē), *n.*

con·trac·tion (kən trak′shən), *n.* **1.** an act or instance of contracting. **2.** the quality or state of being contracted. **3.** a shortened form of a word or group of words, as *e'er* for *ever, can't* for *cannot, dep't* for *department.* **4.** *Physiol.* the change in a muscle by which it becomes thickened and shortened. **5.** a restriction or withdrawal, as of currency or of funds available or loaned on call. [< L *contractiōn-* (s. of *contractiō*)] **—con·trac′tion·al,** *adj.*

—Usage. 3. In some writing, particularly correspondence, contractions serve as an excellent device to inject informality. But teachers and editors who are concerned with a more formal style generally require that full forms be retained unless, of course, direct discourse is being transcribed.

con·trac·tive (kən trak′tiv), *adj.* **1.** serving or tending to contract. **2.** capable of contracting. **—con·trac′tive·ly,** *adv.* **—con·trac′tive·ness,** *n.*

con·trac·tor (kon′trak tər, kən trak′tər), *n.* **1.** a person who contracts to furnish supplies or perform work at a certain price or rate. **2.** something that contracts, esp. a muscle. **3.** *Bridge.* **a.** the player who makes the final bid. **b.** this player's partner. [< LL]

con·trac·tu·al (kən trak′cho͞o əl), *adj.* of, pertaining to, or secured by a contract. [< L *contractu(s)* CONTRACT + -AL[1]] **—con·trac′tu·al·ly,** *adv.*

con·trac·ture (kən trak′chər, -shər), *n.* *Pathol.* a shortening or distortion of muscular tissue due to spasm, scar, or paralysis of the antagonist of the contracting muscle. [< L *contractūra*] **—con·trac′tured,** *adj.*

con·tra·dance (kon′trə dans′, -däns′), *n.* contredanse.

con·tra·dict (kon′trə dikt′), *v.t.* **1.** to assert the contrary or opposite of; deny directly and categorically. **2.** to speak contrary to the assertions of: *to contradict oneself.* **3.** (of an action or event) to imply a denial of: *His way of life contradicts his stated principles.* **4.** *Obs.* to speak or declare against; oppose. **—*v.i.*** **5.** to utter a contrary statement. [< L *contrādict(us)* spoken against (ptp. of *contrādīcere*) = *contrā-* CONTRA- + *dic-* (ptp. s. of *dīcere* to speak) + *-tus* ptp. suffix] **—con′tra·dict′a·ble,** *adj.* **—con′tra·dict′er, con′tra·dic′tor,** *n.* **—Syn. 1, 2.** controvert, dispute. See **deny.**

con·tra·dic·tion (kon′trə dik′shən), *n.* **1.** the act of contradicting; gainsaying or opposition. **2.** assertion of the opposite; denial. **3.** a statement that contradicts or denies another or itself and is logically incongruous. **4.** direct opposition between things compared; inconsistency. **5.** a contradictory act, fact, etc. [ME *contradiccioun* < L *contrādictiōn-* (s. of *contrādictiō*)]

con·tra·dic·tious (kon′trə dik′shəs), *adj.* **1.** inclined to contradict; disputatious. **2.** *Archaic.* self-contradictory.

con·tra·dic·tive (kon′trə dik′tiv), *adj.* tending to contradict; involving contradiction. [CONTRADICT(IOUS) + -IVE]

con·tra·dic·to·ry (kon′trə dik′tə rē), *adj., n., pl.* **-ries.** **—*adj.*** **1.** asserting the contrary or opposite; inconsistent; logically opposite: *contradictory statements.* **2.** tending to contradict. **—*n.*** **3.** *Logic.* a proposition so related to a second that it is impossible for both to be true or both to be false. [ME < LL *contrādictōri(us)*] **—con′tra·dic′to·ri·ly,** *adv.* **—con′tra·dic′to·ri·ness,** *n.* **—Syn. 1.** opposing, irreconcilable.

con·tra·dis·tinc·tion (kon′trə di stingk′shən), *n.* distinction by opposition or contrast: *plants and animals in contradistinction to man.* **—con′tra·dis·tinc′tive,** *adj.* **—con′tra·dis·tinc′tive·ly,** *adv.*

con·tra·dis·tin·guish (kon′trə di sting′gwish), *v.t.* to distinguish by contrasting opposite qualities.

con·trail (kon′trāl), *n.* a visible condensation of water droplets or ice crystals from the atmosphere, occurring in the wake of an aircraft, rocket, or missile under certain conditions. Also called **condensation trail, vapor trail.** [CON(DENSATION) TRAIL]

con·tra·in·di·cate (kon′trə in′də kāt′), *v.t.,* **-cat·ed, -cat·ing.** *Med.* (of a symptom or condition) to give indication against the advisability of (a particular or usual remedy or treatment). [prob. back formation from *contraindication*] **—con·tra·in·di·cant** (kon′trə in′də kənt), *n.* **—con′tra·in′di·ca′tion,** *n.*

con·tral·to (kən tral′tō), *n., pl.* **-tos,** *adj. Music.* **—*n.*** **1.** the lowest female voice or voice part, between soprano and tenor. **2.** a singer with a contralto voice. **—*adj.*** **3.** pertaining to the contralto voice or its compass. [< It = *contr(a)* against + *alto* ALTO]

con·tra·oc·tave (kon′trə ok′tiv, -tāv), *n.* *Music.* the octave between the second and third C's below middle C.

con·tra·pose (kon′trə pōz′), *v.t.,* **-posed, -pos·ing.** to place in contraposition. [back formation from *contraposed* < L *contrāpositus,* ptp. of *contrāpōnere* to place against, with -ED[2] for L *-itus* ptp. suffix]

con·tra·po·si·tion (kon′trə pə zish′ən), *n.* **1.** placement opposite or against. **2.** opposition, contrast, or antithesis. [< LL *contrāpositiōn-* (s. of *contrāpositiō*)]

con·trap·tion (kən trap′shən), *n.* *Informal.* a mechanical contrivance; gadget; device. [? CONTR(IVANCE) + *(ad)aption,* var. of ADAPTATION]

con·tra·pun·tal (kon′trə pun′təl), *adj.* *Music.* **1.** of or pertaining to counterpoint. **2.** composed of two or more relatively independent melodies sounded together. [< It *contrappunt(o)* COUNTERPOINT + -AL[1]] **—con′tra·pun′tal·ly,** *adv.*

con·tra·pun·tist (kon′trə pun′tist), *n.* a person skilled in the practice of counterpoint. [< It *contrappuntist(a)*]

con·trar·i·an (kən trâr′ē ən), *n.* a person who takes an opposing view, esp. one who rejects the majority opinion, as in economic matters.

con·tra·ri·e·ty (kon′trə rī′i tē), *n., pl.* **-ties** for 2. **1.** the quality or state of being contrary. **2.** something contrary or of opposite character; a contrary fact or statement. **3.** *Logic.* the relation between contraries. [late ME *contrariete* < LL *contrārietās*]

con·trar·i·ous (kən trâr′ē əs), *adj.* *Archaic.* perverse; refractory. [ME < L *contrārius* CONTRARY] **—con·trar′i·ous·ly,** *adv.* **—con·trar′i·ous·ness,** *n.*

con·tra·ri·wise (kon′trer ē wīz′, kən trâr′ē wīz′), *adv.* **1.** in the opposite way. **2.** on the contrary; in direct opposition to a statement, attitude, etc. **3.** perversely. [ME *contrarywyse*]

con·tra·ry (kon′trer ē; *for 5 also* kən trâr′ē), *adj., n., pl.* **-ries,** *adv.* **—*adj.*** **1.** opposite in nature or character; diametrically or mutually opposed: *contrary to fact; contrary propositions.* **2.** opposite in direction or position: *departures in contrary directions.* **3.** being the opposite one of two: *I will make the contrary choice.* **4.** unfavorable or adverse. **5.** perverse; stubbornly opposed or willful. **6.** *Bot.* at right angles. **—*n.*** **7.** something that is contrary or opposite: *to prove the contrary of a statement.* **8.** either of two contrary things. **9.** *Logic.* a proposition so related to another proposition that both may not be true though both may be false, as with the propositions "All judges are male" and "No judges are male." **10. on the contrary, a.** in opposition to what has been stated. **b.** from another point of view: *On the contrary, there may be some who would agree with you.* **11. to the contrary,** to the opposite effect: *He may be blameless, but the evidence points to the contrary.* **—*adv.*** **12.** in opposition; oppositely; counter: *to act contrary to one's own principles.* [ME *contrarie* < L *contrāri(us).* See CONTRA-, -ARY] **—con′tra·ri·ly,** *adv.* **—con′tra·ri·ness,** *n.*

—Syn. 1. contradictory, conflicting, counter. See **opposite. 4.** unfriendly, hostile. CONTRARY, ADVERSE both describe that which unfavorably opposes. CONTRARY conveys an idea of something impersonal and objective whose opposition happens to be unfavorable: *contrary winds.* ADVERSE suggests something more personally unfriendly or even hostile; it emphasizes the idea of the resulting misfortune to that which is opposed: *The judge rendered a decision adverse to the defendant.* **5.** intractable, obstinate, refractory, headstrong, stubborn.

con·trast (*v.* kən trast′; *n.* kon′trast), *v.t.* **1.** to compare in order to show unlikeness or differences; note the opposite natures, purposes, etc., of. **—*v.i.*** **2.** to exhibit unlikeness on comparison with something else; form a contrast. **—*n.*** **3.** act or state of contrasting. **4.** state of being contrasted. **5.** a striking exhibition of unlikeness. **6.** a thing or person that is strikingly unlike in comparison. **7.** opposition or juxtaposition of different forms, lines, or colors in a work of art to increase intensity. **8.** *Photog.* the relative difference between light and dark areas of a print or negative. [(v.) < F *contrast(er)* < It *contrastare* to contest < L *contrā-* CONTRA- + *stāre* to stand; (n.) earlier *contraste* < F < It *contrasto* conflict < the verb] **—con·trast′a·ble,** *adj.* **—con·trast′a·bly,** *adv.* **—con·trast′ed·ly,** *adv.* **—con·trast′ing·ly,** *adv.* **—Syn. 1.** differentiate, distinguish. See **compare.**

con·tras·tive (kən tras′tiv), *adj.* marked by or indicating contrast; contrasting. **—con·tras′tive·ly,** *adv.*

con·trast·y (kən tras′tē, kon′tras-), *adj.* (of a photograph) having coarse or sharp gradations of tone, esp. between dark and light areas.

con·tra·val·la·tion (kon′trə və lā′shən), *n. Fort.* a chain of redoubts and breastworks raised by besiegers around a besieged place as protection against outside attacks, as by a relief force. [CONTRA- + VALLATION; cf. F *contrevallation*, It *contravvallazione*]

con·tra·vene (kon′trə vēn′), *v.t.*, **-vened, -ven·ing. 1.** to come or be in conflict with; go or act counter to; oppose: *to contravene a statement.* **2.** to violate, infringe, or transgress. [< LL *contrāven(īre)* = L *contrā* CONTRA- + *venīre* to come] —**con′tra·ven′er,** *n.*

con·tra·ven·tion (kon′trə ven′shən), *n.* an act of contravening; action counter to something; violation. [CONTRAVENE + -TION; cf. MF *contrevention*]

con·tre·danse (kon′tri dans′, -däns′; *Fr.* kôN trə däNs′), *n., pl.* **-dans·es** (-dan′siz, -dän′-; *Fr.* -däNs′). a variation of the quadrille in which the dancers face each other. Also, **contradance.** [< F = *contre-* COUNTER- + *danse* DANCE, mistranslation of COUNTRY-DANCE]

con·tre·temps (kon′trə tän′; *Fr.* kôN trə tän′), *n., pl.* **-temps** (-tänz′; *Fr.* -tän′). an inopportune occurrence; an embarrassing mischance. [< F = *contre-* COUNTER- + *temps* time (< L *tempus*); perh. alter. (by folk etym.) of MF *contrestant*, prp. of *contrester* to oppose; see CONTRAST]

contrib., 1. contribution. **2.** contributor.

con·trib·ute (kən trib′yo͞ot), *v.*, **-ut·ed, -ut·ing.** —*v.t.* **1.** to give (money, time, knowledge, assistance, etc.) along with others to a common supply, fund, etc., as for charitable purposes. **2.** to furnish (an original written work) for publication. —*v.i.* **3.** to give (money, food, etc.) to a common supply, fund, etc.: *He contributes to many charities.* **4.** to furnish works for publication: *He contributes to many magazines.* [< L *contribūt(us)* classified together, ptp. of *contribuere*] —**con·trib′ut·a·ble,** *adj.* —**con·trib′u·tive,** *adj.* —**con·trib′u·tive·ly,** *adv.* —**con·trib′u·tive·ness,** *n.* —**Syn. 1.** provide, furnish, donate.

con·tri·bu·tion (kon′trə byo͞o′shən), *n.* **1.** the act of contributing. **2.** something contributed. **3.** an article, story, etc., furnished to a magazine or other publication. **4.** an impost or levy. **5.** *Insurance.* the method of distributing liability, in case of loss, among several insurers whose policies attach to the same risk. [ME *contribucio(u)n* < LL *contribūtiōn-* (s. of *contribūtiō*)] —**con′tri·bu′tion·al,** *adj.*

con·trib·u·tor (kən trib′yə tər), *n.* **1.** a person who contributes. **2.** a person who contributes an article, story, etc., to a newspaper, magazine, or the like. [late ME *contributour* < AF] —**con·trib·u·to·ri·al** (kən trib′yə tôr′ē əl, -tôr′-), *adj.*

con·trib·u·to·ry (kən trib′yə tôr′ē, -tôr′ē), *adj., n., pl.* **-ries.** —*adj.* **1.** pertaining to or of the nature of contribution; contributing. **2.** furnishing something toward a result: *a contributory factor.* **3.** of, pertaining to, or constituting an insurance or pension plan the premiums of which are paid partly by an employer and partly by his employees. **4.** subject to contribution or levy. —*n.* **5.** a person or thing that contributes. [late ME *contributorie* < ML *contribūtōri(us)*] —**Syn. 2.** accessory, ancillary; secondary, incidental.

con·trite (kən trīt′, kon′trīt), *adj.* **1.** overcome by a sense of guilt and desirous of atonement; penitent. **2.** caused by or showing remorse. [ME *contrit* < L *contrīt(us)* worn down, crushed, ptp. of *conterere*] —**con·trite′ly,** *adv.* —**con·trite′ness,** *n.*

con·tri·tion (kən trish′ən), *n.* **1.** sincere penitence or remorse. **2.** *Theol.* sorrow for and detestation of sin with a true purpose of amendment. [ME *contricio(u)n* < LL *contrītiōn-* (s. of *contrītiō*)] —**Syn. 1.** compunction, regret.

con·triv·ance (kən trī′vəns), *n.* **1.** something contrived, esp. a mechanical device. **2.** the act or manner of contriving; the faculty or power of contriving. **3.** a plan or scheme; expedient.

con·trive (kən trīv′), *v.*, **-trived, -triv·ing.** —*v.t.* **1.** to plan with ingenuity; devise; invent. **2.** to plot (evil, treachery, etc.). **3.** to bring about or effect by a device, stratagem, plan, or scheme. —*v.i.* **4.** to form schemes or designs; plan. **5.** to plot. [ME *contreve(n)* < MF *contreuv-*, tonic s. of *controver* < LL *contropāre* to compare] —**con·triv′a·ble,** *adj.* —**con·triv′er,** *n.* —**Syn. 1.** design, concoct. **2.** conspire.

con·trived (kən trīvd′), *adj.* obviously planned or forced; artificial. [late ME *contrevede*]

con·trol (kən trōl′), *v.*, **-trolled, -trol·ling,** *n.* —*v.t.* **1.** to exercise restraint or direction over; dominate; command. **2.** to hold in check; curb: *to control a horse; to control one's emotions.* **3.** to test or verify (a scientific experiment) by a parallel experiment or other standard of comparison. **4.** to eliminate or prevent the flourishing or spread of: *to control a forest fire; to control rats.* **5.** *Obs.* to check or regulate (transactions), originally by means of a duplicate register. —*n.* **6.** the act or power of controlling. **7.** the situation of being controlled. **8.** a standard of comparison in scientific experimentation; check. **9.** a person or thing that provides a standard of comparison, esp. in a control experiment: *Half the students drank fluoridated water, the others were used as a control.* **10.** a device for regulating and guiding a machine. **11. controls,** a coordinated arrangement of such devices. **12.** prevention of the flourishing or spread of something undesirable: *rodent control.* **13.** a spiritual agency believed to assist a medium at a seance. [late ME *co(u)ntrolle* (v.) < AF *contreroll(er)* < *contrerolle* (n.). See COUNTER-, ROLL] —**con·trol′la·bil′i·ty, con·trol′la·ble·ness,** *n.* —**con·trol′la·ble,** *adj.* —**con·trol′la·bly,** *adv.* —**Syn. 1.** manage, govern, rule. **2.** restrain, bridle. **6.** See **authority.**

control′ chart′, *Statistics.* a chart on which observations are plotted as ordinates in the order in which they are obtained and on which control lines are constructed to indicate whether the population from which the observations are being drawn is remaining the same.

control′ exper′iment, an experiment in which the variables are controlled so that the effects of varying one factor at a time may be observed.

con·trol·ler (kən trō′lər), *n.* **1.** a person who checks expenditures, finances, etc., of a business firm; comptroller. **2.** a person who regulates, directs, or restrains. **3.** a regulating mechanism. [late ME *co(u)nt(re)rollo(u)r* < AF *countrero(u)llour*, MF *contrerolleur* = *contrerolle* duplicate roll (see CONTROL) + *-eur, -our* -OR²] —**con·trol′ler·ship′,** *n.*

control′ stick′, *Aeron.* a lever by which a pilot controls the ailerons and elevator of an aircraft.

control′ sur′face, any movable airfoil, as an aileron, for guiding or controlling an aircraft or missile in flight.

control′ tow′er, a glass-enclosed, elevated structure for the visual observation and control of the air and ground traffic at an airport.

con·tro·ver·sial (kon′trə vûr′shəl), *adj.* **1.** of, pertaining to, or characteristic of controversy; polemical. **2.** subject to controversy; debatable. **3.** given to controversy; disputatious. [< LL *contrōversiāl(is)*] —**con′tro·ver′sial·ism,** *n.* —**con′tro·ver′sial·ist,** *n.* —**con′tro·ver′sial·ly,** *adv.*

con·tro·ver·sy (kon′trə vûr′sē), *n., pl.* **-sies. 1.** dispute, debate, or contention. **2.** contention, strife, or quarrel. [ME *controversie* < L *contrōversia* = *contrōvers(us)* turned against, disputed (*contro-* var. of *contrā* CONTRA- + *versus* ptp. of *vertere* to turn) + *-ia* -Y³] —**Syn. 2.** See **argument.**

con·tro·vert (kon′trə vûrt′, kon′trə vûrt′), *v.t.* **1.** to argue against; oppose. **2.** to argue about; debate; discuss. [alter. of earlier *controverse* (< L *contrōversus*; see CONTROVERSY) with *-vert* from ADVERT, CONVERT, etc.] —**con′tro·vert′er,** *n.* —**con′tro·vert′i·ble,** *adj.* —**con′tro·vert′i·bly,** *adv.* —**Syn. 1.** refute, rebut.

con·tu·ma·cious (kon′to͝o mā′shəs, -tyo͝o-), *adj.* stubbornly perverse or rebellious; obstinately disobedient. —**con′tu·ma′cious·ly,** *adv.* —**con′tu·ma′cious·ness, con·tu·mac·i·ty** (kon′to͝o mas′i tē, -tyo͝o-), *n.* —**Syn.** contrary.

con·tu·ma·cy (kon′to͝o mə sē, -tyo͝o-), *n., pl.* **-cies.** stubborn perverseness or rebelliousness. [< L *contumācia* arrogance, stubbornness = *contumāc-* (s. of *contumāx* defiant, lit., puffed up; see CON-, TUMOR) + *-ia* -Y³]

con·tu·me·ly (kon′to͝o mə lē, -tyo͝o-; kən to͞o′mə lē, -tyo͞o′-; kon′təm lē; *formerly* kon′tyo͝o mē′lē), *n., pl.* **-lies. 1.** an insulting display of contempt. **2.** a humiliating insult. [ME *contumelie* < L *contumēlia* insult, abuse = *con-* CON- + *tumē(re)* (to) be swollen (with rage) + *-l-* (< ?) + *-ia* -Y³] —**con·tu·me·li·ous** (kon′to͝o mē′lē əs, -tyo͝o-), *adj.* —**con′tu·me′li·ous·ly,** *adv.* —**con′tu·me′li·ous·ness,** *n.*

con·tuse (kən to͞oz′, -tyo͞oz′), *v.t.*, **-tused, -tus·ing.** to injure (tissue), esp. without breaking the skin; bruise. [late ME < L *contūs(us)* bruised, crushed (ptp. of *contundere*) = *con-* CON- + *tūd-* (ptp. s. of *tundere* to beat) + *-tus* ptp. suffix] —**con·tu·sive** (kən to͞o′siv, -tyo͞o′-), *adj.*

con·tu·sion (kən to͞o′zhən, -tyo͞o′-), *n.* an injury in which the subsurface tissue is injured but the skin is not broken; bruise. [late ME < L *contūsiōn-* (s. of *contūsiō*). See CONTUSE, -ION] —**con·tu′sioned,** *adj.*

co·nun·drum (kə nun′drəm), *n.* **1.** a riddle whose answer involves a pun. **2.** anything that puzzles. [?]

con·ur·ba·tion (kon′ûr bā′shən), *n.* an extensive urban area resulting from the expansion of several cities or towns so that they coalesce but retain their separate identities. [CON- + URB(AN) + ATION]

con·va·lesce (kon′və les′), *v.i.*, **-lesced, -lesc·ing.** to progress toward recovery of health after illness. [< L *convalesce(re)* (to) grow fully strong = *con-* CON- + *valescere* to grow strong (*val-* strong + *-escere* -ESCE)]

con·va·les·cence (kon′və les′əns), *n.* **1.** the gradual recovery of health and strength after illness. **2.** the period of such recovery. [< LL *convalescentia*]

con·va·les·cent (kon′və les′ənt), *adj.* **1.** convalescing. **2.** of or pertaining to convalescence or convalescing persons. —*n.* **3.** a convalescent person. [< L *convalescent-* (s. of *convalescēns*), prp. of *convalescere* to CONVALESCE; see -ENT] —**con′va·les′cent·ly,** *adv.*

con·vect (kən vekt′), *v.t.* **1.** to transfer (heat or a fluid) by convection. —*v.i.* **2.** (of a fluid) to transfer heat by convection. [< L *convect(us)* carried together (ptp. of *convehere*)] —**con·vec′tive,** *adj.* —**con·vec′tive·ly,** *adv.*

con·vec·tion (kən vek′shən), *n.* **1.** *Physics.* the transfer of heat by the circulation or movement of the heated parts of a liquid or gas. **2.** *Meteorol.* the vertical transport of atmospheric properties, esp. upward (distinguished from *advection*). **3.** the act of conveying or transmitting. [< LL *convectiōn-* (s. of *convectiō*) a bringing together] —**con·vec′tion·al,** *adj.*

con·ve·nance (kon′və näns′; *Fr.* kônvə näNs′), *n., pl.* **-nanc·es** (-nän′siz; *Fr.* -näNs′). **1.** suitability; propriety. **2. convenances,** the social proprieties. [< F = *conven(ir)* (to) be proper + *-ance* -ANCE]

con·vene (kən vēn′), *v.*, **-vened, -ven·ing.** —*v.i.* **1.** to come together; assemble. —*v.t.* **2.** to cause to assemble; convoke. **3.** to summon to appear, as before a judicial officer. [late ME < L *conven(īre)* (to) come together = *con-* CON- + *venīre* to come] —**con·ven′a·ble,** *adj.* —**con·ven′a·bly,** *adv.* —**con·ven′er,** *n.* —**Syn. 1.** congregate, meet.

con·ven·ience (kən vēn′yəns), *n.* **1.** the quality of being convenient; suitability. **2.** a convenient situation or time: *to await one's convenience.* **3.** advantage or accommodation: *a shelter for the convenience of travelers.* **4.** anything that saves or simplifies work, adds to a person's ease or comfort, etc. **5.** *Chiefly Brit.* See **water closet** (def. 1). [ME < L *convenientia* harmony, agreement]

conven′ience store′, a retail store that carries basic food, drug, and household items and is open longer hours than other stores for the convenience of shoppers.

con·ven·ien·cy (kən vēn′yən sē), *n., pl.* **-cies.** *Archaic.* convenience. [ME < L *convenientia*]

con·ven·ient (kən vēn′yənt), *adj.* **1.** agreeable to the needs or purpose. **2.** at hand: *convenient to all transportation.* **3.** *Obs.* fitting; suitable. [ME < L *convenient-* (s. of *conveniēns*), prp. of *convenīre* to be suitable] —**con·ven′ient·ly,** *adv.* —**Syn. 1.** serviceable, advantageous. **2.** handy.

con·vent (kon′vent), *n.* **1.** a community of persons devoted to religious life under a superior: now usually said of a society of nuns. **2.** the building or buildings occupied by such a society. [late ME < L *convent(us)* assembly (ML: convent, n. use of ptp. of *convenīre* to CONVENE); r. ME *covent* < AF] —**Syn. 1.** abbey, priory, cloister.

con·ven·ti·cle (kən ven′ti kəl), *n.* **1.** a secret or unauthorized meeting, esp. for religious worship. **2.** a place of meeting or assembly, esp. a Nonconformist meeting house. **3.** *Obs.* a meeting or assembly. [ME < L *conventicul(um)* (place of) assembly] —**con·ven′ti·cler,** *n.* —**con·ven·tic·u·lar** (kon′ven tik′yə lər), *adj.*

con·ven·tion (kən ven′shən), *n.* **1.** a meeting or formal assembly, as of representatives or delegates, for discussion of and action on particular matters of common concern. **2.** *U.S. Politics.* a representative party assembly to nominate candidates and adopt platforms and party rules. **3.** an agreement, compact, or contract. **4.** an international agreement, esp. one dealing with a specific matter. **5.** general agreement or consent; accepted usage. **6.** conventionalism. **7.** a rule, method, etc., established by general consent or usage; custom. [late ME *convencio(u)n* < L *conventiōn-* (s. of *conventiō*) agreement, lit., a coming together]

con·ven·tion·al (kən ven′shə n^{ə}l), *adj.* **1.** conforming or adhering to accepted standards, as of conduct or taste. **2.** pertaining to convention or general agreement; established by general consent or accepted usage: *conventional symbols.* **3.** ordinary: *conventional phraseology.* **4.** (of figurative art) represented in a generalized or simplified manner. **5.** of or pertaining to a convention, agreement, or compact. **6.** *Law.* resting on consent. **7.** of or pertaining to a convention or assembly. [< LL *conventiōnāl(is)*] —**con·ven′tion·al·ist,** *n.* —**con·ven′tion·al·ly,** *adv.* —**Syn. 1.** See **formal**[1]. **2.** usual, habitual, customary.

con·ven·tion·al·ise (kən ven′shə n^{ə}līz′), *v.t.*, **-ised, -is·ing.** *Chiefly Brit.* conventionalize. —**con·ven′tion·al·i·sa′tion,** *n.*

con·ven·tion·al·ism (kən ven′shə n^{ə}liz′əm), *n.* **1.** adherence to or advocacy of conventional attitudes or practices. **2.** a conventional expression, attitude, etc. **3.** *Philos.* the view that fundamental principles are validated by definition, agreement, or convention.

con·ven·tion·al·i·ty (kən ven′shə nal′i tē), *n., pl.* **-ties** for 3, 4. **1.** conventional quality or character. **2.** adherence to convention. **3.** a conventional practice, principle, form, etc. **4. conventionalities,** conventional rules of behavior.

con·ven·tion·al·ize (kən ven′shə n^{ə}līz′), *v.t.*, **-ized, -iz·ing.** **1.** to make conventional. **2.** *Art.* to represent in a conventional manner. Also, *esp. Brit.,* **conventionalise.** —**con·ven′tion·al·i·za′tion,** *n.*

con·ven·tio·neer (kən ven′shə nēr′), *n.* a person who attends a convention.

con·ven·tu·al (kən ven′cho͞o əl), *adj.* **1.** of, belonging to, or characteristic of a convent. —*n.* **2.** a member of a convent or monastery. [late ME < ML *conventuāl(is)* = *conventu(s)* CONVENT + *-ālis* -AL[1]] —**con·ven′tu·al·ly,** *adj.*

con·verge (kən vûrj′), *v.*, **-verged, -verg·ing.** —*v.i.* **1.** to tend to meet in a point or line; incline toward each other, as lines that are not parallel. **2.** to tend to a common result, conclusion, etc. —*v.t.* **3.** to cause to converge. [< LL *converge(re)* (to) incline together]

con·ver·gence (kən vûr′jəns), *n.* **1.** an act or instance of converging. **2.** a convergent state or quality. **3.** the degree to which or point at which lines, objects, etc., converge. **4.** *Physiol.* a coordinated turning of the eyes to bear upon a near point. **5.** *Meteorol.* **a.** the contraction of a vector field. **b.** a measure of this. **c.** a net flow of air into a given region. Cf. **divergence** (def. 2). **6.** *Biol.* similarity of form or structure caused by environment rather than heredity. Also, **con·ver′gen·cy** (for defs. 1–3).

con·ver·gent (kən vûr′jənt), *adj.* characterized by convergence; tending to come together; merging. [< ML *convergent-* (s. of *convergēns,* prp. of *convergere*)] —**con·ver′gent·ly,** *adv.*

conver′gent evolu′tion, the appearance of apparently similar structures in organisms of different lines of descent.

con·vers·a·ble (kən vûr′sə bəl), *adj.* **1.** easy and pleasant to talk with; agreeable. **2.** able or disposed to converse. **3.** pertaining to or proper for conversation. [< ML *conversābil(is)*] —**con·vers′a·ble·ness,** *n.* —**con·vers′a·bly,** *adv.*

con·ver·sant (kən vûr′sənt, kon′vər-), *adj.* **1.** familiar by use or study (usually fol. by *with*): *to be conversant with Spanish history.* **2.** intimately associated; acquainted. [ME *conversa(u)nt* < L *conversant-* (s. of *conversāns*), prp. of *conversārī* to associate with] —**con·ver′sance, con·ver′san·cy,** *n.* —**con·ver′sant·ly,** *adv.* —**Syn. 1.** versed, practiced.

con·ver·sa·tion (kon′vər sā′shən), *n.* **1.** oral communication between persons; talk; colloquy. **2.** an instance of this. **3.** association or social intercourse. **4.** See **criminal conversation. 5.** the ability to talk socially with others. **6.** *Archaic.* behavior or manner of living. **7.** *Obs.* close familiarity. [ME *conversacio(u)n* < L *conversātiōn-* (s. of *conversātiō*) society, intercourse = *conversāt(us)* associated with (ptp. of *conversārī;* see CONVERSE[1], -ATE[1]) + *-iōn-* -ION]

con·ver·sa·tion·al (kon′vər sā′shə n^{ə}l), *adj.* **1.** of, pertaining to, or characteristic of conversation: *a conversational tone of voice.* **2.** able or ready to converse. —**con′ver·sa′tion·al·ly,** *adv.* —**Syn. 1.** See **colloquial.**

con·ver·sa·tion·al·ist (kon′vər sā′shə n^{ə}list), *n.* a person who enjoys and contributes to good conversation.

conversa′tion piece′, **1.** *Fine Arts.* group portraiture representing fashionable people either in an interior or landscape setting. **2.** any object that arouses comment because of some striking quality.

con·ver·sa·zi·o·ne (kôn′ver sä tsyô′ne; *Eng.* kon′vər sät′sē ō′nē), *n., pl.* **-zio·ni** (-tsyô′nē), *Eng.* **-zi·o·nes.** *Italian.* a social gathering for conversation, esp. on literary or scholarly subjects. [lit., conversation]

con·verse[1] (*v.* kən vûrs′; *n.* kon′vûrs), *v.*, **-versed, -vers·ing,** *n.* —*v.i.* **1.** to talk informally with another or others. **2.** *Obs.* **a.** to maintain a familiar association (usually fol. by *with*). **b.** to have sexual intercourse (usually fol. by *with*). **c.** to commune spiritually (usually fol. by *with*). —*n.* **3.** familiar discourse or talk; conversation. **4.** *Obs.* spiritual communion. [ME *converse(n)* < L *conversārī* to associate with. See CON-, VERSE] —**con·vers′er,** *n.* —**Syn. 1.** talk, chat, discuss. See **speak.**

con·verse[2] (*adj.* kən vûrs′, kon′vûrs; *n.* kon′vûrs), *adj.* **1.** opposite or contrary in direction, action, sequence, etc.; turned around. —*n.* **2.** something that is the opposite or contrary of another. **3.** *Logic.* a proposition obtained from another proposition by conversion. **4.** a group of words correlative with a preceding group but having a significant pair of terms interchanged, as "hot in winter but cold in summer" and "cold in winter but hot in summer." [< L *convers(us)* turned around, ptp. of *convertere;* see CONVERT] —**con·verse·ly** (kən vûrs′lē, kon′vûrs-), *adv.*

con·ver·sion (kən vûr′zhən, -shən), *n.* **1.** the act of converting. **2.** the state or process of being converted. **3.** an alteration of form, substance, etc. **4.** an adaptation to different means or uses. **5.** a change in a person's beliefs or attitudes. **6.** the act of obtaining equivalent value, as of money or units of measurement, in an exchange or calculation. **7.** *Math.* a change in the form or units of an expression. **8.** *Logic.* the transposition of the subject and predicate of a proposition. **9.** *Law.* **a.** unauthorized assumption and exercise of rights of ownership over personal property belonging to another. **b.** change from realty into personalty, or vice versa. **10.** *Football.* a score made on a try for point after touchdown. **11.** *Psychoanal.* the process by which a repressed idea, feeling, etc., is represented by a bodily change, as a simulated physical illness. **12.** *Physics.* the production of radioactive material in a process in which one nuclear fuel is converted into a second nuclear fuel by the capture of neutrons. Cf. **breeding** (def. 6). **13.** *Computer Technol.* **a.** a change from one code or symbolic system to another. **b.** a change from one physical or recording system to another. [ME *conversio(u)n* < L *conversiōn-* (s. of *conversiō*) a complete change. See CONVERSE[2], -ION] —**con·ver′sion·al, con·ver·sion·ar·y** (kən vûr′zhə ner′ē, -shə-), *adj.*

conver′sion ta′ble, a tabular arrangement of the equivalent values of the weight or measure units.

con·vert (*v.* kən vûrt′; *n.* kon′vûrt), *v.t.* **1.** to change (something) into a different form, substance, etc.; transmute; transform. **2.** to cause to acquire different beliefs, attitudes, etc., esp. ones believed to be better. **3.** to adapt to different means or uses (usually fol. by *to* or *into*): *to convert a bedroom into a den.* **4.** to obtain an equivalent value for in an exchange or calculation, as money or units of measurement. **5.** to appropriate wrongfully to one's own use. **6.** to invert or transpose. **7.** *Law.* **a.** to assume unlawful rights of ownership of (personal property). **b.** to change from realty to personalty, or vice versa. **8.** *Logic.* to transpose the subject and predicate of (a proposition) by conversion. **9.** *Finance.* to exchange voluntarily (a bond or preferred stock) into another security, usually common stock. —*v.i.* **10.** to become converted. **11.** *Football.* to make a conversion. —*n.* **12.** a person who has been converted, as to a religion or an opinion. [ME *converte(n)* < L *converte(re)* (to) change completely = *con-* CON- + *vertere* to turn round] —**con·ver′tive,** *adj.* —**Syn. 2.** proselytize. **12.** proselyte, neophyte, disciple.

con·vert·er (kən vûr′tər), *n.* **1.** a person or thing that converts. **2.** a person who converts textile fabrics, esp. cotton cloths into finished products, as by bleaching and dyeing. **3.** *Elect.* a device that converts alternating current to direct current, or vice versa. **4.** *Metall.* a chamber or vessel through which an oxidizing blast of air is forced, as in the Bessemer process. **5.** *Physics.* a reactor for converting one kind of fuel into another kind. Also, **con·ver′tor.**

con·vert·i·ble (kən vûr′tə bəl), *adj.* **1.** capable of being converted. **2.** having a folding top, as an automobile or pleasure boat. —*n.* **3.** an automobile or boat having such a top. [ME < ML *convertibil(is)*] —**con·vert′i·bil′i·ty, con·vert′i·ble·ness,** *n.* —**con·vert′i·bly,** *adv.*

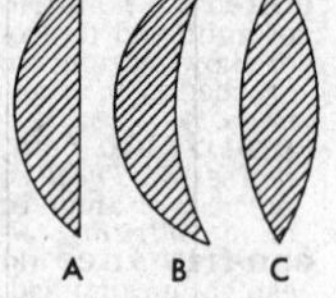

A, Convex or plano-convex lens; B, Convexo-concave lens; C, Convexo-convex lens

con·vert·i·plane (kən vûr′tə plān′), *n.* a plane designed to change its configuration, permitting both vertical and short conventional take-off and landing, and high-speed flight. Also, **con·ver′ta·plane′, con·ver′to·plane′.**

con·vert·ite (kon′vər tīt′), *n. Archaic.* a convert.

con·vex (*adj.* kon veks′, kən-, kon′veks; *n.* kon′veks), *adj.* **1.** having a surface that is curved or rounded outward. Cf. **concave** (def. 1). **2.** *Math.* (of a polygon) having all interior angles less than or equal to 180°. —*n.* **3.** a convex surface, part, or thing. [< L *convex(us)* = *con-* CON- + *vec-*, var. of *vac-* bend + *-sus* ptp. suffix] —**con·vex′ly,** *adv.*

con·vex·i·ty (kən vek′si tē), *n., pl.* **-ties** for 2. **1.** the state of being convex. **2.** a convex surface or thing. [< L *convexitās*]

convexo-, a combining form of **convex:** *convexo-concave.*

con·vex·o-con·cave (kən vek′sō kon kāv′), *adj.* **1.** convex on one side and concave on the other. **2.** *Optics.* pertaining to or noting a lens in which the convex face has a greater degree of curvature than the concave face. Cf. **concavo-convex.**

con·vex·o-con·vex (kən vek′sō kon veks′), *adj.* convex on both sides; biconvex.

con·vex·o-plane (kən vek′sō plān′), *adj.* plano-convex.

con·vey (kən vā′), *v.t.* **1.** to carry, bring, or take from one place to another. **2.** to lead or conduct, as a channel or medium. **3.** to impart, as information. **4.** *Law.* to transfer; pass the title to. **5.** *Archaic.* steal; purloin. **6.** *Obs.* to take away secretly. [ME *convey(en)* < AF *conveie(r)* < VL **conviāre* = *con-* CON- + *viāre* < *via* way; see VIA] —**con·vey′a·ble,** *adj.* —**Syn. 1.** bring. See **carry.**

con·vey·ance (kən vā′əns), *n.* **1.** the act of conveying. **2.** a means of transporting, esp. a vehicle. **3.** *Law.* **a.** the transfer of property from one person to another. **b.** the instrument or document by which this is effected.

con·vey·anc·er (kən vā′ən sər), *n.* a person engaged in conveyancing.

con·vey·anc·ing (kən vā′ən sing), *n.* the branch of law practice consisting of examining titles, drawing deeds, etc., for the conveyance of property.

con·vey·or (kən vā′ər), *n.* **1.** a person or thing that conveys. **2.** *Mach.* an endless chain or belt, set of rollers, etc., for carrying materials. Also, **con·vey′er.**

convey′or belt′, *Mach.* a conveyor consisting of an endless belt or chain.

con·vict (*v., adj.* kən vikt′; *n.* kon′vikt), *v.t.* **1.** to prove or declare guilty of an offense, esp. after a legal trial. **2.** to impress with a sense of guilt. —*n.* **3.** a person proved or declared guilty of an offense. **4.** a person serving a prison sentence. —*adj.* **5.** *Archaic.* convicted. [ME *convict(e)* (ptp.) < L *convict(us)* proved guilty (ptp. of *convincere*) = *con-* CON- + *vic-* (ptp. s. of *vincere* to overcome) + *-tus* ptp. suffix] —**con·vict′a·ble, con·vict′i·ble,** *adj.* —**con·vic′tive,** *adj.* —**con·vic′tive·ly,** *adv.*

con·vic·tion (kən vik′shən), *n.* **1.** the act of convicting. **2.** the state of being convicted. **3.** the act of convincing. **4.** the state of being convinced. **5.** a fixed belief. [late ME < LL *convictiōn-* (s. of *convictiō*) proof (of guilt)] —**con·vic′tion·al,** *adj.* —**Syn. 5.** See **belief.** —**Ant. 4.** doubt.

con·vince (kən vins′), *v.t.*, **-vinced, -vinc·ing. 1.** to persuade by argument or proof (often fol. by *of*): *to convince a man of his folly.* **2.** *Obs.* to prove or find guilty. **3.** *Obs.* to overcome; vanquish. [< L *convince(re)* (to) prove (something) false or true, (somebody) right or wrong = *con-* CON- + *vincere* to overcome] —**con·vinc·ed·ly** (kən vin′sid lē), *adv.* —**con·vinc′ed·ness,** *n.* —**con·vinc′er,** *n.* —**con·vinc′i·bil′i·ty,** *n.* —**con·vin′ci·ble,** *adj.* —**con·vinc′ing·ly,** *adv.* —**con·vinc′ing·ness,** *n.* —**Syn. 1.** See **persuade.**

con·viv·i·al (kən viv′ē əl), *adj.* **1.** fond of feasting, drinking, and companionship. **2.** of or befitting a feast; festive. [< LL *convīviāl(is)* festal = L *convīvi(um)* feast (*convīv(ere)* to feast with = *con-* CON- + *vīvere* to live well + *-ium* n. suffix) + *-ālis* -AL[1]] —**con·viv′i·al·ist,** *n.* —**con·viv′i·al′i·ty,** *n.* —**con·viv′i·al·ly,** *adv.*

con·vo·ca·tion (kon′və kā′shən), *n.* **1.** the act of convoking. **2.** the state of being convoked. **3.** a group of people gathered in answer to a summons; assembly. **4.** *Ch. of Eng.* one of the two provincial synods or assemblies of the clergy. **5.** *Prot. Episc. Ch.* **a.** an assembly of the clergy of part of a diocese. **b.** the area represented at such an assembly. [ME *convocacio(u)n* < L *convocātiōn-* (s. of *convocātiō*). See CONVOKE, -ATION] —**con′vo·ca′tion·al,** *adj.* —**con′vo·ca′tion·al·ly,** *adv.*

con·voke (kən vōk′), *v.t.*, **-voked, -vok·ing.** to call together; summon to meet. [< L *convoc(āre)* = *con-* CON- + *vocāre* to call] —**con·voc·a·tive** (kən vok′ə tiv), *adj.* —**con·vok′er, con′vo·cant,** *n.*

con·vo·lute (kon′və lo͞ot′), *v.*, **-lut·ed, -lut·ing,** *adj.* —*v.t., v.i.* **1.** to coil up; twist. —*adj.* **2.** rolled up together or with one part over another. **3.** *Bot.* coiled up longitudinally, as the petals of cotton. [< L *convolūt(us)* rolled up, ptp. of *convolvere* to CONVOLVE] —**con′vo·lute′ly,** *adv.*

con·vo·lut·ed (kon′və lo͞o′tid), *adj.* **1.** twisted; coiled. **2.** complicated; involved. —**con′vo·lut′ed·ly,** *adv.* —**con′vo·lut′ed·ness,** *n.*

con·vo·lu·tion (kon′və lo͞o′shən), *n.* **1.** a rolled up or coiled condition. **2.** a rolling or coiling together. **3.** a turn of anything coiled; whorl; sinuosity. **4.** *Anat.* one of the sinuous folds or ridges of the surface of the brain. [< L *convolūt(us)* (see CONVOLUTE) + -ION] —**con′vo·lu′tion·al, con·vo·lu·tion·ar·y** (kon′və lo͞o′shə ner′ē), *adj.*

con·volve (kən volv′), *v.i., v.t.*, **-volved, -volv·ing.** to roll or wind together; coil; twist. [< L *convolve(re)* = *con-* CON- + *volvere* to roll,turn, twist] —**con·volve′ment,** *n.*

con·vol·vu·la·ceous (kən vol′vyə lā′shəs), *adj.* belonging to the *Convolvulaceae*, or morning-glory family of plants.

con·vol·vu·lus (kən vol′vyə ləs), *n., pl.* **-lus·es, -li** (-lī′). any plant of the genus *Convolvulus*, which comprises erect, twining, or prostrate herbs having trumpet-shaped flowers. Cf. **morning-glory.** [< NL, L: bindweed]

con·voy (*v.* kon′voi, kən voi′; *n.* kon′voi), *v.t.* **1.** to accompany or escort, usually for protection. —*n.* **2.** the act of convoying. **3.** the protection provided by an escort. **4.** an armed force, warship, etc., that escorts. **5.** a ship, fleet, group of vehicles, etc., accompanied by a protecting escort. **6.** any group of military vehicles traveling together under the same orders. [ME *convoy(en)* < MF *convoie(r)*, AF *conveier* to CONVEY] —**Syn. 1.** See **accompany.**

con·vulse (kən vuls′), *v.t.*, **-vulsed, -vuls·ing. 1.** to shake violently. **2.** to cause to shake violently with laughter, anger, pain, etc. **3.** to cause to suffer violent, spasmodic contractions of the muscles. [< L *convuls(us)* shattered, torn loose (ptp. of *convellere*) = *con-* CON- + *vul-* (ptp. s. of *vellere* to pull, tear) + *-sus*, var. of *-tus* ptp. suffix]

con·vul·sion (kən vul′shən), *n.* **1.** *Pathol.* contortion of the body caused by violent, involuntary muscular contractions. **2.** violent agitation or disturbance; commotion. **3.** an outburst of laughter. [< medical L *convulsiōn-* (s. of *convulsiō*)]

con·vul·sion·ar·y (kən vul′shə ner′ē), *adj., n., pl.* **-ar·ies.** —*adj.* **1.** of or affected with convulsion. —*n.* **2.** a person subject to convulsions.

con·vul·sive (kən vul′siv), *adj.* of the nature of or characterized by convulsions or spasms. [< medical L *convulsīv(us)*] —**con·vul′sive·ly,** *adv.* —**con·vul′sive·ness,** *n.*

co·ny (kō′nē, kun′ē), *n., pl.* **-nies. 1.** the fur of a rabbit. **2.** the daman or some other animal of the same genus. **3.** the pika. **4.** a rabbit. Also, **coney.** [ME, back formation from *conyes* < OF *conis*, pl. of *conil* < L *cunīcul(us)* rabbit, burrowing, mine, prob. of Iberian origin]

coo[1] (ko͞o), *v.*, **cooed, coo·ing,** *n.* —*v.i.* **1.** to utter or imitate the murmur of pigeons or doves. **2.** to murmur amorously. —*v.t.* **3.** to utter by cooing. —*n.* **4.** a cooing sound. [imit.] —**coo′er,** *n.* —**coo′ing·ly,** *adv.*

coo[2] (ko͞o), *interj.* *Brit. Slang.* (used to express surprise.) [?]

Co·o (kô′ô), *n.* Italian name of **Kos.**

Cooch Be·har (ko͞och′ bə här′), a former state in NE India; now part of West Bengal. 1334 sq. mi.

coo·ee (ko͞o′ē), *n., v.*, **coo·eed, coo·ee·ing.** —*n.* **1.** a prolonged, shrill, clear call or cry used as a signal by Australian aborigines. —*v.i.* **2.** to utter this call. [< native Austral]

coo·ey (ko͞o′ē), *n., pl.* **-eys,** *v.i.*, **-eyed, -ey·ing.** cooee.

cook (ko͝ok), *v.t.* **1.** to prepare (food) by the action of heat, as by boiling, baking, roasting, etc. **2.** to subject (anything) to the action of heat. **3.** *Slang.* to falsify, as accounts. —*v.i.* **4.** to prepare food by the action of heat. **5.** (of food) to undergo cooking. **6.** *Informal.* to take place; occur: *What's cooking at the club?* **7. cook one's goose.** See **goose** (def. 6). **8. cook up,** *Informal.* to concoct; contrive: *She hastily cooked up an excuse.* —*n.* **9.** a person who cooks. [v. < n.: ME *cok(e)*, OE *cōc* (cf. Icel *kokkr*, G *Koch*, D *kok*) < L *coc(us)*, var. of *coquus* < *coquere* to cook; akin to Gk *péptein* to cook] —**cook′a·ble,** *adj.* —**cook′less,** *adj.*

Cook (ko͝ok), *n.* **1. Frederick Albert,** 1865–1940, U.S. physician and polar explorer. **2. Captain James,** 1728–79, English navigator and explorer in the S Pacific, Antarctic Ocean, and along the coasts of New Zealand and Australia. **3. Mount.** Also called **Aorangi.** a mountain in New Zealand, on South Island. 12,349 ft.

cook·book (ko͝ok′bo͝ok′), *n.* a book containing recipes and instructions for cooking. Also called, *Brit.*, **cook′ery book′**

cook·er (ko͝ok′ər), *n.* **1.** an appliance or utensil for cooking: *a fireless cooker.* **2.** a person employed in certain industrial processes, as in brewing, distilling, etc., to operate cooking apparatus.

cook·er·y (ko͝ok′ə rē), *n., pl.* **-er·ies** for 2. **1.** the art or practice of cooking. **2.** a place equipped for cooking. [ME]

cook·house (ko͝ok′hous′), *n., pl.* **-hous·es** (-hou′ziz). a building or place for cooking, esp. a ship's galley or a camp kitchen.

cook·ie (ko͝ok′ē), *n.* **1.** *U.S.* a small cake made from stiff, sweet dough dropped, rolled, or sliced and then baked. **2.** *Scot.* a bun. **3.** *Slang.* a person: *a smart cookie.* Also, **cooky.** [< D *koekie*, var. of *koekje* = *koek* cake (MD *coeke*) + *-je* -Y[2]]

cook·ing (ko͝ok′ing), *n.* **1.** the act of a person or thing that cooks. **2.** cookery (def. 1). —*adj.* **3.** used in preparing foods. **4.** fit to eat when cooked (distinguished from *eating*): *cooking apples.*

Cook′ In′let, an inlet of the Gulf of Alaska. 150 mi. long.

Cook′ Is′lands, a group of islands in the S Pacific belonging to New Zealand. 19,214 (1963); 99 sq. mi.

cook·out (ko͝ok′out′), *n.* a party featuring the cooking and eating of a meal out of doors. Also, **cook′-out′.** [n. use of v. phrase *cook out*]

Cook's′ tour′, a guided but cursory tour of the major features of a place or area. [after Thomas *Cook* (1808–92), English travel agent]

cook·stove (ko͝ok′stōv′), *n.* a stove for use in cooking.

Cook′ Strait′, a strait in New Zealand between North and South Islands.

cook·top (ko͝ok′top′), *n.* a cooking surface consisting of a flat sheet of heat-transmitting glass-ceramic material over heating elements, generally electric.

cook·y (ko͝ok′ē), *n., pl.* **cook·ies.** cookie.

cool (ko͞ol), *adj.* **1.** moderately free of heat. **2.** moderately cold when felt. **3.** feeling comfortably free of heat. **4.** allowing one to feel so, as clothes. **5.** unaffected by emotions, as anger or fear. **6.** lacking in enthusiasm or cordiality. **7.** *Informal.* (of a number or sum) without exaggeration or qualification: *a cool million dollars.* **8.** (of colors) with green, blue, or violet predominating. **9.** *Slang.* great; fine; excellent: *a real cool comic.* —*adv.* **10.** *Informal.* coolly. —*n.* **11.** something that is cool: *in the cool of the evening.* **12.** *Slang.* calmness; composure: *Don't lose your cool.* —*v.i.* **13.** to become cool. **14.** to become less emotional, enthusiastic, etc. —*v.t.* **15.** to make cool; impart a sensation of coolness to. **16.** to lessen the ardor or intensity of, as emotions. **17. cool it,** *Slang.* to calm down; take it easy. **18. cool off,** *Informal.* to become calmer or more reasonable. **19. cool one's heels.** See **heel**[1] (def. 13). [ME *cole*, OE *cōl*; c. MLG *kōl*, OHG *kuoli* (G *kühl*)] —**cool′ing·ly,** *adv.* —**cool′ing·ness,** *n.* —**cool′ly,** *adv.* —**cool′ness,** *n.* —**Syn. 1.** See **cold. 5.** composed, collected, unruffled, placid, quiet. **6.** apathetic, indifferent, lukewarm; distant. **16.** temper, abate. —**Ant. 1, 2, 4, 6.** warm.

cool·ant (ko͞o′lənt), *n.* **1.** a substance, usually a liquid or a gas, used to reduce the temperature of a system below a specified level. **2.** a lubricant that dissipates the heat caused by friction.

cool·er (ko͞o′lər), *n.* **1.** a container or apparatus in which something may be cooled or kept cool. **2.** anything that cools or makes cool; refrigerant. **3.** *Informal.* an air conditioner. **4.** a tall, iced drink. **5.** See **water cooler. 6.** *Slang.* jail.

cool-head·ed (ko͞ol′hed′id), *adj.* not easily excited; calm. —**cool′-head′ed·ly,** *adv.* —**cool′-head′ed·ness,** *n.*

Cool·idge (ko͞o′lij), *n.* **Calvin,** 1872–1933, 30th president of the U.S. 1923–29.

coo·lie (ko͞o′lē), *n.* an unskilled, cheaply employed laborer in or from the Orient, esp. India and China. [< Urdu *kūlī* < Tamil *kūli* hire, hireling]

cool·ish (ko͞o′lish), *adj.* somewhat cool.

coo·ly (ko͞o′lē), *n., pl.* **-lies.** coolie.

coomb (ko͞om, kōm), *n.* combe. Also, **coombe.**

coon (ko͞on), *n.* raccoon. [aph. form]

coon·can (ko͞on′kan′), *n.* *Cards.* a variety of rummy for two players. [popular alter. of CONQUIAN]

coon′ dog′, any dog trained to hunt raccoons.

Coon′ Rap′ids, a city in SE Minnesota, near Minneapolis. 30,505 (1970).

coon's′ age′, *Informal.* a long time.

coon·skin (ko͞on′skin′), *n.* the pelt of a raccoon.

coon·tie (ko͞on′tē), *n.* **1.** either of two arrowroots, *Zamia integrifolia* or *Z. floridana*, of Florida. **2.** the flour produced from its starch. [< Seminole *kunti* the flour (from the plant)]

co-op (kō′op, kō op′), *n.* a cooperative store, society, dwelling, etc. Also, **co′op.** [shortened form]

coop (ko͞op, ko͝op), *n.* **1.** an enclosure, cage, or pen for fowls or other small animals. **2.** any small or narrow place. **3. fly the coop,** *Slang.* to escape, as from a prison; flee. —*v.t.* **4.** to place in or as in a coop. —*v.i.* **5.** *Slang.* (of a policeman) to sleep inside a parked patrol car while on duty. [ME *coupe* basket, perh. < Scand; cf. Norw *kaup* wooden can; akin to OE *cȳpa* basket]

coop., cooperative. Also, **co-op., coöp.**

coop·er (ko͞o′pər, ko͝op′ər), *n.* **1.** a person who makes or repairs casks, barrels, etc. —*v.t.* **2.** to make or repair (casks, barrels, etc.). —*v.i.* **3.** to work as a cooper. [ME *couper* < MLG *kūper* or MD *cūper* < ML *cūpār(ius)* (L *cūp(a)* cask, vat + *-ārius* -ER[2])]

Coo·per (ko͞o′pər, ko͝op′ər), *n.* **1. Anthony Ash·ley** (ash′lē). See **Shaftesbury, Anthony Ashley Cooper. 2. James Fen·i·more** (fen′ə mōr′, -môr′), 1789–1851, U.S. novelist. **3. Peter,** 1791–1883, U.S. inventor, manufacturer, reformer, and philanthropist.

coop·er·age (ko͞o′pər ij, ko͝op′ər-), *n.* **1.** the work, business, or place of business of a cooper. **2.** the articles made by a cooper.

co·op·er·ate (kō op′ə rāt′), *v.i.*, **-at·ed, -at·ing.** to work together, esp. willingly, for a common purpose. Also, **co-op′er·ate′, co·öp′er·ate′.** [< LL *cooperāt(us)* busied with, ptp. of *cooperārī*] —**co·op′er·a′tor, co-op′er·a′tor, co·öp′er·a′tor,** *n.*

co·op·er·a·tion (kō op′ə rā′shən), *n.* **1.** an act or instance of working or acting together for a common purpose. **2.** more or less active assistance from a person, organization, etc. **3.** willingness to cooperate. **4.** *Econ.* the combination of persons for purposes of production, purchase, or distribution for their joint benefit. **5.** *Ecol.* mutually beneficial interaction among organisms living in a limited area. Also, **co-op′er·a′tion, co·öp′er·a′tion.** [< LL *cooperātiōn-* (s. of *cooperātiō*)] —**co·op′er·a′tion·ist, co-op′er·a′tion·ist, co·öp′er·a′tion·ist,** *n.*

co·op·er·a·tive (kō op′ə rā′tiv, -ər ə tiv), *adj.* **1.** working or acting together willingly for a common purpose. **2.** demonstrating a willingness to cooperate. **3.** pertaining to economic cooperation. —*n.* **4.** a jointly owned means of production or distribution of goods or services operated by the consumers. **5.** an apartment house in which the apartments are individually owned, usually with each tenant owning his own. **6.** an apartment in such a building. Also, **co-op′er·a′tive, co·öp′er·a′tive.** [< LL *cooperātīv(us)*] —**co·op·er·a·tive·ly, co-op·er·a·tive·ly, co·öp·er·a·tive·ly** (kō op′ə rā′tiv lē, -ər ə tiv-), *adv.* —**co·op′er·a′tive·ness, co-op′er·a′tive·ness, co·öp′er·a′tive·ness,** *n.*

coop′erative store′, a retail store owned and managed by consumer-customers who supply the capital and share in the profits.

Coo·pers·town (ko͞o′pərz toun′, ko͝op′ərz-), *n.* a town in central New York: baseball Hall of Fame. 2403 (1970).

co·opt (kō opt′), *v.t.* **1.** preempt. **2.** to elect into a body by the votes of the members. **3.** to elect or appoint. Also, **co-opt′.** [< L *coopt(āre)*] —**co′op·ta′tion, co′-op·ta′tion, co·op·tion, co-op·tion** (kō op′shən), *n.* —**co·op·ta·tive, co-op·ta·tive** (kō op′tə tiv), *adj.*

co·or·di·nal (kō ôr′dənəl), *adj.* *Bot., Zool.* belonging to the same order. Also, **co·ör′di·nal.**

co·or·di·nate (*adj., n.* kō ôr′dənit, -dənāt′; *v.* kō ôr′dənāt′), *adj., n., v.,* **-nat·ed, -nat·ing.** —*adj.* **1.** of the same order or degree. **2.** involving coordination. **3.** *Math.* using or pertaining to systems of coordinates. **4.** *Gram.* of the same rank in a grammatical construction, as "*Jack*" and "*Jill*" in the phrase "*Jack and Jill.*" —*n.* **5.** a person or thing of equal rank or importance; an equal. **6.** *Math.* any of the magnitudes that serve to define the position of a point, line, or the like, by reference to a fixed figure, system of lines, etc. **7. coordinates,** *Clothing.* women's outer garments, harmonizing in color, fabric, and style, designed to be worn together. —*v.t.* **8.** to place or class in the same order, rank, etc. **9.** to place or arrange in proper order or position. **10.** to combine in harmonious relation or action. —*v.i.* **11.** to become coordinate. **12.** to assume proper order or relation. **13.** to act in harmonious combination. Also, **co-or′di·nate, co·ör′di·nate.** [CO- + (SUB)ORDINATE] —**co·or′di·nate·ly, co-or′di·nate·ly, co·ör′di·nate·ly,** *adv.* —**co·or·di·na·tive, co-or·di·na·tive, co·ör·di·na·tive** (kō ôr′dənā′tiv, -ôr′dənə-), *adj.* —**co·or′di·na′tor, co-or′di·na′tor, co·ör′di·na′tor,** *n.*

coor′dinate cova′lences, *Chem.* a covalent bond in which both of the shared electrons are contributed by one of the atoms. Also called **coor′dinate cova′lent bond′.**

coor′dinating conjunc′tion, *Gram.* a conjunction that connects two grammatical elements of identical construction, as "*and*" in "*Sue and Barbara.*" Cf. **subordinating conjunction.**

co·or·di·na·tion (kō ôr′dənā′shən), *n.* **1.** the act of coordinating. **2.** the state of being coordinated. **3.** proper order or relationship. **4.** harmonious combination or interaction, as of functions or parts. Also, **co-or′di·na′tion, co·ör′di·na′tion.** [< LL *coordinātiōn-* (s. of *coordinātiō*)]

coordina′tion com′pound, *Chem.* a compound in which a central atom is surrounded by others coordinately covalently bonded to it.

coordina′tion num′ber, *Crystall.* the number of anions surrounding a single cation in a stable crystal structure.

Coorg (ko͝org), *n.* a former province in SW India; now part of Mysore state. 1593 sq. mi. Also, **Kurg.**

Coos (ko͞os), *n.* a language of a group of American Indians indigenous to the coast of Oregon.

coot (ko͞ot), *n.* **1.** any aquatic bird of the genus *Fulica*, as *F. americana*, of North America, and *F. atra*, of the Old World, characterized by lobate toes and short wings and tail. **2.** any of various other swimming or diving birds, esp. the scoters. **3.** *Informal.* a foolish or crotchety old man. [ME *cote*; c. D *koet*]

Coot, *Fulica americana* (Length 15 in.)

coot·ie (ko͞o′tē), *n.* a louse, esp. the body louse. [? < Malay *kut(u)* louse + -IE]

co-own (kō′ōn′), *v.t.* to own in conjunction with (another person). —**co′-own′er,** *n.* —**co′-own′er·ship′,** *n.*

cop[1] (kop), *v.t.*, **copped, cop·ping.** *Slang.* **1.** to catch; nab. **2.** to steal; filch. **3. cop out,** *Slang.* **a.** to fail to keep one's promise or do one's share; renege; back out or give up. **b.** Also, **cop a plea.** to plead guilty to a criminal charge, esp. to avoid trial on a graver charge. [akin to OE *copian* to plunder, steal, hence modern take, lay hold of]

cop[2] (kop), *n.* *Informal.* a policeman. [from COPPER[2]]

cop[3] (kop), *n.* a conical mass of thread, yarn, etc., wound on a spindle. [ME, OE *cop* tip, top, prob. c. G *Kopf* head]

cop., **1.** copper. **2.** copyright; copyrighted.

co·pa·cet·ic (kō′pə set′ik, -sē′tik), *adj.* *Slang.* fine; completely satisfactory; O.K.: *If I just had some cash, everything would be copacetic.* Also, **copasetic, copesetic.** [?]

co·pai·ba (kō pā′bə, -pī′bə), *n.* an oleoresin obtained from several tropical, chiefly South American, caesalpiniaceous trees of the genus *Copaifera*: used in varnishes and lacquers and formerly in medicine. Also called **copai′ba bal′sam, copai′ba res′in.** [< Sp < Pg < Tupi]

co·pal (kō′pəl, -pal), *n.* a hard, lustrous resin obtained from various tropical trees, used chiefly in making varnishes. [< Sp < Nahuatl *copal(li)* kind of resin]

co·palm (kō′päm′), *n.* See **sweet gum** (defs. 1, 2). [? < MexSp *copalme* < LaF **copalmé*, b. *copal* COPAL and *palmé* PALMATE]

Co·pán (*Sp.* kô pän′), *n.* See **Santa Rosa de Copán.**

co·par·ce·nar·y (kō pär′sə ner′ē), *n.* *Law.* joint ownership, esp. upon the descent of real property to several female heirs. Also, **co·par·ce·ny** (kō pär′sə nē).

co·par·ce·ner (kō pär′sə nər), *n.* a member of a coparcenary.

co·part·ner (kō pärt′nər, kō′pärt′-), *n.* a fellow partner or associate, as in a business. —**co·part′ner·ship′,** *n.*

co·pa·set·ic (kō′pə set′ik, -sē′tik), *adj.* copacetic.

cope[1] (kōp), *v.*, **coped, cop·ing.** —*v.i.* **1.** to struggle or contend, esp. on fairly even terms or with some degree of success (usually fol. by *with*). **2.** *Archaic.* to come into contact; meet (usually fol. by *with*). —*v.t.* **3.** *Obs.* to come into contact with. [ME *coupe(n)* < MF, OF *couper* (to) strike < *coup* COUP[1]]

A, Cope[2]
B, Crosier

cope[2] (kōp), *n., v.,* **coped, cop·ing.** —*n.* **1.** a long mantle worn by ecclesiastics, esp. in processions. **2.** any cloaklike or canopylike covering. —*v.t.* **3.** to furnish with or as with a cope or coping. [ME, OE *cāp* < ML *cāp(a)*, var. of *cappa* CAP[1]]

cope[3] (kōp), *v.t.*, **coped, cop·ing.** **1.** *Building Trades.* to join (two molded wooden members) by undercutting the end of one of them to the profile of the other so that the joint produced resembles a miter joint (usually fol. by *in* or *together*). **2.** to form (a joint between such members) in this way. **3.** to undercut the end of (a molded wooden member) in order to form a coped joint. [< F *coup(er)* (to) cut; see COPE[1]]

co·peck (kō′pek), *n.* kopeck.

cope·mate (kōp′māt′), *n.* *Obs.* **1.** an antagonist. **2.** a comrade.

Co·pen·ha·gen (kō′pən hā′gən, -hä′-, kō′pən hā′-, -hä′-), *n.* a seaport in and the capital of Denmark, on the E coast of Zealand. 802,391. Danish, **København.**

co·pe·pod (kō′pə pod′), *n.* **1.** any minute crustacean of the subclass *Copepoda.* —*adj.* **2.** belonging or pertaining to the *Copepoda.* [< NL *Copepod(a)* name of the order < Gk *kṓpē* a handle, oar + *-poda* -PODA]

Co·per·ni·can (kō pûr′nə kən, kə-), *adj.* of or pertaining to Copernicus or his theories, esp. the theory that the planets revolve around the sun.

Co·per·ni·cus (kō pûr′nə kəs, kə-), *n.* **1. Nic·o·la·us** (nik′ə lā′əs), (*Mikolaj Kopernik*), 1473–1543, Polish astronomer. **2.** a crater in the second quadrant of the face of the moon, having an extensive ray system. ab. 56 mi. in diam. with walls rising ab. 12,000 ft. from its floor; having several central mountains, the highest being ab. 2400 ft.

co·pe·set·ic (kō′pə set′ik, -sē′tik), *adj.* copacetic.

cope·stone (kōp′stōn′), *n.* **1.** the top stone of a building or other structure. **2.** a stone used for or in coping. **3.** the crown or completion; finishing touch.

A

B

Copings
A, Stone; B, Tile

cop·i·er (kop′ē ər), *n.* **1.** a person or thing that copies. **2.** Also called **photocopier, photocopying machine.** any electrically operated machine using a photographic method, as the electrostatic process, for making instant copies of written, drawn, or printed material.

co·pi·lot (kō′pī′lət), *n.* a pilot who is second in command of an aircraft. Also called **first officer.**

cop·ing (kō′ping), *n.* a finishing course or cap to an exterior masonry wall or the like.

cop′ing saw′, a saw having a light, ribbonlike blade held in a U-shaped frame: used for cutting curves in wood.

co·pi·ous (kō′pē əs), *adj.* **1.** large in quantity or number; abundant. **2.** having or yielding an abundant supply. **3.** exhibiting abundance or fullness, as of thoughts or words. [ME < L *cōpiōs(us)* plentiful, rich = *cōpi(a)* wealth (*co-* CO- + (*o*)*p-* (s. of *ops*) wealth + *-ia* -IA) + *-ōsus* -OUS] —**co′pi·ous·ly,** *adv.* —**co′pi·ous·ness, co·pi·os·i·ty** (kō′pē os′i tē), *n.* —**Syn. 2.** See **ample.**

Coping saw

co·pla·nar (kō plā′nər), *adj.* *Math.* being or operating in the same plane. —**co·pla·nar·i·ty** (kō′plā nar′i tē), *n.*

Cop·ley (kop′lē), *n.* **John Sin·gle·ton** (sing′gəl tən), 1738–1815, U.S. painter.

co·pol·y·mer (kō pol′ə mər), *n.* *Chem.* a compound of high molecular weight produced by polymerizing two or more different monomers together.

co·pol·y·mer·ize (kō pol′ə mə rīz′), *v.t., v.i.,* **-ized, -iz·ing.** *Chem.* to subject to or undergo a change analogous to polymerization but with a union of two or more different monomers. —**co·pol′y·mer·i·za′tion,** *n.*

cop-out (kop′out′), *n.* *Slang.* **1.** an evasion of one's responsibility or a compromising with one's principles. **2.** a person who gives up easily or habitually evades responsibility.

cop·per[1] (kop′ər), *n.* **1.** *Chem.* a metallic element having a characteristic light reddish-brown color: used in large quantities as an electrical conductor and in the manufacture of alloys, as brass and bronze. *Symbol:* Cu; *at. wt.:* 63.54; *at. no.:* 29; *sp. gr.:* 8.92 at 20°C. **2.** a coin composed of copper, bronze, or the like, as the U.S. cent or the British penny. **3.** a container made of copper. **4.** a tool partly or wholly made of copper. **5.** *Brit.* a large kettle, now usually made of iron. —*v.t.* **6.** to cover, coat, or sheathe with copper. —*adj.* **7.** made of copper. **8.** resembling copper. [ME *coper,* OE *coper, copor* (c. Icel *koparr,* G *Kupfer*) < LL *cuprum* for L (*aes*) *Cyprium* CYPRIAN (metal)]

cop·per² (kop′ər), *n. Slang.* a policeman. [COP¹ + -ER¹]

Cop′per Age′, a cultural period intermediate between the Neolithic and the Bronze Ages, marked by the development and use of copper tools.

cop′per ar′senite, *Chem.* a poisonous powder, $CuHAsO_3$, used chiefly as a pigment and as an insecticide.

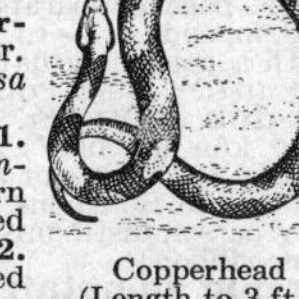

Copperhead (Length to 3 ft.)

cop·per·as (kop′ər əs), *n.* See **ferrous sulfate.** [late ME *coperas,* var. of ME *coperose* < ML (*aqua*) *cuprōsa* coppery (water)]

cop·per·head (kop′ər hed′), *n.* **1.** a venomous snake, *Ancistrodon contortrix,* of the eastern and southeastern U.S., having a brown to copper-red body marked with darker bands. **2.** (*cap.*) a Northerner who sympathized with the South during the American Civil War.

Cop·per·mine (kop′ər mīn), *n.* river in NW Canada, flowing N to the Arctic Ocean. 525 mi. long.

cop·per·plate (kop′ər plāt′), *n.* **1.** a plate of polished copper used for engraving or etching. **2.** a print or impression from such a plate. **3.** engraving or printing of this kind. **4.** a fine, elegant style of handwriting.

cop′per pyri′tes, chalcopyrite.

cop·per·smith (kop′ər smith′), *n.* a person who works in copper. [ME *copresmythe*]

cop′per sul′fate, *Chem.* See **blue vitriol.**

cop·per·tone (kop′ər tōn′), *n.* **1.** a moderate reddish-brown coppery color. —*adj.* **2.** of or having such color: *coppertone appliances.*

cop·per·y (kop′ə rē), *adj.* of, like, or containing copper.

cop·pice (kop′is), *n. Chiefly Brit.* copse. [late ME *copies* < MF *copeis,* OF *copeiz* < VL **colpātīc*(*ium*) cutover area = **colpāt*(*us*) cut (ptp. of **colpāre;* see COPE¹) + *-īcium* -ICE] —**cop′piced,** *adj.*

cop·ra (kop′rə), *n.* the dried, oil-bearing kernel or meat of the coconut. [< Pg < Malayalam *koppara* < Hindi *khoprā* coconut]

copro-, a learned borrowing from Greek, used with the meaning "dung," "filth," "obscenity," in forming compound words. [< Gk *kopro-,* comb. form of *kópros* dung]

cop·ro·lite (kop′rə līt′), *n.* a roundish, stony mass consisting of petrified fecal matter of animals. —**cop·ro·lit·ic** (kop′rə lit′ik), *adj.*

co·prol·o·gy (ko prol′ə jē), *n.* scatology. —**cop′ro·log′i·cal,** *adj.*

co·proph·a·gous (ko prof′ə gəs), *adj.* feeding on dung, as certain beetles. —**co·proph·a·gy** (ko prof′ə jē), *n.*

cop·ro·phil·i·a (kop′rə fil′ē ə, -fēl′yə), *n. Psychiatry.* an extreme interest in feces. [COPRO- + -PHILIA] —**cop′ro·phil′ic,** *adj.*

co·proph·i·lous (kə prof′ə ləs), *adj.* living or growing on dung, as certain fungi.

co-pros·per·i·ty (kō′pro sper′i tē), *n.* joint economic prosperity with another nation or nations.

copse (kops), *n.* a thicket of small trees or bushes; a small wood. Also, *esp. Brit.,* **coppice.** [alter. of COPPICE]

Copt (kopt), *n.* **1.** a member of the Coptic Church. **2.** a native Egyptian claiming descent from the ancient Egyptians. Also, **Copht.** [< Ar *qubt,* back formation from *qubtī* < Coptic *kypti*(*os*), var. of *gyptios* < Gk *Aigýptios* EGYPTIAN]

cop·ter (kop′tər), *n. Informal.* helicopter. [short form]

Cop·tic (kop′tik), *n.* **1.** the extinct language of Egypt that developed from ancient Egyptian, now used liturgically by the Coptic Church. —*adj.* **2.** of or pertaining to Coptic or the Copts.

Cop′tic Church′, the Christian church in Egypt, governed by a patriarch and characterized by an adherence to Monophysitism.

cop·u·la (kop′yə lə), *n., pl.* **-las, -lae** (-lē′). **1.** something that connects or links together. **2.** *Gram., Logic.* a word or set of words, as the English verbs *be* and *seem,* that acts as a connecting link between subject and predicate. [< L = *co-* CO- + *ap-* fasten (see APT) + *-ula* -ULE] —**cop′u·lar,** *adj.*

cop·u·late (*v.* kop′yə lāt′; *adj.* kop′yə lit), *v.,* **-lat·ed, -lat·ing,** *adj.* —*v.i.* **1.** to engage in sexual intercourse. —*adj.* **2.** connected; joined. [late ME < L *copulāt*(*us*) bound together]

cop·u·la·tion (kop′yə lā′shən), *n.* **1.** a joining together or coupling. **2.** sexual union or intercourse. [ME *copulacion* < L *copulātiōn-* (s. of *copulātio*) a binding together]

cop·u·la·tive (kop′yə lā′tiv, -lə tiv), *adj.* **1.** serving to unite or couple. **2.** *Gram.* **a.** involving or consisting of connected words or clauses: *a copulative sentence.* **b.** serving to connect subject and predicate: *a copulative verb.* **c.** serving to connect nouns, noun phrases, verbs, clauses, etc.: *a copulative conjunction.* **3.** of or pertaining to copulation. —*n.* **4.** *Gram.* a copulative word. [ME *copulatif* < LL *copulātīv*(*us*)] —**cop′u·la′tive·ly,** *adv.*

cop·y (kop′ē), *n., pl.* **cop·ies** for 1, 4–6, *v.,* **cop·ied, cop·y·ing.** —*n.* **1.** an imitation, reproduction, or transcript of an original. **2.** written matter or artwork to be reproduced in printed form. **3.** text to be read or heard, as distinguished from pictures to be seen, in newspapers, magazines, television commercials, etc. **4.** one of the various examples or specimens of the same book, engraving, or the like. **5.** *Brit. Informal.* (in schools) a composition; a written assignment. **6.** *Archaic.* something that is to be reproduced; an example or pattern. —*v.t.* **7.** to make a copy of; transcribe; reproduce. **8.** to follow as a pattern or model. —*v.i.* **9.** to make a copy or copies. **10.** to make or do something in imitation of something else. [ME *copie* < ML *cōpia* abundance, something written, L: wealth, abundance; see COPIOUS] —**Syn. 1.** duplicate, carbon, facsimile. **8.** See **imitate.**

cop·y·book (kop′ē bŏŏk′), *n.* **1.** a book containing models, usually of penmanship, for learners to imitate. **2.** a book containing copies, as of documents.

cop·y·boy (kop′ē boi′), *n.* an office boy employed by a newspaper.

cop·y·cat (kop′ē kat′), *n. Informal.* a person who imitates the actions or work of another.

cop′y desk′, *Journalism.* a desk at which copy is edited and prepared for printing.

cop·y-ed·it (kop′ē ed′it), *v.t.* to edit (a manuscript, document, text, etc.) for publication, esp. for punctuation, spelling, grammatical structure, etc. [back formation from COPY EDITOR] —**cop′y ed′itor.**

cop·y·hold (kop′ē hōld′), *n.* (formerly) a type of ownership of land in England, evidenced by a copy of the roll of a manorial court. [late ME]

cop·y·hold·er (kop′ē hōl′dər), *n.* **1.** a device for holding copy in its place. **2.** a proofreader's assistant who reads copy aloud or follows it while proof is read.

cop·y·ist (kop′ē ist), *n.* **1.** a person who transcribes copies, esp. of documents. **2.** an imitator.

cop·y·read·er (kop′ē rē′dər), *n. Journalism.* an editor who prepares copy for the typesetter and printer.

cop·y·right (kop′ē rīt′), *n.* **1.** the exclusive right, granted by law for a certain number of years, to make and dispose of copies of a literary, musical, or artistic work. —*adj.* **2.** Also, **cop′y·right′ed.** protected by copyright. —*v.t.* **3.** to secure a copyright on. —**cop′y·right′a·ble,** *adj.* —**cop′y·right′er,** *n.*

cop·y·writ·er (kop′ē rī′tər), *n.* a writer of copy, esp. for advertisements or publicity releases. —**cop′y·writ′ing,** *n.*

coq au vin (*Fr.* kôk ō VAN′), chicken stewed in a sauce of wine, diced pork, onions, garlic, and mushrooms. [< F: lit., cock with wine]

co·quet (kō ket′), *v.,* **-quet·ted, -quet·ting,** *adj., n.* —*v.i.* **1.** to behave as a coquette; flirt. —*adj.* **2.** coquettish. —*n.* **3.** *Obs.* a male flirt. [< F; lit., cockerel = *coq* cock + *-et* -ET]

co·quet·ry (kō′ki trē, kō ke′trē), *n., pl.* **-ries.** the behavior or arts of a coquette; flirtation. [< F *coquetterie*]

co·quette (kō ket′), *n.* a girl or woman who flirts frivolously with men. [< F; fem. of COQUET] —**co·quet′tish,** *adj.* —**co·quet′tish·ly,** *adv.* —**co·quet′tish·ness,** *n.*

Co·quil·hat·ville (kô kē YA vēl′), *n.* former name of **Mbandaka.**

co·quil′la nut′ (ko kēl′yə, -kē′yə), the hard-shelled oval fruit or nut of a South American palm, *Attalea funifera.* [< Pg *coquilho,* dim. of *côco* coco]

co·quille (kō kil′; *Fr.* kô kē′yᵊ), *n.* **1.** any of various meat or fish dishes baked in a shell or a shell-shaped serving dish. **2.** the utensil for baking such dishes, usually a scallop shell or shell-like casserole. [< F: lit., shell. See COCKLE¹]

co·qui·na (kō kē′nə), *n.* a soft, whitish rock made up of fragments of marine shells and coral, used as a building material. [< Sp: lit., shellfish = OSp *coc*(*a*) shellfish (< L *concha;* see CONCH) + *-ina* -INE¹]

cor-, var. of **com-** before *r: correlate.*

Cor., **1.** Corinthians. **2.** Coroner.

cor., **1.** corner. **2.** cornet. **3.** coroner. **4.** corpus. **5.** correct. **6.** corrected. **7.** correction. **8.** correlative.

cor·a·ci·i·form (kôr′ə sī′ə fôrm′, kor′-), *adj.* belonging or pertaining to the *Coraciiformes,* the order of birds that includes the kingfishers, motmots, rollers, bee-eaters, and hornbills. [back formation from NL *Coraciiformes* = *Coraci*(*as*) genus name (< Gk *korakías* grackle) + *-i-* -I- + *-formes,* pl. of *-formis* -FORM]

cor·a·cle (kôr′ə kəl, kor′-), *n.* a small, rounded boat made of wickerwork or interwoven laths covered with skin, canvas, or the like: used in Wales, Ireland, and parts of western England. [< Welsh *corwgl* = *corwg* (earlier *corwc*) coracle + *-l* suffix; akin to Ir *curach* boat]

cor·a·coid (kôr′ə koid′, kor′-), *Anat., Zool.* —*adj.* **1.** pertaining to the bone that in reptiles, birds, and monotremes articulates with the scapula and the sternum and that in man and other higher mammals is a reduced bony process of the scapula having no connection with the sternum. —*n.* **2.** a coracoid bone or process. [back formation from NL *coracoīdēs* < Gk *korakoeidḗs* ravenlike, hooked like a raven's beak = *korak-* (s. of *kórax*) raven + *-oeidēs* -OID]

cor·al (kôr′əl, kor′-), *n.* **1.** the hard, calcareous skeleton secreted by certain anthozoan animals. **2.** such skeletons collectively, forming reefs, islands, etc. **3.** an anthozoan animal. **4.** something made of coral. **5.** a light yellowish red or pink. **6.** the unimpregnated roe or eggs of the lobster. —*adj.* **7.** made of coral. **8.** making coral. **9.** resembling coral, esp. in color. [ME *coral*(*l*) < L *corāl*(*l*)*um* < Gk *korállion* red coral = *korall-* (< Sem; cf. Heb *gōrāl* pebble) + *-ion* dim. suffix] —**cor′al·like′,** *adj.*

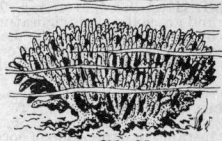

Reef-building coral

Cor·al Ga·bles (kôr′əl gā′bəlz, kor′-), a city in SE Florida, on Biscayne Bay, near Miami. 42,494 (1970).

coralli-, a combining form of **coral:** *coralliferous.* [repr. L *corāllium* CORAL]

cor·al·lif·er·ous (kôr′ə lif′ər əs, kor′-), *adj.* containing or bearing coral.

cor·al·line (kôr′ə lin, -līn′, kor′-), *adj.* **1.** consisting of or containing deposits of calcium carbonate. **2.** corallike. —*n.* **3.** any red alga that is impregnated with lime. **4.** any of various corallike animals or calcareous algae. [< LL *corallīn*(*us*) coral red]

cor′al reef′, a reef composed mainly of coral and other organic matter of which parts have solidified into limestone.

Cor′al Sea′, a part of the S Pacific, bounded by NE Australia, New Guinea, the Solomon Islands, and the New Hebrides: U.S. naval victory over Japanese, May 1942.

cor′al snake′, 1. any of numerous venomous snakes of the family *Elapidae*, found chiefly in the New World tropics, as *Micrurus fulvius*, of the southeastern U.S., often brilliantly marked with bands of red, yellow, and black. **2.** any of several other snakes, as of the genus *Callophis*, of Asia, having red markings.

co·ram po·pu·lo (kō′räm pō′po͝o lō′; *Eng.* kōr′am pop′yə lō′, kôr′-), *Latin.* before the public; publicly.

cor an·glais (kôr′ ôn glā′, ôn̄g-, än-, än̄g-). See **English horn.** [< F = *cor* horn + *anglais* English]

cor·ban (kôr′bən; *Heb.* kôʀ bän′), *n. Chiefly Biblical.* an offering to God. [< Heb *qorbān*, lit., a drawing near]

cor·beil (kôr′bəl; *Fr.* kôʀ bā′), *n.* a sculptured ornament, esp. on a capital, having the form of a basket. [< F *corbeille* < LL *corbicul(a)* dim. of L *corbi(s)* basket; see -CULE]

cor·beille (kôr′bəl; *Fr.* kôʀ be′yᵊ), *n., pl.* **-beilles** (-bəlz; *Fr.* -be′yᵊ). corbeil.

cor·bel (kôr′bəl), *n., v.,* **-beled, -bel·ing** or (*esp. Brit.*) **-belled, -bel·ling.** *Archit.* —*n.* **1.** any bracket, esp. one of brick or stone, usually of slight extent. —*v.t.* **2.** to set (bricks, stones, etc.) so as to form a corbel or corbels. **3.** to support by means of a corbel or corbels. [ME < MF < ML *corvell(us)* = L *corv(us)* RAVEN[1] + *-ellus* dim. suffix]

Corbel (def. 1)

cor′bel arch′, a construction resembling an arch in form but composed of courses of masonry corbeled out until they meet.

cor·bel·ing (kôr′bə lin̄g), *n.* **1.** the construction of corbels. **2.** a system of corbels. Also, *esp. Brit.,* **cor′bel·ling.**

Cor·bett (kôr′bit), *n.* **James John** ("*Gentleman Jim*"), 1866–1933, U.S. boxer: heavyweight champion 1892–1897.

cor·bie (kôʀ′bē), *n. Scot.* a raven or crow. [ME *corbin* < OF < L *corvīn(us)* CORVINE]

cor·bie·step (kôr′bē step′), *n.* any of a series of steplike portions of a masonry gable that terminate the gable above the surface of the roof. Also called **cor′bel step′, crowstep.**

cor·bi·na (kôr bī′nə), *n.* **1.** a game fish, *Menticirrhus undulatus*, of the croaker family, found along the Pacific coast of North America. **2.** any of various related fish. [< Sp *corvina*, fem. of *corvino* < L *corvīn(us)* CORVINE; so named from its color]

Cor·co·va·do (kôʀ′kô vä′do͞o *for 1;* kôʀ′kô vä′thô *for 2*), *n.* **1.** a mountain in SE Brazil, S of Rio de Janeiro. 2310 ft.: statue of Christ on peak. **2.** a volcano in S Chile. 7550 ft.

Cor·cy·ra (kôr sī′rə), *n.* ancient name of **Corfu.** —**Cor·cy·rae·an** (kôr′si rē′ən), *adj., n.*

cord (kôrd), *n.* **1.** a string or thin rope made of several strands braided, twisted, or woven together. **2.** *Elect.* a small, flexible, insulated cable. **3.** a ribbed fabric, esp. corduroy. **4.** a cordlike rib on the surface of cloth. **5.** any influence that binds or restrains. **6.** *Anat.* a cordlike structure: *the spinal cord.* **7.** a unit of volume used chiefly for fuel wood, equal to 128 cubic feet, and usually specified as 8 feet long, 4 feet wide, and 4 feet high. *Abbr.:* cd, cd. —*v.t.* **8.** to bind or fasten with a cord or cords. **9.** to pile or stack up (wood) in cords. **10.** to furnish with a cord. [ME *coord(e)*, OE **corde* (see CORDED) < L *chord(a)* < Gk *chordḗ* gut] —**cord′er,** *n.* —**cord′like′,** *adj.*

cord·age (kôr′dij), *n.* ropes, lines, hawsers, etc., taken collectively, esp. with reference to the rigging and other equipment of a vessel.

cor·date (kôr′dāt), *adj.* heart-shaped, as certain leaves. [< NL *cordāt(us)* heart-shaped = L *cord-* (s. of *cor*) heart + *-ātus* -ATE[1]] —**cor′date·ly,** *adv.*

Cordate leaf

Cor·day d'Ar·mont (kôr dā′ där môN; *Fr.* kôʀ de′ dAʀ môN′), **(Ma·rie Anne) Char·lotte** (mə rē′ an shär′lət; *Fr.* mA rē′ An shAʀ lôt′), 1768–93, French revolutionary heroine who assassinated Jean Paul Marat.

cord·ed (kôr′did), *adj.* **1.** furnished with or made of cords. **2.** ribbed, as a fabric. **3.** bound with cords. **4.** (of wood) stacked up in cords. **5.** stringy or ribbed in appearance. [ME; OE *gecorded*]

Cor·de·liers (kôr′dᵊlērz′), *n.* a radical political club in Paris at the time of the French Revolution. [< MF = *cordelle* (dim. of *corde* CORD) + *-ier* -IER; r. ME *cordeler;* see -ER[2]; so called from the convent where they met (Franciscan friars wear a knotted cord at the waist)]

cor·dial (kôr′jəl *or, esp. Brit.,* -dē əl), *adj.* **1.** courteous and gracious. **2.** invigorating the heart; stimulating. **3.** *Obs.* of or pertaining to the heart. —*n.* **4.** anything that invigorates. **5.** a strong, sweetened, aromatic alcoholic liquor; a liqueur. **6.** a stimulating medicine. [ME < ML *cordiāl(is)* = L *cordi-* (s. of *cor*) heart + *-ālis* -AL[1]] —**cor′dial·ly,** *adv.* —**cor′dial·ness,** *n.* —**Syn. 1.** genial. **2.** cheering.

cor·dial·i·ty (kôr jal′i tē, kôr′jē al′- *or, esp. Brit.,* -dē al′-), *n., pl.* **-ties** for 2. **1.** cordial quality or feeling. **2.** an instance or expression of cordial feeling.

cor·di·er·ite (kôr′dē ə rīt′), *n.* a strongly dichroic blue mineral consisting of a silicate of magnesium, aluminum, and iron. Also called **iolite.** [named after Pierre L. A. *Cordier* (1777–1861), French geologist; see -ITE[1]]

cor·di·form (kôr′də fôrm′), *adj.* heart-shaped; cordate. [< L *cordi-* (s. of *cor*) heart + -FORM]

cor·dil·le·ra (kôr′dil yâr′ə, kôr dil′ər ə), *n.* a chain of mountains, usually the principal mountain system or mountain axis of a large land mass. [< Sp < *cordilla*, dim. of *cuerda* string, mountain range (< L *chorda*); see CORD] —**cor′dil·le′ran,** *adj.*

Cor·dil·le·ras (kôr′dil yâr′əz, kôr dil′ər əz; *Sp.* kôʀ′dē ye′räs), *n.* **1.** a mountain system in W South America: the Andes and its component ranges. **2.** a mountain system in W North America, including the Sierra Nevada, Coast Range, Cascade Range, Rocky Mountains, etc. **3.** the entire chain of mountain ranges parallel to the Pacific coast, extending from Cape Horn to Alaska. —**Cor′dil·le′ran,** *adj.*

cord·ite (kôr′dīt), *n.* a smokeless, slow-burning powder composed of nitroglycerin, cellulose nitrate, and mineral jelly. [CORD + -ITE[1], so called from its cordlike form]

cord·less (kôrd′lis), *adj.* **1.** lacking a cord or cords. **2.** (of an electrical appliance) requiring no wire leading to an external source of electricity because of a self-contained, often rechargeable power supply: *a cordless electric toothbrush.* [CORD + -LESS]

cor·do·ba (kôr′də bə), *n.* a silver coin and monetary unit of Nicaragua equal to 100 centavos.

Cór·do·ba (kôʀ′thô vä), *n.* **1.** Also, **Cor′do·ba, Cordova.** a city in S Spain on the Guadalquivir River. 189,566 (est. 1960). **2.** a city in central Argentina. 589,153 (1965).

cor·don (kôr′dᵊn), *n.* **1.** a cord or braid worn for ornament or as a fastening. **2.** a ribbon worn usually diagonally across the breast as a badge of a knightly or honorary order. **3.** a line of sentinels, military posts, or the like, enclosing or guarding an area. **4.** *Fort.* **a.** a projecting course of stones at the base of a parapet. **b.** the coping of a scarp. **5.** *Archit.* a stringcourse. —*v.t.* **6.** to surround or blockade with or as with a cordon (usually fol. by *off*): *The police cordoned off the street.* [< MF, dim. of *corde*]

cor·don bleu (*Fr.* kôʀ dôN blœ′), *pl.* **cor·dons bleus** (*Fr.* kôʀ dôN blœ′). **1.** the sky-blue ribbon worn as a badge by knights of the highest order of French knighthood under the Bourbons. **2.** some similar high distinction. **3.** any person distinguished in his field, esp. a chef. [< F: lit., blue ribbon]

cor·don sa·ni·taire (*Fr.* kôʀ dôN sA nē teʀ′), *pl.* **cor·dons sa·ni·taires** (*Fr.* kôʀ dôN sA nē teʀ′). **1.** a guarded line or barricade around a quarantined area. **2.** a group of neighboring states forming a barrier between two states that are hostile to each other. [< F: sanitary cordon]

Cor·do·va (kôr′də və), *n.* Córdoba (def. 1).

Cor·do·van (kôr′də vən), *n.* **1.** a native or inhabitant of Córdoba, Spain. **2.** (*l.c.*) a soft, smooth leather originally made at Córdoba of goatskin but later made also of split horsehide, pigskin, etc. —*adj.* **3.** of or pertaining to Córdoba, Spain. **4.** (*l.c.*) designating or made of cordovan.

cor·du·roy (kôr′də roi′, kôr′də roi′), *n.* **1.** a cotton-filling pile fabric with lengthwise cords or ridges. —*adj.* **2.** of, pertaining to, or resembling corduroy. **3.** constructed of logs laid together transversely, as a road across swampy ground. —*v.t.* **4.** to form (a road or the like) by laying logs transversely. [? orig. proper name]

cord·wain (kôrd′wān), *n. Archaic.* cordovan leather. [ME *cordewan* < MF < Sp *cordován* CORDOVAN]

cord·wain·er (kôrd′wā nər), *n. Archaic.* a person who makes shoes, esp. from cordovan leather. [ME *cordewaner* < OF *cordewan(i)er*] —**cord′wain·er·y,** *n.*

cord·wood (kôrd′wo͝od′), *n.* **1.** wood for fuel stacked in cords. **2.** trees suitable only for fuel.

core[1] (kōr, kôr), *n., v.,* **cored, cor·ing.** —*n.* **1.** the central part of a fleshy fruit, containing the seeds. **2.** the central, innermost, or most essential part of anything. **3.** the ferrous material forming the central or inner portion in an electromagnet, induction coil, transformer, or the like. **4.** (in mining, geology, etc.) a sample taken from the ground by means of a corer. **5.** *Geol.* the central portion of the earth, having a radius of ab. 2100 mi. and believed to be composed mainly of molten iron and nickel. Cf. **crust** (def. 6), **mantle** (def. 7). **6.** *Physics.* the region in a reactor that contains its fissionable material. **7.** Also called **magnetic core.** *Computer Technol.* a small ring or loop of ferromagnetic material with two possible states of polarization, used to store one bit of information or to perform switching or logical functions. —*v.t.* **8.** to remove the core of (fruit). **9.** to remove a cylindrical sample from the interior, as of the earth. [ME, perh. var. of *coren*, itself var. of CORN[2]] —**core′less,** *adj.*

core[2] (kōr, kôr), *n. Chiefly Scot.* a small company or team of men. [ME *chor(e)*, OE *chor(a)* dance, company of dancers or singers. See CHORUS]

CORE (kōr, kôr), *n.* Congress of Racial Equality. Also, **C.O.R.E.**

core′ cit′y. See **central city.**

core′ curric′ulum, *Educ.* a curriculum in which the subjects are correlated to a central theme.

co·re·la·tion (kôr′ə lā′shən, kō′ri-), *n. Chiefly Brit.* correlation. —**co′re·la′tion·al,** *adj.*

co·rel·a·tive (kə rel′ə tiv), *adj., n. Chiefly Brit.* correlative. —**co·rel′a·tive·ly,** *adv.*

co·re·li·gion·ist (kō′ri lij′ə nist), *n.* an adherent of the same religion as another.

Co·rel·li (kō rel′ē, kō-; *It.* kô ʀel′lē), *n.* **Ar·can·ge·lo** (äʀ kän′je lô′), 1653–1713, Italian violinist and composer.

co·re·op·sis (kōr′ē op′sis, kôr′-), *n.* any composite plant of the genus *Coreopsis*, including familiar garden species having yellow, brownish, or yellow-and-red flowers. [< NL < Gk *kore-* (s. of *kóris*) bedbug + *-opsis* -OPSIS; so named from the shape of seed]

cor·er (kōr′ər, kôr′-), *n.* **1.** a person or thing that cores. **2.** a knife for coring apples, pears, etc. **3.** a device having a hollow cylindrical drill for taking samples from the earth.

co·re·spond·ent (kō′ri spon′dənt, kōr′i-, kôr′-, kor′-), *n. Law.* a joint defendant, charged along with the respondent, as in cases of adultery.

corf (kôrf), *n., pl.* **corves** (kôrvz). *Mining. Brit.* a small wagon for carrying coal, ore, etc. [ME < MD (c. G *Korb*) < L *corb(is)* basket. See CORBEIL]

Cor·fu (kôr′fo͞o, -fyo͞o; *It.* kôʀ fo͞o′), *n.* **1.** Ancient, **Corcyra.** one of the Ionian Islands, off the NW coast of Greece. 101,770 (1961); 229 sq. mi. **2.** a seaport on this island. 26,991 (1961). Greek, **Kerkyra.**

cor·gi (kôr′gē), *n.* See **Welsh corgi.** [< Welsh = *cor* dwarf + *-gi*, var. of *ci* dog; c. Ir *cu;* see HOUND[1]]

co·ri·a·ceous (kōr′ē ā′shəs, kôr′-, kor′-), *adj.* of or like leather. [< LL *coriāceus* leathern. See CORIUM, -ACEOUS]

co·ri·an·der (kōr′ē an′dər, kôr′-, kor′-), *n.* a herbaceous plant, *Coriandrum sativum*, bearing seeds and seedlike fruit used in cookery and medicine. [ME *coriandre* < L *coriandr(um)* < Gk *koríandron*, var. of *koríannon*]

Cor·inth (kôr′inth, kor′-), *n.* **1.** an ancient city in Greece, on the Isthmus of Corinth. **2.** a port in the NE Peloponnesus, in S Greece, NE of the site of ancient Corinth. 15,892 (1961). **3. Gulf of.** Also called **Gulf of Lepanto.** an arm of the Ionian Sea, N of the Peloponnesus. **4. Isthmus**

of, an isthmus at the head of the Gulf of Corinth, connecting the Peloponnesus with central Greece.

Co·rin·thi·an (kə rin′thē ən), *adj.* **1.** of, pertaining to, or characteristic of Corinth. **2.** luxurious or licentious. **3.** ornate, as literary style. **4.** *Archit.* noting or pertaining to one of the five classical orders, characterized by a deep capital with a round bell decorated with acanthus leaves. Cf. **composite** (def. 3), **Doric** (def. 2), **Ionic** (def. 1), **Tuscan** (def. 2). See illus. at **order.** —*n.* **5.** a native or inhabitant of Corinth. **6.** a man about town, esp. one who lives luxuriously or dissolutely. **7.** an amateur yachtsman.

Co·rin·thi·ans (kə rin′thē ənz), *n.* (*construed as sing.*) either of two books of the New Testament, I Corinthians or II Corinthians, written by Paul.

Cor·i·o·la·nus (kôr′ē ə lā′nəs, kor′-), *n.* **Ga·ius** (or **Gnae·us**) **Mar·ci·us** (gā′əs *or* nē′əs, mär′shē əs), fl. late 5th century B.C., legendary Roman military hero.

co·ri·um (kôr′ē əm, kôr′-), *n., pl.* **co·ri·a** (kôr′ē ə, kôr′). *Anat.* the sensitive vascular layer of the skin beneath the epidermis; derma. [< L: skin, hide, leather]

cork (kôrk), *n.* **1.** the outer bark of an oak, *Quercus Suber*, of Mediterranean countries, used for making stoppers, floats, etc. **2.** Also called **cork oak.** the tree itself. **3.** something made of cork, as a stopper or float. **4.** Also called **phellem.** *Bot.* an outer tissue of bark produced by and exterior to the phellogen. —*v.t.* **5.** to provide or fit with cork or a cork. **6.** to stop with or as if with a cork. **7.** to blacken with burnt cork. [ME *cork(e)* < Ar *qurq* < L *querc(us)* oak] —**cork′like′,** *adj.*

Cork (kôrk), *n.* **1.** a county in Munster province, in S Republic of Ireland. 330,443 (1961); 2881 sq. mi. **2.** a seaport in and the county seat of Cork, in the S part. 77,980 (1961).

cork·age (kôr′kij), *n.* a fee charged, as in a restaurant, for serving wine or liquor brought in by the patron.

cork·board (kôrk′bōrd′, -bôrd′), *n.* an insulating material made of cork, used in building, for industrial purposes, etc.

cork′ cam′bium, *Bot.* phellogen.

corked (kôrkt), *v.* **1.** a pt. and pp. of **cork.** —*adj.* **2.** corky.

cork·er (kôr′kər), *n.* **1.** a person or thing that corks. **2.** *Slang.* someone or something of astonishing or excellent quality.

cork·ing (kôr′king), *Informal.* —*adj.* **1.** excellent; fine. —*adv.* **2.** very: *a corking good time.*

cork′ oak′, cork (def. 2).

cork·screw (kôrk′skrōō′), *n.* **1.** an augerlike, spiral instrument used for drawing corks from bottles. —*adj.* **2.** resembling a corkscrew in shape; spiral. —*v.t., v.i.* **3.** to move in a spiral or zigzag course.

cork·wood (kôrk′wŏŏd′), *n.* **1.** a stout shrub or small tree, *Leitneria floridana*, having shiny deciduous leaves, densely pubescent aments, and a drupaceous fruit. **2.** any of certain trees and shrubs yielding a light and porous wood, as the balsa.

cork·y (kôr′kē), *adj.,* **cork·i·er, cork·i·est.** **1.** of the nature of cork; corklike. **2.** (of wine, brandy, etc.) spoiled, esp. by a tainted cork. Also, **corked.** —**cork′i·ness,** *n.*

corm (kôrm), *n. Bot.* a fleshy, bulblike base of a stem, as in the crocus. [< NL *corm(us)* < Gk *kormós* a tree trunk with boughs lopped off, akin to *keírein* cut off, hew] —**corm′like′.** **cor′moid,** *adj.* —**cor′mous,** *adj.*

Corm of crocus

cor·mo·phyte (kôr′mə fīt′), *n.* any of the *Cormophyta*, an old primary division or group of plants having an axis differentiated into stem and root and including all phanerogams and the higher cryptogams. —**cor·mo·phyt·ic** (kôr′mə fit′ik), *adj.*

cor·mo·rant (kôr′mər ənt), *n.* **1.** any of several voracious, totipalmate sea birds of the family *Phalacrocoracidae*, as *Phalacrocorax carbo*, of America, Europe, and Asia, having a long neck and a distensible pouch under the bill for holding captured fish. **2.** a greedy or rapacious person. —*adj.* **3.** greedy; rapacious; gluttonous. [ME *cormera(u)nt* < MF *cormorant*, OF *cormareng* < LL *cor(vus) marīnus* sea raven. See CORBEL, MARINE]

Cormorant, *Phalacrocorax carbo* (Length 3 ft.)

corn[1] (kôrn), *n.* **1.** Also called **Indian corn;** *esp. technical and Brit.,* **maize.** *U.S., Canadian, Australian.* **a.** a tall, annual cereal plant, *Zea Mays*, having a jointed, solid stem and bearing the kernels on large ears. **b.** the kernels, used as food. **c.** the ears. **2.** the edible seed of certain other cereal plants, esp. wheat in England and oats in Scotland. **3.** the plants themselves. **4.** *U.S.* (loosely) sweet corn. **5.** See **corn whiskey.** **6.** *Slang.* old-fashioned, trite, or mawkishly sentimental entertainment material. —*v.t.* **7.** to preserve and season with salt in grains. **8.** to preserve and season with brine. [ME, OE; c. D *koren*, Icel, G *Korn*, Goth *kaúrn;* akin to L *grānum*, Russ *zerno* GRAIN]

corn[2] (kôrn), *n. Pathol.* a horny callosity of the epidermis, usually with a central core, formed esp. on the toes or feet. [late ME *corne* < MF < L *corn(ū)* horn, hence a horny hardening of the cuticle]

-corn, a learned borrowing from Latin meaning "horn," "horned," used in the formation of compound words: *longicorn.* [repr. L *-cornis* horned]

Corn., **1.** Cornish. **2.** Cornwall.

cor·na·ceous (kôr nā′shəs), *adj.* belonging to the *Cornaceae*, a family of plants, mostly shrubs and trees, including the dogwood. [< NL *Cornāce(ae)* name of the order (*Corn(us)* CORNEL + *-āceae* -ACEAE) + -OUS]

corn·ball (kôrn′bôl′), *n.* **1.** popcorn rolled into a ball and flavored with molasses or caramel. **2.** *Slang.* a country bumpkin; hick. —*adj.* **3.** corny. [CORN[1] + BALL[1]; defs. 2, 3, influenced by slang sense of *corn.* Cf. SCREWBALL, ODDBALL]

Corn′ Belt′, a region in the midwestern U.S., esp. Iowa, Illinois, and Indiana, where corn is raised.

corn′ bord′er, any of several pyralid moths, as *Pyrausta nubilalis*, whose larvae bore into the stem and crown of corn and other plants.

corn′ bread′, a bread made of corn meal. Also called **Indian bread.**

corn′ cake′, *U.S.* a cake made of corn meal.

corn·cob (kôrn′kob′), *n.* **1.** the elongated woody core in which the grains of an ear of corn are embedded. **2.** Also called **corn′cob pipe′.** a tobacco pipe with a bowl made from a corncob.

corn′ crake′, a short-billed, Eurasian rail, *Crex crex*, found in grain fields.

corn·crib (kôrn′krib′), *n.* a ventilated structure for the storage of unhusked corn.

corn′ dodg′er, *Chiefly Southern U.S.* a stiff or hard bread made of fried or baked corn meal.

cor·ne·a (kôr′nē ə), *n. Anat.* the transparent anterior part of the external coat of the eye covering the iris and the pupil and continuous with the sclera. [< ML *cornea* (*tēla*, later *tunica*) horny (web or tunic), fem. of *corneus* CORNEOUS] —**cor′ne·al,** *adj.*

corn′ ear′worm, a noctuid moth, *Heliothis zea*, the larvae of which are highly destructive to crops of corn, cotton, tomatoes, etc.

corned (kôrnd), *adj.* preserved or cured with salt: *corned beef.*

Cor·neille (kôr nā′; *Fr.* kôʀ ne′yᵊ), *n.* **Pierre** (pē âr′; *Fr.* pyeʀ), 1606–84, French dramatist and poet.

cor·nel (kôr′nᵊl), *n.* any tree or shrub of the genus *Cornus;* dogwood. [late ME *corneille* < MF < VL **cornicul(a)* = L *corn(um)* cornel + *-cula*, pl. of *-culum* -CULE; r. OE *corntreōw* cornel tree]

Cor·nel·ia (kôr nēl′yə), *n.* **1.** fl. 2nd century B.C., Roman matron: mother of Gaius and Tiberius Gracchus. **2.** fl. 1st century B.C., first wife of Julius Caesar 83–67? Cf. **Calpurnia, Pompeia.**

cor·nel·ian (kôr nēl′yən), *n.* carnelian.

Cor·ne·li·us (kôr nēl′yəs, -nē′lē əs; *for 2 also Ger.* kôʀnā′lē ŏŏs′), *n.* **1. Saint,** died A.D. 253, Italian ecclesiastic: pope 251–253. **2. Pe·ter von** (pā′təʀ fən), 1783–1867, German painter.

Cor·nell (kôr nel′), *n.* **1. Ezra,** 1809–74, U.S. capitalist and philanthropist. **2. Katharine,** 1898–1974, U.S. actress.

cor·ne·ous (kôr′nē əs), *adj.* consisting of a horny substance; horny. [< L *corneus* horny = *corn(ū)* horn + *-eus* -EOUS]

cor·ner (kôr′nər), *n.* **1.** the meeting place of two converging lines or surfaces. **2.** the space between two converging lines or surfaces near their intersection; angle: *a chair in the corner of the room.* **3.** a projecting angle, esp. of a rectangular figure or object. **4.** the point where two streets meet. **5.** an end; margin; edge. **6.** a narrow, secluded, or secret place. **7.** an awkward or embarrassing position, esp. one from which escape is impossible. **8.** *Finance.* a monopolizing of the available supply of a stock or commodity to a point permitting control of price. **9.** region; part; quarter: *from every corner of the empire.* **10.** a piece to protect the corner of anything. **11. cut corners, a.** to use a shorter route or method. **b.** to reduce costs or care in execution. —*adj.* **12.** situated on or at a corner. **13.** made for use in a corner. —*v.t.* **14.** to furnish with corners. **15.** to place in or drive into a corner. **16.** to force into an awkward or difficult position or one from which escape is impossible: *He finally cornered the hoodlum. She cornered him with a perfectly timed retort.* **17.** to gain control of (a stock, commodity, etc.). —*v.i.* **18.** to form a corner in a stock or commodity. **19.** (of an automobile) to turn, esp. at a speed relatively high for the angle of the turn involved. [ME < AF (OF *cornier*) = OF *corne* corner, horn (< L *corn(ū)* horn) + *-er* -ER[2]]

cor·nered (kôr′nərd), *adj.* **1.** having corners (usually used in combination): *a five-cornered figure.* **2.** having a given number of positions; sided (usually used in combination): *a four-cornered debate.* **3.** forced into an awkward, embarrassing, or inescapable position. [ME]

cor·ner·stone (kôr′nər stōn′), *n.* **1.** a stone uniting two masonry walls at an intersection. **2.** a stone representing the starting place in the construction of a building, usually carved with the date. **3.** something that is essential, indispensable, or basic: *A free press is a cornerstone of democracy.*

cor·ner·wise (kôr′nər wīz′), *adv.* **1.** with the corner in front. **2.** so as to form a corner. **3.** from corner to corner; diagonally. Also, **cor·ner·ways** (kôr′nər wāz′). [late ME]

cor·net (kôr net′ *for 1;* kôr′nit, kôr net′ *for 2–4*), *n.* **1.** *Music.* a valved wind instrument of the trumpet family. **2.** a small cone of paper twisted at the end and used for holding candy, nuts, etc. **3.** *Brit.* a conical wafer, as for ice cream; cone. **4.** a large white headdress worn by the members of some sisterhoods of nuns. [late ME < MF, OF = *corn* horn (< L *cornū*) + *-et* -ET]

Cornet

cor·net-à-pis·tons (kôr net′ə pis′tənz; *Fr.* kôʀ ne′Apē stôɴ′), *n., pl.* **cor·nets-à-pis·tons** (kôr nets′ə pis′tənz; *Fr.* kôʀ ne′zA pē stôɴ′). cornet (def. 1). [< F: lit., cornet with valves]

cor·net·ist (kôr net′ist), *n.* a musician who plays the cornet. Also, **cor·net′tist.**

corn·fed (kôrn′fed′), *adj.* **1.** fed on corn. **2.** having a healthy and guileless appearance.

corn·flakes (kôrn′flāks′), *n.pl.* a breakfast cereal in the form of small toasted flakes made from corn, for serving cold with milk, sugar, etc. Also, **corn′ flakes′.**

corn′ flour′, **1.** flour prepared from corn. **2.** *Chiefly Brit.* cornstarch.

corn·flow·er (kôrn′flou′ər), *n.* **1.** Also called **bluebottle.** a European, composite plant, *Centaurea cyanus,* found in grainfields, having blue to white flowers, often cultivated as an ornamental. **2.** Also called **corn′flower blue′.** a deep, vivid blue. [ME *cornflor*]

corn′ grits′, (*construed as sing. or pl.*) *U.S.* hominy.

corn·husk (kôrn′husk′), *n.* *U.S.* the husk of an ear of corn.

Corn′husker State′, Nebraska (used as a nickname).

corn·husk·ing (kôrn′hus′king), *n.* *U.S.* **1.** the removing of the husks from corn. **2.** See **husking bee.** —**corn′-husk′er,** *n.*

cor·nice (kôr′nis), *n., v.,* **-niced, -nic·ing.** —*n.* **1.** *Archit.* **a.** a projecting, continuous, prominent horizontal feature, located at or near the top of an architectural composition. **b.** the uppermost section of a classical entablature, consisting mainly of a bed molding and a corona, with intervening features. **2.** any of various other ornamental horizontal moldings or bands, as for concealing hooks or rods from which curtains are hung or for supporting picture hooks. —*v.t.* **3.** to furnish or finish with a cornice. [< It: lit., crow (< L *cornix*); for the meaning, cf. Gk *korṓnē* crow, CROWN]

cor·ni·cle (kôr′ni kəl), *n.* any of various small, horn-shaped processes, esp. one of a pair of tubes at the posterior end of the abdomen of aphids, from which a waxy fluid is emitted. [< L *cornicul(um)* little horn]

cor·nic·u·late (kôr nik′yə lāt′, -lit), *adj.* **1.** resembling a small horn in appearance. **2.** having horns or hornlike parts; horned. [< L *corniculāt(us)* horned = *cornicul(um)* little horn (see CORN², -CULE) + *-ātus* -ATE¹]

Cor·ning (kôr′ning), *n.* a city in S New York. 15,792 (1970).

Cor·nish (kôr′nish), *adj.* **1.** of, pertaining to, or characteristic of Cornwall, England, its inhabitants, or the Cornish language. —*n.* **2.** the Celtic language of Cornwall, extinct since c1800. **3.** one of an English breed of chickens raised chiefly for crossing with other breeds to produce roasters. [ME *Cornyssh,* var. of ME *Cornwelisse*]

Cor·nish·man (kôr′nish mən), *n., pl.* **-men.** a native or inhabitant of Cornwall.

Corn′ Law′, *Eng. Hist.* any of the laws regulating domestic and foreign trade in grain, the last of which was repealed in 1846.

corn′ liq′uor. See **corn whiskey.**

corn′ meal′, **1.** meal made of corn. **2.** *Scot.* oatmeal. —**corn′meal′,** *adj.*

corn′ muf′fin, a muffin made from corn meal.

corn′ oil′, the oil obtained by expressing the germs of corn kernels, used in the preparation of foods (esp. salad dressing), lubricants, soaps, etc. Also called **maize oil.**

corn′ pone′, *Southern U.S.* **1.** corn bread, esp. of a plain or simple kind. **2.** a cake or loaf of this.

corn′ pop′py, a common, Old World poppy, *Papaver Rhoeas,* having bright-red flowers.

corn·row (kôrn′rō′), *n.* **1.** a type of braid, originating in Africa, in which the hair, usually parted in sections front to back, is plaited in thin, tight parallel rows close along the scalp. **2.** Usually, **cornrows.** a hair style employing such braids. —*v.t.* **3.** to arrange (hair) in cornrows. [fig. use of CORN¹ + ROW¹]

corn′ sal′ad, any of several plants of the genus *Valerianella,* esp. *V. olitoria* and *V. eriocarpa,* that sometimes grow wild in grainfields and may be used in salads.

corn′ shock′, a stack of upright cornstalks.

corn′ silk′, the long, threadlike, silky styles on an ear of corn.

corn′ smut′, a disease of corn that is characterized by blackish, powdery masses of spores on the affected parts and is caused by a fungus, *Ustilago maydis.*

corn′ snake′, a North American rat snake, *Elaphe guttata,* yellow or gray with dark red blotches, often found in cornfields. Also called **red rat snake.**

corn′ snow′, *Skiing.* snow in the form of small pellets or grains produced by the alternate melting and freezing of a snow layer.

corn·stalk (kôrn′stôk′), *n.* the stalk or stem of corn.

corn·starch (kôrn′stärch′), *n.* a starch or a starchy flour made from corn and used for thickening gravies and sauces, making puddings, etc. Also called, *esp. Brit.,* **corn flour.**

corn′ sug′ar, dextrose.

corn′ syr′up, the syrup prepared from corn.

cor·nu (kôr′no͞o, -nyo͞o), *n., pl.* **-nu·a** (-no͞o ə, -nyo͞o ə). a horn, esp. a bony part that resembles a horn. [< L: a horn] —**cor′nu·al,** *adj.*

cor·nu·co·pi·a (kôr′nə kō′pē ə), *n.* **1.** *Class. Myth.* a horn containing food, drink, etc., in endless supply, said to have been a horn of the goat Amalthaea. **2.** a representation of this horn, used as a symbol of abundance. **3.** an abundant, overflowing supply. **4.** a horn-shaped or conical receptacle or ornament. [< LL = L *cornū* horn + *cōpiae* of plenty (gen. of *cōpia*)] —**cor′nu·co′pi·an,** *adj.*

Cornucopia

cor·nut·ed (kôr no͞o′tid, -nyo͞o′-), *adj.* **1.** having horns. **2.** shaped like a horn. [< L *cornūt(us)* horned]

cor·nu·to (kôr no͞o′tō, -nyo͞o′-), *n., pl.* **-tos.** *Archaic.* a cuckold. [< It: lit., horned one < L *cornūt(us)* horned]

Corn·wall (kôrn′wôl *or, esp. Brit.,* -wəl), *n.* a county in SW England. 397,200; 1357 sq. mi. *Co. seat:* Bodmin.

Corn·wal·lis (kôrn wô′lis, -wol′is), *n.* **Charles, 1st Marquis,** 1738–1805, British general and statesman: surrendered to Washington at Yorktown, Virginia, October 19, 1781.

corn′ whis′key, whiskey made from at least 80 percent corn. Also called **corn, corn liquor.**

corn·y (kôr′nē), *adj.,* **corn·i·er, corn·i·est.** *Informal.* old-fashioned; obvious; trite: *corny jokes.* [ME]

cor·o·dy (kôr′ə dē, kor′-), *n., pl.* **-dies.** *Old Eng. Law.* **1.** the right of a sovereign or lord to receive housing, food, or clothing, as from a religious house. **2.** the housing, food, or clothing so received. Also, **corrody.** [late ME < ML *corrōdi(um)* outfit, provision, var. of *conrēdium* < VL *conrēdāre* to outfit, provide with = *con-* CON- + *rēdāre* < Gmc; cf. OE *rǣdan* to equip]

coroll., corollary. Also, **corol.**

co·rol·la (kə rol′ə), *n.* *Bot.* the internal envelope of floral leaves of a flower; the petals considered collectively. [< L: little garland = *corōn(a)* garland (see CORONA) + *-ula* -ULE] —**co·rol·late** (kə rol′āt, -it, kôr′ə lāt′, -lit, kor′-), **co·rol·lat·ed** (kə rol′ā tid, kôr′ə lā′-, kor′-), *adj.*

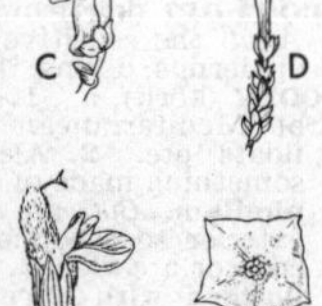

cor·ol·la·ceous (kôr′ə lā′shəs, kor′-), *adj.* of, pertaining to, or resembling a corolla.

cor·ol·lar·y (kôr′ə ler′ē, kor′-; *esp. Brit.,* kə rol′ə rē), *n., pl.* **-lar·ies.** **1.** *Math.* a proposition that is incidentally proved in proving another proposition. **2.** an immediate consequence or easily drawn conclusion. **3.** a natural consequence or result. [ME < LL *corollāri(um)* corollary, in L: money paid for a garland, a gift, gratuity]

Cor′o·man′del Coast′ (kôr′ə man′dəl, kor′-, kôr′-, kor′-), a coastal region in SE India, south of the Kistna River.

co·ro·na (kə rō′nə), *n., pl.* **-nas, -nae** (-nē). **1.** a white or colored circle or set of concentric circles seen around a luminous body, esp. the sun or moon. **2.** *Meteorol.* such a circle or circles attributable to diffraction by thin clouds, mist, or sometimes dust. **3.** Also called **aureole, aureola.** *Astron.* a faintly luminous envelope outside of the sun's chromosphere, the inner part consisting of highly ionized elements. **4.** *Archit.* the projecting, slablike member of a classical cornice. **5.** *Anat.* the upper portion or crown of a part, as of the head. **6.** *Bot.* a crownlike appendage, esp. one on the inner side of a corolla, as in the narcissus. **7.** *Elect.* See **corona discharge.** **8.** a chandelier of wrought metal, having the form of one or more concentric hoops. **9.** a long, straight cigar. [< L *corōna* garland, crown < Gk *korṓnē* crown, curved object, akin to *korōnís* wreath, *kórax* crow, raven]

Corollas
Polypetalous corollas:
A, Papilionaceous;
B, Cruciate;
Gamopetalous corollas:
C, Personate;
D, Tubular;
E, Bilabiate;
F, Rotate

Co·ro·na (kə rō′nə), *n.* a city in S California, SE of Los Angeles. 27,519 (1970).

Co·ro·na Aus·tra·lis (kə rō′nə ô strā′lis), *gen.* **Co·ro·nae Aus·tra·lis** (kə rō′nē ô strā′lis). the Southern Crown, a southern constellation touching the southern part of Sagittarius. [< L; see CORONA, AUSTRAL]

Co·ro·na Bo·re·al·is (kə rō′nə bōr′ē al′is, -ā′lis, bôr′-), *gen.* **Co·ro·nae Bo·re·al·is** (kə rō′nē bōr′ē al′is, -ā′lis, bôr′-). the Northern Crown, a northern constellation between Hercules and Boötes. [< L; see CORONA, BOREAL]

cor·o·nach (kôr′ə nəKH, kor′-), *n.* (in Scotland and Ireland) a lamentation for the dead; dirge. [< ScotGael *corranach,* Ir *coránach* dirge]

coro′na dis′charge, *Elect.* a discharge, frequently luminous, at the surface of a conductor or between two conductors of the same transmission line. Also called **corona, St. Elmo's fire.** Cf. **brush discharge.**

Co·ro·na·do (kôr′ə nä′dō, kor′-; *Sp.* kô′RÔ nä′thô), *n.* **Fran·cis·co Vás·quez de** (fran sis′kō vas kwez′ də; *Sp.* fRän thēs′kô bäs′keth the), 1510–54?, Spanish explorer in North America.

co·ro·na·graph (kə rō′nə graf′, -gräf′), *n.* *Astron.* an instrument for observing and often photographing the sun's corona. Also, **coronograph.**

cor·o·nal (*n.* kôr′ə nəl, kor′-; *adj.* kə rōn′əl, kôr′ə nəl, kor′-), *n.* **1.** a crown or coronet. **2.** a garland. —*adj.* **3.** of or pertaining to a coronal. **4.** *Anat.* **a.** of or pertaining to a corona. **b.** (of a plane along the long axis of the body) lying in the direction of the coronal suture. [< L *corōnāl(is)*]

coro′nal su′ture, *Anat.* a suture extending across the skull between the frontal bone and the parietal bones.

cor·o·nar·y (kôr′ə ner′ē, kor′-), *adj., n., pl.* **-nar·ies.** —*adj.* **1.** *Med.* **a.** encircling like a crown, as certain blood vessels. **b.** pertaining to the arteries that supply the heart tissues and originate in the root of the aorta. **2.** of or pertaining to the human heart, with respect to health. **3.** of or like a crown. —*n.* **4.** *Pathol.* an attack of coronary occlusion, esp. coronary thrombosis. **5.** a coronary artery. [< L *corōnāri(us)* of a crown or wreath]

cor′onary occlu′sion, *Pathol.* partial or total obstruction of a coronary artery, as by a thrombus, usually resulting in infarction of the myocardium.

cor′onary thrombo′sis, *Pathol.* a coronary occlusion in which there is blockage of a coronary arterial branch by a blood clot within the vessel.

cor·o·na·tion (kôr′ə nā′shən, kor′-), *n.* the act or ceremony of crowning a king, queen, or other sovereign. [late ME *coronacio(u)n* < MF *coronation* < L *corōnāt(us)* crowned (ptp. of *corōnāre;* see CORONA, -ATE¹) + MF *-ion* -ION]

cor·o·ner (kôr′ə nər, kor′-), *n.* an officer, as of a county or municipality, whose chief function is to investigate by inquest, as before a jury, any death not clearly resulting from natural causes. [ME < AF *corouner* Crown official = *coroune* CROWN + *-er* -ER²] —**cor′o·ner·ship′,** *n.*

cor·o·net (kôr′ə nit, -net′, kor′-, kôr′ə net′, kor′-), *n.* **1.** a small crown. **2.** a crown worn by noblemen or peers. **3.** a crownlike ornament for the head, as of gold or jewels. **4.** the lowest part of the pastern of a horse, just above the hoof. [alter. of ME *crownet*]

cor·o·net·ed (kôr′ə nit id, -net′id, kor′-, kôr′ə net′id, kor′-), *adj.* **1.** wearing or entitled to wear a coronet. **2.** of noble birth. Also, **cor′o·net′ted.**

co·ro·no·graph (kə rō′nə graf′, -gräf′), *n.* coronagraph.

Co·rot (kō rō′, kə-; *Fr.* kô RŌ′), *n.* **Jean Bap·tiste Camille** (zhäN bA tēst′ kA mē′yə), 1796–1875, French painter.

corp., **1.** corporal. **2.** corporation. Also, **Corp.**

corpl., corporal. Also, **Corpl.**

cor·po·ra (kôr′pər ə), *n.* pl. of **corpus.**

cor·po·ral[1] (kôr′pər əl, -prəl), *adj.* **1.** of the human body; bodily; physical: *corporal pleasure.* **2.** personal: *corporal possession.* **3.** *Zool.* of the body proper, as distinguished from the head and limbs. **4.** *Obs.* corporeal; belonging to the material world. [late ME *corporall* < L *corporāl(is)* bodily = *corpor-* (s. of *corpus* CORPUS) + *-ālis* -AL[1]] **—cor′po·ral′i·ty,** *n.* **—cor′po·ral·ly,** *adv.* **—Syn. 1.** See **physical.**

cor·po·ral[2] (kôr′pər əl, -prəl), *n.* **1.** a noncommissioned officer of lowest rank in the U.S. Army or Marine Corps. **2.** *Brit. Navy.* (formerly) a petty officer who assists the master-at-arms. **3.** (*cap.*) *U.S.* a surface-to-surface, single-stage ballistic missile. [< MF, var. of *caporal* < It *caporal(e),* appar. contr. of phrase *capo corporale* corporal head, i.e., head of a body (of soldiers). See CAPUT, CORPORAL[1]]

cor·po·ral[3] (kôr′pər əl, -prəl), *n.* *Eccles.* a fine cloth, usually of linen, on which the consecrated elements are placed during the Eucharist. [ME *corporalle* < ML *corporale* (*pallium*) eucharistic (altar cloth); r. earlier *corporas* < OF]

cor′poral pun′ishment, *Law.* bodily punishment, as flogging, inflicted on a person convicted of a crime.

cor′poral's guard′, *Mil. Informal.* any small detachment, as one commanded by a corporal.

cor·po·rate (kôr′pər it, -prit), *adj.* **1.** forming a corporation. **2.** of or belonging to a corporation. **3.** united or combined into one. **4.** pertaining to a united group, as of persons. **5.** corporative. [< L *corporāt(us)* made into a body = *corporā-* (s. of *corporāre* to incorporate; see CORPUS) + *-tus* ptp. suffix] **—cor′po·rate·ly,** *adv.*

cor·po·ra·tion (kôr′pə rā′shən), *n.* **1.** an association of individuals, created by law and existing as an entity with powers and liabilities independent of those of its members. **2.** (*cap.*) the group of principal officials of a borough or other municipal division in England. **3.** any group of persons united or regarded as united in one body. [late ME < LL *corporātiōn-* (s. of *corporātiō*)]

cor·po·rat·ism (kôr′pə rə tiz′əm, -prə tiz′-), *n.* the principles, doctrine, or system of corporative organization of a political unit. Also, **cor·po·rat·iv·ism** (kôr′pə rā′tə-viz′əm, -pər ə tə-). **—cor′po·rat·ist,** *adj.*

cor·po·ra·tive (kôr′pə rā′tiv, -pər ə tiv, -prə-), *adj.* **1.** of or pertaining to a corporation. **2.** of or pertaining to a political system under which the principal economic functions, as banking, industry, labor, etc., are organized as corporate unities. Also, **corporate.** [< LL *corporātīv(us)*]

cor·po·ra·tor (kôr′pə rā′tər), *n.* a member of a corporation, esp. one of the original members.

cor·po·re·al (kôr pōr′ē əl, -pôr′-), *adj.* **1.** of the nature of the physical body; bodily. **2.** material; tangible: *corporeal property.* [< L *corpore(us)* bodily (*corpor-* (s. of *corpus*) body + *-eus* adj. suffix) + -AL[1]] **—cor·po′re·al′i·ty, cor·po′re·al·ness,** *n.* **—cor·po′re·al·ly,** *adv.* **—Syn. 1.** See **physical. —Ant. 1.** spiritual.

cor·po·re·i·ty (kôr′pə rē′i tē), *n.* material or physical nature or quality; materiality. [< ML *corporeitās.* See CORPOREAL, -ITY]

cor·po·sant (kôr′pə zant′), *n.* See **corona discharge.** [< Pg *corpo-sant(o)* < L *corpus sanctum,* lit., holy body. See CORPS, SAINT]

corps (kōr, kôr), *n., pl.* **corps** (kōrz, kôrz). **1.** *Mil.* **a.** a military organization consisting of officers and men or of officers alone: *the medical corps; a corps of cadets.* **b.** a military unit of ground combat forces consisting of two or more divisions and other troops. **2.** a group of persons associated or acting together: *the press corps.* **3.** *Obs.* corpse. [late ME < MF, sp. var. of *cors* < L *corp(us)* body]

corps de bal·let (kôr′ də ba lā′, bal′ā; *Fr.* kôR də bᴀ le′), the dancers in a ballet company who perform as a group and have no solo parts. [< F]

corpse (kôrps), *n.* **1.** a dead body, usually of a human being. **2.** *Obs.* a human or animal body, whether alive or dead. [orig. sp. var. of CORSE but the *p* is now sounded] **—Syn. 1.** See **body.**

corps·man (kōr′mən, kôr′-), *n., pl.* **-men. 1.** *U.S. Navy.* an enlisted man working as a pharmacist or hospital assistant. **2.** *U.S. Army.* an enlisted man in the medical corps who accompanies combat troops into battle to give first aid, carry the wounded to safety, etc. **3.** a member of any corps.

cor·pu·lence (kôr′pyə ləns), *n.* obesity; fatness; portliness. Also, **cor′pu·len·cy.** [late ME < L *corpulentia*]

cor·pu·lent (kôr′pyə lənt), *adj.* obese; portly; stout; fat. [ME < L *corpulent(us).* See CORPUS, -LENT] **—cor′pu·lent·ly,** *adv.*

cor·pus (kôr′pəs), *n., pl.* **-po·ra** (-pər ə). **1.** a large or complete collection of writings. **2.** the body of a man or animal, esp. when dead. **3.** *Anat.* a body, mass, or part having a special character or function. **4.** a principal or capital sum, as opposed to interest or income. [< L: body]

cor·pus cal·lo·sum (kôr′pəs kə lō′səm), *pl.* **cor·po·ra cal·los·a** (kôr′pər ə kə lō′sə). *Anat., Zool.* a band of deeply situated transverse white fibers uniting the halves of the cerebrum in mammals. [< NL: lit., firm body]

Cor·pus Chris·ti (kôr′pəs kris′tē), a seaport in S Texas. 204,525 (1970).

Cor·pus Chris·ti (kôr′pəs kris′tē), *Rom. Cath. Ch.* a festival in honor of the Eucharist, celebrated on the Thursday after Trinity Sunday. [ME < ML: lit., body of Christ]

cor·pus·cle (kôr′pə səl, -pus əl), *n.* **1.** *Anat.* a cell, esp. a blood cell. **2.** a minute body forming a more or less distinct part of an organism. **3.** *Physical Chem.* a minute or elementary particle of matter, as an electron, proton, or atom. Also, **cor·pus·cule** (kôr pus′kyōōl). [< L *corpuscul(um).* See CORPUS, -CLE] **—cor·pus·cu·lar** (kôr pus′kyə lər), *adj.*

corpus′cular the′ory, *Physics.* the theory that light is transmitted as a stream of particles. Cf. **wave theory.**

cor·pus de·lic·ti (kôr′pəs di lik′tī), *Law.* the basic element of a crime, as, in murder, the death of the murdered person. [< NL: lit., body of the offense]

cor·pus ju·ris (kôr′pəs jŏŏr′is), the collected law of a nation, state, etc. [< LL: lit., body of law]

Cor·pus Ju·ris Ca·no·ni·ci (kôr′pəs jŏŏr′is kə non′i-sī′), the body of church law by which the Roman Catholic Church was governed until 1918. [< ML: lit., body of canon law]

Cor·pus Ju·ris Ci·vi·lis (kôr′pəs jŏŏr′is si vī′lis), the collective title of the body of ancient Roman law as collected and codified under the emperor Justinian in the 6th century A.D. [< NL: lit., body of civil law]

cor·pus lu·te·um (kôr′pəs lōō′tē əm), *pl.* **cor·po·ra lu·te·a** (kôr′pər ə lōō′tē ə). **1.** *Anat., Zool.* a ductless gland developed within the ovary by the reorganization of a Graafian follicle following ovulation. **2.** *Pharm.* an extract of this gland of the hog or cow, the chief principle of which is progesterone. [< NL: yellow body]

cor·pus stri·a·tum (kôr′pəs strī ā′təm), *pl.* **cor·po·ra stri·a·ta** (kôr′pər ə strī ā′tə). *Anat.* a mass of gray matter beneath the cortex and in front of the thalamus in each cerebral hemisphere. [< NL: striated body]

corr., 1. corrected. **2.** correspond. **3.** correspondence. **4.** correspondent. **5.** corresponding.

cor·rade (kə rād′, kô-), *v.t., v.i.* **-rad·ed, -rad·ing.** to wear down by corrasion. [< L *corrādere* (to) scrape together = *cor-* COR- + *rādere* to scrape; see ERASE, RAZE]

cor·ral (kə ral′), *n., v.,* **-ralled, -ral·ling.** **—***n.* **1.** an enclosure or pen for horses, cattle, etc. **2.** an enclosure formed of wagons during an encampment, for defense against attack. **—***v.t.* **3.** to confine in a corral. **4.** *U.S. Informal.* to seize; capture. [< Sp < LL **currāl(e)* enclosure for carts = L *curr(us)* wagon, cart (< *currere* to run) + *-āle* neut. of *-ālis* -AL[1]]

cor·ra·sion (kə rā′zhən, kô-), *n.* the process in which the earth's surface is abraded by the action of water, wind, etc. [< L *corrās(us)* ptp. of *corrādere* + -ION] **—cor·ra·sive** (kə rā′siv, -ziv, kô-), *adj.*

cor·rect (kə rekt′), *v.t.* **1.** to set or make right; remove the errors or faults from: *The new glasses corrected his eyesight.* **2.** to point out or mark the errors in: *The teacher corrected the examination papers.* **3.** to rebuke or punish in order to improve: *A mother should correct her children when they develop bad habits.* **4.** to counteract the operation or effect of (something hurtful). **5.** *Math., Physics.* to adjust so as to bring into accordance with a standard or required condition. **—***adj.* **6.** free from error; conforming to fact or truth; accurate. **7.** in accordance with an acknowledged or accepted standard; proper: *correct behavior.* [ME *correct(en)* < L *corrēct(us)* made straight (ptp. of *corrigere* = *cor-* COR- + *rēc-,* var. of *rēg-,* past s. of *regere* to direct) + *-tus* ptp. suffix] **—cor·rect′a·ble, cor·rect′i·ble,** *adj.* **—cor·rect′ing·ly,** *adv.* **—cor·rect′ly,** *adv.* **—cor·rect′ness,** *n.* **—cor·rec′tor,** *n.*

—Syn. 1. rectify, amend, emend, remedy. **3.** chasten, castigate. **6.** faultless, perfect, exact. CORRECT, ACCURATE, PRECISE imply conformity to fact, standard, or truth. A CORRECT statement is one free from error, mistakes, or faults: *Columbus was correct when he claimed the earth was round.* An ACCURATE statement is one that, as a result of an active effort to comprehend and verify, shows careful conformity to fact, truth, or spirit: *The two witnesses said his account of the accident was accurate.* A PRECISE statement shows scrupulously strict and detailed conformity to fact: *The chemist gave a precise account of the experiment.* **—Ant. 6.** faulty, inaccurate. **7.** solecistic.

cor·rec·tion (kə rek′shən), *n.* **1.** the act of correcting. **2.** something that is substituted or proposed for what is wrong; emendation. **3.** punishment or chastisement. **4.** *Math., Physics.* a quantity that is applied in order to increase accuracy, as in the use of an instrument or the solution of a problem. [ME *correccio(u)n* < L *corrēctiōn-* (s. of *corrēctiō*) a setting straight] **—cor·rec′tion·al,** *adj.*

cor·rect·i·tude (kə rek′ti tōōd′, -tyōōd′), *n.* correctness, esp. of manners and conduct. [b. CORRECT and RECTITUDE]

cor·rec·tive (kə rek′tiv), *adj.* **1.** tending to correct or rectify; remedial. **—***n.* **2.** a means of correcting; corrective agent. [< ML *corrēctīv(us)*] **—cor·rec′tive·ly,** *adv.*

Cor·reg·gio (kə rej′ō, -rej′ē ō′; *It.* kôR ʀed′jô), *n.* **An·to·nio Al·le·gri da** (än tô′nyô äl le′grē dä), 1494–1534, Italian painter.

Cor·reg·i·dor (kə reg′i dôr′, -dōr′; *Sp.* kôR ʀe′hē dôR′), *n.* an island in Manila Bay, in the Philippines: Americans defeated by the Japanese, May, 1942. 2 sq. mi.

correl., correlative.

cor·re·late (kôr′ə lāt′, kor′-), *v.,* **-lat·ed, -lat·ing,** *adj., n.* **—***v.t.* **1.** to place in or bring into mutual or reciprocal relation; establish in orderly connection. **—***v.i.* **2.** to have a mutual or reciprocal relation; stand in correlation: *The results of the two tests correlate to a high degree.* **—***adj.* **3.** mutually or reciprocally related; correlated. **—***n.* **4.** either of two related things, esp. when one implies the other. [prob. back formation from CORRELATION and CORRELATIVE] **—cor′re·lat′a·ble,** *adj.*

cor·re·la·tion (kôr′ə lā′shən, kor′-), *n.* **1.** mutual relation of two or more things, parts, etc. **2.** the act or state of correlating. **3.** the state of being correlated. **4.** *Statistics.* the degree of correlation between two or more attributes or measurements on the same group of elements. **5.** *Physiol.* the interdependence or reciprocal relations of organs or functions. Also, *esp. Brit.,* **corelation.** [< ML *correlātiōn-* (s. of *correlātiō*)] **—cor′re·la′tion·al,** *adj.*

correla′tion coeffi′cient, *Statistics.* one of a number of measures of correlation, usually assuming values from +1 to −1.

cor·rel·a·tive (kə rel′ə tiv), *adj.* **1.** so related that each implies or complements the other. **2.** being in correlation; mutually related. **3.** *Gram.* having a mutual relation; complementing one another, as *either* and *or, where* and *there.* **4.** *Biol.* (of a typical structure of an organism) found in correlation with another. **—***n.* **5.** either of two things, as two terms, that are correlative. **6.** *Gram.* a correlative expression. Also, *esp. Brit.,* **corelative.** [< ML *correlātīv(us)*] **—cor·rel′a·tive·ly,** *adv.*

correl′ative conjunc′tion, *Gram.* a conjunction grammatically similar to a coordinating conjunction but occurring as a member of a matched pair, as *either . . . or, neither . . . nor,* or *both . . . and.*

corresp., correspondence.

cor·re·spond (kôr′i spond′, kor′-), *v.i.* **1.** to be in agreement or conformity (often fol. by *with* or *to*): *His actions do*

not correspond with his words. **2.** to be similar or analogous; be equivalent in function, position, amount, etc., (usually fol. by *to*): *The U.S. Congress corresponds to the British Parliament.* **3.** to communicate by exchange of letters. [< ML *correspond(ēre)*]
—Syn. 1. harmonize, match, tally. CORRESPOND, AGREE, ACCORD imply comparing persons or things and finding that they harmonize. CORRESPOND suggests having an obvious similarity, though not agreeing in every detail: *Part of this report corresponds with the facts.* AGREE implies having or arriving at a condition in which no essential difference of opinion or detail is evident: *All the reports agree.* ACCORD emphasizes agreeing exactly, both in fact and in point of view: *This report accords with the other.*

cor·re·spond·ence (kôr′i spon′dəns, kor′-), *n.* **1.** Also, **correspondency.** an instance of corresponding. **2.** similarity or analogy. **3.** agreement; conformity. **4.** communication by exchange of letters. **5.** letters that pass between correspondents. [late ME < ML *corrēspondentia*] **—Syn. 3.** accord, consonance. **—Ant. 2.** difference.

correspond′ence course′, a course of instruction provided by a correspondence school.

correspond′ence school′, a school in which study materials and tests are mailed to the students, who in turn mail their work back to the school for grading.

cor·re·spond·en·cy (kôr′i spon′dən sē, kor′-), *n., pl.* **-cies.** correspondence (def. 1).

cor·re·spond·ent (kôr′i spon′dənt, kor′-), *n.* **1.** a person who communicates by letters. **2.** a person employed by a news agency, periodical, or the like, to gather, report, or contribute news, articles, etc., regularly from a distant place. **3.** a thing that corresponds to something else. **4.** a person or firm that has regular business relations with another, esp. at a distance. **—*adj.*** **5.** corresponding; conforming, similar, or analogous. [late ME < ML *corrēspondent-* (s. of *corrēspondēns*), prp. of *corrēspondēre* to CORRESPOND; see -ENT]

cor·re·spond·ing (kôr′i spon′diṅg, kor′-), *adj.* **1.** identical in all essentials or respects: *corresponding fingerprints.* **2.** similar in position, purpose, form, etc.: *corresponding officials in two states.* **3.** associated in a working or other relationship: *a bolt and its corresponding nut.* **4.** dealing with correspondence: *a corresponding secretary.* **5.** sending letters. **6.** employing the mails as a means of association: *a corresponding member of a club.* **—cor′re·spond′ing·ly,** *adv.*

cor·re·spon·sive (kôr′i spon′siv, kor′-), *adj.* responsive to effort or impulse; answering; corresponding. [< ML *corrēspons(us)* (ptp. of *corrēspondēre* to CORRESPOND) + -IVE]

cor·ri·da (kô rē′də), *n.* a bullfight. [< Sp, short for *corrida de toros*, lit., chasing of bulls; *corrida*, fem. of *corrido*, ptp. of *correr* < L *currere* to run]

cor·ri·dor (kôr′i dər, -dôr′, kor′-), *n.* **1.** a gallery or passage connecting parts of a building. **2.** a passage into which several rooms or apartments open. **3.** a narrow tract of land forming a passageway, as one belonging to an inland country and affording an outlet to the sea. [< MF < It *corridor(e)* < Sp *corredor*, lit., runner < *correr* to run < L *currere*]

cor·rie (kôʀ′ē, koʀ′ē), *n. Scot.* a circular hollow in the side of a hill or mountain. [< Gael *coire* cauldron, whirlpool, hollow]

Cor·rie·dale (kôr′ē dāl′, kor′-), *n.* one of a breed of sheep raised originally in New Zealand and noted for its high-quality wool and good market lambs.

Cor·ri·en·tes (kôʀ′ʀē en′tes), *n.* a port in NE Argentina, on the Paraná River. 112,725 (1965).

cor·ri·gen·dum (kôr′i jen′dəm, kor′-), *n., pl.* **-da** (-də). **1.** an error to be corrected, esp. an error in print. **2. corrigenda,** a list of corrections of errors in a book or other publication. [< L: lit., (something) to be corrected (neut. ger. of *corrigere*); see CORRECT]

cor·ri·gi·ble (kôr′i jə bəl, kor′-), *adj.* capable of being corrected, reformed, or improved. [late ME < ML *corrigibil(is)* = *corrig(ere)* (to) CORRECT + *-ibilis* -IBLE] **—cor′ri·gi·bil′i·ty,** *n.* **—cor′ri·gi·bly,** *adv.*

cor·rob·o·rant (kə rob′ər ənt), *Archaic.* **—*adj.*** **1.** strengthening; invigorating. **—*n.*** **2.** a strengthening medicine. [< L *corrōborant-* (s. of *corrōborāns*) strengthening, prp. of *corrōborāre*]

cor·rob·o·rate (*v.* kə rob′ə rāt′; *adj.* kə rob′ər it), *v.,* **-rat·ed, -rat·ing,** *adj.* **—*v.t.*** **1.** to confirm; make more certain: *He corroborated my account of the accident.* **—*adj.*** **2.** *Archaic.* corroborated. [< L *corrōborāt(us)* strengthened (ptp. of *corrōborāre*) = *cor-* COR- + *rōbor(āre)* (to) make strong (< *rōbor, rōbur* oak, hence strength) + *-ātus* -ATE[1]] **—cor·rob·o·ra·tive** (kə rob′ə rā′tiv, -ər ə tiv), **cor·rob·o·ra·to·ry** (kə rob′ər ə tôr′ē, -tōr′ē), *adj.* **—cor·rob′o·ra′tive·ly, cor·rob′o·ra·to′ri·ly,** *adv.* **—cor·rob′o·ra′tor,** *n.* **—Syn. 1.** verify, substantiate.

cor·rob·o·ra·tion (kə rob′ə rā′shən), *n.* **1.** the act of corroborating. **2.** a corroboratory fact, statement, etc. [< LL *corrobōrātiōn-* (s. of *corrobōrātiō*)]

cor·rob·o·ree (kə rob′ə rē), *n. Australian.* **1.** a sacred, festive, or warlike assembly among the aborigines. **2.** any large or noisy gathering. [< Austral native word]

cor·rode (kə rōd′), *v.,* **-rod·ed, -rod·ing.** **—*v.t.*** **1.** to eat away gradually as if by gnawing, esp. by chemical action. **2.** to impair or deteriorate: *Jealousy corroded his character.* **—*v.i.*** **3.** to become corroded. [late ME < L *corrōde(re)* (to) gnaw to pieces = *cor-* COR- + *rōdere* to gnaw; akin to RAT] **—cor·rod′ant,** *n.* **—cor·rod′er,** *n.* **—cor·rod′i·bil′i·ty,** *n.* **—cor·rod′i·ble,** *adj.* **—Syn. 1.** erode. **3.** rust.

cor·ro·dy (kôr′ə dē, kor′-), *n., pl.* **-dies.** corody.

cor·ro·sion (kə rō′zhən), *n.* **1.** the act or process of corroding. **2.** the condition of being corroded. **3.** a product of corroding, as rust. [late ME < LL *corrōsiōn-* (s. of *corrōsiō*) a gnawing away = L *corrōs(us)* (ptp. of *corrōdere* to CORRODE) + *-iōn-* -ION]

cor·ro·sive (kə rō′siv), *adj.* **1.** having the quality of corroding or consuming. **—*n.*** **2.** something corrosive, as an acid, drug, etc. [late ME < ML *corrōsīv(us)* = (see CORROSION, -IVE); r. ME *corosif* < MF] **—cor·ro′sive·ly,** *adv.* **—cor·ro′sive·ness,** *n.*

corro′sive sub′limate. See **mercuric chloride.**

cor·ru·gate (*v.* kôr′ə gāt′, kor′-; *adj.* kôr′ə git, -gāt′, kor′-), *v.,* **-gat·ed, -gat·ing,** *adj.* **—*v.t., v.i.*** **1.** to draw or bend into folds or alternate furrows and ridges. **—*adj.*** **2.** corrugated; wrinkled; furrowed. [late ME < L *corrūgāt(us)* wrinkled (ptp. of *corrūgāre*) = *cor-* COR- + *rūg(āre)* (to) wrinkle + *-ātus* -ATE[1]]

cor′rugated i′ron, a type of galvanized sheet iron or steel strengthened for use in construction by having a series of alternating grooves and ridges forced into it.

cor′rugated pa′per, heavy paper with alternating ridges and grooves for use in packing fragile articles.

cor·ru·ga·tion (kôr′ə gā′shən, kor′-), *n.* **1.** the act of corrugating. **2.** the state of being corrugated. **3.** a wrinkle; fold; furrow; ridge. [< ML *corrūgātiōn-* (s. of *corrūgātiō*) a wrinkling]

cor·rupt (kə rupt′), *adj.* **1.** guilty of dishonest practices, as bribery; without integrity; crooked: *a corrupt judge.* **2.** debased in character; depraved. **3.** decayed; putrid. **4.** infected; tainted. **5.** made inferior by errors or alterations, as a text. **—*v.t.*** **6.** to cause to be dishonest, disloyal, etc., esp. by bribery. **7.** to lower morally; pervert; deprave. **8.** to infect; taint. **9.** to make putrid or putrescent. **10.** to alter (a language, text, etc.) for the worse; debase. **—*v.i.*** **11.** to become corrupt. [ME < L *corrupt(us)* broken in pieces, corrupted (ptp. of *corrumpere*). See COR-, RUPTURE] **—cor·rupt′ed·ly,** *adv.* **—cor·rupt′ed·ness,** *n.* **—cor·rupt′er, cor·rup′tor,** *n.* **—cor·rup′tive,** *adj.* **—cor·rup′tive·ly,** *adv.* **—cor·rupt′ly,** *adv.* **—cor·rupt′ness,** *n.*
—Syn. 1. false, untrustworthy. CORRUPT, DISHONEST, VENAL apply to a person, esp. in public office, who acts on mercenary motives, without regard to honor, right, or justice. A CORRUPT politician is one originally honest who has succumbed to temptation and begun questionable practices. A DISHONEST politician is one lacking native integrity and thoroughly untrustworthy. A VENAL politician is one so debased that he frankly sells his patronage. **3, 4.** putrescent, rotten, spoiled. **4, 5.** contaminated. **6.** demoralize, bribe. **7.** debase, vitiate. **8.** contaminate, pollute, defile. **9.** putrefy.

cor·rupt·i·ble (kə rup′tə bəl), *adj.* capable of being corrupted. [ME < LL *corruptibil(is)*] **—cor·rupt′i·bil′i·ty,** *n.* **—cor·rupt′i·bly,** *adv.*

cor·rup·tion (kə rup′shən), *n.* **1.** the act of corrupting. **2.** the state of being corrupt. **3.** moral perversion; depravity. **4.** perversion of integrity. **5.** corrupt or dishonest proceedings. **6.** bribery. **7.** debasement or alteration, as of language or a text. **8.** a debased form of a word. **9.** putrefactive decay; rottenness. **10.** any corrupting influence or agency. [ME *corrupcio(u)n* < L *corruptiōn-* (s. of *corruptiō*)] **—Syn. 3.** immorality. **5.** baseness, dishonesty. **9.** rot, putrefaction, putrescence. **—Ant. 2–4** purity. **4, 5.** honesty.

cor·rup·tion·ist (kə rup′shə nist), *n.* a person who practices or endorses corruption, esp. in politics.

cor·sage (kôr säzh′), *n.* **1.** a small bouquet worn at the waist, on the shoulder, etc., by a woman. **2.** the body or waist of a dress; bodice. [late ME < MF: bodily shape (later: bust, bodice, corsage) = *cors* body (< L *corpus*) + *-age* -AGE]

cor·sair (kôr′sâr), *n.* **1.** a privateer, esp. one of the Barbary Coast. **2.** a pirate. **3.** a fast vessel used for piracy. [< MF *corsaire* < Pr *corsari* < ML *cursāri(us)*. See COURSE, -ARY]

corse (kôrs), *n. Obs.* corpse. [ME *cors* < OF < L *corp(us)* body]

Corse (kôʀs), *n.* French name of **Corsica.**

cor·se·let (kôr′sə let′ *for 1;* kôrs′lit *for 2*), *n.* **1.** a supporting undergarment, combining brassiere and girdle. **2.** Also, **corslet.** *Armor.* **a.** a suit of light half armor or three-quarter armor of the 16th century or later. **b.** cuirass (def. 1). [< MF *cors* bodice, body + *-elet* -LET]

C, Corselet of English pikeman (17th century)
M, Morion

cor·set (kôr′sit), *n.* **1.** Often, **corsets.** a shaped, close-fitting, and usually boned undergarment, worn by women, to shape and support the body. **—*v.t.*** **2.** to dress or furnish with or as with a corset. [ME < OF = *cors* bodice, body + *-et* -ET]

Cor·si·ca (kôr′si kə), *n.* an island in the Mediterranean, SE of and forming a department of France. 275,465 (1962); 3367 sq. mi. *Cap.:* Ajaccio. French, **Corse.** **—Cor′si·can,** *adj., n.*

cors·let (kôrs′lit), *n.* corselet (def. 2).

cor·tege (kôr tezh′, -tāzh′), *n.* **1.** a line or train of attendants; retinue. **2.** a procession, esp. a ceremonial one. [< F *cortège* < It *cortegg(io)* courtly retinue < *corte* COURT]

cor·tège (kôr tezh′, -tāzh′; *Fr.* kôʀ tezh′), *n., pl.* **-tèg·es** (-tezh′iz, -tā′zhiz; *Fr.* -tezh′). cortege.

Cor·tes (kôr′tiz; *Sp.* kôʀ′tes), *n.* (in Spain or Portugal) the national legislative body. [< Sp, pl. of *corte* COURT]

Cor·tés (kôr tez′; *Sp.* kôʀ tes′), *n.* **Her·nan·do** (hûr nan′dō; *Sp.* eʀ nän′dô) or **Her·nán** (eʀ nän′), 1485–1547, Spanish conqueror of Mexico. Also, **Cor·tez′.**

cor·tex (kôr′teks), *n., pl.* **-ti·ces** (-ti sēz′). **1.** *Bot.* the portion of a stem between the epidermis and the vascular tissue; bark. **2.** *Anat., Zool.* **a.** the rind of an organ, as the outer wall of the kidney. **b.** the layer of gray matter that invests the surface of the cerebral hemispheres and the cerebellum. [< L: bark, rind, shell, husk]

cor·ti·cal (kôr′ti kəl), *adj.* **1.** *Anat.* of, pertaining to, resembling, or consisting of cortex. **2.** *Physiol., Pathol.* resulting from the function or condition of the cerebral cortex. **3.** *Bot.* of or pertaining to the cortex. [< NL *corticāl(is)*] **—cor′ti·cal·ly,** *adv.*

cor·ti·cate (kôr′tə kit, -kāt′), *adj.* having a cortex. Also, **cor′ti·cat′ed.** [< L *corticāt(us)*] **—cor′ti·ca′tion,** *n.*

cortico-, a combining form of **cortex:** *corticosteroid.* Also, *esp. before a vowel,* **cortic-.** [< L *cortic-* (s. of *cortex*) + -o-]

cor·ti·co·ster·oid (kôr′tə kō ster′oid, -stēr′-), *n. Biochem.* any of a class of steroids, as aldosterone, hydrocortisone, or cortisone, occurring in nature as a product of the adrenal cortex, or synthesized. Also called **cor·ti·coid** (kôr′tə koid′). [< L *cortic-* (s. of *cortex*) CORTEX + -o- + STEROID]

cor·tin (kôr′tᵊn, -tin), *n.* *Biochem.* a hormone essential to life, secreted by the adrenal glands. [CORT(EX) + -IN[2]]

cor·ti·sol (kôr′ti sôl′, -sōl′), *n.* *Pharm.* hydrocortisone. [CORTIS(ONE) + -OL[1]]

cor·ti·sone (kôr′ti sōn′, -zōn′), *n.* **1.** *Biochem.* a hormone of the adrenal cortex, $C_{21}H_{28}O_5$, active in carbohydrate and protein metabolism. **2.** *Pharm.* a commercial form of this compound, used chiefly in the treatment of arthritis and certain allergies. Also called **Compound E.** [alter. of *corticosterone* = CORTICO- + STER(OL) + -ONE]

Cor·to·na (kôʀ tô′nä), *n.* **Pie·tro da** (pye′tʀô dä), (*Pietro Berrettini*), 1596–1669, Italian painter and architect.

Co·ru·ña (kô ʀōō′nyä), *n.* See **La Coruña.** Also, **Co·run·na** (kə run′ə).

co·run·dum (kə run′dəm), *n.* a common mineral, aluminum oxide, Al_2O_3, notable for its hardness: transparent varieties used as gems, other varieties, as abrasives; often made synthetically. [< Tamil *kuruntam, kurundam;* akin to Skt *kuruvinda* ruby]

co·rus·cant (kə rus′kənt, kôr′əs-, kor′-), *adj.* sparkling or gleaming; flashing; scintillating; coruscating. [late ME < L *coruscant-* (s. of *coruscāns*) quivering, flashing (prp. of *coruscāre*); see -ANT]

cor·us·cate (kôr′ə skāt′, kor′-), *v.i.,* **-cat·ed, -cat·ing.** to emit vivid flashes of light; sparkle; scintillate; gleam. [< L *coruscāt(us)* quivered, flashed, ptp. of *coruscāre*]

cor·us·ca·tion (kôr′ə skā′shən, kor′-), *n.* **1.** the act of coruscating. **2.** a sudden gleam or flash of light. **3.** a striking display of brilliance or wit. [late ME < LL *coruscātiōn-* (s. of *coruscātiō*)]

Cor·val·lis (kôr val′is), *n.* a city in W Oregon. 35,056 (1970).

cor·vée (kôr vā′), *n.* **1.** unpaid labor for one day, as on the repair of roads, exacted by a feudal lord. **2.** an obligation imposed on inhabitants of a district to perform services, as repair of roads, bridges, etc., for little or no remuneration. [ME < MF < LL *corrogāta* contribution, collection, n. use of fem. of L *corrogātus,* ptp. of *corrogāre* to collect by asking]

corves (kôrvz), *n.* pl. of **corf.**

cor·vette (kôr vet′), *n.* **1.** a warship of the old sailing class, having a flush deck and usually one tier of guns. **2.** *Brit.* a small, lightly armed, fast vessel used mostly for convoy escort and ranging between a destroyer and a gunboat in size. Also, **cor·vet** (kôr vet′, kôr′vet). [< MF < Pg *corvet(a),* irreg. < L *corbīta* merchant vessel, short for *corbīta nāvis,* lit., basketed ship; said to be so named from the basket hoisted as an ensign, marking it a cargo vessel]

cor·vi·na (kôr vē′nə), *n.* any of several sciaenoid fishes, as *Cynoscion parvipinnis,* a food fish found off the coast of California. [< MexSp, Sp: kind of fish, special use of *corvino* CORVINE; so called from its color]

cor·vine (kôr′vīn, -vin), *adj.* **1.** pertaining to or resembling a crow. **2.** belonging or pertaining to the *Corvidae,* a family of birds including the crows, ravens, and jays. [< L *corvīn(us)* = *corv(us)* raven + *-īnus* -INE[1]]

Cor·y·bant (kôr′ə bant′, kor′-), *n., pl.* **Cor·y·ban·tes** (kôr′ə ban′tēz, kor′-), **Cor·y·bants. 1.** *Class. Myth.* any of the spirits or secondary divinities attending Cybele with wild music and dancing. **2.** an ancient Phrygian priest of Cybele. [ME < L *Corybant-* (s. of *Corybās*) < Gk *Korybant-* (s. of *Korýbas*)] —**Cor·y·ban·tic** (kôr′ə ban′tik, kor′-), *adj.*

co·ryd·a·lis (kə rid′ᵊlis), *n.* any papaveraceous plant of the genus *Corydalis* (*Capnoides*), comprising erect or climbing herbs with divided leaves, tuberous or fibrous roots, and irregular spurred flowers. [< NL < Gk *korydallís,* extended var. of *korydós* crested lark < *koryd-,* var. of *koryth-* (s. of *kórys*) helmet, head, crest, akin to *kára* head]

cor·ymb (kôr′imb, -im, kor′-), *n.* *Bot.* a form of inflorescence resembling a raceme but having a relatively shorter rachis and longer lower pedicles so that the flowers form a flat-topped or convex cluster, the outermost flowers being the first to expand. [< L *corymb(us)* < Gk *kórymbos* head, top, cluster of fruit or flowers] —**cor′ymbed,** *adj.* —**cor′ymb·like′,** *adj.*

co·rym·bose (kə rim′bōs), *adj.* characterized by or growing in corymbs; corymblike. [< NL *corymbōs(us)*] —**co·rym′bose·ly,** *adv.*

cor·y·phae·us (kôr′ə fē′əs, kor′-), *n., pl.* **-phae·i** (-fē′ī). **1.** the leader of the chorus in the ancient Greek drama. **2.** (in modern use) the leader of an operatic chorus or any group of singers. [< L < Gk *koryphaîos* leader (n.), leading (adj.) = *koryph(ḗ)* head, top + *-aios* adj. suffix]

cor·y·phée (kôr′ə fā′, kor′-; *Fr.* kô ʀē fā′), *n., pl.* **-phées** (-fāz′; *Fr.* -fā′). a member of a ballet company who dances usually as part of a small group and who ranks above the members of the corps de ballet but below the soloists. [< F < L *coryphae(us)* CORYPHAEUS]

co·ry·za (kə rī′zə), *n.* **1.** *Pathol.* acute inflammation of the mucous membrane of the nasal cavities; cold in the head. **2.** *Vet. Pathol.* a contagious disease of birds, esp. poultry, characterized by the secretion of a thick mucus in the mouth and throat. [< LL < Gk *kóryza* catarrh]

cos[1] (kos, kôs), *n.* romaine. [named after Kos from which it originally came]

cos[2] (kōs), *n.* cosine.

Cos (kôs), *n.* Kos.

cos., 1. companies. **2.** counties.

C.O.S., cash on shipment. Also, **c.o.s.**

Co·sa Nos·tra (kō′zə nō′strə), a secret criminal organization in the U.S., modeled after and associated with the Mafia. [< It: lit., our thing]

co·sec (kō′sēk′), *n.* cosecant.

co·se·cant (kō sē′kənt, -kant), *n.* *Trig.* **1.** (in a right triangle) the ratio of the hypotenuse to the side opposite a given angle. **2.** the secant of the complement, or the reciprocal of the sine, of a given angle or arc. *Abbr.:* cosec, csc [< NL *cosecant-* (s. of *cosecāns*)]

Cosecant
ACB being the angle, the ratio of BC to BA, or that of CL to CD, is the cosecant; or, CD being taken as unity, the cosecant is LC

co·seis·mal (kō sīs′məl, -sīz′-), *adj.* of, pertaining to, or being in a line, curve, etc., connecting or comprising points on the earth's surface at which an earthquake wave arrives simultaneously. Also, **co·seis′mic.**

Co·sen·za (kô zen′tsä), *n.* a city in S Italy. 78,941 (1961).

Cos·grave (koz′grāv), *n.* **William Thomas,** 1880–1965, Irish political leader: president of the executive council of the Irish Free State 1922–32.

cosh[1] (kosh), *Chiefly Brit. Slang.* —*n.* **1.** a blackjack; bludgeon. —*v.t.* **2.** to hit (someone) on the head with a blackjack. [perh. < Romany *kosh, koshter* stick]

cosh[2] (kosh), *n.* hyperbolic cosine. [COS(INE) + H(YPERBOLIC)]

co·sig·na·to·ry (kō sig′nə tōr′ē, -tôr′ē), *adj., n., pl.* **-ries.** —*adj.* **1.** signing jointly with another or others. —*n.* **2.** a person or party who signs a document jointly with another or others.

co·sign·er (kō′sī′nər, kō′sī′-), *n.* a comaker.

co·sine (kō′sīn), *n.* *Trig.* **1.** (in a right triangle) the ratio of the side adjacent to a given angle to the hypotenuse. **2.** the sine of the complement of a given angle or arc. *Abbr.:* cos [< NL *cosin(us)*]

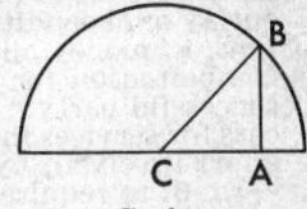

Cosine
ACB being the angle, the ratio of AC to BC is the cosine; or, BC being taken as unity, the cosine is AC

cos′ let′tuce (kos, kôs), romaine.

cosm-, var. of **cosmo-** before a vowel: *cosmic.*

-cosm, var. of **cosmo-** as final element of a compound word: *microcosm.*

cos·met·ic (koz met′ik), *n.* **1.** a powder, lotion, or other preparation for beautifying the complexion, skin, hair, nails, etc. —*adj.* **2.** imparting or improving beauty, esp. of the face. **3.** correcting or concealing physical defects or injuries: *cosmetic surgery.* **4.** used superficially to make something look better, more attractive, or more impressive. [< Gk *kosmētik(ós)* relating to adornment = *kosmēt(ós)* adorned, arranged (verbid of *kosmein* < *kósmos;* see COSMOS) + *-ikos* -IC] —**cos·met′i·cal·ly,** *adv.*

cos·me·ti·cian (koz′mi tish′ən), *n.* **1.** a person who manufactures or sells cosmetics. **2.** an expert, usually professional, in the application of cosmetics.

cos·met·i·cize (koz met′i sīz′), *v.t.,* **-cized, -ciz·ing.** to make appear better, more attractive, or more impressive, usually by superficial means. [COSMETIC + -IZE]

cos·me·tize (koz′mi tīz′), *v.t.,* **-tized, -tiz·ing.** cosmeticize. [COSMET(IC) + -IZE]

cos·me·tol·o·gy (koz′mi tol′ə jē), *n.* the art or profession of applying cosmetics. [< Gk *kosmētó(s)* adorned, arranged (see COSMETIC) + -LOGY, appar. modeled on F *cosmétologie*] —**cos′me·tol′o·gist,** *n.*

cos·mic (koz′mik), *adj.* **1.** of or pertaining to the cosmos: *cosmic laws.* **2.** immeasurably extended in time and space; vast. **3.** forming a part of the material universe, esp. outside of the earth. Also, **cos′mi·cal.** [< Gk *kosmik(ós)* worldly, universal] —**cos′mi·cal·ly,** *adv.*

cos′mic dust′, fine particles of matter in space.

cos′mic ray′, *Astron.* a radiation of extremely high penetrating power that originates in outer space and consists partly of high-energy atomic nuclei.

cosmo-, a learned borrowing from Greek meaning "world," "universe," used in the formation of compound words: *cosmonaut.* Also, **cosm-, -cosm.** [< Gk *kosmo-,* comb. form of *kósmos* COSMOS]

cos·mog·o·ny (koz mog′ə nē), *n., pl.* **-nies.** a theory of the origin and development of the universe. [< Gk *kosmogonía* the creation of the world] —**cos·mo·gon·ic** (koz′mə gon′ik), *adj.* —**cos·mog′o·nist,** *n.*

cos·mog·ra·phy (koz mog′rə fē), *n., pl.* **-phies. 1.** a science that describes and maps the main features of the heavens and the earth, including astronomy, geography, and geology. **2.** a description or representation of the main features of the universe. [< Gk *kosmographía* description of the world] —**cos·mog′ra·pher, cos·mog′ra·phist,** *n.* —**cos·mo·graph·ic** (koz′mə graf′ik), **cos′mo·graph′i·cal,** *adj.* —**cos′mo·graph′i·cal·ly,** *adv.*

cos·mo·line (koz′mə lēn′), *n., v.,* **-lined, -lin·ing.** —*n.* **1.** heavy grease used to preserve weapons from the elements. —*v.t.* **2.** to grease (weapons) against the elements. [COSM(ETIC) + -OL[2] + -INE[2]]

cos·mol·o·gy (koz mol′ə jē), *n.* **1.** the branch of philosophy dealing with the origin and general structure of the universe, with its parts, elements, and laws, and esp. with such of its characteristics as space, time, causality, and freedom. **2.** the branch of astronomy that deals with the general structure and evolution of the universe. [< NL *cosmologia*] —**cos·mo·log·i·cal** (koz′mə loj′i kəl), **cos′mo·log′ic,** *adj.* —**cos′mo·log′i·cal·ly,** *adv.* —**cos·mol′o·gist,** *n.*

cos·mo·naut (koz′mə nôt′, -not′), *n.* an astronaut, esp. a Russian one. [COSMO- + *-naut,* as in *Argonaut;* first coined in Russian]

cos·mop·o·lis (koz mop′ə lis), *n.* an internationally important city inhabited by many different peoples. [COSMO- + -POLIS, modeled on *metropolis*]

cos·mo·pol·i·tan (koz′mə pol′i tᵊn), *adj.* **1.** belonging to all the world; not limited to just one part of the political, social, commercial, or intellectual world. **2.** *Bot., Zool.* widely distributed over the globe. **3.** free from local, provincial, or national ideas, prejudices, or attachments. **4.** of or characteristic of a cosmopolite. —*n.* **5.** a person who is free from local, provincial, or national prejudices, etc.; citizen of the world; cosmopolite. —**cos′mo·pol′i·tan·ism,** *n.*

cos·mop·o·lite (koz mop′ə līt′), *n.* **1.** a person who is cosmopolitan in his ideas, life, etc.; citizen of the world. **2.** an animal or plant of world-wide distribution. [< Gk *kosmopolítē(s)* citizen of the world] —**cos·mop′o·lit′ism,** *n.*

cos·mos (koz′məs, -mōs), *n., pl.* **-mos, -mos·es** for 2, 4. **1.** the world or universe regarded as an orderly, harmonious system. **2.** a complete, orderly, harmonious system. **3.** order or harmony. **4.** any composite plant of the genus *Cosmos,* of tropical America, some species of which, as *C. bipannatus* and *C. sulphureus,* are cultivated for their showy flowers. [ME *cossmos* world < Gk *kósmos* order, form, arrangement, the world or universe]

Cos·mo·tron (kos′mə tron′), *n. Physics.* a proton accelerator. [*cosmo-* (repr. COSMIC RAY) + -TRON]

Cos·sack (kos′ak, -ək), *n.* a member of various tribes of Slavic warriors living chiefly in SE Russia and forming an elite corps of horsemen in czarist Russia. [< Russ *kazak* < Turk *kazak*, soldier, adventurer]

cos·set (kos′it), *v.t.* **1.** to treat as a pet; pamper; coddle. —*n.* **2.** a lamb brought up without its dam; pet lamb. **3.** any pet. [akin to OE *cossetung* kissing, verbal n. based on **cossettan* to kiss < *coss* kiss; c. Icel *koss*, G *Kuss*]

cost (kôst, kost), *n., v.,* **cost, cost·ing.** —*n.* **1.** the price paid to acquire, produce, accomplish, or maintain anything. **2.** a sacrifice, loss, or penalty: *to work at the cost of one's health.* **3.** outlay or expenditure of money, time, trouble, etc. **4. costs,** *Law.* **a.** money allowed to a successful party in a lawsuit in compensation for his legal expenses, chargeable to the unsuccessful party. **b.** money due to a court or one of its officers for services in a cause. **5. at all costs,** regardless of the effort involved; by any means necessary. Also, **at any cost.** —*v.t.* **6.** to require the payment of (money or something else of value in an exchange): *That camera cost $40.* **7.** to result in or entail the loss or injury of: *Carelessness costs lives.* **8.** to entail (effort or inconvenience): *Courtesy costs little.* **9.** to estimate or determine the cost of (manufactured articles, new processes, etc.). —*v.i.* **10.** to estimate or determine costs, as of manufacturing something. [ME *cost(en)* < MF *coste(r)* < L *constāre* to stand with, cost; see CONSTANT] —**Syn. 1.** charge, expense, expenditure. See **price. 2.** detriment.

cost-, var. of **costo-** before a vowel: *costate.*

cos·ta (kos′tə, kô′stə), *n., pl.* **cos·tae** (kos′tē, kô′stē). **1.** a rib or riblike part. **2.** the midrib of a leaf in mosses. **3.** a ridge. **4.** Also called **cos′tal vein′.** *Entomol.* a vein, usually marginal, in the wing of certain insects. [< L: rib, side. See COAST]

Cos·ta Bra·va (kos′tə brä′və, kô′stə, kō′-; *Sp.* kôs′ tä brä′vä), a coastal region in NE Spain, extending NE along the Mediterranean from Barcelona to the border of France.

cost′ account′ing, an accounting system itemizing the costs involved in production. —**cost′ account′ant.**

cos·tal (kos′tᵊl, kôs′tᵊl), *adj. Anat.* pertaining to the ribs or the side of the body: *costal nerves.* [< ML *costāl(is)*]

Cos·ta Me·sa (kos′tə mā′sə, kô′stə, kō′-), a city in SW California, near Los Angeles. 72,660 (1970).

co-star (*n.* kō′stär′; *v.* kō′stär′), *n., v.,* **-starred, -star·ring.** —*n.* **1.** an actor or actress who shares star billing with another. —*v.i.* **2.** to share star billing with another. —*v.t.* **3.** to present (two or more stars) with equal billing.

cos·tard (kos′tərd, kô′stərd), *n.* **1.** *Hort.* a large variety of English apple. **2.** *Archaic.* the head. [ME, perh. *cost* quality (OE: choice) + -ARD]

Cos·ta Ri·ca (kos′tə rē′kə, kô′stə, kō′-; *Sp.* kôs′tä rē′kä), a republic in Central America, between Panama and Nicaragua. 2,012,000; 19,238 sq. mi. *Cap.:* San José. —**Cos′ta Ri′can.**

cos·tate (kos′tāt, kô′stāt), *adj.* having a rib or ribs. [< L *costāt(us)*]

cost-ef·fec·tive (kôst′i fek′tiv), *adj.* producing optimum results for the expenditure, as in military procurement. —**cost′-ef·fec′tive·ness,** *n.*

Cos·ter·mans·ville (kos′tər mənz vil′, kô′stər-), *n.* former name of **Bukavu.**

cos·ter·mon·ger (kos′tər muŋ′gər, -moŋ′-, kô′stər-), *n. Chiefly Brit.* a hawker of fruit, vegetables, fish, etc. [earlier *costerdmonger.* See COSTARD, MONGER]

cos·tive (kos′tiv, kô′stiv), *adj.* **1.** suffering from constipation. **2.** *Archaic.* slow in action or speech. [late ME < MF: constipated (ptp. of *costiver*) < L *constip(ātus)* (see CONSTIPATE); MF *-ive* (modern *-ivé*) was taken as fem. adj. suffix *-ive* -IVE] —**cos′tive·ly,** *adv.* —**cos′tive·ness,** *n.*

cost·ly (kôst′lē, kost′-), *adj.* **-li·er, -li·est. 1.** costing much; high-priced. **2.** resulting in great detriment: *a costly mistake.* **3.** of great value; sumptuous. **4.** *Archaic.* lavish; extravagant. —**cost′li·ness,** *n.* —**Syn. 1.** See **expensive.**

cost·mar·y (kost′mâr′ē, kôst′-), *n., pl.* **-mar·ies.** a perennial plant, *Chrysanthemum Balsamita,* that has fragrant leaves and is used in salads and as a flavoring. [ME *costmarie* = *cost* (OE: costmary < L *cost(um)* some oriental aromatic plant < Gk *kóstos*) + *Marie* (the Virgin) Mary]

costo-, a learned borrowing from Latin meaning "rib," used in the formation of compound words: *costotomy.* Also, *esp. before a vowel,* **cost-.** [comb. form repr. L *costa*]

cost′ of liv′ing, the average cost of food, clothing, and other necessities paid by a person, family, etc.

cos·tot·o·my (ko stot′ə mē), *n., pl.* **-mies.** *Surg.* incision of a rib.

cost-plus (kôst′plus′, kost′-), *n.* the cost of production plus an agreed rate of profit.

cost-push (kôst′pŏŏsh′), *adj.* of or denoting the positive rate of change in prices caused by rising costs of material, labor, etc. Cf. **demand-pull.**

cos·trel (kos′trəl, kô′strəl), *n.* a flask of leather, earthenware, or wood, usually with an ear or ears by which to suspend it, as from the waist. [ME < MF *costerel* = *costier* at the side (< VL **costār(ius)*; see COSTA, -ARY) + *-el* dim. suffix]

cos·tume (*n.* kos′to͞om, -tyo͞om; *v.* ko sto͞om′, -styo͞om′), *n., v.,* **-tumed, -tum·ing.** —*n.* **1.** a style of dress, including accessories and hairdos, esp. that typical of a nation, social class, or historical period. **2.** dress or garb of another period, place, etc., esp. as worn on the stage, at balls, etc. **3.** a set of garments, esp. women's garments, selected for wear at a single time; outfit; ensemble. **4.** fashion of dress appropriate to a particular occasion or season: *dancing costume.* —*v.t.* **5.** to furnish with a costume; dress. [< F < It: usage, habit, dress; in origin, doublet of CUSTOM]

cos′tume jew′elry, jewelry made of nonprecious metals, sometimes gold-plated or silver-plated, often set with imitation or semiprecious stones.

cos·tum·er (ko sto͞o′mər, -styo͞o′-), *n.* **1.** a person who makes, sells, or rents costumes, as for theaters, masquerade parties, etc. **2.** *U.S.* a clothes tree.

cos·tum·i·er (ko sto͞o′mē ər, -styo͞o′-; *Fr.* kôs ty myā′), *n., pl.* **cos·tum·i·ers** (ko sto͞o′mē ərz, -styo͞o′-; *Fr.* kôs ty myā′). costumer (def. 1).

co·sy (kō′zē), *adj.,* **-si·er, -si·est,** *n., pl.* **-sies.** cozy. —**co′si·ly,** *adv.* —**co′si·ness,** *n.*

Co·sy·ra (kō sī′rə), *n.* ancient name of **Pantelleria.**

cot[1] (kot), *n.* a light portable bed, esp. one of canvas stretched on a frame. [< AInd < Hindi *khāt* < Prakrit *khaṭṭā;* akin to Tamil *kaṭṭil* bedstead]

cot[2] (kot), *n.* **1.** a small house; cottage; hut. **2.** a small place of shelter or protection. **3.** a sheath or protective covering, as for an injured finger. [ME, OE *cot(e);* c. Icel *kot* hut]

cot, cotangent.

co·tan (kō′tan′), *n.* cotangent.

co·tan·gent (kō tan′jənt, kō′tan′-), *n. Trig.* **1.** (in a right triangle) the ratio of the side adjacent to a given angle to the side opposite. **2.** the tangent of the complement, or the reciprocal of the tangent, of a given angle or arc. *Abbr.:* cot, ctn [< NL *cotangent-* (s. of *cotangēns*)]

B D L C A

Cotangent
ACB being the angle, the ratio of AC to AB, or that of DL to CD, is the cotangent; or, CD being taken as unity, the cotangent is DL

cote[1] (kōt), *n.* **1.** a shelter for sheep, pigs, pigeons, etc. **2.** *Brit. Dial.* a cottage; small house. [var. of COT[2]]

cote[2] (kōt), *v.t.,* **cot·ed, cot·ing.** *Obs.* to pass by; outstrip; surpass. [?]

Côte d'A·zur (kōt da zyr′), French name of the **Riviera.**

Côte d'Or (kōt dôr′), a department in E France. 387,869 (1962); 3393 sq. mi. *Cap.:* Dijon.

co·te·rie (kō′tə rē), *n.* **1.** a group of people who associate closely because of common social purposes, interests, etc. **2.** a clique. [< F, MF: an association of tenant farmers < ML *coter(ius)* COTTER[2] + MF *-ie* -Y[3]]

co·ter·mi·nous (kō tûr′mə nəs), *adj.* conterminous.

coth, hyperbolic cotangent. [COT(ANGENT) + H(YPERBOLIC)]

co·thur·nus (kō thûr′nəs), *n., pl.* **-ni** (-nī) for 2. **1.** the grave and elevated style of ancient tragedy. **2.** buskin (def. 2). Also, **co·thurn** (kō′thûrn, kō thûrn′). [< L < Gk *kóthornos* buskin]

co·tid·al (kō tīd′ᵊl), *adj.* **1.** pertaining to a coincidence of tides. **2.** (on a chart or map) showing or indicating points having a coincidence of tides.

co·til·lion (kō til′yən, kə-), *n.* **1.** any of various dances resembling the quadrille. **2.** a complex, formalized dance for a large number of people, in which a head couple leads the other dancers through elaborate and stately figures. **3.** a formal ball given esp. for debutantes. [< F *cotillon* kind of dance, OF: petticoat = *cote* COAT + *-illon* dim. suffix]

co·til·lon (kə til′yən, kō-; *Fr.* kô tē yôn′), *n., pl.* **-til·lons** (-til′yənz; *Fr.* -tē yôn′). cotillion.

Co·to·nou (kō′tə no͞o′), *n.* a seaport in SE Benin. 109,328 (1964).

Co·to·pax·i (kō′tə pak′sē; *Sp.* kô′tô pä′hē), *n.* a volcano in central Ecuador, in the Andes range: the highest active volcano in the world. 19,498 ft.

cot·quean (kot′kwēn′), *n.* **1.** *Archaic.* a man who busies himself with women's household affairs. **2.** *Obs.* a coarse woman. [COT[2] + QUEAN]

Cots·wold (kots′wōld, -wəld), *n.* one of an English breed of large sheep having coarse, long wool. [after the COTSWOLDS, where the breed originated]

Cots·wolds (kots′wōldz, -wəldz), *n.* (*construed as pl.*) a range of hills in SW England, in Gloucestershire: sheepherding. Also called **Cots′wold Hills′.**

cot·ta (kot′ə, kô′tə), *n. Eccles.* a short surplice, sleeveless or with short sleeves. [< ML, var. of *cota* kind of tunic. See COAT]

cot·tage (kot′ij), *n.* **1.** a small house, usually of only one story. **2.** a small, modest house, as at a resort, used as a vacation home. **3.** one of a group of small, separate houses, as for patients at a hospital or students at a boarding school. [ME *cotage.* See COT[2], -AGE; cf. ML *cotagium,* said to be < AF] —**Syn. 1, 2.** COTTAGE, CABIN, LODGE, HUT, SHACK, SHANTY formerly meant small, simple, often crude dwellings. During recent years the first three words have gained great currency as terms for the often elaborate structures maintained for recreational purposes. HUT, SHACK, and SHANTY, however, still have the former meaning as their most frequent one.

cot′tage cheese′, a loose, white, mild-flavored cheese made from skim-milk curds, usually without rennet.

cot′tage in′dustry, an industry in which the product is made in a self-employed worker's home (in contrast with a factory).

cot′tage pud′ding, a pudding made by covering plain cake with a sweet sauce, often of fruit.

cot·tag·er (kot′i jər), *n.* **1.** a person who lives in a cottage. **2.** Also called **cotter, cottier.** *Brit.* a rural laborer.

cot·ter[1] (kot′ər), *n. Mach.* **1.** a pin, wedge, key, or the like, fitted or driven into an opening to secure something or hold parts together. **2.** See **cotter pin.** [late ME *coter,* akin to *coterel* (late ME *coterell* iron bracket) < ?]

cot·ter[2] (kot′ər), *n.* cottager (def. 2). [ME *cotere*]

cot′ter pin′, *Mach.* a cotter having a split end that is spread after being pushed through a hole to prevent the cotter from working loose. Also called **cot′ter way′.**

Cot′ti·an Alps′ (kot′ē ən), a mountain range in SW Europe, on the boundary between France and Italy: a part of the Alps. Highest peak, Monte Viso, 12,602 ft.

cot·ti·er (kot′ē ər), *n.* **1.** (formerly, in Ireland) a tenant renting land directly from the landowner, the rental price being fixed by public competition. **2.** *Brit.* cottager (def. 2). [ME *cotier* < OF < ML *cotār(ius).* See COTE[1], -ER[2]]

cot·ton (kot′ᵊn), *n.* **1.** a soft, white, downy substance consisting of the hairs or fibers attached to the seeds of malvaceous plants of the genus *Gossypium,* used in making fabrics, thread, wadding, etc. **2.** the plant itself, having an upright manner of growth, spreading branches, and broad, lobed leaves. **3.** such plants collectively as a cultivated crop. **4.** cloth, thread, a garment, etc., of cotton. **5.** any soft, downy substance resembling cotton, but growing on some other plant. —*v.i.* **6.** *Informal.* to get on well together; agree. **7.** *Obs.* to prosper or succeed. **8. cotton to,** *Informal.* **a.** to become fond of; begin to like. **b.** to approve of; agree with:

Cotton boll

to cotton to a suggestion. [ME *coton* < MF < OIt *coton(e)* < Ar *quṭun,* var. of *quṭn*]

Cot·ton (kot′ən), *n.* **John,** 1584–1652, American clergyman and author (grandfather of Cotton Mather).

cot·ton·ade (kot′ənād′), *n.* a heavy, coarse fabric of cotton or mixed fibers, used esp. for work clothes. [< F *cotonnade.* See COTTON, -ADE[1]]

cot′ton belt′, the cotton-growing part of Southern U.S.

cot′ton cake′, a mass of compressed cottonseed after the oil has been extracted: used chiefly to feed cattle.

cot′ton can′dy, a fluffy confection of spun sugar, gathered or wound around a stick or cone-shaped paper holder.

cot′ton flan′nel. See **Canton flannel.**

cot′ton gin′, a machine for separating the fibers of cotton from the seeds.

cot′ton grass′, any rushlike, cyperaceous plant of the genus *Eriophorum,* common in swampy places and bearing spikes resembling tufts of cotton.

cot·ton·mouth (kot′ən mouth′), *n., pl.* **-mouths** (-mouths′, -mouthz′). a venomous snake, *Ancistrodon piscivorous,* of swamps of the southeastern U.S., that grows to a length of about six feet. Also called **water moccasin.** [so called from the whiteness of lips and mouth]

cot·ton·pick·in′ (kot′ən pik′ən), *adj.* *U.S. Slang.* **1.** fit for nothing better than picking cotton; unworthy. **2.** damned; confounded: *Get your cottonpickin′ hands off my book.* Also, **cot·ton·pick·ing** (kot′ən pik′ən, -pik′ing). [alter. of *cotton picking*]

cot·ton·seed (kot′ən sēd′), *n., pl.* **-seeds,** (*esp. collectively*) **-seed.** the seed of the cotton plant, yielding an oil.

cot′tonseed oil′, a brown-yellow, viscid oil with a nutlike odor, obtained from the seed of the cotton plant: used in the manufacture of soaps, hydrogenated fats, lubricants, and cosmetics, as a cooking and salad oil, and in medicine chiefly as a laxative.

cot′ton stain′er, any of several bugs of the genus *Dysdercus,* esp. *D. suturellus,* that feed on cotton, staining the fibers an indelible reddish or yellowish color.

Cot′ton State′, Alabama (used as a nickname).

cot·ton·tail (kot′ən tāl′), *n.* any of several North American rabbits of the genus *Sylvilagus,* having a fluffy white tail.

cot·ton·weed (kot′ən wēd′), *n.* any of certain plants having stems and leaves covered with a soft, hoary pubescence, as those of the composite genus *Gnaphalium* or of various allied genera.

cot·ton·wood (kot′ən wo͝od′), *n.* any of several American poplars, as *Populus deltoides,* having cottonlike tufts on the seeds.

cot′ton wool′, **1.** cotton in its raw state, as on the boll or gathered but unprocessed. **2.** *Brit.* See **absorbent cotton.**

cot·ton·y (kot′ənē), *adj.* **1.** of or like cotton; soft. **2.** covered with a down or nap resembling cotton.

Cot·tus (kot′əs), *n.* *Class. Myth.* one of the Hecatonchires.

cot·y·le·don (kot′əlēd′ən), *n.* *Bot.* the primary or rudimentary leaf of the embryo of seed plants. [< L: navelwort (a plant) < Gk *kotylēdṓn* a plant (prob. navelwort), lit., a cuplike hollow < *kotýlē* cup] —**cot′y·le′don·al, cot·y·le·don·ar·y** (kot′əlēd′ənerē), **cot′y·le′do·noid′, cot′y·le′don·ous,** *adj.*

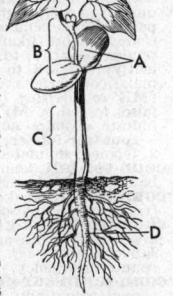

A, Cotyledons of a bean plant; B, Epicotyl; C, Hypocotyl; D, Root

couch (kouch *or, for 3, 9,* ko͞och), *n.* **1.** a piece of furniture for seating usually two to four persons, typically in the form of a bench with a back, sometimes having an armrest at one or each end, and partly or wholly upholstered and often fitted with springs, tailored cushions, skirts, etc.; sofa. **2.** the lair of a wild beast. **3.** *Papermaking.* the board or felt blanket on which wet pulp is laid for drying into paper sheets. —*v.t.* **4.** to put into words; express: *a simple request couched in respectful language.* **5.** to express indirectly or obscurely: *the threat couched under his polite speech.* **6.** to lower or bend down, as the head. **7.** to lower (a spear, lance, etc.) to a horizontal position, as for attack. **8.** to put or lay down, as for rest or sleep; cause to lie down. **9.** *Papermaking.* to transfer (a sheet of pulp) from the wire to the couch. **10.** to embroider by couching. **11.** *Surg.* to remove (a cataract) by inserting a needle and pushing the opaque crystalline lens downward in the vitreous humor below the axis of vision. **12.** *Obs.* to hide; conceal. —*v.i.* **13.** to lie at rest or asleep; repose; recline. **14.** to crouch; bend; stoop. **15.** to lie in ambush or in hiding; lurk. **16.** to lie in a heap for decomposition or fermentation, as leaves. [(n.) ME *couche* < MF, OF < v.; (v.) ME *couche(n)* < MF, OF *couche(r),* OF *colche(r)* < L *collocāre* to put into place. See COL-, LOCATE]

couch·ant (kou′chənt), *adj.* **1.** lying down; crouching. **2.** *Heraldry.* (of an animal) represented as lying on its stomach with its legs pointed forward. [ME < MF, prp. of *coucher* to lay or lie]

couch′ grass′ (kouch, ko͞och), any of various grasses, esp. *Agropyron repens,* known chiefly as troublesome weeds and characterized by creeping rootstocks which spread rapidly. Also called **quitch.** [var. of QUITCH (GRASS)]

couch·ing (kou′ching), *n.* **1.** the act of a person or thing that couches. **2.** a method of embroidering in which heavy threads, laid upon the material, are stitched down at intervals with another thread.

Cou·é (ko͞o ā′), *n.* **É·mile** (ā mēl′), 1857–1926, French psychotherapist.

Cou·é·ism (ko͞o ā′iz əm, ko͞o′ā iz′-), *n.* a method of self-help stressing autosuggestion, popular esp. in the U.S. c1920 and featuring the slogan, "Every day in every way I am getting better and better." [< F *couéisme.* See COUÉ, -ISM]

cou·gar (ko͞o′gər), *n., pl.* **-gars,** (*esp. collectively*) **-gar.** a large, tawny cat, *Felis concolor,* of North and South America. Also called **mountain lion, panther, puma.** [var. of *couguar* < F, alter. of NL *cuguacuara* < Pg < Tupi *çuaçu ara* + Guarani *guaçu ara*]

Cougar (Total length 8 ft.; tail to 3 ft.)

cough (kôf, kof), *v.i.* **1.** to expel air from the lungs suddenly with a harsh noise, often involuntarily. **2.** to make a sound resembling this, as a machine gun firing in spurts. —*v.t.* **3.** to expel by coughing (usually fol. by *up* or *out*): *to cough up a fish bone.* **4. cough up,** *Slang.* to hand over, give, contribute, esp. reluctantly. —*n.* **5.** the act or sound of coughing. **6.** an illness characterized by frequent coughing. **7.** a sound similar to that made by coughing. [ME *cogh(en),* back formation from OE *cohhettan* to cough; akin to D *kuchen* to cough, G *keuchen* to wheeze] —**cough′er,** *n.*

cough′ drop′, a small, medicinal lozenge for relieving a cough, sore throat, etc.

cough′ syr′up, a thick medicated solution, often flavored and usually nonnarcotic, for relieving coughs or soothing irritated throats.

could (ko͝od; *unstressed* kəd), *v.* pt. of **can**[1]. [ME *coude,* OE *cūthe;* modern *-l-* from *would, should*]

could·n′t (ko͝od′ənt), contraction of *could not: We couldn′t get away for the weekend.*

couldst (ko͝odst), *v.* *Archaic.* 2nd pers. sing. of **could.**

cou·lee (ko͞o′lē), *n.* **1.** *Western North America.* a deep ravine or gulch, usually dry, that has been worn away by running water. **2.** a small valley. **3.** a small intermittent stream. **4.** a stream of lava. [< CanF, F: a flowing, n. use of fem. of *coulé,* ptp. of *couler* to flow < L *cōlāre* to filter, strain < *cōlum* strainer, sieve]

cou·lisse (ko͞o lēs′), *n.* a timber or the like having a groove for guiding a sliding panel. [< F: groove, something that slides in a groove; see PORTCULLIS]

cou·loir (ko͞ol wär′; *Fr.* ko͞o lwar′), *n., pl.* **cou·loirs** (ko͞ol-wärz′; *Fr.* ko͞o lwar′). a steep gorge or gully on the side of a mountain. [< F: lit., colander < LL *cōlātōr(ium)* strainer = L *cōlāt(us)* strained (ptp. of *cōlāre;* see COULEE) + *-ōrium* -ORY[2]]

cou·lomb (ko͞o′lom, -lōm, ko͞o lom′), *n.* the meter-kilogram-second unit of electric charge, equal to the quantity of charge transferred in one second by a constant current of one ampere. *Abbr.:* C [named after COULOMB]

Cou·lomb (ko͞o′lom, -lōm, ko͞o lom′; *Fr.* ko͞o lôN′), *n.* **Charles Au·gus·tin de** (sharl ō gy staN′ də), 1736–1806, French physicist and inventor.

coul·ter (kōl′tər), *n.* colter.

cou·ma·rin (ko͞o′mə rin), *n.* *Chem.* a substance, $C_9H_6O_2$, having a vanillalike odor, used chiefly for flavoring and in perfumery. Also, **cumarin.** [< F *coumarine* = *coumar(ou)* tonka-bean tree (< Sp *cumarú* < Pg < Tupi) + *-ine* -IN[2]]

cou·ma·rone (ko͞o′mə rōn′), *n.* *Chem.* a colorless liquid, C_6H_4OCHCH, used chiefly in the synthesis of thermoplastic resins. [COUMAR(IN) + -ONE]

coun·cil (koun′səl), *n.* **1.** an assembly of persons summoned or convened for consultation, deliberation, or advice. **2.** *New Testament.* the Sanhedrin or other authoritative body. **3.** a body of persons specially designated or selected to act in an advisory, administrative, or legislative capacity: *the governor's council on housing.* [ME *co(u)nsile* (< OF *concile* < L *concil(ium)* assembly = *con-* CON- + *-cil-,* var. of *cal-* call + *-ium* n. suffix) + *counseil* < AF < L *consil(ium);* see COUNSEL]

Coun′cil Bluffs′, a city in SW Iowa, across the Missouri River from Omaha, Nebraska. 60,348 (1970).

coun′cil house′, (in Britain) a low-rent house or apartment building constructed to provide housing for low-income families by a local governing authority.

coun·cil·lor (koun′sə lər, -slər), *n.* **1.** councilor. **2.** counselor. —**coun′cil·lor·ship′,** *n.*

coun·cil·man (koun′səl mən), *n., pl.* **-men.** a member of a council, esp. the local legislative body of a city.

coun′cil-man′ag·er plan′ (koun′səl man′ə jər), a system of municipal government in which the administrative powers of the city are entrusted to a manager selected by the city council.

coun′cil of war′, **1.** a conference of high-ranking military officers, usually for discussing major war problems. **2.** any conference for discussing or deciding upon a course of action.

coun·ci·lor (koun′sə lər, -slər), *n.* **1.** a member of a council. **2.** counselor. Also, **councillor.** [COUNCIL + -OR[2]; r. ME *conseiler* < AF: adviser; see COUNSELOR] —**coun′ci·lor·ship′,** *n.*

coun′cil school′, (in Britain) a school provided by public tax moneys, similar to a U.S. public school.

coun·cil·wom·an (koun′səl wo͝om′ən), *n., pl.* **-wom·en.** a female councilman.

coun·sel (koun′səl), *n., v.,* **-seled, -sel·ing** or (*esp. Brit.*) **-selled, -sel·ling.** —*n.* **1.** advice; opinion or instruction given in directing the judgment or conduct of another. **2.** interchange of opinions as to future procedure; consultation; deliberation. **3.** deliberate purpose; plan or design. **4.** (*construed as sing. or pl.*) *Law.* the advocate or advocates engaged in the direction of a cause in court; a legal adviser: *Is counsel for the defense present? Are counsel ready?* **5.** *Archaic.* wisdom; prudence. **6.** *Obs.* a private or secret opinion or purpose. **7. keep one's own counsel,** to conceal one's ideas or opinions; keep silent. —*v.t.* **8.** to give advice to; advise. **9.** to urge the adoption of, as a course of action; recommend (a plan, policy, etc.). —*v.i.* **10.** to give counsel or advice. **11.** to get or take counsel or advice. [ME *counseil* < AF (OF *conseil*) < L *consil(ium)* a taking counsel, consultative body, advice; akin to CONSUL, CONSULT] —**coun′sel·a·ble;** *esp. Brit.,* **coun′sel·la·ble,** *adj.* —**Syn. 1.** recommendation, suggestion, admonition, warning, caution. See **advice. 4.** lawyer, attorney; solicitor, barrister.

coun·se·lor (koun′sə lər), *n.* **1.** a person who counsels; adviser. **2.** a faculty member, as in a high school, who advises students on personal and academic problems. **3.** one of a number of supervisors at a children's camp. **4.** a lawyer, esp. a trial lawyer. **5.** an official of an embassy or legation who ranks below an ambassador or minister. Also, *esp. Brit.*, **coun′sel·lor.** [ME *counseiler* < AF; OF *conseilleor*] —**coun′se·lor·ship′;** *esp. Brit.*, **coun′sel·lor·ship′,** *n.* —**Syn. 4.** counsel, attorney; solicitor, barrister.

coun·se·lor-at-law (koun′sə lər ət lô′), *n., pl.* **coun·se·lors-at-law.** counselor (def. 4).

count[1] (kount), *v.t.* **1.** to check over one by one to determine the total number; enumerate. **2.** to reckon up; calculate; compute. **3.** to list or name the numerals up to: *When angry, count ten.* **4.** to include in a reckoning; take into account: *Count me in if you want to know how many are going.* **5.** to reckon to the credit of another; ascribe; impute. **6.** to consider or regard: *He counted himself lucky to have survived the crash.* —*v.i.* **7.** to count the items of a collection to determine the total. **8.** to list or name numerals in order: *Count up to 100 by fives.* **9.** to have a specified numerical value. **10.** to be worth something: *This book counts as a masterpiece.* **11.** to have merit, value, etc.: *Every bit of help counts.* **12. count down,** to count backward, usually by ones, from a given integer to zero. **13. count off,** (often used imperatively, as in the army) to count aloud by turns, as to arrange positions within a group of persons; divide or become divided into groups: *Close up ranks and count off from the left by threes.* **14. count on** or **upon,** to depend or rely on; trust in: *You can always count on him to lend you money.* **15. count out, a.** *Boxing.* to declare (a boxer) a loser because of inability to stand up before the referee has counted 10 seconds. **b.** to exclude. —*n.* **16.** the act of counting; enumeration. **17.** the number obtained by counting; total. **18.** an accounting. **19.** *Baseball.* the number of balls and strikes, usually designated in that order, that have been called on a batter during his turn at bat: *a count of two balls and one strike.* **20.** *Law.* a distinct charge in a declaration or indictment: *The defendant was found guilty on two of the three counts.* **21.** *Textiles.* **a.** a number representing the size or quality of yarn, esp. the number based on the relation of weight to length of the yarn and indicating its degree of coarseness. **b.** the number of warp and filling threads per inch in woven material, representing the texture of the fabric. **22.** *Physics.* **a.** a single ionizing reaction registered by an ionization chamber, as in a Geiger counter. **b.** the indication of the total number of ionizing reactions registered by an ionization chamber in a given period of time. **23.** *Archaic.* regard; notice. **24. the count,** *Boxing.* the counting aloud of the seconds from 1 to 10 over a downed boxer. Also, **the full count.** —*adj.* **25.** noting a number of items determined by an actual count: *The box is labeled 50 count.* [ME *count(en)* < AF *counte(r)* = MF *conter* < L *computāre* to COMPUTE] —**count′a·ble,** *adj.*

count[2] (kount), *n.* (in some European countries) a nobleman equivalent in rank to an English earl. [< AF *counte* < MF *conte, comte* < L *comitem* (acc. of *comes* companion), lit., he who goes with (someone) = *com-* COM- + *-it(us)*, ptp. of *īre* to go + *-em* acc. ending]

count·down (kount′doun′), *n.* **1.** the backward counting in fixed time units from the initiation of a project, as a rocket launching or the like, with the moment of firing designated as zero. **2.** the final preparations made during this period.

coun·te·nance (koun′tᵊnəns), *n., v.,* **-nanced, -nanc·ing.** —*n.* **1.** appearance, esp. the expression of the face: *a sad countenance.* **2.** the face; visage. **3.** calm facial expression; composure. **4.** approval or favor; encouragement; moral support. **5.** *Obs.* bearing; behavior. —*v.t.* **6.** to permit or tolerate. **7.** to approve, support, or encourage. [ME *contenaunce* behavior, bearing, self-control < AF (OF *contenance*) < L *continentia;* see CONTINENCE] —**coun′te·nanc′er,** *n.* —**Syn. 2.** See **face. 4.** sanction, approbation. **6.** approve.

count·er[1] (koun′tər), *n.* **1.** a table or display case on which goods can be shown, business transacted, etc. **2.** (in restaurants, lunchrooms, etc.) a long, narrow table with stools or chairs along one side for the patrons, behind which refreshments or meals are prepared and served. **3.** a surface for the preparation of food in a kitchen, esp. on a low cabinet. **4.** anything used in keeping account, as a disk of metal or wood, esp. as used in some games, as checkers. **5. over the counter, a.** (of the sale of stock) through a broker's office rather than through the stock exchange. **b.** (of the sale of merchandise) through a retail store rather than through a wholesaler. **6. under the counter,** in a clandestine manner, esp. illegally. [ME *countour* < AF (MF *comptoir*) < ML *computātōr(ium)* place for computing = L *computāt(us)* computed (ptp. of *computāre*) + *-ōrium* -ORY[2]; see COUNT[1], COMPUTE]

count·er[2] (koun′tər), *n.* **1.** a person who counts. **2.** a device for counting revolutions of a wheel, items produced, etc. **3.** *Physics.* an instrument for detecting ionizing radiations and for registering counts. Cf. **Geiger counter.** [ME *countour* < AF (MF *conteor*) < L *computātor*]

coun·ter[3] (koun′tər), *adv.* **1.** in the wrong way; in the reverse direction. **2.** contrary; in opposition. —*adj.* **3.** opposite; opposed; contrary. —*n.* **4.** something that is opposite or contrary to something else. **5.** a blow delivered in receiving or parrying another blow, as in boxing. **6.** *Fencing.* a circular parry. **7.** *Naut.* the part of a stern that overhangs and projects aft of the sternpost of a vessel. **8.** Also called **void.** *Typography.* any part of the face of a type that is less than type-high and is therefore not inked. **9.** a stiffener of leather or other material inserted between the lining and outside leather of a shoe or boot. **10.** the part of a horse's breast that lies between the shoulders and under the neck. —*v.t.* **11.** to meet or answer (a move, blow, etc.) by another in return. **12.** to go counter to; oppose. —*v.i.* **13.** to make a counter or opposing move. **14.** to give a blow while receiving or parrying one, as in boxing. [late ME *countre* < AF (MF *contre*) < L *contrā* against]

coun·ter[4] (koun′tər), *v.t. Obs.* to encounter in opposition or combat. [ME *countre,* aph. var. of *acountre* < MF *acontre* (n.), *acontrer* (v.). See A-[5], ENCOUNTER]

counter-, a combining form of **counter**[3], used with the meanings "against," "contrary," "opposite," "in opposition or response to" (*countermand*); "complementary," "in reciprocation," "corresponding," "parallel" (*counterfoil; counterbalance*); "substitute," "duplicate" (*counterfeit*). [ME *countre-* < AF (MF *contre*) < L *contrā* against]

coun·ter·act (koun′tər akt′), *v.t.* to act in opposition to; frustrate by contrary action. —**coun′ter·ac′tion,** *n.* —**coun′ter·ac′tive,** *adj.* —**Syn.** neutralize, counterbalance.

coun·ter·at·tack (*n.* koun′tər ə tak′; *v.* koun′tər ə tak′), *n.* **1.** an attack made as an offset or reply to another attack. —*v.t., v.i.* **2.** to deliver a counterattack.

coun·ter·bal·ance (*n.* koun′tər bal′əns; *v.* koun′tər bal′əns), *n., v.,* **-anced, -anc·ing.** —*n.* **1.** a weight balancing another weight; a weight or influence equally opposing another; counterpoise. —*v.t., v.i.* **2.** to oppose with an equal weight, force, or influence; offset.

coun·ter·blow (koun′tər blō′), *n.* a blow given in retaliation, as in boxing. Also called **counterpunch.**

coun·ter·change (koun′tər chānj′), *v.t.,* **-changed, -chang·ing. 1.** to cause to change places, qualities, etc.; interchange. **2.** to diversify; checker.

coun·ter·charge (*n.* koun′tər chärj′; *v.* koun′tər chärj′), *n., v.,* **-charged, -charg·ing.** —*n.* **1.** a charge by an accused person against his accuser. **2.** *Mil.* a retaliatory charge. —*v.t.* **3.** to make an accusation against (one's accuser). **4.** *Mil.* to charge in retaliation.

coun·ter·check (*n.* koun′tər chek′; *v.* koun′tər chek′), *n.* **1.** a check that opposes or restrains. **2.** a check controlling or confirming another check. —*v.t.* **3.** to oppose or restrain (a tendency, force, trend, etc.) by contrary action. **4.** to control or confirm by a second check.

coun·ter·claim (*n.* koun′tər klām′; *v.* koun′tər klām′), *n.* **1.** a claim made to offset another claim, esp. in law. —*v.t., v.i.* **2.** to claim so as to offset a previous claim. —**coun′ter·claim′ant,** *n.*

coun·ter·clock·wise (koun′tər klok′wīz′), *adj., adv.* in a direction opposite to that of the normal rotation of the hands of a clock; not clockwise. Also, **contraclockwise.**

coun·ter·cul·ture (koun′tər kul′chər), *n.* the culture of those people, esp. among the young, who reject the traditional values and behavior of society. —**coun′ter·cul′tur·al,** *adj.*

coun·ter·dem·on·stra·tion (koun′tər dem′ən strā′shən), *n.* a demonstration intended to offset the effect of a preceding or concurrent demonstration.

coun·ter·es·pi·o·nage (koun′tər es′pē ə näzh′, -nij), *n.* the detection and frustration of enemy espionage.

coun·ter·feit (koun′tər fit′), *adj.* **1.** made in imitation with intent to deceive; not genuine; forged. **2.** pretended; unreal: *counterfeit grief.* —*n.* **3.** an imitation intended to be passed off as genuine; forgery. **4.** *Archaic.* a copy. **5.** *Archaic.* a close likeness; portrait. **6.** *Obs.* impostor; pretender. —*v.t.* **7.** to make a counterfeit of; imitate fraudulently; forge. **8.** to resemble. **9.** to simulate. —*v.i.* **10.** to make counterfeits, as of money. **11.** to feign; dissemble. [ME *countrefeten* (v.), *countrefet* (adj.), var. of *contrefet* false, forged < MF *contrefait,* ptp. of *contrefaire* to copy, imitate = *contre-* COUNTER- + *faire* to make, do < L *facere*] —**coun′ter·feit′er,** *n.* —**Syn. 1.** spurious, bogus. See **false. 2.** feigned, simulated, fraudulent. **3.** falsification, sham.

coun·ter·foil (koun′tər foil′), *n. Chiefly Brit.* a part of a bank check, etc., that is kept by the issuer as a record.

coun·ter·glow (koun′tər glō′), *n. Astron.* gegenschein. [trans. of G *Gegenschein*]

coun·ter·in·sur·gen·cy (koun′tər in sûr′jən sē), *n.* **1.** a program or an act of combating guerrilla warfare and subversion. —*adj.* **2.** of, pertaining to, or designed for counterinsurgency.

coun·ter·in·sur·gent (koun′tər in sûr′jənt), *n.* **1.** a person who fights or is trained to fight guerrilla forces. —*adj.* **2.** counterinsurgency (def. 2).

coun·ter·in·tel·li·gence (koun′tər in tel′i jəns), *n.* **1.** the activity of an intelligence service employed in thwarting the efforts of an enemy's intelligence agents to gather information or commit sabotage. **2.** an organization engaged in counterintelligence.

coun·ter·ir·ri·tant (koun′tər ir′i tənt), *Med.* —*n.* **1.** an agent for producing irritation in one part to counteract irritation or relieve pain or inflammation elsewhere. —*adj.* **2.** of or acting as a counterirritant.

count·er·man (koun′tər man′), *n., pl.* **-men.** a man who waits on customers from behind a counter, as in a cafeteria or other eating place.

coun·ter·mand (*v.* koun′tər mand′, -mänd′; *n.* koun′tər mand′, -mänd′), *v.t.* **1.** to revoke or cancel (a command, order, etc.). **2.** to recall or stop by a contrary order. —*n.* **3.** a command, order, etc., revoking a previous one. [late ME *countermaund(en)* < MF *contremande(r)* = *contre-* COUNTER- + *mander* to command < L *mandāre;* see MANDATE]

coun·ter·march (*n.* koun′tər märch′; *v.* koun′tər märch′), *n.* **1.** a march back over the same ground. —*v.i.* **2.** to execute a countermarch. —*v.t.* **3.** to cause to countermarch.

coun·ter·meas·ure (koun′tər mezh′ər), *n.* an opposing or retaliatory measure.

coun·ter·mine (*n.* koun′tər mīn′; *v.* koun′tər mīn′), *n., v.,* **-mined, -min·ing.** —*n.* **1.** *Mil.* a mine intended to intercept or destroy an enemy mine. **2.** a counterplot. —*v.t.* **3.** to oppose by a countermine. —*v.i.* **4.** to make a countermine. **5.** *Mil.* to intercept or destroy enemy mines. [late ME]

coun·ter·move (*n.* koun′tər mōōv′; *v.* koun′tər mōōv′), *n., v.,* **-moved, -mov·ing.** —*n.* **1.** an opposing or retaliatory move. —*v.t., v.i.* **2.** to move in opposition or retaliation. —**coun′ter·move′ment,** *n.*

coun·ter·of·fen·sive (koun′tər ə fen′siv), *n. Mil.* an attack by an army against an attacking enemy force.

coun·ter·pane (koun′tər pān′), *n.* a quilt or coverlet for a bed; bedspread. [COUNTER- + PANE (in obs. sense bedspread); r. late ME *counterpoynte* < MF *contre-pointe* quilt, alter. of *coute pointe* < L *culcita puncta* pricked pillow. See QUILT, POINT]

coun·ter·part (koun′tər pärt′), *n.* **1.** a copy or duplicate. **2.** a part that answers to another, as each part of a document executed in duplicate. **3.** one of two parts that fit, complete, or complement each other. **4.** a person or thing closely resembling another. [late ME]

coun·ter·plot (*n., v.* koun′tər plot′; *v. also* koun′tər plot′), *n., v.,* **-plot·ted, -plot·ting.** —*n.* **1.** a plot directed against another plot. **2.** *Literature.* a secondary theme in a play or other literary work. Cf. **subplot.** —*v.i.* **3.** to devise a counterplot; plot in opposition. —*v.t.* **4.** to plot against (a plot or plotter); frustrate by a counterplot.

coun·ter·point (koun′tər point′), *n.* **1.** *Music.* the art of combining melodies. **2.** *Music.* the texture resulting from the combining of individual melodic lines. **3.** a melody composed to be combined with another melody. **4.** Also called **coun′terpoint rhythm′.** *Pros.* syncopation (def. 2). [late ME, appar. trans. of ML (*cantus*) *contrapunctus,* lit., (song) pointed against, the orig. notation of the accompaniment being points set against those of the primary melody]

coun·ter·poise (koun′tər poiz′), *n., v.,* **-poised, -pois·ing.** —*n.* **1.** a counterbalancing weight. **2.** any equal and opposing power or force. **3.** the state of being in equilibrium; balance. —*v.t.* **4.** to balance by an opposing weight. **5.** to counteract or offset by an opposing force. **6.** *Archaic.* to weigh (one thing) against something else; consider carefully. [COUNTER- + POISE¹; r. late ME *countrepeis* < AF, MF *contrepois*]

coun·ter·pro·pos·al (koun′tər prə pō′zəl, -pō′-), *n.* a proposal offered to offset or substitute for a preceding one.

coun·ter·punch (koun′tər punch′), *n.* counterblow.

Coun′ter Reforma′tion, the movement within the Roman Catholic Church that followed the Protestant Reformation of the 16th century.

coun·ter·ref·or·ma·tion (koun′tər ref′ər mā′shən), *n.* a reformation opposed to or counteracting a previous reformation.

coun·ter·rev·o·lu·tion (koun′tər rev′ə lo͞o′shən), *n.* **1.** a revolution against a government recently established by a revolution. **2.** a political movement that resists revolutionary tendencies.

coun·ter·rev·o·lu·tion·ar·y (koun′tər rev′ə lo͞o′shə ner′ē), *n., pl.* **-ar·ies,** *adj.* —*n.* **1.** Also, **coun′ter·rev′o·lu′tion·ist.** a person who advocates or engages in a counterrevolution. —*adj.* **2.** characteristic of or resulting from a counterrevolution. **3.** opposing a revolution or revolutionary government.

coun·ter·ro·tat·ing (koun′tər rō′tā ting, koun′-), *adj.* *Mach.* (of two corresponding or similar moving parts) rotating in opposite directions, as propellers.

coun·ter·scarp (koun′tər skärp′), *n.* *Fort.* **1.** the exterior slope or wall of the ditch of a fort, supporting the covered way. **2.** this slope with the covered way and glacis.

coun·ter·shaft (koun′tər shaft′, -shäft′), *n.* jackshaft (def. 1). —**coun′ter·shaft′ing,** *n.*

coun·ter·sign (*n., v.* koun′tər sīn′; *v. also* koun′tər sīn′), *n.* **1.** *Mil.* a secret sign that must be given in order to pass through a guarded area. **2.** a sign used in reply to another sign. **3.** a signature added to another signature, esp. for authentication. —*v.t.* **4.** to sign (a document that has been signed by someone else), esp. in confirmation or authentication.

coun·ter·sig·na·ture (koun′tər sig′nə chər), *n.* a signature added by way of countersigning.

coun·ter·sink (*v., n.* koun′tər singk′; *v. also* koun′tər singk′), *v.,* **-sank, -sunk, -sink·ing,** *n.* —*v.t.* **1.** to enlarge the upper part of (a hole or cavity) to receive the cone-shaped head of a screw, bolt, etc. **2.** to cause (the head of a screw, bolt, etc.) to sink into a prepared depression so as to be flush with or below the surface. —*n.* **3.** a tool for countersinking a hole. **4.** a countersunk hole.

coun·ter·spy (koun′tər spī′), *n., pl.* **-spies.** a person who spies against or investigates spies of an enemy nation, competing organization, etc.

coun·ter·state·ment (koun′tər stāt′mənt), *n.* a statement made to deny or refute another statement.

coun·ter·ten·or (koun′tər ten′ər), *n.* *Music.* **1.** an adult male voice or voice part higher than that of a tenor. **2.** a singer with such a voice. [ME *cownturtenur,* appar. < AF; cf. MF *contreteneur,* OIt *contratenore*]

coun·ter·thrust (koun′tər thrust′), *n.* a thrust made in opposition or return.

coun·ter·type (koun′tər tīp′), *n.* **1.** a corresponding type. **2.** an opposite type.

coun·ter·vail (koun′tər vāl′), *v.t.* **1.** to oppose with equal power, force, or effect; counteract. **2.** to compensate for; offset. **3.** *Archaic.* to equal. —*v.i.* **4.** to be of equal force in opposition; avail. [ME *contrevail(en)* (v.), late ME *countrevaile* (n.) < AF *countrevail-,* tonic s. (subj.) of *countrevaloir* < L phrase *contrā valēre* to be worth against. See COUNTER-, -VALENT]

coun·ter·weigh (koun′tər wā′), *v.t., v.i.* to counterbalance. [late ME *countreweye(en)*]

coun·ter·weight (koun′tər wāt′), *n.* **1.** a weight that equals or balances another; counterpoise. —*v.t.* **2.** to fit with a counterweight; counterbalance. —**coun′ter·weight′ed,** *adj.*

coun·ter·word (koun′tər wûrd′), *n.* a word used with a meaning much less specific than it had originally, as *swell, awful, terrific.*

coun·ter·work (*n.* koun′tər wûrk′; *v.* koun′tər wûrk′), *n.* **1.** work or action to oppose some other work or action. —*v.i.* **2.** to work in opposition. —*v.t.* **3.** to work in opposition to; hinder or frustrate. —**coun′ter·work′er,** *n.*

count·ess (koun′tis), *n.* **1.** the wife or widow of a count in the nobility of Continental Europe or of an earl in the British peerage. **2.** a woman having the rank of a count or earl in her own right. [ME *c(o)untesse* < AF]

count′ing house′, *Chiefly Brit.* a building or office used by the accounting and bookkeeping department of a business.

count′ing room′, a room used as a counting house.

count·less (kount′lis), *adj.* too numerous to count; innumerable.

count′ noun′, *Gram.* a noun that typically refers to a countable thing and that in English can be used with the indefinite article and in the plural, as *apple, table, birthday.* Cf. **mass noun.**

count′ pal′atine, *pl.* **counts palatine. 1.** (formerly, in Germany) a count having jurisdiction in his fief or province. **2.** *Eng. Hist.* an earl or other county proprietor who exercised royal prerogatives within his county.

coun·tri·fied (kun′tri fīd′), *adj.* rustic or rural in appearance, dress, conduct, etc. Also, **countryfied.**

coun·try (kun′trē), *n., pl.* **-tries,** *adj.* —*n.* **1.** any considerable territory demarcated by specific conditions; region or district: *mountainous country.* **2.** the territory of a nation. **3.** a state. **4.** the people of a district, state, or nation: *The whole country backed the President in his decision.* **5.** the public. **6.** *Law.* the public at large, as represented by a jury. **7.** the land of one's birth or citizenship. **8.** rural districts, as opposed to cities or towns. **9. go to the country,** *Brit.* to dissolve a Parliament that has cast a majority vote disagreeing with the prime minister and cabinet and to call for the election of a new House of Commons. Also, **appeal to the country.** —*adj.* **10.** of the country; rural: *a country road.* **11.** rude; unpolished; rustic: *country manners.* **12.** of a country. **13.** *Dial.* of one's own country. [ME *cuntree* < OF < ML *contrāta,* lit., that which is opposite, hence landscape = L *contr(ā)* against, opposite + *-āta,* fem. of *-ātus* -ATE¹]

coun′try club′, a suburban club with facilities for outdoor sports, social activities, etc.

coun′try cous′in, a person from the country, to whom city life is novel and bewildering.

coun·try-dance (kun′trē dans′, -däns′), *n.* a dance of rural English origin in which the dancers form circles or squares or in which they face each other in two rows.

coun·try·fied (kun′tri fīd′), *adj.* countrified.

coun·try·folk (kun′trē fōk′), *n.* **1.** people living or raised in the country; rustics. **2.** people from the same country; compatriots. Also called **coun·try·peo·ple** (kun′trē pē′pəl).

coun′try gen′tleman, a wealthy man living in his country home or estate.

coun′try house′, a house, usually large and impressive, on an estate in the country.

coun·try·man (kun′trē mən), *n., pl.* **-men. 1.** a native or inhabitant of one's own country. **2.** a native or inhabitant of a particular country. **3.** a person who lives in a rural area. [ME *contre man*] —**Syn. 1.** compatriot, fellow citizen. —**Ant. 1.** foreigner.

coun·try·seat (kun′trē sēt′), *n.* *Brit.* a country mansion or estate.

coun·try·side (kun′trē sīd′), *n.* **1.** a rural section. **2.** its inhabitants.

coun·try·wom·an (kun′trē wo͝om′ən), *n., pl.* **-wom·en.** a woman who is a native or inhabitant of one's own country. [late ME]

coun·ty¹ (koun′tē), *n., pl.* **-ties. 1.** the largest administrative division of a U.S. state. **2.** one of the chief territorial administrative divisions in Great Britain, Ireland, Canada, and New Zealand. **3.** the inhabitants of a county. **4.** *Obs.* the domain of a count or earl. [ME *counte* < AF (MF *comte*) < L *comitāt(us)* retinue, in LL: office of a count > jurisdiction, territory = *comitāt-* (ptp. s. of *comitārī* to go with < *comes* companion) + *-us* n. suffix (4th decl.)]

coun·ty² (koun′tē), *n.* *Obs.* count². [< AF *counte* COUNT²; -*y,* by confusion with COUNTY¹]

coun′ty a′gent, *U.S.* a governmental official employed chiefly to advise farmers on farming and marketing techniques. Also called **agricultural agent.**

coun′ty clerk′, *U.S.* an elective county official in most states who generally keeps records of property titles, distributes ballots, issues licenses, etc.

coun′ty col′lege, (in England) a part-time continuation school with compulsory attendance for boys and girls from 15 to 18 years of age, created under the Education Act (1944).

coun′ty court′, **1.** *U.S.* **a.** an administrative board in counties in some states. **b.** a judicial tribunal in some states with jurisdiction extending over one or more counties. **2.** (in England) the lowest civil tribunal, having limited jurisdiction, mostly for the recovery of small debts.

coun′ty fair′, a competitive exhibition of farm products, livestock, etc., often held annually in the same place in the county.

coun′ty pal′atine, *pl.* **counties palatine.** the territory of a count palatine.

coun′ty seat′, the seat of government of a county. Also called, *esp. Brit.,* **coun′ty town′.**

coup (ko͞o), *n., pl.* **coups** (ko͞oz; *Fr.* ko͞o). **1.** a highly successful stroke, act, or move; a clever action or accomplishment. **2.** See **coup d'état.** [< F: lit., blow, stroke, OF *colp* < LL *colpus,* L *colaphus* < Gk *kólaphos*]

coup de grâce (ko͞od^ə gräs′), *pl.* **coups de grâce** (ko͞od^ə gräs′). *French.* **1.** a death blow, esp. one delivered mercifully to end suffering. **2.** any finishing or decisive stroke. [lit., blow of mercy]

coup de main (ko͞od^ə man′), *pl.* **coups de main** (ko͞od^ə man′). *French.* a surprise attack; a sudden development. [lit., blow from the hand]

coup d'é·tat (ko͞o′ dā tä′; *Fr.* ko͞o dā ta′), *pl.* **coups d'é·tat** (ko͞oz′ dā tä′; *Fr.* ko͞o dā ta′). a sudden and decisive action in politics, esp. one effecting a change of government illegally or by force. [< F: lit., stroke concerning the state]

coup de thé·â·tre (ko͞od^ə tā ä′tr^ə), *pl.* **coups de thé·â·tre** (ko͞od^ə tā ä′tr^ə). *French.* **1.** a surprising or unexpected turn of events in a play. **2.** any theatrical trick intended to have a sensational effect. [lit., stroke concerning the theater]

coup d'oeil (ko͞o dœ′y^ə), *pl.* **coups d'oeil** (ko͞o dœ′y^ə). *French.* a quick glance. [lit., stroke of the eye]

coupe (ko͞op), *n.* **1.** Also, **coupé.** a closed, two-door automobile with a body shorter than that of a sedan of the same model. **2.** coupé (defs. 1, 2).

cou·pé (ko͞o pā′ *or, for 1, 3,* ko͞op), *n.* **1.** a short, four-wheeled, closed carriage, usually with a single seat for two passengers and with an outside seat for the driver. **2.** the end compartment in a European diligence or railroad car. **3.** coupe (def. 1). Also, **coupe** (for defs. 1, 2). [< F, short for *carrosse coupé* cut (i.e., shortened) coach; see COUPED]

Cou·pe·rin (ko͞op^ə ran′), *n.* **Fran·çois** (fräN swa′), 1668–1733, French organist and composer.

cou·ple (kup′əl), *n., v.,* **-pled, -pling.** —*n.* **1.** a combination of two of a kind; pair. **2.** a man and woman considered together, as a married pair, lovers, etc. **3.** any two persons considered together. **4.** *Mech.* a pair of equal, parallel forces acting in opposite directions and tending to produce rotation. **5.** a leash for holding two hounds together. **6. a couple of,** *Informal.* a small number of; a few. —*v.t.* **7.** to fasten, link, or associate together in a pair or pairs. **8.** to join; connect. **9.** to unite in marriage or in sexual union. **10.** *Radio.* to join or associate by means of a coupler. —*v.i.* **11.** to join in a pair; unite. **12.** to copulate. [ME < MF < L *copula* a tie, bond. See COPULA] —**Syn. 1.** See **pair.**

cou·ple·ment (kup′əl mənt), *n.* *Obs.* the act or result of coupling; union. [< MF]

cou·pler (kup′lər), *n.* **1.** a person or thing that couples or links together. **2.** a connecting device in an organ or harpsichord by which keys, manuals, or a manual and pedals, are played together. **3.** *Radio.* a device for transferring electrical energy from one circuit to another, as a transformer that joins parts of a radio apparatus together by induction. **4.** *Mach.* a rod or link transmitting force and motion between a rotating part and a rotating or oscillating part. **5.** Also called **coupling.** *Railroads.* a device for joining pieces of rolling stock.

cou·plet (kup′lit), *n.* **1.** a pair of successive lines of verse, esp. a pair that rhyme and are of the same length. **2.** a pair; couple. **3.** *Music.* any of the contrasting sections of a rondo occurring between statements of the refrain. [< MF]

cou·pling (kup′ling), *n.* **1.** the act of linking, joining, or coming together. **2.** *Mach.* a device for joining two rotating shafts semipermanently at their ends so as to transmit torque from one to the other. Cf. **clutch**[1] (def. 10a). **3.** *Railroads.* coupler (def. 5). **4.** *Elect.* **a.** the association of two circuits permitting transfer of power from one to the other. **b.** a device or expedient to insure this. **5.** the part of the body between the tops of the shoulder blades and the tops of the hip joints in a dog, horse, etc. [ME]

cou·pon (ko͞o′pon, kyo͞o′-), *n.* **1.** a detachable portion of a certificate, ticket, or the like, entitling the holder to a gift or discount, or for use as an order blank, a contest entry form, etc. **2.** a separate certificate, ticket, etc., for the same purpose. **3.** one of a number of small certificates calling for periodical interest payments on a bond. [< F, OF *colpon* piece cut off = *colp(er)* (to) cut (see COPE[1]) + *-on* n. suffix]

cour·age (kûr′ij, kur′-), *n.* **1.** the quality of mind or spirit that enables a person to face difficulty, danger, pain, etc., with firmness and without fear; bravery. **2. have the courage of one's convictions,** to act in accordance with one's beliefs, esp. in spite of criticism. [ME *corage* < OF = *cuer* heart (< L *cor*) + *-age* -AGE]
—**Syn. 1.** fearlessness, dauntlessness, intrepidity, fortitude, pluck, spirit. COURAGE, BRAVERY, VALOR, BRAVADO refer to qualities of spirit and conduct. COURAGE permits a person to face extreme dangers and difficulties without fear: *to take (or lose) courage.* BRAVERY implies true courage together with daring and an intrepid boldness: *bravery in a battle.* VALOR implies continuous, active bravery in the face of personal danger, and a noble and lofty quality of courage: *valor throughout a campaign; valor in fighting for the right.* BRAVADO is now usually a boastful and ostentatious pretense of courage or bravery: *empty bravado.* —**Ant. 1.** cowardice.

cou·ra·geous (kə rā′jəs), *adj.* possessing or characterized by courage; brave or valiant. [ME *corageous* < OF *corageus*] —**cou·ra′geous·ly,** *adv.* —**cou·ra′geous·ness,** *n.* —**Syn.** See **brave.**

cou·rant (ko͝o ränt′; *Fr.* ko͞o RÄN′), *n., pl.* **-rants** (-ränts′; *Fr.* -RÄN′). courante. [< F: lit., running, masc. prp. of *courir* to run]

cou·rante (ko͝o ränt′; *Fr.* ko͞o RÄNT′), *n., pl.* **-rantes** (-ränts′; *Fr.* -RÄNT′). **1.** a 17th-century dance characterized by a running or gliding step. **2.** *Music.* a movement following the allemande in the classical suite. [< MF: lit., running, fem. prp. of *courir* to run]

Cour·bet (ko͞oR be′), *n.* **Gus·tave** (GY STAV′), 1819–77, French painter.

Cour·be·voie (ko͞oR bə VWA′), *n.* a city in N France, WNW of Paris. 59,941 (1962).

cou·ri·er (kûr′ē ər, ko͝or′-), *n.* **1.** a messenger, usually traveling in haste, bearing diplomatic messages, important reports, etc. **2.** *Chiefly Brit.* a person hired by travelers to take charge of the arrangements of a journey. [< MF *cour(r)ier* < It *corrier(e)* = *corr(ere)* (to) run (< L *currere*) + *-iere* -ER[2]; r. ME *corour* < OF *coreor*]

cour·lan (ko͝or′lən), *n.* the limpkin. [< F < Carib; akin to Carib *kurliri* (Galibi dial.)]

Cour·land (ko͝or′lənd), *n.* a former duchy on the Baltic: later, a province of Russia and, in 1918, incorporated into Latvia. Also, **Kurland.**

course (kōrs, kôrs), *n., v.,* **coursed, cours·ing.** —*n.* **1.** advance or progression in a particular direction; onward movement. **2.** a direction or route taken or to be taken. **3.** the path, route, or channel along which anything moves: *the course of a stream.* **4.** the ground, water, etc., on which a race is run, sailed, etc. **5.** the continuous passage through time or a succession of stages: *in the course of a year.* **6.** a customary manner of procedure; regular or natural order of events: *as a matter of course.* **7.** a mode of conduct; behavior. **8.** a particular manner of proceeding: *Try another course of action.* **9.** a systematized or prescribed series: *a course of lectures.* **10.** a program of instruction, as in a college or university. **11.** a prescribed number of classes in a particular field of study. **12.** a part of a meal served at one time: *The main course was steak.* **13.** *Navig.* the line along the earth's surface upon or over which a vessel, an aircraft, etc., proceeds. **14.** *Naut.* the lowermost sail on a fully square-rigged mast: designated by a special name, as foresail or mainsail, or by the designation of the mast itself, as forecourse or main course. **15.** *Building Trades.* a continuous and usually horizontal range of bricks, stones, clapboards, shingles, etc., as in a wall or roof. **16.** *Knitting.* the row of stitches going across from side to side (opposed to *wale*). **17.** Often, **courses.** the menses. **18.** a charge by knights in a tournament. **19.** a pursuit of game with dogs by sight rather than by scent. **20.** See **golf course.** **21.** *Archaic.* a race. **22. in due course,** in the proper or natural order of events; eventually. **23. of course, a.** certainly; definitely. **b.** in the usual or natural order of things. —*v.t.* **24.** to run through or over. **25.** to chase; pursue. **26.** to hunt (game) with dogs by sight rather than by scent. **27.** to cause (dogs) to pursue game by sight. **28.** *Masonry.* to lay (bricks, stones, etc.) in courses. —*v.i.* **29.** to follow a course; direct one's course. **30.** to run, race, or move swiftly. **31.** to take part in a hunt with hounds, a tilting match, etc. [ME *co(u)rs* < OF < L *curs(us)* a running, course, n. use of ptp. of *currere* to run] —**Syn. 1, 13.** bearing. **3.** way, road, track, passage. **6.** process, career. **8.** method, mode.

cours·er[1] (kōr′sər, kôr′-), *n.* **1.** a person who courses. **2.** a dog for coursing. [COURSE + -ER[1]]

cours·er[2] (kōr′sər, kôr′-), *n.* *Literary.* a swift horse. [ME < OF *coursier*]

cours·er[3] (kōr′sər, kôr′-), *n.* any of several swift-footed, ploverlike birds of the genera *Cursorius* and *Pluvianus,* chiefly of the desert regions of Asia and Africa. [irreg. < L *cursōr(ius)* fitted for running]

course·ware (kōrs′wâr′), *n.* *Computer Technol.* educational software designed esp. for use with classroom computers.

cours·ing (kōr′sing, kôr′-), *n.* **1.** the act of a person or thing that courses. **2.** the sport of pursuing game with dogs that follow by sight rather than by scent.

court (kōrt, kôrt), *n.* **1.** an open area mostly or entirely surrounded by buildings, walls, etc. **2.** a high interior usually having a glass roof and surrounded by several stories of galleries or the like. **3.** a short street. **4.** a smooth, level quadrangle on which to play tennis, handball, basketball, etc. **5.** one of the divisions of such an area. **6.** the residence of a sovereign; palace. **7.** a sovereign with his councilors and retinue. **8.** a formal assembly held by a sovereign. **9.** homage paid, as to a king. **10.** special or devoted attention in order to win favor, affection, etc.: *to pay court to a pretty woman.* **11.** *Law.* **a.** a place where justice is administered. **b.** a judicial tribunal duly constituted for the hearing and determination of cases. **c.** a session of a judicial assembly. **12.** a branch or lodge of a fraternal society. **13. out of court,** without a hearing; privately: *The case will be settled out of court.* —*v.t.* **14.** to try to win the favor of. **15.** to seek the affections of; woo. **16.** to attempt to gain (applause, favor, etc.). **17.** to hold out inducements to; invite. **18.** to act in such a manner as to cause, lead to, or provoke: *to court disaster by reckless driving.* —*v.i.* **19.** to seek another's love; woo. [ME *co(u)rt* < OF < L *cohort-* (s. of *cohors*) courtyard; see COHORT]

court-bar·on (kōrt′bar′ən, kôrt′-), *n.* *Old Eng. Law.* a court presided over by the lord of a manor or his steward, for the redress of misdemeanors within the manor and the adjudication of disputes between tenants.

court′ card′, *Brit.* See **face card.**

cour·te·ous (kûr′tē əs), *adj.* having or showing good manners; polite. [COURT + -EOUS; r. ME *co(u)rteis* < AF; see -ESE] —**cour′te·ous·ly,** *adv.* —**cour′te·ous·ness,** *n.* —**Syn.** gracious, courtly. See **civil.** —**Ant.** rude.

cour·te·san (kōr′ti zən, kôr′-, kûr′-), *n.* a prostitute or paramour, esp. one associating with noblemen or men of wealth. Also, **cour′te·zan.** [< MF *courtisane* < It *cortigiana* = *cort(e)* COURT + *-igiana* (*-igi-* -ESE + *-ana,* fem. of *-ano* -AN)]

cour·te·sy (kûr′ti sē *or, for 5,* kûrt′sē), *n., pl.* **-sies. 1.** excellence of manners or social conduct; polite behavior. **2.** a courteous, respectful, or considerate act or expression. **3.** indulgence, consent, or acquiescence: *a "colonel" by courtesy rather than by right.* **4.** favor, help, or generosity: *The costumes for the play were by courtesy of the museum.* **5.** a curtsy. [ME *curteisie*] —**Syn. 1.** courteousness, civility.

cour′tesy card′, a card identifying the bearer and making him eligible for special consideration, as at a club, hotel, or bank.

cour′tesy ti′tle, *Brit.* a title allowed by custom, as to the children of dukes.

court′ hand′, a style of handwriting formerly used in the English law courts.

court·house (kōrt′hous′, kôrt′-), *n., pl.* **-hous·es** (-hou′ziz). **1.** a building in which courts of law are held. **2.** *U.S.* a county seat. [late ME]

cour·ti·er (kōr′tē ər, kôr′-), *n.* **1.** a person in attendance at a royal court. **2.** a person who seeks favor by flattery. [< MF; OF *cortei(er)* (to) be at court + *-ier* -ER[2]; r. ME *courteour* < AF]

court·ly (kōrt′lē, kôrt′-), *adj.,* **-li·er, -li·est,** *adv.* —*adj.* **1.** polite, refined, or elegant. **2.** flattering or obsequious. **3.** pertaining to or suitable for the court of a sovereign. —*adv.* **4.** in a courtly manner; politely or flatteringly. [late ME] —**court′li·ness,** *n.*

court′ly love′, a highly stylized medieval code of behavior that prescribed the rules of conduct between lovers, advocating idealized but illicit love.

court-mar·tial (kōrt′mär′shəl, -mär′-, kôrt′-), *n., pl.* **courts-mar·tial, court-mar·tials,** *v.,* **-tialed, -tial·ing** or (*esp. Brit.*) **-tialled, -tial·ling.** —*n.* **1.** a court consisting of military personnel appointed to try offenses by members of the armed forces against military law. **2.** a trial by such a court. **3.** a conviction by such a court. —*v.t.* **4.** to arraign and try by courtmartial. [alter. of phrase *martial court*]

court′ of appeals′, *Law.* **1.** (in the federal court system and some state court systems) an appellate court intermediate between the trial courts and the court of last resort. **2.** the highest appellate court of New York State. **3.** Also, **Court′ of Appeal′.** *Brit.* See under **Supreme Court of Judicature.** Also, **Court′ of Appeals′** (for defs. 1, 2).

court′ of chan′cery, *Law.* chancery (def. 4a).

court′ of com′mon pleas′, *Law.* **1.** (formerly in England) a court to hear civil cases between common citizens. **2.** *U.S.* (in some states) a court with general civil jurisdiction. Also, **Court′ of Com′mon Pleas′.**

Court′ of Exchequ′er, exchequer (def. 2b).

court′ of rec′ord, a court whose judgments and proceedings are kept on permanent record and that has the power to impose penalties for contempt.

Court of St. James's, the British royal court. Also, **Court of St. James.**

court′ plas′ter, cotton or other fabric coated on one side with an adhesive preparation, as of isinglass and glycerin, used on the skin for medical and cosmetic purposes. [so called because used in courtly circles for making beauty spots]

Cour·trai (*Fr.* ko͞oR TRE′), *n.* a city in W Belgium, on the Lys River. 44,814 (est. 1964). Flemish, **Kortrijk.**

court·room (kōrt′ro͞om′, -ro͝om′, kôrt′-), *n.* a room in which the sessions of a law court are held.

court·ship (kōrt′ship, kôrt′-), *n.* **1.** the wooing of a woman by a man. **2.** the period during which such wooing takes place. **3.** solicitation of favors, applause, etc. **4.** *Obs.* courtly behavior; courtesy; gallantry.

court′ ten′nis, a variety of tennis played indoors on a specially constructed court having high cement walls off which the ball may be played, points being made chiefly by stroking the ball into any of three openings in the walls of the court.

court·yard (kōrt′yärd′, kôrt′-), *n.* a court open to the sky, esp. one enclosed on all sides.

cous·in (kuz′ən), *n.* **1.** Also called **first cousin, cousin-german.** the child of an uncle or aunt. **2.** a person related by descent in a diverging line from a known common ancestor. **3.** a kinsman or kinswoman. **4.** a person or thing related to another by similar natures, languages, geographical proximity, etc.: *our Canadian cousins.* **5.** a term of address used by a sovereign to another sovereign or to a high-ranking noble. [ME *cosin* < OF < L *consōbrīn(us)* = *con-* CON- + *sōbrīnus,* contr. of **sorōrīnus* cousin on the mother's side (*soror* sister + *-īnus* -INE[1])] —**cous′in·ly,** *adj.*

Cou·sin (ko͞o zaN′), *n.* **Vic·tor** (vēk tôR′), 1792–1867, French philosopher and educational reformer.

cous·in-ger·man (kuz′ən jûr′mən), *n., pl.* **cous·ins-ger·man.** cousin (def. 1).

cous·in·ry (kuz′ən rē), *n., pl.* **-ries.** cousins or relatives collectively.

Cous·teau (ko͞o stō′), *n.* **Jacques Yves** (zhäk ēv), born 1910, French naval officer and underseas explorer: developed the aqualung.

cou·teau (ko͞o tō′), *n., pl.* **-teaux** (-tōz′; *Fr.* -tō′). a knife, esp. a large double-edged one formerly carried as a weapon. [< F; OF *coutel* < L *cultell(us)* = *cult(er)* knife + *-ellus* dim. suffix]

cou·ter (ko͞o′tər), *n.* *Armor.* a piece of plate armor for the elbow. [ME < AF = **coute* (c. OF *coute* elbow < L *cubit(um)* n. use of neut. of ptp. of *cubāre* to lie down) + *-er* -ER[2]]

couth (ko͞oth), *adj.* **1.** *Facetious.* showing distinction or sophistication; smooth. **2.** *Archaic.* known or acquainted with. [(def. 1) back formation from UNCOUTH; (def. 2) ME; OE *cūth* known, ptp. of *cunnan* to know (see CAN[1])]

couth·ie (ko͞o′thē), *adj.* *Scot.* agreeable; genial; kindly. [*couth* (OE *cūth* known, friendly, ptp. of *cunnan* to know; see CAN[1]) + *-ie,* Scot var. of -Y[1]]

cou·ture (ko͞o to͝or′; *Fr.* ko͞o TYR′), *n.* **1.** the occupation of a couturier; dressmaking and designing. **2.** fashion designers or couturiers collectively. [< F: lit., sewing, seam]

cou·tu·ri·er (ko͞o to͝or′ē ā′, -ē ər, -to͝or′yā; *Fr.* ko͞o TY-RYĀ′), *n., pl.* **-tu·riers** (-to͝or′ē āz′, -ē ərz, -to͝or′yāz; *Fr.* -TY RYĀ′). a person who designs, makes, and sells fashionable clothes for women. [< F: lit., one who sews]

cou·tu·ri·ère (ko͞o to͝or′ē ər, -ē er′; *Fr.* ko͞o TY RYER′), *n., pl.* **-tu·ri·ères** (-to͝or′ē ərz, -ē erz′; *Fr.* -TY RYER′). a female couturier. Also, **cou·tu·ri·ere** (ko͞o to͝or′ē ər, -ē er′). [< F]

cou·vade (ko͞o väd′; *Fr.* ko͞o VAD′), *n.* a practice among some primitive peoples in which a man, immediately preceding the birth of his child, ritualistically imitates the pregnancy and delivery of the mother. [< F (now obs.), lit., a hatching, sitting on eggs = *couv(er)* (to) hatch (< L *cubāre* to lie down) + *-ade* -ADE[1]]

co·va·lence (kō vā′ləns), *n.* *Chem.* **1.** the number of electron pairs that an atom can share with other atoms. **2.** Also called **cova′lent bond′.** the bond formed by the sharing of a pair of electrons by two atoms. —**co·va′lent,** *adj.*

Co·var·ru·bias (kō′və ro͞o′bē əs; *Sp.* kô′väR Ro͞o′byäs), *n.* **Mi·guel** (mē gel′), 1904–57, Mexican caricaturist, illustrator, and painter.

cove[1] (kōv), *n., v.,* **coved, cov·ing.** —*n.* **1.** a small indentation or recess in the shoreline of a sea, lake, or river. **2.** a sheltered nook. **3.** a hollow or recess in a mountain; cave; cavern. **4.** a narrow pass between woods or hills. **5.** a sheltered area, usually prairie, between woods or hills. **6.** *Archit.* **a.** a concave surface or molding. **b.** a concave surface forming part of a ceiling at its edge so as to eliminate the usual interior angle between the wall and ceiling. —*v.t., v.i.* **7.** to make or become a cove. [ME; OE *cofa* cave, den, closet; c. Icel *kofi* hut, Gk *gýpē* cave]

cove[2] (kōv), *n.* **1.** *Brit. Slang.* a person; fellow. **2.** *Australian Slang.* a boss or manager, esp. a manager of a sheep station. [? < Romany *kova* creature]

cov·en (kuv′ən, kō′vən), *n.* an assembly of witches, esp. a group numbering 13. [ME *covin* band]

cov·e·nant (kuv′ə nənt), *n.* **1.** an agreement, usually formal, between two or more persons to do or not do something specified. **2.** *Law.* an incidental clause in such an agreement. **3.** the conditional promises made to man by God, as revealed in the Scripture. **4.** *Law.* **a.** a formal agreement of legal validity, esp. one under seal. **b.** an early English form of action in suits involving sealed contracts. —*v.i.* **5.** to enter into a covenant. —*v.t.* **6.** to agree to by covenant; pledge. **7.** to stipulate. [ME < OF, n. use of prp. of *covenir* < L *convenīre* to come together, agree; see -ANT] —**cov·e·nan·tal** (kuv′ə nan′tᵊl), *adj.* —**Syn. 1.** treaty, pact, convention, compact.

cov·e·nan·tee (kuv′ə nən tē′, -nan-), *n.* a person to whom something is promised in a covenant.

cov·e·nant·er (kuv′ə nən tər; *for 2 also Scot.* kuv′ə-nan′tər), *n.* **1.** a person who makes a covenant. **2.** (*cap.*) *Scot. Hist.* an adherent of the National Covenant, an agreement (1638) among Scottish Presbyterians to uphold their faith.

cov·e·nan·tor (kuv′ə nən tər), *n.* *Law.* the party who is to perform the obligation expressed in a covenant.

Cov′ent Gar′den (kuv′ənt, kov′-), **1.** a district in central London, England: vegetable and flower market. **2.** a theater in this district, first built 1731–32, important in English theatrical history.

Cov·en·try (kuv′ən trē, kov′-), *n.* a city in NE Warwickshire, in central England: heavily bombed 1940. 305,060 (1961). **2. send to Coventry,** to refuse to associate with: *His friends sent him to Coventry after he was court-marshaled.*

cov·er (kuv′ər), *v.t.* **1.** to place something over or upon, as for protection or concealment. **2.** to be or serve as a covering for; extend over: *Snow covered the fields.* **3.** to provide with a covering: *Cover the pot with a lid.* **4.** to protect or conceal (the body, head, etc.) with clothes, a hat, etc. **5.** to bring upon (oneself): *He covered himself with honors at college.* **6.** to shelter; protect; serve as a defense to. **7.** *Mil.* **a.** to be in line with by occupying a position directly before or behind. **b.** to protect (a soldier, force, or military position) by taking a position from which any hostile troops can be fired upon. **8.** to take charge of or responsibility for. **9.** to hide from view; screen. **10.** to spread with; put over the surface of: *to cover bread with honey.* **11.** to aim at, as with a pistol. **12.** to have within range, as a fortress does adjacent territory. **13.** to include, deal with, or provide for: *The book covers the subject well.* **14.** to suffice to defray or meet (a charge, expense, etc.). **15.** to offset (an outlay, loss, liability, etc.). **16.** *Insurance.* to insure against risk or loss. **17.** to deposit the equivalent of (money deposited), as in wagering. **18.** to accept the conditions of (a bet, wager, etc.). **19.** *Journalism.* **a.** to gather news of: *She covers Wall Street.* **b.** to publish or broadcast a report or reports of: *The press covered the entire campaign.* **20.** to pass or travel over: *We covered 600 miles a day on our trip.* **21.** *Baseball.* to take a position close to or at (a base) so as to catch a ball thrown to the base. **22.** *Sports.* to guard (an opponent on offense). **23.** (of a male animal) to copulate with. **24.** (of a hen) to brood or sit on (eggs or chicks). **25.** to play a card higher than (the one previously played). —*v.i.* *Informal.* **26.** to serve as a substitute for someone who is absent. **27.** to play a card higher than one previously played in the round. **28.** to hide the wrongful or embarrassing action of another by providing an alibi or acting in the other's place: *They covered for him when he missed roll call.* **29. cover up, a.** to cover completely; enfold. **b.** to keep secret; conceal: *She tried to cover up her lack of knowledge.* —*n.* **30.** something that covers, as the lid of a vessel or the binding of a book. **31.** protection, shelter, or concealment. **32.** a pretense; feigning. **33.** woods, underbrush, etc., serving to shelter and conceal wild animals or game; a covert. **34.** anything that veils or shuts from sight: *under cover of darkness.* **35.** a set of eating utensils, as plate, knife, fork, napkin, etc., for one person. **36.** See **cover charge. 37.** *Philately.* **a.** an envelope or outer wrapping for mail. **b.** a letter folded so that the address may be placed on the outside. **38. break cover,** to emerge, esp. suddenly, from a place of concealment: *The fox broke cover and the chase was on.* **39. take cover,** to seek shelter or safety. **40. under cover, a.** under a pretense; secretly. **b.** within an envelope. [ME *cover(en)* < OF *covr(ir)* < L *cooperīre* to cover up = *co-* CO- + *operīre* to cover over (*o-* (var. of *ob-* OB-) + *-perīre* to cover); cf. *aperīre* to uncover] —**cov′er·a·ble,** *adj.* —**cov′er·er,** *n.* —**cov′er·less,** *adj.*
—**Syn. 1.** overlay, overspread, envelop. **9.** cloak, conceal. **15.** counterbalance.

cov·er·age (kuv′ər ij), *n.* **1.** *Insurance.* protection provided by a policy against risks or a risk. **2.** *Finance.* the value of funds held to back up or meet liabilities. **3.** the extent to which something is covered. **4.** the area or the number of persons reached by a communications medium. **5.** *Journalism.* the reporting and subsequent publishing or broadcasting of news.

cov·er·all (kuv′ər ôl′), *n.* Often, **coveralls.** a one-piece work garment, worn to protect other clothing.

cov′er charge′, a fee charged by a restaurant, night club, etc., for entertainment or service. Also called **cover.**

cov′er crop′, a crop, preferably leguminous, planted to keep nutrients from leaching and soil from eroding, as during the winter.

Cov·er·dale (kuv′ər dāl′), *n.* **Miles,** 1488–1569, English divine: translator of the Bible into English 1535.

cov′ered wag′on, 1. *U.S.* a large wagon with a high, bonnetlike canvas top, esp. such a wagon used by the pioneers during the westward migrations in the 19th century. **2.** *Railroads Brit.* a boxcar.

cov′er girl′, an attractive girl whose picture is featured on a magazine cover.

cov·er·let (kuv′ər lit), *n.* **1.** the top covering of a bed; bedspread. **2.** any covering or cover. Also, **cov·er·lid** (kuv′ər-lid). [ME *coverlite* < AF *cuver-lit* bedspread = *cuver* to COVER + *lit* bed < L *lect(us)*]

cov′er plate′, *Building Trades.* a reinforcing plate attached to the outer surface of a flange of a metal beam.

cov′er point′, *Cricket, Lacrosse.* the position and the player stationed near the point.

cov·ert (kuv′ərt, kō′vərt), *adj.* **1.** covered; sheltered. **2.** concealed or secret. **3.** *Law.* (of a woman) under protection of her husband. —*n.* **4.** a covering or cover. **5.** a shelter or hiding place. **6.** concealment or disguise. **7.** *Hunting.* a thicket giving shelter to wild animals or game. **8.** Also called **tectrix.** *Ornith.* one of the small feathers that cover the bases of the large feathers of the wings and tail. See diag. under **bird. 9.** See **covert cloth.** [ME < OF < L *cooper-t(us),* ptp. of *cooperīre* to COVER] —**cov′ert·ly,** *adv.* —**cov′ert·ness,** *n.* —**Syn. 2.** clandestine, surreptitious, furtive.

cov′ert cloth′ (kuv′ərt, kō′vərt), a cotton, woolen, or worsted cloth of twill weave, the warp being of ply yarns one of which may be white. Also called **covert.**

cov·er·ture (kuv′ər chər), *n.* **1.** a cover or covering; shelter; concealment. **2.** *Law.* the status of a married woman considered as under the protection and authority of her husband. [ME < OF. See COVERT, -URE]

cov·er-up (kuv′ər up′), *n.* any action or other means of concealing or preventing investigation or exposure. [n. use of v. phrase *cover up*]

cov·et (kuv′it), *v.t.* **1.** to desire (another's property) inordinately or wrongfully. **2.** to wish for, esp. eagerly: *He won the prize they all coveted.* —*v.i.* **3.** to have an inordinate or wrongful desire. [ME *coveit(en)* < OF *coveit(i)e(r),* irreg. < VL **cupiditāre* to covet < L *cupiditās* CUPIDITY] —**cov′et·a·ble,** *adj.* —**cov′et·er,** *n.* —**Syn. 1.** See **envy.**

cov·et·ous (kuv′i təs), *adj.* **1.** inordinately or wrongfully desirous. **2.** eagerly desirous. [ME *coveitous* < OF < VL **cupiditōs(us).* See CUPIDITY, -OUS] —**cov′et·ous·ly,** *adv.* —**cov′et·ous·ness,** *n.* —**Syn. 1.** greedy, grasping, avaricious.

cov·ey (kuv′ē), *n., pl.* **-eys. 1.** a brood or small flock of partridges or similar birds. **2.** a group, set, or company. [ME, var. of *covee* < MF, OF, n. use of fem. of ptp. of *cover* to hatch < L *cubāre* to lie down]

Co·vi·na (kə vē′nə), *n.* a city in SW California, near Los Angeles. 30,380 (1970).

Cov·ing·ton (kuv′ing tən), *n.* a city in N Kentucky, on the Ohio River. 52,535 (1970).

cow[1] (kou), *n., pl.* **cows,** (*Archaic*) **kine. 1.** the mature female of a bovine animal, esp. of the genus *Bos.* **2.** the female of various other large animals, as the elephant, whale, etc. **3.** *Slang.* an obese and slovenly woman. **4. till the cows come home,** for a long time; forever. [ME *cou,* OE *cū;* c. G *Kuh,* D *koe,* Icel *kȳr;* akin to L *bōs,* Gk *boûs* ox]

cow[2] (kou), *v.t.* to frighten with threats, violence, etc.; intimidate; overawe. [< Scand; cf. Icel *kūga* to oppress, tyrannize over, Dan *kue* to cow]

cow·age (kou′ij), *n.* **1.** a tropical leguminous vine, *Stizolobium pruritum,* bearing reddish or blackish pods. **2.** the pod itself, covered with bristlelike hairs that are irritating to the skin and cause intense itching. **3.** the hairs of the cowage mixed with a liquid vehicle and used to expel intestinal worms. Also, **cowhage.** [< Hindi *kawāch* (also transliterated *kavāc, kavānc*) by folk etymology]

cow·ard (kou′ərd), *n.* **1.** a person who lacks courage in facing danger, difficulty, pain, etc.; a timid or easily intimidated person. **—*adj.* 2.** lacking courage; timid. **3.** proceeding from or expressive of fear or timidity: *a coward cry.* [ME < OF *couard-, couart* cowardly = *coue* tail (< L *cauda*) + *-art* -ARD] **—Syn. 1.** craven, poltroon, dastard, milksop.

Cow·ard (kou′ərd), *n.* **Noel,** 1899–1973, English playwright, composer, and actor.

cow·ard·ice (kou′ər dis), *n.* lack of courage to face danger, difficulty, opposition, etc. [ME *cowardise* < OF *co(u)ardise*] **—Syn.** poltroonery, pusillanimity, timidity. **—Ant.** bravery.

cow·ard·ly (kou′ərd lē), *adj.* **1.** lacking courage; contemptibly timid. **2.** characteristic of or befitting a coward: *a cowardly attack.* **—*adv.* 3.** like a coward. [ME (adv.)] **—cow′ard·li·ness,** *n.*
—Syn. 1. craven, dastardly, pusillanimous, fainthearted, fearful, afraid, scared. COWARDLY, TIMID, TIMOROUS refer to a lack of courage or self-confidence. COWARDLY means weakly or basely fearful in the presence of danger: *The cowardly wretch deserted his comrades in battle.* TIMID means lacking in boldness or self-confidence even when there is no danger present: *A timid person stands in the way of his own advancement.* TIMOROUS suggests a timidity based on an exaggeration of dangers or on an imaginary creation of dangers: *timorous as a mouse.* **—Ant. 1.** brave.

cow·bane (kou′bān′), *n.* any of several umbelliferous plants supposed to be poisonous to cattle, as the European water hemlock, *Cicuta virosa,* or an American swamp plant, *Oxypolis rigidior.*

cow·bell (kou′bel′), *n.* **1.** a bell hung around a cow's neck to indicate its whereabouts. **2.** *U.S.* the bladder campion.

cow·ber·ry (kou′ber′ē, -bə rē), *n., pl.* **-ries. 1.** the berry or fruit of any of various shrubs, as *Vaccinium Vitis-Idaea,* growing in pastures. **2.** any of these shrubs. [cow[1] + BERRY, trans. of L *vaccīnium* plant name, in NL: genus name < *vaccīnus* of cows; see VACCINE]

cow·bind (kou′bīnd′), *n.* either the black-berried white bryony, *Bryonia alba,* or the red-berried bryony, *B. dioica.* [cow[1] + *-bind;* see WOODBINE]

cow·bird (kou′bûrd′), *n.* any of several American blackbirds of the genus *Molothrus,* esp. *M. ater,* of North America, that accompany herds of cattle. Also called **cow′ black′bird.**

cow·boy (kou′boi′), *n.* **1.** a man, usually on horseback, who herds and tends cattle on a ranch, esp. in the western U.S. **2.** a man who exhibits the skills attributed to cowboys, esp. in rodeos, as by roping cattle, riding broncos, etc. **3.** *Informal.* a reckless or speedy driver.

cow·catch·er (kou′kach′ər), *n. U.S.* a triangular frame at the front of a locomotive, streetcar, etc., designed for clearing the track of obstructions. Also called **pilot.**

cow′ col′lege, *U.S. Slang.* **1.** an agricultural college. **2.** a small, obscure rural college.

Cow·ell (kou′əl), *n.* **Henry (Dix·on)** (dik′sən), 1897–1965, U.S. composer.

cow·er (kou′ər), *v.i.* **1.** to crouch in fear. **2.** *Brit. Dial.* to bend with the knees and back; stand or squat in a bent position. [ME *cour(en)* < Scand; cf. Icel *kūra* to mope, Norw *kura* to cower; c. G *kauern*]

Cowes (kouz), *n.* a seaport on the Isle of Wight, in S England: resort. 16,974 (1961).

cow·fish (kou′fish′), *n., pl.* (*esp. collectively*) **-fish,** (*esp. referring to two or more kinds or species*) **-fish·es. 1.** any of several marine fishes having hornlike projections over the eyes, esp. a trunkfish, *Lactophrys quadricornus,* found in the warm waters of the Atlantic Ocean. **2.** a sirenian, as the manatee. **3.** any of various small cetaceans, as a porpoise or dolphin or the grampus, *Grampus griseus.*

cow·girl (kou′gûrl′), *n.* a girl who assists in herding and handling cattle on a ranch.

cow·hage (kou′ij), *n.* cowage.

cow·hand (kou′hand′), *n.* a person employed on a cattle ranch; cowboy.

cow·herd (kou′hûrd′), *n.* a person who tends cows. [ME *couherde,* OE *cūhierde*]

cow·hide (kou′hīd′), *n., v.,* **-hid·ed, -hid·ing. —*n.* 1.** the hide of a cow. **2.** the leather made from it. **3.** a strong, flexible whip made of rawhide or of braided leather. **—*v.t.* 4.** to whip with a cowhide.

co·win·ner (kō win′ər), *n.* one of two or more joint winners.

cowl (koul), *n.* **1.** a hooded garment worn by monks. **2.** the hood of this garment. **3.** part of a garment that is draped to resemble a cowl or hood. **4.** a hoodlike covering for increasing the draft of a chimney or ventilator. **5.** the forward part of the automobile body supporting the rear of the hood and the windshield and housing the pedals and instrument panel. **6.** *Aeron.* a cowling. **—*v.t.* 7.** to put a monk's cowl on. **8.** to cover with or as with a cowl. [ME *cou(e)le,* OE *cugele* < LL *cucull(a)* monk's hood]

Cowl

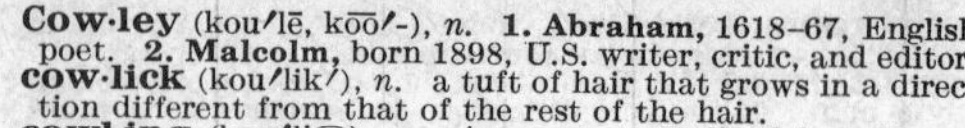

Cow·ley (kou′lē, ko͞o′-), *n.* **1. Abraham,** 1618–67, English poet. **2. Malcolm,** born 1898, U.S. writer, critic, and editor.

cow·lick (kou′lik′), *n.* a tuft of hair that grows in a direction different from that of the rest of the hair.

cowl·ing (kou′ling), *n. Aeron.* a streamlined housing for an aircraft engine.

cow·man (kou′mən), *n., pl.* **-men. 1.** (in the western U.S.) a man who owns cattle; rancher. **2.** *Brit.* a farmer or farm worker who tends cows.

co-work·er (kō′wûr′kər, kō′wûr′-), *n.* a fellow worker.

cow′ pars′nip, any umbelliferous plant of the genus *Heracleum,* as *H. Spondylium,* of Europe, or *H. lanatum,* of North America.

cow·pea (kou′pē′), *n.* **1.** an annual plant, *Vigna sinensis,* extensively cultivated in the southern U.S. for forage, soil improvement, etc. **2.** the seed of this plant, used for food. Also called **black-eyed pea.**

Cow·per (ko͞o′pər, kou′-), *n.* **William,** 1731–1800, English poet and hymnologist.

Cow′per's gland′ (kou′pərz, ko͞o′-), *Anat., Zool.* either of two small glands on either side of the urethra in males, that secrete a mucous substance into the urethra. [named after William *Cowper* (1666–1709), English anatomist who discovered them]

cow·poke (kou′pōk′), *n. U.S. Slang.* a cowboy.

cow′ po′ny, a horse used by cowboys in herding cattle.

cow·pox (kou′poks′), *n. Vet. Pathol.* an eruptive disease of cows that forms in small pustules containing a virus used in smallpox vaccine.

cow·punch·er (kou′pun′chər), *n. U.S. Informal.* a cowboy.

cow·rie (kou′rē), *n.* **1.** the highly polished, usually brightly colored shell of a marine gastropod of the genus *Cypraea,* as that of *C. moneta,* used as money in certain parts of Asia and Africa. **2.** the gastropod itself. [< Hindi *kaurī,* var. of *kaudī* < Tamil or Malayalam *kavaṭi*]

cow·ry (kou′rē), *n., pl.* **-ries.** cowrie.

cow·skin (kou′skin′), *n.* **1.** the skin of a cow. **2.** the leather made from it.

cow·slip (kou′slip′), *n.* **1.** an English primrose, *Primula officinalis* (*P. veris*), having yellow flowers. **2.** the marsh marigold. **3.** See **Virginia cowslip.** [ME *cowslyppe,* OE *cūslyppe* = *cū* cow[1] + *slyppe, slypa* slime; see SLIP[3]]

cow′ town′, a small, provincial town or center, esp. in a cattle-raising district in the western U.S.

cox (koks), *Informal.* **—*n.* 1.** coxswain. **—*v.t.* 2.** to act as coxswain to (a boat). [short form]

Cox (koks), *n.* **James Middleton,** 1870–1957, U.S. journalist and politician.

cox·a (kok′sə), *n., pl.* **cox·ae** (kok′sē). **1.** *Anat.* **a.** See **innominate bone. b.** the joint of the hip. **2.** *Zool.* the first or proximal segment of the leg of insects and other arthropods. [< L: hip] **—cox′al,** *adj.*

A, Coxa of beetle leg; B, Trochanter; C, Femur; D, Tibia; E, Tarsus

cox·al·gi·a (kok sal′jē ə, -jə), *n. Pathol.* pain in the hip. Also, **cox·al·gy** (kok′sal jē). [COX(A) + -ALGIA] **—cox·al′gic,** *adj.*

cox·comb (koks′kōm′), *n.* **1.** a conceited, foolish dandy; pretentious fop. **2.** *Archaic.* head; pate. [sp. var. of COCKSCOMB] **—cox·comb·i·cal** (koks kom′i kəl, -kō′mi-), **cox·comb′ic,** *adj.* **—cox·comb′i·cal·ly,** *adv.*

cox·comb·ry (koks′kōm′rē), *n., pl.* **-ries. 1.** the manners or behavior of a coxcomb. **2.** a foppish trait.

Cox·ey (kok′sē), *n.* **Jacob Sech·ler** (sech′lər), 1854–1951, U.S. political reformer: led a group of marchers (**Cox′ey's ar′my**) in 1894 to Washington to petition Congress for legislation to help the unemployed.

Cox·sack′ie vi′rus (ko͝ok sä′kē), any of a group of viruses closely related to the virus of poliomyelitis, causing certain diseases of man. [named after *Coxsackie,* town in New York, where the first known case appeared]

cox·swain (kok′sən, -swān′), *n.* **1.** the steersman of a racing shell. **2.** a seaman in charge of a ship's boat in the absence of an officer. Also, **cockswain.** [ME *cokeswayne.* See COCKBOAT, SWAIN]

coy (koi), *adj.* **1.** shy; modest. **2.** artfully or affectedly shy or reserved; coquettish. **3.** *Archaic.* quiet; reserved. **4.** *Obs.* disdainful; aloof. **—*v.i.* 5.** *Archaic.* to act in a coy manner. **—*v.t.* *Obs.* 6.** to quiet; soothe. **7.** to pat; caress. [ME < MF *coi* calm, earlier *quei* < VL **quēt(us),* var. of L *quiētus* QUIET[1]] **—coy′ly,** *adv.* **—coy′ness,** *n.* **—Syn. 1.** retiring, diffident, bashful, demure.

coy·ote (kī′ōt, kī ō′tē), *n., pl.* **-tes,** (*esp. collectively*) **-te.** a carnivorous, wolflike mammal, *Canis latrans,* of western North America. Also called **prairie wolf.** [< MexSp < Nahuatl *coyotl*]

Coyote (1½ ft. high at shoulder; total length 3½ ft.; tail 1 ft.)

Coyo′te State′, South Dakota (used as a nickname).

co·yo·til·lo (kō′yō tēl′yō, kī′ō-; *Sp.* kô′yô tē′yô), *n., pl.* **-til·los** (-tēl′yōz; *Sp.* -tē′yôs). any rhamnaceous plant of the genus *Karwinskia,* of Mexico, bearing poisonous fruit. [< MexSp; dim. of COYOTE]

coy·pu (koi′po͞o), *n., pl.* **-pus,** (*esp. collectively*) **-pu.** a large, South American, aquatic rodent, *Myocastor* (or *Myopotamus*) *coypus,* yielding the fur nutria. [< AmerSp *coipú* < Araucanian *coypu*]

Coypu (Total length 3½ ft.; tail to 16 in.)

coz (kuz), *n. Informal.* cousin. [short form]

coz·en (kuz′ən), *v.t., v.i.* to cheat; deceive; trick, swindle, or defraud. [?] **—coz′en·er,** *n.*

coz·en·age (kuz′ə nij), *n.* **1.** the practice of cozening. **2.** the condition of being cozened.

co·zey (kō′zē), *adj.,* **-zi·er, -zi·est,** *n., pl.* **-zeys.** cozy.

co·zy (kō′zē), *adj.,* **-zi·er, -zi·est,** *n., pl.* **-zies. —*adj.* 1.** snugly warm and comfortable. **2.** convenient or beneficial, esp. as a result of dishonesty or connivance: *a cozy agreement between competing firms.* —*n.* **3.** a padded covering for a teapot, etc., to retain the heat. Also, **cosy, cozey, co′zie.** [orig. Scot; prob. < Scand; cf. Norw *koselig* smug, *kose sig* to make oneself comfortable] —**co′zi·ly,** *adv.* —**co′zi·ness,** *n.*

CP, command post.

cp, candlepower.

cp., compare.

C.P., **1.** Common Prayer. **2.** Communist party.

c.p., **1.** candlepower. **2.** chemically pure. **3.** circular pitch.

C.P.A., See **certified public accountant.**

cpd., compound.

CPI, Consumer Price Index.

cpl., corporal.

c.p.m., **1.** *Music.* common particular meter. **2.** cycles per minute.

c.p.o., See **chief petty officer.** Also, **C.P.O.**

CPR, cardiopulmonary resuscitation.

cps, cycles per second. Also, **c.p.s.**

cpt., counterpoint.

CQ, **1.** *Radio.* a signal sent at the beginning of radiograms of general information or sent by an amateur as an invitation for any other amateur to reply. **2.** *Mil.* charge of quarters.

CR, critical ratio.

Cr, *Chem.* chromium.

cr., **1.** credit. **2.** creditor.

C.R., Costa Rica.

craal (kräl), *n.* kraal.

crab[1] (krab), *n., v.,* **crabbed, crab·bing.** —*n.* **1.** any decapod crustacean of the suborder *Brachyura,* having the eyes on short stalks and a short, broad, more or less flattened body, the abdomen being small and folded under the thorax. **2.** any of various other crustaceans, as the hermit crab, or other animals, as the horseshoe crab, resembling the true crabs. **3.** (*cap.*) *Astron., Astrol.* the zodiacal constellation or sign Cancer. **4.** any of various mechanical contrivances for hoisting or pulling. **5.** *Aeron.* the maneuver of crabbing. **6.** the crab louse. See under **louse** (def. 1). **7. catch a crab,** to make a faulty stroke in rowing, so that the oar strikes the water forcibly on the backstroke. —*v.i.* **8.** to catch crabs. **9.** *Aeron.* (of an aircraft) to head partly into the wind to compensate for drift. **10.** *Naut.* to drift or advance with some movement sideways, esp. when under tow. —*v.t.* **11.** *Aeron.* to head (an aircraft) partly into the wind to compensate for drift. [ME *crabbe,* OE *crabba;* c. D *krab,* Icel *krabbi;* akin to G *Krebs*] —**crab′ber,** *n.*

Crab, *Callinectes sapidus* (Length 3 in.)

crab[2] (krab), *n., v.,* **crabbed, crab·bing.** *Informal.* —*n.* **1.** an ill-tempered or grouchy person. —*v.i.* **2.** to find fault; complain. —*v.t.* **2.** to find fault with. [late ME; back formation from CRABBED] —**crab′ber,** *n.*

crab′ ap′ple, **1.** a small, sour, wild apple. **2.** any of various small, tart, cultivated varieties of apple, used for making jelly and preserves. **3.** any tree bearing such fruit. [ME *crabbe;* perh. special use of CRAB[1]]

Crabb (krab), *n.* **George,** 1778–1851, English author and philologist.

Crabbe (krab), *n.* **George,** 1754–1832, English poet.

crab·bed (krab′id), *adj.* **1.** grouchy or irritable. **2.** perverse; contrary; obstinate. **3.** hard to understand; intricate and obscure. **4.** difficult to read or decipher, as handwriting. [ME] —**crab′bed·ly,** *adv.* —**crab′bed·ness,** *n.*

crab·by (krab′ē), *adj.,* **-bi·er, -bi·est.** grouchy; ill-natured; irritable.

crab′ grass′, an annual grass, *Digitaria sanguinalis,* common in cultivated and waste grounds and often occurring as a weedy pest in lawns.

crab′ louse′. See under **louse** (def. 1).

crab·stick (krab′stik′), *n.* **1.** a stick, cane, or club made of wood, esp. of the crab-apple tree. **2.** an ill-tempered, grouchy person.

crack (krak), *v.i.* **1.** to make a sudden, sharp sound in or as in breaking; snap. **2.** to break with a sudden, sharp sound. **3.** to break without complete separation of parts; become fissured. **4.** (of the voice) to break abruptly and discordantly, esp. into an upper register. **5.** *Chem.* to decompose as a result of being subjected to heat. **6.** *Informal.* to fail; give way; succumb, esp. to severe psychological pressure, torture, or the like: *They questioned him for 24 hours before he finally cracked.* **7.** *Chiefly Dial.* to brag; boast. —*v.t.* **8.** to cause to make a sudden sharp sound. **9.** to strike with a sharp noise. **10.** to break without complete separation of parts; break into fissures. **11.** to break with a sudden, sharp sound: *to crack walnuts.* **12.** *Informal.* to break into (a safe, vault, etc.). **13.** *Informal.* to solve; decipher: *to crack the code.* **14.** to damage or impair: *The unexpected evidence cracked his composure.* **15.** to make unsound mentally. **16.** to make (the voice) harsh or unmanageable. **17.** to break with grief; affect deeply. **18.** to utter or tell: *to crack jokes.* **19.** to subject to the process of cracking as in the distillation of petroleum. **20. crack a book,** *Slang.* to open a book in order to read or study. **21. crack a smile,** *Slang.* to smile. **22. crack down,** *U.S. Informal.* to take severe measures, esp. in enforcing laws or regulations. Also, **crack down on. 23. crack up, a.** *Slang.* to suffer a mental or emotional breakdown. **b.** *Informal.* to crash, as in a vehicle. **c.** *Slang.* to laugh or cause to laugh unrestrainedly. **d.** *Informal.* to wreck an automobile, airplane, etc. **24. crack wise,** *Slang.* to wisecrack. —*n.* **25.** a sudden, sharp noise, as of something breaking. **26.** the snap of or as of a whip. **27.** a resounding blow. **28.** a break without complete separation of parts; fissure. **29.** a slight opening, as between floorboards. **30.** a flaw or defect. **31.** a mental defect or deficiency. **32.** a broken or changing tone of the voice. **33.** *Informal.* opportunity; chance; try: *Give him a crack at the game.* **34.** *Informal.* a gibe; wisecrack. **35.** *Slang.* pellet-size pieces of purified cocaine, prepared with other ingredients for smoking: highly addictive. **36.** *Chiefly Brit.* a person or thing that excels in some respect. **37.** *Brit. Dial.* boasting; braggadocio. **38.** *Archaic.* a burglar. —*adj.* **39.** *Informal.* first-rate; excellent: *a crack salesman.* [ME *crakk(en),* var. of *craken,* OE *cracian* to resound; akin to G *krachen,* D *kraken* and perh. also to CREAK] —**Syn. 2.** snap. **3.** craze. **25.** snap, report.

crack·a·jack (krak′ə jak′), *n., adj.* crackerjack.

crack·brain (krak′brān′), *n.* a foolish, senseless, or insane person. [CRACK(ED) + BRAIN]

crack·brained (krak′brānd′), *adj.* foolish or insane.

crack·down (krak′doun′), *n.* *U.S. Informal.* a severe enforcing of laws or regulations.

cracked (krakt), *adj.* **1.** broken: *a container of cracked ice.* **2.** broken without separation of parts; fissured. **3.** damaged or injured. **4.** *Informal.* eccentric; mad; insane. **5.** broken in tone, as the voice. [late ME *crachyd*] —**cracked′ness,** *n.*

crack·er (krak′ər), *n.* **1.** a thin, crisp biscuit. **2.** a firecracker. **3.** Also called **crack′er bon′bon.** a small paper roll used as a party favor, that usually contains candy, trinkets, etc., and that pops when pulled sharply at one or both ends. **4.** (*cap.*) a native or inhabitant of Georgia (the **Cracker State**) (used as a nickname). **5.** *Disparaging.* one of a class of poor whites in parts of the southeastern U.S. **6.** *Dial.* braggart; boaster. **7.** a person or thing that cracks. —*adj.* **8. crackers,** *Brit. Informal.* wild or crazy.

crack·er-bar·rel (krak′ər bar′əl), *adj.* of or suggesting the simple rustic informality and directness thought to be characteristic of a country store: *homespun, cracker-barrel philosophy.* [adj. use of *cracker barrel,* symbol of talkers who supposedly gathered around it in old-style country stores]

Crack·er′ Jack′, *Trademark.* a confection of caramel-coated popcorn.

crack·er·jack (krak′ər jak′), *Slang.* —*n.* **1.** a person or thing of marked ability or excellence. —*adj.* **2.** of marked ability; exceptionally fine. Also, **crackajack.** [earlier *crackajack,* rhyming compound based on CRACK (adj.); *-a-* as in BLACKAMOOR; JACK[1] in sense chap, fellow]

Crack′er State′, Georgia (used as a nickname).

crack·ing (krak′ing), *n.* **1.** (in the distillation of petroleum or the like) the process of breaking down certain hydrocarbons into simpler ones of lower boiling points, as by excess heat, distillation under pressure, etc. —*adv.* **2.** extremely; unusually: *We saw a cracking good game at the stadium.* —*adj.* **3.** done with precision; smart: *A cracking salute from the honor guard.* **4. get cracking,** *Slang.* to begin moving or working; start: *Let's get cracking on these dirty dishes!* [ME]

crack·le (krak′əl), *v.,* **-led, -ling,** *n.* —*v.i.* **1.** to make slight, sudden, sharp noises, rapidly repeated. **2.** to form a network of fine cracks on the surface. **3.** (of ceramic glaze) to craze. —*v.t.* **4.** to cause to crackle. **5.** to break with a crackling noise. **6.** to craze (ceramic glaze). —*n.* **7.** the act of crackling. **8.** a crackling noise. **9.** a network of fine cracks, as in some glazes. **10.** crackleware.

crack·le·ware (krak′əl wâr′), *n.* ceramic ware having a crackled glaze. Also called **crackle.**

crack·ling (krak′ling), *n.* **1.** slight cracking sounds rapidly repeated. **2.** the crisp browned skin or rind of roast pork. **3.** Usually, **cracklings.** *Dial.* the crisp residue left when fat, esp. hog fat, is rendered.

crack·ly (krak′lē), *adj.,* **-li·er, -li·est.** apt to crackle.

crack·nel (krak′nəl), *n.* **1.** a hard, brittle cake or biscuit. **2. cracknels,** small bits of fat pork fried crisp. [ME *crak(e)nele* < MF **craquenelle,* metathetic alter. of *craquelin* < MD *crākelinc* = *crāke(n)* (to) CRACK + *-linc* -LING[1]]

crack′ of doom′, **1.** the signal that will announce the Day of Judgment. **2.** the end of the world; doomsday.

crack·pot (krak′pot′), *Informal.* —*n.* **1.** an eccentric. —*adj.* **2.** eccentric; impractical; insane: *crackpot ideas.* [CRACK(ED) + POT[1] (referring to the head)]

crack-up (krak′up′), *n.* **1.** a crash; collision. **2.** *Informal.* a breakdown in health; esp. a mental breakdown. **3.** collapse or disintegration.

Crac·ow (krak′ou, krä′kou, krā′kō), *n.* a city in S Poland, on the Vistula: the capital of Poland 1320–1609. 500,000 (est. 1963). German, **Krakau.** Polish, **Kraków.**

-cracy, a word element occurring in loan words from Greek (*aristocracy; democracy*); on this model used, with the meaning "rule," "government," "governing body," to form abstract nouns from stems of other origin: *mobocracy; bureaucracy.* Cf. **-crat.** [< MF *-cracie* (F *-cratie*) < LL *-cratia* < Gk *-kratia.* See -CRAT, -Y[3]]

cra·dle (krād′əl), *n., v.,* **-dled, -dling.** —*n.* **1.** a little bed or cot for an infant, usually built on rockers. **2.** a place of origin. **3.** any of various contrivances similar to a child's cradle, as the framework on which a ship rests during construction or repair. **4.** *Agric.* a frame of wood with a row of long curved teeth projecting above and parallel to a scythe, for laying grain in bunches as it is cut. **5.** *Mining.* a box on rockers for washing sand or gravel to separate gold or other heavy metal. **6.** *Aeron.* a docklike structure in which a rigid or semirigid airship is built or is supported during inflation. **7.** an engraver's tool for laying mezzotint grounds. **8.** *Med.* a frame that prevents the bedclothes from touching an injured limb of a bedridden patient. **9. rob the cradle,** *Informal.* to keep company with or marry a person much younger than oneself. —*v.t.* **10.** to place or rock in or as in a cradle. **11.** to nurture during infancy. **12.** to cut (grain) with a cradle. **13.** to place (a vessel) on a cradle. **14.** *Mining.* to wash (sand or gravel) in a cradle; rock. **15.** to receive or hold as a cradle. —*v.i.* **16.** to lie in or as in a cradle. [ME *cradel,* OE *cradol;* akin to OHG *cratto* basket] —**cra′dler,** *n.*

cra·dle·song (krād′əl sông′, -song′), *n.* a lullaby.

craft (kraft, kräft), *n.* **1.** skill or dexterity. **2.** skill in deception; cunning; guile. **3.** a trade or occupation requiring manual skill. **4.** the members of a trade or profession collectively; a guild. **5.** ships or other vessels collectively. **6.** a single ship or other vessel. **7.** aircraft collectively. **8.** a single aircraft. —*v.t.* **9.** to make or manufacture (an object, objects, product, etc.) with skill and careful attention to detail. [ME; OE *cræft* strength, skill; c. G *Kraft*, D *kracht*, Icel *kraptr*] —**Syn. 1.** talent, ability. **2.** craftiness, artifice, deceitfulness, deception. See **cunning. 3.** vocation, calling, métier.

-craft, a combining form of **craft:** *handicraft.*

crafts·man (krafts′mən, kräfts′-), *n., pl.* **-men. 1.** a person who practices a craft; artisan. **2.** an artist. [ME *craftes man* man of skill, earlier *craftman;* r. OE *cræftiga* craftsman, workman; see CRAFTY] —**crafts′man·ship′,** *n.*

craft′ un′ion, a labor union composed only of people in the same craft. —**craft′ un′ionist.**

craft·y (kraf′tē, kräf′-), *adj.,* **craft·i·er, craft·i·est. 1.** cunning; deceitful; sly. **2.** *Archaic.* skillful; ingenious; dexterous. [ME; OE *cræftig* skilled] —**craft′i·ly,** *adv.* —**craft′i·ness,** *n.* —**Syn. 1.** artful, wily, tricky, scheming.

crag (krag), *n.* a steep, rugged rock; a rough, broken, projecting part of a rock. [ME < Celt; cf. Welsh *craig* rock]

crag·gy (krag′ē), *adj.,* **-gi·er, -gi·est. 1.** full of crags. **2.** rugged; harsh; rough. Also, **crag·ged** (krag′id). [ME] —**crag′gi·ness,** *n.*

crags·man (kragz′mən), *n., pl.* **-men.** a person accustomed to or skilled in climbing crags.

Craig·a·von (krāg ā′vən, -av′ən), *n.* **James Craig, 1st Viscount,** 1871–1940, 1st prime minister of Northern Ireland 1921–40.

Crai·gie (krā′gē), *n.* **Sir William (Alexander),** 1867–1957, Scottish lexicographer and philologist.

Craik (krāk), *n.* **Dinah Maria,** nee **Mulock,** 1826–87, English novelist.

Cra·io·va (krä yô′vä), *n.* a city in SW Rumania. 122,108 (est. 1964).

crake (krāk), *n.* any of several short-billed rails, esp. the corn crake. [ME < Scand; cf. Icel *krāka* crow, *krākr* raven]

cram (kram), *v.,* **crammed, cram·ming,** *n.* —*v.t.* **1.** to fill (something) by force with more than it can conveniently hold. **2.** to force or stuff (usually fol. by *into, down,* etc.). **3.** to fill or stuff with or as with food; overfeed. **4.** *Informal.* to study (a subject) hastily, esp. before an examination. **5.** *Archaic.* to tell lies to. —*v.i.* **6.** to eat greedily or to excess. **7.** *Informal.* to study for an examination by hastily memorizing facts at the last minute. —*n.* **8.** a crammed state. **9.** a dense crowd; throng. [ME *cramm(en),* OE *crammian* to stuff, akin to *crimman* to put in] —**cram′mer,** *n.* —**Syn. 2.** crowd, pack, squeeze, compress, overcrowd. **3.** glut. **6.** gorge.

cram·bo (kram′bō), *n., pl.* **-boes. 1.** a game in which one person or side must find a rhyme to a word or a line of verse given by another. **2.** inferior rhyme. [earlier *crambe,* lit., cabbage < L (< Gk *krámbē*), short for *crambē repetīta* cabbage repeated, i.e., rhyming game]

cram-full (kram′fo͝ol′), *adj.* as full as possible; chock-full.

cram·oi·sy (kram′oi zē, -ə zē), *Archaic.* —*adj.* **1.** crimson. —*n.* **2.** crimson cloth. Also, **cram′oi·sie.** [< F *cramoisi,* earlier *crameisi* < Sp *carmesí* < Ar *qirmizī* = *qirmiz* KERMES + *-ī-* suffix of appurtenance; r. late ME *cremesye* < It *cremisi* < Ar, as above]

cramp[1] (kramp), *n.* **1.** Often, **cramps. a.** a sudden, involuntary, persistent contraction of a muscle or group of muscles, esp. of the extremities, sometimes associated with severe pain. **b.** a piercing pain in the abdomen. **c.** an intermittent, painful contraction of structures of a wall containing involuntary muscle, as in biliary colic or in the uterine contractions of menstruation or of labor. **2.** *Pathol.* See **writer's cramp.** —*v.t.* **3.** to affect with or as with a cramp. [ME *crampe* < MD]

cramp[2] (kramp), *n.* **1.** a portable frame or tool with a movable part that can be tightened to hold things together; clamp. **2.** anything that confines or restrains. **3.** a cramped state or part. —*v.t.* **4.** to fasten or hold with a cramp. **5.** to confine; restrain; hamper. **6.** to steer; to turn the front wheel of a vehicle by means of the steering gear. **7. cramp one's style,** *Slang.* to prevent a person from showing his best abilities; thwart. —*adj.* **8.** hard to decipher or understand; difficult. **9.** contracted; narrow. [late ME *crampe* < MD]

cramp·fish (kramp′fish′), *n., pl.* **-fish·es,** (*esp. collectively*) **-fish.** See **electric ray.** [CRAMP[1] + FISH]

cram·pon (kram′pən), *n.* **1.** a grappling iron, esp. one of a pair for raising heavy weights. **2.** a spiked iron plate worn on the shoe to prevent slipping on ice, snow, etc. Also, **cram·poon** (kram po͞on′). [ME *cra(u)mpon* < MF *crampon* = *crampe* hook (< MD; see CRAMP[2]) + *-on* n. suffix]

Cra·nach (krä′näкн), *n.* **Lucas** (*"the Elder"*), 1472–1553, German painter and graphic artist.

cran·ber·ry (kran′ber′ē, -bə rē), *n., pl.* **-ries. 1.** the red, acid fruit or berry of any ericaceous plant of the genus *Vaccinium,* used in making sauce, jelly, etc. **2.** the plant itself. [< LG *kraanbere.* See CRANE, BERRY]

cran′berry tree′, a caprifoliaceous tree or shrub, *Viburnum Opulus,* bearing red berries and white cymose flowers.

crane (krān), *n., v.,* **craned, cran·ing.** —*n.* **1.** any of several large wading birds of the family *Gruidae,* having long legs, bill, and neck and an elevated hind toe. **2.** (not used scientifically) any of various similar birds of other families, as the great blue heron. **3.** *Mach.* a device for lifting and moving heavy weights. **4.** any of various similar devices, as a horizontally swinging arm by a fireplace, for suspending pots, kettles, etc. —*v.t.* **5.** to hoist, lower, or move by or as by a crane. **6.** to stretch (the neck) as a crane does. —*v.i.* **7.** to stretch out one's neck, esp. to see better. **8.** *Informal.* to hesitate at danger, difficulty, etc. [ME; OE *cran;* c. G *Kran,* Gk *géranos*] —**crane′like′,** *adj.*

Crane,
Grus americana
(Height about 5 ft.; wingspread 7½ ft.)

Crane (krān), *n.* **1. (Harold) Hart,** 1899–1932, U.S. poet. **2. Stephen,** 1871–1900, U.S. novelist, poet, and short-story writer.

crane′ fly′, any of numerous dipterous insects of the family *Tipulidae* that resemble a large mosquito with extremely long legs. —**crane′-fly′,** *adj.*

crane's-bill (krānz′bil′), *n.* any plant of the genus *Geranium,* bearing long, slender, beaked fruit. Also, **cranes′bill′, crane′bill′.** [trans. of D *kranebek* geranium (now obs.)]

Cran·ford (kran′fərd), *n.* a township in NE New Jersey. 27,391 (1970).

cra·ni·al (krā′nē əl), *adj.* of or pertaining to the cranium or skull. —**cra′ni·al·ly,** *adv.*

cra′nial in′dex, *Craniom.* the ratio of the greatest breadth of a skull to its greatest length from front to back, multiplied by 100.

cra′nial nerve′, *Anat.* any member of 12 pairs of nerves that emerge from the brain through openings in the skull.

cra·ni·ate (krā′nē it, -āt′), *adj.* **1.** having a cranium or skull. **2.** belonging or pertaining to the subphylum *Vertebrata* (or *Craniata*); vertebrate. —*n.* **3.** a craniate animal.

cranio-, a combining form of **cranium:** *craniology.* Also, *esp. before a vowel,* **crani-.**

craniol., craniology.

cra·ni·ol·o·gy (krā′nē ol′ə jē), *n.* the science that deals with the size, shape, and other characteristics of human skulls. —**cra·ni·o·log·i·cal** (krā′nē ə loj′i kəl), *adj.* —**cra′ni·ol′o·gist,** *n.*

craniom., craniometry.

cra·ni·om·e·try (krā′nē om′i trē), *n.* the science of measuring skulls. —**cra·ni·o·met·ric** (krā′nē ə me′trik), **cra′ni·o·met′ri·cal,** *adj.* —**cra′ni·om′e·trist,** *n.*

cra·ni·o·tome (krā′nē ə tōm′), *n. Surg.* an instrument for performing a craniotomy.

cra·ni·ot·o·my (krā′nē ot′ə mē), *n., pl.* **-mies.** *Surg.* the operation of opening the skull, as for operations on the brain.

cra·ni·um (krā′nē əm), *n., pl.* **-ni·ums, -ni·a** (-nē ə). **1.** the skull of a vertebrate. **2.** the part of the skull that encloses the brain. [< ML < Gk *krānion* skull]

crank[1] (krangk), *n.* **1.** *Mach.* any of several types of arms or levers for imparting rotary or oscillatory motion to a rotating shaft, one end being fixed to the shaft and the other end receiving reciprocating motion from hand, connecting rod, etc. **2.** *Informal.* an ill-tempered, grouchy person. **3.** an eccentric or overzealous person (often used attributively): *crank letters; a crank phone call.* **4.** an eccentric notion. **5.** a clever turn of speech or play on words. **6.** *Obs.* a bend. —*v.t.* **7.** to bend into or make in the shape of a crank. **8.** to furnish with a crank. **9.** *Mach.* to rotate (a shaft) by means of a crank. **10.** to start (an internal-combustion engine) by turning the crankshaft manually or by means of a small motor. —*v.i.* **11.** to turn a crank, as in starting an engine. **12.** *Archaic.* to turn and twist; zigzag. **13. crank up,** *Informal.* to get started or ready. —*adj.* **14.** unstable; shaky; unsteady. **15.** *Brit. Dial.* cranky[1] (def. 5). [ME *cranke,* OE *cranc-,* in *crancstæf* crank; see STAFF[1]] —**crank′less,** *adj.*

crank[2] (krangk), *adj. Naut.* having a tendency to roll easily, as a boat, ship, etc.; tender (opposed to *stiff*). [short for *crank-sided;* cf. D *krengd* careened]

crank[3] (krangk), *adj. Dial.* lively; high-spirited. [ME *cranke* < ?] —**crank′ly,** *adv.* —**crank′ness,** *n.*

crank·case (krangk′kās′), *n.* (in an internal-combustion engine) the housing that encloses the crankshaft, the connecting rods, and allied parts.

crank′ disk′. See **disk crank.**

cran·kle (krang′kəl), *n., v.t., v.i.,* **-kled, -kling.** crinkle. [CRANK[1] + -LE]

crank·pin (krangk′pin′), *n. Mach.* a short cylindrical pin at the outer end of a crank, held by and moving with a connecting rod or link. Also, **crank′ pin′.** Cf. **web** (def. 8).

A, Crankpin
B, Disk crank
C, Connecting rod

crank·plate (krangk′plāt′), *n.* See **disk crank.**

crank·shaft (krangk′shaft′, -shäft′), *n. Mach.* a shaft having one or more cranks, usually formed as integral parts.

crank·y[1] (krang′kē), *adj.,* **crank·i·er, crank·i·est. 1.** ill-tempered; grouchy; cross: *a cranky old man.* **2.** eccentric; queer. **3.** shaky; unsteady; out of order. **4.** full of bends or windings; crooked. **5.** *Brit. Dial.* sickly; in unsound or feeble condition; infirm. [CRANK[1] + -Y[1]] —**crank′i·ly,** *adv.* —**crank′i·ness,** *n.* —**Syn. 1.** crotchety, cantankerous. —**Ant. 1.** good-natured.

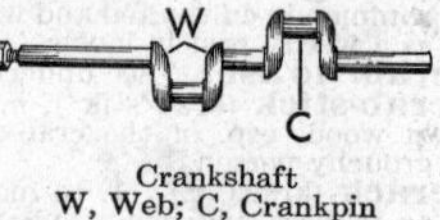

Crankshaft
W, Web; C, Crankpin

crank·y[2] (krang′kē), *adj.* tending to lurch or capsize. [CRANK + -Y[1]]

Cran·mer (kran′mər), *n.* **Thomas,** 1489–1556, 1st Protestant archbishop of Canterbury: leader in the English Protestant Reformation in England.

cran·ne·quin (kran′ə kin), *n.* a portable device for bending a crossbow. See illus. at **crossbow.** [alter. of CRANNOG, with *-quin,* var. of -KIN]

cran·nog (kran′əg), *n.* (in ancient Ireland and Scotland) a small, artificial, fortified island constructed in bogs. Also, **cran·noge** (kran′əj). [< Ir: wooden structure = *crann* beam, tree + *-ōg* n. suffix]

cran·ny (kran′ē), *n., pl.* **-nies.** a small, narrow opening in a wall, rock, etc.; a chink; crevice; fissure: *They searched every nook and cranny for the missing ring.* [late ME *crany* < MF *cran* fissure; see -Y[2]] —**cran′nied,** *adj.*

cran·reuch (krän′rəкн), *n. Scot.* hoarfrost. [appar. < Gael phrase *crann reodhach* frosty tree = *crann* tree + *reodh* frost, hoarfrost + *-ach* adj. suffix]

Cran·ston (kran′stən), *n.* a city in E Rhode Island, near Providence. 74,287 (1970).

crap[1] (krap), *n.* **1.** (in craps) a losing throw, in which the total on the two dice is 2, 3, or 12. **2.** craps. —*v.* **3. crap out, a.** *Slang.* to abandon a project, activity, etc., because of fear or exhaustion. **b.** *Slang.* to rest, relax, nap, or the like. **c.** *Craps.* to roll a seven rather than make one's point. [back formation from CRAPS]

crap[2] (krap), *n., v.,* **crapped, crap·ping.** *Slang.* —*n.* **1.** *Vulgar.* excrement. **2.** nonsense; drivel. **3.** a lie; exaggeration. **4.** refuse; rubbish; junk; litter. —*v.i.* **5.** *Vulgar.* to defecate. [late ME *crappe* chaff < MFlem]

crape (krāp), *n., v.t.,* **craped, crap·ing.** crepe.

crape·hang·er (krāp′haŋ′ər), *n.* *U.S. Slang.* a gloomy person; pessimist. Also, **crepehanger.**
crape′ myr′tle, a tall Chinese shrub, *Lagerstroemia indica,* having showy pink, purple, red, or white flowers, grown as an ornamental in the southern and western U.S. Also, **crepe myrtle.**
crap·per (krap′ər), *n.* *Slang (usually vulgar).* a toilet.
crap·pie (krap′ē, krä′pē), *n.* either of two small sunfishes found in the central U.S., *Pomoxis nigro-maculatus* (**black crappie**) or *P. annularis* (**white crappie**). [< CanF *crapet*]
crap·py (krap′ē), *adj.,* **-pi·er, -pi·est.** *Slang.* disgusting; base or inferior.
craps (kraps), *n.* (*usually construed as sing.*) a gambling game in which two dice are thrown and in which a first throw of 7 or 11 wins, a first throw of 2, 3, or 12 loses, and a first throw of 4, 5, 6, 8, 9, or 10 can be won only by repeating the number thrown before a seven appears. [appar. < F, var. of *crabs* double-ace (lowest throw at hazard) < 18th-century English slang: pl. of CRAB¹]
crap·shoot·er (krap′shoo͞′tər), *n.* a person who plays the game of craps.
crap·u·lent (krap′yo͝o lənt, -yə-), *adj.* sick from gross excess in drinking or eating. [< LL *crāpulent(us)* drunk < L *crāpul(a)* drunkenness < Gk *kraipálē* a hangover; see -ENT] —**crap′u·lence, crap′u·len·cy,** *n.*
crap·u·lous (krap′yo͝o ləs, -yə-), *adj.* **1.** given to or characterized by gross excess in drinking or eating. **2.** suffering from such excess. [< LL *crāpulōs(us).* See CRAPULENT, -OUS]
crash¹ (krash), *v.t.* **1.** to break into pieces violently and noisily; shatter. **2.** to force or drive with violence and noise (usually fol. by *in, through, out,* etc.). **3.** *Informal.* **a.** to gain admittance to though uninvited: *to crash a party.* **b.** to enter without a ticket, permission, etc.: *to crash the gate at a football game.* **4.** *Aeron.* to crash-land. —*v.i.* **5.** to break or fall to pieces noisily. **6.** to make a loud, clattering noise, as if from being dashed to pieces. **7.** to collapse or fail suddenly, as a financial enterprise or the stock market. **8.** to move or go with a crash; strike with a crash. **9.** *Aeron.* to fall or to crash-land. **10.** *Slang.* **a.** to sleep. **b.** to have a night's lodging. —*n.* **11.** a breaking or falling to pieces with loud noise. **12.** the shock of collision and breaking. **13.** a collision or crashing, as of automobiles, an airplane, etc. **14.** a sudden collapse of a business enterprise, the stock market, etc. **15.** a sudden loud noise: *the crash of thunder.* **16.** *Slang.* **a.** sleep. **b.** a night's lodging. —*adj.* **17.** *Informal.* characterized by an intensive effort, esp. to meet an emergency: *a crash program to produce vaccine.* [late ME *crasche;* b. *crase* to break (see CRAZE) and MASH] —**crash′er,** *n.* —**Syn. 1.** smash. **13.** smash-up; accident. **14.** failure, ruin.
crash² (krash), *n.* a plain-weave fabric of rough, irregular, or lumpy yarns, for toweling, dresses, etc. [?]
Crash·aw (krash′ô), *n.* **Richard,** 1613–49, English poet.
crash′ dive′, a rapid, steep-angle dive by a submarine, made esp. to avoid attack from a surface vessel or airplane.
crash-dive (krash′dīv′, -dīv′), *v.i., v.t.,* **-dived** or **-dove, -dived, -div·ing.** (of a submarine) to dive rapidly at a steep angle.
crash-land (krash′land′), *v.t.* **1.** to land (an aircraft), in an emergency, in such a way as to damage the aircraft. —*v.i.* **2.** to crash-land an aircraft. —**crash′-land′ing,** *n.*
cra·sis (krā′sis), *n., pl.* **-ses** (-sēz). *Archaic.* composition; constitution; make-up. [< Gk *krâsis* mixture, blend = *krā-* (root of *kerannýnai* to mix) + *-sis* -SIS]
crass (kras), *adj.* **1.** without refinement, delicacy, or sensitivity; gross. **2.** *Archaic.* thick; coarse: *a crass texture.* [< L *crass(us)* thick, dense, fat, heavy] —**crass′ly,** *adv.* —**crass′ness,** *n.*
cras·si·tude (kras′i to͞od′, -tyo͞od′), *n.* **1.** gross ignorance or stupidity. **2.** thickness; grossness. [< L *crassitūd(ō)* thickness]
cras·su·la·ceous (kras′yo͝o lā′shəs, -yə-), *adj.* belonging to the *Crassulaceae,* a family of mostly fleshy or succulent herbs, including the houseleek and sedum. [< NL *Crassul(a)* genus name (ML *crassula;* see CRASS, -ULE), + -ACEOUS]
Cras·sus (kras′əs), *n.* **Marcus Li·cin·i·us** (li sin′ē əs), c115–53 B.C., Roman general: member of the first triumvirate.
-crat, a learned borrowing from Greek meaning "ruler," "member of a ruling body," "advocate of a particular form of rule," used in the formation of compound words: *autocrat; plutocrat; technocrat.* Cf. **-cracy.** [< Gk *-kratēs* as in *autokratēs* AUTOCRAT; r. *-crate* < F < Gk]
cratch (krach), *n.* *Archaic.* a crib to hold fodder; manger. [ME *cracche* manger < OF *crache,* var. of *creche,* CRÈCHE]
crate (krāt), *n., v.,* **crat·ed, crat·ing.** —*n.* **1.** a box or framework, usually made of wooden slats, for packing and transporting fruit, furniture, etc. **2.** any solid packing case. **3.** *Informal.* something rickety and dilapidated, esp. an automobile. **4.** a quantity, esp. of fruit that a crate approximately 2 ft. × 1 ft. × 1 ft. holds. —*v.t.* **5.** to put in a crate. [ME < L *crāt(is)* wickerwork, hurdle]
cra·ter (krā′tər), *n.* **1.** the cup-shaped depression marking the orifice of a volcano. **2.** (in the surface of the earth, moon, etc.) a bowl-shaped depression with a raised rim, formed by the impact of a meteorite. **3.** (on the surface of the moon) a circular or almost circular area having a depressed floor, almost always containing a central mountain and usually completely enclosed by walls that are often higher than those of a walled plain; ring formation; ring. Cf. **walled plain. 4.** the bowllike orifice of a geyser. **5.** the hole or pit in the ground where a military mine, shell, or bomb has exploded. [< L < Gk *krātḗr* mixing bowl, lit., mixer = *krā-* (root of *kerannýnai* to mix) + *-tēr* agentive suffix] —**cra′ter·less,** *adj.* —**cra′ter·like′,** *adj.*
Cra·ter (krā′tər), *n.* **Joseph Force** (fōrs, fôrs), 1889–?, a judge of the New York State Supreme Court: disappeared August 6, 1930.
Cra′ter Lake′, a lake in the crater of an extinct volcano in SW Oregon, in Crater Lake National Park. 20 sq. mi.; 1996 ft. deep.
Cra′ter Lake′ Na′tional Park′, a national park in SW Oregon, in the Cascade Range: Crater Lake. 250 sq. mi.
craunch (krônch, kränch), *v.t., v.i., n.* crunch. [var. of *cranch,* itself perh. nasalized var. of CRASH¹ in its orig. sense of to break up, shatter] —**craunch′ing·ly,** *adv.*
cra·vat (krə vat′), *n.* **1.** necktie. **2.** a cloth, often made of or trimmed with lace, worn about the neck by men, esp. in the 17th century. [< F *cravate* neckcloth, lit., Croat; so called because worn by Croats in French army]
crave (krāv), *v.t.* **craved, crav·ing. 1.** to long for or desire eagerly. **2.** to require; need. **3.** to ask earnestly for (something). **4.** to long (usually fol. by *for* or *after*). [ME *crave(n),* OE *crafian;* akin to Icel *krefja* to demand, lay claim to] —**crav′er,** *n.* —**Syn. 3.** beseech, entreat, implore.
cra·ven (krā′vən), *adj.* **1.** cowardly; contemptibly timid. —*n.* **2.** a coward. —*v.t.* **3.** to make cowardly. [ME *cravant* overthrown, unexplained alter. of *creant* RECREANT] —**cra′ven·ly,** *adv.* —**cra′ven·ness,** *n.* —**Ant. 1.** brave.
crav·ing (krā′viŋ), *n.* deep longing; great or eager desire; yearning. [ME] —**Syn.** See **desire.**
craw (krô), *n.* **1.** the crop of a bird or insect. **2.** the stomach of an animal. **3. stick in one's craw,** to be irritating or intolerable to one. [ME *crawe,* OE **craga*]
craw·fish (krô′fish′), *n., pl.* (*esp. collectively*) **-fish,** (*esp. referring to two or more kinds or species*) **-fish·es.** crayfish.
crawl¹ (krôl), *v.i.* **1.** to move slowly with the body resting on the ground, as a worm, or on the hands and knees, as a young child. **2.** (of plants or vines) to extend tendrils; creep. **3.** to progress slowly or laboriously. **4.** to move stealthily or abjectly. **5.** to be overrun with or as with crawling things: *The hut crawled with insects.* —*n.* **6.** the act of crawling; a slow, crawling motion. **7.** *Swimming.* a stroke in a prone position, characterized by alternate overarm movements combined with the flutter kick. [ME *crawl(en)* < Scand; cf. Dan *kravle* to crawl, creep] —**crawl′er,** *n.* —**crawl′ing·ly,** *adv.*
—**Syn. 1.** CRAWL, CREEP refer to methods of moving like reptiles or worms, or on all fours. They are frequently interchangeable, but CRAWL is used of a more prostrate movement than CREEP: *A dog afraid of punishment crawls toward his master.* CREEP expresses slow progress: *A baby creeps before walking.* —**Ant. 1.** stride.
crawl² (krôl), *n.* an enclosure in shallow water on the seacoast, for confining fish, turtles, etc. [< D *kraal* KRAAL]
crawl·y (krô′lē), *adj.,* **crawl·i·er, crawl·i·est.** *Informal.* creepy.
cray·fish (krā′fish′), *n., pl.* (*esp. collectively*) **-fish,** (*esp. referring to two or more kinds or species*) **-fish·es. 1.** any fresh-water decapod crustacean of the genera *Astacus* and *Cambarus,* closely related to but smaller than the lobsters. **2.** any of several similar marine crustaceans, esp. the spiny lobster. Also, **crawfish.** [alter. (by folk etym.) of ME *crevis* < MF *crevice* < OHG *krebiz* CRAB¹]

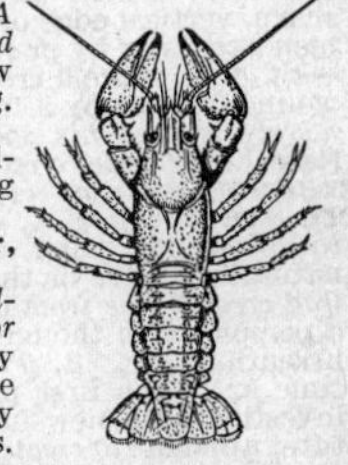

Crayfish,
Cambarus diogenes
(Length 3½ in.)

cray·on (krā′on, -ən), *n., v.,* **-oned, -on·ing.** —*n.* **1.** a pointed stick or pencil of colored clay, chalk, wax, etc., used for drawing. **2.** a drawing in crayons. —*v.t.* **3.** to draw or color with crayons. [< F = *craie* chalk (< L *crēta* clay) + *-on* n. suffix] —**cray′on·ist,** *n.*
craze (krāz), *v.,* **crazed, craz·ing,** *n.* —*v.t.* **1.** to derange or impair the mind of; make insane. **2.** to make small cracks on the surface of (a ceramic glaze, paint, or the like); crackle. **3.** *Brit. Dial.* to crack. **4.** *Archaic.* to weaken; impair. **5.** *Obs.* to break; shatter. —*v.i.* **6.** to become insane. **7.** to become minutely cracked, as a ceramic glaze; crackle. **8.** *Metall.* (of a casehardened object) to develop reticulated surface markings. **9.** *Archaic.* to fall to pieces; break. —*n.* **10.** a widespread fad. **11.** insanity; an insane condition. **12.** a minute crack or pattern of cracks in the glaze of a ceramic object. **13.** *Obs.* flaw; defect. [ME *crase(n)* (to) crush < Scand] —**Syn. 10.** vogue, mode.
cra·zy (krā′zē), *adj.,* **-zi·er, -zi·est,** *n., pl.* **-zies.** —*adj.* **1.** Also, **crazed** (krāzd). demented; insane. **2.** senseless; impractical: *a crazy scheme.* **3.** *Informal.* intensely enthusiastic; passionately excited: *crazy about baseball.* **4.** very enamored or infatuated (usually fol. by *about*): *He was crazy about her.* **5.** intensely anxious or eager; impatient. **6.** unusual; bizarre; singular. **7.** likely to break or fall to pieces. **8.** weak; infirm. **9. like crazy,** *Slang.* with great enthusiasm or energy; to an extreme. —*n.* **10.** *Slang.* an unpredictable, nonconforming person. —**cra′zi·ly,** *adv.* —**cra′zi·ness,** *n.* —**Syn. 1.** lunatic. See **mad. 7.** rickety, shaky, tottering.
cra′zy bone′. See **funny bone.**
cra′zy quilt′, a patchwork quilt made of irregular patches combined with little or no regard to pattern.
cra·zy·weed (krā′zē wēd′), *n.* locoweed.
creak (krēk), *v.i.* **1.** to make a harsh grating or squeaking sound. **2.** to move with creaking. —*v.t.* **3.** to cause to creak. —*n.* **4.** a creaking sound. [ME *crek(en)* (to) croak, appar. back formation from OE *crǣcettan,* var. of *crācettan* to CROAK]
creak·y (krē′kē), *adj.,* **creak·i·er, creak·i·est. 1.** creaking; apt to creak. **2.** old and rundown; dilapidated. —**creak′i·ly,** *adv.* —**creak′i·ness,** *n.*
cream (krēm), *n.* **1.** the part of whole milk that is rich in butterfat. **2.** a soft solid or thick liquid containing medicaments or other specific ingredients, applied externally for a prophylactic, therapeutic, or cosmetic purpose. **3.** Usually, **creams.** a soft-centered confection of fondant or fudge coated with chocolate. **4.** a purée or soup containing cream or milk. **5.** the best part of anything: *the cream of society.* **6.** a yellowish white. **7. cream of the crop,** *Informal.* the best or choicest. —*v.i.* **8.** to form cream. **9.** to froth; foam. —*v.t.* **10.** to work (butter and sugar, or the like) to a smooth, creamy mass. **11.** to prepare (chicken, oysters, vegetables, etc.) with cream, milk, or a cream sauce. **12.** to allow (milk) to form cream. **13.** to skim (milk). **14.** to separate as cream. **15.** to take the cream or best part of. **16.** to use a cosmetic cream on. **17.** *Slang.* to thrash, beat, or defeat. —*adj.* **18.** of the color cream; cream-

colored. [ME *creme* < MF, OF *cresme* < eccl. L *chrisma* CHRISM] —**cream′like′,** *adj.*

cream′ cheese′, a soft, white, smooth-textured, unripened cheese made of sweet milk and sometimes cream.

cream·cups (krēm′kups′), *n., pl.* **-cups.** (*construed as sing. or pl.*) a papaveraceous plant, *Platystemon californicus,* of California, having small, pale-yellow or cream-colored flowers.

cream·er (krē′mər), *n.* **1.** a person or thing that creams. **2.** a small jug, pitcher, etc., for holding cream. **3.** a refrigerator in which milk is placed to facilitate the formation of cream. **4.** a container or apparatus for separating cream from milk.

cream·er·y (krē′mə rē), *n., pl.* **-er·ies. 1.** a place where milk and cream are processed and where butter and cheese are produced. **2.** a place for the sale of milk and its products. **3.** a place where milk is set to form cream.

cream′ ice′, *Brit.* See **ice cream.**

cream′ of tar′tar, a water-soluble powder, $KHC_4H_4O_6$, used chiefly as an ingredient in baking powders and in galvanic tinning of metals. Also called **potassium bitartrate, potassium acid tartrate.**

cream′ puff′, 1. a baked, hollow pastry filled with custard sauce or whipped cream. **2.** *Slang.* **a.** a sissy. **b.** a man who lacks physical strength or stamina.

cream′ sauce′, a white sauce made of cream or milk, flour, and butter.

cream′ so′da, a soft drink made with vanilla-flavored carbonated water colored light brown by caramel.

cream·y (krē′mē), *adj.,* **cream·i·er, cream·i·est. 1.** resembling cream in appearance, consistency, or taste; soft and smooth. **2.** cream-colored. —**cream′i·ly,** *adv.* —**cream′i·ness,** *n.*

crease[1] (krēs), *n., v.,* **creased, creas·ing.** —*n.* **1.** a ridge or groove produced in anything by folding, heat, pressure, etc.; fold; furrow. **2.** a wrinkle, esp. one on the face. **3.** the sharp, vertical edge or line produced in the front and back of men's trousers by pressing, as with a steam presser, iron, etc. —*v.t.* **4.** to make a crease or creases in or on; wrinkle. **5.** to wound or stun by a furrowing or superficial shot: *The bullet merely creased his shoulder.* —*v.i.* **6.** to become creased. [late ME *creeste, crest*] —**crease′less,** *adj.*

crease[2] (krēs), *n.* creese.

cre·ate (krē āt′), *v.,* **-at·ed, -at·ing,** *adj.* —*v.t.* **1.** to cause to come into being, as something unique that would not naturally evolve or that is not made by ordinary processes: *God created Eve from one of Adam's ribs.* **2.** to evolve from a person's own thought or imagination, as a work of art, an invention, etc. **3.** *Theat.* to perform (a role) for the first time or in the first production of a play. **4.** to make by investing with new functions, rank, character, etc.; constitute; appoint: *to create a peer.* **5.** to be the cause or occasion of; give rise to. **6.** to cause to happen; bring about; arrange, as by intention or design: *He wanted to create an opportunity to ask for a raise in his allowance; to create a revolution.* —*v.i.* **7.** to do something creative or constructive. —*adj.* **8.** *Archaic.* created. [ME *creat* (ptp.) < L *creāt(us)* = *creā-* (s. of *creāre* to make) + *-tus* ptp. suffix] —**cre·at′a·ble,** *adj.* —**cre·at′ed·ness,** *n.* —**Syn. 2.** originate, invent.

cre·a·tine (krē′ə tēn′, -tin), *n. Biochem.* an alkaloid or amino acid, $HN{-}C(NH_2)N(CH_3)CH_2COOH$, found in the muscles of vertebrates. [*creat-* (< Gk *kreat-,* s. of *kréas* flesh) + -INE[2]]

cre·at·i·nine (krē at′ᵊnēn′, -at′ᵊnin), *n. Biochem.* the anhydride of creatine, $C_4H_7N_3O$, used chiefly in research. [< G *Kreatinin.* See CREATINE, -INE[2]]

cre·a·tion (krē ā′shən), *n.* **1.** the act of creating; act of producing or causing to exist. **2.** the fact of being created. **3. the Creation,** the original bringing into existence of the universe by God. **4.** a thing that is or has been created. **5.** the world; universe. **6.** creatures collectively. **7.** an original product of the mind, esp. an imaginative artistic work. **8.** a specially designed dress, hat, or other article of women's clothing. [ME *creaccion* < L *creātiōn-* (s. of *creātiō*)]

cre·a·tion·ism (krē ā′shə niz′em), *n.* **1.** the belief that God created the universe, including all life, in its present form precisely as set forth in the Bible in the opening chapter of Genesis. **2.** (*sometimes cap.*) the doctrine that God immediately creates out of nothing a new human soul for each individual born. Cf. **traducianism.** —**cre·a′·tion·ist,** *n.* —**cre·a′tion·is′tic,** *adj.*

cre·a·tive (krē ā′tiv), *adj.* **1.** having the quality or power of creating. **2.** resulting from originality of thought, expression, etc.: *creative writing.* **3.** originative; productive (usually fol. by *of*). —**cre·a′tive·ly,** *adv.* —**cre·a′tive·ness,** *n.*

crea′tive evolu′tion, (in the philosophy of Bergson) the continuous formation of the world as the passive, inert product of the élan vital.

cre·a·tiv·i·ty (krē′ā tiv′i tē), *n.* **1.** the state or quality of being creative. **2.** creative ability or process.

cre·a·tor (krē ā′tər), *n.* **1.** a person or thing that creates. **2. the Creator,** God. [ME *creato(u)r* < eccl. L *creātor*] —**cre·a′tor·ship′,** *n.*

crea·ture (krē′chər), *n.* **1.** anything created, whether animate or inanimate. **2.** an animate being. **3.** an animal, esp. an animal other than man. **4.** a person; human being. **5.** a person who owes his position or fortune to someone or something under whose control or influence he continues. [ME *creature* < eccl. L *creātūr(a)*] —**crea′tur·al,** *adj.* —**crea′ture·ly,** *adv.* —**crea′ture·li·ness,** *n.*

crèche (kresh, krāsh; *Fr.* KRESH), *n., pl.* **crèch·es** (kresh′iz, krā′shiz; *Fr.* KRESH). **1.** *Brit.* a nursery where children are cared for while their mothers work; day nursery. **2.** a home for foundlings. **3.** a tableau of Mary, Joseph, and others around the crib of Jesus in the stable at Bethlehem. [< F << OHG *kripja* CRIB]

Cré·cy (kres′ē; *Fr.* KRĀ sē′), *n.* a village in N France, NW of Reims: English victory over the French 1346. 1419 (1962). Also, **Cressy.**

cre·dence (krēd′ᵊns), *n.* **1.** belief as to the truth of something: *to give credence to a statement.* **2.** something giving a claim to belief or confidence: *letter of credence.* **3.** Also called **cre′dence ta′ble, credenza.** *Eccles.* a small side table, shelf, or niche for holding articles used in the Eucharist service. **4.** credenza (def. 1). [ME < ML *crēdentia*]

cre·den·dum (kri den′dəm), *n., pl.* **-da** (-də). a doctrine that requires belief; article of faith. [< L, neut. of *crēdendus,* ger. of *crēdere* to believe]

cre·dent (krēd′ᵊnt), *adj.* **1.** believing. **2.** *Obs.* credible. [< L *crēdent-* (s. of *crēdēns*), prp. of *crēdere* to believe]

cre·den·tial (kri den′shəl), *n.* **1.** anything that provides the basis for confidence, belief, credit, etc. **2.** Usually, **credentials.** evidence of authority, status, rights, entitlement to privileges, or the like, usually in written form. —*adj.* **3.** providing the basis for confidence, belief, etc. [< ML *crēdenti(a)* CREDENCE + -AL[1]] —**cre·den′tialed,** *adj.*

cre·den·za (kri den′zə), *n.* **1.** Also, **credence.** a sideboard or buffet. **2.** *Eccles.* credence (def. 3). [< It < ML *crēdentia* belief, credit, sideboard; see CREDENCE]

cred·i·ble (kred′ə bəl), *adj.* **1.** capable of being believed; believable. **2.** worthy of belief or confidence; trustworthy: *a credible witness.* [< L *crēdibil(is)* = *crēd(ere)* (to) believe + *-ibilis* -IBLE] —**cred′i·bil′i·ty,** *n.* —**cred′i·bly,** *adv.*

cred·it (kred′it), *n.* **1.** trustworthiness; credibility: *a witness of credit.* **2.** commendation or honor given for some action, quality, etc.: *Give credit where it is due.* **3.** a source of commendation or honor: *You are a credit to your school.* **4.** the ascription or acknowledgment of something as due or properly attributable to a person, institution, etc. **5.** *Educ.* **a.** official acceptance and recording of the work of a student in a particular course of study. **b.** hour (def. 10b). **6.** time allowed for payment for goods or services obtained on trust: *90 days' credit.* **7.** confidence in a purchaser's ability and intention to pay, displayed by entrusting him with goods or services without immediate payment. **8.** reputation of solvency and probity, entitling a person to be trusted in buying or borrowing: *Your credit is good.* **9.** a sum of money due to a person; anything valuable standing on the credit side of an account: *He has an outstanding credit of $50.* **10.** *Bookkeeping.* **a.** an entry of payment or value received on an account. **b.** the right-hand side of an account on which such entries are made (opposed to *debit*). **c.** an entry or the total shown on the credit side. **11.** any deposit or sum of money against which a person may draw. **12. on credit,** by deferred payment: *Everything they have was bought on credit.* —*v.t.* **13.** to believe; put confidence in; trust; have faith in. **14.** to bring honor, esteem, etc., to; reflect credit upon. **15.** *Bookkeeping.* to enter upon the credit side of an account; give credit for or to. **16.** *Educ.* to award educational credits to (often fol. by *with*): *They credited me with three hours in history.* **17. credit to** or **with,** to ascribe to (a thing, person, etc.): *In former times many herbs were credited with healing powers.* [< MF < It *credito* < L *crēditum* loan, n. use of neut. of ptp. of *crēdere* to believe, credit] —**cred′it·less,** *adj.* —**Syn. 2.** merit.

cred·it·a·ble (kred′i tə bəl), *adj.* bringing or deserving credit, honor, reputation, or esteem. —**cred′it·a·ble·ness, cred′it·a·bil′i·ty,** *n.* —**cred′it·a·bly,** *adv.* —**Syn.** praiseworthy, honorable, reputable, respectable.

cred′it card′, a card, issued by a business or agency, allowing the bearer to charge certain purchases or services.

cred′it hour′, hour (def. 10b).

cred′it line′, 1. a line of copy acknowledging the source or origin of published or exhibited material. **2.** Also called **cred′it lim′it.** the maximum amount of credit that a customer of a store, bank, etc., is authorized to use.

cred·i·tor (kred′i tər), *n.* **1.** a person to whom money is due. **2.** *Bookkeeping.* credit (defs. 10b, c). [late ME *creditour* < L *crēditor*]

cred′it un′ion, a cooperative group that makes loans to its members at low interest rates.

cre·do (krē′dō, krā′-), *n., pl.* **-dos. 1.** (*usually cap.*) the Apostles' Creed or the Nicene Creed. **2.** (*usually cap.*) a musical setting of the creed, usually of the Nicene Creed. **3.** any creed or formula of belief. [ME < L: lit., I believe; first word of the Apostles' and Nicene Creeds in Latin]

cre·du·li·ty (kri dōō′li tē, -dyōō′-), *n.* willingness to believe or trust too readily, esp. without proper or adequate evidence; gullibility. [late ME *credulite* < L *crēdulitās*]

cred·u·lous (krej′ə ləs), *adj.* **1.** unduly willing to believe or trust; gullible. **2.** marked by or arising from credulity: *a credulous rumor.* [< L *crēdulus* = *crēd(ere)* (to) believe + *-ulus* -ULOUS] —**cred′u·lous·ly,** *adv.* —**cred′u·lous·ness,** *n.* —**Syn. 1.** believing, trustful, unsuspecting. —**Ant. 1.** cautious, suspicious.

Cree (krē), *n., pl.* **Crees,** (*esp. collectively*) **Cree. 1.** a member of an American Indian people of Ontario, Manitoba, Saskatchewan, and Montana. **2.** an Algonquian language, the language of the Cree Indians.

creed (krēd), *n.* **1.** an authoritative formulated statement of the chief articles of Christian belief. **2. the creed.** See **Apostles' Creed. 3.** an accepted system of religious belief. **4.** any system of belief or of opinion. [ME *crede,* OE *crēda* < L *crēdō* I believe] —**creed′al,** *adj.*

creek (krēk, krik), *n.* **1.** a watercourse smaller than a river. **2.** *Chiefly Brit.* a recess or inlet in the shore of the sea. **3. up the creek,** *Slang.* in a predicament. [ME *creke,* var. of *crike* < Scand; cf. Icel *kriki* nook]

Creek (krēk), *n., pl.* **Creeks,** (*esp. collectively*) **Creek. 1.** a member of a powerful confederacy of Muskogean Indians that formerly occupied most of Alabama and Georgia. **2.** Also called **Muskogee.** a Muskogean language, the language of the Creek Indians.

creel (krēl), *n.* **1.** a basket made of wicker or other material, for holding fish, lobsters, etc. **2.** a trap for fish, lobster, etc. [ME *crele,* perh. < MF **creille,* var. of *greille* GRILLE]

creep (krēp), *v.,* **crept, creep·ing,** *n.* —*v.i.* **1.** to move with the body on or close to the ground, as a reptile or an insect or a child on hands and knees. **2.** to move slowly, imperceptibly, or stealthily: *We crept up and peeked over the wall.* **3.** to sneak up behind someone or without someone's knowledge (usually fol. by *up on*): *We crept up on the guard and knocked him out.* **4.** to move or behave timidly or servilely. **5.** to slip or move along: *The automobile crept through the heavy traffic.* **6.** to enter undetected or unobserved (often fol. by *in* or *into*): *A mood of sadness creeps into the book here and there.* **7.** to slip, slide, or shift slowly along. **8.** to grow along the ground, a wall, etc., as a plant. **9.** (of a metal object) to become deformed, as under continuous loads or at high temperatures. **10. make one's flesh creep,** to be frightening or repellent; cause one to experience uneasiness: *The eerie stories made our flesh creep.* —*n.* **11.** the act of creeping. **12.** *Slang.* a boring, disturbingly eccentric or painfully introverted person. **13.** *Mech.* the gradual, permanent deformation produced by a continued application of heat or stress. **14.** *Geol.* the gradual movement downhill of loose soil, rock, gravel, etc. **15.** a grappling iron; grapnel. **16. the creeps,** *Slang.* a sensation of horror, fear, disgust, etc. [ME *crep(en),* OE *crēopan;* c. D *kruipen,* Icel *krjūpa*] —**Syn. 1.** See **crawl.**

creep·er (krē′pər), *n.* **1.** a person or thing that creeps. **2.** Often, **creepers.** a one-piece garment for an infant. **3.** *Bot.* a plant that grows upon or just beneath the surface of the ground or upon any other surface, sending out rootlets from the stem, as ivy and couch grass. **4.** any of various birds that creep or climb about on trees, esp. of the family *Certhiidae,* of the Northern Hemisphere. **5.** a spiked iron plate worn on the shoe to prevent slipping on ice, rock, etc. [ME *crepere,* OE *crēopere*]

creep′ing erup′tion, *Pathol.* a skin condition caused by the burrowing of dog or cat hookworm larvae under the dermal tissue.

creep·y (krē′pē), *adj.,* **creep·i·er, creep·i·est. 1.** that creeps, as an insect. **2.** having or causing a creeping sensation of the skin, as from horror or fear: *a creepy ghost story.*

creese (krēs), *n.* a short sword or heavy dagger with a wavy blade, used by the Malays. Also, **crease, kris.** [< Malay *kris* dagger]

creesh (krēsh), *n., v.t. Scot.* grease. [late ME *cresche* < MF *creisse,* var. of *greisse* GREASE]

Cre·feld (krā′feld; *Ger.* krā′felt), *n.* Krefeld.

cre·mate (krē′māt), *v.t.,* **-mat·ed, -mat·ing. 1.** to reduce (a dead body) to ashes by fire, esp. as a funeral rite. **2.** to consume by fire; burn. [< L *cremāt(us)* burnt to ashes = *crem(āre)* + *-ātus* -ATE[1]] —**cre·ma·tion** (kri mā′shən), *n.* —**cre·ma′tion·ism,** *n.* —**cre·ma′tion·ist,** *n.* —**cre′ma·tor,** *n.*

cre·ma·to·ri·um (krē′mə tōr′ē əm, -tôr′-, krem′ə-), *n., pl.* **-to·ri·ums, -to·ri·a** (-tōr′ē ə, -tôr′-). a crematory.

cre·ma·to·ry (krē′mə tōr′ē, -tôr′ē, krem′ə-), *n., pl.* **-ries,** *adj.* —*n.* **1.** a place, as a funeral establishment, at which cremation is done. **2.** a furnace for cremating. —*adj.* **3.** of or pertaining to cremation.

crème (krem, krēm, krām; *Fr.* krem), *n., pl.* **crèmes** (kremz, krēmz, krāmz; *Fr.* krem). **1.** cream. **2.** one of a class of liqueurs of a thickish consistency. [< F]

crème de ca·ca·o (krem′ də kä kä′ō, kō′kō, krēm′, krām′; *Fr.* krem də ka ka ō′), a liqueur flavored with cacao and vanilla beans. [< F: lit., cream of cacao]

crème de la crème (krem′ də la krem′), *French.* the very best; choicest part. [lit., cream of the cream]

crème de menthe (krem′ də menth′, mint′, krēm′, krām′; *Fr.* krem də mänt′), a white or green liqueur flavored with mint. [< F: lit., cream of mint]

Cre·mer (krē′mər), *n.* **Sir William Randal,** 1838–1908, English union organizer: Nobel peace prize 1903.

Cre·mo·na (kri mō′nə; *It.* kre mô′nä), *n.* **1.** a city in N Italy, on the Po River. 74,242 (1961). **2.** one of a class of violins of superior quality made there during the 16th, 17th, and 18th centuries.

cre·nate (krē′nāt), *adj.* having the margin notched or scalloped so as to form rounded teeth, as a leaf or a shrunken erythrocyte. Also, **cre′nat·ed.** [< NL *crēnāt(us)* = *crēn(a)* a notch, groove (? back formation from ML *crenellus* CRENEL) + *-ātus* -ATE[1]] —**cre′nate·ly,** *adv.*

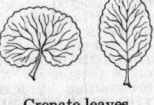

Crenate leaves

cre·na·tion (kri nā′shən), *n.* **1.** a rounded projection or tooth, as on the margin of a leaf. **2.** a notch between teeth.

cren·a·ture (kren′ə chər, krē′nə-), *n.* **1.** a crenation. **2.** a notch or indentation between crenations.

cren·el (kren′ᵊl), *n., v.,* **-eled, -el·ing** or (*esp. Brit.*) **-elled, -el·ling.** —*n.* **1.** any of the open spaces between the merlons of a battlement. **2.** a crenature. —*v.t.* **3.** to crenelate. [late ME < MF, OF, appar. dim. of **cren* notch (recorded from 16th century) < ?]

cren·el·ate (kren′ᵊlāt′), *v.,* **-at·ed, -at·ing,** *adj.* —*v.t.* **1.** to furnish with crenels or battlements. —*adj.* **2.** crenelated. [< F *crénel(er)* (to) crenelate (see CRENEL) + -ATE[1]]

cren·el·at·ed (kren′ᵊlā′tid), *adj.* furnished with crenelations, as a parapet or molding, in the manner of a battlement. Also, *esp. Brit.,* **cren′el·lat′ed.**

Crenelated molding

cren·el·a·tion (kren′ᵊlā′shən), *n.* **1.** act of crenelating. **2.** state of being crenelated. **3.** a battlement or a crenel. **4.** a notch; indentation, as in a garment, wall, piece of furniture, etc. Also, *esp. Brit.,* **cren′el·la′tion.**

cren·el·late (kren′ᵊlāt′), *v.t.,* **-lat·ed, -lat·ing,** *adj. Chiefly Brit.* crenelate.

cren·u·late (kren′yə lāt′, -lit), *adj.* minutely crenate, as the margin of certain leaves. Also, **cren′u·lat′ed.** [< NL *crēnul(ātus)* = *crēnul(a)* (dim. of *crēna* notch; see CRENATE) + *-ātus* -ATE[1]] —**cren′u·la′tion,** *n.*

cre·o·dont (krē′ə dont′), *n.* one of the primitive carnivorous mammals of the extinct suborder *Creodonta,* from the Paleocene to Pleistocene epochs. [< NL *Creodont(a)* = *cre-* (< Gk *kréas* flesh) + *-odont-* -ODONT + *-a* pl. ending]

Cre·ole (krē′ōl), *n.* **1.** a person born in the West Indies or Latin America but of European, esp. Spanish, ancestry. **2.** a person of French ancestry born in Louisiana. **3.** the French patois spoken in parts of Louisiana. Cf. **Cajun. 4.** See **Haitian Creole. 5.** (*l.c.*) a person of mixed Spanish and Negro or French and Negro ancestry. **6.** (*l.c.*) *Archaic.* a native-born Negro, as distinguished from a Negro brought from Africa. —*adj.* **7.** (*sometimes l.c.*) of, pertaining to, or characteristic of a Creole or Creoles. **8.** *Cookery.* (of a sauce or dish) made with tomatoes, peppers, seasonings, etc., and often served with rice. [< F < Sp *criollo* < Pg *crioulo* native < *criar* to bring up < L *creāre;* see CREATE]

Cre·on (krē′on), *n. Class. Myth.* a king of Thebes, the brother of Jocasta and the uncle of Eteocles, Polynices, and Antigone. He defeated the Seven against Thebes.

cre·o·sol (krē′ə sōl′, -sôl′, -sol′), *n. Chem.* a colorless oily liquid, $C_8H_{10}O_2$, having an agreeable odor and a burning taste, obtained from wood tar and guaiacum resin. [CREOS(OTE) + -OL[2]]

cre·o·sote (krē′ə sōt′), *n., v.,* **-sot·ed, -sot·ing.** —*n.* **1.** an oily liquid having a burning taste and a penetrating odor, obtained by the distillation of wood tar and used as a preservative and antiseptic. —*v.t.* **2.** to treat with creosote. [< Gk *kré(as)* flesh + -o- + *sōtḗr* preserver]

cre′osote bush′, an evergreen, zygophyllaceous shrub, *Larrea mexicana,* of northern Mexico and the southwest U.S., bearing resinous foliage with a strong odor of creosote.

crepe (krāp), *n., v.,* **creped, crep·ing.** —*n.* **1.** a thin, light fabric of silk, cotton, or other fiber, with a finely crinkled or ridged surface. **2.** Also called **crepe paper.** thin paper densely wrinkled to resemble this fabric, used for decorating, wrapping, etc. **3.** a silk fabric, usually black, used for mourning veils, bands, etc. **4.** See **crepe rubber. 5.** a thin, light, delicate pancake. —*v.t.* **6.** to cover, clothe, or drape with crepe. Also, **crape.** [< F *crêpe* < L *crīsp(us)* curled, wrinkled]

crêpe (krāp; *for 2 also Fr.* krep), *n., pl.* **crêpes** (krāps; *for 2 also Fr.* krep). **1.** crepe (defs. 1, 3). **2.** crepe (def. 5).

crepe de Chine (krāp′ də shēn′), a light, soft, thin silk or rayon fabric with minute irregularities of surface. [< F: lit., crepe from China]

crepe·hang·er (krāp′hang′ər), *n. U.S. Slang.* crapehanger.

crepe′ myr′tle. See **crape myrtle.**

crepe′ pa′per, crepe (def. 2).

crepe′ rub′ber, 1. a type of crude rubber pressed into crinkled sheets. **2.** a similar type of synthetic rubber used esp. in making shoe soles. Also called **crepe.**

crêpe su·zette (krāp′ sōō zet′; *Fr.* krep sy zet′), *pl.* **crêpe su·zettes** (krāp′ sōō zets′), *Fr.* **crêpes su·zette** (krep sy zet′). a thin dessert pancake, flavored with liqueur and served flambé. Also, **crepe′ su·zette′.** [< F = *crêpe* pancake (see CREPE) + *suzette* special use of proper name]

crep·i·tant (krep′i tᵊnt), *adj.* crackling. [< L *crepitant-* (s. of *crepitāns*) clattering, prp. of *crepitāre,* freq. of *crepāre* to clatter; see -ANT]

crep·i·tate (krep′i tāt′), *v.i.,* **-tat·ed, -tat·ing.** to make a crackling sound; crackle. [< L *crepitāt(us),* ptp. of *crepitāre.* See CREPITANT, -ATE[1]] —**crep′i·ta′tion,** *n.*

crept (krept), *v.* pt. and pp. of **creep.**

cre·pus·cu·lar (kri pus′kyə lər), *adj.* **1.** of, pertaining to, or resembling twilight; dim; indistinct. **2.** *Zool.* appearing or flying in the twilight.

cre·pus·cule (kri pus′kyōōl, krep′ə skyōōl′), *n.* twilight; dusk. Also, **cre·pus·cle** (kri pus′əl). [< L *crepscul(um)* = *crepus-* (var. of *creper* dark) + *-culum* -CULE]

cres., *Music.* crescendo. Also, **cresc.**

cre·scen·do (kri shen′dō, -sen′dō; *It.* kre shen′dô), *n., pl.* **-dos,** *It.* **-di** (-dē), *adj., adv., v.* —*n.* **1.** a gradual increase in force, volume, or loudness. **2.** *Music.* a crescendo passage. —*adj., adv.* **3.** *Music.* gradually increasing in force, volume, or loudness (opposed to *decrescendo*). —*v.i.* **4.** to grow in force or loudness. [< It: lit., growing < L *crescendum,* ger. of *crescere* to grow]

cres·cent (kres′ənt), *n.* **1.** *Astron.* the figure of the moon in its first or last quarter, resembling a segment of a ring tapering to points at the ends. See diag. at **moon. 2.** a shape resembling this. **3.** the emblem of Turkey or of Islam. **4.** the power of Turkey or of Islam. **5.** any crescent-shaped object, as a bun or roll. **6.** a musical percussion instrument of Turkish origin, consisting of a pole bearing a crescent-shaped metal plate, topped with a pavillon, and hung with small bells. —*adj.* **7.** shaped like the moon in its first quarter. **8.** increasing; growing. [< L *crescent-* (s. of *crescēns*) growing, prp. of *crescere;* r. late ME *cressaunt* < AF] —**cres·cen·tic** (krə sen′tik), *adj.*

cre·scit e·un·do (kres′kit e ōōn′dō; *Eng.* kres′it ē un′dō), *Latin.* it grows as it goes: motto of New Mexico.

cres·cive (kres′iv), *adj.* increasing; growing. [< L *cresc(ere)* (to) increase + -IVE]

cre·sol (krē′sōl, -sôl, -sol), *n. Chem.* any of three isomeric compounds having the formula $CH_3C_6H_4OH$, used chiefly as a disinfectant. [*cres-* (irreg. < CREOSOTE) + -OL[2]]

cress (kres), *n.* any of various plants of the mustard family, esp. the watercress, having pungent-tasting leaves often used for salad and as a garnish. [ME *cresse,* OE *cress(a) cresse;* c. D *kers,* G *Kresse*]

cres·set (kres′it), *n.* a metal cup or basket often mounted on a pole or suspended from above, containing oil, pitch, etc., burned as a light or beacon. [ME < MF; OF *craisset* = *craisse* GREASE + -ET]

Cres·si·da (kres′i də), *n.* (in medieval adaptations of the story of the Trojan wars) a new character developed from the characters of Chryseis and Bryseis and portrayed as the lover of the Trojan hero, Troilus, whom she deserts for Diomedes, a Greek. Also, **Criseyde.**

Cres·sy (kres′ē), *n.* Crécy.

crest (krest), *n.* **1.** a tuft or other natural growth on the top of the head of an animal, as the comb of a cock. **2.** anything resembling or suggesting such a tuft. **3.** the ridge of the neck of a horse, dog, etc. **4.** the mane growing from this ridge. **5.** an ornament, ridge, or heraldic device surmounting a helmet. **6.** *Heraldry.* a figure borne above the escutcheon in an achievement of arms, often on a helmet or the like or else by itself as a distinguishing device. **7.** the head or top of anything. **8.** the highest part of a hill or mountain range. **9.** a ridge or ridgelike formation. **10.** the foamy top of a wave. **11.** the point of highest flood, as of a river. **12.** the highest or best of the kind. **13.** a ridge or other prominence on any part of the body of an animal. —*v.t.* **14.** to furnish with a crest. **15.** to serve as a crest for; crown. **16.** to reach the crest of (a hill, mountain, etc.). —*v.i.* **17.** to form or rise to a crest, as a wave or river. [ME *creste* < MF < L *crist(a)*] —**crest′ed,** *adj.* —**crest′less,** *adj.*

crest·fall·en (krest′fô′lən), *adj.* **1.** dejected; dispirited; depressed. **2.** with drooping crest. —**crest′fall′en·ly,** *adv.*

crest·ing (kres′ting), *n.* **1.** *Archit.* a decorative coping, balustrade, etc., usually designed to give an interesting skyline. **2.** *Furniture.* ornamentation carved or sawed in or added to the top rail of a piece of furniture.

cre·ta·ceous (kri tā′shəs), *adj.* **1.** of the nature of, resembling, or containing chalk. **2.** (*cap.*) *Geol.* noting or pertaining to a period of the Mesozoic era occurring from 70,000,000 to 135,000,000 years ago and characterized by the extinction of the giant reptiles and the advent of modern insects. See table at **era.** —*n.* **3.** (*cap.*) *Geol.* the Cretaceous period or system. [< L *crētāceus* = *crēt(a)* chalk (lit., Cretan earth) + *-āceus* -ACEOUS] —**cre·ta′ceous·ly,** *adv.*

Crete (krēt), *n.* a Greek island in the Mediterranean, SE of Greece. 483,258 (1961); 3235 sq. mi. *Cap.:* Canea. Also called **Candia.** —**Cre′tan,** *adj., n.*

cre·tin (krēt′ən, krē′tin), *n.* **1.** a person suffering from cretinism. **2.** a stupid, obtuse, or mentally defective person. [< F; SwissF *creitin, crestin* lit., Christian, i.e., a human being though an idiot] —**cre′ti·noid′,** *adj.* —**cre′tin·ous,** *adj.*

cre·tin·ism (krēt′əniz′əm), *n.* *Pathol.* a chronic disease due to absence or deficiency of the normal thyroid secretion, characterized by physical deformity, dwarfism, idiocy, and, often, goiter. [< F *crétinisme*]

cre·tonne (kri ton′, krē′ton), *n.* a heavy cotton material in printed designs, used esp. for drapery and slip covers. [< F, after *Creton,* Norman village where it was produced]

Cre·ü·sa (krē o͞o′sə), *n.* *Class. Myth.* **1.** Also called **Glauce.** the bride of Jason, slain by the magic of the jealous Medea. **2.** a daughter of Priam and the wife of Aeneas.

cre·val·le (krə val′ē, -val′ə), *n., pl.* (*esp. collectively*) **-le,** (*esp. referring to two or more kinds or species*) **-les.** any of several marine fishes of the jack family, *Carangidae.* [var. of *cavalla* < Sp *caballa* horse mackerel < *caballo* horse < L *caballus*]

cre·vasse (krə vas′), *n., v.,* **-vassed, -vas·sing.** —*n.* **1.** a fissure or deep cleft in glacial ice or the earth's surface. **2.** a breach in an embankment or levee. —*v.t.* **3.** to fissure with crevasses. [< F; see CREVICE]

Crève·coeur (krev kœr′), *n.* **Mi·chel Guil·laume Jean de** (mē shel′ gē yōm′ zhäN də), (pen name: *J. Hector St. John*), 1735–1813, French writer, statesman, and agriculturalist; in U.S. after 1754.

crev·ice (krev′is), *n.* a crack forming an opening; cleft; fissure. [ME *crevace* < MF, OF < *crev(er)* (to) crack (< L *crepāre*) + *-asse* n. suffix] —**crev′iced,** *adj.*

crew[1] (kro͞o), *n.* **1.** a group of persons involved in a particular kind of work or working together: *the crew of a train; a wrecking crew.* **2.** *Naut.* **a.** the company of men who man a ship or boat. **b.** one or all of the common sailors of a ship's company. **3.** the team that mans a racing shell: *varsity crew.* **4.** the sport of racing with racing shells: *He went out for crew in his freshman year.* **5.** *Archaic.* any force or band of armed men. **6.** *Informal.* a company; crowd. —*v.i.* **7.** to serve as crew. [late ME *crewe* augmentation, hence reinforcements, body of soldiers < MF *creue* increase, n. use of fem. of OF *creu,* ptp. of *creistre* to grow < L *crescere;* see CRESCENT]

crew[2] (kro͞o), *v.* a pt. of **crow**[2].

crew′ cut′, a man's haircut in which the hair is closely cropped.

crew·el (kro͞o′əl), *n.* **1.** Also called **crew′el yarn′.** a worsted yarn for embroidery and edging. **2.** crewelwork. [late ME *crule*] —**crew′el·ist,** *n.* —**crew′el·like′,** *adj.*

crew·el·work (kro͞o′əl wûrk′), *n.* decorative embroidery done with worsted yarn on cotton or linen, using simple stitches worked in floral designs. [late ME *crule* yarn]

crew′ neck′, a collarless neckline, as on a sweater or jersey, that fits snugly at the base of the neck. —**crew′-neck′, crew′-necked′,** *adj.*

crib (krib), *n., v.,* **cribbed, crib·bing.** —*n.* **1.** a child's bed with enclosed sides. **2.** a stall or pen for cattle. **3.** a rack or manger for fodder, as in a stable or barn. **4.** a small house or room. **5.** any confined space. **6.** a wicker basket. **7.** *Building Trades, Civil Engineering.* any of various cellular frameworks assembled in layers at right angles, used in the construction of foundations, dams, retaining walls, etc. **8.** a lining for a well or other shaft. **9.** a bin for storing grain, salt, etc. **10.** a barrier projecting part of the way into a river and then upward, acting to reduce the flow of water and as a storage place for logs being floated downstream. **11.** *Brit., Australian.* lunch carried from home and eaten by a laborer on the job; snack. **12.** *Informal.* a petty theft, plagiarism, etc. **13.** *Informal.* a translation, list of correct answers, or other illicit aid used by students, as while reciting, taking exams, or the like; pony. **14.** *Cribbage.* a set of cards made up by equal contributions from each player's hand and belonging to the dealer. —*v.t.* **15.** to confine in or as in a crib. **16.** to provide with a crib or cribs. **17.** to line with timber or planking. **18.** *Informal.* to pilfer or steal, esp. to plagiarize (another's writings or ideas). —*v.i.* **19.** *Informal.* to use a crib in translating. **20.** (of a horse) to practice cribbing. **21.** *Informal.* to steal; plagiarize. [ME *cribbe,* OE *crib(b);* c. D *krib,* G *Krippe*] —**crib′ber,** *n.*

crib·bage (krib′ij), *n.* a card game, basically for two players in which the object is to make counting combinations for points that are scored on a small board (**crib′bage board′**) having holes for pegs.

crib·bing (krib′ing), *n.* **1.** Also called **crib-bit·ing** (krib′bī′ting), **wind-sucking.** an injurious habit in which a horse bites its manger and as a result swallows air. **2.** *Mining.* **a.** a timber lining, closely spaced, as in a shaft. **b.** pieces of timber for lining a shaft, raise, etc. **3.** a system of cribs, as for a building or the like having its foundations rebuilt.

crib·ri·form (krib′rə fôrm′), *adj.* sievelike. Also, **crib·rous** (krib′rəs). [< L *cribr(um)* a sieve + -I- + -FORM]

Crich·ton (krīt′ən), *n.* **James** ("*the Admirable Crichton*"), 1560?–82, Scottish scholar, adventurer, and linguist.

crick[1] (krik), *n.* **1.** a sharp, painful spasm of the muscles, as of the neck or back, making it difficult to move the part. —*v.t.* **2.** to give a crick or wrench to (the neck, back, etc.). [late ME *crikke,* perh. akin to CRICK[2]]

crick[2] (krik), *n.* *U.S. Dial.* creek (def. 1).

Crick (krik), *n.* **Francis Harry Compton,** born 1916, English biophysicist: Nobel prize for medicine 1962.

crick·et[1] (krik′it), *n.* **1.** any of several saltatorial, orthopterous insects of the family *Gryllidae,* characterized by long antennae and stridulating organs on the forewings of the male. **2.** a metal toy consisting of a convex metal piece with a flat metal spring fastened to it at one side that snaps back and forth with a clicking, cricketlike noise when pressed. [ME *criket* insect < MF *criquet* = *criqu(er)* (to) creak (imit.) + *-et* -ET]

Cricket, *Gryllus domesticus* (Length ¾ in.)

crick·et[2] (krik′it), *n.* **1.** a game for two teams of 11 members each that is played on a large field having two wickets 22 yards apart, the object being to score runs by batting the ball far enough so that one is enabled to exchange wickets with the batsman defending the opposite wicket before the ball is recovered. **2.** fair play; gentlemanly conduct: *It wouldn't be cricket to give away his secret.* —*v.i.* **3.** to play cricket. [< MF *criquet* goal post < MFlem *krick* kind of stick; see -ET] —**crick′et·er,** *n.*

crick·et[3] (krik′it), *n.* a small, low stool. [?]

cri·coid (krī′koid), *Anat.* —*n.* **1.** a ring-shaped cartilage at the lower part of the larynx. —*adj.* **2.** of or pertaining to the cricoid cartilage. [< NL *cricoīd(es)* < Gk *krikoeidēs* ring-shaped]

cried (krīd), *v.* pt. of **cry.**

cri·er (krī′ər), *n.* **1.** a person who cries. **2.** a court or town official who makes public announcements. **3.** a hawker. [ME *criere* < OF]

crim., criminal.

crime (krīm), *n.* **1.** an action or an instance of negligence that is deemed injurious to the public welfare or morals or to the interests of the state and that is legally prohibited. **2.** the habitual or frequent performance of crimes: *a life of crime.* **3.** criminal activity and those engaged in it. **4.** any offense, esp. one of grave character. **5.** serious wrongdoing; sin. **6.** *Informal.* a foolish, senseless, or shameful act: *It's a crime to overfeed a dog like that.* [ME < OF < L *crīmin-* (s. of *crīmen*) charge, guilt, crime]
—**Syn. 1.** wrong; misdemeanor, tort, felony. CRIME, OFFENSE agree in meaning a breaking of law. CRIME usually means any serious violation of human laws: *the crime of treason, of robbery.* OFFENSE is used of an infraction of either human or divine law: *an offense leading to a jail sentence; an offense against morals.*

Cri·me·a (krī mē′ə, kri-), *n.* **1.** a peninsula in the SW Soviet Union in Europe, between the Black Sea and the Sea of Azov. **2.** a former autonomous republic of the Soviet Union, now a region of the Ukraine. ab. 10,000 sq. mi. —**Cri·me′an,** *adj.*

Crime′an War′, a war (1853–56) fought by Great Britain, France, Turkey, and Sardinia against Russia, chiefly in the Crimea.

crim·i·nal (krim′ə nəl), *adj.* **1.** *Law.* of or pertaining to crime or its punishment. **2.** of the nature of or involving crime. **3.** guilty of crime. **4.** *Informal.* senseless; foolish: *It's criminal to waste so much time.* —*n.* **5.** a person guilty or convicted of a crime. [late ME < LL *crīmināl(is)*] —**crim′i·nal·ly,** *adv.* —**Syn. 2.** felonious, unlawful, illegal. **5.** convict, culprit, felon, crook, gangster. —**Ant. 2.** lawful. **3.** innocent.

crim′inal assault′, *Law.* **1.** an attack by physical force on a person for which the attacker is liable to criminal prosecution. **2.** a similar act with intent to commit rape.

crim′inal contempt′, *Law.* an act considered to be committed against the dignity or authority of a court and liable to punishment imposed by a judge.

crim′inal conversa′tion, *Civil Law.* adultery.

crim·i·nal·i·ty (krim′ə nal′i tē), *n., pl.* **-ties** for 2. **1.** the quality or state of being criminal. **2.** a criminal act or practice. [< ML *crīminālitās*]

crim′inal law′, laws dealing with criminal offenses and their punishments.

crim·i·nate (krim′ə nāt′), *v.t.,* **-nat·ed, -nat·ing.** **1.** to charge with a crime. **2.** to incriminate. **3.** to censure (something) as criminal; condemn. [< L *crīmināt(us)* accused, ptp. of *crīminārī*] —**crim′i·na′tion,** *n.* —**crim′i·na′tive, crim·i·na·tor·y** (krim′ə nə tōr′ē, -tôr′ē), *adj.* —**crim′i·na′tor,** *n.*

crim·i·nol·o·gy (krim′ə nol′ə jē), *n.* the study of crime and criminals. [< L *crīmin-* (s. of *crīmen;* see CRIME) + -O- + -LOGY] —**crim·i·no·log·i·cal** (krim′ə nəloj′i kəl), **crim′i·no·log′ic,** *adj.* —**crim′i·no·log′i·cal·ly,** *adv.* —**crim′i·nol′o·gist,** *n.*

crim·mer (krim′ər), *n.* krimmer.

crimp[1] (krimp), *v.t.* **1.** to press into small, regular folds; make wavy; corrugate. **2.** to bend (leather) into shape. **3.** to curl (hair), esp. with the use of a curling iron. **4.** *Metalworking.* **a.** to bend the edges of (skelp) before forming into a tube. **b.** to fold the edges of (sheet metal) to make a lock seam. **5.** to produce a corrugated surface in; corrugate, as sheet metal, cardboard, etc. **6.** to press or draw together, as the ends of something. **7.** *Cookery.* to gash (the flesh of a fish) with a knife to make it more crisp when cooked. **8.** to check; arrest; hinder: *The shortage of materials crimped production.* —*n.* **9.** the act of crimping. **10.** a crimped condition or form. **11.** Usually, **crimps.** waves or curls, esp. in hair that has been crimped or that displays a crimped pattern. **12.** the waviness of wool fibers as naturally grown on sheep. **13.** a crease formed in sheet metal or plate metal for fastening purposes or to make the material less flexible. [ME *crymp(en),* OE *(ge)crympan* to curl < *crump* crooked] —**crimp′er,** *n.*

crimp[2] (krimp), *n.* **1.** a person engaged in enlisting seamen, soldiers, etc., by persuasion, swindling, or coercion. —*v.t.* **2.** to enlist (seamen, soldiers, etc.) by such means. [special use of CRIMP[1]]

crim·ple (krim′pəl), *v.t., v.i.,* **-pled, -pling.** to wrinkle, crinkle, or curl. [ME *crymple*]

crimp·y (krim′pē), *adj.,* **crimp·i·er, crimp·i·est.** of a crimped form or appearance.

crim·son (krim′zən, -sən), *adj.* **1.** deep purplish-red. —*n.* **2.** a crimson color, pigment, or dye. —*v.t., v.i.* **3.** to make or become crimson. [late ME *crym(e)syn* < OSp *cremesin* < Ar *qirmizī* (*qirm(iz)* KERMES + -ī suffix of appurtenance) + OSp *-in* -INE[1]; see CRAMOISY] —**crim′son·ly,** *adv.* —**crim′son·ness,** *n.*

cringe (krinj), *v.,* **cringed, cring·ing,** *n.* —*v.i.* **1.** to bend, or crouch, esp. from fear or servility; cower. **2.** to fawn. —*n.* **3.** servile or fawning deference. [ME *crenge(n),* OE **crengan,* causative of *cringan* to yield, fall (in battle)] —**cring′er,** *n.* —**cring′ing·ly,** *adv.*

crin·gle (kriŋ′gəl), *n. Naut.* **1.** an eye or grommet formed on the boltrope of a sail to permit the attachment of lines, consisting of a thimble surrounded by a strop of rope or wire. **2.** the thimble itself. [< LG *kringel* = *kring* circle + *-el* dim. suffix; c. ME *Cringle* (in place-names), Icel *kringla* circle]

cri·nite[1] (krī′nīt), *adj.* **1.** hairy. **2.** *Bot., Entomol.* having long hairs or tufts of long, weak hairs. [< L *crīnīt(us)* = *crīn(is)* hair + *-ītus* -ITE[2]]

cri·nite[2] (krī′nīt, krin′īt), *n.* a fossil crinoid. [CRIN(UM) + -ITE[1]]

crin·kle (kriŋ′kəl), *v.,* **-kled, -kling,** *n.* —*v.t., v.i.* **1.** to turn or wind in many little bends and twists. **2.** to wrinkle; crimple; ripple. **3.** to make slight, sharp sounds; rustle. —*n.* **4.** a turn or twist; wrinkle; ripple. **5.** a crinkling sound. [ME *crinkle(n)*; akin to OE *crincan* to bend, yield, D *krinkelen* to crinkle; see CRINGLE, CRINGE, CRANK[1]]

crin·kle·root (kriŋ′kəl rōōt′, -rŏŏt′), *n.* any of several North American, cruciferous plants of the genus *Dentaria,* esp. *D. diphylla.*

crin·kly (kriŋ′klē), *adj.,* **-kli·er, -kli·est. 1.** having crinkles. **2.** making a rustling noise.

crin·kum-cran·kum (kriŋ′kəm kraŋ′kəm), *n. Archaic.* something full of twists and turns. [humorous var. of *crinkle-crankle,* gradational compound based on CRINKLE; see CRANK[1]]

Crinoid (def. 3)
Sea lily

cri·noid (krī′noid, krin′oid), *adj.* **1.** belonging or pertaining to the *Crinoidea.* **2.** lilylike. —*n.* **3.** any echinoderm of the class *Crinoidea,* having a cup-shaped body to which are attached branched, radiating arms, comprising the sea lilies, feather stars, and various fossil forms. [< Gk *krinoeid(ḗs).* See CRINUM, -OID]

crin·o·line (krin′ᵊlin, -ᵊlēn′), *n.* **1.** a petticoat of haircloth or other stiff material, worn to bell out a skirt. **2.** a hoop skirt. **3.** a stiff, coarse cotton material for interlining. [< F < It *crinolin(o)* = *crino* horsehair (< L *crīn(is)* hair) + *lino* flax < L *līnum*]

cri·num (krī′nəm), *n.* any of the tropical and subtropical, amaryllidaceous plants of the genus *Crinum,* usually having umbels of large, showy flowers. [< NL < Gk *krínon* lily]

cri·ol·lo (krē ō′lō; *Sp.* krē ô′yô), *n., pl.* **-ol·los** (-ō′lōz; *Sp.* -ô′yôs), *adj.* —*n.* **1.** a person born in Latin America but of European, esp. Spanish, ancestry. Cf. **Creole** (def. 1). **2.** a domestic animal of any of several strains or breeds developed in Latin America. —*adj.* **3.** of, pertaining to, or characteristic of a criollo or criollos. [< Sp; see CREOLE]

crip·ple (krip′əl), *n., v.,* **-pled, -pling.** —*n.* **1.** a lame person or animal. **2.** a person who is disabled in any way: *a mental cripple.* **3.** *U.S. Dial.* a swampy, densely overgrown tract of land. —*v.t.* **4.** to make a cripple of; lame. **5.** to disable; impair. [ME *cripel,* OE *crypel;* akin to CREEP] —**crip′pler,** *n.*
—**Syn. 4, 5.** maim. CRIPPLE, DISABLE mean to injure permanently or temporarily, to a degree that interferes with normal activities. To CRIPPLE is to injure in such a way as to deprive of the use of a member, particularly a leg or arm. DISABLE, a more general word, implies such illness, injury, or impairment as makes a person incapable of engaging in his normal activities: *A broken arm cripples but does not disable a judge or an announcer.*

Crip′ple Creek′, a town in central Colorado: gold rush 1891. 425 (1970); 9600 ft. above sea level.

Cripps (krips), *n.* **Sir Stafford,** 1889–1952, British statesman and socialist leader.

Cri·sey·de (kri sā′də), *n.* Cressida.

cri·sis (krī′sis), *n., pl.* **-ses** (-sēz). **1.** a stage in a sequence of events at which the trend of all future events is determined; turning point. **2.** *Lit.* the point at which hostile elements are most tensely opposed. **3.** *Med.* **a.** the point in the course of a serious disease at which a decisive change occurs, leading either to recovery or to death. **b.** the change itself. **4.** a condition of instability, as in social, economic, or political affairs, leading to a decisive change. [< L < Gk *krísis* decision = *krí(nein)* (to) decide + *-sis* -SIS] —**cri′sic,** *adj.* —**Syn. 1.** climax, juncture, exigency.

crisp (krisp), *adj.* **1.** hard but easily breakable; brittle: *crisp toast.* **2.** firm and fresh; not soft or wilted: *a crisp leaf of lettuce.* **3.** brisk; sharp; decided: *a crisp manner.* **4.** lively; pithy; sparkling: *crisp repartee.* **5.** clean and neat; well-groomed. **6.** invigorating: *crisp air.* **7.** crinkled or rippled, as skin or water. **8.** in small, stiff, or firm curls; curly. —*v.t., v.i.* **9.** to make or become crisp. **10.** to curl. —*n.* **11.** *Chiefly Brit.* See **potato chip.** [ME, OE < L *crisp(us)* curled] —**crisp′er,** *n.* —**crisp′ly,** *adv.*

cris·pate (kris′pāt), *adj.* crisped or curled. Also, **cris′pat·ed.** [< L *crispāt(us)* curled, ptp. of *crispāre*]

cris·pa·tion (kri spā′shən), *n.* **1.** the act or state of crisping. **2.** the state of being crisped. **3.** a slight contraction or undulation.

crisp·en (kris′pən), *v.t., v.i.* to make or become crisp.

Cri·spi (krē′spē), *n.* **Fran·ce·sco** (fràn che′skô), 1819–1910, prime minister of Italy 1887–91, 1893–96.

Cris·pin (kris′pin), *n.* **Saint,** with his brother, Saint Crispinian, martyred A.D. c285, Roman Christian missionaries in Gaul: patron saints of shoemakers.

crisp·y (kris′pē), *adj.,* **crisp·i·er, crisp·i·est. 1.** brittle; crisp. **2.** curly or wavy. **3.** brisk. —**crisp′i·ly,** *adv.* —**crisp′i·ness,** *n.*

cris·sal (kris′əl), *adj.* of or pertaining to the crissum. [< NL *crissāl(is)*]

criss·cross (kris′krôs′, -kros′), *adj.* **1.** having many crossing lines, paths, etc. —*n.* **2.** a crisscross mark, pattern, etc. **3.** tick-tack-toe. —*adv.* **4.** in a crisscross manner; crosswise. —*v.t., v.i.* **5.** to mark with or form crossing lines. **6.** to move or cause to move in a crisscross manner. [var. of *christ-cross*]

cris·sum (kris′əm), *n., pl.* **cris·sa** (kris′ə). *Ornith.* **1.** the region surrounding the cloacal opening beneath the tail of a bird. **2.** the feathers of this region collectively. [< NL = L *criss(āre)* (to) move the haunches + *-um* n. suffix]

cris·tate (kris′tāt), *adj.* **1.** having a crest; crested. **2.** forming a crest. Also, **cris′tat·ed.** [< L *cristāt(us).* See CREST, -ATE[1]]

Cris·to·bal (kri stō′bəl), *n.* a seaport in the Canal Zone at the Atlantic end of the Panama Canal, adjacent to Colón. 388 (1970). Spanish, **Cris·tó·bal** (krēs tô′bäl).

Cris·tophe (krē stôf′), *n.* **Henry.** See **Christophe.**

crit., 1. critical. **2.** criticism. **3.** criticized.

cri·te·ri·on (krī tēr′ē ən), *n., pl.* **-te·ri·a** (-tēr′ē ə), **-te·ri·ons.** a standard of judgment or criticism; an established rule or principle for testing anything. [< Gk *kritḗrion* a standard = *krit-* (verbid s. of *krínein* to separate, decide) + *-ērion* neut. suffix of means] —**cri·te·ri·on·al** (krī tēr′ē ə nᵊl), *adj.* —**Syn.** measure, touchstone, test. See **standard.**

crit·ic (krit′ik), *n.* **1.** a person who judges, evaluates, or criticizes. **2.** a person who customarily, as for his occupation, judges the qualities or merits of some class of things, esp. of literary or artistic works, dramatic or musical performances, etc. **3.** a person who tends too readily to make captious, trivial, or harsh judgments. **4.** *Obs.* **a.** criticism. **b.** critique. [< L *critic(us)* < Gk *kritikós* skilled in judging (adj.), critic (n.) = *krī(nein)* (to) separate, decide + *-tikos* -TIC] —**Syn. 2.** reviewer, judge, connoisseur.

crit·i·cal (krit′i kəl), *adj.* **1.** inclined to find fault or to judge with severity, often too readily. **2.** occupied with or skilled in criticism. **3.** involving skillful judgment as to truth, merit, etc.; judicial: *a critical analysis.* **4.** of or pertaining to critics or criticism: *critical essays.* **5.** providing textual variants, proposed emendations, etc.: *a critical edition of Chaucer.* **6.** pertaining to or of the nature of a crisis; crucial: *a critical moment.* **7.** involving grave uncertainty, peril, etc.; dangerous: *a critical wound.* **8.** *Physics.* pertaining to a state, value, or quantity at which one or more properties of a substance or system undergo a change. **9.** *Math.* indicating a point on a curve at which a transition or change takes place. —**crit′i·cal·ly,** *adv.* —**crit′i·cal·ness,** *n.* —**Syn. 1.** carping, faultfinding, caviling. **3.** discriminating, nice, exact, precise. **6.** decisive, climacteric. **7.** hazardous, precarious, perilous. —**Ant. 6.** unimportant.

crit′ical an′gle, 1. *Optics.* the minimum angle of incidence beyond which total internal reflection occurs. **2.** Also called **crit′ical an′gle of attack′.** *Aeron.* the angle of attack, greater than or equal to the angle of attack for maximum lift, at which there is a sudden change in the airflow around an airfoil with a subsequent decrease in lift and increase in drag.

crit′ical mass′, *Physics.* the amount of a given radioactive material necessary to sustain a chain reaction at a constant rate.

crit′ical point′, *Physics.* the point at which a substance in one phase has the same density, pressure, and temperature as in another phase.

crit′ical tem′perature, *Physics.* the temperature of a pure element or compound at a critical point.

crit·ic·as·ter (krit′i kas′tər), *n.* an inferior or incompetent critic. —**crit′ic·as′try,** *n.*

crit·i·cise (krit′i sīz′), *v.i., v.t.,* **-cised, -cis·ing.** *Chiefly Brit.* criticize. —**crit′i·cis′a·ble,** *adj.* —**crit′i·cis′er,** *n.* —**crit′i·cis′ing·ly,** *adv.*

crit·i·cism (krit′i siz′əm), *n.* **1.** the act or art of analyzing and judging the quality of something, esp. a literary or artistic work, musical performance, dramatic production, etc. **2.** the act of passing severe judgment; censure; faultfinding. **3.** a critical comment, article, or essay; critique. **4.** any of various methods of studying texts or documents for the purpose of dating or reconstructing them, evaluating their authenticity, etc. —**Syn. 2.** animadversion. **3.** See **review.**

crit·i·cize (krit′i sīz′), *v.,* **-cized, -ciz·ing.** —*v.i.* **1.** to make judgments as to merits and faults. **2.** to find fault. —*v.t.* **3.** to judge or discuss the merits and faults of. **4.** to censure or find fault with. Also, *esp. Brit.,* **criticise.** —**crit′i·ciz′a·ble,** *adj.* —**crit′i·ciz′er,** *n.* —**crit′i·ciz′ing·ly,** *adv.* —**Syn. 2.** cavil, censure. **3.** appraise. **4.** condemn, blame.

cri·tique (kri tēk′), *n., v.,* **-tiqued, -tiqu·ing.** —*n.* **1.** an article or essay criticizing a literary, architectural, or some other work; review. **2.** a criticism or critical comment on some problem, subject, etc. —*v.t.* **3.** to review or analyze critically. [< F < Gk *kritik(ḗ)* the art of criticism, n. use of fem. of *kritikós* critical; r. CRITIC]

crit·ter (krit′ər), *n. Dial.* a person or animal; creature. Also, **crit′tur.** [var. of CREATURE]

croak (krōk), *v.i.* **1.** to utter a low, hoarse cry, as a frog. **2.** *Slang.* to die. —*v.t.* **3.** to utter or announce by croaking. —*n.* **4.** the act or sound of croaking. [? ME **croke(n),* **crake,* back formation from OE *crācettan* to croak]

croak·er (krō′kər), *n.* **1.** a person or thing that croaks. **2.** any of several sciaenoid fishes that make a croaking noise, esp. *Micropogon undulatus,* found off the Atlantic coast of the southern U.S. **3.** *Slang.* doctor.

croak·y (krō′kē), *adj.,* **croak·i·er, croak·i·est.** low and hoarse: *the croaky call of a frog.*

Cro·at (krō′at), *n.* a native or inhabitant of Croatia; Croatian.

Cro·a·tia (krō ā′shə, -shē ə), *n.* a constituent republic of Yugoslavia, in the NW part: a medieval kingdom; now corresponding to a former Austrian crown land **(Croa′tia and Slavo′nia).** 4,218,000 (est. 1960); 21,835 sq. mi. *Cap.:* Zagreb. Serbo-Croatian, **Hrvatska.**

Cro·a·tian (krō ā′shən, -shē ən), *adj.* **1.** of or pertaining to Croatia, its people, or their language. —*n.* **2.** a Croat. **3.** Serbo-Croatian.

Cro·ce (krô′che), *n.* **Be·ne·det·to** (be′ne det′tô), 1866–1952, Italian statesman, philosopher, and historian.

cro·ce·in (krō′sē in), *n. Chem.* any of several acid azo dyes producing orange or scarlet colors. Also, **cro·ce·ine** (krō′sē-in, -ēn′). [< L *croce(us)* saffron-colored (see CROCUS, -EOUS) + -IN²]

cro·chet (krō shā′; *Brit.* krō′shā, -shē), *n., v.,* **-cheted** (-shād′; *Brit.* -shād, -shēd), **-chet·ing** (-shā′ing; *Brit.* -shā ing, -shē ing). —*n.* **1.** needlework done with a needle having a small hook at one end for drawing the thread or yarn to form intertwined loops. —*v.t., v.i.* **2.** to form by crochet. [< F: knitting needle, lit., small hook, dim. of *croche, croc* < ME or Scand. See CROOK, -ET] —**cro·chet·er** (krō shā′ər; *Brit.* krō′shā ər, -shē-), *n.*

cro·cid·o·lite (krō sid′əlīt′), *n.* a bluish asbestos mineral, essentially a sodium iron silicate. [< Gk *krokid-* (s. of *krokís*) nap, wool + -o- + -LITE]

crock¹ (krok), *n.* **1.** an earthen pot, jar, or other container. **2.** *Brit. Dial.* a metal pot, esp. an iron cooking pot. [ME *crokke,* OE *croc(c), crocca* pot; c. Icel *krukka* jug]

crock² (krok), *n.* **1.** an old ewe. **2.** an old worn-out horse. **3.** *Disparaging.* an old person, esp. if feeble, disabled, or ugly. [late ME *crok* old ewe, perh. akin to obs. *crack* whore and CRACK (v.); cf. LG *krakke* broken-down horse]

crock³ (krok), *n.* **1.** *Dial.* soot; smut. **2.** soil or marking from imperfectly dyed cloth. —*v.t.* **3.** *Dial.* to soil with soot. —*v.i.* **4.** (of cloth) to give off crock when rubbed. [?]

crocked (krokt), *adj. Slang.* drunk.

crock·er·y (krok′ə rē), *n.* crocks collectively; earthenware.

crock·et (krok′it), *n. Archit.* a medieval ornament, almost always suggesting a plant form, and used on the bells of capitals, the copings of gables, etc., that curves up and away from the supporting surface and returns partially upon itself in a knoblike termination. [late ME *croket* hook < AF = *croc* hook (< Gmc; see CROOK¹) + *-et* -ET. See CROCHET]

Crockets on coping of a gable

Crock·ett (krok′it), *n.* **David** ("*Davy*"), 1786–1836, U.S. frontiersman, politician, and folklore hero.

croc·o·dile (krok′ə dīl′), *n.* **1.** any of several crocodilians of the genus *Crocodylus,* found in sluggish waters and swamps of the tropics, having a pointed snout. **2.** any reptile of the order *Crocodilia;* crocodilian. **3.** the tanned skin or hide of this animal. [< L *crocodīl(us)* < Gk *krokódeilos* lizard; r. ME *cocodrille* < ML *cocodrill(us)*]

croc′odile bird′, an African courser, *Pluvianus aegyptius* that often sits upon basking crocodiles and feeds on their insect parasites.

Croc′odile Riv′er, Limpopo.

croc′odile tears′, a hypocritical show of sorrow; false or insincere tears.

Crocodile, *Crocodylus niloticus* (Length 20 ft.)

croc·o·dil·i·an (krok′ə dil′ē ən), *n.* **1.** any reptile of the order *Crocodilia,* comprising the true crocodiles and the alligators, caimans, and gavials. —*adj.* **2.** of or pertaining to the crocodiles.

cro·co·ite (krō′kō īt′), *n.* a mineral, lead chromate, $PbCrO_4$; red lead ore. Also called **cro·co·i·site** (krō′kō i-zīt′). [< Gk *krokó(eis)* saffron-colored + -ITE¹; see CROCUS]

cro·cus (krō′kəs), *n., pl.* **-cus·es. 1.** any of the small, bulbous, iridaceous plants of the genus *Crocus,* cultivated for their showy, solitary flowers. **2.** Also called **cro′cus mar′tis** (mär′tis). a polishing powder consisting of iron oxide. [< L < Gk *krókos* saffron, crocus < Sem; cf. Ar *kurkum* saffron]

Croe·sus (krē′səs), *n., pl.* **-sus·es, -si** (-sī) for 2. **1.** died 546 B.C., king of Lydia 560–546: noted for his great wealth. **2.** a very rich man.

croft (krôft, kroft), *n. Brit.* **1.** a small plot of ground adjacent to a house and used as a kitchen garden, pasture, etc. **2.** a small farm, as one worked by a Scottish crofter. [ME, OE: small field]

croft·er (krôf′tər, krof′-), *n. Brit.* a person who rents and works a very small farm. [ME]

crois·sant (*Fr.* KRWÄ SÄN′), *n., pl.* **-sants** (-SÄN′). a crescent-shaped roll of leavened dough or puff paste. [< F: lit., CRESCENT]

Croix de Guerre (KRWÄDᵊ GER′), a French military award for heroism in battle. [< F: lit., cross of war]

Cro-Mag·non (krō mag′nən, -non, -man′yən; *Fr.* KRŌ-MA NYŌN′), *n.* **1.** an Upper Paleolithic race of men, inhabiting Europe during the Aurignacian-Magdalenian periods, regarded as the prototype of modern European man. See illus. at **Pithecanthropus. 2.** a member of the Cro-Magnon race. [named after the cave (near Périgueux, France) where the first remains were found]

Cro·mer (krō′mər), *n.* **1st Earl of.** See **Baring, Evelyn.**

crom·lech (krom′lek), *n. Archaeol.* **1.** a circle of upright stones or monoliths. **2.** a dolmen. [< Welsh = *crom* bent, curved, crooked (fem. of *crwm*) + *llech* flat stone]

Cromp·ton (kromp′tən), *n.* **Samuel,** 1753–1827, English inventor of the spinning mule.

Crom·well (krom′wəl, -wel, krum′-), *n.* **1. Oliver,** 1599–1658, British general, Puritan statesman, and Lord Protector of England 1653–58. **2.** his son, **Richard,** 1626–1712, British soldier, politician, Lord Protector of England 1658–1659. **3. Thomas, Earl of Essex,** 1485?–1540, British statesman.

crone (krōn), *n.* an ugly, withered old woman. [ME < MD *croonie* old ewe < ONF *caronie* CARRION]

Cro·nin (krō′nin), *n.* **A(rchibald) J(oseph),** 1896–1981, Scottish novelist and physician in the U.S.

Cron·jé (*Du.* KRÔN′yā), *n.* **Piet Ar·nol·dus** (*Du.* pēt är nôl′do͝os), 1835?–1911, Boer general.

Cro·nus (krō′nəs), *n. Class. Myth.* a Titan, son of Uranus and Gaea, who dethroned his father and was in turn dethroned by his own son, Zeus: identified by the Romans with the god Saturn. Also, **Kronos.**

cro·ny (krō′nē), *n., pl.* **-nies.** an intimate friend or companion; chum. [?]

crook (kro͝ok), *n.* **1.** a bent or curved implement, piece, appendage, etc.; hook. **2.** the hooked part of anything. **3.** an instrument or implement having a bent or curved part, as a shepherd's staff or a bishop's crosier. **4.** act of crooking or bending. **5.** any bend, turn, or curve: *a crook in the road.* **6.** *Informal.* a dishonest person, esp. a swindler or thief. **7.** Also called **shank.** a piece of tubing for changing the pitch of a musical wind instrument. —*v.t.* **8.** to bend; curve; make a crook in. —*v.i.* **9.** to bend or curve. [ME *crok(e),* appar. back formation from *croked* CROOKED, but perh. < Scand; cf. Icel *krōkr* hook]

crook·back (kro͝ok′bak′), *n.* a humpback. —**crook′-backed′,** *adj.*

crook·ed (kro͝ok′id; kro͝okt *for 5*), *adj.* **1.** not straight; bending or curved. **2.** askew; awry. **3.** deformed: *a man with a crooked back.* **4.** not straightforward; dishonest. **5.** bent and often raised or moved to one side, as a person's finger or neck. [ME *croked,* OE *crōcod* curved, bent] —**crook′-ed·ly,** *adv.* —**crook′ed·ness,** *n.* —**Syn. 1.** winding, devious, sinuous, spiral, twisted. **3.** misshapen. **4.** unscrupulous, fraudulent.

Crookes (kro͝oks), *n.* **Sir William,** 1832–1919, English chemist and physicist.

crook·neck (kro͝ok′nek′), *n.* any of several varieties of squash having a long, recurved neck.

croon (kro͞on), *v.i.* **1.** to sing or hum in a low, soothing, evenly modulated voice. **2.** to utter a low murmuring sound. —*v.t.* **3.** to sing (a song) in a crooning manner. **4.** to lull by singing to in a low, soothing voice. —*n.* **5.** the act or sound of crooning. [late ME *croyn* < MD *kron(en)* (to) murmur] —**croon′er,** *n.*

crop (krop), *n., v.,* **cropped, crop·ping.** —*n.* **1.** the cultivated produce of the ground, while growing or when gathered. **2.** the yield of such produce for a particular season. **3.** the yield of some other product in a season: *the crop of diamonds.* **4.** a supply produced. **5.** a group of persons or things appearing or occurring together: *a crop of lies.* **6.** the stock or handle of a whip. **7.** Also called **riding crop.** a short riding whip consisting of a stock without a lash. **8.** the act of cropping. **9.** a mark produced by clipping the ears, as of an animal. **10.** a close-cropped hair style. **11.** a special pouchlike enlargement of the gullet of many birds, in which food is held and may undergo partial preparation for digestion. **12.** a digestive organ in other animals; craw. **13. cream of the crop.** See **cream** (def. 7). —*v.t.* **14.** to cut off or remove the head or top of (a plant, grass, etc.). **15.** to cut off the ends or a part of. **16.** to clip the ears, hair, etc., of. **17.** *Photog.* to trim (a print or negative). **18.** to cause to bear a crop or crops. —*v.i.* **19.** to bear or yield a crop or crops. **20. crop out, a.** to rise to the surface. **b.** to become evident or visible; occur: *A few cases of tuberculosis still crop out every now and then.* **21. crop up,** to appear, esp. suddenly or unexpectedly; occur: *A new problem cropped up.* [ME, OE (c. G *Kropf*); basic meaning, protuberance. See CROUP²] —**crop′less,** *adj.*

crop-dust (krop′dust′), *v.t.* to subject (a field) to crop-dusting. —**crop′-dust′er,** *n.*

crop-dust·ing (krop′dus′ting), *n.* the spraying of powdered fungicides or insecticides on crops, as from an airplane.

crop·per (krop′ər), *n.* **1.** a person or thing that crops. **2.** a person who raises a crop. **3.** a person who cultivates land for its owner in return for part of the crop. **4.** a plant that furnishes a crop. **5.** a cloth-shearing machine. **6. come a cropper,** *Informal.* **a.** to fall headlong, esp. from a horse. **b.** to fail suddenly or decisively.

cro·quet (krō kā′; *Brit.* krō′kā, -kē), *n., v.,* **-queted,** (-kād′; *Brit.* -kād, -kēd), **-quet·ing** (-kā′ing; *Brit.* -kā ing, -kē ing). —*n.* **1.** an outdoor game played by knocking wooden balls through a series of wire wickets by means of mallets. **2.** (in croquet) the act of driving away an opponent's ball by striking one's own when the two are in contact. —*v.t.* **3.** to drive away (a ball) by a croquet. [< F (dial.): hockey stick, lit., little hook; see CROCKET]

cro·quette (krō ket′), *n.* a small mass of minced meat, fish, etc., usually coated with bread crumbs and fried in deep fat. [< F, *croqu(er)* (to) crunch (imit.) + *-ette* -ETTE]

cro·qui·gnole (krō′kə nōl′, -kin yōl′), *n.* a type of permanent wave in which the hair is wound around rods from the ends inward and chemically treated. Also called **cro′quignole wave′.** [< F, perh. alter. of **craquenelle* CRACKNEL, influenced by *croquer* to crunch]

crore (krôr, krōr), *n.* (in India) ten millions; one hundred lacs: *a crore of rupees.* [< Hindi *k(a)rōr* < Prakrit *kroḍi*]

cro·sier (krō′zhər), *n.* **1.** the pastoral staff of a bishop or an abbot. See illus. at **cope². 2.** *Bot.* the coiled frond of a fern. Also, **crozier.** [short for *crosier-staff;* late ME *crosier* staff bearer < MF; r. ME *crocer* < AF. See CROSSE, -ER²]

cross (krôs, kros), *n.* **1.** a structure consisting essentially of an upright and a transverse piece, upon which persons were formerly put to death. **2. the Cross,** the cross upon which Jesus died. **3.** a figure of the Cross as a Christian emblem, badge, etc. **4.** a crucifix. **5.** the sign of the Cross made with the right hand as an act of devotion. **6.** a structure or monument in the form of a cross. **7.** Christianity, or those who accept it; Christendom. **8.** any object, figure, or mark resembling a cross, as two intersecting lines. **9.** a mark resembling a cross made instead of a signature by a person unable to write. **10.** a crossing. **11.** a place of crossing. **12.** a thwarting or frustration. **13.** any misfortune or trouble. **14.** a crossing of animals or plants; a mixing of breeds. **15.** an animal, plant, breed, etc., produced by crossing; crossbreed. **16.** a person or thing that is intermediate in character between two others. **17.** *Boxing.* a punch thrown across and over the lead of an opponent: *The champion knocked him out with a right cross to the chin.* **18.** (*cap.*) *Astron.* See **Southern Cross. 19. bear one's cross,** to accept trials or troubles patiently. —*v.t.* **20.** to make the sign of the cross upon or over, as in devotion. **21.** to mark with a cross. **22.** to cancel by marking with a cross or with a line or lines (often fol. by *off* or *out*). **23.** to place in the form of a cross or crosswise. **24.** to put or draw (a line, lines, etc.) across. **25.** *Naut.* to set (a yard) in its proper position on a mast. **26.** to lie or pass across; intersect. **27.** to move, pass, or extend from one side to the other side of (a street, river, etc.). **28.** to transport across something. **29.** to meet and pass. **30.** *Slang.* to betray; double-cross. **31.** to oppose openly; thwart; frustrate. **32.** *Biol.* to cause (members of different species, breeds, or the like) to interbreed. **33.** *Archaic.* to confront in a hostile manner. —*v.i.* **34.** to lie or be athwart; intersect. **35.** to move, pass, or extend from one side or place to another. **36.** to meet and pass. **37.** to interbreed. **38.** *Theat.* to move from one side of the stage to the other, esp. by passing downstage of another actor. **39. cross someone's palm.** See **palm**[1] (def. 10). —*adj.* **40.** lying or passing crosswise or across each other; athwart; transverse: *cross timbers.* **41.** involving interchange; reciprocal. **42.** contrary; opposite. **43.** adverse; unfavorable. **44.** angry and annoyed; snappish. **45.** crossbred; hybrid. [ME, OE *cros* < OIr < L *crux.* See CRUX] —**Syn. 26.** traverse, span, bridge. **31.** baffle, foil, contradict. **44.** petulant, irascible, cantankerous, cranky, ill-tempered, irritable, testy. CROSS, ILL-NATURED, PEEVISH, SULLEN refer to being in a bad mood or ill temper. CROSS means temporarily in an irritable or fretful state, and sometimes somewhat angry: *a cross reply; cross and tired.* ILL-NATURED implies a more permanent condition, without definite cause, and means unpleasant, unkind, inclined to snarl or be spiteful: *an ill-natured dog; ill-natured spite.* PEEVISH means complaining and snappish: *a peevish and whining child.* SULLEN suggests a kind of glowering silent gloominess and means refusing to speak because of bad humor, anger, or a sense of injury or resentment: *sullen and vindictive.* —**Ant. 31.** aid. **44.** good-natured, agreeable.

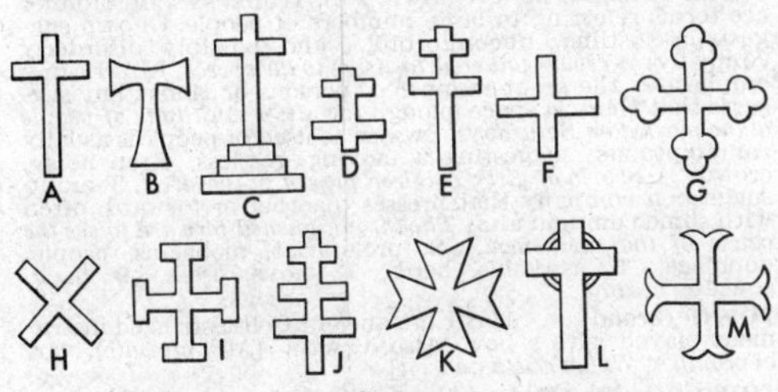

Crosses
A, Latin cross; B, Tau cross or St. Anthony's cross; C, Cross of Calvary; D, Cross of Lorraine; E, Patriarchal cross; F, Greek cross; G, Botonee; H, St. Andrew's cross; I, Jerusalem cross; J, Papal cross; K, Maltese cross; L, Celtic cross; M, Moline

cross·arm (krôs′ärm′, kros′-), *n.* a horizontal arm, bar, line, etc., that crosses or is fastened to a vertical counterpart. —**cross′-armed′,** *adj.*

cross·bar (krôs′bär′, kros′-), *n.* **1.** a transverse bar, line, or stripe. **2.** a horizontal bar used for gymnastics.

cross·beam (krôs′bēm′, kros′-), *n.* a transverse beam in a structure, as a joist.

cross-bed·ded (krôs′bed′id, kros′-), *adj. Geol.* having irregular laminations, as strata of sandstone, inclining in various directions not coincident with the general stratification. [CROSS + *bedded* (see BED, -ED[2])]

cross·bill (krôs′bil′, kros′-), *n.* any fringilline bird of the genus *Loxia,* characterized by mandibles curved so that the tips cross each other when the bill is closed.

cross′ bond′, a brickwork bond having courses of headers alternating with courses of stretchers in such a way that the joints of each course of stretchers are in line with the centers of the next courses of stretchers above and below.

cross·bones (krôs′bōnz′, kros′-), *n.pl.* two bones placed crosswise, usually below a skull, symbolizing death.

cross·bow (krôs′bō′, kros′-), *n.* a weapon consisting of a bow fixed transversely on a stock, the string of which is released by a trigger mechanism. [late ME *crossebowe*]

A, Crossbow (15th century)
B, Crannequin

cross·bow·man (krôs′bō′mən, -bō′-, kros′-), *n., pl.* **-men. 1.** a person equipped with or skilled in the use of a crossbow, as a soldier or hunter. **2.** (in medieval warfare) a foot soldier armed with a crossbow.

cross·bred (krôs′bred′, kros′-), *adj.* **1.** produced by crossbreeding. —*n.* **2.** an animal or group of animals produced by hybridization.

cross·breed (krôs′brēd′, kros′-), *v.,* **-bred, -breed·ing,** *n.* —*v.t.* **1.** to produce (a hybrid) within a species, using two breeds or varieties. —*v.i.* **2.** to undertake or engage in hybridizing, esp. within a single species. —*n.* **3.** a crossbreed.

cross-country (*adj.* krôs′kun′trē, kros′-; *n.* krôs′kun′trē, -kun′-, kros′-), *adj.* **1.** directed or proceeding over fields, through woods, etc., rather than on a road or path: *a cross-country race.* **2.** from one end of the country to the other: *a cross-country flight.* —*n.* **3.** a cross-country sport or sports.

cross·cur·rent (krôs′kûr′ənt, -kur′-, kros′-), *n.* **1.** a current, as in a stream, moving across the main current. **2.** Often, **crosscurrents.** a conflicting tendency or movement.

cross·cut (krôs′kut′, kros′-), *adj., n., v.,* **-cut, -cut·ting.** —*adj.* **1.** made or used for cutting crosswise. **2.** cut across the grain or on the bias. —*n.* **3.** a transverse cut or course. **4.** a shortcut. **5.** *Mining.* an underground passageway, usually from a shaft to a vein of ore or crosswise of a vein of ore. —*v.t.* **6.** to cut or go across.

cross′cut saw′, a saw for cutting wood across the grain.

crosse (krôs, kros), *n.* See under **lacrosse.** [< F: lit., hooked stick, OF *croce* < Gmc; see CRUTCH, CROOK]

cross-ex·am·ine (krôs′ig zam′in, kros′-), *v.t.,* **-ined, -in·ing. 1.** to examine by questions intended to check a previous examination; examine closely or minutely. **2.** *Law.* to examine (a witness called by the opposing side), as for the purpose of discrediting his testimony. —**cross-ex·am·i·na·tion** (krôs′ig zam′ə nā′shən, kros′-), *n.* —**cross′-ex·am′in·er,** *n.*

cross-eye (krôs′ī′, kros′ī′), *n.* strabismus, esp. the form in which both eyes turn toward the nose.

cross-eyed (krôs′īd′, kros′-), *adj.* suffering from cross-eye or strabismus. —**cross′-eyed′ness,** *n.*

cross-fer·ti·li·za·tion (krôs′fûr′t^{ə}li zā′shən, kros′-), *n.* **1.** *Biol.* the fertilization of an organism by the fusion of an egg from one individu al with a sperm or male gamete from a different individual. **2.** *Bot.* fertilization of the flower of one plant by a gamete from the flower of a closely related plant (opposed to *self-fertilization*). **3.** (not used technically) cross-pollination.

cross-fer·ti·lize (krôs′fûr′t^{ə}līz′, kros′-), *v.t.,* **-lized, -liz·ing.** to cause the cross-fertilization of.

cross′ fire′, 1. a brisk exchange, as of words or opinions. **2.** a predicament arising from conflicting claims on one's attention, help, sympathy, etc. **3.** *Mil.* lines of fire from two or more positions, crossing one another. Also, **cross′fire′.**

cross-gar·net (krôs′gär′nit, kros′-), *n.* a T-shaped strap hinge with the crosspiece as the stationary member. See illus. at **hinge.**

cross-grained (krôs′grānd′, kros′-), *adj.* **1.** having the grain running transversely or diagonally, or having an irregular or gnarled grain, as timber. **2.** stubborn; perverse.

cross′ hairs′, fine wires or threads crossing in a focal plane of an optical instrument and serving to define a line of sight. Also called **cross wires.**

cross·hatch (krôs′hach′, kros′-), *v.t.* to hatch or shade with two or more intersecting series of parallel lines. —**cross′hatch′ing,** *n.*

cross·head (krôs′hed′, kros′-), *n. Mach.* a sliding member of a reciprocating engine for keeping the motion of the joint between a piston rod and a connecting rod in a straight line.

cross·ing (krô′sing, kros′ing), *n.* **1.** the act of a person or thing that crosses. **2.** an intersection, as of lines, streets, railroad tracks, etc. **3.** a place at which a road, river, etc., may be crossed. **4.** the act of opposing or thwarting; frustration; contradiction. **5.** *Railroads.* a track structure permitting two tracks to cross one another at grade with sufficient clearance for wheel flanges. **6.** hybridization; crossbreeding.

cross′ing o′ver, *Genetics.* the interchange of corresponding chromatid segments of homologous chromosomes with their linked genes.

cross·jack (krôs′jak′, kros′-; *Naut.* krô′jik, kroj′ik), *n. Naut.* the lowermost square sail set on the mizzenmast of a ship; mizzen course. See diag. at **ship.**

cross-leg·ged (krôs′leg′id, -legd′, kros′-), *adj.* having the legs crossed; having one leg laid across the other.

cross·let (krôs′lit, kros′-), *n.* a small cross, as one used as a heraldic charge. [late ME *croslet*]

cross-link (*n.* krôs′lingk′, kros′-; *v.* krôs′lingk′, kros′-), *Chem.* —*n.* **1.** a bond, atom, or group linking the chains of atoms in a polymer, protein, or other complex organic molecule. —*v.t.* **2.** to attach by a cross-link.

cross·ly (krôs′lē, kros′-), *adv.* in a cross or angry manner.

cross·ness (krôs′nis, kros′-), *n.* the quality or condition of being cross or irritable; irritability.

cross′ of Cal′vary, a Latin cross with a representation of steps beneath it. See illus. at **cross.**

cross′ of Lorraine′, a cross having two crosspieces, the upper shorter than the lower. See illus. at **cross.**

cros·sop·te·ryg·i·an (kro sop′tə rij′ē ən), *n.* any fish of the group *Crossopterygii,* extinct except for the coelacanth, regarded as being ancestral to amphibians and other land vertebrates. [< NL *Crossopterygi(ī)* (< Gk *krosso(ī)* tassels, fringe + *pterýgi(on)* little wing or fin = *pteryg-* (s. of *ptéryx*) wing, fin + *-ion* dim. suffix) + -AN]

cross·o·ver (krôs′ō′vər, kros′-), *n.* **1.** a bridge or other structure for crossing a river, highway, etc. **2.** an act or instance of crossing over. **3.** *Genetics.* **a.** See **crossing over. b.** a genotype resulting from crossing over. **4.** *Railroads.* a track structure composed of two or more turnouts. **5.** (in plumbing) a U-shaped pipe for by-passing another pipe.

cross·patch (krôs′pach′, kros′-), *n. Informal.* a bad-tempered person.

cross·piece (krôs′pēs′, kros′-), *n.* a piece of any material placed across something; transverse piece.

cross-pol·li·nate (krôs′pol′ə nāt′, kros′-), *v.t.,* **-nat·ed, -nat·ing.** to subject to cross-pollination.

cross-pol·li·na·tion (krôs′pol′ə nā′shən, kros′-), *n. Bot.* the transfer of pollen from the flower of one plant to the flower of a plant having a different genetic constitution. Cf. **self-pollination.**

cross′ prod′uct, *Math.* See **vector product.**

cross-pur·pose (krôs′pûr′pəs, kros′-), *n.* **1.** an opposing or contrary purpose. **2. at cross-purposes,** in a way that involves or produces mutual misunderstanding or frustration, usually unintentionally.

cross-ques·tion (krôs′kwes′chən, kros′-), *v.t.* **1.** to cross-examine. —*n.* **2.** a question that is asked by way of cross-examination. —**cross′-ques′tion·ing,** *n.*

cross-re·fer (krôs′ri fûr′, kros′-), *v.t., v.i.,* **-ferred, -fer·ring.** to refer by a cross reference.

cross′ ref′erence, a reference from one part of a book, index, or the like, to another part.

cross·road (krôs′rōd′, kros′-), *n.* **1.** a road that crosses another road, or one that runs transversely to main roads. **2.** a by-road. **3.** Often, **crossroads.** (*construed as sing. or pl.*) **a.** the place where roads intersect. **b.** a point at which a vital decision must be made. **c.** a main center of activity.

cross′ sec′tion, 1. a section made by a plane cutting anything transversely, esp. at right angles to the longest axis. **2.** a piece so cut off. **3.** a pictorial representation of such a section. **4.** the act of cutting anything across. **5.** a typical selection; a sample showing all characteristic parts, relationships, etc.: *a cross section of American opinion.* **6.** *Survey.* a vertical section of the ground surface taken at right angles to a survey line. **7.** *Naval Archit.* station (def. 13). **8.** Also called **nuclear cross section.** *Physics.* a quantity expressing the effective area that a given nucleus presents as a target to a bombarding particle, giving a measure of the probability that the particle will induce a reaction. —**cross′-sec′tion·al,** *adj.*

cross-stitch (krôs′stich′, kros′-), *n.* **1.** a stitch forming an ×. —*v.t., v.i.* **2.** to work in cross-stitch.

cross′ street′, a street crossing another street, or one running transversely to main streets.

cross′ talk′, interference by or reception of other sound, radio, or similar waves or frequencies on a telephone, radio, or other receiving apparatus.

cross·tie (krôs′tī′, kros′-), *n.* **1.** a transverse timber forming a foundation or support; sleeper. **2.** *Railroads.* a tie. —**cross′-tied′,** *adj.*

cross·town (krôs′toun′, kros′-), *adj.* **1.** situated or traveling in a direction extending across a town or city. —*adv.* **2.** in a direction extending across a town or city: *The car sped crosstown.*

cross·tree (krôs′trē′, kros′-), *n.* *Naut.* either of a pair of timbers or metal bars placed either athwart the trestletrees at a masthead to spread the shrouds leading to the mast above, or on the head of a lower mast to support the platform or top.

cross·walk (krôs′wôk′, kros′-), *n.* a lane, usually marked, for pedestrians crossing a street or highway.

cross·way (krôs′wā′, kros′-), *n.* a crossroad. [ME *crosswey*]

C, Crosstree

cross′ wind′ (wind), a wind blowing across the course of a ship, aircraft, etc. Also, **cross′-wind′.**

cross′ wires′. See **cross hairs.**

cross·wise (krôs′wīz′, kros′-), *adv.* **1.** across; transversely. **2.** in the form of a cross. **3.** contrarily. Also, **cross·ways** (krôs′wāz′, kros′-). [ME *a crosse wise* in the form of a cross]

cross′word puz′zle (krôs′wûrd′, kros′-), a puzzle in which words corresponding to numbered clues or definitions are fitted into a pattern of horizontal and vertical squares so that most letters form part of two words.

crotch (kroch), *n.* **1.** a forked piece, part, support, etc. **2.** a forking or place of forking, as of the human body between the legs. **3.** the part of a pair of trousers, panties, or the like, formed by the joining of the two legs. **4.** *Naut.* crutch (def. 5). [var. of CRUTCH] —**crotched** (krocht), *adj.*

crotch·et (kroch′it), *n.* **1.** a small hook. **2.** a hooklike device or part. **3.** a curved surgical instrument with a sharp hook. **4.** an odd fancy or whimsical notion. **5.** *Music Chiefly Brit.* a quarter note. See illus. at **note.** [ME *crochet* hook, staff with hook at end; doublet of CROCKET] —**Syn. 4.** caprice, whimsy, humor; eccentricity.

crotch·et·y (kroch′i tē), *adj.* **1.** given to odd notions, whims, grouchiness, etc. **2.** of the nature of a crotchet. —**crotch′et·i·ness,** *n.*

cro·ton (krōt′ən), *n.* **1.** any of the chiefly tropical, euphorbiaceous plants of the genus *Croton,* many species of which, as *C. Tiglium,* have important medicinal properties. **2.** (among florists) any plant of the related genus *Codiaeum* (or *Phyllaurea*) cultivated for the ornamental foliage. [< NL < Gk *krotōn* a tick, also the castor-oil plant, which has berries likened to ticks]

Cro′ton bug′ (krōt′ən). See **German cockroach.** Also, **cro′ton·bug′.** [named after the *Croton* Aqueduct water, introduced into New York City in 1842]

cro·ton′ic ac′id (krō ton′ik, -tō′nik), *Chem.* a solid, $CH_3CH{=}CHCOOH$, used chiefly in organic synthesis.

cro′ton oil′, a brownish-yellow oil expressed from the seeds of the croton, *Croton Tiglium,* that is a drastic purgative and counterirritant.

crouch (krouch), *v.i.* **1.** to stoop or bend low. **2.** to bend close to the ground, as an animal preparing to spring. **3.** to bow or stoop servilely; cringe. —*v.t.* **4.** to bend low. —*n.* **5.** the act of crouching; a stooping or bending low. [ME *crouche(n),* perh. b. *couchen* to lie down (see COUCH) and *croken* to CROOK]

croup[1] (kro͞op), *n.* *Pathol.* any condition of the larynx or trachea characterized by a hoarse cough and difficult breathing. [n. use of *croup* to cry hoarsely (now dial.), b. CROAK and WHOOP] —**croup′ous,** *adj.*

croup[2] (kro͞op), *n.* the highest part of the rump of a horse. [ME *croupe* < OF < Gmc; see CROP]

crou·pi·er (kro͞o′pē ər, -pē ā′, *Fr.* kro͞o pyā′), *n., pl.* **-pi·ers** (-pē ərz, -pē āz′; *Fr.* -pyā′). **1.** an attendant who collects and pays the money at a gaming table. **2.** an assistant chairman at a public dinner. [< F: lit., one who sits behind another on horseback. See CROUP[2], -ER[2]]

croup·y (kro͞o′pē), *adj.,* **croup·i·er, croup·i·est. 1.** pertaining to or resembling croup. **2.** affected with croup. —**croup′i·ly,** *adv.* —**croup′i·ness,** *n.*

crouse (kro͞os), *adj.* *Scot. and North Eng.* bold; brisk; lively. [ME *crus, crous* fierce, bold, violent < MLG or Fris *krūs* crisp; c. G *kraus*] —**crouse′ly,** *adv.*

crou·ton (kro͞o′ton, kro͞o ton′), *n.* a small, crisp piece of fried or toasted bread, used in soups, as a garnish, etc. [< F, dim. of *croûte* CRUST]

crow[1] (krō), *n.* **1.** any of several oscine birds of the genus *Corvus,* of the family *Corvidae,* having lustrous black plumage, as the common *C. brachyrhynchos,* of North America. **2.** crowbar. **3. as the crow flies,** in a straight line; by the most direct route. **4. eat crow,** *Informal.* to be forced to accept or perform something embarrassing to one, as to retract an emphatic statement or admit that one is wrong; suffer humiliation. [ME *crowe,* OE *crāwe,crāwa;*c.OHG *krāwa;* akin to D *kraai,*G *Krähe*]

Crow, *Corvus brachyrhynchos* (Length 19 in.; wingspread 3 ft.)

crow[2] (krō), *v.,* **crowed** or, for 1 (*esp. Brit.*) **crew; crowed;**

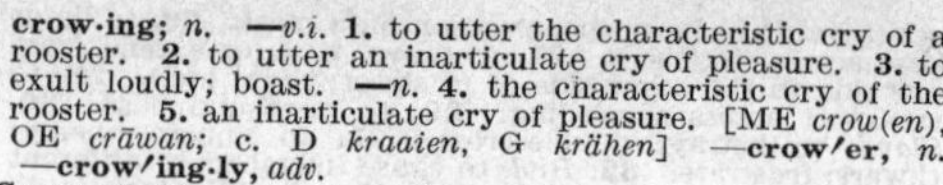

crow·ing; *n.* —*v.i.* **1.** to utter the characteristic cry of a rooster. **2.** to utter an inarticulate cry of pleasure. **3.** to exult loudly; boast. —*n.* **4.** the characteristic cry of the rooster. **5.** an inarticulate cry of pleasure. [ME *crow(en),* OE *crāwan;* c. D *kraaien,* G *krähen*] —**crow′er,** *n.* —**crow′ing·ly,** *adv.*

Crow (krō), *n.* **1.** a member of a Siouan people of eastern Montana. **2.** a Siouan language closely related to Hidatsa. [trans. (through F (*gens de*) *corbeaux* (the people) of the crow) of their own name *Absaroke* crow, sparrow hawk, bird people]

crow·bar (krō′bär′), *n.* a steel bar, usually flattened and slightly bent at one or both ends, used as a lever. Also called **crow.** [CROW[1] + BAR[1]; r. ME *crowe,* so called because one end was beak-shaped]

crow·ber·ry (krō′ber′ē, -bə rē), *n., pl.* **-ries. 1.** the black or reddish berry of a heathlike, evergreen shrub, *Empetrum nigrum,* of northern regions. **2.** the plant itself. **3.** any of certain other fruits or the plants bearing similar berries, as the bearberry. [CROW[1] + BERRY, prob. trans. of G *Krähenbeere*]

crowd[1] (kroud), *n.* **1.** a large number of persons gathered closely together; throng. **2.** the common people; the masses. **3.** any group or class of persons: *They cater to a society crowd.* **4.** a large number of things gathered or considered together. **5.** audience; attendance: *Opening night drew a good crowd.* —*v.i.* **6.** to gather in large numbers. **7.** to press forward; advance by pushing. —*v.t.* **8.** to push; shove. **9.** to press closely together; force into a confined space; cram: *to crowd clothes into a suitcase.* **10.** to fill to excess; fill by pressing or thronging into. [ME *crowd(en),* OE *crūden* to press, hurry; c. MD *crūden* to push (D *kruien*)] —**Syn. 1.** horde, herd. CROWD, MULTITUDE, SWARM, THRONG are terms referring to large numbers of people. CROWD suggests a jostling, uncomfortable, and possibly disorderly company: *A crowd gathered to listen to the speech.* MULTITUDE emphasizes the great number of persons or things but suggests that there is space enough for all: *a multitude of people at the market on Saturdays.* SWARM as used of people is usually contemptuous, suggesting a moving, restless, often noisy, crowd: *A swarm of dirty children played in the street.* THRONG suggests a company that presses together or forward, often with some common aim: *The throng pushed forward to see the cause of the excitement.* **2.** proletariat, plebeians, people, populace. **6.** assemble, herd. **7.** shove, press. **9.** pack, squeeze, cramp.

crowd[2] (kroud), *n.* *Music.* an ancient Celtic stringed instrument played with a bow. Also, **crwth.** [ME *crowd(e),* var. of *crouth* < Welsh *crwth* CRWTH]

crowd·ed (krou′did), *adj.* **1.** filled to excess; filled with a crowd; packed. **2.** uncomfortably close together: *crowded passengers on a bus.*

crow·dy (kro͞o′dē, krō′-, kro͝od′ē), *n., pl.* **-dies.** *Scot. and North Eng.* porridge. Also, **crow′die.** [?]

crow·foot (krō′fo͝ot′), *n., pl.* **-foots** for 1, 2, **-feet** for 3, 4. **1.** any plant of the genus *Ranunculus,* esp. one with divided leaves suggestive of a crow's foot; buttercup. **2.** any of various other plants with leaves or other parts suggestive of a bird's foot, as certain species of the genus *Geranium.* **3.** caltrop (def. 2). **4.** *Naut.* an arrangement of ropes for supporting an awning. [late ME *crowefote*]

crown (kroun), *n.* **1.** any of various types of symbolic headgear worn by a king, queen, emperor, etc., as a symbol of sovereignty. **2.** an ornamental wreath or circlet for the head, conferred by the ancients as a mark of victory, athletic or military distinction, etc. **3.** the distinction that comes from a great achievement. **4. the Crown,** the sovereign as head of the state, or the supreme power of a monarch. **5.** any of various coins bearing the figure of a crown or crowned head. **6.** a former silver coin of the United Kingdom, equal to five shillings. **7.** the monetary unit of Denmark, Iceland, Norway, and Sweden: a krona or krone. **8.** the koruna of Czechoslovakia. **9.** something having the form of a crown, as the corona of a flower. **10.** *Bot.* **a.** the leaves and living branches of a tree. **b.** the point at which the root of a seed plant joins the stem. **11.** the top or highest part of anything, as of the head, a hat, a mountain, etc. **12.** the highest point of any construction of convex outline, as an arch. **13.** the top of the head. **14.** the crest, as of a bird. **15.** *Dentistry.* **a.** the part of a tooth that is covered by enamel. **b.** an artificial substitute, as of gold or porcelain, for the crown of a tooth. **16.** the highest or most nearly perfect state of anything. **17.** an exalting or chief attribute. **18.** Also called **button.** *Horol.* a knurled knob for winding a watch. **19.** Also called **head.** *Naut.* the part of an anchor at which the arms join the shank. **20.** Also called **bezel, top.** *Jewelry.* the part of a cut gem above the girdle. **21.** *Naut., Mach.* swallow[1] (def. 12). **22.** *Knots.* a knot made by interweaving the strands at the end of a rope. —*v.t.* **23.** to place a crown or garland upon the head of. **24.** to invest with or as with a regal crown or with regal dignity and power. **25.** to surmount as with a crown. **26.** to complete worthily; bring to a successful or triumphant conclusion: *The Nobel prize crowned his career as an author.* **27.** *Informal.* to hit on the top of the head. **28.** to give to (a construction) an upper surface of convex section or outline. **29.** to cap (a tooth) with a false crown. **30.** *Checkers.* to change (a checker) into a king by putting another checker of the same color on top of it. **31.** *Knots.* to form a crown on (the end of a rope). [ME *c(o)roune* < AF < L *corōn(a)* wreath; see CORONA] —**crown′less,** *adj.*

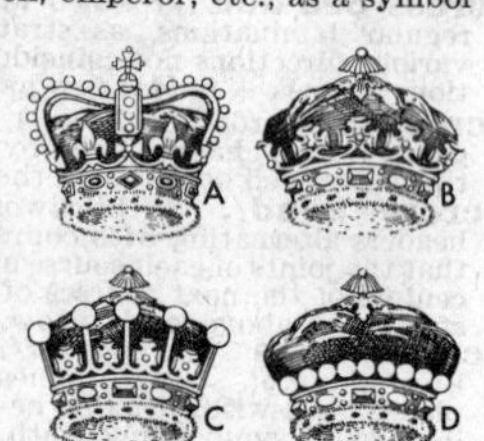

Crowns of British royalty and nobility: A, Sovereign; B, Duke; C, Earl; D, Viscount

crown′ ant′ler, the topmost prong of a stag's antler. Also called **sur-royal.**

crown′ col′ony, a colony in which the Crown controls legislation and administration, as distinguished from one in which there is a constitution and representative government.

crown·er[1] (krou′nər), *n.* a person or thing that crowns. [late ME; see CROWN, -ER[1]]

crown·er[2] (krou′nər, kro͞o′-), *n. Brit. Dial.* coroner. [late ME; see CROWN, -ER[2]]

crown′ glass′, **1.** an optical glass of low dispersion and generally low index of refraction. **2.** an old form of window glass formed by blowing a globe and whirling it into a disk.

crown′ jew′els, the ceremonial objects of a sovereign, as the crown, scepter, etc., that are heavily jeweled.

crown′ land′, land belonging to the Crown, the revenue of which goes to the reigning sovereign.

crown′ lens′, *Optics.* a lens made of crown glass, usually the converging lens component of an achromatic lens.

crown·piece (kroun′pēs′), *n.* **1.** a piece or part forming or fitting the crown or top of anything. **2.** the strap of a bridle that fits across the head of a horse.

Crown′ Point′, a village in NE New York, on Lake Champlain: the site of a fort in the French and Indian and the Revolutionary wars.

crown′ prince′, the heir apparent of a monarch.

crown′ prin′cess, **1.** the wife of a crown prince. **2.** a female heir presumptive.

crown′ saw′, a rotary saw consisting of a hollow cylinder with teeth formed on one end or edge.

crow's-foot (krōz′fo͝ot′), *n., pl.* **-feet.** **1.** Usually **crow's-feet.** wrinkles at the outer corner of the eye. **2.** *Aeron.* a method by which one main cord exerts pressure or pull at several points simultaneously through smaller ropes. [so called because likened to a crow's foot or footprint]

crow's-nest (krōz′nest′), *n.* **1.** *Naut.* a platform or shelter for a lookout at or near the top of a mast. **2.** any similar station ashore, as for a traffic officer. Also, **crow's′ nest′.**

crow·step (krō′step′), *n.* corbiestep.

Croy·don (kroid′ən), *n.* a city in N Surrey, in SE England, near London: airport. 252,387 (1961).

croze (krōz), *n.* the groove at either end of a barrel stave into which the edge of the head fits. [? special use of *crose, croze* (var. of CROSS) in sense cross groove]

cro·zier (krō′zhər), *n.* crosier.

CRT, See **cathode-ray tube.**

cru·ces (kro͞o′sēz), *n.* a pl. of **crux.**

cru·cial (kro͞o′shəl), *adj.* **1.** involving a final and supreme decision; decisive; critical. **2.** severe; trying. **3.** of the form of a cross; cross-shaped. [< L *cruci-* (s. of *crux*) CROSS + -AL[1]] —**cru′cial·ly,** *adv.* —**Syn. 1.** determining, vital.

cru·ci·ate (kro͞o′shē it, -āt′), *adj.* **1.** cross-shaped. **2.** *Bot.* having the form of a cross with equal arms, as the flowers of mustard. **3.** *Entomol.* crossing diagonally when at rest, as the wings of certain insects. [< NL *cruciāt(us).* See CRUCIAL, -ATE[1]] —**cru′ci·ate·ly,** *adv.*

cru·ci·ble (kro͞o′sə bəl), *n.* **1.** a vessel of metal or refractory material employed for heating substances to high temperatures. **2.** *Metall.* a hollow area at the bottom of a furnace in which the metal collects. **3.** a severe, searching test. [late ME *crusible* pot for melting metals < ML *crūcibul(um), -balum* crucible, night lamp, perh. orig. cruse.]

cru·ci·fer (kro͞o′sə fər), *n.* **1.** a person who carries a cross, as in ecclesiastical processions. **2.** *Bot.* a cruciferous plant. [< LL; see CRUCIAL, -FER]

cru·cif·er·ous (kro͞o sif′ər əs), *adj.* **1.** bearing a cross. **2.** *Bot.* belonging or pertaining to the *Cruciferae* or *Brassicaceae,* a family of plants having flowers with a crosslike, four-petaled corolla. [< LL *crucifer* CRUCIFER + -OUS]

cru·ci·fix (kro͞o′sə fiks), *n.* **1.** a cross with the figure of Jesus crucified upon it. **2.** any cross. [ME < eccl. L *crucifix(us)* the crucified one (i.e., Christ), n. use of masc. of ptp. of *crucifīgere* to CRUCIFY]

cru·ci·fix·ion (kro͞o′sə fik′shən), *n.* **1.** the act of crucifying. **2.** the state of being crucified. **3.** (*cap.*) the death of Jesus by being nailed upon a cross. **4.** a picture or other representation of this. **5.** severe punishment or gross injustice. [late ME < eccl. L *crucifixiōn-* (s. of *crucifixiō*)]

cru·ci·form (kro͞o′sə fôrm′), *adj.* **1.** cross-shaped. —*n.* **2.** a cross. [< L *cruci-* (s. of *crux*) cross + -FORM]

cru·ci·fy (kro͞o′sə fī′), *v.t.,* **-fied, -fy·ing.** **1.** to put to death by nailing or binding a person to a cross. **2.** to treat with gross injustice; persecute. [ME *crucifie(n)* < OF *crucifie(r)* < LL *crucifīgere* = L *cruci-* (s. of *crux*) CROSS + *fīgere* to fix, bind fast] —**cru′ci·fi′er,** *n.*

Cru·cis (kro͞o′sis), *n. Astron.* gen. of **Crux.** [L]

crud (krud), *v.,* **crud·ded, crud·ding,** *n.* —*v.t., v.i.* **1.** *Dial.* to curd. —*n. Slang.* **2.** a deposit or coating of refuse or of an impure or alien substance. **3.** a filthy, repulsive, or contemptible person. **4.** *Slang.* anything that is worthless, objectionable, or repugnant. [ME; earlier form of CURD] —**crud′dy,** *adj.*

crude (kro͞od), *adj.,* **crud·er, crud·est,** *n.* —*adj.* **1.** in a raw or unprepared state; unrefined. **2.** lacking in intellectual subtlety, perceptivity, etc.; rudimentary; undeveloped. **3.** lacking finish, polish, proper arrangement, or completeness: *a crude summary.* **4.** lacking culture, refinement, tact, etc. **5.** undisguised; blunt; bare: *a crude answer.* —*n.* **6.** See **crude oil.** [ME < L *crūd(us)* (for *cruidus = *cru(or)* blood, gore + *-idus* -ID[4]) bloody, hence raw, ruthless, unripe; see RAW] —**crude′ly,** *adv.* —**crude′ness,** *n.* —**Syn. 1.** unprepared, coarse. See **raw. 4.** uncouth, coarse.

crude′ oil′, petroleum before refining.

cru·di·tés (kro͞o′di tā′; *Fr.* KRY dē tā), *n.pl.* sliced raw vegetables, as carrots, cucumbers, etc., served esp. as an appetizer and usually accompanied by a dip. [< F, pl. of *crudité* raw vegetables or fruit, indigestibility < MF < L *crūditās* indigestion *crūdus* raw]

cru·di·ty (kro͞o′di tē), *n., pl.* **-ties** for 2. **1.** state or quality of being crude. **2.** an instance of this; anything crude. [ME *crudite* < L *crūditās*]

cru·el (kro͞o′əl), *adj.* **1.** willfully or knowingly causing pain or distress to others. **2.** enjoying the pain or distress of others: *the cruel spectators of the gladiatorial contests.* **3.** causing or marked by great pain or distress: *a cruel remark.* **4.** rigid; stern; unrelentingly severe. [ME < OF < L *crūdēl(is)* = *crūd(us)* bloody, ruthless (see CRUDE) + *-ēlis* adj. suffix] —**cru′el·ly,** *adv.* —**cru′el·ness,** *n.* —**Syn. 1.** barbarous, bloodthirsty, merciless. CRUEL, PITILESS, RUTHLESS, BRUTAL, SAVAGE imply readiness to cause pain to others. CRUEL implies willingness to cause pain, and indifference to suffering: *a cruel stepfather; cruel to animals.* PITILESS adds the idea of hard-heartedness and positive refusal to show compassion: *pitiless to captives; fate that seems pitiless.* RUTHLESS implies cruelty and unscrupulousness, letting nothing stand in one's way, and using any methods necessary: *ruthless in pressing an advantage; ruthless greed.* BRUTAL implies cruelty which takes the form of physical violence: *a brutal master.* SAVAGE suggests fierceness and brutality: *savage battles, jealousy.* —**Ant. 1.** kind.

cru·el·heart·ed (kro͞o′əl här′tid), *adj.* having a cruel heart; lacking kindness, compassion, etc.

cru·el·ty (kro͞o′əl tē), *n., pl.* **-ties** for 3. **1.** state or quality of being cruel. **2.** cruel disposition or conduct. **3.** a cruel act. [ME *cruelte* < OF < L *crūdēlitāt-* (s. of *crūdēlitās*)] —**Syn. 1.** harshness, barbarity, inhumanity. —**Ant. 2, 3.** kindness.

cru·et (kro͞o′it), *n.* a glass bottle, esp. one for holding vinegar, oil, etc., for the table. [ME < AF = OF *crue* pot (< Gmc; cf. OE *crūce* pot) + *-et* -ET]

Cruik·shank (kro͝ok′shangk′), *n.* **George,** 1792–1878, English illustrator, caricaturist, and painter.

cruise (kro͞oz), *v.,* **cruised, cruis·ing,** *n.* —*v.i.* **1.** to sail about without proceeding directly from one point to another, as a yacht on a pleasure trip or a warship in search of hostile vessels. **2.** to travel about without a particular purpose or destination. **3.** *Aeron.* to fly at moderate speed, esp. at the speed that permits maximum operating efficiency. **4.** to travel about slowly, looking for customers or for something demanding attention: *Taxis cruise in the downtown area.* **5.** to travel along at a moderately fast, easily controllable speed. —*v.t.* **6.** to cruise in (a specified area): *to cruise the Caribbean.* —*n.* **7.** the act of cruising; a voyage made by cruising. [< D *kruise(n)* (to) cross, cruise < *kruis* CROSS]

cruise′ mis′sile, a small, winged, rocket- or jet-propelled guided missile that travels in the lower atmosphere and that may be launched from aircraft, ships, or submarines.

cruis·er (kro͞o′zər), *n.* **1.** a person or thing that cruises. **2.** one of a class of warships of medium tonnage, designed for high speed and long cruising radius. **3.** a pleasure vessel, esp. a power-driven one, for cruising. [< D *kruiser*]

crul·ler (krul′ər), *n.* a light, sweet cake fried in deep fat, often having a ring-shaped or twisted form. Also, **kruller.** [< D *krulle* kind of cake (< *krullen* to curl) + -ER[1]]

crumb (krum), *n.* **1.** a small particle of bread, cake, etc., such as breaks or falls off. **2.** a small particle or portion of anything. **3.** the soft inner portion of a bread (distinguished from *crust*). **4.** *Slang.* an objectionable or worthless person. —*v.t.* **5.** *Cookery.* to dress or prepare with crumbs. **6.** to break into crumbs or small fragments. —*adj.* **7.** *Cookery.* baked with a topping of crumbled sugar, butter, and spice: *crumb cake.* [ME *crome, crume,* OE *cruma;* akin to D *kruim,* G *Krume* crumb, L *grūmus* small heap of earth] —**crumb′er,** *n.*

crum·ble (krum′bəl), *v.,* **-bled, -bling.** —*v.t.* **1.** to break into small fragments or crumbs. —*v.i.* **2.** to fall or break into small fragments. **3.** to decay or disintegrate gradually: *The ancient walls had crumbled.* [late ME *crumme* (var. of *crimme,* OE *gecrymman* < *cruma* CRUMB) + -LE]

crum·bly (krum′blē), *adj.,* **-bli·er, -bli·est.** apt to crumble; friable. —**crum′bli·ness,** *n.*

crumb·y (krum′ē), *adj.,* **crumb·i·er, crumb·i·est.** **1.** full of crumbs. **2.** soft.

crum·mie (KRUM′ē, KRo͝om′ē), *n. Chiefly Scot.* a cow with crooked horns. Also **crum′my.** [obs. *crum* crooked (ME, OE *crumb;* c. G *Krumm*) + -IE]

crum·my (krum′ē), *adj.,* **-mi·er, -mi·est.** *Slang.* **1.** maintained in a dirty, run-down condition; shabby; seedy: *a crummy hotel.* **2.** of little or no value; cheap; worthless: *crummy furniture.* **3.** wretchedly inadequate; measly or picayune: *They pay crummy salaries.* [perh. obs. *crum* crooked (see CRUMMIE) + -Y[1]]

crump (krump, kro͝omp), *v.t.* **1.** to crunch with the teeth. —*v.i.* **2.** (of an artillery shell) to land and explode with a heavy, muffled sound. **3.** to make a crunching sound, as in walking over snow. —*n.* **4.** a crunching sound. **5.** a large explosive shell or bomb. —*adj.* **6.** *Brit. Dial.* brittle. [imit.]

crum·pet (krum′pit), *n. Chiefly Brit.* a soft bread resembling a muffin. [short for *crumpetcake* curled cake = ME *crompid* (ptp. of obs. *crump,* var. of CRIMP[1]) + CAKE]

crum·ple (krum′pəl) *v.,* **-pled, -pling,** *n.* —*v.t.* **1.** to press into irregular folds; rumple; wrinkle. **2.** to cause to collapse or give way suddenly. —*v.i.* **3.** to contract into wrinkles; shrink or shrivel. **4.** to give way suddenly; collapse. —*n.* **5.** a wrinkle produced by crumpling. [ME; var. of CRIMPLE] —**crum′ply,** *adj.*

crum·pled (krum′pəld), *adj.* **1.** rumpled; wrinkled. **2.** bent in a spiral curve: *a crumpled ram's horn.* [ME; var. of *crimpled,* ptp. of CRIMPLE]

crunch (krunch), *v.t.* **1.** to crush with the teeth; chew with a crushing noise. **2.** to crush or grind noisily. —*v.i.* **3.** to chew with a crushing sound. —*n.* **4.** act or sound of crunching. **5.** *Slang.* a shortage or reduction of something needed or wanted: *a monetary crunch; the energy crunch.* **6.** *Slang.* distress or depressed conditions due to such a shortage or reduction: *a budget crunch.* **7.** *Slang.* a situation of extreme stress, pressure, or danger; critical test: *When the crunch comes, we all have to do our best.* Also, **craunch.** [b. CRAUNCH and CRUSH] —**crunch′a·ble,** *adj.* —**crunch′ing·ly,** *adv.*

crunch·y (krun′chē), *adj.,* **crunch·i·er, crunch·i·est.** that crunches; crispy. —**crunch′i·ly,** *adv.* —**crunch′i·ness,** *n.*

crup·per (krup′ər, kro͝op′-), *n.* **1.** a leather strap fastened to the saddle of a harness and looping under the horse's tail to prevent the harness from slipping forward. **2.** the rump or buttocks of a horse. **3.** armor for a horse's rump. [ME *cro(u)per,* var. of *cruper* < AF. See CROUP[2], -ER[2]]

cru·ra (kro͝or′ə), *n.* pl. of *crus.*

cru·ral (kro͝or′əl), *adj.* **1.** of or pertaining to the leg or the hind limb. **2.** *Anat., Zool.* of or pertaining to the leg proper, or crus. [< L *crūrāl(is)* belonging to the legs = *crūr-* (s. of *crūs*) leg + *-ālis* -AL[1]]

crus (krus, kro͞os), *n., pl.* **cru·ra** (kro͝or′ə). *Anat., Zool.* **1.** the part of the leg or hind limb between the femur or thigh and the ankle or tarsus; shank. **2.** any leglike part. [< L: leg, shank]

cru·sade (kro͞o sād′), *n., v.,* **-sad·ed, -sad·ing.** —*n.* **1.** (*often cap.*) any of the military expeditions undertaken by the Christians of Europe in the 11th, 12th, and 13th centuries for the recovery of the Holy Land from the Muslims. **2.** any war carried on under papal sanction. **3.** any vigorous, aggressive movement for the defense or advancement of an idea, cause, etc.: *a crusade against crime.* —*v.i.* **4.** to go on or engage in a crusade. [earlier *crusada* < Sp *cruzada;* r. 16th-century *croisade* < MF. See CROSS, -ADE[1]] —**cru·sad′er,** *n.*

cru·sa·do (kro͞o sā′dō, -zā′-), *n., pl.* **-does, -dos.** an early Portuguese coin of gold or silver, bearing the figure of a cross. Also, **cruzado.** [< Pg *cruzado* crossed, marked with a cross. See CROSS -ADE[1]]

cruse (kro͞oz, kro͞os), *n.* an earthen pot, bottle, etc., for liquids. [ME *crouse* (OE *crūse;* c. G *Krause* pot with lid) + ME *croo* (OE *crōg, crōh;* c. G *Krug* jug)]

crush (krush), *v.t.* **1.** to press with a force that destroys or deforms. **2.** to squeeze or pound into small fragments or particles, as ore, stone, etc. **3.** to force out by pressing or squeezing; extract: *to crush cottonseeds to produce oil.* **4.** to hug or embrace forcibly or strongly. **5.** to destroy, subdue, or suppress utterly: *to crush a revolt.* **6.** to overwhelm with confusion, chagrin, or humiliation, as by argumentation or a slighting action or remark; squelch. **7.** to oppress grievously: *to crush the poor.* —*v.i.* **8.** to become crushed. **9.** to advance with crushing; press or crowd forcibly. —*n.* **10.** the act of crushing. **11.** the state of being crushed. **12.** a great crowd. **13.** *Informal.* **a.** an intense infatuation. **b.** the object of such an infatuation. [ME *crusche(n)* < MF *cruis(ir)* < Gmc; cf. MLG *krossen* to crush] —**crush′a·bil′i·ty,** *n.* —**crush′a·ble,** *adj.* —**crush′er,** *n.* —**Syn. 1.** crumple, rumple. **2.** shatter, pulverize, granulate, powder. See **break. 5.** quell, overcome, quash.

crust (krust), *n.* **1.** the hard outer portion of a loaf of bread, roll, etc. (distinguished from *crumb*). **2.** a piece of this. **3.** the baked shell or other outside covering of a pie. **4.** any more or less hard external covering or coating: *a crust of snow.* **5.** the hard outer shell or covering of an animal. **6.** *Geol.* the outer portion of the earth, about 22 miles deep under the continents and 6 miles deep under the oceans. Cf. **core**[1] (def. 5), **mantle** (def. 7). **7.** a scab or eschar. **8.** a deposit on the inside of wine bottles. **9.** *Slang.* unabashed self-assertiveness; nerve; gall. —*v.t.* **10.** to cover with or as with a crust; encrust. **11.** to form (something) into a crust. —*v.i.* **12.** to form or contract a crust. [ME < L *crūst(a)* hard surface (of a body); r. ME *cro(u)ste* < MF < L *crūst(a)*]

Crus·ta·ce·a (kru stā′shē ə, -shə), *n.* the class comprising the crustaceans. [< NL; see CRUSTACEAN]

crus·ta·cean (kru stā′shən), *n.* any chiefly aquatic arthropod of the class *Crustacea,* typically having the body covered with a hard shell or crust, including the lobsters, shrimps, crabs, barnacles, wood lice, etc. [< NL *Crūstāce(a)* (neut. pl.) hard-shelled ones (see CRUST, -ACEA) + -AN]

crus·ta·ceous (kru stā′shəs), *adj.* **1.** of the nature of or pertaining to a crust or shell. **2.** crustacean. **3.** having a hard covering or crust. [< NL *crūstāceus* (adj.) hard-shelled]

crus·tal (krus′tᵊl), *adj.* of or pertaining to a crust, as that of the earth. [< L *crūst(a)* shell, crust + -AL[1]]

crust·y (krus′tē), *adj.,* **crust·i·er, crust·i·est. 1.** of the nature of or resembling a crust; having a crust. **2.** harsh; surly; rude: *a crusty person; a crusty remark.* [late ME] —**crust′i·ly,** *adv.* —**crust′i·ness,** *n.* —**Syn. 2.** testy, touchy; curt, brusque.

crutch (kruch), *n.* **1.** a staff or support to assist a lame or infirm person in walking, usually with a crosspiece fitting under the armpit. **2.** a forked support or part. **3.** a forked device on the left side of a sidesaddle for supporting the legs. **4.** the crotch of the human body. **5.** Also, **crotch.** *Naut.* a forked support for a boom or spar that is not in use. **6.** anything that serves to support or sustain artificially or as an expedient to supplement insufficient resources: *This works program is basically a crutch for the economy.* —*v.t.* **7.** to support on crutches; prop; sustain. [ME *crucche,* OE *cryce* (obl. *crycce*); c. Norw *krykkja,* Dan *krykke,* G *Krücke,* D *kruk.* See CROOK]

crutched (krucht), *adj.* having or bearing a cross: *a crutched friar.* [earlier *crouched* = *crouch* cross (ME *cruche,* OE *crūc* < L *cruci-,* s. of *crux*) + -ED[3]]

crux (kruks), *n., pl.* **crux·es, cru·ces** (kro͞o′sēz). **1.** a basic or decisive point: *the crux of the matter.* **2.** a cross. **3.** something that torments by its puzzling nature; a perplexing difficulty. [< L: a cross, torment, trouble]

Crux (kruks), *n., gen.* **Cru·cis** (kro͞o′sis). *Astron.* See **Southern Cross.** [< L: a cross]

crux an·sa·ta (kruks′ an sā′tə), *pl.* **cru·ces an·sa·tae** (kro͞o′sēz an sā′tē). a T-shaped cross with a loop at the top; ankh. [< L: cross with a handle]

cru·za·do (kro͞o zā′dō; *Port.* kro͞o zä′tho͝o), *n., pl.* **-does, -dos.** crusado.

cru·zei·ro (kro͞o zâr′ō; *Port.* kro͞o ze′ro͝o), *n., pl.* **-zei·ros** (-zâr′ōz; *Port.* -ze′ro͝os). a monetary unit of Brazil, equal to 100 centavos. [< Pg = *cruz* CROSS + *-eiro* -ER[2]]

crwth (kro͞oth), *n. Music.* crowd[2]. [< Welsh; c. Ir *cruit* harp, lyre]

cry (krī), *v.,* **cried, cry·ing,** *n., pl.* **cries.** —*v.i.* **1.** to utter inarticulate sounds, esp. of lamentation, grief, or suffering, usually with tears. **2.** to weep; shed tears, with or without sound. **3.** to shout or yell (sometimes fol. by *out*). **4.** to give forth vocal sounds or characteristic calls, as animals; yelp; bark. **5.** (of a hound or pack) to bay continuously and excitedly in following a scent. —*v.t.* **6.** to utter or pronounce loudly; call out. **7.** to announce publicly as for sale: *to cry one's wares.* **8.** to beg or plead for; implore. **9.** to bring (oneself) to a specified state by weeping: *She cried herself to sleep.* **10. cry havoc.** See **havoc** (def. 2). **11. cry one's eyes** or **heart out,** to cry excessively or inconsolably. **12. cry over spilled** or **spilt milk.** See **milk** (def. 4). —*n.* **13.** the act or sound of crying; a shout, scream, or wail. **14.** clamor or outcry. **15.** an entreaty; appeal. **16.** an oral proclamation or announcement. **17.** a call of wares for sale, services available, etc., as by a street vendor. **18.** public report. **19.** an opinion generally expressed. **20.** See **battle cry. 21.** a political or party slogan. **22.** a fit of weeping. **23.** the utterance or call of an animal. **24.** *Fox Hunting.* **a.** a pack of hounds. **b.** a continuous baying of a hound or a pack in following a scent. **25. a far cry, a.** quite some distance; a long way. **b.** only remotely related; very different. **26. in full cry,** in hot pursuit. [ME *crie(n)* < OF *crie(r)* < VL **critāre* for L *quirītāre* to cry for aid (from a Roman citizen) < *Quirīt-* (s. of *Quirīs*) a citizen of Rome, orig. an inhabitant of the Sabine town Cures]
—**Syn. 1.** wail, keen, moan, **2.** sob, bawl, blubber, whimper. **3.** yowl, clamor, exclaim, scream. CRY, SHOUT, BELLOW, ROAR refer to kinds of loud articulate or inarticulate sounds. CRY is the general word: *to cry out.* To SHOUT is to raise the voice loudly in uttering words or other articulate sounds: *He shouted back to his companions.* BELLOW esp. refers to the loud, deep cry of a bull, moose, etc., or, somewhat in deprecation, to human utterance that suggests such a sound: *The speaker bellowed his answer.* ROAR refers to a deep, hoarse, rumbling or vibrant cry; it often implies tumultuous volume: *The crowd roared approval.*

cry·ba·by (krī′bā′bē), *n., pl.* **-bies. 1.** a person who cries readily for very little reason. **2.** a person who complains too much about losses, defeats, etc.

cry·ing (krī′ing), *adj.* **1.** that cries; clamorous; wailing; weeping. **2.** demanding attention or remedy: *a crying evil.* [ME *cryenge*] —**cry′ing·ly,** *adv.*

cry·mo·ther·a·py (krī′mō ther′ə pē), *n. Med.* cryotherapy. [< Gk *krȳmó(s)* frost, cold + THERAPY]

cryo-, a learned borrowing from Greek meaning "icy cold," "frost," used in the formation of compound words: *cryogenics.* [< Gk *kryo-* comb. form of *krýos*]

cry·o·gen (krī′ə jən), *n.* a substance for producing low temperatures; freezing mixture.

cry·o·gen·ics (krī′ō jen′iks), *n.* (*construed as sing.*) the branch of physics that deals with very low temperatures, esp. those at or near absolute zero. —**cry′o·gen′ic,** *adj.* —**cry′o·gen′i·cal·ly,** *adv.* —**cry′o·gen′i·cist,** *n.*

cry·o·hy·drate (krī′ō hī′drāt), *n.* a mixture of ice and another substance in definite proportions such that a minimum melting or freezing point is attained.

cry·o·lite (krī′ə līt′), *n.* a mineral, sodium aluminum fluoride, Na_3AlF_6, used as a flux in the electrolytic production of aluminum.

cry·om·e·ter (krī om′i tər), *n.* a thermometer for measuring low temperatures. —**cry·om′e·try,** *n.*

cry·on·ics (krī on′iks), *n.* (*construed as sing.*) the deep-freezing of human bodies at death for preservation and possible eventual revival in the future. —**cry·on′ic,** *adj.*

cry·os·co·py (krī os′kə pē), *n., pl.* **-pies. 1.** the determination of the freezing points of liquids or solutions, or of the lowering of the freezing points by dissolved substances. **2.** *Med.* the determination of the freezing points of certain bodily fluids, as urine, for diagnosis. —**cry·o·scop·ic** (krī′ə skop′ik), *adj.*

cry·o·stat (krī′ə stat′), *n.* an apparatus, usually automatic, maintaining a very low constant temperature.

cry·o·sur·ger·y (krī′ō sûr′jə rē), *n.* the use of extreme cold to destroy tissue for therapeutic purposes.

cry·o·ther·a·py (krī′ō ther′ə pē), *n. Med.* treatment by means of applications of cold. Also, **crymotherapy.**

cry·o·tron (krī′ə tron′), *n.* a cryogenic device used as a switch and as a computer-memory element.

crypt (kript), *n.* **1.** a subterranean chamber or vault, esp. one beneath the main floor of a church, used as a burial place. **2.** *Anat.* a slender pit or recess; a small glandular cavity. [< L *crypt(a)* < Gk *krýptē* hidden place, n. use of fem. of *kryptós* hidden, verbid of *krýptein* to hide] —**crypt′al,** *adj.*

crypt·a·nal·y·sis (krip′tə nal′i sis), *n.* **1.** the procedures, processes, methods, etc., used to translate or interpret secret writings, as codes and ciphers, for which the key is unknown: *He subjected the manuscript to cryptanalysis.* **2.** the science or study of such procedures; cryptanalytics. Cf. **cryptography.** [CRYPT(OGRAM) + ANALYSIS] —**crypt·an·a·lyt·ic** (krip′tan ᵊlit′ik), *adj.* —**crypt·an·a·lyst** (krip-tan′ᵊlist), *n.*

crypt·an·a·lyt·ics (krip′tanᵊlit′iks), *n.* (*construed as sing.*) cryptanalysis. [formation from CRYPTANALYSIS, modeled after *analysis, analytics*]

crypt·an·a·lyze (krip tan′ᵊlīz′), *v.t.,* **-lyzed, -lyz·ing.** to study (a cryptogram) for the purpose of discovering the clear meaning; break (a code, cipher, etc.). [back formation from CRYPTANALYSIS]

cryp·tic (krip′tik), *adj.* **1.** hidden; secret; occult: *a cryptic writing.* **2.** mysterious; puzzling; ambiguous: *a cryptic message.* **3.** *Zool.* fitted for concealing. **4.** abrupt; terse; short: *a cryptic note.* **5.** involving or using cipher, code, etc. Also, **cryp′ti·cal.** [< LL *cryptic(us)* < Gk *kryptikós* hidden] —**cryp′ti·cal·ly,** *adv.*

crypto-, a learned borrowing from Greek meaning "hidden," "secret," used in the formation of compound words: *cryptograph.* [comb. form repr. Gk *kryptós* hidden. See CRYPT]

cryp·to·a·nal·y·sis (krip′tō ə nal′i sis), *n.* cryptanalysis. —**cryp·to·an·a·lyt·ic** (krip′tō an′ᵊlit′ik), *adj.* —**cryp·to·an·a·lyst** (krip′tō an′ᵊlist), *n.*

cryp·to·crys·tal·line (krip′tō kris′tᵊlin, -tᵊlīn′), *adj. Mineral.* having a microscopic crystalline structure, indistinguishable to the naked eye.

cryp·to·gam (krip′tə gam′), *n.* **1.** any of the *Cryptogamia,* an old primary division of plants comprising those without true flowers and seeds, as the ferns, mosses, and thallophytes. **2.** a plant without a true seed (opposed to *phanerogam*). [back formation from NL *Cryptogamia.* See CRYPTO-, -GAMY] —**cryp′to·gam′ic, cryp·tog·a·mous** (krip tog′ə məs), *adj.*

cryp·to·gen·ic (krip′tə jen′ik), *adj.* of obscure or unknown origin, as a disease.

cryp·to·gram (krip′tə gram′), *n.* **1.** a message or writing in code or cipher; cryptograph. **2.** an occult symbol or representation. —**cryp′to·gram′mic,** *adj.*

cryp·to·graph (krip′tə graf′, -gräf′), *n.* **1.** cryptogram (def. 1). 2. a system of secret writing; cipher. 3. a device for translating clear text into cipher.

cryp·tog·ra·phy (krip tog′rə fē), *n.* 1. the science or study of secret writing, esp. code and cipher systems. 2. the procedures, processes, methods, etc., of making and using secret writing, as codes and ciphers. Cf. **cryptanalysis.** —**cryp·tog′ra·pher, cryp·tog′ra·phist,** *n.* —**cryp·to·graph·ic** (krip′tə graf′ik), **cryp′to·graph′i·cal, cryp·tog′ra·phal,** *adj.* —**cryp′to·graph′i·cal·ly,** *adv.*

cryp·tol·o·gy (krip tol′ə jē), *n.* 1. cryptography. 2. the science and study of cryptanalysis and cryptography. [< NL *cryptologia*] —**cryp·tol′o·gist,** *n.*

cryp·to·mer·i·a (krip′tə mēr′ē ə), *n.* the Japan cedar, *Cryptomeria japonica.* [< NL; see CRYPTO-, -MERE, -IA]

cryp·to·zo·ic (krip′tə zō′ik), *adj., n.* Precambrian.

cryp·to·zo·ite (krip′tə zō′īt), *n.* a malarial parasite in the stage of development during which it lives in tissue cells. [CRYPTO- + -ZO(A) + -ITE[1]]

cryst., 1. crystalline. 2. crystallography.

crys·tal (kris′tᵊl), *n., adj.* —*n.* 1. a clear, transparent mineral or glass resembling ice. 2. the transparent form of crystallized quartz. 3. *Chem., Mineral.* a solid having a characteristic internal structure and enclosed by symmetrically arranged plane surfaces, intersecting at definite and characteristic angles. 4. anything made of or resembling such a substance. 5. a single grain or mass of a crystalline substance. 6. glass of a high degree of brilliance. 7. the glass or plastic cover over the face of a watch. 8. *Radio.* a. the piece of germanium, silicon, galena, or the like, forming the essential part of a crystal detector. b. the crystal detector itself. —*adj.* 9. composed of crystal. 10. resembling crystal; clear or transparent. 11. *Radio.* pertaining to or employing a crystal detector. 12. indicating a 15th anniversary. [ME *cristal(le)*, OE *cristalla* < ML *cristall(um)*, L *crystallum* < Gk *krýstallos* clear ice, rock crystal < *krystaínein* to freeze] —**crys′tal·like′,** *adj.*

Crys·tal (kris′tᵊl), *n.* a city in SE Minnesota, near Minneapolis. 30,925 (1970).

crys′tal ball′, a ball of clear crystal, glass, or the like, used in crystal gazing.

crys′tal detec′tor, *Radio.* a device in a receiving apparatus, consisting essentially of a fine metal wire touching a crystal of germanium, silicon, galena, or the like, that permits a current to pass freely in one direction only.

crys′tal gaz′ing, the practice of staring into a crystal ball in order to see distant happenings, future events, etc. —**crys′tal gaz′er.**

crystall-, var. of **crystallo-** before a vowel: *crystallite.*

crystall., crystallography.

crys′tal lat′tice, lattice (def. 4).

crystalli-, var. of **crystallo-** before an element of Latin origin: *crystalliferous.*

crys·tal·lif·er·ous (kris′tᵊlif′ər əs), *adj.* bearing, containing, or yielding crystals. Also, **crys·tal·lig·er·ous** (kris′tᵊlij′ər əs).

crys·tal·line (kris′tᵊlin, -tᵊlīn′), *adj.* 1. of or like crystal; clear; transparent. 2. formed by crystallization. 3. composed of crystals. 4. pertaining to crystals or their formation. [< L *crystallin(us)* < Gk *krystállinos*] —**crys·tal·lin·i·ty** (kris′tᵊlin′i tē), *n.*

crys′talline lens′, *Anat.* a doubly convex, transparent, lenslike body in the eye, situated behind the iris, that focuses incident light on the retina.

crys·tal·li·sa·tion (kris′tᵊli zā′shən *or, esp. Brit.,* -tᵊlī-), *n.* *Chiefly Brit.* crystallization.

crys·tal·lise (kris′tᵊlīz′), *v.t., v.i.,* **-lised, -lis·ing.** *Chiefly Brit.* crystallize.

crys·tal·lite (kris′tᵊlīt′), *n.* *Mineral.* a minute body in igneous rock, showing incipient crystallization. —**crys·tal·lit·ic** (kris′tᵊlit′ik), *adj.*

crys·tal·li·za·tion (kris′tᵊli zā′shən, *or, esp. Brit.,* -tᵊlī-), *n.* 1. the act or process of crystallizing. 2. a crystallized body or formation. Also, *esp. Brit.,* **crystallisation.**

crys·tal·lize (kris′tᵊlīz′), *v.,* **-lized, -liz·ing.** —*v.t.* 1. to form into crystals; cause to assume crystalline form. 2. to give definite or concrete form to: *to crystallize an idea.* 3. to coat with sugar. —*v.i.* 4. to form crystals; become crystalline in form. 5. to assume definite or concrete form. Also, *esp. Brit.,* **crystallise.**

crystallo-, a learned borrowing from Greek meaning "crystal," used in the formation of compound words: *crystallography.* Also, **crystall-, crystalli-.** [< Gk *krystallo-*, comb. form of *krýstallos* CRYSTAL]

crys·tal·lo·graph·ic (kris′tᵊlə graf′ik), *adj.* of, pertaining to, or dealing with crystals or crystallography. Also, **crys′tal·lo·graph′i·cal.** —**crys′tal·lo·graph′i·cal·ly,** *adv.*

crys·tal·log·ra·phy (kris′tᵊlog′rə fē), *n.* the science dealing with crystallization and the forms and structure of crystals. —**crys′tal·log′ra·pher,** *n.*

crys·tal·loid (kris′tᵊloid′), *adj.* 1. resembling a crystal, of the nature of a crystalloid. —*n.* 2. a usually crystallizable substance that, when dissolved in a liquid, will diffuse readily through vegetable or animal membranes. 3. *Bot.* one of certain minute crystallike granules of protein, found in the tissues of various seeds. [< Gk *krystalloeid(ēs)*] —**crys′tal·loi′dal,** *adj.*

crys′tal set′, *Radio.* a tubeless receiving set with a crystal detector.

crys′tal sys′tem, *Crystall.* any of the six main classifications of crystals and of crystal lattices according to their symmetry.

crys′tal vi′olet. See **gentian violet.**

Cs, *Chem.* cesium.

cS, centistoke. Also, **cs**

cs., case; cases.

C.S., 1. Christian Science. 2. civil service.

c.s., 1. capital stock. 2. civil service.

C.S.A., Confederate States of America.

csc, cosecant.

csch, hyperbolic cosecant.

csk., cask.

CST, Central Standard Time. Also, **C.S.T., c.s.t.**

Ct., 1. Connecticut. 2. Count.

ct., 1. carat. 2. cent. 3. centum. 4. certificate. 5. county. 6. court.

CT, Connecticut (approved esp. for use with zip code).

C.T., Central Time.

cteno-, a learned borrowing from Greek meaning "comb," used in the formation of compound words: *Ctenophora.* Also, *esp. before a vowel,* **cten-.** [< Gk *kteno-*, comb. form of *kteís* comb (gen. *ktenós*)]

cte·noid (tē′noid, ten′oid), *adj.* *Zool.* 1. comblike or pectinate; rough-edged. 2. having rough-edged scales. [< Gk *ktenoeid(ēs)* like a comb]

Cte·noph·o·ra (ti nof′ər ə), *n.* the phylum comprising the ctenophores. [< NL, neut. pl. of *ctenophorus* CTENOPHORE]

cte·noph·o·ran (ti nof′ər ən), *n.* 1. ctenophore. —*adj.* 2. Also, **cten·o·phor·ic** (ten′ə fôr′ik, -for′-), **cte·noph·o·rous** (ti nof′ər əs), belonging or pertaining to the *Ctenophora.*

cten·o·phore (ten′ə fōr′, -fôr′, tē′nə-), *n.* any marine, swimming invertebrate of the phylum *Ctenophora,* having rounded, oval, or band-shaped, gelatinous bodies and eight meridional rows of ciliated plates; comb jelly. [< NL *ctenophor(us)*]

Ctes·i·phon (tes′ə fon′), *n.* a ruined city in Iraq, on the Tigris, near Baghdad: an ancient capital of Parthia.

ctn, cotangent.

ctr., center.

cts., 1. centimes. 2. cents. 3. certificates.

CT scan′ner. See **CAT scanner.**

CU, close-up.

Cu, *Chem.* copper. [< L *cuprum*]

Cu., cumulus.

cu., 1. cubic. 2. cumulus.

cub (kub), *n.* 1. the young of certain animals, as the fox, bear, etc. 2. a young and inexperienced person, esp. a callow youth or young man. 3. an apprentice. 4. See **cub scout.** [perh. < Scand; cf. Icel *kobbi* young seal, *kubbr* stump, hence short, thickset person] —**cub′bish,** *adj.*

Cu·ba (kyo͞o′bə; *Sp.* ko͞o′vä), *n.* a republic in the Caribbean, S of Florida: largest island in the West Indies. 9,405,000; 44,218 sq. mi. *Cap.:* Havana. —**Cu′ban,** *adj., n.*

cub·age (kyo͞o′bij), *n.* cubic content, displacement, or volume. [CUBE[1] + -AGE]

Cu·ba li·bre (kyo͞o′bə lē′brə), a highball consisting of rum and a cola drink. [< Sp: lit., free Cuba (a toast given by revolutionists before 1940)]

Cu′ban heel′, a broad heel of medium height, slightly tapered at the back.

cu·ba·ture (kyo͞o′bə chər), *n.* 1. the determination of the cubic contents of a thing. 2. cubic contents. [CUBE[1] + *-ature,* after *quadrature*]

cub·by (kub′ē), *n., pl.* **-bies.** a cubbyhole. [dial. *cub* stall, shed (akin to COVE[1]) + -Y[2]]

cub·by·hole (kub′ē hōl′), *n.* 1. a pigeonhole. 2. a small, snug place, room, or cabin.

cube[1] (kyo͞ob), *n., v.,* **cubed, cub·ing.** —*n.* 1. a solid bounded by six equal squares, the angle between any two adjacent faces being a right angle. 2. a cubical piece of anything: *a cube of cheese.* 3. *Math.* the third power of a quantity, expressed as $a^3 = a \cdot a \cdot a$. 4. *Slang.* one of a pair of dice; die. 5. *Informal.* flashcube. —*v.t.* 6. to make into a cube or cubes. 7. to measure the cubic contents of. 8. *Math.* to raise to the third power. 9. to tenderize (meat) by scoring the fibers in a pattern of squares. [ME *cub(us)* < L < Gk *kýbos* cube, die] —**cub′er,** *n.*

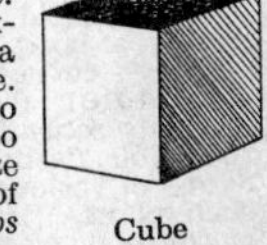
Cube

cu·be[2] (kyo͞o′bā), *n.* any of several tropical, leguminous plants used in making fish poisons and insecticides. [< AmerSp *cubé* < ?]

cu·beb (kyo͞o′beb), n. the spicy fruit or drupe of an East Indian, piperaceous, climbing shrub, *Piper Cubeba,* dried in an unripe but fully grown state and used in the treatment of urinary and bronchial disorders. [< ML *cubēb(a)* < Ar *kubābah* (classical Ar *kabābah*); r. ME *cucube, quibibe* < MF]

cube′ root′, *Math.* a quantity of which a given quantity is the cube: *The cube root of 64 is 4.*

cu·bic (kyo͞o′bik), *adj.* 1. having three dimensions; solid. 2. having the form of a cube; cubical. 3. pertaining to the measurement of volume. 4. pertaining to a unit of linear measure that is multiplied by itself twice to form a unit of measure for volume: *a cubic foot.* 5. *Math.* of or pertaining to the third degree. 6. *Crystall.* belonging or pertaining to the isometric system of crystallization. —*n.* 7. *Math.* a cubic polynomial or equation. [late ME *cubike* < L *cubic(us)* < Gk *kybikós*] —**cu·bic·i·ty** (kyo͞o bis′i tē), *n.*

cu·bi·cal (kyo͞o′bi kəl), *adj.* 1. having the form of a cube. 2. of or pertaining to volume.

cu·bi·cle (kyo͞o′bi kəl), *n.* 1. a bedroom, esp. one of a number of small ones in a divided dormitory, as in English public schools. 2. any small space or compartment formed by partitioning. [late ME < L *cubicul(um)* bedchamber = *cub(āre)* (to) lie down + *-i-* -I- + *-culum* -CLE]

cu′bic meas′ure, 1. the measurement of volume or space by means of cubic units. 2. a system of such units, esp. that in which 1728 cubic inches = 1 cubic foot, and 27 cubic feet = 1 cubic yard.

cu·bic·u·lum (kyo͞o bik′yə ləm), *n., pl.* **-la** (-lə). *Archaeol.* a burial chamber, as in catacombs. [< L. See CUBICLE]

cu·bi·form (kyo͞o′bə fôrm′), *adj.* shaped like a cube.

Cub·ism (kyo͞o′biz əm), *n.* (*often l.c.*) *Fine Arts.* a style of painting and sculpture developed in the early 20th century, characterized chiefly by an emphasis on the formal structure of a work of art, the reduction of natural forms to their geometrical equivalents, and the organization of the planes of a represented object independently of representational requirements. —**cub′ist,** *n.* —**cu·bis′tic,** *adj.* —**cu·bis′ti·cal·ly,** *adv.*

cu·bit (kyo͞o′bit), *n.* an ancient linear unit based on the length of the forearm, usually from 17 to 21 inches. [ME, OE < L *cubit(um)* elbow, cubit; akin to *cubāre* to lie down, c. Goth *hups*, OE *hype* hip, haunch, Gk *kȳphŏs* bent, stooped]

cu·boid (kyo͞o′boid), *adj.* Also, **cu·boi′dal.** **1.** resembling a cube in form. **2.** *Anat.* noting or pertaining to the outermost bone of the distal row of tarsal bones. —*n.* **3.** *Math.* a rectangular parallelepiped. **4.** *Anat.* the cuboid bone. [< Gk *kyboeid(ēs)*]

cub′ report′er, an apprentice newspaper reporter.

cub′ scout′, a member of the junior division (ages 8–11) of the Boy Scouts.

cu·chi·fri·to (ko͞o′chē frē′ tō), *n.* *American Spanish.* a cube of deep-fried pork. [Sp. *cuchi* hog + *frito* (pp. of *freír*) fried]

Cu·chul·ainn (ko͞o kul′in, ko͞o′ḵʜo͝o lin), *n.* *Irish Legend.* a hero of Ulster and the subject of many legends. Also, **Cu·chul′lain.**

cuck′ing stool′ (kuk′ing), a former instrument of punishment consisting of a chair in which an offender was strapped, to be jeered at and pelted by his neighbors, or, sometimes, to be ducked. [ME *cucking stol*, lit., defecating stool = *cucking*, prp. of *cukken* to defecate (< Scand; cf. dial. Sw *kukka*) + *stol* STOOL]

cuck·old (kuk′əld), *n.* **1.** the husband of an unfaithful wife. —*v.t.* **2.** to make a cuckold of. [ME *cokewold, cukeweld*]

cuck·old·ry (kuk′əl drē), *n.* **1.** the act of making someone a cuckold. **2.** the state or quality of being a cuckold.

cuck·oo (ko͞o′ko͞o, ko͝ok′o͞o), *n., pl.* **-oos,** *v.t.,* **-ooed, -oo·ing,** *adj.* —*n.* **1.** a common, European bird, *Cuculus canorus*, of the family *Cuculidae*, noted for its characteristic call and its habit of laying its eggs in the nests of other birds to be hatched. **2.** any of several other birds of the family *Cuculidae.* **3.** the call of the cuckoo, or an imitation of it. —*v.t.* **4.** to repeat monotonously. —*adj.* **5.** *Slang.* crazy or foolish. [ME *cuc(c)u, cuccuk(e)* (imit.); cf. L *cucūlus*, F *coucou*, G *Kuckuk*, D *koekoek*, ModGk *koûko*, etc.]

cuck′oo clock′, a clock that announces the hours by sounds resembling the call of the cuckoo, often accompanied by the appearance of an imitation bird through a little door.

cuck·oo·flow·er (ko͞o′ko͞o flou′ər, ko͝ok′o͞o-), *n.* any of various plants, as the lady's-smock or the ragged robin. [so called because it is found in bloom when the cuckoo is heard]

cuck·oo·pint (ko͞o′ko͞o pīnt′, ko͝ok′o͞o-), *n.* a common European arum, *Arum maculatum.* [apocopated var. of obs. *cuckoopintle*, late ME *cokkupyntel* (see CUCKOO, PINTLE); its spadix is pintleshaped]

cuck·oo-spit (ko͞o′ko͞o spit′, ko͝ok′o͞o-), *n.* **1.** a frothy secretion found on plants, exuded as a protective covering by the young of certain insects. **2.** an insect that produces this secretion. [late ME *cokkowespitle* cuckoopint; so called from the spitlike secretion found on the plant, thought to be left by the bird]

cu. cm., cubic centimeter; cubic centimeters.

cu·cu·li·form (kyo͞o kyo͞o′lə fôrm′), *adj.* pertaining to or resembling the order *Cuculiformes*, comprising the cuckoos, roadrunners, anis, etc. [< L *cucūl(us)* cuckoo + -I- + -FORM]

cu·cul·late (kyo͞o′kə lāt′, kyo͞o kul′āt), *adj.* **1.** cowled; hooded. **2.** resembling a cowl or hood. Also, **cu·cul·lat·ed** (kyo͞o′kə lā′tid, kyo͞o kul′ā-). [< LL *cucullāt(us)* hooded, having a hood = L *cucull(us)* a covering, hood + *-ātus* -ATE[1]] —**cu′cul·late′ly,** *adv.*

cu·cum·ber (kyo͞o′kum bər), *n.* **1.** a creeping plant, *Cucumis sativus*, occurring in many cultivated forms. **2.** the edible, fleshy, usually long, cylindrical fruit of this plant. **3.** any of various allied or similar plants. **4.** the fruit of any such plant. [late ME *cucumbre*, ME, OE *cucumer* < L *cucumer-* (s. of *cucumis*) < ?]

cu′cumber tree′, **1.** any of several American magnolias, esp. *Magnolia acuminata.* **2.** any of certain other trees, as an East Indian tree of the genus *Averrhoa.* [so called from the resemblance of its fruit to cucumbers]

cu·cu·mi·form (kyo͞o kyo͞o′mə fôrm′), *adj.* shaped like a cucumber. [< L *cucumi(s)* cucumber + -FORM]

cu·cur·bit (kyo͞o kûr′bit), *n.* **1.** a gourd. **2.** any cucurbitaceous plant. **3.** *Chem.* a gourd-shaped, matrasslike vessel formerly used in distilling. [ME *cucurbit(a)* gourd < L]

cu·cur·bi·ta·ceous (kyo͞o kûr′bi tā′shəs), *adj.* belonging to the *Cucurbitaceae*, or gourd family of plants, which includes the pumpkin, squash, cucumber, muskmelon, watermelon, etc. [< NL *Cucurbit(aceae)* + -ACEOUS]

Cú·cu·ta (ko͞o′ko͞o tä′), *n.* a city in E Colombia. 147,250 (est. 1964).

cud (kud), *n.* **1.** the portion of food that a ruminant returns from the first stomach to the mouth to chew a second time. **2. chew one's or the cud,** to meditate or muse. [ME; OE *cudu*, var. of *curidu, cwidu;* akin to OHG *quiti* glue, Skt *jatu* resin, gum. See QUID[1]]

cud·bear (kud′bâr′), *n.* a violet coloring matter obtained from various lichens, esp. *Lecanora tartarea.* [coinage based on his own name by Dr. *Cuthbert* Gordon, 18th-century Scottish chemist; see CUDDY[2]]

cud·dle (kud′əl), *v.,* **-dled, -dling,** *n.* —*v.t.* **1.** to draw or hold close in an affectionate manner; hug tenderly. —*v.i.* **2.** to lie close and snug; nestle. —*n.* **3.** act of cuddling; hug; embrace. [? back formation from ME *cudliche* intimate, affectionate, OE *cūthlīc*, or from ME *cuthlechen*, OE *cūthlǣcan* to make friends with] —**cud·dle·some** (kud′əl səm), **cud′dly,** *adj.* —**Syn. 1.** caress. **2.** snuggle.

cud·dy[1] (kud′ē), *n., pl.* **-dies.** **1.** a small cabin at the bow or stern of a vessel. **2.** a galley or pantry in a small vessel. **3.** a small locker in an open boat, esp. one at the bow. **4.** a small room, cupboard, or closet. [?]

cud·dy[2] (kud′ē, ko͝od′ē), *n., pl.* **-dies.** *Chiefly Scot.* **1.** a donkey. **2.** a stupid fellow. [? special use of *Cuddy*, short for *Cuthbert*, man's name]

cudg·el (kuj′əl), *n., v.,* **-eled, -el·ing,** or (*esp. Brit.*) **-elled, -el·ling.** —*n.* **1.** a short, thick stick used as a weapon; club. —*v.t.* **2.** to strike with a cudgel; beat. [ME *cuggel*, OE *cycgel;* akin to G *Kugel* ball]

cud·weed (kud′wēd′), *n.* **1.** any of the woolly, composite herbs of the genus *Gnaphalium.* **2.** any of various plants of allied genera.

cue[1] (kyo͞o), *n., v.,* **cued, cu·ing.** —*n.* **1.** *Theat.* anything said or done, on or behind the stage, that is followed by a specific line or action. **2.** a hint or intimation. **3.** the part one is to play; a prescribed or necessary course of action. **4.** anything that excites to action; stimulus. **5.** *Archaic.* frame of mind; mood. —*v.t.* **6.** to provide with a cue or indication; give a cue to. **7.** to insert, or direct to come in, in a specific place in a musical or dramatic performance (usually fol. by *in* or *into*). [name of the letter *q* as an abbreviation (found in acting scripts) of L *quando* when]

cue[2] (kyo͞o), *n., v.,* **cued, cu·ing.** —*n.* **1.** a long, tapering rod, tipped with leather, used to strike the ball in billiards, pool, etc. **2.** a queue of hair. **3.** a queue or file, as of persons awaiting their turn. —*v.t.* **4.** to tie into a queue or tail. [< F *queue* tail, OF *coue* < L *cōda*, var. of *cauda* tail]

cue′ ball′, *Billiards, Pool.* the ball struck by the cue as distinguished from the other balls on the table.

Cuen·ca (kweng′kä), *n.* a city in SW Ecuador. 60,021 (1962).

Cuer·na·va·ca (kwer′nə vä′kə; *Sp.* kweʀ′nä vä′kä), *n.* a city in and the capital of Morelos, in central Mexico. 37,144 (1960).

cues·ta (kwes′tə), *n.* a long, low ridge with a relatively steep face or escarpment on one side and a long, gentle slope on the other. [< Sp: shoulder, sloping land < L *costa* side (of a hill), rib; see COAST]

cuff[1] (kuf), *n.* **1.** a fold, band, etc., used as a trimming or finish for the bottom of a sleeve. **2.** a turned-up fold, as at the bottom of a trouser leg. **3.** the part of a gauntlet or long glove that extends over the wrist. **4.** a separate or detachable band or piece of linen or other material worn about the wrist, inside or outside of the sleeve. **5.** a handcuff. **6. off the cuff,** *Slang.* **a.** extemporaneously; on the spur of the moment. **b.** unofficially; informally: *I'm telling you this strictly off the cuff.* **7. on the cuff,** *Slang.* **a.** with the promise of future payment; on credit. **b.** without charge; with no payment expected. —*v.t.* **8.** to make a cuff or cuffs on. [ME *cuffe* mitten, OE *cuffie* cap < ML *cuphia* COIF]

cuff[2] (kuf), *v.t.* **1.** to strike with the open hand; beat; buffet. —*n.* **2.** a blow with the fist or the open hand; buffet. [? < Scand; cf. Sw *kuffa* to thrust]

cuff′ link′, a pair of linked buttons or a piece of jewelry for fastening a shirt cuff.

Cu·fic (kyo͞o′fik), *adj., n.* Kufic.

cu. ft., cubic foot; cubic feet.

Cu·ia·bá (ko͞o′yə bä′), *n.* **1.** a river in SW Brazil. ab. 300 mi. long. **2.** a port in W Brazil, on the Cuiabá River. 45,875 (1960). Also, **Cuyabá.**

cu·i bo·no (ko͞o′ē bō′nō; *Eng.* kwē′ bō′nō, kī′-), *Latin.* **1.** for whose benefit? **2.** for what use?; of what good?

cu. in., cubic inch; cubic inches.

cui·rass (kwi ras′), *n.* **1.** Also called **corselet.** defensive armor for the torso comprising a breastplate and backplate, originally made of leather. **2.** either of the plates forming such armor. **3.** *Zool.* a hard shell or other covering forming an indurated defensive shield. —*v.t.* **4.** to equip or cover with a cuirass. [< F *cuirasse* < ML *coriācea*, n. use of fem. of LL *coriāceus* (adj.) leathern = L *cori(um)* leather + *-āceus* -ACEOUS; r. late ME *curas* < MF *curasse*, var. of *cuirasse*]

cui·ras·sier (kwēr′ə sēr′), *n.* a cavalry soldier wearing a cuirass. [< F; see CUIRASS, -ER[2]]

cui·sine (kwi zēn′), *n.* **1.** a style or quality of cooking; cookery. **2.** *Archaic.* the kitchen or culinary department of a house, hotel, etc. [< F: lit., kitchen < LL *coquīn(a)*. See KITCHEN]

cuisse (kwis), *n.* *Armor.* a piece of armor or padding for defending the thigh. Also, **cuish** (kwish). [back formation from *cuisses* (pl.), ME *quyssewes, quysseaux* < MF *cuisseaux* thigh pieces = *cuisse* thigh (< L *coxa* hipbone) + *-eaux*, pl. of *-el* n. suffix]

cuit·tle (kʏ′təl), *v.t.,* **-tled, -tling.** *Scot.* to wheedle or coax.

cuke (kyo͞ok) *n.* *Informal.* cucumber. [by shortening]

culch (kulch), *n.* **1.** the stones, old shells, etc., forming an oyster bed and furnishing the points of attachment for the spawn of oysters. **2.** the spawn. **3.** *Dial.* rubbish; refuse. Also, **cultch.** [perh. metathetic var. of CLUTCH[1]; but note OF *culche* COUCH]

cul-de-sac (kul′də sak′, -sak′, ko͝ol′-; *Fr.* kʏdᵊsᴀk′), *n., pl.* **culs-de-sac** (kulz′də sak′, -sak′, ko͝olz′-; *Fr.* kʏdᵊsᴀk′). **1.** a street, lane, etc., closed at one end; blind alley. **2.** a saclike cavity, tube, or the like, open only at one end, as the caecum. **3.** any situation in which further progress is impossible. [< F: lit., bottom of the sack]

-cule, a suffix with the meaning "small," occurring in loan words from Latin (*ridicule*), used as a diminutive in the formation of compound words: *animalcule.* Also, **-cle.** [repr. L *-culus, -cula, -culum* dim. suffix]

Cu·le′bra Cut′ (ko͞o lā′brə; *Sp.* ko͞o le′vʀä), former name of **Gaillard Cut.**

cu·let (kyo͞o′lit), *n.* **1.** *Jewelry.* a small face forming the bottom of a faceted gem. **2.** *Armor.* a piece below the backplate, composed of lames and corresponding to the fauld in front. [< F (obs.) = *cul* bottom (< L *cūl(us)* buttocks) + *-et* -ET]

cu·lex (kyo͞o′leks), *n., pl.* **-li·ces** (-li sēz′). any mosquito of the genus *Culex*, as the common house mosquito, *C. pipiens.* [< L: gnat, midge]

Cu·lia·cán (ko͞o′lyä kän′), *n.* a city in and the capital of Sinaloa, in NW Mexico. 48,963 (1960).

cu·lic·id (kyo͞o lis′id), *n.* **1.** any of numerous dipterous insects of the family *Culicidae*, comprising the mosquitoes. —*adj.* **2.** belonging or pertaining to the family *Culicidae.* [back formation from NL *Culicidae* = L *culic-* (s. of *culex*) CULEX + *-idae* -ID[2]]

cu·li·nar·y (kyo͞o′lə ner′ē, kul′ə-), *adj.* pertaining to or used in the kitchen or cookery. [< L *culīnāri(us)* of the kitchen = *culīn(a)* kitchen, food + *-ārius* -ARY] —**cu′li·nar′i·ly,** *adv.*

Cu·lion (ko͞o lyōn′), *n.* an island of the Philippines, N of Palawan: leper colony. 150 sq. mi.

cull[1] (kul), *v.t.* **1.** to choose; select; pick; gather the choice things or parts from. **2.** to collect; gather; pluck. —*n.* **3.** act of culling. **4.** anything picked out and put aside as inferior. [ME *cul(en)* (late ME *culle*) < OF *cuill(ir)* < L *colligere* to gather. See COLLECT[1]]

cull[2] (kul), *n.* *Brit. Dial.* dupe; fool. [perh. from CULLY]

Cul·len (kul′ən), *n.* **Coun·tee** (koun tā′, -tē′), 1903–46, U.S. poet.

cul·len·der (kul′ən dər), *n.* colander.

cul·let (kul′it), *n.* broken or waste glass suitable for remelting. [var. of *collet* < It *collett(o)* glass blower's term, lit., little neck. See COL, -ET]

cul·lion (kul′yən), *n.* *Archaic.* a base or vile fellow. [ME *culyon,* var. of *coil(i)on* < MF *coillon* testicle < L *cole(us)* bag, scrotum (< Gk *koleós* sheath) + F *-on* dim. suffix]

cul·lis (kul′is), *n.* *Archit.* a gutter, as at the eaves of a roof. [< F *coulisse* groove, COULISSE]

cul·ly (kul′ē), *n., pl.* **-lies,** *v.,* **-lied, -ly·ing.** *Archaic.* —*n.* **1.** a dupe. —*v.t.* **2.** to trick or cheat. [? shortening of CULLION]

culm[1] (kulm), *n.* **1.** coal dust; slack. **2.** anthracite, esp. of inferior grade. **3.** (*cap.*) *Geol.* a series of Lower Carboniferous rocks, mainly developed in parts of Europe and mostly dark-colored and siliceous. [ME *colme,* prob. < *col* COAL]

culm[2] (kulm), *n.* **1.** a stem or stalk, esp. the jointed and usually hollow stem of grasses. —*v.i.* **2.** to grow or develop into a culm. [< L *culm(us)* stalk; akin to CALAMUS, HAULM]

cul·mif·er·ous (kul mif′ər əs), *adj.* having or producing culms.

cul·mi·nant (kul′mə nənt), *adj.* culminating; topmost. [< ML *culminant-* (s. of *culminans*), prp. of *culmināre*]

cul·mi·nate (kul′mə nāt′), *v.,* **-nat·ed, -nat·ing.** —*v.i.* **1.** to terminate at the highest point, summit, or highest development (usually fol. by *in*). **2.** to end or conclude; arrive at a final stage (usually fol. by *in*): *The argument culminated in a fistfight.* **3.** *Astron.* (of a celestial body) to be on the meridian or reach its highest point in the sky. —*v.t.* **4.** to bring to a close; complete; climax. [< ML *culmināt(us)* brought to a peak (ptp. of *culmināre*) = L *culmin-* (s. of *culmen*) peak, top + *-ātus* -ATE[1]]

cul·mi·na·tion (kul′mə nā′shən), *n.* **1.** act or fact of culminating. **2.** that in which anything culminates; highest point; acme. **3.** *Astron.* the position of a celestial body when it is on the meridian.

cu·lottes (ko͞o lots′, kyo͞o-; ko͞o′lots, kyo͞o′-), *n.pl.* women's casual trousers cut full to resemble a skirt. Also, **cu·lotte′.** [< F: lit., breeches = *cul* rump + *-ottes,* pl. of *-otte,* fem. of *-ot* n. suffix. See CULET]

Culottes

cul·pa (kul′pə; *Lat.* ko͝ol′pä), *n., pl.* **-pae** (-pē; *Lat.* -pī). **1.** *Roman and Civil Law.* negligence; neglect. **2.** guilt; sin. [OE < L: fault, liability, blame]

cul·pa·ble (kul′pə bəl), *adj.* deserving blame or censure. [ME < L *culpābil(is)* = *culpā(re)* (to) hold liable (see CULPA) + *-bilis* -BLE; r. ME *coupable* < MF] —**cul′pa·bil′i·ty,** *n.* —**cul′pa·bly,** *adv.* —**Syn.** censurable, reprehensible. —**Ant.** praiseworthy.

Cul·pep·er (kul′pep′ər), *n.* **Thomas** (*2nd Baron Culpeper of Thoresway*), 1635–89, British colonial governor of Virginia 1680–83.

cul·prit (kul′prit), *n.* **1.** a person arraigned for an offense. **2.** a person or other agent guilty of or responsible for an offense or fault. [traditionally explained as made up of *cul* (repr. L *culpābilis* guilty) + *prit* (repr. AF *prest* ready), marking the prosecution as ready to prove the defendant's guilt. See CULPABLE, PRESTO]

cult (kult), *n.* **1.** a particular system of religious worship, esp. with reference to its rites and ceremonies. **2.** an instance of great veneration of a person, ideal, or thing, esp. as manifested by a body of admirers: *a cult of Napoleon.* **3.** the object of such devotion. **4.** a group or sect bound together by devotion to or veneration of the same thing, person, ideal, etc. **5.** *Sociol.* a group having a sacred ideology and a set of rites centering around their sacred symbols. **6.** a religion that is considered or held to be false or unorthodox, or its members. [< L *cult(us)* tilling, care, refinement, worship, n. use of ptp. of *colere* to cultivate, worship, dwell] —**cul′tic,** *adj.* —**cult′ism,** *n.* —**cult′ist,** *n.*

cultch (kulch), *n.* culch.

cul·ti·va·ble (kul′tə və bəl), *adj.* capable of being cultivated. Also, **cul·ti·vat·a·ble** (kul′tə vā′tə bəl). [CULTIV(ATE) + -ABLE] —**cul′ti·va·bil′i·ty,** *n.*

cul·ti·var (kul′tə vär′, -vər), *n.* a variety of plant that has been produced only under cultivation. [CULTI(VATED) + VAR(IETY)]

cul·ti·vate (kul′tə vāt′), *v.t.,* **-vat·ed, -vat·ing.** **1.** to prepare and work on (land) in order to raise crops; till. **2.** to use a cultivator on. **3.** to promote or improve the growth of (a plant, crop, etc.) by labor and attention. **4.** to produce by culture. **5.** to develop or improve by education or training; refine. **6.** to promote the growth or development of (an art, science, etc.); foster. **7.** to devote oneself to (an art, science, etc.). **8.** to seek to promote or foster (friendship, love, etc.). **9.** to seek the acquaintance or friendship of (a person). [< ML *cultivāt(us)* tilled (ptp. of *cultivāre*) = *cultīv(us)* (L *cult(us),* ptp. of *colere* to till + *-īvus* -IVE) + *-ātus* -ATE[1]]

cul·ti·vat·ed (kul′tə vā′tid), *adj.* **1.** subjected to cultivation. **2.** produced or improved by cultivation, as a plant. **3.** educated or refined; cultured.

cul·ti·va·tion (kul′tə vā′shən), *n.* **1.** act or art of cultivating. **2.** state of being cultivated. **3.** culture; refinement.

cul·ti·va·tor (kul′tə vā′tər), *n.* **1.** a person or thing that cultivates. **2.** an implement drawn between rows of growing plants to loosen the earth and destroy weeds.

cul·trate (kul′trāt), *adj.* sharp-edged and pointed, as a leaf. Also, **cul′trat·ed.** [< L *cultrāt(us)* knife-shaped = *cultr-* (s. of *culter*) knife + *-ātus* -ATE[1]]

cul·tur·al (kul′chər əl), *adj.* of or pertaining to culture or cultivation. —**cul′tur·al·ly,** *adv.*

cul′tural anthropol′ogy, the branch of anthropology dealing with the origins, history, and development of human culture. Also called **social anthropology.** Cf. **physical anthropology.** —**cul′tural anthropol′ogist.**

cul′tural lag′, slowness in development of one part of a culture in respect to another part. Also, **culture lag.**

cul·ture (kul′chər), *n., v.,* **-tured, -tur·ing.** —*n.* **1.** the quality in a person or society that arises from an interest in and acquaintance with what is generally regarded as excellence in arts, letters, manners, scholarly pursuits, etc. **2.** a particular form or stage of civilization: *Greek culture.* **3.** *Sociol.* the sum total of ways of living built up by a group of human beings and transmitted from one generation to another. **4.** *Biol.* **a.** the cultivation of microorganisms, as bacteria, or of tissues, for scientific study, medicinal use, etc. **b.** the product or growth resulting from such cultivation. **5.** the act or practice of cultivating the soil; tillage. **6.** the raising of plants or animals, esp. with a view to their improvement. **7.** the product or growth resulting from such cultivation. **8.** development or improvement of the mind by education or training. —*v.t.* **9.** to subject to culture; cultivate. **10.** *Biol.* **a.** to develop (microorganisms, tissues, etc.) in an artificial medium. **b.** to introduce (living material) into a culture medium. [ME: tilling, place tilled < L *cultūr(a).* See CULT, -URE] —**cul′ture·less,** *adj.* —**Syn. 8.** See **education.**

cul·tured (kul′chərd), *adj.* **1.** cultivated. **2.** enlightened; refined. **3.** artificially nurtured or grown. **4.** made with the aid of a bacterial culture, as sour cream.

cul′tured pearl′, a pearl formed by a pearl oyster or mussel around an object, as around a seed pearl, bead, or piece of mantle tissue, inserted in its body. Also, **cul′ture pearl′.**

cul′ture he′ro, **1.** a mythical or mythicized historical figure who embodies the aspirations or ideals of a society. **2.** a mythical figure who is considered by a people to have furnished it the means of existence or survival, as by inventing its alphabet, stealing fire from the gods, etc.

cul′ture lag′. See **cultural lag.**

cul′ture me′dium, *Bacteriol.* medium (def. 8).

cul′ture shock′, a state of bewilderment, anxiety, and distress in an individual suddenly exposed to a social and cultural environment radically different from his own.

cul·tur·ist (kul′chər ist), *n.* **1.** a cultivator. **2.** an advocate or devotee of culture.

cul·tus (kul′təs), *n., pl.* **-tus·es, -ti** (-tī). a cult. [< L; see CULT]

Cul′ver Cit′y (kul′vər), a city in SW California, W of Los Angeles. 34,526 (1970).

cul·ver·in (kul′vər in), *n.* **1.** a medieval form of musket. **2.** a kind of heavy cannon used in the 16th and 17th centuries. [late ME < MF *coulevrine* < L *colubrīna,* fem. of *colubrīnus* COLUBRINE]

cul·vert (kul′vərt), *n.* a drain or channel crossing under a road, sidewalk, etc.; sewer; conduit. [?]

cum (kum, ko͝om), *prep.* with; together with; along with (usually used in combination): *My garage-cum-workshop is well equipped.* [< L: with, together (prep.)]

Cu·mae (kyo͞o′mē), *n.* an ancient city in SW Italy, on the coast of Campania: believed to be the earliest Greek colony in Italy or in Sicily. —**Cu·mae′an,** *adj.*

Cumae′an sib′yl, *Class. Myth.* a famous prophetess at Cumae who guided Aeneas through the underworld.

cu·ma·rin (ko͞o′mə rin), *n.* *Chem.* coumarin.

cum·ber (kum′bər), *v.t.* **1.** to hinder; hamper. **2.** to overload; burden. **3.** to inconvenience; trouble. —*n.* **4.** a hindrance. **5.** something that cumbers. **6.** *Archaic.* embarrassment; trouble. [ME *cumbren* (v.), aph. var. of *acumbren* to harass, defeat; see ENCUMBER]

Cum·ber·land (kum′bər lənd), *n.* **1.** a county in NW England. 294,162 (1961); 1520 sq. mi. *Co. seat:* Carlisle. **2.** a city in NW Maryland, on the Potomac River. 29,724 (1970). **3.** a city in NE Rhode Island. 26,605 (1970). **4.** a river flowing W from SE Kentucky through N Tennessee into the Ohio River. 687 mi. long.

Cum′berland Gap′, a pass in the Cumberland Mountains at the junction of the Virginia, Kentucky, and Tennessee boundaries. 1315 ft. high.

Cum′berland Moun′tains, a plateau largely in Kentucky and Tennessee, a part of the Appalachian Mountains: highest point, ab. 4000 ft. Also called **Cum′berland Plateau′.**

cum·ber·some (kum′bər səm), *adj.* **1.** burdensome; troublesome. **2.** unwieldy; clumsy. Also, **cum·brous** (kum′brəs). [ME *cummyrsum*] —**cum′ber·some·ly, cum′brous·ly,** *adv.* —**cum′ber·some·ness, cum′brous·ness,** *n.*

cum·brance (kum′brəns), *n.* **1.** trouble; bother. **2.** burden; encumbrance. [ME *combraunce,* aph. var. of *acombraunce* defeat, harassment; see ENCUMBRANCE]

cum′ div′idend, *Stock Exchange.* with or including a dividend that has been previously declared. Cf. **ex dividend.**

cum gra·no sa·lis (ko͝om grä′nō sä′lis; *Eng.* kum grā′nō sā′lis), *Latin.* with a grain of salt; not too seriously.

cum·in (kum′ən), *n.* **1.** a small, apiaceous plant, *Cuminum Cyminum,* bearing aromatic, seedlike fruit, used in cookery and medicine. **2.** the fruit or seeds of this plant. [ME *comin,* OE *cymen* << L *cumīn(um)* < Gk *kýminon* < Sem; cf. Ar *kammūn,* Heb *kammōn* cumin]

cum lau·de (ko͝om lou′dā, -də, -dē; kum lô′dē), with honor: used in diplomas to grant the lowest of three special honors for grades above the average. Cf. **magna cum laude, summa cum laude.** [< L: with praise]

cum·mer·bund (kum′ər bund′), *n.* a wide sash worn as a waistband, esp. one with horizontal pleats, worn beneath a dinner jacket. Also, **kummerbund.** [< Urdu *kamarband* loin band < Pers]

Cum·mings (kum′ingz), *n.* **Edward Est·lin** (est′lin), (pen name: *e e cummings*), 1894–1962, U.S. poet.

cum·quat (kum′kwot), *n.* kumquat.

cum·shaw (kum′shô), *n.* a present; gratuity; tip. [< Chin (Amoy dial.) *kam siā,* c. Mandarin *kan hsieh* grateful thanks]

cu·mu·late (*v.* kyo͞o′myə lāt′; *adj.* kyo͞o′myə lit, -lāt′), *v.,* **-lat·ed, -lat·ing,** *adj.* —*v.t.* **1.** to heap up; amass; accumulate. —*adj.* **2.** heaped up. [< L *cumulāt(us)* heaped up, piled up, accumulated (ptp. of *cumulāre*). See CUMULUS, -ATE[1]] —**cu′mu·late·ly,** *adv.* —**cu′mu·la′tion,** *n.*

cu·mu·la·tive (kyo͞o′myə lā′tiv, -lə tiv), *adj.* **1.** increasing or growing by accumulation or successive additions: *cumulative evidence.* **2.** formed by or resulting from accumulation or the addition of successive parts or elements. **3.** of or pertaining to interest or dividends that, if not paid when due, become a prior claim for payment in the future. —**cu′mu·la′tive·ly,** *adv.* —**cu′mu·la′tive·ness,** *n.*

cumulo-, a combining form of **cumulus.**

cu·mu·lo·cir·rus (kyo͞o′myə lō sir′əs), *n., pl.* **-rus.** cirrocumulus.

cu·mu·lo·nim·bus (kyo͞o′myə lō nim′bəs), *n., pl.* **-bus.** a cloud of a class indicative of thunderstorm conditions, characterized by large, dense, and very tall towers. Also called **thundercloud, thunderclouds, thunderhead.**

cu·mu·lo·stra·tus (kyo͞o′myə lō strā′təs, -strat′əs), *n., pl.* **-tus.** stratocumulus.

cu·mu·lus (kyo͞o′myə ləs), *n., pl.* **-lus. 1.** a heap; pile. **2.** a cloud of a class exhibiting great vertical development and characterized by dense individual elements in the form of puffs, mounds, or towers and flat bases. [< NL (L: mass, pile)]

Cu·nax·a (kyo͞o nak′sə), *n.* an ancient town in Babylonia, near the Euphrates: battle between Cyrus the Younger and Artaxerxes II in 401 B.C.

cunc·ta·tion (kuŋgk tā′shən), *n.* delay; tardiness. [< L *cunctātiōn-* (s. of *cunctātiō*) delay = *cunctāt(us)* delayed (ptp. of *cunctārī*) + *-iōn-* -ION]

Cuneate leaf

cunc·ta·tor (kuŋgk tā′tər), *n.* a procrastinator. [< L = *cunctāt(us)* delayed (ptp. of *cunctārī*) + *-or* -OR[2]]

cu·ne·ate (kyo͞o′nē it, -āt′), *adj.* **1.** Also, **cu·ne·al** (kyo͞o′nē əl). wedge-shaped. **2.** (of leaves) triangular and tapering to a point at the base. Also, **cu′ne·at′ed.** [< L *cuneāt(us)* = *cune(us)* a wedge + *-ātus* -ATE[1]] —**cu′ne·ate·ly,** *adv.*

cu·ne·at·ic (kyo͞o′nē at′ik), *adj.* cuneiform; cuneate.

cu·ne·i·form (kyo͞o nē′ə fôrm′, kyo͞o′nē ə-), *adj.* **1.** having the form of a wedge; wedge-shaped. **2.** composed of slim triangular elements, as the characters used in writing by the ancient Assyrians, Babylonians, and others. **3.** written in cuneiform characters: *cuneiform inscription.* **4.** *Anat.* noting or pertaining to any of various wedge-shaped bones, as of the tarsus. —*n.* **5.** cuneiform characters or writing. **6.** a cuneiform bone. [< L *cune(us)* a wedge + -I- + -FORM]

Cuneiform inscription (Persian)

Cu·ne·o (ko͞o′ne ô), *n.* a city in NW Italy. 46,287 (1961).

cun·ner (kun′ər), *n.* a small fish, *Tautogolabrus adspersus,* commonly found on the North Atlantic coast of the U.S. [?]

cun·ni·lin·gus (kun′ᵊliŋ′gəs), *n.* oral stimulation of the female genitalia. Also, **cun·ni·linc·tus** (kun′ᵊliŋgk′təs). [< NL, L: one who licks the vulva = *cunni-* (comb. form of *cunnus* vulva) + *-lingus* (< *lingere* to lick)]

cun·ning (kun′iŋ), *n.* **1.** skill employed in a crafty manner, as in deceiving; craftiness; guile. **2.** adeptness in performance; dexterity. —*adj.* **3.** showing or made with ingenuity. **4.** artfully subtle or shrewd; crafty; sly. **5.** *Informal.* charmingly cute: *a cunning little baby.* **6.** *Archaic.* skillful; expert. —*v.* **7.** *Obs.* prp. of **can**[1]. [(n.) ME, OE *cunnung* = *cunn(an)* (to) know (see CAN[1]) + *-ung* -ING[1]; (adj., v.) ME, prp. of *cunnan* to know (see CAN[1] (def. 6), -ING[2])] —**cun′ning·ly,** *adv.* —**cun′ning·ness,** *n.*

—**Syn. 1.** shrewdness, artfulness, wiliness, slyness, trickery, deception. CUNNING, ARTIFICE, CRAFT imply an inclination toward deceit, slyness, and trickery. CUNNING implies a shrewd, often instinctive skill in concealing or disguising the real purposes of one's actions: *not intelligence but a low kind of cunning.* An ARTIFICE is a clever, unscrupulous ruse, used to mislead others: *a successful artifice to conceal one's motives.* CRAFT suggests underhand methods and the use of deceptive devices and tricks to attain one's ends: *craft and deceitfulness in every act.* **2.** adroitness. **3.** ingenious, skillful. **4.** artful, wily, tricky, foxy. —**Ant. 2.** inability.

cunt (kunt), *n. Slang (usually vulgar).* **1.** the vagina. **2.** a woman, esp. as an object of sex. **3.** sexual intercourse. [ME *cunte;* c. ON *kunta,* OFris *kunte;* cf. L *cunnus,* Gk *kusthos*]

Cuo·mo (kwō′mō), *n.* **Mario (Matthew),** born 1932, U.S. political leader: governor of New York since 1982.

cup (kup), *n., v.,* **cupped, cup·ping.** —*n.* **1.** a small, open container, of china, glass, metal, etc., usually having one handle and used chiefly as a vessel from which to drink tea, soup, etc. **2.** an ornamental vessel, esp. of precious metal, offered as a prize for a contest. **3.** the quantity contained in a cup. **4.** a unit of capacity, equal to 8 fluid ounces or 16 tablespoons. **5.** any of various beverages, as a mixture of wine and various ingredients: *claret cup.* **6.** the chalice or the wine used in communion. **7.** one's portion, as of joy or suffering. **8.** any cuplike utensil, organ, part, cavity, etc. **9.** *Golf.* **a.** the metal receptacle within the hole. **b.** the hole itself. **10.** See **cupping glass. 11. in one's cups,** intoxicated; drunk. —*v.t.* **12.** to take or place in or as in a cup. **13.** to form into a cuplike shape: *He cupped his hands.* **14.** to use a cupping glass on. [ME, OE *cuppe* < LL *cuppa,* var. of L *cūpa* tub, cask]

cup·bear·er (kup′bâr′ər), *n.* an attendant who fills and passes cups in which drink is served. [late ME *cupberer*]

cup·board (kub′ərd), *n.* **1.** a closet with shelves for dishes, cups, etc. **2.** *Chiefly Brit.* any small closet or cabinet, as for clothes, food, etc. [ME *cuppebord*]

cup·cake (kup′kāk′), *n.* a small cake baked in a cup-shaped pan.

cu·pel (kyo͞o′pəl, kyo͞o pel′), *n., v.,* **-peled, -pel·ing** or (*esp. Brit.*) **-pelled, -pel·ling.** —*n.* **1.** a small, cuplike, porous vessel, usually made of bone ash, used in assaying, as for separating gold and silver from lead. **2.** a receptacle or furnace bottom in which silver is refined. —*v.t.* **3.** to heat or refine in a cupel. [< ML *cūpell(a),* dim. of L *cūp(a)* tub] —**cu·pel·er** (kyo͞o′pə lər), **cu·pel·ler** (kyo͞o pel′ər), *n.* —**cu·pel·la·tion** (kyo͞o′pə lā′shən), *n.*

cup·ful (kup′fo͝ol′), *n., pl.* **-fuls. 1.** the amount a cup can hold. **2.** *Cookery.* a volumetric measure equal to eight fluid ounces; half pint. [ME *cuppefulle*]

cup·hold·er (kup′hōl′dər), *n.* a competitor who has won or successfully defended a specific trophy, title, etc.

Cu·pid (kyo͞o′pid), *n.* **1.** the ancient Roman god of love, usually represented as a winged, naked, infant boy with a bow and arrows. **2.** (*l.c.*) a similar winged being, or a representation of one, esp. as symbolic of love. [ME *Cupide,* var. of *Cupido* < L: lit., desire, love = *cup(ere)* (to) long for, desire + *-īdō* n. suffix]

cu·pid·i·ty (kyo͞o pid′i tē), *n.* eager or inordinate desire, esp. for wealth; greed or avarice. [late ME *cupidite* < L *cupiditās* = *cupid(us)* eager, desirous + *-itās* -ITY]

Cu′pid's bow′ (bō), **1.** a classical bow; the bow Cupid is traditionally pictured as bearing. **2.** a line resembling this, esp. the line of the upper lip. —**Cu′pid's-bow′,** *adj.*

cup′ of tea′, *Informal.* **1.** a subject, person, etc., to one's taste or liking. **2.** *Brit.* **a.** one's fate or destiny. **b.** something or someone to be warned against or suspicious of.

cu·po·la (kyo͞o′pə lə), *n.* **1.** *Archit.* **a.** a light structure on a dome or roof, serving as a belfry, lantern, or belvedere. **b.** a dome, esp. one covering a circular or polygonal area. **2.** any of various domelike structures. **3.** *Foundry.* a vertical furnace for melting iron to be cast. [< It < L *cūpula.* See CUP, -ULE.] —**cu·po·lat·ed** (kyo͞o′pə lā′tid), *adj.*

Cupola

cupped (kupt), *adj.* hollowed out like a cup.

cup·per (kup′ər), *n.* a person who performs the operation of cupping.

cup·ping (kup′iŋ), *n.* the process of drawing blood to the surface by the application of a cupping glass, as for relieving internal congestion. [ME *cuppinge*]

cup′ping glass′, a glass vessel, used in cupping, in which a partial vacuum is created, as by heat.

cupr-, var. of **cupri-** before a vowel: *cupreous.*

cu·pre·ous (kyo͞o′prē əs, ko͞o′-), *adj.* containing or resembling copper. [< LL *cupreus*]

cupri-, a learned borrowing from Latin meaning "copper," used in the formation of compound words: *cupriferous.* Also, **cupr-, cupro-.** [comb. form of LL *cuprum* COPPER[1]]

cu·pric (kyo͞o′prik, ko͞o′-), *adj. Chem.* of or containing copper, esp. in the bivalent state, as cupric oxide, CuO.

cu′pric sul′fate, *Chem.* See **blue vitriol.**

cu·prif·er·ous (kyo͞o prif′ər əs, ko͞o-), *adj.* containing or yielding copper.

cu·prite (kyo͞o′prīt, ko͞o′-), *n.* a mineral, cuprous oxide, Cu_2O, an ore of copper.

cu·pro·nick·el (kyo͞o′prə nik′əl, ko͞o′-), *n. Metall.* any of various alloys of copper with up to 40 percent nickel.

cu·prous (kyo͞o′prəs, ko͞o′-), *adj. Chem.* containing copper in the univalent state, as cuprous oxide, Cu_2O.

cu·pu·late (kyo͞o′pyə lāt′, -lit), *adj.* shaped like a cupule. Also, **cu·pu·lar** (kyo͞o′pyə lər).

cu·pule (kyo͞o′pyo͞ol), *n.* **1.** *Bot.* **a.** a cup-shaped involucre consisting of indurated, cohering bracts, as in the acorn. See illus. at **acorn. b.** a cup-shaped outgrowth of the thallus of certain liverworts. **2.** *Zool.* a small cup-shaped sucker or similar organ or part. [< NL *cūpul(a),* LL: small tub. See CUP, -ULE]

cur (kûr), *n.* **1.** a mongrel dog, esp. a worthless or unfriendly one. **2.** a low, despicable person. [ME *curre,* appar. shortened from *curdogge.* See CURR, DOG]

cur., 1. currency. **2.** current.

cur·a·ble (kyo͝or′ə bəl), *adj.* that can be cured. [ME < L *cūrābil(is)*] —**cur′a·bil′i·ty, cur′a·ble·ness,** *n.* —**cur′a·bly,** *adv.*

Cu·ra·çao (ko͝or′ə sou′, -sō′, kyo͝or′ə-), *n.* **1.** the main island of the Netherlands Antilles, off the NW coast of Venezuela. 131,000 (est. 1963); 173 sq. mi. *Cap.:* Willemstad. **2.** a former name of **Netherlands Antilles. 3.** (*l.c.*) Also, **cu·ra·çoa** (kyo͝or′ə sō′, -sō′ə). a cordial or liqueur flavored with the peel of the sour orange.

cu·ra·cy (kyo͝or′ə sē), *n., pl.* **-cies.** the office or position of a curate. [CURATE + -CY]

cu·ra·re (kyo͝o rär′ē), *n.* **1.** a resinlike substance derived from tropical plants of the genus *Strychnos,* esp. *S. toxifera,* and from the root of pareira, used by South American Indians for poisoning arrows and in medicine for arresting the action of the motor nerves. **2.** a plant yielding this substance. Also, **cu·ra′ri.** [< Pg < Carib *kurari*]

cu·ra·rize (kyo͝or′ə rīz′, kyo͝o rär′īz), *v.t.,* **-rized, -riz·ing.** to treat with curare, as in vivisection. —**cu′ra·ri·za′tion,** *n.*

cu·ras·sow (kyo͝or′ə sō′, kyo͝o ras′ō), *n.* any of several large, arboreal, gallinaceous birds of the family *Cracidae,* of South and Central America. [after CURAÇAO]

cu·rate (kyo͝or′it), *n.* **1.** *Chiefly Brit.* a clergyman employed to assist a rector or vicar. **2.** any ecclesiastic entrusted with the cure of souls, as a parish priest. [ME *curat* < ML *cūrāt(us).* See CURE, -ATE[1]]

cur·a·tive (kyo͝or′ə tiv), *adj.* **1.** serving to cure or heal; remedial. —*n.* **2.** a curative agent; remedy. [late ME < L *cūrāt(us)* cared for, attended to (ptp. of *cūrāre;* see CURE); see -IVE] —**cur′a·tive·ly,** *adv.* —**Syn. 1.** healing.

cu·ra·tor (kyo͝o rā′tər, kyo͝or′ā-), *n.* **1.** the person in charge of a museum, art collection, etc. **2.** a manager or overseer; superintendent. [< L (see CURATIVE, -OR[2]); r. ME *curatour* < AF] —**cu·ra·to·ri·al** (kyo͝or′ə tōr′ē əl, -tôr′-), *adj.* —**cu·ra′tor·ship′,** *n.*

curb (kûrb), *n.* **1.** a rim, esp. of concrete or joined stones, forming an edge for a sidewalk. **2.** the framework around the top of a well. **3.** *U.S.* (formerly) a secondary stock exchange where securities not listed by a primary exchange were traded. **4.** Also called **curb′ bit′.** a bit used with a bridoon for control or restraint of a horse. **5.** an enclosing framework or border. **6.** anything that restrains or controls; a check. **7.** *Vet. Pathol.* a swelling on the lower part of the back of the hock of a horse, often causing lameness. —*v.t.* **8.** to restrain or check. **9.** to put a curb on (a horse). **10.** to furnish with or protect by a curb. Also, *Brit.,* **kerb** (for defs. 1, 10). [ME *curb, courbe* curved piece of wood (n.), stooped, hunchbacked (adj.) < MF *courbe* < L *curv(us)* crooked, bent, curved. See CURVE] —**Syn. 8.** bridle, repress. See **check.** —**Ant. 8.** encourage.

curb·ing (kûr′bing), *n.* **1.** the material forming a curb. **2.** a curb or a section of a curb.

curb′ roof′, a roof divided on each side of the ridge into two or more slopes, as a mansard or gambrel roof.

curb′ serv′ice, service given to people seated in parked cars, as at a roadside eating place.

curb·stone (kûrb′stōn′), *n.* a stone or series of stones forming a curb.

curch (kûrch), *n.* a kerchief worn by Scottish women. [late ME *kerche, c(o)urche,* back formation from *courche(i)s* (pl.) < MF *couvrech(i)es,* pl. of *couvrechef* KERCHIEF; the final *e* of the sing. form, orig. long, was later lost]

cur·cu·li·o (kûr kyo͞o′lē ō′), *n., pl.* **-li·os.** any of several weevils that feed on plums, cherries, and other fruits. [< L: weevil, corn worm]

cur·cu·ma (kûr′kyo͝o mə), *n.* any chiefly Old World, zingiberaceous plant of the genus *Curcuma,* as *C. longa,* yielding turmeric, or *C. Zedoaria,* yielding zedoary. [< NL < Ar *kurkum* saffron, turmeric]

curd (kûrd), *n.* **1.** Often, **curds.** a substance consisting mainly of casein and the like, obtained from milk by coagulation, and used as food or made into cheese. **2.** any substance resembling this. —*v.t., v.i.* **3.** to turn into curd; coagulate; congeal. [ME *crud;* see CROWD[1]]

cur·dle (kûr′dəl), *v.t., v.i.,* **-dled, -dling. 1.** to change into curd; coagulate or congeal. **2. curdle the** or **one's blood,** to fill a person with horror or fear; terrify. —**cur′dler,** *n.*

curd·y (kûr′dē), *adj.,* **curd·i·er, curd·i·est.** like curd; containing curd; coagulated. —**curd′i·ness,** *n.*

cure (kyo͝or), *n., v.,* **cured, cur·ing.** —*n.* **1.** a method or course of remedial treatment, as for disease. **2.** successful remedial treatment; restoration to health. **3.** a means of restoring to health; remedy. **4.** a method or process of preserving meat, fish, etc., as smoking or salting. **5.** *Eccles.* **a.** spiritual charge of the people in a certain district. **b.** the office or district of a curate or parish priest. —*v.t.* **6.** to restore to health. **7.** to relieve or rid of something troublesome or detrimental, as an illness, a bad habit, etc. **8.** to prepare (meat, fish, etc.) for preservation, esp. by salting or drying. **9.** to promote hardening of (fresh concrete or mortar) by keeping it damp. —*v.i.* **10.** to effect a cure. **11.** to become cured. [(n.) ME < OF *cure* and its source L *cūra* care; in religious sense < ML *cūra;* (v.) ME *cure(n)* < MF *cure(r)* and its source L *cūrāre* to take care of < *cūr(a)* care] —**cure′less,** *adj.* —**cur′er,** *n.*
—**Syn. 1.** remedy, restorative, antidote. **7.** CURE, HEAL, REMEDY imply making well, whole, or right. CURE is esp. applied to the eradication of disease or sickness: *to cure a fever, a headache.* HEAL suggests the making whole of wounds, sores, etc.: *to heal a cut or a burn.* REMEDY is a more general word that includes both the others and applies also to making wrongs right: *to remedy a mistake, a misunderstanding.*

cu·ré (kyo͝o rā′, kyo͝or′ā; *Fr.* KY RĀ′), *n., pl.* **cu·rés** (kyo͝o rāz′, kyo͝or′āz; *Fr.* KY RĀ′). (in France) a parish priest. [< F, OF; modeled on eccl. L *cūrātus* parish priest; see CURATE]

cure-all (kyo͝or′ôl′), *n.* a cure for all ills; panacea.

cu·ret (kyo͝o ret′), *n., v.t.,* **-ret·ted, -ret·ting.** curette.

cu·ret·tage (kyo͝o ret′ij, kyo͝or′i täzh′), *n. Surg.* the process or operation of curetting. Also, **cu·rette·ment** (kyo͝o ret′mənt). [< F]

cu·rette (kyo͝o ret′), *n., v.,* **-ret·ted, -ret·ting.** —*n.* **1.** a scoop-shaped surgical instrument for removing tissues from body cavities, as the uterus. —*v.t.* **2.** to scrape with a curette. [< F]

curf (kûrf), *n.* kerf.

cur·few (kûr′fyo͞o), *n.* **1.** an order establishing a specific period of time, usually at night, during which certain restrictions apply, esp. that no unauthorized persons may be outdoors or that places of public assembly must be closed. **2.** the time at which such a daily period starts. **3.** (in medieval Europe) the ringing of a bell at a fixed hour in the evening as a signal for covering or extinguishing fires. [ME < MF *cuevre-feu,* lit., cover (the) fireplace (impv.). See COVER, FOCUS]

cu·ri·a (kyo͝or′ē ə), *n., pl.* **cu·ri·ae** (kyo͝or′ē ē′). **1.** one of the political subdivisions of each of the three tribes of ancient Rome. **2.** (*sometimes cap.*) See **Curia Romana. 3.** the papal court. [< L, contr. of **coviria* = *co-* CO- + *vir* man + *-ia* -IA] —**cu′ri·al,** *adj.*

Cu′ria Ro·ma′na (rō mä′nə, -mä′-), *Roman Cath. Ch.* the body of congregations, offices, etc., that assist the pope in the government and administration of the church. [< ML, L: lit., (the) Roman curia]

Cu·ri·a·ti·i (kyo͝or′ē ā′shē ī′), *n.pl. Rom. Legend.* See under **Horatii.**

cu·rie (kyo͝or′ē, kyo͝o rē′), *n. Physics, Chem.* the unit of radioactivity, equivalent to 3.70×10^{10} disintegrations per second. *Abbr.:* Ci, c [named after Marie CURIE]

Cu·rie (kyo͝or′ē, kyo͝o rē′; *Fr.* KY RĒ′), *n.* **1. I·rène** (*Fr.* Ē REN′). See **Joliot-Curie, Irène. 2. Ma·rie** (mə rē′; *Fr.* MA RĒ′), 1867–1935, Polish physicist and chemist in France: codiscoverer of radium 1898; Nobel prize for physics 1903, for chemistry 1911. **3.** her husband, **Pierre** (pē âr′; *Fr.* PYER), 1859–1906, French physicist and chemist: codiscoverer of radium; Nobel prize for physics 1903.

Cu′rie point′, *Physics.* the temperature beyond which a ferromagnetic substance exhibits paramagnetism. Also called **Cu′rie tem′perature.** [named after Pierre CURIE]

cu·ri·o (kyo͝or′ē ō′), *n., pl.* **-ri·os.** any article, object of art, etc., valued as a curiosity [shortened from CURIOSITY]

cu·ri·o·sa (kyo͝or′ē ō′sə), *n.pl.* **1.** books, pamphlets, etc., dealing with unusual subjects. **2.** erotica. [< NL: unusual things, special use of neut. pl. of L *cūriōsus*]

cu·ri·os·i·ty (kyo͝or′ē os′i tē), *n., pl.* **-ties. 1.** the desire to learn or know about anything; inquisitiveness. **2.** a strange, curious, or interesting quality. **3.** a curious, rare, or novel thing. **4.** *Obs.* carefulness; fastidiousness. [ME *curiosite* < L *cūriōsitās*] —**Syn. 3.** curio, rarity, freak.

cu·ri·ous (kyo͝or′ē əs), *adj.* **1.** desirous of learning or knowing; inquisitive. **2.** prying or meddlesome. **3.** arousing interest or attention through being inexplicable or highly unusual; odd; strange: *a curious sort of person.* **4.** *Archaic.* **a.** made or prepared skillfully. **b.** done with painstaking accuracy or attention to detail. **5.** *Obs.* **a.** careful; fastidious. **b.** marked by intricacy or subtlety. [ME < L *cūriōsus* careful, inquisitive = *cūri-* (comb. form of *cūra* care; see CURE) + *-ōsus* -OUS] —**cu′ri·ous·ly,** *adv.* —**cu′ri·ous·ness,** *n.*
—**Syn. 1.** inquiring, interested. **2.** spying, peeping. CURIOUS, INQUISITIVE, MEDDLESOME, PRYING refer to taking an undue (and petty) interest in others' affairs. CURIOUS implies a desire to know what is not properly one's concern: *curious about a neighbor's habits.* INQUISITIVE implies asking impertinent questions in an effort to satisfy curiosity: *inquisitive in asking about a neighbor's habits.* MEDDLESOME implies thrusting oneself into and taking an active part in other people's affairs (or handling their possessions) entirely unasked and unwelcomed: *a meddlesome aunt who tries to run the affairs of a family.* PRYING implies a meddlesome and persistent inquiring into others' affairs: *a prying reporter inquiring into the secrets of a business firm.* **3.** unusual, singular, novel, rare, exotic. —**Ant. 1, 2.** indifferent.

Cu·ri·ti·ba (ko͞o′RĒ tē′bə; *Eng.* ko͝or′i tē′bə), *n.* a city in and the capital of Paraná, in SE Brazil. 351,259 (1960). Also, **Cu′ri·ty′ba.**

cu·ri·um (kyo͝or′ē əm), *n. Chem.* a radioactive element not found in nature but found among the products of plutonium after bombardment by high-energy helium ions. *Symbol:* Cm; *at. no.:* 96. [< NL; named after Marie and Pierre CURIE; see -IUM]

curl (kûrl), *v.t.* **1.** to form into coils or ringlets, as the hair. **2.** to form into a spiral or curved shape; coil. **3.** *Obs.* to adorn with or as with curls or ringlets. —*v.i.* **4.** to grow in or form curls or ringlets, as the hair. **5.** to coil. **6.** to become curved or undulated. **7.** to play at the game of curling. **8.** to move in a curving direction or path. **9. curl up,** to sit or lie down cozily: *to curl up with a good book.* —*n.* **10.** a coil or ringlet of hair. **11.** anything of a spiral or curved shape, as a lettuce leaf, wood shaving, etc.; coil. **12.** the act of curling. **13.** the state of being curled. **14.** *Plant Pathol.* **a.** the distortion, fluting, or puffing of a leaf, resulting from the unequal development of its two sides. **b.** a disease so characterized. **15.** *Math.* **a.** a vector obtained from a given vector by taking its cross product with the vector whose coordinates are the partial derivative operators with respect to each coordinate. **b.** the operation that produces this vector. [appar. back formation from *curled,* metathetic var. of ME *crulled* (ptp.), *crul* (adj.); cf. MD *crullen* to curl]

Curlew, *Numenius arquatus* (Length 23 in.; wingspread 3¼ ft.)

curl·er (kûr′lər), *n.* **1.** a person or thing that curls. **2.** any of various pins, clasps, or rollers on which locks of hair are wound or clamped for curling. **3.** a player at the game of curling.

cur·lew (kûr′lo͞o), *n.* any of several shore birds of the genus *Numenius,* having a long, slender, downward curved bill, as the common *N. arquatus,* of Europe. [ME < AF *curleu,* c. MF *corleu;* ? imit.]

Cur·ley (kûr′lē), *n.* **James M(ichael),** 1874–1958, U.S. politician.

curl·i·cue (kûr′lə kyo͞o′), *n.* an ornamental, fancy curl or twist. Also, **curlycue.** [CURLY + CUE[2]]

curl·ing (kûr′ling), *n.* a game played on ice in which two teams of four players each compete in sliding curling stones toward a mark in the center of a circle. [?]

curl′ing i′ron, a rod of iron, used when heated for curling the hair. Also, **curl′ing i′rons.** Also called **curl′ing tongs′.**

curl′ing stone′, a large, heavy, ellipsoidal stone or a similar object made of iron, having a handle on the top by which it is released in the game of curling.

Curling stone

curl·pa·per (kûrl′pā′pər), *n.* a piece of paper on which a lock of hair is rolled up tightly until fixed in a curl.

curl·y (kûr′lē), *adj.,* **curl·i·er, curl·i·est. 1.** curling or tending to curl: *curly hair.* **2.** having curls (usually used in combination): *curlyheaded.* —**curl′i·ness,** *n.*

cur·ly·cue (kûr′lə kyo͞o′), *n.* curlicue.

cur·mudg·eon (kər muj′ən), *n.* an irascible, churlish person. [unexplained; perh. *cur-* repr. CUR] —**cur·mudg′eon·ly,** *adj.*

curn (kûrn), *n. Scot.* **1.** a grain. **2.** a small quantity or number. [ME; akin to CORN[1], KERNEL]

curr (kûr), *v.i.* to make a low, murmuring sound, like the purring of a cat. [akin to Icel *kurra* to grumble, murmur, MHG *kurren,* MD *curren* to growl]

cur·rach (kur′əKH, kur′ə), *n. Scot., Irish.* a coracle. Also, **cur′ragh.** [late ME *currok* < ScotGael *curach,* IrGael *currach* boat; see CORACLE]

cur·ra·jong (kur′ə jông′), *n.* kurrajong.

cur·rant (kûr′ənt, kur′-), *n.* **1.** a small seedless raisin, produced chiefly in California and in the Levant. **2.** the small, edible, acid, round fruit or berry of certain wild or cultivated shrubs of the genus *Ribes.* **3.** the shrub itself. [shortened from ME *raysons of Coraunte* raisins of CORINTH, the port in Greece whence they chiefly came]

cur·ren·cy (kûr′ən sē, kur′-), *n., pl.* **-cies. 1.** something that is used as a medium of exchange; money. **2.** general acceptance; prevalence; vogue. 3. a time or period during which something is widely accepted and circulated. 4. circulation, as of coin. [< ML *currentia*]

cur·rent (kûr′ənt, kur′-), *adj.* **1.** passing in time, or belonging to the time actually passing: *the current month.* **2.** passing from one to another; circulating, as a coin. **3.** publicly reported or known: *a rumor that is current.* **4.** prevalent or customary: *the current practice.* **5.** popular; in vogue: *the current fashions.* **6.** *Obs.* genuine; authentic. —*n.* **7.** a flowing; flow, as of a river. **8.** a large portion of air, large body of water, etc., moving in a certain direction. **9.** the speed at which such flow moves; velocity of flow. **10.** *Elect.* **a.** the movement or flow of electric charge. **b.** the rate of flow, usually measured in amperes. **11.** the general tendency; trend. [< L *current-* (s. of *currēns*) running (prp. of *currere*); r. ME *curraunt* < AF; see -ENT] —**cur′rent·ness,** *n.* —**Syn. 4.** common, widespread, rife. CURRENT, PRESENT, PREVAILING, PREVALENT refer to something generally or commonly in use. That which is CURRENT is in general circulation or a matter of common knowledge or acceptance: *current usage in English.* PRESENT refers to that which is in general use now; it is more limited than current, as to time: *present customs.* That which is PREVAILING is something that has superseded others: *prevailing fashion.* That which is PREVALENT exists or is spread widely: *a prevalent idea.* **5.** stylish, fashionable, modish.

cur′rent as′sets, *Com.* assets that are readily convertible into cash.

cur′rent liabil′ities, *Com.* indebtedness maturing within one year.

cur·rent·ly (kûr′ənt lē, kur′-), *adv.* now; at present.

cur·ri·cle (kûr′i kəl), *n.* a light, two-wheeled, open carriage drawn by two horses abreast. [< L *curricul(um)* racing chariot = *curr(us)* chariot, wagon (< *currere* to run) + *-i-* -I- + *-culum* -CLE]

cur·ric·u·lum (kə rik′yə ləm), *n., pl.* **-la** (-lə), **-lums. 1.** the aggregate of courses of study given in a school, college, etc. **2.** the regular or a particular course of study in a school, college, etc. [< L: course, career (lit., a running) = *curri-* (s. of *currere* to run) + *-culum* -CULE] —**cur·ric′u·lar,** *adj.*

cur·ric·u·lum vi·tae (kə rik′yə ləm vī′tē; *Lat.* ko͝or-rik′o͞o lo͞om′ wē′tī), *pl.* **cur·ric·u·la vi·tae** (kə rik′yə lə vī′tē; *Lat.* ko͝or rik′o͞o lä′ wē′tī). **1.** Also called **vita, vitae.** a brief biographical résumé of one's career. **2.** (*italics*) *Latin.* the course of one's life or career.

cur·rie (kûr′ē, kur′ē), *n., v.t.,* **-ried, -ry·ing.** curry[1].

cur·ri·er (kûr′ē ər, kur′-), *n.* **1.** a person who dresses and colors leather after it is tanned. **2.** a person who curries horses. [CURRY[2] + -ER[1]; r. ME *corayour,* etc. < AF << L *coriār(ius)* = *cori(um)* leather + *-ārius* -ARY]

Cur·ri·er (kûr′ē ər, kur′-), *n.* **Nathaniel,** 1813–88, U.S. lithographer. Cf. **Ives** (def. 2).

cur·ri·er·y (kûr′ē ə rē, kur′-), *n., pl.* **-er·ies. 1.** the occupation or business of a currier of leather. **2.** the place where it is carried on.

cur·rish (kûr′ish), *adj.* **1.** of or pertaining to a cur. **2.** curlike; snarling; quarrelsome. **3.** contemptible; base. [late ME *kuresshe*] —**cur′rish·ly,** *adv.* —**cur′rish·ness,** *n.*

cur·ry[1] (kûr′ē, kur′ē), *n., pl.* **-ries,** *v.,* **-ried, -ry·ing.** —*n.* **1.** *East Indian Cookery.* a dish, as meat, vegetables, etc., flavored with curry powder. **2.** See **curry powder.** —*v.t.* **3.** to prepare (food) as a curry: *to curry eggs.* Also, **currie.** [< Tamil *kari* sauce]

cur·ry[2] (kûr′ē, kur′ē), *v.t.,* **-ried, -ry·ing. 1.** to rub and clean (a horse) with a currycomb. **2.** to dress (tanned hides) by soaking, scraping, etc. **3.** to beat or thrash. **4. curry favor,** to seek to advance oneself through flattery or fawning. [ME *cor(r)ay(en), cor(r)ey(en),* etc. < AF *curreier,* c. OF *correer,* earlier *conreer* to make ready = *con-* CON- + *-reer* < VL **rēdāre* < Gmc; cf. OE *rǣdan* to equip, provide for, put in order, READ[1]]

cur·ry·comb (kûr′ē kōm′, kur′-), *n.* **1.** a comb, usually with rows of metal teeth, for currying horses. —*v.t.* **2.** to rub or clean with such a comb.

cur′ry pow′der, a powdered mixture of turmeric, coriander, and other spices.

curse (kûrs), *n., v.,* **cursed** or **curst, curs·ing.** —*n.* **1.** the expression of a wish that misfortune, evil, etc., befall another. **2.** a formula or charm intended to cause such misfortune to another. **3.** an ecclesiastical censure or anathema. **4.** a profane oath. **5.** an evil that has been invoked upon a person. **6.** something accursed. **7.** the cause of evil, misfortune, or trouble. —*v.t.* **8.** to wish or invoke calamity or destruction upon. **9.** to swear at. **10.** to blaspheme. **11.** to afflict with great evil. **12.** to excommunicate. —*v.i.* **13.** to utter curses; swear profanely. [ME *curs* (n.), *cursen* (v.), OE *curs* (n.), *cursian* (v.), of disputed orig.; cf. OIr *cūrsagim* I blame] —**Syn. 1, 3.** imprecation, execration, fulmination, malediction. **5.** misfortune, calamity, trouble. **5, 7.** bane, scourge, plague, affliction, torment. **8–10.** CURSE, BLASPHEME, SWEAR are often interchangeable in the sense of using profane language. However, CURSE is the general word for the heartfelt invoking or violent or angry calling down of evil on another: *They called down curses on their enemies.* To BLASPHEME is to speak contemptuously or with abuse of God or of sacred things: *to blaspheme openly.* To SWEAR is to use the name of God or of some holy person or thing as an exclamation to add force or show anger: *to swear in every sentence.* **11.** plague, scourge, afflict, doom. —**Ant. 1, 3.** blessing, benediction. **8.** bless.

curs·ed (kûr′sid, kûrst), *adj.* **1.** under a curse; damned. **2.** deserving a curse; hateful or abominable. **3.** *Chiefly Dial.* cantankerous; ill-tempered; cross. [ME] —**curs′ed·ly,** *adv.* —**curs′ed·ness,** *n.*

cur·sive (kûr′siv), *adj.* **1.** *Print.* in flowing strokes resembling handwriting. **2.** (of handwriting) in flowing strokes with the letters joined together. —*n.* **3.** *Print.* a style of typeface simulating handwriting. **4.** a cursive letter or character. [< ML *cursīv(us)* flowing (said of penmanship). See COURSE, -IVE] —**cur′sive·ly,** *adv.*

cur·sor (kûr′sər), *n. Computer Technol.* a movable, sometimes blinking, symbol used to indicate where data may be inserted on a computer screen. [< L: runner < *cursus* course, ptp. of *currere* to run]

cur·so·ri·al (kûr sôr′ē əl, -sōr′-), *adj. Zool.* **1.** adapted for running, as the feet and skeleton of dogs or horses. **2.** having limbs adapted for running, as certain birds or insects. [< LL *cursōri(us)* of running (see CURSORY) + -AL[1]]

cur·so·ry (kûr′sə rē), *adj.* performed rapidly without noticing details; hasty; superficial. [< LL *cursōri(us)* running. See COURSE, -ORY[1]] —**cur′so·ri·ly,** *adv.* —**cur′so·ri·ness,** *n.*

curst (kûrst), *v.* **1.** a pt. and pp. of **curse.** —*adj.* **2.** cursed.

curt (kûrt), *adj.* **1.** short; shortened. **2.** brief or terse. **3.** rudely brief; abrupt or brusque. [< L *curt(us)* shortened, short, cut short] —**curt′ly,** *adv.* —**curt′ness,** *n.* —**Syn. 1.** abbreviated. **2.** See **blunt. 3.** snappish, sharp, rude.

cur·tail[1] (kər tāl′), *v.t.* to cut short; cut off a part of; abridge; reduce. [late ME *curtayle* to restrict (said of inheritance); appar. CURT + TAIL[2]] —**cur·tail′er,** *n.* —**cur·tail′ment,** *n.* —**Syn.** lessen, dock. See **shorten.**

cur·tail[2] (kûr′tāl′), *n. Archit.* **1.** a horizontal, spiral termination to the lower end of a stair railing. **2.** Also called **cur′tail step′.** a starting step having a scroll termination to one or both ends of the tread. [? CUR + TAIL[1]]

cur·tain (kûr′tᵊn, -tin), *n.* **1.** a hanging piece of fabric used to shut out the light from a window, adorn a room, etc. **2.** *Theat.* **a.** drapery hanging immediately back of the proscenium arch and concealing the stage from the audience. **b.** the start or end of a performance, scene, act, or play: *an 8:30 curtain; first-act curtain.* **c.** an effect, line, or plot solution at the end of a performance or play. **3.** anything that shuts off, covers, or conceals: *a curtain of artillery fire.* **4.** *Fort.* the part of a wall or rampart connecting two bastions, towers, or the like. **5. curtains,** *Slang.* the end; death, esp. by violence. —*v.t.* **6.** to provide, shut off, conceal, or adorn with or as with a curtain. [ME *co(u)rtine* < OF < LL *cortīn(a)* < ?] —**Syn. 1.** drapery, portiere, valance.

cur′tain call′, the appearance of the performers at the conclusion of a theatrical or other performance in response to the applause of the audience.

cur′tain rais′er, 1. a short play acted before a main play. **2.** *Informal.* **a.** the first of two or more performances, contests, or the like, scheduled on the same program. **b.** the first event in a series.

cur′tain speech′, *Theat.* a brief speech by an actor, producer, author, or the like, immediately following a performance, usually delivered in front of the closed curtains on the stage.

cur′tain wall′, (in a framed building) an exterior wall having no structural function.

cur·tal (kûr′tᵊl), *adj.* **1.** *Archaic.* wearing a short frock: *a curtal friar.* **2.** *Obs.* brief; curtailed. [earlier *courtault* an animal with a docked tail < MF = *court* short (see CURT) + *-ault,* var. of *-ald* n. suffix < Gmc]

cur·tal·ax (kûr′tᵊl aks′), *n. Archaic.* cutlass. Also called **cur′tle ax′.** [var. (by folk etym.) of earlier *curtilace,* appar. < dial. It *cortelaz(o),* metathetic var. of It *coltellaccio* hunting knife = *coltell(o)* (< L *cultellus,* dim. of *culter* knife, COLTER) + *-accio* n. suffix. See CUTLASS]

cur·te·sy (kûr′ti sē), *n., pl.* **-sies.** *Law.* the life tenure formerly enjoyed by a husband in his wife's land inheritance after her death, provided they had issue able to inherit. [var. of COURTESY]

cur·ti·lage (kûr′tᵊlij), *n. Law.* the area of land occupied by a dwelling and its outbuildings. [ME *courtelage* < OF *cortillage* = *cortil* yard (dim. of *cort* COURT) + *-age* -AGE]

Cur·tis (kûr′tis), *n.* **1. Charles,** 1860–1936, vice president of the U.S. 1929–33. **2. Cyrus Her·mann Kotzsch·mar** (hûr′mən koch′mär), 1850–1933, U.S. publisher.

Cur·tiss (kûr′tis), *n.* **Glenn Hammond,** 1878–1930, U.S. inventor: pioneer in the field of aviation.

Cur·ti·us (ko͝or′tsē o͝os′), *n.* **Ernst** (ernst), 1814–96, German archaeologist and historian.

curt·sey (kûrt′sē), *n., pl.* **-seys,** *v.i.,* **-seyed, -sey·ing.** curtsy.

curt·sy (kûrt′sē), *n., pl.* **-sies,** *v.,* **-sied, -sy·ing.** —*n.* **1.** a bow by women in recognition or respect, consisting of bending the knees and lowering the body. —*v.i.* **2.** to make a curtsy. [var. of COURTESY]

cu·rule (kyo͝or′o͞ol), *adj.* **1.** privileged to sit in a curule chair. **2.** of the highest rank. [< L *curūl(is),* var. of *currūlis* = *currū-* (s. of *currus* triumphal car) + *-lis,* var. of *-alis* -AL[1]]

cu′rule chair′, (in ancient Rome) a seat similar to a campstool, used only by certain high officials.

cur·va·ceous (kûr vā′shəs), *adj. Informal.* (of a woman) having a well-shaped figure with pronounced, voluptuous curves. Also, **cur·va′cious.**

cur·va·ture (kûr′və chər), *n.* **1.** act of curving. **2.** curved condition, often abnormal: *curvature of the spine.* **3.** the degree of curving of a line or surface. **4.** *Math.* **a.** (at a point on a curve) the derivative of the inclination of the tangent with respect to arc length. **b.** the absolute value of this derivative. **5.** something curved. [< L *curvātūr(a)* = *curvāt(us)* bent, curved (ptp. of *curvāre*) + *-ūra* -URE]

curve (kûrv), *n., v.,* **curved, curv·ing,** *adj.* —*n.* **1.** a continuously bending line, without angles. **2.** a curving movement or path. **3.** any curved outline, form, thing, or part. **4.** a curved guide used by draftsmen. **5.** *Baseball.* **a.** Also called **curve′ ball′.** a pitched ball that veers from a normal straight path. **b.** the course of such a pitched ball. **6.** *Math.* a collection of points whose coordinates are continuous functions of a single independent variable. **7.** a graphic representation of the variations effected by changing conditions; graph. **8.** a misleading or deceptive trick. **9.** *Educ.* a grading system based on the scale of performance of a group, so that those performing better, regardless of their actual knowledge of the subject, receive high grades: *The new professor marks on the curve.* Cf. **absolute** (def. 10). —*v.t., v.i.* **10.** to bend in a curve; take or cause to take the course of a curve. —*adj.* **11.** curved. [< L *curv(us)* crooked, bent, curved] —**curv·ed·ly** (kûr′vid lē), *adv.* —**curv′ed·ness,** *n.*

cur·vet (*n.* kûr′vit; *v.* kər vet′, kûr′vit), *n., v.,* **-vet·ted** or **-vet·ed, -vet·ting** or **-vet·ing.** —*n.* **1.** *Dressage.* a leap of a horse from a rearing position, in which it springs up with the hind legs outstretched as the forelegs descend. —*v.i.* **2.** to leap in a curvet, as a horse. **3.** to leap and frisk. —*v.t.* **4.** to cause to make a curvet. [earlier *curvetto* < It *corvetta* leap (of a horse) = *corv(o), corv(a)* bent, arched (see CURVE) + *-etta* -ET]

cur·vi-, a combining form of **curve**: *curvilinear*. [< LL, comb. form of *curvus* curved]

cur·vi·lin·e·ar (kûr′və lin′ē ər), *adj.* **1.** consisting of or bounded by curved lines: *a curvilinear figure.* **2.** formed or characterized by curved lines. Also, **cur′vi·lin′e·al.** —**cur·vi·lin·e·ar·i·ty** (kûr′və lin′ē ar′i tē), *n.* —**cur′vi·lin′e·ar·ly,** *adv.*

curv·y (kûr′vē), *adj.*, **curv·i·er, curv·i·est. 1.** curved. **2.** *Informal.* curvaceous. Also, **curv′ey.**

Cur·zon (kûr′zən), *n.* **George Nathaniel, 1st Marquis Curzon of Ked·le·ston** (ked′əl stən), 1859–1925, British statesman: viceroy of India 1899–1905.

Cus·co (*Sp.* ko͞os′kô), *n.* Cuzco.

cu·sec (kyo͞o′sek), *n.* one cubic foot per second. [*cu(bic foot per) sec(ond)*]

Cush (kush), *n.* **1.** the eldest son of Ham. Gen. 10:6. **2.** an area mentioned in the Bible, sometimes identified with Upper Egypt.

cush·at (kush′ət, ko͝osh′-), *n. Brit. Dial.* the ringdove, *Colomba palumbus.* [ME *couschot*, OE *cūscote* wood pigeon]

cu·shaw (kə shô′), *n.* any of several squashes having long, curved necks, esp. varieties of *Cucurbita moschata.* [? < Algonquian]

Cush·ing (ko͝osh′ing), *n.* **1. Caleb,** 1800–79, U.S. statesman and diplomat. **2. Harvey (Williams),** 1869–1939, U.S. surgeon and author. **3. Richard James,** 1895–1970, U.S. Roman Catholic clergyman: cardinal 1958–70; archbishop of Boston 1944–70.

cush·ion (ko͝osh′ən), *n.* **1.** a soft pad or a bag of cloth, leather, or rubber, filled with feathers, air, etc., on which to sit, kneel, or lie. **2.** anything used for absorbing shocks, jolts, etc., or preventing excessive pressure or chafing. **3.** a pillow used in lacemaking. **4.** the elastic raised rim encircling the top of a billiard table. —*v.t.* **5.** to place on or support by a cushion. **6.** to furnish with a cushion or cushions. **7.** to check the motion of (a piston or the like) by a cushion, as of steam. **8.** to form (steam or the like) into a cushion. **9.** to suppress, lessen, or soften the effects of: *to cushion the blow to his pride.* [ME *cuisshin* < MF *coussin* << L *cox(a)* hip + *-īnus* -INE[1]]

Cush·it·ic (kə shit′ik), *n.* **1.** a subfamily of the Afro-Asiatic family of languages, including Somali, Galla, and other languages of Somalia and Ethiopia. —*adj.* **2.** of or pertaining to Cushitic. [*Cushite* (see CUSH, -ITE[1]) + -IC]

Cush·man (ko͝osh′mən), *n.* **Charlotte (Saun·ders)** (sôn′dərz, son′-), 1816–76, U.S. actress.

cush·y (ko͝osh′ē), *adj.*, **cush·i·er, cush·i·est.** *Slang.* easy; pleasant: *a cushy job.* [CUSH(ION) + -Y[1]]

cusk (kusk), *n., pl.* **cusks,** (*esp. collectively*) **cusk. 1.** an edible marine fish, *Brosmius brosme*, of the North Atlantic. **2.** the burbot. [prob. var. of *tusk* kind of fish < Scand; cf. Norw *tosk*, var. of *torsk*, c. Icel *thorskr* codfish]

cusp (kusp), *n.* **1.** a point; pointed end. **2.** *Anat., Zool., Bot.* a point, projection, or elevation, as on the crown of a tooth. **3.** *Geom.* a point where two branches of a curve meet, end, and are tangent. **4.** *Archit.* a decorative device, used esp. in Gothic architecture, consisting of a pair of curves tangent to the line defining the area decorated and meeting at a point within it. **5.** *Astron.* a point of a crescent, esp. of the moon. **6.** *Astrol.* the first part of a house, esp. in nativity calculations. [< L *cusp(is)* a point]

cusped (kuspt), *adj.* having a cusp or cusps. Also, **cus·pate** (kus′pit, -pāt), **cus′pat·ed.**

cus·pid (kus′pid), *n.* (in man) a tooth with a single projection point or elevation; canine. [< L *cuspid-* (s. of *cuspis*) point]

cus·pi·date (kus′pi dāt′), *adj.* **1.** having a cusp or cusps. **2.** furnished with or ending in a sharp point or cusp: *cuspidate leaves; a cuspidate tooth.* Also, **cus′pi·dat′ed, cus′pi·dal.** [< NL *cuspidāt(us)*]

cus·pi·da·tion (kus′pi dā′shən), *n.* decoration with cusps, as in architecture.

cus·pi·dor (kus′pi dôr′), *n.* a bowl-shaped receptacle for spit, tobacco ash, etc. [< Pg: lit., spitter = *cuspid-* (ptp. s. of *cuspir* to spit < L *conspuere* to cover with spit) + *-or* -OR[2]]

cuss (kus), *U.S. Informal.* —*n.* **1.** curse word; oath. **2.** a person or animal: *a strange but likable cuss.* —*v.t.* **3.** to swear at; curse. **4.** to criticize or reprimand in harsh terms (often fol. by *out*): *The coach cussed out the team for losing.* —*v.i.* **5.** to use profanity; curse; swear. [early var. of CURSE]

cuss·ed (kus′id), *adj. U.S. Informal.* cursed. —**cuss′ed·ly,** *adv.*

cuss·ed·ness (kus′id nis), *n. Informal.* intractable temperament; obstinacy.

cus·tard (kus′tərd), *n.* a dish made of eggs and milk folded together, sweetened, and baked, boiled, or frozen. [late ME, var. of *crustade* kind of pie. See CRUST, -ADE[1] and cf. OPr *cr(o)ustado*]

cus′tard ap′ple, 1. the fruit of any of various shrubs and trees native to tropical America, having a soft, edible pulp, esp. *Annona reticulata.* **2.** the shrub or tree itself. **3.** some related tree, as *Asimina triloba*, the North American papaw, or its fruit.

Cus·ter (kus′tər), *n.* **George Arm·strong** (ärm′strông, -strong), 1839–76, U.S. general and Indian fighter.

cus·to·di·an (ku stō′dē ən), *n.* a person who has custody; keeper; guardian. [< L *custōdi(a)* watchman (see CUSTODY) + -AN] —**cus·to′di·an·ship′,** *n.*

cus·to·dy (kus′tə dē), *n., pl.* **-dies. 1.** guardianship or care: *in the custody of her father.* **2.** the keeping or charge of officers of the law: *The car was held in the custody of the police.* **3.** imprisonment; legal restraint. [late ME *custodye* < L *custōdia* a watching, watchman = *custōd-* (s. of *custōs*) keeper + *-ia* -Y[3]] —**cus·to·di·al** (ku stō′dē əl), *adj.*
—**Syn. 1.** keeping, charge, watch. CUSTODY, KEEPING, POSSESSION imply a guardianship or care for something. CUSTODY denotes a strict keeping, as by a formally authorized and responsible guardian or keeper: *in the custody of the sheriff.* KEEPING denotes having in one's care or charge, as for guarding or preservation: *in a bank for safekeeping.* POSSESSION means holding, ownership, or mastery: *Leave it in possession of its owner.* **3.** confinement, detention.

cus·tom (kus′təm), *n.* **1.** a habitual practice; the usual way of acting in given circumstances. **2.** habits or usages collectively; convention. **3.** a practice so long established that it has the force of law. **4.** such practices collectively. **5.** *Sociol.* a group pattern of habitual activity usually transmitted from one generation to another. **6.** toll; duty. **7. customs, a.** (*construed as sing. or pl.*) duties imposed by law on imported or, less commonly, exported goods. **b.** (*construed as sing.*) the government department that collects these duties. **8.** habitual patronage of a particular shop, restaurant, etc. **9.** the customers or patrons of a business firm, collectively. —*adj.* **10.** made specially for individual customers: *custom shoes.* **11.** dealing in things so made, or doing work to order: *a custom tailor.* [ME *custume* < OF, var. of *costume* < LL **co(n)s(uē)tūmin-*, r. L *consuētūdin-* (s. of *consuētūdō*) = *consuēt(us)* accustomed, ptp. of *consuēscere* (*con-* CON- + *suē-* (akin to *suus* one's own) + *-tus* ptp. suffix) + *-ūdin-* n. suffix]
—**Syn. 1, 2.** CUSTOM, HABIT, PRACTICE mean an established way of doing things. CUSTOM, applied to a community or to an individual, implies a more or less permanent continuance of a social usage: *It is the custom to give gifts at Christmas time.* HABIT, applied particularly to an individual, implies such repetition of the same action as to develop a natural, spontaneous, or rooted tendency or inclination to perform it: *to make a habit of reading the newspapers.* PRACTICE applies to a set of fixed habits or an ordered procedure in conducting activities: *It is his practice to verify all statements; secret practice of a cult.*

cus·tom·ar·y (kus′tə mer′ē), *adj., n., pl.* **-ar·ies.** —*adj.* **1.** according to or depending on custom; usual; habitual. **2.** of or established by custom rather than law. **3.** *Law.* defined by long continued practices. —*n.* **4.** a document containing the legal customs or customary laws of a locality. [< ML *custumāri(us)* = *costum(i)a* custom (also in VL; see CUSTOM) + *-ārius* -ARY] —**cus·tom·ar·i·ly** (kus′tə mer′ə lē; *for emphasis,* kus′tə mâr′ə lē), *adv.* —**Syn. 1.** accustomed, conventional, common, regular. See **usual.** —**Ant. 1.** uncommon.

cus·tom-built (kus′təm bilt′), *adj.* built to individual order: *a custom-built limousine.*

cus·tom·er (kus′tə mər), *n.* **1.** a patron, buyer, or shopper. **2.** *Informal.* a person one has to deal with: *a tough customer; a cool customer.* [late ME (see CUSTOM, -ER[1]); cf. ME *customer* collector of customs < AF; OF *costumier*, c. ML *custumārius;* see CUSTOMARY]

cus′tom house′, a government office, often at a seaport, for collecting customs, clearing vessels, etc. Also, **cus′toms house′.**

cus·tom·house (kus′təm hous′), *n., pl.* **-hous·es** (-hou′ziz). See **custom house.** Also, **cus·toms·house** (kus′təmz-hous′).

cus·tom-made (kus′təm mād′), *adj.* made to individual order: *custom-made shoes.*

cus′toms bro′ker, a person or firm whose business is to clear goods or merchandise through customs for a consignee or shipper. Also called **cus′tomhouse bro′ker.**

cus′toms un′ion, a union of nations for regulating customs and tariffs.

cus·tu·mal (kus′cho͞o məl), *n.* a customary. [< ML *custumāl(is)*, a Latinization of OF *costumel* customary, usual. See CUSTOM, -AL[1]]

cut (kut), *v.*, **cut, cut·ting,** *adj., n.* —*v.t.* **1.** to penetrate with or as with a sharp-edged instrument. **2.** to strike sharply, as with a whip. **3.** to wound the feelings of severely. **4.** to divide with or as with a sharp-edged instrument: *to cut bread into slices.* **5.** to hew or saw down; fell: *to cut timber.* **6.** to detach with or as with a sharp-edged instrument: *to cut a slice from a loaf of bread.* **7.** to reap; mow; harvest: *to cut grain or hay.* **8.** to trim by clipping, shearing, paring, or pruning: *to cut one's nails.* **9.** to intersect; cross: *One line cuts another at right angles.* **10.** to abridge or shorten; edit by omitting a part or parts: *to cut a speech.* **11.** *Radio and Television.* to stop the recording or transmitting of. **12.** to lower, reduce, diminish, or curtail (sometimes fol. by *down*): *to cut prices; to cut down the TV sound.* **13.** to dissolve, dilute, or make less thick: *to cut wine.* **14.** to make or fashion by cutting, as a statue, jewel, garment, etc. **15.** to hollow out; excavate: *to cut a trench.* **16.** to grow (a tooth or teeth) through the gum: *The baby is cutting his teeth.* **17.** *Informal.* to cease; discontinue (often fol. by *out*): *Cut the kidding. Let's cut out the pretense.* **18.** (in motion pictures, television, etc.) **a.** to suspend or terminate (a program, motion picture, or scene) by stopping the action of the cameras or players. **b.** to edit (a film) by deleting unwanted footage. **19.** to refuse to recognize socially. **20.** to absent oneself from: *allowed to cut a class three times.* **21.** *Cards.* **a.** to mix (a pack of cards) by dividing it into two or more parts and combining them into a new order. **b.** to take (a card) from a deck. **22.** *Sports.* to hit (a ball) so as to deflect it or cause it to spin. **23.** to record a selection on (a phonograph record or tape). **24.** to make a recording of. **25.** to switch off or reduce the speed of (an engine or motor).
—*v.i.* **26.** to penetrate or divide something, as with a sharp-edged instrument. **27.** to admit of being cut: *Butter cuts easily.* **28.** to traverse or cross, esp. in the most direct way (usually fol. by *across, through, in,* etc.): *to cut across an empty lot.* **29.** to shift suddenly from one scene, episode, etc., to another, as in film making or a novel. **30.** to make a sudden or sharp change in direction; swerve. **31.** to strike a person, animal, etc., sharply, as with a whip. **32.** to wound the feelings severely: *His criticism cut deep.* **33.** (of the teeth) to grow through the gums. **34.** *Cards.* to cut the cards. **35. cut across,** to precede or go beyond considerations of; transcend: *The new tax program cuts across party lines.* **36. cut and run, a.** *Naut.* to cut the anchor cable and set sail, as in an emergency. **b.** to leave hurriedly; flee: *After breaking the window, they cut and ran.* **37. cut back, a.** to shorten by cutting off the end. **b.** to curtail or discontinue: *Steel production has been cut back in recent months.* **38. cut down, a.** Also, **cut down on.** to lessen; decrease: *She cut down her between-meal snacks.* **b.** to remodel, remake, or reduce in size, as a garment: *She cut down her old coat to*

fit her daughter. **39. cut in, a.** to move or thrust oneself, a vehicle, etc., abruptly between or in: *A speeding car cut in and nearly caused an accident.* **b.** to interpose; interrupt: *to cut in with a remark.* **c.** *Informal.* (of a man) to stop a dancing couple in order to take the woman for one's own partner. **40. cut it out,** *Slang.* to stop doing something. **41. cut off, a.** to intercept. **b.** to interrupt. **c.** to bring to a sudden end; stop or shut off. **d.** to disinherit or leave an unexpectedly small sum to someone. **e.** to sever; separate: *After graduation, she was cut off from her college friends.* **42. cut out, a.** to omit; delete. **b.** to part an animal from a herd. **c.** to move out of one's lane of traffic. **d.** *Slang.* to leave suddenly. **e.** *Informal.* to refrain from; stop: *to cut out smoking.* **43. cut up, a.** to cut into pieces or sections. **b.** *Informal.* to play pranks; misbehave: *They got a scolding for cutting up in church.*
—*adj.* **44.** that has been subjected to cutting; divided into pieces or detached by cutting: *cut flowers.* **45.** *Bot.* incised; cleft. **46.** fashioned by cutting; having the surface shaped or ornamented by grinding, polishing, or the like: *cut diamonds.* **47.** reduced by or as by cutting: *cut whiskey; cut prices.* **48** castrated; gelded. **49. cut and dried, a.** fixed or settled in advance. **b.** lacking freshness, original thought, or spontaneity. **50. cut out for,** *Informal.* fitted for; capable of: *He wasn't cut out for military service.*
—*n.* **51.** the act of cutting; a stroke or a blow, as with a knife, whip, etc. **52.** a piece cut off: *a cut of a pie.* **53.** *Butchering.* part of an animal usually cut as one piece. **54.** *Informal.* share: *His agent's cut is 10%.* **55.** a quantity cut, esp. of lumber. **56.** the result of cutting, as an incision, wound, passage, channel, etc. **57.** the manner or fashion in which anything is cut: *the cut of a dress.* **58.** style; manner; kind: *We need a man of his cut in this firm.* **59.** a passage or course straight across or through: *a cut through the woods.* **60.** an excision or omission of a part. **61.** a part or quantity of text deleted or omitted. **62.** a reduction in price, salary, etc. **63.** an act, speech, etc., that wounds the feelings. **64.** an engraved plate or block used for printing. **65.** a printed picture or illustration. **66.** a refusal to recognize an acquaintance. **67.** an absence, as from a school class. **68.** *Sports.* **a.** the act of cutting a ball. **b.** the spin imparted. **69.** *Cards.* a cutting of the cards. **70.** *Motion Pictures, Television.* a sudden shift from one shot to another. **71. a cut above,** *Informal.* somewhat superior to another (thing, person, etc.) in some respect: *Her pies are a cut above any others I've tasted.* [ME *cutten, kytten, kitten,* OE **cyttan;* akin to OSw *kotta* to cut, Icel *kuti* little knife]
—**Syn. 1.** gash, slash, slit, lance. **3.** hurt, slight, insult. **5.** cleave, sunder, bisect. CUT, CHOP, HEW, HACK refer to giving a sharp blow or stroke. CUT is a general word for this: *to cut the grass.* To CHOP is to cut by giving repeated blows with something sharp, as an ax. To CHOP and to HEW are practically interchangeable, but CHOP may refer to a more or less undirected action, whereas HEW, more formal, suggests keeping to a definite purpose: *to chop or hew down a tree; to hew a line.* To HACK is to cut or chop roughly and unevenly: *to hack off a limb.* **10.** abbreviate, curtail. **13.** thin. **56.** gash, slash, slit.

cu·ta·ne·ous (kyo͞o tā′nē əs), *adj.* of, pertaining to, or affecting the skin. [< ML *cutāne(us)* = L *cut(is)* the skin + *-āneus* (*-ān(us)* -AN + *-eus* -EOUS). See HIDE[2]] —**cu·ta′ne·ous·ly,** *adv.*

cut·a·way (kut′ə wā′), *adj.* **1.** (of a coat) tapering from the front waist downward toward tails at the back. **2.** having a part cut away, as an outer section of something illustrated so that the inside may be shown. —*n.* **3.** a cutaway coat, as that worn by a man for formal daytime dress.

Cutaway coat

cut·back (kut′bak′), *n.* **1.** a return in the course of a story, motion picture, etc., to earlier events. **2.** reduction in rate, quantity, etc.: *a cutback in production.* **3.** *Football.* a play in which the ball-carrier abruptly reverses direction.

cutch (kuch), *n.* catechu.

Cutch (kuch), *n.* **1.** a former state in W India, now part of Gujarat state. 8461 sq. mi. **2. Rann of** (ren), a salt marsh NE of this area. 9000 sq. mi. Also, **Kutch.**

cut·cher·ry (kə cher′ē, kuch′ə rē), *n., pl.* **-ries. 1.** (in India) a public administrative or judicial office. **2.** any administrative office. [< Hindi *kacerī,* var. of *kacahrī* audience house, courthouse, office]

cut·cher·y (kə cher′ē, kuch′ə rē), *n., pl.* **-ries.** cutcherry.

cut·down (kut′doun′), *n.* reduction; decrease; diminution.

cute (kyo͞ot), *adj.,* **cut·er, cut·est. 1.** *Chiefly U.S. Informal.* pleasingly pretty or dainty: *a cute hat.* **2.** affectedly or mincingly pretty or clever; precious: *intolerably cute mannerisms.* **3.** *Informal.* mentally keen; clever; shrewd. [aph. var. of ACUTE] —**cute′ly,** *adv.* —**cute′ness,** *n.*

cut·ey (kyo͞o′tē), *n., pl.* **-eys.** cutie.

cut′ glass′, glass ornamented or shaped by cutting or grinding with abrasive wheels. —**cut′-glass′,** *adj.*

cut-grass (kut′gras′, -gräs′), *n.* any of several grasses having blades with rough edges, esp. grasses of the genus *Leersia* (*Homalocenchrus*).

Cuth·bert (kuth′bərt), *n.* **Saint,** A.D. c635–687, English monk and bishop.

cu·ti·cle (kyo͞o′ti kəl), *n.* **1.** the epidermis. **2.** a superficial integument, membrane, or the like. **3.** the nonliving epidermis that surrounds the edges of the fingernail or toenail. **4.** *Bot.* a very thin hyaline film covering the surface of plants, derived from the outer surfaces of the epidermal cells. [< L *cuticul(a)* the skin. See CUTIS, -CLE] —**cu·tic·u·lar** (kyo͞o tik′yə lər), *adj.*

cu·tic·u·la (kyo͞o tik′yə lə), *n., pl.* **-lae** (-lē′). *Zool.* the outer, noncellular layer of the arthropod integument, composed of a mixture of chitin and protein, but commonly containing other hardening substances. [< NL, L; see CUTICLE]

cut·ie (kyo͞o′tē), *n.* **1.** *Informal.* a charmingly pretty or cute girl (often used as a form of address). **2.** *Slang.* **a.** a person who tries to outsmart an opponent, as an athlete who outmaneuvers an opposing player. **b.** a clever or cunning maneuver: *He pulled a cutie.* Also, **cutey.**

cut′ie pie′, *Informal.* sweetheart; sweetie (often used as a term of endearment).

cu·tin (kyo͞o′tin), *n.* a transparent, waxy substance constituting, together with cellulose, the cuticle of plants. [< L *cut(is)* skin + -IN[2]]

cu·tin·ise (kyo͞ot′ᵊnīz′), *v.t., v.i.,* **-ised, -is·ing.** *Chiefly Brit.* cutinize. —**cu′tin·i·sa′tion,** *n.*

cu·tin·ize (kyo͞ot′ᵊnīz′), *v.t., v.i.,* **-ized, -iz·ing.** to make into or become cutin. —**cu′tin·i·za′tion,** *n.*

cu·tis (kyo͞o′tis), *n., pl.* **-tes** (-tēz), **-tis·es.** the corium or true skin. [< L: skin; akin to Gk *skŷtos* HIDE[2]]

cut·lass (kut′ləs), *n.* a short, heavy, slightly curved sword. Also, **cut′las.** [earlier *coutelace* < MF *coutelas* = *coutel* knife (now *couteau*) (< L *cultell(us),* dim. of *culter* COLTER) + *-as* aug. suffix; c. It *coltellaccio* big knife]

cut·ler (kut′lər), *n.* a person who makes, sells, or repairs knives and other cutting instruments. [ME *cuteler* < AF, c. MF *coutelier* < LL *cultellār(ius)* = L *cultell(us)* (dim. of *culter* COLTER) + *-ārius* -ER[2]]

cut·ler·y (kut′lə rē), *n.* **1.** the trade or business of a cutler. **2.** cutting instruments collectively, esp. those for use in serving or eating food. [ME *cutellerie* < MF *coutelerie*]

cut·let (kut′lit), *n.* **1.** a slice of meat, esp. of veal or mutton, for broiling or frying. **2.** a flat croquette of minced chicken, lobster, or the like. [< F *côtelette,* OF *costelette* double dim. of *coste* rib < L *costa;* see -LET]

cut′ nail′, a nail having a tapering, rectangular form with a blunt point, made by cutting from a thin sheet of iron or steel. See illus. at **nail.**

cut·off (kut′ôf′, -of′), *n.* **1.** an act or instance of cutting off. **2.** something that is cut off. **3.** the point, time, or stage for a cutting off. **4.** a road, passage, etc., that leaves another, usually providing a shortcut: *There is the cutoff to Baltimore.* **5.** a new and shorter channel formed in a river by the water cutting across a bend in its course. **6.** *Mach.* arrest of the steam moving the pistons of an engine.

cut·out (kut′out′), *n.* **1.** that which is cut out from something else. **2.** something that cuts out. **3.** an act or instance of cutting out.

cut·o·ver (kut′ō′vər), *adj.* (esp. of timberland) cleared of trees.

cut·purse (kut′pûrs′), *n.* **1.** a pickpocket. **2.** (formerly) a person who steals by cutting purses from the belt. [ME *cutte-purs*]

cut′ rate′, *U.S.* a price, fare, or rate below the standard charge. —**cut′-rate′,** *adj.*

Cut·tack (kut′ək), *n.* a city in E Orissa, in NE India. 165,288 (est. 1965).

cut·ter (kut′ər), *n.* **1.** a person or thing that cuts. **2.** a single-masted sailing vessel, very similar to a sloop but having its mast set somewhat farther astern. **3.** a ship's boat having double-banked oars and one or two lugsails. **4.** Also called **revenue cutter.** a lightly armed vessel, used by a government to prevent smuggling and enforce customs regulations. **5.** a small, light sleigh. [ME *kittere, cuttere*]

cut′ter bar′, 1. (in a mower, binder, or combine) a bar with triangular guards along which the knife or blade runs. **2.** a bar holding the cutting tool in a boring machine or lathe.

cut·throat (kut′thrōt′), *n.* **1.** a person who cuts throats; murderer. —*adj.* **2.** murderous. **3.** ruthless: *cutthroat competition.* **4.** (of a card game) played by three persons, each scoring as an individual.

cut′ time′, *Music.* See **alla breve.**

cut·ting (kut′ing), *n.* **1.** the act of a person or thing that cuts. **2.** something cut, cut out, or cut off. **3.** *Hort.* a piece, as a root, stem, or leaf, cut from a plant and used for propagation. **4.** *Chiefly Brit.* a clipping from a newspaper, magazine, etc. —*adj.* **5.** penetrating or dividing by, or as by, a cut. **6.** piercing, as a wind. **7.** wounding the feelings severely; sarcastic. [ME] —**cut′ting·ly,** *adv.* —**Syn. 7.** caustic, biting.

cut·tle[1] (kut′ᵊl), *n.* **1.** cuttlefish. **2.** cuttlebone. [apocopated form]

cut·tle[2] (kut′ᵊl), *v.t.,* **-tled, -tling.** *Textiles.* **1.** to fold (cloth) face to face after finishing. **2.** to allow (cloth) to lie without further treatment after fulling, milling, scouring, etc. [?]

cut·tle·bone (kut′ᵊl bōn′), *n.* the calcareous internal shell or plate of true cuttlefishes, used to make powder for polishing and fed to pet birds to supply their diet with lime. [CUTTLE(FISH) + BONE[1]]

cut·tle·fish (kut′ᵊl fish′), *n., pl.* (*esp. collectively*) **-fish,** (*esp. referring to two or more kinds or species*) **-fish·es.** any of several decapod, dibranchiate cephalopods, esp. of the genus *Sepia,* having arms with suckers and ejecting an inklike fluid when in danger. [late ME *codel,* OE *cudele* cuttlefish (akin to COD[1]) + FISH]

Cuttlefish,
Sepia officinialis
(Length 5 in.)

cut′ty stool′ (kut′ē), *Scot.* **1.** a low stool. **2.** a seat in old churches, where offenders against chastity or other delinquents sat and received public rebuke. [Scot *cutty* cut short, stubby = CUT (n.) + -Y[2]]

cut·up (kut′up′), *n.* *Informal.* a show-off or prankster.

cut·wa·ter (kut′wô′tər, -wot′ər), *n.* **1.** *Naut.* the forward edge of the stem of a vessel. **2.** a sharply pointed upstream face of a bridge pier, for resisting the effects of moving water or ice.

cut·work (kut′wûrk′), *n.* **1.** openwork embroidery in which the ground fabric is cut out about the pattern. **2.** fretwork formed by perforation or cut in low relief. **3.** ornamental needlework in which spaces cut from a ground material are filled with decorative figures. **4.** See **point coupé** (def. 1).

cut′work lace′. See **point coupé** (def. 2).

cut·worm (kut′wûrm′), *n.* the caterpillar of any of several noctuid moths that feeds at night on the stems of young herbaceous plants.

cu·vette (ko͞o vet′, kyo͞o-), *n.* *Chem.* a small tube or vessel used in laboratory experiments. [< F, dim. of *cuve* vat << L *cūpa.* See CUP, -ETTE]

Cu·vi·er (kyo͞o′vē ā′, ko͞ov yā′; *Fr.* kʏ vyā′), *n.* **Georges Lé·o·pold Chré·tien Fré·dé·ric Da·go·bert** (zhôʀzh lā ô pôld′ kʀā tyaɴ′ fʀā dā ʀēk′ dᴀ gō beʀ′), **Baron,** 1769–1832, French naturalist.

Cux·ha·ven (ko͝oks′hä′fən), *n.* a seaport in N West Germany, at the mouth of the Elbe River. 44,900 (1963).

Cu·ya·bá (ko͞o′yä bä′), *n.* Cuiabá.

Cuy′a·hog′a Falls′ (kī′ə hog′ə; *older* kī′ə hō′gə), a city in NE Ohio, near Akron. 49,678 (1970).

Cuyp (koip), *n.* **Ael·bert** (äl′bəʀt), 1620–91, Dutch painter. Also, **Kuyp.**

Cuz·co (ko͞os′kō; *Sp.* ko͞os′kô), *n.* a city in S Peru: ancient Inca ruins. 78,289 (1961). Also, **Cusco.**

CW, *Radio.* continuous wave.

cwm (ko͞om), *n.* cirque (def. 1). [< Welsh: valley. See COMBE]

Cwm·bran (ko͝om bʀän′), *n.* a town in central Monmouthshire, in SE Wales. 30,043 (1961).

CWO, *Mil.* chief warrant officer.

c.w.o., cash with order.

cwt, hundredweight.

cy, *Computer Technol.* cycle; cycles.

-cy, 1. a suffix used to form abstract nouns from adjectives with stems in *-t, -te, -tic,* and esp. *-nt* (*democracy; accuracy; expediency; stagnancy; necromancy*), also forming nouns from other adjectives (*fallacy*) and from nouns (*lunacy*), and sometimes used to form action nouns (*vacancy; occupancy*). 2. a suffix of nouns denoting rank or office, sometimes attached to the stem of a word rather than to the word itself: *captaincy; colonelcy; magistracy.* [repr. F *-cie, -tie,* L *-cia, -tia,* Gk *-kia, -keia, -tia, -teia;* in most cases to be analyzed as consonant + -Y[3], the consonant making the whole or the last member of the preceding morpheme]

Cy., county.

cy., 1. capacity. 2. currency. 3. *Computer Technol.* cycle; cycles.

cy·an (sī′an, sī′ən), *n.* a hue between blue and green. [< Gk *kýan(os)* dark blue]

cyan-[1], var. of **cyano-**[1], usually before a vowel or *h: cyanamide.*

cyan-[2], var. of **cyano-**[2], before a vowel.

cyan-[3], var. of **cyano-**[3], before a vowel.

cy·an·a·mide (sī an′ə mid, -mīd′, sī′ə nam′īd, -id), *n.* *Chem.* 1. an unstable solid, HN=C=NH. 2. (not in technical use) See **calcium cyanamide.** Also, **cy·an·a·mid** (sī an′ə mid, sī′ə nam′id).

cy·a·nate (sī′ə nāt′), *n.* *Chem.* a salt or ester of cyanic acid.

cy·an·ic (sī an′ik), *adj.* blue: applied esp. to a series of colors in flowers, including the blues and colors tending toward blue.

cyan′ic ac′id, *Chem.* a poisonous acid, HOCN, isomeric with fulminic acid.

cy·a·nide (sī′ə nīd′, -nid), *n., v.,* **-nid·ed, -nid·ing.** —*n.* Also, **cy·a·nid** (sī′ə nid). *Chem.* 1. a salt of hydrocyanic acid, as potassium cyanide, KCN. 2. a nitrile, as methyl cyanide, CH_3CN. —*v.t.* 3. to treat with a cyanide, as an ore in order to extract gold.

cy′anide proc′ess, a process of extracting gold or silver from ore by dissolving the ore in an alkaline solution of sodium cyanide or potassium cyanide.

cy·a·nine (sī′ə nēn′, -nin), *n.* any of several groups of dyes that make silver halide photographic plates sensitive to a wider color range. Also, **cy·a·nin** (sī′ə nin).

cy·a·nite (sī′ə nīt′), *n.* a mineral, aluminum silicate, Al_2SiO_5, used as a refractory. Also, **kyanite.** —**cy·a·nit·ic** (sī′ə nit′ik), *adj.*

cy·a·no (sī′ə nō′), *adj.* *Chem.* containing the cyano group. [independent use of CYANO-[3]]

cyano-[1], a learned borrowing from Greek, indicating dark-blue coloring, used in the formation of compound words: *cyanotype.* Also, *esp. before a vowel,* **cyan-.** [< Gk *kýano(s)* dark blue (adj.), dark-blue substance (n.)]

cyano-[2], a combining form of **cyanide:** *cyanogen.* Also, *esp. before a vowel,* **cyan-.**

cyano-[3], *Chem.* a word element referring to the cyanogen group, CN. Also, *esp. before a vowel,* **cyan-.**

cy·a·no·co·bal·a·min (sī′ə nō kō bal′ə min), *n.* *Biochem.* See **vitamin B_{12}.** [CYANO-[3] + COBAL(T) + (VIT)AMIN]

cy·an·o·gen (sī an′ə jən), *n.* *Chem.* 1. a poisonous gas, $(CN)_2$, having an almondlike odor: used chiefly in organic synthesis. 2. See **cyano group.** [CYANO-[2] + -GEN; from the fact that CN makes part of the pigment Prussian blue]

cyan′ogen bro′mide, *Chem.* a poisonous solid, BrCN, used chiefly as a fumigant and a pesticide.

cy′ano group′, *Chem.* the univalent group, –C≡N; cyanogen. Also called **cy′ano rad′ical.**

cy·a·no·hy·drin (sī′ə nō hī′drin), *n.* *Chem.* any of a class of organic compounds that contains both the –CN and the –OH group, usually linked to the same carbon atom. [CYANO-[3] + HYDR-[2] + -IN[2]]

cy·a·no·sis (sī′ə nō′sis), *n.* *Pathol.* blueness or lividness of the skin, as from imperfectly oxygenated blood. [< NL < Gk *kyánōsis* dark-blue color] —**cy·a·not·ic** (sī′ə not′ik), *adj.*

cy′a·nu′ric ac′id (sī′ə no͝or′ik, -nyo͝or′-, sī′-), *Chem.* a water-soluble solid, $C_3H_3O_3N_3 \cdot 2H_2O$, used chiefly in organic synthesis.

Cyb·e·le (sib′ə lē′), *n.* a nature goddess of Phrygia and Asia Minor, identified by the Greeks with Rhea and by the Romans with Ops. Also, **Cy·be·be** (sī bē′bē).

cy·ber·net·ics (sī′bər net′iks), *n.* (*construed as sing.*) the study of human control functions and of mechanical and electric systems designed to replace them. [< Gk *kybernḗt(ēs)* helmsman, steersman (*kybern(ân)* (to) steer + *-ētēs* agent suffix) + -ICS] —**cy′ber·net′ic,** *adj.* —**cy′ber·net′i·cist, cy·ber·ne·ti·cian** (sī′bər ni tish′ən), *n.*

cy·cad (sī′kad), *n.* any gymnospermous plant of the order *Cycadales,* intermediate in appearance between ferns and the palms, many species having a thick, unbranched, columnar trunk bearing a crown of large, leathery, pinnate leaves. [< NL *Cycad-* (s. of *Cycas*) genus name < Gk *kýkas,* dial. var. of *kóïkas,* acc. pl. of *kóïx* kind of palm, but taken as a synonym (s. *kykad-*) in nom. sing.] —**cy′cad·like′,** *adj.*

cyc·a·da·ceous (sik′ə dā′shəs), *adj.* belonging or pertaining to the order *Cycadales.* [< NL *Cycad-* (see CYCAD) + -ACEOUS]

cycl-, var. of **cyclo-,** before a vowel: *cycloid.*

Cyc·la·des (sik′lə dēz′), *n.* a group of Greek islands in the S Aegean. 99,959 (1961); 1023 sq. mi.

Cy·clad·ic (si klad′ik, sī-), *adj.* 1. of or pertaining to the Cyclades. 2. of or pertaining to the Bronze Age culture of the Cyclades, c3000–c1100 B.C.

cy·cla·mate (sī′klə māt′, sik′lə māt′), *n.* any of a group of artificial sweetening agents, as calcium cyclamate or sodium cyclamate. [CYCL- + AM(IDE) + -ATE[2]]

cyc·la·men (sik′lə mən, -men′), *n.* any low, primulaceous herb of the genus *Cyclamen,* having tuberous rootstocks and white, purple, pink, or crimson flowers. [< ML < Gk *kykláminos* bulbous plant, akin to *kýklos* CYCLE]

cy·cle (sī′kəl), *n., v.,* **-cled, -cling.** —*n.* 1. a round of years or a recurring period of time, esp. one in which certain events or phenomena repeat themselves in the same order and at the same intervals. 2. any complete round or series of occurrences that repeats or is repeated: *the gasoline-engine cycle; a cycle of alternating current.* 3. any long period of years; age. 4. *Literature.* any group of poems, dramas, prose narratives, etc., about a central theme, figure, or the like: *the Arthurian cycle.* 5. a bicycle, tricycle, or the like. 6. *Computer Technol.* a. the smallest interval of time required to complete an action in a computer. b. a series of computer operations repeated as a unit. *Abbr.:* c, c., cy, cy. —*v.i.* 7. to ride or travel by bicycle, tricycle, or similar vehicle. 8. to move or revolve in cycles; pass through cycles. [ME *cicle* < LL *cycl(us)* < Gk *kýklos* cycle, circle, wheel, ring, disk, orb, etc.; see WHEEL]

cy·cle·car (sī′kəl kär′), *n.* a light automobile, open like a motorcycle. [(MOTOR)CYCLE + CAR]

cy·clic (sī′klik, sik′lik), *adj.* 1. of, pertaining to, or constituting a cycle or cycles. 2. revolving or recurring in cycles; characterized by recurrence in cycles. 3. *Chem.* of or pertaining to a compound whose structural formula contains a closed chain or ring of atoms. 4. *Bot.* a. arranged in whorls, as the parts of a flower. b. (of a flower) having the parts so arranged. [< L *cyclic(us)* < Gk *kyklikós* circular] —**cy·clic·i·ty** (sī klis′i tē), *n.*

cy·cli·cal (sī′kli kəl, sik′li-), *adj.* 1. cyclic. 2. of or denoting a business or stock whose earnings fluctuate widely according to variations in the economy: *a cyclical corporation; cyclical stocks.* —*n.* 3. Usually, **cyclicals.** stocks of cyclical companies. —**cy′cli·cal·ly,** *adv.* —**cy·cli·cal·i·ty** (sī′klə kal′i tē), *n.*

cy·cling (sī′kliŋ), *n.* 1. the act or sport of riding or traveling by bicycle, tricycle, or similar vehicle. 2. Also called **bicycle race, bicycle racing.** *Sports.* a race on lightweight bicycles with low handlebars.

cy·clist (sī′klist), *n.* a person who rides or travels by bicycle, tricycle, etc. Also, **cy′cler.** —**cy·clis′tic,** *adj.*

cyclo-, a learned borrowing from Greek meaning "cycle," used in the formation of compound words: *cyclohexane.* Also, *esp. before a vowel,* **cycl-.** [< Gk *kyklo-,* comb. form of *kýklos* circle, ring; c. Skt *cakra,* WHEEL]

cyclo., 1. cyclopedia. 2. cyclotron.

cy·clo·graph (sī′klə graf′, -gräf′, sik′lə-), *n.* arcograph.

cy·clo·hex·ane (sī′klə hek′sān, sik′lə-), *n.* *Chem.* a flammable liquid, C_6H_{12}, composed of a ring of six methylene groups, used chiefly as a solvent.

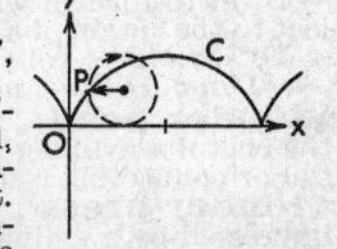

Cycloid (def. 6)
P, Point on rolling circle tracing out cycloid C

cy·cloid (sī′kloid), *adj.* 1. resembling a circle; circular. 2. (of the scale of a fish) smooth-edged, more or less circular in form, and having concentric striations. 3. (of a fish) having such scales. 4. *Psychiatry.* of or noting a personality type characterized by wide fluctuation in mood within the normal range. —*n.* 5. a cycloid fish. 6. *Geom.* a curve generated by a point on the circumference of a circle that rolls on a straight line. [< Gk *kykloeid(ḗs)* like a circle] —**cy·cloi′dal,** *adj.*

cy·clom·e·ter (sī klom′i tər), *n.* 1. an instrument that measures circular arcs. 2. a device for recording the revolutions of a wheel and hence the distance traversed by a wheeled vehicle; odometer.

cy·clone (sī′klōn), *n.* 1. a large-scale, atmospheric wind-and-pressure system characterized by low pressure at its center and by circular wind motion, counterclockwise in the Northern Hemisphere, clockwise in the Southern Hemisphere. Cf. **anticyclone.** 2. (not in technical use) tornado. [< Gk *kyklôn* revolving (prp. of *kyklóein* to revolve) = *kýkl(os)* a circle + *-ōn* prp. suffix] —**cy·clon·ic** (sī klon′ik), **cy·clon′i·cal, cy·clo′nal,** *adj.* —**cy·clon′i·cal·ly,** *adv.*

Cy·clo·pe·an (sī′klə pē′ən), *adj.* 1. of or characteristic of the Cyclops. 2. (*sometimes l.c.*) gigantic; vast. 3. (*usually l.c.*) *Archit., Building Trades.* formed with or containing large, undressed stones: *a cyclopean wall.* [< L *Cyclōpē(us)* (< Gk *Kyklṓpeios;* see CYCLOPS, -EOUS) + -AN]

cy·clo·pe·di·a (sī′klə pē′dē ə), *n.* an encyclopedia. Also, **cy′clo·pae′di·a.** [by aphesis] —**cy′clo·pe′dist, cy′clo·pae′dist,** *n.*

cy·clo·pe·dic (sī′klə pē′dik), *adj.* like an encyclopedia in character or contents; broad and varied; exhaustive. Also, **cy′clo·pae′dic.** [aph. var. of ENCYCLOPEDIC] —**cy′clo·pe′di·cal·ly, cy′clo·pae′di·cal·ly,** *adv.*

cy·clo·pen·tane (sī′klə pen′tān, sik′lə-), *n.* *Chem.* a water-insoluble liquid, C_5H_{10}, used chiefly as a solvent.

cy·clo·pro·pane (sī′klə prō′pān, sik′lə-), *n.* *Chem., Pharm.* a flammable gas, C_3H_6, used in organic synthesis and as an anesthetic.

Cy·clops (sī′klops), *n., pl.* **Cy·clo·pes** (sī klō′pēz). 1. *Class. Myth.* a member of a family of giants having a single round eye in the middle of the forehead. 2. (*l.c.*) a fresh-water copepod of the genus *Cyclops,* having a median eye in the front of the head. [< Gk *Kýklōps*, lit., round eye = *kýkl(os)* a circle, round + *ōps* EYE]

cy·clo·ram·a (sī′klə ram′ə, -rä′mə), *n.* *Theat.* a curved backdrop or rear wall of a stage, for creating an illusion of unlimited space or for obtaining uniform lighting effects. [CYCL- + Gk *(h)órama* view] —**cy′clo·ram′ic,** *adj.*

cy·clo·stom·a·tous (sī′klə stom′ə təs, -stō′mə-, sik′lə-), *adj.* **1.** having a circular mouth. **2.** belonging or pertaining to the cyclostomes. Also, **cy·clos·to·mate** (sī klos′tə-mit, -māt′).

cy·clo·stome (sī′klə stōm′, sik′lə-), *adj.* **1.** belonging or pertaining to the *Cyclostomata*, a subclass of eellike, aquatic, agnathous vertebrates comprising the lampreys and hagfishes. **2.** having a circular mouth. —*n.* **3.** a cyclostome vertebrate; a lamprey or hagfish.

cy·clo·style (sī′klə stīl′, sik′lə-), *n.* a manifolding device, consisting of a pen with a small toothed wheel at one end, that forms a stencil by cutting minute holes in a specially prepared paper stretched over a smooth surface. [formerly trademark] —**cy′clo·sty′lar,** *adj.*

cy·clo·thy·mi·a (sī′klə thī′mē ə, sik′lə-), *n.* *Psychiatry.* a mild, manic-depressive psychosis involving recurring cycles of exhilaration and depression. [CYCLO- + *-thymia* < Gk *thȳm(ós)* spirit + *-ia* -IA] —**cy′clo·thy′mic,** *adj.* —**cy′-clo·thy′mi·ac,** *n.*

cy·clo·tron (sī′klə tron′, sik′lə-), *n.* *Physics.* an accelerator in which particles move in a spiral path under the influence of an alternating voltage and a magnetic field.

Cy·co·lac (sī′kə lak′), *n.* *Trademark.* a lightweight, heavy-duty plastic used for automobile bodies and parts, housings for appliances, etc.

cy·der (sī′dər), *n.* *Brit.* cider.

Cyd·nus (sid′nəs), *n.* a river in SE Asia Minor, in Cilicia.

cyg·net (sig′nit), *n.* a young swan. [late ME *signet* < L *cygn(us)*, var. of *cycnus* (< Gk *kýknos* swan); see -ET]

Cyg·nus (sig′nəs), *n.*, *gen.* **-ni** (-nī). *Astron.* the Swan, a northern constellation southwest of Draco, containing the bright star Deneb. [< L: swan]

cyl., cylinder.

cyl·in·der (sil′in dər), *n.* **1.** *Geom.* a surface or solid bounded by two parallel planes and generated by a line tracing a closed curve perpendicular to the given planes; a surface congruent with and perpendicular to two closed curves. **2.** any cylinderlike object or part, whether solid or hollow. **3.** the rotating part of a revolver, containing the chambers for the cartridges. **4.** (in a pump) a cylindrical chamber in which a piston slides to move or compress a fluid. **5.** (in an engine) a cylindrical chamber in which the pressure of a gas or liquid moves a sliding piston. **6.** (in certain printing presses) **a.** a rotating cylinder that produces the impression and under which passes a flat form to be printed. **b.** either of two cylinders, one carrying a curved form or plate to be printed from, that rotate against each other in opposite directions. **7.** *Archaeol.* a cylindrical or somewhat barrel-shaped object of stone or clay bearing a cuneiform inscription or a carved design. —*v.t.* **8.** to furnish with a cylinder or cylinders. **9.** to subject to the action of a cylinder or cylinders. [< L *cylindr(us)* < Gk *kýlindros* roller, cylinder, akin to *kylíndein* to roll] —**cyl′in·der·like′,** *adj.*

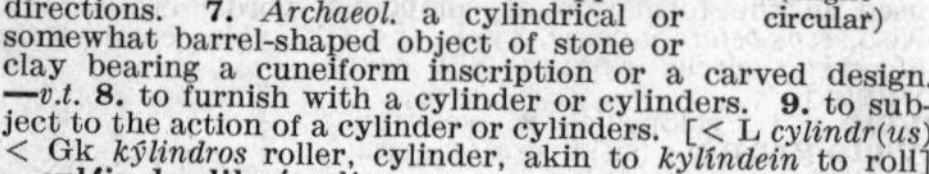

Cylinder (Right circular)

cyl′inder head′, (in a reciprocating engine or pump) the end of a cylinder opposite to that from which the piston rod or connecting rod projects.

cyl′inder press′, a printing press in which paper is impressed by a cylinder against type on a flat plane.

cy·lin·dri·cal (si lin′dri kəl), *adj.* of, pertaining to, or having the form of a cylinder. Also, **cy·lin′dric.** [< NL *cylindric(us)* (< Gk *kylindrikós*; see CYLINDER, -IC) + -AL[1]] —**cy·lin·dri·cal·i·ty** (si lin′dri kal′i tē), **cy·lin′dri·cal·ness,** *n.* —**cy·lin′dri·cal·ly,** *adv.*

cyl·in·droid (sil′in droid′), *n.* **1.** a solid having the form of a cylinder, esp. one with an elliptical, as opposed to a circular, cross section. —*adj.* **2.** resembling a cylinder. [< Gk *kylindroeid(ḗs)*]

cy·lix (sī′liks, sil′iks), *n.*, *pl.* **cyl·i·ces** (sil′ə sēz′). kylix.

Cyl·le·ne (si lē′nē), *n.* **1.** *Class. Myth.* a nymph who nursed Hermes. **2.** a mountain in S Greece. 7789 ft.

Cyl·le·ni·an (si lē′nē ən), *adj.* of or pertaining to Mount Cyllene in Arcadia, Greece, or to the god Hermes, reputed to have been born there.

Cym., Cymric.

cy·ma (sī′mə), *n.*, *pl.* **-mae** (-mē), **-mas.** **1.** *Archit.* either of two moldings having a partly convex and partly concave curve for an outline: used esp. in classical architecture. **2.** *Bot.* a cyme. [< NL < Gk *kŷma* something swollen, a wave, wavy molding, sprout = *ký(ein)* (to) be pregnant, swollen with child + *-ma* n. suffix]

cy′ma rec′ta (rek′tə), *Archit.* a cyma whose concave part projects beyond the convex part. See illus. at **molding.** [< NL: straight cyma]

cy′ma re·ver′sa (ri vûr′sə), *Archit.* a cyma whose convex part projects beyond the concave part. See illus. at **molding.** [< NL: reversed cyma]

cy·ma·ti·um (si mā′shē əm), *n.*, *pl.* **-ti·a** (-shē ə). *Archit.* the uppermost member of a classical cornice or of a cornice of similar form: usually a cyma recta in classical examples. [< L < Gk *kȳmátion* = *kȳmat-* (s. of *kŷma* wave; see CYMA) + *-ion* dim. suffix]

cym·bal (sim′bəl), *n.* a concave plate of brass or bronze that produces a sharp, ringing sound when struck: played either in pairs, by being struck together, or singly, by being struck with a drumstick or the like. [ME; OE *cymbala* < ML, var. of *cymbalum* < L < Gk *kýmbalon*, var. of *kýmbos*, *kýmbē* hollow object] —**cym′bal·er, cym′-bal·eer′, cym′bal·ist,** *n.* —**cym′bal·like′,** *adj.*

Cymbals

cyme (sīm), *n.* **1.** an inflorescence in which the primary axis bears a single terminal flower that develops first, the inflorescence being continued by secondary, tertiary, and other axes. **2.** a flat or convex inflorescence of this type. [< L *cȳma* cabbage sprout < Gk *kŷma*; see CYMA]

cy·mene (sī′mēn), *n.* *Chem.* a colorless, pleasant-smelling benzene derivative, $CH_3C_6H_4CH(CH_3)_2$, occurring in the volatile oil of the common cumin, *Cuminum cyminium*, and existing in three forms, the ortho, meta, and para isomers. Cf. **para-cymene.** [< Gk *kým(inon)* CUMIN + -ENE]

cymo-, a learned borrowing from Greek meaning "wave," used in the formation of compound words: *cymograph.* [< Gk *kymo-*, comb. form of *kŷma* wave]

cy·mo·gene (sī′mə jēn′), *n.* *Chem.* a mixture of very volatile, flammable hydrocarbons, constituting the fraction boiling at about 0°C, obtained in distilling crude petroleum and containing a large percentage of butane. [CYM(ENE) + -O- + -GENE]

cy·mo·graph (sī′mə graf′, -gräf′), *n.* kymograph. —**cy-mo·graph·ic** (sī′mə graf′ik), *adj.*

cy·moid (sī′moid), *adj.* **1.** resembling a cyma. **2.** resembling a cyme.

cy·mo·phane (sī′mə fān′), *n.* *Mineral.* chrysoberyl.

cy·mose (sī′mōs, sī mōs′), *adj.* *Bot.* **1.** bearing a cyme or cymes. **2.** of or of the nature of a cyme. [< L *cymōs(us)* full of shoots] —**cy′mose·ly,** *adv.*

Cym·ric (kim′rik, sim′-), *adj.* **1.** of or pertaining to the Cymry. —*n.* **2.** Welsh (def. 3). Also, **Kymric.**

Cym·ry (kim′rē), *n.* (*construed as pl.*) the Welsh, or the branch of the Celtic race to which the Welsh belong, comprising also the Cornish people and the Bretons. Also, **Kymry.** [< Welsh *Cymry* Welshmen, pl. of *Cymro*, prob. repr. OWelsh **combrox* compatriot = *com-* COM- + **brox* (Welsh *bro* district, region); akin to L *margo* margin]

Cyn·e·wulf (kin′ə wo͝olf′), *n.* fl. early 9th century A.D., Anglo-Saxon poet. Also, **Cynwulf, Kynewulf.**

cyn·ic (sin′ik), *n.* **1.** a person who believes that only selfishness motivates human actions and who disbelieves in or minimizes selfless acts or disinterested points of view. **2.** (*cap.*) one of a sect of Greek philosophers of the 4th century B.C., who advocated the doctrines that virtue is the only good, that the essence of virtue is self-control, and that surrender to any external influence is beneath the dignity of man. —*adj.* **3.** cynical. **4.** (*cap.*) Also, **Cynical.** of or pertaining to the Cynics or their doctrines. [< L *Cynic(us)* < Gk *Kynikós* Cynic, lit., doglike, currish = *kyn-* (s. of *kýōn*) dog + *-ikos* -IC]

cyn·i·cal (sin′i kəl), *adj.* **1.** like or characteristic of a cynic; distrusting or disparaging the motives of others. **2.** showing contempt for accepted standards of honesty or morality by one's actions, esp. by actions that exploit the scruples of others. **3.** (*cap.*) cynic (def. 4). —**cyn′i·cal·ly,** *adv.* —**cyn′-i·cal·ness,** *n.*

—**Syn. 1.** distrustful, disbelieving, sneering, contemptuous, derisive. CYNICAL, PESSIMISTIC, SARCASTIC, SATIRICAL imply holding a low opinion of mankind. CYNICAL suggests a disbelief in the sincerity of human motives: *cynical about honesty.* PESSIMISTIC implies a more or less habitual disposition to look on the dark side of things, and to believe that the worst will happen: *pessimistic about the future.* SARCASTIC refers to sneering or making cutting gibes: *sarcastic about a profession of faith.* SATIRICAL suggests expressing scorn or ridicule by saying the opposite of what one means: *satirical about the way in which actions differ.*

cyn·i·cism (sin′i siz′əm), *n.* **1.** cynical disposition, character, or belief. **2.** a cynical remark. **3.** (*cap.*) any of the doctrines or practices of the Cynics.

cy·no·sure (sī′nə sho͝or′, sin′ə-), *n.* **1.** something that strongly attracts attention by its brilliance, interest, etc.: *the cynosure of all eyes.* **2.** something serving for guidance or direction. **3.** (*cap.*) *Astron. Obs.* **a.** See **Ursa Minor.** **b.** Polaris. [< L *Cynosūra* < Gk *Kynósoura* the constellation Ursa Minor = *kynós* dog's (gen. of *kýōn*) + *ourá* tail] —**cy′no·sur′al,** *adj.*

Cyn·thi·a (sin′thē ə), *n.* **1.** Artemis: so called from her birth on Mount Cynthus, on Delos. **2.** *Literary.* the moon, the emblem of Artemis.

Cyn·wulf (kin′wo͝olf), *n.* Cynewulf.

cy·per·a·ceous (sī′pə rā′shəs, sip′ə-), *adj.* belonging or pertaining to the *Cyperaceae*, or sedge family of plants. [< NL *Cypēr(us)* the typical genus (L: kind of rush < Gk *kýpeiros* a marsh plant) + -ACEOUS]

cy·pher (sī′fər), *n.*, *v.i.*, *v.t.* *Chiefly Brit.* cipher.

cy pres (sē′ prā′), *Law.* **1.** as near as possible. **2.** the doctrine, applied esp. to cases of charitable trusts, that allows the nearest practicable condition to be substituted for an illegal or impossible one. Also, **cy′pres′.** [< AF: lit., as near (c. F *si près*)]

cy·press[1] (sī′prəs), *n.* **1.** any of several evergreen coniferous trees of the genus *Cupressus*, having dark-green, scalelike, overlapping leaves. **2.** any of various other coniferous trees allied to the true cypress, as the bald cypress. **3.** any of various unrelated plants resembling the true cypress. [ME, OE *cypresse* < LL *cypress(us)*, appar. b. L *cupressus* and *cyparissus* < Gk *kypárissos*; r. ME *cipres* < OF]

cy·press[2] (sī′prəs), *n.* *Obs.* a fine, thin fabric resembling lawn or crepe, formerly much used in black for mourning garments and trimmings. Also, **cyprus.** [ME *cipre(s)*, *cyprus*, after CYPRUS]

Cy·press (sī′prəs), *n.* a city in S California, near Long Beach. 31,569 (1970).

cy′press vine′, a convolvulaceous plant, *Quamoclit pennata*, having finely parted leaves and scarlet or white, tubular flowers.

Cyp·ri·an (sip′rē ən), *n.* **Saint** (*Thascius Caecillus Cyprianus*), A.D. c200–258, church father, bishop, and martyr.

Cyp·ri·an (sip′rē ən), *adj.* **1.** noting or pertaining to the worship of Aphrodite or to conduct inspired by Aphrodite. **2.** lewd; licentious. **3.** Cypriote. —*n.* **4.** Cypriote. **5.** a lewd person, esp. a prostitute. **6. the Cyprian,** Aphrodite: so called because her cult was centered on Cyprus. [< L *Cypri(us)* of Cyprus (< Gk *Kýprios* < *Kýpros* CYPRUS) + -AN]

cy·pri·nid (si prī′nid, sip′rə nid), *n.* **1.** any fish belonging to the *Cyprinidae*, or minnow family. —*adj.* **2.** carplike in form or structure. [back formation from NL *Cyprīnidae* = *Cyprīn(us)* genus name (< L < Gk *kyprînos* carp) + *-idae* -ID[2]]

cy·prin·o·dont (si prin′ə dont′, si prī′nə-), *n.* any soft-rayed fish of the order *Cyprinodontes,* found esp. in fresh and brackish waters of North America, including the killifishes, topminnows, and guppies. [< L *cyprīn(us)* (< Gk *kyprînos* carp) + -ODONT]

cyp·ri·noid (sip′rə noid′, si prī′noid), *adj.* **1.** resembling a carp; belonging to the *Cyprinoidea,* a group of fishes including the carps, suckers, and loaches. —*n.* **2.** a cyprinoid fish. [< L *cyprīn(us)* < Gk *kyprînos* carp + -OID]

Cyp·ri·ot (sip′rē ət), *n.* **1.** a native or inhabitant of Cyprus. **2.** the Greek dialect of Cyprus. —*adj.* **3.** of, pertaining to, or characteristic of Cyprus, its people, or their language. Also, **Cyp·ri·ote** (sip′rē ōt′, -ət). [< Gk *Kypriṓtē(s)*]

cyp·ri·pe·di·um (sip′rə pē′dē əm), *n.* any plant of the genus *Cypripedium,* comprising the lady's-slippers. [< NL = L *Cypri(a)* Venus + *-pedi-* -PED + *-um* neut. ending]

Cypro-, a combining form of **Cyprian.**

cy·prus (sī′prəs), *n. Obs.* cypress[2].

Cy·prus (sī′prəs), *n.* an island republic in the Mediterranean, S of Turkey: formerly a British colony; independent since 1960. 639,000; 3572 sq. mi. *Cap.:* Nicosia.

cyp·se·la (sip′sə lə), *n., pl.* **-lae** (-lē′). *Bot.* an achene with an adherent calyx, as in the composite plants. [< NL < Gk *kypsélē* hollow vessel, chest, box]

Cyr·a·no de Ber·ge·rac (sir′ə nō′ də bûr′jə rak′, -zhə rak′, bär′-; *Fr.* sē RA nō′ də beR zhe RAK′). See **Bergerac, Savinien Cyrano de.**

Cyr·e·na·ic (sir′ə nā′ik, sī′rə-), *adj.* **1.** of or pertaining to Cyrenaica or its chief city, Cyrene. **2.** noting or pertaining to a school of philosophy founded by Aristippus of Cyrene, who taught that pleasure is the only rational aim of life. —*n.* **3.** a native or inhabitant of Cyrenaica. **4.** a disciple of the Cyrenaic school of philosophy. [< L *Cȳrēnaic(us)* < Gk *Kȳrēnaïkós* = *Kȳrēna-* (comb. form of *Kȳrḗnē* CYRENE) + *-ikos* -IC]

Cyr·e·na·i·ca (sir′ə nā′ə kə, sī′rə-), *n.* an ancient district in N Africa now the E part of Libya. Also, **Cirenaica.** Also called **Barca.**

Cy·re·ne (sī rē′nē), *n.* an ancient Greek city and colony in N Africa, in Cyrenaica.

Cyr·il (sir′əl), *n.* **Saint** (*"Apostle of the Slavs"*), A.D. 827–869, Greek missionary to the Moravians.

Cy·ril·lic (si ril′ik), *adj.* **1.** noting or pertaining to a script derived from Greek uncials, used for writing Old Church Slavonic and adopted with minor modifications as the alphabet of Russian, Bulgarian, Serbian, etc. **2.** of or pertaining to St. Cyril. [< L *Cyrill(us)* (Saint) CYRIL (said to have been the inventor of this alphabet) + -IC]

Cy·rus (sī′rəs), *n.* **1.** (*"the Great"*) c600–529 B.C., king of Persia 558?–529: founder of the Persian empire. **2.** (*"the Younger"*) 424?–401 B.C., Persian prince and satrap: leader of the armed conspiracy against his brother King Artaxerxes II.

cyst (sist), *n.* **1.** *Pathol.* a closed, bladderlike sac formed in animal tissues, containing fluid or semifluid matter. **2.** a bladder, sac, or vesicle. **3.** *Bot.* **a.** a sporelike cell with a resistant, protective wall. **b.** a cell or cavity enclosing reproductive bodies. **4.** *Zool.* **a.** a sac, usually spherical, surrounding a minute organism that has passed into a dormant condition. **b.** such a sac plus the contained organism. **c.** a capsule or resistant covering. [< NL *cyst(is)* < Gk *kýstis* bag, pouch, the bladder]

cyst-, var. of **cysto-** before a vowel: *cystectomy.*

-cyst, var. of **cysto-** as final element in a compound word: *statocyst.*

cys·tec·to·my (si stek′tə mē), *n., pl.* **-mies.** *Surg.* excision of a cyst or bladder, as the urinary bladder.

cys·te·ine (sis′tē ēn′, -in), *n. Biochem.* a crystalline amino acid, $HSCH_2CH(NH_2)COOH$, a component of nearly all proteins. [alter. of CYSTINE] —**cys′te·in′ic,** *adj.*

cysti-, var. of **cysto-:** *cysticercus.*

cyst·ic (sis′tik), *adj.* **1.** pertaining to, of the nature of, or having a cyst or cysts; encysted. **2.** *Anat.* belonging or pertaining to the urinary bladder or gall bladder.

cys·ti·cer·coid (sis′ti sûr′koid), *n. Zool.* the larva of certain tapeworms, a bladderlike structure with a retracted head or scolex and often with a taillike appendage. [CYSTICERC(US) + -OID]

cys·ti·cer·cus (sis′ti sûr′kəs), *n., pl.* **-cer·ci** (-sûr′sī). *Zool.* the larva of certain tapeworms, a fluid-filled, bladderlike structure with an invaginated head or scolex. [< NL < (Gk *kýsti(s)* bladder + *kérkos* tail]

cys′tic fibro′sis, *Pathol.* a hereditary, chronic disease of the pancreas, lungs, etc., beginning in infancy, in which there is an inability to digest foods and difficulty in breathing.

cys·tine (sis′tēn, -tin), *n. Biochem.* a crystalline amino acid, $C_6H_{12}O_4N_2S_2$, occurring in most proteins, esp. the keratins in hair, wool, and horn. [CYST- + -INE[2]; so called because found in stone of the bladder]

cys·ti·tis (si stī′tis), *n. Pathol.* inflammation of the urinary bladder.

cysto-, a combining form of **cyst:** *cystoscope.* Also, **cyst-, -cyst, cysti-.**

cys·to·carp (sis′tə kärp′), *n.* the mass of carpospores formed as a result of fertilization in red algae, with or without a special envelope. —**cys′to·car′pic,** *adj.*

cyst·oid (sis′toid), *adj.* **1.** resembling a cyst. —*n.* **2.** a cystlike structure or formation.

cys·to·scope (sis′tə skōp′), *n. Med.* a slender, cylindrical instrument for examining the interior of the urinary bladder and for the introduction of medication therein.

cys·tos·co·py (si stos′kə pē), *n., pl.* **-pies.** *Med.* an examination by means of a cystoscope. —**cys·to·scop·ic** (sis′tə skop′ik), *adj.*

cys·tos·to·my (si stos′tə mē), *n., pl.* **-mies.** *Surg.* formation of a permanent or semipermanent opening in the urinary bladder.

cys·to·tome (sis′tə tōm′), *n. Surg.* an instrument for performing a cystotomy.

cys·tot·o·my (si stot′ə mē), *n., pl.* **-mies.** *Surg.* the operation of cutting into the urinary bladder.

cy·tas·ter (sī tas′tər, sī′tas-), *n. Biol.* aster.

-cyte, var. of **cyto-** as final element in a compound word: *leucocyte.*

Cyth·er·a (sith′ər ə, si thēr′ə), *n.* Cerigo.

Cyth·er·e·a (sith′ə rē′ə), *n.* Aphrodite: so called because of her birth in the sea near Cythera. —**Cyth′er·e′an,** *adj.*

cyto-, a learned borrowing from Greek used, with the meaning "cell," in the formation of compound words: *cytoplasm.* Also, **-cyte.** [< Gk *kyto-,* comb. form of *kýtos* container, receptacle, body]

cy·to·chem·is·try (sī′tə kem′i strē), *n.* the branch of cytology dealing with the chemistry of living cells. —**cy′to·chem′i·cal,** *adj.*

cy·to·chrome (sī′tə krōm′), *n. Biochem.* any of several enzymes found in plants and animals, composed of iron, a protein, and a porphyrin, that catalyze intracellular oxidations.

cy·to·gen·e·sis (sī′tə jen′i sis), *n.* the origin and development of cells.

cy·to·ge·net·ics (sī′tō jə net′iks), *n.* (*construed as sing.*) the branch of biology dealing with the study of heredity from the points of view of cytology and genetics. —**cy′to·ge·net′ic, cy′to·ge·net′i·cal,** *adj.* —**cy′to·ge·net′i·cal·ly,** *adv.* —**cy′to·ge·net′i·cist,** *n.*

cy·to·ki·ne·sis (sī′tō ki nē′sis, -kī-), *n.* the changes in the cytoplasm during mitosis, meiosis, and fertilization.

cy·tol·o·gy (sī tol′ə jē), *n.* **1.** the branch of biology dealing with the study of cells, esp. their formation, structure, and functions. **2.** cytological phenomena, processes, etc.: *the cytology of cancer.* —**cy·to·log·ic** (sīt′ᵊloj′ik), **cy′to·log′i·cal,** *adj.* —**cy′to·log′i·cal·ly,** *adv.* —**cy·tol′o·gist,** *n.*

cy·tol·y·sin (sī tol′i sin, sīt′ᵊlī′sin), *n. Biochem.* an antibody that partially or completely destroys animal cells.

cy·tol·y·sis (sī tol′i sis), *n. Physiol.* the dissolution or degeneration of cells. —**cy·to·lyt·ic** (sīt′ᵊlit′ik), *adj.*

cy·ton (sīt′ᵊn), *n.* the body of a nerve cell. [CYT- + *-on* (Gk neut. ending), modeled on *proton*]

cy·to·plasm (sī′tə plaz′əm), *n. Biol.* the protoplasm of a cell exclusive of the nucleus. —**cy′to·plas′mic,** *adj.*

cy·to·plast (sī′tə plast′), *n. Biol.* the intact, cytoplasmic content of a cell. —**cy′to·plas′tic,** *adj.*

cy·to·tech·nol·o·gy (sī′tə tek nol′ə jē), *n.* the study of human cells to detect signs of cancer. —**cy′to·tech·no·log′ic,** *adj.* —**cy′to·tech·nol′o·gist,** *n.*

Cyz·i·cus (siz′ə kəs), *n.* an ancient city in Mysia.

CZ, Canal Zone (approved esp. for use with zip code).

C.Z., Canal Zone.

czar (zär), *n.* **1.** an emperor or king. **2.** (*often cap.*) the former emperor of Russia. **3.** an autocratic ruler or leader. **4.** any person in a position of power, as a high public official. Also, **tsar, tzar.** [< Russ *tsar′,* ORuss *tsĭsarĭ* emperor, king (c. OSlav *tsĭsarĭ*) < Goth *kaisar* emperor (< Gk or L); Gk *kaîsar* < L *Caesar*] —**czar′dom,** *n.*

czar·das (chär′däsh), *n.* a Hungarian dance in two movements, one slow and the other fast. [< Hung *csárdás*]

czar·e·vitch (zär′ə vich), *n.* **1.** a son of a czar. **2.** the eldest son of a czar. Also, **tsarevitch, tzarevitch.** [< Russ *tsarevich* = *tsar′* CZAR + *-evich* patronymic suffix]

cza·rev·na (zä rev′nə), *n.* a daughter of a czar. Also, **tsarevna, tzarevna.** [< Russ *tsarevna* = *tsar′* CZAR + *-evna* fem. patronymic suffix]

cza·ri·na (zä rē′nə), *n.* the wife of a czar; Russian empress. Also, **tsarina, tzarina.** [CZAR + *-ina* fem. suffix (as in *Christina*), modeled on G *Zarin* empress = *Zar* Czar + *-in* fem. suffix]

czar·ism (zär′iz əm), *n.* dictatorship; autocratic government. Also, **tsarism, tzarism.**

czar·ist (zär′ist), *adj.* Also, **czar·is·tic** (zä ris′tik), **tsaristic, tzaristic. 1.** of, pertaining to, or characteristic of a czar or the system and principles of government under a czar. **2.** autocratic; dictatorial. —*n.* **3.** an adherent of a czar or of czarism. Also, **tsarist, tzarist.**

cza·rit·za (zä rit′sə), *n.* a czarina. Also, **tsaritza, tzaritza.** [< Russ *tsaritsa,* fem. of *tsar′*]

Czech (chek), *n.* **1.** a member of the most westerly branch of the Slavs, comprising the Bohemians, or Czechs proper, and, sometimes, the Moravians. **2.** the language of Bohemia and Moravia, a Slavic language similar to Slovak. **3.** (loosely) Czechoslovak. —*adj.* **4.** of or pertaining to Czechoslovakia, its people, or their language.

Czech., Czechoslovakia. Also, **Czechosl.**

Czech·o·slo·vak (chek′ə slō′vak, -väk), *n.* **1.** a member of the branch of the Slavic race comprising the Czechs proper, the Moravians, and the Slovaks. **2.** a native or inhabitant of Czechoslovakia. —*adj.* **3.** of or pertaining to Czechoslovakia, its people, or their language. Also, **Czech′o-Slo′vak.**

Czech·o·slo·va·ki·a (chek′ə slə vä′kē ə, -vak′ē ə), *n.* a republic in central Europe: formed after World War I; comprises the former countries of Bohemia, Moravia, Silesia, and Slovakia. 14,890,000; 49,379 sq. mi. *Cap.:* Prague. Also, **Czech′o-Slo·va′ki·a.** Official name, **Chech′o·slo′vak So′cialist Repub′lic.** —**Czech′o·slo·va′ki·an, Czech′o-Slo·va′ki·an,** *adj., n.*

Czer·no·witz (cheR′nô vits), *n.* German name of **Cernăuţi.**

Czer·ny (cher′nē), *n.* **Carl,** 1791–1857, Austrian composer, esp. of exercises in piano technique.

Czę·sto·cho·wa (cheN′stô KHô′vä), *n.* a city in S Poland. 170,000 (est. 1963).

D

DEVELOPMENT OF MAJUSCULE								
NORTH SEMITIC	GREEK		ETR.	LATIN		MODERN		
						GOTHIC	ITALIC	ROMAN
◁	Δ	Δ	D	D	D	𝔇	*D*	D

DEVELOPMENT OF MINUSCULE					
ROMAN CURSIVE	ROMAN UNCIAL	CAROL. MIN.	MODERN		
			GOTHIC	ITALIC	ROMAN
d	∂	d	𝔡	*d*	d

The fourth letter of the English alphabet developed from North Semitic *daleth* and Greek *delta*. The capital (D) corresponds generally to the North Semitic *daleth* and Greek *delta* (Δ), arriving at its present form in Latin. The minuscule (d) corresponds closely to the Greek *delta* (δ), acquiring its present form from the Roman cursive *d*.

D, d (dē), *n., pl.* **D's or Ds, d's** or **ds.** **1.** the fourth letter of the English alphabet, a consonant. **2.** any spoken sound represented by the letter *D* or *d*, as in *dog, ladder* or *ladle.* **3.** something having the shape of a D. **4.** a written or printed representation of the letter *D* or *d*. **5.** a device, as a printer's type, for reproducing the letter *D* or *d*.

D, **1.** *Elect.* debye. **2.** Dutch (def. 7).

D, **1.** the fourth in order or in a series. **2.** (*sometimes l.c.*) (in some grading systems) a grade or mark, as of academic work, that indicates poor or barely acceptable quality. **3.** *Music.* **a.** the second tone in the scale of C major, or the fourth tone in the relative minor scale, A minor. **b.** a written or printed note representing this tone. **c.** a string, key, or pipe tuned to this tone. **d.** the tonality having D as the tonic note. **4.** (*sometimes l.c.*) the Roman numeral for 500. Cf. **Roman numerals.** **5.** *Chem.* deuterium.

d'[1], *prep.* **1.** de (used in French names as an elided form of *de*): *Charles Louis d'Albert.* **2.** di (used in Italian names as an elided form of *di*): *Gabriele d'Annunzio.*

d'[2], *Informal.* contraction of the second person sing. and pl. of *do* or *did: How d'you like your eggs cooked?*

'd, **1.** contraction of *had: I was glad they'd gone.* **2.** contraction of *did: Where'd they go?* **3.** contraction of *should* or *would: He'd like to go. I'd like to remind you of your promise.*

D., **1.** day. **2.** December. **3.** Democrat. **4.** Democratic. **5.** *Physics.* density. **6.** Deus. **7.** *Optics.* diopter. **8.** Dutch.

d., **1.** date. **2.** daughter. **3.** degree. **4.** *Brit.* pence. [< L *dēnārii*] **5.** *Brit.* penny. [< L *dēnārius*] **6.** *Physics.* density. **7.** dialect. **8.** dialectal. **9.** diameter. **10.** died. **11.** dollar; dollars. **12.** dose.

da (da; *It.* dä; *Port.* də, dä), *prep.* (used in Italian or Portuguese names, often to indicate *of* or *from.*)

da., **1.** daughter. **2.** day; days.

D/A, **1.** (*sometimes l.c.*) days after acceptance. **2.** deposit account. **3.** documents for acceptance.

D.A., **1.** District Attorney. **2.** documents for acceptance. **3.** doesn't answer; don't answer.

dab[1] (dab), *v.,* **dabbed, dab·bing,** *n.* **—*v.t.*** **1.** to pat or tap gently, as with something soft or moist. **2.** to apply (a substance) by light strokes: *He dabbed the salve on his burned finger.* **3.** to strike, esp. lightly, as with the hand. **—*v.i.*** **4.** to strike lightly; make a dab; pat. **—*n.*** **5.** a quick or light blow; a pat, as with the hand or something soft. **6.** a small moist lump or mass. **7.** a small quantity. [ME *dabbe(n);* cf. Norw *dabbe* shuffle along, walk slowly, G *Tappe* pat, *tappen* to feel along, grope]

dab[2] (dab), *n.* **1.** a European flatfish, *Limanda limanda.* **2.** any of several other flatfishes of the genus *Limanda.* [? special use of DAB[1]]

DAB, Dictionary of American Biography.

dab·ber (dab′ər), *n.* **1.** a person or thing that dabs. **2.** a cushionlike article used for applying ink, as by printers and engravers.

dab·ble (dab′əl), *v.,* **-bled, -bling.** **—*v.t.*** **1.** to wet slightly in or with a liquid; splash; spatter. **—*v.i.*** **2.** to play and splash in or as if in water. **3.** to work at anything in an irregular or superficial manner: *to dabble in literature.* [prob. DAB[1] + -LE; cf. D *dabbelen, dabben*] **—dab′bler,** *n.*

dab·chick (dab′chik′), *n.* any of various small grebes, as the pied-billed grebe. [earlier *dapchick* (see DAP, CHICK); cf. *dopp(ened)* moorhen (lit., dipping duck)]

da ca·po (dä kä′pō; *It.* dä kä′pô), repeated from the beginning (used as a musical direction). [< It: lit., from the head]

Dac·ca (dak′ə), *n.* a city in and the capital of Bangladesh, in the central part. 1,310,972.

d'ac·cord (dA kôR′), *adv. French.* agreed; granted.

dace (dās), *n., pl.* (*esp. collectively*) **dace,** (*esp. referring to two or more kinds or species*) **dac·es.** **1.** a small, fresh-water cyprinoid fish, *Leuciscus leuciscus,* of Europe, having a stout, fusiform body. **2.** any of several similar or related fishes of the U.S. [ME *darce, darse* < OF *dars* < LL *dars(us)*]

da·cha (dä′chə), *n.* (in Russia) a country house or villa. Also, **datcha.** [< Russ: lit., payment, a giving]

Da·chau (dä′kou; *Ger.* dä′KHou), *n.* a city in SE West Germany, near Munich: site of Nazi concentration camp. 30,000 (1963).

Dachshund (8 in. high at shoulder)

dachs·hund (däks′ho͝ond′, -ənd, dash′-; *Ger.* däks′ho͝ont′), *n.* one of a German breed of dogs having short legs, a long body and ears, and a usually tan or black-and-tan coat. [< G = *Dachs* badger + *Hund* dog]

Da·ci·a (dā′shē ə, -shə), *n.* an ancient kingdom and later a Roman province between the Carpathian Mountains and the Danube.

da·coit (də koit′), *n.* (in India and Burma) one of a class of criminals who engage in organized robbery and murder. Also, **dakoit.** [< Hindi *ḍakait* < *ḍākā* dacoity < Skt *dashṭaka* crowded]

da·coit·y (də koi′tē), *n., pl.* **-coit·ies.** (in India and Burma) gang robbery; robbery by dacoits. Also, **dakoity.** [< Hindi *ḍakaitī* < *ḍakait* DACOIT]

Da·cron (dā′kron, -krən, dak′ron, -rən), *n. Trademark.* a synthetic textile fiber that is wrinkle-resistant and strong.

dac·tyl (dak′təl, -til), *n.* **1.** *Pros.* a foot of three syllables, one long followed by two short in quantitative meter, or one stressed followed by two unstressed in accentual meter, as in *humanly.* **2.** a finger or toe. [< L *dactyl(us)* < Gk *dáktylos* finger, dactyl, referring to the three finger joints]

-dactyl, var. of **dactylo-** as final element in a compound word: *pterodactyl.*

dac·tyl·ic (dak til′ik), *adj.* **1.** of, containing, or characterized by dactyls: *dactylic hexameter.* **—*n.*** **2.** a dactylic verse. [< L *dactylic(us)* < Gk *daktylikós*] **—dac·tyl′i·cal·ly,** *adv.*

dactylo-, a learned borrowing from Greek meaning "finger," "toe," used in the formation of compound words: *dactylogram.* Also, **dactyl-, -dactyl, -dactyly.** [< Gk, comb. form repr. *dáktylos* finger, toe]

dac·tyl·o·gram (dak til′ə gram′), *n.* a fingerprint.

dac·ty·log·ra·phy (dak′təlog′rə fē), *n.* the study of fingerprints for purposes of identification. **—dac′ty·log′ra·pher,** *n.* **—dac·tyl·o·graph·ic** (dak til′ə graf′ik, dak′təl ə-), *adj.*

dac·ty·lol·o·gy (dak′təlol′ə jē), *n., pl.* **-gies.** the technique of communicating by signs made with the fingers, as in the manual alphabets used by the deaf.

-dactyly, a combination of **-dactyl** and **-y**[3], used to form nouns to stems in **-dactyl.** [< NL *-dactylia*]

dad (dad), *n. Informal.* **1.** father. **2.** fellow; buddy; pal (usually used in addressing a stranger). [childish alter.]

Da·da (dä′dä), *n.* (*sometimes l.c.*) the style and techniques of a group of artists, writers, etc., of the early 20th century who exploited accidental and incongruous effects in their work and programmatically challenged established canons of art, thought, morality, etc. [< F: hobby-horse, childish redupl. of *da* giddap] **—Da′da·ism,** *n.* **—Da′da·ist,** *n.* **—Da′da·is′tic,** *adj.* **—Da′da·is′ti·cal·ly,** *adv.*

dad·dy (dad′ē), *n., pl.* **-dies.** a diminutive of dad.

Daddy-longlegs, *Phalangium opilio*

dad·dy-long·legs (dad′ē lông′legz′, -long′-), *n.* (*construed as sing. or pl.*) **1.** Also called **harvestman.** any of numerous arachnids of the order *Phalangida,* having a compact rounded body and extremely long, slender legs. **2.** *Brit.* a crane fly.

da·do (dā′dō), *n., pl.* **-does, -dos.** **1.** *Archit.* the part of a pedestal between the base and the cornice or cap. **2.** the lower broad part of an interior wall finished in wallpaper, a fabric, paint, etc. **3.** *Carpentry.* a groove or rectangular section for receiving the end of a board. [< It: die, cube, pedestal, perh. < Ar *dad* game]

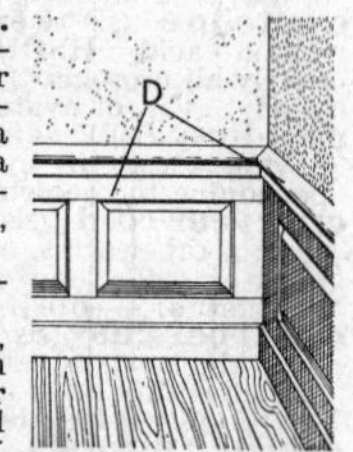

D, Dado (def. 2)

D.A.E., Dictionary of American English. Also, **DAE**

Daed·a·lus (ded′ələs *or, esp. Brit.,* dēd′ələs), *n. Class. Myth.* an Athenian architect who built the labyrinth for Minos and made wings for himself and his son Icarus to escape from Crete. [< L < Gk *Daídalos,* lit., skillful] **—Dae·da·li·an, Dae·da·le·an** (di dā′lē ən, -dāl′yən), **Dae·dal·ic** (di dal′ik), *adj.*

dae·mon (dē′mən), *n.* demon (def. 5). [< L: a spirit, an evil spirit < Gk *daímōn* a deity, fate, fortune < *daí(esthai)* (to) distribute + *-mōn* n. suffix] **—dae·mon·ic** (di mon′ik), **dae·mon·is·tic** (dē′mə nis′tik), *adj.*

dae·mo·ni·an (di mō′nē ən), *n.* demonian.

dae·mon·ol·o·gy (dē′mə nol′ə jē), *n.* demonology.

daff (daf), *v.t.* **1.** *Archaic.* to turn or thrust aside. **2.** *Obs.* to doff. [alter. of DOFF]

daf·fo·dil (daf′ə dil), *n.* **1.** a plant, *Narcissus Pseudo-Narcissus,* having yellow, nodding flowers that bloom in the spring. **2.** (formerly) any plant of this genus. [unexplained var. of ME *affodile* < ML *affodill(us),* var. of L *asphodelus* < Gk: ASPHODEL]

Daffodil, *Narcissus Pseudo-Narcissus*

daff·y (daf′ē), *adj.,* **daff·i·er, daff·i·est.** *Informal.* silly, weak-minded; crazy. [obs. *daff* a fool (ME *daffe;* see DAFT) + -Y[1]]

daft (daft, däft), *adj.* **1.** insane; crazy. **2.** simple or foolish. **3.** *Scot.* merry; playful; frolicsome. [ME *dafte* uncouth, awkward; earlier, gentle, meek, OE *gedæfte;* cf. DEFT] **—daft′ly,** *adv.* **—daft′ness,** *n.*

Da·fydd ap Gwi·lym (dä′vith äp gwi′lim), c1340–c1400, Welsh poet.

dag (dag), *n.* one of a series of decorative scallops or foliations along the edge of a garment, cloth, etc. [ME *dagge* < ?; cf. MF *dague* dagger]

Dag·da (däg′də, -ᵺə), *n. Irish Myth.* a god, the chief of the Tuatha De Danann, the father of Angus Og and Brigit, and the leader of the battle against the Fomorians. Also, **Daghda.**

Dag·en·ham (dag′ə nəm), *n.* a city in SE England, part of greater London. 108,363 (1961).

Dagger with scabbard

dag·ger (dag′ər), *n.* **1.** a short, swordlike weapon with a pointed blade and a handle, used for stabbing. **2.** Also called **obelisk.** *Print.* a mark (†) used esp. for references. —*v.t.* **3.** to stab with or as if with a dagger. **4.** *Print.* to mark with a dagger. [ME, prob. m. MF *dague* < OPr or OIt *daga*]

dag·gle (dag′əl), *v.t., v.i.,* **-gled, -gling.** *Archaic.* to drag or trail through mud, water, etc.; draggle; bemire. [dial. *dag* to bemire + -LE]

Dagh·da (däg′də, -ᵺə), *n. Irish Myth.* Dagda.

da·go (dā′gō), *n., pl.* **-gos, -goes.** (*often cap.*) *Disparaging.* a person of Spanish or esp. of Italian origin or descent. [alter. of *Diego* < Sp: a given name]

Dag·ö (däg′œ′), *n.* Danish name of **Hiiumaa.**

da·go·ba (dä′gə bə), *n.* a dome-shaped memorial alleged to contain relics of Buddha or a Buddhist saint; stupa; chaitya. [< Singhalese *dāgoba* < Pali *dhātugabbha* < Skt *dhātugarbha* = *dhātu* relics + *garbha* womb, inside]

Dag·o·bert I (dag′ə bərt; *Fr.* dA gô beR′), A.D. 602?–639, Merovingian king of the Franks 628–639.

Da·guerre (də gâr′; *Fr.* DA geR′), *n.* **Louis Jacques Man·dé** (lwē zhäk mäɴ dā′), 1789–1851, French painter and inventor of the daguerreotype.

da·guerre·o·type (də ger′ə tīp′, -ē ə tīp′), *n.* **1.** an obsolete photographic process, invented in 1839, in which a picture made on a silver surface sensitized with iodine was developed by exposure to mercury vapor. **2.** a picture made by this process. [named after L. J. M. DAGUERRE]

Dag′wood sand′wich, a huge sandwich in which a large variety of meats, cheeses, dressings, and condiments have been used. [after a character in comic strip *Blondie*]

dah (dä), *n.* an echoic word, the referent of which is a tone interval approximately three times the length of the dot, used to designate the dash of Morse code, International Morse code, etc. Cf. **dit.**

da·ha·be·ah (dä′hə bē′ə), *n.* a large boat used on the Nile as a houseboat or for transporting passengers. Also, **da′ha·bee′yah, da′ha·bi′ah, da′ha·bi′eh, da′ha·bi′ya.** [< Ar *dhahabīyah,* lit., the golden]

Dahl·gren (dal′grən), *n.* **John Adolphus Bernard,** 1809–1870, U.S. naval officer and inventor.

dahl·ia (dal′yə, däl′- *or, esp. Brit.,* dāl′-), *n.* **1.** any composite plant of the genus *Dahlia,* widely cultivated for its showy, variegated flowers. **2.** the flower or tuberous root of a dahlia. [< NL, named after Anders *Dahl* (d. 1789), Swedish botanist; see -IA]

Dah·na (däᴋʜ′nä), *n.* See **Rub′ al Khali.**

Da·ho·mey (də hō′mē; *Fr.* dA ô mā′), *n.* former name of **Benin** (def. 1). —**Da·ho·man** (də hō′mən), *adj., n.*

dai·ly (dā′lē), *adj., n., pl.* **-lies,** *adv.* —*adj.* **1.** of, done, occurring, or issued each day or each weekday. **2.** computed by the day. —*n.* **3.** a newspaper appearing each day or each weekday. **4.** Often, **dailies.** *Motion Pictures.* rush[1] (def. 21). **5.** *Brit.* **a.** a nonresident servant who comes to work every day; a permanently employed servant who sleeps out. **b.** a woman employed to do cleaning or other household work by the day. —*adv.* **6.** every day; day by day. [ME *daily,* OE *dæglīc*] —**dai′li·ness,** *n.*

dai′ly dou′ble, a betting system in horse racing and dog racing in which one bet is made in a special pool on the outcome of two consecutive races.

dai′ly doz′en, *Informal.* a set of 12 or more calisthenic exercises to be done each day.

dai·mon (dī′mōn), *n.* demon (def. 5). —**dai·mon·ic** (dī mon′ik), **dai·mon·is·tic** (dī′mə nis′tik), *adj.*

dai·myo (dī′myô), *n., pl.* **-myo, -myos.** *Japanese Hist.* one of the great feudal lords who were vassals of the emperor. Also, **dai′mio.** [< Jap = *dai* great + *mio* name]

dain·ty (dān′tē), *adj.,* **-ti·er, -ti·est,** *n., pl.* **-ties.** —*adj.* **1.** of delicate beauty; exquisite. **2.** pleasing to the taste; delicious. **3.** of delicate discrimination or taste; excessively particular or fastidious. —*n.* **4.** something delicious to the taste; a delicacy. [ME *deinte* worthiness, happiness, delicacy < AF (OF *deint(i)e*) < L *dignitāt-* (s. of *dignitās*); see DIGNITY] —**dain′ti·ly** *adv.* —**dain′ti·ness,** *n.* —**Syn. 1.** fine. See **delicate. 2.** tender, delectable. **3.** scrupulous.

dai·qui·ri (dī′kə rē, dak′ə-), *n., pl.* **-ris.** a cocktail consisting of rum, lemon or lime juice, and sugar. [after *Daiquirí,* town on the east coast of Cuba]

Dai·ren (dī′ren′), *n.* a city in S Liaoning, in NE China: capital of the former Japanese leased territory of Kwantung in S Manchuria. 4,000,000. Chinese, **Talien.**

dair·y (dâr′ē), *n., pl.* **dair·ies. 1.** an establishment, as a room, building, or buildings, where milk and cream are kept and butter and cheese are made. **2.** a shop or company that sells milk, butter, etc. **3.** the business of a dairy farm, concerned with the production and treatment of milk and cream and the manufacture of butter and cheese. **4.** See **dairy farm.** —*adj.* **5.** (in Jewish dietary laws) of or pertaining to those foods, including all milk products, eggs, fish, vegetables, etc., that may be eaten at a meal in which milk is served, in contrast to meat and meat products, which may not. [ME *daierie* = *daie, deie* dairymaid (OE *dǣge* maker of bread; c. Icel *deigja;* see LADY) + *-erie* -ERY]

dair′y cat′tle, cows raised mainly for their milk.

dair′y farm′, a farm devoted chiefly to the production of milk and the manufacture of butter and cheese.

dair·y·ing (dâr′ē ing), *n.* the business of a dairy.

dair·y·maid (dâr′ē mād′), *n.* a girl or woman employed in a dairy.

dair·y·man (dâr′ē mən), *n., pl.* **-men. 1.** an owner or manager of a dairy. **2.** an employee in a dairy.

da·is (dā′is, dī′-, dās), *n.* a raised platform, as at the end of a room, for a throne, seats of honor, a lecturer's desk, etc. [ME *deis* < AF (OF *dois*) < L *discus* quoit; see DISCUS]

dai·sy (dā′zē), *n., pl.* **-sies. 1.** any of various composite plants whose flowers have a yellow disk and white rays, as the English daisy and the oxeye daisy. **2.** Also called **dai′sy ham′,** a small section of pork shoulder, usually smoked and boned. **3.** *Slang.* someone or something of first-rate quality. **4. push up daisies,** *Informal.* to be dead: *Another year of this and I'll be pushing up daisies.* [ME *dayesye,* OE *dægesēge* the day's eye] —**dai′sied,** *adj.*

dai′sy wheel′, a metal or plastic wheel with raised, fully-formed symbols or alphanumeric characters on the tips of petal-like spokes: used in a printer **(dai′sy wheel′ print′er)** or an electronic typewriter to produce print of superior quality.

dak (dôk, däk), *n.* **1.** transportation by relays of men or horses, esp. in the East Indies. **2.** mail delivered by such transportation. [< Hindi *dāk*]

Dak., Dakota.

Da·kar (dä kär′), *n.* a seaport in and the capital of Senegal; capital of former French West Africa. 978,553; 68 sq. mi.

da·koit (də koit′), *n.* dacoit.

da·koit·y (də koi′tē), *n., pl.* **-koit·ies.** dacoity.

Da·ko·ta (də kō′tə), *n.* **1.** a former territory in the United States: divided into the states of North Dakota and South Dakota 1889. **2. the Dakotas,** North Dakota and South Dakota. **3.** a Sioux Indian. **4.** a division of the Siouan stock of North American Indians, whose former habitat was in and near North and South Dakota. **5.** a Siouan language spoken by the Dakota and Assiniboin Indians. —**Da·ko′tan,** *adj., n.*

Da·la·dier (dA lA dyā′), *n.* **É·douard** (ā dwAR′), 1884–1970, premier of France 1933, 1934, 1938–40.

Da·lai La·ma (dä′lī lä′mə, də lī′), the title of the religious and political leader of Tibet from the 17th century to 1959. Also called **Grand Lama.** [< Mongolian = *dalai* ocean + *lama* a celibate priest]

Dal·croze (*Fr.* dAl kRôz′), *n.* Jaques-Dalcroze.

dale (dāl), *n.* a valley, esp. a broad valley. [ME *dal,* OE *dæl;* c. G *Tal,* Icel *dalr,* Goth *dals*]

Dale (dāl), *n.* **Sir Thomas,** died 1619, British colonial administrator in America: governor of Virginia 1614–16.

dales·man (dālz′mən), *n., pl.* **-men.** a person living in a dale, esp. in the northern counties of England.

da·leth (dä′lid; *Heb.* dä′let), *n.* the fourth letter of the Hebrew alphabet. [< Heb *dāleth,* prob. var. of *deleth* door, as pronounced before a pause]

Dal·hou·sie (dal ho͞o′zē, -hou′-), *n.* **1. George Ramsay, Earl of,** 1770–1838, British general: governor of the Canadian colonies 1819–28. **2. James Andrew Broun Ramsay, 1st Marquis and 10th Earl of,** 1812–60, British statesman: viceroy of India 1848–56.

Da·li (dä′lē), *n.* **Sal·va·dor** (sal′və dôr′; *Sp.* säl′vä ᵺôR′), born 1904, Spanish painter and illustrator; in U.S. after 1940.

Dal·las (dal′əs), *n.* **1. George Miff·lin** (mif′lin), 1792–1864, lawyer and diplomat, vice president of the U.S. 1845–49. **2.** a city in NE Texas. 844,401 (1970).

dalles (dalz), *n.pl.* the rapids of a river running between the walls of a canyon or gorge. Also, **dells.** [< CanF, pl. of F *dalle* flagstone, gutter << Gmc; cf. OE *dæl* DALE]

dal·li·ance (dal′ē əns, dal′yəns), *n.* **1.** a trifling away of time; dawdling. **2.** amorous toying; flirtation.

Dall's′ sheep′ (dôlz), a white-haired wild sheep, *Ovis dalli,* of mountainous regions of northwestern North America, having curved horns. [named after William H. *Dall* (1845–1927), American naturalist]

dal·ly (dal′ē), *v.,* **-lied, -ly·ing.** —*v.i.* **1.** to sport or play, esp. amorously. **2.** to play mockingly; trifle. **3.** to waste time; loiter; delay. —*v.t.* **4.** to waste (time). [ME *dalien* < AF *dalier* to chat << LG *dallen* to talk foolishly] —**dal′li·er,** *n.* —**dal′ly·ing·ly,** *adv.* —**Syn. 1.** fondle, caress, pet. **2.** toy. **3.** See **loiter.**

Dal·ma·tia (dal mā′shə), *n.* a region in W Yugoslavia, along the Adriatic.

Dalmatian (21 in. high at shoulder)

Dal·ma·tian (dal mā′shən), *adj.* **1.** of or pertaining to Dalmatia or its people. —*n.* **2.** an inhabitant of Dalmatia, esp. a member of the native Slavic-speaking people of Dalmatia. **3.** Also called **coach dog, Dalma′tian dog′.** one of a breed of short-haired dogs having a white coat marked with black or liver-colored spots. **4.** a Romance language of Dalmatia, extinct since 1898.

dal·mat·ic (dal mat′ik), *n.* **1.** *Eccles.* a vestment worn over the alb by a deacon or by a bishop. **2.** a similar vestment worn by the king of England at his coronation. [< LL *dalmatic(a),* special use of L *Dalmatica,* fem. of *Dalmaticus* Dalmatian]

Dal·ny (däl′nē), *n.* former name of **Dairen.**

Dal·rym·ple (dal rim′pəl, dal′rim-), *n.* **Sir James, 1st Viscount Stair** (stâr), 1619–95, Scottish jurist.

dal se·gno (däl sān′yō; *It.* däl se′nyô), go back to the sign marking the beginning of a repeat (used as a musical direction). [< It: from the sign]

Dal·ton (dôl′tᵊn), *n.* **1. John,** 1766–1844, English chemist and physicist. **2.** a city in NW Georgia. 18,872 (1970).

Dal′ton's law′, *Physics, Chem.* the law that the total pressure exerted by a mixture of gases is equal to the sum of the partial pressures of the gases of the mixture. Also called **Dal′ton's law′ of par′tial pres′sures.**

Da·ly (dā′lē), *n.* **(John) Au·gus·tin** (ô gus′tin), 1838–99, U.S. playwright, critic, and theatrical manager.

Da′ly Cit′y, a city in central California, S of San Francisco. 66,922 (1970).

dam[1] (dam), *n., v.,* **dammed, dam·ming.** —*n.* **1.** a barrier to

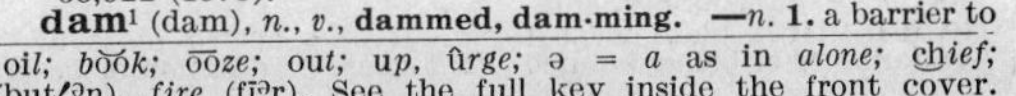

obstruct the flow of water, esp. one built across a stream. **2.** any barrier resembling a dam. —*v.t.* **3.** to furnish with a dam; obstruct or confine with a dam. **4.** to stop up; block up. [ME, prob. < ON; cf. OIcel *damm(a);* akin to OE *demman* to stop up, block]

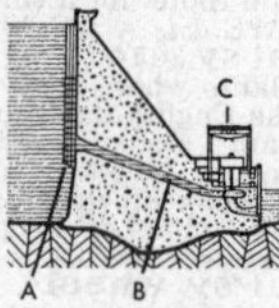

dam^2 (dam), *n.* a female parent (used esp. of four-footed animals). [ME; var. of DAME]

dam·age (dam′ij), *n., v.,* **-aged, -ag·ing.** —*n.* **1.** injury or harm that impairs value or usefulness. **2. damages,** *Law.* the estimated money equivalent for detriment or injury sustained. **3.** Often, **damages.** *Informal.* cost; expense; charge. —*v.t.* **4.** to injure or harm; cause damage to; impair the usefulness of. —*v.i.* **5.** to become damaged. [ME < OF = *dam* (< L *damnum* damage, fine) + *-age* -AGE; see DAMN] —**dam′age·a·ble,** *adj.* —**dam′age·a·ble·ness, dam′age·a·bil′i·ty,** *n.* —**dam′ag·er,** *n.*

A B C

Dam^1 (def. 1)
A, Trash rack
B, Penstock
C, Powerhouse

—**Syn. 1.** loss. DAMAGE, DETRIMENT, HARM, MISCHIEF refer to injuries of various kinds. DAMAGE is the kind of injury or the effect of injury which directly impairs appearance, value, usefulness, soundness, etc.: *Fire causes damage to property. Property suffers damage.* DETRIMENT is a falling off from an original condition as the result of damage, depreciation, devaluation, etc.: *detriment to health because of illness, to property because of neglect.* HARM is the kind of injury that connotes sorrow or a sense of evil; it may denote either physical hurt or mental, moral, or spiritual injury: *bodily harm; harm to one's self-confidence.* MISCHIEF may be damage, harm, trouble, or misfortune caused by a person, esp. if maliciously: *an enemy who would do one mischief.* **4.** hurt, mar. —**Ant. 1.** improvement. **4.** improve.

dam·ag·ing (dam′i jing), *adj.* causing or capable of causing damage; harmful; injurious: *a damaging statement.* —**dam′ag·ing·ly,** *adv.*

Dam·an (də män′), *n.* **1.** a union territory in W India: formerly a district of Portuguese India; annexed by India December, 1961. 23,093 (1961); 176 sq. mi. **2.** the capital of this territory. 22,390 (1961). Portuguese, **Da·mão** (dä-moun′).

Da·man·hur (dä′män hoor′), *n.* a city in N Egypt, near Alexandria. 175,900.

dam·ar (dam′är, -ər, də mär′), *n.* dammar.

Da·ma·ra·land (dä mär′ə land′), *n.* a region in the central part of SW Africa.

Dam·a·scene (dam′ə sēn′, dam′ə sēn′), *adj., n., v.,* **-scened, -scen·ing.** —*adj.* **1.** of or pertaining to the city of Damascus. **2.** (*l.c.*) of or pertaining to the art of damascening. —*n.* **3.** an inhabitant of Damascus. **4.** (*l.c.*) work or patterns produced by damascening. —*v.t.* **5.** (*l.c.*) to produce wavy lines on (watered steel). [ME < L *Damascēn(us)* of Damascus < Gk *Damaskēnós*]

Da·mas·cus (də mas′kəs), *n.* a city in and the capital of Syria, in the SW part: reputed to be the oldest continuously existing city in the world. 936,567. French, **Da·mas** (dA mä′).

Damas′cus steel′. See **watered steel.**

dam·ask (dam′əsk), *n.* **1.** a reversible fabric of linen, silk, cotton, or wool, woven with patterns. **2.** napery of this material. **3.** the pink color of the damask rose. —*adj.* **4.** made of or resembling damask: *damask cloth.* **5.** of the pink color of the damask rose. —*v.t.* **6.** to damascene. **7.** to weave or adorn with elaborate design, as damask cloth. [ME *damaske* < ML *damasc(us),* after DAMASCUS where such fabrics were first made]

dam′ask rose′, a fragrant pink rose, *Rosa damascena.*

Dam·a·sus I (dam′ə səs), **Saint,** pope A.D. 366–384.

Damasus II, died 1048, pope 1048.

dame (dām), *n.* **1.** (formerly) a form of address to any woman of rank or authority. **2.** (*cap.*) (in Britain) **a.** the official title of the wife of a knight or baronet. **b.** the title of a female member of the Order of the British Empire, equivalent to that of a knight. **3.** a matronly woman of advanced age; matron. **4.** *Slang.* a woman. **5.** *Archaic.* the mistress of a household. [ME < OF < L *domina,* fem. of *dominus* lord, master]

dame's′ rock′et, a rocket, *Hesperis matronalis,* of Europe and Asia, having showy purple or white fragrant flowers. Also called **dame's′ vi′olet.**

Da·mien (dā′myen; *Fr.* dA myAN′), *n.* **Father (Jo·seph de Veu·ster)** (*Fr.* zho zef′ də vœ steR′), 1840–89, Belgian Roman Catholic missionary to the lepers of Molokai.

Dam·i·et·ta (dam′ē et′ə), *n.* a city in NE Egypt, in the Nile delta. 110,000. Arabic, **Dumyat.**

dam·mar (dam′är, -ər, də mär′), *n.* **1.** a resin derived largely from dipterocarpaceous trees of southern Asia, and used for making colorless varnish. **2.** any of various similar resins from trees of other families. Also, **damar, dam·mer** (dam′ər). [< Malay *damar*]

damn (dam), *v.t.* **1.** to declare (something) to be bad, invalid, or illegal. **2.** to bring condemnation upon; ruin. **3.** *Theol.* to condemn to eternal punishment in hell. **4.** to swear at or curse, using the word "damn." —*v.i.* **5.** to use the word "damn"; swear. **6. damn with faint praise,** to praise so moderately as, in effect, to condemn. —*interj.* **7.** (used as an expletive to express anger, annoyance, disgust, etc.) —*n.* **8.** the utterance of "damn" in swearing or for emphasis. **9.** something of negligible value: *not worth a damn.* **10. give a damn,** *Informal.* to care; be concerned; consider as important. Also, **give a darn.** —*adj.* **11.** damned (def. 2). —*adv.* **12.** damned. [ME *dam(p)n(en)* < OF *dam(p)ne(r)* < L *damnāre* to condemn < *damnum* damage, fine, harm] —**damn′er,** *n.*

dam·na·ble (dam′nə bəl), *adj.* **1.** worthy of damnation. **2.** detestable, abominable, or outrageous. [ME *dam(p)nable* < MF *damnable* < LL *damnābil(is)* = L *damn(āre)* (see DAMN) + *-ābilis* -ABLE] —**dam′na·ble·ness, dam′na·bil′i·ty,** *n.* —**dam′na·bly,** *adv.*

dam·na·tion (dam nā′shən), *n.* **1.** the act or state of damning or of being damned. **2.** a cause or occasion of being damned. **3.** *Theol.* condemnation to eternal punishment as a consequence of sin. **4.** an oath expressing anger, disappointment, etc. —*interj.* **5.** (used in exclamatory phrases to express anger, disappointment, etc.) [ME *dam(p)nacioun* < OF *damnation* < L *damnātiōn-* (s. of *damnātiō*) = *damnāt(us)* (ptp. of *damnāre;* see DAMN) + *-iōn-* -ION]

dam·na·to·ry (dam′nə tōr′ē, -tôr′ē), *adj.* expressing or causing condemnation. [< L *damnātōri(us)*]

damned (damd), *adj., superl.* **damned·est, damnd·est,** *adv.* —*adj.* **1.** condemned or doomed, esp. to eternal punishment. **2.** detestable; loathsome. **3.** utter: *a damned fool.* —*adv.* **4.** extremely; very; absolutely. [ME *dam(p)ned*]

damned·est (dam′dist), *adj.* **1.** superl. of **damned. 2.** most extraordinary or amazing: *It was the damnedest thing I'd ever seen.* —*n.* **3.** *Informal.* best; utmost: *They did their damnedest to finish on time.*

dam·ni·fy (dam′nə fī′), *v.t.,* **-fied, -fy·ing.** *Law.* to cause loss or damage to. [< MF, OF *damnifi(er)* < LL *damnificāre* < L *damnific(us)* harmful = *damn(um)* damage + *-ificus* (see -I-, -FIC); see -IFY]

damn·ing (dam′ing, dam′ning), *adj.* incriminating: *damning evidence.* —**damn′ing·ly,** *adv.* —**damn′ing·ness,** *n.*

Dam·o·cles (dam′ə klēz′), *n.* a flatterer who, having extolled the happiness of Dionysius, tyrant of Syracuse, was seated at a banquet with a sword suspended over his head by a single hair to show him the perilous nature of that happiness. —**Dam·o·cle·an** (dam′ə klē′ən), *adj.*

dam·oi·selle (dam′ə zel′), *n.* *Archaic.* damsel. Also, **dam′o·sel′, dam′o·zel′.**

Da′mon and Pyth′ias (dā′mən), *Class. Myth.* two young friends whose mutual loyalty was shown by Damon's pledging his life so that Pythias, condemned to death for rebellion by Dionysius, the tyrant of Syracuse, might be granted a respite in order to settle his affairs at home. At the time set for the execution, Pythias returned, and Dionysius relented, pardoning them both.

damp (damp), *adj.* **1.** moderately wet; moist: *damp weather.* **2.** unenthusiastic; dejected; depressed; lifeless. —*n.* **3.** moisture; humidity; moist air. **4.** a noxious or stifling vapor or gas, esp. in a mine. **5.** depression of spirits; dejection. **6.** a restraining or discouraging force or factor. —*v.t.* **7.** to make damp; moisten. **8.** to check or retard the energy, action, etc., of. **9.** to stifle or suffocate; extinguish: *to damp a furnace.* **10.** *Acoustics, Music.* to check or retard the action of (a vibrating string); dull; deaden. **11.** *Physics.* to cause a decrease in amplitude of (successive oscillations or waves). **12. damp off,** to undergo damping-off. [ME; cf. MD *damp,* MHG *dampf* vapor, smoke] —**damp′ish,** *adj.* —**damp′ish·ly,** *adv.* —**damp′ish·ness,** *n.* —**damp′ly,** *adv.* —**damp′ness,** *n.* —**Syn. 1.** dank, steamy, humid. **3.** dankness, dampness, fog, vapor. **7.** humidify. **8.** slow, inhibit, restrain, moderate, abate. —**Ant. 1.** dry.

damp-dry (damp′drī′, -drī′), *v.,* **-dried, -dry·ing,** *adj.* —*v.t.* **1.** (of laundry) to dry partially so that some moisture remains. —*adj.* **2.** of or pertaining to laundry so dried.

damp·en (dam′pən), *v.t.* **1.** to make damp; moisten. **2.** to dull or deaden; depress. **3.** damp (def. 10). —*v.i.* **4.** to become damp. —**damp′en·er,** *n.*

damp·er (dam′pər), *n.* **1.** a person or thing that damps. **2.** a movable plate for regulating the draft in a stove, furnace, etc. **3.** *Music.* **a.** a device in stringed keyboard instruments to deaden the vibration of the strings. **b.** the mute of a brass instrument, as a horn. **4.** *Elect.* an attachment to keep the indicator of a measuring instrument from oscillating excessively, usually a set of vanes in an air space or fluid or a short-circuited winding in a magnetic field.

Dam·pi·er (dam′pē ər, damp′yər), *n.* **William,** 1652–1715, English explorer, buccaneer, and writer.

damp·ing-off (dam′ping ôf′, -of′), *n.* *Plant Pathol.* a disease of seedlings, characterized by wilting and collapse of the plant and caused by several soil fungi.

Dam·rosch (dam′rosh), *n.* **Walter (Jo·han·nes)** (jō-han′əs), 1862–1950, U.S. conductor and composer, born in Germany.

dam·sel (dam′zəl), *n.* a maiden, originally one of gentle or noble birth. [ME *damisel* < AF (OF *damoisele*) < VL **domicella,* dim. of L *domin(a)* lady; see DAME]

dam·sel·fish (dam′zəl fish′), *n., pl.* (*esp. collectively*) **-fish,** (*esp. referring to two or more kinds or species*) **-fish·es.** any of several chiefly tropical, brilliantly colored, marine fishes of the family *Pomacentridae,* found among coral reefs.

dam·sel·fly (dam′zəl flī′), *n., pl.* **-flies.** any of numerous slender, slow-flying insects of the order *Odonata* (suborder *Zygoptera*), distinguished from the dragonflies by having the wings held together over the body when at rest.

dam·son (dam′zən), *n.* **1.** Also called **dam′son plum′.** the small dark-blue or purple fruit of a plum, *Prunus insititia,* introduced into Europe from Asia Minor. **2.** the tree bearing it. [ME *damascene, damson* < L (*prūnum*) *Damascēn(um)* (plum) of Damascus; see DAMASCENE]

Dan (dan), *n.* **1.** a son of Jacob and Bilhah. Gen. 30:6. **2.** one of the 12 tribes of Israel, traditionally descended from him. **3.** the northernmost city of ancient Palestine. **4. from Dan to Beersheba,** from one outermost extreme or limit to the other. Judges 20:1.

Dan (dan), *n.* *Archaic.* a title of honor equivalent to *master* or *sir: Dan Chaucer; Dan Cupid.* [ME < MF *dan(z)* < OF < ML *domn(us),* contr. of L *dominus* lord, master]

Dan, Danish (def. 2).

Dan., **1.** Daniel. **2.** Danish. **3.** Danzig.

Da·na (dā′nə), *n.* **1. Charles Anderson,** 1819–97, U.S. journalist, editor, and publisher. **2. James Dwight,** 1813–95, U.S. geologist and mineralogist. **3. Richard Henry, Jr.,** 1815–82, U.S. jurist, author, and sailor.

Dan·a·ë (dan′ə ē′), *n.* *Class. Myth.* a maiden who bore a son, Perseus, after Zeus came to her in the form of a shower of gold. —**Dan·a·än** (dan′ē ən), *adj.*

Dan·a·i (dan′ā ī′), *n.pl.* *Class. Myth.* **1.** the Argives. **2.** the Greeks.

Da·na·i·des (də nā′i dēz′), *n.pl.* *Class. Myth.* the 50 daughters of Danaus, 49 of whom were condemned to pour water forever into a leaky vessel for having murdered their husbands. Also, **Da·na·i·dae** (də nā′i dē′), **Da·na·ids** (dənā/idz). Cf. **Hypermnestra.** —**Dan·a·id·e·an** (dan/ē id/ē ən, dan/ē i dē/ən), *adj.*

Da·nang (dä/näng/, də nang/), *n.* a seaport in E South Vietnam. 121,400 (est. 1962). Formerly, **Tourane.**

Dan·a·us (dan/ē əs), *n. Class. Myth.* a ruler of Argos who ordered his 50 daughters to kill their husbands on their wedding night. Cf. **Danaides.**

Dan·bur·y (dan/ber/ē, -bə rē), *n.* a city in SW Connecticut. 50,781 (1970).

dance (dans, däns), *v.*, **danced, danc·ing,** *n.* —*v.i.* **1.** to move one's feet, or body, or both, rhythmically in a pattern of steps, esp. to the accompaniment of music. **2.** to leap, skip, etc., as from excitement or emotion. **3.** to bob up and down. —*v.t.* **4.** to perform or take part in (a dance). **5.** to cause to dance. —*n.* **6.** a successive group of rhythmical steps or bodily motions, or both, usually executed to music. **7.** an act or round of dancing; set. **8.** a social gathering for dancing; ball. **9.** a piece of music suited in rhythm or style to a particular form of dancing. **10. the dance,** ballet, interpretive dancing, and other dancing of an artistic nature. [ME *da(u)nce(n)* < OF *dancie(r)*, perh. < VL **deantiāre* = LL *deante* before (see DE-, ANTE-) + *-āre* inf. suffix] —**danc/ing·ly,** *adv.*

dance/ hall/, a public establishment that, for an admission fee, provides music and space for dancing and, sometimes, dancing partners and refreshments.

dance/ of death/, (in medieval art) an allegorical dance in which Death is represented as leading people to the grave. Also called **danse macabre.**

danc·er (dan/sər, dän/-), *n.* a person who dances, usually professionally on the stage. [ME]

D and C, *Med.* a surgical method for the removal of diseased tissue from the lining of the uterus by means of scraping. [*d(ilation) and c(urettage)*]

dan·de·li·on (dan/dᵊlī/ən), *n.* **1.** a weedy composite plant, *Taraxacum officinale*, having deeply notched leaves and golden-yellow flowers. **2.** any other plant of the genus *Taraxacum.* [< MF, m. *dent de lion*, lit., tooth of (a) lion, trans. of ML *dēns leōnis*, in allusion to the toothed leaves]

dan·der[1] (dan/dər), *n.* **1.** dandruff or other scaly particles of hair, fur, feathers, or skin that may cause an allergic reaction. **2.** *Informal.* anger; temper. [alter. of DANDRUFF]

dan·der[2] (dan/dər), *n. Scot.* a stroll; saunter. [?]

Dan·die Din·mont (dan/dē din/mont), one of a breed of small terriers having short legs, pendulous ears, and a long, wiry, pepper- or mustard-colored coat. [after a character who owned two terriers in Walter Scott's novel, *Guy Mannering*, (1815)]

dan·di·fy (dan/də fī/), *v.t.*, **-fied, -fy·ing.** to make into a dandy or fop. —**dan/di·fi·ca/tion,** *n.*

dan·di·prat (dan/dē prat/), *n.* **1.** a silver coin of 16th-century England, equal to about twopence. **2.** *Archaic.* **a.** a child or midget. **b.** a person of childish mind. [?]

dan·dle (dan/dᵊl), *v.t.*, **-dled, -dling. 1.** to move (a baby, child, etc.) lightly up and down, as on one's knee or in one's arms. **2.** to pet. [prob. < It *dandol(are)*] —**dan/dler,** *n.*

dan·druff (dan/drəf), *n.* a seborrheic scurf that forms on the scalp and comes off in small scales. Also, **dan·driff** (dan/drif). [?] —**dan/druff·y, dan/driff·y,** *adj.*

dan·dy (dan/dē), *n., pl.* **-dies,** *adj.*, **-di·er, -di·est.** —*n.* **1.** Also called **jack-a-dandy.** a man who is excessively concerned about clothes and appearance; a fop. **2.** *Informal.* something or someone of exceptional quality. **3.** *Naut. Brit.* **a.** a yawl or ketch. **b.** the jigger or mizzen sail of this vessel. —*adj.* **4.** characteristic of a dandy; foppish. **5.** *U.S. Informal.* fine; first-rate. [?] —**dan/di·ly, dan·di·a·cal·ly** (dan dī/ək lē), *adv.* —**dan/dy·ish, dan·di/a·cal,** *adj.* —**dan/dy·ism,** *n.*

dan/dy roll/, *Papermaking.* a light, open cylinder of wire gauze for impressing a watermark. Also called **dan/dy roll/er.**

Dane (dān), *n.* **1.** a native or inhabitant of Denmark. **2.** a person of Danish descent. **3.** See **Great Dane.** [ME *Dane-*, OE *Dene* (pl.), influenced by ON *Danir* (pl.)]

Dane·geld (dān/geld/), *n.* (*sometimes l.c.*) (in medieval England) an annual tax believed to have been levied originally as a tribute to the Danish invaders but later continued as a land tax. Also, **Dane·gelt** (dān/gelt/). [ME]

Dane·law (dān/lô/), *n.* **1.** the body of laws in force in the northeast of England where the Danes settled in the 9th century A.D. **2.** the part of England under this law. Also, **Dane·la·ge** (dān/lä/gə, dä/nə lä/gə), **Dane·lagh** (dān/lô/). [ME *Dane-lawe*, earlier *Dene-lawe*, OE *Dena lagu*]

dan·ger (dān/jər), *n.* **1.** liability or exposure to harm or injury; risk; peril. **2.** an instance or cause of peril. **3.** *Obs.* power; jurisdiction; domain. [ME *da(u)nger* < AF, c. OF *dangier*, alter. of *dongier* (by influence of *dam* DAMAGE) < VL **domniār(ium)* = L *domini(um)* DOMINION + *-ārium*, neut. of *-ārius* -ARY] —**dan/ger·less,** *adj.*

—**Syn. 1.** DANGER, HAZARD, PERIL, JEOPARDY imply some evil or harm which one may encounter. DANGER is the general word for liability to all kinds of injury or evil consequences, either near at hand and certain, or remote and doubtful: *to be in danger of catching cold or of being killed.* HAZARD suggests a danger which one can foresee but cannot avoid: *A soldier is exposed to many hazards.* PERIL usually denotes great and imminent danger: *The passengers on the disabled ship were in great peril.* JEOPARDY, a less common word, has essentially the same meaning as peril, but emphasizes exposure to the chances of a situation: *To save his friend he put his life in jeopardy.* —**Ant. 1.** safety.

dan·ger·ous (dān/jər əs), *adj.* full of danger or risk; causing danger; perilous; hazardous; unsafe. [ME *da(u)ngerous* domineering, fraught with danger < OF *dangereus* threatening, difficult] —**dan/ger·ous·ly,** *adv.* —**dan/ger·ous·ness,** *n.*

dan·gle (dang/gəl), *v.*, **-gled, -gling,** *n.* —*v.i.* **1.** to hang loosely, esp. with a jerking or swaying motion. **2.** to hover around or wait for a person, as if seeking favor. —*v.t.* **3.** to cause to dangle; hold or carry swaying loosely. —*n.* **4.** the act of dangling. **5.** something that dangles. [< Scand; cf. Dan *dangle* to bob up and down] —**dan/gler,** *n.* —**dan/gling·ly,** *adv.*

dan/gling par/ticiple, *Gram.* a participle or participial phrase, often found at the beginning of a sentence, that from its position appears to modify an element of the sentence other than the one intended, as *plunging* in *Plunging 1000 feet into the gorge, we saw Yosemite Falls.* Cf. **misplaced modifier.**

Dan·iel (dan/yəl), *n.* **1.** *Bible.* **a.** a prophet living in Babylon during the Captivity. **b.** the book of the Bible bearing his name. **2. Samuel,** 1562–1619, English poet and historian: poet laureate 1599–1619.

Dan·iels (dan/yəlz), *n.* **1. Jonathan Worth** (wûrth), born 1902, U.S. journalist and author. **2.** his father, **Jo·se·phus** (jō sē/fəs), 1862–1948, U.S. editor and statesman.

Da·ni·lo·va (də nē/lə və, -lō-; *Russ.* dä nē/lo vä), *n.* **Al·ex·an·dra** (al/ig zan/drə, -zän/-; *Russ.* ä/le ksän/drə), born 1904?, Russian ballet dancer.

dan·i·o (dā/nē ō/), *n., pl.* **-i·os.** any of several cyprinid aquarium fishes of the genus *Danio*, found in India and Ceylon. [< NL]

Dan·ish (dā/nish), *adj.* **1.** of or pertaining to the Danes, their country, or their language. —*n.* **2.** a Germanic language, the language of Denmark, closely related to Norwegian, Swedish, and Icelandic. *Abbr.:* Dan, Dan. **3.** *Informal.* See **Danish pastry.** [ME, alter. of *Denish* (by influence of *Dan* DANE), OE *Denisc* = *Den* Danes + *-isc* -ISH[1]]

Dan/ish pas/try, a light pastry leavened with yeast and often filled with cheese, fruit, etc.

Dan/ish West/ In/dies, former name of the **Virgin Islands of the United States.** Also called **Dan/ish Vir/gin Is/lands.**

Dan·ite (dan/īt), *n.* **1.** a member of the tribe of Dan. **2.** a member of an alleged secret order of Mormons.

dank (dangk), *adj.* unpleasantly moist or humid; damp: *a dank cellar.* [ME (adj. and n.), prob. < Scand; cf. OIcel *dökk* pool] —**dank/ly,** *adv.* —**dank/ness,** *n.*

dan·ke (däng/kə), *interj. German.* thank you.

dan·ke schön (däng/kə shœn/), *German.* thank you very much.

Danl., Daniel.

D'An·nun·zio (də no͞on/sē ō; *It.* dän no͞on/tsyô), *n.* **Ga·bri·e·le** (*It.* gä/brē e/le), 1863–1938, Italian soldier, novelist, and poet.

danse ma·ca·bre (*Fr.* däns ma ka/brᵊ). See **dance of death.** [< F]

dan·seur (*Fr.* dän sœr/), *n., pl.* **-seurs** (*Fr.* -sœr/). a male ballet dancer. [< F: lit., dancer]

dan·seuse (*Fr.* dän sœz/), *n., pl.* **-seuses** (*Fr.* -sœz/). a female ballet dancer. [< F; fem. of *danseur*]

Dan·te (dan/tē, dän/tā; *It.* dän/te), *n.* (*Dante Alighieri*), 1265–1321, Italian poet: author of the allegorical epic poem, *Divine Comedy.* —**Dan·te·an** (dan/tē ən, dan tē/ən), *adj.*, *n.* —**Dan·tesque/,** *adj.*

Dan·ton (dan/tᵊn; *Fr.* dän tôn/), *n.* **Georges Jacques** (zhôrzh zhäk), 1759–94, leader in the French Revolution.

Dan·ube (dan/yo͞ob), *n.* a river in central and SE Europe, flowing E from SW West Germany to the Black Sea. 1725 mi. long. German, **Donau.** Hungarian, **Duna.** Rumanian, **Dunărea.** Czech and Slovak, **Dunaj.**

Dan·u·bi·an (dan yo͞o/bē ən), *adj.* of, pertaining to, or characteristic of a Neolithic culture of the Danube basin.

Dan·vers (dan/vərz), *n.* a town in NE Massachusetts, near Boston. 26,151 (1970).

Dan·ville (dan/vil), *n.* **1.** a city in S Virginia. 46,391 (1970). **2.** a city in E Illinois. 42,570 (1970).

Dan·zig (dan/sig; *Ger.* dän/tsikh), *n.* **1.** a seaport in N Poland, on the Bay of Danzig. 306,000 (est. 1963). **2. Free City of,** a former self-governing territory including the seaport of Danzig: constituted by the treaty of Versailles, 1920; now in Poland. 754 sq. mi. Polish, **Gdańsk.**

dap (dap), *v.i.*, **dapped, dap·ping. 1.** to fish by letting the bait fall lightly on the water. **2.** to dip lightly or suddenly into water. **3.** to bounce or skip. [prob. var. of DAB[1]]

Daph·ne (daf/nē), *n.* **1.** *Class. Myth.* a nymph who, when pursued by Apollo, was saved by being changed into a laurel tree. **2.** (*l.c.*) *Bot.* **a.** the laurel, *Laurus nobilis.* **b.** any thymelaeaceous shrub of the genus *Daphne*, of Europe and Asia, certain species of which, as *D. Mezereum*, are cultivated for their fragrant flowers. [< L < Gk: laurel]

Daph·nis (daf/nis), *n. Class. Myth.* a son of Hermes and a nymph: he was regarded by the Greeks as the originator of pastoral poetry.

Daph/nis and Chlo/e, two lovers in pastoral literature, esp. in a Greek romance attributed to Longus.

dap·per (dap/ər), *adj.* **1.** neat; trim; smart. **2.** small and active. [ME *daper* < MD *dapper* nimble, strong; cf. G *tapfer* brave] —**dap/per·ly,** *adv.* —**dap/per·ness,** *n.*

dap·ple (dap/əl), *n., adj., v.*, **-pled, -pling.** —*n.* **1.** a spot or mottled marking, usually occurring in clusters. **2.** an animal with a mottled skin or coat. —*adj.* **3.** dappled; spotted: *a dapple horse.* —*v.t., v.i.* **4.** to mark or become marked with spots. [prob. back formation from DAPPLED]

dap·pled (dap/əld), *adj.* having spots of a different shade, tone, or color from the background; mottled. [ME, prob. < ON; akin to OIcel *depill* spot]

dap·ple-gray (dap/əl grā/), *adj.* gray with ill-defined mottling of a darker shade. [ME, perh. **appelgrei*, with *d-* from DAPPLED; cf. OIcel *apal-grār, apli* dapple-gray horse]

Dap·sang (dup sung/), *n.* See **K2.**

D.A.R., See **Daughters of the American Revolution.**

Dar/by and Joan/ (där/bē; jōn), a happily married elderly couple who lead a placid, uneventful life. [after a couple mentioned in an 18th-century song]

Dar·dan (där/dᵊn), *adj., n.* Trojan. Also, **Dar·da·ni·an** (där dā/nē ən).

Dar·da·nelles (där/dᵊnelz/), *n.* (*construed as pl.*) the strait between European and Asian Turkey, connecting the Aegean Sea with the Sea of Marmara. 40 mi. long; 1–5 mi. wide. Ancient, **Hellespont.**

Dar·da·nus (där′dᵊnəs), *n.* *Class. Myth.* the ancestor of the Trojans.

dare (dâr), *v.*, **dared** or (*Archaic*) **durst, dared, dar·ing,** *n.* —*v.i.* **1.** to have the necessary courage or boldness for something; be bold enough. —*v.t.* **2.** to have the necessary courage (to do something). **3.** to meet defiantly. **4.** to challenge or provoke (a person) to make a show of his courage; defy: *to dare a man to fight.* —*n.* **5.** an act of daring; defiance; challenge. [ME *dar*, OE *dear(r)*, 1st and 3rd pers. sing. pres. indic. of *durran;* akin to OHG *(gi)tarran*] —**dar′er,** *n.*

Dare (dâr), *n.* **Virginia,** 1587–?, first child born of English parents in the Western Hemisphere.

dare·dev·il (dâr′dev′əl), *n.* **1.** a recklessly daring person. —*adj.* **2.** recklessly daring. —**dare′dev′il·ry, dare′dev′il·try,** *n.*

dare·say (dâr′sā′), *v.i.*, *v.t.* to venture to say (something); assume (something) as probable: *I daresay we will soon finish.* [ME *dar sayen* I dare to say]

Dar es Sa·laam (där′ es sə läm′), a seaport in and the capital of Tanzania, on the Indian Ocean. 430,000. Also, **Dar′-es-Sa·laam′.**

Dar·fur (där fo͝or′), *n.* a province in the W Sudan. 1,538,712 (est. 1961); 191,650 sq. mi. *Cap.:* El Fasher.

dar·ic (dar′ik), *n.* a gold coin and monetary unit of ancient Persia. [< Gk *Dāreik(ós)* (*statḗr*) Persian (stater)]

Dar·i·en (dâr′ē en′, dâr′ē en′), *n.* **1. Gulf of,** an arm of the Caribbean between NE Panama and NW Colombia. **2. Isthmus of,** former name of the Isthmus of Panama. Spanish, **Da·rién** (dä ʀyen′).

dar·ing (dâr′ing), *n.* **1.** adventurous courage; boldness. —*adj.* **2.** bold; intrepid; adventurous. —**dar′ing·ly,** *adv.* —**dar′ing·ness,** *n.* —**Syn. 1.** audacity, bravery. **2.** dauntless, venturesome, audacious, brave. —**Ant. 2.** timid, withdrawing, retiring.

Da·ri·us I (də rī′əs), (*Darius Hystaspes*) (*"the Great"*) 558?–486? B.C., king of Persia 521–486.

Dar·jee·ling (där jē′ling), *n.* **1.** a town in West Bengal, in NE India: mountain resort. 40,700 (1961). **2.** Also called **Darjee′ling tea′.** a tea grown in mountainous areas around the town of Darjeeling.

dark (därk), *adj.* **1.** having very little or no light: *a dark room.* **2.** radiating, admitting, or reflecting little light: *a dark color.* **3.** somber in hue: *a dark brown; a dark red.* **4.** not pale or fair; swarthy. **5.** brunette; dark-haired. **6.** gloomy; cheerless; dismal. **7.** sullen; frowning. **8.** evil; iniquitous; wicked. **9.** destitute of knowledge or culture; unenlightened. **10.** hard to understand; obscure. **11.** hidden or secret. **12.** silent or reticent. **13.** (of coffee) containing only a small amount of milk or cream. —*n.* **14.** the absence of light; darkness. **15.** night; nightfall. **16.** a dark place. **17.** a dark color. **18. in the dark, a.** in ignorance; uninformed: *As usual, he was in the dark about our plans for the evening.* **b.** in secrecy; concealed; obscure. —*v.i.* **19.** *Obs.* to grow dark; darken. [ME *derk*, OE *deorc;* cf. MHG *terken* to darken, hide] —**dark′ish,** *adj.* —**dark′ish·ness,** *n.*
—**Syn. 1.** DARK, DIM, OBSCURE, GLOOMY, MURKY refer to absence or insufficiency of light. DARK implies a more or less complete absence of light: *a dark night.* DIM implies faintness of light or indistinctness of form (resulting from the lack of light or from imperfect vision): *a dim outline.* OBSCURE implies dimness that may arise also from factors that interfere with light or vision: *obscure because of haze, smoke, fog.* GLOOMY means cloudy, ill-lighted, dusky: *a gloomy hall.* MURKY implies a thick, cloudy, or misty darkness: *a murky cave.* **4.** dusky, black. **10.** recondite, abstruse. —**Ant. 1.** lighted. **2.** bright. **6.** cheerful. **7.** pleasant.

Dark′ Ag′es, 1. the period in European history from about A.D. 476 to about 1000. **2.** the whole of the Middle Ages, from about A.D. 476 to the Renaissance.

Dark′ Con′tinent, The, Africa: so called, esp. during the 19th century, because little was known about it.

dark·en (där′kən), *v.t.* **1.** to make dark or darker. **2.** to make obscure. **3.** to make less white or clear in color. **4.** to make gloomy; sadden. **5.** to make blind. —*v.i.* **6.** to become dark or darker. **7.** to become obscure. **8.** to become less white or clear in color. **9.** to grow clouded, as with gloom or anger. [ME *derknen*] —**dark′en·er,** *n.*

dark·ey (där′kē), *n.*, *pl.* **-eys.** *Offensive.* darky.

dark-field (därk′fēld′), *adj.* *Optics.* of or pertaining to the illumination of an object seen through a microscope as bright against a dark background.

dark′ horse′, 1. a race horse, competitor, etc., about whom little is known or who unexpectedly wins. **2.** a person unexpectedly nominated, esp. in a political convention.

dark·ie (där′kē), *n.* *Offensive.* darky.

dark′ lan′tern, a lantern with a shutter that can be slid across its opening to obscure the light.

dar·kle (där′kəl), *v.i.*, **-kled, -kling. 1.** to appear dark; show indistinctly. **2.** to grow dark, gloomy, etc. [back formation from DARKLING, adv. taken as prp.]

dark·ling (därk′ling), *Chiefly Literary.* —*adv.* **1.** in the dark. —*adj.* **2.** growing dark. **3.** being or occurring in the dark; dark; obscure. [ME *derkeling*]

dark′ling bee′tle, any brown or black beetle of the family *Tenebrionidae*, the larvae of which feed on dead or decaying plant material, stored grain, etc.

dark·ly (därk′lē), *adv.* **1.** so as to appear dark. **2.** vaguely; mysteriously; menacingly. **3.** imperfectly; faintly. [ME *derkly*, OE *deorclīce* (in fig. sense only)]

dark′ meat′, meat that is dark-colored after cooking, as a turkey leg. Cf. **white meat** (def. 2).

dark·ness (därk′nis), *n.* **1.** the state or quality of being dark. **2.** absence or deficiency of light. **3.** wickedness or evil. **4.** obscurity; concealment. **5.** lack of knowledge. **6.** lack of sight; blindness. [ME *derknesse*, OE *deorcnysse*]

dark·room (därk′ro͞om′, -ro͝om′), *n.* *Photog.* a room in which film or the like is made, handled, or developed and from which the actinic rays of light are excluded.

dark·some (därk′səm), *adj.* *Chiefly Literary.* dark; darkish. —**dark′some·ness,** *n.*

dark′ star′, *Astron.* an invisible member of a binary or multiple star system.

dark·y (där′kē), *n.*, *pl.* **dark·ies.** *Offensive.* a Negro. Also, **darkey, darkie.**

Dar·lan (dar län′), *n.* **Jean Louis Xa·vier Fran·çois** (zhäɴ lwē gza vyā′ fräɴ swa′), 1881–1942, French naval officer and politician, active in the Vichy government.

dar·ling (där′ling), *n.* **1.** a person very dear to another; one dearly loved (often used in direct address). **2.** a person or thing in great favor. —*adj.* **3.** very dear; dearly loved. **4.** favorite; cherished. **5.** *Informal.* charming; lovable. [ME *derling*, OE *dēorling.* See DEAR[1], -LING[1]] —**dar′ling·ly,** *adv.* —**dar′ling·ness,** *n.*

Dar′ling Riv′er, a river in SE Australia, flowing SW into the Murray River. 1160 mi. long.

Dar·ling·ton (där′ling tən), *n.* a city in S Durham, in NE England. 84,162 (1961).

Darm·stadt (därm′stat; *Ger.* däʀm′shtät′), *n.* a city in central West Germany, S of Frankfort: former capital of Hesse. 139,600 (1963).

darn[1] (därn), *v.t.* **1.** to mend, esp. by interweaving stitches. —*n.* **2.** a darned place, as in a garment. [? ME *dern(en)*, OE *dernan* to hide] —**darn′er,** *n.*

darn[2] (därn), *Informal.* —*adj.*, *adv.* **1.** darned. —*v.t.* **2.** to curse; damn. —*n.* **3. give a darn.** See **damn** (def. 10). [var. of DAMN]

darned (därnd), *U.S. Informal.* —*adj.* **1.** irritating; damned; confounded. —*adv.* **2.** extremely; remarkably. [var. of DAMNED]

dar·nel (där′nᵊl), *n.* any of several annual or perennial grasses of the genus *Lolium*, having simple culms, flat leaves. [ME; cf. F (Walloon) *darnelle*, prob. < Gmc]

darn·ing (där′ning), *n.* **1.** the act of a person or thing that darns. **2.** the result produced. **3.** articles darned or to be darned.

darn′ing egg′, a smooth, egg-shaped piece of wood, ivory, marble, jade, or the like, for holding under a hole or tear to serve as a backing while darning.

darn′ing nee′dle, 1. a long needle with a long eye used in darning. **2.** *U.S. Dial.* a dragonfly.

Darn·ley (därn′lē), *n.* **Lord Henry Stewart** or **Stuart,** 1545–67, Scottish nobleman: second husband of Mary, Queen of Scots (father of James I of England).

Dar·row (dar′ō), *n.* **Clarence (Seward),** 1857–1938, U.S. lawyer.

dart (därt), *n.* **1.** a small, slender, pointed missile, usually feathered, that is propelled by hand or by a blowgun, rifle, etc. **2.** something resembling such a weapon, as the stinging member of an insect. **3. darts,** (*construed as sing.*) a game in which darts are thrown at a target having a bull's-eye in the center. **4.** an act of darting; a sudden swift movement. **5.** a tapered seam of fabric for adjusting the fit of a garment. —*v.i.* **6.** to move swiftly; spring or start suddenly and run swiftly. —*v.t.* **7.** to thrust or move suddenly or rapidly. **8.** to throw with a sudden thrust, as a dart. [ME < MF < Gmc] —**dart′ing·ly,** *adv.* —**dart′ing·ness,** *n.* —**Syn. 1.** arrow, barb. **6.** dash, bolt, shoot.

dart·board (därt′bōrd′, -bôrd′), *n.* the target used in the game of darts.

dart·er (där′tər), *n.* **1.** a person or thing that darts or moves swiftly. **2.** snakebird. **3.** any of several small, darting, fresh-water fishes of the perch family of eastern North America.

dar·tle (där′tᵊl), *v.t.*, *v.i.*, **-tled, -tling.** to dart or shoot forth repeatedly.

Dart·moor (därt′mo͝or, -mōr, -môr), *n.* **1.** a rocky plateau in SW England, in Devonshire. ab. 20 mi. long. **2.** a prison on this plateau.

Dar·win (där′win), *n.* **1. Charles (Robert),** 1809–82, English naturalist and author. **2.** his grandfather, **Erasmus,** 1731–1802, English naturalist and poet. **3.** a seaport in and the capital of Northern Territory, in N Australia. 12,326 (1961).

Dar·win·i·an (där win′ē ən), *adj.* **1.** pertaining to Charles Darwin or his doctrines. —*n.* **2.** a follower of Charles Darwin; a person who accepts Darwinism.

Darwin′ian the′ory, Darwinism.

Dar·win·ism (där′wə niz′əm), *n.* the Darwinian theory that the origin of species is derived by descent, with variation, from parent forms, through the natural selection of those best adapted to survive in the struggle for existence. —**Dar′win·ist, Dar·win·ite** (där′wə nīt′), *n.*, *adj.* —**Dar′win·is′tic,** *adj.*

dash (dash), *v.t.* **1.** to strike violently, esp. so as to break to pieces. **2.** to throw or thrust violently or suddenly. **3.** to splash violently; bespatter (with water, mud, etc.). **4.** to apply roughly, as by splashing. **5.** to mix or adulterate by adding another substance: *to dash wine with water.* **6.** to ruin or frustrate (hopes, plans, etc.). **7.** to depress; dispirit. **8.** to confound or abash. **9.** to accomplish quickly: *to dash a letter off.* —*v.i.* **10.** to strike with violence. **11.** to move with violence; rush. **12. dash off, a.** to hurry away; leave: *I must dash off now.* **b.** Also, **dash down.** to write, make, sketch, etc., hastily. —*n.* **13.** the throwing or splashing of liquid against something. **14.** the sound of such splashing. **15.** a small quantity of anything thrown into or mixed with something else: *a dash of salt.* **16.** a hasty stroke, esp. of a pen. **17.** the sign (—) used to note an abrupt break or pause in a sentence or hesitation in an utterance, to begin and end a parenthetic word, phrase, or clause, etc. **18.** an impetuous movement; a rush; a sudden onset. **19.** *Track.* a short race: *a 100-yard dash.* **20.** spirited action; élan; vigor in action or style. **21.** a dashboard. **22.** *Telegraphy.* a signal of longer duration than a dot, used in groups of dots, dashes, and spaces to represent letters, as in Morse code. **23.** *Archaic.* a violent and rapid blow or stroke. [ME *dassh(en)*, prob. < ON; cf. Dan *daske* slap, flap, Sw *daska*] —**Syn. 11.** dart, bolt. **15.** pinch, bit; touch, tinge; suggestion, soupçon. **20.** flourish.

dash·board (dash′bōrd′, -bôrd′), *n.* **1.** (in an automobile or similar vehicle) an instrument panel beneath the front window. **2.** a board or panel at the front of an open carriage or the like to protect the occupants from mud, dirt, etc.

da·sheen (da shēn′), *n.* the taro plant, *Colocasia esculenta,* native to tropical Asia, now cultivated in the southern U.S. for its edible tubers. [m. F *de Chine* of China]

dash·er (dash′ər), *n.* **1.** a person or thing that dashes. **2.** a kind of plunger with paddles at one end, for stirring and mixing liquids or semisolids in a churn, ice-cream freezer, etc.

da·shi·ki (də shē′kē), *n.* a loose, colorfully patterned pullover shirt for men, originally worn mainly in western Africa. [< Yoruba *danshiki*]

dash·ing (dash′ing), *adj.* **1.** impetuous; lively. **2.** brilliant; showy; stylish. —**dash′ing·ly,** *adv.*

dash·y (dash′ē), *adj.,* **dash·i·er, dash·i·est.** showy; dashing.

das·tard (das′tərd), *n.* **1.** a mean, sneaking coward. —*adj.* **2.** of or befitting a dastard; mean and cowardly. [late ME, prob. < ON **dasat,* neut. ptp. of *dasa* to get tired]

das·tard·ly (das′tərd lē), *adj.* cowardly; meanly; base; sneaking. —**das′tard·li·ness,** *n.*

das·y·ure (das′ē yŏŏr′), *n.* **1.** any of several nocturnal, carnivorous marsupials of the genus *Dasyurus* and related genera, of Australia, Tasmania, etc., typically having a spotted reddish or olive-brown coat. **2.** any of several related animals, as the Tasmanian devil or ursine dasyure. [< NL *Dasyūr(us)* < Gk *dasý(s)* hairy, shaggy (see DENSE) + *our(á)* tail + NL *-us* n. suffix] —**das·y·u·rine** (das′i yŏŏr′in, -in), *adj.* —**das′y·u′roid,** *adj., n.*

dat., dative.

da·ta (dā′tə, dat′ə, dä′tə), *n.* a pl. of **datum.**

da′ta bank′, **1.** the total fund of information gathered and stored by an organization for access and use, generally by computer, and contained in data bases, files, libraries, etc. **2.** See **data base.**

da′ta base′, a comprehensive collection of related data organized for quick access, generally in a computer. Also, **da·ta·base** (dā′tə bās′), **da′ta·base′.**

da′ta proc′essing, processing of information, esp. the handling of information by electronic machines in accordance with strictly defined systems of procedure.

da·ta·ry (dā′tə rē), *n., pl.* **-ries.** *Rom. Cath. Ch.* **1.** the office of the Curia Romana that investigates candidates for papal benefices. **2.** the cardinal who heads this office. [< ML **datāria* the office (where documents were dated); *datārius* the officer (who gave the dates)]

dat·cha (dä′chə), *n.* dacha.

date[1] (dāt), *n., v.,* **dat·ed, dat·ing.** —*n.* **1.** a particular point or period of time at which some event has happened or will happen. **2.** an inscription on a writing, coin, etc., that shows the time, or time and place, of writing, casting, delivery, etc. **3.** the time or period to which any event or thing belongs; period in general. **4.** the time during which anything lasts; duration. **5.** an appointment for a particular time. **6.** a social appointment, engagement, or occasion arranged with a person of the opposite sex. **7.** a person of the opposite sex with whom one has such an appointment. **8. dates,** the birth and death dates, usually in years, of a person. **9. down** or **up to date,** in agreement with or inclusive of the latest information; modern. **10. to date,** up to the present time; up to now. —*v.i.* **11.** to have a date: *The letter dates from 1873.* **12.** to belong to or originate in a particular period: *That dress dates from the 19th century.* **13.** to reckon from some point in time. **14.** to show age or become obsolescent: *Most fashions soon date.* **15.** to go out on dates with persons of the opposite sex. —*v.t.* **16.** to mark or furnish with a date. **17.** to ascertain or fix the period or point in time of; assign a period or point in time to. **18.** to show the age of; show to be old-fashioned. **19.** to make a date with; go out on dates with. [ME < MF < LL *dat(a),* n. use of fem. of *datus* (ptp. of *dare* to give), from the phrase *data* (*Romae*) written, given (at Rome)] —**dat′a·ble, date′a·ble,** *adj.* —**dat′a·ble·ness, date′a·ble·ness,** *n.* —**dat′er,** *n.*

date[2] (dāt), *n.* **1.** the oblong, fleshy fruit of the date palm, a staple food in northern Africa, Arabia, etc., and an important export. **2.** See **date palm.** [ME < OF < OPr *dat(il)* < L *dactyl(us)*; see DACTYL]

dat·ed (dā′tid), *adj.* **1.** having or showing a date. **2.** out-of-date; old-fashioned.

date·less (dāt′lis), *adj.* **1.** without a date; undated. **2.** endless; limitless. **3.** so old as to be undatable. **4.** of permanent interest regardless of age.

date′ line′. See **International Date Line.**

date·line (dāt′līn′), *n.* *Journalism.* a line giving the place of origin and usually the date of a news dispatch or the like.

date′ palm′, the date-bearing palm, *Phoenix dactylifera,* having a stem reaching a height of 60 feet and terminating in a crown of pinnate leaves.

da·tive (dā′tiv), *Gram.* —*adj.* **1.** noting a case that indicates the indirect object of a verb. —*n.* **2.** the dative case. **3.** a word or form in that case. [ME *datif* < L *datīv(us)* (*casus*) dative (case), lit., pertaining to giving case = *dat(us)* given (see DATE[1]) + *-īvus* -IVE; trans. of Gk *dotikḗ* (*ptôsis*)] —**da·ti·val** (dā tī′vəl), *adj.* —**da′tive·ly,** *adv.*

da·tum (dā′təm, dat′əm, dä′təm), *n., pl.* **da·ta** (dā′tə, dat′ə, dä′tə) for 1–4, **da·tums** for 3. **1. data,** (*often construed as sing.*) an individual fact, statistic, or piece of information or a group or body of facts, information, statistics, or the like, either historical or derived by calculation or experimentation: *Additional data is available from the president of the firm. These data represent the results of our analyses.* **2.** *Philos.* **a.** any fact assumed to be a matter of direct observation. **b.** any proposition assumed or given, from which conclusions may be drawn. **3.** *Survey., Civ. Eng.* any level surface, line, or point used as a reference in measuring elevations. **4.** Also called **sense datum.** *Epistemology.* the object of knowledge as presented to the mind. [< L: a thing given, neut. ptp. of *dare* to give]

da′tum plane′, *Survey.* See **tidal datum.**

da·tu·ra (də tŏŏr′ə, -tyŏŏr′ə), *n.* any solanaceous plant of the genus *Datura,* the species having funnel-shaped flowers, prickly pods, and narcotic properties. [< NL < Hindi *dhatūra* Jimson weed < Skt *dhattūra*] —**da·tu′ric,** *adj.*

dau., daughter.

daub (dôb), *v.t.* **1.** to cover or coat with soft, adhesive matter, such as plaster, mud, etc. **2.** to spread (plaster, mud, etc.) on or over something. **3.** to smear, soil, or defile. **4.** to paint unskillfully. —*v.i.* **5.** to daub something. **6.** to paint unskillfully. —*n.* **7.** material, esp. of an inferior kind, for daubing walls. **8.** anything daubed on. **9.** the act or an instance of daubing. **10.** a crude, inartistic painting. [ME *daube(n)* < OF *daube(r)* (to) whiten, paint < L *dealbāre*] —**daub′er,** *n.* —**daub′ing·ly,** *adv.* —**daub′y,** *adj.*

Dau·bi·gny (dō bē nyē′), *n.* **Charles Fran·çois** (shärl fräɴ swa′), 1817–78, French painter.

Dau·det (dō dā′, dô-; *Fr.* dō de′), *n.* **1. Al·phonse** (al fôɴs′), 1840–97, French novelist and short-story writer. **2.** his son, **Lé·on** (lā ôɴ′), 1867–1942, French novelist.

Dau·ga·va (dou′gä vä′), *n.* Lettish name of **Dvina.**

Dau·gav·pils (dou′gäf pēls′), *n.* a city in SE Latvia, in the W Soviet Union in Europe. 114,000. German, **Düna·burg.** Russian, **Dvinsk.**

daugh·ter (dô′tər), *n.* **1.** a female child or person in relation to her parents. **2.** any female descendant. **3.** a female related as if by the ties binding daughter to parent: *daughter of the church.* **4.** anything personified as female and considered with respect to its origin. [ME *doughter,* OE *dohtor;* c. G *Tochter,* Gk *thygátēr,* Skt *duhitā́*] —**daugh′ter·less,** *adj.* —**daugh′ter·like′,** *adj.*

daugh·ter-in-law (dô′tər in lô′), *n., pl.* **daugh·ters-in-law.** the wife of one's son. [ME *doughter in lawe*]

daugh·ter·ly (dô′tər lē), *adj.* pertaining to, befitting, or like a daughter. —**daugh′ter·li·ness,** *n.*

Daugh′ters of the Amer′ican Revolu′tion, a patriotic society of women descended from Americans of the Revolutionary period, organized in 1890. *Abbr.:* D.A.R.

Dau·mier (dō myā′), *n.* **Ho·no·ré** (ô nô rā′), 1808–79, French painter, cartoonist, and lithographer.

daunt (dônt, dänt), *v.t.* **1.** to overcome with fear; intimidate. **2.** to lessen the courage of; dishearten. [ME *da(u)nte(n)* < OF *dante(r),* alter. of *donter* (prob. by influence of *dangier* power, authority) < L *domitāre* to tame < *domit(us),* ptp. of *domāre* to tame] —**daunt′ing·ly,** *adv.* —**daunt′ing·ness,** *n.* —**Syn. 1.** overawe, subdue, dismay, frighten. **2.** discourage, dispirit. —**Ant. 2.** encourage.

daunt·less (dônt′lis, dänt′-), *adj.* not to be daunted; fearless; intrepid; bold. —**daunt′less·ly,** *adv.* —**daunt′less·ness,** *n.* —**Syn.** undaunted, daring, indomitable, brave.

dau·phin (dô′fin; *Fr.* dō faɴ′), *n., pl.* **-phins** (-finz; *Fr.* -faɴ′). the eldest son of a king of France, used as a title from 1349 to 1830. [< F; MF *dalphin,* after DAUPHINÉ, from an agreement to honor thus the province after its cession to France]

dau·phine (dô′fēn; *Fr.* dō fēn′), *n., pl.* **-phines** (-fēnz; *Fr.* -fēn′). the wife of a dauphin. [< F; MF *dalfine,* fem. of *dalphin* DAUPHIN]

Dau·phi·né (dō fē nā′), *n.* a region and former province of SE France. See map at **Provence.**

dau·phin·ess (dô′fi nis), *n.* dauphine. [earlier *daulphiness*]

D.A.V., Disabled American Veterans. Also, **DAV**

Da·vao (dä vou′), *n.* a seaport on SE Mindanao, in the S Philippines. 515,520.

D'Av·e·nant (dav′ə nənt), *n.* **Sir William,** 1606–68, English dramatist and producer: poet laureate 1638–68. Also, **Dav′e·nant.**

dav·en·port (dav′ən pōrt′, -pôrt′), *n.* **1.** *U.S.* a large sofa, often one convertible into a bed. **2.** *Chiefly Brit.* a small writing desk. [the desk is said to be named after a Captain *Davenport* who first commissioned it]

Dav·en·port (dav′ən pōrt′, -pôrt′), *n.* **1. John,** 1597–1670, Puritan clergyman: one of the founders of New Haven. **2.** a city in E Iowa, on the Mississippi River. 98,469 (1970).

Da·vid (dā′vid *for 1, 2;* da vēd′ *for 3*), *n.* **1.** died c970 B.C., the second king of Israel, reigned c1010–c970, successor to Saul. **2. Saint.** Also called **Saint Dewi.** A.D. c510–601?, Welsh bishop: patron saint of Wales. **3. Jacques Louis** (zhäk lwē), 1748–1825, French painter.

Da·vid I (dā′vid), 1084–1153, king of Scotland 1124–53.

Da·vid·son (dā′vid sən), *n.* **Jo** (jō), 1883–1952, U.S. sculptor.

Da·vies (dā′vēz), *n.* **Arthur Bow·en** (bō′ən), 1862–1928, U.S. painter.

da Vin·ci (də vin′chē; *It.* dä vēn′chē), **Le·o·nar·do** (lē′ə när′dō; *It.* le′ô när′dô). See **Vinci, Leonardo da.**

Da·vis (dā′vis), *n.* **1. Alexander Jackson,** 1803–92, U.S. architect. **2. Jefferson,** 1808–89, U.S. statesman: president of the Confederate States of America 1861–65. **3.** Also, **Davys. John,** c1550–1605, English navigator and explorer. **4. Owen,** 1874–1956, U.S. playwright. **5. Richard Harding,** 1864–1916, U.S. journalist, novelist, and playwright. **6. Stuart,** 1894–1964, U.S. painter and illustrator.

Da′vis Strait′, a strait between Canada and Greenland, connecting Baffin Bay and the Atlantic. 200–500 mi. wide.

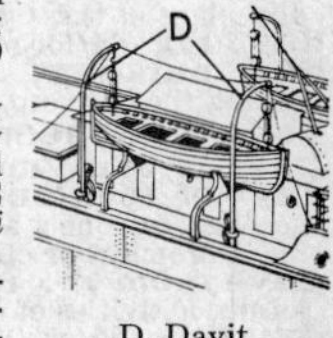

D, Davit

dav·it (dav′it, dā′vit), *n.* *Naut.* any of various cranelike devices used singly or in pairs for supporting, raising, and lowering boats, anchors, etc. [ME *daviot* < AF, appar. dim. of *Davi* David]

Da·vout (da vōō′), *n.* **Louis Ni·co·las** (lwē nē kô lä′), **Duke of Au·er·stadt** (ou′ər stat′), **Prince of Eck·mühl** (ek′myōōl), 1770–1823, marshal of France.

Da·vy (dā′vē), *n.* **Sir Humphry,** 1778–1829, English chemist.

Da′vy Jones′ (jōnz), *Naut.* the spirit of the sea; the sailors' devil. [?]

Da′vy Jones′s lock′er, the ocean's bottom, esp. as the grave of all who perish at sea.

Da′vy lamp′, a safety lamp formerly used by miners. [named after Sir H. DAVY]

Da·vys (dā′vis), *n.* **John.** See **Davis, John.**

daw (dô), *n.* **1.** jackdaw. **2.** *Obs.* simpleton; fool. [ME *dawe;* cf. OHG *taha*]

daw·dle (dôd′əl), *v.,* **-dled, -dling.** —*v.i.* **1.** to waste time; idle; trifle; loiter. —*v.t.* **2.** to waste (time) by trifling (usually fol. by *away*): *to dawdle away the morning.* [var. of *daddle* to TODDLE] —**daw′dler,** *n.* —**daw′dling·ly,** *adv.* —**Syn. 1.** See **loiter.**

Dawes (dôz), *n.* **Charles Gates,** 1865–1951, U.S. financier and diplomat: vice president of the U.S. 1925–29.

dawn (dôn), *n.* **1.** the first appearance of daylight in the morning. **2.** the beginning or rise of anything; advent. **3.** *Informal.* a sudden realization, understanding, or enlightenment. —*v.i.* **4.** to begin to grow light in the morning. **5.** to begin to open or develop. **6.** to begin to be perceived (usually fol. by *on*). [ME *dawen,* OE *dagian;* c. OIcel *daga,* MHG *tagen;* akin to DAY] —**dawn′like′,** *adj.* —**Syn. 1.** daybreak, sunrise. **6.** appear. —**Ant. 1.** sunset.

Daw·son (dô′sən), *n.* **1. Sir John William,** 1820–99, Canadian geologist and educator. **2.** a town in NW Canada, at the confluence of the Yukon and Klondike rivers: former capital of the Yukon Territory. 881 (1961).

Daw′son Creek′, a village in NE British Columbia, Canada, at SE terminus of Alaska Highway. 10,528.

Dax (däks), *n.* a city in SW France: mineral hot springs. 20,294.

day (dā), *n.* **1.** the interval of light between two successive nights; the time between sunrise and sunset. **2.** the light of day; daylight. **3.** *Astron.* **a.** Also called **mean solar day.** a division of time equal to 24 hours and representing the average length of the period during which the earth makes one rotation on its axis. **b.** a division of time equal to the time elapsed between two consecutive returns of the same terrestrial meridian to the sun. **c.** Also called **civil day.** a division of time equal to 24 hours but reckoned from one midnight to the next. Cf. **sidereal day. 4.** an analogous division of time for a planet other than the earth: *the Martian day.* **5.** the portion of a day allotted to labor: *an eight-hour day.* **6.** (*often cap.*) a day assigned to a particular purpose or observance: *New Year's Day.* **7.** a time considered as propitious or opportune. **8.** Often, **days.** a particular time or period: *the present day; in days of old.* **9.** period of existence, power, or influence: *in the day of the dinosaurs.* **10. call it a day,** to stop one's activity temporarily or permanently. **11. day in, day out,** every day without fail; continuously. [ME; OE *dæg;* c. G *Tag;* akin to Skt *dāha* heat]

Day·ak (dī′ak, -ək), *n., pl.* **-aks,** (*esp. collectively*) **-ak.** a member of any of the Malay peoples of interior Borneo. Also, **Dyak.**

Da·yan (dä yän′), *n.* **Mo·she** (mô she′), 1915–81, Israeli political and military leader.

day′ bed′, an armless couch that has a mattress with a removable cover for its seat, for use as a couch by day and as a bed at night. Also, **day′bed′.**

day′ blind′ness, hemeralopia (def. 1).

day·book (dā′bo͝ok′), *n.* **1.** *Bookkeeping.* a journal in which the transactions of the day are entered in the order of their occurrence. **2.** an appointment book.

day′ boy′, *Chiefly Brit.* a boarding-school student who lives at home.

day·break (dā′brāk′), *n.* the first appearance of daylight in the morning; dawn: *After a long, cold night, we finally rode off at daybreak.*

day′ camp′, a camp for children providing no sleeping facilities and attended only on weekdays. Cf. **summer camp.**

day′-care cen′ter, a day nursery, esp. one operated by private or public funds to provide child care at low cost.

day′ coach′, an ordinary railroad passenger car, as distinguished from a sleeping car, parlor car, etc.

day·dream (dā′drēm′), *n.* **1.** a visionary fancy indulged in while awake; reverie. —*v.i.* **2.** to indulge in such reveries. —**day′dream′er,** *n.* —**day′dream′y,** *adj.*

Day-Glo (dā′glō′), *n.* *Trademark.* a brilliant fluorescent paint.

day′ la′borer, an unskilled worker paid by the day.

day′ let′ter, a telegram sent during the day that is cheaper and slower than a regular telegram.

day·light (dā′līt′), *n.* **1.** the light of day. **2.** openness; publicity: *The scandal was brought into the daylight by a newspaper article.* **3.** the time of day; daytime. **4.** daybreak; dawn. —*adj.* **5.** noting, pertaining to, or simulating daylight. **6.** for use in or by daylight: *daylight film.* [ME]

day′light-sav′ing time′ (dā′līt′sā′ving), time one or more hours later than standard time, usually used in summer to give more hours of daylight to the working day.

day′ lil′y, 1. any liliaceous plant of the genus *Hemerocallis,* having yellow or orange flowers that commonly last only for a day. **2.** any liliaceous plant of the genus *Hosta* (*Funkia*), having white or blue flowers. **3.** the flower of any plant of these genera.

day·long (dā′lông′, -long′), *adj.* lasting all day.

day′ nurs′ery, a nursery for the care of small children during the day, esp. while their mothers are at work.

Day′ of Atone′ment, *Judaism.* See **Yom Kippur.**

Day′ of Judg′ment. See **Judgment Day.**

day′ of reck′oning, 1. the time when one is called to account for one's actions, to pay one's debts, or to fulfill one's promises or obligations. **2.** See **Judgment Day.**

day′ room′, a room on a military or air base for the leisure activities of enlisted personnel.

day·side (dā′sīd′), *n.* the side of a planet or the moon illuminated by the sun.

days (dāz), *adv.* in or during the day regularly: *They slept days and worked nights.*

day′ school′, 1. a school open for instruction on week days only. **2.** a school conducted in the daytime. **3.** a private school for pupils living outside the school (distinguished from *boarding school*).

days′ of grace′, days, usually three, allowed for payment after a bill or note falls due. [trans. of L *diēs grātiae*]

day·spring (dā′spring′), *n.* *Archaic.* daybreak. [ME]

day·star (dā′stär′), *n.* **1.** See **morning star. 2.** *Archaic.* the sun. [ME *daysterre,* OE *daegsteorra*]

day·time (dā′tīm′), *n.* the time between sunrise and sunset; day.

day-to-day (dā′tə dā′), *adj.* **1.** occurring each day; daily: *day-to-day chores; day-to-day worries.* **2.** concerned only with immediate needs or desires.

Day·ton (dāt′ən), *n.* a city in SW Ohio. 243,601 (1970).

Day·to′na Beach′ (dā tō′nə), a city in NE Florida: seashore resort. 45,327 (1970).

daze (dāz), *v.,* **dazed, daz·ing,** *n.* —*v.t.* **1.** to stun or stupefy, as with a blow or shock. **2.** to confuse; bewilder; dazzle: *The splendor of the palace dazed him.* —*n.* **3.** a dazed condition. [ME *dase(n)* < OIcel *dasa-* (as in *dasask* to become weary); cf. Dan *dase* to doze, mope] —**daz·ed·ly** (dā′zid lē), *adv.*

daz·zle (daz′əl), *v.,* **-zled, -zling,** *n.* —*v.t.* **1.** to overpower or dim the vision of by intense light. **2.** to bewilder, impress, or confuse by brilliance, splendor, etc. —*v.i.* **3.** to shine or reflect brilliantly. **4.** to be overpowered by light: *Her eyes dazzled in the glare.* **5.** to excite admiration by brilliance. —*n.* **6.** an act or instance of dazzling: *the dazzle of the spotlights.* **7.** something that dazzles; bewildering brightness, brilliance, or splendor. [DAZE + -LE] —**daz′zler,** *n.* —**daz′zling·ly,** *adv.*

dB, decibel; decibels. Also, **db**

D.B., 1. Bachelor of Divinity. **2.** Domesday Book.

d.b., daybook.

DBA, doing business as. Also, **dba**

D.B.E., Dame Commander of the Order of the British Empire.

DBI, *Trademark.* a compound, $C_{10}H_{15}N_5$, used in the form of its hydrochloride for the treatment of diabetes. Also called **phenformin.** [orig. *DB1,* a laboratory coinage, misunderstood as *DBI*]

D.Bib., Douay Bible.

dbl., double.

DC, 1. dental corps. **2.** Also, **D.C., dc, d-c, d.c.** *Elect.* direct current: an electric current of constant direction, having a magnitude that does not vary or varies only slightly. Cf. **AC. 3.** District of Columbia (approved esp. for use with zip code).

D.C., 1. *Music.* da capo. **2.** See **DC** (def. 2). **3.** See **District of Columbia.**

D.C.M., *Brit.* See **Distinguished Conduct Medal.**

DD, dishonorable discharge.

dd, 1. *Law.* today's date. [< L *dē datō*] **2.** delayed delivery. **3.** demand draft.

dd., delivered.

D.D., 1. demand draft. **2.** Doctor of Divinity.

D-day (dē′dā′), *n.* **1.** the day, usually unspecified, set for beginning or carrying out some enterprise or action, as launching a military offensive. **2.** June 6, 1944, the day of the Allied invasion of western Europe in World War II. Also, **D-Day.** [D (for *day*) + DAY; cf. H-HOUR]

D.D.S., Doctor of Dental Surgery.

D.D.Sc., Doctor of Dental Science.

DDT, a water-insoluble solid, $(ClC_6H_4)_2CHCCl_3$, used as an insecticide and as a scabicide and pediculicide. Also called **dichlorodiphenyltrichloroethane, chlorophenothane.** [*d*(*ichloro*)*d*(*iphenyl*)*t*(*richloroethane*)]

de (də; *Fr.* də; *Sp., It., Port.* de), *prep.* from; of: used in French, Spanish, Italian, and Portuguese personal names, originally to indicate place of origin: *Comte de Rochambeau; Don Ricardo de Aragón.* [< F, Sp, It, Pg < L]

DE, 1. Delaware (approved esp. for use with zip code). **2.** destroyer escort.

de' (də; *It.* de), *prep.* dei (used in Italian names as an elided form of *dei*): *de' Medici.*

de-, a formal element occurring in loan words from Latin (*decide*), also used as a prefix to indicate privation, removal, and separation (*dehumidify*), negation (*demerit; derange*), descent (*degrade; deduce*), reversal (*detract*), and intensity (*decompound*). Cf. **di-**[2], **dis-**[1]. [ME < L, comb. form repr. *de* (prep.) from, away from, of, out of, etc.; in some words, < F < L *dē-* or *dis-* DIS-[1]]

D.E., Doctor of Engineering.

Dea., Deacon.

dea·con (dē′kən), *n.* **1.** (in hierarchical churches) a member of the clerical order next below that of a priest. **2.** (in other churches) an appointed or elected officer having variously defined duties. **3.** (in Freemasonry) one of two officers in a masonic lodge. —*v.t.* **4.** to falsify (something), esp. to pack (vegetables or fruit) with only the finest pieces visible. [ME *deken,* OE *diacon* < LL *diācon(us)* < Gk *diākonos* servant, minister, deacon = *diā-* DIA- + *-konos* service] —**dea′con·ship′,** *n.*

dea·con·ess (dē′kə nis), *n.* (in certain Protestant churches) a woman belonging to an order or sisterhood dedicated to social service. [earlier *deaconisse,* m. LL *diāconissa,* fem. of *diāconus* DEACON; see -ESS]

dea·con·ry (dē′kən rē), *n., pl.* **-ries. 1.** the office of a deacon. **2.** deacons collectively. [ME *dekenry*]

de·ac·ti·vate (dē ak′tə vāt′), *v.,* **-vat·ed, -vat·ing.** —*v.t.* **1.** to cause to be inactive; end the effectiveness of. **2.** to demobilize or disband (a military unit). **3.** to render (a bomb, shell, or the like) inoperative. **4.** *Chem.* to render (a chemical, catalyst, etc.) inactive. —*v.i.* **5.** *Physical Chem.* to lose radioactivity. —**de·ac′ti·va′tion,** *n.* —**de·ac′ti·va′tor,** *n.*

dead (ded), *adj.* **1.** no longer living; deprived of life. **2.** not endowed with life; inanimate; inorganic: *dead stones.* **3.** resembling death; deathlike: *a dead sleep.* **4.** bereft of sensation; numb. **5.** lacking sensitivity of feeling; insensitive: *dead to all sense of shame.* **6.** incapable of being moved emotionally. **7.** (of an emotion) no longer felt: *a dead passion.* **8.** no longer current or prevalent; obsolete: *a dead controversy.* **9.** (of a language) no longer in general use as a means of oral communication among a people, as Latin. **10.** utterly tired; exhausted. **11.** infertile; barren: *dead land.* **12.** not moving or circulating, as air or water; stagnant. **13.** no longer functioning, operating, or productive. **14.** put out; extinguished. **15.** tasteless or flat, as liquor. **16.** flat, rather than glossy, bright, or brilliant. **17.** without resonance; anechoic. **18.** without resilience or bounce: *a dead tennis ball.* **19.** lacking the customary activity; dull; inactive: *a dead market.* **20.** without vitality, spirit, enthusiasm, or the like: *a dead party.* **21.** complete; absolute: *The plan was a dead loss.* **22.** sudden or abrupt, as the complete stoppage of an action. **23.** accurate; sure; unerring: *a dead shot.* **24.** direct; straight: *a dead line.* **25.** exact; precise: *the dead center of a circle.* **26.** not fruitful; unproductive: *dead capital.* **27.** *Sports.* out of play: *a dead ball.* **28.** (of a golf ball) lying so close to the hole as to make holing on the next stroke a virtual certainty. **29.** *Elect.* **a.** free from electric charge and from any electric connection to a source of potential difference. **b.** not having a potential different from that of the earth. **30.** (of a lock or bolt) not closing automatically. **31.** (of the mouth of a horse) no longer sensitive to the pressure of a bit. **—*n.* 32.** the period of greatest darkness, coldness, etc.: *the dead of night; the dead of winter.* **33.** (*construed as pl.*) dead persons collectively (usually prec. by *the*): *prayers for the dead.* **—*adv.* 34.** absolutely; completely. **35.** with abrupt and total stoppage of motion, action, or the like: *He stopped dead.* **36.** directly; exactly; diametrically: *dead ahead.* [ME *deed,* OE *dēad;* c. Goth *dauths,* G *tot,* OIcel *daudh*(*r*); orig. ptp. See DIE[1]] **—dead′ness,** *n.*

—Syn. 1. defunct. DEAD, DECEASED, LIFELESS refer to a being or thing that does not have or appear to have life. DEAD is usually applied to that which had life but from which life is now gone: *dead trees, animals; They recovered the dead bodies.* DECEASED, a more formal word than dead, is applied to human beings who no longer have life: *a deceased member of the church.* LIFELESS is applied to that which may have had life but which does not have it or appear to have it now, or to that which is inanimate: *The lifeless body of a child was taken out of the water. She lay lifeless in a faint. Minerals consist of lifeless materials.* **5.** unfeeling, indifferent, callous, cold. **11.** sterile. **12.** still, motionless, inert. **13.** inoperative. **21.** utter, entire, total. **—Ant. 1.** living, alive, quick.

dead·beat (*adj.* ded′bēt′; *n.* ded′bēt′), *adj.* **1.** *Horol.* noting any of various escapements acting without recoil of the locking parts from the shock of contact. See diag. at **escapement. —*n.* 2.** *Informal.* a person who avoids paying his debts or share of expenses; sponger.

dead′ cen′ter, 1. (in a reciprocating engine) either of two positions at which the crank cannot be turned by the connecting rod, occurring at each end of a stroke when the crank and connecting rod are in the same line. **2.** See under **center** (def. 15). **—dead′-cen′ter,** *adj.*

dead·en (ded′ᵊn), *v.t.* **1.** to make less sensitive, active, energetic, or forcible; dull; weaken. **2.** to make impervious to sound, as a floor. **—*v.i.* 3.** to become dead. **—dead′en·er,** *n.*

dead′ end′, 1. a street, water pipe, etc., that is closed at one end. **2.** a position that offers no hope of progress. **—dead′-end′,** *adj.*

dead·en·ing (ded′ᵊning), *n.* **1.** a device or material employed to deaden or render dull. **2.** a device or material preventing the transmission of sound.

dead·eye (ded′ī′), *n., pl.* **-eyes.** *Naut.* either of a pair of disks of hardwood having holes through which a lanyard is reeved and concave rims to receive a strop from a shroud, stay, etc., or from a chain or chain plate, the disks and lanyard being used to tighten the shroud or stay.

Deadeyes

dead·fall (ded′fôl′), *n.* a trap in which a weight falls on and crushes the prey.

dead′ hand′, 1. the inhibiting effect of the past. **2.** *Law.* mortmain.

dead·head (ded′hed′), *Informal.* **—*n.* 1.** a person who uses a ticket, as for a train ride, without paying for it. **2.** a stupid person; dullard. **3.** *Railroads.* a car or train being moved while empty. **—*v.t.* 4.** *Railroads.* to move (an empty car or train). **—*v.i.* 5.** (of a plane, truck, etc.) to return empty or without a payload. **6.** to act or serve as a deadhead.

dead′ heat′, a race ending in a tie.

dead′ let′ter, 1. a law, ordinance, etc., that has lost its force but has not been formally repealed or abolished. **2.** a letter that cannot reach the addressee or be returned to the sender, usually because of incorrect address, and that is sent to and handled in a special division or department (**dead′-let′ter of′fice**) of a general post office. **—dead′-let′ter,** *adj.*

dead·light (ded′līt′), *n.* *Naut.* **1.** a strong shutter able to be screwed against the interior of a porthole in heavy weather. **2.** a thick pane of glass set in the hull or deck to admit light.

dead·line (ded′līn′), *n.* **1.** the latest time for finishing something, as copy for a publication. **2.** a line or limit that must not be passed.

dead′ load′. See under **load** (def. 5).

dead·lock (ded′lok′), *n.* **1.** a complete standstill, as in a dispute. **—*v.t.* 2.** to bring to a deadlock. **—*v.i.* 3.** to come to a deadlock.

dead·ly (ded′lē), *adj.,* **-li·er, -li·est,** *adv.* **—*adj.* 1.** causing or tending to cause death; fatal: *a deadly poison.* **2.** seeking to kill or destroy; implacable: *a deadly enemy.* **3.** like death: *a deadly pallor.* **4.** excessive; inordinate: *deadly haste.* **5.** extremely accurate: *deadly aim.* **6.** excruciatingly boring. **—*adv.* 7.** in a manner resembling or suggesting death: *deadly pale.* **8.** excessively; completely: *deadly dull.* [ME *deedli*(*ch*), OE *dēadlīce*] **—dead′li·ness,** *n.* **—Syn. 1.** See **fatal.**

dead′ly night′shade, 1. belladonna (def. 1). **2.** See **black nightshade.**

dead′ly sins′, the seven sins of pride, covetousness, lust, anger, gluttony, envy, and sloth. Also called **seven deadly sins.** [ME *deedly synnes*]

dead′-man's float′ (ded′manz′), the act of floating face down, with the arms and legs loosely extended.

dead′ march′, a piece of solemn music for a funeral procession.

dead·pan (ded′pan′), *adj., adv., v.,* **-panned, -pan·ning. —*adj.* 1.** marked by a careful pretense of seriousness or calm detachment: *deadpan humor.* **2.** displaying no emotional or personal involvement: *a deadpan style.* **—*adv.* 3.** in a deadpan manner. **—*v.i., v.t.* 4.** to behave or perform in a deadpan manner.

dead′ reck′oning, *Navig.* **1.** calculation of one's position on the basis of distance run on various headings since the last precisely observed position, as accurate allowance as possible being made for wind, currents, compass errors, etc. **2.** position as so calculated.

Dead′ Sea′, a salt lake between Israel and Jordan: the lowest lake in the world. 46 mi. long; 10 mi. wide; 1293 ft. below sea level.

Dead′ Sea′ Scrolls′, a number of scrolls dating from c100 B.C. to A.D. 135, containing liturgical writings and some Old Testament books in Hebrew and Aramaic, found in 1947 and thereafter in caves near the Dead Sea.

dead′ set′, determined; resolute: *His family was dead set against the marriage.*

dead′ weight′, 1. the heavy, unrelieved weight of anything inert. **2.** a heavy or oppressive burden.

dead′weight ton′nage (ded′wāt′), *Naut.* the capacity in long tons of cargo, passengers, fuel, stores, etc. (**dead′weight tons′**), of a vessel: the difference between the loaded and light displacement tonnage of the vessel. Also called **dead′weight capac′ity.**

dead·wood (ded′wŏŏd′), *n.* **1.** the dead branches on a tree; dead branches or trees. **2.** *Bowling.* pins remaining on the alley after having been knocked down by the ball. **3.** useless and burdensome persons or things: *He cut the deadwood from his team.* **4.** *Naut.* the relatively narrow, vertical, solid construction serving only as reinforcement and filling for the space between the keel of a vessel and the stem or sternpost and not as an integral part of the structure of the hull.

deaf (def), *adj.* **1.** partially or wholly lacking or deprived of the sense of hearing; unable to hear. **2.** refusing to listen; heedless (often fol. by *to*): *deaf to all advice.* [ME *deef,* OE *dēaf;* c. MLG *dōf,* D *doof,* OHG *toub*] **—deaf′ly,** *adv.* **—deaf′ness,** *n.*

deaf-and-dumb (def′ən dum′), *adj.* unable to hear or speak.

deaf′-and-dumb′ al′phabet, the manual alphabet used by deaf-mutes as a substitute for speech.

deaf·en (def′ən), *v.t.* **1.** to make deaf. **2.** to stun with noise. **—deaf′en·ing·ly,** *adv.*

deaf-mute (def′myōōt′, -myōōt′), *n.* a deaf-and-dumb person. [trans. of F *sourd-muet*] **—deaf′-mute′ness, deaf′-mut′ism,** *n.*

deal[1] (dēl), *v.,* **dealt, deal·ing,** *n.* **—*v.i.* 1.** to treat, handle, or be concerned with some subject or matter (usually fol. by *with* or *in*): *He dealt with the first question. Botany deals with the study of plants.* **2.** to take action with respect to a thing or person (usually fol. by *with*): *Law courts must deal with lawbreakers.* **3.** to behave in a specified manner: *He deals fairly with all people.* **4.** to trade or do business. **5.** to distribute the cards in a game. **—*v.t.* 6.** to give to one as his share; apportion. **7.** to distribute among a number of recipients, as the cards required in a game. **8.** to give a player (a specific card) in dealing. **9.** to deliver; administer: *to deal a blow.* **—*n.* 10.** *Informal.* **a.** a business transaction. **b.** a bargain or arrangement for mutual advantage. **c.** a secret or underhand agreement or bargain. **d.** treatment received in dealing with another: *a raw deal.* **11.** an indefinite but large quantity, amount, extent, or degree (usually prec. by *good* or *great*): *a good deal of work; a great deal of money.* **12.** an act of dealing or distributing. **13.** *Cards.* **a.** the distribution of cards to the players. **b.** the set of cards in one's hand. **c.** the turn of a player to deal. **d.** the duration of a deal. [ME *dele*(*n*), OE *dǣlan* (c. G *teilen,* etc.) < *dǣl* part (c. G *Teil*)] **—Syn. 3.** act. **4.** traffic. **7.** allot, assign, dole, mete, dispense. **10b.** pact, contract. **—Ant. 7.** collect.

deal[2] (dēl), *n.* **1.** a board or plank, esp. of fir or pine, cut to any of various standard sizes. **2.** such boards collectively. **3.** fir or pine wood. **—*adj.* 4.** made of deal. [ME *dele* < MLG or MD; see THILL]

de·a·late (dē′ā lāt′, -lit), *Entomol.* **—*adj.* 1.** Also, **de·a·lat·ed** (dē′ā lā′tid). having no wings as a result of having bitten or rubbed them off. **—*n.* 2.** a dealate insect. **—de′a·la′tion,** *n.*

deal·er (dē′lər), *n.* **1.** a person who conducts himself toward another or others in a specified manner: *a plain dealer.* **2.** a person whose business is buying and selling, esp. wholesale; trader; merchant. **3.** *Cards.* the player distributing the cards. [ME *delere,* OE *dǣlere*]

deal·er·ship (dē′lər ship′), *n.* **1.** authorization to sell a commodity. **2.** a sales agency or distributor having such authorization.

deal·fish (dēl′fish′), *n., pl.* **-fish·es,** (*esp. collectively*) **-fish.** a ribbonfish, esp. *Trachipterus arcticus.*

deal·ing (dē′ling), *n.* Usually, **dealings.** relations; business: *frequent dealings; commercial dealings.* [ME *deling*]

dealt (delt), *v.* pt. and pp. of **deal**[1].

de·am·i·nate (dē am′ə nāt′), *v.t.,* **-nat·ed, -nat·ing.** *Chem.* to remove the amino from (a compound). **—de·am′i·na′tion,** *n.*

dean[1] (dēn), *n.* **1.** *Educ.* **a.** the head of a faculty in a university or college. **b.** the official in charge of undergraduate students at an English university. **c.** any official in an American college or university having charge of some aspect of administration, as counseling, discipline, or admissions. **2.** *Eccles.* **a.** the head of the chapter of a cathedral or a collegiate church. **b.** Also called **vicar forane.** a priest in the Roman Catholic Church appointed by a bishop to take care of the affairs of a division of a diocese. **3.** the senior member, in length of service, of any group, profession, etc.: *the dean of American journalists.* **—*v.i.* 4.** to serve as an academic dean. [ME *deen* < MF *deien* < LL *decān*(*us*) chief of ten = L *dec*(*em*) ten + *-ānus* -AN] **—dean′ship,** *n.*

dean[2] (dēn), *n.* *Brit.* dene.

dean·er·y (dē′nə rē), *n., pl.* **-er·ies.** the office, jurisdiction, district, or residence of an ecclesiastical dean. [ME *denerie*]

dean's′ list′, a list of students of high scholastic standing, compiled by a college or university usually at the end of each semester or academic year.

dear[1] (dēr), *adj.* **1.** beloved or loved. **2.** (in the salutation of a letter) highly esteemed: *Dear Sir.* **3.** precious in one's regard: *our dearest possessions.* **4.** heartfelt; earnest: *one's dearest wish.* **5.** high-priced; expensive. **6.** excessive; high: *a dear price to pay for one's independence.* **7.** *Obs.* difficult to get; scarce. **8.** *Obs.* worthy; honorable. **—*n.* 9.** a person who is good, kind, or generous: *You're a dear to help me do the work.* **10.** a beloved one (often used in direct address): *my dear.* **—*adv.* 11.** dearly; fondly. **12.** at a high price. —*interj.* **13.** (used as an exclamation of surprise, distress, or the like.) [ME *dere,* OE *dēore;* c. OHG *tiuri,* OIcel *dȳrr*] —**dear′ly,** *adv.* —**dear′ness,** *n.* —**Syn. 1.** darling.

dear[2] (dēr), *adj. Archaic.* hard; grievous. [ME *dere,* OE *dēor* wild; cf. OHG *tiorīh* wild]

Dear·born (dēr′bərn, -bôrn), *n.* **1.** a city in SE Michigan near Detroit. 104,199 (1970). **2.** See **Fort Dearborn.**

Dear′born Heights′, a city in SE Michigan, W of Detroit. 80,069 (1970).

Dear′ John′, *Slang.* a letter from a girl or woman informing her boyfriend or fiancé that she is jilting him.

dearth (dûrth), *n.* **1.** an inadequate supply of something; scarcity; lack. **2.** scarcity and dearness of food; famine. [ME *derthe.* See DEAR[1], -TH[1]]

dear·y (dēr′ē), *n., pl.* **dear·ies.** *Informal.* darling (usually used by women as a term of address): *Mabel, deary, you just don't understand men.* Also, **dear′ie.** [DEAR[1] + -Y[2]]

death (deth), *n.* **1.** the act of dying; the end of life; the total and permanent cessation of all the vital functions of an animal or plant. **2.** an instance of this. **3.** the state of being dead. **4.** (*usually cap.*) the agent of death personified, usually represented as a man or a skeleton carrying a scythe. Cf. **Grim Reaper. 5.** extinction; destruction. **6.** manner of dying: *a hero's death.* **7.** *Law.* See **civil death. 8.** Also called **spiritual death.** loss or absence of Divine Grace; eternal damnation. **9.** bloodshed or murder. **10.** a cause of death: *You'll be the death of me!* **11.** *Archaic.* pestilence; plague. Cf. **Black Death. 12. be death on,** *Informal.* **a.** to be excessively critical of. **b.** to be snobbish toward. **c.** *Baseball.* to be able to cope with easily: *He's death on curves.* **13. do to death, a.** to kill, esp. to murder. **b.** to repeat to the point of monotony. **14. put to death,** to kill; execute. **15. to death,** to an extreme degree; thoroughly: *sick to death of the heat.* [ME *deeth,* OE *dēath;* c. G *Tod,* Goth *dauth(us);* akin to OIcel *deya* to die] —**death′ful,** *adj.* —**death′like′,** *adj.* —**Syn. 1.** decease, demise, passing. —**Ant. 1.** life.

death·bed (deth′bed′), *n.* **1.** the bed on which a person dies. —*adj.* **2.** of, pertaining to, or during the last few hours before a person dies: *a deathbed confession.* [ME *deethbed*]

death′ ben′efit, money to be paid under the terms of an insurance policy to the designated beneficiary of a deceased.

death·blow (deth′blō′), *n.* a blow causing death.

death′ cam′as, **1.** any of several liliaceous herbs of the genus *Zygadenus,* of the Southern and Western U.S. and Canada. **2.** the root of any of these herbs, poisonous to sheep and other animals.

death′ certif′icate, a certificate signed by a doctor, giving information, as age, sex, etc., about a deceased person and the time, place, and cause of death.

death′ cup′, **1.** a poisonous mushroom of the genus *Amanita,* part of which persists around the base of the stipe as a definite membranous cup. **2.** the cup.

death′ dut′y, *Brit. Law.* an inheritance tax.

death′ house′, a building or part of a prison in which persons condemned to death await execution.

death′ in′stinct, **1.** predisposition to self-destruction. **2.** Also called **death wish.** (in psychoanalytic theory) a suicidal impulse as manifested by passivity, withdrawal, or the compulsive repetition of a task.

death′ knell′, **1.** a harbinger of the end, death, or destruction of something. **2.** See **passing bell.**

death·less (deth′lis), *adj.* **1.** not subject to death; immortal. **2.** unceasing; perpetual. **3.** likely to endure because of superior quality, timelessness, etc. (often used ironically): *deathless prose.* —**death′less·ly,** *adv.* —**death′less·ness,** *n.*

death·ly (deth′lē), *adj.* **1.** causing death; deadly; fatal. **2.** like death. **3.** of, pertaining to, or indicating death: *a deathly odor from the sepulcher.* —*adv.* **4.** in the manner of death. **5.** very; utterly: *deathly afraid.* [ME *dethlich,* OE *dēathlīc*] —**death′li·ness,** *n.*

death′ mask′, a cast taken of a person's face after death. Cf. **life mask.**

death′ rat′tle, a sound produced by a dying person, caused by the passage of air through the mucus in the throat.

death′ row′, a row of prison cells for prisoners awaiting execution.

death′ sen′tence, a sentence condemning a convicted felon to execution by the state. Cf. **life sentence.**

death's-head (deths′hed′), *n.* a human skull, esp. as a symbol of mortality.

death's′-head moth′, a European hawk moth, *Acherontia atropos,* having markings on the back of the thorax that resemble a human skull.

deaths·man (deths′mən), *n., pl.* **-men.** *Archaic.* an executioner.

death·trap (deth′trap′), *n.* a structure or situation involving imminent risk of death: *They escaped from the deathtrap just before it exploded.*

Death′ Val′ley, an arid basin in E California and S Nevada: lowest land in North America. ab. 1500 sq. mi.; 280 ft. below sea level.

death′ war′rant, **1.** an official order authorizing the execution of the sentence of death. **2.** anything that ends hope, expectation, etc.

death·watch (deth′woch′, -wôch′), *n.* **1.** a vigil beside a dying or dead person. **2.** a guard set over a condemned person before execution. **3.** any of several beetles of the family *Anobiidae* that make a ticking sound as they bore through wood.

death′ wish′. See **death instinct** (def. 2).

Deau·ville (dō′vil; *Fr.* dō vēl′), *n.* a coastal resort in NW France, S of Le Havre. 5239 (1962).

deb (deb), *n. Informal.* a debutante. [by shortening]

deb., debenture.

de·ba·cle (dā bä′kəl, -bak′əl, də-), *n.* **1.** a general breakup or dispersion; sudden collapse. **2.** a breaking up of ice in a river. **3.** a violent rush of waters or ice. [< F *débâcle* < *débâcl(er)* (to) unbar, clear = *dé-* DIS-[1] + *bâcler* to bar << L *bacul(um)* stick, rod]

de·bar (di bär′), *v.t.,* **-barred, -bar·ring. 1.** to shut out or exclude from a place or condition. **2.** to hinder or prevent; prohibit. [late ME < MF, OF *desbarr(er)* (to) lock out, bar. See DIS-[1], BAR[1]] —**de·bar′ment,** *n.* —**Syn. 1.** See **exclude.**

de·bark[1] (di bärk′), *v.t., v.i.* to disembark. [< F *débarque(r).* See DIS-[1], BARK[3]] —**de·bar·ka·tion** (dē′bär kā′shən), *n.*

de·bark[2] (dē bärk′), *v.t.* to remove the bark from (a log). [DE- + BARK[2]]

de·base (di bās′), *v.t.,* **-based, -bas·ing. 1.** to reduce in quality or value; adulterate. **2.** to lower in rank, dignity, or significance. [DE- + BASE[2]; cf. ABASE] —**de·bas·ed·ness** (di bā′sid nis, -bāst′-), *n.* —**de·base′ment,** *n.* —**de·bas′er,** *n.* —**de·bas′ing·ly,** *adv.* —**Syn. 1.** lower, vitiate, corrupt; contaminate, pollute, defile. **2.** degrade, reduce.

de·bat·a·ble (di bā′tə bəl), *adj.* **1.** in dispute; open to question; doubtful: *Whether he is qualified for the job is debatable.* **2.** capable of being debated: *to be willing to discuss debatable issues.* [late ME < MF]

de·bate (di bāt′), *n., v.,* **-bat·ed, -bat·ing.** —*n.* **1.** a discussion, esp. of a public question in an assembly. **2.** deliberation; consideration. **3.** a contest in which the affirmative and negative sides of a proposition are advocated by opposing speakers. **4.** *Archaic.* strife; contention. —*v.i.* **5.** to engage in discussion, esp. in a legislative or public assembly. **6.** to deliberate; consider; discuss or argue. **7.** *Obs.* to fight; quarrel. —*v.t.* **8.** to discuss or argue (a question, issue, or the like), as in a legislative assembly. **9.** to dispute about. **10.** to engage in formal argumentation or disputation with (another person, group, etc.). **11.** to deliberate upon; consider. **12.** *Archaic.* to contend for or over. [ME *debate(n)* < MF *debat(re).* See DE-, BATE[2]] —**de·bat′er,** *n.* —**de·bat′ing·ly,** *adv.* —**Syn. 1.** argument, controversy, disputation, contention. **6.** dispute, contend.

de·bauch (di bôch′), *v.t.* **1.** to corrupt by sensuality, intemperance, etc.; debase. **2.** *Archaic.* to lead away, as from allegiance or duty. —*v.i.* **3.** to indulge in debauchery. —*n.* **4.** a period of debauchery. **5.** intemperance; debauchery. [< F *débauche(r),* OF *desbaucher* to seduce from duty, corrupt = *des-* DE- + *baucher* < ?] —**de·bauch′er,** *n.* —**de·bauch′ment,** *n.*

de·bauched (di bôcht′), *adj.* **1.** displaying the effect of excessive indulgence in sensual pleasure. **2.** corrupt; debased: *debauched morals; a debauched nation.* —**de·bauch·ed·ly** (di bô′chid lē), *adv.* —**de·bauch′ed·ness,** *n.*

deb·au·chee (deb′ô chē′, -shē′), *n.* a person given to debauchery. [< F *débauché* (ptp. of *débaucher*)]

de·bauch·er·y (di bô′chə rē), *n., pl.* **-er·ies. 1.** excessive indulgence in sensual pleasures; intemperance. **2.** *Archaic.* seduction from duty, allegiance, or virtue.

de·ben·ture (di ben′chər), *n.* **1.** See **debenture bond. 2.** a certificate of drawback issued at a custom house. [ME *debentur* < L *dēbentur (mihi)* there are owing (to me) = *dēb-* owe + *-entur* 3rd pers. pl. indic. pass. suffix] —**de·ben′tured,** *adj.*

deben′ture bond′, a corporation bond unsecured by any mortgage, dependent on the credit of the issuer.

de·bil·i·tate (di bil′i tāt′), *v.t.,* **-tat·ed, -tat·ing.** to make weak or feeble; enfeeble. [< L *dēbilitāt(us)* (ptp. of *dēbilitāre*) = *dēbil(is)* weak + *-ātus* -ATE[1]] —**de·bil′i·ta′tion,** *n.* —**de·bil′i·ta′tive,** *adj.*

de·bil·i·ty (di bil′i tē), *n., pl.* **-ties. 1.** the state of being weak or feeble; weakness: *The old man's debility prevented him from getting out of bed.* **2.** *Pathol.* a condition of the body in which there is weakening of the vital functions. [ME *debylite* < MF *debilite* < L *dēbilitās*]

deb·it (deb′it), *n.* **1.** the recording of debt in an account. **2.** *Bookkeeping.* **a.** that which is entered in an account as a debt; a recorded item of debt. **b.** any entry or the total shown on the debit, or left-hand, side of a ledger. **c.** the left-hand side of an account on which such entries are made (opposed to *credit*). —*v.t.* **3.** to charge (a person, account, etc.) with a debt. **4.** to charge as a debt: *The store debited the purchase to her account.* **5.** *Bookkeeping.* to enter upon the debit side of an account. [ME < OF < L *dēbit(um)* DEBT]

deb·o·nair (deb′ə nâr′), *adj.* **1.** of pleasant manners; courteous, gracious, and charming. **2.** gay; carefree. Also, **deb′o·naire′, deb′on·naire′.** [ME *debonaire, debonere,* OF *debonaire,* orig. phrase *de bon aire* of good lineage] —**deb′o·nair′ly,** *adv.* —**deb′o·nair′ness,** *n.*

de·bone (dē bōn′), *v.t.,* **-boned, -bon·ing.** to remove the bones from; bone.

Deb·o·rah (deb′ər ə), *n.* a prophetess and judge of Israel. Judges 4, 5. Also, *Douay Bible,* **Deb′bo·ra.**

de·bouch (di bo͞osh′, -bouch′), *v.i.* **1.** to march out from a narrow or confined place into open country, as a body of troops. **2.** *Phys. Geog.* **a.** to emerge from a relatively narrow valley upon an open plain, as a river. **b.** to flow from a small valley into a larger one. **3.** to come forth; emerge. [< F *déboucher* = *dé-* DIS-[1] + *bouche* mouth (< L *bucca* cheek, mouth) + *-er* inf. suffix] —**de·bouch′ment,** *n.*

De·bre·cen (de′bʀe tsen′), *n.* a city in E Hungary. 129,671 (1960).

de·bride·ment (di brēd′mənt, dā-), *n.* surgical removal of foreign matter and dead tissue from a wound. [< F = *débrid(er)* (to) take away the bridle, MF *desbrider.* See DE-, BRIDLE, -MENT]

de·brief (dē brēf′), *v.t.* to interrogate (a soldier, astronaut, etc.) on return from a mission. —**de·brief′ing,** *n.*

de·bris (də brē′, dā′brē *or, esp. Brit.,* deb′rē), *n.* **1.** the remains of anything broken down or destroyed; ruins; fragments; rubbish. **2.** *Geol.* an accumulation of loose fragments of rock. Also, **dé·bris′.** [< F *débris,* MF *debris* < *debris(er)* (to) break up (in pieces), OF *debrisier.* See DE-, BRUISE]

de Bro·glie (*Fr.* də bʀô′yᵊ), **Louis Vic·tor** (*Fr.* lwē vēk tôr′). See **Broglie, Louis Victor de.**

de·bruise (də bro͞oz′, dē-), *v.t.,* **-bruised, -bruis·ing.** *Heraldry.* to overlay (a charge) other than an ordinary with an ordinary. [ME *debruse(n), debrise(n)* (to) break down, crush < OF *debr(u)is(ier).* See DEBRIS]

Debs (debz), *n.* **Eugene V(ictor),** 1855–1926, U.S. labor leader: five times Socialist candidate for president 1900–20.

debt (det), *n.* **1.** something that is owed; something that one person is bound to pay to or perform for another: *a debt of five dollars.* **2.** a liability or obligation to pay or render something: *My debt to her for advice is not to be discharged easily.* **3.** the condition of being under such an obligation: *His gambling losses put him deeply in debt.* **4.** *Theol.* an offense requiring reparation; a sin; a trespass. [ME *dette* < OF < VL *dēbit(a)* (neut. pl.), L *dēbit(um)* (neut. sing.), n. use of *dēbitus* (ptp. of *dēbēre* to owe) = *dē-* DE- + *(ha)bēre* to have] —**debt′less,** *adj.* —**Syn. 1.** obligation, duty.

debt′ of hon′or, a gambling debt.

debt·or (det′ər), *n. Accounting.* **1.** a person who is in debt to another. **2. debtors,** receivables. [ME *detto(u)r* < OF *detor* < L *dēbitor*]

debt′ serv′ice, the amount set aside annually in a fund to pay the interest and the part of the principal due on a debt.

de·bug (dē bug′), *v.t.,* **-bugged, -bug·ging.** *Informal.* **1.** to detect and remove defects or errors from. **2.** to remove electronic bugs from (a room or building).

de·bunk (di buŋk′), *v.t. Informal.* to strip or divest of pretentious, false, or exaggerated opinions, sentiments, or claims: *to debunk advertising slogans.* —**de·bunk′er,** *n.*

De·bus·sy (deb′yo͞o sē′, dā′byo͞o-, də byo͞o′sē; *Fr.* də bʏ sē′), *n.* **Claude A·chille** (klōd ə s͟hēl′; *Fr.* klōd A s͟hēl′), 1862–1918, French composer.

de·but (dā byo͞o′, di-, dā′byo͞o, deb′yo͞o), *n.* **1.** a first public appearance, as on a stage. **2.** a formal introduction and entrance into society, esp. of a girl or woman. **3.** the beginning of a profession, career, etc. —*v.i.* **4.** to make a debut. —*v.t.* **5.** to perform (a dance, composition, or the like) for the first time before an audience; introduce. Also, **dé·but′.** [< F *début* < *début(er)* (to) make the first stroke in a game, make one's first appearance. See DE-, BUTT[2]]

deb·u·tant (deb′yo͝o tänt′, -yə-), *n.* a person who makes a debut into a professional career or before the public. Also, **déb′u·tant′.** [< F *débutant,* prp. of *débuter*]

deb·u·tante (deb′yo͝o tänt′, -tant′), *n.* **1.** a girl making a debut, esp. into society. **2.** a girl who has made a debut. Also, **déb′u·tante′.** [< F; fem. of DEBUTANT]

de·bye (di bī′), *n. Elect.* a unit of measure for electric dipole moments, equal to 10^{-18} statcoulomb-centimeters. *Abbr.:* D

dec-, var. of **deca-** before a vowel: *decare.*

Dec., December.

dec., **1.** deceased. **2.** decimeter. **3.** declaration. **4.** declension. **5.** decrease. **6.** *Music.* decrescendo.

deca-, a learned borrowing from Greek meaning "ten," used in the formation of compound words (*decapod*), specialized in the metric system so that *deca-* gives the multiplication by 10 (*decaliter*) and *deci-* the division by 10 (*deciliter*). Also, **dec-, dek-, deka-.** Cf. **deci-.** [< Gk *deka-,* comb. form of *déka* TEN; c. L *decem*]

dec·ade (dek′ād), *n.* **1.** a period of 10 years: *the three decades from 1921 to 1951.* **2.** a group, set, or series of 10. [ME < MF < LL *decad-* (s. of *decas*) < Gk *dekad-* (s. of *dekás*) group of ten] —**dec·a·dal** (dek′ə dᵊl), *adj.* —**dec′a·dal·ly,** *adv.*

dec·a·dence (dek′ə dəns, di kād′ᵊns), *n.* **1.** the act or process of falling into an inferior condition or state; decay; deterioration. **2.** moral decay; self-indulgence. Also, **dec·a·den·cy** (dek′ə dən sē, di kād′ᵊn-). [< MF < ML *dēcadentia* = LL *dēcadent-* (s. of *dēcadēns*), prp. of *dēcadere* to fall away (*dē-* DE- + *cad-* fall + *-ent-* -ENT) + *-ia;* see -ENCE] —**Syn. 1.** decline, degeneration, retrogression.

dec·a·dent (dek′ə dənt, di kād′ᵊnt), *adj.* **1.** characterized by decadence. **2.** of or like the literary decadents of the 19th century. —*n.* **3.** a person who is decadent. **4.** (*often cap.*) a member of a group of French and English writers of the latter part of the 19th century whose works were characterized by great refinement or subtlety of style and a marked tendency toward the artificial and abnormal in content. [back formation from DECADENCE] —**dec′a·dent·ly,** *adv.*

de·caf·fein·ate (dē kaf′ə nāt′, -kaf′ē ə-), *v.t.,* **-at·ed, -at·ing.** to extract caffeine from.

dec·a·gon (dek′ə gon′), *n. Geom.* a polygon having 10 angles and 10 sides. [< ML *decagōn(um)*] —**de·cag·o·nal** (də kag′ə nᵊl), *adj.*

144°

Decagon (Regular)

dec·a·gram (dek′ə gram′), *n. Metric System.* a unit of 10 grams, equivalent to 0.3527 ounce avoirdupois. Also, *esp. Brit.,* **dec′a·gramme′.** [< F *décagramme*]

dec·a·he·dron (dek′ə hē′drən), *n., pl.* **-drons, -dra** (-drə). *Geom.* a solid figure having 10 faces. [< NL] —**dec·a·he·dral** (dek′ə hē′drəl), *adj.*

de·cal (dē′kal, di kal′, dek′əl), *n.* **1.** the art or process of transferring pictures or designs from specially prepared paper to wood, metal, china, glass, etc. **2.** the paper bearing such a picture or design. [shortened form of DECALCOMANIA]

de·cal·ci·fy (dē kal′sə fī′), *v.t.,* **-fied, -fy·ing.** to deprive of lime or calcareous matter, as a bone. —**de·cal·ci·fi·ca·tion** (dē kal′sə fə kā′s͟hən), *n.* —**de·cal′ci·fi′er,** *n.*

de·cal·co·ma·ni·a (di kal′kə mā′nē ə, -mān′yə), *n.* decal. [< F *décalcomanie* = *décalco-* (repr. *décalquer* to transfer a tracing of = *dé-* DE- + *calquer* to trace) + *-manie* -MANIA]

de·ca·les·cence (dē′kə les′əns), *n. Metall.* the increased absorption of heat by a piece of heated metal as a result of structural changes in the metal. [< L *dēcalescent-* (s. of *dēcalescēns*) becoming warm] —**de′ca·les′cent,** *adj.*

dec·a·li·ter (dek′ə lē′tər), *n. Metric System.* a unit of 10 liters equivalent to 9.08 quarts U.S. dry measure or 2.64 gallons U.S. liquid measure. Also, **dekaliter;** *esp. Brit.,* **dec′a·li′tre.** [< F *décalitre*]

Dec·a·logue (dek′ə lôg′, -log′), *n.* See **Ten Commandments.** Also, **dec′a·logue′, Dec′a·log′, dec′a·log′.** [ME *decalog* < LL *decalog(us)* < MGk, Gk *dekálogos*]

dec·a·me·ter (dek′ə mē′tər), *n. Metric System.* a measure of length equal to 10 meters. Also, **dekameter;** *esp. Brit.,* **dec′a·me′tre.** [< F *décamètre*]

de·camp (di kamp′), *v.i.* **1.** to depart from a camp; pack up equipment and leave a camping ground. **2.** to depart quickly, secretly, or unceremoniously. [< F *décamp(er).* See DIS-[1], CAMP[1]] —**de·camp′ment,** *n.*

dec·a·nal (dek′ə nᵊl, di kān′ᵊl), *adj.* of or pertaining to a dean or deanery: *decanal duties.* [< LL *decān(us)* DEAN + -AL[1]] —**dec′a·nal·ly, de·can·i·cal·ly** (di kan′ik lē), *adv.*

de·cant (di kant′), *v.t.* **1.** to pour (wine or other liquid) gently so as not to disturb the sediment. **2.** to pour (a liquid) from one container to another. [< ML *dēcanth(āre)* = L *dē-* DE- + ML *canth(us)* spout, rim of a vessel (in L: iron band around a wheel < Gk *kánthos* corner of the eye, tire) + *-āre* inf. suffix] —**de·can·ta·tion** (dē′kan tā′s͟hən), *n.*

de·cant·er (di kan′tər), *n.* **1.** a bottle used for decanting. **2.** a vessel, usually an ornamental glass bottle, for holding and serving wine, brandy, or the like.

Decanter

de·cap·i·tate (di kap′i tāt′), *v.t.,* **-tat·ed, -tat·ing.** to cut off the head of; behead. [< LL *dēcapitāt(us),* ptp. of *dēcapitāre* (see -ATE[1]) = *dē-* DE- + *capitāre* < L *capit-* (s. of *caput*) head] —**de·cap′i·ta′tion,** *n.* —**de·cap′i·ta′tor,** *n.*

dec·a·pod (dek′ə pod′), *n.* **1.** any crustacean of the order *Decapoda,* having five pairs of walking legs, including the crabs, lobsters, crayfish, prawns, and shrimps. **2.** any dibranchiate cephalopod having 10 arms, as the cuttlefish or squid. —*adj.* **3.** belonging or pertaining to the *Decapoda.* **4.** having 10 feet or legs. [< NL *Decapod(a)*] —**de·cap·o·dous** (də kap′ə dəs), *adj.*

De·cap·o·da (də kap′ə də), *n.* the order comprising the decapods. [< NL]

De·cap·o·lis (di kap′ə lis), *n.* a region in the NE part of ancient Palestine: confederacy of 10 cities in the 1st century B.C.

de·car·bon·ate (dē kär′bə nāt′), *v.t.,* **-at·ed, -at·ing.** to remove carbon dioxide from. —**de·car′bon·a′tion,** *n.*

de·car·bon·ise (dē kär′bə nīz′), *v.t.,* **-ised, -is·ing.** *Chiefly Brit.* decarbonize. —**de·car′bon·i·sa′tion,** *n.* —**de·car′bon·is′er,** *n.*

de·car·bon·ize (dē kär′bə nīz′), *v.t.,* **-ized, -iz·ing.** decarburize. —**de·car′bon·i·za′tion,** *n.* —**de·car′bon·iz′er,** *n.*

de·car·box·yl·ase (dē′kär bok′sə lās′), *n. Biochem.* any of the class of enzymes that catalyze the release of carbon dioxide from the carboxyl group of certain organic acids. Also called **carboxylase.** [DECARBOXYL(ATE) + -ASE]

de·car·box·yl·ate (dē′kär bok′sə lāt′), *v.t.,* **-at·ed, -at·ing.** *Chem.* to remove the carboxyl group from (an organic compound). —**de′car·box′yl·a′tion,** *n.*

de·car·bu·rise (dē kär′bə rīz′, -byə-), *v.t.,* **-rised, -ris·ing.** *Chiefly Brit.* decarburize. —**de·car′bu·ri·sa′tion,** *n.*

de·car·bu·rize (dē kär′bə rīz′, -byə-), *v.t.,* **-rized, -riz·ing.** to remove carbon from (molten steel, automobile cylinder heads, etc.). —**de·car′bu·ri·za′tion, de·car′bu·ra′tion,** *n.*

dec·are (dek′âr, de kâr′), *n. Metric System.* a unit of area equal to 10 ares. Also, **dekare.** [< F *décare*]

dec·a·stere (dek′ə stēr′), *n. Metric System.* a unit of volume equal to 10 steres. Also, **dekastere.** [< F *décastère*]

dec·a·syl·la·ble (dek′ə sil′ə bəl), *n.* a word or line of verse of 10 syllables. —**dec·a·syl·lab·ic** (dek′ə si lab′ik), *adj.*

de·cath·lon (di kat͟h′lon), *n.* an athletic contest comprising 10 different track-and-field events and won by the contestant amassing the highest total score. [DEC- + Gk *âthlon* a contest]

De·ca·tur (di kā′tər), *n.* **1. Stephen,** 1779–1820, U.S. naval officer. **2.** a city in central Illinois. 90,397 (1970). **3.** a city in N Alabama. 38,044 (1970).

de·cay (di kā′), *v.i.* **1.** to become decomposed; rot. **2.** to decline in excellence, prosperity, health, etc.; deteriorate. **3.** *Physics.* to undergo radioactive disintegration. —*v.t.* **4.** to cause to decay or decompose; rot. —*n.* **5.** a progressive decline; deterioration. **6.** loss of strength, health, intellect, etc.: *His mental decay is distressing.* **7.** decomposition; rot. **8.** Also called **disintegration, radioactive decay.** *Physics.* a radioactive process in which a nucleus emits radiation and undergoes spontaneous transformation into one or more different nuclei. [ME *decay(en)* < ONF *decai(ir)* = *de-* DE- + *cair* to fall < VL *cadēre,* r. L *cadere*] —**de·cay′a·ble,** *adj.*
—**Syn. 1.** putrefy. **2.** degenerate, wither. DECAY, DECOMPOSE, DISINTEGRATE, ROT imply a deterioration or falling away from a sound condition. DECAY implies either entire or partial dissolution or deterioration by progressive natural changes: *Teeth decay.* DECOMPOSE suggests the reduction of a substance, through natural change or human agency, to its component elements: *Moisture makes some chemical compounds decompose.* DISINTEGRATE emphasizes the breaking up, going to pieces, or wearing away of anything, so that its original wholeness is impaired: *Rocks disintegrate.* ROT is a stronger word than decay and is esp. applied to decaying vegetable matter, which may or may not emit offensive odors: *Potatoes rot.* **7.** putrefaction. —**Ant. 2.** flourish.

Dec·can (dek′ən), *n.* **1.** the entire peninsula of India S of the Narbada River. **2.** a plateau region in S India between the Narbada and Kristna rivers.

decd., deceased.

de·cease (di sēs′), *n., v.,* **-ceased, -ceas·ing.** —*n.* **1.** departure from life; death. —*v.i.* **2.** to depart from life; die. [ME *deces* < OF < L *dēcess(us)* departure, death, ptp. of *dēcēdere* to go away. See DE-, CEDE]

de·ceased (di sēst′), *adj.* **1.** no longer living; dead. —*n.* **the deceased. 2.** the particular dead person referred to. **3.** dead persons collectively. —**Syn. 1.** See **dead.**

de·ce·dent (di sēd′ᵊnt), *n. Law.* a deceased person. [< L *dēcēdent-* (s. of *dēcēdēns*) departing, withdrawing, prp. of *dēcēdere.* See DECEASE, -ENT]

de·ceit (di sēt′), *n.* **1.** the act or practice of deceiving; fraud; cheating. **2.** an act or device intended to deceive; trick; stratagem. **3.** the quality of being deceitful; falseness: *a man full of deceit.* [ME *deceite* < OF, n. use of fem. of *deceit,* ptp. of *deceivre* to DECEIVE]
—**Syn. 1.** deception, dissimulation. **1, 3.** DECEIT, GUILE, HYPOCRISY, DUPLICITY, FRAUD, TRICKERY refer, with greater or lesser degrees of opprobrium, either to practices designed to mislead or to the qualities that produce those practices. DECEIT is the quality that prompts intentional concealment or perversion of truth for the purpose of misleading: *honest and without deceit.* The quality of GUILE leads to craftiness in the use of deceit: *using guile and trickery to*

attain one's ends. HYPOCRISY is the pretense of possessing qualities of sincerity, goodness, devotion, etc.: *It was sheer hypocrisy for him to go to church.* DUPLICITY involves double-dealing: *the duplicity of a false friend who betrays one's secrets.* FRAUD refers usually to the practice of deceit or duplicity by which one may benefit himself at another's expense: *an advertiser convicted of fraud.* TRICKERY is the quality which leads to the use of tricks and habitual deception: *notorious for his trickery in business deals.* **—Ant. 3.** honesty, sincerity.

de·ceit·ful (di sēt′fəl), *adj.* **1.** full of deceit; given to deceiving: *a deceitful boaster.* **2.** misleading; deceptive: *a deceitful trick.* [ME] **—de·ceit′ful·ly,** *adv.* **—de·ceit′ful·ness,** *n.* **—Syn. 1.** insincere, false, tricky, wily. **2.** illusory, fallacious. **—Ant. 1.** honest. **2.** genuine.

de·ceive (di sēv′), *v.,* **-ceived, -ceiv·ing.** **—***v.t.* **1.** to mislead by a false appearance or statement; delude. **2.** *Archaic.* to pass or while away (time). **—***v.i.* **3.** to practice deceit; act deceitfully. [ME *deceive(n)* < OF *deceiv(re)* < VL **dēcipēre,* r. L *dēcipere* = *dē-* DE- + *-cipere,* comb. var. of *capere* to take] **—de·ceiv′a·ble·ness, de·ceiv′a·bil′i·ty,** *n.* **—de·ceiv′a·bly,** *adv.* **—de·ceiv′er,** *n.* **—de·ceiv′ing·ly,** *adv.* **—Syn. 1.** fool, trick, defraud, betray. See **cheat.**

de·cel·er·ate (dē sel′ə rāt′), *v.t., v.i.,* **-at·ed, -at·ing.** to slow down. [DE- + (AC)CELERATE] **—de·cel′er·a′tion,** *n.* **—de·cel′er·a′tor,** *n.*

De·cem·ber (di sem′bər), *n.* the 12th month of the year, containing 31 days. [ME *decembre* < OF < L *december* the tenth month of the early Roman year = *decem* ten + *-ber* < ?]

De·cem·brist (di sem′brist), *n. Russ. Hist.* a participant in the conspiracy and insurrection against Nicholas I on his accession in December, 1825. [trans. of Russ *dekabrist*]

de·cem·vir (di sem′vər), *n., pl.* **-virs, -vi·ri** (-və rī′). **1.** a member of a permanent board or a special commission of 10 members in ancient Rome. **2.** a member of any council or ruling body of 10. [< L, orig. pl. *decemvirī* = *decem* ten + *virī* men] **—de·cem′vi·ral,** *adj.* **—de·cem′vi·rate,** *n.*

de·cen·cy (dē′sən sē), *n., pl.* **-cies** for 2–4. **1.** the state or quality of being decent. **2.** conformity to the recognized standard of propriety, good taste, modesty, etc. **3.** something decent or proper. **4. decencies,** the requirements of decent living and conduct. [< L *dēcentia* comeliness, decency]

de·cen·na·ry (di sen′ə rē), *n., pl.* **-ries,** *adj.* **—***n.* **1.** a decennium. **—***adj.* **2.** pertaining to a period of 10 years; decennial. [< L *decenn(is)* of ten years (*dec(em)* ten + *-ennis,* comb. form of *annus* a year) + -ARY]

de·cen·ni·al (di sen′ē əl), *adj.* **1.** of or for 10 years. **2.** occurring every 10 years. **—***n.* **3.** a decennial anniversary. **4.** its celebration. [< L *decenni(um)* a period of ten years (*decenn(is)* of ten years = *dec(em)* ten + *-ennis* comb. form of *annus* year + *-ium* n. suffix) + -AL[1]] **—de·cen′ni·al·ly,** *adv.*

de·cen·ni·um (di sen′ē əm), *n., pl.* **-cen·ni·ums, -cen·ni·a** (-sen′ē ə). a period of 10 years; decade. [< L]

de·cent (dē′sənt), *adj.* **1.** fitting; appropriate. **2.** conforming to the recognized standard of propriety, good taste, modesty, etc., as in behavior or speech. **3.** respectable; worthy: *a decent family.* **4.** of fairly attractive appearance: *a decent face.* **5.** adequate; fair; passable: *a decent wage.* **6.** kind; obliging; generous: *Very decent of him to lend me his watch.* [< L *decent-* (s. of *decēns*) fitting (prp. of *decēre;* see -ENT), akin to *decus* honor] **—de′cent·ly,** *adv.* **—de′cent·ness,** *n.* **—Syn. 1.** suitable, apt, fit. **2.** seemly, proper. **—Ant. 1.** inappropriate. **2.** unseemly.

de·cen·tral·ise (dē sen′trə līz′), *v.t.,* **-ised, -is·ing.** *Chiefly Brit.* decentralize. **—de·cen′tral·i·sa′tion,** *n.*

de·cen·tral·ize (dē sen′trə līz′), *v.t.,* **-ized, -iz·ing.** **1.** to distribute the administrative powers or functions of over a less concentrated area. **2.** to disperse (something) from an area of concentration. **—de·cen′tral·ist,** *n.* **—de·cen′tral·i·za′tion,** *n.*

de·cep·tion (di sep′shən), *n.* **1.** the act or state of deceiving or the state of being deceived. **2.** something that deceives or is intended to deceive; fraud; artifice. [ME *decepcioun* < OF < LL *dēceptiōn-* (s. of *dēceptiō*) = L *dēcept(us)* (ptp. of *dēcipere;* see DECEIVE) + *-iōn-* -ION] **—Syn. 2.** trick, stratagem, ruse, hoax, subterfuge.

de·cep·tive (di sep′tiv), *adj.* apt or tending to deceive. [< ML *dēceptīv(us)*] **—de·cep′tive·ly,** *adv.* **—de·cep′tive·ness,** *n.*

de·cer·e·brate (dē ser′ə brāt′), *v.t.,* **-brat·ed, -brat·ing.** *Surg.* to sever the connection between the brain and the spinal cord. [DE- + CEREBR- + -ATE[1]] **—de·cer′e·bra′tion,** *n.*

de·cern (di sûrn′), *v.i.* **1.** *Scots Law.* to enter a judicial decree. **—***v.t.* **2.** *Obs.* to discern. [ME *decern(en)* (to) decide < OF *decerne(r)* < L *dēcernere* = *dē-* DE- + *cernere* to separate, decide]

de·cer·ti·fy (dē sûr′tə fī′), *v.t.,* **-fied, -fy·ing.** to withdraw certification from. **—de·cer·ti·fi·ca·tion** (dē sûr′tə fə kā′shən, dē′sər tif′ə-), *n.*

deci-, a learned borrowing from French meaning "tenth," introduced as part of the various units of the metric system (*deciliter*); on this model, extended to other systems (*decibel*). Cf. **deca-.** [< F *déci-* < L *decimus* tenth]

dec·i·are (des′ē âr′, -är′), *n. Metric System.* a unit of area equivalent to 10 square meters or 11.96 square yards; $^1/_{10}$ are. [< F *déciare*]

dec·i·bel (des′ə bel′), *n. Physics.* **1.** a unit of power ratio, proportional to the common logarithm of the intensities of two sources. **2.** a unit used to compare two voltages or currents, equal to 20 times the common logarithm of their ratio. **3.** a unit of intensity of sound, equal to 20 times the common logarithm of the ratio of the pressure produced by the sound wave to a reference pressure. *Abbr.:* dB, db

de·cide (di sīd′), *v.,* **-cid·ed, -cid·ing.** **—***v.t.* **1.** to determine or settle (a question, controversy, or struggle) by giving victory to one side: *The judge decided the case in favor of the plaintiff.* **2.** to adjust or settle (anything in dispute or doubt): *to decide an argument.* **3.** to bring (a person) to a decision: *The new evidence decided him.* **—***v.i.* **4.** to settle something in dispute or doubt. **5.** to pronounce a formal judgment. [ME *decide(n)* < MF *decide(r)* < L *dēcīdere,* lit., to cut off = *dē-* DE- + *-cīdere* (comb. var. of *caedere* to cut)] **—de·cid′er,** *n.*

—Syn. 1. conclude. DECIDE, RESOLVE, DETERMINE imply settling upon a purpose. To DECIDE is to make up one's mind clearly and firmly as to what to do: *He decided to buy a new car.* To RESOLVE is usually positively or actively to show firmness of purpose: *He resolved to ask for a promotion.* To DETERMINE is to make up one's mind and then doggedly, and sometimes obstinately, to stick to a fixed or settled purpose: *determined to maintain his position.* **—Ant. 1.** hesitate.

de·cid·ed (di sī′did), *adj.* **1.** free from ambiguity; unquestionable; unmistakable. **2.** free from hesitation or wavering; resolute; determined. **—de·cid′ed·ly,** *adv.* **—de·cid′ed·ness,** *n.* **—Syn. 1.** undeniable, indisputable, emphatic, definite. **2.** unhesitating, unwavering.

de·cid·u·a (di sij′o͞o ə), *n., pl.* **-cid·u·as, -cid·u·ae** (-sij′o͞o ē′). *Embryol.* the uterine mucosa that in many of the higher mammals is cast off at parturition. [< NL (fem. n.), L *dēciduus*) falling down (n. and adj.); see DECIDUOUS] **—de·cid′u·al,** *adj.*

de·cid·u·ate (di sij′o͞o it), *adj. Anat., Zool.* **1.** having or characterized by a decidua. **2.** (of a placenta) partly formed from the decidua. [< NL *deciduāt(us)*]

de·cid·u·ous (di sij′o͞o əs), *adj.* **1.** shedding the leaves annually, as trees and shrubs. **2.** falling off or shed at a particular season, stage of growth, etc., as leaves, horns, or teeth. **3.** not permanent; transitory. [< L *dēcidu(us)* (adj.) falling down = *dēcid(ere)* (to) fall down (*dē-* DE- + *-cidere,* comb. form of *cadere* to fall) + *-us* -OUS] **—de·cid′u·ous·ly,** *adv.* **—de·cid′u·ous·ness,** *n.*

decid′uous tooth′. See **milk tooth.**

dec·i·gram (des′ə gram′), *n. Metric System.* a unit of weight of $^1/_{10}$ gram, equivalent to 1.543 grains. *Abbr.:* dg Also, *esp. Brit.,* **dec′i·gramme′.** [< F *décigramme*]

dec·ile (des′il, -īl), *n. Statistics.* one of the values of a variable that divides the distribution of the variable into 10 groups having equal frequencies.

dec·i·li·ter (des′ə lē′tər), *n. Metric System.* a unit of capacity of $^1/_{10}$ liter, equivalent to 6.102 cubic inches, or 3.381 U.S. fluid ounces. *Abbr.:* dl Also, *esp. Brit.,* **dec′i·li′tre.** [< F *décilitre*]

de·cil·lion (di sil′yən), *n.* **1.** a cardinal number represented in the U.S. and France by the number one followed by 33 zeros and in Great Britain and Germany by the number one followed by 60 zeros. **—***adj.* **2.** amounting to one decillion in number. [< L *dec(em)* ten + *-illion,* as in *million*] **—de·cil′lionth,** *adj., n.*

dec·i·mal (des′ə məl), *adj.* **1.** pertaining to tenths or to the number 10. **2.** based on ten: *a decimal system.* **—***n.* **3.** See **decimal fraction.** [< ML *decimāl(is)* of tenths = L *decim(a)* tenth (< *decem* ten) + *-ālis* -AL[1]] **—dec′i·mal·ly,** *adv.*

dec′imal frac′tion, *Arith.* a fraction whose denominator is some power of 10, usually indicated by a dot **(decimal point)** written before the numerator: 0.4 = $^4/_{10}$; 0.126 = $^{126}/_{1000}$. Cf. **common fraction.**

dec·i·mal·ise (des′ə mə līz′), *v.t.,* **-ised, -is·ing.** *Chiefly Brit.* decimalize. **—dec′i·mal·i·sa′tion,** *n.*

dec·i·mal·ize (des′ə mə līz′), *v.t.,* **-ized, -iz·ing.** to reduce or convert to a decimal system. **—dec′i·mal·i·za′tion,** *n.*

dec′imal point′. See under **decimal fraction.**

dec·i·mate (des′ə māt′), *v.t.,* **-mat·ed, -mat·ing.** **1.** to destroy a great number or proportion of. **2.** to select by lot and kill every tenth person of. **3.** to take a tenth of or from. [< L *decimāt(us)* (ptp. of *decimāre*) = *decim(us)* tenth + *-ātus* -ATE[1]] **—dec′i·ma′tion,** *n.* **—dec′i·ma′tor,** *n.*

dec·i·me·ter (des′ə mē′tər), *n. Metric System.* a unit of length equal to $^1/_{10}$ meter. *Abbr.:* dm Also, *esp. Brit.,* **dec′i·me′tre.** [< F *décimètre*]

de·ci·pher (di sī′fər), *v.t.* **1.** to make out the meaning of: *to decipher a person's handwriting.* **2.** to interpret by the use of a key, as something written in cipher: *to decipher a secret message.* **3.** *Obs.* to depict; portray. [trans. of F *déchiffrer*] **—de·ci′pher·a·bil′i·ty,** *n.* **—de·ci′pher·a·ble,** *adj.* **—de·ci′pher·er,** *n.*

de·ci·sion (di sizh′ən), *n.* **1.** the act of deciding, as on a question or problem, by making a judgment. **2.** a judgment, as one formally pronounced by a court. **3.** the act of making up one's mind. **4.** something that is decided; resolution. **5.** the quality of being decided; firmness. [< MF < L *dēcīsiōn-* (s. of *dēcīsiō*), lit., a cutting off = *dēcīs(us)* (ptp. of *dēcīdere;* see DECIDE) + *-iōn-* -ION] **—de·ci′sion·al,** *adj.*

de·ci·sive (di sī′siv), *adj.* **1.** having the power or quality of determining; putting an end to controversy. **2.** characterized by or displaying decision; resolute; determined. [< ML *dēcīsīv(us)*] **—de·ci′sive·ly,** *adv.* **—de·ci′sive·ness,** *n.* **—Syn. 1.** conclusive, final. **2.** firm.

dec·i·stere (des′i stēr′), *n. Metric System.* a unit of volume equal to $^1/_{10}$ stere. [< F *décistère*]

De·cius (dē′shəs, desh′əs), *n.* (*Gaius Messius Quintus Trajanus Decius*) A.D. c201–251, emperor of Rome 249–251.

deck (dek), *n.* **1.** *Naut.* **a.** a floorlike surface wholly or partially occupying one level of a hull, superstructure, or deckhouse, generally cambered, and often serving as a member for strengthening the structure of a vessel. **b.** the space between such a surface and the next such surface above. **2.** any open platform suggesting an exposed deck of a ship. **3.** a pack of playing cards. **4. clear the decks, a.** to prepare for combat, as by removing all unnecessary gear. **b.** to prepare for some activity or work, as by getting rid of hindrances. **5. hit the deck,** *Slang.* **a.** to rise from bed. **b.** to fall or be knocked to the ground or floor. **6. on deck,** *Informal.* **a.** prepared to act or work; ready. **b.** next in line, coming up. **—***adj.* **7.** (of a bridge truss) having a deck or floor upon or above the structure. **—***v.t.* **8.** to clothe or attire (the person) or array (rooms, houses, etc.) in something ornamental or decorative (often fol. by *out*): *She was all decked out in her Sunday best.* **9.** to furnish with a deck. **10.** *Informal.* to knock down; floor. [(n.) ME *dekke* material for covering < MD *dec* roof, covering; (v.) < D, MD *dekke(n)*; c. MLG *decken;* cf. THATCH] **—deck′er,** *n.* **—Syn. 8.** bedeck, trim, bedizen, adorn, embellish; dress.

deck′ chair′, a folding chair, usually with arms and a full-length leg rest, commonly used on the decks of ships. Also called **steamer chair.**

deck·el (dek′əl), *n.* deckle.

Deck·er (dek′ər), *n.* **Thomas.** See **Dekker, Thomas.**

deck′ hand′, *Naut.* a seaman belonging to the deck department of a vessel.

deck·house (dek′hous′), *n., pl.* **-hous·es** (-hou′ziz). *Naut.* any enclosed structure projecting above the weather deck of a vessel and surrounded by exposed deck area on all sides. Cf. **superstructure** (def. 3).

deck·le (dek′əl), *n.* **1.** *Papermaking.* a board, usually of stainless steel, fitted under part of the wire in a Fourdrinier machine for supporting the pulp stack on the wire before it is sufficiently formed to support itself. **2.** See **deckle edge.** Also, **deckel.** [< G *Deckel* cover, lid]

deck′le edge′, the irregular, untrimmed edge of handmade paper, now often produced artificially on paper made by machine. Also called **deckle.** —**deck′le-edged′,** *adj.*

deck′ of′ficer, *Naut.* any officer whose responsibilities include navigation, cargo handling, etc.

decl., declension.

de·claim (di klām′), *v.i.* **1.** to speak aloud rhetorically; make a formal speech. **2.** to inveigh (usually fol. by *against*): *He declaimed against the high rents.* **3.** to speak or write for oratorical effect, without sincerity or sound argument. —*v.t.* **4.** to utter aloud in a rhetorical manner: *to declaim a speech.* [ME *declam(en)* < L *dēclām(āre)*] —**de·claim′er,** *n.*

dec·la·ma·tion (dek′lə mā′shən), *n.* **1.** the act or art of declaiming. **2.** speech or writing for oratorical effect. **3.** *Music.* the proper enunciation of the words, as in recitative. [< L *dēclāmātiōn-* (s. of *dēclāmātiō*) = *dēclāmāt(us)* (ptp. of *dēclāmāre* to DECLAIM; see -ATE[1]) + *-iōn-* -ION]

de·clam·a·tor·y (di klam′ə tôr′ē, -tôr′ē), *adj.* **1.** pertaining to or characterized by declamation. **2.** merely rhetorical; stilted. [< L *dēclāmātōr(ius)* = *dēclāmāt(us)* (see DECLAMATION) + *-ōrius* -ORY[1]]

de·clar·ant (di klâr′ənt), *n.* a person who declares or makes a declaration or statement.

dec·la·ra·tion (dek′lə rā′shən), *n.* **1.** the act of declaring; announcement. **2.** a positive, explicit, or formal statement; proclamation: *a declaration of war.* **3.** something that is announced, avowed, or proclaimed: *The declaration will affect everyone.* **4.** a document embodying an announcement or proclamation. **5.** *Law.* **a.** a formal statement in which a plaintiff presents his claim in an action. **b.** a complaint. **c.** a statement, as by a witness. **6.** *Cards.* **a.** *Bridge.* a bid, esp. the successful bid. **b.** (in bezique and some other games) the statement during the game of the points earned by a player. **7.** a statement of goods, income, etc., esp. for the assessment of duty, tax, or the like. [ME *declaracioun* < L *dēclārātiōn-* (s. of *dēclārātiō*) explanation = *dēclārāt(us)* (ptp. of *dēclārāre* to DECLARE; see -ATE[1]) + *-iōn-* -ION]

Declara′tion of Indepen′dence, 1. the public act by which the Second Continental Congress, on July 4, 1776, declared the Colonies to be free and independent of England. **2.** the document embodying it.

de·clar·a·tive (di klar′ə tiv), *adj.* serving to declare, make known, or explain: *a declarative statement.* Also, **de·clar·a·to·ry** (di klar′ə tôr′ē, -tôr′ē). [< L *dēclārātīv(us)* = *dēclārāt(us)* (see DECLARATION) + *-īvus* -IVE] —**de·clar′a·tive·ly,** *adv.*

de·clare (di klâr′), *v.,* **-clared, -clar·ing.** —*v.t.* **1.** to make known clearly, esp. in explicit or formal terms: *to declare one's position in a controversy.* **2.** to announce officially; proclaim: *to declare a state of emergency.* **3.** to state emphatically. **4.** to manifest; reveal; show. **5.** to make due statement of, esp. goods for duty or income for taxation. **6.** to make (a dividend) payable. **7.** *Bridge.* to bid (a trump suit or no-trump). —*v.i.* **8.** to make a declaration. **9.** to proclaim oneself (usually fol. by *for* or *against*): *He declared against the proposal.* [ME *declare(n)* < L *dēclār(āre)* (to) explain. See DE-, CLEAR] —**de·clar′a·ble,** *adj.* —**de·clar′er,** *n.*
—**Syn. 3.** aver, asseverate. DECLARE, AFFIRM, ASSERT, PROTEST imply making something known emphatically, openly, or formally. To DECLARE is to make known, sometimes in the face of actual or potential contradiction: *to declare someone the winner of a contest.* To AFFIRM is to make a statement based on one's reputation for knowledge or veracity, or so related to a generally recognized truth that denial is not likely: *to affirm the necessity of high standards.* To ASSERT is to state boldly, usually without other proof than personal authority or conviction: *to assert that the climate is changing.* To PROTEST is to affirm publicly, as if in the face of doubt: *to protest that a newspaper account is misleading.* **4.** disclose, publish. —**Ant. 3.** deny.

de·clared (di klârd′), *adj.* avowed; professed: *a declared liberal.* —**de·clar·ed·ly** (di klâr′id lē), *adv.*

de·class (dē klas′, -kläs′), *v.t.* to remove or degrade from one's social class, rank, or the like. [trans. of F *déclasser*]

dé·clas·sé (dā′klə sā′, -kla-; *Fr.* dā klA sā′), *adj.* reduced to or having low status: *a déclassé neighborhood.* [< F, ptp. of *déclasser*]

de·clas·si·fy (dē klas′ə fī′), *v.t.,* **-fied, -fy·ing.** *U.S. Govt., Mil.* to remove the classification from (information, a document, etc.). Cf. **classification** (def. 5). —**de·clas·si·fi·ca·tion** (dē klas′ə fə kā′shən), *n.*

de·clen·sion (di klen′shən), *n.* **1.** *Gram.* **a.** the inflection of nouns, pronouns, and adjectives for categories such as case and number. **b.** the complete series of inflected forms of such a word, or the recital thereof in a fixed order. **c.** a class of such words having similar sets of inflected forms, as the Latin second declension. **2.** an act or instance of declining. **3.** a bending, sloping, or moving downward: *land with a gentle declension toward the sea.* **4.** deterioration; decline. [irreg. < L *dēclīnātiōn-*, lit., a turning aside] —**de·clen′sion·al,** *adj.* —**de·clen′sion·al·ly,** *adv.*

dec·li·nate (dek′lə nāt′, -nit), *adj.* having a downward curve or slope; bending away, as from the horizontal: *a declinate flower.* [< L *dēclīnāt(us)*, ptp. of *dēclīnāre*]

dec·li·na·tion (dek′lə nā′shən), *n.* **1.** a bending, sloping, or moving downward. **2.** deterioration; decline. **3.** a swerving or deviating, as from a standard. **4.** a polite refusal. **5.** *Astron.* the angular distance of a heavenly body from the celestial equator, measured on the great circle passing through the celestial pole and the body. **6.** the horizontal angle between the direction of true north and magnetic north: variable according to geographic location. [ME *declinacioun* < OF *declinacion* < L *dēclīnātiōn-* (s. of *dēclīnātiō*) = *dēclīnāt(us)*, lit., turned aside (ptp. of *dēclīnāre;* see DECLINE, -ATE[1]) + *-iōn-* -ION] —**dec′li·na′tion·al,** *adj.*

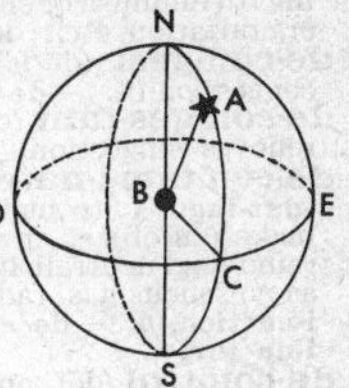

Declination
A, Star; B, Earth; Angle ABC, Declination of star; N, North celestial pole; S, South celestial pole; DE, Celestial equator

de·cline (di klīn′), *v.,* **-clined, -clin·ing,** *n.* —*v.t.* **1.** to withhold or deny consent to do, enter into or upon, etc.; refuse: *He declined to say more about it.* **2.** to express inability or reluctance to accept; refuse with courtesy. **3.** to cause to slope or incline downward. **4.** *Gram.* to recite or display the inflected forms of (a noun, pronoun, or adjective) in a fixed order. —*v.i.* **5.** to express courteous refusal; refuse. **6.** to bend or slant down; slope downward; descend. **7.** to follow a downward course or path. **8.** to draw toward the close, as the day. **9.** to stoop; condescend, as to an unworthy object or level. **10.** to fail in strength, vigor, character, value, etc.; deteriorate. **11.** to dwindle, sink, or fade away: *to decline in popularity.* **12.** *Gram.* to be characterized by declension. —*n.* **13.** a downward slope; declivity. **14.** a failing or gradual loss, as in strength, character, or value; deterioration. **15.** a downward movement, as of prices or population; diminution. **16.** progress downward or toward the close, as of the sun or the day. [ME *decline(n)* < OF *declin(er)* (to) inflect, turn aside, sink < L *dēclīnāre* to slope, incline, bend; c. Gk *klinein*] —**de·clin′a·ble,** *adj.* —**de·clin′er,** *n.* —**Syn. 1.** reject. See **refuse**[1]. **10.** degenerate, decay, weaken. **13.** hill. **14.** degeneration. —**Ant. 6.** rise. **10.** improve.

dec·li·nom·e·ter (dek′lə nom′i tər), *n.* an instrument for measuring magnetic declination. [comb. form repr. L *dēclīnāre* (see DECLINE) + -O- + -METER]

de·cliv·i·ty (di kliv′i tē), *n., pl.* **-ties.** a downward slope. [< L *dēclīvitāt-* (s. of *dēclīvitās*) a slope, hill = *dēclīv(us)* sloping downward (*dē-* DE- + *clīvus* slope, hill) + *-itāt-* -ITY] —**de·cliv′i·tous,** *adj.* —**de·cliv′i·tous·ly,** *adv.*

de·cli·vous (di klī′vəs), *adj.* sloping downward. Also, **de·cli′vent.** [< L *dēclīv(us)* (see DECLIVITY) + -OUS]

de·coct (di kokt′), *v.t.* to extract the flavor or essence of by boiling. [< L *dēcoct(us)* boiled down; see DECOCTION]

de·coc·tion (di kok′shən), *n.* **1.** the act of decocting. **2.** *Pharm.* **a.** an extract obtained by decocting. **b.** water in which a crude vegetable drug has been decocted. [ME *decoccioun* < OF *decoction* < LL *dēcoctiōn-* (s. of *dēcoctiō*) a boiling down = *dēcoct(us)*, ptp. of *dēcoquere* (see DE-, COOK) + *-iōn-* -ION] —**de·coc′tive,** *adj.*

de·code (dē kōd′), *v.,* **-cod·ed, -cod·ing.** —*v.t.* **1.** to translate (a message) from code into the original language or form. —*v.i.* **2.** to work at decoding. —**de·cod′er,** *n.*

de·col·late (di kol′āt), *v.t.,* **-lat·ed, -lat·ing.** to behead; decapitate. [< L *dēcollāt(us)* beheaded (ptp. of *dēcollāre*). See DE-, COLLAR, -ATE[1]] —**de·col·la·tion** (dē′kə lā′shən), *n.*

dé·colle·tage (dā′kol täzh′, -kol ə-, dek′ə lə-; *Fr.* dā kôl-täzh′), *n.* **1.** the neckline of a dress cut low in the front or back and often across the shoulders. **2.** a décolleté garment. Also, **de′colle·tage′.** [< F; see DÉCOLLETÉ, -AGE]

dé·colle·té (dā′kol tā′, -kol ə-, dek′ə lə-; *Fr.* dā kôl tā′), *adj.* **1.** (of a garment) low-necked. **2.** wearing a low-necked garment. Also, **de′colle·te′.** [< F, ptp. of *décolleter* to bare the neck = *dé-* DE- + *collet* COLLAR (see -ET) + *-er* inf. suffix]

de·col·or·ise (dē kul′ə rīz′), *v.t.,* **-ised, -is·ing.** *Chiefly Brit.* decolorize. —**de·col′or·i·sa′tion,** *n.* —**de·col′or·is′er,** *n.*

de·col·or·ize (dē kul′ə rīz′), *v.t.,* **-ized, -iz·ing.** to deprive of color. —**de·col′or·i·za′tion,** *n.* —**de·col′or·iz′er,** *n.*

de·col·our·ise (dē kul′ə rīz′), *v.t.,* **-ised, -is·ing.** *Chiefly Brit.* decolorize. —**de·col′our·i·sa′tion,** *n.* —**de·col′our·is′er,** *n.*

de·col·our·ize (dē kul′ə rīz′), *v.t.,* **-ized, -iz·ing.** *Chiefly Brit.* decolorize. —**de·col′our·i·za′tion,** *n.* —**de·col′our·iz′er,** *n.*

de·com·mis·sion (dē′kə mish′ən), *v.t.* to retire (a ship, airplane, etc.) from active service.

de·com·pen·sate (dē kom′pən sāt′), *v.i.,* **-sat·ed, -sat·ing. 1.** *Pathol.* to suffer loss of adequate heart function due to the heart's inability to compensate for its defects. **2.** to suffer loss of ability to maintain normal or appropriate compensatory mechanisms. —**de′com·pen·sa′tion,** *n.*

de·com·pose (dē′kəm pōz′), *v.,* **-posed, -pos·ing.** —*v.t.* **1.** to separate or resolve into constituent parts or elements; disintegrate. —*v.i.* **2.** to rot; putrefy. [< F *décompose(r).* See DIS-[1], COMPOSE] —**de′com·pos′a·bil′i·ty,** *n.* —**de′com·pos′a·ble,** *adj.* —**de′com·pos′er,** *n.* —**de·com·po·si·tion** (dē′kom pə zish′ən), *n.* —**Syn. 1.** distill, fractionate, analyze. **2.** See **decay.**

de·com·pound (dē′kəm pound′), *v.t.* **1.** to decompose. —*adj.* **2.** *Bot.* divided into compound divisions. **3.** composed of things that are themselves compound.

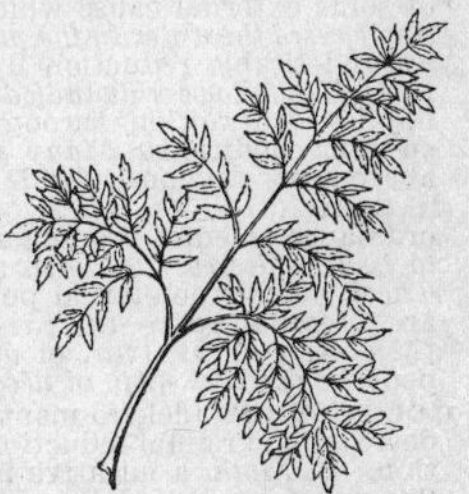
Decompound leaves

de·com·press (dē′kəm pres′), *v.t., v.i.* to undergo or cause to undergo decompression. [trans. of F *décomprimer*] —**de′com·pres′sive,** *adj.*

de·com·pres·sion (dē′kəm presh′ən), *n.* **1.** the act or process of releasing from pressure. **2.** the gradual return of persons, as divers or construction workers, to conditions of normal atmospheric pressure after working in deep water or in air under compression. [prob. < F *décompression*]

de·con·cen·trate (dē kon′sən trāt′), *v.t.*, **-trat·ed, -trat·ing.** to diminish or end the concentration of or within (a group, organization, etc.); decentralize. —**de′con·cen·tra′tion,** *n.*

de·con·gest (dē′kən jest′), *v.t.* to diminish or end the congestion of. —**de′con·ges′tion,** *n.*

de·con·ges·tant (dē′kən jes′tənt), *n. Med.* an agent that relieves congestion.

de·con·tam·i·nate (dē′kən tam′ə nāt′), *v.t.*, **-nat·ed, -nat·ing. 1.** to make free of contamination; purify. **2.** to make (an object or area) safe for unprotected personnel by removing, neutralizing, or destroying any harmful substance, as poisonous gas, radioactive material, etc. —**de′con·tam′i·na′tion,** *n.* —**de′con·tam′i·na′tive,** *adj.* —**de′con·tam′i·na′tor,** *n.*

de·con·trol (dē′kən trōl′), *v.*, **-trolled, -trol·ling,** *n.* —*v.t.* **1.** to remove controls or restraints from: *to decontrol prices or rents.* —*n.* **2.** the removal of control.

dé·cor (dā kôr′, di-, dā′kôr), *n.* **1.** style or mode of decoration, as of a room, building, or the like: *an office having modern décor.* **2.** decoration in general; ornamentation. **3.** *Theat.* scenic decoration; scenery. Also, **de·cor′.** [< F < *décorer* to DECORATE]

dec·o·rate (dek′ə rāt′), *v.t.*, **-rat·ed, -rat·ing. 1.** to furnish or adorn; embellish: *to decorate walls with murals.* **2.** to plan and execute the design, furnishings, and ornamentation of the interior of (a house, office, apartment, etc.), esp. by selecting colors, fabrics, and styles of furniture, by making minor structural changes, etc. **3.** to confer distinction upon by a decoration. [ME (adj.) < L *decorāt(us)* (ptp. of *decorāre*) = *decor-* (s. of *decus*) an ornament, splendor, honor (see DECENT) + *-ātus* -ATE[1]] —**dec·o·ra·tive** (dek′ər ə tiv, dek′rə-, dek′ə rā′-), *adj.* —**dec′o·ra·tive·ly,** *adv.* —**dec′o·ra·tive·ness,** *n.*

dec·o·ra·tion (dek′ə rā′shən), *n.* **1.** the act of decorating. **2.** adornment; embellishment. **3.** a badge, medal, etc., conferred and worn as a mark of honor. [< LL *decorātiōn-* (s. of *decorātiō*) an ornament]

Decora′tion Day′. See **Memorial Day.**

dec·o·ra·tor (dek′ə rā′tər), *n.* **1.** a person who decorates. **2.** See **interior decorator.** —*adj.* **3.** harmonizing with a scheme of interior decoration: *a decorator fireplace.*

dec·o·rous (dek′ər əs, di kōr′əs, -kôr′-), *adj.* characterized by propriety in conduct, manners, appearance, etc. [< L *decōrus* seemly] —**dec′o·rous·ly,** *adv.* —**dec′o·rous·ness,** *n.* —**Syn.** proper, seemly, becoming, decent, sedate.

de·cor·ti·cate (dē kôr′tə kāt′), *v.t.*, **-cat·ed, -cat·ing. 1.** to remove the bark, husk, or outer covering from. **2.** *Surg.* to remove the cortex from (an organ or structure). [< L *decorticāt(us)* peeled (ptp. of *decorticāre*)] —**de·cor′ti·ca′tion,** *n.* —**de·cor′ti·ca′tor,** *n.*

de·co·rum (di kōr′əm, -kôr′-), *n.* **1.** propriety of behavior, speech, dress, etc. **2.** (esp. in Neoclassicism) literary or artistic appropriateness or suitability, as of form to content; congruence of style to subject. **3.** an observance or requirement of polite society. [< L, n. use of neut. of *decōrus*] —**Syn. 1.** politeness, manners, dignity. See **etiquette.**

de·cou·page (dā′ko͞o päzh′), *n.* **1.** the art, technique, or method of decorating something with cutouts of paper, linoleum, plastic or other flat materials. **2.** something produced by this technique. Also, **dé·cou·page** (dā′ko͞o päzh′; *Fr.* dā ko͞o päzh′). [< F *découpage* a cutting out = MF *decoup(er)* (to) cut out (*de-* from, out of (see DE-) + *couper* to cut) + *-age* -AGE]

de·coy (*n.* di koi′, dē′koi; *v.* di koi′), *n.* **1.** a person or thing that entices or lures, as into danger. **2.** anything used as a lure. **3.** a trained bird, or the likeness of one, used to entice game into a trap or within gunshot. **4.** a pond into which wild fowl are lured for capture. **5.** an object capable of reflecting radar waves, used as a spurious aircraft, missile, etc., for the deception of radar detectors. —*v.t.* **6.** to lure by or as if by a decoy. —*v.i.* **7.** to become decoyed. [var. of *coy* (now dial.) < D, m. (*de*) *kooi* (the) cage, MD *côie* < L *cavea* CAGE] —**de·coy′er,** *n.*

de·crease (*v.* di krēs′; *n.* dē′krēs, di krēs′), *v.*, **-creased, -creas·ing,** *n.* —*v.i.* **1.** to lessen, or lessen by degrees, in extent, quantity, strength, power, etc. —*v.t.* **2.** to make less; cause to diminish. —*n.* **3.** the act or process of decreasing; condition of being decreased; gradual reduction. **4.** the amount by which a thing is lessened: *The decrease in sales was almost 20 percent.* [ME *decrese(n)* < OF *decreiss-*, long s. of *decreistre* < L *dēcresc(ere).* See DE-, CRESCENT] —**de·creas′ing·ly,** *adv.*

—**Syn. 1.** wane, lessen, decline, contract, abate. DECREASE, DIMINISH, DWINDLE, SHRINK imply becoming smaller or less in amount. DECREASE commonly implies a gradual and sustained reduction, esp. of bulk, size, volume, or quantity, often from some imperceptible cause or inherent process: *The swelling decreased daily.* DIMINISH usually implies the action of some external cause which keeps taking away: *Evaporation caused the water in the pool to diminish.* DWINDLE implies an undesirable reduction by degrees, resulting in attenuation: *His followers dwindled to a mere handful.* SHRINK esp. implies contraction through an inherent property under specific conditions: *Many fabrics shrink in hot water.* **3.** abatement, decline, subsidence, shrinkage, dwindling.

de·cree (di krē′), *n.*, *v.*, **-creed, -cree·ing.** —*n.* **1.** an ordinance or edict promulgated by civil or other authority: *to issue a decree.* **2.** *Law.* a judicial decision or order. **3.** *Theol.* one of the eternal purposes of God, by which events are foreordained. —*v.t., v.i.* **4.** to ordain or decide by decree. [ME *decre* < OF (var. of *decret*) < L *dēcrēt(um)*, n. use of neut. of *dēcrētus*, ptp. of *dēcernere*; see DECERN]

dec·re·ment (dek′rə mənt), *n.* **1.** the act or process of decreasing; gradual reduction. **2.** the amount lost by reduction. **3.** *Math.* a negative increment. [< L *dēcrēment(um).* See DECREASE, -MENT]

de·crep·it (di krep′it), *adj.* **1.** weakened by old age; feeble; infirm. **2.** worn out by long use; dilapidated: *a decrepit stove.* [ME < L *dēcrepit(us)*, lit., broken down = *dē-* DE- + *crepitus*, ptp. of *crepāre* to crack] —**de·crep′it·ly,** *adv.* —**Syn. 1.** enfeebled. See **weak.** —**Ant. 1.** vigorous.

de·crep·i·tate (di krep′i tāt′), *v.*, **-tat·ed, -tat·ing.** —*v.t.* **1.** to roast or calcine (salt, minerals, etc.) so as to cause crackling or until crackling ceases. —*v.i.* **2.** to crackle, as salt in roasting. [< NL *dēcrepitāt(us)* crackled, ptp. of *dēcrepitāre* = L *dē-* DE- + *crepitāre* to crackle (freq. of *crepāre* to crack); see -ATE[1]] —**de·crep′i·ta′tion,** *n.*

de·crep·i·tude (di krep′i to͞od′, -tyo͞od′), *n.* decrepit condition; dilapidated state; feebleness, esp. from old age. [< F *décrépitude* < L *dēcrepit(us)* DECREPIT; see -TUDE]

decresc., *Music.* decrescendo.

de·cre·scen·do (dē′kri shen′dō, dā′-; *It.* de′kre shen′dô), *adj., adv., n., pl.* **-dos,** *It.* **-di** (-dē). *Music.* —*adj., adv.* **1.** gradually reducing force of loudness; diminuendo (opposed to *crescendo*). —*n.* **2.** a gradual reduction in force or loudness. **3.** a decrescendo passage. [< It, prp. of *decrescere*]

de·cres·cent (di kres′ənt), *adj.* **1.** diminishing; decreasing. **2.** waning, as the moon. [< L *dēcrescent-* (s. of *dēcrescēns*), prp. of *dēcrescere* to DECREASE; see -ENT] —**de·cres′cence,** *n.*

de·cre·tal (di krēt′əl), *adj.* **1.** pertaining to, of the nature of, or containing a decree or decrees. —*n.* **2.** a papal decree authoritatively determining some point of doctrine or church law. **3. Decretals,** the body or collection of such decrees as a part of the canon law. [ME < OF < LL *dēcrētāl(is).* See DECREE, -AL[1]]

de·cre·tive (di krē′tiv), *adj.* pertaining to or having the force of a decree. [< L *dēcrēt(um)* DECREE + -IVE]

dec·re·to·ry (dek′ri tōr′ē, -tôr′ē), *adj.* **1.** pertaining to or following a decree. **2.** established by a decree; judicial; definitive. [< L *dēcrētōri(us).* See DECREE, -ORY[1]]

de·cri·al (di krī′əl), *n.* decrying; noisy censure.

de·crim·i·nal·ize (dē krim′ə nəlīz′), *v.t.*, **-ized, -iz·ing.** to eliminate criminal penalties for possession or use of: *to decriminalize marijuana.* —**de·crim′i·nal·i·za′tion,** *n.*

de·cry (di krī′), *v.t.*, **-cried, -cry·ing. 1.** to speak disparagingly of; express open censure of. **2.** to depreciate by proclamation, as foreign or obsolete coins. [< F *décri(er)*, OF *descrier.* See DIS-[1], CRY] —**de·cri′er,** *n.*

dec·u·man (dek′yo͞o mən), *adj.* large or immense, as a wave. [< L *decumān(us)* of the tenth, var. of *decimānus* (by metonymy: large) = *decim(us)* tenth + *-ānus* -AN]

de·cum·bent (di kum′bənt), *adj.* **1.** lying down; recumbent. **2.** *Bot.* (of stems, branches, etc.) lying or trailing on the ground with the extremity tending to ascend. [< L *dēcumbent-* (s. of *dēcumbēns*), prp. of *dēcumbere.* See DE-, INCUMBENT] —**de·cum′bence, de·cum′ben·cy,** *n.*

de·cu·ri·on (di kyo͝or′ē ən), *n. Rom. Hist.* **1.** a commander of 10 men. **2.** a senator of an ancient Roman town or colony. [ME < L *decuriōn-* (s. of *decuriō*) = *decur(ia)* a division of ten (*dec(em)* ten + *-uria* -URE) + *-iōn-* -ION]

de·curved (dē kûrvd′), *adj.* curved downward, as the bill of a bird.

dec·u·ry (dek′yo͞o rē), *n., pl.* **-ries.** *Rom. Hist.* **1.** a division, company, or body of 10 men. **2.** any larger body of men, esp. the curiae. [< L *decuria* a company of ten. See DECURION, -Y[3]]

Decussate leaves

de·cus·sate (*v.* di kus′āt, dek′ə sāt′; *adj.* di kus′āt, -it), *v.*, **-sat·ed, -sat·ing,** *adj.* —*v.t., v.i.* **1.** to cross in the form of the letter X; intersect. —*adj.* **2.** in the form of the letter X; crossed; intersected. **3.** *Bot.* arranged along the stem in pairs, each pair at right angles to the pair next above or below, as leaves. [< L *decussāt(us)* divided in the form of an X (ptp. of *decussāre*) = *decuss(is)* the number ten (*dec(em)* ten + *-ass* AS[2]) + *-ātus* -ATE[1]] —**de·cus′sate·ly,** *adv.* —**de·cus·sa·tion** (dē′kə sā′shən, dek′ə-), *n.*

D.Ed., Doctor of Education.

de·dans (də däN′), *n., pl.* **-dans** (-däN′). (*construed as sing.*) *Court Tennis.* **1.** a netted winning opening of rectangular shape at the service side of the court. Cf. **grille** (def. 5), **winning gallery. 2.** the body of spectators behind this opening. [< F: (the) inside]

De·de Ag·ach (*Turk.* de′de ä äch′), former name of **Alexandroupolis.**

Ded·ham (ded′əm), *n.* a town in E Massachusetts, near Boston. 26,938 (1970).

ded·i·cate (ded′ə kāt′), *v.*, **-cat·ed, -cat·ing,** *adj.* —*v.t.* **1.** to set apart and consecrate to a deity or to a sacred purpose. **2.** to devote wholly and earnestly, as to some person or purpose: *He dedicated his life to fighting corruption.* **3.** to inscribe (a book, piece of music, etc.) to a person, cause, or the like, in testimony of affection or respect. —*adj.* **4.** *Archaic.* dedicated. [< L *dēdicāt(us)* declared, devoted, ptp. of *dēdicāre* = *dē-* DE- + *dicāre* to proclaim, var. of *dicere* to say, speak (see DICTATE)] —**ded′i·ca′tor,** *n.*

ded·i·cat·ed (ded′ə kā′tid), *adj.* **1.** wholly committed, as to an ideal or cause. **2.** designed, used, or reserved for a specific purpose: *a dedicated word processor.*

ded·i·ca·tion (ded′ə kā′shən), *n.* **1.** the act of dedicating. **2.** the state of being dedicated. **3.** an inscription prefixed or attached to a book, piece of music, etc., dedicating it to a person, cause, etc. [ME *dedicacioun* < L *dēdicātiōn-* (s. of *dēdicātiō*)] —**ded′i·ca′tion·al,** *adj.*

ded·i·ca·to·ry (ded′ə kə tōr′ē, -tôr′ē), *adj.* of or pertaining to dedication; serving as a dedication. Also, **ded·i·ca·tive** (ded′ə kā′tiv).

de·dif·fer·en·ti·a·tion (dē dif′ə ren′shē ā′shən), *n. Biol.* (of cells or tissues) reversion to a more primitive or general state.

de·duce (di do͞os′, -dyo͞os′), *v.t.*, **-duced, -duc·ing. 1.** to derive as a conclusion from something known or assumed; infer. **2.** to trace the derivation of; trace the course of: *to deduce one's lineage.* [< L *dēdūc(ere)* (to) lead down, derive] —**de·duc′i·bil′i·ty, de·duc′i·ble·ness,** *n.* —**de·duc′i·ble,** *adj.* —**de·duc′i·bly,** *adv.*

de·duct (di dukt′), *v.t.* **1.** to take away, as from a sum or amount. **2.** detract; abate (usually fol. by *from*). [< L *dēduct(us)* brought down, withdrawn, ptp. of *dēdūcere*]

de·duct·i·ble (di duk′tə bəl), *adj.* **1.** that can be deducted. **2.** *U.S.* allowable as a tax deduction. —*n.* **3.** an insurance policy having a deductible clause. —**de·duct′i·bil′i·ty,** *n.*

de·duc·tion (di duk′shən), *n.* **1.** the act or process of deducting; subtraction. **2.** something that is deducted. **3.** the act or process of deducing: *His deduction led him to the correct conclusion.* **4.** something that is deduced. **5.** *Logic.* **a.** a process of reasoning in which a conclusion follows necessarily from the premises presented. **b.** a conclusion reached by this process. Cf. **induction** (def. 2). [ME < L *dēductiōn-* (s. of *dēductiō*) a leading away]

de·duc·tive (di duk′tiv), *adj.* based on deduction from accepted premises: *deductive argument; deductive reasoning.* [< L *dēductīv(us)* derivative] —**de·duc′tive·ly,** *adv.*
—**Syn.** DEDUCTIVE and INDUCTIVE refer to two distinct logical processes. DEDUCTIVE reasoning is a logical process in which a conclusion drawn from a set of premises contains no more information than the premises taken collectively. *All dogs are animals; this is a dog; therefore, this is an animal:* The truth of the conclusion is dependent only on the method. *All men are apes; this is a man; therefore, this is an ape:* The conclusion is logically true, although the premise is absurd. INDUCTIVE reasoning is a logical process in which a conclusion is proposed that contains more information than the observations or experience on which it is based. *Every crow that has ever been seen is black; all crows are black:* The truth of the conclusion is verifiable only in terms of future experience and certainty is attainable only if all possible instances have been examined. In the example, there is no certainty that a white crow will not be found tomorrow, but experience would make such an occurrence seem extremely unlikely.

Dee (dē), *n.* **1. John,** 1527–1608, English mathematician and astrologer. **2.** a river in NE Scotland, flowing E into the North Sea at Aberdeen. 90 mi. long. **3.** a river in N Wales and W England, flowing NE into Irish Sea. 70 mi. long.

deed (dēd), *n.* **1.** something that is done, performed, or accomplished; an act. **2.** an exploit or achievement: *Brave men's deeds live after them.* **3.** action or performance, esp. as illustrative of intentions, promises, or the like: *His deeds speak for themselves.* **4.** *Law.* a writing or document executed under seal and delivered to effect a conveyance, esp. of real estate. —*v.t.* **5.** to convey or transfer by deed. [ME *dede,* OE *dēd,* var. of *dǣd;* c. G *Tat,* Goth *(ga)dēth(s);* see DO[1]] —**Syn. 1.** See **action.**

dee·jay (dē′jā′, -jā′), *n.* *Slang.* See **disk jockey.** [pronunciation of initials D.J.]

deem (dēm), *v.t.* **1.** to hold as an opinion; think; regard: *He deemed it wise to refuse the offer.* —*v.i.* **2.** to form or have an opinion; judge. [ME *dem(en),* OE *dēman;* c. Goth *dōmjan,* OHG *tuomen;* see DOOM] —**Syn. 1.** consider, hold.

de-em·pha·sis (dē em′fə sis), *n., pl.* **-ses** (-sēz). a reduction in emphasis.

de-em·pha·size (dē em′fə sīz′), *v.t.,* **-sized, -siz·ing.** to place less emphasis upon; reduce in size, scope, etc.

deep (dēp), *adj.* **1.** extending far down from the top or surface: *a deep well; a deep scratch.* **2.** extending far in or back from the front: *a deep shelf; a deep piece of land.* **3.** extending far in width; broad: *a deep border.* **4.** ranging far from the earth and sun: *a deep space probe.* **5.** having a specified dimension in depth: *a tank eight feet deep.* **6.** situated far down, in, or back: *deep below the surface; deep in the woods.* **7.** reaching or advancing far down: *a deep dive.* **8.** coming from far down: *a deep breath.* **9.** made with the body bent or lowered to a considerable degree: *a deep bow* **10.** difficult to understand; abstruse: *a deep allegory.* **11.** grave or serious: *deep disgrace.* **12.** heartfelt; sincere: *deep affections.* **13.** absorbing; engrossing: *deep study.* **14.** sound and heavy; profound: *deep sleep.* **15.** (of colors) dark and vivid: *a deep red.* **16.** low in pitch, as sound or voice: *deep, sonorous tones.* **17.** having penetrating intellectual powers. **18.** profoundly cunning or artful: *a deep and crafty scheme.* **19.** mysterious; obscure: *deep, dark secrets.* **20.** immersed or involved; enveloped: *a man deep in debt.* **21.** absorbed; engrossed: *deep in thought; deep in a book.* **22. in deep water,** in difficult or serious circumstances; in trouble: *He's been in deep water ever since he got fired from his job.* —*n.* **23.** the deep part of the sea, a river, etc. **24.** a vast extent, as of space, time, etc. **25.** the part of greatest intensity, as of winter. **26.** *Naut.* any of the unmarked levels, one fathom apart, on a deep-sea lead line. Cf. **mark**[1] (def. 14). **27. the deep,** *Chiefly Literary.* the sea or ocean: *on the bosom of the briny deep.* —*adv.* **28.** to or at a considerable or specified depth: *The boat rode deep in the water.* **29.** to or at a considerable or specified distance in or removed from the perimeter: *We walked deep into the woods.* **30.** far on in time: *He claimed he could see deep into the future.* **31.** profoundly; intensely: *He went deep into the matter.* **32. in deep,** inextricably involved. [ME *dep,* OE *dēop;* akin to Goth *diup(s),* OIcel *djup(r),* OHG *tiof*] —**deep′ness,** *n.* —**Syn. 10.** recondite, mysterious, obscure. **17.** sagacious, wise, profound.

deep-dish (dēp′dish′), *adj.* *Cookery.* baked in a deep dish, often with a pastry top: *a deep-dish peach pie.*

deep-dyed (dēp′dīd′), *adj.* thorough; unmitigated: *a deep-dyed villain.*

deep·en (dē′pən), *v.t., v.i.* to make or become deep or deeper.

deep′ fat′, hot fat used for deep-frying food.

deep-freeze (dēp′frēz′), *v.t.,* **-freezed** or **-froze, -freezed** or **-fro·zen, -freez·ing.** to quick-freeze (food).

Deep·freeze (dēp′frēz′), *n.* *Trademark.* a freezer designed for the quick-freezing and cold storage of food.

deep-fry (dēp′frī′), *v.t.,* **-fried, -fry·ing.** to fry in a quantity of fat sufficient to cover the food being cooked.

deep·ly (dēp′lē), *adv.* **1.** at or to a considerable extent downward; well within or beneath a surface. **2.** to a thorough extent or profound degree: *deeply pained; deeply committed.* **3.** with depth of color, tone, sound, etc. **4.** with great cunning, skill, and subtlety. [ME *deply,* OE *dēoplīce,* (adv.) < *dēoplīc* (adj.)]

deep-root·ed (dēp′ro͞o′tid, -ro͝ot′id), *adj.* deeply rooted; firmly implanted: *a deep-rooted patriotism.*

deep-sea (dēp′sē′), *adj.* of, pertaining to, in, or associated with the deeper parts of the sea.

deep-seat·ed (dēp′sē′tid), *adj.* firmly implanted: *a deep-seated sense of propriety; a deep-seated fear of snakes.*

deep′ six′, **1.** *Informal.* burial at sea. **2.** *Slang.* complete rejection: *They gave his ideas the deep six.*

deep-six (dēp′siks′), *v.t.* *Informal.* **1.** to throw overboard. **2.** to get rid of; abandon. [v. use of DEEP SIX]

Deep′ South′, the southeastern part of the U.S., including esp. those states that border the Gulf of Mexico.

deer (dēr), *n., pl.* **deer,** (*occasionally*) **deers. 1.** any of several ruminants of the family *Cervidae,* most of the males of which have solid, deciduous horns or antlers. **2.** any of the smaller species of this family, as distinguished from the moose, elk, etc. [ME *der,* OE *dēor* beast; akin to Goth *dius* beast, OHG *tior*]

Virginia deer, *Odocoileus virginianus* (3½ ft. high at shoulder; length 6½ ft.)

deer′ fly′, any of several tabanid flies of the genus *Chrysops,* the female of which bites and sucks the blood of deer, livestock, and man.

deer·hound (dēr′hound′), *n.* one of a Scottish breed of large dogs having a shaggy, gray or brindled coat.

Deer′ Park′, a town on central Long Island, in SE New York. 32,274 (1970).

deer·skin (dēr′skin′), *n.* **1.** the skin of a deer. **2.** leather made from this. **3.** a garment made of such leather. —*adj.* **4.** made of deerskin: *a deerskin jacket.* [ME *dereskin,* var. of *deres skin*]

Deerhound (2½ ft. high at shoulder)

deer·stalk·er (dēr′stô′kər), *n.* **1.** a person who stalks deer. **2.** a hunting cap having peaks in front and back, with earflaps usually raised and tied on top of the crown.

de·es·ca·late (dē es′kə lāt′), *v.t., v.i.,* **-lat·ed, -lat·ing.** to decrease in intensity, magnitude, etc. Also, **de-es′ca·late′.** —**de·es′ca·la′tion, de-es′ca·la′tion,** *n.*

def., **1.** defective. **2.** defendant. **3.** deferred. **4.** defined. **5.** definition.

de·face (di fās′), *v.t.,* **-faced, -fac·ing. 1.** to mar the face or appearance of; disfigure. **2.** to efface, obliterate, or injure the surface of, as to make illegible, invalid, etc.: *to deface a bond.* [ME *deface(n)* < OF *desfacie(r).* See DIS-[1], FACE] —**de·face′a·ble,** *adj.* —**de·face′ment,** *n.* —**de·fac′er,** *n.* —**Syn. 1.** spoil. See **mar.**

de fac·to (dē fak′tō), **1.** in fact; in reality. **2.** actually existing, esp. when without lawful authority (distinguished from *de jure*). [< L: lit., from the fact]

de·fal·cate (di fal′kāt, -fôl′-), *v.i.,* **-cat·ed, -cat·ing.** *Law.* to be guilty of defalcation. [< ML *dēfalcāt(us)* cut off (ptp. of *dēfalcāre*)] —**de·fal′ca·tor,** *n.*

de·fal·ca·tion (dē′fal kā′shən, -fôl-), *n.* *Law.* **1.** misappropriation of money held by an official, trustee, or other fiduciary. **2.** the sum misappropriated. [< ML *dēfalcātiōn-* (s. of *dēfalcātiō*) a taking away]

def·a·ma·tion (def′ə mā′shən, dē′fə-), *n.* the act of defaming; false or unjustified injury of the good reputation of another as by slander or libel; calumny. [ME *defamatioun;* r. (by analogy with DEFAME) ME *diffamacioun* < ML *diffāmātiōn-* (s. of *diffāmātiō*) = L *diffāmāt(us)* (ptp. of *diffāmāre*) + *-iōn-* -ION]

de·fam·a·to·ry (di fam′ə tōr′ē, -tôr′ē), *adj.* containing defamation; injurious to reputation; slanderous. [ML *diffāmātōri(us)* = L *diffāmāt(us)* (ptp. of *diffāmāre;* see DEFAME) + *-ōrius* -ORY[1]]

de·fame (di fām′), *v.t.,* **-famed, -fam·ing. 1.** to attack the good name or reputation of; slander or libel. **2.** *Archaic.* to disgrace; bring dishonor upon. **3.** *Archaic.* to accuse. [ME *defame(n)* < L *dēfām(āre)* (see DE-, FAME); r. ME *diffame(n)* < OF *diffame(r)* < L *diffāmāre* = *dif-* DIF- + *fām(a)* FAME + *-āre* inf. suffix] —**de·fam′er,** *n.*

de·fault (di fôlt′), *n.* **1.** failure to act; neglect. **2.** failure to meet financial obligations. **3.** *Law.* failure to perform an act or obligation legally required. **4.** *Sports.* failure to participate in or complete a scheduled match. **5.** want; lack; absence: *owing to default of water.* —*v.i.* **6.** to fail in fulfilling or satisfying an engagement, claim, or obligation. **7.** to fail to meet financial obligations. **8.** *Law.* to fail to appear in court. **9.** *Sports.* **a.** to fail to participate in or complete a match. **b.** to lose a match or game by such failure. —*v.t.* **10.** to fail to perform or pay: *to default a debt.* **11.** to declare (a person) to be in default, esp. legally. **12.** *Sports.* **a.** to fail to compete in (a game, race, etc.). **b.** to lose by default. **13.** *Law.* to lose by failure to appear in court. [ME *defau(l)te* < OF *defaute* (AF *defalte*) < *defaillir,* after *faute, faillir.* See DE-, FAULT, FAIL] —**de·fault′er,** *n.*

de·fea·sance (di fē′zəns), *n.* *Law.* **1.** a rendering null and void. **2.** a condition on the performance of which a deed or other instrument is defeated or rendered void. [ME *defesance* < AF *defesaunce,* OF *defesance* = *desfes-* (see DEFEAT) + *-ance* -ANCE]

de·fea·si·ble (di fē′zə bəl), *adj.* that may be annulled or terminated. [< AF *defesible.* See DEFEASANCE, -IBLE] —**de·fea′si·ble·ness, de·fea′si·bil′i·ty,** *n.*

de·feat (di fēt′), *v.t.* **1.** to overcome in a contest, battle, etc.; vanquish. **2.** to frustrate or thwart. **3.** *Law.* to annul. —*n.* **4.** the act of overcoming in a contest. **5.** an overthrow; vanquishment: *the defeat of a government.* **6.** an instance of defeat: *He considered his defeat a personal affront.* **7.** a bringing to naught; frustration: *the defeat of all his hopes.* **8.** *Obs.* undoing; destruction; ruin. [ME *defete(n)* < OF *desfait,* ptp. of *desfaire* to undo, destroy < ML *disfacere* = L *dis-* DIS-[1] + *facere* to do]
—**Syn. 1.** overwhelm, overthrow, rout, check. DEFEAT, CONQUER, OVERCOME, SUBDUE imply gaining a victory or control over an opponent. DEFEAT suggests beating or frus-

trating, sometimes only temporarily: *to defeat an enemy in battle.* CONQUER, more formal, implies finally gaining control over, usually after a series of efforts or against systematic resistance: *to conquer a country, one's inclinations.* OVERCOME emphasizes surmounting difficulties in prevailing over an antagonist: *to overcome opposition, bad habits.* SUBDUE means to conquer so completely that the spirit of resistance is broken: *to subdue an uprising, a rebellious spirit.* **2.** foil, baffle, balk. **5.** downfall.

de·feat·ism (di fē′tiz əm), *n.* the attitude, policy, or conduct of a person who admits or expects defeat. **—de·feat′ist,** *n., adj.*

def·e·cate (def′ə kāt′), *v.,* **-cat·ed, -cat·ing.** **—***v.i.* **1.** to void excrement from the bowels through the anus. **—***v.t.* **2.** to clear of dregs, impurities, etc.; purify; refine. [< L *dēfaecāt(us)* cleansed, refined (ptp. of *dēfaecāre*) = *dē-* DE- + *faec-* (s. of *faex* dregs, sediment) + *-ātus* -ATE[1]] **—def′e·ca′tion,** *n.*

de·fect (*n.* dē′fekt, di fekt′; *v.* di fekt′), *n.* **1.** a fault or imperfection. **2.** want or lack, esp. of something essential to perfection or completeness; deficiency: *a defect in hearing.* **—***v.i.* **3.** to desert a cause, country, etc., esp. in order to adopt another (often fol. by *to*): *He defected to the enemy.* [ME *defect* a falling short < L *dēfect(us)* = *dēfect-* (ptp. s. of *dēficere* to be DEFICIENT) + *-us,* 4th decl. suffix] **—Syn. 1.** DEFECT, BLEMISH, FLAW refer to faults which detract from perfection. DEFECT is the general word for any kind of shortcoming or imperfection, whether literal or figurative: *a defect in eyesight, in character, in a plan.* A BLEMISH is usually a defect on a surface, which mars the appearance: *A mole or scar on a cheek* (*or a scratch on a table*) *is a blemish.* FLAW is applied to a defect in quality, caused by imperfect structure (as in a diamond) or brought about during manufacture (as in texture of cloth, in clearness of glass, etc.).

de·fec·tion (di fek′shən), *n.* **1.** desertion from allegiance, loyalty, duty, or the like; apostasy. **2.** failure; lack; loss. [< L *dēfectiōn-* (s. of *dēfectiō*)]

de·fec·tive (di fek′tiv), *adj.* **1.** having a defect; faulty: *a defective machine.* **2.** *Psychol.* characterized by subnormal intelligence or behavior. **3.** *Gram.* (of an inflected word or its inflection) lacking one or more of the inflected forms proper to most words of the same class in the language, as English *must,* which occurs only in the present tense. **—***n.* **4.** a defective person or thing. [< LL *dēfectīv(us)* (see DEFECT, -IVE), r. ME *defectif* < MF] **—de·fec′tive·ly,** *adv.* **—de·fec′tive·ness,** *n.* **—Syn. 1.** imperfect. **—Ant. 1.** perfect.

defec′tive year′. See under **Jewish calendar.**

de·fec·tor (di fek′tər), *n.* a person who defects from a cause, country, etc. [< L: deserter]

de·fence (di fens′), *n. Chiefly Brit.* defense. **—de·fence′a·ble,** *adj.* **—de·fence′less,** *adj.*

de·fend (di fend′), *v.t.* **1.** to ward off attack from; guard against assault or injury (usually fol. by *from* or *against*): *She defended her children from the mad dog. The sentry defended the platoon against sudden attack.* **2.** to maintain by argument, evidence, etc.; uphold: *He defended his point successfully.* **3.** to contest (a legal charge, claim, etc.). **4.** *Law.* to serve as attorney for (a defendant). **5.** to support (an argument, theory, etc.) in the face of criticism; prove the validity of (a dissertation, thesis, or the like) by answering arguments and questions put by a committee of specialists. **—***v.i.* **6.** *Law.* to enter or make a defense. [ME *defende(n)* < OF *defendre* < L *dēfendere* to ward off = *dē-* DE- + *-fendere* to strike] **—de·fend′er,** *n.* **—Syn. 1.** shelter, shield. DEFEND, GUARD, PRESERVE, PROTECT all mean to keep safe. To DEFEND is to strive to keep safe by resisting attack: *to defend a position in battle; to defend one's country.* To GUARD is to watch over in order to keep safe: *to guard a camp, a secret.* To PRESERVE is to keep safe in the midst of danger, either in a single instance or continuously: *to preserve a city, a spirit of conciliation.* To PROTECT is to keep safe by interposing a shield or barrier: *to protect books by means of heavy paper covers; to protect the reputation of a friend.* **2.** vindicate. **—Ant. 1.** attack.

de·fend·ant (di fen′dənt), *n.* **1.** *Law.* a person against whom a claim or charge is brought in a court (opposed to *plaintiff*). **—***adj.* **2.** defending; making one's defense: *a defendant corporation.* **3.** *Obs.* defensive. [ME *defendaunt* < AF (MF, OF *defendant*)]

Defend′er of the Faith′, a title conferred on Henry VIII by Pope Leo X in 1521, and retained by English sovereigns. [trans. of NL *Fidei defensor*]

de·fen·es·tra·tion (dē fen′i strā′shən), *n.* the act of throwing a person or thing out of a window. [DE- + L *fenestr(a)* a window + -ATION]

de·fense (di fens′ *or, for 1, 6,* dē′fens), *n.* **1.** resistance against attack; protection. **2.** something that defends, esp. a fortification. **3.** the defending of a cause or the like by speech, argument, etc.: *He spoke in defense of the nation's foreign policy.* **4.** a speech, argument, etc., in vindication. **5.** *Law.* **a.** the denial or pleading of the defendant in answer to the claim or charge against him. **b.** a defendant and his legal agents collectively. **6.** *Sports.* **a.** the practice or art of defending oneself or one's goal against attack. **b.** the team attempting to thwart the attack of the team having the ball or puck. Also, *esp. Brit.,* **defence.** [ME < OF < LL *dēfensa* a forbidding, n. use of fem. of ptp. of L *dēfendere* to DEFEND; r. ME *defens* < OF < ML *dēfens(um)* (thing) forbidden, neut. ptp. of L *dēfendere*] **—de·fense′less,** *adj.* **—de·fense′less·ly,** *adv.* **—de·fense′less·ness,** *n.*

defense′ mech′anism, 1. *Physiol.* the defensive reaction of an organism, as against a pathogenic microorganism. **2.** *Psychol.* an unconscious process that opposes the entrance into consciousness or the acting out of unacceptable or painful ideas and impulses.

de·fen·si·ble (di fen′sə bəl), *adj.* **1.** capable of being defended against assault or injury. **2.** that may be defended in argument; justifiable. [ME < LL *dēfensibil(is)* (see DEFENSE, -IBLE); r. ME *defensable* < OF < LL *dēfensābil(is)* = *dēfens(āre)* (freq. of *dēfendere* to DEFEND) + *-ābilis* -ABLE] **—de·fen′si·bil′i·ty, de·fen′si·ble·ness,** *n.* **—de·fen′si·bly,** *adv.*

de·fen·sive (di fen′siv), *adj.* **1.** serving to defend; protective: *defensive armament.* **2.** made or carried on for the purpose of resisting attack: *defensive treaty; a defensive attitude.* **3.** of or pertaining to defense. **—***n.* **4.** a position or attitude of defense: *to be on the defensive about one's mistakes.* **5.** *Obs.* something that serves to defend. [< ML *dēfensīv(us)* (see DEFENSE, -IVE); r. ME *defensif* < MF] **—de·fen′sive·ly,** *adv.* **—de·fen′sive·ness,** *n.*

de·fer[1] (di fûr′), *v.,* **-ferred, -fer·ring.** **—***v.t.* **1.** to put off (action, consideration, etc.) to a future time. **2.** to exempt temporarily from induction into military service. **—***v.i.* **3.** to put off action; delay. [ME *deferre(n),* var. of *differre(n)* (to) DIFFER] **—de·fer′rer,** *n.*

de·fer[2] (di fûr′), *v.i.,* **-ferred, -fer·ring. 1.** to yield in judgment or opinion (usually fol. by *to*): *We all defer to him in these matters.* **2.** to submit for decision; refer. [late ME *deferre(n)* < L *dēferre* to carry from or down, report, accuse = *dē-* DE- + *ferre* to bear]

de·fer·a·ble (di fûr′ə bəl), *adj., n.* deferrable.

def·er·ence (def′ər əns), *n.* **1.** submission or yielding to the judgment, opinion, will, etc., of another. **2.** respectful or courteous regard: *in deference to his wishes.* [< F *déférence*]

def·er·ent[1] (def′ər ənt), *adj.* marked by or showing deference. [DEFER[2] + -ENT]

def·er·ent[2] (def′ər ənt), *adj.* *Anat.* **1.** conveying away; efferent. **2.** of or pertaining to the vas deferens. **—***n.* **3.** *Astron.* (in the Ptolemaic system) the circle around the earth in which a celestial body or the center of the epicycle of its orbit was thought to move. [< L *dēferent-* (s. of *dēferēns*), prp. of *dēferre.* See DEFER[2], -ENT]

def·er·en·tial (def′ə ren′shəl), *adj.* deferent; respectful. [after DEFERENCE, by analogy with such sets as *residence, residential*] **—def′er·en′tial·ly,** *adv.*

de·fer·ment (di fûr′mənt), *n.* **1.** the act of deferring or putting off; postponement. **2.** a temporary exemption from induction into military service.

de·fer·ra·ble (di fûr′ə bəl), *adj.* **1.** capable of being deferred or postponed. **2.** qualified or eligible to receive a military deferment. **—***n.* **3.** a person eligible for deferment from compulsory military service. Also, **deferable.**

de·fer·ral (di fûr′əl), *n.* a deferment.

de·ferred (di fûrd′), *adj.* **1.** postponed or delayed. **2.** suspended or withheld for or until a certain time: *a deferred payment.* **3.** classified as temporarily exempt from induction into military service.

de·fi·ance (di fī′əns), *n.* **1.** a daring or bold resistance to authority or to any opposing force. **2.** open disregard; contempt (often fol. by *of*): *defiance of danger; His refusal amounted to defiance.* **3.** a challenge to meet in combat or in a contest. [ME < OF]

de·fi·ant (di fī′ənt), *adj.* characterized by defiance, bold opposition, or antagonism: *a defiant attitude.* [< F *défiant;* see DEFY, -ANT] **—de·fi′ant·ly,** *adv.* **—Syn.** insubordinate, refractory, recalcitrant, rebellious, insolent. **—Ant.** obedient.

de·fi·cien·cy (di fish′ən sē), *n., pl.* **-cies. 1.** the state of being deficient; incompleteness; insufficiency. **2.** the amount lacked; deficit. [< LL *dēficientia*]

defi′ciency disease′, *Pathol.* an illness due to an insufficiency of one or more essential nutrients.

de·fi·cient (di fish′ənt), *adj.* **1.** lacking some element or characteristic; defective: *deficient in taste.* **2.** insufficient; inadequate: *deficient knowledge.* [< L *dēficient-* (s. of *dēficiēns,* prp. of *dēficere*) = *dē-* DE- + *fic-* make, do (sp. var. of *fac-*) + thematic *-i-* + *-ent-* -ENT] **—de·fi′cient·ly,** *adv.*

def·i·cit (def′i sit; *Brit. also* di fis′it), *n.* the amount by which a sum of money falls short of the required amount. [< L: there is wanting, 3rd pers. sing. pres. indic. of *dēficere;* see DEFICIENT] **—Syn.** shortage, deficiency. **—Ant.** surplus.

def′icit spend′ing, the practice of spending funds in excess of income, esp. by a government.

de fi·de (de fē′de; *Eng.* dē fī′dē), *Latin.* of the faith: a phrase used in the Roman Catholic Church to qualify certain teachings as being divinely revealed, belief in them therefore being obligatory.

de·fi·er (di fī′ər), *n.* a person who defies.

def·i·lade (def′ə lād′), *n., v.,* **-lad·ed, -lad·ing.** **—***n.* **1.** protection or shielding from hostile ground observation and flat projecting fire provided by an artificial or natural obstacle, as a hill. **—***v.t.* **2.** to shield from enemy fire by using natural or artificial obstacles. [< F *défil(er),* orig. to unthread = *dé-* DIS-[1] + *(en)filer* to thread << L *fīl(um)* thread + F *-ade* -ADE[1]]

de·file[1] (di fīl′), *v.t.,* **-filed, -fil·ing. 1.** to make foul, dirty, or unclean; pollute; taint. **2.** to violate the chastity of. **3.** to make impure for ceremonial use; desecrate. **4.** to sully, as a person's reputation. [ME *defile(n), defele(n),* alter. of *defoilen* (by assoc. with *filen* to FILE[3]) < OF *defoule(r)* (to) trample on, violate; cf. OE *befȳlan* to befoul] **—de·file′ment,** *n.* **—de·fil′er,** *n.*

de·file[2] (di fīl′, dē′fīl), *n., v.,* **-filed, -fil·ing.** **—***n.* **1.** any narrow passage, esp. between mountains. **—***v.i.* **2.** to march in a line or by files. [< F *défilé,* n. use of ptp. of *défiler* to march by files; see DEFILADE]

de·fine (di fīn′), *v.t.,* **-fined, -fin·ing. 1.** to state or set forth the meaning of (a word, phrase, etc.). **2.** to explain the nature or essential qualities of; describe: *to define judicial functions.* **3.** to determine or fix the boundaries or extent of: *to define property with stakes.* **4.** to make clear the outline or form of: *The roof of the barn was boldly defined against the sky.* **5.** to specify distinctly: *to define one's responsibilities.* [ME *def(f)ine(n)* < AF, OF *define(r)* (to) put an end to < L *dēfīnīre* to limit, explain. See DE-, FINISH] **—de·fin′a·ble,** *adj.* **—de·fin′a·bil′i·ty,** *n.* **—de·fin′a·bly,** *adv.* **—de·fin′er,** *n.*

de·fin·i·en·dum (di fin′ē en′dəm), *n., pl.* **-da** (-də). **1.** that which is or is to be defined, esp. the term at the head of a dictionary entry. **2.** *Logic.* an expression to be defined in terms of another expression previously defined. Cf. **definiens.** [< L, neut. ger. of *dēfīnīre* to terminate, decide, DEFINE]

de·fin·i·ens (di fin′ē ənz), *n., pl.* **de·fin·i·en·tia** (di fin′ē-en′chə, -chē ə). **1.** that which defines, esp. the defining part of a dictionary entry. **2.** *Logic.* an expression in terms of which another may be adequately defined. Cf. **definiendum.** [< L, prp. of *dēfīnīre;* see DEFINE]

def·i·nite (def′ə nit), *adj.* **1.** clearly defined or determined; precise; exact: *a definite quantity; definite directions.* **2.** having fixed limits; bounded with precision: *a definite area.* **3.** positive; certain; sure: *It is definite that he will take the job.* **4.** defining; limiting. **5.** *Bot.* (of an inflorescence) determinate. [< L *dēfīnīt(us)* bounded, precise, ptp. of *dēfīnīre;* see DEFINE] —**def′i·nite·ness,** *n.* —**Syn. 1.** specific, particular. —**Ant. 1.** inexact.

def′inite ar′ticle, an article, as English *the,* which particularizes the noun it modifies. Cf. **indefinite article.**

def′inite in′tegral, *Math.* the representation, usually in symbolic form, of the difference in values of a primitive of a given function evaluated at two designated points. Cf. **indefinite integral.**

def·i·nite·ly (def′ə nit lē), *adv.* **1.** in a definite manner. **2.** unequivocally; positively. —*interj.* **3.** certainly; surely.

def·i·ni·tion (def′ə nish′ən), *n.* **1.** the act of defining or making definite or clear. **2.** the formal statement of the meaning or significance of a word, phrase, etc. **3.** condition of being definite. **4.** *Optics.* sharpness of the image formed by an optical system. [ME *diffinicioun* < OF *diffinition* < L *dēfīnītiōn-* (s. of *dēfīnītiō*)]

de·fin·i·tive (di fin′i tiv), *adj.* **1.** most reliable or complete, as of a text, author, criticism, study, or the like: *a definitive biography; a definitive performance of a Beethoven sonata.* **2.** serving to define; fix or specify definitely: *to clarify with a definitive statement.* **3.** having its fixed and final form; providing a solution or final answer: *a definitive answer to a dilemma.* —*n.* **4.** a defining or limiting word, as an article, a demonstrative, or the like. [ME *diffinitif* < OF < L *dēfīnītīv(us)*] —**de·fin′i·tive·ly,** *adv.* —**de·fin′i·tive·ness,** *n.*

de·fin·i·tude (di fin′i to͞od′, -tyo͞od′), *n.* definiteness; exactitude; precision.

def·la·grate (def′lə grāt′, dē′flə-), *v.t., v.i.,* **-grat·ed, -grat·ing.** to burn, esp. suddenly and violently. [< L *dēflagrāt(us)* burned down (ptp. of *dēflagrāre*). See DE-, FLAGRANT, -ATE[1]] —**def′la·gra′tion,** *n.*

de·flate (di flāt′), *v.,* **-flat·ed, -flat·ing.** —*v.t.* **1.** to release the air or gas from (something inflated, as a balloon). **2.** to reduce (currency, prices, etc.) from an inflated condition. **3.** to depress or reduce (a person or a person's ego, hopes, spirits, etc.): *Her rebuff thoroughly deflated him.* —*v.i.* **4.** to become deflated. [< L *dēflāt(us)* blown off, away (ptp. of *dēflāre*) = *dē-* DE- + *fl(āre)* (to) blow + *-ātus* -ATE[1]] —**de·fla′tor,** *n.*

de·fla·tion (di flā′shən), *n.* **1.** the act of deflating. **2.** the state of being deflated. **3.** an abnormal decline in the level of commodity prices, esp. one not accompanied by an equal reduction in the costs of production. —**de·fla·tion·ar·y** (di flā′shə ner′ē), *adj.*

de·flect (di flekt′), *v.t., v.i.* to bend or turn aside; turn from a true course or straight line; swerve. [< L *dēflect(ere)* (to) bend down, turn aside = *dē-* DE- + *flectere* to bend, turn] —**de·flec′tor,** *n.*

de·flec·tion (di flek′shən), *n.* **1.** the act or state of deflecting. **2.** the state of being deflected. **3.** amount of deviation. **4.** *Physics.* the deviation of the indicator of an instrument from the position taken as zero. Also, *Brit.,* **de·flexion.** [< LL *dēflexiōn-* s. of *dēflexiō*) = L *dēflex(us)* (ptp. of *dēflectere;* see DEFLECT) + *-iōn-* -ION]

de·flec·tive (di flek′tiv), *adj.* causing deflection.

de·flex·ion (di flek′shən), *n. Brit.* deflection.

def·lo·ra·tion (def′lə rā′shən, dē′flə-), *n.* the act of deflowering. [ME *defloracioun* < OF *defloracion,* LL *dēflōrātiōn-* (s. of *dēflōrātiō*) a plucking of flowers = *dēflōrāt(us),* lit., deprived of flowers, ptp. of *dēflōrāre* to DEFLOWER + *-iōn-* -ION]

de·flow·er (di flou′ər), *v.t.* **1.** to deprive or strip of flowers. **2.** to deprive (a woman) of virginity; ravish; violate. **3.** to despoil of beauty, sanctity, etc. [ME *defloure(n)* < OF *desflore(r)* < L *dēflōrāre*] —**de·flow′er·er,** *n.*

De·foe (di fō′), *n.* **Daniel,** 1659?–1731, English novelist, journalist, and essayist. Also, **De Foe′.**

de·fog (dē fog′), *v.t.,* **-fogged, -fog·ging.** to remove the fog or moisture from (a car window, mirror, etc.). —**de·fog′ger,** *n.*

de·fo·li·ant (dē fō′lē ənt), *n.* a preparation for defoliating plants. [DEFOLI(ATE) + -ANT]

de·fo·li·ate (*v.* dē fō′lē āt′; *adj.* dē fō′lē it, -āt′), *v.,* **-at·ed, -at·ing,** *adj.* —*v.t.* **1.** to strip of leaves. **2.** to destroy (an area of jungle, forest, etc.), as by chemical sprays or incendiary bombs in order to give enemy troops or guerrilla forces no place of concealment. —*v.i.* **3.** to lose leaves. —*adj.* **4.** (of a tree) having lost its leaves, esp. by a natural process. [< ML *dēfoliāt(us),* ptp. of *dēfoliāre.* See DE-, FOLIATE] —**de·fo′li·a′tion,** *n.* —**de·fo′li·a′tor,** *n.*

de·force (di fōrs′, fôrs′), *v.t.,* **-forced, -forc·ing.** *Law.* to withhold (property, esp. land) by force or violence, as from the rightful owner. [ME < AF *deforc(er),* OF *de(s)forc(ier)* See DE-, FORCE] —**de·force′ment,** *n.*

de·for·ciant (di fōr′shənt, -fôr′-), *n. Law.* a person who deforces. [< AF, prp. of *deforcer*]

De For·est (di fôr′ist, for′-), **Lee,** 1873–1961, U.S. inventor of radio, telegraphic, and telephonic equipment.

de·for·est (dē fôr′ist, -for′-), *v.t.* to divest of forests or trees. —**de·for′est·a′tion,** *n.* —**de·for′est·er,** *n.*

de·form (di fôrm′), *v.t.* **1.** to mar the natural form or shape of; put out of shape; disfigure. **2.** to make ugly, ungraceful, or displeasing; mar the beauty of; spoil. **3.** to change the form of; transform. **4.** *Mech.* to subject to deformation: *The metal was deformed under stress.* [ME *deform(en)* < L *dēform(āre)*] —**de·form′er,** *n.* —**Syn. 1.** misshape. See **mar. 2.** ruin.

de·for·ma·tion (dē′fôr mā′shən, def′ər-), *n.* **1.** the act of deforming; distortion. **2.** result of deforming; change of form, esp. for the worse. **3.** *Mech.* a change in the shape or dimensions of a body, resulting from stress; strain. **4.** an altered form. [ME *deformacioun* < L *dēformātiōn-* (s. of *dēformātiō*) = *dēformāt(us)* (ptp. of *dēformāre;* see DEFORM) + *-iōn-* -ION]

de·formed (di fôrmd′), *adj.* having the form changed, with loss of beauty, etc.; misshapen; disfigured. [ME]

de·form·i·ty (di fôr′mi tē), *n., pl.* **-ties. 1.** the quality or state of being deformed, disfigured, or misshapen. **2.** *Pathol.* an abnormally formed part of the body. **3.** a deformed person or thing. [ME *deformite* < OF < L *dēformitās*]

de·fraud (di frôd′), *v.t.* to deprive of a right or property by fraud; cheat. [ME *defraud(en)* < OF *defraud(er)* < L *dēfraudāre*] —**de·frau·da·tion** (dē′frô dā′shən), *n.* —**de·fraud′er,** *n.*

de·fray (di frā′), *v.t.* to bear or pay (the costs, expenses, etc.): *The grant helped defray the expenses of the trip.* [< F *défray(er),* OF *deffroier* to pay costs = *de-* DIS-[1] + *frai* cost] —**de·fray′er,** *n.*

de·fray·al (di frā′əl), *n.* payment of charges or expenses. Also, **de·fray′ment.**

de·frock (dē frok′), *v.t.* to unfrock. [< F *défroqu(er).* See DIS-[1], FROCK]

de·frost (di frôst′, -frost′), *v.t.* **1.** to remove the frost or ice from. **2.** to thaw or partially thaw (frozen food). —*v.i.* **3.** to become free of ice or frost; thaw. —**de·frost′er,** *n.*

defs., definitions.

deft (deft), *adj.* dexterous; nimble; skillful; clever: *deft hands; a deft mechanic.* [ME; var. of DAFT] —**deft′ly,** *adv.* —**deft′ness,** *n.*

de·funct (di fungkt′), *adj.* **1.** deceased; dead; extinct. **2.** no longer in effect or use; not operating or functioning: *a defunct law.* [< L *dēfunct(us)* discharged, dead (ptp. of *dēfungī*). See DE-, FUNCTION]

de·fuse (dē fyo͞oz′), *v.t.,* **-fused, -fus·ing. 1.** defuze. **2.** to deprive of the means or intent to harm: *to defuse tension in a labor dispute.*

de·fuze (dē fyo͞oz′), *v.t.,* **-fuzed, -fuz·ing.** to remove the fuze from (a bomb, mine, etc.).

de·fy (di fī′), *v.t.,* **-fied, -fy·ing. 1.** to challenge the power of; resist boldly or openly. **2.** to offer effective resistance to: *a fort that defies attack.* **3.** to challenge to do something deemed impossible. **4.** *Archaic.* to challenge to a combat or contest. [ME *defie(n)* < OF *desfi(er)* = *des-* DE- + *fier* to trust < VL **fīdāre,* var. of L *fīdere*]

deg., degree; degrees.

dé·ga·gé (dā ga zhā′), *adj. French.* **1.** unconstrained; easy, as in manner. **2.** without emotional involvement; detached. [lit., disengaged]

de·gas (dē gas′), *v.t.,* **-gassed, -gas·sing. 1.** to free from gas. **2.** to treat (a gas or its harmful properties) with chemical agents. **3.** to complete the evacuation of gases in (a vacuum tube).

De·gas (də gä′), *n.* **Hi·laire Ger·main Ed·gar** (ē lɛʀ′ zhɛʀ maɴ′ ed gaʀ′), 1834–1917, French impressionist painter.

de Gaulle (də gōl′, gôl′), **Charles An·dré Jo·seph Ma·rie** (chärlz än′drā jō′zəf mə rē′; *Fr.* shaʀl äɴ dʀā′ zhō zef′ ma ʀē′), 1890–1970, French general and statesman: president 1959–69.

de·gauss (dē gous′), *v.t.* to neutralize (the magnetic field of a ship's hull, electrical equipment, etc.) by means of electric coils that create a magnetic field cancelling that of the hull, chassis, etc. [DE- + GAUSS] —**de·gauss′er,** *n.*

de·gen·er·ate (*v.* di jen′ə rāt′; *adj., n.* di jen′ər it), *v.,* **-at·ed, -at·ing,** *adj., n.* —*v.i.* **1.** to decline in physical, mental, or moral qualities; deteriorate. **2.** *Biol.* to revert to a less highly organized or simpler type. —*adj.* **3.** having declined in physical or moral qualities; deteriorated; degraded. **4.** characterized by or associated with degeneracy: *degenerate times.* —*n.* **5.** a person who has declined, as in morals or character, from standards considered normal. **6.** a sexual deviate. **7.** *Pathol.* a person exhibiting either congenital or acquired morbid physical or mental traits or tendencies. [< L *dēgenerāt(us)* departed from its race (ptp. of *dēgenerāre*) = *dēgener-* (s. of *dēgener*) not genuine + *-ātus* -ATE[1]] —**de·gen·er·a·cy** (di jen′ər ə sē), *n.* —**de·gen′er·ate·ly,** *adv.* —**de·gen′er·ate·ness,** *n.*

de·gen·er·a·tion (di jen′ə rā′shən), *n.* **1.** the process of degenerating. **2.** the condition or state of being degenerate. **3.** *Biol.* reversion to a less highly organized or simpler type. **4.** *Pathol.* **a.** a process by which a tissue deteriorates, loses functional activity, and may become converted into or replaced by other kinds of tissue. **b.** the condition thus produced. [< LL *dēgenerātiōn-* (s. of *dēgenerātiō*)]

de·gen·er·a·tive (di jen′ə rā′tiv, -ər ə tiv), *adj.* **1.** tending to degenerate. **2.** characterized by degeneration.

de·glu·ti·nate (dē glo͞ot′ənāt′), *v.t.,* **-nat·ed, -nat·ing.** to extract the gluten from. —**de·glu′ti·na′tion,** *n.*

de·glu·ti·tion (dē′glo͞o tish′ən), *n. Physiol.* the act or process of swallowing. [< F *déglutition* < L *dēglūtīt(us)* swallowed down, ptp. of *dēglūt(īre)* = *dē-* DE- + *glūtīre* to swallow; see GLUTTON[1], -ION]

deg·ra·da·tion (deg′rə dā′shən), *n.* **1.** the act of degrading. **2.** the state of being degraded. **3.** *Phys. Geog.* the wearing down of the land by the action of water, wind, or ice; erosion. **4.** *Chem.* the breakdown of a compound, esp. an organic hydrocarbon. [< LL *dēgradātiōn-* (s. of *dēgradātiō*) = *dēgradāt(us)* (ptp. of *dēgradāre* to DEGRADE) + *-iōn-* -ION] —**Syn. 2.** humiliation, disgrace, debasement.

de·grade (di grād′; *also, for 1,* dē grād′), *v.,* **-grad·ed, -grad·ing.** —*v.t.* **1.** to reduce (someone) to a lower rank, degree, etc.; deprive of office, rank, degree, or title, esp. as a punishment. **2.** to lower in character or quality; debase; deprave. **3.** to lower in dignity or estimation; bring into contempt: *He felt they were degrading him by making him wash the dishes.* **4.** to reduce in amount, strength, intensity, etc. **5.** *Phys. Geog.* to wear down by erosion, as hills (opposed to *aggrade*). **6.** *Chem.* to break down (a compound, esp. an organic hydrocarbon). —*v.i.* **7.** *Chem.* (esp. of an organic hydrocarbon compound) to break down or decompose. [ME *degrade(n)* < LL *dēgrad(āre)*] —**Syn. 1.** demote, downgrade, lower. **3.** See **humble.** —**Ant. 1.** promote.

de·grad·ed (di grā′did), *adj.* **1.** reduced in rank, position, reputation, etc. **2.** reduced in quality or value; debased; vulgarized. [late ME] —**de·grad′ed·ly,** *adv.* —**de·grad′ed·ness,** *n.*

de·grad·ing (di grā′ding), *adj.* that degrades; debasing. —**de·grad′ing·ly,** *adv.* —**de·grad′ing·ness,** *n.*

de·gree (di grē′), *n.* **1.** any of a series of steps or stages, as in a process or course of action; a point in any scale. **2.** a stage or point, in or as if in progression or retrogression: *He grew weaker by degrees.* **3.** a stage in a scale of rank or station; relative standing in society, business, etc. **4.** a stage in a scale of intensity or amount: *a high degree of mastery.* **5.** extent, measure, scope, or the like: *To what degree will he cooperate?* **6.** *Geom.* the 360th part of a complete circle or turn, often indicated by the sign °, as 45°. **7.** a unit of measure, as of temperature or pressure, marked off on the scale of a measuring instrument. **8.** *Geog., Astron.* a line or point on the earth or the celestial sphere, the position of which is defined by its angular distance from the equator, the equinoctial, or from a given meridian. **9.** the distinctive classification of a crime according to its gravity: *murder in the first degree.* **10.** *Educ.* an academic title conferred by universities and colleges as an indication of the completion of a course of study, or as an honorary recognition of achievement. **11.** *Gram.* one of the parallel formations of adjectives and adverbs used to express differences in quality, quantity, or intensity. In English, *low* and *careful* are the positive degree, *lower* and *more careful* are the comparative degree, *lowest* and *most careful* are the superlative degree. **12.** *Math.* **a.** the sum of the exponents of the variables in an algebraic expression: x^3 *and* $2x^2y$ *are terms of degree three.* **b.** the term of highest degree of a given equation or polynomial. **13.** *Music.* a tone or step of the scale. **14.** *Genetics.* a certain distance or remove in the line of descent, determining the proximity of relationship: *a cousin of the second degree.* **15.** *Obs.* a step, as of a stair. [ME *degre* < OF < L *dē-* DE- + *grad(us)* GRADE] —**de·gree′less,** *adj.*

de·gree-day (di grē′dā′), *n.* one degree of deviation, on a single day, of the daily mean temperature from a given standard temperature.

degree′ of free′dom, *Physics, Chem.* one of the independent variables designating a way in which the configuration in space of a system can change.

de·gres·sion (di gresh′ən), *n.* a downward movement; descent. [late ME < ML *dēgressiōn-* (s. of *dēgressiō*) descent = L *dēgress(us)* having gone aside, down (ptp. of *dēgredī; dē-* DE- + *gre-* go (ptp. s. of *gradī*) + *-ss-* ptp. suffix) + *-iōn-* -ION]

de Groot (də KHRŌT′), **Huig** (hoiKH). See **Grotius, Hugo.**

de·gust (di gust′), *v.t.* taste; savor. Also, **de·gus·tate** (di gus′tāt). [< L *dēgust(āre)* (to) taste, try = *dē-* DE- + *gustāre* to taste < *gust(us)* a tasting] —**de·gus·ta·tion** (dē′gu stā′shən), *n.*

de gus·ti·bus non est dis·pu·tan·dum (de gōōs′ti bōōs′ nōn est dis′pōō tän′dōōm; *Eng.* dē gus′tə bəs non est dis′pyōō tan′dəm), *Latin.* there is no disputing about tastes.

de·hisce (di his′), *v.i.*, **-hisced, -hisc·ing.** to gape; burst open, as capsules of plants. [< L *dēhisc(ere)* (to) gape, part = *dē-* DE- + *hiscere* to gape, yawn (*hi(āre)* (to) yawn + *-scere* inceptive suffix)]

de·his·cence (di his′əns), *n.* **1.** the natural bursting open of capsules, fruits, anthers, etc., for the discharge of their contents. **2.** *Biol.* the release of materials by the splitting open of an organ or tissue. [< NL *dēhiscentia* = L *dēhiscent-* (s. of *dēhiscēns*) gaping (prp. of *dēhiscere;* see DEHISCE, -ENT) + *-ia;* see -ENCE] —**de·his′cent,** *adj.*

de·horn (dē hôrn′), *v.t.* to deprive (cattle) of horns. —**de·horn′er,** *n.*

de·hort (di hôrt′), *v.t. Archaic.* to seek to dissuade. [< L *dēhort(ārī)* (to) dissuade = *dē-* DE- + *hortārī* to urge (freq. pass. form of *horīrī* to urge)]

Deh·ra Dun (dā′rə dōōn′), a city in NW Uttar Pradesh, in N India. 126,900 (1961).

de·hu·man·ize (dē hyōō′mə nīz′ *or, often,* -yōō′-), *v.t.*, **-ized, -iz·ing.** to deprive of human qualities or attributes; divest of individuality. Also, *esp. Brit.,* **de·hu′man·ise′.** —**de·hu′man·i·za′tion,** *n.*

de·hu·mid·i·fi·er (dē′hyōō mid′ə fī′ər, *or, often,* -yōō-), *n.* an electrical appliance for removing moisture from the air.

de·hu·mid·i·fy (dē′hyōō mid′ə fī′ *or, often,* -yōō-), *v.t.*, **-fied, -fy·ing.** to remove moisture from. —**de′hu·mid′i·fi·ca′tion,** *n.*

de·hy·drate (dē hī′drāt), *v.*, **-drat·ed, -drat·ing.** —*v.t.* **1.** to deprive (a chemical compound) of water or the elements of water. **2.** to free (fruit, vegetables, etc.) from moisture for preservation. **3.** to remove water from (the body or a tissue). —*v.i.* **4.** to lose water or moisture. —**de′hy·dra′tion,** *n.* —**de·hy′dra·tor,** *n.* —**Syn. 2.** See **evaporate.**

de·hy·dro·gen·ase (dē hī′drə jə nās′), *n. Biochem.* any of a class of oxide-reductase enzymes that catalyze the removal of hydrogen.

de·hy·dro·gen·ate (dē hī′drə jə nāt′, -hī droj′ə-), *v.t.*, **-at·ed, -at·ing.** *Chem.* to remove hydrogen from (a compound). —**de·hy′dro·gen·a′tion,** *n.*

de·hyp·no·tize (dē hip′nə tīz′), *v.t.*, **-tized, -tiz·ing.** to bring out of the hypnotic state.

dei (dā; *It.* de′ē), *prep.* (used in Italian names originally to indicate *of* or *from.*)

D.E.I., Dutch East Indies.

De·ia·ni·ra (dē′yə nī′rə), *n. Class. Myth.* the wife of Hercules, whom she killed unwittingly.

de·ice (dē īs′), *v.t.*, **-iced, -ic·ing.** **1.** to free or keep free of ice. **2.** to prevent or remove ice formation on (the wing of an airplane or the like). Also, **de-ice′.** —**de·ic′er, de-ic′er,** *n.*

de·i·cide (dē′i sīd′), *n.* **1.** a person who kills a god. **2.** the act of killing a god. [< NL *deicīd(a), -cīd(ium)* = L *dei-* (comb. form of *deus* god) + *-cīda, -ium* -CIDE] —**de′i·ci′dal,** *adj.*

deic·tic (dīk′tik), *adj.* **1.** *Logic.* proving directly. **2.** *Gram.* pointing; demonstrative. [< Gk *deiktik(ós)* relating to proof = *deikt(ós)* able to be proved + *-ikos* -IC] —**deic′ti·cal·ly,** *adv.*

de·if·ic (dē if′ik), *adj.* making divine; deifying. [< LL *deific(us)* = L *dei-* (comb. form of *deus* god) + *-fic-* -FIC]

de·i·fi·ca·tion (dē′ə fə kā′shən), *n.* **1.** the act of deifying. **2.** the state of being deified. **3.** the result of deifying. [ME *deificacion* < LL *deificātiōn-* (s. of *deificātiō*) = *deificāt(us)* (ptp. of *deificāre;* see DEIFIC, -ATE[1]) + *-iōn-* -ION]

de·i·form (dē′ə fôrm′), *adj.* godlike; divine. [< ML *deiform(is)* = L *dei-* (comb. form of *deus* god) + *-formis* -FORM]

de·i·fy (dē′ə fī′), *v.t.*, **-fied, -fy·ing.** **1.** to make a god of; exalt to the rank of or personify as a deity. **2.** to adore or regard as a deity: *to deify prudence.* [ME *deifi(en)* < OF *deifi(er)* < LL *deificāre* = *dei-* (comb. form of *deus* god) + *-fic(āre)* -FY] —**de′i·fi′er,** *n.*

deign (dān), *v.i.* **1.** to think fit or in accordance with one's dignity; condescend: *He would not deign to discuss the matter with us.* —*v.t.* **2.** to condescend to give, grant or accept: *He deigned no reply.* [ME *dein(en)* < OF *deign(ier)* < L *dignārī* to judge worthy < *dign(us)* worthy]

De·i gra·ti·a (de′ē grä′tē ä′; *Eng.* dē′ī grā′shē ə), *Latin.* by the grace of God.

deil (dēl), *n. Scot.* devil. [ME *del, dule*]

De·ïph·o·bus (dē if′ə bəs), *n. Class. Myth.* a son of Priam and Hecuba who married Helen after the death of Paris and was slain by Menelaus.

Deir·dre (dēr′drē, -drə; *Irish* dâR′dRā), *n. Irish Legend.* the wife of Naoise, who killed herself after her husband had been murdered by his uncle, King Conchobar.

de·ism (dē′iz əm), *n.* **1.** belief in the existence of a God on the evidence of reason and nature only, with rejection of supernatural revelation (distinguished from *theism*). **2.** belief in a God who created the world but has since remained indifferent to his creation. [< F *déisme* < L *de(us)* god + F *-isme* -ISM]

de·ist (dē′ist), *n.* a person who believes in deism. [< F *déiste* < L *de(us)* god + F *-iste* -IST] —**de·is′tic, de·is′ti·cal,** *adj.* —**de·is′ti·cal·ly,** *adv.*

de·i·ty (dē′i tē), *n., pl.* **-ties.** **1.** a god or goddess. **2.** divine character or nature; divinity: *Her deity is manifest in her actions.* **3.** the estate or rank of a god: *The king attained deity after his death.* **4.** the character or nature of the Supreme Being: *the deity of Christ.* **5.** a person or thing revered as a god or goddess: *a society in which money is the only deity.* **6. the Deity,** God; Supreme Being. [ME *deite* < OF < LL *deitāt-* (s. of *deitās*) = L *dei-* (comb. form of *deus* god) + *-itāt-* -ITY, formed after L *dīvinitās* divinity]

dé·jà vu (dā zhA vY′), **1.** (*italics.*) *French.* already seen; unoriginal; trite. **2.** *Psychol.* the illusion of having previously experienced something actually being encountered for the first time.

de·ject (di jekt′), *v.t.* **1.** to depress the spirits of; dispirit; dishearten. —*adj.* **2.** *Archaic.* dejected; downcast. [ME < L *dēject(us)* thrown down (ptp. of *dējicere*) = *dē-* DE- + *jec-* throw (ptp. s. of *jacere*) + *-t(us)* ptp. suffix]

de·jec·ta (di jek′tə), *n.pl.* excrements. [< NL, neut. pl. of L *dēject(us)*]

de·ject·ed (di jek′tid), *adj.* depressed in spirits; disheartened; low-spirited. —**de·ject′ed·ly,** *adv.* —**de·ject′ed·ness,** *n.* —**Syn.** discouraged, despondent, dispirited, downhearted, unhappy. See **sad.** —**Ant.** happy.

de·jec·tion (di jek′shən), *n.* **1.** depression or lowness of spirits. **2.** *Med., Physiol.* **a.** evacuation of the bowels; fecal discharge. **b.** excrement. [ME *deieccion* < L *dējectiōn-* (s. of *dējectiō*) a throwing down] —**Ant. 1.** exhilaration.

dé·jeu·ner (dā zhœ nā′; *Eng.* dā′zhə nā′), *n., pl.* **-ners** (-nā′; *Eng.* -nāz′). *French.* lunch; luncheon.

de ju·re (dē jŏŏr′ē; *Lat.* de yōō′Re), by right; according to law (distinguished from *de facto*). [< L]

dek-, var. of **dec-.**

deka-, var. of **deca-.**

de Kalb (di kalb′), **1. Baron.** See **Kalb, Johann. 2.** a city in N Illinois. 32,949 (1970).

dek·a·li·ter (dek′ə lē′tər), *n.* decaliter. *Abbr.:* dkl

dek·a·me·ter (dek′ə mē′tər), *n.* decameter. *Abbr.:* dkm

dek·are (dek′âr, de kâr′), *n.* decare.

dek·a·stere (dek′ə stēr′), *n.* decastere. *Abbr.:* dks

deki-, var. of **deci-.**

Dek·ker (dek′ər), *n.* **Thomas,** 1572?–1632?, English dramatist. Also, **Decker.**

de Koo·ning (də kōō′ning), **Wil·lem** (vil′əm, wil′-), born 1904, U.S. painter, born in the Netherlands.

De Ko·ven (di kō′vən), **(Henry Louis) Reginald,** 1861–1920, U.S. composer, conductor, and music critic.

de Kruif (də krīf′), **Paul,** 1890–1971, U.S. bacteriologist and author.

del[1] (del), **1.** (in names of Spanish derivation) a contraction of *de* and the article *el: Estanislao del Campo.* **2.** (in names of Italian derivation) a contraction of *di* and the article *il: Giovanni del Monte.*

del[2] (del), *Math.* a differential operator. *Symbol:* ∇ [short form of DELTA]

Del., Delaware.

del., **1.** delegate. **2.** delineavit.

De·la·croix (də lA krwä′), *n.* **(Fer·di·nand Vic·tor) Eu·gène** (fer dē näN′ vēk tôR′ œ zhen′), 1798–1863, French painter.

Del′a·go′a Bay′ (del′ə gō′ə, del′-), an inlet of the Indian Ocean, in S Mozambique. 55 mi long

de·laine (də lān′), *n.* **1.** a combing wool of high quality often used in worsteds. **2.** a high-grade worsted dress goods formerly in use. [< F (*mousseline*) *de laine* (muslin) of wool]

de la Ma·drid Hur·ta·do (de lä mä thRēth′ ōōR tä′thō), **Mi·guel** (mē gel′), born 1934, Mexican political leader: president since 1982.

de la Mare (də lə mâr′, del′ə mâr′), **Walter (John),** 1873–1956, English poet, novelist, and short-story writer.

de·lam·i·nate (dē lam′ə nāt′), *v.i.*, **-nat·ed, -nat·ing.** to split into laminae or thin layers.

de·lam·i·na·tion (dē lam′ə nā′shən), *n.* **1.** a splitting apart into layers. **2.** *Embryol.* the separation of a primordial cell layer into two layers by a process of cell migration.

De·la·roche (də lA rôsh′), *n.* **(Hip·po·lyte) Paul** (ē pô lēt′ pôl′), 1797–1856, French historical and portrait painter.

de·late (di lāt′), *v.t.*, **-lat·ed, -lat·ing.** **1.** *Chiefly Scot.* to inform against; denounce or accuse. **2.** *Archaic.* to relate; report: *to delate an offense.* [< L *dēlāt(us)* brought down, reported, accused (ptp. of *dēferre*) = *dē-* DE- + *lā-* carry (ptp. s. of *ferre*) + *-t(us)* ptp. suffix] —**de·la′tion,** *n.* —**de·la′tor,** *n.*

De·lau·nay (də lō ne′), *n.* **Ro·bert** (Rō beR′), 1885–1941, French painter.

De·la·vigne (də lᴀ vēn′yᵊ), *n.* **(Jean Fran·çois) Ca·si·mir** (zhäɴ fʀäɴ swᴀ′ kᴀ zē mēʀ′), 1793–1843, French poet and dramatist.

Del·a·ware (del′ə wâr′), *n., pl.* **-wares,** (*esp. collectively*) **-ware** for 5. **1. Lord.** See **De La Warr, Baron. 2.** a state in the eastern United States, on the Atlantic coast. 548,104 (1970); 2057 sq. mi. *Cap.:* Dover. *Abbr.:* Del., DE **3.** former name of **Cherry Hill. 4.** a river flowing S from SE New York, along the boundary between Pennsylvania and New Jersey into Delaware Bay. 296 mi. long. **5.** a member of an Indian people formerly occupying the drainage basin of the Delaware River and the greater part of New Jersey. **6.** the Algonquian language of the Delaware Indians.

Del′aware Bay′, an inlet of the Atlantic between E Delaware and S New Jersey. ab. 70 mi. long.

Del′aware Wa′ter Gap′, a gorge on the boundary between E Pennsylvania and NW New Jersey.

De La Warr (del′ə wâr′; *Brit.* del′ə wər), **Thomas West, Baron,** 1577–1618, 1st British colonial governor of Virginia. Also, **Delaware.**

de·lay (di lā′), *v.t.* **1.** to put off to a later time; defer; postpone: *The pilot delayed the flight until the weather cleared.* **2.** to impede the progress of; retard or hinder: *The dense fog delayed the plane's landing.* —*v.i.* **3.** to put off action; linger; loiter. —*n.* **4.** the act of delaying; procrastination; loitering. **5.** an instance of being delayed: *There were five delays during the train trip.* [ME *delai(en)* < OF *delaie(r),* b. L *dīlātāre* (freq. of L *diferre* to DEFER[1]) and L var. (unrecorded) of *dēliquāre* to strain, clear off] —**de·lay′er,** *n.* —**Syn. 2.** slow, detain. **3.** procrastinate, tarry. **4.** tarrying.

Del′ Cit′y (del), a city in central Oklahoma, E of Oklahoma City. 27,133 (1970).

de·le (dē′lē), *v.,* **de·led, de·le·ing,** *n. Print.* —*v.t.* **1.** to delete. —*n.* **2.** a mark, as ♈ or ♉, used to indicate matter to be deleted. [< L *dēlē* (2nd pers. sing. pres. act. impv. of *dēlēre*) = *dēl-* destroy + *-ē-* impv. suffix]

de·lec·ta·ble (di lek′tə bəl), *adj.* **1.** delightful; highly pleasing. **2.** delicious. [ME < L *dēlectābil(is)* delightful = *dēlect(āre)* to delight + *-ābilis* -ABLE] —**de·lec′ta·ble·ness, de·lec′ta·bil′i·ty,** *n.* —**de·lec′ta·bly,** *adv.*

de·lec·tate (di lek′tāt), *v.t.,* **-tat·ed, -tat·ing.** to please; delight. [< L *dēlectāt(us)* delighted, ptp. of *dēlectāre*]

de·lec·ta·tion (dē′lek tā′shən), *n.* delight; enjoyment. [ME *delectacioun* < L *dēlectātiōn-* s. of *dēlectātiō*)]

del·e·ga·cy (del′ə gə sē), *n., pl.* **-cies. 1.** the position or commission of a delegate. **2.** the appointing or sending of a delegate. **3.** a body of delegates; delegation.

del·e·gate (*n.* del′ə gāt′, -git; *v.* del′ə gāt′), *n., v.,* **-gat·ed, -gat·ing.** —*n.* **1.** a person designated to act for or represent another or others; a deputy; a representative, as in a political convention. **2.** *U.S. Govt.* **a.** the representative of a Territory in the House of Representatives of the U.S. **b.** a member of the lower house of the state legislatures of Maryland, Virginia, and West Virginia. —*v.t.* **3.** to send or appoint (a person) as deputy or representative. **4.** to commit (powers, functions, etc.) to another as agent or deputy. [ME < ML *dēlēgāt(us),* n. use of L: assigned (ptp. of *dēlēgāre*) = *dē-* DE- + *lēgātus* deputed; see LEGATE] —**del·e·ga·ble** (del′ə gə bəl), *adj.* —**Syn. 1.** envoy. **4.** depute, entrust, commission.

del·e·ga·tion (del′ə gā′shən), *n.* **1.** the act of delegating. **2.** the state of being delegated. **3.** a group or body of delegates. **4.** the body of delegates chosen to represent a political unit in an assembly. [< L *dēlēgātiōn-* (s. of *dēlēgātiō*)] —**Syn. 4.** commission.

de Les·seps (də les′eps; *Fr.* də le seps′), **Vicomte Fer·di·nand Ma·rie** (fûr′dᵊnand′ mə rē′; *Fr.* fer dē näɴ′ mᴀ rē′). See **Lesseps, Ferdinand Marie, Vicomte de.**

de·lete (di lēt′), *v.t.,* **-let·ed, -let·ing.** to strike out or remove (something written or printed); erase; expunge. [< L *dēlēt(us)* destroyed, ptp. of *dēlēre*] —**Syn.** eradicate. See **cancel.**

del·e·te·ri·ous (del′i tēr′ē əs), *adj.* **1.** injurious to health: *deleterious gases.* **2.** hurtful; harmful; injurious: *deleterious influences.* [< NL *dēlētēri(us)* < Gk *dēlētḗrios* destructive = *dēlētḗr* destroyer (*dēlē(esthai)* (to) hurt, injure + *-tēr* agent suffix) + *-ios* -IOUS] —**del′e·te′ri·ous·ly,** *adv.* —**del′e·te′ri·ous·ness,** *n*

de·le·tion (di lē′shən), *n.* **1.** an act or instance of deleting. **2.** the state of being deleted. **3.** a deleted word, passage, etc. [< L *dēlētiōn-* (s. of *dēlētiō*) a destroying]

delft (delft), *n.* **1.** an earthenware having an opaque white glaze with an overglaze decoration, usually blue. **2.** any pottery resembling this. Also, **delf** (delf). Also called **delft′ ware′.** [after DELFT]

Delft (delft), *n.* a city in the W Netherlands. 75,125 (1962).

Del·ga·do (del gä′dō), *n.* **Cape,** a cape at the NE extremity of Mozambique.

Del·hi (del′ē *or, for 2,* del′hī), *n.* **1.** a union territory in N India. 2,658,612 (1961); 574 sq. mi. **2.** Also called **Old Delhi.** a city in and the capital of this territory: former capital of the old Mogul Empire; administrative headquarters of British India 1912–29. 2,061,800 (1961). Cf. **New Delhi.**

del·i (del′ē), *n., pl.* **del·is** (del′ēz). *Informal.* a delicatessen. [by shortening]

De·li·an (dē′lē ən, dēl′yən), *adj.* **1.** pertaining to Delos. —*n.* **2.** a native or inhabitant of Delos.

de·lib·er·ate (*adj.* di lib′ər it; *v.* di lib′ə rāt′), *adj., v.,* **-at·ed, -at·ing.** —*adj.* **1.** carefully weighed or considered; studied; intentional: *a deliberate lie.* **2.** characterized by deliberation; careful or slow in deciding: *a deliberate decision.* **3.** leisurely and steady in movement or action; slow and even; unhurried: *He took deliberate aim and fired.* —*v.t.* **4.** to weigh in the mind; consider: *to deliberate a question.* —*v.i.* **5.** to think carefully or attentively; reflect. **6.** to consult or confer formally: *The jury deliberated for three hours.* [ME < L *dēlīberāt(us)* considered (ptp. of *dēlīberāre*) = *dē-* DE- + *lībr(āre)* (to) balance, weigh (< *lībra* balance, scales) + *-ātus* -ATE[1]] —**de·lib′er·ate·ly,** *adv.* —**de·lib′er·ate·ness,** *n.* —**de·lib′er·a′tor,** *n.*
—**Syn. 1.** purposeful; willful. DELIBERATE, INTENTIONAL, PREMEDITATED, VOLUNTARY refer to something not happening by chance. DELIBERATE is applied to what is done not hastily but with full realization of what one is doing: *a deliberate attempt to evade justice.* INTENTIONAL is applied to what is definitely intended or done on purpose: *an intentional omission.* PREMEDITATED is applied to what has been planned in advance: *a premeditated crime.* VOLUNTARY is applied to what is done by a definite exercise of the will and not because of outward pressures: *a voluntary enlistment.* **2.** methodical, thoughtful. **3.** See **slow. 4.** ponder. —**Ant. 1.** accidental. **2.** impulsive, precipitate.

de·lib·er·a·tion (di lib′ə rā′shən), *n.* **1.** careful consideration before decision. **2.** formal consultation or discussion. **3.** deliberate quality; leisureliness of movement or action; slowness. [ME *deliberacion* < L *dēlīberātiōn-* (s. of *dēlīberātiō*)]

de·lib·er·a·tive (di lib′ə rā′tiv, -ər ə tiv), *adj.* **1.** having the function of deliberating, as a legislative assembly: *a deliberative body.* **2.** having to do with policy; dealing with the wisdom and expediency of a proposal: *a deliberative speech.* [< L *dēlīberātīv(us)*] —**de·lib′er·a′tive·ly,** *adv.* —**de·lib′er·a′tive·ness,** *n.*

De·libes (də lēb′), *n.* **(Clé·ment Phi·li·bert) Lé·o** (klā-mäɴ′ fē lē beʀ′ lā ō′), 1836–91, French composer.

del·i·ca·cy (del′ə kə sē), *n., pl.* **-cies. 1.** fineness of texture, quality, etc.; softness: *the delicacy of lace.* **2.** something delightful or pleasing; esp. a choice food considered with regard to its rarity, costliness, or the like. **3.** fineness of perception or feeling; sensitiveness: *the delicacy of her sensibilities.* **4.** the quality of being easily broken or damaged; fragility. **5.** the quality of requiring or involving great care or tact: *negotiations of great delicacy.* **6.** extreme sensitivity; precision of action or operation; minute accuracy: *the delicacy of a skillful surgeon's touch.* **7.** fineness of feeling with regard to what is fitting, proper, etc.: *Delicacy would not permit her to be rude.* **8.** sensitivity with regard to the feelings of others: *She criticized him with such delicacy that he was not offended.* **9.** bodily weakness; liability to sickness; frailty. **10.** *Obs.* sensuous indulgence; luxury. [ME *delicasie.* See DELICATE, -CY]

del·i·cate (del′ə kit), *adj.* **1.** fine in texture, quality, construction, etc. **2.** fragile; easily damaged; frail. **3.** so fine as to be scarcely perceptible; subtle: *a delicate flavor.* **4.** soft or faint, as color: *a delicate shade of pink.* **5.** exquisite or refined in perception or feeling. **6.** distinguishing subtle differences: *a delicate sense of smell.* **7.** fine or precise in action or execution: *a delicate instrument.* **8.** requiring great care, caution, or tact: *a delicate situation.* **9.** regardful of what is becoming, proper, etc.: *a delicate sense of propriety.* **10.** mindful of or sensitive to the feelings of others. **11.** dainty or choice, as food: *delicate tidbits.* **12.** primly fastidious; squeamish: *not a movie for the delicate viewer.* **13.** *Obs.* sensuous; voluptuous. —*n.* **14.** *Archaic.* a choice food; delicacy. **15.** *Obs.* a source of pleasure; luxury. [ME *delicat* < L *dēlicāt(us)* delightful, dainty; akin to DELICIOUS] —**del′i·cate·ly,** *adv.* —**del′i·cate·ness,** *n.*
—**Syn. 1.** DELICATE, DAINTY, EXQUISITE imply beauty such as might belong in rich surroundings or need careful treatment. DELICATE, used of an object, suggests fragility, small size, and often very fine workmanship: *a delicate piece of carving.* DAINTY, in concrete references, suggests a smallness, gracefulness, and beauty which forbid rough handling; there is a connotation of attractiveness: *a dainty handkerchief;* of persons, it refers to fastidious sensibilities: *dainty in eating habits.* EXQUISITE suggests an outstanding beauty, daintiness, and elegance, or a discriminating sensitivity and ability to perceive fine distinctions: *exquisite tact.* **2.** tender, slight, weak. **7.** exact, accurate. **8.** critical, precarious. —**Ant. 1, 2.** coarse. **3.** hard, crude.

del·i·ca·tes·sen (del′ə kə tes′ən), *n.* **1.** a store selling foods already prepared or requiring little preparation for serving, as cooked meats, cheese, relishes, and the like. **2.** *Informal.* the food products sold in such a store. [< G, pl. of *Delikatesse* dainty < F *délicatesse*]

de·li·cious (di lish′əs), *adj.* **1.** highly pleasing to the senses, esp. to taste or smell: *a delicious dinner; a delicious aroma.* **2.** very pleasing; delightful: *a delicious sense of humor.* —*n.* **3.** (*cap.*) a red variety of apple. **4.** (*cap.*) the tree bearing this fruit, grown in the U.S. [ME < OF < LL *dēliciōs(us)* = L *dēlici(ae)* delights + *-ōsus* -OUS] —**de·li′cious·ly,** *adv.* —**de·li′cious·ness,** *n.* —**Syn. 1.** savory, delectable.

de·light (di līt′), *n.* **1.** a high degree of pleasure or enjoyment; joy; rapture. **2.** something that gives great pleasure. —*v.t.* **3.** to give great pleasure, satisfaction, or enjoyment to; please highly. —*v.i.* **4.** to have great pleasure; take pleasure (fol. by *in* or an infinitive): *She delights in cooking fancy dishes.* [erroneous 16th-century sp. after *light;* r. ME *delit* < OF < *delit(ier)* < L *dēlectāre;* see DELECTABLE] —**Syn. 1.** transport, delectation. See **pleasure. 3.** charm, enrapture.

de·light·ed (di lī′tid), *adj.* **1.** highly pleased. **2.** *Obs.* delightful. —**de·light′ed·ly,** *adv.*

de·light·ful (di līt′fəl), *adj.* affording delight; highly pleasing: *a delightful surprise.* —**de·light′ful·ly,** *adv.* —**de·light′ful·ness,** *n.* —**Syn.** pleasurable, enjoyable; enchanting, agreeable. —**Ant.** disagreeable.

de·light·some (di līt′səm), *adj. Literary.* highly pleasing; delightful. —**de·light′some·ly,** *adv.*

De·li·lah (di lī′lə), *n.* **1.** Samson's mistress, who betrayed him to the Philistines. Judges 16. **2.** a seductive and treacherous woman.

de·lim·it (di lim′it), *v.t.* to fix or mark the limits of; demarcate. [< F *délimit(er)* < L *dēlimitāre*]

de·lim·i·tate (di lim′i tāt′), *v.t.,* **-tat·ed, -tat·ing.** delimit. [< L *dēlimitāt(us),* ptp. of *dēlimitāre*] —**de·lim′i·ta′tion,** *n.* —**de·lim′i·ta′tive,** *adj.*

de·lin·e·ate (di lin′ē āt′), *v.t.,* **-at·ed, -at·ing. 1.** to trace the outline of; sketch or trace in outline; represent pictorially. **2.** to portray in words; describe or outline with precision: *In his speech he delineated the ideal suburban dwelling.* [< L *dēlineāt(us)*] —**de·lin·e·a·ble** (di lin′ē ə bəl), *adj.*

de·lin·e·a·tion (di lin′ē ā′shən), *n.* **1.** the act or process of delineating. **2.** a chart or diagram; a sketch; a rough draft. 3. a description. [< LL *dēlīneātiōn-* (s. of *dēlīneātiō*) a sketch] —**de·lin·e·a·tive** (di lin′ē ā′tiv, -ē ə tiv), *adj.*

de·lin·e·a·tor (di lin′ē ā′tər), *n.* **1.** a person or thing that delineates. **2.** a tailor's pattern which can be adjusted for cutting garments of different sizes.

de·li·ne·a·vit (de lin′e ä′wit; *Eng.* di lin′ē ā′vit), *Latin.* he drew (this); she drew (this). *Abbr.:* del.

de·lin·quen·cy (di liŋ′kwən sē), *n., pl.* **-cies. 1.** failure in or neglect of duty or obligation; dereliction; fault; guilt. **2.** a misdeed or offense; a misdemeanor. Cf. **juvenile delinquency.** [< LL *dēlinquentia* fault, crime = L *dēlinquent-* (s. of *dēlinquēns*), prp. of *dēlinquere* (*dē-* DE- + *linqu(ere)* (to) leave) + *-ia;* see -ENCY]

de·lin·quent (di liŋ′kwənt), *adj.* **1.** failing in or neglectful of a duty or obligation; guilty of a misdeed or offense. **2.** (of an account, tax, debt, etc.) past due. **3.** of or pertaining to delinquents or delinquency. —*n.* **4.** a person who is delinquent, esp. a juvenile delinquent. [< L *dēlinquent-;* see DELINQUENCY] —**de·lin′quent·ly,** *adv.*

del·i·quesce (del′ə kwes′), *v.i.,* **-quesced, -quesc·ing. 1.** to melt away. **2.** to become liquid by absorbing moisture from the air, as certain salts. **3.** *Bot.* to form many small divisions or branches. [< L *dēliquēsce(re)* (to) become liquid. See DE-, LIQUESCENT]

del·i·ques·cence (del′ə kwes′əns), *n.* **1.** the act or process of deliquescing. **2.** the liquid produced when a substance deliquesces. —**del′i·ques′cent,** *adj.*

de·lir·i·ous (di lēr′ē əs), *adj.* **1.** *Pathol.* affected with or characteristic of delirium. **2.** wild with excitement, enthusiasm, etc. [DELIRI(UM) + -OUS] —**de·lir′i·ous·ly,** *adv.* —**de·lir′i·ous·ness,** *n.*

de·lir·i·um (di lēr′ē əm), *n., pl.* **-lir·i·ums, -lir·i·a** (-lēr′ē ə). **1.** *Pathol.* a more or less temporary disorder of the mental faculties, as in fevers, disturbances of consciousness, or intoxication, characterized by excitement, delusions, hallucinations, etc. **2.** a state of violent excitement or emotion. [< L *dēlīrium* frenzy, lit., going out of the furrow = *dēlīr(āre)* (*dē-* DE- + *līr(a)* furrow) + *-ium* (neut. n. suffix)]

delir′ium tre′mens (trē′mənz), *Pathol.* a violent restlessness due to excessive and prolonged use of alcohol, characterized by trembling, terrifying visual hallucinations, etc. [< NL: trembling delirium]

del·i·tes·cent (del′i tes′ənt), *adj.* concealed; hidden; latent. [< L *dēlitescent-* (s. of *dēlitescēns*) hiding away (prp. of *dēlitescere*)] —**del′i·tes′cence, del′i·tes′cen·cy,** *n.*

De·li·us (dē′lē əs, dēl′yəs), *n.* **Frederick,** 1862–1934, English composer.

de·liv·er (di liv′ər), *v.t.* **1.** to carry and turn over (letters, goods, etc.) to the intended recipient or recipients: *to deliver a package.* **2.** to give into another's possession or keeping; surrender: *to deliver a prisoner to the police.* **3.** to give forth in words; utter or pronounce: *to deliver a speech.* **4.** to give forth or emit. **5.** to direct or throw: *to deliver a blow.* **6.** to set free, liberate, or save: *They were delivered from bondage. Deliver me from such tiresome people!* **7.** to assist (a female) in bringing forth young: *The doctor delivered Mrs. Jones of twins.* **8.** to assist at the birth of: *The doctor delivered three sets of twins last year.* **9.** to give birth to: *She delivered twins at 4 a.m.* **10.** to disburden (oneself) of thoughts, opinions, etc. **11.** *Obs.* to make known; assert. —*v.i.* **12.** to give birth. **13.** to provide a delivery service for goods and products: *The store delivers free of charge.* —*adj.* **14.** *Archaic.* agile; quick. [ME *delivre(n)* < OF *delivr(er)* < LL *dēlīberāre* to set free. See DE-, LIBERATE] —**de·liv′er·a·ble,** *adj.* —**de·liv′er·er,** *n.* —**Syn. 1, 2.** transfer. **3.** proclaim, publish. **6.** emancipate, release, redeem, rescue.

de·liv·er·ance (di liv′ər əns), *n.* **1.** an act or instance of delivering. **2.** the state of being delivered; liberation. **3.** salvation. **4.** a thought or judgment expressed; a formal pronouncement. [ME *deliveraunce* < OF *delivrance*]

de·liv·er·y (di liv′ə rē), *n., pl.* **-er·ies. 1.** the delivering of letters, goods, etc. **2.** a giving up or handing over; surrender. **3.** the utterance or enunciation of words. **4.** vocal and bodily behavior during the presentation of a speech: *a speaker's fine delivery.* **5.** the act or manner of giving or sending forth: *the pitcher's fine delivery of the ball.* **6.** release or rescue; liberation. **7.** the state of being delivered of or giving birth to a child; parturition. **8.** something delivered: *The delivery is late today.* **9.** *Com.* a shipment of goods from the seller to the buyer. **10.** *Law.* a legally effective transfer of property. [ME < AF *delivrée* (n.) = *delivré,* ptp. of *delivr(er)* (to) DELIVER + *-ée* -Y[3]]

deliv′ery room′, 1. an area in a hospital equipped for delivering babies. **2.** a room or area in which deliveries are made or received.

dell (del), *n.* a small valley; vale. [ME *delle,* OE *dell;* akin to DALE]

dell′ (del), (in names of Italian derivation) an elided form of *della* (*Giovanni dell'Anguillara*) or a combining form of *del* (*Franceso dell'Aiolle*).

del·la (del′lä), (in names of Italian derivation) a contraction of *di* and the article *la: Andrea della Robbia.*

del·la Rob·bia (del′ə rō′bē ə; *It.* del′lä RÔb′byä), **Lu·ca** (lo͞o′kä). See **Robbia, Luca della.**

Del·lo Joi·o (del′ō joi′ō), **Norman,** born 1913, U.S. composer and pianist.

dells (delz), *n.pl.* dalles. [by folk etym.]

Del·mar′va Penin′sula (del mär′və), a peninsula between Chesapeake and Delaware bays including most of Delaware and those parts of Maryland and Virginia E of Chesapeake Bay. Cf. **Eastern shore.**

de·lo·cal·ise (dē lō′kə līz′), *v.t.,* **-ised, -is·ing.** *Chiefly Brit.* delocalize. —**de·lo′cal·i·sa′tion,** *n.*

de·lo·cal·ize (dē lō′kə līz′), *v.t.,* **-ized, -iz·ing. 1.** to remove from the proper or usual locality. **2.** to free or remove from the restrictions of locality; free of localism, provincialism, or the like: *to delocalize an industry; to delocalize a person's accent.* —**de·lo′cal·i·za′tion,** *n.*

De·los (dē′los, del′ōs), *n.* a Greek island in the Cyclades, in the SW Aegean: site of an oracle of Apollo.

de·louse (dē lous′, -louz′), *v.t.,* **-loused, -lous·ing.** to free of lice; remove lice from.

Del·phi (del′fī), *n.* an ancient city in central Greece, in Phocis: the site of the Delphic oracle.

Del·phi·an (del′fē ən), *adj.* Delphic.

Del·phic (del′fik), *adj.* **1.** of or pertaining to Delphi. **2.** of or pertaining to Apollo, or to his temples or oracles. **3.** oracular; obscure; ambiguous: *Delphic pronouncements.*

Del′phic or′acle, the oracle of Apollo at Delphi, noted for giving ambiguous answers.

del·phin·i·um (del fin′ē əm), *n., pl.* **-i·ums, -i·a** (-ē ə). any of numerous ranunculaceous plants of the genus *Delphinium,* esp. a cultivated one, comprising the larkspurs. [< NL < Gk *delphínion* larkspur < *delphín-* DOLPHIN; so called from the shape of the nectary]

del·ta (del′tə), *n.* **1.** the fourth letter of the Greek alphabet (Δ, δ). **2.** anything triangular, like the Greek capital delta (Δ). **3.** a nearly flat plain of alluvial deposit between diverging branches of the mouth of a river, often triangular. **4.** a word used in communications to represent the letter *D.* **5.** (*cap.*) *Astron.* a star that is usually the fourth brightest of a constellation: *The fourth brightest star in the Southern Cross is Delta Crucis.* [ME *deltha* < L *delta* < Gk *délta;* akin to Heb *dāleth*]

del·ta·ic (del tā′ik), *adj.* **1.** pertaining to or like a delta. **2.** forming or having a delta.

del′ta ray′, *Physics.* a low-energy electron emitted by a substance after bombardment by high-energy particles, as alpha particles.

del′ta wave′, Usually **delta waves.** *Med.* slow brain waves present during deep sleep of normal individuals.

del′ta wing′, the triangular surface that serves as both wing and horizontal stabilizer of some supersonic aircraft.

del·toid (del′toid), *n.* **1.** *Anat.* a large, triangular muscle covering the joint of the shoulder, the action of which raises the arm away from the side of the body. —*adj.* **2.** in the shape of a Greek capital delta (Δ); triangular. [< Gk *deltoeid(ēs)* delta-shaped]

Deltoid leaf

de·lude (di lo͞od′), *v.t.,* **-lud·ed, -lud·ing. 1.** to mislead the mind or judgment of; deceive. **2.** *Obs.* to mock or frustrate the hopes or aims of. **3.** *Obs.* to elude; evade. [ME < L *dēlūde(re)* (to) play false = *dē-* DE- + *lūdere* to play] —**de·lud′er,** *n.* —**de·lud′ing·ly,** *adv.* —**Syn. 1.** dupe, trick.

del·uge (del′yo͞oj), *n., v.,* **-uged, -ug·ing.** —*n.* **1.** a great flood of water; inundation; flood. **2.** a drenching rain; downpour. **3.** anything that overwhelms like a flood: *a deluge of mail.* **4. the Deluge,** flood (def. 2). —*v.t.* **5.** to flood; inundate. **6.** to overrun; overwhelm: *She was deluged with offers of modeling jobs.* [ME < OF < L *dīluv(ium)* flood < *dīluere* to wash off = *dī-* DIS-[1] + *-luere* (var. of *lavere* to wash)]

de·lu·sion (di lo͞o′zhən), *n.* **1.** an act or instance of deluding. **2.** the state of being deluded. **3.** a false belief or opinion: *delusions of grandeur.* **4.** *Psychiatry.* a fixed, dominating, or persistent false mental conception resistant to reason. [ME < L *dēlūsiōn-* (s. of *dēlūsiō*) = *dēlūs(us)* (ptp. of *dēlūdere;* see DELUDE) + *-iōn-* -ION] —**de·lu′sion·al,** *adj.* —**Syn. 2.** See **illusion.**

de·lu·sive (di lo͞o′siv), *adj.* **1.** tending to delude; deceptive: *a delusive reply.* **2.** of the nature of a delusion; false; unreal: *a delusive belief.* Also, **de·lu·so·ry** (di lo͞o′sə rē). —**de·lu′sive·ly,** *adv.* —**de·lu′sive·ness,** *n.*

de·luxe (də lo͝oks′, -luks′), *adj.* **1.** of special elegance or sumptuousness. —*adv.* **2.** in a luxurious or sumptuous manner. Also, **de luxe′.** [< F *de luxe* of luxury]

delve (delv), *v.,* **delved, delv·ing.** —*v.i.* **1.** to carry on intensive and thorough research for data, information, or the like. **2.** *Archaic.* to dig, as with a spade. —*v.t.* **3.** *Archaic.* to dig; excavate. **4.** *Archaic.* to obtain by digging. [ME *delve(n),* OE *delfan;* c. D *delven,* OHG *telban*] —**delv′er,** *n.*

Dem., 1. Democrat. **2.** Democratic.

de·mag·net·ise (dē mag′ni tīz′), *v.t.,* **-ised, -is·ing.** *Chiefly Brit.* demagnetize. —**de·mag′net·i·sa′tion,** *n.* —**de·mag′net·is′er,** *n.*

de·mag·net·ize (dē mag′ni tīz′), *v.t.,* **-ized, -iz·ing.** to remove magnetization from. —**de·mag′net·i·za′tion,** *n.* —**de·mag′net·iz′er,** *n.*

dem·a·gog·ic (dem′ə goj′ik, -gog′-), *adj.* of, pertaining to, or characteristic of a demagogue or demagoguery. Also, **dem′a·gog′i·cal.** [< Gk *dēmagōgik(ós)*] —**dem′a·gog′i·cal·ly,** *adv.*

dem·a·gogue (dem′ə gôg′, -gog′), *n., v.,* **-gogued, -gogu·ing.** —*n.* **1.** a person, esp. an orator or political leader, who gains power and popularity by arousing the emotions, passions, and prejudices of the people. **2.** (in ancient times) a leader of the people. —*v.i.* **3.** to speak or act like a demagogue. Also, **dem′a·gog′.** [< Gk *dēmagōg(ós)* a leader of the people, popular leader = *dêm(os)* people + *agōgós* -AGOGUE]

dem·a·gogu·er·y (dem′ə gô′gə rē, -gog′ə rē), *n.* the methods or practices of a demagogue.

dem·a·go·gy (dem′ə gō′jē, -gô′jē, -goj′ē), *n.* *Chiefly Brit.* demagoguery.

de·mand (di mand′, -mänd′), *v.t.* **1.** to ask for with authority; claim as a right: *He demanded payment of the debt.* **2.** to ask for peremptorily or urgently: *She demanded that we let her in.* **3.** to call for or require as just, proper, or necessary: *This task demands patience.* **4.** *Law.* **a.** to lay formal legal claim to. **b.** to summon, as to court. —*v.i.* **5.** to make a demand; inquire; ask. —*n.* **6.** the act of demanding. **7.** something that is demanded. **8.** an urgent or pressing requirement: *demands upon one's time.* **9.** *Econ.* **a.** the desire to purchase coupled with the power to do so. **b.** the quantity of goods that buyers will purchase at a given price. **10.** the state of being in request for purchase or use: *an article in great demand.* **11.** *Archaic.* inquiry or question. **12. on demand,** (of a note, loan, etc.) payable upon presentation or request for payment. [ME *demaund(en)* < AF *demaund(er)* < ML *dēmandāre* to demand, L: to entrust = *dē-* DE- + *mandāre* to commission, order; see MANDATE] —**de·mand′a·ble,** *adj.* —**de·mand′er,** *n.*

—**Syn. 1.** exact. DEMAND, CLAIM, REQUIRE imply making an authoritative request. To DEMAND is to ask in a bold, authoritative way: *to demand an explanation.* To CLAIM is to assert a right to something: *He claimed it as his due.* To REQUIRE is to ask for something as being necessary; to compel: *The Army requires absolute obedience of its soldiers.*

demand′ depos′it, *Banking.* a deposit subject to withdrawal at the demand of the depositor without prior notice.
de·mand·ing (di man′ding), *adj.* claiming more than is generally felt by others to be due. —**de·mand′ing·ly,** *adv.*
demand′ loan′. See **call loan.**
demand′ note′, a note payable upon presentation.
de·mand-pull (di mand′ po͝ol′), *adj.* of or denoting the positive rate of change in prices resulting from an unusually strong consumer demand for a limited supply of goods and services. Cf. **cost-push.**
de·man·toid (di man′toid), *n. Mineral.* a brilliant green variety of andradite, used as a gem. Also called **Uralian emerald.** [< G = (obs.) *Demant* DIAMOND (< MHG *diemant* < OF *diamant*) + *-oid* -OID]
de·mar·cate (di mär′kāt, dē′mär kāt′), *v.t.,* **-cat·ed, -cat·ing. 1.** to mark off the boundaries of. **2.** to separate distinctly. [back formation from DEMARCATION]
de·mar·ca·tion (dē′mär kā′shən), *n.* **1.** the determining and marking off of the boundaries of something. **2.** separation by distinct boundaries. Also, **de′mar·ka′tion.** [Latinization of Sp *demarcación* < *demarcar* to mark out the bounds of = *de-* DE- + *marcar* < It *marcare* < Gmc; see MARK[1], -TION]
dé·marche (dā marsh′), *n., pl.* **-marches** (-marsh′). *French.* **1.** a plan or mode of procedure. **2.** a change in a course of action. [lit., gait]
deme (dēm), *n.* one of the administrative divisions of ancient Attica and of modern Greece. [< Gk *dêm(os)* a district, the people, commons]
de·mean[1] (di mēn′), *v.t.* to lower in dignity or standing; debase. [DE- + MEAN[2], modeled on *debase*]
de·mean[2] (di mēn′), *v.t.* to conduct or behave (oneself) in a specified manner. [ME *deme(i)n(en)* < OF *demen(er)* = *de-* DE- + *mener* to lead, conduct < L *mināre* to drive, *minārī* to threaten]
de·mean·or (di mē′nər), *n.* **1.** conduct; behavior; deportment. **2.** facial appearance; mien. Also, *esp. Brit.,* **de·mean′-our.** [ME *demenure.* See DEMEAN[2], -OR[1]]
de·ment (di ment′), *v.t. Obs.* to make mad or insane. [< LL *dēment(āre)* (to) deprive of mind = L *dēment-* (s. of *dēmēns*) out of one's mind (*dē-* DE- + *ment-* (s. of *mēns*) mind) + *-āre* inf. suffix]
de·ment·ed (di men′tid), *adj.* affected with dementia; insane. —**de·ment′ed·ly,** *adv.* —**de·ment′ed·ness,** *n.*
de·men·tia (di men′shə, -shē ə), *n.* **1.** *Psychiatry.* severe impairment or loss of intellectual capacity and personality integration. **2.** *Pathol.* mental deterioration, esp. when due to physical causes. [< L: madness = *dēment-* (see DEMENT) + *-ia* n. suffix]
demen′tia prae′cox (prē′koks), *Psychiatry.* schizophrenia. [< NL: precocious dementia]
de·merge (dē mûrj′), *v.,* **-merged, -merg·ing.** —*v.t.* **1.** to remove (a component division or company) from a corporation, usually by sale or by spinoff. —*v.i.* **2.** to be removed in such a way.
de·merg·er (dē mûr′jər), *v.t., v.i.* demerge.
de·mer·it (dē mer′it), *n.* **1.** a mark against a person for misconduct or deficiency. **2.** the quality of being censurable or punishable; fault; culpability. **3.** *Obs.* merit or desert. [ME < L *dēmerit(um)* (ML: fault), prob. n. use of neut. of ptp. of *dēmerērī* to deserve (esp. well)]
Dem·e·rol (dem′ə rōl′, -rôl′, -rol′), *n. Pharm., Trademark.* meperidine.
de·mesne (di mān′, -mēn′), *n.* **1.** the possession of land as one's own. **2.** an estate or part of an estate occupied, controlled, and worked by the owner. **3.** land belonging to and adjoining a manor house; estate. **4.** the territory of a state; domain. **5.** a district; region. [ME *demeine* < AF *demesne,* OF *demein;* see DOMAIN]
De·me·ter (di mē′tər), *n.* the ancient Greek goddess of agriculture and the protectress of marriage and the social order, identified by the Romans with Ceres.
demi-, a word element appearing in loan words from French meaning "half" (*demivolt*), "lesser" (*demitasse*), or sometimes used with a pejorative sense (*demimonde*); on this model, also prefixed to words of English origin (*demigod*). [< F, comb. form repr. *demi* (adj.; also n. and adv.) < L *dīmedius,* r. *dīmidius* half]
dem·i·god (dem′ē god′), *n.* **1.** a mythological being who is partly divine and partly human; an inferior deity. **2.** a deified mortal. Also, *referring to a woman,* **dem·i·god·dess** (dem′ē god′is). [trans. of L *semideus*]
dem·i·john (dem′i jon′), *n.* a large bottle having a short, narrow neck and usually encased in wickerwork. [< F *dame-jeanne* (by folk etym.), appar. special use of proper name]
de·mil·i·ta·rise (dē mil′i tə rīz′), *v.t.,* **-rised, -ris·ing.** *Chiefly Brit.* demilitarize. —**de·mil′i·ta·ri·sa′tion,** *n.*
de·mil·i·ta·rize (dē mil′i tə rīz′), *v.t.,* **-rized, -riz·ing. 1.** to deprive of military character; free from militarism. **2.** to place under civil instead of military control. **3.** to forbid military use of (a border zone). —**de·mil′i·ta·ri·za′tion,** *n.*
De Mille (də mil′), **1. Agnes,** born 1908, U.S. choreographer and dancer, esp. of modern dance. **2.** her uncle, **Cecil B(lount)** (blunt), 1881–1959, U.S. motion-picture producer and director.
dem·i·mon·daine (dem′ē mon dān′; *Fr.* də mē môɴ-den′), *n., pl.* **-daines** (-dānz′; *Fr.* -den′). a woman of the demimonde. [< F = DEMIMONDE + *-aine* fem. adj. suffix]
dem·i·monde (dem′ē mond′; *Fr.* də mē môɴd′), *n.* a class of women who have lost their standing in respectable society, usually because of their indiscreet behavior or sexual promiscuity. [< F: lit., half-world]
dem·i·pique (dem′i pēk′), *n.* an 18th-century military saddle with a low pommel.
dem·i·qua·ver (dem′ē kwā′vər), *n. Music.* a sixteenth note; semiquaver.
dem·i·re·lief (dem′ē ri lēf′), *n.* mezzo-relievo.
de·mise (di mīz′), *n., v.,* **-mised, -mis·ing.** —*n.* **1.** death or decease. **2.** termination of existence or operation: *the demise of the French monarchy.* **3.** *Law.* **a.** a death or decease occasioning the transfer of an estate. **b.** a conveyance or transfer of an estate. **4.** *Govt.* transfer of sovereignty, as by death or abdication. —*v.t.* **5.** *Law.* to transfer (an estate or the like) for a limited time; lease. **6.** *Govt.* to transfer (sovereignty), as by death or abdication. [ME *dimise, demise, dimisse* < OF *demis* (ptp. of *desmetre*) < L *dīmiss(um)* (ptp. of *dīmittere*); see DEMIT, DISMISS]
dem·i·sem·i·qua·ver (dem′ē sem′ē kwā′vər), *n. Music Chiefly Brit.* a thirty-second note. See illus. at **note.**
de·mis·sion (di mish′ən), *n. Archaic.* abdication. [ME *dimissioun* < AF < L *dīmissiōn-* (s. of *dīmissiō*)]
de·mit (di mit′), *v.t.,* **-mit·ted, -mit·ting.** *Chiefly Scot.* to resign (a job, public office, etc.); relinquish; give up. [< L *dīmitt(ere)* (to) send down = *dī-* DI-[2] + *mittere* to send]
dem·i·tasse (dem′i tas′, -täs′; *Fr.* də mē täs′), *n., pl.* **-tass·es** (-tas′iz, -tä′siz; *Fr.* -täs′). **1.** a small cup for serving strong black coffee after dinner. **2.** the coffee contained in such a cup. [< F: lit., half-cup]
dem·i·urge (dem′ē ûrj′), *n. Philos.* **1.** *Platonism.* the artificer of the world. **2.** (in the Gnostic and certain other systems) a supernatural being imagined as creating the world in subordination to the Supreme Being. [< Gk *dēmiourg(ós)* a worker for the people, skilled worker = *dēmio(s)* of the people (< *dêmos* the people) + *-ergos* a worker < *érgon* work] —**dem·i·ur·geous** (dem′ē ûr′jəs), **dem′i·ur′gic, dem′i·ur′gi·cal,** *adj.* —**dem′i·ur′gi·cal·ly,** *adv.*
dem·i·volt (dem′ē vōlt′), *n.* a half turn made by a horse with forelegs raised. Also, **dem′i·volte′.** [< F *demi-volte*]
dem·o (dem′ō), *n., pl.* **dem·os.** *Informal.* **1.** demonstration. **2.** a phonograph or tape recording of a new song distributed to demonstrate its merits.
demo-, a prefix occurring in loan words from Greek, where it meant "people" (*democratic*); on this model, used in the formation of compound words (*demography*). [< Gk, comb. form of *dêmos*]
de·mob (dē mob′), *n., v.,* **-mobbed, -mob·bing.** *Brit. Informal.* —*n.* **1.** demobilization. **2.** a person who has an honorable discharge from the armed forces; one who has been demobilized. —*v.t.* **3.** to discharge or demobilize (a person) from the armed forces. [orig. short for DEMOBILIZE]
de·mo·bi·lise (dē mō′bə līz′), *v.t.,* **-lised, -lis·ing.** *Chiefly Brit.* demobilize. —**de·mo′bi·li·sa′tion,** *n.*
de·mo·bi·lize (dē mō′bə līz′), *v.t.,* **-lized, -liz·ing. 1.** to disband (an army, troop unit, etc.). **2.** to discharge (a person) from military service. —**de·mo′bi·li·za′tion,** *n.*
de·moc·ra·cy (di mok′rə sē), *n., pl.* **-cies. 1.** government by the people; a form of government in which the supreme power is vested in the people and exercised directly by them or by their elected agents under a free electoral system. **2.** a state having such a form of government. **3.** political or social equality; democratic spirit. **4.** the common people with respect to their political power. [< F *démocratie,* LL *democratia* < Gk *dēmokratía* popular government]
dem·o·crat (dem′ə krat′), *n.* **1.** an advocate of democracy. **2.** one who maintains social equality. **3.** (*cap.*) *U.S.* a member of the Democratic party. [< F *démocrate,* back formation from *démocratie* DEMOCRACY; see -CRAT]
dem·o·crat·ic (dem′ə krat′ik), *adj.* **1.** pertaining to or of the nature of democracy or a democracy. **2.** pertaining to or characterized by social equality. **3.** advocating or upholding democracy. **4.** (*cap.*) *U.S.* **a.** of, pertaining to, or characteristic of the Democratic party. **b.** of, pertaining to, or belonging to the Democratic-Republican party. Also, **dem′o·crat′i·cal.** [< F *démocratique,* ML *dēmocratic(us)* < Gk *dēmokratikós*] —**dem′o·crat′i·cal·ly,** *adv.*
Dem′ocrat′ic par′ty, one of the two major political parties in the U.S., founded in 1828.
Democrat′ic-Repub′lican par′ty, *U.S. Hist.* a political party opposed to the old Federalist party.
de·moc·ra·tize (di mok′rə tīz′), *v.t., v.i.,* **-tized, -tiz·ing.** to make or become democratic. Also, *Brit.,* **de·moc′ra·tise′.** [< F *démocratis(er)*] —**de·moc′ra·ti·za′tion,** *n.*
De·moc·ri·tus (di mok′ri təs), *n.* ("*the Laughing Philosopher*") c460–370 B.C., Greek philosopher. —**De·moc·ri·te·an** (di mok′ri tē′ən), *adj.*
dé·mo·dé (dā mô dā′), *adj. French.* no longer in fashion; out of date; outmoded.
de·mod·ed (dē mō′did), *adj.* out of date; outmoded. [trans. of F *démodé*]
de·mod·u·late (dē moj′ə lāt′, -mod′yə-), *v.t.,* **-lat·ed, -lat·ing.** *Radio.* detect (def. 4). —**de·mod′u·la′tion,** *n.*
De·mo·gor·gon (dē′mə gôr′gən, dem′ə-), *n.* a vague, mysterious, infernal power or divinity of ancient mythology. [< LL < Gk]
de·mo·graph·ics (dē′mə graf′iks, dem′ə-), *n.* **1.** (*construed as sing.*) the statistical data of a population, esp. those showing average age, income, education, etc. **2.** (*construed as pl.*) the facts shown by such data.
de·mog·ra·phy (di mog′rə fē), *n.* the science of vital and social statistics, as of the births, deaths, marriages, etc., of populations. —**de·mog′ra·pher,** *n.* —**de·mo·graph·ic** (dē′mə graf′ik, dem′ə-), *adj.* —**de′mo·graph′i·cal·ly,** *adv.*
dem·oi·selle (dem′wä zel′, dem′ə-; *Fr.* də mwa zel′), *n., pl.* **-selles** (-zelz′; *Fr.* -zel′). **1.** a girl or young woman. **2.** a damselfly, esp. of the genus *Agrion.* [< F; see DAMSEL]
de·mol·ish (di mol′ish), *v.t.* **1.** to tear down (a building or other structure); raze. **2.** to put an end to; destroy; finish. **3.** to lay waste to; ruin utterly: *The fire demolished the town.* [< F *démoliss-,* long s. of *démolir* < L *dēmōlīrī* to destroy = *dē-* DE- + *mōlīrī* to set in motion, struggle (*mōl(ēs)* mass, bulk + *-īrī* pass. inf. suffix)] —**de·mol′ish·er,** *n.* —**de·mol′ish·ment,** *n.*
dem·o·li·tion (dem′ə lish′ən, dē′mə-), *n.* **1.** the act or an instance of demolishing. **2.** the state of being demolished; destruction. **3. demolitions,** explosives, esp. as used in war. —*adj.* **4.** of, pertaining to, or working with explosives: *a demolition squad.* **5.** of or pertaining to tearing down or demolishing: *Demolition work had begun on the old building.* [< L *dēmōlītiōn-* (s. of *dēmōlītiō*) = *dēmōlīt(us)* (ptp. of *dēmōlīrī;* see DEMOLISH) + *-iōn-* -ION] —**dem′o·li′tion·ist,** *n.*
de·mon (dē′mən), *n.* **1.** an evil spirit; devil. **2.** an evil passion or influence. **3.** a person considered extremely wicked, evil, or cruel. **4.** a person with great energy, drive, etc.: *He's a demon for work.* **5.** Also, **daemon, daimon.**

Class. Myth. **a.** a god. **b.** a subordinate deity, as the genius of a place or a person's attendant spirit. [defs. 1–4: ME, for L *daemon(ium)* < Gk *daimónion,* thing of divine nature (in Jewish and Christian writers, evil spirit), neut. of *daimónios* < *daímōn;* def. 5 < L; see DAEMON]

demon-, var. of **demono-** before a vowel: *demonism.*

de·mon·e·tise (dē mon′i tīz′, -mun′-), *v.t.,* **-tised, -tis·ing.** *Chiefly Brit.* demonetize. —**de·mon′e·ti·sa′tion,** *n.*

de·mon·e·tize (dē mon′i tīz′, -mun′-), *v.t.,* **-tized, -tiz·ing. 1.** to divest (a monetary standard) of value. **2.** to withdraw (money or the like) from use. [< Fr *démonétise(r).* See DE-, MONETIZE] —**de·mon′e·ti·za′tion,** *n.*

de·mo·ni·ac (di mō′nē ak′, dē′mə nī′ak), *adj.* Also, **de·mo·ni·a·cal** (dē′mə nī′ə kəl). **1.** of, pertaining to, or like a demon; demonic. **2.** possessed by or as by an evil spirit; raging; frantic. —*n.* **3.** a person seemingly possessed by a demon or evil spirit. [ME *demoniak* < LL *daemoniac(us)* < Gk *daimoniakós.* See DEMON-, -I-, -AC] —**de·mo·ni·a·cal·ly** (dē′mə nī′ik lē), *adv.*

de·mo·ni·an (di mō′nē ən), *adj.* demoniac (def. 1). Also, **daemonian.**

de·mon·ic (di mon′ik), *adj.* **1.** inspired as if by a demon, indwelling spirit, or genius. **2.** demoniac (def. 1). Also, **daemonic, de·mon′i·cal.** [< LL *daemonic(us)* < Gk *daimonikós.* See DEMON-, -IC]

de·mon·ise (dē′mə nīz′), *v.t.,* **-ised, -is·ing.** *Chiefly Brit.* demonize.

de·mon·ism (dē′mə niz′əm), *n.* **1.** belief in or worship of demons. **2.** demonology. —**de′mon·ist,** *n.*

de·mon·ize (dē′mə nīz′), *v.t.,* **-ized, -iz·ing. 1.** to turn into a demon or make demonlike. **2.** to subject to the influence of demons. Also, *esp. Brit.,* **demonise.** [< ML *daemonizāre*)]

demono-, a combining form of **demon:** *demonology.* Also, *esp. before a vowel,* **demon-.**

de·mon·og·ra·phy (dē′mə nog′rə fē), *n., pl.* **-phies.** a treatise on demons. —**de′mon·og′ra·pher,** *n.*

de·mon·ol·a·ter (dē′mə nol′ə tər), *n.* a person who worships demons. [back formation from DEMONOLATRY]

de·mon·ol·a·try (dē′mə nol′ə trē), *n.* the worship of demons.

de·mon·ol·o·gy (dē′mə nol′ə jē), *n.* **1.** the study of demons or of beliefs about demons. **2.** the doctrine of demons. Also, **daemonology.** —**de′mon·ol′o·gist,** *n.*

de·mon·stra·ble (di mon′strə bəl, dem′ən-), *adj.* capable of being demonstrated. [ME < OF < L *dēmonstrābil(is)* = *dēmonstr(āre)* (see DEMONSTRATE) + *-ābilis* -ABLE] —**de·mon′stra·bil′i·ty, de·mon′stra·ble·ness,** *n.* —**de·mon′stra·bly,** *adv.*

de·mon·strant (də mon′strənt), *n.* demonstrator (def. 2). [< L *dēmonstrant-* (s. of *dēmonstrāns*) showing, prp. of *dēmonstrāre*]

dem·on·strate (dem′ən strāt′), *v.,* **-strat·ed, -strat·ing.** —*v.t.* **1.** to describe, explain, or illustrate by examples, specimens, experiments, or the like. **2.** to manifest or exhibit; show. **3.** to make evident or establish by arguments or reasoning; prove. —*v.i.* **4.** to make, give, or take part in a demonstration. [< L *dēmonstrāt(us),* ptp. of *dēmonstrāre* to show, point out = *dē-* DE- + *monstrāre* to show (*monstr(um)* a portent (see MONSTER) + *-ātus* -ATE[1]]

dem·on·stra·tion (dem′ən strā′shən), *n.* **1.** the act of proving, as by reasoning, an experiment, or a show of evidence. **2.** something serving as proof or supporting evidence. **3.** a description or explanation, as of a process, illustrated by examples, specimens, or the like. **4.** the act of exhibiting the operation or use of a device, machine, or the like, as to a prospective buyer. **5.** an exhibition, as of feeling; display; manifestation: *demonstrations of affection.* **6.** a public exhibition of the attitude of a group of persons toward a controversial issue or other matter, made by picketing, parading, etc. [ME *demonstracion* < L *dēmonstrātiōn-* (s. of *dēmonstrātiō*)] —**dem′on·stra′tion·al,** *adj.*

de·mon·stra·tive (də mon′strə tiv), *adj.* **1.** characterized by or given to open exhibition or expression of one's emotions, attitudes, etc., esp. of love or affection. **2.** serving to demonstrate; explanatory or illustrative. **3.** serving to prove the truth of anything; conclusive. **4.** *Gram.* indicating or singling out the thing referred to. *This* is a demonstrative pronoun. —*n.* **5.** *Gram.* a demonstrative word, as *this* or *there.* [ME *demonstratif* < L *dēmonstrātīv(us)*] —**de·mon′stra·tive·ly,** *adv.* —**de·mon′stra·tive·ness,** *n.*

dem·on·stra·tor (dem′ən strā′tər), *n.* **1.** a person or thing that demonstrates. **2.** Also, **demonstrant.** a person who takes part in a public demonstration. **3.** a person who exhibits the use and application of a product, service, etc., to a prospective customer. **4.** a product, service, etc., used in demonstrations to prospective customers. [< L]

de·mor·al·ise (di môr′ə līz′, -mor′-), *v.t.,* **-ised, -is·ing.** *Chiefly Brit.* demoralize. —**de·mor′al·i·sa′tion,** *n.* —**de·mor′al·is′er,** *n.*

de·mor·al·ize (di môr′ə līz′, -mor′-), *v.t.,* **-ized, -iz·ing. 1.** to deprive (a person or persons) of spirit, courage, discipline, etc.; destroy the morale of: *The continuous barrage demoralized the infantry.* **2.** to throw (a person) into disorder or confusion; bewilder. **3.** to corrupt or undermine the morals of. [< F *démoralise(r)*] —**de·mor′al·i·za′tion,** *n.* —**de·mor′al·iz′er,** *n.*

De Mor·gan (di môr′gən), **1. Augustus,** 1806–71, English mathematician and logician. **2.** his son, **William Frend** (frend), 1839–1917, English novelist and ceramist.

de mor·tu·is nil ni·si bo·num (dā mōr′to͞o is′ nil nē′sē bō′no͝om; *Eng.* dē môr′cho͞o is nil nī′sī bō′nəm), *Latin.* of the dead (say) nothing unless (it is) good.

de·mos (dē′mos), *n.* **1.** (in ancient Greece) the people. **2.** the common people; populace. [< Gk: district, people]

De·mos·the·nes (di mos′thə nēz′), *n.* 384?–322 B.C., Athenian statesman and orator.

de·mote (di mōt′), *v.t.,* **-mot·ed, -mot·ing.** to reduce to a lower grade or class (opposed to *promote*). [DE- + (PRO)MOTE] —**de·mo′tion,** *n.*

de·moth·ball (dē môth′bôl′, -moth′-), *v.t.* to remove (a naval vessel) from storage or reserve, usually for active duty; reactivate.

de·mot·ic (di mot′ik), *adj.* **1.** of or pertaining to the common people; popular. **2.** of, pertaining to, or noting the simplified form of hieratic writing used in ancient Egypt. —*n.* **3.** (*cap.*) Also called **Romaic.** the Modern Greek vernacular (opposed to *Katharevusa*). [< Gk *dēmotik(ós)* popular, plebeian = *dēmót(ēs)* a plebeian (see DEMO-) + *-ikos* -IC]

de·mount (dē mount′), *v.t.* **1.** to remove from a mounting, setting, etc., as a gun. **2.** to take apart; disassemble. —**de·mount′a·ble,** *adj.*

Demp·sey (demp′sē, dem′-), *n.* **Jack** (*William Harrison Dempsey*), 1895–1983, U.S. boxer: world heavyweight champion 1919–26.

de·mul·cent (di mul′sənt), *adj.* **1.** soothing or mollifying, as a medicinal substance. —*n.* **2.** a demulcent substance for soothing an irritated mucous membrane. [< L *dēmulcent-* (s. of *dēmulcēns,* prp. of *dēmulcēre*) stroking down, softening = *dē-* DE- + *mulc(ēre)* (to) soothe + *-ent-* -ENT]

de·mul·si·fy (dē mul′sə fī′), *v.t.,* **-fied, -fy·ing.** *Physical Chem.* to break down (an emulsion) into separate substances incapable of re-forming the same emulsion. —**de·mul′si·fi·ca′tion,** *n.* —**de·mul′si·fi′er,** *n.*

de·mur (di mûr′), *v.,* **-murred, -mur·ring,** *n.* —*v.i.* **1.** to make objection, esp. on the grounds of scruples; take exception; object. **2.** *Law.* to interpose a demurrer. **3.** *Archaic.* to linger; hesitate. —*n.* **4.** the act of making objection. **5.** an objection raised. **6.** *Law. Obs.* a demurrer. **7.** *Archaic.* hesitation. [ME *demur(en)* < OF *demur-, demuer-,* var. s. of *demorer* < L *dēmorārī* to linger = *dē-* DE- + *morārī* to delay (*mor(a)* delay + *-ārī* pass. inf. suffix)]

de·mure (di myo͝or′), *adj.,* **-mur·er, -mur·est. 1.** shy and modest; reserved. **2.** coyly decorous or sedate. [ME, prob. < AF; cf. OF *meur* ripe, mature < L *matūr(us)*] —**de·mure′ly,** *adv.* —**de·mure′ness,** *n.* —**Syn. 1.** retiring. See **modest.**

de·mur·rage (di mûr′ij, -mur′-), *n.* *Com.* **1.** the detention of a vessel, as in loading or unloading, beyond the time agreed upon. **2.** the similar detention of a railroad car, truck, etc. **3.** a charge for such detention.

de·mur·ral (di mûr′əl, -mur′-), *n.* the act or an instance of demurring; demur.

de·mur·rer (di mûr′ər, -mur′-), *n.* **1.** a person who demurs; objector. **2.** *Law.* a pleading that the facts alleged by the opposite party do not sustain the contention based on them. **3.** an objection or demur. [< AF, var. of OF *demorer*]

De·muth (di mo͞oth′), *n.* **Charles,** 1883–1935, U.S. painter and illustrator.

de·my (di mī′), *n., pl.* **-mies. 1.** (in England) a size of printing paper, 17½ × 22½ inches. **2.** a size of drawing or writing paper, 16 × 21 inches in the U.S. **3.** Also called **demy′ octa′vo.** a size of book, about 5½ × 8¾ inches, untrimmed. *Abbr.:* demy 8vo **4.** Also called **demy′ quar′to.** *Chiefly Brit.* a size of book, about 8¾ × 11 inches, untrimmed. *Abbr.:* demy 4to [ME *demi, demy.* See DEMI-]

de·my·thol·o·gise (dē′mi thol′ə jīz′), *v.t.,* **-gised, -gis·ing.** *Chiefly Brit.* demythologize.

de·my·thol·o·gize (dē′mi thol′ə jīz′), *v.t.,* **-gized, -giz·ing.** to rid of mythological attributes in an attempt to appraise more accurately. —**de′my·thol′o·gi·za′tion,** *n.*

den (den), *n.* **1.** a secluded place, as the lair of a predatory animal. **2.** a cave used as a place of shelter or concealment. **3.** a squalid or vile abode or place: *dens of misery.* **4.** a small, secluded room in a house or apartment, designed to provide a quiet, comfortable, and informal atmosphere for conversation, reading, writing, etc. **5.** one of the units of a cub-scout pack, analogous to a patrol in the Boy Scouts. [ME; OE *denn;* cf. early D *denne* floor, cave, den, G *Tenne* floor]

Den., Denmark.

De·na′li Na′tional Park′ (də nä′lē), a national park in S central Alaska, including Mount McKinley. 3030 sq. mi. Formerly, **Mount McKinley National Park.**

de·nar·i·us (di nâr′ē əs), *n., pl.* **-nar·i·i** (-nâr′ē ī′). **1.** a silver coin and monetary unit of ancient Rome, first issued in the latter part of the 3rd century B.C. **2.** a gold coin of ancient Rome equal to 25 silver denarii; aureus. [< L, orig. adj.: containing ten (asses)]

den·a·ry (den′ə rē, dē′nə-), *adj.* **1.** containing ten; tenfold. **2.** proceeding by tens; decimal. [< L *dēnāri(us)* containing ten = *dēn(ī)* ten at a time (< *decem* ten) + *-ārius* -ARY]

de·na·tion·al·ise (dē nash′ə nᵊlīz′), *v.t.,* **-ised, -is·ing.** *Chiefly Brit.* denationalize. —**de·na′tion·al·is·a′tion,** *n.*

de·na·tion·al·ize (dē nash′ə nᵊ līz′), *v.t.,* **-ized, -iz·ing. 1.** to remove (an industry or the like) from government control or ownership. **2.** to deprive of national status. —**de·na′tion·al·i·za′tion,** *n.*

de·nat·u·ral·ize (dē nach′ər ə līz′), *v.t.,* **-ized, -iz·ing. 1.** to deprive of proper or true nature; make unnatural. **2.** to deprive of naturalization or citizenship. —**de·nat′u·ral·i·za′tion,** *n.*

de·na·ture (dē nā′chər), *v.t.,* **-tured, -tur·ing. 1.** to deprive (something) of its natural character, properties, etc. **2.** to render (any of various alcohols) unfit for drinking by adding an unwholesome substance that does not alter the alcohol's usefulness for other purposes. **3.** *Biochem.* to alter (a protein or the like) by chemical or physical means. —**de·na′tur·ant,** *n.* —**de·na′tur·a′tion,** *n.*

dena′tured al′cohol, *Chem.* alcohol, esp. ethyl alcohol, that has been denatured: used chiefly as a solvent.

Den·bigh (den′bē), *n.* **1.** a municipal borough in and the county seat of Denbighshire, in N Wales. 8044 (1963). **2.** Denbighshire.

Den·bigh·shire (den′bē shēr′, -shər), *n.* a county in N Wales. 173,843 (1961); 669 sq. mi. *Co. seat:* Denbigh. Also called **Denbigh.**

dendr-, var. of **dendro-** before a vowel: *dendrite.*

dendri-, var. of **dendro-** before elements of Latin origin: *dendriform.*

den·dri·form (den′drə fôrm′), *adj.* treelike in form.

Dendrite (def. 1)

den·drite (den′drīt), *n.* **1.** *Geol.* **a.** a branching figure or marking, resembling moss or a shrub or tree in form, found on or in certain stones or minerals due to the presence of a foreign material. **b.** any arborescent crystalline growth. **2.** *Anat.* the branching process of a neuron which conducts impulses toward the cell. [< Gk *dendrít(ēs)* pertaining to a tree]

den·drit·ic (den drit′ik), *adj.* **1.** formed or marked like a dendrite. **2.** of a branching form; arborescent. Also, **den·drit′i·cal.** —**den·drit′i·cal·ly,** *adv.*

dendro-, a learned borrowing from Greek meaning "tree," used in the formation of compound words: *dendrology.* Also, **dendr-, dendri-, -dendron.** [< Gk, comb. form of *déndron*]

den·dro·chro·nol·o·gy (den′drō krə nol′ə jē), *n.* the science dealing with the study of the annual growth rings of trees in determining the dates and chronological order of past events.

den·droid (den′droid), *adj.* treelike; branching like a tree; arborescent. Also, **den·droi′dal.** [< Gk *dendroeid(ḗs)* treelike]

den·drol·o·gy (den drol′ə jē), *n.* the branch of botany dealing with trees and shrubs. —**den·dro·log·i·cal** (den′drə loj′i kəl), **den′dro·log′ic,** *adj.* —**den·drol·o·gist** (den drol′ə jist), *n.*

-dendron, var. of **dendro-** as final element of a compound word: *rhododendron.*

dene (dēn), *n. Brit.* a bare, sandy tract or low sand hill near the sea. Also, **dean.** [ME; OE *denu* valley]

Den·eb (den′eb), *n. Astron.* a first-magnitude star in the constellation Cygnus. [< Ar *dhanab* a tail]

den·e·ga·tion (den′ə gā′shən), *n.* denial; contradiction. [late ME *denegacion* < LL *dēnegātiōn-*]

den·gue (deng′gā, -gē), *n. Pathol.* an infectious, eruptive fever of warm climates, characterized esp. by severe pains in the joints and muscles. Also called **den′gue fe′ver, breakbone fever.** [< Sp; ? of Afr orig.]

Deng Xiao·ping (dœng′ shyou′ping′), born 1904, vice chairman of the Chinese Communist party since 1977.

deni·a·ble (di nī′ə bəl), *adj.* capable of being or liable to be denied or contradicted.

de·ni·al (di nī′əl), *n.* **1.** an assertion that an allegation is false. **2.** refusal to believe a doctrine, theory, or the like. **3.** disbelief in the existence or reality of a thing. **4.** the refusal to satisfy a claim, request, desire, etc., or of a person making it. **5.** refusal to recognize or acknowledge; a disowning or disavowal: *Peter's denial of Christ.* **6.** *Law.* refusal to acknowledge the validity of a claim, suit, or the like; a plea that denies allegations of fact in an adversary's plea. **7.** sacrifice of one's own wants or needs; self-denial.

de·ni·er[1] (di nī′ər), *n.* a person who denies. [ME]

de·nier[2] (də nēr′ *or, esp. for 1,* den′yər; *Fr.* də nyā′), *n.* **1.** a unit of weight indicating the fineness of fiber filaments and yarns, and equal to a yarn weighing one gram per each 9000 meters: used esp. in indicating the fineness of women's hosiery. **2.** any of various coins issued in French-speaking regions, esp. a French coin used from the 8th century A.D. until 1794. [ME < OF < L *dēnār(ius)* DENARIUS]

den·i·grate (den′ə grāt′), *v.t.*, **-grat·ed, -grat·ing.** **1.** to speak damagingly of; sully or defame: *to denigrate someone's good reputation.* **2.** to make black; blacken: *rain clouds denigrating the sky.* [< L *dēnigrāt(us)* blackened (ptp. of *dēnigrāre*) = *dē-* DE- + *nigr(āre)* (to) make black + *-ātus* -ATE[1]] —**den′i·gra′tion,** *n.* —**den′i·gra′tor,** *n.*

De·ni·ker (de nē ker′), *n.* **Jo·seph** (zhô zef′), 1852–1918, French anthropologist and naturalist.

den·im (den′əm), *n.* **1.** a heavy twill cotton for work and leisure garments. **2.** a similar fabric of finer quality for upholstery. **3. denims,** (*construed as pl.*) a garment, esp. overalls or trousers, made of denim. [< F, short for *serge de Nîmes* serge of NÎMES]

Den·is (den′is; *Fr.* də nē′), *n.* **Saint,** died A.D. c280, 1st bishop of Paris: patron saint of France. Also, **Denys.**

Den·i·son (den′i sən), *n.* a city in NE Texas. 24,923 (1970).

de·ni·tri·fy (dē nī′trə fī′), *v.t.*, **-fied, -fy·ing.** to reduce (nitrates) to nitrites, ammonia, and free nitrogen, as in soil by microorganisms. —**de·ni′tri·fi·ca′tion,** *n.*

den·i·zen (den′i zən), *n.* **1.** an inhabitant; resident: *denizens of the deep.* **2.** *Brit.* an alien admitted to residence and to certain rights of citizenship in a country. **3.** an animal, plant, etc., adapted to a new place, condition, or the like. [ME *denisein* < AF = *deinz* within (< L *de intus*) + *-ein* -AN]

Den·mark (den′märk), *n.* a kingdom in N Europe, on the Jutland peninsula and adjacent islands. 5,079,000; 16,576 sq. mi. *Cap.:* Copenhagen.

Den′mark Strait′, a strait between Iceland and Greenland. 130 mi. wide.

den′ moth′er, (in the Boy Scouts) a woman who serves as an adult leader of a cub-scout den.

de·nom·i·nate (di nom′ə nāt′), *v.t.*, **-nat·ed, -nat·ing.** to give a name to; denote; designate. [< L *dēnōmināt(us)* (ptp. of *dēnōmināre*)]

de·nom·i·na·tion (di nom′ə nā′shən), *n.* **1.** a name or designation, esp. one for a class of things. **2.** a class or kind of persons or things having a specific name. **3.** a religious group, usually including many local churches. **4.** the act of naming or designating a person or thing. **5.** one of the grades or degrees in a series of values, measures, weights, etc.: *bills of small denomination.* [ME *denominacioun* < LL *dēnōminātiōn-* (s. of *dēnōminātiō*), in L: metonymy]

de·nom·i·na·tion·al (di nom′ə nā′shə nᵊl), *adj.* **1.** of or pertaining to a denomination or denominations. **2.** founded, sponsored, or controlled by a particular religious denomination or sect: *denominational schools.* **3.** limited, conditioned, originating in, or influenced by the beliefs, attitudes, or interests of a religious sect, political party, etc.: *denominational prejudice.* —**de·nom′i·na′tion·al·ly,** *adv.*

de·nom·i·na·tion·al·ism (di nom′ə nā′shə nᵊliz′əm), *n.* denominational or sectarian spirit or policy; the tendency to divide into denominations or sects. —**de·nom′i·na′tion·al·ist,** *n.*

de·nom·i·na·tive (di nom′ə nā′tiv, -nə tiv), *adj.* **1.** conferring or constituting a distinctive designation or name. **2.** *Gram.* (esp. of verbs) formed from a noun, as English *to man* from the noun *man.* —*n.* **3.** *Gram.* a denominative word, esp. a verb. [< LL *dēnōminātīv(us)*] —**de·nom·i·na·tive·ly** (di nom′ə nā′tiv lē, -nə tiv-), *adv.*

de·nom·i·na·tor (di nom′ə nā′tər), *n.* **1.** *Arith.* the term of a fraction, usually written under the line, that indicates the number of equal parts into which the unit is divided; divisor. **2.** something shared or held in common; standard. **3.** *Archaic.* a person or thing that denominates. [< ML]

de·no·ta·tion (dē′nō tā′shən), *n.* **1.** the association or set of associations that a word or expression usually elicits. Cf. **connotation. 2.** a specific term or name. **3.** the act or fact of denoting; indication. **4.** something that denotes; mark; symbol. **5.** *Logic.* **a.** the class of particulars to which a term is applicable. **b.** that which is represented by a sign. [< L *dēnotātiōn-* (s. of *dēnotātiō*) a marking out = *dēnotāt(us)* (ptp. of *dēnotāre;* see DENOTE) + *-iōn-* -ION]

de·no·ta·tive (dē′nō tā′tiv, di nō′tə tiv), *adj.* able or tending to denote; denoting. —**de′no·ta′tive·ly,** *adv.*

de·note (di nōt′), *v.t.*, **-not·ed, -not·ing.** **1.** to be a mark or sign of; indicate. **2.** to be a name or designation for; mean. **3.** to represent by a symbol; stand as a symbol for. [< F *dénot(er),* L *dēnot(āre)* (to) mark out. See DE-, NOTE] —**de·not′a·ble,** *adj.* —**de·note′ment,** *n.*

de·no·tive (di nō′tiv), *adj.* used or serving to denote; denotative.

de·noue·ment (dā′nōō mäN′), *n.* **1.** the final resolution of a plot, as of a drama or novel. **2.** the point at which this occurs. **3.** the outcome or resolution of a doubtful series of occurrences. Also, **dé′noue·ment′.** [< F: lit., an untying = *dénou(er)* (to) untie < OF *desnoer* (*des-* DE- + *noe(r)* (to) knot < L *nodāre* < *nod(us)* knot) + *-ment* -MENT]

de·nounce (di nouns′), *v.t.*, **-nounced, -nounc·ing.** **1.** to censure or condemn openly or publicly. **2.** to make a formal accusation against, as to the police or in a court. **3.** to give formal notice of the termination or denial of (a treaty, pact, or the like). **4.** *Archaic.* to announce or proclaim, esp. as something evil or calamitous. **5.** *Obs.* to portend. [ME *denounce(n)* < OF *denonc(ier)* (to) speak out < L *dēnuntiāre* to threaten (*dē-* DE- + *nuntiāre* to announce < *nunti(us)* messenger)] —**de·nounce′ment,** *n.* —**de·nounc′er,** *n.* —**Syn. 1.** attack. —**Ant. 1.** praise, commend.

de no·vo (de nō′wō; *Eng;* dē nō′vō), *Latin.* anew; afresh; again; from the beginning.

dense (dens), *adj.*, **dens·er, dens·est.** **1.** having the component parts closely compacted together; crowded or compact: *a dense forest.* **2.** stupid; slow-witted; dull. **3.** intense; extreme. **4.** relatively opaque; transmitting little light, as a photographic negative, optical glass, color, etc. [< L *dens(us)* thick] —**dense′ly,** *adv.* —**dense′ness,** *n.*

den·sim·e·ter (den sim′i tər), *n. Chem., Physics.* any instrument for measuring density. [< L *dens(us)* DENSE + -I- + -METER] —**den·si·met·ric** (den′sə me′trik), *adj.* —**den·sim′e·try,** *n.*

den·si·tom·e·ter (den′si tom′i tər), *n.* **1.** *Photog.* an instrument for measuring the density of negatives. **2.** a densimeter. —**den·si·to·met·ric** (den′si tə me′trik), *adj.* —**den′si·tom′e·try,** *n.*

den·si·ty (den′si tē), *n., pl.* **-ties.** **1.** the state or quality of being dense; compactness. **2.** stupidity; obtuseness. **3.** *Physics.* mass per unit volume. **4.** the degree of opacity of a substance, medium, etc., that transmits light. **5.** *Photog.* the relative opacity of an area of a negative or transparency. [< L *densitāt-* (s. of *densitās*)]

dent[1] (dent), *n.* **1.** a hollow or depression in a surface, as from a blow. —*v.t.* **2.** to make a dent in or on; indent. —*v.i.* **3.** to sink in, making a dent. **4.** become indented: *Tin dents more easily than steel.* [ME *dente,* var. of DINT]

dent[2] (dent), *n.* a toothlike projection, as a tooth of a gear-wheel. [< F < L *dent-* (s. of *dēns*) tooth]

dent-, var. of **denti-** before a vowel: *dentin.*

dent., **1.** dentist. **2.** dentistry.

den·tal (den′tᵊl), *adj.* **1.** of or pertaining to the teeth. **2.** of or pertaining to dentistry or a dentist. **3.** *Phonet.* **a.** (of a speech sound) articulated with the tongue tip touching the back of the upper front teeth or immediately above them, as French *t.* **b.** alveolar, as English *t.* —*n.* **4.** *Phonet.* a dental sound. [< ML *dentāl(is)*]

den′tal floss′, *Dentistry.* a soft, waxed thread for cleaning the spaces between the teeth.

den·tal·ise (den′tᵊlīz′), *v.t.*, **-ised, -is·ing.** *Chiefly Brit.* dentalize. —**den′tal·i·sa′tion,** *n.*

den·ta·li·um (den tā′lē əm), *n., pl.* **-li·ums, -li·a** (-lē ə). any tooth shell of the genus *Dentalium.* [< NL = ML *dentāl(is)* DENTAL + *-ium* neut. n. suffix]

den·tal·ize (den′tᵊlīz′), *v.t.*, **-ized, -iz·ing.** *Phonet.* to change into or pronounce as a dental sound. Also, *esp. Brit.,* **dentalise.** —**den′tal·i·za′tion,** *n.*

den·tate (den′tāt), *adj. Bot., Zool.* having a toothed margin or toothlike projections. [< L *dentāt(us)*] —**den′tate·ly,** *adv.*

den·ta·tion (den tā′shən), *n. Bot., Zool.* **1.** dentate state or form. **2.** an angular projection of a margin.

denti-, a learned borrowing from Latin meaning "tooth," used in the formation of compound words: *dentiform.* Also, *esp. before a vowel,* **dent-.** Cf. **odont-.** [< L, comb. form of *dent-* (s. of *dēns*)]

den·ti·cle (den′ti kəl), *n.* a small tooth or toothlike part. [ME < L *denticul(us)*]

Dentate leaf

den·tic·u·late (den tik′yə lit, -lāt′), *adj. Bot., Zool.* finely dentate, as a leaf. Also, **den·tic′u·lat′ed.** [< L *denticulāt(us)* having small teeth] —**den·tic′u·late·ly,** *adv.*

den·tic·u·la·tion (den tik′yə lā′shən), *n.* **1.** denticulate state or form. **2.** a denticle. **3.** a series of denticles.

den·ti·form (den′tə fôrm′), *adj.* having the form of a tooth; tooth-shaped.

den·ti·frice (den′tə fris), *n.* a powder, paste, or other preparation for cleaning the teeth. [< F < L *dentifric(ium)* tooth powder. See DENTI-, FRICTION]

den·til (den′tᵊl, -til), *n. Archit.* any of a series of small, closely spaced rectangular blocks beneath the corona of a cornice. [< F < *dentille* (obs.), fem. dim. of *dent* tooth]

den·ti·la·bi·al (den′ti lā′bē əl), *adj., n.* labiodental.

den·ti·lin·gual (den′ti liŋ′gwəl), *adj. Phonet.* interdental (def. 2).

den·tin (den′tᵊn, -tin), *n. Dentistry.* the hard, calcareous tissue, similar to but denser than bone, that forms the major portion of a tooth. Also, **den·tine** (den′tēn). —**den′tin·al,** *adj.*

den·tist (den′tist), *n.* a person whose profession is dentistry. [< F *dentiste*]

den·tist·ry (den′ti strē), *n.* the profession or science dealing with the prevention and treatment of diseases and malformations of the teeth, gums, and oral cavity.

den·ti·tion (den tish′ən), *n.* **1.** the kind, number, and arrangement of the teeth of man and animals. **2.** the eruption or cutting of the teeth; teething. [< L *dentītiōn-* (s. of *dentītiō*) a teething = *dentīt(us)* teethed (ptp. of *dentīre;* see DENT[2]) + *-iōn-* -ION]

den·toid (den′toid), *adj.* resembling a tooth.

Den·ton (den′tən), *n.* a city in N Texas. 39,874 (1970).

den·ture (den′chər), *n.* an artificial replacement of one or more teeth. [< F = *dent* tooth + *-ure* -URE]

de·nu·cle·ar·ize (dē no͞o′klē ə rīz′), *v.t.,* **-ized, -iz·ing.** to forbid the deployment or construction of nuclear weapons in (a country or zone). —**de·nu′cle·ar·i·za′tion,** *n.*

den·u·date (*v.* den′yo͝o dāt′, di no͞o′dāt, -nyo͞o′-; *adj.* di-no͞o′dāt, -nyo͞o′-, den′yo͝o dāt′), *v.,* **-dat·ed, -dat·ing,** *adj.* —*v.t.* **1.** to make bare; strip; denude. —*adj.* **2.** denuded; bare. [< L *dēnūdāt(us),* ptp. of *dēnūdāre* to DENUDE]

den·u·da·tion (den′yo͝o dā′shən, dē′no͞o-, -nyo͞o-), *n.* **1.** the act of denuding. **2.** the state of being denuded. **3.** *Geol.* **a.** the laying bare of rock by erosive processes. **b.** erosion. [< LL *dēnūdātiōn-* (s. of *dēnūdātiō*)]

de·nude (di no͞od′, -nyo͞od′), *v.t.,* **-nud·ed, -nud·ing. 1.** to make naked or bare; strip. **2.** *Geol.* to subject to denudation. [< L *dēnūd(āre)*] —**de·nud′er,** *n.*

de·nu·mer·a·ble (di no͞o′mər ə bəl, -nyo͞o′-), *adj. Math.* (of sets) having elements that form a one-to-one correspondence with the natural numbers; countable; enumerable.

de·nun·ci·ate (di nun′sē āt′, -shē-), *v.t., v.i.,* **-at·ed, -at·ing.** to denounce; condemn openly. [< L *dēnuntiāt(us)* declared (ptp. of *dēnuntiāre*)] —**de·nun′ci·a′tor,** *n.*

de·nun·ci·a·tion (di nun′sē ā′shən, -shē-), *n.* **1.** an act or instance of denouncing. **2.** an accusation of crime before a public prosecutor or tribunal. **3.** notice of the termination or the renouncement of an international agreement or part thereof. [< L *dēnuntiātiōn-* (s. of *dēnuntiātiō*)]

de·nun·ci·a·to·ry (di nun′sē ə tôr′ē, -tōr′ē, -shē-), *adj.* characterized by or given to denunciation. Also, **de·nun·ci·a·tive** (di nun′sē ā′tiv, -shē-). —**de·nun′ci·a′tive·ly,** *adv.*

Den·ver (den′vər), *n.* a city in and the capital of Colorado, in the central part. 514,678 (1970).

de·ny (di nī′), *v.t.,* **-nied, -ny·ing. 1.** to state that (something declared or believed to be true) is not true: *to deny an accusation.* **2.** to refuse to agree or accede to: *to deny a petition.* **3.** to withhold the possession, use, or enjoyment of: *to deny a man his rights.* **4.** to withhold something from, or refuse to grant a request to: *to deny a beggar.* **5.** to refuse to recognize or acknowledge; disown; repudiate. **6.** to withhold access to. **7.** *Obs.* **a.** to refuse to take or accept. **b.** to refuse (to do something). [ME *deni(en)* < OF *deni(er)* < L *dēnegāre;* see DE-, NEGATE]
—**Syn. 1.** controvert, oppose, gainsay. DENY, CONTRADICT both imply objecting to or arguing against something. To DENY is to say that something is not true, or that it would not hold in practice: *to deny an allegation.* To CONTRADICT is to declare that the contrary is true: *to contradict a claim.*

Den·ys (den′is; *Fr.* də nē′), *n.* **Saint.** See **Denis, Saint.**

de·o·dar (dē′ə där′), *n.* a large Himalayan cedar, *Cedrus Deodara,* yielding a durable wood. [< Hindi *deodār* < Skt *devadāru* wood of the gods = *deva* god + *dāru* wood]

de·o·dor·ant (dē ō′dər ənt), *n.* **1.** an agent for destroying odors. **2.** a substance for inhibiting or masking perspiration odors. —*adj.* **3.** capable of destroying odors.

de·o·dor·ize (dē ō′də rīz′), *v.t.,* **-ized, -iz·ing.** to rid of odor, esp. of unpleasant odor. Also, *Brit.,* **de·o′dor·ise′.** —**de·o′dor·i·za′tion,** *n.* —**de·o′dor·iz′er,** *n.*

De·o gra·ti·as (dā′ō grät′sē äs′), *Latin.* thanks be to God.

de·on·tol·o·gy (dē′on tol′ə jē), *n.* ethics, esp. that branch dealing with duty, moral obligation, and right action. [< Gk *deont-* that which is binding (s. of *déon,* neut. prp. of *dein*) = *de-* binding + *-ont-* (prp. suffix) + -o- + -LOGY] —**de·on·to·log·i·cal** (dē on′tᵊloj′i kəl), *adj.*

de·or·bit (dē ôr′bit), *v.i.* **1.** to come out of an orbit. —*v.t.* **2.** to put out of an orbit. —*n.* **3.** the act or instance of putting or coming out of an orbit.

De·o vo·len·te (dā′ō vō len′tā), *Latin.* God willing.

de·ox·i·dize (dē ok′si dīz′), *v.t.,* **-dized, -diz·ing.** to remove oxygen from; reduce from the state of an oxide. —**de·ox′i·di·za′tion,** *n.* —**de·ox′i·diz′er,** *n.*

de·ox·y·gen·ate (dē ok′si jə nāt′), *v.t.,* **-at·ed, -at·ing.** to remove oxygen from. —**de·ox′y·gen·a′tion,** *n.*

de·ox·y·ri′bo·nu·cle′ic ac′id (dē ok′si rī′bō no͞o klē′-ik, -nyo͞o-, -rī′-), *Biochem.* See **DNA.**

de·ox·y·ri·bose (dē ok′si rī′bōs), *n. Biochem.* **1.** any of certain carbohydrates having the formula $C_5H_{10}O_4$, derived from ribose by the replacement of a hydroxyl group with a hydrogen atom. **2.** the sugar, $HOCH_2(CHOH)_2CH_2CHO$, obtained from DNA by hydrolysis. Also, **desoxyribose.** [DE- + OXY-[2] + RIBOSE]

dep., **1.** department. **2.** departs. **3.** departure. **4.** deponent. **5.** depot. **6.** deputy.

de·part (di pärt′), *v.i.* **1.** to go away; leave. **2.** to diverge or deviate (usually fol. by *from*): *The new method departs from the old in several respects.* **3.** to pass away, as from life or existence. —*v.t.* **4.** to go away from; leave. —*n.* **5.** *Archaic.* departure; death. [ME *depart(en)* < OF *departir*]
—**Syn. 1.** DEPART, RETIRE, RETREAT, WITHDRAW imply leaving a place. DEPART is a somewhat literary word, implying going away from a definite place: *to depart on a journey.* RETIRE emphasizes the reason or purpose for absenting oneself or drawing back from a place: *to retire from a position in battle.* RETREAT implies a necessary withdrawal, esp. as a result of adverse fortune in war: *to retreat to secondary lines of defense.* WITHDRAW suggests leaving some specific place or situation, usually for some definite and often unpleasant reason: *to withdraw from a hopeless task.*

de·part·ed (di pär′tid), *adj.* **1.** deceased; dead. **2.** gone; past. —*n.* **the departed, 3.** the dead person referred to. **4.** dead persons collectively.

de·part·ee (dē pär tē′), *n.* a person who leaves (an area, country, etc.).

de·part·ment (di pärt′mənt), *n.* **1.** a distinct part of anything arranged in divisions; a division of a complex whole or organized system. **2.** a division of official business, duties, or functions. **3.** (*cap.*) *U.S.* one of the principal divisions of the federal government, headed by a Secretary who is a member of the President's cabinet: *the Department of Commerce.* **4.** one of the principal administrative districts in France. **5.** one of the principal branches of a governmental organization: *the sanitation department.* **6.** a division of a business enterprise dealing with a particular area of activity: *the production department.* **7.** a section of a retail store selling a particular class or kind of goods: *the sportswear department.* **8.** one of the sections of a school or college dealing with a particular field of knowledge: *the department of English.* [< F *département*] —**de·part·men·tal** (di pärt men′tᵊl, dē′pärt-), *adj.* —**de·part·men′tal·ly,** *adv.*

de·part·men·tal·ise (di pärt men′tᵊlīz′, dē′pärt-), *v.t.,* **-ised, -is·ing.** *Chiefly Brit.* departmentalize.

de·part·men·tal·ize (di pärt men′tᵊlīz′, dē′pärt-), *v.t.,* **-ized, -iz·ing.** to divide into departments. —**de·part·men′tal·ism,** *n.* —**de′part·men′tal·i·za′tion,** *n.*

Depart′ment of Ag′riculture, *U.S.* the department of the federal government that institutes and administers all federal programs dealing with agriculture.

Depart′ment of Com′merce, *U.S.* the department of the federal government that promotes and administers domestic and foreign commerce.

Depart′ment of Defense′, *U.S.* the department of the federal government charged with ensuring that the military capacity of the U.S. is adequate to safeguard the national security.

Depart′ment of Educa′tion, *U.S.* the department of the federal government that institutes and administers all federal programs dealing with education: created in 1979 by transfer from part of the former Department of Health, Education, and Welfare.

Depart′ment of En′ergy, *U.S.* the department of the federal government that sets forth and maintains the national energy policy, including energy conservation, environmental protection, etc.

Depart′ment of Health′ and Hu′man Serv′ices, *U.S.* the department of the federal government that institutes and administers all federal programs dealing with public health and welfare: created in 1979 from the reorganized Department of Health, Education, and Welfare.

Depart′ment of Hous′ing and Ur′ban Devel′opment, *U.S.* the department of the federal government that institutes and administers all federal programs dealing with housing, urban renewal, and metropolitan planning.

Depart′ment of Jus′tice, *U.S.* the department of the federal government charged with the responsibility for the enforcement of federal laws.

Depart′ment of La′bor, *U.S.* the department of the federal government charged with improving the welfare, opportunities, and working conditions of wage earners.

Depart′ment of State′, *U.S.* the department of the federal government that sets forth and maintains the foreign policy of the U.S., esp. in negotiations with foreign governments and international organizations.

Depart′ment of the Inte′rior, *U.S.* the department of the federal government charged with the conservation and development of the natural resources of the U.S.

Depart′ment of the Treas′ury, *U.S.* the department of the federal government that collects revenue and administers the national finances.

Depart′ment of Transporta′tion, *U.S.* the department of the federal government that coordinates and institutes national transportation programs.

depart′ment store′, a large retail store organized into various departments of merchandise.

de·par·ture (di pär′chər), *n.* **1.** an act or instance of departing. **2.** divergence or deviation, as from a standard, rule, etc.: *a departure from accepted teaching methods.* **3.** *Navig.* the distance due east or west made by a vessel or aircraft. **4.** *Survey.* the length of the projection, on the east-west reference line, of a survey line. **5.** *Archaic.* death. [ME < OF *departeure;* cf. AF *departir* (n. use of inf.)]

de·pend (di pend′), *v.i.* **1.** to rely; place trust (usually fol. by *on* or *upon*): *to depend on the accuracy of a report.* **2.** to rely for support, maintenance, help, etc. (usually fol. by *on* or *upon*): *Children depend on their parents.* **3.** to be conditioned or contingent (usually fol. by *on* or *upon*): *His success here depends upon effort and ability.* **4.** *Gram.* (of a word or other linguistic form) to be subordinate to another linguistic form in the same construction; to form a part of a construction other than the head. **5.** to hang down; be suspended (usually fol. by *from*): *The chandelier depends from the ceiling.* **6.** to be undetermined or pending: *I may go or I may not, it all depends.* [ME *depend(en)* < OF *depend(re)* < L *dēpendēre* to hang down = *dē-* DE- + *pendere* to hang]

de·pend·a·ble (di pen′də bəl), *adj.* worthy of trust; reliable. —**de·pend′a·bil′i·ty, de·pend′a·ble·ness,** *n.* —**de·pend′a·bly,** *adv.*

de·pend·ence (di pen′dəns), *n.* **1.** the state of depending on or needing someone or something for aid, support, or the like. **2.** reliance; confidence; trust. **3.** the state of being conditional or contingent on something: *the dependence of an effect upon a cause.* **4.** subordination or subjection. **5.** an object of reliance or trust. Also, **de·pend′ance.** [ME *dependaunce* < ML *dēpendentia,* OF *dependance*]

de·pend·en·cy (di pen′dən sē), *n., pl.* **-cies. 1.** the state of being dependent; dependence. **2.** something dependent or subordinate. **3.** an outbuilding or annex. **4.** a subject territory that is not part of the ruling country. Also, **de·pend′an·cy.**

de·pend·ent (di pen′dənt), *adj.* **1.** depending on someone or something else for aid, support, etc. **2.** conditioned or determined by something else; contingent. **3.** subordinate; subject: *a dependent territory.* **4.** *Gram.* not used in isolation;

used only in connection with other forms. In *I walked out when the bell rang, when the bell rang* is a dependent clause. Cf. **independent** (def. 12), **main**[1] (def. 4). **5.** hanging down; pendent. **—***n.* **6.** a person who depends on or needs someone or something for aid, support, etc. **7.** (in U.S. federal income-tax law) a child, parent, or certain other relative for whom the taxpayer furnishes more than half of the total support, provided such a person has less than $600 gross income for the tax year. **8.** *Archaic.* a subordinate part. Also, **de·pend′ant.** [ME *dependaunt*] **—de·pend′ent·ly, de·pend′ant·ly,** *adv.*

depend′ent var′iable, *Math.* a variable in a functional relation whose value is determined by the values assumed by other variables in the relation, as *y* in the relation $y = 3x^2$. Cf. **independent variable.**

de·per·son·al·ise (dē pûr′sə nᵊlīz′), *v.t.*, **-ised, -is·ing.** *Chiefly Brit.* depersonalize.

de·per·son·a·li·za·tion (dē pûr′sə nᵊli zā′shən *or, esp. Brit.*, -nᵊlī-), *n.* **1.** the act of depersonalizing. **2.** the state of being depersonalized. **3.** *Psychiatry.* a state in which an individual no longer perceives the reality of self or of his environment. Also, *esp. Brit.*, **de·per′son·al·i·sa′tion.**

de·per·son·al·ize (dē pûr′sə nᵊlīz′), *v.t.*, **-ized, -iz·ing.** **1.** to make impersonal. **2.** to deprive of personality or individuality: *a mechanistic society which is depersonalizing its members.* Also, *esp. Brit.*, **depersonalise.**

De·pew (də pyōō′), *n.* **Chauncey Mitchell,** 1834–1928, U.S. lawyer, legislator, and orator.

de·pict (di pikt′), *v.t.* **1.** to represent by or as by painting; portray; delineate. **2.** to represent or characterize in words; describe. [< L *dēpict(us)* (ptp. of *dēpingere*) = *dē-* DE- + *pic-* paint (ptp. s. of *pingere*) + *-t(us)* ptp. suffix] **—de·pic′tor,** *n.* **—de·pic′tion,** *n.*

—Syn. 1. reproduce, draw, paint. **1, 2.** DEPICT, PORTRAY, SKETCH imply an actual reproduction of an object or scene by colors or lines, or by words. DEPICT emphasizes vividness of detail: *to depict the confusion of departure.* PORTRAY emphasizes faithful representation: *We could not portray the anguish of the exiles.* SKETCH suggests the drawing of the outlines of the most prominent features, or of the fundamental details, often in a preparatory way: *to sketch a scene to be painted later; to sketch the plans for an advertising campaign.*

de·pic·ture (di pik′chər), *v.t.*, **-tured, -tur·ing.** to picture; depict. [< L *dēpict(us)* (see DEPICT) + -URE]

dep·i·late (dep′ə lāt′), *v.t.*, **-lat·ed, -lat·ing.** to remove the hair from (hides, skin, etc.). [< L *dēpilāt(us)* plucked (ptp. of *dēpilāre*) = *dē-* DE- + *pil(āre)* (to) deprive of hair (< *pil(us)* a hair) + *-ātus* -ATE[1]] **—dep′i·la′tion,** *n.* **—dep′i·la′tor,** *n.*

de·pil·a·to·ry (di pil′ə tōr′ē, -tôr′ē), *adj.*, *n.*, *pl.* **-ries.** **—***adj.* **1.** capable of removing hair. **—***n.* **2.** a depilatory agent. **3.** such an agent in a mild liquid or cream form for temporarily removing unwanted hair from the body. [< ML *dēpilātōr(ius)*]

de·plane (dē plān′), *v.i.*, **-planed, -plan·ing.** to disembark from an airplane.

de·plete (di plēt′), *v.t.*, **-plet·ed, -plet·ing.** **1.** to decrease seriously or exhaust the abundance or supply of. **2.** *Surg.* to empty or relieve (overcharged vessels), as by bloodletting or purging. [< L *dēplēt(us)* emptied out (ptp. of *dēplēre*) = *dē-* DE- + *pl(ēre)* (to) fill + *-ē-* thematic vowel + *-t(us)* ptp. suffix] **—de·ple′tion,** *n.* **—de·ple′tive,** *adj.*

de·plor·a·ble (di plōr′ə bəl, -plôr′-), *adj.* **1.** causing grief or regret; lamentable. **2.** worthy of censure or disapproval; wretched; bad: *This room is in deplorable order.* [< F *déplorable*, MF] **—de·plor′a·ble·ness,** *n.* **—de·plor′a·bly,** *adv.*

de·plore (di plōr′, -plôr′), *v.t.*, **-plored, -plor·ing.** **1.** to regret deeply or strongly; lament. **2.** to disapprove of. [< L *dēplōr(āre)* (to) weep bitterly, complain = *dē-* DE- + *plōrāre* to wail, prob. of imit. orig.]

de·ploy (di ploi′), *v.t.* **1.** *Mil.* to spread out (troops) so as to form an extended front or line. **2.** to arrange, place, or move strategically or appropriately. **—***v.i.* **3.** to spread out strategically or in an extended front or line. [< F *déploy(er)*. See DIS-[1], PLOY] **—de·ploy′ment,** *n.*

de·plume (dē plōōm′), *v.t.*, **-plumed, -plum·ing.** **1.** to deprive of feathers; pluck. **2.** to strip of honor, wealth, etc. [ME < ML *dēplūm(āre)*] **—de′plu·ma′tion,** *n.*

de·po·lar·ise (dē pō′lə rīz′), *v.t.*, **-ised, -is·ing.** *Chiefly Brit.* depolarize. **—de·po′lar·i·sa′tion,** *n.* **—de·po′lar·is′er,** *n.*

de·po·lar·ize (dē pō′lə rīz′), *v.t.*, **-ized, -iz·ing.** to deprive of polarity or polarization. **—de·po′lar·i·za′tion,** *n.* **—de·po′lar·iz′er,** *n.*

de·po·lym·er·ize (dē′pə lim′ə rīz′, dē pol′ə mə-), *v.t.*, **-ized, -iz·ing.** *Chem.* to break down (a polymer) into monomers. **—de·po·lym·er·i·za·tion** (dē′pə lim′ər i zā′shən, dē pol′ə mər i-), *n.*

de·pone (di pōn′), *v.t.*, *v.i.*, **-poned, -pon·ing.** to testify under oath; depose. [< L *dēpōne(re)* (to) put away, down, aside (ML: to testify) = *dē-* DE- + *pōne(re)* (to) put]

de·po·nent (di pō′nənt), *adj.* **1.** *Classical Gk. and Lat. Gram.* (of a verb) appearing only in the passive or Greek middle-voice forms, but with active meaning. **—***n.* **2.** *Law.* a person who testifies, esp. under oath. **3.** *Classical Gk. and Lat. Gram.* a deponent verb, as Latin *loquor.* [< L *dēpōnent-* (s. of *dēpōnēns*) putting away (ML: testifying), prp. of *dēpōnere*]

de·pop·u·late (dē pop′yə lāt′), *v.t.*, **-lat·ed, -lat·ing.** to remove or reduce the number of inhabitants of, as by destruction or expulsion. [< L *dēpopulāt(us)* devastated (ptp. of *dēpopulārī*)] **—de·pop′u·la′tion,** *n.* **—de·pop′u·la′tor,** *n.*

de·port (di pōrt′, -pôrt′), *v.t.* **1.** to expel (an alien) from a country; banish. **2.** to bear, conduct, or behave (oneself) in a particular manner. **—***n.* **3.** *Obs.* deportment. [< F *déport(er)*, L *dēport(āre)* (to) carry away, banish oneself] **—de·port′a·ble,** *adj.*

de·por·ta·tion (dē′pōr tā′shən, -pôr-), *n.* **1.** the lawful expulsion of an undesired alien or other person from a state. **2.** the act or an instance of deporting. [< L *dēportātiōn-* (s. of *dēportātiō*) = *dēportāt(us)* (ptp. of *dēportāre* to DEPORT) + *-iōn-* -ION]

de·por·tee (dē′pōr tē′, -pôr-), *n.* a person who is or who is about to be deported, as from a country.

de·port·ment (di pōrt′mənt, -pôrt′-), *n.* demeanor; conduct; behavior. [< F *déportement*] **—Syn.** See **behavior.**

de·pos·al (di pō′zəl), *n.* the act of deposing or removing from office; deposition. [ME]

de·pose (di pōz′), *v.*, **-posed, -pos·ing.** **—***v.t.* **1.** to remove from office or position, esp. high office. **2.** to declare or testify, esp under oath, usually in writing. **—***v.i.* **3.** to bear witness; give sworn testimony, esp. in writing. [ME *depos(en)* < OF *depos(er)* (to) put down = *de-* DE- + *poser* < VL *posāre*, LL *pausāre;* see POSE[1]] **—de·pos′a·ble,** *adj.* **—de·pos′er,** *n.*

de·pos·it (di poz′it), *v.t.* **1.** to put, place, or set down, esp. carefully or exactly. **2.** to insert (a coin) in a coin-operated device: *Deposit a quarter and push the button.* **3.** to lay or throw down by a natural process; precipitate: *The river deposited soil at its mouth.* **4.** to deliver and leave (an item): *Please deposit your returned books with the librarian.* **5.** to place for safekeeping or in trust, esp. in a bank account. **6.** to give as security or in part payment. **—***v.i.* **7.** to be placed, inserted, left for safekeeping, etc. **—***n.* **8.** something precipitated, delivered and left, or thrown down, as by a natural process; sediment. **9.** a coating of metal deposited on something, usually by an electric current. **10.** a natural accumulation or occurrence, esp. of oil or ore: *a mountain range with many rich deposits of gold.* **11.** anything laid away or entrusted to another for safekeeping. **12.** money placed in a bank account or an instance of placing money in a bank account. **13.** anything given as security or in part payment: *The boy returned the pop bottle and got his two-cent deposit back. He made a deposit on the house and signed a ten-year mortgage.* **14.** depository. [< L *dēposit(us)* laid down, ptp. of *dēpōnere;* see DEPONE] **—Syn. 5.** bank, save, store. **10.** lode, vein.

de·pos·i·tar·y (di poz′i ter′ē), *n.*, *pl.* **-tar·ies.** **1.** a person to whom anything is given in trust. **2.** depository. [< LL *dēpositāri(us)* a trustee]

dep·o·si·tion (dep′ə zish′ən, dē′pə-), *n.* **1.** removal from an office or position. **2.** the act or process of depositing. **3.** something that is deposited. **4.** *Law.* a statement under oath, taken down in writing, to be used in court in place of the spoken testimony of the witness. [ME < OF, LL *dēpositiōn-* (s. of *dēpositiō*) a putting aside, testimony, burial = *dēposit(us)* laid down (see DEPOSIT) + *-iōn-* -ION] **—dep′o·si′tion·al,** *adj.*

de·pos·i·tor (di poz′i tər), *n.* **1.** a person or thing that deposits. **2.** a person who deposits money in a bank or who has a bank account. [< LL]

de·pos·i·to·ry (di poz′i tōr′ē, -tôr′ē), *n.*, *pl.* **-ries.** **1.** a place where anything is deposited or stored, as for safekeeping, future shipment, etc. **2.** a depositary; trustee. [(def. 1) < ML *dēpositōri(um);* (def. 2) DEPOSIT + -ORY[1] (n. use of adj. suffix)]

de·pot (dē′pō; *Mil. or Brit.* dep′ō), *n.* **1.** a railroad or bus station. **2.** *Mil.* a place to which supplies and materials are shipped and stored for distribution. **3.** a storehouse or warehouse. [< F *dépôt* < L *dēposit(um)* (neut.), n. use of *dēpositus;* see DEPOSIT] **—Syn. 1.** terminal. See **station.**

de·prave (di prāv′), *v.t.*, **-praved, -prav·ing.** **1.** to make bad or worse; vitiate; corrupt. **2.** *Obs.* to defame. [ME *deprave(n)* < L *dēprāv(āre)* (to) pervert, corrupt = *dē-* DE- + *prāv(us)* crooked + *-āre* inf. suffix] **—dep·ra·va·tion** (dep′rə vā′shən), *n.* **—de·prav′er,** *n.*

de·praved (di prāvd′), *adj.* corrupt, wicked, or perverted. **—de·praved·ly** (di prāvd′lē, -prā′vid-), *adv.* **—de·praved′ness,** *n.* **—Syn.** debased, degenerate; dissolute, profligate; licentious, lascivious, lewd. See **immoral.**

de·prav·i·ty (di prav′i tē), *n.*, *pl.* **-ties** for 2. **1.** the state of being depraved. **2.** a depraved act or practice.

dep·re·cate (dep′rə kāt′), *v.t.*, **-cat·ed, -cat·ing.** **1.** to express earnest disapproval of. **2.** to protest against (a scheme, purpose, etc.). **3.** to depreciate or belittle. **4.** *Archaic.* to pray for deliverance from. [< L *dēprecāt(us)* prayed against, warded off (ptp. of *dēprecārī*). See DE-, PRAY, -ATE[1]] **—dep′re·cat′ing·ly,** *adv.* **—dep′re·ca′tion,** *n.* **—dep′re·ca′tor,** *n.*

dep·re·ca·tive (dep′rə kā′tiv, -kə tiv), *adj.* serving to deprecate; deprecatory. [< LL *dēprecātīv(us)*] **—dep′re·ca′tive·ly,** *adv.*

dep·re·ca·to·ry (dep′rə kə tōr′ē, -tôr′ē), *adj.* **1.** of the nature of or expressing disapproval, protest, or depreciation. **2.** apologetic; making apology. [< LL *dēprecātōri(us)*] **—dep′re·ca·to′ri·ly,** *adv.* **—dep′re·ca·to′ri·ness,** *n.*

de·pre·ci·a·ble (di prē′shē ə bəl), *adj.* **1.** capable of depreciating or being depreciated in value. **2.** *U.S.* capable of being depreciated for tax purposes.

de·pre·ci·ate (di prē′shē āt′), *v.*, **-at·ed, -at·ing.** **—***v.t.* **1.** to reduce the purchasing value of (money). **2.** to lessen the value or price of. **3.** *U.S.* to claim depreciation on (a property) for tax purposes. **4.** to represent as of little value or merit; belittle. **—***v.i.* **5.** to decline in value. [< LL *dēpretiāt(us)* undervalued (ptp. of *dēpretiāre*, sp. var. of *dēpreciāre*). See DE-, PRICE, -ATE[1]] **—de·pre′ci·at′ing·ly,** *adv.* **—de·pre′ci·a′tor,** *n.* **—Syn. 4.** disparage, decry, minimize.

de·pre·ci·a·tion (di prē′shē ā′shən), *n.* **1.** a decrease in value due to wear and tear, decay, decline in price, etc. **2.** *U.S.* such a decrease as allowed in computing the value of property for tax purposes. **3.** a decrease in the purchasing or exchange value of money. **4.** a lowering in estimation; disparagement.

de·pre·ci·a·to·ry (di prē′shē ə tōr′ē, -tôr′ē), *adj.* tending to depreciate. Also, **de·pre·ci·a·tive** (di prē′shē ā′tiv).

dep·re·date (dep′ri dāt′), *v.*, **-dat·ed, -dat·ing.** **—***v.t.* **1.** to plunder or lay waste to; pillage; ravage. **—***v.i.* **2.** to plunder or pillage. [< LL *dēpraedāt(us)* plundered (ptp. of *depraedārī*). See DE-, PREY, -ATE[1]] **—dep′re·da′tor,** *n.* **—dep·re·da·to·ry** (dep′ri dā′tə rē, di pred′ə tōr′ē, -tôr′ē, dep′ri də-), *adj.*

dep·re·da·tion (dep′ri dā′shən), *n.* the act of preying upon or plundering; robbery; ravage. [ME *depredacion* < LL *dēpraedātiōn-* (s. of *dēpraedātiō*) a plundering]

de·press (di pres′), *v.t.* **1.** to lower in spirits; deject; dispirit; make sad or gloomy. **2.** to lower in force, vigor, activity, etc.; weaken. **3.** to lower in amount or value **4.** to put into a lower position; press down. [ME *depress(en)* < OF *depress(er)* < L *dēpress(us)* pressed down (ptp. of *dēprimere* = *dē-* DE- + *-primere,* comb. form of *premere* to press); see PRESSURE] —**de·press′i·ble,** *adj.* —**de·press′·ing·ly,** *adv.* —**Syn. 1.** dishearten, discourage, sadden. See **oppress. 3.** devalue, cheapen. —**Ant. 4.** raise, elevate.

de·pres·sant (di pres′ənt), *adj.* **1.** *Med.* having the quality of depressing or lowering the vital activities; sedative. **2.** causing a lowering in spirits; dejecting. —*n.* **3.** *Med.* a sedative. Cf. **stimulant.**

de·pressed (di prest′), *adj.* **1.** dejected; downcast; sad; gloomy. **2.** pressed down, or situated lower than the general surface. **3.** lowered in force, amount, etc. **4.** undergoing economic hardship, esp. poverty and unemployment. **5.** *Bot., Zool.* flattened down; greater in width than in height. —**Syn. 1.** morose, despondent, miserable; blue. See **sad.**

depressed′ ar′ea, a region where unemployment and a low standard of living prevail. Also called, *Brit.,* **distressed area.**

de·pres·sion (di presh′ən), *n.* **1.** the act of depressing. **2.** the state of being depressed. **3.** a depressed or sunken place or part. **4.** dejection; sadness; gloom. **5.** *Psychiatry.* emotional dejection greater and more prolonged than that warranted by any objective reason. **6.** dullness or inactivity, as of trade. **7.** a period during which business, employment, and stock-market values decline or remain at a low level of activity. **8. the Depression.** See **Great Depression. 9.** *Pathol.* a low state of vital powers or functional activity. **10.** *Astron.* the angular distance of a celestial body below the horizon; negative altitude. **11.** *Survey.* the angle between the line from an observer or instrument to an object below him or it and a horizontal line. **12.** *Meteorol.* an area of low atmospheric pressure. **13.** an area wholly or mostly surrounded by higher land, ordinarily having interior drainage and not conforming to the valley of a single stream. [ME < ML *dēpressiōn-* (s. of *dēpressiō*), LL: a pressing down] —**Syn. 4.** discouragement, despondency.

de·pres·sive (di pres′iv), *adj.* **1.** tending to depress. **2.** characterized by depression, esp. mental depression. —**de·pres′sive·ly,** *adv.* —**de·pres′sive·ness,** *n.*

de·pres·so·mo·tor (di pres′ō mō′tər), *adj. Physiol.* causing a retardation of motor activity: *depressomotor nerves.*

de·pres·sor (di pres′ər), *n.* **1.** a person or thing that depresses. **2.** *Surg.* an instrument for pressing down a protruding part. **3.** *Anat.* **a.** a muscle that draws down some part of the body. **b.** a nerve, the stimulation of which decreases the heartbeat and blood pressure. [< LL]

de·pres·su·rize (dē presh′ə rīz′), *v.t.,* **-rized, -riz·ing.** to remove air pressure from (a pressurized compartment of an aircraft or spacecraft). —**de·pres·su′ri·za′tion,** *n.*

dep·ri·va·tion (dep′rə vā′shən), *n.* **1.** the act of depriving. **2.** the fact of being deprived. **3.** dispossession; loss. **4.** removal from office. **5.** privation. Also, **de·priv·al** (di prī′vəl). [< ML *dēprīvātiōn-* (s. of *dēprīvātiō*) = *dēprīvāt(us)* deprived (ptp. of *dēprīvāre* to DEPRIVE) + *-iōn-* -ION]

de·prive (di prīv′), *v.t.,* **-prived, -priv·ing. 1.** to remove or withhold something from the enjoyment or possession of: *to deprive a man of life.* **2.** to remove from office. [ME *deprive(n)* < OF *depriv(er)* < ML *dēprīvāre.* See DE-, PRIVATE] —**de·priv′a·ble,** *adj.* —**de·priv′er,** *n.*

de pro·fun·dis (dā prō fo͝on′dis), *Latin.* from the depths (of sorrow, despair, etc.).

de·pro·gram (dē prō′gram), *v.t.,* **gramed, -gram·ing** or (*esp. Brit.*) **-grammed, -gram·ming.** to free (a convert) from the influence of a religious cult, political indoctrination, etc., as by intensive persuasion or reeducation. —**de·pro′gram·er, de·pro′gram·mer,** *n.*

dept., department.

depth (depth), *n.* **1.** a dimension taken through an object or body of material, usually downward or horizontally inward. **2.** the quality of being deep; deepness. **3.** complexity or obscurity, as of a subject. **4.** gravity; seriousness. **5.** emotional profundity. **6.** intensity, as of silence, color, etc. **7.** lowness of tonal pitch: *the depth of a voice.* **8.** Often, **depths.** a deep part or place. **9.** Sometimes, **depths.** the farthest, innermost, or extreme part or state: *the depth of space; the depths of the forest; the depths of despair.* **10.** Usually, **depths.** a low intellectual or moral condition: *How could he sink to such depths?* **11.** the part of greatest intensity, as of night or winter. **12. in depth,** extensively or thoroughly. —*adj.* **13.** done or conducted in depth: *a depth study; a depth interview.* [ME *depthe.* See DEEP, -TH[1]]

depth′ charge′, an explosive device for use against submarines and other underwater targets.

depth′ of field′, *Optics.* the range of distances along the axis of an optical instrument, usually a camera lens, through which an object will produce a relatively distinct image.

dep·u·rate (dep′yə rāt′), *v.t., v.i.,* **-rat·ed, -rat·ing.** to make or become free from impurities; purify; cleanse. [< ML *dēpūrāt(us)* purified (ptp. of *dēpūrāre*)] —**dep′u·ra′tion,** *n.* —**dep′u·ra′tor,** *n.*

dep·u·ra·tive (dep′yə rā′tiv), *adj.* **1.** purifying or cleansing. —*n.* **2.** a depurative agent or substance.

dep·u·ta·tion (dep′yə tā′shən), *n.* **1.** the act of appointing a person or persons to represent or act for another or others. **2.** the person or body of persons so appointed or authorized. [ME *deputacioun* < ML *dēputātiōn-* (s. of *dēputātiō*), LL: delegation = *dēputāt(us)* (ptp. of *dēputāre;* see DEPUTE, -ATE[1]) + *-iōn-* -ION]

de·pute (də pyo͞ot′), *v.t.,* **-put·ed, -put·ing. 1.** to appoint as one's substitute or agent. **2.** to assign (authority, a function, etc.) to a deputy. [ME *depute(n)* < OF *deput(er)* (to) assign < LL *dēputāre* to allot, L: to consider = *dē-* DE- + *putāre* to think; see PUTATIVE]

dep·u·tize (dep′yə tīz′), *v.,* **-tized, -tiz·ing.** —*v.t.* **1.** to appoint as deputy. —*v.i.* **2.** to act as a deputy; substitute.

dep·u·ty (dep′yə tē), *n., pl.* **-ties,** *adj.* —*n.* **1.** a person appointed or authorized to act as a substitute for another or others. **2.** a person appointed or elected as assistant to a public official. **3.** a person representing a constituency in certain legislative bodies. —*adj.* **4.** appointed, elected, or serving as an assistant, subordinate, or second-in-command: *a deputy sheriff.* [ME *depute* < OF, n. use of ptp. of *deputer*]

De Quin·cey (di kwin′sē), **Thomas,** 1785–1859, English essayist.

der., **1.** derivation. **2.** derivative. **3.** derive. **4.** derived.

de·rac·in·ate (di ras′ə nāt′), *v.t.,* **-nat·ed, -nat·ing. 1.** to pull up by the roots; uproot. **2.** to isolate or alienate (a person or persons) from a native or customary environment. [< F *déracin(er)* = *dé-* DIS-[1] + *racine* root < LL *rādīcīn(a)* (dim. of L *rādīc-,* s. of *rādīx*) + -ATE[1]] —**de·rac′i·na′tion,** *n.*

de·raign (di rān′), *v.t. Law.* to dispute or contest (a claim, suit, etc.). [ME *derein(er)* < OF *deraisn(ier)* (to) render an account = *de-* DE- + *raisnier* to discourse < VL **ratiōnāre;* see REASON, ARRAIGN] —**de·raign′ment,** *n.*

de·rail (dē rāl′), *v.t.* **1.** to cause (a train, streetcar, etc.) to run off the rails of a track. —*v.i.* **2.** (of a train, streetcar, etc.) to run off the rails of a track. [< F *déraill(er)* = *dé-* DIS-[1] + *rail* RAIL[1] (< E)] —**de·rail′ment,** *n.*

de·rail·leur (də rā′lər), *n.* **1.** a gear mechanism on a bicycle in which the chain can readily be switched among sprockets of different sizes to vary the ratio of wheel revolutions to pedal strokes. **2.** a bicycle with such a mechanism: *a ten-speed derailleur.* [< F]

De·rain (də RAN′), *n.* **An·dré** (äN drā′), 1880–1954, French painter.

de·range (di rānj′), *v.t.,* **-ranged, -rang·ing. 1.** to throw into disorder; disarrange. **2.** to disturb the condition, action, or function of. **3.** to make insane. [< F *dérang(er),* OF *desrengier.* See DIS-[1], RANGE]

de·ranged (di rānjd′), *adj.* **1.** disordered. **2.** insane.

de·range·ment (di rānj′mənt), *n.* **1.** the act of deranging. **2.** disarrangement; disorder. **3.** insanity or a mental disturbance. [< F *dérangement*]

Der·by (dûr′bē; *Brit.* där′bē), *n.* a city in and the county seat of Derbyshire, in central England. 215,200.

Der·by (dûr′bē; *Brit.* där′bē), *n., pl.* **-bies. 1.** a race for three-year-old horses run annually at Epsom Downs, near London, England **2.** a race for three-year-old horses run annually at Churchill Downs, Louisville, Kentucky. **3.** any of certain other important annual horse races, usually for three-year-old horses. **4.** (*l.c.*) a race or contest, usually one open to all who wish to enter. **5.** (*l.c.*) Also called, *esp. Brit.,* **bowler.** a man's stiff felt hat with rounded crown and narrow brim. [after Edward Stanley, 12th Earl of *Derby* (d. 1834), who instituted the English Derby race]

Der·by·shire (dûr′bē shēr′, -shər; *Brit.* där′bi shēr′, -shər), *n.* a county in central England. 877,400; 1006 sq. mi. *Co. seat:* Derby.

de·reg·u·late (dē reg′yə lāte′), *v.t., v.i.* **-lat·ed, -lat·ing.** to remove or reduce government regulation (of), esp. as an official policy: *the consequences of deregulating the airline industry.* —**de·reg′u·la′tion,** *n.*

der·e·lict (der′ə likt), *adj.* **1.** left or abandoned, as by the owner or guardian: *a derelict ship.* **2.** neglectful of duty; delinquent; negligent. —*n.* **3.** personal property abandoned by the owner. **4.** *Naut.* a vessel abandoned in open water. **5.** a person abandoned by society; vagrant; bum. **6.** a person guilty of neglect of duty. **7.** *Law.* land left dry by a change of the water line. [< L *dērelict(us)* forsaken (ptp. of *dērelinquere*) = *dē-* DE- + *relict(us)* ptp. of *relinquere* to leave, abandon; see RELINQUISH]

der·e·lic·tion (der′ə lik′shən), *n.* **1.** deliberate or conscious neglect; negligence: *dereliction of duty.* **2.** the act of abandoning something. **3.** the state of being abandoned. **4.** *Law.* a leaving dry of land by recession of the water line. [< L *dērelictiōn-* (s. of *dērelictiō*) an abandoning]

de·ride (di rīd′), *v.t.,* **-rid·ed, -rid·ing.** to scoff or jeer at; mock. [< L *dērīd(ēre)* (to) mock = *dē-* DE- + *rīdēre* to laugh] —**de·rid′er,** *n.* —**de·rid′ing·ly,** *adv.* —**Syn.** See **ridicule.**

de ri·gueur (də RĒ gœr′; *Eng.* də ri gûr′), *French.* strictly required, as by etiquette, usage, or fashion.

der·in·ger (der′in jər), *n.* derringer.

de·ri·sion (di rizh′ən), *n.* **1.** the act of deriding; ridicule; mockery. **2.** an object of ridicule. [ME *derisioun* < OF *derision* < LL *dērīsiōn-* (s. of *dērīsiō*) = L *dērīs(us)* mocked (ptp. of *dērīdēre;* see DERIDE) + *-iōn-* -ION]

de·ri·sive (di rī′siv), *adj.* characterized by or expressing derision; ridiculing; mocking. Also, **de·ri·so·ry** (di rī′sə rē, -zə-). —**de·ri′sive·ly,** *adv.* —**de·ri′sive·ness,** *n.*

deriv., **1.** derivation. **2.** derivative. **3.** derive. **4.** derived.

der·i·va·tion (der′ə vā′shən), *n.* **1.** the act or fact of deriving or of being derived. **2.** the process of deriving. **3.** the source from which something is derived; origin. **4.** something that is or has been derived; derivative. **5.** *Math.* **a.** development of a theorem. **b.** differentiation. **6.** *Gram.* the process or device of adding affixes to or changing the shape of a base, thereby assigning the result to a form class that may undergo further inflection or participate in different syntactic constructions. [ME < L *dērīvātiōn-* (s. of *dērīvātiō*) a turning away = *dērīvāt(us)* (ptp. of *dērīvāre;* see DERIVE, -ATE[1]) + *-iōn-* -ION] —**der′i·va′tion·al,** *adj.*

de·riv·a·tive (di riv′ə tiv), *adj.* **1.** derived. **2.** not original; secondary. —*n.* **3.** something derived or derivative. **4.** *Gram.* a form that has undergone derivation from another, as *atomic* from *atom.* **5.** *Chem.* a substance or compound obtained from, or regarded as derived from, another substance or compound. **6.** Also called **derived′ func′tion;** *esp. Brit.,* **differential coefficient.** *Math.* the limit of the ratio of the increment of a function to the increment of a variable in it as the latter tends to 0; the instantaneous change of one quantity with respect to another, as velocity, which is the instantaneous change of distance with respect to time. **7.** *Psychoanal.* behavior that allows expression of an id impulse with a minimum of anxiety. [ME < LL *dērīvātīv(us)*] —**de·riv′a·tive·ly,** *adv.*

de·rive (di rīv′), *v.,* **-rived, -riv·ing.** —*v.t.* **1.** to receive or obtain from a source or origin (usually fol. by *from*). **2.** to trace from a source or origin. **3.** to reach or obtain by reasoning; deduce; infer. **4.** *Chem.* to produce or obtain (a substance) from another. —*v.i.* **5.** to originate (often fol. by *from*). [ME *dirive(n), derive(n)* (to) flow, draw from, spring < OF *derive(r)* < L *dērīvāre* to lead off = *dē-* DE- + *rīv(us)* a stream + *-āre* inf. suffix] —**de·riv′a·ble,** *adj.*

derm-, var. of **dermato-:** *dermoid.*

-derm, var. of **dermato-** as final element of compound words: *endoderm.*
der·ma[1] (dûr′mə), *n. Anat., Zool.* **1.** the corium or true skin. **2.** skin; integument. [< NL < Gk: skin = *dér(ein)* (to) skin + *-ma* n. suffix] **—der′mal,** *adj.*
der·ma[2] (dûr′mə), *n.* **1.** beef or fowl intestine used as a casing in preparing certain savory dishes, esp. kishke. **2.** kishke. [< Yiddish *derme,* pl. of *darm* intestine < MHG < OHG; akin to OE *thearm* gut]
derm·a·bra·sion (dûr′mə brā′zhən), *n. Surg.* the removal of acne scars, dermal nevi, or the like, by abrading with wire brushes, sandpaper, or other abrasives. Also called **skin planing.**
dermat-, var. of **dermato-** before a vowel: *dermatitis.*
der·ma·ti·tis (dûr′mə tī′tis), *n. Pathol.* inflammation of the skin.
dermato-, a learned borrowing from Greek meaning "skin," used in the formation of compound words: *dermatology.* Also, **derm-, -derm, dermat-, dermo-.** [< Gk, comb. form of *dermat-,* (s. of *dérma*)]
der·mat·o·gen (dər mat′ə jən, dûr′mə tə jən), *n. Bot.* a thin layer of meristem in embryos and growing ends of stems and roots, that gives rise to the epidermis.
der·ma·toid (dûr′mə toid′), *adj.* resembling skin; skinlike.
der·ma·tol·o·gist (dûr′mə tol′ə jist), *n.* a specialist in dermatology, esp. a doctor who specializes in the treatment of diseases of the skin.
der·ma·tol·o·gy (dûr′mə tol′ə jē), *n.* the science dealing with the skin and its diseases. **—der·ma·to·log·i·cal** (dûr′mə tᵊloj′i kəl), *adj.*
der·ma·tome (dûr′mə tōm′), *n. Embryol.* the part of a mesodermal somite contributing to the development of the dermis. [DERMA[1] + -TOME] **—der·ma·tom·ic** (dûr′mə tom′ik), *adj.*
der·ma·to·phyte (dûr′mə tə fīt′, dər mat′ə-), *n. Pathol.* any fungus parasitic on the skin causing a skin disease, as ringworm, in man or animals. **—der·mat·o·phyt·ic** (dûr′mə tə fit′ik, dər mat′ə fit′-), *adj.*
der·ma·to·plas·ty (dûr′mə tə plas′tē, dər mat′ə-), *n. Surg.* See **skin grafting. —der′ma·to·plas′tic,** *adj.*
der·ma·to·sis (dûr′mə tō′sis), *n., pl.* **-to·ses** (-tō′sēz). *Pathol.* any disease of the skin. [< NL]
der·mis (dûr′mis), *n. Anat., Zool.* derma[1]. [< NL; abstracted from EPIDERMIS] **—der′mic,** *adj.*
dermo-, var. of **dermato-.**
der·ni·er (dεʀ nyā′; *Eng.* dûr′nē ər, dern yā′), *adj. French.* last; final; ultimate.
der·nier cri (dεʀ nyā kʀē′), *French.* **1.** the latest word. **2.** the latest fashion. [lit., last cry]
der·o·gate (*v.* der′ə gāt′; *adj.* der′ə git, -gāt′), *v.,* **-gat·ed, -gat·ing,** *adj.* **—*v.i.*** **1.** to detract, as from authority, estimation, etc. (usually fol. by *from*). **2.** to stray in character or conduct; degenerate (usually fol. by *from*). **—*v.t.*** **3.** *Archaic.* to take away (a part) so as to impair the whole. **—*adj.*** **4.** *Archaic.* debased. [ME < L *dērogāt(us)* repealed, restricted (ptp. of *dērogāre*) = *dē-* DE- + *rog(āre)* (to) ask + *-ātus* -ATE[1]] **—der′o·gate′ly,** *adv.* **—der′o·ga′tion,** *n.*
de·rog·a·tive (di rog′ə tiv), *adj.* lessening; belittling; derogatory. [< MF *derogatif* < L *dērogāt(us)* + MF *-if* -IVE] **—de·rog′a·tive·ly,** *adv.*
de·rog·a·to·ry (di rog′ə tôr′ē, -tōr′ē), *adj.* tending to derogate or detract, as from authority or estimation; disparaging: *a derogatory remark.* [< LL *dērogātōri(us)* of a derogation] **—de·rog·a·to·ri·ly** (di rog′ə tôr′ə lē, -tōr′-, -rog′ə tôr′-, -tōr′-), *adv.* **—de·rog′a·to′ri·ness,** *n.*
der·rick (der′ik), *n.* **1.** *Mach.* a jib-equipped crane having a boom hinged near the base of the mast so as to rotate about the mast, for moving a load toward or away from the mast by raising or lowering the boom. **2.** the towerlike framework over an oil well or the like. **3.** *Naut.* a boom for lifting cargo or the like, pivoted at its inner end to a mast or king post, and raised and supported at its outer end by topping lifts. [after *Derrick,* 17th-century hangman at Tyburn, London]
der·ri·ère (der′ē âr′; *Fr.* de ʀyεʀ′), *n.* the buttocks; rump; behind. Also, **der′ri·ere′.** [< F; OF *deriere* < L *de retrō* from the back, backward; see ARREAR]
der·ring-do (der′ing dōō′), *n.* daring deeds; heroic daring. [ME *durringdo,* lit., daring to do, erroneously taken as n. phrase. See DARE, DO[1]]
der·rin·ger (der′in jər), *n.* a short-barreled pocket pistol. Also, **deringer.** [named after Henry *Deringer,* mid-19th-century American gunsmith who invented it]

Derringer

der·ris (der′is), *n.* any East Indian, leguminous plant of the genus *Derris,* esp. *D. elliptica,* the roots of which contain rotenone and are used as an insecticide. [< NL < Gk: a covering < *déros* skin, hide; akin to *dérma* (see DERMATO-)]
der·ry (der′ē), *n., pl.* **-ries.** a meaningless refrain or chorus in old songs. Also called **der·ry-down** (der′ē doun′).
Der·ry (der′ē), *n.* Londonderry.
der·vish (dûr′vish), *n.* a member of any of various Muslim ascetic orders, some of which carry on ecstatic observances, such as dancing and whirling or chanting or shouting. [< Turk: beggar < Pers *darvīsh* religious mendicant] **—der′vish·like′,** *adj.*
Der·went (dûr′wənt), *n.* **1.** a river flowing N and W into Solway Firth, in N England. **2.** a river flowing S and SE past Derby to the Trent, in central England. **3.** a river flowing into the Ouse, in Yorkshire in NE England. **4.** a river flowing NE to the Tyne, in N England. **5.** a river in S Australia, in S Tasmania, flowing SE to the Tasman Sea. 107 mi. long.
des (de), *prep.* (used in French names as a contraction of *de* and the article *les*): *François des Adrets.*
de·sal·i·nate (dē sal′ə nāt′), *v.t.,* **-nat·ed, -nat·ing.** desalt. **—de·sal′i·na′tion,** *n.*
de·sa·lin·ize (dē sā′lə nīz′, -lī-, -sal′ə-), *v.t.,* **-ized, -iz·ing.** desalt. **—de·sa′lin·i·za′tion,** *n.*
de·salt (dē sôlt′), *v.t.* to remove the salt from (esp. sea water), usually to make it drinkable. **—de·salt′er,** *n.*
De·sargues (dā zaʀg′, *Eng.* dā zärg′), *n.* **Gé·rard** (zhā ʀaʀ′), 1593–1662, French mathematician.
desc., descendant.
des·cant (*n., adj.* des′kant; *v.* des kant′, dis-), *n.* **1.** *Music.* **a.** a melody or counterpoint accompanying a simple theme and usually written above it. **b.** (in part music) the soprano. **c.** a song or melody. **2.** a variation upon anything; comment on a subject. **—*adj.*** *Music Chiefly Brit.* **3.** soprano: *a descant recorder.* **4.** treble: *a descant viol.* **—*v.i.*** **5.** *Music.* to sing. **6.** to comment or discourse at great length. Also, **discant.** [ME *discant, descaunt* < ONF, ML *discanth(us).* See DIS-[1], CHANT] **—des·cant′er,** *n.*
Des·cartes (dā kärt′; *Fr.* de kaʀt′), *n.* **Re·né** (rə nā′; *Fr.* ʀə nā′), 1596–1650, French philosopher and mathematician.
de·scend (di send′), *v.i.* **1.** to move or pass from a higher to a lower place; climb or come down. **2.** to pass from higher to lower in any scale or series. **3.** to go from generals to particulars, as in a discussion. **4.** to slope, tend, or lead downward. **5.** to be inherited or transmitted, as through succeeding generations of a family: *The title descends through eldest sons.* **6.** to have a specific person or family among one's ancestors (usually fol. by *from*): *He is descended from Cromwell.* **7.** to be derived from something past; come down from: *This festival descends from a druidic rite.* **8.** to approach or pounce upon, esp. in a greedy or hasty manner (fol. by *on* or *upon*): *Heirs descended upon the rich man's estate.* **9.** to settle, as a cloud or vapor. **10.** to attack, esp. with violence and suddenness (usually fol. by *on* or *upon*): *to descend upon enemy soldiers.* **11.** to sink or come down from a certain intellectual, moral, or social standard. **12.** *Astron.* to move toward the horizon, as the sun or a star. **—*v.t.*** **13.** to move downward upon or along; go or climb down (stairs, a hill, etc.). **14.** to extend or lead down along: *The path descends the hill.* [ME *descend(en)* < OF *descend(re)* < L *dēscendere* = *dē-* DE- + *scend-* climb (sp. var. of *scandere;* see SCAN) + *-ere* inf. suffix]
de·scend·ant (di sen′dənt), *n.* **1.** a person who is descended from a specific ancestor; an offspring. **2.** something deriving from an earlier form. **—*adj.*** **3.** descending; descendent. [ME *descendaunt* (adj.) < OF *descendant,* prp. of *descendre*]
de·scend·ent (di sen′dənt), *adj.* **1.** descending; going or coming down. **2.** deriving or descending from an ancestor. [< L *dēscendent-* (s. of *dēscendēns*), prp. of *dēscendere*]
de·scend·er (di sen′dər), *n.* **1.** a person or thing that descends. **2.** *Print.* **a.** (in any of most lower-case letters) the part that goes below the body. **b.** a letter having such a part, as *p, q, j,* or *y.*
de·scend·i·ble (di sen′də bəl), *adj.* **1.** capable of being transmitted by inheritance. **2.** permitting descent: *a descendible hill.* Also, **de·scend′a·ble.** [ME *descendable* < OF]
de·scen·sion (di sen′shən), *n.* **1.** *Astrol.* the part of the zodiac in which the influence of a planet is weakest. **2.** *Archaic.* descent. [ME *descensioun* < OF *descension,* L *dēscensiōn-* (s. of *dēscensiō*) = *dēscens(us)* (ptp. of *dēscendere* to DESCEND) + *-iōn-* -ION]
de·scent (di sent′), *n.* **1.** the act or process of descending. **2.** a downward inclination or slope. **3.** a passage or stairway leading down. **4.** lineage. **5.** any decline in degree or state. **6.** a sudden raid. **7.** *Law.* transmission of real property by intestate succession. [ME < OF *descente* < *descendre* to DESCEND] **—Syn. 1.** falling, sinking. **2.** decline, grade. **4.** ancestry, parentage. **6.** assault, foray. **—Ant. 1, 2.** ascent, rise.
Des·chutes (dā shōōt′), *n.* a river flowing N from the Cascade Range in central Oregon to the Columbia River. 250 mi. long.
de·scribe (di skrīb′), *v.t.,* **-scribed, -scrib·ing.** **1.** to tell or depict in written or spoken words; give an account of. **2.** to pronounce, as by a designating term; label. **3.** to indicate; be a sign of; denote. **4.** to represent or delineate by a picture or figure; draw or trace the outline of: *to describe an arc.* [ME *describe(n)* < L *dēscrībe(re).* See DE-, SCRIBE[1]] **—de·scrib′a·ble,** *adj.* **—de·scrib′er,** *n.* **—Syn. 1.** portray, represent; recount, tell, relate, narrate.
de·scrip·tion (di skrip′shən), *n.* **1.** a statement, account, or picture in words that describes; descriptive representation. **2.** the act or method of describing. **3.** sort; kind; variety. **4.** *Geom.* the act or process of describing a figure. [ME *descripcioun* < L *dēscriptiōn-* (s. of *dēscriptiō*) = *dēscript(us)* (ptp. of *dēscrībere* to DESCRIBE) + *-iōn-* -ION] **—Syn. 3.** species; nature, character, condition; ilk.
de·scrip·tive (di skrip′tiv), *adj.* **1.** having the quality of describing; characterized by description. **2.** *Gram.* **a.** (of an adjective or other modifier) expressing a quality of the word it modifies, as *fresh* in *fresh milk.* Cf. **limiting. b.** (of a clause) nonrestrictive. Cf. **restrictive** (def. 4). **3.** noting, concerned with, or based upon fact or experience. **4.** characterized by or based upon the classification and description of material in a given field: *descriptive botany.* [< LL *dēscriptīv(us)*] **—de·scrip′tive·ly,** *adv.* **—de·scrip′tive·ness,** *n.*
descrip′tive clause′, a relative clause that describes or supplements but does not identify the antecedent, and that is usually set off by commas in English; a nonrestrictive clause. In *This year, which has been dry, is bad for crops* the clause *which has been dry* is a descriptive clause. Cf. **restrictive clause.**
descrip′tive geom′etry, **1.** the theory of making projections of any accurately defined figure such that from them can be deduced not only its projective, but also its metrical, properties. **2.** geometry in general, treated by means of projections.
descrip′tive linguis′tics, the study of the grammar, classification, and arrangement of the features of language or of a language, without reference to their history or origin.

de·scry (di skrī′), *v.t.*, **-scried, -scry·ing.** **1.** to make out (something unclear or distant) by looking carefully; discern. **2.** to discover; detect. [ME *descrie(r)* < OF *decri(er)* (to) proclaim, DECRY. See DIS-[1], CRY] —**de·scri′er,** *n.*

des·e·crate (des′ə krāt′), *v.t.*, **-crat·ed, -crat·ing.** **1.** to divert from a sacred to a profane use or purpose. **2.** to treat with sacrilege; profane. [DE- + (CON)SECRATE] —**des′e·crat′er, des′e·cra′tor,** *n.* —**des′e·cra′tion,** *n.*

de·seg·re·gate (dē seg′rə gāt′), *v.*, **-gat·ed, -gat·ing.** —*v.t.* **1.** to eliminate racial segregation in: *to desegregate all schools.* —*v.i.* **2.** to eliminate racial segregation.

de·seg·re·ga·tion (dē′seg rə gā′shən, dē seg′-), *n.* the elimination of laws, customs, or practices that restrict different races, groups, etc., to specific or separate schools and other public facilities, neighborhoods, etc.

de·sen·si·tize (dē sen′si tīz′), *v.t.*, **-tized, -tiz·ing.** **1.** to lessen the sensitiveness of. **2.** to make indifferent in feeling, unaware, or the like. **3.** *Physiol.* to eliminate the natural or acquired reactivity or sensitivity of (an animal, organ, tissue, etc.) to an external stimulus, as an allergen. **4.** *Photog.* to make less sensitive or wholly insensitive to light, as the emulsion on a film. —**de·sen′si·ti·za′tion,** *n.* —**de·sen′si·tiz′er,** *n.*

des·ert[1] (dez′ərt), *n.* **1.** a region so arid that it supports only sparse vegetation or none at all. **2.** any area in which few forms of life can exist because of lack of water, permanent frost, or absence of soil. **3.** any place lacking in something, usually as specified: *The town was a cultural desert.* —*adj.* **4.** of, pertaining to, or like a desert; desolate; barren. **5.** occurring, living, or flourishing in the desert: *a desert tribe.* [ME < OF < eccl. L *dēsert(um)* (neut.), n. use of ptp. of *dēserere* to abandon, forsake = *dē-* DE- + *serere* to join together (in a line); cf. SERIES]
—**Syn. 1.** DESERT, WASTE, WILDERNESS refer to areas that are uninhabited. DESERT emphasizes lack of water; it refers to a dry, barren, treeless region, usually sandy: *an oasis in a desert; the Sahara Desert.* WASTE emphasizes lack of inhabitants and of cultivation; it is used of wild, barren land, but figuratively the word is also applied to turbulent seas: *a desolate waste; a terrifying waste of water.* WILDERNESS emphasizes the difficulty of finding one's way because of barrenness or of luxuriant vegetation; it is also applied to the ocean, esp. in stormy weather: *a trackless wilderness.*

de·sert[2] (di zûrt′), *v.t.* **1.** to leave (a person, place, etc.) without intending to return, esp. in violation of a duty, promise, or the like; abandon; forsake: *He deserted his wife.* **2.** (of military personnel) to run away from (service, duty, etc.) with the intention of never returning. **3.** to fail (someone) at a time of need: *All his friends had deserted him.* —*v.i.* **4.** to forsake or leave one's duty, obligations, or the like (sometimes fol. by *from, to,* etc.). [< F *déserte(r)* < LL *dēsertāre,* freq. of L *dēserere;* see DESERT[1]] —**de·sert′er,** *n.*
—**Syn. 1.** DESERT, ABANDON, FORSAKE mean to leave behind persons, places, or things. DESERT implies intentionally violating an oath, formal obligation, or duty: *to desert campaign pledges.* ABANDON suggests giving up wholly and finally, whether of necessity, unwillingly, or through shirking responsibilities: *to abandon a hopeless task.* FORSAKE has emotional connotations, since it implies violating obligations of affection or association: *to forsake a noble cause.*

de·sert[3] (di zûrt′), *n.* **1.** Often, **deserts.** reward or punishment that is deserved: *to get one's just deserts.* **2.** the fact of deserving reward or punishment. **3.** merit or virtue. [ME < OF *deserte,* n. use of fem. ptp. of *deservir* to DESERVE]

de·sert·ed (di zûr′tid), *adj.* **1.** abandoned; forsaken. **2.** untenanted; without inhabitants. **3.** unfrequented; lonely.

de·ser·tion (di zûr′shən), *n.* **1.** the act of deserting. **2.** the state of being deserted. **3.** *Law.* willful abandonment, esp. of one's spouse without consent, in violation of legal or moral obligations. **4.** *Mil.* leaving or running away from service or duty without the intention of returning. Cf. **A.W.O.L.** [< LL *dēsertiōn-* (s. of *dēsertiō*)]

de·serve (di zûrv′), *v.*, **-served, -serv·ing.** —*v.t.* **1.** to merit or have a claim to (reward, assistance, punishment, etc.) because of one's acts, qualities, or situation. —*v.i.* **2.** to be worthy of, qualified for, or have a claim to reward, punishment, recompense, etc. [ME *deserve(n)* < OF *deserv(ir),* L *dēservīre* to serve zealously] —**de·serv′er,** *n.*

de·served (di zûrvd′), *adj.* justly earned; merited. —**de·serv·ed·ness** (di zûr′vid nis), *n.*

de·serv·ed·ly (di zûr′vid lē), *adv.* justly; rightly.

de·serv·ing (di zûr′ving), *adj.* worthy of reward, praise, or help. —**de·serv′ing·ly,** *adv.* —**de·serv′ing·ness,** *n.*

de·sex (dē seks′), *v.t.* **1.** to castrate or spay. **2.** to deprive of sex, sex appeal, or sexual interest.

de·sex·u·al·ize (dē sek′shōō ə līz′), *v.t.*, **-ized, -iz·ing.** desex. —**de·sex′u·al·i·za′tion,** *n.*

des·ha·bille (dez′ə bēl′, -bē′), *n.* dishabille.

des·ic·cant (des′ə kənt), *adj.* **1.** desiccating, as a medicine. —*n.* **2.** a drying substance or agent. [< L *dēsiccant-* (s. of *dēsiccāns*), prp. of *dēsiccāre* to dry up]

des·ic·cate (des′ə kāt′), *v.*, **-cat·ed, -cat·ing.** —*v.t.* **1.** to dry thoroughly; dry up. **2.** to preserve (food) by removing moisture; dehydrate. —*v.i.* **3.** to become thoroughly dried or dried up. [< L *dēsiccāt(us)* dried up, ptp. of *dēsiccāre* = *dē-* DE- + *siccāre* < *sicc(us)* dry; see -ATE[1]] —**des′ic·ca′tion,** *n.* —**des′ic·ca′tive,** *adj.*

des·ic·cat·ed (des′ə kā′tid), *adj.* dehydrated.

des·ic·ca·tor (des′ə kā′tər), *n.* **1.** a person or thing that desiccates. **2.** an apparatus for drying fruit, milk, etc. **3.** *Chem.* an apparatus for absorbing moisture in a substance, esp. an airtight, usually glass container containing calcium chloride or some other drying agent.

de·sid·er·a·ta (di sid′ə rā′tə), *n.* pl. of **desideratum.**

de·sid·er·ate (di sid′ə rāt′), *v.t.*, **-at·ed, -at·ing.** to wish or long for; want; desire. [< L *dēsīderāt(us)* longed for (ptp. of *dēsīderāre*) = *dē-* DE- + *sīder-* (s. of *sīdus*) star + *-ātus* -ATE[1]] —**de·sid′er·a′tion,** *n.*

de·sid·er·a·tive (di sid′ə rā′tiv, -ər ə tiv), *adj.* **1.** having or expressing desire. **2.** *Gram.* (of a verb derived from another verb) expressing desire to perform the action denoted by the underlying verb. —*n.* **3.** *Gram.* a desiderative verb.

de·sid·er·a·tum (di sid′ə rā′təm), *n.*, *pl.* **-ta** (-tə). something wanted or needed. [< L, n. use of neut. ptp. of *dēsīderāre;* see DESIDERATE]

de·sign (di zīn′), *v.t.* **1.** to prepare the preliminary sketch or the plans for (a work to be executed), esp. to plan the form and structure of: *to design a new bridge.* **2.** to plan and fashion artistically or skillfully. **3.** to intend for a definite purpose: *a scholarship designed for medical students.* **4.** to form or conceive in the mind; contrive; plan. **5.** to assign in thought or intention; purpose. **6.** *Archaic.* to mark out, as by a sign; indicate. —*v.i.* **7.** to make drawings, preliminary sketches, or plans. **8.** to plan and fashion the form and structure of an object, work of art, decorative scheme, etc. —*n.* **9.** an outline, sketch, or plan, as of the form and structure of a work of art. **10.** the organization or structure of formal elements in a work of art; composition. **11.** the pattern or motif of an artistic work. **12.** the art of designing. **13.** a plan or project. **14.** a plot or intrigue. **15.** intention; purpose; end. [ME *design(en)* < L *dēsign(āre)* (to) mark out] —**Syn. 4.** devise, project. **13.** See **plan.**

des·ig·nate (*v.* dez′ig nāt′; *adj.* dez′ig nit, -nāt′), *v.*, **-nat·ed, -nat·ing,** *adj.* —*v.t.* **1.** to mark or point out; specify. **2.** to denote; indicate. **3.** to name; entitle; style. **4.** to nominate or select for a duty, office, purpose, etc. —*adj.* **5.** named or selected for an office, position, etc., but not yet installed (often used in combination following the noun it modifies): *ambassador-designate.* [ME < L *dēsignāt(us),* ptp. of *dēsignāre*] —**des′ig·na′tive, des·ig·na·to·ry** (dez′ig nə tôr′ē, -tōr′ē, dez′ig nā′tə rē), *adj.* —**des′ig·na′tor,** *n.*

des′ignated hit′ter, *Baseball.* a hitter selected prior to the start of the game to bat for the starting pitcher and all subsequent pitchers without otherwise affecting the status of the pitchers in the game. *Abbr.:* dh

des·ig·na·tion (dez′ig nā′shən), *n.* **1.** the act of designating. **2.** the fact of being designated. **3.** a distinctive name or title. **4.** a nomination, appointment, or election. [ME *designacioun* < L *dēsignātiōn-* (s. of *dēsignātiō*) a marking out]

de·signed (di zīnd′), *adj.* made or done by design; intended; planned. —**de·sign·ed·ly** (di zī′nid lē), *adv.*

des·ig·nee (dez′ig nē′), *n.* a person who is designated. [DESIGN(ATE) + -EE]

de·sign·er (di zī′nər), *n.* **1.** a person who devises or executes designs for works of art, dresses, machines, or stage sets. **2.** a schemer, intriguer, or plotter.

de·sign·ing (di zī′ning), *adj.* **1.** scheming; intriguing; artful; crafty. **2.** showing or using forethought. —*n.* **3.** the act or art of making designs. —**de·sign′ing·ly,** *adv.*

des·i·nence (des′ə nəns), *n.* **1.** a termination or ending, as the final line of a verse. **2.** *Gram.* a termination, ending, or suffix of a word. [< F < ML *dēsinentia* = L *dēsinent-* (s. of *dēsinēns*), prp. of *dēsinere* to put down, leave (*dē-* DE- + *sinere* to leave) + *-ia;* see -ENCE] —**des′i·nent, des·i·nen·tial** (des′ə nen′shəl), *adj.*

de·sir·a·ble (di zīər′ə bəl), *adj.* **1.** worth desiring; pleasing, excellent, or fine. **2.** arousing desire or longing: *a desirable woman.* **3.** advisable; recommendable: *a desirable law.* —*n.* **4.** a person or thing that is desirable. [ME *desirable* < OF] —**de·sir′a·bil′i·ty,** *n.* —**de·sir′a·bly,** *adv.*

de·sire (di zīər′), *v.*, **-sired, -sir·ing,** *n.* —*v.t.* **1.** to wish or long for; crave; want. **2.** to express a wish to obtain; ask for; request. —*n.* **3.** a longing or craving: *a desire for fame.* **4.** an expressed wish; request. **5.** something desired. **6.** sexual appetite or a sexual urge. [ME *desire(n)* < OF *desir(er)* < L *dēsīderāre;* see DESIDERATE] —**de·sir′er,** *n.*
—**Syn. 1.** covet, fancy. See **wish. 2.** solicit. **3.** aspiration, hunger, appetite, thirst. DESIRE, CRAVING, LONGING, YEARNING suggest feelings that impel a person to the attainment or possession of something. DESIRE is a strong feeling, worthy or unworthy, that impels to the attainment or possession of something: *a desire for success.* CRAVING implies a deep and imperative wish for something, based on a sense of need and hunger (literally or figuratively). A LONGING is an intense wish, generally repeated or enduring, for something that is at the moment beyond reach but may be attainable at some future time: *a longing to visit Europe.* YEARNING suggests persistent, uneasy, and sometimes wistful or tender longing. —**Ant. 1.** reject, loathe.

de·sir·ous (di zīər′əs), *adj.* having or characterized by desire; desiring. [ME < OF *desireus*] —**de·sir′ous·ly,** *adv.* —**de·sir′ous·ness,** *n.*

de·sist (di zist′, -sist′), *v.i.* to cease, as from some action or proceeding; stop. [ME < OF *desist(er)* < L *dēsistere* to leave off = *dē-* DE- + *sistere* to stand, place, redupl. form of *stare* to stand] —**de·sist′ance, de·sist′ence,** *n.*

desk (desk), *n.* **1.** an article of furniture having a broad, usually level, writing surface, as well as drawers or compartments for papers, writing materials, etc. **2.** a frame for supporting a book from which the service is read in a church. **3.** a pulpit. **4.** the section of a large organization, as a governmental bureau, newspaper, etc., having responsibility for particular operations: *news desk.* **5.** a stand used to support sheet music; music stand. —*adj.* **6.** of or pertaining to a writing desk: *a desk drawer.* **7.** made for use on a desk: *a desk dictionary.* **8.** done at or based on a desk: *a desk job.* [ME *deske* < ML *desc(a)* table < L *disc(us)* desk, dish]

desk-size (desk′sīz′), *adj.* of a size suitable for use at a desk: *a desk-size dictionary.*

desk′top pub′lishing (desk′top′), the writing, assembling, and design of publications, as business reports, newsletters, and trade journals, in a business or editorial office by the use of computers, esp. microcomputers.

D. ès L., Doctor of Letters. [< F *Docteur ès Lettres*]

des·man (des′mən), *n.*, *pl.* **-mans.** either of two aquatic, insectivorous mammals, *Myogale moschata,* of southeastern Russia, or *M. pyrenaica,* of the Pyrenees, related to shrews. [< Sw, short for *desman-råtta* muskrat]

des·mid (des′mid), *n.* any of the microscopic freshwater algae belonging to the family *Desmidiaceae.* [< NL *Desmid(ium)* name of the genus < Gk *desm(ós)* a band, chain + NL *-id-* dim. suffix] —**des·mid′i·an,** *adj.*

des·moid (des′moid), *adj.* *Anat., Zool.* **1.** resembling a fascia or fibrous sheet. **2.** resembling a ligament. [< Gk *desm(ós)* (see DESMID) + -OID]

Des Moines (də moin′, moinz′), **1.** a city in and the capital of Iowa, in the central part, on the Des Moines River. 201,404 (1970). **2.** a river flowing SE from SW

Minnesota through Iowa to the Mississippi River. ab. 530 mi. long.

Des·mou·lins (de mo͞o laN′), *n.* **(Lu·cie Sim·plice) Ca·mille (Be·noit)** (lʏ sē′ saN plēs′ kA mē′yə bə nwA′), 1760–94, journalist, pamphleteer, and leader in the French Revolution.

des·o·late (*adj.* des′ə lit; *v.* des′ə lāt′), *adj., v.,* **-lat·ed, -lat·ing.** —*adj.* **1.** barren or laid waste; devastated. **2.** destitute of inhabitants; uninhabited. **3.** isolated, as a place; lonely. **4.** feeling abandoned, as by friends. **5.** dreary; dismal: *desolate prospects.* —*v.t.* **6.** to lay waste; devastate. **7.** to depopulate. **8.** to make disconsolate. **9.** to forsake or abandon. [ME < L *dēsōlāt(us)* forsaken, ptp. of *dēsōlāre* = *dē-* DE- + *sōlāre* to make lonely < *sōl(us)* SOLE[1]; see -ATE[1]] —**des′o·late·ly,** *adv.* —**des′o·lat′er, des′o·la′tor,** *n.*

—**Syn. 1.** ravaged. **2.** desert. **4.** lonesome, lost; miserable, wretched, woebegone, woeful, inconsolable, cheerless, hopeless. DESOLATE, DISCONSOLATE, FORLORN suggest a person who is in a sad and wretched condition. The DESOLATE person or place gives a feeling or impression of isloation or of being deprived of human consolation, relationships, or presence: *desolate and despairing.* The DISCONSOLATE person is aware of the efforts of others to console and comfort him, but is unable to be relieved or cheered by them: *She remained disconsolate even in the midst of friends.* The FORLORN person has the feeling or gives the impression of being lost or deserted or forsaken, as by friends: *wretched and forlorn in a strange city.* **6.** ravage, ruin. **8.** sadden, depress. **9.** desert. —**Ant. 4.** delighted, happy.

des·o·la·tion (des′ə lā′shən), *n.* **1.** the act or an instance of desolating. **2.** the state of being desolated. **3.** devastation; ruin. **4.** depopulation. **5.** dreariness; barrenness. **6.** loneliness. **7.** sorrow. **8.** a desolate place. [ME < LL *dēsōlātiōn-* (s. of *dēsōlātiō*) a desolating]

De So·to (də sō′tō; *Sp.* de sô′tô), **Her·nan·do** (hər nan′dō; *Sp.* eʀ nän′dô) or **Fer·nan·do** (fər nan′dō; *Sp.* feʀ nän′dô), c1500–42, Spanish soldier and explorer in America.

des·ox′y·ri′bo·nu·cle′ic ac′id (des ok′si rī′bō no͞o klē′ik, -nyo͞o-, -rī′-), *Biochem.* See **DNA.**

des·ox·y·ri·bose (des ok′si rī′bōs), *n.* *Biochem.* deoxyribose.

de·spair (di spâr′), *n.* **1.** loss of hope; hopelessness. **2.** something causing this. —*v.i.* **3.** to lose, give up, or be without hope (often fol. by *of*): *to despair of humanity.* —*v.t.* **4.** *Obs.* to give up hope of. [ME *despeir* (n.), *despeir(en)* (v.) < AF *despeir,* OF *despoir* (n.), *despeir-,* tonic s. of *desperer* < L *dēspērāre* to be without hope = *dē-* DE- + *spērāre* to hope, akin to *spes* hope]

—**Syn. 1.** gloom, disheartenment. DESPAIR, DESPERATION, DESPONDENCY, DISCOURAGEMENT, HOPELESSNESS refer to a state of mind caused by circumstances which seem too much to cope with. DESPAIR suggests total loss or abandonment of hope, which may be passive or may drive a person to furious efforts, even if at random: *in the depths of despair; courage born of despair.* DESPERATION is usually an active state, the abandonment of hope impelling to a furious struggle against adverse circumstances, with utter disregard of consequences: *an act of desperation when everything else had failed.* DESPONDENCY is usually a temporary state of deep gloom and disheartenment: *a spell of despondency.* DISCOURAGEMENT is a temporary loss of courage, hope, and ambition because of obstacles, frustrations, etc.: *His optimism yielded to discouragement.* HOPELESSNESS is a loss of hope so complete as to result in a more or less permanent state of passive despair. —**Ant. 1.** hope.

de·spair·ing (di spâr′ing), *adj.* affected with or showing despair. —**de·spair′ing·ly,** *adv.* —**Syn. 1.** See **hopeless.**

des·patch (di spach′), *v.t., v.i., n.* dispatch.

des·per·a·do (des′pə rä′dō, -rā′-), *n., pl.* **-does, -dos.** a bold, reckless criminal. [prob. pseudo-Sp alter. of obs. n. DESPERATE, in same sense]

des·per·ate (des′pər it, -prit), *adj.* **1.** reckless or dangerous because of despair or urgency: *a desperate killer.* **2.** having an urgent need, desire, etc.: *desperate for attention.* **3.** very serious or dangerous. **4.** extremely bad; intolerable or shocking. **5.** extreme or excessive. **6.** making a final, intense effort. **7.** actuated by a feeling of hopelessness. **8.** giving in to despair. [ME < L *dēspērāt(us),* ptp. of *dēspērāre* to DESPAIR; see -ATE[1]] —**des′per·ate·ly,** *adv.* —**des′per·ate·ness,** *n.* —**Syn. 1.** rash, frantic. **3.** grave. See **hopeless. 8.** forlorn, desolate. —**Ant. 1.** careful.

des·per·a·tion (des′pə rā′shən), *n.* **1.** the state of being desperate. **2.** the act or fact of despairing; despair. [ME *desperacioun* < L *dēspērātiōn-* (s. of *dēspērātiō*)] —**Syn. 1.** See **despair.**

des·pi·ca·ble (des′pi kə bəl; *for emphasis* di spik′ə bəl), *adj.* deserving to be despised; contemptible. [< LL *dēspicābil(is)* = L *dēspic(ārī)* (to) despise, *dēspic(ere)* (to) look down (*dē-* DE- + *spic-* look, comb. form of *specere*) + *-ābilis* -ABLE] —**des′pi·ca·ble·ness,** *n.* —**des′pi·ca·bly,** *adv.* —**Syn.** worthless, base, vile, mean. —**Ant.** admirable.

de·spise (di spīz′), *v.t.,* **-spised, -spis·ing.** to regard with contempt or disdain; loathe. [ME *despise(n)* < OF *despis-,* s. of *despire* < L *dēspicere;* see DESPICABLE] —**de·spis′er,** *n.* —**Syn.** contemn, detest. —**Ant.** admire.

de·spite (di spīt′), *prep., n., v.,* **-spit·ed, -spit·ing.** —*prep.* **1.** in spite of; notwithstanding. —*n.* **2.** contemptuous treatment; insult. **3.** *Archaic.* malice or spite. **4. in despite of,** in defiance of; in spite of. —*v.t.* **5.** *Obs.* to vex; spite. [orig. *in despite of;* ME *despit* < OF < L *dēspect(us)* a looking down upon, ptp. of *dēspicere;* see DESPICABLE] —**Syn. 1.** See **notwithstanding.**

de·spite·ful (di spīt′fəl), *adj.* malicious; spiteful.

des·pit·e·ous (di spit′ē əs), *adj.* *Archaic.* malicious; spiteful. [var. of ME *despitous* < AF; OF *despiteus*]

Des Plaines (des plānz′), a city in NE Illinois, near Chicago. 57,239 (1970).

de·spoil (di spoil′), *v.t.* to strip of possessions, things of value, etc.; rob; plunder; pillage. [ME *despoil(en)* < OF *despoill(ier)* < L *dēspoliāre* to strip, rob, plunder] —**de·spoil′er,** *n.* —**de·spoil′ment,** *n.* —**Syn.** dispossess; rifle.

de·spo·li·a·tion (di spō′lē ā′shən), *n.* **1.** the act of despoiling. **2.** the fact or circumstance of being despoiled. [< LL *dēspoliātiōn-* (s. of *dēspoliātiō*) = L *dēspoliāt(us)* (ptp. of *dēspoliāre;* see DESPOIL) + *-iōn-* -ION]

de·spond (di spond′ *or, esp. for 2,* des′pond), *v.i.* **1.** to be depressed by loss of hope or courage. —*n.* **2.** *Archaic.* despondency. [< L *dēspond(ēre)* (to) give up, lose heart, promise = *dē-* DE- + *spondēre* to promise] —**de·spond′er,** *n.* —**de·spond′ing·ly,** *adv.*

de·spond·en·cy (di spon′dən sē), *n.* depression of spirits from loss of courage or hope; dejection. Also, **de·spond′ence.** —**Syn.** discouragement, melancholy, gloom, desperation. See **despair.** —**Ant.** joy.

de·spond·ent (di spon′dənt), *adj.* feeling or showing profound hopelessness, dejection, or discouragement. [< L *dēspondent-* (s. of *dēspondēns*), prp. of *dēspondēre*] —**de·spond′ent·ly,** *adv.* —**Syn.** discouraged, disheartened, downhearted. See **hopeless.** —**Ant.** happy, hopeful.

des·pot (des′pət, -pot), *n.* **1.** a ruler having absolute power; autocrat. **2.** any tyrant or oppressor. **3.** honorary title of a Byzantine emperor. [< Gk *despót(ēs)* master]

des·pot·ic (di spot′ik), *adj.* of, pertaining to, or of the nature of a despot or despotism. Also, **des·pot′i·cal.** [< F *despotique* < Gk *despotik(ós)*] —**des·pot′i·cal·ly,** *adv.* —**des·pot′i·cal·ness,** *n.*

des·pot·ism (des′pə tiz′əm), *n.* **1.** the rule of a despot; the exercise of absolute authority. **2.** absolute power or control; tyranny. **3.** an absolute or autocratic government. **4.** a country ruled by a despot. [< F *despotisme*]

des·qua·mate (des′kwə māt′), *v.i.,* **-mat·ed, -mat·ing.** *Pathol.* to come off in scales, as the skin. [< L *dēsquāmāt(us)* scaled (ptp. of *dēsquāmāre*)] —**des′qua·ma′tion,** *n.*

Des·sa·lines (dā sA lēn′), *n.* **Jean Jacques** (zhäN zhäk), 1758–1806, Haitian revolutionary: emperor of Haiti as Jacques I, 1804–06.

Des·sau (des′ou), *n.* a city in central East Germany, SW of Berlin. 94,300 (est. 1959).

des·sert (di zûrt′), *n.* **1.** *U.S.* pastry, ice cream, etc., served as the final course of a meal. **2.** *Brit.* a serving of fruit, nuts, candy, etc., after the final course of a meal. [< F < *desserv(ir)* (to) clear the table. See DIS-[1], SERVE]

des·sert·spoon (di zûrt′spo͞on′), *n.* a spoon intermediate in size between a tablespoon and a teaspoon, used in eating pudding, ice cream, etc.

de·sta·bi·lize (dē stā′bə līz′), *v.t.,* **-lized, -liz·ing.** to make unstable; upset or destroy the stability of: *to destabilize world peace.*

de-Sta·lin·i·za·tion (dē stä′li ni zā′shən), *n.* the policy of eradicating the memory or influence of Stalin and Stalinism.

Des·ter·ro (*Port.* des teʀ′ʀo͞o), *n.* former name of **Florianópolis.**

des·ti·na·tion (des′tə nā′shən), *n.* **1.** the place to which a person or thing travels or is sent. **2.** an ultimate end or design. [ME < L *dēstinātiōn-* (s. of *dēstinātiō*) an establishing, purpose = *dēstināt(us)* (ptp. of *dēstināre;* see DESTINE) + *-iōn-* -ION]

des·tine (des′tin), *v.t.,* **-tined, -tin·ing. 1.** to set apart for a particular purpose; intend. **2.** to foreordain, as by divine decree; predetermine. [ME *destin(en)* < OF *destin(er)* < L *dēstināre* to establish, determine = *dē-* DE- + **stanāre* < *stāre* to stand]

des·tined (des′tind), *adj.* **1.** bound for a certain destination. **2.** having as one's destiny to be or do something.

des·ti·ny (des′tə nē), *n., pl.* **-nies. 1.** something that is to happen or has happened to a particular person or thing; lot or fortune. **2.** the predetermined course of events. **3.** the power or agency that determines the course of events. [ME *destinee* < OF (n. use of ptp. of *destiner*) < L *dēstināta,* fem. ptp. of *dēstināre*] —**Syn. 1.** fate. **2.** future. See **fate.**

des·ti·tute (des′ti to͞ot′, -tyo͞ot′), *adj.* **1.** without means of subsistence. **2.** deprived; lacking (often fol. by *of*): *destitute of children.* **3.** *Obs.* abandoned; deserted. [ME < L *dēstitūt(us)* put away, abandoned (ptp. of *dēstituere*) = *dē-* DE- + *stit-* place, put (sp. var. of *statuere;* see STATUTE) + *-ū-* thematic vowel + *-t(us)* ptp. suffix] —**Syn. 1.** needy, poor, indigent, necessitous, penniless, impoverished. **2.** deficient. —**Ant. 1.** affluent.

des·ti·tu·tion (des′ti to͞o′shən, -tyo͞o′-), *n.* **1.** lack of the means of subsistence; utter poverty. **2.** deprivation, lack, or absence. [ME < L *dēstitūtiōn-* (s. of *dēstitūtiō*) an abandoning] —**Syn. 1.** See **poverty.**

des·tri·er (des′trē ər, de strēr′), *n.* *Archaic.* a war-horse; charger. [ME *destrer* < AF, var. of OF *destrier,* lit., (horse) led at the right hand < *destre* right hand < L *dextera;* see -ARY]

de·stroy (di stroi′), *v.t.* **1.** to injure beyond repair or renewal. **2.** to put an end to; extinguish. **3.** to kill. **4.** to render ineffective or useless. —*v.i.* **5.** to engage in destruction. [ME *destroy(en)* < OF *destruire* < VL **dēstrūgere,* var. of L *dēstruere* (*dē-* DE- + *struere* to pick up, build)] —**Syn. 1.** smash, level, waste, ravage, devastate, demolish, raze. **2.** extirpate, annihilate, uproot. —**Ant. 1, 2.** create.

de·stroy·er (di stroi′ər), *n.* **1.** a person or thing that destroys. **2.** *U.S.* a fast, relatively small warship used as an escort in convoys, in antisubmarine duties, etc. [ME *destroiere* (cf. OF *destruiere*)]

de·struct (di strukt′), *Rocketry.* —*adj.* **1.** serving or designed to destroy, as a destructor. —*n.* **2.** the intentional destruction of a missile. —*v.t.* **3.** to destroy. [back formation from DESTRUCTION]

de·struct·i·ble (di struk′tə bəl), *adj.* capable of being destroyed. [< LL *dēstructibil(is)*] —**de·struct′i·bil′i·ty,** *n.*

de·struc·tion (di struk′shən), *n.* **1.** the act of destroying. **2.** the fact or condition of being destroyed. **3.** a cause or means of destroying. [ME < L *dēstructiōn-* (s. of *dēstructiō*) = *dēstruct(us)* (ptp. of *dēstruere;* see DESTROY) + *-iōn-* -ION] —**de·struc′tion·ist,** *n.* —**Syn. 1.** extinction, extermination, eradication, devastation. See **ruin.**

de·struc·tive (di struk′tiv), *adj.* **1.** tending to destroy; causing much damage (often fol. by *of* or *to*). **2.** tending to disprove or discredit (opposed to *constructive*): *destructive criticism.* [< MF < LL *dēstructīv(us)*] —**Syn. 1.** ruinous, baleful, pernicious, deleterious, fatal, deadly, lethal. **2.** unfavorable, unfriendly, adverse, negative. —**Ant. 1.** creative.

destruc′tive distilla′tion, *Chem.* the decomposition of a substance, as wood or coal, by heating with a minimal exposure to air and the subsequent collection of the volatile products.

de·struc·tor (di struk′tər), *n.* **1.** *Brit.* a furnace for the burning of refuse; incinerator. **2.** *Rocketry.* a destruct mechanism or device for destroying an errant missile. [< LL *dēstructor.* See DESTRUCTION, -OR[2]]

des·ue·tude (des′wi to͞od′, -tyo͞od′), *n.* the state of being no longer used or practiced. [ME < L *dēsuētūdo* = *dēsuēt(us),* ptp. of *dēsuescere* to lay aside (*dē-* DE- + *suescere* to become accustomed) + *-ūdo* n. suffix]

de·sul·fur (dē sul′fər), *v.t.* to free from sulfur; desulfurize. Also, **de·sul′phur.**

de·sul·fu·rise (dē sul′fyə rīz′, -fə-), *v.t.*, **-rised, -ris·ing.** *Chiefly Brit.* desulfurize. —**de·sul′fu·ri·sa′tion,** *n.* —**de·sul′fu·ris′er,** *n.*

de·sul·fu·rize (dē sul′fyə rīz′, -fə-), *v.t.*, **-rized, -riz·ing.** to free from sulfur. —**de·sul′fu·ri·za′tion,** *n.* —**de·sul′fu·riz′er,** *n.*

des·ul·to·ry (des′əl tōr′ē, -tôr′ē), *adj.* **1.** lacking in consistency, constancy, or visible order; disconnected; fitful. **2.** digressing; random. [< L *dēsultōri(us)* of a jumper, superficial = *dēsult(us),* ptp. of *dēsilīre* to leap down (*dē-* DE- + *sul-,* var. of *sal-* leap + *-tus* ptp. suffix) + *-ōrius* -ORY[1]] —**des′ul·to′ri·ly,** *adv.* —**des′ul·to′ri·ness,** *n.* —**Ant. 1.** methodical. **2.** pertinent.

de·tach (di tach′), *v.t.* **1.** to unfasten and separate. **2.** *Mil.* to send away (a regiment, ship, etc.) on a special mission. [< F *détach(er),* OF *destachier* = *des-* DIS-[1] + *tache* (<< Romanic *tacca* nail)] —**de·tach′a·ble,** *adj.*

de·tached (di tacht′), *adj.* **1.** separated; not attached. **2.** disinterested; unbiased: *a detached judgment.* **3.** aloof; not involved or concerned. —**Syn. 2.** uninvolved, uninterested, impartial, dispassionate, unprejudiced. —**Ant. 1.** attached. **2.** involved.

de·tach·ment (di tach′mənt), *n.* **1.** the act of detaching. **2.** the condition of being detached. **3.** aloofness. **4.** freedom from prejudice or partiality. **5.** the act of sending out a detached force of troops or naval ships. **6.** the force sent. [< F *détachement*]

de·tail (*n.* di tāl′, dē′tāl; *v.* di tāl′), *n.* **1.** an individual or minute part; an item or particular. **2.** particulars collectively; minutiae. **3.** attention to or treatment of a subject in individual or minute parts. **4.** intricate, finely wrought decoration. **5.** any small section of a larger structure or whole, considered as a unit. **6.** *Mil.* **a.** an appointment or assignment for a special task. **b.** the party or person so selected: *the kitchen detail.* **c.** a particular assignment of duty. **7. in detail,** item by item; with particulars. —*v.t.* **8.** to relate or report with complete particulars. **9.** to mention one by one; specify; list. **10.** *Mil.* to appoint or assign for some particular duty. **11.** to provide with intricate, finely wrought decoration. [< F *détail* < OF *detaill(er)* (to) cut in pieces. See DIS-[1], TAILOR]

de·tailed (di tāld′, dē′tāld), *adj.* **1.** having numerous details. **2.** thorough in the treatment of details. —**Syn. 1.** involved, complex, complicated. **2.** exhaustive, thorough, comprehensive.

de·tain (di tān′), *v.t.* **1.** to keep from proceeding; keep waiting; delay. **2.** to keep under restraint or in custody. **3.** *Archaic.* to withhold, as from a person. [ME *detain(en)* < OF *deten(ir)* < L *dētinēre* = *dē-* DE- + *-tinēre,* comb. form of *tenēre* to hold] —**de·tain′a·ble,** *adj.* —**de·tain′ment,** *n.* —**Syn. 1.** retard, stop, slow, stay, check. **2.** confine, arrest. **3.** retain. —**Ant. 1.** promote, advance.

de·tain·er (di tā′nər), *n.* *Law.* **1.** the wrongful detaining or withholding of what belongs to another. **2.** a writ for the further detention of a person already in custody. [< AF *detener* (n. use of inf.), var. of OF *detenir;* see DETAIN]

de·tect (di tekt′), *v.t.* **1.** to discover or catch (a person) in the performance of some act: *to detect someone cheating.* **2.** to find out the true character or activity of: *to detect a spy.* **3.** to discover the presence, existence, or fact of: *to detect the odor of gas.* **4.** *Radio.* to subject to the action of a detector; demodulate. [ME *detect* (ptp.) < L *dētect(us)* (ptp. of *dētegere*) = *dē-* DE- + *tec-* cover (var. of *tegere*) + *-t(us)* ptp. suffix] —**de·tect′a·ble, de·tect′i·ble,** *adj.* —**Syn. 1.** descry, find.

de·tec·tion (di tek′shən), *n.* **1.** the act of detecting. **2.** the fact of being detected. **3.** discovery, as of error or crime. **4.** *Radio.* **a.** rectification of alternating currents in a radio receiver. **b.** the conversion of an alternating carrier wave or current into a direct pulsating current equivalent to the transmitted signal. [ME < LL *dētectiōn-* (s. of *dētectiō*)]

de·tec·tive (di tek′tiv), *n.* **1.** a member of the police force or a private investigator whose function it is to obtain information and evidence, as of offenses against the law. —*adj.* **2.** of or pertaining to detection or detectives: *a detective story.* **3.** serving to detect; detecting.

de·tec·tor (di tek′tər), *n.* **1.** a person or thing that detects. **2.** *Radio.* **a.** a device for detecting electric oscillations or waves. **b.** a device, as a crystal detector or a vacuum tube, that rectifies the alternating currents in a radio receiver. [< LL *dētector* an uncoverer]

de·tent (di tent′), *n.* *Mach.* a mechanism for temporarily keeping one part in a certain position relative to another, released by application of force to one of the parts. [< F *détente,* OF *destente* < *destendre* to relax. See DIS-[1], TENDER[2]]

dé·tente (dā tänt′; *Fr.* dā täNt′), *n., pl.* **-tentes** (-tänts′; *Fr.* -täNt′). a relaxation of international tension. [< F; see DETENT]

de·ten·tion (di ten′shən), *n.* **1.** the act of detaining. **2.** the state of being detained. **3.** maintenance of a person in custody or confinement, esp. while awaiting a court decision. **4.** the withholding of what belongs to or is claimed by another. —*adj.* **5.** of or pertaining to detention or used to detain: *the detention room of a police station.* [ME < L *dētentiōn-* (s. of *dētentiō*) = *dētent(us)* detained (ptp. of *dētinēre;* see DETAIN) + *-iōn-* -ION]

deten′tion home′, a house of correction or detention for juvenile offenders or delinquents, usually under the supervision of a juvenile court.

de·ter (di tûr′), *v.t.*, **-terred, -ter·ring.** **1.** to discourage or restrain from acting or proceeding, as through fear or doubt. **2.** to prevent; check; arrest. [< L *dēterr(ēre)* (to) prevent, hinder = *dē-* DE- + *terrēre* to frighten] —**de·ter′ment,** *n.* —**Syn. 1.** dissuade, hinder, stop.

de·terge (di tûrj′), *v.t.*, **-terged, -terg·ing.** **1.** to wipe or wash away; cleanse. **2.** to cleanse of impurities or undesirable matter, as a wound. [< L *dēterg(ēre)* (to) wipe off = *dē-* DE- + *tergēre* to wipe]

de·ter·gent (di tûr′jənt), *adj.* **1.** cleansing; purging. —*n.* **2.** any of a group of water-soluble cleaning agents that have wetting and emulsifying properties. **3.** a similar substance that is oil-soluble and capable of holding insoluble foreign matter in suspension, used in lubricating oils, dry-cleaning preparations, etc. **4.** any cleansing agent, including soap. [< L *dētergent-* (s. of *dētergēns*) wiping off (prp. of *dētergēre*)]

de·te·ri·o·rate (di tēr′ē ə rāt′), *v.t., v.i.*, **-rat·ed, -rat·ing.** **1.** to make or become worse; make or become lower in character, quality, value, etc. **2.** to disintegrate or wear away. [< LL *dēteriōrāt(us)* made worse (ptp. of *dēteriōrāre*) = L *dēterior* worse, comp. of **deter* poor + *-ātus* -ATE[1]] —**Syn. 1.** degenerate, decline, weaken, retrogress, worsen, diminish.

de·te·ri·o·ra·tion (di tēr′ē ə rā′shən), *n.* **1.** the act or process of deteriorating. **2.** the state or condition of having deteriorated. **3.** a gradual decline, as in quality, serviceability or vigor. [< LL *dēteriōrātiōn-* (s. of *dēteriōrātiō*) = *dēteriōrāt(us)* (see DETERIORATE) + *-iōn-* -ION]

de·ter·mi·nant (di tûr′mə nənt), *n.* **1.** a determining agent or factor. **2.** *Math.* an algebraic expression of the sum of products of elements, usually written in a square array and used in the solution of systems of linear equations. [< L *dēterminant-* (s. of *dēterminans*), prp. of *dētermināre*]

de·ter·mi·nate (di tûr′mə nit), *adj.* **1.** having defined limits; definite. **2.** settled; positive. **3.** conclusive; final. **4.** resolute. **5.** *Bot.* (of an inflorescence) having the primary and each secondary axis ending in a flower or bud, thus preventing further elongation. **6.** *Engineering.* able to be analyzed completely by means of the principles of statics. [ME < L *dēterminat(us),* ptp. of *dēterminare*]

de·ter·mi·na·tion (di tûr′mə nā′shən), *n.* **1.** the act of coming to a decision or of fixing or settling a purpose. **2.** ascertainment, as after observation or investigation. **3.** the information ascertained; solution. **4.** the settlement of a dispute, question, etc. **5.** the decision or settlement arrived at or pronounced. **6.** the quality of being resolute. **7.** a fixed purpose or intention. **8.** the fixing or settling of amount, limit, character, etc. **9.** fixed direction or tendency toward some object or end. **10.** *Chiefly Law.* conclusion or termination. **11.** *Embryol.* the fixation of the nature of morphological differentiation in a group of cells before actual, visible differentiation. **12.** *Logic.* **a.** the act of rendering a notion more precise by the addition of differentiating characteristics. **b.** the definition of a concept in terms of its constituent elements. [ME *determinacioun* < L *dēterminātiōn-* (s. of *dēterminātiō*) a boundary, conclusion]

de·ter·mi·na·tive (di tûr′mə nā′tiv, -nə tiv), *adj.* **1.** serving to determine; determining. —*n.* **2.** something that determines. [prob. < ML *dēterminātīv(us)* fixed, LL: crucial (of a disease)] —**Syn. 1.** conclusive, deciding, settling. **2.** determinant, determiner.

de·ter·mine (di tûr′min), *v.*, **-mined, -min·ing.** —*v.t.* **1.** to settle or decide (a dispute, question, etc.) by an authoritative or conclusive decision. **2.** to conclude or ascertain, as after reasoning or observation. **3.** *Geom.* to fix the position of. **4.** to cause, affect, or control; fix or decide causally. **5.** to give direction or tendency to; impel. **6.** *Logic.* to limit (a notion) by adding differentiating characteristics. **7.** *Chiefly Law.* to put an end to; terminate. **8.** to lead or bring (a person) to a decision. **9.** to decide upon. —*v.i.* **10.** to come to a decision or resolution; decide. **11.** *Chiefly Law.* to come to an end. [ME *determine(n)* < OF *determin(er)* < L *dētermināre.* See DE-, TERMINATE] —**de·ter′mi·na·ble,** *adj.* —**de·ter′mi·na·bil′i·ty,** *n.* —**de·ter′mi·na·bly,** *adv.* —**Syn. 1.** resolve. See **decide. 5.** induce, lead.

de·ter·mined (di tûr′mind), *adj.* **1.** resolute; unwaveringly decided. **2.** settled; resolved. —**de·ter′mined·ly,** *adv.* —**de·ter′mined·ness,** *n.* —**Syn. 1.** inflexible, rigid.

de·ter·min·er (di tûr′mə nər), *n.* **1.** a person or thing that determines. **2.** *Gram.* a member of a subclass of English adjectival words that limit the nouns they modify in a special way and that usually are placed before descriptive adjectives, as *a, an, the, your, their.*

de·ter·min·ism (di tûr′mə niz′əm), *n.* **1.** the doctrine that all facts and events exemplify natural laws. **2.** the doctrine that all events, including human choices and decisions, have sufficient causes. —**de·ter′min·ist,** *n., adj.* —**de·ter′min·is′tic,** *adj.*

de·ter·rent (di tûr′ənt, -tur′-, -ter′-), *adj.* **1.** serving or tending to deter. —*n.* **2.** something that deters. [< L *dēterrent-* (s. of *dēterrēns*), prp. of *dēterrēre*]

de·ter·sive (di tûr′siv), *adj.* **1.** cleansing; detergent. —*n.* **2.** a detergent agent or medicine. [< F *détersif* < L (medical) *dētersīv(us)* = L *dēters(us)* (ptp. of *dētergēre;* see DETERGE) + *-īvus* -IVE]

de·test (di test′), *v.t.* to feel abhorrence of; hate; dislike intensely. [< MF *detest(er)* < L *dētestārī,* lit., to curse while calling a deity to witness = *dē-* DE- + *testārī* to bear witness; see TESTATE] —**de·test′er,** *n.* —**Syn.** abhor, loathe, abominate, execrate, despise. See **hate.** —**Ant.** love, like.

de·test·a·ble (di tes′tə bəl), *adj.* deserving to be detested; abominable; hateful. [ME < OF < L *dētestābil(is)*] —**de·test′a·bil′i·ty, de·test′a·ble·ness,** *n.* —**de·test′a·bly,** *adv.* —**Syn.** abhorrent, loathsome, odious, vile.

de·tes·ta·tion (dē′te stā′shən), *n.* **1.** abhorrence; hatred. **2.** a person or thing detested. [ME *detestacion* < L *dētestātiōn-* (s. of *dētestātiō*) = *dētestāt(us)* (ptp. of *dētestārī* to DETEST; see -ATE[1]) + *-iōn-* -ION]

de·throne (dē thrōn′), *v.t.*, **-throned, -thron·ing.** to remove from a throne; depose. —**de·throne′ment,** *n.*

det·i·nue (det′ⁿno͞o′, -ⁿnyo͞o′), *n.* *Law.* an old common-law form of action to recover possession of personal property wrongfully detained. [ME *detenu* < OF *detenue* detention, orig. fem. ptp. of *detenir* to DETAIN]

det·o·nate (det′ⁿnāt′), *v.*, **-nat·ed, -nat·ing.** —*v.i.* **1.** to explode with suddenness and violence. —*v.t.* **2.** to cause to explode. [< L *dētonāt(us)* thundered forth (ptp. of *dētonāre*) = *dē-* DE- + *ton(āre)* (to) THUNDER + *-ātus* -ATE[1]]

det·o·na·tion (det′ᵊnā′shən), *n.* **1.** the act of detonating. **2.** an explosion. [< ML *dētonātiōn-* (s. of *dētonātiō*)] —**det′o·na′tive,** *adj.*

det·o·na·tor (det′ᵊnā′tər), *n.* **1.** a device, as a percussion cap or an explosive, used to make another substance explode. **2.** something that explodes.

de·tour (dē′to͝or, di to͝or′), *n.* **1.** a roundabout or circuitous way or course, esp. one used temporarily instead of the main one. —*v.i.* **2.** to make a detour. —*v.t.* **3.** to cause to make a detour. **4.** to make a detour around. [< F *détour,* OF *destor* < *destor(ner)* (to) turn aside. See DE-, TURN]

de·tox·i·cate (dē tok′sə kāt′), *v.t.,* **-cat·ed, -cat·ing.** to detoxify. [DE- + L *toxic(um)* poison (see TOXIC) + -ATE[1]] —**de·tox·i·cant** (dē tok′sə kənt), *adj., n.* —**de·tox′i·ca′tion,** *n.* —**de·tox′i·ca′tor,** *n.*

de·tox·i·fy (dē tok′sə fī′), *v.t.,* **-fied, -fy·ing.** to rid of poison or the effect of poison. [back formation from DETOXIFICATION, alter. of DETOXICATION] —**de·tox′i·fi·ca′tion,** *n.*

de·tract (di trakt′), *v.t.* **1.** to draw away or divert; distract. **2.** *Archaic.* to take away (a part); abate. —*v.i.* **3.** to take away a part, as from quality, value, or reputation (usually fol. by *from*). [ME < L *dētract(us)* drawn away (ptp. of *dētrahere*)] —**de·tract′ing·ly,** *adv.* —**de·trac′tor,** *n.*

de·trac·tion (di trak′shən), *n.* the act of disparaging or belittling the reputation or worth of a person, work, etc. [ME *detraccion* < LL *dētractiōn-* (s. of *dētractiō*)] —**de·trac′tive,** *adj.* —**de·trac′tive·ly,** *adv.*

de·train (dē trān′), *v.i.* **1.** to alight from a railroad train. —*v.t.* **2.** to remove from a railroad train. —**de·train′ment,** *n.*

det·ri·ment (de′trə mənt), *n.* **1.** loss, damage, disadvantage, or injury. **2.** a cause of loss or damage. [ME < L *dētrīment(um)* loss, damage. See DETRITUS, -MENT] —**Syn. 1.** harm, hurt, impairment, prejudice. See **damage.**

det·ri·men·tal (de′trə men′tᵊl), *adj.* causing detriment; damaging or injurious.

de·tri·tion (di trish′ən), *n.* the act of wearing away by rubbing. [< ML *dētrītiōn-* (s. of *dētrītiō*). See DETRITUS, -ION]

de·tri·tus (di trī′təs), *n.* **1.** rock in small particles or other material broken away from a mass, as by the action of water or glacial ice. **2.** debris. [< F *détritus* < L: a rubbing away, n. use of ptp. of *dēterere* = *dē-* DE- + *terere* to rub] —**de·tri·tal** (di trīt′ᵊl), *adj.*

De·troit (di troit′), *n.* **1.** a city in SE Michigan, on the Detroit River. 1,513,601 (1970). **2.** a river in SE Michigan, flowing S from Lake St. Clair to Lake Erie, forming part of the boundary between the U.S. and Canada. ab. 32 mi. long.

de trop (də trō′), *French.* **1.** too much; too many. **2.** in the way; not wanted.

de·trude (di tro͞od′), *v.t.,* **-trud·ed, -trud·ing.** **1.** to thrust out or away. **2.** to thrust or force down. [ME < L *dētrūd(ere)* (to) thrust down, drive away = *dē-* DE- + *trūdere* to thrust, drive, force]

de·trun·cate (di trung′kāt), *v.t.,* **-cat·ed, -cat·ing.** to reduce by cutting off a part; cut down. [< L *dētruncāt(us)* (ptp. of *dētruncāre*). See DE-, TRUNCATE] —**de′trun·ca′tion,** *n.*

de·tu·mes·cence (dē′to͞o mes′əns, -tyo͞o-), *n.* subsidence of swelling. [< L *dētumesc(ere)* (to) cease swelling (*dē-* DE- + *tumescere* to swell + -ENCE)]

Deu·ca·li·on (do͞o kā′lē ən, dyo͞o-), *n.* *Class. Myth.* a son of Prometheus who survived the deluge with his wife, Pyrrha, to become the founder of the renewed human race.

deuce[1] (do͞os, dyo͞os), *n.* **1.** *Cards.* a card having two pips; a two, or two spot. **2.** *Dice.* **a.** the face of a die having two pips. **b.** a cast or point of two. **3.** *Tennis.* a tie that can be broken by a player scoring two successive points to win the game or two successive games to win the set. —*adj.* **4.** (esp. in games, sports, and gambling) two. [< MF *deus* two < L *duōs* (m. acc. of *duo*)]

deuce[2] (do͞os, dyo͞os), *n.* *Informal.* devil; dickens (used as a mild oath): *Where the deuce did they hide it?* [ME *deus,* special use of DEUCE[1]]

deuc·ed (do͞o′sid, dyo͞o′-; do͞ost, dyo͞ost), *adj.* *Chiefly Brit. Informal.* confounded; damned. —**deuc′ed·ly,** *adv.*

De·us (dē′əs, dā′-; *Lat.* de′o͝os), *n.* God. *Abbr.:* D. [< L *deus* god; c. Gk *Zeús* Zeus, Skt *dēva* god, OE *Tēw* Tiu, ON *Tyr* Tyr]

De·us·ded·it (dē′əs ded′it, -dē′dit), *n.* **Saint,** died A.D. 618, Italian ecclesiastic: pope 615–618. Also called **Adeodatus I.**

de·us ex ma·chi·na (de′o͝os eks mä′ki nä′; *Eng.* dē′əs eks mak′ə nə, dā′-), *Latin.* **1.** (in Greek drama) a god who resolves the entanglements of the play by his supernatural intervention. **2.** an artificial, forced, or improbable device used to resolve the difficulties of a plot. [lit., god from a (stage) machine]

De·us vo·bis·cum (dā′o͝os vō bis′ko͝om), *Latin.* God be with you.

De·us vult (dā′o͝os vo͝olt′), *Latin.* God wills (it): cry of the Crusaders.

deut-, var. of **deuto-** before a vowel.

Deut., Deuteronomy.

deuter-, var. of **deutero-** before a vowel: *deuteron.*

deu·ter·ag·o·nist (do͞o′tə rag′ə nist, dyo͞o′-), *n.* (in classical Greek drama) the character second in importance to the protagonist, esp. one serving as the antagonist. [< Gk *deuteragōnist(ēs)*]

deu·ter·an·ope (do͞o′tər ə nōp′, dyo͞o′-), *n.* *Ophthalm.* a person who has deuteranopia. [back formation from DEUTERANOPIA]

deu·ter·a·no·pi·a (do͞o′tər ə nō′pē ə, dyo͞o′-), *n.* *Ophthalm.* a defect of vision in which the retina fails to respond to green. [< NL; see DEUTER-, ANOPIA] —**deu·ter·an·op·ic** (do͞o′tər ə nop′ik, dyo͞o′-), *adj.*

deu·te·ri·um (do͞o tēr′ē əm, dyo͞o-), *n.* *Chem.* an isotope of hydrogen, having twice the mass of ordinary hydrogen; heavy hydrogen. *Symbol:* D; *at. no.:* 1; *at. wt.:* 2.01. [< NL < Gk *deúter(ion)* of second quality (neut. of *deutereîos*) = *deúter(os)* second (see DEUTER-) + *-ei* adj. suffix + *-on* neut. sing. suffix]

deute′rium ox′ide, *Chem.* heavy water, D_2O.

deutero-, a combining form meaning "second" (*deuterocanonical*), sometimes specialized as a combining form of **deuterium** (*deuteron*). Also, **deut-, deuter-, deuto-.** [< Gk, comb. form of *deúteros*]

deu′ter·o·ca·non′i·cal books′ (do͞o′tə rō kə non′i kəl, dyo͞o′-, do͞o′-, dyo͞o′-), the books of the Bible regarded by the Roman Catholic Church as canonical but not universally acknowledged as such in the early church or by Protestants.

deu·ter·og·a·my (do͞o′tə rog′ə mē, dyo͞o′-), *n.* digamy. [< Gk *deuterogamía* a second marriage] —**deu′ter·og′a·mist,** *n.*

deu·ter·on (do͞o′tə ron′, dyo͞o′-), *n.* *Physics.* a positively charged particle consisting of a proton and a neutron, equivalent to the nucleus of an atom of deuterium. Cf. **triton.**

Deu·ter·on·o·my (do͞o′tə ron′ə mē, dyo͞o′-), *n.* the fifth book of the Pentateuch. [< LL *Deuteronomi(um)* < Gk *Deuteronómion* (see DEUTERO-, -NOMY); r. earlier *Deutronome,* ME *Deutronomie* < LL]

deuto-, var. of **deutero-:** *deutoplasm.* Also, *esp. before a vowel,* **deut-.**

deu·to·plasm (do͞o′tə plaz′əm, dyo͞o′-), *n.* *Embryol.* the nonliving, nutritive material, as a yolk granule, in the ovarian cytoplasm. —**deu′to·plas′mic,** *adj.*

Deutsch (doich), *n.* **Babette,** born 1895, U.S. poet, novelist, and critic.

Deut′sche mark′ (doi′chə), the monetary unit of West Germany, equal to 100 pfennigs. *Abbr.:* DM Also, **Deut′sche·mark′.** Cf. **ostmark.** [< G: German mark]

Deut·sches Reich (doi′chəs rīkh′), a former German name of **Germany.**

Deutsch·land (doich′länt′), *n.* German name of **Germany.**

deut·zi·a (do͞ot′sē ə, dyo͞ot′-, doit′-), *n.* any saxifragaceous shrub of the genus *Deutzia,* having showy white, bluish, pink, or purplish flowers, grown as an ornamental. [< NL, named after Jean *Deutz,* 18th-century Dutch patron of botany; see -IA]

de·va (dā′və), *n.* *Hindu Myth.* a god or divinity; one of an order of good spirits. [< Skt]

De Va·le·ra (dev′ə lâr′ə, -lēr′ə; *Irish.* de vä lā′rä), **Ea·mon** (ā′mən), 1882–1975, Irish political leader and statesman, born in the U.S.: prime minister of the Republic of Ireland 1932–48, 1951–54, 1957–59; president 1959–73.

de·val·u·ate (dē val′yo͞o āt′), *v.t.,* **-at·ed, -at·ing.** **1.** to deprive of value; reduce the value of. **2.** to fix a lower legal value on (a currency).

de·val·u·a·tion (dē val′yo͞o ā′shən), *n.* **1.** an official lowering of the legal exchange value of a country's currency by reducing the currency's gold equivalency. **2.** a reduction of a value, status, etc.

de·val·ue (dē val′yo͞o), *v.t.,* **-val·ued, -val·u·ing.** to devaluate.

De·va·na·ga·ri (dā′və nä′gə rē′), *n.* an alphabetical script of India, used for the writing of Hindi, Sanskrit, etc. Also called **Nagari.** [< Skt: lit., Nagari (an alphabet of India) of the gods]

dev·as·tate (dev′ə stāt′), *v.t.,* **-tat·ed, -tat·ing.** **1.** to lay waste; render desolate. **2.** to overwhelm. [< L *dēvastāt(us)* laid waste (ptp. of *dēvastāre*) = *dē-* DE- + *vast(āre)* (to) lay waste (akin to *vastus* empty) + *-ātus* -ATE[1]] —**dev′as·ta′tive,** *adj.* —**dev′as·ta′tor,** *n.* —**Syn. 1.** destroy, sack, despoil. See **ravage.**

dev·as·ta·tion (dev′ə stā′shən), *n.* **1.** the act of devastating; destruction. **2.** devastated state; desolation. [ME < LL *dēvastātiōn-* (s. of *dēvastātiō*)]

de Ve·ga (də vā′gə; *Sp.* de be′gä), **Lo·pe** (lō′pā, -pē; *Sp.* lô′pe), (*Lope Félix de Vega Carpio*), 1562–1635, Spanish dramatist and poet.

de·vein (dē vān′), *v.t.* to remove the dorsal vein of (a shrimp).

devel., development.

de·vel·op (di vel′əp), *v.t.* **1.** to bring out the capabilities or possibilities of; bring to a more advanced or effective state. **2.** to cause to grow or expand. **3.** to elaborate or expand in detail: *to develop a theory.* **4.** to bring into being or activity; generate; evolve. **5.** to transfer the details of (a two-dimensional design, pattern, or the like) from one surface onto another without altering the distances between points. **6.** *Math.* to express in an extended form, as in a series. **7.** *Photog.* **a.** to render visible (the latent image on an exposed film or the like). **b.** to treat (an exposed film or the like) with chemicals so as to make visible its latent image. **8.** *Chess.* to bring (a piece) into effective play. —*v.i.* **9.** to grow into a more mature or advanced state; advance; expand. **10.** to come gradually into existence or operation; be evolved. **11.** to be disclosed; become evident or manifest. **12.** *Biol.* to undergo differentiation in ontogeny or progress in phylogeny. **13.** to undergo developing, as a photographic film. [< F *développ(er),* OF *desveloper* = *des-* DIS-[1] + *veloper* to wrap up; see ENVELOPE] —**de·vel′op·a·bil′i·ty,** *n.* —**de·vel′op·a·ble,** *adj.*

de·vel·ope (di vel′əp), *v.t., v.i.,* **-oped, -op·ing.** develop.

de·vel·op·er (di vel′ə pər), *n.* **1.** a person or thing that develops. **2.** *Photog.* a reducing agent or solution for developing a film or the like. **3.** a person who invests in and develops the urban or suburban potentialities of real estate, esp. by subdividing the land into home sites and then building houses and selling them.

de·vel·op·ing (di vel′ə ping), *adj.* (of a nation or geographical area) having a standard of living and level of industrial production that are rising fairly quickly but are still considerably below the potential levels that could be obtained with the continuing aid of capital and skilled technicians to develop resources and industries.

de·vel·op·ment (di vel′əp mənt), *n.* **1.** the act or process of developing; progress. **2.** a developed state, form, or product. **3.** *Music.* the part of a movement or composition in which a theme or themes are developed. **4.** a large group of dwellings constructed as a unified community. **5.** *Chess.* the act or process of developing chess pieces. Also, **de·vel′ope·ment.** —**de·vel′op·men′tal,** *adj.* —**de·vel′op·men′tal·ly,** *adv.* —**Syn. 1.** expansion, elaboration, growth, evolution; unfolding, maturing, maturation. **2.** maturity, ripeness. —**Ant. 1.** deterioration, disintegration.

De·ven·ter (dā′vən tər), *n.* a city in the E Netherlands. 57,973 (1962).

Dev·e·reux (dev′ə ro͞o′), *n.* **Robert, 2nd Earl of Essex,** 1556–1601, British statesman and soldier: courtier of Queen Elizabeth I.

de·vest (di vest′), *v.t.* **1.** *Law.* to divest. **2.** *Obs.* to remove the clothes from; undress. [< MF *desvest(er),* var. of OF *desvestir* = *des-* DIS-¹ + *vestir* to clothe < L *vestīr(e)*; see DIVEST]

De·vi (dā′vē), *n. Hinduism.* **1.** a mother goddess having various forms. **2.** Also called **Annapurna, Parvati.** the consort of Shiva, identified with Shakti and Kali as a goddess of love, maternity, and death. [< Skt, fem. of *deva* DEVA]

de·vi·ant (dē′vē ənt), *adj.* **1.** deviating from the norm. —*n.* **2.** a person or thing that deviates markedly from the accepted norm. [ME < L *dēviant-* (s. of *dēviāns,* prp. of *dēviāre*). See DE-, VIA, -ANT]

de·vi·ate (*v.* dē′vē āt′; *adj., n.* dē′vē it), *v.,* **-at·ed, -at·ing,** *adj., n.* —*v.i.* **1.** to turn aside, as from a route, way, or course. **2.** to depart or swerve, as from a course of action or acceptable norm. **3.** to digress. —*v.t.* **4.** to cause to swerve; turn aside. —*adj.* **5.** characterized by deviation from an accepted norm, as of behavior. —*n.* **6.** a person or thing that departs from the accepted norm or standard. **7.** a sexual pervert. [< LL *dēviāt(us)* turned from the straight road, ptp. of *dēviāre*] —**de′vi·a′tor,** *n.* —**de·vi·a·to·ry** (dē′vē ə tôr′ē, -tōr′ē), **de′vi·a′tive,** *adj.*
—**Syn. 1.** veer, wander, stray. DEVIATE, DIGRESS, DIVERGE imply turning or going aside from a path. To DEVIATE is to turn or wander, often by slight degrees, from what is considered the most direct or desirable approach to a given physical, intellectual, or moral end: *Fear caused him to deviate from the truth.* To DIGRESS is primarily to wander from the main theme or topic in writing or speaking, esp. for explanation or illustration: *A speaker may digress to relate an amusing anecdote.* Two paths DIVERGE when they proceed from a common point in such directions that the distance between them increases: *The sides of an angle diverge from a common point. Their interests gradually diverged.*

de·vi·a·tion (dē′vē ā′shən), *n.* **1.** the act of deviating; divergence. **2.** departure from a standard or norm. **3.** *Statistics.* the difference between one of a set of values and some fixed value, usually the mean of the set. **4.** *Navig.* the error of a magnetic compass, as a result of local magnetism: expressed in plus degrees east or minus degrees west of magnetic north. Cf. **variation** (def. 8). **5.** departure or divergence from an established dogma or ideology, esp. a communist one. [ME < ML *dēviātiōn-* (s. of *dēviātiō*)]

de·vice (di vīs′), *n.* **1.** something made, usually for a particular working purpose; an invention or contrivance, esp. a mechanical or electrical one. **2.** a plan, scheme, or trick for effecting a purpose. **3.** a representation or design used as a heraldic charge or as an emblem, badge, trademark, or the like. **4.** a motto. **5.** something elaborately or fancifully designed. **6.** *Literary.* a particular word pattern, combination of word sounds, etc., used to arouse a desired reaction in the reader. **7.** *Archaic.* devising; invention. **8. leave to one's own devices,** to leave alone to do as one pleases. [b. ME *devis* division, discourse and *devise* heraldic device, will; both < OF < L *dīvīs(a),* fem. of *dīvīsus;* see DIVISION] —**Syn. 1.** gadget. **2.** project, design; stratagem, maneuver. **4.** slogan, legend.

dev·il (dev′əl), *n., v.,* **-iled, -il·ing** or (*esp. Brit.*) **-illed, -il·ling.** —*n.* **1.** *Theol.* **a.** (*sometimes cap.*) the supreme spirit of evil: Satan. **b.** a subordinate evil spirit at enmity with God. **2.** an atrociously wicked, cruel, or ill-tempered person. **3.** a person of great cleverness, energy, or recklessness. **4.** *Print.* an errand boy or the youngest apprentice in a printing office. **5.** a person, esp. one in unfortunate or pitiable circumstances: *The poor devil kept losing jobs.* **6.** any of various mechanical devices, as a machine for tearing rags, a machine for manufacturing wooden screws, etc. **7.** any of various portable furnaces or braziers used in construction and foundry work. **8. between the devil and the deep blue sea,** between two undesirable alternatives. **9. devil of a,** extremely difficult or annoying; hellish: *We had a devil of a time getting home.* **10. raise the devil, a.** to cause a commotion. **b.** to make an emphatic protest or take drastic measures. —*v.t.* **11.** *Informal.* to annoy; harass; pester. **12.** to tear (rags, cloth, etc.) with a devil. **13.** *Cookery.* to prepare (food, usually finely chopped) with hot or savory seasoning. [ME *devel,* OE *dēofol* < L *diabolus* < Gk *diábolos* slanderer, enemy, Satan (eccl.)]

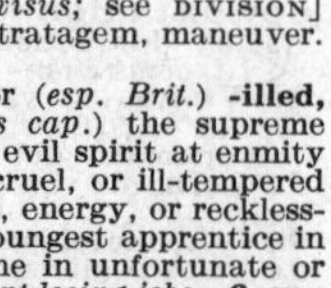

dev·iled (dev′əld), *adj. Cookery.* prepared with hot or savory seasoning, usually after being finely chopped.

dev·il·fish (dev′əl fish′), *n., pl.* (*esp. collectively*) **-fish,** (*esp. referring to two or more kinds or species*) **-fish·es. 1.** any of several huge rays of the family *Mobulidae,* esp. of the genus *Manta,* found in tropical waters, having a pair of fleshy horns on the head. **2.** an octopus.

Devilfish,
Manta hamiltoni
(18 ft. across "wing tips"; total length 20 ft.; tail 6 ft.)

dev·il·ish (dev′ə lish, dev′lish), *adj.* **1.** of, like, or befitting a devil; diabolical; fiendish. **2.** *Informal.* excessive; very great: *He's in a devilish mess.* —*adv.* **3.** *Informal.* excessively; extremely: *He's devilish proud of himself.* —**dev′il·ish·ly,** *adv.* —**dev′il·ish·ness,** *n.* —**Syn. 1.** satanic, demoniac, infernal.

dev·il·kin (dev′əl kin), *n.* a little devil; imp.

dev·il-may-care (dev′əl mā kâr′), *adj.* reckless; careless; rollicking.

dev·il·ment (dev′əl mənt), *n.* devilish action or conduct; mischief.

dev·il·ry (dev′əl rē), *n., pl.* **-ries.** deviltry. [ME]

dev′il's ad′vocate, 1. a person who advocates an opposing or bad cause for the sake of argument. **2.** *Rom. Cath. Ch.* an official whose duty is to argue against a proposed beatification or canonization. [trans. of NL *advocātus diabolī*]

dev′il's darn′ing nee′dle, a dragonfly.

dev′il's food′ cake′, a rich, chocolate cake. [modeled on ANGEL FOOD CAKE]

Dev′il's Is′land, one of the Safety Islands, off the coast of French Guiana: former French penal colony. French, **Île du Diable.**

dev·il·try (dev′əl trē), *n., pl.* **-tries. 1.** reckless or mischievous behavior; mischief. **2.** extreme wickedness. **3.** an act or instance of mischievous or wicked behavior. **4.** diabolic magic or art. **5.** demonology. Also, **devilry.** [var. of DEVILRY]

de·vi·ous (dē′vē əs), *adj.* **1.** departing from the shortest way; circuitous; indirect. **2.** without definite course; vagrant. **3.** departing from the proper or accepted way; roundabout. **4.** not straightforward; shifty or crooked. [< L *dēvi(us)* lying off the road. See DE-, VIA, -OUS] —**de′vi·ous·ly,** *adv.* —**de′vi·ous·ness,** *n.* —**Syn. 1.** roundabout. **4.** cunning, crafty, sly, stealthy, furtive.

de·vis·a·ble (di vī′zə bəl), *adj.* **1.** capable of being devised, invented, or contrived. **2.** *Law.* capable of being transferred. [ME < AF: assignable by will, OF: that which may be divided. See DEVISE, -ABLE]

de·vis·al (di vī′zəl), *n.* the act of devising.

de·vise (di vīz′), *v.,* **-vised, -vis·ing,** *n.* —*v.t.* **1.** to contrive, plan, or elaborate; invent from existing principles or ideas: *to devise a method.* **2.** *Law.* to assign or transmit (property, esp. real property) by will. **3.** *Archaic.* to imagine; suppose. —*v.i.* **4.** to form a plan; contrive. —*n. Law.* **5.** the act of disposing of property by will. **6.** a will or clause in a will disposing of property, esp. real property. **7.** the property disposed of. [ME *devise(n)* < OF *devis(er)* < VL **dīvīsāre,* freq. of L *dīvidere* to DIVIDE] —**de·vis′er,** *n.* —**Syn. 1.** concoct, scheme, project, design.

de·vi·see (di vī zē′, dev′i zē′), *n. Law.* a person to whom a devise is made.

de·vi·sor (di vī′zər), *n. Law.* a person who makes a devise. [ME < AF *devisour* (OF *deviseur*)]

de·vi·tal·ise (dē vīt′ᵊlīz′), *v.t.,* **-ised, -is·ing.** *Chiefly Brit.* devitalize. —**de·vi′tal·i·sa′tion,** *n.*

de·vi·tal·ize (dē vīt′ᵊlīz′), *v.t.,* **-ized, -iz·ing.** to deprive of vitality or vital properties; make lifeless; weaken. —**de·vi′tal·i·za′tion,** *n.* —**Ant.** invigorate.

de·vit·ri·fy (dē vi′trə fī′), *v.t.,* **-fied, -fy·ing.** to deprive, wholly or partly, of vitreous character or properties. —**de·vit′ri·fi·ca′tion,** *n.*

de·vo·cal·ise (dē vō′kə līz′), *v.t.,* **-ised, -is·ing.** *Chiefly Brit.* devocalize. —**de·vo′cal·i·sa′tion,** *n.*

de·vo·cal·ize (dē vō′kə līz′), *v.t.,* **-ized, -iz·ing.** *Phonet.* to unvoice. —**de·vo′cal·i·za′tion,** *n.*

de·voice (dē vois′), *v.t., v.i.,* **-voiced, -voic·ing.** *Phonet.* to unvoice.

de·void (di void′), *adj.* not possessing, untouched by, void, or destitute (usually fol. by *of*): *a man devoid of humor.* [ME, orig. ptp. < OF *desvuid(ier)* (to) empty out. See DIS-¹, VOID]

de·voir (də vwär′, dev′wär; *Fr.* də VWAR′), *n., pl.* **de·voirs** (də vwärz′, dev′wärz; *Fr.* də VWAR′). **1.** an act of civility or respect. **2. devoirs,** respects or compliments. **3.** something for which one is responsible; duty. [ME *devoir, deveir, dever* < OF *devoir* (AF *deveir, dever*) < L *dēbēre* to owe; see DEBT]

dev·o·lu·tion (dev′ə lo͞o′shən), *n.* **1.** the act or fact of devolving. **2.** the passing on to a successor of an unexercised right. **3.** *Law.* the passing of property upon death, as to an heir. **4.** *Biol.* degeneration; retrograde evolution. **5.** the transfer of power or authority from a central government to a local government. [< ML *dēvolūtiōn-* (s. of *dēvolūtiō*) a rolling down = L *dēvolūt(us)* rolled down (ptp. of *dēvolvere;* see DEVOLVE) + *-iōn-* -ION]

de·volve (di volv′), *v.,* **-volved, -volv·ing.** —*v.t.* **1.** to transfer or delegate (a duty, responsibility, etc.) to or upon another; pass on. **2.** *Archaic.* to cause to roll downward. —*v.i.* **3.** to be transferred or passed on from one to another, as an obligation. **4.** *Archaic.* to roll or flow downward. [ME *devolve(n)* < L *dēvolv(ere)* (to) roll down = *dē-* DE- + *volvere* to roll] —**de·volve′ment,** *n.*

Dev·on (dev′ən), *n.* **1.** Devonshire. **2.** one of an English breed of red cattle, bred for beef and milk.

De·vo·ni·an (də vō′nē ən), *adj.* **1.** *Geol.* noting or pertaining to a period of the Paleozoic era, occurring from 350,000,000 to 400,000,000 years ago, characterized by the dominance of fishes and the advent of amphibians and ammonites. See table at **era. 2.** of or pertaining to Devonshire, England. —*n.* **3.** *Geol.* the Devonian period or system.

Dev·on·shire (dev′ən shēr′, -shər), *n.* a county in SW England. 822,906 (1961); 2612 sq. mi. *Co. seat:* Exeter. Also called **Devon.**

de·vote (di vōt′), *v.,* **-vot·ed, -vot·ing,** *adj.* —*v.t.* **1.** to give up or appropriate to or concentrate on a particular pursuit, occupation, purpose, cause, etc.: *devoting himself to science.* **2.** to appropriate by or as by a vow; set apart or dedicate by a solemn or formal act; consecrate. **3.** *Archaic.* to commit to evil or destruction; doom. —*adj.* **4.** *Archaic.* devoted. [< L *dēvōt(us)* vowed (ptp. of *dēvovēre*). See DE-, VOTE, VOW] —**Syn. 1.** assign, apply, consign.

de·vot·ed (di vō′tid), *adj.* **1.** zealous or ardent in attachment. **2.** dedicated; consecrated. **3.** *Archaic.* accursed or doomed. —**de·vot′ed·ly,** *adv.* —**de·vot′ed·ness,** *n.* —**Syn. 1.** faithful, constant, loyal, devout.

dev·o·tee (dev′ə tē′), *n.* **1.** a person devoted to or enthusiastic over something. **2.** a person who is extremely devoted to his religion.

de·vo·tion (di vō′shən), *n.* **1.** profound dedication; consecration. **2.** earnest attachment to a cause, person, etc. **3.** an assignment or appropriation to any purpose, cause, etc. **4.** *Theol.* the ready will to serve God. **5.** Often, **devotions.** *Eccles.* religious observance or worship; a form of prayer or

worship for special use. [ME *devocioun* < LL *dēvōtiōn-* (s. of *dēvōtiō*). See DEVOTE, -ION] **—Syn. 2.** zeal, ardor. See **love.**
de·vo·tion·al (di vō′shə nᵊl), *adj.* **1.** characterized by devotion; used in devotions. **—***n.* **2.** Often, **devotionals.** a short religious service, esp. as part of a meeting, convocation, or the like. **—de·vo′tion·al′i·ty, de·vo′tion·al·ness,** *n.* **—de·vo′tion·al·ly,** *adv.*
De Vo·to (də vō′tō), **Bernard (Augustine),** 1897–1955, U.S. novelist and critic.
de·vour (di vour′), *v.t.* **1.** to swallow or eat up voraciously. **2.** to consume wantonly: *Fire devoured the old museum.* **3.** to engulf or swallow up. **4.** to take in greedily with the senses or intellect. **5.** to absorb or engross wholly: *a mind devoured by fears.* [ME *devour(en)* < OF *devour(er)* < L *dēvorāre* to swallow down = *dē-* DE- + *vorāre* to eat up] **—de·vour′er,** *n.* **—de·vour′ing·ly,** *adv.*
de·vout (di vout′), *adj.* **1.** devoted to divine worship or service; pious; religious. **2.** expressing devotion or piety: *devout prayer.* **3.** earnest or sincere; hearty. [ME < OF *devo(u)t* < LL *dēvot(us),* L: devoted; see DEVOTE] **—de·vout′ly,** *adv.* **—de·vout′ness,** *n.* **—Syn. 1.** worshipful, holy, saintly. See **religious. —Ant. 1.** irreverent.
De Vries (də vrēs′; *Du.* də vʀēs′), **Hu·go** (hyo͞o′gō; *Du.* hʏ′gō), 1848–1935, Dutch botanist and student of organic heredity.
dew (do͞o, dyo͞o), *n.* **1.** moisture condensed from the atmosphere, esp. at night, and deposited in the form of small drops upon any cool surface. **2.** something like or compared to such drops of moisture, as in purity or refreshing quality. **3.** moisture in small drops on a surface, as tears or perspiration. **—***v.t.* **4.** to wet with or as with dew. [ME; OE *dēaw;* c. G *Tau,* OIcel *dögg*] **—dew′less,** *adj.*
Dew (do͞o, dyo͞o), *n.* **Bay of.** See **Sinus Roris.**
DEW (do͞o, dyo͞o), *adj.* distant early warning. Cf. **DEW line.**
De·wa·li (də wä′lē), *n.* Diwali.
de·wan (di wän′, -wôn′), *n.* (in India) any of certain officials, as a finance minister or prime minister of a native colony. Also, **diwan.** [< Hindi: minister (of state) < Pers *dēvan* register; see DIVAN]
Dew′ar ves′sel (do͞o′ər, dyo͞o′-), a container with an evacuated space between two highly reflective walls, used to keep substances at near-constant temperature; thermos. Also called **Dew′ar, Dew′ar flask′.** [named after Sir James *Dewar* (1842–1923), Scottish chemist and physicist, its inventor]
dew·ber·ry (do͞o′ber′ē, -bə rē, dyo͞o′-), *n., pl.* **-ries. 1.** (in North America) the fruit of any of several trailing blackberries of the genus *Rubus.* **2.** (in England) the fruit of a bramble, *Rubus caesius.* **3.** a plant bearing either fruit.
dew·claw (do͞o′klô′, dyo͞o′-), *n.* **1.** a functionless inner claw or digit in the foot of some dogs, not reaching the ground in walking. **2.** an analogous false hoof of deer, hogs, etc.
dew·drop (do͞o′drop′, dyo͞o′-), *n.* a drop of dew.
De Wet (*Du.* də wet′), **Chris·ti·an Ru·dolph** (*Du.* kʀis′tē än′ ʀʏ′dolf), 1854–1922, Boer general and politician.
Dew·ey (do͞o′ē, dyo͞o′ē), *n.* **1. George,** 1837–1917, U.S. admiral: defeated Spanish fleet in Manila Bay during the Spanish-American War. **2. John,** 1859–1952, U.S. philosopher and educator. **3. Mel·vil** (mel′vil), (*Melvil Louis Kossuth Dewey*), 1851–1931, U.S. educator, administrator, and innovator in library science. **4. Thomas E(dmund),** 1902–71, U.S. political leader: governor of New York 1943–55.
Dew′ey dec′imal classifica′tion, *Library Science.* a system of classifying published works using the numbers of a decimal system, devised by Melvil Dewey in 1876. Also called **Dew′ey dec′imal sys′tem.**
dew·fall (do͞o′fôl′, dyo͞o′fôl′), *n.* **1.** formation of dew. **2.** the time at which dew begins to form.
De·wi (dā′wē), *n.* **Saint.** See **David, Saint.**
De Witt (də wit′), **Jan** (yän), 1625–72, Dutch statesman.
dew·lap (do͞o′lap′, dyo͞o′-), *n.* **1.** a pendulous fold of skin under the throat of a bovine animal. **2.** any similar part, as the loose skin under the throat of some dogs or the wattle of fowls. [ME *dew(e)lappe; -lappe,* OE *læppa* pendulous piece; *dew(e)-* prob. akin to DEW]
DEW′ line′, a 3000-mile-long network of radar stations north of the Arctic Circle, maintained by the U.S. and Canada for providing advance warning of the approach of hostile planes, missiles, etc.
dew′ point′, the temperature to which air must be cooled for dew to form. Also called **dew′-point tem′perature.** Cf. **absolute humidity, relative humidity.**
dew·y (do͞o′ē, dyo͞o′ē), *adj.* **dew·i·er, dew·i·est. 1.** moist with or as with dew. **2.** having the quality of dew: *dewy tears.* **3.** *Literary.* falling gently or refreshing like dew: *dewy sleep.* **4.** of dew. **—dew′i·ly,** *adv.* **—dew′i·ness,** *n.*
dew·y-eyed (do͞o′ē īd′, dyo͞o′-), *adj.* romantically naïve or credulous; innocent and trusting.
Dex·a·myl (dek′sə mil), *n. Pharm., Trademark.* a mixture of dextroamphetamine and amobarbital that curbs the appetite and raises the spirits, used in the treatment of obesity and mental depression.
Dex·e·drine (dek′si drēn′, -drin), *n. Pharm., Trademark.* dextroamphetamine.
dex·ter (dek′stər), *adj.* **1.** on the right side; right. **2.** *Heraldry.* noting the side of an escutcheon or achievement of arms to the right of the bearer and to the left of the spectator (opposed to *sinister*). **3.** *Obs.* favorable. [< L: right, favorable; c. Gk *dexiós*]
dex·ter·i·ty (dek ster′i tē), *n.* **1.** skill or adroitness in using the hands or body; agility. **2.** mental adroitness or skill. **3.** right-handedness. [< L *dexteritās* readiness]
dex·ter·ous (dek′strəs, -stər əs), *adj.* **1.** skillful or adroit in the use of the hands or body. **2.** having mental adroitness or skill; clever. **3.** done with dexterity. **4.** right-handed. Also, **dextrous.** [< L *dexter* right, skillful + -OUS] **—dex′ter·ous·ly,** *adv.* **—dex′ter·ous·ness,** *n.* **—Syn. 1.** deft, nimble, handy. **—Ant. 1.** clumsy. **2.** inept.
dextr-, var. of **dextro-** before a vowel: *dextral.*
dex·tral (dek′strəl), *adj.* **1.** of, pertaining to, or on the right side; right (opposed to *sinistral*). **2.** right-handed. **3.** *Zool.* (of certain gastropod shells) coiling from left to right, as seen from the apex. **—dex·tral′i·ty,** *n.* **—dex′tral·ly,** *adv.*
dex·trin (dek′strin), *n.* a gummy, dextrorotatory substance formed from starch, used chiefly as a thickening agent and a mucilage, and as a substitute for gum arabic and other natural substances. Also, **dex·trine** (dek′strin, -strēn). Also called **British gum.** [< F *dextrine*]
dex·tro (dek′strō), *adj. Chem.* dextrorotatory.
dextro-, 1. a learned borrowing from Latin meaning "right," used in the formation of compound words: *dextrogyrate.* **2.** *Chem.* a word element meaning "turning clockwise": *dextroglucose.* Also, *esp. before a vowel,* **dextr-.** [< L, comb. form of *dexter*]
dex·tro·am·pheta·mine (dek′strō am fet′ə mēn′, -min), *n. Pharm.* a solid, $C_6H_5CH_2CH(NH_2)CH_3$, that stimulates the central nervous system, used chiefly to lift the mood and to control the appetite.
dex·tro·glu·cose (dek′strō glo͞o′kōs), *n. Chem.* See under **glucose** (def. 1).
dex·tro·gy·rate (dek′strō jī′rit, -rāt), *adj. Optics, Crystall.* dextrorotatory. Also, **dex·tro·gyre** (dek′strō jīᵊr′).
dex·tro·ro·ta·tion (dek′strō rō tā′shən), *n. Optics, Crystall.* a turning to the right of the plane of polarization.

dex·tro·ro·ta·to·ry (dek′strō rō′tə tôr′ē, -tōr′ē), *adj. Optics, Chem., Crystall.* turning to the right, as the rotation to the right of the plane of polarization of light in certain crystals and the like; dextrogyrate. Cf. **levorotatory.**
dex·trorse (dek′strôrs, dek strôrs′), *adj. Bot.* (of a climbing plant) rising helically from right to left, as seen from outside the helix (opposed to *sinistrorse*). Also, **dextror′sal.** [< L *dextrors(um)* toward the right, contr. of *dextro-* DEXTRO- + *vors(us)* turned (ptp. of *vortere,* var. of *vertere*) + *-um* adv. suffix] **—dex′trorse·ly,** *adv.*

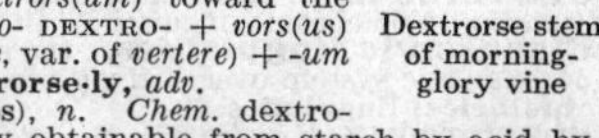

Dextrorse stem of morning-glory vine

dex·trose (dek′strōs), *n. Chem.* dextroglucose, commercially obtainable from starch by acid hydrolysis. Also called **corn sugar, grape sugar.** Cf. **glucose** (def. 1).
dex·trous (dek′strəs), *adj.* dexterous.
dey (dā), *n.* (formerly) a title of a governor or ruler in North Africa. [< F < Turk *dayi,* orig. maternal uncle]
Dezh·nev (dezh nyôf′), *n.* **Cape,** a cape in the NE Soviet Union in Asia, on the Bering Strait: the northeasternmost point of Asia. Also called **East Cape.**
D.F.C., See **Distinguished Flying Cross.**
dg, decigram; decigrams.
d-glu·cose (dē′glo͞o′kōs), *n.* See **glucose** (def. 1).
DH., (in Morocco) dirham; dirhams.
dh, *Baseball.* See **designated hitter.**
Dhah·ran (dä rän′), *n.* a city in E Saudi Arabia: oil center. 12,500 (est. 1962).
dhar·ma (där′mə, dur′-), *n. Hinduism, Buddhism.* **1.** essential quality or character, as of the cosmos or one's own nature. **2.** conformity to religious law, custom, duty, or one's own quality or character. **3.** virtue. **4.** religion. **5.** law, esp. religious law. [< Skt: decree, custom, akin to *dhārāyati* he holds]
dhar·na (där′nə, dur′-), *n.* (in India) the practice of exacting justice or compliance with a just demand by sitting and fasting at the doorstep of an offender. Also, **dhurna.** [< Hindi: placing]
Dhau·la·gi·ri (dou′lə gēr′ē), *n.* a mountain in W central Nepal: a peak of the Himalayas. 26,826 ft.
dhole (dōl), *n.* a fierce, wild dog, *Cuon rutilus,* of India, that hunts in packs which attack large game. [?]
dhoo·ly (do͞o′lē), *n., pl.* **-lies.** dooly.
dho·ti (dō′tē), *n., pl.* **-tis. 1.** a loincloth worn by Hindu men in India. **2.** the cotton fabric of which it is made. Also, **dhoo·ti, dhoo·tie, dhu·ti** (do͞o′tē). [< Hindi]
dhow (dou), *n.* any of various types of sailing vessels used by Arabs on the east African, the Arabian, and the Indian coasts, generally lateen-rigged on two or three masts. [< Ar *dāwa*]

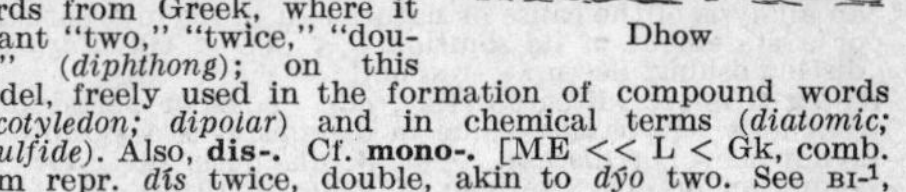

Dhow

dhur·na (dur′nə), *n.* dharna.
DI, 1. Department of the Interior. **2.** drill instructor.
Di, *Chem.* didymium.
di-[1], a prefix occurring in loan words from Greek, where it meant "two," "twice," "double" (*diphthong*); on this model, freely used in the formation of compound words (*dicotyledon; dipolar*) and in chemical terms (*diatomic; disulfide*). Also, **dis-.** Cf. **mono-.** [ME << L < Gk, comb. form repr. *dís* twice, double, akin to *dýo* two. See BI-[1], TWI-]
di-[2], var. of **dis-**[1] before *b, d, l, m, n, r, s, v,* and sometimes *g* and *j: digest; divide.*
di-[3], var. of **dia-** before a vowel: *diorama.*
di., diameter. Also, **dia.**
dia-, a prefix occurring in loan words from Greek (*diabetes; dialect*) and used, in the formation of compound words, to mean "passing through" (*diathermy*), "thoroughly," "completely" (*diagnosis*), "going apart" (*dialysis*), and "opposed in moment" (*diamagnetism*). Also, **di-.** [< Gk, comb. form repr. *diá* (prep.) through, between, across, by, of, akin to *dýo* two and *di-* DI-[1]]
di·a·base (dī′ə bās′), *n.* **1.** *U.S.* a dark igneous rock occurring as minor intrusive rocks composed essentially of labradorite and pyroxene. **2.** *Brit.* a dark igneous rock consisting

essentially of augite and feldspar. 3. *Obs.* diorite. [< F = *dia-* (error for *di-* two) + *base* BASE[1]] —**di′a·ba′sic,** *adj.*

di·a·be·tes (dī′ə bē′tis, -tēz), *n.* *Pathol.* 1. Also called **diabe′tes mel·li′tus** (mə lī′təs). a disease that impairs the ability of the body to use sugar and causes sugar to appear abnormally in the urine. 2. Also called **diabe′tes in·sip′i·dus** (in sip′i dəs). a disease in which there is a persistent, abnormal amount of urine. [< NL, L < Gk: lit., a passer through = *diabē-* (var. s. of *diabaínein* = *dia-* DIA- + *baínein* to pass) + *-tēs* agent suffix]

di·a·bet·ic (dī′ə bet′ik), *adj.* 1. of, pertaining to, or for diabetes or persons having diabetes. 2. having or resulting from diabetes. —*n.* 3. a person who has diabetes. [< L *diabētic(us)*]

di·a·ble·rie (dē ä′blə rē; *Fr.* dyᴀ blə ʀē′), *n., pl.* **-ries** (-rēz; *Fr.* -ʀē′). 1. diabolic magic or art; sorcery; witchcraft. 2. the domain or realm of devils. 3. the lore of devils; demonology. 4. reckless mischief; deviltry; diabolism. [< F, OF = *diable* DEVIL + *-erie* -ERY]

di·a·ble·ry (dē ä′blə rē), *n., pl.* **-ries.** diablerie.

di·a·bol·ic (dī′ə bol′ik), *adj.* 1. having the qualities of a devil; fiendish; outrageously wicked: *a diabolic plot.* 2. pertaining to or actuated by the devil or a devil. Also, **di′a·bol′i·cal.** [ME *diabolik* < LL *diabolic(us)* < Gk *diabolikós.* See DEVIL, -IC] —**di′a·bol′i·cal·ly,** *adv.* —**di′a·bol′i·cal·ness,** *n.*

di·ab·o·lise (dī ab′ə līz′), *v.t.,* **-lised, -lis·ing.** *Chiefly Brit.* diabolize.

di·ab·o·lism (dī ab′ə liz′əm), *n.* 1. *Theol.* **a.** action aided or caused by the devil; sorcery; witchcraft. **b.** the character or condition of a devil. **c.** a belief in or worship of devils. 2. action befitting the devil; deviltry. [< Gk *diábol(os)* DEVIL + -ISM] —**di·ab′o·list,** *n.*

di·ab·o·lize (dī ab′ə līz′), *v.t.,* **-lized, -liz·ing.** 1. to make diabolical. 2. to represent as diabolical. 3. to subject to diabolical influences. Also, *esp. Brit.,* **diabolise.** [< Gk *diábol(os)* DEVIL + -IZE]

di·a·ce·tyl (dī′ə sēt′^{ə}l, -as′i t^{ə}l), *n.* *Chem.* biacetyl.

di·a·chron·ic (dī′ə kron′ik), *adj.* *Linguistics.* of or pertaining to diachronic linguistics. Cf. **synchronic.**

diachron′ic linguis′tics, the study of the changes in a linguistic system over a given period of time. Also called **historical linguistics.**

di·ach·ro·ny (dī ak′rə nē), *n., pl.* **-nies.** 1. *Linguistics.* change or development in a linguistic system over a period of time. 2. historical change. [DIACHRON(IC) + -Y[3]]

di·ac·id (dī as′id), *adj.* *Chem.* 1. capable of combining with two molecules of a monobasic acid. 2. (of an acid or a salt) having two replaceable hydrogen atoms.

di·ac·o·nal (dī ak′ə n^{ə}l), *adj.* pertaining to a deacon; decanal. [< LL *diāconāl(is)*]

di·ac·o·nate (dī ak′ə nit, -nāt′), *n.* 1. the office or dignity of a deacon. 2. a body of deacons. [< LL *diāconāt(us)*]

di·a·crit·ic (dī′ə krit′ik), *n.* 1. Also called **diacrit′ical mark′.** a mark, point, or sign added or attached to a letter or character to distinguish it from another of similar form, to give it a particular phonetic value, to indicate stress, etc., as a cedilla, tilde, circumflex, or macron. —*adj.* 2. diacritical. 3. *Med.* diagnostic. [< Gk *diakritik(ós)* distinctive]

di·a·crit·i·cal (dī′ə krit′i kəl), *adj.* 1. serving to distinguish; distinctive. 2. capable of distinguishing. 3. *Phonet.* serving as a diacritic. —**di′a·crit′i·cal·ly,** *adv.*

di·ac·tin·ic (dī′ak tin′ik), *adj.* *Physics.* capable of transmitting actinic rays. —**di·ac′tin·ism,** *n.*

di·a·del·phous (dī′ə del′fəs), *adj.* *Bot.* 1. (of stamens) united into two sets by their filaments. 2. (of plants) having the stamens so united.

di·a·dem (dī′ə dem′), *n.* 1. a crown. 2. a cloth headband worn as a symbol of power. 3. royal dignity or authority. —*v.t.* 4. to adorn with or as if with a diadem; crown. [ME *diademe* < L *diadēma* < Gk *diádēma* fillet, band = *diadē-* (verbid s. of *diadeîn* to bind round) + *-ma* n. suffix]

di·ad·ro·mous (dī ad′rə məs), *adj.* 1. *Bot.* (of a leaf) having a fanlike venation. 2. (of fish) migrating between fresh and salt waters. Cf. **anadromous, catadromous.**

di·aer·e·sis (dī er′i sis), *n., pl.* **-ses** (-sēz′). dieresis. —**di·ae·ret·ic** (dī′ə ret′ik), *adj.*

diag. diagram.

Dia·ghi·lev (dyä′gi lef′), *n.* **Ser·gei Pa·vlo·vich** (sᴇʀ gā′ pä vlô′vich), 1872–1929, Russian ballet producer.

di·ag·nose (dī′əg nōs′, -nōz′, dī′əg nōs′, -nōz′), *v.,* **-nosed, -nos·ing.** —*v.t.* 1. to determine the identity of (an illness) by a medical examination. 2. to classify or determine on the basis of scientific examination. 3. to ascertain or analyze the cause or nature of (a problem or situation). —*v.i.* 4. to make a diagnosis. [back formation from DIAGNOSIS] —**di′ag·nos′a·ble,** *adj.*

di·ag·no·sis (dī′əg nō′sis), *n., pl.* **-ses** (-sēz). 1. *Med.* **a.** the process of determining by examination the nature and circumstances of a diseased condition. **b.** the decision reached from such an examination. 2. *Biol.* scientific determination; a description that classifies precisely. 3. an analysis of the cause or nature of a problem or situation, or a statement of its solution. [< NL < Gk *diágnōsis* a distinguishing. See DIA-, -GNOSIS]

di·ag·nos·tic (dī′əg nos′tik), *adj.* 1. of or pertaining to diagnosis. 2. having value in diagnosis, as a symptom or syndrome of a disease. —*n.* 3. diagnosis (def. 1). 4. a symptom or characteristic of value in diagnosis. [< Gk *diagnōstik(ós)* = *diagnōs-* (see DIAGNOSIS) + *-tikos* -TIC] —**di′ag·nos′ti·cal·ly,** *adv.*

di·ag·nos·ti·cian (dī′əg no stish′ən), *n.* an expert in making diagnoses.

di·ag·nos·tics (dī′əg nos′tiks), *n.* (*construed as sing.*) the art or science of diagnosis.

di·ag·o·nal (dī ag′ə n^{ə}l), *adj.* 1. *Math.* **a.** connecting two nonadjacent angles or vertices of a polygon or polyhedron, as a straight line. **b.** extending from one edge of a solid figure to an opposite edge, as a plane. 2. having an oblique direction. 3. having oblique lines, ridges, markings, etc. —*n.* 4. something that is diagonal. 5. virgule. 6. *Math.* a set of entries in a square matrix running either from upper left to lower right or lower left to upper right. 7. *Chess.* one of the oblique lines of squares on a chessboard. [< L *diagonāl(is)* < Gk *diagṓn(ios)* from angle to angle (see DIA-, -GON) + L *-ālis* -AL[1]] —**di·ag′o·nal·ly,** *adv.*

di·a·gram (dī′ə gram′), *n., v.,* **-gramed, -gram·ing** or (*esp. Brit.*) **-grammed, -gram·ming.** —*n.* 1. a drawn figure illustrating a geometrical theorem, mathematical demonstration, etc. 2. a drawing or plan that outlines and explains the parts, operation, etc., of something. 3. a chart, plan, or scheme. —*v.t.* 4. to represent by a diagram; make a diagram of. [< L *diagram(ma)* < Gk: that which is marked out by lines. See DIA-, -GRAM[1]]

di·a·gram·mat·ic (dī′ə grə mat′ik), *adj.* 1. in the form of a diagram. 2. pertaining to diagrams. Also, **di′a·gram·mat′i·cal.** [DIAGRAM + *-atic* as in *problem, problematic*] —**di′a·gram·mat′i·cal·ly,** *adv.*

di·a·graph (dī′ə graf′, -gräf′), *n.* 1. a device for drawing, used in reproducing outlines, plans, etc., mechanically on any desired scale. 2. a combined protractor and scale. [< F *diagraphe* < Gk *diagráph(ein)* (to) draw. See DIA-, -GRAPH]

di·a·ki·ne·sis (dī′ə ki nē′sis, -kī-), *n.* *Biol.* the last stage in prophase, prior to the dissolution of the nuclear membrane. [< NL = *dia-* DIA- + Gk *kínēsis* movement = *kin(ein)* (to) move + *-ē-* thematic vowel + *-sis* -SIS]

di·al (dī′əl, dīl), *n., v.,* **di·aled, di·al·ing** or (*esp. Brit.*) **di·alled, di·al·ling.** —*n.* 1. a graduated plate, disk, or face upon which time is indicated by pointers or shadows, as of a clock or sundial. 2. a plate or disk with graduations or figures for indicating some measurement or number, usually by means of a pointer. 3. a rotatable plate or disk having a knob used for regulating a mechanism, making and breaking electrical connections, etc. 4. a rotatable plate or disk on a telephone, fitted with finger holes marked with letters and numbers, used in making calls through an automatic switchboard. —*v.t.* 5. to indicate or register on or as on a dial. 6. to regulate, select, or tune to by means of a dial, as on a radio. 7. to work the dial of a telephone in order to call (another telephone, person, etc.). —*v.i.* 8. to use a telephone dial. 9. to tune in or regulate by means of a dial. [ME < ML *diāl(is)* daily (L *di(ēs)* day + *-ālis* -AL[1])] —**di′al·er;** *esp. Brit.,* **di′al·ler,** *n.*

dial., 1. dialect. 2. dialectal.

di·a·lect (dī′ə lekt′), *n.* 1. *Linguistics.* a variety of a language that is distinguished from other varieties of the same language by features of phonology, grammar, and vocabulary, and by its use by a group of speakers who are set off from others geographically or socially. 2. a variety of a language that differs from the standard language, esp. when considered a substandard. 3. a language considered as one of a group that have a common ancestor: *Persian, Latin, and English are Indo-European dialects.* 4. jargon or cant. [< L *dialect(us)* < Gk *diálekt(os)* discourse, language, dialect, = *dialég(esthai)* (to) converse (*dia-* DIA- + *lég(ein)* (to) speak) + *-t(os)* ptp. suffix] —**di′a·lec′tal,** *adj.* —**di′a·lec′tal·ly,** *adv.* —**Syn. 2.** idiom, patois. See **language.**

di′alect at′las, *Linguistics.* a collection of maps indicating the distribution of various phonological, morphological, lexical, or other features of the dialects of a specified area.

di′alect geog′raphy, *Linguistics.* the study of regional dialect variation. —**di′alect geog′rapher.**

di·a·lec·tic (dī′ə lek′tik), *adj.* Also, **dialectical.** 1. of, pertaining to, or of the nature of logical argumentation. 2. dialectal. —*n.* 3. the art or practice of logical discussion, as of the truth of a theory or opinion. 4. logical argumentation. 5. Often, **dialectics.** logic or any of its branches. 6. See **Hegelian dialectic.** 7. **dialectics,** (*often construed as sing.*) the arguments or bases of dialectical materialism, including the elevation of matter over mind and a constantly changing reality with a material basis. [< L *dialectic(a)* < Gk *dialektikḗ* (*téchnē*) argumentative (art), fem. of *dialektikós*] —**di′a·lec′ti·cal·ly,** *adv.*

di·a·lec·ti·cal (dī′ə lek′ti kəl), *adj.* 1. dialectic. 2. dialectal.

dialec′tical mate′rialism, a form of materialism, developed chiefly by Karl Marx, noted especially for the application of the Hegelian dialectic in its philosophy of history. —**dialec′tical mate′rialist.**

di·a·lec·ti·cian (dī′ə lek tish′ən), *n.* 1. a person skilled in dialectic; logician. 2. a dialectologist. [alter. of F *dialecticien*]

di·a·lec·ti·cism (dī′ə lek′ti siz′əm), *n.* 1. dialectal speech or influence. 2. a dialectal word or expression.

di·a·lec·tol·o·gy (dī′ə lek tol′ə jē), *n., pl.* **-gies** for 2. 1. *Linguistics.* the study dealing with dialects and dialect features. 2. the linguistic features of a dialect. —**di·a·lec·to·log·ic** (dī′ə lek′t^{ə}loj′ik), **di′a·lec′to·log′i·cal,** *adj.* —**di′a·lec′to·log′i·cal·ly,** *adv.* —**di′a·lec·tol′o·gist,** *n.*

di·al′lyl sul′fide (dī al′il), *Chem.* See **allyl sulfide.** [DI-[1] + ALLYL]

di·a·log·ic (dī′ə loj′ik), *adj.* 1. of, pertaining to, or characterized by dialogue. 2. participating in dialogue. Also, **di′a·log′i·cal.** [< ML *dialogic(us)* < Gk *dialogikós.* See DIALOGUE, -IC] —**di′a·log′i·cal·ly,** *adv.*

di·al·o·gise (dī al′ə jīz′), *v.i.,* **-gised, -gis·ing.** *Chiefly Brit.* dialogize.

di·al·o·gism (dī al′ə jiz′əm), *n.* the discussion of a subject in an imaginary dialogue. [< LL *dialogism(os)* < Gk *dialogismós* a consideration]

di·al·o·gist (dī al′ə jist), *n.* 1. a speaker in a dialogue. 2. a writer of dialogue. [< LL *dialogist(a)* < Gk *dialogist(ḗs)*] —**di·a·lo·gis·tic** (dī′ə lō jis′tik), *adj.*

di·al·o·gize (dī al′ə jīz′), *v.i.,* **-gized, -giz·ing.** to carry on a dialogue. Also, *esp. Brit.,* **dialogise.** [< Gk *dialogíz(esthai)* (to) converse]

di·a·logue (dī′ə lôg′, -log′), *n., v.,* **-logued, -logu·ing.** —*n.* 1. conversation between two or more persons or between characters in a novel, drama, etc. 2. an exchange of ideas, esp. on a political issue, with a view to reaching an amicable agreement. 3. a literary work in the form of a conversation: *a dialogue of Plato.* —*v.i.* 4. to converse. —*v.t.* 5. to put into the form of a dialogue. Also, **di′a·log′.** [ME *dialoge* < OF < L *dialog(us)* < Gk *diálogos*] —**di′a·logu′er,** *n.*

di′al tone′, (in a dial or push-button telephone) a steady humming sound which indicates that the line is ready for dialing.

di·a·lyse (dī′ə līz′), *v.t., v.i.,* **-lysed, -lys·ing.** *Chiefly Brit.* dialyze. —**di′a·lys′a·bil′i·ty,** *n.* —**di′a·lys′a·ble,** *adj.* —**di′a·ly·sa′tion,** *n.*

di·al·y·sis (dī al′i sis), *n., pl.* **-ses** (-sēz′). *Physical Chem.,*

Physiol. the separation of crystalloids from colloids in a solution by diffusion through a membrane. [< LL < Gk: a separation] —**di·a·lyt·ic** (dī′ə lit′ik), *adj.* —**di′a·lyt′i·cal·ly,** *adv.*

di·a·lyze (dī′ə līz′), *v.*, **-lyzed, -lyz·ing.** *Physical Chem., Physiol.* —*v.t.* **1.** to subject to dialysis; separate or procure by dialysis. —*v.i.* **2.** to undergo dialysis. Also, *esp. Brit.*, **dialyse.** —**di′a·lyz′a·bil′i·ty,** *n.* —**di′a·lyz′a·ble,** *adj.* —**di′a·ly·za′tion,** *n.*

di·a·lyz·er (dī′ə lī′zər), *n.* **1.** Also, **di·al·y·za·tor** (dī al′i-zā′tər). *Physical Chem.* an apparatus containing a semipermeable membrane for dialysis. **2.** *Med.* an apparatus substituted for the kidney to filter waste products from the blood artificially. Also, *esp. Brit.*, **di′a·lys′er.**

diam., diameter.

di·a·mag·net (dī′ə mag′nit), *n.* *Physics.* a diamagnetic substance. [back formation from DIAMAGNETIC]

di·a·mag·net·ic (dī′ə mag net′ik), *adj.* *Physics.* noting or pertaining to a class of substances, as bismuth and copper, whose permeability is less than that of a vacuum: in a magnetic field, their induced magnetism is in a direction opposite to that of iron. Cf. **antiferromagnetic, ferromagnetic, paramagnetic.** —**di′a·mag·net′i·cal·ly,** *adv.* —**di·a·mag·net·ism** (dī′ə mag′ni tiz′əm), *n.*

di·am·e·ter (dī am′i tər), *n.* **1.** *Geom.* **a.** a straight line passing through the center of a circle or sphere and meeting at each end the circumference or surface. **b.** a straight line passing from side to side of any figure or body, through its center. **2.** the length of such a line. **3.** the width of a circular or cylindrical object. [ME *diametre* < ML *diametrus,* L *diametros* < Gk: diagonal, diameter. See DIA-, METER[1]]

di·am·e·tral (dī am′i trəl), *adj.* **1.** of a diameter. **2.** forming a diameter. [ME < ML *diametrāl(is)* < L *diametr(os)* DIAMETER + *-ālis* -AL[1]] —**di·am′e·tral·ly,** *adv.*

di·a·met·ri·cal (dī′ə me′tri kəl), *adj.* **1.** of, pertaining to, or along a diameter. **2.** direct; complete; absolute: *diametrical opposites.* Also, **di′a·met′ric.** [< Gk *diametrik(ós)* (see DIAMETER, -IC) + -AL[1]] —**di′a·met′ri·cal·ly,** *adv.*

di·am·ine (dī′ə mēn′, -min, dī′ə mēn′), *n.* *Chem.* a compound containing two amino groups.

dia·mond (dī′mənd, dī′ə-), *n.* **1.** a pure or nearly pure form of carbon, naturally crystallized in the isometric system, of extreme hardness. **2.** a piece of this stone, esp. when cut and polished and valued as a precious gem or when used in a drill or cutting tool. **3.** a ring or other piece of jewelry containing such a precious stone. **4.** a tool provided with such a stone, used for cutting glass. **5.** crystallized carbon, or a piece of it, artificially produced. **6.** *Geom.* an equilateral quadrilateral, esp. as placed with its diagonals vertical and horizontal; a lozenge or rhombus. **7.** a red lozenge-shaped figure on a playing card. **8.** a card of the suit bearing such figures. **9.** **diamonds,** (*construed as sing. or pl.*) the suit so marked. **10.** *Baseball.* **a.** the space enclosed by home plate and the three bases; infield. **b.** the entire playing field. **11.** *Print.* a 4½-point type of a size between brilliant and pearl. —*adj.* **12.** made of or set with a diamond or diamonds: *a diamond ring; a diamond necklace.* **13.** having the shape of a diamond: *a dress with a diamond print.* **14.** indicating the 75th, or sometimes the 60th, event of a series, as of a wedding anniversary. —*v.t.* **15.** to adorn with or as with diamonds. [ME *diamaunde* < MF *diamande,* var. of *diamant* < ML *diamant-* (s. of *diamas*), alter. of L *adamas* ADAMANT, diamond] —**dia′mond·like′,** *adj.*

Diamond (def. 6)

Dia·mond (dī′mənd, dī′ə-), *n.* **Cape,** a hill in Canada, in S Quebec, on the St. Lawrence River.

dia·mond·back (dī′mənd bak′, dī′ə-), *n.* **1.** See **diamondback rattlesnake. 2.** See **diamondback terrapin.**

dia′mondback rat′tlesnake, any of several large, highly venomous rattlesnakes having diamond-shaped markings on the back.

dia′mondback ter′rapin, any of several edible turtles of the genus *Malaclemys,* found in tidewaters of the eastern and southern U.S., having diamond-shaped markings on the back.

Dia′mond Head′, a promontory on SE Oahu Island, in central Hawaii. 761 ft. high.

dia′mond ring′ effect′, *Astron.* a phenomenon, sometimes observed immediately before and after a total eclipse, in which one of Baily's beads is much brighter than the others, resembling a diamond ring around the moon.

Dia′mond State′, Delaware (used as a nickname).

Di·an·a (dī an′ə), *n.* **1.** (*Princess of Wales*) (*Lady Diana Spencer*), born 1961, wife of Charles, Prince of Wales. **2.** an ancient Roman deity, goddess of the moon and of hunting, and protectress of women, identified by the Romans with the Greek Artemis. **3.** the moon personified as a goddess.

Diana

di·an·drous (dī an′drəs), *adj.* *Bot.* **1.** (of a flower) having two stamens. **2.** (of a plant) having flowers with two stamens. [< NL *diandrus*]

di·a·no·et·ic (dī′ə nō et′ik), *adj.* pertaining to thought or reasoning, esp. discursive reasoning. [< Gk *dianoētik(ós)* = *diánoi(a)* the intellect, a thought, belief (*dia-* DIA- + *nó(ein)* (to) think + *-ia* -IA) + *-ē-* thematic vowel + *-tikos* -TIC]

di·an·thus (dī an′thəs), *n.*, *pl.* **-thus·es.** any caryophyllaceous plant of the genus *Dianthus,* as the carnation or sweet william. [< NL < Gk *Di(ós)* of Zeus (gen. of *Zeús*) + *ánthos* flower]

di·a·pa·son (dī′ə pā′zən, -sən), *n.* *Music.* **1.** a full, rich outpouring of melodious sound. **2.** the compass of a voice or instrument. **3.** a fixed standard of pitch. **4.** either of two principal timbres or stops of a pipe organ, one of full, majestic tone **(open diapason)** and the other of a lighter, more flutelike tone **(stopped diapason). 5.** any of several other organ stops. **6.** a tuning fork. [< L: the whole octave < Gk *diā pasôn* (*chordôn*) through all (the notes), short for *hē diā pasôn chordôn symphōnía* the concord through all the notes of the scale] —**di′a·pa′son·al,** *adj.*

di·a·pause (dī′ə pôz′), *Zool.* —*n.* **1.** a period of quiescence between periods of growth or reproductive activity, as in arthropods or adult annelids. —*v.i.* **2.** to undergo diapause. [< Gk *diápausis*]

dia·per (dī′pər, dī′ə pər), *n.* **1.** a piece of cloth or other absorbent material that forms part of a baby's underclothing; a baby's breechcloth. **2.** a linen or cotton fabric with a woven pattern of small, constantly repeated figures, as diamonds. **3.** Also called **dia′per pat′tern.** such a pattern, originally used in the Middle Ages in weaving silk and gold. —*v.t.* **4.** to put a diaper on (a baby). **5.** to ornament with a diaperlike pattern. [ME *diapre* < MF, var. of *diaspre* < ML *diaspr(us)* made of diaper < MGk *díaspros* pure white = *dia-* DIA- + *áspros* white]

di·aph·a·nous (dī af′ə nəs), *adj.* **1.** very sheer and light; almost completely transparent or translucent. **2.** delicately hazy. [< ML *diaphanus* < Gk *diaphanḗs* transparent = *diaphan-* (s. of *diaphaínein* to show through; see DIA-, -PHANE) + L *-us* -OUS] —**di·aph′a·nous·ly,** *adv.* —**di·aph·a·ne·i·ty** (dī af′ə nē′i tē, dī′ə fə-), **di·aph′a·nous·ness,** *n.*

di·a·phone (dī′ə fōn′), *n.* a foghorn producing a low-pitched, two-toned signal.

di·a·pho·re·sis (dī′ə fə rē′sis), *n.* *Med.* perspiration, esp. when artificially induced. [< LL < Gk: a sweating = *diaphorē-* (verbid s. of *diaphoreîn* to carry off or through) + *-sis* -SIS]

di·a·pho·ret·ic (dī′ə fə ret′ik), *Med.* —*adj.* **1.** producing perspiration. —*n.* **2.** a diaphoretic medicine. [< LL *diaphorētic(us)* < Gk *diaphorētikós* promoting perspiration]

di·a·phragm (dī′ə fram′), *n.* **1.** *Anat.* **a.** a muscular, membranous or ligamentous wall separating two cavities or limiting a cavity. **b.** the partition separating the thoracic cavity from the abdominal cavity in mammals. **2.** *Physical Chem.* **a.** a porous plate separating two liquids, as in a galvanic cell. **b.** a semipermeable membrane. **3.** a thin disk that vibrates when receiving or producing sound waves, as in a telephone, microphone, or the like. **4.** Also called **pessary.** a contraceptive device, usually of rubber, that fits over the uterine cervix. **5.** *Optics.* a ring or a plate with a hole in the center that is placed on the axis of an optical instrument, as a camera, and that controls the amount of light entering the instrument. **6.** a plate or web for stiffening metal-framed constructions. —*v.t.* **7.** to furnish with a diaphragm. [< LL *diaphragm(a)* < Gk *diáphragma* the diaphragm, midriff = *dia-* DIA- + *phrágma* a fence]

di·a·phrag·mat·ic (dī′ə frag mat′ik), *adj.* **1.** of the diaphragm. **2.** like a diaphragm. [< Gk *diaphragmat-* (s. of *diáphragma* DIAPHRAGM) + -IC] —**di′a·phrag·mat′i·cal·ly,** *adv.*

di·aph·y·sis (dī af′i sis), *n.*, *pl.* **-ses** (-sēz′). *Anat.* the shaft of a long bone. [< NL < Gk = *diaphý(esthai)* (to) grow between + *-sis* -SIS] —**di·a·phys·i·al** (dī′ə fiz′ē əl), *adj.*

di·a·poph·y·sis (dī′ə pof′i sis), *n.*, *pl.* **-ses** (-sēz′). *Anat., Zool.* the upper part of the transverse process of a vertebra. [< NL; see DI-[3], APOPHYSIS] —**di·ap·o·phys·i·al** (dī′ap ə-fiz′ē əl), *adj.*

Di·ar·bek·r (dē är bek′ər), *n.* Diyarbekir.

di·ar·chy (dī′är kē), *n.*, *pl.* **-chies.** a government in which power is vested in two rulers. Also, **dyarchy.** —**di·ar′chi·al, di·ar′chic,** *adj.*

di·ar·rhe·a (dī′ə rē′ə), *n.* *Pathol.* an intestinal disorder characterized by abnormal frequency and fluidity of fecal evacuations. Also, **di′ar·rhoe′a.** [< LL *diarrhoea* < Gk *diárrhoia* a flowing through = *diarrho-* (var. s. of *diarrheîn* to flow through) + *-ia* -IA] —**di′ar·rhe′al, di′ar·rhe′ic, di·ar·rhet·ic** (dī′ə ret′ik), *adj.*

di·ar·thro·sis (dī′är thrō′sis), *n.*, *pl.* **-ses** (-sēz). *Anat.* a form of articulation that permits maximal motion, as the knee joint. [< NL = *di-* DI-[3] + Gk *árthrōsis;* see ARTHRO-, -SIS] —**di·ar·thro·di·al** (dī′är thrō′dē əl), *adj.*

di·a·ry (dī′ə rē), *n.*, *pl.* **-ries. 1.** a daily record, esp. of the writer's own experiences, observations, attitudes, etc. **2.** a book for keeping such a record. [< L *diāri(um)* daily allowance, journal = *di(ēs)* day + *-ārium* -ARY] —**di′a·rist,** *n.*

Di·as (dē′əs; *Port.* dē′əsh), *n.* **Bar·tho·lo·me·u** (bär′to͞o-lo͞o me′o͞o), c1450–1500, Portuguese navigator and discoverer of the Cape of Good Hope. Also, **Diaz.**

Di·as·po·ra (dī as′pər ə), *n.* **1.** the scattering of the Jews to countries outside of Palestine after the Babylonian captivity. **2.** the body of Jews living in such countries. **3.** such countries collectively. [< Gk: dispersion. See DIA-, SPORE]

di·a·spore (dī′ə spōr′, -spôr′), *n.* a mineral, aluminum hydroxide, $HAlO_2$. [< Gk *diasporá;* see DIASPORA]

di·a·stal·sis (dī′ə stal′sis, -stôl′-), *n.*, *pl.* **-ses** (-sēz). *Physiol.* the downward wave of contraction of the alimentary canal that forms part of peristalsis. [< NL = Gk *dia-* DIA- + *stálsis* contraction; see PERISTALSIS]

di·a·stase (dī′ə stās′), *n.* *Biochem.* an enzyme that converts starch into dextrin and maltose, present in germinated barley, potatoes, etc. [< F < Gk *diástasis*]

di·as·ta·sis (dī as′tə sis), *n.*, *pl.* **-ses** (-sēz′). *Physiol.* the diastolic rest period immediately preceding systole. [< NL < Gk: separation. See DIA-, STASIS]

di·a·stat·ic (dī′ə stat′ik), *adj.* *Biochem.* **1.** of or pertaining to diastase. **2.** having the properties of diastase: *diastatic action.* Also, **di·a·sta·sic** (dī′ə stā′sik). [< Gk *diastatik(ós)* separative]

di·a·ste·ma (dī′ə stē′mə), *n.*, *pl.* **-ma·ta** (-mə tə). *Dentistry.* a space between two teeth. [< LL < Gk: interval = *diastē(nai)* to stand apart + *-ma* n. suffix]

di·as·ter (dī as′tər), *n.* *Biol.* the stage in mitosis at which the chromosomes, after their division and separation, are grouped near the poles of the spindle. —**di·as′tral,** *adj.*

di·as·to·le (dī as′tᵊlē′), *n.* **1.** *Physiol.* the normal rhythmical dilatation of the heart during which the chambers are filling with blood. Cf. **systole** (def. 1). **2.** *Pros.* the lengthening of a syllable regularly short. [< LL < Gk: a putting asunder, dilation, lengthening; cf. *diastéllein* to set apart (*dia-* DIA- + *stéllein* to put, place)] —**di·as·tol·ic** (dī′ə stol′ik), *adj.*

di′astol′ic pres′sure, *Med.* the lowest arterial pressure of the blood, occurring at the end of diastole.

di·as·tro·phism (dī as′trə fiz′əm), *n. Geol.* **1.** the action of the forces that cause the earth's crust to be deformed, producing continents, mountains, changes of level, etc. **2.** any such deformation. [< Gk *diastroph(ḗ)* a distortion (see DIA-, STROPHE) + -ISM] —**di·a·stroph·ic** (dī′ə strof′ik), *adj.*

di·a·tes·sa·ron (dī′ə tes′ə ron′), *n.* (*sometimes cap.*) a harmony of the four Gospels, arranged to form a single narrative. [< LL: the interval of a fourth, L: (a medicine) made of four < Gk *dià tessárōn* through four]

di·a·ther·man·cy (dī′ə thûr′mən sē), *n., pl.* **-cies.** the ability to transmit infrared radiation. [< F *diathermansie* < Gk *dia-* DIA- + *thérmansis* a heating < *thermaínein* to heat] —**di′a·ther′man·ous,** *adj.*

di·a·ther·mic (dī′ə thûr′mik), *adj.* of or pertaining to diathermy. [< F *diathermique*]

di·a·ther·my (dī′ə thûr′mē), *n. Med.* the production of heat in body tissues by electric currents, for therapeutic purposes. Also, **di·a·ther·mi·a** (dī′ə thûr′mē ə). [< NL *diathermia.* See DIA-, -THERMY]

di·ath·e·sis (dī ath′i sis), *n., pl.* **-ses** (-sēz′). **1.** *Pathol.* a constitutional predisposition or tendency, as to a particular disease or affection. **2.** *Gram. Rare.* voice (def. 12). [< NL < Gk: arrangement, disposition. See DIA-, THESIS] —**di·a·thet·ic** (dī′ə thet′ik), *adj.*

di·a·tom (dī′ə təm, -tom′), *n.* any of numerous microscopic, unicellular, marine or fresh-water algae having siliceous cell walls. [< NL *Diatom(a)* name of the genus < Gk *diátom(os)* cut in two. See DIA-, -TOME]

di·a·to·ma·ceous (dī′ə tə mā′shəs), *adj.* consisting of or containing diatoms or their fossil remains. [< NL *Diatomā-ce(ae)* name of the family (see DIATOM, -ACEAE) + -OUS]

di′atoma′ceous earth′, a fine siliceous earth composed chiefly of the cell walls of diatoms: used in filtration, as an abrasive, etc. Also called **di·at·o·mite** (dī at′ə mīt′), **kieselguhr.**

di·a·tom·ic (dī′ə tom′ik), *adj. Chem.* **1.** having two atoms in the molecule. **2.** containing two replaceable atoms or groups; binary. —**di·at·o·mic·i·ty** (dī′at ə mis′i tē), *n.*

di·a·ton·ic (dī′ə ton′ik), *adj. Music.* **1.** using a scale composed of five whole tones and two semitones, as the major, minor, and certain modal scales. **2.** of or pertaining to the tones, intervals, or harmonies of such a scale. [< LL *diatonic(us)* < Gk *diatonikós*] —**di′a·ton′i·cal·ly,** *adv.*

di·a·tribe (dī′ə trīb′), *n.* a bitter, abusive denunciation. [< L *diatrib(a)* < Gk *diatribḗ* pastime, study, discourse < *diatrī́b(ein)* (to) rub away (*dia-* DIA- + *trī́bein* to rub)]

di·at·ro·pism (dī a′trə piz′əm), *n. Bot.* the tendency of some plant organs to take a transverse position to the line of action of an outside stimulus. —**di·a·trop·ic** (dī′ə trop′ik), *adj.*

Di·az (dē′əs; *Port.* dē′əsh), *n.* **Bar·tho·lo·me·u** (bäʀ′tōō lōō me′ōō). See **Dias, Bartholomeu.**

Dí·az (dē′äs), *n.* **(Jo·sé de la Cruz) Por·fi·rio** (hô se′ the lä kʀōōs′ pôʀ fē′ʀyô), 1830–1915, president of Mexico 1877–80, 1884–1911.

diaz-, var. of **diazo-** before a vowel: *diazine.*

Dí·az de Bi·var (dē′äth the bē vär′), **Ro·dri·go** (ʀô thʀē′gô) or **Ruy** (ʀwē). See **Cid, The.** Also, **Dí·az de Vi·var** (dē′äth the bē vär′).

di·az·e·pam (dī az′ə pam′), *n.* a tranquilizer, $C_{16}H_{13}ClN_2O$, that relieves anxiety, depression, and muscular tension. [DI-[1] + AZ- + EP- + *am* (orig. uncert.)]

di·a·zine (dī′ə zēn′, dī az′ēn, -in), *n. Chem.* any of three isomeric compounds having the formula $C_4H_4N_2$, containing a ring of four carbon and two nitrogen atoms.

di·az·o (dī az′ō, -ā′zō), *adj. Chem.* containing the diazo group. [DI-[1] + AZO-]

diazo-, *Chem.* a combining form of **diazo:** *diazomethane.* Also, *esp. before a vowel,* **diaz-.**

di·az′o·a·mi′no group′ (dī az′ō ə mē′nō, -am′ə nō′, -ā′zō-), *Chem.* the divalent group, –N=NNH–.

diaz′o group′, *Chem.* the bivalent group, –N=N–, united with one hydrocarbon group and another atom or group, as in benzenediazo hydroxide, $C_6H_5N{=}NOH$, or the bivalent group =N–N united with one hydrocarbon group, as in diazomethane, $CH_2{-}N{=}N$. Also called **diazo radical.**

di·a·zole (dī′ə zōl′, dī az′ōl), *n. Chem.* any of a group of organic compounds containing three carbon and two nitrogen atoms arranged in a ring.

di·az·o·meth·ane (dī az′ō meth′ān, -ā′zō-), *n. Chem.* a toxic, explosive gas, CH_2N_2, used chiefly as a methylating agent and in organic synthesis.

di·a·zo·ni·um (dī′ə zō′nē əm), *adj. Chem.* of or derived from a diazonium compound. [DIAZ- + *-onium,* as in *ammonium*]

diazo′nium com′pound, *Chem.* any of a series of compounds that contain the group Ar–N–, in which Ar represents an aryl group.

diazo′nium salt′, *Chem.* any of a group of salts of the general formula ArN_2X, in which Ar represents an aryl group and X an anion, as benzenediazonium chloride, $(C_6H_5N{-}N)Cl$.

diaz′o rad′ical. See **diazo group.**

Dí·az Or·daz (dē′äs ôʀ thäs′), **Gus·ta·vo** (gōōs tä′vô), 1911–79, Mexican public official: president 1964–70.

dib (dib), *v.i.,* **dibbed, dib·bing.** to fish by letting the bait bob lightly on the water. [? var. of DAB[1]]

Di·bai (di bī′), *n.* Dubai.

di·ba·sic (dī bā′sik), *adj. Chem.* **1.** containing two replaceable or ionizable hydrogen atoms: *dibasic acid.* **2.** having two univalent, basic atoms, as dibasic sodium phosphate, Na_2HPO_4. —**di·ba·sic·i·ty** (dī′bā sis′i tē), *n.*

dib·ble (dib′əl), *n., v.,* **-bled, -bling.** —*n.* **1.** Also, **dib·ber** (dib′ər). a pointed implement for making holes in the ground for planting seeds, bulbs, etc. —*v.t.* **2.** to make a hole (in the ground) with a dibble. [? akin to DIB]

dib·buk (dib′ək; *Heb.* dē bŏŏk′), *n., pl.* **dib·buks, dib·buk·im** (di bŏŏk′im; *Heb.* dē bŏŏ kēm′). *Jewish Folklore.* dybbuk.

di·bran·chi·ate (dī brang′kē it, -kē āt′), *adj.* **1.** belonging or pertaining to the *Dibranchiata,* a subclass or order of cephalopods with two gills, including the decapods and octopods. —*n.* **2.** a dibranchiate cephalopod. [< NL *Dibranchiāt(a)*]

di·car′box·yl′ic ac′id (dī kär′bok sil′ik, -kär′-), *Chem.* any of the organic compounds that contain two carboxyl groups.

di·cast (dī′kast, dik′ast), *n.* (in ancient Athens) a citizen eligible to be chosen by lot to sit as a judge. [< Gk *dikast(ḗs)* a juryman < *dikáz(ein)* (to) judge, determine (< *díkē* right, law, order) + *-tēs* agentive suffix] —**di·cas′tic,** *adj.*

dice (dīs), *n.pl., sing.* **die,** *v.,* **diced, dic·ing.** —*n.* **1.** small cubes, marked on each side with one to six spots, usually used in pairs in games or gambling. **2.** any of various games played by shaking and throwing such cubes. Cf. **craps. 3.** any small cubes. **4. no dice,** *Slang.* a negative response; refusal; being without success: *He asked for a raise, but it was no dice.* —*v.t.* **5.** to cut into small cubes. **6.** to decorate with cubelike figures. —*v.i.* **7.** to play at dice. [ME *dyce,* unexplained var. of *dees,* pl. of *de* DIE[2]] —**dic′er,** *n.*

di·cen·tra (dī sen′trə), *n.* any plant of the genus *Dicentra,* having racemes of drooping flowers, as the Dutchman's-breeches or the bleeding heart. [< NL < Gk *díkentr(os)* with two stings or spurs = *di-* DI-[1] + *kéntr(on)* a spur, point, sting (< *kent(ein)* (to) prick, sting) + L *-a* n. suffix]

di·ceph·a·lous (dī sef′ə ləs), *adj.* two-headed. [< Gk *diképhal(os)* two-headed] —**di·ceph′a·lism,** *n.*

dice·y (dī′sē), *adj.,* **dic·i·er, dic·i·est.** *Informal.* perilous; hazardous; risky.

di·chlo·ride (dī klōr′īd, -id, -klôr′-), *n.* (chiefly in organic chemistry) bichloride.

di·chlo′ro·di·eth′yl sul′fide (dī klōr′ō dī eth′əl, -klôr′-, -klōr′-, -klôr′-), *Chem.* See **mustard gas.**

di·chlo·ro·di·flu·o·ro·meth·ane (dī klōr′ō dī flōō′ə rō-meth′ān, -flŏŏr′ō-, -flōr′-, -flôr′-, dī klôr′-), *n. Chem.* a nonflammable gas, CCl_2F_2, that boils at −29°C: used chiefly as a propellant in aerosols and as a refrigerant.

di·chlo·ro·di·phen·yl·tri·chlor·o·eth·ane (dī klōr′ō-dī fen′il trī klōr′ō eth′ān, -trī klôr′-, dī klôr′-), *n. Chem.* See **DDT.**

di·chlo′ro·phe·nox′y·a·ce′tic ac′id (dī klōr′ō fi-nok′sē ə sē′tik, -ə set′ik, -ə sē′tik, -ə set′ik, -fi nok′-, dī-klōr′-, dī klôr′-), *Chem.* See **2, 4-D.**

dicho-, a prefix occurring in loan words from Greek (*dichotomy*), on this model used, with the meaning "in two parts," "in pairs," in the formation of compound words (*dichogamy*). [< Gk, comb. form of *dícha* in two, asunder]

di·chog·a·mous (dī kog′ə məs), *adj. Bot.* having the stamens and pistils maturing at different times, therefore preventing self-pollination, as a monoclinous flower (opposed to *homogamous*). Also, **di·cho·gam·ic** (dī′kō gam′ik).

di·chog·a·my (dī kog′ə mē), *n.* a dichogamous condition.

di·chot·o·mise (dī kot′ə mīz′), *v.t., v.i.,* **-mised, -mis·ing.** *Chiefly Brit.* dichotomize. —**di·chot′o·mi·sa′tion,** *n.*

di·chot·o·mize (dī kot′ə mīz′), *v.,* **-mized, -miz·ing.** —*v.t.* **1.** to divide or separate into two parts, kinds, etc. —*v.i.* **2.** to become divided into two parts; form a dichotomy. [< LL *dichotom(os)* DICHOTOMOUS + -IZE] —**di·chot·o·mist** (dī kot′ə mist), *n.* —**di·chot′o·mi·za′tion,** *n.*

di·chot·o·mous (dī kot′ə məs), *adj.* **1.** divided or dividing into two parts. **2.** of or pertaining to dichotomy. [< LL *dichotomos* < Gk; see DICHO-, -TOMOUS] —**di·chot′o·mous·ly,** *adv.*

di·chot·o·my (dī kot′ə mē), *n., pl.* **-mies.** **1.** division into two parts, kinds, etc.; subdivision into halves or pairs. **2.** a difference of opinion; a schism or split. **3.** *Logic.* classification by division into two mutually exclusive groups. **4.** *Bot.* a mode of branching by constant bifurcation, as in some stems, in veins of leaves, etc. **5.** *Astron.* the phase of the moon or of an inferior planet when half of its disk is visible. [< Gk *dichotomía*]

Dichotomy (def. 4)

di·chro·ic (dī krō′ik), *adj.* **1.** characterized by dichroism: *dichroic crystal.* **2.** dichromatic. Also, **di·chro·it·ic** (dī′krō-it′ik). [< Gk *díchro(os)* of two colors + -IC]

di·chro·i·scope (dī krō′i skōp′), *n.* dichroscope. —**di·chro·i·scop·ic** (dī krō′i skop′ik), *adj.*

di·chro·ism (dī′krō iz′əm), *n.* **1.** *Crystall.* pleochroism of a uniaxial crystal such that it exhibits two different colors when viewed from two different directions under transmitted light. **2.** *Chem.* the exhibition of essentially different colors by certain solutions in different degrees of dilution or concentration. [< Gk *díchro(os)* (see DICHROIC) + -ISM]

di·chro·mate (dī krō′māt), *n. Chem.* a salt of the hypothetical acid, $H_2Cr_2O_7$, as potassium dichromate, $K_2Cr_2O_7$. Also, **bichromate.**

di·chro·mat·ic (dī′krō mat′ik, -krə-), *adj.* **1.** having or showing two colors; dichromic. **2.** *Zool.* exhibiting two color phases within a species not due to age or season.

di·chro·mat·i·cism (dī′krō mat′i siz′əm, -krə-), *n.* dichroism (def. 1).

di·chro·ma·tism (dī krō′mə tiz′əm), *n.* **1.** the quality or state of being dichromatic. **2.** Also, **di·chro·ma·top·si·a** (dī krō′mə top′sē ə). *Ophthalm.* a defect of vision in which the retina responds to only two of the three primary colors. Cf. **monochromatism** (def. 2), **trichromatism** (def. 3). [DICHROMAT(IC) + -ISM]

di·chro·mic[1] (dī krō′mik), *adj.* pertaining to or involving two colors only: *dichromic vision.* [DI-[1] + CHROMIC]

di·chro·mic[2] (dī krō′mik), *adj. Chem.* (of a compound) containing two chromium atoms. [DI-[1] + CHROM(IUM) + -IC]

dichro′mic ac′id, *Chem.* the hypothetical acid, $H_2Cr_2O_7$, from which dichromates are derived. [DI-[1] + CHROM(IUM) + -IC]

di·chro·scope (dī′krə skōp′), *n.* an instrument for observing the dichroism or pleochroism of crystals. Also, **dichroiscope, di·chro·o·scope** (dī krō′ə skōp′). [DICHRO(ISM) + -SCOPE] —**di·chro·scop·ic** (dī′krə skop′ik), **di·chro·o·scop·ic** (dī krō′ə skop′ik), *adj.*

dick (dik), *n.* **1.** *U.S. Slang.* a detective. **2.** *Slang* (*vulgar*). penis. [generic use of the proper name]

dick·cis·sel (dik sis′əl), *n.* a bunting, *Spiza americana,* of the eastern and central U.S., having a brownish back streaked with black, a black patch on the throat, and a yellowish breast. [imit. of its call]

dick·ens (dik′inz), *n.* devil; deuce (usually prec. by *the* and often used in exclamations and as a mild imprecation): *What the dickens!* [prob. substitute for *devil;* ? special use of *Dicken,* earlier form of *Dick,* proper name]

Dick·ens (dik′inz), *n.* **Charles (John Huf·fam)** (huf′əm), (pen name: *Boz*), 1812–70, English novelist. —**Dick·en·si·an** (di ken′zē ən), *adj., n.*

dick·er[1] (dik′ər), *v.i.* **1.** to trade with petty bargaining; haggle. **2.** to barter. **3.** to try to arrange matters by mutual bargaining. —*v.t.* **4.** to swap or trade, esp. with bargaining or haggling. —*n.* **5.** a petty bargain. **6.** a barter or swap. **7.** an item or goods bartered or swapped. **8.** a deal, esp. a political deal. [? v. use of DICKER[2]]

dick·er[2] (dik′ər), *n.* the number or quantity ten, esp. a lot of ten hides or skins. [ME *diker* (c. MHG *techer*) << L *decuria* DECURY]

dick·ey (dik′ē), *n., pl.* **-eys.** **1.** a woman's blouse without sides or sleeves, for wearing under a dress or suit. **2.** a detachable insert worn to simulate the front of a shirt, as in clerical dress or formal attire. Cf. **vest** (def. 2), **vestee.** **3.** a bib or pinafore worn by a child. **4.** a small bird. **5.** a donkey, esp. a male. [< *Dicky,* dim. of *Dick,* proper name]

Dick·in·son (dik′in sən), *n.* **1. Emily (Elizabeth),** 1830–1886, U.S. poet. **2. John,** 1732–1808, U.S. statesman.

Dick′ test′, *Med.* a test for determining immunity or susceptibility to scarlet fever in which scarlet-fever toxin is injected into the skin. [named after G. F. DICK who devised it]

dick·y (dik′ē), *n., pl.* **dick·ies.** dickey.

di·cli·nous (dī′klə nəs, dī klī′-), *adj.* *Bot.* **1.** (of a plant species, variety, etc.) having the stamens and the pistils in separate flowers, either on the same plant or on different plants; either monoecious or dioecious. **2.** (of a flower) having only stamens or only pistils; unisexual. [DI-[1] + CLIN- + -OUS] —**di′cli·nism,** *n.*

di·cot (dī′kot), *n.* a dicotyledon. Also, **di·cot·yl** (dī kot′əl). [by shortening]

di·cot·y·le·don (dī kot′əlēd′ən, dī′kotəlēd′-), *n.* an angiospermous plant of the subclass *Dicotyledoneae,* characterized by producing seeds with two cotyledons and an exogenous manner of growth. Cf. **monocotyledon.** [< NL *Dicotyledon-(ēs)* name of the class. See DI-[1], COTYLEDON] —**di·cot·y·le·don·ous** (dī kot′əlēd′ənəs, -əled′-; dī′kotəlēd′ənəs, -kotəled′-), *adj.*

di·cou·ma·rin (dī ko͞o′mər in, -kyo͞o′-), *n.* *Pharm.* a powder, $C_{19}H_{12}O_6$, used chiefly to prevent the coagulation of blood and in the treatment of arterial thrombosis. Also, **di·cou·ma·rol** (dī ko͞o′mə rôl′, -rōl′, -kyo͞o′-). [DI-[1] + COUMARIN]

di·crot·ic (dī krot′ik), *adj.* *Physiol.* **1.** having two arterial beats for one heartbeat, as certain pulses. **2.** pertaining to such a pulse. [< Gk *díkrot(os)* double-beating (*di-* DI- + *krótos* a clapping, rattling noise) + -IC] —**di·cro·tism** (dī′krə tiz′əm), *n.*

dict., **1.** dictation. **2.** dictator. **3.** dictionary.

dic·ta (dik′tə), *n.* a pl. of **dictum.**

dic·ta·graph (dik′tə graf′, -gräf′), *n.* Dictograph.

Dic·ta·phone (dik′tə fōn′), *n.* *Trademark.* a phonographic instrument that records and reproduces dictation.

dic·tate (*v.* dik′tāt, dik tāt′; *n.* dik′tāt), *v.,* **-tat·ed, -tat·ing,** *n.* —*v.t.* **1.** to say or read aloud (something) for another to transcribe or for a machine to record. **2.** to prescribe positively; command with authority. —*v.i.* **3.** to say or read aloud something to be taken down. **4.** to give orders. —*n.* **5.** an authoritative order or command. **6.** a guiding or governing principle, requirement, etc.: *to follow the dictates of one's conscience.* [< L *dictāt(us)* pronounced, repeated, dictated, ptp. of *dictāre,* freq. of *dīcere* to say, speak; see -ATE[1]] —**dic′tat·ing·ly,** *adv.*

dic·ta·tion (dik tā′shən), *n.* **1.** the act or manner of dictating for reproduction in writing. **2.** the act or manner of transcribing words uttered by another. **3.** words that are dictated or that are reproduced from dictation. **4.** the act of ordering or commanding authoritatively. **5.** something commanded. [< LL *dictātiōn-* (s. of *dictātiō*) a dictating]

dic·ta·tor (dik′tā tər, dik tā′tər), *n.* **1.** a person exercising absolute power, esp. one who assumes absolute control without the free consent of the people. **2.** (in ancient Rome) a person invested with supreme authority during a crisis. **3.** a person who authoritatively prescribes conduct, usage, etc.: *a dictator of fashion.* **4.** a person who dictates, as to a secretary. Also, *referring to a woman,* **dic·ta·tress** (dik tā′tris). [< L: a chief magistrate, dictator]

dic·ta·to·ri·al (dik′tə tôr′ē əl, -tōr′-), *adj.* **1.** of or pertaining to a dictator or dictatorship. **2.** appropriate to, or characteristic of, a dictator; absolute; unlimited. **3.** inclined to dictate or command; imperious; overbearing. [< L *dictātōri(us)* (see DICTATE, -ORY[1]) + -AL[1]] —**dic′ta·to′ri·al·ly,** *adv.* —**dic′ta·to′ri·al·ness,** *n.* —**Syn. 2.** totalitarian. **3.** despotic, tyrannical.

dic·ta·tor·ship (dik tā′tər ship′, dik′tā-), *n.* **1.** a country, government, or the form of government in which absolute power is exercised by a dictator. **2.** absolute, imperious, or overbearing power or control. **3.** the office or position held by a dictator.

dic·tion (dik′shən), *n.* **1.** style of speaking or writing as dependent upon choice of words. **2.** the accent, inflection, intonation, and speech-sound quality manifested by an individual speaker; enunciation. [< LL, L *dictiōn-* (s. of *dictiō*) word, oratory = *dict(us)* said, spoken (ptp. of *dīcere* + *-iōn-* -ION]
—**Syn. 1.** usage, language. DICTION, PHRASEOLOGY, WORDING refer to the means and the manner of expressing ideas. DICTION usually implies a high level of usage; it refers chiefly to the choice of words, their arrangement, and the force, accuracy, and distinction with which they are used: *The speaker was distinguished for his excellent diction; poetic diction.* PHRASEOLOGY refers more to the manner of combining the words into related groups, and esp. to the peculiar or distinctive manner in which certain technical, scientific, and professional ideas are expressed: *legal phraseology.* WORDING refers to the exact words or phraseology used to convey thought: *the wording of a will.*

dic·tion·ar·y (dik′shə ner′ē), *n., pl.* **-ar·ies.** **1.** a book containing a selection of the words of a language, usually arranged alphabetically, giving information about their meanings, pronunciations, etymologies, etc.; lexicon. **2.** a book giving information on particular subjects or on a particular class of words, names, or facts, usually arranged alphabetically: *a biographical dictionary.* [< ML *dictiōnāri(um),* lit., a wordbook]

Dic·to·graph (dik′tə graf′, -gräf′), *n.* *Trademark.* a telephonic device for listening to conversations secretly or obtaining a record of them.

dic·tum (dik′təm), *n., pl.* **-ta** (-tə), **-tums.** **1.** an authoritative pronouncement; judicial assertion. **2.** a saying; maxim. **3.** See **obiter dictum.** [< L: something said, a saying, command, word, n. use of neut. ptp. of *dīcere*]

did (did), *v.* pt. of **do**[1].

di·dac·tic (dī dak′tik), *adj.* **1.** intended for instruction; instructive: *didactic poetry.* **2.** inclined to teach or lecture others too much; preaching or moralizing. **3. didactics,** (*construed as sing.*) the art or science of teaching. Also, **di·dac′ti·cal.** [< Gk *didaktik(ós)* apt at teaching, instructive = *didak-* (verbal s. of *didáskein* to teach) + *-tikos* -TIC] —**di·dac′ti·cal·ly,** *adv.* —**di·dac′ti·cism,** *n.*

di·dap·per (dī′dap′ər), *n.* *U.S. Dial.* a dabchick. [ME *dydoppar;* shortened form of *dive-dapper;* see DAP]

did·dle[1] (did′əl), *v.,* **-dled, -dling.** *Informal.* —*v.t.* **1.** to cheat; swindle. —*v.i.* **2.** to waste time. [? akin to OE *dydrian* to deceive] —**did′dler,** *n.*

did·dle[2] (did′əl), *v.t., v.i.,* **-dled, -dling.** *Informal.* to move rapidly up and down or backward and forward. [akin to DODDER[1]]

Di·de·rot (dē′də rō′; *Fr.* dēdə rō′), *n.* **De·nis** (də nē′), 1713–84, French philosopher, critic, and encyclopedist.

did·n't (did′ənt), contraction of *did not.*

di·do (dī′dō), *n., pl.* **-dos, -does.** Usually, **didos, didoes.** *Informal.* a prank; antic. [?]

Di·do (dī′dō), *n.* *Class. Myth.* a queen of Carthage who killed herself when abandoned by Aeneas.

didst (didst), *v.* *Archaic.* 2nd pers. sing. pt. of **do**[1].

di·dym·i·um (dī dim′ē əm, di-), *n.* *Chem.* a mixture of neodymium and praseodymium, formerly thought to be an element. *Symbol:* Di [< NL < Gk *dídym(os)* twin. See DIDYMOUS, -IUM]

did·y·mous (did′ə məs), *adj.* *Bot.* occurring in pairs; paired; twin. [< Gk *dídym(os)* twin, double, (akin to *dís* twice, double) + -OUS]

die[1] (dī), *v.i.,* **died, dy·ing.** **1.** to cease to live; expire. **2.** (of something inanimate) to cease to exist: *The secret died with him.* **3.** to lose force or active qualities: *Superstitions die slowly.* **4.** to cease to function; stop: *The motor died.* **5.** to be no longer subject; become indifferent: *to die to worldly matters.* **6.** to pass gradually; fade (usually fol. by *away, out,* or *down*): *The storm slowly died down.* **7.** *Theol.* to lose spiritual life. **8.** to faint or languish. **9.** to suffer as if dying: *I'm dying of boredom!* **10.** to pine with desire, love, etc. **11.** *Informal.* to desire or want keenly or greatly: *I'm dying for a cup of coffee.* **12. die hard,** to yield only after a bitter struggle; cling stubbornly. **13. die off,** to die one after another until the number is greatly reduced: *Her friends are all dying off.* **14. never say die,** never give up hope or effort. [ME *dien, deien,* OE *dīegan,* prob. < Scand; cf. Icel *deyja;* akin to DEAD, DEATH]
—**Syn. 1.** depart. DIE, PERISH mean to relinquish life. To DIE is to become dead from any cause and in any circumstances. It is the simplest, plainest, and most direct word for this idea, and is used figuratively of anything that has once displayed activity: *An echo, flame, storm, rumor dies.* PERISH, a more literary term, implies death under harsh circumstances such as hunger, cold, neglect, etc.; figuratively, PERISH connotes utter extinction: *Hardship caused many pioneers to perish. Ancient Egyptian civilization has perished.* **2.** end, vanish, disappear. **3.** weaken, fail. **6.** decline, wither, decay.

die[2] (dī), *n., pl.* **dies** for 1, 2, **dice** for 3; *v.,* **died, die·ing.** —*n.* **1.** *Mach.* **a.** any of various devices for cutting or forming material in a press or a stamping or forging machine. **b.** a hollow device of steel, often composed of several pieces to be fitted into a stock, for cutting the threads of bolts or the like. **c.** one of the separate pieces of such a device. **d.** a steel block or plate with small conical holes through which wire, plastic rods, etc., are drawn. **2.** an engraved stamp for impressing a design upon some softer material, as in coining money. **3.** sing. of **dice.** **4. the die is cast,** the irrevocable decision has been made. —*v.t.* **5.** to impress, shape, or cut with a die. [back formation from DICU; r. ME *de* < OF < L *dat(um),* orig. neut. ptp. of *dare* to give (appar. in the sense of given by fortune)]

A

B

Die[2] (def. 2)
A, Greek drachma, 4th century B.C.;
B, Die

die·back (dī′bak′), *n.* *Plant Pathol.* a condition in a plant in which the branches or shoots die from the tip inward, caused by any of several parasites, environmental conditions, etc.

die′ cast′ing, *Metall.* **1.** a process in which molten metal is forced into metallic molds under hydraulic pressure to shape it, form objects, etc. **2.** an article made by this process. —**die′-cast′ing,** *adj.*

di·e·cious (dī ē′shəs), *adj.* *Biol.* dioecious. —**di·e′cious·ly,** *adv.*

Die·fen·ba·ker (dē′fən bā′kər), *n.* **John George,** 1895–1979, prime minister of Canada 1957–63.

Die·go-Sua·rez (dyā′gō swär′es), *n.* a seaport in N Madagascar. 28,772 (1960). Also called **Antsirane.**

die-hard (dī′härd′), *n.* **1.** a person who vigorously maintains or defends a hopeless position, outdated attitude, lost cause, or the like. —*adj.* **2.** resisting vigorously and stubbornly to the last. Also, **die′hard′.**

diel·drin (dēl′drin), *n.* *Chem.* a poison, $C_{12}H_8OCl_6$, used as an insecticide. [DIEL(S-AL)D(E)R (REACTION) + -IN]

di·e·lec·tric (dī′i lek′trik), *Elect.* —*n.* **1.** a nonconducting substance; insulator. —*adj.* **2.** of or pertaining to a dielectric substance. [DI-³ + ELECTRIC] —**di′e·lec′tri·cal·ly,** *adv.*

di′elec′tric con′stant, *Elec.* a measure of the ability of a dielectric to store an electric charge, as when in a capacitor.

Dien Bien Phu (dyen′ byen′ fo͞o′), a town in North Vietnam: defeat of French forces by Viet Minh 1954.

di·en·ceph·a·lon (dī′en sef′ə lon′), *n., pl.* **-lons, -la** (-lə). *Anat.* the posterior section of the forebrain. [< NL; see DI-³, ENCEPHALON] —**di·en·ce·phal·ic** (dī′en sə fal′ik), *adj.*

di·ene (dī′ēn, dī ēn′), *n.* *Chem.* any compound containing two double bonds, as 1,3-butadiene, $CH_2{=}CH{-}CH{=}CH_2$. [DI-¹ + -ENE]

-dienes, *Chem.* a combining form of **diene.** [DIENE + -S³]

die′ plate′, diestock.

Di·eppe (dē ep′; *Fr.* dyep), *n.* a seaport in N France, on the English Channel: raided by an Allied expeditionary force August 1942. 30,327 (1962).

di·er·e·sis (dī er′i sis), *n., pl.* **-ses** (-sēz′). **1.** the separation of two adjacent vowels, dividing one syllable into two. **2.** a sign (¨) placed over the second of two adjacent vowels to indicate separate pronunciation, as in *naïve.* **3.** *Pros.* the division made in a line or verse by coincidence of the end of a foot and the end of a word. Also, **diaeresis.** [< L *diaerēsis* the division of a syllable into two < Gk *diaíresis* a dividing, division = *diair(eîn)* (to) divide (*di-* DI-³ + *hair(eîn)* (to) take) + *-e-* thematic vowel + *-sis* -SIS] —**di·e·ret·ic** (dī′ə ret′ik), *adj.*

Dies (dīz), *n.* **Martin,** 1901–72, U.S. politician; member of the House of Representatives 1931–44; chairman of a special House committee investigating subversive activities 1938–44.

die·sel (dē′zəl), *n.* **1.** (*sometimes cap.*) See **diesel engine.** —*adj.* **2.** of, pertaining to, or for a diesel engine: *diesel fuel.* [named after Rudolf DIESEL]

Die·sel (dē′zəl), *n.* **Ru·dolf** (ro͞o′dolf; *Ger.* ro͞o′dôlf), 1858–1913, German automotive engineer.

die′sel en′gine, a compression-ignition engine in which a spray of fuel, introduced into air heated by compression to 1000°F, ignites at a virtually constant pressure.

Di·es I·rae (dē′äs ēr′ā), a Latin hymn on the Day of Judgment, commonly sung in a Requiem Mass.

di·e·sis (dī′i sis), *n., pl.* **-ses** (-sēz′). See **double dagger.** [ME < L < Gk *díesis* a quarter-tone, a sending through = *die-* (verbid s. of *diiénai* to send through: (*di-* DI-³ + *hiénai* to send) + *-sis* -SIS; the double dagger was formerly used to denote the diesis in music]

di·es non (dī′ēz non′), *Law.* a day on which no courts can be held. [short for L *diēs non jūridicus* a day not juridical (for legal business)]

die·stock (dī′stok′), *n.* a frame for holding a number of standard threaded dies for cutting screw threads. Also, **die′ stock′.** Also called **die plate, screw stock.**

di·et¹ (dī′it), *n., v.,* **-et·ed, -et·ing.** —*n.* **1.** food considered in terms of its qualities, composition, and effects on health. **2.** a particular selection of food, esp. as prescribed to cure a disease, gain or lose weight, etc. **3.** the usual or regular foods a person eats most frequently. **4.** food habitually provided. **5.** anything that is habitually provided or partaken of: *a steady diet of quiz shows and murder mysteries.* —*v.t.* **6.** to regulate the food of, esp. in order to improve the physical condition. **7.** to feed. —*v.i.* **8.** to select or limit the food one eats to improve one's physical condition or to lose weight. **9.** *Archaic.* to eat; feed. [ME *diete* ML *diēta,* L *diaet(a)* < Gk *díaita* prescribed way of living = *dia-* DIA- + *-aita* (akin to *aîsa* share, lot)] —**di′et·er,** *n.*

di·et² (dī′it), *n.* **1.** the legislative body of certain countries, as Japan. **2.** the general assembly of the estates of the former Holy Roman Empire. [late ME < ML *diēt(a)* public assembly, appar. the same word as L *diaeta* (see DIET¹) with sense affected by L *diēs* day]

di·e·tar·y (dī′i ter′ē), *adj., n., pl.* **-tar·ies.** —*adj.* **1.** of or pertaining to diet: *a dietary cure.* —*n.* **2.** a regulated allowance of food. **3.** *Obs.* a system of diet. [ME *dietarie* system of diet]

di′etary law′, *Judaism.* any of the body of laws dealing with the foods and combinations of foods permitted or forbidden to be eaten, the vessels to be used in preparing and serving different types of foods, and the procedure to be followed in treating certain foods prior to use.

di·e·tet·ic (dī′i tet′ik), *adj.* Also, **di′e·tet′i·cal. 1.** pertaining to diet or to regulation of the use of food. **2.** prepared or suitable for special diets, esp. those requiring a restricted sugar intake. —*n.* **3. dietetics,** (*construed as sing.*) the science concerned with the nutritional planning and preparation of foods. [< L *diaetetic(us)* < Gk *diaitētikós* = *diait(a)* (see DIET¹) + *-ē-* thematic vowel + *-tikos* -TIC]

di·eth·yl·stil·bes·trol (dī eth′əl stil bes′trōl, -trôl, -trol), *n.* *Pharm.* a synthetic estrogen, $[HOC_6H_4C(C_2H_5){=}]_2$, used chiefly in the treatment of menopausic symptoms and in animal feeds for caponization. Also, **di·eth′yl·stil·bes′trol.** Also called **stilbestrol, stilboestrol.** [DI-¹ + ETHYL + STILBESTROL]

di·e·ti·tian (dī′i tish′ən), *n.* a person who is an expert in nutrition or dietetics. Also, **di′e·ti′cian.** [DIET¹ + *-itian;* see -ICIAN]

Die·trich (dē′trik, -trikh), *n.* **Mar·le·ne** (mär lā′nə), born 1904, U.S. actress and singer, born in Germany.

Dieu et mon droit (dyœ′ ā môN drwa′), *French.* God and my right: motto on the royal arms of England.

dif-, var. of **dis-¹** before *f: differ.*

diff., 1. difference. **2.** different.

dif·fer (dif′ər), *v.i.* **1.** to be unlike, dissimilar, or distinct in nature or qualities. **2.** to disagree in opinion, belief, etc.; be at variance; disagree. **3.** *Obs.* to dispute; quarrel. [ME *differ(en)* (to) be unlike < L *differre* to bear apart, put off, delay (see DEFER¹), be different = *dif-* DIF- + *ferre* to bear]

dif·fer·ence (dif′ər əns, dif′rəns), *n., v.,* **-enced, -enc·ing.** —*n.* **1.** the state or relation of being different; dissimilarity. **2.** an instance or point of unlikeness or dissimilarity. **3.** a significant change in a situation. **4.** a distinguishing characteristic; distinctive quality, feature, etc. **5.** the degree in which one person or thing differs from another. **6.** discrimination; distinction. **7.** a disagreement in opinion. **8.** a dispute or quarrel. **9.** the amount by which one quantity is greater or less than another. **10.** *Logic.* a differentia. **11. split the difference, a.** to compromise, esp. to make equal concessions. **b.** to divide the remainder equally. —*v.t.* **12.** to cause difference in or between; make different. **13.** to perceive the difference in or between; discriminate. **14.** *Heraldry.* to add a charge to (a coat of arms) to identify a particular branch of a family. [ME < MF < L *differentia* = *different-* carrying different ways (see DIFFERENT) + *-ia;* see -ENCE]

—**Syn. 1.** inconsistency, variation, diversity, inequality, divergence, contrariety. DIFFERENCE, DISCREPANCY, DISPARITY, DISSIMILARITY imply perceivable unlikeness, variation, or diversity. DIFFERENCE refers to a complete or partial lack of identity or a degree of unlikeness: *a difference of opinion; a difference of six inches.* DISCREPANCY usually refers to the difference or inconsistency between things that should agree, balance, or harmonize: *a discrepancy between the statements of two witnesses.* DISPARITY implies inequality, often where a greater approximation to equality might reasonably be expected: *a great disparity between the ages of husband and wife.* DISSIMILARITY indicates an essential lack of resemblance between things in some respect comparable: *a dissimilarity between social customs of China and Japan.* **6.** See **distinction.** —**Ant. 1.** similarity.

dif·fer·ent (dif′ər ənt, dif′rənt), *adj.* **1.** differing in character or quality; not alike; dissimilar. **2.** not identical; separate or distinct. **3.** various; several. **4.** unusual; not ordinary. [ME < MF < L *different-* (s. of *differēns*), prp. of *differre.* See DIFFER, -ENT] —**dif′fer·ent·ly,** *adv.* —**Syn. 1.** unlike, diverse, divergent, altered, changed, contrary, deviant, variant. **3.** sundry, divers. See **various.**

—**Usage.** Most grammarians, chiefly on semantic grounds, regard any preposition but FROM after DIFFERENT as a solecism: *He is different from me. His handwriting is different from mine.* But in the comparative of the sense "unusual, not ordinary," DIFFERENT is used in the same way as other adjectives: *He is more different than you are.*

dif·fer·en·ti·a (dif′ə ren′shē ə), *n., pl.* **-ti·ae** (-shē ē′). **1.** the character or attribute by which one species is distinguished from all others of the same genus. **2.** the character or basic factor by which one entity is distinguished from another. [< L: DIFFERENCE]

dif·fer·en·ti·a·ble (dif′ə ren′shē ə bəl), *adj.* capable of being differentiated.

dif·fer·en·tial (dif′ə ren′shəl), *adj.* **1.** of or pertaining to difference or diversity. **2.** constituting a difference; distinguishing; distinctive: *a differential feature.* **3.** exhibiting or depending upon a difference or distinction. **4.** *Physics, Mach.* pertaining to or involving the difference of two or more motions, forces, etc. **5.** *Math.* pertaining to or involving a derivative or derivatives. —*n.* **6.** a difference or the amount of difference, as in cost, salary, quantity, degree, or quality, between things that are comparable. **7.** Also called **differential gear.** *Mach.* an epicyclic train of gears designed to permit two or more shafts to revolve at different speeds, as a set of gears in an automobile permitting the rear wheels to be driven at different speeds when the car is turning. **8.** *Math.* **a.** a function of two variables that is obtained from a given function, $y = f(x)$, and that expresses the approximate increment in the given function as the derivative of the function times the increment in the independent variable, written as $dy = f'(x)dx$. **b.** any generalization of this function to higher dimensions. **9.** *Com.* the difference between various rates applicable. **10.** *Physics.* the quantitative difference between two or more forces, motions, etc.: *a pressure differential.* [< ML *differentiāl(is)*] —**dif′fer·en′tial·ly,** *adv.*

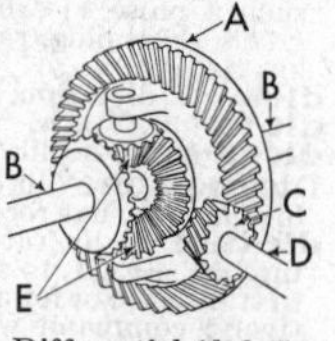

Differential (def. 7)
A, Ring gear;
B, Axle; C, Drive
shaft gear; D, Drive
shaft; E, Pinion gear

dif′feren′tial cal′culus, the branch of mathematics that deals with differentials and derivatives.

differen′tial coeffic′ient, *Chiefly Brit.* derivative (def. 6).

differen′tial equa′tion, *Math.* an equation involving differentials or derivatives.

dif′feren′tial gear′, *Mach.* **1.** differential (def. 7). **2.** any of various comparable arrangements of gears, as an epicyclic train.

differen′tial psychol′ogy, the branch of psychology dealing with the study of characteristic differences or variations of groups or individuals.

dif′feren′tial wind′lass, a windlass employing a larger winding drum and a smaller unwinding drum, turning at the same rate, to raise a freely suspended load.

dif·fer·en·ti·ate (dif′ə ren′shē āt′), *v.,* **-at·ed, -at·ing.** —*v.t.* **1.** to form or mark differently from other such things; distinguish. **2.** to change; alter. **3.** to perceive the difference in or between. **4.** to make different by modification, as a biological species. **5.** *Math.* to obtain the differential or the derivative of. —*v.i.* **6.** to become unlike or dissimilar; change in character. **7.** to make a distinction. **8.** *Biol.* (of cells or tissues) to change from relatively generalized to specialized kinds, during development. [< ML *differentiāt(us)* distinguished (ptp. of *differentiāre*)] —**dif′fer·en′ti·a′tion,** *n.* —**dif′fer·en′ti·a′tor,** *n.* —**Syn. 1.** set off. See **distinguish. 3.** separate.

dif·fi·cile (dif′i sēl′; *Fr.* dē fē sēl′), *adj.* **1.** hard to deal with, satisfy, or please. **2.** *Archaic.* hard to do; difficult. [< F < L *difficilis* difficult. See DIF-, FACILE]

dif·fi·cult (dif′ə kult′, -kəlt), *adj.* **1.** requiring much labor or skill to be accomplished; not readily done; hard. **2.** hard to understand or solve: *a difficult problem.* **3.** hard to deal with or get on with: *a difficult pupil.* **4.** hard to please or satisfy. **5.** hard to persuade or induce; stubborn. **6.** disadvantageous; trying; hampering. **7.** fraught with hardship, esp. financial hardship. [back formation from DIFFICULTY] —**dif′fi·cult′ly,** *adv.* —**Syn. 1.** arduous. See **hard. 2.** obscure, complex, intricate, perplexing, involved, knotty. **4.** particular, finical, fussy. **5.** obdurate, uncompromising. —**Ant. 1.** easy. **2.** simple.

dif·fi·cul·ty (dif′ə kul′tē, -kəl tē), *n., pl.* **-ties. 1.** the fact or condition of being difficult. **2.** Often, **difficulties.** an embarrassing situation, esp. of financial affairs. **3.** a trouble. **4.** a cause of trouble or embarrassment. **5.** reluctance; unwillingness. **6.** a demur; objection. **7.** something that is hard to do, understand, or surmount; an impediment or obstacle. [ME *difficulte* < L *difficultās,* b. *difficilis* DIFFICILE and *facultās* FACULTY] —**Syn. 2.** dilemma, predicament, quandary, plight, fix. **3.** problem.

dif·fi·dence (dif′i dəns), *n.* distrust of one's own ability, worth, or fitness; timidity; shyness. [< L *diffīdentia* mistrust, want of confidence]

dif·fi·dent (dif′i dənt), *adj.* **1.** lacking confidence in oneself; timid; shy. **2.** *Archaic.* distrustful. [< L *diffīdent-* (s. of *diffīdēns* mistrusting, despairing, prp. of *diffīdere*) = *dif-* DIF- + *fīd-* trust + *-ent-* -ENT] —**dif′fi·dent·ly,** *adv.* —**Syn. 1.** self-conscious, self-effacing, modest, unassuming. —**Ant. 1.** self-confident, forward.

dif·fract (di frakt′), *v.t.* to break up or bend by diffraction. [back formation from DIFFRACTION]

dif·frac·tion (di frak′shən), *n.* *Physics.* **1.** the phenomenon exhibited by wave fronts that, passing the edge of an opaque body, are modulated, thereby causing a redistribution of energy within the front: it is detectable in light waves by the presence of minute dark and light bands at the edge of a shadow. **2.** the bending of waves, esp. sound and light waves, around obstacles in their path. [< NL *diffractiōn-* (s. of *diffractiō* a breaking up) = L *diffract(us)* broken up (ptp. of *diffringere*) + *-iōn-* -ION]

diffrac′tion grat′ing, *Physics.* a band of equidistant parallel lines, usually more than 5000 to the inch, ruled on a glass or polished metal surface for diffracting light to produce optical spectra. Also called **grating.**

dif·frac·tive (di frak′tiv), *adj.* causing or pertaining to diffraction. —**dif·frac′tive·ly,** *adv.* —**dif·frac′tive·ness,** *n.*

dif·fuse (*v.* di fyōōz′; *adj.* di fyōōs′), *v.,* **-fused, -fus·ing,** *adj.* —*v.t.* **1.** to pour out and spread, as a fluid. **2.** to spread or scatter widely or thinly; disseminate. **3.** *Physics.* to spread by diffusion. —*v.i.* **4.** to spread. **5.** *Physics.* to intermingle by diffusion. —*adj.* **6.** characterized by great length or discursiveness in speech or writing; wordy. **7.** widely spread or scattered; dispersed. **8.** *Bot.* widely or loosely spreading. **9.** (of reflection) scattered, like that from a rough surface (opposed to *specular*). [ME < L *diffūs(us)* spread, poured forth] —**dif·fuse·ly** (di fyōōs′lē), *adv.* —**dif·fuse′ness,** *n.* —**dif·fus′er, dif·fu′sor,** *n.*

dif·fus·i·ble (di fyōō′zə bəl), *adj.* capable of being diffused. —**dif·fus′i·bil′i·ty,** *n.*

dif·fu·sion (di fyōō′zhən), *n.* **1.** the act of diffusing. **2.** the state of being diffused. **3.** diffuseness or prolixity of speech or writing; discursiveness. **4.** *Physics.* **a.** an intermingling of molecules, ions, etc., resulting from random thermal agitation, as in the dispersion of a vapor in air. **b.** a reflection or refraction of light or other electromagnetic radiation from an irregular surface or an erratic dispersion through a surface; scattering. **5.** *Anthropol., Sociol.* the transmission of elements or features of one culture to another. [ME < L *diffūsiōn-* (s. of *diffūsiō*) a spreading out]

dif·fu·sive (di fyōō′siv), *adj.* **1.** tending to diffuse. **2.** characterized by diffusion. **3.** diffuse; prolix. —**dif·fu′sive·ly,** *adv.* —**dif·fu′sive·ness,** *n.*

dig (dig), *v.,* **dug** or (*Archaic*) **digged; dig·ging;** *n.* —*v.i.* **1.** to break up, turn over, or remove earth, sand, etc., as with a spade; make an excavation. **2.** to make one's way or work by or as by removing or turning over material: *to dig through the files.* —*v.t.* **3.** to break up, turn over, or loosen (earth, sand, etc.), as with a spade. **4.** to form or excavate (a hole, tunnel, etc.) by removing material. **5.** to unearth, obtain, or remove by digging. **6.** to find or discover by effort or search (often fol. by *out*). **7.** to poke, thrust, or force (usually fol. by *in* or *into*): *He dug his heel into the ground.* **8.** *Slang.* **a.** to understand and appreciate. **b.** to take notice of; note. **9. dig in, a.** to dig trenches, as in order to defend a position in battle. **b.** to maintain one's opinion or position. **c.** to dig into. **10. dig into,** *Informal.* to attack, work, or apply oneself vigorously. **11. dig up, a.** to discover in the course of digging. **b.** *Informal.* to obtain or find by chance. —*n.* **12.** thrust; poke. **13.** a cutting, sarcastic remark. **14. digs,** *Chiefly Brit. Informal.* diggings (def. 2). [ME *diggen,* ? dissimilated var. of **dingen* to hollow out; see DINGLE]

dig., digest.

di·gam·ma (dī gam′ə), *n.* a letter of the early Greek alphabet that represented a sound similar to English *w.* [< L < Gk *dígamma* (see DI-[1], GAMMA); from its shape, taken as gamma (Γ) with two bars]

dig·a·my (dig′ə mē), *n.* a second marriage, after the death or divorce of the first husband or wife; deuterogamy. Cf. **monogamy** (def. 3). [< LL *digamia* < Gk. See DI-[1], -GAMY] —**dig′a·mous,** *adj.*

di·gas·tric (dī gas′trik), *Anat.* —*adj.* **1.** (of a muscle) having two bellies with an intermediate tendon. —*n.* **2.** a muscle of the lower jaw, the action of which assists in lowering the jaw. [< NL *digastric(us).* See DI-[1], GASTRIC]

Dig·by (dig′bē), *n.* **Sir Ken·elm** (ken′elm), 1603–65, English writer, naval commander, and diplomat.

di·gen·e·sis (dī jen′i sis), *n.* *Zool.* See **alternation of generations.** [< NL; see DI-[1], GENESIS] —**di·ge·net·ic** (dī′jə net′ik), *adj.*

di·gest (*v.* di jest′, dī-; *n.* dī′jest), *v.t.* **1.** to prepare and convert (food) in the alimentary canal for assimilation into the system. **2.** to promote the digestion of (food). **3.** to assimilate mentally, as an argument. **4.** to arrange methodically in the mind; think over: *to digest a plan.* **5.** to bear with patience; endure. **6.** to arrange in convenient or methodical order; reduce to a system; classify. **7.** to condense, abridge, or summarize. —*v.i.* **8.** *Chem.* to soften or disintegrate a substance by means of moisture, heat, chemical action, or the like. **9.** to digest food. **10.** to undergo digestion, as food. —*n.* **11.** a collection or compendium, usually of literary, historical, legal, or scientific matter, esp. when classified or condensed. **12. the Digest,** a collection in 50 books of the body of Roman law, being the largest part of the Corpus Juris Civilis; the Pandects. [(v.) ME *digest(en)* < L *dīgest(us)* separated, dissolved (ptp. of *dīgerere*) = *dī-* DI-[2] + *ges-* carry, bear (perf. s. of *gerere*) + *-t-* ptp. suffix; (n.) ME: collection of laws < LL *dīgest(a)* (pl.) < L: collection of writings < *dīgest(us),* as above] —**Syn. 4.** study, ponder. **6.** systematize, codify. **11.** abstract, conspectus, abridgment. See **summary.**

di·gest·ant (di jes′tənt, dī-), *n.* *Med.* an agent that promotes digestion.

di·gest·er (di jes′tər, dī-), *n.* **1.** a person or thing that digests. **2.** Also, **digestor.** *Chem.* an apparatus in which substances are softened or disintegrated by moisture, heat, chemical action, or the like.

di·gest·i·ble (di jes′tə bəl, dī-), *adj.* capable of being digested; readily digested. [ME < LL *dīgestibil(is)*] —**di·gest′i·bil′i·ty, di·gest′i·ble·ness,** *n.* —**di·gest′i·bly,** *adv.*

di·ges·tion (di jes′chən, -jesh′-, dī-), *n.* **1.** the process in the alimentary canal by which food is converted into a substance suitable for absorption and assimilation into the body. **2.** the function or power of digesting food: *My digestion is bad.* **3.** the act of digesting or being digested. [ME *digestioun* < MF *digestion* < L *dīgestiōn-* (s. of *dīgestiō*)] —**di·ges′tion·al,** *adj.*

di·ges·tive (di jes′tiv, dī-), *adj.* **1.** serving for or pertaining to digestion; having the function of digesting food: *the digestive system.* **2.** promoting digestion. —*n.* **3.** an agent or medicine promoting digestion. [ME < MF *digestif,* L *dīgestīv(us)*] —**di·ges′tive·ly,** *adv.*

diges′tive bis′cuit, *Brit.* a large, round, semisweet dessert cookie, similar to a graham cracker.

di·ges·tor (di jes′tər, dī-), *n.* digester (def. 2).

digged (digd), *v.* a pt. of **dig.**

dig·ger (dig′ər), *n.* **1.** a person or an animal that digs. **2.** a tool, part of a machine, etc., for digging. **3.** (*cap.*) Also called **Dig′ger In′dian.** a member of any of several Indian peoples of western North America, esp. of a tribe that dug roots for food. [late ME]

dig′ger wasp′, any of numerous solitary wasps of the family *Sphecidae* that excavate a nest in soil, wood, etc., which they provision with prey paralyzed by stinging.

dig·gings (dig′iṅgz *for 1;* dig′ənz *for 2*), *n.* **1.** (*usually construed as sing.*) a place where digging is carried on. **2.** Also called **digs.** (*construed as pl.*) *Chiefly Brit. Informal.* living quarters; lodgings.

dight (dīt), *v.t.,* **dight** or **dight·ed, dight·ing.** *Archaic.* **1.** to equip; furnish. **2.** to dress; adorn. [ME *dight(en),* OE *dihtan* to arrange, compose < L *dictāre* (see DICTATE); c. G *dichten*]

dig·it (dij′it), *n.* **1.** a finger or toe. **2.** the breadth of a finger used as a unit of linear measure, usually equal to ¾ inch. **3.** a whole number from one to nine. **4.** any of the Arabic figures of 1 through 9 and 0. **5.** index (def. 5). [ME < L *digit(us)* finger, toe]

dig·it·al (dij′i tᵊl), *adj.* **1.** of or pertaining to a digit. **2.** resembling a digit or finger. **3.** *Computer Technol.* using numerical digits to represent discretely all variables occurring in a problem. **4.** having digits or digitlike parts. —*n.* **5.** one of the keys or finger levers of keyboard instruments. [ME < L *digitāl(is)*] —**dig′it·al·ly,** *adv.*

dig′ital comput′er, a computer that processes information in digital form. Cf. **analog computer.**

dig·i·tal·in (dij′i tal′in, -tā′lin), *n.* *Pharm.* **1.** a glucoside obtained from digitalis. **2.** any of several extracts of mixtures of glucosides obtained from digitalis. [DIGITAL(IS) + -IN[2]]

dig·i·tal·is (dij′i tal′is, -tā′lis), *n.* **1.** any scrophulariaceous plant of the genus *Digitalis,* esp. the common foxglove, *D. purpurea.* **2.** the dried leaves of the foxglove, *Digitalis purpurea,* used as a heart stimulant. [< NL, special use of L *digitālis* (Latinization of the German name of the plant *Fingerhut*); see DIGITAL]

dig·i·tal·ism (dij′i tᵊliz′əm), *n.* *Pathol.* the abnormal condition resulting from an overconsumption of digitalis.

dig·i·tate (dij′i tāt′), *adj.* **1.** *Zool.* having digits or digitlike processes. **2.** *Bot.* having radiating divisions or leaflets resembling the fingers of a hand. **3.** like a digit or finger. Also, **dig′i·tat′ed.** [< L *digitāt(us)*] —**dig′i·tate′ly,** *adv.*

Digitate leaf

dig·i·ta·tion (dij′i tā′shən), *n.* *Biol.* **1.** digitate formation. **2.** a digitlike process or division.

digiti-, a learned borrowing from Latin meaning "finger," used in the formation of compound words: *digitigrade.* [comb. form repr. L *digitus*]

dig·i·ti·grade (dij′i tə grād′), *adj.* **1.** walking on the toes, as most quadruped mammals. —*n.* **2.** a digitigrade animal. [< F]

dig·i·tox·in (dij′i tok′sin), *n.* *Pharm.* a cardiac glycoside, $C_{41}H_{64}O_{13}$, or a mixture of cardiac glycosides of which this is the chief constituent, obtained from digitalis and used as a heart stimulant. [DIGI(TALIS) + TOXIN]

di·glot (dī′glot), *adj.* **1.** bilingual. —*n.* **2.** a bilingual book or edition. [< Gk *díglōtt(os).* See DI-[1], -GLOT] —**di·glot′tic,** *adj.*

dig·ni·fied (dig′nə fīd′), *adj.* marked by dignity of aspect or manner; noble; stately: *dignified conduct.* —**dig·ni·fied·ly** (dig′nə fīd′lē, -fī′id-), *adv.* —**dig′ni·fied′ness,** *n.* —**Syn.** grave, august.

dig·ni·fy (dig′nə fī′), *v.t.,* **-fied, -fy·ing. 1.** to confer honor or dignity upon; honor; ennoble. **2.** to give a high-sounding title or name to; confer unmerited distinction upon. [< MF *dignifier* < LL *dignificāre* = L dign(us) worthy + *-ificāre* -IFY]

dig·ni·tar·y (dig′ni ter′ē), *n.*, *pl.* **-tar·ies.** a person who holds a high rank or office, as in the government. —**dig·ni·tar·i·al** (dig′ni târ′ē əl), *adj.*

dig·ni·ty (dig′ni tē), *n.*, *pl.* **-ties. 1.** formal, grave, or noble bearing, conduct, or speech. **2.** nobility or elevation of character; worthiness. **3.** elevated rank, office, station, etc. **4.** *Archaic.* **a.** a person of high rank or title. **b.** such persons collectively. [ME *dignite* < OF < L *dignitāt-* (s. of *dignitās*) worthiness = *dign(us)* worthy + *-itāt-* -ITY] —**Syn. 1.** decorum.

di·graph (dī′graf, -gräf), *n.* a pair of letters representing a single speech sound, as *ea* in *meat*, or *th* in *path*.

di·gress (di gres′, dī-), *v.i.* **1.** to wander away from the main topic. **2.** *Archaic.* to turn aside. [< L *dīgress(us)* having departed or gone aside (ptp. of *dīgredī*) = *dī-* DI-[2] + *gre-* go (perf. s. of *gradī* to go) + *-ss(us)* ptp. suffix] —**di·gress′er,** *n.* —**di·gress′ing·ly,** *adv.* —**Syn. 1.** ramble, stray. See **deviate.**

di·gres·sion (di gresh′ən, dī-), *n.* **1.** the act of digressing. **2.** a passage or section that deviates from the central theme of a discourse. [< L *dīgressiōn-* (s. of *dīgressiō*) a going away or aside; r. ME *disgressioun* < AF] —**di·gres′sion·al,** *adj.*

di·gres·sive (di gres′iv, dī-), *adj.* tending to digress; departing from the main subject. [< L *dīgressīv(us)*] —**di·gres′sive·ly,** *adv.* —**di·gres′sive·ness,** *n.*

di·he·dral (dī hē′drəl), *adj.* **1.** having or formed by two planes. **2.** of or pertaining to a dihedron. —*n.* **3.** dihedron. **4.** *Aeron.* the angle at which the right and left wings or the halves of any other horizontal surface of an airplane or the like are inclined upward or downward.

D, Dihedral angle included between planes AA and BB

di·he·dron (dī hē′drən), *n.* *Geom.* a figure formed by two intersecting planes.

di·hy·brid (dī hī′brid), *Biol.* —*n.* **1.** the offspring of parents differing in two specific pairs of genes. —*adj.* **2.** of or pertaining to such an offspring. —**di·hy′brid·ism,** *n.*

di·hy·drate (dī hī′drāt), *n.* *Chem.* a hydrate that contains two molecules of water, as potassium sulfite, $K_2SO_3 \cdot 2H_2O$. —**di·hy′drat·ed,** *adj.*

Di·jon (dē zhôN′), *n.* a city in E central France. 141,104 (1962).

dik-dik (dik′dik′), *n.* any of several small antelopes of the genera *Madoqua* and *Rhynchotragus*, of eastern and southwestern Africa, being about 14 inches high at the shoulder. [native EAfr name]

dike[1] (dīk), *n.*, *v.*, **diked, dik·ing.** —*n.* **1.** an embankment for controlling the waters of the sea or a river. **2.** a ditch. **3.** a bank of earth formed of material being excavated. **4.** a causeway. **5.** an obstacle; barrier. **6.** *Geol.* **a.** a long, narrow, crosscutting mass of igneous or eruptive rock intruded into a fissure in older rock. **b.** a similar mass of rock composed of other kinds of material, as sandstone. —*v.t.* **7.** to furnish or drain with a dike. **8.** to enclose, restrain, or protect by a dike: *to dike a tract of land.* Also, **dyke.** [ME *dik(e)*, var. of *dich* DITCH; *-k-* perh. < Scand; cf. Icel *dīki* ditch] —**dik′er,** *n.*

dike[2] (dīk), *n.* *Slang.* dyke[2].

dil., dilute.

di·lac·er·ate (di las′ə rāt′, dī-), *v.t.*, **-at·ed, -at·ing.** to tear apart or to pieces. [< L *dīlacerāt(us)* torn to pieces (ptp. of *dīlacerāre*)] —**di·lac′er·a′tion,** *n.*

di·lap·i·date (di lap′i dāt′), *v.*, **-dat·ed, -dat·ing.** —*v.t.* **1.** to bring into a state of disrepair, as by misuse or neglect. **2.** *Archaic.* to squander; waste. —*v.i.* **3.** to fall into ruin or decay. [< L *dīlapidāt(us)* thrown away, consumed, scattered (ptp. of *dīlapidāre*)] —**di·lap′i·da′tion,** *n.* —**di·lap′i·da′tor,** *n.*

di·lap·i·dat·ed (di lap′i dā′tid), *adj.* fallen into partial ruin or decay, as from misuse or neglect.

di·lat·ant (di lāt′ᵊnt, dī-), *adj.* dilating; expanding. [< L *dīlātant-* (s. of *dīlātāns*), prp. of *dīlātāre* to DILATE; see -ANT] —**di·lat′an·cy,** *n.*

dil·a·ta·tion (dil′ə tā′shən, dī′lə-), *n.* **1.** the act of dilating. **2.** the state of being dilated. **3.** a dilated formation or part. **4.** *Pathol.* an abnormal enlargement of an aperture or a canal of the body. **5.** *Surg.* **a.** an enlargement made in a body aperture or canal for surgical or medical treatment. **b.** a restoration to normal patency of an abnormally small body opening or passageway, as of the anus or esophagus. Also, **dilation.** [ME *dilatacioun* < MF *dilatacion* < L *dīlātātiōn-* (s. of *dīlātātiō*) = *dīlātāt(us)* spread out (ptp. of *dīlātāre* to DILATE) + *-iōn-* -ION]

di·late (dī lāt′, di-), *v.*, **-lat·ed, -lat·ing.** —*v.t.* **1.** to make wider or larger; cause to expand. **2.** *Archaic.* to describe or develop at length. —*v.i.* **3.** to spread out; expand. **4.** to speak at length; expatiate (often fol. by *on* or *upon*). [ME *dilate(n)* < MF *dilat(er)*, L *dīlāt(āre)* (to) spread out = *dī-* DI-[2] + *lāt(us)* broad + *-āre* inf. suffix] —**di·lat′a·bil′i·ty,** *n.* —**di·lat′a·ble,** *adj.* —**di·lat′a·bly,** *adv.* —**Syn. 1.** enlarge, widen. **3.** swell. —**Ant. 1.** constrict.

di·lat·er (dī lā′tər, di-), *n.* dilator.

di·la·tion (dī lā′shən, di-), *n.* dilatation.

di·la·tive (dī lā′tiv, di-), *adj.* serving or tending to dilate.

dil·a·tom·e·ter (dil′ə tom′i tər), *n.* *Physics.* a device for measuring expansion caused by changes in temperature in substances. —**dil·a·to·met·ric** (dil′ə tə me′trik), *adj.* —**dil′a·to·met′ri·cal·ly,** *adv.* —**dil′a·tom′e·try,** *n.*

di·la·tor (dī lā′tər, di-), *n.* **1.** a person or thing that dilates. **2.** *Anat.* a muscle that dilates some cavity of the body. **3.** *Surg.* an instrument for dilating body canals, orifices, or cavities.

dil·a·to·ry (dil′ə tôr′ē, -tōr′ē), *adj.* **1.** inclined to delay or procrastinate; slow; tardy. **2.** intended to bring about delay: *a dilatory strategy.* [< LL *dīlātōri(us)* delaying < L *dīlātōr-* (s. of *dīlātor* delayer) = L *dīlāt(us)* put off, delayed (ptp. of *diferre;* see DIFFER) + *-ōr-* -OR[2]] —**dil′a·to′ri·ly,** *adv.* —**dil′a·to′ri·ness,** *n.*

dil·do (dil′dō), *n.*, *pl.* **-dos.** *Slang.* an artificial erect penis. Also, **dil′doe.** [?]

di·lem·ma (di lem′ə), *n.* **1.** a situation requiring a choice between equally undesirable alternatives. **2.** any difficult or perplexing situation or problem. **3.** *Logic.* a form of syllogism in which the major premise is formed of two or more hypothetical propositions and the minor premise is a disjunctive proposition, as "If A, then B; if C then D. Either A or C. Therefore, either B or D." [< LL < Gk = *di-* DI-[1] + *lêmma* an assumption, premise < *lambánein* to take] —**dil·em·mat·ic** (dil′ə mat′ik), **dil′em·mat′i·cal, dil·em′mic,** *adj.* —**dil′em·mat′i·cal·ly,** *adv.* —**Syn. 1.** See **predicament. 2.** question, difficulty.

dil·et·tante (dil′i tänt′, dil′i tänt′, dil′i tan′tē, -tän′tā), *n.*, *pl.* **-tantes, -tan·ti** (-tän′tē), *adj.* —*n.* **1.** a person who takes up an art, activity, or subject merely for amusement; dabbler. **2.** a lover of an art or science, esp. of a fine art. —*adj.* **3.** of or pertaining to dilettantes. [< It, n. use of prp. of *dilettare* < L *dēlectāre* to DELIGHT] —**dil′et·tan′tish, dil′et·tan′te·ish,** *adj.*

dil·et·tant·ism (dil′i tän′tiz əm, -tan′-), *n.* the practices or characteristics of a dilettante. Also, **dil·et·tan·te·ism** (dil′i tan′tē iz′əm, -tän′-).

dil·i·gence[1] (dil′i jəns), *n.* **1.** constant and earnest effort to accomplish what is undertaken; persistent exertion of body or mind. **2.** *Obs.* care; caution. [ME *deligence* < MF, L *dīligentia*] —**Syn. 1.** application, industry, assiduity, perseverance.

Diligence

dil·i·gence[2] (dil′i jəns; *Fr.* dē lē zhäNs′), *n.*, *pl.* **-gen·ces** (-jən siz; *Fr.* -zhäNs′). a public stagecoach, esp. as formerly used in France. [short for F *carosse de diligence* speed coach]

dil·i·gent (dil′i jənt), *adj.* **1.** constant in effort to accomplish something. **2.** done or pursued with persevering attention; painstaking: *a diligent search.* [ME < MF, L *dīligent-* (s. of *dīligēns*), prp. of *dīligere* to choose, like = *dī-* DI-[2] + *-ligere* (sp. var. of *legere* to choose, read); see -ENT] —**dil′i·gent·ly,** *adv.* —**Syn. 1.** industrious, assiduous, sedulous. See **busy. 2.** persevering, untiring, tireless.

dill (dil), *n.* **1.** an apiaceous plant, *Anethum graveolens*, bearing a seedlike fruit used in medicine, in cookery, for flavoring pickles, etc. **2.** its aromatic seeds or leaves used as a common food flavoring. **3.** See **dill pickle.** [ME *di(l)le*, OE *dile;* akin to G *Dill*, Sw *dill*]

Dil·lin·ger (dil′in jər), *n.* **John,** 1902–34, U.S. bank robber and murderer.

dill′ pick′le, a cucumber pickle flavored with dill or with dill and garlic.

dil·ly (dil′ē), *n.*, *pl.* **-lies.** *Informal.* something remarkable of its kind: *a dilly of a movie.* [? special use of *Dilly*, girl's given name]

dil·ly·dal·ly (dil′ē dal′ē, -dal′-), *v.i.*, **-lied, -ly·ing.** to waste time, esp. by indecision; trifle; loiter. [gradational redupl. of DALLY]

dil·u·ent (dil′yo͞o ənt), *adj.* **1.** serving to dilute; diluting. —*n.* **2.** a diluting substance. [< L *dīluent-* (s. of *dīluēns*), prp. of *dīluere* to DILUTE; see -ENT]

di·lute (di lo͞ot′, dī-; *adj. also* dī′lo͞ot), *v.*, **-lut·ed, -lut·ing,** *adj.* —*v.t.* **1.** to make (a liquid) thinner or weaker by the addition of water or the like. **2.** to reduce the strength, force, or efficiency of by admixture. —*v.i.* **3.** to become diluted. —*adj.* **4.** reduced in strength, as a chemical by admixture; weak: *a dilute solution.* [< L *dīlūt(us)* washed away, dissolved (ptp. of *dīluere*) = *dī-* DI-[2] + *lū-* ptp. s. of *luere* to wash + *-t(us)* ptp. suffix]

di·lu·tion (di lo͞o′shən, dī-), *n.* **1.** the act or state of diluting. **2.** the state of being diluted. **3.** something diluted; a diluted form of anything.

di·lu·vi·al (di lo͞o′vē əl), *adj.* **1.** pertaining to or caused by a flood or deluge, esp. the Biblical flood. **2.** *Geol.* pertaining to or consisting of diluvium. Also, **di·lu′vi·an.** [< LL *dīluviāl(is)*. See DILUVIUM, -AL[1]]

di·lu·vi·um (di lo͞o′vē əm), *n.*, *pl.* **-vi·a** (-vē ə), **-vi·ums.** *Geol.* the coarse superficial deposit of glaciers; glacial drift. Also, **di·lu′vi·on** (di lo͞o′vē ən). [< L: flood = *dīlu(ere)* (to) DILUTE + connecting *-v-* + *-ium* n. suffix]

dim (dim), *adj.*, **dim·mer, dim·mest,** *v.*, **dimmed, dim·ming,** *n.* —*adj.* **1.** not bright; obscure from lack of light or from weakness of emitted light: *dim illumination; a dim, flickering lamp.* **2.** not seen clearly or in detail; indistinct. **3.** not clear to the mind; vague: *a dim idea.* **4.** not brilliant; dull in luster: *a dim color.* **5.** not clear or distinct to the senses; faint: *a dim sound.* **6.** not seeing clearly: *eyes dim with tears.* **7.** tending to be unfavorable; not likely to happen, succeed, etc. **8.** not understanding clearly. **9. take a dim view of,** to regard with pessimism, skepticism, etc. —*v.t.* **10.** to make dim or dimmer. **11.** to switch (the headlights of a vehicle) from the high to the low beam. —*v.i.* **12.** to become or grow dim or dimmer. —*n.* **13. dims,** the low-beam headlights or parking lights of an automobile or truck. [ME, OE *dimm;* c. OFris *dim*, Icel *dimm(r)*] —**dim′ly,** *adv.* —**dim′ness,** *n.* —**Syn. 1.** See **dark. 10.** darken, cloud. **12.** blur, dull, fade.

dim., **1.** diminuendo. **2.** diminutive. Also, **dimin.**

Di·Mag·gi·o (də mä′jē ō′, -maj′ē ō′), *n.* **Joseph Paul** ("*Joe*"), born 1914, U.S. baseball player.

dime (dīm), *n.* **1.** a silver coin of the U.S., the 10th part of a dollar, equal to 10 cents. **2. a dime a dozen,** *Slang.* readily available; common. [ME < MF (var. of *disme*) < L *decima* tenth part, tithe, n. use of fem. of *decimus* tenth < *decem* ten]

di·men·hy·dri·nate (dī′men hī′drə nāt′), *n.* *Pharm.* a synthetic antihistamine, $C_{17}H_{22}NO \cdot C_7H_6ClN_4O_2$, used in the treatment of allergies and as a preventive for seasickness and airsickness. [DIME(THYL + AMI)N(E) + HYDR(AM)IN(E) + -ATE[2]]

dime′ nov′el, a cheap melodramatic novel, popular esp. from c1850 to c1920.

di·men·sion (di men′shən, dī-), *n.* **1.** magnitude measured in a particular direction, or along a diameter or principal axis. **2.** Usually, **dimensions. a.** measurement in width, length, and thickness. **b.** scope or importance: *the dimensions* of a problem. **3.** magnitude; size. **4.** *Topology.* a magnitude that serves to define the location of an element within a given set, as of a point on a line, an object in a space, or an event in space-time. **5. dimensions,** *Informal.* measurement (def. 5). [ME *dimensioun* < MF *dimension,* L *dīmensiōn-* (s. of *dīmensiō*) a measuring = *dīmens(us)* measured out (ptp. of *dīmētīrī;* see DI-², METER²) + *-iōn-* -ION] —**di·men′sion·al,** *adj.* —**di·men′sion·al′i·ty,** *n.*

di·mer (dī′mər), *n.* *Chem.* **1.** a molecule composed of two identical molecules. **2.** a polymer derived from two identical monomers.

di·mer·cap·rol (dī′mər kap′rōl, -rôl, -rol), *n.* *Chem.* a viscous liquid, $CH_2(SH)CH(SH)CH_2OH$, developed as an antidote to lewisite and now used in treating bismuth, mercury, and arsenic poisoning. [alter. of *dimercaptopropanol* (*mercapto-* comb. form of MERCAPTAN)]

Dimerous flower

dim·er·ous (dim′ər əs), *adj.* **1.** consisting of or divided into two parts. **2.** *Bot.* (of flowers) having two members in each whorl. [< NL *dimerus* < Gk *dimer(ḗs)* bipartite] —**dim′er·ism,** *n.*

dime′ store′, five-and-ten.

dim·e·ter (dim′i tər), *n.* *Pros.* a verse or line of two measures or feet. [< LL: < Gk *dímetr(os)* of two measures]

di·meth′yl sulf·ox′ide (dī meth′əl sulf ok′sīd), *Chem.* See **DMSO.**

di·met·ric (dī me′trik), *adj.* tetragonal [DI-¹ + METRIC²]

di·mid·i·ate (di mid′ē āt′, dī-; *adj. also* di mid′ē it), *v.,* **-at·ed, -at·ing,** *adj.* —*v.t.* **1.** *Heraldry.* to combine (two coats of arms) so that the dexter half of one coat is placed beside the sinister half of the other. —*adj.* **2.** divided into halves. [< L *dīmidiāt(us)* divided in half (ptp. of *dīmidiāre*) = *dīmidi(us)* half or *dīmidi(um)* a half (see DI-², MEDIUM) + *-ātus* -ATE¹] —**di·mid′i·a′tion,** *n.*

di·min·ish (di min′ish), *v.t.* **1.** to make or cause to seem smaller, less important, etc.; lessen; reduce. **2.** *Music.* to make (an interval) smaller by a half step. **3.** to detract from the authority, honor, stature, or reputation of; disparage. —*v.i.* **4.** to lessen; decrease. [ME; b. *diminue* (< ML *dīminuere* for L *dēminuere* to make smaller) and MINISH] —**di·min′ish·a·ble,** *adj.* —**di·min′ish·ing·ly,** *adv.* —**Syn. 1.** contract, decrease. **4.** ebb, dwindle, abate. See **decrease.**

di·min·ished (di min′isht), *adj.* *Music.* **1.** (of an interval) smaller by a half tone than the corresponding perfect or minor interval. **2.** (of a triad) having a minor third and a diminished fifth above the root.

dimin′ishing returns′, 1. *Econ.* the fact, often stated as a law or principle, that when any factor of production, as labor, is increased while other factors, as capital and land, are held constant in amount, the output per unit of the variable factor will eventually diminish. **2.** any rate of profit, production, benefits, etc., that, beyond a certain point, fails to increase proportionately with added investment, effort, skill, or the like.

di·min·u·en·do (di min′yo͞o en′dō), *adj., n., pl.* **-dos.** *Music.* —*adj.* **1.** gradually reducing in force or loudness; decrescendo (opposed to *crescendo*). —*n.* **2.** a gradual reduction of force or loudness. **3.** a diminuendo passage. *Symbol:* > [< It, prp. of *diminuire* to DIMINISH]

dim·i·nu·tion (dim′ə no͞o′shən, -nyo͞o′-), *n.* **1.** the act, fact, or process of diminishing; lessening; reduction. **2.** *Music.* the imitation of a subject or theme in notes of shorter duration than those first used. [ME *diminucion* < L *dīminūtiōn-* (s. of *dīminūtiō*) for *dēminūtiōn-* (s. of *dēminūtiō*) = *dēminūt(us)* (ptp. of *dēminuere*: *dē-* DE- + *minuere* to lessen) + *-iōn-* -ION]

di·min·u·tive (di min′yə tiv), *adj.* **1.** small; little; tiny: *a diminutive house.* **2.** *Gram.* pertaining to or productive of a form denoting smallness, familiarity, affection, or triviality, as the suffix *-let,* in *droplet* from *drop.* —*n.* **3.** a small thing or person. **4.** *Gram.* a diminutive element or formation. [ME < ML *dīminūtīv(us)* = L *dīminūt(us)* lessened (for *dēminūtus;* see DIMINUTION) + *-īvus* -IVE] —**di·min′u·tive·ly,** *adv.* —**di·min′u·tive·ness,** *n.* —**Syn. 1.** See **little.**

dim·i·ty (dim′i tē), *n., pl.* **-ties.** a thin, cotton fabric woven with a stripe or check of heavier yarn. [< ML *dimit(um)* (< Gk *dímiton,* n. use of neut. of *dímitos* double-threaded = *di-* DI-¹ + *mít(os)* warp thread + *-os* adj. suffix) + -Y²; r. ME *demyt*]

dim·mer (dim′ər), *n.* **1.** a person or thing that dims. **2.** a rheostat or similar device for varying the intensity of illumination, esp. in stage lighting. **3. dimmers,** dim (def. 13).

di·morph (dī′môrf), *n.* *Crystall.* either of the two forms assumed by a substance exhibiting dimorphism. [< Gk *dímorph(os)* having two shapes = *di-* DI-¹ + *morphḗ* form; see -MORPH]

di·mor·phism (dī môr′fizəm), *n.* **1.** *Zool.* the occurrence of two forms distinct in structure, coloration, etc., among animals of the same species. **2.** *Bot.* the occurrence of two different forms of flowers, leaves, etc., on the same plant or on different plants of the same species. **3.** *Crystall.* the property of some substances of crystallizing in two chemically identical but crystallographically distinct forms.

Dimorphism (def. 2) Submerged and floating leaves of fanwort, genus *Cabomba*

di·mor·phite (dī môr′fīt), *n.* a mineral, arsenic sulfide.

di·mor·phous (dī môr′fəs), *adj.* exhibiting dimorphism. Also, **di·mor′phic.** [< Gk *dímorph(os)* (see DIMORPH)]

dim-out (dim′out′), *n.* a reduction or concealment of night lighting, as of a city, a ship, etc., to make it less visible to an enemy from the air or sea. Also, **dim′out′.**

dim·ple (dim′pəl), *n., v.,* **-pled, -pling.** —*n.* **1.** a small, natural hollow area, permanent or transient, in some soft part of the human body, esp. one formed in the cheek in smiling. **2.** any similar slight depression. —*v.t.* **3.** to mark with or as with dimples. **4.** *Metalworking.* to dent (a metal sheet) so as to permit use of bolts or rivets with countersunk heads. —*v.i.* **5.** to form or show dimples. [ME *dimpel;* c. G *Tümpel* pool] —**dim′ply,** *adj.*

dim sum (dim′ sum′), *Chinese Cookery.* small dumplings, usually steamed or fried and filled with meat, vegetables, condiments, etc., and served as appetizers or as a light meal. [< Chin (Cantonese dial.) heart's delight (lit., dot on the heart)]

dim·wit (dim′wit′), *n.* *Slang.* a stupid or slow-thinking person. —**dim′-wit′ted,** *adj.* —**dim′-wit′ted·ly,** *adv.* —**dim′-wit′ted·ness,** *n.*

din (din), *n., v.,* **dinned, din·ning.** —*n.* **1.** a loud, confused noise; a continued, loud, or tumultuous sound; noisy clamor. —*v.t.* **2.** to assail with din. **3.** to sound or utter with clamor or persistent repetition. —*v.i.* **4.** to make a din. [ME *din(e),* OE *dyne, dynn;* c. OIcel *dynr* noise, OHG *tuni*]

Din., (in Yugoslavia) dinar; dinars.

Di·nah (dī′nə), *n.* the daughter of Jacob and Leah. Gen. 30:21. Also, *Douay Bible,* **Di′na.**

di·nar (di när′), *n.* **1.** any of various former coins of the Near East, esp. gold coins issued by Islamic governments. **2.** a money of account of Iran, the 100th part of a rial. **3.** a copper coin and monetary unit of Yugoslavia, equal to 100 paras. *Abbr.:* Din. **4.** a paper money and monetary unit of Iraq and Jordan, equal to 1000 fils. **5.** a paper money and monetary unit of Kuwait, equal to 1000 fils. *Abbr.:* KD. **6.** a paper money and monetary unit of Tunisia, equal to 1000 millimes. [< Ar, Pers < LGk *dēnár(ion)* < L *dēnāri(us)*]

Dinar′ic Alps′ (di nar′ik), a mountain range in W Yugoslavia: part of the Alps.

d'In·dy (daN dē′), *n.* **Vin·cent** (vaN säN′). See **Indy, d'.**

dine (dīn), *v.,* **dined, din·ing.** —*v.i.* **1.** to eat the principal meal of the day; have dinner. **2.** to take any meal. —*v.t.* **3.** to entertain at dinner. **4. dine out,** to take a meal, esp. the principal meal of the day, away from home, as in a hotel or restaurant. [ME *dine(n)* < OF *di(s)n(er)* < VL **disjējūnāre* to break one's fast = *dis-* DIS-¹ + *jējūnāre*]

din·er (dī′nər), *n.* **1.** a person who dines. **2.** a railroad dining car. **3.** a restaurant built like such a car. **4.** any roadside restaurant.

di·ner·ic (dī ner′ik, di-), *adj.* *Physics.* of or pertaining to the face of separation of two immiscible liquid phases. [DI-¹ + LGk *nēr(ón)* water + -IC]

di·ner·o (di nâr′ō *for 2;* Sp. dē ne′rô *for 1*), *n.* **1.** a former silver coin of Peru, equal to ¹⁄₁₀ of a sol. **2.** *U.S. Slang.* money. [< Sp < L *dēnārius* DENARIUS]

Din·e·sen (din′i sən), *n.* **I·sak** (ī′zək), (pen name of *Baroness Karen Blixen*), 1885–1962, Danish author.

di·nette (dī net′), *n.* **1.** a small space, often in or near the kitchen, serving as an informal dining room. **2.** Also called **dinette′ set′.** a small table and set of matching chairs for such a space.

ding (ding), *v.t., v.i.* **1.** to sound as a bell; ring, esp. with wearisome continuance. **2.** *Informal.* to keep repeating; impress by reiteration. —*n.* **3.** the sound of a bell or the like. [see DING-DONG]

ding-a-ling (ding′ə ling′), *n.* *Informal.* a stupid, befuddled, dim-witted person.

ding·bat (ding′bat′), *n.* **1.** *Informal.* dingus. **2.** *Print.* an ornamental piece of type for borders, decorations, etc. **3.** *Archaic.* an object, as a brick, serving as a missile. [?]

ding-dong (ding′dông′, -dong′), *n.* **1.** the sound of a bell. **2.** any similar sound of repeated strokes. —*adj.* **3.** characterized by or resembling the sound of a bell. **4.** marked by rapid alternation of retaliatory action: *a ding-dong struggle between the two teams.* [gradational compound based on *ding,* appar. b. DIN and RING²]

din·gey (ding′ē, ding′gē), *n., pl.* **-geys.** dinghy.

din·ghy (ding′ē, ding′gē), *n., pl.* **-ghies. 1.** a ship's small boat. **2.** any of various rowing or sailing boats used in sheltered waters along the Indian coasts to transport passengers and freight. Also, **dingey, dingy, dinky.** [< Bengali *diṅgi,* Hindi *diṅgī,* dim. of *diṅgā* boat]

Dingo (21 in. high at shoulder; total length 3½ ft.; tail 14 in.)

din·gle (ding′gəl), *n.* a narrow valley or shady dell. [ME: a deep dell, hollow; akin to OE *dung* dungeon, OHG *tunc* cellar]

din·go (ding′gō), *n., pl.* **-goes.** a wolflike, wild dog, *Canis dingo,* of Australia, having a reddish-brown coat. [< native Austral]

ding·us (ding′əs), *n., pl.* **-us·es.** *Informal.* a gadget or object whose name is unknown or forgotten. [< D *dinges,* c. G *Dings,* gen. of *Ding* THING¹]

din·gy¹ (din′jē), *adj.,* **-gi·er, -gi·est. 1.** of a dark, dull, or dirty color or aspect; lacking brightness or freshness. **2.** shabby; dismal. [?] —**din′gi·ness,** *n.*

din·gy² (ding′gē), *n., pl.* **-gies.** dinghy.

din′ing car′, a railroad car equipped as a restaurant and supplied with a kitchen, pantry, etc.

din′ing room′, a room in which meals are eaten, as in a home or hotel.

din′ing ta′ble, a table, esp. one seating several persons, where meals are served and eaten.

di·ni·tro·ben·zene (dī nī′trō ben′zēn, -ben zēn′), *n.* *Chem.* any of three isomeric benzene derivatives having the formula $C_6H_4(NO_2)$ the most important of which is the meta form: used chiefly in the manufacture of dyes.

dink¹ (dingk), *Scot.* —*adj.* **1.** neatly dressed; dressed in one's finest or newest clothes. —*v.t.* **2.** to decorate; array. [?] —**dink′ly,** *adv.*

dink² (dingk), *n.* dinghy. [by apocope and unvoicing]

dink[3] (dingk), *n.* a small, close-fitting cap, often worn by college freshmen; beanie. [? back formation from DINKY[1]]
dink·ey (ding′kē), *n., pl.* **-eys.** anything small, esp. a small locomotive. Also, **dinky.** [DINK[1] + -EY[2]]
din·kum (ding′kəm), *Australian.* —*adj.* **1.** genuine; authentic. **2.** honest; fair. —*adv.* **3.** honestly, truly. [dial. E: work]
dink·y[1] (ding′kē), *adj.*, **dink·i·er, dink·i·est,** *n., pl.* **dink·ies.** —*adj.* **1.** *Informal.* of small size or importance. —*n.* **2.** dinkey. [DINK[1] + -Y[1]]
dink·y[2] (ding′kē), *n., pl.* **dink·ies.** dinghy.
din·ner (din′ər), *n.* **1.** the main meal of the day, eaten in the evening or at midday. **2.** a formal meal in honor of some person or occasion. **3.** See **table d'hôte.** [ME *diner* < OF *disner* (n. use of v.); see DINE]
din′ner jack′et, 1. a man's jacket for semiformal evening dress; tuxedo. **2.** the complete semiformal outfit, including this jacket, dark trousers, a bow tie, and, usually, a cummerbund.
din·ner·ware (din′ər wâr′), *n.* china, glasses, and silver used for table service.
dino-, a learned borrowing from Greek, where it meant "terrible," used in the formation of compound words: *dinothere.* [< Gk *deino-*, comb. form of *deinós*]
Di·noc·er·as (dī nos′ər əs), *n.* an extinct genus of huge, horned, ungulate mammals of the Eocene epoch of North America. [< NL DINO- + Gk *kéras* horn]
din·o·flag·el·late (din′ə flaj′ə lāt′), *n.* any of numerous chiefly marine, plantlike flagellates of the order *Dinoflagellata*, which are important elements of plankton and have usually two flagella, one being in a groove around the body and the other extending from the center of the body.
di·no·saur (dī′nə sôr′), *n.* any chiefly terrestrial, herbivorous, or carnivorous reptile of the extinct orders *Saurischia* and *Ornithischia*, from the Mesozoic era, certain species of which are the largest known land animals. [< NL *dinosaur(us)*. See DINO-, -SAUR]

Dinosaur, *Tyrannosaurus rex* (Height 20 ft.; length 50 ft.)

di·no·sau·ri·an (dī′nə sôr′ē ən), *adj.* **1.** pertaining to or of the nature of a dinosaur. —*n.* **2.** a dinosaur. [< NL *Dinosauri(a)* name of the group (see DINO-, -SAUR) + -AN]
di·no·there (dī′nə thēr′), *n.* any elephantlike mammal of the extinct genus *Dinotherium*, from the later Tertiary period of Europe and Asia, having downward-curving tusks in the lower jaw. [< NL *dinother(ium)* = *dino-* DINO- + Gk *thēríon* a wild beast < *thēr-* a beast, wild animal]
dint (dint), *n.* **1.** force; power: *by dint of argument.* **2.** a dent. **3.** *Archaic.* a blow; stroke. —*v.t.* **4.** to make a dent or dents in. **5.** to impress or drive in with force. [ME]
Din·wid·die (din wid′ē, din′wid ē), *n.* **Robert,** 1693–1770, British colonial administrator in America: lieutenant governor of Virginia 1751–58.
di·oc·e·san (dī os′i sən), *adj.* **1.** of or pertaining to a diocese. —*n.* **2.** the bishop in charge of a diocese. [ME < ML *diocēsān(us)*]
di·o·cese (dī′ə sēs′, -sis), *n.* an ecclesiastical district under the jurisdiction of a bishop. [ME *diocise, diocese* < MF < LL *diocēsis*, var. of *dioecēsis*, L: a governor's jurisdiction < Gk *dioíkēsis* housekeeping, administration, province, diocese = *dioik(eîn)* (to) keep house, administer, govern (*di-* DI-[3] + *oikeîn* to dwell, occupy, manage < *oîkos* house) + *-ē-* thematic vowel + *-sis* -SIS]
Di·o·cle·tian (dī′ə klē′shən), *n.* (*Gaius Aurelius Valerius Diocletianus*) A.D. 245–316, Illyrian soldier: emperor of Rome 284–305.
di·ode (dī′ōd), *n.* *Electronics.* a device, as a two-element electron tube or semiconductor, through which current can pass only in one direction. [DI-[1] + -ODE[2]]
di·oe·cious (dī ē′shəs), *adj.* *Biol.* (esp. of plants) having the male and female organs in separate and distinct individuals; having separate sexes. [< NL *Dioeci(a)* name of the class (*di-* DI-[1] + Gk *oikía* a house, dwelling < *oîkos*) + -OUS]
Di·og·e·nes (dī oj′ə nēz′), *n.* 412?–323 B.C., Greek Cynic philosopher. —**Di·o·gen·ic** (dī′ə jen′ik), *adj.*
Di′o·mede Is′lands (dī′ə mēd′), two islands in Bering Strait, one belonging to the Soviet Union **(Big Diomede),** ab. 15 sq. mi., and one belonging to the U.S. **(Little Diomede),** ab. 4 sq. mi.: separated by the International Date Line and the U.S.-Soviet Union boundary.
Di·o·me·des (dī′ə mē′dēz), *n.* *Class. Myth.* **1.** the son of Tydeus, next in prowess to Achilles at the siege of Troy. **2.** a Thracian king who fed his wild mares on human flesh and was himself fed to them by Hercules. Also, **Di·o·mede** (dī′ə mēd′).
Di·o·ne (dī ō′nē), *n.* *Class. Myth.* the consort of Zeus: sometimes believed to be the mother of Aphrodite.
Di·o·ny·si·a (dī′ə nish′ē ə, -nis′-), *n.pl.* the orgiastic and dramatic festivals held periodically in honor of Dionysus, esp. those in Attica, from which Greek comedy and tragedy developed. [< L < Gk]
Di·o·nys·i·ac (dī′ə nis′ē ak′), *adj.* **1.** pertaining to the Dionysia or to Dionysus; Bacchic. **2.** Dionysian (def. 2). [< L *Dionȳsiac(us)* < Gk *Dionysiakós*. See DIONYSUS, -AC]
Di·o·ny·sian (dī′ə nish′ən, -nis′ē ən), *adj.* **1.** pertaining to Dionysus or Bacchus. **2.** recklessly uninhibited; frenzied; orgiastic. Cf. **Apollonian.**
Di·o·ny·si·us (dī′ə nish′ē əs, -nis′-), *n.* **1.** ("*the Elder*") 431?–367 B.C., Greek soldier: tyrant of Syracuse 405–367. **2. Saint,** died A.D. 268, pope 259–268.
Diony′sius Ex·ig′u·us (eg zig′yo͞o əs, ek sig′-), died A.D. 556?, Scythian monk, chronologist, and scholar: devised the current system of reckoning the Christian era.
Diony′sius of Alexan′dria, Saint ("*the Great*"), A.D. c190–265, patriarch of Alexandria 247?–265?.
Diony′sius of Halicarnas′sus, died 7? B.C., Greek rhetorician and historian in Rome.
Di·o·ny·sus (dī′ə nī′səs), *n.* *Class. Myth.* the god of fertility, wine, and drama; Bacchus. Also, **Di′o·ny′sos.**
di′o·phan′tine equa′tion (dī′ə fan′tīn, -tēn, -fan′tᵊn, dī′-), *Math.* an equation involving more than one variable in which the coefficients of the variables are integers and for which integral solutions are sought. [named after *Diophantus* 3rd-century A.D. Greek mathematician; see -INE[1]]
di·op·side (dī op′sīd, -sid), *n.* *Mineral.* a common variety of pyroxene. [DI-[3] + Gk *óps(is)* appearance + -IDE]
di·op·tase (dī op′tās), *n.* a mineral, hydrous copper silicate, $CuSiO_3 \cdot H_2O$. [< F = *di-* DI-[3] + Gk *optasía* view]
di·op·ter (dī op′tər), *n.* *Optics.* a unit of measure of the refractive power of a lens. *Abbr.:* D. Also, *esp. Brit.,* **di·op′tre.** [< L *dioptra* < Gk: instrument for measuring height or levels = *di-* DI-[3] + **op-* (for *ópsesthai* to see) + *-tra*]
di·op·tom·e·ter (dī′op tom′i tər), *n.* an instrument for measuring the refraction of the eye. [DI-[3] + OPT(IC) + -O- + -METER]
di·op·tric (dī op′trik), *adj.* **1.** *Optics.* pertaining to dioptrics: *dioptric images.* **2.** *Optics, Ophthalm.* noting or pertaining to refraction or refracted light. Also, **di·op′tri·cal.** [< Gk *dioptrik(ós)*] —**di·op′tri·cal·ly,** *adv.*
di·op·trics (dī op′triks), *n.* (*construed as sing.*) the branch of geometrical optics dealing with the formation of images by lenses. [see DIOPTRIC, -ICS]
di·o·ram·a (dī′ə ram′ə, -rä′mə), *n.* **1.** a scene reproduced in three dimensions by placing objects, figures, etc., in front of a painted background. **2.** a spectacular picture, partly translucent, for exhibition through an aperture. [< F = *di-* DI-[3] + Gk (*h*)*órama* view (*hor(ân)* (to) see, look + *-a-* thematic vowel + *-ma* n. suffix)] —**di′o·ram′ic,** *adj.*
di·o·rite (dī′ə rīt′), *n.* a granular igneous rock consisting essentially of plagioclase feldspar and hornblende. [< F, irreg. < Gk *dior(ízein)* (to) distinguish; see -ITE[1]] —**di·o·rit·ic** (dī′ə rit′ik), *adj.*
Di·os·cu·ri (dī′ə skyo͝or′ī), *n.pl.* *Class. Myth.* Castor and Pollux, the twin sons of Zeus and Leda.
di·os·gen·in (dī′oz jen′in, dī oz′jə nin), *n.* *Biochem.* a compound, $C_{27}H_{42}O_3$, used in the synthesis of steroidal hormones, as of progesterone. [< NL *Dios(corea)* name of the genus, irreg. after *Dioscorides* 1st-century A.D. Greek physician + -GEN + -IN[2]]
di·ox·ide (dī ok′sīd, -sid), *n.* *Chem.* an oxide containing two atoms of oxygen, each of which is bonded directly to an atom of a second element, as nitrogen dioxide, NO_2.
di·ox·in (dī ok′sən), *n.* *Chem.* a highly toxic chlorinated hydrocarbon, 2,3,7,8 tetrachlorodibenzo-p-dioxin, formed by acid runoff and as an impurity or byproduct in herbicide manufacture and other industrial processes: believed to be carcinogenic.
dip (dip), *v.,* **dipped** or (*Archaic*) **dipt; dip·ping,** *n.* —*v.t.* **1.** to plunge (something, as a cloth or a sponge) temporarily into a liquid, so as to moisten it, dye it, or cause it to take up some of the liquid. **2.** to raise or take up by bailing, scooping, or ladling. **3.** to lower and raise: *to dip a flag in salutation.* **4.** to immerse (cattle, sheep, hogs, etc.) in a solution to destroy germs, parasites, or the like. **5.** to make (a candle) by repeatedly plunging a wick into melted wax. —*v.i.* **6.** to plunge briefly into water or other liquid: *The boat dipped into the waves.* **7.** to put the hand, a dipper, etc., down into a liquid or a container, esp. in order to remove something: *He dipped into the jar for an olive.* **8.** to sink or drop down: *The sun dipped below the horizon.* **9.** to incline or slope downward. **10.** to decrease slightly or temporarily: *Stock-market prices often dip on Fridays.* **11.** to engage slightly in a subject: *to dip into astronomy.* **12.** to read here and there in a book. —*n.* **13.** the act of dipping or plunging into or as into a liquid. **14.** that which is taken up by dipping. **15.** a scoop of ice cream. **16.** a liquid or soft substance into which something is dipped. **17.** a creamy mixture of savory foods for scooping with potato chips, crackers, and the like, often served as an hors d'oeuvre, esp. with cocktails. **18.** a momentary lowering; a sinking down. **19.** a moderate or temporary decrease: *a dip in stock-market prices.* **20.** a downward extension, inclination, slope, or course. **21.** the amount of such extension. **22.** a hollow or depression in the land. **23.** a brief swim. **24.** *Geol., Mining.* the downward inclination of a vein or stratum with reference to a horizontal plane. **25.** the angular amount by which the horizon lies below the level of the eye. **26.** Also called **magnetic dip.** the angle that a magnetized needle pivoted on a horizontal axis makes with the plane of the horizon. **27.** a short, downward plunge, as of an airplane. **28.** *Gymnastics.* an exercise on the parallel bars in which a person bends his elbows until his chin is on a level with the bars, then elevates himself by straightening his arms. [ME *dipp(en)*, OE *dyppan;* akin to G *taufen* to baptize, and to DEEP]
—**Syn. 1.** duck. DIP, IMMERSE, PLUNGE refer literally to putting something into water (or any liquid). To DIP is to put down into a liquid quickly or partially and lift out again: *to dip a finger into water to test the temperature.* IMMERSE denotes a gradual lowering into a liquid until covered by it, sometimes for a moment or two only (as in certain forms of baptism): *to immerse meat in salt water.* PLUNGE adds a suggestion of force or suddenness: *to plunge a chicken into boiling water before plucking it.* **2.** scoop, ladle, bail.
di·phase (dī′fāz′), *adj.* *Elect.* having two phases; two-phase. Also, **di·phas·ic** (dī fā′zik).
di·phen·yl (dī fen′ᵊl, -fēn′-), *n.* *Chem.* biphenyl.
di·phen·yl·a·mine (dī fen′ᵊl ə mēn′, -am′in, -fēn′-), *n.* *Chem.* a benzene derivative, $(C_6H_5)_2NH$, used in the preparation of dyes, as a stabilizer for nitrocellulose propellants, and in chemical analysis.
di·phos·gene (dī fos′jēn), *n.* *Chem.* a toxic liquid, $ClOOCCl_3$: a World War I poison gas now used chiefly in organic synthesis. [DI-[1] + PHOSGENE]
diph·the·ri·a (dif thēr′ē ə, dip-), *n.* *Pathol.* a febrile, infectious disease caused by the bacillus *Corynebacterium diphtheriae*, and characterized by the formation of a false membrane in the air passages, esp. the throat. [< NL < F *diphthérie* = *diphthér-* < Gk *diphthér(a)* skin, leather + *-ia* -IA] —**diph·the·rit·ic** (dif′thə rit′ik, dip′-), **diph·the′ri·al, diph·ther·ic** (dif ther′ik, dip-), *adj.*

diph·thong (dif′thông, -thong, dip′-), *n.* **1.** *Phonet.* an unsegmentable, gliding speech sound varying continuously in phonetic quality but held to be a single sound or phoneme as the *oi*-sound of *toy* or *boil.* **2.** (not in technical use) **a.** a digraph, as the *ea* of *meat.* **b.** a ligature, as *æ.* [< LL *diphthong(us)* < Gk *díphthongos*, lit., having two sounds (*di-* DI-¹ + *phthóngos* voice, sound)] —**diph·thon·gal** (dif-thông′gəl, -thong′-, dip-), *adj.*

diph·thong·ise (dif′thông īz′, -gīz′, -thong-, dip′-), *v.t., v.i.*, **-ised, -is·ing.** *Chiefly Brit.* diphthongize. —**diph′-thong·i·sa′tion,** *n.*

diph·thong·ize (dif′thông īz′, -gīz′, -thong-, dip′-), *v.*, **-ized, -iz·ing.** *Phonet.* —*v.t.* **1.** to change into or pronounce as a diphthong. —*v.i.* **2.** to become a diphthong. —**diph′-thong·i·za′tion,** *n.*

diph·y·o·dont (dif′ē ə dont′), *adj.* *Zool.* having two successive sets of teeth, as most mammals. [< Gk *diphy(ḗs)* double, twofold (*di-* DI-¹ + *phyḗ* growth, nature < *phýein* to produce, grow) + -ODONT]

dipl., **1.** diplomat. **2.** diplomatic.

di·plex (dī′plex), *adj.* pertaining to or noting a telegraphic or telephonic system permitting the sending or receiving of two signals or messages simultaneously. [DI-¹ + *-plex*, modeled on *duplex*]

diplo-, a combining form meaning "double," "in pairs": *diplococcus.* [< Gk, comb. form of *diplóos* twofold]

dip·lo·blas·tic (dip′lə blas′tik), *adj.* having two germ layers, the ectoderm and entoderm, as the embryos of sponges and coelenterates.

dip·lo·coc·cus (dip′lə kok′əs), *n.*, *pl.* **-coc·ci** (-kok′sī). *Bacteriol.* any of several spherical bacteria occurring in pairs, as *Diplococcus pneumoniae.* [< NL]

di·plod·o·cus (di plod′ə kəs), *n.*, *pl.* **-cus·es.** a huge, herbivorous dinosaur of the genus *Diplodocus*, from the upper Jurassic period of western North America, growing to a length of about 87 feet. [< NL = *diplo-* DIPLO- + Gk *dokós* beam, bar, shaft]

dip·lo·ë (dip′lō ē′), *n.* *Anat.* the cancellate bony tissue between the hard inner and outer walls of the bones of the cranium. [< Gk: a fold < *diplóos* DIPLO-] —**di·plo·ic** (di plō′ik), **di·plo·et·ic** (dip′lō et′ik), *adj.*

dip·loid (dip′loid), *adj.* **1.** double; twofold. **2.** *Biol.* having two similar complements of chromosomes. —*n.* **3.** *Biol.* an organism or cell having double the haploid number of chromosomes. **4.** *Crystall.* a solid belonging to the isometric system and having 24 trapezoidal planes. —**dip·loi′dic,** *adj.*

di·plo·ma (di plō′mə), *n.*, *pl.* **-mas, -ma·ta** (-mə tə), *v.*, **-maed, -ma·ing.** —*n.* **1.** a document given by an educational institution conferring a degree on a person or certifying his satisfactory completion of a course of study. **2.** a document conferring some honor, privilege, or power. **3.** a public or official document, esp. one of historical interest. —*v.t.* **4.** to furnish with a diploma. [< L: a letter of recommendation, an official document < Gk: a letter folded double = *diplō(os)* DIPLO- + *-ma* n. suffix]

di·plo·ma·cy (di plō′mə sē), *n.* **1.** the conduct by government officials of negotiations and other relations between nations. **2.** the art or science of conducting such negotiations. **3.** skill in managing negotiations, handling people, etc., so that there is little or no ill will; tact. [< F *diplomatie* (with *t* pronounced as *s*)]

dip·lo·mat (dip′lə mat′), *n.* **1.** a person employed by a national government to conduct official negotiations and maintain political, economic, and social relations with another country or countries. **2.** a person who is tactful and skillful in managing a delicate situation, handling people, etc. [< F *diplomate*, back formation from *diplomatique* DIPLOMATIC]

dip·lo·mate (dip′lə māt′), *n.* a person who has received a diploma, esp. a doctor, engineer, etc., who has been certified as a specialist by a board within his profession. [DIPLOM(A) + -ATE¹]

dip·lo·mat·ic (dip′lə mat′ik), *adj.* **1.** of, pertaining to, or engaged in diplomacy: *diplomatic officials; diplomatic immunity.* **2.** skilled in diplomacy; tactful. **3.** of or pertaining to diplomatics: *a diplomatic edition of a text.* [< F *diplomatique* < NL *diplōmatic(us)* = L *diplōmat-* (s. of *diplōma*) DIPLOMA + *-icus* -IC] —**dip′lo·mat′i·cal·ly,** *adv.*

diplomat′ic corps′, the entire body of diplomats accredited to and resident at a capital or court.

diplomat′ic immu′nity, exemption from taxation, arrest, customs duties, etc., enjoyed by diplomatic officials and their dependents under international law.

dip·lo·mat·ics (dip′lə mat′iks), *n.* (*construed as sing.*) the science of deciphering old official documents and of determining their authenticity.

di·plo·ma·tist (di plō′mə tist), *n.* *Chiefly Brit.* a diplomat [DIPLOMAT(IC) + -IST]

di·plo·pi·a (di plō′pē ə), *n.* *Ophthalm.* a pathological condition of vision in which a single object appears double (opposed to *haplopia*). [< NL] —**di·plop·ic** (di plop′ik), *adj.*

dip·lo·pod (dip′lə pod′), *adj.* **1.** belonging or pertaining to the *Diplopoda.* —*n.* **2.** any arthropod of the class *Diplopoda*, comprising the millipedes. [< NL *Diplopod(a)*. See DIPLO-, -POD]

di·plo·sis (di plō′sis), *n.* *Biol.* the doubling of the chromosome number by the union of the haploid sets in the union of gametes. [< Gk *díplōsis* a doubling = *dipl(oûn)* (to) double (< *diplóos* DIPLO-) + *-ōsis* -OSIS]

dip·no·an (dip′nō ən), *adj.* **1.** belonging or pertaining to the group *Dipnoi*, comprising the lungfishes. —*n.* **2.** a dipnoan fish. [< NL *Dipno(i)* name of the class, n. use of pl. of *dipnous* (adj.) (< Gk *dípno(os)* double-breathing: *di-* DI-¹ + *pno(ḗ)* breathing, breath, air < *pneîn* to breathe) + -AN]

dip·o·dy (dip′ə dē), *n.*, *pl.* **-dies.** *Pros.* a group of two feet, esp., in accentual verse, in which one of the two accented syllables bears primary stress and the other bears secondary stress. [< LL *dipodia* < Gk: the quality of having two feet = *dipod-* (s. of *dípous*) two-footed (see DI-¹, -POD) + *-ia* -Y] —**di·pod·ic** (dī pod′ik), *adj.*

di·pole (dī′pōl′), *n.* **1.** *Physics, Elect.* a pair of electric point charges or magnetic poles of equal magnitude and opposite signs, separated by an infinitesimal distance. **2.** *Physical Chem.* a molecule in which the centroid of the positive charges is different from the centroid of the negative charges. **3.** Also called **di′pole anten′na.** *Radio, Television.* an antenna of a transmitter or receiver consisting of two equal rods extending in opposite directions. [DI-¹ + POLE²] —**di·po′lar,** *adj.*

dip·per (dip′ər), *n.* **1.** a person or thing that dips. **2.** a cuplike container with a long, straight handle, used for dipping liquids. **3.** (*cap.*) *Astron.* **a.** Also called **Big Dipper.** the group of seven bright stars in Ursa Major resembling such a vessel in outline. **b.** Also called **Little Dipper.** a similar group in Ursa Minor. **4.** any of various diving birds, esp. the water ouzels. [ME: diving bird]

dip·py (dip′ē), *adj.*, **-pi·er, -pi·est.** *Slang.* mad; foolish; silly. [?]

dip·so·ma·ni·a (dip′sə mā′nē ə), *n.* an irresistible, typically periodic, craving for intoxicating drink. [< NL < Gk *díps(a)* thirst + *-o-* -O- + *manía* -MANIA]

dip·so·ma·ni·ac (dip′sə mā′nē ak′), *n.* a person with an abnormal, irresistible, and insatiable craving for liquor. —**dip·so·ma·ni·a·cal** (dip′sə mə nī′ə kəl), *adj.* —**Syn.** See **drunkard.**

dipt (dipt), *v.* *Archaic.* pt. of **dip¹.**

Dip·ter·a (dip′tər ə, -trə), *n.* **1.** (*italics*) the order comprising the dipterous insects. **2.** (*l.c.*) pl. of dipteron. [< NL < Gk, neut. pl. of *dípteros* two-winged; see DIPTEROUS]

dip·ter·an (dip′tər ən), *adj.* **1.** dipterous (def. 1). —*n.* **2.** a dipterous insect.

dip·ter·o·car·pa·ceous (dip′tə rō kär pā′shəs), *adj.* belonging to the *Dipterocarpaceae*, a family of trees, chiefly of tropical Asia. [< NL *Dipterocarpace(ae)* (*Dipterocarp(us)* (see DIPTERA, -O-, -CARP) + *-aceae* -ACEAE) + -OUS]

dip·ter·on (dip′tə ron′), *n.*, *pl.* **-ter·a** (-tər ə). a dipterous insect: a fly. [< Gk, neut. of *dípteros*; see DIPTEROUS]

dip·ter·ous (dip′tər əs), *adj.* **1.** *Entomol.* belonging or pertaining to the order *Diptera*, comprising the houseflies, mosquitoes, gnats, etc., characterized typically by a single, anterior pair of membranous wings with the posterior pair reduced to small, knobbed structures. **2.** *Bot.* having two winglike appendages, as seeds, stems, or the like. [< NL *dipter(us)* < Gk *dípteros* two-winged. See DI-¹, -PTEROUS]

dip·tych (dip′tik), *n.* **1.** a hinged two-leaved tablet used in ancient times for writing on with a stylus. **2.** a pair of pictures or carvings on two panels, usually hinged together. [< LL *diptych(a)* writing tablet with two leaves < Gk, neut. pl. of *díptychos* folded together = *di-* DI-¹ + *ptych(ḗ)* a fold (< *ptýssein* to fold) + *-a* neut. pl. ending]

Di·rac (di rak′), *n.* **Paul A·dri·en Maurice** (ā′drē ən), born 1902, English physicist: Nobel prize 1933.

Di·rae (dī′rē) *n.pl.* *Rom. Myth.* Furiae.

dire (dīᵊr), *adj.*, **dir·er, dir·est.** **1.** causing or involving great fear or suffering; dreadful; terrible: *a dire calamity.* **2.** indicating misfortune or disaster: *a dire prediction.* **3.** urgent; desperate: *in dire need of food.* [< L *dīr(us)* fearful, unlucky] —**dire′ly,** *adv.* —**dire′ness,** *n.*

di·rect (di rekt′, dī-), *v.t.* **1.** to guide by advice, helpful information, instruction, etc. **2.** to regulate the course of; control. **3.** to administer; manage; supervise: *He directs the affairs of the company.* **4.** to give authoritative instructions to; command; order or ordain (something): *I directed him to leave the room.* **5.** to serve as director for (a musical work, play, motion picture, etc.). **6.** to tell or show (a person) the way to a place; guide. **7.** to aim or send toward a place or object: *to direct radio waves around the globe.* **8.** to cause to move, act, or work toward a given end or result (often fol. by *to* or *toward*): *He directed his energies toward the accomplishment of the work.* **9.** to address (words, a remark, etc.) to a person or persons. **10.** to mark (a letter, package, etc.) with the name and address of the intended recipient. —*v.i.* **11.** to act as a guide. **12.** to give commands or orders. **13.** to serve as the director of a play, orchestra, etc. —*adj.* **14.** proceeding in a straight line or by the shortest course: *a direct route.* **15.** proceeding in an unbroken line of descent: *a direct descendant.* **16.** *Math.* (of a proportion) containing terms of which an increase (or decrease) in one results in an increase (or decrease) in another: a term is said to be in direct proportion to another term if one increases (or decreases) as the other increases (or decreases). **17.** personal or immediate: *direct contact with the voters; direct exposure to a disease.* **18.** straightforward; frank; candid. **19.** absolute; exact: *the direct opposite.* **20.** consisting exactly of the words originally used: *direct quotation.* **21.** *Govt.* of or by action of voters, which takes effect without any intervening agency such as representatives. **22.** inevitable; consequential: *a direct result of political action.* **23.** allocated for or arising from a particular known agency, process, job, etc.: *The new machine was listed by the accountant as a direct cost.* **24.** *Elect.* of or pertaining to direct current. **25.** *Astron.* **a.** moving in an orbit in the same direction as the earth in its revolution round the sun. **b.** appearing to move on the celestial sphere in the direction of the natural order of the signs of the zodiac, from west to east. Cf. **retrograde** (def. 4). **26.** (of dye colors) working without the use of a mordant; substantive. —*adv.* **27.** in a direct manner; directly; straight: *Answer me direct.* [ME *direct(en)* < L *dīrect(us)* made straight (ptp. of *dīrigere* to arrange) = *dī-* DI-² + *rec-* (perf. s. of *regere* to guide) + *-t(us)* ptp. suffix] —**di·rect′ness,** *n.*

—**Syn. 1.** See **guide. 4.** DIRECT, ORDER, COMMAND mean to issue instructions. DIRECT suggests also giving explanations or advice; the emphasis is not on the authority of the director, but on steps necessary for the accomplishing of a purpose. ORDER connotes a personal relationship, in which a person in a superior position imperatively instructs a subordinate (or subordinates) to do something. COMMAND, less personal and, often, less specific in detail, suggests greater formality and, sometimes, a more fixed authority on the part of the superior. **18.** open, sincere, outspoken. —**Ant. 14.** devious, roundabout.

direct′ ac′tion, any action seeking to achieve a result

directly, esp. an action against an established authority or powerful institution, as a strike, picketing, etc.

direct′ cur′rent. See DC (def. 2).

direct′ dis′course, quotation of a speaker using his exact words. Cf. **indirect discourse.**

di·rect·ed (di rek′tid, dī-), *adj.* **1.** having direction; guided; regulated: *a carefully directed program.* **2.** subject to direction, guidance, etc.

direct′ ev′idence, evidence of a witness who testifies to the truth of the fact to be proved (contrasted with *circumstantial evidence*).

direct′ examina′tion, *Law.* the first interrogation of a witness by the side that has called him (contrasted with *cross-examination*).

di·rec·tion (di rek′shən, dī-), *n.* **1.** the act or an instance of directing. **2.** the line along which anything lies, faces, moves, etc., with reference to the point or region toward which it is directed. **3.** the point or region itself: *The direction is north.* **4.** a position on a line extending from a specific point toward a point of the compass or toward the nadir or the zenith. **5.** a line of thought or action or a tendency or inclination: *the direction of contemporary thought.* **6.** instruction or guidance for making, using, etc.: *directions for baking a cake.* **7.** order; command. **8.** management; control; guidance; supervision: *a company under good direction.* **9.** a directorate. **10.** the name and address of the intended recipient as written on a letter, package, etc. **11.** decisions in a stage or film production as to stage business, speaking of lines, lighting, and general presentation. **12.** the technique, act, or business of making such decisions, managing and training a cast of actors, etc. **13.** the technique, act, or business of directing an orchestra, play, motion picture, etc. **14.** *Music.* a symbol or phrase which indicates in a score the proper tempo, style of performance, mood, etc. [ME *direccioun* < L *dīrectiōn-* (s. of *dīrectiō*) a making straight]

di·rec·tion·al (di rek′shə nəl, dī-), *adj.* **1.** of or pertaining to direction in space. **2.** *Radio.* adapted for determining the direction of signals received, or for transmitting signals in a given direction.

direc′tion find′er, *Radio.* a contrivance on a receiver, usually based on a loop antenna rotating on a vertical axis, that permits ascertaining the direction of incoming radio waves. —**direc′tion find′ing.**

di·rec·tive (di rek′tiv, dī-), *adj.* **1.** serving to direct; directing. —*n.* **2.** an authoritative instruction or direction: *the directives of the bishop.* [ME < ML *dīrectīv(us)*]

direct′ light′ing, lighting in which most of the light is cast directly from the fixture or source to the illumined area.

di·rect·ly (di rekt′lē, dī-), *adv.* **1.** in a direct line, way, or manner; straight. **2.** at once; immediately: *Do that directly.* **3.** presently; shortly; soon: *They will be here directly.* **4.** absolutely; exactly; precisely: *directly opposite the store.* **5.** without intervening space; next in order: *The truck was parked directly behind my car.* **6.** *Math.* in direct proportion. —*conj.* **7.** as soon as: *Directly he arrived, he mentioned the subject.* [ME *directli*] —**Syn. 2.** See **immediately.**

direct′ mail′, mail, usually consisting of advertising matter, appeals for donations, or the like, sent individually to large numbers of people.

direct′ ob′ject, a word or group of words representing the person or thing upon which the action of a verb is performed or toward which it is directed: in English, generally coming after the verb, without a preposition. In *He saw it* the pronoun *it* is the direct object of *saw.*

Di·rec·toire (dē rek twär′), *adj.* **1.** noting or pertaining to the style of French furnishings and decoration of the mid-1790's. —*n.* **2.** *Fr. Hist.* directory (def. 4). [< F]

di·rec·tor (di rek′tər, dī-), *n.* **1.** a person or thing that directs. **2.** one of a body of persons chosen to control or govern the affairs of a company or corporation: *a board of directors.* **3.** the person responsible for the interpretive aspects of a stage, film, television, or radio production. **4.** the musical conductor of an orchestra, chorus, etc. **5.** the manager or chief executive of certain schools, institutes, government bureaus, etc. **6.** *Mil.* a mechanical or electronic device that continuously calculates firing data for use against an airplane or other moving target. [< LL] —**di·rec′tor·ship′,** *n.*

di·rec·to·rate (di rek′tər it, dī-), *n.* **1.** the office of a director. **2.** a body of directors. [< F *directorat* < LL *dīrector* DIRECTOR + F *-at* -ATE[1]]

di·rec·to·ri·al (di rek tôr′ē əl, -tōr′-, dī′-), *adj.* pertaining to a director or directorate. [< LL *dīrectōri(us)* (see DIRECTOR, -ORY[1]) + -AL[1]] —**di·rec·to′ri·al·ly,** *adv.*

di·rec·to·ry (di rek′tə rē, -trē, dī-), *n., pl.* **-ries,** *adj.* —*n.* **1.** a book containing an alphabetical index of the names and addresses of persons in a city, district, organization, etc., or of a particular class of people. **2.** a board or tablet on a wall of a building listing the room and floor numbers of the occupants. **3.** a book of directions. **4. the Directory,** *Fr. Hist.* the body of five directors forming the executive power of France from 1795 to 1799. —*adj.* **5.** serving to direct; directing; directive. [defs. 1, 2, 3, 5: < ML *dīrectōrium,* neut. n. use of LL *dīrectōrius* DIRECTORIAL; def. 4: trans. of F *Directoire* < ML, as above]

direct′ pri′mary, *U.S. Politics.* a primary in which a party nominates its candidates by direct vote.

di·rec·tress (di rek′tris, dī-), *n.* a female director.

di·rec·trix (di rek′triks, dī-), *n., pl.* **di·rec·trix·es, di·rec·tri·ces** (di rek′tri sēz′, dī-; dī′rek trī′sēz). *Math.* a fixed line used in the description of a curve or surface. [< NL]

direct′ tax′, *Govt.* a tax exacted directly from the persons being taxed, as an income tax.

Di·re·da·wa (dē′rā də wä′), *n.* a city in E Ethiopia. 30,000 (est. 1962). Also, **Di′re Da·wa′.**

dire·ful (dīər′fəl), *adj.* **1.** dreadful; terrible. **2.** indicating misfortune or disaster. —**dire′ful·ly,** *adv.* —**dire′ful·ness,** *n.*

dirge (dûrj), *n.* **1.** a funeral song or a song in commemoration of the dead. **2.** *Eccles.* the office of the dead, or the funeral service as sung. **3.** any composition resembling this, as a lament for the dead. **4.** a mournful sound resembling a dirge. [ME *dir(i)ge* < L: DIRECT, syncopated var. of *dīrige* (impv. of *dīrigere*), first word of the antiphon sung in the Latin office of the dead (Psalm V, 8)]

dir·ham (dir ham′), *n.* the monetary unit of Morocco, equal to 100 francs. *Abbr.:* DH. [< Ar *dirham* < L *drachm(a)*; see DRACHMA]

dir·i·gi·ble (dir′i jə bəl, di rij′ə-), *n.* **1.** an airship. —*adj.* **2.** designed for or capable of being directed, controlled, or steered. [< L *dīrig(ere)* (to) DIRECT + -IBLE]

di·ri·go (dē′ri gō′; *Eng.* dir′i gō′), *Latin.* I direct: motto of Maine.

dir·i·ment (dir′ə mənt), *adj.* causing to become wholly void; nullifying. [< L *diriment-* (s. of *dirimēns,* prp. of *dirimere*) parting, dividing = *dir-* (var. of *dis-* DIS-[1]) + *emere* to buy, take; see -ENT]

dir′iment imped′iment, *Law.* a fact or circumstance that renders a marriage void from the beginning.

dirk (dûrk), *n.* **1.** a dagger. —*v.t.* **2.** to stab with a dirk. [alter. of Scot *durk*]

dirn·dl (dûrn′dəl), *n.* **1.** a dress with a close-fitting bodice and full skirt, often with short, full sleeves and a low neck. **2.** a full skirt in such a colorful style.

dirt (dûrt), *n.* **1.** any foul or filthy substance, as mud, grime, dust, excrement, etc. **2.** earth or soil, esp. when loose. **3.** something or someone vile, mean, or worthless. **4.** moral filth; vileness; corruption. **5.** obscene or licentious language. **6.** gossip, esp. of a malicious nature. **7.** *Mining.* **a.** crude, broken ore or waste. **b.** (in placer mining) the material from which gold is separated by washing. **8. do someone dirt,** *Slang.* to do something mean or vicious to another. [ME *dirt, drit* < Scand; cf. OIcel *drit* excrement; c. OE *drītan*]

dirt-cheap (dûrt′chēp′), *adj.* very inexpensive.

dirt′ farm′er, *Informal.* a farmer who works on the soil, distinguished from one who operates a farm with hired hands or tenants. —**dirt′ farm′.** —**dirt′ farm′ing.**

dirt′ poor′, extremely poor; poverty-stricken.

dirt·y (dûr′tē), *adj.,* **dirt·i·er, dirt·i·est,** *v.,* **dirt·ied, dirt·y·ing.** —*adj.* **1.** soiled with dirt; foul; unclean: *dirty laundry.* **2.** spreading or imparting dirt; soiling: *dirty smoke.* **3.** vile; mean; contemptible. **4.** obscene or lewd: *a dirty joke.* **5.** undesirable or unpleasant; tedious: *He left the dirty work for me.* **6.** very unfortunate or regrettable: *That's a dirty shame!* **7.** not fair or sportsmanlike; unscrupulous: *a dirty fighter; to play a dirty trick.* **8.** insulting, contemptuous, or resentful: *a dirty look; a dirty crack about the cooking.* **9.** *Physics.* (of a nuclear weapon) producing a relatively large amount of radioactive fallout. **10.** (of the weather) stormy; squally. **11.** appearing as if soiled; dark-colored; dingy; murky. —*v.t., v.i.* **12.** to make or become dirty. —**dirt′i·ly,** *adv.* —**dirt′i·ness,** *n.*
—**Syn. 1.** grimy, defiled. DIRTY, FILTHY, FOUL, SQUALID refer to that which is not clean. DIRTY is applied to that which is filled or covered with dirt so that it is unclean or defiled: *dirty streets; dirty clothes.* FILTHY is an emphatic word suggesting something that is offensively defiled or is excessively soiled or dirty: *a filthy hovel.* FOUL implies an uncleanness that is grossly offensive to the senses: *a foul odor.* SQUALID, applied usually to dwellings or surroundings, implies dirtiness that results from slovenly indifference or poverty: *a whole family living in one squalid room.* **3.** base, vulgar, low, shabby, groveling. **4.** nasty, lascivious, lecherous. **10.** rainy, foul, sloppy, disagreeable, nasty. **11.** dull, dark.

dirt′y tricks′, *Politics Informal.* unethical or illegal campaign practices or pranks intended to disrupt or sabotage the campaigns of opposing candidates.

Dis (dis), *n. Class. Myth.* **1.** a god of the underworld, identified with Orcus or the Greek god Pluto. **2.** the underworld; Orcus; Hades.

dis-[1], a learned borrowing from Latin meaning "apart," "asunder," "away," "utterly," or having a privative, negative, or reversing force (see **de-, un-**[2]); used freely, esp. with these latter significations, as an English formative: *disability; disaffirm; disbar; disbelief; discontent; dishearten; dislike; disown.* Also, **di-.** [< L (akin to *bis,* Gk *dís* twice); before *f, dif-;* before some consonants, *di-;* often r. obs. *des-* < OF]

dis-[2], var. of **di-**[1] before *s: dissyllable.*

dis·a·bil·i·ty (dis′ə bil′i tē), *n., pl.* **-ties** for 2. **1.** lack of competent power, strength, or physical or mental ability; incapacity. **2.** a physical or mental handicap, esp. one that prevents a person from living a normal life or from performing a specific job. **3.** anything that disables or puts one at a disadvantage. **4.** the state or condition of being disabled. **5.** legal incapacity; legal disqualification.
—**Syn. 1.** disqualification, incompetence, incapability, impotence. DISABILITY, INABILITY imply a lack of power or ability. A DISABILITY is some disqualifying deprivation or loss of power, physical or other: *excused because of a physical disability; a temporary disability.* INABILITY is a lack of ability, usually because of an inherent lack of talent, power, etc.: *inability to talk, to do well in higher mathematics.*

dis·a·ble (dis ā′bəl), *v.t.,* **-bled, -bling.** **1.** to make unable; weaken or destroy the capability of; cripple; incapacitate. **2.** to make legally incapable; disqualify. [ME] —**dis·a′ble·ment,** *n.* —**Syn. 1.** See **cripple. 2.** eliminate.

dis·a·bled (dis ā′bəld), *adj.* crippled; incapacitated.

dis·a·buse (dis′ə byōōz′), *v.t.,* **-bused, -bus·ing.** to free (a person) from deception or error; set right. [< F *désabuse(r)*] —**dis′a·bus′al,** *n.*

di·sac·cha·ride (dī sak′ə rīd′, -rid), *n. Chem.* any of a group of carbohydrates, as sucrose or lactose, that yield monosaccharides on hydrolysis.

dis·ac·cord (dis′ə kôrd′), *v.i.* **1.** to be out of accord; disagree. —*n.* **2.** lack of accord; disagreement. [ME *disaccord(en)* < OF *desaccord(er)* (v.) < *desacort* (n.)]

dis·ac·cus·tom (dis′ə kus′təm), *v.t.* to cause to lose a habit. [< MF *desacoustum(er),* OF *desacostumer*]

dis·ad·van·tage (dis′əd van′tij, -vän′-), *n., v.,* **-taged, -tag·ing.** —*n.* **1.** absence or deprivation of advantage or equality. **2.** the state or an instance of being in an unfavorable circumstance or condition: *to be at a disadvantage.* **3.** something that puts one into an unfavorable position or condition: *His bad temper is a disadvantage.* **4.** injury to interest, reputation, etc.; loss. —*v.t.* **5.** to subject to disadvantage. [ME *disavauntage* < OF *desavantage*] —**Syn. 1.** drawback, inconvenience, hindrance.

dis·ad·van·taged (dis′əd van′tijd, -vän′-), *adj.* lacking the normal or usual advantages, comforts, etc.

dis·ad·van·ta·geous (dis ad′vən tā′jəs, dis′ad-), *adj.* characterized by or involving disadvantage; detrimental. **—dis·ad′van·ta′geous·ly,** *adv.* **—dis·ad′van·ta′geous·ness,** *n.*

dis·af·fect (dis′ə fekt′), *v.t.* to alienate the affection of; make discontented or disloyal. **—dis′af·fect′ed·ly,** *adv.* **—dis′af·fect′ed·ness,** *n.*

dis·af·fec·tion (dis′ə fek′shən), *n.* absence or alienation of affection or good will; estrangement; disloyalty.

dis·af·fil·i·ate (dis′ə fil′ē āt′), *v.*, **-at·ed, -at·ing.** **—***v.t.* **1.** to sever affiliation with; disassociate. **—***v.i.* **2.** to sever an affiliation. **—dis′af·fil′i·a′tion,** *n.*

dis·af·firm (dis′ə fûrm′), *v.t.* **1.** to deny; contradict. **2.** *Law.* to annul; reverse; repudiate. **—dis·af·fir·ma·tion** (dis′af ər mā′shən), **dis′af·fir′mance,** *n.*

dis·a·gree (dis′ə grē′), *v.i.*, **-greed, -gree·ing.** **1.** to fail to agree; differ. **2.** to differ in opinion; dissent. **3.** to quarrel. **4.** to cause physical discomfort or ill effect (usually fol. by *with*): *The oysters disagreed with her.* [ME < MF *desagre(er)*]

dis·a·gree·a·ble (dis′ə grē′ə bəl), *adj.* **1.** contrary to one's taste or liking; unpleasant; repugnant. **2.** unpleasant in manner or nature: *a thoroughly disagreeable person.* **—***n.* **3.** an unpleasant or repugnant circumstance, attribute, etc. [ME < MF *desagreable*] **—dis′a·gree′a·ble·ness, dis′a·gree′a·bil′i·ty,** *n.* **—dis′a·gree′a·bly,** *adv.*

dis·a·gree·ment (dis′ə grē′mənt), *n.* **1.** the act, state, or fact of disagreeing. **2.** lack of agreement; diversity; unlikeness: *a disagreement of colors.* **3.** difference of opinion; dissent. **4.** quarrel; argument.

dis·al·low (dis′ə lou′), *v.t.* **1.** to refuse to allow; reject; veto. **2.** to refuse to admit the truth or validity of. [ME < OF *desallou(er)*] **—dis′al·low′a·ble,** *adj.* **—dis′al·low′ance,** *n.*

dis·an·nul (dis′ə nul′), *v.t.*, **-nulled, -nul·ling.** to annul utterly; make void: *to disannul a contract.* **—dis′an·nul′ment,** *n.*

dis·ap·pear (dis′ə pēr′), *v.i.* **1.** to cease to be seen; vanish from sight. **2.** to cease to exist or be known; pass away; end gradually.
—Syn. 1. DISAPPEAR, VANISH suggest that something passes from sight. DISAPPEAR is used of whatever suddenly or gradually goes out of sight: *We watched him turn down a side street and then disappear.* VANISH suggests complete, generally rapid, and often mysterious disappearance: *A mirage can vanish as suddenly as it appears.*

dis·ap·pear·ance (dis′ə pēr′əns), *n.* the act of disappearing; a ceasing to be seen or to exist.

dis·ap·point (dis′ə point′), *v.t.* **1.** to fail to fulfill the expectations or wishes of: *His gross ingratitude disappointed us.* **2.** to defeat the fulfillment of (hopes, plans, etc.); thwart; frustrate. [ME < MF *desappoint(er)*] **—dis′ap·point′er,** *n.* **—dis′ap·point′ing·ly,** *adv.*

dis·ap·point·ed (dis′ə poin′tid), *adj.* **1.** depressed or discouraged by the failure of one's hopes or expectations. **2.** *Obs.* inadequately appointed; ill-equipped. **—dis′ap·point′ed·ly,** *adv.*

dis·ap·point·ment (dis′ə point′mənt), *n.* **1.** the act or fact of disappointing. **2.** the state or feeling of being disappointed. **3.** a person or thing that disappoints: *The play was a disappointment.* **—Syn. 1.** failure, defeat, frustration.

dis·ap·pro·ba·tion (dis′ap rə bā′shən), *n.* disapproval; condemnation.

dis·ap·prov·al (dis′ə proo͞′vəl), *n.* the act or state of disapproving; a condemnatory feeling, look, or utterance. **—Syn.** disapprobation, dislike, condemnation, censure.

dis·ap·prove (dis′ə proo͞v′), *v.*, **-proved, -prov·ing.** **—***v.t.* **1.** to think (something) wrong or reprehensible; censure or condemn in opinion. **2.** to withhold approval from; decline to sanction: *The court disapproved the verdict.* **—***v.i.* **3.** to have an unfavorable opinion (usually fol. by *of*). **—dis′ap·prov′er,** *n.* **—dis′ap·prov′ing·ly,** *adv.* **—Ant. 1.** praise.

dis·arm (dis ärm′), *v.t.* **1.** to deprive of a weapon or weapons. **2.** to deprive of means of attack or defense: *to disarm an argument.* **3.** to divest of hostility, suspicion, etc.; make friendly: *His smile disarmed us.* **—***v.i.* **4.** to lay down one's weapons. **5.** (of a country) to reduce or limit the size of the armed forces. [ME < OF *desarm(er)*]

dis·ar·ma·ment (dis är′mə mənt), *n.* **1.** the act or an instance of disarming. **2.** the reduction or limitation of the size, equipment, armament, etc., of the armed forces of a country. [DISARM + *-ament,* modeled on *armament*]

dis·arm·ing (dis är′ming), *adj.* removing hostility, suspicion, etc., as by being charming: *a disarming smile.* **—dis·arm′ing·ly,** *adv.*

dis·ar·range (dis′ə rānj′), *v.t.*, **-ranged, -rang·ing.** to disturb the arrangement of; disorder; unsettle. **—dis′ar·range′ment,** *n.*

dis·ar·ray (dis′ə rā′), *v.t.* **1.** to put out of array or order; throw into disorder. **2.** to undress. **—***n.* **3.** disorder; confusion: *The army retreated in disarray.* **4.** disorder of apparel; disorderly dress. [ME *disaraie(n)* < OF *desarroy* (n.) < *desarroyer, desareer* (v.)]

dis·ar·tic·u·late (dis′är tik′yə lāt′), *v.t., v.i.*, **-lat·ed, -lat·ing.** to make or become disjointed, as the bones of a body, stems of a plant, etc. **—dis′ar·tic′u·la′tion,** *n.*

dis·as·sem·ble (dis′ə sem′bəl), *v.t.*, **-bled, -bling.** to take apart.

dis·as·sem·bly (dis′ə sem′blē), *n.* **1.** the act of disassembling. **2.** the state of being disassembled.

dis·as·so·ci·ate (dis′ə sō′shē āt′, -sē-), *v.t.*, **-at·ed, -at·ing.** to dissociate. **—dis′as·so′ci·a′tion,** *n.*

dis·as·ter (di zas′tər, -zä′stər), *n.* **1.** a calamitous event, esp. one occurring suddenly and causing great damage or hardship. **2.** *Obs.* an unfavorable aspect of a star or planet. [< MF *desastre,* It *disastr(o)* = *dis-* DIS-[1] + *astro* star < L *astrum* < Gk *ástron*]
—Syn. 1. mischance, misfortune, misadventure, mishap, accident, blow, reverse, adversity, affliction. DISASTER, CALAMITY, CATASTROPHE, CATACLYSM refer to adverse happenings often occurring suddenly and unexpectedly. A DISASTER may be caused by carelessness, negligence, bad judgment, or the like; or by natural forces, as a hurricane, flood, etc.: *a railway disaster.* CALAMITY suggests great affliction, either personal or general; the emphasis is on the grief or sorrow caused: *the calamity of losing a dear child.* CATASTROPHE refers esp. to the tragic outcome of a personal or public situation; the emphasis is on destruction or irreplaceable loss: *the catastrophe of a defeat in battle.* CATACLYSM, physically an earth-shaking change, refers to a personal or public upheaval of extreme violence: *a cataclysm that turned his life in a new direction.* **—Ant. 1.** success.

disas′ter ar′ea, *U.S.* **1.** a region or locality affected by a major disaster, as a flood. **2.** such a region or locality eligible for emergency governmental relief. Also called **distressed area.**

dis·as·trous (di zas′trəs, -zä′strəs), *adj.* **1.** causing great distress or injury; ruinous; calamitous. **2.** *Archaic.* foreboding disaster. [< MF *desastreux,* It *disastros(o)*] **—dis·as′trous·ly,** *adv.* **—dis·as′trous·ness,** *n.*

dis·a·vow (dis′ə vou′), *v.t.* to disclaim knowledge of, connection with, or responsibility for; repudiate. [ME *disavou(en), desavou(en)* < OF *desavou(er)*] **—dis′a·vow′ed·ly,** *adv.*

dis·a·vow·al (dis′ə vou′əl), *n.* a repudiation or denial.

dis·band (dis band′), *v.t.* **1.** to break up or dissolve (an organization): *They disbanded the corporation.* **2.** to dissolve (a military body) by dismissing it from service. **—***v.i.* **3.** to break up or disperse, as a band or company. [< MF *desband(er)* = *des-* DIS-[1] + *bande* troop, BAND[1] + *-er* inf. suffix] **—dis·band′ment,** *n.* **—Syn. 1.** disperse, dismiss, scatter. **2.** demobilize. **—Ant. 1.** organize, unite.

dis·bar (dis bär′), *v.t.*, **-barred, -bar·ring.** *Law.* to expel from the legal profession. **—dis·bar′ment,** *n.*

dis·be·lief (dis′bi lēf′), *n.* refusal to believe or to accept as true. **—Syn.** unbelief, incredulity.

dis·be·lieve (dis′bi lēv′), *v.t.*, **-lieved, -liev·ing.** to refuse or reject belief in. **—dis′be·liev′er,** *n.*

dis·bow·el (dis bou′əl), *v.t.*, **-eled, -el·ing** or (*esp. Brit.*) **-elled, -el·ling.** to disembowel. [ME]

dis·bur·den (dis bûr′dᵊn), *v.t.* **1.** to remove a burden from; rid of a burden. **2.** to relieve of anything oppressive or annoying: *to disburden one's mind of doubt.* **3.** to get rid of (a burden). **—***v.i.* **4.** to unload a burden. **—dis·bur′den·ment,** *n.*

dis·burse (dis bûrs′), *v.t.*, **-bursed, -burs·ing.** **1.** to pay out (money); expend. **2.** to distribute or scatter. [< MF *desbours(er),* OF *desborser* = *des-* DIS-[1] + *-borser* < *borse* PURSE < LL *bursa* bag] **—dis·burs′a·ble,** *adj.* **—dis·burs′er,** *n.* **—Syn. 1.** lay out. See **spend.**

dis·burse·ment (dis bûrs′mənt), *n.* **1.** the act or an instance of disbursing. **2.** money paid out or spent. [< MF *desboursement*]

disc (disk), *n., v.t.* disk.

disc., **1.** discount. **2.** discovered.

dis·calced (dis kalst′), *adj.* without shoes; barefoot: applied esp. to members of certain religious orders. Also, **dis·cal·ce·ate** (dis kal′sē it, -āt′). [part trans. of L *discalceātus* = *dis-* DIS-[1] + *calceātus* shod, ptp. of *calceāre* (*calce(us)* a shoe < *calc-* (s. of *calx*) heel + *-ātus* -ATE[1])]

dis·cant (*n.* dis′kant; *v.* dis kant′), *n., v.i.* descant. [ME < ML *discanth(us)*] **—dis·cant′er,** *n.*

dis·card (*v.* di skärd′; *n.* dis′kärd), *v.t.* **1.** to cast aside; dismiss, esp. from use. **2.** *Cards.* **a.** to throw out (a card or cards) from one's hand. **b.** to play (a card, not a trump, of a different suit from that of the card led). **—***v.i.* **3.** *Cards.* to discard a card or cards. **—***n.* **4.** the act of discarding. **5.** a person or thing that is cast out or rejected. **6.** *Cards.* a card or cards discarded. **—Ant. 1.** retain.

dis·case (dis kās′), *v.t.*, **-cased, -cas·ing.** to take the case or covering from; uncase.

dis·cern (di sûrn′, -zûrn′), *v.t.* **1.** to perceive by the sight or some other sense or by the intellect; see, recognize, or apprehend. **2.** to distinguish mentally; recognize as distinct or different; discriminate. **—***v.i.* **3.** to distinguish or discriminate. [ME *discern(en)* < L *discern(ere)* (to) separate = *dis* -DIS-[1] + *cernere* to separate] **—dis·cern′er,** *n.* **—Syn. 1.** discover, espy. See **notice. 2, 3.** differentiate, judge.

dis·cern·i·ble (di sûr′nə bəl, -zûr′-), *adj.* capable of being discerned; distinguishable. Also, **dis·cern′a·ble.** [< L *discernibil(is)* (see DISCERN, -IBLE); r. earlier *discernable* < MF] **—dis·cern′i·bly,** *adv.*

dis·cern·ing (di sûr′ning, -zûr′-), *adj.* showing good judgment and understanding. **—dis·cern′ing·ly,** *adv.*

dis·cern·ment (di sûrn′mənt, -zûrn′-), *n.* **1.** the faculty of discerning; discrimination; acuteness of judgment and understanding. **2.** the act or an instance of discerning. [< MF *discernement*] **—Syn. 1.** judgment, perspicacity, insight. **2.** differentiation, comparison, evaluation.

dis·charge (*v.* dis chärj′; *n.* dis′chärj, dis chärj′), *v.*, **-charged, -charg·ing,** *n.* **—***v.t.* **1.** to relieve of a charge or load; unload: *to discharge a ship.* **2.** to remove or send forth: *They discharged the cargo at New York.* **3.** to fire or shoot (a firearm or missile). **4.** to pour forth; emit: *to discharge oil.* **5.** to relieve oneself of (an obligation, burden, etc.). **6.** to relieve of obligation, responsibility, etc. **7.** to fulfill, perform, or execute (a duty, function, etc.). **8.** to relieve or deprive of office, employment, etc.; dismiss from service. **9.** to release, send away, or allow to go (often fol. by *from*): *They discharged him from prison.* **10.** to pay (a debt). **11.** *Law.* **a.** to release (a defendant, esp. one under confinement). **b.** to release (a bankrupt) from former debts. **12.** *Elect.* to rid (a battery, capacitor, etc.) of a charge of electricity. **13.** *Dyeing.* to free from a dye, as by chemical bleaching. **—***v.i.* **14.** to get rid of a burden or load. **15.** to deliver a charge or load. **16.** to pour forth. **17.** to blur or run, as a color or dye. **18.** *Elect.* to lose or give up a charge of electricity. **—***n.* **19.** the act of discharging a ship, load, etc. **20.** the act of firing a weapon. **21.** a sending or coming forth, as of water from a pipe; ejection; emission. **22.** the rate or amount of such issue. **23.** something sent forth or emitted. **24.** a relieving, ridding, or getting rid of something of the nature of a charge. **25.** *Law.* **a.** an acquittal or exoneration. **b.** an annulment, as of a court order. **c.** the freeing of one held under legal process. **26.** a relieving or being relieved of obligation or liability; fulfillment of an obligation. **27.** the payment of a debt. **28.** a release or dismissal, as from prison, an office, employment, etc. **29.** a certificate of such a release or a certificate of release from obligation or liability. **30.** *Mil.* **a.** the separation of a person from military service. **b.** a certificate of such separation. **31.** *Elect.* **a.** the removal or transference of an electric charge, as by the conversion of chemical energy to electrical energy. **b.** the equalization of a difference of potential, as between two terminals. **c.** the spark, flash, or glow produced by an electric current passing through a vapor or gas. [ME *descharge(n)* < OF *descharg(ier)* < LL *discarricāre*] —**dis·charge′a·ble,** *adj.* —**dis·charg′er,** *n.* —**Syn. 1.** unburden, disburden. **4.** expel, eject, exude. **6, 9.** See **release. 7.** See **perform. 8.** cashier, fire, remove. **9.** dismiss. **10.** settle, liquidate. **20.** detonation, shooting. **26.** execution, performance.

dis·ci·ple (di sī′pəl), *n., v.,* **-pled, -pling.** —*n.* **1.** *Relig.* any professed follower of Christ in His lifetime, esp. one of the 12 apostles. **2.** a pupil or an adherent of another; follower: *a disciple of Freud.* —*v.t.* **3.** *Archaic.* to convert into a disciple. **4.** *Obs.* to teach; train. [ME < OF < L *discipul(us)* = **discip(ere)* (to) grasp (*dis-* DIS-[1] + *-cipere,* comb. form of *capere* to take) + *-ulus* -ULE; r. ME *deciple* < OF; r. OE *discipul* < L, as above] —**dis·ci′ple·ship′,** *n.* —**Syn. 2.** See **pupil**[1].

Disci′ples of Christ′, a Christian denomination, founded in the U.S. by Alexander Campbell in the early 19th century, that rejects all creeds, holds the Bible as a sufficient rule of faith and practice, and baptizes by immersion.

dis·ci·plin·a·ble (dis′ə plin′ə bəl), *adj.* **1.** subject to or meriting disciplinary action: *a disciplinable breach of rules.* **2.** capable of being instructed. [ME < MF < LL *disciplīnābil(is)*]

dis·ci·pli·nal (dis′ə plə nəl, -plin′əl, dis′ə plīn′əl), *adj.* of, pertaining to, or of the nature of discipline: *disciplinal rigor.*

dis·ci·pli·nar·i·an (dis′ə plə nâr′ē ən), *n.* **1.** a person who enforces or advocates discipline: *The teacher was a formidable disciplinarian.* —*adj.* **2.** disciplinary.

dis·ci·pli·nar·y (dis′ə plə ner′ē), *adj.* of, for, or constituting discipline; promoting discipline.

dis·ci·pline (dis′ə plin), *n., v.,* **-plined, -plin·ing.** —*n.* **1.** training to act in accordance with rules; drill: *military discipline.* **2.** instruction and exercise designed to train to proper conduct or action. **3.** punishment inflicted by way of correction and training. **4.** the training effect of experience, adversity, etc.: *the harsh discipline of poverty.* **5.** behavior in accord with rules of conduct. **6.** a set or system of rules and regulations. **7.** a whip or scourge, used in the practice of mortification or as an instrument of chastisement in certain religious communities. **8.** a branch of instruction or learning: *the disciplines of history and economics.* —*v.t.* **9.** to train by instruction and exercise; drill. **10.** to bring to a state of order and obedience by training and control. **11.** to punish or penalize in order to train and control; correct; chastise. [ME < L *disciplīna* instruction, tuition. See DISCIPLE, -INE[2]] —**dis′ci·plin′er,** *n.* —**Syn. 3.** chastisement, castigation, correction.

disc′ jock′ey. See **disk jockey.**

dis·claim (dis klām′), *v.t.* **1.** to repudiate or deny interest in or connection with; disavow; disown. **2.** *Law.* to renounce a claim or right to. **3.** to reject the claims or authority of. —*v.i.* **4.** *Law.* to renounce or repudiate a legal claim or right. **5.** *Obs.* to disavow interest. [ME < AF *disclaim(er), desclam(er)*]

dis·claim·er (dis klā′mər), *n.* **1.** the act of disclaiming; the repudiating or denying of a claim; disavowal. **2.** a person who disclaims. **3.** a statement, document, or the like, that disclaims. [ME < AF: to DISCLAIM]

dis·cla·ma·tion (dis′klə mā′shən), *n.* the act of disclaiming; renunciation; disavowal. [< ML *disclamāt(us)* (ptp. of *disclamāre* to DISCLAIM, prob. < AF *disclaime;* see -ATE[1]) + -ION]

dis·close (di sklōz′), *v.,* **-closed, -clos·ing,** *n.* —*v.t.* **1.** to make known; reveal or uncover. **2.** to cause to appear; lay open to view. **3.** *Obs.* to open up; unfold. —*n.* **4.** *Obs.* disclosure. [ME *disclose(n), desclosen* < OF *desclos-,* s. of *desclore* = *des-* DIS-[1] + *clore* to CLOSE < L *claudere*] —**dis·clos′er,** *n.* —**Syn. 1.** show, tell, unveil. See **reveal. 2.** expose. —**Ant. 1.** conceal.

dis·clo·sure (di sklō′zhər), *n.* **1.** the act or an instance of disclosing; exposure; revelation. **2.** something that is disclosed; a revelation.

dis·co (dis′kō), *n., pl.* **-cos.** *Informal.* **1.** discotheque. **2. a.** a style of popular music for dancing, usually recorded and with complex electronic instrumentation, in which simple, repetitive lyrics are subordinated to a heavy, pulsating, rhythmic beat. **b.** any of various forms of dance, often improvisational, performed to such music.

dis·cob·o·lus (di skob′ə ləs), *n., pl.* **-li** (-lī′, -lē′). *Chiefly Class. Antiq.* a discus thrower. [< L < Gk *diskobólos* = *dísk(os)* DISCUS + *-o-* -O- + *-bolos* thrower < *bállein* to throw]

dis·cog·ra·pher (di skog′rə fər), *n.* a person who compiles discographies.

dis·cog·ra·phy (di skog′rə fē), *n.* **1.** a selective or complete list of phonograph recordings. **2.** the analysis, history, or classification of phonograph recordings. [< F *discographie*]

dis·coid (dis′koid), *adj.* Also, **dis·coi′dal. 1.** having the form of a discus or disk; flat and circular. **2.** *Bot.* (of a composite flower) consisting of a disk only, without rays. —*n.* **3.** something in the form of a disk. [< LL *discoīd(ēs)* < Gk *diskoeidḗs* quoit-shaped]

dis·col·or (dis kul′ər), *v.t.* **1.** to change or spoil the color of; fade or stain. —*v.i.* **2.** to change color; become faded or stained. Also, *esp. Brit.,* **dis·col′our.** [ME *discolour(en)* < OF *descolor(er)* < LL *discolōrā(ī)* (to) change color < L *discolor* of another color]

dis·col·or·a·tion (dis kul′ə rā′shən), *n.* **1.** the act or fact of discoloring. **2.** the state of being discolored. **3.** a discolored marking or area; stain. Also called **dis·col′or·ment.**

dis·com·bob·u·late (dis′kəm bob′yə lāt′), *v.t.,* **-lat·ed, -lat·ing.** *Informal.* to upset; confuse; frustrate. [? by alter. from DISCOMPOSE or DISCOMFORT]

dis·com·fit (dis kum′fit), *v.t.* **1.** to defeat utterly; rout. **2.** to frustrate the plans of; thwart; foil. **3.** to confuse and deject; disconcert. —*n.* **4.** *Archaic.* rout; defeat. [ME < OF *desconfit,* ptp. of *desconfire* = *des-* DIS-[1] + *confire* to make, accomplish < L *conficere;* see CONFECT] —**dis·com′fit·er,** *n.* —**Syn. 3.** discompose, embarrass, disturb.

dis·com·fi·ture (dis kum′fi chər), *n.* **1.** defeat in battle; rout. **2.** frustration of hopes or plans. **3.** confusion; embarrassment. [ME *desconfiture* < OF: defeat]

dis·com·fort (dis kum′fərt), *n.* **1.** uneasiness, hardship, or mild pain. **2.** anything that disturbs the comfort. —*v.t.* **3.** to disturb the comfort or happiness of; make uncomfortable or uneasy. [ME *discomfort(en)* < OF *desconfort(er)*]

dis·com·fort·a·ble (dis kum′fər tə bəl, -kumf′tə-), *adj.* *Archaic.* **1.** physically uncomfortable; comfortless. **2.** causing unease or discouragement. [ME < OF *desconfortable*]

dis·com·mend (dis′kə mend′), *v.t.* **1.** to express disapproval of. **2.** to bring into disfavor.

dis·com·mode (dis′kə mōd′), *v.t.,* **-mod·ed, -mod·ing.** to cause inconvenience to; disturb, trouble, or incommode. [< MF *discommod(er)*] —**dis′com·mo′di·ous,** *adj.* —**dis′com·mo′di·ous·ly,** *adv.*

dis·com·mod·i·ty (dis′kə mod′i tē), *n., pl.* **-ties.** *Archaic.* **1.** inconvenience. **2.** a source of inconvenience or trouble.

dis·com·pose (dis′kəm pōz′), *v.t.,* **-posed, -pos·ing. 1.** to upset the order of; disarrange. **2.** to disturb the composure of; perturb. —**dis′com·pos′ed·ly,** *adv.* —**Syn. 2.** disconcert.

dis·com·po·sure (dis′kəm pō′zhər), *n.* the state of being discomposed; disorder; agitation; perturbation.

dis·con·cert (dis′kən sûrt′), *v.t.* **1.** to disturb the self-possession of; perturb; ruffle. **2.** to throw into disorder or confusion; disarrange. [< obs. F *disconcert(er)*] —**dis′con·cert′ing·ly,** *adv.* —**dis′con·cert′ment,** *n.* —**Syn. 1.** discompose, perplex, bewilder, abash, discomfit.

dis·con·cert·ed (dis′kən sûr′tid), *adj.* confused, ruffled, abashed, or uneasy. —**dis′con·cert′ed·ly,** *adv.* —**dis′con·cert′ed·ness,** *n.*

dis·con·form·i·ty (dis′kən fôr′mi tē), *n., pl.* **-ties. 1.** *Geol.* the surface of a division between parallel rock strata, indicating interruption of sedimentation: a type of unconformity. **2.** *Archaic.* nonconformity.

dis·con·nect (dis′kə nekt′), *v.t.* to sever or interrupt the connection of or between; detach. —**dis′con·nect′er,** *n.* —**dis′con·nec′tive,** *adj.*

dis·con·nect·ed (dis′kə nek′tid), *adj.* **1.** disjointed; broken. **2.** not coherent; seemingly irrational: *a disconnected argument.* —**dis′con·nect′ed·ly,** *adv.* —**dis′con·nect′ed·ness,** *n.*

dis·con·nec·tion (dis′kə nek′shən), *n.* **1.** the act of disconnecting. **2.** the state of being disconnected; lack of connection. Also, *Brit.,* **dis′con·nex′ion.**

dis·con·sid·er (dis′kən sid′ər), *v.t.* to discredit. —**dis′con·sid′er·a′tion,** *n.*

dis·con·so·late (dis kon′sə lit), *adj.* **1.** without consolation or solace; inconsolable. **2.** characterized by or causing dejection; cheerless; gloomy. [ME < ML *disconsōlāt(us)* = L *dis-* DIS-[1] + *consōlātus* consoled, ptp. of *consōlārī* to CONSOLE[1]; see -ATE[1]] —**dis·con′so·late·ly,** *adv.* —**dis·con·so·la·tion** (dis kon′sə lā′shən), **dis·con′so·late·ness,** *n.* —**Syn. 1.** heartbroken, dejected. **1, 2.** sad, melancholy, sorrowful, miserable. See **desolate.**

dis·con·tent (dis′kən tent′), *adj.* **1.** not content; dissatisfied; discontented. —*n.* **2.** Also, **dis′con·tent′ment.** lack of content; dissatisfaction. **3.** a restless desire for something one does not have. **4.** a malcontent. —*v.t.* **5.** to make discontented. —**Syn. 2.** uneasiness, inquietude, restlessness, displeasure. See **dissatisfaction.**

dis·con·tent·ed (dis′kən ten′tid), *adj.* uneasy in mind; dissatisfied; restlessly unhappy. —**dis′con·tent′ed·ly,** *adv.* —**dis′con·tent′ed·ness,** *n.*

dis·con·tin·u·ance (dis′kən tin′yo͞o əns), *n.* **1.** the act or state of discontinuing. **2.** the state of being discontinued; cessation. **3.** *Law.* the termination of a suit by the act of the plaintiff. [ME]

dis·con·tin·u·a·tion (dis′kən tin′yo͞o ā′shən), *n.* breach or interruption of continuity or unity. [< MF < ML *discontinuātiōn-* (s. of *discontinuātiō*) = *discontinuāt(us)* (ptp. of *discontinuāre* to DISCONTINUE; see -ATE[1]) + *-iōn-* -ION]

dis·con·tin·ue (dis′kən tin′yo͞o), *v.,* **-tin·ued, -tin·u·ing.** —*v.t.* **1.** to cause to cease; put an end to; stop. **2.** to cease to take, use, etc.: *to discontinue a newspaper.* **3.** *Law.* to terminate or abandon (a suit, claim, or the like). —*v.i.* **4.** to stop; cease; desist. [ME < MF *discontinu(er)* < ML *discontinuāre*] —**dis′con·tin′u·er,** *n.* —**Syn. 1.** See **interrupt.**

dis·con·ti·nu·i·ty (dis′kon tənо͞o′i tē, -tənyo͞o′-), *n., pl.* **-ties. 1.** lack of continuity; absence of uninterrupted connection; irregularity. **2.** a break or gap. **3.** *Geol.* a zone between layers within the earth where the velocity of earthquake waves changes radically. [< ML *discontinuitās.* See DISCONTINUOUS, -ITY]

dis·con·tin·u·ous (dis′kən tin′yo͞o əs), *adj.* not continuous; broken; intermittent: *a discontinuous argument.* [< ML *discontinuus*] —**dis′con·tin′u·ous·ly,** *adv.*

dis·co·phile (dis′kə fīl′), *n.* a person who studies and collects phonograph records.

dis·cord (*n.* dis′kôrd; *v.* dis kôrd′), *n.* **1.** lack of concord or harmony between persons or things; disagreement. **2.** difference of opinion. **3.** strife; dispute; war: *martial discord.* **4.** *Music.* an inharmonious combination of musical tones sounded together. **5.** any confused or harsh noise; dissonance. —*v.i.* **6.** to disagree; be at variance. [(n.) ME *descorde, discorde* < OF *descort* (< *descorder*), *descorde* < L *discord(ia)* < *discord-* (s. of *discors*) discordant (*dis-* DIS-[1] + *cord-,* s. of *cors* heart); (v.) ME *discord(en)* < OF *descord(er)* < L *discordāre* < *discord-,* as above] —**Syn. 3.** conflict, struggle, argument, contention.

dis·cord·ance (dis kôr′dəns), *n.* **1.** a discordant state; disagreement; discord. **2.** an instance of this. **3.** dissonance. **4.** *Geol.* lack of parallelism between superjacent strata. [ME < OF]

dis·cor·dan·cy (dis kôr′dən sē), *n., pl.* **-cies.** discordance (defs. 1–3).

dis·cord·ant (dis kôr′dənt), *adj.* **1.** being at variance; disagreeing. **2.** disagreeable to the ear; dissonant; harsh. [ME *discordaunt* < OF *discordant* < L *discordant-* (s. of *discordāns*), prp. of *discordāre*] —**dis·cord′ant·ly,** *adv.*

dis·co·theque (dis′kō tek′, dis′kō tek′, -kə-), *n.* a cabaret in which patrons may dance to popular music, esp. on recordings. Also, **dis′co·thèque′.** [< F *discothèque.* See DISC, -O-, THECA]

dis·count (*v.* dis′kount, dis kount′; *n.* dis′kount), *v.t.* **1.** to deduct (an amount) from a bill, charge, etc. **2.** to offer for sale or sell at a reduced price. **3.** to advance or lend money with deduction of interest on (commercial paper not immediately payable). **4.** to purchase or sell (a bill or note) before maturity at a reduction based on the interest still to be earned. **5.** to leave out of account; disregard. **6.** to take into account in advance, often so as to diminish the effect of. —*v.i.* **7.** to advance or lend money after deduction of interest. —*n.* **8.** the act or an instance of discounting. **9.** an amount deducted, esp. for prompt payment. **10.** any deduction from the nominal value. **11.** a payment of interest in advance upon a loan of money. **12.** the amount of interest obtained. **13.** an allowance made for exaggeration or bias, as in a report, story, etc. **14. at a discount, a.** *Com.* below par. **b.** below the usual list price. [DIS-¹ + COUNT¹, modeled on F *décompt(er),* OF *desconter* < ML *discomputāre*] —**dis′count·a·ble,** *adj.*

dis·coun·te·nance (dis koun′tᵊnəns), *v.,* **-nanced, -nanc·ing,** *n.* —*v.t.* **1.** to disconcert or embarrass. **2.** to show disapproval of; treat with disfavor. —*n.* **3.** disapproval; disapprobation.

dis·count·er (dis′koun tər), *n.* **1.** a person who discounts. **2.** a person who operates a discount house.

dis′count house′, a store that sells merchandise for less than the usual price. Also called **dis′count store′.**

dis′count rate′, *Finance.* **1.** the rate of interest charged in discounting commercial paper. **2.** the rediscount rate.

dis·cour·age (di skûr′ij, -skur′-), *v.t.,* **-aged, -ag·ing.** **1.** to deprive of courage, hope, or confidence; dishearten; dispirit. **2.** to dissuade (usually fol. by *from*). **3.** to hinder. **4.** to express disapproval of. [ME *discorage(n)* < MF *descorag(er),* OF *descoragier*] —**dis·cour′ag·er,** *n.* —**dis·cour′ag·ing·ly,** *adv.*
—**Syn. 1.** daunt, depress, deject. DISCOURAGE, DISMAY, INTIMIDATE may imply the attempt to dishearten or frighten a person so as to prevent some action, or any further action. To DISCOURAGE is to dishearten by expressing disapproval or by suggesting that a contemplated action or course will probably fail: *He was discouraged from giving up his job.* To DISMAY is to dishearten completely, by the disclosure of unsuspected facts, so that the action contemplated seems useless or dangerous: *to dismay a prosecutor by revealing his brother's connection with a crime.* To INTIMIDATE is to frighten, as by threats of force, violence, or dire consequences: *to intimidate a witness.* —**Ant. 1.** encourage.

dis·cour·age·ment (di skûr′ij mənt, -skur′-), *n.* **1.** the act or an instance of discouraging. **2.** the state of being discouraged. **3.** something that discourages. [< MF *descouragement,* OF *descoragement*] —**Syn. 2.** depression, dejection, hopelessness. See **despair. 3.** deterrent, obstacle, obstruction. —**Ant. 1–3.** encouragement.

dis·course (*n.* dis′kōrs, -kôrs, dis kōrs′, -kôrs′; *v.* dis kōrs′, -kôrs′), *n., v.,* **-coursed, -cours·ing.** —*n.* **1.** communication of thought by words; talk; conversation. **2.** a formal discussion of a subject in speech or writing, as a dissertation, treatise, sermon, etc. —*v.i.* **3.** to communicate thoughts orally; talk; converse. **4.** to treat a subject formally in speech or writing. —*v.t.* **5.** to give forth (musical sounds). [ME *discours* < ML *discurs(us)* (sp. by influence of ME *cours* course), LL: conversation, L: a running to and fro (n. use of ptp. of *discurrere*) = *dis-* DIS-¹ + *cursus* (see COURSE)] —**dis·cours′er,** *n.*

dis·cour·te·ous (dis kûr′tē əs), *adj.* impolite; rude. —**dis·cour′te·ous·ly,** *adv.* —**dis·cour′te·ous·ness,** *n.*

dis·cour·te·sy (dis kûr′ti sē), *n., pl.* **-sies.** **1.** lack or breach of courtesy; incivility; rudeness. **2.** a discourteous or impolite act.

dis·cov·er (di skuv′ər), *v.t.* **1.** to gain sight or knowledge of (something previously unseen or unknown): *to discover America; to discover electricity.* **2.** *Archaic.* to make known; reveal; disclose. **3.** *Archaic.* to make manifest unintentionally; give away; betray. [ME *discover(en)* < OF *descovr(ir)* < LL *discooperīre*] —**dis·cov′er·a·ble,** *adj.* —**dis·cov′er·er,** *n.*
—**Syn. 1.** detect, ascertain, unearth, notice. DISCOVER, INVENT, ORIGINATE suggest bringing to light something previously unknown. To DISCOVER may be to find some existent thing that was previously unknown: *to discover a new continent, a planet, electricity;* it may also refer to devising a new use for something already known: *to discover the value of coal tar as a source of organic chemicals.* To INVENT is to make or create something new, esp. something ingeniously devised to perform mechanical operations: *to invent a device for detecting radioactivity.* To ORIGINATE is to begin something new, esp. new ideas, methods, etc.: *to originate a religious or political movement.* See also **learn.**

dis·cov·er·y (di skuv′ə rē), *n., pl.* **-er·ies.** **1.** the act or an instance of discovering. **2.** something discovered. **3.** *Law.* compulsory disclosure, as of facts or documents.

Discov′ery Day′. See **Columbus Day.**

Discov′ery In′let, an inlet of the Ross Sea, in Antarctica.

dis·cred·it (dis kred′it), *v.t.* **1.** to injure the credit or reputation of: *an effort to discredit certain politicians.* **2.** to destroy confidence in: *Later research discredited earlier theories.* **3.** to give no credence to; disbelieve: *There was good reason to discredit the witness.* —*n.* **4.** loss or lack of belief or confidence; distrust. **5.** loss or lack of repute or esteem; disrepute. **6.** something that damages a good reputation.

dis·cred·it·a·ble (dis kred′i tə bəl), *adj.* bringing discredit; disgraceful. —**dis·cred′it·a·bly,** *adv.*

dis·creet (di skrēt′), *adj.* judicious in one's conduct or speech, esp. with regard to maintaining silence about something of a delicate nature; prudent; circumspect. [ME *discret* < OF < ML *discrēt(us),* L: separated, ptp. of *discernere;* see DISCERN] —**dis·creet′ly,** *adv.* —**dis·creet′ness,** *n.*

dis·crep·an·cy (di skrep′ən sē), *n., pl.* **-cies** for 2. **1.** the state or quality of being discrepant; inconsistency. **2.** an instance of difference or inconsistency. Also, **dis·crep′ance.** [< L *discrepantia.* See DISCREPANT, -ANCY] —**Syn. 1.** incongruity, disagreement. See **difference. 2.** variation. —**Ant. 1.** consistency.

dis·crep·ant (di skrep′ənt), *adj.* differing; disagreeing; discordant; inconsistent. [ME < L *discrepant-* (s. of *discrepāns*), prp. of *discrepāre* to sound discordant = *dis-* DIS-¹ + *crepāre* to crack, creak; see -ANT] —**dis·crep′ant·ly,** *adv.*

dis·crete (di skrēt′), *adj.* **1.** detached from others; separate; distinct. **2.** consisting of or characterized by distinct or individual parts; discontinuous. [ME < L *discrēt(us)* separated; see DISCREET] —**dis·crete′ly,** *adv.* —**dis·crete′ness,** *n.*

dis·cre·tion (di skresh′ən), *n.* **1.** the power or right to decide or act according to one's own judgment. **2.** quality of being discreet; prudence: *Throwing all discretion to the winds, he blurted out the truth.* [ME *discrecioun* < LL *discrētiōn-* (s. of *discrētiō*)]

dis·cre·tion·ar·y (di skresh′ə ner′ē), *adj.* subject or left to one's own discretion. Also, **dis·cre·tion·al** (di skresh′ə nᵊl). —**dis·cre′tion·al·ly,** *adv.*

dis·crim·i·nant (di skrim′ə nənt), *n. Math.* a relatively simple expression that determines some of the properties, as the nature of the roots, of a given equation or function. [< L *discrīminant-* (s. of *discrīmināns*) separating (prp. of *discrīmināre*) = *discrīmin-,* s. of *discrīmen* (*dis-* DIS-¹ + *crīmin-,* perf. s. of *cernere* to distinguish) + *-ant-* -ANT]

dis·crim·i·nate (*v.* di skrim′ə nāt′; *adj.* di skrim′ə nit), *v.,* **-nat·ed, -nat·ing,** *adj.* —*v.i.* **1.** to make a distinction in favor of or against a person or thing on a categorical basis rather than according to actual merit. **2.** to note or observe a difference; distinguish accurately. —*v.t.* **3.** to make or constitute a distinction in or between; differentiate. **4.** to note or distinguish as different. —*adj.* **5.** marked by discrimination; making nice distinctions. [< L *discrīmināt(us)* separated, ptp. of *discrīmināre*] —**dis·crim′i·nate·ly,** *adv.* —**dis·crim′i·na′tor,** *n.* —**Syn. 3.** See **distinguish.**

dis·crim·i·nat·ing (di skrim′ə nā′ting), *adj.* **1.** differentiating; analytical. **2.** noting differences or distinctions with nicety; possessing discrimination. **3.** having excellent taste or judgment. **4.** differential, as a tariff. **5.** possessing distinctive features. —**dis·crim′i·nat′ing·ly,** *adv.*

dis·crim·i·na·tion (di skrim′ə nā′shən), *n.* **1.** the act or an instance of discriminating. **2.** the resulting state. **3.** treatment or distinction not based on individual merit in favor of or against a person, group, etc. **4.** the power of making fine distinctions; discriminating judgment. **5.** *Archaic.* something that serves to differentiate. [< L *discrīminātiōn-* (s. of *discrīminātiō*) a distinguishing] —**dis·crim′i·na′tion·al,** *adj.*

dis·crim·i·na·tive (di skrim′ə nā′tiv, -nə tiv), *adj.* **1.** making distinctions; discriminating. **2.** discriminatory (def. 1). —**dis·crim′i·na′tive·ly,** *adv.*

dis·crim·i·na·to·ry (di skrim′ə nə tōr′ē, -tôr′ē), *adj.* **1.** characterized by or exhibiting prejudice, racial bias, or the like: *discriminatory practices.* **2.** discriminative (def. 1).

dis·cur·sive (di skûr′siv), *adj.* **1.** digressive; rambling. **2.** proceeding by reasoning or argument; not intuitive. [< ML *discursīv(us).* See DISCOURSE, -IVE] —**dis·cur′sive·ly,** *adv.* —**dis·cur′sive·ness,** *n.*

Discus

dis·cus (dis′kəs), *n., pl.* **dis·cus·es, dis·ci** (dis′ī). **1.** a circular disk, usually wooden with a metal rim, for throwing for distance in athletic competition. **2.** the sport of throwing this disk. [< L < Gk *dískos* a quoit, discus, disk < *dikeîn* to throw]

dis·cuss (di skus′), *v.t.* **1.** to consider or examine by argument, comment, etc.; talk over or write about; debate. **2.** *Rare.* to consume (food or drink) enthusiastically. **3.** *Civil Law.* to collect a debt from (the person primarily liable) before proceeding against the person secondarily liable. **4.** *Obs.* to make known; reveal. [ME *discuss(en)* < L *discuss(us)* struck asunder, shaken, scattered, ptp. of *discutere* = *dis-* DIS-¹ + *-cutere* (comb. form of *quatere* to shake, strike)] —**dis·cuss′er,** *n.* —**dis·cuss′i·ble, dis·cuss′a·ble,** *adj.*
—**Syn. 1.** reason, deliberate.

dis·cus·sant (di skus′ənt), *n.* a person who participates in a formal discussion or symposium.

dis·cus·sion (di skush′ən), *n.* the act or an instance of discussing; consideration or examination by argument, comment, etc.; debate. [ME < OF *discucion* < LL *discussiōn-* (s. of *discussiō*) inquiry, examination, L: a shaking] —**dis·cus′sion·al,** *adj.*

dis·dain (dis dān′), *v.t.* **1.** to look upon or treat with contempt; despise; scorn. **2.** to think unworthy of notice, performance, etc.; consider beneath oneself. —*n.* **3.** a feeling of contempt for anything regarded as unworthy; haughty contempt; scorn. [ME *disdain(en)* < OF *desdeign(ier).* See DIS-¹, DEIGN] —**Syn. 1.** contemn, spurn. **3.** contemptuousness, haughtiness, arrogance. See **contempt.** —**Ant. 1.** accept. **3.** admiration.

dis·dain·ful (dis dān′fəl), *adj.* full of or showing disdain; scornful. —**dis·dain′ful·ly,** *adv.* —**dis·dain′ful·ness,** *n.*
—**Syn.** contemptuous, haughty, supercilious.

dis·ease (di zēz′), *n., v.,* **-eased, -eas·ing.** —*n.* **1.** *Pathol.* a condition of the body in which there is incorrect function resulting from the effect of heredity, infection, diet, or environment; illness; sickness; ailment. **2.** any abnormal condition in a plant that interferes with its normal, vital physiological processes, caused by pathogenic microorganisms, parasites, unfavorable environmental, genetic, or nutritional factors, etc. **3.** any deranged or depraved condition, as of the mind, society, etc. **4.** decomposition of a material under special circumstances: *tin disease.* —*v.t.* **5.** to affect with disease; make ill. [ME *disese* < OF *desaise*]
—**Syn. 1.** morbidity, ailment, indisposition, infirmity. DISEASE, MALADY, DISORDER imply a deviation of the body, or an organ of it, from health or normality. DISEASE and MALADY apply to organic deviations involving structural change. A DISEASE is a serious, active, prolonged, and deep-rooted condition. A MALADY is a lingering, chronic disease, usually painful and often fatal. A DISORDER is a physical or

mental derangement, frequently a slight or transitory one. —**Ant. 1.** health. **5.** cure.

dis·em·bark (dis′em bärk′), *v.t., v.i.* to put or go on shore from a ship; land. [< MF *desembarqu(er)*] —**dis-em·bar·ka·tion** (dis em′bär kā′shən), **dis′em·bark′ment,** *n.*

dis·em·bar·rass (dis′em bar′əs), *v.t.* **1.** to free from embarrassment. **2.** to relieve; rid. **3.** to extricate from something troublesome, embarrassing, or the like. —**dis′-em·bar′rass·ment,** *n.*

dis·em·bod·y (dis′em bod′ē), *v.t.*, **-bod·ied, -bod·y·ing.** to divest (a soul, spirit, etc.) of a body. —**dis′em·bod′i-ment,** *n.*

dis·em·bogue (dis′em bōg′), *v.*, **-bogued, -bogu·ing.** —*v.i.* **1.** to discharge contents by pouring forth. **2.** to discharge water, as at the mouth of a stream. **3.** *Phys. Geog.* debouch (def. 2). —*v.t.* **4.** to discharge; cast forth. [< Sp *desemboc(ar)* = *des-* DIS-[1] + *embocar* to enter by the mouth (*em-* in + *boc(a)* mouth + *-ar* inf. suffix)] —**dis′em·bogue′-ment,** *n.*

dis·em·bow·el (dis′em bou′əl), *v.t.*, **-eled, -el·ing** or (*esp. Brit.*) **-elled, -el·ling.** to remove the bowels or entrails from; eviscerate. —**dis′em·bow′el·ment,** *n.*

dis·en·a·ble (dis′en ā′bəl), *v.t.*, **-bled, -bling.** to deprive of ability; make unable; prevent.

dis·en·chant (dis′en chant′, -chänt′), *v.t.* to deprive of or to free from enchantment; disillusion. [< MF *desenchant(er)*] —**dis′en·chant′er,** *n.* —**dis′en·chant′ing·ly,** *adv.* —**dis′en·chant′ment,** *n.*

dis·en·cum·ber (dis′en kum′bər), *v.t.* to free from encumbrance; disburden. [< MF *desencombr(er)*] —**Syn.** disentangle, unburden.

dis·en·dow (dis′en dou′), *v.t.* to deprive (a church, school, etc.) of endowment. —**dis′en·dow′er,** *n.* —**dis′-en·dow′ment,** *n.*

dis·en·fran·chise (dis′en fran′chīz), *v.t.*, **-chised, -chis·ing.** to disfranchise. —**dis·en·fran·chise·ment** (dis′en-fran′chiz mənt, -chīz-), *n.*

dis·en·gage (dis′en gāj′), *v.*, **-gaged, -gag·ing.** —*v.t.* **1.** to release from attachment or connection; unfasten; free. **2.** *Mil.* to break off action with (an enemy). —*v.i.* **3.** to become disengaged. [< MF *desengag(er)*]

dis·en·gage·ment (dis′en gāj′mənt), *n.* **1.** the act or process of disengaging. **2.** the state of being disengaged. **3.** freedom from obligation or occupation; leisure.

dis·en·tail (dis′en tāl′), *v.t. Law.* to free (an estate) from entail. —**dis′en·tail′ment,** *n.*

dis·en·tan·gle (dis′en taŋ′gəl), *v.t., v.i.*, **-gled, -gling.** to free or become free from entanglement; untangle; extricate (often fol. by *from*).

dis·en·thral (dis′en thrôl′), *v.t.*, **-thralled, -thral·ling.** disenthrall. —**dis′en·thral′ment,** *n.*

dis·en·thrall (dis′en thrôl′), *v.t.* to free from bondage; liberate. —**dis′en·thrall′ment,** *n.*

dis·es·tab·lish (dis′e stab′lish), *v.t.* **1.** to deprive of the character of being established. **2.** to withdraw exclusive state recognition or support from (a church). —**dis′es-tab′lish·ment,** *n.*

dis·es·tab·lish·men·tar·i·an (dis′e stab′lish mən târ′ē-ən), *n.* **1.** a person who favors the separation of church and state, esp. the withdrawal of special rights, status, and support granted an established church by a state. —*adj.* **2.** of, pertaining to, or favoring the disestablishment of a state church. —**dis′es·tab′lish·men·tar′i·an·ism,** *n.*

dis·es·teem (dis′ə stēm′), *v.t.* **1.** to hold in low regard; think unfavorably of. —*n.* **2.** lack of esteem; disfavor; low regard.

dis·fa·vor (dis fā′vər), *n.* **1.** unfavorable regard; displeasure; dislike: *The minister incurred the king's disfavor.* **2.** lack of favor; state of being regarded unfavorably. **3.** an unkind or detrimental act: *The pianist did himself a disfavor in trying to sing.* —*v.t.* **4.** to regard or treat with disfavor. Also, *esp. Brit.*, **dis·fa′vour.** [prob. < obs. F *desfaveur*]

dis·fea·ture (dis fē′chər), *v.t.*, **-tured, -tur·ing.** to mar the features of; disfigure. —**dis·fea′ture·ment,** *n.*

dis·fig·ure (dis fig′yər), *v.t.*, **-ured, -ur·ing.** **1.** to deface or deform; mar the appearance or beauty of. **2.** to mar the effect or excellence of. [ME *disfigur(en)* < OF *desfigur(er)*] —**dis·fig′ur·er,** *n.* —**Syn. 1.** spoil, blemish. See **mar.**

dis·fig·ure·ment (dis fig′yər mənt), *n.* **1.** the act or an instance of disfiguring. **2.** a disfigured condition. **3.** something that disfigures, as a scar. Also called **dis·fig′ur·a′-tion.**

dis·fran·chise (dis fran′chīz), *v.t.*, **-chised, -chis·ing.** **1.** to deprive (a person) of a right of citizenship, as of the right to vote. **2.** to deprive of a franchise, privilege, or right. [ME] —**dis·fran·chise·ment** (dis fran′chiz mənt, -chīz-), *n.*

dis·frock (dis frok′), *v.t. Eccles.* to unfrock.

dis·fur·nish (dis fûr′nish), *v.t.* to deprive of something with which a person or thing is furnished; strip. [< MF *desfourniss-*, s. of *desfournir*] —**dis·fur′nish·ment,** *n.*

dis·gorge (dis gôrj′), *v.*, **-gorged, -gorg·ing.** —*v.t.* **1.** to eject or throw out from the throat, mouth, or stomach; vomit forth. **2.** to surrender or yield (something, esp. something illicitly obtained). **3.** to discharge forcefully or as a result of force. —*v.i.* **4.** to eject, yield, or discharge something. [late ME < MF *desgorg(er)*]

dis·grace (dis grās′), *n.*, *v.*, **-graced, -grac·ing.** —*n.* **1.** the state of being in dishonor; ignominy; shame. **2.** a person, act, or thing that is dishonorable or shameful. **3.** the state of being out of favor; exclusion from favor, confidence, or trust: *courtiers and ministers in disgrace.* —*v.t.* **4.** to bring or reflect shame or reproach upon: *to be disgraced by cowardice.* **5.** to treat with disfavor. [< MF < It *disgrazia* = *dis-* DIS-[1] + *grazia* < L *gratia*] —**dis·grac′er,** *n.* —**Syn. 1.** notoriety, taint. DISGRACE, DISHONOR, IGNOMINY, INFAMY imply a very low position in the opinion of others. DISGRACE implies the disfavor, with a greater or less degree of reproachful disapprobation, of others: *He brought disgrace on his family; to be in disgrace.* DISHONOR implies a stain on honor or honorable reputation; it relates esp. to the conduct of the person himself: *He preferred death to dishonor.* IGNOMINY is disgrace in which one's situation invites contempt: *the ignominy of being discovered cheating.* INFAMY is shameful notoriety, or baseness of action or character which is widely known and recognized: *The children never outlived the father's infamy.* **3.** disfavor, obloquy. **5.** humiliate, degrade. —**Ant. 1.** honor.

dis·grace·ful (dis grās′fəl), *adj.* bringing or deserving disgrace; shameful; dishonorable; disreputable. —**dis-grace′ful·ly,** *adv.* —**dis·grace′ful·ness,** *n.*

dis·grun·tle (dis grun′tᵊl), *v.t.*, **-tled, -tling.** to put into a state of sulky dissatisfaction; make discontent. —**dis-grun′tle·ment,** *n.* [DIS-[1] + *gruntle*, freq. of GRUNT; see -LE]

dis·guise (dis gīz′, di skīz′), *v.*, **-guised, -guis·ing,** *n.* —*v.t.* **1.** to change the appearance or guise of so as to conceal identity or mislead: *The king was disguised as a peasant.* **2.** to conceal or cover up the real state or character of; misrepresent: *to disguise one's intentions.* —*n.* **3.** something that disguises; a thing that serves or is intended for concealment of identity, character, or quality; a deceptive covering, condition, manner, etc. **4.** the make-up, mask, or costume of an entertainer. **5.** the act of disguising. **6.** the state of being disguised: *His illness proved to be a blessing in disguise.* [ME *disg(u)ise(n)* < OF *desguis(er)*] —**dis·guis′a·ble,** *adj.* —**dis·guis′ed·ly,** *adv.* —**dis-guis′er,** *n.* —**Syn. 2.** cloak, mask.

dis·gust (dis gust′, di skust′), *v.t.* **1.** to cause nausea or loathing in. **2.** to offend the good taste, moral sense, etc., of. —*n.* **3.** a strong distaste; nausea; loathing. **4.** repugnance caused by something offensive; strong aversion. [< MF *desgoust(er)* = *des-* DIS-[1] + *gouster* to taste, relish < *goust* taste < L *gust(a)*; see CHOOSE] —**dis·gust′ed·ly,** *adv.* —**dis·gust′ed·ness,** *n.* —**Syn. 1.** sicken, nauseate. **2.** repel, revolt. **4.** abhorrence, detestation. See **dislike.** —**Ant. 1.** delight. **4.** relish.

dis·gust·ful (dis gust′fəl, di skust′-), *adj.* causing disgust; nauseous; offensive. —**dis·gust′ful·ly,** *adv.*

dis·gust·ing (dis gus′ting, di skus′-), *adj.* causing disgust; offensive to the physical, moral, or aesthetic taste. —**dis-gust′ing·ly,** *adv.* —**Syn.** loathsome, sickening, repulsive, revolting, repugnant, abhorrent, detestable.

dish (dish), *n.* **1.** an open, more or less shallow container of pottery, glass, etc., used esp. for holding or serving food. **2.** any container used at table. **3.** something that is served or contained in a dish. **4.** a particular article or preparation of food: *Rice is an inexpensive dish.* **5.** the quantity held by a dish; dishful: *a dish of applesauce.* **6.** concavity or the degree of concavity, as of a wheel. **7.** *Slang.* an attractive girl or woman. —*v.t.* **8.** to put into or serve in a dish, as food. **9.** to fashion like a dish; make concave. **10. dish it out,** *Informal.* to dispense abusive language, punishment, or praise, enthusiastic approval, etc. **11. dish out,** *Informal.* to deal out; distribute. [ME; OE *disc* dish, plate, bowl (akin to G *Tisch* table) < L *disc(us)* dish, DISCUS]

dis·ha·bille (dis′ə bēl′, -bē′), *n.* **1.** the state of being carelessly or partly dressed. **2.** a state of disarray or disorder. **3.** *Archaic.* a loose morning dress; negligee. **4.** a disorderly or disorganized state of mind or way of thinking. Also, **des-habille.** [< F *déshabillé*, n. use of ptp. of *déshabiller* to undress = *dés-* DIS-[1] + *habiller* to dress; see HABILIMENT]

dish′ anten′na, an antenna with a dish-shaped reflector, esp. for receiving satellite and microwave transmissions.

dis·har·mo·ni·ous (dis′här mō′nē əs), *adj.* inharmonious; discordant.

dis·har·mo·nize (dis här′mə nīz′), *v.t., v.i.*, **-nized, -niz-ing.** to make or be inharmonious. —**dis·har·mo·nism** (dis-här′mə niz′əm), *n.*

dis·har·mo·ny (dis här′mə nē), *n.*, *pl.* **-nies.** **1.** lack of harmony; discord. **2.** something discordant.

dish·cloth (dish′klôth′, -kloth′), *n.*, *pl.* **-cloths** (-klôthz′, -klothz′, -klôths′, -kloths′). a cloth for washing dishes. Also called *Brit.*, **dish·clout** (dish′klout′).

dish′cloth gourd′, luffa (def. 1).

dis·heart·en (dis här′tᵊn), *v.t.* to depress the hope, courage, or spirits of; discourage. —**dis·heart′en·ing·ly,** *adv.* —**dis·heart′en·ment,** *n.*

dished (disht), *adj.* **1.** concave: *a dished face.* **2.** *Slang.* (no longer current) exhausted. **3.** (of a parallel pair of vehicle wheels) farther apart at the top than at the bottom.

dis·her·it (dis her′it), *v.t.* to disinherit. [ME *deserit(en)* < OF *deserit(er)*. See DIS-[1], INHERIT]

di·shev·el (di shev′əl), *v.t.*, **-eled, -el·ing** or (*esp. Brit.*) **-elled, -el·ling.** **1.** to let down, as hair, or wear or let hang in loose disorder, as clothing. **2.** to cause untidiness and disarray in. [back formation from DISHEVELED] —**di·shev′el-ment,** *n.*

di·shev·eled (di shev′əld), *adj.* **1.** hanging loosely or in disorder; unkempt: *disheveled hair.* **2.** untidy; disarranged: *disheveled appearance.* Also, *esp. Brit.*, **di·shev′elled.** [ME *discheveled* < OF *deschevele*, ptp. of *descheveler* to dishevel the hair = *des-* DIS-[1] + *chevel* hair < L *capill(us)*, dim. form, akin to *caput* head]

dish·ful (dish′fo͝ol), *n.*, *pl.* **-fuls.** the amount a dish will hold.

dis·hon·est (dis on′ist), *adj.* **1.** not honest; disposed to lie, cheat, or steal; untrustworthy. **2.** proceeding from or exhibiting lack of honesty; fraudulent. [ME *dishoneste* < OF *deshoneste*] —**dis·hon′est·ly,** *adv.* —**Syn. 1.** unscrupulous, perfidious. See **corrupt.** —**Ant. 1, 2.** honest.

dis·hon·es·ty (dis on′i stē), *n.*, *pl.* **-ties.** **1.** lack of honesty; a disposition to lie, cheat, or steal. **2.** a dishonest act; fraud. [ME *deshonestee*]

dis·hon·or (dis on′ər), *n.* **1.** lack or loss of honor; disgraceful or dishonest character or conduct. **2.** disgrace; ignominy; shame. **3.** an indignity; insult: *to do someone a dishonor.* **4.** a cause of shame or disgrace. **5.** *Com.* failure or refusal to accept or pay a draft, check, etc. —*v.t.* **6.** to deprive of honor; disgrace, bring reproach or shame on. **7.** *Com.* to fail or refuse to honor or pay (a draft, check, etc.). **8.** to rape or seduce. Also, *esp. Brit.*, **dis·hon′our.** [ME *dishonour* < OF *deshonor*] —**dis·hon′or·er;** *esp. Brit.*, **dis·hon′our·er,** *n.*

dis·hon·or·a·ble (dis on′ər ə bəl), *adj.* **1.** showing lack of honor; ignoble; base; disgraceful; shameful. **2.** having no honor or good repute. Also, *esp. Brit.*, **dis·hon′our·a·ble.** —**dis·hon′or·a·ble·ness;** *esp. Brit.*, **dis·hon′our·a·ble·ness,** *n.* —**dis·hon′or·a·bly;** *esp. Brit.*, **dis·hon′our·a·bly,** *adv.* —**Syn. 1.** shameless, false. **2.** unscrupulous, disgraceful, scandalous, ignominious.

dishon′orable dis′charge, *U.S. Mil.* **1.** the discharge of a person from military service for an offense more serious than one for which a bad conduct discharge is given. **2.** a certificate of such a discharge.

dish·pan (dish′pan′), *n.* a large pan in which dishes, pots, etc., are washed.

dish·rag (dish′rag′), *n.* a dishcloth.

dish·tow·el (dish′tou′el), *n.* a towel for drying dishes.

dish·wash·er (dish′wosh′ər, -wô′shər), *n.* **1.** a person who washes dishes. **2.** a machine for washing dishes, kitchen utensils, etc.

dish·wa·ter (dish′wô′tər, -wot′ər), *n.* **1.** water in which dishes are, or have been, washed. **2. dull as dishwater** (or **ditchwater**), extremely dull; boring.

dis·il·lu·sion (dis′i lo͞o′zhən), *v.t.* **1.** to free from or deprive of illusion; disenchant. **—***n.* **2.** a freeing or a being freed from illusion; disenchantment. **—dis′il·lu′sion·ment,** *n.*

dis·in·cli·na·tion (dis in′klə nā′shən, dis′in-), *n.* the state of being disinclined; aversion; distaste; unwillingness.

dis·in·cline (dis′in klīn′), *v.t., v.i.,* **-clined, -clin·ing.** to make or be averse or unwilling.

dis·in·fect (dis′in fekt′), *v.t.* to cleanse (clothing, wounds, etc.) in order to destroy harmful microorganisms; free from infection. [< MF *desinfect(er)*] **—dis′in·fec′tion,** *n.*

dis·in·fect·ant (dis′in fek′tənt), *n.* **1.** any chemical agent that destroys harmful organisms. **—***adj.* **2.** serving as a disinfectant. [< F *désinfectant,* n. use of prp. of *désinfect(er),* MF]

dis·in·fest (dis′in fest′), *v.t.* to rid of insects, rodents, etc. **—dis·in′fes·ta′tion,** *n.*

dis·in·flate (dis′in flāt′), *v.t.,* **-flat·ed, -flat·ing.** to reduce (the general price level) from an inflated state. **—dis′in·fla′tion,** *n.*

dis·in·for·ma·tion (dis′in fər mā′shən, di sin′-), *n.* false information about a country's military, political, or economic strength and plans, publicly announced or planted in the news media of other countries to mislead or to discredit foreign intelligence agents, leaders, or institutions. [< Russ *dezinformatsiya* disinformation, used in name of department in Soviet intelligence]

dis·in·gen·u·ous (dis′in jen′yo͞o əs), *adj.* not ingenuous; lacking in frankness, candor, or sincerity; insincere. **—dis′in·gen′u·ous·ly,** *adv.* **—dis′in·gen′u·ous·ness,** *n.*

dis·in·her·it (dis′in her′it), *v.t.* **1.** *Law.* to exclude from inheritance (an heir or a next of kin). **2.** to deprive of a heritage, country, right, privilege, etc. **—dis′in·her′i·tance,** *n.*

dis·in·te·grate (di sin′tə grāt′), *v.,* **-grat·ed, -grat·ing.** **—***v.i.* **1.** to separate into component parts; break up. **2.** *Physics.* **a.** to decay. **b.** (of a nucleus) to change into one or more different nuclei after being bombarded by high energy particles. **—***v.t.* **3.** to reduce to particles, fragments, or parts; break up or destroy the cohesion of: *Rocks are disintegrated by frost and rain.* **—dis·in·te·gra·ble** (di sin′tə grə bəl), *adj.* **—dis·in′te·gra′tive,** *adj.* **—dis·in′te·gra′tor,** *n.*

dis·in·te·gra·tion (di sin′tə grā′shən), *n.* **1.** the act or process of disintegrating. **2.** *Physics.* decay (def. 8).

dis·in·ter (dis′in tûr′), *v.t.,* **-terred, -ter·ring.** **1.** to take out of the place of interment; exhume; unearth. **2.** to bring from obscurity into view. **—dis′in·ter′ment,** *n.*

dis·in·ter·est (dis in′tər ist, -trist), *n.* **1.** absence of interest; indifference. **—***v.t.* **2.** to divest of interest or concern.

dis·in·ter·est·ed (dis in′tə res′tid, -tri stid), *adj.* **1.** unbiased by personal interest or advantage; not influenced by selfish motives: *a judge's disinterested decision.* **2.** *Nonstandard.* not interested; indifferent. **—dis·in′ter·est′ed·ly,** *adv.* **—dis·in′ter·est′ed·ness,** *n.*
—Syn. DISINTERESTED, UNINTERESTED are not properly synonyms. DISINTERESTED today stresses absence of prejudice or of selfish interests: *a disinterested report.* UNINTERESTED suggests aloofness and indifference: *completely uninterested and taking no part in the proceedings.*

dis·in·vest (dis′in vest′), *v.i.* **1.** to engage in disinvestment. **—***v.t.* **2.** to subject (funds, goods, etc.) to disinvestment.

dis·in·vest·ment (dis′in vest′mənt), *n.* the withdrawal of invested funds or the cancellation of financial aid, subsidies, or the like, as in a foreign country.

dis·join (dis join′), *v.t.* **1.** to undo the union of; disunite; separate. **—***v.i.* **2.** to become disunited; separate. [ME < OF *desjoind(re)* < L *disjungere*] **—dis·join′a·ble,** *adj.*

dis·joint (dis joint′), *v.t.* **1.** to separate or disconnect the joints or joinings of. **2.** to put out of order; derange. **—***v.i.* **3.** to come apart. **4.** to be dislocated; be out of joint. **—***adj.* **5.** *Obs.* disjointed; out of joint. [ME *disjoint* < OF *desjoint,* ptp. of *desjoindre* to DISJOIN]

dis·joint·ed (dis join′tid), *adj.* **1.** having the joints or connections separated: *a disjointed fowl.* **2.** disconnected; incoherent: *a disjointed discourse.* **—dis·joint′ed·ly,** *adv.* **—dis·joint′ed·ness,** *n.*

dis·junct (dis jungkt′), *adj.* **1.** disjoined; separated. **2.** *Music.* progressing melodically by intervals larger than a second. **3.** *Entomol.* having the head, thorax, and abdomen separated by deep constrictions. [ME < L *disjunct(us)* separated, ptp. of *disjungere* to DISJOIN; see JUNCTION]

dis·junc·tion (dis jungk′shən), *n.* **1.** the act of disjoining. **2.** the state of being disjoined: *a disjunction between thought and action.* **3.** *Logic.* **a.** an expression of the relationship between alternatives in a propositional statement. **b.** a connective symbol, as v, usually read as "or." [late ME *disjunccioun* < L *disjunctiōn-* (s. of *disjunctiō*) separation]

dis·junc·tive (dis jungk′tiv), *adj.* **1.** serving or tending to disjoin; separating; dividing; distinguishing. **2.** *Gram.* **a.** syntactically setting two or more expressions in opposition to each other, as *but* in *poor but happy,* or expressing an alternative, as *or* in *this or that.* **b.** not syntactically dependent upon some particular expression. **3.** *Logic.* **a.** characterizing propositions that include alternatives. **b.** (of a syllogism) containing at least one disjunctive proposition as a premise. **—***n.* **4.** a statement, course of action, etc., involving alternatives. **5.** *Logic.* disjunction (def. 3). [ME < LL *disjunctīv(us)* placed in opposition] **—dis·junc′tive·ly,** *adv.*

disk (disk), *n.* **1.** any thin, flat, circular plate or object. **2.** any surface that is flat and round, or seemingly so: *the disk of the sun.* **3.** a phonograph record. **4.** *Bot., Zool.* any of various roundish, flat structures or parts. **5.** See **intervertebral disk. 6.** *Bot.* (in the daisy and other composite plants) the central portion of the flower head, composed of tubular florets. **7.** *Math.* the domain bounded by a circle. **8.** *Computer Technol.* **a.** a thin, round plate of plastic or metal with magnetic recording surfaces on one or both sides, used to store and retrieve data. **b.** See **disk pack. 9.** *Archaic.* discus. **—***v.t.* **10.** to cultivate (soil) with a disk harrow. Also, **disc.** [< L *disc(us)* DISCUS]

disk′ crank′, *Mach.* a crank having the form of a disk with a crankpin mounted off center. Also called **crank disk, crankplate.**

disk·ette (dis′ket, dis ket′), *n.* See **floppy disk.**

disk′ flow′er, *Bot.* one of a number of small tubular flowers composing the disk of certain composite plants. Also called **disk′ flo′ret.** Cf. **ray flower.**

disk′ har′row, a harrow having a number of sharp-edged, concave disks set at an angle so as to turn the soil, pulverize it, and destroy weeds.

disk′ jock′ey, a performer who conducts a radio program featuring recorded music and informal talk.

disk′ pack′, *Computer Technol.* a cylinder containing several magnetic disks that can be handled as a unit: used for data storage and retrieval.

disk′ wheel′, a spokeless vehicular wheel, esp. on automobiles.

dis·like (dis līk′), *v.,* **-liked, -lik·ing,** *n.* **—***v.t.* **1.** to regard with displeasure, antipathy, or aversion. **—***n.* **2.** a feeling of aversion; antipathy. **—dis·lik′a·ble, dis·like′a·ble,** *adj.*
—Syn. 2. disrelish. DISLIKE, DISGUST, DISTASTE, REPUGNANCE imply antipathy toward something. DISLIKE is a general word, the strength of the feeling being indicated by the context. It expresses a positive (not necessarily strong), sometimes inherent or permanent feeling of antipathy for something: *to have a dislike for crowds, for someone.* DISGUST is a very strong word, expressing a feeling of loathing for what is offensive to the physical taste or to the feelings and sensibilities: *The taste of spoiled food fills one with disgust. He feels disgust at seeing snobbery and ostentation.* DISTASTE, though etymologically equal to disgust, is weaker; it implies a more or less settled dislike for what is naturally uncongenial or has been made so by association: *to have distaste for spicy foods, for hard work, for unconventional art.* REPUGNANCE is a strong feeling of aversion for something: *to feel repugnance for (or toward) low criminals, for hypocritical conduct.*

dis·lo·cate (dis′lō kāt′), *v.t.,* **-cat·ed, -cat·ing.** **1.** to put out of place; displace. **2.** *Surg.* to put out of joint or out of position, as a limb. **3.** to throw out of order; derange; upset; disorder. [< ML *dislocāt(us)* (ptp. of *dislocāre*)]

dis·lo·ca·tion (dis′lō kā′shən), *n.* **1.** the act or an instance of dislocating. **2.** the state of being dislocated. [ME]

dis·lodge (dis loj′), *v.,* **-lodged, -lodg·ing.** **—***v.t.* **1.** to remove or force out of a particular place. **2.** to drive out of a hiding place, a military position, etc. **—***v.i.* **3.** to go from a place of lodgment. [late ME *dislogg(en)* < OF *deslog(er)*] **—dis·lodg′ment;** *esp. Brit.,* **dis·lodge′ment,** *n.*

dis·loy·al (dis loi′əl), *adj.* not loyal; false to one's obligations or allegiances; faithless; treacherous. [< MF *desloial* < OF *desleal*] **—dis·loy′al·ly,** *adv.* **—Syn.** unfaithful.

dis·loy·al·ty (dis loi′əl tē), *n., pl.* **-ties.** **1.** the quality of being disloyal; lack of loyalty; unfaithfulness. **2.** violation of allegiance or duty, as to a government. **3.** a disloyal act. [ME < MF *desloiaute* < OF *desleaute*]
—Syn. 1. faithlessness, subversion. DISLOYALTY, PERFIDY, TREACHERY, TREASON imply betrayal of trust, and esp. traitorous acts against one's country. DISLOYALTY applies to any violation of loyalty, whether to a person, a cause, or one's country, and whether in thought or in deeds: *to suspect disloyalty in a friend.* PERFIDY implies deliberate breaking of faith or of one's pledges and promises, on which others are relying: *It is an act of perfidy to cheat innocent persons.* TREACHERY implies being secretly traitorous but seeming friendly and loyal: *In treachery deceit is added to disloyalty.* TREASON is wishing harm to one's country or government and performing overt acts to help its enemies: *Acting to aid a hostile power is treason.* **—Ant. 1.** loyalty.

dis·mal (diz′məl), *adj.* **1.** causing gloom or dejection; dreary; cheerless. **2.** characterized by ineptness or lack of interest. **3.** *Obs.* **a.** disastrous; calamitous. **b.** unlucky; sinister. **—***n.* **4. the dismals,** *Informal.* low spirits; the dumps. **5.** *Southern U.S.* a tract of swampy land along the coast. [ME < OF phrase **dis mal* unlucky days, trans. of L *diēs malī*] **—dis′mal·ly,** *adv.* **—dis′mal·ness,** *n.*

Dis′mal Swamp′, a swamp in SE Virginia and NE North Carolina. ab. 30 mi. long; ab. 600 sq. mi.

dis·man·tle (dis man′tᵊl), *v.t.,* **-tled, -tling.** **1.** to deprive or strip of apparatus, furniture, equipment, defenses, etc.: *to dismantle a ship.* **2.** to pull down; take apart. **3.** to divest of dress, covering, etc. [< MF *desmantel(er)*] **—dis·man′tle·ment,** *n.* **—dis·man′tler,** *n.*

dis·mast (dis mast′, -mäst′), *v.t.* to deprive (a ship) of masts; break off the masts of.

dis·may (dis mā′), *v.t.* **1.** to break down the courage of completely, as by sudden danger; daunt. **2.** to surprise in such a manner as to perturb or disillusion. **—***n.* **3.** sudden or complete loss of courage; utter disheartenment. **4.** sudden disillusionment. **5.** agitation of mind; perturbation; alarm. [ME *dismai(en),* prob. < OF **desmai(er)* = *des-* DIS-[1] + *-maier* << Gmc *mag-* be able; see MAY[1]] **—Syn. 1.** frighten.

dis·mem·ber (dis mem′bər), *v.t.* **1.** to deprive of members or limbs; divide limb from limb. **2.** to divide into parts; cut to pieces; mutilate. [ME *dismembr(en)* < OF *desmembr(er)*] **—dis·mem′ber·ment,** *n.*

dis·miss (dis mis′), *v.t.* **1.** to direct or allow (a person or a group of persons) to disperse; bid to depart. **2.** to discharge, as from office or service: *to dismiss an employee.* **3.** to discard or reject; put aside from consideration: *He dismissed the story as mere rumor.* **4.** *Law.* to put out of court, as a complaint or appeal. [ME < ML *dismiss(us)* sent away (for L *dimissus,* ptp. of *dīmittere*) = L *dis-* DIS-[1] + *mi-* send (s. of *mittere*) + *-ss-* ptp. suffix] **—dis·miss′i·ble,** *adj.* **—dis·miss′ive,** *adj.*

dis·miss·al (dis mis′əl), *n.* **1.** the act or an instance of dismissing. **2.** the state of being dismissed. **3.** a discharge from employment, service, etc.

dis·mount (*v.* dis mount′; *n.* dis′mount′, dis mount′), *v.i.*

1. to get off or alight from a horse, bicycle, etc. —*v.t.* 2. to bring or throw down, as from a horse; unhorse. 3. to remove (a thing) from its mounting, support, etc. 4. to take (a mechanism) to pieces. —*n.* 5. the act or process of dismounting. [prob. modeled on ML *dismontāre* or F *démonter*] —**dis·mount′a·ble,** *adj.*

Dis·ney (diz′nē), *n.* **Walt(er E.),** 1901–66, U.S. creator and producer of animated cartoons, motion pictures, etc.

dis·o·be·di·ence (dis′ə bē′dē əns), *n.* lack of obedience; neglect or refusal to obey. [ME < OF *desobedience*]

dis·o·be·di·ent (dis′ə bē′dē ənt), *adj.* neglecting or refusing to obey. [ME < OF *desobedient*] —**dis′o·be′di·ent·ly,** *adv.* —**Syn.** insubordinate, rebellious.

dis·o·bey (dis′ə bā′), *v.t., v.i.* to neglect or refuse to obey. [ME *disobei(en)* < OF *desobeir*] —**dis′o·bey′er,** *n.* —**Syn.** violate; defy.

dis·o·blige (dis′ə blīj′), *v.t.,* **-bliged, -blig·ing.** 1. to refuse or neglect to oblige; act contrary to the desire of. 2. to give offense to; affront. 3. to cause inconvenience to; incommode. [< MF *desoblig(er)*] —**dis′o·blig′ing·ly,** *adv.* —**dis′o·blig′ing·ness,** *n.*

dis·or·der (dis ôr′dər), *n.* 1. lack of order or regular arrangement; disarrangement; confusion. 2. an irregularity: *a disorder in legal proceedings.* 3. breach of order; a public disturbance. 4. a derangement of physical or mental health: *a mild stomach disorder.* —*v.t.* 5. to destroy the order or regular arrangement of; disarrange. 6. to derange the physical or mental health of.

—**Syn.** 1. disorderliness, disarray, jumble. 3. riot, turbulence. DISORDER, BRAWL, DISTURBANCE, UPROAR are disruptions or interruptions of a peaceful situation. DISORDER refers to unrest within a city or state, and to any scene in which there is confusion or fighting among individuals or groups: *The police went to the scene of the disorder.* A BRAWL is a noisy, unseemly quarrel, usually in a public place: *a tavern brawl.* A DISTURBANCE refers to an instance of disorder that inconveniences many people: *Hecklers at the inauguration created a disturbance.* An UPROAR refers to tumult and clamor: *The announcement of victory caused an uproar in the waiting crowd.* 4. ailment, malady, complaint, sickness. See **disease.** 5. disarray, disorganize.

dis·or·dered (dis ôr′dərd), *adj.* 1. in confusion; disarranged. 2. suffering from a physical or mental disorder. —**dis·or′dered·ly,** *adv.* —**dis·or′dered·ness,** *n.*

dis·or·der·ly (dis ôr′dər lē), *adj.* 1. characterized by disorder; untidy; confused: *a disorderly desk.* 2. unruly; tumultuous. 3. *Law.* violating or opposing constituted order; contrary to public order or morality. —*adv.* 4. irregularly or confusedly. —**dis·or′der·li·ness,** *n.*

disor′derly con′duct, *Law.* any of various petty misdemeanors, generally including nuisances, breaches of the peace, offensive or immoral conduct in public, etc.

disor′derly house′, 1. a house of prostitution; brothel. 2. a gambling place.

dis·or·gan·ise (dis ôr′gə nīz′), *v.t.,* **-ised, -is·ing.** *Chiefly Brit.* disorganize. —**dis·or′gan·is′er,** *n.*

dis·or·gan·i·za·tion (dis ôr′gə ni zā′shən *or, esp. Brit.,* -nī-), *n.* 1. a breaking up of order or system; disunion or disruption of constituent parts. 2. the absence of organization or orderly arrangement; disarrangement; disorder. Also, *esp. Brit.,* **dis·or′gan·i·sa′tion.** [< F *désorganisation*]

dis·or·gan·ize (dis ôr′gə nīz′), *v.t.,* **-ized, -iz·ing.** to destroy the organization, systematic arrangement, or orderly connection of; throw into confusion or disorder. Also, *esp. Brit.,* **disorganise.** [< F *désorganis(er)*] —**dis·or′gan·iz′er,** *n.*

dis·o·ri·ent (dis ōr′ē ent′, -ôr′-), *v.t.* 1. to cause to lose one's way. 2. to confuse by removing or obscuring something that has guided a person, group, or culture, as customs, moral standards, etc. 3. *Psychiatry.* to cause to lose perception of time, place, or one's personal identity. [< F *désorient(er)*]

dis·o·ri·en·tate (dis ōr′ē ən tāt′, -ôr′-), *v.t.,* **-tat·ed, -tat·ing.** to disorient. —**dis·o′ri·en·ta′tion,** *n.*

dis·own (dis ōn′), *v.t.* to refuse to acknowledge as belonging or pertaining to oneself; deny the ownership of or responsibility for; repudiate.

dis·par·age (di spar′ij), *v.t.,* **-aged, -ag·ing.** 1. to speak of or treat slightingly; depreciate; belittle. 2. to bring reproach or discredit upon; lower the estimation of. [ME *disparage(n)* < OF *desparag(ier)* (to) match equally = *des-* DIS-^{1} + *parage* equality = *par(er)* (to) equalize (< L *parāre;* see PEER^{1}) + *-age* -AGE)] —**dis·par′ag·er,** *n.* —**dis·par′ag·ing·ly,** *adv.* —**Syn. 1.** decry, minimize.

dis·par·age·ment (di spar′ij mənt), *n.* 1. the act or an instance of disparaging. 2. something that causes loss of dignity or reputation. [< MF *desparagement*]

dis·pa·rate (dis′pər it, di spar′-), *adj.* distinct in kind; essentially different; dissimilar; unlike. [< L *disparāt(us)* separated (ptp. of *disparāre*). See DIS-^{1}, PARE, -ATE^{1}] —**dis′pa·rate·ly,** *adv.* —**dis′pa·rate·ness,** *n.* —**Syn.** separate, divergent, incommensurable.

dis·par·i·ty (di spar′i tē), *n., pl.* **-ties.** lack of similarity or equality; difference. [< MF *desparite* < LL *disparitāt-* (s. of *disparitās*)] —**Syn.** See **difference.**

dis·part (dis pärt′), *v.t., v.i.* to separate; divide into parts. [appar. < It *dispart-,* s. of *dispartire* < L to part, separate, divide]

dis·pas·sion (dis pash′ən), *n.* 1. freedom from passion. 2. the state or quality of being unemotional.

dis·pas·sion·ate (dis pash′ə nit), *adj.* free from or unaffected by passion; devoid of personal feeling or bias; impartial. —**dis·pas′sion·ate·ly,** *adv.* —**dis·pas′sion·ate·ness,** *n.* —**Syn.** cool, unemotional, uninvolved.

dis·patch (di spach′), *v.t.* 1. to send off or away with speed, as a messenger, telegram, body of troops, etc. 2. to put to death; kill. 3. to transact or dispose of (a matter) promptly or speedily. —*v.i.* 4. *Archaic.* to hasten; be quick. —*n.* 5. the sending off of a messenger, letter, etc., to a destination. 6. act of putting to death; execution. 7. prompt or speedy action. 8. a message or communication sent in haste, by special messenger, etc. 9. *Journalism.* a news account hastily transmitted by a reporter. Also, **despatch.** [< It *dispacci(are)* (to) hasten, speed, or < Sp *despach(ar)* << OF *despeechier.* See DIS-^{1}, IMPEACH]

dispatch′ case′. See **attaché case.**

dis·patch·er (di spach′ər), *n.* 1. a person who dispatches. 2. a person who oversees the departure of trains, planes, buses, etc., as for a transportation company, railroad, etc. Also, **despatcher.**

dis·pel (di spel′), *v.t.,* **-pelled, -pel·ling.** to drive off in various directions; scatter; disperse; dissipate. [< L *dispell(ere)* (to) drive asunder = *dis-* DIS-^{1} + *pellere* to drive] —**Syn.** See **scatter.**

dis·pend (di spend′), *v.t.* *Obs.* to pay out; expend; spend. [ME *dispend(en)* < OF *despend(re)* < L *dispendere* to weigh out; see DISPENSE]

dis·pen·sa·ble (di spen′sə bəl), *adj.* 1. capable of being dispensed with or done without; not essential. 2. capable of being dispensed or administered. 3. *Rom. Cath. Ch.* capable of being permitted or forgiven, as an offense or sin. [< ML *dispensābil(is)*] —**dis·pen′sa·bil′i·ty, dis·pen′sa·ble·ness,** *n.*

dis·pen·sa·ry (di spen′sə rē), *n., pl.* **-ries.** 1. a place where something is dispensed, esp. medicines. 2. a charitable or public institution where medicines are furnished and medical advice is given gratuitously or for a small fee. [< ML *dispensāria* storeroom]

dis·pen·sa·tion (dis′pən sā′shən, -pen-), *n.* 1. the act or an instance of dispensing; distribution. 2. something that is distributed or given out. 3. a specified order, system, or arrangement; administration or management: *Things were managed differently under the dispensation of the last ministry.* 4. *Theol.* a. the divine ordering of the affairs of the world. b. a divinely appointed order or age. 5. a dispensing with, doing away with, or doing without something. 6. *Rom. Cath. Ch.* a. a relaxation of law in a particular case granted by a competent superior. b. an official document authorizing such a relaxation of law. [ME *dispensacioun* < ML *dispensātiōn-* (s. of *dispensātiō*) a pardon, relaxation, LL: order, system, divine grace, L: distribution = *dispensāt(us)* (ptp. of *dispensāre* to DISPENSE; see -ATE^{1}) + *-iōn-* -ION] —**dis′pen·sa′tion·al,** *adj.*

dis·pen·sa·tor (dis′pən sā′tər, -pen-), *n.* *Archaic.* a person who dispenses; distributor; administrator. [ME *dispensatour* < ML *dispensātor,* L: manager, steward]

dis·pen·sa·to·ry (di spen′sə tōr′ē, -tôr′ē), *n., pl.* **-ries.** 1. a book describing the composition, preparation, and uses of medicinal substances; a nonofficial pharmacopoeia. 2. a dispensary. [< ML *dispensātōri(um),* n. use of neut. of LL *dispensātōri(us)* of management]

dis·pense (di spens′), *v.,* **-pensed, -pens·ing,** *n.* —*v.t.* 1. to deal out; distribute. 2. to administer: *to dispense the law without bias.* 3. *Pharm.* to prepare and distribute (medicine), esp. on prescription. 4. *Rom. Cath. Ch.* to grant a dispensation to. —*v.i.* 5. to grant dispensation. 6. **dispense with, a.** to do without; forgo. **b.** to do away with; rid of. **c.** to grant exemption from a law or promise. —*n.* 7. *Obs.* expenditure. [ME *dispens(en)* < ML *dispens(āre)* (to) pardon, exempt, LL: to distribute (by weight), freq. of *dispendere* to weigh out = *dis-* DIS-^{1} + *pend-* weigh] —**Syn.** 1. allot.

dis·pens·er (di spen′sər), *n.* 1. a person or thing that dispenses. 2. a container, package, device, or vending machine for holding and dispensing something in small amounts, as facial tissue, paper cups, candy, etc. [ME]

dis·peo·ple (dis pē′pəl), *v.t.,* **-pled, -pling.** to deprive of people; depopulate.

dis·perse (di spûrs′), *v.,* **-persed, -pers·ing,** *adj.* —*v.t.* 1. to drive or send off in various directions; scatter. 2. to spread widely; disseminate: *to disperse knowledge.* 3. to dispel; cause to vanish: *The wind dispersed the fog.* —*v.i.* 4. to become scattered. 5. to be dispelled; vanish. —*adj.* 6. *Physical Chem.* noting the dispersed particles in a dispersion. [< L *dispers(us)* (ptp. of *dispergere*) = *di-* DI-^{2} + *spēr-* scatter (s. of *-spergere,* comb. form of *spargere* to SPARGE) + *-sus* ptp. suffix; r. ME *disparse* < MF < L] —**dis·pers·ed·ly** (di spûr′sid lē), *adv.* —**dis·pers′er,** *n.* —**Syn.** 1. See **scatter.** —**Ant.** 1. combine, collect.

dis·per·sion (di spûr′zhən, -shən), *n.* 1. Also called **dis·per·sal** (di spûr′səl). the act, state, or an instance of dispersing. 2. the state of being dispersed. 3. *Optics.* **a.** the variation of the index of refraction of a transparent substance, with the wavelength of light. **b.** the separation of white or compound light into its respective colors, as in the formation of a spectrum by a prism. 4. *Statistics.* the scattering of values of a variable around the mean or median of a distribution. 5. *Mil.* a scattered pattern of hits of bombs dropped under identical conditions, or of shots fired from the same gun with the same firing data. 6. *Chem.* a system of dispersed particles suspended in a solid, liquid, or gas. 7. (*cap.*) Diaspora (def. 1). [< L *dispersiōn-* (s. of *dispersiō*)]

dis·per·sive (di spûr′siv), *adj.* serving or tending to disperse. —**dis·per′sive·ness,** *n.*

dis·per·soid (di spûr′soid), *n.* *Physical Chem.* the suspended particles in a dispersion.

dis·pir·it (di spir′it), *v.t.* to deprive of spirit, hope, enthusiasm, etc.; discourage; dishearten. [DI-^{2} + SPIRIT]

dis·pir·it·ed (di spir′i tid), *adj.* discouraged; dejected; disheartened; gloomy. —**dis·pir′it·ed·ly,** *adv.* —**dis·pir′it·ed·ness,** *n.*

dis·pit·e·ous (dis pit′ē əs), *adj.* *Archaic.* cruel; pitiless. [var. of DESPITEOUS, with *dis-* (< L) for *des-* (< F)]

dis·place (dis plās′), *v.t.,* **-placed, -plac·ing.** 1. to compel (a person or persons) to leave home, country, etc. 2. to move or put out of the usual or proper place. 3. to take the place of; supplant. 4. to remove from a position, office, or dignity. 5. *Obs.* to make oneself rid of; banish from oneself. —**dis·plac′er,** *n.* —**Syn.** 4. depose, oust, dismiss.

displaced′ per′son, a person driven or expelled from his homeland by war or tyranny. *Abbr.:* DP, D.P.

dis·place·ment (dis plās′mənt), *n.* 1. the act of displacing. 2. the state of being displaced or the amount or degree to which something is displaced. 3. *Physics.* **a.** the displacing in space of one mass by another. **b.** the weight or the volume of fluid displaced by a floating or submerged body. Cf. **Archimedes' principle. c.** the linear or angular distance in a given direction between a body or point and a reference position. **d.** the distance of an oscillating body from its central position or point of equilibrium at any given moment. 4. *Geol.* the offset of rocks caused by movement along a fault. **5.** *Mech.* the total volume of space through which the pistons of an engine travel. **6.** *Naut.* the amount of water that a vessel displaces, expressed in displacement tons. **7.** *Psychoanal.* the transfer of an emotion from its original focus to another object, person, situation, etc.

displace′ment hull′, *Naut.* a hull that displaces a significant volume of water when under way. Cf. **planing hull.**

displace′ment ton′, *Naut.* a unit for measuring the displacement of a vessel, equal to a long ton of 2240 pounds or 35 cubic feet of sea water.

displace′ment ton′nage, *Naut.* the number of long tons of water displaced by a vessel.

dis·plant (dis plant′, -plänt′), *v.t. Obs.* **1.** to dislodge. **2.** to transplant. [DIS-[1] + PLANT, modeled on MF *desplanter*]

dis·play (di splā′), *v.t.* **1.** to show; exhibit; make visible: *to display a sign.* **2.** to reveal; betray: *to display fear.* **3.** to unfold; open out; spread out: *to display a sail.* **4.** to show ostentatiously; flaunt. **5.** *Print.* to give special prominence to (words, captions, etc.) by choice and arrangement of type. —*n.* **6.** the act or an instance of displaying; exhibition: *a display of courage.* **7.** an ostentatious show: *a vulgar display of wealth.* **8.** *Print.* **a.** the giving of prominence to particular words, sentences, etc., by the choice and arrangement of types and position. **b.** printed matter thus displayed. **9.** an arrangement, as of merchandise designed to advertise, attract buyers, etc. [ME *desplay(en)* < AF *desplei(er)* < LL *displicāre* to unfold. See DIS-[1], PLICATE] —**dis·play′er,** *n.*
—**Syn. 1.** DISPLAY, EXHIBIT, EVINCE, MANIFEST mean to show or bring to the attention of another or others. To DISPLAY is literally to spread something out so that it may be most completely and favorably seen: *to display goods for sale.* To EXHIBIT is to put something in plain view and usually in a favorable position for particular observation: *to exhibit the best flowers at a special show.* They may both be used of showing (off) one's qualities or feelings: *He displayed his wit, his ignorance. He exhibited great surprise.* To EVINCE and to MANIFEST have only this latter reference, MANIFEST being the stronger word: *to evince or manifest surprise, interest, sympathy.* **4.** flourish, parade, air. **6.** See **show.** —**Ant. 1.** conceal.

display′ type′, *Print.* type larger than body type, as for headings.

dis·please (dis plēz′), *v.,* **-pleased, -pleas·ing.** —*v.t.* **1.** to incur the dissatisfaction, dislike, or disapproval of; offend; annoy. —*v.i.* **2.** to be unpleasant; cause displeasure. [ME *desplese(n)* < AF, MF *desplais(ir)* < VL **displacēre*] —**dis·pleas′ing·ly,** *adv.*

dis·pleas·ure (dis plezh′ər), *n., v.,* **-ured, -ur·ing.** —*n.* **1.** dissatisfaction, disapproval, or annoyance. **2.** *Archaic.* discomfort, uneasiness, or pain. **3.** *Archaic.* a cause of offense, annoyance, or injury. —*v.t.* **4.** *Archaic.* to displease. [DIS-[1] + PLEASURE; r. late ME *desplaisir* < MF (n. use of inf.); see DISPLEASE] —**Syn. 1.** distaste, dislike; indignation, vexation. See **dissatisfaction.** —**Ant. 1.** pleasure.

dis·plode (dis plōd′), *v.t., v.i.,* **-plod·ed, -plod·ing.** *Archaic.* to explode. [< L *displōd(ere)* = *dis-* DIS-[1] + *plaudere* to make a sudden loud noise]

dis·plume (dis plo͞om′), *v.t.,* **-plumed, -plum·ing. 1.** to strip of plumes; deplume. **2.** to strip of honors.

dis·port (di spōrt′, -spôrt′), *v.t.* **1.** to divert or amuse (oneself). **2.** to display (oneself) in a sportive manner. —*v.i.* **3.** to divert oneself; sport. —*n.* **4.** diversion; amusement; play; sport. [ME *disporte, desporte* < AF *desport(er)*]

dis·pos·a·ble (di spō′zə bəl), *adj.* **1.** designed for or capable of being disposed of: *a disposable paper plate.* **2.** free for use; available: *disposable profits.*

dis·pos·al (di spō′zəl), *n.* **1.** the act or an instance of disposing; arrangement: *the disposal of the troops.* **2.** a disposing of or getting rid of something: *the disposal of waste material.* **3.** a disposing of, as by gift or sale; bestowal. **4.** power or right to dispose of a thing; control: *left at his disposal.*

dis·pose (di spōz′), *v.,* **-posed, -pos·ing,** *n.* —*v.t.* **1.** to put in a particular or the proper order or arrangement; adjust; arrange. **2.** to put in a particular or suitable place. **3.** to give a tendency or inclination to; incline. **4.** to make fit or ready; prepare. —*v.i.* **5.** to arrange or decide matters. **6.** *Obs.* to make terms. **7. dispose of, a.** to deal with conclusively; settle. **b.** to get rid of; discard; give away. **c.** to do away with; destroy. —*n.* **8.** *Archaic.* disposition; habit. **9.** *Obs.* arrangement; regulation; disposal. [ME < MF *dispos(er)*] —**dis·pos′er,** *n.*

dis·posed (di spōzd′), *adj.* having a certain inclination or disposition; inclined (usually fol. by *to* or an infinitive).

dis·po·si·tion (dis′pə zish′ən), *n.* **1.** the predominant or prevailing tendency of one's spirits; mental outlook or mood: *a girl with a pleasant disposition.* **2.** a state of mind regarding something; inclination: *a disposition to gamble.* **3.** physical inclination or tendency: *the disposition of ice to melt when heated.* **4.** arrangement or placing, as of troops or buildings. **5.** the final settlement of a matter. **6.** bestowal, as by gift or sale. **7.** power to dispose of a thing; control: *funds at one's disposition.* **8.** *Archaic.* regulation; management; dispensation: *the disposition of God.* [< L *dispositiōn-* (s. of *dispositiō*) = *disposit(us)* (ptp. of *dispōnere* to distribute; see DISPOSE, -ITE[2]) + *-iōn-* -ION; r. ME *disposicioun* < AF]
—**Syn. 1.** nature, character, humor. DISPOSITION, TEMPER, TEMPERAMENT refer to the aspects and habits of mind that one displays over a length of time. DISPOSITION is the natural or prevailing aspect of one's mind as shown in behavior and in relationships with others: *a happy disposition; a selfish disposition.* TEMPER sometimes denotes the essential quality of one's nature: *a glacial temper;* usually it has to do with propensity toward anger: *an even temper; a quick or hot temper.* TEMPERAMENT refers to the particular, often unusual, balance of emotions determining a person's character: *an artistic temperament; an unstable temperament.* **2.** bent, tendency, predisposition, proclivity. **4.** order, grouping, placement. **5.** outcome, result. **7.** direction.

dis·pos·sess (dis′pə zes′), *v.t.* to put (a person) out of possession, esp. of real property; oust. [DIS-[1] + POSSESS; r. ME *disposseden* = DIS-[1] + MF *posseder* < L *possidēre* (*por-* (?) + *sedēre* to SIT)] —**dis′pos·ses′sion,** *n.* —**dis′pos·ses′sor,** *n.* —**dis·pos·ses·so·ry** (dis′pə zes′ə rē), *adj.* —**Syn.** See **strip**[1].

dis·pos·sessed (dis′pə zest′), *adj.* **1.** evicted; ousted. **2.** without property, status, etc., as wandering or displaced persons. **3.** having suffered a loss of expectations, prospects, etc.; disinherited; alienated: *Modern man is spiritually dispossessed.*

dis·po·sure (di spō′zhər), *n. Archaic.* disposal; disposition.

dis·praise (dis prāz′), *v.,* **-praised, -prais·ing,** *n.* —*v.t.* **1.** to speak of as undeserving or unworthy; censure; disparage. —*n.* **2.** the act or an instance of dispraising; censure. [ME < OF *despreis(i)er*] —**dis·prais′er,** *n.* —**dis·prais′ing·ly,** *adv.*

dis·pread (di spred′), *v.t., v.i.,* **-pread, -pread·ing.** *Archaic.* to spread out; extend. Also, **disspread.** [DI-[2] + SPREAD] —**dis·pread′er,** *n.*

dis·prize (dis prīz′), *v.t.,* **-prized, -priz·ing.** *Archaic.* to hold in small esteem; disdain. [ME *disprise(n)* < MF *despris(er),* late var. of *despreis(i)er* to DISPRAISE]

dis·proof (dis pro͞of′), *n.* **1.** the act of disproving. **2.** proof to the contrary; refutation.

dis·pro·por·tion (dis′prə pōr′shən, -pôr′-), *n.* **1.** lack of proportion; lack of proper relationship in size, number, etc. **2.** something out of proportion. —*v.t.* **3.** to make disproportionate. —**dis′pro·por′tion·a·ble,** *adj.* —**dis′pro·por′tion·a·ble·ness,** *n.* —**dis′pro·por′tion·a·bly,** *adv.*

dis·pro·por·tion·al (dis′prə pōr′shə nəl, -pôr′-), *adj.* not in proportion; disproportionate. —**dis′pro·por′tion·al′i·ty,** *n.* —**dis′pro·por′tion·al·ly,** *adv.*

dis·pro·por·tion·ate (dis′prə pōr′shə nit, -pôr′-), *adj.* not proportionate; out of proportion, as in size, number, etc. —**dis′pro·por′tion·ate·ly,** *adv.* —**dis′pro·por′tion·ate·ness,** *n.*

dis·prove (dis pro͞ov′), *v.t.,* **-proved, -prov·ing.** to prove (an assertion, claim, etc.) to be false or wrong; refute; invalidate. [ME *disprove(n)* < OF *desprov(er)*] —**dis·prov′a·ble,** *adj.*

dis·put·a·ble (di spyo͞o′tə bəl, dis′pyo͝o-), *adj.* capable of being disputed; debatable; questionable. [< L *disputābil(is)*] —**dis·put′a·bil′i·ty,** *n.* —**dis·put′a·bly,** *adv.*

dis·pu·tant (di spyo͞ot′ənt), *n.* **1.** a person who disputes; debater. —*adj.* **2.** engaged in dispute; disputing. [< L *disputant-* (s. of *disputāns,* prp. of *disputāre*)]

dis·pu·ta·tion (dis′pyo͝o tā′shən), *n.* **1.** the act of disputing or debating; verbal controversy; discussion or debate. **2.** an academic exercise consisting of the arguing of a thesis between its maintainer and his opponents. **3.** *Obs.* conversation. [< L *disputātiōn-* (s. of *disputātiō*) = *disputāt(us)* (ptp. of *disputāre;* see DISPUTE, -ATE[1]) + *-iōn-* -ION; r. ME *desputisoun* < OF]

dis·pu·ta·tious (dis′pyo͝o tā′shəs), *adj.* given to disputation; argumentative; contentious. Also, **dis·put·a·tive** (di spyo͞o′tə tiv). —**dis′pu·ta′tious·ly,** *adv.* —**dis′pu·ta′tious·ness,** *n.*

dis·pute (di spyo͞ot′), *v.,* **-put·ed, -put·ing,** *n.* —*v.i.* **1.** to engage in argument or debate. **2.** to argue vehemently; wrangle or quarrel. —*v.t.* **3.** to argue or debate about; discuss. **4.** to argue against; call in question: *to dispute a proposal.* **5.** to quarrel or fight about; contest. **6.** to strive against; oppose: *to dispute an advance of troops.* —*n.* **7.** a debate or controversy: *An increase in taxes was the subject of the dispute.* **8.** a quarrel. [ME < LL *disput(āre)* (to) dispute (L: to discuss) = *dis-* DIS-[1] + *putāre* to reckon, consider; see PUTATIVE] —**dis·put′er,** *n.* —**Syn. 8.** disputation, altercation, squabble. See **argument.**

dis·qual·i·fi·ca·tion (dis kwol′ə fə kā′shən), *n.* **1.** the act or an instance of disqualifying. **2.** the state of being disqualified. **3.** something that disqualifies.

dis·qual·i·fy (dis kwol′ə fī′), *v.t.,* **-fied, -fy·ing. 1.** to deprive of qualification or fitness; render unfit. **2.** to deprive of legal or other rights or privileges; declare ineligible or unqualified. **3.** *Sports.* to deprive of the right to participate in or win a contest because of a violation of the rules. —**dis·qual′i·fi′a·ble,** *adj.*

dis·qui·et (dis kwī′it), *n.* **1.** lack of calm, peace, or ease; anxiety; uneasiness. —*v.t.* **2.** to deprive of quiet, rest, or peace; disturb. —*adj.* **3.** *Archaic.* uneasy; disquieted. —**dis·qui′et·ed·ly, dis·qui′et·ly,** *adv.*

dis·qui·et·ing (dis kwī′i ting), *adj.* causing anxiety or uneasiness; disturbing: *disquieting news.* —**dis·qui′et·ing·ly,** *adv.*

dis·qui·e·tude (dis kwī′i to͞od′, -tyo͞od′), *n.* the state of disquiet; uneasiness.

dis·qui·si·tion (dis′kwi zish′ən), *n.* a formal discourse or treatise in which a subject is examined and discussed; dissertation. [< L *disquīsītiōn-* (s. of *disquīsītiō*) = *disquīsīt(us)* (ptp. of *disquīrere* to inquire diligently, investigate = *dis-* DIS-[1] + *quaerere* to seek, ask) + *-iōn-* -ION]

Dis·rae·li (diz rā′lē), *n.* **Benjamin, 1st Earl of Beaconsfield,** 1804–81, British statesman and novelist: prime minister 1867, 1874–80.

dis·rate (dis rāt′), *v.t.,* **-rat·ed, -rat·ing.** to reduce to a lower rating or rank.

dis·re·gard (dis′ri gärd′), *v.t.* **1.** to pay no attention to; leave out of consideration. —*n.* **2.** lack of regard or attention; neglect. —**Syn. 1.** ignore. See **slight. 2.** inattention, oversight; indifference. —**Ant. 1.** notice.

dis·re·gard·ful (dis′ri gärd′fəl), *adj.* neglectful; careless. —**dis′re·gard′ful·ly,** *adv.* —**dis′re·gard′ful·ness,** *n.*

dis·rel·ish (dis rel′ish), *v.t.* **1.** to have a distaste for; dislike. —*n.* **2.** distaste; dislike.

dis·re·mem·ber (dis′ri mem′bər), *v.t. Dial.* to fail to remember; forget.

dis·re·pair (dis′ri pâr′), *n.* the condition of needing repair; an impaired or neglected state.

dis·rep·u·ta·ble (dis rep′yə tə bəl), *adj.* **1.** not reputable; having a bad reputation. **2.** discreditable; dishonorable. **3.** shabby or shoddy. —**dis·rep′u·ta·bil′i·ty, dis·rep′u·ta·ble·ness,** *n.* —**dis·rep′u·ta·bly,** *adv.*

dis·re·pute (dis′ri pyo͞ot′), *n.* bad repute; discredit; low regard (usually prec. by *in* or *into*): *These theories have fallen into disrepute.* —**Syn.** disfavor, disgrace.

dis·re·spect (dis′ri spekt′), *n.* **1.** lack of respect; discourtesy; rudeness. —*v.t.* **2.** to regard or treat with contempt or rudeness.

dis·re·spect·a·ble (dis′ri spek′tə bəl), *adj.* not respectable. —**dis′re·spect′a·bil′i·ty,** *n.*

dis·re·spect·ful (dis′ri spekt′fəl), *adj.* showing disrespect; lacking courtesy or esteem. —**dis′re·spect′ful·ly,** *adv.* —**dis′re·spect′ful·ness,** *n.* —**Syn.** discourteous, impolite, rude, impudent, impertinent, irreverent.

dis·robe (dis rōb′), *v.t., v.i.,* **-robed, -rob·ing.** to undress. —**dis·robe′ment,** *n.* —**dis·rob′er,** *n.*

dis·root (dis ro͞ot′, -ro͝ot′), *v.t.* to uproot; dislodge.

dis·rupt (dis rupt′), *v.t.* **1.** to cause disorder or turmoil in. **2.** to destroy, usually temporarily, the normal continuance or unity of; interrupt: *Telephone service was disrupted for hours.* **3.** to break apart. —*adj.* **4.** disrupted; broken apart. [< L *disrupt(us)* (var. of *dīruptus,* ptp. of *dīrumpere*). See DI-², RUPTURE] —**dis·rupt′er, dis·rup′tor,** *n.*

dis·rup·tion (dis rup′shən), *n.* **1.** forcible separation or division into parts: *the disruption of rock.* **2.** a disrupted condition: *The state was in disruption.* [< L *disruptiōn-* (s. of *disruptiō*)]

dis·rup·tive (dis rup′tiv), *adj.* causing, tending to cause, or caused by disruption; disrupting. —**dis·rup′tive·ly,** *adv.*

dis·sat·is·fac·tion (dis′sat is fak′shən, dis sat′-), *n.* the state or attitude of not being satisfied; displeasure. —**Syn.** disappointment, disapproval, uneasiness. DISSATISFACTION, DISCONTENT, DISPLEASURE imply a sense of dislike for, or unhappiness in, one's surroundings and a wish for other conditions. DISSATISFACTION results from contemplating what falls short of one's wishes or expectations and is usually only temporary: *dissatisfaction with the results of a morning's work.* DISCONTENT is a sense of lack and a general feeling of uneasy dislike for the conditions of one's life, which colors one's entire outlook: *feeling a continual vague discontent.* DISPLEASURE, a more positive word, suggests a certain amount of anger as well as dissatisfaction: *displeasure at being kept waiting.* —**Ant.** satisfaction.

dis·sat·is·fac·to·ry (dis′sat is fak′tə rē, dis sat′-), *adj.* causing dissatisfaction; unsatisfactory.

dis·sat·is·fied (dis sat′is fīd′), *adj.* **1.** not satisfied or pleased; discontented. **2.** showing dissatisfaction: *a dissatisfied look.* —**dis·sat′is·fied′ly,** *adv.*

dis·sat·is·fy (dis sat′is fī′), *v.t.,* **-fied, -fy·ing.** to cause to be displeased, esp. by failing to provide something expected or desired.

dis·seat (dis sēt′), *v.t. Archaic.* to unseat.

dis·sect (di sekt′, dī-), *v.t.* **1.** to cut apart (an animal body, plant, etc.) to examine the structure, relation of parts, or the like. **2.** to examine minutely part by part; analyze: *to dissect an idea.* [< L *dissect(us)* (ptp. of *dissecāre* to cut up) = *dis-* DIS-¹ + *sec-* cut + *-tus* ptp. suffix] —**dis·sec′ti·ble,** *adj.* —**dis·sec′tor,** *n.*

dis·sect·ed (di sek′tid, dī-), *adj.* **1.** *Bot.* deeply divided into numerous parts, as a leaf. **2.** *Phys. Geog.* separated, by erosion, into many closely spaced valleys, as a plateau.

dis·sec·tion (di sek′shən, dī-), *n.* **1.** the act of dissecting. **2.** something that has been dissected. **3.** a detailed, part-by-part analysis. [< L *dissectiōn-* (s. of *dissectiō*)]

dis·seise (dis sēz′), *v.t.,* **-seised, -seis·ing.** *Law.* to deprive (a person) of seizin, or of the possession of a freehold interest in land, esp. wrongfully or by force; oust. [ME *disseise* < AF *disseis(ir).* See DIS-¹, SEIZE] —**dis·sei′sor,** *n.*

dis·sei·see (dis′sē zē′, dis sē zē′), *n. Law.* a person who is disseised. Also, **dis′sei·zee′.**

dis·sei·sin (dis sē′zin), *n. Law.* **1.** the act of disseising. **2.** the state of being disseised. Also, **dis·sei′zin.** [ME *disseisine* < AF]

dis·seize (dis sēz′), *v.t.,* **-seized, -seiz·ing.** *Law.* disseise. —**dis·sei′zor,** *n.*

dis·sem·blance¹ (di sem′bləns), *n.* dissimilarity; unlikeness. [late ME < MF *dessemblance.* See DIS-¹, SEMBLANCE]

dis·sem·blance² (di sem′bləns), *n.* dissembling; dissimulation. [DISSEMBLE + -ANCE]

dis·sem·ble (di sem′bəl), *v.,* **-bled, -bling.** —*v.t.* **1.** to give a false appearance to; conceal the real nature of. **2.** to put on the appearance of; feign. **3.** *Archaic.* to let pass unnoticed; ignore. —*v.i.* **4.** to conceal one's true motives, thoughts, etc., by some pretense; speak or act hypocritically. [alter. (? by assoc. with obs. *semble* to RESEMBLE) of ME *dissimulen* < L *dissimulāre.* See DIS-¹, SIMULATE] —**dis·sem′bler,** *n.* —**dis·sem′bling·ly,** *adv.*

dis·sem·i·nate (di sem′ə nāt′), *v.t.,* **-nat·ed, -nat·ing.** to scatter or spread widely; promulgate extensively. [< L *dissēmindruminat(us)* (ptp. of *dissēmināre; dis-* DIS-¹ + *sēmināre* to sow) = *dis-* + *sēmin-* (s. of *sēmen* seed) + *-ātus* -ATE¹] —**dis·sem′i·na′tion,** *n.* —**dis·sem′i·na′tive,** *adj.* —**dis·sem′i·na′tor,** *n.*

dis·sen·sion (di sen′shən), *n.* **1.** strong disagreement; discord; a contention or quarrel. **2.** difference in sentiment or opinion; disagreement. [< L *dissēnsiōn-* (s. of *dissēnsiō*) = *dissēns(us)* (ptp. of *dissentīre;* see DISSENT) + *-iōn-* -ION; r. ME *dissencioun* < AF] —**Syn. 1.** strife. See **quarrel¹.**

dis·sent (di sent′), *v.i.* **1.** to differ in sentiment or opinion; disagree (often fol. by *from*). **2.** to reject the doctrines or authority of an established church. —*n.* **3.** difference in sentiment or opinion. **4.** separation from an established church, esp. the Church of England; nonconformity. [ME *dissent(en)* < L *dissent(īre)* = *dis-* DIS-¹ + *sentīre* to feel] —**dis·sent′ing·ly,** *adv.*
—**Syn. 3.** disagreement, dissatisfaction, opposition. DISSENT, DISSIDENCE mean disagreement with the majority opinion. DISSENT may express either withholding of agreement or open disagreement. DISSENTERS may withdraw from a group, but if so, they merely go their own way. DISSIDENCE, formerly much the same as DISSENT, has come to suggest not only strong dissatisfaction but a determined opposition. If DISSIDENTS withdraw, they continue actively to oppose the original group.

dis·sent·er (di sen′tər), *n.* **1.** a person who dissents; nonconformist. **2.** (*often cap.*) a person who dissents from the Church of England.

dis·sen·tient (di sen′shənt), *adj.* **1.** dissenting, esp. from the opinion of the majority. —*n.* **2.** a person who dissents. [< L *dissentient-* (s. of *dissentiēns,* prp. of *dissentīre*)] —**dis·sen′tience, dis·sen′tien·cy,** *n.* —**dis·sen′tient·ly,** *adv.*

dis·sen·tious (di sen′shəs), *adj.* contentious; quarrelsome.

dis·sep·i·ment (di sep′ə mənt), *n.* **1.** a partition or septum. **2.** *Bot.* one of the partitions formed within ovaries and fruits by the coherence of the sides of the constituent carpels. [< L *dissaepīment(um)* = *dis-* DIS-¹ + *saepīmentum* hedge (*saepī(re)* (to) fence + *-mentum* -MENT)] —**dis·sep′i·men′tal,** *adj.*

D, Dissepiment

dis·sert (di sûrt′), *v.i. Archaic.* to discourse on a subject. [< L *dissert(āre)* to set forth at length (freq. of *disserere* to arrange in order) = *dis-* DIS-¹ + *ser-* put together + freq. *-t-* + *-āre* inf. suffix]

dis·ser·tate (dis′ər tāt′), *v.i.,* **-tat·ed, -tat·ing.** to discuss a subject fully and learnedly; discourse. [prob. back formation from DISSERTATION] —**dis′ser·ta′tor,** *n.*

dis·ser·ta·tion (dis′ər tā′shən), *n.* **1.** a written essay, treatise, or thesis, esp. one written by a candidate for the degree of Doctor of Philosophy. **2.** any formal discourse in speech or writing. [< L *dissertātiōn-* (s. of *dissertātiō*) = *dissertāt(us)* (ptp. of *dissertāre;* see DISSERT, -ATE¹) + *-iōn-* -ION] —**dis′ser·ta′tion·al,** *adj.* —**dis′ser·ta′tion·ist,** *n.*

dis·serve (dis sûrv′), *v.t.,* **-served, -serv·ing.** to serve harmfully or injuriously.

dis·serv·ice (dis sûr′vis), *n.* harmful or injurious service; an ill turn.

dis·sev·er (di sev′ər), *v.t.* **1.** to sever; separate. **2.** to divide into parts. —*v.i.* **3.** to part; separate. [ME *des(s)ever(en)* < OF *dessevr(er)* < LL *dissēparāre.* See DIS-¹, SEPARATE] —**dis·sev′er·ance, dis·sev′er·ment, dis·sev′er·a′tion,** *n.*

dis·si·dence (dis′i dᵊns), *n.* disagreement. [< L *dissidentia*] —**Syn.** See **dissent.**

dis·si·dent (dis′i dᵊnt), *adj.* **1.** disagreeing or dissenting, as in opinion or attitude. —*n.* **2.** a person who dissents. [< L *dissident-* (s. of *dissidēns,* prp. of *dissidēre* to sit apart) = *dis-* DIS-¹ + *sid-* (var. of *sed-* SIT) + *-ent-* -ENT] —**dis′si·dent·ly,** *adv.*

dis·sil·i·ent (di sil′ē ənt), *adj.* flying or bursting apart; bursting open. [< L *dissilient-* (s. of *dissiliēns,* prp. of *dissilīre* to leap apart) = *dis-* DIS-¹ + *sili-* (var. of *sali-* leap; see SALLY) + *-ent-* -ENT] —**dis·sil′i·en·cy, dis·sil′i·ence,** *n.*

dis·sim·i·lar (di sim′ə lər, dis sim′-), *adj.* not similar; unlike; different. —**dis·sim′i·lar·ly,** *adv.*

dis·sim·i·lar·i·ty (di sim′ə lar′i tē), *n., pl.* **-ties. 1.** unlikeness; difference. **2.** a point of difference.

dis·sim·i·late (di sim′ə lāt′), *v.t.,* **-lat·ed, -lat·ing.** *Phonet.* to modify by dissimilation. [DIS-¹ + (AS)SIMILATE] —**dis·sim′i·la′tive,** *adj.* —**dis·sim·i·la·to·ry** (di sim′ə lə tôr′ē, -tōr′ē), *adj.*

dis·sim·i·la·tion (di sim′ə lā′shən), *n.* **1.** the act of making or becoming unlike. **2.** *Phonet.* the phonetic process by which a speech sound becomes different from or less like a neighboring sound, as *pilgrim* (pil′grim) from Latin *peregrīnus* (peʀ′e grē′no͝os), or disappears entirely because of a like sound in another syllable, as in the pronunciation (guv′ə nər) for *governor.* Cf. **assimilation** (def. 6). **3.** *Biol.* catabolism.

dis·si·mil·i·tude (dis′si mil′i to͞od′, -tyo͞od′), *n.* **1.** unlikeness; difference; dissimilarity. **2.** a point of difference; dissimilarity. [< L *dissimilitūdō*]

dis·sim·u·late (di sim′yə lāt′), *v.,* **-lat·ed, -lat·ing.** —*v.t.* **1.** to disguise or conceal under a false appearance; dissemble. —*v.i.* **2.** to conceal one's true motives, thoughts, etc., by some pretense; speak or act hypocritically. [< L *dissimulāt(us)* (ptp. of *dissimulāre* to feign)] —**dis·sim′u·la′tive,** *adj.* —**dis·sim′u·la′tor,** *n.*

dis·sim·u·la·tion (di sim′yə lā′shən), *n.* **1.** the act of dissimulating; feigning; hypocrisy. **2.** *Psychiatry.* the ability or the tendency to appear normal when actually suffering from a disorder: a characteristic of the paranoiac. [< L *dissimulātiōn-* (s. of *dissimulātiō*) a feigning (see DIS-¹, SIMULATION); r. ME *dissimulacioun* < AF]

dis·si·pate (dis′ə pāt′), *v.,* **-pat·ed, -pat·ing.** —*v.t.* **1.** to scatter in various directions; disperse. **2.** to scatter or spread wastefully or extravagantly; squander. —*v.i.* **3.** to become scattered or dispersed; be dispelled. **4.** to indulge in extravagant, intemperate, or dissolute pleasure. [< L *dissipāt(us)* (ptp. of *dissipāre* to scatter) = *dis-* DIS-¹ + *sip-* (root of *supāre* to throw) + *-ātus* -ATE¹] —**dis′si·pat′er, dis′si·pa′tor,** *n.* —**dis′si·pa′tive,** *adj.* —**Syn. 3.** disappear, vanish. —**Ant. 1, 3.** unite.

dis·si·pat·ed (dis′ə pā′tid), *adj.* indulging in or characterized by excessive devotion to pleasure; dissolute. —**dis′si·pat′ed·ly,** *adv.* —**dis′si·pat′ed·ness,** *n.*

dis·si·pa·tion (dis′ə pā′shən), *n.* **1.** the act of dissipating. **2.** the state of being dissipated; dispersion; disintegration. **3.** a wasting by misuse: *the dissipation of a fortune.* **4.** amusement or diversion. **5.** dissolute mode of living, esp. excessive drinking of liquor; intemperance. **6.** *Physics, Mech.* a process in which energy is used or lost without accomplishing useful work, as friction causing loss of mechanical energy. [< L *dissipātiōn-* (s. of *dissipātiō*)]

dis·so·ci·a·ble (di sō′shē ə bəl, -shə bəl *or, for 1,* -sē ə-), *adj.* **1.** capable of being dissociated; separable. **2.** not sociable; unsociable. **3.** incongruous; not reconcilable. [< L *dissociābil(is)*] —**dis·so′ci·a·bil′i·ty,** *n.*

dis·so·cial (di sō′shəl), *adj.* disinclined toward society; unsocial. [< LL *dissociāl(is)* irreconcilable] —**dis·so′ci·al′i·ty,** *n.*

dis·so·ci·ate (di sō′shē āt′, -sē-), *v.,* **-at·ed, -at·ing.** —*v.t.* **1.** to sever the association of; disunite; separate. **2.** *Physical Chem.* to subject to dissociation. —*v.i.* **3.** to withdraw from association. **4.** *Physical Chem.* to undergo dissociation. [DIS-¹ + (AS)SOCIATE, modeled on L *dissociātus,* ptp. of *dissociāre* to divide, sever] —**dis·so′ci·a′tive,** *adj.*

dis·so·ci·a·tion (di sō′sē ā′shən, -shē ā′-), *n.* **1.** the act or an instance of dissociating. **2.** the state of being dissociated; disunion. **3.** *Physical Chem.* the reversible resolution or decomposition of a complex substance into simpler constituents caused by variation in physical conditions, as when water gradually decomposes into hydrogen and oxygen under great heat in such a way that when the temperature is lowered the liberated elements recombine to form water. **4.** *Psychiatry.* the splitting off of a group of mental processes from the main body of consciousness, as in amnesia or certain forms of hysteria. [DIS-[1] + (AS)SOCIATION, modeled on L *dissociātiō* separation]

dis·sol·u·ble (di sol′yə bəl), *adj.* capable of being dissolved. [< L *dissolūbil(is)* = *dissolū-*, perf. s. of *dissolvere* to DISSOLVE + *-bilis* -BLE] —**dis·sol′u·bil′i·ty, dis·sol′u·ble·ness,** *n.*

dis·so·lute (dis′ə lo͞ot′), *adj.* indifferent to moral restraints; given to immoral or improper conduct; licentious. [< L *dissolūt(us)* (ptp. of *dissolvere* to DISSOLVE)] —**dis′so·lute′ly,** *adv.* —**dis′so·lute′ness,** *n.*

dis·so·lu·tion (dis′ə lo͞o′shən), *n.* **1.** the act or process of resolving or dissolving into parts or elements. **2.** the resulting state. **3.** the undoing or breaking of a bond, tie, etc. **4.** the breaking up of an assembly or organization; dismissal; dispersal. **5.** death; decease. **6.** a bringing or coming to an end; disintegration; termination. **7.** legal termination, esp. of business activity. **8.** *Chem.* the act by which a solid, gas, or liquid is dispersed homogeneously in a gas, solid, or, esp., a liquid. **9.** dissoluteness. [< L *dissolūtiōn-* (s. of *dissolūtiō*); r. ME *dissolucioun* < AF]

dis·solve (di zolv′), *v.,* **-solved, -solv·ing,** *n.* —*v.t.* **1.** to make a solution of, as by mixing with a liquid; pass into solution: *to dissolve salt in water.* **2.** to melt; liquefy. **3.** to undo (a tie or bond); break up (a connection, union, etc.). **4.** to break up or order the termination of (an assembly or organization); dismiss; disperse. **5.** to bring to an end; terminate; destroy: *to dissolve one's hopes.* **6.** to separate into parts or elements; disintegrate. **7.** to destroy the binding power or influence of: *to dissolve a spell.* **8.** *Law.* to deprive of force; abrogate; annul: *to dissolve a marriage.* —*v.i.* **9.** to become dissolved, as in a solvent. **10.** to become melted or liquefied. **11.** to disintegrate or disperse. **12.** to lose intensity or strength. **13.** *Motion Pictures.* to fade out one shot or scene while simultaneously fading in the next. —*n.* **14.** Also called **lap dissolve.** *Motion Pictures.* a transition from one scene to the next made by dissolving. [< L *dissolv(ere)*] —**dis·solv′a·bil′i·ty,** *n.* —**dis·solv′a·ble,** *adj.* —**Syn. 1.** See **melt.**

dis·sol·vent (di zol′vənt), *adj.* **1.** capable of dissolving another substance. —*n.* **2.** a solvent. [< L *dissolvent-* (s. of *dissolvēns*, prp. of *dissolvere*)]

dis·so·nance (dis′ə nəns), *n.* **1.** an inharmonious or harsh sound; discord. **2.** *Music.* a simultaneous combination of tones conventionally accepted as being in a state of unrest and needing completion. Cf. **consonance** (def. 3). See illus. at **resolution.** **3.** incongruity. [< LL *dissonantia*]

dis·so·nan·cy (dis′ə nən sē), *n., pl.* **-cies.** dissonance.

dis·so·nant (dis′ə nənt), *adj.* **1.** disagreeing or harsh in sound; discordant. **2.** out of harmony; incongruous; at variance. [< L *dissonant-* (s. of *dissonāns*, prp. of *dissonāre* to sound harsh) = *disson-* (< *dissonus* discordant; see DIS-[1], SOUND[1]) + *-ant-* -ANT; r. ME *dissonaunte* < AF] —**dis′so·nant·ly,** *adv.*

dis·spread (di spred′), *v.t., v.i.,* **-spread, -spread·ing.** dispread.

dis·suade (di swād′), *v.t.,* **-suad·ed, -suad·ing.** **1.** to deter by advice or persuasion; persuade not to do something (usually fol. by *from*): *She dissuaded him from leaving home.* **2.** *Archaic.* to advise or urge against. [< L *dissuād(ēre)* = *dis-* DIS-[1] + *suādēre* to persuade] —**dis·suad′a·ble,** *adj.* —**dis·suad′er,** *n.*

dis·sua·sion (di swā′zhən), *n.* the act or an instance of dissuading. [< L *dissuāsiōn-* (s. of *dissuāsiō*) a speaking against = *dissuās(us)* (ptp. of *dissuādēre* to DISSUADE) + *-iōn-* -ION]

dis·sua·sive (di swā′siv), *adj.* tending or liable to dissuade. —**dis·sua′sive·ly,** *adv.* —**dis·sua′sive·ness,** *n.*

dis·syl·la·ble (di sil′ə bəl, dis′sil′-, dī′sil-), *n.* disyllable. —**dis·syl·lab·ic** (dis′i lab′ik, dis′si-), *adj.*

dis·sym·me·try (di sim′i trē, dis sim′-), *n.* absence or lack of symmetry. —**dis·sym·met·ric** (dis′i me′trik, dis′si-), **dis′sym·met′ri·cal,** *adj.* —**dis′sym·met′ri·cal·ly,** *adv.*

dist., **1.** distance. **2.** district.

dis·taff (dis′taf, -täf), *n.* **1.** a staff with a cleft end for holding wool, flax, etc., from which the thread is drawn in spinning by hand. **2.** a similar attachment on a spinning wheel. **3.** the female sex. **4.** woman's work. —*adj.* **5.** noting, pertaining to, characteristic of, or suitable for a woman; female. [ME *distaf*, OE *distæf* = *dis-* (c. LG *diesse* bunch of flax on a distaff; cf. DIZEN) + *stæf* STAFF[1]]

dis′taff side′, the female side of a family (distinguished from *spear side*).

dis·tain (di stān′), *v.t.* *Archaic.* to discolor; stain; sully. [ME *desteigne* < MF *destein(dre)* = *des-* DIS-[1] + *teindre* < L *tingere* to dye, TINGE]

dis·tal (dis′t^əl), *adj.* situated away from the point of origin or attachment, as of a limb or bone; terminal. Cf. **proximal.** [DIST(ANT) + -AL[1]] —**dis′tal·ly,** *adv.*

dis·tance (dis′təns), *n., v.,* **-tanced, -tanc·ing.** —*n.* **1.** the extent or amount of space between two things, points, lines, etc. **2.** the state or fact of being apart in space, as of one thing from another; remoteness. **3.** a linear extent of space: *Seven miles is a distance too great to walk in an hour.* **4.** an expanse; area: *A vast distance of water surrounded the ship.* **5.** the interval between two points of time; an extent of time: *His vacation period was a good distance away.* **6.** remoteness or difference in any respect: *We agree on a few things but our philosophies are a long distance apart.* **7.** an amount of progress: *We've come a long distance on the project.* **8.** a distant point, place, or region. **9.** the distant part of a field of view: *a tree in the distance.* **10.** *Music.* interval (def. 5). **11.** *Obs.* disagreement or dissension; a quarrel. **12.** **keep one's distance,** to avoid becoming familiar with; remain cool or aloof. Also, **keep at a distance.** —*v.t.* **13.** to leave behind at a distance, as at a race; surpass. **14.** to place at a distance. **15.** *Rare.* to cause to appear distant. [ME < L *distantia* (see DISTANT, -Y[3], -ANCE); r. ME *destaunce* < AF]

dis·tant (dis′tənt), *adj.* **1.** far off or apart in space; not near at hand; remote or removed (often followed by *from*). **2.** separate or apart; distinct; not joined. **3.** apart or far off in time. **4.** remote or far apart in any respect: *a distant relative.* **5.** reserved or aloof; not familiar or cordial. **6.** arriving from or going to a distance. [ME < L *distant-* (s. of *distāns*, prp. of *distāre* to stand apart) = *di-* DI-[2] + *stā-* stand + *-nt-* prp. suffix; r. ME *distaunt* < AF] —**dis′tant·ly,** *adv.* —**dis′tant·ness,** *n.*

dis·taste (dis tāst′), *n., v.,* **-tast·ed, -tast·ing.** —*n.* **1.** dislike; disinclination. **2.** dislike for food or drink. —*v.t.* **3.** *Archaic.* to dislike. —**Syn. 1.** aversion, disgust. See **dislike.**

dis·taste·ful (dis tāst′fəl), *adj.* **1.** unpleasant, offensive, or causing dislike. **2.** unpleasant to the taste. —**dis·taste′ful·ly,** *adv.* —**dis·taste′ful·ness,** *n.* —**Syn. 1.** disagreeable, displeasing.

Dist. Atty., district attorney.

dis·tem·per[1] (dis tem′pər), *n.* **1.** *Vet. Pathol.* **a.** a specific infectious disease of dogs, caused by a filterable virus and characterized by lethargy, fever, loss of appetite, vomiting, diarrhea, nervous tics, and convulsions. **b.** Also called **strangles.** an infectious febrile disease of horses, caused by the organism *Streptococcus equi* and characterized by catarrh of the upper air passages and the formation of pus by the submaxillary and other lymphatic glands. **c.** Also called **cat distemper, feline distemper, panleucopenia, panleukopenia.** a usually fatal disease of cats, caused by a virus and characterized by fever, refusal of food, vomiting, and diarrhea. **d.** (formerly) any of several diseases characterized by fever and catarrhal symptoms. **2.** a deranged condition of mind or body; a disorder or disease: *a feverish distemper.* **3.** disorder or disturbance, esp. of a political nature. —*v.t.* **4.** *Obs.* to derange physically or mentally. [ME *distemp(e)re(n)* < ML *distemper(āre)* (see DIS-[1], TEMPER); r. ME *destempre* < MF]

dis·tem·per[2] (dis tem′pər), *Art.* —*n.* **1.** a painting or technique of decorative painting in which glue or gum is used as a binder or medium to achieve a mat surface and rapid drying. **2.** (formerly) the tempera technique. —*v.t.* **3.** to paint in distemper. [ME *distempere(n)* < MF *destempr(er).* See DISTEMPER[1]]

dis·tem·per·a·ture (dis tem′pər ə chər), *n.* a distempered or disordered condition; disturbance of health, mind, or temper. [obs. *distemperate* (DIS-[1] + TEMPERATE) + -URE]

dis·tend (di stend′), *v.t., v.i.* **1.** to spread in all directions; expand; swell. **2.** to expand by stretching, as something hollow or elastic. [< L *distend(ere)*] —**Syn. 1, 2.** enlarge, bloat. —**Ant. 1, 2.** shrink, contract.

dis·ten·si·ble (di sten′sə bəl), *adj.* capable of being distended. [< L *distens(us)* (ptp. of *distendere* to DISTEND) + -IBLE] —**dis·ten′si·bil′i·ty,** *n.*

dis·tent (di stent′), *adj.* *Obs.* distended. [< L *distent(us)* distended, ptp. of *distendere* to DISTEND]

dis·ten·tion (di sten′shən), *n.* **1.** the act of distending. **2.** the state of being distended. Also, **dis·ten′sion.** [< L *distentiōn-* (s. of *distentiō*)]

dis·tich (dis′tik), *n.* *Pros.* **1.** a unit of two lines of verse, usually a self-contained statement; couplet. **2.** a rhyming couplet. [< L *distich(on)*, n. use of neut. of Gk *dístichos* having two lines. See DI-[1], STICH]

dis·ti·chous (dis′tə kəs), *adj.* **1.** *Bot.* arranged alternately in two vertical rows on opposite sides of an axis, as leaves. **2.** *Zool.* divided into two parts, as antennae. [< L *distichus* (< Gk *dístichos* DISTICH); see -OUS] —**dis′ti·chous·ly,** *adv.*

dis·til (di stil′), *v.t., v.i.,* **-tilled, -til·ling.** *Chiefly Brit.* distill.

dis·till (di stil′), *v.t.* **1.** to subject to a process of vaporization and subsequent condensation, as for purification or concentration. **2.** to extract, concentrate, or purify by distillation. **3.** to obtain by or as by distillation. **4.** to remove by distillation (usually fol. by *off* or *out*). —*v.i.* **5.** to undergo or perform distillation. **6.** to become vaporized and then condensed in distillation. **7.** to drop, pass, or condense as a distillate. [ME *distille(n)* < L *distill(āre)*, var. of *dēstillāre* = *dē-* DE- + *stillāre* to drop] —**dis·till′a·ble,** *adj.*

dis·til·land (dis′t^əland′), *n.* a substance that undergoes distillation. Cf. **distillate.** [< L *distillānd(um)*, neut. ger. of *distillāre* to DISTILL]

dis·til·late (dis′t^əlit, -t^əlāt′, di stil′it), *n.* **1.** the product obtained from the condensation of vapors in distillation. **2.** any concentration, essence, or abstraction. [< L *distillāt(us)*, ptp. of *distillāre* to trickle down]

dis·til·la·tion (dis′t^əlā′shən), *n.* **1.** the volatilization or evaporation and subsequent condensation of a liquid, as when water is boiled in a retort and the steam is condensed in a cool receiver. **2.** the purification or concentration of a substance by such a process. **3.** a product of distilling; distillate. **4.** the act or fact of distilling. **5.** the state of being distilled. [< L *distillātiōn-* (s. of *distillātiō*) (see DISTILLATE, -ION); r. ME *distillacioun* < AF] —**dis·til·la·to·ry** (di stil′ə tôr′ē, -tōr′ē), *adj.*

dis·tilled (di stild′), *adj.* obtained, produced, or purified by distillation.

dis·till·er (di stil′ər), *n.* **1.** an apparatus for distilling, as a condenser or still. **2.** a person whose business it is to extract alcoholic liquors by distillation.

dis·till·er·y (di stil′ə rē), *n., pl.* **-er·ies.** a place or establishment where distilling, esp. of liquors, is done.

dis·till·ment (di stil′mənt), *n.* *Archaic.* distillation. Also, *esp. Brit.,* **dis·til′ment.**

dis·tinct (di stiŋkt′), *adj.* **1.** distinguished as not being the same; not identical; separate (sometimes fol. by *from*). **2.** different in nature or quality; dissimilar (sometimes fol. by *from*): *Gold is distinct from iron.* **3.** clear to the senses or intellect; plain; definite; unmistakable: *The ship appeared as a distinct silhouette.* **4.** distinguishing or perceiving clearly: *distinct vision.* **5.** unusual; rare; notable: *His praise is a distinct honor.* **6.** *Archaic.* distinctively decorated or adorned. [ME < L *distinct(us)* (ptp. of *distinguere* to DISTINGUISH) *di-* DI-[2] + *sting-* prod, mark + *-tus* ptp. suffix]

—**dis·tinct′ness,** *n.* —**Syn. 1.** individual. See **various. 3.** well-defined, unconfused. —**Ant. 3, 4.** indistinct.

dis·tinc·tion (di stiŋk′shən), *n.* **1.** a distinguishing as different. **2.** the recognizing of differences; discrimination: *to make a distinction between right and wrong.* **3.** a discrimination made between things as different: *Death comes to all without distinction.* **4.** the condition of being different; difference: *There is a distinction between what he says and what he does.* **5.** a distinguishing quality or characteristic: *It has the distinction of being the oldest house in the town.* **6.** a distinguishing or treating with special honor, attention, or favor. **7.** marked superiority; note; eminence. **8.** distinguished appearance. **9.** *Obs.* division; separation. [< L *distinctiōn-* (s. of *distinctiō*); see DISTINCT, -ION; r. ME *distinccioun* < AF]
—**Syn. 3.** DISTINCTION and DIFFERENCE may both refer to perceivable dissimilarities and, in this meaning, may be used interchangeably: *There is a distinction (difference) between the two.* DISTINCTION, however, usually suggests the perception of dissimilarity, as the result of analysis and discrimination: *a carefully made distinction between two treatments of the same theme;* whereas DIFFERENCE refers only to the condition of being dissimilar: *the difference between Gothic and Roman architecture.* **7.** renown, importance. —**Ant. 4.** resemblance.

dis·tinc·tive (di stiŋk′tiv), *adj.* distinguishing; serving to distinguish; characteristic. [< ML *distinctīv(us)*] —**dis·tinc′tive·ly,** *adv.* —**dis·tinc′tive·ness,** *n.*

dis·tinct·ly (di stiŋkt′lē), *adv.* **1.** in a distinct manner; clearly. **2.** without doubt; unmistakably. —**Syn. 1.** See **clearly.**

dis·tin·gué (dis′taŋ gā′, di staŋ′gā; *Fr.* dē stäɴ gā′), *adj.* distinguished; having an air of distinction. Also, *referring to a woman,* **dis′tin·guée′.** [< F, adj. use of ptp. of *distinguer* to DISTINGUISH]

dis·tin·guish (di stiŋ′gwish), *v.t.* **1.** to mark off as different (often fol. by *from*): *He was distinguished from the other boys by his height.* **2.** to recognize as distinct or different; recognize the individual features or characteristics of: *It is hard to distinguish her from her sister.* **3.** to perceive clearly by sight or other sense; discern; recognize: *I cannot distinguish things so far away.* **4.** to make prominent, conspicuous, or eminent: *to distinguish oneself in battle.* **5.** to divide into classes; classify. **6.** *Archaic.* to single out for or honor with special attention. —*v.i.* **7.** to indicate or show a difference (usually fol. by *between*). **8.** to recognize or note differences; discriminate. [ME *distingu(en)* (< L *distinguere*) + -ISH²; r. ME *distingen* < MF *distinguer;* see DISTINCT] —**dis·tin′guish·a·ble,** *adj.* —**dis·tin′guish·a·bly,** *adv.* —**dis·tin′guish·er,** *n.* —**dis·tin′guish·ing·ly,** *adv.* —**dis·tin′guish·ment,** *n.*
—**Syn. 2.** DISTINGUISH, DISCRIMINATE, DIFFERENTIATE suggest a positive attempt to analyze characteristic features or qualities of things. To DISTINGUISH is to recognize the characteristic features belonging to a thing: *to distinguish a light cruiser from a heavy cruiser.* To DISCRIMINATE is to perceive the particular, nice, or exact differences between things, to determine wherein these differences consist, and to estimate their significance: *to discriminate prejudiced from unprejudiced testimony.* To DIFFERENTIATE is especially to point out exactly and in detail the differences between (usually) two things: *The symptoms of both diseases are so similar that it is hard to differentiate one from the other.* —**Ant. 2.** confuse.

dis·tin·guished (di stiŋ′gwisht), *adj.* **1.** conspicuous; marked. **2.** noted or eminent. **3.** having an air of distinction; distingué. —**Syn. 2.** renowned, illustrious. See **famous.**

Distin′guished Con′duct Med′al, *Brit. Mil.* a decoration awarded for distinguished conduct in operations in the field against an enemy. *Abbr.:* D.C.M.

Distin′guished Fly′ing Cross′, **1.** *U.S. Mil.* a decoration awarded for heroic or extraordinary achievement while on aerial duty. **2.** *Brit. Mil.* a decoration awarded for similar achievement while in flying operations against an enemy. *Abbr.:* D.F.C.

Distin′guished Serv′ice Cross′, *U.S. Army.* a bronze medal awarded to an officer or enlisted man for extraordinary heroism in military action against an armed enemy. *Abbr.:* D.S.C.

Distin′guished Serv′ice Med′al, **1.** *U.S. Mil.* a decoration awarded for exceptionally meritorious performance of a duty of great responsibility. **2.** *Brit. Mil.* a decoration awarded for distinguished conduct in war. *Abbr.:* D.S.M.

Distin′guished Serv′ice Or′der, *Brit. Mil.* a decoration awarded for distinguished service in action. *Abbr.:* D.S.O.

dis·tort (di stôrt′), *v.t.* **1.** to misrepresent; to give a false, perverted, or disproportionate meaning to: *to distort the facts.* **2.** to twist awry or out of shape; make crooked or deformed. [< L *distort(us)* (ptp. of *distorquēre* to distort) = *dis-* DIS-¹ + *tor(qu)-* (s. of *torquēre* to twist) + *-tus* ptp. suffix] —**dis·tort′er,** *n.* —**dis·tor′tive,** *adj.*

dis·tort·ed (di stôr′tid), *adj.* **1.** not truly or completely representing the facts or reality; perverted; false: *a distorted view of life.* **2.** twisted, deformed, or misshapen. **3.** lacking the true proportions or clarity of the original image, sound, etc., as an image seen through an imperfect lens or sound heard from a defective record player. —**dis·tort′ed·ly,** *adv.* —**dis·tort′ed·ness,** *n.*

dis·tor·tion (di stôr′shən), *n.* **1.** the act of distorting. **2.** the state of being distorted. **3.** anything distorted. [< L *distortiōn-* (s. of *distortiō*)] —**dis·tor′tion·al,** *adj.*

distr., **1.** distribution. **2.** distributor.

dis·tract (di strakt′), *v.t.* **1.** to draw away or divert, as the mind or attention: *The music distracted him from his work.* **2.** to divide (the mind, attention, etc.) between objects. **3.** to disturb or trouble greatly in mind: *Grief distracted him.* **4.** to amuse; provide a pleasant diversion for. —*adj.* **5.** *Obs.* distracted. [< L *distract(us)* (ptp. of *distrahere* to draw apart)] —**dis·tract′er,** *n.* —**dis·tract′i·bil′i·ty,** *n.* —**dis·tract′i·ble,** *adj.* —**dis·tract′ing·ly,** *adv.* —**dis·trac′tive,** *adj.* —**dis·trac′tive·ly,** *adv.*

dis·tract·ed (di strak′tid), *adj.* **1.** having the attention diverted; not concentrating. **2.** rendered incapable of behaving, reacting, or thinking normally, as by worry or remorse. —**dis·tract′ed·ly,** *adv.*

dis·trac·tion (di strak′shən), *n.* **1.** the act of distracting. **2.** the state of being distracted. **3.** mental distress or derangement. **4.** that which divides the attention or prevents concentration: *The distractions of the city hinder my studies.* **5.** something that amuses or diverts: *Fishing is his major distraction.* **6.** division or disorder caused by dissension; tumult. [< L *distractiōn-* (s. of *distractiō*) separation]

dis·train (di strān′), *Law.* —*v.t.* **1.** to constrain by seizing and holding goods, etc., in pledge for rent, damages, etc., or in order to obtain satisfaction of a claim. —*v.i.* **2.** to levy a distress. [ME *distreine(n)* < OF *destreind(re)* < L *distringere* to stretch out = *di-* DI-² + *stringere* to draw tight; see STRAIN¹] —**dis·train′a·ble,** *adj.* —**dis·train′ment,** *n.* —**dis·trai′nor, dis·train′er,** *n.*

dis·traint (di strānt′), *n.* *Law.* the act of distraining; a distress. [DISTRAIN + *-t,* modeled on *constraint, restraint*]

dis·trait (di strā′; *Fr.* dēs tʀe′), *adj.* inattentive because of distracting worries, fears, etc.; absent-minded. Also, *referring to a female,* **dis·traite** (di strāt′; *Fr.* dēs tʀet′). [< F < L *distract(us);* see DISTRACT]

dis·traught (di strôt′), *adj.* **1.** distracted; bewildered; deeply agitated. **2.** mentally deranged; crazed. [var. of obs. *distract* distracted, by assoc. with *straught,* old ptp. of STRETCH]

dis·tress (di stres′), *n.* **1.** acute physical or mental suffering; pain, anxiety, or sorrow. **2.** anything that causes pain, anxiety, trouble, or sorrow; affliction; trouble. **3.** a state of extreme necessity, misfortune, or trouble. **4.** the state of a ship or airplane requiring immediate assistance, as when on fire in transit. **5.** *Law.* **a.** the act of distraining. **b.** the thing seized in distraining. —*v.t.* **6.** to afflict with great pain, anxiety, or sorrow; trouble; worry; bother. **7.** to subject to pressure, stress, or strain; embarrass or exhaust by strain: *to be distressed by excessive work.* **8.** to compel by pain or force of circumstances. **9.** to dent, scratch, or stain (lumber, furniture, or the like) to give an appearance of age. [(n.) *destresse* < OF < LL **districtia* = L *district(us)* (see DISTRICT) + *-ia* -Y³; (v.) ME *destress(en)* < AF *destress(er)* (OF *destrecier*) < *destresse* (n.) + *-er* inf. suffix] —**dis·tress′ful,** *adj.* —**dis·tress′fully,** *adv.* —**dis·tress′ing·ly,** *adv.* —**Syn. 1.** agony, anguish, adversity, hardship, tribulation. —**Ant. 1.** comfort.

dis·tressed (di strest′), *adj.* affected with distress.

distressed′ ar′ea, **1.** *U.S.* See **disaster area. 2.** *Brit.* See **depressed area.**

dis·tress·ful (di stres′fəl), *adj.* **1.** causing or involving distress: *the distressful circumstances of poverty.* **2.** full of distress; feeling or indicating distress. —**dis·tress′ful·ly,** *adv.* —**dis·tress′ful·ness,** *n.*

distress′ mer′chandise, *Com.* goods offered for sale by a commercial firm, esp. a retail store, at reduced prices to raise cash quickly.

dis·trib·u·tar·y (di strib′yo͞o ter′ē), *n., pl.* **-tar·ies.** a branch of a river flowing away from the main stream and not rejoining it (opposed to *tributary*).

dis·trib·ute (di strib′yo͞ot), *v.t.,* **-ut·ed, -ut·ing. 1.** to divide and give out in shares; allot. **2.** to disperse through a space or over an area; spread; scatter. **3.** to sell, offer for sale, or deliver (an item or line of merchandise) to individual customers, esp. in a specified region or area. **4.** to divide into classes or into groups or parts of distinct character: *The work is distributed for speedier handling.* **5.** *Logic.* to employ (a term) so as to refer to all individuals denoted by it. [< L *distribūt(us),* ptp. of *distribuere* to divide up] —**dis·trib′ut·a·ble,** *adj.* —**Syn. 1.** assign, mete, apportion.

dis·trib·u·tee (di strib′yo͞o tē′), *n.* *Law.* a person who shares in a decedent estate.

dis·tri·bu·tion (dis′trə byo͞o′shən), *n.* **1.** the act or an instance of distributing. **2.** the state or manner of being distributed. **3.** arrangement; classification. **4.** that which is distributed. **5.** the frequency of occurrence or the natural geographic range or place where any item or category of items occur: *That particular pronunciation has too wide a distribution to be considered as part of an accent. What is the distribution of coniferous forests in the world?* **6.** placement, location, or disposition. **7.** apportionment; the way in which items, a quantity, or the like, is divided or apportioned: *the distribution of property among heirs; the distribution of trumps in a game of bridge.* **8.** the delivery or giving out of an item or items to the intended recipients, as mail, newspapers, etc. **9.** the total number of an item delivered, sold, or given out: *The distribution of our school paper is now 800.* **10.** the marketing, transporting, merchandising, and selling of any item: *We have a good product but our distribution is bad.* **11.** *Econ.* **a.** the division of the aggregate income of any society among its members. **b.** the system of dispersing goods throughout a community. **12.** *Statistics.* a set of values or measurements of a set of elements, each measurement being associated with an element. [< L *distribūtiōn-* (s. of *distribūtiō*)] —**dis′tri·bu′tion·al,** *adj.*

distribu′tion curve′, *Statistics.* the curve or line of a graph in which cumulative frequencies are plotted as ordinates and values of the variate as abscissas.

distribu′tion func′tion, *Statistics.* a function of a variate for which the functional value corresponding to a given value of the variate is the number of or the proportion of values of the variate equal to or less than the given value.

dis·trib·u·tive (di strib′yə tiv), *adj.* **1.** serving to distribute, assign, allot, or divide; characterized by or pertaining to distribution. **2.** *Gram.* referring to the members of a group individually, as the adjectives *each* and *every.* **3.** *Logic.* (of a term) distributed in a given proposition. **4.** *Math.* **a.** (of a binary operation) having the property that terms in an expression may be expanded in a particular way to form an equivalent expression, as $a(b + c) = ab + ac$. **b.** having reference to this property: *distributive law for multiplication over addition.* —*n.* **5.** a distributive word or expression. [< LL *distribūtīv(us)* (see DISTRIBUTE, -IVE); r. ME *distributif* < MF] —**dis·trib′u·tive·ly,** *adv.* —**dis·trib′u·tive·ness,** *n.*

dis·trib·u·tor (di strib′yə tər), *n.* **1.** a person or thing that distributes. **2.** *Com.* a person or firm, esp. a wholesaler, that markets, sells, or delivers an item or line of merchandise, esp. to individual customers in a specific region or area. **3.** *Mach.* a device in a multicylinder engine for distributing the igniting voltage to the spark plugs in a definite sequence. Also, **dis·trib/ut·er.** [< L]

dis·trib·u·tor·ship (di strib/yə tər ship/), *n.* *Com.* a franchise held by a distributor.

dis·trict (dis/trikt), *n.* **1.** a division of territory, as of a country, state, or county, marked off for administrative, electoral, or other purposes. **2.** a region or locality: *the theater district.* **3.** *Brit.* a subdivision of a county or a town, roughly equal to a U.S. ward or precinct. **—*v.t.*** **4.** to divide into districts. [< ML *district(us)* exercise of justice, (area of) jurisdiction, n. use of L ptp. of *distringere* to stretch out; see DISTRAIN]

dis/trict attor/ney, an officer who acts as attorney for the people or government within a specified district.

dis/trict court/, *U.S. Law.* **1.** (in many states) the court of general jurisdiction. **2.** the federal trial court sitting in each district of the United States.

Dis/trict of Colum/bia, a federal area in the E United States, on the Potomac, coextensive with the federal capital, Washington: governed by Congress. 756,510 (1970); 69 sq. mi. *Abbr.:* D.C., DC

dis·trust (dis trust/), *v.t.* **1.** to regard with doubt or suspicion; have no trust in. **—*n.*** **2.** lack of trust; suspicion; doubt. **—dis·trust/er,** *n.* **—Syn. 2.** See **suspicion.**

dis·trust·ful (dis trust/fəl), *adj.* unable or unwilling to trust; doubtful; suspicious. **—dis·trust/ful·ly,** *adv.* **—dis·trust/ful·ness,** *n.*

dis·turb (di stûrb/), *v.t.* **1.** to interrupt the quiet, rest, or peace of. **2.** to interfere with; interrupt; hinder. **3.** to throw into commotion or disorder; agitate; unsettle. **4.** to perplex; trouble: *to be disturbed by strange behavior.* [ME *disturbe(n)* < L *disturb(āre)* (to) destroy = *dis-* DIS-[1] + *turbāre* to confuse; r. ME *disto(u)rben* < OF *desto(u)rb(er)*] **—dis·turb/er,** *n.*

dis·turb·ance (di stûr/bəns), *n.* **1.** the act of disturbing. **2.** the state of being disturbed. **3.** an instance of being disturbed. **4.** something that disturbs. **5.** an outbreak of disorder; a breach of public peace: *Political disturbances shook the city.* **6.** *Geol.* a crustal movement of moderate intensity, somewhat restricted in area. [ME *disto(u)rbance,* etc. < OF] **—Syn. 2.** perturbation, confusion. See **agitation. 5.** confusion, tumult, riot. See **disorder. —Ant. 3.** order.

dis·turbed (di stûrbd/), *adj.* **1.** marked by symptoms of neurosis or psychosis: *a disturbed personality.* **2.** agitated; distressed; disrupted; bothered: *disturbed seas; disturbed feelings.*

di·sul·fate (dī sul/fāt), *n.* *Chem.* a salt of pyrosulfuric acid, as sodium disulfate, $Na_2S_2O_7$. Also, **di·sul/phate.**

di·sul·fide (dī sul/fīd, -fid), *n.* *Chem.* **1.** (in inorganic chemistry) a sulfide containing two atoms of sulfur, as carbon disulfide, CS_2. **2.** (in organic chemistry) a sulfide containing the bivalent group –SS–, as diethyl disulfide, $C_2H_5SSC_2H_5$. Also, **di·sul/phide.**

di·sul·fu·ric (dī/sul fyŏŏr/ik), *adj.* *Chem.* pyrosulfuric. Also, **di/sul·phu/ric.**

dis·un·ion (dis yōōn/yən), *n.* **1.** a severance of union; separation; disjunction. **2.** lack of unity; dissension.

dis·un·ion·ist (dis yōōn/yə nist), *n.* **1.** a person who advocates or causes disunion. **2.** *U.S. Hist.* a secessionist during the period of the Civil War. **—dis·un/ion·ism,** *n.*

dis·u·nite (dis/yōō nīt/), *v.,* **-nit·ed, -nit·ing. —*v.t.*** **1.** to sever the union of; separate; disjoin. **2.** to set at variance; alienate: *The issue disunited the party members.* **—*v.i.*** **3.** to part; fall apart. **—dis·u·nit/er,** *n.*

dis·u·ni·ty (dis yōō/ni tē), *n., pl.* **-ties.** lack of unity or accord.

dis·use (*n.* dis yōōs/; *v.* dis yōōz/), *n., v.,* **-used, -us·ing. —*n.*** **1.** discontinuance of use or practice: *Some customs are falling into disuse.* **—*v.t.*** **2.** to cease to use.

dis·u·til·i·ty (dis/yōō til/i tē), *n.* the quality of causing inconvenience, harm, distress, etc.

dis·val·ue (dis val/yōō), *n., v.,* **-ued, -u·ing. —*n.*** **1.** disesteem; disparagement. **—*v.t.*** **2.** *Archaic.* to depreciate; disparage.

di·syl·lab·ic (dī/si lab/ik, dis/i-), *adj.* consisting of or pertaining to two syllables. Also, **dissyllabic.** [DI-[1] + SYLLABIC]

di·syl·la·ble (dī/sil ə bəl, di sil/-), *n.* a word of two syllables. Also, **dissyllable.** [DI-[1] + SYLLABLE; cf. Gk *disýllabos;* var. *dissyllable* has *ss* < MF *dissilabe*]

dis·yoke (dis yōk/), *v.t.,* **-yoked, -yok·ing.** to free from or as from a yoke.

dit (dit), *n.* an echoic word, the referent of which is a click or brief tone interval, used to designate the dot of Morse code, International Morse code, etc. Cf. **dah.**

di·tat De·us (dē/tät de/ŏŏs; *Eng.* dī/tat dē/əs), *Latin.* God enriches: motto of Arizona.

ditch (dich), *n.* **1.** a long, narrow excavation made in the ground by digging, as for draining or irrigating land; trench. **2.** any open passage or trench, as a natural channel or waterway. **—*v.t.*** **3.** to dig a ditch or ditches in or around. **4.** to derail (a train) or drive or force (an automobile, bus, etc.) off the road. **5.** to crash-land (a land-based aircraft) on water and abandon it. **6.** *Slang.* **a.** to get rid of; discard. **b.** to escape from: *to ditch the cops.* **—*v.i.*** **7.** to dig a ditch. **8.** (of the crew of an aircraft) to crash-land in water. [ME *dich,* OE *dīc;* c. G *Teich.* See DIKE] **—ditch/less,** *adj.*

ditch·wa·ter (dich/wô/tər, -wot/ər), *n.* **1.** water, esp. stagnant and dirty water, that has collected in a ditch. **2. dull as ditchwater.** See **dishwater** (def. 2).

di·the·ism (dī/thē iz/əm), *n.* **1.** the doctrine of or belief in two equally powerful gods. **2.** belief in the existence of two independent antagonistic principles, one good and the other evil, as in Zoroastrianism. [DI-[1] + THEISM] **—di/the·ist,** *n.* **—di/the·is/tic, di/the·is/ti·cal,** *adj.*

dith·er (dith/ər), *n.* **1.** a trembling; vibration. **2.** *Informal.* a state of flustered excitement or fear. **—*v.i.*** **3.** to act irresolutely; vacillate. [var. of *didder* (ME *diddere*); cf. DODDER[1]]

dith·y·ramb (dith/ə ram/, -ramb/), *n.* **1.** a Greek choral song or chant of vehement or wild character and usually of irregular form. **2.** any poem or other composition having similar characteristics, as an impassioned or exalted theme or irregular form. [< L *dithyramb(us)* < Gk *dithýrambos*]

dith·y·ram·bic (dith/ə ram/bik), *adj.* **1.** of, pertaining to, or of the nature of a dithyramb. **2.** wildly irregular in form. **3.** wildly enthusiastic. [< L *dithyrambic(us)* < Gk *dithyrambikós*] **—dith/y·ram/bi·cal·ly,** *adv.*

dit·ta·ny (dit/ənē), *n., pl.* **-nies. 1.** a labiate plant, *Origanum Dictamnus,* of Crete, formerly believed to have medicinal qualities. **2.** a labiate plant, *Cunila origanoides,* of North America, bearing clusters of purplish flowers. **3.** Also called **burning-bush, fraxinella, gas-plant.** a perennial, rutaceous plant, *Dictamnus albus,* having foliage and flowers that emit an inflammable vapor. [ME *ditane, detany* < OF *ditan* < L *dictamn(us), dictamn(um)* < Gk *díktamnon,* perh. akin to *Diktē,* a mountain in Crete where the herb abounded]

dit·to (dit/ō), *n., pl.* **-tos,** *adv., v.,* **-toed, -to·ing. —*n.*** **1.** the aforesaid; the above; the same (used in accounts, lists, etc., to avoid repetition). *Abbr.:* do. *Symbol:* ". Cf. **ditto mark. 2.** another of the same. **3.** *Informal.* the same thing or a close copy. **—*adv.*** **4.** as already stated; likewise. **—*v.t.*** **5.** to duplicate or repeat the statement of. [< It, var. of *detto* < L *dictus* said, ptp. of *dīcere* to say; see DICTUM]

dit/to mark/, Often, **ditto marks.** two small marks (") indicating the repetition of something, usually placed beneath the thing repeated.

dit·ty (dit/ē), *n., pl.* **-ties. 1.** a poem intended to be sung. **2.** a short, simple song. [ME *dite* < OF *dit(i)e* poem, n. use of ptp. of *ditier* to compose < L *dictāre;* see DICTATE]

dit/ty bag/, a bag used by sailors to hold sewing implements and other necessities. [?]

dit/ty box/, a small box used like a ditty bag.

Di·u (dē/ōō), *n.* a former district in Portuguese India, comprising a small island and seaport at the extremity of Kathiawar peninsula: annexed by India in December, 1961. 24,342 (1950); 14 sq. mi.

di·u·re·sis (dī/yŏŏ rē/sis), *n.* increased discharge of urine. [< NL < Gk *diourē-* (verbid s. of *diourein* to urinate) + *-sis* -SIS; see DIURETIC]

di·u·ret·ic (dī/yŏŏ ret/ik), *Med.* **—*adj.*** **1.** increasing the volume of the urine excreted, as by a medicinal substance. **—*n.*** **2.** a diuretic medicine or agent. [< NL *diurētic(us)* < Gk *diourētikós* = *di-* DI-[3] + *ourē-* (verbid s. of *ourein* to urinate) + *-tikos* -TIC] **—di/u·ret/i·cal·ly,** *adv.* **—di/u·ret/i·cal·ness,** *n.*

di·ur·nal (dī ûr/nəl), *adj.* **1.** of or pertaining to a day or each day; daily. **2.** of or belonging to the daytime (opposed to *nocturnal*). **3.** *Bot.* showing a periodic alteration of condition with day and night, as certain flowers that open by day and close by night. **4.** active by day, as certain birds and insects (opposed to *nocturnal*). **—*n.*** **5.** *Liturgy.* a service book containing offices for the daily hours of prayer. **6.** *Archaic.* a diary. **7.** *Archaic.* a newspaper, esp. a daily one. [ME < L *diurnāl(is)* = *diurn(us)* daily + *-ālis* -AL[1]] **—di·ur/nal·ly,** *adv.* **—di·ur/nal·ness,** *n.*

diur/nal par/allax. See under **parallax** (def. 2).

div, *Math.* divergence.

Div., **1.** divine. **2.** divinity.

div., **1.** divided. **2.** dividend. **3.** division. **4.** divisor.

di·va (dē/vä), *n., pl.* **-vas, -ve** (-ve). a distinguished female singer; prima donna. [< It < L, fem. of *dīvus* god; cf. DIVINE]

di·va·gate (dī/və gāt/), *v.i.,* **-gat·ed, -gat·ing. 1.** to wander; stray. **2.** to digress in speech. [< L *dīvagāt(us)* (ptp. of *dīvagārī* to wander off) = *dī-* DI-[2] + *vag-* (s. of *vagārī* to wander) + *-ātus* -ATE[1]] **—di/va·ga/tion,** *n.*

di·va·lent (dī vā/lənt), *adj.* *Chem.* having a valence of two, as the ferrous ion, Fe^{++}. **—di·va/lence,** *n.*

Di·va·li (di vä/lē), *n.* Diwali.

di·van (di van/, -vän/ *or, esp. for 1,* dī/van), *n.* **1.** a sofa or couch. **2.** (esp. in the Orient) a long, cushioned seat, usually without arms or back, placed against a wall. **3.** a council of state in Turkey and other countries of the Middle East. **4.** any council, committee, or commission. **5.** (in the Middle East) a council chamber or audience chamber. **6.** a smoking room, as in connection with a tobacco shop. **7.** a collection of poems, esp. a collection in Arabic or Persian of poems by one poet. [< Turk < Pers *dīwān,* orig. *dēvan* booklet (whence the meanings account book, office, council, bench)]

di·var·i·cate (*v.* dī var/ə kāt/, di-; *adj.* dī var/ə kit, -kāt/, di-), *v.,* **-cat·ed, -cat·ing,** *adj.* **—*v.i.*** **1.** to spread apart; branch; diverge. **2.** *Bot., Zool.* to branch at a wide angle. **—*adj.*** **3.** spread apart; widely divergent. **4.** *Bot., Zool.* branching at a wide angle. [< L *dīvāricāt(us)* (ptp. of *dīvāricāre*) = *dī-* DI-[2] + *vāric-* (base of *vāricāre* to straddle; see PREVARICATE) + *-ātus* -ATE[1]] **—di·var/i·cate·ly,** *adv.* **—di·var/i·cat/ing·ly,** *adv.* **—di·var/i·ca/tion,** *n.* **—di·var/i·ca/tor,** *n.*

dive (dīv), *v.,* **dived** or **dove, dived, div·ing,** *n.* **—*v.i.*** **1.** to plunge, esp. headfirst, as into water. **2.** to submerge, as a submarine. **3.** to plunge, fall, or descend through the air, into a tunnel in the earth, etc.: *The acrobats dived into nets.* **4.** to penetrate suddenly into something, as with the hand: *to dive into a purse.* **5.** to dart: *to dive into a doorway.* **6.** to enter deeply or plunge into a subject, business, activity, etc. **—*v.t.*** **7.** to cause to plunge, submerge, or descend. **—*n.*** **8.** the act or an instance of diving. **9.** a jump or plunge into water, esp. in a prescribed way from a diving board. **10.** the vertical or almost vertical descent of an airplane at a speed surpassing the possible speed of the same plane in level flight. **11.** a submerging, as of a submarine, skindiver, etc. **12.** a dash, plunge, or lunge, as if throwing oneself at or into something: *The right end made a dive for the football.* **13.** a sudden or sharp decline, as of stock prices or atmospheric temperature. **14.** *Informal.* a dingy or disreputable bar or nightclub. **15.** *Boxing Slang.* a false show of being knocked out, usually in a bout whose result has been prearranged. [ME *dīve(n)* (to) dive, dip, OE *dȳfan* to dip (causative of *dūfan* to dive, sink); c. Icel *dȳfa* dip, G *taufen* to baptize; akin to DIP]

dive-bomb (dīv/bom/), *v.i., v.t.* to attack with or as with a dive bomber.

dive′ bomb′er, an airplane of the fighter-bomber type that drops its bombs while diving at the enemy.

div·er (dī′vər), *n.* **1.** a person or thing that dives. **2.** a person who makes a business of diving in water, as for pearl oysters, to examine sunken vessels, etc. **3.** *Brit.* a loon. **4.** any of several other birds noted for their skill in diving.

di·verge (di vûrj′, dī-), *v.*, **-verged, -verg·ing.** —*v.i.* **1.** to move, lie, or extend in different directions from a common point; branch off. **2.** to differ in opinion, character, form, etc.; deviate. **3.** *Math.* (of a sequence, series, etc.) to have no unique limit; to have infinity as a limit. **4.** to turn aside or digress, as from a path, discussion, or plan. —*v.t.* **5.** to deflect or turn aside. [< ML *dīverg(ere)* = L *dī-* DI-[2] + *vergere* to incline] —**Syn. 4.** See **deviate.**

di·ver·gence (di vûr′jəns, dī-), *n.* **1.** the act, an instance, or amount of diverging: *a divergence in opinion.* **2.** (in physics, meteorology, etc.) the total amount of flux escaping an infinitesimal volume at a point in a vector field, as the net flow of air from a given region. **3.** *Math.* **a.** the limiting ratio of the flux passing through an area surrounding a given point to this area as the area decreases to zero for a given vector at the given point in the vector field; the scalar product of the given vector and the vector whose components are the partial derivatives with respect to each coordinate. *Abbr.:* div **b.** the operation of obtaining this quantity. [< ML *dīvergentia*] —**Syn. 1.** separation, division, variation, deviation.

di·ver·gen·cy (di vûr′jən sē, dī-), *n.*, *pl.* **-cies.** divergence; deviation. [< ML *dīvergentia*]

di·ver·gent (di vûr′jənt, dī-), *adj.* **1.** diverging; differing, deviating. **2.** pertaining to or causing divergence. [< ML *dīvergent-* (s. of *dīvergēns,* prp. of *dīvergere*)] —**di·ver′gent·ly,** *adv.*

di·vers (dī′vərz), *adj.* **1.** several; sundry. —*pron.* **2.** (*construed as pl.*) some indefinite number, or quantity; some; several. [ME < OF < L *dīvers(us)* DIVERSE]

di·verse (di vûrs′, dī-, dī′vûrs), *adj.* **1.** of various kinds or forms; multiform. **2.** of a different kind, form, character, etc.; unlike. [ME < L *dīvers(us),* ptp. of *dīvertere* to DIVERT] —**di·verse′ly,** *adv.* —**Syn. 1.** varied, manifold, divergent.

di·ver·si·fi·ca·tion (di vûr′sə fə kā′shən), *n.* **1.** the act or state of diversifying. **2.** the act or practice of manufacturing a variety of products, investing in a variety of securities, selling a variety of merchandise, etc., so that a failure in or an economic slump affecting one will not be disastrous. [< ML *dīversificātiōn-* (s. of *dīversificātiō*)]

di·ver·si·fied (di vûr′sə fīd′, dī-), *adj.* **1.** distinguished by various forms or by a variety of objects: *diversified activity.* **2.** varied; distributed among or producing several types: *diversified investments.*

di·ver·si·fy (di vûr′sə fī′, dī-), *v.*, **-fied, -fy·ing.** —*v.t.* **1.** to make diverse, as in form or character; give variety or diversity to; variegate. —*v.i.* **2.** to invest in different types of securities, investments, etc., or produce different types of manufactured products, crops, etc. [late ME < MF *diversifi(er)* < ML *dīversificāre*] —**di·ver′si·fi′a·bil′i·ty,** *n.* —**di·ver′si·fi′a·ble,** *adj.* —**di·ver′si·fi′er,** *n.*

di·ver·sion (di vûr′zhən, -shən, dī-), *n.* **1.** the act of diverting, or turning aside, as from a course or purpose. **2.** *Brit.* a detour on a highway or road. **3.** distraction from business, care, etc.; recreation; entertainment; amusement. **4.** *Mil.* a feint intended to draw off attention from the point of main attack. [< ML *dīversiōn-* (s. of *dīversiō*)] —**di·ver′sion·al,** *adj.* —**di·ver′sion·ar′y,** *adj.*

di·ver·si·ty (di vûr′si tē, dī-), *n.*, *pl.* **-ties.** **1.** the state or fact of being diverse; difference; unlikeness. **2.** variety; multiformity. **3.** a point of difference. [ME *diversite* < MF < L *dīversitās*]

di·vert (di vûrt′, dī-), *v.t.* **1.** to turn aside or from a path or course; deflect. **2.** to draw off to a different course, purpose, etc. **3.** to distract from serious occupation; amuse. [late ME < L *dīvert(ere)* = *dī-* DI-[2] + *vertere* to turn] —**di·vert′ed·ly,** *adv.* —**di·vert′er,** *n.* —**di·vert′i·ble,** *adj.* —**Syn. 3.** entertain. See **amuse.** —**Ant. 3.** bore.

di·ver·tic·u·lum (dī′vər tik′yə ləm), *n.*, *pl.* **-la** (-lə). *Anat.* a blind, tubular sac or process branching off from a canal or cavity. [< L, var. of *dēverticulum* = *dēverti-* (comb. form of *dēvertere* = *dē-* DE- + *vertere* to turn) + *-culum* -CULE] —**di′ver·tic′u·lar,** *adj.*

di·ver·ti·men·to (di vûr′tə men′tō; *It.* dē ver′tē men′tō), *n.*, *pl.* **-ti** (-tē). *Music.* an instrumental composition in several movements, light and diverting in character, similar to a serenade. Also called **divertissement.** [< It]

di·vert·ing (di vûr′ting, dī-), *adj.* serving to divert; entertaining; amusing. —**di·vert′ing·ly,** *adv.*

di·ver·tisse·ment (di vûr′tis mənt; *Fr.* dē ver tēs mäN′), *n.*, *pl.* **-ments** (-mənts; *Fr.* -mäN′). **1.** a diversion or entertainment. **2.** *Music.* divertimento. **3.** a short ballet or other performance serving as an interlude in a play, opera, etc. **4.** a series of such performances. [< F = *divertiss(e)-* (s. of *divertir* to DIVERT) + *-ment* -MENT]

di·ver·tive (di vûr′tiv, dī-), *adj.* diverting; amusing.

Di·ves (dī′vēz), *n.* **1.** the rich man of the parable in Luke 16:19–31. **2.** any rich man. [< L: rich, rich man]

di·vest (di vest′, dī-), *v.t.* **1.** to strip of clothing, ornament, etc. **2.** to strip or deprive of anything; dispossess. **3.** to rid of or free from: *to divest oneself of responsibility.* **4.** *Com.* to sell off. **5.** *Law.* to take away (property, rights, etc.). [< ML *dīvest(īre)*] —**di·vest′i·ble,** *adj.* —**Syn. 1.** unclothe, denude. **2.** See **strip**[1].

di·vest·i·ture (di ves′ti chər, dī-), *n.* **1.** the act of divesting; state of being divested. **2.** property or investments that have been divested. **3.** Also, **di·ves·ture** (di ves′chər, dī-). the sale of business holdings, a subsidiary, etc., esp. under legal compulsion. [DI-[2] + (IN)VESTITURE]

di·vide (di vīd′), *v.*, **-vid·ed, -vid·ing,** *n.* —*v.t.* **1.** to separate into parts, groups, sections, etc. **2.** to separate or part from something else; sunder; cut off. **3.** to deal out in parts; apportion; distribute in shares. **4.** to cleave; part. **5.** to separate in opinion or feeling; cause to disagree: *The issue divided the senators.* **6.** to distinguish the kinds of; classify. **7.** *Math.* **a.** to separate into equal parts by the process of mathematical division; apply the mathematical process of division to. **b.** to be a divisor of, without a remainder. **8.** to mark a uniform scale on (a ruler, thermometer, etc.). **9.** *Brit. Govt.* to separate (a legislature, assembly, etc.) into two groups in ascertaining the vote on a question. —*v.i.* **10.** to become divided or separated. **11.** to share something with others: *We all divide equally.* **12.** to diverge; branch; fork: *The road divides six miles from here.* **13.** to perform the mathematical process of division. **14.** *Brit. Govt.* to vote by separating into two groups. —*n.* **15.** a division: *a divide in the road.* **16.** *Archaic.* the act of dividing. **17.** Also called **height of land.** *Phys. Geog.* the line or zone of higher ground between two adjacent streams or drainage basins. [< L *dīvid(ere)* = *dī-* DI-[2] + *vid-* separate, a root found also in *vidua* WIDOW] —**di·vid′a·ble,** *adj.* —**Syn. 1.** See **separate. 2.** sever, shear. **3.** partition, portion. **5.** alienate, estrange. **6.** sort, arrange, distribute.

di·vid·ed (di vī′did), *adj.* **1.** separated; separate. **2.** disunited. **3.** shared; apportioned. **4.** *Bot.* (of a leaf) cut into distinct portions by incisions extending to the midrib or the base. —**di·vid′ed·ly,** *adv.* —**di·vid′ed·ness,** *n.*

divid′ed high′way, a superhighway with a broad median strip, designed to prevent collisions, headlight glare, etc., between vehicles moving in opposite directions.

di·vi·de et im·pe·ra (dē′wi de′ et im′pe rä′; *Eng.* div′ə dē′ et im′pər ə), *Latin.* divide and rule: political maxim of Machiavelli.

div·i·dend (div′i dend′), *n.* **1.** *Finance.* **a.** a pro rata share in an amount to be distributed. **b.** a sum of money paid to shareholders of a corporation out of earnings. **2.** *Banking.* the interest paid on deposits by a mutual savings bank. **3.** *Math.* a number that is to be divided by a divisor. **4.** *Law.* a sum out of an insolvent estate paid to creditors. **5.** *Insurance.* (in participating insurance) a distribution to a policyholder of a portion of the premium not needed by the company to pay claims or to meet expenses. **6.** a share of anything divided. **7.** anything received as a bonus, reward, or in addition to or beyond what is expected. [< L *dīviden-d(um)* thing to be divided, neut. ger. of *dīvidere* to DIVIDE] —**Syn. 6.** allotment, portion.

di·vid·er (di vī′dər), *n.* **1.** a person or thing that divides. **2. dividers, a.** a pair of compasses, as used for dividing lines, measuring, etc. **b.** a set of colored pages or the like used to separate sections in notebooks, files, etc. **3.** a partition between two areas or dividing one area into two, as a piece of cardboard in a box or a bookcase jutting out from a wall. **4.** See **room divider.**

Dividers

div·i-div·i (div′ē div′ē), *n.*, *pl.* **div·i-div·is, div·i-div·i. 1.** a shrub or small tree, *Caesalpinia coriaria,* of tropical America, the astringent pods of which are used in tanning and dyeing. **2.** the related species *C. tinctoria.* **3.** the pods of either plant. [< Sp < *Carib*]

di·vid·u·al (di vij′o͞o əl), *adj.* *Archaic.* **1.** divisible or divided. **2.** separate; distinct. **3.** distributed; shared. [< L *dīvidu(us)* divisible (see DIVIDE) + -AL[1]] —**di·vid′u·al·ly,** *adv.*

div·i·na·tion (div′ə nā′shən), *n.* **1.** the attempt to foretell future events or discover hidden knowledge by occult or supernatural means. **2.** augury; prophecy: *The divination of the high priest was fulfilled.* **3.** perception by intuition; instinctive foresight. [< L *dīvīnātiōn-* (s. of *dīvīnātiō*) = *dīvīnāt(us),* ptp. of *dīvīnāre* to soothsay (see DIVINE, -ATE[1]) + *-iōn-* -ION; r. ME *divinacioun* < AF] —**di·vin·a·to·ry** (di vin′ə tôr′ē, -tōr′ē), *adj.*

di·vine (di vīn′), *adj.*, *n.*, *v.*, **-vined, -vin·ing.** —*adj.* **1.** of, pertaining to, or proceeding from a god, esp. the Supreme Being. **2.** addressed, appropriated, or devoted to God or a god; religious; sacred: *divine worship.* **3.** godlike; characteristic of or befitting a deity: *divine magnanimity.* **4.** heavenly; celestial: *the divine kingdom.* **5.** *Informal.* extremely good; unusually lovely. **6.** being God; being a god: *a divine person.* **7.** of superhuman or surpassing excellence. **8.** *Archaic.* of or pertaining to divinity or theology. —*n.* **9.** a theologian; scholar in religion. **10.** a priest or clergyman. **11. the Divine, a.** God. **b.** (*sometimes l.c.*) the spiritual aspect of man; the group of attributes and qualities of mankind regarded as godly or godlike. —*v.t.* **12.** to discover or declare (something obscure or in the future) by divination; prophesy. **13.** to discover (water, metal, etc.) by means of a divining rod. **14.** to perceive by intuition or insight; conjecture. **15.** *Archaic.* to portend. —*v.i.* **16.** to use or practice divination; prophesy. **17.** to have perception by intuition or insight; conjecture. [ME < L *dīvīn(us)* = *dīv(us)* god + *-īnus* -INE[1]; r. ME *devin(e)* < OF *devin* < L, as above] —**di·vin′a·ble,** *adj.* —**di·vine′ly,** *adv.* —**Syn. 12, 16.** foretell, predict, foresee, forecast. **14, 17.** discern, understand. —**Ant. 4.** worldly, mundane.

Divine′ Lit′urgy, *Chiefly Eastern Ch.* See under **liturgy** (def. 3).

divine′ of′fice, (*sometimes caps.*) *Eccles.* office (def. 11c).

di·vin·er (di vī′nər), *n.* a person who divines; soothsayer; prophet. [DIVINE + -ER[1]; r. ME *divinour* < AF < LL *dīvīnātor* soothsayer]

divine′ right′ of kings′, the right to rule derived directly from God, not from the consent of the people.

divine′ serv′ice, service[1] (def. 15).

div′ing bell′, an open-bottomed chamber in which persons can go underwater, the water being excluded from the upper part of the chamber by the equal pressure of the air.

div′ing board′, a springboard.

div′ing suit′, any of various waterproof costumes for underwater swimming or diving, esp. one that is weighted, hermetically sealed, and supplied with air under pressure. Also called **div′ing dress′.**

divin′ing rod′, a rod, esp. a forked stick, commonly of hazel, supposed to be useful in locating underground water, metal deposits, etc. Also called **dowsing rod.**

di·vin·i·ty (di vin′i tē), *n.*, *pl.* **-ties. 1.** the quality of being divine; divine nature. **2.** deity; godhood. **3.** a divine being; God. **4. the Divinity,** (*sometimes l.c.*) the Deity. **5.** a being having divine attributes. **6.** theology. **7.** godlike character; supreme excellence: *the divinity of Beethoven's music.* **8.** Also called **divin′ity fudge′.** a fluffy white or artificially tinted fudge made usually of sugar, corn syrup, egg whites, and flavoring, often with nuts. [ME *divinite* < MF < L *dīvīnitāt-* (s. of *dīvīnitās*)]

divin′ity school′, a Protestant seminary.

di·vi·nize (div′ə nīz′), *v.t.*, **-nized, -niz·ing.** to make divine; deify. Also, *esp. Brit.*, **divinise.** [DIVINE + -IZE; cf. F *diviniser*] —**div′i·ni·za′tion,** *n.*

di·vis·i·bil·i·ty (di viz′ə bil′i tē), *n.* **1.** the capacity of being divided. **2.** *Math.* the capacity of being evenly divided, without remainder. [< LL *dīvisibil(is)* DIVISIBLE + -ITY]

di·vis·i·ble (di viz′ə bəl), *adj.* **1.** capable of being divided. **2.** *Math.* capable of being evenly divided, without remainder. [< LL *dīvisibil(is)* = L *dīvīs(us)* (ptp. of *dīvidere* to DIVIDE) + *-ibilis* -IBLE] —**di·vis′i·ble·ness,** *n.* —**di·vis′i·bly,** *adv.*

di·vi·sion (di vizh′ən), *n.* **1.** the act of dividing. **2.** the state of being divided. **3.** *Arith.* the operation, inverse to multiplication, of determining the number of times or the extent to which one number or quantity, the divisor, is contained in another, the dividend, the result being the quotient. **4.** something that divides or separates; partition. **5.** something that marks a division; dividing line or mark. **6.** one of the parts into which a thing is divided; section. **7.** separation by difference of opinion or feeling; disagreement; dissension. **8.** *Govt.* the separation of a legislature into two groups in taking a vote. **9.** one of the parts into which a country or an organization is divided for political, judicial, military, or other purposes. **10.** *Mil.* **a.** (in the army) a major administrative and tactical unit, larger than a regiment or brigade and smaller than a corps, usually commanded by a major general. **b.** (in the navy) a number of ships, usually four, forming a tactical group that is part of a fleet or squadron. **11.** an administrative unit of an industrial enterprise, government bureau, transportation system, or university. **12.** *Sports.* a group composed of all the teams or competitors of comparable standing, skill, weight, age, rating, or the like: *the heavyweight division in boxing.* **13.** *Biol.* a major primary subdivision of the plant kingdom, consisting of one or more classes. Cf. **phylum** (def. 1). **14.** *Zool.* any subdivision of a classificatory group or category. **15.** *Hort.* a type of propagation in which new plants are grown from segments separated from the parent plant. [ME < L *dīvīsiōn-* (s. of *dīvīsiō*) (see DIVISIBLE, -ION); r. ME *devisioun* < AF] —**di·vi′sion·al, di·vi′sion·ar′y,** *adj.* —**di·vi′sion·al·ly,** *adv.*
—**Syn. 1.** separation, apportionment, allotment, distribution. DIVISION, PARTITION suggest the operation of dividing into parts or one part from another. DIVISION usually means little more than the marking off or separation of a whole into parts. PARTITION often adds the idea of sharing, of an allotting or assigning of parts following division: *partition of an estate, of a country.* **5.** boundary, demarcation.

Di·vi·sion·ism (di vizh′ə niz′əm), *n.* (*sometimes l.c.*) Pointillism. —**Di·vi′sion·ist,** *n., adj.*

divi′sion sign′, *Arith.* the symbol (÷) placed between two expressions to denote division of the first by the second.

di·vi·sive (di vī′siv), *adj.* **1.** forming or expressing division or distribution. **2.** creating dissension or discord. [< LL *dīvīsīv(us)*] —**di·vi′sive·ly,** *adv.* —**di·vi′sive·ness,** *n.*

di·vi·sor (di vī′zər), *n.* *Math.* **1.** a number by which another number, the dividend, is divided. **2.** a number contained in another given number a certain integral number of times, without a remainder. [< L *dīvīsor*]

di·vorce (di vōrs′, -vôrs′), *n.*, *v.* **-vorced, -vorc·ing.** —*n.* **1.** *Law.* a judicial declaration dissolving a marriage in whole or in part. Cf. **judicial separation. 2.** any formal separation of man and wife according to established custom, as among uncivilized tribes. **3.** total separation; disunion: *a divorce between thought and action.* —*v.t.* **4.** to separate by divorce: *The judge divorced the couple.* **5.** to break the marriage contract between oneself and (one's spouse) by divorce. **6.** to separate or isolate: *Some painters divorce art from life.* —*v.i.* to obtain a legal divorce. [ME < MF < L *dīvort(ium)* separation = *divort-* DIVERT + *-ium* -Y[3] (L *-tium* > E *-ce*)] —**di·vorce′a·ble,** *adj.* —**di·vorc′er,** *n.* —**di·vor′cive,** *adj.*

di·vor·cé (di vōr sā′, -vôr-, -vōr′sā, -vôr′-), *n.* a divorced man. [< F, n. use of masc. ptp. of *divorcer* < ML *dīvortiāre* to divorce < L *dīvorti(um)* DIVORCE]

di·vor·cee (di vōr sē′, -sā′, -vôr-, -vōr′sē, -vôr′-), *n.* a divorced woman. Also, **di·vor·cée′.**

di·vorce·ment (di vōrs′mənt, -vôrs′-), *n.* divorce; separation.

div·ot (div′ət), *n.* **1** . *Golf.* a piece of turf gouged out with a club in making a stroke. **2.** *Scot.* a piece of turf; a sod. [?]

di·vul·gate (di vul′gāt), *v.t.*, **-gat·ed, -gat·ing.** *Archaic.* to make publicly known; publish. [< L *dīvulgāt(us)* made common property (ptp. of *dīvulgāre*) = *dīvulg-* (see DIVULGE) + *-ātus* -ATE[1]] —**di·vul′ga·tor, di·vul′gat·er,** *n.* —**div·ul·ga·tion** (div′əl gā′shən), *n.* —**di·vul·ga·to·ry** (di vul′gə tōr′ē, -tôr′ē), *adj.*

di·vulge (di vulj′, dī-), *v.t.*, **-vulged, -vulg·ing.** to disclose or reveal (something private, secret, or previously unknown). [late ME < L *dīvulg(āre)* = *dī-* DI-[2] + *vulgāre* to make general or common, to spread (*vulg(us)* the masses + *-āre* inf. suffix)] —**di·vulge′ment,** *n.* —**di·vulg′er,** *n.* —**Syn.** See **reveal.**

di·vul·gence (di vul′jəns, dī-), *n.* a divulging.

di·vul·sion (di vul′shən, dī-), *n.* a tearing apart; violent separation. [< L *dīvulsiōn-* (s. of *dīvulsiō*) = *dīvuls(us)* (ptp. of *dīvellere* = *dī-* DI-[2] + *vellere* to pluck) + *-iōn-* -ION] —**di·vul·sive** (di vul′siv, dī-), *adj.*

div·vy (div′ē), *v.t., v.i.* **-vied, -vy·ing.** *Informal.* to divide or share; divide and distribute (often fol. by *up*): *They divvied up the profits among themselves.* [short for DIVIDEND]

Di·wa·li (di wä′lē), *n.* the Hindu festival of lights, celebrated as a religious holiday throughout India in mid-November. Also, **Dewali, Divali.**

di·wan (di wän′, -wôn′), *n.* dewan.

Dix·ie (dik′sē), *n.* **1.** Also called **Dixieland, Dixie Land.** the southern states of the United States, esp. those that were part of the Confederacy. **2.** any of several songs with this name, esp. the minstrel song (1859) by D. D. Emmett, popular as a Confederate war song. —*adj.* **3.** of, from, or characteristic of the southern states of the United States. [? (MASON-)DIX(ON LINE) + -IE]

Dix·ie·crat (dik′sē krat′), *n.* a member of a faction of southern Democrats stressing states' rights and opposed to the civil-rights programs of the Democratic party, esp. a southern Democrat who bolted the party in 1948 and voted for the candidates of the States' Rights Democratic party. [DIXIE + (DEMO)CRAT]

Dix′iecrat par′ty. See **States' Rights Democratic party.**

Dix·ie·land (dik′sē land′), *n.* **1.** a style of jazz, originating in New Orleans, played by a small group of instruments, as trumpet, trombone, clarinet, piano, and drums, and marked by strongly accented four-four time and vigorous, quasi-improvisational solos and ensembles. **2.** Also, **Dix′ie Land′.** Dixie (def. 1).

dix·it (dik′sit), *n.* an utterance. [< L: lit., he has said]

Di·yar·be·kir (dē yär′be kir′), *n.* a city in SE Turkey in Asia, on the Tigris River. 169,746. Also, **Diarbekr.**

di·zen (dī′zən, diz′ən), *v.t.* *Archaic.* to deck with clothes or finery; bedizen. [*dis-* bunch of flax on a DISTAFF + -EN[1]]

diz·zy (diz′ē), *adj.*, **-zi·er, -zi·est,** *v.*, **-zied, -zy·ing.** —*adj.* **1.** having a sensation of whirling and a tendency to fall; giddy; vertiginous. **2.** bewildered; confused. **3.** causing giddiness or confusion: *a dizzy height.* **4.** heedless; thoughtless. **5.** *Informal.* foolish; silly: *a dizzy blonde.* —*v.t.* **6.** to make dizzy. [ME *dysy*, OE *dysig* foolish; c. LG *düsig* stupefied] —**diz′zi·ly,** *adv.* —**diz′zi·ness,** *n.*

D.J., 1. disk jockey. **2.** District Judge. **3.** Doctor of Law. [< L *Doctor Juris*]

Dja·kar·ta (jə kär′tə), *n.* a seaport in and the capital of Indonesia, on the NW coast of Java. 4,576,009. Also, **Jacarta, Jakarta.** Formerly, **Batavia.**

Djam·bi (jäm′bē), *n.* a port on SE Sumatra, in W Indonesia. 158,559 . Also, **Jambi.**

Djeb′el Druze′ (jeb′əl). See **Jebel ed Druz.**

djel·la·bah (jə lä′bə), *n.* a loose-fitting hooded gown or robe worn by men in North Africa. [< Ar *jallabah*]

Djer·ba (jer′bə), *n.* an island off the SE coast of Tunisia: Roman ruins. 65,533; 197 sq. mi. Also, **Jerba.**

Dji·bou·ti (ji bo͞o′tē), *n.* **1.** a republic in E Africa, on the Gulf of Aden: formerly an overseas territory of France; independent since 1977. 110,000; 8492 sq. mi. *Cap.:* Djibouti. Formerly, **French Territory of the Afars and Issas, French Somaliland. 2.** a seaport in and the capital of Djibouti, in the SE part. 102,000. Also, **Jibuti.**

Dji·las (ji′läs), *n.* **Mi·lo·van** (mē′lo vän), born 1911, Yugoslavian political leader and author.

djin (jin), *n.*, *pl.* **djins,** (*esp. collectively*) **djin.** *Islam.* jinn. Also, **djinn, djin·ni** (jin′ē).

Djok·ja·kar·ta (jôk′yä kär′tä), *n.* Dutch name of **Jogjakarta.**

D.J.S., Doctor of Juridical Science.

dk., 1. deck. **2.** dock.

dl, deciliter; deciliters.

D/L, demand loan.

D layer, the lowest region of the ionosphere, characterized by mounting electron and ion density: exists, at night only, from about 70–80 kilometers to about 100–120 kilometers of altitude.

D.Lit., Doctor of Literature. [< L *Doctor Litterārum*]

D.Litt., Doctor of Letters. [< L *Doctor Litterārum*]

dlr., dealer.

D.L.S., Doctor of Library Science.

dlvy., delivery.

DM, See **Deutsche mark.** Also, **DM., Dm.**

dm, decimeter; decimeters.

DMSO, *Chem., Pharm.* a colorless, nontoxic, water-soluble liquid, $(CH_3)_2SO$, noted for its unusual capacity for penetrating the skin: used as a solvent, an antifreeze, and in medicine. Also called **dimethyl sulfoxide.** [*d(i)m(ethyl) s(ulf)o(xide)*]

D.Mus., Doctor of Music.

DMZ, demilitarized zone.

DNA, *Biochem.* any of the class of nucleic acids that contains deoxyribose, found chiefly in the nucleus of cells: responsible for transmitting hereditary characteristics and for the building of proteins. Also called **deoxyribonucleic acid, desoxyribonucleic acid.** Cf. **RNA.** [*d(eoxyribo)-n(ucleic) a(cid)*]

D.N.B., Dictionary of National Biography.

Dne·pro·dzer·zhinsk (dnye′prō dzer zhinsk′), *n.* a city in the E central Ukraine, in the SW Soviet Union in Europe, on the Dnieper River. 255,000.

Dne·pro·pe·trovsk (dnye′prō pe trôfsk′), *n.* a city in the E central Ukraine, in the SW Soviet Union in Europe, on the Dnieper River. 1,061,000. Formerly, **Ekaterinoslav.**

Dnie·per (nē′pər, dnye′per), *n.* a river in the W Soviet Union in Europe flowing S to the Black Sea. 1400 mi. long. Russian, **Dne·pr** (dnye′pər).

Dnies·ter (nē′stər, dnyes′ter), *n.* a river in the SW Soviet Union in Europe, flowing SE from the Carpathian Mountains to the Black Sea. ab. 875 mi. long. Russian, **Dnes·tr** (dnyes′tər). Rumanian, **Nistru.**

do[1] (do͞o; *unstressed* do͝o, də), *v.*, *pres. sing. 1st pers.* **do,** *2nd* **do** or (*Archaic*) **do·est** or **dost,** *3rd* **does** or (*Archaic*) **do·eth** or **doth,** *pres. pl.* **do;** *past sing. 1st pers.* **did,** *2nd* **did** or (*Archaic*) **didst,** *3rd* **did,** *past pl.* **did;** *past part.* **done;** *pres. part.* **do·ing;** *n.*, *pl.* **dos, do's.** —*v.t.* **1.** to perform (an act, duty, penance, role, etc.). **2.** to execute (a piece or amount of work): *to do a hauling job.* **3.** to accomplish; finish; complete: *He has already done it.* **4.** to put forth; exert: *Do your best.* **5.** to be the cause of (good, harm, credit, etc.); bring about; effect. **6.** to render, give, or pay (homage, justice, etc.). **7.** to deal with, fix, clean, arrange, move, etc., (anything) as the case may require: *to do the dishes; She did her hair.* **8.** to travel (a distance); traverse: *We did 30 miles today.* **9.** to travel at the rate of (a specified speed in miles per hour): *He was doing 80 when they arrested him.* **10.** to serve (someone); suffice for: *This will do us for the present.* **11.** to make or prepare: *I'll do the salad.* **12.** to serve (a term of time) in prison or, sometimes, in office. **13.** to create, form, or bring into being: *She does lovely oil portraits.* **14.** to study or work at or in the field of: *I have to do my math* *tonight.* **15.** to explore or travel through as a sightseer: *They did Europe in three weeks.* —*v.i.* **16.** to act or conduct oneself; behave; be in action. **17.** to proceed: *to do wisely.* **18.** to get along; fare; manage: *to do without an automobile.* **19.** to be in health, as specified: *Mother and child are doing fine.* **20.** to serve or be satisfactory, as for the purpose; suffice; be enough: *Will this do?* **21.** to finish or be finished. **22.** to happen; transpire; take place: *What's doing at the office?* **23.** (used without special meaning in interrogative, negative, and inverted constructions, in imperatives with *you* or *thou* expressed, and occasionally as a metrical expedient in verse): *Do you think so? I don't agree.* **24.** (used to lend emphasis to a principal verb): *Do visit us!* **25.** (used to avoid repetition of a verb or full verb expression): *I think as you do.* **26. do away with, a.** to put an end to; abolish. **b.** to murder. **27. do for,** *Chiefly Brit.* to cook and keep house for; manage or provide for. **28. do in,** *Slang.* **a.** to murder. **b.** to injure gravely or exhaust: *all done in after the long hike.* **29. do one proud.** See **proud** (def. 9). **30. do or die,** to make a supreme effort. **31. do out of,** *Slang.* to swindle; cheat: *A furniture store did me out of several hundred dollars.* **32. do over,** *Informal.* to redecorate. **33. do time,** *Informal.* to serve a term in prison. **34. do up,** *Informal.* **a.** to wrap and tie up. **b.** to pin up or arrange (the hair). **c.** to fasten (a garment, curtains or drapes, etc.). **35. make do with, a.** to manage; cope. **b.** to manage to get along with what is at hand, despite its inadequacy: *She can't afford a new coat and so will have to make do with the old one.* —*n.* **36.** *Brit. Slang.* a swindle; hoax. **37.** *Chiefly Brit.* a festive social gathering; party. **38. dos and don'ts,** customs, rules, or regulations. [ME, OE *dōn;* c. D *doen,* G *tun;* akin to L *-dere* to put (as in *abdere* to put away)] —**Syn. 1, 17.** act. **3.** Do, ACCOMPLISH, ACHIEVE mean to bring some action to a conclusion. Do is the general word, carrying no implication of success or failure: *He did a great deal of hard work.* ACCOMPLISH and ACHIEVE both have a connotation of successful completion of an undertaking. ACCOMPLISH emphasizes attaining a desired purpose through effort, skill, and perseverance: *to accomplish what one has hoped for.* ACHIEVE emphasizes accomplishing something important, excellent, or great: *to achieve a benefit for mankind.*

do² (dō), *n., pl.* **dos.** *Music.* **1.** the syllable used for the first tone or keynote of a diatonic scale. **2.** (in the fixed system of solmization) the tone C. Cf. **sol-fa** (def. 1), **ut.** [< It]

D/O, delivery order. Also, **d.o.**

D.O., **1.** Doctor of Optometry. **2.** Doctor of Osteopathy.

D.O.A., dead on arrival.

dob·ber (dob′ər), *n. U.S. Dial.* a float for a fishing line; bob. [< D: buoy]

dob·bin (dob′in), *n.* **1.** a horse, esp. a quiet, plodding horse for farm work or for drawing a wagon or coach. **2.** (*cap.*) a conventional name for a quiet, plodding horse. [var. of *Robin,* alter. of *Robert*]

dob·by (dob′ē), *n., pl.* **-bies. 1.** *Brit. Dial.* a fatuous person; fool. **2.** *Textiles.* **a.** an attachment on a loom, used in weaving small patterns. **b.** Also called **dob′by weave′.** a small geometric or floral pattern produced by this attachment. **c.** a fabric having such a pattern. [akin to dial. *dovie* stupid, imbecile < *dove* to doze, dote, OE *dofian, dobian;* c. G *toben* to rage; cf. OE *dobende* decrepit]

Do·ber·man pin·scher (dō′bər mən pin′shər), one of a German breed of medium-sized, short-haired dogs having a black, brown, or blue coat with rusty brown markings. [named after Ludwig *Dobermann,* 19th-century German, original breeder; *pinscher* terrier, a pseudo-G coinage, perh. based on G *Pinzgau* Austrian district noted for its breeding farms]

Doberman pinscher (27 in. high at shoulder)

do·bie (dō′bē), *n.* adobe.

do·bla (dō′blä), *n.* a former gold coin of Spain. [< Sp < L *dupla,* fem. of *duplus* DOUBLE]

do·blón (də blōn′; *Sp.* dô vlōn′), *n., pl.* **-blon·es** (-blō′nēz; *Sp.* -vlô′nes). a former gold coin of Spain and Spanish America, equal to two gold escudos. [< Sp: DOUBLOON]

do·bra (dō′brə), *n.* any of various former Portuguese coins, esp. a gold coin of John V equal to two johannes. [< Pg < L *dupla,* fem. of *duplus* DOUBLE]

Do·bru·ja (dō′brŏŏ jə; *Bulg.* dô′brŏŏ jä′), *n.* a region in SE Rumania and NE Bulgaria, between the Danube River and the Black Sea. 2970 sq. mi. Rumanian, **Do·bro·gea** (dô′brô jä′).

Do·bry·nin (do brē′nin), *n.* **A·na·to·ly F(e·do·ro·vich)** (ä nä tô′li fyô′do ro vich), born 1919, Russian diplomat.

dob·son (dob′sən), *n.* hellgrammite. [after surname *Dobson*]

Dob·son (dob′sən), *n.* **(Henry) Austin,** 1840–1921, English poet, biographer, and essayist.

dob·son·fly (dob′sən flī′), *n., pl.* **-flies.** a large insect, *Corydalus cornutus,* having membranous wings, the male of which has greatly elongated, hornlike mandibles. [after surname *Dobson;* see FLY²]

Dob·zhan·sky (dôb zhan′skē), *n.* **Theodosius,** born 1900, U.S. geneticist, born in Russia.

doc (dok), *n. Informal.* **1.** doctor. **2.** (*usually cap.*) (used as a term of address for a physician, dentist, or veterinarian). [by shortening]

doc., *pl.* **docs.** document.

do·cent (dō′sənt; *Ger.* dō tsent′), *n.* **1.** privatdocent. **2.** a college or university lecturer. [< G *Dozent* < L *docent-* = *doc-* teach + *-ent-* -ENT] —**do′cent·ship′,** *n.*

doch-an-dor·rach (dokн′ən dor′əкн), *n. Scot., Irish.* a stirrup cup. Also, **doch′-an-dor′roch, doch-an-dor·ris** (dokн′ən dor′is). [cf. Ir *deoch an dorais* drink of the door]

doc·ile (dos′əl; *Brit.* dō′sīl), *adj.* **1.** easily managed; tractable: *a docile horse.* **2.** readily trained; teachable. [late ME < L *docilis* readily taught = *doc(ēre)* (to) teach + *-ilis* -ILE] —**doc′ile·ly,** *adv.* —**do·cil·i·ty** (do sil′i tē, dō-), *n.* —**Syn. 1.** manageable; obedient.

dock¹ (dok), *n.* **1.** a wharf. **2.** the space or waterway between two piers or wharves, as for receiving a ship while in port. **3.** such a waterway, enclosed or open, together with the surrounding piers, wharves, etc. **4.** See **dry dock. 5.** a platform for loading and unloading trucks, railroad freight cars, etc. **6.** an airplane hangar or repair shed. —*v.t.* **7.** to bring (a ship or boat) into a dock; lay up in a dock. **8.** to place in dry dock, as for repair or maintenance. —*v.i.* **9.** to come or go into a dock or dry dock. **10.** (of a space vehicle) to join together with another space vehicle in outer space. [< MD, orig. hollow made in sand or mud by grounded ship; c. Norw, Icel *dokk* hollow, Latvian *danga* muddy hole made by traffic]

dock² (dok), *n.* **1.** the solid or fleshy part of an animal's tail, as distinguished from the hair. **2.** the part of a tail left after cutting or clipping. —*v.t.* **3.** to cut off the end of; cut short: *to dock the ears of cattle.* **4.** to cut short the tail of: *to dock a horse.* **5.** to deduct a part from: *to dock one's wages.* **6.** to deduct from the wages of, usually as a punishment: *The boss docked him a day's pay.* **7.** to deduct from (wages): *The boss docked his paycheck $20.* [ME *dok,* OE *-docca,* in *fingirdoccana* (gen. pl.) finger muscles; c. Fris *dok,* LG *docke* bundle, Icel *dokkur* stumpy tail, MHG *tocke* bundle]

dock³ (dok), *n.* the place in a courtroom where a prisoner is placed during trial. [< Flem *dok* cage]

dock⁴ (dok), *n.* **1.** any of various weedy, polygonaceous plants of the genus *Rumex* having long taproots. **2.** any of various other plants, mostly coarse weeds. [ME *dokke,* OE *docce;* c. MD *docke,* MHG *tocke*]

dock·age¹ (dok′ij), *n.* **1.** a charge for the use of a dock. **2.** docking accommodations. **3.** the act of docking a vessel. [DOCK¹ + -AGE]

dock·age² (dok′ij), *n.* **1.** a curtailment; deduction, as from wages. **2.** waste material in wheat and other grains that is easily removed. [DOCK² + -AGE]

dock·er¹ (dok′ər), *n.* a longshoreman; a laborer on shipping docks. [DOCK + -ER¹]

dock·er² (dok′ər), *n.* a person or thing that docks, or cuts short. [DOCK² + -ER¹]

dock·et (dok′it), *n., v.,* **-et·ed, -et·ing.** —*n.* **1.** a list of causes in court for trial. **2.** *Chiefly Brit.* **a.** an official memorandum or entry of proceedings in a legal cause. **b.** a register of such entries. **c.** any of various certificates or warrants giving the holder right to obtain, buy, or move goods that are controlled by the government, as a customhouse docket certifying duty has been paid. **3.** the list of business to be transacted by a board, council, legislative assembly, or the like. **4.** *Brit.* a writing on a letter or document stating its contents; any statement of particulars attached to a package, envelope, etc.; a label or ticket. —*v.t.* **5.** *Law.* to make an entry in the docket of the court. **6.** to endorse (a letter, document, etc.) with a memorandum. [late ME *dogget* < ?]

dock-wal·lop·er (dok′wol′ə pər), *n. Slang.* a casual laborer about docks or wharves. —**dock′-wal′lop·ing,** *n.*

dock·yard (dok′yärd′), *n.* **1.** a waterside area containing docks, workshops, warehouses, etc., for building, outfitting, and repairing ships, for storing naval supplies, etc. **2.** *Brit.* a navy yard.

doc·tor (dok′tər), *n.* **1.** a person licensed to practice medicine; physician, dentist, or veterinarian. **2.** a person who has been awarded a doctor's degree. **3.** See **Doctor of the Church. 4.** *Mach.* any of various minor mechanical devices, esp. one designed to remedy an undesirable characteristic of an automatic process. **5.** *Angling.* any of several artificial flies. **6.** *Archaic.* a man of great learning. **7.** *Archaic.* a loaded die. —*v.t.* **8.** to give medical treatment to; act as a physician to: *He feels he can doctor himself for just a common cold.* **9.** to treat (an ailment); apply remedies to. **10.** to restore to original or working condition; repair; mend. **11.** to tamper with; falsify: *He doctored the information on his passport.* **12.** to revise, alter, or adapt (a photograph, manuscript, etc.), esp. in order to improve the material: *to doctor a play.* —*v.i.* **13.** to practice medicine. **14.** *Dial.* to take medicine; receive medical treatment. [< L = *doc(ēre)* (to) teach + *-tor* -TOR; r. ME *doct(o)ur* < AF < L, as above] —**doc′tor·al, doc·to·ri·al** (dok tōr′ē əl, -tôr′-), *adj.* —**doc′tor·al·ly, doc·to′ri·al·ly,** *adv.*

doc·tor·ate (dok′tər it), *n.* **1.** See **doctor's degree. 2.** See **Doctor of Philosophy** (def. 1). [< ML *doctorāt(us)* degree of doctor]

Doc′tor of Philos′ophy, 1. a doctor's degree awarded for completing advanced graduate studies in the humanities, the social sciences, the behavioral sciences, or the pure sciences. **2.** a person who has been awarded this degree. *Abbr.:* Ph.D.

Doc′tor of the Church′, a title conferred on an ecclesiastic for great learning and saintliness.

doc′tor's degree′, 1. any of numerous academic degrees of the highest rank awarded by universities and some colleges for completing advanced work in graduate school or a professional school, as the M.D. or esp. the Ph.D. **2.** an honorary degree conferring the title of doctor upon the recipient, as with the LL.D. degree. Also called **doctorate.**

doc·tri·naire (dok′trə nâr′), *adj.* **1.** dogmatic; authoritarian. **2.** impractical or merely theoretical. —*n.* **3.** a person who tries to apply a theory without regard for practicalities. [< F = *doctrine* DOCTRINE + *-aire* -ARY]

doc·tri·nal (dok′trə nᵊl; *Brit. also* dok trīn′ᵊl), *adj.* of, pertaining to, or concerned with, doctrine: *a doctrinal dispute.* [< LL *doctrīnāl(is)*] —**doc′tri·nal′i·ty,** *n.* —**doc′tri·nal·ly,** *adv.*

doc·trine (dok′trin), *n.* **1.** a particular principle, position, or policy taught or advocated, as of a religion, government, etc.: *Catholic doctrines.* **2.** that which is taught; teachings collectively: *religious doctrine.* [ME < MF < L *doctrīn(a)* teaching = *doct(o)r* DOCTOR + *-īna* -INE²] —**Syn. 1.** tenet.

doc·u·dra·ma (dok′yə drä′mə, -dram′ə), *n. Television.* a drama in which actual events are re-created, often with the addition of fictional elements to heighten interest. [b. DOCU(MENTARY) + DRAMA]

doc·u·ment (*n.* dok′yə mənt; *v.* dok′yə ment′), *n.* **1.** a written or printed paper furnishing information or evidence, as a passport, deed, etc.; a legal or official paper. **2.** any written item, as a book, article, or letter, esp. of a factual or informative nature. **3.** *Archaic.* evidence; proof. —*v.t.* **4.** to furnish with documents, evidence, or the like: *a carefully* *documented biography.* **5.** to support by documentary evidence: *to document a case.* **6.** *Naut.* to provide (a vessel) with a certificate giving particulars concerning its nationality, ownership, tonnage, dimensions, etc., according to its size and purpose. **7.** *Obs.* to instruct. [late ME < L *documentum* = *docu-* (perf. s. of *docēre* to teach) + *-mentum* -MENT]

doc·u·men·ta·ry (dok′yə men′tə rē), *adj., n., pl.* **-ries.** —*adj.* **1.** Also, **doc·u·men·tal** (dok′yə men′tᵊl). pertaining to, consisting of, or derived from documents: *a documentary history of France.* —*n.* **2.** *Motion Pictures, Television.* a film or program portraying an actual event, life of a real person, period of history, or the like, in a factual way, esp. one containing sections photographed of actual incidents as they occurred. —**doc′u·men′ta·ri·ly,** *adv.*

doc·u·men·ta·tion (dok′yə men tā′shən), *n.* **1.** the use of documentary evidence. **2.** a furnishing with documents, as to substantiate a claim or the data in a book or article. **3.** *Library Science.* **a.** the collecting, recording, and dissemination of specialized knowledge. **b.** a classification system for documents.

DOD, Department of Defense.

do·dad (do͞o′dad), *n.* doodad.

dod·der[1] (dod′ər), *v.i.* to shake; tremble; totter. [cf. DITHER, TOTTER, TEETER, etc.] —**dod′der·er,** *n.*

dod·der[2] (dod′ər), *n.* any of the leafless parasitic plants of the genus *Cuscuta,* having yellowish, reddish, or white threadlike stems that twine about clover, etc. [ME *doder;* c. D, Dan *dodder,* MLG *dod(d)er,* MHG *toter,* G *Dotter*]

dod·dered (dod′ərd), *adj.* infirm; feeble.

dod·der·ing (dod′ər ing), *adj.* shaky or trembling, as from old age; tottering: *a doddering old man.*

dodeca-, a learned borrowing from Greek meaning "twelve," used in the formation of compound words: *dodecahedron.* Also, *esp. before a vowel,* **dodec-.** [< Gk *dōdeka-* comb. form of *dōdekás* twelve = *dō-* TWO + *-dekas* TEN]

do·dec·a·gon (dō dek′ə gon′, -gən), *n.* *Geom.* a polygon having 12 angles and 12 sides. Also, **duodecagon.** —**do·de·cag·o·nal** (dō′de kag′ə nᵊl), *adj.*

do·dec·a·he·dron (dō dek′ə hē′drən, dō′dek-), *n., pl.* **-drons, -dra** (-drə). *Geom.* a solid figure having 12 faces. —**do·dec′a·he′dral,** *adj.*

Dodecahedrons
A, Rhombic; B, Pentagonal

Do·dec·a·nese (dō dek′ə nēs′, -nēz′, dō′dek ə-), *n.* a group of 12 Greek islands in the Aegean, off the SW coast of Turkey: belonged to Italy 1911–1945. 123,021 (1961); 1035 sq. mi.

dodge (doj), *v.,* **dodged, dodg·ing,** *n.* —*v.i.* **1.** to move aside or change position suddenly, as to avoid a blow or get behind something. **2.** to use evasive methods; prevaricate: *When asked a direct question, he dodges.* —*v.t.* **3.** to elude or evade by a sudden shift of position or by strategy: *to dodge a blow; to dodge a question.* —*n.* **4.** a quick, evasive movement; a sudden jump aside or away as to avoid a blow or the like. **5.** *Informal.* an ingenious expedient or contrivance; a shifty trick: *He agreed with you as a dodge to win your confidence.* [?] —**Syn. 2.** equivocate. **3.** elude.

Dodge′ Cit′y (doj), a city in SW Kansas, on the Arkansas River: important frontier town and railhead on the old Santa Fe route. 14,127 (1970).

dodg·er (doj′ər), *n.* **1.** a person who dodges. **2.** a shifty person. **3.** a person who persistently evades a responsibility, as specified: *a tax dodger.* **4.** *Chiefly Southern U.S.* See **corn dodger. 5.** *Australian.* a large slice, lump, or portion of food, esp. of bread.

Dodg·son (doj′sən), *n.* **Charles Lutwidge** (lut′wij). See **Carroll, Lewis.**

do·do (dō′dō), *n., pl.* **-dos, -does. 1.** any of several clumsy, flightless, extinct birds of the genera *Raphus* and *Pezophaps,* related to the pigeons but about the size of a turkey, formerly inhabiting the islands of Mauritius and Réunion. **2.** *Slang.* a dullwitted, slow-reacting person. [< Pg *doudo* < *doudo* silly] —**do′do·ism,** *n.*

Dodo,
Raphus solitarius
(Length 3 ft.)

Do·do·na (də dō′nə), *n.* an ancient town in NW Greece, in Epirus: the site of a famous oracle of Zeus. —**Do·do·nae·an, Do·do·ne·an** (dōd′ᵊnē′ən), *adj.*

doe (dō), *n., pl.* **does,** (*esp. collectively*) **doe.** the female of the deer, antelope, goat, rabbit, and certain other animals. [ME *do,* OE *dā;* c. Dan *daa,* Alemannic *tē;* akin to OE *dēon* to suck]

DOE, Department of Energy.

Doe·nitz (dœ′nits), *n.* **Karl** (kärl), 1891–1980, German admiral: supreme commander of the Nazi military forces.

do·er (do͞o′ər), *n.* **1.** a person or thing that does something, esp. a person who gets things done with vigor and efficiency. **2.** a person characterized by action as distinguished from one given to contemplation.

does[1] (dōz), *n.* pl. of **doe.**

does[2] (duz), *v.* 3rd pers. sing. pres. ind. of **do**[1].

doe·skin (dō′skin′), *n.* **1.** the skin of a doe. **2.** leather made from this. **3.** soft leather made of sheepskin. **4.** a closely woven woolen cloth made with a satin or a small twill weave. **5.** a similar smooth-finished cloth made of cotton or nylon. [ME *doskin*]

Doe of Virginia deer,
Odocoileus virginianus

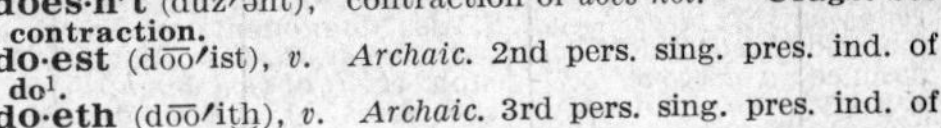

does·n't (duz′ənt), contraction of *does not.* —**Usage.** See **contraction.**

do·est (do͞o′ist), *v.* *Archaic.* 2nd pers. sing. pres. ind. of **do**[1].

do·eth (do͞o′ith), *v.* *Archaic.* 3rd pers. sing. pres. ind. of **do**[1].

doff (dof, dôf), *v.t.* **1.** to remove or take off, as clothing. **2.** to remove or tip (the hat), as in greeting. **3.** to throw off; get rid of. [ME, contr. of *do off;* cf. DON[1]] —**doff′er,** *n.*

dog (dôg, dog), *n., v.,* **dogged, dog·ging.** —*n.* **1.** a domesticated carnivore, *Canis familiaris,* bred in a great many varieties. **2.** any animal belonging to the same family, *Canidae,* including the wolves, jackals, and foxes. **3.** the male of such an animal as contrasted with bitch, vixen, etc. **4.** any of various animals resembling a dog. **5.** *Slang.* a despicable man or youth. **6.** *Informal.* a fellow in general, as specified: *a gay dog.* **7. dogs,** *Slang.* feet. **8.** *Slang.* something worthless or of extremely poor quality: *That used car you bought is a dog.* **9.** *Slang.* an ugly, boring, or crude girl or woman. **10.** *Informal.* See **hot dog. 11.** (*cap.*) *Astron.* either of two constellations, Canis Major or Canis Minor. **12.** *Mach.* **a.** any of various mechanical devices, as for gripping or holding something. **b.** a projection on a moving part for moving steadily or for tripping another part with which it engages. **13. go to the dogs,** *Informal.* to deteriorate; degenerate morally or physically; go to ruin. **14. lead a dog's life,** to have an unhappy or harassed existence. **15. put on the dog,** *U.S. Slang.* to assume an attitude of wealth or importance; put on airs. —*v.t.* **16.** to follow or track like a dog, esp. with hostile intent; hound. **17.** to drive or chase with a dog or dogs. [ME *dogge,* OE *docga* < ?] —**dog′like′,** *adj.*

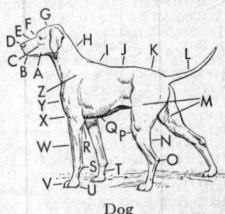

Dog
A, Jaw; B, Flews; C, Cheek; D, Nose; E, Muzzle; F, Stop; G, Forehead; H, Neck; I, Withers; J, Back; K, Croup or rump; L, Tail; M, Thigh; N, Breech; O, Hock; P, Stifle; Q, Chest; R, Elbow; S, Knee; T, Pastern; U, Pad; V, Paw; W, Forearm; X, Upper arm; Y, Brisket; Z, Shoulder

dog·bane (dôg′bān′, dog′-), *n.* any plant of the genus *Apocynum,* esp. *A. androsaemifolium,* a perennial herb yielding an acrid milky juice and having an intensely bitter root.

dog·ber·ry (dôg′ber′ē, -bə rē, dog′-), *n., pl.* **-ries. 1.** the berry or fruit of any of various plants, as the European dogwood, *Cornus sanguinea,* the chokeberry, *Aronia arbutifolia,* or the mountain ash, *Sorbus americana.* **2.** the plant itself. **3.** any of several plants, esp. the dog rose or bearberry.

dog′ bis′cuit, a hard biscuit for dogs, usually containing ground meat, bones, etc.

dog·cart (dôg′kärt′, dog′-), *n.* **1.** a light, two-wheeled, horse-drawn vehicle with two seats set back to back. **2.** a cart drawn by a dog or dogs.

dog·catch·er (dôg′kach′ər, dog′-), *n.* a person employed by a municipal pound or the like to find and impound stray or homeless dogs, cats, etc.

dog′ col′lar, 1. a collar used to restrain and identify a dog. **2.** *Informal.* a close-fitting necklace. **3.** *Slang.* a collar of the type worn by some clergymen, having the opening at the back; clerical collar.

dog′ days′, 1. a sultry part of the summer associated with the period in which Sirius, the Dog Star, rises at the same time as the sun, now often reckoned from July 3 to August 11. **2.** any period of quiescence. [trans. of L *diēs caniculārēs;* see CANICULAR]

doge (dōj), *n.* the chief magistrate in the former republics of Venice and Genoa. [< It, Venetian var. of *duce* leader < s. of L *dux;* see DUKE] —**doge′dom,** *n.* —**doge′ship,** *n.*

dog-ear (dôg′ēr′, dog′-), *n.* **1.** (in a book) the corner of a page folded over like a dog's ear, as by careless use, or to mark a place. —*v.t.* **2.** to fold the corner of (a page). Also, **dog's-ear.** —**dog′-eared′,** *adj.*

do·gey (dō′gē), *n., pl.* **-geys.** dogie.

dog·face (dôg′fās′, dog′-), *n.* *Slang.* an enlisted man in the U.S. Army, esp. an infantryman in World War II.

dog′ fen′nel, 1. mayweed. **2.** a composite weed, *Eupatorium capillifolium,* having heads of greenish-white to bronze flowers.

dog·fight (dôg′fīt′, dog′-), *n.* **1.** a violent fight between or as if between dogs, esp. a violent engagement of highly maneuverable warplanes at close quarters. —*v.t.* **2.** to engage in a dogfight with.

dog·fish (dôg′fish′, dog′-), *n., pl.* (*esp. collectively*) **-fish,** (*esp. referring to two or more kinds or species*) **-fish·es. 1.** any of several small sharks, esp. of the genera *Mustelus* and *Squalus,* that are destructive to food fishes. **2.** any of various other fishes, as the bowfin. [earlier *dokefyche*]

dog·ged (dô′gid, dog′id), *adj.* persistent in effort; stubbornly tenacious: *a dogged scholar.* —**dog′ged·ly,** *adv.* —**dog′ged·ness,** *n.* —**Syn.** See **stubborn.**

Dog′ger Bank′ (dô′gər, dog′ər), a shoal in the North Sea, between N England and Denmark: fishing grounds; naval battle 1915.

dog·ger·el (dô′gər əl, dog′ər-), *adj.* **1.** (of verse) comic or burlesque, and usually loose or irregular in measure. **2.** rude; crude; poor. —*n.* **3.** doggerel verse. Also, **dog·grel** (dô′grəl, dog′rəl). [ME; see DOG, -REL; cf. DOG LATIN]

dog·ger·y (dô′gə rē, dog′ə-), *n., pl.* **-ger·ies. 1.** doglike behavior or conduct, esp. when surly. **2.** dogs collectively. **3.** rabble; canaille; mob.

dog′gie bag′, a small bag provided by a restaurant in which a customer can carry home leftovers of a meal, esp. meat, usually to feed a dog or other pet. Also, **dog′gy bag′.**

dog·gish (dô′gish, dog′ish), *adj.* **1.** like a dog; canine: *doggish affection.* **2.** surly; mean. **3.** stylish and showy. [ME] —**dog′gish·ly,** *adv.* —**dog′gish·ness,** *n.*

dog·gone (dôg′gôn′, -gon′, dog′-), *v.t.,* **-goned, -gon·ing,**

adj., superl. **-gon·est,** *adv. Informal.* **—*v.t.* 1.** to damn: *Doggone your silly ideas.* **—*adj.* 2.** Also, **doggoned.** damned; confounded: *Well, I'll be doggoned.* **—*adv.* 3.** Also, **doggoned.** damned: *a doggone fool.* [euph. alter. of *God damn(ed)*]

dog·gy[1] (dô′gē, dog′ē), *n., pl.* **-gies. 1.** a little dog or a puppy. **2.** (used as a pet term for any dog.) Also, **dog′gie.** [DOG + -Y[2]]

dog·gy[2] (dô′gē, dog′ē), *adj.,* **-gi·er, -gi·est. 1.** of or pertaining to a dog: *a doggy smell.* **2.** pretentious; ostentatious. Also, **dog′gie.** [ME; see DOG, -Y[1]]

dog′gy bag′. See **doggie bag.**

dog·house (dôg′hous′, dog′-), *n., pl.* **-hous·es** (-hou′ziz). **1.** a small shelter for a dog. **2.** (on a yacht) a small cabin that presents a relatively high profile and gives the appearance of a box. **3. in the doghouse,** *Slang.* in disfavor or disgrace: *He's in the doghouse because he forgot his wife's birthday.*

do·gie (dō′gē), *n. Western U.S.* a motherless calf in a cattle herd. Also, **dogey, dogy.**

dog′ in the man′ger, a person who selfishly keeps something so that others may not use or enjoy it.

dog′ Lat′in, 1. mongrel or spurious Latin. **2.** a jargon imitating Latin.

dog·leg (dôg′leg′, dog′-), *n.* **1.** something bent at a sharp angle. **—*adj.* 2.** dog-legged.

dog′leg fence′. See **snake fence.**

dog-leg·ged (dôg′leg′id, -legd′, dog′-), *adj.* bent like the hind leg of a dog. Also, **dogleg.**

dog·ma (dôg′mə, dog′-), *n., pl.* **-mas, -ma·ta** (-mə tə). **1.** a system of principles or tenets, as of a church. **2.** a specific tenet or doctrine authoritatively put forth, as by a church: *the dogma of the Assumption.* **3.** prescribed doctrine: *political dogma.* **4.** a settled or established opinion, belief, or principle: *the dogma that might makes right.* [< L < Gk = *dok(ein)* (to) seem, think, seem good + *-ma* n. suffix]

dog·mat·ic (dôg mat′ik, dog-), *adj.* **1.** of, pertaining to, or of the nature of a dogma or dogmas; doctrinal. **2.** asserting opinions in a doctrinaire or arrogant manner; opinionated. Also, **dog·mat′i·cal.** [< LL *dogmatic(us)* < Gk *dogmatikós* = *dogmat-* (s. of *dógma*) + *-ikos* -IC] **—dog·mat′i·cal·ly,** *adv.*

dog·mat·ics (dôg mat′iks, dog-), *n.* (*construed as sing.*) the science that treats of the arrangement and statement of religious doctrines, esp. of the doctrines received in and taught by the Christian church. Also called **dogmat′ic theol′ogy.** [see DOGMATIC, -ICS]

dog·ma·tise (dôg′mə tīz′, dog′-), *v.i., v.t.,* **-tised, -tis·ing.** *Chiefly Brit.* dogmatize. **—dog′ma·ti·sa′tion,** *n.* **—dog′ma·tis′er,** *n.*

dog·ma·tism (dôg′mə tiz′əm, dog′-), *n.* dogmatic character; unfounded positiveness in matters of opinion; arrogant assertion of opinions as truths. [< ML *dogmatism(us)* (see DOGMATIC, -ISM); r. *dogmatisme* < F]

dog·ma·tist (dôg′mə tist, dog′-), *n.* **1.** a person who asserts his opinions in an unduly positive or arrogant manner; a dogmatic person. **2.** a person who lays down dogmas. [< ML *dogmatist(a)* = *dogmat(izāre)* (to) DOGMATIZE + *-ista* -IST]

dog·ma·tize (dôg′mə tīz′, dog′-), *v.,* **-tized, -tiz·ing. —*v.i.* 1.** to make dogmatic assertions; speak or write dogmatically. **—*v.t.* 2.** to assert or deliver as a dogma. Also, *esp. Brit.,* **dogmatise.** [< LL *dogmatiz(āre)*] **—dog′ma·ti·za′tion,** *n.* **—dog′ma·tiz′er,** *n.*

do-good·er (do͞o′go͝od′ər), *n.* a well-intentioned but naïve or ineffectual social reformer.

dog′ pad′dle, a simple swimming stroke mainly used to stay afloat while remaining almost stationary in the water, done by paddling both arms underwater while kicking the legs.

dog-pad·dle (dôg′pad′əl, dog′-), *v.i.,* **-dled, -dling.** to swim by use of the dog-paddle stroke.

dog′ rose′, an Old World wild rose, *Rosa canina,* having pale-red flowers.

dog's-ear (dôgz′ēr′, dogz′-), *n., v.t.* dog-ear. **—dog's′-eared′,** *adj.*

dog′ sled′, a sled pulled by dogs over snow or ice, as in the Arctic. Also called **dog′ sledge′.**

Dog′ Star′, 1. the bright star Sirius, in Canis Major. **2.** the bright star Procyon, in Canis Minor.

dog's-tongue (dôgz′tung′, dogz′-), *n.* hound's-tongue.

dog′ tag′, 1. *U.S. Slang.* either of a pair of metal identification tags that are worn on a chain around the neck by a member of the armed forces and that are stamped with the wearer's name, Social Security number (formerly serial number), blood type, and, often, religious affiliation. **2.** a small disk or strip attached to a dog's collar stating owner, home, etc.

dog-tired (dôg′tīərd′, dog′-), *adj. Informal.* utterly exhausted; worn out.

dog·tooth (dôg′to͞oth′, dog′-), *n.* **1.** Also, **dog′ tooth′.** a canine tooth. **2.** *Archit.* any of a series of small pyramidal ornaments, usually formed by a radiating arrangement of four sculptured leaves, set close together in a concave molding, used esp. in England in the 13th century.

dog′tooth vi′olet, 1. a bulbous, liliaceous plant, *Erythronium dens-canis,* of Europe, having purple flowers. **2.** any of several American plants of the genus *Erythronium,* as *E. americanum,* having yellow flowers, or *E. albidum,* having pinkish-white flowers. Also, **dog's′-tooth vi′olet.**

dog·trot (dôg′trot′, dog′-), *n.* a gentle trot, like that of a dog.

dog·watch (dôg′woch′, -wôch′, dog′-), *n. Naut.* either of two two-hour watches, the first from 4 to 6 P.M., the latter from 6 to 8 P.M. Also, **dog′ watch′.**

dog·wood (dôg′wo͝od′, dog′-), *n.* **1.** any tree or shrub of the genus *Cornus,* esp. *C. sanguinea,* of Europe, or *C. florida,* of America. **2.** the wood of any such tree.

do·gy (dō′gē), *n., pl.* **-gies.** dogie.

Do·ha (dō′hə, -ha), *n.* a town in and the capital of the sheikdom of Qatar, on the Persian Gulf. 100,000.

Doh·nā·nyi (dôh′nä nyi), *n.* **Ernst von** (ERNST fən) or **Er·nö** (ER′nœ), 1877–1960, Hungarian composer in the U.S.

doi·ly (doi′lē), *n., pl.* **-lies. 1.** any small, ornamental mat, as of embroidery or lace. **2.** *Archaic.* a small napkin, as one used during a dessert course. Also, **doyley.** [named after a London draper of the late 17th century]

do·ing (do͞o′ing), *n.* **1.** action; performance; execution: *Your misfortune is not of my doing.* **2. doings,** deeds; proceedings; happenings; events. [ME]

doit (doit), *n.* **1.** Also, **duit.** a former small copper coin of the Netherlands and its colonies: first issued in the 17th century. **2.** a bit or trifle. [< D *duit;* akin to Icel *thveiti* small coin, E *thwait* clearing (< Scand), *thwite* to WHITTLE]

do-it-your·self (do͞o′it yər self′ *or, commonly,* -i chər-), *adj.* **1.** of or designed for construction or use by amateurs without special training. **—*n.* 2.** the activity or hobby of building or repairing by oneself.

dol., dollar.

do·lab·ri·form (dō lab′rə fôrm′), *adj. Bot., Zool.* shaped like an ax or a cleaver. [< L *dolābr(a)* mattock, pickax + -I- + -FORM]

Dolabriform leaf

Dol′by Sys′tem (dōl′bē), *Trademark.* a device with a simplified electronic circuit that reduces the background noise added to a sound signal by the medium in which it is recorded or transmitted, as magnetic tape recording. [named after Ray *Dolby* (b. 1933), U.S. inventor] **—Dol·by·ized** (dōl′bē īzd′), *adj.*

dol·ce (dōl′chā; *It.* dôl′che), *adj. Music.* sweet; soft. [< It < L *dulcis* savory, sweet; see DULCET]

dol·ce far nien·te (dôl′che fär nyen′te) *Italian.* pleasing inactivity. [lit: (it is) sweet to do nothing]

dol·ce vi·ta (dôl′che vē′tä; *Eng.* dōl′chā vē′tə), *Italian.* sweet life; the good life perceived as one devoted to pleasure or excessive self-indulgence (usually prec. by *the* or *la*).

dol·drums (dōl′drəmz, dol′-), *n.* (*construed as pl.*) **1.** a state of inactivity or stagnation, as in business, art, etc. **2. the doldrums, a.** a belt of calms and light variable winds near the equator. **b.** the weather prevailing in this area. **3.** a dull, listless, depressed mood; low spirits. [? obs. *dold* stupid (see DOLT) + *-rum(s)* (pl.) n. suffix (see TANTRUM)]

dole[1] (dōl), *n., v.,* **doled, dol·ing. —*n.* 1.** a portion or allotment of money, food, etc., esp. as given at regular intervals in charity or for maintenance. **2.** a dealing out or distributing, esp. in charity. **3.** a form of payment to the unemployed instituted by the British government in 1918. **4.** any similar payment by a government to an unemployed person. **5.** *Archaic.* one's fate or destiny. **—*v.t.* 6.** to distribute in charity. **7.** to give out sparingly or in small quantities (usually fol. by *out*). [ME *dōl,* OE *(ge)dāl* sharing; cf. DEAL[1]]

dole[2] (dōl), *n. Archaic.* grief or sorrow; lamentation. [ME *do(e)l* < OF < LL *dol(us),* var. of *dolor* DOLOR]

Dole (dōl), *n.* **Robert J(oseph),** born 1932, U.S. politician: senator since 1969.

dole·ful (dōl′fəl), *adj.* sorrowful; mournful; melancholy. [ME *dolful*] **—dole′ful·ly,** *adv.* **—dole′ful·ness,** *n.*

dol·er·ite (dol′ə rīt′), *n.* **1.** a coarse-grained variety of basalt. **2.** any of various other igneous rocks, as diabase. **3.** any basaltlike igneous rock whose composition can be determined only by microscopic examination. [< F *dolérite* < Gk *doler(ós)* deceitful (< *dólos* wile) + F *-ite* -ITE[1]] **—dol·er·it·ic** (dol′ə rit′ik), *adj.*

dole·some (dōl′səm), *adj. Literary.* doleful.

dolicho-, a combining form meaning "long" or "narrow": *dolichocephalic.* [< NL < Gk *dolichós* long]

dol·i·cho·ce·phal·ic (dol′ə kō sə fal′ik), *adj.* (in cephalometry) **1.** long-headed; having a breadth of head small in proportion to the length from front to back. Cf. **brachycephalic. 2.** having a cephalic index of 75 or under. Also, **dol·i·cho·ceph·a·lous** (dol′ə kō sef′ə ləs). **—dol′i·cho·ceph′a·lism, dol′i·cho·ceph′a·ly,** *n.*

doll (dol), *n.* **1.** a toy representing a baby or other human being, esp. a child's toy. **2.** *Slang.* **a.** a girl or woman, esp. one who is very attractive. **b.** a boy or man who is considered attractive by a woman. **3.** *Slang.* a generous or helpful person: *Be a doll and pit these dates for me.* **—*v.t., v.i.* 4. doll up,** *Slang.* to dress in an elegant or ostentatiously stylish manner. [special use of *Doll,* short form of *Dorothy*] **—doll′ish,** *adj.* **—doll′ish·ly,** *adv.*

dol·lar (dol′ər), *n.* **1.** a currency bill and monetary unit of the U.S., equal to 100 cents. **2.** a silver coin and monetary unit of Canada, equal to 100 cents. **3.** any of the monetary units of various other nations and territories, as Australia, Barbados, Belize, Hong Kong, Liberia, New Zealand, Singapore, Trinidad and Tobago, etc., equal to 100 cents. **4.** a thaler. **5.** a peso. **6.** See **Levant dollar. 7.** yuan (def. 1). [earlier *daler* < LG, D *daler;* c. G *Taler,* short for *Joachimsthaler* coin minted in Joachimsthal, in Bohemia]

dol′lar-a-year′ man′ (dol′ər ə yēr′), *U.S.* a federal appointee serving for a token salary.

dol′lar cost′ av′eraging, a system of buying securities at regular intervals, using a fixed amount of cash over a considerable period of time regardless of the prevailing prices of the securities. Also called **dol′lar av′eraging.**

dol′lar diplo′macy, 1. a government policy of promoting the business interests of its citizens in other countries. **2.** diplomacy or foreign relations strengthened by the power of a nation's financial resources.

dol′lar gap′, the difference, measured in U.S. dollars, between the earnings of a foreign country through sales and investments in the U.S. and the payments made by that country to the U.S.

dol·lars-and-cents (dol′ərs and′ sents′), *adj.* considered strictly in terms of money: *from a dollars-and-cents viewpoint.*

doll·house (dol′hous′), *n., pl.* **-hous·es** (-hou′ziz). a miniature toy house built to the scale of children's dolls. Also, *esp. Brit.,* **doll's′ house′.**

dol·lop (dol′əp), *n.* **1.** a lump or blob, as of paint or mud. **2.** a serving or portion, esp. a small one: *Add a dollop of soda water to the mixture.* [cf. Norw (dial.) *dolp* lump]

dol·ly (dol′ē), *n., pl.* **dol·lies,** *v.,* **dol·lied, dol·ly·ing. —*n.* 1.** *Baby Talk.* a doll. **2.** a low truck or cart with small wheels for moving loads too heavy to be carried by hand. **3.** a small locomotive operating on narrow-gauge tracks, esp. in quarries and construction sites. **4.** *Brit. Dial.* a short wooden pole with a hollow dishlike base for stirring clothes while laundering them. **5.** *Motion Pictures, Television.* a mobile platform for moving a camera about a set. **—*v.t.* 6.** to transport or convey (a camera) by means of a dolly. **—*v.i.* 7.** to move a camera on a dolly, esp. toward or away from the subject being filmed or televised. **8.** (of a camera) to be transported or conveyed on a dolly.

Dol·ly Var·den (dol′ē vär′d^{ə}n), a woman's costume of the 19th century, including a flower-trimmed, broad-brimmed hat and a dress consisting of a tight bodice and bouffant panniers in a flower print over a calf-length quilted petticoat. [named after a character in Dickens' novel *Barnaby Rudge* (1841)]

dol·man (dōl′mən, dol′-), *n., pl.* **-mans. 1.** a woman's mantle with capelike arm pieces instead of sleeves. **2.** a long outer robe worn by Turks. [syncopated var. of *doliman, dolyman* < Turk *dolaman* (obs.) < *dolamak* to wind round]

dol′man sleeve′, a sleeve tapered from a very large armhole to fit closely at the wrist.

dol·men (dōl′men, -mən, dol′-), *n. Archaeol.* a structure usually regarded as a tomb, consisting of two or more large, upright stones set with a space between and capped by a horizontal stone. Cf. **cromlech** (def. 1). [< F < Cornish, lenited form of *tolmen* hole of stone (taken by French archaeologists to mean cromlech)]

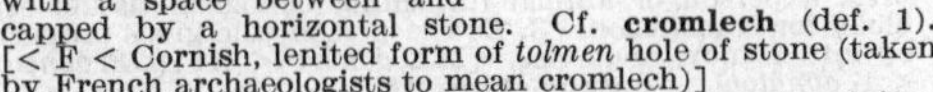

Dolmen

do·lo·mite (dō′lə mīt′, dol′ə-), *n.* **1.** a mineral, calcium magnesium carbonate, $CaMg(CO_3)_2$. **2.** a rock consisting essentially or largely of this mineral. [< F, named after D. de *Dolom(ieu)* (1750–1801), French mineralogist; see -ITE[1]] —**dol·o·mit·ic** (dol′ə mit′ik), *adj.*

Do·lo·mites (dō′lə mīts′, dol′ə-), *n.* (*construed as pl.*) a mountain range in N Italy: a part of the Alps. Highest peak, Marmolada, 10,965 ft. Also called **Do′lomite Alps′.**

do·lor (dō′lər), *n.* sorrow; grief; anguish. Also, *esp. Brit.,* **do′lour.** [< L = *dol(ēre)* (to) feel pain + *-or* -OR[1]; r. ME *dolour* < AF]

do·lo·ro·so (dō′lə rō′sō; *It.* dô′lô Rô′sô), *adj. Music.* plaintive, as if expressing sorrow. [< It]

do·lor·ous (dō′lər əs, dol′ər-), *adj.* full of, expressing, or causing pain or sorrow; grievous; mournful: *a dolorous melody; dolorous news.* [DOLOR + -OUS; r. ME *dolerous* < AF] —**do′lor·ous·ly,** *adv.* —**do′lor·ous·ness,** *n.*

dol·phin (dol′fin, dôl′-), *n.* **1.** any of several chiefly marine, cetacean mammals of the family *Delphinidae,* having a fishlike body, numerous teeth, and a head elongated into a beaklike snout. **2.** either of two large, slender fishes, *Coryphaena hippurus* or *C. equisetis,* found in warm and temperate seas. **3.** *Naut.* **a.** a pile, cluster of piles, or buoy to which a vessel may be moored in open water. **b.** a cluster of piles used as a fender, as at the entrance to a dock. [ME *dolphyn* < OF *dauphin, doffin* < OPr *dalfin* < VL *dalfīn(us),* L *delphīnus* < Gk *delphī́n*]

Bottle-nosed dolphin, *Tursiops truncatus* (Length 8½ ft.)

dol′phin strik′er, *Naut.* See **martingale boom.**

dols., dollars.

dolt (dōlt), *n.* a dull, stupid person; blockhead. [var. of obs. *dold* stupid, orig. ptp. of ME *dollen, dullen* to DULL] —**dolt′ish,** *adj.* —**dolt′ish·ly,** *adv.* —**dolt′ish·ness,** *n.*

Dol·ton (dōl′t^{ə}n), *n.* a city in NE Illinois, near Chicago. 25,937 (1970).

dom (dom; *for 2 also Port.* dôN), *n.* **1.** (*sometimes cap.*) a title of a monk in the Benedictine, Carthusian, Cistercian, and certain other monastic orders. **2.** (*usually cap.*) a title formerly given to certain Portuguese and Brazilian dignitaries. [(def. 1) short for L *dominus* lord, master; (def. 2) < Pg < L]

-dom, a native English suffix referring to domain (*kingdom*), collection of persons (*officialdom*), rank or station (*earldom*), or general condition (*freedom*). [OE *-dōm;* c. Icel *-dōmr,* G *-tum;* see DOOM]

Dom., 1. Dominica. **2.** Dominican.

dom., 1. domain. **2.** domestic.

D.O.M., to God, the Best, the Greatest. [< L *Deō Optimō Maximō*]

do·main (dō mān′), *n.* **1.** *Law.* ultimate ownership and control over the use of land. **2.** the territory governed by a single ruler or government; realm. **3.** a field of action, knowledge, influence, etc.: *the domain of science.* **4.** a region characterized by a specific feature, type of growth or wildlife, etc. **5.** *Math.* the set of values assigned to the independent variables of a function. **6.** *Physics.* one of many small magnetically polarized regions in a ferromagnetic body. [< F *domaine,* OF *demeine* < LL *dominicum,* n. use of neut. of L *dominicus* of a master = *domin(us)* lord + *-icus* -IC]

dome (dōm), *n., v.,* **domed, dom·ing.** —*n.* **1.** *Archit.* **a.** a vault, having a circular plan and usually in the form of a portion of a sphere, so constructed as to exert an equal thrust in all directions. **b.** a domical roof or ceiling. **c.** a polygonal vault, ceiling, or roof. **2.** something resembling or shaped like the hemispherical vault of a building or room: *the great dome of the sky.* **3.** *Crystall.* a form having planes that intersect the vertical axis and are parallel to one of the lateral axes. **4.** *Slang.* a person's head. —*v.t.* **5.** to cover with or as with a dome. **6.** to shape like a dome. —*v.i.* **7.** to rise or swell as a dome. [< MF < It *duomo* < eccl. L *domus (Dei)* house of God, church; akin to TIMBER] —**dome′like′,** *adj.*

domes·day (do͞omz′dā′, dōmz′-), *n.* doomsday.

Domes′day Book′ (do͞omz′dā′, dōmz′-), a record of a survey of the lands of England made by order of William the Conqueror about 1086, giving ownership, extent, value, etc., of the properties. Also, **Doomsday Book.**

do·mes·tic (də mes′tik), *adj.* **1.** of or pertaining to the home, the household, household affairs, or the family. **2.** devoted to home life or household affairs: *a domestic woman.* **3.** tame; domesticated: *a domestic animal.* **4.** of or pertaining to one's own or a particular country. **5.** indigenous to or produced within one's own country; not foreign; native: *domestic goods.* —*n.* **6.** a hired household servant. [< L *domestic(us)* = *domes-* (var. s. of *domus* house; see DOME) + *-ticus* (cf. RUSTIC); r. *domestique* < F] —**do·mes′ti·cal·ly,** *adv.*

do·mes·ti·cate (də mes′tə kāt′), *v.,* **-cat·ed, -cat·ing.** —*v.t.* **1.** to convert to domestic uses; tame. **2.** to accustom to household life or affairs. **3.** to cause to be or feel at home; naturalize. —*v.i.* **4.** to be domestic. [< ML *domesticāt(us)* (ptp. of *domesticāre*)] —**do·mes·ti·ca·ble** (də mes′tə kə bəl), *adj.* —**do·mes′ti·ca′tion,** *n.* —**do·mes′ti·ca′tive,** *adj.* —**do·mes′ti·ca′tor,** *n.*

domes′tic fowl′, 1. a bird of any breed of chicken. **2.** poultry.

do·mes·tic·i·ty (dō′me stis′i tē), *n., pl.* **-ties. 1.** the state of being domestic; domestic or home life. **2.** a domestic activity or chore.

domes′tic sci′ence. See **home economics.**

do·mi·cal (dō′mi kəl, dom′i-), *adj.* **1.** domelike. **2.** having a dome or domes. Also, **do′mic.** —**do′mi·cal·ly,** *adv.*

dom·i·cile (dom′i sīl′, -səl, dō′mi-), *n., v.,* **-ciled, -cil·ing.** —*n.* **1.** a place of residence; an abode; house or home. **2.** *Law.* a permanent legal residence. —*v.t.* **3.** to establish in a domicile. Also, **dom′i·cil.** [< MF < L *domicil(ium)* = *domi-* (see DOME) + *-cilium* (*cil-* (see CONCEAL) + *-ium* -Y[3])] —**dom·i·cil·i·ar·y** (dom′i sil′ē er′ē, dō′mi-), *adj.*

dom·i·cil·i·ate (dom′i sil′ē āt′), *v.,* **-at·ed, -at·ing.** —*v.t.* **1.** to domicile. —*v.i.* **2.** to establish a residence for oneself or one's family. [< L *domicili(um)* DOMICILE + -ATE[1]] —**dom′i·cil′i·a′tion,** *n.*

dom·i·nance (dom′ə nəns), *n.* **1.** rule; control; authority. **2.** the condition of being dominant. Also, **dom′i·nan·cy.**

dom·i·nant (dom′ə nənt), *adj.* **1.** ruling; controlling; exerting authority or influence: *dominant motives in human behavior.* **2.** occupying a commanding position: *the dominant points of the globe.* **3.** predominant; main; chief: *Corn is the dominant crop of Iowa.* **4.** *Genetics.* of or pertaining to a dominant. **5.** *Music.* pertaining to or based on the dominant. —*n.* **6.** *Genetics.* **a.** the one of a pair of alleles that masks the effect of the other when both are present in the same cell or organism. **b.** the trait or character determined by such an allele. Cf. **recessive** (defs. 3, 4). **7.** *Music.* the fifth tone of a scale. **8.** *Ecol.* any plant or animal that exerts so important an influence on the conditions of an area as to determine what other organisms can live there. [< L *dominant-* (s. of *dominans,* prp. of *dominārī* to DOMINATE); see -ANT] —**dom′i·nant·ly,** *adv.*

—**Syn. 1.** prevailing, principal. DOMINANT, PREDOMINANT describe something outstanding. DOMINANT describes that which is most influential or important: *the three dominant characteristics of monkeys.* PREDOMINANT describes that which is dominant over all others, or is more widely prevalent: *Curiosity is the predominant characteristic of monkeys.*

dom′inant ten′ement, *Law.* land in favor of which an easement or other servitude exists over another's land. Also called **dom′inant estate′.**

dom·i·nate (dom′ə nāt′), *v.,* **-nat·ed, -nat·ing.** —*v.t.* **1.** to rule over; govern; control. **2.** to tower above; overlook; overshadow. **3.** to predominate, permeate, or characterize. —*v.i.* **4.** to rule; exercise control; predominate. **5.** to occupy a commanding or elevated position. [< L *dominīt(us)* (ptp. of *dominārī* to master, control) = *domin-* (s. of *dominus*) master + *-ātus* -ATE[1]] —**dom′i·nat′ing·ly,** *adv.* —**dom′i·na′tor,** *n.*

dom·i·na·tion (dom′ə nā′shən), *n.* **1.** the act or an instance of dominating. **2.** rule or sway; control, often arbitrary. **3. dominations,** *Theol.* an order of angels. Cf. **angel** (def. 1). [ME < L *dominātiōn-* (s. of *dominātiō*) (see DOMINATE, -ION); r. ME *dominacioun* < AF]

dom·i·na·tive (dom′ə nā′tiv, -nə tiv), *adj.* dominating; controlling. [< ML *dominātiv(us)*]

dom·i·ne (dom′ə nē′, dō′mə-), *n. Obs.* lord; master (used as a title of address). [voc. of L *dominus* master, lord]

dom·i·neer (dom′ə nēr′), *v.i.* **1.** to rule arbitrarily or despotically; tyrannize. —*v.t.* **2.** to tower over or above. [< D *domineer(en)* < F *dominer* < L *dominārī* to DOMINATE]

dom·i·neer·ing (dom′ə nēr′ing), *adj.* inclined to rule arbitrarily or despotically; overbearing; tyrannical. —**dom′i·neer′ing·ly,** *adv.* —**dom′i·neer′ing·ness,** *n.* —**Syn.** arrogant; despotic, oppressive.

Dom·i·nic (dom′ə nik), *n.* **Saint,** 1170–1221, Spanish priest: founder of the Dominican order.

Dom·i·ni·ca (dom′ə nē′kə, də min′ə kə), *n.* one of the Windward Islands, in the E West Indies: formerly a British colony; independent since 1978. 78,000; 290 sq. mi. *Cap.:* Roseau.

do·min·i·cal (də min′i kəl), *adj.* **1.** of or pertaining to Jesus Christ as Lord. **2.** of or pertaining to the Lord's Day, or Sunday. [< LL *dominicāl(is).* See DOMAIN, -AL[1]]

domin′ical let′ter, any one of the letters from A to G used in church calendars to mark the Sundays throughout any particular year, serving primarily to aid in determining the date of Easter.

Do·min·i·can (də min′ə kən), *adj.* **1.** of or pertaining to St. Dominic or the Dominicans. —*n.* **2.** a member of one of the mendicant religious orders founded by St. Dominic; Black Friar. [*Dominic-* (s. of *Dominicus* Latinized form of *Domingo* de Guzman, founder of the order) + -AN]

Do·min·i·can (də min′i kən), *adj.* **1.** of or pertaining to the Dominican Republic. —*n.* **2.** a native or inhabitant of the Dominican Republic.

Domin′ican Repub′lic, a republic in the West Indies, occupying the E part of the island of Hispaniola. 4,835,000; 19,129 sq. mi. *Cap.:* Santo Domingo. Formerly, **Santo Domingo.**

dom·i·nie (dom′ə nē, dō′mə-), *n.* **1.** *Chiefly Scot.* a schoolmaster. **2.** *Dial.* a pastor or minister. [var. of DOMINE]

do·min·ion (də min′yən), *n.* **1.** the power or right of governing and controlling; sovereign authority. **2.** rule; control; domination. **3.** a territory, usually of considerable size, under a single rulership. **4.** lands or domains subject to sovereignty or control. **5.** *Govt.* one of the self-governing member nations of the British Commonwealth. **6. the Dominion,** Canada. **7. dominions,** *Theol.* domination (def. 3). [late ME < MF < ML **dominiōn-* (s. of **dominiō*) lordship. See DOMINIUM, -ION]

Domin′ion Day′, (in Canada) a legal holiday, July 1, celebrating the formation of the Dominion on July 1, 1867.

Dom·i·nique (dom′ə nēk′), *n.* one of an American breed of chickens, raised for meat and eggs. [named after F *Dominique* DOMINICA]

dom·i·no[1] (dom′ə nō′), *n., pl.* **-noes, -nos. 1.** a large, loose cloak, usually hooded, worn with a small mask by persons in masquerade. **2.** the mask. **3.** a person wearing such dress. [< It: hood and mask costume < ML or MF: black hood worn by priests in winter < L]

dom·i·no[2] (dom′ə nō′), *n., pl.* **-noes. 1.** a flat, thumb-sized, rectangular piece of ivory, bone, wood, or plastic, the face of which is divided into two parts, each left blank or bearing from one to six pips or dots arranged as on the faces of dice. **2. dominoes,** (*construed as sing.*) any of various games usually played with 28 such pieces. [? DOMINO[1]]

dom′ino the′ory, a theory that if one country, esp. in Southeast Asia, is taken over by communism, nearby nations will be taken over one after another.

Do·mi·nus (dō′mi no͝os′, dom′i-), *n. Latin.* Lord; God.

Do·mi·nus vo·bis·cum (dō′mi no͝os′ vō bis′ko͝om, dom′-i-), *Latin.* the Lord be with you.

Do·mi·tian (də mish′ən, -ē ən), *n.* (*Titus Flavius Domitianus Augustus*) A.D. 51–96, Roman emperor 81–96.

Dom·nus (dom′nəs), *n.* Donus.

Dom·ré·my-la-Pu·celle (dôɴ ʀə mē′lᴀ ᴘʏ sel′), *n.* a village in NE France, SW of Nancy: birthplace of Joan of Arc. 257 (1962). Also called **Dom·ré·my′.**

Dom. Rep., Dominican Republic.

don[1] (don; *It., Sp.* dôn), *n.* **1.** (*cap.*) Mr.; Sir: a Spanish title prefixed to a man's Christian name. **2.** a Spanish lord or gentleman. **3.** a person of great importance. **4.** (in the English universities) a head, fellow, or tutor of a college. **5.** (*cap.*) a title of address for an Italian priest. [< Sp, It < L *dominus*]

don[2] (don), *v.t.,* **donned, don·ning.** to put on or dress in: *to don one's clothes.* [contr. of DO[1] + ON; cf. DOFF]

Don (don; *for 1 also Russ.* dôn), *n.* **1.** a river flowing generally S from the central Soviet Union in Europe, to the Sea of Azov. ab. 1200 mi. long. **2.** a river in NE Scotland, flowing E from Aberdeen county to the North Sea. 62 mi. long. **3.** a river in central England, flowing NE from S Yorkshire to the Humber estuary. 60 mi. long.

do·na (dô′nä), *n.* Portuguese form of **doña.** [< Pg < L *domina,* fem. of *dominus*]

do·ña (dô′nyä), *n.* **1.** (*cap.*) Madam: a Spanish title of respect prefixed to a married woman's Christian name. **2.** a Spanish lady. [< Sp < L *domina,* fem. of *dominus*]

Do·nar (dō′när), *n. Germanic Myth.* the god of thunder, corresponding to Thor. [< OHG *thonar, donar;* c. OE *Thunor,* Icel *Thōrr;* see THUNDER, THURSDAY]

do·nate (dō′nāt, dō nāt′), *v.,* **-nat·ed, -nat·ing.** —*v.t.* **1.** to present as a gift; contribute; make a donation of, as to a fund or cause. —*v.i.* **2.** to give a gift, grant, or contribution: *They donate to the Red Cross every year.* [prob. back formation from DONATION] —**do′na·tor,** *n.*

Don·a·tel·lo (don′ə tel′ō; *It.* dô′nä tel′lô), *n.* (*Donato di Niccolo di Betto Bardi*) 1386?–1466, Italian sculptor. Also, **Do·na·to** (də nä′tō; *It.* dô nä′tô).

do·na·tion (dō nā′shən), *n.* **1.** the act of presenting something as a gift, grant, or contribution. **2.** a gift, as to a fund; contribution. [< L *dōnātiōn-* (s. of *dōnātiō*) = *dōnāt(us),* ptp. of *dōnāre* to give (*dōn-,* s. of *dōnum* gift, + *-ātus* -ATE[1]) + *-iōn-* -ION] —**Syn. 2.** See **present**[2].

Don·a·tist (don′ə tist, dō′nə-), *n.* a member of a Christian sect which developed in northern Africa in A.D. 311, and which maintained that it alone constituted the whole and only true church and that baptisms and ordinations of the orthodox clergy were invalid. —**Don′a·tism,** *n.*

don·a·tive (don′ə tiv, dō′nə-), *n.* a gift or donation. [< L *dōnātīv(um),* n. use of neut. of *dōnātīvus* gratuitous. See DONATION, -IVE]

Do·na·tus (dō nā′təs), *n.* early 4th-century bishop of Casae Nigrae in northern Africa: leader of a heretical Christian group. Cf. **Donatist.**

Do·nau (dō′nou), *n.* German name of **Danube.**

Don·cas·ter (doŋ′kas tər; *Brit.* doŋ′kə stər), *n.* a city in S Yorkshire, in N England. 86,402 (1961).

done (dun), *v.* **1.** pp. of **do**[1]. **2. be** or **have done with,** to break off relations or connections with; stop. —*adj.* **3.** completed; through. **4.** cooked sufficiently. **5.** worn out; exhausted; used up. **6.** in conformity with fashion, good taste, or propriety; acceptable: *It isn't done.* **7. done for,** *Informal.* **a.** tired; exhausted. **b.** deprived of one's means; ruined. **c.** dead or close to death. **8. done in,** *Informal.* very tired; exhausted.

do·nee (dō nē′), *n. Law.* a person to whom a gift is made. [DON(OR) + -EE]

Don·e·gal (don′i gôl′, don′i gôl′), *n.* a county in the N Republic of Ireland. 113,842 (1961); 1865 sq. mi. *Co. seat:* Lifford.

Don·el·son, Fort (don′əl sən). See **Fort Donelson.**

Do·nets (do nets′), *n.* **1.** a river in the SW Soviet Union in Europe, flowing SE to the Don River. ab. 650 mi. long. **2.** Also called **Donets′ Ba′sin.** an area S of this river, in the E Ukraine: coal-mining and industrial region. 9650 sq. mi.

Do·netsk (do netsk′), *n.* a city in SW Soviet Union, in the Donets Basin. 809,000 (1965). Formerly, **Stalin, Stalino, Yuzovka.**

dong[1] (dôŋ, doŋ), *n.* a deep sound like that of a large bell. [imit.; see DING-DONG]

dong[2] (dôŋ, doŋ), *n. Slang* (*usually vulgar*). penis. [?]

Don·go·la (doŋ′gə lə), *n.* a former province in the N Sudan, now part of the northern province.

Don·i·zet·ti (don′i zet′ē; *It.* dô′nē dzet′tē), *n.* **Ga·e·ta·no** (gä′e tä′nô), 1797–1848, Italian operatic composer.

don·jon (dun′jən, don′-), *n.* the inner tower, keep, or stronghold of a castle. [var. of DUNGEON]

Don Juan (don wän′ *or, also,* don jo͞o′ən; *Sp.* dôn hwän′), **1.** a legendary Spanish nobleman famous for his many seductions and dissolute life. **2.** a libertine or rake. **3.** a ladies' man or womanizer.

don·key (doŋ′kē, duŋ′-), *n., pl.* **-keys,** *adj.* —*n.* **1.** the ass, *Equus asinus.* **2.** a stupid, silly, or obstinate person. —*adj.* **3.** *Mach.* auxiliary: *donkey engine.* [var. of *Dunkey,* pet var. of *Duncan,* man's name]

don·na (dôn′nä), *n.* **1.** (*cap.*) Madam: an Italian title of respect prefixed to a married woman's Christian name. **2.** an Italian lady. [< It < L *domina,* fem. of *dominus*]

Donne (dun), *n.* **John,** 1573–1631, English poet and clergyman.

don·nish (don′ish), *adj.* resembling or characteristic of a university don, esp. stuffily academic. —**don′nish·ly,** *adv.* —**don′nish·ness,** *n.*

don·ny·brook (don′ē bro͝ok′), *n.* (*often cap.*) a wild, noisy fight; brawl; free-for-all. Also called **Don′nybrook Fair′.** [after *Donnybrook Fair,* held annually until 1855 in County Dublin, Ireland, and famous for riots]

do·nor (dō′nər), *n.* **1.** a person who gives or donates. **2.** *Med.* a person or animal furnishing biological tissue, esp. blood for transfusion. **3.** *Law.* a person who gives property by gift, legacy, or devise. [ME *donour* < AF (OF *doneur*) < L *dōnātor*] —**do′nor·ship′,** *n.*

do-noth·ing (do͞o′nuth′ing), *n.* **1.** a lazy or worthless person. —*adj.* **2.** characterized by unwillingness to work; idle. —**do′-noth′ing·ism,** *n.*

Don Quix·o·te (don′ kē hō′tē, don kwik′sət; *Sp.* dôn kē hô′te), a person who is inspired by lofty and chivalrous but impractical ideals. [from the hero of Cervantes' romance, *Don Quixote de la Mancha* (1605 and 1615)]

don·sie (don′sē), *adj.* **1.** *Scot.* unfortunate; ill-fated; unlucky. **2.** *Brit. Dial.* fastidious; neat; tidy. Also, **don′sy.** [perh. < ScotGael *donas* harm, ill + -IE]

don't (dōnt), **1.** contraction of *do not.* **2.** *Nonstandard.* contraction of *does not.* —*n.* **3. don'ts,** customs or regulations that forbid something. Cf. **do**[1] (def. 38). —**Usage.** See **contraction.**

Do·nus (dō′nəs), *n.* died A.D. 678, pope 676–678. Also, **Domnus.**

do·nut (dō′nət, -nut′), *n.* doughnut.

don·zel (don′zəl), *n. Archaic.* a young gentleman not yet knighted; squire or page. [< It *donzell(o)* < OPr *donzel* < VL **dom(i)nicell(us),* dim. of L *dominus* lord]

doo·dad (do͞o′dad), *n. Informal.* **1.** a decorative embellishment; trinket; bauble. **2.** dingus; gadget. Also, **do-dad.** [repetitive compound with gradation, based on dial. *dad* piece, flake]

doo·dle (do͞od′əl), *v.,* **-dled, -dling,** *n.* —*v.t., v.i.* **1.** to draw or scribble idly. **2.** to waste (time) in aimless or foolish activity. —*n.* **3.** a design, figure, or the like, made by idle scribbling. [orig., fool (n.)] —**doo′dler,** *n.*

doo·dle·bug[1] (do͞od′əl bug′), *n. U.S. Dial.* the larva of an antlion. [DOODLE + BUG[1]]

doo·dle·bug[2] (do͞od′əl bug′), *n.* a divining rod or similar device supposedly useful in locating underground water, oil, minerals, etc. [? special use of DOODLEBUG[1]]

doo·hick·ey (do͞o′hik′ē), *n., pl.* **-eys.** *Informal.* dingus; thingumbob; gadget. [*doo* (alter. of DO[1]; see DOODAD) + HICKEY]

Doo·lit·tle (do͞o′lit′əl), *n.* **1. Hilda** (pen name: *H.D.*), 1886–1961, U.S. poet. **2. James Harold,** born 1896, U.S. aviator and general.

doo·ly (do͞o′lē), *n., pl.* **-lies.** (in India) a simple litter, used to transport sick or wounded persons. Also, **doo′lie, dhooly.** [< Hindi *dōlī* litter]

doom (do͞om), *n.* **1.** fate or destiny, esp. adverse fate. **2.** ruin; death: *to fall to one's doom.* **3.** a judgment, decision, or sentence, esp. an unfavorable one. **4.** the Last Judgment. —*v.t.* **5.** to destine, esp. to an adverse fate. **6.** to pronounce judgment against; condemn. **7.** to ordain or fix as a sentence or fate. [ME *dome, dōm,* OE *dōm* judgment, law; c. Icel *dōmr,* Goth *dōms;* cf. Skt *dhāman,* Gk *thémis* law; see DO[1], DEEM]

dooms·day (do͞omz′dā′), *n.* **1.** the day of the Last Judgment, at the end of the world. **2.** any day of judgment or sentence. Also, **domesday.** [OE *dōmesdæg* Judgment Day]

Dooms′day Book′ (do͞omz′dā′). See **Domesday Book.**

Doon (do͞on), *n.* a river in SW Scotland, flowing NW from Ayr county to the Firth of Clyde. ab. 30 mi. long.

door (dōr, dôr), *n.* **1.** a movable, usually solid barrier for opening and closing an entranceway, cupboard, cabinet, or the like, commonly swinging on hinges or sliding in grooves. **2.** a doorway. **3.** the building, house, etc., to which a door belongs: *two doors down the street.* **4.** any means of approach, access, or exit: *the doors to learning.* **5. lay at someone's door,** to hold someone accountable for: *We laid the blame for the mistake at his door.* **6. out of doors,** outside of buildings; in the open: *We couldn't wait to get out of doors again after the long winter.* **7. show someone the door,** to request or order someone to leave. [ME *dore,* OE *duru* door, *dor* gate; akin to G *Tür,* Icel *dyrr,* Gk *thýra,* L *foris,* etc.]

door·bell (dōr′bel′, dôr′-), *n.* a bell at a door rung by persons outside seeking admittance.

door′ chain′, a short, removable chain for attaching between a doorjamb and the door to restrict its opening.

door′ check′, a device, usually hydraulic or pneumatic, for controlling the closing of a door. Also called **door′clos′er.**

do-or-die (do͞o′ər dī′), *adj.* **1.** determined to succeed at all costs; desperate; all-out: *a do-or-die attempt to halt the invaders.* **2.** involving a potentially fatal crisis or crucial emergency.

door·frame (dōr′frām′, dôr′-), *n.* the frame of a doorway, including two jambs and a lintel or head.

door·jamb (dōr′jam′, dôr′-), *n.* either of the two side-pieces of a doorframe. Also called **doorpost.**

door·keep·er (dōr′kē′pər, dôr′-), *n.* **1.** a person who guards the entrance of a building. **2.** *Brit.* a janitor; hall porter, as in an apartment house or hotel.

door·knob (dōr′nob′, dôr′-), *n.* the handle or knob for opening a door.

door·man (dōr′man′, -mən, dôr′-), *n., pl.* **-men** (-men′, -mən). the door attendant of an apartment house, night club, etc.

door·mat (dōr′mat′, dôr′-), *n.* a mat, usually placed before a door or other entrance, for scraping mud or dirt from shoes.

Doorn (dōrn, dôrn), *n.* a village in the central Netherlands, SE of Utrecht: the residence of Wilhelm II of Germany after his abdication. 9357 (1964).

door·nail (dōr′nāl′, dôr′-), *n.* **1.** a large-headed nail formerly used for strengthening or ornamenting doors. **2. dead as a doornail,** undoubtedly dead. [ME *dornail*]

door·plate (dōr′plāt′, dôr′-), *n.* a small identification plate on the outside door of a house or room.

door·post (dōr′pōst′, dôr′-), *n.* doorjamb.

door′ prize′, a prize given to a person attending a show, dance, or the like, esp. on a drawing of ticket numbers.

door·sill (dōr′sil′, dôr′-), *n.* the sill of a doorway.

door·step (dōr′step′, dôr′-), *n.* a step or one of a series of steps leading to a door from the ground outside.

door·stop (dōr′stop′, dôr′-), *n.* **1.** a device for holding a door open in a desired position. **2.** a small rubber-covered knob or other device for preventing a door from striking a wall.

door-to-door (dōr′tə dōr′, dôr′tə dôr′), *adj.* **1.** canvassing, selling, calling, etc., on prospective customers in person. **2.** shipped direct from the point of pickup to the point of delivery.

door·way (dōr′wā′, dôr′-), *n.* **1.** the passage or opening into a building, room, etc., commonly closed and opened by a door; portal. **2.** a means of access: *a doorway to success.*

door·yard (dōr′yärd′, dôr′-), *n.* a yard in front of the door of a house.

dope (dōp), *n., v.,* **doped, dop·ing.** —*n.* **1.** any thick liquid or pasty preparation, as a lubricant, used in preparing a surface. **2.** an absorbent material used to hold a liquid, as in the manufacture of dynamite. **3.** *Aeron.* **a.** any of various varnishlike products used esp. for waterproofing and strengthening the fabric of airplane wings. **b.** a similar product used to coat the fabric of a balloon to reduce gas leakage. **4.** any narcotic or narcoticlike drug. **5.** *Slang.* a narcotic preparation given surreptitiously to a horse to improve or impair its performance in a race. **6.** *Slang.* information, data, or news: *What's the latest dope on the weather?* **7.** *Slang.* a stupid person. **8.** *Southern U.S.* a carbonated drink, esp. Coca-Cola. —*v.t.* **9.** *Slang.* to affect with dope or drugs. **10.** to apply or treat with dope. **11. dope out,** *Slang.* to figure out, deduce, calculate, or devise: *to dope out a plan; to dope out a solution to a problem.* [< D *doop* sauce, a dipping, gravy < *doopen* to DIP¹] —**dop′er,** *n.*

dope·sheet (dōp′shēt′), *n.* a bulletin of the entries in various horse races, including the name, jockey, past performances, etc.

dope·ster (dōp′stər), *n.* a person who undertakes to predict the outcome of elections, sports events, or other contests.

dope·y (dō′pē), *adj.,* **dop·i·er, dop·i·est.** *Informal.* **1.** sluggish or befuddled from or as from the use of narcotics or alcohol. **2.** stupid; inane. Also, **dopy.** —**dop′i·ness,** *n.*

Dop·pel·gäng·er (dop′əl gang′ər; *Ger.* dô′pəl geng′ər), *n.* a supposed ghostly double or counterpart of a living person. Also called **doubleganger.** [< G: lit., double-walker]

Dop′pler effect′ (dop′lər), *Physics.* the apparent change in the frequency of a wave, as a light wave or sound wave, resulting from relative motion of the source and the receiver. [named after C. J. *Doppler* (1803–53), Austrian physicist]

Dop′pler shift′, *Physics.* the magnitude of the change in frequency or wavelength of waves caused by the Doppler effect.

dop·y (dō′pē), *adj.,* **dop·i·er, dop·i·est.** dopey.

dor¹ (dôr), *n.* a common European dung beetle, *Geotrupes stercorarius.* Also called **dor·bee·tle** (dôr′bēt′əl). [ME *dor(r)e,* OE *dora;* cf. MLG *dorte* DRONE²]

dor² (dôr), *n. Archaic.* mockery; scorn. [< Icel *dār* mockery; cf. G *Tor* fool]

Dor., 1. Dorian. **2.** Doric.

DORAN (dōr′an, dôr′-), *n.* an electronic device for determining range and assisting navigation, employing the principle of the Doppler effect. [*Do(ppler) ran(ge)*]

Dor·cas (dôr′kəs), *n.* a Christian woman at Joppa who made clothing for the poor. Acts 9:36–41.

Dor·ches·ter (dôr′ches′tər, -chi stər), *n.* a town in and the county seat of Dorsetshire. 12,266 (1961).

Dor·dogne (dôr dôn′yə), *n.* a river in SW France, flowing W to the Gironde estuary. 300 mi. long.

Dor·drecht (dôr′drekht), *n.* a city in the SW Netherlands, on the Waal River. 85,711 (1962). Also called **Dort.**

Dore (dôr), *n.* **Monts,** a group of mountains in central France: highest peak, 6188 ft.

Do·ré (dô rā′; *Fr.* dô rā′), *n.* **(Paul) Gus·tave** (pôl gʏ stav′), 1832?–83, French painter, illustrator, and sculptor.

Do·ri·an (dōr′ē ən, dôr′-), *adj.* **1.** of or pertaining to the ancient Greek region of Doris or to the Dorians. —*n.* **2.** a member of a people who entered Greece about the 12th century B.C.: one of the four main divisions of the prehistoric Greeks. Cf. **Achaean** (def. 5), **Aeolian** (def. 2), **Ionian** (def. 3). [< L *Dōri(us)* (< Gk *Dṓrios*) + -AN]

Dor·ic (dôr′ik, dor′-), *adj.* **1.** of or pertaining to Doris, its inhabitants, or their dialect. **2.** *Archit.* noting or pertaining to one of the five classical orders, developed in Greece and altered by the Romans and consisting typically of a channeled column having as a capital an ovolo molding supporting a square abacus, above which come a plain architrave, a frieze of triglyphs and metopes, and a cornice whose corona often has mutules on its soffit. Cf. **composite** (def. 3), **Corinthian** (def. 4), **Ionic** (def. 1), **Tuscan** (def. 2). See illus. at **order.** —*n.* **3.** a dialect of ancient Greek spoken in the Peloponnesus, Crete, Sicily, Rhodes, and other Dodecanese islands. [< L *Dōric(us)* < Gk *Dōrikós* Dorian]

Do·ris (dōr′is, dôr′-, dor′-), *n. Class. Myth.* the wife of Nereus and mother of the Nereids.

Do·ris (dōr′is, dôr′-, dor′-), *n.* an ancient region in central Greece: the earliest home of the Dorians.

Dor·king (dôr′king), *n.* one of an English breed of chickens having five toes on each foot, instead of the usual four. [after *Dorking,* town in Surrey, England]

dorm (dôrm), *n. Informal.* dormitory. [by shortening]

dor·man·cy (dôr′mən sē), *n.* the state of being dormant.

dor·mant (dôr′mənt), *adj.* **1.** lying asleep or as if asleep; inactive; torpid. **2.** in a state of rest or inactivity; inoperative; in abeyance: *The project is dormant for the time being.* **3.** undisclosed; unasserted: *dormant talent.* **4.** (of a volcano) not erupting. **5.** *Bot.* temporarily inactive: *dormant buds.* [ME *dorma(u)nt* < AF, prp. of *dormir* < L *dormīre* to sleep; see -ANT] —**Syn. 3.** latent. —**Ant. 1.** awake, active.

Dormer

dor·mer (dôr′mər), *n.* **1.** Also called **dor′mer win′dow.** a vertical window in a projection built out from a sloping roof. **2.** the entire projecting structure. [< MF *dormoir* DORMITORY]

dor·mie (dôr′mē), *adj. Golf.* (of a player or side) being in the lead by as many holes as are still to be played. Also, **dor′my.** [?]

dor·mi·ent (dôr′mē ənt), *adj.* sleeping; dormant. [< L *dormient-* (s. of *dormiēns,* prp. of *dormīre*); see -ENT]

dor·mi·to·ry (dôr′mi tōr′ē, -tôr′ē), *n., pl.* **-ries. 1.** a residence hall, as at a college, providing living and recreational facilities. **2.** a room containing a number of beds and serving as communal sleeping quarters. [< L *dormītōri(um)* (neut. of *dormītōrius*) = *dormīt(us)* (ptp. of *dormīre* to sleep) + *-ōrium* -ORY²]

dor·mouse (dôr′mous′), *n., pl.* **-mice** (-mīs′). any small, furry-tailed, Old World rodent of the family *Gliridae,* resembling a small squirrel. [*dor-* (? < Scand; cf. Icel *dūra* to nap, Sw (dial.) *dorsk* sleepy) + MOUSE]

Dormouse, *Muscardinus avellanarius* (Length 6 in.)

dor·nick¹ (dôr′nik), *n.* a stout linen cloth, esp. one of a damask linen. Also, **dor′neck.** [ME *dornyk,* after *Doornik* (F *Tournai*), where the cloth was first made]

dor·nick² (dôr′nik), *n.* **1.** a boulder, esp. one of iron ore found in limonite deposits. **2.** a small stone that is easy to throw. [? < Ir *dornōg* small casting stone (lit., fistful)]

do·ron·i·cum (də ron′ə kəm), *n.* any plant of the genus *Doronicum,* of Europe and Asia, having alternate, usually clasping leaves and heads of yellow flowers. [< NL < Ar *dorūn(aj)* + L *-icum,* neut. of *-icus* -IC]

dorp (dôrp), *n.* a village; hamlet. [< D: village; c. THORP]

Dor·pat (dôr′pät), *n.* German name of **Tartu.**

dor·sal (dôr′səl), *adj.* **1.** *Zool., Anat.* of, pertaining to, or situated on the back, as of an organ or part: *dorsal nerves.* **2.** *Bot.* pertaining to the surface away from the axis, as of a leaf; abaxial. **3.** *Phonet.* (of a speech sound) articulated with the dorsum of the tongue. —*n.* **4.** *Phonet.* a dorsal speech sound. [< ML *dorsāl(is)* = L *dors(um)* back + *-ālis* -AL¹] —**dor′sal·ly,** *adv.*

dor′sal fin′, the fin or finlike integumentary expansion generally developed on the backs of aquatic vertebrates.

dor·ser (dôr′sər), *n.* dosser.

Dor·set (dôr′sit), *n.* **1. 1st Earl of.** See **Sackville, Thomas. 2.** Dorsetshire.

Dor·set·shire (dôr′sit shēr′, -shər), *n.* a county in S England. 309,176 (1961); 973 sq. mi. *Co. seat:* Dorchester. Also called **Dorset.**

dorsi-, a combining form of **dorsum, dorsal:** *dorsiventral.* Also, **dorso-.**

dor·si·ven·tral (dôr′sə ven′trəl), *adj.* **1.** *Bot.* having distinct dorsal and ventral sides, as most foliage leaves. **2.** *Zool.* dorsoventral. —**dor′si·ven·tral′i·ty,** *n.* —**dor′si·ven′tral·ly,** *adv.*

dor·so·ven·tral (dôr′sō ven′trəl), *adj.* **1.** *Zool.* pertaining to the dorsal and ventral aspects of the body; extending from the dorsal to the ventral side. **2.** *Bot.* dorsiventral. —**dor′so·ven′tral·ly,** *adv.*

dor·sum (dôr′səm), *n., pl.* **-sa** (-sə). *Anat., Zool.* **1.** the back, as of the body. **2.** the back or outer surface of an organ, part, etc. [< L]

Dort (dôrt), *n.* Dordrecht.

Dort·mund (dôrt′mənd; *Ger.* dôrt′mŏŏnt′), *n.* a city in W West Germany. 650,900 (1963).

dort·y (dôr′tē), *adj. Scot.* sullen; sulky. [*dort* sulkiness (< ?) + -Y¹] —**dor′ti·ness,** *n.*

do·ry¹ (dōr′ē, dôr′ē), *n., pl.* **-ries.** a boat with a narrow, flat bottom, high bow, and flaring sides. [< *dōri,* native name for a dugout on Mosquito Coast of Central America]

do·ry² (dōr′ē, dôr′ē), *n., pl.* **-ries.** any compressed marine fish of the family *Zeidae,* esp. *Zeus faber.* [late ME *dorre, dorray* < MF *doree* (fem. ptp. of *dorer* to gild) < LL *deaurāta* (fem. ptp. of *deaurāre* to gild). See DE-, AUREATE]

dos-à-dos (dō′sē dō′, -zi- *for 1–3; Fr.* dō zä dō′ *for 4*), *n., pl.* **-dos** (-dōz′), *v.,* **-dosed** (-dōd′), **-dos·ing** (-dō′ing), *adv.* —*n.* **1.** a figure in square-dancing, in which two persons advance, pass around each other back to back, and return to their places. —*v.t.* **2.** to dance this figure around (one's partner). —*v.i.* **3.** to execute a dos-à-dos. —*adv.* **4.** *Archaic.* back to back. Also, **do-si-do** (for defs. 1–3). [< F: back to back]

dos·age (dō′sij), *n.* **1.** the administration of medicine in doses. **2.** the amount of medicine to be given. **3.** *Physics.* dose.

dose (dōs), *n., v.,* **dosed, dos·ing.** —*n.* **1.** a quantity of medicine prescribed to be taken at one time. **2.** a quantity of anything analogous to medicine, esp. of something nauseous or disagreeable: *Failing the exam was a hard dose to swallow.* **3.** an amount of sugar added in the production of champagne. **4.** *Physics.* the quantity of radiation absorbed by a given mass of material, esp. tissue. **5.** *Slang.* a case of gonorrhea or syphilis. —*v.t.* **6.** to administer in or apportion for doses. **7.** to give a dose of medicine to. **8.** to add sugar to (champagne) during production. —*v.i.* **9.** to take medicine. [earlier *dos* < ML *dos(is)* < Gk *dósis* a giving]

do·si·do (dō′sē dō′, -zi-), *n., pl.* **-dos,** *v.t., v.i.,* **-doed, -do·ing.** dos-à-dos (defs. 1–3).

do·sim·e·ter (dō sim′i tər), *n.* a device carried on the person for measuring the quantity of radiation, as gamma rays, to which one has been exposed. [< Gk *dósi(s)* DOSE + -METER]

do·sim·e·try (dō sim′i trē), *n.* **1.** the process or method of measuring the dosage of radiation. **2.** the measurement of the doses of medicines. [< Gk *dósi(s)* DOSE + -METRY] —**do·si·met·ric** (dō′sə me′trik), *adj.* —**do·si·me·tri·cian** (dō′sə mi trish′ən), **do·sim′e·trist,** *n.*

Dos Pas·sos (dōs pas′ōs), **John (Rod·er·i·go)** (ro drē′gō), 1896–1970, U.S. novelist.

doss (dos), *Brit. Slang.* —*n.* **1.** a place to sleep, esp. in a cheap lodging house. —*v.i.* **2.** to sleep or lie down in any convenient place. [? < Scand; cf. Sw *dorsk* sleepy]

dos·sal (dos′əl), *n.* an ornamental hanging placed at the back of an altar or at the sides of the chancel. Also, **dos′sel.** [< ML *dossal(e),* var. of *dorsale,* neut. of L *dorsālis* DORSAL]

dos·ser (dos′ər), *n.* **1.** a basket for carrying objects on the back; pannier. **2.** an ornamental covering for a wall, back of a seat, etc. Also, **dorser.** [ME < AF; MF *dossier* < ML *dosser(ium),* var. of *dorserium* = *dors(um)* back + *-erium* -ERY; r. ME *dorser* < ML *dorser(ium)*]

dos·se·ret (dos′ə ret′), *n.* *Archit.* a supplementary capital or thickened abacus, as in Byzantine architecture. [< F, MF, dim. of DOSSER]

dos·si·er (dos′ē ā′, -ē ər, dô′sē ā′, -sē ər; *Fr.* dô syā′), *n., pl.* **dos·si·ers** (dos′ē āz′, -ē ərz, dô′sē āz′, -sē ərz; *Fr.* dô syā′). a group of documents on the same subject, esp. a complete group containing detailed information. [< F: bundle of documents with a label attached to the back or spine) = *dos* (< L *dorsum*) back + *-ier* -ER[2]]

D, Dosseret (On capital supporting arches)

dost (dust), *v.* *Archaic.* 2nd pers. sing. pres. ind. of **do**[1].

Dos·to·ev·sky (dos′tə yef′skē, -toi-, dus′-; *Russ.* do sto yef′ski), *n.* **Feo·dor Mi·khai·lo·vich** (fyô′dor mi khī′lo vich), 1821–81, Russian novelist. Also, **Dos′to·yev′sky, Dos′to·ev′ski, Dos′to·yev′ski, Dos′toi·ev′ski.**

dot[1] (dot), *n., v.,* **dot·ted, dot·ting.** —*n.* **1.** a minute or small spot; speck. **2.** a small, roundish mark made with or as with a pen. **3.** a small specimen or amount: *a dot of butter.* **4.** *Music.* **a.** a point placed after a note or rest, to indicate that the duration of the note or rest is to be increased one half. **b.** a point placed under or over a note to indicate that it is to be played staccato. **5.** *Telegraphy.* a signal of shorter duration than a dash, used in groups with dashes and spaces to represent letters, as in Morse code. **6. on the dot,** *Informal.* precisely on time; prompt; punctual: *The guests arrived at eight o'clock on the dot.* —*v.t.* **7.** to mark with or as with a dot or dots. **8.** to stud or diversify with or as with dots: *Trees dot the landscape.* **9.** to form or cover with dots. —*v.i.* **10.** to make a dot or dots. **11. dot one's i's and cross one's t's,** to be meticulous or precise. [OE *dott* head of a boil; c. OHG *tutta* nipple; *dit* < OE *dyttan* to stop up (prob. < *dott*)] —**dot′ter,** *n.*

dot[2] (dot, dôt), *n.* *Civil Law.* dowry (def. 1). [< F < L *dōt-* (s. of *dōs*) dower, *dōtāre* to endow, akin to *dāre* to give] —**do·tal** (dōt′əl), *adj.*

dot·age (dō′tij), *n.* **1.** feebleness of mind, esp. resulting from old age; senility. **2.** foolish affection. [ME]

do·tard (dō′tərd), *n.* a person whose mind is feeble, esp. from old age. [ME] —**do′tard·ly,** *adv.*

do·ta·tion (dō tā′shən), *n.* an endowment. [< L *dōtātiōn-* (s. of *dōtātiō*) = *dōtāt(us),* ptp. of *dōtāre* (see DOT[2], -ATE[1]) + *-iōn-* -ION; r. ME *dotacioun* < AF]

dote (dōt), *v.i.,* **dot·ed, dot·ing.** **1.** to bestow excessive love or fondness regularly (usually fol. by *on* or *upon*): *She dotes on her youngest son.* **2.** to be weak-minded, esp. from old age. [ME *dot(i)e(n)* (obs.), *dote* (n.); c. MD *doten;* see DOTTY[1]] —**dot′er,** *n.*

doth (duth), *v.* *Archaic.* 3rd pers. sing. pres. ind. of **do**[1].

Do·than (dō′thən), *n.* a city in SE Alabama. 36,733 (1970).

dot·ing (dō′ting), *adj.* **1.** excessively fond: *doting parents.* **2.** weak-minded, esp. from old age. —**dot′ing·ly,** *adv.* —**dot′ing·ness,** *n.*

dot′ prod′uct, *Math.* See **scalar product.**

dot·ted (dot′id), *adj.* **1.** marked with a dot or dots. **2.** consisting or constructed of dots. **3.** having objects scattered or placed in a random manner (often fol. by *with*): *a landscape dotted with small houses.*

dot′ted swiss′. See under **Swiss muslin.**

dot·ter·el (dot′ər əl), *n.* **1.** any of several plovers, esp. *Eudromias morinellus,* of Europe and Asia, which is easily captured. **2.** *Brit. Dial.* a silly, stupid person; dupe. Also, **dot·trel** (do′trəl). [late ME *dotrelle.* See DOTE, -REL]

dot·tle (dot′əl), *n.* a plug of half-burnt tobacco in the bottom of a pipe after smoking. Also, **dot′tel.** [dial. *dot* small lump (prob. identical with DOT[1]) + -LE]

dot·ty[1] (dot′ē), *adj.,* **-ti·er, -ti·est.** *Informal.* **1.** crazy; eccentric. **2.** feeble or unsteady in gait. [dial. *dot* to confuse (cf. Icel *dotta* to doze, nap, be half asleep) + -Y[1]] —**dot′ti·ly,** *adv.*

dot·ty[2] (dot′ē), *adj.* marked with dots; dotted. [DOT[1] + -Y[1]] —**dot′ti·ness,** *n.*

Dou (dou), *n.* **Ge·rard** (gā′rärt), 1613–75, Dutch painter. Also, **Douw, Dow.**

Dou·ai (do͞o ā′; *Fr.* dwe), *n.* a city in N France, SE of Calais. 50,104 (1962). Also, **Dou·ay′.**

Dou·a·la (do͞o ä′lä), *n.* a seaport in W Cameroon. 150,000 (est. 1964). Also, **Duala.**

Dou′ay Bi′ble (do͞o′ā), an English translation of the Bible, prepared by Roman Catholic scholars from the Vulgate, the New Testament published at Reims in 1582 and the Old Testament at Douai in 1609–10. Also called **Dou′ay Ver′sion.**

dou·ble (dub′əl), *adj., n., v.,* **-bled, -bling,** *adv.* —*adj.* **1.** twice as large, heavy, strong, etc.: *double pay.* **2.** twofold in form, number, extent, etc.: *a double blanket.* **3.** composed of two like parts; paired. **4.** *Bot.* (of flowers) having many more than the normal number of petals. **5.** (of musical instruments) producing a tone an octave lower than indicated in a score. **6.** twofold in character, meaning, or conduct; dual or ambiguous: *a double interpretation.* **7.** deceitful; hypocritical; insincere. **8.** duple, as time or rhythm. **9.** folded in two; having one half folded over the other. —*n.* **10.** something that is twice the usual size, amount, strength, etc. **11.** a duplicate or counterpart; something exactly or closely resembling another: *This dress is the double of that. He is the double of his cousin.* **12.** Also called **double room.** a type of hotel accommodation with a double bed for occupancy by two persons. Cf. **twin** (def. 3). **13.** a fold or plait. **14.** a sudden backward turn; reversal. **15.** a trick or artifice. **16.** a substitute actor or singer; understudy. **17.** *Motion Pictures.* a substitute who performs hazardous feats for a star. **18.** *Theat.* an actor having two roles in one play. **19.** *Baseball.* a base hit that enables a batter to reach second base safely; two-base hit. **20. doubles,** (*construed as sing.*) a game between two pairs of players, as in tennis. **21.** (in bridge or other card games) **a.** a challenge by an opponent that the declarer cannot fulfill his contract, increasing the points to be won or lost. **b.** a hand which warrants such a challenge. **22.** *Bridge.* a conventional bid informing one's partner that a player's hand is of a certain strength. **23.** See **daily double.** **24.** *Bowling.* two strikes in succession. **25.** *Music.* a variation. **26. on the double,** *Informal.* **a.** in double time, as marching troops. **b.** without delay; at once.
—*v.t.* **27.** to make double or twice as great; add an equal amount to: *The baby doubled its weight in a year.* **28.** to bend or fold with or as with one part over another (often fol. by *over, up, back,* etc.): *Double over the edge before sewing. A left jab doubled him up.* **29.** to clench (the fist). **30.** *Naut.* to sail around (a projecting area of land): *to double Cape Horn.* **31.** to pair; couple. **32.** *Music.* to reduplicate by means of a tone in another part, either at the unison or at an octave above or below. **33.** (in bridge and other card games) **a.** to challenge (the bid of an opponent) by making a call that increases the value of tricks to be won or lost. **b.** to challenge the bid of (an opponent). **34.** *Baseball.* **a.** to cause the advance of (a base runner) by a two-base hit. **b.** to cause (a run) to be scored by a two-base hit (often fol. by *in*): *He doubled in the winning run.* **c.** to put out (a base runner) as the second out of a double play.
—*v.i.* **35.** to become double. **36.** to bend or fold (often fol. by *up* or *over*): *to double over with pain.* **37.** to turn back on a course or reverse direction (often fol. by *back*). **38.** to serve in two capacities or in an additional capacity: *The girl doubles as secretary and receptionist.* **39.** *Music.* to play an instrument besides one's regular instrument (usually fol. by *on*): *The saxophonist doubles on drums.* **40.** (in bridge and other card games) to double the bid of an opponent. **41.** *Baseball.* to make a two-base hit. **42.** to double-date. **43. double in brass,** *Slang.* to serve in two capacities; do work different from one's own: *It is a small firm, and everyone doubles in brass when emergencies arise.* **44. double up, a.** to share quarters planned for only one person or family. **b.** to bend over, as from pain.
—*adv.* **45.** twofold; doubly. [ME < OF < L *dupl(us)* = *du(o)* two + *-plus* -FOLD] —**dou′ble·ness,** *n.* —**dou′bler,** *n.*

dou·ble-act·ing (dub′əl ak′ting), *adj.* **1.** (of a reciprocating engine, pump, etc.) having pistons accomplishing work in both directions. Cf. **single-acting.** **2.** having twice the usual effectiveness, strength, use, etc.

dou′ble a′gent, a spy in the service of two rival countries, companies, etc.

dou′ble bar′, *Music.* a double vertical line on a staff indicating the conclusion of a piece of music or a subdivision of it.

dou·ble-bar·reled (dub′əl bar′əld), *adj.* **1.** having two barrels mounted side by side, as a shotgun. **2.** serving a double purpose or having two parts or aspects. **3.** very strong; extremely forceful.

dou′ble bass′ (bās), the largest instrument of the violin family, having three or, usually, four strings, rested vertically on the floor when played. Also called **bass fiddle, bass viol, contrabass, string bass.** —**dou′ble-bass′,** *adj.*

dou′ble bassoon′, a bassoon an octave lower in pitch than the ordinary bassoon: the largest and deepest-toned instrument of the oboe class; contrabassoon.

dou′ble bed′, a bed large enough for two adults.

dou′ble boil′er, a cooking utensil consisting of two pots, one of which fits into the other: water is boiled in the lower pot to cook or warm food in the upper.

dou′ble bond′, *Chem.* a chemical linkage consisting of two covalent bonds between two atoms of a molecule, represented in chemical formulas by two lines, two dots, or four dots, as $CH_2{=}CH_2$, $CH_2{:}CH_2$, or $CH_2{::}CH_2$.

dou·ble-breast·ed (dub′əl bres′tid), *adj.* **1.** (of a coat, jacket, etc.) overlapping sufficiently in front to allow for two rows of buttons. **2.** (of a suit) having a coat or jacket that so overlaps. Cf. **single-breasted.**

dou·ble-check (dub′əl chek′, -chek′), *v.t., v.i.* **1.** to check twice or again; recheck. —*n.* **2.** a second examination or verification to assure accuracy, proper functioning, or the like.

dou′ble chin′, a fold of fat beneath the chin. —**dou′ble-chinned′,** *adj.*

dou′ble cross′, **1.** *Informal.* **a.** a betrayal or swindle of a colleague. **b.** an attempt to win a contest that a person has agreed beforehand to lose. **2.** *Genetics.* a cross in which both parents are first-generation hybrids resulting from single crosses, thus involving four inbred lines.

dou·ble-cross (dub′əl krôs′, -kros′), *v.t. Informal.* to prove treacherous to; betray. —**dou′ble-cross′er,** *n.*
dou′ble dag′ger, *Print.* a mark (‡) used for references, as footnotes. Also called **diesis.**
dou′ble date′, *U.S. Informal.* a date which two couples go on together.
dou·ble-date (dub′əl dāt′), *v.,* **-dat·ed, -dat·ing.** *U.S. Informal.* —*v.i.* **1.** to take part in a double date. —*v.t.* **2.** to accompany (someone) on a double date.
Dou·ble·day (dub′əl dā′), *n.* **Abner,** 1819–93, U.S. army officer and reputed inventor of the game of baseball.
dou·ble-deal·ing (dub′əl dē′ling), *n.* **1.** duplicity; deception. —*adj.* **2.** using duplicity; treacherous. —**dou′ble-deal′er,** *n.*
dou·ble-deck·er (dub′əl dek′ər), *n.* **1.** something with two decks, tiers, or the like, as two beds one above the other, a ship with two decks above the water line, or a bus with two decks. **2.** a food item consisting of two main layers, as a sandwich made with three slices of bread and two layers of filling, a cake of two layers, etc.
dou′ble decomposi′tion, *Chem.* a reaction whose result is the interchange of two parts of two substances to form two new substances, as $AgNO_3 + NaCl \rightarrow AgCl + NaNO_3$. Also called **metathesis.**
dou·ble-dig·it (dub′əl dij′it), *adj.* of or denoting a percentage greater than ten, esp. with reference to rates traditionally below that level: *double-digit inflation.*
dou·ble-dip (dub′əl dip′), *v.i.* **-dipped, -dip·ping.** *Informal.* to earn a salary from one position while collecting a pension from the same employer or organization, esp. to be a wage earner on the federal payroll while receiving a military retiree's pension. —**dou′ble-dip′per,** *n.* —**dou′ble-dip′ping,** *n.*
dou′ble ea′gle, a gold coin of the U.S., issued from 1849 to 1933, equal to 2 eagles or 20 dollars.
dou·ble-edged (dub′əl ejd′), *adj.* **1.** having two cutting edges, as a razor blade or knife. **2.** capable of acting two ways or having opposite effects: *a double-edged argument.*
dou·ble-end·ed (dub′əl en′did), *adj.* **1.** having the two ends alike. **2.** *Naut.* **a.** operating equally well with either end as the bow, as a ferryboat. **b.** noting a vessel having a stern curved or pointed so as to resemble or suggest a bow. **3.** noting a vehicle, as a streetcar, designed to be operated with either end serving as the front.
dou·ble en·ten·dre (dub′əl än tän′drə, -tänd′; *Fr.* do͞o blän tän′drᵊ), *pl.* **dou·ble en·ten·dres** (dub′əl än tän′drəz, -tändz′; *Fr.* do͞o blän tän′drᵊ). **1.** a word or expression with two meanings, one of which is usually risqué. **2.** a double meaning. [< obs. F; see DOUBLE, INTEND]
dou·ble en·tente (do͞o blän tänt′), *pl.* **dou·bles en·tentes** (do͞o blə zän tänt′). *French.* a double meaning; ambiguity.
dou′ble en′try, *Bookkeeping.* a method in which each transaction is entered twice in the ledger, once to the debit of one account, and once to the credit of another. Cf. **single entry.**
dou′ble expo′sure, *Photog.* **1.** the act of exposing the same film, frame, plate, etc., twice. **2.** the resulting picture.
dou′ble fea′ture, a motion-picture program consisting of two features.
dou′ble first′, *Brit. Univ.* **1.** a first in two subjects. **2.** a student who earns a first in two subjects.
dou′ble flat′, *Music.* a symbol (𝄫) that lowers the pitch of the note following it by two semitones.
dou·ble·gang·er (dub′əl gang′ər), *n.* Doppelgänger. [partial trans. of G *Doppelgänger*]
dou·ble·head·er (dub′əl hed′ər), *n.* **1.** *Sports.* two games between the same teams or two different pairs of teams, in immediate succession. **2.** a railroad train pulled by two locomotives.
dou′ble he′lix, the helical arrangement of the two complementary strands that make up the DNA molecules found in chromosomes.
dou·ble-hung (dub′əl hung′), *adj.* (of a window) having two vertically sliding sashes, each closing a different part of the opening.
dou′ble indem′nity, a clause in a life-insurance or accident-insurance policy providing for payment of twice the face value of the policy in the event of accidental death.
dou′ble in′tegral, *Math.* an integral in which the integrand involves a function of two variables and which requires two integrations to evaluate.
dou′ble jeop′ardy, *Law.* the subjecting of a person to a second trial for the same offense the person has already been tried for.
dou·ble-joint·ed (dub′əl join′tid), *adj.* (of people and animals) having unusually flexible joints that can bend in unusual ways or to an abnormally great extent.
dou·ble-knit (dub′əl nit′), *n.* **1.** a weft-knit fabric which consists of two single-knit fabrics intimately interlooped together. **2.** a garment made of such a fabric.
dou′ble mag′num, Jeroboam (def. 2).
dou′ble neg′ative, a syntactic construction in which two negative words are used in the same clause to express a single negation.
—**Usage.** The double negative is today regarded as nonstandard: *He didn't go anywhere* (not *nowhere*). *We don't want any* (not *none*). *They don't ever* (not *never*) *visit us any* (not *no*) *more.*
dou·ble·ness (dub′əl nis), *n.* **1.** the quality or condition of being double. **2.** deception or dissimulation.
dou·ble-park (dub′əl pärk′), *v.t., v.i.* to park alongside another automobile already parked parallel to the curb.
dou′ble play′, *Baseball.* a play in which two put-outs are made.
dou′ble pneumo′nia, *Pathol.* pneumonia affecting both lungs.
dou′ble posses′sive, *Gram.* a possessive consisting of a prepositional phrase with *of* containing a substantive in the possessive case, as *of father's* in *He is a friend of father's.*
dou′ble pur′chase. See **gun tackle.**
dou·ble-quick (*adj., adv.* dub′əl kwik′; *n., v.* dub′əl-kwik′), *adj.* **1.** very quick or rapid. —*adv.* **2.** in a very quick or rapid manner. —*n.* **3.** See **double time.** —*v.t., v.i.* **4.** to double-time.
dou′ble quotes′, quotation marks (" "), as usually appear around quoted material. Cf. **single quotes.**
dou·ble-reed (dub′əl rēd′), *adj. Music.* of or pertaining to wind instruments producing sounds by means of a pair of reeds fastened together, as the oboe.
dou′ble refrac′tion, *Optics.* the separation of a ray of light into two unequally refracted, polarized rays, occurring in crystals in which the velocity of light rays is not the same in all directions. Also called **birefringence.**
dou′ble rhyme′. See under **feminine rhyme.**
dou′ble room′, double (def. 12).
dou′ble salt′, *Chem.* a salt that crystallizes as a single substance but ionizes as two distinct salts when dissolved.
dou′ble sharp′, *Music.* a symbol (× or 𝄪) that raises by two semitones the pitch of the corresponding note.
dou·ble-space (dub′əl spās′), *v.t., v.i.,* **-spaced, -spac·ing.** to typewrite leaving a full space between lines.
dou′ble stand′ard, any set of principles containing different provisions for one group of people than for another, esp. the unwritten code of sexual behavior that permits men more freedom than women.
dou′ble star′, *Astron.* two stars that appear as one if not viewed through a telescope with adequate magnification, such as two stars that are separated by a great distance but are nearly in line with each other and an observer, or those that are relatively close together and comprise a single physical system. Cf. **binary star.**
dou′ble stop′, *Music.* two notes bowed simultaneously on a stringed instrument, as the violin.
dou·ble-stop (dub′əl stop′), *v.,* **-stopped, -stop·ping.** *Music.* —*v.t.* **1.** to play a double stop on (a stringed instrument). —*v.i.* **2.** to play a double stop.
dou·blet (dub′lit), *n.* **1.** a close-fitting jacket, sometimes with a short skirt, worn by men in the Renaissance. **2.** a pair of like things; couple. **3.** one of a pair of like things; duplicate. **4.** one of two or more words in a language that are derived from the same source, as *coy* and *quiet,* both taken from the same Latin word, *quiet* directly, and *coy* by way of Old French. **5.** *Print.* an unintentional repetition in printed matter or proof. **6. doublets,** a throw of a pair of dice in which the same number of spots turns up on each die. **7.** *Jewelry.* a counterfeit gem made of two pieces, either of smaller gemstones, inferior stones, or glass. [ME < MF; see DOUBLE, -ET]

Doublets (def. 1)
Elizabethan period

dou′ble tack′le, a pulley having two grooved wheels.
dou′ble take′, a rapid or surprised second look, either literal or figurative, at a person or situation whose significance had not been completely grasped at first.
dou·ble-talk (dub′əl tôk′), *n.* **1.** speech using nonsense syllables along with words in a rapid patter. **2.** evasive or ambiguous language. —*v.t.* **3.** to accomplish or persuade by double-talk.
dou′ble tape′. See under **magnetic tape.**
dou·ble·think (dub′əl thingk′), *n.* the acceptance as valid of two inconsistent versions of a factual matter at the same time, consciously disciplining the mind to ignore the conflict between them.
dou′ble tide′, agger.
dou′ble time′, **1.** *U.S. Army.* the fastest rate of marching troops, a slow jog in which 180 paces, each of 3 feet, are taken in a minute. **2.** a slow run by troops in step. **3.** a rate of overtime pay that is twice the regular wage rate.
dou·ble-time (dub′əl tīm′), *v.,* **-timed, -tim·ing.** —*v.t.* **1.** to cause to move in double time. —*v.i.* **2.** to move in double time; jog.
dou·ble·ton (dub′əl tən), *n. Chiefly Bridge.* a set of only two cards of the same suit in a hand. [mod. on SINGLETON]
dou·ble-tongue (dub′əl tung′), *v.i.,* **-tongued, -tongu·ing.** *Music.* (in playing a wind instrument) to apply the tongue rapidly to the teeth and the hard palate alternately so as to produce a rapid series of detached notes.
dou·ble-tongued (dub′əl tungd′), *adj.* deceitful; hypocritical. [ME *dowble tungid*]
dou·ble·tree (dub′əl trē′), *n.* a pivoted bar with a whiffletree attached to each end, used in harnessing two horses abreast. See illus. at **whiffletree.** [modeled on SINGLETREE]
dou′ble whip′. See under **whip** (def. 20).
dou·bloon (du blo͞on′), *n.* a former gold coin of Spain and Spanish America, originally equal to two escudos. [< Sp *doblón* = *dobla* a former gold coin + *-ón* aug. suffix]
dou·blure (də blo͝or′, do͞o-; *Fr.* do͞o blyr′), *n., pl.* **-blures** (-blo͝orz′; *Fr.* -blyr′). an ornamental lining of a book cover. [< F: a lining]
dou·bly (dub′lē), *adv.* **1.** to a double measure or degree: *to be doubly cautious.* **2.** in a double manner. **3.** *Obs.* with duplicity. [ME]
Doubs (do͞o), *n.* a river in E France, flowing into the Saône River. ab. 260 mi. long.
doubt (dout), *v.t.* **1.** to be uncertain about; hold questionable; hesitate to believe. **2.** to distrust. **3.** *Archaic.* to fear; be apprehensive about. —*v.i.* **4.** to be uncertain or undecided about something. —*n.* **5.** a feeling of uncertainty about the truth, reality, or nature of something. **6.** distrust. **7.** a state of affairs such as to cause uncertainty. **8.** *Obs.* fear; dread. **9. beyond the shadow of a doubt,** with certainty; definitely. Also, **beyond a doubt, beyond doubt.** [ME *dout(en)* < OF *dout(er)* < L *dubitāre* to waver, hesitate, be uncertain (freq. of OL *dubāre*)] —**doubt′a·ble,** *adj.* —**doubt′a·bly,** *adv.* —**doubt′er,** *n.* —**doubt′ing·ly,** *adv.*
doubt·ful (dout′fəl), *adj.* **1.** admitting of or causing doubt; uncertain. **2.** of uncertain outcome or result. **3.** of equivocal character. **4.** unsettled in opinion or belief; undecided;

hesitating. **5.** unlikely; improbable. [ME *douteful*] —**doubt′ful·ly,** *adv.* —**doubt′ful·ness,** *n.*
—**Syn. 1.** unsure, indeterminate. **2.** undetermined, unsettled, indecisive, dubious, problematic. **3.** shady, questionable. **4.** irresolute, vacillating, hesitant. DOUBTFUL, DUBIOUS imply reluctance or unwillingness to be convinced. To be DOUBTFUL about something is to feel that it is open to question or that more evidence is needed to prove it: *to be doubtful about the statements of witnesses.* DUBIOUS implies greater vacillation, vagueness, or suspicion: *dubious about suggested methods of manufacture, about future plans.*

doubt′ing Thom′as, a person who refuses to believe without proof; skeptic. John 20:24–29.

doubt·less (dout′lis), *adv.* Also, **doubt′less·ly. 1.** without doubt; unquestionably. **2.** probably or presumably. —*adj.* **3.** free from doubt or uncertainty. [ME *douteles*] —**doubt′less·ness,** *n.*

douce (do͞os), *adj. Scot. and North Eng.* sedate; modest; quiet. [ME < OF (fem.) < L *dulci-*, s. of *dulcis* sweet] —**douce′ly,** *adv.* —**douce′ness,** *n.*

dou·ceur (do͞o sûr′; *Fr.* do͞o sœʀ′), *n., pl.* **-ceurs** (-sûrz′; *Fr.* -sœʀ′). **1.** a gratuity; tip. **2.** a conciliatory gift or bribe. **3.** *Archaic.* sweetness; agreeableness. [< F: sweetness < LL *dulcor.* See DOUCE, -OR[1]]

douche (do͞osh), *n., v.,* **douched, douch·ing.** —*n.* **1.** a jet or current of water applied to a body part, organ, or cavity for medicinal or hygienic purposes. **2.** the application of such a jet. **3.** an instrument, as a syringe, for administering it. —*v.t.* **4.** to apply a douche to. —*v.i.* **5.** to use a douche; undergo douching. [< F < It *doccia* water pipe, abstracted from *doccione* big drainpipe (where *-one* was taken as aug. suffix) < L *ductiōn-* (s. of *ductiō*) a leading, conveying]

dough (dō), *n.* **1.** flour or meal combined with water, milk, etc., in a mass for baking into bread, cake, etc.; paste of bread. **2.** any soft, pasty mass. **3.** *Slang.* money. [ME *dowgh*, etc., OE *dāg, dāh;* c. D *deeg*, Icel *deig*, Goth *daigs*, G *Teig*]

dough·boy (dō′boi′), *n. Informal.* **1.** an American infantryman, esp. one in Europe in World War I. **2.** any infantryman. [DOUGH + BOY; prob. so called from the buttons (resembling dumplings, the orig. sense of doughboy) on infantry uniforms in the Civil War]

dough·face (dō′fās′), *n. U.S. Hist.* **1.** (before and during the Civil War) a Northerner sympathetic to the South. **2.** a congressman from a Northern state not opposed to slavery in the South.

dough·nut (dō′nət, -nut′), *n.* **1.** a small, usually ring-shaped cake of sweetened dough fried in deep fat. **2.** anything shaped like a thick ring; an annular object; toroid. Also, **donut.**

dought (dout), *v.* a pt. of **dow.**

dough·ty (dou′tē), *adj.,* **-ti·er, -ti·est.** steadfastly courageous and resolute. [ME; OE *dohtig* worthy = **doht* worth (c. OHG *toht;* see DOW) + *-ig* -Y[1]; r. OE *dyhtig*, c. G *tüchtig*] —**dough′ti·ly,** *adv.* —**dough′ti·ness,** *n.*

dough·y (dō′ē), *adj.,* **dough·i·er, dough·i·est.** of or like dough, esp. in being soft and heavy or pallid and flabby. —**dough′i·ness,** *n.*

Doug·las (dug′ləs), *n.* **1. Sir James** (*"the Black Douglas"*), 1286–1330, Scottish military leader. **2. James, 2nd Earl of,** 1358?–88, Scottish military leader. **3. Stephen A(rnold),** 1813–61, U.S. political leader and statesman. **4. William O(r·ville)** (ôr′vil), 1898–1980, associate justice of the U.S. Supreme Court 1939–75. **5.** a city on and the capital of the Isle of Man: resort. 18,837 (1961).

Doug′las fir′, a coniferous tree, *Pseudotsuga taxifolia* (*P. mucronata* or *P. Douglasii*), of western North America, often over 200 feet high, and yielding a strong, durable timber: the state tree of Oregon. Also called **Doug′las pine′, Doug′las spruce′, Oregon pine.** [named after David *Douglas* (1798–1834), Scottish botanist and traveler in America]

Doug·lass (dug′ləs), *n.* **Frederick,** 1817–95, U.S. ex-slave, abolitionist, and orator.

Dou·kho·bor (do͞o′kō bôr′), *n., pl.* **-bors, -bor·tsy** (-bôrt′sē). a member of a religious sect originating in Russia in the 18th century, believing in the supreme authority of the inner voice, rejecting the establishing of churches, and opposing civil authority. Also, **Dukhobor.** [< Russ *dukhoborets* = *dukh* spirit + *borets* wrestler, contender (*bor-*, s. of *borot'sja* to contend + *-ets* agent suffix)]

dou·ma (do͞o′mä), *n.* duma.

dour (do͝or, dour, dou′ər), *adj.* **1.** sullen; gloomy. **2.** severe; stern. [ME < L *dūr(us)* DURE[1]] —**dour′ly,** *adv.* —**dour′ness,** *n.*

dou·ra (do͝or′ə), *n.* durra. Also, **dou′rah.**

dou·rine (do͝o rēn′), *n. Vet. Pathol.* an infectious disease of horses, affecting the genitals and hind legs, caused by a protozoan parasite, *Trypanosoma equiperdum.* [< F; cf. Ar *darin* scabby]

Dou·ro (*Port.* dō′ʀo͞o), *n.* a river in SW Europe, flowing W from N Spain through N Portugal to the Atlantic. ab. 475 mi. long. Spanish, **Duero.**

douse (dous), *v.,* **doused, dous·ing,** *n.* —*v.t.* **1.** to plunge into water or other liquid; drench. **2.** to splash or throw water or other liquid on. **3.** *Informal.* to extinguish: *She doused the candle flame with her fingertips.* —*v.i.* **4.** to plunge or be plunged into a liquid. —*n.* **5.** *Brit. Dial.* a stroke or blow. Also, **dowse.** [?]

Douw (*Du.* dou), *n.* **Ger·rard** (*Du.* gä′ʀäʀt). See **Dou.**

dove[1] (duv), *n.* **1.** any bird of the family *Columbidae*, usually the smaller species with pointed tails. Cf. **pigeon**[1] (def. 1). **2.** a symbol of peace, innocence, and gentleness. **3.** (*cap.*) a symbol for the Holy Ghost. **4.** an innocent, gentle, or tender person. **5.** Also called **peace dove.** *Informal.* a person, esp. one in public office, who advocates peace or a conciliatory national attitude. [ME; OE *dūfe-* (in *dūfedoppa* dip-diver); c. D *duif*, G *Taube*, Icel *dūfa*, Goth *dūbo*, diver] —**dove′like′,** *adj.* —**dov′ish,** *adj.*

dove[2] (dōv), *v.* a pt. of **dive.**

dove·cote (duv′kōt′), *n.* a structure, usually at a height above the ground, for housing domestic pigeons. Also, **dove·cot** (duv′kot′).

dove·kie (duv′kē), *n.* a small, short-billed, black and white auk, *Plautus alle*, of the northern part of the Atlantic and Arctic oceans. Also, **dove′key.** [DOVE + *-kie* compound suffix (see -OCK, -IE)]

Do·ver (dō′vər), *n.* **1.** a seaport in E Kent, in SE England: point nearest the coast of France. 35,248 (1961). **2. Strait of.** French, **Pas de Calais.** a strait between England and France, connecting the English Channel and the North Sea: least width 20 mi. **3.** a city in and the capital of Delaware, in the central part. 17,488 (1970).

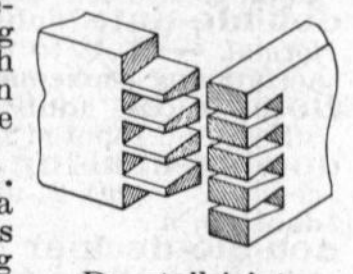
Dovetail joint

dove·tail (duv′tāl′), *n. Carpentry.* **1.** a tenon of tapered cross section. **2.** a joint formed of one or more such tenons fitting tightly within corresponding mortises. —*v.t., v.i.* **3.** *Carpentry.* to join or fit together by means of a dovetail or dovetails. **4.** to join or fit together compactly or harmoniously. [so named from its shape] —**dove′tail′er,** *n.*

dow (dou, dō), *v.i.,* **dowed** or **dought** (dout), **dow·ing.** *Scot. and North Eng.* **1.** to be able. **2.** to thrive; prosper; do well. [ME *dowen, doghen*, OE *dugan* to be worthy; c. G *taugen;* cf. DOUGHTY]

Dow (*Du.* dou), *n.* **Ger·rard** (*Du.* gä′ʀäʀt). See **Dou.**

Dow., dowager. Also, **dow.**

dow·a·ble (dou′ə bəl), *adj. Law.* **1.** subject to the provision of a dower: *dowable land.* **2.** entitled to dower. [< AF; see ENDOW, -ABLE]

dow·a·ger (dou′ə jər), *n.* **1.** a woman who holds some title or property from her deceased husband, esp. the widow of a king, duke, etc. (often used as an additional title to differentiate her from the wife of the present king, duke, etc.): *a queen dowager.* **2.** an elderly woman of stately dignity, esp. one of elevated social position: *a wealthy dowager.* [< MF *douag(i)ere* = *douage* dower (see ENDOW, -AGE) + *-ier* -ER[2]]

Dow·den (doud′ən), *n.* **Edward,** 1843–1913, Irish critic and poet.

dow·dy[1] (dou′dē), *adj.,* **-di·er, -di·est,** *n., pl.* **-dies.** —*adj.* **1.** not neat or stylish; frumpy: *dowdy clothes.* **2.** not smartly done; old-fashioned: *a dowdy apartment.* —*n.* **3.** a dowdy woman. [ME *doude* unattractive woman + -Y[1] or -Y[2]] —**dow′di·ly,** *adv.* —**dow′di·ness,** *n.* —**dow′dy·ish,** *adj.* —**Syn. 1, 2.** shabby. —**Ant. 1.** fashionable, chic.

dow·dy[2] (dou′dē), *n., pl.* **-dies.** pandowdy. [short form]

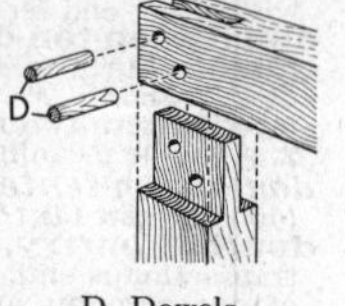

D, Dowels

dow·el (dou′əl), *n., v.,* **-eled, -el·ing** or (*esp. Brit.*) **-elled, -el·ling.** —*n.* **1.** Also called **dow′el pin′.** *Carpentry.* a pin, usually round, fitting into holes in two adjacent pieces to prevent their slipping or to align them. **2.** a round wooden rod of relatively small diameter. —*v.t.* **3.** to reinforce or furnish with a dowel or dowels. [ME *dowle* < MLG *dövel* plug; cf. G *Döbel, Dübel*, OHG *tubili*]

dow·er (dou′ər), *n.* **1.** *Law.* the portion of a deceased husband's real property allowed to his widow for her lifetime. **2.** dowry (def. 1). **3.** a natural gift or endowment. —*v.t.* **4.** to provide with a dower or dowry. **5.** to give as a dower or dowry. [ME *dowere* < OF *do(u)aire* < ML *dō(t)ār-(ium).* See DOT[2], -ARY]

dow·er·y (dou′ə rē), *n., pl.* **-er·ies.** *Rare.* dowry.

dow·itch·er (dou′ich ər), *n.* any of several long-billed, snipelike shore birds of North America, esp. *Limnodromus griseus.* [*dowitch* < Iroquoian (cf. Onondaga *tawish*); see -ER[1]]

down[1] (doun), *adv.* **1.** from higher to lower; in descending direction or order; toward, into, or in a lower position. **2.** on or to the ground, floor, or bottom: *He fell down.* **3.** to or in a sitting or lying position. **4.** to or in a position, area, or district considered geographically lower, as to the south on a map or globe: *We drove down from San Francisco to Los Angeles.* **5.** to or at a lower value or rate. **6.** to a lesser pitch or volume: *Turn down the TV.* **7.** in or to a calmer, less active state. **8.** from an earlier to a later time: *down to the present.* **9.** from a greater to a lesser strength, amount, etc.: *to water down liquor.* **10.** in an attitude of earnest application: *to get down to work.* **11.** on paper or in a book: *Write down the address.* **12.** in cash at the time of purchase; at once: *We paid $40 down.* **13.** to the point of defeat, submission, inactivity, etc.: *They shouted down the opposition.* **14.** to the source or actual position: *The dogs tracked down the bear.* **15.** confined to bed with illness: *He's down with a cold.* **16.** in or into a lower status or condition. **17. down with! a.** on or toward the ground: *Down with your rifles!* **b.** away with! cease!: *Down with tyranny!*
—*prep.* **18.** in a descending or more remote direction or place on, over, or along: *They ran off down the street.*
—*adj.* **19.** going or directed downward. **20.** being at a low position or on the ground, floor, or bottom. **21.** toward, associated with, or serving the south, a business district, etc.: *the down train.* **22.** downcast; dejected. **23.** being the portion of the full price paid at the time of purchase or delivery. **24.** *Football.* (of the ball) not in play. **25.** behind an opponent or opponents in points, games, etc. **26.** *Baseball.* out. **27.** losing or having lost the amount indicated, esp. at gambling: *After an hour at poker, he was down $10.* **28.** finished or done: *five down and one to go.* **29. down and out,** without friends, money, or prospects; destitute. **30. down in the mouth,** discouraged; depressed. **31. down on,** *Informal.* hostile or averse to.
—*n.* **32.** a downward movement; descent. **33.** a turn for the worse; reverse: *The business cycle experienced a sudden down.* **34.** *Football.* **a.** one of a series of four plays during which a team must advance the ball at least 10 yards to keep possession of it. **b.** the declaring of the ball as down or out of play, or the play immediately preceding this. **35.** *Slang.* downer.
—*v.t.* **36.** to cause to fall, esp. to knock, throw, or shoot down: *The boxer downed his opponent in the third round. Antiaircraft guns downed three bombers.* **37.** *Informal.* to defeat in a game or contest: *The Mets downed the Dodgers in today's game.* **38.** to drink down, esp. quickly or in one gulp: *to down a tankard of ale.*
—*v.i.* **39.** (often used imperatively) to get down; go down:

Down, boy! Down! They're shooting at us! [ME *doune,* OE *dūne,* aph. var. of *adūne* for *of dūne* off (the) hill; see DOWN³]

down² (doun), *n.* **1.** the soft, first plumage of many young birds. **2.** the soft under plumage of birds as distinct from the contour feathers. **3.** a growth of soft, fine hair or the like. **4.** *Bot.* **a.** a fine, soft pubescence on plants and some fruits. **b.** the light, feathery pappus or coma on some seeds by which they are borne on the wind, as on the dandelion and thistle. [ME *downe* < Scand; cf. Icel *dūnn*]

down³ (doun), *n.* **1.** *Archaic.* a hill, esp. a sand dune. **2.** Usually, **downs.** (used esp. in southern England) open, rolling, upland country with fairly smooth, grassy slopes. **3.** (*cap.*) any sheep of several breeds, raised originally in the downs of southern England, as the Southdown, Suffolk, etc. [ME: OE *dūn* hill; c. D *duin* DUNE]

Down (doun), *n.* a county in SW Northern Ireland. 311,876; 952 sq. mi. *Co. seat:* Downpatrick.

down-at-heel (doun′at hēl′), *adj.* shabby; run-down; seedy: *He is rapidly becoming a down-at-heel drifter.* Also, **down′at-the-heel′, down′-at-heels′, down′-at-the-heels′.**

down·beat (doun′bēt′), *n.* *Music.* **1.** the downward stroke of a conductor's arm or baton indicating the first or accented beat of a measure. **2.** the first beat of a measure. —*adj.* **3.** *Informal.* gloomy; pessimistic.

down-bow (doun′bō′), *n.* *Music.* (in bowing on a stringed instrument) a stroke bringing the tip of the bow toward the strings, indicated by the symbol ⊓ (opposed to *up-bow*).

down·cast (doun′kast′, -käst′), *adj.* **1.** dejected in spirit; depressed. **2.** directed downward, as the eyes. —*n.* **3.** overthrow or ruin. **4.** a shaft down which air passes, as into a mine (opposed to *upcast*). [ME *douncaste(n)*]

down·come (doun′kum′), *n.* *Archaic.* descent or downfall; comedown. [ME *douncome*]

down·court (doun′kōrt′, -kôrt′), *adv., adj.* *Basketball.* in, into, or toward a team's offensive half of the court.

down′ East′, **1.** New England. **2.** the state of Maine. —**down′-east′er,** *n.*

down·er (dou′nər), *n.* *Slang.* **1.** a depressant or sedative drug, esp. a barbiturate. **2.** a depressing experience, person, or thing.

Dow′ners Grove′ (dou′nərz), a city in NE Illinois, near Chicago. 32,751 (1970).

Dow·ney (dou′nē), *n.* a city in SW California, near Los Angeles. 88,445 (1970).

down·fall (doun′fôl′), *n.* **1.** descent to a lower position or standing; overthrow; ruin. **2.** something causing this. **3.** a fall, as of rain, snow, or the like, often sudden or heavy. **4.** a trap using a falling weight for killing or imprisoning the prey. [ME] —**down′fall′en,** *adj.*

down·grade (doun′grād′), *n., adj., adv., v.,* **-grad·ed, -grad·ing.** —*n.* **1.** a downward slope, esp. of a road. **2.** **on the downgrade,** falling from success, wealth, etc.; failing. —*adj., adv.* **3.** downhill. —*v.t.* **4.** to reduce in rank, income, etc. **5.** to minimize the importance of; denigrate.

down·haul (doun′hôl′), *n.* *Naut.* a line for pulling or holding down a sail or boom.

down·heart·ed (doun′här′tid), *adj.* dejected; depressed; discouraged. —**down′heart′ed·ly,** *adv.* —**down′heart′ed·ness,** *n.* —**Syn.** downcast, disheartened.

down·hill (doun′hil′), *adv.* **1.** down the slope of a hill; downward. **2.** into a worse condition. —*adj.* **3.** going or tending downward on or as on a hill.

Down′ing Street′ (dou′ning), a street in W central London, England: government offices; residence of the prime minister.

down′ pay′ment, an initial amount paid at the time of purchase, in installment buying, time sales, etc. Also, **down′-pay′ment.**

down·play (doun′plā′), *v.t.* to treat or speak of (something) so as to reduce its importance, value, strength, etc.

down·pour (doun′pōr′, -pôr′), *n.* a heavy, drenching rain.

down·range (*adj.* doun′rānj′; *adv.* doun′rānj′), *adj., adv.* *Rocketry.* in the designated path from a launch pad to the point taken as the target.

down·right (doun′rīt′), *adj.* **1.** thorough; absolute; out-and-out. **2.** frankly direct; straightforward. **3.** *Archaic.* directed straight downward: *a downright blow.* —*adv.* **4.** completely or thoroughly. [ME] —**down′right′ness,** *n.*

Downs (dounz), *n.* **the, 1.** a range of low ridges in S and SW England. **2.** a roadstead in the Strait of Dover, between SE England and Goodwin Sands.

down·shift (doun′shift′), *v.i.* **1.** to shift the automobile transmission into a lower gear. —*n.* **2.** the act or instance of downshifting.

down·size (doun′sīz′), *v.,* **-sized, -siz·ing,** *adj.* —*v.t.* **1.** to design and manufacture a smaller version of (a standard product, such as a car). —*adj.* **2.** Also, **down·sized** (doun′sīzd′). being or of a smaller version: *a downsized car.* [DOWN¹ + SIZE (v.)]

down·spout (doun′spout′), *n.* a pipe for conveying rain water from a roof or gutter to the ground or to a drain. Also called **drainspout.**

Down's′ syn′drome (dounz), *Pathol.* the abnormal condition of a child born with a wide, flattened skull, epicanthic folds at the eyelids, and usually a moderate to severe mental deficiency and other organic problems: caused by a chromosomal abnormality. Formerly, **Mongolism.** [named after J.L.H. *Down* (1828–96), English physician]

down·stage (*adv., n.* doun′stāj′; *adj.* doun′stāj′), *Theat.* —*adv.* **1.** at or toward the front of the stage. —*adj.* **2.** of or pertaining to the front of the stage. —*n.* **3.** the front half of the stage.

down·stairs (*adv., n.* doun′stârz′; *adj.* doun′stârz′), *adv.* **1.** down the stairs. **2.** to or on a lower floor. —*adj.* **3.** Also, **down′stair′.** pertaining to or situated on a lower floor, esp. the ground floor. —*n.* **4.** (*construed as sing.*) the lower floor or floors of a building.

down·state (*n., adv.* doun′stāt′; *adj.* doun′stāt′), *U.S.* —*n.* **1.** the southern part of a state. —*adj.* **2.** located in or characteristic of this part. —*adv.* **3.** in, to, or into the downstate area. —**down′stat′er,** *n.*

down·stream (doun′strēm′), *adv.* with or in the direction of the current of a stream.

down·swing (doun′swing′), *n.* **1.** a downward swing, as of a golf club in driving a ball. **2.** a downward trend or decrease, as of business, a nation's birth rate, etc.

down·throw (doun′thrō′), *n.* a throwing down or being thrown down; overthrow.

down·time (doun′tīm′), *n.* an interval during which a machine is not productive, as during loading, maintenance, repairs, or the like.

down-to-earth (doun′to͞o ûrth′, -tə-), *adj.* practical and realistic.

down·town (doun′toun′), *adv.* **1.** to or in the central business section of a city. —*adj.* **2.** of, pertaining to, or situated in the central business section of a city. —*n.* **3.** the central business section of a city. —**down′town′er,** *n.*

down·trod·den (doun′trod′ən), *adj.* **1.** tyrannized over; oppressed. **2.** trodden down; trampled. Also, **down′trod′.**

down·turn (doun′tûrn′), *n.* **1.** an act or instance of turning down or the state of being turned down. **2.** a turn or trend downward; decline. [n. use of v. phrase *turn down*]

down′ un′der, *Informal.* Australia or New Zealand.

down·ward (doun′wərd), *adv.* **1.** Also, **down′wards.** from a higher to a lower place or condition. **2.** down from a source or beginning. **3.** from a past time, predecessor, or ancestor. —*adj.* **4.** moving or tending to a lower place or condition. **5.** descending from a source or beginning. [ME *dounward*] —**down′ward·ly,** *adv.* —**down′ward·ness,** *n.*

down′ward mobil′ity. See under **vertical mobility** (def. 1).

down·wind (doun′wind′), *adv.* **1.** in the same direction that the wind is blowing. **2.** on or toward the lee side.

down·y (dou′nē), *adj.,* **down·i·er, down·i·est.** **1.** of or resembling down; fluffy; soft. **2.** made of or covered with down. —**down′i·ness,** *n.*

down′y mil′dew, **1.** any fungus of the family *Peronosporaceae,* which causes many plant diseases and produces a white, downy mass of conidiophores, usually on the undersurface of the leaves of the host plant. **2.** *Plant Pathol.* a disease caused by any of several fungi of the family *Peronosporaceae,* as of the genera *Peronospora* and *Phytophthora.*

dow·ry (dou′rē), *n., pl.* **-ries.** **1.** Also, **dower.** the money, goods, or estate that a woman brings to her husband at marriage. **2.** a natural gift, endowment, talent, etc. **3.** *Obs.* a widow's dower. Also, *Rare,* **dowery.** [ME *dowerie* < AF]

dow·sa·bel (dou′sə bel′), *n.* *Obs.* sweetheart. [< L *Dulcibella* woman's name. See DULCET, BELLE]

dowse¹ (dous), *v.t., v.i.,* **dowsed, dows·ing,** *n.* douse.

dowse² (douz), *v.i.,* **dowsed, dows·ing.** to search for underground supplies of water, metal, etc., by the use of a divining rod. [?] —**dows′er,** *n.*

dows′ing rod′ (dou′zing). See **divining rod.**

Dow·son (dou′sən), *n.* **Ernest (Christopher),** 1867–1900, English poet.

dox·ol·o·gy (dok sol′ə jē), *n., pl.* **-gies.** **1.** a hymn or form of words containing an ascription of praise to God. **2.** **the Doxology,** the metrical formula beginning "Praise God from whom all blessings flow." [< ML *doxologia* < Gk = *doxo-* (comb. form of *dóxa* honor, glory) + *-logia* -LOGY] —**dox·o·log·i·cal** (dok′sə loj′i kəl), *adj.* —**dox′o·log′i·cal·ly,** *adv.*

dox·y¹ (dok′sē), *n., pl.* **dox·ies.** **1.** opinion; doctrine. **2.** religious views. Also, **dox′ie.** [from (ORTHO)DOXY, etc.]

dox·y² (dok′sē), *n., pl.* **dox·ies.** *Slang.* **1.** a mistress or paramour. **2.** a prostitute. [< MFlem *docke* doll + *-sy,* affectionate dim. suffix]

doy·en (doi en′, doi′ən; *Fr.* dwa yan′), *n., pl.* **doy·ens** (doi enz′, doi′enz; *Fr.* dwa yan′). the senior member, as in age or rank, of a group, class, etc. [< F; see DEAN]

doy·enne (doi en′; *Fr.* dwa yen′), *n., pl.* **doy·ennes** (doi enz′; *Fr.* dwa yen′). a female doyen. [< F]

Doyle (doil), *n.* **Sir Arthur Co·nan** (kō′nən, kō′-), 1859–1930, British physician, novelist, and detective-story writer.

doy·ley (doi′lē), *n., pl.* **-leys.** doily.

D'Oy·ly Carte (doi′lē kärt′), **Richard,** 1844–1901, English theatrical producer.

doz., dozen; dozens.

doze (dōz), *v.,* **dozed, doz·ing,** *n.* —*v.i.* **1.** to sleep lightly, fitfully, or for a brief period. **2.** to fall into a light sleep unintentionally (often fol. by *off*). **3.** to be half asleep. —*v.t.* **4.** to pass or spend (time) in drowsiness (often fol. by *away*): *He dozed away the afternoon.* —*n.* **5.** a light or fitful sleep. [< Scand; cf. obs. Dan *daase* to be idle, OIcel *dūsi* lazy, sleepy, dull person, Icel *dosa,* c. *dasa* to exhaust, tire out; cf. DAZE] —**doz′er,** *n.*

doz·en (duz′ən), *n., pl.* **doz·ens,** (*as after a numeral*) **doz·en,** *adj.* —*n.* **1.** a group of twelve. —*adj.* **2.** twelve. [ME *dozeine* < OF *do(u)zaine*]

doz·enth (duz′ənth), *adj.* twelfth.

doz·y (dō′zē), *adj.,* **doz·i·er, doz·i·est.** drowsy; half asleep. —**doz′i·ly,** *adv.* —**doz′i·ness,** *n.*

D/P, documents against payment.

D.P., See **displaced person.** Also, **DP**

dpt., **1.** department. **2.** deponent.

D.P.W., Department of Public Works.

dr, door.

Dr, *Chiefly Brit.* Doctor.

Dr., **1.** Doctor. **2.** Drive (used in street names).

dr., **1.** debit. **2.** debtor. **3.** drachma; drachmas. **4.** dram; drams. **5.** drawer. **6.** drum.

drab¹ (drab), *n., adj.,* **drab·ber, drab·best.** —*n.* **1.** dull gray; dull brownish or yellowish gray. **2.** any of several fabrics of this color, esp. of thick wool or cotton. —*adj.* **3.** having a drab color. **4.** dull; cheerless. [< MF *drap* < LL *drapp(us)* piece of cloth] —**drab′ly,** *adv.* —**drab′ness,** *n.*

drab² (drab), *n., v.,* **drabbed, drab·bing.** —*n.* **1.** a dirty, untidy woman; slattern. **2.** a prostitute. —*v.i.* **3.** to associate with drabs. [?; cf. D *drab* dregs, lees, obs. D *drablen* to run or tramp about, Ir *drabóg* slattern = *drab* spot, stain + *-óg* n. suffix; see DRABBLE, DRAFF]

drab·bet (drab′it), *n.* a coarse, drab linen. [DRAB¹ + -ET]

drab·ble (drab′əl), *v.t., v.i.,* **-bled, -bling.** to draggle; make or become wet and dirty. [ME *drabele(n)* < MLG *drabbeln* to bespatter = *drabbe* liquid mud + *-eln* -LE]

dra·cae·na (drə sē′nə), *n.* **1.** any liliaceous tree of the genus *Dracaena*, of tropical regions. **2.** any tree of the closely related genus *Cordyline*. [< NL < Gk *drákaina*, fem. of *drákōn* DRAGON]

drachm[1] (dram), *n.* *Brit.* a dram in apothecaries' and troy weights, and sometimes in avoirdupois weights. [learned sp. of DRAM]

drachm[2] (dram), *n.* drachma.

drach·ma (drak′mə), *n., pl.* **-mas, -mae** (-mē). **1.** a cupronickel coin and monetary unit of modern Greece, equal to 100 lepta. *Abbr.:* dr., drch. **2.** the principal silver coin of ancient Greece. **3.** a small unit of weight in ancient Greece, approximately equivalent to the U.S. and British apothecaries' dram. **4.** any of various modern weights, esp. a dram. [< L < Gk *drachmḗ*, prob. = *drach-* root of *drássesthai* to grasp + *-mē* n. suffix (hence, lit., handful)]

Dra·co (drā′kō), *n.* a late 7th-century B.C. Athenian statesman noted for the severity of his code of laws. Also called **Dra·con** (drā′kon).

Dra·co (drā′kō), *n., gen.* **Dra·co·nis** (drā kō′nis). *Astron.* the Dragon, a northern circumpolar constellation between Ursa Major and Cepheus. [< L < Gk *drákō(n)* DRAGON]

Dra·co·ni·an (drā kō′nē ən), *adj.* **1.** of, pertaining to, or characteristic of Draco or his code of laws. **2.** (*sometimes l.c.*) rigorous; unusually severe or cruel: *Draconian forms of punishment.* Also, **Draconic.** [< L *Dracōn-* (s. of *Draco*) + -IAN] —**Dra·co′ni·an·ism,** *n.*

dra·con·ic (drā kon′ik), *adj.* of or like a dragon. [< L *dracōn-* (s. of *dracō*) DRAGON + -IC] —**dra·con′i·cal·ly,** *adv.*

Dra·con·ic (drā kon′ik), *adj.* (*sometimes l.c.*) Draconian. [< L *Dracōn-* (s. of *Draco*) + -IC] —**Dra·con′i·cal·ly,** *adv.*

draff (draf), *n.* dregs, as in a brewing process; lees; refuse. [ME *draf;* c. Icel, D *draf;* akin to D *drab* (see DRAB[2]), G *Treber* draff] —**draff′y,** *adj.*

draft (draft, dräft), *n.* **1.** a drawing, sketch, or design. **2.** a first or preliminary form of any writing, subject to revision, copying, etc. **3.** act of drawing; delineation. **4.** a current of air in any enclosed space, esp. in a room, chimney, or stove. **5.** a device for regulating the current of air in a stove, fireplace, etc. **6.** a selection or drawing of persons for military service; levy. **7.** the act of drawing or pulling loads. **8.** that which is drawn or pulled; a haul. **9.** an animal or team of animals used to pull a load. **10.** the force required to pull a load. **11.** the taking of supplies, forces, money, etc., from a given source. **12.** a written order drawn by one person upon another for payment of money; bill of exchange. **13.** a drain or demand made on anything. **14.** draught (defs. 1–4). **15.** *Naut.* the depth to which a vessel is immersed when bearing a given load. **16.** *Foundry.* the slight taper given to a pattern so that it may be drawn from the sand without injury to the mold. **17.** *Masonry.* a line or border chiseled at the edge of a stone, to serve as a guide in leveling the surfaces. **18.** *Chiefly Brit.* a short stream or creek. **19.** *Obs.* an allowance granted to a buyer for waste of goods sold by weight. **20. on draft,** available to be drawn from a cask: *imported beer on draft.* —*v.t.* **21.** to draw the outlines or plan of; sketch. **22.** to draw up in written form; compose. **23.** to draw or pull. **24.** *U.S.* to take or select by draft, esp. for military service. —*adj.* **25.** used or suited for drawing loads: *a draft ox.* **26.** drawn or available to be drawn from a cask or tasting as if it comes from a cask: *draft beer.* **27.** being a tentative or preliminary outline, version, design, or sketch. Also, *esp. Brit.,* **draught** (for defs. 1, 3–5, 7–10, 15–27). [later sp. of DRAUGHT] —**draft′er,** *n.* —**draft′a·ble,** *adj.*

draft′ board′, *U.S.* a board of civilians responsible for selecting men for military service.

draft′ dodg′er, a person who evades or attempts to evade compulsory military service.

draft·ee (draf tē′, dräf-), *n.* a person who is drafted into military service. Cf. **enlistee** (def. 1).

draft′ horse′, a horse used for pulling heavy loads.

drafts·man (drafts′mən, dräfts′-), *n., pl.* **-men. 1.** a person employed in making mechanical drawings, as of machines, structures, etc. **2.** a person who draws sketches, plans, or designs. **3.** an artist exceptionally skilled in drawing. **4.** a person who draws up documents. **5.** draughtsman (def. 1). Also, **draughtsman** (for defs. 1–4). —**drafts′man·ship′,** *n.*

draft·y (draf′tē, dräf′-), *adj.,* **draft·i·er, draft·i·est.** characterized by or admitting drafts of air. Also, **draughty.** —**draft′i·ly,** *adv.* —**draft′i·ness,** *n.*

drag (drag), *v.,* **dragged, drag·ging,** *n., adv., adj.* —*v.t.* **1.** to draw with force, effort, or difficulty; pull heavily or slowly along; haul; trail. **2.** to search or catch with a drag, grapnel, or the like. **3.** to level and smooth (land) with a drag or harrow. **4.** to introduce or bring in, as an irrelevant matter. **5.** to protract (something) or pass (time) tediously or painfully (often fol. by *out* or *on*): *They dragged the discussion out for three hours.* —*v.i.* **6.** to be drawn or hauled along. **7.** to trail on the ground. **8.** to move heavily or with effort. **9.** to proceed or pass with tedious slowness. **10.** to lag behind. **11.** to use a drag or grapnel; dredge. —*n.* **12.** *Naut.* any device for dragging the bottom of a body of water to recover or detect objects. **13.** a heavy harrow. **14.** *Slang.* **a.** a painfully boring person. **b.** something tedious; a bore. **15.** a stout sledge or sled. **16.** *Aeron.* the aerodynamic force exerted on an airfoil, airplane, or other aerodynamic body, that tends to retard its forward motion. **17.** a four-horse sporting and passenger coach with seats inside and on top. **18.** anything that retards progress. **19.** the act of dragging. **20.** slow, laborious movement or procedure; retardation. **21.** *Informal.* a puff or inhalation on a cigarette, pipe, etc. **22.** *Hunting.* **a.** the scent left by a fox or other animal. **b.** something, as aniseed, dragged over the ground to leave an artificial scent. **c.** Also called **drag hunt.** a hunt, esp. a fox hunt, in which the hounds follow an artificial scent. **23.** *Angling.* **a.** a brake on a fishing reel. **b.** the sideways pull on a fishline, as caused by a cross current. **24.** *Slang.* transvestite attire. **25.** *Slang.* a girl whom one escorts to a dance, party, etc.; date. **26.** *U.S. Slang.* See **drag race.** —*adv.* **27.** with a girl: *Are you going stag or drag?* —*adj.* **28.** *Slang.* of, noting, or pertaining to transvestites or transvestite attire. [both n. and v. prob. < MLG *dragge* grapnel, *draggen* to dredge < *drag-* DRAW]

dra·gée (dra zhā′), *n.* **1.** a piece of sugar-coated candy. **2.** a small, beadlike piece of candy used for decorating cakes. **3.** a sugar-coated medicine. [< F; see DREDGE[2]]

drag·ger (drag′ər), *n.* **1.** *U.S.* any of various small motor trawlers. **2.** a person or thing that drags.

drag·ging (drag′ing), *adj.* **1.** extremely tired or slow; lethargic; sluggish. **2.** tediously slow in progressing, terminating, etc. **3.** used in dragging, hoisting, etc. —**drag′ging·ly,** *adv.*

drag·gle (drag′əl), *v.,* **-gled, -gling.** —*v.t.* **1.** to soil by dragging over damp ground or in mud. —*v.i.* **2.** to trail on the ground; be or become draggled. **3.** to follow slowly.

drag·gle·tail (drag′əl tāl′), *n.* **1.** a dirty, untidy person. **2.** slut; slattern.

drag·gle·tailed (drag′əl tāld′), *adj.* **1.** untidy; bedraggled. **2.** sluttish. **3.** having bedraggled clothes.

drag·hound (drag′hound′), *n.* a hound for use in following a hunting drag.

drag′ hunt′, drag (def. 22c).

drag·line (drag′līn′), *n.* **1.** a rope dragging from something. **2.** an excavating machine having a bucket that is dropped from a boom and dragged toward the machine by a cable.

drag′ link′, a link connecting cranks on parallel shafts.

drag·net (drag′net′), *n.* **1.** a net to be drawn along the bottom of a river, pond, etc., or along the ground, to catch fish, small game, etc. **2.** a system or network for finding or catching someone, as a criminal by the police. [OE *drægnet*]

drag·o·man (drag′ə mən), *n., pl.* **-mans, -men.** (in the Near East) a professional interpreter. [< F; r. ME *drogman* < MF *drog(o)man, dragoman* < OIt *dragomann(o)* < MGk *dragómanos* < Ar *targumān* interpreter]

drag·on (drag′ən), *n.* **1.** a fabulous monster variously represented, generally as a huge, winged reptile, often spouting fire. **2.** *Bible.* a large animal, possibly a large snake or crocodile. **3.** a fierce, violent person. **4.** a very watchful and strict female chaperon; duenna. **5.** *Bot.* any of several araceous plants, as *Arisaema Dracontium* **(green dragon),** the flowers of which have a long, slender spadix and a green, shorter spathe. **6.** a short musket carried by a mounted infantryman in the 16th and 17th centuries. **7.** *Mil. Slang.* a heavy vehicle for transporting a tank. **8.** (*cap.*) *Astron.* the constellation Draco. **9.** *Archaic.* a huge serpent or snake. [ME < OF < L *dracōn-* (s. of *dracō*) < Gk *drákōn* kind of serpent, prob. orig. epithet, the (sharp-) sighted one, akin to *dérkesthai* to look] —**drag′on·ish,** *adj.*

drag·on·ess (drag′ə nis), *n.* a female dragon.

drag·on·et (drag′ə net′, drag′ə nit), *n.* any small, usually brightly colored, shore fish of the genus *Callionymus.* [ME < MF]

drag·on·fly (drag′ən flī′), *n., pl.* **-flies.** any of numerous stout-bodied, harmless insects of the order *Odonata* (suborder *Anisoptera*) that prey on other insects, and are distinguished from the damselflies by the horizontal position of the wings at rest.

Dragonfly,
Plathemis lybia
(Length 1½ in.;
wingspread 2½ in.)

drag·on·head (drag′ən hed′), *n.* any of several mints of the genus *Dracocephalum.* Also, **drag′on's head′.** [trans. of NL *Dracocephalum*]

drag′on la′dy, (*often caps.*) *Informal.* a ruthless, aggressive, and powerful woman, esp. in the Orient.

drag′on liz′ard. See **Komodo dragon.**

drag′on's blood′, a deep-red resin formerly used in medicine, now used chiefly in the preparation of varnishes.

drag′on tree′, a liliaceous tree, *Dracaena Draco,* of the Canary Islands, yielding a variety of dragon's blood.

dra·goon (drə go͞on′), *n.* **1.** a cavalryman of a heavily armed troop. **2.** a member of a military unit formerly composed of such cavalrymen, as in the British army. **3.** a mounted infantryman armed with a short musket. —*v.t.* **4.** to set dragoons or soldiers upon; persecute by armed force; oppress. **5.** to force by rigorous and oppressive measures; coerce. [< F *dragon,* special use of *dragon* DRAGON, applied first to a pistol hammer (because of its shape), then to the firearm, then to troops so armed] —**dra·goon′age,** *n.*

drag′ race′, *U.S. Slang.* a short race between two or more automobiles starting from a standstill, the winner being the car that can accelerate the fastest. Also called **drag.** —**drag′ rac′er.** —**drag′ rac′ing.**

drag·rope (drag′rōp′), *n.* **1.** a rope for dragging something, as a piece of artillery. **2.** a rope dragging from something, as the guide rope from a balloon.

drag′ strip′, a straight, paved area or course where drag races are held.

drain (drān), *v.t.* **1.** to withdraw or draw off (a liquid) gradually; remove slowly or by degrees, as by filtration. **2.** to withdraw liquid gradually from; empty by drawing off liquid: *to drain a crankcase.* **3.** to draw off or take away completely. **4.** to deprive of possessions, resources, spiritual strength, etc., by gradual withdrawal or exhaustion; exhaust. —*v.i.* **5.** to flow off gradually. **6.** to become empty or dry by the gradual flowing off of liquid or moisture. —*n.* **7.** that by which anything is drained, as a pipe or conduit. **8.** *Surg.* a material or appliance for maintaining the opening of a wound to permit free exit of fluid contents. **9.** gradual or continuous outflow or expenditure. **10.** that which causes such an outflow or expenditure. **11.** the act of draining. **12.** *Phys. Geog.* **a.** an artificial watercourse, as a ditch or trench. **b.** a natural watercourse modified to increase its flow of water. **13. go down the drain,** to become worthless or profitless. [ME *dreyne,* OE *drēhn(ian), drēahnian* to strain, filter; akin to DRY] —**drain′a·ble,** *adj.* —**drain′er,** *n.*

drain·age (drā′nij), *n.* **1.** the act or process of draining. **2.** a system of drains, artificial or natural. **3.** See **drainage basin. 4.** that which is drained off. **5.** *Surg.* the drainage of fluids, as bile, urine, etc., from the body, or of pus and other diseased products from a wound.

drain′age ba′sin, the area drained by a river and all its tributaries. Also called **drain′age ar′ea.**

drain·board (drān′bōrd′, -bôrd′), *n.* a working surface beside or on a kitchen sink, formed and inclined to drain into the sink.

drain·pipe (drān′pīp′), *n.* a large pipe that carries away the discharge of soil pipes, waste pipes, etc.

drain·spout (drān′spout′), *n.* downspout.

drake[1] (drāk), *n.* a male duck. Cf. **duck**[1] (def. 2). [ME; c. LG *drake,* dial. HG *drache;* cf. OHG *(an)trahho, (anu)-trehho* male duck]

drake[2] (drāk), *n.* **1.** a small cannon, used esp. in the 17th and 18th centuries. **2.** *Obs.* a dragon. [ME; OE *drac(a)* < L *dracō* DRAGON]

Drake (drāk), *n.* **Sir Francis,** c1540–96, English admiral and explorer: sailed around the world 1577–80.

Dra·kens·berg (drä′kənz bûrg′), *n.* a mountain range in the E Republic of South Africa: highest peak, 10,988 ft. Also called **Quathlamba.**

Drake′ Pas′sage, a strait between S South America and the South Shetland Islands, connecting the Atlantic and Pacific oceans.

dram (dram), *n., v.,* **drammed, dram·ming.** —*n.* **1.** a unit of apothecaries' weight, equal to 60 grains, or 1/8 ounce. **2.** 1/16 ounce, avoirdupois weight (27.34 grains). **3.** See **fluid dram. 4.** a small drink of liquor. **5.** a small quantity of anything. —*v.i.* **6.** *Archaic.* to drink drams; tipple. —*v.t.* **7.** *Archaic.* to ply with drink. [ME *dramme,* assimilated var. of *dragme* < OF < LL *dragma,* L *drachma* DRACHMA]

dra·ma (drä′mə, dram′ə), *n.* **1.** a composition in prose or verse presenting in dialogue or pantomime a story involving conflict or contrast of character, esp. one intended to be acted on the stage; a play. **2.** the branch of literature having such compositions as its subject; dramatic art or representation. **3.** the art dealing with the writing and production of plays. **4.** any series of events having vivid, emotional, conflicting, or striking interest or results: *the drama of a murder trial.* [< LL < Gk: action (of a play) = *drâ(n)* to do + *-ma* n. suffix]

Dram·a·mine (dram′ə mēn′), *n. Pharm., Trademark.* dimenhydrinate.

dra·mat·ic (drə mat′ik), *adj.* **1.** of or pertaining to the drama. **2.** employing the form or manner of the drama. **3.** characteristic of or appropriate to the drama, esp. in involving conflict or contrast of character; vivid; moving. **4.** highly effective; striking. [< LL *drāmatic(us)* < Gk *drāmatikós* = *drāmat-* (s. of *drâma*) DRAMA + *-ikos* -IC] —**dra·mat′i·cal·ly,** *adv.* —**Syn. 1.** theatrical. **4.** startling, sensational.

dramat′ic i′rony, *Theat.* an irony derived from the audience's understanding of a speech or a situation not grasped by the characters in a dramatic work.

dramat′ic mon′ologue, a poetic form in which a single character, addressing a silent auditor at a critical moment, reveals himself and the dramatic situation.

dra·mat·ics (drə mat′iks), *n.* **1.** (*construed as sing. or pl.*) the art of producing or acting dramas. **2.** (*construed as pl.*) dramatic productions, esp. by amateurs. **3.** (*construed as pl.*) dramatic, overemotional, or insincere behavior.

dram·a·tise (dram′ə tīz′, drä′mə-), *v.t.,* **-tised, -tis·ing.** *Chiefly Brit.* dramatize. —**dram′a·tis′a·ble,** *adj.* —**dram′-a·tis′er,** *n.*

dram·a·tis per·so·nae (dram′ə tis pər sō′nē, drä′mə-), **1.** (*construed as pl.*) the characters in a play. **2.** (*construed as sing.*) a list of the characters preceding the text of a play. [< L: characters of the play]

dram·a·tist (dram′ə tist, drä′mə-), *n.* a writer of dramas or dramatic poetry; playwright. [< Gk *drāmat-* (see DRAMATIC) + -IST]

dram·a·ti·za·tion (dram′ə ti zā′shən, drä′mə- *or, esp. Brit.,* -tī-), *n.* **1.** the act of dramatizing. **2.** construction or representation in dramatic form. **3.** a dramatized version of a novel, a historic incident, etc. Also, *esp. Brit.,* **dram′a-ti·sa′tion.**

dram·a·tize (dram′ə tīz′, drä′mə-), *v.t.,* **-tized, -tiz·ing. 1.** to put into a form suitable for acting on a stage. **2.** to express or represent vividly, emotionally, or strikingly. Also, *esp. Brit.,* **dramatise.** [< Gk *drāmat-* (see DRAMATIC) + -IZE] —**dram′a·tiz′a·ble,** *adj.* —**dram′a·tiz′er,** *n.*

dram·a·turge (dram′ə tûrj′, drä′mə-), *n.* a dramatist. Also, **dram′a·tur′gist.** [? back formation from DRAMATURGY, but cf. F *dramaturge,* G *Dramaturg*]

dram·a·tur·gy (dram′ə tûr′jē, drä′mə-), *n.* **1.** the craft or the techniques of dramatic composition considered collectively. **2.** the dramatic art. [< Gk *drāmatourgía* dramatic composition = *drāmatourg(ós)* playwright + *-ia* -Y[3]. See DRAMATIC, -URGY] —**dram′a·tur′gic, dram′a·tur′gi·cal,** *adj.* —**dram′a·tur′gi·cal·ly,** *adv.* —**dram′a·tur′gist,** *n.*

dram·mock (dram′ək), *n. Chiefly Scot.* an uncooked mixture of meal, usually oatmeal, and cold water. [cf. Gael *dramag* foul mixture]

dram. pers., See **dramatis personae.**

dram·shop (dram′shop′), *n. Archaic.* barroom.

drank (draŋk), *v.* a pt. and pp. of **drink.**

drape (drāp), *v.,* **draped, drap·ing,** *n.* —*v.t.* **1.** to cover or hang with cloth or other fabric, esp. in graceful folds; adorn with drapery. **2.** to adjust (curtains, clothes, etc.) into graceful folds, attractive lines, etc. **3.** to arrange, hang, or let fall carelessly. —*v.i.* **4.** to hang, fall, or become arranged in folds, as drapery: *This silk drapes well.* —*n.* **5.** a draped curtain or hanging. **6.** manner or style of hanging: *the drape of a skirt.* [late ME < MF *drap(er)* < *drap* cloth (see DRAB[1])] —**drap′a·ble, drape′a·ble,** *adj.*

drap·er (drā′pər), *n. Brit.* **1.** a dealer in cloth; a retail merchant or clerk who sells piece goods. **2.** a retail merchant or clerk who sells clothing and dry goods. [ME < AF; OF *drapier*]

Dra·per (drā′pər), *n.* **1. Henry,** 1837–82, U.S. astronomer. **2.** his father, **John William,** 1811–82, U.S. chemist, physiologist, historian, and writer; born in England.

dra·per·y (drā′pə rē), *n., pl.* **-per·ies. 1.** coverings, hangings, clothing, etc., of fabric, esp. as arranged in loose, graceful folds. **2.** long curtains, usually of heavy fabric and often designed to open and close across a window. **3.** the draping or arranging of hangings, clothing, etc., in graceful folds. **4.** cloths or textile fabrics collectively. **5.** *Brit.* **a.** See **dry goods. b.** the stock, shop, or business of a draper. [ME *draperie* < OF] —**dra′per·ied,** *adj.*

dras·tic (dras′tik), *adj.* **1.** acting with force or violence; violent. **2.** extremely severe or extensive. [< Gk *drastik(ós)* active = *drast(ós)* (verbal adj. of *drân* to do) + *-ikos* -IC] —**dras′ti·cal·ly,** *adv.*

drat (drat), *v.,* **drat·ted, drat·ting,** *interj.* —*v.t.* **1.** *Informal.* to damn; confound. —*interj.* **2.** (used to express mild disgust, disappointment, or the like.) [alter. of *(o)d rot* God rot (i.e., may God rot him, her, it)]

drat·ted (drat′id), *adj. Informal.* damned; confounded (used as a mild oath).

draught (draft, dräft), *n.* Also, **draft** (for defs. 1–4). **1.** the drawing of a liquid from its receptacle, as of ale from a cask: *ale on draught.* **2.** the act of drinking or inhaling. **3.** that which is taken in by drinking or inhaling; a drink; dose. **4.** a quantity of fish caught. **5. draughts,** (*construed as sing.*) *Brit.* checker[1] (def. 2). **6.** *Chiefly Brit.* draft (defs. 1, 3–5, 7–10, 15–20). —*v.t.* **7.** *Chiefly Brit.* draft (defs. 21–24). —*adj.* **8.** *Chiefly Brit.* draft (defs. 25–27). [ME *draht* (c. D *dragt,* G *Tracht,* Icel *dráttr*); akin to OE *dragan* to DRAW, *drōht* a pull (at the oars)] —**draught′er,** *n.*

draught·board (draft′bōrd′, -bôrd′, dräft′-), *n. Brit.* checkerboard (def. 1). Also, **draughts·board** (drafts′bōrd′, -bôrd′, dräfts′-).

draughts·man (drafts′mən, dräfts′-), *n., pl.* **-men. 1.** *Brit.* a checker, as used in the game of checkers. **2.** draftsman (defs. 1–4).

draught·y (draf′tē, dräf′-), *adj.,* **draught·i·er, draught·i·est.** drafty. —**draught′i·ly,** *adv.* —**draught′i·ness,** *n.*

Dra·va (drä′və), *n.* a river in S central Europe, flowing E and SE from S Austria along a part of the boundary between Hungary and SE Yugoslavia into the Danube. 450 mi. long. Also, **Dra′ve.** German, **Drau** (drou).

drave (drāv), *v.* a pt. of **drive.**

Dra·vid·i·an (drə vid′ē ən), *n.* **1.** a great linguistic family of India, wholly distinct from Indo-European. **2.** a member of an Australoid race occupying parts of southern India and Ceylon. —*adj.* **3.** Also, **Dra·vid′ic.** of or pertaining to this people or their language. [< Skt *Draviḍ(a)* folk name + -IAN]

draw (drô), *v.,* **drew, drawn, draw·ing,** *n.* —*v.t.* **1.** to cause to move in a particular direction by or as by a pulling force; pull; drag (often fol. by *along, away, in, out, off,* etc.). **2.** to bring, take, or pull out, as from a receptacle. **3.** to bring toward oneself or itself, as by inherent force or influence; attract: *The concert drew a large audience.* **4.** to sketch (someone or something) in lines or words; delineate; depict: *to draw a vase.* **5.** to compose or create (a picture) in lines. **6.** to mark or lay out; trace: *to draw perpendicular lines.* **7.** to frame or formulate (as a distinction or the like). **8.** to write out in legal form (sometimes fol. by *up*): *to draw up a contract.* **9.** to inhale or suck in. **10.** to derive or use, as from a source. **11.** to deduce; infer: *to draw a conclusion.* **12.** to get, take, or receive, as from a source: *He drew a salary of $100 a week.* **13.** to withdraw funds from a drawing account against future commissions on sales. **14.** to produce; bring in: *The deposits draw interest.* **15.** to disembowel: *to draw a turkey.* **16.** to drain: *to draw a pond.* **17.** to pull out to full or greater length; stretch; make by attenuating: *to draw filaments of molten glass.* **18.** to bend (a bow) by pulling back its string in preparation for shooting an arrow. **19.** to choose or to have assigned to one at random, by or as by picking an unseen number, item, etc.: *Let's draw straws to see who has to wash the car.* **20.** *Metalworking.* to make or reduce the sectional area of (a wire, tube, etc.) by pulling its material through a die. **21.** to wrinkle or shrink by contraction. **22.** *Med.* to digest and cause to discharge: *to draw an abscess by a poultice.* **23.** *U.S. Army.* to obtain (rations, clothing, equipment, weapons, or ammunition) from an issuing agency, such as the quartermaster. **24.** *Naut.* (of a vessel) to need (a specific depth of water) to float in: *She draws six feet.* **25.** to leave (a contest) undecided; tie. **26.** *Cards.* **a.** to take or be dealt (a card or cards) from the pack. **b.** *Bridge.* to remove the outstanding cards in (a given suit) by leading that suit. **27.** *Billiards.* to cause (a cue ball) to recoil after impact by giving it a backward spin on the stroke. **28.** *Hunting.* to search (a covert) for game. **29.** *Cricket.* to play (a ball) with a bat held at an angle in order to deflect the ball between the wicket and the legs. **30.** *Curling.* to slide (the stone) gently. **31.** to steep (tea) in boiling water. **32.** to form or shape (heated glass) by stretching. —*v.i.* **33.** to exert a pulling, moving, or attracting force. **34.** to move, go, or pass, esp. slowly or continuously, as under a pulling force (often fol. by *on, off, out,* etc.): *The day draws near.* **35.** to take out a sword, pistol, etc., for action (often fol. by *on*). **36.** to hold a drawing, lottery, or the like: *to draw for prizes.* **37.** to sketch or to trace figures; create a picture or depict by sketching. **38.** to be skilled in or practice the art of sketching. **39.** to shrink or contract (often fol. by *up*). **40.** to make a draft or demand (usually fol. by *on* or *upon*): *to draw on one's imagination.* **41.** to levy or call on for money, supplies, etc. **42.** to produce or permit a draft, as a pipe or flue. **43.** to leave a contest undecided; tie. **44.** *Hunting.* (of a hound) **a.** to search a covert for game. **b.** to follow a game animal by its scent. **45.** to attract customers, an audience, etc. **46.** to pull back the string of a bow in preparation for shooting an arrow. **47. draw ahead, a.** to pass (something moving in the same direction) gradually. **b.** *Naut.* (of the wind) to blow from a direction closer to that in which a vessel is moving; haul forward. Cf. **veer**[1] (def. 2). **48. draw on, a.** to come nearer; approach. **b.** to clothe oneself in. **c.** *Naut.* (of a vessel) to gain on (another vessel). **49. draw oneself up,** to assume an erect posture. **50. draw out, a.** to pull out; remove. **b.** to prolong; lengthen. **c.** to persuade someone to speak with or confide in one. **d.** *Naut.* (of a vessel) to move away from (sometimes fol. by *from*). **e.** to take (money, esp. all one's money) from a place of deposit. **51. draw up, a.** to devise or formulate; draft, esp. in legal form: *to draw up a will.* **b.** to put into position; arrange: *The officer drew up his men.* **c.** to stop or halt: *His car drew up at the curb.*

—*n.* **52.** the act of drawing. **53.** something that attracts customers, an audience, etc. **54.** that which is moved by being drawn, as the movable part of a drawbridge. **55.** that which is chosen or drawn at random, as a lot or chance. **56.** *Informal.* drawing (defs. 5, 6). **57.** a contest that ends in a tie; an undecided contest. **58.** *Poker.* **a.** a card or cards taken or dealt from the pack. **b.** See **draw poker. 59.** *Phys. Geog.* **a.** a small, natural drain passage with a shallow bed; gully. **b.** the dry bed of a stream. **60.** the pull necessary to draw a bow to its full extent. **61.** an amount regularly made available from a drawing account for a salesman as an advance against commissions. **62. beat to the draw, a.** to outdraw an opponent. **b.** to outdo someone else by taking advantage of an opportunity before he can. [ME *draw(en),* OE *dragan;* c. Icel *draga* to draw, G *tragen* to carry; cf. DRAG] —**draw′a·ble,** *adj.*

draw·back (drô′bak′), *n.* **1.** a hindrance or disadvantage; an undesirable or objectionable feature. **2.** *Govt.* a refund of tariff or other tax, as when imported goods are re-exported.

draw·bar (drô′bär′), *n.* *Railroads.* a metal rod or bar for connecting two pieces of rolling stock, as a steam locomotive and a tender.

draw·bridge (drô′brij′), *n.* a bridge of which the whole or a section may be drawn up, let down, or drawn aside, to prevent access or to leave a passage open for boats, barges, etc. [ME *drawebrigge*]

Drawbridge

draw·ee (drô ē′), *n.* *Finance.* the person on whom an order, draft, or bill of exchange is drawn.

draw·er (drôr *for 1, 2;* drô′ər *for 3–5*), *n.* **1.** a sliding, lidless, horizontal compartment, as in a piece of furniture, that may be drawn out in order to gain access to it. **2. drawers,** an undergarment, with legs, that covers the lower part of the body. **3.** a person or thing that draws. **4.** *Finance.* a person who draws an order, draft, or bill of exchange. **5.** *Archaic.* a tapster. [ME]

draw·ing (drô′ing), *n.* **1.** the act of a person or thing that draws. **2.** a representation by lines; a delineation of form without reference to color. **3.** a sketch, plan, or design, esp. one made with pen, pencil, or crayon. **4.** the art or technique of making these. **5.** something decided by drawing lots; lottery. **6.** the selection, or time of selection, of the winning chance or chances sold by lottery or raffle. [ME]

draw′ing account′, *Com.* **1.** an account used by a partner or employee for cash withdrawals. **2.** an account that is charged with advances of money for expenses, on salaries, against earnings, etc., esp. for salesmen.

draw′ing board′, a rectangular board on which paper is placed or mounted for making drawings.

draw′ing card′, a speaker, entertainer, performance, sale, item, etc., that attracts many customers, patrons, or the like.

draw′ing room′, **1.** a formal reception room. **2.** *U.S.* (in a railroad car) a private room for two or three passengers. **3.** *Brit.* a formal reception, esp. at court. [(*with*)*drawing*] —**draw′ing-room′,** *adj.*

draw·knife (drô′nīf′), *n., pl.* **-knives.** *Carpentry.* a knife with a handle at each end at right angles to the blade, used by drawing over a surface. Also called **draw′ing knife′, drawshave.**

Drawknife

drawl (drôl), *v.t., v.i.* **1.** to say or speak in a slow manner, usually prolonging the vowels. —*n.* **2.** the act or utterance of a person who drawls. [< D or LG *dralen* to linger] —**drawl′er,** *n.* —**drawl′ing·ly,** *adv.* —**drawl′ing·ness,** *n.* —**drawl′y,** *adj.*

drawn (drôn), *v.* **1.** pp. of **draw.** —*adj.* **2.** tense; haggard. **3.** eviscerated, as a fowl.

drawn′ but′ter, **1.** melted butter, clarified and often seasoned with herbs. **2.** a sauce of melted butter, flour, vegetable or fish stock, and lemon juice.

drawn′ work′, ornamental work done by drawing threads from a fabric.

draw·plate (drô′plāt′), *n.* *Metalworking.* a small plate containing tapered holes used as dies for drawing wire, small tubing, etc.

draw′ pok′er, a variety of poker in which each player can, after an initial bet, discard several of the five cards dealt to him and receive substitutes.

draw·shave (drô′shāv′), *n.* *Carpentry.* drawknife.

draw·string (drô′string′), *n.* a string, cord, etc., that tightens or closes an opening, as of a bag, clothing, or the like, when one or both ends are pulled. Also, **draw′ string′.**

draw·tube (drô′to͞ob′, -tyo͞ob′), *n.* a tube sliding within another tube, as the tube carrying the eyepiece in a microscope.

dray (drā), *n.* **1.** a low, strong cart without fixed sides, for carrying heavy loads. **2.** a sledge or sled. **3.** (loosely) a truck or other vehicle used to haul goods. —*v.t.* **4.** to transport (goods) by dray. [ME *draye* sledge; cf. OE *draeg-* (in *drægnet* dragnet), akin to *dragan* to DRAW]

dray·age (drā′ij), *n.* **1.** transportation by dray. **2.** a charge made for it.

dray·man (drā′mən), *n., pl.* **-men.** a man who drives a dray.

Dray·ton (drāt′ən), *n.* **1. Michael,** 1563–1631, English poet. **2. William Henry,** 1742–1779, American member of Continental Congress, 1778–79.

drch., (in Greece) drachma; drachmas.

dread (dred), *v.t.* **1.** to fear greatly; be in extreme apprehension of: *to dread death.* **2.** to be reluctant to do, meet, or experience: *I dread going to big parties.* **3.** *Archaic.* to hold in respectful awe. —*v.i.* **4.** to be in great fear. —*n.* **5.** terror or apprehension, as of something in the future; great fear. **6.** a person or thing dreaded. **7.** *Archaic.* deep awe or reverence. —*adj.* **8.** greatly feared; frightful; terrible. **9.** held in awe or reverential fear. [ME *drede(n),* OE *drǣdan,* aph. var. of *adrǣdan, ondrǣdan;* c. OHG *intrātan* to fear] —**Syn. 5.** See **fear. 8.** dreadful, horrible.

dread·ful (dred′fəl), *adj.* **1.** causing great dread, fear, or terror; terrible. **2.** inspiring awe or reverence. **3.** extremely bad, unpleasant, or ugly. —*n. Brit.* **4.** See **penny dreadful. 5.** *Brit.* a periodical given to highly sensational matter. [ME *dredful*] —**dread′ful·ly,** *adv.* —**dread′ful·ness,** *n.* —**Syn. 1.** frightful, dire.

dread·locks (dred′loks′), *n.* (*construed as pl.*) a hair style, esp. among Rastafarians, in which the hair is worn in long, ropelike locks.

dread·nought (dred′nôt′), *n.* **1.** a type of battleship armed with heavy-caliber guns in turrets: so called from the British battleship *Dreadnought,* launched in 1906, the first of this type. **2.** an outer garment of heavy woolen cloth. **3.** a thick cloth with a long pile. Also, **dread′naught′.**

dream (drēm), *n., v.,* **dreamed** or **dreamt, dream·ing,** *adj.* —*n.* **1.** a succession of images, thoughts, or emotions passing through the mind during sleep. **2.** an object seen in a dream. **3.** an involuntary vision occurring to a person awake. **4.** a vision voluntarily indulged in while awake; daydream; reverie. **5.** an aspiration; goal; aim. **6.** a wild or vain fancy. **7.** something of an unreal beauty or charm. **8.** the sleeping state in which a dream occurs. —*v.i.* **9.** to have a dream or dreams. **10.** to indulge in daydreams or reveries. **11.** to think or conceive of something in a very remote way (usually fol. by *of*): *I wouldn't dream of asking her.* —*v.t.* **12.** to see or imagine in sleep or in a vision. **13.** to imagine as in a dream; fancy; suppose. **14.** to pass or spend (time) in dreaming (often fol. by *away*): *to dream away the afternoon.* **15. dream up,** *Informal.* to form an idea or plan of action in the imagination; devise. —*adj.* **16.** *Informal.* ideal; desirable: *a dream trip.* [ME *dreem,* OE *drēam;* c. OS *drōm* mirth, dream, Icel *draumr,* OHG *troum* dream; modern sense first recorded in ME but presumably current in OE too, as in OS] —**dream′er,** *n.* —**dream′ing·ly,** *adv.* —**dream′less,** *adj.*

dream·boat (drēm′bōt′), *n.* *Slang.* a person or thing that is extremely attractive or desirable.

dream·land (drēm′land′), *n.* **1.** a pleasant, lovely land that exists only in the imagination. **2.** sleep (def. 11).

dreamt (dremt), *v.* a pt. and pp. of **dream.**

dream′ world′, the world of imagination or illusion rather than of objective reality.

dream·y (drē′mē), *adj.,* **dream·i·er, dream·i·est. 1.** abounding in dreams; characterized by or causing dreams. **2.** of the nature of or characteristic of dreams. **3.** vague; dim. **4.** soothing; restful; quieting. **5.** *Informal.* wonderful; marvelous. —**dream′i·ly,** *adv.* —**dream′i·ness,** *n.*

drear (drēr), *adj.* *Literary.* dreary. [back formation from DREARY]

drear·y (drēr′ē), *adj.,* **drear·i·er, drear·i·est,** *n., pl.* **drear·ies.** —*adj.* **1.** causing sadness or gloom. **2.** dull; boring. **3.** sorrowful; sad. —*n.* **4.** a dull, drab, tedious, or unpleasant person, writer, etc. [ME *drery,* OE *drēorig* bloody, G *traurig* sad] —**drear′i·ly,** *adv.* —**drear′i·ness,** *n.* —**Syn. 1.** gloomy, dismal, drear, cheerless, depressing.

dredge[1] (drej), *n., v.,* **dredged, dredg·ing.** —*n.* **1.** any of various powerful machines for removing earth, as from the bottom of a river, by means of a scoop, a suction pipe, or the like. **2.** a barge on which such a machine is mounted. **3.** a dragnet or other contrivance for gathering material or objects from the bottom of a river, bay, etc. —*v.t.* **4.** to clear out with a dredge; remove sand, silt, mud, etc., from the bottom of. **5.** to take, catch, or gather with a dredge; obtain or remove by a dredge. —*v.i.* **6.** to use a dredge. [late ME *dreg-* (Scot), OE **drecg(e)*; see DRAY, DRAW]

dredge[2] (drej), *v.t.,* **dredged, dredg·ing.** *Cookery.* to sprinkle or coat with some powdered substance, esp. flour. [ME *drage, dreg(g)e* < OF *drag(i)e* << Gk *tragēmata,* pl. of *trágēma* sweetmeat, dried fruit]

dredg·er[1] (drej′ər), *n.* **1.** *Chiefly Brit.* dredge[1] (def. 1). **2.** a person who uses a dredge.

dredg·er[2] (drej′ər), *n.* a container with a perforated top for sprinkling flour, sugar, etc., on food for cooking.

dree (drē), *adj., v.,* **dreed, dree·ing.** *Scot. and North Eng.* —*adj.* **1.** tedious; dreary. —*v.t.* **2.** to suffer; endure. [ME; OE *drēog(an)* (to) endure; c. Goth *driugan* to serve (in arms)]

dreg (dreg), *n.* **1. dregs,** the sediment of liquors; lees; grounds. **2.** Usually, **dregs.** the least valuable part of anything: *the dregs of society.* **3.** a small remnant; any small quantity. [ME < Scand; cf. Icel *dreggjar* dregs; akin to L *fracēs* oil grounds]

drei·del (drād′əl), *n., pl.* **-dels, -del.** a four-sided top bearing the Hebrew letters *nun, gimel, he,* and *shin,* used chiefly in a children's game traditionally played on the Jewish festival of Hanukkah. [< Yiddish, Galician dial. for standard *dreydl* < G *dreh(en)* (to) turn + instrumental suffix *-dl*]

Dreidel

Drei·ser (drī′sər, -zər), *n.* **Theodore,** 1871–1945, U.S. novelist.

drench (drench), *v.t.* **1.** to wet thoroughly; soak. **2.** to saturate by immersion in a liquid; steep. **3.** to cover or fill completely; bathe. **4.** *Vet. Med.* to administer a draft of medicine to (an animal), esp. by force. **5.** *Archaic.* to cause to drink. —*n.* **6.** the act of drenching. **7.** something that drenches: *a drench of rain.* **8.** a preparation for drenching or steeping. **9.** a solution, esp. one of fermenting bran, for drenching hides or skins. **10.** a large drink or draft. **11.** a draft of medicine, esp. one administered to an animal by force. [ME *drenche(n),* OE *drencan,* causative of *drincan* to DRINK; c. D *drenken,* G *tränken* to water, give to drink] —**drench′er,** *n.* —**drench′ing·ly,** *adv.* —**Syn. 1.** See **wet.**

Dren·the (dren′tə), *n.* a province in the E Netherlands. 324,517 (1962); 1011 sq. mi. Also, **Dren′te.**

Dres·den (drez′dən; *Ger.* drās′dən), *n.* a city in SE East Germany, on the Elbe River. 503,859 (1964).

Dres′den chi′na, porcelain ware produced at Meissen, Germany, near Dresden, after 1710.

dress (dres), *n.* **1.** the most common outer garment of women, consisting of waist and skirt in one piece. **2.** clothing; apparel; garb: *The dress of the 18th century was colorful.* **3.** formal attire. **4.** outer covering, as the plumage of birds. **5.** a particular form of appearance; guise. —*adj.* **6.** of or for a dress or dresses. **7.** of or for a formal occasion. **8.** requiring formal dress. —*v.t.* **9.** to put clothing upon. **10.** to design clothing for or sell clothes to. **11.** to trim; ornament; adorn. **12.** *Angling.* to prepare (bait or a fishhook) for use. **13.** to cut up, trim, and remove the skin, feathers, viscera, etc., from (an animal, meat, fowl, or flesh of a fowl). **14.** to prepare (skins, fabrics, ore, etc.) by special processes. **15.** to comb out and do up (hair). **16.** to cultivate (land, fields, etc.). **17.** to apply medication or a dressing to (a wound or sore). **18.** to make straight; bring (troops) into line: *to dress the ranks.* **19.** *Theat.* to arrange (a stage) by effective placement of properties, scenery, actors, etc. **20.** *Print.* to fit (furniture) around and between pages in a chase. —*v.i.* **21.** to clothe or attire oneself; put on one's clothes. **22.** to put on or wear formal or fancy clothes: *to dress for dinner.* **23.** to come into line, as troops. **24.** to align oneself with the next soldier, marcher, dancer, etc., in line. **25. dress down,** *Informal.* **a.** to reprimand; scold. **b.** to thrash; beat. **26. dress ship, a.** to decorate a ship by hoisting lines of flags running its full length. **b.** *U.S. Navy.* to display the national ensigns at each masthead and a larger ensign on the flagstaff. **27. dress up,** to put on one's best or fanciest clothing; dress relatively formally. [ME *dresse(n)* < MF *dresse(r)* (to) arrange, prepare, OF *drecier* < VL **dīrēctiāre* < L *dīrēct(us)* DIRECT]

dres·sage (drə säzh′; *Fr.* dre sazh′), *n.* the art or method of training a horse in obedience and in precision of movement. [< F; see DRESS, -AGE]

dress′ cir′cle, a circular or curving division of seats in a theater, opera house, etc., usually the first gallery, originally set apart for spectators in evening dress.

dress′ coat′. See **tail coat.** —**dress′-coat′ed,** *adj.*

dress·er[1] (dres′ər), *n.* **1.** a person who dresses. **2.** a person employed to dress others, care for costumes, etc. **3.** *Chiefly Brit.* a surgeon's assistant. **4.** a person who dresses in a particular manner, as specified: *a fancy dresser.* **5.** any of several tools or devices used in dressing materials. **6.** *Metalworking.* **a.** a block, fitting into an anvil, on which pieces are forged. **b.** a mallet for shaping sheet metal. [DRESS + -ER[1]]

dress·er[2] (dres′ər), *n.* **1.** a dressing table or bureau. **2.** a sideboard or set of shelves for dishes and cooking utensils. **3.** *Obs.* a table or sideboard on which food is dressed for serving. [ME *dresso(u)r* sideboard < AF; MF *dresseur,* OF *dreceor(e).* See DRESS, -ORY[2]]

dress·ing (dres′ing), *n.* **1.** the act of a person or thing that dresses. **2.** that with which something is dressed. **3.** a sauce for food: *salad dressing.* **4.** stuffing for a fowl: *turkey dressing.* **5.** material used to dress a wound. **6.** manure, compost, or other fertilizers. [ME]

dress·ing-down (dres′ing doun′), *n.* *Informal.* **1.** a severe reprimand; scolding. **2.** a thrashing; beating.

dress′ing gown′, a tailored robe worn for lounging or when dressing.

dress′ing room′, a room for use in getting dressed, esp. backstage in a theater, television studio, etc.

dress′ing sta′tion, *Mil.* a post or center near a combat area that gives first aid to the wounded.

dress′ing ta′ble, **1.** a table or stand, usually surmounted by a mirror, in front of which a person sits while dressing, applying make-up, etc. **2.** *Chiefly Brit.* a side table, similar in appearance to a lowboy, having a shaped apron containing one or two rows of drawers.

dress·mak·er (dres′mā′kər), *n.* **1.** a person whose occupation is the making of women's dresses, coats, etc. —*adj.* **2.** (of women's clothing) having soft, feminine lines or elaborate detail. Cf. **tailored** (def. 1). —**dress′mak′ing,** *n.*

dress′ parade′, the formal, ceremonial parade at which soldiers in dress uniforms take formation under arms.

dress′ rehears′al, a rehearsal of a play, often the final one, in costume and with scenery, properties, and lights arranged and operated as for a performance.

dress′ shield′, a thin pad for attaching under the arm of a garment to protect it from perspiration stains. Also called **shield.**

dress′ shirt′, **1.** a man's white shirt, usually having French cuffs and a stiff or pleated front to be fastened with studs, worn for semiformal or formal evening dress. **2.** a man's white or light-colored shirt, buttoning down the front and typically having long sleeves with barrel or French cuffs, and a soft or starched collar, worn with a necktie, esp. to business. Cf. **sport shirt.**

dress′ suit′, a man's suit for formal evening dress, with tail coat and open-front waistcoat.

dress′ u′niform, **1.** *U.S. Air Force.* a uniform consisting of the coat and trousers of the service uniform, with a white shirt and black bow tie, worn for formal occasions. **2.** *U.S. Army.* a blue uniform worn for formal occasions. **3.** *U.S. Navy.* a dark blue uniform worn in cool seasons or climates.

dress-up (dres′up′), *adj.* being an occasion, situation, etc., for which a person must be somewhat formally well-dressed: *the first dress-up dinner of the season.*

dress·y (dres′ē), *adj.,* **dress·i·er, dress·i·est.** *Informal.* **1.** showy in dress; stylish. **2.** appropriate to somewhat formal occasions. —**dress′i·ly,** *adv.* —**dress′i·ness,** *n.*

drest (drest), *v.* *Obs.* a pt. and pp. of **dress.**

drew (drōō), *v.* pt. of **draw.**

Drew (drōō), *n.* **1. John,** 1827–62, U.S. actor, born in Ireland. **2.** his son, **John,** 1853–1927, U.S. actor.

Drey·fus (drā′fəs, drī′-; *Fr.* drɛ fys′), *n.* **Al·fred** (al′frid; *Fr.* al fred′), 1859–1935, French army officer of Jewish descent: convicted of treason 1894, 1899; acquitted 1906.

drib (drib), *n.* a small or minute quantity; bit. [back formation from DRIBLET]

drib·ble (drib′əl), *v.,* **-bled, -bling,** *n.* —*v.i.* **1.** to fall or flow in drops or small quantities; trickle. **2.** to drivel; slaver. **3.** *Sports.* to advance a ball or puck by bouncing it or giving it a series of short kicks or pushes. —*v.t.* **4.** to let fall in drops. **5.** *Sports.* **a.** *Basketball.* to bounce (the ball) as in advancing or keeping control of it. **b.** (esp. in ice hockey and soccer) to move (the ball or puck) along by a rapid succession of short kicks or pushes. —*n.* **6.** a small trickling stream or a drop. **7.** a small quantity of anything: *a dribble of revenue.* **8.** the act or an instance of dribbling a ball or puck. **9.** *Scot.* a drizzle; a light rain. [obs. *drib* (v.) prob. var. of DRIP + -LE] —**drib′bler,** *n.*

drib·let (drib′lit), *n.* **1.** a small portion or part. **2.** a small or petty sum. Also, **drib′blet.** [obs. *drib* (v.) (see DRIBBLE) + -LET]

dribs′ and drabs′, small and usually irregular amounts: *He repaid the loan in dribs and drabs.*

dried (drīd), *v.* pt. and pp. of **dry.**

dried-up (drīd′up′), *adj.* **1.** depleted of moisture; gone dry. **2.** shriveled with age; wizened.

dri·er[1] (drī′ər), *n.* **1.** a person or thing that dries. **2.** any substance added to paints, varnishes, etc., to make them dry quickly. **3.** dryer (def. 1). [DRY + -ER[1]]

dri·er[2] (drī′ər), *adj.* comparative of **dry.**

dri·est (drī′ist), *adj.* superlative of **dry.**

drift (drift), *n.* **1.** a driving movement or force; impulse; impetus; pressure. **2.** *Navig.* (of a vessel) the component of the movement that is due to the force of wind and currents. **3.** *Phys. Geog.* a broad, shallow ocean current that advances at the rate of 10 or 15 miles a day. **4.** the speed in knots of an ocean current. **5.** *Aeron.* the deviation of an aircraft from a set course due to cross winds. **6.** the course along which something moves; tendency; aim. **7.** a meaning; intent; purport: *the drift of a statement.* **8.** something driven, as animals, rain, etc. **9.** a heap of any matter driven together. **10.** a snowdrift. **11.** *Geol.* **a.** a deposit of detritus. **b.** the deposit of a continental ice sheet. **12.** the state or process of being driven. **13.** overbearing power or influence. **14.** *Mining.* an approximately horizontal passageway in underground mining. **15.** *Physics.* the movement of charged particles under the influence of an electric field. **16.** the gradual deviation of a rocket or guided missile from its intended trajectory. —*v.i.* **17.** to be carried along by currents of water or air, or by the force of circumstances. **18.** to wander aimlessly: *He drifts from town to town.* **19.** to be driven into heaps, as by the wind: *drifting sand.* **20.** to deviate or vary from a set course or adjustment. —*v.t.* **21.** to carry along. **22.** to drive into heaps. [ME, verbal abstract of OE *drīfan* to DRIVE; c. D *drift* herd, flock, G *Trift* herd, pasturage, road to pasture] —**drift′ing·ly,** *adv.*

drift·age (drif′tij), *n.* **1.** the action or an amount of drifting. **2.** drifted matter. **3.** *Navig.* the amount of drift away from a set course as a result of wind and currents. **4.** windage.

drift′ an′chor, a sea anchor or drag.

drift·bolt (drift′bōlt′), *n.* a spike, having a round shank, for fastening heavy timbers together. Also called **drift·pin** (drift′pin′).

drift·er (drif′tər), *n.* **1.** a person who or thing that drifts. **2.** a person who goes from place to place, job to job, etc., remaining in each for a very short period. **3.** a tramp, hobo, or bum. **4.** Also called **drift′ boat′.** a boat used in fishing with vertical nets that drift with the current or tide.

drift′ ice′, floating ice in masses that drift with the wind or ocean currents, as in the polar seas.

drift·wood (drift′wŏŏd′), *n.* wood floating on or cast ashore by the water.

drift·y (drif′tē), *adj.,* **drift·i·er, drift·i·est.** of the nature of or characterized by drifts.

drill[1] (dril), *n.* **1.** *Mach., Building Trades.* **a.** a shaftlike tool with two or more cutting edges for making holes in firm materials, esp. by rotation. **b.** a machine operating such a tool. **2.** *Mil.* **a.** training in formal marching or other precise military movements. **b.** an exercise in such training: *gun drill.* **3.** any strict, methodical training, instruction, or exercise: *a drill in spelling.* **4.** a gastropod, *Urosalpinx cinera,* destructive to oysters. —*v.t.* **5.** to pierce or bore a hole in (something). **6.** to make (a hole) by boring. **7.** *Mil.* to instruct and exercise in formation marching, handling of arms, or the like. **8.** to impart (knowledge) by strict training, discipline, or repetition. —*v.i.* **9.** to pierce or bore something with or as with a drill. **10.** to go through exercise in military or other training. [< D *dril* (n.), *drillen* (v.)] —**drill′a·ble,** *adj.* —**drill′er,** *n.* —**Syn. 3.** See **exercise.**

drill[2] (dril), *n.* **1.** a small furrow made in the soil in which to sow seeds. **2.** a machine for sowing in rows and for covering the seeds when sown. **3.** a row of seeds or plants thus sown. —*v.t.* **4.** to sow (seed) in drills. **5.** to sow or plant (soil, a plot of ground, etc.) in drills. —*v.i.* **6.** to sow seed in drills. [cf. dial. *drill* rill, G *Rille* furrow, *rillen* to groove] —**drill′er,** *n.*

drill[3] (dril), *n.* a strong, twilled cotton fabric. [short for DRILLING[2]]

drill[4] (dril), *n.* a baboon, *Papio leucophaeus,* of western Africa, smaller than the mandrill. [appar. native name; see MANDRILL]

drill·ing[1] (dril′ing), *n.* the act of a person or thing that drills. [DRILL[1] + -ING[1]]

drill·ing[2] (dril′ing), *n.* drill[3]. [alter. of G *Drillich,* itself alter. of L *trilīx* triple-twilled (G *dri-* three- r. L *tri-*)]

drill·mas·ter (dril′mas′tər, -mä′stər), *n.* **1.** a person who trains others in anything, esp. routinely or mechanically. **2.** *Mil.* a person who instructs in marching drill.

drill′ press′, a drilling machine having a single vertical spindle.

drill·stock (dril′stok′), *n.* a device for holding a drill.

dri·ly (drī′lē), *adv.* dryly.

Drin (drēn), *n.* a river in S Europe, flowing generally NW from N Yugoslavia through N Albania into the Adriatic. 180 mi. long.

Dri·na (drē′nə, -nä), *n.* a river in central Yugoslavia, flowing N to the Sava River. 160 mi. long.

drink (driŋk), *v.*, **drank** or (*Nonstandard*) **drunk; drunk** or, often, **drank; drink·ing;** *n.* **—*v.i.* 1.** to take water or other liquid into the mouth and swallow it; imbibe. **2.** to imbibe alcoholic liquors, esp. habitually or to excess; tipple. **3.** to propose or participate in a toast. **—*v.t.* 4.** to take into the mouth and swallow (a liquid). **5.** to take in (a liquid) in any manner; absorb. **6.** to take in through the senses, esp. with eagerness and pleasure (often fol. by *in*): *He drank in the beauty of the scene.* **7.** to swallow the contents of (a cup, glass, etc.). **8.** to drink to (a person, thing, or event): *to drink one's health.* **—*n.* 9.** any liquid that is swallowed to quench thirst, for nourishment, etc.; beverage. **10.** alcoholic liquor. **11.** excessive indulgence in alcoholic liquor: *Drink was his downfall.* **12.** a draft of liquid: *to take a drink.* **13.** *Informal.* a large body of water (usually prec. by *the*): *to fall in the drink.* [ME *drinke(n),* OE *drincan;* c. D *drinken,* G *trinken,* Goth *drinkan,* Icel *drekka*]

drink·a·ble (driŋ′kə bəl), *adj.* **1.** suitable for drinking. **—*n.* 2.** Usually, **drinkables.** substances that are drinkable; liquids for drinking.

drink·er (driŋ′kər), *n.* **1.** a person who drinks. **2.** a person who drinks alcoholic liquors habitually or to excess. [ME *drinkere,* OE *drincere*]

drink·ing (driŋ′kiŋ), *adj.* **1.** suitable or safe to drink: *drinking water.* **2.** used in drinking: *drinking glass.* **3.** addicted to or indulging excessively in alcoholic liquor: *Is he a drinking man?* [ME]

Drink·wa·ter (driŋk′wô′tər, -wot′ər), *n.* **John,** 1882–1937, English poet, playwright, and critic.

drip (drip), *v.*, **dripped** or **dript, drip·ping,** *n.* **—*v.i.* 1.** to let drops fall; shed drops. **2.** to fall in drops, as a liquid. **—*v.t.* 3.** to let fall in drops. **—*n.* 4.** the act of dripping. **5.** the liquid that drips. **6.** the sound made by falling drops: *I heard the drip of a faucet.* **7.** *Slang.* an unattractive, colorless person. **8.** *Archit., Building Trades.* any device, as a molding, for shedding rain water. **9.** Also called **intravenous drip.** *Med.* the continuous, slow introduction of a fluid into a vein of the body. [ME *dryppe,* OE *drypp(an)* < *dropa* DROP]

drip′ cof′fee, a beverage prepared in a vessel in which boiling water filters from a top compartment through the coffee into a pot below.

drip-dry (*adj.* drip′drī′; *v.* drip′drī′, -drī′), *adj., v.,* **-dried, -dry·ing.** **—*adj.* 1.** wash-and-wear. **—*v.i.* 2.** (of a cloth item) to dry into its desired form and shape when hung dripping wet after washing.

drip′ grind′, finely ground coffee beans, used in making drip coffee.

drip·o·la·tor (drip′ə lā′tər), *n.* a pot for making drip coffee. [DRIP + (PERC)OLATOR]

drip′ pan′, 1. a pan, tray, etc., for collecting liquid waste: *Put a drip pan under the crankcase.* **2.** See **dripping pan.**

drip·ping (drip′iŋ), *n.* **1.** the act of anything that drips. **2.** Often, **drippings. a.** the liquid that drips. **b.** fat and juices exuded from meat in cooking. [ME]

drip′ping pan′, a shallow metal pan used under roasting meat to receive the dripping. Also called **drip pan.**

drip·py (drip′ē), *adj.*, **-pi·er, -pi·est. 1.** dripping or tending to drip: *a drippy faucet.* **2.** tending to be rainy, wet, or drizzly. **3.** *Informal.* revoltingly sentimental; mawkish.

drip·stone (drip′stōn′), *n.* **1.** *Archit.* a stone molding used as a drip. **2.** calcium carbonate, $CaCO_3$, occurring in the form of stalactites and stalagmites.

drive (drīv), *v.*, **drove** or (*Archaic*) **drave; driv·en; driv·ing;** *n.* **—*v.t.* 1.** to send, expel, or otherwise cause to move by force or compulsion (often fol. by *away, off,* etc.): *to drive away the flies.* **2.** to force to work or act; overwork. **3.** to cause and guide the movement of (a vehicle, an animal, etc.): *to drive a car; to drive a mule.* **4.** to transport in a vehicle, esp. an automobile: *He drove her to the station.* **5.** to keep (machinery) going. **6.** to impel; constrain; urge; compel. **7.** to carry (business, an agreement, etc.) vigorously through: *He drove a hard bargain.* **8.** (in mining, construction, etc.) to dig (a mine shaft, tunnel, etc.) horizontally. **9.** *Sports.* to hit or propel (a ball, puck, shuttlecock, etc.) very hard. **10.** *Golf.* to hit (a golf ball), esp. from the tee, as with a driver or driving iron. **11.** *Hunting.* **a.** to chase (game). **b.** to search (a district) for game. **12.** to float (logs) down a river or stream. **—*v.i.* 13.** to go along before an impelling force; be impelled: *The ship drove before the wind.* **14.** to rush or dash violently. **15.** to cause and guide the movement of a vehicle or animal. **16.** to know how to operate an automobile. **17.** to possess a valid driver's license: *In this state, you can't drive until you're 18 years old.* **18.** to go or travel in a driven vehicle; ride: *He drives to work with me.* **19.** *Golf.* to hit a golf ball, esp. from the tee, as with a driver or driving iron. **20.** to strive vigorously toward an objective. **21. drive at,** to attempt or intend to convey; allude to; suggest: *What is he driving at?* **—*n.* 22.** the act of driving. **23.** a trip in a vehicle, esp. a short pleasure trip. **24.** an impelling along, as of game, cattle, or floating logs, in a particular direction. **25.** the animals, logs, etc., thus driven. **26.** *Psychol.* an inner urge that stimulates a response, inciting or repressing action; a basic or instinctive need. **27.** a vigorous onset or onward course toward a goal or objective. **28.** a strong military offensive. **29.** a united effort to accomplish some specific purpose, esp. to raise money, as for a charity. **30.** energy and initiative: *a person with great drive.* **31.** vigorous pressure or effort, as in business. **32.** a road for vehicles, esp. a broad or scenic highway. **33.** *Mach.* a driving mechanism, as of an automobile: *gear drive; chain drive.* **34.** *Auto.* the point or points of power application to the roadway: *four-wheel drive.* **35.** *Sports.* a propelling, forcible stroke. **36.** *Golf.* a shot, esp. with a driver or driving iron from the tee, that is intended to carry a great distance. **37.** a hunt in which game is driven toward stationary hunters. [ME *drive(n),* OE *drīfan;* c. D *drijven,* Icel *drīfa,* Goth *dreiban,* G *treiben*] **—driv′a·ble, drive′a·ble,** *adj.* **—Syn. 1.** push, force. **30.** enterprise.

drive-in (drīv′in′), *n.* **1.** a motion-picture theater, bank, etc., designed to accommodate patrons in their automobiles. **—*adj.* 2.** of or pertaining to such an establishment.

driv·el (driv′əl), *v.*, **-eled, -el·ing** or (*esp. Brit.*) **-elled, -el·ling,** *n.* **—*v.i.* 1.** to let saliva flow from the mouth or mucus from the nose; slaver. **2.** to talk childishly or idiotically. **3.** *Archaic.* to issue like spittle. **—*v.t.* 4.** to utter childishly or idiotically. **5.** to waste foolishly. **—*n.* 6.** childish, silly, or meaningless talk or thinking; nonsense; twaddle. **7.** saliva flowing from the mouth, or mucus from the nose; slaver. [ME *dryvele,* var. of *drevele(n),* OE *dreflian;* akin to DRAFF] **—driv′el·er;** *esp. Brit.,* **driv′el·ler,** *n.* **—driv′el·ing·ly;** *esp. Brit.,* **driv′el·ling·ly,** *adv.*

driv·en (driv′ən), *v.* pp. of **drive.**

driv·er (drī′vər), *n.* **1.** a person or thing that drives. **2.** a coachman, chauffeur, etc. **3.** a person who drives an animal or animals, as a drover or cowboy. **4.** *Brit.* a locomotive engineer. **5.** *Mach.* **a.** a part transmitting force or motion. **b.** the member of a pair of connected pulleys, gears, etc., nearest the power source. **6.** See **driving wheel** (def. 2). **7.** *Golf.* a club whose face has almost no slope, for hitting long, low drives from the tee. [ME *drivere*] **—driv′er·less,** *adj.*

driv′er ant′. See **army ant.**

driv′er's seat′, any position of power or control.

drive′ screw′, a fastener with a helical thread of coarse pitch that can be driven into wood with a hammer and removed with a screwdriver. Also called **screw nail.** See illus. at **nail.**

drive′ shaft′, *Mach.* a shaft for imparting torque from a power source or prime mover to machinery.

drive·way (drīv′wā′), *n.* **1.** a road, esp. a private one, leading from a street or other thoroughfare to a building, house, garage, etc. **2.** any road for driving on.

driv·ing (drī′viŋ), *adj.* **1.** energetic; vigorously active: *a driving young salesman.* **2.** having force and violence: *a driving storm.* **3.** relaying or transmitting power. [ME]

driv′ing i′ron, *Golf.* a driver with an iron head.

driv′ing wheel′, 1. *Mach.* a main wheel which communicates motion to others. **2.** Also called **driver.** *Railroads.* one of the wheels of a locomotive transmitting the power of an engine or motor into tractive effort.

driz·zle (driz′əl), *v.*, **-zled, -zling,** *n.* **—*v.t., v.i.* 1.** to rain gently and steadily in fine drops; sprinkle (often used impersonally with *it* as subject): *It drizzled throughout the night.* **—*n.* 2.** a very light rain. **3.** *Meteorol.* precipitation consisting of numerous, minute droplets of water. [? back formation from *dryseling,* dissimilated var. of ME *drysning* fall (of dew); akin to OE *drēosan* to fall; c. OS *driosan,* Goth *driusan*] **—driz′zling·ly,** *adv.* **—driz′zly,** *adj.*

Drog·he·da (drô′i də), *n.* a seaport in the NE Republic of Ireland, near the mouth of the Boyne River: the town was captured and its inhabitants massacred by Cromwell 1649. 17,085 (1961).

drogue (drōg), *n.* **1.** a canvas bag used as a sea anchor. **2.** a parachutelike device for braking. [earlier *drug,* common dial. var. of DRAG]

droit (droit; *Fr.* drwa), *n., pl.* **droits** (droits; *Fr.* drwa). a legal right or claim. [< F < ML *dīrēct(um)* legal right, law, n. use of neut. of L *dīrēctus* DIRECT]

droll (drōl), *adj.* **1.** amusing in an odd way; whimsically humorous; waggish. **—*n.* 2.** a droll person; jester; wag. **—*v.i.* 3.** *Archaic.* to play the droll or wag; jest; joke. [< MF *drolle* pleasant rascal < MD *drol* a fat little man] **—droll′ness,** *n.* **—drol′ly,** *adv.* **—Syn. 1.** See **amusing.**

droll·er·y (drō′lə rē), *n., pl.* **-er·ies. 1.** something droll. **2.** an oddly amusing story or jest. **3.** a droll quality or manner; whimsical humor. **4.** the action or behavior of a droll person; jesting; whimsy. **5.** *Archaic.* a comic picture. **6.** *Archaic.* a puppet show. [DROLL + -ERY; cf. F *drôlerie*]

-drome, a suffix occurring in loan words from Greek, meaning "running," "course," "race course" (*hippodrome*), on this model used to refer to other large structures (*airdrome*). [comb. form of Gk *drómos*]

Dromedary (6 ft. high at shoulder; length 9½ ft.)

drom·e·dary (drom′i der′ē, drum′-), *n., pl.* **-dar·ies.** the one-humped camel, *Camelus dromedarius,* of Arabia and northern Africa. [ME *dromedarie, -ary* < LL *dromedāri(us)* (*camēlus*) < Gk *dromad-* (s. of *dromás*) running + L *-ārius* -ARY]

drom·ond (drom′ənd, drum′-), *n.* a large, fast-sailing vessel of the Middle Ages. Also, **drom·on** (drom′ən, drum′-). [ME *dromund* < AF << Gk *drómōn* swift ship < *drómos* a running]

-dromous, a word element used to form adjectives from nouns ending in **-drome.**

drone[1] (drōn), *n.* **1.** the male of the honeybee and other bees, stingless and making no honey. See illus. at **bee**[1]. **2.** a person who lives on the labor of others; parasitic loafer. **3.** a remote-control mechanism, as a radio-controlled airplane or boat. [ME *drone, drane,* OE *dran, dron;* akin to OHG *treno,* G *Drohne*] **—dron′ish,** *adj.*

drone[2] (drōn), *v.*, **droned, dron·ing,** *n.* **—*v.i.* 1.** to make a dull, continued, monotonous sound; hum; buzz. **2.** to speak in a monotonous tone. **—*v.t.* 3.** to say in a dull, monotonous tone. **—*n.* 4.** *Music.* **a.** a continuous low tone produced by the bass pipes or bass strings of musical instruments. **b.** the pipes (esp. of the bagpipe) or strings producing this tone. **c.** a bagpipe equipped with such pipes. **5.** a monotonous tone; humming or buzzing sound. **6.** a person who speaks in a monotonous tone. [see DRONE[1] and cf. ME *droun* to roar, Icel *drynja* to bellow, Goth *drunjus* noise] **—dron′ing·ly,** *adv.*

drool (drōōl), *v.i.* **1.** to water at the mouth, as in anticipation of food. **2.** to show excessive pleasure or anticipation of pleasure. **3.** to talk foolishly. **—*n.* 4.** drivel. [var. of *driule,* itself var. of DRIVEL]

droop (drōōp), *v.i.* **1.** to sag, sink, bend, or hang down, as from weakness, exhaustion, or lack of support. **2.** *Literary.* to sink; descend, as the sun. **3.** to fall into a state of physical weakness; flag; fail. **4.** to lose spirit or courage. —*v.t.* **5.** to let sink or drop: *an eagle drooping its wings.* —*n.* **6.** a sagging, sinking, bending, or hanging down, as from weakness, exhaustion, or lack of support. [ME *drupe(n), drowpe(n)* < Icel *drūpa;* akin to DROP] —**droop′i·ness,** *n.* —**droop′ing·ly,** *adv.* —**Syn. 3.** decline, wilt, fade.

droop·y (drōō′pē), *adj.,* **droop·i·er, droop·i·est. 1.** hanging down; sagging. **2.** lacking in spirit or courage; disheartened; dejected.

drop (drop), *n., v.,* **dropped** or **dropt, drop·ping.** —*n.* **1.** a small quantity of liquid that falls or is produced in a more or less spherical mass; a liquid globule. **2.** the quantity of liquid contained in such a globule. **3.** a very small quantity of liquid. **4.** a minute quantity of anything: *not even a drop of mercy.* **5.** Usually, **drops.** liquid medicine given in a dose or form of globules from a medicine dropper. **6.** something resembling or likened to a liquid globule, as certain ornaments, a spherical earring, etc. **7.** a small, usually spherical, piece of candy; lozenge. **8.** a pendant. **9.** the act or an instance of dropping; fall; descent. **10.** the distance or depth to which anything drops. **11.** a steep slope. **12.** that which drops or is used for dropping. **13.** a central depository where items are left or transmitted: *a mail drop.* **14.** a decline in amount, degree, quality, value, etc. **15.** *Mil.* **a.** a group of men dropped by parachute in one military action. **b.** an instance of dropping supplies by parachute. **c.** a descent by parachute. **16.** *Theat.* See **drop curtain. 17.** See **trap door. 18.** a gallows. **19.** a slit or opening through or into which something can be dropped in depositing it, as in a mailbox. **20.** *Naut.* the vertical dimension amidships of any sail that is bent to a standing yard. Cf. **hoist** (def. 5a). **21.** the newborn young of an animal. **22. at the drop of a hat,** at the slightest provocation or without delay. **23. get** or **have the drop on,** *Informal.* **a.** to aim and be ready to shoot a gun at an antagonist before he can draw his gun. **b.** to get or have at a disadvantage.
—*v.i.* **24.** to fall in globules or small portions, as water or other liquid. **25.** to fall vertically; have an abrupt descent. **26.** to sink or fall to the ground, as if inanimate. **27.** to fall wounded, dead, etc. **28.** to come to an end; cease; lapse. **29.** *Informal.* to withdraw; quit (often fol. by *out*): *to drop out of a race; to drop from a game.* **30.** to cease to appear or be seen; vanish: *to drop from sight or notice.* **31.** to squat or crouch, as a dog at the sight of game. **32.** to fall lower in condition, degree, value, etc.; sink; diminish or lessen. **33.** to pass or enter without effort into some condition, activity, or the like: *to drop asleep.* **34.** to move gently, as with the tide or a light wind. **35.** to fall or move to a position that is lower, farther back, inferior, etc.: *to drop back in line; to drop to the rear.* **36.** to make an unexpected or unannounced stop at a place; pay an informal visit or call (usually fol. by *in, by,* or *over*): *Let's drop in at Tom's.*
—*v.t.* **37.** to let fall in drops or small portions: *to drop lemon juice into tea.* **38.** to let or cause to fall. **39.** to cause or allow to sink to a lower position. **40.** to cause to decrease in value, amount, quality, etc.; reduce. **41.** to utter or express casually or incidentally: *to drop a hint.* **42.** to send or mail (a note, message, etc.): *Drop me a line.* **43.** to bring to the ground by a blow or shot. **44.** to set down or unload, as from a ship, car, etc.: *Drop me at the corner.* **45.** to omit (a letter or syllable) in pronunciation or writing: *He dropped his h's.* **46.** to lower (the voice) in pitch or loudness. **47.** to cease to keep up or have to do with. **48.** to cease to employ; dismiss. **49.** *Sports.* **a.** to throw, shoot, hit, kick, or roll (a ball, puck, etc.) through or into a basket, hole, or other goal. **b.** to lose (a game or contest). **50.** *Football.* **a.** to drop-kick (a ball). **b.** to score with a drop kick. **51.** (of animals) to give birth to. **52.** to parachute (men, supplies, etc.). **53.** to lengthen by lowering or letting out: *to drop the hem of a skirt.* **54.** *Naut.* to outdistance; pass out of sight of. **55.** *Cookery.* to poach (an egg). **56. drop behind,** to fall short of the required pace or progress. **57. drop off, a.** to fall asleep. **b.** to decrease; decline. [(v.) ME *dropp(en),* OE *droppian;* (n.) ME *droppe* < v.; r. ME *drope,* OE *dropa;* c. Icel *dropi*]

drop′ cloth′, a sheet of cloth, paper, plastic, or the like, laid over furniture, a floor, etc., for protection while the room is being painted.

drop′ cook′y, a cooky made by dropping batter from a spoon onto a greased cooky sheet for baking.

drop′ cur′tain, *Theat.* a curtain that is lowered into position from the flies.

drop′ forge′, a device for making large forgings in which a heavy object is allowed to fall vertically upon a piece of work placed on an anvil or between dies. Also called **drop′ ham′mer, drop press.**

drop-forge (drop′fōrj′, -fôrj′), *v.t.,* **-forged, -forg·ing.** *Metalworking.* to form in a drop forge. —**drop′forg′er,** *n.*

drop′ kick′, *Football.* a kick made by dropping a football to the ground and kicking it as it starts to bounce up. Cf. **place kick, punt**[1] (def. 1).

drop-kick (drop′kik′), *Football.* —*v.t.* **1.** to score (a field goal or point after touchdown) by a drop kick. **2.** to kick (the ball as dropped for a drop kick). —*v.i.* **3.** to make a drop kick. —**drop′-kick′er,** *n.*

drop′ leaf′, *Furniture.* an extension attached to a table and folded vertically when not needed. —**drop′-leaf′,** *adj.*

drop·let (drop′lit), *n.* a little drop.

drop·light (drop′līt′), *n.* a lamp suspended from the ceiling or wall by a flexible cord or tube.

drop-off (drop′ôf′, -of′), *n.* **1.** a vertical or very steep descent. **2.** a decline or decrease.

drop·out (drop′out′), *n.* **1.** an act or instance of dropping out. **2.** a student who withdraws before completing a course of instruction. **3.** a person who withdraws from high school after having reached the legal age to do so. Also, **drop′-out′.**

dropped′ scone′, scone (def. 3).

drop·per (drop′ər), *n.* **1.** a person who or thing that drops. **2.** a glass tube with a hollow rubber bulb at one end and a small orifice at the other, for drawing in a liquid and expelling it in drops; a medicine dropper.

drop·ping (drop′ing), *n.* **1.** the act of a person or thing that drops. **2.** something that is dropped or falls in drops. **3. droppings,** dung of animals. [ME; OE *droppung*]

drop′ press′. See **drop forge.**

drop′ ship′ment, *Com.* a shipment of goods made directly from the manufacturer to the retailer but billed through the wholesaler or distributor.

drop′ shot′, 1. (in tennis, badminton, etc.) a ball or shuttlecock so softly hit that it falls to the playing surface just after clearing the net. **2.** (in squash, handball, etc.) a ball so softly hit that it falls suddenly to the ground just after striking the front wall.

drop·si·cal (drop′si kəl), *adj.* of, like, or affected with dropsy. —**drop′si·cal·ly,** *adv.* —**drop′si·cal·ness,** *n.*

drop′ sid′ing, weatherboarding having its upper edges narrowed to fit into grooves or rabbets in its lower edges, and its backs flat against the sheathing or studs of the wall. Also called **novelty siding.** See illus. at **siding.**

drop·sy (drop′sē), *n. Pathol.* an excessive accumulation of serous fluid in a serous cavity or in the subcutaneous cellular tissue. [ME *drop(e)sie,* aph. var. of *ydropesie* < OF < ML *(h)ydrōpisīa* = L *hydrōpis(is)* (< Gk *hydrôpi-,* s. of *hýdrōps* HYDROPS + *-sis* -SIS) + *-ia* -Y[3]] —**drop·sied** (drop′sēd), *adj.*

dropt (dropt), *v.* a pt. and pp. of **drop.**

drop′ ta′ble, a table top hinged to a wall, held in a horizontal position by a bracket while in use.

drop·wort (drop′wûrt′), *n.* **1.** a European rosaceous herb, *Filipendula hexapetala,* bearing small, odorless white or reddish flowers. **2.** any North American, umbelliferous plant of the genus *Oxypolis,* as *O. rigidior,* found in ditches and marshes.

drosh·ky (drosh′kē), *n., pl.* **-kies. 1.** a light, low, four-wheeled, open vehicle used mainly in Russia. **2.** any of various similar carriages. [< Russ *drozhki*]

dros·ky (dros′kē), *n., pl.* **-kies.** droshky.

dro·soph·i·la (drō sof′ə lə, drə-), *n., pl.* **-las, -lae** (-lē′). a fly of the genus *Drosophila,* esp. *D. melanogaster,* used in laboratory studies of heredity. [< NL < Gk *drósо(s)* dew + *phíla,* neut. pl. of *phílos* -PHILE]

dross (drôs, dros), *n.* waste matter; refuse. [ME *dros(se),* OE *drōs;* c. MD *droes* dregs; cf. ME *drōsen,* OE *drōsna;* c. MHG *truosen* husks]

dross·y (drô′sē, dros′ē), *adj.,* **dross·i·er, dross·i·est. 1.** containing dross. **2.** resembling dross; worthless. [ME] —**dross′i·ness,** *n.*

drought (drout), *n.* **1.** an extended period of dry weather, esp. one injurious to crops. **2.** an extended shortage: *a drought of good writing.* **3.** *Dial.* thirst. Also, **drouth** (drouth). [ME; OE *drūgath* = *drūg-* (base of *drȳge* DRY) + *-ath* -TH[1]; c. D *droogte* dryness]

drought·y (drou′tē), *adj.,* **drought·i·er, drought·i·est. 1.** dry. **2.** lacking rain. **3.** *Dial.* thirsty. —**drought′i·ness,** *n.*

drouth·y (drou′thē), *adj.,* **drouth·i·er, drouth·i·est.** droughty. —**drouth′i·ness,** *n.*

drove[1] (drōv), *v.* pt. of **drive.**

drove[2] (drōv), *n., v.,* **droved, drov·ing.** —*n.* **1.** a number of oxen, sheep, or swine driven in a group; herd; flock. **2.** a large crowd of human beings, esp. in motion: *They came to Yankee Stadium in droves.* **3.** Also called **drove′ chis′el.** *Masonry.* a chisel, from two to four inches broad at the edge, for dressing stones to an approximately true surface. —*v.t., v.i.* **4.** to drive or deal in (cattle) as a drover; herd. **5.** *Masonry.* to work or smooth (stone) with a drove. [ME; OE *drāf* that which is driven, i.e., herd, flock; akin to DRIVE] —**Syn. 1.** See **flock**[1].

dro·ver (drō′vər), *n.* a person who drives cattle, sheep, etc., to market.

drown (droun), *v.i.* **1.** to be suffocated by immersion in water or other liquid. —*v.t.* **2.** to suffocate by immersion in water or other liquid. **3.** to destroy or get rid of as if by immersion: *He drowned his sorrows in drink.* **4.** to overwhelm, as by a flood; overpower. **5.** to add too much water or liquid to (a mixture). [ME *drounne,* etc., OE *druncnian,* perh. by loss of *c* between nasals and shift of length from *nn* to *ou*] —**drown′er,** *n.*

drowse (drouz), *v.,* **drowsed, drows·ing,** *n.* —*v.i.* **1.** to be sleepy or half asleep. **2.** to be dull or sluggish. —*v.t.* **3.** to pass or spend (time) in drowsing (often fol. by *away*): *He drowsed away the morning.* **4.** to make sleepy or drowsy. —*n.* **5.** a sleepy condition; state of being half asleep; drowsiness. [OE *drūs(ian)* (to) droop, become sluggish, akin to *drēosan* to fall]

drow·si·head (drou′zē hed′), *n. Archaic.* drowsiness.

drow·sy (drou′zē), *adj.,* **-si·er, -si·est. 1.** half asleep; sleepy. **2.** marked by or resulting from sleepiness. **3.** dull; sluggish. **4.** inducing lethargy or sleepiness: *drowsy spring weather.* —**drow′si·ly,** *adv.* —**drow′si·ness,** *n.*

drub (drub), *v.,* **drubbed, drub·bing,** *n.* —*v.t.* **1.** to beat with a stick or the like; cudgel; flog; thrash. **2.** to drive in or out as if by flogging. *Latin was dubbed into them.* **3.** to defeat decisively, as in a game or contest. **4.** to stamp (the feet). —*n.* **5.** a blow with a stick or the like. [prob. connected with Ar *ḍarb* blow, beating] —**drub′ber,** *n.*

drub·bing (drub′ing), *n.* **1.** a sound thrashing. **2.** a decisive defeat, as in a game or contest.

drudge (druj), *n., v.,* **drudged, drudg·ing.** —*n.* **1.** a person who does menial, distasteful, dull, or hard work. **2.** a person who works in a routine, unimaginative way. —*v.i.* **3.** to perform menial, distasteful, dull, or hard work. [cf. OE man's name *Drycghelm* helmet maker = *drycg* (akin to *drēogan* to work) + *helm* HELM[2]] —**drudg′er,** *n.* —**drudg′ing·ly,** *adv.*

drudg·er·y (druj′ə rē), *n.* menial, distasteful, dull, or hard work. —**Syn.** See **work.**

drug (drug), *n., v.,* **drugged, drug·ging.** —*n.* **1.** *Pharm.* a chemical substance administered to a person or animal to prevent or cure disease or otherwise enhance physical or mental welfare. **2.** a habit-forming medicinal substance, esp. a narcotic. **3. drugs,** *U.S.* any personal hygienic items sold in a drugstore, as toothpaste, mouthwash, etc. **4.** *Obs.* any ingredient used in chemistry, pharmacy, dyeing, or the like. **5. drug on the market,** a commodity that is overabundant or in excess of demand in the market. Also, **drug in the market.** —*v.t.* **6.** to mix (food or drink) with a drug, esp.

a stupefying, narcotic, or poisonous drug. **7.** to stupefy or poison with a drug. **8.** to administer a medicinal drug to. **9.** to administer anything nauseous to. [ME *drogges* (pl.) < MF *drogue* < Gmc; cf. MD *droge* DRY]

drug·get (drug′it), *n.* **1.** Also called **India drugget.** a rug from India of coarse hair with cotton or jute. **2.** *Obs.* a fabric woven wholly or partly of wool, used for clothing. [< MF *droguet* worthless stuff (textile) = *drogue* trash (see DRUG) + *-et* -ET]

drug·gist (drug′ist), *n.* **1.** a person who compounds or prepares drugs according to medical prescriptions; apothecary; pharmacist; dispensing chemist. **2.** the owner or operator of a drugstore. [DRUG + -IST; cf. F *droguiste*]

drug·store (drug′stōr′, -stôr′), *n.* *U.S.* the place of business of a druggist or pharmacist, usually also selling cosmetics, stationery, cigarettes, etc. Also, **drug′ store′.**

Dru·id (drōō′id), *n.* (*often l.c.*) a member of a pre-Christian religious order of priests among the ancient Celts of Gaul, Britain, and Ireland. Also, *referring to a woman,* **Dru·id·ess** (drōō′i dis). [< L *druid(ae)* < Gaulish *druid(es)* (pl.); r. *druide* < F; cf. OIr *drui* (nom.), *druid* (dat., acc.)] —**dru·id′ic, dru·id′i·cal,** *adj.* —**dru′id·ism,** *n.*

Dru′id stone′, sarsen.

drum[1] (drum), *n., v.,* **drummed, drum·ming.** —*n.* **1.** a musical percussion instrument consisting of a hollow, usually cylindrical body covered at one or both ends with a tightly stretched membrane, or head, and which produces a booming, tapping, or hollow sound when struck with the hand, a stick, or a pair of sticks. **2.** any hollow tree or similar object or device used in this way. **3.** the sound produced by such an instrument, object, or device. **4.** any rumbling or deep booming sound. **5.** a natural organ by which an animal produces a loud or bass sound. **6.** *Anat., Zool.* **a.** See **middle ear. b.** See **tympanic membrane. 7.** any cylindrical object with flat ends. **8.** a cylindrical part of a machine. **9.** a cylindrical box or receptacle, esp. a large, metal one for storing or transporting liquids. **10.** any of several cylindrical or nearly cylindrical stones laid one above the other to form a column or pier. **11.** any of several marine and fresh-water fishes of the family *Sciaenidae* that produce a drumming sound. **12.** *Computer Technol.* See **magnetic drum.** —*v.i.* **13.** to beat or play a drum. **14.** to beat on anything rhythmically, esp. to tap one's fingers rhythmically on a hard surface. **15.** to make a sound like that of a drum; resound. —*v.t.* **16.** to beat (a drum) rhythmically; perform by beating a drum. **17.** to call or summon by, or as by, beating a drum. **18.** to drive or force by persistent repetition: *to drum an idea into someone.* **19. drum out, a.** (formerly) to expel or dismiss in disgrace from a military service to the beat of a drum. **b.** to dismiss in disgrace. **20. drum up,** to obtain or create (customers, enthusiasm, etc.) through vigorous effort. [back formation from *drumslade* drum, drummer, alter. (by mishearing) of D or LG *trommelslag* drumbeat = *trommel* drum + *slag* beat (akin to *slagen* to beat; c. SLAY)]

drum[2] (drum), *n.* *Scot., Irish Eng.* a long, narrow hill or ridge. [< Ir and ScotGael *druim*]

drum·beat (drum′bēt′), *n.* the sound of a drum.

drum′ corps′, a band of drum players under the direction of a drum major.

drum·fire (drum′fīᵊr′), *n.* gunfire so heavy and continuous as to sound like the beating of drums.

drum·fish (drum′fish′), *n., pl.* (*esp. collectively*) **-fish,** (*esp. referring to two or more kinds or species*) **-fish·es.** drum[1] (def. 11).

drum·head (drum′hed′), *n.* **1.** the membrane stretched upon a drum. **2.** *Naut.* the top part of a capstan. —*adj.* **3.** characteristic of a drumhead court-martial; carried out in summary fashion: *a drumhead execution.*

drum′head court′-martial, a court-martial held for the summary trial of charges of offenses committed during military operations.

drum·lin (drum′lin), *n.* *Geol.* a long, narrow or oval, smoothly rounded hill of unstratified glacial drift. [DRUM[2] + *-lin,* var. of -LING[1]]

drum′ ma′jor, the marching leader of a drum corps or band.

drum′ majorette′, a girl who twirls a baton, esp. while marching with a band or drum corps, as in a parade. Also called **majorette.**

drum·mer (drum′ər), *n.* **1.** a person who plays a drum. **2.** *U.S.* a commercial traveler or traveling salesman.

Drum·mond (drum′ənd), *n.* **1. Henry,** 1851–97, Scottish clergyman and writer. **2. William,** 1585–1649, Scottish poet.

Drum′mond light′. See **calcium light.** [named after Capt. T. *Drummond* (1797–1840), British engineer]

drum·stick (drum′stik′), *n.* **1.** a stick for beating a drum. **2.** the meaty leg of a fowl.

drunk (drungk), *adj.* **1.** having one's faculties impaired by an excess of alcoholic liquor; intoxicated. **2.** overcome or dominated by a strong feeling or emotion: *drunk with power.* **3.** pertaining to or caused by intoxication or inebriated persons. —*n.* **4.** a drunken person. **5.** a spree; drinking party. —*v.* **6.** pp. and a nonstandard pt. of **drink.** [ME *drunke(n),* OE *druncen* (n., adj.), ptp. of *drincan* to DRINK] —**Syn. 1.** inebriated. —**Ant. 1–3.** sober.

drunk·ard (drungk′ərd), *n.* a person who is habitually or frequently drunk.
—**Syn.** toper, sot, tippler, drinker. DRUNKARD, INEBRIATE, DIPSOMANIAC are terms for a person who drinks hard liquors habitually. DRUNKARD connotes willful indulgence to excess. INEBRIATE, once a more formal word, is now applied only humorously. DIPSOMANIAC is the term for a person who, because of some psychological or physiological illness, has an irresistible craving for liquor. The DIPSOMANIAC is popularly called an ALCOHOLIC. —**Ant.** teetotaler.

drunk·en (drungk′kən), *adj.* **1.** intoxicated; drunk. **2.** given to drunkenness. **3.** pertaining to, proceeding from, or marked by intoxication: *a drunken quarrel.* [var. of DRUNK adj. and ptp.] —**drunk′en·ly,** *adv.* —**drunk′en·ness,** *n.* —**Syn. 1.** inebriated, tipsy, besotted.

drunk·om·e·ter (drungk kom′i tər), *n.* a device for chemically analyzing a person's breath to determine the amount of alcohol in his blood.

dru·pa·ceous (drōō pā′shəs), *adj.* *Bot.* **1.** resembling or relating to a drupe; consisting of drupes. **2.** producing drupes: *drupaceous trees.*

drupe (drōōp), *n.* *Bot.* a fruit, as a peach, cherry, or plum, consisting of an outer skin, or epicarp, a usually pulpy and succulent layer, or mesocarp, and a hard and woody inner shell, or endocarp, usually enclosing a single seed. [< L *drūpa, druppa* overripe olive < Gk *drýppa* olive]

drupe·let (drōōp′lit), *n.* *Bot.* a little drupe, as one of the individual pericarps composing the blackberry.

Dru′ry Lane′ (drŏŏr′ē), a street in London, England, famous for its theaters.

Druse (drōōz), *n.* a member of a sect living chiefly in Syria and Lebanon, having a faith combining elements of Christianity, Judaism, and Islam. [< F < Ar *durūz* pl. of *darazī,* after *Ismail ad-Darazī* (Ismail the tailor), 11th-century founder of the sect] —**Dru′se·an, Dru′si·an,** *adj.*

Dru·sus (drōō′səs), *n.* **Nero Claudius** ("*Germanicus*"), 38–9 B.C., Roman general.

druth·ers (druth′ərz), *n.* (*usually construed as sing.*) *Dial.* one's own way, choice, or preference: *If I had my druthers, I'd go swimming.* [pl. of *druther,* alter. of *would rather*]

Druze (drōōz), *n.* Druse.

dry (drī), *adj.,* **dri·er, dri·est,** *v.,* **dried, dry·ing,** *n., pl.* **drys.** —*adj.* **1.** free from moisture or excess moisture; not moist or wet: *a dry towel; dry air.* **2.** having or characterized by little or no rain: *a dry climate.* **3.** characterized by absence, deficiency, or failure of natural or ordinary moisture. **4.** not under, in, or on water: *It was good to be on dry land.* **5.** not now containing or yielding water or other liquid: *The well is dry.* **6.** not yielding milk: *a dry cow.* **7.** free from tears: *dry eyes.* **8.** drained or evaporated away: *a dry river.* **9.** desiring drink; thirsty. **10.** causing thirst: *dry work.* **11.** served or eaten without butter, jam, etc.: *dry toast.* **12.** (of cooked food) lacking enough moisture or juice to be satisfying or succulent. **13.** (of bread and bakery products) stale. **14.** *Building Trades.* **a.** (of masonry construction) built without fresh mortar or cement. **b.** (of a wall, ceiling, etc., in an interior) finished without the use of fresh plaster. **15.** *Art.* hard and formal in outline, or lacking mellowness and warmth in color. **16.** plain; bald; unadorned: *dry facts.* **17.** dull; uninteresting: *a dry subject.* **18.** expressed in a straight-faced, matter-of-fact way: *dry humor.* **19.** indifferent; cold; unemotional: *a dry answer.* **20.** unproductive: *The greatest of artists have dry years.* **21.** (of wines) not sweet. **22.** of or pertaining to nonliquid substances or commodities: *dry provisions.* **23.** *U.S.* characterized by or favoring prohibition of the manufacture and sale of alcoholic liquors for use as beverages: *a dry state.* **24.** (of lumber) fully seasoned. **25. not dry behind the ears,** immature; callow; inexperienced. —*v.t.* **26.** to make dry; free from moisture: *to dry the dishes.* —*v.i.* **27.** to become dry; lose moisture. **28. dry up, a.** to make or become completely dry. **b.** to cease to exist; evaporate. **c.** *Informal.* to stop talking. —*n.* **29.** *Informal.* a prohibitionist. **30.** a dry area. [ME *drie,* OE *dryge;* akin to D *droog,* G *trocken;* see DROUGHT] —**dry′a·ble,** *adj.* —**dry′ly,** *adv.* —**dry′ness,** *n.*
—**Syn. 1.** DRY, ARID both mean without moisture. DRY is the general word indicating absence of water or freedom from moisture (which may be favorable): *a dry well; dry clothes* or *land.* ARID suggests great or intense dryness in a region or climate, esp. such as results in bareness or in barrenness: *arid tracts of desert.* **17.** tedious, barren, boring, tiresome, jejune. **26.** See **evaporate.** —**Ant. 1.** wet.

dry·ad (drī′əd, -ad), *n., pl.* **-ads, -a·des** (-ə dēz′). (*often cap.*) *Class. Myth.* a deity or nymph of the woods. Cf. **hamadryad.** [abstracted from Gk *Dryádes,* pl. of *Dryás* = *drý(s)* tree, oak + *-as* fem. suffix] —**dry·ad·ic** (drī ad′ik), *adj.*

dry-as-dust (drī′əz dust′), *adj.* dull and boring.

dry′ bat′tery, *Elect.* a dry cell or a voltaic battery consisting of a number of dry cells.

dry′-bulb′ thermom′eter (drī′bulb′), an ordinary thermometer used in conjunction with one having a wet bulb, in a psychrometer. Cf. **wet-bulb thermometer.**

dry′ cell′, *Elect.* a cell in which the electrolyte exists in the form of a paste, is absorbed in a porous medium, or is otherwise restrained from flowing.

dry-clean (drī′klēn′), *v.t.* to subject to dry cleaning. [back formation from DRY CLEANING] —**dry′ clean′er.**

dry′ clean′ing, 1. the cleaning of garments, fabrics, draperies, etc., with a liquid other than water, as benzine or gasoline. **2.** garments for cleaning in this way.

Dry·den (drīd′ᵊn), *n.* **John,** 1631–1700, English poet, dramatist, and critic.

dry′ distilla′tion. See **destructive distillation.**

dry′ dock′, a structure able to contain a vessel and to be drained or lifted so as to leave the vessel free of water with all parts of the hull accessible for repairs, painting, etc. Cf. **floating dock, graving dock.**

dry-dock (drī′dok′), *v.t.* **1.** to place (a ship) in dry dock. —*v.i.* **2.** (of a ship) to go into dry dock.

dry·er (drī′ər), *n.* **1.** a machine, appliance, or apparatus for removing moisture, as by forced ventilation or heat: *a hair dryer; a clothes dryer.* **2.** drier (defs. 1, 2).

dry′ farm′ing, a mode of farming practiced in regions of slight or insufficient rainfall, depending largely upon tillage methods that render the soil more receptive of moisture and reduce evaporation. —**dry′ farm′er.**

dry′ fly′, *Angling.* an artificial fly designed for use on the surface of the water. Cf. **wet fly.**

dry′ fres′co. See **fresco secco.**

dry′ goods′, textile fabrics and related merchandise.

Dry′ Ice′, *Trademark.* solidified carbon dioxide, CO_2, used as a refrigerant.

dry·ing (drī′ing), *adj.* **1.** causing dryness: *a drying breeze.* **2.** designed to or capable of becoming dry and hard on exposure to air. [ME]

dry′ing oil′, any of a group of oily, organic liquids, as linseed oil, that when applied as a thin coating absorb atmospheric oxygen, forming a tough, elastic layer.

dry′ kiln′, an oven for the controlled drying and seasoning of cut lumber.

dry′ law′, *U.S.* a law prohibiting the sale of alcoholic beverages.

dry′ meas′ure, the system of units of capacity used esp. in measuring dry commodities, such as grain or fruit.
dry′ milk′. See **powdered milk.**
dry′ nurse′, **1.** a nurse who takes care of but does not suckle another's infant. Cf. **wet nurse. 2.** *Informal.* a person who tutors or guides an inexperienced superior.
dry-nurse (drī′nûrs′), *v.t.*, **-nursed, -nurs·ing.** to act as a dry nurse to.
dry·point (drī′point′), *n.* **1.** a technique of engraving, esp. on copper, in which a pointed needle is used to make furrows that produce a print characterized by soft, velvety black lines. **2.** a print made by this technique.
dry′ rot′, **1.** *Plant Pathol.* **a.** a decay of seasoned timber, resulting in its becoming brittle and crumbling to a dry powder, caused by various fungi. **b.** any of various diseases of plants in which the rotted tissues are dry. **2.** any concealed or unsuspected inner decay.
dry′ run′, **1.** *Mil.* practice in firing arms without using live ammunition. **2.** a rehearsal.
dry-shod (drī′shod′), *adj., adv.* having or keeping the shoes dry. [OE *drȳgsceod*]
Dry′ Tor·tu′gas (tôr to͞o′gəz), a group of 10 small islands at the entrance to the Gulf of Mexico: a part of Florida; the site of Fort Jefferson.
dry·wall (drī′wôl), *n.* a prefabricated panel of dried plaster between paper sheets, used in wall construction.
dry′ wash′, **1.** clothes, curtains, etc., washed and dried but not yet ironed. **2.** wash (def. 33).
D.S., *Music.* See **dal segno.**
d.s., daylight saving.
D.Sc., Doctor of Science.
D.S.C., See **Distinguished Service Cross.**
D.S.M., See **Distinguished Service Medal.**
D.S.O., See **Distinguished Service Order.**
DST, Daylight Saving Time. Also, **D.S.T.**
D. Surg., Dental Surgeon.
d.t., See **delirium tremens.** Also, **d.t.'s.**
D.Th., Doctor of Theology. Also, **D.Theol.**
du (do͞o, dyo͞o; *Fr.* dʏ), (in names of French derivation) a contraction of *de* and the article *le: Joachim du Bellay.*
Du., 1. Duke. **2.** Dutch.
du·ad (do͞o′ad, dyo͞o′-), *n.* a group of two; pair. [< L *du(o)* two + -AD[1]]
du·al (do͞o′əl, dyo͞o′-), *adj.* **1.** of, pertaining to, or noting two. **2.** composed or consisting of two people, items, parts, etc., together; twofold; double: *dual ownership; dual controls on a plane.* **3.** having a twofold, or double, character or nature. **4.** *Gram.* noting or pertaining to a member of the category of number denoting two referents. **—***n.* *Gram.* **5.** the dual number. **6.** a form in the dual. [< L *duāl(is)* containing two, relating to a pair = *du(o)* two + *-ālis* -AL[1]] **—du′al·ly,** *adv.*
Du·a·la (do͞o ä′lä), *n.* Douala.
Du′al Alli′ance, **1.** the alliance between France and Russia (1890), strengthened by a military convention (1892–93) and lasting until the Bolshevik Revolution in 1917. **2.** the alliance between Germany and Austria-Hungary against Russia 1879–1918.
du·al·ism (do͞o′ə liz′əm, dyo͞o′-), *n.* **1.** the state of being dual or consisting of two parts; division into two. **2.** *Philos.* **a.** a theory that there are two basic substances or principles, as mind and body. Cf. **monism** (def. 1a), **pluralism** (def. 1a). **b.** (in epistemology) a theory that the idea or sense datum present to the mind is not identical with the object known. Cf. **monism** (def. 1b). **3.** *Theol.* **a.** the doctrine that there are two eternal principles, one good and the other evil. **b.** the belief that man embodies two parts, as body and soul. **—du′al·ist,** *n.* **—du′al·is′tic,** *adj.* **—du′al·is′ti·cal·ly,** *adv.*
du·al·i·ty (do͞o al′i tē, dyo͞o-), *n.* a dual state or quality. [ME *dualitie* < LL *duālitās*]
du′al personal′ity, *Psychol.* a disorder in which an individual possesses two dissociated personalities.
du·al-pur·pose (do͞o′əl pûr′pəs, dyo͞o′-), *adj.* **1.** serving two functions. **2.** (of cattle) bred for two purposes, as to provide beef and milk.
Duar·te Fuen·tes (dwär′te fwen′tes), **Jo·sé Na·po·le·ón** (hô se′ nä pô le ôn′), born 1926, Salvadoran political leader: president since 1984.
dub[1] (dub), *v.t.*, **dubbed, dub·bing. 1.** to strike lightly with a sword in the ceremony of conferring knighthood; make, or designate as, a knight: *The king dubbed him a knight.* **2.** to invest with any name, character, dignity, or title; style; name; call: *He was dubbed a charlatan.* **3.** to strike, cut, rub, or make smooth, as leather or timber. [ME *dubb(en),* OE *dubbian* < unrecorded n.; c. HG (dial.) *tuppe* big piece of wood, Norw *dubb* peg; cf. Icel *dubba,* OF *adub-(b)er* to dub (< E), LG *dubben* to strike; see DOWEL]
dub[2] (dub), *n.* *Slang.* an awkward, unskillful person. [?]
dub[3] (dub), *v.*, **dubbed, dub·bing,** *n.* **—***v.t., v.i.* **1.** to thrust; poke. **—***n.* **2.** a thrust; poke. **3.** a drumbeat. [appar. same word (with older sense) as DUB[1]]
dub[4] (dub), *v.*, **dubbed, dub·bing,** *n.* **—***v.t.* **1.** to furnish (a film or tape) with a new sound track, as one recorded in the language of the country of import. **2.** to add (music, speech, etc.) to a film or tape (often fol. by *in*). **3.** to copy (a tape or disk recording). **—***n.* **4.** the new sounds added to a film or tape. [short for DOUBLE]
dub[5] (dub), *n.* *Scot. and North Eng.* a pool of water; puddle. [?; cf. G *Tümpel* pond, puddle]
Du·bai (do͞o bī′), *n.* **1.** a member state of the United Arab Emirates. **2.** a seaport in and the capital of this state, in NE United Arab Emirates, on the Persian Gulf. 206,861.
Du Bar·ry (do͞o bar′ē, dyo͞o; *Fr.* dʏ bᴀ ʀē′), **Comtesse** (*Marie Jeanne Bécu*), 1746–93, mistress of Louis XV.
dub·bin (dub′in), *n.* a mixture of tallow and oil used in dressing leather. Also, **dubbing.** [var. of DUBBING]
dub·bing (dub′ing), *n.* **1.** the conferring of knighthood; accolade. **2.** *Angling.* the material used for the body of an artificial fly. **3.** dubbin. [ME]
du Bel·lay (do͞o bə lā′, dyo͞o; *Fr.* dʏ be lā′), **Joachim.** See **Bellay, Joachim du.**
du·bi·e·ty (do͞o bī′i tē, dyo͞o-), *n., pl.* **-ties. 1.** doubtfulness; doubt. **2.** a matter of doubt. Also called **dubiosity.** [< L *dubietās*]
Du·bin·sky (do͞o bin′skē), *n.* **David,** 1892–1982, U.S. labor leader, born in Poland: president of the I.L.G.W.U. 1932–66.
du·bi·os·i·ty (do͞o′bē os′i tē, dyo͞o′-), *n., pl.* **-ties.** dubiety.
du·bi·ous (do͞o′bē əs, dyo͞o′-), *adj.* **1.** doubtful; marked by or occasioning doubt: *a dubious reply.* **2.** of doubtful quality or propriety; questionable: *a dubious transaction; a dubious compliment.* **3.** of uncertain outcome: *in dubious battle.* **4.** wavering or hesitating in opinion; inclined to doubt. [< L *dubi(us)* + -OUS] **—du′bi·ous·ly,** *adv.* **—du′bi·ous·ness** *n.* **—Syn. 4.** See **doubtful.**
du·bi·ta·ble (do͞o′bi tə bəl, dyo͞o′-), *adj.* open to doubt; doubtful; uncertain. [< L *dubitābil(is).* See DOUBT, -BLE] **—du′bi·ta·bly,** *adv.*
du·bi·ta·tion (do͞o′bi tā′shən, dyo͞o′-), *n.* doubt. [late ME < L *dubitātiōn-* (s. of *dubitātiō*) = *dubitāt(us)* (ptp. of *dubitāre* to DOUBT; see -ATE[1]) + *-iōn-* -ION]
Dub·lin (dub′lin), *n.* **1.** a seaport in and the capital of the Republic of Ireland, in the E part, on the Irish Sea. 567,866. **2.** a county in E Republic of Ireland. 849,542; 356 sq. mi. *Co. seat:* Dublin.
Dub′lin Bay′, an inlet of the Irish Sea at Dublin.
Du Bois (do͞o bois′), **William E(dward) B(urg·hardt)** (bûrg′härd), 1868–1963, U.S. educator and writer.
Du·bon·net (do͞o′bə nā′, dyo͞o′-), *n.* **1.** *Trademark.* a sweet, red or white, aromatized wine, used chiefly as an aperitif. **2.** (*l.c.*) a deep purple-red color.
Du·brov·nik (do͞o′bʀôv nik), *n.* a seaport in S Yugoslavia, on the Adriatic. 25,000 (est. 1964). Italian, **Ragusa.**
Du·buf·fet (dʏ bʏ fe′), *n.* **Jean** (zhäɴ), 1901–85, French painter.
Du·buque (də byo͞ok′), *n.* a city in E Iowa, on the Mississippi River. 62,309 (1970).
duc (dʏk), *n., pl.* **ducs** (dʏk). *French.* duke.
du·cal (do͞o′kəl, dyo͞o′-), *adj.* of or pertaining to a duke. [< LL *ducāl(is)* of a leader. See DUKE, -AL[1]] **—du′cal·ly,** *adv.*
duc·at (duk′ət), *n.* **1.** any of various gold coins formerly issued in various parts of Europe, esp. that first issued in Venice in 1284. **2.** *Slang.* a ticket to a public performance. [ME < MF < OIt *ducat(o)* = *duc(a)* DUKE + *-ato* -ATE[1] (from the portrait of a duke (or doge) stamped on it)]
du·ce (do͞o′chā; *It.* do͞o′che), *n., pl.* **-ces,** *It.* **-ci** (-chē). **1.** a leader or dictator. **2. il Duce,** the leader: applied to Benito Mussolini. [< It < L *dūci-* (s. of *dux*) leader]
Du Chail·lu (do͞o shī′yo͞o, -shal′-, dyo͞o-; *Fr.* dʏ shᴀ yʏ′), **Paul Bel·lo·ni** (pôl bə lō′nē; *Fr.* pôl be lô nē′), 1835–1903, U.S. explorer in Africa, traveler, and writer; born in France.
Du·champ (dʏ shäɴ′), *n.* **Mar·cel** (mᴀʀ sel′), 1887–1968, French painter, in U.S. after 1915.
duch·ess (duch′is), *n.* **1.** the wife or widow of a duke. **2.** a woman who holds in her own right the sovereignty of a duchy. [ME *duchesse* < MF, fem. of *duc* DUKE; see -ESS]
duch·y (duch′ē), *n., pl.* **duch·ies.** the territory ruled by a duke or duchess. [ME *duche, duchie* < MF *duche* < LL *ducāt(us)* leadership. See DUKE, -ATE[1]]
duck[1] (duk), *n., pl.* **ducks,** (*esp. collectively for 1–3*) **duck. 1.** any of numerous wild or domesticated web-footed swimming birds of the family *Anatidae,* esp. of the genus *Anas* and allied genera, characterized by a broad, flat bill, short legs, and depressed body. **2.** the female of this bird, as distinguished from the male. Cf. **drake**[1]. **3.** the flesh of this bird, eaten as food. **4.** Often, **ducks.** (*construed as sing.*) *Brit. Slang.* ducky[2]. [ME *duk, doke,* OE *dūce* diver, duck; akin to DUCK[2]]
duck[2] (duk), *v.i.* **1.** to plunge the whole body or the head momentarily under water. **2.** to stoop or bend suddenly; bob. **3.** to avoid or evade a blow, unpleasant task, etc.; dodge. **—***v.t.* **4.** to plunge or dip in water momentarily. **5.** to lower (the head, body, etc.) suddenly. **6.** to avoid or evade (a blow, unpleasant task, etc.); dodge: *to duck an embarrassing question.* **—***n.* **7.** the act or an instance of ducking. [ME *duke(n), douken;* c. G *tauchen* to dive, *ducken* to duck] **—duck′er,** *n.* **—Syn. 1.** dive, dip, souse. **2.** bow, dodge.
duck[3] (duk), *n.* **1.** a heavy, plain-weave cotton fabric for tents, clothing, etc. **2. ducks,** (*construed as pl.*) slacks or trousers made of this material. [< D *doek* cloth; c. G *Tuch*]
duck[4] (duk), *n.* (in World War II) an amphibious military truck. [alter. of DUKW, code name]

Duckbill
(Total length 2 ft.; tail 6 in.)

duck·bill (duk′bil′), *n.* a small, aquatic, egg-laying monotreme, *Ornithorhynchus anatinus,* of Australia and Tasmania, having webbed feet and a bill like that of a duck. Also called **duck′bill plat′ypus, duck′-billed plat′ypus, platypus.**
duck·board (duk′bōrd′, -bôrd′), *n.* a board or number of boards laid as a floor over wet or muddy ground.
duck′ foot′, *Furniture.* See **web foot.**
duck·ie (duk′ē), *adj.* ducky[1].
duck′ing stool′, a former instrument of punishment consisting of a chair in which offenders were tied to be plunged into water.

Ducking stool

duck·ling (duk′ling), *n.* a young duck. [late ME; see DUCK[1], -LING[1]]
duck·pin (duk′pin′), *n.* **1.** *Bowling.* a short pin of relatively large diameter, used in a game resembling tenpins and bowled at with small balls. **2. duckpins,** (*construed as sing.*) the game. [so called from the pin's resemblance to the shape of a duck]

ducks′ and drakes′, 1. a pastime in which flat stones or shells are skipped over the surface of water. 2. **play ducks and drakes with,** to handle recklessly; squander. Also, **make ducks and drakes of.** [from a fancied likeness to a waterfowl's movements]
duck′ soup′, *Slang.* something that is easy to accomplish.
duck·tail (duk′tāl′), *n.* a style of haircut in which the hair is worn long on the sides and combed to meet at the back. Also called **duck′tail hair′cut.**
duck·weed (duk′wēd′), *n.* any plant of the family *Lemnaceae,* esp. of the genus *Lemna,* comprising small aquatic plants that float free on still water. [late ME *dockewede;* so called because eaten by ducks]
duck·y[1] (duk′ē), *adj.,* **duck·i·er, duck·i·est.** *Informal.* 1. fine; excellent. 2. dear; darling. Also, **duckie.** [DUCK[1] + -Y[1]]
duck·y[2] (duk′ē), *n., pl.* **duck·ies.** *Brit. Slang.* (used as a term of endearment or familiarity) dear; sweetheart; darling; pet. [DUCK[1] + -Y[2] (? altered by folk etymology < MFlem *docke* doll; see DOXY[2])]
duct (dukt), *n.* 1. any tube, canal, pipe, or conduit by which a fluid, air, or other substance is conducted or conveyed. 2. *Anat., Zool.* a tube, canal, or vessel conveying a body fluid, esp. a glandular secretion or excretion. 3. *Bot.* a cavity or vessel formed by elongated cells or by many cells. 4. *Elect.* a single enclosed runway for conductors or cables. 5. *Print.* (in a press) the reservoir for ink. [< L *duct(us)* leadership, a conducting, a drawing off (as of water), hence channel (in ML), n. use of ptp. of *dūcere* to lead] —**duct′less,** *adj.*
duc·tile (duk′tᵊl, -til), *adj.* 1. capable of being hammered out thin, as certain metals; malleable. 2. capable of being drawn out into wire or threads, as gold. 3. able to undergo change of form without breaking. 4. capable of being molded or shaped; plastic. [< L, neut. of *ductilis.* See DUCT, -ILE] —**duc′tile·ly,** *adv.* —**duc·til′i·ty, duc′tile·ness,** *n.*
duct′less gland′. See **endocrine gland.**
dud (dud), *n. Informal.* 1. a person or enterprise that proves to be a failure. 2. *Mil.* a shell that fails to explode after being fired. [? special use of *dud,* sing. of DUDS]
dude (do͞od, dyo͞od), *n.* 1. a man excessively concerned with his clothes, grooming, and manners. 2. *Western U.S.* an Easterner vacationing on a ranch. [?] —**dud′ish,** *adj.* —**dud′ish·ly,** *adv.*
du·deen (do͞o dēn′), *n. Irish Eng.* a short clay tobacco pipe. [< Ir *dúidín* = *dúd* pipe + *-ín* dim. suffix]
dude′ ranch′, a ranch operated as a vacation resort.
Du·de·vant (*Fr.* dʏdᵊ väɴ′), *n.* **Madame A·man·dine Lu·cile Au·rore** (*Fr.* A mäɴ dēn′ lʏ sēl′ ō rôr′). See **Sand, George.**
dudg·eon[1] (duj′ən), *n.* a feeling of offense or resentment; anger: *We left in high dudgeon.* [?]
dudg·eon[2] (duj′ən), *n. Obs.* 1. a wood used esp. for the handles of knives, daggers, etc. 2. a handle or hilt made of this wood. [late ME; cf. AF *digeon*]
Dud·ley (dud′lē), *n.* 1. **Robert, 1st Earl of Leicester,** 1532?–88, British statesman and favorite of Queen Elizabeth. 2. **Thomas,** 1576–1653, English governor of Massachusetts Bay Colony 1634–35, 1640–41, 1645–46, 1650–51. 3. a city in central England, near Birmingham. 61,748 (1961).
duds (dudz), *n.pl. Informal.* 1. clothes, esp. a suit of clothes. 2. belongings in general. [ME *dudde;* akin to LG *dudel* coarse sackcloth; cf. OE *Dudda,* man's name]
due (do͞o, dyo͞o), *adj.* 1. immediately owed: *This bill is due.* 2. owing or owed, irrespective of whether the time of payment has arrived. 3. owing or observed as a moral or natural right. 4. rightful; proper; fitting: *due care; in due time.* 5. adequate; sufficient: *a due margin for delay.* 6. under engagement as to time; expected to be ready, be present, or arrive; scheduled: *The plane is due at noon.* 7. **due to,** attributable, as to a cause: *The delay was due to heavy traffic.* —*n.* 8. something due, owed, or naturally belonging to someone. 9. Usually, **dues.** a regular fee or charge payable at specific intervals, esp. to a group or organization: *membership dues.* 10. **give someone his due, a.** to give what justice demands; treat fairly. **b.** to credit a disliked or dishonorable person with something meritorious. —*adv.* 11. directly or exactly: *a due east course.* 12. *Obs.* duly. [ME < MF *deu,* ptp. of *devoir* < L *debēre* to owe; see DEBT] —**due′ness,** *n.*
due′ bill′, a written acknowledgment of indebtedness.
du·e·cen·to (do͞o′ə chen′tō, dyo͞o′-; *It.* do͞o′e chen′tô), *n.* (*often cap.*) the 13th century, with reference to Italy, esp. to its art or literature. [< It, short for *milduecento* 1200, used for the period 1200–99] —**du′e·cen′tist,** *n.*
due′ course′ of law′. See **due process of law.**
du·el (do͞o′əl, dyo͞o′-), *n., v.,* **-eled, -el·ing** or (*esp. Brit.*) **-elled, -el·ling.** —*n.* 1. a prearranged combat between two persons, fought with deadly weapons according to an accepted code of procedure, esp. to settle a private quarrel. 2. any contest between two persons or parties. —*v.t., v.i.* 3. to fight in a duel. [earlier *duell* < ML *duell(um),* L, archaic var. of *bellum* war] —**du′el·is′tic;** *esp. Brit.,* **du′el·lis′tic,** *adj.*
du·el·ist (do͞o′ə list, dyo͞o′-), *n.* a person who participates in a duel. Also, *esp. Brit.,* **du′el·list.** Also called **du′el·er;** *esp. Brit.,* **du′el·ler.**
du·el·lo (do͞o el′ō, dyo͞o-; *It.* do͞o el′lô), *n., pl.* **-los,** *It.* **-li** (-lē). 1. the practice or art of dueling. 2. the code of rules regulating dueling. [< It; see DUEL]
du·en·na (do͞o en′ə, dyo͞o-), *n.* 1. (in Spain and Portugal) an older woman serving as escort or chaperon of a young lady. 2. a governess. [< Sp (now *dueña*) < L *domina,* fem. of *dominus* master]
due′ proc′ess of law′, the regular administration of the law, according to which no citizen may be denied his legal rights and all laws must conform to fundamental, accepted legal principles, as the right of the accused to confront his accusers. Also called **due′ proc′ess, due course of law.**
Due·ro (dwe′rô), *n.* Spanish name of **Douro.**
du·et (do͞o et′, dyo͞o-), *n. Music.* a composition for two voices or instruments. [earlier *duett* < It *duett(o).* See DUO, -ET] —**du·et′tist,** *n.*
duff[1] (duf), *n.* organic matter in various stages of decomposition on the floor of the forest. [fig. use of DUFF[2]]
duff[2] (duf), *n.* a stiff flour pudding, boiled or steamed and often flavored with currants, citron, spices, etc. [var. of DOUGH]
duff[3] (duf), *n. Slang.* the buttocks or rump. [special use of DUFF[2]]
duf·fel (duf′əl), *n.* 1. a sportsman's clothing and equipment. 2. a coarse woolen cloth having a thick nap. Also, **duf′fle.** [after *Duffel,* a town near Antwerp]
duf′fel bag′, a large, cylindrical canvas bag, used esp. by sportsmen and military personnel for carrying personal effects.
duff·er (duf′ər), *n. Informal.* 1. a plodding, clumsy, incompetent person. 2. a dull, indecisive old man. [? Scot dial. *duffar, dowfart* dullard < *dowf* dull, DEAF]
duf′fle coat′, a hooded overcoat of sturdy wool, usually knee-length and with frog fasteners. Also, **duf′fel coat′.** [var. of DUFFEL]
Duf·fy (duf′ē), *n.* **Sir Charles Gav·an** (gav′ən), 1816–1903, Irish and Australian politician.
Du·fy (dʏ fē′), *n.* **Ra·oul** (RA o͞ol′), 1877–1953, French painter.
dug[1] (dug), *v.* a pt. and pp. of **dig.**
dug[2] (dug), *n.* the breast or nipple of a female mammal. [< Scand; cf. Dan *dægge* to coddle; c. Goth *daddjan* to give suck]
Du Gard (*Fr.* dʏ GAR′), **Ro·ger Mar·tin** (*Fr.* Rô zhā′ MAR taN′). See **Martin Du Gard, Roger.**

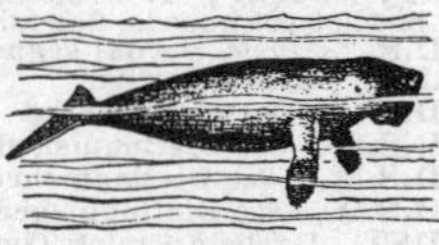
Dugong
(Length 9 ft.)

du·gong (do͞o′gong), *n.* a herbivorous, aquatic mammal, *Dugong dugon,* of the Red Sea and Indian Ocean, having a fishlike body, flipper-like forelimbs, no hind limbs, and a paddlelike tail. [alter. of Malay *duyong*]
dug·out (dug′out′), *n.* 1. a rough shelter or dwelling formed by an excavation in the ground, esp. one used by soldiers. 2. a boat made by hollowing out a log. 3. *Baseball.* a roofed structure, usually below ground level, in which the players sit when not on the field.
Du Gues·clin (dʏ ge klaN′), **Ber·trand** (ber tRäN′), ("*the Eagle of Brittany*"), c1320–80, French military leader: constable of France 1370–80.
Du·ha·mel (do͞o′ə mel′, dyo͞o′-; *Fr.* dʏ A mel′), *n.* **Georges** (zhôRzh), (pen name: *Denis Thévenin*), 1884–1966, French novelist, physician, poet, and essayist.
dui·ker (dī′kər), *n., pl.* **-kers,** (*esp. collectively*) **-ker.** any of several small African antelopes of the *Cephalophus, Sylvicapra,* and related genera, of which usually only the males have short, spikelike horns. [< SAfrD, D *duiker* diver = *duik(en)* (to) dive (see DUCK[2]) + *-er* -ER]
Duis·burg (dʏs′bo͝ork′), *n.* a city in W West Germany, at the junction of the Rhine and Ruhr rivers: the largest river port in Europe. 501,100 (1963). Formerly, **Duis·burg-Ham·born** (dʏs′bo͝ork′häm′bôrn).
duit (doit, dīt), *n.* doit (def. 1).
du jour (də zho͝or′, do͞o; *Fr.* dʏ zho͞oR′), of the kind being served today: *soup du jour.* [< F: of the day]
Du·kas (dʏ kA′), *n.* **Paul (Ab·ra·ham)** (pôl A bRA Am′), 1865–1935, French composer.
duke (do͞ok, dyo͞ok), *n.* 1. (in Continental Europe) the male ruler of a duchy; the sovereign of a small state. 2. a British nobleman holding the highest hereditary title outside the royal family, ranking immediately below a prince and above a marquis. 3. a nobleman of corresponding rank in certain other countries. 4. **dukes,** *Slang.* fists; hands: *Put up your dukes.* [ME *duke, duc* < OF *duc* < L *dūc-* (s. of *dux* leader); akin to TUG, TOW[1]]
Duke (do͞ok, dyo͞ok), *n.* 1. **Benjamin Newton,** 1855–1929, U.S. industrialist. 2. his brother, **James Buchanan,** 1856–1925, U.S. industrialist.
duke·dom (do͞ok′dəm, dyo͞ok′-), *n.* 1. a duchy. 2. the office or rank of a duke. [late ME]
Du·kho·bor (do͞o′kə bôr′), *n., pl.* **Du·kho·bors, Du·kho·bor·tsy** (do͞o′kə bôrt′sē). Doukhobor.
dul·cet (dul′sit), *adj.* 1. pleasant to the ear; melodious. 2. pleasant or agreeable to the eye or the feelings; soothing. 3. *Archaic.* sweet to the taste or smell. [obs. *dulce* (< L *dulc(is)* sweet) + -ET; r. ME *doucet* < MF; see DOUCE] —**dul′cet·ly,** *adv.* —**dul′cet·ness,** *n.*

Dulcimer

dul·ci·fy (dul′sə fī′), *v.t.,* **-fied, -fy·ing.** 1. to make more agreeable; mollify; appease. 2. to sweeten. [< LL *dulcificāre,* with -FY for *-ficāre*] —**dul′ci·fi·ca′tion,** *n.*
dul·ci·mer (dul′sə mər), *n.* a trapezoidal zither with metal strings that are struck with light hammers. [alter. of ME *dowcemere* < MF *doulcemer,* dissimilated var. of *doulcemele* < OIt *dolcimel(o), dolzemele* < L *dulce melos* sweet song. See DULCET, MELIC]
dul·cin·e·a (dul sin′ē ə, dul′sə nē′ə), *n.* a ladylove; sweetheart. [after *Dulcinea* the ladylove of Don Quixote]
du·li·a (do͞o lī′ə, dyo͞o-), *n. Rom. Cath. Theol.* veneration given to saints. Cf. **hyperdulia, latria.** [< ML: service, work done < Gk *douleía* slavery = *doûl(os)* slave + *-eia* -Y[3]]
dull (dul), *adj.* 1. mentally slow; lacking brightness of mind; obtuse; somewhat stupid. 2. lacking keenness of perception in the senses or feelings; insensible; unfeeling. 3. not intense or acute: *a dull pain.* 4. slow in motion or action; not brisk; sluggish. 5. not lively or spirited; listless. 6. causing boredom; tedious; uninteresting: *a dull sermon.* 7. not sharp; blunt: *a dull knife.* 8. having very little depth of color; lacking in richness or intensity of color. 9. not bright, intense, or clear; dim: *a dull day; a dull sound.* —*v.t., v.i.* 10. to make or become dull. [ME; akin to OE *dol* foolish, stupid; c. G *toll*] —**dull′ish,** *adj.* —**dull′ness, dul′ness,** *n.* —**dul′ly,** *adv.*
—**Syn.** 1. unimaginative, unintelligent, stolid. DULL,

SLOW, STUPID are applied figuratively to mental qualities. DULL implies obtuseness, inability to receive clear impressions, lack of imagination: *a dull child.* SLOW applies to a sluggish intellect not able rapidly to take in or understand, although its eventual action may be good: *a slow mind.* STUPID implies slowness of mental processes, but also applies to lack of intelligence, wisdom, prudence, etc.: *a stupid person, thing to do.* **5.** apathetic, torpid, inactive, inert. **6.** boring, tiresome, dreary, vapid. **7.** DULL, BLUNT refer to the edge or point of an instrument, tool, or the like. DULL implies a lack or a loss of keenness or sharpness: *a dull razor or saw.* BLUNT may mean the same or may refer to an edge or point not intended to be keen or sharp: *a blunt or stub pen; a blunt foil.* **10.** blunt, deaden, benumb; depress, dishearten, discourage. **—Ant. 1, 5.** bright. **6.** interesting.

dull·ard (dul′ərd), *n.* a somewhat stupid person.

Dul·les (dul′əs), *n.* **John Foster,** 1888–1959, U.S. statesman: Secretary of State 1953–59.

dulse (duls), *n.* a coarse, edible, red seaweed, *Rhodymenia palmata.* [< Scot < Gael *duileasg* (by syncope, and loss of final, as in SCOTS, etc.)]

Du·luth (də lo͞oth′), *n.* a port in E Minnesota, on Lake Superior. 100,578 (1970).

du·ly (do͞o′lē, dyo͞o′-), *adv.* **1.** in a proper or fitting manner. **2.** in due time; punctually. [ME *duelich(e).* See DUE, -LY]

du·ma (do͞o′mə; *Russ.* do͞o′mä), *n.* **1.** (in Russia prior to 1917) a council or official assembly. **2.** (*cap.*) an elective legislative assembly, established in 1905 by Nicholas II, constituting the lower house of parliament. Also, **douma.** [< Russ: thought, meditation, council]

Du·mas (dʏ mä′), *n.* **1. A·le·xan·dre** (A lek säN′dRᵊ), ("*Dumas père*"), 1802–70, French dramatist and novelist. **2.** his son, **Alexandre** ("*Dumas fils*"), 1824–95, French dramatist and novelist.

Du Mau·ri·er (do͞o môr′ē ā′, dyo͞o′; *Fr.* dʏ mō Ryā′), **1. Dame Daphne** (*Lady Browning*), born 1907, English novelist. **2.** her grandfather, **George Louis Pal·mel·la Bus·son** (pal mel′ə bo͞o sôn′; *Fr.* bʏ sôN′), 1834–96, English illustrator and novelist.

dumb (dum), *adj.* **1.** *Informal.* stupid; dull-witted. **2.** without the power of speech: *a dumb animal.* **3.** temporarily unable to speak: *dumb with astonishment.* **4.** refraining from speech; silent. **5.** made, done, etc., without speech. **6.** lacking some usual property, characteristic, etc. **7.** performed in pantomime; mimed. [OE; c. Icel *dumbr,* Goth *dumbs,* OS *dumb,* OHG *tump,* G *dumm*] **—dumb′ly,** *adv.* **—dumb′ness,** *n.*

—Syn. 2, 3. DUMB, MUTE, SPEECHLESS, VOICELESS describe a condition in which speech is absent. DUMB was formerly used to refer to persons unable to speak; it is now used almost entirely of the inability of animals to speak: *dumb beasts of the field.* The term MUTE is now the one more often applied to persons who, usually because of congenital deafness, have never learned to talk: *With training most mutes learn to speak well enough to be understood.* Either of the foregoing terms or SPEECHLESS may describe a temporary inability to speak, caused by emotion, etc.: *dumb with amazement; mute with terror; left speechless by surprise.* VOICELESS means literally having no voice, either from natural causes or from injury: *Turtles are voiceless.*

dumb′ a′gue, *Pathol.* an irregular form of intermittent malarial fever, lacking the usual chill.

Dum·bar·ton (dum bär′tᵊn), *n.* **1.** Also, **Dunbarton.** Also called **Dum·bar·ton·shire** (dum bär′tᵊn sh̲ēr′, -sh̲ər). a county in W Scotland. 184,546 (1961); 241 sq. mi. **2.** its county seat, near the Clyde River. 26,496 (est. 1964).

Dum′bar·ton Oaks′ (dum′bär tᵊn), an estate in the District of Columbia: site of conferences held to discuss proposals for creation of the United Nations August–October, 1944.

dumb·bell (dum′bel′), *n.* **1.** a gymnastic device consisting of two weighted balls connected by a bar, used for exercising. **2.** *Slang.* a stupid person.

dumb′ show′, **1.** (esp. in early English drama) a part of a play given in pantomime. **2.** gestures without speech. **—dumb′-show′,** *adj.*

dumb·struck (dum′struk′), *adj.* temporarily deprived of the power of speech, as by surprise or confusion; dumfounded. Also, **dumb′-struck′, dumb·strick·en** (dum′-strik′ən), **dumb′-strick′en.**

dumb·wait·er (dum′wā′tər), *n.* **1.** *U.S.* a small elevator used in apartment houses, restaurants, etc., for moving food, garbage, etc., between floors. **2.** *Brit.* **a.** an auxiliary serving table. **b.** a serving stand with tiers of revolving shelves. **c.** a serving cart.

dum·dum (dum′dum′), *n.* a hollow-nosed or soft-nosed bullet that expands greatly on impact. Also called **dum′dum bul′let.** [after *Dum-Dum,* town in India where the bullets were made]

dum-dum (dum′dum′), *n.* *Slang.* a silly, stupid person. [redupl. of DUM(B)]

dum·found (dum found′, dum′found′), *v.t.* to make speechless with amazement; astonish. Also, **dumb·found′, dum·found′er, dumb·found′er.** [DUMB + (CON)FOUND]

Dum·fries (dum frēs′), *n.* **1.** Also called **Dum·fries·shire** (dum frēs′sh̲ēr′, -sh̲ər, -frēsh̲′-). a county in S Scotland. 88,423 (1961); 1047 sq. mi. **2.** its county seat: burial place of Robert Burns. 27,574 (est. 1964).

dumm·kopf (do͝om′kôf′, -kŏpf′, dum′-), *n.* *Slang.* a stupid person; blockhead. [< G: lit. stupid head]

dum·my (dum′ē), *n., pl.* **-mies,** *adj., v.,* **-mied, -my·ing.** **—***n.* **1.** a representation or copy of something, as for displaying. **2.** a representation of a human figure, as for displaying clothes in store windows; mannequin. **3.** *Informal.* a stupid person; dolt. **4.** a person who has nothing to say or who takes no active part in affairs. **5.** a person put forward to act for others while ostensibly acting for himself. **6.** *Slang.* a person who lacks the power of speech; mute. **7.** *Bridge.* **a.** the declarer's partner, whose hand is exposed and played by the declarer. **b.** the hand of cards so exposed. **8.** *Print.* sheets folded and made up to show the size, shape, form, sequence, and general style of a contemplated piece of printing. **—***adj.* **9.** noting or pertaining to an imitation, representation, or copy. **10.** counterfeit; sham; fictitious. **11.** put forward to act for others while ostensibly acting for oneself. **—***v.t.* **12.** *Print.* to prepare a dummy of (a contemplated piece of printing) (often fol. by *up*). **13.** to represent in a dummy (often fol. by *in*): *to dummy in an illustration.* [DUMB + -Y³]

dump¹ (dump), *v.t.* **1.** to drop or let fall in a mass; fling down or drop heavily or suddenly. **2.** to empty out, as from a container by tilting or overturning. **3.** to unload or empty out (a container). **4.** *Informal.* to be dismissed, fired, or released from a contract. **5.** *Informal.* to transfer or rid oneself of suddenly and irresponsibly: *Don't dump your troubles on me!* **6.** *Com.* to put (goods) on the market in large quantities and at a low price, esp. in a foreign country. **7.** *Computer Technol.* **a.** to record (data stored in an internal storage unit at a given instant of time) on an ouput device, usually as an aid in detecting program errors. **b.** to cut off the electric power of (a computer) accidentally or intentionally. **—***v.i.* **8.** to fall or drop down suddenly. **9.** to throw away or discard garbage, refuse, etc. **10.** to offer goods for sale at a low price, esp. in large quantities. **—***n.* **11.** an accumulation of discarded garbage, refuse, etc. **12.** a place where garbage, refuse, etc., is deposited. **13.** *Mil.* a collection of ammunition, stores, etc., deposited at some point, as near a battlefront, to be distributed for use. **14.** the act of dumping. **15.** *Slang.* a place, house, or town that is dilapidated, dirty, or disreputable. **16.** *Computer Technol.* a printed listing of all the information contained in the storage of a computer or on a computer tape, or both. [ME < Scand: cf. Icel *dumpa* to thump, Dan *dumpe* to fall with a thump] **—dump′er,** *n.*

dump² (dump), *n.* **1. dumps,** *Informal.* a depressed state of mind (usually prec. by *in the*): *to be in the dumps over money problems.* **2.** *Obs.* a plaintive melody. [cf. G *dumpf* dull, MD *domp* haze]

dump·cart (dump′kärt′), *n.* a cart with a body that can be tilted, or a bottom that can be opened downward to discharge its load.

dump·ish (dum′pish), *adj.* **1.** depressed; sad. **2.** *Obs.* dull; stupid. **—dump′ish·ly,** *adv.* **—dump′ish·ness,** *n.*

dump·ling (dump′liŋ), *n.* **1.** a ball of steamed and seasoned dough, often served in soup or with stewed meat. **2.** a boiled or baked dessert consisting of a wrapping of dough enclosing an apple or other fruit. [*dump* (< ?) + -LING¹]

dump′ truck′, a truck having a body that can be tilted to discharge its load through an open tailgate.

dump·y¹ (dum′pē), *adj.,* **dump·i·er, dump·i·est.** dumpish; dejected; sulky.

dump·y² (dum′pē), *adj.,* **dump·i·er, dump·i·est.** short and stout; squat: *a dumpy woman.* [? akin to DUMPLING] **—dump′i·ly,** *adv.* **—dump′i·ness,** *n.*

Dum·yat (do͝om yät′), *n.* Arabic name of **Damietta.**

dun¹ (dun), *v.,* **dunned, dun·ning,** *n.* **—***v.t.* **1.** to make repeated and insistent demands upon, esp. for the payment of a debt. **—***n.* **2.** a person who duns another. **3.** a demand for payment, esp. a written one. [? special use of ME *don(i)e(n)* (to) make a din < Scand; cf. Icel *duna* to make a thundering noise; akin to OE *dynian;* see DIN]

dun² (dun), *adj.* **1.** dull, grayish brown. **2.** dark; gloomy. **—***n.* **3.** a dun color. **4.** a horse of a dun color, with a black mane and tail. **5.** a mayfly. [ME *dun(ne),* OE *dunn;* c. OS *dun*]

Du·na (do͝o′no), *n.* Hungarian name of the **Danube.**

Dü·na (dʏ′nä), *n.* German name of the **Dvina.**

Dü·na·burg (dʏ′nä bo͝oRk′), *n.* German name of **Daugavpils.**

Du·naj (do͝o′nī), *n.* Czech and Slovak name of the **Danube.**

Du·nant (*Fr.* dʏ näN′), *n.* **Jean Hen·ri** (*Fr.* zhäN äN Rē′), 1828–1910, Swiss banker: founder of the Red Cross.

Du·nă·rea (do͝o′nə Ryä), *n.* Rumanian name of **Danube.**

Dun·bar (dun′bär *for 1;* dun bär′ *for 2, 3*), *n.* **1. Paul Laurence,** 1872–1906, U.S. poet. **2. William,** c1460–c1520, Scottish poet. **3.** a town in SE Scotland, at the mouth of the Firth of Forth: Cromwell's defeat of the Scots 1650. 4292 (est. 1964).

Dun·bar·ton (dun bär′tᵊn), *n.* Dumbarton (def. 1).

Dun·can (duŋ′kən), *n.* **Isadora,** 1878–1927, U.S. dancer: pioneer in modern dance.

Duncan I, died 1040, king of Scotland 1030–40: murdered by Macbeth.

Dun·can Phyfe (duŋ′kən fīf′), of, pertaining to, or resembling the furniture made by Duncan Phyfe, esp. the earlier pieces in the Sheraton and Directoire styles.

dunce (duns), *n.* a dull-witted, stupid, or ignorant person; dolt. [after John DUNS SCOTUS, whose writings were attacked by the humanists as foolish] **—dun′ci·cal, dunc′ish,** *adj.* **—dunc′ish·ly,** *adv.* **—Syn.** blockhead, ignoramus.

dunce′ cap′, a tall, cone-shaped hat formerly worn in school by slow or lazy students as a punishment. Also, **dunce′s cap′.** Also called **fool's cap.**

Dun·dalk (dun′dôk), *n.* a town in central Maryland, near Baltimore. 85,377 (1970).

Dun·dee (dun dē′, dun′dē), *n.* a seaport in E Scotland, on the Firth of Tay. 182,959 (1961).

dun·der·head (dun′dər hed′), *n.* a dunce; blockhead; numskull. Also called **dun·der·pate** (dun′dər pāt′). [< D *donderbol* cannon ball, lit., thunder ball; *-bol* means head in D slang; cf. BLOCKHEAD] **—dun′der·head′ed,** *adj.* **—dun′der·head′ed·ness,** *n.*

dune (do͞on, dyo͞on), *n.* a sand hill or sand ridge formed by the wind. [< F, OF < MD *dūna;* c. DOWN³]

dune′ bug′gy, a rugged, lightweight motor vehicle with oversized tires that can drive up and down sand dunes easily. Also called **dune′ wag′on.**

Dun·e·din (dun ē′din), *n.* a seaport on SE South Island, in New Zealand. 73,245 (1961).

Dun·ferm·line (dun fûrm′lin, -ferm′-, dum-), *n.* a city in SW Fife, in E Scotland, near the Firth of Forth. 47,159 (1961).

dung (duŋ), *n.* **1.** manure; excrement, esp. of animals. **—***v.t.* **2.** to cover (ground) with or as with dung. [ME,

OE; c. LG, G *dung;* cf. Icel *dyngja* heap, dung, Sw *dynga* dung, muck, OHG *tunga* manuring] —**dung′y,** *adj.*

dun·ga·ree (dung′gə rē′), *n.* **1. dungarees, a.** work clothes, overalls, etc., of blue denim. **b.** See **blue jeans. 2.** blue denim. [< Hindi *dungrī*]

dung′ bee′tle, any of various scarabaeid beetles that feed upon or breed in dung.

dun·geon (dun′jən), *n.* **1.** any strong, close prison or cell, usually underground, as in a medieval castle. **2.** the keep or stronghold of a castle; donjon. [ME *dungeo(u)n, donjon,* etc. < MF *donjon* < ML **dominiōn-* (s. of **dominiō*) keep, mastery, syncopated var. of **dominiōn-* DOMINION]

dung·hill (dung′hil′), *n.* **1.** a heap of dung. **2.** a repugnantly filthy or degraded place or condition. [ME]

dunk (dungk), *v.t.* **1.** to dip (a doughnut, cake, etc.) into coffee, milk, or the like, before eating. **2.** to submerge in a liquid. —*v.i.* **3.** to dip something in a liquid. [< G *dunk(en),* nasalized var. of *ducken* to DUCK[2]] —**dunk′er,** *n.*

Dunk·er (dung′kər), *n.* a member of the Church of the Brethren, a denomination of Christians characterized by the practice of trine immersion, and opposition to military service and the taking of oaths. Also, **Dun·kard** (dung′kərd), **Tunker.** [< G: lit., ducker, dipper, i.e., baptizer by immersion]

Dun·kirk (dun′kûrk), *n.* a seaport in N France: evacuation of British forces under German fire May 29–June 4, 1940. 83,759. French, **Dun·kerque** (dœn kerk′).

Dun Laoghai·re (dun lâr′ə), a seaport in E Republic of Ireland, near Dublin. 53,171 (1970). Also called **Dun-lea′ry.**

dun·lin (dun′lin), *n.* a common sandpiper, *Erolia alpina,* which breeds in the northern parts of the Northern Hemisphere. [var. of *dunling.* See DUN[2], -LING[1]]

Dun·lop (dun lop′, dun′lop), *n.* **John Boyd,** 1840–1921, Scottish inventor of the pneumatic tire.

Dun·more (dun mōr′, -môr′; dun′mōr, -môr), *n.* **John Murray, 4th Earl of,** 1732–1809, Scottish colonial governor in America.

dun·nage (dun′ij), *n.* **1.** baggage or personal effects, esp. of a sailor. **2.** loose material laid beneath or wedged among objects carried by ship or rail to prevent injury from chafing or moisture or to provide ventilation. [cf. D (*het is*) *dunnetjes* (it is) poor stuff]

Dunne (dun), *n.* **Fin·ley Peter** (fin′lē), 1867–1936, U.S. humorist.

dunn·ite (dun′īt), *n.* an ammonium picrate explosive used as a bursting charge for armor-piercing projectiles and in high-explosive shells. [named after Col. B. W. *Dunn* (1860–1936), U.S. Army, the inventor; see -ITE[1]]

Du·nois (dʏ nwa′), *n.* **Jean** (zhäN), **Comte de** ("*Bastard of Orleans*"), 1403?–68; French military leader.

Dun·sa·ny (dun sā′nē), *n.* **Edward John More·ton Drax Plun·kett** (môr′tᵊn draks plung′ket, -kit, môr′-), **18th Baron** ("*Lord Dunsany*"), 1878–1957, Irish dramatist, poet, and essayist.

Dun·si·nane (dun′sə nān′, dun′sə nān′), *n.* a hill NE of Perth, in central Scotland. 1012 ft.

Duns Sco·tus (dunz skō′təs), **John** ("*Doctor Subtilis*"), 1265?–1308, Scottish scholastic theologian.

Dun·sta·ble (dun′stə bəl), *n.* **John,** c1390–1453, English composer. Also, **Dun·sta·ple** (dun′stə pəl).

Dun·stan (dun′stən), *n.* **Saint,** A.D. c925–988, English statesman: archbishop of Canterbury 961–978.

du·o (do͞o′ō, dyo͞o′ō), *n., pl.* **du·os. 1.** *Music.* duet. **2.** two persons commonly associated with one another; couple. **3.** two animals or objects of the same sort; two things ordinarily placed or found together; a pair: *a duo of lovebirds.* [< It < L: two]

duo-, an element borrowed from Greek and Latin meaning "two," used in the formation of compound words: *duologue.* [comb. form of Gk *dýo,* L *duo* TWO]

du·o·dec·a·gon (do͞o′ə dek′ə gon′, dyo͞o′-), *n. Geom.* dodecagon.

du·o·de·cil·lion (do͞o′ō di sil′yən, dyo͞o′-), *n., pl.* **-lions,** (*as after a numeral*) **-lion,** *adj.* —*n.* **1.** a cardinal number represented in the U.S. and France by one followed by 39 zeros, and in Great Britain and Germany by one followed by 72 zeros. —*adj.* **2.** amounting to one duodecillion in number. [< L *duodec(im)* twelve + *-illion,* as in *million*] —**du′o·de·cil′lionth,** *n., adj.*

du·o·dec·i·mal (do͞o′ə des′ə məl, dyo͞o′-), *adj.* **1.** pertaining to twelfths or to the number twelve. **2.** proceeding by twelves. —*n.* **3.** one of a system of numbers based on the number 12. **4.** one of twelve equal parts. [< L *duodecim* twelve + -AL[1]] —**du′o·dec′i·mal′i·ty,** *n.* —**du′o·dec′i·mal·ly,** *adv.*

du·o·dec·i·mo (do͞o′ə des′ə mō′, dyo͞o′-), *n., pl.* **-mos,** *adj.* —*n.* **1.** Also called **twelvemo.** a book size of about 5 x 7½ inches, determined by printing on sheets folded to form 12 leaves or 24 pages. *Abbr.:* 12mo, 12° **2.** a book of this size. —*adj.* **3.** in duodecimo; twelvemo. [short for L *in duodecimō* in twelfth]

duoden-, a combining form of **duodenum:** *duodenary.*

du·o·de·nal (do͞o′ə dēn′ᵊl, dyo͞o′-; do͞o od′ᵊnᵊl, dyo͞o-), *adj.* of, pertaining to, or affecting the duodenum.

du·o·den·a·ry (do͞o′ə den′ə rē, -dē′nə rē, dyo͞o′-), *adj.* duodecimal.

du·o·de·num (do͞o′ə dē′nəm, dyo͞o′-; do͞o od′ᵊnəm, dyo͞o-), *n., pl.* **du·o·de·na** (do͞o′ə dē′nə, dyo͞o′-; do͞o od′ᵊnə, dyo͞o-), **du·o·de·nas.** *Anat. Zool.* the first portion of the small intestine, from the stomach to the jejunum. See diag. at **intestine.** [< ML; L *duodēn(ī)* twelve each, so called from its length, about twelve fingerbreadths]

du·o·logue (do͞o′ə lôg′, -log′, dyo͞o′-), *n.* a conversation between two persons; dialogue. [DUO- + (MONO)LOGUE]

duo·mo (dwô′mô), *n., pl.* **-mi** (-mē). *Italian.* cathedral. [lit., dome]

du·o·tone (do͞o′ə tōn′, dyo͞o′-), *adj.* **1.** of two tones or colors. —*n.* **2.** a picture in two tones or colors. **3.** *Print.* **a.** a method of printing an illustration in two shades of the same color. **b.** an illustration printed by this method.

dup (dup), *v.t.,* **dupped, dup·ping.** *Brit. Dial.* to open; push or swing open. [contr. of DO[1] + UP, cf. DOFF, DON[2]]

dup., duplicate.

dupe (do͞op, dyo͞op), *n., v.,* **duped, dup·ing.** —*n.* **1.** a person who is easily deceived or fooled; gull. **2.** a person who unquestioningly or unwittingly serves a cause or another person: *a dupe of the communists.* —*v.t.* **3.** to make a dupe of; deceive; delude; trick. [< F; MF *duppe,* for **(tête) d'uppe* head of hoopoe, i.e., fool (cf. *tête de fou*) < VL **uppa,* L *upupa* hoopoe, a bird thought to be especially stupid (F *huppe* hoopoe < aspirated var.)] —**dup′a·bil′i·ty,** *n.* —**dup′a·ble,** *adj.* —**dup′er,** *n.*

dup·er·y (do͞o′pə rē, dyo͞o′-), *n., pl.* **-er·ies** for 1. **1.** the act, practice, or an instance of duping. **2.** the state of being duped. [< F *duperie*]

du·ple (do͞o′pəl, dyo͞o′-), *adj.* **1.** having two parts; double; twofold. **2.** *Music.* having two or sometimes a multiple of two beats in a measure: *duple meter.* [< L *dupl(us)* double]

Du·pleix (dʏ pleks′), *n.* **Jo·seph Fran·çois** (zhō zef′ fräN swa′), **Marquis,** 1697–1763, French colonial governor of India 1724–54.

Du·ples·sis-Mor·nay (*Fr.* dʏ ple sē′môʀ nā′), *n.* **Philippe** (fē lēp′). See **Mornay, Philippe de.**

du′ple time′, *Music.* characterized by two beats to the measure.

du·plex (do͞o′pleks, dyo͞o′-), *adj.* **1.** having two parts; double; twofold. **2.** (of a machine) having two identical working units, operating together or independently, in a single framework or assembly. **3.** pertaining to or noting a telegraphic system permitting the simultaneous transmission of two messages in opposite directions over one channel. —*n.* **4.** See **duplex apartment. 5.** See **duplex house. 6.** paper or cardboard having different colors, finishes, or stocks on opposite sides. [< L: twofold, double = *du(o)* two + *-plex* -FOLD] —**du·plex′i·ty,** *n.*

du′plex apart′ment, an apartment, or a suite of rooms, on two connected stories. Also called **duplex.**

du′plex house′, a house having separate apartments for two families. Also called **duplex.**

du·pli·ca·ble (do͞o′plə kə bəl, dyo͞o′-), *adj.* capable of being duplicated. [DUPLIC(ATE) + -ABLE] —**du′pli·ca·bil′i·ty,** *n.*

du·pli·cate (*adj., n.* do͞o′plə kit, dyo͞o′-; *v.* do͞o′plə kāt′, dyo͞o′-), *n., v.,* **-cat·ed, -cat·ing,** *adj.* —*n.* **1.** a copy exactly like an original. **2.** anything corresponding in all respects to something else. **3. in duplicate,** in two copies, esp. two copies made at one time. —*v.t.* **4.** to make a copy of (something). **5.** to make twice as great, as by multiplying. **6.** to repeat; do again. —*adj.* **7.** having or consisting of two identical parts; twofold; double. **8.** exactly like something else. **9.** *Cards.* noting a game in which each team plays a series of identical hands, the winner being the team making the best total score: *duplicate bridge.* [< L *duplicāt(us)* (ptp. of *duplicāre* to make double) = *duplic-* (s. of *duplex*) DUPLEX + *-ātus* -ATE[1]] —**du′pli·ca′tive,** *adj.* —**Syn. 1.** facsimile, replica, reproduction. **4.** See **imitate.** —**Ant. 1.** original.

du·pli·ca·tion (do͞o′plə kā′shən, dyo͞o′-), *n.* **1.** the act or an instance of duplicating. **2.** the state of being duplicated. **3.** a duplicate. [< L *duplicātiōn-* (s. of *duplicātiō;* see DUPLICATE, -ION); r. ME *duplicacioun* < AF]

du·pli·ca·tor (do͞o′plə kā′tər, dyo͞o′-), *n.* a machine for making duplicates, as a mimeograph. Cf. **copier** (def. 2). Also called **du′plicating machine′.** [< LL]

du·plic·i·ty (do͞o plis′i tē, dyo͞o-), *n., pl.* **-ties** for 1. **1.** deceitfulness in speech or conduct; double-dealing. **2.** a twofold or double state or quality. [ME *duplicite* < MF < LL *duplicitāt-* (s. of *duplicitās*) = L *duplic-* (s. of *duplex*) DUPLEX + *-itāt-* -ITY] —**Syn. 1.** deception. See **deceit.**

du·Pont (do͞o pont′, dyo͞o-, do͞o′pont, dyo͞o′-; *also Fr.* dʏ pôN′), *n.* **1. E·leu·thère I·ré·née** (e lœ teʀ′ ē ʀā nā′), 1771–1834, U.S. industrialist, born in France. **2.** his father, **Pierre Samuel** (pē âr′ sam′yo͞o əl; *Fr.* pyeʀ sa mʏ el′), 1739–1817, French economist and statesman. Also, **Du Pont′.**

Du·pré (dʏ pʀā′), *n.* **1. Jules** (zhʏl), 1812–89, French painter. **2. Mar·cel** (maʀ sel′), 1886–1971, French organist.

Du·quesne (do͞o kān′, dyo͞o-; *for 1 also Fr.* dʏ ken′), *n.* **1. A·bra·ham** (a bʀa am′), 1610–88, French naval commander. **2.** a city in SW Pennsylvania, on the Monongahela River. 11,410 (1970). **3. Fort.** See **Fort Duquesne.**

Du Quoin (do͞o koin′), a town in SW Illinois: site of the Hambletonian. 6691 (1970).

dur (do͞oʀ), *adj. German.* (in music) written in a major key; major.

Dur., Durango.

du·ra (do͝or′ə, dyo͝or′ə), *n.* See **dura mater.** —**du′ral,** *adj.*

du·ra·ble (do͝or′ə bəl, dyo͝or′-), *adj.* **1.** highly resistant to wear, decay, etc.; lasting; enduring. —*n.* **2. durables.** See **durable goods.** [ME < MF < L *dūrābil(is).* See DURE[2], -ABLE] —**du′ra·bil′i·ty, du′ra·ble·ness,** *n.* —**dur′a·bly,** *adv.*

du′rable goods′, goods that are not consumed or destroyed in use and can be used over a number of years, as appliances and machinery.

du′rable press′. See **permanent press.**

Du·ral·u·min (do͝o ral′yə min, dyo͝o-), *n. Trademark.* an alloy of aluminum that is four percent copper and contains small amounts of magnesium, manganese, iron, and silicon: used for applications requiring lightness and strength, as in airplane construction.

du′ra ma′ter, *Anat.* the tough, fibrous membrane forming the outermost of the three coverings of the brain and spinal cord. Also called **dura.** Cf. **arachnoid** (def. 2), **pia mater.** [late ME < ML: lit., hard mother]

du·ra·men (do͝o rā′min, dyo͝o-), *n. Bot.* the hard central wood, or heartwood, of an exogenous tree. [< L: hardness, hardened vine branch = *dūrā(re)* (to) harden + *-men* n. suffix]

dur·ance (do͝or′əns, dyo͝or′-), *n.* **1.** imprisonment, esp. long confinement. **2.** *Archaic.* **a.** duration. **b.** endurance. [late ME < MF. See DURE[2], -ANCE]

Du·ran·go (do͝o rang′gō; *Sp.* do͞o ʀäng′gô), *n.* **1.** a state in N Mexico. 1,122,000 (1970); 47,691 sq. mi. **2.** a city in and the capital of this state, in the S part. 209,000 (1970).

Du·rant (də rant′), *n.* **Will(iam James),** 1885–1981, U.S. author and historian.

du·ra·tion (do͝o rā′shən, dyo͝o-), *n.* **1.** continuance in time. **2.**

the length of time during which something continues or exists. [< ML *dūrātiōn-* (s. of *dūrātiō*) = L *dūrāt(us)* (ptp. of *dūrāre* to last; see DURE²) + *-iōn-* -ION] —**du·ra′tion·al,** *adj.*

du·ra·tive (dŏŏr′ə tiv, dyŏŏr′-), *adj.* *Gram.* noting or pertaining to a verb aspect expressing incomplete or continued action. *Beat* and *walk* are durative in contrast with *strike* and *step.* [DURAT(ION) + -IVE]

Du·raz·zo (də rät′sō; *It.* dōō rät′tsô), *n.* a seaport in W Albania, on the Adriatic: important ancient city. 47,870 (est. 1964). Albanian, **Durrës.**

Dur·ban (dûr′bən), *n.* a seaport in SE Natal, in the E Republic of South Africa. 560,010 (1960).

dur·bar (dûr′bär), *n.* (in India) **1.** the court of a native ruler. **2.** a public audience or levee held by a native prince or by a British governor or viceroy; an official reception. **3.** the hall or place of audience. [alter. of Urdu *darbār* court < Pers = *dar* door + *bār* entry]

dure¹ (dŏŏr, dyŏŏr), *adj.* *Archaic.* hard; severe. [ME < MF < L *dūr(us)* hard]

dure² (dŏŏr, dyŏŏr), *v.i., v.t.,* **dured, dur·ing.** *Archaic.* endure. [ME < OF *dur(er)* < L *dūrāre* to last; see DURE¹]

Dü·rer (dŏŏr′ər, dyŏŏr′-; *Ger.* dʏ′rəʀ), *n.* **Al·brecht** (äl′brekHt), 1471–1528, German painter and engraver.

du·ress (dŏŏ res′, dyŏŏ-, dŏŏr′is, dyŏŏr′-), *n.* **1.** compulsion by threat; coercion; constraint. **2.** forcible restraint, esp. imprisonment. [ME *duresse* < MF *duresse, -esce, -ece* < L *dūritia* hardness, harshness, oppression. See DURE¹, -ICE]

Dur·ham (dûr′əm), *n.* **1.** a county in NE England. 1,517,039 (1961); 1015 sq. mi. **2.** its county seat. 20,484 (1961). **3.** a city in N North Carolina. 95,438 (1970). **4.** *Stockbreeding.* Shorthorn.

du·ri·an (dŏŏr′ē ən), *n.* **1.** the edible fruit of a tree, *Durio zibethinus,* of southeastern Asia, having a hard, prickly rind, a highly flavored, pulpy flesh, and an offensive odor. **2.** the tree itself. Also, **du′ri·on.** [< Malay < *duri* thorn]

dur·ing (dŏŏr′ing, dyŏŏr′-), *prep.* **1.** throughout the duration, continuance, or existence of: *He lived in Florida during the winter.* **2.** at some time or point in the course of: *They departed during the night.* [ME; orig. DURE² + -ING²]

Durk·heim (dûrk′hīm; *Fr.* dʏʀ kem′), *n.* **É·mile** (ā mēl′), 1858–1917, French sociologist and philosopher.

dur·mast (dûr′mast′, -mäst′), *n.* a European oak, *Quercus petraea,* yielding a heavy, elastic wood used for furniture and in the construction of buildings. [short for *durmast oak,* i.e., ? oak yielding MAST² even in times of dearth; see DEAR²]

du·ro (dŏŏr′ō; *Sp.* dōō′ʀô), *n., pl.* **-ros** (-rōz; *Sp.* -ʀôs). a peso of Spain or Spanish America. [< Sp, short for *peso duro* hard piastre; see DURE¹]

Du·roc (dŏŏr′ok, dyŏŏr′-), *n.* one of an American breed of hardy red hogs having drooping ears. Also called **Du·roc-Jer·sey** (dŏŏr′ok jûr′zē, dyŏŏr′-). [named after a horse owned by breeder]

dur·ra (dŏŏr′ə), *n.* a type of grain sorghum with slender stalks, cultivated in Asia and Africa and introduced into the U.S. Also, **doura, dourah.** Also called **Indian millet, Guinea corn.** [< Ar *dhura(h)*]

Dur·rës (dōōʀ′ʀəs), *n.* Albanian name of **Durazzo.**

durst (dûrst), *v.* *Archaic.* pt. of **dare.**

du′rum wheat′ (dŏŏr′əm, dyŏŏr′-), a wheat, *Triticum durum,* the grain of which yields flour used in making macaroni, spaghetti, etc. Also called **du′rum.** [< NL (*trīticum*) *dūrum* hard (wheat). See DURE¹]

Dur·yea (dŏŏr′yā, dŏŏr′ē ā′), *n.* **Charles Edgar,** 1861–1938, U.S. inventor and automobile manufacturer.

Du·se (dōō′ze), *n.* **E·le·o·no·ra** (e′le ô nô′ʀä), 1859–1924, Italian actress.

dusk¹ (dusk), *n.* **1.** the state or period of partial darkness between day and night; the dark part of twilight. **2.** partial darkness; shade; gloom. [back formation from DUSKY]

dusk² (dusk), *adj.* **1.** dark; tending to darkness. —*v.t., v.i.* **2.** to make or become dusk; darken. [ME *duske* (adj.), *dusken* (v.); metathetic alter. of OE *dox* dusky, *doxian* to turn dark; c. L *fuscus* dark] —**dusk′ish,** *adj.*

dusk·y (dus′kē), *adj.,* **dusk·i·er, dusk·i·est. 1.** somewhat dark; having little light; dim; shadowy. **2.** having dark skin. **3.** of a dark color. **4.** gloomy. —**dusk′i·ly,** *adv.* —**dusk′i·ness,** *n.* —**Syn. 2.** dark; swarthy. —**Ant. 3.** fair, blond.

Düs·sel·dorf (dŏŏs′əl dôrf′; *Ger.* dʏs′əl dôʀf′), *n.* a port in and the capital of North Rhine-Westphalia, in W West Germany, on the Rhine. 704,000 (1963).

dust (dust), *n.* **1.** earth or other matter in fine, dry particles. **2.** any finely powdered substance, as sawdust. **3.** a cloud of finely powdered earth or other matter in the air. **4.** the ground; the earth's surface. **5.** that to which anything, as the human body, is ultimately reduced by disintegration or decay. **6.** *Brit.* **a.** ashes, refuse, etc. **b.** junk¹ (def. 1). **7.** a low or humble condition. **8.** anything worthless. **9.** disturbance; turmoil. **10.** See **gold dust. 11.** *Archaic.* the mortal body of man. **12.** *Archaic.* a single particle or grain. **13.** *Archaic.* money; cash. **14. bite the dust, a.** to be killed, esp. in battle; die. **b.** to suffer defeat; be unsuccessful; fail. **15. lick the dust, a.** to be killed; die. **b.** to humble oneself abjectly; grovel. —*v.t.* **16.** to wipe the dust from: *to dust a table.* **17.** to sprinkle with a powder or dust: *to dust rosebushes with an insecticide.* **18.** to strew or sprinkle (a powder, dust, or other fine particles): *to dust insecticide on a rosebush.* **19.** to soil with dust; make dusty. —*v.i.* **20.** to wipe dust from furniture, woodwork, etc. **21.** to become dusty. **22.** to apply dust or powder to a plant, one's body, etc. [ME; OE *dūst;* c. G *Dunst* vapor] —**dust′less,** *adj.*

dust·bin (dust′bin′), *n.* *Chiefly Brit.* an ashcan; garbage can.

dust′ bowl′, an area subject to dust storms, esp. the region in S central U.S. that suffered such storms in the 1930's.

dust′ cart′, *Brit.* a garbage truck.

dust′ cov′er, 1. a cloth covering, often of muslin, used to protect furniture or furnishings during an extended period of nonuse. **2.** See **book jacket.**

dust′ dev′il, a small whirlwind, common in dry regions, made visible by the dust, debris, and sand it picks up from the ground.

dust·er (dus′tər), *n.* **1.** a person or thing that removes or applies dust. **2.** an apparatus or device for sprinkling dust, powder, insecticide, or the like. **3.** a long, lightweight overgarment, worn to protect the clothing from dust. **4.** a woman's lightweight housecoat. **5.** a light summer coat for women, loose-fitting and often unlined. **6.** See **dust storm. 7.** *Baseball Slang.* a ball purposely thrown by a pitcher at or dangerously close to a batter.

dust′ jack′et. See **book jacket.**

dust·man (dust′man′, -mən), *n., pl.* **-men** (-men′, -mən). **1.** *Brit.* a garbage man; one employed to remove or cart away garbage, refuse, ashes, etc. **2.** sandman.

dust·off (dust′ôf′, -of′), *n.* *U.S. Mil. Slang.* medevac (def. 1).

dust·pan (dust′pan′), *n.* a short-handled, shovellike utensil into which dust is swept for removal.

dust′ storm′, a storm of strong winds and dust-filled air over an extensive area of normally arable land during a period of drought (distinguished from *sandstorm*). Also, **dust′storm′.** Also called **duster.**

dust·up (dust′up′), *n.* *Informal.* a quarrel; argument; row.

dust·y (dus′tē), *adj.,* **dust·i·er, dust·i·est. 1.** filled, covered, or clouded with or as with dust. **2.** of the nature of dust; powdery. **3.** of the color of dust; having a grayish cast: *dusty pink.* [ME] —**dust′i·ly,** *adv.* —**dust′i·ness,** *n.*

dust′y mil′ler, any of various flowering plants and herbs of the Mediterranean region, having white downy foliage.

Dutch (duch), *adj.* **1.** of, pertaining to, or characteristic of the Netherlands, its people, or their language. **2.** *U.S.* of, pertaining to, or characteristic of the Pennsylvania Dutch. **3.** *Slang.* German; Teutonic. **4. go Dutch,** *Informal.* to have each participant treat himself or pay his own expenses. —*n.* **5.** the people of the Netherlands and their immediate descendants elsewhere, collectively. **6.** *U.S.* See **Pennsylvania Dutch. 7.** the language of the Netherlands, a Germanic language. *Abbr.:* D **8. in Dutch,** *Slang.* **a.** in trouble. **b.** in disfavor (with someone). [ME *Du(c)ch* < MD *du(u)tsch;* c. OHG *diutisc* popular (as opposed to learned), trans. of L *vulgāris* vernacular; akin to OE *theodisc* speech]

Dutch′ Bor′neo, the former name of the southern and larger part of the island of Borneo: now part of Indonesia.

Dutch′ cour′age, *Informal.* courage inspired by drunkenness or drinking liquor.

Dutch′ door′, a door consisting of two units horizontally divided so that the upper part can be opened while the lower remains closed.

Dutch door

Dutch′ East′ In′dies, a former name of the Republic of Indonesia.

Dutch′ elm′ disease′, *Plant Pathol.* a serious disease of elms, characterized by wilting, yellowing, and falling of the leaves, caused by a fungus, *Ceratostomella ulmi,* transmitted by bark beetles.

Dutch′ Guian′a, Surinam.

Dutch′ Har′bor, a U.S. naval base on Unalaska Island, in the Aleutian Islands.

Dutch·man (duch′mən), *n., pl.* **-men. 1.** a native or inhabitant of the Netherlands. **2.** *Building Trades.* a piece or wedge inserted to hide the fault in a badly made joint, to stop an opening, etc. **3.** *Archaic.* a German. [ME]

Dutch·man's-breech·es (duch′mənz brich′iz), *n., pl.* **-breech·es.** an herb, *Dicentra* (or *Bicuculla*) *cucullaria,* having pale-yellow, two-spurred flowers. Also called **white eardrop.** [so called from the shape of the flowers]

Dutch·man's-pipe (duch′mənz-pīp′), *n.* a climbing, vine *Aristolochia durior,* having large curved leaves and flowers suggesting a tobacco pipe.

Dutchman's-pipe, *Aristolochia durior*

Dutch′ New′ Guin′ea, a former name of **West Irian.**

Dutch′ ov′en, 1. a heavily constructed kettle with a close-fitting lid, used for pot roasts, stews, etc. **2.** a metal utensil, open in front, for roasting before an open fire. **3.** a brick oven in which the walls are preheated for cooking.

Dutch′ treat′, a meal or entertainment for which each person pays his own share.

Dutch′ un′cle, *Informal.* a person who criticizes or reproves with unsparing severity and frankness: *He talked to her like a Dutch uncle.*

Dutch′ West′ In′dies, a former name of **Netherlands Antilles.**

du·te·ous (dōō′tē əs, dyōō′-), *adj.* dutiful; obedient. —**du′te·ous·ly,** *adv.* —**du′te·ous·ness,** *n.*

du·ti·a·ble (dōō′tē ə bəl, dyōō′-), *adj.* subject to customs duty, as imported goods. —**du′ti·a·bil′i·ty,** *n.*

du·ti·ful (dōō′ti fəl, dyōō′-), *adj.* **1.** performing the duties expected or required of one; characterized by doing one's duty: *a dutiful citizen; a dutiful child.* **2.** required by duty; proceeding from or expressive of a sense of duty: *dutiful attention.* —**du′ti·ful·ly,** *adv.* —**Syn. 1.** respectful, duteous.

du·ty (dōō′tē, dyōō′-), *n., pl.* **-ties. 1.** something that one is expected or required to do by moral or legal obligation. **2.** the binding or obligatory force of something that is morally or legally right; moral or legal obligation. **3.** action or a task required by one's position or occupation; function: *the duties of a clergyman.* **4.** the respectful and obedient conduct due to a parent, superior, elder, etc. **5.** an act or expression of respect. **6.** a task or chore that one is expected to perform. **7.** *Mil.* **a.** an assigned task, occupation, or place of service: *He was on radar duty for two years.* **b.** the military service required of a citizen by a country: *After graduation, he began his duty.* **8.** *Com.* a tax imposed by law on the import or export of goods. **9.** *Chiefly Brit.* a tax: *income duty.* **10.** *Mach.*

a. the amount of work done by an engine per unit amount of fuel consumed. b. the measure of effectiveness of any machine. 11. *Agric.* the amount of water necessary to provide for the crop in a given area. 12. **do duty,** to serve the same function; substitute for: *bookcases that do duty as room dividers.* 13. **off duty,** not at one's post or work; at liberty. 14. **on duty,** at one's post or work; occupied; engaged. [ME *du(e)te* < AF *duete.* See DUE, -TY²]
—**Syn.** 1. DUTY, OBLIGATION refer to what one feels bound to do. DUTY is what a person performs, or avoids doing, in fulfillment of the permanent dictates of conscience, piety, right, or law: *duty to one's country; one's duty to tell the truth, to raise children properly.* An OBLIGATION is what a person is bound to do to fulfill the dictates of usage, custom, or propriety, and to carry out a particular, specific, and often personal promise or agreement: *financial or social obligations.* 3. responsibility, business. 4. deference, reverence.

du·um·vir (do͞o um′vər, dyo͞o-), *n., pl.* **-virs, -vi·ri** (-və rī′). *Rom. Hist.* one of two officers or magistrates jointly exercising a public function. [< L, back formation from *duumvirōrum,* gen. pl. of *duovirī* two men = *duo-* DUO- + *virī,* pl. of *vir* man, c. OE *wer* (see WEREWOLF)]

du·um·vi·rate (do͞o um′vər it, dyo͞o-), *n.* 1. a coalition of two men holding the same office, as in ancient Rome. 2. the office or government of two such persons. [< L *duumvirāt(us)*]

Du·va·lier (do͞o′väl yā′; *Fr.* dʏ va lyā′), *n.* **Fran·çois** (fräɴ swa′) ("*Papa Doc*"), 1907–71, Haitian politician: president 1957–71.

du·ve·tyn (do͞o′vi tēn′), *n.* a napped fabric, in a twilled or plain weave, of cotton, wool, silk, or rayon. Also, **du′ve·tine′, du′ve·tyne′.** [< F *duvetine* = *duvet* down + *-ine* -INE²]

Du·vi·da (*Port.* do͞o′vē də), *n.* **Rí·o da** (*Port.* ʀē′o͝o də), former name of Río Roosevelt.

D.V., 1. Deo volente. 2. Douay Version (of the Bible).

Dvi·na (dvi nä′), *n.* 1. Lettish, **Daugava.** German, **Düna.** a river in the W Soviet Union in Europe, flowing NW to the Baltic Seat at Riga. ab. 640 mi. long. 2. **Northern,** a river in the N Soviet Union in Europe, flowing NW into the White Sea. ab. 470 mi. long.

Dvina′ Bay′, an arm of the White Sea, in the NW Soviet Union in Europe. Formerly, **Gulf of Archangel.**

Dvinsk (dvēnsk), *n.* Russian name of **Daugavpils.**

D.V.M., Doctor of Veterinary Medicine.

Dvo·řák (*Eng.* dvôr′zhäk, -zhak; *Czech.* dvô′ʀzhäk), *n.* **An·ton** (*Eng.* an′tən, -ton; *Czech.* än′tôn), 1841–1904, Czech composer.

D/W, dock warrant.

dwarf (dwôrf), *n.* 1. a person who is considerably smaller than the average in stature or size, esp. one who is not normally proportioned. 2. an animal or plant much below the ordinary size of its kind or species. 3. a legendary being in the form of a small, often misshapen and ugly man, usually having magic powers. 4. See **dwarf star.** —*adj.* 5. of unusually small stature or size; diminutive. —*v.t.* 6. to cause to appear or seem small in size, extent, character, etc., as by being much larger or better. 7. to make dwarf or dwarfish; prevent the due development of. —*v.i.* 8. to become stunted or smaller. [ME *dwerf,* OE *dweorh;* r. ME *dwerg,* OE *dweorg;* c. OHG *twerg,* Icel *dvergr*] —**dwarf′ish,** *adj.* —**dwarf′ish·ly,** *adv.* —**dwarf′ish·ness,** *n.* —**dwarf′ism,** *n.*
—**Syn.** 1. DWARF, MIDGET, PYGMY are terms for a very small person. A DWARF is one checked in growth, or stunted; he usually has a large head or is in some way not normally formed: *In the past, dwarfs were considered very comical.* A MIDGET is one perfect in form and normal in function, but like a tiny replica of the ordinary species: *Some midgets are like handsome dolls.* A PYGMY is properly a member of one of certain small-sized peoples of Africa and Asia, but the word is often used to mean dwarf or midget. 2. runt, miniature.
—**Ant.** 1, 5. giant.

dwarf′ al′der, a small buckthorn, *Rhamnus alnifolia,* having leaves resembling those of an alder.

dwarf′ cher′ry, any of various low, shrubby cherries, as the sand cherry.

dwarf′ cor′nel, the bunchberry.

dwarf′ star′, *Astron.* a star of relatively small volume but often of very high density. Cf. **white dwarf.**

dwell (dwel), *v.i.,* **dwelt** or **dwelled, dwell·ing.** 1. to live or stay as a permanent resident; reside. 2. to live or continue in a given condition or state: *to dwell in happiness.* 3. to linger over or emphasize in thought, speech, or writing (often fol. by *on* or *upon*): *to dwell on a particular point in an argument.* [ME *dwell(en)* (to) lead astray, stun, abide, OE *dwellan* to lead or go astray, hinder; c. Icel *dvelja*] —**dwell′er,** *n.*

dwell·ing (dwel′ing), *n.* a building or place of shelter to live in; place of residence. [ME] —**Syn.** See **house.**

dwelt (dwelt), *v.* a pt. and pp. of **dwell.**

Dwight (dwīt), *n.* **Timothy,** 1826–1916, U.S. ecclesiastic: president of Yale University 1886–98.

dwin·dle (dwin′dəl), *v.,* **-dled, -dling.** —*v.i.* 1. to become smaller and smaller; shrink; waste away. 2. to fall away, as in quality; degenerate. —*v.t.* 3. to make smaller and smaller; cause to shrink. [DWINE + -LE] —**Syn.** 1. diminish, wane. See **decrease.** 3. lessen. —**Ant.** 1. increase.

dwine (dwīn), *v.i.,* **dwined, dwin·ing.** *Chiefly Dial.* to waste away; fade. [ME; OE *dwīn(an)* (to) waste away; c. MD *dwīnen* to languish, Icel *dvīna* to pine away]

dwt, pennyweight; pennyweights.

DX, *Radio.* distance (used esp. to designate difficult short-wave reception).

Dy, *Chem.* dysprosium.

dy·ad (dī′ad), *n.* 1. a group of two; couple, pair. 2. *Biol.* a. a secondary morphological unit, consisting of two monads: *a chromosome dyad.* b. the double chromosomes resulting from the separation of the four chromatids of a tetrad. 3. *Chem.* an element, atom, or group having a valence of two. Cf. **monad** (def. 2), **triad** (def. 2a). —*adj.* 4. of two parts; dyadic. [< Gk *dyad-* (s. of *dyás*) pair. See DUO-, -AD¹]

dy·ad·ic (dī ad′ik), *adj.* 1. of or consisting of two parts. 2. pertaining to the number two. [< Gk *dyadik(ós)*]

dyad′ic sys′tem. See **binary system.**

Dy·ak (dī′ak), *n.* Dayak.

dy·ar·chy (dī′är kē), *n., pl.* **-chies.** diarchy. —**dy·ar′chic, dy·ar′chi·cal,** *adj.*

dyb·buk (dib′ək; *Heb.* dē bo͞ok′), *n., pl.* **dyb·buks, dyb·buk·im** (di bo͞ok′im; *Heb.* dē bo͞o kēm′). *Jewish Folklore.* a demon or the soul of a dead person that enters the body of a living person and controls him. Also, **dibbuk.** [< Yiddish *dibbūk* devil < Heb *dābhūq,* akin to *dābhaq* to hang on]

dye (dī), *n., v.,* **dyed, dye·ing.** —*n.* 1. a coloring material or matter. 2. a liquid containing coloring matter, for imparting a particular hue to cloth, paper, etc. 3. color or hue, esp. as produced by dyeing. 4. **of the deepest** or **blackest dye,** of the most extreme or the worst sort: *a liar of the deepest dye.* —*v.t.* 5. to color or stain; treat with a dye; color (cloth, hair, etc.) with a substance containing coloring matter: *to dye a dress green.* 6. to impart (color) by means of a dye. —*v.i.* 7. to impart color, as a dye: *This brand dyes well.* 8. to become colored or absorb color when treated with a dye: *This cloth dyes easily.* [ME *die(n),* OE *dēagian* < *dēag* a dye] —**dy′a·ble, dye′a·ble,** *adj.* —**dy′er,** *n.*

dyed-in-the-wool (dīd′ən thə wo͝ol′), *adj.* 1. through-and-through; complete: *a dyed-in-the-wool Democrat.* 2. dyed before weaving.

dy·er's-broom (dī′ərz bro͞om′, -bro͝om′), *n.* woadwaxen.

dy·er's-weed (dī′ərz wēd′), *n.* any of various plants yielding dyes, as the weld, *Reseda Luteola,* the dyeweed, *Genista tinctoria,* or the woad, *Isatis tinctoria.*

dye·stuff (dī′stuf′), *n.* a material yielding or used as a dye. [prob. trans. of G *Farbstoff*]

dye·weed (dī′wēd′), *n.* a fabaceous shrub, *Genista tinctoria,* of the Old World, having yellow flowers and yielding a yellow dye.

dye·wood (dī′wo͝od′), *n.* any wood yielding a coloring matter used for dyeing.

dy·ing (dī′ing), *adj.* 1. ceasing to live; approaching death: *a dying man.* 2. of, pertaining to, or associated with death: *his dying hour.* 3. given, uttered, or manifested just before death: *her dying words.* 4. drawing to a close: *the dying year.* —*n.* 5. the act or process of ceasing to live or of ending or drawing to a close. [late ME (n., adj.), ME (n.)]

dyke¹ (dīk), *n., v.,* **dyked, dyk·ing.** dike¹.

dyke² (dīk), *n. Slang.* a female homosexual; lesbian. Also, **dike.**

dyn, *Physics.* dyne; dynes.

dyn., dynamics. Also, **dynam.**

dyna-, a learned borrowing from Greek meaning "power," used in the formation of compound words: *dynamotor.* Also, **dynam-, dynamo-.** [comb. form of Gk *dýnamis* power, *dýnasthai* to be able]

dy·nam·e·ter (dī nam′i tər), *n. Optics.* an instrument for determining the magnifying power of telescopes.

dy·nam·ic (dī nam′ik), *adj.* Also, **dy·nam′i·cal.** 1. pertaining to or characterized by energy or effective action; vigorously active or forceful; energetic. 2. *Physics.* a. of or pertaining to force or power. b. of or pertaining to force related to motion. 3. pertaining to dynamics. 4. of or pertaining to the range of volume of musical sound. —*n.* 5. a dynamic power or force. [< F *dynamique* < Gk *dynamik(ós).* See DYNA-, -IC] —**dy·nam′i·cal·ly,** *adv.*

dy·nam·ics (dī nam′iks), *n.* 1. (*construed as sing.*) *Physics.* the branch of mechanics that deals with the motion and equilibrium of systems under the action of forces, usually from outside the system. 2. (*construed as pl.*) the motivating or driving forces, physical or moral, in any field. 3. (*construed as pl.*) the pattern or history of growth, change, and development in any field. 4. (*construed as pl.*) variation and gradation in the volume of musical sound.

dy·na·mism (dī′nə miz′əm), *n.* 1. any of various theories or philosophical systems that seek to explain phenomena of nature by the action of force. Cf. **mechanism** (def. 8), **vitalism** (def. 1). 2. great force or power; vigor. 3. *Psychol.* a habitual mode of reducing or eliminating tension. —**dy′na·mist,** *n.* —**dy′na·mis′tic,** *adj.*

dy·na·mite (dī′nə mīt′), *n., v.,* **-mit·ed, -mit·ing.** —*n.* 1. a high explosive, originally consisting of nitroglycerin, now usually of ammonium nitrate, mixed with an absorbent substance, as kieselguhr. 2. *Slang.* any person or thing having a spectacular effect. —*v.t.* 3. to blow up, shatter, or destroy with dynamite: *Saboteurs dynamited the dam.* 4. to mine or charge with dynamite. [DYNAM- + -ITE¹] —**dy′na·mit′er,** *n.* —**dy·na·mit·ic** (dī′nə mit′ik), *adj.* —**dy′na·mit′i·cal·ly,** *adv.*

dy·na·mo (dī′nə mō′), *n., pl.* **-mos.** 1. an electric generator, esp. for direct current. 2. *Informal.* an energetic, hard-working, forceful person. [short for DYNAMOELECTRIC]

dynamo-, var. of **dyna-:** *dynamometer.* Also, **dynam-.**

dy·na·mo·e·lec·tric (dī′nə mō i lek′trik), *adj.* pertaining to or effecting the conversion of mechanical energy into electric energy, or vice versa: *a dynamoelectric machine.* Also, **dy′na·mo·e·lec′tri·cal.**

dy·na·mom·e·ter (dī′nə mom′i tər), *n. Mech.* 1. a device for measuring mechanical force, as a balance. 2. a device for measuring mechanical power, esp. one that measures the output or driving torque of a rotating machine. —**dy′na·mom′e·try,** *n.*

dy·na·mo·tor (dī′nə mō′tər), *n.* an electric machine for transforming direct current into alternating current or for altering the voltage of direct current, having two armature windings on the same core and a common magnetic field.

dy·nast (dī′nast, -nəst; *Brit. also* din′ast), *n.* a ruler or potentate, esp. a hereditary ruler. [< L *dynast(ēs)* < Gk. See DYNA-, -IST]

dy·nas·ty (dī′nə stē; *Brit. also* din′ə stē), *n., pl.* **-ties.** 1. a sequence of rulers from the same family, stock, or group: *the Ming dynasty.* 2. the rule of such a sequence. [late ME < LL *dynastīa* < Gk *dynasteia*] —**dy·nas·tic** (dī nas′tik; *Brit. also* di nas′tik), **dy·nas′ti·cal,** *adj.* —**dy·nas′ti·cal·ly,** *adv.*

dy·na·tron (dī′nə tron′), *n. Electronics.* a tetrode, frequently used as an oscillator in radio, in which an increase in the plate voltage results in a decrease in the plate current because of emission of electrons from the plate.

dyne (dīn), *n. Physics.* the standard centimeter-gram-second unit of force, equal to the force that produces an acceleration of one centimeter per second per second on a mass of one gram. *Abbr.:* dyn [< F < Gk *dýn(amis)* force, power]

dys-, a learned borrowing from Greek meaning "ill," "bad," used in the formation of technical terms: *dysfunction.* [< Gk; c. Icel *tor-*, G *zer-*, Skt *dus-*]

dys·en·ter·y (dis′ən ter′ē), *n.* **1.** *Pathol.* an infectious disease marked by inflammation and ulceration of the lower part of the bowels, with diarrhea that becomes mucous and hemorrhagic. **2.** *Informal.* diarrhea. [< ML *dysenteria* < Gk = *dysénter(a)* bad bowels + *-ia* -IA; r. ME *dissenterie* < OF] —**dys′en·ter′ic,** *adj.*

dys·func·tion (dis fuŋgk′shən), *n.* *Med.* malfunctioning, as of an organ of the body.

dys·gen·ic (dis jen′ik), *adj.* pertaining to or causing degeneration in the type of offspring produced. Cf. **eugenic.**

dys·gen·ics (dis jen′iks), *n.* (*construed as sing.*) *Biol.* the study of the operation of factors that cause degeneration in offspring.

dys·lex·i·a (dis lek′sē ə), *n.* *Pathol.* an impairment of the ability to read due to a brain defect. [< NL < Gk *dys-* DYS- + *léx(is)* word + *-ia* -IA]

dys·lo·gis·tic (dis′lə jis′tik), *adj.* conveying disapproval or censure; not complimentary or eulogistic. [DYS- + (EU)-LOGISTIC] —**dys′lo·gis′ti·cal·ly,** *adv.*

dys·men·or·rhe·a (dis′men ə rē′ə), *n.* *Med.* painful menstruation. Also, **dys′men·or·rhoe′a.** [< NL] —**dys′-men·or·rhe′al, dys′men·or·rhoe′al,** *adj.*

dys·pep·sia (dis pep′shə, -sē ə), *n.* deranged or impaired digestion; indigestion (opposed to *eupepsia*). Also, **dys-pep·sy** (dis pep′sē). [< L < Gk = *dys-* DYS- + *péps(is)* digestion + *-ia* -IA]

dys·pep·tic (dis pep′tik), *adj.* Also, **dys·pep′ti·cal.** **1.** pertaining to, subject to, or suffering from dyspepsia. **2.** gloomy and irritable. —*n.* **3.** a person subject to or suffering from dyspepsia. —**dys·pep′ti·cal·ly,** *adv.*

dys·pha·gia (dis fā′jə, -jē ə), *n.* *Pathol.* difficulty in swallowing. [< NL; see DYS-, -PHAGIA] —**dys·phag·ic** (dis faj′ik), *adj.*

dys·pha·sia (dis fā′zhə, -zhē ə, -zē ə), *n.* *Pathol.* inability to speak or understand words because of a brain lesion. [DYS- + (A)PHASIA] —**dys·pha·sic** (dis fā′zik), *adj.*

dys·pho·ni·a (dis fō′nē ə), *n.* any disturbance of normal vocal function. [< NL < Gk: roughness of sound. See DYS-, -PHONE, -IA] —**dys·phon·ic** (dis fon′ik), *adj.*

dys·pho·ri·a (dis fōr′ē ə, -fôr′-), *n.* *Pathol.* a state of dissatisfaction, anxiety, restlessness, or fidgeting. [< NL < Gk: malaise, discomfort. See DYS-, -PHORE, -IA] —**dys-phor·ic** (dis fôr′ik, -for′-), *adj.*

dysp·ne·a (disp nē′ə), *n.* *Pathol.* difficult or labored breathing (opposed to *eupnea*). Also, **dysp·noe′a.** [< L *dyspnoea* < Gk *dýspnoia* = *dys-* DYS- + *pno(ē)* breath + *-ia* -IA] —**dysp·ne′al, dysp·ne′ic, dysp·noe′al, dysp-noe′ic, dysp·no·ic** (disp nō′ik), *adj.*

dys·pro·si·um (dis prō′sē əm, -shē-), *n.* *Chem.* a rare-earth metallic element. *Symbol:* Dy; *at. wt.:* 162.50; *at. no.:* 66. [< NL < Gk *dysprôs(itos)* hard to get at (*dys-* DYS- + *pros-* to + *itós*, ptp. of *iénai* to go) + -IUM]

dys·tel·e·ol·o·gy (dis′tel ē ol′ə jē, -tē lē-), *n.* **1.** *Philos.* a doctrine denying the existence of a final cause or purpose. **2.** the assumed absence of purpose in life or nature. **3.** the evasion or frustration of a natural or normal function or purpose. —**dys·tel·e·o·log·i·cal** (dis′tel ē ə loj′i kəl, -tē lē-), *adj.* —**dys′tel·e·ol′o·gist,** *n.*

dys·thy·mi·a (dis thī′mē ə), *n.* despondency or a tendency to be despondent. [< NL < Gk = *dys-* DYS- + *thym(ós)* spirit + *-ia* -IA] —**dys·thy′mic,** *adj.*

dys·tro·phy (dis′trə fē), *n.* **1.** *Med.* faulty or inadequate nutrition or development. **2.** *Pathol.* any of a number of disorders characterized by weakening, degeneration, or abnormal development of muscle. Also, **dys·tro·phi·a** (di-strō′fē ə). [< NL *dystrophia*]

dys·u·ri·a (dis yŏŏr′ē ə), *n.* *Pathol.* difficult or painful urination. [< NL < Gk *dysouría*] —**dys·u′ric,** *adj.*

Dyu·sham·be (dyŏŏ shäm′be), *n.* a city in and the capital of Tadzhikistan, in the SW Soviet Union in Asia. 310,000 (1965). Formerly, **Stalinabad.**

dz., dozen; dozens.

Dzer·zhinsk (dzer zhinsk′), *n.* a city in the central Soviet Union in Europe, NE of Moscow. 180,000 (est. 1962).

Dzhu·gash·vi·li (*Russ.* jŏŏ′gäsh vē′li), *n.* **Io·sif Vis-sa·ri·o·no·vich** (*Russ.* yō′sif vis sä ri ô′no vich). See **Stalin, Joseph.** Also, **Dzu′gash·vi′li.**

dzig·ge·tai (jig′i tī′), *n.* chigetai.

Dzun·ga·ri·a (dzŏŏŋ gâr′ē ə, zŏŏŋ-), *n.* a region in N Sinkiang, China: a Mongol kingdom 11th to 14th centuries.

DEVELOPMENT OF MAJUSCULE								
NORTH SEMITIC	GREEK		ETR.	LATIN		MODERN		
						GOTHIC	ITALIC	ROMAN
∃	∃	E	∃	∃	E	𝕰	*E*	E

DEVELOPMENT OF MINUSCULE					
ROMAN CURSIVE	ROMAN UNCIAL	CAROL. MIN.	MODERN		
			GOTHIC	ITALIC	ROMAN
ϵ	є	e	𝖊	*e*	e

The fifth letter of the English alphabet developed from North Semitic *he.* Originally a consonant with an *h*-sound, it was transformed into a vowel in Greek, although in Classical Greek and in certain local alphabets North Semitic *heth* (see **H**) was used to represent *eta* (long e). The minuscule (e) was derived from the capital (E) through the uncial form.

E, e (ē), *n., pl.* **E's** or **Es, e's** or **es.** **1.** the fifth letter of the English alphabet, a vowel. **2.** any spoken sound represented by the letter *E* or *e,* as in *met, meet,* or *mere.* **3.** a written or printed representation of the letter *E* or *e.* **4.** a device, as a printer's type, for reproducing the letter *E* or *e.*

E, **1.** east. **2.** eastern. **3.** English (def. 4). **4.** excellent.

E, **1.** the fifth in order or in a series. **2.** (*sometimes l.c.*) (in some grading systems) a grade or mark, as of academic work, that indicates work that is unacceptable or that needs improvement in order to be passing. **3.** *Music.* **a.** the third tone in the scale of C major or the fifth tone in the relative minor scale, A minor. **b.** a written or printed note representing this tone. **c.** a string, key, or pipe tuned to this tone. **d.** the tonality having E as the tonic note. **4.** *Elect.* See **electromotive force.** **5.** *Physics.* energy.

e, *Math.* a transcendental constant equal to 2.7182818 . . ., used as the base of natural logarithms; the limit of the expression $(1 + \frac{1}{n})^n$ as *n* approaches infinity.

e-, var. of **ex-**[1], occurring in words of Latin origin before consonants other than *c, f, p, q, s,* and *t: emit.*

E., **1.** Earl. **2.** east. **3.** eastern. **4.** English.

e., **1.** eldest. **2.** *Football.* end. **3.** entrance. **4.** *Baseball.* error; errors.

E·a (ā′ä), *n.* the Akkadian god of wisdom, the father of Marduk.

ea., each.

each (ēch), *adj.* **1.** every one of two or more considered individually or one by one: *each stone in a building; a hallway with a door at each end.* —*pron.* **2.** each one: *Each went his way.* —*adv.* **3.** to, from, or for each; apiece: *The new typewriters cost over a hundred dollars each.* [ME *eche,* OE *ǣlc* = *ā* ever (see AY[1]) + (*ge*)*līc* (A)LIKE; c. OHG *ēo-gilīh,* OFris *ellīk,* D, LG *elk*]
—**Syn. 1.** EACH, EVERY are alike in having a distributive meaning. Of two or more members composing a (usually) definite aggregate, EACH directs attention to the separate members in turn: *Each child* (of those considered and enumerated) *received a large apple.* EVERY emphasizes the idea of inclusiveness or universality; it is also used of an indefinite number, all being regarded singly and separately: *Every child present received an apple* (no child was omitted). *Every child* (of all in existence) *likes to play.*
—**Usage. 2.** Careful writers and speakers make certain that EACH, which is a singular pronoun, is always used with a singular verb: *Each child has his own book. Each of the houses is painted a different color.*

each′ oth′er, **1.** each the other: *to love each other.* **2.** one another (used as a compound reciprocal pronoun in oblique cases): *They struck at each other.* [ME *ech other,* OE *ǣlc ōther*]

Ead·mund I (ed′mənd). See **Edmund I.**

Eadmund II. See **Edmund II.**

Eads (ēdz), *n.* **James Buchanan,** 1820–87, U.S. engineer and inventor.

Ead·wine (ed′win), *n.* Edwin.

ea·ger (ē′gər), *adj.* **1.** keen or ardent in desire or feeling; impatiently longing: *I am eager for news.* **2.** characterized by or revealing great earnestness: *an eager look.* **3.** *Archaic.* keen; sharp; biting. [ME *egre* < OF *egre, aigre* < L *acer* sharp] —**ea′ger·ly,** *adv.* —**ea′ger·ness,** *n.* —**Syn. 1.** fervent, zealous, enthusiastic.

ea·gle (ē′gəl), *n.* **1.** any of several large, diurnal, accipitrine birds of prey, noted for their size, strength, and powers of flight and vision. **2.** a figure or representation of an eagle, much used as an emblem: *the Roman eagle.* **3.** a standard, seal, or the like, bearing such a figure. **4.** one of a pair of silver insignia in the shape of eagles with outstretched wings worn by a colonel in the U.S. Army, Air Force, and Marine Corps, and by a captain in the U.S. Navy. **5.** a gold coin of the U.S., issued until 1933, equal to 10 dollars, having on its reverse the figure of an eagle. **6.** (*cap.*) *Astron.* the constellation Aquila. **7.** *Golf.* a score of two below par on any hole. [ME *egle* < OF *egle, aigle* < OPr *aigla* < L *aquila,* n. use of fem. of *aquilus* dark-colored]

ea·gle-eyed (ē′gəl īd′), *adj.* sharp-sighted.

ea′gle scout′, a boy scout who has earned 21 merit badges.

ea·glet (ē′glit), *n.* a young eagle. [< F *aiglette* (in heraldry)]

ea·gre (ē′gər, ā′gər), *n.* *Chiefly Brit.* a tidal bore flood. [earlier *eager, eagar* = OE *ēa* river + *gār* storm]

Ea·ker (ā′kər), *n.* **Ira Clarence,** born 1896, U.S. Air Force general.

Ea·kins (ā′kinz), *n.* **Thomas,** 1844–1916, U.S. painter.

eal·der·man (ôl′dər mən), *n., pl.* **-men.** *Obs.* alderman.

eal·dor·man (ôl′dər mən), *n., pl.* **-men.** *Obs.* alderman.

Ea·ling (ē′ling), *n.* a city in SE England, part of Greater London, 183,151 (1961).

-ean, an element used to form adjectives from nouns with stems in **-ea:** *trachean.* [< L *-ē*(*us*) (Gk *-eios*), *-ae*(*us*) (Gk *-aios*), *-e*(*us*) + -AN]

E. and P., extraordinary and plenipotentiary.

ean·ling (ēn′ling), *n.* *Obs.* a young lamb; kid. [var. of YEANLING]

ear[1] (ēr), *n.* **1.** the organ of hearing in man and other vertebrates, in man consisting of the external ear, which receives sound vibrations that are passed into the middle ear, causing a vibration of its bones which in turn causes a movement of the fluid in the internal ear, the hair cells of which stimulate the auditory nerve which transmits the impulse to the brain. **2.** the external part alone. **3.** the sense of hearing: *sounds pleasing to the ear.* **4.** keen or sensitive perception of the differences of sound, esp. musical sounds: *an ear for music.* **5.** attention; heed: *to gain a person's ear.* **6.** *Journalism.* a small box in either upper corner of a newspaper page, usually the front page, containing the name of or a symbol for the edition, a weather bulletin, etc. **7. be all ears,** to listen with all one's attention. **8. bend an ear,** to listen attentively. **9. bend one's ear,** *Slang.* to talk to someone uninterruptedly and often so as to induce

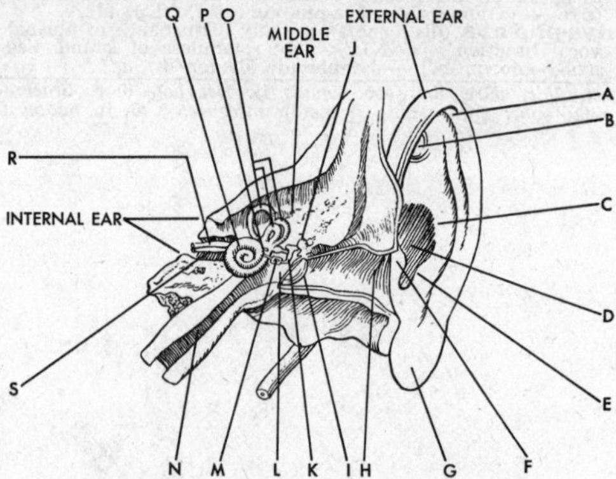

Human ear (transverse section)
External ear: A, Helix; B, Fossa of antihelix; C, Antihelix; D, Concha; E, Antitragus; F, Tragus; G, Lobe; H, External auditory meatus. Middle ear: I, Tympanic membrane; J, Malleus; K, Incus; L, Tympanic cavity; M, Stapes; N, Eustachian tube. Internal ear: O, Semicircular canals; P, Vestibule; Q, Cochlea; R, Nerves; S, Internal auditory meatus

boredom: *He'll bend your ear for hours.* **10. play by ear.** See **play** (def. 53). **11. play it by ear.** See **play** (def. 59). **12. up to one's ears,** deeply involved or immersed: *up to our ears in work.* **13. wet behind the ears.** See **wet** (def. 9). [ME *ere,* OE *ēare;* c. Icel *eyra,* G *Ohr,* Goth *auso,* L *auris,* Lith *ausis,* Gk *oûs*]

ear[2] (ēr), *n.* **1.** the part of a cereal plant, as corn, wheat, etc., that contains the flowers and hence the fruit, grains, or kernels. —*v.i.* **2.** to form or put forth ears, as a cereal plant. [ME *ere,* OE *ēar, ǣhher;* c. G *Ähre,* Icel *ax,* Goth *ahs* ear, L *acus* husk]

ear·ache (ēr′āk′), *n.* pain in the middle or internal ear or an instance of it.

ear·drop (ēr′drop′), *n.* an earring with a pendant.

ear′ drops′, drops for use in the ear, esp. to relieve earache.

ear·drum (ēr′drum′), *n.* See **tympanic membrane.**

eared (ērd), *adj.* having ears or earlike appendages. [ME *ered,* OE *ēarede*]

ear·ful (ēr′fŏŏl), *n., pl.* **-fuls.** *U.S. Informal.* **1.** an amount of oral information or advice, esp. when given without solicitation. **2.** a sharp verbal rebuke; a dressing-down.

Ear·hart (âr′härt), *n.* **Amelia (Mary),** 1897–1937, U.S. aviatrix: disappeared on Pacific flight 1937.

ear·ing (ēr′ing), *n.* *Naut.* any of various short ropes attached to cringles and used for bending a corner of a sail to a yard, boom, or gaff, for reefing a sail, or for bending a corner of an awning to a spar or stanchion.

earl (ûrl), *n.* **1.** a British nobleman of a rank next below that of marquis and next above that of viscount. An earl was called a count for a time after the Norman Conquest: an earl's wife is called a countess. **2.** (in Anglo-Saxon England) a governor of one of the great divisions of England, including East Anglia, Mercia, Northumbria, and Wessex. [ME *erl,* OE *eorl;* c. OS *erl* man, Icel *jarl* chieftain]

earl·dom (ûrl′dəm), *n.* **1.** the rank or title of an earl. **2.** *Obs.* the territory or jurisdiction of an earl. [ME *erldom,* OE *eorldōm*]

earl·ship (ûrl′ship), *n.* earldom (def. 1). [OE *eorlscipe*]

ear·ly (ûr′lē), *adv.*, **-li·er, -li·est,** *adj.*, **-li·er, -li·est.** —*adv.* **1.** in or during the first part of a period of time, a course of action, a series of events, etc.: *early in the year.* **2.** in the early part of the morning: *to get up early.* **3.** before the usual or appointed time; ahead of time. **4.** far back in time: *Man early learned the usefulness of weapons.* —*adj.* **5.** occurring in the first part of a period of time, a course of action, a series of events, etc.: *an early hour of the day.* **6.** occurring before the usual or appointed time: *an early dinner.* **7.** belonging to a period far back in time: *early French architecture.* **8.** occurring in the near future: *I look forward to an early reply.* [ME *erlich* (adj.) *erliche* (adv.), OE *ǣrlīc, ǣrlīce,* mutated var. of *ārlīc, ārlīce* = *ār-* early (positive of *ǣr* ERE) + *līc(e)* -LY] —**ear′li·ness,** *n.* —**Ant. 1–3, 5–7.** late.

Ear·ly (ûr′lē), *n.* **Ju·bal Anderson** (jo͞o′bəl), 1816–94, Confederate general in the U.S. Civil War.

Ear′ly Amer′ican, 1. (of furniture, buildings, utensils, etc.) built or made in the U.S. in the colonial period or soon after. **2.** made in imitation of the Early American style.

ear′ly bird′, 1. *Informal.* a person who arises or arrives before others. **2.** (*caps.*) a commercial communications satellite for relaying television, telephone, and other signals between the U.S. and Europe.

Ear′ly Chris′tian, noting or pertaining to the style of religious architecture developed chiefly in Italy from the 3rd century A.D. through the 5th century, but evolving in the Eastern Roman Empire into the Byzantine style by the end of this period.

Ear′ly Eng′lish, noting or pertaining to the first style of Gothic architecture in Great Britain, ending in the latter half of the 13th century, characterized by the use of lancet arches, plate tracery, and narrow openings.

Ear′ly Ren′aissance, a style of art developed principally in Florence during the 15th century and characterized chiefly by the development of linear perspective, chiaroscuro, and geometrical compositions. Cf. **High Renaissance.**

ear·mark (ēr′märk′), *n.* **1.** a mark of identification made on the ear of an animal. **2.** any identifying or distinguishing mark or characteristic. —*v.t.* **3.** to mark with an earmark. **4.** to set aside for a specific purpose, use, recipient, etc.: *to earmark goods for export.*

ear·muff (ēr′muf′), *n.* *U.S.* one of a pair of adjustable coverings for protecting the ears in cold weather.

earn[1] (ûrn), *v.t.* **1.** to gain or get in return for one's labor or service: *to earn one's living.* **2.** to merit as compensation, as for service; deserve: *to receive more than one has earned.* **3.** to acquire through merit; bring about or cause deservedly: *to earn a reputation for honesty.* **4.** to gain as due return or profit: *Savings bonds earn interest.* —*v.i.* **5.** to gain income. [ME *ern(i)en,* OE *earnian;* akin to OHG *arnēn* to earn] —**earn′er,** *n.* —**Syn. 1.** See **gain**[1].

earn[2] (ûrn), *v.t., v.i.* *Obs.* to yearn.

earned′ in′come, income from wages, salaries, fees, or the like.

ear·nest[1] (ûr′nist), *adj.* **1.** serious in intention, purpose, or effort; sincerely zealous: *an earnest worker.* **2.** showing depth and sincerity of feeling: *earnest words; an earnest entreaty.* **3.** seriously important; demanding or receiving serious attention: *earnest consideration of measures to be adopted.* —*n.* **4.** full seriousness, as of intention or purpose: *in earnest.* [ME *erneste,* OE *eornoste* (adj.); ME *ernest,* OE *eornost* (n.); c. D, G *ernst*] —**ear′nest·ly,** *adv.* —**ear′nest·ness,** *n.* —**Syn. 1.** fervent. EARNEST, RESOLUTE, SERIOUS, SINCERE imply having qualities of depth, firmness, and stability. EARNEST implies having a purpose and being steadily and soberly eager in pursuing it: *an earnest student.* RESOLUTE adds somewhat more of a quality of determination; a person who is resolute is very difficult to sway or turn aside from a purpose: *resolute in defending the right.* SERIOUS implies having depth and a soberness of attitude which contrasts with gaiety and frivolity; it may include the qualities of both earnestness and resolution: *serious and thoughtful.* SINCERE suggests genuineness, trustworthiness, and absence of deceit or superficiality: *a sincere interest in music.* **3.** purposeful. —**Ant. 1.** frivolous.

ear·nest[2] (ûr′nist), *n.* **1.** a portion of something, given or done in advance as a pledge of the remainder. **2.** anything that gives pledge, promise, assurance, or indication of what is to follow. [ME *ernes(t),* alter. of OF *erres,* pl. of *erre* earnest money < L *arrha,* short for *arrhabō* < Gk *arrhabṓn* < Sem (cf. Heb *'ērābōn* security, pledge)]

earn·ing (ûr′ning), *n.* **1.** the act of a person who earns. **2. earnings,** money earned; wages; profits. [ME *erning,* OE *earning, earnung* merit, pay]

Earp (ûrp), *n.* **Wy·att (Ber·ry Stapp)** (wī′ət ber′ē stap′), 1848–1929, U.S. frontiersman, law officer, and gunfighter.

ear·phone (ēr′fōn′), *n.* the sound receiver in a headset, as of a radio, telephone, etc.

ear·piece (ēr′pēs′), *n.* **1.** a piece that covers or passes over the ear, as on a cap, eyeglasses, etc. **2.** an earphone.

ear·plug (ēr′plug′), *n.* a plug for the opening of the outer ear to keep out water or noise.

ear·ring (ēr′ring′, -ing), *n.* an ornament worn on the lobe of the ear. [ME *erering,* OE *ēarhring*]

ear′ shell′, abalone.

ear·shot (ēr′shot′), *n.* the range or distance within which a sound, voice, etc., can be heard.

ear·split·ting (ēr′split′ing), *adj.* very loud; deafening.

earth (ûrth), *n.* **1.** (*often cap.*) the planet third in order from the sun, having an equatorial diameter of 7926 miles and a polar diameter of 7900 miles, a mean distance from the sun of 92.9 million miles, and a period of revolution of 365.26 days, and having one satellite. **2.** the inhabitants of this planet, esp. the human inhabitants: *The whole earth rejoiced.* **3.** this planet as the habitation of man, often in contrast to heaven and hell: *to create a hell on earth.* **4.** the surface of this planet: *to fall to earth.* **5.** the solid matter of this planet; dry land; ground. **6.** soil and dirt, as distinguished from rock and sand. **7.** *Fox Hunting.* any hole in the ground in which a fox takes refuge. **8.** worldly matters, as distinguished from spiritual matters. **9.** *Chem.* any of several metallic oxides that are difficult to reduce, as alumina, zirconia, yttria, etc. Cf. **alkaline earth, rare earth. 10.** Also called **earth′ col′or.** *Fine Arts.* any of various pigments consisting chiefly of iron oxides and tending toward brown in hue. **11.** *Elect.* a ground. **12.** *Obs.* a land or country. [ME *erthe,* OE *eorthe;* c. G *Erde,* D *aarde,* Icel *jörth,* Dan *jord,* Goth *airtha*]

earth·born (ûrth′bôrn′), *adj.* **1.** born on or sprung from the earth; of earthly origin. **2.** mortal; human.

earth·bound (ûrth′bound′), *adj.* **1.** firmly set in or attached to the earth. **2.** limited to the earth or its surface. **3.** having only earthly interests. **4.** lacking in imagination, sophistication, or the like: *an earthbound style of writing.* Also, **earth′-bound′.**

earth·en (ûr′thən), *adj.* **1.** composed of earth. **2.** made of baked clay. [ME *erthen,* OE *eorthen*]

earth·en·ware (ûr′thən wâr′), *n.* **1.** pottery of baked or hardened clay, esp. any of the coarse, opaque varieties. **2.** clay for making such pottery.

earth·i·ness (ûr′thē nis), *n.* **1.** earthy nature or properties. **2.** the quality of being unaffectedly realistic, direct, or down-to-earth. **3.** the quality of being unrefined, coarse, or scatological: *I don't like the earthiness of his jokes.* [ME *erthynesse*]

earth·light (ûrth′līt′), *n.* *Astron.* earthshine.

earth·ling (ûrth′ling), *n.* **1.** an inhabitant of earth; mortal. **2.** a person attached to earthly or worldly things. [EARTH + -LING[1]; cf. OE *eorthling* plowman]

earth·ly (ûrth′lē), *adj.,* **-li·er, -li·est. 1.** of or pertaining to the earth, esp. as opposed to heaven; worldly. **2.** possible or conceivable: *of no earthly use.* [ME *erth(e)ly,* OE *eorthlīc*] —**earth′li·ness,** *n.*
—**Syn. 1.** earthy. EARTHLY, TERRESTRIAL, WORLDLY, MUNDANE refer to that which is concerned with the earth literally or figuratively. EARTHLY now almost always implies a contrast to that which is heavenly: *earthly pleasures; our earthly home.* TERRESTRIAL, from Latin, is the more formal equivalent of EARTHLY, and it applies to the earth as a planet or to the land as opposed to the water, and is contrasted with that which is celestial: *terrestrial areas; the terrestrial globe.* WORLDLY is commonly used in the derogatory sense of being devoted to the vanities, cares, advantages, or gains of this present life to the exclusion of spiritual interests or the life to come: *worldly success; worldly standards.* MUNDANE, from Latin, is a formal equivalent of WORLDLY and suggests that which is bound to the earth, is not exalted, and therefore is commonplace: *mundane affairs, pursuits, etc.* **2.** imaginable. —**Ant. 1.** spiritual, divine.

earth·man (ûrth′man′, -mən), *n., pl.* **-men** (-men′, -mən). a human inhabitant or native of the planet earth.

earth′ moth′er, the earth conceived of as the female principle of fertility and the source of all life. Also, **Earth′ Moth′er.**

earth·nut (ûrth′nut′), *n.* **1.** any of various roots, tubers, or underground growths, as the peanut and the truffle. **2.** any of the plants producing these. [ME *erthenote,* OE *eorthnutu*]

earth·quake (ûrth′kwāk′), *n.* a vibration or movement of a part of the earth's surface, due to the faulting of rocks, to volcanic forces, etc. [ME *erthequake* (see EARTH, QUAKE), r. OE *eorthdyne;* see DIN]

earth′ sci′ence, any of various sciences, as geography, geology, etc., that deal with the earth, its composition, or any of its changing aspects.

earth·shak·ing (ûrth′shā′king), *adj.* imperiling, challenging, or affecting basic beliefs, attitudes, etc.

earth·shine (ûrth′shīn′), *n.* *Astron.* the faint illumination of the part of the moon not illuminated by sunlight, as during a crescent phase, caused by the reflection of light from the earth. Also called **earthlight.**

earth·star (ûrth′stär′), *n.* a fungus of the genus *Geaster,* having a covering which splits into the form of a star.

earth·ward (ûrth′wərd), *adv.* **1.** Also, **earth′wards.** toward the earth. —*adj.* **2.** directed toward the earth. [ME *ertheward*]

earth·work (ûrth′wûrk′), *n.* **1.** excavation and piling of earth in an engineering operation. **2.** *Mil.* a construction formed chiefly of earth for protection against enemy fire, used in both offensive and defensive operations.

earth·worm (ûrth′wûrm′), *n.* **1.** any one of numerous annelid worms that burrow in soil and feed on soil and decaying organic matter. **2.** *Archaic.* a mean or groveling person. [ME *ertheworm*]

earth·y (ûr′thē), *adj.,* **earth·i·er, earth·i·est. 1.** of the nature of or consisting of earth or soil. **2.** characteristic of earth: *an earthy smell.* **3.** realistic; practical. **4.** coarse or unrefined: *an earthy sense of humor.* **5.** direct; robust; unaffected. **6.** *Archaic.* worldly; pertaining to the earth. [ME *erthy*] —**earth′i·ly,** *adv.*

ear′ trum′pet, a trumpet-shaped device for holding to the ear to amplify sound, formerly used as an aid to a person with defective hearing.

ear·wax (ēr′waks′), *n.* cerumen. [ME *erewax*]

ear·wig (ēr′wig′), *n., v.,* **-wigged, -wig·ging.** —*n.* **1.** any of numerous elongate, nocturnal insects of the order *Dermaptera,* having a pair of large, movable pincers at the rear of the abdomen. —*v.t.* **2.** to fill the mind of with prejudice by insinuations. [ME *erwigge,* OE *ēarwicga* ear insect; from the superstition that they enter people's ears. See WIGGLE]

ease (ēz), *n., v.,* **eased, eas·ing.** —*n.* **1.** freedom from labor, pain, or discomfort. **2.** freedom from concern or anxiety; a quiet state of mind: *to be at ease about one's health.* **3.** freedom from difficulty or great effort; facility: *It can be done with ease.* **4.** freedom from financial need; plenty: *a life of ease.* **5.** freedom from stiffness, constraint, or formality: *to be at ease with others.* **6. at ease,** *Mil.* in a position of rest in which soldiers may relax but may not leave their places or talk. —*v.t.* **7.** to give rest or relief to; make comfortable. **8.** to free from anxiety or care. **9.** to mitigate, lighten, or lessen: *to ease pain.* **10.** to move or shift with great care: *to ease a car into a narrow parking space.* **11.** to render less difficult; facilitate: *I'll help if it will ease* your job. 12. *Naut.* a. to bring (the helm or rudder of a vessel) slowly amidships. b. to bring the head of (a vessel) into the wind. —*v.i.* 13. to abate in severity, pressure, tension, etc. (often fol. by *off* or *up*). 14. to become less painful, burdensome, etc. 15. to move, shift, or be moved or be shifted with great care. 16. **ease out,** to remove from authority or a job tactfully. [ME *ese, eise* < OF *aise,* perh. < VL **adiaces,* var. of L *adiacēns* ADJACENT] —**eas′er,** *n.* —**Syn.** 1. repose, contentment, effortlessness. EASE, COMFORT refer to a sense of relaxation or of well-being. EASE implies a relaxed condition with an absence of effort or pressure: *a life of ease; ease after the day's work.* COMFORT suggests a sense of well-being, along with ease, which produces a quiet happiness and contentment: *comfort in one's old age.* 2. tranquillity, serenity, calmness, peace. 5. naturalness, informality. 7, 8. comfort, relieve. 8. tranquilize, soothe. 9. alleviate, assuage, allay. —**Ant.** 1. discomfort, effort. 2. disturbance. 5. constraint.

ease·ful (ēz′fəl), *adj.* quiet; peaceful; restful. [ME *eisefull*] —**ease′ful·ly,** *adv.*

ea·sel (ē′zəl), *n.* 1. a stand or frame for supporting an artist's canvas, a blackboard, or the like. 2. any stand or frame for displaying objects, as paintings, china, etc. [< D *ezel* ass, easel (c. G *Esel,* OE *esel* ass) < VL **asilus,* var. of L *asellus,* dim. of *asinus* ASS[1]]

ease·ment (ēz′mənt), *n.* 1. an easing; relief. 2. something that gives ease; convenience. 3. *Law.* a right held by one person to make use of the land of another for a limited purpose, as right of passage. [ME *esement* < OF *aisement*]

eas·i·er (ē′zē ər), *adj.* comparative of **easy.**

eas·i·est (ē′zē ist), *adj.* superlative of **easy.**

eas·i·ly (ē′zə lē, ēz′lē), *adv.* 1. in an easy manner; with ease; without trouble. 2. beyond question; by far: *easily the best.* 3. likely; well: *It may easily rain.* [ME *esily*]

eas·i·ness (ē′zē nis), *n.* 1. the quality or condition of being easy. 2. ease of manner; carelessness; indifference. [ME *esinesse*]

east (ēst), *n.* 1. a cardinal point of the compass, 90° to the right of north. *Abbr.:* E 2. the direction in which this point lies. 3. (*usually cap.*) a quarter or territory situated in this direction. 4. **the East, a.** the Orient; the Far East. **b.** the countries east of Europe. **c.** the part of the U.S. east of the Mississippi River. **d.** the part of the U.S. east of the Allegheny Mountains. **e.** New England. **f.** *Ancient and Medieval Hist.* the Eastern Roman Empire. —*adj.* 5. lying toward or situated in the east: *the east end of town.* 6. in the direction of or toward the east. 7. coming from the east, as a wind. —*adv.* 8. toward the east: *heading east.* 9. from the east. [ME *est,* OE *ēast;* c. G *ost,* Icel *austr;* akin to L *aurora,* Gk *aúōs* (var. of *ēōs*) dawn. See EASTER]

East., eastern. Also, **east.**

East′ An′glia, an early English kingdom in SE Britain: modern Norfolk and Suffolk. See map at **Mercia.** —**East′ An′glian.**

East′ A′sia, the countries and land area of the People's Republic of China, Hong Kong, Japan, Korea, Macao, Mongolia, Ryukyu islands, Taiwan, and the Soviet Union in Asia.

East′ Bengal′, the part of Bengal in Bangladesh: formerly part of the Indian province of Bengal. Cf. **Bengal** (def. 1).

East′ Berlin′. See under **Berlin** (def. 2).

east·bound (ēst′bound′), *adj.* traveling, proceeding, or headed east: *eastbound traffic.*

East·bourne (ēst′bôrn, -bərn), *n.* a seaport in E Sussex, in SE England. 60,897 (1961).

East′ Bruns′wick, a township in central New Jersey. 34,166 (1970).

east′ by north′, *Navig., Survey.* a point on the compass 11°15′ north of east. *Abbr.:* EbN

east′ by south′, *Navig., Survey.* a point on the compass 11°15′ south of east. *Abbr.:* EbS

East′ Cape′. See **Dezhnev, Cape.**

East′ Chica′go, a port in NW Indiana, on Lake Michigan, near Chicago. 46,982 (1970).

East′ Chi′na Sea′, a part of the N Pacific, bounded by China, Japan, Korea, the Ryukyus, and Taiwan. 480,000 sq. mi.

East′ Cleve′land, a city in NE Ohio, near Cleveland. 39,600 (1970).

East′ Detroit′, a city in SE Michigan. 45,920 (1970).

East′ End′, a section of E London, England.

East·er (ē′stər), *n.* 1. an annual Christian festival in commemoration of the resurrection of Jesus Christ, observed on the first Sunday after the first full moon after the vernal equinox. 2. the day on which this festival is celebrated. [ME *ester,* OE *ēastre;* c. G *Ostern;* orig. name of a goddess and her festival; akin to EAST]

East′er egg′, 1. an egg that is dyed or decorated as an Easter gift or decoration. 2. an imitation of this, as one made of chocolate, candy, etc.

East′er Is′land, an island in the S Pacific, W of and belonging to Chile. ab. 45 sq. mi. Also called **Rapa Nui.**

East′er lil′y, any of several white-flowered lilies, esp. *Lilium longiflorum,* that are artificially brought into bloom in early spring.

east·er·ly (ē′stər lē), *adj., adv., n., pl.* **-lies.** —*adj.* 1. of, pertaining to, or situated in the east. 2. in the direction of or toward the east. 3. coming from the east, as a wind. —*adv.* 4. toward the east. 5. from the east, as a wind. —*n.* 6. an easterly wind. [obs. *easter* eastern + -LY]

East′er Mon′day, the day after Easter, a legal holiday in North Carolina and parts of the British Commonwealth.

east·ern (ē′stərn), *adj.* 1. lying toward or situated in the east. 2. directed or proceeding toward the east: *an eastern route.* 3. coming from the east: *an eastern wind.* 4. (*often cap.*) of or pertaining to the East: *an Eastern Congressman.* 5. (*cap.*) of or pertaining to the Eastern Church or to any of the churches comprising it. 6. (*usually cap.*) Oriental. [ME *esterne,* OE *ēasterne;* akin to Icel *austroenn,* OHG *ōstrōni*]

East′ern Church′, 1. any of the churches originating in countries formerly comprising the Eastern Roman Empire, observing an Eastern rite and adhering to the Nicene Creed; Byzantine Church. 2. See **Orthodox Church** (def. 2).

East′ern Em′pire. See **Eastern Roman Empire.**

east·ern·er (ē′stər nər), *n.* (*often cap.*) a native or inhabitant of an eastern area, esp. of the eastern U.S.

East′ern Ghats′, a low mountain range in S India along the E margin of the Deccan plateau and parallel to the coast of the Bay of Bengal.

East′ern Hem′isphere, the eastern part of the terrestrial globe, including Asia, Africa, Australia, and Europe.

east′ern hem′lock, a hemlock, *Tsuga canadensis,* of eastern North America: the state tree of Pennsylvania.

east·ern·ize (ē′stər nīz′), *v.t.,* **-ized, -iz·ing.** 1. to influence with ideas, customs, etc., characteristic of the Orient. 2. *U.S.* to influence with ideas, customs, etc., characteristic of the eastern U.S., esp. cosmopolitan ideas or customs. —**east′ern·i·za′tion,** *n.*

east·ern·most (ē′stərn mōst′ *or, esp. Brit.,* -məst), *adj.* farthest east.

East′ern Or′thodox, of or pertaining to the Orthodox Church.

east′ern red′ ce′dar. See **red cedar** (def. 1).

East′ern rite′, 1. the rite of an Eastern Church, usually observed in the national language of the country where the church is located. 2. a Uniat church.

East′ern Ro′man Em′pire, the eastern part of the Roman Empire, esp. after the division by Theodosius I in A.D. 395, and having its capital at Constantinople. Also called **Eastern Empire.** Cf. **Western Roman Empire.**

East′ern shore′, the eastern shore of Chesapeake Bay, including parts of Maryland, Delaware, and Virginia. Cf. **Delmarva Peninsula.**

East′ern Slavs′. See under **Slav** (def. 1).

East′ern Thrace′. See under **Thrace** (def. 2).

East′ern time′. See under **standard time.**

East′ern Tur′kestan. See under **Turkestan.**

East′er sep′ulcher, sepulcher (def. 2).

East′er Sun′day, Easter (def. 2).

East·er·tide (ē′stər tīd′), *n.* 1. Easter time. 2. the week following Easter. 3. the 50 days between Easter and Whitsuntide. [late ME *Estertyde*]

East′ Flan′ders, a province in W Belgium. 1,289,011 (est. 1964); 1150 sq. mi. *Cap.:* Ghent.

East′ German′ic, an extinct branch of the Germanic languages comprising Gothic and probably others of which there are no written records. *Abbr.:* EGmc.

East′ Ger′many, a country in central Europe: consists of the Soviet zone of occupied Germany, created by the division of Germany in 1945. 16,028,000 (est. 1964); 41,535 sq. mi. *Cap.:* East Berlin. Official name, **German Democratic Republic.** —**East′ Ger′man.**

East′ Goth′, an Ostrogoth.

East′ Ham′, a city in SE England, near London. 105,359 (1961).

East′ Hart′ford, a town in central Connecticut. 57,583 (1970).

East′ In′dia Com′pany, 1. the company chartered by the British government in 1600 to carry on trade in the East Indies: dissolved in 1874. 2. any similar company, as one chartered by the Dutch (1602–1798), the French (1664–1769), or the Danes (1729–1801).

East′ In′dies, 1. the Malay Archipelago. 2. Also called **the Indies, Indonesia.** SE Asia, including Indonesia and the Malay Archipelago. Also called **East′ In′dia.** —**East′ In′dian.**

east·ing (ē′sting), *n.* 1. *Navig.* the distance due east made good on any course tending eastward; easterly departure. 2. a shifting eastward; easterly direction. 3. *Survey.* a distance east from a north-south reference line.

East′ Kil′bride (kil′brīd), a town in W Lanark, in E Scotland. 31,972 (1961).

East′ Lan′sing, a city in S Michigan. 47,540 (1970).

East′ Lon′don, a seaport in the SE Cape of Good Hope province, in the S Republic of South Africa. 113,746 (1960).

East′ Los′ An′geles, a city in SW California, near Los Angeles. 105,033 (1970).

East′ Lo′thi·an (lō′thē ən, -thē-), a country in SE Scotland. 52,653 (1961); 267 sq. mi. *Co. seat:* Haddington. Formerly, **Haddington.**

East·man (ēst′mən), *n.* **George,** 1854–1932, U.S. philanthropist and inventor in the field of photography.

East′ Mead′ow, a town on W Long Island, in SE New York. 46,290 (1970).

East′ Mill′creek′ (mil′krēk′), a town in N Utah, near Salt Lake City. 26,579 (1970).

east-north·east (ēst′nôrth′ēst′), *n.* 1. the point on a compass midway between east and northeast. —*adj.* 2. in the direction of or toward this point. 3. from this point, as a wind. —*adv.* 4. toward this point. 5. from this point. *Abbr.:* ENE, E.N.E.

Eas·ton (ē′stən), *n.* a city in E Pennsylvania, on the Delaware River. 30,256 (1970).

East′ Or′ange, a city in NE New Jersey, near Newark. 75,471 (1970).

East′ Pak′istan, former name of **Bangladesh.**

East′ Point′, a city in N Georgia, near Atlanta. 39,315 (1970).

East′ Prov′idence, a city in NE Rhode Island, near Providence. 48,207 (1970).

East′ Prus′sia, a former province in NE Germany: an enclave separated from Germany by the Polish Corridor; now divided between Poland and the Soviet Union. 14,283 sq. mi. *Cap.:* Königsberg. German, **Ostpreussen.** —**East′ Prus′sian.**

East′ Punjab′, the eastern part of the former province of Punjab: now part of Punjab state.

East′ Rid′ing, an administrative division of Yorkshire, in NE England. 527,051 (1961); 1172 sq. mi. *Co. seat:* Beverley.

East′ Riv′er, a strait in SE New York separating Manhattan Island from Long Island and connecting New York Bay and Long Island Sound.

east-south·east (ēst′south/ēst′), —*n.* **1.** the point on a compass midway between east and southeast. —*adj.* **2.** in the direction of or toward this point. **3.** from this point, as a wind. —*adv.* **4.** toward this point. **5.** from this point. *Abbr.:* ESE, E.S.E.

East St. Louis, a city in SW Illinois, across the Mississippi River from St. Louis, Missouri. 69,996 (1970). —**East St. Louisan.**

East′ Suf′folk, an administrative division of Suffolk county, in E England. 342,696 (1961); 871 sq. mi. *Co. seat:* Ipswich.

East′ Sus′sex, an administrative division of Sussex county, in SE England. 664,669 (1961); 829 sq. mi. *Co. seat:* Lewes.

east·ward (ēst′wərd), *adj.* **1.** moving, facing, or situated toward the east. —*adv.* **2.** Also, **eastwards.** toward the east. —*n.* **3.** the east. [ME *estward,* OE *ēasteweard*]

east·ward·ly (ēst′wərd lē), *adj., adv.* toward the east.

eas·y (ē′zē), *adj.,* **eas·i·er, eas·i·est,** *adv., n.* —*adj.* **1.** not difficult; requiring little effort or labor: *a book that is easy to read; an easy victory.* **2.** free from pain, discomfort, worry, or care: *an easy mind.* **3.** providing or conducive to ease or comfort; comfortable: *an easy life.* **4.** fond of or given to ease; easygoing: *an easy disposition.* **5.** not harsh or strict; lenient. **6.** not burdensome or oppressive: *easy terms on a loan.* **7.** not difficult to influence or overcome; compliant: *an easy prey.* **8.** free from formality, constraint, or embarrassment: *an easy manner.* **9.** effortlessly clear and fluent: *an easy style of writing.* **10.** not tight or constricting: *an easy fit.* **11.** not forced or hurried; moderate: *an easy pace.* —*adv.* **12.** *Informal.* in an easy manner; comfortably: *to go easy; to take it easy.* —*n.* **13.** a word formerly used in communications to represent the letter *E.* [ME *aisie, esy* < OF *aaisie,* ptp. of *aaisier* to put (someone) at his ease (orig. adv. phrase *a aise* at EASE)] —**Syn. 2.** tranquil, untroubled, contented. **7.** accommodating, agreeable. —**Ant. 1.** difficult. **3.** uncomfortable.

eas′y chair′, **1.** an upholstered armchair for lounging. **2.** *Obs.* See **wing chair.**

eas·y·go·ing (ē′zē gō′ing), *adj.* **1.** calm and unworried; relaxed and rather casual. **2.** going easily, as a horse. Also, **eas′y-go′ing.**

eas′y mark′, a person who is easily exploited, deceived, or swindled.

eas′y ri′der, *Slang.* a man supported by a prostitute.

eas′y street′, *Slang.* a footing of wealth, financial independence, or ease: *If the book sells, next year we'll be on easy street.* Also, **Eas′y Street′.**

eat (ēt), *v.,* **ate** (āt; *esp. Brit.* et) or (*Archaic*) **eat** (et, ēt); **eat·en** or (*Archaic*) **eat** (et, ēt); **eat·ing;** *n.* —*v.t.* **1.** to take into the mouth and swallow for nourishment; chew and swallow (food). **2.** to consume gradually; wear away; corrode. **3.** to ravage or devastate. **4.** to make (a hole, passage, etc.), as by gnawing or corrosion. —*v.i.* **5.** to consume food; take a meal. **6.** to make a way, as by gnawing or corrosion: *Acid ate through the linoleum.* **7. eat crow.** See **crow**[1] (def. 4). **8. eat one's words.** See **word** (def. 12). **9. eat out,** to have a meal at a restaurant rather than at home. **10. eat up, a.** to consume wholly. **b.** to show enthusiasm for; take pleasure in: *The audience ate up everything he said.* **c.** to believe without question. —*n.* **11. eats,** *Slang.* food. [ME *ete(n),* OE *etan;* c. G *essen,* Goth *itan,* L *edere*] —**eat′er,** *n.*

eat·a·ble (ē′tə bəl), *adj.* **1.** fit to be eaten; edible. —*n.* **2.** Usually, **eatables.** articles of food.

eat·en (ēt′ᵊn), *v.* a pp. of **eat.**

eat·er·y (ē′tə rē), *n., pl.* **-er·ies.** *Slang.* a restaurant or other commercial establishment serving food.

eat·ing (ē′ting), *n.* **1.** the act of a person or thing that eats. **2.** food with reference to the quality it reveals when eaten: *This fish is delicious eating.* —*adj.* **3.** good or fit to eat, esp. raw (distinguished from *cooking*): *eating apples.* **4.** used in eating: *eating utensils.* [ME]

Ea·ton (ēt′ᵊn), *n.* **The·oph·i·lus** (thē of′ə ləs), 1590–1658, English colonist and colonial administrator in America.

eau (ō), *n., pl.* **eaux** (ō). *French.* water.

Eau Claire (ō′ klâr′), a city in W Wisconsin. 44,619 (1970).

eau de Co·logne (ō′ də kə lōn′), cologne.

eau de Ja·velle (ō′ də zhə vel′, zhə-; *Fr.* ōdᵊ zhA-vel′). See **Javel water.**

eau de vie (ōdᵊ vē′; *Eng.* ō′də vē′), *French.* brandy, esp. a coarser and less purified variety. [lit., water of life]

eave (ēv), *n.* Usually, **eaves.** the overhanging lower edge of a roof. [ME *eves,* OE *efes;* c. OHG *obisa,* Goth *ubizwa* hall] —**eaved,** *adj.*

eaves·drop (ēvz′drop′), *v.,* **-dropped, -drop·ping.** —*v.i.* **1.** to listen secretly to a private conversation. —*v.t.* **2.** to eavesdrop on. [lit., to be on the *eavesdrop* (ME *evesdrope,* var. of *evesdripe,* OE *yfesdrype*) of a house, i.e., on the ground to which falls the drip from the eaves. See EAVE, DROP, DRIP] —**eaves′drop′per,** *n.*

ebb (eb), *n.* **1.** the flowing back of the tide as the water returns to the sea (opposed to *flood, flow*). **2.** a flowing backward or away; decline or decay. **3.** a point of decline: *His fortunes were at a low ebb.* —*v.i.* **4.** to flow back or away, as the water of a tide (opposed to *flow*). **5.** to decline or decay; waste or fade away: *His life is ebbing.* [ME *eb(be),* OE *ebba;* c. OFris *ebba,* D *eb(be),* OS *ebbia,* G *Ebbe* ebb, Icel *efja* place where water backs up; akin to OFF] —**Syn. 2.** wane. **4.** subside, abate, recede. **5.** sink, wane.

ebb′ tide′, the reflux of the tide or the tide at ebb.

E·ber·hart (ā′bər härt′, eb′ər-), *n.* **Richard,** born 1904, U.S. poet.

Eb·lis (eb′lis), *n.* *Islamic Myth.* an evil spirit or devil, the chief of the wicked jinns. Also, **Iblis.** [< Ar *Iblīs* < Gk *diábolos* slanderer, the Devil; *di-* lost by confusion with Aram *di-* of]

EbN, See **east by north.**

eb·on·ise (eb′ə nīz′), *v.t.,* **-ised, -is·ing.** *Chiefly Brit.* ebonize.

eb·on·ite (eb′ə nīt′), *n.* vulcanite. [EBON(Y) + -ITE[1]]

eb·on·ize (eb′ə nīz′), *v.t.,* **-ized, -iz·ing.** to stain or finish black in imitation of ebony. Also, *esp. Brit.,* **ebonise.**

eb·on·y (eb′ə nē), *n., pl.* **-on·ies,** *adj.* —*n.* **1.** a hard, heavy wood, most highly prized when black, from various tropical trees of the genus *Diospyros,* as *D. Ebenum* of southern India and Ceylon. **2.** any tree yielding such wood. **3.** a deep, lustrous black. —*adj.* **4.** Also, **eb·on** (eb′ən). made of ebony. **5.** of a deep, lustrous black. [*ebon* ebony (ME < L *eben(us)* < Gk *(h)ébenos*) + -Y[1]; r. ME *hebenyf* < L *hebeninus* of ebony (misread as *hebeniuus*) < Gk *ebéninos*]

Eb·o·ra·cum (eb′ə rā′kəm), *n.* ancient Latin name of York, England.

E·bro (ē′brō; *Sp.* e′brô), *n.* a river flowing SE from N Spain to the Mediterranean. ab. 470 mi. long.

EbS, See **east by south.**

e·bul·lient (i bul′yənt), *adj.* **1.** overflowing with fervor, enthusiasm, or excitement; high-spirited. **2.** boiling up; bubbling up like a boiling liquid. [< L *ēbullient-* (s. of *ēbulliēns* boiling up, prp. of *ēbullīre*). See E-, BULLA, -ENT] —**e·bul′lience, e·bul′lien·cy,** *n.* —**e·bul′lient·ly,** *adv.*

eb·ul·li·tion (eb′ə lish′ən), *n.* **1.** a seething or overflowing, as of passion or feeling; outburst. **2.** the state of being ebullient. **3.** the act or process of boiling up. [< L *ēbullītiōn-* (s. of *ēbullītiō*) = *ēbullīt(us)* (ptp. of *ēbullīre* to boil up) = *ēbullī-* (see EBULLIENT) + *-t-* ptp. suffix + *-iōn-* -ION]

e·bur·na·tion (ē′bər nā′shən, eb′ər-), *n.* *Pathol.* an abnormal condition in which bone becomes hard and dense like ivory. [< L *eburn(us)* of ivory (*ebur* ivory + *-nus* adj. suffix) + -ATION]

ec-, var. of **ex-**[3] before a consonant: *eccentric.*

E.C., **1.** Engineering Corps. **2.** Established Church.

é·car·té (ā′kär tā′; *Brit.* ā kär′tā; *Fr.* ā KAR tā′), *n.* a card game for two players. [< F, n. use of ptp. of *écarter* to discard. See EX-[1], CARD[1], -EE]

e·cau·date (ē kô′dāt), *adj.* *Zool.* having no tail. [< NL *ecaudat(us)*]

Ec·bat·a·na (ek bat′ᵊnə), *n.* ancient name of **Hamadan.**

ec·bol·ic (ek bol′ik), *Med.* —*adj.* **1.** promoting labor by increasing uterine contractions. —*n.* **2.** an ecbolic agent. [< Gk *ekbol(ē)* expulsion (*ek-* EC- + *-bolē* a throwing) + -IC]

ec·ce ho·mo (ech′ā hō′mō), *Latin.* "Behold the man!": the words with which Pilate presented Christ, crowned with thorns, to his accusers. John 19:5.

ec·cen·tric (ik sen′trik, ek-), *adj.* **1.** deviating from the recognized or customary character, practice, etc.; irregular; erratic; peculiar; odd. **2.** *Geom.* not having the same center; not concentric: used esp. of two circles or spheres at least one of which contains the centers of both. **3.** (of an axis, axle, etc.) not situated in the center. **4.** (of a wheel, cam, etc.) having the axis or support away from the center. **5.** *Astron.* deviating from a circular form, as an elliptic orbit. —*n.* **6.** a person who has an unusual or odd personality, set of beliefs, or behavior pattern. **7.** something that is unusual, peculiar, or odd. **8.** *Mach.* a device for converting circular motion into reciprocating rectilinear motion, consisting of a disk fixed somewhat out of center to a revolving shaft, and working freely in a surrounding collar (**eccen′tric strap′**), to which a rod (**eccen′tric rod′**) is attached. [< ML *eccentric(us)* < Gk *ékkentr(os)* out of center (see EC-, CENTER) + L *-icus* -IC] —**ec·cen′tri·cal,** *adj.* —**ec·cen′tri·cal·ly,** *adv.* —**Ant. 1.** normal, ordinary.

Eccentric circles A, Center of small circle; B, Center of large circle

ec·cen·tric·i·ty (ek′sən tris′i tē, ek′sen-), *n., pl.* **-ties.** **1.** an oddity or peculiarity, as of conduct. **2.** the quality of being eccentric. **3.** the amount by which something is eccentric. **4.** *Math.* a constant expressed as the ratio of the distance from a point on a conic to a focus and the distance from the point to the directrix. [< ML *eccentricitās*] —**Syn. 2.** queerness, freakishness, aberration.

ec·chy·mo·sis (ek′ə mō′sis), *n., pl.* **-ses** (-sēz). *Pathol.* a discoloration due to extravasation of blood, as in a bruise. [< NL < Gk *ekchýmōsis* extravasation. See EC-, CHYME, -OSIS] —**ec·chy·mot·ic** (ek′ə mot′ik), *adj.*

Eccl., Ecclesiastes. Also, **Eccles.**

eccl., ecclesiastical. Also, **eccles.**

ecclesi-, var. of **ecclesio-** before a vowel: *ecclesiarch.*

ec·cle·si·a (i klē′zhē ə, -zē ə), *n., pl.* **-si·ae** (-zhē ē′, -zē ē′). **1.** an assembly, esp. the popular assembly of ancient Athens. **2.** a congregation; church. [< LGk *ekklēsía* assembly = *ekklē(tós)* summoned (*ek-* EC- + *klē-,* var. of *kal-,* s. of *kalein* to call + *-tos* ptp. suffix) + *-sia* n. suffix]

ec·cle·si·arch (i klē′zē ärk′), *n.* *Eastern Ch.* a sacristan, esp. of a monastery. [< MGk *ekklēsiárchēs*]

Ec·cle·si·as·tes (i klē′zē as′tēz), *n.* a book of the Bible. [< LL < Gk *ekklēsiastḗs* assemblyman]

ec·cle·si·as·tic (i klē′zē as′tik), *n.* **1.** a clergyman or other person in religious orders. —*adj.* **2.** ecclesiastical. [< LL *ecclēsiastic(us)* < Gk *ekklēsiastikós*]

ec·cle·si·as·ti·cal (i klē′zē as′ti kəl), *adj.* of or pertaining to the church or the clergy; churchly; clerical; not secular; not lay: *ecclesiastical discipline; ecclesiastical writings.* [late ME] —**ec·cle′si·as′ti·cal·ly,** *adv.*

ec·cle·si·as·ti·cism (i klē′zē as′ti siz′əm), *n.* **1.** ecclesiastical principles, practices, or spirit. **2.** devotion, esp. excessive devotion, to the principles or interests of the church.

Ec·cle·si·as·ti·cus (i klē′zē as′ti kəs), *n.* a book of the Apocrypha. Also called **Wisdom of Jesus, Son of Sirach.**

ecclesio-, a combining form meaning "church": *ecclesiology.* Also, *esp. before a vowel,* **ecclesi-.** [repr. MGk *ekklēsía* church (Gk: assembly)]

ec·cle·si·ol·a·try (i klē′zē ol′ə trē), *n.* excessive reverence for churchly forms and traditions. —**ec·cle′si·ol′a·ter,** *n.*

ec·cle·si·ol·o·gy (i klē′zē ol′ə jē), *n.* **1.** the study of ecclesiastical adornments and furnishings. **2.** the study of church doctrine. —**ec·cle·si·o·log·ic** (i klē′zē ə loj′ik), **ec·cle′si·o·log′i·cal,** *adj.* —**ec·cle′si·o·log′i·cal·ly,** *adv.* —**ec·cle′si·ol′o·gist,** *n.*

ec·dys·i·ast (ek diz′ē ast′), *n.* stripper (def. 2). [ECDYSI(S) + *-ast,* var. of -IST; coined by H. L. Mencken]

ec·dy·sis (ek′di sis), *n., pl.* **-ses** (-sēz′). the shedding or casting off of an outer coat or integument by snakes, crustaceans, etc. [< NL < Gk *ékdysis* a getting out = *ek-* EC- + *dý(ein)* (to) enter + *-sis* -SIS] —**ec·dys·i·al** (ek diz′ē əl, -dizh′-, -dizh′əl), *adj.*

e·ce·sis (i sē′sis), *n.* *Ecol.* the establishment of an immigrant plant in a new environment. [< Gk *oíkēsis* an inhabiting = *oik(eîn)* (to) inhabit (akin to *oîkos* house, home) + *-ē-* thematic vowel + *-sis* -SIS]

ECG, electrocardiogram. Also, **E.C.G.**

ech·e·lon (esh′ə lon′), *n.* **1.** a level of command, authority, or rank. **2.** a formation of troops, airplanes, etc., in which a group of men or an individual craft or vehicle is disposed to the right or left of the one in front. **3.** one of the groups of a formation so disposed. —*v.t., v.i.* **4.** to form in an echelon. [< F *échelon,* orig. rung of a ladder, OF *eschelon* = *esch(i)ele* ladder (< L *scāla* SCALE[3]) + *-on* n. suffix]

E·che·ver·rí·a Al·va·rez (ā′che ve-rē′ə äl′vä reth′), **Luís** (lo͞o ēs′), born 1922, Mexican statesman: president 1970–76.

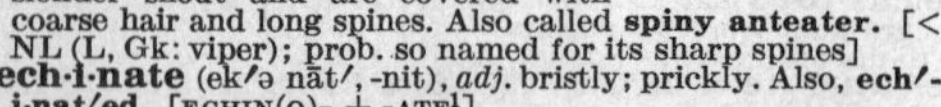
Echidna, *Tachyglossus aculeatus* (Length to 1½ ft.)

e·chid·na (i kid′nə), *n.* any of several insectivorous monotremes of the genera *Tachyglossus,* of Australia, Tasmania, and New Guinea, and *Zaglossus,* of New Guinea, that have claws and a slender snout and are covered with coarse hair and long spines. Also called **spiny anteater.** [< NL (L, Gk: viper); prob. so named for its sharp spines]

ech·i·nate (ek′ə nāt′, -nit), *adj.* bristly; prickly. Also, **ech′i·nat′ed.** [ECHIN(O)- + -ATE[1]]

echino-, a learned borrowing from Greek meaning "sea urchin," used in the formation of compound words: *echinoderm.* Also, *esp. before a vowel,* **echin-.** [< Gk *echîno(s)* ECHINUS]

e·chi·no·derm (i kī′nə dûrm′, ek′i nə-), *n.* any marine animal of the phylum *Echinodermata,* having a radiating arrangement of parts and a body wall stiffened by calcareous pieces that may protrude as spines and including the starfishes, sea urchins, etc.

E·chi·no·der·ma·ta (i kī′nə dûr′mə tə, ek′ə-), *n.* the phylum comprising the echinoderms. [< NL]

e·chi·no·der·ma·tous (i kī′nə dûr′mə təs, ek′i nə-), *adj.* belonging or pertaining to the *Echinodermata.*

e·chi·noid (i kī′noid, ek′ə noid′), *adj.* **1.** belonging or pertaining to the *Echinoidea.* **2.** resembling a sea urchin. —*n.* **3.** any echinoderm of the class *Echinoidea.*

Ech·i·noi·de·a (ek′ə noi′dē ə), *n.* the class comprising the sea urchins, sand dollars, etc. [< NL]

e·chi·nus (i kī′nəs), *n., pl.* **-ni** (-nī). **1.** a sea urchin of the genus *Echinus.* **2.** *Archit.* an ovolo molding, esp. one having an outline with several radii or one carved with an egg-and-dart pattern. See illus. at **molding.** [ME < L < Gk *echînos* hedgehog, sea urchin]

ech·o (ek′ō), *n., pl.* **ech·oes,** *v.,* **ech·oed, ech·o·ing.** —*n.* **1.** a repetition of sound produced by the reflection of sound waves from an obstructing surface. **2.** a sound heard again near its source after being reflected. **3.** any repetition or close imitation, as of the ideas or opinions of another. **4.** a person who reflects or imitates another. **5.** (*cap.*) *Class. Myth.* a mountain nymph who pined away for love of the beautiful youth Narcissus until only her voice remained. **6.** *Electronics.* the reflection of a radio wave, as in radar. **7.** a word used in communications to represent the letter E. —*v.i.* **8.** to emit an echo; resound with an echo. **9.** to be repeated by an echo. —*v.t.* **10.** to repeat by or as by an echo; emit an echo of. **11.** to repeat or imitate the words, sentiments, etc., of. **12.** to repeat or imitate (words, sentiments, etc.). [ME *ecco* < L *ēchō* < Gk, akin to *ēchḗ* sound] —**ech′o·er,** *n.* —**ech′o·less,** *adj.*

e·cho·ic (e kō′ik), *adj.* **1.** resembling an echo. **2.** onomatopoetic. [< L *ēchōic(us)*]

ech·o·la·li·a (ek′ō lā′lē ə), *n.* **1.** *Psychiatry.* the uncontrollable and immediate repetition of words spoken by another person. **2.** the imitation by a baby of the vocal sounds produced by others, occurring as a natural phase of development. —**ech·o·lal·ic** (ek′ō lal′ik, -lā′lik), *adj.*

ech·o·lo·ca·tion (ek′ō lō kā′shən), *n.* *Electronics.* the general method of locating objects by determining the time for an echo to return and the direction from which it returns, as by radar and sonar.

Eck (ek), *n.* **Jo·hann** (yō′hän), (*Johann Mayer*), 1486–1543, German Roman Catholic theologian: opponent of Martin Luther.

Eck·er·mann (ek′ər män), *n.* **Jo·hann Pe·ter** (yō′hän pā′tər), 1792–1854, German writer.

Eck·hart (ek′härt), *n.* **Jo·han·nes** (yō hä′nəs), ("*Meister Eckhart*"), c1260–1327?, Dominican theologian and preacher: founder of German mysticism. Also, **Eck·ardt, Eck·art** (ek′ärt).

é·clair (ā klâr′, i klâr′, ā′klâr; *Fr.* ā kler′), *n., pl.* **é·clairs** (ā klârz′, i klârz′, ā′klârz; *Fr.* ā kler′). a cream puff of oblong shape, usually filled with whipped cream or custard and coated with icing. [< F: lit., lightning (flash), OF *esclair,* appar. back formation from *esclairier* to light, flash, < VL **exclariāre,* alter. of L *exclārāre*]

É·clair·cisse·ment (ā kler sēs mäN′), *n., pl.* **-ments** (-mäN′) for 2. *French.* **1.** *European Hist.* the Enlightenment. **2.** (*l.c.*) clarification; explanation.

ec·lamp·si·a (i klamp′sē ə), *n.* *Pathol.* a form of toxemia of pregnancy, characterized by convulsions. [< NL < Gk *éklamps(is)* sudden development (*ek-* EC- + *lámp(ein)* (to) shine + *-sis* -SIS) + *-ia* -IA]

é·clat (ā klä′; *Fr.* ā klA′), *n.* **1.** brilliance of success, reputation, etc.: *the éclat of a great achievement.* **2.** showy or elaborate display; fanfare. **3.** acclamation; acclaim. [< F, OF *esclat* splinter, akin to *esclater* to splinter, of disputed orig.]

ec·lec·tic (i klek′tik), *adj.* **1.** selecting; choosing from various sources. **2.** made up of what is selected from different sources. **3.** not following any one system, as of philosophy, medicine, etc., but selecting and using what are considered the best elements of all systems. **4.** noting or pertaining to works of architecture, art, decoration, etc., produced by a certain person or during a certain period, that derive from a wide range of historic styles. —*n.* **5.** Also, **ec·lec·ti·cist** (i klek′ti sist). a person who follows an eclectic method, as in architecture. [< Gk *eklektik(ós)* selective = *éklekt(os)* chosen, select (*ékleg(ein)* (to) pick out + *-tos* ptp. suffix; see EC-) + *-ikos* -IC] —**ec·lec′ti·cal·ly,** *adv.*

ec·lec·ti·cism (i klek′ti siz′əm), *n.* **1.** the use or advocacy of an eclectic method. **2.** an eclectic system.

e·clipse (i klips′), *n., v.,* **e·clipsed, e·clips·ing.** —*n.* **1.** *Astron.* **a.** the obscuration of the light of the moon by the intervention of the earth between it and the sun (**lunar eclipse**) or the obscuration of the light of the sun by the intervention of the moon between it and a point on the earth (**solar eclipse**). **b.** a similar phenomenon with respect to any other planet and either its satellite or the sun. **c.** the partial or complete interception of the light of one component of a binary star by the other. **2.** any obscuration of light. **3.** a reduction or loss of status, reputation, etc. —*v.t.* **4.** to cause to undergo eclipse: *The moon eclipses the sun.* **5.** to cast a shadow upon; obscure; darken. **6.** to make dim or obscure by comparison; surpass. [ME, back formation (cf. ELLIPSE) from OE *eclypsis* (or its pl.) < L *eclīpsis* < Gk *ékleipsis* = *ekleíp(ein)* (to) leave out, forsake, fail to appear (see EC-) + *-sis* -SIS]

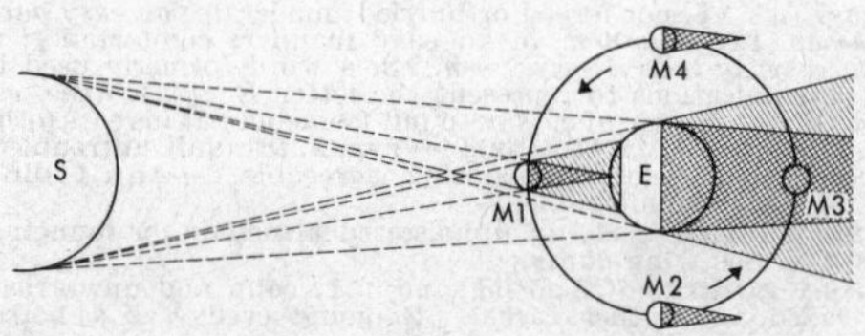

Eclipse
S, Sun; E, Earth; M1, Eclipse of the sun; M3, Eclipse of the moon; M2, M4, Intermediate phases

e·clip·tic (i klip′tik), *n.* *Astron.* **1.** the great circle formed by the intersection of the plane of the earth's orbit with the celestial sphere; the apparent annual path of the sun in the heavens. **2.** an analogous great circle on a terrestrial globe. —*adj.* Also, **e·clip′ti·cal. 3.** pertaining to an eclipse. **4.** pertaining to the ecliptic. [ME < ML *eclīptic(a),* fem. of *eclīpticus* < Gk *ekleiptikós* = *ekleipt-* (verbal s. of *ekleípein;* see ECLIPSE) + *-ikos* -IC] —**e·clip′ti·cal·ly,** *adv.*

ec·lo·gite (ek′lə jīt′), *n.* a rock consisting of granular aggregate of green pyroxene and red garnet, often containing cyanite, silvery mica, quartz, and pyrite. [< Gk *eklog(ḗ)* selection (see ECLOGUE) + -ITE[1]]

ec·logue (ek′lôg, -log), *n.* a pastoral or idyllic poem, often in dialogue form. [late ME *eclog* < L *ecloga* < Gk *eklogḗ* selection, akin to *eklégein* to select; see EC-]

eco-, **1.** a combining form meaning "household," "environment": *economy; ecocide.* **2.** a combining form of **ecology:** *ecolaw; ecopolitics.* [< Gk *oîko(s)* house]

ec·o·cide (ek′ə sīd′, ē′kə-), *n.* destruction of the earth's ecology or environment, as by the indiscriminate use of natural resources, dumping of chemical wastes, etc. [ECO- + -CIDE] —**ec′o·cid′al,** *adj.*

ecol., **1.** ecological. **2.** ecology.

é·cole (ā kôl′), *n., pl.* **é·coles** (ā kôl′). *French.* school[1].

e·col·o·gy (i kol′ə jē), *n.* **1.** the branch of biology dealing with the relations between organisms and their environment. **2.** the branch of sociology concerned with the spacing and interdependence of people and institutions. Also, **oecology.** [earlier *oecology* < Gk *oîko(s)* house + -LOGY; modeled on G *Ökologie*] —**ec·o·log·i·cal** (ek′ə loj′i kəl, ē′kə-), **ec′o·log′ic,** *adj.* —**ec′o·log′i·cal·ly,** *adv.* —**e·col′o·gist,** *n.*

econ., **1.** economic. **2.** economics. **3.** economy.

e·con·o·met·rics (i kon′ə me′triks), *n.* (*construed as sing.*) *Econ.* the application of statistical and mathematical techniques in testing and demonstrating economic theories. [see ECONOMY, -METRIC, -ICS] —**e·con′o·met′ric, e·con′o·met′ri·cal,** *adj.*

e·co·nom·ic (ē′kə nom′ik, ek′ə-), *adj.* **1.** pertaining to the production, distribution, and use of income, wealth, and commodities. **2.** of or pertaining to the science of economics. **3.** pertaining to an economy. **4.** pertaining to one's personal finances. **5.** pertaining to application in human economy: *economic botany.* **6.** affecting or apt to affect the welfare of material resources: *weevils and other economic pests.* [< L *oeconomic(us)* < Gk *oikonomikós* relating to household management = *oikonóm(os)* steward (*oîko(s)* house + *nómos* manager) + *-ikos* -IC]

e·co·nom·i·cal (ē′kə nom′i kəl, ek′ə-), *adj.* **1.** avoiding waste or extravagance; thrifty. **2.** economic.
—**Syn. 1.** saving, provident, sparing, parsimonious. ECONOMICAL, THRIFTY, FRUGAL imply careful and saving use of resources. ECONOMICAL implies prudent planning in the disposition of resources so as to avoid unnecessary waste or expense: *economical in budgeting household expenditures.* THRIFTY is a stronger word than economical, and adds to it the idea of industry and successful management: *a thrifty housewife looking for bargains.* FRUGAL emphasizes being saving, sometimes excessively saving, esp. in such matters as food, dress, or the like: *frugal almost to the point of being stingy.* —**Ant. 1.** wasteful.

e·co·nom·i·cal·ly (ē′kə nom′ik lē, ek′ə-), *adv.* **1.** in a thrifty or frugal manner; with economy. **2.** as regards the efficient use of income and wealth. **3.** as regards one's personal resources of money: *He's quite well off economically.*

econom′ic deter′minism, the doctrine that all social, cultural, political, and intellectual forms are determined by or result from economic factors such as the quality of natural resources, productive capability, technological development, or the distribution of wealth. —**econom′ic deter′minist.**

e·co·nom·ics (ē′kə nom′iks, ek′ə-), *n.* **1.** (*construed as sing.*) the science treating of the production, distribution, and consumption of goods and services, or the material welfare of mankind. **2.** (*construed as pl.*) financial considerations; economically significant aspects.

e·con·o·mise (i kon′ə mīz′), *v.t., v.i.,* **-mised, -mis·ing.** *Chiefly Brit.* economize. —**e·con′o·mis′er,** *n.*

e·con·o·mism (i kon′ə miz′əm), *n.* (in Chinese Communist ideology) the practice of letting farmers keep a larger share of their products, giving workers increased wages and benefits, etc., in order to improve productivity. [ECONOM(Y) + -ISM]

e·con·o·mist (i kon′ə mist), *n.* **1.** an expert in economics. **2.** *Archaic.* a thrifty or frugal person.

e·con·o·mize (i kon′ə mīz′), *v.,* **-mized, -miz·ing.** —*v.t.* **1.** to manage economically; use sparingly or frugally. —*v.i.* **2.** to practice economy; avoid waste or extravagance. Also, *esp. Brit.,* **economise.** —**e·con′o·miz′er,** *n.*

e·con·o·my (i kon′ə mē), *n., pl.* **-mies,** *adv.* —*n.* **1.** thrifty management; frugality in the expenditure or consumption of money, materials, etc. **2.** an act or means of thrifty saving; a saving. **3.** the management of the resources of a community, country, etc., esp. with a view to its productivity. **4.** the prosperity or earnings of a place: *the national economy.* **5.** the disposition or regulation of the parts or functions of any organic whole; an organized system or method. **6.** the efficient, sparing, or concise use of something: *an economy of movement.* **7.** *Theol.* **a.** the divine plan for man. **b.** any method of divine administration. **8.** *Archaic.* the management of household affairs. —*adv.* **9.** in economy-class accommodations, or by economy-class conveyance: *to travel economy.* [< L *oeconomia* < Gk *oikonomía* household management = *oîko(s)* house + *-nomia* -NOMY] —**Syn. 1.** thriftiness, thrift, saving. —**Ant. 1.** lavishness.

econ′omy class′, a type of low-priced fare accommodation for travel, esp. on an airplane.

ec·o·spe·cies (ek′ō spē′shēz, -sēz, ē′kō-), *n. Ecol.* a taxon consisting of one or more interbreeding ecotypes; equivalent to a taxonomic species. [ECO(LOGY) + SPECIES] —**ec′o·spe·cif′ic,** *adj.*

ec·o·sys·tem (ek′ō sis′təm, ē′kō-), *n. Ecol.* a system formed by the interaction of a community of organisms with their environment. [ECO(LOGY) + SYSTEM]

ec·o·tone (ek′ə tōn′, ē′kə-), *n. Ecol.* the transition zone between two different plant communities, as that between forest and prairie. [ECO(LOGY) + *tone* < Gk *tónos* tension] —**ec′o·ton′al,** *adj.*

ec·o·type (ek′ə tīp′, ē′kə-), *n. Ecol.* a subspecies or race that is especially adapted to a particular set of environmental conditions. [ECO(LOGY) + TYPE] —**ec·o·typ·ic** (ek′ə tip′ik, ē′kə-), *adj.* —**ec′o·typ′i·cal·ly,** *adv.*

ec·ru (ek′rōō, ā′krōō), *adj.* **1.** a pale tan in color, as raw silk, unbleached linen, etc. —*n.* **2.** an ecru color. Also, **é·cru** (*Fr.* ā KRY′). [< F = *é-* completely (< L *ex-* EX-1) + *cru* raw (< L *crūdus;* see CRUDE)]

ec·sta·sy (ek′stə sē), *n., pl.* **-sies. 1.** an overpowering emotion or exaltation; a state of sudden, intense feeling. **2.** rapturous delight. **3.** the frenzy of poetic inspiration. **4.** mental transport or rapture from the contemplation of divine things. [ME *extasie* < OF < ML *extasis* < Gk *ékstasis* displacement, trance. See EC-, STASIS]

ec·stat·ic (ek stat′ik), *adj.* **1.** of, pertaining to, or characterized by ecstasy. **2.** subject to or in a state of ecstasy; rapturous. —*n.* **3.** a person subject to fits of ecstasy. **4. ecstatics,** ecstatic delights; raptures. [< Gk *ekstatik(ós).* See EC-, STATIC, ECSTASY] —**ec·stat′i·cal·ly,** *adv.*

ect-, var. of **ecto-** before a vowel: *ectostosis.*

ec·ta·sis (ek′tə sis), *n., pl.* **-ses** (-sēz′). *Pros.* the lengthening of an ordinarily short syllable. [< LL < Gk *éktasis* a stretching out] —**ec·tat·ic** (ek tat′ik), *adj.*

ecto-, a learned borrowing from Greek meaning "outer," "outside," "external," used in the formation of compound words: *ectoderm.* Also, *esp. before a vowel,* **ect-.** [comb. form of Gk *ektós* outside]

ec·to·blast (ek′tə blast′), *n. Embryol.* **1.** the ectoderm. **2.** epiblast (def. 2). —**ec′to·blas′tic,** *adj.*

ec·to·derm (ek′tə dûrm′), *n. Embryol.* the outer germ layer in the embryo of a metazoan. —**ec′to·der′mal, ec′to·der′mic,** *adj.*

ec·to·en·zyme (ek′tō en′zīm), *n. Biochem.* exoenzyme.

ec·tog·e·nous (ek toj′ə nəs), *adj.* growing outside the body of the host, as certain bacteria and other parasites. Also, **ec·to·gen·ic** (ek′tō jen′ik).

ec·to·mere (ek′tə mēr′), *n. Embryol.* any of the blastomeres that participate in the development of the ectoderm. —**ec·to·mer·ic** (ek′tō mer′ik), *adj.*

ec·to·morph (ek′tə môrf′), *n.* a person of the ectomorphic type.

ec·to·mor·phic (ek′tə môr′fik), *adj.* having a thin body build characterized by the relative prominence of structures developed from the embryonic ectoderm (contrasted with *endomorphic, mesomorphic*). —**ec′to·morph′y,** *n.*

-ectomy, a combining form meaning "excision (of a specified part)": *tonsilectomy.* [< NL *-ectomia*]

ec·to·par·a·site (ek′tō par′ə sīt′), *n.* an external parasite (opposed to *endoparasite*). —**ec·to·par·a·sit·ic** (ek′tō par′ə sit′ik), *adj.*

ec·top·ic (ek top′ik), *adj. Pathol.* occurring in an abnormal position or place; displaced. [< NL *ectop(ia)* displacement of an organ or part (< Gk *éktop(os)* out of place + -IA) + -IC]

ectop′ic preg′nancy, *Med.* the development of a fertilized ovum outside the uterus, as in a fallopian tube. Also called **extrauterine pregnancy.**

ec·to·plasm (ek′tə plaz′əm), *n.* **1.** *Biol.* the outer portion of the cytoplasm of a cell. Cf. **endoplasm. 2.** *Spiritualism.* the supposed emanation from the body of a medium. —**ec′to·plas′mic,** *adj.*

ec·to·sarc (ek′tə särk′), *n. Biol.* the ectoplasm of a protozoan. [ECTO- + *-sarc* (see SARCO-)] —**ec′to·sar′cous,** *adj.*

ec·tos·to·sis (ek′tos tō′sis, -tə-), *n.* the ossification of cartilage that begins under the perichondrium and proceeds inward. [ECT- + OSTOSIS] —**ec·tos·te·al** (ek tos′tē əl), *adj.* —**ec·tos′te·al·ly,** *adv.*

ec·to·zo·a (ek′tə zō′ə), *n.pl., sing.* **-zo·on** (-zō′on). (*often cap.*) *Biol.* parasites on the body of an animal, as lice. [ECTO- + -ZOA] —**ec′to·zo′an,** *adj., n.*

ec·type (ek′tīp), *n.* a reproduction; copy (opposed to *prototype.* [< Gk *éktyp(os)* wrought in relief = *ek-* EC- + *týp(os)* figure (on a wall) + *-os* adj. suffix; akin to TYPE] —**ec·ty·pal** (ek′tə pəl), *adj.*

é·cu (ā kyōō′; *Fr.* ā KY′), *n., pl.* **é·cus** (ā kyōōz′; *Fr.* ā KY′). any of various gold and silver coins of France, issued from the reign of Louis IX until 1794, bearing the figure of a shield. [< F; MF, OF *escu* < L *scūtum* shield]

Ecua., Ecuador.

Ec·ua·dor (ek′wə dôr′), *n.* a republic in NW South America. 6,500,845; 104,510 sq. mi. *Cap.:* Quito. —**Ec′ua·do′ran, Ec′ua·do′ri·an,** *adj., n.*

ec·u·men·i·cal (ek′yŏŏ men′i kəl *or, esp. Brit.,* ē′kyŏŏ-), *adj.* **1.** general; universal. **2.** pertaining to the whole Christian church. **3.** promoting or fostering Christian unity throughout the world. **4.** of or pertaining to a movement (**ec′umen′ical move′ment**), esp. among Protestant groups since the 1800's, aimed at achieving universal Christian unity and church union through international interdenominational organizations that cooperate on matters of mutual concern. Also, **ec′u·men′ic, oecumenical, oecumenic.** [< LL *oecumenic(us)* belonging to the whole inhabited world (< Gk *oikoumenikós* = *oikoumen-* (s. of prp. pass. of *oikeîn* to inhabit) + *-ikos* -IC) + -AL1] —**ec′u·men′i·cal·ly,** *adv.*

ec′umen′ical coun′cil, a solemn assembly in the Roman Catholic Church, convoked and presided over by the pope, composed of cardinals, bishops, and certain other prelates whose decrees, when confirmed by the pope, become binding. Also, **Ec′umen′ical Coun′cil.**

ec·u·men·i·cal·ism (ek′yŏŏ men′i kə liz′əm), *n.* the doctrines and practices of the ecumenical movement. Also, **e·cu·men·i·cism** (ek′yŏŏ men′i siz′əm).

ec′umen′ical pa′triarch, the patriarch of Constantinople, regarded as the highest dignitary of the Greek Orthodox Church.

ec·ze·ma (ek′sə mə, eg′zə-, ig zē′-), *n. Pathol.* an inflammatory disease of the skin attended with itching and the exudation of serous matter. [< NL < Gk *ékzema* = *ek-* EC- + *ze-* (s. of *zeîn* to boil, ferment) + *-ma* n. suffix] —**ec·zem·a·tous** (ig zem′ə təs), *adj.*

-ed1, a suffix forming the past tense of weak verbs: *He waited.* [OE *-de, -ede, -ode, -ade;* orig. disputed]

-ed2, a suffix forming the past participle of weak verbs (*he had crossed the river*), and of participial adjectives indicating a condition or quality resulting from the action of the verb (*inflated balloons*). [OE *-ed, -od, -ad;* orig. disputed]

-ed3, a suffix forming adjectives from nouns: *bearded; moneyed; tender-hearted.* [OE *-ede*]

ed., 1. edited. **2.** *pl.* **eds.** edition. **3.** *pl.* **eds.** editor.

E.D., 1. election district. **2.** ex dividend.

e·da·cious (i dā′shəs), *adj.* devouring; voracious; consuming.

e·dac·i·ty (i das′i tē), *n.* the state of being edacious; voraciousness; appetite. [< L *edācitās* = *edāci-* (s. of *edāx*) gluttonous = *ed-* EAT + *-āci-* adj. suffix + *-tāt-* -TY2]

E·dam (ē′dəm, ē′dam; *Du.* ā däm′), *n.* a mild, hard, yellow cheese, produced in a round shape and coated with red wax. Also called **E′dam cheese′.** [after *Edam,* town in Netherlands, where it originated]

e·daph·ic (i daf′ik), *adj.* related to or caused by particular soil conditions, as of texture or drainage, rather than by physiographic or climatic factors. [< Gk *édaph(os)* ground, bottom + -IC] —**e·daph′i·cal·ly,** *adv.*

Ed.B., Bachelor of Education.

EDC, European Defense Community.

Ed.D., Doctor of Education.

Ed·da (ed′ə), *n., pl.* **Ed·das.** either of two old Icelandic literary works, one a collection of poems on mythical and religious subjects erroneously attributed to Saemund Sigfusson (c1055–1133), the other a collection of ancient Scandinavian myths and legends, rules and theories of versification, poems, etc., compiled and written in part by Snorri Sturluson (1179–1241). —**Ed′dic, Ed·da·ic** (e dā′ik), *adj.*

Ed·ding·ton (ed′ing tən), *n.* **Sir Arthur (Stanley),** 1882–1944, English astronomer and physicist.

ed·dy (ed′ē), *n., pl.* **-dies,** *v.,* **-died, -dy·ing.** —*n.* **1.** a current at variance with the main current in a stream of liquid or gas, esp. one having a rotary or whirling motion. **2.** a small whirlpool. **3.** any similar current, as of air, dust, or fog. —*v.t., v.i.* **4.** to move or whirl in eddies. [late ME; OE *ed-* turning + *ēa* water; akin to Icel *itha*]

Ed·dy (ed′ē), *n.* **Mary (Morse) Baker,** 1821–1910, U.S. founder of the Christian Science Church.

Ed′dy·stone Rocks′ (ed′i stən), a group of rocks near the W end of the English Channel, SW of Plymouth, England: lighthouse.

E·de (ā′də), *n.* city in central Netherlands. 61,872 (1962).

e·del·weiss (ād′əl vīs′, -wīs′), *n.* a small composite herb, *Leontopodium alpinum,* having white woolly leaves and flowers, growing in the high altitudes of the Alps. [< G = *edel* noble + *weiss* WHITE]

e·de·ma (i dē′mə), *n., pl.* **-ma·ta** (-mə tə). *Pathol.* effusion of serous fluid into the interstices of cells in tissue spaces or into body cavities. Also, **oedema.** [< NL *oedēma* < Gk *oídēma* a swelling = *oidē-* (s. of *oideîn* to swell) + *-ma* n. suffix] —**e·dem·a·tous** (i dem′ə təs), **e·dem·a·tose** (i dem′ə tōs′), *adj.*

E·den (ēd′ən), *n.* **1.** the place where Adam and Eve lived before the Fall. Gen. 2:8–24. **2.** any delightful region or abode; a paradise. **3.** a state of perfect happiness. Also called **Garden of Eden.** [< Heb *'ēden* delight, pleasure] —**E·den·ic** (ē den′ik), *adj.*

E·den·ta·ta (ē′den tā′tə, -tä′-), *n.* the order comprising the edentates. [< NL, neut. pl. of L *ēdentātus*]

e·den·tate (ē den′tāt), *adj.* **1.** belonging or pertaining to the *Edentata,* an order of New World mammals, comprising the armadillos, the sloths, and the South American anteaters. **2.** toothless. —*n.* **3.** an edentate mammal. [< L *ēdentāt(us)* deprived of teeth. See E-, DENTATE]

E·des·sa (i des′ə), *n.* an ancient city in NW Mesopotamia, on the modern site of Urfa.

edge (ej), *n.*, *v.*, **edged, edg·ing·** —*n.* **1.** a line at which a surface terminates; border: *Grass grew along the edges of the road. The paper had deckle edges.* **2.** a brink or verge: *the edge of a precipice.* **3.** any of the narrow surfaces of a thin, flat object: *a book with gilt edges.* **4.** a line at which two surfaces of a solid object meet: *an edge of a box.* **5.** the thin, sharp side of the blade of a cutting instrument or weapon. **6.** the sharpness proper to a blade: *The knife has lost its edge.* **7.** sharpness or keenness of language, argument, tone of voice, appetite, desire, etc. **8.** *Brit. Dial.* a hill or cliff. **9.** *Informal.* an improved position; advantage: *He gained the edge on his opponent.* **10.** *Cards.* advantage, esp. the advantage gained by being the age or eldest hand. **11. on edge, a.** (of a person or a person's nerves) acutely sensitive; nervous; tense. **b.** impatient; eager. —*v.t.* **12.** to put an edge on; sharpen. **13.** to provide with an edge or border: *to edge a skirt with lace.* **14.** to make or force (one's way) gradually by moving edgewise or sideways. —*v.i.* **15.** to move sideways: *to edge through a crowd.* **16.** to advance gradually: *The car edged up to the curb.* **17. edge out,** to defeat or vanquish (rivals or opponents) by a small margin. [ME *egge,* OE *ecg;* c. G *Ecke* corner; akin to L *aciēs,* Gk *akís* point] —**edg′er,** *n.*
—**Syn. 1.** rim, lip. EDGE, BORDER, MARGIN refer to a boundary. An EDGE is the boundary line of a surface or plane: *the edge of a table.* BORDER is the boundary of a surface or the strip adjacent to it, inside or out: *a border of lace.* MARGIN is a limited strip, generally unoccupied, at the extremity of an area: *the margin of a page.*

edge′ tool′, a tool with a cutting edge. [ME *egge tol*]

edge·wise (ej′wīz′), *adv.* **1.** with the edge forward; toward the edge. **2.** sideways. Also, **edge·ways** (ej′wāz′).

Edge·worth (ej′wûrth′), *n.* **Maria,** 1767–1849, English novelist.

edg·ing (ej′ing), *n.* **1.** the act of one who edges. **2.** something that forms or is placed along an edge or border.

edg·y (ej′ē), *adj.*, **edg·i·er, edg·i·est. 1.** sharp-edged; sharply defined, as outlines. **2.** nervously irritable; impatient and anxious. —**edg′i·ly,** *adv.* —**edg′i·ness,** *n.*

edh (eth), *n.* eth.

ed·i·ble (ed′ə bəl), *adj.* **1.** fit to be eaten as food; eatable. —*n.* **2.** Usually, **edibles.** edible articles; food. [< LL *edibil(is)* = *ed(ere)* (to) EAT + *-ibilis* -IBLE] —**ed′i·bil′i·ty, ed′i·ble·ness,** *n.*

e·dict (ē′dikt), *n.* **1.** a decree issued by a sovereign or other authority. **2.** any authoritative proclamation or command. [< L *ēdictum,* n. use of neut. of *ēdictus* (ptp. of *ēdicere* to say out). See E-, DICTUM] —**e·dic′tal,** *adj.* —**e·dic′tal·ly,** *adv.*

ed·i·fi·ca·tion (ed′ə fə kā′shən), *n.* **1.** an act of edifying. **2.** the state of being edified; uplift; enlightenment. **3.** moral improvement. [< L *aedificātiōn-* (s. of *aedificātiō*) = *aedificāt(us)* (ptp. of *aedificāre* to EDIFY; see -ATE[1]) + *-iōn-* -ION]

ed·i·fice (ed′ə fis), *n.* a building, esp. one of large size or imposing appearance. [ME < MF < L *aedificium* = *aedific(āre)* (to) build (see EDIFY) + *-ium* neut. suffix] —**ed·i·fi·cial** (ed′ə fish′əl), *adj.*

ed·i·fy (ed′ə fī′), *v.t.*, **-fied, -fy·ing.** to build up or increase the faith, morality, etc., of; instruct or benefit, esp. morally; uplift. [ME *edifie(n)* < OF *edifier* < L *aedificāre* to build = *aedi-* (s. of *aedēs*) house, temple + *-ficāre* -FY] —**e·dif·i·ca·to·ry** (i dif′ə kə tōr′ē, -tôr′ē, ed′ə fə kā′tə rē), *adj.* —**ed′i·fi′er,** *n.* —**ed′i·fy′ing·ly,** *adv.*

e·dile (ē′dīl), *n.* *Rom. Hist.* aedile.

E·di·na (i dī′nə), *n.* a city in SE Minnesota, near Minneapolis. 44,046 (1970).

Ed·in·burgh (ed′ən bûr′ō, -bur′ō *or, esp. Brit.,* -brə), *n.* **1. Duke of.** Philip (def. 4). **2.** a city in and the capital of Scotland, in the SE part. 470,085. **3.** former name of **Midlothian.**

E·dir·ne (e dēr′ne), *n.* a city in NW European Turkey. 86,542 (1965). Also called **Adrianople.**

Ed·i·son (ed′i sən), *n.* **1. Thomas Al·va** (al′və), 1847–1931, U.S. inventor, esp. of the electric light, phonograph, etc. **2.** a township in central New Jersey. 67,120 (1970).

ed·it (ed′it), *v.t.* **1.** to supervise or direct the preparation of (a newspaper, magazine, book, etc.); serve as editor of. **2.** to collect, prepare, and arrange (materials) for publication. **3.** to revise or correct, as a manuscript. **4.** to omit; eliminate (often fol. by *out*): *The author has edited out all references to his own family.* **5.** to prepare (motion-picture or television film) by deleting, arranging, and splicing shots, by synchronizing the sound record with the film, etc. [partly back formation from EDITOR, partly < L *ēdit(us)* given out, published, ptp. of *ēdere* = *ē-* E- + *dăre* to give]

edit., **1.** edited. **2.** edition. **3.** editor.

e·di·tion (i dish′ən), *n.* **1.** one of a series of printings of the same book, newspaper, etc., each issued at a different time and differing from another by alterations, additions, etc. (distinguished from *impression*). **2.** the format in which a literary work is published: *a one-volume edition of Shakespeare.* **3.** the whole number of impressions or copies of a book, newspaper, etc., printed from one set of type at one time. [< L *ēditiōn-* (s. of *ēditiō*) publication]

ed·i·tor (ed′i tər), *n.* **1.** a person having managerial and sometimes policy-making responsibility for the editorial part of a publishing firm or of a newspaper, magazine, or the like. **2.** the supervisor of a department of a newspaper, magazine, etc.: *the music editor.* **3.** a person who edits material for publication, films, etc. [< L]

ed·i·to·ri·al (ed′i tōr′ē əl, -tôr′-), *n.* **1.** an article in a newspaper or other periodical presenting the opinion of the publisher, editor, or editors. **2.** a statement broadcast on radio or television that presents the opinion of the owner, manager, or the like, of the station or channel. —*adj.* **3.** of or pertaining to an editor or to editing: *editorial policies.* **4.** of, pertaining to, or involved in the preparation of an editorial or editorials: *editorial page.* **5.** of or pertaining to the literary contents, policies, and activities of a publication, as distinguished from its commercial contents or business activities. —**ed·i·to·ri·al·ist** (ed′i tōr′ē ə list, -tôr′-), *n.*

ed·i·to·ri·al·ize (ed′i tōr′ē ə līz′, -tôr′-), *v.i.*, **-ized -iz·ing. 1.** to set forth one's position or opinion on some subject in, or as if in, an editorial. **2.** to inject personal opinions into a factual account. —**ed′i·to′ri·al·i·za′tion,** *n.* —**ed′i·to′ri·al·iz′er,** *n.*

ed·i·to·ri·al·ly (ed′i tōr′ē ə lē, -tôr′-), *adv.* **1.** in an editorial manner; as an editor does. **2.** in an editorial.

ed′itor in chief′, *pl.* **editors in chief.** the principal policy-making executive or ranking editor of a publishing house, publication, etc.

ed·i·tor·ship (ed′i tər ship′), *n.* **1.** the office or function of an editor. **2.** editorial direction.

Ed. M., Master of Education.

Ed·mon·ton (ed′mən tən), *n.* **1.** a city in and the capital of Alberta, in the central part, in SW Canada. 357,696 (1965). **2.** a city in NE Middlesex, in SE England, near London. 92,062 (1961).

Ed·mund I (ed′mənd), A.D. 921?–946, king of England 940–946. Also, **Eadmund I.**

Edmund II, ("*Ironside*") A.D. c980–1016, English king defeated by Canute 1016. Also, **Eadmund II.**

E·do (ed′ō; *Jap.* e′dô′), *n.* a former name of **Tokyo.**

E·dom (ē′dəm), *n.* **1.** Esau, the brother of Jacob. **2.** Greek, **Idumaea, Idumea.** an ancient region between the Dead Sea and the Gulf of Aqaba, bordering ancient Palestine. See map at **Philistia. 3.** the kingdom of the Edomites located in this region.

E·dom·ite (ē′də mīt′), *n.* a descendant of Edom. Num. 20:14–21. —**E′dom·it′ish, E·dom·it·ic** (ē′də mit′ik), *adj.*

EDP, See **electronic data processing.**

eds., **1.** editions. **2.** editors.

Ed′sel Ford′ Range′ (ed′səl), a mountain range in Antarctica, E of the Ross Sea.

EDT, Eastern daylight time. Also, **E.D.T.**

educ., **1.** educated. **2.** education. **3.** educational.

ed·u·ca·ble (ej′ŏŏ kə bəl, ed′yŏŏ-), *adj.* capable of being educated. Also, **ed·u·cat·a·ble** (ej′ŏŏ kā′tə bəl, ed′yŏŏ-). —**ed′u·ca·bil′i·ty, ed′u·cat′a·bil′i·ty,** *n.*

ed·u·cate (ej′ŏŏ kāt′, ed′yŏŏ-), *v.t.*, **-cat·ed, -cat·ing. 1.** to develop the faculties and powers of (a person) by teaching, instruction, or schooling. **2.** to qualify by instruction or training for a particular calling, practice, etc.; train: *to educate someone for law.* **3.** to provide education for; send to school. **4.** to develop or train (the ear, taste, etc.). —*v.i.* **5.** to educate a person or group. [< L *ēducāt(us)* brought up, taught (ptp. of *ēducāre*) = *ē-* E- + *duc-* lead + *-ātus* -ATE[1]]
—**Syn. 1.** teach, instruct, school, drill.

ed·u·cat·ed (ej′ŏŏ kā′tid, ed′yŏŏ-), *adj.* **1.** having undergone education. **2.** characterized by or displaying qualities of culture and learning. **3.** based on some information or experience: *an educated estimate of sales.*

ed·u·ca·tion (ej′ŏŏ kā′shən, ed′yŏŏ-), *n.* **1.** the act or process of imparting or acquiring general knowledge and of developing the powers of reasoning and judgment. **2.** the act or process of imparting or acquiring particular knowledge or skills, as for a trade or profession. **3.** a degree, level, or kind of schooling: *a university education.* **4.** the result produced by instruction, training, or study. **5.** the science or art of teaching; pedagogics. [< L *ēducātiōn-* (s. of *ēducātiō*)]
—**Syn. 1.** instruction, schooling, tuition. EDUCATION, TRAINING imply a discipline and development by means of study and learning. EDUCATION is the development of the special and general abilities of the mind (learning to know): *a liberal education.* TRAINING is practical education (learning to do) or practice, usually under supervision, in some art, trade, or profession: *training in art, teacher training.* **4.** learning, knowledge, enlightenment. EDUCATION, CULTURE are often used interchangeably to mean the results of schooling. EDUCATION, however, suggests chiefly the information acquired. CULTURE is a mode of thought and feeling encouraged by education (the process and the acquirement). It suggests an aspiration toward, and an appreciation of, high intellectual and aesthetic ideals: *The level of culture in a country depends upon the education of its people.* —**Ant. 4.** illiteracy.

ed·u·ca·tion·al (ej′ŏŏ kā′shə nəl, ed′yŏŏ-), *adj.* **1.** pertaining to education. **2.** tending or intended to educate, instruct, or inform. —**ed′u·ca′tion·al·ly,** *adv.*

educa′tional park′, a group of elementary and high schools, usually in a parklike setting, that accommodates students from a large, diversified area rather than from individual neighborhoods.

educa′tional tel′evision, any television program that is educational, whether on a commercial or a noncommercial station.

ed·u·ca·tion·ist (ej′ŏŏ kā′shə nist, ed′yŏŏ-), *n.* a specialist in the theory and methods of education. Also, **ed′u·ca′tion·al·ist.**

ed·u·ca·tive (ej′ŏŏ kā′tiv, ed′yŏŏ-), *adj.* **1.** serving to educate. **2.** pertaining to or productive of education: *the educative process.*

ed·u·ca·tor (ej′ŏŏ kā′tər, ed′yŏŏ-), *n.* **1.** a person or thing that educates, esp. a teacher, principal, or other person involved in planning or directing education. **2.** an educationist. [< L]

ed·u·ca·to·ry (ej′ŏŏ kə tōr′ē, -tôr′ē, ed′yŏŏ-), *adj.* serving to educate; educative.

e·duce (i dōōs′, i dyōōs′), *v.t.*, **e·duced, e·duc·ing. 1.** to draw forth or bring out, as something potential or latent; elicit; develop. **2.** to infer or deduce. [ME < L *ēdūce(re)* = *ē-* E- + *dūcere* to lead] —**e·duc′i·ble,** *adj.*

e·duct (ē′dukt), *n.* something educed; eduction. [< L *ēduct(um)* something educed, n. use of neut. of *ēductus* educed, ptp. of *ēdūcere* to EDUCE]

e·duc·tion (i duk′shən), *n.* **1.** the act of educing. **2.** something educed. [< L *ēductiōn-* (s. of *ēductiō*)]

e·duc·tive (i duk′tiv), *adj.* educing; serving to educe.

Ed·ward (ed′wərd), *n.* **1. Prince of Wales and Duke of Cornwall** ("*The Black Prince*"), 1330–76, English military leader (son of Edward III). **2. Lake,** a lake in central Africa, between Uganda and Zaïre: a source of the Nile. 830 sq. mi.

Edward I, ("*Edward Longshanks*") 1239–1307, king of England 1272–1307 (son of Henry III).

Edward II, 1284–1327, king of England 1307–27 (son of Edward I).

Edward III, 1312–77, king of England 1327–77 (son of Edward II).

Edward IV, 1442–83, king of England 1461–70, 1471–83: 1st king of the house of York.

Edward V, 1470–83, king of England 1483 (son of Edward IV).

Edward VI, 1537–53, king of England 1547–53 (son of Henry VIII and Jane Seymour).

Edward VII, (*Albert Edward*) ("*the Peacemaker*") 1841–1910, king of Great Britain and Ireland 1901–10 (son of Queen Victoria).

Edward VIII, (*Duke of Windsor*) 1894–1972, king of Great Britain 1936 (son of George V; brother of George VI).

Ed·ward·i·an (ed wôr′dē ən, -wär′-), *adj.* of, pertaining to, or characteristic of the reign of Edward VII, esp. its opulence and self-satisfaction. —**Ed·ward′i·an·ism,** *n.*

Ed·wards (ed′wərdz), *n.* **Jonathan,** 1703–58, American clergyman and theologian.

Ed′wards Plateau′, a highland area in SW Texas. 2000–5000 ft. high.

Ed′ward the Confes′sor, Saint, 1002?–66, English king 1042–66: founder of Westminster Abbey.

Ed·win (ed′win), *n.* A.D. 585?–633. king of Northumbria 617–633. Also, **Eadwine.**

-ee, a suffix of nouns denoting one who is the object of some action, or undergoes or receives something (often as opposed to the person acting): *assignee; employee.* [< F *-é* (masc.), *-ée* (fem.), ptp. endings < L *-ātus, -āta* -ATE[1]]

E.E., 1. Early English. **2.** Electrical Engineer. **3.** Electrical Engineering.

E.E. & M.P., Envoy Extraordinary and Minister Plenipotentiary.

EEC, European Economic Community.

EEE, the widest proportional shoe size.

EEG, electroencephalogram. Also, **E.E.G.**

eel (ēl), *n., pl.* (*esp. collectively*) **eel,** (*esp. referring to two or more kinds or species*) **eels. 1.** any of numerous elongated, snakelike, marine or fresh-water fishes of the order *Apodes,* having no ventral fins. **2.** any of several similar but unrelated fishes, as the lamprey. [ME *ele,* OE *ēl, ǣl;* c. D, G *Aal,* Icel *āll*] —**eel′like′,** *adj.*

Eel (def. 1), *Anguilla rostrata* (Length to 6 ft.)

eel·grass (ēl′gras′, -gräs′), *n.* **1.** a grasslike marine herb, *Zostera marina,* having narrow, ribbonlike leaves. **2.** See **tape grass.**

eel·pout (ēl′pout′), *n.* **1.** any blennioid fish of the family *Zoarcidae,* esp. *Zoarces viviparus,* of Europe. **2.** the burbot. [OE *ǣlepūte*]

eel·worm (ēl′wûrm′), *n.* any small nematode worm of the family *Anguillulidae,* including the minute vinegar eel, *Anguillula aceti.*

e'en (ēn), *adv. Chiefly Literary.* even[1].

e'er (âr), *adv. Chiefly Literary.* ever.

-eer, a suffix of nouns denoting one who is concerned with, or employed in connection with, or busies himself with something: *auctioneer; engineer; profiteer.* Also, **-ier.** [var. of *-ier* < F < L *-ārius* -ARY; see -ER[2]]

ee·rie (ēr′ē), *adj.,* **-ri·er, -ri·est. 1.** uncanny, so as to arouse superstitious fear; weird. **2.** *Brit. Dial.* affected with superstitious fear. [ME *eri,* dial. var. of *argh,* OE *earg* cowardly; c. OFris *erg,* Icel *argr* evil, G *arg* cowardly] —**ee′ri·ly,** *adv.* —**ee′ri·ness,** *n.* —**Syn. 1.** See **weird.**

ee·ry (ēr′ē), *adj.,* **-ri·er, -ri·est.** eerie.

ef-, var. of **ex-**[1] (by assimilation) before *f: efficient.*

ef·fa·ble (ef′ə bəl), *adj.* utterable; expressible. [< MF < L *effābil(is)* = *eff(ārī)* (to) speak out (*ef-* EF- + *fārī* to speak) + *-ābilis* -ABLE]

ef·face (i fās′), *v.t.,* **-faced, -fac·ing. 1.** to wipe out; destroy; do away with: *to efface a memory.* **2.** to rub out, erase, or obliterate (outlines, traces, inscriptions, etc.). **3.** to make (oneself) inconspicuous; withdraw (oneself) modestly or shyly. [< F *efface(r)*] —**ef·face′a·ble,** *adj.* —**ef·face′ment,** *n.* —**ef·fac′er,** *n.*

ef·fect (i fekt′), *n.* **1.** something that is produced by an agency or cause; result; consequence. **2.** power to produce results; efficacy; influence: *His protest had no effect.* **3.** the state of being effective or operative; operation or execution; accomplishment or fulfillment: *to bring a plan into effect.* **4.** a mental impression produced, as by a painting or a speech. **5.** main idea or meaning; gist: *He disapproved of the proposal and wrote to that effect.* **6.** the making of a desired impression. **7.** an illusory phenomenon: *a three-dimensional effect.* **8.** a scientific phenomenon (usually named for its discoverer): *the Doppler effect.* **9.** the result intended; purport; intent. **10. in effect,** for practical purposes; virtually. **11. take effect, a.** to go into operation; begin to function. **b.** to produce a result. —*v.t.* **12.** to produce as an effect; bring about; accomplish. **13.** to produce or make. [ME < L *effect(us)* (4th decl.), n. use of ptp. of *efficere* to effect = *ef-* EF- + *fec-* (var. of *fac-*) do + *-tus* ptp. suffix] —**ef·fect′i·ble,** *adj.*
—**Syn. 1.** outcome, issue. EFFECT, CONSEQUENCE(S), RESULT refer to something produced by an action or a cause. An EFFECT is that which is produced, usually more or less immediately and directly: *The effect of morphine is to produce sleep. Morphine produces the effect of sleep.* A CONSEQUENCE, something that follows naturally or logically, as in a train of events or sequence of time, is less intimately connected with its cause than is an effect: *Punishment is the consequence of disobedience. Take the consequences.* A RESULT may be near or remote, and often is the sum of effects or consequences as making an end or final outcome: *The English language is the result of the fusion of many different elements.* **12.** achieve, realize, fulfill, perform, consummate. —**Ant. 1.** cause.

ef·fect·er (i fek′tər), *n.* effector.

ef·fec·tive (i fek′tiv), *adj.* **1.** adequate to accomplish a purpose; producing the intended or expected result: *effective measures.* **2.** actually in operation or in force; functioning: *The law becomes effective at midnight.* **3.** producing a deep or vivid impression; striking: *an effective photograph.* **4.** prepared and available for service, esp. military service. —*n.* **5.** a soldier or sailor fit for duty or active service. **6.** the effective total of a military force. [ME < L *effectīv(us)* practical] —**ef·fec′tive·ly,** *adv.* —**ef·fec′tive·ness, ef·fec·tiv′i·ty,** *n.*
—**Syn. 1.** capable, competent. EFFECTIVE, EFFECTUAL, EFFICIENT refer to that which is able to produce a (desired) effect. EFFECTIVE is applied to that which has the power to, or which actually does, produce an (often lasting) effect: *an effective action, remedy, speech.* EFFECTUAL is used esp. of that which produces the effect desired or intended, or a decisive result: *An effectual bombardment silenced the enemy.* EFFICIENT (applied also to persons) is the most active of these words, and implies the skillful use of energy or industry to accomplish desired results with little waste of effort: *efficient methods; an efficient manager.* **2.** operative. **3.** telling. —**Ant. 1.** futile.

ef·fec·tor (i fek′tər), *n.* **1.** *Physiol.* an organ tissue or cell that carries out a response to a nerve impulse. **2.** a person or thing that effects. Also, **effecter.** [< L]

ef·fects (i fekts′), *n.pl.* goods; movables; personal property. —**Syn.** See **property.**

ef·fec·tu·al (i fek′cho͞o əl), *adj.* **1.** producing or capable of producing an intended effect; adequate. **2.** valid or binding, as an agreement or document. [late ME < ML *effectuāl(is)* (see EFFECT, -AL[1]); r. ME *effectuel* < MF] —**ef·fec′tu·al·ly,** *adv.* —**ef·fec′tu·al·ness, ef·fec′tu·al′i·ty,** *n.* —**Syn. 1.** See **effective.**

ef·fec·tu·ate (i fek′cho͞o āt′), *v.t.,* **-at·ed, -at·ing.** to bring about; effect. [< ML *effectuāt(us)* brought to pass (ptp. of *effectuāre*). See EFFECT, -ATE[1]] —**ef·fec′tu·a′tion,** *n.*

ef·fem·i·na·cy (i fem′ə nə sē), *n.* the state or quality of being effeminate. [EFFEMIN(ATE) + -ACY]

ef·fem·i·nate (i fem′ə nit), *adj.* **1.** (of a man) soft or delicate to an unmanly degree in traits, tastes, habits, etc. **2.** characterized by unmanly softness, delicacy, etc. [< L *effēminātus)*. See EF-, FEMININE, -ATE[1]] —**ef·fem′i·nate·ly,** *adv.* —**ef·fem′i·nate·ness,** *n.* —**Syn. 1.** See **female.**

ef·fem·i·nise (i fem′ə nīz′), *v.t.,* **-nised, -nis·ing.** *Chiefly Brit.* effeminize. —**ef·fem′i·ni·sa′tion,** *n.*

ef·fem·i·nize (i fem′ə nīz′), *v.t.,* **-nized, -niz·ing.** to make effeminate. [EFFEMIN(ATE) + -IZE] —**ef·fem′i·ni·za′tion,** *n.*

ef·fen·di (i fen′dē), *n., pl.* **-dis. 1.** a former Turkish title of respect, esp. for government officials. **2.** (in eastern Mediterranean countries) a man who is well-educated or a member of the aristocracy. [< Turk *efendi* < ModGk *aphentēs* for Gk *authentēs* doer, master. See AUTHENTIC]

ef·fer·ent (ef′ər ənt), *Anat., Physiol.* —*adj.* **1.** conveying or conducting away from an organ or part (opposed to *afferent*). —*n.* **2.** an efferent part, as a nerve or blood vessel. [< L *efferent-* (s. of *efferēns* carrying off, prp. of *efferre*) = *ef-* EF- + *ferent-* carrying (*fer-* carry + *-ent-* -ENT)] —**ef′fer·ence,** *n.* —**ef′fer·ent·ly,** *adv.*

ef·fer·vesce (ef′ər ves′), *v.i.,* **-vesced, -vesc·ing. 1.** to give off bubbles of gas, as fermenting liquors; bubble and hiss. **2.** to issue forth in bubbles. **3.** to show enthusiasm, excitement, liveliness, etc. [< L *effervesce(re).* See E-, FERVENT, -ESCE] —**ef′fer·ves′cence, ef′fer·ves′cen·cy,** *n.*

ef·fer·ves·cent (ef′ər ves′ənt), *adj.* **1.** effervescing; bubbling. **2.** gay; lively. [< L *effervescent-* (s. of *effervescēns*), prp. of *effervescere* to EFFERVESCE; see -ENT] —**ef′fer·ves′cent·ly, ef′fer·vesc′ing·ly,** *adv.*

ef·fete (i fēt′), *adj.* **1.** exhausted of vigor or energy; worn out. **2.** lacking in wholesome vigor; decadent. **3.** unable to produce; sterile. [< L *effēta* exhausted from bearing = *ef-* EF- + *fēta* having brought forth, fem. ptp. of lost v.; see FETUS] —**ef·fete′ly,** *adv.* —**ef·fete′ness,** *n.*

ef·fi·ca·cious (ef′ə kā′shəs), *adj.* having or showing the desired result or effect; effective as a means, measure, remedy, etc. [< L *efficāci-* (s. of *efficāx*) effectual. See EFFICIENT, -ACIOUS] —**ef′fi·ca′cious·ly,** *adv.* —**ef′fi·ca′cious·ness,** *n.*

ef·fi·ca·cy (ef′ə kə sē), *n.* capacity for producing a desired result or effect; effectiveness. [< L *efficācia.* See EFFICACIOUS, -Y[3]]

ef·fi·cien·cy (i fish′ən sē), *n., pl.* **-cies. 1.** the state or quality of being efficient; competency in performance. **2.** accomplishment of or ability to accomplish a job with a minimum expenditure of time and effort. **3.** the ratio of the work done or energy developed by a machine, engine, etc., to the energy supplied to it, usually expressed as a percentage. [< L *efficientia.* See EFFICIENT, -Y[3]]

effi′ciency ex′pert, a person who studies the methods, procedures, and job characteristics of a business or factory to increase the efficiency of equipment and personnel. Also called **effi′ciency engineer′.**

ef·fi·cient (i fish′ənt), *adj.* **1.** performing or functioning in the best possible and least wasteful manner; competent; capable. **2.** satisfactory and economical to use. **3.** producing an effect, as a cause; causative. [< L *efficient-* (s. of *efficiēns*). See EF-, -FIC, -ENT] —**ef·fi′cient·ly,** *adv.* —**Syn. 1.** See **effective.**

ef·fig·i·ate (i fij′ē āt′), *v.t.,* **-at·ed, -at·ing.** *Archaic.* to make an image or effigy of. [< LL *effigiāt(us)* imagined (ptp. of *effigiāre*)] —**ef·fig·i·a·tion** (i fij′ē ā′shən), *n.*

ef·fi·gy (ef′i jē), *n., pl.* **-gies. 1.** a representation or image, esp. sculptured, as on a monument. **2.** a crude representation of someone disliked, used for purposes of ridicule. **3. burn** or **hang in effigy,** to burn or hang an image of a despised person as a public expression of indignation, ridicule, or contempt. [< L *effigia* = *effig-* (*ef-* EF- + *fig-* shape, form; see FIGURE) + *-ia* -Y[3]] —**ef·fig′i·al,** *adj.*

ef·flo·resce (ef′lə res′), *v.i.,* **-resced, -resc·ing. 1.** to burst into bloom; blossom. **2.** *Chem.* **a.** to change to a mealy or powdery substance upon exposure to air. **b.** to become incrusted or covered with crystals of salt or the like through evaporation or chemical change. [< L *efflōresce(re)* (to) blossom out = *ef-* EF- + *flōrescere* to begin to bloom]

ef·flo·res·cence (ef′lə res′əns), *n.* **1.** the state or a period of flowering. **2.** an example or result of growth and development. **3.** *Chem.* **a.** the act or process of efflorescing. **b.** the resulting powdery substance or incrustation. **4.** *Pathol.* a rash or eruption of the skin. [< MF < ML *efflōrescentia*]

ef·flo·res·cent (ef′lə res′ənt), *adj.* **1.** efflorescing; blossoming. **2.** *Chem.* **a.** subject to efflorescence. **b.** covered with or forming an efflorescence. [< L *efflōrescent-* (s. of *efflōrescēns*), prp. of *efflōrescere* to EFFLORESCE; see -ENT]

ef·flu·ence (ef′lo͞o əns), *n.* **1.** the process or action of flowing out; efflux. **2.** something that flows out; emanation. [< L *efflu-* outflow (= *ef-* EF- + *flu-* flow) + -ENCE]

ef·flu·ent (ef′lo͞o ənt), *adj.* **1.** flowing out or forth. —*n.* **2.** something that flows out or forth; outflow; effluence. **3.** a stream flowing out of a larger stream, lake, reservoir, etc. [< L *effluent-* (s. of *effluēns* flowing out, prp. of *effluere*)]

ef·flu·vi·um (i flo͞o′vē əm), *n., pl.* **-vi·a** (-vē ə), **-vi·ums.** a slight or invisible exhalation or vapor, esp. one that is disagreeable or noxious. [< L = *ef-* EF- + *fluv-* (var. of *flu-*) flow (see EFFLUENT) + *-ium* -Y[3]] —**ef·flu′vi·al,** *adj.*

ef·flux (ef′luks), *n.* **1.** outward flow, as of water. **2.** something that flows out; effluence. [< L *efflux(us)*, ptp. of *effluere* to flow out. See EFFLUVIUM]

ef·fort (ef′ərt), *n.* **1.** deliberate exertion of physical or mental power. **2.** a strenuous attempt. **3.** something done by exertion; an achievement. **4.** the amount of exertion necessary to achieve a specified aim: *the war effort.* **5.** *Chiefly Brit.* **a.** an organized community drive or achievement. **b.** a fund-raising drive, as for charity. **6.** *Mech.* the force or energy that is applied to a machine for the accomplishment of useful work. [late ME < MF; OF *esfort, esforz* < *esforcier* to force (*es-* EX-[1] + *forcier* to FORCE)]
—**Syn. 1.** struggle, striving. EFFORT, APPLICATION, ENDEAVOR, EXERTION imply actions directed or force expended toward a definite end. EFFORT is an expenditure of energy to accomplish some usually single and definite object: *He made an effort to control himself.* APPLICATION is continuous effort plus careful attention: *constant application to duties.* ENDEAVOR means a continued and sustained series of efforts to achieve some end, often worthy and difficult: *a constant endeavor to be useful.* EXERTION is the vigorous and often strenuous expenditure of energy, frequently without conscious reference to a definite end: *out of breath from exertion.*

ef·fort·less (ef′ərt lis), *adj.* **1.** requiring or involving no effort; easy. **2.** making no effort; passive. —**ef′fort·less·ly,** *adv.* —**ef′fort·less·ness,** *n.* —**Syn. 1.** smooth, facile.

ef·fron·ter·y (i frun′tə rē), *n., pl.* **-ter·ies. 1.** shameless or impudent boldness; barefaced audacity. **2.** an act or instance of this. [< F *effronterie* = OF *esfront* shameless (see EX [1], FRONT) + *-erie* -ERY] —**Syn. 1.** impudence.

ef·ful·gent (i ful′jənt), *adj.* shining forth brilliantly; radiant. [< L *effulgent-* (s. of *effulgēns*, prp. of *effulgēre*) = *ef-* EF- + *fulg-* shine + *-ent-* -ENT] —**ef·ful′gence.**

ef·fuse (*v.* i fyo͞oz′; *adj.* i fyo͞os′), *v.*, **-fused, -fus·ing,** *adj.* —*v.t.* **1.** to pour out or forth; shed; disseminate. —*v.i.* **2.** to exude; flow out. **3.** *Physics.* (of a gas) to flow through a very small orifice. —*adj.* **4.** *Bot.* spread out loosely. **5.** (of certain shells) having the lips separated by a gap or groove. [ME < L *effūs(us)* (ptp. of *effundere*) poured out]

ef·fu·sion (i fyo͞o′zhən), *n.* **1.** the act of effusing or pouring forth. **2.** something that is effused. **3.** an unrestrained expression of feelings: *sentimental effusions.* **4.** *Pathol.* **a.** the escape of a fluid from its natural vessels into a body cavity. **b.** the fluid that escapes. [ME < L *effūsiōn-* (s. of *effūsiō*)]

ef·fu·sive (i fyo͞o′siv), *adj.* **1.** unduly demonstrative; lacking reserve. **2.** pouring out; overflowing. **3.** *Geol.* noting or pertaining to igneous rocks which have solidified near or on the surface of the earth (opposed to *plutonic*). —**ef·fu′sive·ly,** *adv.* —**ef·fu′sive·ness,** *n.*

eft[1] (eft), *n.* **1.** a newt, esp. the common newt, *Diemictylus viridescens* **(red eft),** in its immature terrestrial stage. **2.** *Obs.* a lizard. [ME *evete*, OE *efete*]

eft[2] (eft), *adv.* *Archaic.* **1.** again. **2.** afterward. [OE; akin to AFT, AFTER]

EFT, electronic funds transfer: a method of transferring bank funds by electronic means, as from one corporate bank account to another or by withdrawal from one's own account to deposit in a creditor's, esp. so as to pay bills. Also, **EFTS** [e(lectronic) f(unds) t(ransfer) (system)]

eft·soon (eft so͞on′), *adv.* *Archaic.* **1.** soon afterward. **2.** again. **3.** forthwith. Also, **eft·soons′.** [ME *eftsone*, OE *eftsōna*]

Eg., 1. Egypt. **2.** Egyptian.

e.g., for example; for the sake of example; such as. [< L *exemplī grātia*]

e·gad (i gad′, ē′gad′), *interj.* (used as an expletive or mild oath): *Egad, that's true!* [euphemistic alter. of *ah God!*]

E·ga·di (eg′ə dē), *n.* a group of islands in the Mediterranean Sea off the coast of W Sicily. 15 sq. mi.

e·gal·i·tar·i·an (i gal′i târ′ē ən), *adj.* **1.** asserting, resulting from, or characterized by belief in the equality of all men. —*n.* **2.** a person who adheres to egalitarian beliefs. [alter. of EQUALITARIAN with F *égal* r. EQUAL] —**e·gal′i·tar′i·an·ism,** *n.*

é·ga·li·té (ā gȧ lē tā′), *n.* *French.* equality.

Eg·bert (eg′bərt), *n.* A.D. 775?–839, king of the West Saxons 802–839; 1st king of the English 828–839.

E·ger (ā′gəʀ), *n.* German name of **Ohře.**

E·ge·ri·a (i jēr′ē ə), *n.* *Rom. Legend.* one of the Camenae, the wife and instructress of Numa Pompilius.

e·gest (ē jest′), *v.t.* to discharge, as from the body; void (opposed to *ingest*). [< L *ēgest(us)* (ptp. of *ēgerere*) carried out = *ē-* E- + *ges-* (var. of *ger-*) carry + *-tus* ptp. suffix] —**e·ges·tion** (ē jes′chən, -jesh′-), *n.* —**e·ges′tive,** *adj.*

e·ges·ta (ē jes′tə), *n.pl.* matter egested from the body, as excrement. [neut. pl. of L *ēgestus* carried out. See EGEST]

egg[1] (eg), *n.* **1.** the roundish reproductive body produced by the female of certain animals, as birds and some snakes, consisting of an ovum and its envelopes. **2.** such a body produced by a domestic bird, esp. the hen. **3.** the contents of an egg or eggs. **4.** anything resembling a hen's egg. **5.** Also called **egg′ cell′.** *Biol.* the ovum or female reproductive cell. **6.** *Slang.* person: *He's a good egg.* **7. lay an egg,** *Slang.* to be unsuccessful, esp. in front of an audience. **8. put all one's eggs in one basket,** to venture everything in a single enterprise. —*v.t.* **9.** to prepare (food) by dipping in beaten egg. [ME < Scand; cf. Icel *egg*; c. ME *ey*, OE *ǣg*, G *Ei* egg]

egg[2] (eg), *v.t.* to incite or urge; encourage (usually fol. by *on*). [ME < Scand; cf. Icel *eggja* to incite < *egg* EDGE]

egg′ and dart′, *Archit.* an ornament for enriching an ovolo or echinus, consisting of a closely set, alternating series of oval and pointed forms. Also called **egg′ and an′chor, egg′ and tongue′.**

egg·beat·er (eg′bē′tər), *n.* a small rotary device for beating eggs, whipping cream, etc.

egg′drop soup′ (eg′drop′), a soup made by stirring eggs into a simmering broth.

egg·head (eg′hed′), *n.* *Informal.* an intellectual.

Eg·gle·ston (eg′əl stən), *n.* **Edward,** 1837–1902, U.S. author, editor, and clergyman.

egg·nog (eg′nog′), *n.* a drink made of eggs, milk or cream, sugar, and, usually, liquor.

egg·plant (eg′plant′, -plänt′), *n.* **1.** a plant, *Solanum Melongena*, cultivated for its edible, dark-purple or occasionally white or yellow fruit. **2.** the fruit of this plant, used as a table vegetable.

egg′ roll′, (in Chinese and Chinese-American cuisine) a dish consisting of a cylindrical casing of egg dough filled with a minced mixture of roast pork, bamboo shoots, onions, etc., and browned in deep fat.

eggs′ Ben′edict, (*sometimes l.c.*) a dish consisting of toast or toasted halves of English muffin covered with a slice of ham, poached eggs, and hollandaise sauce.

egg-shaped (eg′shāpt′), *adj.* having an oval form, usually with one end larger than the other.

egg·shell (eg′shel′), *n.* **1.** the shell of a bird's egg, consisting of keratin fibers and calcite crystals. **2.** a pale yellow-tan color. **3.** rather bulky paper having a slightly rough finish. —*adj.* **4.** like an eggshell, as in thinness and delicacy; very brittle. **5.** being pale yellow-tan in color. **6.** having little or no gloss: *eggshell white paint.* [ME *ayschelle*]

egg′shell por′celain, very thin, translucent porcelain.

egg′ white′, the white of an egg, esp. a hen's; albumen.

e·gis (ē′jis), *n.* aegis.

eg·lan·tine (eg′lən tīn′, -tēn′), *n.* **1.** the sweetbrier. **2.** the Austrian briar, *Rosa foetida.* [ME < MF; OF *aiglent* (< VL **aculentum*, neut. of **aculentus* prickly = L *acu(s)* needle + *-lentus* adj. suffix) + *-ine* -INE[1]]

EGmc, East Germanic.

e·go (ē′gō, eg′ō), *n., pl.* **e·gos. 1.** the "I" or self of any person; a person as thinking, feeling, and willing, and distinguishing itself from the selves of others and from objects of its thought. **2.** (*often cap.*) *Philos.* **a.** the enduring and conscious element that knows experience. **b.** *Scholasticism.* the complete man comprising both body and soul. **3.** *Psychoanal.* the part of the psychic apparatus that experiences and reacts to the outside world and thus mediates between the primitive drives of the id and the demands of the social and physical environment. **4.** egotism or self-importance. **5.** self-esteem or self-image. [< L: I]

e·go·cen·tric (ē′gō sen′trik, eg′ō-), *adj.* **1.** having or regarding the self as the center of all worldly things. **2.** having little or no regard for interests, beliefs, or attitudes other than one's own; self-centered. —*n.* **3.** an egocentric person. —**e·go·cen·tric·i·ty** (ē′gō sen tris′i tē, eg′ō-), *n.* —**e′go·cen′trism,** *n.*

e′go ide′al, *Psychoanal.* a more or less conscious ideal of personal excellence toward which an individual strives.

e·go·ism (ē′gō iz′əm, eg′ō-), *n.* **1.** the habit of valuing everything only in reference to one's personal interest; selfishness (opposed to *altruism*). **2.** egotism or self-conceit. **3.** *Phil.* any of various theories that regard the ego as the starting point or basic entity in epistemology, ethics, or metaphysics. **4.** *Ethics.* the view that each person should regard his own welfare as the supreme end of his actions. [< NL *egōism(us)*] —**Syn. 1.** See **egotism.**

e·go·ist (ē′gō ist, eg′ō-), *n.* **1.** a self-centered or selfish person (opposed to *altruist*). **2.** an egotist; an arrogantly conceited person. **3.** *Obs.* an adherent of the metaphysical principle of the ego or self. [< NL *egōist(a)*]

e·go·is·tic (ē′gō is′tik, eg′ō-), *adj.* **1.** pertaining to or of the nature of egoism. **2.** being centered in or preoccupied with oneself and the gratification of one's own desires; self-centered (opposed to *altruistic*). Also, **e′go·is′ti·cal.** —**e′go·is′ti·cal·ly,** *adv.*

e·go·ma·ni·a (ē′gō mā′nē ə, -mān′yə, eg′ō-), *n.* psychologically abnormal egotism. —**e′go·ma′ni·ac′,** *n.* —**e·go·ma·ni·a·cal** (ē′gō mə nī′i kəl), *adj.*

e·go·tism (ē′gə tiz′əm, eg′ə-), *n.* **1.** excessive and objectionable reference to oneself, in conversation or writing; self-conceit; boastfulness. **2.** self-centeredness or selfishness; egoism. [alter. of L *idiōtismus* common way of speaking, idiom, with L *ego* r. *idio-*]
—**Syn. 1.** EGOTISM, EGOISM refer to preoccupation with one's ego or self. EGOTISM is the common word for obtrusive and excessive reference to and emphasis upon oneself and one's own importance, in conversation and writing, often to the extent of monopolizing attention and showing disregard for others' opinions: *His egotism alienated all his friends.* EGOISM, a less common word, is used esp. in epistemology, ethics, and metaphysics, where it emphasizes the importance of self. See also **pride.** —**Ant. 1.** humility.

e·go·tist (ē′gə tist, eg′ə-), *n.* **1.** a conceited, boastful person. **2.** an egoist. [EGOT(ISM) + -IST]

e·go·tis·tic (ē′gə tis′tik, eg′ə-), *adj.* **1.** pertaining to or characterized by egotism. **2.** given to talking about oneself; vain; boastful; opinionated. **3.** indifferent to the well-being of others; selfish; egoistic. Also, **e′go·tis′ti·cal.** —**e′go·tis′ti·cal·ly,** *adv.*

e′go trip′, an act undertaken primarily to satisfy one's vanity or self-image: *Her charitable activity was one long ego trip.*

e·go-trip (ē′gō trip′, e′gō-), *v.i.*, **-tripped, -trip·ping.** to do something or conduct oneself primarily to satisfy one's vanity or self-image.

e·gre·gious (i grē′jəs, -jē əs), *adj.* **1.** remarkable or extraordinary in some bad way; glaring; flagrant; notorious. **2.** *Archaic.* distinguished or eminent. [< L *ēgregius* preeminent = *ē*- E- + *gregi*- (s. of *grex*) flock + -*us* -OUS] —**e·gre′gious·ly,** *adv.* —**e·gre′gious·ness,** *n.*

e·gress (*n.* ē′gres; *v.* i gres′), *n.* **1.** the act or an instance of going, esp. from an enclosed place. **2.** a means or place of going out; an exit. **3.** the right or permission to go out. **4.** *Astron.* emersion (def. 1). —*v.i.* **5.** to go out; emerge. [< L *ēgress*(*us*) departure = *ē*- E- + *gress*- (ptp. s. of *gradī* to step; see -GRADE) + -*us* n. suffix (4th decl.)]

e·gres·sion (i gresh′ən), *n.* a going out; egress. [< L *ēgressiōn*- (s. of *ēgressiō*) a going out. See EGRESS, -ION]

e·gret (ē′grit, eg′rit), *n.* **1.** any of several usually white herons that grow long, ornamental plumes during the breeding season. **2.** a plume of an egret; aigrette. —*adj.* **3.** made of or covered with egret plumes. [ME *egrete* < MF < OPr *aigreta* = *aigr*- (< OHG *heiger* HERON) + -*eta* -ET]

Egret, *Casmerodius albus egretta* (Length 3½ ft.)

E·gypt (ē′jipt), *n.* **1.** an ancient kingdom in NE Africa, along the Nile River: divided into the Nile Delta **(Lower Egypt)** and the area from Cairo S to the Sudan **(Upper Egypt)**. **2.** See **Arab Republic of Egypt.**

Egypt, Egyptian (def. 4). Also, **Egypt.**

E·gyp·tian (i jip′shən), *adj.* **1.** of or pertaining to Egypt or its people. **2.** *Obs.* of or pertaining to the Gypsies. —*n.* **3.** a native or inhabitant of Egypt. **4.** the extinct, Afro-Asiatic language of the ancient Egyptians. *Abbr.:* Egypt **5.** *Obs.* a Gypsy. [ME (see EGYPT, -IAN); r. *Egiptish,* OE *Egiptisc;* see -ISH[1]]

Egyp′tian cal′endar, the calendar of ancient Egypt, having a year consisting of twelve 30-day months, with five additional days at the end, leap year not being considered.

Egyp′tian cot′ton, a cotton, *Gossypium barbadense,* having long, silky, strong fibers, now grown chiefly in Egypt and the southwestern U.S.

E·gyp·tol·o·gy (ē′jip tol′ə jē), *n.* the scientific study of Egyptian antiquities. —**E·gyp·to·log·i·cal** (i jip′tə loj′i kəl), *adj.* —**E′gyp·tol′o·gist,** *n.*

eh (ā, e), *interj.* (an interrogative utterance, usually expressing surprise or doubt or seeking confirmation): *Eh? What did you say?*

EHF, See **extremely high frequency.**

Eh·ren·burg (ā′rən bo͝ork′), *n.* **Il·ya Gri·gor·ie·vich** (il yä′ gri gôr′yə vich), 1891–1967, Russian novelist and journalist.

Ehr·lich (âr′likh), *n.* **Paul** (poul), 1854–1915, German physician, bacteriologist, and chemist: Nobel prize 1908.

E.I., **1.** East Indian. **2.** East Indies.

Eich·mann (īk′mən, īkh′-; *Ger.* īkh′män′), *n.* **Ad·olf** (ad′olf, ā′dolf; *Ger.* ä′dôlf), 1906–62, German Nazi concentration-camp official: executed in Israel for World War II war crimes.

ei·der (ī′dər), *n.* **1.** See **eider duck.** **2.** eiderdown. [< ModIcel *æthar* (18th-century sp. *ædar*), gen. sing. of *æthur* eider duck, in phrase *ædar dūnn* down of the eider duck; sp. *eider* < G or Sw]

ei·der·down (ī′dər doun′), *n.* **1.** down, or soft feathers, from the breast of the female eider duck. **2.** a heavy quilt or comforter, esp. one filled with eiderdown. **3.** *U.S.* a fabric of cotton with wool nap. —*adj.* **4.** filled with down, or feathers of the breast of the female eider duck.

ei′der duck′, any of several large sea ducks of the genus *Somateria* and allied genera of the Northern Hemisphere, the females of which yield eiderdown.

Eider duck, *Somateria mollissima* (Length 2 ft.)

ei·det·ic (ī det′ik), *adj.* **1.** of, pertaining to, or constituting visual imagery retained in the memory and readily reproducible with great accuracy and in great detail. **2.** of, pertaining to, or of the nature of an abstraction, pure form, or essence. [< Gk *eidētik*(*ós*). See EIDOS, -ETIC]

ei·do·lon (ī dō′lən), *n., pl.* **-la** (-lə), **-lons.** **1.** a phantom; apparition; image. **2.** an ideal. [see IDOL]

ei·dos (ī′dos, ā′-), *n. pl.* **ei·de** (ī′dē, ā′dā). *Philos.* form; idea; essence; ideal. [< Gk *eîdos* something seen, form; akin to *ideîn,* L *vidēre* to see]

Eif·fel (ī′fəl; *Fr.* e fel′), *n.* **A·le·xan·dre Gus·tave** (A lek sän′drᵊ gys tav′), 1832–1923, French civil engineer.

eight (āt), *n.* **1.** a cardinal number, seven plus one. **2.** a symbol for this number, as 8 or VIII. **3.** a set of this many persons or things, as the crew of an eight-oared racing shell. **4.** a playing card the face of which bears eight pips. —*adj.* **5.** amounting to eight in number. [ME *eighte,* OE *eahta;* c. D, G *acht,* Icel *ātta,* Goth *ahtau,* L *octō,* Gk *oktō*]

eight·ball (āt′bôl′), *n.* **1.** *Pool.* **a.** a black ball bearing the number eight. **b.** a game in which one player or side must pocket all of either the solid-color balls or the striped ones before pocketing the eightball. **2. behind the eight-ball,** *Slang.* in a disadvantageous or uncomfortable situation.

eight·een (ā′tēn′), *n.* **1.** a cardinal number, ten plus eight. **2.** a symbol for this number, as 18 or XVIII. **3.** a set of this many persons or things. —*adj.* **4.** amounting to 18 in number. [ME *ehtetene,* OE *eahtatēne;* c. Icel *āttjān,* G *achtzehn*]

eight·een·mo (ā′tēn′mō), *n., pl.* **-mos,** *adj. Bookbinding.* octodecimo.

eight·eenth (ā′tēnth′), *adj.* **1.** next after the seventeenth; being the ordinal number for 18. **2.** being one of 18 equal parts. —*n.* **3.** an eighteenth part, esp. of one (1/18). **4.** the eighteenth member of a series. [ME *eightenthe, eightethe,* OE *eahtatēotha*]

eight·fold (āt′fōld′), *adj.* **1.** comprising eight parts or members. **2.** eight times as great or as much. —*adv.* **3.** in eightfold measure.

eighth (ātth), *adj.* **1.** next after the seventh; being the ordinal number for eight. **2.** being one of eight equal parts. —*n.* **3.** an eighth part, esp. of one (⅛). **4.** the eighth member of a series. **5.** *Music.* octave. —*adv.* **6.** in the eighth place; eighthly. [ME *eighthe,* OE *eahtotha;* c. OHG *ahtoda,* Icel *āttandi,* Goth *ahtud*-] —**eighth′ly,** *adv.*

eighth′ note′, *Music.* a note having one eighth of the time value of a whole note; a quaver. See illus. at **note.**

eighth′ rest′, *Music.* a rest equal in value to an eighth note. See illus. at **rest**[1].

eight·i·eth (ā′tē ith), *adj.* **1.** next after the seventy-ninth; being the ordinal number for 80. **2.** being one of 80 equal parts. —*n.* **3.** an eightieth part, esp. of one (1/80). **4.** the eightieth member of a series. [ME *eightetithe,* OE (*hund*)*eahtatigotha* eightieth]

eight·pen·ny (āt′pen′ē), *adj.* **1.** noting a nail 2½ inches long. *Abbr.:* 8d **2.** costing or amounting to the sum of eight pennies.

eight-track (āt′trak′), *n.* a magnetic-tape cartridge, esp. one carrying eight parallel tracks of prerecorded sound or music. Also, **8′-track′.**

eight·y (ā′tē), *n., pl.* **eight·ies,** *adj.* —*n.* **1.** a cardinal number, ten times eight. **2.** a symbol for this number, as 80 or LXXX. **3.** a set of this many persons or things. **4. eighties,** the numbers, years, degrees, or the like, between 80 and 89, as in referring to numbered streets, indicating the years of a lifetime or of a century, or degrees of temperature. —*adj.* **5.** amounting to 80 in number. [ME *eighteti,* OE *eahtatig*]

eight·y-six (ā′tē siks′), *v.t. Slang.* to refuse to serve (an undesirable or unwelcome customer in a restaurant or bar).

ei·kon (ī′kon), *n.* icon (defs. 1, 2).

Ei·lat (ā lät′), *n.* Elath.

E. Ind., East Indian.

Eind·ho·ven (īnt′hō′vən), *n.* a city in the S Netherlands. 174,612 (1962).

Ein·stein (īn′stīn; *Ger.* īn′shtīn′), *n.* **Al·bert** (al′bərt; *Ger.* äl′bert), 1879–1955, German physicist, U.S. citizen from 1940: formulator of the theories of relativity; Nobel prize for physics 1921.

Ein′stein equa′tion, *Physics.* any of several equations formulated by Einstein, esp. the mass-energy equation.

Ein·stein·i·an (īn stī′nē ən), *adj.* pertaining to Albert Einstein or his theories, esp. the theory of relativity.

ein·stein·i·um (īn stī′nē əm), *n. Chem.* a synthetic, radioactive, metallic element. *Symbol:* Es; *at. no.:* 99. [named after Albert EINSTEIN; see -IUM]

Ein′stein shift′, *Physics, Astron.* the shift toward longer wavelengths in radiation subjected to a strong gravitational force by the body emitting the radiation.

Ein′stein the′ory, *Physics.* relativity (def. 2). Also called **Ein′stein's the′ory of relativ′ity.**

Eir·e (âr′ə, ī′rə), *n.* a former name of the Republic of Ireland.

Ei·sen·how·er (ī′zən hou′ər), *n.* **Dwight David,** 1890–1969, U.S. general and statesman: 34th president of the U.S. 1953–61.

Ei·sen·stein (ī′zən stīn′; *Russ.* ī′zen shtān′), *n.* **Ser·gei Mi·khai·lo·vich** (ser gā′ mi khī′lo vich), 1898–1948, Russian theatrical and motion-picture director.

Eisk (āsk), *n.* Yeisk.

eis·tedd·fod (ā steth′vod, ī steth′-), *n., pl.* **eis·tedd·fods, eis·tedd·fod·au** (ā′steth vod′ī, ī′steth-). (in Wales) an annual competition among poets and minstrels. [< Welsh: lit., session = *eistedd* sit(ting) + *fod,* var. of *bod* be(ing)] —**eis′tedd·fod′ic,** *adj.*

ei·ther (ē′thər, ī′thər), *adj.* **1.** one or the other of two: *You may sit at either end of the table.* **2.** each of two; the one and the other: *There are trees on either side of the river.* —*pron.* **3.** one or the other. —*conj.* **4.** (a coordinating conjunction that, when preceding a word or statement followed by the disjunctive *or,* serves to emphasize the possibility of choice): *Either come or write.* —*adv.* **5.** also; too; as well; to the same degree (used after negative clauses coordinated by *and, or,* or *nor,* or after negative subordinate clauses): *He is not fond of parties, and I am not either.* [ME; OE *ǣgther,* contr. of *ǣghwæther* each of two, both] —**Usage.** The pronoun EITHER is commonly followed by a singular verb: *Either is good enough.*

e·jac·u·late (*v.* i jak′yə lāt′; *n.* i jak′yə lit), *v.,* **-lat·ed, -lat·ing,** *n.* —*v.t.* **1.** to utter suddenly and briefly; exclaim. **2.** to eject suddenly and swiftly; discharge. **3.** to eject (semen). —*v.i.* **4.** to eject semen. —*n.* **5.** the semen emitted in an ejaculation. [< L *ējaculāt*(*us*) (ptp. of *ējaculārī*) shot out = *ē*- E- + *jacul*(*um*) javelin (*jac*(*ere*) (to) throw + -*ulum* -ULE) + -*ātus* -ATE[1]] —**e·jac′u·la′tor,** *n.*

e·jac·u·la·tion (i jak′yə lā′shən), *n.* **1.** an abrupt, exclamatory utterance. **2.** the act or process of ejaculating, esp. the discharge of semen.

e·jac·u·la·to·ry (i jak′yə lə tōr′ē, -tôr′ē), *adj.* **1.** pertaining to or of the nature of an exclamatory utterance. **2.** *Physiol.* pertaining to ejaculation. Also, **e·jac·u·la·tive** (i jak′yə lā′tiv, -lə tiv).

e·ject (i jekt′), *v.t.* **1.** to drive or force out; expel, as from a place or position. **2.** to dismiss, as from office, occupancy, etc. **3.** to evict, as from property. **4.** to throw out, as from within; throw off. —*v.i.* **5.** to propel oneself, in an emergency, from a damaged or malfunctioning airplane, as by an ejection seat. [< L *ēject*(*us*) (ptp. of *ēicere*) thrown out = *ē*- E- + *jec*- (var. s. of *jacere*) throw + -*tus* ptp. suffix]

e·jec·ta (i jek′tə), *n.pl.* matter ejected, as from a volcano in eruption. [neut. pl. of L *ējectus.* See EJECT]

e·jec·tion (i jek′shən), *n.* **1.** the act or an instance of ejecting. **2.** the state of being ejected. **3.** something ejected, as lava. [< L *ējectiōn-* (s. of *ējectiō*) a throwing out]

ejec′tion seat′, an airplane seat that can be ejected with the pilot in an emergency. Also called **ejec′tor seat′.**

e·jec·tive (i jek′tiv), *adj.* **1.** serving to eject. **2.** *Phonet.* (of a voiceless stop, affricate, or fricative) produced with air compressed above the closed glottis. **—***n.* **3.** *Phonet.* an ejective stop, affricate, or fricative. **—e·jec′tive·ly,** *adv.*

e·ject·ment (i jekt′mənt), *n.* **1.** the act of ejecting. **2.** *Law.* a possessory action wherein the title to real property may be tried and the possession recovered.

e·jec·tor (i jek′tər), *n.* **1.** a person or thing that ejects. **2.** (in a firearm or gun) the mechanism that after firing throws out the empty cartridge or shell.

E·ka·te·rin·burg (*Russ.* e kä′te rēn bŏŏrkh′), *n.* former name of **Sverdlovsk.**

E·ka·te·ri·no·dar (*Russ.* e kä′te rē′no där′), *n.* former name of **Krasnodar.**

E·ka·te·ri·no·slav (*Russ.* e kä′te rē′no släf′), *n.* former name of **Dnepropetrovsk.**

eke[1] (ēk), *v.t.,* **eked, ek·ing.** **1.** *Archaic.* to increase; enlarge; lengthen. **2. eke out, a.** to supply by some expedient what is lacking; supplement. **b.** to make (a living) or support (existence) laboriously. [ME *eke(n)*, OE *ēac(i)an* (v.i.) < *ēaca* (n.) increase; ME *echen*, OE *ēcan*, var. of *īecan* (v.t.) < WGmc **aukjan;* both akin to Icel *auka*, Goth *aukan*, L *augēre*, Gk *auxánein* to increase, amplify]

eke[2] (ēk), *adv.* *Archaic.* also. [ME *eek*, OE *ēc, ēac;* c. G *auch*, Icel, Goth *auk*]

EKG, electrocardiogram. Also, **E.K.G.** [< G *E(lectro)-k(ardio)g(ramme)*]

el (el), *n.* See **elevated railroad.**

El Aai·ún (*Arab.* el′ ī yōōn′), a city in and the capital of Spanish Sahara. 9000 (est. 1963).

e·lab·o·rate (*adj.* i lab′ər it; *v.* i lab′ə rāt′), *adj., v.,* **-rat·ed, -rat·ing.** **—***adj.* **1.** worked out with great care and nicety of detail; executed with great minuteness. **2.** marked by intricate and often excessive detail; complicated. **—***v.t.* **3.** to work out carefully or minutely; develop to perfection. **4.** to produce or develop by labor. **—***v.i.* **5.** to add details in writing, speaking, etc.; give additional or fuller treatment (usually fol. by *on* or *upon*): *to elaborate upon a theme.* [< L *ēlabōrāt(us)* (ptp. of *ēlabōrāre*) worked out. See E-, LABOR, -ATE[1]] **—e·lab′o·rate·ly,** *adv.* **—e·lab′o·rate·ness,** *n.* **—e·lab′o·ra′tive,** *adj.* **—e·lab′o·ra′tor,** *n.*
—Syn. 1. perfected, painstaking. **2.** ornate, intricate. ELABORATE, LABORED, STUDIED apply to that which is worked out in great detail. That which is ELABORATE is characterized by great, sometimes even excessive, nicety or minuteness of detail: *elaborate preparations for a banquet; an elaborate apology.* That which is LABORED is marked by excessive, often forced or uninspired, effort: *a labored explanation, style of writing.* That which is STUDIED is accomplished with care and deliberation, and is done purposely, sometimes even having been rehearsed: *a studied pose.* **3, 5.** refine, improve. **—Ant. 1.** simple.

e·lab·o·ra·tion (i lab′ə rā′shən), *n.* **1.** the act or an instance of elaborating. **2.** the state of being elaborated; elaborateness. **3.** something that is elaborated. [< L *ēlabōrātiōn-* (s. of *ēlabōrātiō*)]

el·ae·op·tene (el′ē op′tēn), *n.* *Chem.* eleoptene.

El·a·gab·a·lus (el′ə gab′ə ləs, ē′lə-), *n.* Heliogabalus.

E·laine (i lān′), *n.* any of several women in Arthurian romance, as the daughter of King Pelles and the mother, by Lancelot, of Sir Galahad.

El A·la·mein (el ä′lä mān′, -lə-), a town on the N coast of the Arab Republic of Egypt, ab. 70 mi. W of Alexandria: decisive British victory October, 1942. Also called **Alamein.**

E·lam (ē′ləm), *n.* an ancient kingdom E of Babylonia and N of the Persian Gulf. *Cap.:* Susa. See map at **Chaldea.**

E·lam·ite (ē′lə mīt′), *n.* **1.** a native or inhabitant of ancient Elam. **2.** a language of unknown affinities, spoken by the Elamites as late as the 1st century B.C., written c3500–c2500 B.C. in a linear script and thereafter in a cuneiform script. **—***adj.* **3.** of or pertaining to Elam, its people, or their language.

E·lam·it·ic (ē′lə mit′ik), *n.* Elamite (def. 2).

é·lan (ā län′, ā lan′; *Fr.* ā läN′), *n.* dash; impetuous ardor. [< F; MF *eslan* a dash, rush, appar. back formation from *eslancer* to dart. See EX-[1], LANCE[1]]

e·land (ē′lənd), *n., pl.* **e·lands,** (*esp. collectively*) **e·land.** either of two large, African antelopes of the genus *Taurotragus*, having long, spirally twisted horns. [< SAfrD, special use of D *eland* elk < obs. G *Elen(d)*, prob. < Lith *élnis;* akin to ELK]

Eland, *Taurotragus oryx* (5½ ft. high at shoulder; horns to 3½ ft.; length to 11 ft.)

é·lan vi·tal (*Fr.* ā läN vē tal′), (esp. in Bergsonian philosophy) the creative force within an organism that is able to build physical form and to produce growth and necessary or desirable adaptations. [< F: lit., vital ardor]

e·lapse (i laps′), *v.,* **e·lapsed, e·laps·ing,** *n.* **—***v.i.* **1.** (of time) to slip by or pass away. **—***n.* **2.** the passage or termination of a period of time; lapse. [< L *ēlāps(us)* (ptp. of *ēlābī* to slip away)]

e·las·mo·branch (i las′mə brangk′, i laz′-), *adj.* **1.** belonging or pertaining to the *Elasmobranchii*, the group of cartilaginous fishes comprising the sharks and rays. **—***n.* **2.** an elasmobranch fish. [< NL *elasmobranch(ii)* < Gk *elasmó(s)* plate metal + *bránchia* (neut. pl.) gills]

e·las·tic (i las′tik), *adj.* **1.** capable of returning to its original length, shape, etc., after being stretched, deformed, or expanded. **2.** spontaneously expansive, as gases. **3.** flexible; accommodating; tolerant: *an elastic conscience.* **4.** springing back or rebounding; springy; resilient. **5.** *Physics.* of, pertaining to, or noting a body having the property of elasticity. **—***n.* **6.** webbing, or material in the form of a band, made elastic with strips of rubber. **7.** something made from this material, as a garter. [< NL *elastic(us)* expansive < Gk *elastikós* = *elast(ós)* beaten (*elas-*, var. s. of *elaúnein* to beat, + *-tos* ptp. suffix) + *-ikos* -IC] **—e·las′ti·cal·ly,** *adv.*

elas′tic deforma′tion, *Physics.* the temporary change in length, volume, or shape produced in an elastic substance by a stress that is less than the elastic limit of the substance.

e·las·tic·i·ty (i la stis′i tē, ē′la stis′-), *n.* **1.** the state or quality of being elastic. **2.** flexibility; resilience. **3.** buoyancy; ability to resist or overcome depression. **4.** *Physics.* the property of a substance that enables it to change its length, volume, or shape in direct response to a force and to recover its original form upon the removal of the force.

e·las·ti·cize (i las′ti sīz′), *v.t.,* **-cized, -ciz·ing.** to make elastic, as by stitching with bands of elastic.

elas′tic lim′it, *Physics.* the greatest stress that can be applied to an elastic body without causing permanent deformation.

e·las·tin (i las′tin), *n.* *Biochem.* a protein constituting the basic substance of elastic tissue. [ELAST(IC) + -IN[2]]

e·las·to·mer (i las′tə mər), *n.* *Chem.* a natural or synthetic elastic substance, as rubber or neoprene. [ELAST(IC) + -O- + -MER] **—e·las·to·mer·ic** (i las′tə mer′ik), *adj.*

e·late (i lāt′), *v.,* **e·lat·ed, e·lat·ing,** *adj.* **—***v.t.* **1.** to make very happy or proud; cause to be in high spirits. **—***adj.* **2.** *Literary.* elated. [< L *ēlāt(us)* carried away, lifted up (ptp. of *efferre*) = *ē-* E- + *lā-* carry, lift + *-tus* ptp. suffix]

e·lat·ed (i lā′tid), *adj.* very happy or proud; jubilant; in high spirits. **—e·lat′ed·ly,** *adv.* **—e·lat′ed·ness,** *n.*

el·a·ter (el′ə tər), *n.* **1.** *Bot.* an elastic filament serving to disperse spores. **2.** *Zool.* elaterid. **3.** *Obs.* elasticity. [< NL < Gk: driver = *ela-* (s. of *elaúnein* to drive; see ELASTIC) + *-tēr* n. suffix]

e·lat·er·id (i lat′ər id), *n.* **1.** any beetle of the family *Elateridae*, comprising the click beetles. **—***adj.* **2.** belonging or pertaining to the family *Elateridae.*

e·lat·er·ite (i lat′ə rīt′), *n.* an elastic, rubbery, brownish, natural asphalt.

el·a·te·ri·um (el′ə tēr′ē əm), *n.* *Pharm.* a grayish-green, bitter solid obtained from the juice of *Ecballium elaterium*, the squirting cucumber, and used as a cathartic. [< L < Gk *elatḗrion* squirting cucumber, neut. of *elatḗrios* purgative = *elatḗr* (see ELATER) + *-ios* adj. suffix]

E·lath (ā lät′), *n.* a seaport at the N tip of the Gulf of Aqaba, in S Israel. 9,700 (est. 1965). Also, **Eilat.**

e·la·tion (i lā′shən), *n.* a feeling or state of great joy or pride; exultant gladness; high spirits. [< L *ēlātiōn-* (s. of *ēlātiō*), (see ELATE, -ION); r. ME *elacioun* < AF]

e·la·tive (ē′lə tiv, el′ə-), *n.* (in Arabic grammar) an adjectival form denoting intensity or superiority, approximately equivalent to the comparative and superlative of other languages. [< L *ēlāt(us)* (see ELATE) + -IVE]

El·ba (el′bə), *n.* an Italian island in the Mediterranean, between Corsica and Italy: the scene of Napoleon's first exile 1814–15. 25,402 (1961); 94 sq. mi.

El·be (el′bə, elb), *n.* a river in central Europe, flowing NW from W Czechoslovakia through East and West Germany to the North Sea. 725 mi. long. Czech, **Labe.**

El·ber·feld (el′bər felt′), *n.* a former city in W West Germany, now incorporated into Wuppertal.

El·bert (el′bərt), *n.* **Mount,** a mountain in central Colorado, in the Sawatch range: second highest peak of the Rocky Mountains in the U.S. 14,431 ft.

El·ber·ta (el bûr′tə), *n.* **1.** a freestone peach having reddish-yellow skin. **2.** the tree bearing this fruit.

El·bląg (el′blôNg), *n.* a seaport in N Poland: formerly in Germany. 82,000 (est. 1963). Also, **El·bing** (el′bing).

el·bow (el′bō), *n.* **1.** the bend or joint of the human arm between upper arm and forearm. **2.** the joint at the upper end of the forearm of a quadruped. **3.** something bent like an elbow, as a sharp turn in a road or river, or a piece of pipe bent at an angle. **4.** Also called **ell.** a plumbing pipe or pipe connection having a right-angled bend. **5. out at the elbows, a.** poorly dressed; shabby. **b.** impoverished. Also, **out at elbows. 6. rub elbows with,** to mingle socially with; associate with. **—***v.t.* **7.** to push with or as with the elbow; jostle. **8.** to make (one's way) by so pushing. **—***v.i.* **9.** to elbow one's way. [ME *elbowe*, OE *el(n)boga;* c. G *Ellenbogen*, Icel *ǫlnbogi.* See ELL[2], BOW[1]]

el′bow grease′, *Informal.* strenuous physical exertion, as in manual labor.

el·bow·room (el′bō rōōm′, -rŏŏm′), *n.* ample room; space in which to move freely.

El·brus (el′brōōs), *n.* a mountain in the S Soviet Union in Europe, in the Caucasus range: the highest peak in Europe, 18,465 ft. Also, **El′bruz.**

El·burz′ Moun′tains (el bŏŏrz′), a mountain range in N Iran, along the S coast of the Caspian Sea. Highest peak Mt. Demavend, 18,606 ft.

El Ca·jon (el′ kə hōn′), a city in SW California. 52,273 (1970).

El Cap·i·tan (el kap′i tan′), a mountain in E California, in the Sierra Nevada Mountains: precipice that rises over 3300 ft. above Yosemite Valley.

El Cer·ri·to (el′ sə rē′tō), a city in W California, on San Francisco Bay. 25,190 (1970).

El·che (el′che), *n.* a city in E Spain. 67,088 (1955).

El Cid Cam·pe·a·dor (*Sp.* el thēd′ käm′pe ä thôr′, sēd′). See **Cid, The.**

eld (eld), *n.* *Archaic.* **1.** age. **2.** old age. **3.** antiquity. [ME *elde*, OE *eldo, ieldo* < *(e)ald* OLD; see WORLD]

eld·er[1] (el′dər), *adj.* *a compar. of* **old** *with* **eldest** *as superl.* **1.** of greater age; older. **2.** of higher rank; senior. **3.** of or pertaining to former times; earlier. **—***n.* **4.** a person who is older or higher in rank than oneself. **5.** an aged person. **6.** one of the older and more influential men of a tribe or community, often a chief or ruler. **7.** a presbyter. **8.** (in certain Protestant churches) a layman who is a governing officer, often assisting the pastor in services. [ME; OE *eldra*, comp. of *eald* OLD] **—Syn. 1.** See **older.**

el·der[2] (el′dər), *n.* any caprifoliaceous tree or shrub of the genus *Sambucus*, having clusters of white flowers and red or black, berrylike fruit. [ME *eldre, elrene, ellerne*, OE *ellærn;* c. MLG *ellern*]

el·der·ber·ry (el′dər ber′ē, -bə rē), *n., pl.* **-ries. 1.** the drupaceous fruit of the elder, used in making wine and jelly. **2.** elder[2]. [ME *eldreberie*]
eld·er·ly (el′dər lē), *adj.* **1.** somewhat old; between middle and old age. **2.** of or pertaining to persons in later life. —**eld′er·li·ness,** *n.* —**Syn. 1.** See **old.**
eld′er states′man, 1. an influential elderly citizen, often a retired statesman, whose advice is sought by government leaders. **2.** any influential member of a company, group, etc., whose advice is deeply respected. **3.** *Japanese Hist.* any of the retired political leaders who continued to exert a strong influence in the government and who controlled the emperor's privy council, esp. 1898–1914.
eld·est (el′dist), *adj.* *a superl. of* **old** *with* **elder** *as compar.* oldest; first-born; of greatest age: *eldest brother; eldest sister; eldest born.* [OE *eldesta,* superl. of (*e*)*ald* OLD]
El Do·ra·do (el′ də rä′dō, -rā′- *or, Sp.,* el dô ʀä′t͟hô *for 1, 2;* el′ də rā′dō *for 3*), **1.** a legendary treasure city of South America, sought by the early Spanish explorers. **2.** any fabulously wealthy place. **3.** a city in S Arkansas. 25,283 (1970).
el·dritch (el′drich), *adj.* eerie; weird; spooky. Also, **el′drich.** [earlier *elrich* = OE *el-* foreign, strange, uncanny + *-rīc* creature (as in *gāsrīc*); cf. *ælwiht* alien creature]
E·le·a (ē′lē ə), *n.* an ancient Greek city in SW Italy.
El′eanor of Aq′uitaine (el′ə nər, -nôr′), 1122?–1204, queen of Louis VII of France 1137–52; queen of Henry II of England 1154–89.
El·e·at·ic (el′ē at′ik), *adj.* **1.** of or pertaining to Elea. **2.** noting or pertaining to a school of philosophy, founded by Parmenides, that developed systematic methods of inquiry into the phenomenal world, esp. with reference to the phenomena of plurality and change. —*n.* **3.** a philosopher of the Eleatic school. [< L *Eleātic(us)* < Gk *Eleātikós*] —**El′e·at′i·cism,** *n.*
el·e·cam·pane (el′ə kam pān′), *n.* a composite plant, *Inula Helenium,* having large yellow flowers and aromatic leaves and root. [ME; OE *ele(ne), eolone* (metathetic alter. of ML *enula,* L *inula* elecampane) + ME *campane* < ML *campāna;* see CAMP[1], -ANE, -AN]
e·lect (i lekt′), *v.t.* **1.** to select by vote, as for an office. **2.** to determine in favor of (a method, course of action, etc.). **3.** to pick out; choose: *to elect a course in school.* **4.** *Theol.* to select for divine mercy or favor, esp. for eternal salvation. —*v.i.* **5.** to choose or select someone or something, as by voting. —*adj.* **6.** selected for an office, but not yet inducted (usually used in combination following a noun): *the governor-elect.* **7.** picked out; chosen. **8.** select or choice. **9.** *Theol.* chosen by God, esp. for eternal life. —*n.* **the elect, 10.** a person or the persons chosen or worthy to be chosen. **11.** *Theol.* a person or persons chosen by God, esp. for eternal life. [< L *ēlect(us)* chosen (ptp. of *ēligere*) = *ē-* E- + *leg-* choose + *-tus* ptp. suffix] —**Syn. 3.** See **choose.** —**Ant. 1, 2.** reject.
elect., 1. electric. **2.** electrical. **3.** electricity. Also, **elec.**
e·lect·a·ble (i lek′tə bəl), *adj.* capable of being elected, as to public office. —**e·lect·a·bil·i·ty** (i lek′tə bil′i tē), *n.*
e·lect·ee (i lek tē′), *n.* a person who has been elected.
e·lec·tion (i lek′shən), *n.* **1.** the selection of a person or persons for office by vote. **2.** a public vote upon a proposition submitted. **3.** the act of electing; choice. **4.** *Theol.* the choice by God of individuals, as for a particular work, or esp. for salvation or eternal life. [< L *ēlectiōn-* (s. of *ēlectiō;* see ELECT, -ION); r. ME *eleccioun* < AF]
Elec′tion Day′, 1. *U.S.* the first Tuesday after the first Monday in November on which national elections are held for electors of the President and Vice-President in those years evenly divisible by four. On even years constituents elect members of the House of Representatives for two-year terms and one third of the Senate for six-year terms. **2.** (*often l.c.*) any day designated for the election of public officials.
elec′tion dis′trict, precinct (def. 2).
e·lec·tion·eer (i lek′shə nēr′), *v.i.* to work for the success of a candidate, party, ticket, etc., in an election. —**e·lec′tion·eer′er,** *n.*
e·lec·tive (i lek′tiv), *adj.* **1.** pertaining to the principle of electing to an office, position, etc. **2.** appointed by election, as an official. **3.** bestowed by or derived from election, as an office. **4.** having the power or right of electing to office, as a body of persons. **5.** open to choice; optional; not required. —*n.* **6.** an optional study; a course that a student may select from among alternatives. [< ML *ēlectīv(us)*] —**e·lec′tive·ly,** *adv.* —**e·lec′tive·ness,** *n.*
e·lec·tor (i lek′tər), *n.* **1.** a person who elects or may elect, esp. a qualified voter. **2.** *U.S.* a member of the electoral college. **3.** (*usually cap.*) one of the German princes entitled to elect the emperor of the Holy Roman Empire. [late ME *electo(u)r* < L *ēlector*]
e·lec·tor·al (i lek′tər əl), *adj.* **1.** pertaining to electors or election. **2.** consisting of electors. —**e·lec′tor·al·ly,** *adv.*
elec′toral col′lege, *U.S.* a body of electors chosen by the voters in each state to elect the President and Vice-President.
elec′toral vote′, *U.S.* the formal vote cast by the electoral college to reflect the popular vote of each state in a presidential election.
e·lec·tor·ate (i lek′tər it), *n.* **1.** the body of persons entitled to vote in an election. **2.** the dignity or territory of an Elector.
electr-, var. of **electro-** before a vowel: *electrode.*
E·lec·tra (i lek′trə), *n.* *Class. Myth.* the daughter of Agamemnon and Clytemnestra who incited her brother Orestes to kill Clytemnestra and her lover Aegisthus.
Elec′tra com′plex, *Psychoanal.* the unresolved desire of a daughter for sexual gratification from her father.
e·lec·tress (i lek′tris), *n.* **1.** a female elector. **2.** (*usually cap.*) the wife or widow of an Elector.
e·lec·tric (i lek′trik), *adj.* **1.** pertaining to, derived from, produced by, or involving electricity: *an electric current; an electric shock.* **2.** producing, transmitting, or operated by electric currents: *an electric bell.* **3.** electrifying; thrilling; exciting; stirring. **4.** (of a musical instrument) **a.** producing sound by electrical or electronic means: *an electric organ.* **b.** equipped with connections to an amplifier-loudspeaker system: *an electric guitar.* [< NL *electric(us)* = L *ēlectr(um)* amber (< Gk *ēlektron*) + *-icus* -IC]
e·lec·tri·cal (i lek′tri kəl), *adj.* **1.** electric. **2.** concerned with electricity. —**e·lec′tri·cal·ly,** *adv.* —**e·lec′tri·cal·ness,** *n.*
elec′trical storm′, thunderstorm. Also, **electric storm.**
elec′trical transcrip′tion, 1. a radio broadcast from a phonograph record. **2.** the phonograph record itself.
elec′tric chair′, 1. an electrified chair used to execute criminals. **2.** the penalty of legal electrocution.
elec′tric charge′, *Physics.* charge (def. 39a).
elec′tric eel′, an eellike, fresh-water fish, *Electrophorus electricus,* found in the Amazon and Orinoco rivers and tributaries, sometimes over six feet in length, capable of emitting strong electric discharges.
elec′tric eye′, See **photoelectric cell** (def. 1).
elec′tric field′, *Physics.* a condition of space in the vicinity of an electric charge, manifesting itself as a force on an electric charge within that space.
elec′tric fur′nace, a furnace in which the heat required is produced through electricity.
e·lec·tri·cian (i lek trish′ən, ē′lek-), *n.* a person who installs, operates, maintains, or repairs electric devices or electrical wiring. [irreg. ELECTR(ICITY) + -ICIAN]
e·lec·tric·i·ty (i lek tris′i tē, ē′lek-), *n.* **1.** a fundamental physical agency caused by the presence and motion of electrons, protons, and other charged particles, manifesting itself as attraction, repulsion, magnetic, luminous and heating effects, and the like. **2.** the science dealing with this agency. **3.** electric current. **4.** a state or feeling of excitement, anticipation, tension, etc.
elec′tric nee′dle, *Surg.* an acusector.
elec′tric ray′, any ray of the family *Torpedinidae,* capable of emitting strong electric discharges.
elec′tric storm′. See **electrical storm.**
elec′tric torch′, *Brit.* torch (def. 4).
e·lec·tri·fy (i lek′trə fī′), *v.t.,* **-fied, -fy·ing. 1.** to charge with or subject to electricity; apply electricity to. **2.** to supply (a region, community, etc.) with electric power. **3.** to equip for the use of electric power, as a railroad. **4.** to startle greatly; excite or thrill. —**e·lec′tri·fi·ca′tion,** *n.* —**e·lec′tri·fi′er,** *n.*
e·lec·tro (i lek′trō), *n., pl.* **-tros.** electrotype.
electro-, a combining form of **electric** or **electricity:** *electromagnetic.* Also, *esp. before a vowel,* **electr-.** [< Gk *elektro-,* comb. form of *ēlektron* amber]
e·lec·tro·a·cous·tic (i lek′trō ə ko͞o′stik), *adj.* of or pertaining to electroacoustics. Also, **e·lec′tro·a·cous′ti·cal.** —**e·lec′tro·a·cous′ti·cal·ly,** *adv.*
e·lec·tro·a·cous·tics (i lek′trō ə ko͞o′stiks), *n.* (*construed as sing.*) the branch of electronics that deals with the conversion of electricity into acoustical energy and vice versa.
e·lec·tro·a·nal·y·sis (i lek′trō ə nal′i sis), *n.* analysis by electrochemical methods. —**e·lec·tro·an·a·lyt·ic** (i lek′trō-an′əlit′ik), **e·lec′tro·an′a·lyt′i·cal,** *adj.*
e·lec·tro·car·di·o·gram (i lek′trō kär′dē ə gram′), *n.* the graphic record produced by an electrocardiograph. Also called **EKG, E.K.G., ECG, E.C.G., cardiogram.**
e·lec·tro·car·di·o·graph (i lek′trō kär′dē ə graf′, -gräf′), *n.* a galvanometric device that detects and records the minute differences in potential between different parts of the body caused by heart action: used in the detection and diagnosis of heart disease. Also called **cardiograph.** —**e·lec·tro·car·di·o·graph·ic** (i lek′trō kär′dē ə graf′ik), *adj.* —**e·lec′tro·car′di·o·graph′i·cal·ly,** *adv.* —**e·lec·tro·car·di·og·ra·phy** (i lek′trō kär′dē og′rə fē), *n.*
e·lec·tro·chem·is·try (i lek′trō kem′i strē), *n.* the branch of chemistry that deals with the chemical changes produced by electricity and the production of electricity by chemical changes. —**e·lec·tro·chem·i·cal** (i lek′trō kem′i-kəl), *adj.* —**e·lec′tro·chem′i·cal·ly,** *adv.* —**e·lec′tro-chem′ist,** *n.*
e·lec·tro·cute (i lek′trə kyo͞ot′), *v.t.,* **-cut·ed, -cut·ing. 1.** to kill by electricity. **2.** to execute (a criminal) by electricity, as in an electric chair. [ELECTRO- + (EXE)CUTE] —**e·lec′-tro·cu′tion,** *n.*
e·lec·trode (i lek′trōd), *n.* *Elect.* a conductor through which a current enters or leaves an electric or electronic device, as an electrolytic cell, arc generator, vacuum tube, gaseous discharge tube, etc. [ELECTR- + -ODE[2]]
e·lec·tro·de·pos·it (i lek′trō di poz′it), *Physical Chem.* —*n.* **1.** a deposit, usually of metal, produced by electrolysis. —*v.t.* **2.** to deposit by electrolysis. —**e·lec·tro·dep·o·si·tion** (i lek′trō dep′ə zish′ən, -dē′pə-), *n.*
e·lec·tro·di·al·y·sis (i lek′trō dī al′i sis), *n., pl.* **-ses** (-sēz′). *Physical Chem.* dialysis in which electrodes of opposite charge are placed on either side of a membrane to accelerate diffusion.
e·lec·tro·dy·nam·ic (i lek′trō dī nam′ik), *adj.* **1.** pertaining to the force of electricity in motion. **2.** pertaining to electrodynamics. Also, **e·lec′tro·dy·nam′i·cal.**
e·lec·tro·dy·nam·ics (i lek′trō dī nam′iks), *n.* (*construed as sing.*) the branch of physics that deals with the interactions of electric, magnetic, and mechanical phenomena.
e·lec·tro·dy·na·mom·e·ter (i lek′trō dī′nə mom′i tər), *n.* an instrument that uses the interaction between the magnetic fields produced by the currents in two coils to measure current, voltage, or power.
e·lec·tro·en·ceph·a·lo·gram (i lek′trō en sef′ə lə gram′), *n.* a graphic record produced by an electroencephalograph. Also called **EEG, E.E.G.**
e·lec·tro·en·ceph·a·lo·graph (i lek′trō en sef′ə lə graf′, -gräf′), *n.* *Med.* an instrument for measuring and recording the electric activity of the brain. —**e·lec·tro·en·ceph·a·lo·graph·ic** (i lek′trō en sef′ə lə graf′ik), *adj.* —**e·lec·tro·en·ceph·a·log·ra·phy** (i lek′trō en sef′ə log′rə fē), *n.*
e·lec·tro·form (i lek′trə fôrm′), *v.t.* to form (an object) by the electrodeposition of a metal upon a mold.
e·lec·tro·form·ing (i lek′trō fôr′ming), *n.* the act or

process of forming a metallic object by electroplating a removable mandrel or matrix.

e·lec·tro·graph (i lek′trə graf′, -gräf′), *n.* **1.** a curve or plot automatically traced by the action of an electric device, as an electrometer or an electrically-controlled pen. **2.** an apparatus for engraving metal plates on cylinders used in printing. **3.** an apparatus for electrically transmitting pictures. **4.** a picture produced by such a device. —**e·lec·tro·graph·ic** (i lek′trō graf′ik), *adj.* —**e·lec·trog·ra·phy** (i lek-trog′rə fē, ē′lek-), *n.*

e·lec·tro·jet (i lek′trə jet′), *n.* a current of ions in the upper atmosphere, moving with respect to the surface of the earth, and causing various auroral phenomena.

e·lec·tro·ki·net·ics (i lek′trō ki net′iks, -kī-), *n.* (*construed as sing.*) the branch of physics that deals with electricity in motion. —**e·lec′tro·ki·net′ic,** *adj.*

e·lec·trol·o·gist (i lek trol′ə jist), *n.* a person skilled in the use of electrolysis for removing moles, warts, or excess hair. [ELECTRO(LYSIS) + -LOG(Y) + -IST]

e·lec·tro·lu·mi·nes·cence (i lek′trō lo͞o′mə nes′əns), *n.* luminescence produced by the activation of a dielectric phosphor by an alternating current. —**e·lec′tro·lu′mi·nes′cent,** *adj.*

e·lec·trol·y·sis (i lek trol′i sis, ē′lek-), *n.* **1.** the passage of an electric current through an electrolyte with subsequent migration of ions to the electrodes. **2.** the destruction of tumors, hair roots, etc., by an electric current.

e·lec·tro·lyte (i lek′trə līt′), *n.* **1.** a conducting medium in which the flow of current is accompanied by the movement of ions. **2.** *Physical Chem.* any substance that dissociates into ions when dissolved in a suitable medium or melted and thus forms a conductor of electricity.

e·lec·tro·lyt·ic (i lek′trə lit′ik), *adj.* **1.** pertaining to or derived by electrolysis. **2.** pertaining to an electrolyte. Also, **e·lec′tro·lyt′i·cal.** —**e·lec′tro·lyt′i·cal·ly,** *adv.*

elec′trolyt′ic cell′. See under **cell.** (def. 8).

e·lec·tro·lyze (i lek′trə līz′), *v.t.*, **-lyzed, -lyz·ing.** *Physical Chem.* to decompose by electrolysis. Also, *esp. Brit.*, **e·lec′tro·lyse′.** —**e·lec′tro·ly·za′tion,** *n.* —**e·lec′tro·lyz′er,** *n.*

e·lec·tro·mag·net (i lek′trō mag′nit), *n.* a device consisting of an iron or steel core that is magnetized by electric current in a coil surrounding it.

e·lec·tro·mag·net·ic (i lek′trō mag-net′ik), *adj.* **1.** of or pertaining to an electromagnet. **2.** pertaining to electromagnetism.

Electromagnet A, DC power source or battery; B, Core; C, Coil carrying current; D, Armature; E, Load

electromagnet′ic radia′tion, *Physics.* radiation consisting of electromagnetic waves, including radio waves, light, x-ray, and gamma rays.

e·lec·tro·mag·net·ics (i lek′trō-mag net′iks), *n.* (*construed as sing.*) electromagnetism (def. 2).

elec′tromagnet′ic spec′trum, the entire spectrum of all kinds of electric and magnetic radiation, including the visible spectrum.

elec′tromagnet′ic wave′, *Physics.* a wave produced by the acceleration of an electric charge and propagated by the periodic variation of intensities of usually perpendicular electric and magnetic fields.

e·lec·tro·mag·net·ism (i lek′trō mag′ni tiz′əm), *n.* **1.** the phenomena associated with the relations between electric current and magnetism. **2.** Also, **electromagnetics.** the science that deals with these phenomena.

e·lec·tro·me·chan·i·cal (i lek′trō mə kan′i kəl), *adj.* of or pertaining to mechanical devices or systems electrically actuated, as by a solenoid.

e·lec·tro·met·al·lur·gy (i lek′trō met′əlûr′jē, -mə tal′ər jē), *n.* the branch of metallurgy dealing with the processing of metals by means of electricity. —**e·lec′tro·met′al·lur′gi·cal,** *adj.* —**e·lec′tro·met′al·lur′gist,** *n.*

e·lec·trom·e·ter (i lek trom′i tər, ē′lek-), *n.* a device for determining a potential difference between two charged bodies by measuring the electrostatic force between them. —**e·lec·tro·met·ric** (i lek′trō me′trik), *adj.*

e·lec·tro·mo·tive (i lek′trə mō′tiv), *adj.* pertaining to, producing, or tending to produce a flow of electricity.

elec′tromo′tive force′, *Elect.* the potential difference between the terminals of a source of electrical energy; the energy per unit of charge passing through the source: expressed in volts. *Abbr.:* emf; *Symbol:* E

e·lec·tro·mo·tor (i lek′trə mō′tər), *n.* an electric motor.

e·lec·tron (i lek′tron), *n.* **1.** Also called **negatron.** *Physics, Chem.* an elementary particle that is a fundamental constituent of matter, having a negative charge of 1.602×10^{-19} coulomb, a mass of 9.108×10^{-31} kilogram, and spin of ½, and existing independently or as the component outside the nucleus of an atom. **2.** *Elect.* a unit of charge equal to the charge on one electron. [< Gk *ēlektron* amber]

elec′tron cam′era, *Electronics.* an apparatus that converts an optical image into a corresponding electric current by electronic means without the intervention of mechanical scanning.

e·lec·tro·neg·a·tive (i lek′trō neg′ə tiv), *adj.* *Physical Chem.* **1.** containing negative electricity; tending to migrate to the positive pole in electrolysis. **2.** assuming negative potential when in contact with a dissimilar substance. **3.** nonmetallic. —**e·lec′tro·neg′a·tiv′i·ty,** *n.*

elec′tron gun′, *Television.* the cathode in a cathode ray tube that emits electrons, and the surrounding electrostatic or electromagnetic apparatus that controls and focuses the electron stream.

e·lec·tron·ic (i lek tron′ik, ē′lek-), *adj.* **1.** of or pertaining to electronics or to devices, circuits, or systems developed through electronics. **2.** of or pertaining to electrons or to an electron. **3.** (of a musical instrument) using electric or electronic means to produce or modify the sound. —**e·lec·tron′i·cal·ly,** *adv.*

electron′ic da′ta proc′essing, the use of electronic computers in the processing of information. *Abbr.:* EDP

electron′ic mail′, messages from one individual to another sent via telecommunications links between computers or terminals.

electron′ic mu′sic, electronically produced sounds recorded on tape, and arranged into combinations by the composer.

e·lec·tron·ics (i lek tron′iks, ē′lek-), *n.* (*construed as sing.*) the science dealing with the development and application of devices and systems involving the flow of electrons in a vacuum, in gaseous media, and in semiconductors.

electron′ic spread′sheet, a type of software for microcomputers that offers the user a visual display of a simulated work sheet and the means of using it for financial plans, budgets, etc.

electron′ic surveil′lance, the gathering of information by surreptitious use of electronic devices, esp. by wiretapping, as in crime detection, espionage, etc.

elec′tron lens′, a combination of electric and magnetic fields, used to focus streams of electrons.

elec′tron mi′croscope, a microscope of extremely high power that uses beams of electrons instead of rays of light, the magnified image being formed on a fluorescent screen or recorded on a photographic plate.

elec′tron op′tics, the study and use of the physical and optical properties of beams of electrons under the influence of electric or magnetic fields.

elec′tron tel′escope, a telescope in which an invisible infrared image of a distant object is focused on the photosensitive cathode of an image converter tube.

elec′tron tube′, an electronic device that typically consists of a sealed glass bulb containing two or more electrodes: used to generate, amplify, and rectify electric oscillations and alternating currents. Cf. **gas tube, vacuum tube.**

e·lec·tron-volt (i lek′tron vōlt′), *n.* *Physics.* a unit of energy, equal to the energy acquired by an electron accelerating through a potential difference of one volt and equivalent to 1.602×10^{-19} joules. *Abbr.:* EV, ev

e·lec·tro·pho·re·sis (i lek′trō fə rē′sis), *n.* *Physical Chem.* the motion of colloidal particles suspended in a fluid medium, due to the influence of an electric field on the medium. Also called **cataphoresis.** [ELECTRO- + Gk *phórēsis* a being borne; see -PHORE, -SIS] —**e·lec·tro·pho·ret·ic** (i lek′trō fə ret′ik), *adj.*

e·lec·troph·o·rus (i lek trof′ər əs, ē′lek-), *n.*, *pl.* **-o·ri** (-ə rī′). a device for generating static electricity by means of induction. [ELECTRO- + -*phorus*, Latinization of -PHORE]

e·lec·tro·plate (i lek′trə plāt′), *v.*, **-plat·ed, -plat·ing,** *n.* —*v.t.* **1.** to coat with a metal by electrolysis. —*n.* **2.** electroplated articles. —**e·lec′tro·plat′er,** *n.*

e·lec·tro·pos·i·tive (i lek′trə poz′i tiv), *adj.* *Physical Chem.* **1.** containing positive electricity; tending to migrate to the negative pole in electrolysis. **2.** assuming positive potential when in contact with a dissimilar substance. **3.** basic, as an element or group.

e·lec·tro·scope (i lek′trə skōp′), *n.* a device, usually consisting of two pieces of gold leaf enclosed in a glass-walled chamber, for detecting the presence and determining the sign of electric charges by means of electrostatic attraction and repulsion. —**e·lec·tro·scop·ic** (i lek′trə skop′ik), *adj.*

e·lec·tro·shock (i lek′trə shok′), *n.* *Psychiatry.* shock therapy administered by means of electrical currents.

e·lec·tro·stat·ic (i lek′trə stat′ik), *adj.* *Elect.* of or pertaining to static electricity. —**e·lec′tro·stat′i·cal·ly,** *adv.*

elec′trostat′ic gen′erator, *Physics, Elect.* See **Van de Graaff generator.**

e·lec·tro·stat·ics (i lek′trə stat′iks), *n.* (*construed as sing.*) the branch of physics dealing with electric phenomena not associated with electricity in motion.

e·lec·tro·sur·ger·y (i lek′trō sûr′jə rē), *n.* the use in surgery of an electric instrument, as an acusector, or of an electric current; surgical diathermy. —**e·lec·tro·sur·gi·cal** (i lek′trō sûr′ji kəl), *adj.*

e·lec·tro·tech·nics (i lek′trō tek′niks), *n.* (*construed as sing.*) the study or science of practical and industrial applications of electricity. Also, **e·lec·tro·tech·nol·o·gy** (i lek′trō-tek nol′ə jē).

e·lec·tro·ther·a·peu·tics (i lek′trō ther′ə pyo͞o′tiks), *n.* (*construed as sing.*) therapeutics based on the curative effects of electricity. —**e·lec′tro·ther′a·peu′tic,** *adj.*

e·lec·tro·ther·a·py (i lek′trō ther′ə pē), *n.* treatment of diseases by means of electricity; electrotherapeutics. —**e·lec′tro·ther′a·pist,** *n.*

e·lec·trot·o·nus (i lek trot′ənəs, ē′lek-), *n.* *Physiol.* the altered state of a nerve during the passage of an electric current through it. [< NL; see ELECTRO-, TONUS] —**e·lec·tro·ton·ic** (i lek′trə ton′ik), *adj.*

e·lec·tro·type (i lek′trə tīp′), *n.*, *v.*, **-typed, -typ·ing.** —*n.* **1.** facsimile, for use in printing, of a block of type, an engraving, or the like, consisting of a thin copper or nickel shell deposited by electrolytic action in a wax, lead, or plastic mold of the original and backed with lead alloy. **2.** electrotypy. —*v.t.* **3.** to make an electrotype or electrotypes of. —**e·lec′tro·typ′er,** *n.*

e·lec·tro·typ·y (i lek′trə tī′pē), *n.* the process of making electrotypes. —**e·lec·tro·typ·ic** (i lek′trō tip′ik), *adj.* —**e·lec·tro·typ·ist** (i lek′trō tī′pist), *n.*

e·lec·tro·va·lence (i lek′trō vā′ləns), *n.* *Chem.* **1.** the valance of an ion, equal to the number of positive or negative charges acquired by an atom through a loss or gain of electrons. **2.** Also called **elec′trova′lent bond′, ionic bond.** the bond formed between two ions through the transfer of electrons. Also, **e·lec′tro·va′len·cy.** —**e·lec′tro·va′lent,** *adj.* —**e·lec′tro·va′lent·ly,** *adv.*

e·lec·trum (i lek′trəm), *n.* **1.** an amber-colored alloy of gold and silver used in ancient times. **2.** German silver; nickel silver. [< L < Gk *ēlektron*]

e·lec·tu·ar·y (i lek′cho͞o er′ē), *n.*, *pl.* **-ar·ies.** *Pharm., Vet. Med.* a pasty mass comprised of a medicine, usually in powder form, mixed in a palatable medium, as syrup: used esp. for animals and administered by application to the teeth, tongue, or gums. [ME *electuarie* < LL *ēlect(u)ārī(um)* irreg. < Gk *ekleiktón* electuary (n. use of neut. of *ekleiktós*, verbal adj. of *ekleíchein* to lick out) + L *-ārium* -ARY]

el·ee·mos·y·nar·y (el′ə mos′ə ner′ē, -moz′-, el′ē ə-), *adj.* of, pertaining to, or supported by gifts, charity, or charitable donations. [< ML *eleēmosynāri(us)* = LL *eleēmosyn(a)* (see ALMS) + *-ārius* -ARY]

el·e·gance (el′ə gəns), *n.* **1.** elegant quality: *elegance of dress.* **2.** something elegant; a refinement. [< MF < L *ēlegantia* choiceness]

el·e·gan·cy (el′ə gən sē), *n., pl.* **-cies.** elegance. [< L *ēlegantia*]

el·e·gant (el′ə gənt), *adj.* **1.** tastefully fine or luxurious in dress, style, design, etc.: *elegant furnishings.* **2.** gracefully refined and dignified, as in tastes, habits, or literary style. **3.** nice, choice, or pleasingly superior in quality or kind, as a preparation or process. **4.** excellent; fine; superior: *an absolutely elegant wine.* [late ME < L *ēlegant-* (s. of *ēlegāns*) tasteful, choice = *ēleg-* (akin to *ēlig-* select; see ELECT) + *-ant-* -ANT; orig. prp. of lost v.] —**el′e·gant·ly,** *adv.* —**Syn. 1.** See **fine. 2.** polished, courtly. —**Ant. 1.** ordinary.

el·e·gi·ac (el′ə jī′ək, -ak, i lē′jē ak′), *adj.* Also, **el′e·gi′a·cal. 1.** expressing sorrow or lamentation: *elegiac strains.* **2.** used in, suitable for, or resembling an elegy. **3.** *Class. Pros.* noting a distich the first line of which is a dactylic hexameter and the second a pentameter. —*n.* **4.** an elegiac verse. **5.** a poem or poems in such verses. [< L *elegīac(us)* < Gk *elegeiakós*]

elegi′ac pentam′eter, *Class. Pros.* pentameter (def. 2).

el·e·gise (el′i jīz′), *v.t., v.i.,* **-gised, -gis·ing.** *Chiefly Brit.* elegize.

el·e·gist (el′i jist), *n.* the author of an elegy.

e·le·git (i lē′jit), *n. Law.* a writ of execution against a judgment debtor's goods, property, or land, held by the judgment creditor until payment of the debt, as from rents on the land. [< L: he has chosen, perf. 3rd pers. sing. ind. of *ēligere;* so called from wording of writ]

el·e·gize (el′i jīz′), *v.,* **-gized, -giz·ing.** —*v.t.* **1.** to lament in or as if in an elegy. —*v.i.* **2.** to compose an elegy. Also, *esp. Brit.,* **elegise.**

el·e·gy (el′i jē), *n., pl.* **-gies. 1.** a mournful, melancholy, or plaintive poem, esp. a lament for the dead. **2.** poetry or a poem written in elegiac meter. **3.** a sad or mournful musical composition. [< L *elegī(a)* < Gk *elegeía,* orig. neut. pl. of *elegeîos* elegiac = *éleg(os)* a lament + *-eios* adj. suffix]

elem., 1. element. **2.** elements.

el·e·ment (el′ə mənt), *n.* **1.** a component or constituent of a whole or one of the parts into which a whole may be resolved by analysis. **2.** one of the substances, esp. earth, water, air, and fire, formerly regarded as constituting the material universe. **3.** the natural habitat of something: *Water is the element of fish.* **4.** the sphere of activity, environment, etc., regarded as naturally suited to any person or thing: *to be in one's element.* **5. elements, a.** atmospheric agencies or forces, as wind, rain, and cold: *a ruddy complexion from exposure to the elements.* **b.** the rudimentary principles of an art, science, etc.: *the elements of grammar.* **c.** the bread and wine of the Eucharist. **6.** *Chem.* any of a class of substances, of which 103 are now recognized, that cannot be separated into simpler substances by chemical means. See **Periodic Table of the Elements** on the following page. **7.** *Math.* **a.** an infinitesimal and indivisible part of a given quantity. **b.** an entity that satisfies all the conditions of belonging to a given set. **8.** *Geom.* one of the points, lines, planes, or other geometrical forms of which a figure is composed. **9.** *Elect.* an electric device with terminals for connection to other electrical devices. **10.** *Radio.* an electrode in a vacuum tube. [ME < L *element(um)* letter of the alphabet, first principle, rudiment]
—**Syn. 1.** ELEMENT, COMPONENT, CONSTITUENT, INGREDIENT refer to the units which build up substances and compounds or mixtures. ELEMENT denotes a fundamental, ultimate part: *the elements of matter, of a discussion.* COMPONENT and CONSTITUENT denote that which goes into the making of a compound, COMPONENT suggesting one of a number of parts, and CONSTITUENT an active and necessary participation: *The turntable and speaker are components of an audio system. Hydrogen and oxygen are the constituents of water.* INGREDIENT denotes something essential or nonessential which enters into a mixture or compound: *the ingredients of a cake.* **4.** medium, milieu.

el·e·men·tal (el′ə men′tᵊl), *adj.* **1.** of the nature of an ultimate constituent; simple; uncompounded. **2.** pertaining to rudiments or first principles. **3.** starkly simple or primitive; basic: *a spare, elemental prose style; hate, lust, and other elemental emotions.* **4.** of, pertaining to, or of the nature of the four elements. **5.** pertaining to the agencies, forces, or phenomena of physical nature. **6.** comparable to the great forces of nature, as in power or magnitude: *elemental grandeur.* **7.** pertaining to chemical elements. [< ML *elementāl(is)*] —**el′e·men′tal·ly,** *adv.*

el·e·men·ta·ry (el′ə men′tə rē, -trē), *adj.* **1.** pertaining to or dealing with elements, rudiments, or first principles: *elementary education; an elementary grammar.* **2.** of or pertaining to an elementary school: *elementary teachers.* **3.** of the nature of an ultimate constituent; simple or uncompounded. **4.** pertaining to the four elements or to the great forces of nature; elemental. **5.** (of a function) expressible by the operations of addition, subtraction, multiplication, division, or taking powers and roots applied a finite number of times each. **6.** *Chem.* of or noting one or more elements. [ME *elementari(e)* < L *elementāri(us)*] —**el·e·men·ta·ri·ly** (el′ə men ter′ə lē), *adv.* —**el′e·men′ta·ri·ness,** *n.*
—**Syn. 1.** ELEMENTARY, PRIMARY, RUDIMENTARY refer to what is basic and fundamental. ELEMENTARY refers to the introductory, simple, easy facts, steps, or parts of a subject that must be learned first in order to understand succeeding ones: *elementary facts about geography; elementary arithmetic.* PRIMARY may mean much the same as ELEMENTARY; however, it usually emphasizes the idea of what comes first even more than that of simplicity: *the primary grades in school.* RUDIMENTARY applies to what is undeveloped or imperfect: *a rudimentary form of government.*

el′emen′tary par′ticle, *Physics.* any of several entities that are less complex than an atom and are the constituents of all matter.

elemen′tary school′, the lowest school giving formal instruction, teaching elementary subjects and extending variously from six to eight years. Also called **primary school.**

el·e·mi (el′ə mē), *n., pl.* **-mis.** any of various fragrant resins used chiefly in the manufacture of varnishes, ointments, and perfumes. Also called **gum elemi.** [short for *gum elemi* < NL *gummi elimī;* cf. Ar *al lāmi* the elemi]

e·len·chus (i leng′kəs), *n., pl.* **-chi** (-kī, -kē). a logical refutation; an argument that refutes another. [< L < Gk *élenchos* refutation] —**e·lenc·tic** (i lengk′tik), *adj.*

el·e·op·tene (el′ē op′tēn), *n. Chem.* the liquid part of a volatile oil (opposed to *stearoptene*). Also, **elaeoptene.** [< Gk *élaio(n)* oil + *ptēn(ós)* winged, akin to *pétesthai* to fly]

el·e·phant (el′ə fənt), *n., pl.* **-phants,** (*esp. collectively*) **-phant. 1.** any of several large, five-toed mammals, with the nose and upper lip elongated into a prehensile trunk, of the family *Elephantidae* of Africa, having large, flapping ears and tusks of ivory in both males and females, or, *Elephas* of India, having comparatively small ears and tusks in the males only. **2.** See **white elephant. 3.** *Chiefly Brit.* a size of drawing or writing paper, 23 × 28 inches. [ME < L *elephant(us)* < Gk *elephant-* (s. of *eléphās*) elephant; r. ME *olifaunt* < AF] —**el′e·phan·toid′,** *adj.*

Elephant (African), *Loxodonta africana* (11 ft. high at shoulder; tusks 6 to 8 ft.)

el′ephant gun′, a gun of very large caliber, as .410 or greater, used in killing elephants or other big game.

el·e·phan·ti·a·sis (el′ə fən tī′ə sis, -fan-), *n. Pathol.* a chronic disease resulting from lymphatic obstruction, characterized by enormous enlargement of the parts affected, esp. of the legs and scrotum, and usually caused by a filarial infection. [< L < Gk *elephantíasis.* See ELEPHANT, -IASIS] —**el·e·phan·ti·as·ic** (el′e fan′tē as′ik, -fən tī′ə sik′), *adj.*

Elephant (Indian), *Elephas maximus* (9 ft. high at shoulder; tusks 4 to 5 ft.)

el·e·phan·tine (el′ə fan′tin, -tīn, -tēn), *adj.* **1.** pertaining to or resembling an elephant. **2.** huge; ponderous; clumsy: *elephantine movements; elephantine humor.* [< L *elephantin(us)* < Gk *elephántinos*]

el·e·phant's-ear (el′ə fənts ēr′), *n.* the taro plant.

el·e·phant's-foot (el′ə fənts fŏŏt′), *n., pl.* **-foots.** any climbing vine of the genus *Testudinaria,* of southern Africa, as *T. Elephantipes,* having a massive, edible, yamlike tuber. Also called **Hottentot's bread.**

El·eu·sin′i·an mys′teries (el′yŏŏ sin′ē ən), the mysteries, celebrated annually at Eleusis and Athens in ancient times, in memory of the abduction and return of Persephone and in honor of Demeter and Bacchus. [< L *Eleusini(us)* < Gk *Eleusínios* of Eleusis + -AN]

E·leu·sis (i lōō′sis), *n.* a city in ancient Greece, in Attica.

El·eu·the·ri·us (el′yŏŏ thēr′ē əs), *n.* **Saint,** pope A.D. 175–189.

el·e·vate (el′ə vāt′), *v.,* **-vat·ed, -vat·ing,** *adj.* —*v.t.* **1.** to move or raise to a higher place or position; lift up. **2.** to raise to a higher state, rank, or office; exalt; promote: *to elevate an archbishop to cardinal.* **3.** to raise to a higher intellectual or spiritual level: *to elevate the mind.* **4.** to raise the spirits; put in high spirits. —*adj.* **5.** *Archaic.* raised; elevated. [< L *ēlevāt(us)* lightened, lifted up (ptp. of *ēlevāre*) = *ē-* E- + *lev(is)* light + *-ātus* -ATE[1]] —**el′e·vat′ing·ly,** *adv.*
—**Syn. 1.** lift, hoist. **2.** promote, advance, dignify. ELEVATE, ENHANCE, EXALT mean to raise or make higher in some respect. To ELEVATE is to raise something up to a relatively higher level, position, or state: *to elevate the living standards of a group.* To ENHANCE is to add to the attractions or desirability of something: *Landscaping enhances the beauty of the grounds. Paved streets enhance the value of real estate.* To EXALT is to raise very high in rank, character, estimation, mood, etc.: *A king is exalted above his subjects.*

el·e·vat·ed (el′ə vā′tid), *adj.* **1.** raised up, esp. above the ground: *an elevated platform.* **2.** exalted or noble: *elevated thoughts.* **3.** elated; joyful. —*n.* **4.** an elevated railroad.

el′evated rail′road, a railway system operating on an elevated structure, as over streets. Also called **el.**

el·e·va·tion (el′ə vā′shən), *n.* **1.** the height to which something is elevated or to which it rises. **2.** the altitude of a place above sea level or ground level. **3.** an elevated place, thing, or part; an eminence. **4.** loftiness; grandeur or dignity; nobleness: *elevation of mind.* **5.** the act of elevating. **6.** the state of being elevated. **7.** *Archit.* a drawing or design that represents an object or structure as being projected geometrically on a vertical plane parallel to one of its sides. **8.** *Survey.* **a.** the angle between the line from an observer or instrument to an object above him or it and a horizontal line. **b.** the distance above a datum level. **9. the Elevation,** *Rom. Cath. Ch.* the lifting of the Eucharistic elements immediately after consecration, for adoration. [< L *ēlevātiōn-* (s. of *ēlevātiō*) (see ELEVATE, -ION); r. ME *elevacioun* < AF]
—**Syn. 1.** See **height. 3.** height; hill; mountain; plateau.

el·e·va·tor (el′ə vā′tər), *n.* **1.** a person or thing that elevates or raises. **2.** a moving platform or cage for conveying goods, persons, etc., from one level to another, as in a building. **3.** a building in which grain is stored and handled by means of mechanical elevator and conveyor devices. **4.** *Aeron.* a hinged horizontal surface on an airplane or the like,

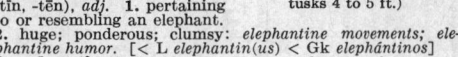

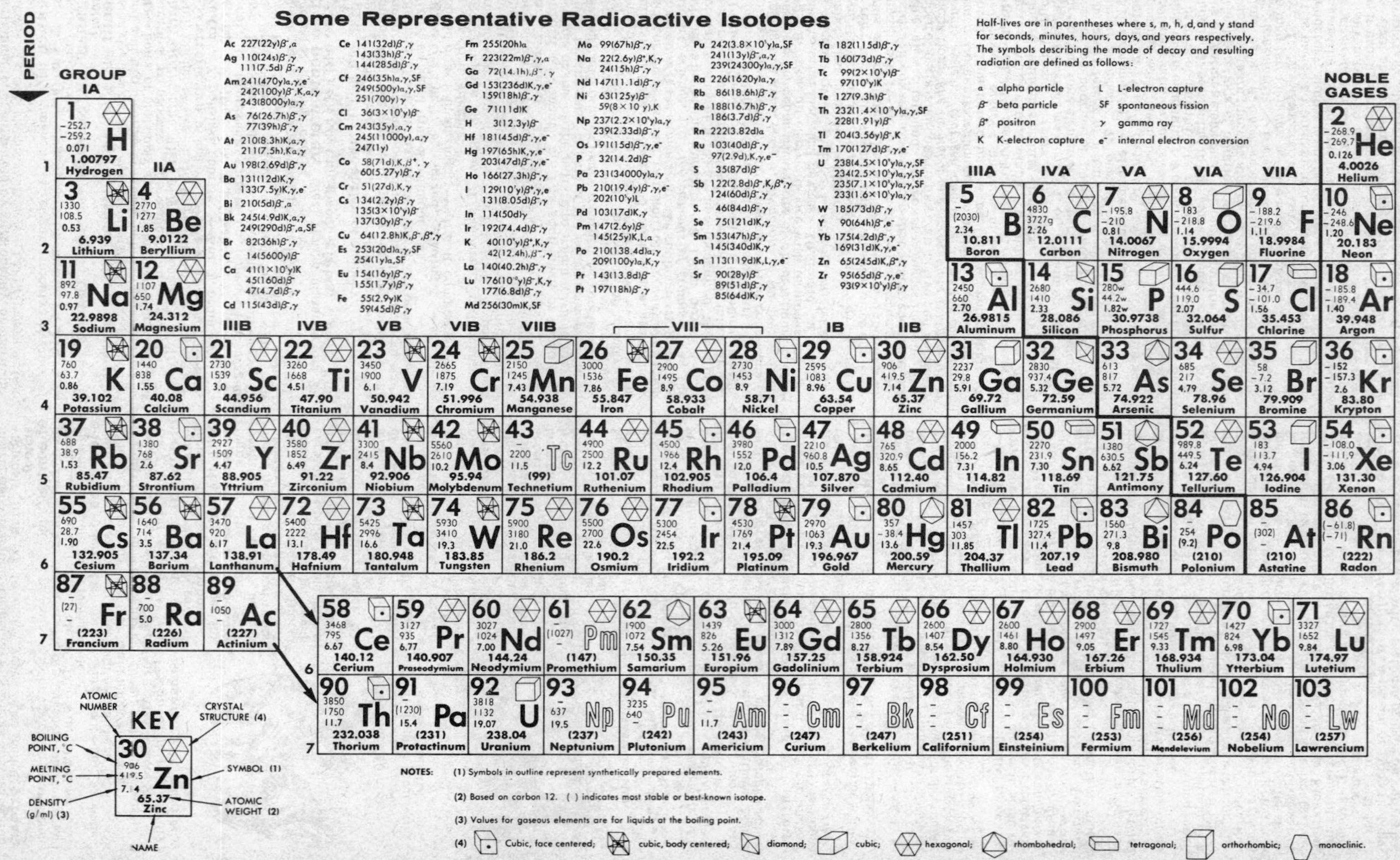
PERIODIC TABLE OF THE ELEMENTS
Some Representative Radioactive Isotopes
Ac 227(22y)β⁻,α
Ag 110(24s)β⁻,γ 111(7.5d)β⁻,γ
Am 241(470y)α,γ,e⁻ 242(100y)β⁻,K,α,γ 243(8000y)α,γ
As 76(26.7h)β⁻,γ 77(39h)β⁻,γ
At 210(8.3h)K,α,γ 211(7.5h)K,α,γ
Au 198(2.69d)β⁻,γ
Ba 131(12d)K,γ 133(7.5y)K,γ,e⁻
Bi 210(5d)β⁻,α
Bk 245(4.9d)K,α,γ 249(290d)β⁻,α,SF
Br 82(36h)β⁻,γ
C 14(5600y)β⁻
Ca 41(1×10⁵y)K 45(160d)β⁻ 47(4.7d)β⁻,γ
Cd 115(43d)β⁻,γ
Ce 141(32d)β⁻,γ 143(33h)β⁻,γ 144(285d)β⁻,γ
Cf 246(35h)α,γ,SF 249(500y)α,γ,SF 251(700y)γ
Cl 36(3×10⁵y)β⁻
Cm 243(35y)α,γ 245(11000y)α,γ 247(1y)
Co 58(71d)K,β⁺,γ 60(5.27y)β⁻,γ
Cr 51(27d)K,γ
Cs 134(2.2y)β⁻,γ 135(3×10⁶y)β⁻ 137(30y)β⁻,γ
Cu 64(12.8h)K,β⁻,β⁺,γ
Es 253(20d)α,γ,SF 254(1y)α,SF
Eu 154(16y)β⁻,γ 155(1.7y)β⁻,γ
Fe 55(2.9y)K 59(45d)β⁻,γ
Fm 255(20h)α
Fr 223(22m)β⁻,γ,α
Ga 72(14.1h)β⁻,γ
Gd 153(236d)K,γ,e⁻ 159(18h)β⁻,γ
Ge 71(11d)K
H 3(12.3y)β⁻
Hf 181(45d)β⁻,γ,e⁻
Hg 197(65h)K,γ,e⁻ 203(47d)β⁻,γ,e⁻
Ho 166(27.3h)β⁻,γ
I 129(10⁷y)β⁻,γ,e 131(8.05d)β⁻,γ
In 114(50d)γ
Ir 192(74.4d)β⁻,γ
K 40(10⁹y)β⁻,K,γ 42(12.4h)β⁻,γ
La 140(40.2h)β⁻,γ
Lu 176(10¹⁰y)β⁻,K,γ 177(6.8d)β⁻,γ
Md 256(30m)K,SF
Mo 99(67h)β⁻,γ
Na 22(2.6y)β⁺,K,γ 24(15h)β⁻,γ
Nd 147(11.1d)β⁻,γ
Ni 63(125y)β⁻ 59(8×10⁴y)K
Np 237(2.2×10⁶y)α,γ 239(2.33d)β⁻,γ
Os 191(15d)β⁻,γ,e⁻
P 32(14.2d)β⁻
Pa 231(34000y)α,γ
Pb 210(19.4y)β⁻,γ,e⁻ 202(10⁵y)L
Pd 103(17d)K,γ
Pm 147(2.6y)β⁻ 145(25y)K,L,α
Po 210(138.4d)α,γ 209(100y)α,K,γ
Pr 143(13.8d)β⁻
Pt 197(18h)β⁻,γ
Pu 242(3.8×10⁵y)α,SF 241(13y)β⁻,α,γ 239(24300y)α,γ,SF
Ra 226(1620y)α,γ
Rb 86(18.6h)β⁻,γ
Re 188(16.7h)β⁻,γ 186(3.7d)β⁻,γ
Rn 222(3.82d)α
Ru 103(40d)β⁻,γ 97(2.9d)K,γ,e⁻
S 35(87d)β⁻
Sb 122(2.8d)β⁻,K,β⁺,γ 124(60d)β⁻,γ
S 46(84d)β⁻,γ
Se 75(121d)K,γ
Sm 153(47h)β⁻,γ 145(340d)K,γ
Sn 113(119d)K,L,γ,e⁻
Sr 90(28y)β⁻ 89(51d)β⁻,γ 85(64d)K,γ
Ta 182(115d)β⁻,γ
Tb 160(73d)β⁻,γ
Tc 99(2×10⁵y)β⁻ 97(10⁶y)K
Te 127(9.3h)β⁻
Th 232(1.4×10¹⁰y)α,γ,SF 228(1.91y)β⁻
Tl 204(3.56y)β⁻,K
Tm 170(127d)β⁻,γ,e⁻
U 238(4.5×10⁹y)α,γ,SF 234(2.5×10⁵y)α,γ,SF 235(7.1×10⁸y)α,γ,SF 233(1.6×10⁵y)α,γ
W 185(73d)β⁻,γ
Y 90(64h)β⁻,e⁻
Yb 175(4.2d)β⁻,γ 169(31d)K,γ
Zn 65(245d)K,β⁺,γ
Zr 95(65d)β⁻,γ,e⁻ 93(9×10⁵y)β⁻,γ
Half-lives are in parentheses where s, m, h, d, and y stand for seconds, minutes, hours, days, and years respectively. The symbols describing the mode of decay and resulting radiation are defined as follows:
α alpha particle
β⁻ beta particle
β⁺ positron
K K-electron capture
L L-electron capture
SF spontaneous fission
γ gamma ray
e⁻ internal electron conversion
PERIOD
GROUP IA
IIA
IIIB
IVB
VB
VIB
VIIB
VIII
IB
IIB
IIIA
IVA
VA
VIA
VIIA
NOBLE GASES
1 H −252.7 −259.2 0.071 1.00797 Hydrogen
2 He −268.9 −269.7 0.126 4.0026 Helium
3 Li 1330 108.5 0.53 6.939 Lithium
4 Be 2770 1277 1.85 9.0122 Beryllium
5 B (2030) 2.34 10.811 Boron
6 C 4830 3727g 2.26 12.0111 Carbon
7 N −195.8 −210 0.81 14.0067 Nitrogen
8 O −183 −218.8 1.14 15.9994 Oxygen
9 F −188.2 −219.6 1.11 18.9984 Fluorine
10 Ne −246 −248.6 1.20 20.183 Neon
11 Na 892 97.8 0.97 22.9898 Sodium
12 Mg 1107 650 1.74 24.312 Magnesium
13 Al 2450 660 2.70 26.9815 Aluminum
14 Si 2680 1410 2.33 28.086 Silicon
15 P 280w 44.2w 1.82w 30.9738 Phosphorus
16 S 444.6 119.0 2.07 32.064 Sulfur
17 Cl −34.7 −101.0 1.56 35.453 Chlorine
18 Ar −185.8 −189.4 1.40 39.948 Argon
19 K 760 63.7 0.86 39.102 Potassium
20 Ca 1440 838 1.55 40.08 Calcium
21 Sc 2730 1539 3.0 44.956 Scandium
22 Ti 3260 1668 4.51 47.90 Titanium
23 V 3450 1900 6.1 50.942 Vanadium
24 Cr 2665 1875 7.19 51.996 Chromium
25 Mn 2150 1245 7.43 54.938 Manganese
26 Fe 3000 1536 7.86 55.847 Iron
27 Co 2900 1495 8.9 58.933 Cobalt
28 Ni 2730 1453 8.9 58.71 Nickel
29 Cu 2595 1083 8.96 63.54 Copper
30 Zn 906 419.5 7.14 65.37 Zinc
31 Ga 2237 29.8 5.91 69.72 Gallium
32 Ge 2830 937.4 5.32 72.59 Germanium
33 As 613 817 5.72 74.922 Arsenic
34 Se 685 217 4.79 78.96 Selenium
35 Br 58 −7.2 3.12 79.909 Bromine
36 Kr −152 −157.3 2.6 83.80 Krypton
37 Rb 688 38.9 1.53 85.47 Rubidium
38 Sr 1380 768 2.6 87.62 Strontium
39 Y 2927 1509 4.47 88.905 Yttrium
40 Zr 3580 1852 6.49 91.22 Zirconium
41 Nb 3300 2415 8.4 92.906 Niobium
42 Mo 5560 2610 10.2 95.94 Molybdenum
43 Tc — 2200 11.5 (99) Technetium
44 Ru 4900 2500 12.2 101.07 Ruthenium
45 Rh 4500 1966 12.4 102.905 Rhodium
46 Pd 3980 1552 12.0 106.4 Palladium
47 Ag 2210 960.8 10.5 107.870 Silver
48 Cd 765 320.9 8.65 112.40 Cadmium
49 In 2000 156.2 7.31 114.82 Indium
50 Sn 2270 231.9 7.30 118.69 Tin
51 Sb 1380 630.5 6.62 121.75 Antimony
52 Te 989.8 449.5 6.24 127.60 Tellurium
53 I 183 113.7 4.94 126.904 Iodine
54 Xe −108.0 −111.9 3.06 131.30 Xenon
55 Cs 690 28.7 1.90 132.905 Cesium
56 Ba 1640 714 3.5 137.34 Barium
57 La 3470 920 6.17 138.91 Lanthanum
72 Hf 5400 2222 13.1 178.49 Hafnium
73 Ta 5425 2996 16.6 180.948 Tantalum
74 W 5930 3410 19.3 183.85 Tungsten
75 Re 5900 3180 21.0 186.2 Rhenium
76 Os 5500 2700 22.6 190.2 Osmium
77 Ir 5300 2454 22.5 192.2 Iridium
78 Pt 4530 1769 21.4 195.09 Platinum
79 Au 2970 1063 19.3 196.967 Gold
80 Hg 357 −38.4 13.6 200.59 Mercury
81 Tl 1457 303 11.85 204.37 Thallium
82 Pb 1725 327.4 11.4 207.19 Lead
83 Bi 1560 271.3 9.8 208.980 Bismuth
84 Po — 254 (9.2) (210) Polonium
85 At — (302) — (210) Astatine
86 Rn (−61.8) (−71) — (222) Radon
87 Fr — (27) — (223) Francium
88 Ra — 700 5.0 (226) Radium
89 Ac — 1050 — (227) Actinium
58 Ce 3468 795 6.67 140.12 Cerium
59 Pr 3127 935 6.77 140.907 Praseodymium
60 Nd 3027 1024 7.00 144.24 Neodymium
61 Pm — (1027) — (147) Promethium
62 Sm 1900 1072 7.54 150.35 Samarium
63 Eu 1439 826 5.26 151.96 Europium
64 Gd 3000 1312 7.89 157.25 Gadolinium
65 Tb 2800 1356 8.27 158.924 Terbium
66 Dy 2600 1407 8.54 162.50 Dysprosium
67 Ho 2600 1461 8.80 164.930 Holmium
68 Er 2900 1497 9.05 167.26 Erbium
69 Tm 1727 1545 9.33 168.934 Thulium
70 Yb 1427 824 6.98 173.04 Ytterbium
71 Lu 3327 1652 9.84 174.97 Lutetium
90 Th 3850 1750 11.7 232.038 Thorium
91 Pa — (1230) 15.4 (231) Protactinium
92 U 3818 1132 19.07 238.04 Uranium
93 Np — 637 19.5 (237) Neptunium
94 Pu 3235 640 — (242) Plutonium
95 Am — — 11.7 (243) Americium
96 Cm (247) Curium
97 Bk (247) Berkelium
98 Cf (251) Californium
99 Es (254) Einsteinium
100 Fm (253) Fermium
101 Md (256) Mendelevium
102 No (254) Nobelium
103 Lw (257) Lawrencium
KEY
ATOMIC NUMBER
CRYSTAL STRUCTURE (4)
BOILING POINT, °C
MELTING POINT, °C
DENSITY (g/ml) (3)
SYMBOL (1)
ATOMIC WEIGHT (2)
NAME
30 906 419.5 7.14 Zn 65.37 Zinc
NOTES:
(1) Symbols in outline represent synthetically prepared elements.
(2) Based on carbon 12. ( ) indicates most stable or best-known isotope.
(3) Values for gaseous elements are for liquids at the boiling point.
(4) Cubic, face centered; cubic, body centered; diamond; cubic; hexagonal; rhombohedral; tetragonal; orthorhombic; monoclinic.

used to control the longitudinal inclination and usually placed at the tail end of the fuselage. [< LL]

e·lev·en (i lev′ən), *n.* **1.** a cardinal number, ten plus one. **2.** a symbol for this number, as 11 or XI. **3.** a set of this many persons or things, esp. a football team. **—***adj.* **4.** amounting to eleven in number. [ME *elleven(e)*, OE *ellefne, endleofan;* c. OHG *einlif* (G *elf*), Icel *ellifu*, Goth *ainlib-*, lit., one remaining (after counting 10). See ONE, LEAVE[1]]

e·lev·enth (i lev′ənth), *adj.* **1.** next after the tenth; being the ordinal number for 11. **2.** being one of 11 equal parts. **—***n.* **3.** an eleventh part, esp. of one ($^1/_{11}$). **4.** the eleventh member of a series. [ME *enleventh, enlefte*, OE *endlyfta* (akin to OFris *andlofta*, OS *ellifto*)]

elev′enth hour′, the last possible moment for doing something: *to change plans at the eleventh hour.*

el·e·von (el′ə von′), *n.* *Aeron.* a control surface functioning both as an elevator and as an aileron. [ELEV(ATOR + AILER)ON]

elf (elf), *n., pl.* **elves** (elvz). one of a class of imaginary beings, with magical powers, given to capricious interference in human affairs: usually represented in diminutive human form; sprite; fairy. [ME, back formation from *elven*, OE *elfen* nymph (i.e., female elf), var. of *ælfen;* see ELFIN] **—Syn. 1.** See **fairy.**

Elf, extremely low frequency. Also, **elf.**

El Fai·yum (el′ fī yōōm′), Faiyum (def. 2). Also, **El′ Fa·yum′.**

El Fa·sher (el fash′ər), a city in W Sudan. 30,000 (est. 1964).

El Fer·rol (el fer rôl′), a seaport in NW Spain: naval arsenal and dockyard. 79,593 (1965). Also called **Ferrol.**

elf·in (el′fin), *adj.* **1.** of or like elves. **2.** small and charmingly sprightly, merry, or mischievous. **—***n.* **3.** an elf. [alter. of ME *elven* elf, OE *elfen, ælfen* nymph = *ælf* elf + *-en* fem. suffix (c. G *-in*); *ælf* c. G *Alp* nightmare, puck, Icel *alfr* elf, L *albus* white]

elf·ish (el′fish), *adj.* elflike; elfin; small and mischievous; impish. Also, **elvish.** [alter. of ME; see ELVISH] **—elf′·ish·ly,** *adv.* **—elf′ish·ness,** *n.*

elf·lock (elf′lok′), *n.* a tangled lock of hair.

El·gar (el′gər, -gär), *n.* **Sir Edward,** 1857–1934, English composer.

El·gin (el′jin *for 1;* el′gin *for 2*), *n.* **1.** a city in NE Illinois. 55,691 (1970). **2.** former name of **Moray.**

El·gon (el′gon), *n.* an extinct volcano in E Africa, on the boundary between Uganda and Kenya. 14,176 ft.

El Gre·co (el grek′ō; *Sp.* el gre′kô), (*Domenikos Theotocopoulos*) 1541–1614, Spanish painter, born in Crete.

El Ha·sa (el hä′sə), Hasa.

E·li (ē′lī), *n.* a Hebrew judge and priest. I Sam. 1–3.

E·li·a (ē′lē ə), *n.* See **Lamb, Charles.**

E·li·as (i lī′əs), *n.* *Douay Bible.* Elijah.

e·lic·it (i lis′it), *v.t.* to draw or bring out or forth; educe; evoke. [< L *ēlicit(us)* drawn out (ptp. of *ēlicere*) = *ē-* E- + *lici-* draw, lure + *-tus* ptp. suffix] **—e·lic′it·a·ble,** *adj.* **—e·lic′i·ta′tion,** *n.* **—e·lic′i·tor,** *n.*

e·lide (i līd′), *v.t.,* **e·lid·ed, e·lid·ing. 1.** to omit (a vowel, consonant, or syllable) in pronunciation. **2.** to pass over; omit; ignore. **3.** *Law.* to annul or quash. [< L *ēlīd(ere)* (to) strike out = *ē-* E- + *-līdere* var. of *laedere* to strike, wound]

el·i·gi·bil·i·ty (el′i jə bil′i tē), *n.* the quality or state of being eligible, esp. legal qualification for election or appointment.

el·i·gi·ble (el′i jə bəl), *adj.* **1.** fit or proper to be chosen; worthy of choice; desirable: *to marry an eligible bachelor.* **2.** legally qualified to be elected or appointed to office. **—***n.* **3.** a person or thing that is eligible: *Of the eligibles, only he is running for office.* [< LL *ēligibil(is)* = L *ē-* E- + *ligi-* select + *-bilis* -BLE] **—el′i·gi·bly,** *adv.*

El·i·hu (el′ə hyōō′, i lī′hyōō), *n.* a young man who entered into discourse with Job. Job. 32–37. [< Heb: my God is he]

E·li·jah (i lī′jə), *n.* a Hebrew prophet of the 9th century B.C. I Kings 17; II Kings 2. Also, *Douay Bible,* **Elias.** [< Heb: my God is Yahweh]

Eli′jah Muham′mad, (*Elijah Poole*) 1897–1975, U.S. religious leader, head of the Black Muslims 1934–75.

e·lim·i·nate (i lim′ə nāt′), *v.t.,* **-nat·ed, -nat·ing. 1.** to remove or get rid of, esp. as being incorrect, offensive, or in some other way undesirable: *to eliminate smudges.* **2.** to omit, esp. as being unimportant or irrelevant. **3.** *Physiol.* to void or expel from an organism. **4.** *Math.* to remove (a quantity) from a simultaneous equation. [< L *ēlīmināt(us)* turned out of doors (ptp. of *ēlīmināre*) = *ē-* E- + *līmen* threshold + *-ātus* -ATE[1]] **—e·lim·i·na·bil·i·ty** (i lim′ə nə bil′i tē), *n.* **—e·lim′i·na·ble,** *adj.* **—e·lim′i·nant,** *n.* **—e·lim′i·na′tive,** *adj.* **—e·lim′i·na′tor,** *n.* **—Syn. 1.** See **exclude.**

e·lim·i·na·tion (i lim′ə nā′shən), *n.* **1.** the act of eliminating. **2.** the state of being eliminated.

El·i·ot (el′ē ət, el′yət), *n.* **1. Charles William,** 1834–1926, U.S. educator: president of Harvard University 1869–1909. **2. George** (pen name of *Mary Ann Evans*), 1819–80, English novelist. **3. John** (*"the Apostle of the Indians"*), 1604–90, American colonial missionary. **4. Sir John,** 1592–1632, British statesman. **5. T(homas) S(tearns)** (stûrnz), 1888–1965, British poet, critic, and playwright; born in the U.S.: Nobel prize 1948.

E·lis (ē′lis), *n.* an ancient country on the Peloponnesus.

E·lis·a·beth (i liz′ə bəth), *n.* the mother of John the Baptist. Luke 1:5–25. Also, *Douay Bible,* **Elizabeth.**

E·lis·a·beth·ville (i liz′ə bəth vil′), *n.* former name of **Lubumbashi.**

E·li·sa·vet·grad (*Russ.* e lē zä vet′grät), *n.* former name of **Kirovograd.**

E·li·sa·vet·pol (*Russ.* e lē zä vet′pol yᵊ), *n.* former name of **Kirovabad.**

E·li·sha (i lī′shə), *n.* a Hebrew prophet of the 9th century B.C., the successor of Elijah. II Kings 3–9. Also, *Douay Bible,* **El·i·se·us** (el′i sē′əs). [< Heb: God has saved]

e·li·sion (i lizh′ən), *n.* **1.** the omission of a vowel, consonant, or syllable in pronunciation. **2.** (in verse) the omission of a vowel at the end of a word when the next word begins with a vowel, as *th'orient.* [< L *ēlīsiōn-* (s. of *ēlīsiō*) a striking out = *ēlīs(us)* (ptp. of *ēlīdere;* see ELIDE) + *-iōn-* -ION]

e·lite (i lēt′, ā lēt′), *n.* **1.** (*often construed as pl.*) the choice or best of anything considered collectively, esp. of a group or class of persons: *the elite of the intellectual community.* **2.** (*construed as pl.*) persons of the highest class: *Only the elite were there.* **3.** a group of persons exercising the major share of authority or control within a larger organization: *the power elite in the U.S.* **4.** a type, approximately 10-point and having 12 characters to the inch, widely used in typewriters. Cf. **pica**[1]. **—***adj.* **5.** representing the choicest or best. Also, **é·lite′.** [< F *élite,* OF *e(s)lite,* n. use of fem. of *e(s)lit* ptp. of *e(s)lire* to choose; see ELECT]

Elite′ Guard′. See **SS Troops.**

e·lit·ism (i lē′tiz əm, ā lē′-), *n.* **1.** practice of or belief in rule by an elite. **2.** consciousness of or pride in belonging to a select or favored group. Also, **é·lit′ism.** **—e·lit′ist,** *n.*

e·lix·ir (i lik′sər), *n.* **1.** *Pharm.* a sweetened, aromatic solution of alcohol and water used as a vehicle for medicinal substances. **2.** an alchemic preparation supposedly capable of transmuting base metals into gold or of prolonging life. **3.** the quintessence or absolute embodiment of anything. **4.** a panacea; cure-all. [ME < ML < Ar *al iksīr* alchemical preparation < LGk *xḗrion* drying powder (for wounds) = Gk *xēr(ós)* dry + *-ion,* neut. of *-ios* adj. suffix]

Eliz., Elizabethan.

E·liz·a·beth (i liz′ə bəth), *n.* **1.** *Douay Bible.* Elisabeth. **2.** (*Pauline Elizabeth Ottilie Luise, Princess of Wied*) ("*Carmen Sylva*") 1843–1916, queen of Rumania 1881–1914 and author. **3.** (*Elizaveta Petrovna*) 1709–62, empress of Russia 1741–62 (daughter of Peter the Great). **4. Saint,** 1207–31, Hungarian princess and religious mystic. **5.** a city in NE New Jersey. 112,654 (1970).

Elizabeth I, (*Elizabeth Tudor*) 1533–1603, queen of England 1558–1603 (successor to Mary I; daughter of Henry VIII and Anne Boleyn).

Elizabeth II, (*Elizabeth Alexandra Mary Windsor*) born 1926, queen of Great Britain since 1952 (daughter of George VI).

E·liz·a·be·than (i liz′ə bē′thən, -beth′ən), *adj.* **1.** of or pertaining to Elizabeth I, queen of England, or to her times. **2.** noting or pertaining to an English Renaissance style of architecture of the reign of Elizabeth I, characterized by fantastic ornament of German or Flemish origin. Cf. **Jacobean** (def. 2). **—***n.* **3.** a person who lived in England during the Elizabethan period, esp. a poet or dramatist.

Elk, *Cervus canadensis* (5 ft. high at shoulder; antlers 5 ft.; length 8 ft.)

elk (elk), *n., pl.* **elks,** (*esp. collectively*) **elk** for 1, 2. **1.** the largest living deer, *Alces alces,* of Europe and Asia, resembling but smaller than the North American moose, having large, palmate antlers. **2.** Also called **wapiti.** a large, North American deer, *Cervus canadensis,* the male of which has large, spreading antlers. **3.** a pliable leather, usually of calfskin or cowhide, tanned and smoked to resemble elk hide. **4.** (*cap.*) a member of a fraternal organization **(Benev′olent and Protec′tive Or′der of Elks′)** that supports or contributes to various charitable causes. [ME; OE *eolc,* appar. = *eol(a)* elk + *-k* suffix, r. OE *eolh;* c. G *Elch* (OHG *el(a)ho*), L *alcēs,* Gk *álkē*]

Elk·hart (elk′härt, el′kärt), *n.* a city in N Indiana. 43,152 (1970).

elk·hound (elk′hound′), *n.* See **Norwegian elkhound.**

ell[1] (el), *n.* an extension usually at right angles to one end of a building. [ME *ele* transept, lit., wing, old form of AISLE]

ell[2] (el), *n.* a measure of length, now little used, varying in different countries: in England equal to 45 inches. [ME, OE *eln;* c. Icel *eln,* OHG *elina,* Goth *aleina,* L *ulna,* Gk *ōlénē.* See ELBOW]

ell[3] (el), *n.* **1.** elbow (def. 4). **2.** something that is L-shaped. [by shortening; also partly from the shape of the letter L]

El·las (e läs′), *n.* Modern Greek name of **Greece.**

Elles′mere Is′land (elz′mēr), an island in the Arctic Ocean, NW of Greenland: a part of Canada. 76,600 sq. mi.

El′lice Is′lands (el′is), a group of islands in the central Pacific, S of the equator: a part of the British colony of Gilbert and Ellice Islands. 16½ sq. mi. Also called **Lagoon Islands.**

El·ling·ton (el′ing tən), *n.* **Edward Kennedy** ("*Duke*"), 1899–1974, U.S. jazz pianist, composer, arranger, and conductor.

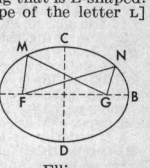

Ellipse
AB, CD, Axes of ellipse; F, G, Foci; FM+MG=GN+NF, M and N being arbitrary points on the ellipse

el·lipse (i lips′), *n.* *Geom.* a plane curve such that the sums of the distances of each point in its periphery from two fixed points, the foci, are equal. It is a conic section formed by the intersection of a right circular cone by a plane that cuts obliquely the axis and the opposite sides of the cone. Equation: $\frac{x^2}{a^2} + \frac{y^2}{b^2} = 1$. See also diag. at **conic section.** [back formation from earlier ELLIPSIS (or its pl.)]

el·lip·sis (i lip′sis), *n., pl.* **-ses** (-sēz). **1.** *Gram.* the omission from a sentence of a word or words that would complete the construction. **2.** *Print.* a mark or marks as ——, . . ., or * * *, to indicate an omission or suppression of letters or words. [< L < Gk *élleipsis* an omission = *el-* (var. of *en-* EN-[2]) + *leip-* (s. of *leípein* to leave) + *-sis* -SIS]

Ellipsoid

el·lip·soid (i lip′soid), *n.* **1.** *Geom.* a solid figure all plane sections of which are ellipses or circles. **—***adj.* **2.** ellipsoidal.

el·lip·soi·dal (i lip soid′əl, el′ip-), *adj.* pertaining to or having the form of an ellipsoid.

el·lip·ti·cal (i lip′ti kəl), *adj.* **1.** pertaining to or having the form of an ellipse. **2.** pertaining to or marked by grammatical ellipsis. **3.** (of speech or writing) expressed with extreme or excessive economy. **4.** (of a style of speaking or writing) tending to be ambiguous, cryptic, or obscure in the use of ellipsis. Also, **el·lip′tic.** [< Gk *elleiptik(ós)* defective (see ELLIPSIS, -TIC) + -AL[1]] **—el·lip′ti·cal·ly,** *adv.* **—el·lip′ti·cal·ness,** *n.*

ellip′tic geom′etry. See **Riemannian geometry** (def. 1).

el·lip·tic·i·ty (i lip tis′i tē, el′ip-), *n.* the degree of divergence of an ellipse from a circle. [*elliptic-* (see ELLIPTICAL) + -ITY]

El·lis (el′is), *n.* **(Henry) Have·lock** (hav′lok), 1859–1939, English psychologist and writer.

El′lis Is′land, an island in upper New York Bay: a former U.S. immigrant examination station.

El·li·son (el′i sən), *n.* **Ralph (Waldo),** born 1914, U.S. novelist, essayist, and lecturer.

El·lo·ra (e lōr′ə, e lôr′ə), *n.* a village in S central India: important Hindu archaeological site. Also, **Elura.**

Ells·worth (elz′wûrth), *n.* **Lincoln,** 1880–1951, U.S. polar explorer.

elm (elm), *n.* **1.** any tree of the genus *Ulmus,* as *U. procera* **(English elm),** characterized by the gradually spreading columnar manner of growth of its branches. Cf. **American elm. 2.** the wood of such a tree. [ME, OE; c. OHG *elm;* akin to Icel *almr,* L *ulmus*]

El Man·su·ra (el′ man so͝or′ə), a city in the NE Arab Republic of Egypt, in the Nile delta: defeat of the Crusaders 1250 and the capture of Louis IX by the Mamelukes. 172,600 (est. 1962). Also called **Mansura.**

elm′ blight′. See **Dutch elm disease.**

Elm·hurst (elm′hûrst), *n.* a city in NE Illinois, W of Chicago. 48,887 (1970).

El·mi·ra (el mī′rə), *n.* a city in S central New York. 39,945 (1970).

El Mis·ti (el mēs′tē), a volcano in S Peru, in the Andes. 19,200 ft. Also called **Misti.**

El·mont (el′mont), *n.* a town on W Long Island, in SE New York. 29,363 (1970).

El Mon·te (el mon′tē), a city in SW California, near Los Angeles. 69,852 (1970).

Elm′wood Park′ (elm′wo͝od′), a city in NE Illinois. 26,160 (1970).

El O·beid (el ō bād′), a city in central Sudan: Egyptian army defeated by the Mahdi 1883. 60,000 (est. 1964). Also called **Obeid.**

el·o·cu·tion (el′ə kyo͞o′shən), *n.* **1.** a person's manner of speaking or reading aloud. **2.** *Speech.* the study and practice of public speaking. [< L *ēlocūtiōn-* (s. of *ēlocūtiō*) a speaking out] **—el·o·cu·tion·ar·y** (el′ə kyo͞o′shə ner′ē), *adj.* **—el′o·cu′tion·ist,** *n.*

E·lo·him (e′lō him′, e lō′him; *in liturgical use* e lô kēm′), *n.* God, esp. as used in the Hebrew text of the Old Testament. [< Heb, pl. of *elōh* God] **—El·o·him·ic** (el′ō him′ik), *adj.* **—E·lo′hism,** *n.*

E·lo·hist (e lō′hist), *n.* a writer of one of the major sources of the Hexateuch, in which God is characteristically referred to as *Elohim* rather than *Yahweh.* Cf. **Yahwist.** [< Heb *elōh* God + -IST] **—El′o·his′tic,** *adj.*

e·loign (i loin′), *v.t.* *Archaic.* to remove (oneself) to a distance. Also, **e·loin′.** [late ME *e(s)loi(g)ne* < AF *e(s)loigner* to go or take far = *es-* EX-[1] + *loigner* < *loing* < L *longē* afar = *long(us)* distant (see LONG[1]) + *-ē* adv. suffix] **—e·loign′er, e·loin′er,** *n.* **—e·loign′ment, e·loin′ment,** *n.*

e·lon·gate (i lông′gāt, i long′-, ē′lông gāt′, ē′long-), *v.,* **-gat·ed, -gat·ing,** *adj.* **—***v.t.* **1.** to draw out to greater length; lengthen; extend. **—***v.i.* **2.** to increase in length. **—***adj.* **3.** extended; lengthened; elongated. [< LL *ēlongāt(us)* lengthened out, ptp. of *ēlongāre,* orig. to remove (*ē-* E- + *long(ē)* far off + *-āre* inf. ending), later taken as if *ē-* E- + *long(us)* LONG + *-āre,* hence to lengthen out] **—e·lon·ga·tive** (ē′lông gā′tiv, ē′long-), *adj.*

e·lon·ga·tion (i lông gā′shən, i long-, ē′lông-, ē′long-), *n.* **1.** the act of elongating. **2.** the state of being elongated. **3.** something that is elongated, or an elongated part. [ME < LL *ēlongātiōn-* (s. of *ēlongātiō*) orig. removal = *ēlongāt(us)* (see ELONGATE) + *-iōn-* -ION]

e·lope (i lōp′), *v.i.,* **e·loped, e·lop·ing. 1.** to run off secretly to be married, usually without the consent or knowledge of one's parents. **2.** to run away with a lover. **3.** to abscond or escape. [ME **alope(n)* (to) run away (> AF *aloper*). See A-[3], LOPE] **—e·lope′ment,** *n.* **—e·lop′er,** *n.*

el·o·quence (el′ə kwəns), *n.* **1.** the action, practice, or art of using language with fluency, power, and aptness. **2.** eloquent language or discourse. [ME < MF < L *ēloquentia*]

el·o·quent (el′ə kwənt), *adj.* **1.** having or exercising the power of fluent, forceful, and appropriate speech: *an eloquent orator.* **2.** characterized by forceful and appropriate expression: *an eloquent speech.* **3.** movingly expressive: *looks eloquent of disgust.* [ME < L *ēloquent-* (s. of *ēloquēns,* prp. of *ēloquī*) speaking out, eloquent = *ē-* E- + *loqu-* speak + *-ent-* -ENT] **—el′o·quent·ly,** *adv.* **—el′o·quent·ness,** *n.*

El Pas·o (el pas′ō), a city in W Texas, on the Rio Grande. 322,261 (1970).

El Sal·va·dor (el sal′və dôr′; *Sp.* el säl′vä t͟hôr′), a republic in NW Central America. 4,200,000; 13,176 sq. mi. *Cap.:* San Salvador. Also called **Salvador.**

else (els), *adj.* **1.** other than the persons or things mentioned or implied: *What else could I have done?* **2.** in addition to the persons or things mentioned or implied: *Who else was there?* **3.** other or in addition (used in the possessive following an indefinite pronoun): *someone else's money.* **—***adv.* **4.** if not (usually prec. by *or*): *It's a macaw, or else I don't know birds.* **5.** in some other way; otherwise: *How else could I have acted?* **6.** at some other place or time: *Where else might I find this book?* **7. or else,** or suffer the consequences: *Do what I say, or else.* [ME, OE *elles* (c. OHG *elles*) = *ell-* other (c. Goth *aljis,* L *alius,* Gk *állos*) + *-es* 's[1]] **—Usage.** The possessive forms of SOMEBODY ELSE, EVERYBODY ELSE, etc., are *somebody else's, everybody else's,* the forms *somebody's else, everybody's else* being considered nonstandard in present day English. One exception is the possessive for WHO ELSE, which is occasionally formed as *whose else* when a noun does not immediately follow: *Is this book yours? Whose else could it be? No, it's somebody else's.*

El·se·ne (el′sə nə), *n.* Flemish name of **Ixelles.**

El·se·vier (el′zə vēr′, -vər), *n., adj.* Elzevir.

else·where (els′hwâr′ -wâr′), *adv.* somewhere else; in or to some other place. [ME *elleswher,* OE *elles hwǣr*]

El·si·nore (el′sə nōr′, -nôr′), *n.* Helsingör.

e·lu·ci·date (i lo͞o′si dāt′), *v.t.,* **-dat·ed, -dat·ing.** to make lucid or clear; throw light upon; explain. [< LL *ēlūcidāt(us)* (ptp. of *ēlūcidāre*) enlightened] **—e·lu′ci·da′tion,** *n.* **—e·lu′ci·da′tive,** *adj.* **—e·lu′ci·da′tor,** *n.* **—Syn.** explicate, clarify. See **explain.**

e·lude (i lo͞od′), *v.t.,* **e·lud·ed, e·lud·ing. 1.** to avoid or escape by speed, cleverness, trickery, etc. **2.** to slip away from; evade: *The answer eludes me.* **3.** *Obs.* to baffle or puzzle. [< L *ēlūde(re)* (to) deceive, evade = *ē-* E- + *lūdere* to play, deceive] **—e·lud′er,** *n.* **—Syn. 1.** See **escape.**

E′lul (el′o͝ol; *Heb.* e lo͞ol′), *n.* the twelfth month of the Jewish calendar. Cf. **Jewish calendar.**

E·lu·ra (e lo͝or′ə), *n.* Ellora.

e·lu·sion (i lo͞o′zhən), *n.* the act of eluding; evasion; clever escape. [< LL *ēlūsiōn-* (s. of *ēlūsiō*) deception, evasion = *ēlūs(us),* ptp. of *ēlūdere* to ELUDE (*ē-* E- + *lūd-* play + *-tus* ptp. suffix) + *-iōn-* -ION]

e·lu·sive (i lo͞o′siv), *adj.* **1.** eluding clear perception or complete mental grasp; hard to express or define: *an elusive concept.* **2.** cleverly or skillfully evasive: *a fish too elusive to catch.* [< L *ēlūs(us)* (ptp. of *ēlūdere* to ELUDE) + -IVE] **—e·lu′sive·ly,** *adv.* **—e·lu′sive·ness,** *n.*

e·lute (ē lo͞ot′, i lo͞ot′), *v.t.,* **e·lut·ed, e·lut·ing.** *Physical Chem.* to remove by dissolving, as absorbed material from an adsorbent. [< L *ēlūt(us)* (ptp. of *ēluere*) washed out = *ē-* E- + *lū-* (var. of *lau-*) LAVE[1] + *-tus* ptp. suffix]

e·lu·tri·ate (i lo͞o′trē āt′), *v.t.,* **-at·ed, -at·ing. 1.** to purify by washing and straining or decanting. **2.** to separate the light and heavy particles of by washing. [< L *ēlutriāt(us)* (ptp. of *ēlutriāre*) washed out = *ē-* E- + *lutri-* wash (< ?) + *-ātus* -ATE[1]] **—e·lu′tri·a′tion,** *n.* **—e·lu′tri·a′tor,** *n.*

e·lu·vi·al (i lo͞o′vē əl, -vyəl), *adj.* of or pertaining to eluviation or eluvium. [< NL; see ELUVIUM, -AL[1]]

e·lu·vi·a·tion (i lo͞o′vē ā′shən), *n.* the movement through the soil of materials brought into suspension or dissolved by the action of water. [ELUVI(UM) + -ATION]

e·lu·vi·um (i lo͞o′vē əm), *n., pl.* **-vi·a** (-vē ə). *Geol.* a deposit of soil, dust, etc., formed from the decomposition of rock and found in its place of origin. [< NL; see E-, ALLUVIUM]

el·ver (el′vər), *n.* a young eel, esp. one that is migrating up a stream from the ocean. [var. of *ellfare,* lit., eel-journey. See EEL, FARE]

elves (elvz), *n.* pl. of **elf.**

elv·ish (el′vish), *adj.* elfish. [ME; see ELF, -ISH[1]] **—elv′ish·ly,** *adv.*

E·ly (ē′lē), *n.* **Isle of,** a former administrative county in E England: now part of Cambridgeshire. 375 sq. mi. *Co. seat:* March.

El·y·ot (el′ē ət, el′yət), *n.* **Sir Thomas,** c1490–1546, English scholar and diplomat.

E·lyr·i·a (i lēr′ē ə), *n.* a city in N Ohio. 53,427 (1970).

É·ly·sée (ā lē zā′), *n.* a palace in Paris: the official residence of the president of France.

E·ly·sian (i lizh′ən, i lē′zhən), *adj.* **1.** of or like Elysium. **2.** blissful; delightful. [ELYSI(UM) + -AN]

E·ly·si·um (i lizh′ē əm, i lē′zhē-, i liz′-, i lē′zē-, i lizh′əm), *n.* **1.** Also called **Ely′sian Fields′.** *Class. Myth.* the abode of the blessed after death. **2.** any similarly conceived abode or state of the dead. **3.** any place or state of perfect happiness. [< L < Gk *ēlýsion* (*pedíon*) blest (plain)]

E·ly·tis (e lē′tis), *n.* **Odysseus** (*Odysseus Alepoudelis*), born 1911, Greek poet: Nobel prize 1979.

el·y·tra (el′i trə), *n.* pl. of **elytron.**

el·y·tron (el′i tron′), *n., pl.* **-tra** (-trə). one of the pair of hardened forewings of certain insects, as beetles, forming a protective covering for the posterior, or flight, wings. [< NL < Gk: a covering] **—el·y·troid** (el′i troid), *adj.* **—el·y·trous** (el′i trəs), *adj.*

El·ze·vir (el′zə vēr′, -vər), *n.* **1. Louis,** c1540–1617, Dutch printer. **2.** a style of printing type with firm hairlines and stubby serifs. Also, **Elsevier, El′ze·vier′.** **—El′ze·vir′i·an,** *adj.*

em (em), *n., pl.* **ems. 1.** the letter *M, m.* **2.** Also called **mutton, mut.** *Print.* **a.** the square of any size of type, used as the unit of measurement for matter printed in that type size. **b.** (originally) the portion of a line of type occupied by the letter *M* in type of the same size. **3.** See **em pica.**

EM, enlisted man; enlisted men.

'em (əm), *pron.* *Informal.* them: *Put 'em down there.* [ME *hem,* OE *heom,* dat. pl. of HE[1]]

em-[1], var. of **en-[1]** before *b, p,* and sometimes *m: embalm.* Cf. **im-[1]**.

em-[2], var. of **en-[2]** before *b, m, p, ph: embolism, emphasis.*

Em., *Physical Chem.* emanation (def. 3).

e·ma·ci·ate (i mā′shē āt′), *v.t.,* **-at·ed, -at·ing.** to make lean by a gradual wasting away of flesh. [< L *ēmaciāt(us)* wasted away = *ē-* E- + *maciātus,* ptp. of *maciāre* to produce leanness (*maci(ēs)* leanness + *-ātus* -ATE[1])]

e·ma·ci·at·ed (i mā′shē ā′tid), *adj.* characterized by emaciation.

e·ma·ci·a·tion (i mā′shē ā′shən, -sē-), *n.* **1.** abnormal thinness caused by lack of nutrition or by disease. **2.** the process or a period of emaciating. [< L *ēmaciāt(us)* (see EMACIATE) + -ION]

em·a·nate (em′ə nāt′), *v.*, **-nat·ed, -nat·ing.** —*v.i.* **1.** to flow out, issue, or proceed, as from a source or origin; come forth; originate. —*v.t.* **2.** to send forth; emit. [< L *ēmānāt(us)* having flowed out (ptp. of *ēmānāre*) = *ē-* E- + *mān-* flow + *-ātus* -ATE[1]] —**em′a·na′tive,** *adj.* —**em′a·na′tor,** *n.* —**em·a·na·to·ry** (em′ə nə tōr′ē, -tôr′ē), *adj.* —**Syn. 1.** arise, spring, flow. See **emerge.**

em·a·na·tion (em′ə nā′shən), *n.* **1.** the act or an instance of emanating. **2.** something that emanates or is emanated. **3.** *Physical Chem.* a gaseous product of radioactive disintegration, as radon. [< LL *ēmānātiōn-* (s. of *ēmānātiō*)] —**em′a·na′tion·al,** *adj.*

e·man·ci·pate (i man′sə pāt′), *v.t.*, **-pat·ed, -pat·ing. 1.** to free from restraint, influence, or the like. **2.** to free (a slave) from bondage. **3.** *Roman and Civil Law.* to terminate paternal control over. [< L *ēmancipāt(us)* (ptp. of *ēmancipāre*) freed from control = *ē-* E- + *man(us)* hand + *cip-* (var. s. of *capere* to seize) + *-ātus* -ATE[1]] —**e·man′ci·pa′tive,** *adj.* —**e·man′ci·pa′tor,** *n.* —**e·man·ci·pa·to·ry** (i man′sə pə tōr′ē, -tôr′ē), *adj.* —**Syn. 1, 2.** See **release.**

e·man·ci·pat·ed (i man′sə pā′tid), *adj.* **1.** freed, as from slavery, bondage, or the like. **2.** not constrained or restricted by custom, tradition, superstition, etc.; uninhibited.

e·man·ci·pa·tion (i man′sə pā′shən), *n.* **1.** the act of emancipating. **2.** the state or fact of being emancipated. [< L *ēmancipātiōn-* (s. of *ēmancipātiō*) = *ēmancipāt(us)* (see EMANCIPATE) + *-iōn-* -ION] —**e·man′ci·pa′tion·ist,** *n.*

Emancipa′tion Proclama′tion, *U.S. Hist.* the proclamation issued by President Lincoln on January 1, 1863, freeing the slaves in those territories still in rebellion against the Union.

Emarginate leaves

e·mar·gi·nate (i mär′jə nāt′), *adj.* **1.** notched at the margin. **2.** *Bot.* notched at the apex, as a petal or leaf. Also, **e·mar′gi·nat′ed.** [< L *ēmargināt(us)* deprived of its edge] —**e·mar′gi·nate′ly,** *adv.* —**e·mar′gi·na′tion,** *n.*

e·mas·cu·late (*v.* i mas′kyə lāt′; *adj.* i mas′kyə lit, -lāt′), *v.*, **-lat·ed, -lat·ing,** *adj.* —*v.t.* **1.** to castrate. **2.** to deprive of strength or vigor; weaken. **3.** to render effeminate. —*adj.* **4.** emasculated. **5.** effeminate. [< L *ēmasculāt(us)* (ptp. of *ēmasculāre*). See E-, MASCULINE, -ATE[1]] —**e·mas′cu·la′tion,** *n.* —**e·mas′cu·la′tive,** *adj.* —**e·mas′cu·la′tor,** *n.* —**e·mas·cu·la·to·ry** (i mas′kyə lə tōr′ē, -tôr′ē), *adj.*

em·balm (em bäm′), *v.t.* **1.** to treat (a dead body) so as to preserve it, as with chemicals, drugs, or balsams. **2.** to preserve from oblivion; keep in memory. **3.** to prevent the development of. **4.** to impart a balmy fragrance to: *lilacs embalming the evening air.* [ME *embalme(n)*, *embaume(n)* < MF *embalmer*, *embaumer*, OF *emba(u)smer*] —**em·balm′er,** *n.* —**em·balm′ment,** *n.*

em·bank (em bangk′), *v.t.* to enclose, confine, or protect with a bank, mound, dike, or the like. [EM-[1] + BANK[1]]

em·bank·ment (em bangk′mənt), *n.* **1.** a bank, mound, dike, or the like, raised to hold back water, carry a roadway, etc. **2.** the act of embanking.

em·bar·go (em bär′gō), *n.*, *pl.* **-goes,** *v.*, **-goed, -go·ing.** —*n.* **1.** an order of a government prohibiting the movement of merchant vessels from or into its ports. **2.** an injunction from a government control agency to refuse freight for shipment. **3.** any legal restriction imposed upon commerce. **4.** a restraint or hindrance; prohibition. —*v.t.* **5.** to impose an embargo on. [< Sp < *embargar* to hinder, embarrass < VL **imbarricāre* = *im-* IM-[1] + *-barricāre* (**barr(a)* BAR[1] + *-icāre* causative suffix)]

em·bark (em bärk′), *v.t.* **1.** to put or receive on board a ship. **2.** to involve (someone) in an enterprise. **3.** to venture or invest (something) in an enterprise. —*v.i.* **4.** to board a ship, as for a voyage. **5.** to engage in an enterprise, business, etc. [< MF *embarqu(er)* < OPr *embarcar*]

em·bar·ka·tion (em′bär kā′shən), *n.* the act, process, or an instance of embarking. [< F *embarcation*]

em·bark·ment (em bärk′mənt), *n.* an embarkation.

em·bar·ras de ri·chesses (äN BA RÄ də RĒ shes′), *French.* an embarrassment of riches; overabundance, as of material goods, choices, or the like.

em·bar·rass (em bar′əs), *v.t.* **1.** to make uncomfortably self-conscious; cause confusion and shame to; disconcert; abash: *His bad manners embarrassed her.* **2.** to make difficult or intricate, as a question or problem; complicate. **3.** to put obstacles or difficulties in the way of; impede. **4.** to beset with financial difficulties; burden with debt. —*v.i.* **5.** to become disconcerted, abashed, or confused: *She embarrasses easily.* [< F *embarrass(er)* < Sp *embarazar* < Pg *embaraçar* = *em-* EM-[1] + *baraç(a)* noose + *-ar* inf. suffix] —**em·bar·rassed·ly** (em bar′əst lē, -ə sid lē), *adv.* —**em·bar′rass·ing·ly,** *adv.* —**Syn. 1.** discompose, chagrin.

em·bar·rass·ment (em bar′əs mənt), *n.* **1.** the state of being embarrassed; abashment. **2.** the act or an instance of embarrassing. **3.** something that embarrasses. **4.** excessive amount; overabundance: *an embarrassment of riches.* [< F *embarrassement*] —**Syn. 1.** discomposure. See **shame.**

em·bas·sa·dor (em bas′ə dər), *n.* *Archaic.* ambassador.

em·bas·sage (em′bə sij), *n.* *Archaic.* embassy. [var. of *ambassage* < OF *ambasse* (< ML *ambactia* office; see EMBASSY) + -AGE]

em·bas·sy (em′bə sē), *n.*, *pl.* **-sies. 1.** an ambassador and his staff. **2.** the official headquarters of an ambassador. **3.** the function or office of an ambassador. **4.** a group of persons sent on a diplomatic mission. [var. of *ambassy* < MF *ambassee* < VL **ambactiāta* = ML *ambacti(a)* office (< Gallic L *ambact(us)* vassal, servant = *amb-* AMBI- + *-act(us)* mover, ACTOR + *-ia* -Y[3]) + *-āta* fem. suffix]

em·bat·tle[1] (em bat′ᵊl), *v.t.*, **-tled, -tling. 1.** to arrange in order of battle; prepare for battle; arm. **2.** to fortify (a town, camp, etc.). [ME *embataile(n)* < MF *embataillier.* See EM-[1], BATTLE[1]]

em·bat·tle[2] (em bat′ᵊl), *v.t.*, **-tled, -tling.** to furnish with battlements. [ME *embataile(n).* See EM-[1], BATTLE[2]]

em·bat·tled (em bat′ᵊld), *adj.* **1.** disposed or prepared for battle. **2.** *Heraldry.* noting a charge, as an ordinary, having a series of square indentations suggesting crenelation.

em·bay (em bā′), *v.t.* **1.** to enclose in or as in a bay; surround or envelop. **2.** to form into a bay.

em·bay·ment (em bā′mənt), *n.* **1.** a bay. **2.** *Physical Geog.* the process by which a bay is formed.

em·bed (em bed′), *v.t.*, **-bed·ded, -bed·ding. 1.** to fix into a surrounding mass: *to embed stones in cement.* **2.** to place in or as in a bed. Also, **imbed.** —**em·bed′ment,** *n.*

em·bel·lish (em bel′ish), *v.t.* **1.** to beautify by or as by ornamentation; ornament; adorn. **2.** to enhance (a statement or narrative) with fictitious additions. [ME *embelisshe(n)* < MF *embeliss-* (long s. of *embelir*). See EM-[1], BELLE, -ISH[2]] —**em·bel′lish·er,** *n.* —**Syn. 1.** decorate, garnish, embroider. —**Ant. 1.** disfigure.

em·bel·lish·ment (em bel′ish mənt), *n.* **1.** an ornament or decoration. **2.** a fictitious addition, as to a factual statement. **3.** *Music.* ornament (def. 7). **4.** act of embellishing.

em·ber (em′bər), *n.* **1.** a small live coal, brand of wood, etc., as in a dying fire. **2. embers,** the smoldering remains of a fire. [ME *eemer, emeri,* OE *ǣmerge, ǣmyrie* (c. Icel *eimyrja,* OHG *eimuria*) = *ǣm-* (c. Icel *eimr* steam) + *-erge, -yrie,* akin to OE *ys(e)le* ember, L *ūrere* to burn]

Em′ber day′, any of the days in the quarterly three-day period of prayer and fasting (the Wednesday, Friday, and Saturday after the first Sunday in Lent, after Whitsunday, after Sept. 14, and after Dec. 13) observed in the Roman Catholic church and other Western churches. [ME *ymber day,* OE *ymbrendæg*]

em·bez·zle (em bez′əl), *v.t.*, **-zled, -zling.** to appropriate fraudulently to one's own use, as money or property entrusted to one's care. [late ME *embesile(n)* < AF *embeseiller* to destroy, make away with = *em-* EM-[1] + *beseiller,* OF *beseiller* to destroy < ?] —**em·bez′zle·ment,** *n.* —**em·bez′zler,** *n.*

em·bit·ter (em bit′ər), *v.t.* **1.** to make bitter or more bitter. **2.** to cause to feel bitter or hostile. Also, **imbitter.** —**em·bit′ter·er,** *n.* —**em·bit′ter·ment,** *n.*

Em·bla (em′blä), *n.* *Scand. Myth.* the first woman, made by the gods from a tree. Cf. **Ask.**

em·blaze (em blāz′), *v.t.*, **-blazed, -blaz·ing. 1.** to illuminate, as by a blaze. **2.** to kindle. —**em·blaz′er,** *n.*

em·bla·zon (em blā′zən), *v.t.* **1.** to depict, as on an escutcheon in heraldry. **2.** to decorate with brilliant colors. **3.** to proclaim; celebrate or extol. —**em·bla′zon·er,** *n.*

em·bla·zon·ment (em blā′zən mənt), *n.* **1.** the act of emblazoning. **2.** something that is emblazoned.

em·bla·zon·ry (em blā′zən rē), *n.* **1.** the act or art of emblazoning; heraldic decoration. **2.** brilliant representation or embellishment.

em·blem (em′bləm), *n.* **1.** an object or its representation, symbolizing a quality, state, class of persons, etc. **2.** a sign, design, or figure that identifies or represents something: *the emblem of a school.* **3.** an allegorical picture, often inscribed with a motto supplemental to the visual image with which it forms a single unit of meaning. —*v.t.* **4.** to represent with an emblem. [ME < L *emblēma* inlaid or mosaic work < Gk: something put on = *em-* EM-[2] + *blēma* something thrown or put, cf. *embállein* to throw in or on] —**Syn. 1.** token, sign, figure, image. **2.** device, badge.

em·blem·at·ic (em′blə mat′ik), *adj.* pertaining to, of the nature of, or serving as an emblem; symbolic. Also, **em′blem·at′i·cal.** [< Gk *emblēmat-* s. of *émblēma* (see EMBLEM) + -IC] —**em′blem·at′i·cal·ly,** *adv.* —**em′blem·at′i·cal·ness,** *n.*

em·blem·a·tise (em blem′ə tīz′), *v.t.*, **-tised, -tis·ing.** *Chiefly Brit.* emblematize.

em·blem·a·tize (em blem′ə tīz′), *v.t.*, **-tized, -tiz·ing.** to serve as an emblem of; represent by an emblem. [*emblemat-* (see EMBLEMATIC) + -IZE]

em·ble·ments (em′blə mənts), *n.pl.* *Law.* the products or profits of land that has been sown or planted. [pl. of *emblement* < AF, MF *emblaement* = *emblae(r)* (< ML *imblādāre* to sow with grain = *im-* IM-[1] + *blād(a)* grain (F *blé*) < Gmc (cf. MD *blaad,* OE *blǣd*) + *-āre* v. suffix) + *-ment* -MENT]

em·bod·i·ment (em bod′ē mənt), *n.* **1.** the act of embodying. **2.** the state or fact of being embodied. **3.** a thing, being, or person embodying a spirit, principle, abstraction, etc.; incarnation. **4.** comprehensive organization: *The Constitution is the embodiment of American democratic principles.*

em·bod·y (em bod′ē), *v.t.*, **-bod·ied, -bod·y·ing. 1.** to provide with a body; incarnate. **2.** to give a concrete form to. **3.** to collect into or include in a body; organize; incorporate. Also, **imbody.** —**em·bod′i·er,** *n.*

em·bold·en (em bōl′dᵊn), *v.t.* to make bold or bolder; hearten; encourage. Also, **imbolden.**

em·bo·lec·to·my (em′bə lek′tə mē), *n.*, *pl.* **-mies.** *Surg.* removal of an embolus from an artery that it is obstructing. [EMBOL(US) + -ECTOMY]

em·bol·ic (em bol′ik), *adj.* **1.** *Pathol.* pertaining to an embolus or to embolism. **2.** *Embryol.* of, pertaining to, or resulting from emboly. [EMBOL(US) + -IC]

em·bo·lism (em′bə liz′əm), *n.* **1.** intercalation, as of a day in a year. **2.** a period of time intercalated. **3.** *Pathol.* the occlusion of a blood vessel by an embolus. [< ML *embolism(us)* < LGk *embolismós.* See EMBOLUS, -ISM] —**em′bo·lis′mic,** *adj.*

em·bo·lus (em′bə ləs), *n.*, *pl.* **-li** (-lī′). *Pathol.* undissolved material carried by the blood current and impacted in some part of the vascular system, as thrombi, tissue fragments, clumps of bacteria, fat globules, or gas bubbles. [< L: piston < Gk *émbolos* stopper = *em-* EM-[2] + *bólos* a throw, akin to *bállein* to throw]

em·bo·ly (em′bə lē), *n.*, *pl.* **-lies.** *Embryol.* the pushing or growth of one part into another, as in the formation of certain gastrulas. [< Gk *embolḗ* a putting into its place, a setting, akin to *embállein* to throw in]

em·bon·point (äN bôN pwaN′), *n.* *French.* excessive plumpness; stoutness. [lit., in good condition]

em·bosk (em bosk′), *v.t.* to hide or conceal (something, oneself, etc.) with or as with foliage, greenery, or the like: *to embosk oneself within a grape arbor.*

em·bos·om (em bo͝oz′əm, -bo͞o′zəm), *v.t.* **1.** to enfold, envelop, or enclose. **2.** to take into or hold in the bosom; embrace. **3.** to cherish; foster. Also, **imbosom.**

em·boss (em bôs′, -bos′), *v.t.* **1.** to raise (surface designs); represent in relief. **2.** to cause to bulge out; make protuberant. **3.** *Metalworking.* to raise a design on (a blank) with dies of similar pattern, one the negative of the other. **4.** to decorate (a surface) with raised ornament. [ME *embose(n)* < MF *embocer*] —**em·boss′er,** *n.* —**em·boss′ment,** *n.*

em·bou·chure (äm′bo͞o sho͝or′, äm′bo͞o sho͝or′; *Fr.* äN bo͞o shʏʀ′), *n., pl.* **-chures** (-sho͝orz′; *Fr.* -shʏʀ′). **1.** the mouth of a river. **2.** the opening out of a valley into a plain. **3.** *Music.* **a.** the mouthpiece of a wind instrument, esp. when of metal. **b.** the adjustment of a player's mouth to such a mouthpiece. [< F = *embouch(er)* (to) put to mouth (*em-* EM-[1] + *bouche* mouth < L *bucca* puffed cheek) + *-ure* -URE]

em·bowed (em bōd′), *adj.* vaulted; arched. [ME *embow(en)* (see EM-[1], BOW[2]) + -ED[2]]

em·bow·el (em bou′əl, -boul′), *v.t.,* **-eled, -el·ing** or (*esp. Brit.*) **-elled, -el·ling. 1.** to disembowel. **2.** *Obs.* to enclose, bury deep within.

em·bow·er (em bou′ər), *v.t., v.i.* to shelter in or as in a bower; cover or surround with foliage. Also, **imbower.**

em·brace[1] (em brās′), *v.,* **-braced, -brac·ing,** *n.* —*v.t.* **1.** to take or clasp in the arms; press to the bosom; hug. **2.** to take or receive gladly or eagerly; accept willingly: *to embrace an idea.* **3.** to avail oneself of: *to embrace an opportunity.* **4.** to adopt (a profession, a religion, etc.): *to embrace Buddhism.* **5.** to take in with the eye or the mind. **6.** to encircle; surround; enclose. **7.** to include or contain. —*v.i.* **8.** to join in an embrace. —*n.* **9.** the act or an instance of embracing; hug. [ME < OF *embrac(ier)*] —**em·brace′a·ble,** *adj.* —**em·brace′ment,** *n.* —**em·brac′er,** *n.* —**Syn. 2.** adopt, espouse, welcome. **3.** seize. **7.** cover, embody. See **include.** —**Ant. 7.** exclude.

em·brace[2] (em brās′), *v.t.,* **-braced, -brac·ing.** *Law.* to attempt to influence (a judge or jury) through corrupt means. [late ME < AF *embrac(er)* (-c- < EMBRACE[1]), OF *embraser* to instigate (lit., set fire to). See EM-[1], BRAISE]

em·brace·or (em brā′sər), *n.* *Law.* a person guilty of embracery. [late ME < AF; MF *embraseor* instigator]

em·brac·er·y (em brā′sə rē), *n., pl.* **-er·ies.** *Law.* an attempt to influence a judge or jury by corrupt means, as by bribery, threats, or promises. [ME *embracerie*]

em·branch·ment (em branch′mənt, -bränch′-), *n.* **1.** a branching or ramification. **2.** a branch. [< F *embranchement*]

em·bran·gle (em brang′gəl), *v.t.,* **-gled, -gling.** to confuse; entangle. [EM-[1] + *brangle* (b. BRAWL and WRANGLE)] —**em·bran′gle·ment,** *n.*

em·bra·sure (em brā′zhər), *n.* **1.** (in fortification) an opening, as a loophole or crenel, through which missiles may be discharged. **2.** *Archit.* a splayed enlargement of a door or window toward the inner face of a wall. [< F = obs. *embras(er)* (to) chamfer, widen (*em-* EM-[1] + ?) + *-ure* -URE] —**em·bra′sured,** *adj.*

em·brit·tle (em brit′əl), *v.t., v.i.,* **-tled, -tling.** to make or become brittle. —**em·brit′tle·ment,** *n.*

em·bro·cate (em′brō kāt′), *v.t.,* **-cat·ed, -cat·ing.** to moisten and rub with a liniment or lotion. [< ML *embrocāt(us)* (ptp. of *embrocāre*) = LL *embroch(a)* (< Gk *embrochē* infusion = *em-* EM-[2] + *brochē* a making wet) + *-ātus* -ATE[1]]

em·bro·ca·tion (em′brō kā′shən), *n.* **1.** the act of embrocating a bruised or diseased part of the body. **2.** the liquid used for this; a liniment or lotion.

em·broi·der (em broi′dər), *v.t.* **1.** to decorate with ornamental needlework. **2.** to produce or form in needlework. **3.** to adorn or embellish rhetorically, esp. with fictitious additions. —*v.i.* **4.** to do embroidery. [EM-[1] + BROIDER; r. ME *embrodere(n),* freq. of *embroden* < MF *embro(u)der* = *em-* EM-[1] + OF *brosder* < *brosd* < EGmc (see BRAD)] —**em·broi′der·er,** *n.*

em·broi·der·y (em broi′də rē, -drē), *n., pl.* **-der·ies. 1.** the art of working ornamental designs with a needle and thread. **2.** embroidered work or ornamentation. **3.** elaboration or embellishment, as in telling a story. [ME *embrouderie* needlework on cloth < MF *embroud(er)* + ME *-erie* -ERY; *oi* < EMBROIDER]

em·broil (em broil′), *v.t.* **1.** to bring into discord or conflict; involve in contention or strife. **2.** to throw into confusion; complicate. [< MF *embrouill(er)*] —**em·broil′er,** *n.* —**em·broil′ment,** *n.*

em·brue (em bro͞o′), *v.t.,* **-brued, -bru·ing.** imbrue.

em·brute (em bro͞ot′), *v.t., v.i.,* **-brut·ed, -brut·ing.** imbrute.

embry-, var. of **embryo-** before a vowel.

em·bry·ec·to·my (em′brē ek′tə mē), *n., pl.* **-mies.** *Surg.* removal of an embryo.

em·bry·o (em′brē ō′), *n., pl.* **-os. 1.** an organism in the earlier stages of its development, as before emergence from the egg or before metamorphosis. **2.** the young of a viviparous animal, esp. of a mammal, in the early stages of development within the womb. Cf. **fetus. 3.** *Bot.* the rudimentary plant usually contained in the seed. **4.** the beginning or rudimentary stage of anything. [< ML *embryon-, embryo* < Gk *émbryon,* n. use of neut. of *émbryos* ingrowing = *em-* EM-[2] + *bry-* (s. of *brýein* to swell) + *-os* adj. suffix] —**em·bry·oid** (em′brē oid′), *adj.*

embryo-, a combining form of **embryo:** *embryology.* Also, *esp. before a vowel,* **embry-.**

em·bry·og·e·ny (em′brē oj′ə nē), *n.* the formation and development of the embryo. Also, **em·bry·o·gen·e·sis** (em′brē ō jen′i sis). —**em·bry·o·gen·ic** (em′brē ō jen′ik), **em·bry·o·ge·net·ic** (em′brē ō jə net′ik), *adj.*

embryol., embryology.

em·bry·ol·o·gist (em′brē ol′ə jist), *n.* a specialist in embryology.

em·bry·ol·o·gy (em′brē ol′ə jē), *n., pl.* **-gies. 1.** the science dealing with the formation, development, structure, and functional activities of embryos. **2.** the origin, growth, and development of an embryo. —**em·bry·o·log·i·cal** (em′brē ə loj′i kəl), **em′bry·o·log′ic,** *adj.* —**em′bry·o·log′i·cal·ly,** *adv.*

em·bry·on·ic (em′brē on′ik), *adj.* **1.** pertaining to or in the state of an embryo. **2.** rudimentary; undeveloped. [*embryon-* (see EMBRYO) + -IC] —**em′bry·on′i·cal·ly,** *adv.*

em′bryo sac′, *Bot.* the megaspore of a seed-bearing plant, being situated within the ovule, giving rise to the endosperm or supposed female prothallium, and forming the egg cell or nucleus from which the embryo plant develops after fertilization of the egg.

em·cee (em′sē′), *n., v.,* **-ceed, -cee·ing.** —*n.* **1.** master of ceremonies. —*v.t.* **2.** to act as master of ceremonies for. —*v.i.* **3.** to act as a master of ceremonies. [from M.C.]

em′ dash′, *Print.* a dash one em long.

Em·den (em′dən), *n.* a seaport in NW West Germany. 46,100 (1963).

-eme, a suffix denoting a basic structural element (of a specified type) in a language: *morpheme.* [< Gk *-ēma* as in *phṓnēma* PHONEME]

e·meer (ə mēr′), *n.* emir.

e·meer·ate (ə mēr′it, -āt), *n.* emirate.

e·mend (i mend′), *v.t.* **1.** to edit (a text) by removing errors, flaws, etc. **2.** to free from faults or errors; correct. [ME *emende(n)* < L *ēmendāre* to correct = *ē-* E- + *mend(um)* fault + *-āre* v. suffix] —**e·mend′a·ble,** *adj.* —**Syn.** See **amend.**

e·men·date (ē′mən dāt′, i men′dāt), *v.t.,* **-dat·ed, -dat·ing.** to emend (a text). [< L *ēmendāt(us),* ptp. of *ēmendāre*] —**e·men·da·tor** (ē′mən dā′tər, em′ən-), *n.*

e·men·da·tion (ē′mən dā′shən, em′ən-), *n.* **1.** a correction. **2.** the act of emending. [< L *ēmendātiōn-* (s. of *ēmendātiō*)] —**e·men·da·to·ry** (i men′də tôr′ē, -tōr′ē), *adj.*

em·er·ald (em′ər əld, em′rəld), *n.* **1.** a rare, green variety of beryl valued as a gem. **2.** a clear, deep green. **3.** *Print. Brit.* a 6½-point type of a size between nonpareil and minion. [ME *emeraude, emeralde* < OF *esmeraude, esmeralde, esmeragde* < L *smaragdus* < Gk *smáragdos;* akin to Skt *marakata* emerald]

em′erald cut′, *Jewelry.* a type of cut, used esp. on emeralds and diamonds, in which the girdle is a square or rectangle with truncated corners.

Em′erald Isle′, Ireland (def. 1).

e·merge (i mûrj′), *v.i.,* **e·merged, e·merg·ing. 1.** to rise or come forth from or as from water or other liquid. **2.** to come forth into view or notice, as from concealment or obscurity. **3.** to come up or arise, as a question or difficulty. **4.** to come into existence; develop: *New political problems emerge every day.* **5.** to rise, as from an inferior or unfortunate state or condition: *to emerge from a depression.* [< L *ēmerge(re)* (to) arise out of. See E-, MERGE]
—**Syn. 2.** EMERGE, EMANATE, ISSUE mean to come forth from a place or source. EMERGE is used of coming forth from something that envelops or encloses, from a place shut off from view, or from concealment, obscurity, retirement, or the like, into sight and notice: *The sun emerges from behind the clouds.* EMANATE is used esp. of intangible or immaterial things, as light, vapor, ideas, news, etc., spreading or streaming from a source. ISSUE is most often used of a number of persons, a mass of matter, or a volume of smoke, sound, or the like, coming forth through any outlet or outlets.

e·mer·gence (i mûr′jəns), *n.* **1.** the act or process of emerging. **2.** an outgrowth, as a prickle, on the surface of a plant. **3.** an unpredictable development, as in evolution. [EMERGENCY, with -ENCE r. -ENCY]

e·mer·gen·cy (i mûr′jən sē), *n., pl.* **-cies.** a sudden, urgent, usually unforeseen occurrence or occasion requiring immediate action. [< ML *ēmergentia.* See EMERGE, -ENCY, EMERGENT]
—**Syn.** exigency, extremity, pinch, quandary, plight. EMERGENCY, CRISIS refer to situations in which quick action and judgment are necessary, although they may not avert undesirable consequences. An EMERGENCY is a situation demanding immediate action: *A power failure created an emergency in transportation.* A CRISIS is a vital or decisive turning point in a condition or state of affairs, and everything depends on the outcome of it: *Help arrived when affairs had reached a crisis.*

e·mer·gent (i mûr′jənt), *adj.* **1.** emerging; rising from a liquid or other surrounding medium. **2.** coming into view or notice; issuing. **3.** coming into existence, esp. through gaining political independence: *the emergent nations of Africa.* **4.** arising casually or unexpectedly. **5.** calling for immediate action; urgent. —*n.* **6.** *Ecol.* an aquatic plant having its stem, leaves, etc., extending above the surface of the water. [< L *ēmergent-* (s. of *ēmergēns*) arising out of, prp. of *ēmergere* to EMERGE] —**e·mer′gent·ly,** *adv.* —**e·mer′gent·ness,** *n.*

emer′gent evolu′tion, *Biol., Philos.* the unpredictable appearance of entirely new properties at certain critical stages or levels in the course of evolution, as of multicellular organisms, nervous systems, or psychic processes.

e·mer·i·tus (i mer′i təs), *adj., n., pl.* **-ti** (-tī′, -tē′). —*adj.* **1.** retired or honorably discharged from active duty because of age, infirmity, or long service, but retained on the rolls: *a professor emeritus.* —*n.* **2.** an emeritus professor, minister, etc. [< L: having fully earned (ptp. of *ēmerēre*). See E-, MERIT]

e·mersed (i mûrst′), *adj.* *Bot.* risen or standing out of water, surrounding leaves, etc. [< L *ēmers(us)* (ptp. of *ēmergere* to EMERGE) + -ED[2]]

e·mer·sion (i mûr′zhən, -shən), *n.* **1.** Also called **egress.** *Astron.* the emergence of a heavenly body from an eclipse by another body, an occultation, or a transit. Cf. **immersion** (def. 5). **2.** *Archaic.* the act of emerging. [< L *ēmers(us)* (ptp. of *ēmergere* to EMERGE) + -ION]

Em·er·son (em′ər sən), *n.* **Ralph Waldo,** 1803–82, U.S. essayist and poet. —**Em·er·so·ni·an** (em′ər sō′nē ən), *adj.*

em·er·y (em′ə rē, em′rē), *n.* a granular mineral substance consisting typically of corundum mixed with magnetite or hematite, used powdered, crushed, or consolidated for grinding and polishing. [late ME < MF *emeri* < OF *esmeril* VL **smericul(um)* = MGk *smēri* (< Gk *smýris* rubbing powder; akin to SMEAR) + L *-culum* -CULE]

em′ery board′, a small, stiff strip, as of paper or cardboard, coated with powdered emery, used in manicuring.

em′ery wheel′. See **grinding wheel.**
em·e·sis (em′i sis), *n.* *Pathol.* vomiting. [< NL < Gk: a vomiting = *eme-* (s. of *emeîn* to vomit) + *-sis* -SIS]
e·met·ic (ə met′ik), *adj.* **1.** inducing vomiting, as a medicinal substance. —*n.* **2.** an emetic medicine or agent. [< L *emetic(us)* < Gk *emetikós* = *émet(os)* vomiting + *-ikos* -IC]
em·e·tine (em′i tēn′, -tin), *n.* *Pharm.* a colorless, crystalline or white, powdery substance, $C_{29}H_{40}N_2O_4$, the active principle of ipecac: used chiefly in the treatment of amoebic dysentery and as an emetic and expectorant. [< Gk *éme-t(os)* vomiting + -INE²; cf. F *émétine*]
e·meu (ē′myōō), *n.* emu.
é·meute (ā mœt′), *n., pl.* **é·meutes** (ā mœt′). *French.* a riot.
emf, See **electromotive force.** Also, **E.M.F., EMF, e.m.f.**
-emia, *Med.* a suffix referring to the state of the blood: *hyperemia.* Also, **-aemia, -haemia, -hemia.** [< NL < Gk *-(h)aimia* (as in *anaimia* want of blood) = *haim-* (s. of *haîma*) blood + *-ia* -IA]
em·i·grant (em′ə grənt), *n.* **1.** a person who emigrates, as from his native country. —*adj.* **2.** emigrating. [< L *ēmīgrant-* (s. of *ēmīgrāns*) moving away (prp. of *ēmīgrāre*). See E-, MIGRANT]
em·i·grate (em′ə grāt′), *v.i.*, **-grat·ed, -grat·ing.** to leave one country or region to settle in another; migrate: *to emigrate to Australia.* [< L *ēmīgrāt(us)* moved away (ptp. of *ēmīgrāre*). See E-, MIGRATE] —**em′i·gra′tive,** *adj.* —**Syn.** See **migrate.**
em·i·gra·tion (em′ə grā′shən), *n.* **1.** the act or an instance of emigrating. **2.** a body of emigrants; emigrants collectively: *The emigration settled in large cities.* [< LL *ēmīgrātiōn-* (s. of *ēmīgrātiō*) removal] —**em′i·gra′tion·al,** *adj.*
é·mi·gré (em′ə grā′; *Fr.* ā mē grā′), *n., pl.* **-grés** (-grāz′; *Fr.* -grā′). an emigrant, esp. a person who flees from his native land because of political conditions. [< F: lit., emigrated, ptp. of *émigrer* < L *ēmīgrāre* to EMIGRATE]
E·mi·lia-Ro·ma·gna (e mē′lyä rô mä′nyä), *n.* a region in N Italy. 3,646,507 (1961); 8547 sq. mi.
em·i·nence (em′ə nəns), *n.* **1.** high station, rank, or repute: *philosophers of eminence.* **2.** a high place or part; a hill or elevation; height. **3.** (*cap.*) a title of honor applied to cardinals (usually prec. by *His* or *Your*). **4.** *Anat.* an elevation or projection, esp. on a bone. [late ME < MF < L *ēminentia*] —**Syn. 1.** note, fame. **2.** prominence.
é·mi·nence grise (ā mē näns grēz′), *pl.* **é·mi·nences grises** (ā mē näns grēz′). *French.* See **gray eminence.**
em·i·nen·cy (em′ə nən sē), *n., pl.* **-cies.** eminence.
em·i·nent (em′ə nənt), *adj.* **1.** high in station, rank, or repute; distinguished: *eminent statesmen.* **2.** conspicuous, signal, or noteworthy: *eminent fairness.* **3.** lofty; high. **4.** prominent; projecting; protruding. [ME < L *ēminent-* (s. of *ēminēns*) outstanding (prp. of *ēminēre*) = *ē-* E- + *min-* project(ion) + *-ent-* -ENT] —**em′i·nent·ly,** *adv.* —**Syn. 1.** prominent, celebrated, renowned, illustrious, outstanding. See **famous. 2.** noted; notable.
em′inent domain′, *Law.* the power of the state to take private property for public use upon compensating the owner.
e·mir (ə mēr′), *n.* **1.** an Arab chieftain or prince. **2.** a title of honor of the descendants of Muhammad. Also, **emeer.** [< Ar *amīr* commander]
e·mir·ate (ə mēr′it, -āt), *n.* the office or rank of an emir. Also, **emeerate.**
em·is·sar·y (em′i ser′ē), *n., pl.* **-sar·ies. 1.** an agent, esp. of a national government, sent on a mission or errand. **2.** a spy or other agent sent on a secret mission. [< L *ēmissāri(us)* one sent out. See EMISSION, -ARY]
e·mis·sion (i mish′ən), *n.* **1.** the act or an instance of emitting. **2.** something that is emitted; discharge; emanation. **3.** the act or an instance of issuing, as paper money. **4.** *Electronics.* a measure of the number of electrons emitted by the heated filament or cathode of a vacuum tube. **5.** an ejection or discharge of semen or other fluid from the body. **6.** the fluid ejected or discharged. [< L *ēmissiōn-* (s. of *ēmissiō*) = *ēmiss(us)* (ptp. of *ēmittere* to EMIT) + *-iōn-* -ION] —**e·mis·sive** (i mis′iv), *adj.*
emis′sion spec′trum, *Physics.* the spectrum formed by electromagnetic radiation emitted by a given source, characteristic of the source and the type of excitation inducing the radiation.
em·is·siv·i·ty (em′i siv′i tē), *n.* *Thermodynamics.* the ability of a surface to emit radiant energy compared to that of a black body at the same temperature and with the same area.
e·mit (i mit′), *v.t.*, **e·mit·ted, e·mit·ting. 1.** to send forth (liquid, light, heat, sound, particles, etc.); discharge. **2.** to issue, as an order or a decree. **3.** to issue formally for circulation, as paper money. **4.** to utter or voice, as sounds or opinions. [< L *ēmitte(re)* (to) send forth = *ē-* E- + *mittere* to send] —**e·mit′ter,** *n.* —**Syn. 1.** exude, expel, eject.
Em·man·u·el (i man′yōō əl), *n.* Immanuel.
Em·men (em′ən), *n.* a city in the NE Netherlands. 69,474 (1962).
em·men·a·gogue (ə men′ə gôg′, -gog′, ə mē′nə-), *Med.* —*n.* **1.** a medicine that promotes the menstrual discharge. —*adj.* **2.** Also, **em·men·a·gog·ic** (ə men′ə goj′ik, -gog′-, ə mē′nə-). stimulating the menstrual flow. [< Gk *émmēn(a)* menses (neut. pl. of *emmēnios* monthly = *em-* EM-² + *mēn* month + *-ios* adj. suffix) + -AGOGUE]
em·mer (em′ər), *n.* a wheat, *Triticum dicoccum,* having a two-grained spikelet, grown as a forage crop in Europe, Asia, and the western U.S. [< G; OHG *amari* spelt]
em·met (em′it), *n.* *Chiefly Dial.* an ant. [ME *emete,* OE *ǣmette* ANT]
Em·met (em′it), *n.* **Robert,** 1778–1803, Irish patriot.
e·mol·lient (i mol′yənt), *adj.* **1.** having the power of softening or relaxing living tissues, as a medicinal substance; soothing, esp. to the skin. —*n.* **2.** *Med.* an emollient medicine or agent. [< L *ēmollient-* (s. of *ēmolliēns*) softening up (prp. of *ēmollīre*) = *ē-* E- + *molli(s)* soft + *-ent-* -ENT] —**e·mol′lience,** *n.*
e·mol·u·ment (i mol′yə mənt), *n.* profit arising from office or employment; compensation for services; salary or fees. [< L *ēmolument(um)* gain, profit (orig. miller's fee) = *ē-* E- + *molu-* (var. of *moli-,* comb. form of *molere* to grind) + *-mentum* -MENT]
e·mote (i mōt′), *v.i.*, **e·mot·ed, e·mot·ing. 1.** to show or affect emotion. **2.** to portray emotion in acting, esp. exaggeratedly or ineptly. [back formation from EMOTION] —**e·mot′er,** *n.*
e·mo·tion (i mō′shən), *n.* **1.** an affective state of consciousness in which joy, sorrow, fear, hate, or the like, is experienced, as distinguished from cognitive and volitional states of consciousness: usually accompanied by certain physiological changes, as increased heartbeat, respiration, or the like, and often overt manifestation, as crying, shaking, or laughing. **2.** an instance of this, as love, hate, sorrow, or fear. **3.** something that causes or effects such a reaction: *the powerful emotion of a great symphony.* [< ML *ēmōtiōn-* (s. of *ēmōtiō*) a moving away = L *ēmōt(us)* (ptp. of *ēmovēre;* see E-, MOVE) + *-iōn-* -ION] —**e·mo′tion·a·ble,** *adj.* —**e·mo′tion·less,** *adj.* —**Syn. 1.** See **feeling.**
e·mo·tion·al (i mō′shə nəl), *adj.* **1.** pertaining to or involving emotion or the emotions. **2.** subject to or easily affected by emotion. **3.** appealing to the emotions: *an emotional request for contributions.* **4.** showing or revealing very strong emotions: *an emotional scene in a play.* **5.** actuated, effected, or determined by emotion rather than reason: *an emotional decision.* —**e·mo′tion·al·ly,** *adv.*
e·mo·tion·al·ise (i mō′shə nəlīz′), *v.t.*, **-ised, -is·ing.** *Chiefly Brit.* emotionalize.
e·mo·tion·al·ism (i mō′shə nəliz′əm), *n.* **1.** excessively emotional character: *the emotionalism of sentimental fiction.* **2.** excessive appeal to the emotions: *the emotionalism of patriotic propaganda.* **3.** a tendency to display or respond with undue emotion, esp. morbid emotion. **4.** unwarranted expression or display of emotion.
e·mo·tion·al·ist (i mō′shə nəlist), *n.* **1.** a person who appeals to the emotions, esp. unduly. **2.** a person easily affected by emotion. **3.** a person who bases conduct or the theory of conduct upon feelings rather than reason. —**e·mo′-tion·al·is′tic,** *adj.*
e·mo·tion·al·i·ty (i mō′shə nal′i tē), *n.* emotional state or quality: *the emotionality of the artistic temperament.*
e·mo·tion·al·ize (i mō′shə nəlīz′), *v.t.*, **-ized, -iz·ing.** to make emotional; treat as a matter of emotion: *to emotionalize religion.* Also, *esp. Brit.,* **emotionalise.**
e·mo·tive (i mō′tiv), *adj.* **1.** characterized by or pertaining to emotion: *the emotive and rational capacities of man.* **2.** productive of or directed toward the emotions. [< L *ēmōt(us)* (see EMOTION) + -IVE] —**e·mo′tive·ly,** *adv.* —**e·mo′tive·ness,** *n.*
Emp., 1. Emperor. **2.** Empire. **3.** Empress.
em·pale (em pāl′), *v.t.*, **-paled, -pal·ing.** impale. —**em·pale′ment,** *n.* —**em·pal′er,** *n.*
em·pan·el (em pan′əl), *v.t.*, **-eled, -el·ing** or (*esp. Brit.*) **-elled, -el·ling.** impanel.
em·pa·thize (em′pə thīz′), *v.i.*, **-thized, -thiz·ing.** to experience empathy (often fol. by *with*): *to empathize with those in distress.*
em·pa·thy (em′pə thē), *n.* *Psychol.* **1.** intellectual identification with or vicarious experiencing of the feelings, thoughts, or attitudes of another person. **2.** the imaginative ascribing to an object, as a natural object or work of art, feelings or attitudes present in oneself. [< Gk *empátheia* affection (see EM-², -PATHY); present meaning influenced by G *Einfühlung*] —**em·path·ic** (em path′ik), *adj.* —**em·path′i·cal·ly,** *adv.*
Em·ped·o·cles (em ped′ə klēz′), *n.* c490–c430 B.C., Greek philosopher and statesman.
em·pen·nage (äm′pə näzh′; *Fr.* än pe nazh′), *n., pl.* **-nag·es** (-nä′zhiz; *Fr.* -nazh′). the rear part of an airplane or airship, usually comprising the stabilizer, elevator, vertical fin, and rudder. [< F: lit., feathering]
em·per·or (em′pər ər), *n.* the sovereign or supreme ruler of an empire. [ME *empero(u)r* < OF *empereor* < L *imperātor* leader = *imperāt(us)* imposed, ordered, ptp. of *imperāre* (*im-* IM-¹ + *per-,* var. of *par-* set, put + *-ātus* -ATE¹) + *-or* -OR²] —**em′per·or·ship′,** *n.*
em′peror pen′guin, the largest of the penguins, *Aptenodytes forsteri,* of the coasts of Antarctica. See illus. at **penguin.**
em·per·y (em′pə rē), *n., pl.* **-per·ies.** absolute dominion; empire. [ME *emperie* < AF < L *imperi(um)* mastery, sovereignty, empire = *imper(āre)* (to) rule (see EMPEROR) + *-ium* -Y³]
em·pha·sis (em′fə sis), *n., pl.* **-ses** (-sēz′). **1.** stress laid upon, or importance or significance attached to, anything: *The president's statement gave emphasis to the crisis.* **2.** something that is given stress or importance: *Morality was the emphasis of his speech.* **3.** *Rhet.* stress laid on particular words by means of position, repetition, voice, etc. **4.** intensity or force of expression, action, etc.: *Determination lent emphasis to his proposals.* **5.** prominence, as of form or outline: *The background detracts from the emphasis of the figure.* [< L < Gk: indication]
em·pha·sise (em′fə sīz′), *v.t.*, **-sised, -sis·ing.** *Chiefly Brit.* emphasize.
em·pha·size (em′fə sīz′), *v.t.*, **-sized, -siz·ing.** to give emphasis to; lay stress upon; stress: *to emphasize a point; to emphasize the eyes with mascara.* [EMPHAS(IS) + -IZE]
em·phat·ic (em fat′ik), *adj.* **1.** uttered, or to be uttered, with emphasis; strongly expressive. **2.** using emphasis in speech or action. **3.** forceful; insistent. **4.** forcibly significant; strongly marked; striking. **5.** clearly or boldly outlined. [< Gk *emphatik(ós)* indicative, forceful = **em-phat(ós)* (*em-* EM-² + *phatós,* var. of *phantós* visible = *phan-,* s. of *phaínesthai* to appear + *-tos* adj. suffix) + *-ikos* -IC] —**em·phat′i·cal·ly,** *adv.* —**em·phat′i·cal·ness,** *n.* —**Syn. 3.** positive, decided, unequivocal, definite. —**Ant. 3.** weak.
em·phy·se·ma (em′fi sē′mə, -zē′-), *n.* *Pathol.* abnormal distention of an organ or a part of the body, esp. the lungs, with air or other gas. [< NL < Gk: inflation = *em-* EM-² + *physē-* (var. s. of *physân* to blow) + *-ma* n. suffix denoting result of action] —**em·phy·sem·a·tous** (em′fi sem′ə təs, -sē′mə-, -zem′ə-, -zē′mə-), *adj.*

em′ pi′ca, *Print.* about one sixth of an inch, generally used as the unit of measurement in printing.

em·pire (em′pīər; *for 8 also* om pēr′), *n.* **1.** an aggregate of nations, tribes, clans, or peoples ruled over by one supreme sovereign: usually a territory of greater extent than a kingdom. **2.** a government under an emperor. **3.** (*often cap.*) the historical period during which a nation is under such a government: *a history of French decorative arts of the Second Empire.* **4.** imperial power; sovereignty. **5.** supreme control; absolute sway: *to have empire over the minds of men.* **6.** a powerful and important enterprise or holding: *an oil empire.* —*adj.* **7.** (*cap.*) characteristic of or developed during the first French empire, 1804–15. **8.** (*cap.*) noting or pertaining to the style of architecture, furnishings, decoration, and fashion prevailing in France and imitated in various other countries c1800–c1830. [ME < OF < L *imper(ium)*; see EMPERY] —**Syn. 4.** dominion, rule, supremacy.

Empire méridienne

Em′pire Day′, former name of **Commonwealth Day.**

Em′pire State′, the state of New York (used as a nickname).

em·pir·ic (em pir′ik), *n.* **1.** anyone who follows an empirical method. **2.** *Archaic.* a quack; charlatan. —*adj.* **3.** empirical. [< L *empīric(us)* < Gk *empeirikós* experienced = *em-* EM-[2] + *peir-* (s. of *peirân* to attempt) + *-ikos* -IC]

em·pir·i·cal (em pir′i kəl), *adj.* **1.** derived from or guided by experience or experiment. **2.** depending upon experience or observation alone, without using science or theory, as formerly in medicine. **3.** verifiable by experience or experiment. —**em·pir′i·cal·ly,** *adv.* —**em pir′i·cal·ness,** *n.*

empir′ical for′mula, *Chem.* a chemical formula indicating the elements of a compound and their relative proportions, as $(CH_2O)_n$. Cf. **molecular formula, structural formula.**

em·pir·i·cism (em pir′i siz′əm), *n.* **1.** empirical method or practice. **2.** *Philos.* the doctrine that all knowledge is derived from sense experience. Cf. **rationalism** (def. 2). **3.** undue reliance upon experience, as formerly in medicine; quackery. **4.** an empirical conclusion. —**em·pir′i·cist,** *n., adj.*

em·place (em plās′), *v.t.,* **-placed, -plac·ing.** to put in place or position. [back formation from EMPLACEMENT]

em·place·ment (em plās′mənt), *n.* **1.** *Fort.* the space, platform, or the like, for a gun or battery and its accessories. **2.** a putting in place or position; location: *the emplacement of a wall.* [< F = obs. *emplac(er)* (to) place (see EM-[1], PLACE) + *-ment* -MENT]

em·ploy (em ploi′), *v.t.* **1.** to hire or engage the services of (a person or persons); provide employment for. **2.** to keep busy or at work; engage the attentions of: *He employs himself by reading after work.* **3.** to make use of (an instrument, means, etc.); use; apply: *to employ a hammer to drive a nail.* **4.** to occupy or devote (time, energies, etc.). —*n.* **5.** employment; service: *to be in someone's employ.* [late ME *employe* < MF *emploie(r)* << L *implicāre* to infold (LL: to engage); see IMPLICATE] —**em·ploy′a·bil′i·ty,** *n.* —**em·ploy′a·ble,** *adj.* —**Syn. 1.** retain; occupy, use.

em·ploy·ee (em ploi′ē, em′ploi ē′), *n.* a person working for another person or a business firm for pay; worker. Also, **em·ploy′e, em·ploy′é.** [< F *employé* employed, ptp. of *employer* to EMPLOY]

em·ploy·er (em ploi′ər), *n.* a person who employs, esp. for wages.

em·ploy·ment (em ploi′mənt), *n.* **1.** the act or an instance of employing. **2.** the state of being employed; employ; service: *to begin or terminate employment.* **3.** an occupation by which a person earns a living; work; business. **4.** an activity that occupies a person's time. —**Syn. 3.** vocation, calling; job, trade, profession.

employ′ment a′gency, an agency that finds jobs for persons seeking employment or assists employers in finding persons to fill positions that are open.

em·poi·son (em poi′zən), *v.t.* **1.** to corrupt. **2.** to embitter. **3.** *Obs.* to poison. [ME *empoysone(n)* < OF *empoisone(r)*] —**em·poi′son·ment,** *n.*

Em·po·ri·a (em pôr′ē ə, -pôr′-), *n.* a city in E Kansas. 23,327 (1970).

em·po·ri·um (em pôr′ē əm, -pôr′-), *n., pl.* **-po·ri·ums, -po·ri·a** (-pôr′ē ə, -pôr′-). **1.** a place, town, or city of important commerce; a principal center of trade. **2.** a large store, esp. one selling a great variety of articles. [< L < Gk *empórion* market = *empor-* (s. of *émporos*) merchant (*em-* EM-[2] + *póros* voyage) + *-ion* n. suffix of place]

em·pov·er·ish (em pov′ər ish, -pov′rish), *v.t. Obs.* impoverish.

em·pow·er (em pou′ər), *v.t.* **1.** to give power or authority to; authorize. **2.** to enable or permit. —**em·pow′er·ment,** *n.*

em·press (em′pris), *n.* **1.** a female ruler of an empire. **2.** the consort of an emperor. [ME *emperice, emperesse* < OF *emperesse, empereriz* < L *imperātrix,* fem. of *imperātor*]

em·prise (em prīz′), *n. Archaic.* **1.** an adventurous enterprise. **2.** knightly daring or prowess. Also, **em·prize′.** [ME < MF, n. use of fem. of *empris* (ptp. of *emprendre* to undertake)]

Emp·son (emp′sən), *n.* **William,** 1906–84, English critic and poet.

emp·ty (emp′tē), *adj.,* **-ti·er, -ti·est,** *v.,* **-tied, -ty·ing,** *n., pl.* **-ties.** —*adj.* **1.** containing nothing; void of the usual or appropriate contents: *an empty bottle.* **2.** vacant; unoccupied: *an empty house.* **3.** without burden or load. **4.** destitute of people or human activity: *empty streets.* **5.** destitute of some quality or qualities; devoid (usually fol. by *of*): *a life empty of happiness.* **6.** without force, effect, or significance; hollow; meaningless: *empty compliments; empty pleasures.* **7.** hungry. **8.** without knowledge or sense; frivolous; foolish: *an empty head.* **9.** completely spent of emotion. —*v.t.* **10.** to make empty; discharge the contents of. **11.** to discharge (contents): *to empty the water out of a bucket.* —*v.i.* **12.** to become empty. **13.** to discharge contents, as a river. —*n.* **14.** something that is empty, as a box, bottle, can, etc. [ME (with intrusive *-p-*); OE *ǣm(et)tig* (*ǣmett(a)* leisure + *-ig* -Y[1])] —**emp′ti·a·ble,** *adj.* —**emp′ti·er,** *n.* —**emp′ti·ly,** *adv.* —**emp′ti·ness,** *n.*

—**Syn. 1.** vacuous. EMPTY, VACANT, BLANK denote absence of content or contents. EMPTY means without appropriate or accustomed contents: *empty barrel; The house is empty* (has no furnishings). VACANT is usually applied to that which is temporarily unoccupied: *vacant chair; vacant* (uninhabited) *house.* BLANK applies to surfaces free from any marks or lacking appropriate markings, openings, etc.: *blank paper; a blank wall.* **6.** delusive, vain. **10.** unload. —**Ant. 1.** full.

emp·ty-hand·ed (emp′tē han′did), *adj., adv.* **1.** having nothing in the hands, as in doing no work. **2.** having gained nothing: *to come back from fishing empty-handed.*

emp·ty-head·ed (emp′tē hed′id), *adj.* lacking intelligence or knowledge; foolish; brainless.

emp′ty nest′er, *Informal.* a couple without children or whose grownup children no longer live with them.

em·pur·ple (em pûr′pəl), *v.t.,* **-pled, -pling.** to tinge or color with purple.

em·py·e·ma (em′pē ē′mə, -pī-), *n. Pathol.* a collection of pus in a body cavity, esp. in the pleural cavity. [< LL < Gk: abscess = *em-* EM-[2] + *pyē-* (var. s. of *pyeîn* to suppurate, akin to *pýon, pýos* pus) + *-ma* n. suffix denoting result of action] —**em′py·e′mic,** *adj.*

em·pyr·e·al (em pir′ē əl, em′pə rē′əl, -pī-), *adj.* **1.** Also, **empyrean.** pertaining to the highest heaven in the cosmology of the ancients. **2.** pertaining to the sky; celestial. **3.** formed of pure fire or light. [< LL *empyre(us),* var. of *empyrius* (< Gk *empýrios* fiery; see EM-[2], PYR-) + -AL[1]]

em·py·re·an (em′pə rē′ən, -pī-, em pir′ē ən), *n.* **1.** the highest heaven, supposed by the ancients to contain the pure element of fire. **2.** the visible heavens; the firmament. —*adj.* **3.** empyreal (def. 1). [< LL *empyre(us)* EMPYREAL + -AN]

Emu (Height 5 ft.; length 6 ft.)

em′ quad′, **1.** a square unit of area, one em on each side. **2.** a piece of type consisting of a box one em on each side, as □.

e·mu (ē′myōō), *n.* a large, flightless, ratite bird, *Dromiceius novaehollandiae,* of Australia, resembling the ostrich but smaller and having a feathered head and neck and rudimentary wings. Also, **emeu.** [alter. of Pg *ema* ostrich (orig. crane)]

em·u·late (*v.* em′yə lāt′; *adj.* em′yə lit), *v.,* **-lat·ed, -lat·ing,** *adj.* —*v.t.* **1.** to try to equal or excel; imitate with effort to equal or surpass. **2.** to rival with some degree of success. —*adj.* **3.** *Obs.* emulous. [< L *aemulāt(us),* ptp. of *aemulārī* to rival] —**em′u·la′tive,** *adj.* —**em′u·la′tive·ly,** *adv.* —**em′u·la′tor,** *n.*

em·u·la·tion (em′yə lā′shən), *n.* **1.** effort or desire to equal or excel others. **2.** *Obs.* jealous rivalry. [< L *aemulātiōn-* (s. of *aemulātiō*)] —**Syn. 1.** competition, rivalry.

em·u·lous (em′yə ləs), *adj.* **1.** desirous of equaling or excelling; filled with emulation. **2.** arising from or of the nature of emulation, as actions, attitudes, etc. **3.** *Obs.* jealous; envious. [< L *aemulus* vying with; see -OUS] —**em′u·lous·ly,** *adv.* —**em′u·lous·ness,** *n.*

e·mul·si·fy (i mul′sə fī′), *v.t.,* **-fied, -fy·ing.** to make into an emulsion. [< L *ēmuls(us)* (see EMULSION) + -IFY] —**e·mul′si·fi′a·ble, e·mul′si·ble,** *adj.* —**e·mul′si·fi·ca′tion,** *n.* —**e·mul′si·fi′er,** *n.*

e·mul·sion (i mul′shən), *n.* **1.** a liquid preparation of the color and consistency of milk. **2.** *Physical Chem.* any colloidal suspension of a liquid in another liquid. **3.** *Pharm.* a liquid preparation consisting of two completely immiscible liquids, one of which, as minute globules, is dispersed throughout the other: used as a means of making a medicine palatable. **4.** *Photog.* a photosensitive composition, consisting of one or more of the silver halides suspended in gelatin for coating one surface of a film or the like. [< NL *ēmulsiōn-* (s. of *ēmulsiō*) = L *ēmuls(us)* milked out (*ē-* E- + *mulsus,* ptp. of *mulgēre* to milk) + *-iōn-* -ION] —**e·mul′sive,** *adj.*

e·mul·soid (i mul′soid), *n. Physical Chem.* a sol having a liquid disperse phase. Cf. **suspensoid.** [< L *ēmuls(us)* + -OID] —**e·mul·soi·dal** (i mul soid′əl, ē′mul-), *adj.*

e·munc·to·ry (i mungk′tə rē), *n., pl.* **-ries,** *adj.* —*n.* **1.** a part or organ of the body, as the skin, a kidney, etc., carrying off waste products. —*adj.* **2.** excretory. [< NL *ēmunctōri(um)* = L *ēmunct(us)* wiped off (*ē-* E- + *munc-,* var. s. of *mungere* to wipe + *-tus* ptp. suffix) + *-ōrium* -ORY[2]]

en (en), *n.* **1.** the letter *N, n.* **2.** *Print.* half of the width of an em.

en-[1], **1.** a prefix meaning primarily "in," "into," occurring first in words from French, but now used freely as an English formative with the old concrete force of putting the object into or on something or of bringing the object into a specified condition, often serving to form transitive verbs from nouns or adjectives: *enable; enact; endear; engulf; enshrine; enslave.* **2.** a prefix attached to verbs in order to make them transitive or, if they are already transitive, to give them the transitive sign: *enkindle; entwine; engird; engrave.* Also, **em-**[1]. Cf. **in-**[2]. [ME < OF < L *in-* IN-[2]]

en-[2], a prefix representing Greek *en-,* corresponding to **en-**[1] and occurring chiefly in combinations already formed in Greek: *energy; enthusiasm.* Also, **em-**[2]. [< Gk (often through L); c. IN-[1], IN-[2]]

-en[1], a suffix formerly used to form transitive and intransitive verbs from adjectives (*fasten; harden; sweeten*), or from nouns (*heighten; lengthen; strengthen*). [ME, OE *-n-* (as in ME *fast-n-e(n),* OE *fæst-n-ian* to make fast, fasten); morphemic now; c. *-n-* of like verbs in other Gmc languages (Icel *fastna*)]

-en[2], a suffix formerly used to form adjectives from nouns: *ashen; golden; oaken.* [ME, OE; c. OHG *-īn,* Goth *-eins,* L *-īnus,* etc.; see -INE[1]]

-en[3], a suffix used to mark the past participle in many

strong and some weak verbs: *taken; proven.* [ME, OE; c. G *-en*, Icel *-inn*, etc.]
-en[4], a suffix used in forming the plural of some nouns: *brethren; children; oxen.* [ME; OE *-an*, case ending of n-stem nouns, as in *naman* obl. sing., and nom. and acc. pl. of *nama* name; akin to n-stem forms in other IE languages, as in L *nomen, nomin-* name]
-en[5], a diminutive suffix: *kitten; maiden.* [ME, OE, from neut. of -EN[2]]
en·a·ble (en ā′bəl), *v.t.*, **-bled, -bling.** **1.** to make able; give power, means, or ability to; make competent; authorize. **2.** to make possible or easy. [ME] —**en·a′bler,** *n.*
en·act (en akt′), *v.t.* **1.** to make into an act or statute. **2.** to act the part of: *to enact Hamlet.* [ME *enacte(n)*] —**en·act′a·ble,** *adj.* —**en·ac′tor,** *n.*
en·ac·tive (en ak′tiv), *adj.* having power to enact or establish, as a law.
en·act·ment (en akt′mənt), *n.* **1.** the act of enacting. **2.** the state or fact of being enacted. **3.** something that is enacted; a law or statute.
en·ac·to·ry (en ak′tə rē), *adj. Law.* of or pertaining to an enactment.
e·nam·el (i nam′əl), *n.*, *v.*, **-eled, -el·ing** or (*esp. Brit.*) **-elled, -el·ling.** —*n.* **1.** a glassy substance, usually opaque, applied by fusion to the surface of metal, pottery, etc., as an ornament or for protection. **2.** enamelware. **3.** any of various enamellike varnishes, paints, etc. **4.** any enamellike surface with a bright luster. **5.** an artistic work executed in enamel. **6.** *Dentistry.* the hard, glossy, calcareous covering of the crown of a tooth. —*v.t.* **7.** to inlay or overlay with enamel. **8.** to form an enamellike surface upon: *to enamel cardboard.* **9.** to decorate as with enamel; variegate with colors. [ME *enamele(n)* < AF, MF *enamele(r)* = *en-* EN-[1] + *ameler*, contr. of *esmaillier* to enamel < *esma(i)l* enamel < ML *smalt(um)* < Gmc; cf. SMELT[1]] —**e·nam′el·er;** *esp. Brit.*, **e·nam′el·ler,** *n.* —**e·nam′el·ist;** *esp. Brit.*, **e·nam′el·list,** *n.* —**e·nam′el·work′,** *n.*
e·nam·el·ing (i nam′ə liŋ), *n.* **1.** the art, act, or work of a person who enamels. **2.** a decoration or coating of enamel. Also, *esp. Brit.*, **e·nam′el·ling.** [late ME]
e·nam·el·ware (i nam′əl wâr′), *n.* metalware, as cooking utensils, covered with an enamel surface.
en·am·or (en am′ər), *v.t.* to inflame with love; charm; captivate (usually used in the passive and fol. by *of*): *to be enamored of a lady.* Also, *esp. Brit.*, **en·am′our.** [ME *enamoure(n)* < OF *enamoure(r)*] —**Syn.** fascinate, enchant.
en ar·rière (äN NA RYER′), *French.* backward.
en·ar·thro·sis (en′är thrō′sis), *n.*, *pl.* **-ses** (-sēz). *Anat.* a joint, as at the shoulder, in which a convex end of one bone is socketed in a concavity of another; ball-and-socket joint. [< NL < Gk. See EN-[2], ARTHRO-, -OSIS] —**en·ar·thro·di·al** (en′är thrō′dē əl), *adj.*
e·nate (ē′nāt), *n.* **1.** a kinsman related on one's mother's side. Cf. **agnate, cognate.** —*adj.* **2.** Also, **e·nat·ic** (ē nat′ik). related on one's mother's side. [< L *ēnāt(us)*, ptp. of *ēnāscī* to issue forth, be born]
en a·vant (äN NA väN′), *French.* forward; onward.
en bloc (äN blôk′; *Eng.* en blok′), *French.* as a whole.
enc., **1.** enclosed. **2.** enclosure. **3.** encyclopedia.
en·cae·nia (en sēn′yə, -sē′nē ə), *n.* **1.** (*construed as pl.*) festive ceremonies commemorating the founding of a city or the consecration of a church. **2.** (*often cap.*) (*often construed as sing.*) ceremonies at Oxford University in honor of founders and benefactors. [ME < LL < Gk *enkaínia* consecration festivities, neut. pl. of *enkaínios* = *en-* EN-[2] + *-kainios* bound, var. of *kainós* new]
en·cage (en kāj′), *v.t.*, **-caged, -cag·ing.** to confine in or as in a cage; coop up.
en·camp (en kamp′), *v.i.*, **1.** to settle or lodge in a camp. —*v.t.* **2.** to make into a camp. **3.** to lodge in a camp.
en·camp·ment (en kamp′mənt), *n.* **1.** the act or an instance of encamping; lodgment in a camp. **2.** the place or quarters occupied in camping; camp.
en·cap·su·late (en kap′sə lāt′), *v.t.*, *v.i.*, **-lat·ed, -lat·ing.** to make, form, or place in or as in a capsule. —**en·cap′su·la′tion,** *n.*
en·cap·sule (en kap′səl), *v.t.*, *v.i.*, **-suled, -sul·ing.** encapsulate.
en·car·nal·ise (en kär′nᵊlīz′), *v.t.*, **-ised, -is·ing.** *Chiefly Brit.* encarnalize.
en·car·nal·ize (en kär′nᵊlīz′), *v.t.*, **-ized, -iz·ing.** to invest with a worldly or sensual nature or form; make carnal.
en·case (en kās′), *v.t.*, **-cased, -cas·ing.** to enclose in or as in a case. Also, **incase.**
en·case·ment (en kās′mənt), *n.* **1.** the act of encasing. **2.** the state of being encased. **3.** *Biol., Embryol.* the theory that the germs of succeeding generations of a given species are enclosed, one within the other, in the germ cell of one of the parents. **4.** something that encases; case. Also, **incasement.**
en·caus·tic (en kô′stik), *adj.* **1.** painted with wax colors fixed with heat, or with any process in which colors are burned in. —*n.* **2.** a work of art produced by an encaustic process. [< L *encausticus(us)* < Gk *enkaustikós* for burning in] —**en·caus′ti·cal·ly,** *adv.*
-ence, a noun suffix equivalent to **-ance,** corresponding to the suffix **-ent** in adjectives: *abstinence; continence; dependence; difference.* [ME < OF < L *-entia.* See -ENT, -Y[3]]
en·ceinte[1] (en sänt′; *Fr.* äN SANT′), *adj.* pregnant; with child. [< F, irreg. < L *incient-* (s. of *inciēns*) pregnant; akin to Gk *énkyos* = *en-* EN-[2] + *ký(ein)* (to) be great with child]
en·ceinte[2] (en sänt′; *Fr.* äN SANT′), *n.*, *pl.* **-ceintes** (-sänts′; *Fr.* -SANT′). **1.** a wall or enclosure, as of a fortified place. **2.** the place enclosed. [< F: enclosure, also girding fence or rampart < L *incincta*, n. use of fem. of *incinctus* girded in (ptp. of *incingere*) = *in-* IN-[2] + *cing-* gird + *-tus* ptp. suffix]
En·cel·a·dus (en sel′ə dəs), *n. Class. Myth.* a giant thought to lie buried under Mount Etna, in Sicily.
encephal-, var. of **encephalo-** before a vowel: *encephalic.*
en·ce·phal·ic (en′sə fal′ik), *adj.* of or pertaining to the encephalon or brain.
en·ceph·a·li·tis (en sef′ə lī′tis), *n. Pathol.* inflammation of the substance of the brain. —**en·ceph·a·lit·ic** (en sef′ə lit′ik), *adj.*
encephalo-, a learned borrowing from Greek meaning "brain," used in the formation of compound words: *encephalograph.* Also, *esp. before a vowel,* **encephal-.** [< Gk *enképhalo(s).* See ENCEPHALON]
en·ceph·a·lo·gram (en sef′ə lə gram′), *n. Med.* an x-ray photograph of the brain.
en·ceph·a·lo·graph (en sef′ə lə graf′, -gräf′), *n. Med.* **1.** an encephalogram. **2.** an electroencephalograph.
en·ceph·a·log·ra·phy (en sef′ə log′rə fē), *n. Med.* the production of encephalograms, following replacement of the cerebrospinal fluid with air. —**en·ceph·a·lo·graph·ic** (en sef′ə lə graf′ik), *adj.* —**en·ceph′a·lo·graph′i·cal·ly,** *adv.*
en·ceph·a·lo·ma·la·cia (en sef′ə lō mə lā′shə, -shē ə), *n. Pathol.* a softness or degeneration of brain tissue, as caused by impairment of blood supply. [ENCEPHALO- + Gk *malak(ós)* soft + -IA]
en·ceph·a·lo·my·e·li·tis (en sef′ə lō mī′ə lī′tis), *n. Pathol.* inflammation of the brain and spinal cord. —**en·ceph·a·lo·my·e·lit·ic** (en sef′ə lō mī′ə lit′ik), *adj.*
en·ceph·a·lon (en sef′ə lon′), *n.*, *pl.* **-la** (-lə). the brain. [< NL, alter. (*-on* for *-os*) of Gk *enképhalos* brain]
en·chain (en chān′), *v.t.* **1.** to fasten with or as with a chain or chains; fetter; restrain. **2.** to hold fast, as the attention. [ME *enchaine(n)* < OF *enchaine(r), -chaener*] —**en·chain′ment,** *n.*
en·chant (en chant′, -chänt′), *v.t.* **1.** to subject to magical influence; cast a spell over; bewitch. **2.** to impart a magic quality or effect to. **3.** to delight to a high degree; charm. [ME *enchante(n)* < MF *enchante(r)* < L *incantāre* to bespell; see INCANTATION] —**Syn. 3.** fascinate; captivate.
en·chant·er (en chan′tər, -chän′-), *n.* **1.** a person who enchants or delights. **2.** a magician; sorcerer. [ENCHANT + -ER[1]; r. ME *enchantour* < AF; OF *enchanteor* < L *incantātor.* See INCANTATION, -OR[2]]
en·chant·ing (en chan′tiŋ, -chän′-), *adj.* charming; bewitching.
en·chant·ment (en chant′mənt, -chänt′-), *n.* **1.** the art, act, or an instance of enchanting. **2.** the state of being enchanted. **3.** something that enchants. [ME *enchantement* < OF < L *incantāment(um)*] —**Syn. 1.** magic, sorcery, fascination. **3.** spell, charm.
en·chant·ress (en chan′tris, -chän′-), *n.* **1.** a woman who enchants; sorceress. **2.** a fascinating woman. [ME *enchaunteresse* < MF *enchanteresse*]
en·chase (en chās′), *v.t.*, **-chased, -chas·ing.** **1.** to place (gems) in an ornamental setting. **2.** to decorate with inlay, embossing, or engraving. [late ME < MF *enchasse(r)* (to) case in = *en-* EN-[1] + *chasse*, var. of *casse* CASE[2]] —**en·chas′er,** *n.*
en·chi·la·da (en′chə lä′də, -lad′ə), *n. Mexican Cookery.* a rolled tortilla filled with beef, chicken, etc., and served with cheese and a chili-flavored sauce. [< AmerSp, fem. of Sp *enchilado* spiced with chili (ptp. of *enchilar*). See EN-[1], CHILI, -ATE[1]]
en·chi·rid·i·on (en′kī rid′ē ən, -ki-), *n.*, *pl.* **-rid·i·ons, -rid·i·a** (-rid′ē ə). a handbook; manual. [< LL < Gk *encheirídion* handbook. See EN-[2], CHIRO-, -IDION]
en·cho·ri·al (en kōr′ē əl, -kôr′-), *n.* (esp. of demotic writing) belonging to or used in a particular country; native; domestic. Also, **en·chor·ic** (en kôr′ik, -kor′-). [< LL *enchōri(us)* (< Gk *enchṓrios* = *en-* EN-[2] + *chṓr(ā)* country + *-ios* adj. suffix) + -AL[1]]
en·ci·pher (en sī′fər), *v.t.* to convert (a message, communication, etc.) into cipher. —**en·ci′pher·er,** *n.* —**en·ci′pher·ment,** *n.*
en·cir·cle (en sûr′kəl), *v.t.*, **-cled, -cling.** **1.** to form a circle around; surround; encompass. **2.** to make a circling movement around. [ME] —**en·cir′cle·ment,** *n.*
encl., **1.** enclosed. **2.** enclosure.
en·clasp (en klasp′, -kläsp′), *v.t.* to hold in or as in a clasp or embrace.
en·clave (en′klāv; *Fr.* äN KLAV′), *n.*, *pl.* **-claves** (-klāvz; *Fr.* -KLAV′). a country, or esp., an outlying portion of a country, entirely or mostly surrounded by the territory of another country. [< F, appar. back formation from *enclaver* < VL **inclāvāre* to lock in. See IN-[2], CLAVICLE]
en·clit·ic (en klit′ik), *adj.* **1.** (of a word) closely connected with the preceding word and not having an independent accent or phonological status. —*n.* **2.** an enclitic word, as Latin *que* "and" in *arma virumque,* "arms and the man." [< LL *encliticus(us)* < Gk *enklitikós* = *en-* EN-[2] + *klít(os)* slope + *-ikos* -IC] —**en·clit′i·cal·ly,** *adv.*
en·close (en klōz′), *v.t.*, **-closed, -clos·ing.** **1.** to shut or hem in; close in on all sides. **2.** to surround, as with a fence or wall. **3.** to insert in the same envelope, package, or the like, with the main letter, consignment, etc. **4.** to hold or contain. Also, **inclose.** [ME *en-, inclose(n)* (to) close in] —**en·clos′a·ble,** *adj.* —**en·clos′er,** *n.* —**Syn. 1.** surround, encircle, encompass.
en·clo·sure (en klō′zhər), *n.* **1.** the act or an instance of enclosing. **2.** the state of being enclosed. **3.** the separation and appropriation of land by means of a fence. **4.** a tract of land surrounded by a fence. **5.** something that encloses, as a fence or wall. **6.** something that is enclosed, as a paper sent in a letter. Also, **inclosure.**
en·code (en kōd′), *v.t.*, **-cod·ed, -cod·ing.** to convert (a message, information, etc.) into code. —**en·code′ment,** *n.* —**en·cod′er,** *n.*
en·co·mi·ast (en kō′mē ast′), *n.* a person who utters or writes an encomium; eulogist. [< Gk *enkōmiast(ḗs).* See ENCOMIUM, -IST] —**en·co′mi·as′tic, en·co′mi·as′ti·cal,** *adj.* —**en·co′mi·as′ti·cal·ly,** *adv.*
en·co·mi·um (en kō′mē əm), *n.*, *pl.* **-mi·ums, -mi·a** (-mē ə). a formal expression of high praise; eulogy. [< L < Gk *enkṓmion* = *en-* EN-[2] + *kôm(os)* a revel + *-ion* -Y[3]]
en·com·pass (en kum′pəs), *v.t.* **1.** to form a circle about; encircle; surround. **2.** to enclose; envelop. **3.** to include comprehensively. **4.** *Obs.* to outwit. —**en·com′pass·ment,** *n.*
en·core (äng′kōr, -kôr, än′-), *interj.*, *n.*, *v.*, **-cored, -cor·ing.** —*interj.* **1.** again; once more (used by an audience in

calling for a repetition of a song, act, etc., or for an additional number or piece). —*n.* **2.** a demand, as by applause, for a repetition of a song, act, etc., or for a performance of an additional number or piece. **3.** the performance or selection given in response to such a demand. —*v.t.* **4.** to call for an encore from (a performer). [< F: still, yet, besides < L (*in*) *hanc horām* until this hour]

en·coun·ter (en koun′tər), *v.t.* **1.** to come upon; meet with, esp. unexpectedly. **2.** to meet with or contend against (difficulties, opposition, etc.). **3.** to meet (a person, military force, etc.) in conflict. —*v.i.* **4.** to meet, esp. in conflict. —*n.* **5.** a meeting with a person or thing, esp. casually or unexpectedly. **6.** a meeting of persons or groups that are in conflict or opposition; combat; battle. **7.** *Obs.* manner of meeting; behavior. [ME *encountre(n)* < OF *encontre(r)* < ML *incontrāre* < LL *incontr(ā)* facing = L *in* + *contrā*; see COUNTER[3]] —**en·coun′ter·er,** *n.* —**Syn. 1–3.** confront, face.

encoun′ter group′, a group of persons who meet regularly (usually over a short period of time), with or without a trained professional in charge, to increase self- and social-awareness and to change behavior through openness, honesty, interpersonal confrontation, self-disclosure and strong emotional expression.

en·cour·age (en kûr′ij, -kur′-), *v.t.*, **-aged, -ag·ing. 1.** to inspire with courage, spirit, or confidence. **2.** to stimulate by assistance, approval, etc. [late ME *encorage* < MF *encorag(ier)*] —**en·cour′ag·er,** *n.* —**en·cour′ag·ing·ly,** *adv.* —**Syn. 1.** embolden, hearten, reassure, incite. **2.** aid, help; promote, advance, foster. —**Ant. 1.** dishearten.

en·cour·age·ment (en kûr′ij mənt, -kur′-), *n.* **1.** the act of encouraging. **2.** the state of being encouraged. **3.** something that encourages. —**Ant. 1.** disapproval.

en·crim·son (en krim′zən), *v.t.* to make crimson.

en·cri·nite (en′krə nīt′), *n.* a crinoid, esp. a fossil crinoid. [< NL *encrin(us)* (< Gk *en-* EN-[2] + *krínon* lily) + -ITE[1]]

en·croach (en krōch′), *v.i.* **1.** to advance beyond proper limits; make gradual inroads. **2.** to trespass upon the property, domain, or rights of another, esp. stealthily or by gradual advances. [ME *encroche(n)* < OF *encrochie(r)* (to) hook in, seize = *en-* EN-[1] + *croc* hook < Gmc; see CROOK] —**en·croach′er,** *n.* —**Syn. 1, 2.** See **trespass.**

en·croach·ment (en krōch′mənt), *n.* **1.** the act or an instance of encroaching. **2.** anything taken by encroaching.

en·crust (en krust′), *v.t.*, *v.i.* incrust. —**en·crust′ant,** *adj.*, *n.*

en·crus·ta·tion (en′kru stā′shən), *n.* incrustation.

en·cul·tu·ra·tion (en kul′chə rā′shən), *n.* the process by which a person adapts to a culture and assimilates its values. [EN-[1] + (AC)CULTURATION]

en·cum·ber (en kum′bər), *v.t.* **1.** to impede or hinder; hamper; retard. **2.** to block up or fill with what is obstructive or superfluous. **3.** to burden or weigh down. **4.** to burden with obligations, debt, etc. Also, **incumber.** [ME *encombre(n)* < MF *encombre(r)* = *en-* EN-[1] + *combre* barrier < LL *combr(us)* < Gaulish **comberos* a bringing together; see COM-, BEAR[1]] —**en·cum′ber·ing·ly,** *adv.* —**Syn. 4.** oppress.

en·cum·brance (en kum′brəns), *n.* **1.** something that encumbers; something burdensome, useless, or superfluous; burden; hindrance. **2.** a dependent person, esp. a child. **3.** *Law.* a burden or claim on property, as a mortgage. Also, **incumbrance.** [ME *encombraunce* < MF *encombrance*]

en·cum·branc·er (en kum′brən sər), *n.* *Law.* a person who holds an encumbrance.

-ency, a noun suffix, equivalent to **-ence:** *consistency; dependency; exigency.* [< L *-entia.* See -ENT, -Y[3]]

ency., encyclopedia. Also, **encyc., encycl.**

en·cyc·li·cal (en sik′li kəl, -sī′kli-), *n.* **1.** *Rom. Cath. Ch.* a letter addressed by the pope to all the bishops of the church. —*adj.* **2.** (of a letter) intended for wide or general circulation. Also, **en·cyc′lic.** [< LL *encyclic(us)* (< Gk *enkýklios,* with *-icus* -IC for *-ios;* see EN-[2], CYCLE) + -AL[1]]

en·cy·clo·pe·di·a (en sī′klə pē′dē ə), *n.* **1.** a book or set of books containing articles on various topics, usually in alphabetical arrangement, covering all branches of knowledge or all aspects of one subject. **2.** (*cap.*) the 18th-century French work edited by Diderot and D'Alembert, distinguished by its advanced or radical character. Also, **en·cy′clo·pae′di·a.** [< NL *encyclopaedia,* by mistake for Gk *enkýklios paideía* circular (i.e., well-rounded) education. See ENCYCLICAL, PEDI-[2]]

en·cy·clo·pe·dic (en sī′klə pē′dik), *adj.* **1.** pertaining to or of the nature of an encyclopedia; relating to all branches of knowledge. **2.** comprehending a wide variety of information; comprehensive: *an encyclopedic memory.* Also, **en·cy′clo·pae′dic, en·cy′clo·pe′di·cal, en·cy′clo·pae′di·cal.** —**en·cy′clo·pe′di·cal·ly, en·cy′clo·pae′di·cal·ly,** *adv.*

en·cy·clo·pe·dism (en sī′klə pē′diz əm), *n.* **1.** encyclopedic learning. **2.** (*often cap.*) the doctrines and influence of the Encyclopedists. Also, **en·cy′clo·pae′dism.**

en·cy·clo·pe·dist (en sī′klə pē′dist), *n.* **1.** a compiler of or contributor to an encyclopedia. **2.** (*often cap.*) one of the collaborators on the French Encyclopedia. Also, **en·cy′clo·pae′dist.**

en·cyst (en sist′), *v.t.*, *v.i.* *Biol.* to enclose or become enclosed in a cyst. —**en·cyst′ment, en′cys·ta′tion,** *n.*

end[1] (end), *n.* **1.** the extremity of anything that is longer than it is wide or broad: *the end of a street; the end of a rope.* **2.** a point, line, or limitation that indicates the full extent, degree, etc., of something; limit; bounds. **3.** a part or place at or adjacent to an extremity. **4.** the furthermost imaginable place or point. **5.** a termination or conclusion. **6.** the concluding part. **7.** a purpose or aim: *to gain one's ends.* **8.** the purpose for which something exists. **9.** an issue or result. **10.** termination of existence; death. **11.** a cause of death, destruction, or ruin. **12.** a remnant or fragment: *mill end; ends and trimmings.* **13.** a share or part in something. **14.** *Football.* either of the linemen stationed farthest from the center. **15.** *Slang.* **a.** that which finally exhausts one's patience. **b.** the peak of quality; acme. **16. at loose ends, a.** without an occupation; unsettled. **b.** without definite plans; confused; uncertain. **17. make both ends meet,** to live within one's means. Also, **make ends meet.** —*v.t.* **18.** to bring to an end or conclusion. **19.** to form the end of. **20.** to cause the demise of; kill. **21.** to constitute the most outstanding or greatest possible example or instance of (usually used in the infinitive): *the blunder to end all blunders.* —*v.i.* **22.** to come to an end; terminate; cease. **23.** to issue or result. **24.** to reach or arrive at a final condition, circumstance, or goal (often fol. by *up*): *to end up in the army.* [ME, OE *ende;* c. G *Ende,* Icel *endir,* Goth *andeis* end; akin to Skt *ánta* end] —**end′er,** *n.*

—**Syn. 4.** tip, bound, limit, terminus. **5.** END, CLOSE, CONCLUSION, FINISH, OUTCOME refer to the termination of something. END implies a natural termination, completion of an action or process, or attainment of purpose: *the end of a day, of a race; to some good end.* CLOSE implies a planned rounding off of something in process: *the close of a conference.* CONCLUSION suggests a decision or arrangement: *All evidence leads to this conclusion; the conclusion of peace terms.* FINISH emphasizes completion of something begun: *a fight to the finish.* OUTCOME suggests the issue of something that was in doubt: *the outcome of a game.* **6.** finale, peroration. **7.** intent, intention, goal. See **aim. 9.** outcome, consequence. **10.** destruction, extermination, annihilation, ruin. **18.** conclude, complete, close. **18, 22.** stop. —**Ant. 5.** beginning, start. **18, 22.** begin.

end[2] (end), *v.t.* *Brit. Dial.* to put wheat, hay, or other grain into a stack or barn. [? var. of *in* to harvest (OE *innian* to lodge, put up). See INN]

end-, var. of **endo-** before a vowel: *endamoeba.*

end., endorsed.

end-all (end′ôl′), *n.* **1.** the end of everything; ultimate conclusion. **2.** something that brings things to such an end.

en·dam·age (en dam′ij), *v.t.*, **-aged, -ag·ing.** to damage. [ME] —**en·dam′age·ment,** *n.*

en·da·moe·ba (en′də mē′bə), *n.*, *pl.* **-bae** (-bē), **-bas.** any protozoan of the genus *Endamoeba,* a species of which causes dysentery in man. Also, **en′da·me′ba.** —**en′da·moe′bic, en′da·me′bic,** *adj.*

en·dan·ger (en dān′jər), *v.t.* to expose to danger; imperil. [late ME] —**en·dan′ger·ment,** *n.*

en·dan·gered (en dān′jərd), *adj.* **1.** threatened with danger: *endangered lives of trapped coal miners.* **2.** threatened with extinction: *endangered wildlife.*

en′ dash′, *Print.* a dash one en long.

end·brain (end′brān′), *n.* the telencephalon.

en·dear (en dēr′), *v.t.* **1.** to make dear, esteemed, or beloved. **2.** *Obs.* to make costly. —**en·dear′ing·ly,** *adv.*

en·dear·ment (en dēr′mənt), *n.* **1.** the act of endearing. **2.** the state of being endeared. **3.** something that endears; an action or utterance showing affection.

en·deav·or (en dev′ər), *v.i.* **1.** to exert oneself to do or effect something; make an effort; strive. **2.** to attempt; try. —*v.t. Obs.* **3.** to try to reach or achieve (something). **4.** to exert (one's mind, powers, etc.) to achieve something. —*n.* **5.** a strenuous effort; attempt. Also, *esp. Brit.,* **en·deav′our.** [ME *endevere(n).* See EN-[1], DEVOIR] —**en·deav′or·er;** *esp. Brit.,* **en·deav′our·er,** *n.* —**Syn. 1.** struggle, labor. **1, 2.** See **try. 2.** essay, undertake. **5.** See **effort.**

En·de·cott (en′də kət, -kot′), *n.* **John,** 1588?–1665, colonial governor of Massachusetts 1644–65, born in England. Also, **Endicott.**

en·dem·ic (en dem′ik), *adj.* **1.** Also, **en·dem′i·cal.** peculiar to a particular people or locality; indigenous. —*n.* **2.** an endemic disease. [< NL *endēmic(us)* = Gk *éndēm(os)* endemic (see EN-[2], DEMOS) + L *-icus* -IC] —**en·dem′i·cal·ly,** *adv.* —**en·de·mism** (en′də miz′əm), **en·de·mic·i·ty** (en′də mis′i tē), *n.*

En′der·by Land′ (en′dər bē), a part of the coast of Antarctica, E of Queen Maud Land: discovered 1831.

en·der·mic (en dûr′mik), *adj.* acting through the skin by absorption, as a medicine. —**en·der′mi·cal·ly,** *adv.*

En·di·cott (en′də kət, -kot′), *n.* **John.** See **Endecott.**

end·ing (en′ding), *n.* **1.** a bringing or coming to an end; termination; close. **2.** the final or concluding part; conclusion. **3.** death; destruction. **4.** *Gram.* an inflectional morpheme at the end of a word, as *-s* in *cuts* or *-ed* in *granted.* **5.** (not in technical use) any final word part, as the *-ow* of *widow.* [ME *endyng,* OE *endung*]

en·dive (en′dīv, än′dēv; *Fr.* äN dēv′), *n.*, *pl.* **-dives** (-dīvz, -dēvz; *Fr.* -dēv′). **1.** a plant, *Cichorium endivia,* of two main types, one having finely divided, curled leaves and one with broad, fleshy leaves, both used for salads. **2.** chicory (defs. 1, 2). [ME < MF < ML *endīv(ia),* L *intibus, intubus,* etc. < ?]

end·less (end′lis), *adj.* **1.** having or seeming to have no end, limit, or conclusion; boundless; infinite; interminable. **2.** made continuous, as by joining the two ends of a single length. [ME *endelees,* OE *endelēas*] —**end′less·ly,** *adv.* —**end′less·ness,** *n.* —**Syn. 1.** limitless, unending, unceasing, continuous, continual, perpetual, everlasting. See **eternal.** —**Ant. 1.** finite.

end′ line′, **1.** *Football.* a line at each end of the field parallel to and 10 yards behind the goal line. **2.** *Basketball.* a line at each end of the court at right angles to the sidelines.

end·long (end′lông′, -long′), *adv.* *Archaic.* **1.** lengthwise. **2.** on end. [ME *endelong;* r. OE *andlong* ALONG]

end′ man′, **1.** a man at one end of a row or line. **2.** a man at either end of the line of performers of a minstrel troupe who carries on a dialogue with the interlocutor.

end′ mat′ter, *Print.* See **back matter.**

end·most (end′mōst′), *adj.* furthest; most distant; last.

endo-, a learned borrowing from Greek meaning "within," used in the formation of compound words: *endocardial.* Also, *esp. before a vowel,* **end-.** [< Gk, comb. form of *éndon* within]

en·do·blast (en′də blast′), *n.* *Embryol.* **1.** entoderm. **2.** hypoblast (def. 2). —**en′do·blas′tic,** *adj.*

en·do·car·di·al (en′dō kär′dē əl), *adj.* **1.** situated within the heart. **2.** of or pertaining to the endocardium.

en·do·car·di·tis (en′dō kär dī′tis), *n.* *Pathol.* inflammation of the endocardium. —**en·do·car·dit·ic** (en′dō kär dit′ik), *adj.*

en·do·car·di·um (en′dō kär′dē əm), *n.*, *pl.* **-di·a** (-dē ə). *Anat.* the serous membrane that lines the cavities of the heart. [< NL = *endo-* ENDO- + *-cardium* < Gk *-kardion* = *kard(ía)* heart + *-ion,* neut. of *-ios* adj. suffix]

en·do·carp (en′də kärp′), *n.* *Bot.* the inner layer of a pericarp, as the stone of certain fruits. —**en′do·car′pal, en′do·car′pic,** *adj.*

en·do·cen·tric (en′dō sen′trik), *adj. Gram.* (of a construction or compound) having the same syntactic function in the sentence as one of its immediate constituents, as *cold water*, which functions as would the noun *water*. Cf. **exocentric.**

en·do·crine (en′də krin, -krīn′, -krēn′), *Anat., Physiol.* —*adj.* Also, **en·do·cri·nal** (en′də krīn′əl), **en′do·crin′ic, en·doc·ri·nous** (en dok′rə nəs). **1.** secreting internally. **2.** of or pertaining to an endocrine gland or its secretion: *an endocrine imbalance.* —*n.* **3.** an internal secretion; hormone. **4.** See **endocrine gland.** [ENDO- + Gk *krī́n(ein)* (to) separate]

en′docrine gland′, any of various glands, as the thyroid, adrenals, and pituitary, that secrete hormones directly into the blood or lymph; ductless gland.

en·do·cri·nol·o·gy (en′dō krə nol′ə jē, -krī-), *n.* the science dealing with the endocrine glands and their secretions, esp. in relation to their processes or functions. —**en·do·crin·o·log·ic** (en′dō krin′əloj′ik), **en′do·crin′o·log′i·cal,** *adj.* —**en′do·cri·nol′o·gist,** *n.*

en·do·derm (en′də dûrm′), *n. Embryol.* entoderm. [ENDO- + -DERM, modeled on F *endoderme*] —**en′do·der′mal, en′do·der′mic,** *adj.*

en·do·der·mis (en′dō dûr′mis), *n. Bot.* a specialized tissue in the roots and stems of vascular plants, composed of a single layer of modified parenchyma cells forming the inner boundary of the cortex. [< NL]

en·do·don·tics (en′dō don′tiks), *n.* (*construed as sing.*), the branch of dentistry dealing with the cause, diagnosis, prevention, and treatment of diseases of the dental pulp, usually by removal of the nerve and other tissue of the pulp cavity and its replacement with suitable filling material; root canal therapy. Also, **en·do·don·tia** (en′dō don′shə, -shē ə), **en·do·don·tol·o·gy** (en′dō don tol′ə jē). [< NL *endodont(ia)* (see END-, -ODONT, -IA) + -ICS]—**en′do·don′tist,** *n.*

en·do·en·zyme (en′dō en′zīm), *n. Biochem.* an enzyme that functions within a cell. Cf. **exoenzyme.**

en·dog·a·my (en dog′ə mē), *n.* marriage within a specific tribe or similar social unit. Cf. **exogamy** (def. 1). —**en·dog′a·mous, en·do·gam·ic** (en′dō gam′ik), *adj.*

en·do·gen (en′də jen′, -jən), *n. Bot.* any plant of the obsolete class *Endogenae*, including the monocotyledons, whose stems were erroneously supposed to grow from within. [ENDO- + -GEN, modeled on F *endogène*]

en·dog·e·nous (en doj′ə nəs), *adj.* **1.** *Biol.* growing or proceeding from within; originating within. **2.** *Physiol., Biochem.* pertaining to the metabolism of nitrogenous elements of cells and tissues. —**en·do·ge·nic·i·ty** (en′do jə nis′i tē), *n.*

en·dog·e·ny (en doj′ə nē), *n. Biol.* development or growth from within. Also, **en·do·gen·e·sis** (en′dō jen′i sis).

en·do·lymph (en′də limf′), *n. Anat.* the fluid contained within the membranous labyrinth of the ear. —**en·do·lym·phat·ic** (en′dō lim fat′ik), *adj.*

en·do·morph (en′də môrf′), *n.* **1.** a mineral enclosed within another mineral. Cf. **perimorph. 2.** a person of the endomorphic type.

en·do·mor·phic (en′də môr′fik), *adj.* **1.** *Mineral.* **a.** occurring in the form of an endomorph. **b.** of or pertaining to endomorphs. **c.** taking place within a rock mass. **2.** having a heavy body build characterized by the relative prominence of structures developed from the embryonic entoderm (contrasted with *ectomorphic, mesomorphic*). —**en′do·mor′phy,** *n.*

en·do·mor·phism (en′dō môr′fiz əm, -də-), *n. Mineral.* a change brought about within the mass of an intrusive igneous rock. [ENDOMORPH(IC) + -ISM]

en·do·par·a·site (en′dō par′ə sīt′), *n.* an internal parasite (opposed to *ectoparasite*). —**en·do·par·a·sit·ic** (en′dō par′ə sit′ik), *adj.*

en·do·phyte (en′də fīt′), *n. Bot.* a plant living within another plant, usually as a parasite. —**en·do·phyt·ic** (en′də fit′ik), *adj.* —**en′do·phyt′i·cal·ly,** *adv.* —**en·doph·y·tous** (en dof′i təs), *adj.*

en·do·plasm (en′də plaz′əm, -dō-), *n. Biol.* the inner portion of the cytoplasm of a cell. Cf. **ectoplasm** (def. 1). —**en′do·plas′mic,** *adj.*

en·dop·o·dite (en dop′ə dīt′), *n. Zool.* the inner or medial branch of a biramous crustacean appendage. Also called **en·do·pod** (en′də pod′). Cf. **exopodite.** [ENDO- + -POD + -ITE[1]] —**en·dop·o·dit·ic** (en dop′ə dit′ik), *adj.*

end′ or′gan, *Physiol.* one of several specialized structures found at the peripheral end of sensory or motor nerve fibers.

en·dorse (en dôrs′), *v.t.*, **-dorsed, -dors·ing. 1.** to approve, support, or sustain: *to endorse a statement.* **2.** to write (something) on the back of a document, paper, etc. **3.** to designate oneself as payee of (a check) by signing, usually on the reverse side of the instrument. **4.** to sign one's name on (a commercial document or other instrument). **5.** to make over (a stated amount) to another as payee by one's endorsement. **6.** to acknowledge (payment) by placing one's signature on a bill, draft, etc. Also, **indorse.** [var. (with *en-* for *in-*) of earlier *indorse* < ML *indors(āre)* (to) put on the back = L *in-* IN-[2] + *dors(um)* back; r. *endoss*, ME *endosse(n)* < OF *endosse(r)* = *en-* EN-[1] + *dos* < L *dors(um)*] —**en·dors′a·ble,** *adj.* —**en·dors′er, en·dor′sor,** *n.* —**en·dors′ing·ly,** *adv.* —**Syn. 1.** sanction, uphold, back.

en·dor·see (en dôr sē′, en′dôr-), *n.* a person to whom a negotiable document is endorsed. Also, **indorsee.**

en·dorse·ment (en dôrs′mənt), *n.* **1.** approval or sanction. **2.** the placing of one's signature, instructions, etc., on a document. **3.** the signature, instructions, etc., placed on the reverse of a commercial document assigning the interest therein to another. **4.** *Insurance.* a clause under which the stated coverage of an insurance policy may be altered. Also, **indorsement.**

en·do·scope (en′də skōp′), *n.* a slender, tubular instrument used to examine the interior of a body cavity or hollow organ. —**en·do·scop·ic** (en′də skop′ik), *adj.* —**en·dos·co·pist** (en dos′kə pist), *n.* —**en·dos′co·py,** *n.*

en·do·skel·e·ton (en′dō skel′i tᵊn), *n. Zool.* the internal skeleton or framework of the body of an animal (opposed to *exoskeleton*). —**en′do·skel′e·tal,** *adj.*

en·dos·mo·sis (en′dos mō′sis, -doz-), *n. Physical Chem.* **1.** osmosis from the outside toward the inside. **2.** the flow of a substance from an area of lesser concentration to one of greater concentration (opposed to *exosmosis*). Also, **en·dos·mos** (en′dos mōs′, -doz-). —**en·dos·mot·ic** (en′dos mot′ik, -doz-), *adj.* —**en′dos·mot′i·cal·ly,** *adv.*

en·do·sperm (en′də spûrm′), *n. Bot.* nutritive matter in seed-plant ovules, derived from the embryo sac. [ENDO- + -SPERM, modeled on F *endosperme*]

en·do·spore (en′də spōr′, -spôr′), *n.* **1.** *Bot.* the inner coat of a spore. **2.** *Bacteriol.* a spore formed within a cell of a rod-shaped organism. —**en·dos·por·ous** (en dos′pər əs, en′dō spōr′-, -spôr′-), *adj.* —**en·dos′por·ous·ly,** *adv.*

en·do·spo·ri·um (en′də spōr′ē əm, -spôr′-), *n., pl.* **-spo·ri·a** (-spōr′ē ə, -spôr′-). *Bot.* endospore (def. 1). [ENDO- + NL *-sporium* < Gk *spor(á)* seed + *-ion* dim. suffix]

en·dos·te·um (en dos′tē əm), *n., pl.* **-te·a** (-tē ə). *Anat.* the membrane lining the medullary cavity of a bone. [END- + NL *osteum* < Gk *ostéon* bone]

en·do·the·ci·um (en′dō thē′shē əm, -sē əm), *n., pl.* **-ci·a** (-shē ə, -sē ə). *Bot.* **1.** the lining of the cavity of an anther. **2.** (in mosses) the central mass of cells in the rudimentary capsule, from which the archespore is generally developed. **3.** (in bryophytes) the central mass of cells in the capsule, including the spores and columella. —**en·do·the·ci·al** (en′dō thē′shē əl, -shəl, -sē əl), *adj.*

en·do·the·li·um (en′dō thē′lē əm), *n., pl.* **-li·a** (-lē ə). a type of epithelium composed of a single layer of smooth, thin cells which lines the heart, blood vessels, lymphatics, and serous cavities. [ENDO- + NL *-thelium*; cf. EPITHELIUM] —**en′do·the′li·al,** *adj.* —**en′do·the′li·oid′,** *adj.*

en·do·ther·mic (en′dō thûr′mik), *adj. Chem.* noting or pertaining to a chemical change that is accompanied by an absorption of heat (opposed to *exothermic*). Also, **en′do·ther′mal.** —**en′do·ther′mi·cal·ly,** *adv.* —**en′do·ther′mism,** *n.*

en·do·tox·in (en′dō tok′sin), *n. Biochem.* the toxic protoplasm liberated when a microorganism dies and disintegrates, as in *Eberthella typhi*, the causative agent of typhoid fever. Cf. **exotoxin.** —**en′do·tox′ic,** *adj.*

en·dow (en dou′), *v.t.* **1.** to provide with a permanent fund or source of income. **2.** to furnish, as with some gift, faculty, or quality; equip. **3.** *Archaic.* to provide with dower. [ME *endowe(n)* < OF *endoue(r)* = *en-* EN-[1] + *douer* < L *dōtāre* to dower = *dōt-* (s. of *dōs*) dowry + *-āre* v. suffix] —**en·dow′er,** *n.*

en·dow·ment (en dou′mənt), *n.* **1.** the act of endowing. **2.** the property, funds, etc., with which an institution or person is endowed. **3.** Usually, **endowments.** an attribute of mind or body; a gift of nature. [late ME] —**Syn. 2.** gift, grant, bequest. **3.** capacity, talent, faculties, ability, capability. —**Ant. 3.** incapacity.

endow′ment insur′ance, life insurance providing for the payment of a stated sum to the insured if he lives beyond the maturity date of the policy, or to a beneficiary if the insured dies before that date.

end′ pa′per, *Bookbinding.* a sheet of paper folded to form two leaves, one of which is pasted flat inside each cover of a book, the other forming a flyleaf. Also called **end′ sheet′.**

end′ point′, *Chem.* the point in a titration usually noting the completion of a reaction and marked by a change of some kind, as of the color of an indicator.

end′ prod′uct, the final or resulting product, as of an industry, process of growth, etc.

end′ run′, *Football.* a running play in which the ball-carrier attempts to outflank the defensive end. Also called **end′ sweep′.**

end-stopped (end′stopt′), *adj. Pros.* (of a line of verse) ending at the end of a syntactic unit that is usually followed by a pause in speaking and a punctuation mark in writing.

end′ ta′ble, a small table placed beside a chair or at the end of a sofa.

en·due (en do͞o′, -dyo͞o′), *v.t.*, **-dued, -du·ing. 1.** to invest or endow with some gift, quality, or faculty. **2.** to put on; assume. **3.** to clothe. Also, **indue.** [ME *endewe(n)* (to) induct, cover < OF *enduire* < L *indūcere*. See INDUCE]

en·dur·a·ble (en do͝or′ə bəl, -dyo͝or′-), *adj.* capable of being endured. —**en·dur′a·bly,** *adv.* —**Syn.** bearable, tolerable.

en·dur·ance (en do͝or′əns, -dyo͝or′-), *n.* **1.** the fact or power of enduring or bearing anything. **2.** lasting quality; duration. **3.** something endured, as a hardship; trial. —**Syn. 1.** See **patience.**

en·dure (en do͝or′, -dyo͝or′), *v.*, **-dured, -dur·ing.** —*v.t.* **1.** to hold out against; sustain or undergo without impairment or yielding. **2.** to bear without resistance or with patience; tolerate. **3.** to admit of; allow; bear. —*v.i.* **4.** to continue to exist; last. **5.** to support adverse force or influence of any kind; suffer without yielding; suffer patiently. [ME *endure(n)* < OF *endure(r)* < L *indūrāre* to harden, steel, make lasting. See IN-[2], DURE[2]] —**Syn. 2.** stand, suffer, brook. See **bear**[1]. **4.** abide. See **continue.**

en·dur·ing (en do͝or′ing, -dyo͝or′-), *adj.* **1.** lasting; permanent. **2.** patient; long-suffering. —**en·dur′ing·ly,** *adv.* —**en·dur′ing·ness,** *n.*

end·ways (end′wāz′), *adv.* **1.** on end. **2.** with the end upward or forward. **3.** toward the ends or end; lengthwise. Also, **end·wise** (end′wīz′).

En·dym·i·on (en dim′ē ən), *n. Class. Myth.* a young man who was kept immortally youthful and beautiful through eternal sleep: beloved of the goddess Selene.

end′ zone′, *Football.* an area at each end of the field between the goal line and the end line.

-ene, *Chem.* a combining form indicating unsaturated hydrocarbons (*anthracene; benzene*), esp. those of the alkene series (*butylene*). [< Gk *-ēnē*, fem. of *-ēnos*, adj. suffix denoting origin or source]

ENE, east-northeast. Also, **E.N.E.**

en·e·ma (en′ə mə), *n. Med.* **1.** the injection of a fluid into the rectum. **2.** the fluid injected. [< LL < Gk: injection = *en-* EN-[2] + *(h)e-* (s. of *hiénai* to throw) + *-ma* n. suffix]

en·e·my (en′ə mē), *n., pl.* **-mies,** *adj.* —*n.* **1.** a person who feels hatred for or fosters harmful designs against another; an

adversary or opponent. **2.** an armed foe; an opposing military force. **3.** a hostile nation or state. **4.** a citizen of such a state. **5. enemies,** persons, nations, etc., that are hostile to one another. **6.** something harmful or prejudicial. **7. the Enemy,** the Devil; Satan. **—***adj.* **8.** belonging to a hostile power or to any of its nationals: *enemy property.* **9.** *Obs.* inimical; ill-disposed. [ME *enemi* < OF < L *inimic(us)* unfriendly. See IN-[3], AMICABLE]
—Syn. 1. antagonist. ENEMY, FOE refer to a dangerous public or personal adversary. ENEMY emphasizes the idea of hostility: *to overcome the enemy; a bitter enemy.* FOE, a more literary word, may be used interchangeably with enemy, but emphasizes somewhat more the danger to be feared from such a one: *deadly foe.* **—Ant. 1.** friend. **2.** ally.

en′emy al′ien, an alien residing in a country at war with the one of which he is a citizen.

E·ne·o·lith·ic (ē′nē ō lith′ik), *adj.* Chalcolithic. Also, **Aeneolithic.**

en·er·get·ic (en′ər jet′ik), *adj.* **1.** possessing or exhibiting energy; forcible; vigorous. **2.** powerful in action or effect; effective. Also, **en′er·get′i·cal.** [< Gk *energētik(ós)*] **—en′er·get′i·cal·ly,** *adv.* **—Syn. 1.** See **active. 2.** effectual.

en·er·get·ics (en′ər jet′iks), *n.* (*construed as sing.*) the branch of physics that deals with energy. **—en′er·get′i·cist,** *n.* **—en·er·ge·tis·tic** (en′ər ji tis′tik), *adj.*

en·er·gise (en′ər jīz′), *v.t., v.i.,* **-gised, -gis·ing.** *Chiefly Brit.* energize. **—en′er·gis′er,** *n.*

en·er·gize (en′ər jīz′), *v.,* **-gized, -giz·ing.** **—***v.t.* **1.** to give energy to; rouse into activity. **—***v.i.* **2.** to be in operation; put forth energy. **—en′er·giz′er,** *n.*

en·er·gu·men (en′ər gyo͞o′mən), *n.* **1.** a person possessed by an evil spirit; demoniac. **2.** a fanatical enthusiast. [< LL *energūmen(os)* possessed of an evil spirit < Gk *energoúmenos* pass. participle of *energein* to be active. See ENERGY]

en·er·gy (en′ər jē), *n., pl.* **-gies. 1.** Often, **energies. a.** the capacity for vigorous activity; available power. **b.** a feeling of tension caused or seeming to be caused by an excess of such power. **2.** an adequate or abundant amount of such power. **3.** an exertion of such power. **4.** the habit of vigorous activity; vigor as a characteristic. **5.** the ability to act, lead others, effect, etc., forcefully. **6.** forcefulness of expression. **7.** *Physics.* the capacity to do work; the property of a system that diminishes, when the system does work on any other system, by an amount equal to the work so done. *Symbol:* E [< LL *energīa* < Gk *enérgeia* activity = *energé-* (s. of *energeîn* to be active; see EN-[2], ERGO-[1]) + *-ia* -Y[3]] **—Syn. 1a, 2.** vigor, force, potency. **4.** zeal, push.

en′ergy lev′el, *Physics.* one of a quantized series of states in which matter may exist, each having constant energy and separated from others in the series by finite quantities of energy. Also called **en′ergy state′.**

en·er·vate (*v.* en′ər vāt′; *adj.* i nûr′vit), *v.,* **-vat·ed, -vat·ing,** *adj.* **—***v.t.* **1.** to deprive of nerve, force, or strength; destroy the vigor of; weaken. **—***adj.* **2.** enervated. [< L *ēnervāt(us)* weakened (ptp. of *ēnervāre*)] **—en′er·va′tion,** *n.* **—en′er·va′tive,** *adj.* **—en′er·va′tor,** *n.* **—Syn. 1.** enfeeble, exhaust.

en·er·vat·ed (en′ər vā′tid), *adj.* without vigor, force, or strength; languid.

E·nes·co (e nes′kō), *n.* **Georges** (zhôrzh), 1881–1955, Rumanian violinist, composer, and conductor. Also, **E·nes·cu** (e nes′ko͞o).

en·face (en fās′), *v.t.,* **-faced, -fac·ing. 1.** to write, print, or stamp something on the face of (a note, draft, etc.). **2.** to write, print, or stamp (something) on the face of a note, draft, etc. **—en·face′ment,** *n.*

en fa·mille (äɴ fa mē′yᵊ), *French.* in the family.

en·fant ter·ri·ble (äɴ fäɴ te rē′blᵊ), *pl.* **en·fants ter·ri·bles** (äɴ fäɴ te rē′blᵊ). *French.* **1.** an incorrigible child. **2.** a person who says and does indiscreet or irresponsible things.

en·fee·ble (en fē′bəl), *v.t.,* **-bled, -bling.** to make feeble; weaken. [ME *enfeble(n)* < OF *enfebl(ir)*] **—en·fee′ble·ment,** *n.* **—en·fee′bler,** *n.* **—Syn.** enervate, debilitate.

en·feoff (en fef′, -fēf′), *v.t.* **1.** to invest with a freehold estate in land. **2.** to give as a fief. [ME *enfe(o)ffe(n)* < AF *enfe(o)ffe(r)*] **—en·feoff′ment,** *n.*

en·fet·ter (en fet′ər), *v.t.* to bind with or as with fetters.

En·field (en′fēld′), *n.* **1.** a city in N Middlesex, in SE England, N of London. 109,524 (1961). **2.** a town in N Connecticut. 46,189 (1970).

en·fi·lade (en′fə lād′, en′fə lād′), *n., v.,* **-lad·ed, -lad·ing. —***n.* **1.** *Mil.* **a.** a position of works, troops, etc., making them subject to a sweeping fire from along the length of a line of troops, a trench, a battery, etc. **b.** the fire thus directed. **—***v.t.* **2.** *Mil.* to attack with an enfilade. [< F = *enfil(er)* (to) thread, string (see EN-[1], FILE[1]) + *-ade* -ADE[1]]

en·fin (äɴ faɴ′), *adv.* *French.* in conclusion; finally. [lit., in (the) end]

en·flame (en flām′), *v.t., v.i.,* **-flamed, -flam·ing.** inflame.

en·fleu·rage (*Fr.* äɴ flœ razh′), *n.* a process of extracting perfumes by exposing inodorous oils or fats to the exhalations of flowers. [< F = *enfleur(er)* (to) impregnate with scent of flowers (see EN-[1], FLOWER) + *-age* -AGE]

en·fold (en fōld′), *v.t.* **1.** to wrap up; envelop. **2.** to surround as if with folds. **3.** to clasp; embrace. **4.** to form into a fold or folds. Also, **infold. —en·fold′er,** *n.* **—en·fold′ment,** *n.*

en·force (en fōrs′, -fôrs′), *v.t.,* **-forced, -forc·ing. 1.** to put or keep in force; compel obedience to: *to enforce laws strictly.* **2.** to obtain (payment, obedience, etc.) by force or compulsion. **3.** to impose (a course of action) upon a person. **4.** to support (a demand, claim, etc.) by force. **5.** to impress or urge (an argument, contention, etc.) forcibly; lay stress upon. [ME *enforce(n)* < OF *enforc(ier), enforc(ir)* = *en-* EN-[1] + *forci(e)r* to FORCE] **—en·force′a·bil′i·ty,** *n.* **—en·force′a·ble,** *adj.* **—en·forc·ed·ly** (en fōr′sid lē, -fôr′-), *adv.* **—en·forc′er,** *n.* **—en·forc′ive,** *adj.*

en·force·ment (en fōrs′mənt, -fôrs′-), *n.* **1.** the act or process of enforcing. **2.** *Archaic.* something that enforces. [late ME < AF, OF]

en·fran·chise (en fran′chīz), *v.t.,* **-chised, -chis·ing. 1.** to grant a franchise to; admit to citizenship, esp. to the right of voting. **2.** to set free; liberate, as from slavery. Also called **franchise.** [< MF, OF *enfranchiss-* (long s. of *enfranchir* to free). See EN-[1], FRANK[1], -ISH[2]] **—en·fran·chise·ment** (en fran′chiz mənt, -chīz-), *n.* **—en·fran′chis·er,** *n.*

eng (eng), *n.* the symbol, ŋ, that, in the International Phonetic Alphabet and in the pronunciation alphabets of some dictionaries, represents the voiced velar nasal consonant indicated in this dictionary by ng, as in the pronunciations of *cling* (kling), and *clink* (klingk). Also called **agma.**

Eng., 1. England. **2.** English.

eng., 1. engine. **2.** engineer. **3.** engineering. **4.** engraved. **5.** engraver. **6.** engraving.

En·ga·dine (eng′gə dēn′), *n.* the valley of the Inn River in E Switzerland: resorts. 60 mi. long.

en·gage (en gāj′), *v.,* **-gaged, -gag·ing. —***v.t.* **1.** to occupy the attention or efforts of (a person or persons): *He engaged her in conversation.* **2.** to secure for aid, employment, use, etc.; hire: *to engage a workman; to engage a room.* **3.** to attract and hold fast: *The novel engaged his attention and interest.* **4.** to attract or please: *His good nature engages everyone.* **5.** to bind, as by pledge, promise, contract, or oath; make liable. **6.** to betroth (usually used in the passive). **7.** to bring (troops) into conflict; enter into conflict with. **8.** *Mech.* to cause (gears or the like) to become interlocked; interlock with. **9.** *Archaic.* to entangle or involve. **10.** *Archaic.* to attach or secure. **—***v.i.* **11.** to occupy oneself; become involved. **12.** to take employment. **13.** to pledge one's word; assume an obligation. **14.** to cross weapons; enter into conflict. **15.** *Mech.* (of gears or the like) to interlock. [< MF *engag(er),* OF *engagier.* See EN-[1], GAGE[1]] **—en·gag′er,** *n.*

en·ga·gé (*Fr.* äɴ ga zhā′), *adj.* having chosen to involve oneself in or commit oneself to something, as opposed to remaining aloof or indifferent. [< F: lit., engaged]

en·gaged (en gājd′), *adj.* **1.** busy or occupied; involved. **2.** under engagement; pledged. **3.** pledged to be married; betrothed. **4.** entered into conflict with. **5.** *Mech.* **a.** interlocked. **b.** (of wheels) in gear with each other. **6.** *Archit.* (of a distinct member) built so as to be truly or seemingly attached in part to the structure before which it stands: *an engaged column.* **—en·gag·ed·ly** (en gā′jid lē, -gājd′-), *adv.* **—en·gag′ed·ness,** *n.*

en·gage·ment (en gāj′mənt), *n.* **1.** the act of engaging. **2.** the state of being engaged. **3.** a pledge; an obligation or agreement. **4.** betrothal. **5.** employment, or a period or post of employment. **6.** an appointment or arrangement. **7.** an encounter, conflict, or battle. **8.** *Mech.* the act or state of interlocking. **—Syn. 3.** contract, promise.

en·gag·ing (en gā′jing), *adj.* winning; attractive; pleasing: *her engaging smile.* **—en·gag′ing·ly,** *adv.* **—en·gag′ing·ness,** *n.*

en garde (än gärd′; *Fr.* äɴ gard′), *Fencing.* (used as the call to assume the position for action.) [< F: on guard]

en·gar·land (en gär′lənd), *v.t.* to encircle with or as with a garland.

En·gels (eng′əls *for 1;* eng′gels *for 2*), *n.* **1. Frie·drich** (frē′drikh), 1820–95, German socialist writer and systematizer of Marxism: spent much of his life in England. **2.** a city in the E Soviet Union in Europe, on the Volga River. 106,000 (est. 1962).

en·gen·der (en jen′dər), *v.t.* **1.** to produce, cause, or give rise to: *Hatred engenders violence.* **2.** to beget; procreate. **—***v.i.* **3.** to be produced or caused; come into existence. [ME *engendre(n)* < OF *engendre(r)* < L *ingenerāre.* See EN-[1], GENERATE] **—en·gen′der·er,** *n.* **—en·gen′der·ment,** *n.* **—Syn. 1.** beget, occasion. **1, 2.** create, generate, breed.

engin., engineering.

en·gine (en′jən), *n.* **1.** a machine for converting thermal energy into mechanical energy or power to produce force and motion. **2.** a railroad locomotive. **3.** a fire engine. **4.** any mechanical contrivance. **5.** a machine or instrument used in warfare, as a battering ram, catapult, piece of artillery, etc. **6.** *Obs.* an instrument of torture, esp. the rack. [ME *engin* < OF < L *ingen(ium)* nature, innate quality, esp. mental power, hence a clever invention = *in-* IN-[2] + *-genium* = *gen-* begetting (see KIN) + *-ium* -Y[3]] **—en′gine·less,** *adj.*

en′gine driv′er, *Brit.* an engineer on a locomotive.

en·gi·neer (en′jə nēr′), *n.* **1.** a person versed in the design, construction, and use of engines or machines, or in any of various branches of engineering. **2.** a person who manages an engine or a locomotive. **3.** a member of an army, navy, or air force specially trained in engineering work. **4.** a skillful manager: *a political engineer.* **—***v.t.* **5.** to plan, construct, or manage as an engineer. **6.** to arrange, manage, or carry through by skillful or artful contrivance. [ENGINE + -EER; r. ME *engyn(e)our* < OF *engigneor* < ML *ingeniātor* = *ingeniāt(us),* ptp. of *ingeniāre* to design, devise (see -ATE[1]) + *-or* -OR[2]]

en·gi·neer·ing (en′jə nēr′ing), *n.* **1.** the art or science of making practical application of the knowledge of pure sciences, as physics, chemistry, etc., as in the construction of engines, bridges, buildings, mines, chemical plants, and the like. **2.** the action, work, or profession of an engineer. **3.** skillful or artful contrivance; maneuvering. **—en′gi·neer′ing·ly,** *adv.*

engineer's′ chain′. See under **chain** (def. 8a).

en·gine·ry (en′jən rē), *n., pl.* **-ries. 1.** engines collectively; machinery. **2.** engines of war collectively. **3.** skillful or artful contrivance.

en·gi·nous (en′jə nəs), *adj.* *Obs.* clever; crafty. [ME < MF *engigneus* < L *ingeniōs(us)* INGENIOUS]

en·gird (en gûrd′), *v.t.,* **-girt** or **-gird·ed, -gird·ing.** to encircle; encompass.

en·gir·dle (en gûr′dᵊl), *v.t.,* **-dled, -dling.** to engird.

en·gla·cial (en glā′shəl), *adj.* *Geol.* **1.** within the ice of a glacier. **2.** believed to have been formerly within the ice of a glacier. **—en·gla′cial·ly,** *adv.*

Eng·land (ing′glənd *or, often,* -lənd), *n.* the largest division of the United Kingdom, constituting, with Scotland and Wales, the island of Great Britain. 43,430,972 (1961); 50,327 sq. mi. *Cap.:* London. Latin, **Anglia. —Eng′land·er,** *n.*

En·gle·wood (eng′gəl wo͝od′), *n.* **1.** a city in central Colorado. 33,695 (1970). **2.** a city in NE New Jersey. 24,985 (1970).

Eng·lish (ing′glish *or, often,* -lish), *adj.* **1.** of, pertaining to, or characteristic of England or its inhabitants, institutions, etc. **2.** belonging or pertaining to, or spoken or written in, the English language. —*n.* **3.** the people of England collectively, esp. as distinguished from the Scots, Welsh, and Irish. **4.** the Germanic language of the British Isles, standard in the U.S. and most of the British Commonwealth. *Abbr.:* E, E. Cf. **Middle English, Modern English, Old English.** **5.** (*sometimes l.c.*) *Sports.* a spinning motion imparted to a ball, esp. in billiards. **6.** *Print.* a 14-point type of a size between pica and Columbian. **7.** *U.S.* a grade of calendered paper having a smooth matte finish. —*v.t.* **8.** to translate into English: *to English Euripides.* **9.** to adopt (a foreign word) into English; anglicize. **10.** *Sports.* to impart English to (a ball). [ME; OE *englisc* = *Engle* (pl.) the English (see ANGLES) + *-isc* -ISH[1]] —**Eng′lish·ness,** *n.*

Eng′lish bond′, a brickwork bond having alternate courses of headers and stretchers.

Eng′lish Cana′dian, *Chiefly Canadian.* **1.** a Canadian of pure British stock. **2.** an English-speaking Canadian. **3.** of or pertaining to Canadians of British descent.

Eng′lish Chan′nel, an arm of the Atlantic between S England and N France, connected with the North Sea by the Strait of Dover. 350 mi. long; 20–100 mi. wide.

Eng′lish Civ′il War′, the war (1642–46) between the Parliamentarians and the Royalists, sometimes extended to include the events of the period 1646–48.

Eng′lish dai′sy, *Chiefly U.S.* the common European daisy, *Bellis perennis.*

Eng′lish elm′. See under **elm** (def. 1).

Eng′lish horn′, a large oboe, a fifth lower in pitch than the ordinary oboe, having a pear-shaped bell. Also called **cor anglais.**

English horn

Eng·lish·ism (iṉg′gli shiz′əm *or, often,* -li-), *n.* **1.** a Briticism. **2.** attachment to what is English.

Eng′lish i′vy, ivy (def. 1).

Eng·lish·man (iṉg′glish mən *or, often,* -lish-), *n., pl.* **-men.** a native or a naturalized citizen of England. [ME; OE *engliscman*]

Eng′lish muf′fin, a muffin made from yeast dough and baked on a griddle.

Eng′lish Pale′, pale[2] (def. 6).

Eng′lish Revolu′tion, the events of 1688–89 by which James II was expelled and the sovereignty conferred on William and Mary. Also called **Glorious Revolution.**

Eng·lish·ry (iṉg′glish rē *or, often,* -lish-), *n.* **1.** the fact of being English, esp. by birth. **2.** a population that is English or of English descent: *the Englishry of Ireland.* [late ME *Englisherie* < AF *Englescherie.* See ENGLISH, -ERY]

Eng′lish sad′dle, a saddle having a fairly low cantle and pommel, full side flaps usually set forward, and a well-padded leather seat. See illus. at **saddle.**

English setter
(2 ft. high at shoulder)

Eng′lish set′ter, one of a breed of medium-sized, long-haired bird dogs having a flat, usually black-and-white or tan-and-white coat.

Eng′lish son′net. See **Shakespearean sonnet.**

Eng′lish spar′row. See **house sparrow.**

Eng′lish spring′er span′iel, one of an English breed of springer spaniels having a flat, medium-length, usually black-and-white or liver-and-white coat. See illus. at **springer spaniel.**

Eng′lish toy′ span′iel, one of an English breed of toy spaniels having a long, silky coat, a rounded head, and a short, upturned muzzle.

Eng′lish wal′nut, **1.** a walnut tree, *Juglans regia.* **2.** the nut of this tree, widely used in cookery.

Eng·lish·wom·an (iṉg′glish wo͝om′ən *or, often,* -lish-), *n., pl.* **-wom·en.** a woman who is a native or citizen of England.

en·glut (en glut′), *v.t.,* **-glut·ted, -glut·ting.** to gulp down. [< MF *englot(ir)* < LL *ingluttīre* to swallow = L *in-* IN-[2] + *gluttīre* to swallow; see GLUTTON[1]]

en·gorge (en gôrj′), *v.t., v.i.,* **-gorged, -gorg·ing.** **1.** to swallow greedily; glut or gorge. **2.** *Pathol.* to congest with blood. [< F *engorge(r)*] —**en·gorge′ment,** *n.*

engr., **1.** engineer. **2.** engraved. **3.** engraver. **4.** engraving.

en·graft (en graft′, -gräft′), *v.t.* to insert, as a scion of one tree or plant into another, for propagation. Also, **ingraft.** —**en·graft′ment,** *n.*

en·grail (en grāl′), *v.t.* to ornament the edge of (a coin, medal, etc.) with curved indentations or raised dots. [ME *engrele(n)* < MF *engresle(r)* = *en-* EN-[1] + *gresler* to make slender << L *gracil(is)* GRACILE; cf. F *grêle* kind of file < *grêl(er)*] —**en·grail′ment,** *n.*

en·grain (en grān′), *v.t., adj.* ingrain (defs. 1, 2).

en·grained (en grānd′, en′grānd′), *adj.* ingrained. —**en·grain·ed·ly** (en grā′nid lē, -grānd′-), *adv.*

en·gram (en′gram), *n.* **1.** *Biol.* the durable mark caused by a stimulus upon protoplasm. **2.** *Neurol., Psychol.* trace[1] (def. 6). —**en·gram′mic,** *adj.*

en·grave (en grāv′), *v.t.,* **-graved, -grav·ing.** **1.** to chase (letters, designs, etc.) on a hard surface, as of metal, stone, or the end grain of wood. **2.** to print from such a surface. **3.** to mark or ornament with incised letters, designs, etc. **4.** to impress deeply; infix. [EN-[1] + GRAVE[3], modeled on F *engraver*] —**en·grav′er,** *n.*

en·grav·ing (en grā′ving), *n.* **1.** the act of a person or thing that engraves. **2.** the art of forming designs by cutting, corrosion by acids, a photographic process, etc., on the surface of metal plates, blocks of wood, or the like, for or as for the purpose of taking off impressions or prints of the design so formed. **3.** the design engraved. **4.** an engraved plate or block. **5.** an impression or print from this.

en·gross (en grōs′), *v.t.* **1.** to occupy completely, as the mind or attention; absorb. **2.** to write or copy in a large script or in a formal manner, as a public document or record: *to engross a deed.* **3.** to acquire enough of (a commodity) to monopolize it. [ME *engros(s)e(n),* partly < ML *ingross(āre)* (to) thicken, write large and thick (see IN-[2], GROSS); partly < AF, MF *en gros* in quantity, wholesale < L *in* + *grossus*] —**en·gros·sed·ly** (en grō′sid lē, -grōst′-), *adv.* —**en·gross′er,** *n.*

en·gross·ing (en grō′siṉg), *adj.* **1.** fully occupying the mind or attention; absorbing. **2.** having complete control; monopolizing. —**en·gross′ing·ly,** *adv.*

en·gross·ment (en grōs′mənt), *n.* **1.** the act of engrossing. **2.** the state of being engrossed or absorbed. **3.** an engrossed copy of a document.

en·gulf (en gulf′), *v.t.* **1.** to swallow up in or as in a gulf; submerge. **2.** to plunge or immerse. **3.** to overwhelm by or as if by flood. Also, **ingulf.** —**en·gulf′ment,** *n.*

en·hance (en hans′, -häns′), *v.t.,* **-hanced, -hanc·ing.** **1.** to raise to a higher degree; intensify; magnify. **2.** to raise the value or price of. [ME *enhaunce(n)* < AF *enhaunce(r),* nasalized var. of OF *enhaucier* = *en-* EN-[1] + *haucier* to raise = *haut* high (b. Gmc **hauh* + L *altus*) + *-ier* v. suffix] —**en·hance′ment,** *n.* —**en·hanc′er,** *n.* —**en·hanc′ive,** *adj.* —**Syn. 2.** See **elevate.** —**Ant. 2.** reduce.

en·har·mon·ic (en′här mon′ik), *adj.* *Music.* having the same pitch in the tempered scale but written in different notation, as G sharp and A flat. [< LL *enharmonic(us)* < Gk *enarmónios* (-*icus* -IC r. *-ios*)] —**en′har·mon′i·cal·ly,** *adv.*

en·heart·en (en här′tᵊn), *v.t.* to inspire or renew courage, hope, fortitude, etc., in.

E·nid (ē′nid), *n.* a city in N Oklahoma. 44,986 (1970).

e·nig·ma (ə nig′mə), *n., pl.* **-mas, -ma·ta** (-mə tə). **1.** a puzzling or inexplicable occurrence or situation. **2.** a saying, question, picture, etc., containing a hidden meaning; riddle. **3.** a person of puzzling or contradictory character. [< L *aenigma* < Gk *aínigma* = *ainig-* (var. s. of *ainíssesthai* to speak in riddles < *aîn(os)* fable) + *-ma* n. suffix of result] —**Syn. 1.** problem. See **puzzle.**

en·ig·mat·ic (en′ig mat′ik, ē′nig-), *adj.* resembling an enigma; perplexing; mysterious. Also, **en′ig·mat′i·cal.** [< LL *aenigmatic(us)* < Gk *ainigmatikós* = *ainigmat-* (s. of *aínigma*) ENIGMA + *-ikos* -IC] —**en′ig·mat′i·cal·ly,** *adv.*

en·isle (en īl′), *v.t.,* **-isled, -isl·ing.** **1.** to make an island of. **2.** to place on an island. **3.** to isolate.

En·i·we·tok (en′ə wē′tok, ə nē′wi tôk′), *n.* an atoll in the NW Marshall Islands: atomic and hydrogen bomb tests 1947–52.

en·jambe·ment (en jam′mənt, -jamb′-; *Fr.* äɴ zhäɴb-mäɴ′), *n., pl.* **-ments** (-mənts; *Fr.* -mäɴ′). enjambment.

en·jamb·ment (en jam′mənt, -jamb′-), *n.* *Pros.* the running on of the thought from one line, couplet, or stanza to the next without a syntactical break. [< F *enjambement* = *enjamb(er)* (to) stride over, project, encroach (see EN-[1], JAMB[1]) + *-ment* -MENT] —**en·jambed′,** *adj.*

en·join (en join′), *v.t.* **1.** to direct or order (someone) to do something. **2.** to prescribe (a course of action) with authority or emphasis. **3.** *Law.* to prohibit or restrain by an injunction. [ME *enjoi(g)ne(n)* < OF *enjoind(re)* < L *injungere* to fasten to, bring upon. See IN-[2], JOIN] —**en·join′er,** *n.* —**en·join′ment,** *n.* —**Syn. 1.** charge, bid, command, require. **3.** proscribe, interdict, ban.

en·joy (en joi′), *v.t.* **1.** to experience with joy; take pleasure in. **2.** to have and use with satisfaction; have the benefit of. **3.** to find or experience pleasure for (oneself). [ME *enjoye(n)* (to) make joyful < OF *enjoie(r)* (to) give joy to] —**en·joy′er,** *n.* —**en·joy′ing·ly,** *adv.*

en·joy·a·ble (en joi′ə bəl), *adj.* giving or capable of giving enjoyment; affording enjoyment: *a very enjoyable film.* —**en·joy′a·ble·ness,** *n.* —**en·joy′a·bly,** *adv.* —**Syn.** delightful, pleasant, agreeable, pleasurable.

en·joy·ment (en joi′mənt), *n.* **1.** the act of enjoying. **2.** the possession, use, or occupancy of anything with satisfaction or pleasure. **3.** a particular form or source of pleasure: *Hunting is his greatest enjoyment.* **4.** *Law.* the exercise of a right. —**Syn. 3.** delight, gratification. See **pleasure.**

en·kin·dle (en kin′dᵊl), *v.t., v.i.,* **-dled, -dling.** to kindle into flame, ardor, activity, etc. —**en·kin′dler,** *n.*

enl., **1.** enlarge. **2.** enlarged. **3.** enlisted.

en·lace (en lās′), *v.t.,* **-laced, -lac·ing.** **1.** to bind or encircle with or as with a lace or cord: *Vines enlaced the tree.* **2.** to interlace; intertwine: *to enlace strands of rope.* [ME *enlace(n)* < OF *enlacie(r)*] —**en·lace′ment,** *n.*

en·large (en lärj′), *v.,* **-larged, -larg·ing.** —*v.t.* **1.** to make larger; increase in extent, bulk, or quantity; add to. **2.** to increase the capacity or scope of; expand. **3.** to make (a photographic print) larger than the negative. —*v.i.* **4.** to grow larger; increase; expand. **5.** to speak or write at large; expatiate. [ME *enlarge(n)* < OF *enlargi(e)(r)*] —**en·large′a·ble,** *adj.* —**en·larg′er,** *n.* —**Syn. 1.** extend, magnify, amplify, dilate. See **increase.** —**Ant. 1.** diminish.

en·large·ment (en lärj′mənt), *n.* **1.** the act of enlarging; increase; expansion; amplification. **2.** anything, as a photograph, that is an enlarged form of something else. **3.** anything that enlarges something else; addition.

en·light·en (en līt′ᵊn), *v.t.* **1.** to give intellectual or spiritual light to; instruct; impart knowledge to. **2.** *Archaic.* to shed light upon. [ME *enli(g)htene(n)*] —**en·light′ened·ly,** *adv.* —**en·light′en·er,** *n.* —**Syn. 1.** edify, teach, inform.

en·light·en·ment (en līt′ᵊn mənt), *n.* **1.** the act of enlightening. **2.** the state of being enlightened. **3. the Enlightenment,** a philosophical movement of the 18th century characterized by belief in the power of human reason and by innovations in political, religious, and educational doctrine.

en·list (en list′), *v.i.* **1.** to engage for military service by enrolling after mutual agreement. **2.** to enter into some cause, enterprise, etc. —*v.t.* **3.** to engage for military service. **4.** to secure (a person, services, etc.) for some cause, enterprise, etc. —**en·list′er,** *n.*

enlist′ed man′, any male member of the U.S. armed services who is not a commissioned officer or a warrant officer.

en·list·ee (en lis tē′), *n.* **1.** a person who enlists for military service. Cf. **draftee. 2.** an enlisted man or woman.

en·list·ment (en list′mənt), *n.* **1.** the period of time for which one is committed to a military service. **2.** the act of enlisting.

en·liv·en (en lī′vən), *v.t.* **1.** to make vigorous or active; invigorate. **2.** to make sprightly, gay, or cheerful; brighten. [obs. *enlive* to give life to (EN-1 + LIFE) + -EN1] **—en·liv′en·er,** *n.* **—en·liv′en·ing·ly,** *adv.* **—en·liv′en·ment,** *n.* **—Syn. 1.** animate, inspirit, vivify, quicken. **2.** exhilarate, gladden. **—Ant. 2.** depress.

en masse (än mas′, en; *Fr.* äN MAS′), in a mass; all together; as a group. [< F]

en·mesh (en mesh′), *v.t.* to catch, as in a net; entangle. Also, **immesh, inmesh. —en·mesh′ment,** *n.*

en·mi·ty (en′mi tē), *n., pl.* **-ties.** a feeling or condition of hostility; hatred; ill will; animosity; antagonism. [ME *enemite* < MF < OF *enemiste* < VL **inimīcitāt-* (s. of **inimīcitās*). See ENEMY, -ITY]

ennea-, a learned borrowing from Greek meaning "nine," used in the formation of compound words: *enneahedron.* [< Gk, comb. form of *ennéa* NINE]

en·ne·ad (en′ē ad′), *n.* a group of nine persons or things. [< Gk *ennead-* (s. of *enneás*) = *enné(a)* nine + *-ad-* -AD1] **—en′ne·ad′ic,** *adj.*

en·ne·a·gon (en′ē ə gon′), *n.* nonagon. [< Gk *enneá-gōn(os)*]

en·ne·a·he·dron (en′ē ə hē′drən), *n., pl.* **-dra** (-drə). a solid figure having nine faces. **—en′ne·a·he′dral,** *adj.*

En·ni·us (en′ē əs), *n.* **Quin·tus** (kwin′təs), 239–169? B.C., Roman poet.

en·no·ble (en nō′bəl), *v.t.,* **-bled, -bling. 1.** to elevate in degree, excellence, or respect; dignify; exalt: *a personality ennobled by true generosity.* **2.** to confer a title of nobility on. [late ME *ennobele(n)* < MF, OF *ennobli(r)*] **—en·no′ble·ment,** *n.* **—en·no′bler,** *n.* **—en·no′bling·ly,** *adv.*

en·nui (än wē′, än′wē; *Fr.* äN nwē′), *n.* a feeling of weariness and discontent resulting from satiety or lack of interest; boredom. [< F: boredom; OF *enui* displeasure; see ANNOY]

E·noch (ē′nək), *n.* **1.** the father of Methuselah. Gen. 5:22. **2.** a son of Cain. Gen. 4:17.

e·nol (ē′nōl, ē′nôl, ē′nol), *n. Chem.* an organic compound containing a hydroxyl group attached to a doubly linked carbon atom, as in >C=C(OH)–. [appar. < Gk (*h*)*én* one (neut.) + -OL1] **—e·nol·ic** (ē nol′ik), *adj.*

e·nol·o·gy (ē nol′ə jē), *n.* oenology.

e·norm (ē nôrm′), *adj. Archaic.* enormous; huge; vast. [late ME *enorme* < MF < L *ēnorm(is).* See E-, NORM]

e·nor·mi·ty (i nôr′mi tē), *n., pl.* **-ties. 1.** outrageous or heinous character; atrociousness. **2.** something outrageous or heinous, as an offense. **3.** *Nonstandard.* greatness of size, scope, extent, or influence; immensity. [late ME *enormite* < MF < L *ēnormitāt-* (s. of *ēnormitās*)]
—Usage. 3. Although ENORMITY was once standard as a synonym for ENORMOUSNESS, its present use in any sense other than those given in definitions 1 and 2 is now usually regarded as incorrect.

e·nor·mous (i nôr′məs), *adj.* **1.** greatly exceeding the common size, extent, etc.; huge; immense. **2.** outrageous or atrocious: *enormous wickedness.* [ENORM + -OUS] **—e·nor′mous·ly,** *adv.* **—e·nor′mous·ness,** *n.* **—Syn. 1.** vast, colossal, gigantic. See **huge.**

E·nos (ē′nəs), *n.* the son of Seth. Gen. 5:6.

e·nough (i nuf′), *adj.* **1.** adequate for the want or need; sufficient for the purpose or to satisfy desire. **—***n.* **2.** an adequate quantity or number; sufficiency. **—***adv.* **3.** in a quantity or degree that answers a purpose or satisfies a need or desire; sufficiently. **4.** fully or quite: *ready enough.* **5.** tolerably or passably: *He sings well enough.* **—***interj.* **6.** No more! Stop! That will do! [ME *enogh,* OE *genōh;* c. G *genug,* Goth *ganohs,* Icel *nōgr;* akin to OE *geneah* it suffices, Skt *naśati* (he) reaches]

e·nounce (i nouns′), *v.t.,* **e·nounced, e·nounc·ing. 1.** to announce, declare, or proclaim. **2.** to state definitely, as a proposition. **3.** to utter or pronounce, as words; enunciate. [E- + (AN)NOUNCE, modeled on F *énoncer* < L *ēnuntiāre* to tell; see ENUNCIATE] **—e·nounce′ment,** *n.*

e·now (i nou′; *formerly* i nō′), *adj., adv. Archaic.* enough. [ME *inow,* OE *genōg* (var. of *genōh* ENOUGH); ME *inowe,* OE *genōge,* pl. of *genōg* ENOUGH]

en pa·pil·lote (äN pa pē yôt′), *French.* (of food, esp. meat or fish) cooked and served in a wrapping of foil or oiled paper.

en pas·sant (än′ pa sänt′; *Fr.* äN pä säN′), **1.** (*italics*) *French.* in passing; by the way. **2.** *Chess.* a method by which a pawn that is moved two squares can be captured by an opponent's pawn commanding the square that was passed.

en·phy·tot·ic (en′fī tot′ik), *adj.* (of a disease) regularly affecting but not destroying the plants in a given area. [EN-2 + -PHYTE + -OTIC]

en·plane (en plān′), *v.i.,* **-planed, -plan·ing.** to enter an airplane.

en prise (än′ prēz′; *Fr.* äN PRĒZ′), *Chess.* in line for capture; likely to be captured. [< F; see PRIZE1]

en′ quad′, *Print.* a piece of type consisting of a box one en on the top and bottom, and type-high on the sides: ▯ *is an en quad.*

en·quire (en kwīər′), *v.t., v.i.,* **-quired, -quir·ing.** inquire.

en·quir·y (en kwīər′ē, en′kwə rē), *n., pl.* **-quir·ies.** inquiry.

en·rage (en rāj′), *v.t.,* **-raged, -rag·ing.** to put into a rage; infuriate. [< MF *enrage(r)*] **—en·rag·ed·ly** (en rā′jid lē, -rājd′-), *adv.* **—en·rage′ment,** *n.* **—Syn.** anger, inflame.

en rap·port (äN RA pôR′; *Eng.* än′ ra pôr′, -pōr′, rə-), *French.* in sympathy or accord; in agreement; congenial.

en·rapt (en rapt′), *adj.* rapt; transported; enraptured.

en·rap·ture (en rap′chər), *v.t.,* **-tured, -tur·ing.** to move to rapture; delight beyond measure. **—en·rap′tured·ly,** *adv.*

en·rav·ish (en rav′ish), *v.t.* to enrapture.

en·reg·is·ter (en rej′i stər), *v.t.* to register; record. [< MF *enregistre(r)*] **—en·reg′is·tra′tion,** *n.*

en·rich (en rich′), *v.t.* **1.** to supply with riches, wealth, abundant or valuable possessions, etc. **2.** to supply with abundance of anything desirable: *to enrich the mind with knowledge.* **3.** to add greater value or significance to. **4.** to adorn or decorate. **5.** to make finer in quality, as by supplying desirable elements or ingredients. [ME *enriche(n)* < OF *enrichi(r)*] **—en·rich′er,** *n.* **—en·rich′ing·ly,** *adv.*

en·rich·ment (en rich′mənt), *n.* **1.** the act of enriching. **2.** the state of being enriched. **3.** something that enriches.

en·robe (en rōb′), *v.t.,* **-robed, -rob·ing.** to dress; attire. **—en·rob′er,** *n.*

en·rol (en rōl′), *v.t., v.i.,* **-rolled, -rol·ling.** enroll.

en·roll (en rōl′), *v.t.* **1.** to write (a name), or insert the name of (a person), in a roll or register; place upon a list. **2.** to enlist (oneself). **3.** to put in a record; record. **4.** to roll or wrap up. **—***v.i.* **5.** to enroll oneself. [ME *enrolle(n)* < OF *enrolle(r)*] **—en·roll′er,** *n.*

en·roll·ee (en rō lē′, -rō′lē), *n.* a person who enrolls, or has enrolled, in a class, school, course of study, etc.

en·roll·ment (en rōl′mənt), *n.* **1.** the act or process of enrolling. **2.** the state of being enrolled. **3.** the number of persons enrolled, as for a course or in a school. Also, **en·rol′ment.**

en·root (en rōōt′, -ro͝ot′), *v.t.* **1.** to fix by the root. **2.** to attach or place securely; implant deeply.

en route (än rōōt′, en; *Fr.* äN RŌŌT′), on the way. [< F]

ens (enz), *n., pl.* **en·ti·a** (en′shē ə). *Metaphys.* an existing or real thing; an entity. [< LL, prp. of *esse* to be]

Ens., Ensign.

en·sam·ple (en sam′pəl), *n. Archaic.* example. [ME < MF, var. (*en-* r. *es-*) of *essample* < OF < L *exempl(um)* EXAMPLE]

en·san·guine (en sang′gwin), *v.t.,* **-guined, -guin·ing.** to stain or cover with or as with blood.

En·sche·de (en′sKHə dā′), *n.* a city in the E Netherlands. 130,256 (1962).

en·sconce (en skons′), *v.t.,* **-sconced, -sconc·ing. 1.** to cover or shelter; hide securely. **2.** to settle securely or snugly: *I found him ensconced in an armchair.* [EN-1 + SCONCE2]

en·scroll (en skrōl′), *v.t.* **1.** to commemorate or record permanently. **2.** to write or inscribe on a scroll. Also, **inscroll.**

en·sem·ble (än säm′bəl, -sämb′; *Fr.* äN säN′blə), *n., pl.* **-sem·bles** (-säm′bəlz, -sämbz′; *Fr.* -säN′blə), *adv.* **—***n.* **1.** all the parts of a thing taken together, so that each part is considered only in relation to the whole. **2.** a person's entire costume. **3.** the general effect, as of a work of art. **4.** *Music.* **a.** the united performance of an entire group of singers, musicians, etc. **b.** the group so performing: *a string ensemble.* **5.** a group of supporting performers in a theatrical production. **—***adv.* **6.** together; all at once; simultaneously. [< F: together < L *insimul.* See IN-2, SIMULTANEOUS]

En·se·na·da (en′se nä′thä; *Eng.* en′se nä′də), *n.* a seaport in N Lower California, in NW Mexico. 42,561 (1960).

en·sheathe (en shēth′), *v.t.,* **-sheathed, -sheath·ing.** to enclose in or as in a sheath; sheathe. Also, **en·sheath′, insheathe, insheath.**

en·shrine (en shrīn′), *v.t.,* **-shrined, -shrin·ing. 1.** to place in or as in a shrine. **2.** to cherish as sacred: *to enshrine the nation's ideals.* Also, **inshrine. —en·shrine′ment,** *n.*

en·shroud (en shroud′), *v.t.* to shroud; conceal.

en·si·form (en′sə fôrm′), *adj. Biol.* sword-shaped; xiphoid. [< L *ensi(s)* sword + -FORM]

en·sign (en′sīn; *Mil.* en′sən), *n.* **1.** a flag or banner, as a military or naval standard used to indicate nationality. **2.** a badge of office or authority, as heraldic arms. **3.** a sign, token, or emblem: *the dove, an ensign of peace.* **4.** *U.S. Navy.* the lowest commissioned officer, ranking next below a lieutenant, junior grade, and equal to a second lieutenant in the Army. **5.** *Brit. Army.* (formerly) an officer who carried the standard or flag of a regiment or company. [ME *ensigne* < OF *enseigne* < L *insignia.* See INSIGNIA] **—en′sign·ship′, en′sign·cy,** *n.*

en·si·lage (en′sə lij), *n., v.,* **-laged, -lag·ing. —***n.* **1.** the preservation of green fodder in a silo or pit. **2.** silage. **—***v.t.* **3.** ensile. [< F]

en·sile (en sīl′, en′sīl), *v.t.,* **-siled, -sil·ing. 1.** to preserve (green fodder) in a silo. **2.** to make into silage. [< F *ensile(r)* < Sp *ensilar.* See EN-1, SILO] **—en·si′la·bil′i·ty,** *n.*

en·slave (en slāv′), *v.t.,* **-slaved, -slav·ing.** to make a slave of; reduce to or as to slavery. **—en·slave′ment,** *n.* **—en·slav′er,** *n.*

en·snare (en snâr′), *v.t.,* **-snared, -snar·ing.** to capture or trap in or as in a snare. Also, **insnare. —en·snare′ment,** *n.* **—en·snar′er,** *n.* **—Syn.** entrap, entangle, enmesh.

En·sor (en′sôr), *n.* **James,** 1860–1949, Belgian painter.

en·sor·cell (en sôr′səl), *v.t.* to bewitch. Also, **en·sor′cel.** [< MF *ensorcele(r)* (to) bewitch, dissimilated var. of *ensorcerer* < OF; see EN-1, SORCERER] **—en·sor′cell·ment,** *n.*

en·soul (en sōl′), *v.t.* **1.** to endow with a soul. **2.** to cherish in the soul. Also, **insoul.**

en·sphere (en sfēr′), *v.t.,* **-sphered, -spher·ing. 1.** to enclose in or as in a sphere. **2.** to form into a sphere. Also, **insphere.**

en·sta·tite (en′stə tīt′), *n. Mineral.* a yellow-green fibrous magnesium silicate. [< Gk *enstát(ēs)* adversary + -ITE1] **—en·sta·tit·ic** (en′stə tit′ik), *adj.*

en·sue (en sōō′), *v.i.,* **-sued, -su·ing. 1.** to follow in order; come afterward, esp. in immediate succession. **2.** to follow as a consequence; result. [ME *ensue(n)* < AF *ensue(r)* (c. OF *ensui(v)re*)] **—en·su′ing·ly,** *adv.* **—Syn. 1, 2.** See **follow.**

en suite (äN swēt′), *French.* in succession; in a series or set.

en·sure (en sho͝or′), *v.t.,* **-sured, -sur·ing. 1.** to secure or guarantee: *This letter will ensure you a hearing.* **2.** to make sure or certain. **3.** to make secure or safe. **4.** insure (defs. 1, 2). [ME *ensure(n)* < AF *enseure(r)*] **—en·sur′er,** *n.*

en·swathe (en swoth′, -swāth′), *v.t.,* **-swathed, -swath·ing.** to swathe. Also, **inswathe. —en·swathe′ment,** *n.*

-ent, a formal element, equivalent to **-ant,** appearing in nouns and adjectives of Latin origin: *accident; different.* [< L *-ent-* (s. of *-ēns*), prp. of conjugations 2, 3, 4]

en·tab·la·ture (en tab′lə chər), *n. Archit.* the part of a classical temple between the columns and the eaves, usually composed of an architrave, a frieze, and a cornice. [< MF < It *intavolatura,* lit., something tabled, i.e., laid flat = *in-* IN-2 + *tavolat-* tabled (*tavol-* table + *-at-* -ATE1) + *-ura* -URE]

en·ta·ble·ment (en tā′bəl mənt), *n.* the platform above the dado on a pedestal. [< F]

en·tail (en tāl′), *v.t.* **1.** to cause or involve by necessity or as a consequence: *a loss entailing no regret.* **2.** to limit the passage of (a landed estate) to a specified line of heirs. **3.** to cause (anything) to descend to a fixed series of possessors. —*n.* **4.** the act of entailing. **5.** the state of being entailed. **6.** any predetermined order of succession. **7.** something that is entailed. [ME *entaile(n)*] —**en·tail′er,** *n.* —**en·tail′ment,** *n.*

en·tan·gle (en taŋ′gəl), *v.t.*, **-gled, -gling.** **1.** to make tangled; ensnarl; intertwine. **2.** to involve in anything like a tangle; ensnare; enmesh: *to be entangled by intrigue.* **3.** to confuse or perplex. —**en·tan′gler,** *n.* —**Syn. 3.** bewilder.

en·tan·gle·ment (en taŋ′gəl mənt), *n.* **1.** the act of entangling. **2.** the state of being entangled. **3.** something that entangles; snare; involvement; complication.

en·ta·sis (en′tə sis), *n.* *Archit.* a slight convexity given to a column, tower, etc. [< Gk = *enta-* (var. of *entein-*, s. of *enteínein* to stretch tight = *en-* EN-^{2} + *ta-* (*tein-*) stretch) + *-sis* -SIS]

En·teb·be (en teb′e), *n.* a town in S Uganda, on Lake Victoria: former capital of Uganda. 10,941 (1959).

en·tel·e·chy (en tel′ə kē), *n., pl.* **-chies.** **1.** a realization or actuality as opposed to a potentiality. **2.** (in vitalist philosophy) a vital agent or force directing growth and life. [< LL *entelechīa* < Gk *entelécheia* = *en-* EN-^{2} + *tél(os)* goal + *éch(ein)* (to) have + *-eia* -Y^3] —**en·te·lech·i·al** (en′tə lek′ē əl), *adj.*

en·tente (än tänt′; *Fr.* äɴ täɴt′), *n., pl.* **-tentes** (-tänts′; *Fr.* -täɴt′). **1.** an understanding between nations in respect to international policy. **2.** an alliance of parties to such an understanding. [< F: understanding, OF: intention, n. use of fem. of *entent*, ptp. of *entendre* to INTEND]

en·tente cor·diale (än tänt′ kôr dyäl′; *Fr.* äɴ täɴt′ kôʀ dyal′), a friendly understanding, esp. between governments. [< F]

en·ter (en′tər), *v.i.* **1.** to come or go in. **2.** *Theat.* to make an entrance (used in stage directions): *Enter Othello.* **3.** to be admitted into a school, competition, etc. **4.** to make a beginning (often fol. by *on* or *upon*): *We have entered upon a new phase in man's history.* —*v.t.* **5.** to come or go into. **6.** to penetrate or pierce: *The bullet entered the bone.* **7.** to put in or insert: *to enter a wedge under a door.* **8.** to become a member of; join. **9.** to cause to be admitted, as into a competition. **10.** to engage or become involved in: *He entered the medical profession.* **11.** to share in; have an intuitive understanding of: *to enter the spirit of a novel.* **12.** to record or register, as in a ledger. **13.** *Law.* **a.** to make a formal record of (a fact). **b.** to occupy or to take possession of (lands). **c.** to file an application for (public lands). **14.** to put forward, submit, or register formally: *to enter a bid for a contract.* **15.** to report (a vessel, cargo, etc.) at the custom house. **16.** **enter into, a.** to begin participation in; engage in. **b.** to investigate; consider. **c.** to sympathize with; share in. **d.** to form a constituent part or ingredient of. [ME *entre(n)* < OF *entre(r)* < L *intrāre* to enter < *intrā* within] —**en′ter·a·ble,** *adj.* —**en′ter·er,** *n.* —**Ant. 1.** leave. **7.** remove.

enter-, var. of **entero-** before a vowel: *enteritis.*

en·ter·ic (en ter′ik), *adj.* of or pertaining to the enteron; intestinal. Also, **en·ter·al** (en′tər əl). [< Gk *enterik(ós)*] —**en′ter·al·ly,** *adv.*

enter′ic fe′ver, *Pathol.* typhoid (def. 1).

en·ter·i·tis (en′tə rī′tis), *n.* *Pathol.* inflammation of the intestines, esp. the small intestine. [< NL]

entero-, a learned borrowing from Greek meaning "intestine," used in the formation of compound words: *enterotoxemia.* Also, *esp. before a vowel,* **enter-.** [< Gk, s. of *énteron* intestine]

en·ter·on (en′tə ron′), *n., pl.* **-ter·a** (-tər ə). *Anat., Zool.* the alimentary canal. [< NL < Gk: intestine]

en·ter·os·to·my (en′tə ros′tə mē), *n., pl.* **-mies.** *Surg.* the making of an artificial opening into the intestine through the abdominal wall.

en·ter·o·tox·e·mi·a (en′tə rō tok sē′mē ə), *n.* **1.** *Pathol.* the presence in the blood of toxins from the intestines. **2.** *Vet. Pathol.* a disease of sheep caused by bacterial toxins of *Clostridium perfringens* in the intestinal tract.

en·ter·prise (en′tər prīz′), *n.* **1.** a project, esp. an important or difficult one. **2.** a plan for such a project. **3.** participation in such projects. **4.** dynamic boldness or ingenuity. **5.** a company organized for commercial purposes; business firm. [late ME < MF *entreprise*, n. use of fem. of *entrepris* (ptp. of *entreprendre* to undertake) < L *inter-* INTER- + *prēnsus* grasped, seized, contr. of *prehēnsus* = *pre-* PRE- + *hend-* take hold of + *-tus* ptp. suffix] —**Syn. 1.** plan, undertaking, venture.

en·ter·pris·ing (en′tər prī′ziŋ), *adj.* full of or characterized by great initiative, ingenuity, and energy. —**en′ter·pris′ing·ly,** *adv.* —**en′ter·pris′er,** *n.* —**Syn.** venturesome, resourceful, adventurous. See **ambitious.**

en·ter·tain (en′tər tān′), *v.t.* **1.** to hold the attention of agreeably; divert; amuse. **2.** to treat as a guest; show hospitality to. **3.** to admit into or hold in the mind; consider. **4.** *Archaic.* to maintain or keep up. **5.** *Obs.* to give admittance or reception to; receive. —*v.i.* **6.** to exercise hospitality; entertain company. [late ME *entertene* to hold mutually < MF *entreten(ir)*, irreg. < ML *intertenēre* = L *inter-* INTER- + *tenēre* to hold] —**Syn. 1.** See **amuse.**

en·ter·tain·er (en′tər tā′nər), *n.* **1.** a singer, comedian, reciter, or the like, esp. a professional one. **2.** a person who entertains, esp. lavishly and often.

en·ter·tain·ing (en′tər tā′niŋ), *adj.* affording entertainment; amusing. —**en′ter·tain′ing·ly,** *adv.*

en·ter·tain·ment (en′tər tān′mənt), *n.* **1.** the act of entertaining. **2.** a diversion or amusement. **3.** something affording diversion or amusement, esp. a performance. **4.** hospitable provision for guests. **5.** *Obs.* maintenance in service.

en·thal·py (en′thal pē, en thal′-), *n., pl.* **-pies.** *Thermodynamics.* a quantity associated with a thermodynamic system, expressed as the internal energy of a system plus the product of the pressure and volume of the system. *Symbol:* H [< Gk *enthálp(ein)* (to) warm in (*en-* EN-^{2} + *thálpein* to warm) + -Y^3]

en·thral (en thrôl′), *v.t.*, **-thralled, -thral·ling.** enthrall. —**en·thral′ment,** *n.*

en·thrall (en thrôl′), *v.t.* **1.** to captivate or charm. **2.** to put or hold in thralldom; subjugate. Also, **inthral, inthrall.** —**en·thrall′er,** *n.* —**en·thrall′ing·ly,** *adv.* —**en·thrall′ment,** *n.*

en·throne (en thrōn′), *v.t.*, **-throned, -thron·ing.** **1.** to place on or as on a throne. **2.** to invest with sovereign or episcopal authority. **3.** to exalt. Also, **inthrone.** —**en·throne′ment,** *n.*

en·thuse (en thōōz′), *v.*, **-thused, -thus·ing.** —*v.i.* **1.** to show enthusiasm. —*v.t.* **2.** to move to enthusiasm. [back formation from ENTHUSIASM]
—**Usage.** Although it is too widely encountered in the speech and writing of reputable teachers and authors to be listed as anything short of standard, ENTHUSE is nonetheless felt by many to be poor style, and in formal writing it would be best to paraphrase it.

en·thu·si·asm (en thōō′zē az′əm), *n.* **1.** lively, absorbing interest; excited involvement. **2.** an activity in which such interest is shown. **3.** any of various forms of extreme religious devotion, usually associated with intense emotionalism and a break with orthodoxy. [< LL *enthūsiasm(us)* < Gk *enthousiasmós* = *enthousí(a)* possession by a god (*énthous*, var. of *éntheos* having a god within = *en-* EN-^{2} + *-thous, -theos* god-possessing + *-ia* -Y) + *-asmos* (akin to *-ismos* -ISM)] —**Syn. 1.** eagerness, fervor, zeal, ardor, passion. —**Ant. 1.** indifference.

en·thu·si·ast (en thōō′zē ast′), *n.* **1.** a person who is filled with enthusiasm for something: *a sports enthusiast.* **2.** a religious visionary or fanatic; a person accused individually, or as a result of group membership, of enthusiasm in religious practice. [< Gk *enthousiast(ḗs)* one inspired = *enthousi-* (see ENTHUSIASM) + *-astēs*, akin to *-istēs* -IST]

en·thu·si·as·tic (en thōō′zē as′tik), *adj.* full of or characterized by enthusiasm; eager; fervent. [< Gk *enthousiastik(ós)*] —**en·thu′si·as′ti·cal·ly,** *adv.* —**Syn.** zealous, passionate, fervid, impassioned.

en·thy·meme (en′thə mēm′), *n.* *Logic.* **1.** a syllogism in which one premise or the conclusion is unexpressed. **2.** (in Aristotle) a rhetorical syllogism with probable premises, used to persuade. [< L *enthȳmēma* < Gk = *en-* EN-^{2} + *thȳm(ós)* spirit, thought + *-ēma* -EME] —**en·thy·me·mat·ic** (en′thə mē mat′ik), *adj.*

en·tice (en tīs′), *v.t.*, **-ticed, -tic·ing.** to lead on by exciting desire; allure; inveigle. [ME *entice(n)* < OF *enticie(r)* (to) incite < VL **intītiāre* = L *in-* IN-^{2} + *tītī(o)* firebrand] —**en·tic′ing·ly,** *adv.* —**en·tic′ing·ness,** *n.* —**Syn.** lure, attract, decoy, tempt. —**Ant.** repel.

en·tice·ment (en tīs′mənt), *n.* **1.** the act or practice of enticing. **2.** the state of being enticed. **3.** something that entices. [ME < MF]

en·tire (en tī^{ə}r′), *adj.* **1.** having all its parts or elements; whole; complete. **2.** not broken, mutilated, or decayed; intact. **3.** unimpaired or undiminished. **4.** being of one piece; undivided; continuous. **5.** *Bot.* without notches or indentations, as leaves. **6.** full or thorough. **7.** not gelded. **8.** *Obs.* wholly of one kind; unmixed or pure. —*n.* **9.** the whole; entirety. **10.** *Obs.* an ungelded animal, esp. a stallion. [ME *entere* < MF *entier* < L *integrum*, acc. of *integer* whole. See INTEGER] —**en·tire′ness,** *n.* —**Syn. 1.** See **complete.** —**Ant. 1.** partial.

en·tire·ly (en tī^{ə}r′lē), *adv.* **1.** wholly or fully. **2.** solely or exclusively. [ME]

en·tire·ty (en tī^{ə}r′tē), *n., pl.* **-ties.** **1.** the state of being entire; completeness. **2.** something that is whole or entire. [ME *enter(e)te* < MF *entierete* < L *integritāt-* (s. of *integritās*) INTEGRITY]

en·ti·tle (en tīt′^{ə}l), *v.t.*, **-tled, -tling.** **1.** to give (a person or thing) a title, right, or claim to something; furnish with grounds for laying claim. **2.** to call by a particular title or name; address. **3.** to designate (a person) by an honorary title. Also, **intitle.** [ME *entitle(n)* < AF *entitle(r)*, var. of MF *entituler* < LL *intitulāre.* See IN-^{2}, TITLE] —**en·ti′tlement,** *n.*

en·ti·ty (en′ti tē), *n., pl.* **-ties.** **1.** something that has a real existence; thing: *corporeal entities.* **2.** being or existence, esp. when considered as distinct or self-contained. **3.** essential nature. [< ML *entitās* = *enti-* (s. of *ēns*) being (prp. of *esse*) + *-tās* -TY^2]

ento-, a learned borrowing from Greek meaning "within," used in the formation of compound words: *entoderm.* [comb. form repr. Gk *entós*]

en·to·blast (en′tə blast′), *n.* *Embryol.* **1.** entoderm. **2.** hypoblast (def. 2). —**en·to·blas·tic** (en′tō blas′tik), *adj.*

en·to·derm (en′tə dûrm′), *n.* *Embryol.* the inner germ layer in the embryo of a metazoan. Also, **endoderm.** —**en·to·der·mal** (en′tō dûr′məl) **en′to·der′mic,** *adj.*

en·toil (en toil′), *v.t.* *Archaic.* to take in toils; ensnare.

en·tomb (en tōōm′), *v.t.* **1.** to place in a tomb; bury; inter. **2.** to serve as a tomb for. Also, **intomb.** [late ME *entoumbe(n)* < MF *entombe(r)*] —**en·tomb′ment,** *n.*

entomo-, a learned borrowing from Greek used, with the meaning "insect," in the formation of compound words: *entomology.* Also, *esp. before a vowel,* **entom-.** [comb. form of Gk *éntomos* notched; in neut. pl., insects (verbid of *entémnein* to cut in or up). See EN-^{2}, -TOMY]

entomol., entomology. Also, **entom.**

en·to·mol·o·gise (en′tə mol′ə jīz′), *v.i.*, **-gised, -gis·ing.** *Chiefly Brit.* entomologize.

en·to·mol·o·gize (en′tə mol′ə jīz′), *v.i.*, **-gized, -giz·ing.** **1.** to study entomology. **2.** to gather entomological specimens.

en·to·mol·o·gy (en′tə mol′ə jē), *n., pl.* **-gies.** the branch of zoology dealing with insects. —**en·to·mo·log·i·cal** (en′tə mə loj′i kəl), **en′to·mo·log′ic,** *adj.* —**en′to·mo·log′i·cal·ly,** *adv.* —**en′to·mol′o·gist,** *n.*

en·to·moph·a·gous (en′tə mof′ə gəs), *adj.* feeding on insects; insectivorous.

en·to·mos·tra·can (en′tə mos′trə kən), *adj.* **1.** belonging or pertaining to the *Entomostraca.* —*n.* **2.** any small crustacean of the group *Entomostraca,* including the copepods, ostracods, phyllopods, etc. [< NL *Entomostrac(a)* (see ENTOM-, OSTRACIZE) + -AN] —**en′to·mos′tra·cous,** *adj.*

en·to·phyte (en′tə fīt′), *n. Bot.* endophyte. —**en·to·phyt·ic** (en′tə fit′ik), *adj.*

en·tou·rage (än′to͞o räzh′; *Fr.* äN to͞o RAzh′), *n.* **1.** a body of personal attendants. **2.** surroundings; environment. [< F = *entour(er)* (to) surround (< *entour* around; see EN-[1], TOUR) + *-age* -AGE]

en·to·zo·a (en′tə zō′ə), *n.pl., sing.* **-zo·on** (-zō′on). (*often cap.*) *Biol.* animals, esp. the intestinal worms, living as parasites within a body. —**en′to·zo′an,** *adj., n.*

en·to·zo·ic (en′tə zō′ik), *adj. Biol.* living parasitically within an animal. Also, **en′to·zo′al.**

en·tr′acte (än trakt′; *Fr.* äN trAkt′), *n., pl.* **-tr′actes** (-trakts′; *Fr.* -trAkt′). **1.** the interval between two acts of a theatrical or operatic performance. **2.** a performance of music, dancing, etc., during such an interval. [< F: between-act. See INTER-, ACT]

en·trails (en′trālz, -trəlz), *n.pl.* **1.** the internal parts of an animal, esp. the intestines. **2.** the internal parts of anything; insides. [ME *entrailles* < MF < ML *intrālia* (by dissimilation and syncope) < L *interānea* internals, i.e., entrails]

en·train[1] (en trān′), *v.i.* **1.** to board a train. —*v.t.* **2.** to put aboard a train. [EN-[1] + TRAIN]

en·train[2] (en trān′), *v.t.* **1.** *Chem.* (of a substance, as a vapor) to carry along (a dissimilar substance, as drops of liquid) during a given process, as evaporation or distillation. **2.** (of a liquid) to trap (bubbles) produced either mechanically through turbulence or chemically through a reaction. [< MF *entraine(r).* See EN-[1], TRAIN]

en·trance[1] (en′trəns), *n.* **1.** the act of entering, as into a place or upon new duties. **2.** a point or place of entering, as a doorway. **3.** the power or liberty of entering; admission. **4.** *Theat.* the moment or place in a play at which an actor appears on the stage. **5.** *Music.* the point in a musical score at which a voice or instrument joins the ensemble. **6.** the manner, means, or style of entering. [ME *entraunce* < MF *entrance*]
—**Syn. 1, 2.** entry, ingress. **3.** ENTRANCE, ADMITTANCE, ADMISSION refer to the possibility of entering a place or a group. ENTRANCE may refer to either possibility and carries the least suggestion of permission or supervision: *Entrance is by way of the side door.* ADMITTANCE refers more to place and suggests that permission may be denied: *no admittance.* ADMISSION refers more to social groups and suggests entrance by payment, by formal or special permission, privilege, and the like: *admission to a baseball game, to the bar.* —**Ant. 2.** exit.

en·trance[2] (en trans′, -träns′), *v.t.,* **-tranced, -tranc·ing. 1.** to fill with delight or wonder; enrapture. **2.** to put into a trance. [EN-[1] + TRANCE[1]] —**en·trance′ment,** *n.* —**en·tranc′ing·ly,** *adv.*

en·trance·way (en′trəns wā′), *n.* an entryway.

en·trant (en′trənt), *n.* **1.** a person who enters. **2.** a new member, as of an association, a university, etc. **3.** a competitor in a contest. [< F, n. use of prp. of *entrer* to ENTER]

en·trap (en trap′), *v.t.,* **-trapped, -trap·ping. 1.** to catch in or as in a trap; ensnare. **2.** to draw into contradiction or damaging admission. [< MF *entrape(r)*] —**en·trap′ment,** *n.* —**en·trap′per,** *n.* —**en·trap′ping·ly,** *adv.*

en·treat (en trēt′), *v.t* **1.** to ask (a person) earnestly; beseech; implore; beg. **2.** to ask earnestly for (something). —*v.i.* **3.** to make an earnest petition. [ME *entrete(n)* < MF *entraite(r), entraitier*] —**en·treat′ing·ly,** *adv.* —**en·treat′ment,** *n.* —**Syn. 1.** pray, sue, solicit. See **appeal.**

en·treat·y (en trē′tē), *n., pl.* **-treat·ies.** earnest request or petition; supplication. —**Syn.** appeal, suit, plea, solicitation.

en·tre·chat (*Fr.* äN trə shA′), *n., pl.* **-chats** (*Fr.* -shA′). *Ballet.* a jump in which the dancer crosses his feet a number of times while in the air. [< F, alter. of It (*capriola*) *intrecciata* intwined (caper). See IN-[2], TRESS, -ATE[1]]

en·trée (än′trā), *n.* **1.** the act of entering; entrance. **2.** the privilege of entering; access. **3.** a means of obtaining entry, as into a particular social or professional world. **4.** *U.S.* See **main course** (def. 1). **5.** a dish served at dinner before the main course or between the regular courses. Also, **en′tree.** [< F, n. use of fem. ptp. of *entrer* to enter; see ENTRY]

en·tre·mets (än′trə mā′; *Fr.* äN trə me′), *n., pl.* **-mets** (-māz′; *Fr.* -me′). (*construed as sing. or pl.*) a dish or dishes served with the main course of a meal; side dish. [< F: lit., between-course; OF *entremes.* See INTER-, MESS]

en·trench (en trench′), *v.t.* **1.** to dig trenches for defensive purposes around (oneself, a military position, etc.). **2.** to place in a position of strength: *safely entrenched behind undeniable facts.* —*v.i.* **3.** to trespass or infringe (usually fol. by *on* or *upon*): *to entrench on the rights of another.* Also, **intrench.** —**en·trench′er,** *n.*

entrench′ing tool′. See **intrenching tool.**

en·trench·ment (en trench′mənt), *n.* **1.** the act of entrenching. **2.** an entrenched position. **3.** Usually, **entrenchments.** an earth breastwork or ditch for protection against enemy fire. Also, **intrenchment.**

en·tre nous (än′trə no͞o′; *Fr.* äN trə no͞o′), between ourselves; confidentially. [< F]

en·tre·pôt (än′trə pō′; *Fr.* äN trə pō′), *n., pl.* **-pôts** (-pōz′; *Fr.* -pō′). a center or warehouse for the distribution or transshipment of goods. Also, **en′tre·pot′.** [< F = *entre* INTER- + *pôt* < L *posit(um),* n. use of neut. ptp. of *pōnere* to put, place (modeled on *dépôt* DEPOT)]

en·tre·pre·neur (än′trə prə nûr′, -no͝or′; *Fr.* äN trə prə nœr′), *n., pl.* **-neurs** (-nûrz′, -no͝orz′; *Fr.* -nœr′). **1.** a person who organizes, manages, and assumes responsibility for a business or other enterprise. **2.** an employer of productive labor; contractor. [< F: lit., one who undertakes (some task) = *entrepren(dre)* (to) undertake (< L *inter-* INTER- + *prendere* to take, var. of *prehendere*) + *-eur* -OR[2]. See ENTERPRISE] —**en′tre·pre·neur′i·al,** *adj.* —**en′tre·pre·neur′ship,** *n.*

en·tre·sol (en′tər sol′, än′trə-; *Fr.* äN trə sôl′), *n., pl.* **-sols** (-solz′; *Fr.* -sôl′). *Archit.* an intermediate story between two stories; mezzanine. [< F: lit., between-floor = *entre-* INTER- + *sol* floor < L *sol(um)* ground]

en·tro·py (en′trə pē), *n.* **1.** *Thermodynamics.* a measure of the amount of energy unavailable for work during a natural process. *Symbol:* S **2.** the measure of the frequency with which an event occurs within a system; measure of probability of distribution in a closed or isolated system; measure of randomness. **3.** hypothesized tendency toward uniform inertness, esp. of the universe.

en·trust (en trust′), *v.t.* **1.** to invest with a trust or responsibility. **2.** to commit (something) in trust (usually fol. by *to*). Also, **intrust.** —**en·trust′ment,** *n.*

en·try (en′trē), *n., pl.* **-tries. 1.** the act of entering; entrance. **2.** a place of entrance. **3.** the right to enter; access. **4.** the act of recording something in a book, register, etc. **5.** the item so recorded. **6.** a person or thing entered in a contest or competition. **7.** *Law.* act of taking possession of lands by setting foot on them. **8.** the giving of an account of a ship's cargo at a custom house. **9.** *Bookkeeping.* **a.** See **double entry. b.** See **single entry. 10.** Also called **en′try card′.** *Bridge.* a winning card in one's hand or the hand of one's partner that gives the lead to one hand or the other. [ME *entre(e)* < MF *entree* < L *intrāta;* n. use of fem. of *intrātus,* ptp. of *intrāre* to ENTER; see -ATE[1]]

en·try·way (en′trē wā′), *n.* a passage affording entrance.

en·twine (en twīn′), *v.t., v.i.,* **-twined, -twin·ing.** to twine with, around, or together. Also, **intwine.** —**en·twine′ment,** *n.*

en·twist (en twist′), *v.t.* to twist together. Also, **intwist.**

e·nu·cle·ate (*v.* i no͞o′klē āt′, i nyo͞o′-; *adj.* i no͞o′klē it, -āt′, i nyo͞o′-), *v.,* **-at·ed, -at·ing,** *adj.* —*v.t.* **1.** *Biol.* to deprive of the nucleus. **2.** to remove (a kernel, tumor, eyeball, etc.) from its enveloping cover. **3.** *Archaic.* to bring out; disclose; explain. —*adj.* **4.** having no nucleus. [< L *ēnucleāt(us)* (ptp. of *ēnucleāre*)] —**e·nu′cle·a′tion,** *n.*

E·nu·gu (ā no͞o′go͞o), *n.* a city in SE Nigeria. 138,457 (1963).

e·nu·mer·a·ble (i no͞o′mər ə bəl, i nyo͞o′-), *adj.* denumerable. [ENUMER(ATE) + -ABLE]

e·nu·mer·ate (i no͞o′mə rāt′, i nyo͞o′-), *v.t.,* **-at·ed, -at·ing. 1.** to mention separately as if in counting; name one by one; specify, as in a list. **2.** to ascertain the number of; count. [< L *ēnumerāt(us)* (ptp. of *ēnumerāre*). See E-, NUMBER, -ATE[1]] —**e·nu·mer·a·tive** (i no͞o′mə rā′tiv, -rə tiv, i nyo͞o′-), *adj.* —**e·nu′mer·a′tor,** *n.*

e·nu·mer·a·tion (i no͞o′mə rā′shən, i nyo͞o′-), *n.* **1.** the act of enumerating. **2.** a catalog or list. [< L *ēnumerātiōn-* (s. of *ēnumerātiō*)]

e·nun·ci·ate (i nun′sē āt′, -shē-), *v.,* **-at·ed, -at·ing.** —*v.t.* **1.** to pronounce (words, sentences, etc.), esp. in an articulate manner. **2.** to state or declare definitely. **3.** to proclaim. —*v.i.* **4.** to pronounce words, esp. in an articulate manner. [< L *ēnuntiāt(us)* (ptp. of *ēnuntiāre*). See E-, NUNCIO, -ATE[1]] —**e·nun′ci·a′tive, e·nun′ci·a·to′ry,** *adj.* —**e·nun′ci·a′tive·ly,** *adv.* —**e·nun′ci·a′tor,** *n.*

e·nun·ci·a·tion (i nun′sē ā′shən, -shē-), *n.* **1.** the act or the manner of enunciating. **2.** utterance or pronunciation. **3.** a formal announcement. [< L *ēnuntiātiōn-* (s. of *ēnuntiātiō*)]

en·ure (en yo͝or′), *v.t., v.i.,* **-ured, -ur·ing.** inure.

en·u·re·sis (en′yə rē′sis), *n. Med.* involuntary urination; incontinence. [< NL < Gk *en-* EN-[2] + *ourē-* (s. of *ourein* to urinate) + *-sis* -SIS] —**en·u·ret·ic** (en′yə ret′ik), *adj.*

en·vel·op (en vel′əp), *v.t.* **1.** to wrap in or as in a covering. **2.** to serve as a wrapping or covering for. **3.** to surround entirely. **4.** *Mil.* to attack an enemy's flank. [ME *envolupe(n)* < OF *envolupe(r),* by dissimilation < L *involvere* to wrap up. See INVOLVE] —**en·vel′op·er,** *n.* —**Syn. 1.** enfold, cover, conceal. **3.** encompass, enclose.

en·ve·lope (en′və lōp′, än′-), *n.* **1.** a flat paper container, as for a letter, usually having a gummed flap or other means of closure. **2.** a wrapper, integument, etc. **3.** *Biol., Bot.* a surrounding or enclosing part, as a corolla. **4.** *Geom.* a curve or surface tangent to each member of a set of curves or surfaces. **5.** the fabric structure enclosing the gasbag of a dirigible, blimp, etc. **6.** the gasbag itself. [< F *enveloppe;* see ENVELOP]

en·vel·op·ment (en vel′əp mənt), *n.* **1.** the act of enveloping. **2.** the state of being enveloped. **3.** a wrapping or covering. **4.** *Mil.* an attack on an enemy's flank.

en·ven·om (en ven′əm), *v.t.* **1.** to impregnate with venom; make poisonous. **2.** to embitter. [ME *envenime(n)* < OF *envenime(r)*]

En·ver Pa·sha (en veR′ pä shä′), 1881–1922, Turkish soldier and statesman.

en·vi·a·ble (en′vē ə bəl), *adj.* to be envied; desirable. —**en′vi·a·bly,** *adv.*

en·vi·ous (en′vē əs), *adj.* **1.** full of, feeling, or expressing envy. **2.** *Obs.* emulous. [ME < AF; OF *envieus* < L *invidiōs(us)* INVIDIOUS] —**en′vi·ous·ly,** *adv.* —**en′vi·ous·ness,** *n.*

en·vi·ron (en vī′rən, -vī′ərn), *v.t.* to form a circle or ring round; surround; envelop. [ME *enviroune(n)* < OF *environne(r)* < *environ* around (*en-* EN-[1] + *viron* a circle)]

en·vi·ron·ment (en vī′rən mənt, -vī′ərn-), *n.* **1.** the aggregate of surrounding things, conditions, or influences. **2.** the act of environing. **3.** the state of being environed. **4.** something that environs. —**en·vi′ron·men′tal,** *adj.* —**en·vi′ron·men′tal·ly,** *adv.*

en·vi·ron·men·tal·ist (en vī′rən men′tə list), *n.* **1.** an expert on environmental problems. **2.** any person who advocates or works to protect the air, water, animals, plants, and other natural resources from pollution or its effects. [ENVIRONMENTAL + -IST] —**en·vi′ron·men′tal·ism,** *n.*

en·vi·rons (en vī′rənz, -vī′ərnz, en′vər ənz, -vī ərnz), *n.pl.* surrounding parts or districts, as of a city; outskirts; suburbs. [< F (pl.); r. ME *environ* < OF; n. pl. use of ENVIRON]

en·vis·age (en viz′ij), *v.t.,* **-aged, -ag·ing. 1.** to contemplate; visualize: *He envisages an era of scientific discovery.* **2.** *Archaic.* to look in the face of; face. [< F *envisag(er)*] —**en·vis′age·ment,** *n.*

en·vi·sion (en vizh′ən), *v.t.* to picture mentally.

en·voy[1] (en′voi, än′-), *n.* **1.** a diplomatic agent. **2.** any accredited messenger or representative. **3.** Also called **en′voy extraor′dinary and min′ister plenipoten′tiary.** a diplomatic agent next in dignity after an ambassador. [< F *envoyé* (n. use of ptp. of *envoyer* to send) < LL *inviāt(us)* sent on a journey (lit., way, road). See IN [1], VIA, -ATE[1]]

en·voy[2] (en′voi), *n.* *Literature.* a short concluding or summarizing stanza, often containing the dedication or a similar postscript to a prose work. Also, **en′voi.** [ME *envoye* < OF < *envoy(er)* (to) send; see ENVOY[1]]

en·vy (en′vē), *n., pl.* **-vies,** *v.,* **-vied, -vy·ing.** —*n.* **1.** a sense of discontent or jealousy with regard to another's advantages, success, possessions, etc. **2.** desire for an advantage possessed by another. **3.** an object of envious feeling. **4.** *Obs.* ill will. —*v.t.* **5.** to regard with envy; be envious of. —*v.i.* **6.** *Obs.* to be affected with envy. [ME *envie* < OF < L *invidia* = *invid(us)* envious (< *invidēre* to envy) + *-ia* -Y[3]] —**en′vi·er,** *n.* —**en′vy·ing·ly,** *adv.*
—**Syn. 1.** jealousy, enviousness, covetousness. **5.** resent. ENVY, BEGRUDGE, COVET refer to one's attitude concerning the possessions or attainments of others. To ENVY is to feel resentful because someone else possesses or has achieved what one wishes oneself to possess or to have achieved: *to envy the wealthy, a girl's beauty.* To BEGRUDGE is simply to be unwilling that another should have the possessions, honors, or credit he deserves: *to begrudge a man a reward for heroism.* To COVET is to long jealously to possess what someone else possesses: *I covet your silverware.*

en·wind (en wīnd′), *v.t.,* **-wound, -wind·ing.** to wind or coil about; encircle. Also, **inwind.**

en·womb (en wōōm′), *v.t.* to enclose in or as in the womb.

en·wrap (en rap′), *v.t.,* **-wrapped, -wrap·ping. 1.** to envelop. **2.** to engross. Also, **inwrap.** [ME]

en·wreathe (en rēth′), *v.t.,* **-wreathed, -wreath·ing.** to surround with or as with a wreath. Also, **inwreathe.**

en·zo·ot·ic (en′zō ot′ik), *adj.* *Vet. Med.* **1.** (of diseases) afflicting animals in a particular locality. Cf. **endemic.** —*n.* **2.** an enzootic disease. Also, **en′zo·öt′ic.** [EN-[2] + ZO- + -OTIC, modeled on *epizootic*] —**en′zo·ot′i·cal·ly, en′zo·öt′i·cal·ly,** *adv.*

en·zy·mat·ic (en′zī mat′ik, -zi-), *adj.* of or pertaining to an enzyme. Also, **en·zy·mic** (en zī′mik, -zim′ik). —**en′zy·mat′i·cal·ly,** *adv.*

en·zyme (en′zīm), *n.* *Biochem.* any of various complex organic substances, originating from living cells and capable of producing certain chemical changes in organic substances by catalytic action, as in digestion. [< MGk *énzym(os)* leavened]

en·zy·mol·o·gy (en′zī mol′ə jē, -zi-), *n.* the science that deals with the chemistry, biochemistry, and biology of enzymes. —**en′zy·mol′o·gist,** *n.*

en·zy·mol·y·sis (en′zī mol′i sis, -zi-), *n.* *Biochem.* the decomposition of a chemical compound catalyzed by an enzyme. —**en·zy·mo·lyt·ic** (en′zi mə lit′ik), *adj.*

eo-, a learned borrowing from Greek meaning "primeval," used in the formation of compound words: *Eocene.* [< Gk, comb. form of *ēōs* dawn. See EAST, AURORA]

e.o., ex officio.

E·o·cene (ē′ə sēn′), *Geol.* —*adj.* **1.** noting or pertaining to an epoch of either the Tertiary or Paleogene period. See table under **era.** —*n.* **2.** the Eocene period or series.

e·o·hip·pus (ē′ō hip′əs), *n., pl.* **-pus·es.** an extinct horse of the genus *Hyracotherium,* from the early Eocene epoch of the western U.S. [< NL = *eo-* EO- + Gk *híppos* horse]

Eohippus
(9 in. high at shoulder; length 18 in.)

EOKA (e ô′kä), *n.* the Greek Cypriot liberation movement in Cyprus. [ModGk *E(lliniki) O(rganosis) K(iprion) A(gonis-ton)* Greek Organization of Cypriot fighters]

E·o·li·an (ē ō′lē ən), *adj.* **1.** (*l.c.*) *Geol.* **a.** noting or pertaining to sand or rock material carried or arranged by the wind. **b.** formed or eroded by the wind. **2.** Aeolian. —*n.* **3.** Aeolian.

E·ol·ic (ē ol′ik), *n., adj.* Aeolian. Also, **Aeolic.**

e·ol·i·pile (ē ol′ə pīl′), *n.* aeolipile.

e·o·lith (ē′ə lith), *n.* a chipped flint thought to have been used as a tool by early man.

e·o·lith·ic (ē′ə lith′ik), *adj.* of, pertaining to, or characteristic of the earliest stage of human culture, marked chiefly by the use of eoliths.

e.o.m., *Chiefly Com.* end of the month.

e·on (ē′ən, ē′on), *n.* **1.** Also, **aeon.** a division of geologic time comprising two or more eras. **2.** aeon (def. 1).

e·o·ni·an (ē ō′nē ən), *adj.* aeonian.

E·os (ē′os), *n.* the ancient Greek goddess of the dawn, identified by the Romans with Aurora.

e·o·sin (ē′ə sin), *n.* *Chem.* **1.** a red solid, $C_{20}H_8Br_4O_5$, derived from fluorescein, used esp. in dyeing. **2.** any of a variety of eosinlike, acid dyes. Also, **e·o·sine** (ē′ə sin, -sēn′). [< Gk *ēōs* dawn (see EO-) + -IN[2]] —**e′o·sin′ic,** *adj.* —**e′o·sin·like′,** *adj.*

e·o·sin·o·phil (ē′ə sin′ə fil), *Biol.* —*n.* **1.** an eosinophilic cell, tissue, organism, or substance. **2.** a leukocyte having eosinophilic granules in the cytoplasm and usually a bilobate nucleus. —*adj.* **3.** eosinophilic. Also, **e·o·sin·o·phile** (ē′ə-sin′ə fīl′). Also called **acidophil.**

e·o·sin·o·phil·ic (ē′ə sin′ə fil′ik), *adj.* *Biol.* having an affinity for eosin and other acid dyes; acidophilic. Also, **e·o·si·noph·i·lous** (ē′ə si nof′ə ləs).

-eous, var. of **-ous,** occurring in adjectives borrowed from Latin or (infrequently) derived from Latin nouns: *arboreous.* [< L *-e(us)* adj. suffix + -OUS]

E·o·zo·ic (ē′ə zō′ik), *adj.* *Geol. Obs.* noting or pertaining to the Precambrian era, esp. the period including the beginnings of animal life.

ep-, var. of **epi-** before a vowel or *h: epencephalon.*

Ep., Epistle.

e·pact (ē′pakt), *n.* **1.** the difference in days between the lengths of the solar and lunar years. **2.** the number of days since new moon at the beginning of the calendar year, January 1. [< LL *epact(a)* < Gk *epaktḗ,* n. use of fem. of *epaktós* added = *ep-* EP- + *ag-* (s. of *ágein* to lead) + *-tos* ptp. suffix]

E·pam·i·non·das (i pam′ə non′dəs), *n.* 418?–362 B.C., Theban general and statesman.

ep·arch (ep′ärk), *n.* **1.** the prefect or governor of an eparchy. **2.** *Gk. Ch.* a bishop or metropolitan of an eparchy. [< Gk *éparch(os)* commander, governor, prefect]

ep·ar·chy (ep′är kē), *n., pl.* **-chies. 1.** (in modern Greece) one of the administrative subdivisions of a province. **2.** (in ancient Greece) a province. [< Gk *eparchía* prefecture, province] —**ep·ar′chi·al,** *adj.*

ep·au·let (ep′ə let′, -lit, ep′ə let′), *n.* an ornamental shoulder piece worn on uniforms. Also, **ep′au·lette′.** [< F *épaulette* = *épaule* shoulder (< L *spatula* blade; see SPATULA) + *-ette* -ET]

E·pe·ans (i pē′ənz), *n.pl.* *Class. Myth.* the descendants of Epeus, a son of Endymion.

é·pée (ā pā′), *n.* *Fencing.* a rapier with a three-sided blade and a guard over the tip. Also, **e·pee′.** [< F: sword < L *spatha* sword < Gk *spáthē* blade. See SPADE[1]]

é·pée·ist (ā pā′ist), *n.* *Fencing.* a person who fences with an épée. [< F *épéiste*]

ep·ei·rog·e·ny (ep′ī roj′ə nē), *n.* *Geol.* vertical or tilting movement of the earth crust, generally affecting broad areas of a continent. Also, **e·pei·ro·gen·e·sis** (i pī′rō jen′i-sis), **epirogeny.** [< Gk *ēpeiro(s)* mainland, continent + -GENY] —**e·pei·ro·gen·ic** (i pī′rō jen′ik), **e·pei·ro·ge·net·ic** (i pī′rō jə net′ik), *adj.*

ep·en·ceph·a·lon (ep′ən sef′ə lon′), *n., pl.* **-lons, -la** (-lə). *Anat.* the hindbrain. —**ep·en·ce·phal·ic** (ep′ən sə-fal′ik), *adj.*

ep·en·the·sis (e pen′thi sis), *n., pl.* **-ses** (-sēz′). the insertion of one or more sounds in the middle of a word. [< LL: insertion of a letter < Gk. See EP-, EN-[2], THESIS] —**ep·en·thet·ic** (ep′ən thet′ik), *adj.*

e·pergne (i pûrn′, ā pârn′), *n.* an ornamental dish for holding fruit, flowers, etc. [? < F *épargne* treasury, saving < *épargner* to save < Gmc; cf. G *sparen* to save]

ep·ex·e·ge·sis (ep ek′si jē′sis), *n., pl.* **-ses** (-sēz). *Rhet.* **1.** the addition of a word or words to explain a preceding word or sentence. **2.** the word or words so added. [< Gk: explanation. See EP-, EXEGESIS] —**ep·ex·e·get·ic** (ep ek′-si jet′ik), **ep·ex′e·get′i·cal,** *adj.* —**ep·ex′e·get′i·cal·ly,** *adv.*

eph-, var. of **epi-** before an aspirate: *ephedrine.*

Eph., Ephesians.

e·phah (ē′fə), *n.* a Hebrew unit of dry measure, equal to about a bushel. Also, **e′pha.** [< Heb]

e·phebe (i fēb′, ef′ēb), *n.* (in ancient Greece) a young man, esp. one just enrolled as a citizen. [< L *ephēb(us)* < Gk *éphēbos* = *ep-* EP- + *hḗbē* manhood] —**e·phe′bic,** *adj.*

e·phed·rine (i fed′rin; *Chem.* ef′i drēn′, -drin), *n.* *Pharm.* a crystalline alkaloid, $C_6H_5CHOHCH(CH_3)NHCH_3$, used chiefly for the treatment of respiratory ailments. [< NL *Ephedr(a)* name of the plant genus from which it is obtained, L: the plant horsetail < Gk: horsetail, lit., sitting on (*eph-* EPH- + *hédra* seat, chair) + -INE[2]]

e·phem·er·a (i fem′ər ə), *n., pl.* **-er·as, -er·ae** (-ə rē′). **1.** anything short-lived or transitory. **2.** an ephemerid. [< Gk, neut. pl. of *ephḗmeros,* taken as sing.; see EPHEMERAL]

e·phem·er·al (i fem′ər əl), *adj.* **1.** lasting a very short time; transitory. **2.** lasting but one day: *an ephemeral flower.* —*n.* **3.** anything short-lived, as certain insects. [< Gk *ephḗmer(os)* short-lived, lasting but a day (*ep-* EP- + *hēmér(a)* day + *-os* adj. suffix) + -AL[1]] —**e·phem′er·al·ly,** *adv.* —**e·phem′er·al′i·ty, e·phem′er·al·ness,** *n.*

e·phem·er·id (i fem′ər id), *n.* an insect of the order *Ephemeroptera,* comprising the mayflies. [< NL *Ephēmerid(ae).* See EPHEMERAL, -ID[2]]

e·phem·er·is (i fem′ər is), *n., pl.* **eph·e·mer·i·des** (ef′-ə mer′i dēz′). **1.** a table showing the positions of a heavenly body at regular intervals in time. **2.** an astronomical almanac containing such tables. **3.** *Obs.* an almanac or calendar. [< L: daybook, diary < Gk: diary, account book < *ephḗmer(os);* see EPHEMERAL]

e·phem·er·on (i fem′ə ron′, -ər ən), *n., pl.* **-er·a** (-ər ə), **-er·ons.** ephemera (def. 2). [< Gk: short-lived insect, n. use of neut. of *ephḗmeros*]

Ephes., Ephesians.

E·phe·sians (i fē′zhənz), *n.* (*construed as sing.*) a book of the New Testament, written by Paul.

Eph·e·sus (ef′i səs), *n.* an ancient city in W Asia Minor, S of Izmir. —**E·phe·sian** (i fē′zhən), *adj., n.*

eph·od (ef′od, ē′fod), *n.* *Judaism.* a richly embroidered vestment worn by the high priest. Ex. 28:6, 7, 25–28. [ME < ML < Heb *ēphōd,* appar. meaning "idol" in some passages]

eph·or (ef′ôr, ef′ər), *n., pl.* **-ors, -or·i** (-ə rī′). one of a body of magistrates in an ancient Dorian state, as Sparta. [< L *ephor(us)* < Gk *éphoros* overseer, guardian, ruler (cf. *ephorân* to look over = *ep-* EP- + *horân* to see, look)] —**eph′or·al,** *adj.*

E·phra·im (ē′frē əm, ē′frəm), *n.* **1.** the younger son of Joseph. Gen. 41:52. **2.** the tribe of Israel descended from him. Gen. 48:1. **3.** the Biblical kingdom of the Hebrews in N Palestine. Cf. **Judah** (def. 3). [< LL < Gk < Heb *Ephrajim* very fruitful]

E·phra·im·ite (ē′frē ə mīt′), *n.* **1.** a member of the tribe of Ephraim. **2.** an inhabitant of the Northern kingdom of Israel. —*adj.* **3.** Also, **E·phra·i·mit·ic** (ē′frē ə mit′ik). of or pertaining to the tribe of Ephraim or the Ephraimites.

epi-, a prefix occurring in loan words from Greek, where it meant "upon," "on," "over," "near," "at," "before," "after" (*epicedium; epidermis; epigene; epitome*), on this model, used in the formation of new compound words (*epicardium; epinephrine*). Also, **ep-, eph-.** [< Gk, comb. form of *epí,* prep. and adv.]

ep·i·blast (ep′ə blast′), *n.* *Embryol.* **1.** the ectoderm. **2.** the primordial outer layer of a young embryo before the segregation of the germ layers, capable of becoming the ectoderm. —**ep′i·blas′tic,** *adj.*

e·pib·o·ly (i pib′ə lē), *n., pl.* **-lies.** *Embryol.* the growth of one part so that it overlies or surrounds another. [< Gk *epibolḗ* a throwing on = *epi-* EPI- + *bol-* (var. s. of *bállein* to throw) + *-ē* n. suffix] —**ep·i·bol·ic** (ep′ə bol′ik), *adj.*

ep·ic (ep′ik), *adj.* Also, **ep′i·cal. 1.** noting or pertaining to a poetic composition, usually centered upon a hero, in which a series of great achievements or events is narrated in elevated style: *Homer's* Iliad *is an epic poem.* **2.** resembling or suggesting such poetry: *an epic novel.* **3.** heroic; majestic; impressively great: *the epic events of the war.* **4.** of unusually great size or extent. **—*n.* 5.** an epic poem. **6.** epic poetry. **7.** any composition resembling an epic poem. **8.** something worthy to form the subject of an epic. **9.** (*cap.*) Also called **Old Ionic.** the Greek dialect represented in the *Iliad* and the *Odyssey,* apparently Aeolic modified by Ionic. [< L *epic(us)* < Gk *epikós*] **—ep′ic·like′,** *adj.*

ep·i·ca·lyx (ep′ə kā′liks, -kal′iks), *n., pl.* **-ca·lyx·es, -ca·ly·ces** (-kā′li sēz′, -kal′i-). *Bot.* an involucre resembling an outer calyx, as in the mallow.

A, Epicalyx
B, Calyx

ep·i·can·thus (ep′ə kan′thəs), *n., pl.* **-thi** (-thī, -thē). *Anat.* a fold of skin extending from the eyelid over the inner canthus of the eye, common in members of the Mongolian race. Also called **Mongolian fold.** [< NL] **—ep′i·can′thic,** *adj.*

ep·i·car·di·um (ep′ə kär′dē əm), *n., pl.* **-di·a** (-dē ə). *Anat.* the inner serous layer of the pericardium, lying directly upon the heart. [< NL; see EPI-, PERICARDIUM] **—ep′i·car′di·al, ep′i·car′di·ac′,** *adj.*

ep·i·carp (ep′ə kärp′), *n. Bot.* the outermost layer of a pericarp, as a rind or peel.

Ep·i·cas·te (ep′ə kas′tē), *n. Homeric Legend.* Jocasta.

ep·i·ce·di·um (ep′i sē′dē əm, -si dī′əm), *n., pl.* **-se·di·a** (-sē′dē ə, -si dī′ə). a funeral song; dirge. [< L < Gk *epikḗdeion,* n. use of neut. of *epikḗdeios* of a funeral = *epi-* EPI- + *kēde-* (s. of *kêdos* care, sorrow) + *-ion* neut. n. suffix] **—ep′i·ce′di·al, ep′i·ce′di·an,** *adj.*

ep·i·cene (ep′i sēn′), *adj.* **1.** belonging to, or partaking of the characteristics of, both sexes. **2.** flaccid; feeble; weak. **3.** effeminate; nonmasculine. **4.** (of Greek and Latin nouns) of the same grammatical gender regardless of the sex of the being referred to. **—*n.* 5.** an epicene person or thing. [ME < L *epicoen(us)* of both genders < Gk *epíkoinos* common to many. See EPI-, CENO-²] **—ep′i·cen′ism,** *n.*

ep·i·cen·ter (ep′i sen′tər), *n. Geol.* a point, directly above the true center of disturbance, from which the shock waves of an earthquake apparently radiate. Also, *Brit.,* **ep′i·cen′tre.** [< NL *epicentr(um)* < Gk *epíkentros* on the center] **—ep′i·cen′tral,** *adj.*

ep·i·cot·yl (ep′ə kot′əl, -il), *n. Bot.* (in the embryo of a plant) the part of the stem above the cotyledons. [EPI- + Gk *kotýl(ē)* cup]

e·pic·ri·sis (i pik′ri sis), *n.* a critical study or evaluation. [< Gk *epíkrisis* a judgment (cf. *epikrínein* to judge)]

ep·i·crit·ic (ep′ə krit′ik), *adj. Physiol.* noting or pertaining to a discriminating responsiveness to small variations in pain or temperature stimuli (opposed to *protopathic*). [< Gk *epikritik(os)* determinative]

Ep·ic·te·tus (ep′ik tē′təs), *n.* A.D. c60–c120, Greek Stoic philosopher and teacher, mainly in Rome.

ep·i·cure (ep′ə kyŏŏr′), *n.* **1.** a person who cultivates a refined taste, as in food, art, music, etc.; connoisseur. **2.** *Archaic.* a sensualist. [ME < L *Epicūr(us)* < Gk *Epíkouros* EPICURUS] **—Syn. 1.** gastronome, gourmet, epicurean. **2.** voluptuary. **—Ant. 1.** ascetic.

ep·i·cu·re·an (ep′ə kyŏŏ rē′ən, -kyŏŏr′ē-), *adj.* **1.** having luxurious tastes or habits, esp. in eating and drinking. **2.** fit for an epicure: *epicurean delicacies.* **3.** (*cap.*) of, pertaining to, or characteristic of Epicurus or Epicureanism. **—*n.* 4.** a person devoted to the pursuit of pleasure; epicure. **5.** (*cap.*) a disciple of Epicurus. [ME < L *Epicūre(us)* of Epicurus (< Gk *Epikoúreios*) + -AN]

Ep·i·cu·re·an·ism (ep′ə kyŏŏ rē′ə niz′əm, -kyŏŏr′ē-), *n.* **1.** the philosophical system of Epicurus, holding that the world is a series of fortuitous combinations of atoms and that the highest good is pleasure. **2.** (*l.c.*) epicurean indulgence or habits. Also, **Ep·i·cur·ism** (ep′ə kyŏŏ riz′əm, ep′ə kyŏŏr′iz əm).

Ep·i·cu·rus (ep′ə kyŏŏr′əs), *n.* 342?–270 B.C., Greek philosopher.

ep·i·cy·cle (ep′i sī′kəl), *n.* **1.** *Astron.* a small circle, the center of which moves around in the circumference of a larger circle: used in Ptolemaic astronomy. **2.** *Math.* a circle that rolls, externally or internally, on another circle. [ME < MF < LL *epicycl(us)* < Gk *epíkyklos*] **—ep·i·cy·clic** (ep′ə sī′klik, -sik′lik), *adj.*

ep′icyclic train′, *Mach.* a train of gears or pulleys in which one or more of the axes revolve about a central axis.

ep·i·cy·cloid (ep′i sī′kloid), *n. Geom.* a curve generated by the motion of a point on the circumference of a circle that rolls externally on a fixed circle. **—ep′i·cy·cloi′dal,** *adj.*

E, Epicycloid; P, Point tracing epicycloid as small circle rolls on fixed circle

Ep·i·daur·us (ep′i dôr′əs), *n.* an ancient town in Argolis: sanctuary of Asclepius.

ep·i·dem·ic (ep′i dem′ik), *adj.* **1.** Also, **ep′i·dem′i·cal.** affecting at the same time a large number of persons in a locality, as a contagious disease. **—*n.* 2.** a temporary prevalence of a disease. **3.** a rapid spread or sudden prevalence of something. [obs. *epidem(y)* (< LL *epidēmia* < Gk: staying in one place, among the people; see EPI-, DEMOS, -Y³) + -IC] **—ep′i·dem′i·cal·ly,** *adv.*

epidem′ic encephali′tis, *Pathol.* See **sleeping sickness** (def. 2).

ep·i·de·mi·ol·o·gy (ep′i dē′mē ol′ə jē), *n.* the branch of medicine dealing with epidemic diseases. **—ep·i·de·mi·o·log·i·cal** (ep′i dē′mē ə loj′i kəl), *adj.* **—ep′i·de′mi·o·log′i·cal·ly,** *adv.* **—ep′i·de′mi·ol′o·gist,** *n.*

ep·i·der·mis (ep′i dûr′mis), *n.* **1.** *Anat.* the outer, nonvascular, nonsensitive layer of the skin, covering the true skin or corium. **2.** *Zool.* the outermost living layer of an animal, usually composed of one or more layers of cells. **3.** *Bot.* a thin layer of cells forming the outer integument of seed plants and ferns. [< LL: surface skin < Gk: upper skin] **—ep′i·der′mal, ep′i·der′mic,** *adj.*

ep·i·der·moid (ep′i dûr′moid), *adj.* resembling epidermis. Also, **ep′i·der·moi′dal.**

ep·i·did·y·mis (ep′i did′ə mis), *n., pl.* **-di·dym·i·des** (-di dim′i dēz′). *Anat.* an elongated organ on the posterior surface of a testis that constitutes the convoluted beginning of the vas deferens. [< Gk; see EPI-, DIDYMOUS] **—ep′i·did′y·mal,** *adj.*

ep·i·dote (ep′i dōt′), *n.* a mineral, calcium aluminum iron silicate, $Ca_2(Al, Fe)_3Si_3O_{12}(OH)$. [< F *épidote* < Gk *epídot(os)* given besides, increased (ptp. of *epididónai*) = *epi-* EPI- + *dotós* given (ptp. of *didónai*); so named from the length of its crystals] **—ep·i·dot·ic** (ep′i dot′ik), *adj.*

ep·i·fo·cal (ep′ə fō′kəl), *adj. Geol.* epicentral.

ep·i·gas·tric (ep′ə gas′trik), *adj.* lying on, distributed over, or pertaining to the epigastrium. [EPIGASTR(IUM) + -IC]

ep·i·gas·tri·um (ep′ə gas′trē əm), *n., pl.* **-tri·a** (-trē ə). *Anat.* the part of the abdomen lying over the stomach. [< NL < Gk *epigástrion,* n. use of neut. of *epigástrios* over the stomach]

ep·i·ge·al (ep′i jē′əl), *adj.* **1.** *Entomol.* living near the surface of the ground, as on low-growing surface vegetation. **2.** *Bot.* epigeous. Also, **ep′i·ge′an.** [EPIGE(OUS) + -AL¹]

ep·i·gene (ep′i jēn′), *adj. Geol.* formed or originating on the earth's surface (opposed to *hypogene*). [< F *épigène* < Gk *epigen(ḗs)* born after, growing after]

ep·i·gen·e·sis (ep′i jen′i sis), *n.* **1.** *Biol.* the theory that an embryo develops from the successive differentiation of an originally undifferentiated structure. **2.** *Geol.* ore deposition subsequent to the original formation of the enclosing rock. **—ep′i·gen′e·sist, e·pig·e·nist** (i pij′ə nist), *n.* **—ep·i·ge·net·ic** (ep′i jə net′ik), *adj.* **—ep′i·ge·net′i·cal·ly,** *adv.*

e·pig·e·nous (i pij′ə nəs), *adj. Bot.* growing on the surface, esp. the upper surface, as fungi on leaves.

ep·i·ge·ous (ep′i jē′əs), *adj. Bot.* growing on or close to the ground. [< Gk *epígei(os)* on, of the world = *epi-* EPI- + *-geios* (*gê* earth + *-ios* adj. suffix); see -OUS]

ep·i·glot·tis (ep′ə glot′is), *n., pl.* **-glot·tis·es, -glot·ti·des** (-glot′i dēz′). *Anat.* a thin, valvelike, cartilaginous structure that covers the glottis during swallowing. [< Gk] **—ep′i·glot′tal, ep′i·glot′tic,** *adj.*

ep·i·gone (ep′ə gōn′), *n.* an undistinguished imitator of an important writer, painter, etc. Also **ep·i·gon** (ep′ə gon′). [< L *epigon(us)* < Gk *epígonos* (one) born afterwards; in pl. the Epigoni = *epi-* EPI- + *-gonos,* akin to *gígnesthai* to be born] **—ep·i·gon·ic** (ep′ə gon′ik), *adj.* **—e·pig·o·nism** (i pig′ə niz′əm, e pig′-, ep′ə gō′niz əm, -gon′iz-), *n.*

E·pig·o·ni (i pig′ə nī′), *n.pl., sing.* **-o·nus** (-ə nəs). *Class. Myth.* the sons of the Seven against Thebes.

ep·i·gram (ep′ə gram′), *n.* **1.** any witty, ingenious, or pointed saying tersely expressed. **2.** epigrammatic expression: *Wilde had a genius for epigram.* **3.** a short, concise poem, often satirical, displaying a witty or ingenious turn of thought. [ME < L *epigram(ma)* inscription < Gk: inscription, epigram. See EPI-, -GRAM¹]

ep·i·gram·mat·ic (ep′ə grə mat′ik), *adj.* **1.** of or like an epigram; terse and ingenious in expression. **2.** given to epigrams. [< L *epigrammatic(us)* < Gk *epigrammatikós* = *epigrammat-* (s. of *epígramma*) EPIGRAM + *-ikos* -IC] **—ep′i·gram·mat′i·cal·ly,** *adv.*

ep·i·gram·ma·tise (ep′ə gram′ə tīz′), *v.t., v.i.,* **-tised, -tis·ing.** *Chiefly Brit.* epigrammatize.

ep·i·gram·ma·tism (ep′ə gram′ə tiz′əm), *n.* epigrammatic character or style. [< L *epigrammat-* (s. of *epigramma;* see EPIGRAM) + -ISM]

ep·i·gram·ma·tist (ep′ə gram′ə tist), *n.* a maker of epigrams. [< LL *epigrammatist(a)* < Gk *epigrammatistḗs*]

ep·i·gram·ma·tize (ep′ə gram′ə tīz′), *v.,* **-tized, -tiz·ing.** **—*v.t.* 1.** to express in epigrams. **2.** to make epigrams about (a person or thing). **—*v.i.* 3.** to make epigrams. Also, *esp. Brit.,* **epigrammatise.** [EPIGRAMMAT(IC) + -IZE]

ep·i·graph (ep′ə graf′, -gräf′), *n.* **1.** an inscription, esp. on a building, statue, or the like. **2.** an apposite quotation at the beginning of a book, chapter, etc. [< Gk *epigraph(ḗ)* inscription]

ep·i·graph·ic (ep′ə graf′ik), *adj.* **1.** of or pertaining to epigraphs. **2.** of or pertaining to epigraphy. **3.** of the style characteristic of epigraphs. Also, **ep′i·graph′i·cal.** **—ep′i·graph′i·cal·ly,** *adv.*

e·pig·ra·phy (i pig′rə fē), *n.* **1.** the study or science of epigraphs or inscriptions, esp. of ancient inscriptions. **2.** inscriptions collectively. **—e·pig′ra·phist, e·pig′ra·pher,** *n.*

e·pig·y·nous (i pij′ə nəs), *adj. Bot.* **1.** (of flowers) having all floral parts conjoint and generally divergent from the ovary at or near its summit. **2.** (of stamens, petals, etc.) having the parts so arranged.

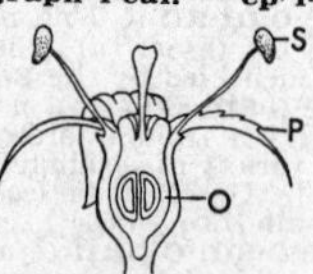

Epigynous stamens
S, Stamen; P, Petal; O, Ovary

ep·i·lep·sy (ep′ə lep′sē), *n. Pathol.* a disorder of the nervous system, usually characterized by fits of convulsions that end with loss of consciousness. Also, **ep′i·lep′si·a.** Cf. **grand mal, petit mal.** [< LL *epilēpsia* < Gk: epileptic seizure (akin to *epilambánein* to get hold of, attack) = *epi-* EPI- + *-lēp-* take + *-sia* suffix denoting result] **—ep·i·lep·toid** (ep′i lep′toid), **ep′i·lep′ti·form,** *adj.*

ep·i·lep·tic (ep′ə lep′tik), *adj. Pathol.* **1.** pertaining to or symptomatic of epilepsy. **—*n.* 2.** a person affected with epilepsy. [< L *epilēptic(us)* < Gk *epilēptikós*] **—ep′i·lep′ti·cal·ly,** *adv.*

ep·i·logue (ep′ə lôg′, -log′), *n., v.,* **-logued, -logu·ing.** **—*n.*** Also, **ep′i·log′. 1.** a speech delivered by one of the actors at the end of a play. **2.** a concluding part added to a literary work. **—*v.t.* 3.** to provide with an epilogue. [ME < L *epilog(us)* < Gk *epílogos* peroration of a speech] **—e·pil·o·gist** (i pil′ə jist), *n.*

Ep·i·me·the·us (ep′ə mē′thē əs, -thōōs), *n. Class. Myth.* a Titan, son of Iapetus and brother of Prometheus and Atlas; the husband of Pandora.

ep·i·mor·pho·sis (ep′ə môr′fə sis, -môr fō′-), *n. Zool.* a form of development in which body segmentation is completed before hatching. —**ep′i·mor′phic,** *adj.*

ep·i·na·os (ep′ə nā′os), *n., pl.* **-na·oi** (-nā′oi). a rear vestibule, as of a classical temple.

ep·i·neph·rine (ep′ə nef′rin, -rēn), *n.* **1.** Also called **adrenaline.** *Biochem.* a hormone, $C_6H_3(OH)_2CHOHCH_2NHCH_3$, produced by the adrenal glands and causing a rise in blood pressure. **2.** *Pharm.* a commercial form of this substance, used chiefly as a heart stimulant, to constrict the blood vessels, and to relax the bronchi in asthma. Also, **ep′i·neph′rin.** [EPI- + Gk *nephr(ós)* kidney + -INE[2]]

Epiph., Epiphany.

Ep·i·pha·ni·a (ep′ə fə nī′ə), *n.* ancient name of **Hama.**

E·piph·a·ny (i pif′ə nē), *n., pl.* **-nies.** **1.** a Christian festival, observed on January 6, commemorating the manifestation of Christ to the gentiles in the persons of the Magi. **2.** (*l.c.*) an appearance or manifestation, esp. of a deity. [ME *epiphanie* < eccl. L *epiphania* < LGk *epipháneia,* Gk: apparition = *epi-* EPI- + *-phan-* appear (s. of *phaínein*) + *-eia* -Y[3]] —**ep·i·phan·ic** (ep′ə fan′ik), *adj.*

ep·i·phe·nom·e·nal·ism (ep′ē fə nom′ə nəliz′əm), *n.* the doctrine that consciousness is merely an epiphenomenon of physiological processes. —**ep′i·phe·nom′e·nal·ist,** *n.*

ep·i·phe·nom·e·non (ep′ē fə nom′ə non′, -nən), *n.* **1.** any secondary phenomenon. **2.** *Pathol.* a secondary complication arising during an illness. —**ep′i·phe·nom′e·nal,** *adj.* —**ep′i·phe·nom′e·nal·ly,** *adv.*

e·piph·y·sis (i pif′i sis), *n., pl.* **-ses** (-sēz′). *Anat.* **1.** a part or process of a bone separated from the main body of the bone by a layer of cartilage, and subsequently uniting with the bone through further ossification. **2.** See **pineal body.** [< NL < Gk: growth upon. See EPI-, PHYSIS] —**ep·i·phys·e·al** (ep′ə fiz′ē əl, i pif′i sē′əl, -zē′-), **ep′i·phys′i·al,** *adj.*

ep·i·phyte (ep′ə fīt′), *n.* *Bot.* a plant that grows nonparasitically upon another, deriving its nutrients and water from rain, the air, dust, etc.; an air plant or aerophyte. —**ep·i·phyt·ic** (ep′ə fit′ik), **ep′i·phyt′i·cal,** *adj.* —**ep′i·phyt′i·cal·ly,** *adv.*

ep·i·phy·tot·ic (ep′ə fī tot′ik), *adj.* (of a disease) destroying a large number of plants in an area at the same time. [EPI- + -PHYT(E) + -OTIC]

ep·i·rog·e·ny (ep′ī roj′ə nē), *n.* *Geol.* epeirogeny. —**e·pi·ro·gen·ic** (i pī′rə jen′ik), **e·pi·ro·ge·net·ic** (i pī′rō jə net′ik), *adj.*

E·pi·rus (i pī′rəs), *n.* **1.** an ancient district in NW Greece and S Albania. **2.** a modern region in NW Greece. 352,604 (1961); 3573 sq. mi. —**E·pi·rote** (i pī′rōt), **E·pei·rot** (i pī′rət), *n.*

Epis., **1.** Episcopal. **2.** Episcopalian. **3.** Epistle.

Episc., **1.** Episcopal. **2.** Episcopalian.

e·pis·co·pa·cy (i pis′kə pə sē), *n., pl.* **-cies.** **1.** government of the church by bishops. **2.** the office or incumbency of a bishop. **3.** the order of bishops.

e·pis·co·pal (i pis′kə pəl), *adj.* **1.** of or pertaining to a bishop. **2.** based on or recognizing a governing order of bishops. **3.** (*cap.*) designating the Anglican Church or some branch of it, as the Protestant Episcopal Church. [ME < LL *episcopāl(is).* See BISHOP, -AL[1]] —**e·pis′co·pal·ly, E·pis′co·pal·ly,** *adj.*

E·pis·co·pa·lian (i pis′kə pāl′yən, -pā′lē ən), *adj.* **1.** pertaining or adhering to the Protestant Episcopal Church of the Anglican communion. **2.** (*l.c.*) pertaining or adhering to the episcopal form of church government. —*n.* **3.** a member of an episcopal church. **4.** (*l.c.*) an adherent of episcopal church government. —**E·pis′co·pa′lian·ism,** *n.*

e·pis·co·pal·ism (i pis′kə pə liz′əm), *n.* the theory of church polity that vests the supreme authority in the episcopal order as a whole.

e·pis·co·pate (i pis′kə pit, -pāt′), *n.* **1.** the office and dignity of a bishop; bishopric. **2.** the order or body of bishops. **3.** the incumbency of a bishop. [< LL *episcopāt(us)* the office of a bishop]

ep·i·si·ot·o·my (ə pē′zē ot′ə mē, ep′i sī-), *n., pl.* **-mies.** *Obstet., Surg.* incision of the vulva to allow sufficient clearance for birth. [< Gk *epísio(n)* pubic region + -TOMY]

ep·i·sode (ep′i sōd′, -zōd′), *n.* **1.** an incident in the course of a person's life or experience. **2.** an incident, scene, etc., within a narrative, usually fully developed and either integrated within the main story or digressing from it. **3.** a dramatic section in an ancient Greek tragedy between two choral odes. **4.** *Music.* an intermediate or digressive passage. **5.** any one of the separate installments that constitute a serial. [< Gk *epeisód(ion)* addition, episode, n. use of neut. of *epeisódios* coming in addition = *epi-* EPI- + *eísod(os)* entrance (*eis-* into + *hodós* road, way) + *-ios* adj. suffix] —**Syn. 1.** See **event.**

ep·i·sod·ic (ep′i sod′ik, -zod′-), *adj.* **1.** pertaining to or of the nature of an episode. **2.** divided into separate or loosely connected parts or sections. Also, **ep′i·sod′i·cal.** —**ep′i·sod′i·cal·ly,** *adv.*

e·pis·ta·sis (i pis′tə sis), *n.* *Genetics.* a form of interaction between nonallelic genes in which one combination of such genes has a dominant effect over other combinations. [< Gk: stopping, stoppage] —**ep·i·stat·ic** (ep′i stat′ik), *adj.*

ep·i·stax·is (ep′i stak′sis), *n.* *Pathol.* nosebleed. [< Gk: a dripping = *epi-* EPI- + *stag-* drop + *-sis* -SIS]

e·pis·te·mol·o·gy (i pis′tə mol′ə jē), *n.* a branch of philosophy that investigates the origin, nature, methods, and limits of human knowledge. [< Gk *epistḗm(ē)* knowledge + -O- + -LOGY] —**e·pis·te·mo·log·i·cal** (i pis′tə mə loj′i kəl), *adj.* —**e·pis′te·mo·log′i·cal·ly,** *adv.* —**e·pis′te·mol′o·gist,** *n.*

ep·i·ster·num (ep′i stûr′nəm), *n., pl.* **-na** (-nə). **1.** *Anat.* the manubrium. **2.** *Entomol.* the anterior portion of a pleuron.

e·pis·tle (i pis′əl), *n.* **1.** a letter, esp. a formal or didactic one. **2.** (*usually cap.*) one of the apostolic letters in the New Testament. **3.** (*often cap.*) an extract, usually from one of the Epistles of the New Testament, forming part of the Eucharistic service in certain churches. [ME; OE *epistol* < L *epistula, epistola* < Gk *epistolḗ* message, letter = *epi-* EPI- + *stol-* (var. s. of *stéllein* to send) + *-ē* n. suffix]

e·pis·to·lar·y (i pis′tə ler′ē), *adj.* Also, **ep·i·stol·ic** (ep′i stol′ik), **ep′i·stol′i·cal.** **1.** contained in or carried on by letters. **2.** of, pertaining to, or consisting of letters: *an epistolary novel.* [ME < L *epistolār(is)* of, belonging to a letter. See EPISTLE, -ARY]

e·pis·to·ler (i pis′tᵊlər), *n.* **1.** Also, **e·pis′to·list.** a writer of an epistle. **2.** the person who reads or chants the epistle in the Eucharistic service. Also, **e·pis·tler** (i pis′lər, i pist′lər). [< L *epistol(a)* EPISTLE + -ER[1]]

ep·i·style (ep′i stīl′), *n.* the architrave of a classical building. [< L *epistȳl(ium)* the crossbeam resting on the column < Gk *epistȳ́lion* crossbeam of architrave (*epi-* EPI- + *styl(os)* a column + *-ion* dim. suffix)] —**ep′i·sty′lar,** *adj.*

ep·i·taph (ep′i taf′, -täf′), *n.* **1.** a commemorative inscription on a tomb. **2.** a brief writing in praise of a deceased person. [ME *epitaphe* < L *epitaph(ium)* < Gk *epitáphion* over a tomb = *epi-* EPI- + *táph(os)* tomb + *-ion* n., adj. suffix] —**ep·i·taph·ic** (ep′i taf′ik), *adj.* —**ep′i·taph′ist,** *n.*

e·pit·a·sis (i pit′ə sis), *n.* the part of an ancient drama, following the protasis, containing the main action. Cf. **catastasis, catastrophe** (def. 4), **protasis** (def. 2). [< Gk: emphasis, increase of intensity, stretching = *epi-* EPI- + *-ta-* (var. s. of *teínein* to stretch) + *-sis* -SIS]

ep·i·tha·la·mi·on (ep′ə thə lā′mē ən), *n., pl.* **-mi·a** (-mē ə). a song or poem in honor of a bride and bridegroom. [< Gk: nuptial, n. use of neut. of *epithalámios* nuptial. See EPI-, THALAMUS]

ep·i·tha·la·mi·um (ep′ə thə lā′mē əm), *n., pl.* **-mi·ums, -mi·a** (-mē ə). epithalamion.

ep·i·the·li·o·ma (ep′ə thē′lē ō′mə), *n., pl.* **-mas, -ma·ta** (-mə tə). *Pathol.* a growth or tumor consisting chiefly of epithelial cells. —**ep·i·the·li·om·a·tous** (ep′ə thē′lē om′ə təs), *adj.*

ep·i·the·li·um (ep′ə thē′lē əm), *n., pl.* **-li·ums, -li·a** (-lē ə). *Biol.* any tissue that covers a surface, lines a cavity, or the like, and that performs protective, secreting, or other functions, as the epidermis. [< NL; see EPI-, THELITIS, -IUM] —**ep′i·the′li·al,** *adj.* —**ep′i·the′li·oid′,** *adj.*

ep·i·thet (ep′ə thet′), *n.* **1.** any word or phrase replacing or added to the name of a person or thing to describe a characteristic attribute. **2.** a word, phrase, etc., used invectively as a term of abuse or contempt, to express hostility, or the like. [< L *epithet(on)* epithet, adjective < Gk: epithet, something added = *epi-* EPI- + *the-* (var. s. of *tithénai* to put) + *-ton* neut. ptp. suffix] —**ep′i·thet′ic, ep′i·thet′i·cal,** *adj.*

e·pit·o·me (i pit′ə mē), *n.* **1.** a person or thing that is typical of or possesses to a high degree the features of a whole class: *He is the epitome of goodness.* **2.** a summary or condensed account. [< L: abridgment (var. of *epitoma*) < Gk *epitomḗ* abridgment, surface incision] —**ep·i·tom·i·cal** (ep′i tom′i kəl), **ep′i·tom′ic,** *adj.*

e·pit·o·mise (i pit′ə mīz′), *v.t.,* **-mised, -mis·ing.** *Chiefly Brit.* epitomize. —**e·pit′o·mi·sa′tion,** *n.* —**e·pit′o·mis′er,** *n.*

e·pit·o·mist (i pit′ə mist), *n.* a person who writes an epitome.

e·pit·o·mize (i pit′ə mīz′), *v.t.,* **-mized, -miz·ing.** **1.** to represent ideally; typify. **2.** to make an epitome of. Also, *esp. Brit.,* **epitomise.** —**e·pit′o·mi·za′tion,** *n.* —**e·pit′o·miz′er,** *n.*

ep·i·zo·ic (ep′i zō′ik), *adj.* *Biol.* dwelling on the surface of an animal. [EPIZO(ON) + -IC] —**ep′i·zo′ism,** *n.* —**ep·i·zo·ite** (ep′i zō′īt), *n.*

ep·i·zo·on (ep′i zō′on, -ən), *n., pl.* **-zo·a** (-zō′ə). *Biol.* an external parasite or commensal on the body of an animal; ectozoon. Also, **ep′i·zo′ön.** [< NL]

ep·i·zo·ot·ic (ep′i zō ot′ik), *Vet. Med.* —*adj.* **1.** (of diseases) spreading quickly among animals. —*n.* **2.** an epizootic disease. Also, **ep′i·zo·öt′ic.** [EPI + ZO(O)- + -OTIC] —**ep′i·zo·ot′i·cal·ly, ep′i·zo·öt′i·cal·ly,** *adv.*

e plu·ri·bus u·num (e plo͞o′ri bo͝os′ o͞o′no͝om; *Eng.* ē′ plo͝or′ə bəs yo͞o′nəm), *Latin.* out of many, one. (motto of the U.S.).

ep·och (ep′ək *or, esp. Brit.,* ē′pok), *n.* **1.** a particular period of time marked by distinctive features, events, etc.: *an epoch of peace and good will.* **2.** the beginning of a distinctive period in the history of anything. **3.** a memorable date. **4.** *Geol.* any of several divisions of a geological period during which a geological series is formed. Cf. **age** (def. 11). **5.** *Astron.* **a.** an arbitrarily fixed instant of time or date, usually the beginning of a century or half century, used as a reference in giving the elements of a planetary orbit or the like. **b.** the mean longitude of a planet as seen from the sun at such an instant or date. [< NL *epoch(a)* < Gk *epochḗ* pause, check, fixed time = *ep-* EP- + *-och-* (var. s. of *échein* to have) + *-ē* n. suffix] —**Syn. 1.** era. See **age.**

ep·och·al (ep′ə kəl), *adj.* **1.** of, pertaining to, or like an epoch or epochs. **2.** epoch-making. —**ep′och·al·ly,** *adv.*

ep·och-mak·ing (ep′ək mā′king), *adj.* opening a new era, as in human history, thought, or knowledge.

ep·ode (ep′ōd), *n.* **1.** *Class. Pros.* a kind of lyric poem in which a long verse is followed by a short one. **2.** the part of a lyric ode following the strophe and antistrophe. [< L *epōd(os)* < Gk *epōidós* an aftersong, singing after]

ep·o·nym (ep′ə nim), *n.* a person, real or imaginary, from whom something, as a tribe, nation, or place, takes or is said to take its name. [back formation from EPONYMOUS] —**ep′o·nym′ic,** *adj.*

ep·on·y·mous (e pon′ə məs), *adj.* giving one's name to a tribe, place, etc. [< Gk *epṓnymos* giving name. See EP-, -ONYM, -OUS]

ep·on·y·my (e pon′ə mē), *n.* the derivation of names from eponyms. [< Gk *epōnymía* surname, derived name]

ep·o·pee (ep′ə pē′, ep′ə pē′), *n.* **1.** an epic. **2.** epic poetry. Also, **ep·o·poe·ia** (ep′ə pē′ə). [< F *épopée* < Gk *epopoiía* = *épo(s)* EPOS + *poi(eîn)* (to) make + *-ia* -IA]

ep·os (ep′os), *n.* **1.** an epic. **2.** epic poetry. **3.** a group of poems, transmitted orally, concerned with parts of a common epic theme. **4.** a series of events suitable for treatment in epic poetry. [< L < Gk: speech, tale, song; akin to L *vox* VOICE, Skt *vácas* word, hymn]

ep·ox·y (e pok′sē), *adj., n., pl.* **-ox·ies.** *Chem.* **—***adj.* **1.** containing an oxygen atom bound to two atoms already connected, usually carbon atoms, thus forming a ring, as in ethylene oxide or epoxy ethane, $H_2C(O)CH_2$. **—***n.* **2.** Also called **epox′y res′in.** any of a class of substances derived by polymerization from certain epoxy chemicals: used in adhesives, coatings, etc. [EP- + OXY-[2]]

ep·si·lon (ep′sə lon′, -lən *or, esp. Brit.,* ep sī′lən), *n.* the fifth letter of the Greek alphabet (Ε, ε). [< Gk *ē psilón* bare, simple *e* (i.e., unaspirated)]

Ep·som (ep′səm), *n.* a town in SE England, S of London: site of annual Derby. 71,177 (1961). Official name, **Ep′som and Ew′ell.**

Ep′som salt′, Often, **Epsom salts.** *Chem., Pharm.* hydrated magnesium sulfate, $MgSO_4 \cdot 7H_2O$: used in the dyeing of fabrics, leather tanning, fertilizers, etc., and as a cathartic. [after EPSOM; so called from its presence in the local mineral water at Epsom]

Ep·stein (ep′stīn), *n.* **Sir Jacob,** 1880–1959, English sculptor, born in the U.S.

eq., 1. equal. **2.** equation. **3.** equivalent.

eq·ua·ble (ek′wə bəl, ē′kwə-), *adj.* **1.** uniform, as motion or temperature. **2.** uniform in operation or effect, as laws. **3.** tranquil, as the mind. [< L *aequābil(is)* that can be made equal, similar. See EQUAL, -ABLE] **—eq′ua·bil′i·ty, eq′ua·ble·ness,** *n.* **—eq′ua·bly,** *adv.* **—Syn. 3.** steady, regular, temperate. **—Ant. 1.** variable.

e·qual (ē′kwəl), *adj., n., v.,* **e·qualed, e·qual·ing** or (*esp. Brit.*) **e·qualled, e·qual·ling.** **—***adj.* **1.** of the same in quantity, degree, merit, etc.: *two students of equal brilliance.* **2.** evenly proportioned or balanced: *an equal contest.* **3.** uniform in operation or effect. **4.** sufficient in quantity or degree. **5.** adequate in power, ability, etc. (fol. by *to*): *He wasn't equal to the task.* **6.** level, as a plain. **7.** *Archaic.* tranquil or undisturbed. **8.** *Archaic.* impartial or equitable. **—***n.* **9.** a person or thing that is equal. **—***v.t.* **10.** to be or become equal to; match. **11.** to make or do something equal to. **12.** *Archaic.* to equalize. [ME < L *aequāl(is)* equal, like = *aequ(us)* even, plain, just + *-ālis* -AL[1]] **—Syn. 1.** proportionate, commensurate, coordinate, correspondent. EQUAL, EQUIVALENT imply a correspondence between two or more things. EQUAL indicates a correspondence in all respects, unless a particular respect (or respects) is stated or implied: *A dime is equal to 10 cents* (that is, in purchasing power, which is implied). EQUIVALENT indicates a correspondence in one or more respects, but not in all: *An egg is said to be the equivalent of a pound of meat* (that is, in nutritive value). **3.** even, regular. **5.** suited, fitted. **9.** peer, match, fellow. **—Ant. 1.** different. **4, 5.** inadequate.

e′qual-ar′e·a projec′tion (e′kwəl âr′ē ə), *Cartog.* a projection in which regions on the earth's surface that are of equal area are represented as equal in size.

e·qual·ise (ē′kwə līz′), *v.t.,* **-ised, -is·ing.** *Chiefly Brit.* equalize. —**e′qual·i·sa′tion,** *n.*

e·qual·i·tar·i·an (i kwol′i târ′ē ən), *adj.* **1.** pertaining or adhering to the doctrine of equality among men. **—***n.* **2.** a person who adheres to the doctrine of equality among men. **—e·qual′i·tar′i·an·ism,** *n.*

e·qual·i·ty (i kwol′i tē), *n., pl.* **-ties. 1.** the state or quality of being equal. **2.** uniform character, as of motion or surface. [ME < L *aequālitāt-* (s. of *aequālitās*)]

Equal′ity State′, Wyoming (used as a nickname).

e·qual·ize (ē′kwə līz′), *v.t.,* **-ized, -iz·ing. 1.** to make equal: *to equalize tax burdens.* **2.** to make uniform. Also, *esp. Brit.,* **equalise.** **—e′qual·i·za′tion,** *n.*

e·qual·iz·er (ē′kwə lī′zər), *n.* **1.** a person or thing that equalizes. **2.** a device or appliance for equalizing strains, pressures, etc. Also, *esp. Brit.,* **e′qual·is′er.**

e·qual·ly (ē′kwə lē), *adv.* **1.** in an equal or identical manner: *to treat rich and poor equally.* **2.** to an equal degree or extent: *The two of you are equally matched.*

e′qual sign′, *Math.* the symbol (=), used in a mathematical expression to indicate that the terms it separates are equal. Also, **e′quals sign′.**

e′qual time′, *U.S.* a doctrine which stipulates that a television or radio station must give or sell equal time on the air to all legally qualified political candidates for a particular office if it gives or sells any time to one of them.

E·qua·nil (ē′kwə nil), *n. Pharm., Trademark.* meprobamate.

e·qua·nim·i·ty (ē′kwə nim′i tē, ek′wə-), *n.* composure, esp. under tension; equilibrium. [< L *aequanimitāt-* (s. of *aequanimitās*). See EQUAL, ANIMUS, -ITY]

e·quan·i·mous (i kwan′ə məs), *adj.* having or showing equanimity; even-tempered. [< LL *aequanim(us)* (see EQUANIMITY) + -OUS] **—e·quan′i·mous·ly,** *adv.*

e·quate (i kwāt′), *v.t.,* **e·quat·ed, e·quat·ing. 1.** to state the equality of or between, as in an equation. **2.** to reduce to an average or to a common standard of comparison. **3.** to regard, treat, or represent as equivalent: *We cannot equate might with right.* [ME < L *aequāt(us)* made equal (ptp. of *aequāre*)] **—e·quat′a·bil′i·ty,** *n.,* **—e·quat′a·ble,** *adj.*

e·qua·tion (i kwā′zhən, -shən), *n.* **1.** the act of equating. **2.** equally balanced state; equilibrium. **3.** *Math.* an expression or a proposition, often algebraic, asserting the equality of two quantities. **4.** *Chem.* a symbolic representation showing the kind and amount of the starting materials and products of a reaction.

e·qua·tion·al (i kwā′zhə nəl, -shə-), *adj.* **1.** of, using, or involving equations. **2.** *Gram.* (of a sentence or predication) consisting of a subject and a complement with or without a copula. "*Very interesting, those books*" is an equational sentence. **—e·qua′tion·al·ly,** *adv.*

e·qua·tor (i kwā′tər), *n.* **1.** the great circle on a sphere or heavenly body whose plane is perpendicular to the polar axis. **2.** the great circle of the earth that is equidistant from the North Pole and South Pole. **3.** a circle separating a surface into two congruent parts. **4.** See **celestial equator.** [ME < ML *aequātor,* lit., equalizer (of day and night, as when the sun crosses the equator)]

e·qua·to·ri·al (ē′kwə tôr′ē əl, -tōr′-, ek′wə-), *adj.* **1.** of, pertaining to, or near an equator, esp. the equator of the earth. **2.** of, like, or typical of the regions at the earth's equator. **—***n.* **3.** a telescope mounting having two axes of motion, one parallel to the earth's axis, and one at right angles to it. **—e′qua·to′ri·al·ly,** *adv.*

Equato′rial Guin′ea, a republic in W equatorial Africa, comprising Río Muni and Fernando Po: formerly a Spanish colony. 400,000; 10,824 sq. mi. *Cap.:* Malabo. Formerly, **Spanish Guinea.**

eq·uer·ry (ek′wə rē), *n., pl.* **-ries. 1.** an officer of a royal or similar household in charge of the horses. **2.** an officer who attends on the British sovereign. [alter. (influenced by L *equus* horse) of earlier *esquiry, escuirie* < MF *escuirie* stable, squires collectively < *escuyer* SQUIRE; see -Y[3]]

e·ques·tri·an (i kwes′trē ən), *adj.* **1.** of or pertaining to horsemen or horsemanship. **2.** mounted on horseback. **3.** of or pertaining to the ancient Roman equites. **4.** representing a person mounted on a horse: *an equestrian statue.* **5.** pertaining to or composed of knights or mounted warriors. **—***n.* **6.** a person who rides horses. [< L *equestri(s)* (cf. *eques* horseman) + -AN] **—e·ques′tri·an·ism,** *n.*

e·ques·tri·enne (i kwes′trē en′), *n.* a female equestrian. [EQUESTRI(AN) + *-enne,* as in *comedienne*]

equi-, a combining form meaning "equal": *equidistant.* [ME < L *aequi-,* comb. form repr. *aequus* equal]

e·qui·an·gu·lar (ē′kwē aŋ′gyə lər), *adj.* having all the angles equal. **—e′qui·an′gu·lar′i·ty,** *n.*

e·qui·dis·tance (ē′kwi dis′təns), *n.* equal distance.

e·qui·dis·tant (ē′kwi dis′tənt), *adj.* equally distant. [< MF < LL *aequidistant-* (s. of *aequidistāns*)] **—e′qui·dis′tant·ly,** *adv.*

e·qui·lat·er·al (ē′kwə lat′ər əl), *adj.* **1.** having all the sides equal. **—***n.* **2.** a figure having all its sides equal: *an equilateral triangle.* See diag. at **triangle. 3.** a side that is equivalent, or equal to others. [< LL *aequilaterāl(is)*] **—e′qui·lat′er·al·ly,** *adv.*

e·quil·i·brant (i kwil′ə brənt), *n. Physics.* a counterbalancing force or system of forces. [< F *équilibrant*]

e·quil·i·brate (i kwil′ə brāt′, ē′kwə lī′brāt), *v.,* **-brat·ed, -brat·ing.** **—***v.t.* **1.** to balance equally; keep in equipoise or equilibrium. **2.** to be in equilibrium with; counterpoise. **—***v.i.* **3.** to be in equilibrium; balance. [< LL *aequilībrāt(us),* ptp. of *aequilībrāre* to be in EQUILIBRIUM; see -ATE] **—e·qui·li·bra·tion** (ē′kwə lə brā′shən, i kwil′ə-), *n.* **—e·qui·li·bra·tor** (ē′kwə lī′brā tər, i kwil′ə brā′-), *n.*

e·quil·i·brist (i kwil′ə brist), *n.* a performer skilled at balancing, as a tightrope walker. [< F *équilibriste*] **—e·quil′i·bris′tic,** *adj.*

e·qui·lib·ri·um (ē′kwə lib′rē əm), *n., pl.* **-ri·ums, -ri·a** (-rē ə). **1.** a state of rest or balance due to the equal action of opposing forces. **2.** equal balance between any powers, influences, etc.; equality of effect. **3.** mental or emotional balance; equanimity. **4.** *Chem.* the condition existing when a chemical reaction and its reverse reaction proceed at equal rates. [< L *aequilībrium* = *aequi-* EQUI- + *lībr(a)* balance + *-ium* -IUM] **—e·quil·i·bra·to·ry** (i kwil′ə brə tôr′ē, -tōr′ē, ē′kwə lib′rə-), *adj.* **—e′qui·lib′ri·ous,** *adj.*

e·qui·mo·lec·u·lar (ē′kwə mə lek′yə lər), *adj. Physics, Chem.* containing equal numbers of molecules.

e·quine (ē′kwīn), *adj.* **1.** of or resembling a horse. **—***n.* **2.** a horse. [< L *equīn(us)* = *equ(us)* horse + *-īnus* -INE[1]] **—e′quine·ly,** *adv.* **—e·quin′i·ty,** *n.*

e·qui·noc·tial (ē′kwə nok′shəl), *adj.* **1.** pertaining to an equinox or the equinoxes. **2.** pertaining to the celestial equator. **3.** occurring at or about the time of an equinox. **4.** *Bot.* (of a flower) opening regularly at a certain hour. **—***n.* **5.** See **celestial equator. 6.** See **equinoctial storm.** [ME < L *aequinoctiāl(is);* see EQUINOX, -AL[1]]

equinoc′tial cir′cle, *Astron.* See **celestial equator.**

equinoc′tial line′. See **celestial equator.**

equinoc′tial point′, either of the two points at which the celestial equator and the ecliptic intersect each other; the position of the sun's center at the equinoxes.

equinoc′tial storm′, a storm of violent winds and rain occurring at or near the time of an equinox but not physically related to the equinox. Also called **equinoctial, line gale, line storm.**

equinoc′tial year′, year (def. 3b).

e·qui·nox (ē′kwə noks′, ek′wə-), *n.* **1.** the time when the sun crosses the plane of the earth's equator, making night and day of equal length all over the earth, occurring about March 21 **(vernal equinox)** and September 22 **(autumnal equinox). 2.** either of the equinoctial points. [ME < ML *equinox(ium)* for L *aequinoctium* the time of equal days and nights. See EQUI-, NOCTI-, -IUM]

e·quip (i kwip′), *v.t.,* **e·quipped, e·quip·ping. 1.** to furnish or provide with whatever is needed. **2.** to dress out; array. [< MF *equip(er),* OF *esquiper* to fit out, equip, prob. < Scand; cf. Icel *skipa* to put in order, arrange, man (a ship)] **—e·quip′per,** *n.* **—Syn. 1.** outfit, rig. See **furnish.**

eq·ui·page (ek′wə pij), *n.* **1.** a carriage. **2.** a carriage with its horses and attendants. **3.** outfit, as of a ship, an army, or a soldier; equipment. **4.** a set of small household articles, as of china. [< MF]

e·quip·ment (i kwip′mənt), *n.* **1.** anything kept, furnished, or provided for a specific purpose. **2.** the act of equipping. **3.** the state of being equipped. **4.** the knowledge and skill necessary for a task, occupation, etc. **5.** the rolling stock of a railroad. **—Syn. 1.** apparatus, gear.

e·qui·poise (ē′kwə poiz′, ek′wə-), *n., v.,* **-poised, -pois·ing.** **—***n.* **1.** an equal distribution of weight; even balance. **2.** a counterpoise. **—***v.t.* **3.** to equal or offset in weight, balance.

e·qui·pol·lent (ē′kwə pol′ənt), *adj.* **1.** equal in power, effect, etc.; equivalent. **2.** *Logic.* (of two propositions, statements, etc.) logically equivalent in any of various specified ways. **—***n.* **3.** an equivalent. [ME < L *aequipollent-* (s. of *aequipollēns*) of equal value = *aequi-* EQUI- + *pollent-* (s. of *pollēns*) able, prp. of *pollere* to be strong] **—e′qui·pol′lence, e′qui·pol′len·cy,** *n.* **—e′qui·pol′lent·ly,** *adv.*

e·qui·pon·der·ance (ē′kwə pon′dər əns), *n.* equality of weight; equipoise. Also, **e′qui·pon′der·an·cy.** [*equiponder(ant)* (< ML *aequiponderant-,* s. of *aequiponderāns,* prp. of *aequiponderāre;* see EQUI-, PONDER, -ANT) + -ANCE] **—e′qui·pon′der·ant,** *adj.*

e·qui·pon·der·ate (ē′kwə pon′də rāt′), *v.t.,* **-at·ed, -at·ing.** to counterbalance. [< ML *aequiponderāt(us),* ptp. of *aequiponderāre*]

e·qui·po·tent (ē′kwə pōt′ənt), *adj.* equal in power, ability, or effect.

ERA	YEARS AGO	PERIOD		EPOCH	CHARACTERIZED BY
Archeozoic	5,000,000,000-1,500,000,000				earth's crust formed; unicellular organisms; earliest known life
Proterozoic	1,500,000,000-600,000,000				bacteria, algae, and fungi; primitive multicellular organisms
Paleozoic	600,000,000-500,000,000	Cambrian			marine invertebrates
	500,000,000-440,000,000	Ordovician			conodonts, ostracods, algae, and seaweeds
	440,000,000-400,000,000	Silurian			air-breathing animals
	400,000,000-350,000,000	Devonian			dominance of fishes; advent of amphibians and ammonites
	350,000,000-300,000,000	Mississippian	Carboniferous		increase of land areas; primitive ammonites; development of winged insects
	300,000,000-270,000,000	Pennsylvanian			warm climates; swampy lands; development of large reptiles and insects
	270,000,000-220,000,000	Permian			many reptiles
Mesozoic	220,000,000-180,000,000	Triassic			volcanic activity; marine reptiles, dinosaurs
	180,000,000-135,000,000	Jurassic			dinosaurs, conifers
	135,000,000-70,000,000	Cretaceous			extinction of giant reptiles; advent of modern insects; flowering plants
Cenozoic	70,000,000-60,000,000	Paleogene	Tertiary	Paleocene	advent of birds, mammals
	60,000,000-40,000,000			Eocene	presence of modern mammals
	40,000,000-25,000,000			Oligocene	saber-toothed cats
	25,000,000-10,000,000	Neocene		Miocene	grazing mammals
	10,000,000-1,000,000			Pliocene	growth of mountains; increase in size and numbers of mammals; gradual cooling of climate
	1,000,000-10,000	Quaternary		Pleistocene	widespread glacial ice
	10,000-present			Recent	development of man

e·qui·po·ten·tial (ē′kwə pə ten′shəl), *adj. Physics.* of the same or uniform potential at every point: *an equipotential surface.* —**e′qui·po·ten′ti·al′i·ty,** *n.*

eq·ui·se·tum (ek′wi sē′təm), *n., pl.* **-tums, -ta** (-tə). any plant of the genus *Equisetum,* comprising the horsetails or scouring rushes. [< NL; L *equisaetum* = *equi-* horse + *saeta* bristle] —**eq′ui·se′tic,** *adj.*

eq·ui·ta·ble (ek′wi tə bəl), *adj.* **1.** characterized by equity or fairness; just and right; reasonable. **2.** *Law.* **a.** pertaining to or valid in equity. **b.** pertaining to the system of equity, as distinguished from the common law. —**eq′ui·ta·ble·ness,** *n.* —**eq′ui·ta·bly,** *adv.*

eq·ui·tant (ek′wi tənt), *adj. Bot.* straddling or overlapping, as leaves whose bases overlap the leaves above or within them. [< L *equitant-* (s. of *equitāns*) riding (prp. of *equitāre*) = *equit-* (s. of *eques;* see EQUITES) + *-ant-* -ANT]

eq·ui·ta·tion (ek′wi tā′shən), *n.* the act or skill of riding on horseback. [< L *equitātiōn-* (s. of *equitātiō*) = *equitāt(us)* (ptp. of *equitāre* to ride) + *-iōn-* -ION]

eq·ui·tes (ek′wi tēz′), *n., pl. Rom. Hist.* **1.** cavalry. **2.** members of a privileged class derived from the ancient Roman cavalry. [< L, pl. of *eques* horseman < *equus* horse]

eq·ui·ty (ek′wi tē), *n., pl.* **-ties. 1.** the quality of being fair or impartial; fairness; impartiality. **2.** something that is fair and just. **3.** *Law.* **a.** the application of the dictates of conscience or the principles of natural justice to the settlement of controversies. **b.** a system of jurisprudence serving to supplement and remedy the limitations and the inflexibility of the common law. **c.** an equitable right or claim. **4.** the value, less liabilities, of a property or business; net worth. **5.** (*cap.*) See **Actors' Equity Association.** [ME *equite* < L *aequitās*]

equiv., equivalent.

e·quiv·a·lence (i kwiv′ə ləns *or, esp. for 3,* ē′kwə vā′ləns), *n.* **1.** the state or fact of being equivalent; equality in value, force, significance, etc. **2.** an instance of this; an equivalent. **3.** *Chem.* the quality of having equal valence. **4.** *Logic.* (of two propositions, statements, etc.) the fact of being equipollent. [< MF < ML *aequivalentia.* See EQUIVALENT, -IA, -ENCE]

e·quiv·a·len·cy (i kwiv′ə lən sē), *n., pl.* **-cies.** equivalence (defs. 1, 2). [< ML *aequivalentia*]

e·quiv·a·lent (i kwiv′ə lənt *or, esp. for 5,* ē′kwə vā′lənt), *adj.* **1.** equal in value, measure, force, significance, etc. **2.** corresponding in position, function, etc. **3.** *Geom.* having the same extent, as a triangle and a square of equal area. **4.** *Math.* capable of being set into one-to-one correspondence. **5.** *Chem.* having the same capacity to combine chemically. —*n.* **6.** something that is equivalent. [late ME < LL *aequivalent-* (s. of *aequivalēns*), prp. of *aequivalēre*] —**e·quiv′a·lent·ly,** *adv.* —**Syn. 1.** See **equal.**

equiv′alent weight′, *Chem.* the combining power, esp. in grams (**gram equivalent**), of an element or compound, equivalent to hydrogen as a standard of 1.00797 or oxygen as a standard of 8; the atomic weight divided by the valence.

e·quiv·o·cal (i kwiv′ə kəl), *adj.* **1.** of uncertain significance; not determined. **2.** of doubtful nature or character; questionable; dubious. **3.** having different meanings equally possible, as a word or phrase; susceptible of double interpretation; ambiguous. [ME *equivoc* < LL *aequivoc(us)* ambiguous (L *aequi-* EQUI- + *vōc-,* s. of *vōx* VOICE + *-us* adj. suffix) + -AL[1]] —**e·quiv′o·cal′i·ty, e·quiv·o·ca·cy** (i kwiv′ə kə sē), *n.* —**e·quiv′o·cal·ly,** *adv.* —**e·quiv′o·cal·ness,** *n.* —**Syn. 3.** See **ambiguous.**

e·quiv·o·cate (i kwiv′ə kāt′), *v.i.,* **-cat·ed, -cat·ing.** to use ambiguous or unclear expressions, usually to avoid a direct answer or in order to mislead; hedge. [late ME < ML *aequivocāt(us),* ptp. of *aequivocāre*] —**e·quiv′o·cat′ing·ly,** *adv.* —**e·quiv′o·ca′tor,** *n.*

e·quiv·o·ca·tion (i kwiv′ə kā′shən), *n.* **1.** the use of equivocal or ambiguous expressions, esp. in order to mislead or hedge. **2.** an equivocal or ambiguous expression; equivoque. **3.** *Logic.* a fallacy caused by the double meaning of a word. [late ME *equivocacion* < LL *aequivocātiōn-* (s. of *aequivocātiō*)]

eq·ui·voque (ek′wə vōk′, ē′kwə-), *n.* **1.** an equivocal term; an ambiguous expression. **2.** a play upon words; pun. **3.** double meaning; ambiguity. Also, **eq′ui·voke′.** [ME *equivoc* (adj.)]

er (ə, ər), *interj.* (used to express or represent a pause hesitation, uncertainty, etc.)

Er, *Chem.* erbium.

-er[1], **1.** a suffix used in forming nouns designating persons from the object of their occupation or labor (*hatter; tiler; tinner; moonshiner*), or from their place of origin or abode (*Icelander; southerner; villager*), or designating either persons or things from some special characteristic or circumstance (*six-footer; three-master; teetotaler; fiver; tenner*). **2.** a suffix serving as the regular English formative of agent nouns, being attached to verbs of any origin (*bearer; creeper; employer; harvester; teacher; theorizer*). [OE *-ere;* c. G *-er;* akin to L *-ārius*]

-er[2], a suffix of nouns denoting persons or things concerned or connected with something: *butler; grocer; garner.* [ME < AF *-er* = OF *-er, -ier* < L *-ārius, -ārium.* Cf. -ARY]

-er[3], a termination of nouns denoting action or process: *dinner; rejoinder; remainder; trover.* [< F, orig. inf. suffix]

-er[4], a suffix regularly used in forming the comparative degree of adjectives: *harder; smaller.* [OE *-ra, -re;* c. G *-er*]

-er[5], a suffix regularly used in forming the comparative degree of adverbs: *faster.* [OE *-or;* c. OHG *-or,* G *-er*]

-er[6], a formal element appearing in verbs having frequentative meaning: *flicker; flutter; shiver; shudder.* [OE *-r-;* c. G *-(e)r-*]

E.R., 1. King Edward. [< L *Edwardus Rex*] **2.** Queen Elizabeth. [< L *Elizabeth Rēgīna*]

e·ra (ēr′ə, er′ə), *n.* **1.** a period of time marked by distinctive character, events, etc. **2.** the period of time to which anything belongs or is assigned. **3.** a system of chronological notation reckoned from a given date. **4.** a point of time from which succeeding years are numbered, as at the beginning of a system of chronology. **5.** a date or an event forming the beginning of any distinctive period. **6.** *Geol.* a major division of geological time composed of a number of periods.

[< LL *aera* fixed date, era, epoch (from which time is reckoned), prob. special use of L *aera* counters (pl. of *aes* piece of metal, money, brass); c. Goth *aiz*, OE *ār* ORE, Skt *ayas* metal] —**Syn. 1.** See **age.**

ERA, Equal Rights Amendment (to the U.S. Constitution, esp. referring to sexual equality).

e·ra·di·ate (i rā′dē āt′), *v.i., v.t.*, **-at·ed, -at·ing.** to radiate. —**e·ra′di·a′tion,** *n.*

e·rad·i·cate (i rad′ə kāt′), *v.t.*, **-cat·ed, -cat·ing. 1.** to destroy utterly; exterminate; annihilate: *to eradicate an army.* **2.** to erase or remove. **3.** to pull up by the roots. [< L *ērādīcāt(us)* rooted out (ptp. of *ērādīcāre*). See E-, RADICAL, -ATE¹] —**e·rad′i·ca·ble,** *adj.* —**e·rad′i·ca·bly,** *adv.* —**e·rad·i·cant** (i rad′ə kənt), *adj., n.* —**e·rad′i·ca′tion,** *n.* —**e·rad′i·ca′tive,** *adj.* —**e·rad′i·ca′tor,** *n.* —**Syn. 1.** obliterate. See **abolish. 2.** expunge. **3.** uproot.

e·rase (i rās′), *v.*, **e·rased, e·ras·ing.** —*v.t.* **1.** to rub or scrape out, as letters or characters written, engraved, etc.; efface. **2.** to rub off or scrape out from (a blackboard, piece of paper, etc.). —*v.i.* **3.** to give way to effacement readily or easily. **4.** to obliterate characters, letters, markings, etc., from something. [< L *ērās(us)* (ptp. of *ērādere*). See E-, RAZE] —**e·ras′a·ble,** *adj.* —**Syn. 1.** expunge. See **cancel.** —**Ant. 1.** restore.

e·ras·er (i rā′sər), *n.* an instrument, as a piece of rubber or cloth or a motor-driven device for erasing marks made with pen, pencil, chalk, etc.

e·ra·sion (i rā′zhən), *n.* *Surg.* **1.** the scraping away of tissue, esp. of bone. **2.** excision of a joint.

E·ras·mus (i raz′məs), *n.* **Des·i·de·ri·us** (dez′i dēr′ē əs), 1466?–1536, Dutch scholar, theologian, and writer.

E·ras·tian (i ras′chən, -tē ən), *adj.* **1.** of or pertaining to Thomas Erastus or Erastianism. —*n.* **2.** an advocate of Erastianism.

E·ras·tian·ism (i ras′chə niz′əm, -tē ə niz′-), *n.* the doctrine, advocated by Thomas Erastus, of the supremacy of the state over the church in ecclesiastical matters.

E·ras·tus (i ras′təs; *Ger.* ā räs′to͝os), *n.* **Thom·as** (tom′əs; *Ger.* tō′mäs), 1524–83, a Swiss-German theologian.

e·ras·ure (i rā′shər), *n.* **1.** the act or an instance of erasing. **2.** a spot or mark left after erasing.

Er·a·to (er′ə tō′), *n.* *Class. Myth.* the Muse of love poetry.

Er·a·tos·the·nes (er′ə tos′thə nēz′), *n.* 276?–195? B.C., Greek mathematician and astronomer at Alexandria.

Er·bil (ir′bil), *n.* a town in N Iraq: built on the site of ancient Arbela. 35,000 (est. 1962). Also, **Arbil, Irbil.**

er·bi·um (ûr′bē əm), *n.* *Chem.* a rare-earth metallic element, having pink salts. *Symbol:* Er; *at. wt.:* 167.26; *at. no.:* 68. [< NL, named after *(Ytt)erb(y)*, Sweden, where it is found; see -IUM]

Er·cill·a (eʀ thē′lyä, -sē′yä), *n.* **A·lon·so de** (ä lôn′sô the), 1533–94, Spanish epic poet; soldier in the conquest of Chile.

Erck·mann-Cha·tri·an (eʀk mаɴ′shа tʀē äɴ′), *n.* joint pen name of **É·mile Erckmann** (ā mēl′), 1822–99, and **A·le·xan·dre Chatrian** (а lek säɴ′dʀᵊ), 1826–90, collaborating French novelists and dramatists.

ere (âr), *prep., conj.* *Poetic.* before. [ME; OE *ǣr*, *ēr* (c. G *ehr*), comp. of *ār* soon, early; c. Goth *air.* See ERST, EARLY]

Er·e·bus (er′ə bəs), *n.* **1.** *Class. Myth.* the darkness under the earth, imagined either as the abode of sinners after death or of all the dead. **2. Mount,** a volcano in Antarctica, on Ross Island. 13,202 ft. [< L < Gk *Érebos;* c. Skt *rājas* darkness, Arm *erek* evening, Goth *riquis* darkness]

E·rech·the·um (i rek′thē əm, er′ək thē′əm), *n.* a temple at Athens, begun c420 B.C., having two Ionic porches and a porch of caryatids: regarded as one of the finest examples of classical architecture. Also, **E·rech·the·ion** (i rek′thē ən, er′ək thē′ən).

E·rech·the·us (i rek′thē əs, -thyo͞os), *n.* *Gk. Legend.* a king of Athens and the father of Procris.

e·rect (i rekt′), *adj.* **1.** upright in position or posture: *to stand or sit erect.* **2.** raised or directed upward: *a dog with ears erect.* **3.** *Bot.* vertical throughout; not spreading or declined: *an erect stem; an erect leaf or ovule.* **4.** *Heraldry.* **a.** (of a charge) represented palewise: *a sword erect.* **b.** (of an animal or part of an animal) represented upright: *a boar's head erect.* **5.** *Optics.* (of an image) having the same position as the object; not inverted. —*v.t.* **6.** to build; construct; raise: *to erect a house.* **7.** to raise and set in an upright or vertical position: *to erect a telegraph pole.* **8.** to construct (something) upon a given base: *to erect a philosophical system.* **9.** *Geom.* to draw or construct (a line or figure) upon a given line, base, or the like. **10.** *Optics.* to change (an inverted image) to the normal position. **11.** to set up or establish, as an institution; found. —*v.i.* **12.** to become erect; stand up or out. [< L *ērect(us)* raised up (ptp. of *ērigere*) = *e-* E- + *reg-* guide, direct (see ROYAL) + *-tus* ptp. suffix] —**e·rect′a·ble,** *adj.* —**e·rect′ly,** *adv.* —**e·rect′ness,** *n.* —**Syn. 1.** standing, vertical. See **upright.**

e·rec·tile (i rek′tᵊl, -til, -tīl), *adj.* **1.** capable of being erected or set upright. **2.** *Anat.* capable of being distended with blood and becoming rigid, as tissue. [< F *érectile*] —**e·rec·til·i·ty** (i rek til′i tē, ē′rek-), *n.*

e·rec·tion (i rek′shən), *n.* **1.** the act of erecting. **2.** the state of being erected. **3.** something erected, as a building or other structure. **4.** *Physiol.* a distended and rigid state of an organ or part containing erectile tissue, esp. of the penis or the clitoris. [< LL *ērectiōn-* (s. of *ērectiō*)]

e·rec·tive (i rek′tiv), *adj.* tending to erect.

e·rec·tor (i rek′tər), *n.* **1.** Also, **e·rect′er.** a person or thing that erects. **2.** *Anat.* a muscle that erects the body or one of its parts.

-erel, var. of **-rel.**

ere·long (âr lông′, -long′), *adv.* *Archaic.* before long; soon.

er·e·mite (er′ə mīt′), *n.* a hermit or recluse, esp. one under a religious vow. [< LL *erēmīt(a)* HERMIT] —**er·e·mit·ic** (er′ə mit′ik), **er′e·mit′i·cal, er·e·mit·ish** (er′ə mī′tish), *adj.* —**er′e·mit′ism,** *n.*

ere·now (âr nou′), *adv.* *Archaic.* before this time. [ME *ar now*]

e·rep·sin (i rep′sin), *n.* *Biochem.* a mixture of proteolytic enzymes, consisting of peptidases and occurring in the intestinal secretions. [< L *ēr(ipere)* (to) take away (*ē-* E- + *rapere* to take) + (P)EPSIN]

er·e·thism (er′ə thiz′əm), *n.* *Physiol.* an unusual or excessive degree of irritability or stimulation in an organ or tissue. [< F *éréthisme* < Gk *erethism(ós)* irritation = *ereth(ízein)* (to) irritate + *-ismos* -ISM] —**er′e·this′mic, er·e·this·tic** (er′ə this′tik), **er′e·thit′ic, e·reth·ic** (ə reth′ik, e reth′-), *adj.*

ere·while (âr hwīl′, -wīl′), *adv.* *Archaic.* a while before; formerly. [ME]

Er·furt (eʀ′fo͝oʀt), *n.* a city in SW East Germany. 189,770 (1964).

erg (ûrg), *n.* *Physics.* the centimeter-gram-second unit of work or energy, equal to the work done by a force of one dyne when its point of application moves through a distance of one centimeter in the direction of the force; 10^{-7} joule. [< Gk *érg(on)* work]

erg-, var. of **ergo-** before a vowel: *ergodic.*

er·go (ûr′gō, er′gō), *conj., adv.* therefore. [< L]

ergo-¹, a combining form meaning "work." Also, *esp. before a vowel,* **erg-.** [comb. form repr. Gk *érgon*]

ergo-², a combining form of **ergot:** *ergosterol.* [< F]

er·god·ic (ûr god′ik), *adj.* *Math., Statistics.* of or pertaining to the condition that, in an interval of sufficient duration, a system will return to states which are closely similar to previous ones. [ERG- + Gk *hod(ós)* way, road + -IC] —**er·go·dic·i·ty** (ûr′gə dis′i tē), *n.*

er·go·nom·ics (ûr′gə nom′iks), *n.* (*construed as sing. or pl.*) biotechnology. [ERG- + (EC)ONOMICS] —**er′go·nom′ic,** *adj.*

er·gos·ter·ol (ûr gos′tə rōl′, -rôl′, -rol′), *n.* *Biochem.* a water-insoluble sterol, $C_{28}H_{43}OH$, that occurs in ergot and yeast and that, when irradiated with ultraviolet light, is converted into vitamin D.

er·got (ûr′gət, -got), *n.* **1.** *Plant Pathol.* **a.** a disease of rye and other cereal grasses, caused by a fungus that replaces the affected grain with a long, hard, hornlike, dark-colored, sclerotial body. **b.** the sclerotial body itself. **2.** *Pharm.* the sclerotium developed on rye plants: used chiefly to prevent or check postpartum hemorrhage. [< F: lit., a rooster's spur; OF *argos, argoz, argot* spur(s)]

er·got·ism (ûr′gə tiz′əm), *n.* *Pathol.* a condition caused by eating grain that is infected with ergot or by taking an overdose of medicinal ergot: characterized by cramps, spasms, and a form of gangrene.

er·i·ca·ceous (er′ə kā′shəs), *adj.* belonging to the *Ericaceae*, or heath family of plants, which includes the heath, arbutus, azalea, rhododendron, American laurel, etc. [< NL *Ericāce(ae)* (L *erīc(a)* heath, broom (< Gk *ereíkē*) + *-āceae* -ACEAE) + -OUS]

Er·ic·son (er′ik sən), *n.* **Leif** (lēf; *Icel.* lāv), fl. A.D. c1000, Norse mariner: according to Icelandic saga, discoverer of Vinland (son of Eric the Red). Also, **Ericsson.**

Er·ics·son (er′ik sən), *n.* **1. John,** 1803–89, Swedish engineer and inventor, in the U.S. after 1839. **2.** See **Ericson, Leif.**

Er′ic the Red′, born A.D. c950, Norse mariner: explorer and colonizer of Greenland c985.

E·rid·a·nus (i rid′ᵊnəs), *n., gen.* **-a·ni** (-ᵊnī′). *Astron.* the River, a large southern constellation between Cetus and Orion.

E·ri·du (ā′ri do͞o), *n.* an ancient Sumerian and Babylonian city near the Euphrates: center for the worship of Ea.

E·rie (ēr′ē), *n., pl.,* for 3, **E·ries,** (*esp. collectively*) **E·rie. 1. Lake,** a lake between the NE central United States and SE central Canada: the southernmost lake of the Great Lakes; Commodore Perry's defeat of the British in 1813. 239 mi. long; 9940 sq. mi. **2.** a port in NW Pennsylvania, on Lake Erie. 129,231 (1970). **3.** a member of a tribe of American Indians formerly living along the southern shore of Lake Erie.

E′rie Canal′, a canal in New York between Albany and Buffalo, connecting the Hudson River with Lake Erie: completed in 1825. Cf. **New York State Barge Canal** (def. 2).

E·rig·e·na (e rij′ə nə), *n.* **Jo·han·nes Sco·tus** (jō han′ēz skō′təs, -han′is), A.D. c810–c877, Irish philosopher and theologian.

Er·in (er′in, ēr′in, âr′in), *n.* *Literary.* Ireland.

er·i·na·ceous (er′ə nā′shəs), *adj.* of the hedgehog kind or family. [< L *ērināce(us)* hedgehog + -OUS]

e·rin·go (i ring′gō), *n., pl.* **-goes, -gos.** eryngo.

Er·in go bragh (âr′in gō bʀä′, ēʀ′in, eʀ′in), *Gaelic.* Ireland forever.

E·rin·ys (i rin′is, i rī′nis), *n., pl.* **E·rin·y·es** (i rin′ē ēz′). *Class. Myth.* any of the Furies.

E·ris (ēr′is, er′is), *n.* the ancient Greek goddess of discord and sister of Ares: identified by the Romans with Discordia.

er·is·tic (e ris′tik), *adj.* **1.** Also, **er·is′ti·cal.** pertaining to controversy or disputation. —*n.* **2.** a person who engages in disputation; controversialist. [< Gk *eristik(ós)* = *erist(ós)* (verbid of *erízein* < *éris* discord) + *-ikos* -IC] —**er·is′ti·cal·ly,** *adv.*

Er·i·tre·a (er′i trē′ə; *It.* e′ʀē tʀe′ä), *n.* a governorate of Ethiopia, in NE Africa, on the Red Sea: formerly an Italian colony. 1,422,300 (est. 1962); 47,076 sq. mi. *Cap.:* Asmara. —**Er′i·tre′an,** *adj., n.*

E·ri·van (*Russ.* ye ʀi vän′), *n.* a city in and the capital of Armenia, in the S Soviet Union in Asia Minor. 623,000 (1965). Also, **Yerevan.**

Er·lan·der (eʀ′län dəʀ), *n.* **Ta·ge (Fri·tiof)** (tä′gə fʀē′chəf), 1901–69, Swedish statesman: prime minister 1946–69.

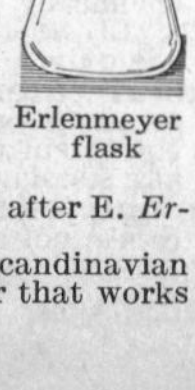

Er′len·mey·er flask′ (ûr′lən mī′ər, er′-), a flask having a wide base, narrow neck, and conical form, convenient in laboratory experimentation for swirling liquids by hand. [named after E. *Erlenmeyer* (d. 1909), German chemist]

Erlenmeyer flask

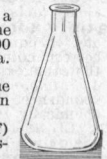

erl·king (ûrl′king′), *n.* (in German and Scandinavian mythology) a spirit or personified natural power that works mischief, esp. to children. [< G *Erlkönig* alder (tree) king, Herder's mistrans. of Dan *ellerkonge*, var. of *elverkonge* king of the elves]

er·mine (ûr′min), *n., pl.* **-mines,** (*esp. collectively*) **-mine. 1.** an Old World weasel, *Mustela erminea*, having a white winter coat with black at the tip of the tail. Cf. **stoat. 2.** *U.S.* any of various weasels having a white winter coat. **3.** the white winter fur of the ermine. **4.** the rank or position of a person who wears a robe trimmed with ermine on official or state occasions, as a king, peer, or judge. [ME < OF (*h*)*ermine*, n. use of fem. of (*h*)*ermin* (masc. adj.) < L *Armen(ius)*, short for *Armenius* (*mūs*) Armenian (rat)]

Ermine, *Mustela erminea* (Total length 1 ft.; tail 4½ in.)

er·mined (ûr′mind), *adj.* covered or adorned with ermine.

-ern, an adjective suffix occurring in names of directions: *northern; southern.* [ME, OE *-erne*; c. OHG *-rōni* (as in *nordrōni* northern)]

erne (ûrn), *n.* See **sea eagle.** Also, **ern.** [ME *ern, arn,* OE *earn*; c. OHG *arn* (G *Aar*), MLG *arn(e)*; akin to Lith *erelis* eagle, Gk *órnīs* bird]

Ernst (ûrnst; *Ger.* ERNST), *n.* **Max** (maks; *Ger.* mäks), 1891–1976, German painter, in the U.S. after 1941.

e·rode (i rōd′), *v.,* **e·rod·ed, e·rod·ing.** —*v.t.* **1.** to eat out or away; destroy by slow consumption. **2.** to form (a channel) by eating or wearing away (used esp. in geology to note the action of all the forces of nature that wear away the earth's surface). —*v.i.* **3.** to become eroded. [< L *ērōd(ere)* = *ē-* E- + *rōdere* to gnaw]

e·rod·ent (i rōd′ᵊnt), *adj.* eroding; erosive. [< L *ērōdent-* (s. of *ērōdēns*)]

e·rog·e·nous (i roj′ə nəs), *adj.* **1.** sexually gratifying or sensitive. **2.** arousing or tending to arouse sexual desire. Also, **er·o·gen·ic** (er′ə jen′ik). [< Gk *érō(s)* love + -GENOUS]

E·ros (ēr′os, er′os), *n., pl.* **E·ro·tes** (ə rō′tēz). **1.** the ancient Greek god of love, identified by the Romans with Cupid. **2.** a representation of this god. **3.** a winged figure of a child representing love or the power of love. **4.** (*sometimes l.c.*) physical love or sexual desire. Cf. **agape**[2] (def. 2). **5.** *Psychiatry.* **a.** the libido. **b.** instincts for self-preservation collectively.

e·rose (i rōs′), *adj* **1.** uneven, as if gnawed away. **2.** *Bot.* (esp. of a leaf) having the margin irregularly incised as if gnawed. [< L *ērōs(us)*, ptp. of *ērōdere* to ERODE] —**e·rose′ly,** *adv.*

e·ro·sion (i rō′zhən), *n.* **1.** the act or state of eroding. **2.** the state of being eroded. **3.** the process by which the surface of the earth is worn away by the action of water, glaciers, winds, waves, etc. [< L *ērōsiōn-* (s. of *ērōsiō*)] —**e·ro′sion·al,** *adj.*

e·ro·sive (i rō′siv), *adj.* serving to erode; causing erosion. [< L *ērōs(us)* (see EROSE) + -IVE] —**e·ro′sive·ness, e·ro·siv′i·ty,** *n.*

e·rot·ic (i rot′ik), *adj.* Also, **e·rot′i·cal. 1.** of, pertaining to, or treating of sexual love; amatory. **2.** arousing or satisfying sexual desire. **3.** subject to or marked by strong sexual desires. —*n.* **4.** an erotic poem. **5.** an erotic person. [< Gk *erōtik(ós)* of love, caused by love, given to love. See EROTO-, -IC] —**e·rot′i·cal·ly,** *adv.*

e·rot·i·ca (i rot′i kə), *n.* literature or art dealing with sexual love. [< Gk, neut. pl. of *erōtikós* EROTIC]

e·rot·i·cism (i rot′i siz′əm), *n.* **1.** the sexual or erotic quality or character of something. **2.** the use of sexually arousing symbolism. **3.** sexual drive or tendency, esp. that which is abnormal. Also, **er·o·tism** (er′ə tiz′əm).

eroto-, a combining form denoting sexual desire: *erotomania.* [< Gk, comb. form = *erōt-* (s. of *érōs*) love + *-o-* -o-]

e·ro·to·gen·ic (i rō′tə jen′ik, i rot′ə-), *adj.* erogenous.

e·ro·to·ma·ni·a (i rō′tə mā′nē ə, -mān′yə, i rot′ə-), *n.* *Psychiatry.* abnormally strong or persistent sexual desire. —**e·ro·to·ma·ni·ac** (i rō′tə mā′nē ak′, i rot′ə-), *n.*

err (ûr, er), *v.i.* **1.** to go astray in thought or belief; be mistaken; be incorrect. **2.** to go astray morally; sin. **3.** to deviate from the true course, aim, or purpose. [ME *erre(n)* < OF *err(er)* < L *errāre*; akin to Goth *airzjan*, OHG *irrôn*, G *irren*]

er·ran·cy (ûr′ən sē), *n., pl.* **-cies. 1.** the state or an instance of erring. **2.** tendency to err. [< L *errantia* a wandering]

er·rand (er′ənd), *n.* **1.** a trip to convey a message or execute a commission; a short journey for a specific purpose. **2.** a special business entrusted to a messenger; commission. **3.** the purpose of any trip or journey. [ME *erande*, OE *ærende*; c. OHG *ārunti*; cf. OE *ār* messenger, Goth *airus*]

er·rant (er′ənt), *adj.* **1.** journeying or traveling, as a medieval knight in quest of adventure. **2.** deviating from the regular or proper course; erring. **3.** moving in an aimless or lightly changing manner: *an errant breeze.* [ME *erraunt* < MF *errant*, prp. of *errer* to travel < VL *iterāre* to journey: b. MF *errant*, prp. of *errer* to ERR] —**er′rant·ly,** *adv.*

er·rant·ry (er′ən trē), *n., pl.* **-ries.** conduct or performance like that of a knight-errant.

er·ra·re hu·ma·num est (ER RÄ′RE hōō mä′nōōm est′; *Eng.* e râr′ē hyōō mā′nəm est′), *Latin.* to err is human.

er·ra·ta (i rā′tə, i rä′-), *n.* pl. of **erratum.**

er·rat·ic (i rat′ik), *adj.* **1.** deviating from the proper or usual course in conduct or opinion; eccentric; queer. **2.** having no certain course; wandering; not fixed: *erratic winds.* **3.** *Geol.* carried by some natural means, as glacial action, from the place of origin. —*n.* **4.** an erratic or eccentric person. **5.** *Geol.* an erratic boulder or the like. [ME < L *errātic(us)* = *errāt(us)* (ptp. of *errāre* to ERR) + *-icus* -IC] —**er·rat′i·cal·ly,** *adv.* —**er·rat′i·cism,** *n.*

er·ra·tum (i rā′təm, i rä′-), *n., pl.* **-ta** (-tə). an error in writing or printing. [< L, n. use of *errātum* wandered, erred, strayed (neut. ptp. of *errāre*)]

erron., **1.** erroneous. **2.** erroneously.

er·ro·ne·ous (ə rō′nē əs, e rō′-), *adj.* **1.** containing error; mistaken; incorrect. **2.** *Archaic.* straying from what is right. [ME < L *errōneus* straying = *errōn-* (s. of *errō*) wanderer (< *err-*; see ERR) + *-eus* -EOUS] —**er·ro′ne·ous·ly,** *adv.* —**er·ro′ne·ous·ness,** *n.* —**Syn. 1.** inaccurate, wrong, false. —**Ant. 1.** accurate.

er·ror (er′ər), *n.* **1.** a deviation from accuracy or correctness; a mistake, as in action or speech. **2.** belief in something untrue; the holding of mistaken opinions. **3.** the condition of believing what is not true: *in error about the date.* **4.** a moral offense; wrongdoing; sin. **5.** *Math.* the difference between the observed or approximately determined value and the true value of a quantity. **6.** *Baseball.* a misplay in fielding that enables a batter or base runner who otherwise would have been put out to reach base safely or that enables a batter to continue batting. **7.** *Law.* a mistake in a matter of fact or law in a case tried in a court of record. [ME *errour* < L *errōr-* (s. of *error*)] —**Syn. 1.** blunder, slip. **4.** transgression, trespass.

ers (ûrs, ârs), *n.* ervil. [MF < OPr < LL *ervus*, var. of L *ervum.* See ERVIL]

er·satz (er′zäts, -sats), *adj.* **1.** serving as a substitute, esp. something synthetic; artificial. —*n.* **2.** an artificial substance or article used to replace something natural or genuine. [< G *Ersatz* a substitute (< *ersetzen* to replace)]

Erse (ûrs), *n.* (not in technical use) Gaelic, esp. Scots Gaelic.

Er·skine (ûr′skin), *n.* **John** (*Erskine of Carnock*), 1695–1768, Scottish writer on law.

erst (ûrst), *adv.* *Archaic.* before the present time; formerly. [ME *erest*, OE *ǣrest* (c. OHG *ērist*, G *erst*). See ERE, -EST[1]]

erst·while (ûrst′hwīl′, -wīl′), *adj.* **1.** former; of times past: *erstwhile enemies.* —*adv.* **2.** *Archaic.* formerly; erst.

er·u·bes·cent (er′ōō bes′ənt), *adj.* becoming red or reddish; blushing. [< L *ērubēscent-* (s. of *ērubēscēns*), prp. of *ērubēscere*] —**er′u·bes′cence,** *n.*

e·ruct (i rukt′), *v.t., v.i.* **1.** to belch forth, as wind from the stomach. **2.** to emit or issue violently, as matter from a volcano. [< L *ēruct(āre)* (to) belch = *ē-* E- + *ructāre* to belch]

e·ruc·tate (i ruk′tāt), *v.t., v.i.,* **-tat·ed, -tat·ing.** to eruct. [< L *ēructāt(us)* belched forth, sent forth] —**e·ruc·ta·tion** (i ruk tā′shən, ē′ruk-), *n.* —**e·ruc·ta·tive** (i ruk′tə tiv), *adj.*

er·u·dite (er′yōō dīt′, er′ōō-), *adj.* characterized by erudition; learned or scholarly: *an erudite professor; an erudite commentary.* [ME < L *ērudīt(us)*. See E-, RUDE, -ITE[2]] —**er′u·dite′ly,** *adv.* —**er′u·dite′ness,** *n.*

er·u·di·tion (er′yōō dish′ən, er′ōō-), *n.* knowledge acquired by study, research, etc.; learning; scholarship. [ME < L *ērudītiōn-* (s. of *ērudītiō*) an instruction] —**Syn.** See **learning.**

e·rum·pent (i rum′pənt), *adj.* **1.** bursting forth. **2.** *Bot.* prominent, as if bursting through the epidermis. [< L *ērumpent-* (s. of *ērumpēns*), prp. of *ērumpere* = *ē-* E- + *rumpere* to break; see -ENT]

e·rupt (i rupt′), *v.i.* **1.** to burst forth, as volcanic matter. **2.** (of a volcano, geyser, etc.) to eject matter. **3.** to break out of a pent-up state, usually in a sudden and violent manner: *His anger erupted.* **4.** to break out in a skin rash: *Hives erupted on his face.* **5.** (of teeth) to break through surrounding hard and soft tissues and become visible in the mouth. —*v.t.* **6.** to cause to burst forth. **7.** (of a volcano, geyser, etc.) to eject (matter). [< L *ērupt(us)* burst forth, broken out (ptp. of *ērumpere*)] —**e·rupt′i·ble,** *adj.*

e·rup·tion (i rup′shən), *n.* **1.** an issuing forth suddenly and violently; outburst; outbreak. **2.** *Geol.* the ejection of molten rock, water, etc., as from a volcano, geyser, etc. **3.** something that is erupted or ejected, as molten rock or volcanic ash. **4.** *Pathol.* **a.** the breaking out of a rash or the like. **b.** a rash or exanthema. [ME < L *ēruptiōn-* (s. of *ēruptiō*)]

e·rup·tive (i rup′tiv), *adj.* **1.** bursting forth, or tending to burst forth. **2.** pertaining to or of the nature of an eruption. **3.** *Geol.* noting a rock formed by the eruption of molten material. **4.** *Pathol.* causing or accompanied by an eruption or rash. —*n.* **5.** *Geol.* an eruptive rock. [< F *éruptif*] —**e·rup′tive·ly,** *adv.* —**e·rup·tiv′i·ty, e·rup′tive·ness,** *n.*

E.R.V., English Revised Version.

er·vil (ûr′vil), *n.* a vetch, *Vicia Ervilia*, grown in Europe for forage. Also called **ers.** [< L *ervilia*, akin to *ervum* bitter vetch; prob. of non-IE orig.]

-ery, a suffix of nouns denoting occupation, business, calling or condition, place or establishment, goods or products, things collectively, qualities, actions, etc.: *archery; bakery; cutlery; fishery; grocery; nunnery; pottery; finery; foolery; prudery; scenery; tracery; trickery; witchery.* [ME < OF *-erie.* See -ER[2], -Y[3]]

Er·y·man′thi·an boar′ (er′ə man′thē ən), *Class. Myth.* a savage boar that plagued Arcadia and was captured by Hercules.

e·ryn·go (i ring′gō), *n., pl.* **-goes, -gos.** any of several umbelliferous herbs of the genus *Eryngium*, as the sea holly. Also, **eringo.** [< L *ēryngion* a kind of thistle < Gk, dim. of *ḗryngos* the eryngo]

er·y·sip·e·las (er′i sip′ə ləs, ēr′i-), *n.* *Pathol.* an acute, febrile infectious disease, caused by a specific streptococcus, characterized by diffusely spreading deep-red inflammation of the skin or mucous membranes. [ME *erisipila* < L *erysipelas* < Gk = *erysi-* prob. akin to *erythrós* red + *-pelas* prob. skin, akin to *pelma* sole of the foot; cf. L *pellis* skin] —**er·y·si·pel·a·tous** (er′i si pel′ə təs, ēr′-), *adj.*

er·y·the·ma (er′ə thē′mə), *n.* *Pathol.* abnormal redness of the skin due to local congestion, as in inflammation. [< NL < Gk = *erythr(ós)* red (*erythaínein* to redden) + *-ēma* n. suffix] —**er·y·the·mat·ic** (er′ə thi mat′ik), **er·y·them·a·tous** (er′ə them′ə təs, -thē′mə-), *adj.*

e·ryth·rism (i rith′riz əm), *n.* abnormal redness, as of plumage or hair. —**er·y·thris·mal** (er′ə thriz′məl), **er·y·thris·tic** (er′ə thris′tik), *adj.*

e·ryth·rite (i rith′rīt), *n.* **1.** a mineral, hydrous cobalt arsenate, $Co_3As_2O_8 \cdot 8H_2O$; cobalt bloom. **2.** erythritol. [ERYTHR(O)- + -ITE[1]]

e·ryth·ri·tol (i rith′ri tōl′, -tôl′, -tol′), *n.* *Chem., Pharm.* a tetrahydroxy compound, $CH_2OHCHOHCHOHCH_2OH$, used chiefly for coronary vasodilatation and in the treatment of hypertension.

erythro-, a learned borrowing from Greek meaning "red," used in the formation of compound words: *erythrocyte.* [< Gk *erythrṓ(s)*]

e·ryth·ro·blast (i rith′rə blast′), *n.* *Anat.* a nucleated cell in the bone marrow from which erythrocytes develop. —**e·ryth′ro·blas′tic,** *adj.*

e·ryth·ro·blas·to·sis (i rith′rō bla stō′sis), *n.* *Pathol.* **1.** the presence of erythroblasts in the blood. **2.** this condition in the fetus or newborn, usually caused by an Rh incompatibility between mother and baby.

e·ryth·ro·cyte (i rith′rə sīt′), *n.* *Physiol.* one of the red cells of the blood that contain hemoglobin and that carry oxygen to the cells and tissues and carbon dioxide back to the respiratory organs. —**e·ryth·ro·cyt·ic** (i rith′rə sit′ik), *adj.*

e·ryth·ro·cy·tom·e·ter (i rith′rō sī tom′i tər), *n.* an apparatus used for counting red blood cells. —**e·ryth′ro·cy·tom′e·try,** *n.*

e·ryth·ro·my·cin (i rith′rō mī′sin), *n.* *Pharm.* an antibiotic, $C_{37}H_{67}NO_{13}$, used chiefly in the treatment of diseases caused by many Gram-positive and some Gram-negative organisms.

e·ryth·ro·phyll (i rith′rə fil′), *n.* *Biochem.* a substance in vegetation, responsible in the autumn for the red coloration in leaves.

Erz′ Moun′tains (ârts), a mountain range in central Europe, on the boundary between East Germany and Czechoslovakia. Highest peak, Keilberg, 4080 ft. German, **Erz·ge·bir·ge** (erts′gə bēr′gə).

Er·zu·rum (er′zə ro͝om′), *n.* a city in NE Turkey in Asia. 106,301 (1965). Also, **Er′ze·rum′.**

Es, *Chem.* einsteinium.

es-, for words with initial **es-,** see also **aes-.**

-es[1], a plural suffix occurring in loan words from Greek: *Hyades.* [< Gk *-es*]

-es[2], var. of **-s**[2] in verbs ending in *s, z, ch, sh,* or postconsonantal *y: passes; buzzes; pitches; dashes; studies.*

-es[3], var. of **-s**[3] in nouns ending in *s, z, ch, sh,* or postconsonantal *y,* and in nouns ending in *f* with *v* in the plural: *losses; mazes; riches; ashes; babies; sheaves.*

E·sau (ē′sô), *n.* a son of Isaac and Rebekah, older brother of Jacob, to whom he sold his birthright. Gen. 25:21–25.

Es·bjerg (es′byer), *n.* a seaport in SW Denmark. 58,225 (1960).

Esc., (in Portugal) escudo; escudos.

es·ca·drille (es′kə dril′; *Fr.* es ka drē′yə), *n., pl.* **-drilles** (-drilz′; *Fr.* -drē′yə). **1.** a squadron or divisional unit of airplanes: *the Lafayette Escadrille of World War I.* **2.** *Obs.* a small naval squadron. [< F: flotilla, MF < Sp *escuadrilla,* dim. of *escuadra* SQUADRON]

es·ca·lade (es′kə lād′), *n., v.,* **-lad·ed, -lad·ing.** —*n.* **1.** a scaling or mounting by means of ladders, esp. in an assault upon a fortified place. —*v.t.* **2.** to mount, pass, or enter by means of ladders. [< F < It *scalata* < *scalare* to SCALE[3]; see -ADE[1]] —**es′ca·lad′er,** *n.*

es·ca·late (es′kə lāt′), *v.t., v.i.,* **-lat·ed, -lat·ing.** to increase in intensity, magnitude, etc.: *to escalate a war; a time when prices escalate.* [back formation from ESCALATOR] —**es′ca·la′tion,** *n.* —**es·ca·la·to·ry** (es′kə lə tōr′ē, -tôr′ē), *adj.*

es·ca·la·tor (es′kə lā′tər), *n.* a continuously moving stairway for carrying passengers up or down. Also called **moving staircase, moving stairway.** [formerly trademark]

es′calator clause′, a provision in a contract calling for adjustments in charges, wages, etc., over a period of time based on fluctuations in production costs, the cost of living, or other variable costs.

es·cal·lop (e skol′əp, e skal′-), *v.t.* **1.** to bake (food cut in pieces) in sauce or other liquid, often with crumbs on top; scallop. **2.** to bake (fish, potatoes, etc.) in scallop shells. —*n.* **3.** scallop. Also, **es·cal′op.** [ME < MF *escalope* shell < Gmc; cf. D *schelp* shell]

es·ca·pade (es′kə pād′, es′kə pād′), *n.* **1.** a reckless adventure or wild prank, esp. one contrary to usual or proper behavior. **2.** an escape from confinement or restraint. [< F < Sp *escapada*]

es·cape (e skāp′), *v.,* **-caped, -cap·ing,** *n.* —*v.i.* **1.** to slip or get away, as from confinement or restraint; gain or regain liberty. **2.** to slip away from pursuit or peril; avoid capture, punishment, or any threatened evil. **3.** to issue from a confining enclosure, as a fluid. **4.** to slip away; fade; elude. **5.** *Bot.* (of an introduced plant) to grow wild. —*v.t.* **6.** to slip away from or elude (pursuers, captors, etc.). **7.** to succeed in avoiding (any threatened or possible danger or evil). **8.** to elude (one's memory, notice, search, etc.). **9.** to slip from or be uttered by (a person, one's lips, etc.) inadvertently, as a remark. —*n.* **10.** the act or an instance of escaping. **11.** the fact of having escaped. **12.** a means of escaping: *We used the tunnel as an escape.* **13.** avoidance of reality: *Mystery stories can be an escape.* **14.** *Bot.* a plant originally cultivated, now growing wild. [ME *escape(n)* < ONF *escap(er)* < L *ex-* EX-[1] + *cappa* cloak] —**es·cap′a·ble,** *adj.* —**es·cap·ee′,** *n.* —**es·cap′er,** *n.*
—**Syn. 1.** flee, abscond, decamp. **6.** shun, fly. ESCAPE, ELUDE, EVADE mean to keep free of something. To ESCAPE is to succeed in keeping away from danger, pursuit, observation, etc.: *to escape punishment.* To ELUDE implies slipping through an apparently tight net, thus avoiding, often by a narrow margin, whatever threatens; it implies, also, using vigilance, adroitness, dexterity, or slyness so as to baffle or foil: *A fox managed to elude the hounds.* To EVADE is to turn aside from or go out of reach of a person or thing (at least temporarily), usually by using artifice or stratagem to direct attention elsewhere: *to evade the police; to evade a direct question.* **10.** flight.

escape′ mech′anism, *Psychol.* a means of avoiding an unpleasant life situation, as by daydreaming.

es·cape·ment (e skāp′mənt), *n.* **1.** *Horol.* the portion of a watch or clock that measures beats and controls the speed of the going train. **2.** a mechanism for regulating the motion of a typewriter carriage, consisting of pawls and a toothed wheel or rack. **3.** a mechanism in a piano that causes a hammer to fall back into rest position immediately after striking a string. **4.** *Archaic.* **a.** an act of escaping. **b.** a way of escape; outlet. [ESCAPE + -MENT; trans. of F *échappement*]

escape′ veloc′ity, *Physics, Rocketry.* the minimum speed an object must have to free itself from the gravitational pull of a body.

escape′ wheel′, *Horol.* a toothed wheel for regulating a going train to which it is geared.

A B

Escapements (def. 1)
A, Anchor escapement
B, Deadbeat escapement

es·cap·ism (e skā′piz əm), *n.* the avoidance of reality by absorption of the mind in entertainment or in an imaginative situation, activity, etc. —**es·cap′ist,** *adj., n.*

es·car·got (e skar gō′), *n., pl.* **-gots** (-gō′). *French.* an edible snail.

es·ca·role (es′kə rōl′), *n.* a broad-leaved chicory, used for salads. [< F < It *scar(i)ola* < LL *ēscāriola* endive = L *ēscāri(us)* fit for eating (L *ēsc(a)* food + *-ārius* -ARY) + *-ola* dim. suffix]

es·carp (e skärp′), *n.* **1.** *Fort.* the inner slope or wall of the ditch surrounding a rampart. **2.** any similar steep slope. —*v.t.* **3.** to make into an escarp; give a steep slope to; furnish with escarps. [< F, MF *escarpe* < It *scarpa* < Gmc]

es·carp·ment (e skärp′mənt), *n.* **1.** a long, precipitous, clifflike ridge of land, rock, or the like, commonly formed by faulting or fracturing of the earth's crust. **2.** *Fort.* ground cut into an escarp. [< F *escarpement*]

Es·caut (es kō′), *n.* French name of **Scheldt.**

-esce, a suffix appearing in verbs borrowed from Latin, where it had an inchoative meaning: *convalesce; putresce.* [< L *-ēscere*]

-escence, a suffix of nouns denoting action or process, change, state, or condition, etc., and corresponding to verbs ending in *-esce* or adjectives ending in *-escent: convalescence; luminescence.* [< L *-ēscentia.* See -ESCE, -ENCE]

-escent, a suffix of adjectives borrowed from Latin, where it had an inchoative force; often corresponding to verbs in *-esce* and nouns in *-escence: convalescent; recrudescent.* [< L, s. of *-ēscēns,* prp. ending]

esch·a·lot (esh′ə lot′, esh′ə lot′), *n.* shallot. [< F, MF *eschalotte,* dim. of *eschaloigne* SCALLION]

es·char (es′kär, -kər), *n.* *Pathol.* a hard crust or scab, as from a burn. [ME *escare* < LL *eschara* < Gk *eschára* hearth, brasier, coals and therefore indication of burning; cf. SCAR[1]]

es·cha·rot·ic (es′kə rot′ik), *Med.* —*adj.* **1.** producing an eschar, as a medicinal substance; caustic. —*n.* **2.** an escharotic agent. [< LL *escharōtic(us)* < Gk *escharōtikós*]

es·cha·tol·o·gy (es′kə tol′ə jē), *n.* *Theol.* any system of doctrines concerning last, or final, matters, as death or the afterlife. [< Gk *éschato(s)* last + -LOGY] —**es·cha·to·log·i·cal** (es′kə tᵊloj′i kəl), *adj.* —**es′cha·to·log′i·cal·ly,** *adv.* —**es′cha·tol′o·gist,** *n.*

es·cheat (es chēt′), *Law.* —*n.* **1.** the reverting of property to the state, or, in England, to the crown, when there is a failure of persons legally qualified to inherit or to claim. **2.** the right to take property subject to escheat. —*v.i.* **3.** to revert by escheat, as to the crown or the state. —*v.t.* **4.** to make an escheat of; confiscate. [ME *eschete* < OF *eschete, escheoite,* fem. ptp. of *escheoir* < LL **excadēre* to fall to a person's share = L *ex-* EX-[1] + *cadere* to fall (VL *cadēre*)] —**es·cheat′a·ble,** *adj.*

es·chew (es cho͞o′), *v.t.* to abstain from; avoid: *to eschew evil.* [ME *eschewe(n)* < OF *eschive(r), escheve(r)* < Gmc; cf. OHG *sciuhen,* G *scheuchen,* SHY[2]] —**es·chew′al,** *n.* —**es·chew′er,** *n.*

Es·con·di·do (es′kən dē′dō), *n.* a city in SW California. 36,792 (1970).

Es·co·ri·al (e skōr′ē əl, -skôr′-; *Sp.* es′kô ryäl′), *n.* an architectural complex in central Spain, 27 miles NW of Madrid, containing a monastery, palace, church, and mausoleum of the Spanish sovereigns: erected 1563–84. Also, **Escurial.**

es·cort (*n.* es′kôrt; *v.* e skôrt′), *n.* **1.** a body of persons, or a single person, accompanying another or others for protection, guidance, or courtesy. **2.** an armed guard, as a body of soldiers, ships, etc. **3.** a man or boy who accompanies a woman or girl in public. **4.** protection, safeguard, or guidance on a journey. —*v.t.* **5.** to attend or accompany as an escort. [< F < It *scorta* < *scorgere* to conduct < VL **excorrigere.* See EX-[1], CORRECT] —**Syn. 4.** convoy. **5.** conduct, usher, guard, guide. See **accompany.**

es·cri·toire (es′kri twär′), *n.* See **writing desk.** [< F, MF < L *scrīptōr(ium).* See SCRIPT, -ORY[2]]

es·crow (es′krō, e skrō′), *n.* *Law.* **1.** a contract, bond, etc., deposited with a third person, by whom it is to be delivered to the grantee on the fulfillment of some condition. **2. in escrow,** in the keeping of a third person for delivery to a given party upon the fulfillment of some condition. [ME < AF *escro(u)we,* OF *escro(u)e.* See SCROLL]

es·cu·age (es′kyo͞o ij), *n.* scutage. [< AF, OF]

es·cu·do (e sko͞o′dō; *Port.* es ko͞o′do͝o; *Sp.* es ko͞o′t͟hō), *n., pl.* **-dos** (-dōz; *Port.* -do͝os; *Sp.* -t͟hōs). **1.** a nickel and bronze coin and monetary unit of Portugal equal to 100 centavos. *Abbr.:* Esc. **2.** a paper money and monetary unit of Chile, equal to 100 centesimos. **3.** any of various former gold coins of Spain and Spanish America. **4.** a former silver coin of Spain: discontinued in 1868. [< Sp: shield < L *scūtum*]

Es·cu·la·pi·an (es′kyo͝o lā′pē ən), *n., adj.* Aesculapian.

es·cu·lent (es′kyə lənt), *adj.* **1.** suitable for use as food; edible. —*n.* **2.** something edible, esp. a vegetable. [< L *ēsculent(us)* edible, full of food = *ēsc(a)* food (see ESCAROLE) + *-ulentus* -ULENT]

Es·cu·ri·al (e skyo͝or′ē əl), *n.* Escorial.

es·cutch·eon (e skuch′ən), *n.* **1.** a shield or shieldlike surface on which a coat of arms is depicted. **2.** an ornamental or protective plate around a keyhole, door handle, drawer pull, light switch, etc. **3.** *Naut.* a panel on the stern of a vessel bearing its name and port of registry. **4. blot on one's escutcheon,** a stain on one's reputation; disgrace. [< ONF *escuchon* << L *scūtum* shield] —**es·cutch′eoned,** *adj.*

Esd., Esdras.

Es·dra·e·lon (es′drā ē′lon, -drə-, ez′-), *n.* the W part of the Plain of Jezreel.

Es·dras (ez′drəs), *n.* **1.** either of the first two books of the Apocrypha, I Esdras or II Esdras. **2.** *Douay Bible.* **a.** Ezra (def. 1). **b.** either of two books, I or II Esdras, corresponding to the books of Ezra and Nehemiah, respectively, in the Authorized Version.

chief A B C base dexter sinister

Escutcheon (def. 1) A, Honor point B, Fess point C, Nombril

ESE, east-southeast. Also, **E.S.E.**

-ese, a suffix of nouns and adjectives referring to locality, nationality, language, literary style, etc.: *Bengalese; Chinese; journalese.* [ME < OF *-eis* << L *-ēnsis*]

Esh·kol (esh′kôl, esh kôl′), *n.* **Le·vi** (lē′vē, lā′vē), (*Levi Shkolnik*), 1895–1969, Israeli statesman, born in Russia: prime minister 1963–69.

Esk., Eskimo.

es·ker (es′kər), *n.* *Geol.* a serpentine ridge of gravelly and sandy drift, believed to have been formed by streams under or in glacial ice. Also, **es·kar** (es′kär, -kər). [< Ir *eiscir* ridge of mountains]

E·skil·stu·na (es′kil styo͞o′nä), *n.* a city in SE Sweden, W of Stockholm. 62,429 (1965).

Es·ki·mo (es′kə mō′), *n., pl.* **-mos, -mo. 1.** a member of a people of Mongoloid stock, inhabiting areas of Greenland, northern Canada, Alaska, and northeastern Siberia. **2.** either of two related polysynthetic languages spoken by the Eskimos, esp. the one spoken in all of the Eskimo territory except southern Alaska. **—***adj.* **3.** Eskimoan. Also, **Esquimau.** [< Dan *Eskimo,* F *Eskimau* < Algonquian name applied to tribes farther north; cf. Abnaki *eskimantsic* eaters of raw flesh] —**Es′ki·mo′an,** *adj.* —**Es·ki·moid** (es′kə moid′), *adj.*

Es′kimo dog′, 1. one of a breed of strong, medium-sized dogs having a dense, coarse coat, used in arctic regions for hunting and drawing sleds. **2.** any dog of the arctic regions of North America used for drawing sleds. Also called **husky.**

Eskimo dog (def. 1) (2 ft. high at shoulder)

Es·ki·se·hir (es kē′she hēʀ′), *n.* a city in W Turkey in Asia. 174,451 (1965). Also, **Es·ki′she·hir′.**

ESL, English as a second language.

e·soph·a·ge·al (i sof′ə jē′əl, ē′sə faj′ē əl), *adj.* pertaining to the esophagus. Also, **oesophageal.** [ESOPHAG(US) + *-eal,* var. of -IAL]

e·soph·a·gus (i sof′ə gəs, ē sof′-), *n., pl.* **-gi** (-jī′). *Anat., Zool.* a tube connecting the mouth or pharynx with the stomach gullet. Also, **oesophagus.** [< NL *oesophagus* < Gk *oisophágos* gullet, lit., channel for eating (*oiso-,* akin to *oísein,* fut. inf. of *phérein* to carry + *-phagos* -PHAGE); r. ME *ysophagus* < ML]

es·o·ter·ic (es′ə ter′ik), *adj.* **1.** understood by or meant for only the select few who have special knowledge or interest; recondite. **2.** belonging to the select few. **3.** private; secret; confidential. [< Gk *esōterik(ós)* inner = *esṓter(os)* inner + *-ikos* -IC] —**es′o·ter′i·cal·ly,** *adv.*

es·o·ter·i·ca (es′ə ter′i kə), *n.pl.* esoteric matters or items. [< NL, n. use of neut. pl. of Gk *esōterikós* ESOTERIC]

ESP, extrasensory perception: perception or communication outside of normal sensory activity, as in telepathy and clairvoyance.

esp., especially.

es·pa·drille (es′pə dril′), *n.* a flat sandal, usually with a canvas upper. [< F < Pr *espardilho,* dim. of *espart* ESPARTO]

es·pal·ier (e spal′yər), *n.* **1.** a trellis or framework on which fruit trees or shrubs are trained to grow flat. **2.** a plant so trained. **—***v.t.* **3.** to train on an espalier. **4.** to furnish with an espalier. [< F, MF: trellis < It *spalliera* back rest, espalier = *spall(a)* shoulder, support + *-iera* -IER]

Espalier

Es·pa·ña (es pä′nyä), *n.* Spanish name of **Spain.**

es·pa·ñol (es pä nyôl′), *n., pl.* **-ño·les** (-nyô′les) for 2, *adj.* *Spanish.* **—***n.* **1.** the Spanish language. **2.** a native or inhabitant of Spain. **—***adj.* **3.** of or pertaining to Spain, the Spanish people, or their language.

Es·par·te·ro (es′pär te′rô), *n.* **Bal·do·me·ro** (bäl′dô me′rô), **Count of Lu·cha·na** (lo͞o chä′nä), 1792–1879, Spanish general and statesman.

es·par·to (e spär′tō), *n., pl.* **-tos.** any of several grasses, esp. *Stipa tenacissima,* of S Europe and N Africa, used for making paper, cordage, etc. Also, **espar′to grass′.** [< Sp < L *spartum* < Gk *spárton* rope made of *spártos* kind of rush]

es·pe·cial (e spesh′əl), *adj.* special. [ME < MF < L *speciāl(is)* pertaining to a particular kind. See SPECIAL]

es·pe·cial·ly (e spesh′ə lē), *adv.* **1.** for a special reason or in a special way. **2.** particularly; exceptionally; markedly: *Be especially watchful.* [late ME]
—Syn. 1. signally, notably; mainly. ESPECIALLY, PARTICULARLY, CHIEFLY, PRINCIPALLY refer to those cases of a class or kind that seem to be significant. ESPECIALLY and PARTICULARLY single out the most prominent case or example (often in order to particularize a general statement): *Winter is especially severe on old people. Corn grows well in the Middle West, particularly in Iowa.* CHIEFLY and PRINCIPALLY imply that the general statement applies to a majority of the cases in question, and have a somewhat comparative force: *Owls fly chiefly at night. Crime occurs principally in large cities.*

es·per·ance (es′pər əns), *n.* *Obs.* hope. [late ME *esperaunce* < MF *esperance* < VL **sperantia* = L *spērant-* (s. of *spērāns*) hoping (prp. of *spērāre* < *spēs* hope) + *-ia* -IA]

Es·pe·ran·to (es′pə rän′tō, -ran′-), *n.* an artificial language based on the most common words in the important European languages and intended for international use. [lit., the hoping one, orig. pseudonym of the inventor, L. L. Zamenhof (1859–1917), Russian philologist. See ESPERANCE] —**Es′pe·ran′tism,** *n.* —**Es′pe·ran′tist,** *n.*

es·pi·al (e spī′əl), *n.* **1.** the act of spying. **2.** the act of keeping watch. [ME *espiaille* < MF. See ESPY, -AL^{2}]

es·piè·gle (e spye′gl^{ə}), *adj.* *French.* roguish; playful.

es·piè·gle·rie (e spye glə ʀē′), *n., pl.* **-ries** (-ʀē′). *French.* a roguish or playful trick.

es·pi·o·nage (es′pē ə näzh′, -nij, es′pē ə näzh′), *n.* **1.** the practice of spying on others. **2.** the systematic use of spies by a government to discover the military and political secrets of other nations. [< F *espionnage,* MF *espionage* = *espionn(er)* (to) spy (< *espion* spy (< It *spione* < Gmc; akin to G *spähen* to look out) + *-age* -AGE]

Es·pí·ri·to San·to (es pē′ʀē to͝o säɴ′to͝o), a state in E Brazil. 1,188,665 (1960); 15,196 sq. mi. *Cap.:* Vitória.

es·pla·nade (es′plə nād′, -näd′), *n.* any open, level space, esp. one serving for public walks or drives. [< F, m. It *spianata* < *spianare* < L *explānāre* to level; see -ADE]

es·pous·al (e spou′zəl), *n.* **1.** adoption or advocacy, as of a cause or principle. **2.** Sometimes, **espousals. a.** a marriage ceremony. **b.** an engagement or betrothal celebration. [ME *espousaille* < MF, OF *espousailles* < L *spōnsālia* (n. use of neut. pl. of *spōnsālis*)]

es·pouse (e spouz′), *v.t.,* **-poused, -pous·ing. 1.** to make one's own; adopt or embrace, as a cause. **2.** to take in marriage; marry. **3.** *Obs.* to give (a woman) in marriage. [< MF *espous(er)* < L *spōnsāre* to betroth, espouse] —**es·pous′er,** *n*

es·pres·so (e spres′ō), *n.* a strong coffee prepared by forcing live steam under pressure, or boiling water, through ground dark-roast coffee beans. [< It (*caffè*) *espresso* pressed (coffee)]

es·prit (e sprē′), *n.* sprightliness of spirit or wit; lively intelligence. [< F < L *spirit(us)* SPIRIT]

es·prit de corps (e sprē′ də kôr′), a sense of union and of common interests and responsibilities, as developed among a group of persons associated together. [< F]

es·py (e spī′), *v.t.,* **-pied, -py·ing.** to see at a distance; catch sight of. [ME *espy(en)* < OF *espi(er)* << Gmc; cf. G *spähen* to spy]

Esq., Esquire.

-esque, an adjective suffix indicating style, manner, or distinctive character: *arabesque; Romanesque.* [< F < It *-esco* << Gmc; see -ISH^{1}]

Es·qui·line (es′kwə līn′), *n.* one of the seven hills on which ancient Rome was built.

Es·qui·mau (es′kə mō′), *n., pl.* **-maux** (-mō′, -mōz′), *adj.* Eskimo. —**Es′qui·mau′an,** *adj.*

es·quire (e skwī^{ə}r′, es′kwī^{ə}r), *n., v.,* **-quired, -quir·ing. —***n.* **1.** (*cap.*) an unofficial title of respect, having no precise significance, sometimes placed, esp. in its abbreviated form, after a man's surname in written address: in the U.S., usually applied to lawyers; in Britain, applied to a commoner considered to have gained the social position of a gentleman. *Abbr.:* Esq. **2.** (in the Middle Ages) a squire attendant upon a knight. **3.** a man belonging to the order of English gentry ranking next below a knight. **—***v.t.* **4.** to raise to the rank of esquire. **5.** to escort or attend in public. [ME *esquier* < MF *escuier* < L *scūtārius* shield bearer. See SCUTUM, -ARY]

ess (es), *n.* **1.** the letter *S, s.* **2.** something shaped like an S.

-ess, a suffix forming distinctively feminine nouns: *countess; hostess; lioness.* [ME *-esse* < OF < LL *-issa* < Gk]

es·say (*n.* es′ā *for 1;* es′ā, e sā′ *for 2–4; v.* e sā′), *n.* **1.** a short literary composition on a particular theme or subject, usually in prose and generally analytic, speculative, or interpretative. **2.** an effort to perform or accomplish something; attempt. **3.** *Philately.* a design for a proposed stamp differing in any way from the design of the stamp as issued. **4.** *Obs.* a tentative effort; trial; assay. **—***v.t.* **5.** to try; attempt. **6.** to put to the test; make trial of. [late ME (v.) < MF *essayer,* c. AF *assayer* to ASSAY < LL *exagium* a weighing = *ex-* EX-^{1} + *-agium* < *agere* to do, act, drive, (influenced by *exigere* to examine, weigh; see EXACT)] —**es·say′er,** *n.* —**es′say·is′tic,** *adj.*

es·say·ist (es′ā ist), *n.* **1.** a writer of essays. **2.** *Rare.* a person who makes essays or trials.

Es·sen (es′ən), *n.* a city in W West Germany: the chief city of the Ruhr River valley; Krupp works. 729,400 (1963).

es·sence (es′əns), *n.* **1.** the basic or necessary constituent of a thing; intrinsic nature, as contrasted with what is accidental, ephemeral, or superficial. **2.** a substance obtained from a plant, drug, or the like, by distillation, infusion, etc., and containing its characteristic properties in concentrated form. **3.** an alcoholic solution of an essential oil; spirit. **4.** a perfume; scent. **5.** something that exists, esp. a spiritual or immaterial entity. [ME *essencia* < ML, for L *essentia* = *ess(e)* (to) be + *-entia* -ENCE]

es′sence of mir′bane (mûr′bān), *Chem.* nitrobenzene. Also, **es′sence of myr′bane.** [?]

Es·sene (es′ēn, e sēn′), *n.* *Judaism.* a member of an ascetic Palestinian sect that flourished from the 2nd century B.C. to the 2nd century A.D. —**Es·se·ni·an** (e sē′nē ən), **Es·sen·ic** (e sen′ik), *adj.*

es·sen·tial (ə sen′shəl), *adj.* **1.** absolutely necessary; indispensable: *Discipline is essential in an army.* **2.** pertaining to or constituting the essence of a thing. **3.** noting or containing an essence of a plant, drug, etc. **4.** being such by its very nature or in the highest sense; natural; spontaneous: *essential happiness.* **—***n.* **5.** a basic, indispensable, or necessary element; chief point. [ME *essencial* < ML *essenciāl(is)* for LL *essentiālis.* See ESSENCE, -AL^{1}] —**es·sen′tial·ly,** *adv.* —**es·sen′tial·ness,** *n.* **—Syn. 1.** fundamental, basic, inherent, intrinsic, vital. See **necessary.**

essen′tial hyperten′sion, *Pathol.* persistent high blood pressure, having no known cause.

es·sen·tial·ism (ə sen′shə liz′əm), *n.* *Educ.* a doctrine that certain traditional concepts, ideals, and skills are essential to society and should be taught methodically to all students, regardless of individual ability, need, etc. Cf. **progressivism.** —**es·sen′tial·ist,** *n.*

es·sen·ti·al·i·ty (ə sen′s͟hē al′i tē), *n., pl.* **-ties** for 2. **1.** the quality of being essential; essential character. **2.** an essential feature, element, or point.

essen′tial oil′, any of a class of volatile oils obtained from plants and possessing the odor and other characteristic properties of the plant: used chiefly in the manufacture of perfumes, flavors, and pharmaceuticals.

Es·se·qui·bo (es′ə kwē′bō), *n.* a river flowing from S Guyana N to the Atlantic. ab. 550 mi. long.

Es·sex (es′iks), *n.* **1. 2nd Earl of.** See **Devereux, Robert. 2.** a county in SE England. 2,286,970 (1961); 1528 sq. mi. *Co. seat:* Chelmsford. **3.** a town in N Maryland, near Baltimore. 38,193 (1970).

es·so·nite (es′ə nīt′), *n.* See **cinnamon stone.** [< F < Gk *hḗssōn* less (from its being less hard than true hyacinth); see -ITE[1]]

EST, Eastern Standard Time. Also, **E.S.T., e.s.t.**

-est[1], a suffix forming the superlative degree of adjectives and adverbs: *warmest; fastest.* [OE *-est, -ost.* Cf. Gk *-isto-*]

-est[2], a native English suffix formerly used to form the second person singular indicative of verbs: *knowest; sayest; goest.* Also, **-st.** [ME; OE *-est, -ast, -st* 2nd pers. sing. pres. indic. endings of some verbs (*-s* earlier verbal ending + *-t,* by assimilation from *thū* THOU) and 2nd pers. sing. past endings of weak verbs (earlier *-es* + *-t*)]

est., 1. established. **2.** estate. **3.** estimated. **4.** estuary.

estab., established.

es·tab·lish (e stab′lis͟h), *v.t.* **1.** to bring into being on a firm or permanent basis; found; institute: *to establish a university.* **2.** to install or settle in a position, place, business, etc.: *to establish one's son in business.* **3.** to cause to be accepted or recognized. **4.** to show to be valid or true; prove: *to establish the facts.* **5.** to enact, appoint, or ordain for permanence, as a law; fix unalterably. **6.** to bring about permanently: *to establish order.* **7.** to make (a church) a national or state institution. **8.** *Cards.* to obtain control of (a suit) so that one can win all the subsequent tricks in it. [ME *establisse(n)* < MF *establiss-,* extended s. of *establir* < L *stabilīre,* akin to *stabilis* STABLE[2]] —**es·tab′lish·er,** *n.* —**Syn. 1.** form, organize. See **fix. 4.** verify, substantiate. **5.** decree. —**Ant. 1.** abolish. **4.** disprove.

estab′lished church′, a church that is recognized by law, and often financially supported, as the official church of a nation. Cf. **national church.**

es·tab·lish·ment (e stab′lis͟h mənt), *n.* **1.** the act or an instance of establishing. **2.** the state or fact of being established. **3.** something established; a constituted order or system. **4. the Establishment,** the existing power structure in society; institutional authority. **5.** a household; place of residence including its furnishings, grounds, etc. **6.** a place of business together with its employees, merchandise, etc. **7.** a permanent civil, military, or other force or organization. **8.** an institution, as a school, hospital, etc. **9.** the recognition by the state of a church as the state church. **10.** the church so recognized, esp. the Church of England. **11.** *Archaic.* a fixed or settled income.

es·tab·lish·men·tar·i·an (e stab′lis͟h mən târ′ē ən), *adj.* **1.** of or pertaining to an established church, esp. the Church of England, or the principle of state religion. **2.** (*cap.*) of, pertaining to, or favoring the Establishment. —*n.* **3.** a supporter or adherent of the principle of the establishment of a church by state law; an advocate of state religion. **4.** (*cap.*) a person who favors or is a member of the Establishment. —**es·tab′lish·men·tar′i·an·ism,** *n.*

Es·taing, d′ (des taN′), **Charles Hec·tor** (s͟hARl ek tôR′), 1729–94, French admiral.

es·ta·mi·net (e stA mē ne′), *n., pl.* **-nets** (-ne′). *French.* a bistro or small café.

es·tan·cia (e stän′sē ə; *Sp.* es tän′syä), *n., pl.* **-cias** (-sē əz; *Sp.* -syäs). (in Spanish America) a landed estate or a cattle ranch. [< AmerSp, Sp: dwelling]

es·tate (e stāt′), *n., v.,* **-tat·ed, -tat·ing.** —*n.* **1.** a piece of landed property, esp. one of large extent with an elaborate house on it: *to have an estate in the country.* **2.** *Law.* **a.** property or possessions. **b.** the legal position or status of an owner, considered with respect to his property in land or other things. **c.** the degree or quantity of interest that a person has in land with respect to the nature of the right, its duration, or its relation to the rights of others. **d.** the property of a deceased person. **3.** *Brit.* a housing development. **4.** a period or condition of life: *to attain to man's estate.* **5.** a major political or social group or class. **6.** condition or circumstances with reference to worldly prosperity, estimation, etc.; social status or rank. **7.** *Archaic.* pomp or state. **8.** *Obs.* high social status or rank. —*v.t.* **9.** *Obs.* to establish in or as in an estate. [ME *estat* < MF; c. Pr *estat.* See STATE] —**Syn. 1.** See **property.**

estate′ a′gent, *Brit.* the steward or manager of a landed estate.

Estates′ Gen′eral, *French Hist.* the States-General.

Es·te (es′te), *n.* a city in NE Italy: medieval fortress; ancient Roman ruins. 14,438 (1951).

es·teem (e stēm′), *v.t.* **1.** to regard highly or favorably; regard with respect or admiration: *I esteem him for his honesty.* **2.** to consider as of a certain value; regard: *I esteem it worthless.* **3.** *Obs.* to set a value on; appraise. —*n.* **4.** favorable opinion or judgment; respect or regard: *to hold a person in esteem.* **5.** *Archaic.* opinion or judgment; estimation; valuation. [ME *esteme(n), estime(n)* (v.) < MF *estime(r)* < L *aestimāre* to fix the value of] —**Syn. 1.** honor, revere, respect. See **appreciate. 4.** favor, admiration, honor. See **respect.** —**Ant. 1.** disdain.

es·ter (es′tər), *n.* *Chem.* a compound produced by the reaction between an acid and an alcohol with the elimination of a molecule of water, as ethyl acetate, $CH_3COOC_2H_5$, or dimethyl sulfate, $(CH_3O)_2SO_2$. [coined by L. Gmelin (1788–1853), German chemist]

es·ter·ase (es′tə rās′), *n.* *Biochem.* any enzyme that hydrolyzes an ester into an alcohol and an acid.

Es·ter·ha·zy (es′tər hä′zē; *Fr.* e steR A zē′), *n.* **Ma·rie Charles Fer·di·nand Wal·sin** (mA Rē′ s͟hARl feR dē näN′ vAl saN′), 1847–1923, French army officer: forged evidence against Alfred Dreyfus.

es·ter·i·fy (e ster′ə fī′), *v.t., v.i.,* **-fied, -fy·ing.** *Chem.* to convert into an ester. —**es·ter′i·fi′a·ble,** *adj.* —**es·ter′i·fi·ca′tion,** *n.*

Es′tes Park′ (es′tiz), a summer resort in N Colorado. 1616 (1970).

Esth., 1. Esther. **2.** Esthonia.

Es·ther (es′tər), *n.* **1.** the wife of Ahasuerus. **2.** a book of the Bible bearing her name. **3.** a number of prayers, visions, interpretations of dreams, etc., that are included in the Douay Bible as chapters 10–16.

es·the·sia (es t͟hē′z͟hə, -z͟hē ə, -zē ə), *n.* capacity for sensation or feeling; sensitivity. Also, **aesthesia.** [< NL < Gk *aísthēs(is)* (see ESTHESIS) + -IA]

es·the·sis (es t͟hē′sis), *n.* sensation; feeling. [< Gk *aísthēsis* sensation, perception]

es·thete (es′t͟hēt), *n.* aesthete.

es·thet·ic (es t͟het′ik), *adj.* aesthetic.

es·thet·i·cal (es t͟het′i kəl), *adj.* aesthetical. —**es·thet′i·cal·ly,** *adv.*

es·the·ti·cian (es′t͟hi tis͟h′ən), *n.* aesthetician.

es·thet·i·cism (es t͟het′i siz′əm), *n.* aestheticism.

es·thet·ics (es t͟het′iks), *n.* aesthetics.

Es·tho·ni·a (e stō′nē ə, es t͟hō′-), *n.* Estonia.

Es·tho·ni·an (e stō′nē ən, es t͟hō′-), *adj., n.* Estonian.

Es·tienne (es tyen′), *n.* a family of French printers, book dealers, and scholars, including esp. **Hen·ri** (äN Rē′), died 1520; his son, **Ro·bert** (Rô beR′), 1503?–59; **Henri** (son of Robert), 1531?–98. Also, **Étienne.**

es·ti·ma·ble (es′tə mə bəl), *adj.* **1.** worthy of esteem; deserving respect or admiration. **2.** capable of being estimated. [ME < MF < L *aestimābil(is).* See ESTEEM, -ABLE] —**es′ti·ma·ble·ness,** *n.* —**es′ti·ma·bly,** *adv.*

es·ti·mate (*v.* es′tə māt′; *n.* es′tə mit, -māt′), *v.,* **-mat·ed, -mat·ing,** *n.* —*v.t.* **1.** to form an approximate judgment or opinion regarding the value, amount, size, weight, etc., of; calculate approximately. **2.** to form an opinion of; judge. —*v.i.* **3.** to make an estimate. —*n.* **4.** an approximate judgment or calculation, as of the value, amount, or weight of something. **5.** a judgment or opinion, as of the qualities of a person or thing. **6.** a statement of the approximate charge for work to be done, submitted by a person ready to undertake the work. [< L *aestimāt(us),* ptp. of *aestimāre* to value, estimate; see -ATE[1]] —**es′ti·ma′tor,** *n.* —**Syn. 1.** reckon, assess, value, evaluate, appraise. **4.** valuation, appraisal.

es·ti·ma·tion (es′tə mā′s͟hən), *n.* **1.** judgment or opinion: *In my estimation the boy is guilty.* **2.** esteem; respect. **3.** approximate calculation; estimate. [ME *estimacioun* < MF < L *aestimātiōn-* (s. of *aestimātiō*)] —**Syn. 2.** appreciation, regard, honor.

es·ti·ma·tive (es′tə mā′tiv), *adj.* **1.** capable of estimating. **2.** pertaining to or based upon estimation; estimated. [ME < ML *aestimātīv(us)*]

e·stip·u·late (ē stip′yə lit, -lāt′), *adj.* *Bot.* exstipulate.

es·ti·val (es′tə vəl, e stī′vəl), *adj.* pertaining or appropriate to summer. Also, **aestival.** [ME < LL *aestīvāl(is)* = L *aestīv(us)* summer + *-ālis* -AL[1]]

es·ti·vate (es′tə vāt′), *v.i.,* **-vat·ed, -vat·ing. 1.** to spend the summer, as at a specific place or in a certain activity. **2.** *Zool.* to pass the summer in a torpid condition. Also, **aestivate.** [< L *aestīvāt(us),* ptp. of *aestīvāre* to reside during the summer (akin to *aestīvus* summer); see -ATE[1]] —**es′ti·va′tor,** *n.*

es·ti·va·tion (es′tə vā′s͟hən), *n.* **1.** *Zool.* the act of estivating. **2.** *Bot.* the arrangement of the parts of a flower in the bud. Also, **aestivation.**

Es·to·ni·a (e stō′nē ə), *n.* a constituent republic of the Soviet Union, on the Baltic, S of the Gulf of Finland: an independent republic 1918–40; annexed by the Soviet Union 1940. 1,300,000 (est. 1965); 18,300 sq. mi. *Cap.:* Tallinn. Also, **Esthonia.** Official name, **Esto′nian So′viet So′cialist Repub′lic.**

Es·to·ni·an (e stō′nē ən), *adj.* **1.** of or pertaining to Estonia or its people. —*n.* **2.** one of a Finnish people inhabiting Estonia, Livonia, and other districts of Russia. **3.** the Uralic language of Estonia, very closely related to Finnish. Also, **Esthonian.**

es·top (e stop′), *v.t.,* **-topped, -top·ping. 1.** *Law.* to hinder or prevent by estoppel. **2.** *Archaic.* to stop. [ME < OF *estop(er)* (to) stop up (AF *estopper* legal sense) < *estoupe* << L *stuppa* tow. Cf. STOP] —**es·top′page,** *n.*

es·to per·pe·tu·a (es′tō peR pet′o͞o ä′; *Eng.* es′tō pər pec͟h′o͞o ə), *Latin.* may she live forever: motto of Idaho.

es·top·pel (e stop′əl), *n.* *Law.* a bar or impediment preventing a party from asserting a fact or a claim inconsistent with a position he previously took. [< MF *estoupail* stopper. See ESTOP, -AL[2]]

Es·tour·nelles de Con·stant, d′ (de sto͞oR nel′ də kôN stäN′), **Paul Hen·ri Ben·ja·min Bal·luat** (pôl äN Rē′ baN z͟hA maN′ bA lwA′), **Baron Constant de Re·becque** (də Rə bek′), 1852–1924, French diplomat: Nobel peace prize 1909.

es·to·vers (e stō′vərz), *n.pl.* *Law.* necessaries allowed by law, as wood and timber to a tenant, alimony to a wife, etc. [ME < AF, n. use of OF *estovoir, estover* to be necessary < L *est opus* there is need]

es·tra·di·ol (es′trə dī′ōl, -ôl, -ol), *n.* **1.** *Biochem.* an estrogenic hormone, $C_{18}H_{24}O_2$, that causes proliferation and thickening of the tissues and blood vessels of the endometrium. **2.** *Pharm.* a commercial form of this compound, used in the treatment of estrogen deficiency and certain menopausal and postmenopausal conditions. Also, **oestradiol.** [*estra-* (comb. form repr. ESTRIN) + DI-[1] + -OL[1]]

es·trange (e strānj′), *v.t.,* **-tranged, -trang·ing. 1.** to turn away in feeling or affection; alienate the affections of. **2.** to remove to or keep at a distance. **3.** to divert from the original use or possessor. [< MF, OF *estranger* < ML *extrāneāre,* L: to treat as a stranger. See STRANGE] —**es·trange′ment,** *n.* —**es·trang′er,** *n.*

es·tray (e strā′), *n.* **1.** anything that has strayed away. **2.** *Law.* a domestic animal found wandering or without an owner. —*v.i.* **3.** to stray. [ME *astrai* < AF *estray.* See STRAY]

Es·tre·ma·du·ra (es′tRe mä t͟ho͞o′Rä), *n.* a region in W Spain, formerly a province. Also, **Extremadura.**

es·trin (es′trin), *n. Biochem.* estrone. [< NL; see ESTRUS, -IN[2]]

es·tri·ol (es′trē ōl′, -ôl′, -ol′), *n.* **1.** *Biochem.* an estrogenic hormone, $C_{18}H_{21}(OH)_3$, occurring in urine during pregnancy. **2.** *Pharm.* a commercial form of this compound, used in conditions involving estrogen deficiency. Also, **oestriol.** [ES(TRIN) + TRI- + -OL[1]]

es·tro·gen (es′trə jən), *n. Biochem.* any of a group of female hormones capable of inducing estrus in immature, spayed mammals. Also, **oestrogen.**

es·tro·gen·ic (es′trə jen′ik), *adj. Biochem.* promoting or producing estrus. —**es′tro·gen′i·cal·ly,** *adv.*

es·trone (es′trōn), *n.* **1.** *Biochem.* an estrogenic hormone, $C_{18}H_{22}O_2$, found during pregnancy in urine and placental tissue. **2.** *Pharm.* a commercial form of this compound, used in the treatment of estrogen deficiency and certain menopausal and postmenopausal conditions. Also, **estrin, oestrin, oestrone.** Also called **theelin.** [ESTR(IN) + -ONE]

es·trous (es′trəs), *adj.* involving or pertaining to the estrus. Also, **oestrous.**

es′trous cy′cle, *Zool.* a recurrent series of physiological changes in sexual and other organs in female mammals, extending from one rutting period to the next.

es·trus (es′trəs), *n. Zool.* **1.** the period of heat or rut; the period of maximum sexual receptivity of the female. **2.** See **estrous cycle.** Also, **es·trum** (es′trəm), **oestrus.** [< L *oestrus* < Gk *oîstros* gadfly, sting, hence frenzy] —**es·tru·al** (es′trōō əl), *adj.*

es·tu·a·rine (es′cho͞o ə rīn′, -ər in), *adj.* **1.** formed in an estuary. **2.** found in estuaries.

es·tu·ar·y (es′cho͞o er′ē), *n., pl.* **-ar·ies.** **1.** the part of the mouth or lower course of a river in which the river's current meets the sea's tide. **2.** an arm or inlet of the sea at the lower end of a river. [< L *aestuāri(um)* channel, creek, inlet = *aestu(s)* tide + *-ārium* -ARY] —**es·tu·ar·i·al** (es′cho͞o âr′ē əl), *adj.*

e·su·ri·ent (i so͝or′ē ənt), *adj.* hungry; greedy. [< L *ēsurient-* (s. of *ēsuriēns,* prp. of *ēsurīre*) hungering = *ēsur-* hunger + *-ent-* -ENT] —**e·su′ri·ence, e·su′ri·en·cy,** *n.* —**e·su′ri·ent·ly,** *adv.*

-et, a noun suffix having properly a diminutive force (now lost in many words): *islet; bullet; midget; owlet; plummet.* Cf. **-ette.** [ME < OF *-et* (masc.), *-ette* (fem.)]

E.T., Eastern Time. Also, **e.t.**

e·ta (ā′tə, ē′tə), *n.* the seventh letter of the Greek alphabet (H, η).

E.T.A., estimated time of arrival. Also, **ETA**

é·ta·gère (ā tA zhER′), *n., pl.* **-gères** (-zhER′). *French.* a series of open shelves for bric-a-brac.

et al. (et al′, äl′, ôl′), **1.** and elsewhere. [< L *et alibi*] **2.** and others. [< L *et aliī*]

et·a·mine (et′ə mēn′), *n.* a lightweight, loosely woven fabric of cotton or worsted. [< F << L *stāminea,* fem. of *stāmineus* made of threads. See STAMEN, -EOUS]

et·a·oin shrd·lu (et′ē oin′ shûrd′lo͞o, ē′tē-), the letters produced by running the finger down the first two vertical rows of keys at the left of the keyboard of a Linotype keyboard: used as a temporary marking slug but sometimes inadvertently cast and printed.

é·tape (ā tap′; *Fr.* ā tAp′), *n., pl.* **é·tapes** (ā taps′; *Fr.* ā tAp′). *Mil.* **1.** a place where troops camp after a day's march. **2.** a day's march. **3.** *Archaic.* supplies issued to troops during a march. [< F; MF *estaple* < MD *stapel* warehouse; see STAPLE[2]]

etc., See **et cetera.** —**Usage.** See **and.**

et cet·er·a (et set′ər ə, se′trə), and others; and so forth; and so on (used to indicate that more of the same sort or class might have been mentioned). *Abbr.:* etc. [< L]

et·cet·er·a (et set′ər ə, -se′trə), *n., pl.* **-ras.** **1.** a number of other things or persons unspecified. **2. etceteras,** extras or sundries. [n. use of ET CETERA]

etch (ech), *v.t.* **1.** to cut, bite, or corrode with an acid or the like, as to form a design from which to print. **2.** to produce (a design, image, etc.) by this method, as on copper or glass. **3.** to outline clearly or sharply; delineate, as a person's features, character, etc. **4.** to fix permanently in or implant firmly on the mind; root in the memory. —*v.i.* **5.** to practice the art of etching. [< D *etse(n)* < G *ätzen* to etch, orig. cause to eat; c. OE *ettan* to graze; akin to EAT] —**etch′er,** *n.*

etch·ing (ech′ing), *n.* **1.** the act or process of making designs or pictures on a metal plate, glass, etc., by the corrosive action of an acid. **2.** a print made from an etched plate. **3.** the design so produced. **4.** a plate bearing such a design.

E.T.D., estimated time of departure. Also, **ETD**

E·te·o·cles (i tē′ə klēz′), *n. Class. Myth.* a son of Oedipus and the brother of Polynices, by whom he was slain. Cf. **Seven against Thebes** (def. 1).

e·ter·nal (i tûr′nəl), *adj.* **1.** lasting forever; without beginning or end; always existing (opposed to *temporal*): *eternal life.* **2.** perpetual; ceaseless; endless: *eternal quarreling.* **3.** enduring; immutable: *eternal principles.* **4.** *Metaphys.* existing outside of all relations of time; not subject to change. —*n.* **5.** something that is eternal. **6. the Eternal,** God. [ME < LL *aeternāl(is)*] —**e·ter′nal·ly,** *adv.* —**e·ter·nal·i·ty** (i′tûr nal′i tē), **e·ter′nal·ness,** *n.*

—**Syn. 1.** permanent, unending. ETERNAL, ENDLESS, EVERLASTING, PERPETUAL imply lasting or going on without ceasing. That which is ETERNAL is, by its nature, without beginning or ending: *God, the eternal Father.* That which is ENDLESS never stops but goes on continually as if in a circle: *an endless succession of years.* That which is EVERLASTING will endure through all future time: *a promise of everlasting life.* PERPETUAL implies continuous renewal as far into the future as one can foresee: *perpetual strife between nations.* **3.** timeless, immortal, imperishable, indestructible.

Eter′nal Cit′y, The, the city of Rome, Italy.

e·terne (i tûrn′), *adj. Archaic.* eternal. [ME < L *aetern(us),* contr. of *aeviternus* = *aev(um)* age + *-i-* -I- + *-ternus* (as in *sempiternus*)]

e·ter·nise (i tûr′nīz), *v.t.,* **-nised, -nis·ing.** *Chiefly Brit.* eternize. —**e·ter′ni·sa′tion,** *n.*

e·ter·ni·ty (i tûr′ni tē), *n., pl.* **-ties.** **1.** infinite time; duration without beginning or end. **2.** eternal existence, esp. as contrasted with mortal life. **3.** the state into which the soul passes at death. **4.** a seemingly endless period of time. [ME *eternite* < L *aeternitās*]

e·ter·nize (i tûr′nīz), *v.t.,* **-nized, -niz·ing.** **1.** to make eternal; perpetuate. **2.** to immortalize. Also, *esp. Brit.,* **eternise.** [< ML *ēterniz(āre)*] —**e·ter′ni·za′tion,** *n.*

e·te·sian (i tē′zhən), *adj.* (of certain Mediterranean winds) occurring annually. [< L *etēsi(ae)* < Gk *etēsíai (ánemoi)* periodic (winds) + -AN]

eth (eth), *n.* a letter in the form of a crossed *d,* written đ or ð, used in Old English writing to represent both voiced and unvoiced *th* and in modern Icelandic and in phonetic alphabets to represent voiced *th.* Also, **edh.**

-eth[1], an ending of the third person singular present indicative of verbs, now occurring only in archaic forms or used in solemn or poetic language: *doeth* or *doth; hopeth; sitteth.* Also, **-th.** [OE *-eth, -ath, -oth, -th;* akin to L *-t*]

-eth[2], var. of **-th[2],** the ordinal suffix, used when the cardinal number ends in *-y: twentieth; thirtieth.*

Eth., Ethiopia.

eth·ane (eth′ān), *n. Chem.* a colorless, odorless, flammable gas, CH_3CH_3, of the methane series, used chiefly as a fuel and in organic synthesis. Also called **bimethyl, methyl methane.** [ETH(YL) + -ANE]

Eth·a·nim (eth′ə nim; *Heb.* e tä nēm′), *n. Chiefly Biblical.* a month equivalent to Tishri of the modern Jewish calendar. I Kings 8:2. [< Heb]

eth·a·nol (eth′ə nōl′, -nôl′, -nol′), *n. Chem.* alcohol (def. 1). [ETHANE + -OL[1]]

Eth·el·bert (eth′əl bûrt′), *n.* A.D. 552?–616, king of Kent 560–616. Ancient, **Æthelbert.**

Eth·el·red II (eth′əl red′), ("*the Unready*") A.D. 968?–1016, king of the English 978–1016.

eth·ene (eth′ēn), *n. Chem.* ethylene (def. 2).

e·ther (ē′thər), *n.* **1.** Also called **ethyl ether.** *Chem., Pharm.* a highly volatile, flammable liquid, $(C_2H_5)_2O$, having a pleasant aromatic odor, used as a solvent and as an inhalant anesthetic. **2.** *Chem.* one of a class of compounds in which two organic groups are attached directly to an oxygen atom, having the general formula, ROR, as ethyl ether. **3.** the upper regions of space; the clear sky; the heavens. **4.** the medium supposed by the ancients to fill the upper regions of space. **5.** *Physics.* a hypothetical substance once supposed to occupy all space, postulated to account for the propagation of electromagnetic radiation through space. Also, **aether** (for defs. 3–5). [ME < L *aether* the upper air, pure air, ether < Gk *aithḗr* < *aíthein* to glow, burn; akin to OE *ād* funeral pyre, L *aestus* heat]

e·the·re·al (i thēr′ē əl), *adj.* **1.** light, airy, or tenuous. **2.** extremely delicate or refined: *ethereal beauty.* **3.** heavenly or celestial. **4.** of the ether or upper regions of space. **5.** *Chem.* pertaining to, containing, or resembling ethyl ether. Also, **aethereal** (for defs. 1–4). [< L *aethere(us)* (< Gk *aithérios*) = *aether* ETHER + *-e(us)* adj. suffix + -AL[1]] —**e·the′re·al′i·ty, e·the′re·al·ness,** *n.* —**e·the′re·al·ly,** *adv.*

e·the·re·al·ise (i thēr′ē ə līz′), *v.t.,* **-ised, -is·ing.** *Chiefly Brit.* etherealize. Also, **etherialise.** —**e·the′re·al·i·sa′tion,** *n.*

e·the·re·al·ize (i thēr′ē ə līz′), *v.t.,* **-ized, -iz·ing.** to make ethereal. Also, **etherialize.** —**e·the′re·al·i·za′tion,** *n.*

Eth·er·ege (eth′ər ij), *n.* **Sir George,** 1635?–91, English dramatist.

e·the·ri·al·ise (i thēr′ē ə līz′), *v.t.,* **-ised, -is·ing.** *Chiefly Brit.* etherealize. —**e·the′ri·al·i·sa′tion,** *n.*

e·the·ri·al·ize (i thēr′ē ə līz′), *v.t.,* **-ized, -iz·ing.** etherealize. —**e·the′ri·al·i·za′tion,** *n.*

e·ther·ize (ē′thə rīz′), *v.t.,* **-ized, -iz·ing.** *Med.* to put under the influence of ether. —**e′ther·i·za′tion,** *n.* —**e′ther·iz′er,** *n.*

eth·ic (eth′ik), *n.* **1.** a body of moral principles or values. —*adj.* **2.** ethical. [ME *ethic, etic* < L *ēthic(us)* < Gk *ēthikós.* See ETHOS, -IC]

eth·i·cal (eth′i kəl), *adj.* **1.** pertaining to or dealing with morals or the principles of morality; pertaining to right and wrong in conduct. **2.** in accordance with the rules or standards for right conduct or practice, esp. the standards of a profession: *It is not considered ethical for physicians to advertise.* **3.** (of drugs) sold only upon medical prescription. —**eth′i·cal·ly,** *adv.* —**eth′i·cal·ness, eth′i·cal′i·ty,** *n.* —**Syn. 2.** moral, upright, honest, righteous, virtuous, honorable. —**Ant. 2.** immoral.

eth·i·cize (eth′i sīz′), *v.t.,* **-cized, -ciz·ing.** to make ethical; treat or regard as ethical.

eth·ics (eth′iks), *n.pl.* **1.** (*construed as sing. or pl.*) a system of moral principles. **2.** the rules of conduct recognized in respect to a particular class of human actions or a particular group, culture, etc.: *medical ethics; Christian ethics.* **3.** moral principles, as of an individual: *His ethics forbade betrayal of a confidence.* **4.** (*usually construed as sing.*) the branch of philosophy dealing with values relating to human conduct, with respect to the rightness and wrongness of certain actions and to the goodness and badness of the motives and ends of such actions. [ETHIC + -S[3], modeled on Gk *tà ēthiká,* neut. pl.] —**e·thi·cian** (e thish′ən), **eth·i·cist** (eth′i sist), *n.* —**Syn. 2.** See **moral.**

E·thi·op (ē′thē op′), *adj., n. Archaic.* Ethiopian. Also, **E·thi·ope** (ē′thē ōp′). [ME < L *Aethiop(s)* < Gk *Aithíops*]

E·thi·o·pi·a (ē′thē ō′pē ə), *n.* **1.** Formerly, **Abyssinia.** a republic in E Africa: a part of the former Italian E Africa 1936–41. 30,200,000; 409,266 sq. mi. Present boundaries include Eritrea. *Cap.:* Addis Ababa. **2.** an ancient region in NE Africa, bordering on Egypt and the Red Sea.

E·thi·o·pi·an (ē′thē ō′pē ən), *adj.* **1.** of or pertaining to Ethiopia or to its inhabitants. **2.** Negro. **3.** belonging to the part of Africa south of the equator. **4.** *Zoogeog.* belonging to a geographical division comprising Africa south of the tropic of Cancer, the southern part of the Arabian peninsula, and Madagascar. —*n.* **5.** a native or inhabitant of Ethiopia. **6.** a member of any of various supposedly dark-skinned peoples regarded by the ancients as coming from a country lying south of Egypt. **7.** a Negro.

E·thi·op·ic (ē′thē op′ik, -ō′pik), *adj.* **1.** Ethiopian. —*n.*

2. Also called **Geez, Ge'ez.** the Semitic language of ancient Ethiopia, now used only as the liturgical language of the Ethiopian Church. [< L *Aethiopic(us)*]

eth·moid (eth′moid), *Anat.* —*adj.* **1.** Also, **eth·moi′dal.** of or pertaining to a bone at the base of the cranium at the root of the nose. —*n.* **2.** the ethmoid bone. [< Gk *ēthmoeid(ēs)* sievelike; see -OID]

eth·narch (eth′närk), *n.* the ruler of a people, tribe, or nation. [< Gk *ethnárchēs*]

eth·nar·chy (eth′när kē), *n., pl.* **-chies.** the government, office, or jurisdiction of an ethnarch. [< Gk *ethnarchía*]

eth·nic (eth′nik), *adj.* Also, **eth′ni·cal. 1.** pertaining to or characteristic of a people, esp. a speech or culture group. **2.** referring to the origin, classification, characteristics, etc., of such groups. **3.** pertaining to non-Christians. **4.** belonging to or deriving from the cultural, racial, religious, or linguistic traditions of a people or country, esp. a primitive one: *ethnic dances.* —*n.* **5.** *U.S.* a member of an ethnic group, esp. one belonging to a minority group that is not part of the white Anglo-Saxon Protestant tradition. [ME *ethnik* heathen < LL *ethnic(us)* < Gk *ethnikós*] —**eth′ni·cal·ly,** *adv.*

eth′nic group′, *Sociol.* a group of people of the same race or nationality who share a common and distinctive culture. Also called **ethnos.**

ethno-, a learned borrowing from Greek meaning "race," "culture," "people," used in the formation of compound words: *ethnography.* [< Gk, comb. form of *éthnos*]

eth·no·cen·trism (eth′nō sen′triz əm), *n.* **1.** *Sociol.* the belief in the inherent superiority of one's own group and culture. **2.** a tendency to view alien groups or cultures in terms of one's own. —**eth′no·cen′tric,** *adj.* —**eth′no·cen′tri·cal·ly,** *adv.* —**eth′no·cen·tric′i·ty,** *n.*

ethnog., ethnography.

eth·nog·e·ny (eth noj′ə nē), *n.* *Anthropol.* a branch of ethnology that studies the origin of distinctive populations or races. —**eth·no·gen·ic** (eth′nō jen′ik), *adj.* —**eth·nog′e·nist,** *n.*

eth·nog·ra·phy (eth nog′rə fē), *n.* a branch of anthropology dealing with the scientific description of individual cultures. —**eth·nog′ra·pher,** *n.* —**eth·no·graph·ic** (eth′nə graf′ik), **eth′no·graph′i·cal,** *adj.* —**eth′no·graph′i·cal·ly,** *adv.*

ethnol., 1. ethnological. **2.** ethnology.

eth·nol·o·gy (eth nol′ə jē), *n.* **1.** a branch of anthropology that analyzes cultures, esp. in regard to their historical development and the similarities and dissimilarities between them. **2.** a branch of anthropology dealing with the origin, distribution, and distinguishing characteristics of the races of mankind. —**eth·no·log·i·cal** (eth′nə loj′i kəl), **eth′no·log′ic,** *adj.* —**eth′no·log′i·cal·ly,** *adv.* —**eth·nol′o·gist,** *n.*

eth·no·mu·si·col·o·gy (eth′nō myōō′zi kol′ə jē), *n.* the study of folk and primitive music and of their relationship to the peoples and cultures to which they belong. —**eth·no·mu·si·co·log·i·cal** (eth′nō myōō′zi kə loj′i kəl), *adj.* —**eth′no·mu′si·col′o·gist,** *n.*

eth·nos (eth′nos), *n.* *Sociol.* See **ethnic group.** [< Gk: race, culture, people]

e·thol·o·gy (e thol′ə jē, ē thol′-), *n.* the scientific study of animal behavior, esp. in relation to habitat. [< Gk *ēthología.* See ETHOS, -LOGY] —**eth·o·log·i·cal** (eth′ə loj′i kəl), *adj.* —**eth′o·log′i·cally,** *adv.* —**e·thol′o·gist,** *n.*

e·thos (ē′thos, eth′os), *n.* **1.** *Sociol.* the fundamental character or spirit of a culture; the underlying sentiment that informs the beliefs, customs, or practices of a group or society. **2.** the moral element in dramatic literature that determines a man's action rather than his thought or emotion. **3.** the character or disposition of a community, group, person, etc. [< Gk: custom, habit, character]

eth·yl (eth′əl), *adj.* **1.** *Chem.* containing the ethyl group, as ethyl ether, $(C_2H_5)_2O$. —*n.* **2.** a type of antiknock fluid, containing tetraethyllead and other ingredients for an even combustion. [ETH(ER) + -YL]

eth′yl ac′etate, *Chem.* a volatile, flammable liquid, $CH_3COOC_2H_5$, having a fragrant, fruitlike odor: used chiefly as a scent in the manufacture of perfume, and as a solvent for paints and lacquers.

eth′yl al′cohol, *Chem.* alcohol (def. 1).

eth·yl·ate (eth′ə lāt′), *v.,* **-at·ed, -at·ing,** *n.* *Chem.* —*v.t.* **1.** to introduce one or more ethyl groups into (a compound). —*n.* **2.** a metallic derivative of ethyl alcohol, as potassium ethylate, KOC_2H_5. —**eth′yl·a′tion,** *n.*

eth·yl·ene (eth′ə lēn′), *Chem.* —*adj.* **1.** containing the ethylene group. —*n.* **2.** Also called **ethene.** a flammable gas, $CH_2{=}CH_2$, the first member of the ethylene series, used to improve the color of citrus fruits, in the synthesis of organic compounds, and as an inhalation anesthetic. —**eth·yl·e·nic** (eth′ə lē′nik, -len′ik), *adj.*

eth′ylene gly′col, *Chem.* glycol (def. 1).

eth′ylene group′, *Chem.* the bivalent group, $-CH_2CH_2-$, derived from ethylene or ethane. Also called **eth′ylene rad′ical.**

eth′ylene ox′ide, *Chem.* a gaseous ring compound C_2H_4O, used chiefly in the synthesis of ethylene glycol and plastics.

eth′ylene se′ries, *Chem.* See **alkene series.**

eth′yl e′ther, *Chem.* ether (def. 1).

eth′yl group′, *Chem.* the univalent group, CH_3CH_2-, derived from ethane. Also called **eth′yl rad′ical.** —**e·thyl·ic** (ə thil′ik), *adj.*

eth·yne (eth′īn, e thīn′), *n.* *Chem.* acetylene. [ETH(YL) + *-yne* (var. of -INE[1])]

-etic, a suffix used in the formation of adjectives: *eidetic.* [< L *-etic(us),* Gk *-etik(os)* = *-et-* a formative occurring in some nouns + *-ikos* -IC]

É·tienne (*Fr.* ā tyen′), *n.* Estienne.

etio-, a combining form of Greek origin meaning "cause": *etiology.* Also, **aetio-.** [< Gk *aitio-,* comb. form repr. *aitía* cause]

e·ti·o·late (ē′tē ə lāt′), *v.t.,* **-lat·ed, -lat·ing.** to cause (a plant) to whiten by excluding light; bleach: *to etiolate celery.* [< F *étiol(er)* (to) make pale (< ?) + -ATE[1]] —**e′ti·o·la′tion,** *n.*

e·ti·ol·o·gy (ē′tē ol′ə jē), *n., pl.* **-gies. 1.** *Pathol.* the study of the causes of diseases. **2.** the cause or origin of a disease. **3.** the study of causation. **4.** any study of causes, causation, or causality. Also, **aetiology.** [< LL *aetiologia* < Gk *aitiología* determining the cause of something] —**e·ti·o·log·i·cal** (ē′tē ə loj′i kəl), *adj.* —**e′ti·o·log′i·cal·ly,** *adv.* —**e′ti·ol′o·gist,** *n.*

et·i·quette (et′ə kit, -ket′), *n.* **1.** conventional requirements as to social behavior. **2.** a prescribed or accepted code of usage in matters of ceremony: *court etiquette.* **3.** the code of ethics of a profession: *medical etiquette.* [< F *étiquette,* MF *estiquette* ticket, memorandum < *estiqu(i)er* to attach, stick < Gmc. See STICK[2], -ETTE]
—**Syn. 1.** ETIQUETTE, DECORUM, PROPRIETY imply observance of the formal requirements governing behavior in polite society. ETIQUETTE refers to conventional forms and usages: *the rules of etiquette.* DECORUM suggests dignity and a sense of what is becoming or appropriate for a person of good breeding: *a fine sense of decorum.* PROPRIETY (usually plural) implies established conventions of morals and good taste: *to observe the proprieties.*

Et·na (et′nə), *n.* **Mount,** an active volcano in E Sicily. 10,758 ft. Also, **Aetna.**

ETO, *Mil.* (in World War II) European Theater of Operations.

é·toile (ā twal′), *n., pl.* **é·toiles** (ā twal′). *French.* **1.** a star or something shaped like a star. **2.** See **prima ballerina.**

E·ton (ēt′ən), *n.* a town in S Buckinghamshire, in S England, on the Thames, W of London: site of Eton College. 3901 (1961).

E′ton col′lar, a broad, stiff collar, as that worn folded outside an Eton jacket.

E′ton Col′lege, a preparatory school for boys in Eton, England, founded in 1440 by Henry VI.

E·to·ni·an (ē tō′nē ən), *n.* **1.** a student or alumnus of Eton College. —*adj.* **2.** of or pertaining to Eton College.

Eton jacket

E′ton jack′et, a short jacket reaching to the waistline and open in front.

Etr., Etruscan (def. 3).

E·tru·ri·a (i trŏŏr′ē ə), *n.* an ancient country located between the Arno and Tiber rivers, roughly corresponding to modern Tuscany in W Italy.

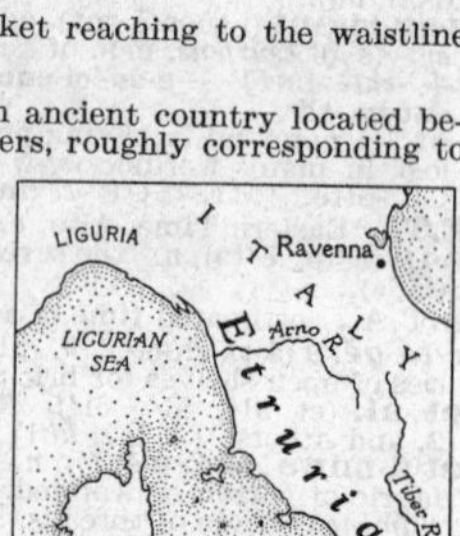

E·trus·can (i trus′kən), *adj.* **1.** pertaining to Etruria, its inhabitants, civilization, art, or language. —*n.* **2.** an inhabitant of ancient Etruria. **3.** the extinct language of Etruria, not known to be related to any other language. *Abbr.:* Etr. Also called **E·tru·ri·an** (i trŏŏr′ē ən). [< L *Etrusc(us)* of Etruria + -AN]

et seq., *pl.* **et seqq., et sqq.** and the following. [< L *et sequēns*]

et seqq., and those following. Also, **et sqq.** [< L *et sequentēs, et sequentia*]

-ette, a noun suffix, the feminine form of *-et,* occurring with the original diminutive force (*cigarette*), as a distinctively feminine ending (*coquette*), in various colloquial or humorous formations (*usherette*), and in trademarks of imitations or substitutes (*Leatherette*). Cf. **-et.** [< F, fem. of *-et* -ET]

et tu, Bru·te (et tōō′ brōō′tā), *Latin.* and thou, Brutus!: alleged dying words of Julius Caesar in accusation as his friend Brutus stabbed him.

é·tude (ā′tōōd, ā′tyōōd, ā tōōd′, ā tyōōd′; *Fr.* ā tyd′), *n., pl.* **é·tudes** (ā′tōōdz, ā′tyōōdz, ā tōōdz′, ā tyōōdz′; *Fr.* ā tyd′). *Music.* a composition intended mainly for the practice of technique. [< F; see STUDY]

e·tui (ā twē′, et′wē), *n., pl.* **e·tuis.** a small, often decorative case, esp. one for needles, toilet articles, or the like. Also, **e·twee′.** [< F *étui,* OF *estui* holder, back formation from *estuier* to keep < VL **studiāre* to treat with care]

ETV, See **educational television.**

etym., 1. etymological. **2.** etymology. Also, **etymol.**

et·y·mol·o·gise (et′ə mol′ə jīz′), *v.t., v.i.,* **-gised, -gis·ing.** *Chiefly Brit.* etymologize.

et·y·mol·o·gize (et′ə mol′ə jīz′), *v.,* **-gized, -giz·ing.** —*v.t.* **1.** to trace the history of (a word). —*v.i.* **2.** to study etymology. **3.** to give or suggest the etymology of words. [< ML *etymologiz(āre)*]

et·y·mol·o·gy (et′ə mol′ə jē), *n., pl.* **-gies. 1.** the study of historical linguistic change, esp. as applied to individual words. **2.** an account of the history of a particular word. **3.** the derivation of a word. [< L *etymologia* < Gk = *etymológ(os)* studying words (see ETYMON, LOGOS) + *-ia* -Y[3]] —**et·y·mo·log·i·cal** (et′ə mə loj′i kəl), *adj.* —**et′y·mo·log′i·cal·ly,** *adv.* —**et′y·mol′o·gist,** *n.*

et·y·mon (et′ə mon′), *n., pl.* **-mons, -ma** (-mə). the linguistic form from which another form is historically derived, as the Latin *cor* "heart," which is the etymon of English *cordial,* or the Indo-European **k(e)rd-,* which is the etymon of Latin *cor,* Greek *kardía,* Russian *serdtse,* and English *heart.* [< L: the origin of a word < Gk: the essential meaning of a word seen in its origin (neut. of *étymos* true, actual, real)]

Et·zel (et′səl), *n.* *Germanic Legend.* Attila: represented in the *Nibelungenlied* as the second husband of Kriemhild after the death of Siegfried. Cf. **Atli.**

Eu, *Chem.* europium.

eu-, a prefix meaning "good," "well," occurring chiefly in words of Greek origin: *eupepsia.* [< Gk, comb. form of *eûs* good (adj.) or *eû* (neut., used as adv.) well]

Eu·boe·a (yōō bē′ə), *n.* a Greek island in the W Aegean Sea. 166,097 (1961); 1586 sq. mi. *Cap.:* Chalcis. Also called **Negropont.** Modern Greek, **Evvoia.** —**Eu·boe′an,** *adj., n.* —**Eu·bo·ic** (yōō bō′ik), *adj.*

eu·caine (yōō kān′), *n.* *Pharm.* a white, crystalline solid, $C_{15}H_{21}NO_2$, used chiefly in the form of its hydrochloride as a local anesthetic. Also called **betacaine.** [EU- + *-caine* (as in COCAINE)]

eu·ca·lyp·tol (yōō′kə lip′tōl, -tôl, -tol), *n.* *Chem.* cineole. Also, **eu·ca·lyp·tole** (yōō′kə lip′tōl). [EUCALYPT(US) + -OL[2]]

eu·ca·lyp·tus (yōō′kə lip′təs), *n., pl.* **-ti** (-tī), **-tus·es.** any of numerous aromatic, evergreen, myrtaceous trees of the genus *Eucalyptus.* Also, **eu·ca·lypt** (yōō′kə lipt′). Also called **blue gum.** [< NL < Gk *eu-* EU- + *kalyptós* covered, wrapped, akin to *kalýptein* to cover] —**eu′ca·lyp′tic,** *adj.*

eu·cha·ris (yōō′kə ris), *n.* any of several South American, amaryllidaceous plants of the genus *Eucharis,* certain species of which are cultivated for their large, fragrant, white flowers. [< NL, special use of Gk *eúcharis* gracious = *eu-* EU- + *cháris* grace, favor; see CHARISMA]

Eu·cha·rist (yōō′kə rist), *n.* **1.** the sacrament of Holy Communion; the sacrifice of the Mass; the Lord's Supper. **2.** the consecrated elements of the Holy Communion, esp. the bread. [ME *eukarist* < eccl. L *eucharist(ia)* < eccl. Gk: gratefulness, thanksgiving. See EU-, CHARISMA, -IA] —**Eu′cha·ris′tic, Eu′cha·ris′ti·cal,** *adj.*

eu·chre (yōō′kər), *n., v.,* **-chred, -chring.** —*n.* **1.** *Cards.* a game played by two, three, or four persons, usually with the 32 highest cards in the pack. **2.** an instance of euchring or being euchred. —*v.t.* **3.** to get the better of (an opponent) in a hand at euchre by his failure to win three tricks after having made the trump. **4.** *Informal.* to outwit; get the better of, as by scheming (usually fol. by *out*). [?]

eu·chro·ma·tin (yōō krō′mə tin), *n.* *Genetics.* the part of a chromosome that is not as compact or as stainable as heterochromatin and is believed to contain the genetically active material of the chromosome. —**eu·chro·mat·ic** (yōō′krə mat′ik), *adj.*

eu·chro·mo·some (yōō krō′mə sōm′), *n.* *Genetics.* autosome.

Euck·en (oi′kən), *n.* **Ru·dolph Chris·toph** (ʀōō′dôlf kʀis′tôf), 1846–1926, German philosopher: Nobel prize 1908.

eu·clase (yōō′klās), *n.* a rare, green or blue mineral, beryllium aluminum silicate, $HBeAl(SiO_5)$, occurring in prismatic crystals. [< F]

Eu·clid (yōō′klid), *n.* **1.** fl. c300 B.C., Greek geometrician and educator at Alexandria. **2.** See **Euclidean geometry. 3.** a city in NE Ohio, near Cleveland. 71,552 (1970).

Eu·clid·e·an (yōō klid′ē ən), *adj.* of or pertaining to Euclid or adopting his postulates. Also, **Eu·clid′i·an.** [< L *Euclīdē(us)* of Euclid (< Gk *Eukleídeios*) + -AN]

Euclid′ean geom′etry, geometry based upon the postulates of Euclid, esp. the postulate that only one line may be drawn through a given point parallel to a given line.

Euclid′ean space′, *Math.* ordinary three-dimensional space.

eu·de·mon (yōō dē′mən), *n.* a good demon or spirit. Also, **eu·dae′mon.** [< Gk *eudaímōn* blessed with a good genius, fortunate, happy. See EU-, DEMON]

eu·de·mo·ni·a (yōō′di mō′nē ə), *n.* happiness. Also, **eu′dae·mo′ni·a.** [< Gk *eudaimonía.* See EUDEMON, -IA]

eu·de·mon·ic (yōō′di mon′ik), *adj.* **1.** pertaining or conducive to happiness. **2.** pertaining to eudemonics or eudemonism. Also, **eu′dae·mon′ic.** [< Gk *eudaimonik(ós)*]

eu·de·mon·ics (yōō′di mon′iks), *n.* (*usually construed as sing.*) **1.** the theory or art of happiness. **2.** the practice of eudemonism. Also, **eu′dae·mon′ics.** [see EUDEMONIC, -ICS]

eu·de·mon·ism (yōō dē′mə niz′əm), *n.* *Ethics.* the doctrine that the basis of moral obligations is to be found in the tendency of right actions to produce happiness. Also, **eu·dae′mon·ism.** —**eu·de′mon·ist, eu·dae′mon·ist,** *n.* —**eu·de′mon·is′tic, eu·dae′mon·is′tic, eu·de′mon·is′ti·cal, eu·dae′mon·is′ti·cal,** *adj.* —**eu·de′mon·is′ti·cal·ly, eu·dae′mon·is′ti·cal·ly,** *adv.*

eu·di·om·e·ter (yōō′dē om′i tər), *n.* *Chem.* a graduated glass measuring tube for gas analysis. [< Gk *eúdio(s)* clear, mild (lit., well skied = *eu-* EU- + *Di-,* s. of *Zeús* god of the sky + *-os* adj. suffix) + -METER] —**eu·di·o·met·ric** (yōō′dē ə me′trik), **eu′di·o·met′ri·cal,** *adj.* —**eu′di·o·met′ri·cal·ly,** *adv.*

Eu·gene (yōō jēn′), *n.* a city in W Oregon. 78,389 (1970).

Eu·gène (œ zhen′), *n.* **Prince** (*François Eugène de Savoie-Carignan*), 1663–1736, Austrian general, born in France.

Eugene I. See **Eugenius I.**

Eugene II. See **Eugenius II.**

Eugene III. See **Eugenius III.**

Eugene IV. See **Eugenius IV.**

eu·gen·ic (yōō jen′ik), *adj.* **1.** of or bringing about improvement in the type of offspring produced. **2.** having good inherited characteristics. Also, **eu·gen′i·cal.** Cf. **dysgenic.** [< Gk *eugen(ḗs)* well born (see EU-, -GEN) + -IC] —**eu·gen′i·cal·ly,** *adv.*

eu·gen·i·cist (yōō jen′i sist), *n.* **1.** a specialist in eugenics. **2.** an advocate of eugenic measures. Also, **eu·ge·nist** (yōō′jə nist).

eu·gen·ics (yōō jen′iks), *n.* (*construed as sing.*) the science of improving the qualities of a breed or species, esp. the human race, by the careful selection of parents. [see EUGENIC, -ICS]

Eu·gé·nie (œ zhā nē′), *n.* **Comtesse de Te·ba** (de tē′bä), (*Marie Eugénie de Montijo de Guzmán*), 1826–1920, wife of Napoleon III, born in Spain: Empress of France 1853–70.

Eu·ge·ni·us I (yōō jē′nē əs, -jēn′yəs), **Saint,** died A.D. 657, pope 654–657. Also, **Eugene I.**

Eugenius II, died A.D. 827, Italian ecclesiastic: pope 824–827. Also, **Eugene II.**

Eugenius III, (*Bernardo Pignatelli* or *Paganelli*) died 1153, Italian ecclesiastic: pope 1145–53. Also, **Eugene III.**

Eugenius IV, (*Gabriele* or *Gabriel Condolmieri* or *Condulmer*) 1383–1447, Italian ecclesiastic: pope 1431–47. Also, **Eugene IV.**

eu·ge·nol (yōō′jə nōl′, -nôl′, -nol′), *n.* *Chem., Pharm.* an aromatic liquid, $C_{10}H_{12}O_2$, used chiefly in perfumery and in dentistry as an antiseptic. Also called **eugen′ic ac′id.** [< NL *Eugen(ia)* name of genus of trees (see EUGENIC) + -OL[2]]

Eu·gle·na (yōō glē′nə), *n.* a genus of green protozoans having a reddish eyespot and a single flagellum, found in fresh, esp. stagnant, water. [< NL < Gk *eu-* EU- + *glḗnē* the pupil, eyeball, socket of a joint]

eu·he·mer·ise (yōō hē′mə rīz′, -hem′ə-), *v.t., v.i.,* **-ised, -is·ing.** *Chiefly Brit.* euhemerize.

eu·he·mer·ism (yōō hē′mə riz′əm, -hem′ə-), *n.* **1.** (*often cap.*) the theory of Euhemerus that the mythologies of the gods arose out of the deification of men. **2.** any interpretation of myths that attributes their origin to historical persons or events. —**eu·he′mer·ist,** *n.* —**eu·he′mer·is′tic,** *adj.* —**eu·he′mer·is′ti·cal·ly,** *adv.*

eu·he·mer·ize (yōō hē′mə rīz′, -hem′ə-), *v.t., v.i.,* **-ized, -iz·ing.** to treat or explain (myths) by euhemerism. Also, *esp. Brit.,* **euhemerise.**

Eu·he·mer·us (yōō hē′mər əs), *n.* fl. c300 B.C., Greek mythographer.

eu·la·chon (yōō′lə kon′), *n.* candlefish. [< Chinook *ulakan*]

Eu·ler (oi′lər; *Ger.* oi′ləʀ), *n.* **Le·on·hard** (*Ger.* lā′ôn härt′), 1707–83, Swiss mathematician.

eu·lo·gi·a (yōō lō′jē ə; *for 2 also Gk.* ev′lô yē′ä), *n.* **1.** Also called **antidoron, holy bread.** *Eastern Ch.* blessed bread given to the congregation during vespers or at the end of the liturgy. **2.** *Gk. Orth. Ch.* a blessing. [< MGk < Gk *eulogía.* See EULOGY]

eu·lo·gise (yōō′lə jīz′), *v.t.,* **-gised, -gis·ing.** *Chiefly Brit.* eulogize. —**eu′lo·gis′er,** *n.*

eu·lo·gist (yōō′lə jist), *n.* a person who eulogizes.

eu·lo·gis·tic (yōō′lə jis′tik), *adj.* pertaining to or containing eulogy; laudatory. Also, **eu′lo·gis′ti·cal.** —**eu′lo·gis′ti·cal·ly,** *adv.*

eu·lo·gi·um (yōō lō′jē əm), *n., pl.* **-gi·ums, -gi·a** (-jē ə). **1.** a eulogy. **2.** eulogistic language. [< ML = L *eu-* EU- + (*ē*)*logium* inscription on a tombstone]

eu·lo·gize (yōō′lə jīz′), *v.t.,* **-gized, -giz·ing.** to praise highly; speak or write a eulogy about. Also, *esp. Brit.,* **eulogise.** —**eu′lo·giz′er,** *n.* —**Syn.** extol, laud, panegyrize.

eu·lo·gy (yōō′lə jē), *n., pl.* **-gies. 1.** a speech or writing in praise of a person or thing, esp. a set oration in honor of a deceased person. **2.** high praise or commendation. [< LL *eulogia* (< Gk: praise, blessing; see EU-, -LOGY) and ML *eulogium* EULOGIUM]

Eu·mae·us (yōō mē′əs), *n.* (in the *Odyssey*) the faithful swineherd of Odysseus.

Eu·men·i·des (yōō men′i dēz′), *n.pl.* *Gk. Myth.* the Furies.

eu·nuch (yōō′nək), *n.* a castrated man, esp. formerly, one employed by Oriental rulers as a harem attendant. [ME *eunuk* < L *eunūch(us)* < Gk *eunoûchos* eunuch, chamberlain = *eun(ḗ)* bed, place of sleeping + *-ouchos* keeping (akin to *échein* to hold)]

eu·on·y·mus (yōō on′ə məs), *n.* any of several shrubs or small trees of the genus *Euonymus,* of northern temperate regions, usually bearing crimson or rose-colored capsules enclosing the seed. Also, **evonymus.** [< L, n. use of Gk *euṓnymos* of good name]

eu·pa·to·ri·um (yōō′pə tōr′ē əm, -tôr′-), *n.* any of numerous composite plants of the genus *Eupatorium,* comprising the bonesets or thoroughworts. [< NL < Gk *eupatórion* hemp agrimony, after *Eupátor,* surname of Mithridates, said to have first used it]

eu·pat·rid (yōō pa′trid, yōō′pə-), *n., pl.* **-pat·ri·dae** (-pa′tri dē′). one of the hereditary aristocrats of ancient Athens and other states of Greece, who at one time formed the ruling class. [< Gk *eupatríd(ēs),* lit., of a good father, of noble descent. See EU-, PATRI-, -ID[2]]

Eu·pen and Mal·mé·dy (*Fr.* œ pen′; *Fr.* mal mā dē′), a district on the Belgian-German border: ceded to Belgium 1919; reannexed to Germany 1940; now part of Belgium.

eu·pep·sia (yōō pep′shə, -sē ə), *n.* good digestion (opposed to *dyspepsia*). Also, **eu·pep·sy** (yōō′pep sē). [< NL < Gk: good digestion. See EU-, PEPSIN, -IA] —**eu·pep·tic** (yōō pep′tik), *adj.*

eu·phe·mise (yōō′fə mīz′), *v.t., v.i.,* **-mised, -mis·ing.** *Chiefly Brit.* euphemize. —**eu′phe·mis′er,** *n.*

eu·phe·mism (yōō′fə miz′əm), *n.* **1.** the substitution of a mild, indirect, or vague expression for one thought to be offensive, harsh, or blunt. **2.** the expression so substituted: *"To pass away" is a euphemism for "to die."* [< Gk *euphēmism(ós)* the use of words of good omen = *eu-* EU- + *phḗm(ē)* speaking, fame + *-ismos* -ISM] —**eu′phe·mist,** *n.* —**eu′phe·mis′tic, eu′phe·mis′ti·cal,** *adj.* —**eu′phe·mis′ti·cal·ly,** *adv.*

eu·phe·mize (yōō′fə mīz′), *v.,* **-mized, -miz·ing.** —*v.t.* **1.** to refer to by means of euphemism. —*v.i.* **2.** to employ euphemism. Also, *esp. Brit.,* **euphemise.** [< Gk *euphēmíz(ein)* (to) use words of good omen] —**eu′phe·miz′er,** *n.*

eu·phon·ic (yōō fon′ik), *adj.* pertaining to or characterized by euphony. Also, **eu·phon′i·cal.** —**eu·phon′i·cal·ly,** *adv.*

eu·pho·ni·ous (yōō fō′nē əs), *adj.* pleasant in sound; agreeable to the ear. —**eu·pho′ni·ous·ly,** *adv.* —**eu·pho′ni·ous·ness,** *n.*

eu·pho·nise (yōō′fə nīz′), *v.t.,* **-nised, -nis·ing.** *Chiefly Brit.* euphonize.

eu·pho·ni·um (yōō fō′nē əm), *n.* a brass musical instrument similar to the baritone tuba but with a wider bore and mellower tone. [EUPH(ONY + HARM)ONIUM]

Euphonium

eu·pho·nize (yōō′fə nīz′), *v.t.,* **-nized, -niz·ing.** to make euphonious. Also, *esp. Brit.,* **euphonise.**

eu·pho·ny (yōō′fə nē), *n., pl.* **-nies. 1.** agreeableness of sound; pleasing effect to the ear, esp. a pleasant-sounding or harmonious combination or succession of words: *the majestic euphony of Milton's poetry.* **2.** *Phonet.* harmoniousness or economy of utterance of speech sounds, supposedly resulting from combinatory phonetic change. [< LL *euphōnia* < Gk]

eu·phor·bi·a (yōō fôr′bē ə), *n.* any plant of the genus *Euphorbia,* comprising the spurges. [ME *euforbia* for L *euphorbea,* an African plant named after *Euphorbos,* a Greek physician]

eu·phor·bi·a·ceous (yōō fôr′bē ā′shəs), *adj.* belonging to the *Euphorbiaceae,* or spurge family of plants, comprising the spurges, the cascarilla, castor oil, and cassava plants, etc. [< NL *Euphorbiace(ae)* (see EUPHORBIA, -ACEAE) + -OUS]

eu·pho·ri·a (yo͞o fôr′ē ə, -fōr′-), *n.* *Psychol.* a feeling of well-being, esp. an exaggerated one having no basis in truth or reality. [< NL < Gk: state of well-being] —**eu·phor·ic** (yo͞o fôr′ik, -for′-), *adj.*

eu·pho·ri·ant (yo͞o fôr′ē ənt), *adj.* **1.** tending to induce euphoria. —*n.* **2.** a euphoriant drug.

eu·phra·sy (yo͞o′frə sē), *n., pl.* **-sies.** the eyebright, *Euphrasia officinalis.* [late ME *eufrasie* < ML *eufrasia* < Gk *euphrasia* cheerfulness (cf. *euphraínein* to cheer)]

Eu·phra·tes (yo͞o frā′tēz), *n.* a river in SW Asia, flowing from E Turkey through Syria and Iraq, joining the Tigris to form the Shatt-al-Arab near the Persian Gulf. 1700 mi. long. —**Eu·phra′te·an,** *adj.*

eu·phu·ism (yo͞o′fyo͞o iz′əm), *n.* **1.** an affected style in imitation of that of Lyly, fashionable in England about the end of the 16th century, characterized chiefly by long series of antitheses, frequent similes relating to fabulous natural history, alliteration, etc. **2.** any similar high-flown, ornate style of writing or speaking. **3.** an instance of such style or language. [after *Euphues,* main character in Lyly's works; see -ISM] —**eu′phu·ist,** *n.* —**eu′phu·is′tic, eu′phu·is′ti·cal,** *adj.* —**eu′phu·is′ti·cal·ly,** *adv.*

eu·plas·tic (yo͞o plas′tik), *adj.* *Physiol.* capable of being transformed into organized tissue. [< Gk *eúplast(os)* malleable + -IC]

eup·ne·a (yo͞op nē′ə), *n.* *Pathol.* easy or normal breathing (opposed to *dyspnea*). Also, **eup·noe′a.** [< NL *eupnoea* < Gk *eúpnoia* ease of breathing = *eu-* EU- + *-pno(os)* breathing + *-ia* -IA] —**eup·ne′ic, eup·noe′ic,** *adj.*

eu·po·tam·ic (yo͞o′pə tam′ik), *adj.* *Ecol.* (of a plant or animal) living or growing in fresh water.

Eur., **1.** Europe. **2.** European.

Eur·a·sia (yo͝o rā′zhə, -shə), *n.* Europe and Asia considered as a whole.

Eur·a·sian (yo͝o rā′zhən, -shən), *adj.* **1.** of or pertaining to Eurasia. **2.** of mixed European and Asian descent. —*n.* **3.** the offspring of a European and an Asian.

Eur·at·om (yo͝o rat′əm), *n.* an organization formed in 1957, comprising France, the Netherlands, Belgium, Luxembourg, Italy, and West Germany, for coordinated action in developing and marketing their nuclear resources. [*Eur(opean) Atom(ic Energy Community)*]

eu·re·ka (yo͝o rē′kə), *interj.* **1.** (*cap.*) I have found (it): motto of California. **2.** (used as an exclamation of triumph at a discovery.) [< Gk *heúrēka,* 1st person sing. perf. indic. act. of *heurískein* to find, discover; attributed to Archimedes on discovering the principle of specific gravity]

eu·rhyth·mic (yo͝o rith′mik), *adj.* **1.** characterized by a pleasing rhythm; harmoniously ordered or proportioned. **2.** of or pertaining to eurhythmics. Also, **eurythmic.** [EURHYTHM(Y) + -IC] —**eu·rhyth′mi·cal,** *adj.*

eu·rhyth·mics (yo͝o rith′miks), *n.* (*construed as sing. or pl.*) the art of interpreting in bodily movements the rhythm of musical compositions. Also, **eurythmics.** [see EURHYTHMIC, -ICS]

eu·rhyth·my (yo͝o rith′mē), *n.* rhythmical movement or order; harmonious motion or proportion. Also, **eurythmy.** [< L *eurythmia* < Gk *eurhythmía* good proportion, gracefulness. See EU-, RHYTHM, -Y[3]]

Eu·rip·i·des (yo͝o rip′i dēz′), *n.* c480–406? B.C., Greek dramatist. —**Eu·rip′i·de′an,** *adj.*

eu·ri·pus (yo͝o rī′pəs), *n., pl.* **-pi** (-pī). a strait, esp. one in which the flow of water is violent. [< L < Gk *eúripos* (applied esp. to the strait between Euboea and Boeotia) = *eu-* EU- + *-rīpos* rusher, akin to *ripḗ* rush]

Euro-, **1.** a combining form meaning "of or in Europe, esp. Western Europe": *Europort.* **2.** a combining form meaning "issued or circulated in Europe and usually denominated in a currency of the country of origin": *Eurobond; Eurosterling.* [< EURO(PEAN)]

Eu·roc·ly·don (yo͝o rok′li don′), *n.* a stormy northeast or north-northeast wind. [< Gk *euroklýdōn* = *Eûro(s)* EURUS + *klýdōn* wave, surge, cf. *klýzein* to dash against, wash]

Eu·ro·com·mu·nism (yo͝or′ō kom′yə niz′əm), *n.* a form of communism emerging in some West European nations (Spain, France, Italy, etc.) and claimed to be independent of the Communist party of the Soviet Union.

Eu·ro·dol·lars (yo͝or′ə dol′ərz), *n.pl.* U.S. dollars deposited abroad, esp. in Europe, and used as a medium of international credit, esp. to finance trade or investment.

Eu·ro·mar·ket (yo͝or′ō mär′kit), *n.* See **Common Market** (def. 1).

Eu·ro·mart (yo͝or′ə märt′), *n.* See **Common Market** (def. 1).

Eu·ro·pa (yo͝o rō′pə), *n.* *Class. Myth.* a sister of Cadmus who was abducted by Zeus in the form of a bull and taken to Crete, where she bore him Rhadamanthys, Minos, and Sarpedon.

Eu·rope (yo͝or′əp), *n.* a continent in the W part of Eurasia, separated from Asia by the Ural Mountains on the E and the Caucasus Mountains and the Black and Caspian seas on the SE. In British usage, *Europe* sometimes contrasts with *England.* Excluding the Soviet Union and Turkey, 473,000,000; ab. 3,754,000 sq. mi.

Eu·ro·pe·an (yo͝or′ə pē′ən), *adj.* **1.** of or pertaining to Europe or its inhabitants. **2.** native to or derived from Europe. —*n.* **3.** a native or inhabitant of Europe. **4.** a person of European descent. [< L *Eurōpae(us)* (see EUROPE, -EOUS) + -AN]

Europe′an Atom′ic En′ergy Commu′nity. See **Euratom.**

Europe′an Econom′ic Commu′nity, official name of the **Common Market.**

Eu·ro·pe·an·ise (yo͝or′ə pē′ə nīz′), *v.t.,* **-ised, -is·ing.** *Chiefly Brit.* Europeanize. —**Eu′ro·pe′an·i·sa′tion,** *n.*

Eu·ro·pe·an·ism (yo͝or′ə pē′ə niz′əm), *n.* **1.** European characteristics, ideas, methods, sympathies, etc. **2.** a European trait or practice. **3.** belief in or advocacy of the unification of Europe.

Eu·ro·pe·an·ize (yo͝or′ə pē′ə nīz′), *v.t.,* **-ized, -iz·ing.** to make European. Also, *esp. Brit.,* **Europeanise.** —**Eu′ro·pe′an·i·za′tion,** *n.*

Europe′an plan′, *U.S.* a hotel rate covering only lodging and service. Cf. **American plan.**

Europe′an Recov′ery Pro′gram, a plan for aiding the European nations in economic recovery after World War II, proposed by U.S. Secretary of State George C. Marshall in 1947 and implemented in 1948 under the Economic Cooperation Administration. Also called **Marshall Plan.**

eu·ro·pi·um (yo͝o rō′pē əm), *n.* *Chem.* a rare-earth metallic element. *Symbol:* Eu; *at. wt.:* 151.96; *at. no.:* 63. [named after EUROPE; see -IUM]

Eu·rus (yo͝or′əs), *n.* the ancient Greek personification of the east or southeast wind. Cf. **Volturnus.**

eury-, a combining form meaning "broad," "wide": *eurythermal.* [< Gk, comb. form of *eurýs* wide]

Eu·ry·a·le (yo͝o rī′ə lē′), *n.* *Class. Myth.* one of the three Gorgons.

Eu·ryd·i·ce (yo͝o rid′i sē′), *n.* *Class. Myth.* the wife of Orpheus.

Eu·rys·the·us (yo͝o ris′thē əs, -tho͞os), *n.* *Class. Myth.* a king of Mycenae and cousin of Hercules, upon whom he imposed 12 labors. Cf. **labors of Hercules.**

eu·ry·ther·mal (yo͝or′ə thûr′məl), *adj.* *Ecol.* (of a plant or animal) able to withstand wide variations in temperature. Also, **eu′ry·ther′mic, eu′ry·ther′mous.** Cf. **stenothermal.**

eu·ryth·mic (yo͝o rith′mik), *adj.* eurhythmic. —**eu·ryth′mi·cal,** *adj.*

eu·ryth·mics (yo͝o rith′miks), *n.* (*construed as sing. or pl.*) eurhythmics.

eu·ryth·my (yo͝o rith′mē), *n.* eurhythmy.

Eu·se·bi·us (yo͞o sē′bē əs), *n.* pope A.D. 309 or 310.

Euse′bius of Caesare′a, (*Pamphili*) A.D. 263?–c340, Christian theologian and historian: Bishop of Caesarea c315–c340.

Eu·sta′chian tube′ (yo͞o stā′shən, -stā′kē ən), *Anat.* a canal extending from the middle ear to the pharynx; auditory canal. [named after B. EUSTACHIO; see -AN]

E·u·sta·chio (e′o͞o stä′kyô), *n.* **Bar·to·lom·me·o** (bär′tô-lôm me′ô), 1524?–1574, Italian anatomist. Latin, **Eu·sta·chi·us** (yo͞o stā′kē əs).

eu·sta·cy (yo͞o′stə sē), *n., pl.* **-cies.** *Geol.* a world-wide change in sea level, usually caused by the advance or retreat of continental glaciers. [EU- + *-stacy* for STASIS] —**eu·stat·ic** (yo͞o stat′ik), *adj.* —**eu·stat′i·cal·ly,** *adv.*

eu·tax·y (yo͞o′tak sē, yo͞o tak′sē), *n.* good or right order. [< Gk *eutaxía* = *eútakt(os)* well arranged (see EU-, TACTIC) + *-ia* -Y[3]]

eu·tec·tic (yo͞o tek′tik), *Physical Chem.* —*adj.* **1.** of greatest fusibility: said of an alloy or mixture whose melting point is lower than that of any other alloy or mixture of the same ingredients. **2.** noting or pertaining to such a mixture or its properties: *a eutectic melting point.* —*n.* **3.** a eutectic substance. [< Gk *eútēkt(os)* easily melted, dissolved (*eu-* EU- + *tēktós* melted) + -IC]

eu·tec·toid (yo͞o tek′toid), *adj.* **1.** resembling a eutectic. —*n.* **2.** a eutectoid alloy.

Eu·ter·pe (yo͞o tûr′pē), *n.* *Class. Myth.* the Muse of music and lyric poetry. —**Eu·ter′pe·an,** *adj.*

eu·tha·na·sia (yo͞o′thə nā′zhə, -zhē ə, -zē ə), *n.* **1.** Also called **mercy killing.** the act of putting to death painlessly a person suffering from an incurable and painful disease or condition. **2.** painless death. [< NL < Gk: an easy death = *eu-* EU- + *thánat(os)* death + *-ia* -Y[3]] —**eu·tha·na·sic** (yo͞o′thə nā′zik), *adj.*

eu·then·ics (yo͞o then′iks), *n.* (*construed as sing.*) a science concerned with bettering the condition of human beings through the improvement of their environment. [< Gk *euthēn(ein)* (to) be well off, prosper + -ICS] —**eu·then′ist,** *n.*

eu·the·ri·an (yo͞o thēr′ē ən), *adj.* **1.** belonging or pertaining to the group *Eutheria,* comprising the placental mammals. —*n.* **2.** a eutherian animal. [< NL *Euthēri(a)* (< Gk *eu-* EU- + *thēría,* pl. of *thēríon* wild beast) + -AN]

Eu·tych·i·a·nus (yo͞o tik′ē ā′nəs), *n.* **Saint,** died A.D. 283, pope 275–283. Also, **Eu·tych·i·an** (yo͞o tik′ē ən).

eux·e·nite (yo͞ok′sə nīt′), *n.* a brownish-black mineral containing yttrium, columbium, titanium, uranium, etc. [< Gk *eúxen(os)* kind to strangers, hospitable (see EU-, XENO-) + -ITE[1]]

Eux′ine Sea′ (yo͞ok′sin, -sīn). See **Black Sea.**

EV, electron-volt. Also, **ev**

E.V., (of the Bible) English Version.

EVA, extravehicular activity.

e·vac·u·ate (i vak′yo͞o āt′), *v.,* **-at·ed, -at·ing.** —*v.t.* **1.** to leave empty; vacate. **2.** to remove (persons or things) from a place, esp. for reasons of safety. **3.** to remove residents from (a city, town, area, etc.), esp. for reasons of safety. **4.** *Mil.* **a.** to remove (troops, wounded soldiers, civilians, etc.) from a place, as a combat area. **b.** to withdraw from or quit (a town, fort, etc., that has been occupied). **5.** *Physiol.* to discharge or eject, esp. from the bowels. **6.** to produce a vacuum in. **7.** to deprive. —*v.i.* **8.** to leave a place because of military or other threats. **9.** to void; defecate. [ME < L *ēvacuāt(us)* (ptp. of *ēvacuāre* to empty out = *ē-* E- + *vacuāre* to empty); see -ATE[1]] —**e·vac′u·a′tor,** *n.*

e·vac·u·a·tion (i vak′yo͞o ā′shən), *n.* **1.** the act or process of evacuating. **2.** the condition of being evacuated; discharge or expulsion, as of contents. **3.** *Physiol.* discharge, as of waste matter through the excretory passages, esp. from the bowels. **4.** that which is evacuated or discharged. **5.** the removal of persons or things from an endangered area. **6.** *Mil.* withdrawal or removal of troops, civilians, etc. [late ME *evacuacioun* < medical L *ēvacuātiōn-* (s. of *ēvacuātiō*)] —**e·vac·u·a·tive** (i vak′yo͞o ā′tiv), *adj.*

e·vac·u·ee (i vak′yo͞o ē′, i vak′yo͞o ē′), *n.* a person who is withdrawn or removed from a place of danger. [< F *évacué,* ptp. of *évacuer* to EVACUATE; see -EE]

e·vade (i vād′), *v.,* **e·vad·ed, e·vad·ing.** —*v.t.* **1.** to escape from by trickery or cleverness: *to evade one's pursuers.* **2.** to get around by trickery: *to evade the law.* **3.** to avoid doing or fulfilling: *to evade a duty.* **4.** to avoid answering directly: *to evade a question.* **5.** to elude; escape: *The solution evaded him.* —*v.i.* **6.** to practice evasion. **7.** to elude or get away by craft or slyness. [< L *ēvād(ere)* (to) pass over, go out = *ē-* E- + *vādere* to go, walk] —**e·vad′er,** *n.* —**e·vad′ing·ly,** *adv.* —**Syn. 1.** dodge. **3.** See **escape. 6.** prevaricate, equivocate, quibble.

e·vag·i·nate (i vaj′ə nāt′), *v.t.*, **-nat·ed, -nat·ing.** to turn inside out, or cause to protrude by eversion, as a tubular organ. [< LL *ēvāgīnāt(us)* (ptp. of *ēvāgīnāre*) unsheathed] —**e·vag′i·na′tion,** *n.*

e·val·u·ate (i val′yo͞o āt′), *v.t.*, **-at·ed, -at·ing. 1.** to determine or set the value or amount of; appraise: *to evaluate property; to evaluate an argument.* **2.** *Math.* to ascertain the numerical value of (a function, relation, etc.). [back formation from EVALUATION < F] —**e·val′u·a′tion,** *n.* —**e·val′u·a′tive,** *adj.* —**e·val′u·a′tor,** *n.*

ev·a·nesce (ev′ə nes′, ev′ə nes′), *v.i.*, **-nesced, -nesc·ing.** to disappear gradually; vanish; fade away. [< L *ēvānēsc(ere)* (to) VANISH] —**ev′a·nes′cence,** *n.*

ev·a·nes·cent (ev′ə nes′ənt), *adj.* **1.** vanishing; passing away; fleeting. **2.** tending to become imperceptible; scarcely perceptible. [< L *ēvānēscent-* (s. of *ēvānēscēns*) vanishing, disappearing] —**ev′a·nes′cent·ly,** *adv.*

Evang., Evangelical.

e·van·gel[1] (i van′jəl), *n.* **1.** gospel (def. 2). **2.** (*usually cap.*) any of the four Gospels. **3.** doctrine taken as a guide or regarded as of prime importance. **4.** good news or tidings. [ME < eccl. L *ēvangel(ium)* < Gk *euangélion* good news (see EU-, ANGEL); r. ME *evangile* < MF]

e·van·gel[2] (i van′jəl), *n.* an evangelist. [< LL *evangelus* < Gk *euángel(os)* (adj.) bringing good news. See EVANGEL]

e·van·gel·i·cal (ē′van jel′i kəl, ev′ən-), *adj.* Also, **e′van·gel′ic. 1.** pertaining to or in keeping with the gospel and its teachings. **2.** belonging to or designating the Christian churches that emphasize the teachings and authority of the Scriptures, esp. of the New Testament, in opposition to the institutional authority of the church itself. **3.** pertaining to certain Protestant movements that stress the importance of personal experience of guilt for sin, and of reconciliation to God through Christ. **4.** marked by ardent or zealous enthusiasm for a cause. **5.** evangelistic. —*n.* **6.** an adherent of evangelical doctrines. [< LL *ēvangelic(us)* (< eccl. Gk *euangelikós*; see EVANGEL[1], -IC) + -AL[1]] —**e′van·gel′i·cal·ly,** *adv.*

e·van·gel·i·cal·ism (ē′van jel′i kə liz′əm, ev′ən-), *n.* **1.** evangelical doctrines or principles. **2.** adherence to evangelical principles or doctrines or to an evangelical church or party.

e·van·ge·lise (i van′jə līz′), *v.t., v.i.*, **-lised, -lis·ing.** *Chiefly Brit.* evangelize. —**e·van′ge·li·sa′tion,** *n.* —**e·van′ge·lis′er,** *n.*

e·van·ge·lism (i van′jə liz′əm), *n.* **1.** the preaching or promulgation of the gospel; the work of an evangelist. **2.** evangelicalism. **3.** missionary zeal, purpose, or activity.

e·van·ge·list (i van′jə list), *n.* **1.** a preacher of the gospel. **2.** (*cap.*) any of the writers (Matthew, Mark, Luke, and John) of the four Gospels. **3.** a revivalist. **4.** an occasional or itinerant preacher. **5.** (*cap.*) *Morman Ch.* a patriarch. **6.** a person marked by zealous enthusiasm for or support of any cause. [ME *evangeliste* < L *evangelis(ta)* < Gk *euangelistēs*]

e·van·ge·lis·tic (i van′jə lis′tik), *adj.* **1.** pertaining to evangelists or to preachers of the gospel. **2.** evangelical. **3.** seeking to evangelize; striving to convert sinners. **4.** designed or fitted to evangelize. **5.** (*often cap.*) of or pertaining to the four Evangelists. —**e·van′ge·lis′ti·cal·ly,** *adv.*

e·van·ge·lize (i van′jə līz′), *v.*, **-lized, -liz·ing.** —*v.t.* **1.** to preach the gospel to. **2.** to convert to Christianity. —*v.i.* **3.** to preach the gospel; act as an evangelist. Also, *esp. Brit.*, **evangelise.** [ME *evangelise(n)* < eccl. L *ēvangelizāre* < LGk *euangelízesthai*] —**e·van′ge·li·za′tion,** *n.* —**e·van′ge·liz′er,** *n.*

e·van·ish (i van′ish), *v.i. Literary.* **1.** to vanish or disappear. **2.** to cease to be. [ME *evanissh(en)* < MF *esvaniss-*, extended s. of *esvanir.* See E-, EVANESCE, VANISH]

Ev·ans (ev′ənz), *n.* **1. Sir Arthur John,** 1851–1941, English archaeologist. **2. Herbert Mc·Lean** (mə klān′), 1882–1971, U.S. embryologist and anatomist. **3. Mary Ann.** See **Eliot, George. 4. Ru·dulph** (ro͞o′dulf), 1878–1960, U.S. sculptor.

Ev·ans·ton (ev′ən stən), *n.* a city in NE Illinois, on Lake Michigan, near Chicago. 79,808 (1970).

Ev·ans·ville (ev′ənz vil′), *n.* a city in SW Indiana, on the Ohio River. 138,764 (1970).

e·vap·o·rate (i vap′ə rāt′), *v.*, **-rat·ed, -rat·ing.** —*v.i.* **1.** to turn to vapor; pass off in vapor. **2.** to give off moisture. **3.** to disappear; vanish; fade: *Her hopes evaporated.* —*v.t.* **4.** to convert into a gaseous state or vapor: *The sun evaporated the dew.* **5.** to extract moisture or liquid from, as by heat, so as to make dry or to reduce to a denser state: *to evaporate fruit.* **6.** to cause to disappear or fade; dissipate. [late ME (ptp.) < L *ēvapōrāt(us)* (ptp. of *ēvapōrāre*) dispersed in vapor] —**e·vap′o·ra′tor,** *n.* —**Syn. 1.** vaporize. **3.** evanesce. **5.** EVAPORATE, DEHYDRATE, DRY mean to abstract moisture from. To EVAPORATE is to remove moisture by means of heat, forced ventilation, or the like, and thus to produce condensation or shriveling: *to evaporate milk, sliced apples.* To DEHYDRATE is to remove all vestiges of moisture: *One may dehydrate foods in order to make them easier to preserve and to transport.* To DRY may mean to wipe moisture off the surface or to withdraw moisture by natural means, such as exposure to air or heat: *to dry a dish, clothes.*

evap′orated milk′, thick, unsweetened milk made by removing some of the water from whole milk.

e·vap·o·ra·tion (i vap′ə rā′shən), *n.* **1.** the act or process of evaporating. **2.** the state of being evaporated. **3.** *Archaic.* matter or the quantity of matter evaporated or passed off in vapor. [ME *evaporacioun* < L *ēvapōrātiōn-* (s. of *ēvapōrātiō*)] —**e·vap·o·ra·tive** (i vap′ə rā′tiv, -ər ə tiv), *adj.*

e·vap·o·rim·e·ter (i vap′ə rim′i tər), *n.* atmometer. Also, **e·vap·o·rom·e·ter** (i vap′ə rom′i tər). Also called **evapora′tion gauge′.**

Ev·a·ris·tus (ev′ə ris′təs), *n.* **Saint,** died A.D. 105, pope 97–105.

Ev·arts (ev′ərts), *n.* **William Maxwell,** 1818–1901, U.S. lawyer and statesman.

e·va·sion (i vā′zhən), *n.* **1.** the act or an instance of escaping, avoiding, or shirking something: *evasion of one's duty; his evasion of responsibilities.* **2.** the avoiding of an argument, accusation, question, or the like, as by a subterfuge: *The old political boss was notorious for his practice of evasion.* **3.** a means of evading; subterfuge; an excuse or trick to avoid or get around something. **4.** physical or mental escape: *summertime evasions of the city.* [late ME < L *ēvāsiōn-* (s. of *ēvāsiō*) = *ēvās(us)* gone out (ptp. of *ēvādere*; see EVADE) + *-iōn-* -ION] —**Syn. 1.** avoidance.

e·va·sive (i vā′siv), *adj.* **1.** tending or seeking to evade; characterized by evasion: *an evasive answer.* **2.** elusive or evanescent. [EVAS(ION) + -IVE] —**e·va′sive·ly,** *adv.* —**e·va′sive·ness,** *n.*

eve (ēv), *n.* **1.** the evening or the day before a holiday, church festival, or any date or event: *Christmas Eve; the eve of election.* **2.** the period preceding or leading up to any event, crisis, etc. **3.** the evening. [ME; var. of EVEN[2]]

Eve (ēv), *n.* the first woman. Gen. 3:20.

e·vec·tion (i vek′shən), *n. Astron.* a periodic irregularity in the moon's motion, caused by the attraction of the sun. [< L *ēvectiōn-* (s. of *ēvectiō*) a going upwards, flight = *ēvect(us)* (ptp. of *ēvehere*) carried forth, moved forth + *-iōn-* -ION] —**e·vec′tion·al,** *adj.*

Ev·e·lyn (ev′ə lin, ēv′lin), *n.* **John,** 1620–1706, English diarist.

e·ven[1] (ē′vən), *adj.* **1.** level; flat; without irregularities; smooth: *an even surface.* **2.** on the same level; in the same plane or line; parallel: *even with the ground.* **3.** free from variations or fluctuations; regular: *even motion.* **4.** uniform in action, character, or quality: *an even color.* **5.** equal in measure or quantity: *even quantities of two substances.* **6.** divisible by two, as a number (opposed to *odd*). **7.** denoted by such a number: *the even pages of a book.* **8.** exactly expressible in integers, or in tens, hundreds, etc., without fractional parts: *an even mile; an even hundred.* **9.** equally balanced or divided; equal: *Check to see if the scales are even.* **10.** leaving no balance of debt on either side; square. **11.** calm; placid; not easily excited or angered: *an even temper.* **12.** equitable, impartial, or fair: *an even bargain.* —*adv.* **13.** evenly: *The road ran even over the fields.* **14.** still; yet (used to emphasize a comparative): *even more suitable.* **15.** (used to suggest that something mentioned as a possibility constitutes an extreme case or an unlikely instance): *Even the slightest noise disturbs him. Even if he attends, he may not participate.* **16.** just (used to emphasize occurrence, coincidence, or simultaneousness of occurrences): *Even as he lay dying, they argued over his estate.* **17.** fully or quite: *even to death.* **18.** indeed (used as an intensive for stressing the identity or truth of something): *He is willing, even eager, to do it.* **19.** *Archaic.* exactly or precisely: *It was even so.* **20. break even,** to have one's profits equal one's losses; neither gain nor lose. **21. get even,** to be revenged; retaliate. —*v.t.* **22.** to make even; level; smooth. **23.** to place in an even state as to claim or obligation; balance (often fol. by *up*): *to even up accounts.* —*v.i.* **24.** to become even: *The odds evened before the race.* [ME; OE *efen;* c. Goth *ibns,* OHG *eban,* ON *jafn* even, equal] —**e′ven·ly,** *adv.* —**e′ven·ness,** *n.* —**Syn. 1.** See **level. 11.** tranquil, peaceful.

e·ven[2] (ē′vən), *n. Archaic.* evening; eve. [ME; OE *ǣfen;* akin to G *Abend,* OFris *āvond*]

e·ven·fall (ē′vən fôl′), *n.* the beginning of evening.

e·ven-hand·ed (ē′vən han′did), *adj.* impartial; equitable. —**e′ven-hand′ed·ly,** *adv.* —**e′ven-hand′ed·ness,** *n.*

eve·ning (ēv′ning), *n.* **1.** the latter part of the day and early part of the night. **2.** the period from sunset to bedtime. **3.** *Chiefly Southern and Midland U.S.* the time between noon and sunset, including the afternoon and twilight. **4.** any concluding or declining period: *the evening of life.* **5.** an evening's reception or entertainment: *Her evenings at home were extremely fashionable.* —*adj.* **6.** of or pertaining to evening. **7.** occurring or seen in the evening: *the evening mist.* [ME; OE *ǣfnung* = *ǣfn-* (s. of *ǣfnian*) draw toward evening + *-ung* -ING[1]] —**Syn. 1.** eventide, dusk, twilight.

eve′ning dress′, formal or semiformal attire for evening wear. Cf. **morning dress.**

eve′ning gown′, a woman's formal dress, usually having a floor-length skirt. Also called **gown.**

Eve′ning Prayer′, *Anglican Ch.* evensong (def. 1).

eve′ning prim′rose, 1. an onagraceous plant, *Oenothera biennis,* having yellow flowers that open at nightfall. **2.** any of various plants of the same or related genera.

eve·nings (ēv′ningz), *adv.* in or during the evening regularly: *He worked days and played evenings.*

eve′ning star′, a bright planet, esp. Venus, seen in the west directly after sunset. [OE *ǣfensteorra*]

e′ven mon′ey, equal odds in a wager.

e·ven·song (ē′vən sông′, -song′), *n.* **1.** (*usually cap.*) Also called **Evening Prayer.** *Anglican Ch.* a form of worship to be said or sung at evening. **2.** vesper (def. 3c). **3.** *Archaic.* evening. [ME; OE *ǣfensang*]

e·vent (i vent′), *n.* **1.** anything that happens or is regarded as happening; an occurrence, esp. one of some importance. **2.** the outcome, issue, or result of anything; consequence. **3.** something that occurs in a certain place during a particular interval of time. **4.** *Sports.* any of the contests in a program. **5. at all events,** regardless of what happens; in any case. Also, **in any event. 6. in the event,** if it should happen; in case: *In the event of rain, the party will be held indoors.* [< L *ēvent(us)* occurrence, outcome = *ēvent-* (ptp. s. of *ēvenīre* to occur, come out) + *-us* n. suffix (4th decl.)] —**Syn. 1.** happening, case, circumstance. EVENT, EPISODE, INCIDENT, OCCURRENCE are terms for a happening. An EVENT is usually an important happening, esp. one that comes out of and is connected with previous happenings: *historical events.* An EPISODE is one of a progressive series of happenings, frequently distinct from the main course of events but arising naturally from them and having a continuity and interest of its own: *an episode in one's life.* An

INCIDENT is usually a happening that takes place in connection with an event or a series of events of greater importance: *an amusing incident in a play.* An OCCURRENCE is something (usually of an ordinary nature) that happens, having no particular connection with (or causation by) antecedent happenings: *His arrival was an unexpected occurrence.*

e·ven-tem·pered (ē′vən tem′pərd), *adj.* not easily ruffled or disturbed; calm: *He is one of the most even-tempered individuals I know.*

e·vent·ful (i vent′fəl), *adj.* **1.** full of events or incidents, esp. of a striking character. **2.** having important results; momentous. —**e·vent′ful·ly,** *adv.* —**e·vent′ful·ness,** *n.*

e·ven·tide (ē′vən tīd′), *n.* evening. [ME; OE *ǣfentīd*]

e·ven·tu·al (i ven′cho͞o əl), *adj.* **1.** happening at some indefinite future time or after a series of occurrences; ultimate: *His mistakes led to his eventual dismissal.* **2.** *Archaic.* depending upon uncertain events; contingent. [modeled on F *éventuel.* See EVENT, -AL[1]]

e·ven·tu·al·i·ty (i ven′cho͞o al′i tē), *n., pl.* **-ties. 1.** a contingent event; a possible occurrence or circumstance: *Rain is an eventuality to be reckoned with in planning the picnic.* **2.** the state or fact of being eventual; contingent character.

e·ven·tu·al·ly (i ven′cho͞o ə lē), *adv.* finally; ultimately; at some time: *Eventually we all must die.*

e·ven·tu·ate (i ven′cho͞o āt′), *v.i.,* **-at·ed, -at·ing. 1.** to have issue; result. **2.** to be the issue or outcome; come about. [< L *eventu(s)* EVENT + -ATE[1]] —**e·ven′tu·a′tion,** *n.*

ev·er (ev′ər), *adv.* **1.** at any time: *Have you ever seen anything like it?* **2.** in any possible case; by any chance; at all: *How did you ever manage to do it?* **3.** continuously: *ever since then.* **4.** at all times; always: *He is ever ready to find fault.* [ME; OE *ǣfre;* perh. akin to AY[1], and to Goth *aiws* time] —**Syn. 4.** constantly. See **always.** —**Ant. 4.** never.

ev·er·bear·ing (ev′ər bâr′ing), *adj.* continuously producing or bringing forth, as a tree or shrub.

ev·er·bloom·ing (ev′ər blo͞o′ming), *adj.* in bloom through most of the growing months of the year.

Ev·er·est (ev′ər ist), *n.* **Mount,** a mountain in S Asia, on the boundary between Nepal and Tibet, in the Himalayas: the highest mountain in the world. 29,028 ft.

Ev·er·ett (ev′ər it, ev′rit), *n.* **1. Edward,** 1794–1865, U.S. statesman, orator, and writer. **2.** a city in E Massachusetts, near Boston. 42,485 (1970). **3.** a seaport in NW Washington on Puget Sound. 53,622 (1970).

ev·er·glade (ev′ər glād′), *n. Southern U.S.* a tract of low, swampy land characterized by clumps of tall grass and numerous branching waterways.

Ev·er·glades (ev′ər glādz′), *n.* (*construed as pl.*) a swampy and partly forested region in S Florida, mostly S of Lake Okeechobee. Over 5000 sq. mi.

Ev′erglades Na′tional Park′, a national park in the Everglades region of S Florida. 2186 sq. mi.

Ev·er·good (ev′ər go͝od′), *n.* **Philip** (*Philip Blashki*), 1901–1973, U.S. painter.

ev·er·green (ev′ər grēn′), *adj.* **1.** (of trees, shrubs, etc.) having green leaves throughout the entire year, the leaves of the past season not being shed until after the new foliage has been completely formed. —*n.* **2.** an evergreen plant. **3. evergreens,** evergreen twigs or branches used for decoration.

Ev′ergreen Park′, a city in NE Illinois, near Chicago. 25,921 (1970).

Ev′ergreen State′, the state of Washington (used as a nickname).

ev·er·last·ing (ev′ər las′ting, -lä′sting), *adj.* **1.** lasting forever; eternal. **2.** lasting or continuing for an indefinitely long time: *the everlasting hills.* **3.** incessant; constantly recurring. **4.** wearisome; tedious: *his everlasting puns.* —*n.* **5.** eternal duration; eternity: *What is the span of one life compared with the everlasting?* **6. the Everlasting,** the Eternal Being; God. **7.** Also called **ev′erlast′ing flow′er.** any of various plants or flowers which retain their shape, color, etc., when dried, as certain asteraceous plants of the genus *Helichrysum,* or various cudweeds of the genus *Gnaphalium.* [ME] —**ev′er·last′ing·ly,** *adv.* —**ev′er·last′ing·ness,** *n.* —**Syn. 1.** See **eternal.**

ev·er·more (ev′ər mōr′, -môr′), *adv.* **1.** always; continually; forever. **2.** at all future times; henceforth. [ME *evermor*]

e·ver·si·ble (i vûr′sə bəl), *adj.* capable of being everted. [< L *ēvers(us)* (ptp. of *ēvertere;* see EVERT) overturned, overthrown + -IBLE]

e·ver·sion (i vûr′zhən, -shən), *n.* a turning or being turned outward or inside out. [late ME < L *ēversiōn-* (s. of *ēversiō*)]

e·vert (i vûrt′), *v.t.* to turn outward or inside out. [ME < L *ēvert(ere)* (to) overturn = *ē-* E- + *vertere* to turn]

e·ver·tor (i vûr′tər), *n. Anat.* a muscle that turns a part toward the outside.

ev·er·y (ev′rē), *adj.* **1.** being one of an aggregate or series taken collectively; each: *We go there every day.* **2.** all possible; the greatest possible degree of: *every prospect of success.* **3. every bit,** *Informal.* in every respect; completely: *This is every bit as good as she says it is.* **4. every now and then,** on occasion; from time to time. Also, **every once in a while, every so often. 5. every other,** every second; every alternate: *milk deliveries every other day.* **6. every which way,** *Informal.* in all directions; in disorganized fashion. [ME *every, everich,* OE *ǣfre ǣlc* EVER, EACH] —**Syn. 1.** See **each.**

ev·er·y·bod·y (ev′rē bod′ē), *pron.* every person.

ev·er·y·day (ev′rē dā′), *adj.* **1.** of or pertaining to every day; daily: *an everyday occurrence.* **2.** of or for ordinary days, as contrasted with Sundays or special occasions: *everyday clothes.* **3.** ordinary; commonplace: *a placid, everyday scene.* [ME *everydayes*] —**eve′ry·day′ness,** *n.*

ev·er·y·man (ev′rē man′), *n.* **1.** an ordinary man; the common man. —*pron.* **2.** everybody; everyone.

ev·er·y·one (ev′rē wun′, wən), *pron.* every person; everybody. [ME *everichon*] —**Usage.** See **anyone.**

ev·er·y·place (ev′rē plās′), *adv.* everywhere. —**Usage.** See **anyplace.**

ev·er·y·thing (ev′rē thing′), *pron.* **1.** every particular of an aggregate or total; all. **2.** something extremely important: *This news means everything to us.* —*n.* **3.** that which is extremely important: *Money is his everything.* [ME]

ev·er·y·way (ev′rē wā′), *adv.* in every way; in every direction, manner, or respect: *They tried everyway to find the information.*

ev·er·y·where (ev′rē hwâr′, -wâr′), *adv.* in every place or part; in all places. [ME *everihwer,* OE *ǣfre* EVER + *gehwǣr* (*ge-* Y- + *hwǣr* WHERE)] —**Usage.** See **anyplace.**

Eve·sham (ēv′shəm, ē′shəm, ē′səm), *n.* a town in SE Worcestershire, in W England: battle 1265. 13,847.

e·vict (i vikt′), *v.t.* **1.** to expel (a person, esp. a tenant) from land, a building, etc., by legal process. **2.** to recover (property, titles, etc.) by virtue of superior legal title. [ME *evict(en)* < LL *ēvict(us)* having recovered one's property by law, L: overcome, conquered, ptp. of *ēvincere;* see EVINCE] —**e·vic′tion,** *n.* —**e·vic′tor,** *n.*

e·vict·ee (i vik tē′, i vik′tē), *n.* a person who has been evicted.

ev·i·dence (ev′i dəns), *n., v.,* **-denced, -denc·ing.** —*n.* **1.** ground for belief; that which tends to prove or disprove something; proof. **2.** something that makes evident; an indication or sign: *His flushed look was visible evidence of his fever.* **3.** *Law.* data presented to a court or jury in proof of the facts in issue and which may include the testimony of witnesses, records, documents, or objects. **4. in evidence,** plainly visible; conspicuous: *The first signs of spring are in evidence.* —*v.t.* **5.** to make evident or clear; show clearly; manifest: *to evidence one's approval.* **6.** to support by evidence: *He evidenced his accusation with incriminating letters.* [ME < MF < LL *ēvidentia*]

—**Syn. 3.** information, deposition, affidavit. EVIDENCE, EXHIBIT, TESTIMONY, PROOF refer to information furnished in a legal investigation to support a contention. EVIDENCE is any information so given, whether furnished by witnesses or derived from documents or from any other source: *Hearsay evidence is not admitted in a trial.* An EXHIBIT in law is a document or article that is presented in court as evidence: *The signed contract is Exhibit A.* TESTIMONY is usually evidence given by witnesses under oath: *The jury listened carefully to the testimony.* PROOF is evidence that is so complete and convincing as to put a conclusion beyond reasonable doubt: *proof of the innocence of the accused.* **5.** demonstrate.

ev·i·dent (ev′i dənt), *adj.* plain or clear to the sight or understanding: *His frown made it evident to all that he was displeased.* [ME < L *ēvident-* (s. of *ēvidēns*) = *ē-* E- + *vident-* (s. of *vidēns*) seeing, prp. of *vidēre* to see; see -ENT] —**Syn.** obvious, manifest, palpable, patent. See **apparent.**

ev·i·den·tial (ev′i den′shəl), *adj.* noting, pertaining to, serving as, or based on evidence. [< LL *ēvidenti(a)* (see EVIDENCE) + -AL[1]] —**ev′i·den′tial·ly,** *adv.*

ev·i·dent·ly (ev′i dənt lē; *for emphasis* ev′i dent′lē), *adv.* obviously; unquestionably. [ME] —**Syn.** See **clearly.**

e·vil (ē′vəl), *adj.* **1.** morally wrong; immoral; wicked: *evil deeds; an evil life.* **2.** harmful; injurious: *evil laws.* **3.** characterized or accompanied by misfortune or suffering; unfortunate; disastrous: *to be fallen on evil days.* **4.** due to actual or imputed bad conduct or character: *an evil reputation.* **5.** marked by anger, irritability, irascibility, etc.: *He is known for his evil disposition.* **6. the evil one,** the devil; Satan. —*n.* **7.** that which is evil; evil quality, intention, or conduct: *to choose the lesser of two evils.* **8.** the force in nature that governs and gives rise to wickedness and sin. **9.** the wicked or immoral part of someone or something: *The evil in his nature has destroyed the good.* **10.** harm; mischief; misfortune: *to wish one evil.* **11.** anything causing injury or harm: *Tobacco is considered by some to be an evil.* **12.** a disease, as king's evil. —*adv.* **13.** in an evil manner; badly; ill: *It went evil with him.* [ME *evel, evil,* OE *yfel;* c. Goth *ubils,* OHG *ubil,* G *übel,* OFris, MD *evel*] —**e′vil·ly,** *adv.* —**e′vil·ness,** *n.* —**Syn. 1.** sinful, iniquitous, depraved, base, vile, nefarious. See **bad**[1]. **2.** pernicious, destructive. **7.** wickedness, depravity, iniquity, unrighteousness, corruption, baseness. —**Ant. 1.** righteous.

e·vil·do·er (ē′vəl do͞o′ər, ē′vəl do͞o′ər), *n.* a person who does evil or wrong. [ME] —**e·vil·do·ing** (ē′vəl do͞o′ing, ē′vəl do͞o′ing), *n.*

e′vil eye′, the power, superstitiously attributed to certain persons, of inflicting injury or bad luck by a look. —**e′vil-eyed′,** *adj.*

e·vil-mind·ed (ē′vəl mīn′did), *adj.* **1.** having an evil disposition or harmful, malicious intentions. **2.** disposed to construe words, phrases, stories, etc., in a lascivious, lewd manner; salacious. —**e′vil-mind′ed·ly,** *adv.* —**e′vil-mind′ed·ness,** *n.*

e·vince (i vins′), *v.t.,* **e·vinced, e·vinc·ing. 1.** to show clearly; make evident or manifest; prove. **2.** to reveal the possession of (a quality, trait, etc.). [< L *ēvince(re)* (to) conquer, overcome, carry one's point = *ē-* E- + *vincere* to conquer] —**e·vin′ci·ble,** *adj.* —**Syn. 1.** See **display.**

e·vin·cive (i vin′siv), *adj.* serving to evince; indicative.

e·vis·cer·ate (i vis′ə rāt′), *v.,* **-at·ed, -at·ing,** *adj.* —*v.t.* **1.** to disembowel: *to eviscerate a chicken.* **2.** to deprive of vital or essential parts: *The censors eviscerated the book.* —*adj.* **3.** *Surg.* disemboweled, usually after a surgical operation on the abdomen when the wound breaks open as the result of a technical error or poor healing. [< L *ēviscerāt(us)* (ptp. of *ēviscerāre*) deprived of entrails, torn to pieces] —**e·vis′cer·a′tion,** *n.* —**e·vis′cer·a′tor,** *n.*

ev·i·ta·ble (ev′i tə bəl), *adj.* that can be avoided. [< L *ēvitābil(is).* See EVITE, -ABLE]

e·vite (i vīt′), *v.t.,* **e·vit·ed, e·vit·ing.** *Archaic.* to avoid; shun. [< L *ēvīt(āre)* = *ē-* E- + *vītāre* to avoid]

E·vi·us (ē′vē əs), *n. Class. Myth.* Dionysus. [< Gk *Evios,* from the cry *evaí, evoí* associated with Dionysus in lyric passages]

ev·o·ca·ble (ev′ə kə bəl), *adj.* that may be evoked.

ev·o·ca·tion (ev′ə kā′shən), *n.* the act or an instance of evoking; a calling forth: *the evocation of old memories.* [ME *evocacioun* < L *ēvocātiōn-* (s. of *ēvocātiō*) calling forth, out = *ēvocāt(us)* (ptp. of *ēvocāre* to EVOKE) + *-iōn-* -ION]

e·voc·a·tive (i vok′ə tiv, -vō′kə-), *adj.* tending to evoke: *perfume evocative of spring.* [< L *ēvocātīv(us)*] —**e·voc′a·tive·ly,** *adv.* —**e·voc′a·tive·ness,** *n.*

ev·o·ca·tor (ev′ə kā′tər), *n.* **1.** a person who evokes, esp. one who calls up spirits. **2.** *Embryol.* the chemical substance in an organizer that functions as a morphogenetic stimulus. [< L: one who calls to arms]

e·voke (i vōk′), *v.t.*, **e·voked, e·vok·ing.** **1.** to call up, produce, or suggest (memories, feelings, etc.): *The music evoked the mood of spring.* **2.** to elicit or draw forth: *His comment evoked protests.* **3.** to call up; cause to appear; summon: *to evoke a spirit from the dead.* [< L *ēvoc(āre)* = *ē-* E- + *vocāre* to call (akin to *vōx* VOICE)] —**e·vok′er,** *n.*

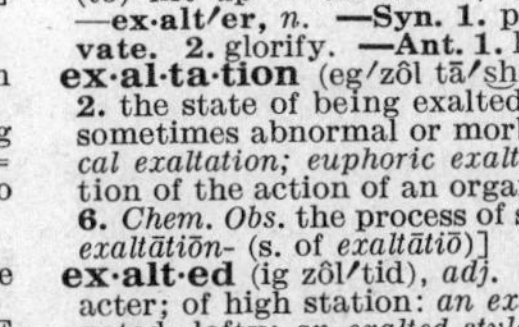

ABC, Evolute of parabolic arc OPQ

ev·o·lute (ev′ə lo͞ot′), *n.* *Geom.* the locus of the centers of curvature of, or the envelope of the normals to, another curve. Cf. **involute** (def. 5). [< L *ēvolūt(us)* (ptp. of *ēvolvere* to EVOLVE) rolled out, unfolded]

ev·o·lu·tion (ev′ə lo͞o′shən or, *esp. Brit.*, ē′və-), *n.* **1.** any process of formation or growth; development: *the evolution of man; the evolution of the drama.* **2.** a product of such development; something evolved: *The space program is the evolution of years of research.* **3.** *Biol.* the continuous genetic adaptation of organisms or species to the environment by the integrating agencies of selection, hybridization, inbreeding, and mutation. **4.** a motion incomplete in itself, but combining with coordinated motions to produce a single action, as in a machine. **5.** a pattern formed by or as by a series of movements: *the evolutions of a figure skater.* **6.** an evolving, or giving off, of gas, heat, etc. **7.** *Math. Obsolesc.* the extraction of roots. Cf. **involution** (def. 9b). [< L *ēvolūtiōn-* (s. of *ēvolūtiō*) an unrolling, opening] —**ev′o·lu′tion·al,** *adj.* —**ev′o·lu′tion·al·ly,** *adv.*

ev·o·lu·tion·ar·y (ev′ə lo͞o′shə ner′ē or, *esp. Brit.*, ē′və-), *adj.* **1.** pertaining to evolution or development; developmental: *the evolutionary origin of species.* **2.** of, pertaining to, or in accordance with a theory of evolution, esp. in biology. **3.** pertaining to or performing evolutions.

ev·o·lu·tion·ist (ev′ə lo͞o′shə nist or, *esp. Brit.*, ē′və-), *n.* **1.** a person who believes in a doctrine of evolution. —*adj.* Also, **ev′o·lu′tion·is′tic. 2.** of or pertaining to evolution or evolutionists. **3.** believing in or supporting a doctrine of evolution. —**ev′o·lu′tion·ism,** *n.*

ev·o·lu·tive (ev′ə lo͞o′tiv or, *esp. Brit.*, ē′və-), *adj.* **1.** of, pertaining to, or promoting evolution; evolutionary: *evolutive conditions; an evolutive process.* **2.** tending to evolve, or toward evolution.

e·volve (i volv′), *v.*, **e·volved, e·volv·ing.** —*v.t.* **1.** to develop gradually: *to evolve a scheme.* **2.** to give off or emit, as odors or vapors. —*v.i.* **3.** to come forth gradually into being; develop; undergo evolution: *The whole idea evolved from a casual remark.* **4.** *Biol.* to develop by a process of evolution to a more highly organized state or condition. [< L *ēvolve(re)* (to) unroll, open, unfold = *ē-* E- + *volvere* to roll, turn] —**e·volv′a·ble,** *adj.* —**e·volve′ment,** *n.* —**e·volv′er,** *n.*

e·von·y·mus (e von′ə məs), *n.* euonymus.

É·vo·ra (e′vo͝o rə), *n.* a city in central Portugal: Roman ruins; cathedral. 34,145 (1960).

e·vul·sion (i vul′shən), *n.* the act of plucking or pulling out; forcible extraction. [< L *ēvulsiōn-* (s. of *ēvulsiō*) = *ēvuls(us)* plucked out (ptp. of *ēvellere* = *ē-* E- + *vellere* to pluck) + *-iōn-* -ION]

Év·voi·a (e′vē ä), *n.* Modern Greek name of **Euboea.**

ev·zone (ev′zōn), *n.* an infantryman belonging to an elite corps in the Greek army. [< NGk, Gk *eúzōn(os)* well girt]

ewe (yo͞o; *Dial.* yō), *n.* an adult female sheep. [ME; OE *ēowu, ēwe;* c. OHG *ou, ouwi,* D *ooi,* L *ovis,* Gk *óis,* Skt *ávi*]

E·we (ā′vā, ā′wā), *n.* a Kwa language of western Africa that is spoken in parts of Togo and Ghana.

Ew·ell (yo͞o′el), *n.* **Richard Stod·dert** (stod′ərt), 1817–72, Confederate lieutenant general in the U.S. Civil War.

ewe-neck (yo͞o′nek′), *n.* a thin hollow neck, low in front of the shoulder, as of a horse or other animal. —**ewe′-necked′,** *adj.*

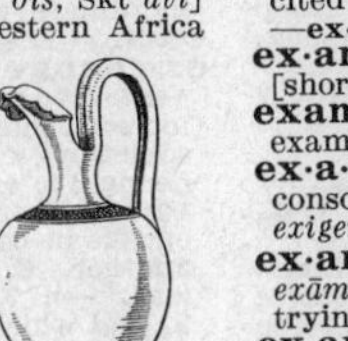
Ewer

ew·er (yo͞o′ər), *n.* **1.** a pitcher with a wide spout. **2.** *Decorative Art.* a vessel having a spout and a handle, esp. a tall, slender vessel with a base. [ME < AF = OF *evier* < L *aquār(ius)* vessel for water. See AQUA, -ARY]

Ew·ing (yo͞o′ing), *n.* a township in W New Jersey. 32,831 (1970).

ex[1] (eks), *prep.* **1.** *Finance.* without, not including, or without the right to have: *ex interest; ex rights.* **2.** *Com.* free of charges to the purchaser until the time of removal from a specified place or thing: *ex ship; ex warehouse.* [< L. See EX-[1]]

ex[2] (eks), *n.* the letter *X, x.*

ex-[1], a prefix meaning "out of," "from," and hence "utterly," "thoroughly," and sometimes imparting a privative or negative force or indicating a former title, status, etc., freely used as an English formative: *exstipulate; exterritorial; ex-president* (former president); *ex-member; ex-wife.* Also, **e-, ef-.** [< L, comb. form of *ex, ē* (prep.) out of, from, beyond]

ex-[2], var. of **exo-.**

ex-[3], a prefix identical in meaning with **ex-**[1], occurring before vowels in words of Greek origin: *exarch; exegesis.* Also, **ec-.** [< Gk; see EX-[1]]

Ex., Exodus.

ex., **1.** examination. **2.** examined. **3.** example. **4.** except. **5.** exception. **6.** exchange. **7.** excursion. **8.** executed.

ex·ac·er·bate (ig zas′ər bāt′, ik sas′-), *v.t.*, **-bat·ed, -bat·ing. 1.** to increase the bitterness or violence of (disease, ill feeling, etc.); aggravate. **2.** to embitter the feelings of (a person); irritate; exasperate. [< L *exacerbāt(us)* (ptp. of *exacerbāre*) exasperated, provoked] —**ex·ac′er·bat′ing·ly,** *adv.* —**ex·ac′er·ba′tion,** *n.*

ex·act (ig zakt′), *adj.* **1.** strictly accurate or correct: *an exact likeness; an exact description.* **2.** precise, as opposed to approximate: *the exact sum; the exact date.* **3.** admitting of no deviation, as laws or discipline; strict or rigorous. **4.** characterized by or using strict accuracy, precision, etc.: *exact instruments; an exact thinker.* —*v.t.* **5.** to call for, demand, or require: *to exact obedience.* **6.** to force or compel the payment, yielding, or performance of: *to exact money; to exact tribute from a conquered people.* [late ME *exacte* (v.) < L *exact(us)* (ptp. of *exigere*) driven out, thrust out = *ex-* EX-[1] + *ag-* (s. of *agere*) drive + *-tus* ptp. suffix] —**ex·act′a·ble,** *adj.* —**ex·act′er, ex·ac′tor,** *n.* —**ex·act′ness,** *n.* —**Syn. 3.** rigid, severe, unbending. **4.** methodical, careful, punctilious, scrupulous. **6.** See **extract.** —**Ant. 1, 2.** imprecise.

ex·act·a (ig zak′tə), *n.* a type of bet, esp. on horse races, in which the bettor must select the first- and second-place finishers in exact order. [AmerSp (QUINIELA) *exacta* exact quiniela]

ex·act·ing (ig zak′ting), *adj.* **1.** unduly severe or rigid in demands or requirements: *an exacting teacher.* **2.** requiring close application or attention: *an exacting task.* **3.** given to or characterized by exaction; extortionate. —**ex·act′ing·ly,** *adv.* —**ex·act′ing·ness,** *n.*

ex·ac·tion (ig zak′shən), *n.* **1.** the act of exacting; extortion: *the exactions of usury.* **2.** something exacted. [ME *exactioun* < L *exactiōn-* (s. of *exactiō*) a demanding]

ex·act·i·tude (ig zak′ti to͞od′, -tyo͞od′), *n.* the quality of being exact; exactness; preciseness; accuracy. [< F]

ex·act·ly (ig zakt′lē), *adv.* **1.** in an exact manner; precisely according to rule, measure, fact, etc.; accurately. **2.** just: *He will do exactly what he wishes.* **3.** quite so; that's right.

exact′ sci′ence, a science, as chemistry or physics, that deals with quantitatively measurable phenomena of the material universe.

ex·ag·ger·ate (ig zaj′ə rāt′), *v.*, **-at·ed, -at·ing.** —*v.t.* **1.** to magnify beyond the limits of truth; overstate; represent disproportionately: *to exaggerate the difficulties of a situation.* **2.** to increase or enlarge abnormally: *Those shoes exaggerate the size of her feet.* —*v.i.* **3.** to employ exaggeration, as in speech or writing. [< L *exaggerāt(us)* (ptp. of *exaggerāre*) heaped up = *ex-* EX-[1] + *agger(āre)* (to) heap + *-ātus* -ATE[1]] —**ex·ag′ger·at′ing·ly,** *adv.* —**ex·ag′ger·a′tor,** *n.*

ex·ag·ger·at·ed (ig zaj′ə rā′tid), *adj.* **1.** unduly magnified: *to have an exaggerated opinion of oneself.* **2.** abnormally increased or enlarged. —**ex·ag′ger·at′ed·ly,** *adv.*

ex·ag·ger·a·tion (ig zaj′ə rā′shən), *n.* **1.** the act of exaggerating or overstating. **2.** an instance of exaggerating; an overstatement: *His statement concerning the size of his income is a gross exaggeration.* [< L *exaggerātiōn-* (s. of *exaggerātiō*)]

ex·ag·ger·a·tive (ig zaj′ə rā′tiv, -ər ə tiv), *adj.* given to or characterized by exaggeration. Also, **ex·ag·ger·a·to·ry** (ig zaj′ər ə tōr′ē, -tôr′ē). —**ex·ag′ger·a′tive·ly,** *adv.*

ex·alt (ig zôlt′), *v.t.* **1.** to elevate in rank, honor, power, character, quality, etc.: *He was exalted to the position of president.* **2.** to praise; extol. **3.** to stimulate, as the imagination: *The lyrics of Shakespeare exalted the audience.* **4.** to intensify, as a color: *complementary colors exalt each other.* **5.** *Obs.* to elate, as with pride or joy. [late ME *exalte* < L *exaltā(re)* (to) lift up = *ex-* EX-[1] + *alt(us)* high + *-āre* inf. ending] —**ex·alt′er,** *n.* —**Syn. 1.** promote, raise, ennoble. See **elevate. 2.** glorify. —**Ant. 1.** humble. **2.** depreciate.

ex·al·ta·tion (eg′zôl tā′shən), *n.* **1.** the act of exalting. **2.** the state of being exalted. **3.** elation of mind or feeling, sometimes abnormal or morbid in character; rapture: *mystical exaltation; euphoric exaltation.* **4.** abnormal intensification of the action of an organ. **5.** *Brit. Obs.* a flight of larks. **6.** *Chem. Obs.* the process of subliming. [ME *exaltacioun* < L *exaltātiōn-* (s. of *exaltātiō*)]

ex·alt·ed (ig zôl′tid), *adj.* **1.** elevated, as in rank or character; of high station: *an exalted personage.* **2.** noble or elevated; lofty: *an exalted style of writing.* **3.** rapturously excited: *He was in an exalted mood.* —**ex·alt′ed·ly,** *adv.* —**ex·alt′ed·ness,** *n.*

ex·am (ig zam′), *n.* *Informal.* an examination, as in school. [short form]

exam., **1.** examination. **2.** examined. **3.** examinee. **4.** examiner.

ex·a·men (ig zā′men), *n.* *Eccles.* an examination, as of conscience. [< L: means of weighing, testing, akin to *exigere* to weigh. See EXACT]

ex·am·i·nant (ig zam′ə nənt), *n.* an examiner. [< L *exāminant-* (s. of *exāminans*, prp. of *exāmināre*) weighing, trying, examining]

ex·am·i·na·tion (ig zam′ə nā′shən), *n.* **1.** the act of examining; inspection; inquiry; investigation. **2.** the state of being examined. **3.** the act or process of testing pupils, candidates, etc., as by questions. **4.** the test itself; the list of questions asked. **5.** the answers, statements, etc., made by one examined. **6.** *Law.* formal interrogation. [ME *examinacioun* < L *exāminātiōn-* (s. of *exāminātiō*)] —**ex·am′i·na′tion·al,** *adj.*
—**Syn. 1.** observation, inquisition. EXAMINATION, INSPECTION, SCRUTINY refer to a looking at something. An EXAMINATION may mean a careful noting of details or may mean little more than a casual glance over something: *An examination of the plumbing revealed a defective pipe.* An INSPECTION is a formal and official examination: *an inspection of records; a military inspection.* SCRUTINY implies a critical and minutely detailed examination: *The papers seemed to be in good order, but they would not stand close scrutiny.* See also **investigation.**

ex·am·ine (ig zam′in), *v.t.*, **-ined, -in·ing. 1.** to inspect or scrutinize carefully: *to examine a prospective purchase.* **2.** to inspect or investigate (a person's body or any part of it), esp. in order to evaluate general health or determine the cause of illness. **3.** to inquire into or investigate: *to examine one's motives.* **4.** to test the knowledge, reactions, or qualifications of (a pupil, candidate, etc.), as by questions or assigning tasks. **5.** to subject to legal inquisition; put to question in regard to conduct or to knowledge of facts; interrogate: *to examine a witness or a suspected person.* [ME < MF *examin(er)* < L *exāmināre* to weigh, examine, test = *exāmin-* (s. of *exāmen* EXAMEN) + *-āre* inf. ending] —**ex·am′in·a·ble,** *adj.* —**ex·am′in·er,** *n.* —**ex·am′in·ing·ly,** *adv.* —**Syn. 1.** probe, explore, study.

ex·am·i·nee (ig zam′ə nē′), *n.* a person who is examined.

ex·am·ple (ig zam′pəl, -zäm′-), *n., v.,* **-pled, -pling.** —*n.* **1.** one of a number of things, or a part of something, taken to show the character of the whole. **2.** a pattern or model, as of something to be imitated or avoided: *to set a good example.* **3.** an instance serving for illustration; specimen. **4.** an instance illustrating a rule or method, as a mathematical problem proposed for solution. **5.** an instance, esp. of punishment, serving as a warning to others; warning: *Public executions were meant to be examples to the populace.* **6.** a precedent; parallel case: *an action without example.* —*v.t.* **7.** *Rare.* to exemplify (used in the passive). [ME *exa(u)mple* < MF *example* < L *exempl(um),* akin to *eximere* to take out (*ex-* EX-[1] + *emere* to buy, orig. take); r. ME *exemple* < L, as above]
—**Syn. 1.** EXAMPLE, SAMPLE, SPECIMEN refer to an individual phenomenon taken as representative of a type, or to a part representative of the whole. EXAMPLE is used of an object, activity, condition, etc., which is assumed to illustrate a certain principle, law, or standard: *a good example of baroque architecture.* SAMPLE, used mainly in a concrete reference, refers to a small portion of a substance or to a single representative of a group or type which is intended to show what the rest of the substance or the group is like: *a sample of yarn.* SPECIMEN usually suggests that the "sample" chosen is intended to serve a scientific or technical purpose: *a blood specimen; zoological specimens.* **2.** See **ideal. 3.** See **case**[1].

ex·an·i·mate (ig zan′ə mit, -māt′), *adj.* **1.** inanimate or lifeless. **2.** spiritless; disheartened. [< L *exanimāt(us)* (ptp. of *exanimāre*) deprived of life]

ex·an·them (eg zan′thəm, ig-, ek san′-), *n. Pathol.* an eruptive disease, esp. one attended with fever, as smallpox or measles. [< LL *exanthēm(a)* < Gk: skin eruption, breaking forth, lit., a bursting into flower = *ex-* EX-[3] + *anthē-* (verbal s. of *anthein* to blossom; see ANTHO-) + *-ma* n. suffix] —**ex·an·the·mat·ic** (eg zan′thə mat′ik, ek san′-), **ex·an·them·a·tous** (eg′zan them′ə təs, ek′san-), *adj.*

ex·an·the·ma (eg′zan thē′mə, ek′san-), *n., pl.* **-them·a·ta** (-them′ə tə, -thē′mə-), **-the·mas.** exanthem.

ex·arch (ek′särk), *n.* **1.** *Eastern Ch.* **a.** a patriarch's deputy. **b.** a title applied to a bishop ranking below a patriarch and above a metropolitan. **2.** the ruler of a province in the Byzantine Empire. [< LL *exarch(us)* superintendent < Gk *éxarchos* overseer, leader] —**ex·arch′al,** *adj.*

ex·ar·chate (ek′sär kāt′, ek sär′kāt), *n.* the office or domain of an exarch. [< ML *exarchāt(us)*]

ex·as·per·ate (ig zas′pə rāt′), *v.t.,* **-at·ed, -at·ing. 1.** to irritate to a high degree; annoy extremely. **2.** to increase the intensity or violence of (disease, pain, feelings, etc.). [< L *exasperāt(us)* (ptp. of *exasperāre*) made rough, provoked = *ex-* EX-[1] + *asper* harsh, rough + *-ātus* -ATE[1]] —**ex·as′per·at′ed·ly,** *adv.* —**Syn. 1.** incense, anger. See **irritate.**

ex·as·per·at·ing (ig zas′pə rā′ting), *adj.* extremely annoying or irritating; infuriating. —**ex·as′per·at′ing·ly,** *adv.*

ex·as·per·a·tion (ig zas′pə rā′shən), *n.* **1.** the act or an instance of exasperating; provocation. **2.** the state of being exasperated; extreme irritation or annoyance. [< L *exasperātiōn-* (s. of *exasperātiō*) roughness, bitterness]

Exc., Excellency.

exc., **1.** except. **2.** exception. **3.** excursion.

Ex·cal·i·bur (ek skal′ə bər), *n. Arthurian Romance.* the magic sword of King Arthur.

ex ca·the·dra (eks kə thē′drə, kath′i drə), *Latin.* from the seat of authority; with authority: used esp. of those pronouncements of the pope which are considered infallible. [lit., from the chair]

ex·ca·vate (eks′kə vāt′), *v.t.,* **-vat·ed, -vat·ing. 1.** to make hollow by removing the inner part; make a hole or cavity in; form into a hollow, as by digging. **2.** to make (a hole, tunnel, etc.) by removing material. **3.** to dig or scoop out (earth, sand, etc.). **4.** to expose or lay bare by digging; unearth. [< L *excavāt(us)* (ptp. of *excavāre*) hollowed out]

ex·ca·va·tion (eks′kə vā′shən), *n.* **1.** a hole or cavity made by excavating. **2.** the act of excavating. [< L *excavātiōn-* (s. of *excavātiō*) a hollowing]

ex·ca·va·tor (eks′kə vā′tər), *n.* **1.** a person or thing that excavates. **2.** a power-driven machine for digging, moving, or transporting loose gravel, sand, or soil.

ex·ceed (ik sēd′), *v.t.* **1.** to go beyond the bounds or limits of. **2.** to go beyond in quantity, degree, rate, etc.: *to exceed the speed limit.* **3.** to surpass; be superior to. —*v.i.* **4.** to be greater, as in quantity or degree. **5.** to excel or be superior. [ME *excede(n)* < L *excēd(ere)* (to) go out or beyond. See EX-[1], CEDE] —**ex·ceed′a·ble,** *adj.* —**ex·ceed′er,** *n.* —**Syn. 1.** overstep, transcend. **3.** outdo, outstrip, beat.

ex·ceed·ing (ik sē′ding), *adj.* **1.** extraordinary; exceptional. —*adv.* **2.** exceedingly.

ex·ceed·ing·ly (ik sē′ding lē), *adv.* extremely.

ex·cel (ik sel′), *v.,* **-celled, -cel·ling.** —*v.i.* **1.** to surpass others or be superior in some respect. —*v.t.* **2.** to surpass; be superior to; outdo. [late ME *excelle(n)* < L *excell(ere)* = *ex-* EX-[1] + **cellere* to rise high, tower]
—**Syn. 2.** outstrip, transcend, exceed, top. EXCEL, OUTDO, SURPASS imply being better than others or being superior in achievement. To EXCEL is to be superior to others in some (usually) good or desirable quality, attainment, or performance: *to excel opponents at playing chess.* To OUTDO is to make more successful effort than others: *to outdo competitors in the high jump.* To SURPASS is to go beyond others (who are definitely pointed out), esp. in a contest as to quality or ability: *to surpass one's classmates in knowledge of history.*

ex·cel·lence (ek′sə ləns), *n.* **1.** the fact or state of excelling; superiority; eminence. **2.** an excellent quality or feature. **3.** (*usually cap.*) excellency (def. 1). [ME < MF < L *excellentia*] —**Syn. 1.** preeminence. **2.** merit, virtue.

ex·cel·len·cy (ek′sə lən sē), *n., pl.* **-cies. 1.** (*usually cap.*) Also, **Excellence.** a title of honor given to certain high officials, as governors and ambassadors. **2.** (*usually cap.*) *Rom. Cath. Ch.* a title given to bishops and archbishops. **3.** (*usually cap.*) a person so entitled. **4.** Usually, **excellencies.** excellent qualities, characteristics, or the like. [ME *excellencie* < L *excellentia*]

ex·cel·lent (ek′sə lənt), *adj.* **1.** possessing excellence or superior merit; remarkably good. **2.** *Obs.* extraordinary; superior. [< L *excellent-* (s. of *excellēns*), prp. of *excellere* to EXCEL; see -ENT] —**ex′cel·lent·ly,** *adv.* —**Ant. 1.** inferior.

ex·cel·si·or (ik sel′sē ər, ek-), *n.* **1.** wood shavings, used for stuffing, packing, etc. **2.** *Print.* a 3-point type. [formerly trademark]

ex·cel·si·or (ek sel′si ōr′; *Eng.* ik sel′sē ôr′), *adj. Latin.* ever upward; motto of New York State.

ex·cept[1] (ik sept′), *prep.* **1.** with the exclusion of; excluding; save; but: *They were all there except me.* —*conj.* **2.** only; with the exception (usually fol. by *that*): *parallel cases, except that one is younger than the other.* **3.** otherwise than; but (fol. by an adv., phrase, or clause): *well fortified except here.* **4.** *Archaic.* unless. [late ME < L *except(us)* (ptp. of *excipere*) taken out = *ex-* EX-[1] + *-ceptus* (comb. form of *captus,* ptp. of *capere* to take)]
—**Syn. 1.** EXCEPT (more rarely EXCEPTING), BUT, SAVE point out something excluded from a general statement. EXCEPT emphasizes the exclusion: *Take any number except six.* BUT merely states the exclusion: *We ate all but one.* SAVE is now mainly found in poetic use: *nothing in sight save sky and sea.*

ex·cept[2] (ik sept′), *v.t.* **1.** to exclude; leave out. —*v.i.* **2.** to object (usually fol. by *to* or *against*): *to except to a statement; to except against a witness.* [ME *except(en)* < MF *except(er)* < L *exceptāre* < *except(us)* (ptp.); see EXCEPT[1]] —**ex·cept′a·ble,** *adj.* —**Usage.** See **accept.**

ex·cept·ing (ik sep′ting), *prep.* **1.** excluding; barring; saving; except. —*conj.* **2.** *Archaic.* except; unless; save. —**Syn. 1.** See **except**[1].

ex·cep·tion (ik sep′shən), *n.* **1.** the act of excepting. **2.** the fact of being excepted. **3.** something excepted; an instance or case not conforming to the general rule. **4.** an adverse criticism, esp. on a particular point; opposition of opinion; objection; demurral. **5.** *Law.* an objection, as to a ruling of the court in the course of a trial. **6. take exception, a.** to make an objection; demur. **b.** to take offense. [ME *excepcioun* < L *exceptiōn-* (s. of *exceptiō*)]

ex·cep·tion·a·ble (ik sep′shə nə bəl), *adj.* liable to exception or objection; objectionable. —**ex·cep′tion·a·ble·ness,** *n.* —**ex·cep′tion·a·bly,** *adv.*

ex·cep·tion·al (ik sep′shə nəl), *adj.* **1.** forming an exception or unusual instance; unusual; extraordinary. **2.** unusually excellent; superior. —**ex·cep′tion·al′i·ty,** *n.* —**ex·cep′tion·al·ness,** *n.* —**ex·cep′tion·al·ly,** *adv.* —**Syn. 1.** uncommon, singular. See **irregular.** —**Ant. 2.** average.

ex·cep·tive (ik sep′tiv), *adj.* **1.** being or making an exception. **2.** disposed to take exception; objecting. [< LL *exceptīv(us)*]

ex·cerpt (*n.* ek′sûrpt; *v.* ik sûrpt′), *n.* **1.** a passage taken out of a book, document, film, or the like; extract. —*v.t.* **2.** to take (a passage) from a book, film, or the like; extract. [late ME < L *excerpt(us)* (ptp. of *excerpere*) picked out, plucked out = *ex-* EX-[1] + *-cerp-* (comb. form of *carpere* to pluck) + *-tus* ptp. suffix] —**ex·cerpt′er, ex·cerp′tor,** *n.* —**ex·cerpt′i·ble,** *adj.* —**ex·cerp′tion,** *n.*

ex·cess (*n.* ik ses′; *adj.* ek′ses, ik ses′), *n.* **1.** the fact of exceeding specified limits in amount or degree. **2.** the amount or degree by which one thing exceeds another. **3.** an extreme or excessive amount or degree; superabundance: *to have an excess of energy.* **4.** the state of going beyond what is regarded as customary or proper: *to talk to excess.* **5.** immoderate indulgence; intemperance in eating, drinking, etc. —*adj.* **6.** more than or above what is necessary, usual, or specified; extra. [ME < L *excess(us),* n. use of ptp. of *excēdere* to EXCEED] —**Syn. 3.** surplus, superfluity. **5.** dissipation. —**Ant. 3.** lack, deficiency.

ex·ces·sive (ik ses′iv), *adj.* exceeding the usual or proper limit or degree; characterized by excess. [late ME (see EXCESS, -IVE); r. ME *excessif* < MF] —**ex·ces′sive·ly,** *adv.* —**ex·ces′sive·ness,** *n.* —**Syn.** extravagant, extreme, inordinate, exorbitant, unreasonable. —**Ant.** reasonable.

exch., **1.** exchange. **2.** exchequer.

ex·change (iks chānj′), *v.,* **-changed, -chang·ing,** *n.* —*v.t.* **1.** to part with for some equivalent; give up (something) for something else. **2.** to change for another; replace with something else. **3.** to give and receive reciprocally; interchange: *to exchange blows.* **4.** to transfer for a recompense; barter: *to exchange goods with foreign countries.* —*v.i.* **5.** to engage in bartering, replacing, or substituting one thing for another. **6.** to pass or be taken in exchange or as an equivalent. —*n.* **7.** the act, process, or an instance of exchanging. **8.** that which is given or received as a replacement or substitution for something else. **9.** a place for buying and selling commodities, securities, etc. **10.** a central office or central station: *a telephone exchange.* **11.** the method or system by which debits and credits in different places are settled without the actual transfer of money, by means of bills of exchange representing money values. **12.** the amount or percentage charged for exchanging money, collecting a draft, etc. **13.** the reciprocal transfer of equivalent sums of money, as in the currencies of two different countries. **14.** the giving or receiving of a sum of money in one place for a bill ordering the payment of an equivalent sum in another. **15.** See **rate of exchange. 16.** the amount of the difference in value between two or more currencies, or between the values of the same currency at two or more places. **17.** the checks, drafts, etc., exchanged at a clearing house. [ME *exchaunge(n)* < AF *eschaungier* < VL **excambiāre*] —**ex·chang′er,** *n.* —**Syn. 1.** interchange, trade, swap. **7.** interchange, trade, traffic, business, commerce, barter. **9.** market.

ex·change·a·ble (iks chān′jə bəl), *adj.* capable of being exchanged. —**ex·change′a·bil′i·ty,** *n.* —**ex·change′a·bly,** *adv.*

ex·chang·ee (iks chān jē′, -chān′jē, eks′chān jē′), *n.* a person who takes part in an exchange, as of students, prisoners, etc.

exchange′ rate′. See **rate of exchange.**

ex·cheq·uer (eks′chek ər, iks chek′ər), *n.* **1.** a treasury, as of a state or nation. **2.** (in Great Britain) **a.** (*often cap.*) the governmental department in charge of the public revenues. **b.** (*cap.*) Also called **Court of Exchequer.** an ancient common-law court of civil jurisdiction in which cases affecting the revenues of the crown were tried, now merged in the King's Bench Division of the High Court of Justice. **3.** *Informal.* funds; finances. [ME *escheker, eschequier* < AF *escheker, eschekier* (OF *eschequier*) chessboard, counting table. See CHECKER[1]]

ex·cide (ik sīd′), *v.t.*, **-cid·ed, -cid·ing.** to cut out; excise. [< L *excīde(re)* (to) cut out = *ex-* EX-[1] + *cīd-* (var. s. of *caedere* to cut)]

ex·cip·i·ent (ik sip′ē ənt), *n. Pharm.* a pharmacologically inert, adhesive substance, as honey, syrup, or gum arabic, used to bind the contents of a pill or tablet. [< L *excipient-* (s. of *excipiēns*, prp. of *excipere*) excepting, taking up = *ex-* EX-[1] + *-cip-* (var. of *capere* to take) + *-i-* -I- + *-ent-* -ENT]

ex·cis·a·ble (ik sī′zə bəl), *adj.* subject to excise duty.

ex·cise[1] (*n.* ek′sīz, -sīs; *v.* ik sīz′), *n.*, *v.*, **-cised, -cis·ing.** —*n.* **1.** an inland tax or duty on certain commodities, as spirits, tobacco, etc., levied on their manufacture, sale, or consumption within the country. **2.** a tax levied for a license to carry on certain employments, pursue certain sports, etc. —*v.t.* **3.** to impose an excise on. [appar. < MD *excijs*, var. of *accijs* < ML *accīsa*, lit. a cut, n. use of fem. ptp. of L *accīdere* to cut into = *ac-* AC- + *cīd-*, var. s. of *caedere* to cut]

ex·cise[2] (ik sīz′), *v.t.*, **-cised, -cis·ing. 1.** to expunge, as a passage or sentence, from a text. **2.** to cut out or off, as a tumor. [< L *excīs(us)* cut out, hewn down, ptp. of *excīdere* to EXCIDE] —**ex·cis′a·ble,** *adj.*

ex·cise·man (ek′sīz mən), *n.*, *pl.* **-men.** *Brit.* an officer who collects excise taxes and enforces excise laws.

ex·ci·sion (ek sizh′ən, ik-), *n.* **1.** the act of removal; an excising. **2.** *Surg.* resection. **3.** excommunication. [< L *excīsiōn-* (s. of *excīsiō*) a cutting out]

ex·cit·a·bil·i·ty (ik sī′tə bil′i tē), *n.* **1.** the quality of being excitable. **2.** *Physiol.* irritability.

ex·cit·a·ble (ik sī′tə bəl), *adj.* **1.** capable of being excited. **2.** easily excited. [< LL *excitābil(is)*] —**ex·cit′a·ble·ness,** *n.* —**ex·cit′a·bly,** *adv.* —**Syn. 2.** emotional, passionate, fiery. —**Ant. 2.** placid.

ex·cit·ant (ik sīt′ənt, ek′si tənt), *adj.* **1.** stimulating —*n.* **2.** *Physiol.* something that excites; stimulant. [< L *excitant-* (s. of *excitāns*) calling forth, arousing]

ex·ci·ta·tion (ek′sī tā′shən, -si-), *n.* **1.** the act of exciting. **2.** the state of being excited. **3.** *Physics.* a process in which a molecule, atom, nucleus, or particle is excited. [ME *excitacioun* < LL *excitātiōn-* (s. of *excitātiō*) = L *excitāt(us)* (ptp. of *excitāre;* see EXCITE) + *-iōn-* -ION]

ex·cit·a·tive (ik sī′tə tiv), *adj.* tending to excite. Also, **ex·cit·a·to·ry** (ik sī′tə tōr′ē, -tôr′ē). [< F *excitatif* < L **excitātīv(us)*]

ex·cite (ik sīt′), *v.t.*, **-cit·ed, -cit·ing. 1.** to arouse or stir up the emotions or feelings of: *to excite a person to anger.* **2.** to arouse or stir up (emotions or feelings): *to excite anger in a person.* **3.** to cause; awaken: *to excite interest or curiosity.* **4.** to stir to action; stir up: *to excite a dog by baiting him.* **5.** *Physiol.* to stimulate: *to excite a nerve.* **6.** *Elect.* to supply with electricity for producing electric activity or a magnetic field. **7.** *Physics.* to raise (an atom, molecule, etc.) to an excited state. [ME < L *excit(āre)*, freq. of *exciēre* to set in motion, awaken, instigate = *ex-* EX-[1] + *ciēre* to set in motion] —**Syn. 1.** stir, awaken, stimulate, animate, kindle, inflame. **4.** disturb, agitate, ruffle. —**Ant. 1.** calm, soothe.

ex·cit·ed (ik sī′tid), *adj.* **1.** stirred emotionally; agitated. **2.** stimulated to activity; brisk. —**ex·cit′ed·ly,** *adv.* —**ex·cit′ed·ness,** *n.* —**Syn. 1.** impassioned. **2.** eager, enthusiastic. —**Ant. 1.** calm.

excit′ed state′, *Physics.* any of the energy levels of a physical system, esp. an atom, molecule, etc., that have higher energy than the lowest energy level.

ex·cite·ment (ik sīt′mənt), *n.* **1.** an excited state or condition. **2.** something that excites. [late ME *excitament* < ML *excitāment(um)*] —**Syn. 1.** perturbation, commotion, ado. See **agitation.**

ex·cit·er (ik sī′tər), *n.* **1.** a person or thing that excites. **2.** *Elect.* an auxiliary generator that supplies energy for the excitation of another electric machine. [ME]

ex·cit·ing (ik sī′ting), *adj.* producing excitement; stirring; thrilling. [EXCITE + -ING[2]] —**ex·cit′ing·ly,** *adv.*

ex·ci·tor (ik sī′tər, -tôr), *n.* **1.** *Physiol.* a nerve whose stimulation excites greater action. **2.** *Archaic.* an exciter.

excl., 1. exclamation. **2.** excluding. **3.** exclusive.

ex·claim (ik sklām′), *v.i.* **1.** to cry out or speak suddenly and vehemently, as in surprise, strong emotion, protest, etc. —*v.t.* **2.** to cry out; say loudly or vehemently. [earlier *exclame* < L *exclām(āre)* (to) cry out] —**ex·claim′er,** *n.*

exclam., 1. exclamation. **2.** exclamatory.

ex·cla·ma·tion (ek′sklə mā′shən), *n.* **1.** the act of exclaiming; outcry; loud complaint or protest. **2.** an interjection. [ME *exclamacio(u)n* < L *exclāmātiōn-* (s. of *exclāmātiō*) a calling out = *exclāmāt(us)* (ptp. of *exclāmāre;* see EXCLAIM) + *-iōn-* -ION] —**ex′cla·ma′tion·al,** *adj.*

exclama′tion point′, the sign (!) used in writing after an exclamation. Also called **exclama′tion mark′.**

ex·clam·a·to·ry (ik sklam′ə tōr′ē, -tôr′ē), *adj.* **1.** using, containing, or expressing exclamation. **2.** pertaining to exclamation. [< L *exclāmāt(us)* called out (see EXCLAMATION) + -ORY[1]]

ex·clave (eks′klāv), *n.* a portion of a country geographically separated from the main part by surrounding alien territory. [EX-[1] + *-clave*, modeled on *enclave*]

ex·clo·sure (ik sklō′zhər), *n.* an area protected against any intruders, as by fences. [EX-[1] + *-closure*, modeled on *enclosure*]

ex·clude (ik sklōōd′), *v.t.*, **-clud·ed, -clud·ing. 1.** to shut or keep out; prevent the entrance of. **2.** to shut out from consideration, privilege, membership, etc. **3.** to expel and keep out; eject. [ME < L *exclūd(ere)* (to) shut out, cut off = *ex-* EX-[1] + *clūd-* (var. s. of *claudere* to close)] —**ex·clud′a·bil′i·ty,** *n.* —**ex·clud′a·ble, ex·clud′i·ble,** *adj.* —**ex·clud′er,** *n.* —**ex·clu·so·ry** (ik sklōō′sə rē), *adj.*
—**Syn. 1.** bar, except, omit, preclude. **2.** EXCLUDE, DEBAR, ELIMINATE mean to remove from a certain place, or from consideration in a particular situation. To EXCLUDE is to set aside as unwanted, unusable, etc.: *words excluded from polite conversation.* To DEBAR is to prohibit, esp. in a legal sense, from a place or from the enjoyment of privileges, rights, or the like: *to debar all candidates lacking the necessary preparation.* To ELIMINATE is to select and remove, esp. as irrelevant, unnecessary, or undesirable: *to eliminate such objections.* **3.** reject. —**Ant. 1.** include.

ex·clu·sion (ik sklōō′zhən), *n.* **1.** the act or an instance of excluding. **2.** the state of being excluded. [late ME < L *exclūsiōn-* (s. of *exclūsiō*) = *exclūs(us)* shut out (ptp. of *exclūdere;* see EXCLUDE) + *-iōn-* -ION] —**ex·clu′sion·ar′y,** *adj.*

ex·clu·sion·ism (ik sklōō′zhə niz′əm), *n.* the principle, policy, or practice of exclusion, as from rights or privileges. —**ex·clu′sion·ist, ex·clu′sion·er,** *n.*

exclu′sion prin′ciple, *Physics.* the principle that no two electrons, protons, or neutrons in a given system can be in states characterized by the same set of quantum numbers. Also called **Pauli exclusion principle.**

ex·clu·sive (ik sklōō′siv), *adj.* **1.** not admitting of something else; incompatible: *mutually exclusive plans of action.* **2.** excluding from consideration or account (often fol. by *of*): *a profit of ten percent, exclusive of taxes.* **3.** limited to that which is designated: *exclusive attention to business.* **4.** excluding all others from a part or share: *an exclusive right to film the novel.* **5.** single or sole. **6.** disposed to resist the admission of outsiders to membership, association, intimacy, etc.: *an exclusive circle of friends.* —*n.* **7.** *Journalism.* a piece of news obtained by a newspaper, along with the privilege of using it first. [late ME < ML *exclūsīv(us)*] —**ex·clu′sive·ly,** *adv.* —**ex·clu′sive·ness, ex·clu·siv·i·ty** (eks′klōō siv′i tē), *n.* —**Syn. 6.** select, clannish, snobbish, cliquish. —**Ant. 1, 2, 4.** inclusive.

ex·cog·i·tate (eks koj′i tāt′), *v.t.*, **-tat·ed, -tat·ing.** to think out; devise; invent. [< L *excogitāt(us)* deduced, devised, invented, ptp. of *excogitāre*] —**ex·cog′i·ta′tion,** *n.* —**ex·cog′i·ta′tive,** *adj.* —**ex·cog′i·ta′tor,** *n.*

ex·com·mu·ni·ca·ble (eks′kə myōō′nə kə bəl), *adj.* **1.** liable or deserving to be excommunicated, as a person. **2.** punishable by excommunication, as an offense.

ex·com·mu·ni·cate (*v.* eks′kə myōō′nə kāt′; *n., adj.* eks′kə myōō′nə kit, -kāt′), *v.*, **-cat·ed, -cat·ing,** *n.*, *adj.* —*v.t.* **1.** to cut off from communion or membership, esp. from the sacraments and fellowship of the church by ecclesiastical sentence. —*n.* **2.** an excommunicated person. —*adj.* **3.** excommunicated. [late ME < LL *excommūnicāt(us)*, lit., put out of the community (ptp. of *excommūnicāre*) = *ex-* EX-[1] + *commūn(is)* COMMON, public + *-ic-* (by analogy with *commūnicāre* to COMMUNICATE) + *-ātus* -ATE[1]] —**ex·com·mu·ni·ca·tive** (eks′kə myōō′nə kā′tiv, -kə tiv), **ex·com·mu·ni·ca·to·ry** (eks′kə myōō′nə kə tōr′ē, -tôr′ē), *adj.* —**ex′com·mu′ni·ca′tor,** *n.*

ex·com·mu·ni·ca·tion (eks′kə myōō′nə kā′shən), *n.* **1.** the act of excommunicating. **2.** the state of being excommunicated. **3.** the ecclesiastical sentence by which a person is excommunicated. [late ME < LL *excommūnicātiōn-* (s. of *excommūnicātiō*)]

ex·co·ri·ate (ik skōr′ē āt′, -skôr′-), *v.t.*, **-at·ed, -at·ing. 1.** to strip off or remove the skin from: *His palms were excoriated by the hard labor of shoveling.* **2.** to denounce or berate severely; flay verbally: *He was excoriated for his mistakes.* [late ME < LL *excoriāt(us)* stripped, skinned (ptp. of *excoriāre*). See EX-[1], CORIUM, -ATE[1]]

ex·co·ri·a·tion (ik skōr′ē ā′shən, -skôr′-), *n.* **1.** the act of excoriating. **2.** the state of being excoriated. **3.** an excoriated place on the body. [ME *excoriacioun* < ML *excoriātiōn-* (s. of *excoriātiō*)]

ex·cre·ment (ek′skrə mənt), *n.* waste matter discharged from the body, esp. feces. [< L *excrēment(um)* = *excrē-* (perf. s. of *excernere* to EXCRETE) + *-mentum* -MENT] —**ex·cre·men·tal** (ek′skrə men′tᵊl), **ex·cre·men·ti·tious** (ek′skrə men tish′əs), *adj.*

ex·cres·cence (ik skres′əns), *n.* **1.** abnormal growth or increase. **2.** an abnormal outgrowth, usually harmless, on an animal or vegetable body. **3.** a normal outgrowth, such as hair, horns, etc. **4.** any disfiguring addition. [late ME < L *excrēscentia*]

ex·cres·cen·cy (ik skres′ən sē), *n.* **1.** something that is excrescent; excrescence. **2.** a state of being excrescent. [var. of EXCRESCENCE; see -ENCY]

ex·cres·cent (ik skres′ənt), *adj.* **1.** growing abnormally out of something else; superfluous. **2.** *Phonet.* (of a speech sound) inserted or added as a result of articulatory interaction or impetus, as the *t*-sound in *sense* (sents), without grammatical or historical justification; intrusive. [< L *excrēscent-* (s. of *excrēscēns*), prp. of *excrēscere*] —**ex·cres′cent·ly,** *adv.*

ex·cre·ta (ik skrē′tə), *n.pl.* excreted matter, as sweat, urine, feces, etc. [< L: things sifted out or separated, neut. pl. of *excrētus*] —**ex·cre′tal,** *adj.*

ex·crete (ik skrēt′), *v.t.*, **-cret·ed, -cret·ing.** to separate and eliminate from an organic body; separate and expel from the blood or tissues, as waste or harmful matters. [< L *excrēt(us)* (ptp. of *excernere*) sifted out, separated = *ex-* EX-[1] + *crē-* (perf. s. of *cernere* to sift) + *-tus* ptp. suffix] —**ex·cret′er,** *n.* —**ex·cre′tive,** *adj.*

ex·cre·tion (ik skrē′shən), *n.* **1.** act of excreting. **2.** the substance excreted, as sweat or urine, or certain plant products. [< LL *excrētiōn-* (s. of *excrētiō*) that which is sifted out]

ex·cre·to·ry (ek′skri tōr′ē, -tôr′ē, ik skrē′tə rē), *adj.* pertaining to or concerned in excretion; having the function of excreting: *excretory organs.*

ex·cru·ci·ate (ik skrōō′shē āt′), *v.t.*, **-at·ed, -at·ing. 1.** to inflict severe pain upon; torture. **2.** to cause mental anguish to. [< L *excruciāt(us)* tormented greatly, tortured, ptp. of *excruciāre* = *ex-* EX-[1] + *cruciāre* to torment, crucify (*cruci-*, s. of *crux* CROSS + *-āre* inf. suffix)]

ex·cru·ci·at·ing (ik skrōō′shē ā′ting), *adj.* **1.** extremely painful; unbearably distressing; torturing. **2.** extreme; intense: *He signed his name with excruciating care.* —**ex·cru′ci·at′ing·ly,** *adv.*

ex·cru·ci·a·tion (ik skrōō′shē ā′shən), *n.* **1.** the act of excruciating. **2.** the state of being excruciated. **3.** an instance of this; torture. [< LL *excruciātiōn-* (s. of *excruciātiō*)]

ex·cul·pate (ek′skul pāt′, ik skul′pāt), *v.t.*, **-pat·ed, -pat·ing.** to clear from a charge of guilt or fault; free from blame; vindicate. [< L *exculpāt(us)* freed from blame = *ex-* EX-[1] + *culpātus* blamed (ptp. of *culpāre;* see CULPABLE)] —**ex·cul·pa·ble** (ik skul′pə bəl), *adj.* —**ex′cul·pa′tion,** *n.*

ex·cul·pa·to·ry (ik skul′pə tōr′ē, -tôr′ē), *adj.* tending to clear from a charge of fault or guilt.

ex·cur·rent (ik skûr′ənt, -skur′-), *adj.* **1.** running out or forth. **2.** *Zool.* giving passage outward; affording exit: *the excurrent canal of certain sponges.* **3.** *Bot.* **a.** having the axis prolonged so as to form an undivided main stem or trunk, as the stem of the spruce. **b.** projecting beyond the apex, as the midrib in certain leaves. [< L *excurrent-* (s. of *excurrēns*) running forth, prp. of *excurrere*]

ex·cur·sion (ik skûr′zhən, -shən), *n.* **1.** a short journey or trip for a special purpose: *a pleasure excursion; a scientific excursion.* **2.** a trip on a train, ship, etc., at a reduced rate: *weekend excursions to the seashore.* **3.** the group of persons making such a journey. **4.** deviation or digression. **5.** *Physics.* the displacement of a body from a mean position or neutral value, as in an oscillation. **6.** an accidental increase in the power level of a reactor, usually forcing its emergency shutdown. **7.** *Obs.* a sally or raid. [< L *excursiōn-* (s. of *excursiō*). See EXCURSUS, -ION]

ex·cur·sion·ist (ik skûr′zhə nist, -shə-), *n.* a person who goes on an excursion.

ex·cur·sive (ik skûr′siv), *adj.* **1.** given to making excursions in speech, thought, etc.; digressive. **2.** of the nature of such excursions; desultory. [< L *excurs(us)* (see EXCURSUS) + -IVE] —**ex·cur′sive·ly,** *adv.* —**ex·cur′sive·ness,** *n.*

ex·cur·sus (ek skûr′səs), *n., pl.* **-sus·es, -sus.** a detailed discussion of some point in a book, esp. one added as an appendix. [< L: a running out, sally, digression (ptp. of *excurrere*). See EX-[1], COURSE]

ex·cus·a·to·ry (ik skyōō′zə tôr′ē, -tōr′ē), *adj.* serving or intended to excuse. [late ME < ML *excūsātōri(us)* = LL *excūsātōr-* (s. of *excūsātor* = *excūsāt(us)*, ptp. of *excūsāre* to EXCUSE + *-or* -OR[2]) + *-ius* adj. suffix; see -ORY[1]]

ex·cuse (*v.* ik skyōōz′; *n.* ik skyōōs′), *v.,* **-cused, -cus·ing,** *n.* —*v.t.* **1.** to regard or judge with indulgence; pardon or forgive; overlook (a fault, error, etc.). **2.** to offer an apology for; apologize for; seek to remove the blame of: *He excused his absence by saying that he was ill.* **3.** to serve as an apology or justification for; justify: *Ignorance of the law excuses no man.* **4.** to release from an obligation or duty: *to be excused from jury duty.* **5.** to seek or obtain exemption or release for (oneself): *to excuse oneself from duty.* **6.** to refrain from exacting; remit; dispense with: *to excuse a debt.* —*n.* **7.** an explanation offered as a reason for being excused; a plea offered in extenuation of a fault or for release from an obligation, promise, etc. **8.** something serving to excuse; a ground or reason for excusing. **9.** the act of excusing. **10.** a pretext or subterfuge. **11.** an inferior or inadequate specimen of something specified: *His latest effort is a poor excuse for a novel.* [ME *excuse(n)* < L *excūsā(re)* (to) put outside, exonerate = *ex-* EX-[1] + *-cūsāre* < *causa* CAUSE; r. ME *escuse(n)* < MF *escuse(r)*] —**ex·cus′a·ble,** *adj.* —**ex·cus′a·ble·ness,** *n.* —**ex·cus′a·bly,** *adv.* —**ex·cus′er,** *n.*
—**Syn. 1.** EXCUSE, FORGIVE, PARDON imply being lenient or giving up the wish to punish. EXCUSE means to overlook some (usually) slight offense, because of circumstance, realization that it was unintentional, or the like: *to excuse bad manners.* FORGIVE is applied to excusing more serious offenses; the person wronged not only overlooks the offense but harbors no ill feeling against the offender: *to forgive and forget.* PARDON usually applies to a specific act of lenience or mercy by an official or superior in remitting all or the remainder of the punishment that belongs to a serious offense or crime: *The governor was asked to pardon the condemned criminal.* **3.** extenuate, palliate. **4.** free. **7.** justification. EXCUSE, APOLOGY both imply an explanation of some failure or failing. EXCUSE implies a desire to avoid punishment or rebuke. APOLOGY usually implies acknowledgment that one has been, at least seemingly, in the wrong; it may aim at setting matters right by alleging extenuating circumstances or by expressing regret. **10.** pretense, evasion.

ex′ div′idend, *Stock Exchange.* without or not including a previously declared dividend. *Abbr.:* ex div. Cf. **cum dividend.**

exec., **1.** executive. **2.** executor.

ex·e·cra·ble (ek′sə krə bəl), *adj.* **1.** utterly detestable; abominable; abhorrent. **2.** very bad: *an execrable stage performance.* [ME: expressing a curse < L *ex(s)ecrābil(is)* accursed, detestable] —**ex′e·cra·ble·ness,** *n.* —**ex′e·cra·bly,** *adv.*

ex·e·crate (ek′sə krāt′), *v.,* **-crat·ed, -crat·ing.** —*v.t.* **1.** to detest utterly; abhor; abominate. **2.** to curse; imprecate evil upon; damn; denounce: *He execrated all who opposed him.* —*v.i.* **3.** to utter curses. [< L *ex(s)ecrāt(us)* cursed (ptp. of *execrārī*) = *ex-* EX-[1] + *sacr-* (root of *sacrāre;* see SACRAMENT) + *-ātus* -ATE[1]] —**ex′e·cra′tor,** *n.*

ex·e·cra·tion (ek′sə krā′shən), *n.* **1** the act of execrating. **2.** a curse or imprecation. **3.** the object execrated; a thing held in abomination. [ME *execracioun* < L *ex(s)ecrātiōn-* (s. of *exsecrātiō*)]

ex·e·cra·tive (ek′sə krā′tiv), *adj.* **1.** pertaining to or characterized by execration. **2.** prone to execrate. —**ex′e·cra′tive·ly,** *adv.*

ex·e·cra·to·ry (ek′sə krə tôr′ē, -tōr′ē, -krā′tə rē), *adj.* **1.** pertaining to execration. **2.** having the nature of or containing an execration.

ex·ec·u·tant (ig zek′yə tənt), *n.* a person who executes or performs, esp. musically. [< F *exécutant*]

ex·e·cute (ek′sə kyōōt′), *v.t.,* **-cut·ed, -cut·ing.** **1.** to carry out; accomplish: *to execute a plan.* **2.** to perform or do: *to execute a gymnastic feat.* **3.** to inflict capital punishment on; put to death according to law. **4.** to produce in accordance with a plan or design. **5.** to perform or play (a piece of music). **6.** *Law.* **a.** to give effect or force to (a law, decree, judicial sentence, etc.). **b.** to carry out the terms of (a will). **c.** to complete and give validity to (a legal instrument) by fulfilling the legal requirements. [ME *execute(n),* back formation from EXECUTOR] —**ex′e·cut′a·ble,** *adj.* —**ex′e·cut′er,** *n.* —**Syn. 1.** achieve, complete. **2.** See **perform. 3.** See **kill**[1]. **6a.** enforce, administer.

ex·e·cu·tion (ek′sə kyōō′shən), *n.* **1.** the act or process of executing. **2.** the state or fact of being executed. **3.** the infliction of capital punishment or, formerly, of any legal punishment. **4.** a mode or style of performance; technical skill, as in music. **5.** *Law.* a judicial writ directing the enforcement of a judgment. [ME *execucioun* < L *execūtiōn-* (s. of *execūtiō*)] —**ex′e·cu′tion·al,** *adj.*

ex·e·cu·tion·er (ek′sə kyōō′shə nər), *n.* **1.** an official who inflicts capital punishment in pursuance of a legal warrant. **2.** a person who executes an act, will, judgment, etc.

ex·ec·u·tive (ig zek′yə tiv), *n.* **1.** a person or group of persons having administrative or supervisory authority, as in a company. **2.** the person or persons in whom the supreme executive power of a government is vested. **3.** the executive branch of a government. —*adj.* **4.** of, for, pertaining to, or suited for carrying out plans, duties, etc.: *executive ability.* **5.** pertaining to or charged with the execution of laws or the administration of public affairs: *executive committees.* **6.** designed for or used by executives. [ME < ML *execūtīv(us)* = L *execūt(us)* followed up, performed (ptp. of *ex(s)equī;* see EX-[1], SEQUENCE) + *-īvus* -IVE] —**ex·ec′u·tive·ly,** *adv.* —**ex·ec′u·tive·ness,** *n.*

Exec′utive Man′sion, *U.S.* **1.** the official residence of the governor of a state. **2.** See **White House** (def. 1).

exec′utive or′der, (*often caps.*) a regulation having the force of law issued by the President of the U.S. to the army, navy, or other part of the executive branch of the government.

exec′utive ses′sion, *Govt.* a session, generally closed to the public, of a legislative body or its leaders.

ex·ec·u·tor (ig zek′yə tər), *n.* **1.** a person who executes, carries out, or performs some duty, job, assignment, artistic work, etc. **2.** *Law.* a person named by a decedent in his will to carry out its provisions. [ME *executour* < L *execūtor* = *execūt(us)* (see EXECUTIVE) + *-or* -OR[2]; r. ME *esecutor* < AF *essecutour*] —**ex·ec·u·to·ri·al** (ig zek′yə tôr′ē əl, -tōr′-), *adj.*

ex·ec·u·to·ry (ig zek′yə tôr′ē, -tōr′ē), *adj.* **1.** executive. **2.** *Law.* to be performed or executed. [ME *executorie* operative, being in effect < LL *ex(s)ecūtōri(us)* executive]

ex·ec·u·trix (ig zek′yə triks), *n., pl.* **ex·ec·u·tri·ces** (ig zek′yə trī′sēz), **ex·ec·u·trix·es.** *Law.* a female executor. [ME < LL]

ex·e·ge·sis (ek′si jē′sis), *n., pl.* **-ses** (-sēz). critical explanation or interpretation, esp. of Scripture. [< Gk: an interpretation, explanation = *ex-* EX-[3] + *ēge-* (verbal s. of *hēgeesthai* to guide) + *-sis* -SIS] —**ex·e·get·ic** (ek′si jet′ik), **ex′e·get′i·cal,** *adj.* —**ex′e·get′i·cal·ly,** *adv.*

ex·e·gete (ek′si jēt′), *n.* a person skilled in exegesis. [< Gk *exēgētēs* guide, director, interpreter = *exēgē-* (see EXEGESIS) + *-tēs* agent suffix]

ex·e·get·ics (ek′si jet′iks), *n.* (*construed as sing.*) the science of exegesis. [< Gk *exēgētik(ós)* explanatory (see EXEGETE) + -ICS]

ex·em·pla (ig zem′plə), *n.* pl. of **exemplum.**

ex·em·plar (ig zem′plər, -plär), *n.* **1.** a model or pattern to be copied or imitated: *He is the exemplar of patriotic virtue.* **2.** a typical example or instance. **3.** an original or archetype: *Plato thought nature but a copy of ideal exemplars.* **4.** a copy of a book or text. [ME < L, var. of *exemplāre,* n. use of neut. of *exemplāris* EXEMPLARY; r. ME *exaumplere* < MF *examplaire*]

ex·em·pla·ry (ig zem′plə rē, eg′zəm pler′ē), *adj.* **1.** worthy of imitation; commendable. **2.** serving as a warning: *an examplary penalty.* **3.** serving as a model or pattern. **4.** serving as an illustration or specimen; illustrative; typical. **5.** of, pertaining to, or composed of exempla: *the exemplary literature of the medieval period.* [< L *exemplār(is)*] —**ex·em′pla·ri·ly,** *adv.* —**ex·em′pla·ri·ness,** **ex′em·plar′i·ty,** *n.*

ex·em·pli·fi·ca·tion (ig zem′plə fə kā′shən), *n.* **1.** the act of exemplifying. **2.** that which exemplifies; an illustration or example. **3.** *Law.* an attested copy of a document, under official seal. [late ME < ML *exemplificātiōn-* (s. of *exemplificātiō*) a setting forth = *exemplificāt(us)* (ptp. of *exemplificāre* to EXEMPLIFY) + *-iōn-* -ION]

ex·em·pli·fi·ca·tive (ig zem′plə fə kā′tiv), *adj.* serving to exemplify. [EXEMPLIFICAT(ION) + -IVE]

ex·em·pli·fy (ig zem′plə fī′), *v.t.,* **-fied, -fy·ing.** **1.** to show or illustrate by example. **2.** to furnish or serve as an example of. **3.** *Law.* to make an attested copy of (a document) under seal. [ME *exemplifie(n)* < MF *exemplifie(r)* < ML *exemplificāre* to copy] —**ex·em′pli·fi′a·ble,** *adj.* —**ex·em′pli·fi′er,** *n.*

ex·em·pli gra·ti·a (ek sem′plē grä′tē ä′; *Eng.* ig zem′plī grā′shē ə), *Latin.* See **e.g.**

ex·em·plum (ig zem′pləm), *n., pl.* **-pla** (-plə). **1.** an anecdote that illustrates or supports a moral point, as in a medieval sermon. **2.** an example. [< LL, L: lit., a pattern, model, copy]

ex·empt (ig zempt′), *v.t.* **1.** to free from an obligation or liability to which others are subject; release. —*adj.* **2.** released from, or not subject to, an obligation, liability, etc.: *He is exempt from the draft.* —*n.* **3.** a person who is exempt from, or not subject to, an obligation, duty, etc. [ME *exempt(en)* < L *exempt(us)* (ptp. of *eximere*) taken out, freed, released = *ex-* EX-[1] + *emptus* (ptp. of *emere* to buy, obtain)] —**ex·empt′i·ble,** *adj.*

ex·emp·tion (ig zemp′shən), *n.* **1.** *U.S.* a person who can be listed on an income-tax form as a deduction, as oneself, one's wife, or a dependent. **2.** the act of exempting. **3.** the state of being exempted; immunity. [late ME < L *exemptiōn-* (s. of *exemptiō*) removal] —**ex·emp′tive,** *adj.*
—**Syn. 3.** exception. EXEMPTION, IMMUNITY imply special privilege or freedom from requirements imposed upon others. EXEMPTION implies release or privileged freedom from sharing with others some (usually arbitrarily imposed) duty, tax, etc.: *exemption from military service.* IMMUNITY implies freedom from a penalty or from some natural or common liability, esp. one that is disagreeable or threatening: *immunity from disease.* —**Ant. 3.** liability.

ex·e·qua·tur (ek′sə kwā′tər), *n.* a written recognition of a consul by the government of the state in which he is stationed authorizing him to exercise his powers. [< L: lit., he may perform, 3rd pers. sing. pres. subj. of *exequī.* See EXEQUY]

ex·e·quy (ek′sə kwē), *n., pl.* **-quies. 1.** Usually, **exequies.** funeral rites or ceremonies; obsequies. **2.** a funeral procession. [ME *exequies* (pl.) < ML, L *exequiae,* lit., train of followers = *exequ-* follow to the grave (s. of *exequī* = *ex-* EX-[1] + *sequī* to follow) + *-ae* n. pl. suffix] —**ex·e·qui·al** (ek sē′kwē əl), *adj.*

ex·er·cise (ek′sər sīz′), *n.*, *v.*, **-cised, -cis·ing.** —*n.* **1.** bodily or mental exertion, esp. for the sake of training or improvement. **2.** something done or performed as a means of practice or training: *exercises for the piano.* **3.** a putting into action, use, operation, or effect: *the exercise of caution.* **4.** a written composition, musical piece, or artistic work whose intrinsic value is technical rather than aesthetic. **5.** Often, **exercises.** a traditional or reoccurring ceremony: *graduation exercises.* **6.** a religious observance or service. —*v.t.* **7.** to put through exercises, or forms of practice or exertion, designed to train, develop, condition, etc. **8.** to put (faculties, rights, etc.) into action, practice, or use: *to exercise one's strength; to exercise freedom of speech.* **9.** to use or display in one's action or procedure: *to exercise caution.* **10.** to make use of (one's privileges, powers, etc.): *to exercise one's constitutional rights.* **11.** to discharge (a function); perform: *to exercise the duties of one's office.* **12.** to worry; make uneasy. —*v.i.* **13.** to go through exercises; take bodily exercise. [ME < MF *exercice* < L *exercitium* = *exercit(us)* drilled, ptp. of *exercēre* to train (*ex-* EX-[1] + *-ercēre*, comb. form of *arcēre* to restrain) + *-ium* n. suffix] —**ex′er·cis′a·ble,** *adj.* —**ex′er·cis′er,** *n.*
—**Syn. 1.** activity; calisthenics, gymnastics. **2.** EXERCISE, DRILL, PRACTICE refer to activities undertaken for training in some skill. An EXERCISE may be either physical or mental, and may be more or less irregular in time and varied in kind: *an exercise in arithmetic.* DRILL is disciplined repetition of set exercises, often performed in a group, directed by a leader: *military drill.* PRACTICE is methodical exercise, usually characterized by much repetition, with a view to becoming perfect in some operation or pursuit and to acquiring further skills: *Even great musicians require constant practice.* **3.** employment, application. **7.** discipline, drill, school. **9.** employ, apply. **12.** try, trouble.

ex·er·ci·ta·tion (ig zûr′si tā′shən), *n.* **1.** exercise or exertion, as of the faculties or powers of the body or mind. **2.** practice or training. **3.** the performance of a religious observance. **4.** a disquisition or discourse performed as a display of skill. [ME *exercitacioun* < L *exercitātiōn-* (s. of *exercitātiō*) exercise, practice = *exercitāt(us)* exercised (ptp. of *exercitāre*, freq. of *exercēre*; see EXERCISE) + *-iōn-* -ION]

ex·ergue (ig zûrg′, ek′sûrg), *n.* the space below the device on a coin or medal, sometimes separated from the field by a line. [< F, appar. < Gk *ex-* EX-[3] + *érg(on)* work] —**ex·ergu·al** (ig zûr′gəl), *adj.*

ex·ert (ig zûrt′), *v.t.* **1.** to put forth, as power; exercise, as ability or influence; put into vigorous action. **2.** to put (oneself) into strenuous, vigorous action or effort. [< L *exert(us)* (ptp. of *exserere*) thrust out = *ex-* EX-[1] + *ser-* bind together + *-tus* ptp. suffix] —**ex·er′tive,** *adj.*

ex·er·tion (ig zûr′shən), *n.* **1.** vigorous action or effort. **2.** an effort: *a great exertion to help others.* **3.** exercise, as of power or faculties. **4.** an instance of this. —**Syn. 1.** endeavor, activity, strain. See **effort. 2.** attempt.

Ex·e·ter (ek′si tər), *n.* a city in and the county seat of Devonshire, in SW England: cathedral. 80,215 (1961).

ex·e·unt (ek′sē ənt), *v.i.* (they) go offstage (used as a stage direction, usually preceding the names of the characters). [< L]

ex fa·ci·e (eks fā′shē ē′), *Law.* (of a document) considered on the basis of its face; apparently: *The contract was ex facie satisfactory.* [< L: on the face, from the face]

ex fac·to (eks fäk′tō; *Eng.* eks fak′tō), *Latin.* according to fact; actually.

ex·fo·li·ate (eks fō′lē āt′), *v.*, **-at·ed, -at·ing.** —*v.t.* **1.** to throw off in scales, splinters, etc. **2.** to remove the surface of (a bone, the skin, etc.) in scales or laminae. —*v.i.* **3.** to throw off scales or flakes; peel off in thin fragments: *The bark of some trees exfoliates.* **4.** *Geol.* **a.** to split or swell into a scaly aggregate, as certain minerals when heated. **b.** to separate into rudely concentric layers or sheets, as certain rocks during weathering. **5.** *Med.* to separate and come off in scales, as scaling skin or any structure separating in flakes. [< LL *exfoliāt(us)* stripped of leaves, ptp. of *exfoliāre*] —**ex·fo·li·a·tive** (eks fō′lē ā′tiv, -ə tiv), *adj.*

ex·fo·li·a·tion (eks fō′lē ā′shən), *n.* **1.** the act or state of exfoliating. **2.** the state of being exfoliated. **3.** that which is exfoliated or scaled or flaked off. [< NL *exfoliātiōn-* (s. of *exfoliātiō*)]

ex·hal·ant (eks hā′lənt, ig zā′-), *adj.* **1.** exhaling; emitting. —*n.* **2.** that which exhales, as the ducts of certain mollusks. Also, **ex·ha′lent.** [< L *exhālant-* (s. of *exhālāns*), prp. of *exhālāre* to EXHALE; see -ANT]

ex·ha·la·tion (eks′hə lā′shən, eg′zə-), *n.* **1.** the act of exhaling. **2.** that which is exhaled; vapor; emanation. [ME *exalacion* < L *exhālātiōn-* (s. of *exhālātiō*)]

ex·hale (eks hāl′, ig zāl′), *v.*, **-haled, -hal·ing.** —*v.i.* **1.** to emit breath or vapor. **2.** to pass off as vapor; pass off as an effluence. —*v.t.* **3.** to breathe out; emit (air, vapor, sound, etc.). **4.** to give off as vapor. **5.** to draw out as a vapor or effluence; evaporate. [late ME *exale* < L *exhāl(āre)* = *ex-* EX-[1] + *hālāre* to breathe]

ex·haust (ig zôst′), *v.t.* **1.** to use up or consume completely; expend the whole of. **2.** to drain of strength or energy, wear out, or fatigue greatly, as a person: *I have exhausted myself working.* **3.** to draw out all that is essential in (a subject, topic, etc.); treat or study thoroughly. **4.** to empty by drawing out the contents. **5.** to create a vacuum in. **6.** to draw out or drain off completely. **7.** to deprive wholly of useful or essential properties, possessions, resources, etc. **8.** to deprive of ingredients by the use of solvents, as a drug. **9.** to destroy the fertility of (soil), as by intensive cultivation. —*v.i.* **10.** to pass out or escape, as spent steam from the cylinder of an engine. —*n. Mach.* **11.** the escape of steam or gases from the cylinder of an engine. **12.** the steam or gases ejected. **13.** the parts of an engine through which the exhaust is ejected. [< L *exhaust(us)* emptied out, drained out, ptp. of *exhaurīre*] —**ex·haust′er,** *n.* —**ex·haust′i·bil′i·ty,** *n.* —**ex·haust′i·ble,** *adj.* —**ex·haust′ing·ly,** *adv.* —**Syn. 2.** tire, enervate, prostrate, debilitate. **12.** fumes, smoke, vapor. —**Ant. 2.** strengthen, invigorate. **4.** fill.

ex·haus·tion (ig zôs′chən, -zôsh′-), *n.* **1.** the act or state of exhausting. **2.** the state of being exhausted. **3.** extreme weakness or fatigue. [< NL *exhaustiōn-* (s. of *exhaustiō*)]

ex·haus·tive (ig zôs′tiv), *adj.* **1.** exhausting a subject, topic, etc.; comprehensive; thorough. **2.** tending to exhaust or drain, as of resources or strength. —**ex·haust′ive·ly,** *adv.* —**ex·haust′ive·ness,** *n.*

ex·haust·less (ig zôst′lis), *adj.* inexhaustible. —**ex·haust′less·ly,** *adv.* —**ex·haust′less·ness,** *n.*

ex·hib·it (ig zib′it), *v.t.* **1.** to offer or expose to view; present for inspection. **2.** to manifest or display: *to exhibit anger.* **3.** to place on show: *to exhibit paintings.* **4.** to make manifest; explain. **5.** *Law.* to submit (a document, object, etc.) in evidence in a court of law. **6.** *Med. Obs.* to administer (something) as a remedy. —*v.i.* **7.** to make or give an exhibition; present something to public view. —*n.* **8.** an act or instance of exhibiting; exhibition. **9.** that which is exhibited. **10.** an object or a collection of objects shown in an exhibition, fair, etc. **11.** *Law.* a document or object exhibited in court and referred to and identified in written evidence. [late ME < L *exhibit(us)* held out, shown (ptp. of *exhibēre*) = *ex-* EX-[1] + *-hib-* (var. s. of *habēre* to have) + *-itus* -ITE[2]] —**ex·hib′i·tor, ex·hib′it·er,** *n.* —**Syn. 1.** show, demonstrate. See **display. 2.** evince, show, reveal. **8.** showing, show, display. **9, 11.** See **evidence. 10.** display.

ex·hi·bi·tion (ek′sə bish′ən), *n.* **1.** an exhibiting, showing, or presenting to view. **2.** a public display, as of the work of artists or craftsmen, the products of farms or factories, objects of general interest, etc. **3.** *Chiefly Brit.* an exposition; a large fair of extended duration, as a World's Fair. **4.** (in England) an allowance given to a student in a college, university, or school, usually upon the result of a competitive examination. [ME *exhibicion* < LL *exhibitiōn-* (s. of *exhibitiō*) a presenting]

ex·hi·bi·tion·er (ek′sə bish′ə nər), *n.* (in England) a student who receives an exhibition.

ex·hi·bi·tion·ism (ek′sə bish′ə niz′əm), *n.* **1.** a tendency to behave in such a way as to attract attention. **2.** *Psychiatry.* a disorder characterized esp. by a compulsion to exhibit the genitals.

ex·hi·bi·tion·ist (ek′sə bish′ə nist), *n.* **1.** a person who desires to make an exhibition of himself or his powers, personality, etc. **2.** *Psychiatry.* a person affected with the compulsions of exhibitionism. —**ex′hi·bi′tion·is′tic,** *adj.*

ex·hib·i·tive (ig zib′i tiv), *adj.* serving for exhibition; tending to exhibit. [< NL *exhibitīv(us)*] —**ex·hib′i·tive·ly,** *adv.*

ex·hib·i·to·ry (ig zib′i tôr′ē, -tōr′ē), *adj.* pertaining to or intended for exhibition or display. [< LL *exhibitōri(us)* relating to showing, displaying]

ex·hil·a·rant (ig zil′ər ənt), *adj.* **1.** exhilarating. —*n.* **2.** something that exhilarates. [< L *exhilarant-* (s. of *exhilarāns*) gladdening, cheering, prp. of *exhilarāre*]

ex·hil·a·rate (ig zil′ə rāt′), *v.t.*, **-rat·ed, -rat·ing.** **1.** to enliven; invigorate; stimulate. **2.** to make cheerful or merry. [< L *exhilarāt(us)* greatly gladdened, cheered, ptp. of *exhilarāre* = *ex-* EX-[1] + *hilarāre* to cheer (see HILARITY); see -ATE[1]] —**ex·hil′a·rat′ing·ly,** *adv.* —**ex·hil′a·ra′tor,** *n.* —**Syn. 1.** elate. **2.** cheer, gladden. —**Ant. 1, 2.** depress.

ex·hil·a·ra·tion (ig zil′ə rā′shən), *n.* **1.** exhilarated condition or feeling. **2.** the act of exhilarating. [< LL *exhilarātiōn-* (s. of *exhilarātiō*)] —**Syn. 1.** joyousness, gaiety, hilarity.

ex·hil·a·ra·tive (ig zil′ə rā′tiv, -ər ə tiv), *adj.* tending to exhilarate. Also, **ex·hil·a·ra·to·ry** (ig zil′ər ə tôr′ē, -tōr′ē).

ex·hort (ig zôrt′), *v.t.* **1.** to urge, advise, or caution earnestly; admonish urgently. —*v.i.* **2.** to give advice; give admonition. [late ME *ex(h)orte* < L *exhort(ārī)* (to) encourage greatly = *ex-* EX-[1] + *hortārī* to urge] —**ex·hort′er,** *n.*

ex·hor·ta·tion (eg′zôr tā′shən, ek′sôr-), *n.* **1.** the act or process of exhorting. **2.** an utterance, discourse, or address conveying urgent advice or recommendations. [ME *exhortacion* < L *exhortātiōn-* (s. of *exhortātiō*) a pleading, urging]

ex·hor·ta·tive (ig zôr′tə tiv), *adj.* **1.** serving or intended to exhort. **2.** pertaining to exhortation. Also, **ex·hor·ta·to·ry** (ig zôr′tə tôr′ē, -tōr′ē). [late ME < L *exhortātīv(us)* = *exhortāt(us)* (ptp. of *exhortārī* to EXHORT) + *-īvus* -IVE] —**ex·hor′ta·tive·ly,** *adv.*

ex·hume (ig zo͞om′, -zyo͞om′, eks hyo͞om′), *v.t.*, **-humed, -hum·ing.** **1.** to dig (something buried, esp. a dead body) out of the earth; disinter. **2.** to revive or restore; bring to light. [late ME < ML *exhumāre* = L *ex-* EX-[1] + *humāre* to inter] —**ex·hu·ma·tion** (eks′hyo͝o mā′shən), *n.* —**ex·hum′er,** *n.*

ex·i·gen·cy (ek′si jən sē), *n.*, *pl.* **-cies.** **1.** exigent state or character; urgency. **2.** Usually, **exigencies.** the need, demand, or requirement intrinsic to a circumstance, condition, etc.: *the exigencies of city life.* **3.** a case or situation which demands prompt action or remedy; emergency: *He promised help in any exigency.* Also, **ex′i·gence.** [< ML *exigentia*]

ex·i·gent (ek′si jənt), *adj.* **1.** requiring immediate action or aid; urgent; pressing. **2.** requiring a great deal, or more than is reasonable. [ME < L *exigent-* (s. of *exigēns*) driving out, demanding (prp. of *exigere*) = *ex-* EX-[1] + *-ig-* drive (var. s. of *agere*) + *-ent-* -ENT] —**ex′i·gent·ly,** *adv.*

ex·i·gi·ble (ek′si jə bəl), *adj.* liable to be exacted; requirable. [< F]

ex·ig·u·ous (ig zig′yo͞o əs, ik sig′-), *adj.* scanty; meager; small. [< L *exiguus* = *exig(ere)* (see EXIGENT) + *-u-* (unexplained) + *-us* -OUS] —**ex·i·gu·i·ty** (ek′sə gyo͞o′i tē), **ex·ig′u·ous·ness,** *n.* —**ex·ig′u·ous·ly,** *adv.*

ex·ile (eg′zīl, ek′sīl), *n.*, *v.*, **-iled, -il·ing.** —*n.* **1.** prolonged separation from one's country or home, as by force of circumstances. **2.** anyone separated from his country or home. **3.** expulsion from one's native land by authoritative decree. **4.** the fact or state of such expulsion. **5.** a person banished from his native land. **6. the Exile,** the Babylonian captivity of the Jews, 597–538 B.C. —*v.t.* **7.** to separate from country, home, etc. **8.** to expel or banish (a person) from his country. [ME *exil* banishment < L *ex(s)il(ium)* = *exsul* banished person + *-ium* n. suffix of state or condition]

ex·il·ic (eg zil′ik, ek sil′-), *adj.* pertaining to exile, as that of the Jews in Babylon. Also, **ex·il′i·an.**

ex·im·i·ous (eg zim′ē əs), *adj. Archaic.* distinguished; eminent; excellent. [< L *eximius* (< *eximere* to take out, remove) = *ex-* EX-[1] + *-im-* (var. s. of *emere* to buy, take) + *-ius* -IOUS] —**ex·im′i·ous·ly,** *adv.*

ex int., without interest.

ex·ist (ig zist′), *v.i.* **1.** to have actual being; be. **2.** to have life or animation; live. **3.** to continue to be or live: *Belief in magic still exists.* **4.** to have being in a specified place or under certain conditions; be found; occur: *Famine exists in many parts of the world.* [< L *ex(s)ist(ere)* (to) exist, appear, emerge = *ex-* EX-[1] + *sistere* to stand]

ex·ist·ence (ig zis′təns), *n.* **1.** the state or fact of existing; being. **2.** continuance in being or life; life: *a struggle for existence.* **3.** mode of existing: *They were working for a better existence.* **4.** all that exists: *Existence shows a universal order.* **5.** something that exists; entity; being. [late ME < LL *ex(s)istentia*]

ex·ist·ent (ig zis′tənt), *adj.* **1.** existing; having existence. **2.** now existing. —*n.* **3.** a person or thing that exists. [< L *existent-* (s. of *existēns*) stepping forth, appearing]

ex·is·ten·tial (eg′zi sten′shəl, ek′si-), *adj.* **1.** pertaining to existence. **2.** of or pertaining to existentialism. [< LL *existentiāl(is)*] —**ex′is·ten′tial·ly,** *adv.*

ex·is·ten·tial·ism (eg′zi sten′shə liz′əm, ek′si-), *n. Philos.* a modern movement encompassing a variety of themes, among them the doctrine that individual existence determines essence, that man has absolute freedom of choice but that there are no rational criteria serving as a basis for choice, and the general claim that the universe is absurd, with an emphasis on the phenomena of anxiety and alienation. —**ex′is·ten′tial·ist,** *adj., n.* —**ex′is·ten′tial·is′tic,** *adj.* —**ex′is·ten′tial·is′ti·cal·ly,** *adv.*

ex·it[1] (eg′zit, ek′sit), *n.* **1.** a way or passage out. **2.** a going out or away; departure: *to make one's exit.* **3.** a departure of an actor from the stage as part of the action of a play. —*v.i.* **4.** to go out; leave. [< L *exit(us)*, n. use of ptp. of *exīre* to go out]

ex·it[2] (eg′zit, ek′sit), *v.i.* (he or she) goes offstage (used as a stage direction, often preceding the name of the character): *Exit Falstaff.* [< L]

ex lib., ex libris.

ex li·bris (eks lī′bris, lē′-), *pl.* **-bris** for 2. **1.** from the library of (a phrase inscribed in a book before the name of the owner). **2.** an inscription in or on a book, to indicate the owner; bookplate. [< L: out of the books (of), from the books (of)]

Ex·moor (eks′mŏŏr′), *n.* a moorland in SW England, in Somersetshire and Devonshire.

ex ni·hi·lo ni·hil fit (eks ni′hi lō′ ni′hil fit′; *Eng.* eks nī′hi lō′ nī′hil fit′), *Latin.* nothing is created from nothing.

exo-, a learned borrowing from Greek meaning "outside," "outer," "external," used in the formation of compound words: *exocentric.* Also, **ex-**[2]. [< Gk, comb. form of *éxō* outside]

ex·o·bi·ol·o·gy (ek′sō bī ol′ə jē), *n.* the study of life beyond the earth's atmosphere, as on other planets. —**ex′o·bi·ol′o·gist,** *n.*

ex·o·carp (ek′sō kärp′), *n. Bot.* epicarp.

ex·o·cen·tric (ek′sō sen′trik), *adj. Gram.* not having the same syntactic function in the sentence as any one of its immediate constituents. *Bittersweet* is an exocentric compound when it functions as a noun, because its elements both usually function as adjectives. Cf. **endocentric.**

ex·o·crine (ek′sə krin, -krīn′, -krēn′), *Anat., Physiol.* —*adj.* **1.** secreting externally. **2.** of or pertaining to an exocrine gland or its secretion. —*n.* **3.** an external secretion. [EXO- + Gk *krīn(ein)* (to) separate]

ex′ocrine gland′, any of several glands, as the salivary glands, that secretes externally through a duct.

Exod., Exodus.

ex·o·don·tics (ek′sə don′tiks), *n.* (*construed as sing.*) the branch of dentistry dealing with the extraction of teeth. Also, **ex·o·don·tia** (ek′sə don′shə, -shē ə).

ex·o·don·tist (ek′sə don′tist), *n.* a specialist in exodontics.

ex·o·dos (ek′sə dos′), *n., pl.* **-doi** (-doi′), *Greek.* the concluding scene in ancient Greek drama, esp. tragedy.

ex·o·dus (ek′sə dəs), *n.* **1.** a going out; a departure or emigration, usually of a large number of people. **2. the Exodus,** the departure of the Israelites from Egypt under Moses. **3.** (*cap.*) the second book of the Bible, containing an account of the Exodus. [< L: a going out < Gk *éxodos* a marching out, going out = *ex-* EX-[3] + *hodós* way]

ex·o·en·zyme (ek′sō en′zīm), *n. Biochem.* an enzyme, as pepsin, that functions outside of the cell producing it. Also called **ectoenzyme.** Cf. **endoenzyme.**

ex·o·er·gic (ek′sō ûr′jik), *adj. Physical Chem.* of or noting a reaction that is accompanied by a liberation of energy; exothermic (opposed to *endoergic*). [EXO- + Gk *érg(on)* work + -IC]

ex off., ex officio.

ex of·fi·ci·o (eks ə fish′ē ō′), by virtue of office or official position. [< L] —**ex′-of·fi′ci·o′,** *adj.*

ex·og·a·my (ek sog′ə mē), *n.* **1.** marriage outside a specific tribe or similar social unit. Cf. **endogamy. 2.** *Biol.* the union of gametes of unrelated parents. —**ex·og·a·mous** (ek sog′ə məs), **ex·o·gam·ic** (ek′sə gam′ik), *adj.*

ex·o·gen (ek′sə jən), *n. Bot.* any plant of the obsolete class *Exogenae*, including the dicotyledons. [< NL *Exogen(a)*]

ex·og·e·nous (ek soj′ə nəs), *adj.* **1.** having its origin external; derived externally. **2.** *Bot.* **a.** (of plants, as the dicotyledons) having stems that grow by the addition of an annual layer of wood to the outside beneath the bark. **b.** pertaining to plants having such stems. **c.** belonging to the exogens. **3.** *Physiol., Biochem.* of or noting the metabolic assimilation of proteins or other metabolites, the elimination of nitrogenous catabolites being in direct proportion to the amount of metabolites taken in. —**ex·og′e·nous·ly,** *adv.*

ex·on·er·ate (ig zon′ə rāt′), *v.t.*, **-at·ed, -at·ing. 1.** to clear, as of a charge; free from blame; exculpate. **2.** to relieve, as from an obligation, duty, or task. [late ME < L *exonerāt(us)* (ptp. of *exonerāre* to unburden, discharge) = *ex-* EX-[1] + *oner-* (s. of *onus*) a burden + *-ātus* -ATE[1]] —**ex·on′er·a′tion,** *n.* —**ex·on′er·a′tive,** *adj.* —**Syn. 1.** vindicate. See **absolve. 2.** release. —**Ant. 1.** blame.

ex·oph·thal·mos (ek′sof thal′məs, -mos), *n. Pathol.* protrusion of the eyeball from the orbit, caused by disease, esp. hyperthyroidism, or injury. Also, **ex·oph·thal·mus** (ek′sof thal′məs), **ex·oph·thal·mi·a** (ek′sof thal′mē ə). [< NL < Gk = *ex-* EX-[3] + *ophthalmós*; see OPHTHALMIC] —**ex′oph·thal′mic,** *adj.*

ex·o·ra·ble (ek′sər ə bəl), *adj.* susceptible of being persuaded or moved by entreaty. [< L *exōrābil(is)* = *exōr(āre)* (to) prevail upon, move by entreaty (*ex-* EX-[1] + *ōrāre* to pray, beg) + *-ābilis* -ABLE] —**ex′o·ra·bil′i·ty,** *n.*

ex·or·bi·tance (ig zôr′bi təns), *n.* the quality of being exorbitant; excessiveness. Also, **ex·or′bi·tan·cy.** [late ME]

ex·or·bi·tant (ig zôr′bi tənt), *adj.* exceeding the bounds of custom, propriety, or reason, esp. in amount or extent: *to charge an exorbitant price.* [late ME < LL *exorbitant-* (s. of *exorbitāns*, prp. of *exorbitāre* to go out of the track)] —**ex·or′bi·tant·ly,** *adv.* —**Syn.** excessive, unreasonable.

ex·or·cise (ek′sôr sīz′), *v.t.*, **-cised, -cis·ing. 1.** to seek to expel (an evil spirit) by adjuration or religious or solemn ceremonies. **2.** to free (a person, place, etc.) of evil spirits or malignant influences. Also, **exorcize.** [late ME < LL *exorciz(āre)* < Gk *exorkíz(ein)* = *ex-* EX-[3] + *horkízein* to cause (someone) to swear an oath] —**ex′or·cis′er,** *n.*

ex·or·cism (ek′sôr siz′əm), *n.* **1.** the act or process of exorcising. **2.** the ceremony or the formula used in exorcising. [ME *exorcism(us)* < LL < Gk *exorkismós* administration of an oath]

ex·or·cist (ek′sôr sist), *n.* **1.** a person who practices exorcism. **2.** *Rom. Cath. Ch.* **a.** a member of the second-ranking of the four minor orders. **b.** the order itself. Cf. **acolyte** (def. 2), **lector** (def. 2), **ostiary** (def. 1). [ME < LL *exorcist(a)* < Gk *exorkistḗs*]

ex·or·cize (ek′sôr sīz′), *v.t.*, **-cized, -ciz·ing.** exorcise. —**ex′or·ciz′er,** *n.*

ex·or·di·um (ig zôr′dē əm, ik sôr′-), *n., pl.* **-di·ums, -di·a** (-dē ə). **1.** the beginning of anything. **2.** the introductory part of an oration or discourse. [< L = *ex-* EX-[1] + *ōrd-* begin (s. of *ōrdīrī*) + *-ium* neut. n. suffix] —**ex·or′di·al,** *adj.*

ex·o·skel·e·ton (ek′sō skel′i tən), *n. Zool.* an external covering or integument, esp. when hard, as the shell of crustaceans, the scales and plates of fishes, etc. (opposed to *endoskeleton*). —**ex′o·skel′e·tal,** *adj.*

ex·os·mo·sis (ek′sos mō′sis, ek′soz-), *n. Physical Chem.* **1.** osmosis from the inside toward the outside. **2.** (in osmosis) the flow of a substance from an area of greater concentration to one of lower concentration (opposed to *endosmosis*). Also, **ex·os·mose** (ek′sos mōs′, -soz-). —**ex·os·mot·ic** (ek′sos-mot′ik, -soz-), **ex·os·mic** (ek sos′mik, -soz′-), *adj.*

ex·o·sphere (ek′sō sfēr′), *n.* the highest, least dense region of the atmosphere. —**ex·o·spher·ic** (ek′sō sfer′ik), *adj.*

ex·o·spore (ek′sə spōr′, -spôr′), *n. Bot.* the outer coat of a spore. —**ex′o·spor′ous,** *adj.*

ex·os·to·sis (ek′sos tō′sis, -sə-), *n., pl.* **-ses** (-sēz). *Pathol.* the abnormal formation of a bony growth on a bone or tooth. [< NL < Gk: an outgrowth] —**ex·os·tot·ic** (ek′sə-stot′ik), *adj.*

ex·o·ter·ic (ek′sə ter′ik), *adj.* **1.** suitable for or communicated to the general public. **2.** not belonging or pertaining to the inner or select circle, as of disciples or intimates. **3.** popular; simple; commonplace. **4.** pertaining to the outside; exterior; external. [< LL *exōteric(us)* external < Gk *exōterikós* = *exōter(os)* inclined outward (*exo-* EXO- + *-teros* comp. suffix) + *-ikos* -IC] —**ex′o·ter′i·cal·ly,** *adv.*

ex·o·ther·mic (ek′sō thûr′mik), *adj. Chem.* noting or pertaining to a chemical change that is accompanied by a liberation of heat (opposed to *endothermic*). Also, **ex′o·ther′mal.** —**ex′o·ther′mi·cal·ly, ex′o·ther′mal·ly,** *adv.*

ex·o·tic (ig zot′ik), *adj.* **1.** of foreign origin or character; not native: *exotic foods.* **2.** striking or unusual in effect or appearance. —*n.* **3.** anything exotic, as a plant. [< L *exōtic(us)* < Gk *exōtikós* foreign] —**ex·ot′i·cal·ly,** *adv.* —**ex·ot′ic·ness,** *n.*

ex·ot·i·cism (ig zot′i siz′əm), *n.* **1.** a tendency to adopt what is exotic. **2.** exotic quality or character. **3.** anything exotic, as a foreign word or idiom.

ex·o·tox·in (ek′sō tok′sin), *n. Biochem.* a soluble toxin excreted by a microorganism. Cf. **endotoxin.** —**ex′o·tox′ic,** *adj.*

exp., 1. expenses. **2.** expired. **3.** export. **4.** express.

ex·pand (ik spand′), *v.t.* **1.** to increase in extent, size, volume, scope, etc. **2.** to spread or stretch out; unfold. **3.** to express in fuller form or greater detail; develop: *to expand a short story into a novel.* **4.** *Math.* **a.** to write (a mathematical expression) so as to show the products of its factors. Cf. **factor** (def. 7). **b.** to rewrite (a mathematical expression) as a sum, product, etc., of terms of a particular kind. —*v.i.* **5.** to increase or grow in extent, bulk, scope, etc. **6.** to spread out; unfold; develop. **7.** to express more fully or in greater detail (usually fol. by *on* or *upon*): *Please expand on that statement.* [late ME *expande(n)* < L *expande(re)* (to) spread out = *ex-* EX-[1] + *pandere* to extend, stretch] —**ex·pand′a·ble, ex·pand′i·ble,** *adj.* —**ex·pand′er,** *n.*

—**Syn. 1.** swell, enlarge, increase. EXPAND, DILATE, DISTEND, INFLATE imply becoming larger and filling more space. TO EXPAND is to spread out, usually in every direction, so as to occupy more space or have more capacity: *to expand one's chest.* TO DILATE is esp. to increase the width or circumference, and applies to space enclosed within confines or to hollow bodies: *to dilate the pupils of the eyes.* To DISTEND is to stretch, often beyond the point of natural expansion: *to distend an artery.* To INFLATE is to blow out or swell a hollow body with air or gas: *to inflate a balloon.*

ex·panse (ik spans′), *n.* **1.** that which is spread out, esp. over a relatively large area; an uninterrupted space or area. **2.** expansion; extension. [< NL *expans(um)*, n. use of neut. of L *expansus*, ptp. of *expandere* to EXPAND]

ex·pan·si·ble (ik span′sə bəl), *adj.* capable of being expanded. [< L *expans(us)* (see EXPANSE) + -IBLE] —**ex·pan′si·bil′i·ty,** *n.*

ex·pan·sile (ik span′sil, -sīl), *adj.* pertaining to or capable of expansion.

ex·pan·sion (ik span′shən), *n.* **1.** the act or state of expanding. **2.** the state of being expanded. **3.** the amount or degree of expanding. **4.** an expanded portion or form of a thing. **5.** anything spread out; expanse. **6.** *Math.* the development at length of an expression indicated in a contracted form, as $a^2 + 2ab + b^2$ of the expression $(a + b)^2$. **7.** *Mach.* that part of the operation of an engine in which the volume of the working medium increases and its pressure decreases. [< LL *expansiōn-* (s. of *expansiō*) a spreading out] —**ex·pan′sion·ar′y,** *adj.*

expan′sion cham′ber, *Physics.* See **cloud chamber.**

ex·pan·sion·ism (ik span′shə niz′əm), *n.* a policy of expansion, as of territory or currency: *the colonial expansionism of Europe in the 19th century.* —**ex·pan′sion·ist,** *n.* —**ex·pan′sion·is′tic,** *adj.*

ex·pan·sive (ik span′siv), *adj.* **1.** tending to expand or capable of expanding. **2.** causing expansion. **3.** having a wide range or extent; comprehensive; extensive. **4.** (of a person or his character, speech, etc.) effusive, unrestrained, or open. **5.** working by expansion, as an engine. **6.** *Psychiatry.* marked by an abnormal euphoristic state and by delusions of grandeur. —**ex·pan′sive·ly,** *adv.*

ex par·te (eks pär′tē), from or on one side only, as in a controversy; in the interest of one party. [< L]

ex·pa·ti·ate (ik spā′shē āt′), *v.i.,* **-at·ed, -at·ing. 1.** to enlarge in discourse or writing; be copious in description or discussion: *to expatiate upon a theme.* **2.** to move or wander about intellectually, imaginatively, etc., without restraint. [< L *expatiāt(us)* wandered, ptp. of *ex(s)patiārī* = *ex-* EX-[1] + *spatiārī* to walk about; see -ATE[1]] —**ex·pa′ti·a′tion,** *n.*

ex·pa·tri·ate (*v.* eks pā′trē āt′; *adj., n.* eks pā′trē it, -āt′), *v.,* **-at·ed, -at·ing,** *adj., n.* —*v.t.* **1.** to banish (a person) from his native country. **2.** to withdraw (oneself) from residence in one's native country. **3.** to withdraw (oneself) from allegiance to one's country. —*adj.* **4.** expatriated; exiled. —*n.* **5.** an expatriated person. [< ML *expatriāt(us)* banished (ptp. of *expatriāre*) = *ex-* EX-[1] + *patri(a)* native land + *-ātus* -ATE[1]] —**ex·pa′tri·a′tion,** *n.*

ex·pect (ik spekt′), *v.t.* **1.** to look forward to; regard as likely to happen; anticipate the occurrence or the coming of: *to expect guests; to expect a hurricane.* **2.** to look for with reason or justification: *We expect obedience.* **3.** *Informal.* to suppose or surmise: *I expect that you are tired from the trip.* —*v.i.* **4.** to be pregnant. [< L *ex(s)pect(āre)* (to) lookout for, await = *ex-* EX-[1] + *spectāre* to look at; see SPECTACLE] —**ex·pect′a·ble,** *adj.* —**ex·pect′a·bly,** *adv.*
—**Syn. 1.** EXPECT, ANTICIPATE all imply looking to some future event. EXPECT implies confidently believing, usually for good reasons, that an event will occur: *to expect a visit from a friend.* ANTICIPATE is to look forward to an event and even to picture it: *Do you anticipate trouble?*

ex·pect·an·cy (ik spek′tᵊn sē), *n., pl.* **-cies. 1.** the quality or state of expecting; expectation; anticipatory belief or desire. **2.** the state of being expected. **3.** an object of expectation; something expected. Also, **ex·pect′ance.** [< ML *ex(s)pectantia*]

ex·pect·ant (ik spek′tᵊnt), *adj.* **1.** having expectations; expecting. **2.** in expectation; expected; prospective: *an expectant fortune.* **3.** pregnant; expecting: *an expectant mother.* **4.** characterized by expectations. —*n.* **5.** a person who expects or who waits in expectation. [ME < L *expectant-* (s. of *expectāns*), prp. of *expectāre* to EXPECT; see -ANT] —**ex·pect′ant·ly,** *adv.*

ex·pec·ta·tion (ek′spek tā′shən), *n.* **1.** the act of expecting. **2.** the state of expecting: *to wait in expectation.* **3.** an expectant mental attitude. **4.** something expected; a thing looked forward to. **5.** Often, **expectations.** a prospect of future good or profit: *to have great expectations.* **6.** the degree of probability of the occurrence of something: *There is little expectation that he will win.* **7.** *Statistics.* See **mathematical expectation. 8.** the state of being expected. [< L *expectātiōn-* (s. of *expectātiō*) an awaiting = *expectāt(us)* (ptp. of *expectāre* to EXPECT) + *-iōn-* -ION] —**Syn. 2.** expectancy, anticipation, hope, trust.

ex·pect·a·tive (ik spek′tə tiv), *adj.* **1.** of or pertaining to expectation. **2.** characterized by expectation. [ME < ML *expectātīv(us)*]

expect′ed val′ue, *Statistics.* **1.** (of any variate) the expectation of a function equal to the variate itself. **2.** the arithmetic mean of a variable over a finite class.

ex·pec·to·rant (ik spek′tər ənt), *Med.* —*adj.* **1.** promoting the secretion of fluid from the respiratory tract. —*n.* **2.** an expectorant medicine. [< L *expectorant-* (s. of *expectorāns*), prp. of *expectorāre* to EXPECTORATE; see -ANT]

ex·pec·to·rate (ik spek′tə rāt′), *v.,* **-rat·ed, -rat·ing.** —*v.t.* **1.** to eject or expel, as phlegm, from the throat or lungs by coughing or hawking and spitting; spit. —*v.i.* **2.** to spit. [< L *expectorāt(us)* (ptp. of *expectorāre* to expel from the breast) = *ex-* EX-[1] + *pector-* (s. of *pectus* breast) + *-ātus* -ATE[1]] —**ex·pec′to·ra′tor,** *n.*

ex·pec·to·ra·tion (ik spek′tə rā′shən), *n.* **1.** the act of expectorating. **2.** matter that is expectorated.

ex·pe·di·en·cy (ik spē′dē ən sē), *n., pl.* **-cies. 1.** the quality of being expedient; advantageousness; advisability. **2.** a regard for what is politic or advantageous rather than for what is right or just. **3.** something expedient. Also, **ex·pe′di·ence.** [< LL *expedientia*]

ex·pe·di·ent (ik spē′dē ənt), *adj.* **1.** tending to promote some proposed or desired object; fit or suitable under the circumstances. **2.** conducive to advantage or interest, as opposed to right. **3.** acting in accordance with expediency. —*n.* **4.** a means to an end. **5.** a means devised or employed in an exigency. [late ME < L *expedient-* (s. of *expediēns*), prp. of *expedīre*] —**ex·pe′di·ent·ly,** *adv.* —**Syn. 1.** advisable, appropriate, desirable. **2.** advantageous, profitable. **5.** device, contrivance, resort.

ex·pe·di·en·tial (ik spē′dē en′shəl), *adj.* pertaining to or regulated by expediency.

ex·pe·dite (ek′spi dīt′), *v.,* **-dit·ed, -dit·ing,** *adj.* —*v.t.* **1.** to speed up the progress of; hasten. **2.** to accomplish promptly, as a piece of business; dispatch. **3.** to issue or dispatch, as an official document, letter, etc. —*adj.* **4.** *Obs.* ready for action; alert. [< L *expedīt(us)* disengaged, set free (the feet) (ptp. of *expedīre*) = *ex-* EX-[1] + *ped-* (s. of *pēs*) foot + *-ītus* -ITE[2]] —**ex′pe·dit′er, ex′pe·di′tor,** *n.* —**Syn. 1.** quicken, accelerate, hurry. —**Ant. 1.** delay.

ex·pe·di·tion (ek′spi dish′ən), *n.* **1.** an excursion, journey, or voyage made for some specific purpose, as of war or exploration. **2.** the body of persons, ships, etc., engaged in such an activity. **3.** promptness or speed in accomplishing something. [late ME < L *expedītiōn-* (s. of *expedītiō*) a (military) traveling] —**Syn. 1.** See **trip. 3.** dispatch.

ex·pe·di·tion·ar·y (ek′spi dish′ə ner′ē), *adj.* pertaining to or composing an expedition.

ex·pe·di·tious (ek′spi dish′əs), *adj.* characterized by promptness; quick. —**ex′pe·di′tious·ly,** *adv.* —**ex′pe·di′tious·ness,** *n.*

ex·pel (ik spel′), *v.t.,* **-pelled, -pel·ling. 1.** to drive or force out or away; discharge or eject: *to expel air from the lungs; to expel an invader from a country.* **2.** to cut off from membership or relations: *to expel a student from a college.* [ME *expelle* < L *expell(ere)* (to) drive out, drive away = *ex-* EX-[1] + *pellere* to push, drive] —**ex·pel′la·ble,** *adj.* —**Syn. 2.** oust, dismiss, exile.

ex·pel·lant (ik spel′ənt), *adj.* **1.** expelling, or having the power to expel. —*n.* **2.** an expellant medicine. Also, **ex·pel′lent.** [var. of *expellent* (see -ANT) < L *expellent-* (s. of *expellēns*), prp. of *expellere* to EXPEL; see -ENT]

ex·pel·lee (ek′spe lē′, -spə-, ik spel′ē), *n.* a person who has been expelled or deported.

ex·pel·ler (ik spel′ər), *n.* **1.** a person or thing that expels. **2.** a press used to extract oil from corn, soybeans, etc.

ex·pend (ik spend′), *v.t.* **1.** to use up: *He expended much energy on his work.* **2.** to pay out; disburse; spend. [late ME < L *expend(ere)* (to) weigh out, lay out, pay] —**ex·pend′er,** *n.* —**Syn. 1.** consume, empty. See **spend.**

ex·pend·a·ble (ik spen′də bəl), *adj.* **1.** capable of being expended. **2.** (of an item of equipment or supply) consumed in use or not reusable. **3.** *Mil.* (of men, equipment, or supplies) capable of being sacrificed in order to accomplish a military objective. —*n.* **4.** Usually, **expendables.** expendable persons or items of equipment, esp. in warfare. —**ex·pend′a·bil′i·ty,** *n.*

ex·pend·i·ture (ik spen′di chər), *n.* **1.** the act of expending; disbursement; consumption. **2.** that which is expended; expense. [< ML *expendit(us)* laid out, paid (var. of *expēnsus,* ptp. of *expendere;* see EXPEND) + -URE]

ex·pense (ik spens′), *n.* **1.** cost or charge. **2.** a cause or occasion of spending: *A car can be a great expense.* **3.** the act of expending; expenditure. **4. expenses,** *Com.* charges incurred in the execution of an undertaking or commission. **5. at the expense of,** at the sacrifice of; to the detriment of: *quantity at the expense of quality.* [ME < LL *expēnsa,* n. use of fem. of *expēnsus,* ptp. of *expendere* to EXPEND] —**Syn. 1.** outlay, expenditure. See **price.**

expense′ account′, an account of expenditures for which an employee will be reimbursed by his employer.

ex·pen·sive (ik spen′siv), *adj.* entailing great expense; very high-priced; costly: *an expensive party.* —**ex·pen′sive·ly,** *adv.* —**ex·pen′sive·ness,** *n.*
—**Syn.** EXPENSIVE, COSTLY apply to that which is higher in price than the average person's usual purchases. EXPENSIVE is applied to whatever entails considerable expense; it suggests a price more than the average person would normally be able to pay or a price paid by the average person only for something special or especially desirable: *an expensive automobile.* COSTLY implies that the price is a large sum, usually because of the fineness, preciousness, etc., of the object: *a costly jewel.* —**Ant.** cheap, low-priced.

ex·pe·ri·ence (ik spēr′ē əns), *n., v.,* **-enced, -enc·ing.** —*n.* **1.** a particular instance of personally encountering or undergoing something. **2.** the process or fact of personally observing, encountering, or undergoing something: *business experience.* **3.** the encountering or undergoing of things generally as they occur in the course of time: *to learn from experience.* **4.** knowledge gained from what one has observed, encountered, or undergone: *men of experience.* —*v.t.* **5.** to meet with; undergo; feel: *to experience nausea.* [ME < L *experientia* = *experient-* (s. of *experiēns,* prp. of *experīrī* to try, test; see EX-[1], PERIL) + *-ia;* see -ENCE] —**Syn. 5.** encounter, know.

ex·pe·ri·enced (ik spēr′ē ənst), *adj.* wise or skillful in a particular field through experience: *an experienced teacher.* —**Syn.** skilled, expert, practiced, veteran, accomplished.

ex·pe·ri·en·tial (ik spēr′ē en′shəl), *adj.* pertaining to or derived from experience. [< ML *experientiāl(is)*] —**ex·pe′ri·en′tial·ly,** *adv.*

ex·per·i·ment (*n.* ik sper′ə mənt; *v.* ek sper′ə ment′), *n.* **1.** a test, trial, or tentative procedure; an act or operation for the purpose of discovering something unknown or of testing a principle, supposition, etc.: *a chemical experiment.* **2.** the conducting of such operations; experimentation. **3.** *Obs.* experience. —*v.i.* **4.** to try or test, esp. in order to discover or prove something. [ME: proof < L *experīment(um)*] —**ex·per′i·ment′er,** *n.* —**Syn. 1.** See **trial. 2.** research, investigation.

ex·per·i·men·tal (ik sper′ə men′tᵊl), *adj.* **1.** pertaining to, derived from, or founded on experiment: *an experimental science.* **2.** based on or derived from experience; empirical. **3.** of the nature of an experiment; tentative: *It is still in an experimental stage.* [late ME < ML *experīmentāl(is)*] —**ex·per′i·men′tal·ly,** *adv.*

ex·per·i·men·tal·ism (ik sper′ə men′tᵊliz′əm), *n.* **1.** doctrine or practice of relying on experimentation; empiricism. **2.** fondness for experimenting or innovating. —**ex·per′i·men′tal·ist,** *n.*

experimen′tal psychol′ogy, the study of emotional and mental activity, as learning, in animals and man by means of experimental methods.

ex·per·i·men·ta·tion (ik sper′ə men tā′shən), *n.* the act, process, practice, or an instance of making experiments.

ex·pert (*n., v.* ek′spûrt; *adj.* ik spûrt′, ek′spûrt), *n.* **1.** a person who has special skill or knowledge in some particular field; specialist; authority. **2.** *U.S. Mil.* the highest rating in rifle marksmanship. —*adj.* **3.** possessing special skill or knowledge; trained by practice; skillful or skilled (often fol. by *in* or *at*): *an expert driver; to be expert at driving a car.* **4.** pertaining to, coming from, or characteristic of an expert: *expert work, expert advice.* [ME < L *expert(us),* ptp. of *experīrī* to try, EXPERIENCE] **—ex·pert′ly,** *adv.* **—ex·pert′ness,** *n.* **—Syn. 1.** master. **3.** experienced, proficient, adroit. **—Ant. 1.** novice. **3.** inept.

ex·per·tise (ek′spər tēz′), *n.* expert skill or knowledge; expertness. [< F: survey, report (made by experts); *-ise* taken to mean *-ness*]

ex·pi·a·ble (ek′spē ə bəl), *adj.* capable of being expiated. [< LL *expiābil(is)*]

ex·pi·ate (ek′spē āt′), *v.t.,* **-at·ed, -at·ing.** to atone for; make amends or reparation for. [< L *expiāt(us)* atoned for, made good (ptp. of *expiāre*) = *ex-* EX-[1] + *piā(re)* (to) propitiate (see PIOUS) + *-tus* ptp. suffix] **—ex′pi·a′tor,** *n.*

ex·pi·a·tion (ek′spē ā′shən), *n.* **1.** the act of expiating. **2.** the means by which atonement or reparation is made. [late ME *expiacion* < L *expiātiōn-* (s. of *expiātiō*) atonement, satisfaction]

ex·pi·a·to·ry (ek′spē ə tōr′ē, -tôr′ē), *adj.* able to make atonement or expiation; offered by way of expiation. [< LL *expiātōri(us)*]

ex·pi·ra·tion (ek′spə rā′shən), *n.* **1.** a coming to an end; termination; close: *the expiration of a contract.* **2.** the act of expiring, or breathing out; emission of air from the lungs. **3.** *Archaic.* death. [late ME *expiracioun* < L *expīrātiōn-* (s. of *expīrātiō*) = *expīrāt(us)* (ptp. of *ex(s)pīrāre* to EXPIRE) + *-iōn-* -ION]

ex·pir·a·to·ry (ik spīər′ə tōr′ē, -tôr′ē), *adj.* pertaining to the expiration of air from the lungs.

ex·pire (ik spīər′), *v.,* **-pired, -pir·ing.** **—v.i. 1.** to come to an end; terminate, as a contract, guarantee, etc. **2.** to die out, as a fire. **3.** to emit the last breath; die. **4.** to breathe out. **—v.t. 5.** to breathe out; emit (air) from the lungs. **6.** *Obs.* to give off or emit. [late ME < L *ex(s)pīr(āre)* (to) breathe out = *ex-* EX-[1] + *spīrāre* to breathe] **—ex·pir′er,** *n.*

ex·pi·ry (ik spīər′ē, ek′spə rē), *n., pl.* **-ries. 1.** expiration of breath. **2.** an end, as of life, a contract, etc.

ex·plain (ik splān′), *v.t.* **1.** to make plain or clear; render intelligible. **2.** to make known in detail: *to explain how to do something; to explain a process.* **3.** to assign a meaning to; interpret: *How can you explain such a silly remark?* **4.** to make clear the cause or reason of; account for: *I cannot explain his behavior.* **—v.i. 5.** to give an explanation. **6. explain away,** to dispel (doubts, difficulties, etc.) by explanation: *She explained away the child's fears.* [late ME *explane(n)* < L *explān(āre)* (to) smooth out, make intelligible, spread out on flat surface. See EX-[1], PLAIN[1]] **—ex·plain′a·ble,** *adj.* **—ex·plain′er,** *n.*
—Syn. 1. explicate. EXPLAIN, ELUCIDATE, EXPOUND, INTERPRET imply making the meaning of something clear or understandable. To EXPLAIN is to make plain, clear, or intelligible something that is not known or understood: *to explain a theory or a problem.* To ELUCIDATE is to throw light on what before was dark and obscure, usually by illustration and commentary and sometimes by elaborate explanation: *They asked him to elucidate his statement.* To EXPOUND is to give a methodical, detailed, scholarly explanation of something, usually Scriptures, doctrines, or philosophy: *to expound the doctrine of free will.* To INTERPRET is to give the meaning of something by paraphrase, by translation, or by an explanation (sometimes involving one's personal opinion and therefore original), which is often of a systematic and detailed nature: *to interpret a poem.*

ex·pla·na·tion (ek′splə nā′shən), *n.* **1.** the act or process of explaining. **2.** that which explains; a statement made to clarify something and make it understandable; exposition. **3.** a meaning or interpretation: *to find an explanation of a mystery.* **4.** a mutual declaration of the meaning of words spoken, actions, motives, etc., with a view to adjusting a misunderstanding or reconciling differences. [ME *explanacioun* < L *explānātiōn-* (s. of *explānātiō*) = *explānāt(us)* (ptp. of *explānāre* to EXPLAIN; see -ATE[1]) + *-iōn-* -ION] **—Syn. 1.** elucidation, explication, interpretation, description. **3.** solution, key, answer.

ex·plan·a·to·ry (ik splan′ə tōr′ē, -tôr′ē), *adj.* serving to explain. Also, **ex·plan′a·tive.** [< LL *explānātōri(us)*] **—ex·plan′a·to′ri·ly, ex·plan′a·tive·ly,** *adv.*

ex·plant (*v.* eks plant′, -plänt′; *n.* eks′plant′, -plänt′), *v.t.* **1.** to take (living material) from an animal or plant and place it in a culture medium. **—n. 2.** a piece of explanted tissue. [< NL *explant(āre)*] **—ex′plan·ta′tion,** *n.*

ex·ple·tive (ek′spli tiv), *n.* **1.** an interjectory word or expression, frequently profane; an exclamatory oath. **2.** *Gram.* a word considered as regularly filling the syntactic position of another, as *it* in *It is his duty to go,* or *there* in *There is nothing here.* **3.** a syllable, word, or phrase serving to fill out. **—adj. 4.** Also, **ex·ple·to·ry** (ek′spli tōr′ē, -tôr′ē). added merely to fill out a sentence or line, give emphasis, etc. [< LL *explētīv(us)* serving to fill out = L *explēt(us)* filled, filled up (ptp. of *explēre*) (*ex-* EX-[1] + *plē(re)* (to) fill) + *-īvus* -IVE] **—ex′ple·tive·ly,** *adv.*

ex·pli·ca·ble (ek′splə kə bəl, ik splik′ə bəl), *adj.* capable of being explained. [< L *explicābil(is)*]

ex·pli·cate (ek′splə kāt′), *v.t.,* **-cat·ed, -cat·ing. 1.** to develop (a principle, theory, etc.). **2.** to make plain or clear; explain; interpret: *to explicate a difficult text.* [< L *explicāt(us)* unfolded, set forth, ptp. of *explicāre.* See EX-[1], -PLY[2], -ATE[1]] **—ex′pli·ca′tor,** *n.*

ex·pli·ca·tion (ek′splə kā′shən), *n.* **1.** the act of explicating. **2.** an explanation; interpretation. [< F < L *explicātiōn-* (s. of *explicātiō*)]

ex·pli·ca·tive (ek′splə kā′tiv, ik splik′ə tiv), *adj.* explanatory; interpretive. Also, **ex·pli·ca·to·ry** (ek′splə kə tōr′ē, -tôr′ē, ik splik′ə-). [< L *explicātīv(us)*] **—ex′pli·ca′tive·ly,** *adv.*

ex·plic·it (ik splis′it), *adj.* **1.** fully and clearly expressed; leaving nothing merely implied; unequivocal. **2.** clearly developed or formulated: *to have an explicit understanding of a problem.* **3.** definite and unreserved in expression; outspoken. [< L *explicit(us)* unfolded, set forth, var. ptp. of *explicāre;* see EXPLICATE] **—ex·plic′it·ly,** *adv.* **—ex·plic′it·ness,** *n.* **—Syn. 1.** definite, precise, exact, unambiguous. **3.** open. **—Ant. 1.** indefinite, ambiguous.

ex·plode (ik splōd′), *v.,* **-plod·ed, -plod·ing. —v.i. 1.** to expand with force and noise because of rapid chemical change or decomposition, as gunpowder, nitroglycerine, etc. (opposed to *implode*). **2.** to burst violently with a loud report, as a boiler from excessive pressure of steam. **3.** to burst forth violently or emotionally, esp. with noise, laughter, violent speech, etc. **4.** *Phonet.* (of plosives) to terminate the occlusive phase with a plosion. Cf. **implode** (def. 2). **—v.t. 5.** to cause (gunpowder, a boiler, etc.) to explode. **6.** to discredit or disprove: *to explode a theory.* **7.** *Phonet.* to end with plosion. **8.** *Obs.* to drive (a player, play, etc.) from the stage by loud expressions of disapprobation. [< L *explōd(ere)* (to) drive off by clapping, drive away = *ex-* EX-[1] + *plod-* var. s. of *plaudere* to clap, beat] **—ex·plod′er,** *n.*

explod′ed view′, a drawing, photograph, or the like, that shows the individual parts of a mechanism separately but indicates their proper relationship.

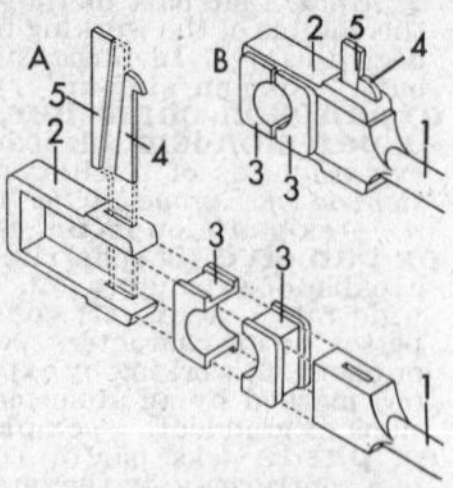

A, Exploded view of marine steam engine connecting rod; B, Assembled; 1, Connecting rod; 2, Strap; 3, Brass; 4, Gib; 5, Cotter

ex·plod·ent (ik splōd′ənt), *n.* an explosive. [< L *explōdent-* (s. of *explōdēns*), prp. of *explōdere* to EXPLODE; see -ENT]

ex·ploit[1] (ek′sploit, ik sploit′), *n.* a striking or notable deed; feat; spirited or heroic act. [ME *exploit, espleit* < OF *esploit,* AF *espleit* < L *explicit(um),* neut. of *explicitus* (ptp.). See EXPLICIT] **—Syn.** accomplishment.

ex·ploit[2] (ik sploit′), *v.t.* **1.** to utilize, esp. for profit; turn to practical account. **2.** to use selfishly for one's own ends. **3.** to promote through advertising and public relations. [< F *exploit(er)* < *exploit* (n.); r. late ME *expleiten* to achieve < AF *espleiter* < *espleit* (n.). See EXPLOIT[1]] **—ex·ploit′a·ble,** *adj.* **—ex·ploit′a·tive,** *adj.* **—ex·ploit′er,** *n.*

ex·ploi·ta·tion (ek′sploi tā′shən), *n.* **1.** utilization for profit: *the exploitation of newly discovered oil fields.* **2.** selfish utilization. **3.** the use of public relations and advertising to promote a person, movie, product, etc. [< F]

ex·plo·ra·tion (ek′splə rā′shən), *n.* **1.** the act or an instance of exploring or investigating; examination. **2.** the investigation of unknown regions. [< L *explōrātiōn-* (s. of *explōrātiō*) an examination = *explōrāt(us)* searched out, examined (ptp. of *explōrāre* to EXPLORE) + *-iōn-* -ION]

ex·plor·a·to·ry (ik splōr′ə tōr′ē, -splôr′ə tôr′ē), *adj.* **1.** pertaining to or concerned with exploration: *an exploratory trip; an exploratory operation.* **2.** inclined to make explorations. Also, **ex·plor′a·tive.** [late ME < L *explōrātōri(us)*]

ex·plore (ik splōr′, -splôr′), *v.,* **-plored, -plor·ing. —v.t. 1.** to traverse or range over (a region, area, etc.) for the purpose of discovery. **2.** to look into closely; scrutinize; examine. **3.** *Surg.* to investigate into, esp. mechanically, as with a probe. **4.** *Obs.* to search for; search out. **—v.i. 5.** to engage in exploration. [< L *explōr(āre)* (to) search out, examine = *ex-* EX-[1] + *plōrāre* to cry out, prob. orig. with reference to hunting cries]

ex·plor·er (ik splōr′ər, -splôr′-), *n.* **1.** a person or thing that explores, esp. a person who investigates unknown regions. **2.** any instrument used in exploring or sounding a wound, a cavity in a tooth, etc. **3.** (*cap.*) *U.S.* one of a series of satellites equipped to study cosmic rays, radiation belts, micrometeorites, gamma radiation, etc.

ex·plo·sion (ik splō′zhən), *n.* **1.** the act or an instance of exploding; a violent expansion or bursting with noise, as of gunpowder or a boiler. **2.** the noise itself. **3.** a violent outburst, as of laughter, anger, etc. **4.** *Phonet.* plosion. [< L *explōsiōn-* (s. of *explōsiō*) = *explōs(us)* driven off by clapping (ptp. of *explōdere* to EXPLODE) + *-iōn-* -ION]

ex·plo·sive (ik splō′siv), *adj.* **1.** tending or serving to explode. **2.** pertaining to or of the nature of an explosion. **3.** *Phonet.* plosive. **—n. 4.** an explosive agent or substance, as dynamite. **5.** *Phonet.* plosive. **—ex·plo′sive·ly,** *adv.* **—ex·plo′sive·ness,** *n.*

ex·po (ek′spō), *n., pl.* **-pos.** (*often cap.*) *Informal.* exposition (def. 1): *Boat Expo; Computer Expo.*

ex·po·nent (ik spō′nənt *or, esp. for 3,* ek′spō nənt), *n.* **1.** a person or thing that expounds or explains; an interpreter. **2.** a person or thing that is a representative, advocate, type, or symbol of something: *Lincoln is an exponent of American democracy.* **3.** *Math.* a symbol placed above and after another symbol to denote the power to which the latter is to be raised, as *n* in the expression x^n. [< L *expōnent-* (s. of *expōnēns*), prp. of *expōnere* to EXPOUND; see -ENT]

ex·po·nen·tial (ek′spō nen′shəl), *adj.* **1.** of or pertaining to an exponent or exponents. **2.** *Math.* **a.** of or pertaining to the constant *e.* **b.** (of an equation) having one or more unknown variables in one or more exponents. **—n. 3.** *Math.* the constant *e* raised to the power equal to a given expression, as e^{3x}, which is the exponential of 3*x*. **—ex′po·nen′tial·ly,** *adv.*

ex·po·ni·ble (ik spō′nə bəl), *Logic.* **—adj. 1.** (of a proposition) requiring an expanded and revised statement to remove some obscurity. **—n. 2.** an exponible proposition. [< ML *expōnibil(is)*]

ex·port (*v.* ik spōrt′, -spôrt′, ek′spōrt, -spôrt; *n., adj.* ek′spōrt, -spôrt), *v.t.* **1.** to send (commodities) to other countries or places for sale, exchange, etc. **—n. 2.** the act of exporting; exportation. **3.** that which is exported; an article exported. **—adj. 4.** of or pertaining to exportation of goods or to exportable goods. [< L *export(āre)* (to) carry out, bear away] **—ex·port′a·ble,** *adj.* **—ex·port′er,** *n.*

ex·por·ta·tion (ek′spōr tā′shən, -spôr-), *n.* **1.** the act of exporting; the sending of commodities out of a country, typically in trade. **2.** something exported. [< L *exportātiōn-* (s. of *exportātiō*) = *exportāt(us)* (ptp. of *exportāre* to EXPORT) + *-iōn-* -ION]

Ex′port-Im′port Bank′ (ek′spōrt im′pōrt, ek′spôrt im′pôrt), *U.S.* a federal bank, established in 1934, authorized to make loans to foreign governments and commercial enterprises, with the provision that such funds be used to purchase U.S. goods.

ex·pos·al (ik spō′zəl), *n.* an exposure.

ex·pose (ik spōz′), *v.t.,* **-posed, -pos·ing. 1.** to lay open to danger, attack, harm, etc.; subject to: *to expose soldiers to gunfire.* **2.** to lay open to something specified: *to expose oneself to bad influences.* **3.** to uncover or bare to the air, cold, etc.: *to expose one's head to the rain.* **4.** to present to view; exhibit; display. **5.** to make known, disclose, or reveal (intentions, secrets, etc.). **6.** to reveal or unmask (a crime, impostor, etc.). **7.** to desert in an unsheltered or open place; abandon, as a child. **8.** to subject, as to the action of something: *to expose a photographic plate to light.* [ME *expose(n)* < OF *expose(r)* (see EX-[1], POSE[1]); but assoc. with deriv. of L *expōnere* to set forth, EXPOUND] —**ex·pos′a·ble,** *adj.* —**ex·pos′er,** *n.* —**Syn. 1.** endanger, imperil, jeopardize. **5.** uncover, unveil. —**Ant. 1.** protect. **4–6.** conceal.

ex·po·sé (ek′spō zā′), *n.* an exposure or revelation, as of something discreditable. [< F, n. use of ptp. of *exposer* to EXPOSE]

ex·posed (ik spōzd′), *adj.* **1.** left or being without shelter or protection. **2.** laid open to view; unconcealed. **3.** susceptible to attack; vulnerable. —**ex·pos·ed·ness** (ik-spō′zid nis), *n.*

ex·po·si·tion (ek′spə zish′ən), *n.* **1.** a public exhibition or show. **2.** the act of expounding, setting forth, or explaining. **3.** a detailed statement or explanation; explanatory treatise. **4.** the act of presenting to view; display. **5.** exposure (def. 6). **6.** the state of being exposed; exposure. **7.** *Music.* the first section of a fugue or a sonata form, in which the principal themes normally are introduced. [ME *exposicioun* < L *expositiōn-* (s. of *expositiō*)] —**ex′po·si′tion·al,** *adj.* —**Syn. 1.** exhibit, demonstration, display, presentation. **3.** elucidation, commentary; critique, interpretation, exegesis, explication.

ex·pos·i·tor (ik spoz′i tər), *n.* a person who expounds or gives an exposition. [ME < LL *expositōr-* (s. of *expositor*)] —**ex·pos·i·to·ri·al** (ik spoz′i tōr′ē əl, -tôr′-), *adj.* —**ex-pos′i·to′ri·al·ly,** *adv.*

ex·pos·i·to·ry (ik spoz′i tōr′ē, -tôr′ē), *adj.* serving to expound, set forth, or explain. Also, **ex·pos′i·tive.** [< ML *expositōri(us)*] —**ex·pos′i·to′ri·ly, ex·pos′i·tive·ly,** *adv.*

ex post fac·to (eks′ pōst′ fak′tō), **1.** from or by subsequent action; subsequently; retrospectively or retroactively. **2.** having retroactive force; made or done subsequently. [< L: from a thing done afterward, from what is done afterward]

ex·pos·tu·late (ik spos′chə lāt′), *v.i.*, **-lat·ed, -lat·ing.** to reason earnestly with a person against something he intends to do or has done; remonstrate. [< L *expostulāt(us)* demanded urgently, required (ptp. of *expostulāre*)] —**ex-pos′tu·lat′ing·ly,** *adv.* —**ex·pos′tu·la′tor,** *n.* —**ex·pos-tu·la·to·ry** (ik spos′chə lə tōr′ē, -tôr′ē), **ex·pos′tu·la′tive,** *adj.*

ex·pos·tu·la·tion (ik spos′chə lā′shən), *n.* **1.** the act of expostulating; remonstrance; earnest and kindly protest. **2.** an expostulatory remark or address. [< L *expostulātiōn-* (s. of *expostulātiō*) complaint]

ex·po·sure (ik spō′zhər), *n.* **1.** the act of exposing. **2.** disclosure, as of something private or secret. **3.** the act or an instance of revealing or unmasking, as an impostor, crime, etc. **4.** a laying open or subjecting to the action or influence of something: *exposure to the elements.* **5.** *Photog.* **a.** the act of presenting a film or the like to the actinic rays of light. **b.** each of the areas exposed on a film. **c.** the length of time that a film is exposed to the light. **6.** a turning out or deserting, esp. of a child, without shelter or protection; abandonment. **7.** state of being exposed. **8.** placement or situation with regard to sunlight or wind; aspect: *a southern exposure.* **9.** an exposed surface: *exposures of rock.* —**Syn. 2.** divulgement, revelation, exposé. —**Ant. 1.** concealment, hiding.

expo′sure me′ter, *Photog.* an instrument that measures the intensity of light in a certain place and indicates the proper exposure. Also called **light meter.**

ex·pound (ik spound′), *v.t.* **1.** to set forth or state in detail: *to expound theories.* **2.** to explain; interpret. [ME *expoune(n), expounde(n)* < OF *espondre* < L *expōnere* to put out, set forth, explain = *ex-* EX-[1] + *pōnere* to put] —**ex-pound′er,** *n.* —**Syn. 2.** See **explain.**

ex·press (ik spres′), *v.t.* **1.** to put (thought) into words: *to express an idea clearly.* **2.** to show, manifest, or reveal. **3.** to set forth the opinions, feelings, etc., of (oneself): *He can express himself eloquently.* **4.** to represent by a symbol or formula. **5.** *U.S.* to send express. **6.** to press or squeeze out: *to express the juice of grapes.* **7.** to exude or emit (a liquid, odor, etc.), as if under pressure. —*adj.* **8.** clearly indicated; explicit: *He defied my express command.* **9.** special; definite. **10.** duly or exactly formed or represented. **11.** pertaining to an express: *an express agency.* **12.** specially direct or fast: *an express bus.* —*n.* **13.** an express train, bus, elevator, etc. **14.** a system of sending freight, parcels, money, etc., that is faster but more expensive than ordinary freight service. **15.** a company engaged in this business. **16.** *Brit.* a messenger or a message specially sent. **17.** something sent by express. —*adv.* **18.** by express. **19.** *Obs.* expressly. [ME *expresse(n)* < L *express(us)* (ptp. of *exprimere*)] —**ex·press′er, ex·pres′sor,** *n.* —**ex·press′i·ble, ex·press′a·ble,** *adj.* —**Syn. 1.** utter, declare, word, state. **2.** indicate. **4.** designate, signify, denote. **8.** unambiguous. **9.** particular, singular. **10.** faithful, exact. **12.** rapid, nonstop.

ex·press·age (ik spres′ij), *n.* **1.** the business of transmitting parcels, money, etc., by express. **2.** the charge for such transmission.

express′ deliv′ery, *Brit.* See **special delivery.**

ex·pres·sion (ik spresh′ən), *n.* **1.** the act of expressing or setting forth in words. **2.** a particular word or phrase. **3.** the manner or form in which a thing is expressed in words; wording. **4.** power of expressing in words: *joy beyond expression.* **5.** indication of feeling, character, etc., as in the voice, or in artistic execution. **6.** a look or intonation expressing personal reaction, feeling, etc. **7.** the quality or power of expressing attitude, emotion, etc.: *a face that lacks expression; to read with expression.* **8.** the act of expressing or representing, as by symbols. **9.** *Math.* a symbol or a combination of symbols representing a value, relation, or the like. **10.** the act of expressing or pressing out. [ME < L *expressiōn-* (s. of *expressiō*) a pressing out] —**ex·pres′-sion·al,** *adj.* —**ex·pres′sion·less,** *adj.* —**ex·pres′sion-less·ly,** *adv.* —**Syn. 1.** utterance, declaration, assertion, statement. **2.** term, idiom. **3.** language, diction, phraseology. **5.** manifestation, sign. **6.** aspect, air, countenance, mien, tone.

Ex·pres·sion·ism (ik spresh′ə niz′əm), *n.* **1.** *Fine Arts.* **a.** (*usually l.c.*) a manner of painting, sculpting, etc., in which natural forms and colors are distorted or exaggerated. **b.** a style of art developed in the 20th century, characterized chiefly by heavy, often black lines that define forms, sharply contrasting, often vivid colors, and subjective or symbolic treatment of thematic material. **2.** (*often l.c.*) a style or manner of literature and theater stressing the subjective element in experience and the symbolic aspects of objects, events, etc. **3.** (*usually l.c.*) a phase in the development of early 20th-century music marked by the use of atonality and complex, unconventional rhythm, melody, and form. [< G *Expressionismus*] —**Ex·pres′sion·ist,** *n., adj.* —**Ex·pres′sion·is′tic,** *adj.* —**Ex·pres′sion·is′-ti·cal·ly,** *adv.*

ex·pres·sive (ik spres′iv), *adj.* **1.** serving to express; indicative of power to express: *a look expressive of gratitude.* **2.** full of expression; meaningful: *an expressive shrug.* **3.** of, pertaining to, or concerned with expression. [ME < MF] —**ex·pres′sive·ly,** *adv.* —**ex·pres′sive·ness,** *n.*

express′ let′ter, *Brit.* a special-delivery letter.

ex·press·ly (ik spres′lē), *adv.* **1.** in an express manner; explicitly. **2.** for the express purpose; specially. [ME *expressli*]

express′ ri′fle, a rifle designed for firing at game at short range.

ex·press·way (ik spres′wā′), *n.* a highway especially planned for high-speed traffic, usually having few if any intersections, limited points of access or exit, and a divider between lanes for traffic moving in opposite directions.

ex·pro·pri·ate (eks prō′prē āt′), *v.t.*, **-at·ed, -at·ing. 1.** to take (property, ideas, etc.) from another, esp. without his permission. **2.** to deprive (a person, business, etc.) of property. [< ML *expropriāt(us)* separated from one's own (ptp. of *expropriāre*). See EX-[1], PROPER, -ATE[1]] —**ex·pro-pri·a·ble** (eks prō′prē ə bəl), *adj.* —**ex·pro′pri·a′tion,** *n.* —**ex·pro′pri·a′tor,** *n.*

ex·pugn·a·ble (ek spyōō′nə bəl, -spug′nə-), *adj.* able to be overcome, conquered, defeated, etc. [< L *expugnābil(is)* = *expugnā(re)* (to) take by storm (*ex-* EX-[1] + *pugnāre* to fight) + *-bilis* -BLE]

ex·pul·sion (ik spul′shən), *n.* **1.** the act of driving out or expelling: *expulsion of air.* **2.** the state of being expelled. [late ME < L *expulsiōn-* (s. of *expulsiō*) = *expuls(us)* driven out (ptp. of *expellere* to EXPEL) + *-iōn-* -ION] —**ex-pul′sive,** *adj.*

ex·punc·tion (ik spungk′shən), *n.* the act of expunging; erasure. [< LL *expunctiōn-* (s. of *expunctiō*) a blotting out = L *expunct(us)* blotted out (ptp. of *expungere* to EXPUNGE) + *-iōn-* -ION]

ex·punge (ik spunj′), *v.t.*, **-punged, -pung·ing. 1.** to strike or blot out; erase. **2.** to efface; wipe out or destroy. [< L *expung(ere)* (to) blot out, erase = *ex-* EX-[1] + *pungere* to prick] —**ex·pung′er,** *n.*

ex·pur·gate (ek′spər gāt′, ik spûr′gāt), *v.t.*, **-gat·ed, -gat·ing. 1.** to amend by removing offensive or objectionable matter: *to expurgate a book.* **2.** to remove (offensive parts) from a book, speech, etc. [< L *expurgāt(us)*, ptp. of *expurgāre* to clean out. See EX-[1], PURGE, -ATE[1]] —**ex′pur-ga′tion,** *n.* —**ex′pur·ga′tor,** *n.* —**ex·pur·ga·to·ri·al** (ik-spûr′gə tōr′ē əl, -tôr′-), *adj.* —**ex·pur′ga·to′ry,** *adj.*

ex·qui·site (ek′skwi zit, ik skwiz′it), *adj.* **1.** of special beauty or charm, or rare and appealing excellence, as a face, flower, etc. **2.** extraordinarily fine; consummate: *exquisite weather.* **3.** intense or keen, as pleasure, pain, etc. **4.** keenly or delicately sensitive or responsive: *an exquisite ear for music.* **5.** of rare excellence of production or workmanship. **6.** of peculiar refinement or elegance: *exquisite taste.* **7.** *Obs.* carefully sought out, ascertained, devised, etc. —*n.* **8.** a person, esp. a man, who is excessively concerned about his clothes, grooming, etc.; dandy; coxcomb. [late ME < L *exquīsīt(us)* sought after (ptp. of *exquīrere*). See EX-[1], QUEST, -ITE[2]] —**ex′qui·site·ly,** *adv.* —**ex′-qui·site·ness,** *n.* —**Syn. 1.** beautiful, elegant. See **delicate. 2.** perfect, matchless. See **fine**[1]. **3.** poignant. **5.** select, choice, precious. **6.** discriminating. —**Ant. 1.** gross. **2.** ordinary.

exr., executor.

ex·san·guine (eks sang′gwin), *adj.* anemic; bloodless. [< L *exsangu(is)* bloodless (see EX-[1], SANGUINE) + -INE[1]] —**ex′san·guin′i·ty,** *n.*

ex·scind (ek sind′), *v.t.* to cut out or off. [< L *exscind(ere)* (to) destroy, tear away = *ex-* EX-[1] + *scindere* to cut, tear; see SCISSION]

ex·sect (ek sekt′), *v.t.* to cut out. [< L *exsect(us)* cut out, cut away, ptp. of *ex(s)ecāre*] —**ex·sec·tile** (ek sek′t^{ə}l, -tīl, -til), *adj.* —**ex·sec′tion,** *n.*

ex·sert (ek sûrt′), *v.t.* **1.** to thrust or force out, esp. beyond surrounding parts. —*adj.* **2.** thrust out; exserted. [< L *exsert(us)* stretched out, put forth, var. of *exertus;* see EXERT] —**ex·ser′tion,** *n.*

ex·ser·tile (eks sûr′t^{ə}l, -til), *adj.* *Biol.* capable of being exserted or protruded. [< F *exertile*]

ex·sic·cate (ek′sə kāt′), *v.*, **-cat·ed, -cat·ing.** —*v.t.* **1.** to dry or remove the moisture from, as a substance. **2.** to dry up, as moisture. —*v.i.* **3.** to dry up. [late ME < L *exsiccāt(us)* dried up, ptp. of *exsiccāre*] —**ex′sic·ca′tion,** *n.* —**ex′sic·ca′tive,** *adj.* —**ex′sic·ca′tor,** *n.*

ex·stip·u·late (eks stip′yə lit, -lāt′), *adj.* *Bot.* having no stipules. Also, **estipulate.**

ext., 1. extension. **2.** external. **3.** extinct. **4.** extra.

ex·tant (ek′stənt, ik stant′), *adj.* **1.** in existence; not destroyed or lost. **2.** *Archaic.* standing out; protruding. [< L *ex(s)tant-* (s. of *ex(s)tāns*) standing out, prp. of *exstāre* = *ex-* EX-[1] + *stāre* to stand]

ex·tem·po·ral (ik stem′pər əl), *adj.* *Archaic.* extemporaneous; extempore. [< L *extemporāl(is)* on the spur of the moment] —**ex·tem′po·ral·ly,** *adv.*

ex·tem·po·ra·ne·ous (ik stem′pə rā′nē əs), *adj.* **1.** done or spoken without special preparation; impromptu. **2.** previously planned but delivered with the help of few or no notes: *extemporaneous lectures.* **3.** speaking or performing with little or no advance preparation: *extemporaneous actors.* **4.** made with anything available, as a shelter. [< LL *extemporāneus* on the spur of the moment] —**ex·tem′po·ra′ne·ous·ly,** *adv.* —**ex·tem′po·ra′ne·ous·ness, ex·tem·po·ra·ne·i·ty** (ik stem′pə rə nē′i tē), *n.*
—**Syn. 1, 2.** EXTEMPORANEOUS (EXTEMPORARY, EXTEMPORE), IMPROMPTU, IMPROVISED are used of (artistic) expression given without preparation or based on only partial preparation. EXTEMPORANEOUS, although often used interchangeably with IMPROMPTU, is applied more precisely to an unmemorized speech given from an outline or notes: *an extemporaneous discussion.* IMPROMPTU is applied to a speech (poem, song, etc.) delivered without preparation, and at a moment's notice: *Called upon without warning, she nevertheless gave an excellent impromptu speech.* IMPROVISED is applied to that which is composed (recited, sung, acted) on a particular occasion, and which demands swift and unwavering inventiveness: *an improvised piano accompaniment.* —**Ant. 1.** memorized.

ex·tem·po·rar·y (ik stem′pə rer′ē), *adj.* **1.** extemporaneous; extempore. **2.** *Obs.* sudden; unexpected. —**ex·tem·po·rar·i·ly** (ik stem′pə râr′ə lē), *adv.* —**Syn. 1.** See **extemporaneous.**

ex·tem·po·re (ik stem′pə rē), *adv.* **1.** on the spur of the moment; without premeditation or preparation; offhand. **2.** without notes: *to speak extempore.* **3.** (of musical performance) by improvisation. —*adj.* **4.** extemporaneous; impromptu. [< L: lit., out of the time, at the moment = *ex-* EX-[1] + *tempore* time (abl. sing. of *tempus*)] —**Syn. 4.** See **extemporaneous.**

ex·tem·po·rise (ik stem′pə rīz′), *v.i., v.t.,* **-rised, -ris·ing.** *Chiefly Brit.* extemporize. —**ex·tem′po·ri·sa′tion,** *n.* —**ex·tem′po·ris′er,** *n.*

ex·tem·po·rize (ik stem′pə rīz′), *v.,* **-rized, -riz·ing.** —*v.i.* **1.** to speak extemporaneously. **2.** *Music.* to improvise. **3.** to do or manage something in a makeshift way. —*v.t.* **4.** to make or devise extempore. **5.** *Music.* to compose offhand; improvise. —**ex·tem′po·ri·za′tion,** *n.* —**ex·tem′po·riz′er,** *n.*

ex·tend (ik stend′), *v.t.* **1.** to stretch out; draw out to the full length. **2.** to stretch or arrange in a given direction, or so as to reach a particular point, as a wall, line of troops, etc. **3.** to stretch or hold out, as the hand. **4.** to place at full length, esp. horizontally, as the body, limbs, etc. **5.** to increase the duration of; prolong. **6.** to stretch out in various or all directions; expand. **7.** to enlarge the scope of, or make more comprehensive. **8.** to hold forth as an offer; grant; give: *to extend aid to needy scholars.* **9.** *Finance.* to postpone (the payment of a debt) beyond the time originally agreed upon. **10.** *Bookkeeping.* to transfer (figures) from one column to another. **11.** *Law.* **a.** *Brit.* to assess or value. **b.** to make a seizure or levy upon, as land, by a writ of extent. **12.** *Obs.* to take by seizure. **13.** *Obs.* to exaggerate. —*v.i.* **14.** to be or become extended; stretch out in length, duration, or in various or all directions. **15.** to reach, as to a particular point. **16.** to increase in length, area, scope, etc. [ME *extend(en)* < L *extend(ere)* (to) stretch out] —**ex·tend′i·bil′i·ty, ex·tend′a·bil′i·ty,** *n.* —**ex·tend′i·ble, ex·tend′a·ble,** *adj.* —**Syn. 5.** See **lengthen. 6.** spread, enlarge. —**Ant. 1.** shorten, contract.

ex·tend·ed (ik sten′did), *adj.* **1.** stretched out. **2.** continued or prolonged. **3.** spread out. **4.** widespread or extensive; having extension or spatial magnitude. **5.** outstretched: *extended arms.* —**ex·tend′ed·ly,** *adv.* —**ex·tend′ed·ness,** *n.*

ex·tend·er (ik sten′dər), *n.* any inert chemical substance added to paint chiefly to increase its volume.

ex·ten·si·ble (ik sten′sə bəl), *adj.* capable of being extended. [EXTENS(ION) + -IBLE] —**ex·ten′si·bil′i·ty, ex·ten′si·ble·ness,** *n.*

ex·ten·sile (ik sten′səl, -sīl), *adj.* *Chiefly Zool., Anat.* capable of being extended; adapted for stretching out; extensible; protrusible. [EXTENS(ION) + -ILE]

ex·ten·sion (ik sten′shən), *n.* **1.** the act of extending. **2.** the state of being extended. **3.** that by which something is extended; prolongation. **4.** an extra telephone that operates on the principal line. **5.** *Com.* an allowance of further time to a debtor for paying the debt. **6.** *Physics.* that property of a body by virtue of which it occupies space. **7.** *Anat.* **a.** the act of straightening a limb. **b.** the position assumed by a straightened limb. **8.** *Surg.* the act of pulling the broken or dislocated part of a limb in a direction from the trunk, in order to bring the ends of the bone into their natural situation. **9.** Also called **extent.** *Logic.* the class of things to which a term is applicable. Cf. **intension** (def. 5). [late ME < LL *extensiōn-* (s. of *extensiō*)] —**ex·ten′sion·al,** *adj.* —**ex·ten′sion·al′i·ty, ex·ten′sion·al·ism,** *n.* —**ex·ten′sion·al·ly,** *adv.* —**ex·ten′sion·less,** *adj.* —**Syn. 1.** stretching, expansion, enlargement, increase. **3.** lengthening, protraction, continuation. —**Ant. 1.** contraction.

exten′sion cours′es, (in many universities and colleges) a program for persons not regularly enrolled as students.

ex·ten·si·ty (ik sten′si tē), *n.* **1.** the quality of having extension. **2.** *Psychol.* the attribute of sensation by which spatial extension is perceived. [< L *extens(us)* (see EXTENSIVE) + -ITY]

ex·ten·sive (ik sten′siv), *adj.* **1.** of great extent; wide; broad: *an extensive area.* **2.** far-reaching; comprehensive: *extensive knowledge.* **3.** lengthy: *an extensive preface.* **4.** great in amount, number, or degree: *an extensive fortune.* **5.** noting or pertaining to a system of agriculture involving the cultivation of large areas of land with a minimum of labor and expense (opposed to *intensive*). [late ME < LL *extensīv(us)* = L *extens(us)* (ptp. of *extendere* to EXTEND) + *-īvus* -IVE] —**ex·ten′sive·ly,** *adv.* —**ex·ten′sive·ness, ex·ten·siv·i·ty** (ek′sten siv′i tē, ik-), *n.* —**Syn. 1.** large, ample, vast. —**Ant. 1, 2.** limited, narrow, confined.

ex·ten·som·e·ter (ek′sten som′i tər), *n.* *Mach.* an instrument for measuring minute degrees of expansion, contraction, or deformation.

ex·ten·sor (ik sten′sər, -sôr), *n.* *Anat.* a muscle that serves to extend or straighten a part of the body. [< NL; see EXTENSIVE, -OR[2]]

ex·tent (ik stent′), *n.* **1.** the degree to which a thing extends; length, area, volume, or scope: *the extent of his lands.* **2.** something extended, as a space, length, area, or volume; something having extension. **3.** *U.S. Law.* a writ giving a creditor possession of a debtor's lands, absolutely or for a term of years. **4.** *Eng. Law.* **a.** Also called **writ of extent.** a writ to recover debts of record due to the crown, under which land, property, etc., may be seized. **b.** a seizure made under such a writ. **5.** *Archaic.* assessment or valuation, as of land. **6.** *Logic.* extension (def. 9). [ME *extente* assessment < ML *extenta,* n. use of fem. of L *extentus,* ptp. of *extendere* to EXTEND] —**Syn. 1.** magnitude, amount, range, expanse.

ex·ten·u·ate (ik sten′yo͞o āt′), *v.t.,* **-at·ed, -at·ing. 1.** to represent (a fault, offense, etc.) as less serious. **2.** to serve to make (a fault, offense, etc.) be or seem less serious. **3.** to underestimate, underrate, or make light of. **4.** *Archaic.* to make thin or emaciated. [late ME (adj.) < L *extenuāt(us),* ptp. of *extenuāre* = *ex-* EX-[1] + *tenuāre* to make thin or small; see -ATE[1]] —**ex·ten′u·at′ing·ly,** *adv.* —**ex·ten′u·a′tor,** *n.* —**ex·ten·u·a·to·ry** (ik sten′yo͞o ə tôr′ē, -tōr′ē), —**ex·ten′u·a′tive,** *adj.*

ex·ten·u·a·tion (ik sten′yo͞o ā′shən), *n.* **1.** the act of extenuating. **2.** the state of being extenuated. **3.** something that extenuates; a partial excuse. [late ME *extenuacioun* < L *extenuātiōn-* (s. of *extenuātiō*)]

ex·te·ri·or (ik stēr′ē ər), *adj.* **1.** outer; being on the outer side: *the exterior surface.* **2.** suitable for outdoor use. **3.** situated outside; pertaining to or connected with what is outside: *exterior territories.* —*n.* **4.** the outer surface or part; outside. **5.** outward form or appearance. [< L, comp. of *exter* or *exterus* on the outside, outward. See EX-[1]] —**ex·te′ri·or·ly,** *adv.* —**Syn. 1.** outward, external. **3.** outlying; extrinsic. **5.** mien, aspect, face. —**Ant. 1, 4.** interior.

exte′rior an′gle, *Geom.* **1.** an angle formed outside parallel lines by a third line that intersects them. Cf. **interior angle. 2.** an angle formed outside a polygon by one side and an extension of an adjacent side; the supplement of an interior angle of the polygon.

ex·te·ri·or·ise (ik stēr′ē ə rīz′), *v.t.,* **-ised, -is·ing.** *Chiefly Brit.* exteriorize. —**ex·te′ri·or·i·sa′tion,** *n.*

ex·te·ri·or·ize (ik stēr′ē ə rīz′), *v.t.,* **-ized, -iz·ing. 1.** to externalize. **2.** *Surg.* to expose (an internal structure) temporarily outside the body, for surgery, experimentation, etc. —**ex·te′ri·or·i·za′tion,** *n.*

ex·ter·mi·nate (ik stûr′mə nāt′), *v.t.,* **-nat·ed, -nat·ing.** to get rid of by destroying; destroy totally; extirpate. [< L *extermināt(us),* ptp. of *extermināre* to EXTERMINE; see -ATE[1]] —**ex·ter·mi·na·ble** (ik stûr′mə nə bəl), *adj.* —**ex·ter′mi·na′tion,** *n.* —**ex·ter·mi·na·to·ry** (ik stûr′mə nə tôr′ē, -tōr′ē), **ex·ter′mi·na′tive,** *adj.* —**Syn.** eradicate, annihilate, eliminate.

ex·ter·mi·na·tor (ik stûr′mə nā′tər), *n.* **1.** a person or thing that exterminates. **2.** a person or establishment engaged in the business of destroying vermin in buildings.

ex·ter·mine (ik stûr′min), *v.t.,* **-mined, -min·ing.** *Obs.* to exterminate. [late ME < L *extermin(āre)* (to) drive beyond the boundaries]

ex·tern (*n.* ek′stûrn; *adj.* ik stûrn′), *n.* **1.** a person connected with an institution but not residing in it, as a doctor or medical student at a hospital, or a day student at a school. —*adj.* **2.** *Archaic.* external; outer. [< L *extern(us)* < *exter, exterus*]

ex·ter·nal (ik stûr′nəl), *adj.* **1.** of or pertaining to the outside or outer part: *an external surface.* **2.** *Med.* to be applied to the outside of a body, as a remedy. **3.** situated outside of something; acting or coming from without: *external influences.* **4.** pertaining to outward or visible appearance; superficial. **5.** pertaining to foreign countries: *external commerce.* **6.** *Zool., Anat.* on the side farthest away from the body, from the median line, or from the center of a radially symmetrical form. **7.** *Metaphys.* of or pertaining to the world of things, considered as independent of the perceiving mind. —*n.* **8.** the outside; outer surface; exterior. **9.** something that is external. **10. externals,** external features, circumstances, etc.; outward appearance; superficialities. [late ME] —**ex·ter′nal·ly,** *adv.*

exter′nal au′ditory mea′tus, *Anat.* the canal extending from the opening in the external ear to the tympanic membrane.

ex·ter·nal-com·bus·tion (ik stûr′nəl kəm bus′chən, -bush′-), *adj.* noting or pertaining to an engine, as a steam engine, in which fuel ignition takes place outside the cylinder.

exter′nal ear′, the outer portion of the ear, consisting of the auricle and the canal extending to the tympanic membrane. Cf. **ear** (def. 1).

ex·ter·nal·ise (ik stûr′nəlīz′), *v.t.,* **-ised, -is·ing.** *Chiefly Brit.* externalize. —**ex·ter′nal·i·sa′tion,** *n.*

ex·ter·nal·ism (ik stûr′nəliz′əm), *n.* attention or devotion to externals; excessive attention to externals, esp. in religion. —**ex·ter′nal·ist,** *n.*

ex·ter·nal·i·ty (ek′stər nal′i tē), *n., pl.* **-ties. 1.** the state or quality of being external. **2.** something external; an outward feature. **3.** excessive attention to externals.

ex·ter·nal·ize (ik stûr′nəlīz′), *v.t.,* **-ized, -iz·ing. 1.** to make external; embody in an outward form. **2.** to regard as consisting of externals. **3.** to regard or treat as being caused by externals; attribute to external causes. **4.** to direct (the personality) outward in social relationships. Also, *esp. Brit.,* **externalise.**

ex·ter·o·cep·tor (ek′stər ə sep′tər), *n.* *Physiol.* a receptor responding to stimuli originating from outside the body. [*extero-* (comb. form of L *exterus* EXTERIOR) + (RE)CEPTOR] —**ex′ter·o·cep′tive,** *adj.*

ex·ter·ri·to·ri·al (eks′ter i tôr′ē əl, -tōr′-), *adj.* extraterritorial. —**ex·ter′ri·to′ri·al′i·ty,** *n.* —**ex′ter·ri·to′ri·al·ly,** *adv.*

ex·tinct (ik stingkt′), *adj.* **1.** not existing now; that has ended or died out: *an extinct species.* **2.** no longer in use; obsolete: *an extinct custom.* **3.** extinguished, as a fire, or having ceased eruption, as a volcano. [late ME < L *ex(s)tinct(us)* put out, quenched, ptp. of *ex(s)tinguere* to EXTINGUISH] —**Syn. 1.** gone, vanished. **2.** archaic, outmoded.

ex·tinc·tion (ik stingk′shən), *n.* **1.** the act of extinguishing. **2.** the fact or condition of being extinguished or extinct. **3.** suppression; abolition; annihilation: *the extinction of hopes.* **4.** *Biol.* the act or process of becoming extinct or dying out. [late ME *extinccio(u)n* < L *ex(s)tinctiōn-* (s. of *ex(s)tinctiō*)]

ex·tinc·tive (ik stingk′tiv), *adj.* tending or serving to extinguish.

ex·tin·guish (ik sting′gwish), *v.t.* **1.** to put out (a fire, light, etc.); put out the flame of (something burning or lighted): *to extinguish a candle.* **2.** to put an end to or bring to an end; annihilate: *to extinguish hope.* **3.** to obscure or eclipse, as by superior brilliance. **4.** *Law.* to discharge (a debt), as by payment. [< L *ex(s)tingu(ere)* (*ex-* EX-[1] + *stinguere* to quench) + -ISH[2]] —**ex·tin′guish·a·ble,** *adj.* —**ex·tin′guish·ment,** *n.*

ex·tin·guish·er (ik sting′gwi shər), *n.* **1.** a person or thing that extinguishes. **2.** See **fire extinguisher.**

ex·tir·pate (ek′stər pāt′, ik stûr′pāt), *v.t.*, **-pat·ed, -pat·ing.** **1.** to remove utterly; destroy totally; exterminate. **2.** to pull up by or as by the roots; root up. [< L *ex(s)tirpāt(us)* plucked up by the stem (ptp. of *ex(s)tirpāre*). See EX-[1], STIRP, -ATE[1]] —**ex′tir·pa′tion,** *n.* —**ex′tir·pa′tive,** *adj.* —**ex′tir·pa′tor,** *n.*

ex·tol (ik stōl′, -stol′), *v.t.*, **-tolled, -tol·ling.** to praise highly; laud; eulogize. Also, **ex·toll′.** [late ME *extolle(n)* < L *extoll(ere)* (to) lift up, raise = *ex-* EX-[1] + *tollere* to lift, raise up] —**ex·tol′ler,** *n.* —**ex·tol′ling·ly,** *adv.* —**ex·tol′ment, ex·toll′ment,** *n.* —**Syn.** glorify, exalt, celebrate. —**Ant.** disparage.

ex·tort (ik stôrt′), *v.t.* *Law.* to wrest or force (money, information, etc.) from a person by violence, intimidation, or abuse of authority. [late ME (adj.) < L *extort(us),* ptp. of *extorquēre*] —**ex·tort′er,** *n.* —**ex·tor′tive,** *adj.* —**Syn. 1.** See **extract.**

ex·tor·tion (ik stôr′shən), *n.* **1.** the act or an instance of extorting. **2.** *Law.* the wrongful taking of a person's money or property with his consent but by the use of threat or violence or under color of office. **3.** oppressive or illegal exaction, as of excessive price or interest. **4.** anything extorted. [ME *extorcion* < LL *extortiōn-* (s. of *extortiō* torture)] —**ex·tor′tion·ar′y,** *adj.* —**Syn. 1, 4.** blackmail.

ex·tor·tion·ate (ik stôr′shə nit), *adj.* **1.** exorbitant; grossly excessive: *extortionate prices.* **2.** characterized by extortion, as persons: *extortionate moneylenders.* —**ex·tor′tion·ate·ly,** *adv.*

ex·tor·tion·ist (ik stôr′shə nist), *n.* a person who practices extortion. Also, **ex·tor′tion·er.** [ME *extorciouner*]

ex·tra (ek′strə), *adj.* **1.** beyond or more than what is expected or necessary; additional. **2.** larger or better than what is usual. —*n.* **3.** something extra or additional. **4.** an additional expense. **5.** a special edition of a newspaper. **6.** something of superior quality. **7.** *Motion Pictures, Television.* a person hired for a minor part, as in a mob scene. **8.** an additional worker. **9.** Usually, **extras.** *Cricket.* a score or run not made from the bat, as a bye or a wide. —*adv.* **10.** in excess of the usual or specified amount: *an extra high price.* **11.** beyond the ordinary degree; unusually: *extra large.* [? by shortening of EXTRAORDINARY]

extra-, a prefix meaning "outside," "beyond," freely used as an English formative: *extrajudicial; extraterritorial.* Also, **extro-.** [< L, comb. form of *extrā* (adv. and prep.) outside (of), without]

ex′tra-base′ hit′ (ek′strə bās′), *Baseball.* a double or a triple.

ex·tra·ca·non·i·cal (ek′strə kə non′i kəl), *adj.* *Eccles.* not included in the canon of Scripture.

ex·tra·cel·lu·lar (ek′strə sel′yə lər), *adj.* *Biol.* outside a cell or cells. —**ex′tra·cel′lu·lar·ly,** *adv.*

ex·tra-con·densed (ek′strə kən denst′), *adj.* *Print.* (of type) narrower than condensed type in proportion to its height.

ex·tract (*v.* ik strakt′; *n.* ek′strakt), *v.t.* **1.** to pull or draw out, esp. by force: *to extract a tooth.* **2.** to deduce (a doctrine, principle, etc.). **3.** to derive or obtain (pleasure, comfort, etc.) from a particular source. **4.** to copy out (matter), as from a book. **5.** to make excerpts from (a book, pamphlet, etc.). **6.** to extort (information, money, etc.). **7.** to separate or obtain (a juice, ingredient, principle, etc.) from a mixture by pressure, distillation, or the like. **8.** *Math.* to determine (the root of a quantity). —*n.* **9.** something extracted. **10.** a passage taken from a book, article, etc.; excerpt; quotation. **11.** a solid, viscid, or liquid substance extracted from a plant, drug, or the like and containing its essence in concentrated form: *beef extract.* [late ME < L *extract(us)* (ptp. of *extrahere*)] —**ex·tract′a·bil′i·ty, ex·tract′i·bil′i·ty,** *n.* —**ex·tract′a·ble, ex·tract′i·ble,** *adj.*
—**Syn. 1.** pry out. **6.** EXTRACT, EXACT, EXTORT, WREST imply using force to remove something. To EXTRACT is to draw forth something as by pulling, importuning, or the like: *to extract a confession by using third-degree methods.* To EXACT is to impose a penalty, or to obtain by force or authority, something to which one lays claim: *to exact payment, obedience.* To EXTORT is usually to wring something by intimidation or threats from an unwilling person: *to extort money by threats of blackmail.* To WREST is to take by force or violence in spite of active resistance: *The courageous minority wrested the power from their oppressors.* **7.** withdraw, distill. **9.** citation, selection.

ex·tract·ant (ik strak′tənt), *n.* *Chem.* a substance extracted.

ex·trac·tion (ik strak′shən), *n.* **1.** an act, instance, or process of extracting: *the extraction of a tooth.* **2.** the state or fact of being extracted. **3.** descent or lineage: *of foreign extraction.* **4.** something extracted; extract. [late ME *extraccioun* < LL *extractiōn-* (s. of *extractiō*)]

ex·trac·tive (ik strak′tiv), *adj.* **1.** tending or serving to extract or based upon extraction: *the coal and other extractive industries.* **2.** capable of being extracted. **3.** of or of the nature of an extract. —*n.* **4.** something extracted.

ex·trac·tor (ik strak′tər), *n.* **1.** a person or thing that extracts. **2.** (in a firearm or cannon) the mechanism that pulls an empty or unfired cartridge or shell case out of the chamber before ejection. **3.** a centrifuge for spinning wet laundry so as to remove excess water. **4.** *Med., Dentistry.* an instrument for drawing out, extracting, or pulling.

ex·tra·cur·ric·u·lar (ek′strə kə rik′yə lər), *adj.* **1.** outside the regular curriculum: *extracurricular reading.* **2.** of or pertaining to school activities exclusive of the regular academic course.

ex·tra·dit·a·ble (ek′strə dī′tə bəl, ek′strə dī′-), *adj.* **1.** capable of being extradited; subject to extradition: *an extraditable person.* **2.** capable of incurring extradition: *an extraditable offense.*

ex·tra·dite (ek′strə dīt′), *v.t.*, **-dit·ed, -dit·ing.** **1.** to give up (a fugitive or prisoner) to another nation or authority. **2.** to obtain the extradition of. [back formation from EXTRADITION]

ex·tra·di·tion (ek′strə dish′ən), *n.* the surrender of a fugitive from justice or a prisoner by one state or authority to another. [< F; see EX-[1], TRADITION]

ex·tra·dos (ek′strə dos′, -dōs′, ek strā′dos, -dōs), *n., pl.* **-dos** (-dōz′, -dōz), **-dos·es.** *Archit.* the exterior curve or surface of an arch or vault. Cf. **intrados.** [< F = *extra-* EXTRA- + *dos* back (< L *dorsum* DORSUM)] —**ex·tra′dosed,** *adj.*

ex·tra·ga·lac·tic (ek′strə gə lak′tik), *adj.* outside the Milky Way system: *an extragalactic nebula.*

ex′tragalac′tic neb′ula, *Astron.* nebula (def. 1c).

ex·tra·ju·di·cial (ek′strə jōō dish′əl), *adj.* outside or beyond the action or authority of a court. —**ex′tra·ju·di′cial·ly,** *adv.*

ex·tra·mar·i·tal (ek′strə mar′i tᵊl), *adj.* pertaining to sexual relations with someone other than one's spouse.

ex·tra·mun·dane (ek′strə mun′dān, -mun dān′), *adj.* beyond the material world or universe. [< LL *extrāmundān(us)* beyond the world]

ex·tra·mu·ral (ek′strə myŏŏr′əl), *adj.* **1.** involving representatives of more than one school: *extramural athletics.* **2.** outside the walls or boundaries, as of a city or university. Cf. **intramural** (defs. 1, 2). —**ex′tra·mu′ral·ly,** *adv.*

ex·tra·ne·ous (ik strā′nē əs), *adj.* **1.** coming from without; external; foreign. **2.** not pertinent; irrelevant: *an extraneous remark.* [< L *extrāneus* external, foreign] —**ex·tra′ne·ous·ly,** *adv.* —**ex·tra′ne·ous·ness,** *n.* —**Syn. 1.** extrinsic, adventitious, alien. **2.** inappropriate, nonessential, superfluous. —**Ant. 1.** intrinsic. **2.** pertinent.

ex·tra·nu·cle·ar (ek′strə nōō′klē ər, -nyōō′-), *adj.* pertaining to or affecting the parts of a cell outside the nucleus.

ex·traor·di·nar·y (ik strôr′dᵊner′ē, ek′strə ôr′dᵊner′ē), *adj.* **1.** beyond what is usual, ordinary, or established: *extraordinary powers of the President; extraordinary costs.* **2.** exceptional in character, degree, etc.; noteworthy; remarkable: *extraordinary beauty.* **3.** (of an official, employee, etc.) outside of or additional to the ordinary staff; having a special, often temporary task or responsibility: *minister extraordinary and plenipotentiary.* [late ME *extraordinarie* < L *extrāordināri(us)* beyond what is ordinary] —**ex·traor·di·nar·i·ly** (ik strôr′dᵊnâr′ə lē, ek′strə ôr′-), *adv.* —**ex·traor′di·nar′i·ness,** *n.* —**Syn. 1.** inordinate. **2.** uncommon, singular, rare, phenomenal, special. —**Ant. 1, 2.** common.

ex·trap·o·late (ik strap′ə lāt′, ek′strə pə-), *v.*, **-lat·ed, -lat·ing.** —*v.t.* **1.** *Statistics.* to estimate the value of a variable outside its tabulated or observed range. **2.** to infer an unknown from something that is known; conjecture. —*v.i.* **3.** to perform extrapolation. [EXTRA- + (INTER)POLATE] —**ex·trap′o·la′tion,** *n.* —**ex·trap′o·la′tive, ex·trap·o·la·to·ry** (ik strap′ə lə tōr′ē, -tôr′ē), *adj.* —**ex·trap′o·la′tor,** *n.*

ex·tra·sen·so·ry (ek′strə sen′sə rē), *adj.* outside of normal sense perception.

ex′trasen′sory percep′tion. See **ESP.**

ex·tra·ter·res·tri·al (ek′strə tə res′trē əl), *adj.* outside, or originating outside, the limits of the earth.

ex·tra·ter·ri·to·ri·al (ek′strə ter′i tōr′ē əl, -tôr′-), *adj.* beyond local territorial jurisdiction. Also, **exterritorial.** —**ex′tra·ter′ri·to′ri·al·ly,** *adv.*

ex·tra·ter·ri·to·ri·al·i·ty (ek′strə ter′i tōr′ē al′i tē, -tôr′-), *n.* the possession or exercise of political rights by a foreign power within a state having its own government. Also, **exterritoriality.**

ex·tra·u·ter·ine (ek′strə yōō′tər in, -tə rīn′), *adj.* being or developing outside the uterus.

ex′trau′terine preg′nancy, *Med.* See **ectopic pregnancy.**

ex·trav·a·gance (ik strav′ə gəns), *n.* **1.** excessive expenditure or outlay of money. **2.** an instance of this. **3.** unrestrained or fantastic excess, as of actions, opinions, etc. **4.** an extravagant action, notion, etc. [< F, MF] —**Syn. 3.** lavishness, profusion. —**Ant. 1.** frugality.

ex·trav·a·gan·cy (ik strav′ə gən sē), *n., pl.* **-cies.** extravagance.

ex·trav·a·gant (ik strav′ə gənt), *adj.* **1.** spending much more than is necessary or prudent; wasteful. **2.** excessively high: *extravagant prices.* **3.** exceeding the bounds of reason, as actions, demands, passions, etc. **4.** going beyond what is justifiable; unrestrained: *extravagant praise.* **5.** *Obs.* wandering beyond bounds. [ME < ML *extrāvagant-* (s. of *extrāvagāns*), prp. of *extrāvagārī* = *extrā-* EXTRA- + *vagārī* to wander] —**ex·trav′a·gant·ly,** *adv.* —**ex·trav′a·gant·ness,** *n.* —**Syn. 1.** imprudent, lavish. **2.** excessive, inordinate, immoderate. **3.** unreasonable, fantastic, wild, absurd, preposterous; unrestrained. —**Ant. 1.** prudent, thrifty. **2.** moderate. **3.** reasonable.

ex·trav·a·gan·za (ik strav′ə gan′zə), *n.* an elaborate musical or dramatic composition, as comic opera or musical comedy. [alter. of It *(e)stravaganza* extravagance]

ex·trav·a·gate (ik strav′ə gāt′), *v.i.*, **-gat·ed, -gat·ing.** *Archaic.* **1.** to wander beyond bounds; stray; roam at will. **2.** to go beyond the bounds of propriety or reason. [< ML *extrāvagāt(us)* strayed, wandered away from, ptp. of *extrāvagārī*] —**ex·trav′a·ga′tion,** *n.*

ex·trav·a·sate (ik strav′ə sāt′), *v.*, **-sat·ed, -sat·ing,** *n.* —*v.t.* **1.** *Pathol.* to force out from the proper vessels, as blood, esp. so as to diffuse through the surrounding tissues. **2.** *Geol.* to pour forth, as molten lava, from a subterranean source. —*v.i.* 3. *Pathol.* to be extravasated, as blood. 4. *Geol.* to pour forth lava or the like. —*n.* 5. *Pathol.* the extravasated material; extravasation. [EXTRA- + VAS + -ATE[1]] —**ex·trav′a·sa′tion,** *n.*

ex·tra·vas·cu·lar (ek′strə vas′kyə lər), *adj. Anat.* situated outside of a blood vessel or vessels.

ex·tra·ve·hic·u·lar (ek′strə vē hik′yə lər), *adj.* of, pertaining to, or being an activity performed by an astronaut outside his space vehicle during a space flight.

ex·tra·ver·sion (ek′strə vûr′zhən, -shən, ek′strə vûr′-), *n. Psychol.* extroversion.

ex·tra·vert (ek′strə vûrt′), *n., adj. Psychol.* extrovert.

Ex·tre·ma·du·ra (*Sp.* es′tʀe mä ᵺōō′ʀä), *n.* Estremadura.

ex·treme (ik strēm′), *adj.,* **-trem·er, -trem·est,** *n.* —*adj.* 1. of a character or kind farthest removed from the ordinary or average: *an extreme case; extreme measures.* 2. utmost or exceedingly great in degree: *extreme joy.* 3. farthest from the center or middle; outermost; endmost. 4. farthest, utmost, or very far in any direction. 5. exceeding the bounds of moderation: *extreme fashions.* 6. going to the utmost or very great lengths in action, opinion, etc.: *an extreme conservative.* 7. last or final: *extreme hopes.* —*n.* 8. the highest or a very high degree: *cautious to an extreme.* 9. one of two things as remote or different from each other as possible: *the extremes of joy and grief.* 10. the utmost length; an excessive length: *extremes in dress.* 11. an extreme act, measure, condition, etc.: *the extreme of poverty.* 12. *Math.* **a.** the first or the last term, as of a proportion or series. **b.** a relative maximum or relative minimum value of a function in a given region. 13. *Logic.* the subject or the predicate of the conclusion of a syllogism. 14. *Archaic.* the utmost point, or extremity, of something. [late ME < L *extrēm(us),* superl. of *exterus* outward. See EXTERIOR] —**ex·treme′ness,** *n.* —**Syn. 2.** greatest, highest. **6.** extravagant, excessive. See **radical.** —**Ant. 6.** moderate.

ex·treme·ly (ik strēm′lē), *adv.* very; exceedingly: *extremely cold; extremely kind.*

extreme′ly high′ fre′quency, *Radio.* any frequency between 30,000 and 300,000 megacycles per second. *Abbr.:* EHF

extreme′ unc′tion, *Rom. Cath. Ch.* a sacrament consisting of anointment with oil and the recitation of prayer, administered by a priest to a person in danger of dying. Also called **last rites.**

ex·trem·ism (ik strē′miz əm), *n.* a tendency to go to extremes or an instance of going to extremes, esp. in politics.

ex·trem·ist (ik strē′mist), *n.* 1. a person who goes to extremes, esp. in political matters. 2. a supporter of extreme doctrines or practices. —*adj.* 3. of extremists.

ex·trem·i·ty (ik strem′i tē), *n., pl.* **-ties.** 1. the extreme or terminal point or part of something. 2. a limb of the body. 3. Usually, **extremities.** the end parts of the limbs, as the hands or feet. 4. Sometimes, **extremities.** a condition or circumstance of extreme need, distress, etc. 5. the utmost or any extreme degree: *the extremity of joy.* 6. an extreme measure, act, etc. 7. extreme character, as of political or religious opinions. 8. *Archaic.* a person's last moment before death. [ME < L *extrēmitās*] —**Syn. 1.** verge, border.

ex·tri·ca·ble (ek′strə kə bəl, ik strik′ə bəl), *adj.* capable of being extricated.

ex·tri·cate (ek′strə kāt′), *v.t.,* **-cat·ed, -cat·ing.** 1. to free or release from entanglement; disengage. 2. to liberate (gas) from combination, as in a chemical process. [< L *extricāt(us)* (ptp. of *extricāre*) = *ex-* EX-[1] + *tric(ae)* perplexities + *-ātus* -ATE[1]] —**ex′tri·ca′tion,** *n.*

ex·trin·sic (ik strin′sik), *adj.* 1. not essential or inherent, extraneous: *extrinsic facts.* 2. outward or external; operating or coming from without: *extrinsic influences.* Also, **ex·trin′si·cal.** [< LL *extrinsec(us)* outward, adj. use of L: on the outward side = *extrin-* (< *exter* outward) + *secus* beside, akin to *sequī* follow] —**ex·trin′si·cal·ly,** *adv.*

extro-, var. of **extra-** (used to contrast with **intro-**): *extrovert.*

ex·trorse (ek strôrs′), *adj. Bot.* turned or facing outward, as anthers that open toward the perianth. [< LL *extrors(us)* in outward direction = *extr(a)-* EXTRA- + *(vo)rsus* (adv.) turned] —**ex·trorse′ly,** *adv.*

ex·tro·ver·sion (ek′strō vûr′zhən, -shən, ek′strō vûr′-, -strə-), *n. Psychol.* the direction of interest outward or to objects outside the self, as toward the external environment. Also, **extraversion.** Cf. **introversion.** [EXTRO- + L *versiōn-* (s. of *versiō*) a turning] —**ex′tro·ver′sive,** *adj.* —**ex′tro·ver′sive·ly,** *adv.*

ex·tro·vert (ek′strō vûrt′, -strə-), *Psychol.* —*n.* 1. a person who is primarily interested in things outside the self, as one who is gregarious. —*adj.* 2. of, pertaining to, or characterized by extroversion. Also, **extravert.** [EXTRO- + L *vert(ere)* (to) turn]

ex·trude (ik strōōd′), *v.,* **-trud·ed, -trud·ing.** —*v.t.* 1. to thrust, force, or press out; expel. 2. to form (metal, plastic, etc.) by forcing through a die. —*v.i.* 3. to protrude. 4. to be extruded: *This metal extrudes easily.* [< L *extrūd(ere)* (to) thrust out, drive out = *ex-* EX-[1] + *trūdere* to thrust, push] —**ex·trud′er,** *n.* —**ex·tru·si·ble** (ik strōō′sə bəl), **ex·tru′sile,** *adj.* —**ex·tru·sion** (ik strōō′zhən), *n.*

ex·tru·sive (ik strōō′siv), *adj.* 1. tending to extrude. 2. pertaining to extrusion. 3. *Geol.* (of rocks) having been forced to the surface of the earth while in a molten or plastic condition (opposed to *intrusive*). [EXTRUS(ION) (< ML *extrūsiōn-,* s. of *extrūsiō* = L *extrūs(us),* ptp. of *extrūdere* to EXTRUDE + *-iōn-* -ION) + -IVE]

ex·u·ber·ance (ig zōō′bər əns), *n.* 1. Also, **ex·u′ber·an·cy.** the state of being exuberant. 2. an instance of this: *His pranks are youthful exuberances.* [< L *exūberantia*] —**Syn. 1.** superabundance, copiousness. —**Ant. 1.** scarcity.

ex·u·ber·ant (ig zōō′bər ənt), *adj.* 1. lavish; unreserved: *an exuberant welcome.* 2. abounding in vitality; extremely joyful and vigorous. 3. profuse in growth; luxuriant: *exuberant vegetation.* [late ME < L *exūberant-* (s. of *exūberāns*), prp. of *exūberāre* = *ex-* EX-[1] + *ūberāre* to be fruitful (< *über* fertile); see -ANT] —**ex·u′ber·ant·ly,** *adv.*

ex·u·ber·ate (ig zōō′bə rāt′), *v.i.,* **-at·ed, -at·ing.** to be exuberant; superabound; overflow. [late ME < L *exūberāt(us)*]

ex·u·date (eks′yōō dāt′, ek′sə-, eg′zə-), *n.* a substance exuded; exudation.

ex·u·da·tion (eks′yōō dā′shən, ek′sə-, eg′zə-), *n.* 1. the act of exuding. 2. something exuded, as sweat. [< LL *ex(s)ūdātiōn-* (s. of *ex(s)ūdātiō*) = *ex(s)ūdāt(us)* (ptp. of *ex(s)ūdāre* to EXUDE) + *-iōn-* -ION] —**ex·u·da·tive** (ig zōō′də tiv, ik-sōō′-), *adj.*

ex·ude (ig zōōd′, ik sōōd′), *v.,* **-ud·ed, -ud·ing.** —*v.i.* 1. to ooze out, as sweat, through the pores. —*v.t.* 2. to send out, as sweat; emit through or as through the pores. [< L *ex(s)ūd(āre)* = *ex-* EX-[1] + *sūdāre* to sweat]

ex·ult (ig zult′), *v.i.* 1. to rejoice exceedingly; be highly elated or jubilant. 2. *Obs.* to leap, esp. for joy. [< L *ex(s)ult(āre)* (to) leap up = *ex-* EX-[1] + *-sultāre* (comb. form of *saltāre* to leap)] —**ex·ult′ing·ly,** *adv.*

ex·ult·ant (ig zul′tᵊnt), *adj.* exulting; highly elated; jubilant. [< L *ex(s)ultant-* (s. of *ex(s)ultāns*), prp. of *ex(s)ultāre* to EXULT; see -ANT] —**ex·ult′ant·ly,** *adv.*

ex·ul·ta·tion (eg′zul tā′shən, ek′sul-), *n.* the act of exulting; lively or triumphant joy, as over success or victory. Also, **ex·ult·an·cy** (ig zul′tᵊn sē), **ex·ult′ance.** [late ME < L *ex(s)ultātiōn-* (s. of *ex(s)ultātiō*) = *ex(s)ultāt(us)* (ptp. of *ex(s)ultāre* to EXULT) + *-iōn-* -ION]

ex·urb (ek′sərb, eg′zərb), *n.* a small, usually fashionable, community situated beyond the suburbs of a city. [EX-[1] + (SUB)URB] —**ex·ur·ban** (eks ûr′bən), *adj.*

ex·ur·ban·ite (eks ûr′bə nīt′), *n.* a person living in an exurb but typically working in the city. [EX-[1] + (SUB)-URBANITE]

ex·ur·bi·a (eks ûr′bē ə), *n.* a generalized area comprising the exurbs. [EX-[1] + (SUB)URBIA]

ex·u·vi·ae (ig zōō′vē ē′, ik sōō′-), *n.pl.* the cast skins, shells, or other coverings of animals. [< L < *exuere* to remove, strip off, divest oneself of = *ex-* EX-[1] + *-uere* to put on] —**ex·u′vi·al,** *adj.*

ex·u·vi·ate (ig zōō′vē āt′, ik sōō′-), *v.t., v.i.,* **-at·ed, -at·ing.** to cast off or shed (exuviae); molt. —**ex·u′vi·a′tion,** *n.*

-ey[1], var. of **-y**[1], esp. after *y: clayey.*

-ey[2], var. of **-y**[2], esp. after *y.*

ey·as (ī′əs), *n.* a nestling, esp. a young falcon. [ME, var. of *nyas, nias* (*a nyas* taken as *an eyas*) < MF *niais* nestling < L *nīdus* nest]

Eyck (īk), *n.* **Hu·bert van** (hyōō′bərt van; *Du.* hʏ′beʀt vän), or **Huy·brecht van** (*Du.* hoi′bʀeкнt vän), 1366–1426, and his brother **Jan van** (*Du.* yän vän), (*Jan van Brugge*), 1385?–1440: Flemish painters.

eye (ī), *n., pl.* **eyes,** (*Archaic*) **ey·en** or **eyne,** *v.,* **eyed, ey·ing** or **eye·ing.** —*n.* 1. the organ of sight, in vertebrates typically one of a pair of spherical bodies contained in an orbit of the skull. 2. the aggregate of structures situated within or near the orbit that assist, support, or protect the eye. 3. this organ with respect to the color of the iris: *blue eyes.* 4. the region surrounding the eye: *a black eye.* 5. sight; vision. 6. appreciative or discriminating visual perception: *the eye of an artist.* 7. look, glance, or gaze: *to cast one's eye on a thing.* 8. an attentive look, close observation, or watch: *to be under the eye of a guard.* 9. regard, view, or intention: *an eye to one's own advantage.* 10. manner or way of looking at a thing; estimation; opinion: *in the eyes of the law.* 11. a center of light, intelligence, influence, etc. 12. something suggesting the eye in appearance, shape, etc., as the opening in the lens of a camera, the bud of a potato, a bull's-eye, or the hole in a needle. 13. *Meteorol.* the approximately circular region of relatively light winds and fair weather found at the center of a severe tropical cyclone. 14. *Naut.* the precise direction from which a wind is blowing. 15. **catch someone's eye,** to draw or attract someone's attention: *to catch a waiter's eye.* 16. **have an eye for,** to be discerning or perceptive of. 17. **have eyes only for,** to see or desire no other person or thing but. Also, **only have eyes for.** 18. **keep an eye on,** to watch over attentively. 19. **keep an eye out for,** to be vigilant; watch for. 20. **lay, clap, or set eyes on,** *Informal.* to catch sight of; see. 21. **make eyes at,** to gaze flirtatiously or amorously at: *to make eyes at the pretty girls.* 22. **see eye to eye,** to have exactly the same opinion; agree. 23. **with an eye to,** with an object or advantage in mind: *with an eye to one's future.* —*v.t.* 24. to fix the eyes upon; view: *to eye a pretty girl.* 25. to observe or watch. 26. to make an eye in: *to eye a needle.* —*v.i.* 27. *Obs.* to appear to the eye. [ME *eie, ie,* OE *ēge,* var. of *ēage;* c. G *Auge;* akin to L *oculus,* Skt *akṣi*] —**eye′a·ble,** *adj.* —**eye′like′,** *adj.* —**ey′er,** *n.*

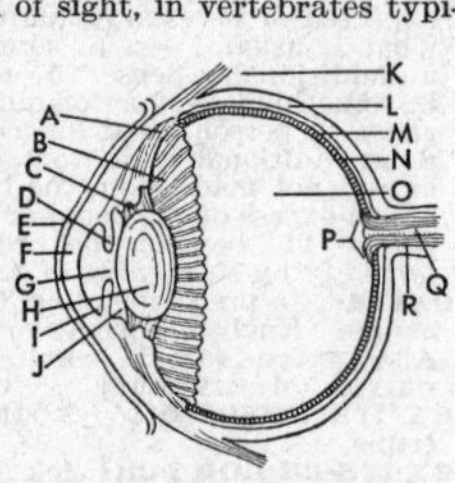

Eye (Human)
A, Ciliary muscle; B, Ciliary processes; C, Suspensory ligament; D, Iris; E, Conjunctiva; F, Cornea; G, Pupil; H, Crystalline lens; I, Anterior chamber; J, Posterior chamber; K, Ocular muscles; L, Sclera; M, Choroid coat; N, Retina; O, Vitreous humor; P, Blind spot; Q, Optic nerve; R, Retinal artery

eye·ball (ī′bôl′), *n.* 1. the ball or globe of the eye. —*v.t.* 2. to look at, check, or observe very closely.

eye·ball-to-eye·ball (ī′bôl′tə ī′bôl′), *adj., adv.* face-to-face, esp. in confrontation.

eye′ bank′, a place for the storage of corneas that have been removed from the eyes of people recently dead, used for transplanting to the eyes of persons having corneal defects.

eye·bolt (ī′bōlt′), *n.* a bolt having an eye at one end.

eye·bright (ī′brīt′), *n.* 1. any of various scrophulariaceous herbs of the genus *Euphrasia,* as *E. officinalis* of Europe, formerly used for treating diseases of the eye. 2. the scarlet pimpernel. See under **pimpernel.**

eye·brow (ī′brou′), *n.* 1. the arch or ridge forming the upper part of the orbit of the eye. 2. the fringe of hair growing on this arch.

eye·cup (ī′kup′), *n.* a cup or glass with a rim shaped to fit snugly about the eye, used for applying lotions. Also called **eye′ bath′.**

eye′ di′alect, the literary use of misspellings that are intended to convey dialectal pronunciations but that are actually phonetic respellings of standard pronunciations, as *wimmin* for "women."

eye·drop·per (ī′drop′ər), *n.* a dropper, esp. one for eye drops.

eye′ drops′, *Med.* drops for use in the eyes.

eye·ful (ī′fo͝ol′), *n., pl.* **-fuls. 1.** an amount of foreign matter in the eye: *an eyeful of dust.* **2.** the amount that a person can or wants to see: *The tourists got an eyeful of slum life.* **3.** *Informal.* a very beautiful woman.

eye·glass (ī′glas′, ī′gläs′), *n.* **1. eyeglasses.** Also called **glasses.** a device to aid defective vision or to protect the eyes from light, dust, and the like, consisting usually of two glass lenses set in a frame that rests on the nose and is held in place by pieces passing over or around the ears (usually used with *pair of*). Cf. **goggle** (def. 1), **pince-nez, spectacle** (def. 3). **2.** a single lens used to aid vision; monocle. **3.** eyepiece. **4.** an eyecup.

eye·hole (ī′hōl′), *n.* **1.** See **eye socket. 2.** a hole to look through, as in a mask or a curtain. **3.** a circular opening for the insertion of a pin, hook, rope, etc.; eye.

eye·lash (ī′lash′), *n.* **1.** one of the short hairs growing on the edge of an eyelid. **2.** the fringe of hairs itself.

eye·less (ī′lis), *adj.* **1.** lacking eyes. **2.** blind.

eye·let (ī′lit), *n., v.,* **-let·ed** or **-let·ted, -let·ing** or **-let·ting.** —*n.* **1.** a small hole, finished along the edge, for the passage of a cord or as in embroidery for decoration. **2.** a metal ring for lining a small hole; grommet. **3.** an eyehole in a wall, mask, etc. **4.** a small eye. —*v.t.* **5.** to make (an eyelet) in. **6.** to insert metal eyelets in. [ME *oillet* < OF *oillet* = *oill* (< L *oculus;* see OCULAR) + *-et* -ET; influenced by EYE]

eye·let·eer (ī′li tēr′), *n.* a small, pointed instrument for making eyelet holes.

eye·lid (ī′lid′), *n.* the movable lid of skin that serves to cover and uncover the eyeball. [ME]

ey·en (ī′ən), *n. Archaic.* pl. of **eye.**

eye·o·pen·er (ī′ō′pə nər), *n.* **1.** a startling or enlightening experience or disclosure. **2.** a drink of liquor taken early in the day.

eye·piece (ī′pēs′), *n.* the lens or combination of lenses in an optical instrument through which the eye views the image; ocular.

eye′ rhyme′. See **sight rhyme.**

eye·shade (ī′shād′), *n.* a visor worn on the head or forehead to shield the eyes from overhead light.

eye′ shad′ow, a cosmetic coloring material applied to the eyelids.

eye·shot (ī′shot′), *n.* **1.** range of vision; view. **2.** *Archaic.* a glance.

eye·sight (ī′sīt′), *n.* **1.** the power or faculty of seeing. **2.** the range of the eye. [ME]

eye′ sock′et, the socket or orbit of the eye.

eye·sore (ī′sōr′, ī′sôr′), *n.* something that mars the beauty or neat appearance of a scene, neighborhood, room, etc., as a dilapidated building, ugly piece of furniture, or the like.

eye′ splice′, a splice made in a rope by turning back one end and interweaving it with the main body of the rope so as to form a loop. See illus. at **splice.**

eye·spot (ī′spot′), *n.* **1.** a sensory organ of lower animals, having a light-perceiving function. **2.** an eyelike spot, as on the tail of a peacock; eye. **3.** *Plant Pathol.* a disease of plants, characterized by lesions, rotting, and stunting of growth.

eye·stalk (ī′stôk′), *n. Zool.* the stalk or peduncle upon which the eye is borne in lobsters, shrimps, etc.

eye·strain (ī′strān′), *n.* discomfort produced in the eyes by their excessive or improper use.

eye·tooth (ī′to͞oth′), *n., pl.* **-teeth** (-tēth′). **1.** a canine tooth of the upper jaw; cuspid: so named from its position under the eye. **2. cut one's eyeteeth,** to gain sophistication or experience. **3. give one's eyeteeth,** to give anything in exchange for that which one desires.

eye·wash (ī′wosh′, ī′wôsh′), *n.* **1.** Also called **collyrium.** *Pharm.* a solution applied locally to the eye for irrigation or administering medication. **2.** *Slang.* nonsense; bunk.

eye·wa·ter (ī′wô′tər, ī′wot′ər), *n. Archaic.* **1.** a lotion for the eyes. **2.** natural tears or a watery discharge from the eye.

eye·wink (ī′wingk′), *n.* **1.** a wink of the eye. **2.** *Obs.* a look or glance.

eye·wink·er (ī′wing′kər), *n.* an eyelash.

eye·wit·ness (*n.* ī′wit′nis, ī′wit′nis; *v.* ī′wit′nis), *n.* **1.** a person who sees some act or occurrence and can give a first-hand account of it. —*v.t.* **2.** to view with one's own eyes: *to eyewitness a murder.*

eyne (īn), *n. Archaic.* pl. of **eye.**

eyre (âr), *n.* **1.** a journey in a circuit. **2.** *Old Eng. Law.* **a.** the circuit made by judges commissioned to hold court in different counties. **b.** a court held by justices in eyre. [ME < AF; OF *erre* < *erre(r)* to journey; see ERR]

Eyre (âr), *n.* **Lake,** a shallow salt lake in S South Australia. 3430 sq. mi.

Eyre′ Penin′sula, a peninsula in S Australia, E of the Great Australian Bight. Also, **Eyre's′ Penin′sula.**

ey·rie (âr′ē, ēr′ē), *n.* aerie. Also, **ey′ry.**

ey·rir (ā′rēr), *n., pl.* **au·rar** (oi′rär). an aluminum bronze coin of Iceland, the 100th part of a krona. [< OIcel < ON: ounce, unit of money; c. Sw *öre* < L *aureus* golden]

Eysk (āsk), *n.* Yeisk.

Ez., Ezra. Also, **Ezr.**

Ezek., Ezekiel.

E·ze·ki·el (i zē′kē əl), *n.* **1.** a Major Prophet of the 6th century B.C. **2.** a book of the Bible bearing his name. Also, *Douay Bible,* **E·ze′chi·el.**

Ezr., Ezra.

Ez·ra (ez′rə), *n.* **1.** Also, *Douay Bible,* **Esdras.** a Jewish scribe and prophet of the 5th century B.C. **2.** Also, *Douay Bible,* **I Esdras.** a book of the Bible bearing his name.

DEVELOPMENT OF MAJUSCULE								
NORTH SEMITIC	GREEK		ETR.	LATIN		MODERN		
						GOTHIC	ITALIC	ROMAN
Y	ᒣ	—	ᖷ	ᒣ	F	𝔉	*F*	F

DEVELOPMENT OF MINUSCULE					
ROMAN CURSIVE	ROMAN UNCIAL	CAROL. MIN.	MODERN		
			GOTHIC	ITALIC	ROMAN
F	F	ſ	𝔣	*f*	f

The sixth letter of the English alphabet developed from North Semitic *waw,* denoted by a symbol resembling Y. A variant (see **U**) was adopted by the Greeks as *digamma* (ϝ), which had a *w*-like sound, but later dropped out of use as an alphabetic character, surviving only as a numeral. In early Latin, the *f*-sound was represented by *fh;* but the *h* was soon discontinued. The minuscule (**f**) is a scribal variant of the capital.

F, f (ef), *n., pl.* **F's** or **Fs, f's** or **fs. 1.** the sixth letter of the English alphabet, a consonant. **2.** any spoken sound represented by the letter *F* or *f*, as in *fat, differ,* or *huff.* **3.** a written or printed representation of the letter *F* or *f.* **4.** a device, as a printer's type, for reproducing the letter *F* or *f.*

F, 1. Fahrenheit. **2.** *Elect.* farad. **3.** fermi. **4.** *Math.* field. **5.** *Genetics.* filial. **6.** firm. **7.** French. **8.** *Math.* function (of).

F, 1. the sixth in order or in a series. **2.** (*sometimes l.c.*) (in some grading systems) a grade or mark that indicates academic work of the lowest quality; failure. **3.** *Music.* **a.** the fourth tone in the scale of C major or the sixth tone in the relative minor scale, A minor. **b.** a written or printed note representing this tone. **c.** a string, key, or pipe tuned to this tone. **d.** the tonality having F as the tonic note. **4.** *Chem.* fluorine. **5.** *Physics.* force.

f, 1. *Elect.* farad. **2.** firm. **3.** *Music.* forte.

f, *Physics.* **1.** force. **2.** frequency.

F-, *U.S. Mil.* (in designations of aircraft) fighter: *F-105.*

F., 1. Fahrenheit. **2.** February. **3.** Fellow. **4.** forint. **5.** franc; francs. **6.** France. **7.** French. **8.** Friday.

f., 1. (in prescriptions) make. [< L *fac*] **2.** *Elect.* farad. **3.** farthing. **4.** father. **5.** fathom. **6.** feet. **7.** female. **8.** feminine. **9.** (in prescriptions) let them be made. [< L *fiant*] **10.** (in prescriptions) let it be made. [< L *fiat*] **11.** filly. **12.** fine. **13.** fluid (ounce). **14.** folio. **15.** following. **16.** foot. **17.** form. **18.** formed of. **19.** franc; francs. **20.** from. **21.** *Math.* function (of). **22.** (in the Netherlands) gulden; guldens.

f/, *Photog.* See **f number.**

fa (fä), *n. Music.* **1.** the syllable used for the fourth tone of a diatonic scale. **2.** (in the fixed system of solmization) the tone F. Cf. **sol-fa** (def. 1). [ME; see GAMUT]

FA, *Mil.* Field Artillery.

FAA, Federal Aviation Agency.

fa·ba·ceous (fə bā′shəs), *adj.* belonging to the *Fabaceae,* or bean family of plants, sometimes included in the *Leguminosae,* including many herbs, shrubs, and trees, that bear seeds in pods or legumes. [< L *fabāceus* of, consisting of beans = *fab*(*a*) bean + *-āceus* -ACEOUS]

Fa·ber·gé (fab′ər zhā′; *Fr.* fa ber zhā′), *n.* **(Peter) Carl (Gus·ta·vo·vitch)** (gə stä′və vich), 1846–1920, Russian goldsmith and jeweler.

Fa·bi·an (fā′bē ən, fāb′yən), *n.* **Saint,** died A.D. 250, pope 236–250.

Fa·bi·an (fā′bē ən), *adj.* **1.** seeking victory by delay and harassment rather than by a decisive battle, as in the manner of Fabius Maximus. **2.** of or pertaining to the Fabian Society. **—***n.* **3.** a member of or sympathizer with the Fabian Society. [< L *Fabiān*(*us*)]

Fa′bian Soci′ety, an organization founded in England in 1884, favoring the gradual spread of socialism by peaceful means.

Fa·bi·us Max·i·mus (fā′bē əs mak′sə məs), (*Quintus Fabius Maximus Verrucosus*) (*Cunctator*) 275–203 B.C., Roman statesman and general.

fa·ble (fā′bəl), *n., v.,* **-bled, -bling. —***n.* **1.** a short tale to teach a moral, often with animals or inanimate objects as characters; apologue. **2.** a story not founded on fact. **3.** a story about supernatural or extraordinary persons or incidents; legend. **4.** legends or myths collectively. **5.** an untruth; falsehood. **6.** *Archaic.* the plot of an epic, dramatic poem, play, etc. **7.** *Archaic.* idle talk. **—***v.i.* **8.** to tell or write fables. **9.** to speak falsely; lie. **—***v.t.* **10.** to describe as if actually so; talk about as if true. [ME, var. of *fabel, fabul* < L *fābula* a story, tale = *fā*(*rī*) (to) speak + *-bula* suffix of means or result] **—fa′bler,** *n.* **—Syn. 1.** parable, allegory. See **legend. 3.** myth. **5.** lie, fib, fabrication.

fa·bled (fā′bəld), *adj.* **1.** having no real existence; fictitious. **2.** celebrated in fables.

fab·li·au (fab′lē ō′; *Fr.* fa blē ō′), *n., pl.* **fab·li·aux** (fab′lē ōz′; *Fr.* fa blē ō′). a short metrical tale, popular in medieval France, and usually ribald and humorous. [< F, irreg. dim. of *fable* FABLE]

Fa·bre (fä′bər; *Fr.* fa′brə), *n.* **Jean Hen·ri** (zhän än rē′), 1823–1915, French entomologist and writer on insect life.

fab·ric (fab′rik), *n.* **1.** a cloth made by weaving, knitting, or felting fibers. **2.** the texture of the woven, knitted, or felted material. **3.** framework; structure. **4.** a building; edifice. **5.** the method of construction. **6.** *Petrog.* the spatial arrangement and orientation of the constituents of a rock. [late ME *fabrike* < L *fabrica* piece of skilled work, workshop. See FORGE[1]]

fab·ri·cant (fab′rə kənt), *n.* a maker or manufacturer. [< L *fabricant-* (s. of *fabricāns*) making, prp. of *fabricāre*]

fab·ri·cate (fab′rə kāt′), *v.t.,* **-cat·ed, -cat·ing. 1.** to make by art and labor; construct. **2.** to make by assembling standard parts or sections. **3.** to devise or invent (a story, lie, etc.). **4.** to fake; forge (a document, signature, etc.). [< L *fabricāt*(*us*) made, ptp. of *fabricāre*] **—fab′ri·ca′tive,** *adj.* **—fab′ri·ca′tor,** *n.* **—Syn. 1.** build. See **manufacture.**

fab·ri·ca·tion (fab′rə kā′shən), *n.* **1.** the act or process of fabricating; manufacture. **2.** something fabricated, esp. an untruthful statement. [ME *fabricacioun* < L *fabricātiōn-* (s. of *fabricātiō*)] **—Syn. 2.** See **fiction.**

fab·u·list (fab′yə list), *n.* **1.** a person who invents or relates fables. **2.** a liar. [< MF *fabuliste*]

fab·u·lous (fab′yə ləs), *adj.* **1.** almost unbelievable; incredible. **2.** exceptionally good or unusual; marvelous; superb. **3.** told or known through fables, myths, or legends. [< L *fābulōs*(*us*)] **—fab′u·lous·ly,** *adv.* **—fab′u·lous·ness,** *n.* **—Syn. 1.** amazing, astonishing, astounding. **3.** fabled. **—Ant. 1.** usual. **3.** actual, historical.

fac., 1. facsimile. **2.** factor. **3.** factory.

Façade

fa·çade (fə säd′, fa-; *Fr.* fa sad′), *n., pl.* **-çades** (-sädz′; *Fr.* -sad′). **1.** *Archit.* the front of a building, esp. an imposing or decorative one. **2.** a false or superficial appearance, often designed to give a favorable impression. Also, **fa·cade′.** [< F < It *facciata.* See FACE, -ADE[1]]

face (fās), *n., v.,* **faced, fac·ing. —***n.* **1.** the front part of the head, from the forehead to the chin. **2.** a look or expression on this part: *a sad face.* **3.** an expression or look that indicates ridicule, disgust, etc.; grimace: *to make a face.* **4.** *Informal.* boldness; impudence. **5.** outward appearance. **6.** outward show or pretense. **7.** good reputation; dignity; prestige. **8.** the amount specified in a bill or note, exclusive of interest. **9.** the manifest sense or express terms, as of a document. **10.** the geographic characteristics or general appearance (of a land surface). **11.** the surface: *face of the earth.* **12.** the side or part of a side upon which the use of a thing depends: *the face of a watch.* **13.** the most important or most frequently seen side; front. **14.** the acting, striking, or working surface of an implement, tool, etc. **15.** *Geom.* any one of the bounding surfaces of a solid figure. **16.** *Mining.* the front or end of a drift or excavation, where the material is or was mined. **17.** *Print.* **a.** the working surface of a type, of a plate, etc. **b.** Also called **typeface.** any design of type. **c.** Also called **typeface.** the general style or appearance of type: *broad or narrow face.* **18.** *Naut., Aeron.* the rear or after side of a propeller blade (opposed to *back*). **19.** *Fort.* either of the two outer sides that form the salient angle of a bastion or the like. **20.** *Crystall.* any of the outer plane surfaces of a crystal. **21.** *Archaic.* sight; presence: *to flee from the face of the enemy.* **22. fly in the face of.** See **fly**[1] (def. 17). **23. in the face of, a.** in spite of; notwithstanding. **b.** when confronted with. **24. show one's face,** to make an appearance; be seen. **25. to one's face,** in one's presence; brazenly; directly. **—***v.t.* **26.** to look toward or in the direction of. **27.** to have the front toward or permit a view of. **28.** to confront directly. **29.** to confront courageously, boldly, or impudently (usually fol. by *down* or *out*): *to face down an opponent.* **30.** to oppose or to meet defiantly. **31.** to cover or partly cover with a different material in front. **32.** to finish the edge of (a garment) with facing. **33.** to turn the face of (a playing card) upward. **34.** to dress or smooth the surface of (a stone or the like). **35.** *Ice Hockey.* (of a referee) to put (the puck) in play by dropping it between two opposing players each having his stick on the ice and facing the goal of the opponent. **—***v.i.* **36.** to turn or be turned (often fol. by *to* or *toward*): *to face toward the sea.* **37.** to be placed with the front in a certain direction (often fol. by *on, to,* or *toward*): *The house faces on the street.* **38.** to turn to the right, left, or in the opposite direction: *Left face!* **39.** *Ice Hockey.* to face the puck (often fol. by *off*). **40. face up to, a.** to acknowledge; admit. **b.** to meet courageously; confront. [ME < OF < VL **facia,* r. L *faciēs* FACIES] **—face′a·ble,** *adj.* **—fac′er,** *n.* **—Syn. 1.** features. FACE, COUNTENANCE, VISAGE refer to the front of the (usually human) head. The FACE is the combination of the features: *a face with broad cheekbones.* COUNTENANCE, a more formal word, denotes the face as it is affected by or reveals the state of mind: *a thoughtful countenance.* VISAGE, still more formal, refers to the face as seen in a certain aspect, esp. as revealing seriousness or severity: *a stern visage.* **2.** appearance, aspect, mien.

face′ card′, the king, queen, or jack of playing cards.

face-cen·tered (fās′sen′tərd), *adj. Crystall.* (of a crystal structure) having lattice points on the faces of the unit cells. Cf. **body-centered.**

face-hard·en (fās′här′dən), *v.t.* to harden the surface of (metal), as by chilling or casehardening.

face·less (fās′lis), *adj.* **1.** without a face. **2.** lacking personal distinction or identity: *a faceless mob.* **3.** unable to be identified; concealing one's identity.

face-lift (fās′lift′), *n.* plastic surgery on the face for elevating sagging tissues and eliminating wrinkles and other signs of age. Also called **face′ lift′ing.**

face-off (fās′ôf′, -of′), *n. Ice Hockey.* the act of facing the puck, as at the start of a game or period.

face·plate (fās′plāt′), *n.* (on a lathe) a perforated plate, mounted on the live spindle, to which the work is attached.

face-sav·ing (fās′sā′ving), *adj.* **1.** serving to save one's prestige or dignity. **—*n.*** **2.** any act that saves one's prestige or dignity.

fac·et (fas′it), *n., v.,* **-et·ed, -et·ing** or (*esp. Brit.*) **-et·ted, -et·ting.** **—*n.*** **1.** one of the small, polished plane surfaces of a cut gem. **2.** an aspect; phase. **3.** *Zool.* one of the corneal lenses of a compound arthropod eye. **—*v.t.*** **4.** to cut facets on. [< F *facette* little face]

fa·cete (fə sēt′), *adj. Archaic.* facetious; witty. [< L *facēt(us)* courteous, elegant, witty] **—fa·cete′ly,** *adv.* **—fa·cete′ness,** *n.*

fa·ce·ti·ae (fə sē′shē ē′), *n.pl.* **1.** amusing or witty remarks or writings. **2.** coarsely witty books, stories, etc. [< L, pl. of *facētia* something witty]

fa·ce·tious (fə sē′shəs), *adj.* frivolously amusing; funny: *a facetious remark; a facetious person.* [FACETE + -IOUS] **—fa·ce′tious·ly,** *adv.* **—fa·ce′tious·ness,** *n.* **—Syn.** comical, droll, jocular. See **humorous.**

face-to-face (fās′tə fās′), *adv.* **1.** in a position with the fronts or faces turned toward each other, esp. when close together. **2.** in a way involving close contact or direct opposition. **—*adj.*** **3.** with the fronts or faces toward each other, esp. when close together. **4.** involving close contact or direct opposition.

face′ val′ue, **1.** the value printed on the face of a stock, bond, etc. **2.** apparent value: *Do not accept promises at face value.*

fa·cial (fā′shəl), *adj.* **1.** of the face: *facial expression.* **2.** for the face: *facial tissues.* **—*n.*** **3.** a massage or other treatment to beautify the face. [< ML *faciāl(is)*] **—fa′cial·ly,** *adv.*

fa′cial an′gle, *Craniom.* the angle formed by the intersection of the axis of the face with the axis of the skull.

Orthognathous Skull — Prognathous Skull

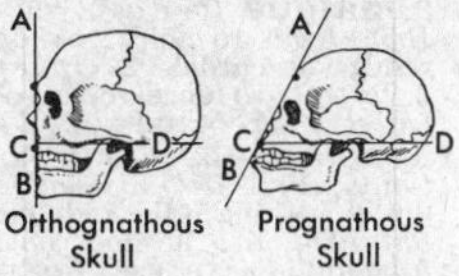

ACD, Facial angle; AB, Axis of face; CD, Axis of skull

fa′cial in′dex, *Craniom.* the ratio of the breadth of the face to its height.

-facient, a learned borrowing from Latin meaning "that makes or causes (something)," used in the formation of compound words: *febrifacient.* [< L *facient-* (s. of *faciēns,* prp. of *facere*) making = *faci-* (s. of *facere*) + *-ent-* -ENT]

fa·ci·es (fā′shē ēz′, -shēz), *n., pl.* **fa·ci·es.** **1.** general appearance, as of an animal or vegetable group. **2.** *Geol.* the composite nature of sedimentary deposits reflecting the conditions and environment of their origin. **3.** *Med.* a facial expression characteristic of a disease or pathological condition. [ME < L: form, figure, appearance, face]

fac·ile (fas′il *or, esp. Brit.,* -īl), *adj.* **1.** moving, acting, working, proceeding, etc., with ease; glib: *a facile mind.* **2.** easily performed, used, etc.: *a facile method.* **3.** easy or unconstrained, as manners or persons; affable, agreeable, or complaisant; easily influenced. [late ME < L *facil(is)* that can be done, easy = *fac(ere)* (to) do, make + *-ilis* -ILE] **—fac′ile·ly,** *adv.* **—fac′ile·ness,** *n.* **—Syn. 1.** smooth, flowing, fluent; superficial.

fa·cil·i·tate (fə sil′i tāt′), *v.t.,* **-tat·ed, -tat·ing.** **1.** to make easier or less difficult; help forward (an action, a process, etc.). **2.** to assist the progress of (a person). **—fa·cil′i·ta′tion,** *n.* **—fa·cil′i·ta′tive,** *adj.* **—fa·cil′i·ta′tor,** *n.*

fa·cil·i·ty (fə sil′i tē), *n., pl.* **-ties.** **1.** something designed, built, installed, etc., to serve a specific function or perform a particular service: *transportation facilities; educational facilities.* **2.** the quality of being easily or conveniently done or performed. **3.** something that permits the easier performance of an action, course of conduct, etc. **4.** freedom from difficulty; ease. **5.** readiness or ease due to skill, aptitude, or practice; dexterity: *He translated with great facility.* **6.** an easy-flowing manner. **7.** ready compliance. [late ME *facilite* < L *facilitās*]

fac·ing (fā′sing), *n.* **1.** a covering in front, as an outer layer of stone on a brick wall. **2.** a lining applied to the edge of a garment for ornament or strengthening. **3.** material turned outward or inward, as a cuff or hem. **4. facings,** coverings on the collar, cuffs, etc., of a military coat.

fa·cin·o·rous (fə sin′ər əs), *adj. Archaic.* dreadfully wicked. [< L *facinorōs(us)* criminal, atrocious]

facsim., facsimile.

fac·sim·i·le (fak sim′ə lē), *n., v.,* **-led, -le·ing.** **—*n.*** **1.** an exact copy, as of a book, painting, manuscript, etc. **2.** a method of transmitting drawings, printed material, or the like, by means of radio or telegraph. **—*v.t.*** **3.** to reproduce in facsimile; make a facsimile of. [earlier *fac simile* make the like = L *fac* (impv. of *facere*) + *simile;* see SIMILE] **—Syn. 1.** replica, reproduction. **1, 3.** duplicate.

fact (fakt), *n.* **1.** the quality of existing or of being real; actuality; truth: *It has no basis in fact.* **2.** something known to exist or to have happened. **3.** a truth known by actual experience or observation; that which is known to be true: *Scientists deal with facts.* **4.** something said to be true or supposed to have happened. **5.** Often, **facts.** *Law.* an actual or alleged event or circumstance, as distinguished from its legal effect or consequence. **6. after the fact,** *Law.* after the commission of a crime: *an accessory after the fact.* **7. before the fact,** *Law.* prior to the commission of a crime: *an accessory before the fact.* **8. in fact,** really; indeed. [< L *fact(um)* something done, deed] **—fact′ful,** *adj.*

fact-find·ing (fakt′fīn′ding), *adj.* **1.** engaged in determining facts. **—*n.*** **2.** determination of facts.

fac·tion (fak′shən), *n.* **1.** a group or clique within a larger group, party, government, organization, or the like. **2.** party strife and intrigue; dissension. [< L *factiōn-* (s. of *factiō*) a doing, company]

fac·tion·al (fak′shə nəl), *adj.* **1.** of a faction or factions. **2.** self-interested; partisan. **—fac′tion·al·ism,** *n.* **—fac′tion·al·ist,** *n.*

fac·tious (fak′shəs), *adj.* **1.** given to faction; dissentious. **2.** pertaining to or proceeding from faction: *factious quarrels.* [< L *factiōs(us)* fond of doing, busy, of a company or party. See FACTION, -OUS] **—fac′tious·ly,** *adv.* **—fac′tious·ness,** *n.*

fac·ti·tious (fak tish′əs), *adj.* artificial or contrived; not spontaneous or natural: *factitious enthusiasm.* [< L *factītius,* var. of *factīcius* made by art, artificial] **—fac·ti′tious·ly,** *adv.* **—fac·ti′tious·ness,** *n.* **—Syn.** forced, feigned, engineered. **—Ant.** genuine, sincere.

fac·ti·tive (fak′ti tiv), *adj. Gram.* noting or pertaining to verbs that take a direct object and an objective complement indicating consequence, as *made* in *They made him king.* [< NL *factitīv(us)* = *factit-* (s. of L *factitāre* to do often, practice, declare (someone) to be) + *-īvus* -IVE] **—fac′ti·tive·ly,** *adv.*

fact′ of life′, **1.** any aspect of human existence that must be confronted or regarded as unalterable or presently existing. **2. facts of life, a.** the facts concerning sex, reproduction, and birth. **b.** any unavoidable fact, situation, etc.

fac·toid (fak′toid), *n.* a lie or half-truth, devised esp. to gain publicity and accepted as a fact because of constant repetition in print, conversation, etc. [FACT + -OID; said to have been coined by N. Mailer in *Marilyn* (1973)]

fac·tor (fak′tər), *n.* **1.** one of the elements contributing to a particular result or situation. **2.** *Math.* one of two or more numbers, algebraic expressions, or the like, that when multiplied together produce a given product; a divisor: *The numbers 6 and 3 are factors of 18.* **3.** *Biol.* a gene, allele, or other determiner for hereditary characters. **4.** *Biochem.* any of certain substances necessary to a biochemical or physiological process, esp. those whose exact nature and function are unknown. **5.** *Com.* a business organization that lends money on accounts receivable or buys and collects accounts receivable. **6.** an agent; a person who acts or transacts business for another. **—*v.t.*** **7.** *Math.* to express (a mathematical quantity) as a product of two or more quantities of like kind, as $30 = 2 \cdot 3 \cdot 5$, or $x^2 - y^2 = (x + y)(x - y)$. Cf. **expand** (def. 4a). [late ME *facto(u)r* < L *factor* a maker, doer, performer] **—fac′tor·a·bil′i·ty,** *n.* **—fac′tor·a·ble,** *adj.* **—fac′tor·ship′,** *n.*

fac·tor·age (fak′tər ij), *n. Com.* **1.** the action or business of a factor. **2.** the allowance or commission paid a factor.

fac·to·ri·al (fak tōr′ē əl, -tôr′-), *n.* **1.** *Math.* the product of a given positive integer multiplied by all lesser positive integers. *Symbol:* $n!$, $\lfloor\underline{n}$, where n is the given integer. **—*adj.*** **2.** *Math.* of or pertaining to factors or factorials. **3.** *Com.* of or pertaining to a factor or a factory. **—fac·to′ri·al·ly,** *adv.*

fac·tor·ing (fak′tər ing), *n.* **1.** *Com.* the business of purchasing and collecting accounts receivable or of advancing cash on the basis of accounts receivable. **2.** the act or process of separating an equation, formula, cryptogram, etc., into its component parts.

fac·tor·ize (fak′tə rīz′), *v.t.,* **-ized, -iz·ing.** *Math.* to resolve into factors. **—fac′tor·i·za′tion,** *n.*

fac·to·ry (fak′tə rē), *n., pl.* **-ries.** **1.** a building or group of buildings with facilities for the manufacture of goods. **2.** *Com.* (formerly) an establishment for factors and merchants carrying on business in a foreign country. [< ML *factōria*] **—fac′to·ry·like′,** *adj.* **—Syn. 1.** manufactory.

fac·to·tum (fak tō′təm), *n.* a person employed to do all kinds of work, as the chief servant of a household. [< ML = L *fac* make, do (impv. of *facere*) + *tōtum,* neut. of *tōtus* all]

fac·tu·al (fak′cho͞o əl), *adj.* **1.** of or pertaining to facts; concerning facts. **2.** based on or restricted to facts: *a factual biography.* [FACT + *-ual* as in *actual*] **—fac′tu·al·ly,** *adv.* **—fac′tu·al′i·ty, fac′tu·al·ness,** *n.*

fac·tu·al·ism (fak′cho͞o ə liz′əm), *n.* **1.** devotion to or extensive reliance upon facts. **2.** a theory emphasizing or relying upon factual information. **—fac′tu·al·ist,** *n.* **—fac′tu·al·is′tic,** *adj.*

fac·ture (fak′chər), *n.* **1.** the act, process, or manner of making anything; construction. **2.** the thing made. [late ME < L *factūra* the making (of something)]

fac·u·la (fak′yə lə), *n., pl.* **-lae** (-lē′). *Astron.* an irregular, unusually bright patch on the sun's surface. [< L: little torch = *fac-* (s. of *fax*) torch + *-ula* -ULE] **—fac′u·lar,** *adj.*

fac·ul·ta·tive (fak′əl tā′tiv), *adj.* **1.** conferring a faculty, privilege, permission, or the power of doing or not doing something: *a facultative enactment.* **2.** left to one's option or choice; optional. **3.** that may or may not take place; that may or may not assume a specified character. **4.** *Biol.* having the capacity to live under more than one specific set of environmental conditions, as an animal or plant that can lead either a parasitic or a nonparasitic life (opposed to *obligate*). **5.** of or pertaining to the faculties. [< NL *facultātīv(us)*] **—fac′ul·ta′tive·ly,** *adv.*

fac·ul·ty (fak′əl tē), *n., pl.* **-ties.** **1.** an ability, natural or acquired, for a particular kind of action. **2.** one of the powers of the mind, as memory, reason, speech, etc. **3.** an inherent capability of the body. **4.** *Educ.* **a.** one of the departments of learning, as theology, medicine, or law, in a university. **b.** the teaching body, sometimes with the students, in any of these departments. **c.** the entire teaching and administrative force of a university, college, or school. **5.** the members of a learned profession: *the medical faculty.* **6.** power or authority conferred by the state, a superior, etc. [ME *facultee* < MF < L *facultāt-* (s. of *facultās*) feasibility, means = *facul* easily (see FACILE) + *-tāt-* -TY²] **—Syn. 1.** capacity, capability, aptitude. See **ability.**

fad (fad), *n.* a temporary fashion, manner of conduct, etc., esp. one followed enthusiastically by a group. [n. use of dial. *fad* to look after things, busy oneself with trifles, back formation from obs. *faddle* to play with, fondle. See FIDDLE] **—fad′dish, fad′dy,** *adj.* **—fad′dish·ness,** *n.* **—fad′dism,** *n.* **—fad′dist,** *n.* **—Syn.** craze, vogue.

fade (fād), *v.,* **fad·ed, fad·ing.** **—*v.i.*** **1.** to lose brightness or vividness of color. **2.** to become dim, as light, or lose brightness of illumination. **3.** to lose freshness, vigor, strength, or health: *The flower faded.* **4.** to disappear or die gradually (often fol. by *away* or *out*): *His anger faded away.* **5.** *Motion Pictures, Television.* to appear or disappear gradually (usually fol. by *in* or *out*). **6.** *Football.* (of an offensive back) to move back toward one's goal line, preparatory to making a forward pass. **—*v.t.*** **7.** to cause to fade: *Sunshine faded the tapestry.* **8.** (in dice throwing) to make a wager against (the caster). **9.** *Motion Pictures, Television.* to cause (a scene) to appear or disappear gradually (usually fol. by *in* or *out*). [ME *fade(n)* < *fade* pale, dull < OF < VL *fatid(us)*, r. L *fatuus* FATUOUS] —**fad′a·ble,** *adj.* —**fad′-ed·ly,** *adv.* —**fad′ed·ness,** *n.* —**fad′er,** *n.* —**Syn. 1.** blanch, bleach, pale. **3.** wither, droop, languish, decline.

fade-in (fād′in′), *n.* **1.** *Motion Pictures, Television.* a gradual increase in the visibility of a scene. **2.** *Broadcasting, Recording.* a gradual increase in the audibility of sound.

fade·less (fād′lis), *adj.* not fading or diminishing; unfading. —**fade′less·ly,** *adv.*

fade-out (fād′out′), *n.* **1.** *Motion Pictures, Television.* a gradual decrease in the visibility of a scene. **2.** *Broadcasting, Recording.* a gradual decrease in the audibility of sound.

fadge (faj), *v.i.*, **fadged, fadg·ing.** *Brit. Dial.* **1.** to fit; suit; agree. **2.** to succeed; thrive; result. [akin to OE *gefæg* acceptable. See FAY[2], FUDGE[3]]

FAdm, Fleet Admiral.

fa·do (fä′dŏŏ; *Eng.* fä′dō), *n.* a Portuguese popular song or dance, typically accompanied on the guitar. [< Pg < L *fatum* FATE]

fae·ces (fē′sēz), *n.pl.* feces. —**fae·cal** (fē′kəl), *adj.*

Fa·en·za (fä en′zə; *It.* fä en′tsä), *n.* a city in N Italy, SE of Bologna. 51,269 (1961).

fa·er·ie (fā′ə rē, fâr′ē), *n.* **1.** the imaginary land of the fairies. **2.** *Archaic.* a fairy. —*adj.* **3.** fairy. Also, **fa′ër·ie, faery, faëry.** [var. of FAIRY]

Faer′oe Is′lands (fâr′ō), a group of 21 islands in the N Atlantic between Great Britain and Iceland, belonging to Denmark but having extensive home rule. 34,596 (1960); 540 sq. mi. *Cap.:* Torshaven. Also, **Faroe Islands.** Also called **Faer′oes.** Danish, **Faer·ö·er·ne** (fer œ′er nə).

Faer·o·ese (fâr′ō ēz′, -ēs′), *n., pl.* **-ese,** *adj.* —*n.* **1.** a native or inhabitant of the Faeroe Islands. **2.** the North Germanic language spoken there. —*adj.* **3.** of or pertaining to the Faeroe Islands, its people, or their language. Also, **Faroese.**

fa·er·y (fā′ə rē, fâr′ē), *n., pl.* **fa·er·ies,** *adj.* faerie. Also, **fa′ër·y.**

Faf·nir (fäv′nir, fôv′-), *n.* *Scand. Myth.* a dragon, a son of Hreidmar: he killed Hreidmar for the cursed treasure of Andvari and was killed in turn by Sigurd.

fag[1] (fag), *v.*, **fagged, fag·ging,** *n.* —*v.t.* **1.** to tire or exhaust (often fol. by *out*): *The long climb fagged us out.* —*v.i.* **2.** *Brit. Informal.* to do menial chores for an older public-school pupil. —*n.* **3.** *Slang.* a cigarette. **4.** a fag end, as of cloth. **5.** *Brit. Informal.* a younger pupil in a British public school required to perform certain menial tasks for, and submit to the hazing of, an older pupil. **6.** a drudge. [late ME *fagge* a loose end, broken thread (in cloth)]

fag[2] (fag), *n.* faggot[2].

fa·ga·ceous (fə gā′shəs), *adj.* belonging to the *Fagaceae,* or beech family of trees and shrubs, which includes the beech, chestnut, oak, etc. [< NL *Fāgāce(ae)* name of the family (L *fāg(us)* beech + *-āceae* -ACEAE) + -OUS]

fag′ end′, 1. the last part or very end of something. **2.** the unfinished end of a piece of cloth; remnant.

fag·got[1] (fag′ət), *n.* *Brit.* fagot.

fag·got[2] (fag′ət), *n.* *Slang.* a male homosexual. [?] —**fag′-got·y,** *adj.*

fag·got·ry (fag′ə trē), *n.* male homosexuality.

fag·ot (fag′ət), *n.* **1.** a bundle of sticks, twigs, or branches bound together and used as fuel, a fascine, etc. **2.** a bundle; bunch. **3.** a bundle of pieces of iron or steel to be welded or rolled together. —*v.t.* **4.** to bind or make into a fagot. **5.** to ornament with fagoting. Also, *Brit.,* **faggot.** [ME < MF; cf. Gk *phákelos* fagot] —**fag′ot·er,** *n.*

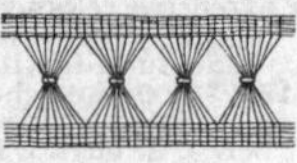

Fagoting

fag·ot·ing (fag′ə ting), *n.* an openwork decoration of fabric in which the thread is drawn in crisscross stitches across an open seam. Also, *Brit.,* **fag′got·ing.**

fahl·band (fäl′band′; *Ger.* fäl′bänt′), *n.* *Mining.* a belt or zone of rock impregnated with metallic sulfides. [< G = *fahl* pale-colored + *Band* ribbon, stripe]

Fahr., Fahrenheit (temperature scale). Also, **Fah.**

Fahr·en·heit (far′ən hīt′; *Ger.* fäʀ′ən hīt′), *n.* **1. Ga·bri·el Da·ni·el** (*Ger.* gä′bʀē el′ dä′nē el′), 1686–1736, German physicist: devised a temperature scale and introduced the use of mercury in thermometers. —*adj.* **2.** noting, pertaining to, or measured according to a temperature scale **(Fahr′-enheit scale′)** in which 32° represents the ice point and 212° the steam point. *Abbr.:* F See illus. at **thermometer.**

fa·ïence (fī äns′, fā-; *Fr.* fA yäɴs′), *n.* glazed earthenware or pottery, esp. a fine variety with highly colored designs. Also, **fa·ience′.** [< F, orig. pottery of FAENZA]

fail (fāl), *v.i.* **1.** to fall short of success or achievement in something expected, attempted, desired, or approved: *The experiment failed.* **2.** to receive less than the passing grade or mark in an examination, class, or course of study. **3.** to be or become deficient or lacking; fall short; be insufficient or absent: *Our supplies failed.* **4.** to dwindle, pass, or die away: *The flowers failed for lack of rain.* **5.** to lose strength or vigor; become weaker. **6.** to become unable to meet or pay debts or business obligations; become insolvent or bankrupt. **7.** (of a building member, structure, machine part, etc.) to break, bend, crush, or be otherwise destroyed or made useless because of an excessive load. **8.** to stop functioning or operating. —*v.t.* **9.** to be unsuccessful in the performance or completion of: *He failed to do his duty.* **10.** to prove of no use or help to, as some expected or usual resource: *His friends failed him. Words failed him.* **11.** to receive less than a passing grade or mark in. **12.** to declare (a person) unsuccessful in a test, course of study, etc.; give less than a passing grade to. —*n.* **13.** *Obs.* failure as to performance, occurrence, etc. **14. without fail,** with certainty; positively. [ME *faile(n)* < OF *faill(ir)* < VL **fallīre,* r. L *fallere* to disappoint, deceive] —**Syn. 5.** decline, fade, sink, wane. **10.** desert, forsake. —**Ant. 1.** succeed. **10.** support.

fail·ing (fā′ling), *n.* **1.** the act of a person or thing that fails; failure. **2.** the state of a person or thing that fails. **3.** a defect; shortcoming; weakness. —*prep.* **4.** in the absence or default of. [ME] —**fail′ing·ly,** *adv.* —**fail′ing·ness,** *n.* —**Syn. 3.** deficiency, frailty, imperfection, flaw.

faille (fīl, fāl; *Fr.* fA′yə), *n.* a soft, transversely ribbed fabric of silk, rayon, or lightweight taffeta. [< F, orig. a veil for the head, hence the cloth of which it was made]

fail-safe (fāl′sāf′), *adj.* **1.** *Electronics.* pertaining to or noting a mechanism built into a system, as in an early warning system or a nuclear reactor, that insures safety if the system fails to operate properly. **2.** equipped with a secondary system that insures continued operation even if the primary system fails. **3.** of, pertaining to, or designating a system of coded military controls to insure that bombers will not pass beyond a prearranged point or arm their nuclear warheads without direct orders from a designated authority. —*n.* **4.** the point beyond which the bombers cannot go without specific instruction; the fail-safe point.

fail·ure (fāl′yər), *n.* **1.** the act or an instance of failing or proving unsuccessful; lack of success. **2.** nonperformance of something due, required, or expected. **3.** an insufficiency; a subnormal quantity or quality: *the failure of crops.* **4.** deterioration or decay, esp. of vigor, strength, etc. **5.** a condition of being bankrupt by reason of insolvency. **6.** a becoming insolvent or bankrupt: *the failure of a bank.* **7.** a person or thing that proves unsuccessful. [FAIL + -URE; r. *failer* a (de)fault < AF (n. use of inf.), c. F *faillir*] —**Syn. 2.** neglect, omission, dereliction. **4.** decline.

fain (fān), *Archaic.* —*adv.* **1.** gladly; willingly: *He fain would accept.* —*adj.* **2.** content; willing. **3.** constrained or obliged. **4.** glad; pleased. **5.** desirous; eager. [ME; OE *fæg(e)n;* c. Icel *feginn* happy; akin to FAIR[1], FAY[2]]

fai·naigue (fə nāg′), *v.*, **-naigued, -nai·guing.** —*v.i.* **1.** *Brit. Dial.* to shirk; evade work or responsibility. **2.** to renege at cards. **3.** *Informal.* to cheat; finagle. —*v.t.* **4.** *Informal.* to deceive, cheat, or trick (someone). [var. of *fenege,* alter. of RENEGE] —**fai·nai′guer,** *n.*

fai·né·ant (fā′nē ənt; *Fr.* fe nā äɴ′), *adj., n., pl.* **-ants** (-ənts; *Fr.* -äɴ′). —*adj.* **1.** Also, **fai·ne·ant** (fā′nē ənt). doing nothing; idle; indolent. —*n.* **2.** an idler. [< F, earlier *fait-nient,* lit., he does nothing, pseudo-etym. alter. of OF *faignant* idler, n. use of prp. of *se faindre* to shirk] —**fai·ne·ance** (fā′nē əns), **fai′ne·an·cy,** *n.*

faint (fānt), *adj.* **1.** lacking brightness, vividness, clearness, loudness, strength, etc. **2.** feeble or slight. **3.** feeling weak, dizzy, or exhausted; about to lose consciousness: *faint with hunger.* **4.** lacking courage; cowardly; timorous. —*v.i.* **5.** to lose consciousness temporarily. **6.** *Archaic.* **a.** to lose brightness. **b.** to grow weak; lose spirit or courage. —*n.* **7.** temporary loss of consciousness; a swoon: *to fall into a faint.* [ME < OF, ptp. of *faindre,* var. of *feindre* to FEIGN] —**faint′-er,** *n.* —**faint′ing·ly,** *adv.* —**faint′ish,** *adj.* —**faint′ish-ness,** *n.* —**faint′ly,** *adv.* —**faint′ness,** *n.* —**Syn. 1.** indistinct, dim, faded, dull. **2.** faltering, weak. **4.** fearful, timid.

faint·heart·ed (fānt′här′tid), *adj.* lacking courage; cowardly; timorous. [late ME *feynt hertyd*] —**faint′-heart′ed·ly,** *adv.* —**faint′heart′ed·ness,** *n.*

faints (fānts), *n.pl.* the impure spirit produced in the first and last stages of the distillation of whiskey. [n. use (in pl.) of FAINT (adj.)]

fair[1] (fâr), *adj.* **1.** free from bias, dishonesty, or injustice. **2.** legitimately sought, pursued, done, given, etc.; proper under the rules: *a fair fight.* **3.** moderately large; ample: *a fair income.* **4.** neither excellent nor poor; moderately good: *fair health.* **5.** marked by favoring conditions; likely; promising: *in a fair way to succeed.* **6.** *Meteorol.* **a.** (of the sky) bright; sunny; cloudless to half-cloudy. **b.** (of the weather) fine; with no aspect of rain, snow, or hail; not stormy. **7.** *Naut.* (of a wind or tide) tending to aid the progress of a vessel. **8.** unobstructed; not blocked up. **9.** without irregularity or unevenness: *a fair surface.* **10.** free from blemish, imperfection, or anything that impairs the appearance, quality, or character. **11.** clear; easy to read. **12.** of a light hue; not dark: *fair skin.* **13.** pleasing in appearance; attractive: *a fair young maiden.* **14.** courteous; civil: *fair words.* **15. fair to middling,** *U.S. Informal.* only tolerably good; so-so. —*adv.* **16.** in a fair manner; fairly: *He doesn't play fair.* **17.** favorably; auspiciously. **18.** *Brit., Australian.* entirely; completely; quite: *It happened so quickly that it fair took my breath away.* **19. bid fair,** to seem likely: *This entry bids fair to win first prize.* **20. fair and square,** *Informal.* **a.** honestly; justly; straightforwardly: *He won the race fair and square.* **b.** honest; just; straightforward: *He was admired for being fair and square in all his dealings.* —*n.* **21.** *Archaic.* something that is fair. **22.** *Archaic.* **a.** a woman. **b.** a beloved woman. —*v.t.* **23.** *Shipbuilding.* to draw and adjust (the lines of a hull being designed) to produce regular surfaces of the correct form. —*v.i.* **24.** *Dial.* (of the weather) to clear. [ME; OE *fæger;* c. OS, OHG *fagar,* Icel *fagr,* Goth *fagrs*] —**fair′ness,** *n.*

—**Syn. 1.** unbiased, equitable, just, honest. FAIR, IMPARTIAL, DISINTERESTED, UNPREJUDICED refer to lack of bias in opinions, judgments, etc. FAIR implies the treating of all sides alike, justly and equitably: *a fair compromise.* IMPARTIAL also implies showing no more favor to one side than another, but suggests particularly a judicial consideration of a case: *an impartial judge.* DISINTERESTED implies a fairness arising particularly from lack of desire to obtain a selfish advantage: *The motives of her guardian were entirely disinterested.* UNPREJUDICED means not influenced or swayed by bias, or by prejudice caused by irrelevant considerations: *an unprejudiced decision.* **4.** passable, tolerable, middling. **8.** open, clear, unencumbered. **10.** clean. **11.** legible, distinct. **12.** blond, pale. **13.** pretty, comely.

fair[2] (fâr), *n.* **1.** *U.S.* a competitive exhibition of farm products, livestock, etc., often combined with carnivallike entertainment and held annually by a county or state. **2.** *Chiefly Brit.* a periodic gathering of buyers and sellers in an appointed place. **3.** an exhibition and sale of articles to raise money, often for some charitable purpose. [ME *feire* < OF < LL *fēria* holiday (ML: market), in L only pl.; akin to FEAST]

fair′ ball′, *Baseball.* a batted ball that is not a foul ball.

Fair·banks (fâr′bangks′), *n.* **1. Charles Warren,** 1852–1918, political leader: vice president of the U.S. 1905–09. **2. Douglas,** 1883–1939, U.S. motion-picture actor. **3.** a town in central Alaska, on the Tanana River. 14,771 (1970).

Fair·born (fâr′bôrn′), *n.* a city in W Ohio, near Dayton. 32,267 (1970).

fair′ catch′, *Football.* a catch of a kicked ball in which the receiver signals that he will not advance the ball and therefore may not be interfered with or tackled.

fair′ cop′y, 1. an exact copy. 2. a copy of a document made after final correction.

Fair′ Deal′, the domestic policies and principles of the liberal wing of the Democratic party under President Harry S Truman. Cf. **Great Society, New Deal, New Frontier.** —**Fair′ Deal′er.**

Fair·fax (fâr′faks), *n.* 1. **Thomas** (*3rd Baron Fairfax of Cameron*), 1612–71, British general: commander in chief of the parliamentary army 1645–50. 2. **Thomas** (*6th Baron Fairfax*), 1692–1782, English colonist in Virginia.

Fair·field (fâr′fēld′), *n.* 1. a town in SW Connecticut. 56,487 (1970). 2. a city in W California, N of Oakland. 44,146 (1970).

fair′ green′, *Golf Obs.* fairway (def. 2).

fair·ground (fâr′ground′), *n.* Often, **fairgrounds.** a place where fairs, horse races, etc., are held: in the U.S. usually an area set aside by a city, county, or state for an annual fair.

fair-haired (fâr′hârd′), *adj.* 1. having light-colored hair. 2. **fair-haired boy,** a youth or man favored by a superior.

fair′ hous′ing, *U.S.* See **open housing.**

fair·ing[1] (fâr′ing), *n.* *Aeron.* a structure on the exterior of an aircraft, for reducing drag. [FAIR[1] + -ING[1]]

fair·ing[2] (fâr′ing), *n.* *Archaic.* a gift, esp. one given at or bought at a fair. [FAIR[2] + -ING[1]]

fair·ish (fâr′ish), *adj.* 1. moderately good, large, or well. 2. moderately light in color.

Fair′ Lawn′, a city in NE New Jersey. 37,975 (1970).

fair·lead (fâr′lēd′), *n.* a pulley, thimble, etc., used to guide a rope forming part of the rigging of a ship, crane, etc., in such a way as to prevent chafing. Also, **fair′lead′er.**

fair·ly (fâr′lē), *adv.* 1. in a fair manner; justly; impartially. 2. moderately; tolerably. 3. actually; completely. 4. properly; legitimately. 5. clearly; distinctly. 6. *Obs.* softly. 7. *Obs.* courteously. [late ME]

fair-mind·ed (fâr′min′did), *adj.* characterized by impartiality; unprejudiced. —**fair′-mind′ed·ness,** *n.*

Fair·mont (fâr′mont), *n.* a city in W West Virginia. 26,093 (1970).

Fair′ Oaks′, a locality in E Virginia, near Richmond: battle 1862. Also called **Seven Pines.**

fair′ play′, just and honorable treatment, action, or conduct.

fair′ sex′, women collectively.

fair-spo·ken (fâr′spō′kən), *adj.* courteous or plausible in speech; smooth-spoken. —**fair′-spo′ken·ness,** *n.*

fair′ trade′, trade carried on under a fair-trade agreement.

fair-trade (fâr′trād′), *adj., v.,* **-trad·ed, -trad·ing.** —*adj.* 1. subject to or resulting from an agreement or contract between a manufacturer and a retailer to sell a branded or trademarked product at no less than a specific price. —*v.t.* 2. to sell (a commodity) under a fair-trade agreement. —**fair′-trad′er,** *n.*

fair·way (fâr′wā′), *n.* 1. an unobstructed passage or area. 2. *Golf.* the mowed part of any hole between the tee and the green. 3. *Naut.* the navigable portion of a river, harbor, etc.; main channel.

fair-weath·er (fâr′weth′ər), *adj.* 1. for fair weather only. 2. weakening or failing in time of trouble: *fair-weather friends.*

Fair·weath·er (fâr′weth′ər), *n.* **Mount,** a mountain in SE Alaska. 15,292 ft.

fair·y (fâr′ē), *n., pl.* **fair·ies,** *adj.* —*n.* 1. one of a class of imaginary supernatural beings, generally conceived as having a diminutive human form, possessing magical powers, and intervening in human affairs. 2. *Slang.* a male homosexual. —*adj.* 3. of or pertaining to fairies: *fairy magic.* 4. of the nature of a fairy; fairylike. [ME *faierie* < OF: fairyland. See FAY[1], -ERY] —**fair′y·like′,** *adj.*
—**Syn. 1.** fay, pixy, leprechaun, nix, nixie. FAIRY, BROWNIE, ELF, SPRITE are terms for imaginary beings usually less than human size, thought to be helpful or harmful to mankind. FAIRY is the most general name for such beings: *a good fairy as a godmother; misadventures caused by an evil fairy.* A BROWNIE is a tiny fellow of limited powers who appears usually at night to do household tasks or play pranks: *The brownies turned the cream to butter.* ELF suggests a mischievous or roguish fairy: *That child is a perfect little elf.* SPRITE suggests a fairy of pleasing appearance, easy and light of movement; it may, however, be impish or even hostile: *a dainty sprite.*

fair·y·land (fâr′ē land′), *n.* 1. the imaginary realm of the fairies. 2. any enchantingly beautiful region.

fair′y ring′, a circle formed on the grass in a field by the growth of certain fungi, formerly supposed to be caused by fairies in their dances.

fair′y tale′, 1. a story, usually for children, about elves, hobgoblins, dragons, fairies, or other magical creatures. 2. an incredible or misleading statement, account, or report. Also called **fair′y sto′ry.**

Fai·sal (fī′səl), *n.* (*Faisal Abdel Aziz al Saud al Faisal*) 1904–75, king of Saudi Arabia 1964–75 (son of ibn-Saud and brother of Saud).

Faisal I, 1885–1933, king of Syria 1920; king of Iraq 1921–33. Also, **Feisal I, Feisul I.**

Faisal II, 1935–58, king of Iraq 1939–58 (grandson of Faisal I). Also, **Feisal II, Feisul II.**

fait ac·com·pli (fe TA kôN plē′), *pl.* **faits ac·com·plis** (fe ZA kôN plē′). *French.* an accomplished fact; a thing already done.

faith (fāth), *n.* 1. confidence or trust in a person or thing. 2. belief that is not based on proof. 3. belief in God or in the doctrines or teachings of religion. 4. belief in anything, as a code of ethics, or the occurrence of a future event. 5. a system of religious belief: *the Jewish faith.* 6. the obligation of loyalty or fidelity to a person, promise, engagement, etc. 7. the observance of this obligation; fidelity to one's promise, oath, allegiance, etc.: *to act in good faith.* 8. *Christian Theol.* the trust in God and in His promises as made through Christ and the Scriptures by which man is justified or saved. 9. **in faith,** in truth; indeed. [ME *feith* < AF *feid* < L *fid(e)-,* s. of *fidēs* trust, akin to *fīdere* to trust]
—**Syn. 5.** doctrine, tenet, creed, dogma, persuasion, religion. —**Ant. 1, 2.** distrust, skepticism.

faith′ cure′, 1. a method of attempting to cure disease by prayer and religious faith. 2. a cure thus effected.

faith·ful (fāth′fəl), *adj.* 1. strict or thorough in the performance of duty: *a faithful worker.* 2. true to one's word, promises, vows, etc. 3. steady in allegiance or affection. 4. reliable, trusted, or believed. 5. adhering or true to fact or an original: *a faithful account; a faithful copy.* 6. *Obs.* full of faith; believing. —*n.* 7. the body of loyal members of any party or group. 8. **the faithful,** the believers, esp. of Christianity or Islam. [ME *feithful*] —**faith′ful·ly,** *adv.* —**faith′ful·ness,** *n.*
—**Syn. 1, 3.** true, devoted, staunch. 3. FAITHFUL, CONSTANT, LOYAL imply qualities of stability, dependability, and devotion. FAITHFUL implies long-continued and steadfast fidelity to whatever one is bound to by a pledge, duty, or obligation: *a faithful friend.* CONSTANT suggests firmness and steadfastness in attachment: *a constant affection.* LOYAL implies unswerving allegiance to a person, organization, cause, or idea: *loyal to one's associates, one's country.* 5. accurate, precise, exact.

faith′ heal′er, a person who claims ability to heal the sick by prayer and religious faith.

faith·less (fāth′lis), *adj.* 1. not adhering to allegiances, promises, vows, or duty. 2. not trustworthy; unreliable. 3. without trust or belief. 4. without religious faith. [ME *faithles*] —**faith′less·ly,** *adv.* —**faith′less·ness,** *n.* —**Syn. 1.** false, inconstant; disloyal, treacherous.

fai·tour (fā′tər), *n.* *Archaic.* impostor; fake. [ME < AF: impostor, c. OF *faitor* perpetrator, lit., doer, maker < L *factor*]

Fai·yum (fī yōōm′), *n.* 1. a province in the E central Arab Republic of Egypt: many archaeological remains. 839,000 (est. 1960); 691 sq. mi. 2. Also called **El Faiyum, El Fayum.** a city in and the capital of this province, SW of Cairo. 117,800 (est. 1962). Also, **Fayum.**

Faiz·a·bad (fī′zä bäd′), *n.* Fyzabad.

fake[1] (fāk), *v.,* **faked, fak·ing,** *n., adj.* —*v.t.* 1. to prepare or make (something specious, deceptive, or fraudulent). 2. to pretend; simulate: *to fake illness.* —*v.i.* 3. to fake something; pretend. —*n.* 4. anything made to appear other than it actually is; counterfeit. 5. a person who fakes; faker. 6. a spurious report or story. —*adj.* 7. designed to deceive or cheat; not real; counterfeit. [orig. vagrants' slang: to do for, rob, kill (someone), shape (something); ? var. of obs. *feak, feague* to beat, akin to D *veeg* a slap, *vegen* to sweep, wipe] —**Syn. 5.** fraud, impostor, charlatan.

fake[2] (fāk), *v.,* **faked, fak·ing,** *n.* *Naut.* —*v.t.* 1. to lay (a rope) in a coil or series of long loops so that it will run freely without fouling or kinking (often fol. by *down*). —*n.* 2. any complete turn of a rope that has been faked down. 3. any of the various ways in which a rope may be faked down. Also, **flake.** [late ME *fake(n)*]

fak·er (fā′kər), *n.* *Informal.* a person who fakes.

fak·er·y (fā′kə rē), *n., pl.* **-er·ies.** the practice or result of faking.

fa·kir (fə kēr′, fā′kər), *n.* 1. a Muslim or Hindu religious ascetic or mendicant monk commonly considered a wonder-worker. 2. a member of any Islamic religious order; dervish. Also, **fa·keer′.** [< Ar *faqīr* poor]

fa-la (fä lä′), *n.* 1. a text or refrain in old songs. 2. a type of part song or madrigal popular in the 16th and 17th centuries.

Fa·lange (fā′lanj; *Sp.* fä län′he), *n.* the fascist party of Spain. [< Sp: PHALANX] —**Fa·lan′gist,** *n.*

fal·cate (fal′kāt), *adj.* hooked; curved like a scythe or sickle; falciform. Also, **fal′cat·ed.** [< L *falcāt(us)* = *falc-* (s. of *falx*) sickle + *-ātus* -ATE[1]]

fal·chion (fôl′chən, -shən), *n.* 1. a broad, short sword having a convex edge curving sharply to the point. 2. *Archaic.* any sword. [< It *falcione* = *falce* sickle (see FALCATE) + *-one* aug. suffix; r. ME *fauchoun* < OF]

fal·ci·form (fal′sə fôrm′), *adj.* sickle-shaped; falcate. [< L *falci-* (s. of *falx*) sickle + -FORM]

fal·con (fal′kən, fôl′-, fô′kən), *n.* 1. any of several diurnal birds of prey of the family *Falconidae,* esp. of the genus *Falco,* having long, pointed wings and a notched bill. 2. *Falconry.* **a.** the female gyrfalcon. **b.** the female peregrine. **c.** any bird of prey trained for use in falconry. Cf. **tercel.** 3. a small cannon in use during the 15th–17th centuries. [< LL *falcōn-* (s. of *falcō*) hawk (akin to *falx* sickle); r. ME *faucon* < OF] —**fal·co·nine** (fôl′kə nīn′, -nin, fal′-, fô′kə-), *adj.*

Peregrine falcon, *Falco peregrinus* (Length 18 in.)

fal·con·er (fôl′kə nər, fal′-, fô′kə-), *n.* 1. a person who hunts with falcons; one who follows the sport of falconry. 2. a person who trains hawks for hunting. [FALCON + -ER[2]; r. ME *falkenar* (< ML *falcōnārius*), *fauconer* < AF, c. OF *fauconier*]

fal·co·net[1] (fôl′kə net′, fal′-, fô′kə-), *n.* any of several small Asian falcons, esp. of the genus *Microhierax.* [FALCON + -ET]

fal·co·net[2] (fôl′kə net′, fal′-, fô′kə-), *n.* a light cannon of the 16th century. [< It *falconett(o)*]

fal·con-gen·tle (fôl′kən jen′tᵊl, fal′-, fô′kən-), *n.* 1. the female of the peregrine falcon. 2. any female falcon. [trans. of F *faucon gentil,* lit., noble falcon; r. ME *gentil fauco(u)n, facon jent,* etc.]

fal·con·i·form (fôl kō′nə fôrm′, fal-, fô kō′-, fôl′kə-nə-, fal′-, fô′kə-), *adj.* of, pertaining to, or belonging to the order *Falconiformes,* comprising the vultures, hawks, eagles, ospreys, falcons, caracaras, etc.

fal·con·ry (fôl′kən rē, fal′-, fô′kən-), *n.* 1. the sport of hunting with falcons, hawks, eagles, etc.; hawking. 2. the art of training birds of prey to hunt. [FALCON + -RY, modeled on F *fauconnerie*]

fal·de·ral (fal′də ral′), *n.* **1.** mere nonsense; foolish talk or ideas. **2.** a trifle; gimcrack; gewgaw. Also, **fal·de·rol** (fal′də rol′), **folderol.** [from meaningless refrains of old songs]

fald·stool (fôld′sto͞ol′), *n.* **1.** a chair or seat, originally one capable of being folded, used by a bishop when away from his throne or in a church not his own. **2.** a movable folding stool or desk at which worshipers kneel during certain acts of devotion. **3.** such a stool as used by sovereigns of England at their coronation. **4.** a desk at which the litany is said or sung. [OE *fealdestōl* folding chair; c. OHG *faltistuol*]

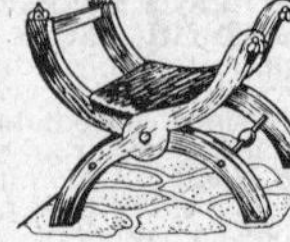
Faldstool (def. 1)

Fa·lie·ri (*It.* fä lye′rē), *n.* **Ma·ri·no** (*It.* mä rē′nô), 1278?–1355, Venetian army commander: doge of Venice 1354–55. Also, **Fa·lie′ro** (*It.* fä lye′rô).

Fa·lis·can (fə lis′kən), *n.* **1.** any one of an ancient people who inhabited southern Etruria. **2.** the Italic dialect spoken by this people, closely related to Latin. —*adj.* **3.** of or pertaining to the Faliscans or their language. [< L *Falisc(i)* the Faliscans + -AN]

Fal·kirk (fôl′kûrk), *n.* a city in central Scotland, W of Edinburgh: Scots under Wallace defeated by the English 1298. 38,042 (est. 1964).

Falk′land Is′lands (fôk′lənd), a group of more than 100 islands in the S Atlantic, ab. 300 mi. E of the Strait of Magellan: a British crown colony; Germans defeated by British in naval battle 1914. 2102 (1964); 4618 sq. mi. *Chief town:* Stanley.

Falk·ner (fôk′nər), *n.* **William.** See **Faulkner, William.**

fall (fôl), *v.*, **fell, fall·en, fall·ing,** *n.* —*v.i.* **1.** to descend under the force of gravity, as to a lower place through loss or lack of support. **2.** to come or drop down suddenly to a lower position, esp. to leave a standing or erect position suddenly, whether voluntarily or not: *to fall on one's knees.* **3.** to move to a lower level, degree, amount, quality, value, number, etc.; become less or lower; decline: *Stock prices fell.* **4.** to subside or abate. **5.** to hang down; extend downward: *Her hair falls to her shoulders.* **6.** to become lowered or directed downward, as the eyes. **7.** to succumb to temptation, esp. to become unchaste or to lose one's innocence. **8.** to lose status, position, dignity, etc. **9.** to succumb to attack: *The city fell to the enemy.* **10.** to be overthrown, as a government. **11.** to drop down wounded or dead, esp. to be slain: *to fall in battle.* **12.** to pass into some physical, mental, or emotional condition: *to fall asleep; to fall in love.* **13.** to envelop or come as if by dropping, as stillness, night, etc. **14.** to issue forth. **15.** to come by lot or chance: *The chore fell to him.* **16.** to come by chance into a particular position: *to fall among thieves.* **17.** to come to pass, occur, or become at a certain time: *Christmas falls on a Monday. The rent falls due today.* **18.** to have its proper place: *The accent falls on the last syllable.* **19.** to come by right: *The inheritance fell to the only living relative.* **20.** to be naturally divisible (usually fol. by *into*): *The story fell into two distinct parts.* **21.** to lose animation; appear disappointed, as the face. **22.** to slope or extend in a downward direction: *The field falls gently to the stream.* **23.** to be directed, as light, sight, etc., on something: *His eyes fell upon the forgotten jewelry.* **24.** to collapse; topple.
—*v.t.* **25.** to fell (a tree, animal, etc.). **26. fall back on** or **upon, a.** Also, **fall back to.** to retreat to. **b.** to have recourse to; rely on. **27. fall behind, a.** to lag in pace or progress. **b.** to fail to pay (a debt, obligation, etc.) at the appointed time. **28. fall down,** *Informal.* to perform disappointingly; disappoint; fail. **29. fall for,** *Slang.* **a.** to be deceived by. **b.** to fall in love with. **30. fall foul** or **afoul of.** See **foul** (def. 20). **31. fall in, a.** to fall to pieces toward the interior; sink inward. **b.** to take one's place in the ranks, as a soldier. **c.** Also, **fall in with.** to become acquainted with, esp. by chance. **32. fall off, a.** to separate from; withdraw. **b.** to deteriorate; decline. **c.** to decrease in number, amount, or intensity; diminish. **d.** *Naut.* to deviate from the heading; fall to leeward. **33. fall on** or **upon, a.** to assault; attack. **b.** to be the obligation of. **c.** to experience; encounter. **d.** to chance upon; come upon. **34. fall out, a.** to quarrel; disagree. **b.** to happen; occur. **c.** to leave one's place in the ranks, as a soldier. **35. fall through,** to come to nothing; fail of realization. **36. fall to, a.** to apply oneself; begin. **b.** to begin to eat. **37. fall under, a.** to be the concern or responsibility of. **b.** to be classified as; be included within.
—*n.* **38.** the act or an instance of falling or dropping from a higher to a lower place or position. **39.** something that falls or drops: *a fall of rain.* **40.** *Chiefly U.S.* autumn. **41.** a decline to a lower level: *a gradual fall in reputation.* **42.** the distance through which anything falls. **43.** Usually, **falls.** a cataract or waterfall. **44.** downward slope or declivity. **45.** a falling from an erect position, as to the ground: *to have a bad fall.* **46.** a hanging down: *a fall of long hair.* **47.** a succumbing to temptation; lapse into sin. **48. the Fall,** *Theol.* the state of sin, loss of innocence, and expulsion from Eden suffered by Adam and Eve because of their disobedience to God. Cf. **original sin. 49.** surrender or capture, as of a city. **50.** proper place: *the fall of an accent on a syllable.* **51.** *Wrestling.* **a.** the act or an instance of holding or forcing an opponent's shoulders against the mat for a specified length of time. **b.** a match or division of a match. **52.** an opaque veil hanging loose from the back of a hat. **53.** See **falling band. 54.** a decorative cascade of lace, ruffles, or the like. **55.** *Mach., Naut.* the part of the rope of a tackle to which the power is applied in hoisting. **56.** *Hunting.* a deadfall. **57.** the long soft hair that hangs over the forehead and eyes of certain terriers. **58.** a hairpiece consisting of long hair, usually hanging at the back of one's hairdo. **59. ride for a fall,** to risk or be destined for disaster, embarrassment, a loss of pride or status, etc. [ME *falle(n)*, OE *feallan;* c. G *fallen,* Icel *falla;* akin to Lith *pùlti* to fall]

Fal·la (fä′yə; *Sp.* fä′lyä), *n.* **Ma·nuel de** (mä nwel′ de), 1876–1946, Spanish composer.

fal·la·cious (fə lā′shəs), *adj.* **1.** deceptive; misleading: *fallacious testimony.* **2.** containing a fallacy; logically unsound: *fallacious reasoning.* **3.** disappointing; delusive: *a fallacious peace.* [< L *fallāciōs(us)* deceitful, deceptive] —**fal·la′cious·ly,** *adv.* —**fal·la′cious·ness,** *n.*

fal·la·cy (fal′ə sē), *n., pl.* **-cies. 1.** a deceptive, misleading, or false notion, belief, etc. **2.** a misleading or unsound argument. **3.** deceptive, misleading, or false nature; erroneousness. **4.** *Logic.* any of various types of erroneous reasoning that render arguments logically unsound. **5.** *Obs.* deception. [< L *fallāci(a)* a trick, deceit = *fallāc-* (s. of *fallax*) deceitful + *-ia* -Y³; r. ME *fallace* < MF]

fal·lal (fal lal′), *n.* a bit of finery; a showy article of dress. Also, **fal-lal.** [? syncopated var. of FALDERAL] —**fal·lal′ish·ly, fal-lal′ish·ly,** *adv.*

fal·lal·er·y (fal lal′ə rē), *n.* fallals collectively; finery. Also, **fal-lal′er·y.**

fall·en (fô′lən), *v.* **1.** pp. of **fall.** —*adj.* **2.** having dropped or come down from a higher place, from an upright position, or from a higher level, degree, amount, quality, value, number, etc. **3.** on the ground; prostrate; down flat. **4.** degraded or immoral. **5.** (of a woman) having lost one's chastity. **6.** overthrown; destroyed; conquered. **7.** dead.

fall·er (fô′lər), *n.* **1.** a person or thing that falls. **2.** any device that operates by falling. [late ME]

fall·fish (fôl′fish′), *n., pl.* **-fish·es,** (*esp. collectively*) **-fish.** a large minnow, *Semotilus corporalis,* found in the eastern U.S.

fall′ guy′, *U.S. Slang.* **1.** an easy victim. **2.** a scapegoat.

fal·li·ble (fal′ə bəl), *adj.* **1.** (of persons) liable to err or to be deceived or mistaken. **2.** liable to be erroneous or false. [< ML *fallibil(is)* = L *fall(ī)* (pass. of *fallere* to deceive) + *-ibilis* -IBLE] —**fal′li·bil′i·ty, fal′li·ble·ness,** *n.* —**fal′li·bly,** *adv.*

fall′ing band′, a large, flat collar, usually trimmed with lace, worn by men in the 17th century. Also called **fall.**

fall·ing-out (fô′ling out′), *n., pl.* **fall·ings-out, fall·ing-outs.** a quarrel or estrangement among persons formerly in close association with one another.

fall′ing rhythm′, *Pros.* a rhythmic pattern created by the succession of metrical feet each of which is composed of one accented syllable followed by one or more unaccented syllables.

fall′ing sick′ness, epilepsy.

fall′ing star′, an incandescent meteor; a shooting star.

fall-off (fôl′ôf′, -of′), *n.* a decline in quantity, vigor, etc.

Fal·lo′pi·an tube′ (fə lō′pē ən), *Anat., Zool.* either of a pair of slender tubes leading from the body cavity to the uterus, that transports ova from the ovary to the uterus; the oviduct of mammals. Also, **fal·lo′pi·an tube′.** [named after Gabriello *Fallopio* (d. 1562), Italian anatomist]

fall·out (fôl′out′), *n.* **1.** the settling to the ground of airborne particles of radioactive dust, soot, and other materials that result from a nuclear explosion. **2.** the particles themselves. **3.** an unexpected or often incidental outcome, effect, or product: *the psychological fallout of the Vietnam War.* Also, **fall′-out′.** Also called **radioactive fallout** (for defs. 1, 2).

fal·low¹ (fal′ō), *adj.* **1.** (of land) plowed and left unseeded for a season or more; uncultivated. —*n.* **2.** land that has undergone plowing and harrowing and has been left unseeded for one or more growing seasons. **3.** the plowing and harrowing of land that is to be left unseeded for a growing season. —*v.t.* **4.** to make (land) fallow for agricultural purposes. [ME *falwe,* OE *fealga* fallow land, pl. of *fealh;* akin to FELLOE] —**fal′low·ness,** *n.*

fal·low² (fal′ō), *adj.* pale-yellow; light-brown; dun. [ME *fal(o)we,* OE *fealu;* c. G *falb*]

fal′low deer′, a Eurasian deer, *Dama dama,* with a fallow or yellowish coat.

Fallow deer (3 ft. high at shoulder; antlers to 2½ ft.; length 5 ft.)

Fall′ Riv′er, a seaport in SE Massachusetts, on an arm of Narragansett Bay. 96,898 (1970).

Falls (fôlz), *n.* a town in NE Pennsylvania, on the Susquehanna River. 35,830 (1970).

Fal·mouth (fal′məth), *n.* a seaport in SW Cornwall, in SW England. 15,427 (1961).

false (fôls), *adj.,* **fals·er, fals·est,** *adv.* —*adj.* **1.** not true or correct; erroneous. **2.** uttering or declaring what is untrue: *a false witness.* **3.** not faithful or loyal; treacherous: *a false friend.* **4.** tending to deceive or mislead; deceptive. **5.** not genuine; counterfeit; fake. **6.** based on mistaken, erroneous, or inconsistent impressions, ideas, or facts: *false pride.* **7.** used as a substitute or supplement, esp. temporarily: *false supports for a bridge.* **8.** *Biol.* having a superficial resemblance to something that properly bears the name: *the false acacia.* **9.** not properly, accurately, or honestly made, done, or adjusted: *a false balance.* **10.** inaccurate in pitch, as a musical note. —*adv.* **11.** dishonestly; faithlessly; treacherously. **12. play someone false,** to betray someone; be treacherous or faithless. [ME, OE *fals* < L *fals(us)* feigned, false, orig. ptp. of *fallere* to deceive] —**false′ly,** *adv.* —**false′ness,** *n.*
—**Syn. 1.** mistaken, incorrect, wrong, untrue. **2.** untruthful, lying, mendacious. **3.** insincere, hypocritical, disloyal, unfaithful, traitorous. **5.** FALSE, SHAM, COUNTERFEIT agree in referring to something that is not genuine. FALSE is used mainly of imitations of concrete objects; it often implies an intent to deceive: *false hair.* SHAM is rarely used of concrete objects and has nearly always the suggestion of intent to deceive: *sham title; sham tears.* COUNTERFEIT always has the implication of cheating; it is used particularly of spurious imitation of coins, paper money, etc.

false′ alarm′, **1.** a false report of fire to a fire department. **2.** something that excites unfounded alarm or expectation.

false′ arrest′, *Law.* arrest or detention of a person contrary to or unauthorized by law.

false′ dawn′, zodiacal light occurring before sunrise.

false′ face′, a mask that covers the entire face.

false-heart·ed (fôls′här′tid), *adj.* having a false or

treacherous heart; deceitful; perfidious. **—false′-heart′ed·ly,** *adv.* **—false′-heart′ed·ness,** *n.*

false·hood (fôls′ho͝od), *n.* **1.** a false statement; lie. **2.** the lack of conformity to truth or fact: *the falsehood of superstitions.* **3.** something false; an untrue idea, belief, etc. **4.** the act of lying or making false statements. **5.** *Obs.* deception. [ME *falshede*]
—Syn. 1. distortion, fabrication, fiction. FALSEHOOD, FIB, LIE, UNTRUTH refer to something untrue or incorrect. A FALSEHOOD is a statement that distorts or suppresses the truth, in order to deceive: *to tell a falsehood about one's ancestry.* A FIB denotes a trivial falsehood, and is often used to characterize that which is not strictly true: *a polite fib.* A LIE is a vicious falsehood: *to tell a lie about one's neighbor.* An UNTRUTH is an incorrect statement, either intentionally misleading or arising from misunderstanding or ignorance: *I'm afraid you are telling an untruth.* **4.** untruthfulness, inveracity, mendacity. **—Ant. 1.** truth.

false′ hori′zon, a line or plane that simulates the horizon, used in altitude-measuring devices or the like.

false′ impris′onment, *Law.* the unlawful imprisonment or detention of a person.

false′ rib′, *Anat.* any of the lower five ribs on either side of the body that are not directly attached to the sternum.

false′ step′, **1.** a stumble. **2.** an unwise act.

false′ teeth′, a denture, esp. a pair of removable full dentures of both jaws.

false′ to′paz, citrine (def. 2).

fal·set·to (fôl set′ō), *n., pl.* **-tos,** *adj., adv.* **—n. 1.** an unnaturally or artificially high-pitched voice or register, esp. in a man. **2.** a person, esp. a man, who sings with such a voice. **—adj. 3.** of, noting, or having the quality and compass of such a voice. **4.** singing in a falsetto **—adv. 5.** in a falsetto: *to speak falsetto.* [< It; see FALSE, -ET]

false′ vam′pire, any of several large carnivorous bats of the families *Megadermatidae* and *Phyllostomatidae,* of Africa, Asia, and Australia, erroneously reputed to suck the blood of animals and man.

fals·ie (fôl′sē), *n.* *Informal.* either of a pair of shaped pads, made of rubber, fabric, or the like, for wearing inside a brassiere to give the breasts a larger or more shapely appearance.

fal·si·fy (fôl′sə fī′), *v.,* **-fied, -fy·ing.** **—v.t. 1.** to make false or incorrect, esp. so as to deceive. **2.** to alter fraudulently. **3.** to represent falsely; misrepresent. **4.** to show or prove to be false; disprove. **—v.i. 5.** to make false statements. [late ME *falsifie(n)* < MF *falsifi(er)* < LL *falsificāre*] **—fal′si·fi′a·ble,** *adj.* **—fal·si·fi·ca·tion** (fôl′sə fə kā′shən), *n.* **—fal′si·fi′er,** *n.*

fal·si·ty (fôl′si tē), *n., pl.* **-ties. 1.** the quality or condition of being false; incorrectness; untruthfulness; treachery. **2.** something false; falsehood. [ME *falsete* < OF < LL *falsitās*]

Fal·staff (fôl′staf, -stäf), *n.* **Sir John,** the jovial, fat knight of brazen assurance and few scruples in Shakespeare's plays *Henry IV,* Parts 1 and 2, and *The Merry Wives of Windsor.* **—Fal·staff′i·an,** *adj.*

Fal·ster (fäl′stər), *n.* an island in SE Denmark. 46,662 (1960); 198 sq. mi.

falt·boat (fält′bōt′), *n.* a small boat having a collapsible wooden frame covered with waterproof cloth. Also, **foldboat.** [< G *Faltboot* folding boat]

fal·ter (fôl′tər), *v.i.* **1.** to hesitate or waver in action, purpose, etc.; give way. **2.** to speak hesitatingly or brokenly. **3.** to move unsteadily; stumble. **—v.t. 4.** to utter hesitatingly or brokenly: *to falter an apology.* **—n. 5.** the act of faltering; an unsteadiness of gait, voice, action, etc. **6.** a faltering sound. [ME *faltre(n)* < Scand; cf. Icel *faltrast* to be uncertain] **—fal′ter·er,** *n.* **—fal′ter·ing·ly,** *adv.* **—Syn. 1.** vacillate. **2.** stammer, stutter.

fam., **1.** familiar. **2.** family.

F.A.M., Free and Accepted Masons. Also, **F. & A.M.**

Fa·ma·gu·sta (fä mə go͞o′stə), *n.* a seaport on the E coast of Cyprus, on an inlet of the Mediterranean: castle; large cathedral (now a mosque). 38,000 (est. 1964).

fame (fām), *n., v.,* **famed, fam·ing.** **—n. 1.** widespread reputation, esp. of a favorable character; renown; public eminence. **2.** reputation; common estimation or opinion generally held of a person or thing. **—v.t. 3.** to spread the renown of; make famous. [ME < L *fāma* talk, public opinion, repute, akin to *fārī* to speak] **—fame′less,** *adj.* **—Syn. 1.** repute, celebrity. **—Ant. 1.** obscurity.

famed (fāmd), *adj.* very well-known; famous.

fa·mil·ial (fə mil′yəl, -mil′ē əl), *adj.* **1.** of, pertaining to, or characteristic of a family. **2.** appearing in individuals by heredity. [< F]

fa·mil·iar (fə mil′yər), *adj.* **1.** commonly or generally known or seen. **2.** well acquainted; thoroughly conversant: *to be familiar with a subject.* **3.** informal; easy; unceremonious; unconstrained. **4.** closely intimate. **5.** unduly intimate; taking liberties. **6.** domesticated; tame. **7.** *Rare.* of or pertaining to a family or household. **—n. 8.** a familiar friend or associate. **9.** See **familiar spirit. 10.** *Rom. Cath. Ch.* **a.** an officer of the Inquisition who arrested accused or suspected persons. **b.** a person who belongs to the household of the pope or of a bishop, rendering domestic service. [ME < L *familiār(is)* of a household (see FAMILY, -AR[1]); r. ME *famulier* < MF] **—fa·mil′iar·ly,** *adv.* **—fa·mil′iar·ness,** *n.*
—Syn. 1. common, well-known, frequent. **3.** free. **4.** close, friendly. FAMILIAR, CONFIDENTIAL, INTIMATE suggest a long association between persons. FAMILIAR means well acquainted with another person: *a familiar friend.* CONFIDENTIAL suggests a sense of mutual trust which extends to the sharing of confidences and secrets: *a confidential adviser.* INTIMATE suggests close acquaintance or connection, often based on interest, sympathy, or affection: *intimate and affectionate letters.* **5.** free, forward, intrusive, bold, presumptuous. **—Ant. 1.** strange. **2.** unacquainted.

fa·mil·iar·ise (fə mil′yə rīz′), *v.t., v.i.,* **-ised, -is·ing.** *Chiefly Brit.* familiarize. **—fa·mil′iar·i·sa′tion,** *n.* **—fa·mil′iar·is′er,** *n.* **—fa·mil′iar·is′ing·ly,** *adv.*

fa·mil·i·ar·i·ty (fə mil′ē ar′i tē), *n., pl.* **-ties. 1.** thorough knowledge of a thing, subject, etc. **2.** the state of being familiar; friendly relationship; close acquaintance. **3.** an absence of ceremony; informality. **4.** undue intimacy; freedom of behavior justified only by the closest relationship. **5.** Often, **familiarities.** an instance or manifestation of such freedom, as in action or speech. **6.** a sexual liberty or impropriety. [ME *familiarite* < OF < L *familiāritāt-* (s. of *familiāritās*) intimacy] **—Syn. 3.** unconstraint. **4.** liberty, freedom, license. **—Ant. 1.** ignorance. **3.** constraint. **4.** reserve.

fa·mil·iar·ize (fə mil′yə rīz′), *v.t.,* **-ized, -iz·ing. 1.** to make (a person) well acquainted or conversant with something. **2.** to make (something) well known; bring into common knowledge or use. **3.** *Archaic.* to make familiar; establish (a person) in friendly intimacy. Also, *esp. Brit.,* **familiarise. —fa·mil′iar·i·za′tion,** *n.* **—fa·mil′iar·iz′er,** *n.* **—fa·mil′iar·iz′ing·ly,** *adv.*

famil′iar spir′it, a supernatural spirit or demon supposed to attend on or serve a person. Also called **familiar.**

fam·i·ly (fam′ə lē, fam′lē), *n., pl.* **-lies,** *adj.* **—n. 1.** parents and their children, whether dwelling together or not. **2.** the children of one person or one couple collectively. **3.** the spouse and children of one person. **4.** any group of persons closely related by blood, as parents, children, uncles, aunts, and cousins. **5.** all those persons considered as descendants of a common progenitor. **6.** *Chiefly Brit.* approved lineage, esp. noble, titled, famous, or wealthy ancestry: *young men of family.* **7.** a group of persons who form a household under one head, including parents, children, servants, etc. **8.** the staff, or body of assistants, of an official: *the office family.* **9.** a group of related things or people. **10.** *Slang.* a unit of the Mafia or Cosa Nostra operating in one area under a local leader. **11.** *Biol.* the usual major subdivision of an order or suborder in the classification of plants and animals, usually consisting of several genera. **12.** *Linguistics.* the largest category into which languages related by common origin can be classified with certainty. Cf. **stock** (def. 13), **subfamily** (def. 2). **—adj. 13.** of, pertaining to, or characteristic of a family: *a family trait.* **14.** belonging to or used by a family: *a family automobile; a family room.* **15. in a** or **the family way,** expecting a child; pregnant. [ME *familie* < L *familia* a household, family servants. See FAMULUS, -Y[3]]

fam′ily cir′cle, 1. the closely related members of a family. **2.** a section in a theater, opera house, etc., containing inexpensive seats, as the topmost gallery.

fam′ily man′, 1. a man who has a family. **2.** a man inclined to lead a domestic life.

fam′ily name′, 1. the hereditary surname of a family. **2.** a given name frequently used in a family.

fam′ily plan′ning, the idea or program of limiting the size of families by spacing or preventing pregnancies, esp. for economic reasons. Cf. **planned parenthood.**

fam′ily tree′, a genealogical chart showing the ancestry, descent, and relationship of all members of a family. Also called **genealogical tree.**

fam·ine (fam′in), *n.* **1.** extreme and general scarcity of food. **2.** any extreme and general scarcity. **3.** extreme hunger; starvation. [ME < MF < VL **famīna* = L *fam(ēs)* hunger + *-īna* -INE[2]]

fam·ish (fam′ish), *v.t., v.i.* *Archaic.* **1.** to suffer or cause to suffer extreme hunger; starve. **2.** to starve to death. [late ME *famisshe* = *fam(en)* (to) starve (< MF *afamer* < VL **affamāre;* see AF-, FAMINE) + *-isshe* -ISH[2]]

fam·ished (fam′isht), *adj.* very hungry. [late ME] **—Syn.** See **hungry.**

fa·mous (fā′məs), *adj.* **1.** having a widespread reputation; renowned; celebrated. **2.** *Informal.* first-rate; excellent. [ME < L *fāmōs(us)*] **—fa′mous·ly,** *adv.* **—fa′mous·ness,** *n.*
—Syn. 1. famed, notable, illustrious. FAMOUS, CELEBRATED, EMINENT, DISTINGUISHED refer to someone or something widely and favorably known. FAMOUS is the general word: *a famous lighthouse.* CELEBRATED originally referred to something commemorated, but now usually refers to someone or something widely known for conspicuous merit, services, etc.: *a celebrated writer.* EMINENT implies high standing among one's contemporaries, esp. in one's own profession or craft: *an eminent physician.* DISTINGUISHED adds to eminent the idea of honors conferred more or less publicly: *a distinguished scientist.* **—Ant. 1.** unknown, obscure.

fam·u·lus (fam′yə ləs), *n., pl.* **-li** (-lī′). a servant or attendant, esp. of a scholar or a magician. [< L: house slave]

fan[1] (fan), *n., v.,* **fanned, fan·ning.** **—n. 1.** any device for causing a current of air by the movement of a broad surface or a number of such surfaces. **2.** an implement, of feathers, paper, etc., often in the shape of a long triangle or of a semicircle, for waving lightly to create a cooling current of air about a person. **3.** anything resembling such an implement, as the tail of a bird. **4.** any of various devices consisting essentially of a series of radiating vanes or blades attached to and revolving with a central hublike portion to produce a current of air: *ceiling fan; wall fan.* **5.** a series of revolving blades supplying air for winnowing or cleaning grain. **—v.t. 6.** to move or agitate (the air) with or as with a fan. **7.** to cause air to blow upon, as from a fan; cool or refresh with or as with a fan. **8.** to stir to activity with or as with a fan: *to fan a flame; to fan emotions.* **9.** (of a breeze, current of air, etc.) to blow upon, as if driven by a fan. **10.** to spread out like a fan. **11.** *Agric.* to winnow, esp. by an artificial current of air. **—v.i. 12.** to strike, swing, or brush lightly at something. **13.** to spread out like a fan (often fol. by *out*): *The forest fire fanned out in all directions.* [ME, OE *fann* < L *vann(us)* winnowing fan] **—fan′like′,** *adj.* **—fan′ner,** *n.*

fan[2] (fan), *n.* an enthusiastic devotee or follower. [short for FANATIC]

fa·nat·ic (fə nat′ik), *n.* **1.** a person with extreme and uncritical enthusiasm or zeal, as in religion, politics, etc. **—adj. 2.** fanatical. [< L *fānātic(us)* pertaining to a temple, inspired, frantic = *fān(um)* temple + *-āticus;* see -ATE[1], -IC] **—Syn. 1.** enthusiast, zealot.

fa·nat·i·cal (fə nat′i kəl), *adj.* actuated or characterized by extreme, uncritical enthusiasm or zeal, as in religion, politics, etc. —**fa·nat′i·cal·ly,** *adv.* —**fa·nat′i·cal·ness,** *n.* —**Syn.** zealous, frenzied. See **intolerant, radical.**

fa·nat·i·cise (fə nat′i sīz′), *v.t., v.i.,* **-cised, -cis·ing.** *Chiefly Brit.* fanaticize.

fa·nat·i·cism (fə nat′i siz′əm), *n.* fanatical character, spirit, or conduct.

fa·nat·i·cize (fə nat′i sīz′), *v.,* **-cized, -ciz·ing.** —*v.t.* **1.** to make fanatical. —*v.i.* **2.** to act with or show fanaticism. Also, *esp. Brit.,* **fanaticise.**

fan·cied (fan′sēd), *adj.* **1.** unreal; imaginary: *to be upset by fancied grievances.* **2.** desired or favored: *She was his fancied bride.*

fan·ci·er (fan′sē ər), *n.* **1.** a person having a liking for or interest in something; enthusiast. **2.** a person who breeds animals, plants, etc., esp. in order to improve the strain.

fan·ci·ful (fan′si fəl), *adj.* **1.** exhibiting fancy; capricious or whimsical in appearance. **2.** suggested by fancy; imaginary; unreal. **3.** led by fancy rather than reason or experience; whimsical. —**fan′ci·ful·ly,** *adv.* —**fan′ci·ful·ness,** *n.* —**Syn. 2.** illusory. **3.** unpredictable.

fan·ci·less (fan′si lis), *adj.* without fancy or imagination.

fan′ club′, a club enthusiastically devoted to a movie star or other celebrity.

fan·cy (fan′sē), *n., pl.* **-cies,** *adj.,* **-ci·er, -ci·est,** *v.,* **-cied, -cy·ing,** *interj.* —*n.* **1.** imagination or inclination, esp. as exercised in a capricious manner. **2.** the artistic ability of creating unreal or whimsical imagery, decorative detail, etc., as in poetry or drawing. **3.** a mental image or conception. **4.** an idea or opinion with little foundation; illusion. **5.** a caprice; whim; vagary. **6.** a capricious preference; inclination; a liking: *to take a fancy to kumquats.* **7.** critical judgment; taste. **8.** the breeding of animals to develop points of beauty or excellence. **9. the fancy,** *Obs.* people deeply interested in a sport, art, etc. **10.** *Obs.* love. —*adj.* **11.** made, designed, grown, adapted, etc., to please the taste or fancy; of superfine quality or exceptional appeal. **12.** ornamental; decorative; not plain. **13.** depending on imagination or caprice; whimsical; irregular. **14.** bred to develop points of beauty or excellence, as an animal. —*v.t.* **15.** to form a conception of; picture to oneself. **16.** to believe without being absolutely sure or certain. **17.** to take a liking to; like. —*interj.* **18.** (used as an exclamation of mild surprise.) [ME *fan(t)sy,* syncopated var. of *fantasie* FANTASY] —**fan′ci·ness,** *n.*

—**Syn. 2.** FANCY, FANTASY, IMAGINATION refer to qualities in literature or other artistic composition. The creations of FANCY are casual, whimsical, and often amusing: *letting one's fancy play freely on a subject; an impish fancy.* FANTASY now usually suggests an unrestrained or extravagant fancy, often resulting in caprice: *The use of fantasy in art creates interesting results.* IMAGINATION suggests that the memories of actual sights and experiences may so blend in the mind of the writer or artist as to produce something that has never existed before—often a hitherto unperceived vision of reality: *to use imagination in portraying character and action.* **3.** thought, notion, impression, idea. **5.** quirk, humor, crotchet. **11.** elegant, choice. **12.** decorated, ornate. **15.** envision, conceive, imagine.

fan′cy div′ing, diving from a springboard into the water in prescribed ways recognized in formal competition. —**fan′cy div′er.**

fan′cy dress′, a costume for a masquerade, chosen to please the fancy, often a costume of a particular period or of a class or type of person.

fan·cy-free (fan′sē frē′), *adj.* free from any influence, esp. that of love.

fan′cy man′, 1. a woman's lover. **2.** a pimp. **3.** a gigolo.

fan′cy wom′an, 1. an immoral woman, esp. a man's mistress. **2.** a prostitute. Also called **fan′cy la′dy.**

fan·cy·work (fan′sē wûrk′), *n.* ornamental needlework.

fan′ dance′, a provocative solo dance performed by a nude or nearly nude woman using a fan or fans for covering and provocation. —**fan′ danc′er.**

fan·dan·go (fan daŋ′gō), *n., pl.* **-gos. 1.** a lively Spanish or Spanish-American dance in triple time, performed by a man and woman playing castanets. **2.** a piece of music for such a dance or one having its rhythm. **3.** (esp. in the southwest U.S.) a ball or dance. [< Sp < ?]

fane (fān), *n. Archaic.* **1.** a temple. **2.** a church. [ME < L *fān(um)* temple, sanctuary]

Fan·euil (fan′əl, -yəl), *n.* **Peter,** 1700–43, American merchant in Boston.

Fan·fa·ni (fän fä′nē), *n.* **A·min·to·re** (ä′mēn tô′re), born 1908, Italian statesman: premier 1958–63.

fan·fare (fan′fâr), *n.* **1.** a flourish or short air played on trumpets or the like. **2.** an ostentatious display or flourish. **3.** *Informal.* publicity or advertising. [< F, back formation from *fanfarer* to blow a fanfare < *fanfaron* FANFARON]

fan·fa·ron (fan′fə ron′), *n.* **1.** a braggart. **2.** a fanfare. [< F < Sp *fanfarrón* braggart < Ar *farfār* talkative]

fan·fa·ron·ade (fan′fə rə nād′), *n.* bragging; bravado; bluster. [< F *fanfaronnade* < Sp *fanfarronada*]

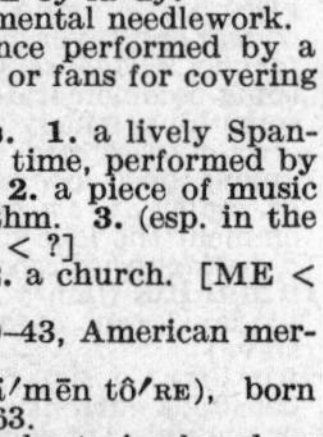

fang (faŋ), *n.* **1.** one of the long, sharp, hollow or grooved teeth of a venomous snake by which poison is injected. **2.** a canine tooth. **3.** a doglike tooth. **4.** the root of a tooth. **5.** a pointed, tapering part of a thing. [ME, OE: something caught; c. G *Fang* capture, booty, Icel *fang* a grasp, hold] —**fanged** (faŋd), *adj.* —**fang′less,** *adj.* —**fang′like′,** *adj.*

F, Fangs (of rattlesnake)

fan·jet (fan′jet′), *n.* **1.** Also called **turbofan.** a jet engine having a large impeller that takes in air only part of which is used for the combustion of fuel, the remainder being mixed with the combustion products to form a low-velocity exhaust jet. **2.** an airplane having one or more of such engines. Also, **fan′ jet′.**

fan·light (fan′līt′), *n.* a transom window, esp. one having the form of a semicircle or of half an ellipse.

fan′ magazine′, a magazine containing information and gossip about celebrities.

fan′ mail′, mail sent to a celebrity by his admirers.

fan·ny (fan′ē), *n., pl.* **-nies.** *Informal.* the buttocks. [? alter. of FANCY vulva (obs. euphemism)]

fan′ palm′, a palm having fan-shaped leaves, as the talipot.

fan·tail (fan′tāl′), *n.* **1.** a tail, end, or part shaped like a fan. **2.** one of a breed of domestic pigeons, having a fan-shaped tail. **3.** an artificially bred variety of goldfish with double anal and caudal fins. **4.** *U.S. Naut.* **a.** the part of a rounded stern extending abaft the aftermost perpendicular; a rounded counter. **b.** the area within this. —**fan′-tailed′,** *adj.*

fan-tan (fan′tan′), *n.* **1.** Also, **fan′ tan′.** Also called **parliament, sevens.** *Cards.* a game in which the cards are played sequentially, the winner being the player who first gets rid of his cards. **2.** a Chinese gambling game in which bets are made on what the remainder will be after a pile of coins or other objects has been counted off in fours. [< Chin *fan t'an* repeated divisions]

fan·ta·sia (fan tā′zhə, -zhē ə, fan′tə zē′ə), *n. Music.* **1.** a composition in fanciful or irregular form. **2.** a potpourri of well-known airs arranged with florid decorations. [< It; see FANTASY]

fan·ta·size (fan′tə sīz′), *v.,* **-sized, -siz·ing.** —*v.i.* **1.** to conceive fanciful or extravagant notions, ideas, suppositions, or the like. —*v.t.* **2.** to create in one's fancy, daydreams, or the like; imagine.

fan·tasm (fan′taz əm), *n.* phantasm.

fan·tas·ma·go·ri·a (fan taz′mə gôr′ē ə, -gōr′-), *n.* phantasmagoria. —**fan·tas′ma·go′ric,** *adj.* —**fan·tas′ma·go′ri·cal·ly,** *adv.*

fan·tast (fan′tast), *n.* a visionary. Also, **phantast.** [< G, var. of *Phantast* < Gk *phantast(ḗs)* boaster; mod. sense by assoc. with FANTASTIC]

fan·tas·tic (fan tas′tik), *adj.* **1.** conceived or appearing as if conceived by an unrestrained imagination; grotesque; eccentric; odd. **2.** fanciful or capricious, as persons or their ideas, actions, etc. **3.** imaginary or groundless: *fantastic fears.* **4.** extravagantly fanciful; irrational. **5.** incredibly great or extreme; exorbitant: *fantastic sums of money.* **6.** *Informal.* extraordinarily good: *a fantastic musical.* Also, **fan·tas′ti·cal.** [ME *fantastik* pertaining to imagination < ML *fantastic(us),* var. of LL *phantasticus* < Gk *phantastikós* able to present or show (to the mind) = *phantáz(ein)* (to) make visible + *-tikos* -TIC] —**fan·tas′ti·cal·ly,** *adv.*

fan·ta·sy (fan′tə sē, -zē), *n., pl.* **-sies. 1.** imagination, esp. when extravagant and unrestrained. **2.** the forming of grotesque mental images. **3.** a mental image, esp. when grotesque. **4.** *Psychol.* an imaginative sequence, esp. one in which desires are fulfilled; daydream. **5.** a hallucination. **6.** a supposition based on no solid foundation. **7.** caprice; whim. **8.** an ingenious or fanciful thought or creation. **9.** *Music.* fantasia. Also, **phantasy.** [ME *fantasie* imaginative faculty, mental image < L *phantasia* < Gk: idea, notion, image, lit., a making visible] —**Syn. 1.** See **fancy.**

Fan·ti (fan′tē, fän′-), *n.* a dialect that is spoken and written in Ghana, belongs to the Kwa group of languages, and is mutually intelligible with Twi.

Fan·tin-La·tour (fäN taN lä to͞or′), *n.* **(Ig·nace) Hen·ri (Jo·seph Thé·o·dore)** (ē nyAs′ äN rē′ zhô zef′ tā ô dôr′), 1836–1904, French painter.

fan·toc·ci·ni (fan′tə chē′nē), *n.pl.* **1.** puppets operated by concealed wires or strings. **2.** dramatic representations in which such puppets are used. [< It: marionettes, pl. of *fantoccino* little doll, dim. of *fantoccio,* aug. of *fante* boy < L *infante-,* s. of *infans* INFANT]

fan·tom (fan′təm), *n., adj.* phantom.

fan′ vault′, a vault composed of concave conoidal surfaces, springing from the corners of the vaulting compartment and touching at the top. See illus. at **vault**[1].

fan·wort (fan′wûrt′), *n.* any aquatic plant of the genus *Cabomba,* having white flowers.

fa·qir (fə kēr′, fā′kər), *n.* fakir. Also, **fa·quir′.**

far (fär), *adv., adj.,* **far·ther** or **fur·ther, far·thest** or **fur·thest.** —*adv.* **1.** at or to a great distance or a remote point; a long way off. **2.** at or to a remote or advanced time. **3.** at or to a definite point of progress, or degree. **4. as far as,** to the degree or extent that: *as far as I can tell.* **5. by far, a.** by a great deal; very much. **b.** plainly; obviously. **6. far and away,** by far; undoubtedly. **7. far and wide,** to great lengths; over great distances. Also, **far and near, near and far. 8. far be it from me,** I do not wish or dare (to interrupt, criticize, etc.). **9. go far, a.** to attain success. **b.** to have a great effect toward; help. **10. how far,** to what distance, extent, or degree. **11. in so far as,** to the extent that. Also, **insofar as, so far as. 12. so far, a.** up to now. **b.** up to a certain point or extent: *We were able to plan only so far.* **13. so far so good,** no difficulty up to the present. —*adj.* **14.** being at a great distance; remote in time or place. **15.** extending to a great distance: *the far frontiers of empire.* **16.** more distant of the two: *the far side.* **17. a far cry from,** greatly different from. **18. few and far between.** See **few** (def. 2). [ME *far, fer,* OE *feorr;* c. OHG *ferr,* Icel *fjar,* Goth *fairra;* akin to G *fern* far, L *porro* far off, long ago, forward, etc.] —**far′ness,** *n.* —**Syn. 14.** distant.

far·ad (far′əd, -ad), *n. Elect.* the unit of capacitance equal to the change in the number of coulombs of charge per volt of change of potential. *Abbr.:* F, f [named after M. FARADAY]

Far·a·day (far′ə dē, -dā′), *n.* **1. Michael,** 1791–1867, English physicist and chemist: discoverer of electromagnetic induction. **2.** a unit of electricity used in electrolysis, equal to 96,500 coulombs.

fa·rad·ic (fə rad′ik), *adj. Elect.* of or pertaining to a discontinuous, asymmetric, alternating current from the secondary winding of an induction coil. [< F *faradique*]

far·a·dise (far′ə dīz′), *v.t.,* **-dised, -dis·ing.** *Chiefly Brit.* faradize. —**far′a·di·sa′tion,** *n.* —**far′a·dis′er,** *n.*

fa·ra·dism (far′ə diz′əm), *n. Med.* the use of faradic current for therapeutic purposes, esp. for treating muscles or nerves. [< F *faradisme*]

far·a·dize (far′ə dīz′), *v.t.,* **-dized, -diz·ing.** *Med.* to stimulate or treat by faradism. Also, *esp. Brit.,* **faradise.** [< F *faradis(er)*] —**far′a·di·za′tion,** *n.* —**far′a·diz′er,** *n.*

far·an·dole (far′ən dōl′; *Fr.* fA räN dôl′), *n., pl.* **-doles** (-dōlz′; *Fr.* -dôl′). a lively dance of Provence in which all the dancers join hands. [< F < Pr *farandoulo* (akin to Sp *farándula* traveling troupe of comedians) < ?]

far·a·way (fär′ə wā′), *adj.* **1.** distant; remote. **2.** abstracted or dreamy: *a faraway look.*

farce (färs), *n., v.,* **farced, farc·ing.** —*n.* **1.** a light, humorous play in which the plot depends upon a skillfully exploited situation rather than upon the development of character. **2.** humor of the type displayed in such works. **3.** a ridiculous sham. **4.** *Cookery.* forcemeat. —*v.t.* **5.** to season (a speech or composition), esp. with witty material. **6.** *Obs.* to stuff; cram. [ME *fars* stuffing < MF *farce* < LL **farsa,* n. use of fem. of *farsus* stuffed]

far·ceur (FAR SŒR′), *n., pl.* **-ceurs** (-SŒR′). *French.* **1.** a writer or player of farces. **2.** a joker or wag.

far·ci (fär sē′; *Fr.* FAR sē′), *adj. Cookery.* stuffed. [< F, ptp. of *farcir* to stuff < L *farcīre*]

far·ci·cal (fär′si kəl), *adj.* **1.** pertaining to or of the nature of farce. **2.** resembling farce; ludicrous; absurd. —**far′ci·cal′i·ty, far′ci·cal·ness,** *n.* —**far′ci·cal·ly,** *adv.* —**Syn. 2.** ridiculous, preposterous, comical.

far·cy (fär′sē), *n., pl.* **-cies.** *Vet. Pathol.* a form of the disease glanders chiefly affecting the superficial lymphatics and the skin of horses. [late ME *farsy,* var. of *farsin* < MF *farcin* < LL *farcīmin(um)* glanders]

far′cy bud′, *Vet. Pathol.* an ulcerated swelling, produced in farcy. Also called **far′cy but′ton.**

fard (färd), *Archaic.* —*n.* **1.** facial cosmetics. —*v.t.* **2.** to apply cosmetics to (the face). [< MF; OF *farde* < Gmc; cf. OS *frataha,* OE *frætwe* adornments]

far·del (fär′dəl), *n. Archaic.* a bundle; burden. [ME < MF, OF, dim. of *farde* bundle < Ar *fardah* load]

fare (fâr), *n., v.,* **fared, far·ing.** —*n.* **1.** the price charged for transporting a passenger. **2.** a paying passenger. **3.** a person who hires a public vehicle and its driver. **4.** food; diet. **5.** something offered to the public, as for entertainment: *theater fare.* **6.** *Archaic.* state of things. —*v.i.* **7.** to eat; dine. **8.** to experience good or bad fortune, treatment, etc.; get on: *He fared well in his profession.* **9.** to go; turn out; happen (used impersonally): *It fared ill with him.* **10.** *Archaic.* to go; travel. [ME *fare(n),* OE *faran;* c. G *fahren,* Icel *fara,* Goth *faran*] —**far′er,** *n.* —**Syn. 4.** See **food.**

Far′ East′, a collective term indicating the countries of East Asia, South Asia, and Southeast Asia. —**Far′ East′ern.**

fare-thee-well (fâr′t͟hē wel′), *n.* **1.** a state of perfection: *The meal was done to a fare-thee-well.* **2.** the maximum effect: *to lie to a fare-thee-well.* Also, **fare-you-well** (fâr′yo͞o-wel′), **fare-ye-well** (fâr′yē wel′).

fare·well (fâr′wel′), *interj.* **1.** may you fare well; good-by; adieu (used by or to someone departing, esp. on an extensive trip). —*n.* **2.** an expression of good wishes at parting. **3.** leave-taking; departure: *a fond farewell.* **4.** a party given to a person who is about to embark on a long journey, retire, etc. —*adj.* **5.** parting; final: *a farewell performance.* [ME *farwel*]

Fare·well (fâr′wel′), *n.* **Cape,** a cape in S Greenland: most southerly point of Greenland.

far-fetched (fär′fecht′), *adj.* improbable; not naturally pertinent; forced; strained: *a far-fetched excuse.* Also, **far′fetched′.**

far-flung (fär′flung′), *adj.* **1.** extending over a great distance. **2.** widely disbursed or distributed.

Far·go (fär′gō), *n.* a city in SE North Dakota. 53,365 (1970).

fa·ri·na (fə rē′nə), *n.* **1.** flour or meal made from cereal grains and cooked as cereal, used in puddings, soups, etc. **2.** *Chiefly Brit.* starch, esp. potato starch. [< L = *fār* spelt + *-īna* -INE[2]]

far·i·na·ceous (far′ə nā′shəs), *adj.* **1.** consisting or made of flour or meal, as food. **2.** containing or yielding starch, as seeds; starchy. **3.** mealy in appearance or nature. [< L *farīnāceus*]

far·i·nose (far′ə nōs′), *adj.* **1.** yielding farina. **2.** resembling farina; farinaceous. **3.** covered with a mealy powder. [< LL *farīnōs(us)* mealy] —**far′i·nose′ly,** *adv.*

far·kle·ber·ry (fär′kəl ber′ē, -bə rē), *n., pl.* **-ries.** a shrub or small tree, *Vaccinium (Batodendron) arboreum,* of the southern U.S., bearing a black, many-seeded berry. [*farkle* (< ?) + BERRY]

farl (färl), *n.* a thin, circular cake of flour or oatmeal. Also, **farle.** [contr. of late ME *fardel* repr. OE *fēortha dǣl* fourth part]

Far·ley (fär′lē), *n.* **James A(loysius),** 1888–1976, U.S. political leader.

farm (färm), *n.* **1.** a tract of land, usually with a house, barn, etc., on which crops and often livestock are raised for livelihood. **2.** land or water devoted to the raising of animals, fish, etc.: *a pig farm; an oyster farm.* **3.** the system, method, or act of collecting revenue by letting out a territory in districts. **4.** a country or district let out for the collection of revenue. **5.** a fixed amount accepted from a person in lieu of taxes or the like that he is authorized to collect. **6.** *Eng. Hist.* **a.** the rent or income from leased property. **b.** the condition of being leased at a fixed rent; a lease; possession under lease. **7.** *Chiefly Baseball.* a team in a minor league affiliated with a team in a major league and used for training players. **8.** *Obs.* a fixed yearly amount payable in the form of rent, taxes, or the like. —*v.t.* **9.** to cultivate (land). **10.** to take the proceeds or profits of (a tax, undertaking, etc.) on paying a fixed sum. **11.** to let or lease (taxes, revenues, an enterprise, etc.) to another for a fixed sum or a percentage (often fol. by *out*): *to farm out the bill collections.* **12.** to let or lease the labor or services of (a person) for hire. **13.** to contract for the maintenance of (a person, institution, etc.): *a county that farms its poor.* **14.** *Chiefly Baseball.* to assign (a player) to a farm (usually fol. by *out*). —*v.i.* **15.** to operate a farm. [ME *ferme* lease, rented land, rent < OF < VL **ferma* < L *firmāre* to make firm, confirm. See FIRM[1]] —**farm′a·ble,** *adj.*

farm·er (fär′mər), *n.* **1.** a person who farms; one who operates a farm or cultivates land. **2.** a person who undertakes some service, as the care of children or the poor, at a fixed price. **3.** a person who undertakes the collection of taxes, duties, etc., paying a fixed sum for the privilege of retaining them. [ME *fermer* < AF, c. OF *fermier* renter]

Far·mer (fär′mər), *n.* **Fannie (Mer·ritt)** (mer′it), 1857–1915, U.S. authority on cooking.

farm′er cheese′, a pressed cheese made from whole milk or partly skimmed milk, similar to dry cottage cheese.

farm·er-gen·er·al (fär′mər jen′ər əl), *n., pl.* **farm·ers-gen·er·al.** (in France, under the old monarchy) a member of a company of capitalists that farmed certain taxes. [trans. of F *fermier-général*] —**far′mer-gen′er·al·ship′,** *n.*

Farm′er-La′bor par′ty (fär′mər lā′bər), **1.** a political party in Minnesota, founded in 1920 and merged with the Democratic party in 1944. **2.** a political party founded in Chicago in 1919 and dissolved in 1924.

Farm′ers Branch′, a city in N Texas, N of Dallas. 27,492 (1970).

farm′ hand′, a person who works on a farm, esp. a hired worker; a hired hand. Also, **farm′hand′.**

farm·house (färm′hous′), *n., pl.* **-hous·es** (-hou′ziz). a house on a farm, esp. the chief dwelling.

farm·ing (fär′ming), *n.* **1.** the business of operating a farm. **2.** the practice of letting or leasing taxes, revenue, etc., for collection.

Farm·ing·ton (fär′ming tən), *n.* a city in NW New Mexico. 21,979 (1970).

farm·land (färm′land′), *n.* land under cultivation or capable of being cultivated.

farm·stead (färm′sted′), *n.* a farm with its buildings.

farm·yard (färm′yärd′), *n.* a yard or enclosure surrounded by or connected with farm buildings.

Far·ne·se (fäʀ ne′ze), *n.* **A·les·san·dro** (ä′les sän′dʀō), **Duke of Parma,** 1545–92, Italian general and statesman.

Farns·worth (färnz′wûrth′), *n.* **Phi·lo Taylor** (fī′lō), 1906–1971, U.S. physicist and inventor: pioneer in television.

far·o (fâr′ō), *n. Cards.* a gambling game in which players bet on cards as they are drawn from the dealer's box. [sp. var. of *Pharaoh,* c. It *Faraone,* F *Pharaon,* name given to game]

Far′oe Is′lands (fâr′ō). See **Faeroe Islands.**

Far·o·ese (fâr′ō ēz′, -ēs′), *n., pl.* **-ese,** *adj.* Faeroese.

far-off (fär′ôf′, -of′), *adj.* distant; remote in space or time.

fa·rouche (FA ro͞osh′), *adj. French.* **1.** fierce. **2.** sullenly unsociable or shy.

Fa·rouk I (fä ro͞ok′). See **Faruk I.**

far-out (fär′out′), *adj. Slang.* **1.** unconventional; offbeat. **2.** radical; extreme. **3.** recondite or esoteric.

Far·quhar (fär′kwər, -kwär, -kər), *n.* **George,** 1678–1707, English playwright, born in Ireland.

far·rag·i·nous (fə raj′ə nəs), *adj.* heterogeneous; mixed. [< L *farrāgin-* (s. of *farrāgō;* see FARRAGO) + -OUS]

far·ra·go (fə rä′gō, -rā′-), *n., pl.* **-goes.** a confused mixture; hodgepodge; medley: *a farrago of doubts, fears, hopes, and wishes.* [< L: lit., mixed fodder, mash = *farr-* (s. of *fār*) spelt, grits + *-āgō* suffix noting kind or nature]

Far·ra·gut (far′ə gət), *n.* **David Glasgow,** 1801–70, U.S. admiral: won the battles of New Orleans and Mobile Bay for the Union in the U.S. Civil War.

Far·rar (fə rär′), *n.* **Geraldine** (*Mrs. Lou Tellegen*), 1882–1967, U.S. operatic soprano.

far-reach·ing (fär′rē′ching), *adj.* extending far in influence, effect, etc.: *the far-reaching effect of his speech.*

Far·rell (far′əl), *n.* **James T(homas),** 1904–79, U.S. novelist.

far·ri·er (far′ē ər), *n. Chiefly Brit.* a blacksmith. [var. of *ferrier* < MF, OF < L *ferrār(ius)* smith (see FERRUM, -ARY); r. late ME *fer(r)our* < AF, c. OF *ferreor* < L **ferrātor*]

far·ri·er·y (far′ē ə rē), *n., pl.* **-er·ies.** the trade or establishment of a farrier.

far·row[1] (far′ō), *n.* **1.** a litter of pigs. —*v.t.* **2.** (of swine) to bring forth (young). —*v.i.* **3.** to produce a litter of pigs. [ME *farwen* to give birth to a litter of pigs < OE *fearh* pig]

far·row[2] (far′ō), *adj.* (of a cow) not pregnant. [late ME *ferow;* akin to Flem *verwe-* (in *verwekoe* barren cow), OE *fearr* ox]

far·see·ing (fär′sē′ing), *adj.* **1.** having foresight; sagacious. **2.** able to see objects distinctly at a great distance.

Far·si (fär′sē), *n.* an Indo-European, Iranian language, the principal language of Iran, written in the Arabic alphabet; Persian.

far·sight·ed (fär′sī′tid, -sī′tid), *adj.* **1.** seeing objects at a distance more clearly than those near at hand; hypermetropic. **2.** seeing to a great distance. **3.** wise, as in foreseeing future developments: *a farsighted statesman.* —**far′-sight′ed·ly,** *adv.* —**far′sight′ed·ness,** *n.*

fart (färt), *Slang (vulgar).* —*n.* **1.** a flatus expelled through the anus. **2.** a contemptible person. —*v.i.* **3.** to expel a flatus through the anus. [ME *ferte(n), farte(n)* (v.), *fert, fart* (n.); c. Gk *pérdein* (v.), *pordḗ* (n.)]

far·ther (fär′t͟hər), *adv., compar. of* **far** *with* **farthest** *as superl.* **1.** at or to a greater distance. **2.** at or to a more advanced point. **3.** at or to a greater degree or extent. **4.** *Nonstandard.* further (def. 3). —*adj., compar. of* **far** *with* **farthest** *as superl.* **5.** more distant or remote. **6.** extending to a greater distance. **7.** *Nonstandard.* further (def. 6). [ME *ferther;* orig. var. of FURTHER]

Far′ther In′dia, Indochina.

far·ther·most (fär′t͟hər mōst′, -məst), *adj.* farthest.

far·thest (fär′t͟hist), *adj., superl. of* **far** *with* **farther** *as compar.* **1.** most distant or remote. **2.** most extended; longest. —*adv., superl. of* **far** *with* **farther** *as compar.* **3.** at or to the greatest distance. **4.** at or to the most advanced point. **5.** at or to the greatest degree or extent. [ME *ferthest;* orig. var. of FURTHEST]

far·thing (fär′t͟hing), *n.* **1.** a former bronze coin of Great Britain, equal to one fourth of a British penny: withdrawn in 1961. **2.** something of very small value. [ME *ferthing,* OE *fēorthing.* See FOURTH, -ING[1]]

far·thin·gale (fär′t͟hing gāl′), *n.* a hoop or framework for expanding a woman's skirt, worn esp. in the 16th century. [earlier *verdynggale* < MF *verdugale,* alter. of OSp *verdugado* = *verdug(o)* tree shoot, rod (lit., something green) + *-ado* -ADE[1]; so called from rod used to extend skirt]

Farthingale (Elizabethan period)

Fa·ruk I (fä ro͞ok′), 1920–65, king of Egypt from 1936 until his abdication in 1952. Also, **Farouk I.**

Far′ West′, the area of the U.S. west of the Great Plains.

F.A.S., *Com.* free alongside ship: without charge to the buyer for delivering goods alongside ship. Also, **f.a.s.**

fas·ces (fas′ēz), *n.* (*usually construed as sing.*) a bundle of rods containing an ax with the blade projecting, borne before Roman magistrates as an emblem of official power. [< L, pl. of *fascis* bundle, pack]

fas·ci·a (fash′ē ə), *n., pl.* **fas·ci·ae** (fash′ē ē′). **1.** a band or fillet, as for binding the hair. **2.** *Surg.* a bandage. **3.** *Archit.* **a.** any broad, flat, horizontal surface, as the outer edge of a cornice, a stringcourse, etc. **b.** any of a series of horizontal bands, usually three in number, each projecting beyond the one below to form the architrave in the Ionic, Corinthian, and Composite orders. **4.** *Anat., Zool.* **a.** a band or sheath of connective tissue investing, supporting, or binding together internal organs or parts of the body. **b.** tissue of this kind. **5.** *Zool., Bot.* a distinctly marked band of color, as on an insect, plant, etc. [< L: band, bandage; akin to FASCES] **—fas′ci·al,** *adj.*

fas·ci·ate (fash′ē āt′), *adj.* **1.** bound with a band, fillet, or bandage. **2.** *Bot.* compressed into a band or bundle, as stems grown together. **3.** *Zool.* **a.** composed of bundles. **b.** bound together in a bundle. **c.** marked with a band or bands. Also, **fas′ci·at′ed.** [FASCI(A) + -ATE[1]] **—fas′ci·ate′ly,** *adv.*

Fasces

fas·ci·a·tion (fash′ē ā′shən), *n.* **1.** the act of binding up or bandaging. **2.** the process of becoming fasciate. **3.** the resulting state. **4.** an abnormality in a plant, in which a stem enlarges into a flat, ribbonlike shape resembling several stems fused together.

fas·ci·cle (fas′i kəl), *n.* **1.** a small bundle, tight cluster, or the like. **2.** a section of a book being published in installments. **3.** *Bot.* a close cluster, as of flowers or leaves. **4.** *Anat.* a small bundle of fibers within a nerve or the central nervous system. [late ME < L *fascicul(us),* dim. of *fascis*]

fas·cic·u·lar (fə sik′yə lər), *adj.* pertaining to or forming a fascicle; fasciculate.

fas·cic·u·late (fə sik′yə lit, -lāt′), *adj.* arranged in a fascicle or fascicles. Also, **fas·cic′u·lat′ed.**

fas·cic·u·la·tion (fə sik′yə lā′shən), *n.* a fascicular condition.

fas·ci·cule (fas′ə kyo͞ol′), *n.* a fascicle, esp. of a book. [var. of FASCICULUS and FASCICLE; see -CULE]

fas·cic·u·lus (fə sik′yə ləs), *n., pl.* **-li** (-lī′). **1.** a fascicle, as of nerve or muscle fibers. **2.** a fascicle of a book. [< L]

fas·ci·nate (fas′ə nāt′), *v.,* **-nat·ed, -nat·ing.** **—***v.t.* **1.** to attract and hold spellbound by a unique power, personal charm, unusual nature, etc. **2.** to arouse the interest or curiosity of; allure. **3.** to transfix as through terror. **4.** *Obs.* to bewitch. **—***v.i.* **5.** to capture the interest or hold the attention. [< L *fascināt(us)* bewitched = *fascin(um)* the evil eye + *-ātus* -ATE[1]] **—fas′ci·nat′ed·ly,** *adv.*

fas·ci·nat·ing (fas′ə nā′ting), *adj.* bewitching; enchanting; charming; captivating. **—fas′ci·nat′ing·ly,** *adv.*

fas·ci·na·tion (fas′ə nā′shən), *n.* **1.** the act of fascinating. **2.** the state or an instance of being fascinated. **3.** a fascinating quality; powerful attraction; charm. **4.** *Cards.* a form of solitaire. [< L *fascinātiōn-* a bewitching]

fas·ci·na·tor (fas′ə nā′tər), *n.* a person or thing that fascinates. **2.** a woman's head scarf of crochet work, lace, or the like. [< L]

fas·cine (fa sēn′, fə-), *n.* *Fort.* a long bundle of sticks bound together, used in building earthworks and batteries and in strengthening ramparts. [< F < L *fascīn(a)* bundle of sticks]

fas·cism (fash′iz əm), *n.* **1.** (*sometimes cap.*) a totalitarian governmental system led by a dictator and emphasizing an aggressive nationalism and often racism. **2.** (*sometimes cap.*) the philosophy, principles, or methods of fascism. **3.** (*cap.*) a fascist movement, esp. the one established by Mussolini in Italy 1922–43. [< It *fascism(o)* = *fasc(io)* bundle, political group (see FASCES) + *-ismo* -ISM]

fas·cist (fash′ist), *n.* **1.** a person who believes in fascism. **2.** (*often cap.*) a member of a fascist movement or party. **3.** a dictatorial person. **—***adj.* **4.** Also, **fa·scis·tic** (fə shis′tik), of or like fascism or fascists. [< It *fascist(a)*] **—fa·scis′ti·cal·ly,** *adv.*

Fa·scis·ta (fə shis′tə; *It.* fä shē′stä), *n., pl.* **Fa·scis·ti** (fə shis′tē; *It.* fä shē′stē). a member of the Fascist movement in Italy. [< It: FASCIST]

fash (fash), *Scot.* **—***n.* **1.** trouble; worry. **—***v.t., v.i.* **2.** to bother; annoy. [< MF *fascher* < LL **fastīdiāre* to disgust = L *fastīdi(um)* disgust + *-āre* inf. suffix]

fash·ion (fash′ən), *n.* **1.** a prevailing custom or style of dress, etiquette, etc.: *the latest fashion in hats.* **2.** conventional usage in dress, manners, etc. **3.** fashionable people collectively. **4.** manner; way; mode. **5.** the make or form of anything. **6.** a kind or sort. **7.** *Obs.* workmanship. **8.** *Obs.* act or process of making. **9. after** or **in a fashion,** in a manner that is careless, inept, or unsatisfactory. **—***v.t.* **10.** to give a particular shape or form to; make: *Primitive man fashioned tools from stones.* **11.** to accommodate or adapt. **12.** *Obs.* to contrive; manage. [ME *facioun* shape, manner < OF *faceon* < L *factiōn-* a doing, company]
—Syn. 1. mode; fad, rage, craze. FASHION, STYLE, VOGUE imply popularity or widespread acceptance of manners, customs, dress, etc. FASHION is that which characterizes or distinguishes the habits, manners, dress, etc., of a period or group: *the fashions of the 18th century.* STYLE is sometimes the equivalent of FASHION, but also denotes conformance to a prevalent standard having distinct characteristics: *a chair in the Queen Anne style.* VOGUE suggests the temporary popularity of certain fashions: *this year's vogue in dancing.*

fash·ion·a·ble (fash′ə nə bəl), *adj.* **1.** observant of or conforming to the fashion. **2.** of, characteristic of, or patronized by the world of fashion. **—***n.* **3.** a fashionable person. **—fash′ion·a·ble·ness,** *n.* **—fash′ion·a·bly,** *adv.*

fash·ion·er (fash′ə nər), *n.* **1.** a person who fashions, forms, or shapes something. **2.** *Obs.* a tailor or modiste.

fash′ion plate′, **1.** a picture showing the prevailing or new fashion in clothes. **2.** a person who consistently wears the latest style in dress.

Fa·sho·da (fə shō′də), *n.* a village in SE Sudan, on the White Nile: conflict of British and French colonial interests 1898 **(Fasho′da In′cident).** Modern name, **Kodok.**

fast[1] (fast, fäst), *adj.* **1.** moving or able to move, operate, function, or take effect quickly; quick; swift; rapid: *a fast horse; a fast pain reliever.* **2.** done in or taking comparatively little time: *a fast race.* **3.** (of time) indicating a time in advance of the correct time, as a clock. **4.** adapted to, allowing, productive of, or imparting rapid movement: *a hull with fast lines.* **5.** characterized by unrestrained conduct or lack of moral conventions. **6.** characterized by extreme energy or activity, esp. in the pursuit of pleasure. **7.** resistant: *acid-fast.* **8.** firmly fixed in place; not easily moved. **9.** held or caught firmly, so as to be unable to escape or be extricated. **10.** firmly tied, as a knot. **11.** closed and made secure. **12.** such as to hold securely: *to lay fast hold on a thing.* **13.** firm in adherence; loyal: *fast friends.* **14.** permanent, lasting, or unfading: *a fast color.* **15.** deep or sound, as sleep. **16.** *Photog.* **a.** (of a lens) able to transmit a relatively large amount of light in a relatively short time. **b.** (of a film) requiring relatively little exposure to attain a given density. **17.** *Horse Racing.* **a.** (of a track condition) completely dry. **b.** (of a track surface) very hard. **18. pull a fast one,** *Slang.* to play an unfair or unscrupulous trick; practice deceit. **—***adv.* **19.** tightly; firmly: *to hold fast.* **20.** soundly: *fast asleep.* **21.** quickly, swiftly, or rapidly. **22.** in quick succession. **23.** in a wild or dissipated way. **24.** ahead of the correct or announced time. **25.** *Archaic.* close; near: *fast by.* **26. play fast and loose.** See **play** (def. 56). [ME; OE *fæst;* c. D *vast,* Icel *fastr* firm, G *fest;* akin to FAST[2]]
—Syn. 1, 2. fleet, speedy. See **quick. 5.** dissolute, immoral; wild. **8.** secure, tight, firm. **9.** inextricable. **13.** faithful, steadfast. **14.** enduring. **19.** securely, tenaciously. **23.** recklessly, wildly. **—Ant. 1, 2.** slow. **8.** loose.

fast[2] (fast, fäst), *v.i.* **1.** to abstain from all food. **2.** to eat only sparingly or of certain kinds of food, esp. as a religious observance. **—***n.* **3.** an abstinence from food, or a limiting of one's food, esp. as a religious observance; fasting. **4.** a day or period of fasting. [ME *faste(n),* OE *fæstan;* c. G *fasten,* Goth *fastan,* Icel *fasta*]

fast[3] (fast, fäst), *n.* a chain or rope for mooring a vessel. [ME *fest* < Scand; cf. Icel *festr* mooring rope; akin to FAST[1]]

fast·back (fast′bak′, fäst′-), *n.* **1.** a form of back for an automobile body consisting of a single, unbroken convex curve from the top to the level of the rear bumper. **2.** a car having such a back.

fast′ day′, a day on which fasting is observed, esp. such a day appointed by some ecclesiastical or civil authority: *Good Friday is a fast day for Catholics.* [ME]

fas·ten (fas′ən, fä′sən), *v.t.* **1.** to attach firmly or securely in place; fix securely to something else. **2.** to make secure, as an article of dress with buttons, clasps, etc., or a door with a lock, bolt, etc. **3.** to enclose securely, as a person or an animal (usually fol. by *in*): *to fasten a monkey in a cage.* **4.** to attach by any connecting agency: *to fasten a nickname on someone.* **5.** to direct (the eyes, thoughts, etc.) intently. **—***v.i.* **6.** to become fast, fixed, or firm. **7.** to close firmly or securely; lock. **8.** to take a firm hold; seize (usually fol. by *on* or *upon*): *to fasten on an idea.* **9.** to focus attention; concentrate (usually fol. by *on* or *upon*): *His gaze fastened on the jewels.* [ME *fasten(en),* OE *fæstnian;* c. Icel *fastna* to betroth; akin to FAST[1]] **—fas′ten·er,** *n.* **—Syn. 1, 2.** connect, link, clinch, bind, tie. **—Ant. 1, 2.** loosen, loose.

fas·ten·ing (fas′ə ning, fä′sə-), *n.* something that fastens, as a lock or clasp. [ME]

fast-food (fast′fo͞od′), *adj.* of or specializing in standardized foods, such as fried chicken, hamburgers, etc., that can be quickly served or taken out: *a fast-food outlet.*

fas·tid·i·ous (fa stid′ē əs), *adj.* **1.** hard to please; excessively critical or demanding: *a fastidious taste in literature.* **2.** requiring or characterized by excessive care or delicacy. [< L *fastīdiōs(us)* squeamish = *fastīdi(um)* disgust (*fast(us)* disdain + *-tidium* for *taedium* TEDIUM) + *-ōsus* -OUS] **—fas·tid′i·ous·ly,** *adv.* **—fas·tid′i·ous·ness,** *n.*

fas·tig·i·ate (fa stij′ē it, -āt′), *adj.* **1.** rising to a pointed top. **2.** *Zool.* joined together in a tapering adhering group. **3.** *Bot.* **a.** erect and parallel, as branches. **b.** having such branches. Also, **fas·tig′i·at′ed.** [< L *fastigi(um)* top, peak + -ATE[1]]

fast·ness (fast′nis, fäst′-), *n.* **1.** a secure or fortified place; stronghold. **2.** the state of being fixed or firm. **3.** the state of being rapid. [ME; OE *fæstnes*]

fast′ track′, **1.** *Informal.* **a.** a racetrack dry and hard enough for optimum speed. **b.** a railroad track for express trains. **2. on a** or **the fast track,** advancing or being promoted more rapidly than usual, esp. in business or other organizational positions: *an executive on the fast track.* **—fast′-track′,** *adj.*

fat (fat), *adj.,* **fat·ter, fat·test,** *n., v.,* **fat·ted, fat·ting.** **—***adj.* **1.** having too much adipose tissue; chubby; corpulent; obese: *a fat woman.* **2.** plump; well-fed: *Buy a fat chicken.* **3.** consisting of or containing fat; greasy; oily: *fat meat.* **4.** abounding in a particular element: *Fat pine is rich in resin.* **5.** (of paint) having more oil than pigment. Cf. **lean**[2] (def. 4). **6.** fertile, as land. **7.** profitable, as an office or position. **8.** affording good opportunities, esp. for gain. **9.** wealthy; prosperous; rich. **10.** thick; big, broad, or extended: *a fat sheaf of bills.* **11.** plentiful. **12.** plentifully supplied; abundant. **13.** dull; stupid. **14. a fat chance,** *Slang.* a very slight chance. **15. a fat lot,** *Slang.* little or not at all. **—***n.* **16.** any of several white or yellowish greasy substances composed of carbon, hydrogen, and oxygen, that form the chief part of adipose tissue of animals and also occur in plants: used in the manufacture of soap and paints and in cooking. **17.** animal tissue containing much of this substance. **18.** the richest or best part of anything. **19.** the condition of being obese; corpulence. **20.** superfluity; an overabundance or excess. **21. chew the fat.** See **chew** (def. 9). **22. the fat is in the fire,** an irrevocable action has been started, whether for good or bad. **23. the fat of the land,** the best or richest of anything. **—***v.t., v.i.* **24.** to make or become fat. [ME; OE *fǣtt,* orig. ptp. of *fǣtan* to cram, load, adorn; c. Goth *fētjan* to adorn; akin to VAT] —**fat′less,** *adj.* —**fat′like′,** *adj.* —**Syn. 1.** portly, pudgy. See **stout. 3.** unctuous, fatty. **6.** rich, fruitful, productive. **7.** lucrative. **11.** abundant. —**Ant. 1.** thin. **3.** lean. **6.** barren.

fa·tal (fāt′ᵊl), *adj.* **1.** causing or capable of causing death: *a fatal accident; a fatal dose.* **2.** causing destruction, misfortune, ruin, or failure. **3.** decisively important; fateful: *The fatal day finally arrived.* **4.** influencing or concerned with fate: *The fatal sisters spun their thread.* **5.** proceeding from or decreed by fate; inevitable. **6.** *Obs.* doomed. **7.** *Obs.* prophetic. [late ME < L *fātāl(is)* of fate] —**fa′tal·ness,** *n.*
—**Syn. 1.** FATAL, DEADLY, LETHAL, MORTAL apply to something that has caused or is capable of causing death. FATAL may refer to either the future or the past; in either case, it emphasizes inevitability and the inescapable—the disastrous, whether death or dire misfortune: *The accident was fatal. Such a mistake would be fatal.* DEADLY looks to the future, and suggests that which is likely to cause death (though not inevitably so): *a deadly poison, disease.* Like DEADLY, LETHAL looks to the future but, like many other words of Latin origin, suggests a more technical usage: *a lethal dose; a gas that is lethal.* MORTAL looks to the past and refers to death that has actually occurred: *He received a mortal wound. The disease proved to be mortal.* **5.** predestined, foreordained. —**Ant. 1.** life-giving.

fa·tal·ism (fāt′ᵊliz′əm), *n.* **1.** *Philos.* the doctrine that all events are predetermined or subject to fate. **2.** the acceptance of or submission to fate. —**fa′tal·ist,** *n.* —**fa′-tal·is′tic,** *adj.* —**fa′tal·is′ti·cal·ly,** *adv.*

fa·tal·i·ty (fā tal′i tē, fə-), *n., pl.* **-ties. 1.** a disaster resulting in death. **2.** a death resulting from a disaster: *a rise in holiday highway fatalities.* **3.** the quality of causing death or disaster; deadliness. **4.** a calamity or misfortune. **5.** predetermined liability to disaster, misfortune, etc. **6.** the quality of being predetermined by or subject to fate. **7.** the fate or destiny of a person or thing. **8.** a fixed, unalterably predetermined course of things. [< LL *fātālitās*]

fa·tal·ly (fāt′ᵊlē), *adv.* **1.** in a manner leading to death or disaster. **2.** by fate; by predetermination. [late ME]

Fa·ta Mor·ga·na (*It.* fä′tä môʀ gä′nä), **1.** a mirage, esp. as seen in the Strait of Messina. **2.** See **Morgan le Fay.** [< It, trans. of MORGAN LE FAY]

fat·back (fat′bak′), *n.* the fat and fat meat from the upper part of a side of pork, usually cured by salting.

fate (fāt), *n., v.,* **fat·ed, fat·ing.** —*n.* **1.** something that unavoidably befalls a person; fortune; lot. **2.** ultimate agency by which the order of things is prescribed. **3.** that which is inevitably predetermined; destiny. **4.** a prophetic declaration of what must be. **5.** death, destruction, or ruin. **6. Fates,** *Class. Myth.* the three goddesses of destiny. —*v.t.* **7.** to predetermine, as by the decree of fate; destine. [ME < L *fāt(um)* utterance, oracle, destiny, orig. neut. of *fātus,* ptp. of *fārī* to speak]
—**Syn. 1.** karma, kismet; chance, luck. FATE, DESTINY refer to the idea of a fortune that is predetermined and inescapable. The two words are frequently interchangeable. FATE stresses the irrationality and impersonal character of events: *It was Napoleon's fate to be exiled.* The word is often lightly used, however: *It was my fate to meet him that very afternoon.* DESTINY emphasizes the idea of an unalterable course of events, and is often used of a propitious fortune: *He became a man of destiny. It was his destiny to save his nation.* **7.** foreordain, preordain.

fat·ed (fā′tid), *adj.* subject to or guided by fate; destined or doomed.

fate·ful (fāt′fəl), *adj.* **1.** involving momentous consequences; decisively important. **2.** fatal, deadly, or disastrous. **3.** controlled by destiny. **4.** prophetic; ominous. —**fate′ful·ly,** *adv.* —**fate′ful·ness,** *n.*

fat′ farm′, *Informal.* a resort that specializes in helping people lose weight.

fath., fathom.

fat·head (fat′hed′), *n.* *Informal.* a stupid person; fool.

fa·ther (fä′t͟hər), *n.* **1.** a male parent. **2.** any male ancestor, esp. the founder of a race, family, or line. **3.** (loosely) a father-in-law, stepfather, or adoptive father. **4.** any man who exercises paternal care over another or others: *a father to the poor.* **5.** a priest. **6.** a title of respect for an old man. **7.** *Chiefly Brit.* the oldest member of a society, profession, etc. Cf. **dean**[1] (def. 3). **8.** one of the leading men in a city, town, etc.: *the city fathers.* **9.** a person who has originated or established something: *the founding fathers.* **10.** a precursor, prototype, or early form: *The horseless carriage was the father of the modern automobile.* **11.** (*cap.*) *Theol.* God. **12. the Father,** *Theol.* the first person of the Trinity. **13.** *Ch. Hist.* any of the chief early Christian writers. **14.** *Eccles.* **a.** (*often cap.*) a title of reverence used to members of the clergy, esp. priests. **b.** a person bearing this title. —*v.t.* **15.** to beget. **16.** to originate. **17.** to act as a father toward. **18.** to acknowledge oneself the father of. **19.** to assume as one's own. **20.** to charge with the begetting of. [ME *fader,* OE *fæder;* c. G *Vater,* L *pater,* Gk *patḗr,* Skt *pitar,* Ir *athair,* Arm *hayr*] —**fa′ther·like′,** *adj.*

Fa′ther Christ′mas, *Brit.* See **Santa Claus.**

fa′ther confes′sor, *Eccles.* confessor (def. 2).

fa′ther fig′ure, a man embodying the qualities of an idealized conception of the male parent. Also called **fa′ther im′age.**

fa·ther·hood (fä′t͟hər ho͝od′), *n.* **1.** the state of being a father. **2.** fathers collectively. **3.** the qualities or spirit of a father. [late ME *faderhode;* r. ME *faderheed*]

fa·ther-in-law (fä′t͟hər in lô′), *n., pl.* **fa·thers-in-law.** the father of one's husband or wife. [ME]

fa·ther·land (fä′t͟hər land′), *n.* **1.** one's native country. **2.** the land of one's ancestors.

fa·ther·less (fä′t͟hər lis), *adj.* **1.** without a living father. **2.** without a known or legally responsible father. [ME *faderles,* OE *fæderlēas*]

fa·ther·ly (fä′t͟hər lē), *adj.* **1.** of, like, or befitting a father. **2.** *Archaic.* in the manner of a father. [ME *faderly,* OE *fæderlic*] —**fa′ther·li·ness,** *n.*
—**Syn. 1.** FATHERLY, PATERNAL refer to the relationship of a male parent to his children. FATHERLY has emotional connotations: it always suggests a kind, protective, tender, or forbearing attitude: *fatherly advice.* PATERNAL may suggest a kindly, more proprietary attitude: *paternal interest;* but it may also be used objectively, as a legal and official term: *his paternal grandmother; paternal estate.*

Fa′ther's Day′, *U.S.* a day, usually the third Sunday in June, set aside in honor of fathers.

Fa′ther Time′, the personification of time as an old man, usually having a beard and carrying a scythe.

fath·om (fat͟h′əm), *n., pl.* **fath·oms,** (*esp. collectively*) **fath·om,** *v.* —*n.* **1.** a unit of length equal to six feet: used chiefly in nautical and mining measurements. *Abbr.:* fath. —*v.t.* **2.** to measure the depth of by means of a sounding line; sound. **3.** to understand thoroughly. [ME *fathme,* OE *fæthm* span of outstretched arms; c. G *Faden* six-foot measure, Icel *fathmr;* akin to PATENT] —**fath′om·a·ble,** *adj.*

fa·thom·e·ter (fa t͟hom′i tər), *n.* See **sonic depth finder.**

fath·om·less (fat͟h′əm lis), *adj.* **1.** impossible to measure the depth of; bottomless. **2.** impossible to understand: *fathomless motives.* —**fath′om·less·ly,** *adv.* —**fath′om·less·ness,** *n.*

fa·tid·ic (fā tid′ik, fə-), *adj.* of or pertaining to prophecy; prophetic. Also, **fa·tid′i·cal.** [< L *fātidic(us)* = *fāti-* (comb. form of *fātum* FATE) + *-dic-* (var. s. of *dīcere* to say) + *-us* adj. suffix] —**fa·tid′i·cal·ly,** *adv.*

fat·i·ga·ble (fat′ə gə bəl), *adj.* easily fatigued or tired. [< L *fatīgābil(is)*] —**fat′i·ga·ble·ness, fat′i·ga·bil′i·ty,** *n.*

fa·tigue (fə tēg′), *n., v.,* **-tigued, -ti·guing.** —*n.* **1.** weariness from bodily or mental exertion. **2.** a cause of weariness; labor; exertion. **3.** *Physiol.* temporary diminution of the irritability or functioning of organs, tissues, or cells after excessive exertion or stimulation. **4.** *Mech.* the weakening or breakdown of material subjected to stress. **5.** Also called **fatigue′ du′ty.** *Mil.* **a.** labor of a generally nonmilitary kind done by soldiers. **b.** the state of being engaged in such labor: *on fatigue.* **6. fatigues,** *Mil.* See **fatigue clothes.** —*v.t.* **7.** to weary with bodily or mental exertion. [< F *fatigue* (n.), *fatiguer* (v.), < L *fatīgāre* to tire] —**fa·tigue′-less,** *adj.* —**Syn. 7.** tire, debilitate, enervate.

fatigue′ clothes′, a military uniform for fatigue duty. Also called **fatigues.**

fa·tigued (fə tēgd′), *adj.* tired; wearied. —**Syn.** See **tired**[1].

Fat·i·ma (fat′i mə, fä′tē mä′), *n.* **1.** A.D. 606?–632, daughter of Muhammad. **2.** the seventh and last wife of Bluebeard.

Fá·ti·ma (fä′ti mə), *n.* a village in central Portugal, N of Lisbon: Roman Catholic shrine.

Fat·i·mid (fat′ə mid), *n.* **1.** any caliph of the North African dynasty, 909–1171, claiming descent from Fatima and Ali. **2.** any descendant of Fatima and Ali. Also, **Fat·i·mite** (fat′ə mīt′).

fat·ling (fat′ling), *n.* a young animal, as a calf or a lamb, fattened for slaughter.

fat·ly (fat′lē), *adv.* **1.** in the manner of a fat person: *to walk fatly.* **2.** clumsily or ponderously. **3.** richly.

fat·ness (fat′nis), *n.* **1.** the state or condition of being fat; corpulence. **2.** richness; fertility: *the fatness of the land.* [ME *fatnesse,* OE *fætnes*]

fats (fats), *n.* **1.** (*cap.*) (*construed as sing.*) *Informal.* (used as an epithet for a fat boy or man): *Fats plays a mean horn.* **2.** (*construed as pl.*) cattle fattened and ready for market.

Fat·shan (fät′shän′), *n.* Nanhai.

fat·so (fat′sō), *n., pl.* **-sos, -soes.** *Often derogatory or facetious.* a fat person. [? alter. of *so fat*]

fat-sol·u·ble (fat′sol′yə bəl), *adj.* *Chem.* soluble in oils or fats.

fat·ten (fat′ᵊn), *v.t.* **1.** to make fat. **2.** to feed for slaughter. **3.** to enrich; increase. —*v.i.* **4.** to grow fat. —**fat′ten·a·ble,** *adj.* —**fat′ten·er,** *n.*

fat·ti ma·schi·i, pa·ro·le fe·mi·ne (fät′tē mä′skē ē′ pä ʀô′le fe′mē ne), *Italian.* deeds (are) manly, words womanish: a motto of Maryland.

fat·tish (fat′ish), *adj.* somewhat fat. [ME] —**fat′tish·ness,** *n.*

fat·ty (fat′ē), *adj.,* **-ti·er, -ti·est. 1.** consisting of, containing, or resembling fat: *fatty tissue.* **2.** *Pathol.* characterized by excessive accumulation of fat. [ME] —**fat′ti·ly,** *adv.* —**fat′ti·ness,** *n.*

fat′ty ac′id, *Chem.* any of a class of aliphatic acids, esp. one such as palmitic, stearic, oleic, or the like, present as glycerides in animal and vegetable fats and oils.

fa·tu·i·ty (fə to͞o′i tē, -tyo͞o′-), *n., pl.* **-ties. 1.** Also, **fa·tu′-i·tous·ness.** foolishness; complacent stupidity. **2.** something foolish, as a fatuous remark. [< L *fatuitās*] —**fa·tu′i·tous,** *adj.*

fat·u·ous (fach′o͞o əs), *adj.* **1.** complacently foolish or inane; silly. **2.** unreal; illusory. [< L *fatuus* silly, lit., gaping, akin to *fatiscere* to gape] —**fat′u·ous·ly,** *adv.* —**fat′u·ous·ness,** *n.* —**Syn. 1.** dense, dim-witted. See **foolish.**

fau·bourg (fō′bo͝or, -bo͝org; *Fr.* fō bo͞oʀ′), *n., pl.* **-bourgs** (-bo͝orz, -bo͝orgz; *Fr.* -bo͞oʀ′). a part of a city outside, or once outside, the walls; suburb. [late ME *faubourgh* < MF *fau(x)bourg,* folk-etym. var. of *forsbourg* < L *foris* outside + MF *bourg* (< Gmc) town, BURG]

fau·cal (fô′kəl), *adj.* **1.** pertaining to the fauces or opening of the throat. **2.** *Phonet.* **a.** pharyngeal. **b.** exploded into the pharynx, as the release of the *t*-sound of *catnip,* the *d*-sound of *madness,* etc. —*n.* **3.** *Phonet.* pharyngeal.

fau·ces (fô′sēz), *n., pl.* **-ces.** *Anat.* the cavity at the back of the mouth, leading into the pharynx. [late ME < L] —**fau·cial** (fô′shəl), *adj.*

fau·cet (fô′sit), *n.* any device for controlling the flow of liquid from a pipe; tap; cock. [late ME < MF *fausset* peg for a vent = *fauss(er)* (to) force in (< LL *falsāre* to falsify) + *-et* -ET]

faugh (pf; *spelling pron.* fô), *interj.* (used to express disgust.)

fauld (fôld), *n.* *Armor.* a piece below the breastplate, composed of lames and corresponding to the culet in back. [var. of FOLD[1]]

Faulk·ner (fôk′nər), *n.* **William,** 1897–1962, U.S. novelist and short-story writer: Nobel prize 1949. Also, **Falkner.**

fault (fôlt), *n.* **1.** a defect or imperfection; flaw; failing. **2.** an error or mistake. **3.** a misdeed or transgression. **4.** responsibility for failure or a wrongful act. **5.** *Geol., Mining.* a break in the continuity of a body of rock or of a vein, with dislocation along the plane of fracture. **6.** *Elect.* a partial or total local failure in the insulation or continuity of a conductor or in the functioning of an electric system. **7.** *Sports.* (in tennis, handball, etc.) **a.** a served ball that does not land in the proper section of an opponent's court. **b.** a failure to serve the ball according to the rules, as from within a certain area. **8.** *Hunting.* a losing of the scent; a check. **9.** *Obs.* lack; want. **10. at fault, a.** Also, **in fault.** open to censure; blameworthy. **b.** in a dilemma; puzzled. **11. find fault,** to seek and make known defects or flaws; complain; criticize. **12. to a fault,** to an almost excessively favorable degree: *to be generous to a fault.* —*v.i.* **13.** *Geol.* to undergo a fault or faults. **14.** to commit a fault; blunder; err. —*v.t.* **15.** *Geol.* to cause a fault in. **16.** to find fault with, blame, or censure. [ME *faute* < MF < VL **fallita,* n. use of fem. of **fallitus,* r. L *falsus,* ptp. of *fallere* to be wrong] —**Syn. 1.** blemish; frailty, shortcoming. FAULT, FOIBLE, WEAKNESS imply shortcomings or imperfections in a person. FAULT is the common word used to refer to any of the ordinary shortcomings of a person; when it is used, condemnation is not necessarily implied: *Of his many faults the greatest is vanity.* FOIBLE, WEAKNESS both tend to excuse the person referred to. Of these FOIBLE is the milder, suggesting a weak point that is slight and often amusing, manifesting itself in eccentricity rather than in wrongdoing: *the foibles of artists.* WEAKNESS suggests that the person in question is unable to control a particular impulse, and gives way to self-indulgence: *a weakness for pretty women.* —**Ant. 1.** virtue.

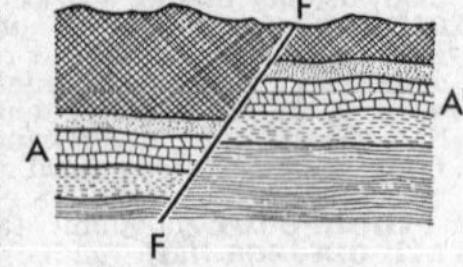

Fault (def.5)
Section of strata displaced by a fault; A and A′, formerly continuous mass of rock; F, Fault line

fault·find·er (fôlt′fīn′dər), *n.* a person who finds fault; one who complains or objects, esp. in a petty way.

fault·find·ing (fôlt′fīn′ding), *n.* **1.** the act of pointing out faults, esp. faults of a petty nature; carping. —*adj.* **2.** given to finding fault; disposed to complain or object; captious. —**Syn. 2.** critical, censorious, caviling.

fault·less (fôlt′lis), *adj.* without fault or defect; perfect. [ME *faultes*] —**fault′less·ly,** *adv.* —**fault′less·ness,** *n.*

fault′ plane′, *Geol.* the plane of fracture in a fault.

fault·y (fôl′tē), *adj.,* **fault·i·er, fault·i·est. 1.** having faults or defects. **2.** *Obs.* culpable; at fault. [ME *fauty*] —**fault′i·ly,** *adv.* —**fault′i·ness,** *n.* —**Syn. 1.** defective, imperfect. —**Ant. 1.** perfect.

faun (fôn), *n.* *Class. Myth.* a rural deity having a human shape, with the ears, horns, tail, and the hind legs of a goat. [ME, back formation from *Faunes* (pl.) < L *Faunī*] —**faun′like′,** *adj.*

fau·na (fô′nə), *n., pl.* **-nas, -nae** (-nē). **1.** the animals of a given region or period. **2.** a treatise on such animals. [< NL, special use of L *Fauna,* name of sister of FAUNUS] —**fau′nal,** *adj.* —**fau′nal·ly,** *adv.*

Fau·nus (fô′nəs), *n.* an ancient Italian woodland deity, later identified with Pan.

Fau·ré (fō rā′), *n.* **Ga·bri·el Ur·bain** (ga brē el′ ōōr-baN′), 1845–1924, French composer.

Faust (foust), *n.* **Jo·hann** (yō′hän), c1480–c1538, German magician, alchemist, and astrologer, represented in medieval legend as selling his soul to the devil in exchange for knowledge and power, and later the subject of many literary and musical works. Also, **Faust·us** (foust′əs).

Faus·ti·an (fou′stē ən), *adj.* **1.** of, pertaining to, or characteristic of Faust: *a Faustian novel.* **2.** characterized by spiritual dissatisfaction; sacrificing spiritual values for power, knowledge, or material gain.

faute de mieux (fōt də myœ′), *French.* for lack of something better.

fau·teuil (fō′til; *Fr.* fō tœ′yə), *n., pl.* **-teuils** (-tilz; *Fr.* -tœ′yə). **1.** *Fr. Furniture.* an upholstered armchair. **2.** *Brit.* stall[1] (def. 11). [< F; OF *faudestuel* < Gmc; see FALDSTOOL]

Fauve (fōv), *n.* **1.** (*sometimes l.c.*) one of a group of French artists of the early 20th century whose works are characterized chiefly by the use of vivid colors in immediate juxtaposition, contours usually in marked contrast to the color of the area defined, and representational images not described by local color. —*adj.* **2.** (*often l.c.*) of, pertaining to, or derived from the Fauves or the style or use of color characteristic of them. [< F: wild beast, n. use of *fauve* wild, lit., tawny < Gmc; see FALLOW[2]] —**Fauv′ism,** *n.* —**Fauv′ist,** *n.*

faux pas (fō pä′), *pl.* **faux pas** (fō päz′; *Fr.* fō pä′). a blunder in manners or conduct. [< F: false step] —**Syn.** error; indiscretion, impropriety.

fa′va bean′ (fä′və). See **broad bean.** [< It *fava* bean < L *faba*]

fa·ve·la (fä ve′lä; *Eng.* fä vel′ə), *n.* *Port.* a shanty town in or near a city, esp. in Brazil; a slum area. [< Pg]

fa·ve·o·late (fə vē′ə lāt′), *adj.* honeycombed; alveolate; pitted. [< NL *faveol(us)* (L *fav(us)* honeycomb + *(alv)eolus* little cavity; see ALVEOLAR) + -ATE[1]]

fa·vo·ni·an (fə vō′nē ən), *adj.* **1.** of or pertaining to the west wind. **2.** mild, favorable, or propitious. [< L *Favōniān(us).* Cf. FOEHN]

Fa·vo·ni·us (fə vō′nē əs), *n.* the ancient Roman personification of the west wind. Cf. **Zephyrus.**

fa·vor (fā′vər), *n.* **1.** a kind act; something done or granted out of good will: *to ask a favor.* **2.** friendly regard or disposition; good will: *to win the favor of the king.* **3.** the state of being approved or held in regard: *to be in favor.* **4.** excessive kindness; unfair partiality. **5.** a gift bestowed as a token of good will, kind regard, love, etc. **6.** a ribbon, badge, etc., worn in evidence of good will or loyalty. **7.** a small gift or decorative or festive item, as a noisemaker or paper hat. **8.** *Rare.* a letter, esp. a commercial one. **9.** Usually, **favors.** sexual intimacy, esp. as permitted by a woman. **10. find favor,** to gain the good will or approval of; meet with approval; be liked. **11. in favor of, a.** on the side of; in support of. **b.** to the advantage of. **c.** (of a check, draft, etc.) payable to. **12. in one's favor,** to one's credit; as an advantage. —*v.t.* **13.** to regard with favor. **14.** to prefer; treat with partiality. **15.** to show favor to; oblige. **16.** to be favorable to; facilitate. **17.** to deal with gently: *to favor a lame leg.* **18.** to aid or support. **19.** *Informal.* to resemble: *to favor one's father.* Also, *esp. Brit.,* **favour.** [ME *favo(u)r* < MF < L *favōr-* (s. of *favor*) good will = *fav(ēre)* (to) befriend + *-ōr* -OR[1]] —**fa′vor·er,** *n.* —**Syn. 5.** present. **13.** approve, countenance, allow. **18.** help, assist.

fa·vor·a·ble (fā′vər ə bəl), *adj.* **1.** providing aid, advantage, or convenience; advantageous: *a favorable position.* **2.** manifesting favor; inclined to aid or approve. **3.** creating or winning favor; pleasing: *to make a favorable impression.* **4.** (of an answer) granting what is desired. **5.** promising well. Also, *esp. Brit.,* **favourable.** [ME < MF < L *favōrābil(is)*] —**fa′vor·a·ble·ness,** *n.* —**fa′vor·a·bly,** *adv.* —**Syn. 1.** helpful, useful. **2.** benign. **5.** propitious, auspicious.

fa·vored (fā′vərd), *adj.* **1.** regarded or treated with preference or partiality: *a favored child.* **2.** enjoying special advantages: *the favored classes.* **3.** of specified appearance (usually used in combination): *ill-favored.* Also, *esp. Brit.,* **favoured.** [ME *favo(u)red*]

fa·vor·ite (fā′vər it), *n.* **1.** a person or thing regarded with special favor or preference. **2.** *Sports.* a competitor considered likely to win. **3.** a person or thing popular with the public. **4.** a person treated with special or undue favor by a king, official, etc.: *favorites at the court.* —*adj.* **5.** regarded with particular favor or preference: *a favorite child.* Also, *esp. Brit.,* **favourite.** [< It *favorit(o),* ptp. of *favorire* to favor]

fa′vorite son′, *U.S. Politics.* a person nominated as a presidential candidate at a national political convention by the delegates from his own state.

fa·vor·it·ism (fā′vər i tiz′əm), *n.* **1.** the unfair favoring of one person or group over others. **2.** the state of being a favorite. Also, *esp. Brit.,* **favouritism.**

fa·vour (fā′vər), *n., v.t.* *Chiefly Brit.* favor. —**fa′vour·er,** *n.*

fa·vour·a·ble (fā′vər ə bəl), *adj.* *Chiefly Brit.* favorable. —**fa′vour·a·ble·ness,** *n.* —**fa′vour·a·bly,** *adv.*

fa·voured (fā′vərd), *adj.* *Chiefly Brit.* favored.

fa·vour·ite (fā′vər it), *n., adj.* *Chiefly Brit.* favorite.

fa·vour·it·ism (fā′vər i tiz′əm), *n.* *Chiefly Brit.* favoritism.

fa·vus (fā′vəs), *n., pl.* **fa·vus·es.** *Pathol.* a skin disease, esp. of the scalp, characterized by dry incrustations due to the fungus *Achorion schoenleinii.* [< NL, special use of L *favus* honeycomb]

Fawkes (fôks), *n.* **Guy,** 1570–1606, English conspirator: leader in the Gunpowder Plot 1605.

Fawn of Virginia deer, *Odocoileus virginianus*

fawn[1] (fôn), *n.* **1.** a young deer, esp. an unweaned one. **2.** a light yellowish-brown color. —*v.i.* **3.** (of deer) to bring forth young. [ME *fawn, foun* < MF *faon, foun, feon* << VL **feton-,* s. of **feto* offspring, var. of L *fētus* FETUS] —**fawn′like′,** *adj.*

fawn[2] (fôn), *v.i.* **1.** to seek notice or favor by servile demeanor. **2.** (esp. of dogs) to show fondness by wagging the tail, licking one's hand, etc. [ME *fawne(n),* OE *fagnian,* var. of *fægnian* to rejoice, make glad < *fægen* happy; see FAIN] —**fawn′er,** *n.* —**fawn′ing·ly,** *adv.* —**fawn′ing·ness,** *n.*

fax (faks), *n.* *Informal.* facsimile (def. 2). [by shortening]

fay[1] (fā), *n.* a fairy. [ME *faie, fei* < MF *feie, fee* << L *Fāta* FATE]

fay[2] (fā), *v.t., v.i.* to fit, esp. closely together, as timbers in shipbuilding. [ME *feie(n)* (to) put together, join, OE *fēgan* (akin to *gefōg* joint); c. G *fügen*]

fay[3] (fā), *n.* *Archaic.* faith. [ME *fai, fei* < AF, var. of *feid* FAITH]

Fa·yal (fä yäl′), *n.* an island in the Azores, in the N Atlantic. 23,923 (1950); 66 sq. mi.

Fay·ette·ville (fā′it vil′), *n.* **1.** a city in S North Carolina. 53,510 (1970). **2.** a city in NW Arkansas. 30,729 (1970).

Fa·yum (fī yōōm′), *n., adj.* Faiyum.

faze (fāz), *v.t.,* **fazed, faz·ing.** *Informal.* to cause to be disconcerted; daunt. [var. of FEEZE]

f.b., **1.** freight bill. **2.** *Sports.* fullback. Also, **fb.**

F.B.A., Fellow of the British Academy.

FBI, *U.S. Govt.* Federal Bureau of Investigation: a federal agency charged with the investigation of certain types of violations for the Attorney General.

f.c., **1.** *Baseball.* fielder's choice. **2.** *Print.* follow copy.

FCA, Farm Credit Administration.

FCC, *U.S. Govt.* Federal Communications Commission: a board charged with regulating broadcasting and interstate communication.

F clef, *Music.* See **bass clef.** See illus. at **clef.**

F.D., **1.** Fidei Defensor. **2.** fire department.

FDA, Food and Drug Administration.

FDIC, See **Federal Deposit Insurance Corporation.**

Fe, *Chem.* iron. [< L *ferrum*]

fe., fecit.

feal (fēl), *adj.* *Archaic.* faithful; loyal. [< MF, OF, var. of *feeil* (with change of suffix) < L *fidēl(is)* faithful. See FIDELITY]

fe·al·ty (fē′əl tē), *n., pl.* **-ties. 1.** *Hist.* fidelity to a lord, usually sworn by a vassal and having the binding force of a contractual obligation. **2.** fidelity; faithfulness. [< MF *fealte* (see FEAL, -TY[2]); r. ME *fe(a)ute* < MF, earlier *feelte* < L *fidēlitāt-* (s. of *fidēlitās*) FIDELITY] —**Syn. 2.** loyalty.

fear (fēr), *n.* **1.** a distressing emotion aroused by an impending pain, danger, evil, etc., or by the illusion of such. **2.** a specific instance of such a feeling. **3.** anxiety; solicitude. **4.** reverential awe, esp. toward God. **5.** something of which one is afraid or that causes fright or apprehension. **6. for fear of,** in order to avoid or prevent. —*v.t.* **7.** to be frightened of. **8.** to have reverential awe of. **9.** *Archaic.* to be afraid (used reflexively). **10.** *Archaic.* to frighten. —*v.i.* **11.**

to be frightened. [ME *fere*, OE *fǣr* sudden attack or danger; c. OS *fār* ambush, D *gevaar*, G *Gefahr* danger, Icel *fār* disaster]
—Syn. 1. apprehension, terror, fright, panic, horror, trepidation. FEAR, DREAD, ALARM all imply a painful emotion experienced when a person is confronted by threatening danger or evil. FEAR and DREAD usually refer more to a condition or state than to an event. FEAR is often applied to an attitude toward something which, when experienced, will cause the sensation of fright: *fear of falling.* DREAD suggests an attitude of anticipating something that will be disagreeable rather than frightening: *She lives in dread of losing her money.* The same is often true of FEAR, when used in a negative statement: *She has no fear of losing her money.* ALARM implies an agitation of the feelings caused by awakening to imminent danger; it names a feeling of fright or panic: *He started up in alarm.* **3.** concern. **7.** apprehend, dread. **—Ant. 1.** courage, bravery. **3.** indifference.

Fear (fēr), *n.* **Cape, 1.** a river in SE North Carolina. 202 mi. long. **2.** a cape at the mouth of this river.

fear·ful (fēr′fəl), *adj.* **1.** causing, or apt to cause, fear. **2.** feeling fear, dread, apprehension, or solicitude. **3.** full of awe or reverence. **4.** showing or caused by fear. **5.** extreme in size, intensity, or badness: *a fearful head cold; fearful poverty.* [ME *ferful*] **—fear′ful·ly,** *adv.* **—fear′ful·ness,** *n.* **—Syn. 2.** afraid, apprehensive, uneasy.

fear·less (fēr′lis), *adj.* without fear; bold or brave. [ME *fereles*] **—fear′less·ly,** *adv.* **—fear′less·ness,** *n.* **—Syn.** intrepid, dauntless, undaunted. See **brave. —Ant.** cowardly, fearful.

fear·nought (fēr′nôt′), *n.* **1.** a stout woolen cloth for overcoats. **2.** a coat made of this. Also, **fear′naught′.**

fear·some (fēr′səm), *adj.* **1.** causing fear or awe. **2.** afraid; timid. **—fear′some·ly,** *adv.* **—fear′some·ness,** *n.*

fea·sance (fē′zəns), *n. Law.* the doing or performing of an act, as of a condition or duty. [< AF *fesa(u)nce*, c. F *faisance* = *fais-* (var. s. of *faire* < L *facere* to do) + *-ance* -ANCE]

fea·si·ble (fē′zə bəl), *adj.* **1.** capable of being done or accomplished: *a feasible plan.* **2.** suitable: *a road feasible for travel.* **3.** probable; likely: *a feasible theory.* [late ME *feseable* (< AF), *faisible* (< MF) = *fes-*, *fais-* (var. s. of *faire* < L *facere* to do) + *-ible* -IBLE] **—fea·si·bil·i·ty** (fē′zə bil′i tē), **fea′si·ble·ness,** *n.* **—fea′si·bly,** *adv.* **—Syn. 1.** workable, practicable. See **possible. 2.** suited, usable.

feast (fēst), *n.* **1.** a periodical celebration or time of celebration, usually of a religious nature, commemorating an event, person, etc.: *a feast in honor of a patron saint.* **2.** a sumptuous meal for many guests. **3.** any rich or abundant meal. **4.** something highly agreeable. **—*v.i.* 5.** to have or partake of a feast. **—*v.t.* 6.** to provide or entertain with a feast. **7.** to gratify or delight. [ME *feste* < OF < L *fēsta*, neut. pl. (taken as fem. sing. n.) of *fēstus* festal, gladsome = *fēs-* (akin to FAIR²) + *-tus* adj. suffix] **—feast′er,** *n.* **—feast′less,** *adj.* **—Syn. 2.** FEAST, BANQUET imply large social events, with an abundance of food. A FEAST is a meal with a plenteous supply of food and drink for a large company. A BANQUET is an elaborate feast for a formal and ceremonious occasion.

feast·ful (fēst′fəl), *adj. Archaic.* festive; joyful. [ME *festful*] **—feast′ful·ly,** *adv.*

feat¹ (fēt), *n.* **1.** a noteworthy or extraordinary act or achievement. **2.** *Obs.* a specialized skill; profession. [ME *fet* (< AF), *fait* (< MF) < L *fact(um)* FACT] **—Syn. 1.** accomplishment.

feat² (fēt), *adj. Brit. Dial.* **1.** apt; skillful; dexterous. **2.** suitable. **3.** neat. [late ME < MF *fait* made (to fit) < L *fact(us).* See FACT]

feath·er (feth′ər), *n.* **1.** one of the horny structures forming the principal covering of birds, consisting typically of a hard, tubular portion attached to the body and tapering into a thinner, stemlike portion bearing a series of slender, barbed processes that interlock to form a flat structure on each side. **2.** condition, as of health, spirits, etc.: *After his vacation he was in fine feather.* **3.** kind; character: *two troublemakers of the same feather.* **4.** something like a feather, as a tuft or fringe of hair. **5.** *Carpentry.* **a.** a spline for joining the grooved edges of two boards. **b.** tongue (def. 15). **6.** a featherlike flaw, esp. in a precious stone. **7.** one of the vanes at the tail of an arrow or dart. **8.** something very light, small, or trivial. **9.** *Rowing.* the act of feathering. **10.** *Archaic.* attire. **11.** *Obs.* plumage. **12.** **a feather in one's cap,** a praiseworthy accomplishment; distinction; honor. **13.** **birds of a feather.** See **bird** (def. 6). **14.** **cut a feather,** *Naut.* (of a vessel) to proceed with speed. **—*v.t.* 15.** to provide with feathers, as an arrow. **16.** to clothe or cover with or as with feathers. **17.** *Rowing.* to turn (an oar) after a stroke so that the blade becomes nearly horizontal, and hold it thus as it is moved back into position for the next stroke. **18.** *Aeron.* **a.** to change the blade angle of (a propeller) so that the chords of the blades are parallel to the line of flight. **b.** to turn off (an engine) while in flight. **—*v.i.* 19.** to grow feathers. **20.** to be or become feathery in appearance. **21.** to move like feathers. **22.** *Rowing.* to feather an oar. **23.** **feather one's nest,** to take advantage of the opportunities to enrich oneself, esp. selfishly or at another's expense. [ME, OE *fether;* c. D *veder*, G *Feder*, Icel *fjöthr;* akin to Gk *pterón*, Skt *pátram* wing, feather] **—feath′er·less,** *adj.* **—feath′er·less·ness,** *n.* **—feath′er·like′,** *adj.*

Feather A, Barb; B, Rachis; C, Web or vane; D, Down; E, Calamus or quill

feath′er bed′, a quilt or sack stuffed with feathers and used as a mattress. [ME *fether bed*]

feath·er·bed·ding (feth′ər bed′ing), *n.* **1.** the practice of requiring an employer to hire unnecessary employees, to assign unnecessary work, or to limit production according to a union rule or a safety statute. **2.** an instance of this.

feath·er·brain (feth′ər brān′), *n.* a foolish or giddy person; scatterbrain. **—feath′er·brained′,** *adj.*

feath′er dust′er, a brush for dusting that is composed of a bundle of feathers attached to a handle.

feath·ered (feth′ərd), *adj.* **1.** clothed, covered, or provided with feathers, as a bird, arrow, etc. **2.** winged; swift.

feath·er·edge (feth′ər ej′), *n.* **1.** an edge that thins out like that of a feather. **2.** the thinner edge of a wedge-shaped board or plank. **—feath′er·edged′,** *adj.*

feath·er·head (feth′ər hed′), *n.* a foolish or giddy person; featherbrain. **—feath′er·head′ed,** *adj.*

feath·er·ing (feth′ər ing), *n.* **1.** a coat or covering of feathers; plumage. **2.** *Music.* a very light and delicate use of the violin bow.

feath′er mer′chant, *Slang.* a person who avoids responsibility and effort; loafer; slacker.

feath′er palm′, any palm having large pinnate or bipinnate leaves, as the date palm or royal palm.

feath′er star′, a free-swimming crinoid.

feath·er·stitch (feth′ər stich′), *n.* **1.** an embroidery stitch in which short branches extend alternately on each side of a central stem. **—*v.t.* 2.** to ornament with featherstitches.

feath·er-veined (feth′ər vānd′), *adj. Bot.* (of a leaf) having a series of veins branching from each side of the midrib toward the margin, pinnately veined.

feath·er·weight (feth′ər wāt′), *n.* **1.** a boxer or other contestant intermediate in weight between a bantamweight and a lightweight, esp. a professional boxer weighing up to 126 pounds. **2.** an insignificant person or thing. **—*adj.* 3.** belonging to the class of featherweights, esp. in boxing. **4.** trifling; slight.

feath·er·y (feth′ə rē), *adj.* **1.** clothed or covered with feathers; feathered. **2.** resembling feathers; light; airy; unsubstantial. **—feath′er·i·ness,** *n.*

feat·ly (fēt′lē), *adv.* **1.** in a feat manner; fitly. **2.** skillfully; nimbly. **3.** neatly; elegantly. **—*adj.* 4.** graceful; elegant. [ME *fetly*] **—feat′li·ness,** *n.*

fea·ture (fē′chər), *n., v.,* **-tured, -tur·ing.** **—*n.* 1.** any part of the face, as the nose, chin, etc. **2.** **features,** the face; countenance. **3.** the form or cast of the face: *delicate of feature.* **4.** a prominent or conspicuous part or characteristic. **5.** something offered as a special attraction. **6.** the main motion picture in a movie program. **7.** a column, cartoon, etc., appearing regularly in a newspaper or magazine. **8.** See **feature story. 9.** *Archaic.* make, form, or shape. **—*v.t.* 10.** to be a feature or distinctive mark of. **11.** to make a feature of; give prominence to. **12.** to delineate the main characteristics of; depict; outline. **13.** *Informal.* to conceive of; imagine. **14.** *Chiefly Dial.* to resemble in features; favor. [ME *feture* < AF, c. MF *faiture* < L *factūra* a making]
—Syn. 4. FEATURE, CHARACTERISTIC, PECULIARITY refer to a distinctive trait of an individual or of a class. FEATURE suggests an outstanding or marked property which attracts attention: *Complete harmony was a feature of the convention.* CHARACTERISTIC means a distinguishing mark or quality (or one of such) always associated in one's mind with a particular person or thing: *Defiance is one of his characteristics.* PECULIARITY means that distinct characteristic which marks off an individual in the class to which he or it belongs: *A blue-black tongue is a peculiarity of the chow chow.*

fea·tured (fē′chərd), *adj.* **1.** made a feature of; given prominence to. **2.** having features or a certain kind of features (usually used in combination): *a well-featured face.* **3.** *Obs.* formed; fashioned. [ME *fetured*]

fea·ture·less (fē′chər lis), *adj.* without distinctive features; uninteresting: *a featureless landscape.*

fea′ture sto′ry, **1.** a newspaper or magazine article or report often having an emotional, personal, or humorous slant. **2.** the most prominent story in a magazine. Also called **feature.**

feaze (fēz, fāz) *n., v.t.,* **feazed, feaz·ing.** feeze.

Feb., February.

febri-, a learned borrowing from Latin meaning "fever," used in the formation of compound words: *febriferous.* [comb. form repr. L *febris* FEVER]

fe·bric·i·ty (fi bris′i tē), *n.* the state of being feverish. [< ML *febricitās* = L **febric(us)* feverish (see FEBRI-, -IC) + *-itās* -ITY]

feb·ri·fa·cient (feb′rə fā′shənt), *adj.* **1.** producing fever. **—*n.* 2.** something that produces fever.

fe·brif·er·ous (fi brif′ər əs), *adj.* producing fever.

fe·brif·ic (fi brif′ik), *adj.* producing or marked by fever.

feb·ri·fuge (feb′rə fyōōj′), *adj.* **1.** serving to dispel or reduce fever, as a medicine. **—*n.* 2.** a febrifuge medicine or agent. [< F < ML *febrifugia* plant good for curing fever] **—fe·brif·u·gal** (fi brif′yə gəl, feb′rə fyōō′gəl), *adj.*

fe·brile (fē′brəl, feb′rəl *or, esp. Brit.,* fē′brīl), *adj.* pertaining to or marked by fever; feverish. [< medical L *febrīl(is)*] **—fe·bril·i·ty** (fi bril′i tē), *n.*

Feb·ru·ar·y (feb′rōō er′ē, feb′yōō er′ē), *n., pl.* **-ar·ies.** the second month of the year, ordinarily containing 28 days but containing 29 days in leap years. [ME; OE *Februarius* < L, short for *Februārius mēnsis* expiatory month, named after *Februa* expiation period, pl. of *februum* purgation; see -ARY]

Feb′ruary Revolu′tion. See **Russian Revolution** (def. 1).

fec., fecit.

fe·cal (fē′kəl), *adj.* of, pertaining to, or being feces.

fe·ces (fē′sēz), *n.pl.* **1.** waste matter discharged from the intestines through the anus; excrement. **2.** dregs; sediment. Also, **faeces.** [late ME < L *faecēs* grounds, dregs, sediment (pl. of *faex*)]

Fech·ner (feKH′nər), *n.* **Gus·tav The·o·dor** (gōōs′täf tā′ô dōr′), 1801–87, German physicist, psychologist, and philosopher.

fe·cit (fā′kit; *Eng.* fē′sit), *v. Latin.* he made (it); she made (it): formerly used on works of art after the name of the artist. *Abbr.:* fe., fec.

feck·less (fek′lis), *adj.* **1.** ineffective; incompetent; feeble: *feckless attempts to repair the plumbing.* **2.** without worth, spirit, or value; indifferent; lazy: *a feckless young man.* [late ME *fek* (var. of *fect*, for EFFECT) + -LESS] **—feck′less·ly,** *adv.* **—feck′less·ness,** *n.*

fec·u·la (fek′yə lə), *n., pl.* **-lae** (-lē′). **1.** fecal matter, esp. of insects. **2.** dregs or foul or muddy matter. [< L *faecula* burnt tartar, the crust of wine. See FECES, -ULE]

fec·u·lent (fek′yə lənt), *adj.* full of dregs or fecal matter; foul; turbid; muddy. [late ME < L *faeculent(us)* full of dregs. See FECES, -ULENT] —**fec′u·lence,** *n.*

fe·cund (fē′kund, -kənd, fek′und, -ənd), *adj.* **1.** producing or capable of producing offspring, or fruit, vegetation, etc., in abundance; prolific; fruitful. **2.** very productive or creative intellectually. [late ME < L *fēcund(us)* = *fē-* (see FETUS) + *-cundus* adj. suffix; r. late ME *fecounde* < AF]

fe·cun·date (fē′kən dāt′, fek′ən-), *v.t.,* **-dat·ed, -dat·ing.** **1.** to make prolific or fruitful. **2.** *Biol.* to impregnate. [< L *fēcundāt(us)* made fruitful, fertilized (ptp. of *fēcundāre*)] —**fe′cun·da′tion,** *n.* —**fe′cun·da′tor,** *n.* —**fe·cun·da·to·ry** (fi kun′də tôr′ē, -tōr′ē), *adj.*

Fe·cun·di·ta·tis (fā ko͝on′di tä′tis, fē-), *n.* **Mare.** See **Mare Fecunditatis.**

fe·cun·di·ty (fi kun′di tē), *n.* **1.** the quality of being fecund; capacity, esp. in female animals, of producing many offspring. **2.** fruitfulness or fertility, as of the earth. **3.** the capacity of abundant creativity. [< L *fēcunditās*]

fed[1] (fed), *v.* **1.** pt. and pp. of **feed.** **2. fed up,** *Informal.* disgusted, bored, or impatient.

fed[2] (fed), *n.* *U.S. Informal.* **1.** a federal official or law-enforcement officer: *to be busted by the feds for income-tax evasion.* **2. the Fed,** the Federal Reserve Board. [FED(ERAL)]

Fed., Federal.

fe·da·yeen (fe dä yēn′), *n.pl.* Palestinian guerrilla commandos, operating esp. against Israel. [Ar, lit., those who sacrifice their lives]

fed·er·a·cy (fed′ər ə sē), *n., pl.* **-cies.** a confederacy. [by aphesis]

fed·er·al (fed′ər əl), *adj.* **1.** of or pertaining to a compact or a league, esp. a league between nations or states. **2.** *Govt.* **a.** pertaining to or of the nature of a union of states under a central government distinct from the individual governments of the separate states. **b.** of, pertaining to, or noting such a central government. **3.** (*cap.*) *U.S. Hist.* **a.** of or pertaining to the Federalists or to the Federalist party. **b.** supporting the principles of the Federalist party. **c.** (in the Civil War) pertaining to or supporting the Union government. —*n.* **4.** an advocate of federation or federalism. **5.** (*cap.*) *U.S. Hist.* (during the Civil War) an adherent of the Union government, esp. a soldier in the Federal army. [earlier *foederal* < L *foeder-* (s. of *foedus*) league + -AL[1]] —**fed′er·al·ly,** *adv.* —**fed′er·al·ness,** *n.*

Fed′eral Bu′reau of Investiga′tion. See **FBI.**

Fed′eral Communica′tions Commis′sion. See FCC.

Fed′eral Depos′it Insur′ance Corpora′tion, *U.S.* a public corporation, established in 1933, which insures, up to a specified amount, all demand deposits of member banks. *Abbr.:* FDIC

Fed′eral Dis′trict, a district in which the central government of a federation is located.

fed·er·al·ise (fed′ər ə līz′), *v.t.,* **-ised, -is·ing.** *Chiefly Brit.* federalize. —**fed′er·al·i·sa′tion,** *n.*

fed·er·al·ism (fed′ər ə liz′əm), *n.* **1.** the federal principle of government. **2.** (*cap.*) *U.S. Hist.* **a.** advocacy of the federal system of government. **b.** the principles of the Federalist party.

fed·er·al·ist (fed′ər ə list), *n.* **1.** an advocate of federalism. **2.** (*cap.*) *U.S. Hist.* a member or supporter of the Federalist party. —*adj.* **3.** Also, **fed′er·al·is′tic.** of federalism or the Federalists.

Fed′eralist par′ty, *U.S. Hist.* **1.** a political group that favored the adoption by the states of the Constitution. **2.** a political party in early U.S. history advocating a strong central government. Also, **Fed′eral par′ty.**

fed·er·al·ize (fed′ər ə līz′), *v.t.,* **-ized, -iz·ing.** **1.** to bring under the control of a federal government. **2.** to bring together in a federal union, as states. Also, *esp. Brit.,* **federalise.** —**fed′er·al·i·za′tion,** *n.*

Fed′eral Repub′lic of Ger′many, official name of West Germany.

Fed′eral Reserve′ Sys′tem, the U.S. federal banking system that is under the control of a central board of governors **(Fed′eral Reserve′ Board′)** with a central bank **(Fed′eral Reserve′ Bank′)** in each of 12 districts. It has wide powers in controlling credit and flow of money.

Fed′eral Trade′ Commis′sion. See **FTC.**

fed·er·ate (*v.* fed′ə rāt′; *adj.* fed′ər it), *v.,* **-at·ed, -at·ing,** *adj.* —*v.t., v.i.* **1.** to unite in a league or federation. **2.** to organize on a federal basis. —*adj.* **3.** federated; allied: *federate nations.* [< L *foederāt(us)* leagued together, allied]

fed·er·a·tion (fed′ə rā′shən), *n.* **1.** the act of federating or uniting in a league. **2.** the formation of a political unity, with a central government, by a number of separate states, each of which retains control of its own internal affairs. **3.** a league or confederacy. **4.** a federated body or government. [< LL *foederātiōn-* (s. of *foederātiō*)]

fed·er·a·tive (fed′ə rā′tiv, fed′ər ə tiv), *adj.* **1.** pertaining to or of the nature of a federation. **2.** inclined to federate. —**fed·er·a·tive·ly** (fed′ə rā′tiv lē, -ər ə tiv-), *adv.*

fe·do·ra (fi dôr′ə, -dōr′ə), *n.* a soft felt hat with a curled brim and a crown creased lengthwise. [said to be named after *Fédora* play by Victorien Sardou (1831–1908)]

fee (fē), *n., v.,* **feed, fee·ing.** —*n.* **1.** a charge or payment for services: *a doctor's fee.* **2.** a sum paid or charged for a privilege: *an admission fee.* **3.** a gratuity; tip. **4.** a charge allowed by law for the service of a public officer. **5.** *Law.* **a.** an estate of inheritance in land, either absolute and without limitation to any particular class of heirs **(fee simple)** or limited to a particular class of heirs **(fee tail).** **b.** an inheritable estate in land held of a feudal lord on condition of the performing of certain services. **c.** a territory so held. —*v.t.* **6.** to give a fee to. **7.** *Chiefly Scot.* to hire; employ. [ME < AF, c. OF *fie,* var. of *fief* FIEF] —**fee′-less,** *adj.* —**Syn. 1.** stipend, emolument; honorarium.

fee·ble (fē′bəl), *adj.,* **-bler, -blest.** **1.** physically weak, as from age, sickness, etc. **2.** weak intellectually or morally. **3.** lacking in volume, loudness, brightness, distinctness, etc. **4.** lacking in force, strength, or effectiveness: *feeble arguments.* [ME *feble* < OF, var. of *fleible* (by dissimilation) < L *flēbil(is)* lamentable = *flē(re)* (to) weep + *-bilis* -BLE] —**fee′ble·ness,** *n.* —**fee′bly,** *adv.* —**Syn. 1.** infirm, frail, debilitated. See **weak. 3.** faint, dim. **4.** ineffective. —**Ant. 1–4.** strong.

fee·ble-mind·ed (fē′bəl mīn′did), *adj.* **1.** lacking the normal mental powers: *congenitally feeble-minded children.* **2.** stupid; dull-witted: *feeble-minded remarks.* —**fee′ble-mind′ed·ly,** *adv.* —**fee′ble-mind′ed·ness,** *n.*

feed (fēd), *v.,* **fed, feed·ing,** *n.* —*v.t.* **1.** to give food to; supply with nourishment. **2.** to yield or serve as food for. **3.** to provide as food. **4.** to furnish for consumption. **5.** to satisfy; minister to; gratify. **6.** to supply for maintenance or operation. **7.** to provide with the necessary materials for development, maintenance, or operation. **8.** to use (land) as pasture. **9.** *Theat. Informal.* **a.** to provide lines or cues to (an actor, esp. a comedian). **b.** *Chiefly Brit.* to prompt. —*v.i.* **10.** to take food; eat. **11.** to be nourished or gratified; subsist. **12. chain feed,** to pass (work) successively into a machine in such a manner that each new piece is held in place by or connected to the one before. —*n.* **13.** food, esp. for farm animals. **14.** an allowance, portion, or supply of such food. **15.** *Informal.* a meal, esp. a lavish one. **16.** the act of feeding. **17.** the act or process of feeding a furnace, machine, etc. **18.** the material, or the amount of it, so fed or supplied. **19.** a feeding mechanism. **20.** *Elect.* feeder (def. 8). **21. off one's feed,** *Slang.* **a.** reluctant to eat; without appetite. **b.** dejected; sad. **c.** unwell; ill. [ME *fede(n),* OE *fēdan;* c. Goth *fodjan,* OS *fōdian.* See FOOD] —**feed′a·ble,** *adj.*

—**Syn. 1, 2, 5.** nourish, sustain. **13.** FEED, FODDER, FORAGE, PROVENDER mean food for animals. FEED is the general word: *chicken feed.* FODDER is esp. applied to dry or green feed, as opposed to pasturage, fed to horses, cattle, etc.: *fodder for winter feeding; Cornstalks are good fodder.* FORAGE is food that an animal obtains (usually grass, leaves, etc.) by searching about for it: *Lost cattle can usually live on forage.* PROVENDER denotes dry feed, such as hay, oats, or corn: *a supply of provender in the haymow.* —**Ant. 1, 2, 5.** starve.

feed·back (fēd′bak′), *n.* **1.** *Electronics.* the returning of some of the energy of the plate circuit of a vacuum tube to the grid circuits, either to oppose the input **(inverse feedback)** or to aid the input **(regenerative feedback).** **2.** automatic furnishing of data concerning the output of a machine to an automatic control device so that errors may be corrected. **3.** the whistling noise that occurs when an output signal of an audio system is picked up at the input. **4.** the reaction of some results of a process serving to alter or reinforce the character of that process.

feed′ bag′, **1.** Also called **nose bag.** a bag for feeding horses, fastened to the head with straps. **2. put on the feed bag,** *Slang.* to have a meal; eat. Also, **feed′bag′.**

feed·box (fēd′boks′), *n.* a box for animal feed.

feed·er (fē′dər), *n.* **1.** a person or thing that supplies or takes food. **2.** a bin or other device from which birds or animals may eat. **3.** a livestock animal that is fed an enriched diet to fatten it for market. **4.** a person or device that feeds a machine, printing press, etc. **5.** a tributary stream. **6.** a branch railroad. **7.** See **feeder line.** **8.** Also, **feed.** *Elect.* a conductor, or group of conductors, connecting primary equipment in an electric power system. **9.** *Brit.* a baby's bib. [ME]

feed′er line′, a branch of a main transportation line, esp. an airline.

feed·lot (fēd′lot′), *n.* a large plot of land where livestock, esp. beef cattle, are fed and fattened prior to slaughter.

feed·stuff (fēd′stuf′), *n.* a substance used for feed. Also, **feed·ing·stuff** (fē′ding stuf′).

feel (fēl), *v.,* **felt, feel·ing,** *n.* —*v.t.* **1.** to perceive or examine by touch. **2.** to have a sensation of (something), other than by sight, hearing, taste, or smell: *to feel a toothache.* **3.** to find or pursue (one's way) by touching, groping, or cautious moves. **4.** to be or become conscious of. **5.** to be emotionally affected by. **6.** to experience the effects of. **7.** to have a particular sensation or impression of (often used reflexively and usually fol. by an adjunct or complement): *to feel oneself slighted.* **8.** to have a general or thorough conviction of. —*v.i.* **9.** to have perception by touch or by any nerves of sensation other than those of sight, hearing, taste, and smell. **10.** to make examination by touch; grope. **11.** to perceive a state of mind or a condition of body: *to feel happy; to feel well.* **12.** to have sympathy or compassion (usually fol. by *with* or *for*): *to feel for someone in distress.* **13.** to have a sensation of being: *to feel warm.* **14.** to make itself perceived or apparent; seem: *How does it feel to be rich?* **15. feel like,** *Informal.* to have a desire for; be favorably disposed to. **16. feel like oneself,** to be in one's usual frame of mind or state of health. Also, **feel oneself.** **17. feel out,** *Informal.* to attempt to ascertain by indirect or subtle means. **18. feel up,** *Slang* (*usually vulgar*). to caress or fondle sexually. **19. feel up to,** *Informal.* to feel or be able to; be capable of. —*n.* **20.** a quality of an object that is perceived by feeling or touching. **21.** a quality that is manifested as a vague mental impression or feeling: *a feel of winter.* **22.** the sense of touch. **23.** native ability or acquired sensitivity: *to have a feel for what is right.* **24.** *Informal.* the act or an instance of touching with the hand or fingers. [ME *fele(n),* OE *fēlan;* c. OS *fōlian,* G *fühlen;* akin to Icel *falma* to grope]

feel·er (fē′lər), *n.* **1.** a person or thing that feels. **2.** a proposal, remark, hint, etc., designed to bring out the opinions or purposes of others: *to put out feelers.* **3.** *Zool.* an organ of touch, as an antenna or a tentacle.

feel·ing (fē′ling), *n.* **1.** the function or the power of perceiving by touch; physical sensation not connected with sight, hearing, taste, or smell. **2.** a particular sensation of this kind. **3.** the general state of consciousness considered independently of particular sensations, thoughts, etc. **4.** a consciousness or vague awareness: *a feeling of inferiority.* **5.** an emotion or emotional perception or attitude: *a feeling of pleasure.* **6.** capacity for emotion, esp. compassion. **7.** a sentiment; opinion. **8. feelings,** sensibilities; susceptibilities. **9.** fine emotional endowment. **10.** (in music, art, etc.) **a.** emotion or sympathetic perception revealed by an artist in his work: *a poem without feeling.* **b.** the general impression conveyed by a work: *a landscape painting with a feeling of spaciousness.* **c.** sympathetic appreciation, as of music: *to play with feeling.* —*adj.* **11.** sensitive; sentient. **12.**

readily affected by emotion; sympathetic: *a feeling heart.* **13.** indicating or characterized by emotion: *a feeling reply to the charge.* [ME] —**feel′ing·ly,** *adv.* —**feel′ing·ness,** *n.* —**Syn. 5.** FEELING, EMOTION, PASSION, SENTIMENT refer to pleasurable or painful sensations experienced when a person is stirred to sympathy, anger, fear, love, grief, etc. FEELING is a general term for a subjective point of view as well as for specific sensations: *to be guided by feeling rather than by facts; a feeling of sadness.* EMOTION is applied to an intensified feeling: *agitated by emotion.* PASSION is strong or violent emotion, often so overpowering that it masters the mind or judgment: *stirred to a passion of anger.* SENTIMENT is a mixture of thought and feeling, esp. refined or tender feeling: *Recollections are often colored by sentiment.* **6.** sympathy, empathy, tenderness. **11.** emotional, tender. **13.** impassioned, passionate. —**Ant. 5, 6.** apathy. **12.** cold.

fee′ sim′ple. See under **fee** (def. 5a). [< AF]

feet (fēt), *n.* **1.** a pl. of **foot. 2. on one's feet, a.** in a standing position. **b.** in a financially independent or secure position. **c.** in a restored or recovered state; able to continue: *The medicine helped her get back on her feet.* **3. sweep one off one's feet,** to impress or overwhelm by ability, charm, etc. —**feet′less,** *adj.*

fee′ tail′. See under **fee** (def. 5a). [< AF]

feeze (fēz, fāz), *n.* **1.** *Dial.* a state of vexation or worry. **2.** *Chiefly Dial.* a violent rush or impact. Also, **feaze.** [ME *fese(n)*; akin to OE *fȳsan* to drive away, put to flight]

feign (fān), *v.t.* **1.** to represent fictitiously; put on an appearance of: *to feign sickness.* **2.** to invent fictitiously or deceptively, as a story or an excuse. **3.** to imitate deceptively: *to feign another's voice.* —*v.i.* **4.** to make believe; pretend: *She feigns to be ill.* [ME *fei(g)ne(n)* < OF *feign-*, present s. of *feindre* < L *fingere* to shape, invent, feign] —**feign′er,** *n.* —**feign′ing·ly,** *adv.* —**Syn. 1.** simulate, affect. **2.** concoct, devise, fabricate. **4.** See **pretend.**

feigned (fānd), *adj.* **1.** pretended; counterfeit: *feigned enthusiasm.* **2.** assumed: *a feigned name.* **3.** disguised: *a feigned voice.* **4.** fictitiously invented. [ME] —**feign·ed·ly** (fā′nid lē), *adv.* —**feign′ed·ness,** *n.*

Fein·ing·er (fī′niŋ ər), *n.* **Ly·o·nel (Charles Adrian)** (lī′ə nəl), 1871–1956, U.S. painter.

feint (fānt), *n.* **1.** an attack aimed at one place or point merely as a distraction from the real place or point of attack: *the feints of a skilled fencer.* —*v.i.* **2.** to make a feint. [< F *feinte*, n. use of fem. of *feint*, ptp. of *feindre* to FEIGN]

Fei·sal I (fī′səl). See **Faisal I.** Also, **Feisul I.**

Feisal II. See **Faisal II.** Also, **Feisul II.**

feist (fīst), *n.* *U.S. Dial.* a small mongrel dog. [short for *feisting cur;* ME, OE *fīsting* breaking wind; akin to MD *vijsten*, Icel *fīsa* to break wind]

feist·y (fī′stē), *adj.* quick-tempered or quarrelsome.

feld·spar (feld′spär′, fel′-), *n.* any of a group of minerals, principally aluminosilicates of potassium, sodium, and calcium: one of the most important constituents of igneous rock. Also, *esp. Brit.,* **felspar.** [*feld-* (< G: field) + SPAR[3]; r. *feldspath* < G (*Feld* field + *Spath* spar)] —**feld·spath·ic** (feld spath′ik, fel-), **feld′spath·ose′,** *adj.*

feld·spath·oid (feld′spa thoid′, fel′-), *Mineral.* —*adj.* **1.** Also, **feld′spath·oi′dal.** of or pertaining to a group of minerals similar in chemical composition to certain feldspars except for a lower silica content. —*n.* **2.** a mineral of this group. [< G *Feldspath* (see FELDSPAR) + -OID]

fe·li·cif·ic (fē′li sif′ik), *adj.* causing or tending to cause happiness. [< L *fēlīci-* (s. of *fēlix*) happy + -FIC]

fe·lic·i·tate (fi lis′i tāt′), *v.,* **-tat·ed, -tat·ing,** *adj.* —*v.t.* **1.** to compliment upon a happy event; congratulate. **2.** *Archaic.* to make happy. —*adj.* **3.** *Obs.* made happy. [< LL *fēlīcitāt(us)* made happy (ptp. of *fēlīcitāre*)] —**fe·lic′i·ta′tor,** *n.*

fe·lic·i·ta·tion (fi lis′i tā′shən), *n.* an expression of good wishes; congratulation.

fe·lic·i·tous (fi lis′i təs), *adj.* **1.** well-suited for the occasion, apt; appropriate. **2.** having a special ability for suitable manner or expression, as a person. —**fe·lic′i·tous·ly,** *adv.* —**fe·lic′i·tous·ness,** *n.* —**Syn. 1.** fit, befitting.

fe·lic·i·ty (fi lis′i tē), *n., pl.* **-ties. 1.** the state of being happy, esp. in a high degree: *marital felicity.* **2.** an instance of this. **3.** a source of happiness. **4.** a skillful faculty or capacity: *felicity of expression.* **5.** an instance or display of this: *the many felicities of the poem.* **6.** *Archaic.* good fortune. [ME *felicite* < L *fēlīcitās* = *fēlīci-* (s. of *fēlix*) happy + *-tās* -TY[2]] —**Syn. 1.** See **happiness.**

fe·lid (fē′lid), *n.* a feline [< NL *Fēlid(ae)* name of the family = L *fēl-* (s. of *fēlēs*) cat + *-idae* -ID[2]]

fe·line (fē′līn), *adj.* **1.** of or pertaining to the cat family, *Felidae,* which includes, besides the domestic cat, the lions, tigers, leopards, lynxes, jaguars, etc. **2.** catlike. **3.** sly, stealthy, or treacherous. —*n.* **4.** an animal of the cat family. [< L *fēlīn(us)* = *fēl(ēs)* cat + *-īnus* -INE[1]] —**fe′line·ly,** *adv.* —**fe′line·ness, fe·lin·i·ty** (fi lin′i tē), *n.*

fe′line distem′per, *Vet. Pathol.* distemper[1] (def. 1c).

Fe·lix I (fē′liks), **Saint,** died A.D. 274, pope 269–274.

Felix III, Saint, died A.D. 492, pope 483–492.

Felix IV, Saint, died A.D. 530, pope 526–530.

fell[1] (fel), *v.,* pt. of **fall.**

fell[2] (fel), *v.t.* **1.** to cause to fall; knock, strike, shoot, or cut down: *to fell a moose; to fell a tree.* **2.** *Sewing.* to finish (a seam) by sewing the edge down flat. —*n.* **3.** *Lumbering.* the amount of timber cut down in one season. **4.** *Sewing.* a seam finished by felling. [ME *felle(n)*, OE *fellan*, causative of *feallan* to FALL; c. Goth *falljan* to cause to fall] —**fell′a·ble,** *adj.*

fell[3] (fel), *adj.* **1.** fierce; cruel; dreadful. **2.** destructive; deadly: *fell poison; fell disease.* [ME *fel* < OF, nom. of *felon* wicked. See FELON[1]] —**fell′ness,** *n.*

fell[4] (fel), *n.* the skin or hide of an animal; pelt. [ME, OE; c. D *vel*, G *Fell*, Icel *-fjall* (in *berfjall* bearskin), Goth *-fill* (in *thrutsfill* scab-skin, leprosy); akin to L *pellis* skin, hide]

fell[5] (fel), *n.* *Scot. and North Eng.* an upland pasture, moor, or thicket; a highland plateau. [ME < Scand; cf. Icel *fjall* mountain, akin to G *Fels(en)* rock, cliff]

fel·la (fel′ə), *n.* *Dial.* fellow.

fel·lah (fel′ə), *n., pl.* **fel·lahs,** *Arab.* **fel·la·hin, fel·la·heen** (fel′ə hēn′). a native peasant or laborer in Egypt, Syria, and other Arabic-speaking countries. [< Ar: peasant]

fel·la·ti·o (fə lā′shē ō′, fe-), *n.* oral stimulation of the penis, esp. to orgasm. Also, **fel·la·tion** (fə lā′shən, fe-). [< NL *fellatiōn-* (s. of *fellatiō*) = L *fellāt(us)*, *felāt(us)* (ptp. of *fellāre, felāre* to suck) + *-iōn-* -ION]

fell·er[1] (fel′ər), *n.* *Dial.* fellow. [FELLOW + hiatus-filling *r;* orig. found only before a word beginning with a vowel]

fell·er[2] (fel′ər), *n.* **1.** a person or thing that fells. **2.** *Sewing.* a person or thing that fells a seam. [ME *fellere.* See FELL[2], -ER[1]]

fell·mon·ger (fel′muŋ′gər, -moŋ′-), *n.* a dealer in skins or hides of animals, esp. sheepskins. —**fell′mon′ger·ing, fell′mon′ger·y,** *n.*

fel·loe (fel′ō), *n.* the circular rim or a part of the rim of a wheel, into which the outer ends of the spokes are inserted. Also, **felly.** [ME *felwe*, OE *felg(e)*; c. G *Felge*]

fel·low (fel′ō), *n.* **1.** a man or boy: *a fine old fellow; a nice little fellow.* **2.** *Informal.* beau; suitor. **3.** *Informal.* person; one: *They don't treat a fellow very well here.* **4.** a companion; comrade; associate. **5.** a person belonging to the same class; equal; peer: *The doctor conferred with his fellows.* **6.** one of a pair; mate; match: *a shoe without its fellow.* **7.** *Educ.* **a.** a graduate student of a university or college to whom an allowance is granted for special study. **b.** *Brit.* an incorporated member of a college, entitled to certain privileges. **c.** a member of the corporation or board of trustees of certain universities or colleges. **8.** a member of any of certain learned societies: *a fellow of the British Academy.* **9.** *Archaic.* a person of small worth or no esteem. **10.** *Obs.* a partner. —*v.t.* **11.** to make or represent as equal with another. **12.** *Archaic.* to produce a fellow to; match. —*adj.* **13.** belonging to the same class or group; united by the same occupation, interests, etc.; being in the same conditon: *fellow students.* [ME *felowe, felawe*, late OE *fēolaga* < Scand; cf. Icel *fēlagi* partner, lit., business associate = *fē* money, property (c. OE *feoh*, G *Vieh*) + *-lagi* bedfellow, comrade; akin to LAIR[1], LIE[2]]

fel·low-man (fel′ō man′), *n., pl.* **-men.** a kindred member of the human race. Also, **fel′low·man′.**

fel′low-serv′ant rule′ (fel′ō sûr′vənt), the common-law doctrine that an employer is not liable to an employee for injuries resulting from the negligence of a fellow employee.

fel·low·ship (fel′ō ship′), *n., v.,* **-shiped, -ship·ing** or (*esp. Brit.*) **-shipped, -ship·ping.** —*n.* **1.** the condition or relation of being a fellow: *the fellowship of mankind.* **2.** friendly relationship; companionship. **3.** community of interest, feeling, etc. **4.** communion, as between members of the same church. **5.** friendliness. **6.** an association of persons having similar tastes, interests, etc. **7.** a company, guild, or corporation. **8.** *Educ.* **a.** the body of fellows in a college or university. **b.** the position or stipend of a fellow of a college or university. **c.** a foundation for the maintenance of fellows in a college or university. —*v.t.* **9.** *Chiefly U.S.* to admit to fellowship, esp. religious fellowship. —*v.i.* **10.** *Chiefly U.S.* to join in fellowship, esp. religious fellowship. [ME *felaweshipe*]

fel′low trav′eler, a nonmember who supports or sympathizes with a political party, esp. the Communist party.

fel·ly (fel′ē), *n., pl.* **-lies.** felloe. [ME *felien* (pl.), var. of *felwe* FELLOE]

fe·lo de se (fē′lō di sē′, fel′ō), *pl.* **fe·lo·nes de se** (fē′lō-nēz′ di sē′, fel′ō), or **fe·los de se** (fē′lōz di sē′, fel′ōz). felo-de-se.

fe·lo-de-se (fē′lō di sē′, fel′ō-), *n., pl.* **fe·lo·nes-de-se** (fē′lō nēz′di sē′, fel′ō-), or **fe·los-de-se** (fē′lōz di sē′, fel′ōz-). **1.** a person who commits suicide or commits an unlawful malicious act resulting in his own death. **2.** the act of suicide. [< AL = *felo* a felon + *dē* in respect to, of + *sē* oneself]

fel·on[1] (fel′ən), *n.* **1.** *Law.* a person who has committed a felony. **2.** *Obs.* a wicked person. —*adj.* **3.** *Archaic.* wicked; malicious; treacherous. [ME *fel(o)un* wicked < AF, c. OF *felon* (obl.), ML *fellōn-*, s. of *fellō* treacherous (adj.), traitor, wicked person (n.); ? orig. same word as FELON[2]]

fel·on[2] (fel′ən), *n.* *Pathol.* an acute and painful inflammation of the deeper tissues of a finger or toe, usually near the nail: a form of whitlow. [late ME *felo(u)n* < ML *fellōn-* (s. of *fellō*) scrofulous tumor, perh. < L *fel* gall, venom]

fe·lo·ni·ous (fə lō′nē əs), *adj.* **1.** *Law.* pertaining to, of the nature of, or involving a felony: *felonious intent.* **2.** *Archaic.* wicked; base; villainous. [FELONY + -OUS; r. ME *felonous*] —**fe·lo′ni·ous·ly,** *adv.* —**fe·lo′ni·ous·ness,** *n.*

fel·on·ry (fel′ən rē), *n.* **1.** the whole body or class of felons. **2.** the convict population of a penal colony.

fel·o·ny (fel′ə nē), *n., pl.* **-nies. 1.** *Law.* any of various offenses, as murder or burglary, of graver character than misdemeanors, esp. those commonly punished in the U.S. by imprisonment for more than a year. **2.** *Early Eng. Law.* any crime punishable by death or mutilation and forfeiture of lands and goods. [ME *felonie* < OF: wickedness]

fel·site (fel′sīt), *n.* a dense, fine-grained, igneous rock consisting typically of feldspar and quartz, both of which may appear as phenocrysts. [FELS(PAR) + -ITE[1]] —**fel·sit·ic** (fel sit′ik), *adj.*

fel·spar (fel′spär′), *n.* *Chiefly Brit.* feldspar. [< G *Fels* rock + SPAR[3], by false etymological analysis] —**fel·spath·ic** (fel spath′ik), **fel′spath·ose′,** *adj.*

felt[1] (felt), *v.* pt. and pp. of **feel.**

felt[2] (felt), *n.* **1.** a nonwoven fabric of wool, fur, or hair, matted together by heat, moisture, and great pressure. **2.** any article made of this material, as a hat. **3.** any matted fabric or material, as a mat of asbestos fibers, rags, old paper, etc., used for insulation and in construction. —*adj.* **4.** pertaining to or made of felt. —*v.t.* **5.** to make into felt; mat or press together. **6.** to cover with or as with felt. —*v.i.* **7.** to become matted together. [ME, OE; c. G *Filz;* see FILTER]

felt·ing (fel′tiŋ), *n.* **1.** felted material. **2.** the act or process of making felt.

fe·luc·ca (fə luk′ə), *n.* a sailing vessel, lateen-rigged on two masts, used on the Mediterranean Sea and along the Spanish and Portuguese coasts. [earlier *falluca* < Sp *faluca*, earlier var. of *falúa* < Ar *fulūk*, pl. of *fulk* ship]

Felucca

fem., 1. female. 2. feminine.

fe·male (fē′māl), *n.* **1.** a human being of the sex that conceives and bears young; a woman or girl. **2.** any animal of corresponding sex, either bearing living young or producing eggs. **3.** *Bot.* a pistillate plant. **—*adj.* 4.** belonging to the sex that bears young or produces eggs. **5.** of, pertaining to, or characteristic of this sex; feminine: *female suffrage; female charm.* **6.** *Bot.* **a.** designating or pertaining to a plant or the reproductive structure of a plant that produces or contains elements that need fertilization. **b.** (of seed plants) pistillate. **7.** *Mach.* noting a part, thread, etc., into which a corresponding male part fits. **8.** *Obs.* womanish; weakly. [ME, var. (by assoc. with *male*) of *femelle* < ML *fēmella* female, L: little woman, dim. of *fēmina;* see FEME] **—fe′male·ness,** *n.*
—Syn. 1. See **woman. 5.** FEMALE, EFFEMINATE, FEMININE refer to attributes of women. FEMALE is both the general and scientific term, and was formerly used to designate anything not male: *female organs in a plant or animal; a female seminary.* EFFEMINATE is seldom applied to women; it refers reproachfully or contemptuously to qualities which, although natural in women, are unmanly and weak when possessed by men, and often suggest homosexuality: *effeminate gestures; an effeminate voice.* FEMININE, corresponding to masculine, applies to the attributes particularly appropriate to women, esp. the softer and more delicate qualities. The word is seldom used merely to denote sex, and, if applied to ideas, objects, or the like, suggests the delicacy and weakness of women: *a feminine figure, point of view, features.* **—Ant. 1–8.** male.

fe′male suf′frage. See **woman suffrage.**

feme (fem), *n. Law.* a woman or wife. [< AF << L *fēmina* woman; akin to FETUS, FECUND]

feme′ cov′ert (kuv′ərt), *Law.* a married woman. [< AF: covered (protected) woman]

feme′ sole′ (sōl), *Law.* an unmarried woman, whether spinster, widow, or divorcée. [< AF]

fem·i·nie (fem′ə nē), *n.* women collectively. [ME < MF, OF = *femin-* (< L *fēmina*) woman + *-ie* -Y[3]]

fem·i·nine (fem′ə nin), *adj.* **1.** pertaining to a woman or girl: *feminine beauty; feminine dress.* **2.** like a woman; weak; gentle. **3.** effeminate; womanish. **4.** belonging to the female sex; female. **5.** *Gram.* noting or pertaining to the gender that has among its members many nouns referring to females, as well as other nouns, as Latin *stella* "star," or German *Zeit* "time." **—*n. Gram.* 6.** the feminine gender. **7.** a noun or other element in that gender. [late ME < L *fēminīnus* = *fēmin(a)* woman (see FEME) + *-īnus* -INE[1]] **—fem′i·nine·ly,** *adv.* **—fem′i·nine·ness,** *n.* **—Syn. 2.** See **female.**

fem′inine end′ing, **1.** *Pros.* an unaccented syllable at the close of a line of poetry. **2.** *Gram.* a termination or final syllable marking a feminine word.

fem′inine rhyme′, *Pros.* a rhyme having either two syllables of which the second is unstressed **(double rhyme),** as in *motion, notion,* or three syllables of which the second and third are unstressed **(triple rhyme),** as in *fortunate, importunate.*

fem·i·nin·i·ty (fem′ə nin′i tē), *n.* **1.** the quality of being feminine; womanliness. **2.** women collectively. Also, **fe·min·i·ty** (fi min′i tē). [ME *femininite*]

fem·i·nise (fem′ə nīz′), *v.t., v.i.,* **-nised, -nis·ing.** *Chiefly Brit.* feminize. **—fem′i·ni·sa′tion,** *n.*

fem·i·nism (fem′ə niz′əm), *n.* **1.** the doctrine advocating social and political rights for women equal to those of men. **2.** (*sometimes cap.*) an organized movement for the attainment of such rights for women. [< L *fēmin(a)* woman + -ISM] **—fem′i·nist,** *n.* **—fem′i·nis′tic,** *adj.*

fem·i·nize (fem′ə nīz′), *v.t., v.i.,* **-nized, -niz·ing.** to make or become feminine. Also, *esp. Brit.,* **feminise.** [< L *fēmin(a)* woman + -IZE] **—fem′i·ni·za′tion,** *n.*

femme (fam; *Eng.* fem), *n., pl.* **femmes** (fam; *Eng.* femz). *French.* **1.** a woman. **2.** a wife.

femme de cham·bre (fam də shäN′brᵊ), *pl.* **femmes de cham·bre** (fam də shäN′brᵊ). *French.* **1.** a lady's maid. **2.** a chambermaid. [lit., woman of (the) bedroom]

femme fa·tale (fam fa tal′; *Eng.* fem′ fə tal′, -täl′), *pl.* **femmes fa·tales** (fam fa tal′; *Eng.* fem fə talz′, -tälz′). *French.* an irresistibly attractive woman who leads men into danger; siren. [lit., fatal woman]

fem·o·ral (fem′ər əl), *adj.* of, pertaining to, or situated near the thigh or femur. [< L *femor-* (s. of *femur*) thigh + -AL[1]]

fem′oral ar′tery, *Anat.* the main artery of the thigh, supplying blood to the leg.

fe·mur (fē′mər), *n., pl.* **fe·murs, fem·o·ra** (fem′ər ə). **1.** *Anat., Zool.* a bone in the leg, extending from the pelvis to the knee; thighbone. **2.** *Zool.* a corresponding bone, of the hind limb, in a quadruped. **3.** *Entomol.* the third segment of the leg of an insect (counting from the base), situated between the trochanter and the tibia. [< L: the thigh]

fen (fen), *n.* **1.** *Brit.* low land covered wholly or partially with water; boggy land; a marsh. **2. the Fens,** a marshy region W and S of The Wash, in E England. [ME, OE; c. Icel *fen* quagmire, Goth *fani* mud, D *ven,* G *Fenn* fen, bog]

fence (fens), *n., v.,* **fenced, fenc·ing.** **—*n.* 1.** a barrier enclosing or bordering a field, yard, etc., usually made of posts and wire or wood, used to prevent entrance, to confine, or to mark a boundary. **2.** the art or sport of fencing. **3.** skill in argument, repartee, etc. **4.** a person who receives and disposes of stolen goods. **5.** the place of business of such a person. **6.** *Archaic.* a means of defense; a bulwark. **7. mend one's fences,** to strengthen or reestablish one's position by conciliation or negotiation. **8. on the fence,** *U.S. Informal.* uncommitted; neutral; undecided. **—*v.t.* 9.** to enclose by some barrier, as for protection, defense, or for establishing exclusive right to possession: *to fence a farm.* **10.** to separate by or as by a fence or fences (often fol. by *in, off, out,* etc.): *to fence off a corner of one's yard.* **11.** *Archaic.* to ward off; keep out. **—*v.i.* 12.** to practice the art or sport of fencing. **13.** to parry arguments; strive to avoid giving direct answers; hedge. **14.** *Obs.* to raise a defense. [late ME *fens,* aph. for *defens* DEFENSE]

fence′ liz′ard, a spiny lizard, *Sceloperus undulatus,* of the eastern U.S., often found on fences, rocks, logs, etc. See illus. at **lizard.**

fenc·er (fen′sər), *n.* **1.** a person who fences. **2.** a person who practices the art or sport of fencing. **3.** a horse trained to jump barriers, as for show or sport. **4.** *Australian.* a person who builds or repairs fences.

fence-sit·ter (fens′sit′ər), *n.* a person who remains neutral in a controversy or who is undecided. **—fence′-sit′ting,** *n.*

fenc·ing (fen′sing), *n.* **1.** the art, practice, or sport in which an épée, foil, or saber is used for defense and attack. **2.** a parrying of arguments; avoidance of direct answers. **3.** an enclosure or railing. **4.** fences collectively. **5.** material for fences. [late ME *fensing* safeguarding, maintenance]

fend (fend), *v.t.* **1.** to ward off (often fol. by *off*): *to fend off blows.* **2.** *Archaic.* to defend. **—*v.i.* 3.** to resist or make defense: *to fend against poverty.* **4.** to parry; fence. **5.** to shift; provide: *to fend for oneself.* [ME *fende(n),* aph. var. of *defenden* to DEFEND]

fend·er (fen′dər), *n.* **1.** a person or thing that wards something off. **2.** a sheet-metal part mounted over the road wheel of an automobile, bicycle, etc., to reduce the splashing of mud, water, and the like. **3.** a device on the front of a locomotive, streetcar, or the like, for clearing the track of obstructions. **4.** *Naut.* a piece of timber, bundle of rope, or the like, hung over the side of a vessel to lessen shock or prevent chafing, as between the vessel and a dock. **5.** a low metal guard before an open fireplace, to keep back falling coals. [ME *fendour,* aph. var. of *defendour* DEFENDER] **—fend′ered,** *adj.*

Fé·ne·lon (fā nᵊ lôN′), *n.* **Fran·çois de Sa·li·gnac de La Mothe** (fräN swa′ də sa lē nyak′ də la môt′), 1651–1715, French theologian and writer.

fe·nes·tra (fi nes′trə), *n., pl.* **-trae** (-trē). **1.** *Anat., Zool.* a small opening or perforation, as in a bone, esp. between the middle and inner ear. **2.** *Entomol.* a transparent spot in an otherwise opaque surface, as in the wings of certain butterflies and moths. [< NL, special use of L *fenestra* window, hole (in a wall)] **—fe·nes′tral,** *adj.*

fe·nes·trat·ed (fi nes′trā tid, fen′i strā′tid), *adj.* *Archit.* having windows; windowed; characterized by windows. Also, **fe·nes′trate.** [< L *fenestrāt(us)* furnished with windows (see FENESTRA, -ATE[1]) + -ED[2]]

fen·es·tra·tion (fen′i strā′shən), *n.* **1.** *Archit.* the design and disposition of windows and other exterior openings of a building. **2.** *Med., Surg.* **a.** a perforation in a structure. **b.** an operation to effect such an opening. **c.** Also called **fenestra′tion opera′tion.** the creation of an artificial opening into the labyrinth of the ear to restore hearing loss from otosclerosis. [< L *fenestrāt(us)* furnished with windows (see FENESTRATED) + -ION]

Feng·kieh (fung′jye′), *n.* a city in central China, on the Yangtze River. ab. 250,000. Also called **Kweichow.**

Feng·tien (fung′tyen′), *n.* **1.** Mukden. **2.** former name of **Liaoning.**

Fe·ni·an (fē′nē ən, fēn′yən), *n.* **1.** (formerly) a member of an Irish revolutionary organization that advocated an independent Irish republic. **2.** *Irish Legend.* a member of a roving band of warriors, the center of a cycle of legends **(Fe′nian cy′cle)** comparable to those of King Arthur and the Round Table. [< IrGael *fēinne* (pl. of *fiann* band of Fenians) + -IAN; infl. by OIr *féne* ancient inhabitant of Ireland] **—Fe′ni·an·ism,** *n.*

fen·nec (fen′ek), *n.* a small, pale yellowish-brown fox, *Vulpes zerda,* of northern Africa, having large, pointed ears. [< Ar *fenek*]

fen·nel (fen′ᵊl), *n.* **1.** an umbelliferous plant, *Foeniculum vulgare,* having yellow flowers. **2.** Also, **fen′nel seed′.** the aromatic fruits of this plant, used in cookery and medicine. [ME *fenel,* OE *fenol,* var. of *finu(g)l* < VL **fenucl(um),* r. L *fēniculum* = *fēni-* (comb. form of *fēnum* hay) + *-culum* -CLE]

fen·ny (fen′ē), *adj.* **1.** marshy; boggy. **2.** inhabiting or growing in fens. [ME; OE *fennig*]

Fen·rir (fen′rir), *n. Scand. Myth.* a wolflike monster, a son of Loki destined to be released at Ragnarok to eat Odin. Also called **Fen·ris-wolf** (fen′ris wo͝olf′).

fen·u·greek (fen′yo͞o grēk′), *n.* a plant, *Trigonella Foenum-Graecum,* indigenous to western Asia but extensively cultivated elsewhere, chiefly for forage and for its mucilaginous seeds, which are used in medicine. [ME *fenugrek,* OE *fēnogrēcum* < L *fēnu(m) Graecum,* lit., Greek hay. See FENNEL]

feoff (fef, fēf), *v.t.* to invest with a fief or fee; enfeoff. [ME *feoffe(n)* < AF *feoffe(r)* (c. OF *feifer*) < *feoff* FIEF] **—feof′for, feoff′er,** *n.*

feoff·ee (fef′ē, fē fē′), *n.* a person invested with a grant of lands, as a fief. [late ME *feoffe* < AF, ptp. of *feoffer* to invest with a FIEF; see -EE]

feoff·er (fef′ər, fē′fər), *n.* a person who invests another with a grant of lands. [ME *feoffor* < AF *feoffour* = *feoff(er)* (to) FEOFF + *-our* -OR[2]]

feoff·ment (fef′mənt, fēf′-), *n.* the act of investing a person with a grant of lands. [ME *feoffement* < AF]
FEPC, Fair Employment Practices Committee.
fer (fûr; *unstressed* fər), *prep., conj.* *Eye Dial.* for.
-fer, a noun suffix borrowed from Latin, meaning "bearing": *conifer.* Cf. **-ferous.** [< L, orig. adj. suffix, akin to *ferre* to BEAR[1]]
fe·ral (fēr′əl, fer′-), *adj.* **1.** existing in a natural state, as animals or plants; not domesticated or cultivated; wild. **2.** having reverted to the wild state, as from domestication. **3.** of or characteristic of wild animals; ferocious; brutal. [< ML *ferāl(is)* = L *fer(a)* wild beast + *-ālis* -AL[1]]
fer·bam (fûr′bam), *n.* *Chem.* a black, fluffy, water-insoluble powder, $[(CH_3)_2NCSS]_3Fe$, used chiefly as a fungicide for protecting certain farm crops. [*fer(ric dimethyldithiocar)bam(ate)*]
Fer·ber (fûr′bər), *n.* **Edna,** 1887–1968, U.S. novelist, short-story writer, and playwright.
fer-de-lance (fer′dᵊlans′, -dᵊläns′), *n.* a large pit viper, *Trimeresurus atrox,* of tropical America. [< F: lit., iron part (i.e., head) of a lance]
Fer·di·nand I (fûr′dᵊnand′; *Ger.* fer′di nänt′), **1.** 1503–64, king of Bohemia and Hungary 1526–64; emperor of the Holy Roman Empire 1558–64 (brother of Emperor Charles V). **2.** (*Prince Maximilian Karl Leopold Maria of Saxe-Coburg*) 1861–1948, king of Bulgaria 1908–18. **3.** Spanish, **Fernando I.** ("*Ferdinand the Great*") died 1065, king of Castile 1033–65, king of Navarre and Leon 1037–65; emperor of Spain 1056–65.
Ferdinand II, 1. 1578–1637, king of Bohemia 1617–19, 1620–37; king of Hungary 1619?–37; emperor of the Holy Roman Empire 1620–37. **2.** ("*the Catholic*") 1452–1516, king of Sicily 1468–1516, king of Aragon 1479–1516; as Ferdinand III, king of Naples 1504–16; as King Ferdinand V, joint sovereign (with Isabella I) of Castile 1474–1504; regent of Castile, 1504–16.
Ferdinand III. See **Ferdinand II** (def. 2).
Ferdinand V. See **Ferdinand II** (def. 2).
Fer·dus (fer′dəs), *n.* Firdausi.
fere (fēr), *n.* *Obs.* a companion; mate. [ME; OE *(ge)fēra* < *fēran* to go; akin to FARE]
Fer·gus (fûr′gəs), *n.* *Irish Legend.* one of the great warrior kings of Ulster: he lost his throne to Conchobar and became a tutor to Cuchulainn.
Fer·gu·son (fûr′gə sən), *n.* a city in E Missouri, near St. Louis. 28,759 (1970).
fe·ri·a (fēr′ē ə), *n., pl.* **fe·ri·ae** (fēr′ē ē′), **fe·ri·as.** *Eccles.* a weekday on which no feast is celebrated. [< LL: day of the week (e.g., *secunda fēria* second day, Monday); in L only pl. *fēriae* holidays; see FAIR[2]] —**fe′ri·al,** *adj.*
fe·rine (fēr′īn, -in), *adj.* feral. [< L *ferīn(us)* = *fer(a)* a wild animal (n. use of fem. of *ferus* wild) + *-īnus* -INE[1]]
fer·i·ty (fer′i tē), *n.* **1.** a wild, untamed, or uncultivated state. **2.** savagery; ferocity. [< L *feritās* = *fer(us)* wild, untamed + *-itās* -ITY]
Fer·man·agh (fər man′ə), *n.* a county in SW Northern Ireland. 51,531 (1961); 653 sq. mi. *Co. seat:* Enniskillen.
Fer·mat (fer mä′; *Eng.* fer mä′), *n.* **Pierre de** (pyer də), 1601–65, French mathematician.
fer·ma·ta (fer mä′tə; *It.* fer mä′tä), *n., pl.* **-tas,** *It.* **-te** (-te). *Music.* **1.** the sustaining of a note, chord, or rest for a duration longer than the indicated time value, with the length of the extension at the performer's discretion. **2.** a symbol, 𝄐 or 𝄑, respectively, placed over or under a note, chord, or rest to indicate a fermata. [< It: stop, pause, n. use of fem. of ptp. of *fermare* to stop < L *firmāre* to make firm. See FIRM[1], -ATE[1]]
fer·ment (*n.* fûr′ment; *v.* fər ment′), *n.* **1.** any of a group of living organisms, as yeasts, molds, or certain bacteria, that cause fermentation. **2.** an enzyme. **3.** fermentation. **4.** agitation; unrest; tumult: *artistic ferment; political ferment.* —*v.t.* **5.** to act upon as a ferment. **6.** *Biochem.* to cause to undergo fermentation. **7.** to inflame; foment: *to ferment prejudiced crowds to riot.* **8.** to cause agitation or excitement in. —*v.i.* **9.** to be fermented; undergo fermentation. **10.** to seethe with agitation or excitement, as of creativity. [late ME < L *ferment(um)* yeast (n.), *ferment(āre)* (to) cause to rise (v.); akin to BARM, L *fervēre* to boil] —**fer·ment′a·bil′i·ty,** *n.* —**fer·ment′a·ble,** *adj.*
fer·men·ta·tion (fûr′men tā′shən), *n.* **1.** the act or process of fermenting. **2.** *Biochem.* a change brought about by a ferment, as yeast enzymes, which convert grape sugar into ethyl alcohol. **3.** agitation; excitement; ferment. [ME *fermentacioun* < LL *fermentātiōn-* (s. of *fermentātiō*)]
fer·ment·a·tive (fər men′tə tiv), *adj.* **1.** tending to produce or undergo fermentation. **2.** pertaining to or of the nature of fermentation. [obs. *fermentate* to cause to ferment (< L *fermentāt(us)*; see FERMENT, -ATE[1]) + -IVE] —**fer·ment′a·tive·ly,** *adv.* —**fer·ment′a·tive·ness,** *n.*
fer·mi (fûr′mē; *It.* fer′mē), *n.* a unit of length, 10^{-13} centimeter. *Abbr.:* F [named after E. FERMI]
Fer·mi (fûr′mē; *It.* fer′mē), *n.* **En·ri·co** (en rē′kō; *It.* en rē′kô), 1901–54, Italian physicist, in the U.S. after 1939: Nobel prize 1938.
fer·mi·um (fûr′mē əm), *n.* *Chem.* a synthetic, radioactive element. *Symbol:* Fm; *at. no.:* 100. [named after E. FERMI; see -IUM]
fern (fûrn), *n.* *Bot.* any of the pteridophytes of the order *Filicales,* distinguished from other pteridophytes in having leaves that are few in number, that are large in proportion to the stems, and that bear sporangia on the undersurface or margin. [ME *ferne,* OE *fearn;* c. G *Farn* fern, Skt *parṇá* feather] —**fern′less,** *adj.* —**fern′like′,** *adj.*

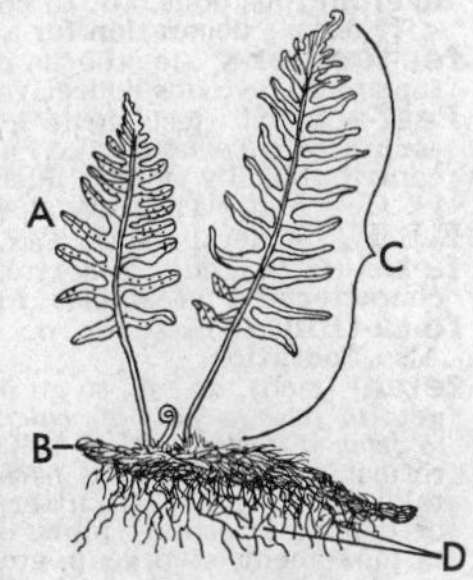

Fern
Mature sporophyte of *Polypodium virginianum*
A, Sori; B, Rhizome (stem); C, Leaf; D, Roots

Fer·nán·dez (fer nan′dez; *Sp.* fer nän′deth), *n.* **Juan** (hwän, wän; *Sp.* hwän), 1536?–1602?, Spanish navigator: explorer in South America and the Pacific.
Fer·nan·do I (fer nan′dô). See **Ferdinand I** (def. 3).
Fer·nan·do de No·ro·nha (fer nänn′dōō də nōō rô′nyä), an island in the S Atlantic, ab. 125 mi. E of easternmost tip of Brazil: a Brazilian penal colony. 10 sq. mi.
Fer·nan·do Po (fər nan′dō pō′), an island in the Bight of Biafra, near the W coast of Africa: a province of Equatorial Guinea. 62,600 (est. 1964); ab. 780 sq. mi. Also, **Fernan′do Po′o** (pō′ō), **Fernan′do Pó′o** (pō′ō).
fern·brake (fûrn′brāk′), *n.* a thicket of ferns.
Fern·dale (fûrn′dāl′), *n.* a city in SE Michigan, near Detroit. 30,850 (1970).
fern·er·y (fûr′nə rē), *n., pl.* **-er·ies. 1.** a place or a glass case in which ferns are grown for ornament. **2.** a collection of ferns in a garden or a potted display.
fern′ seed′, the spores of ferns, formerly supposed to have the power to make persons invisible.
fern·y (fûr′nē), *adj.,* **fern·i·er, fern·i·est. 1.** pertaining to, consisting of, or like ferns: *ferny leaves.* **2.** abounding in or overgrown with ferns: *ferny undergrowth.*
fe·ro·cious (fə rō′shəs), *adj.* **1.** savagely fierce, as a wild beast, person, action, etc.; violently cruel. **2.** extreme or intense: *a ferocious thirst.* —**fe·ro′cious·ly,** *adv.* —**fe·ro′cious·ness,** *n.* —**Syn. 1.** rapacious. See **fierce.** —**Ant. 1.** mild, tame.
fe·roc·i·ty (fə ros′i tē), *n.* a ferocious quality or state; savage fierceness. [< L *ferōcitās* = *ferōci-* (s. of *ferox*) daring, headstrong + *-tās* -TY[2]]
-ferous, a suffix meaning "bearing," "producing," "yielding," "containing," "conveying," used to form adjectives from stems in **-fer:** *coniferous; pestiferous.* [ME; see -FER, -OUS]
Fer·ra·ra (fə rär′ə; *It.* fer rä′rä), *n.* a city in N Italy, near the Po River: medieval university. 151,145.
Fer·ra·ro (fə rär′ō), *n.* **Geraldine Anne** ("*Gerry*"), born 1935, U.S. politician: congresswoman 1978–84; first female vice-presidential nominee of a major political party 1984.
fer·re·ous (fer′ē əs), *adj.* of, resembling, or containing iron. [< L *ferreus* = *ferr(um)* iron + *-eus* -EOUS]
fer·ret[1] (fer′it), *n.* **1.** a domesticated, red-eyed, albinic variety of the polecat, used in Europe for driving rabbits and rats from their burrows. —*v.t.* **2.** to drive out by or as if by means of a ferret (often fol. by *out*): *to ferret out enemies.* **3.** to hunt with ferrets: *to ferret rabbits.* **4.** to search out or bring to light (often fol. by *out*): *to ferret out the facts.* —*v.i.* **5.** to search about. [ME, var. of *furet* < MF << VL **furitt(us)* = *fur* thief (< L) + *-ittus* -ET] —**fer′ret·er,** *n.* —**fer′ret·y,** *adj.*
fer·ret[2] (fer′it), *n.* a narrow ribbon for binding, trimming, etc. [alter. of It *fioretto* floss silk, lit., little flower = *fior(e)* (< L *flōrem;* see FLOWER) + *-etto* -ET]
ferri-, 1. a learned borrowing from Latin meaning "iron," used in the formation of compound words: *ferriferous.* **2.** *Chem.* a combining form of **ferric:** *ferricyanide.* Cf. **ferro-.** [< L, comb. form of *ferrum* iron]
fer·ri·age (fer′ē ij), *n.* **1.** conveyance or transportation by a ferryboat. **2.** the fare or price charged for ferrying.
fer·ric (fer′ik), *adj.* *Chem.* of or containing iron, esp. in the trivalent state. [< L *ferr(um)* iron + -IC]
fer′ric chlo′ride, *Chem.* a solid compound, $FeCl_3$, used chiefly in engraving, for deodorizing sewage, as a mordant, and in medicine as an astringent and styptic.
fer′ric ox′ide, *Chem.* a dark-red solid, Fe_2O_3, occurring naturally, as hematite and rust: used chiefly as a pigment and in the manufacture of polishing compounds.
fer′ri·cy·an′ic ac′id (fer′ī sī an′ik, fer′ē-), *Chem.* an unstable solid, $H_3Fe(CN)_6$, obtained by the interaction of a ferricyanide and an acid.
fer·ri·cy·a·nide (fer′ī sī′ə nīd′, fer′ē-), *n.* *Chem.* a salt of ferricyanic acid, as potassium ferricyanide, $K_3Fe(CN)_6$.
fer·rif·er·ous (fə rif′ər əs), *adj.* producing iron.
Fer′ris wheel′ (fer′is), an amusement ride consisting of a large upright wheel rotating on a permanent stand and having seats suspended freely around its rim so as to remain horizontal as the wheel revolves. [named after G. W. G. *Ferris* (d. 1896), American engineer]
fer·rite (fer′īt), *n.* **1.** *Chem.* a compound, as $NaFeO_2$, formed when ferric oxide is combined with a more basic metallic oxide. **2.** *Metall.* the pure iron constituent of ferrous metals, as distinguished from the iron carbides. **3.** *Petrog.* any of various reddish-brown, indeterminable mineral substances, probably iron compounds, frequently observed in the microscopic examination of certain igneous rocks. [FERR(I)- + -ITE[1]]
ferro-, a combining form meaning "iron": *ferroconcrete.* In chemical terminology, the meanings of **ferri-** and **ferro-** are specialized to correspond to *ferric* and *ferrous.* Cf. **ferri-.** [repr. L *ferrum* iron]
fer·ro·al·loy (fer′ō al′oi, -ə loi′), *n.* an alloy of iron with some other material, used in the manufacture of steel.
fer·ro·chro·mi·um (fer′ō krō′mē əm), *n.* a ferroalloy containing up to 70 percent chromium. Also, **fer·ro·chrome** (fer′ə krōm′).
fer·ro·con·crete (fer′ō kon′krēt, -kong′-, -kon krēt′), *n.* See **reinforced concrete.**
fer′ro·cy·an′ic ac′id (fer′ō sī an′ik), *Chem.* an unstable solid, $H_4Fe(CN)_6$, obtained by the interaction of a ferrocyanide and an acid.
fer·ro·cy·a·nide (fer′ō sī′ə nīd′, -nid), *n.* *Chem.* a salt of ferrocyanic acid, as potassium ferrocyanide, $K_4Fe(CN)_6$.
fer·ro·e·lec·tric (fer′ō i lek′trik), *Physics.* —*adj.* **1.** pertaining to a substance that possesses spontaneous electric polarization that can be reversed by an electric field. —*n.* **2.** a ferroelectric substance. [FERRO- + ELECTRIC; coined on analogy with *ferromagnetic*] —**fer′ro·e·lec′tri·cal·ly,** *adv.* —**fer′ro·e·lec·tric′i·ty,** *n.*
Fer·rol (*Sp.* fer rôl′), *n.* See **El Ferrol.**

fer·ro·mag·ne·sian (fer′ō mag nē′zhən, -shən), *adj. Mineral.* (of minerals and rocks) containing iron and magnesium.
fer·ro·mag·net·ic (fer′ō mag net′ik), *adj. Physics.* noting or pertaining to a substance, as iron, that can possess magnetization in the absence of an external magnetic field. Cf. **antiferromagnetic, diamagnetic, paramagnetic.** —**fer·ro·mag·ne·tism** (fer′ō mag′ni tiz′əm), *n.*
fer·ro·man·ga·nese (fer′ō mang′gə nēs′, -nēz′), *n.* a ferroalloy containing up to 90 percent manganese.
fer·ro·sil·i·con (fer′ō sil′ə kən), *n.* a ferroalloy containing up to 95 percent silicon.
fer·ro·type (fer′ə tīp′), *v.,* **-typed, -typ·ing,** *n. Photog.* —*v.t.* **1.** to put a glossy surface on (a print) by pressing it while wet on a metal sheet (**fer′rotype tin′**). —*n.* **2.** a positive photograph made on a sensitized sheet of enameled iron or tin; tintype.
fer·rous (fer′əs), *adj. Chem.* of or containing iron, esp. in the bivalent state. [FERR(I)- + -OUS]
fer′rous sul′fate, *Chem., Pharm.* a bluish-green solid, $FeSO_4 \cdot 7H_2O$, used chiefly in the manufacture of other iron salts, in water purification, and in the treatment of anemia. Also called **copperas, green vitriol.**
fer·ru·gi·nous (fə rōō′jə nəs), *adj.* **1.** iron-bearing. **2.** of the color of iron rust. [< L *ferrūginus* rust colored = *ferrūgin-* (s. of *ferrūgō* iron rust < *ferrum* iron) + *-us* -OUS]
fer·rule (fer′əl, -ōōl), *n., v.,* **-ruled, -rul·ing.** —*n.* **1.** a ring put around the end of a post, cane, or the like, to prevent splitting. **2.** a short metal sleeve for strengthening a tool handle at the end holding the tool. **3.** a bushing or adapter holding the end of a tube and inserted into a hole in a plate in order to make a tight fit. **4.** a short ring for reinforcing or decreasing the interior diameter of the end of a tube. —*v.t.* **5.** to furnish with a ferrule. Also, **ferule.** [< L *ferr(um)* iron + -ULE; r. late ME *virole* < MF (c. ML *virola*) < L *viriola* = *viri(a)* bracelet + *-ola* dim. suffix]
fer·ry (fer′ē), *n., pl.* **-ries,** *v.,* **-ried, -ry·ing.** —*n.* **1.** a commercial service with terminals and boats for transporting persons, automobiles, etc., across a river, bay, or the like. **2.** a ferryboat. **3.** a service for flying airplanes over a particular route, esp. the delivery of airplanes to an overseas purchaser or base of operations. **4.** the legal right to ferry passengers, baggage, etc., and to charge tolls for the service. —*v.t.* **5.** to carry or convey over water in a boat or plane. —*v.i.* **6.** to pass over water in a boat or by ferry. [ME *ferie(n),* OE *ferian* to carry; c. Icel *ferja,* Goth *farjan;* akin to FARE]
fer·ry·boat (fer′ē bōt′), *n.* a boat for transporting passengers, vehicles, etc., across a river, bay, or the like. [late ME *feryboot*]
fer·tile (fûr′t^{ə}l *or, esp. Brit.,* -tīl), *adj.* **1.** bearing, producing, or capable of producing vegetation, crops, etc., abundantly: *fertile soil.* **2.** bearing or capable of bearing offspring. **3.** abundantly productive: *a fertile imagination.* **4.** producing an abundance (usually fol. by *of* or *in*): *a land fertile of wheat.* **5.** conducive to productiveness: *fertile showers.* **6.** *Biol.* **a.** fertilized, as an egg or ovum; fecundated. **b.** capable of growth or development, as seeds or eggs. **7.** *Bot.* **a.** capable of producing sexual reproductive structures. **b.** capable of causing fertilization, as an anther with fully developed pollen. **c.** having spore-bearing organs, as a frond. **8.** *Physics.* (of an element or substance) convertible into a fissionable material. **9.** *Obs.* produced in abundance. [late ME < L *fertil(is)* fruitful, akin to *ferre* to BEAR[1]; see -ILE] —**fer′tile·ly,** *adv.* —**fer′tile·ness,** *n.* —**Syn. 1–3.** fecund. See **productive.** —**Ant. 1–3.** sterile, barren.
Fer′tile Cres′cent, **1.** an ancient agricultural region extending NE from the Nile to the Tigris and SE to the Persian Gulf. **2.** *Islam.* (formerly) the Arab world in the Middle East.
fer·ti·lise (fûr′t^{ə}līz′), *v.t.,* **-lised, -lis·ing.** *Chiefly Brit.* fertilize. —**fer′ti·lis′a·ble,** *adj.*
fer·ti·lis·er (fûr′t^{ə}lī′zər), *n. Chiefly Brit.* fertilizer.
fer·til·i·ty (fər til′i tē), *n.* **1.** the state or quality of being fertile. **2.** *Biol.* the ability to produce offspring; power of reproduction. [late ME *fertilite* < L *fertilitās*]
Fer·til·i·ty (fər til′i tē), *n.* **Sea of.** See **Mare Fecunditatis.**
fer·ti·li·za·tion (fûr′t^{ə}li zā′shən *or, esp. Brit.,* -t^{ə}lī-), *n.* **1.** the act or process or an instance of fertilizing. **2.** the state of being fertilized. **3.** *Biol.* **a.** the union of male and female gametic nuclei. **b.** fecundation or impregnation of animals or plants. **4.** the enrichment of soil, as for the production of crops. Also, *esp. Brit.,* **fer′ti·li·sa′tion.**
fer·ti·lize (fûr′t^{ə}līz′), *v.t.,* **-lized, -liz·ing.** **1.** *Biol.* **a.** to render (the female or gamete) capable of development by uniting it with the male gamete. **b.** to fecundate or impregnate (an animal or plant). **2.** to make fertile; enrich: *to fertilize farm land.* **3.** to make productive. Also, *esp. Brit.,* **fertilise.** —**fer′ti·liz′a·ble,** *adj.*
fer·ti·liz·er (fûr′t^{ə}lī′zər), *n.* **1.** any substance used to fertilize the soil, esp. a commercial or chemical manure. **2.** a fertilizing agent, esp. of an animal or plant. Also, *esp. Brit.,* **fertiliser.**
fer·u·la (fer′ŏŏ lə, fer′yŏŏ-), *n., pl.* **-las, -lae** (-lē′). **1.** *Bot.* any umbelliferous plant of the genus *Ferula,* chiefly of the Mediterranean region and central Asia, generally tall and coarse with dissected leaves, many of the Asian species yielding strongly scented, medicinal gum resins. **2.** ferule[1] (def. 1). [special uses of L *ferula* giant fennel (NL, plant meaning only)]
fer·u·la·ceous (fer′ŏŏ lā′shəs, fer′yŏŏ-), *adj.* pertaining to reeds or canes; having a stalklike reed: *ferulaceous plants.* [< NL *ferulāceus*]
fer·ule[1] (fer′əl, -ōōl), *n., v.,* **-uled, -ul·ing.** —*n.* **1.** Also, **ferula.** a rod, cane, or flat piece of wood for punishing children, esp. by striking them on the hand. —*v.t.* **2.** to punish with a ferule. [< L *ferula* schoolmaster's rod (lit., stalk of giant fennel); r. OE *ferele* < L *ferula*]
fer·ule[2] (fer′əl, -ōōl), *n., v.t.,* **-uled, -ul·ing.** ferrule.
fer·ven·cy (fûr′vən sē), *n.* warmth or intensity of feeling; ardor; zeal; fervor. [late ME < LL *ferventia* (see FERVENT, -ENCY); r. *fervence* < MF < L *ferventia*]
fer·vent (fûr′vənt), *adj.* **1.** having or showing great warmth or intensity of spirit, feeling, enthusiasm, etc.; ardent: *a fervent admirer; a fervent plea.* **2.** hot; burning; glowing. [ME < L *fervent-* (s. of *fervēns*), prp. of *fervēre* to boil; see -ENT] —**fer′vent·ly,** *adv.* —**fer′vent·ness,** *n.* —**Syn. 1.** fervid, warm; eager, earnest, zealous, impassioned, passionate. —**Ant. 1.** apathetic.
fer·vid (fûr′vid), *adj.* **1.** heated or vehement in spirit, enthusiasm, etc.; fervent: *a fervid orator.* **2.** burning; glowing; hot. [< L *fervid(us)* boiling] —**fer·vid′i·ty,** *n.* —**fer′vid·ly,** *adv.* —**fer′vid·ness,** *n.*
Fer·vi·dor (fûr′vi dôr′; *Fr.* fer vē dôr′), *n.* Thermidor. [< F, appar. b. *ferv(eur)* FERVOR and *(therm)idor* THERMIDOR]
fer·vor (fûr′vər), *n.* **1.** great warmth and earnestness of feeling: *to speak with great fervor.* **2.** intense heat. Also, *esp. Brit.,* **fer′vour.** [late ME < L: heat (see FERVENT, -OR[1]); r. ME *fervour* < AF < L *fervōr-,* s. of *fervor*] —**Syn. 1.** ardor, intensity, passion. —**Ant. 1.** apathy.
Fes·cen·nine (fes′ə nīn′, -nin), *adj.* (*sometimes l.c.*) scurrilous; licentious; obscene: *Fescennine verse.* [< L *Fescennīn(us)* of, belonging to *Fescennia,* a town in Etruria noted for jesting and scurrilous verse; see -INE[1]]
fes·cue (fes′kyōō), *n.* **1.** Also called **fes′cue grass′.** any grass of the genus *Festuca,* some species of which are cultivated for pasture or lawns. **2.** a straw, slender twig, etc., used to point out the letters in teaching children to read. [ME *festu* < MF << VL *festuc(um)* stalk, r. L *festūca*]
fess (fes), *n. Heraldry.* an ordinary in the form of a broad horizontal band across the middle of an escutcheon. Also, **fesse.** [late ME *fesse* < AF << L *fascia* FASCIA]
Fes·sen·den (fes′ən dən), *n.* **William Pitt,** 1806–69, U.S. statesman.
fess′ point′, *Heraldry.* the central point of an escutcheon. Also called **heart point.**
-fest, a combining form denoting a festive occasion, esp. one involving a contest: *songfest.* [< G *Fest,* MHG *vest* < L *festum.* See FEAST]
fes·tal (fes′t^{ə}l), *adj.* pertaining to or befitting a feast, festival, or gala occasion. [late ME < L *fēst(um)* FEAST + -AL[1]] —**fes′tal·ly,** *adv.*
fes·ter (fes′tər), *v.i.* **1.** to form pus; to generate purulent matter; suppurate. **2.** to cause ulceration, as a foreign body in the flesh. **3.** to putrefy or rot. **4.** to rankle, as a feeling of resentment. —*v.t.* **5.** to cause to fester or rankle: *Malice festered his spirit.* —*n.* **6.** an ulcer; a rankling sore. **7.** a small, purulent, superficial sore. [ME < MF *festre* < L *fistula* ulcer (lit., pipe, tube)]
fes·ti·na len·te (fes tē′nä len′te; *Eng.* fe stī′nə len′tē), *Latin.* make haste slowly.
fes·ti·nate (*v.* fes′tə nāt′; *adj.* fes′tə nāt′, -nit), *v.,* **-nat·ed, -nat·ing,** *adj. Obs.* —*v.t., v.i.* **1.** to hurry; hasten. —*adj.* **2.** hurried. [< L *festīnāt(us)* hurried, ptp. of *festīnāre;* see -ATE[1]] —**fes′ti·nate′ly,** *adv.*
fes·ti·val (fes′tə vəl), *n.* **1.** a day or time of religious or other celebration, marked by feasting, ceremonies, or other observances: *the festival of Christmas; a Roman festival.* **2.** a periodic commemoration or celebration. **3.** a period or program of festive activities, cultural events, or entertainment: *a music festival.* **4.** gaiety; merrymaking. —*adj.* **5.** of, pertaining to, or befitting a feast or holiday. [ME < eccl. L *fēstivālis* (*diēs*) holy (day)]
fes·tive (fes′tiv), *adj.* **1.** pertaining to or suitable for a feast or festival: *festive decorations; a festive meal.* **2.** joyous; merry. [< L *fēstīv(us)* merry < *fēst(us)* festal + *-īvus* -IVE] —**fes′tive·ly,** *adv.* —**fes′tive·ness,** *n.*
fes·tiv·i·ty (fe stiv′i tē), *n., pl.* **-ties.** **1.** a festive celebration or occasion. **2.** **festivities,** festive events or activities: *the festivities of Christmas.* **3.** festive character or quality; gaiety. [ME *festivite* < L *fēstivitās*]
fes·toon (fe stōōn′), *n.* **1.** a string or chain of flowers, foliage, ribbon, etc., suspended in a curve between two points. **2.** a decorative representation of this, as in architectural work or on pottery. —*v.t.* **3.** to adorn with or as with festoons: *to festoon a hall.* **4.** to form (flowers, leaves, ribbon, or the like) into festoons. **5.** to connect by festoons. [< F *feston* < It *festone* decoration for a feast < *festa* FEAST]

Festoon

fes·toon·er·y (fe stōō′nə rē), *n.* **1.** a decoration of festoons. **2.** festoons collectively.
Fest·schrift (fest′shrift′), *n., pl.* **-shrift·en** (-shrif′tən), **-schrifts.** (*sometimes l.c.*) a volume of articles, essays, etc., contributed by many authors in honor of a colleague. [< G = *Fest* feast, festival + *Schrift* a writing]
F.E.T., Federal Excise Tax.
fe·tal (fēt′^{ə}l), *adj. Embryol.* of, pertaining to, or having the character of a fetus. Also, **foetal.**
fe·ta·tion (fē tā′shən), *n. Embryol.* pregnancy; gestation. Also, **foetation.**
fetch[1] (fech), *v.t.* **1.** to go for and bring back; return with; get: *to fetch a pail of water.* **2.** to cause to come; bring: *to fetch a doctor.* **3.** to sell for or bring (a price, financial return, etc.): *The horse fetched $50 more than it cost.* **4.** to take (a breath). **5.** to utter (a sigh, groan, etc.). **6.** to deal or deliver (a stroke, blow, etc.). **7.** to perform or execute (a movement, step, leap, etc.). **8.** *Chiefly Naut. or Dial.* to reach; arrive at: *to fetch port.* **9.** *Hunting.* (of a dog) to retrieve (game). —*v.i.* **10.** to go and bring things. **11.** *Chiefly Naut.* to move or maneuver. **12.** *Hunting.* to retrieve game (often used as a command to a dog). **13.** to go by an indirect route (often fol. by *around* or *about*). —*n.* **14.** the act of fetching. **15.** the distance of fetching: *a long fetch.* **16.** an area where ocean waves are being generated by the wind. **17.** the reach of a thing. **18.** the uninterrupted distance traveled by a wind or an ocean wave. **19.** a trick; dodge. [ME *fecche(n),* OE *fecc(e)an,* var. of *fetian,* akin to

-*fat* (in *sīthfat* journey), G *fassen* to grasp] —**fetch′er,** *n.* —**Syn. 1.** See **bring.**

fetch[2] (fech), *n.* the ghost of a living person, often supposed to appear as an omen of that person's death; wraith. [? short for *fetch-life* one sent to fetch the soul of a dying person]

fetch·ing (fech′ing), *adj.* charming; captivating. —**fetch′ing·ly,** *adv.*

fete (fāt, fet), *n., v.,* **fet·ed, fet·ing.** —*n.* **1.** a religious feast or festival. **2.** a festal day; holiday. **3.** a festive celebration or entertainment: *The ball was the greatest fete of the season.* —*v.t.* **4.** to entertain at or honor with a fete: *to fete a visiting celebrity.* Also, **fête** (fāt, fet; *Fr.* fet). [< F, earlier *feste* FEAST]

fête cham·pê·tre (fet shäN pe′trə), *pl.* **fêtes cham·pê·tres** (fet shäN pe′trə). *French.* an outdoor festival or a garden party.

fete′ day′, a festival day.

fet·e·ri·ta (fet′ə rē′tə), *n.* a grain sorghum cultivated for grain and forage. [< Ar (Sudan dial.)]

fet·ich (fet′ish, fē′tish), *n.* fetish.

fet·ich·ism (fet′i shiz′əm, fē′ti-), *n.* fetishism. —**fet′ich·ist,** *n.* —**fet′ich·is′tic,** *adj.*

fe·ti·cide (fē′ti sīd′), *n.* the act of destroying a fetus or causing an abortion. Also, **foeticide.** [*feti-* (comb. form of FETUS) + -CIDE] —**fe′ti·cid′al,** *adj.*

fet·id (fet′id, fē′tid), *adj.* having an offensive odor; stinking. Also, **foetid.** [< L *fētid(us)* = *fēt-* (s. of *fētēre* to stink) + *-idus* -ID[4]] —**fet′id·ly,** *adv.* —**fet′id·ness,** *n.*

fet·ish (fet′ish, fē′tish), *n.* **1.** an object regarded as having magical power. **2.** any object, idea, etc., eliciting unquestioning reverence, respect, or devotion: *to make a fetish of high grades.* **3.** *Psychol.* any object or nongenital part of the body that causes a habitual erotic response or fixation. Also, **fetich.** [earlier *fateish* < Pg *feitiço* charm, sorcery (n.), artificial (adj.) < L *factīcius* FACTITIOUS; r. *fatisso, fetisso* < Pg, as above]

fet·ish·ism (fet′i shiz′əm, fē′ti-), *n.* **1.** belief in or use of fetishes. **2.** *Psychol.* the compulsive use of some object or nongenital part of the body as a stimulus in attaining sexual gratification, as a shoe, a lock of hair, etc. **3.** blind devotion. Also, **fetichism.** —**fet′ish·is′tic,** *adj.*

fet·ish·ist (fet′i shist, fē′ti-), *n.* a person who practices fetishism. Also, **fetichist.**

fet·lock (fet′lok′), *n.* **1.** the projection of the leg of a horse behind the joint between the cannon bone and great pastern bone, bearing a tuft of hair. **2.** the tuft of hair itself. **3.** Also called **fet′lock joint′.** the joint at this point. [ME *fitlok* (c. SwissG *Fisloch*) = *fitl-* (< ?) + *-ok* -OCK]

fe·tor (fē′tər), *n.* any strong offensive smell; stench. Also, **foetor.** [< L = *fēt-* (s. of *fētēre* to stink) + *-or* -OR[1]]

fet·ter (fet′ər), *n.* **1.** a chain or shackle placed on the feet. **2.** Usually, **fetters.** anything that confines or restrains. —*v.t.* **3.** to put fetters upon. **4.** to confine; restrain. [ME, OE *feter;* c. OHG *fezzera,* Icel *fjöturr;* akin to FOOT] —**fet′ter·er,** *n.* —**fet′ter·less,** *adj.*

fet′ter bone′, the great pastern bone. See under **pastern** (def. 2).

fet·ter·bush (fet′ər bo͝osh′), *n.* an evergreen, ericaceous shrub, *Lyonia lucida,* of the southern U.S., having fragrant white flowers. [FETTER + BUSH[1]; so called because it impedes walkers]

fet·tle (fet′əl), *n., v.,* **-tled, -tling.** —*n.* **1.** state; condition: *in fine fettle.* —*v.t.* **2.** *Foundry.* to remove sand from (a casting). **3.** *Metall.* to repair the hearth of (an open-hearth furnace). [ME *fetle* to shape, prepare, back formation from *fetled,* OE **fetelede* girded up = *fetel* belt + *-ede* -ED[2]]

fet·tling (fet′ling), *n.* *Metall.* the material with which the hearth of a puddling furnace is lined, usually a dolomite or refractory mixture.

fet·tu·ci·ni (fet′ə chē′nē), *n.* (*construed as sing. or pl.*) pasta in the form of narrow strips. Also, **fet·tu·ci·ne** (fet′ə-chē′ne), **fet·tuc·ci·ne** (fet′ə chē′ne; *It.* fet′to͞ot chē′ne). [< It]

fe·tus (fē′təs), *n., pl.* **-tus·es.** *Embryol.* (used chiefly of viviparous mammals) the young of an animal while in the womb or egg, esp. in the later stages of development when the body structures are in the recognizable form of its kind, in man being from the latter part of the third month until birth. Also, **foetus.** Cf. **embryo** (def. 2). [< L: offspring = **fē-* breed (see FEME) + *-tus* n. suffix of result]

feud[1] (fyo͞od), *n.* **1.** a bitter, continuous hostility, esp. between two families, clans, etc., often lasting for years or for generations. **2.** a quarrel or contention: *a feud between labor and management.* —*v.i.* **3.** to engage in a feud. [var. of *fead* (*a* being misread as *u*), ME *fede* < MF *fe(i)de* < OHG *fēhida;* c. OE *fǣhth* enmity. See FOE] —**Syn. 2.** argument, difference.

feud[2] (fyo͞od), *n.* fee (def. 5). [< ML *feud(um),* var. of *feodum.* See FEE]

feu·dal[1] (fyo͞od′əl), *adj.* **1.** of, pertaining to, or of the nature of a fief or fee: *a feudal estate.* **2.** of or pertaining to the holding of land in a fief or fee. **3.** of, pertaining to, or like the feudal system, its social and economic structure, etc.: *feudal law.* **4.** of or pertaining to the Middle Ages. [< ML *feudāl(is).* See FEUD[2], -AL[1]]

feu·dal[2] (fyo͞od′əl), *adj.* of or pertaining to a feud. [FEUD[1] + -AL[1]]

feu·dal·ise (fyo͞od′əlīz′), *v.t.,* **-ised, -is·ing.** *Chiefly Brit.* feudalize. —**feu′dal·i·sa′tion,** *n.*

feu·dal·ism (fyo͞od′əliz′əm), *n.* the principles and practices of the feudal system. —**feu′dal·ist,** *n.* —**feu′dal·is′tic,** *adj.*

feu·dal·i·ty (fyo͞o dal′i tē), *n., pl.* **-ties** for 2. **1.** the state or quality of being feudal. **2.** a fief or fee. [FEUDAL[1] + -ITY; r. earlier *feodality* < F *féodalité*]

feu·dal·ize (fyo͞od′əlīz′), *v.t.,* **-ized, -iz·ing.** to bring under the feudal system. Also, *esp. Brit.,* **feudalise.** —**feu′dal·i·za′tion,** *n.*

feu′dal sys′tem, the system of social and economic organization in medieval Europe, based on the holding of lands in fief or fee and on the resulting relations between lord and vassal.

feu·da·to·ry (fyo͞o′də tôr′ē, -tôr′ē), *n., pl.* **-ries,** *adj.* —*n.* **1.** a person who holds his lands by feudal tenure; a feudal vassal. **2.** a fief or fee. —*adj.* **3.** (of a kingdom or state) under the overlordship of another sovereign or state. **4.** (of a feudal estate) holding or held by feudal tenure. [< ML *feudātor* fief-holder + -Y[1]]

feud·ist[1] (fyo͞o′dist), *n.* a person who participates in a feud. [FEUD[1] + -IST]

feud·ist[2] (fyo͞o′dist), *n.* a writer or authority on feudal law. [FEUD[2] + -IST]

Feuil·lant (fœ yäN′), *n.* *Fr. Hist.* a member of a club of constitutional monarchists. [named after the meeting place, the convent of Notre Dame des *Feuillants*]

feuil·le·ton (foi′i tən; *Fr.* fœyə tôN′), *n., pl.* **-tons** (-tənz; *Fr.* -tôN′). **1.** a part of a European newspaper (usually the bottom of one or more pages) containing fiction, criticism, etc. **2.** an item printed in the feuilleton. [< F = *feuillet* little leaf (*feuille* (< L *folium* leaf) + *-et* -ET) + *-on* n. suffix] —**feuil·le·ton·ism** (foi′yi tə niz′əm), *n.* —**feuil′le·ton·ist,** *n.* —**feuil′le·ton·is′tic,** *adj.*

fe·ver (fē′vər), *n.* **1.** an abnormal condition of the body, characterized by undue rise in temperature, quickening of the pulse, and disturbance of various body functions. **2.** an abnormally high body temperature. **3.** any of a group of diseases in which high temperature is a prominent symptom: *scarlet fever.* **4.** intense nervous excitement: *The audience was in a fever of anticipation.* —*v.t.* **5.** to affect with or as if with fever: *The excitement fevered him.* [ME; OE *fefer* < L *febr-* (s. of *febris*) fever] —**fe′ver·less,** *adj.*

fe′ver blis′ter, a vesicular eruption on the face, often accompanying a cold or febrile condition; herpes simplex. Also called **fe′ver sore′.**

fe·ver·few (fē′vər fyo͞o′), *n.* a perennial composite plant, *Chrysanthemum Parthenium,* bearing small white flowers, formerly used as a febrifuge. [late ME < AF **feverfue* (r. early ME *fever fugie,* OE *feferfuge*) < LL *febrifug(ia).* See FEBRIFUGE]

fe′ver heat′, **1.** feverish excitement. **2.** the heat of fever; body heat exceeding 98.6°F.

fe·ver·ish (fē′vər ish), *adj.* **1.** excited or restless, as if from fever. **2.** having fever, esp. a slight degree of fever. **3.** pertaining to, of the nature of, or resembling fever: *a feverish disease; feverish excitement.* **4.** infested with fever, as a region. **5.** having a tendency to produce fever. Also, **fe′ver·ous.** [ME *feverisch*] —**fe′ver·ish·ly, fe′ver·ous·ly,** *adv.* —**fe′ver·ish·ness,** *n.*

fe′ver tree′, **1.** any of several trees that produce or are believed to produce a febrifuge, as the blue gum, which is believed to prevent malaria. **2.** a small rubiaceous tree, *Pinckneya pubens,* of the southeastern U.S., having a bark used as a tonic and febrifuge.

fe·ver·weed (fē′vər wēd′), *n.* any plant of the genus *Eryngium,* esp. *E. foetidum,* of the West Indies, or *E. campestre,* of Europe.

fe·ver·wort (fē′vər wûrt′), *n.* the thoroughwort or boneset.

few (fyo͞o), *adj.* **1.** not many but more than one: *Few artists live luxuriously.* **2. few and far between,** at widely separated intervals; infrequent: *In Nevada the towns are few and far between.* —*n.* **3.** (*construed as pl.*) a small number or amount: *Send me a few.* **4. quite a few,** *Informal.* a fairly large number; many. **5. the few,** a special, limited number; minority: *music that will appeal to the few.* —*pron.* **6.** (*construed as pl.*) a small number of persons or things. [ME *fewe,* OE *fēawe;* c. Goth *fawai;* akin to L *paucus* few, *paulus* little, *pauper* poor, *puer* boy, Gk *paûros* little, few] —**few′ness,** *n.*

few·er (fyo͞o′ər), *adj.* **1.** comparative of **few.** —*pron.* **2.** (*construed as pl.*) a smaller number: *Fewer have come than we anticipated.* [ME *fewere,* OE **fēawran*]

—**Usage. 1.** FEWER, LESS are sometimes confused because both imply a comparison with something larger (in number or in amount). FEWER is used with plural nouns or pronouns and applies only to number: *Fewer street cars are running now than ten years ago.* LESS is used in various ways. It is used with singular nouns and pronouns and is commonly applied to material in bulk, in reference to amount: *There was less gasoline in the tank than we had thought. There is less of it than we need.* It is also used frequently with abstractions, esp. where the idea of amount is figuratively present: *less courage; less wealth.* LESS applies where such attributes as value, degree, etc. (but not size or number), are concerned: *A nickel is less than a dime* (in value).

-fex, a learned borrowing from Latin, where it meant "maker," used in the formation of compound words: *spinifex.* [< L = *fec-* (var. s. of *facere* to make) + *-s* nom. sing. ending. See -FIC]

fey (fā), *adj.* **1.** *Chiefly Scot.* appearing to be under a spell; marked by an apprehension of death, calamity, or evil. **2.** supernatural; unreal; enchanted: *elves, fairies, and other fey creatures.* **3.** being in unnaturally high spirits, a state formerly thought to precede death. **4.** whimsical; strange, otherworldly: *a fey character.* [ME; OE *fǣge* doomed to die; c. Icel *feigr* doomed, G *feig* cowardly]

Feyn·man (fīn′mən), *n.* **Richard Phillips,** born 1918, U.S. physicist: Nobel prize 1965.

fez (fez), *n., pl.* **fez·zes.** a cap, shaped like a truncated cone, usually of red felt and ornamented with a black tassel, worn esp. by men in the Near East. [< Turk *fes,* after *Fes* FEZ] —**fezzed,** *adj.*

Fez (Turkish)

Fez (fez), *n.* a city in N Morocco: formerly one of the traditional capitals of the sultanate in the former French zone. 216,133 (1960).

Fez·zan (fez zän′), *n.* a former province in SW Libya: a portion of the Sahara with numerous oases. 47,000 (est. 1956); 220,000 sq. mi. *Chief town:* Murzuq.

ff, *Music.* fortissimo.

ff., 1. folios. 2. (and the) following (pages, verses, etc.).

FFA, Future Farmers of America.

F.F.A., free from alongside (ship). Also, **f.f.a.**

F.F.I., 1. free from infection. 2. French Forces of the Interior.

F.F.V., First Families of Virginia.

f.g., *Basketball, Football.* field goal; field goals.

FHA, Federal Housing Administration.

F.I., Falkland Islands.

fi·a·cre (fē ä′kər, -äk′; *Fr.* fyA′kʀᵊ), *n., pl.* **-a·cres** (-ä′kərz, -äks′; *Fr.* -kʀᵊ). a small horse-drawn carriage. [< F; after the Hotel de St. *Fiacre* in Paris, where such carriages were first for hire]

fi·an·cé (fē′än sā′, fē än′sā; *Fr.* fyäɴ sā′), *n., pl.* **-cés** (-sāz′, -sāz; *Fr.* -sā′). a man engaged to be married; a man to whom a girl or woman is engaged: *He is the fiancé of Miss Jones.* [< F: betrothed, ptp. of *fiancer,* OF *fiancier* < *fiance* a promise = *fi(er)* (to) trust (<< L *fīdere*) + *-ance* -ANCE]

fi·an·cée (fē′än sā′, fē än′sā; *Fr.* fyäɴ sā′), *n., pl.* **-cées** (-sāz′, -sāz; *Fr.* -sā′). a girl or woman engaged to be married; a girl or woman to whom a man is engaged: *She is the fiancée of Mr. Phelps.* [< F; fem. of FIANCÉ]

fi·as·co (fē as′kō), *n., pl.* **-cos, -coes.** a complete and ignominious failure. [< It: lit., bottle < Gmc; see FLASK[1]]

fi·at (fī′ət, -at), *n.* 1. an authoritative decree, sanction, or order: *a royal fiat.* 2. an arbitrary decree or pronouncement, esp. by a person or group of persons having absolute authority to enforce it: *The king ruled by fiat.* [< L: let it be done, 3rd sing. pres. subj. of *fierī* to come about, become]

fi·at lux (fē′ät lo͝oks′; *Eng.* fī′at luks′), *Latin.* let there be light.

fi′at mon′ey, *U.S.* paper currency made legal tender by law, but not based on or convertible into coin.

fib[1] (fib), *n., v.,* **fibbed, fib·bing.** —*n.* 1. a trivial lie; minor falsehood. —*v.i.* 2. to tell a fib. [short for *fibble-fable* nonsense, gradational compound based on FABLE] —**fib′ber,** *n.* —**Syn. 1.** See **falsehood.**

fib[2] (fib), *v.t.,* **fibbed, fib·bing.** *Brit.* to strike; beat. [?]

fi·ber (fī′bər), *n.* 1. a fine, threadlike piece, as of cotton, jute, or asbestos. 2. a slender filament: *a fiber of platinum.* 3. filaments collectively. 4. matter or material composed of filaments: *a plastic fiber.* 5. something resembling a filament. 6. an essential character, quality, or strength: *people of strong moral fiber.* 7. *Bot.* **a.** filamentous matter from the bast tissue or other parts of plants, used for industrial purposes. **b.** a slender, threadlike root of a plant. **c.** a slender, tapered cell that serves to strengthen tissue. 8. *Anat., Zool.* a slender, threadlike element or cell, as of nerve, muscle, or connective tissue. Also, **fibre.** [ME *fibre* < L *fibra* filament] —**fi′ber·less,** *adj.*

fi·ber·board (fī′bər bōrd′, -bôrd′), *n.* 1. a building material made of wood or other plant fibers compressed and cemented into rigid sheets. 2. a sheet of this.

fi·ber·fill (fī′bər fil′), *n.* lightweight synthetic fibers, such as polyester, used as filling for pillows, padding, etc.

Fi·ber·glas (fī′bər glas′, -gläs′), *n. Trademark.* fiberglass.

fi·ber·glass (fī′bər glas′, -gläs′), *n.* a material consisting of extremely fine filaments of glass that are combined in yarn and woven into fabrics, used in masses as a thermal and acoustical insulator, or embedded in various resins to make boat hulls, fishing rods, and the like. Also, **fi′ber glass′.**

fi′ber op′tics, the technique of transmitting light, images, etc., through long, thin transparent fibers, as of glass, plastic, or the like. —**fi′ber-op′tic,** *adj.*

Fi·bo·nac′ci num′bers (fē′bō nä′chē), *Math.* the unending sequence 1, 1, 2, 3, 5, 8, 13, 21, 34, . . . where each term is defined as the sum of its two predecessors. Also called **Fibonac′ci se′quence.** [named after Leonardo *Fibonacci* (1180?–1250?), It. mathematician]

fibr-, var. of **fibro-** before a vowel: *fibrin.*

fi·bre (fī′bər), *n.* fiber. —**fi′bre·less,** *adj.*

fi·bri·form (fī′brə fôrm′, fib′rə-), *adj.* of the form of a fiber or fibers.

fi·bril (fī′brəl, fib′rəl), *n.* 1. a small or fine fiber or filament. 2. *Bot.* one of the delicate hairs on the young roots of some plants. 3. *Anat.* an extracellular threadlike structure or filament. [< NL *fibril(la),* dim. of L *fibra* FIBER] —**fi′bril·lar,** *adj.* —**fi′bril·lose′,** *adj.*

fi·bril·la (fī bril′ə, fi-), *n., pl.* **-bril·lae** (-bril′ē). a fibril.

fi·bril·late (fī′brə lāt′, fib′rə-), *v.,* **-lat·ed, -lat·ing.** —*v.t.* 1. to cause to undergo fibrillation. —*v.i.* 2. to undergo fibrillation.

fi·bril·la·tion (fī′brə lā′shən, fib′rə-), *n.* 1. the formation of fibrils. 2. *Pathol.* uncontrolled twitching or quivering of muscular fibrils, as of the cardiac muscles.

fi·bril·li·form (fī bril′ə fôrm′, fi-), *adj.* of the form of a fibril.

fi·brin (fī′brin), *n.* 1. *Biochem.* a white, tough, strongly elastic fibrous protein, formed in the coagulation of blood. 2. *Bot.* a substance like fibrin found in some plants; gluten. —**fi′brin·ous,** *adj.*

fibrino-, a combining form of **fibrin:** *fibrinolysis.*

fi·brin·o·gen (fī brin′ə jən), *n. Biochem.* a globulin occurring in blood and yielding fibrin in the coagulation of blood.

fi·brin·o·gen·ic (fī′brə nō jen′ik), *adj. Physiol.* producing fibrin. Also, **fi·bri·nog·e·nous** (fī′brə noj′ə nəs). —**fi′brin·o·gen′i·cal·ly,** *adv.*

fi·bri·nol·y·sin (fī′brə nol′i sin), *n.* 1. Also called **plasmin.** *Biochem.* a proteolytic enzyme that causes fibrinolysis in blood clots. 2. Also called **streptokinase.** *Pharm.* an enzyme used chiefly for the breakdown of blood clots, as in certain cases of thrombosis.

fi·bri·nol·y·sis (fī′brə nol′i sis), *n., pl.* **-ses** (-sēz′). *Biochem.* the disintegration or dissolution of fibrin, esp. by enzymatic action. —**fi·bri·no·lyt·ic** (fī′brə nō lit′ik, fī brin′ᵊlit′-), *adj.*

fibro-, a learned borrowing from Latin meaning "fiber," used in the formation of compound words: *fibroblast; fibrovascular.* Also, *esp. before a vowel,* **fibr-.** [comb. form repr. L *fibra* FIBER]

fi·bro·blast (fī′brə blast′), *n. Anat.* a cell that contributes to the formation of connective tissue fibers. —**fi′bro·blas′tic,** *adj.*

fi·broid (fī′broid), *adj.* 1. resembling fiber or fibrous tissue. 2. composed of fibers, as a tumor. —*n.* 3. *Pathol.* a tumor largely composed of smooth muscle.

fi·bro·in (fī′brō in), *n. Biochem.* an indigestible protein, a principal component of spider webs and silk. [FIBRO- + -IN[2], modeled on F *fibroïne*]

fi·bro·ma (fī brō′mə), *n., pl.* **-ma·ta** (-mə tə), **-mas.** *Pathol.* a tumor consisting essentially of fibrous tissue. —**fi·brom·a·tous** (fī brom′ə təs), *adj.*

fi·bro·sis (fī brō′sis), *n. Pathol.* the development in an organ of excess fibrous connective tissue. —**fi·brot·ic** (fī brot′ik), *adj.*

fi·brous (fī′brəs), *adj.* containing, consisting of, or resembling fibers. —**fi′brous·ly,** *adv.* —**fi′brous·ness,** *n.*

fi·bro·vas·cu·lar (fī′brō vas′kyə lər), *adj. Bot.* composed of fibrous and conductive tissue: *a fibrovascular bundle.*

fib·u·la (fib′yə lə), *n., pl.* **-lae** (-lē′), **-las.** 1. *Anat., Zool.* the outer and thinner of the two bones of the leg, extending from the knee to the ankle. 2. *Zool.* a corresponding bone of the hind limb, in a quadruped, often rudimentary or ankylosed with the tibia. 3. a clasp or brooch, often ornamented, used by the ancient Greeks and Romans. [< L: fastener; akin to FIX; see -ULE] —**fib′u·lar,** *adj.*

-fic, a suffix meaning "making," "producing," "causing," appearing in adjectives borrowed from Latin: *frigorific; honorific; pacific; prolific.* [< L *-fic(us)* making, producing = *-fic-* (var. s. of *facere* to make) + *-us* adj. suffix; in some words r. *-fique* < MF < L *-fic(us)*]

F.I.C.A., Federal Insurance Contributions Act.

-fication, a suffix of nouns of action or state corresponding to verbs ending in **-fy:** *deification; pacification.* [< L *-ficātiōn-* (s. of *-ficātiō*) a making (see -FY, -TION); in some words r. ME *-ficacioun* < AF]

fiche (fēsh), *n.* microfiche.

Fich·te (fiᴋʜ′tə), *n.* **Jo·hann Gott·lieb** (yō′hän gôt′lēp), 1762–1814, German philosopher. —**Fich′te·an,** *adj., n.* —**Fich′te·an·ism,** *n.*

fich·u (fish′o͞o; *Fr.* fē shʏ′), *n., pl.* **fich·us** (fish′o͞oz; *Fr.* fē shʏ′). a light neck scarf or shawl of muslin, lace, or the like. [< F: small shawl]

fick·le (fik′əl), *adj.* 1. casually changeable; capricious: *fickle weather.* 2. not constant or loyal in affections. [ME *fikel,* OE *ficol* deceitful, akin to *fācen* treachery, *fician* to deceive, *gefic* deception] —**fick′le·ness,** *n.* —**Syn. 1.** unstable, variable. **2.** inconstant.

fi·co (fē′kō), *n., pl.* **-coes.** 1. *Archaic.* the merest trifle. 2. *Obs.* fig[1] (def. 5). [< It *fico, fica* FIG[1]]

fict., fiction.

fic·tile (fik′tᵊl; *Brit.* fik′tīl), *adj.* 1. capable of being molded; plastic. 2. molded into form by art. 3. made of earth, clay, etc., by a potter. 4. of or pertaining to pottery. 5. easily led, as a person or a mob; tractable. [< L *fictil(is)* earthen (lit., moldable). See FICTION; -ILE]

fic·tion (fik′shən), *n.* 1. the class of literature comprising works of imaginative narration, esp. in prose form. 2. works of this class, as novels or short stories: *detective fiction.* 3. something feigned, invented, or imagined; a made-up story; falsehood. 4. the act of feigning, inventing, or imagining. 5. *Law.* an allegation that a fact exists which is known not to exist. [< L *fictiōn-* (s. of *fictiō*) a shaping, hence a feigning, fiction = *fict(us)* molded (ptp. of *fingere*) + *-iōn-* -ION]
—**Syn. 3.** fable, fantasy. FICTION, FABRICATION suggest a story that is without basis in reality. FICTION suggests a story invented and fashioned either to entertain or to deceive: *clever fiction; pure fiction.* FABRICATION applies particularly to a false but carefully invented statement or series of statements, in which some truth is sometimes interwoven, the whole usually intended to deceive: *fabrications to lure speculators.* —**Ant. 3.** fact.

fic·tion·al (fik′shə nᵊl), *adj.* of, pertaining to, or of the nature of fiction: *fictional characters.* —**fic′tion·al·ly,** *adv.*

fic·tion·al·ize (fik′shə nᵊlīz′), *v.t.,* **-ized, -iz·ing.** to make into fiction; give a fictional version of: *to fictionalize a biography.* —**fic′tion·al·i·za′tion,** *n.*

fic·tion·ist (fik′shə nist), *n.* a writer of fiction.

fic·ti·tious (fik tish′əs), *adj.* 1. created, taken, or assumed as a convention or hypothesis; false; not genuine: *fictitious names.* 2. of, pertaining to or consisting of fiction; imaginatively produced or set forth; created by the imagination: *a fictitious hero.* [< L *fictīcius* artificial. See FICTION, -ITIOUS] —**fic·ti′tious·ly,** *adv.* —**fic·ti′tious·ness,** *n.* —**Syn. 1.** spurious, feigned, simulated, fake. **2.** fictional.

fic·tive (fik′tiv), *adj.* 1. fictitious; imaginary. 2. pertaining to the creation of fiction. —**fic′tive·ly,** *adv.*

fid (fid), *n. Naut.* 1. a stout bar of wood or metal lying across the trestletrees of a lower spar of a mast and passing through a hole **(fid hole)** or mortise in the heel of an upper spar so as to support the upper spar. 2. any of various tapered wooden or metal pins for parting the strands in a rope or for forming and stretching grommets. [?]

-fid, a suffix meaning "divided," "lobed," occurring in adjectives borrowed from Latin (*bifid*); on this model, used in the formation of compound words (*pinnatifid*). [< L *-fid(us)* divided = *-fid-* (var. s. of *findere* to split) + *-us* adj. suffix]

fid., fiduciary.

fid·dle (fid′ᵊl), *n., v.,* **-dled, -dling.** —*n.* 1. a musical instrument of the viol family. 2. *Informal.* violin. 3. *Naut.* a barrier to keep dishes, pots, etc., from sliding along or off a table. 4. **fit as a fiddle,** in perfect health; very fit. Also, **as fit as a fiddle.** 5. **play second fiddle.** See **second fiddle.** —*v.i.* 6. *Informal.* to play on the fiddle. 7. to make trifling or fussing movements with the hands (often fol. by *with*): *fiddling with his cuffs.* 8. to trifle, waste time, etc. —*v.t.* 9. *Informal.* to play (a tune) on a fiddle. 10. to trifle or waste (usually used with *away*): *to fiddle time away.* [ME, OE *fithele* (c. G *Fiedel,* D *vedel,* OHG *fidula*), perh. < VL *vītula,* akin to L *vītulārī* to rejoice] —**fid′dler,** *n.*

fid·dle-de-dee (fid′ᵊl di dē′), *interj., n.* nonsense. Also, **fid′dle·de·dee′, fid′dle·dee·dee′.** [FIDDLE + *-de-* (redupl. prefix) + (TWEEDLE)DEE in obs. sense of fiddler]

fid·dle-fad·dle (fid′əl fad′əl), *n., v.,* **-dled, -dling.** *Informal.* —*n.* **1.** nonsense. **2.** something trivial. —*v.i.* **3.** to fuss with trifles. [gradational compound based on FIDDLE] —**fid′dle-fad′dler,** *n.*

fid·dle·head (fid′əl hed′), *n. Naut.* a billethead having a form similar to the volute carved at the upper end of a violin.

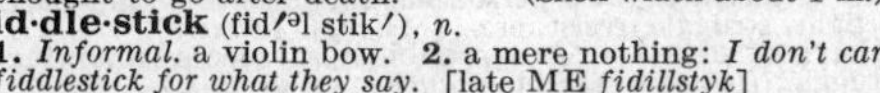

Fiddler crab, *Uca pugilator* (Shell width about 1 in.)

fid′dler crab′, any small, burrowing crab of the genus *Uca,* the male of which has one greatly enlarged claw.

fid′dler's green′, the paradise to which sailors are thought to go after death.

fid·dle·stick (fid′əl stik′), *n.* **1.** *Informal.* a violin bow. **2.** a mere nothing: *I don't care a fiddlestick for what they say.* [late ME *fidillstyk*]

fid·dle·sticks (fid′əl stiks′), *interj.* nonsense. [short for *fiddlestick's end,* i.e., the most worthless part of a worthless weapon]

fid·dling (fid′ling), *adj.* trifling; trivial.

Fi·de·i De·fen·sor (fē′de ē′ de fen′sôr; *Eng.* fī′dē ī′ di fen′sôr), *Latin.* Defender of the Faith: one of the titles of English sovereigns.

fi·del·i·ty (fi del′i tē, fī-), *n., pl.* **-ties. 1.** strict observance of promises, duties, etc. **2.** loyalty. **3.** conjugal faithfulness. **4.** adherence to fact or detail. **5.** accuracy; exactness. **6.** *Electronics.* the ability to transmit or receive signals accurately. [late ME *fidelite* < *fidēlitās* = *fidēli-* (s. of *fidēlis* loyal = *fidē(s)* FAITH + *-lis* adj. suffix) + *-tās* -TY[2]]

fidge (fij), *v.i.,* **fidged, fidg·ing,** *n. Scot.* fidget. [var. of *fitch* to move back and forth; c. Icel *fīkjast* to be eager, MSw *fīkja* to be restless; akin to FICKLE]

fidg·et (fij′it), *v.i.* **1.** to move about restlessly, nervously, or impatiently. —*v.t.* **2.** to cause to fidget; make uneasy. —*n.* **3.** Often, **fidgets.** the condition or an instance of being nervously restless, uneasy, or impatient. **4.** Also, **fidg′et·er.** a person who fidgets. [FIDGE + *-et* (< ?)] —**fidg′et·ing·ly,** *adv.* —**fidg′et·y,** *adj.*

fid′ hole′. See under **fid** (def. 1).

fi·du·cial (fi do͞o′shəl, -dyo͞o′-), *adj.* **1.** *Physics.* accepted as a fixed basis of reference or comparison: *a fiducial point.* **2.** based on or having trust: *fiducial dependence upon God.* [< LL *fīdūciāl(is)* = *fīdūci(a)* trust (akin to *fīdere* to trust) + *-ālis* -AL[1]] —**fi·du′cial·ly,** *adv.*

fi·du·ci·ar·y (fi do͞o′shē er′ē, -dyo͞o′-), *n., pl.* **-ar·ies,** *adj.* —*n.* **1.** *Law.* a person to whom property or power is entrusted for the benefit of another. —*adj.* **2.** *Law.* of or pertaining to the relation between a fiduciary and his principal. **3.** depending on public confidence for value or currency, as fiat money. **4.** *Obs.* like or based on trust or reliance. [< L *fīdūciāri(us)* of something held in trust] —**fi·du′ci·ar′i·ly,** *adv.*

fie (fī), *interj.* (used, now usually facetiously, to express disapproval.) [ME *fi* < MF < L; cf. Icel *fȳ,* L *phy*]

Fied·ler (fēd′lər), *n.* **Arthur,** 1894–1979, U.S. symphony conductor.

fief (fēf), *n.* a fee, feud, or estate in land held of a feudal lord. [< F, var. of OF *fieu, fie,* c. AF *fe* FEE < Gmc; cf. OHG *fihu,* OE *feoh* cattle, property; akin to L *pecū* flock of sheep, *pecus* cattle, *pecūnia* wealth]

field (fēld), *n.* **1.** a piece of open or cleared ground, esp. one suitable for pasture or tillage. **2.** *Sports.* **a.** an area or piece of ground devoted to sports or contests. **b.** the area in which field events are held. **c.** (in betting) all the contestants or numbers that are grouped together as one: *to bet on the field in a horse race.* **d.** the players on the playing ground in football: *to dodge through a broken field.* **3.** *Baseball.* **a.** the team in the field, as opposed to the one at bat. **b.** the outfield. **4.** *Mil.* **a.** the scene or area of active military operations. **b.** a battleground. **c.** a battle. **5.** an expanse of anything: *a field of ice.* **6.** any region characterized by a particular feature, product, mineral, mining activity, etc.: *a gold field.* **7.** the surface of a canvas, coin, shield, etc., on which something is portrayed: *a gold star on a field of blue.* **8.** (in a flag) the ground of each division. **9.** a sphere of activity, interest, etc., esp. within a particular business or profession: *the field of teaching; the field of Shakespearean scholarship.* **10.** the area or region drawn on or serviced by a business or profession; outlying areas where business, selling, mining, etc., is carried on, in contrast to a home or branch office: *our representatives in the field.* **11.** Also called **field of force.** *Physics.* a region of space under the influence of some agent, as electricity or magnetism. **12.** Also called **field of view.** *Optics.* the entire angular expanse visible through an optical instrument at a given time. **13.** *Elect.* the structure in a generator or motor that produces a magnetic field around a rotating armature. **14.** *Math.* a number system that has the same properties relative to the operations of addition, subtraction, multiplication, and division as the number system of all real numbers. **15.** *Photog.* the area of a subject that is viewed by a lens at a particular diaphragm opening. **16.** *Computer Technol.* **a.** a set of one or more characters, not necessarily part of the same machine word, considered as a single unit of information. **b.** Also called **card field.** (in a punch card) any number of columns regularly used for recording the same information. **17.** *Obs.* open country. **18. play the field,** *Informal.* to vary one's activities, esp. to date a number of members of the opposite sex rather than only one. —*v.t. Baseball, Cricket.* **19.** to catch or pick up (the ball) in play. **20.** to place (a player, group of players, or a team) in the field to play. —*v.i. Baseball, Cricket.* **21.** to act as a fielder; field the ball. **22.** to take to the field. —*adj.* **23.** *Sports.* **a.** of, taking place, or competed for on the field and not on the track, as the discus throw or shot put. **b.** of or pertaining to field events. **24.** *Mil.* of or pertaining to campaign and active combat service as distinguished from service in rear areas or at headquarters: *a field soldier.* **25.** of or pertaining to a field. **26.** grown or cultivated in a field. **27.** working as a farm laborer in a field: *a field hand.* **28.** working as a salesman, representative, etc., in the field: *a field agent.* [ME, OE *feld;* c. G *Feld*]

Field (fēld), *n.* **1. Cyrus West,** 1819–92, U.S. financier: projector of the first Atlantic cable. **2. Eugene,** 1850–95, U.S. poet and journalist. **3. Marshall,** 1834–1906, U.S. merchant and philanthropist.

field′ artil′lery, *Mil.* artillery mobile enough to accompany troops in the field.

field′ corn′, feed corn grown for stock.

field′ day′, **1.** a day devoted to outdoor sport or athletic contests. **2.** an outdoor gathering; outing; picnic. **3.** a day for military exercises and display. **4.** an occasion or opportunity for unrestricted activity, amusement, etc.: *The children had a field day with their new skateboards.*

field·er (fēl′dər), *n.* **1.** *Baseball, Cricket.* a player who fields the ball. **2.** *Baseball.* any of the players of the infield or the outfield, esp. an outfielder.

field′er's choice′, *Baseball.* a fielder's putting out of a base runner when a play at first base would put out the batter.

field′ event′, an event in a track meet that involves throwing, as a discus or javelin, or jumping and is not performed on the running track.

field·fare (fēld′fâr′), *n.* a European thrush, *Turdus pilaris,* having reddish-brown plumage with an ashy head and a blackish tail. [ME *feldefare* (with two *f*'s by assimilation), OE *feldeware* field-dweller]

field′ glass′es, a compact, easily portable binocular telescope for use out-of-doors. Also, **field′ glass′.**

field′ goal′, **1.** *Football.* a three-point goal made by place-kicking or drop-kicking the ball over the crossbar between the opponent's goal posts. **2.** *Basketball.* a goal made while the ball is in play.

field′ gun′, *Mil.* a cannon mounted on a carriage for service in the field.

field′ hock′ey, a game, played on a rectangular field, in which two teams of 11 players each compete in driving a small ball into each other's goal, using hockey sticks.

field′ house′, **1.** a building at an athletic field having dressing facilities, storage spaces, etc. **2.** a building sheltering an area used for athletic events.

Field·ing (fēl′ding), *n.* **Henry,** 1707–54, English novelist, dramatist, and essayist.

field′ inten′sity, *Physics.* See **field strength.**

field′ line′, *Physics.* See **line of force.**

field′ mag′net, a magnet for producing a magnetic field, as in a particle accelerator or an electric motor.

field′ mar′shal, an officer of the highest military rank in the British and certain other armies, and of the second highest rank in the French army.

field′ mouse′, any of various short-tailed mice or voles inhabiting fields and meadows.

field′ mush′room. See under **mushroom** (def. 2).

field′ of′ficer, *Mil.* an officer holding the grade of major, lieutenant colonel, or colonel.

field′ of force′, *Physics.* field (def. 11).

field′ of hon′or, the scene of a battle or duel.

field′ of view′, *Optics.* field (def. 12).

field′ of vi′sion, the entire view encompassed by the eye when it is trained in any particular direction. Also called **visual field.**

field·piece (fēld′pēs′), *n. Mil.* a field gun.

field′ ra′tion, *U.S. Army.* ration issued in actual articles to troops in the field.

Fields (fēldz), *n.* **W. C.** (*William Claude Dukenfield*), 1880–1946, U.S. comedian.

field′ span′iel, one of a British breed of hunting spaniels having a flat or slightly waved, usually black coat.

field·stone (fēld′stōn′), *n.* stone found in fields and used for building purposes.

field′ strength′, *Physics.* the vector sum of all forces exerted by a field on a unit mass, unit charge, unit magnetic pole, etc., at a given point within the field. Also called **field intensity.**

field′ the′ory, *Physics.* a detailed mathematical description of the distribution and movement of matter under the influence of one or more fields.

field′ tri′al, a competition among hunting dogs under natural conditions in the field, judged on the basis of performance in hunting.

field′ trip′, **1.** a trip to gain firsthand knowledge away from the classroom, as to a museum, factory, geological area, etc. **2.** a trip by a scholar or researcher to gather data at first hand, as to an archaeological or anthropological site.

field′ wind′ing (wīn′ding), *Elect.* the electrically conducting circuit, usually a number of coils wound on individual poles and connected in series, that produces the magnetic field in a motor or generator.

field′ work′, research or exploration done in the field: *archaeological field work.* —**field′work′er,** *n.*

fiend (fēnd), *n.* **1.** a diabolically cruel or wicked person. **2.** an evil spirit. **3.** Satan; the devil. **4.** *Informal.* a mischievous or annoying person: *Those children are little fiends.* **5.** *Informal.* a person hopelessly addicted to some pernicious habit: *an opium fiend.* **6.** *Informal.* a person excessively interested in some game, sport, etc.; fan; buff: *a bridge fiend.* [ME *feend,* OE *fēond;* c. G *Feind,* Icel *fjandr,* Goth *fijands* foe, orig. prp. of *fijan* to hate]

fiend·ish (fēn′dish), *adj.* diabolically cruel and wicked. —**fiend′ish·ly,** *adv.* —**fiend′ish·ness,** *n.*

fierce (fērs), *adj.,* **fierc·er, fierc·est. 1.** menacingly wild, savage, or hostile. **2.** violent in force or intensity: *fierce winds.* **3.** furiously eager or intense: *fierce competition.* **4.** *Informal.* extremely bad or severe: *a fierce cold.* [ME *fiers* < OF < L *ferus* wild, fierce] —**fierce′ly,** *adv.* —**fierce′ness,** *n.*
—**Syn. 1.** untamed; furious. FIERCE, FEROCIOUS suggest vehemence and violence. FIERCE suggests violence of temper, manner, or action: *fierce in repelling a foe.* FEROCIOUS implies fierceness or cruelty, esp. of a bloodthirsty kind, in disposition or action: *a ferocious glare; ferocious brutality.* —**Ant. 1.** tame, mild.

fi·e·ri fa·ci·as (fī′ə rī′ fā′shē as′), *Law.* a writ commanding a sheriff to levy and sell as much of a debtor's property as necessary to satisfy a creditor's claim. [< L: lit., have it made = *fierī* to be made + *faciās* cause, 2nd sing. pres. subj. of *facere* to bring about]

fier·y (fīər′ē, fī′ə rē), *adj.*, **fier·i·er, fier·i·est.** **1.** consisting of, attended with, or containing fire. **2.** intensely hot. **3.** like or suggestive of fire; flashing; flaming: *a fiery red; angry, fiery eyes.* **4.** intensely impetuous or passionate: *a fiery speech.* **5.** easily angered or provoked. **6.** flammable, as gas in a mine. **7.** inflamed, as a tumor or sore. **8.** causing a burning sensation, as certain liquors or condiments. [ME *fi(e)ry*] —**fier′i·ly,** *adv.* —**fier′i·ness,** *n.* —**Syn. 4.** fervent, vehement, spirited, impassioned. —**Ant. 2–4.** cool, cold.

fier′y cross′, a burning cross, the emblem of several organizations, notably the Ku Klux Klan.

Fie·so·le (*It.* fye′zô le), *n.* **1. Gio·van·ni da** (*It.* jô vän′nē dä). See **Angelico, Fra.** **2.** a town in central Italy, near Florence: Etruscan and ancient Roman ruins; cathedral. 12,481 (1961).

fi·es·ta (fē es′tə; *Sp.* fyes′tä), *n., pl.* **-tas** (-təz; *Sp.* -täs). **1.** (in Spain and Latin America) a festive celebration of a religious holiday. **2.** any festival or festive celebration. [< Sp < L *festa;* see FEAST]

fife (fīf), *n., v.,* **fifed, fif·ing.** —*n.* **1.** a high-pitched transverse flute used commonly in military and marching music. —*v.t., v.i.* **2.** to play on a fife. [< G *Pfeife* PIPE[1]] —**fif′er,** *n.*

Fife

Fife (fīf), *n.* a county in E Scotland. 321,110 (est. 1964); 505 sq. mi. *Cap.:* Cupar. Also called **Fife·shire** (fīf′shēr, -shər).

fife′ rail′, *Naut.* a rail surrounding a mast for holding belaying pins. Cf. **pin rail.**

fif·teen (fif′tēn′), *n.* **1.** a cardinal number, ten plus five. **2.** a symbol for this number, as 15 or XV. **3.** a set of this many persons or things. —*adj.* **4.** amounting to 15 in number. [ME, OE *fiftene*]

fif·teenth (fif′tēnth′), *adj.* **1.** next after the fourteenth; being the ordinal number for 15. **2.** being one of 15 equal parts. —*n.* **3.** a fifteenth part, esp. of one (1/15). **4.** the fifteenth member of a series. **5.** *Music.* the interval of two octaves. [ME *fiftenthe* (see FIFTEEN, -TH[2]); r. ME *fiftethe,* OE *fīftēotha*]

fifth (fifth), *adj.* **1.** next after the fourth; being the ordinal number for five. **2.** being one of five equal parts. —*n.* **3.** a fifth part, esp. of one (1/5). **4.** the fifth member of a series. **5.** a fifth part of a gallon of liquor or spirits; 4/5 of a quart. **6.** *Music.* **a.** a tone on the fifth degree from another tone (counted as the first). **b.** the interval between such tones. **c.** the harmonic combination of such tones. [earlier *fift,* ME *fifte,* OE *fīfta; -th* by analogy with FOURTH, etc.] —**fifth′ly,** *adv.*

Fifth′ Amend′ment, an amendment to the Constitution of the U.S., providing chiefly that no person be required to testify against himself in a criminal case and that no person be subjected to double jeopardy.

fifth′ col′umn, **1.** a group of people who, although residing in a country, act traitorously and subversively out of a secret sympathy with an enemy. **2.** (originally) Falangist sympathizers in Madrid during the Spanish Civil War who were prepared to betray the city which was under attack by four columns of the insurgents' army. —**fifth′ col′umnist.**

Fifth′ Repub′lic, the republic established in France in 1958, the successor of the Fourth Republic.

fifth′ wheel′, **1.** a horizontal ring or segment of a ring placed above the front axle of a carriage and designed to support the forepart of the body while allowing it to turn freely in a horizontal plane. **2.** an extra wheel for a four-wheeled vehicle. **3.** a superfluous or unwanted person or thing.

fif·ti·eth (fif′tē ith), *adj.* **1.** next after the forty-ninth; being the ordinal number for 50. **2.** being one of 50 equal parts. —*n.* **3.** a fiftieth part, esp. of one (1/50). **4.** the fiftieth member of a series. [ME *fiftithe,* OE *fīftigotha*]

fif·ty (fif′tē), *n., pl.* **-ties,** *adj.* —*n.* **1.** a cardinal number, ten times five. **2.** a symbol for this number, as 50 or L. **3.** a set of this many persons or things. **4. fifties,** the numbers, years, degrees, or the like, between 50 and 59, as in referring to numbered streets, indicating the years of a lifetime or of a century, or degrees of temperature. **5.** *Informal.* a fifty-dollar bill. —*adj.* **6.** amounting to 50 in number. [ME; OE *fīftig*]

fif·ty-fif·ty (fif′tē fif′tē), *adv. Informal.* **1.** with equality of shares, as of profits, expenses, etc. —*adj.* **2.** shared equally. **3.** half good, favorable, or likely and half bad, unfavorable, or unlikely: *He has a fifty-fifty chance of winning the game.*

fig[1] (fig), *n.* **1.** any moraceous tree or shrub of the genus *Ficus,* esp. a small tree, *F. Carica,* bearing a turbinate or pear-shaped fruit. **2.** the fruit of such a tree or shrub, or of any related species. **3.** any of various plants having a fruit somewhat resembling this. **4.** a contemptibly trifling or worthless amount; the least bit: *His help wasn't worth a fig.* **5.** a gesture of contempt. [ME *fige* < OF < OPr *figa* < VL **fica,* r. L *ficus;* but note OE *fegīgo* condyloma]

fig[2] (fig), *v.,* **figged, fig·ging,** *n. Informal.* —*v.t.* **1.** to dress or array (usually fol. by *out*). **2.** to furbish (usually fol. by *up*). —*n.* **3.** dress or array: *to appear at a party in full fig.* [earlier *feague* to liven, whip up < G *fegen* to furbish, sweep, clean; akin to FAIR[1]]

fig., **1.** figurative. **2.** figuratively. **3.** figure; figures.

fight (fīt), *n., v.,* **fought, fight·ing.** —*n.* **1.** a battle or combat. **2.** any contest or struggle: *a fight for recovery from an illness.* **3.** an angry argument or disagreement. **4.** *Boxing.* a bout or contest. **5.** ability or inclination to fight: *There was no fight left in him.* —*v.i.* **6.** to engage in combat; attempt to defeat an adversary. **7.** to contend in any manner; strive vigorously for or against something: *He fought against despair.* —*v.t.* **8.** to contend with in battle; war against. **9.** to contend with or against in any manner: *to fight crime.* **10.** to carry on (a battle, duel, etc.). **11.** to make (one's way) by fighting or striving. **12.** to cause or set (a boxer, cock, etc.) to fight. **13.** to manage or maneuver (troops, ships, guns, planes, etc.) in battle. [ME; OE *fe(o)htan;* c. G *fechten;* akin to L *pectere* to comb]
—**Syn. 1, 2.** encounter, engagement, fray, skirmish, melee; scuffle, tussle, row. FIGHT, COMBAT, CONFLICT, CONTEST denote a struggle of some kind. FIGHT connotes a hand-to-hand struggle for supremacy, literally or in a figurative sense. COMBAT suggests an armed encounter to settle a dispute. CONFLICT implies a bodily, mental, or moral struggle caused by opposing views, beliefs, etc. CONTEST applies to either a friendly or a hostile struggle for a definite prize or aim. **6.** struggle. **7.** contest, struggle.

fight·er (fī′tər), *n.* **1.** *Boxing.* a boxer. **2.** *Mil.* an aircraft designed to destroy enemy aircraft in the air and to protect bomber aircraft. **3.** a person having the will or inclination to fight, struggle, resist, etc. [ME; OE *fēohtere*]

fight′ing chance′, a possibility of success following a struggle: *He has a fighting chance to get well.*

fig′ leaf′, **1.** the leaf of a fig tree. **2.** something intended to conceal what may be considered indecorous or indecent.

fig·ment (fig′mənt), *n.* **1.** a mere product of mental invention; a fantastic notion. **2.** a feigned, invented, or imagined story, theory, etc. [late ME < L *figment(um)* something made or feigned = *fig-* (s. of *fingere* to mold, feign) + *-mentum* -MENT]

fig·ur·al (fig′yər əl), *adj.* consisting of human or animal figures: *the figural representations in ancient wall paintings.* [ME < LL *figūrāl(is)*]

fig·u·rant (fig′yo͞o rant′; *Fr.* fē gy rän′), *n., pl.* **-rants** (-rants′; *Fr.* -rän′). a ballet dancer who dances only with others in groups or figures. [< F, n. use of prp. of *figurer* to FIGURE, appear in; see -ANT]

fig·ur·ate (fig′yər it), *adj.* **1.** of a certain determinate figure or shape. **2.** *Music.* characterized by the use of passing notes or other embellishments; florid. [< L *figūrāt(us)* formed, shaped, ptp. of *figūrāre*] —**fig′ur·ate·ly,** *adv.*

fig·u·ra·tion (fig′yə rā′shən), *n.* **1.** the act of shaping into a particular figure. **2.** the resulting figure or shape. **3.** the act of representing figuratively. **4.** a figurative representation: *allegorical figurations.* **5.** *Music.* **a.** the employment of passing notes or other embellishments. **b.** the figuring of a bass part. [late ME *figuracioun* < L *figūrātiōn-* (s. of *figūrātiō*) a shaping]

fig·ur·a·tive (fig′yər ə tiv), *adj.* **1.** of the nature of or involving a figure of speech, esp. a metaphor; metaphorical; not literal: *a figurative expression.* **2.** abounding in or fond of figures of speech. **3.** representing by means of a figure or likeness, as in drawing or sculpture. **4.** representing by a figure or emblem; emblematic. [late ME < LL *figūrātīv(us)* (see FIGURATE, -IVE); r. ME *figuratif* < MF] —**fig′ur·a·tive·ly,** *adv.* —**fig′ur·a·tive·ness,** *n.*

fig·ure (fig′yər; *Brit.* fig′ər), *n., v.,* **-ured, -ur·ing.** —*n.* **1.** a written symbol other than a letter. **2.** a numerical symbol, esp. an Arabic numeral. **3.** an amount or value expressed in numbers. **4. figures,** the use of numbers in calculating; arithmetic: *to be poor at figures.* **5.** the form or shape of something; outline. **6.** the bodily form or frame: *a graceful figure.* **7.** a character or personage, esp. one of distinction: *a well-known figure in society.* **8.** the appearance or impression made by a person or sometimes a thing. **9.** a representation, pictorial or sculptured, esp. of the human form. **10.** an emblem or symbol: *The dove is a figure of peace.* **11.** *Rhet.* a figure of speech. **12.** a design or pattern, as in cloth. **13.** a movement or series of movements in skating. **14.** *Music.* a short succession of musical notes, as either a melody or a group of chords, that produces a single and distinct impression. **15.** *Geom.* a combination of geometric elements disposed in a particular form or shape: *The circle, square, and polygon are plane figures.* **16.** *Logic.* the form of a categorical syllogism with respect to the relative position of the middle term. **17.** *Obs.* a phantasm or illusion. —*v.t.* **18.** to compute or calculate (often fol. by *up*): *to figure up a total.* **19.** to express in figures. **20.** to mark or adorn with a design or pattern. **21.** to represent or express by a figure of speech. **22.** to represent by a pictorial or sculptured figure; picture or depict; trace (an outline, silhouette, etc.). **23.** *Informal.* to conclude, reason, or think about. **24.** *Music.* **a.** to embellish with passing notes or other decorations. **b.** to write figures above or below (a bass part) to indicate accompanying chords. —*v.i.* **25.** to compute or work with numerical figures. **26.** to be or appear, esp. conspicuously: *His name figures in my report.* **27.** (of a situation, act, etc.) to be logical or expected: *He quit the job when he didn't get a raise—it figured.* **28. figure on,** *Informal.* **a.** to count or rely on. **b.** to take into consideration; plan on: *You had better figure on running into heavy traffic leaving the city.* **29. figure out,** *U.S. Informal.* **a.** to calculate; compute. **b.** to understand; solve. [ME < L *figūra* shape, trope = *fig-* (s. of *fingere* to shape) + *-ūra* -URE] —**fig′ure·less,** *adj.* —**fig′ur·er,** *n.* —**Syn. 2.** number. **3.** sum, total; price. **5.** See **form.**

fig·ured (fig′yərd), *adj.* **1.** formed or shaped: *figured stones.* **2.** represented by a pictorial or sculptured figure. **3.** ornamented with a device or pattern. [ME, ptp. of *figuren* to FIGURE; see -ED[2]]

fig′ured bass′ (bās). See **thorough bass.**

fig′ure eight′, a representation in outline of the number eight as traced on ice in figure skating. Also called **figure of eight.**

fig·ure·head (fig′yər hed′), *n.* **1.** a person who is head of a group, company, etc., in title but has no real authority. **2.** *Naut.* a carved figure or bust on a ship's prow.

fig′ure of eight′, **1.** See **figure eight.** **2.** a knot made by forming a bight on the standing part of a rope, turning the end once around the standing part, and passing it through the bight. See illus. at **knot.**

fig′ure of speech′, *Rhet.* any expressive use of language, as a metaphor, simile, antithesis, etc. Cf. **trope** (def. 1).

fig′ure skat′ing, ice skating in which the skater traces patterns on the ice in a prescribed manner. —**fig′ure skat′er.**

fig·ur·ine (fig′yə rēn′), *n.* a small ornamental figure of pottery, metalwork, etc.; statuette. [< F < It *figurina*]

fig·wort (fig′wûrt′), *n.* **1.** any of numerous, usually coarse, herbs of the genus *Scrophularia.* **2.** any scrophulariaceous plant.

Fi·ji (fē′jē), *n.* **1.** an independent archipelago in the S Pacific, N of New Zealand, comprising the **Fi′ji Is′lands** and a smaller group to the NW; formerly a British colony, now a member of the Commonwealth. 585,000; 7040 sq. mi. *Cap.:* Suva. **2.** a native of Fiji.

Fi·ji·an (fē′jē ən, fi jē′ən), *adj.* **1.** of, pertaining to, or characteristic of Fiji, its inhabitants, or their language. —*n.* **2.** a Fiji. **3.** the Austronesian language of the Fijian people.

fil (fil), *n.* fils.

fil·a·gree (fil′ə grē′), *n., adj., v.t.,* **-greed, -gree·ing.** filigree.

fil·a·ment (fil′ə mənt), *n.* **1.** a very fine thread or threadlike structure; a fiber or fibril: *filaments of gold.* **2.** a single fibril of natural or synthetic textile fiber. **3.** *Bot.* **a.** the stalklike portion of a stamen, supporting the anther. **b.** a long slender cell or series of attached cells, as in some algae, fungi, etc. **4.** (in an incandescent lamp) the threadlike conductor, often of tungsten, which is heated to incandescence by the passage of an electric current. **5.** *Electronics.* the heating element (sometimes also acting as a cathode) of an electron tube, resembling the filament in an incandescent lamp. [< NL *fīlāment(um)* = ML *fīlā(re)* (to) wind thread, spin (see FILE[1]) + *-mentum* -MENT] —**fil·a·men·ta·ry** (fil′ə men′tə rē), **fil′a·men′tous,** *adj.*

fi·lar (fī′lər), *adj.* **1.** of or pertaining to a thread or threads. **2.** having threads or the like. [< L *fīl(um)* a thread + -AR[1]]

fi·lar·i·a (fi lâr′ē ə), *n., pl.* **-lar·i·ae** (-lâr′ē ē′). any slender, threadlike, nematode worm of the family *Filariidae* and related families, parasitic when adult in the blood or tissues of vertebrates, and developing as a larva in certain blood-sucking arthropods. [< NL; see FILE[1], -ARIA] —**fi·lar′i·al,** *adj.*

fil·a·ri·a·sis (fil′ə rī′ə sis), *n. Pathol.* the presence of filarial worms in the blood and lymph channels, lymph glands, and other tissues. [< NL]

fil·a·ture (fil′ə chər), *n.* **1.** the act of forming into threads, as the reeling of silk from cocoons. **2.** a reel for drawing off silk from cocoons. **3.** an establishment for reeling silk. [< F < ML *fīlātūra* the spinning art = *fīlāt(us)* spun (ptp. of *fīlāre;* see FILE[1]) + *-ūra* -URE]

fil·bert (fil′bərt), *n.* **1.** the thick-shelled, edible nut of certain cultivated varieties of hazel, esp. of *Corylus Avellana,* of Europe. **2.** a tree or shrub bearing such nuts. [ME, short for *filbert nut,* so called because ripe by Aug. 22 (St. Philbert's day)]

filch (filch), *v.t.* to steal (esp. something of small value); pilfer. [ME *filche(n)* to attack (in a body), take as booty, OE *fylcian* to marshal (troops), draw (soldiers) up in battle array < *gefylce* band of men; akin to FOLK] —**filch′er,** *n.*

file[1] (fīl), *n., v.,* **filed, fil·ing.** —*n.* **1.** a folder, cabinet, or other container in which papers, letters, etc., are arranged in convenient order. **2.** a collection of papers, records, etc., so arranged. **3.** a line of persons or things arranged one behind another, as soldiers in a formation (distinguished from *rank*). **4.** one of the vertical lines of squares on a chessboard. **5.** a list or roll. **6. on file,** arranged in order for convenient reference; in a file. —*v.t.* **7.** to arrange (papers, records, etc.) in convenient order for preservation or reference. **8.** to submit (an application, petition, etc.). —*v.i.* **9.** to march in a file or line, as soldiers. **10.** to make application, as for a job. [late ME *file(n)* < MF *file(r)* (to) string documents on a thread or wire, OF: to wind or spin thread < ML *fīlāre* < L *fīl(um)* thread, string] —**fil′er,** *n.*

file[2] (fīl), *n., v.,* **filed, fil·ing.** —*n.* **1.** a long, narrow tool of steel or other metal having a series of ridges or points on its surfaces for reducing or smoothing surfaces of metal, wood, etc. **2.** a small, similar tool for trimming and cleaning fingernails; nail file. —*v.t.* **3.** to reduce, smooth, cut, or remove with or as with a file. [ME; OE *fīl, fēol;* c. G *Feile;* akin to Gk *pikrós* sharp] —**fil′er,** *n.*

file[3] (fīl), *v.t.,* **filed, fil·ing.** *Archaic.* to defile; corrupt. [ME; OE *fȳlan* to befoul, defile < *fūl* FOUL]

file·fish (fīl′fish′), *n., pl.* (*esp. collectively*) **-fish,** (*esp. referring to two or more kinds or species*) **-fish·es. 1.** any marine fishes of the family *Monacanthidae,* having a leathery skin with small, hard scales. **2.** a triggerfish.

fi·let (fi lā′, fil′ā; *Fr.* fē le′), *n., pl.* **fi·lets** (fi lāz′, fil′āz; *Fr.* fē le′), *v.t.* fillet (defs. 1, 8).

fi·let mi·gnon (fi lā′ min yon′, min′yon; *Fr.* fē le mē-nyôN′), *pl.* **fi·lets mi·gnons** (fi lā′ min yonz′, min′yonz; *Fr.* fē le mē nyôN′). a small, tender round of steak cut from the thick end of a beef tenderloin. [< F: dainty fillet]

fil·i·al (fil′ē əl), *adj.* **1.** of, pertaining to, or befitting a son or daughter: *filial obedience.* **2.** noting or having the relation of a child to a parent. **3.** *Genetics.* pertaining to the sequence of generations following the parental generation, each generation being designated by an F followed by a subscript number indicating its place in the sequence. [ME < LL *fīliāl(is)* = L *fīli(us)* son + *-ālis* -AL[1]] —**fil′i·al·ly,** *adv.* —**fil′i·al·ness,** *n.*

fil·i·ate (fil′ē āt′), *v.t.,* **-at·ed, -at·ing. 1.** *Law.* to determine judicially the paternity of, as a bastard child. **2.** *Archaic.* to affiliate; associate. [< ML *fīlāt(us)* like the father (said of a son) = L *fīli(us)* son + *-ātus* -ATE[1]]

fil·i·a·tion (fil′ē ā′shən), *n.* **1.** the fact of being the child of a certain parent. **2.** descent, as from a parent; derivation. **3.** *Law.* the judicial determination of the paternity of a bastard child. **4.** the relation of one thing to another from which it is derived. **5.** an affiliated branch, as of a society. [late ME *filiacion* < ML *fīliātiōn-* (s. of *fīliātiō*)]

fil·i·beg (fil′ə beg′), *n.* the kilt or pleated skirt worn by Scottish Highlanders. Also, **philibeg.** [< ScotGael = *feile* kilt + *beag* little]

fil·i·bus·ter (fil′ə bus′tər), *n.* **1.** *U.S.* the use of irregular or obstructive tactics, as exceptionally long speeches, by a member of a minority in a legislative assembly to prevent the adoption of a measure generally favored or to force a decision almost unanimously disliked. **2.** *Hist.* an irregular military adventurer; freebooter or buccaneer. **3.** *Hist.* a person who engages in an unauthorized military expedition into a foreign country to foment or support a revolution. —*v.i.* **4.** *U.S.* to impede legislation by a filibuster. **5.** *Hist.* to act as a freebooter or military adventurer. —*v.t.* **6.** *U.S.* to impede by legislative filibustering. [< Sp *filibustero* < F *flibustier,* var. of *fribustier* < FREEBOOTER] —**fil′i·bus′ter·er,** *n.* —**fil′i·bus′ter·ism,** *n.*

fil·i·cide (fil′i sīd′), *n.* **1.** a person who kills his son or daughter. **2.** the act of killing one's son or daughter. [< L *fīli(us)* son (*fīli(a)* daughter) + -CIDE] —**fil′i·cid′al,** *adj.*

fil·i·form (fil′ə fôrm′, fī′lə-), *adj.* threadlike; filamentous. [< L *fīl(um)* a thread + -I- + -FORM]

fil·i·gree (fil′ə grē′), *n., adj., v.,* **-greed, -gree·ing.** —*n.* **1.** ornamental work of fine wires, esp. lacy jewelers' work of scrolls and arabesques. **2.** anything very delicate or fanciful: *a filigree of frost.* —*adj.* **3.** composed of or resembling filigree. —*v.t.* **4.** to adorn with or form into filigree. Also, **filagree, fillagree.** [earlier *filigreen,* var. of FILIGRAIN]

fil·ings (fī′lingz), *n.pl.* particles removed by a file.

Fil·i·pi·no (fil′ə pē′nō), *n., pl.* **-nos,** *adj.* —*n.* **1.** an inhabitant of the Philippines. —*adj.* **2.** Philippine. [< Sp < (*las Islas*) *Filipinas* PHILIPPINE (islands)]

fil·is·ter (fil′i stər), *n.* fillister.

fill (fil), *v.t.* **1.** to make full; put as much as can be held into: *to fill a jar with water.* **2.** to occupy to the full capacity: *The crowd filled the hall.* **3.** to supply plentifully: *to fill a house with furniture.* **4.** to feed fully; satiate. **5.** to put into a receptacle: *to fill sand into a pail.* **6.** to be plentiful throughout: *Fish filled the rivers.* **7.** to pervade completely: *The odor filled the room.* **8.** to furnish (a vacancy or office) with an occupant. **9.** to occupy and perform the duties of (a position, post, etc.). **10.** to execute (a purchase order). **11.** to supply (a blank space) with written matter, decorative work, etc. **12.** to meet satisfactorily, as requirements: *This book fills a great need.* **13.** to make up or compound (a medical prescription). **14.** to stop up or close (a cavity, hole, etc.): *to fill a tooth.* **15.** *Naut.* **a.** to distend (a sail) by pressure of the wind so as to impart headway to a vessel. **b.** to brace (a yard) so that the sail will catch the wind. **16.** to add filler, esp. to adulterate: *filled soaps.* **17.** *Building Trades.* to build up the level of (an area) with earth, stones, etc. —*v.i.* **18.** to become full. **19.** to become distended, as sails with the wind. **20. fill away,** *Naut.* **a.** to fall off the wind and proceed on a course. **b.** to brace the yards, so that the sails will catch the wind. **21. fill in, a.** to supply missing or desired information. **b.** to complete (a document, sketch, etc.) by filling spaces. **c.** to substitute for: *to fill in for a colleague who is ill.* **d.** to fill with some material: *to fill in a crack with putty.* **e.** *Slang.* to supply (someone) with information: *Please fill me in on the news.* **22. fill out, a.** to complete (a document, list, etc.) by supplying missing or desired information. **b.** to become larger, fuller, etc. **23. fill the bill.** See **bill**[1] (def. 11). **24. fill up, a.** to fill completely. **b.** to become completely filled. —*n.* **25.** a full supply; an adequate quantity to satisfy want or desire: *to eat one's fill.* **26.** *Building Trades.* a quantity of earth, stones, etc., for building up the level of an area of ground. [ME *fille(n),* OE *fyllan;* c. G *füllen,* Goth *fulljan* to make full; see FULL[1]]

fill·a·gree (fil′ə grē′), *n., adj., v.t.,* **-greed, -gree·ing.** filigree.

fille (fē′yᵊ), *n., pl.* **filles** (fē′yᵊ). *French.* **1.** a daughter. **2.** a girl. **3.** an unmarried woman; spinster.

fille de joie (fē′yᵊ də zhwä′), *pl.* **filles de joie** (fē′yᵊ də zhwä′). *French.* a prostitute. [lit., girl of pleasure]

filled′ gold′, a composition consisting of gold plating welded to and rolled with a backing of brass or other base metal, at least $^1/_{20}$ of the total weight being that of the gold. Also called **rolled gold.** Cf. **gold-filled.**

fill·er (fil′ər), *n.* **1.** a person or thing that fills. **2.** a substance used to fill cracks, pores, etc., as in a surface before painting. **3.** a liquid, paste, or the like used to coat a surface or to give solidity, bulk, etc., to a substance, as paper, a chemical powder, etc. **4.** *Journalism.* material considered of secondary importance, used to fill out a column or page. **5.** *Building Trades.* a plate, slab, block, etc., connecting two parallel members. **6.** an implement used in filling, as a funnel.

fil·lér (fē′lâr, fil′âr), *n., pl.* **-lér.** a money of account of Hungary, the 100th part of a forint. Also, **fil′ler.** [< Hung]

fil·let (fil′it; *usually* fi lā′, fil′ā *for 1, 8*), *n.* **1.** *Cookery.* **a.** a boneless cut or slice of meat or fish, esp. the beef tenderloin. **b.** a piece of veal or other meat boned, rolled, and tied, for roasting. **2.** a ribbon or the like for binding the hair; headband. **3.** a strip of any material used for binding. **4.** *Bookbinding.* **a.** a decorative line impressed on a book cover. **b.** a rolling tool for impressing such lines. **5.** *Archit.* **a.** a narrow, flat molding or area, raised or sunk between larger moldings or areas. See illus. at **molding. b.** a narrow portion of the surface of a column left between adjoining flutes. **6.** *Anat.* lemniscus. **7.** a raised rim or ridge, as a ring on the muzzle of a gun. —*v.t.* **8.** *Cookery.* **a.** to cut or prepare (meat or fish) as a fillet. **b.** to cut fillets from. **9.** to bind or adorn with or as with a fillet. Also, **filet** (for defs. 1, 8). [ME *filet* < MF = *fil* thread (see FILE[1]) + *-et* -ET]

fill-in (fil′in′), *n.* **1.** a person or thing that fills in, as a substitute, replacement, insertion, etc. **2.** *Informal.* a brief, informative summary.

fill·ing (fil′ing), *n.* **1.** something that is put in as a filler: *the filling of a pie.* **2.** *Dentistry.* a substance in plastic form, as cement, amalgam, gold foil, or the like, used to close a cavity in a tooth. **3.** the act of a person or thing that fills; a making or becoming full. **4.** Also called **pick, weft, woof.** *Textiles.* yarn carried by the shuttle and interlacing at right angles with the warp in woven cloth. [ME]

fill′ing sta′tion, a roadside retail station for servicing motor vehicles with gasoline, oil, etc.

fil·lip (fil′əp), *v.t.* **1.** to strike with the nail of a finger snapped from the end of the thumb. **2.** to tap or strike smartly. **3.** to drive or urge on by or as by a fillip. —*v.i.* **4.** to make a fillip with the fingers. —*n.* **5.** the act or an instance of filliping; a smart tap or stroke. **6.** anything that tends to rouse, excite, or revive; a stimulus. [late ME *philippe* to make a signal or sound with thumb and right forefinger; appar. special use of name *Philip.* See FLIP[1]]

fil·lis·ter (fil′i stər), *n.* *Carpentry.* **1.** a rabbet or groove, as one on a window sash to hold the glass and putty. **2.** Also called **fil′lister plane′,** a plane for cutting rabbets or grooves. Also, **filister.** [?]

fil′lister head′, a cylindrical screwhead. See illus. at **screw.**

Fill·more (fil′mōr, -môr), *n.* **Mil·lard** (mil′ərd), 1800–74, 13th president of the United States 1850–53.

fil·ly (fil′ē), *n., pl.* **-lies. 1.** a young female horse. **2.** *Informal.* a girl. [late ME *fyly* < Scand; cf. Icel *fylja* female FOAL]

film (film), *n.* **1.** a thin layer or coating: *a film of grease.* **2.** *Photog.* **a.** a cellulose nitrate or cellulose acetate composition made in thin sheets or strips and coated with a sensitive emulsion for taking photographs. **b.** a sheet, strip, or roll of this. **3.** *Motion Pictures.* **a.** a reel of motion-picture film. **b.** See **motion picture. 4. films, a.** motion pictures collectively. **b.** the motion-picture industry. **5.** a thin skin or membrane. **6.** a delicate web of filaments or fine threads. **7.** a thin haze, blur, or mist. **—***v.t.* **8.** to cover with a film, thin skin, or pellicle. **9.** *Motion Pictures.* **a.** to photograph with a motion-picture camera. **b.** to reproduce in the form of motion pictures: *to film a novel.* **—***v.i.* **10.** to become covered by a film. **11.** *Motion Pictures.* **a.** to be adaptable for filming. **b.** to engage in the production of motion pictures. [ME *filme,* OE *filmen* membrane; akin to FELL[4]]

film′ clip′, *Television.* a strip of motion-picture film used in a telecast, esp. as supplementary material in a live program.

film·dom (film′dəm), *n.* the realm of motion pictures; the motion-picture industry or its personnel. Also called **film′-land′.**

film·strip (film′strip′), *n.* a length of film containing a series of still pictures or titles for projection on a screen.

film·y (fil′mē), *adj.,* **film·i·er, film·i·est.** of the nature of, resembling, or covered with a film. **—film′i·ly,** *adv.* **—film′i·ness,** *n.*

fil·o·plume (fil′ə plōōm′, fī′lə-), *n.* *Ornith.* a specialized, hairlike feather having a slender shaft with few or no barbs. [< NL *filoplūma.* See FILE[1], -O-, PLUME]

fi·lose (fī′lōs), *adj.* **1.** threadlike. **2.** ending in a threadlike process. [< L *fīl(um)* a thread + -OSE[1]]

fils (fils), *n., pl.* **fils. 1.** a bronze coin of Iraq and Jordan, the thousandth part of a dinar. **2.** a cupronickel coin of Kuwait, the thousandth part of a dinar or the hundredth part of a dirhem. Also, **fil.** [< Ar]

fils (fēs), *n., pl.* **fils.** *French.* son: sometimes used after a name with the meaning of *Jr.,* as in *Dumas fils.* Cf. **père.**

fil·ter (fil′tər), *n.* **1.** any substance, as cloth, paper, porous porcelain, or a layer of charcoal or sand, through which liquid, air, smoke, or the like, is passed to remove suspended impurities or to recover solids. **2.** any device, as a tank, tube, cigarette filter tip, etc., containing such a substance for filtering. **3.** *Informal.* a filter-tipped cigarette. **4.** *Photog.* a screen of dyed gelatin or glass for controlling the rendering of color or for diminishing the intensity of light. **5.** *Physics.* a device that selectively damps oscillations of certain frequencies while not affecting oscillations of other frequencies. **—***v.t.* **6.** to remove by the action of a filter. **7.** to act as a filter for. **8.** to pass (something) through or as through a filter. **—***v.i.* **9.** to pass through or as through a filter. **—***adj.* **10.** *Informal.* filter-tipped: *a filter cigarette.* [late ME *filtre* < ML *filtr(um)* felt, piece of felt used to strain liquids < Gmc; see FELT[2]] **—fil′ter·er,** *n.*

fil·ter·a·ble (fil′tər ə bəl), *adj.* **1.** capable of being filtered. **2.** *Bacteriol.* capable of passing through bacteria-retaining filters: *a filterable virus.* Also, **filtrable. —fil′ter·a·bil′i·ty, fil′ter·a·ble·ness,** *n.*

fil′ter bed′, a pond or tank having a false bottom covered with sand and serving to filter river or pond waters.

fil′ter pa′per, porous paper used in filtering.

fil′ter tip′, 1. a mouthpiece for a cigarette or cigar with a means of filtering the smoke. **2.** a cigarette or cigar with such a mouthpiece. **—fil′ter-tipped′,** *adj.*

filth (filth), *n.* **1.** foul matter; offensive or disgusting dirt or refuse. **2.** a foul condition: *to live in filth.* **3.** moral impurity, corruption, or obscenity. **4.** vulgar or obscene language. [ME; OE *fȳlth*]

filth·y (fil′thē), *adj.,* **filth·i·er, filth·i·est. 1.** characterized by or of the nature of filth; completely or disgustingly dirty. **2.** vulgar; obscene: *filthy language.* **3.** contemptibly offensive, vile, or objectionable. [ME] **—filth′i·ly,** *adv.* **—filth′i·ness,** *n.* **—Syn. 1.** See **dirty. 2.** dirty, pornographic.

fil·tra·ble (fil′trə bəl), *adj.* filterable. **—fil′tra·bil′i·ty,** *n.*

fil·trate (fil′trāt), *v.,* **-trat·ed, -trat·ing,** *n.* **—***v.t., v.i.* **1.** to filter. **—***n.* **2.** liquid that has been passed through a filter. [< ML *filtrāt(us)* filtered, ptp. of *filtrāre*] **—fil′trat·a·ble,** *adj.* **—fil·tra′tion,** *n.*

fi·lum (fī′ləm), *n., pl.* **-la** (-lə). a threadlike structure, object, or part; filament. [< L: thread, filament, fiber]

fim·bri·a (fim′brē ə), *n., pl.* **-bri·ae** (-brē ē′). Often, **fimbriae.** *Bot., Zool.* a fringe or fringed border. [< NL, L: border, edge, fringe] **—fim′bri·al,** *adj.*

fim·bri·ate (fim′brē it, -āt′), *adj.* *Bot., Zool.* having a border of hairs or filiform processes. Also, **fim′bri·at′ed.** [< L *fimbriāt(us)* fringed]

fim·bri·a·tion (fim′brē ā′shən), *n.* *Bot., Zool.* **1.** fimbriate or fringed condition. **2.** a fringe or fringelike part. [< ML *fimbriātiōn-* (s. of *fimbriātiō*)]

Fimbriate petals

fim·bril·late (fim bril′it, -āt), *adj.* *Bot., Zool.* bordered by or having a small or fine fringe. [< NL *fimbrill(a)* little fringe (see FIMBRIA) + -ATE[1]]

fin (fin), *n., v.,* **finned, fin·ning.** **—***n.* **1.** a membranous, winglike or paddlelike organ attached to any of various parts of the body of fishes and certain other aquatic animals, used for propulsion, steering, or balancing. **2.** *Naut.* **a.** a winglike appendage to a hull, as one for controlling the dive of a submarine or for damping the roll of a surface vessel. **b.** See **fin keel. 3.** *Aeron.* **a.** See **vertical stabilizer. b.** any of certain small, subsidiary structures on an aircraft, usually placed parallel to the plane of symmetry. **4.** any of a number of standing ridges, as on a radiator, intended to maximize heat transfer to the surrounding air by exposing a large surface area. **5.** any part, as of a mechanism, resembling a fin. **6.** *Slang.* a five-dollar bill. **7.** Usually, **fins.** flipper (def. 2). **—***v.t.* **8.** to cut off the fins from (a fish). **9.** to provide or equip with a fin or fins. **—***v.i.* **10.** to move the fins; lash the water with the fins, as a whale when dying. [ME, OE *finn;* c. D *vin,* LG *finne;* akin to Sw *fena*] **—fin′less,** *adj.* **—fin′like′,** *adj.*

Fin., 1. Finland. **2.** Finnish.

fin., financial.

fin·a·ble (fī′nə bəl), *adj.* subject to payment of a fine. Also, **fineable. —fin′a·ble·ness,** *n.*

fi·na·gle (fi nā′gəl), *v.,* **-gled, -gling.** *Informal.* **—***v.i.* **1.** to practice deception or fraud. **—***v.t.* **2.** to trick or cheat (a person) (often fol. by *out of*): *He finagled the backers out of a fortune.* **3.** to get or achieve (something) by guile or trickery. **4.** to wangle: *to finagle free tickets.* [*finaig-* (var. of *fenegue,* alter. of RENEGE) + -LE] **—fi·na′gler,** *n.*

fi·nal (fīn′əl), *adj.* **1.** pertaining to or coming at the end; last in place, order, or time. **2.** ultimate: *the final goal.* **3.** conclusive or decisive: *a final decision.* **4.** *Law.* precluding further controversy on the questions passed upon. **5.** constituting the end or purpose: *a final result.* **—***n.* **6.** something that is last or terminal. **7.** Often, **finals, a.** the last and decisive game, contest, or round in a series, as in sports. **b.** the last, usually comprehensive, examination in a course of study. [ME < L *fīnāl(is)* = *fīn(is)* end + *-ālis* -AL[1]] **—Syn. 1.** See **last**[1].

fi·nal·e (fi nal′ē, -nä′lē), *n.* **1.** *Music.* the last piece, division, or movement of a composition. **2.** the concluding part of any performance, course of proceedings, etc. [< It, n. use of *finale* (adj.) < L *fīnālis* FINAL]

fi·nal·ism (fīn′əliz′əm), *n.* the doctrine or belief that all events are determined by ultimate goals or purposes.

fi·nal·ist (fīn′əlist), *n.* a person entitled to take part in the final trial or round, as of an athletic contest.

fi·nal·i·ty (fī nal′i tē), *n., pl.* **-ties** for 2. **1.** state, quality, or fact of being final; conclusiveness or decisiveness. **2.** something that is final; a final act, utterance, etc.

fi·na·lize (fīn′əlīz′), *v.,* **-lized, -liz·ing.** **—***v.t.* **1.** to put into final form; complete all the administrative details of. **—***v.i.* **2.** to complete an agreement; conclude negotiations: *We should finalize by the end of the week.* **—fi′na·li·za′tion,** *n.* **—Usage.** Although FINALIZE is regarded by many as a recent, bureaucratic coinage, the word has been current in both American and British English for at least 40 years, and it appears in all kinds of writing, usually in formal contexts.

fi·nal·ly (fīn′əlē), *adv.* **1.** at the final point or moment. **2.** in a final manner; conclusively or decisively. [ME]

fi·nance (fi nans′, fī′nans), *n., v.,* **-nanced, -nanc·ing.** **—***n.* **1.** the management of public revenues; the conduct or transaction of money matters generally, esp. those affecting the public, as in the fields of banking and investment. **2. finances,** the pecuniary resources, as of a government, company, organization, or individual; revenue. **—***v.t.* **3.** to supply with capital or obtain or furnish credit for. **4.** to manage financially. [late ME *finaunce* < MF *finance* = *fin(er)* (to) end, settle, pay (see FINE[2]) + *-ance* -ANCE]

finance′ com′pany, an institution engaged in such specialized forms of financing as purchasing accounts receivable, extending credit to retailers and manufacturers, discounting installment contracts, and granting loans with goods as security.

fi·nan·cial (fi nan′shəl, fī-), *adj.* **1.** pertaining to money matters; pecuniary: *financial operations.* **2.** of or pertaining to those commonly engaged in dealing with money and credit. **—fi·nan′cial·ly,** *adv.*

—Syn. 1. FINANCIAL, FISCAL, MONETARY, PECUNIARY refer to matters concerned with money. FINANCIAL usually refers to money matters or transactions of some size or importance: *a financial wizard.* FISCAL is used esp. in connection with government funds, or those of any organization: *the end of the fiscal year.* MONETARY relates esp. to money as such: *a monetary system or standard.* PECUNIARY refers to money as used in making ordinary payments: *a pecuniary obligation or reward.*

fin·an·cier (fin′ən sēr′, fī′nən-; *Brit.* fi nan′sē ər), *n.* **1.** a person who is skilled in or engaged in financial operations, whether public, corporate, or individual. **—***v.t.* **2.** to finance. **—***v.i.* **3.** to act as a financier. [< F]

Finback, *Balaenoptera physalus* (Length 60 to 70 ft.)

fin·back (fin′bak′), *n.* any whalebone whale of the genus *Balaenoptera,* having a prominent dorsal fin, esp. *B. physalus,* of Atlantic and Pacific coasts; rorqual. Also called **fin′back whale′.**

finch (finch), *n.* any of numerous small passerine birds of the family *Fringillidae,* including the buntings, sparrows, crossbills, linnets, grosbeaks, etc., most of which have a short, conical bill adapted for eating seeds. [ME; OE *finc;* c. D *vink,* G *Fink;* akin to Gk *spíngos* finch]

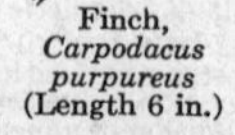

Finch, *Carpodacus purpureus* (Length 6 in.)

find (fīnd), *v.,* **found, find·ing,** *n.* **—***v.t.* **1.** to come upon by chance; meet with: *He found a nickel in the street.* **2.** to learn, attain, or obtain by search or effort: *to find a job; I hope you'll find happiness someday.* **3.** to discover: *Columbus found America.* **4.** to recover (something lost). **5.** to gain or regain the use of: *to find one's voice.* **6.** to learn by experience, or perceive: *to find something to be true.* **7.** to ascertain by study or calculation: *to find the sum of several numbers.* **8.** *Law.* **a.** to determine after judicial inquiry: *to find a person guilty.* **b.** to pronounce as an official act (an indictment, verdict, or judgment). **9.** to provide or furnish: *Come visit; we'll find a bed for you.* **—***v.i.* **10.** to determine an issue after judicial inquiry: *The jury found for* *the plaintiff.* **11. find fault.** See **fault** (def. 11). **12. find oneself,** to discover and follow one's real interests or talents. **13. find out, a.** to discover or confirm the truth of (something). **b.** to detect or expose, as a crime or offense. **c.** to uncover the true nature, identity, or intentions of (someone). —*n.* **14.** act of finding or discovering. **15.** something found, esp. a valuable or gratifying discovery. [ME *finde(n),* OE *findan;* c. G *finden,* D *vinden,* Icel *finna,* Goth *finthan*]

find·er (fīn′dər), *n.* **1.** a person or thing that finds. **2.** Also called **viewfinder.** *Photog.* a camera attachment enabling a photographer to determine what will be included in the picture. **3.** *Astron.* a small, wide-angled telescope attached to a larger one for locating an object. [ME *findere*]

fin de siè·cle (fan də sye′klə), *French.* **1.** end of the century, esp. of or pertaining to the end of the 19th century. **2.** (toward the close of the 19th century) **a.** of, pertaining to, or characterized by sophisticated concepts of art, society, etc. **b.** decadent.

find·ing (fīn′ding), *n.* **1.** the act of a person or thing that finds; discovery. **2.** something that is found or ascertained. **3.** *Law.* a decision or verdict after judicial inquiry. **4. findings,** tools, materials, etc., used by artisans. [ME, OE]

Find·lay (fin′lē, find′-), *n.* a city in NW Ohio. 35,800 (1970).

fine[1] (fīn), *adj.,* **fin·er, fin·est,** *adv., v.,* **fined, fin·ing.** —*adj.* **1.** of superior or best quality; of high or highest grade; excellent: *fine wine.* **2.** consisting of minute particles: *fine sand.* **3.** very thin or slender: *fine thread.* **4.** keen or sharp, as a tool. **5.** of delicate texture or workmanship: *fine tracery.* **6.** highly skilled or accomplished: *a fine musician.* **7.** trained down to the proper degree, as an athlete. **8.** characterized by refinement or elegance; polished or refined: *fine manners; a fine lady.* **9.** affectedly ornate or elegant. **10.** delicate or subtle: *a fine distinction.* **11.** showy or smart; smartly dressed. **12.** good-looking or handsome: *a fine young man.* **13.** free from imperfections; pure. **14.** (of an alloy of precious metal) containing a large or specified amount of pure metal. —*adv.* **15.** *Informal.* in an excellent manner; very well: *She cooks fine.* **16.** finely; delicately. —*v.i.* **17.** to become fine or finer. —*v.t.* **18.** to make fine or finer, esp. by refining or pulverizing. **19.** to reduce the size or proportions of (often used with *down* or *away*): *to fine down the ornamentation on a building.* **20.** to clarify (wines or spirits) by filtration. [ME *fin* < OF < L *fīn(is)* end, utmost limit] —**Syn. 1.** superior; perfect; select. FINE, CHOICE, ELEGANT, EXQUISITE are terms of praise with reference to quality. FINE is a general term: *a fine horse, person, book.* CHOICE implies a discriminating selection of the object in question: *a choice piece of steak.* ELEGANT suggests a refined and graceful superiority that is generally associated with luxury and a cultivated taste: *elegant furnishings.* EXQUISITE suggests an admirable delicacy, finish, or perfection: *exquisite lace.*

fine[2] (fīn), *n., v.,* **fined, fin·ing.** —*n.* **1.** a sum of money exacted as a penalty for an offense or dereliction; mulct: *a parking fine.* **2.** *Law.* a fee paid by a feudal tenant to the landlord, as on the renewal of tenure. **3.** *Eng. Law.* a conveyance of land through decree of a court, based upon a simulated lawsuit. **4.** *Archaic.* a penalty of any kind. **5. in fine, a.** in short; briefly. **b.** in conclusion; finally. —*v.t.* **6.** to subject to a fine or pecuniary penalty. [ME *fin* < OF < L *fīn(is)* end, ML: settlement, payment]

fi·ne[3] (fē′nā), *n.* *Music.* the end of a repeated section, whether da capo or dal segno. [< It < L *finis* end]

fine·a·ble (fī′nə bəl), *adj.* finable. —**fine′a·ble·ness,** *n.*

fine′ art′, visual art considered primarily in relation to aesthetic criteria or judgments of beauty and meaningfulness: specifically, painting, sculpture, drawing, watercolor, graphics, and architecture. Cf. **commercial art.**

fine-cut (fīn′kut′), *adj.* cut into very thin strips: *fine-cut tobacco.*

fine-grain (fīn′grān′), *adj.* *Photog.* **1.** (of an image) having an inconspicuous or invisible grain. **2.** (of a developer or emulsion) permitting the grain of an image to be inconspicuous or invisible.

fine-grained (fīn′grānd′), *adj.* **1.** being of fine grain or texture, as certain woods or leathers. **2.** fine-grain.

fine·ly (fīn′lē), *adv.* **1.** in a fine manner; excellently; elegantly; delicately. **2.** in fine particles or pieces: *finely chopped onions.* [ME *fineliche*]

fine′ nail′, a short, steel finishing nail from 1 to 1½ inches long. Cf. **threepenny** (def. 2b).

fine·ness (fīn′nis), *n.* **1.** state or quality of being fine. **2.** the proportion of pure precious metal in an alloy, often expressed in parts per thousand. [late ME; see FINE[1], -NESS]

fine′ print′, the detailed wording of a contract, lease, insurance policy, or the like, often in type smaller than the main body of the document and including restrictions or qualifications that could be considered disadvantageous or undesirable. Also called **small print.**

fin·er·y[1] (fī′nə rē), *n.* fine or showy dress, ornaments, etc. [FINE[1] + -ERY]

fin·er·y[2] (fī′nə rē), *n., pl.* **-er·ies.** *Metalworking.* a hearth for converting cast iron into wrought iron; refinery. [< MF *finerie* < *finer* to refine. See FINE[1], -ERY]

fines herbes (fēn′ erbz′, ûrbz′; *Fr.* fēn zerb′), *Cookery.* a combination of finely chopped herbs for flavoring soups, sauces, omelets, etc. [< F: fine herbs]

fine·spun (fīn′spun′), *adj.* **1.** spun or drawn out to a fine thread. **2.** highly or excessively refined or subtle. Also, **fine′-spun′.**

fi·nesse (fi nes′), *n., v.,* **-nessed, -ness·ing.** —*n.* **1.** extreme delicacy or subtlety in performance, skill, discrimination, etc. **2.** skill and adroitness in handling a difficult or highly sensitive situation. **3.** a trick, artifice, or stratagem. **4.** *Bridge.* an attempt to win a trick with a card while holding a higher card not in sequence with it, in the hope that the card or cards between will not be played. —*v.i.* **5.** to use finesse or artifice. **6.** *Bridge.* to make a finesse. —*v.t.* **7.** to bring about by finesse or artifice. **8.** *Bridge.* **a.** to make a finesse with (a card). **b.** to force the playing of (a card) by a finesse. [late ME: degree of excellence or purity < MF]

fine′-tooth comb′ (fīn′to͞oth′), **1.** a comb having narrow, closely set teeth. **2. go over** or **through with a fine-tooth comb,** to examine in close detail; search thoroughly. Also, **fine′-toothed comb′** (fīn′to͞otht′, -to͞othd′).

fine-tune (fīn′to͞on′), *v.t.,* **-tuned, -tun·ing. 1.** to adjust (a radio or television receiver) to keep it on the best possible audio or video signal. **2.** *Informal.* to use appropriate methods or controls to produce stability or improvement in: *to fine-tune the nation's economy.*

fin·foot (fin′fo͝ot′), *n., pl.* **-foots.** any of several aquatic birds of the family *Heliornithidae,* of South America, Asia, and Africa, related to the rails and coots and characterized by lobate toes. —**fin′-foot′ed,** *adj.*

Fin′gal's Cave′ (fing′gəlz), a cave on the island of Staffa, in the Hebrides, Scotland. 227 ft. long; 42 ft. wide.

fin·ger (fing′gər), *n.* **1.** any of the terminal members of the hand, esp. one other than the thumb. **2.** a part of a glove made to receive a finger. **3.** the breadth of a finger as a unit of measurement; digit. **4.** the length of a finger: approximately 4½ inches. **5.** something like a finger in form, use, or purpose: *the finger on the speedometer.* **6.** any of various projecting parts of machines. **7. burn one's fingers,** to suffer injury or loss by meddling or by acting rashly. **8. have a finger in the pie, a.** to have an interest or share in. **b.** to meddle in. **9. keep one's fingers crossed,** to wish for good luck or success, as in a specific endeavor. **10. lay** or **put one's finger on, a.** to indicate exactly; remember. **b.** to discover; locate. **11. not lift a finger,** to make no attempt; do nothing. **12. twist around one's little finger,** to exert one's influence easily or successfully upon. —*v.t.* **13.** to touch with the fingers; handle; toy or meddle with. **14.** *Music.* **a.** to play on (an instrument) with the fingers. **b.** to perform or mark (a passage of music) with a certain fingering. —*v.i.* **15.** *Music.* to use the fingers in playing. [ME, OE; c. G *Finger,* D *vinger,* Icel *fingr,* Goth *figgrs*] —**fin′ger·er,** *n.* —**fin′ger·less,** *adj.*

fin′ger board′, 1. (of a violin, cello, etc.) the strip of wood on the neck against which the strings are stopped by the fingers. **2.** keyboard. Also, **fin′ger·board′.**

fin′ger bowl′, a small bowl to hold water for rinsing the fingers at table.

fin·ger·breadth (fing′gər bredth′, -bretth′), *n.* the breadth of a finger: approximately ¾ inch.

fin·gered (fing′gərd), *adj.* **1.** having fingers of a specified kind or number (usually used in combination): *a light-fingered pickpocket.* **2.** spoiled or marred by handling, as merchandise. **3.** *Zool., Bot.* digitate. **4.** (of a musical score) marked to show which fingers to use in playing the notes.

fin·ger·ing (fing′gər ing), *n.* **1.** the act of a person who fingers. **2.** *Music.* **a.** the action or method of using the fingers in playing on an instrument. **b.** the indication of the way the fingers are to be used in performing a piece of music.

Fin′ger Lakes′, a group of elongated glacial lakes in central and W New York: resort region.

fin·ger·ling (fing′gər ling), *n.* **1.** a young or small fish, esp. a very small salmon or trout. **2.** something very small. [late ME: finger stall]

fin·ger·nail (fing′gər nāl′), *n.* the nail at the end of a finger. [ME]

fin′ger paint′, a jellylike paint used chiefly by children in painting with their fingers.

fin·ger-paint (fing′gər pānt′), *v.t., v.i.* to paint by using finger paints on damp or wet paper.

fin′ger paint′ing, 1. the technique of applying paint to wet paper with the fingers to produce a painting. **2.** a painting produced in this way.

fin′ger post′, a guidepost that indicates direction by means of a pointing finger.

fin·ger·print (fing′gər print′), *n.* **1.** an impression of the markings of the inner surface of the fingertip, esp. when made with ink for purposes of identification. —*v.t.* **2.** to take the fingerprints of.

fin·ger·tip (fing′gər tip′), *n.* **1.** the tip of a finger. **2.** a covering used to protect the end joint of a finger. —*adj.* **3.** extending to the fingertips, as a coat, veil, etc. **4. at one's fingertips,** close at hand; easily available.

fin′ger wave′, *Hairdressing.* a wave set by impressing the fingers into hair dampened by lotion or water.

fin·i·al (fin′ē əl, fī′nē-), *n.* **1.** *Archit.* a relatively small, ornamental, terminal feature at the top of a gable, pinnacle, etc. **2.** an ornamental termination to the top of a piece of furniture, or the like. [late ME < L *fīnis* end. See FINE[1], -AL[1]] —**fin′i·aled,** *adj.*

fin·i·cal (fin′i kəl), *adj.* **1.** finicky. **2.** *Archaic.* (of things) overelaborate; too detailed. [FINE[1] + -ICAL] —**fin′i·cal·ness, fin′i·cal′i·ty,** *n.* —**fin′i·cal·ly,** *adv.*

fin·ick·y (fin′ə kē), *adj.* excessively particular or fastidious; difficult to please; fussy. Also, **finnicky, fin·i·king** (fin′ə king), **fin·ick·in** (fin′ə kin). [FINIC(AL) + -Y[1]]

fin·is (fin′is, fē nē′, fī′nis), *n.* end; conclusion. [< L]

fin·ish (fin′ish), *v.t.* **1.** to bring (something) to an end or to completion; complete. **2.** to come to the end of (a course, period of time, etc.): *to finish school.* **3.** to use completely (often fol. by *up* or *off*): *to finish up a can of paint.* **4.** to overcome completely; destroy or kill (often fol. by *off*): *This spray will finish off the cockroaches.* **5.** to complete and perfect in detail; put the final touches on (sometimes fol. by *up*): *She finished up a painting.* **6.** to put a finish on (wood, metal, etc.): *We finished the desk in antique red lacquer.* **7.** to perfect (a person) in education, accomplishments, social graces, etc. —*v.i.* **8.** to come to an end. **9.** to complete a course, project, etc. (sometimes fol. by *up*): *It was nine o'clock when we finished up.* **10.** *Obs.* to die. —*n.* **11.** the end or conclusion; the last stage. **12.** the end of a hunt, race, etc.: *a close finish.* **13.** a decisive ending; death: *a fight to the finish.* **14.** the quality of being finished or completed with smoothness, elegance, etc. **15.** educational or social polish. **16.** the surface coating or texture of wood, metal, etc.: *a glossy finish.* **17.** something used or serving to finish, complete, or perfect a thing. **18.** ornamental woodwork or the like, esp. inside a building. **19.** a final coat of plaster or paint. **20.** a material for application in finishing. [ME *finisshe(n)* < MF *finiss-,* long s. of *finir* < L *fīnīre* to end. See FINE[1]] —**fin′ish·er,** *n.* —**Syn. 1.** terminate, conclude, close. **3.** consume. **11.** termination. See **end**[1]. **14.** polish.

fin·ished (fin′isht), *adj.* **1.** ended or completed. **2.** completed or perfected in all details. **3.** polished to the highest degree of excellence: *a finished piece of writing.* **4.** highly accomplished: *a finished violinist.* **5.** condemned, doomed, or in the process of extinction.

fin′ishing nail′, a slender nail having a small globular head, and used for finish work. See illus. at **nail.**

fin′ishing school′, a private school, usually at the high-school or junior-college level that educates young women for their lives in polite society.

Fin·is·terre (fin′i stâr′; *Sp.* fē′nēs teR′Re), *n.* **Cape,** a headland in NW Spain: the westernmost point of Spain.

fi·nite (fī′nīt), *adj.* **1.** having bounds or limits; not too great or too small to be measurable. **2.** *Math.* **a.** (of a set of elements) capable of being completely counted. **b.** not infinite or infinitesimal. **c.** not zero. **3.** subject to limitations or conditions, as of space, time, circumstances, or the laws of nature: *man's finite existence.* —*n.* **4.** something that is finite. [< L *fīnīt(us)* limited, ptp. of *fīnīre*] —**fi′nite·ly,** *adv.* —**fi′nite·ness,** *n.*

fi′nite verb′, a verb form which distinguishes person, number, and tense, and also mood or aspect, as *opens* in *She opens the door.*

fin·i·tude (fin′i to͞od′, -tyo͞od′, fī′ni-), *n.* state or quality of being finite.

fink (fiŋk), *Slang.* —*n.* **1.** a strikebreaker. **2.** a labor spy. **3.** an informer; stool pigeon. **4.** a contemptible or thoroughly unattractive person. —*v.i.* **5.** to inform to the police; squeal. **6.** to act as a strikebreaker; scab. [< G slang (? < Yiddish): orig., student who does not belong to a club; lit., FINCH]

fin′ keel′, *Naut.* a finlike projection extending downward from the keel of a sailboat, serving to prevent lateral motion and acting as additional ballast.

Fin·land (fin′lənd), *n.* **1.** Finnish, **Suomi.** a republic in N Europe: formerly a province of the Russian Empire. 4,720,300; 130,119 sq. mi. *Cap.:* Helsinki. **2.** **Gulf of,** an arm of the Baltic, S of Finland.

Fin·land·er (fin′lən dər), *n.* an inhabitant of Finland.

Fin·lay (fin′lā), *n.* **Car·los Juan** (kär′lōs wän), 1833–1915, U.S. physician, born in Cuba.

fin·mark (fin′märk′), *n.* the markka of Finland. Also, **finnmark.** [< Sw; see FINN, MARK[2]]

Finn (fin), *n.* **1.** an inhabitant or native of Finland. **2.** any native speaker of Finnish, as in America or Russia. **3.** a native speaker of any Finnic language. [OE *Finnas* (pl.)]

Finn (fin), *n.* *Irish Legend.* a king of the Tuatha De Danann and the father of Ossian: the subject of many legends. Also, **Fionn.**

Finn, Finnish (def. 1). Also, **Finn.**

fin·nan had·die (fin′ən had′ē), smoked haddock. Also called **fin′nan had′dock.** [lit., haddock of *Findhorn,* fishing port in Scotland]

Finn·ic (fin′ik), *adj.* **1.** of or belonging to a branch of the Uralic language family that includes esp. Finnish, Estonian, and Lapp. —*n.* **2.** the Finnic branch of Uralic. Also, **Finnish.**

fin·nick·y (fin′i kē), *adj.* finicky.

Finn·ish (fin′ish), *n.* **1.** the principal language of Finland, a Uralic language related closely to Estonian and remotely to Hungarian. *Abbr.:* Finn, Finn. **2.** Finnic. —*adj.* **3.** of or pertaining to Finland or its inhabitants. **4.** Finnic.

finn·mark (fin′märk′), *n.* finmark.

Fin·no-U·gric (fin′ō o͞o′grik, -yo͞o′-), *n.* **1.** a subfamily of Uralic languages of eastern Europe and western Siberia, including esp. Finnish, Estonian, Lapp, Hungarian, and several languages spoken in the Ural mountains. —*adj.* **2.** of or pertaining to these languages. Also, **Fin′no-U′gri·an.**

fin·ny (fin′ē), *adj.,* **-ni·er, -ni·est. 1.** pertaining to or abounding in fish. **2.** having fins; finned.

Fin·sen (fin′sən), *n.* **Niels Ry·berg** (nēls RY′beR), 1860–1904, Danish physician: Nobel prize 1903.

Fin·ster·aar·horn (fin′stər är′hôrn), *n.* a mountain in S central Switzerland: highest peak of the Bernese Alps, 14,026 ft.

Fionn (fin), *n.* *Irish Legend.* Finn. Also called **Fionn′ Mac-Cumal′** (mə ko͞ol′).

fiord (fyôrd, fyōrd; *Norw.* fyo͝oR, fyōR), *n.* fjord.

fip·ple (fip′əl), *n.* *Music.* a plug stopping the upper end of a pipe, as a recorder or a whistle, and having a narrow slit through which the player blows. [? special use of dial. *fipple* loose lower lip, pouting lip; cf. Icel *flipi* lower lip of a horse, Norw *flipe* flap, lappet]

fip′ple flute′, *Music.* a recorder or other flutelike instrument equipped with a fipple. Cf. **recorder** (def. 5).

fir (fûr), *n.* **1.** any of the pyramidal coniferous trees of the genus *Abies.* **2.** the wood of such a tree. [ME *firre,* OE *fyrh;* c. OS *furie;* akin to OE *furh-* (in *fuhrwudu* pine), Icel *fura* fir, L *quercus* oak]

Fir·dau·si (fēr dou′sē), *n.* (*Abul Qasim Mansu* or *Hasan*) 932–1020, Persian poet. Also, **Ferdus, Fir·dou′si, Fir·du·si** (fēr do͞o′sē).

fire (fīər), *n., v.,* **fired, fir·ing.** —*n.* **1.** the state, process, or an instance of combustion in which ignited fuel or other material combines with oxygen, giving off light, heat, and flame. **2.** a burning mass of material, as on a hearth or in a furnace. **3.** the destructive burning of a building, town, forest, etc.; conflagration. **4.** heat used for cooking, esp. the lighted burner of a stove: *Put the kettle on the fire.* **5.** brilliance, as of a gem. **6.** burning passion; ardor; enthusiasm. **7.** liveliness of imagination. **8.** fever or inflammation. **9.** severe trial or trouble. **10.** exposure to fire as a means of torture or ordeal. **11.** strength, as of an alcoholic beverage. **12.** a spark or sparks. **13.** the discharge of firearms: *to open fire.* **14.** *Literary.* a luminous object, as a star. **15.** *Archaic.* a composition or device for producing a conflagration or a fiery display. **16.** *Archaic.* lightning or a thunderbolt. **17.** **catch fire,** to become ignited; burn. Also, **catch on fire. 18. go through fire and water,** to brave any danger or endure any trial. **19. hang fire, a.** to be delayed in exploding, or fail to explode. **b.** to be undecided, postponed, or delayed: *The new project is hanging fire.* **20. miss fire, a.** to fail to explode or discharge, as a firearm. **b.** to fail to produce the desired effect; be unsuccessful: *The joke missed fire.* **21. on fire, a.** ignited; burning; afire. **b.** eager; ardent; zealous. **22. play with fire,** to trifle with a serious or dangerous matter. **23. set fire to, a.** to cause to burn; ignite. **b.** to excite; arouse; inflame. Also, **set on fire. 24. under fire, a.** under attack, esp. by military forces. **b.** under censure or criticism. —*v.t.* **25.** to discharge (a gun). **26.** to project (a bullet or the like) by or as if by discharging from a gun. **27.** to set on fire. **28.** to supply with fuel; attend to the fire of. **29.** to subject to heat. **30.** to bake in a kiln; burn. **31.** to heat very slowly for the purpose of drying, as tea. **32.** to inflame, as with passion; fill with ardor. **33.** to inspire. **34.** to light or cause to glow as if on fire. **35.** to subject to explosion or explosive force, as a mine. **36.** *Informal.* to dismiss from a job. **37.** *Informal.* to hurl; throw: *to fire a stone through a window.* **38.** *Archaic.* to drive out or away by, or as by, fire. —*v.i.* **39.** to take fire; be kindled. **40.** to glow as if on fire. **41.** to become inflamed with passion; become excited. **42.** to go off, as a gun. **43.** to discharge a gun: *to fire at a fleeing enemy.* **44.** to hurl a projectile. **45.** (of plant leaves) to turn yellow or brown before the plant matures. **46.** (of an internal-combustion engine) to cause ignition of the air-fuel mixture in a cylinder or cylinders. **47. fire away,** *Informal.* to begin to talk and continue without slackening, as to ask a series of questions. [ME; OE *fyr;* c. Icel *fūrr,* G *Feuer,* Gk *pŷr* (see PYRO-)] —**fire′less,** *adj.* —**fir′er,** *n.*

fire′ alarm′, **1.** a signal that a fire has started. **2.** a bell, siren, horn, etc., that provides such a signal.

fire·arm (fīər′ärm′), *n.* a small-arms weapon from which a projectile is fired by gunpowder.

fire·ball (fīər′bôl′), *n.* **1.** a projectile filled with explosive or combustible material. **2.** a ball of fire, as the sun. **3.** a luminous meteor. **4.** globe-shaped lightning. **5.** the highly luminous central portion of a nuclear explosion. **6.** *Informal.* an unusually energetic or ambitious worker.

fire·bird (fīər′bûrd′), *n.* *U.S. Dial.* any of several small birds having bright red or orange plumage, esp. the Baltimore oriole.

fire′ blight′, *Plant Pathol.* a bacterial disease of pears, apples, quinces, etc., characterized by blossom, twig, and fruit blights, and by stem cankers. [so called from the burnt look of the foliage]

fire·boat (fīər′bōt′), *n.* a powered vessel fitted for fire fighting.

fire·box (fīər′boks′), *n.* **1.** the box or chamber containing the fire of a steam boiler, furnace, etc. **2.** the furnace of a locomotive, where coal, oil, or other fuel is burned to generate steam. **3.** a box or panel with a device for notifying the fire station of an outbreak of fire. **4.** *Obs.* a tinderbox.

fire·brand (fīər′brand′), *n.* **1.** a piece of burning wood or other material. **2.** a person who kindles strife and unrest, inflames the passions, etc. **3.** an extremely energetic or impassioned person. [ME]

fire·brat (fīər′brat′), *n.* a bristletail, *Thermobia domestica,* that lives in areas around furnaces, boilers, steampipes, etc.

fire·break (fīər′brāk′), *n.* a strip of ploughed or cleared land made to check the spread of a prairie or forest fire.

fire·brick (fīər′brik′), *n.* a brick made of fire clay.

fire′ brigade′, **1.** a small fire department privately employed by an institution. **2.** *Brit.* a fire department; hook-and-ladder company.

fire·bug (fīər′bug′), *n.* *Informal.* arsonist; pyromaniac.

fire′ clay′, a refractory clay used for making crucibles, firebricks, etc.

fire′ com′pany, **1.** a company of firemen. **2.** a fire-insurance company.

fire′ control′, *Mil.* technical and sometimes automatic supervision of artillery or naval gunfire on a target, as for range, elevation, etc.

fire·crack·er (fīər′krak′ər), *n.* a paper or cardboard cylinder filled with an explosive and having a fuse, for exploding to make a noise, as during a celebration.

fire-cure (fīər′kyo͝or′), *v.t.,* **-cured, -cur·ing.** to cure (tobacco) by means of open fires, the smoke and flame imparting a creosotic flavor.

fire·damp (fīər′damp′), *n.* a combustible gas consisting chiefly of methane, formed esp. in coal mines.

fire′ depart′ment, **1.** the department of a municipal government charged with the prevention and extinguishing of fire. **2.** the men in this department.

fire·dog (fīər′dôg′, -dog′), *n.* an andiron.

fire·drake (fīər′drāk′), *n.* a mythical fiery dragon. [ME *fyrdrake,* OE *fȳrdraca*]

fire′ drill′, a practice drill of duties and procedures to be followed in case of fire.

fire-eat·er (fīər′ē′tər), *n.* **1.** a juggler who pretends to eat fire. **2.** an easily provoked, belligerent person. —**fire′-eat′ing,** *adj., n.*

fire′ en′gine, a motor truck equipped for fire fighting, usually having a motor-driven pump for shooting water or chemical solutions at high pressure.

fire′ escape′, a metal stairway down an outside wall for escaping from a burning building.

fire′ extin′guisher, a portable apparatus, usually containing chemicals, for putting out a fire.

fire′ fight′, *Mil.* a skirmish, as one preceding a major assault.

fire′ fight′er, fireman (def. 1). —**fire′ fight′ing.**

fire·fly (fīər′flī′), *n., pl.* **-flies.** any of several soft-bodied, nocturnal beetles of the family *Lampyridae,* having light-producing organs at the rear of the abdomen. Also called **glowfly, lightning bug.** Cf. **glowworm.**

Firefly, *Photuris pennsylvanica* A, Adult; B, Larva (Length ½ in.)

fire·guard (fīər′gärd′), *n.* a screen or grating placed in front of an open fireplace as a protection; fire screen.

fire·house (fīər′hous′), *n., pl.* **-hous·es** (-hou′ziz). See **fire station.**

fire′ i′rons, the implements used for tending a fireplace, as tongs, poker, etc. [ME *fire-yren*]

fire′less cook′er, an insulated container which seals in heat for a long enough time to cook food.

fire·light (fīər′līt′), *n.* the light from a fire, as on a hearth. [ME *firlight,* OE *fȳrlēoht*]

fire·lock (fīər′lok′), *n.* **1.** a gun having a lock in which the priming is ignited by sparks struck from flint and steel, as the flintlock musket. **2.** *Archaic.* a soldier armed with such a gun.
fire·man (fīər′mən), *n., pl.* **-men.** **1.** a man employed to extinguish or prevent fires. **2.** a man employed to tend fires, as on a locomotive; stoker. **3.** *U.S. Navy.* an enlisted man assigned to the care and operation of a ship's machinery.
Fi·ren·ze (fē ren′dze), *n.* Italian name of **Florence.**
fire′ o′pal, a red, Mexican opal, often with a color play.
fire·place (fīər′plās′), *n.* **1.** the part of a chimney which opens into a room and in which fuel is burned; hearth. **2.** any open structure, usually of masonry, for containing fire, as at a camp site.
fire·plug (fīər′plug′), *n.* a hydrant.
fire′ pot′, the part of a household furnace in which the fire is made.
fire′ pow′er, *Mil.* **1.** the ability to deliver fire. **2.** the amount of fire delivered by a unit, ship, plane, or weapon. Also, **fire′pow′er.**
fire·proof (fīər′pro͞of′), *adj.* **1.** resistant to destruction by fire; incombustible. —*v.t.* **2.** to make fireproof.
fire·proof·ing (fīər′pro͞o′fing), *n.* **1.** the act or process of rendering fireproof. **2.** material for use in making anything fireproof.
fire-re·sist·ant (fīər′ri zis′tənt), *adj.* noting construction meeting standard requirements when exposed to fire of a certain heat for a certain length of time. —**fire′ resist′ance.**
fire′ room′, *Naut.* a chamber in which the boilers of a steam vessel are fired. Also called **stokehold, stokehole.**
fire′ sale′, a special sale of merchandise supposedly damaged by fire or smoke or by water or chemicals used in extinguishing a fire.
fire′ screen′, fireguard.
fire′ ship′, a vessel loaded with combustibles and explosives, ignited, and set adrift to destroy an enemy's ships or constructions.
fire·side (fīər′sīd′), *n.* **1.** Also called **hearthside.** the space about a fire or hearth. **2.** home. **3.** home or family life. —*adj.* **4.** informal and neighborly in manner: *the President's fireside chat.*
fire′ sta′tion, a building in which fire-fighting apparatus and often firemen are housed; firehouse. Also called **station house.**
fire·stone (fīər′stōn′), *n.* a fire-resisting stone, esp. a kind of sandstone used in fireplaces, furnaces, etc. [late ME *fyyrstone,* OE *fȳrstān*]
Fire·stone (fīər′stōn′), *n.* **Harvey Samuel,** 1868–1938, U.S. industrialist and rubber manufacturer.
fire′ tow′er, a tower, as on a mountain, from which a watch for fires is kept.
fire·trap (fīər′trap′), *n.* a building which, because of its age, material, structure, or the like, is especially dangerous in case of fire.
fire′ wall′, **1.** a wall made of fireproof material to prevent the spread of a fire from one part of a building to another. **2.** *Aeron.* a fireproof wall for isolating the engine compartment from the rest of an aircraft.
fire·ward·en (fīər′wôr′dən), *n.* a person having authority in the prevention or extinguishing of fires, as in towns or camps.
fire·wa·ter (fīər′wô′tər, -wot′ər), *n.* *Informal.* alcoholic drink; liquor.
fire·weed (fīər′wēd′), *n.* any of various plants appearing in recently burned clearings or districts, as the willow herb.
fire·wood (fīər′wo͝od′), *n.* wood for fuel. [ME *ferwode*]
fire·work (fīər′wûrk′), *n.* **1.** Often, **fireworks.** a combustible or explosive device for producing a striking display of light or a loud noise, often also used in signaling at night. **2. fireworks, a.** a pyrotechnic display. **b.** a display of violent temper, esp. between two persons.
fir·ing (fīər′ing), *n.* **1.** the act of a person or thing that fires. **2.** material for a fire; fuel. **3.** the act of baking ceramics or glass.
fir′ing line′, *Mil.* **1.** the positions at which troops are stationed to fire upon the enemy or targets. **2.** the troops firing from this line. **3.** the forefront of any action or activity.
fir′ing pin′, *Ordn.* a plunger in the firing mechanism of a firearm or cannon that strikes the cartridge primer, igniting the propelling charge.
fir′ing squad′, **1.** a military detachment assigned to execute a condemned person. **2.** a military detachment assigned to fire a salute at the burial of a person being honored.
fir·kin (fûr′kin), *n.* **1.** a British unit of capacity usually equal to a quarter of a barrel. **2.** a small wooden vessel or tub for butter, lard, etc. [ME *ferdkyn, firdekyn* = *ferde* (var. of *ferthe* FOURTH) + *-kin* -KIN]
firm[1] (fûrm), *adj.* **1.** not soft or yielding when pressed; comparatively solid, hard, stiff, or rigid: *firm ground.* **2.** securely fixed in place. **3.** steady; not shaking or trembling: *a firm hand.* **4.** not likely to change; fixed; settled; unalterable: *a firm belief.* **5.** steadfast or unwavering, as persons or principles. **6.** indicating firmness or determination: *a firm expression.* —*v.t., v.i.* **7.** to make or become firm. —*adv.* **8.** firmly. [< L *firm(us)*; r. ME *ferm* < MF < L] —**firm′ly,** *adv.* —**firm′ness,** *n.*
—**Syn. 1.** FIRM, HARD, SOLID, STIFF are applied to substances that tend to retain their form unaltered in spite of pressure or force. FIRM often implies that something has been brought from a more yielding state to a fixed or elastic one: *The addition of pectin makes jellies firm.* HARD is applied to substances so resistant that it is difficult to make any impression upon their surface or to penetrate their interior: *as hard as a stone.* SOLID is applied to substances that without external support retain their form and resist pressure: *Water in the form of ice is solid.* It sometimes denotes the opposite of hollow: *a solid block of marble.* STIFF implies rigidity that resists a bending force: *as stiff as a poker.* **2.** fast, stable. **4.** established, confirmed. **5.** determined, immovable, resolute. —**Ant. 1.** yielding, soft.
firm[2] (fûrm), *n.* **1.** a partnership or unincorporated association of two or more persons for carrying on a business. **2.** the name or title under which associated parties transact business: *the firm of Smith & Jones.* [< Sp *firma* signature (hence, legal name of a partnership, etc.) back formation from *firmar* to sign < L *firmāre* to strengthen, confirm < *firm(us)* FIRM[1]] —**Syn. 1.** company, business, concern, house.
fir·ma·ment (fûr′mə mənt), *n.* the vault of heaven; sky. [ME < LL *firmāment(um)* sky, L: support, prop, stay = *firmā(re)* (to) strengthen, support (see FIRM[2]) + *-mentum* -MENT] —**fir·ma·men·tal** (fûr′mə men′təl), *adj.*
fir·man (fûr′mən, fər män′), *n., pl.* **-mans.** an edict or administrative order issued by a Middle Eastern sovereign (formerly by an Ottoman Turkish sultan). [< Turk *ferman* < Pers]
fir′mer chis′el (fûr′mər), *Carpentry.* a narrow-bladed chisel for paring and mortising, driven by hand pressure or with a mallet. [*firmer* < F *fermoir,* b. *formoir* that which forms (< *former* to FORM) and *fermer* to make FIRM[1]]
firn (firn), *n.* névé. [< G (Swiss), n. use of *firn* last year's, old; c. OE *fyrn* former, ancient, Goth *fairneis;* akin to Icel *forn* ancient. See BEFORE]
fir·ry (fûr′ē), *adj.* **1.** of or pertaining to the fir. **2.** made of fir. **3.** abounding in firs.
first (fûrst), *adj.* **1.** being before all others with respect to time, order, rank, importance, etc., used as the ordinal number of *one.* **2.** *Music.* highest or chief among several voices or instruments of the same class: *first alto; first horn.* **3.** *Auto.* low[1] (def. 31). **4. first thing,** before anything else; at once; promptly: *I'll call you first thing when I arrive.* —*adv.* **5.** before all others or anything else in time, order, rank, etc. **6.** for the first time. **7.** in preference to something else; rather; sooner: *I'd die first.* **8.** in the first place; firstly. **9. first and last,** everything considered; above all else. **10. first off,** *Informal.* at the outset; at once. —*n.* **11.** something that is first in time, order, rank, etc. **12.** the beginning. **13.** the first part; first member of a series. **14.** *Auto.* low gear; first gear. **15.** the first place in a race or other competition. **16.** *Baseball.* See **first base** (def. 1). **17.** *Brit. Univ.* **a.** a first-class honors. **b.** a person who has won such honors. **18.** Usually, **firsts.** *Com.* a product or goods of the first or highest quality. [ME; OE *fyr(e)st* (see FORE[1], -EST[1]); c. G *Fürst* prince, lit., he who is first in rank]
first′ aid′, emergency aid or treatment given before regular medical services can be obtained. —**first′-aid′,** *adj.*
First′ Bal′kan War′. See **Balkan War** (def. 1).
first′ base′, **1.** *Baseball.* the first in counterclockwise order of the bases from home plate. **2. get to first base,** *Informal.* to succeed in the initial phase of a plan or undertaking.
first-born (fûrst′bôrn′), *adj.* **1.** first in the order of birth; eldest. —*n.* **2.** a first-born child. **3.** a first result or product. [ME]
first′ cause′, **1.** a cause that does not depend upon any other. **2.** (*caps.*) *Theol.* God. **3.** any prime mover.
first′ class′, **1.** the best, finest, or highest class, grade, or rank. **2.** the most expensive and most luxurious class of accommodation on trains, ships, airplanes, etc. **3.** (in the U.S. postal system) the class of mail consisting of letters, postal cards, or the like, together with all mailable matter sealed against inspection.
first-class (fûrst′klas′, -kläs′), *adj.* **1.** of the highest or best class or quality. **2.** best-equipped and most expensive. **3.** given or entitled to preferred treatment, handling, etc. —*adv.* **4.** by first-class transportation.
first′ cous′in, cousin (def. 1).
First′ day′, (among Quakers) Sunday.
first′-de·gree′ burn′ (fûrst′di grē′), *Pathol.* See under **burn**[1] (def. 31).
First′ Em′pire, the empire (1804–14) established in France by Napoleon Bonaparte.
first′ estate′, the first of the three estates: the clergy in France; the Lords Spiritual in England. Cf. **estate** (def. 5).
first′ fam′ily, **1.** a family having the highest or one of the highest social ranks in a given place. **2.** (*often caps.*) *U.S.* the family of the chief executive of a country, state, or city. **3.** a family descended from a colonist or early settler in a country, region, etc.
first′ floor′, **1.** (in the U.S.) the ground floor of a building. **2.** (in foreign countries, and sometimes in the U.S.) the first floor above the ground floor.
first′ fruits′, **1.** the earliest fruits of the season. **2.** the first products or results of anything. [ME]
first-gen·er·a·tion (fûrst′jen′ə rā′shən), *adj.* noting a U.S. citizen either born as a foreigner and naturalized or born as a native American of foreign-born parents.
first·hand (fûrst′hand′), *adv.* **1.** from the first or the original source. —*adj.* **2.** of or pertaining to the first or original source. **3.** direct from the original source. Also, **first′-hand′.**
first′ inten′tion, *Logic.* intention (def. 4a).
First′ Interna′tional, a socialistic organization (1864–1876) formed to unite and promote the interests of workers throughout the world. Cf. **international** (def. 5).
first′ la′dy, **1.** (*often caps.*) *U.S.* the wife of the chief executive of a country, state, or city. **2.** the foremost woman in any art, profession, or the like.
first′ law′ of mo′tion, *Physics.* See under **law of motion.**
first′ law′ of thermodynam′ics. See under **law of thermodynamics.**
first′ lieuten′ant, *Mil.* a U.S. Army, Air Force, or Marine Corps officer ranking above a second lieutenant and below a captain.
first-line (fûrst′līn′), *adj.* **1.** available for immediate service, esp. combat service: *first-line troops.* **2.** of prime importance or quality.
first·ling (fûrst′ling), *n.* **1.** the first of a kind. **2.** first offspring.
First′ Lord′, *Brit.* the head of a board commissioned to perform the duties of a high office of state: *First Lord of the Admiralty.*
first·ly (fûrst′lē), *adv.* in the first place; first.
first′ mate′, the officer of a merchant vessel next in

command beneath the captain. Also called **chief mate, chief officer, first officer, mate.**

first′ mort′gage, a mortgage having priority over all other mortgages on property. —**first′-mort′gage,** *adj.*

first′ name′. See **given name.**

first-night·er (fûrst′nī′tər), *n.* a person who habitually attends the theater, opera, etc., on opening night.

first′ offend′er, a person convicted of an offense of law for the first time.

first′ of′ficer, 1. See **first mate. 2.** copilot.

first′ pa′per, *U.S. Informal.* an official declaration of intention filed by a resident alien desiring to become a citizen: not required by law after 1952.

first′ per′son, *Gram.* **1.** the person used by a speaker in statements referring to himself. In English, *I* and *we* are pronouns of the first person. **2.** a form in the first person.

first′ post′. See under **post**[2] (def. 7).

first′ prin′ciple, any axiom, law, or abstraction assumed and regarded as representing the highest possible degree of generalization.

first′ quar′ter, *Astron.* the instant, approximately one week after a new moon, when one half of the moon's disk is illuminated by the sun. See diag. at **moon.**

first-rate (fûrst′rāt′), *adj.* **1.** of the first rate or class. **2.** excellent; very good. —*adv.* **3.** *Informal.* very well.

First′ Reich′, the Holy Roman Empire until its dissolution in 1806.

First′ Repub′lic, the republic established in France, 1792–1804.

first′ ser′geant, *Mil.* a U.S. Army, Marine Corps or Air Force senior noncommissioned officer responsible for personnel and administration of a company, squadron, etc.

first-string (fûrst′strĭng′), *adj.* **1.** of greatest importance or prestige: *the first-string critics.* **2.** composed of regular members, players, etc.: *the first-string team.*

first′ watch′, *Naut.* the watch from 8 P.M. until midnight.

first′ wa′ter, 1. the highest degree of fineness in a diamond or other precious stone. Cf. **water** (def. 11). **2.** the finest quality; highest rank.

First′ World′ War′. See **World War I.**

firth (fûrth), *n.* *Chiefly Scot.* a long, narrow indentation of the seacoast. Also, **frith.** [< Scand; cf. Icel *firth-*, s. of *fjörthr*, FJORD]

fisc (fisk), *n.* a royal or state treasury; exchequer. [ME *fisc(us)* < L: treasury, lit., basket, bag]

fis·cal (fis′kəl), *adj.* **1.** of or pertaining to the public treasury or revenues. **2.** pertaining to financial matters in general. —*n.* **3.** (in some countries) a prosecuting attorney. **4.** *Philately.* a revenue stamp. [< L *fiscāl(is)*] —**fis′cal·ly,** *adv.* —**Syn. 1.** See **financial.**

fis′cal year′, any yearly period established for accounting purposes.

Fisch·er (fish′ər), *n.* **Robert James** (*"Bobby"*), born 1943, U.S. chess player.

fish (fish), *n., pl.* (*esp. collectively*) **fish,** (*esp. referring to two or more kinds or species*) **fish·es,** *v.* —*n.* **1.** any of various completely aquatic, cold-blooded vertebrates, having gills, commonly fins, and typically an elongated body usually covered with scales. **2.** any of various other aquatic animals. **3.** the flesh of fishes used as food. **4. Fishes,** *Astron., Astrol.* the constellation or sign of Pisces. **5.** *Informal.* a person: *a cold fish; an odd fish.* **6.** a long strip of wood, iron, etc., used to strengthen a mast, joint, etc. **7. fish out of water,** a person out of his proper or accustomed environment. **8. neither fish nor fowl,** having no specific character or conviction; neither one nor the other. **9. other fish to fry,** other matters requiring attention. —*v.t.* **10.** to catch or attempt to catch (any species of fish or the like). **11.** to try to catch fish in (a stream, lake, etc.). **12.** to draw or pull as by fishing (often fol. by *up* or *out*): *He fished out a coin for the boy.* **13.** to search through as by fishing. **14.** *Naut.* **a.** to raise the flukes of (an anchor), after catting or raising to the hawsehole, in order to secure it to the deck or side of a vessel. **b.** to reinforce (a mast or other spar) by fastening a spar, batten, metal bar, or the like, lengthwise over a weak place. —*v.i.* **15.** to catch or attempt to catch fish. **16.** to search for or attempt to catch onto something under water, in mud, etc. **17.** to seek to obtain something indirectly or by artifice. **18. fish in troubled waters,** to take advantage of troubled or uncertain conditions for personal profit. [ME; OE *fisc;* c. D *vis,* G *Fisch,* Icel *fiskr,* Goth *fisks;* akin to L *piscis,* Ir *iasc*] —**fish′a·ble,** *adj.* —**fish′like′,** *adj.*

Fish (External features of yellow perch) A, External nares; B, Operculum; C, Lateral line; D, Spinous dorsal fin; E, Soft dorsal fin; F, Caudal fin; G, Anal fin; H, Pelvic fin; I, Pectoral fin

Fish (fish), *n.* **Hamilton,** 1808–93, U.S. statesman: Secretary of State 1869–77.

fish′ and chips′, *Chiefly Brit.* fried fish fillets and French fried potatoes.

fish·bolt (fish′bōlt′), *n.* a bolt for securing a fishplate or fishplates.

fish′ cake′, a fried ball or cake of shredded fish, esp. salt codfish, and mashed potato. Also called **fish′ ball′.**

fish·er (fish′ər), *n.* **1.** a fisherman. **2.** any animal that catches fish for food. **3.** a dark-brown or blackish, somewhat foxlike marten, *Martes pennanti,* of northern North America. **4.** its fur. [ME *fisscher,* OE *fiscere*]

Fisher, *Martes pennanti* (Total length 3 ft.; tail 14 in.)

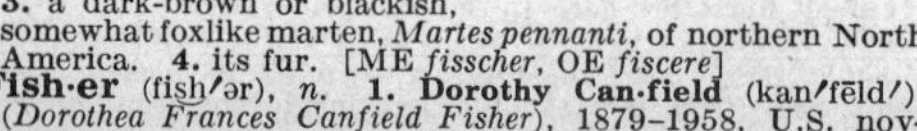

Fish·er (fish′ər), *n.* **1. Dorothy Can·field** (kan′fēld′), (*Dorothea Frances Canfield Fisher*), 1879–1958, U.S. novelist. **2. John Arbuthnot, 1st Baron Fisher of Kil·verstone** (kil′vər stən), 1841–1920, British admiral.

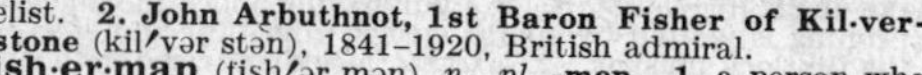

fish·er·man (fish′ər mən), *n., pl.* **-men. 1.** a person who fishes as a livelihood or for pleasure. **2.** a ship employed in fishing. [late ME *fissherman*]

fish′erman's bend′, a knot made by taking a round turn on the object to which the rope is to be fastened, usually an anchor, passing the end of the rope around the standing part and under the round turn, and securing the end. See illus. at **knot.**

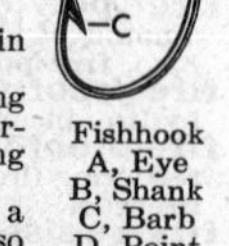

Fishhook A, Eye B, Shank C, Barb D, Point

fish·er·y (fish′ə rē), *n., pl.* **-er·ies. 1.** the occupation or industry of catching fish or taking other products from bodies of water. **2.** a place where such an industry is regularly carried on. **3.** a fishing establishment. **4.** *Law.* the right to fish in certain waters.

fish′ hawk′, osprey.

fish·hook (fish′hŏŏk′), *n.* a hook used in fishing. [ME *fischhook*]

fish·ing (fish′ing), *n.* **1.** the act of catching fish. **2.** the technique, occupation, or diversion of catching fish. **3.** a place for catching fish. [ME *fisshing*]

fish′ing pole′, a long, slender rod with a line and hook at one end, for use in fishing. Also called **fish pole.**

fish′ing rod′, a long, slender, flexible rod for use with a reel and line in catching fish. Cf. **fly rod.**

fish′ing tack′le, the equipment, as rods, lines, hooks, etc., used in fishing.

fish′ joint′, a joint between two structural members, as beams or rails, butted together and joined by fishplates.

fish′ lad′der, a series of ascending pools constructed to enable salmon or other fish to swim upstream around or over a dam.

fish·line (fish′līn′), *n.* a line used in fishing.

fish′ meal′, dried fish that has been ground, used as fertilizer or as an ingredient in foods.

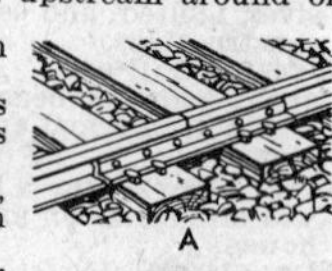

fish·mon·ger (fish′mung′gər, -mong′-), *n.* *Chiefly Brit.* a dealer in fish. [ME *fysshmongere*]

fish·net (fish′net′), *n.* a net for catching fish. [ME, OE *fiscnett*]

fish·plate (fish′plāt′), *n.* a metal or wooden plate or slab, bolted to each of two members that have been butted or lapped together. [*fish,* repr. F *fiche* fastening < *ficher* to fasten, fix (see FICHU) + PLATE[1]]

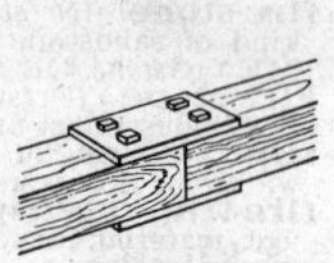

Fishplates A, Railroad fishplate or joint bar; B, Fishplates binding two timbers butted together

fish′ pole′. See **fishing pole.**

fish·pound (fish′pound′), *n.* *U.S.* a submerged net used by commercial fishermen for capturing fish.

fish′skin disease′ (fish′skin′), *Pathol.* ichthyosis.

fish′ sto′ry, *Informal.* an exaggerated or incredible story.

fish·tail (fish′tāl′), *Informal.* —*v.i.* **1.** to slow an airplane by causing its tail to move rapidly from side to side. —*n.* **2.** such a maneuver. **3.** *Jewelry.* a setting consisting of four prominent triangular corner prongs to hold a stone.

fish′ ward′en, a public official who enforces game laws relating to fish.

fish·wife (fish′wīf′), *n., pl.* **-wives. 1.** a woman who sells fish. **2.** a coarse-mannered, vulgar-tongued woman. [ME *fisshwyf*]

fish·y (fish′ē), *adj.,* **fish·i·er, fish·i·est. 1.** like a fish in smell, taste, or the like. **2.** consisting of or abounding in fish. **3.** *Informal.* improbable, as a story. **4.** *Informal.* of questionable character. **5.** dull and expressionless. —**fish′i·ly,** *adv.* —**fish′i·ness,** *n.*

Fiske (fisk), *n.* **1. John** (*Edmund Fisk Green; John Fisk*), 1842–1901, U.S. philosopher and historian. **2. Minnie Mad·dern** (mad′ərn), (*Marie Augusta Davey*), 1865–1932, U.S. actress.

fissi-, a learned borrowing from Latin meaning "cleft," used in the formation of compound words: *fissiparous.* [< L, comb. form of *fissus* cloven, *fissum* fissure, special uses of ptp. of *findere* to split]

fis·sile (fis′əl), *adj.* **1.** capable of being split or divided; cleavable. **2.** fissionable [< L *fissil(is)*]

fis·sion (fish′ən), *n.* **1.** act of cleaving or splitting into parts. **2.** *Biol.* the division of an organism into new organisms as a process of reproduction. **3.** Also called **nuclear fission.** *Physics.* the splitting of the nucleus of an atom into nuclei of lighter atoms, accompanied by the release of energy. Cf. **fusion** (def. 5). [< L *fissiōn-* (s. of *fissiō*) a splitting, dividing]

fis·sion·a·ble (fish′ə nə bəl), *adj.* *Physics.* capable of undergoing fission. Also called **fissile.** —**fis′sion·a·bil′i·ty,** *n.*

fis′sion bomb′. See **atomic bomb.**

fis·sip·a·rous (fi sip′ər əs), *adj.* reproducing by fission. —**fis·sip′a·rous·ly,** *adv.* —**fis·sip′a·rous·ness,** *n.*

fis·si·ros·tral (fis′ə ros′trəl), *adj.* *Ornith.* **1.** having a broad, deeply cleft beak or bill, as the swallows and goatsuckers. **2.** (of the bill) deeply cleft.

fis·sure (fish′ər), *n., v.,* **-sured, -sur·ing.** —*n.* **1.** a narrow opening produced by cleavage or separation of parts; cleft. **2.** cleavage (def. 1). **3.** *Anat.* a natural division or groove in an organ, as in the brain. —*v.t., v.i.* **4.** to cleave; split; open. [late ME < medical L *fissūra*]

fist (fist), *n.* **1.** the hand closed tightly, with the fingers doubled into the palm. **2.** *Print.* index (def. 6). —*v.t.* **3.** to grasp in the fist. [ME; OE *fȳst;* c. G *Faust* fist; ? orig. meaning five (fingers) as one, i.e., clenched]

fist·ful (fist′fŏŏl), *n., pl.* **-fuls.** a handful.

fist·ic (fis′tik), *adj.* of boxing; pugilistic: *fistic heroes.*

fist·i·cuff (fis′tə kuf′), *n.* **1.** a cuff or blow with the fist. **2. fisticuffs,** combat with the fists. —*v.t., v.i.* **3.** to strike or fight with the fists. [earlier *fisty cuff*]

fis·tu·la (fis′chŏŏ lə), *n., pl.* **-las, -lae** (-lē′). **1.** *Pathol.* a narrow passage or duct formed by disease or injury, as one leading from an abscess to a free surface, or from one cavity to another. **2.** *Surg.* an opening made into a hollow organ, as the bladder or eyeball, for drainage. **3.** *Vet. Pathol.* any of various suppurative inflammations, as in the withers of a horse **(fis′tulous with′ers),** characterized by the formation of passages or sinuses through the tissues and to the surface of the skin. **4.** *Obs.* a pipe, as a flute. [ME < L: pipe, tube, reed, ulcer]

fis·tu·lous (fis′cho͝o ləs), *adj.* **1.** *Pathol.* pertaining to or resembling a fistula. **2.** tubelike; tubular. **3.** containing tubes or tubelike parts. Also, **fis′tu·lar, fis·tu·late** (fis′cho͝o lit). [< L *fistulōs(us)*]

fit[1] (fit), *adj.*, **fit·ter, fit·test,** *v.*, **fit·ted** or **fit, fit·ting,** *n.* —*adj.* **1.** adapted or suited: *Is it fit to eat?* **2.** proper or becoming: *fit behavior.* **3.** qualified or competent, as for an office or function: *a fit candidate.* **4.** worthy or deserving. **5.** prepared or ready: *crops fit for gathering.* **6.** in good physical condition or health. —*v.t.* **7.** to be adapted to or suitable for (a purpose, object, occasion, etc.). **8.** to be of the right size or shape for: *The dress fitted her perfectly.* **9.** to adjust or make conform to something. **10.** to make qualified or competent. **11.** to prepare; make ready. **12.** to place with care and precision; adjust: *He fitted the picture into the frame.* **13.** to provide; furnish; equip. —*v.i.* **14.** to be suitable or proper. **15.** to be of the right size or shape, as a garment for the wearer. **16. fit out** or **up,** to furnish with clothing, furniture, or other requisites; supply; equip. —*n.* **17.** the manner in which a thing fits: *a perfect fit.* **18.** something that fits: *The coat is a poor fit.* **19.** the process or a process of fitting. [ME; akin to MD *vitten* to befit] —**fit′ness,** *n.* —**fit′ta·ble,** *adj.* —**Syn. 1.** suitable, appropriate, apt, applicable, apropos. **2.** fitting, befitting.

fit[2] (fit), *n.* **1.** a sudden, acute attack, as of a convulsive disease. **2.** a sudden, temporary spasm, as of activity or of coughing or laughing. **3.** a highly emotional reaction. **4. by fits and starts,** at irregular intervals; intermittently. Also, **by fits, in fits and starts. 5. throw a fit,** *Informal.* to become extremely excited or angry. [ME; OE *fitt* round of fighting. See FIT[3]]

fit[3] (fit), *n.* *Archaic.* **1.** a song, ballad, or story. **2.** a division of a song, ballad, or story. [ME; OE *fitt* round of singing, canto, song, speech]

fitch (fich), *n.* **1.** the European polecat, *Mustela putorius.* **2.** its fur. Also, **fitch·et** (fich′it), **fitch·ew** (fich′o͞o). [late ME *fiche* < MD *vitsche* polecat, named from its stench; akin to dial. G *fietschen* to stink]

Fitch (fich), *n.* **1. John,** 1743–98, U.S. inventor: pioneer in development of the steamboat. **2. (William) Clyde,** 1865–1909, U.S. playwright.

Fitch·burg (fich′bûrg), *n.* a city in N Massachusetts. 43,343 (1970).

fitch·y (fich′ē), *adj.* *Heraldry.* (of a cross) having the lowermost arm, or other arms as specified, terminating in a point. Also, **fitch·ée** (fich′ē, fi chā′). [< MF *fiche,* ptp. of *ficher* to fix. See FICHU]

fit·ful (fit′fəl), *adj.* appearing, acting, etc., in fits; recurring irregularly. —**fit′ful·ly,** *adv.* —**fit′ful·ness,** *n.*

fit·ly (fit′lē), *adv.* **1.** in a fit manner. **2.** at a fit time.

fit·ted (fit′id), *adj.* made so as to follow closely the contours of a form or shape: *a fitted dress.*

fit·ter (fit′ər), *n.* **1.** a person or thing that fits. **2.** a person who fits garments. **3.** a worker who fits together or adjusts the parts of machinery. **4.** a person who supplies and fixes fittings or fixtures. **5.** a person who furnishes whatever is necessary for some purpose.

fit·ting (fit′ing), *adj.* **1.** suitable or appropriate; proper or becoming. —*n.* **2.** the act of a person or thing that fits. **3.** an act or instance of trying on clothes that are being made or altered. **4.** anything provided as equipment, parts, supply, etc. **5.** Usually, **fittings.** furniture, furnishings, fixtures, etc., as of an apartment, automobile, etc. —**fit′ting·ly,** *adv.* —**fit′ting·ness,** *n.* —**Syn. 1.** fit, meet, right, decorous, seemly.

Fitz·ger·ald (fits jer′əld), *n.* **F(rancis) Scott (Key),** 1896–1940, U.S. novelist and short-story writer.

Fitz·Ger·ald (fits jer′əld), *n.* **Edward,** 1809–83, English poet: translator of Omar Khayyám.

Fiu·me (fyo͞o′me), *n.* former name of **Rijeka.**

five (fīv), *n.* **1.** a cardinal number, four plus one. **2.** a symbol for this number, as 5 or V. **3.** a set of this many persons or things. **4.** a playing card, die face, or half of a domino face with five pips. **5. take five,** *Informal.* to rest from what one is doing, esp. for five minutes. **6.** *Informal.* a five-dollar bill. —*adj.* **7.** amounting to five in number. [ME; OE *fīf;* c. D *vijf,* G *fünf,* Icel *fimm,* Goth *fimf,* L *quinque,* Gk *pénte,* Skt *pancha*]

five-and-ten (fīv′ən ten′), *n.* a retail store offering a wide assortment of inexpensive items for personal and household use. Also called **five′-and-ten′-cent store′** (fīv′ən-ten′sent′), **five-and-dime** (fīv′ən dīm′), **dime store, ten-cent store.**

five-fin·ger (fīv′fing′gər), *n.* **1.** any of certain species of potentilla having leaves of five leaflets, as *Potentilla canadensis.* **2.** See **bird's-foot trefoil. 3.** the oxlip. **4.** See **Virginia creeper.** [OE *fīffingre*]

five·fold (fīv′fōld′), *adj.* **1.** comprising five parts or members. **2.** five times as great or as much. —*adv.* **3.** in fivefold measure. [ME *fiffold,* OE *fīffeald*]

five-gait·ed (fīv′gā′tid), *adj.* *Manège.* noting an American saddle horse that has been trained to execute the rack and slow gait in addition to the walk, trot, and canter.

Five′ Na′tions, a confederacy of Iroquoian Indians: the Mohawks, Oneidas, Onondagas, Cayugas, and Senecas, and, after the 18th century, the Tuscarora.

five′-o'clock shad′ow, the visible beard growth on some men toward evening despite the regular morning shave.

five·pen·ny (fīv′pen′ē), *adj.* **1.** *Carpentry.* noting a nail 1¾ inches long. *Abbr.:* 5d **2.** worth five pence.

fiv·er (fī′vər), *n.* *Slang.* **1.** a five-dollar bill. **2.** *Brit.* a five-pound note.

five′ sens′es, sense (defs. 1, 2).

five-spot (fīv′spot′), *n.* **1.** a playing card or the upward face of a die bearing five pips; a domino one half of which bears five pips. **2.** *Slang.* a five-dollar bill.

five-star (fīv′stär′), *adj.* having the highest rank or quality: *a five-star general; five-star brandy.*

Five′ Towns′. See **Potteries, the.**

Five′-Year Plan′ (fīv′yēr′), (*sometimes l.c.*) any plan for national economic or industrial development having goals to be reached in five years, esp. as undertaken by the Soviet Union and the People's Republic of China.

fix (fiks), *v.*, **fixed** or **fixt, fix·ing,** *n.* —*v.t.* **1.** to make fast, firm, or stable. **2.** to attach or place permanently. **3.** to settle definitely; determine: *to fix a price.* **4.** to direct (the eyes, the attention, etc.) steadily. **5.** to attract and hold (the eye, the attention, etc.). **6.** to make set or rigid. **7.** to put into permanent form. **8.** to put or place (responsibility, blame, etc.) on a person. **9.** to assign or refer to a definite place, time, etc. **10.** to repair; mend. **11.** to put in order; adjust or arrange: *Fix your room!* **12.** to provide or supply with (something needed or wanted). **13.** *Informal.* to arrange matters with, or with respect to, esp. privately or dishonestly, so as to secure favorable action: *to fix a jury or a game.* **14.** to prepare (a meal or food). **15.** *Informal.* to get even with; get revenge upon. **16.** *Informal.* to castrate or spay (an animal, esp. a pet). **17.** *Chem.* **a.** to make stable in consistence or condition; reduce from fluidity or volatility to a more permanent state. **b.** to convert atmospheric nitrogen into a useful compound, as a nitrate fertilizer. **18.** *Photog.* to render (an image) permanent by removing the light-sensitive silver halides. **19.** *Microscopy.* to kill, make rigid, and preserve for microscopic study. —*v.i.* **20.** to become fixed. **21.** to become set; assume a rigid or solid form. **22.** to become stable or permanent. **23.** to settle down. **24.** *Dial.* to prepare; plan (usually fol. by an infinitive): *I was just fixing to call you.* **25. fix on** or **upon,** to decide on; determine. **26. fix up,** *U.S. Informal.* **a.** to arrange for. **b.** to provide with; furnish. **c.** to repair; renew. **d.** to smooth over; solve. —*n.* **27.** *Informal.* a position from which it is difficult to escape; predicament. **28.** *Navig.* a charted position of a vessel or aircraft, determined by two or more bearings taken on landmarks, heavenly bodies, etc. **29.** the determining of the position of a ship, plane, etc., by mathematical, electronic, or other means. **30.** *Slang.* an injection of heroin or other narcotic. **31.** *Slang.* an underhanded or illegal arrangement: *the fix is on in the fifth race.* [late ME *fixe(n)* < ML *fixā(re)* < L *fix(us)* fixed, ptp. of *fīgere* to fasten] —**fix′a·ble,** *adj.* —**fix′er,** *n.*
—**Syn. 1, 2.** fasten, secure, stabilize. FIX, ESTABLISH imply making firm or permanent. To FIX is to fasten in position securely or to make more or less permanent against change, esp. something already existing: *to fix a bayonet on a gun; fix a principle in one's mind.* To ESTABLISH is to make firm or permanent something (usually newly) originated, created, or ordained: *to establish a business, a claim to property.* **2.** set, plant, implant. **3.** establish, define. **11.** repair, mend, correct, amend. **27.** dilemma, plight, quandary.
—**Usage. 10.** In the sense of *repair,* FIX appears to have been used first in America, but there is evidence for its use in England as early as the beginning of the 19th century. No formal stigma attaches to such use; those who object to it for reasons of style are groundlessly prejudiced.

fix·ate (fik′sāt), *v.*, **-at·ed, -at·ing.** —*v.t.* **1.** to make stable or stationary. —*v.i.* **2.** to become fixed. **3.** *Psychoanal.* to develop a fixation. [< L *fix(us)* (see FIX) + -ATE[1]]

fix·a·tion (fik sā′shən), *n.* **1.** act of fixing. **2.** state of being fixed. **3.** *Psychoanal.* a partial arrest of emotional and instinctual development at an early point in life. **4.** a preoccupation or obsession; compulsive absorption or involvement. [ME *fixacion* < ML *fixātiōn-* (s. of *fixātiō*) a reduction to a fixed state]

fix·a·tive (fik′sə tiv), *adj.* **1.** serving to fix; making fixed or permanent. —*n.* Also, **fix·a·tif** (fik′sə tiv, -tēf′). **2.** a fixative substance, as a gummy liquid sprayed on a drawing to prevent blurring. **3.** a substance that retards evaporation, as in the manufacture of perfume.

fixed (fikst), *adj.* **1.** fastened, attached, or placed so as to be firm and not readily movable; firmly implanted; stationary; rigid. **2.** rendered stable or permanent, as color. **3.** set or intent upon something; steadily directed: *a fixed stare.* **4.** definitely and permanently placed. **5.** definite; not fluctuating or varying. **6.** coming each year on the same calendar date: *a fixed holiday.* **7.** put in order. **8.** *Informal.* arranged with, or arranged, privately or dishonestly. [ME] —**fix·ed·ly** (fik′sid lē), *adv.* —**fix′ed·ness,** *n.*

fixed′ as′set, any long-term asset, as a building, tract of land, or patent. Also called **capital asset.**

fixed′ charge′, 1. an expense that cannot be modified. **2.** a periodic obligation, as taxes, interest on bonds, etc.

fixed′ ide′a, a persistent or obsessing idea, often delusional, that can, in extreme form, be a symptom of insanity. **2.** *Music.* See **idée fixe** (def. 2).

fixed′ oil′, *Chem.* a natural vegetable or animal oil that is nonvolatile, as lard oil, linseed oil, etc.

fixed′ sat′ellite, *Rocketry.* an earth satellite that remains over a particular point on the earth's surface owing to its 24-hour orbital period.

fixed′ star′, *Astron.* any of the stars that appear always to retain the same position in respect to one another.

fix·ing (fik′sing), *n.* **1.** act of a person or thing that fixes. **2. fixings.** Also, *Dial.*, **fix·in's** (fik′sinz). appropriate accompaniments: *turkey with all the fixings.* [late ME]

fix·i·ty (fik′si tē), *n., pl.* **-ties** for 2. **1.** the state or quality of being fixed; stability; permanence. **2.** something fixed, stable, or permanent. [< NL *fixitās*]

fixt (fikst), *v.* a pt. and pp. of **fix.**

fix·ture (fiks′chər), *n.* **1.** something securely, and usually permanently, attached or appended, as to a wall or ceiling: *a light fixture; kitchen fixture.* **2.** a person or thing long established in the same place or position. **3.** *Law.* a movable chattel, as a machine, which, by reason of annexation to real property, is considered a part of the realty. **4.** *Rare.* the act of fixing. [var. of earlier *fixure* (< LL *fixūra*), with *-t-* from MIXTURE]

fiz·gig (fiz′gig′), *n.* **1.** a frivolous, giddy, restless woman or girl. **2.** a kind of firework that makes a loud hissing sound. **3.** a kind of whirling toy that makes a whizzing noise. [earlier *fisgig* = *fis* (late ME *fise* term of abuse; akin to Icel *fīsa* to break wind) + *gig* (ME *gigge* girl; see GIGGLE)]

fizz (fiz), *v.i.* **1.** to make a hissing or sputtering sound; effervesce. —*n.* **2.** a hissing sound; effervescence. **3.** *U.S.* **a.** soda water or other effervescent water. **b.** its effervescence. **c.** an iced mixed drink made of liquor, lemon juice, sugar, and soda. [back formation from FIZZLE] —**fizz′er,** *n.*

fiz·zle (fiz′əl), *v.*, **-zled, -zling,** *n.* —*v.i.* **1.** to make a hissing or sputtering sound, esp. one that dies out weakly. **2.** *Informal.* to fail ignominiously after a good start. —*n.* **3.** a fizzling, hissing, or sputtering. **4.** *Informal.* a fiasco; a failure. [earlier *fysel* to break wind, freq. of **fise* < Scand; cf. Icel *fīsa* to break wind, akin to FEIST]

fizz·wa·ter (fiz′wô′tər, -wot′ər), *n.* effervescent water; soda water.

fizz·y (fiz′ē), *adj.*, **fizz·i·er, fizz·i·est.** bubbly; fizzing.

fjeld (fyeld; *Norw.* fyel), *n.* a rocky, barren plateau of the Scandinavian peninsula. [< Norw; see FELL[5]]

fjord (fyôrd, fyōrd; *Norw.* fyŏŏr, fyōr), *n.* **1.** a long, narrow arm of the sea bordered by steep cliffs: usually formed by glacial erosion. **2.** (in Scandinavia) a bay. Also, **fiord.** [< Norw; see FIRTH]

FL, Florida (approved esp. for use with zip code).

Fl., **1.** Flanders. **2.** Flemish.

fl., **1.** florin. **2.** flourished [< L *floruit*] **3.** fluid. **4.** (in the Netherlands) gulden; guldens.

Fla., Florida.

flab·ber·gast (flab′ər gast′), *v.t.* *Informal.* to overcome with surprise and bewilderment; astound. [var. of *flabagast* (FLABB(Y) + AGHAST)] —**Syn.** amaze, astonish, stagger, nonplus.

flab·by (flab′ē), *adj.*, **-bi·er, -bi·est.** **1.** hanging loosely or limply, as flesh or muscles; flaccid. **2.** having such flesh. **3.** lacking firmness or determination. [alter. of late ME *flabband* (said of webs) = *flabb-* (< ?) + *-and* prp. ending; see -Y[1]] —**flab′bi·ly,** *adv.* —**flab′bi·ness,** *n.*

fla·bel·late (flə bel′it, -āt), *adj.* *Bot., Zool.* fan-shaped. Also, **fla·bel·li·form** (flə bel′ə fôrm′). [< L *flābell(um)* FLABELLUM + -ATE[1]]

fla·bel·lum (flə bel′əm), *n.*, *pl.* **-bel·la** (-bel′ə). **1.** a fan, esp. one used in religious ceremonies. **2.** a fan-shaped part. [< L: small fan, dim. of *flābra* breezes = *flā(re)* (to) blow + *-bra*, pl. of *-brum* n. suffix of means]

flac·cid (flak′sid), *adj.* soft and limp; not firm; flabby: *flaccid biceps.* [< L *flaccid(us)* flabby = *flacc(us)* flabby + *-idus* -ID[4]] —**flac·cid′i·ty, flac′cid·ness,** *n.* —**flac′cid·ly,** *adv.*

flack[1] (flak), *n.* *Slang.* **1.** See **press agent.** **2.** publicity. [?]

flack[2] (flak), *n.* flak.

flac·on (flak′ən; *Fr.* flᴀ kôɴ′), *n.*, *pl.* **flac·ons** (flak′ənz; *Fr.* flᴀ kôɴ′). a small bottle or flask with a stopper. Cf. **flagon.** [< F; see FLAGON]

flag[1] (flag), *n.*, *v.*, **flagged, flag·ging.** —*n.* **1.** a piece of cloth, varying in design, usually attached at one edge to a staff or cord, and used as the symbol of a nation, state, or organization, as a means of signaling, etc.; ensign; standard; banner; pennant. **2.** *Hunting.* the tail of a deer or of a setter dog. **3.** *Journalism.* **a.** the nameplate of a newspaper. **b.** masthead (def. 2). **4.** *Music.* hook (def. 10). —*v.t.* **5.** to decorate with flags. **6.** to signal or warn (a person, automobile, etc.) with, or as with, a flag (sometimes fol. by *down*): *to flag a taxi; to flag down a passing car.* **7.** to communicate (information) by signaling. **8.** to decoy, as game, by waving a flag or the like. **9.** to mark (a page, file card, etc.) for attention, as by attaching protruding tabs. [? b. FLAP (n.) and FAG[1] (n.) in obs. sense, a flap] —**flag′ger,** *n.* —**flag′less,** *adj.*

flag[2] (flag), *n.* **1.** any of various plants with long, sword-shaped leaves, as the sweet flag. **2.** See **blue flag.** **3.** the long, slender leaf of such a plant or of a cereal plant. [ME *flagge*]

flag[3] (flag), *v.i.*, **flagged, flag·ging.** **1.** to hang loosely or limply; droop. **2.** to diminish in vigor, energy, interest, etc.: *Public enthusiasm tends to flag.* [? b. of FLAP (v.) and FAG[1] (v.) in obs. sense to droop]

flag[4] (flag), *n.*, *v.*, **flagged, flag·ging.** —*n.* **1.** flagstone. —*v.t.* **2.** to pave with flagstones. [late ME *flagge* piece of sod, OE *flæcg* poultice, plaster; akin to Icel *flaga* slab]

Flag′ Day′, June 14, the anniversary of the day (June 14, 1777) when Congress adopted the Stars and Stripes as the national emblem of the United States.

fla·gel·la (flə jel′ə), *n.* pl. of **flagellum.**

flag·el·lant (flaj′ə lənt, flə jel′ənt), *n.* **1.** a person who flagellates or who scourges himself for religious discipline. **2.** (*often cap.*) one of a medieval European sect of fanatics who practiced scourging in public. —*adj.* **3.** flagellating. **4.** severely criticizing. [< L *flagellant-* (s. of *flagellāns*) whipping, prp. of *flagellāre.* See FLAGELLUM, -ANT] —**flag′el·lant·ism,** *n.*

flag·el·late (*v.* flaj′ə lāt′; *adj.*, *n.* flaj′ə lit, -lāt′), *v.*, **-lat·ed, -lat·ing,** *adj.*, *n.* —*v.t.* **1.** to whip; scourge; flog; lash. —*adj.* **2.** Also, **flag′el·lat′ed.** *Biol.* having flagella. **3.** *Bot.* producing filiform runners or runnerlike branches, as the strawberry. **4.** pertaining to or caused by flagellates. —*n.* **5.** any protozoan of the class *Mastigophora* (*Flagellata*), having one or more flagella. [< L *flagellāt(us)* whipped, ptp. of *flagellāre.* See FLAGELLUM, -ATE[1]] —**flag′el·la′tion,** *n.* —**flag′el·la′tor,** *n.*

F

Flagellate, genus *Euglena*; F, Flagellum

fla·gel·li·form (flə jel′ə fôrm′), *adj.* *Biol.* long, slender, and flexible, like the lash of a whip. [FLAGELL(UM) + -I- + -FORM]

fla·gel·lum (flə jel′əm), *n.*, *pl.* **-gel·la** (-jel′ə), **-gel·lums.** **1.** *Biol.* a long, lashlike appendage serving as an organ of locomotion in certain reproductive bodies, bacteria, protozoa, etc. **2.** *Bot.* a runner. **3.** a whip or lash. [< L: little whip, dim. of *flagrum* a whip, scourge]

flag·eo·let (flaj′ə let′, -lā′), *n.* **1.** a small flute with four finger holes in front and two in the rear. **2.** any fipple flute. [< F, sp. var. of OF *flajolet* = *flajol* flute (< VL **flabeolum* < L *flāre* to blow) + *-et* -ET]

Flageolet

Flagg (flag), *n.* **James Montgomery,** 1877–1960, U.S. painter and illustrator.

flag·ging[1] (flag′ing), *adj.* showing a loss of energy, determination, etc.; weakening; failing; drooping. [FLAG[3] + -ING[2]] —**flag′ging·ly,** *adv.*

flag·ging[2] (flag′ing), *n.* **1.** flagstones collectively. **2.** a pavement of flagstones. [FLAG[4] + -ING[1]]

flag·gy[1] (flag′ē), *adj.*, **-gi·er, -gi·est.** without sufficient energy, enthusiasm, determination, etc.; flagging; drooping; limp. [FLAG[3] + -Y[1]]

flag·gy[2] (flag′ē), *adj.* consisting of or resembling flagstone; laminate. [FLAG[4] + -Y[1]]

flag·gy[3] (flag′ē), *adj.* abounding in, consisting of, or resembling flag plants. [ME *flaggi*]

fla·gi·tious (flə jish′əs), *adj.* **1.** shamefully wicked, as persons; villainous. **2.** heinous or flagrant, as a crime; infamous. [ME *flagicious* < L *flāgitiōs(us)* = *flāgiti(um)* shame, scandal + *-ōsus* -OUS] —**fla·gi′tious·ly,** *adv.* —**fla·gi′tious·ness,** *n.* —**Syn.** **1.** profligate, corrupt, depraved, dissolute. **2.** nefarious, vicious, iniquitous, atrocious.

flag·man (flag′mən), *n.*, *pl.* **-men.** **1.** a person who has charge of or carries a flag. **2.** a person who signals with a flag or lantern.

flag′ of′ficer, a naval officer above the rank of captain.

flag′ of truce′, *Mil.* a white flag displayed as an invitation to the enemy to confer.

flag·on (flag′ən), *n.* **1.** a large bottle for wine, liquors, etc. **2.** a container for holding liquids, as for use at table, esp. a container with a handle, a spout, and usually a cover. [late ME, var. of *flakon* < MF *fla(s)con* < LL *flascōn-* (s. of *flascō*) FLASK]

flag·pole (flag′pōl′), *n.* a staff or pole on which a flag is displayed. Also called **flagstaff.**

flag′ rank′, naval rank above that of captain.

fla·grant (flā′grənt), *adj.* **1.** outrageously noticeable or evident: *a flagrant error.* **2.** notorious; scandalous: *a flagrant crime.* **3.** *Archaic.* blazing, burning, or glowing. [late ME < L *flagrant-* (s. of *flagrāns*) burning, prp. of *flagrāre*] —**fla′gran·cy, fla′grance, fla′grant·ness,** *n.* —**fla′grant·ly,** *adv.* —**Syn.** **2.** disgraceful, shocking.

fla·gran·te de·lic·to (flə gran′tē di lik′tō), *Law.* while the crime is, or was, being committed. [< L: lit., while the crime is blazing]

flag·ship (flag′ship′), *n.* **1.** a ship bearing the flag officer or the commander of a fleet, squadron, or the like, and displaying his flag. **2.** the main vessel of a passenger or shipping line.

Flag·stad (flag′stad; *Norw.* fläg′stä), *n.* **Kir·sten Ma·rie** (kûr′stən mə rē′; *Norw.* ᴋʜish′tən mä ʀē′ə, ᴋʜiʀ′stən), 1895–1962, Norwegian operatic soprano.

flag·staff (flag′staf′, -stäf′), *n.*, *pl.* **-staves, -staffs.** flagpole.

Flag·staff (flag′staf′, -stäf′), *n.* a city in central Arizona. 26,117 (1970).

flag′ sta′tion, a railroad station where trains stop only when flagged or when passengers are to be discharged. Also called **flag′ stop′.**

flag·stone (flag′stōn′), *n.* a flat stone slab used esp. for paving. Also called **flag.**

flag-wav·ing (flag′wā′ving), *n.* an ostentatiously emotional display of patriotism or factionalism. —**flag′-wav′er,** *n.*

Fla·her·ty (fla′ər tē, flä′-), *n.* **Robert Joseph,** 1884–1951, U.S. pioneer in the production of documentary motion pictures.

flail (flāl), *n.* **1.** an instrument for threshing grain by hand, consisting of a handle with a freely swinging bar attached to one end. **2.** a similar instrument used as a weapon of war in the Middle Ages. —*v.t.* **3.** to strike with or as if with a flail. —*v.i.* **4.** to toss about. [ME *fleil*, OE **flegel*; c. D *vlegel*, G *Flegel* < WGmc **flagil-* < LL *flagell(um)* flail, L: whip, scourge]

flair (flâr), *n.* **1.** a natural talent or ability; bent; knack. **2.** smartness of style, manner, etc. **3.** keen perception or discernment. [< F, OF: scent, back formation from *flairier* to reek << LL *flagrāre*, dissimilated var. of L *fragrāre.* See FRAGRANT]

flak (flak), *n.* **1.** antiaircraft fire. **2.** *Informal.* annoying criticism or opposition. **3.** *Informal.* a heated discussion or argument. Also, **flack.** [< G *Fl(ieger)a(bwehr)k(anone)* antiaircraft gun = *Flieger* aircraft (lit., flyer) + *Abwehr* defense + *Kanone* cannon]

flake[1] (flāk), *n.*, *v.*, **flaked, flak·ing.** —*n.* **1.** a small, flat, thin piece, esp. one detached from a larger piece. **2.** any small piece or mass. **3.** a stratum or layer. —*v.i.* **4.** to peel off in flakes. —*v.t.* **5.** to break flakes or chips from; break into flakes. **6.** to cover with or as with flakes. **7.** to form into flakes. [ME; akin to OE *flac-* in *flacor* flying (said of arrows), Icel *flakka* to rove, wander, MD *vlacken* to flutter] —**flak′er,** *n.*

flake[2] (flāk), *n.* a frame, as for drying fish. [ME *flake, fleke* < Scand; cf. Icel *flaki, fleki* hurdle]

flake[3] (flāk), *n.*, *v.t.*, **flaked, flak·ing.** *Naut.* fake[2].

flak·y (flā′kē), *adj.*, **flak·i·er, flak·i·est.** **1.** of or like flakes or layers. **2.** peeling off in flakes. **3.** *Slang.* **a.** eccentric, peculiar, or non-conformist. **b.** questionable; unreliable. —**flak′i·ly,** *adv.* —**flak′i·ness,** *n.*

flam (flam), *n.*, *v.*, **flammed, flam·ming.** *Informal.* —*n.* **1.** a falsehood. **2.** a deception or trick. —*v.t.*, *v.i.* **3.** to deceive; delude; cheat. [short for FLIM-FLAM]

flam·bé (fläm bā′; *Fr.* fläɴ bā′), *adj.* (of food) served in flaming liquor, esp. brandy. Also, **flam·béed** (fläm bād′). [< F, ptp. of *flamber* to flame]

flam·beau (flam′bō), *n.*, *pl.* **-beaux** (-bōz), **-beaus.** **1.** a flaming torch. **2.** a large, decorated candlestick, as of bronze. [< F: torch, irreg. < OF *flambe* FLAME]

flam·boy·ant (flam boi′ənt), *adj.* **1.** strikingly bold or brilliant; showy. **2.** conspicuously dashing and colorful. **3.** florid; ornate; elaborately styled: *flamboyant speeches.* **4.** *Archit.* noting or pertaining to French Gothic architecture, esp. of the late 15th century, characterized by the use of elaborate tracery. —*n.* **5.** See **royal poinciana.** [< F, prp. of *flamboyer* to flame, flair < OF *flambe* FLAME; see -ANT] —**flam·boy′ance, flam·boy′an·cy,** *n.* —**flam·boy′ant·ly,** *adv.*

flame (flām), *n., v.,* **flamed, flam·ing.** —*n.* **1.** burning gas or vapor, as from ignited wood or coal. **2.** a portion of ignited gas or vapor. **3.** Often, **flames.** state or condition of blazing combustion. **4.** any flamelike condition; glow; inflamed condition. **5.** brilliant light; scintillating luster. **6.** bright coloring; a streak or patch of color. **7.** intense ardor, zeal, or passion. **8.** *Informal.* an object of love; sweetheart. —*v.i.* **9.** to burn with a flame or flames; burst into flames; blaze. **10.** to glow like flame; shine brilliantly; flash. **11.** to burn as with flame, as passions. **12.** to break into anger, indignation, etc. —*v.t.* **13.** to subject to the action of flame or fire. [ME *flaume* < AF, var. of *flaumbe,* c. OF *flambe,* earlier *flamble* < L *flammula,* dim. of *flamma* flame; see -ULE] —**flam′er,** *n.* —**flame′less,** *adj.* —**flame′like′,** *adj.*
—**Syn. 1.** fire. FLAME, BLAZE, CONFLAGRATION refer to the light and heat given off by combustion. FLAME is the common word, referring to a combustion of any size: *the light of a match flame.* BLAZE usually denotes a quick, hot, bright, and comparatively large flame: *The fire burst into a blaze.* CONFLAGRATION refers to destructive flames that spread over a considerable area: *A conflagration destroyed Chicago.*

flame′ cell′, *Zool.* one of the hollow cells terminating the branches of the excretory tubules of certain lower invertebrates, containing a tuft of continuously moving cilia.

fla·men (flā′mən, -men), *n., pl.* **fla·mens, fla·mi·nes** (flam′ə nēz′). (in ancient Rome) a priest devoted to the service of one deity. [< L (? earlier **flādmen;* akin to OE *blōtan* to sacrifice); r. ME *flamin* < L *flāmin-* (s. of *flāmen*)]

fla·men·co (flə meng′kō), *adj., n., pl.* **-cos.** —*adj.* **1.** of or like a gypsy, esp. like the music and dances of the Andalusian gypsies: *flamenco rhythms.* —*n.* **2.** a strongly rhythmic style of dancing, characteristic of the Andalusian gypsies. **3.** *Music.* **a.** a style of instrumental or vocal music originating in southern Spain and typically of an intensely rhythmic, improvisatory character. **b.** music in this style performed by itself or as an accompaniment to flamenco dancing. [< Sp: gypsylike, orig. Fleming. See FLAMINGO]

flame-out (flām′out′), *n.* the failure of a jet engine due to an interruption of the fuel supply or to faulty combustion. Also, **flame′out′.** Also called **blowout.**

flame·proof (flām′pro͞of′), *adj.* resisting the effect of flames; not readily ignited or burned by flames.

flame·throw·er (flām′thrō′ər), *n.* *Mil.* a weapon that squirts ignited incendiary fuel.

flam·ing (flā′ming), *adj.* **1.** emitting flames; blazing; fiery. **2.** like a flame in brilliance, heat, or shape. **3.** intensely ardent or passionate: *flaming youth.* [ME *flammande*] —**flam′ing·ly,** *adv.*

fla·min·go (flə ming′gō), *n., pl.* **-gos, -goes.** any of several aquatic birds of the family *Phoenicopteridae,* having very long legs and neck, webbed feet, a bill bent downward at the tip, and pinkish to scarlet plumage. [< Pg *flamengo* (c. Sp *flamenco*), lit., Fleming < MD *Vlaming;* name assoc. with *flama* flame and so with bird from its color]

Flamingo, *Phoenicopterus ruber* (Height 5 ft.; length 4 ft.)

Fla·min′i·an Way′ (flə min′ē ən), an ancient Roman road extending N from Rome to what is now Rimini. 215 mi. long.

Fla·min·i·us (flə min′ē əs), *n.* **Ga·ius** (gā′əs), died 217 B.C., Roman statesman and general: defeated by Hannibal.

flam·ma·ble (flam′ə bəl), *adj.* easily set on fire; combustible; inflammable. [< L *flammā(re)* (to) set on fire + -BLE] —**flam′ma·bil′i·ty,** *n.*

Flam·ma·rion (fla ma ryôN′), *n.* **(Ni·co·las) Ca·mille** (nē kô lä′ ka mē′yᵊ), 1842–1925, French astronomer and author.

flam·y (flā′mē), *adj.,* **flam·i·er, flam·i·est.** of or like flame.

flan (flan, flän; *for 1 also Fr.* fläN; *for 2 also Sp.* flän), *n., pl.* **flans** (flanz, flänz; *for 1 also Fr.* fläN), *Sp.* **fla·nes** (flä′nes) for 2. **1.** an open, tartlike pastry filled with custard, cream, fruit, etc., the shell of which is baked in a ring of metal on a baking sheet. **2.** (in Spanish cookery) a sweetened egg custard. **3.** a piece of metal shaped ready to form a coin, but not yet stamped by the die. [< F; OF *flaon* < LL *fladōn-,* s. of *fladō* < OHG: flat cake, G *Fladen*]

Flan·a·gan (flan′ə gən), *n.* **Edward Joseph** ("*Father Flanagan*"), 1886–1948, U.S. Roman Catholic priest, born in Ireland: founder of a farm village for wayward boys.

flan·chard (flang′kərd), *n.* *Armor.* a piece for the middle of one side of a horse, between the peytral and the crupper. Also, **flan′card.** [late ME *flancard* < MF; see FLANK, -ARD]

Flan·ders (flan′dərz), *n.* a medieval country in W Europe, extending along the North Sea from the Strait of Dover to the Scheldt River: the corresponding modern regions include the provinces of East Flanders and West Flanders in W Belgium, and the adjacent parts of N France and SW Netherlands.

flâ·ne·rie (flänᵊ rē′), *n.* *French.* idleness; dawdling.

flâ·neur (flä nœr′), *n., pl.* **-neurs** (-nœr′). *French.* idler; dawdler; loafer.

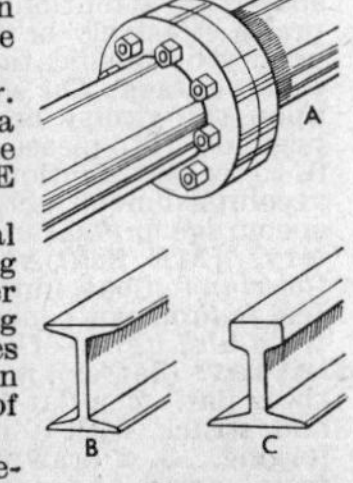

Flanges
A, Flanges on connecting pipe ends; B, Flanges on I beam; C, Flange on foot of rail

flange (flanj), *n., v.,* **flanged, flang·ing.** —*n.* **1.** a projecting rim, collar, or ring on a shaft, pipe, machine housing, etc., cast or formed to give additional strength, stiffness, or supporting area, or to provide a place for the attachment of other objects. **2.** a broad ridge or pair of ridges projecting from the edge of a rolled metal shape generally at right angles, in order to strengthen or stiffen it. **3.** a ring or collar, usually provided with holes for bolts, and screwed or welded over the end of a tube or pipe to permit other objects to be attached to it. —*v.i.* **4.** to project like, or take the form of, a flange. [late ME *flaunche* side charge (on shield face) < MF *flanche,* fem. of *flanc* FLANK] —**flange′less,** *adj.* —**flang′er,** *n.*

flank (flangk), *n.* **1.** the side of an animal or a man between the ribs and hip. **2.** the flesh constituting this part. **3.** a slice of meat from the flank of an animal. **4.** the side of anything, as of a building. **5.** *Mil., Navy.* the extreme right or left side of an army or fleet, or a subdivision of an army or fleet. **6.** *Fort.* **a.** the right or left side of a work or fortification. **b.** the part of a bastion that extends from the curtain to the face and protects the curtain and the opposite face. —*v.t.* **7.** to stand or be placed or posted at the flank or side of. **8.** to defend or guard at the flank. **9.** to pass around or turn the flank of. —*v.i.* **10.** to occupy a position at the flank or side. **11.** to present the flank or side. [ME; OE *flanc* < ML *flanc(us)* side < Gmc; cf. OHG *hlanca* loin]

flank·er (flang′kər), *n.* **1.** a person or thing that flanks. **2.** *Mil.* one of a body of soldiers employed on the flank of an army to guard a line of march. **3.** *Fort.* a fortification projecting so as to defend another work or to command the flank of an assailing body.

flank′ speed′, the full speed of a ship.

flan·nel (flan′ᵊl), *n., v.,* **-neled, -nel·ing** or (*esp. Brit.*), **-nelled, -nel·ling.** —*n.* **1.** a warm, soft, napped fabric of wool or cotton or blends of wool and cotton or rayon, or of cotton warp with wool filling. **2. flannels, a.** an outer garment, esp. trousers, made of flannel. **b.** woolen undergarments. —*v.t.* **3.** to cover or clothe with flannel. **4.** to rub with flannel. [ME *flaunneol,* dissimilated var. of *flanyn* garment for penitents < Welsh; cf. Welsh *gwlanen* a flannel = *gwlân* wool (akin to L *lāna*) + *-en* piece] —**flan′nel·ly,** *adj.*

flan·nel·et (flan′ᵊlet′), *n.* a cotton fabric, plain or printed, napped on one side. Also, **flan′nel·ette′.**

flap (flap), *v.,* **flapped, flap·ping,** *n.* —*v.i.* **1.** to swing or sway about loosely, esp. with noise. **2.** to move up and down, as wings. **3.** to strike a blow with something broad and flexible. —*v.t.* **4.** to move (the wings) up and down, as birds. **5.** to move (the arms) up and down in a similar fashion. **6.** to cause to swing or sway loosely, esp. with noise. **7.** to strike with something broad and flexible. **8.** *Informal.* to toss, fold, shut, etc., smartly, roughly, or noisily. **9.** *Phonet.* to pronounce (a sound) with articulation resembling that of a flap. —*n.* **10.** a flapping motion. **11.** the noise produced by something that flaps. **12.** a blow given with something broad and flexible. **13.** something broad and flexible, or flat and thin, that hangs loosely, attached at one side only. **14.** one leaf of a folding door, shutter, or the like. **15. a.** Also called **flap′ hinge′.** a hinge having a strap or plate for screwing to the face of a door, shutter, or the like. See illus. at **hinge. b.** one leaf of a hinge. **16.** *Surg.* a portion of skin or flesh that is partially separated from the body and may subsequently be transposed by grafting. **17.** *Aeron.* a movable surface used for increasing the lift or drag of an airplane. **18.** *Slang.* **a.** a state of nervous excitement. **b.** an emergency situation. **19.** *Phonet.* **a.** a rapid flip of the tongue tip against the upper teeth or alveolar ridge, as in the *r*-sound in a common British pronunciation of *very,* or the *t*-sound in the common American pronunciation of *water.* **b.** a trill. [ME *flappe* a blow, slap, *flappe(n)* (to) hit, slap; cf. D *flap, flappen*] —**flap′less,** *adj.*

flap·doo·dle (flap′do͞od′ᵊl), *n.* *Informal.* nonsense; bosh. [?]

flap·jack (flap′jak′), *n.* griddlecake.

flap·pa·ble (flap′ə bəl), *adj.* *Slang.* easily upset or confused, esp. in a crisis. [back formation from UNFLAPPABLE]

flap·per (flap′ər), *n.* **1.** something broad and flat for striking with or for making a noise by striking. **2.** a broad, flat, hinged or hanging piece; flap. **3.** a young bird just learning to fly. **4.** a young woman, esp. an unconventional one during the 1920's. —**flap′per·dom,** *n.* —**flap′per·ish,** *adj.*

flare (flâr), *v.,* **flared, flar·ing,** *n.* —*v.i.* **1.** to burn with an unsteady, swaying flame, as a torch in the wind. **2.** to blaze with a sudden burst of flame (often fol. by *up*): *The fire flared up as the paper caught on.* **3.** to develop suddenly, as violence (often fol. by *up*). **4.** to shine or glow. **5.** to spread gradually outward, as the end of a trumpet, the bottom of a wide skirt, etc. —*v.t.* **6.** to cause to flare. **7.** to display conspicuously or ostentatiously. **8.** to signal by flares of fire or light. **9. flare out** or **up,** to become suddenly enraged. —*n.* **10.** a flaring or swaying flame or light, as of torches in the wind. **11.** a sudden blaze or burst of flame. **12.** a bright blaze of fire or light used as a signal, a means of illumination or guidance, etc. **13.** a device or substance used to produce such a blaze of fire or light. **14.** a sudden burst, as of zeal or temper. **15.** a gradual spread outward in form; outward curvature. **16.** something that spreads out. **17.** *Optics.* unwanted light reaching the image plane of an optical instrument, resulting from extraneous reflections, scattering by lenses, and the like. **18.** *Photog.* a fogged appearance given to an image by reflection within a camera lens or within the camera itself. [orig. uncert.] **Syn. 1.** flame. **11.** flash.

flare·back (flâr′bak′), *n.* a blast of flame that sometimes issues from the breech of a large gun or cannon when it is opened after firing.

flare-up (flâr′up′), *n.* **1.** a sudden flaring up of flame or light. **2.** a sudden outburst of anger. **3.** a sudden outbreak of violence, disease, or other condition thought to be inactive.

flar·ing (flâr′ing), *adj.* **1.** blazing; flaming. **2.** glaringly bright or showy. **3.** spreading gradually outward in form: *a flaring skirt.* —**flar′ing·ly,** *adv.*

flash (flash), *n.* **1.** a brief, sudden burst of bright light. **2.** a sudden, brief outburst or display, as of joy or wit. **3.** a very brief moment; instant. **4.** flashlight (def. 1). **5.** ostentatious display; gaudy showiness. **6.** Also called **news flash.** *Journalism.* a brief dispatch sent by a wire service, usually transmitting preliminary news of an important story. **7.** *Photog.* bright artificial light thrown briefly upon a subject

during an exposure. **8.** the sudden flame or intense heat produced by a bomb or other explosive device. **9.** *Archaic.* an artificially induced rush of water for sending a boat down a shallow stream. **10.** *Obs.* the cant or jargon of thieves, vagabonds, etc. **11. flash in the pan, a.** a brief, intense effort that produces no permanent result. **b.** a person who makes such an effort; one who enjoys short-lived success. —*v.i.* **12.** to break forth into sudden flame or light, esp. transiently or intermittently. **13.** to speak or behave with sudden anger, outrage, or the like (often fol. by *out*): *to flash out at a stupid remark.* **14.** to gleam. **15.** to burst suddenly into view or perception. **16.** to move like a flash. **17.** to break into sudden action. **18.** *Archaic.* to make a flash or sudden display. **19.** *Archaic.* to dash or splash, as the sea or waves. —*v.t.* **20.** to emit or send forth (fire or light) in sudden flashes. **21.** to cause to flash, as powder by ignition or a sword by waving. **22.** to send forth like a flash. **23.** to transmit or communicate instantaneously, as by telegraph. **24.** *Informal.* to make an ostentatious display of. **25.** to increase the flow of water in (a river, channel, etc.). **26.** *Glassmaking.* **a.** to coat (plain glass or a glass object) with a layer of colored, opalescent, or white glass. **b.** to apply (such a layer). **c.** to color or make (glass) opaque by reheating. **27.** *Building Trades.* to protect with flashing. —*adj.* **28.** showy or ostentatious. **29.** of or belonging to sporting men; sporty. **30.** sudden and brief: *a flash storm.* **31.** caused by or used as protection against flash: *flash injuries; flash clothing.* **32.** *Informal.* belonging to or connected with thieves, vagabonds, etc., or their cant or jargon. [ME *flasshe(n)* (to) sprinkle; ? b. FLY[1] and WASH] —**flash′er,** *n.* —**flash′ing·ly,** *adv.*
—**Syn. 1.** flare, gleam, glare. **3.** twinkling, wink. **14.** scintillate. FLASH, GLANCE, GLINT, GLITTER mean to send forth a sudden gleam (or gleams) of bright light. To FLASH is to send forth light with a sudden, transient brilliancy: *A shooting star flashed briefly.* To GLANCE is to emit a brilliant flash of light as a reflection from a smooth surface: *Sunlight glanced from the windshield.* To GLINT is to reflect a bright gleam of light as from something polished or burnished: *Light glints from burnished copper.* To GLITTER is to reflect intermittent flashes of light from a hard surface: *Ice glitters in the moonlight.* **28.** flashy, gaudy, tawdry, pretentious.

flash·back (flash′bak′), *n.* a scene representing an earlier event inserted into a current situation depicted in a novel, motion picture, play, etc.

flash′ bulb′, *Photog.* **1.** a glass bulb, burning with a brilliant flash when ignited electrically, for momentarily illuminating a subject. **2.** Also called **flashtube, flash tube.** an electronic flash lamp having a tube containing xenon or krypton. Also, **flash′bulb′.**

flash′ card′, a card bearing words, numerals, or pictures, designed for gaining a rapid response from pupils when held up briefly by a teacher, as in a drill.

flash·cube (flash′kyōōb′), *n.* *Photog.* a cube, for attaching to a camera, that contains a flash bulb in each vertical side and rotates automatically for taking four flash pictures in rapid succession. Also, **flash′ cube′.**

flash′ flood′, a sudden and destructive rush of water down a narrow gully or over a sloping surface.

flash′ gun′, *Photog.* a device that simultaneously discharges a flash bulb and operates a camera shutter.

flash·ing (flash′ing), *n.* **1.** *Building Trades.* sheet metal or the like used to cover and protect certain joints and angles, as where a roof comes in contact with a wall. **2.** the act of creating an artificial flood in a conduit or stream, as in a sewer for cleansing it.

flash′ lamp′, *Photog.* a special lamp for providing momentary illumination for the subject of a photograph. Also, **flash′lamp′.**

flash·light (flash′līt′), *n.* **1.** a small, portable electric lamp powered by dry batteries or a tiny generator. **2.** a flash of light, or a light that flashes. **3.** any source of artificial light as used in flash photography.

flash·o·ver (flash′ō′vər), *n.* *Elect.* a disruptive discharge around or over the surface of a solid or liquid insulator.

flash′ photog′raphy, photography using a momentary flash of artificial light as a source of illumination. Also called **photoflash photography.**

flash′ point′, *Physical Chem.* the lowest temperature at which a liquid will give off sufficient vapor to ignite on application of a flame. Also called **flash′ing point′.**

flash·tube (flash′tōōb′, -tyōōb′), *n.* *Photog.* See **flash bulb** (def. 2). Also, **flash′ tube′.**

flash·y (flash′ē), *adj.*, **flash·i·er, flash·i·est. 1.** briefly and superficially sparkling or brilliant: *a flashy performance.* **2.** pretentiously smart; showy; gaudy: *flashy clothes.* **3.** *Archaic.* flashing with light. —**flash′i·ly,** *adv.* —**flash′i·ness,** *n.* —**Syn. 2.** See **gaudy**[1].

flask (flask, fläsk), *n.* **1.** a bottle, usually of glass, having a rounded body and a narrow neck, used to hold wine, oil, etc. **2.** a flat metal or glass bottle for carrying in the pocket: *a flask full of brandy.* **3.** the quantity contained in a flask. **4.** *Foundry.* a container into which sand is rammed around a pattern to form a mold. [ME; OE *flasce, flaxe;* cf. FLAGON]

flat[1] (flat), *adj.*, **flat·ter, flat·test,** *n.*, *v.*, **flat·ted, flat·ting,** *adv.* —*adj.* **1.** horizontally level. **2.** level, even, or without inequalities of surface, as land, tabletops, etc. **3.** having a surface that is without marked projections or depressions. **4.** lying horizontally and at full length, as a person. **5.** lying wholly on or against something. **6.** thrown down, laid low, or level with the ground, as fallen trees or buildings. **7.** having a generally level shape or appearance; not deep or thick. **8.** spread out, as an unrolled map, the open hand, etc. **9.** deflated; collapsed: *a flat tire.* **10.** without qualification; absolute, downright, or positive: *a flat denial.* **11.** without modification or variation: *a flat price; a flat rate.* **12.** without vitality or animation; lifeless; dull. **13.** having lost its flavor, sharpness, or life, as wine or food; stale. **14.** (of a beverage) having lost its effervescence. **15.** pointless, as a remark or joke. **16.** commercially dull, as trade or the market. **17.** *Painting.* **a.** not having the illusion of volume or depth. **b.** lacking gradations of tone or color. **c.** without gloss; mat. **18.** not clear, sharp, or ringing, as sound, a voice, etc. **19.** lacking resonance and variation in pitch; monotonous. **20.** *Music.* **a.** (of a tone) lowered a half step in pitch: *B flat.* **b.** below an intended pitch, as a note; too low (opposed to *sharp*). **21.** *Gram.* derived without change in form, as English *to brush* from the noun *brush* and adverbs which do not add *-ly* to the adjective form as *fast, cheap, slow,* etc. **22.** *Phonet.* lenis; voiced. **23. flat a,** the *a*-sound (a) of *glad, bat,* or *act.* —*n.* **24.** something flat. **25.** Often, **flats.** a shoe, esp. a woman's shoe, with a flat heel or no heel. **26.** a flat surface, side, or part of anything: *the flat of his hand.* **27.** flat or level ground; a flat area: *salt flats.* **28.** a marsh, shoal, or shallow. **29.** *Music.* **a.** (in musical notation) the character ♭, which when attached to a note or to a staff degree lowers its significance one chromatic half step. **b.** a tone one chromatic half step below another. **30.** *Theat.* a piece of scenery consisting of a wooden frame, usually rectangular, covered with lightweight board or fabric. **31.** a broad, thin book, chiefly for children: *a juvenile flat.* **32.** *Informal.* a deflated automobile tire. **33.** Also called **platform.** *Naut.* **a.** a partial deck between two full decks. **b.** a low, flat barge or lighter. **34.** an iron or steel bar of rectangular section. **35.** *Hort.* a shallow box used for rooting seeds and cuttings. **36.** *Football.* the area of the field immediately inside of or outside of an offensive end, close behind or at the line of scrimmage. —*v.t.* **37.** to make flat. **38.** *Music.* to lower (a pitch), esp. one half step. —*v.i.* **39.** to become flat. **40. flat in,** *Naut.* to pull the clew of (a fore-and-aft sail) as nearly amidships as possible. Also, **flatten in.** —*adv.* **41.** in a flat position; horizontally; levelly. **42.** in a flat manner; positively; absolutely. **43.** completely; utterly: *flat broke.* **44.** exactly; precisely. **45.** *Music.* below the true pitch: *to sing flat.* **46.** *Finance.* without interest. **47. fall flat,** to fail to produce the desired effect; fail completely. [ME < Scand; cf. Icel *flat(r),* Sw *flat;* akin to OE *flet* floor (see FLAT[2]), Gk *platýs* (see PLATE[1], PLATY-)] —**flat′ly,** *adv.* —**flat′ness,** *n.*
—**Syn. 1.** plane. See **level. 4.** supine, prostrate, prone. **10.** categorical. **12.** boring, spiritless, prosaic, insipid. **13.** vapid, unsavory. —**Ant. 1, 4.** upright, vertical.

flat[2] (flat), *n.* an apartment or suite of rooms on one floor, forming a residence, as for a family. [var. of obs. *flet,* OE: floor, house, hall; akin to FLAT[1]]

flat′-bed press′ (flat′bed′). See **cylinder press.**

flat·boat (flat′bōt′), *n.* a large flat-bottomed boat for use in shallow water, esp. for use on rivers.

flat·car (flat′kär′), *n.* *U.S.* a railroad car without sides or top; platform car.

flat·fish (flat′fish′), *n., pl.* (*esp. collectively*) **-fish,** (*esp. referring to two or more kinds or species*) **-fish·es.** any fish of the order *Heterosomata* (*Pleuronectiformes*), including the halibut, sole, flounder, etc., having a greatly compressed body, with both eyes on the upper side in the adult, and swimming on one side.

flat·foot (flat′fōōt′ *or, for 1,* -fōōt′), *n., pl.* **-feet** for 1, **-foots** for 2. **1.** *Pathol.* **a.** a condition in which the arch of the foot is flattened so that the entire sole rests upon the ground. **b.** a foot with such an arch. **2.** *Slang.* a policeman.

flat·foot·ed (flat′fōōt′id), *adj.* **1.** having flatfeet. **2. catch one flatfooted,** *Informal.* to catch one off his guard; surprise: *The amount of the dinner check caught us flatfooted.* —**flat′-foot′ed·ly,** *adv.* —**flat′-foot′ed·ness,** *n.*

flat·head (flat′hed′), *n., pl.* (*esp. collectively*) **-head,** (*esp. referring to two or more kinds or species*) **-heads.** any of several scorpaenoid fishes of the family *Platycephalidae,* found chiefly in the Indo-Pacific region, where they are used for food. [FLAT[1] + HEAD, so called from physical appearance]

Flat·head (flat′hed′), *n.* **1.** a member of a tribe of Salishan Indians of northwest Montana. **2.** a Chinook Indian. [so called from their supposed practice of flattening their children's heads]

flat·i·ron (flat′ī′ərn), *n.* **1.** an iron with a flat bottom, heated for use in pressing clothes, cloth, etc. **2.** *Geol.* a triangular-shaped hogback that resembles a flatiron resting on its base.

flat′ knot′. See **reef knot.**

flat·ling (flat′ling), *adv.* Also, **flat′lings.** *Brit. Dial.* **1.** in a flat position; with the flat side, as of a sword. **2.** flatly or positively. —*adj.* **3.** *Obs.* dealt with the flat side. [ME]

flat′ sil′ver, flatware (def. 1).

flat′ tax′, an income tax levied at the same fixed percentage of income for all, regardless of the taxable base, and that allows no or very few tax exemptions, deductions, or credits.

flat·ten (flat′ən), *v.t.* **1.** to make flat. —*v.i.* **2.** to become flat. **3. flatten in,** *Naut.* See **flat**[1] (def. 40). **4. flatten out,** *Aeron.* to fly into a horizontal position, as after a dive. —**flat′ten·er,** *n.*

flat·ter[1] (flat′ər), *v.t.* **1.** to try to please by complimentary speech or attention. **2.** to compliment insincerely. **3.** to praise effusively or excessively. **4.** to represent favorably; gratify by falsification: *The portrait flatters her.* **5.** to show to advantage: *The black dress flattered her figure.* **6.** to play upon the vanity or susceptibilities of; cajole, wheedle, or beguile. **7.** to please or gratify by compliments or attentions. **8.** to feel satisfaction with (oneself) esp. with reference to an accomplishment, act, or occasion. **9.** to beguile with hope; encourage prematurely, falsely, etc. —*v.i.* **10.** to use flattery. [ME *flat(t)er(en)* (to) float, flutter, fawn upon, OE *floterian* to float, flutter; for sense development, cf. FLICKER[1], Icel *flathra;* not connected with F *flatter* to flatter] —**flat′ter·a·ble,** *adj.* —**flat′ter·er,** *n.* —**flat′ter·ing·ly,** *adv.*

flat·ter[2] (flat′ər), *n.* **1.** a person or thing that makes something flat. **2.** a flat-faced blacksmith's tool, laid on a forging and struck with a hammer to smooth the surface of the forging. **3.** a drawplate with a flat orifice for drawing flat metal strips, as for watch springs. [FLAT[1] + -ER[1]]

flat·ter·y (flat′ə rē), *n., pl.* **-ter·ies** for 2. **1.** the act of flattering. **2.** a flattering compliment or speech; excessive, insincere praise. [ME *flaterie* < MF = *flat(er)* (to) flatter + *-erie* -ERY]

flat·ting (flat′ing), *n.* the act of a person or thing that makes flat, as in the manufacture of sheet metal, flat paint, etc.

flat·tish (flat′ish), *adj.* somewhat flat.

flat·top (flat′top′), *n.* *U.S. Navy Informal.* an aircraft carrier. Also, **flat′-top′.**

flat·u·lent (flach′ə lənt), *adj.* **1.** generating gas in the alimentary canal, as food. **2.** attended with, caused by, or suffering from, such an accumulation of gas. **3.** having unsupported pretentions; pompous; turgid: *a flatulent style.* [< NL *flātulent(us).* See FLATUS, -ULENT] —**flat′u·lence, flat′u·len·cy,** *n.* —**flat′u·lent·ly,** *adv.*

fla·tus (flā′təs), *n., pl.* **-tus·es.** an accumulation of gas in the stomach, intestines, or other body cavity. [< L: a blowing, breathing, breath (4th decl. n.) < *flātus,* ptp. of *flāre* to blow]

flat·ware (flat′wâr′), *n.* **1.** utensils for the table, as knives, forks, and spoons. **2.** dishes or containers for the table, or for other use, that are more or less flat, as plates or saucers (distinguished from *hollowware*).

flat·wise (flat′wīz′), *adv.* with the flat side, rather than the edge, foremost or in contact. Also, **flat·ways** (flat′wāz′).

flat·work (flat′wûrk′), *n.* articles of linen, clothing, etc., that are ordinarily ironed mechanically rather than by hand. Also called **flat′wash′.**

flat·worm (flat′wûrm′), *n.* a platyhelminth.

Flau·bert (flō bâr′; *Fr.* flō bᴇʀ′), *n.* **Gus·tave** (gʏs tᴀv′), 1821–80, French novelist.

flaunt (flônt), *v.t.* **1.** to parade or display ostentatiously. **2.** *Nonstandard.* to treat with disdain; flout: *flaunting military regulations.* —*v.i.* **3.** to parade or display oneself ostentatiously. **4.** to wave conspicuously in the air. —*n.* **5.** the act of flaunting. **6.** *Obs.* something flaunted. [< Scand; cf. Norw *flanta* to gad about < *flana* to roam; akin to Gk *plánē* a roaming (see PLANET)] —**flaunt′er,** *n.* —**flaunt′ing·ly,** *adv.* —**Syn. 1.** flourish.
—**Usage. 2.** This sense of FLAUNT stems from its confusion with FLOUT and, although this confusion is quite common, is regarded as nonstandard usage.

flaunt·y (flôn′tē), *adj.,* **flaunt·i·er, flaunt·i·est. 1.** (of persons) inclined to be ostentatious, showy, or vain. **2.** (of things) gaudy; flashy; ostentatious. —**flaunt′i·ly,** *adv.* —**flaunt′i·ness,** *n.*

flau·tist (flô′tist, flou′-), *n.* flutist. [< It *flautist(a)* = *flaut(o)* FLUTE + *-ista* -IST]

flav-, var. of **flavo-** before a vowel: *flavin.*

fla·ves·cent (flə ves′ənt), *adj.* turning yellow; yellowish. [< L *flāvēscent-* (s. of *flāvēscēns*), prp. of *flāvēscere* to become yellow]

fla·vin (flā′vin), *n. Chem.* **1.** a complex heterocyclic ketone that is common to the nonprotein part of several important yellow enzymes, the flavoproteins. **2.** quercetin. [FLAV- + -IN[2]]

-flavin, *Chem.* a combining form indicating any of a number of natural derivatives of flavin: *riboflavin.*

fla·vine (flā′vin, -vēn), *n. Chem.* flavin.

flavo-, a learned borrowing from Latin meaning "yellow," used in the formation of compound words (*flavopurpurin*); in some chemical terms, specialized in meaning to indicate **flavin** (*flavoprotein*). Also, *esp. before a vowel,* **flav-.** [comb. form repr. L *flāvus*]

fla·vone (flā′vōn), *n. Chem.* **1.** a colorless compound, $C_{15}H_{10}O_2$, the parent substance of a group of derivatives some of which have been used as yellow dyes. **2.** any derivative of this compound.

fla·vo·pro·tein (flā′vō prō′tēn, -tē ən), *n. Biochem.* an enzyme, containing riboflavin and linked with a protein, active in the oxidation of foods in animal cells.

fla·vo·pur·pu·rin (flā′vō pûr′pyə rin), *n. Chem.* a yellow anthraquinone dye, $C_{14}H_5O_2(OH)_3$.

fla·vor (flā′vər), *n.* **1.** taste, esp. the distinctive taste of something as it is experienced in the mouth. **2.** a substance or extract that provides a particular flavor. **3.** the characteristic quality of something: *This movie really catches the flavor of New York.* **4.** a particular quality noticeable in something, as in a style of writing, painting, etc.: *language with a strong nautical flavor.* **5.** *Archaic.* smell, odor, or aroma. —*v.t.* **6.** to give flavor to (something). Also, *esp. Brit.,* **fla′vour.** [ME < MF *fla(o)ur* < LL **flātor* stench, breath, alter. of L *flātus.* See FLATUS, -OR[1]] —**fla′vor·less,** *esp. Brit.,* **fla′vour·less,** *adj.* —**Syn. 1.** See **taste. 3.** essence, spirit.

fla·vor·ful (flā′vər fəl), *adj.* full of flavor; tasty. Also, **fla′vor·ous, fla′vor·some, fla′vor·y;** *esp. Brit.,* **fla′vour·ful, fla′vour·some, fla′vour·y.** —**fla′vor·ful·ly;** *esp. Brit.,* **fla′vour·ful·ly,** *adv.*

fla·vor·ing (flā′vər ing), *n.* something that gives flavor; a substance or preparation used to give a particular flavor to food or drink. Also, *esp. Brit.,* **fla′vour·ing.**

flaw[1] (flô), *n.* **1.** a feature that mars the perfection of something; defect; fault. **2.** a defect impairing legal soundness or validity. **3.** a crack, break, breach, or rift. —*v.t.* **4.** to produce a flaw in. —*v.i.* **5.** to contract a flaw; become cracked or defective. [ME *flaw(e), flage* < Scand; akin to Icel *flaga* thin layer of earth, Dan *flage,* Sw *flaga* sliver, chip, OE *flēan* to FLAY] —**flaw′less,** *adj.* —**flaw′less·ly,** *adv.* —**flaw′less·ness,** *n.* —**Syn. 1.** imperfection. See **defect.**

flaw[2] (flô), *n.* **1.** Also called **windflaw.** a sudden, usually brief windstorm or gust of wind. **2.** a short spell of rough weather. **3.** *Obs.* a burst of feeling, fury, etc. [< Scand; cf. Icel *flaga* sudden onset, Norw *flaga* gust, MLG *vlage*]

flaw·y (flô′ē), *adj.,* **flaw·i·er, flaw·i·est.** characterized by gusts, as wind.

flax (flaks), *n.* **1.** any plant of the genus *Linum,* esp. *L. usitatissimum,* a slender, erect, annual plant having narrow, lance-shaped leaves and blue flowers, cultivated for its fiber and seeds. **2.** the fiber of this plant, manufactured into linen yarn for thread or woven fabrics. **3.** any of various plants resembling flax. [ME; OE *fleax;* c. D, LG *vlas,* G *Flachs*]

flax·en (flak′sən), *adj.* **1.** of, pertaining to, or resembling flax. **2.** of the pale yellowish color of dressed flax. Also, **flax′y.**

Flax·man (flaks′mən), *n.* **John,** 1755–1826, English sculptor and draftsman.

flax·seed (flaks′sēd′, flak′-), *n.* the seed of flax, yielding linseed oil; linseed.

flay (flā), *v.t.* **1.** to strip off the skin or outer covering of, as by whipping. **2.** to criticize or rebuke with scathing severity. **3.** to deprive or strip of money or property; fleece. [ME *fle(n),* OE *flēan;* c. MD *vlaen,* Icel *flā*] —**flay′er,** *n.*

fld., 1. field. **2.** fluid.

fl. dr., See **fluid dram.** Also, **f ʒ**

fldxt., (in prescriptions) fluidextract. [< L *fluidextractum*]

Flea (def. 1), *Ctenocephalides canis* (Length ⅛ in.)

flea (flē), *n.* **1.** any of numerous small, wingless, bloodsucking insects of the order *Siphonaptera,* parasitic upon mammals and birds, and noted for their ability to leap. **2.** any of various small beetles and crustaceans that leap like a flea, or swim in a jumpy manner, as the water flea and beach flea. **3. flea in one's ear,** a rebuke, rebuff, or broad hint: *He put a flea in my ear about the secret meeting.* [ME *fle,* OE *flēah, flēa;* c. G *Floh;* akin to FLEE]

flea·bag (flē′bag′), *n. Slang.* a cheap, run-down hotel or rooming house.

flea·bane (flē′bān′), *n.* any of various composite plants, as *Pulicaria dysenterica,* of Europe, or *Erigeron philadelphicus,* of the U.S., reputed to destroy or drive away fleas.

flea·bite (flē′bīt′), *n.* **1.** the bite of a flea. **2.** the red spot caused by it. **3.** any petty annoyance or irritation, as a trifling wound. [late ME *flee byte*]

flea-bit·ten (flē′bit′ən), *adj.* **1.** bitten by a flea or fleas. **2.** infested with fleas: *a flea-bitten blanket.* **3.** (of a horse) having a light-colored coat with small reddish spots or streaks.

Flèche

fleam (flēm), *n.* **1.** *Surg.* a kind of lancet, as for opening veins. **2.** the beveled leading edge of a sawtooth. [ME *fleme, fleom* < MF *flieme* << LL *phlebotomus,* m. Gk *phlebotómon* neut. n. use of adj. See PHLEBOTOMY]

flea′ mar′ket, an open-air market, esp. in one of the larger cities of Europe, where old or used articles are sold.

flea·wort (flē′wûrt′), *n.* **1.** a rough-leaved composite herb, *Inula Conyza,* of Europe. **2.** a European plantain, *Plantago Psyllium,* whose seeds resemble fleas and are used in medicine. [ME *flewort,* OE *flēawyrt*]

flèche (flāsh; *Fr.* flesh), *n., pl.* **flè·ches** (flā′shiz; *Fr.* flesh). **1.** *Archit.* a steeple or spire, esp. one in the Gothic style, emerging from the ridge of a roof. **2.** *Fort.* a fieldwork consisting of two faces forming a salient angle and having an open gorge. [< F: lit., arrow, prob. < Gmc. Cf. FLY[1]]

flé·chette (flā shet′), *n., pl.* **flé·chettes** (flā shets′; *Fr.* flā shet′). *Mil.* a steel dart for shooting from a gun or releasing from an airplane in strafing. [< F]

fleck (flek), *n.* **1.** a spot or small patch of color, light, etc., esp. on the skin. **2.** a speck; a small bit: *a fleck of dirt.* —*v.t.* **3.** to mark with a fleck or flecks; spot; dapple. [< Scand; c. OIcel *flekk(r)* spot, streak, Sw *fläck,* OHG *flec* (G *Fleck*); akin to OIcel *flekka* to soil, MLG, MD *vlecken*] —**fleck′y,** *adj.*

flec·tion (flek′shən), *n.* **1.** the act of bending. **2.** the state of being bent. **3.** a bend or bent part. **4.** *Anat.* flexion. **5.** *Gram.* inflection (def. 2). Also, *esp. Brit.,* **flexion** (for defs. 1–3). [< L *flexiōn-* (s. of *flexiō*) a bending, turning, change] —**flec′tion·al,** *adj.* —**flec′tion·less,** *adj.*

fled (fled), *v.* pt. and pp. of **flee.**

fledge (flej), *v.,* **fledged, fledg·ing.** —*v.t.* **1.** to raise (a young bird) until it is able to fly. **2.** to furnish with or as with feathers or plumage. **3.** to provide (an arrow) with feathers. —*v.i.* **4.** (of a young bird) to acquire the feathers necessary for flight. [ME *flegge,* OE *-flycge* (in *unflycge* unfledged); c. OHG *flucki,* MLG *vlügge* (G *flügge*). See FLY[1]]

fledg·ling (flej′ling), *n.* **1.** a young bird just fledged. **2.** an inexperienced person. Also, *esp. Brit.,* **fledge′ling.**

fledg·y (flej′ē), *adj.,* **fledg·i·er, fledg·i·est.** feathered or feathery.

flee (flē), *v.,* **fled, flee·ing.** —*v.i.* **1.** to run away, as from danger, pursuers, etc.; take flight. **2.** to move swiftly; fly; speed. —*v.t.* **3.** to run away from (a place, person, etc.). [ME *flee(n),* OE *flēon;* c. OHG *flichan* (G *fliehen*), Goth *thliuhan;* cf. OE *fleogan* to FLY[1]]

fleece (flēs), *n., v.,* **fleeced, fleec·ing.** —*n.* **1.** the coat of wool that covers a sheep or a similar animal. **2.** the amount of wool shorn at one time. **3.** something resembling a fleece. **4.** a fabric with a soft, silky pile, used for warmth, as for lining garments. **5.** the soft nap or pile of such a fabric. —*v.t.* **6.** to remove the fleece of (a sheep). **7.** to deprive of money or belongings by fraud, hoax, or the like; swindle. **8.** to overspread, as with a fleece; fleck with fleecelike masses. [ME *flees,* OE *flēos, flȳs;* c. MD *vlies,* MHG *vlius,* G *Vlies*] —**fleec′er,** *n.*

fleec·y (flē′sē), *adj.,* **fleec·i·er, fleec·i·est.** covered with, consisting of, or resembling a fleece or wool. —**fleec′i·ly,** *adv.* —**fleec′i·ness,** *n.*

fleer[1] (flēr), *v.i.* **1.** to grin or laugh coarsely or mockingly. —*v.t.* **2.** to mock or deride. —*n.* **3.** a fleering look; a jeer or gibe. [ME *fler(ien)* < Scand; cf. Norw *flire* a grin] —**fleer′ing·ly,** *adv.*

fle·er[2] (flē′ər), *n.* a person who flees. [ME]

fleet[1] (flēt), *n.* **1.** the largest organized unit of naval ships grouped for tactical or other purposes. **2.** the largest organization of warships under the command of a single officer. **3.** a number of naval vessels, or vessels carrying armed men. **4.** a large group of ships, airplanes, trucks, etc., operated by a single company or regarded as a unit: *a fleet of cabs.* [ME *flete,* OE *flēot,* flowing water, ship < *flēotan* to float]

fleet[2] (flēt), *adj.* **1.** swift; rapid: *to be fleet of foot.* —*v.i.* **2.** to move swiftly; fly. **3.** *Naut.* to change position; shift. **4.** *Archaic.* to glide away like a stream. **5.** *Archaic.* to fade; vanish. **6.** *Obs.* to float; drift. **7.** *Obs.* to swim. —*v.t.* **8.** to cause (time) to pass lightly or swiftly. **9.** *Naut.* to move or change the position of. [ME *flete(n)* (to) be fleet, OE *flēotan* to FLOAT] —**fleet′ly,** *adv.* —**fleet′ness,** *n.* —**Syn. 8.** speed, hasten; beguile.

fleet[3] (flēt), *n.* *Brit. Dial.* **1.** an arm of the sea; inlet. **2. the Fleet,** a former prison in London, long used for debtors. [ME *flete,* OE *flēot* flowing water; c. G *Fliess* brook]

fleet′ ad′miral, *U.S. Navy.* the highest ranking naval officer, ranking next above admiral.

fleet-foot·ed (flēt′fo͝ot′id), *adj.* able to run fast; swift of foot.

fleet·ing (flē′ting), *adj.* passing swiftly; vanishing quickly; transient; transitory. [ME] —**fleet′ing·ly,** *adv.* —**fleet′ing·ness,** *n.* —**Syn.** passing, flitting, flying, brief, fugitive.

Fleet′ Street′, a street in central London, England: location of many newspaper offices; often used figuratively to mean the entire British newspaper world.

Flem, Flemish (def. 3). Also, **Flem.**

Flem·ing (flem′ing), *n.* **1. Sir Alexander,** 1881–1955, Scottish bacteriologist and physician: codiscoverer, with Sir Howard Florey, of penicillin 1929; Nobel prize for medicine 1945. **2. Ian (Lancaster),** 1908–64, British writer of suspense novels.

Flem·ing (flem′ing), *n.* **1.** a native of Flanders. **2.** a Flemish-speaking Belgian. [ME < MD *Vlaming;* cf. OIcel *flǣming,* OHG *Flaming,* ML *Flamingus,* Sp *flamenco* FLAMENCO]

Flem·ish (flem′ish), *adj.* **1.** of or pertaining to Flanders, its people, or their language. —*n.* **2.** the people of Flanders collectively; the Flemings. **3.** one of the official languages of Belgium, a Germanic dialect mutually intelligible with Dutch. *Abbr.:* Flem, Flem. —*v.t.* **4.** (*sometimes l.c.*) *Naut.* to fake down (rope) in a Flemish coil. [ME < coastal D dial. var. of MD *Vlamisch* (D *Vlaamsch*) = *Vlam-* (see FLEMING) + *-isch* -ISH[1]]

Flem′ish bond′, a brickwork bond having alternate stretchers and headers in each course, each header being centered above and below a stretcher.

Flem′ish coil′, *Naut.* a fake in the form of a flat, closely wound spiral. Also called **Flem′ish fake′.**

flense (flens), *v.t.,* **flensed, flens·ing. 1.** to strip the blubber or the skin from (a whale, seal, etc.). **2.** to strip off (blubber or skin). Also, **flench** (flench), **flinch.** [< D *flense(n)*] —**flens′er,** *n.*

flesh (flesh), *n.* **1.** the soft substance of an animal or human body, consisting of muscle and fat. **2.** muscular and fatty tissue. **3.** this substance or tissue in animals, viewed as an article of food, usually excluding fish and sometimes fowl; meat. **4.** fatness; weight: *to put on flesh.* **5.** the body, esp. as distinguished from the spirit or soul. **6.** man's physical or animal nature, as distinguished from his moral or spiritual nature. **7.** mankind. **8.** living creatures generally. **9.** one's family, relatives, or kindred. **10.** *Bot.* the soft pulpy portion of a fruit, vegetable, etc., as distinguished from the core, skin, shell, etc. **11.** the surface of the human body, esp. with respect to its color or outward appearance. **12. in the flesh,** present before one's eyes; in person: *Her screen idol looked quite different in the flesh.* —*v.t.* **13.** to plunge (a weapon) into the flesh. **14.** *Hunting.* to feed (a hound or hawk) with flesh in order to make it more eager for the chase. Cf. **blood** (def. 17). **15.** to inflame the ardor or passions of by subjecting to a foretaste. **16.** to fill with flesh or fleshly enjoyments; surfeit; glut. **17.** to overlay or cover (a skeleton or skeletal frame) with flesh or with a fleshlike substance. **18.** to remove adhering flesh from (hides), in leather manufacture. —*v.i.* **19.** to become fleshy (often used with *out*). [ME *flesc,* OE *flǣsc;* c. OFris *flēsk,* OHG *fleisk* (G *Fleisch*), OIcel *flesk* bacon]

flesh′ and blood′, 1. offspring or relatives: *one's own flesh and blood.* **2.** the human body or nature: *more than flesh and blood can endure.* [ME *flesh and blod*]

flesh′ fly′, any of several dipterous insects of the family *Sarcophagidae* that deposit their eggs or larvae in carrion or in the flesh of living animals.

flesh·ings (flesh′ingz), *n.* (*construed as pl.*) flesh-colored tights.

flesh·ly (flesh′lē), *adj.,* **-li·er, -li·est. 1.** of or pertaining to the flesh or body; bodily, corporeal, or physical. **2.** carnal; sensual. **3.** worldly, rather than spiritual. **4.** *Obs.* having much flesh; fleshy. [ME; OE *flǣsclic*]

flesh·pot (flesh′pot′), *n.* **1.** a pot or vessel containing flesh or meat. **2.** a place offering luxurious and unrestrained pleasure or amusement.

flesh·y (flesh′ē), *adj.,* **flesh·i·er, flesh·i·est. 1.** having much flesh; plump; fat. **2.** consisting of or resembling flesh. **3.** *Bot.* consisting of fleshlike substance; pulpy, as a fruit; thick and tender, as a leaf. [ME] —**flesh′i·ness,** *n.*

fletch (flech), *v.t.* to provide (an arrow) with a feather. [back formation from FLETCHER]

fletch·er (flech′ər), *n.* a person who makes arrows. [ME *flecchere* < OF *flechier.* See FLECHE, -ER[2]]

Fletch·er (flech′ər), *n.* **John,** 1579–1625, English dramatist: collaborated with Francis Beaumont.

Fletch·er·ism (flech′ə riz′əm), *n.* the practice of chewing food until it is reduced to a finely divided, liquefied mass: advocated by Horace Fletcher, 1849–1919, U.S. nutritionist.

Fleurs-de-lis as used on royal arms of France, before 1376

fleur-de-lis (flûr′dᵊlē′, -lēs′, flo͝or′-; *Fr.* flœr də lēs′), *n., pl.* **fleurs-de-lis** (flûr′dᵊlēz′, flo͝or′-; *Fr.* flœr de lēs′). **1.** a heraldic device somewhat resembling three petals or floral segments of an iris tied by an encircling band. **2.** the distinctive bearing of the royal family of France. **3.** the iris flower or plant. Also, **fleur-de-lys** (for defs. 1, 2). [< F; r. ME *flourdelis* < AF *flour de lis,* lit., lily flower]

fleur-de-lys (flûr′dᵊlē′, -lēs′, flo͝or′-; *Fr.* flœr də lēs′), *n., pl.* **fleurs-de-lys** (flûr′dᵊlēz′, flo͝or′-; *Fr.* flœr də lēs′). fleur-de-lis (defs. 1, 2).

Fleu·ry (flœ rē′), *n.* **1. An·dré Her·cule de** (äN drā′ er kyl′ də), 1653–1743, French cardinal and statesman. **2. Claude** (klōd), 1640–1723, French ecclesiastical historian.

flew[1] (flo͞o), *v.* a pt. of **fly**[1].

flew[2] (flo͞o), *n.* flue[3].

flews (flo͞oz), *n.pl.* the large, pendulous sides of the upper lip of certain dogs, as bloodhounds. [?]

flex (fleks), *v.t., v.i.* **1.** to bend, as a part of the body. —*n.* **2.** the act of flexing. **3.** *Brit.* **a.** any flexible, insulated electric cord. **b.** *Slang.* an elastic band, as a garter. [< L *flex(us),* ptp. of *flectere* to bend, turn]

flex·i·ble (flek′sə bəl), *adj.* **1.** capable of being bent; easily bent. **2.** susceptible of modification or adaptation; adaptable: *a flexible schedule.* **3.** willing or disposed to yield; pliable: *a flexible personality.* [ME < L *flexibil(is)* pliant, easily bent] —**flex′i·bil′i·ty, flex′i·ble·ness,** *n.* —**flex′i·bly,** *adv.* —**Syn. 1.** pliable, elastic, supple. FLEXIBLE, LIMBER, PLIANT refer to that which bends easily. FLEXIBLE refers to that which is capable of being bent and adds sometimes the idea of compressibility or expansibility: *a piece of rubber hose is flexible.* LIMBER is esp. applied to the body to refer to ease of movement: *a young and limber dancer.* PLIANT stresses an inherent quality or tendency to bend or yield that may mean merely adaptable or suggest something derogatory: *a pliant character.* **3.** tractable, compliant.

flex·ile (flek′sil *or, esp. Brit.,* -sīl), *adj.* flexible; pliant; tractable. [< L *flexil(is)* pliant, pliable] —**flex·il′i·ty,** *n.*

flex·ion (flek′shən), *n.* **1.** *Anat.* **a.** the act of bending a limb. **b.** the position which a limb assumes when it is bent. **2.** *Chiefly Brit.* flection (defs. 1–3). [< L *flexiōn-* (s. of *flexiō*) a bending, turning] —**flex′ion·al,** *adj.*

flex·i·time (flek′si tīm′), *n.* a work arrangement under which employees are individually allowed to choose, within limits, their own working hours. Also, **flex·time** (fleks′tīm′). [FLEXI(BLE) + TIME]

Flex·ner (fleks′nər), *n.* **1. Abraham,** 1866–1959, U.S. educator. **2.** his brother, **Simon,** 1863–1946, U.S. pathologist.

flex·or (flek′sər), *n.* *Anat.* a muscle which serves to flex or bend a part of the body. [< NL]

flex·u·ous (flek′sho͞o əs), *adj.* full of bends or curves; winding; sinuous. Also, **flex·u·ose** (flek′sho͞o ōs′). [< L *flexuōs(us)* full of turns, winding, crooked] —**flex′u·ous·ly,** *adv.* —**flex·u·os·i·ty** (flek′sho͞o os′i tē), *n.*

flex·ure (flek′shər), *n.* **1.** act of flexing or bending. **2.** state of being flexed or bent. **3.** the part bent; bend; fold. [< L *flexūra* a bending, turning, winding] —**flex′ur·al,** *adj.*

fley (flā), *v.,* **fleyed, fley·ing.** *Chiefly Scot.* to frighten; terrify. [ME *flaie(n), fleie(n),* OE *-flȳgan* (in *ā-flȳgan*)]

flib·ber·ti·gib·bet (flib′ər tē jib′it), *n.* **1.** a chattering or flighty, light-headed person, usually a woman. **2.** *Archaic.* a gossip. [ME *flepergebet, flipergebet;* appar. imit.]

flick[1] (flik), *n.* **1.** a sudden light blow or stroke, as with a whip or the finger. **2.** the sound made by such a blow or stroke. **3.** a light and rapid movement: *a flick of the wrist.* **4.** something thrown off with or as with a jerk: *a flick of mud.* —*v.t.* **5.** to strike lightly with a whip, the finger, etc. **6.** to remove with such a stroke: *to flick dust from one's coat.* **7.** to move (something) with a sudden stroke or jerk. —*v.i.* **8.** to move with a jerk or jerks. **9.** to flutter. [late ME *flykke;* appar. imit.]

flick[2] (flik), *n.* *Chiefly Brit. Informal.* a motion picture. [back formation from FLICKER[1]]

flick·er[1] (flik′ər), *v.i.* **1.** to burn unsteadily; shine with a wavering light. **2.** to wave to and fro; vibrate; quiver. **3.** to flutter. —*v.t.* **4.** to cause to flicker. —*n.* **5.** an unsteady flame or light. **6.** a flickering; flickering movement. **7.** a brief occurrence or appearance: *a flicker of hope.* [ME *flikere(n),* OE *flicorian* to flutter; c. D *flikkeren*] —**flick′er·ing·ly,** *adv.* —**flick′er·y,** *adj.*

flick·er[2] (flik′ər), *n.* any of several American woodpeckers of the genus *Colaptes,* having the undersides of the wings and tail brightly marked with yellow or red. [imit.]

flied (flīd), *v.* a pt. and pp. of **fly**[1].

fli·er (flī′ər), *n.* **1.** something that flies, as a bird or insect. **2.** an aviator. **3.** a person or thing that moves with great speed. **4.** some part of a machine having a rapid motion. **5.** *Informal.* a flying jump or leap: *He took a flier off the bridge.* **6.** *Informal.* a financial venture outside of one's ordinary business. **7.** *Archit.* one of the steps in a straight flight. Cf. **winder** (def. 2). **8.** *U.S.* a small handbill. **9.** a silvery-green sunfish, *Centrarchus macropterus,* found from Virginia to Florida and through the lower Mississippi valley. Also, **flyer.** [ME]

flight[1] (flīt), *n.* **1.** the act, manner, or power of flying. **2.** the distance covered or the course taken by a flying object: *a 500-mile flight.* **3.** a number of beings or things flying or passing through the air together: *a flight of swallows.* **4.** a trip by an airplane, glider, etc. **5.** a scheduled trip on an airline. **6.** the basic tactical unit of military air forces, consisting of two or more aircraft. **7.** the act, principles, or technique of flying an airplane: *flight training.* **8.** a journey into or through outer space, as of a rocket. **9.** swift movement, transition, or progression: *the flight of time.* **10.** a soaring above or transcending ordinary bounds: *a flight of fancy.* **11.** *Archit.* **a.** a series of steps between any landing and the next. **b.** a series of steps, and sometimes of landings, between any floor and the next. **12.** *Archery.* a light arrow for long-distance shooting. —*v.i.* **13.** (of wild fowls) to fly in flights. [ME; OE *flyht;* c. D *vlucht*]

flight[2] (flīt), *n.* **1.** act of fleeing; hasty departure. **2. put to flight,** to force to flee; rout. **3. take flight,** to retreat; flee. Also, **take to flight.** [ME; c. G *Flucht;* akin to FLEE]

flight′ attend′ant, an airline employee who serves meals, attends to passengers' comfort, etc., during a flight.

flight′ deck′, the upper deck of an aircraft carrier, used as a runway for aircraft.

flight′ feath′er, *Ornith.* one of the large, stiff feathers of the wing and tail of a bird that are essential to flight.

flight·less (flīt′lis), *adj.* incapable of flying.

flight′ path′, the locus of the center of gravity of an airplane during flight.

flight′ pay′, (in the U.S. Air Force) a monthly pay supplement for flight time.

flight′ strip′, *Aeron.* **1.** a strip of cleared land used as an emergency runway for aircraft. **2.** runway.

flight′ sur′geon, a medical officer in the U.S. Air Force who is qualified in aeromedicine.
flight-test (flīt′test′), *v.t.* to test (an airplane or the like) in flight.
flight·wor·thy (flīt′wûr′thē), *adj.* in proper physical or mechanical condition for safe flight: *a flightworthy spacecraft.*
flight·y (flī′tē), *adj.*, **flight·i·er, flight·i·est. 1.** given to flights of fancy; capricious; frivolous. **2.** slightly delirious; light-headed; mildly crazy. **3.** irresponsible. **4.** *Archaic.* swift or fleet. —**flight′i·ly,** *adv.* —**flight′i·ness,** *n.*
flim·flam (flim′flam′), *n., v.,* **-flammed, -flam·ming.** *Informal.* —*n.* **1.** a piece of nonsense; twaddle; bosh. **2.** a trick or deception; humbug. —*v.t.* **3.** to trick, delude, or cheat. [cf. Icel *flimska* mockery] —**flim′flam′mer,** *n.*
flim·sy (flim′zē), *adj.*, **-si·er, -si·est,** *n., pl.* **-sies.** —*adj.* **1.** without material strength or solidity: *a flimsy foundation.* **2.** weak; inadequate; not effective or convincing: *a flimsy excuse.* —*n.* **3.** a thin paper, esp. for use in making carbon copies. **4.** a copy of a report, order, etc., on such paper. [? metathetic var. of FILMY modeled on *tipsy, limpsy*] —**flim′si·ly,** *adv.* —**flim′si·ness,** *n.* —**Syn. 1.** shoddy.
flinch[1] (flinch), *v.i.* **1.** to draw back or shrink from what is dangerous, difficult, or unpleasant. **2.** to shrink under pain; wince. —*n.* **3.** act of flinching. **4.** *Cards.* a game in which the cards are accumulated in orderly fashion on the table. [? nasalized var. of dial. *flitch* to flit, shift one's position] —**flinch′er,** *n.* —**flinch′ing·ly,** *adv.* —**Syn. 1.** recoil.
flinch[2] (flinch), *v.t.* flense.
flin·ders (flin′dərz), *n.pl.* splinters or fragments. [late ME *flendris,* ? < Scand; cf. Norw *flindra* splinter]
fling (fling), *v.,* **flung, fling·ing,** *n.* —*v.t.* **1.** to throw, cast, or hurl with force or violence. **2.** to move (oneself) violently with impatience, contempt, or the like: *She flung herself angrily from the room.* **3.** to put suddenly or violently: *to fling someone into jail.* —*v.i.* **4.** to move with haste or violence; rush; dash. **5.** to fly into violent and irregular motions, as a horse; throw the body about, as a person. **6.** to speak harshly or abusively (usually fol. by *out*): *He flung out in a rage against the whole human race.* —*n.* **7.** act of flinging. **8.** a short period of unrestrained indulgence of one's impulses. **9.** Also called **Highland fling.** a lively Scottish dance characterized by flinging movements of the arms and legs. **10. take a fling at,** to make an attempt at something. [ME; cf. Sw *flänga* to fly, race] —**fling′er,** *n.*
flint (flint), *n.* **1.** a hard kind of stone, a form of silica. **2.** a piece of this, esp. as used for striking fire. —*v.t.* **3.** to furnish with flint. [ME, OE; c. MD *vlint,* Dan *flint;* cf. PLINTH]
Flint (flint), *n.* **1.** a city in SE Michigan. 193,317 (1970). **2.** Flintshire.
flint′ corn′, a variety of corn, *Zea Mays indurata,* having hard-skinned kernels not subject to shrinkage.
flint′ glass′, *Optics.* an optical glass of high dispersion and relatively high index of refraction, composed of alkalis, lead oxide, and silica.
flint·lock (flint′lok′), *n.* **1.** a gunlock in which a piece of flint striking against steel produces sparks that ignite the priming. **2.** an old-fashioned firearm with such a lock.

Flintlock
A, Steel struck by flint; B, Powder pan; C, Touchhole; D, Flint; E, Cock

Flint·shire (flint′shēr, -shər), *n.* a county in NE Wales. 149,888 (1961); 256 sq. mi. *Co. seat:* Mold. Also called **Flint.**
flint·y (flin′tē), *adj.*, **flint·i·er, flint·i·est. 1.** composed of, containing, or resembling flint, esp. in hardness. **2.** unyielding; unmerciful; cruel; obdurate: *his flinty heart.* —**flint′i·ly,** *adv.* —**flint′i·ness,** *n.*
flip[1] (flip), *v.,* **flipped, flip·ping,** *n.* —*v.t.* **1.** to toss or put in motion with a sudden impulse as a snap of a finger and thumb, esp. as to cause to turn over in the air: *to flip a coin.* **2.** to move (something) suddenly or jerkily. **3.** to turn over, esp. with a short rapid gesture: *He flipped the cards as he spoke.* —*v.i.* **4.** to make a flicking movement; snap. **5.** to move with a jerk or jerks, as with the flippers, wings, etc. **6.** *Slang.* to react to something excitedly: *He flipped over his new girl friend.* **7. flip out,** *Slang.* **a.** to go or make insane or irrational. **b.** to get or make excited. —*n.* **8.** an instance of flipping; a smart tap or strike. **9.** a sudden jerk. **10.** a somersault, esp. one performed in the air. [prob. imit.; see FILLIP]
flip[2] (flip), *n.* a mixed drink made with liquor or wine, sugar, and egg, topped with nutmeg. [? n. use of FLIP[1], so called from tossing of ingredients in preparation]
flip[3] (flip), *adj.*, **flip·per, flip·pest.** *Informal.* smart; pert; flippant. [adj. use of FLIP[1]]
flip′ chart′, one of a group of large cardboard charts, usually attached at the top so that they can be flipped over one by one, as for graphic illustration of a lecture.
flip-flop (flip′flop′), *n., v.,* **-flopped, -flop·ping.** —*n.* **1.** a backward somersault. **2.** a banging to and fro. —*v.i.* **3.** to execute a backward somersault. **4.** to bang to and fro.
flip·pant (flip′ənt), *adj.* **1.** frivolously shallow; disrespectful; characterized by levity. **2.** *Chiefly Dial.* nimble, limber, or pliant. **3.** *Obs.* glib; voluble. [? FLIP[3] + -ANT; cf. Icel *fleipa* to babble, Sw *flipa* to cry] —**flip′pan·cy,** *n.* —**flip′pant·ly,** *adv.* —**Syn. 1.** saucy, impertinent, impudent.
flip·per (flip′ər), *n.* **1.** a broad, flat limb, as of a seal, whale, etc., especially adapted for swimming. **2.** Usually, **flippers.** Also called **fin.** one of a pair of paddlelike devices, usually of rubber, worn on the feet as an aid in swimming.
flip′ side′, *Slang.* the reverse and, sometimes, less important side of a phonograph record.
flirt (flûrt), *v.i.* **1.** to court triflingly or act amorously without serious intentions; play at love; coquet. **2.** to trifle or toy, as with an idea: *She flirted with the notion of buying a wig.* **3.** to move with a jerk or jerks; dart about. —*v.t.* **4.** to give a brisk motion to; wave smartly. **5.** to throw or propel with a toss or jerk; fling suddenly. —*n.* **6.** Also, **flirt′er.** a person who flirts. **7.** a quick throw or toss; sudden jerk or darting motion. [imit.] —**flirt′ing·ly,** *adv.*

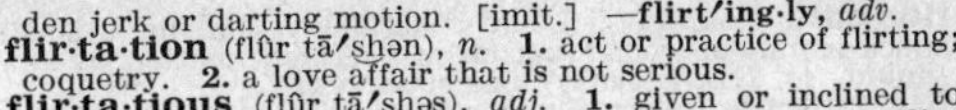

flir·ta·tion (flûr tā′shən), *n.* **1.** act or practice of flirting; coquetry. **2.** a love affair that is not serious.
flir·ta·tious (flûr tā′shəs), *adj.* **1.** given or inclined to flirtation. **2.** pertaining to flirtation. Also, **flirt′y.** —**flir·ta′tious·ly,** *adv.* —**flir·ta′tious·ness,** *n.*
flit (flit), *v.,* **flit·ted, flit·ting,** *n.* —*v.i.* **1.** to move lightly and swiftly; fly, dart, or skim along. **2.** to flutter, as a bird. **3.** to pass away quickly, as time. **4.** *Chiefly Scot. and North Eng.* to depart or die. —*v.t.* **5.** *Archaic.* to remove; transfer; oust or dispossess. —*n.* **6.** a light, swift movement; flutter. **7.** *Slang.* a male homosexual. [ME *flitte(n)* < Scand; c. Icel *flytja* to carry, Sw *flytta.* See FLEET[2]] —**Syn. 1.** See **fly**[1].
flitch (flich), *n.* **1.** the side of a hog (or, formerly, some other animal) salted and cured: *a flitch of bacon.* **2.** a steak cut from a halibut. **3.** *Carpentry.* **a.** a thin piece of wood, as a veneer. **b.** a bundle of veneers, arranged as cut from the log. —*v.t.* **4.** to cut into flitches. [ME *flicche,* OE *flicca;* c. MLG *vlicke,* Icel *flikki*]
flit·ter[1] (flit′ər), *v.i., v.t.* to flutter. [FLIT + -ER[6]]
flit·ter[2] (flit′ər), *n.* a person or thing that flits. [FLIT + -ER[1]]
flit·ter·mouse (flit′ər mous′), *n., pl.* **-mice.** *Archaic.* bat[2] (def. 1). [FLITTER[1] + MOUSE; loan trans. of G *Fledermaus*]
fliv·ver (fliv′ər), *n.* *Facetious.* an old, small, or cheap automobile. [?]
float (flōt), *v.i.* **1.** to rest or remain on the surface of a liquid; be buoyant. **2.** to move gently on the surface of a liquid; drift along: *The canoe floated downstream.* **3.** to rest or move in a liquid, the air, etc.: *a balloon floating on high.* **4.** to move lightly and gracefully: *She floated down the stairs.* **5.** to move or hover before the eyes or in the mind. **6.** to be free from attachment. **7.** to move or drift about: *to float from place to place.* **8.** to vacillate (often fol. by *between*). **9.** (of a currency) to be allowed to fluctuate freely in the foreign-exchange market instead of being exchanged at a fixed rate. —*v.t.* **10.** to cause to float. **11.** to flood or irrigate. **12.** to make smooth with a float, as the surface of plaster. **13.** to cover (a surface) with a liquid. **14.** to launch (a company, scheme, etc.); set going. **15.** to sell on the stock market, as an issue of stocks or bonds. **16.** to let (a currency) float in the foreign-exchange market. —*n.* **17.** something that floats, as a raft. **18.** something for buoying up. **19.** an inflated bag to sustain a person in water; life preserver. **20.** *Plumbing, Mach.* (in certain types of apparatus, cisterns, etc.) a device, as a hollow ball, which through its buoyancy automatically regulates the level, supply, or outlet of a liquid. **21.** *Naut.* a floating platform attached to a wharf, a bank, or the like, and used as a landing. **22.** *Aeron.* a hollow, boatlike structure under the wing or fuselage of an airplane, keeping it afloat in water. **23.** *Angling.* a piece of cork or other material for supporting a baited line in the water and indicating by its movements when a fish bites. **24.** *Zool.* an inflated organ that supports an animal in the water. **25.** Also called **float·board** (flōt′bōrd′, -bôrd′). paddle[1] (def. 5). **26.** a vehicle bearing a display, usually an elaborate tableau, in a parade or procession. **27.** *Building Trades.* a flat tool for spreading and smoothing plaster or stucco. **28.** a single-cut file of moderate smoothness. **29.** the loose yarn on the back of cloth due to a figure weave or brocading. **30.** *Banking.* uncollected checks and commercial paper in process of transfer from bank to bank. **31.** the act of floating in the foreign-exchange market. [ME *flote(n),* OE *flotian;* c. OIcel *flota,* MD *vloten.* See FLEET[2]] —**float′a·ble,** *adj.* —**float′a·bil′i·ty,** *n.*
float·age (flō′tij), *n.* flotage.
float·a·tion (flō tā′shən), *n.* *Chiefly Brit.* flotation.
float·el (flō tel′), *n.* a houseboat that serves as a hotel, sometimes permanently moored to a dock. [FLOAT(ING) + (HOT)EL]
float·er (flō′tər), *n.* **1.** a person or thing that floats. **2.** *Informal.* a person who is continually changing his place of abode, employment, etc. **3.** *U.S.* a person who fraudulently votes, usually for pay, in different places in the same election. **4.** a policy in which property frequently moved from one place to another is insured against theft, damage, etc.
float′ glass′, extremely smooth, nearly distortion-free glass manufactured by pouring molten glass on a surface of molten tin: regarded commercially as a form of plate glass.
float·ing (flō′ting), *adj.* **1.** being buoyed up on water, air, etc. **2.** having little or no attachment. **3.** *Pathol.* away from its proper position, esp. in a downward direction: *a floating kidney.* **4.** not fixed or settled in a definite place or state: *a floating population.* **5.** *Finance.* **a.** not permanently invested, as capital. **b.** composed of sums due within a short time: *a floating debt.* **6.** *Mach.* **a.** having a soft suspension greatly reducing vibrations between the suspended part and its support. **b.** working smoothly.
float′ing dock′, a submersible, floating structure used as a dry dock, having a floor that is submerged, slipped under a floating vessel, and raised so as to raise the vessel entirely out of the water. Also called **float′ing dry′ dock′.**
float′ing is′land, a dessert consisting of boiled custard with portions of meringue, whipped cream, or whipped egg whites and sometimes jelly floating upon it or around it.
float′ing rib′, *Anat.* one member of the two lowest pairs of ribs, which are attached neither to the sternum nor to the cartilages of other ribs.
float·plane (flōt′plān′), *n.* a seaplane having landing gear consisting of one or more floats. Also, **float′ plane′.**
floc (flok), *n.* a tuftlike mass, as in a chemical precipitate. Also, **flock.** [< L *flocc(us)*]
floc·cil·la·tion (flok′sə lā′shən), *n.* *Pathol.* a delirious picking of the bedclothes by the patient, as in certain fevers.
floc·cose (flok′ōs), *adj.* **1.** *Bot.* consisting of or bearing woolly tufts or long soft hairs. **2.** flocculent. [< LL *floccōs(us)* full of tufts of wool. See FLOCK[2], -OSE[1]]
floc·cu·lant (flok′yə lənt), *n.* a chemical for producing flocculation of suspended particles, as to improve the plasticity of clay for ceramic purposes.
floc·cu·late (flok′yə lāt′), *v.,* **-lat·ed, -lat·ing.** —*v.t.* **1.** to form into flocculent masses. —*v.i.* **2.** to form flocculent masses, as a cloud, a precipitate, etc.; form aggregated or compound masses of particles. —**floc′cu·la′tion,** *n.*

floc·cule (flok′yo͞ol), *n.* **1.** something resembling a small flock or tuft of wool. **2.** a bit of flocculent matter, as in a liquid. [< NL *floccul(us).* See FLOC, -ULE]
floc·cu·lent (flok′yə lənt), *adj.* **1.** like a clump or tuft of wool. **2.** covered with a soft, woolly substance. **3.** consisting of or containing loose woolly masses. —**floc′cu·lence, floc′cu·len·cy,** *n.* —**floc′cu·lent·ly,** *adv.*
floc·cu·lus (flok′yə ləs), *n., pl.* **-li** (-lī′). **1.** floccule. **2.** *Astron.* one of the bright or dark patches on the sun's surface, visible in a spectroheliogram. [< NL; see FLOCCULE]
floc·cus (flok′əs), *n., pl.* **floc·ci** (flok′sī), *adj.* —*n.* **1.** a small tuft of woolly hairs. —*adj.* **2.** *Meteorol.* (of a cloud) having small, rounded tufts. [< L: tuft of wool]
flock[1] (flok), *n.* **1.** a number of animals of one kind keeping, feeding, or herded together, as sheep, goats, or birds. **2.** a crowd; large number of people. **3.** the Christian church in relation to Christ. **4.** a single congregation in relation to its pastor. —*v.i.* **5.** to gather or go in a flock, company, or crowd. [ME; OE *floc;* c. Icel *flokkr*]
—**Syn. 1, 2.** bevy, covey, flight, gaggle; brood, hatch, litter; shoal, school, swarm, group, company. FLOCK, DROVE, HERD, PACK refer to a company of animals, often under the care or guidance of someone. FLOCK is the popular term, which applies to groups of animals, esp. of sheep or goats, and companies of birds: *This lamb is the choicest of the flock. A flock of wild geese flew overhead.* DROVE is esp. applied to a number of oxen, sheep, or swine when driven in a group: *A drove of oxen was taken to market.* HERD is usually applied to large animals such as cattle, originally meaning those under the charge of someone; but by extension, to other animals feeding or driven together: *a herd of elephants.* PACK applies to a number of animals kept together or keeping together for offense or defense: *a pack of wolves.* Applied to people, DROVE, HERD, and PACK are contemptuous.
flock[2] (flok), *n.* **1.** a lock or tuft of wool, hair, cotton, etc. **2.** (*sometimes construed as pl.*) wool refuse, shearings of cloth, old cloth torn to pieces, or the like, for upholstering furniture, stuffing mattresses, etc. **3.** (*sometimes construed as pl.*) finely powdered wool, cloth, etc., for decorating wallpaper, covering phonograph turntables, etc. **4.** floc. —*v.t.* **5.** to stuff with flock, as a mattress. **6.** to cover or coat with flock, as wallpaper, phonograph turntables, etc. [ME *flok* < OF *floc* < L *flocc(us)* FLOC. Cf. OHG *floccho*]
floe (flō), *n.* **1.** Also called **ice floe.** a sheet of floating ice, chiefly on the surface of the sea, smaller than an ice field. **2.** a detached floating portion of such a sheet. [? < Norw *flo* layer (cf. Icel *flō* layer, level); c. OE *flōh* piece, flagstone; cf. FLAW[1]]
flog (flog, flôg), *v.t.,* **flogged, flog·ging.** to beat hard with a whip, stick, etc.; whip; castigate; chastise; scourge. [? b. FLAY and *jog,* var. of JAG[1]; but cf. FLAGELLATE] —**flog′ga·ble,** *adj.* —**flog′ger,** *n.* —**Syn.** thrash, lash, belabor.
flog·ging (flog′ing, flô′ging), *n.* punishment by beating or whipping.
flood (flud), *n.* **1.** a great flowing or overflowing of water, esp. over land not usually submerged. **2. the Flood,** the universal deluge recorded as having occurred in the days of Noah. Gen. 7. **3.** any great outpouring or stream: *a flood of words.* **4.** the flowing in of the tide (opposed to *ebb*). **5.** *Informal.* a floodlight. **6.** *Archaic.* a large body of water. —*v.t.* **7.** to overflow in or cover with a flood of water or other liquid; fill to overflowing. **8.** to fill or occupy completely: *roads flooded with cars.* **9.** to overwhelm with an abundance of something. **10.** to floodlight. —*v.i.* **11.** to flow or pour in, or as in, a flood. **12.** to rise in a flood; overflow. [ME *flod,* OE *flōd;* c. Goth *flōd(us),* OHG *fluot* (G *Flut*)] —**flood′a·ble,** *adj.* —**flood′er,** *n.*
flood·gate (flud′gāt′), *n.* *Civ. Eng.* a gate designed to regulate the flow of water. [ME]
flood′ lamp′, a floodlight.
flood·light (flud′līt′), *n., v.,* **-light·ed** or **-lit, -light·ing.** —*n.* **1.** an artificial light so directed or diffused as to give a comparatively uniform illumination over a rather large given area. **2.** a floodlight lamp or projector. —*v.t.* **3.** to illuminate with a floodlight.
flood′ plain′, *Phys. Geog.* a nearly flat plain along the course of a stream that is naturally subject to flooding.
flood′ tide′, **1.** the inflow of the tide; rising tide. **2.** a tide at its greatest height. **3.** a peak or climax.
floor (flōr, flôr), *n.* **1.** that part of a room or the like which forms its lower enclosing surface and upon which one walks. **2.** a continuous, supporting surface extending horizontally throughout a building, having a number of rooms, apartments, or the like, and constituting one level or stage in the structure; story. **3.** a level, supporting surface in any structure: *the elevator floor.* **4.** one of two or more layers of material composing a floor: *rough floor; finish floor.* **5.** a platform or prepared level area for a particular use: *a threshing floor.* **6.** the flat bottom of any more or less hollow place: *the floor of a tunnel.* **7.** a more or less flat extent of surface: *the floor of the ocean.* **8.** the part of a legislative chamber, auditorium, etc., where the members or attendants sit, and from which they speak. **9.** the right of one member to speak from such a place in preference to other members: *The Senator from Alaska has the floor.* **10.** the main part of a stock or commodity exchange or the like, as distinguished from the galleries, platform, etc. **11.** *Naut.* **a.** the bottom of a hull. **b.** any of a number of deep, transverse framing members at the bottom of a steel or iron hull. **c.** the lowermost member of a frame in a wooden vessel. —*v.t.* **12.** to cover or furnish with a floor. **13.** to bring down to the floor or ground; knock down. **14.** *Informal.* to confound; nonplus: *He was floored by the problem.* [ME *flor,* OE *flōr;* c. OIcel *flōr(r),* MLG *vlōr,* MHG *vluor* (G *Flur*)] —**floor′er,** *n.*
floor·age (flōr′ij, flôr′-), *n.* floor space.
floor·board (flōr′bōrd′, flôr′bôrd′), *n.* any of the boards composing a floor.
floor·ing (flōr′ing, flôr′-), *n.* **1.** a floor. **2.** floors collectively. **3.** materials for making floors.
floor′ lamp′, a tall lamp designed to stand on the floor.
floor′ lead′er, *U.S. Govt.* the majority leader or minority leader in either the Senate or the House of Representatives.
floor′ mod′el, **1.** an appliance or the like on exhibition in a store. **2.** a radio, television set, or the like, intended to stand on the floor rather than on a table; console.
floor·shift (flōr′shift′, flôr-), *n.* a gearshift set in the floor of an automobile.
floor′ show′, an entertainment given in a night club or cabaret, usually consisting of a series of singing, dancing, and, often, comic acts.
floor·walk·er (flōr′wô′kər, flôr′-), *n.* a person employed in a store to direct customers, supervise salespeople, etc.
floo·zy (flo͞o′zē), *n., pl.* **-zies.** *Slang.* a gaudily dressed, dissipated, and usually immoral woman, esp. a dowdy prostitute. Also, **floo′zie.** [?]
flop (flop), *v.,* **flopped, flop·ping,** *n.* —*v.i.* **1.** to fall or plump down suddenly, esp. with noise; drop or turn with a sudden bump or thud (sometimes fol. by *down*). **2.** to change suddenly, as from one side or party to another (often fol. by *over*). **3.** *Informal.* to fail; to be unsuccessful: *The play flopped dismally.* **4.** to flap, as in the wind. —*v.t.* **5.** to drop, throw, etc., with a sudden bump or thud. **6.** to flap clumsily and heavily, as wings. —*n.* **7.** an act of flopping. **8.** the sound of flopping; a thud. **9.** *Informal.* a failure. [var. of FLAP] —**flop′per,** *n.*
flop·house (flop′hous′), *n., pl.* **-hous·es** (-hou′ziz). a cheap, rundown hotel, usually for men.
flop·py (flop′ē), *adj.,* **-pi·er, -pi·est,** *n., pl.* **-pies.** —*adj.* **1.** flopping or tending to flop. —*n.* **2.** *Computer Technol.* See **floppy disk.** —**flop′pi·ly,** *adv.* —**flop′pi·ness,** *n.*
flop′py disk′, *Computer Technol.* a thin, round, flexible disk with magnetic surfaces, for storing and retrieving data. Also called **diskette, floppy.**
flor-, var. of **flori-:** *florist.*
flor., flourished. [< L *floruit*]
flo·ra (flōr′ə, flôr′ə), *n., pl.* **flo·ras, flo·rae** (flōr′ē, flôr′ē). **1.** the plants of a particular region or period, listed by species and considered as a whole. **2.** a work systematically describing such plants. **3.** plants, as distinguished from fauna. [< L < *flōr-* (s. of *flōs*) FLOWER]
Flo·ra (flōr′ə, flôr′ə), *n.* the Roman goddess of flowers.
flo·ral (flōr′əl, flôr′-), *adj.* **1.** pertaining to or consisting of flowers. **2.** (*cap.*) of or pertaining to the goddess Flora. [< L *flōrāl(is)* pertaining to *Flōra*] —**flo′ral·ly,** *adv.*
flo′ral en′velope, *Bot.* the calyx and corolla of a flower.
Flo·ré·al (flô rā al′), *n.* (in the French Revolutionary calendar) the eighth month of the year, extending from April 20 to May 19. [< F < L *flōre(us)* of flowers (*flōr-,* s. of *flōs* flower + *-eus* adj. suffix) + F *-al* -AL[1]]
flo·re·at·ed (flōr′ē ā′tid, flôr′-), *adj.* floriated.
Flor·ence (flôr′əns, flor′-), *n.* **1.** Italian, **Firenze.** a city in central Italy, on the Arno River: capital of the former grand duchy of Tuscany. 464,425. **2.** a city in NW Alabama, on the Tennessee River. 34,031 (1970). **3.** a city in E South Carolina. 25,997 (1970).
Flor′ence flask′, *Chem.* a round bottle having a flat bottom and long neck.

Florence flask

Flor·ence-Gra·ham (flôr′əns grā′əm), *n.* a town in SW California, near Los Angeles. 42,895 (1970).
Flor·en·tine (flôr′ən tēn′, -tīn′, flor′-), *adj.* **1.** of or pertaining to Florence, Italy: *the Florentine poets of the 14th century.* **2.** pertaining to or designating the style of art developed in Florence during the late 13th to the 15th centuries. **3.** (of food) served or prepared with spinach: *eggs Florentine.* —*n.* **4.** a native or inhabitant of Florence. [< L *Flōrentīn(us)* pertaining to *Flōrent(ia)* FLORENCE + *-inus* -INE[1]]
Flo·res (*Sp.* flô′res *for 1, 2; Port.* flô′rish *for 3*), *n.* **1. Juan Jo·sé** (hwän hô se′), 1800–64, Ecuadorian general and statesman: president 1830–35, 1839–45. **2.** one of the Lesser Sunda Islands in Indonesia, separated from Celebes by the Flores Sea. 200,000 with adjacent islands; 7753 sq. mi. **3.** the westernmost island of the Azores, in the N Atlantic. 55 sq. mi.
flo·res·cence (flō res′əns, flô-, flə-), *n.* act, state, or period of flowering; bloom. [< NL *flōrēscentia* = L *flōrēscent-* (s. of *flōrēscēns,* prp. of *flōrēscere*) beginning to flower or blossom (see FLOR-, -ESCENT) + *-ia;* see -ENCE] —**flo·res′cent,** *adj.*
Flo′res Sea′ (flōr′is, -ēz, flôr′-), a sea between Celebes and the Lesser Sunda Islands in Indonesia. ab. 180 mi. wide.
flo·ret (flōr′it, flôr′-), *n.* **1.** a small flower. **2.** *Bot.* one of the closely clustered small flowers that make up the flower head of a composite flower, as the daisy. [ME *flouret* < OF *florete,* dim. of *flor* FLOWER; see -ET]
flori-, a learned borrowing from Latin meaning "flower," used in the formation of compound words: *floriferous.* Also, **flor-.** [< L, comb. form = *flōr-* (s. of *flōs*) flower + *-i-* -I-]
Flo·ri·a·nóp·o·lis (flōr′ē ə nop′ə lis, flôr′-; *Port.* flô′ryə-nô′po͝o lēs′), *n.* a seaport in and the capital of Santa Catarina state, on an island off the S coast of Brazil. 115,665. Formerly, **Desterro.**
flo·ri·at·ed (flōr′ē ā′tid, flôr′-), *adj.* made of or decorated with floral ornamentation: *floriated design; floriated china.* Also, **floreated.**
flo·ri·bun·da (flōr′ə bun′də, flôr′-), *n.* any of a class of roses characterized by a long blooming period and the production of large flowers often in thick clusters. [< NL, n. use of fem. of *flōribundus* flowering freely = *flōri-* FLORI- + *-bundus* adj. suffix]
flo·ri·cul·ture (flōr′ə kul′chər, flôr′-), *n.* the cultivation of flowers or flowering plants, esp. under glass. —**flo′ri·cul′tur·al,** *adj.* —**flo′ri·cul′tur·ist,** *n.*
flor·id (flôr′id, flor′-), *adj.* **1.** reddish, ruddy, or rosy: *a florid complexion.* **2.** flowery; excessively ornate; showy. **3.** *Obs.* abounding in or consisting of flowers. [< L *flōrid(us)*] —**flo·rid·i·ty** (flō rid′i tē, flə-), **flor′id ness,** *n.* —**flor′id·ly,** *adv.* —**Syn. 2.** embellished, decorated. —**Ant. 1.** pale, **2.** plain, simple, unaffected.
Flor·i·da (flôr′i də, flor′-), *n.* a state in the SE United States between the Atlantic and the Gulf of Mexico. 6,789,443 (1970); 58,560 sq. mi. *Cap.:* Tallahassee. *Abbr.:* Fla., FL
Flor′ida Cur′rent, the part of the Gulf Stream that extends from the Florida Strait to Cape Hatteras.
Flor′ida Keys′, a chain of small islands and reefs off the coast of S Florida. ab. 225 mi. long.
Flor′ida Strait′, a strait between Florida, Cuba, and the Bahamas, connecting the Gulf of Mexico and the Atlantic.

flo·rif·er·ous (flō rif′ər əs, flô-), *adj.* flower-bearing. [< L *flōrifer* (see FLORI-, -FER) + -OUS] —**flo·rif′er·ous·ly,** *adv.* —**flo·rif′er·ous·ness,** *n.*

flor·in (flôr′in, flor′-), *n.* **1.** a cupronickel coin of Great Britain, equal to two shillings or the tenth part of a pound, first issued in 1849 as a silver coin: not in use after 1971. **2.** the gulden of the Netherlands. **3.** a former gold coin of Florence, first issued in 1252 and widely imitated. **4.** a former gold coin of England, first issued under Edward III. **5.** a former gold coin of Austria, first issued in the middle of the 14th century. [ME < MF < OIt *fiorin(o)* Florentine coin stamped with a lily < *fiore* flower < L *flōr-* FLOR-]

Flo·ri·o (flôr′ē ō′, flōr′-), *n.* **John,** 1553?–1625, English lexicographer and translator.

Flor·is·sant (flôr′i sənt), *n.* a city in E Missouri, near St. Louis. 65,908 (1970).

flo·rist (flôr′ist, flōr′-, flor′-), *n.* a retailer of flowers, ornamental plants, etc.

flo·ris·tic (flō ris′tik, flô-), *adj.* pertaining to flowers or a flora. —**flo·ris′ti·cal·ly,** *adv.*

-florous, a learned borrowing from Latin meaning "-flowered," "having flowers," used in the formation of adjectives: *uniflorous.* [< L *-flōrus* flowered, bloomed]

flo·ru·it (flō′ro͝o it; *Eng.* flôr′yo͞o it, flōr′-, flor′-), *n. Latin.* he (or she) flourished: used to indicate the period during which a person flourished, esp. when the exact birth and death dates are unknown. *Abbr.:* fl., flor.

floss (flôs, flos), *n.* **1.** the cottony fiber yielded by the silk-cotton tree. **2.** silk filaments with little or no twist, used in weaving or in embroidery. **3.** any silky, filamentous matter, as the silk of corn. **4.** See **dental floss.** Also called **floss′ silk′** (for defs. 1, 2). [< Scand; cf. Icel *flos* shag of velvet]

floss·y (flô′sē, flos′ē), *adj.,* **floss·i·er, floss·i·est. 1.** made of or resembling floss; downy. **2.** *Slang.* showily stylish; fancy.

flo·tage (flō′tij), *n.* **1.** the act or state of floating. **2.** floating power; buoyancy. **3.** anything that floats; flotsam. **4.** ships, refuse, etc., afloat on a river. **5.** part of a ship above the water line. Also, **floatage.** [FLOAT + -AGE; cf. F *flottage*]

flo·ta·tion (flō tā′shən), *n.* **1.** the act or state of floating. **2.** the floating or launching of a commercial venture, loan, etc. **3.** *Metall.* a process for separating the different crystalline phases in a mass of powdered ore based on their tendency to sink in, or float on, a given liquid. Also, *esp. Brit.,* **floatation.** [FLOAT + -ATION; cf. F *flottaison* (see FLOTSAM)]

flota′tion col′lar, a large, inflated tubular device that is attached, as by frogmen, around a space vehicle immediately after splashdown to prevent sinking.

flo·til·la (flō til′ə), *n.* **1.** a group of small naval vessels, esp. a naval unit containing two or more squadrons. **2.** a small fleet. [< Sp, dim. of *flota* fleet < F *flotte* < OE *flota*]

Flo·tow (flō′tō), *n.* **Frie·drich von** (frē′drikh fən), 1812–1883, German composer.

flot·sam (flot′səm), *n.* the part of the wreckage of a ship and its cargo found floating on the water. Cf. **jetsam.** [< AF *floteson* < *flote(r)* (to) float < OE *flot(ian)*]

flot′sam and jet′sam, 1. the wreckage of a ship and its cargo found either floating upon the sea or washed ashore. **2.** useless trifles; odds and ends.

flounce[1] (flouns), *v.,* **flounced, flounc·ing,** *n.* —*v.i.* **1.** to go with an impatient, angry, or impertinent movement of the body (usually fol. by *away, off, out,* etc.): *She flounced out of the room in a rage.* **2.** to throw the body about, as in floundering or struggling; twist; turn; jerk. —*n.* **3.** the action of flouncing; a flouncing movement. [< Scand; cf. Norw *flunsa* to hurry]

flounce[2] (flouns), *n., v.,* **flounced, flounc·ing.** —*n.* **1.** a strip of material, wider than a ruffle, gathered at one edge and attached as a trimming, esp. on a woman's skirt. —*v.t.* **2.** to trim with a flounce or flounces. [alter. of FROUNCE]

flounc·ing (floun′sing), *n.* **1.** material used in making flounces. **2.** trimming consisting of a flounce.

floun·der[1] (floun′dər), *v.i.* **1.** to struggle with stumbling or plunging movements (usually fol. by *about, along, on, through,* etc.): *The child was floundering about in the water.* **2.** to struggle clumsily or helplessly in embarrassment or confusion. —*n.* **3.** action of floundering; a floundering movement. [? b. FLOUNCE[1] and FOUNDER[2]] —**floun′der·ing·ly,** *adv.*

floun·der[2] (floun′dər), *n., pl.* (*esp. collectively*) **-der,** (*esp. referring to two or more kinds or species*) **-ders. 1.** a European, marine flatfish, *Platichthys flesus,* used for food. **2.** any of numerous similar or closely related non-European flatfishes. **3.** any flatfish other than soles. [ME < AF *floundre* < Scand; cf. Norw *flundra*]

Winter flounder, *Pseudopleuronectes americanus* (Length to 1½ ft.)

flour (flour, flou′ər), *n.* **1.** the finely ground meal of grain, esp. the finer meal separated by bolting. **2.** the finely ground and bolted meal of wheat. **3.** any fine, soft powder: *flour of emery.* —*v.t.* **4.** to make (grain or the like) into flour; grind and bolt. **5.** *Cookery.* to sprinkle or dredge with flour. —*v.i.* **6.** (of mercury) to refuse to amalgamate with another metal because of some impurity of the metal; lie on the surface of the metal in the form of minute globules. **7.** chalk (def. 9). [ME; special use of FLOWER. Cf. F *fleur de farine* the flower or finest part of the meal]

flour·ish (flûr′ish, flur′-), *v.i.* **1.** to be in a vigorous state; thrive: *a period in which art flourished.* **2.** to be in its or in one's prime; be at the height of fame, excellence, influence, etc. **3.** to be successful; prosper. **4.** to grow luxuriantly, or thrive in growth, as a plant. **5.** to make strokes or flourishes with a brandished weapon or the like. **6.** to make an ostentatious display. **7.** to add embellishments and ornamental lines to writing, letters, etc. **8.** to speak or write in flowery or pretentious language. —*v.t.* **9.** to brandish or wave (a sword, stick, etc.) about in the air. **10.** to parade, flaunt, or display ostentatiously. **11.** to adorn with decorative designs, color, etc. —*n.* **12.** a brandishing or waving, as of a sword, stick, or the like. **13.** an ostentatious display. **14.** a decoration or embellishment in writing. **15.** *Rhet.* a parade of fine language; an expression used merely for effect. **16.** *Music.* **a.** an elaborate passage or addition largely for display. **b.** a trumpet call or fanfare. **17.** *Rare.* the condition of flourishing or thriving: *in full flourish.* **18.** *Obs.* state of flowering. [ME *florisshe(n)* < MF *floriss-,* long s. of *florir* << L *flōrēre* to bloom. See FLOWER] —**flour′ish·er,** *n.* —**Syn. 1.** grow, increase. **6.** flaunt. **11.** ornament. —**Ant. 1.** fade, decline, fail.

flour·y (flour′ē, flou′ə rē), *adj.* **1.** of, pertaining to, or resembling flour. **2.** covered or white with flour.

flout (flout), *v.t.* **1.** to treat with disdain, scorn, or contempt; scoff at; mock. —*v.i.* **2.** to show disdain, scorn, or contempt; scoff, mock, or gibe (often fol. by *at*). —*n.* **3.** a disdainful, scornful, or contemptuous remark, act, etc.; mocking insult; gibe. [ME *floute(n)* (to) play the FLUTE; cf. D *fluiten* to play the flute, jeer] —**flout′er,** *n.* —**flout′ing·ly,** *adv.* —**Usage.** See **flaunt.**

flow (flō), *v.i.* **1.** to move along in a stream, as water or other liquid. **2.** to circulate, as the blood. **3.** to stream or well forth. **4.** to issue or proceed from a source: *Orders flowed from the office.* **5.** to menstruate. **6.** to come or go as in a stream, as persons or things: *A constant stream of humanity flowed by.* **7.** to proceed continuously and smoothly, as thought, speech, etc. **8.** to fall or hang loosely at full length, as hair: *Her hair flowed over her shoulders.* **9.** to overflow or abound with something: *The tavern flowed with wine.* **10.** to rise and advance, as the tide (opposed to *ebb*). —*v.t.* **11.** to cause or permit to flow. **12.** to cover with water or other liquid; flood. —*n.* **13.** act of flowing. **14.** movement in or as in a stream; any continuous movement, as of thought, speech, trade, etc. **15.** the rate of flowing: *an even flow.* **16.** the volume of fluid that flows through a passage of any given section in a unit of time. **17.** something that flows; stream. **18.** an outpouring or discharge of something, as in a stream: *a flow of blood.* **19.** menstruation. **20.** an overflowing. **21.** the rise of the tide (opposed to *ebb*). **22.** *Physics.* the transference of energy: *heat flow.* [ME *flowe(n),* OE *flōwan;* c. MLG *vlōien,* Icel *flōa*]

—**Syn. 1.** FLOW, GUSH, SPOUT, SPURT refer to certain of the movements characteristic of fluids. FLOW is the general term: *Water flows. A stream of blood flows.* To GUSH is to rush forth copiously from a cavity, in as large a volume as can issue therefrom, as the result of some strong impelling force: *The water will gush out if the main breaks.* SPOUT and SPURT both imply the ejecting of a liquid from a cavity by some internal impetus given to it. SPOUT implies a rather steady, possibly well-defined, jet or stream, not necessarily of long duration but always of considerable force: *A whale spouts.* SPURT implies a forcible, possibly sudden, spasmodic, or intermittent issue or jet: *The liquid spurted out suddenly when the bottle cap was pushed in.* **7.** run. **9.** teem. **17.** current.

flow·age (flō′ij), *n.* **1.** act of flowing; flow. **2.** state of being flooded. **3.** flowing or overflowing water, or other liquid. **4.** *Mech.* gradual internal motion or deformation.

flow′ chart′, 1. Also called **flow sheet.** a detailed diagram or chart of the operations and equipment through which material passes, as in a manufacturing process. **2.** *Computer Technol.* a graphic representation, more detailed than a flow diagram, of a sequence of operations in a computer program.

flow′ di′agram, *Computer Technol.* a schematic representation, less detailed than a flow chart, of a sequence of subroutines, indicating the general flow of information for solving a problem by a computer.

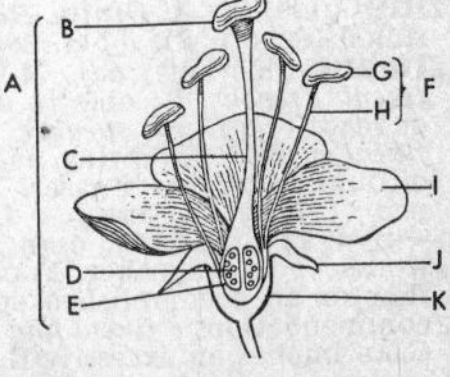

Flower
A, Pistil; B, Stigma; C, Style; D, Ovule; E, Ovary; F, Stamen; G, Anther; H, Filament; I, Petal; J, Sepal; K, Receptacle

flow·er (flou′ər), *n.* **1.** the blossom of a plant. **2.** *Bot.* **a.** that part of a seed plant comprising the reproductive organs and their envelopes if any, esp. when such envelopes are more or less conspicuous in form and color. **b.** an analogous reproductive structure in other plants, as the mosses. **3.** a plant considered with reference to its blossom or cultivated for its floral beauty. **4.** a state of efflorescence or bloom: *Peonies were in flower.* **5.** an ornament representing a flower. **6.** any ornament or adornment. **7.** See **figure of speech. 8.** the finest or most flourishing state or period, as of life or beauty. **9.** the best or finest member or part of a number, body, or whole: *the flower of American youth.* **10.** the finest or choicest product or example. **11. flowers,** (*construed as sing.*) *Chem.* a substance in the form of a fine powder, esp. as obtained by sublimation: *flowers of sulfur.* —*v.i.* **12.** to produce flowers, as a plant; blossom; come to full bloom. **13.** to come out into full development; mature. —*v.t.* **14.** to cover or deck with flowers. **15.** to decorate with a floral design. [ME *flour* flower, best of anything < OF *flor, flour, flur* < L *flōr-* (s. of *flōs*). Cf. BLOSSOM] —**flow′er·like′,** *adj.*

flow·er·age (flou′ər ij), *n.* **1.** flowers collectively. **2.** floral ornament or decoration. **3.** the process or state of flowering.

flow′er bud′. See under **bud**[1] (def. 1a).

flow′er child′, a young person who rejects conventional life styles and values in favor of a simple, idealistic life.

flow·ered (flou′ərd), *adj.* **1.** having flowers. **2.** decorated with flowers or a floral pattern. [ME]

flow·er·er (flou′ər ər), *n.* a plant that flowers at a specific time or in a certain manner: *a late flowerer.*

flow·er·et (flou′ər it), *n.* a small flower; floret. [var. of FLORET]

flow′er girl′, 1. a young girl at a wedding ceremony who precedes the bride and carries or scatters flowers in her path. **2.** *Brit.* a woman who sells flowers in the street.

flow′er head′, *Bot.* an inflorescence consisting of a dense cluster of sessile florets; capitulum.

flow·er·ing (flou′ər ing), *adj.* bearing flowers. [ME]

flow′ering dog′wood, a North American tree, *Cornus*

florida, having small greenish flowers in the spring, surrounded by white or pink bracts that resemble petals: the state flower and the state tree of Virginia.

flow′ering ma′ple, any malvaceous shrub of the genus *Abutilon,* having large, bright-colored flowers.

flow·er·less (flou′ər lis), *adj.* **1.** having no flowers. **2.** *Bot.* having no true seeds; cryptogamic.

flow·er·pot (flou′ər pot′), *n.* a container, usually a clay pot, in which to grow plants.

flow·er·y (flou′ə rē), *adj.* **1.** covered with or having many flowers. **2.** decorated with floral designs. **3.** full of highly ornate language, elaborate figures of speech, etc.: *a flowery style of oratory.* **4.** resembling that of a flower: *a flowery aroma.* [ME] —**flow′er·i·ness,** *n.* —**Syn. 3.** florid, showy, elaborate.

flow·ing (flō′ing), *adj.* **1.** moving in or as in a stream: *flowing water.* **2.** proceeding smoothly or easily; facile: *flowing language.* **3.** long, smooth, graceful, and without sudden interruption or change of direction: *flowing lines; flowing gestures.* **4.** falling or hanging loosely at full length: *flowing hair.* **5.** abounding; having in excess: *a land flowing with riches.* [ME *flowynge,* OE *flōende*] —**flow′ing·ly,** *adv.*

flown[1] (flōn), *v.* a pp. of **fly**[1].

flown[2] (flōn), *adj.* **1.** decorated with colors that have been fluidly blended: *flown ceramic ware.* **2.** *Archaic.* filled to excess. [ME *flōwen;* ptp. of FLOW]

flow′ sheet′. See **flow chart** (def. 1).

fl. oz., See **fluid ounce.**

flu (flo͞o), *n.* influenza. [shortened form]

flub (flub), *v.,* **flubbed, flub·bing,** *n. Informal.* —*v.t., v.i.* **1.** to perform poorly; bungle. —*n.* **2.** a blunder. [?]

flub·dub (flub′dub′), *n. Informal.* pretentious nonsense or show; airs. [?]

fluc·tu·ant (fluk′cho͞o ənt), *adj.* **1.** fluctuating; varying; unstable. **2.** undulating; moving in waves. [< L *fluctuant-* (s. of *fluctuāns*) undulating, moving to and fro (prp. of *fluctuāre*)]

fluc·tu·ate (fluk′cho͞o āt′), *v.,* **-at·ed, -at·ing.** —*v.i.* **1.** to change continually from one position, condition, etc., to another; vary irregularly; be undecided or unstable; vacillate. **2.** to move in waves or like waves. —*v.t.* **3.** to cause to fluctuate. [< L *fluctuāt(us)* undulated, ptp. of *fluctuāre* to flow. See FLUX, -ATE[1]] —**Syn. 1.** See **waver. 2.** undulate, oscillate.

fluc·tu·a·tion (fluk′cho͞o ā′shən), *n.* **1.** continual change from one course, condition, etc., to another; vacillation; instability. **2.** wavelike motion; undulation. **3.** *Genetics.* a body variation due to environmental factors and not inherited. [< L *fluctuātiōn-* (s. of *fluctuātiō*) a fluctuation, wavering]

flue[1] (flo͞o), *n.* **1.** a passage or duct for smoke in a chimney. **2.** any duct or passage for air, gas, or the like. **3.** a tube, esp. a large one, in a fire-tube boiler. **4.** *Music.* **a.** See **flue pipe. b.** Also called **windway.** a narrow slit in the upper end of a pipe through which the air current is directed. [earlier *flew,* ? repr. OE *flēwsa* a flowing, the form *flews* being taken as pl.]

flue[2] (flo͞o), *n.* downy matter; fluff. [? OE *flug-* (in *flugol* swift, fleeting); akin to FLY[1]. Cf. LG *flug*]

flue[3] (flo͞o), *n.* a fishing net. Also, **flew.** [ME *flowe;* cf. MD *vluwe* fishing net]

flue[4] (flo͞o), *n.* **1.** *Ornith. Rare.* a barb of a feather. **2.** *Naut.* fluke[1] (defs. 1, 2). [? cf. Sw *fly*] —**flued,** *adj.*

flu·ent (flo͞o′ənt), *adj.* **1.** spoken or written effortlessly: *fluent French.* **2.** able to speak or write smoothly, easily, or readily: *a fluent speaker.* **3.** easy; graceful: *fluent motion; fluent curves.* **4.** flowing, as a stream. **5.** capable of flowing, or fluid, as liquids or gases. [< L *fluent-* (s. of *fluēns*) flowing, prp. of *fluere;* see -ENT] —**flu′en·cy,** *n.* —**flu′ent·ly,** *adv.* —**Syn. 1, 2.** FLUENT, GLIB, VOLUBLE may refer to a flow of words or to a speaker. FLUENT suggests an easy and ready flow or an accomplished speaker and is usually a term of commendation: *a fluent and interesting speech; a fluent orator.* GLIB implies an excessive fluency divorced from sincerity or profundity; it often suggests talking smoothly and hurriedly to cover up or deceive, not giving the hearer a chance to stop and think; it may also imply a plausible, prepared, and well-rehearsed lie: *He had a glib answer for everything; a glib salesman.* VOLUBLE implies an overcopious and often rapid flow of words, and characterizes a person who loves to talk and will spare his audience no details: *She overwhelmed him with her voluble answer; a voluble gossip.*

flue′ pipe′, *Music.* a pipe, esp. an organ pipe, having a flue.

flue′ stop′, a rank of flue pipes in an organ.

fluff (fluf), *n.* **1.** light, downy particles, as of cotton. **2.** a soft, light, downy mass: *a fluff of summer clouds.* **3.** a light, frivolous thing; trifle. **4.** *Informal.* an error or blunder, esp. one made by a performer in the delivery of his lines. —*v.t.* **5.** to make into fluff; shake or puff out (feathers, hair, etc.) into a fluffy mass. **6.** *Informal.* to make a mistake in: *The leading man fluffed his lines.* —*v.i.* **7.** to become fluffy; move, float, or settle down like fluff. **8.** *Informal.* to make a mistake, esp. in the delivery of lines by a performer; blunder. [? b. FLUE[2] and PUFF]

fluff·y (fluf′ē), *adj.,* **fluff·i·er, fluff·i·est. 1.** of, resembling, or covered with fluff. **2.** light or airy: *a fluffy cake.* **3.** having little or no intellectual weight; frivolous. —**fluff′i·ly,** *adv.* —**fluff′i·ness,** *n.*

flü·gel·horn (flo͞o′gəl hôrn′; *Ger.* flʏ′gəl hôʀn′), *n.* a brass wind instrument with three valves, usually pitched in B flat and used esp. in military bands. [< G = *Flügel* wing + *Horn* horn]

flu·id (flo͞o′id), *n.* **1.** a substance, as a liquid or gas, that is capable of flowing and which changes its shape at a steady rate when acted upon by a force. —*adj.* **2.** pertaining to a substance that easily changes its shape; capable of flowing. **3.** consisting of or pertaining to fluids. **4.** changing readily; not fixed or stable. [< L *fluid(us)* = *flu(ere)* (to) flow + *-idus* -ID[4]] —**flu′id·al,** *adj.* —**flu·id′i·ty, flu′id·ness,** *n.* —**flu′id·ly, flu′id·al·ly,** *adv.* —**Syn. 1.** vapor. —**Ant. 1, 2.** solid.

flu′id dram′, the eighth part of a fluid ounce. *Abbr.:* fl. dr., f℥ Also, **fluid′ drachm′.**

flu′id drive′, *Auto.* a power coupling consisting of two vaned rotors in a sealed casing filled with oil.

flu·id·ex·tract (flo͞o′id ek′strakt), *n. Pharm.* a liquid preparation, containing alcohol as a solvent or as a preservative and having in each cubic centimeter the medicinal activity of one gram of the crude drug in powdered form.

flu·id·ics (flo͞o id′iks), *n.* (*construed as sing.*) the technology dealing with the use of a flowing liquid or gas in various devices, esp. controls, to perform functions, as sensing, amplifying, or computing, usually performed by electric currents in electronic devices. [see FLUID, -ICS] —**flu·id′ic,** *adj.*

flu·id·ise (flo͞o′i dīz′), *v.t.,* **-ised, -is·ing.** *Chiefly Brit.* fluidize. —**flu′id·i·sa′tion,** *n.* —**flu′id·is′er,** *n.*

flu·id·ize (flo͞o′i dīz′), *v.t.,* **-ized, -iz·ing. 1.** to make (something) fluid. **2.** *Chem.* to suspend or transport (finely divided particles) in a stream of gas or air. —**flu′id·i·za′tion,** *n.* —**flu′id·iz′er,** *n.*

flu′id mechan′ics, an applied science dealing with the basic principles of gaseous and liquid matter.

flu′id ounce′, a measure of capacity equal to 1/16 pint or 1.8047 cubic inches in the U.S., and to 1/20 of an imperial pint or 1.7339 cubic inches in Great Britain. *Abbr.:* fl. oz., f℥

flu′id pres′sure, *Physics, Mech.* the pressure exerted by a fluid, directly proportional to the specific gravity at any point and to the height of the fluid above the point.

fluke[1] (flo͝ok), *n.* **1.** the part of an anchor that catches in the ground, esp. the flat, triangular piece at the end of each arm. **2.** the barbed head of a harpoon, spear, arrow, or the like. **3.** either half of the triangular tail of a whale. [? special use of FLUKE[3]] —**fluke′less,** *adj.*

fluke[2] (flo͝ok), *n.* **1.** an accidental advantage; stroke of good luck. **2.** an accidentally successful stroke in billiards or some other game. [?; cf. dial. *fluke* a guess]

fluke[3] (flo͝ok), *n.* **1.** any of several American flounders of the genus *Paralichthys,* esp. *P. dentatus,* found in the Atlantic Ocean. **2.** any of various other flatfishes. **3.** a trematode. [ME *flok(e), fluke,* OE *flōc;* c. OIcel *flōki;* cf. OHG *flah* flat (G *flach*)] —**fluke′less,** *adj.*

fluk·ey (flo͞o′kē), *adj.,* **fluk·i·er, fluk·i·est.** fluky.

fluk·y (flo͞o′kē), *adj.,* **fluk·i·er, fluk·i·est. 1.** *Informal.* obtained by chance rather than skill. **2.** uncertain, as a wind. —**fluk′i·ness,** *n.*

flume (flo͞om), *n., v.,* **flumed, flum·ing.** —*n.* **1.** a deep narrow defile containing a mountain stream or torrent. **2.** an artificial channel or trough for conducting water, as one used for the transportation of logs, fish, or the like. —*v.t.* **3.** to transport (logs, fish, etc.) in a flume. **4.** to divert (a stream) by a flume. [ME *flum* < OF << L *flūmen* stream]

flum·mer·y (flum′ə rē), *n., pl.* **-mer·ies. 1.** oatmeal or flour boiled with water until thick. **2.** a type of fruit custard or blancmange, usually thickened with cornstarch. **3.** any of various dishes made of flour, milk, eggs, sugar, etc. **4.** foolish humbug; empty compliment. [alter. of Welsh *llymru*]

flum·mox (flum′əks), *v.t. Informal.* to bewilder; confuse. [?]

flung (flung), *v.* pt. and pp. of **fling.**

flunk (flungk), *Informal.* —*v.i.* **1.** to fail, as a student in a recitation or examination. **2.** to fail and be unable to continue in, as school or the like (usually fol. by *out*): *He flunked out of flight training and was sent back to the infantry.* —*v.t.* **3.** to fail to get a passing mark in. **4.** to give a failing grade to; remove (a student) as unqualified from a school, course, etc. [? akin to FLINCH[1], FUNK]

flun·key (flung′kē), *n., pl.* **-keys.** flunky.

flun·ky (flung′kē), *n., pl.* **-kies. 1.** *Disparaging.* a male servant in livery; lackey. **2.** a servile follower; toady. [? alter. of FLANKER]

fluo-, var. of **fluoro-:** *fluophosphate.*

flu·o·phos·phate (flo͞o′ə fos′fāt), *n. Chem.* fluorophosphate.

flu·or (flo͞o′ôr, -ər), *n. Mineral.* fluorite. [< L: a flowing; so called from its use as a flux]

fluor-, var. of **fluoro-** before a vowel: *fluorene.*

flu·o·rene (flo͞o′ə rēn′, -rin, flo͝or′ēn, -in, flōr′-, flôr′-), *n. Chem.* a crystalline solid, $C_{13}H_{10}$, used chiefly in the manufacture of resins and dyes.

flu·o·resce (flo͞o′ə res′, flo͝o res′, flō-, flô-), *v.i.,* **-resced, -resc·ing.** to exhibit the phenomenon of fluorescence. [back formation from FLUORESCENCE]

flu·o·res·ce·in (flo͞o′ə res′ē in, flo͝o res′-, flō-, flô-), *n. Chem.* an orange-red solid, $C_{20}H_{12}O_5$, that in alkaline solutions produces an orange color and an intense green fluorescence: used chiefly as an indicator and in dyes. Also, **flu′o·res′ce·ine.** [FLUORESCE + -IN[2]]

flu·o·res·cence (flo͞o′ə res′əns, flo͝o res′-, flō-, flô-), *n. Physics, Chem.* **1.** the emission of radiation, esp. of visible light, by a substance during exposure to external radiation, as light or x-rays. Cf. **phosphorescence** (def. 1). **2.** the property possessed by a substance capable of such emission. **3.** the radiation so produced.

flu·o·res·cent (flo͞o′ə res′ənt, flo͝o res′-, flō-, flô-), *adj.* possessing the property of fluorescence; exhibiting fluorescence.

fluores′cent lamp′, a tubular electric discharge lamp in which light is produced by the fluorescence of phosphors coating the inside of the tube.

fluor·i·date (flo͝or′i dāt′, flōr′-, flôr′-), *v.t.,* **-dat·ed, -dat·ing.** to introduce a fluoride into. [back formation from FLUORIDATION]

fluor·i·da·tion (flo͝or′i dā′shən, flōr′-, flôr′-), *n.* the addition of fluorides to the public water supply to reduce the incidence of tooth decay.

flu·o·ride (flo͞o′ə rīd′, flo͝or′īd, flōr′-, flôr′-), *n. Chem.* **1.** a salt of hydrofluoric acid, as sodium fluoride, NaF. **2.** a compound containing fluorine, as methyl fluoride, CH_3F.

fluor·i·dise (flo͝or′i dīz′, flōr′-, flôr′-), *v.t.,* **-dised, -dis·ing.** *Chiefly Brit.* fluoridize. —**fluor′i·di·sa′tion,** *n.*

fluor·i·dize (flo͝or′i dīz′, flōr′-, flôr′-), *v.t.,* **-dized, -diz·ing.** to treat with a fluoride. —**fluor′i·di·za′tion,** *n.*

fluor·i·nate (flo͝or′ə nāt′, flōr′-, flôr′-), *v.t.,* **-nat·ed, -nat·ing.** *Chem.* to treat or combine with fluorine. —**fluor′i·na′tion,** *n.*

flu·o·rine (flo͞o′ə rēn′, -rin, flo͝or′ēn, -in, flōr′-, flôr′-), *n. Chem.* the most reactive nonmetallic element, a pale-yellow, corrosive toxic gas that occurs combined, esp. in minerals. *Symbol:* F; *at. wt.:* 18.9984; *at. no.:* 9. [FLUOR- + -INE[1]]

flu·o·rite (flo͞o′ə rīt′, flo͝or′īt, flōr′-, flôr′-), *n.* a common

mineral, calcium fluoride, CaF_2, the principal source of fluorine. Also called **fluor, fluorspar, fluor spar.** [< It]
fluoro-, 1. a combining form noting the presence of fluorine: *fluorocarbon.* 2. a combining form of **fluorescence:** *fluoroscopy.* Also, **fluo-, fluor-.** [< NL; see FLUOR, -O-]
flu·o·ro·car·bon (flo͞o′ə rō kär′bən, flo͝or′ō-, flôr′-, flōr′-), *n. Chem.* any of a class of compounds produced by substituting fluorine for hydrogen in a hydrocarbon: used chiefly as a lubricant and fire-extinguishing agent.
flu·o·rom·e·ter (flo͞o′ə rom′i tər, flo͝o rom′-, flō-, flô-), *n.* an instrument for measuring fluorescence, often as a means of determining the nature of the substance emitting the fluorescence. —**flu·o·ro·met·ric** (flo͞o′ər ə me′trik, flo͝or′ə-, flōr′ə-, flôr′ə-), *adj.* —**flu′o·rom′e·try,** *n.*
flu·o·ro·phos·phate (flo͞o′ə rō fos′fāt, flo͝or′ō-, flōr′-, flôr′-), *n. Chem.* a salt or ester of a fluorophosphoric acid. Also, **fluophosphate.**
fluor·o·scope (flo͝or′ə skōp′, flōr′-, flôr′-, flo͞o′ər ə-), *n.* a tube or box fitted with a screen coated with a fluorescent substance, used for viewing objects by means of x-ray or other radiation.
fluor·o·scop·ic (flo͝or′ə skop′ik, flōr′-, flôr′-, flo͞o′ər ə-), *adj.* of or pertaining to the fluoroscope or fluoroscopy. —**fluor′o·scop′i·cal·ly,** *adv.*
fluor·os·co·py (flo͝o ros′kə pē, flō-, flô-, flo͞o′ə ros′-), *n.* the use of or examination by means of a fluoroscope.
fluo·ro·sis (flo͝o rō′sis, flō-, flô-, flo͞o′ə rō′-), *n. Pathol.* poisoning by excessive use of fluorides.
flu·or·spar (flo͞o′ôr spär′, -ər-), *n. Mineral.* fluorite. Also, **flu′or spar′.**
flur·ry (flûr′ē, flur′ē), *n., pl.* **-ries,** *v.,* **-ried, -ry·ing.** —*n.* 1. a shower of snow. 2. sudden commotion, excitement, or confusion. 3. *Stock Exchange.* a brief agitation in prices. 4. *Rare.* a sudden gust of wind. —*v.t.* 5. to put (a person) into a flurry; make nervous; confuse; fluster. [b. FLUTTER and HURRY] —**Syn. 2.** pother, stir, to-do, fuss, ado.
flush[1] (flush), *n.* 1. a blush; rosy glow. 2. a rushing or overspreading flow, as of water. 3. a sudden rise of emotion or excitement: *a flush of anger.* 4. glowing freshness or vigor: *the flush of youth.* 5. the hot stage of a fever. —*v.t.* 6. to redden; cause to blush or glow. 7. to flood with water, as for cleansing purposes. 8. to wash out (a sewer, toilet, etc.) by a sudden rush of water. 9. to animate or excite; inflame. —*v.i.* 10. to blush; redden. 11. to flow with a rush; flow and spread suddenly. [b. FLASH and GUSH; in some senses, further blended with BLUSH] —**flush′er,** *n.*
flush[2] (flush), *adj.* 1. even or level, as with a surface; forming one plane. 2. having direct contact; being right next to; immediately adjacent; contiguous: *The table was flush against the wall.* 3. well-supplied, as with money; affluent; prosperous. 4. abundant; plentiful. 5. having a ruddy color; blushing. 6. full of vigor; lusty. 7. full to overflowing. 8. *Naut.* noting a continuous weather deck that has no superstructure but may have deckhouses, companions, etc. 9. *Print.* even or level with either margin of the page. —*adv.* 10. on the same level; in a straight line; without a change of plane. 11. in direct contact; squarely: *set flush against the edge.* —*v.t.* 12. to make flush or even. —*v.i.* 13. to send out shoots, as plants in spring. —*n.* 14. a fresh growth, as of shoots and leaves. [? special uses of FLUSH[1]] —**flush′ness,** *n.*
flush[3] (flush), *Hunting.* —*v.t.* 1. to rouse and cause to start up or fly off: *to flush a woodcock.* —*v.i.* 2. to fly out or start up suddenly. —*n.* 3. a flushed bird, or flock of birds. [ME *flussh* < ?]
flush[4] (flush), *Cards.* —*adj.* 1. consisting entirely of cards of one suit: *a flush hand.* —*n.* 2. a hand or set of cards all of one suit. Cf. **royal flush, straight flush.** 3. *Pinochle.* a meld of ace, king, queen, jack, and ten of the trump suit. Cf. **marriage** (def. 5). [cf. F (obs.) *flus,* var. of *flux* flow, flush (cf. phrase *run* of cards) < L *flux(us)* FLUX]
flush-deck (flush′dek′), *adj. Naut.* noting a vessel having no shelter deck, poop, forecastle, or other superstructure of any kind above the freeboard deck, but sometimes having deckhouses, companions, etc. Also, **flush′-decked′.**
Flush·ing (flush′ing), *n.* a seaport on Walcheren Island, in the SW Netherlands. 28,856 (1964). Dutch, **Vlissingen.**
flus·ter (flus′tər), *v.t.* 1. to put into a state of nervous, agitated confusion. 2. to excite and confuse with drink. —*v.i.* 3. to become nervously and agitatedly confused. —*n.* 4. nervous excitement; confusion; flurry. [ME *flostre(n);* cf. Icel *flaustr* to hurry, bustle and cf. BLUSTER] —**Syn. 1.** upset, bewilder, disconcert, disturb. 4. turmoil, agitation, upset, bewilderment, distraction.
flus·trate (flus′trāt), *v.t.,* **-trat·ed, -trat·ing.** *Informal.* to fluster. [FLUST(E)R + -ATE[1], modeled on *frustrate*] —**flus·tra′tion,** *n.*
flute (flo͞ot), *n., v.,* **flut·ed, flut·ing.** —*n.* 1. a musical wind instrument consisting of a tube with a series of finger holes or keys, in which the wind is directed against a sharp edge, either directly, as in the modern transverse flute, or through a flue, as in the recorder. 2. *Archit., Furniture.* a channel, groove, or furrow, as on the shaft of a column. 3. a groove or furrow, as in a ruffle of cloth, on a piecrust, or the like. —*v.i.* 4. to produce flutelike sounds. 5. to play on a flute. —*v.t.* 6. to utter in flutelike tones. 7. to form flutes or furrows in. [ME *floute* < MF *flaüte, flahute, fleüte* < OPr *flaüt* (perh. alter. of *flaujol, flauja*) < VL **flabeol(um).* See FLAGEOLET, LUTE] —**flute′like′,** *adj.*

Flute

flut·ed (flo͞o′tid), *adj.* 1. fine, clear, and mellow; flutelike: *fluted notes.* 2. having flutes or grooves, as a ruffle.
flut·er (flo͞o′tər), *n.* 1. a person who makes flutings. 2. *Archaic.* a flutist. [ME *flouter, floutour* < OF *fleuteur, flauteor* = *flaut(er)* (to) play the flute + *-eur, -eor* -ER[1]]
flut·ing (flo͞o′ting), *n.* 1. the act of playing on the flute. 2. the sound made by such playing; a flutelike sound. 3. ornamental grooves or furrows, as in a Greek column. 4. the act of making such grooves or fluted work. 5. a groove, furrow, or flute, or a series of these.
flut·ist (flo͞o′tist), *n.* a flute player. Also, **flautist.** [FLUTE + -IST; see FLAUTIST]
flut·ter (flut′ər), *v.i.* 1. to wave, flap, or toss about in the air, as a flag. 2. (of birds) to flap the wings, or fly with flapping movements. 3. to move in quick, irregular motions; vibrate. 4. to beat rapidly and irregularly, as the heart. 5. to be tremulous or agitated. 6. to go with irregular motions or aimless course. —*v.t.* 7. to cause to flutter; vibrate; agitate. 8. to throw into a state of nervous or tremulous excitement; cause mental agitation; confuse. —*n.* 9. a fluttering movement. 10. a state of nervous excitement or mental agitation. 11. sensation; stir: *to cause a flutter.* 12. *Swimming.* See **flutter kick.** 13. a rapid variation in pitch fidelity resulting from fluctuations in the speed of a recording. [ME *flotere(n),* OE *floterian,* freq. of *flotian* to FLOAT] —**flut′ter·er,** *n.* —**flut′ter·ing·ly,** *adv.* —**Syn. 2.** See **fly**[1].
flut·ter·board (flut′ər bōrd′, -bôrd′), *n.* a kickboard.
flut′ter kick′, *Swimming.* a kick in which the legs make rapid alternate up-and-down movements while the knees remain rigid, as in the crawl.
flu·vi·al (flo͞o′vē əl), *adj.* 1. of or pertaining to a river: *fluvial contour.* 2. produced by or found in a river: *fluvial deposits.* [< L *fluviāl(is)* = *fluvi(us)* river (< *fluere* to flow) + *-ālis* -AL[1]]
flux (fluks), *n.* 1. a flowing or flow. 2. the flowing in of the tide. 3. continuous change, passage, or movement: *His political views are in flux.* 4. lack of certainty, purpose, or direction; instability. 5. *Pathol.* **a.** an abnormal discharge of liquid matter from the bowels. **b.** dysentery. 6. *Physics.* **a.** the rate of flow of fluid, particles, or energy. **b.** a quantity expressing the strength of a field of force in a given area. 7. *Chem., Metall.* **a.** a substance used to refine metals by combining with impurities to form a molten mixture that can be readily removed. **b.** a substance used to remove oxides from and prevent further oxidation of fused metal, as in soldering or hot-dip coating. 8. a melting together; fusion: *metal in flux.* —*v.t.* 9. to melt; make fluid. 10. to fuse by the use of flux. 11. *Obs.* to purge. —*v.i.* 12. *Archaic.* to flow by melting. [ME < L *flux(us)* a flowing, n. use of ptp. of *fluere* to flow]
flux′ den′sity, *Physics.* the magnetic, radiant, or electric flux per unit of cross-sectional area.
flux·ion (fluk′shən), *n.* 1. the act of flowing; a flow or flux. 2. *Math. Obs.* the derivative relative to the time. [< MF < LL *fluxiōn-* (s. of *fluxiō*) a flowing] —**flux′ion·al, flux′ion·ar·y,** *adj.* —**flux′ion·al·ly,** *adv.*
flux·me·ter (fluks′mē′tər), *n. Physics.* an instrument for measuring magnetic flux, consisting essentially of a ballistic galvanometer.
fluyt (flīt), *n.* a small 17th-century merchant ship of northern Europe, having a rounded stern, a flat bottom, and three masts. [var. of *flute* a flyboat < D *fluit* FLUTE]
fly[1] (flī), *v.,* **flew** or, for 8, 15, **flied, flown, fly·ing,** *n., pl.* **flies.** —*v.i.* 1. to move through the air on wings, as a bird. 2. to be carried through the air by the wind or any other force or agency. 3. to float or flutter in the air: *flags flying in the breeze.* 4. to travel through the air or outer space in an aircraft, rocket, or satellite, or as an aircraft, rocket, or satellite does. 5. to move suddenly and quickly; start unexpectedly and rapidly: *He flew from the room.* 6. to flee; take flight; escape. 7. to move or pass swiftly: *How time flies!* 8. *Baseball.* **a.** to bat a fly ball: *He flied into right field.* **b.** to fly out.
—*v.t.* 9. to make (something) float or move through the air: *to fly a kite.* 10. to operate (an aircraft, spaceship, or the like). 11. to hoist aloft, as for display, signaling, etc.: *to fly a flag.* 12. to operate an aircraft over (a particular route): *to fly the Pacific.* 13. to transport or convey (something) by air. 14. to escape from (something): *to fly an enemy's wrath.* 15. *Theat.* to raise (scenery) from the stage or acting area into the flies. 16. **fly at** or **into,** to attack or lash out at, either verbally or physically. 17. **fly in the face of,** to act in defiance of (authority, custom, etc.). 18. **fly off the handle.** See **handle** (def. 6). 19. **fly out,** *Baseball, Softball.* to be put out by hitting a fly ball that is caught by a player of the opposing team. 20. **let fly, a.** to hurl or propel (a weapon, missile, etc.). **b.** to give free rein to an emotion.
—*n.* 21. a strip or fold of material along one edge of a garment opening for concealing buttons or other fasteners, used esp. on a man's trousers; a placket. 22. a flap forming the door of a tent. 23. Also called **tent fly.** a piece of canvas forming the outer roof of a tent. 24. act of flying; a flight. 25. the course of a flying object, as a ball. 26. *Baseball.* See **fly ball.** 27. *Horol.* a regulating device for chime and striking mechanisms, consisting of an arrangement of vanes on a revolving axis. 28. *Print.* (in some presses) the apparatus for removing the printed sheets to the delivery table. 29. (on a flag) **a.** the horizontal dimension of a flag as flown from a vertical staff. **b.** the end of the flag farther from the staff. Cf. **hoist** (def. 6). 30. **flies,** *Theat.* the space above the stage, used chiefly for storing scenery and equipment. 31. **on the fly, a.** during flight; before reaching the ground. **b.** hurriedly; without pausing. [ME *flīe(n),* OE *flēogan;* c. OHG *fliogan,* G *fliegen,* OIcel *fljuga*] —**fly′a·bil′i·ty,** *n.* —**fly′a·ble,** *adj.*
—**Syn. 1.** FLY, FLIT, FLUTTER, HOVER, SOAR refer to moving through the air as on wings. FLY is the general term: *Birds fly. Airplanes fly.* To FLIT is to make short rapid flights from place to place: *A bird flits from tree to tree.* To FLUTTER is to agitate the wings tremulously, either without flying or in flying only short distances: *A young bird flutters out of a nest and in again.* To HOVER is to linger in the air, or to move over or about something within a narrow area or space: *hovering clouds; a hummingbird hovering over a blossom.* To SOAR is to (start to) fly upward to a great height usually with little advance in any other direction, or else to (continue to) fly at a lofty height without visible movement of the wings: *Above our heads an eagle was soaring.* 7. pass, glide, slip, elapse.

fly² (flī), *n., pl.* **flies. 1.** Also called **true fly.** any of numerous two-winged insects of the order *Diptera,* esp. of the family *Muscidae,* as the common housefly. **2.** any of various winged insects, as the mayfly or firefly. **3.** *Angling.* a fishhook dressed with hair, feathers, silk, tinsel, etc., so as to resemble an insect or small fish, for use as a lure or bait. **4. fly in the ointment,** a circumstance, esp. a trifling inconvenience, that detracts from the enjoyment or usefulness of something. [ME *flie,* OE *flēoge, flȳge;* akin to MD *vliege* (D *vlieg*), OHG *flioga* (G *Fliege*)] **—fly′less,** *adj.*

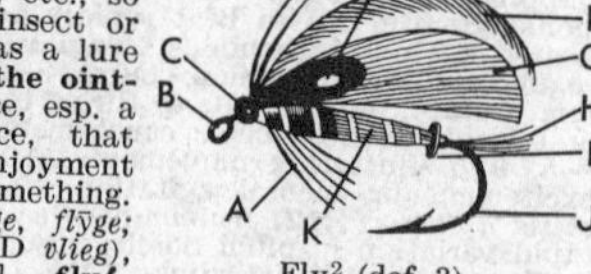

Fly² (def. 3)
A, Hackle; B, Eye; C, Head; D, Horns; E, Cheek; F, Topping; G, Wing; H, Tail; I, Butt; J, Hook; K, Body

fly³ (flī), *adj. Brit. Slang.* **1.** knowing; smart; nimble-minded. **2.** agile; nimble. [? special use of FLY¹]

fly′ ag′aric, a very poisonous mushroom, *Amanita muscaria,* yielding a substance that is toxic to flies.

fly′ ash′, 1. fine particles of ash of a solid fuel carried out of the flue of a furnace with the waste gases produced during combustion. **2.** such ash recovered from the waste gases, used chiefly as a reinforcing agent in the manufacture of bricks, concrete, etc.

fly′ ball′, *Baseball.* a ball that is batted up into the air. Also called **fly.** Cf. **ground ball.**

fly′ block′, *Mach., Naut.* **1.** (in a Spanish burton or the like) a block, supported by a runner, through which the hauling part of the fall is rove. **2.** any block that shifts with the movement of its tackle.

fly·blow (flī′blō′), *v.,* **-blew, -blown, -blow·ing,** *n.* **—*v.t.* 1.** to deposit eggs or larvae on (meat or other food). **—*n.* 2.** the egg or young larva of a blowfly, deposited on meat or other food. [back formation from FLYBLOWN]

fly·blown (flī′blōn′), *adj.* **1.** covered with flyblows: *flyblown meat.* **2.** spoiled; tainted; contaminated.

fly′ book′, *Angling.* a booklike case for storing or carrying artificial flies.

fly-by-night (flī′bī nīt′), *adj.* **1.** not reliable or responsible, esp. in business. **2.** not lasting; brief; impermanent; transitory. **—*n.* 3.** a person or thing that is unreliable.

fly-by-wire (flī′bī wīᵊr′), *adj.* activated entirely by electrical controls connected by fine but strong wires between the device and the controller: *a fly-by-wire helicopter.*

fly′ cast′ing, *Angling.* act or technique of casting with an artificial fly as the lure, the rod used being longer and more flexible than that used in bait casting.

fly·catch·er (flī′kach′ər), *n.* **1.** any of numerous Old World birds of the family *Muscicapidae,* that feed on insects captured in the air. **2.** Also called **tyrant flycatcher.** any of numerous similar American birds of the family *Tyrannidae.*

fly·er (flī′ər), *n.* flier. [late ME]

fly-fish (flī′fish′), *v.i.* to fish with artificial flies as bait.

fly′ gal′lery, *Theat.* a narrow platform at the side of a stage from which ropes are manipulated to raise or lower scenery, battens, etc.

fly·ing (flī′ing), *adj.* **1.** that flies; making flight or passing through the air: *a flying insect; an unidentified flying object.* **2.** floating, fluttering, waving, hanging, or moving freely in the air: *flying banners.* **3.** extending through the air: *a flying leap.* **4.** moving swiftly. **5.** hasty; brief: *a flying visit.* **6.** *Naut.* (of a sail) having none of its edges bent to spars or stays. **—*n.* 7.** the act of moving through the air on wings; flight. **—*adv.* 8.** *Naut.* without being bent to a yard, stay, or the like: *a sail set flying.* [ME (n.), OE *flēogende* (n.)]

fly′ing boat′, a seaplane whose main body consists of a single hull or boat that supports it on water. Cf. **floatplane.**

fly′ing box′car, *Informal.* a large airplane designed to carry cargo.

fly′ing bridge′, *Naut.* an open platform, esp. one on top of a pilothouse, having duplicate controls, as a steering wheel, engine room telegraph, compass, etc.

fly′ing but′tress, *Archit.* a segmental arch transmitting an outward and downward thrust to a solid buttress which through its inertia transforms the thrust into a vertical one. See illus. at **buttress.**

fly′ing cir′cus, 1. a squadron of airplanes operating together, esp. in World War I. **2.** a carnival troupe, or the like, offering exhibitions of stunt flying at fairs, circuses, etc.

fly′ing col′ors, victory; triumph; success.

fly′ing drag′on, any of several arboreal lizards of the genus *Draco,* having an extensible membrane along each side by means of which it makes long, gliding leaps.

Fly′ing Dutch′man, 1. a legendary Dutch ghost ship supposed to be seen at sea, esp. near the Cape of Good Hope. **2.** the captain of this ship, supposed to have been condemned to sail the sea, beating against the wind, till the Day of Judgment.

fly′ing field′, *Aeron.* a small landing field with short runways and facilities for servicing airplanes on a lesser scale than those of an airport.

fly′ing fish′, any of several fishes of the family *Exocoetidae,* having stiff and greatly enlarged pectoral fins enabling it to glide considerable distances through the air after leaping from the water.

Flying fish, *Cypselurus californicus* (Length 1½ ft.)

fly′ing for′tress, a heavy bomber with four radial piston engines, widely used over Europe by the U.S. Army Air Force in World War II.

fly′ing fox′, any large fruit-eating bat of the family *Pteropodidae,* esp. of the genus *Pteropus,* as *P. edulis,* of Old World tropical regions, having a foxlike head.

fly′ing frog′, an East Indian frog, *Rhacophorus nigrapalmatus,* having broadly webbed feet enabling it to make long, gliding leaps.

fly′ing gur′nard, any of several marine fishes of the family *Dactylopteridae,* esp. *Dactylopterus volitans,* having enlarged, colorful pectoral fins that enable it to glide short distances through the air. Also called **butterflyfish.**

fly′ing jib′, *Naut.* the outer or outermost of two or more jibs, set well above the jib boom. See diag. at **ship.**

fly′ing le′mur, either of two lemurlike mammals, *Cynocephalus temminckii,* of southeastern Asia and the East Indies, or *C. volans,* of the Philippines, having broad folds of skin on both sides of the body that aid it in gliding from tree to tree.

fly′ing machine′, a contrivance that sustains itself in and propels itself through the air; an airplane.

fly′ing mare′, *Wrestling.* an attack in which one grasps the opponent's wrist, turns, and throws him over the shoulder and down.

Flying phalanger, genus *Petaurus* (Total length to 2½ ft.; tail 16 in.)

fly′ing phalan′ger, any of various small phalangers of Australia and New Guinea, having a parachutelike fold of skin on each side of the body enabling it to take long gliding leaps.

fly′ing sau′cer, any of various disk-shaped objects allegedly seen flying at high speeds and altitudes, and generally presumed to be from outer space.

fly′ing squir′rel, a squirrellike animal, esp. of the genus *Glaucomys,* as *G. volans* of the eastern U.S., having folds of skin connecting the fore and hind legs, that enable it to take long gliding leaps.

Flying squirrel, *Glaucomys volans* (Total length 1 ft.; tail 4 in.)

fly′ing start′, a vigorous and enthusiastic start or beginning, sometimes with an advantage over competitors.

fly·leaf (flī′lēf′), *n., pl.* **-leaves.** a blank leaf in the front or the back of a book. [FLY¹ (n., in combination: something fastened by the edge) + LEAF]

fly·pa·per (flī′pā′pər), *n.* paper designed to kill flies by poisoning them or catching them on its sticky surface.

Fly′ Riv′er (flī), a river in New Guinea, flowing SE from the central part to the Gulf of Papua. ab. 800 mi. long.

fly′ rod′, a light, extremely flexible fishing rod specially designed for use in fly-fishing.

fly′ sheet′, a sheet of instructions or information.

fly·speck (flī′spek′), *n.* **1.** a speck or tiny stain from the excrement of a fly. **2.** a minute spot. **3.** *Plant Pathol.* a disease of pome fruits, characterized by small, raised, dark spots on the fruit, caused by a fungus, *Leptothyrium pomi.* **—*v.t.* 4.** to mark with flyspecks.

fly′ swat′ter, a device for killing flies, mosquitoes, and other insects, usually a square sheet of wire mesh attached to a long handle and variously ornamented.

fly·trap (flī′trap′), *n.* **1.** any of various plants that entrap insects, esp. Venus's-flytrap. **2.** a trap for catching flies.

fly·way (flī′wā′), *n.* a specific air route taken by birds during migration.

fly·weight (flī′wāt′), *n.* a boxer or other contestant of the lightest competitive class, esp. a professional boxer weighing up to 112 pounds.

fly·wheel (flī′hwēl′, -wēl′), *n. Mach.* a heavy disk or wheel rotating on a shaft so that its momentum gives almost uniform rotational speed to the shaft and to all connected machinery. [FLY¹ (see FLYLEAF) + WHEEL]

FM, 1. *Electronics.* frequency modulation: a method of impressing a signal on a radio carrier wave by varying the frequency of the carrier wave. **2.** *Radio.* a system of radio broadcasting by means of frequency modulation. **3.** of, pertaining to, or utilizing such a system. Cf. **AM.**

Fm, *Chem.* fermium.

fm., 1. fathom. **2.** from.

F.Mk., finmark. Also, **FMk**

fn, footnote.

FNMA, Federal National Mortgage Association.

f number, *Optics, Photog.* a number corresponding to the ratio of the focal length to the diameter of a lens system, esp. a camera lens, a smaller number indicating a larger lens diameter and hence a smaller exposure time: *f*/1.4 signifies that the focal length of the lens is 1.4 times as great as the diameter. *Abbr.: f/* Also called **speed.** Cf. **f-stop.**

fo., folio.

foal (fōl), *n.* **1.** a young horse, mule, or other related animal, esp. one less than one year of age. **—*v.t., v.i.* 2.** to give birth to (a colt or filly). [ME *fole,* OE *fola;* c. OHG *folo* (G *Fohlen*); akin to L *pullu(s)* young animal, Gk *pôlos* foal]

foam (fōm), *n.* **1.** a collection of minute bubbles formed on the surface of a liquid by agitation, fermentation, etc.: *foam on a glass of beer.* **2.** the froth of perspiration, caused by great exertion, formed on the skin of a horse or other animal. **3.** froth formed in the mouth, as in epilepsy and rabies. **4.** (in fire fighting) **a.** a substance that smothers the flames on a burning liquid by forming a layer of minute, stable, heat-resistant bubbles on the liquid's surface. **b.** the layer of bubbles so formed. **—*v.i.* 5.** to form or gather foam; emit foam; froth. [ME *fom,* OE *fām;* c. G *Feim*] **—foam′ing·ly,** *adv.* **—foam′less,** *adj.* **—foam′like′,** *adj.*

foam′ rub′ber, a light, spongy rubber, used for mattresses, cushions, etc.

foam·y (fō′mē), *adj.,* **foam·i·er, foam·i·est. 1.** covered with or full of foam. **2.** consisting of foam. **3.** resembling foam. **4.** pertaining to foam. [ME *fomy,* OE *fāmig*] **—foam′i·ly,** *adv.* **—foam′i·ness,** *n.*

fob[1] (fob), *n.* **1.** a short chain or ribbon with a medallion or similar ornament, attached to a watch and worn hanging from a pocket. **2.** a watch pocket just below the waistline in trousers or breeches. [?; cf. HG (dial.) *fuppe* pocket, *fuppen* to pocket stealthily]

fob[2] (fob), *v.t.,* **fobbed, fob·bing. 1.** *Archaic.* to cheat; deceive. **2. fob off, a.** to cheat someone by substituting something spurious or inferior; palm off (often fol. by *on*). **b.** to put (someone) off by deception or trickery. [ME *fobbe(n)*; c. G *foppen* to delude; cf. FOB[1]]

f.o.b., *Com.* free on board: without charge to the buyer for placing goods on board a carrier at the point of shipment. Also, **F.O.B.**

fo·cal (fō′kəl), *adj.* of or pertaining to a focus. [< NL *focāl(is)*] —**fo′cal·ly,** *adv.*

fo′cal infec′tion, *Pathol., Dentistry.* an infection in which the bacteria are localized in some region, as the tissue around a tooth or a tonsil, from which they may spread to some other organ or structure of the body.

fo·cal·ise (fō′kə līz′), *v.t.,* **-ised, -is·ing.** *Chiefly Brit.* focalize. —**fo′cal·i·sa′tion,** *n.*

fo·cal·ize (fō′kə līz′), *v.t.,* **-ized, -iz·ing.** focus. —**fo′cal·i·za′tion,** *n.*

fo′cal length′, *Optics.* **1.** the distance between a focal point of a lens or mirror and the corresponding principal plane. **2.** the distance between an object lens and its corresponding focal plane in a telescope. Also called **fo′cal dis′tance.**

fo′cal plane′, *Optics.* **1.** a plane through a focal point and normal to the axis of a lens, mirror, or other optical system. **2.** the transverse plane in a telescope where the real image of a distant view is in focus.

fo′cal-plane shut′ter (fō′kəl plān′), *Photog.* a camera shutter situated directly in front of the film.

fo′cal point′, 1. the central or principal point of focus. **2.** the point at which disparate elements converge; center of activity or attention: *The focal point of our discussion was the need for action.* **3.** *Optics.* a point on the axis of an optical system such that rays diverging from the point are deviated parallel to the axis after refraction or reflection by the system and that rays parallel to the axis of the system converge to the point after refraction or reflection by the system.

Foch (fosh; *Fr.* fôsh), *n.* **Fer·di·nand** (fer dē näɴ′), 1851–1929, French marshal.

fo·ci (fō′sī), *n.* a pl. of **focus.**

fo′c's′le (fōk′səl), *n.* *Naut.* forecastle. Also, **fo′c'sle.**

fo·cus (fō′kəs), *n., pl.* **-cus·es, -ci** (-sī), *v.,* **-cused, -cus·ing** or (*esp. Brit.*) **-cussed, -cus·sing.** —*n.* **1.** *Physics.* a point at which rays of light, heat, or other radiation meet after being refracted or reflected. **2.** *Optics.* **a.** the focal point of a lens. **b.** the focal length of a lens. **c.** the clear and sharply defined condition of an image. **d.** the position of a viewed object or the adjustment of an optical device necessary to produce a clear image: *in focus; out of focus.* **3.** a central point, as of attraction, attention, or activity; focal point. **4.** *Geom.* one of the points from which the distances to any point of a given curve are in a linear relation. **5.** the starting place of an earthquake. **6.** *Pathol.* the primary center from which a disease develops or in which it localizes. —*v.t.* **7.** to bring to a focus or into focus: *to focus the lens of a camera.* **8.** to concentrate: *to focus one's thoughts.* —*v.i.* **9.** to become focused. [< L: fireplace, hearth]

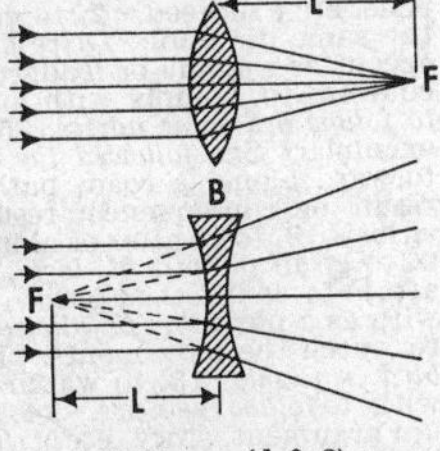

F, Focus (def. 2)
L, Focal distance; A, Convex lens; B, Concave lens

fod·der (fod′ər), *n.* **1.** coarse food for livestock. —*v.t.* **2.** to feed with or as with fodder. [ME; OE *fodder, fōdor*; c. G *Futter*; akin to FOOD] —**Syn. 1.** See **feed.**

fodg·el (foj′əl), *adj.* *Scot.* fat; stout; plump. [*fodge* (var. of FADGE) a short, fat person + *-el* adj. suffix]

foe (fō), *n.* **1.** a person who feels enmity, hatred, or malice toward another; enemy. **2.** an enemy in war; a hostile army or country. **3.** a person belonging to a hostile army or nation. **4.** an opponent in a game or contest; adversary: *a political foe.* **5.** a person who is opposed in feeling, principle, etc., to something: *a foe to progress.* **6.** a thing that is harmful to or destructive of something: *Sloth is the foe of health.* [ME *foo*, OE *fāh* hostile, *gefāh* enemy; c. OHG *gifēh* at war. See FEUD[1]] —**Syn. 1.** See **enemy. 1, 3–5.** opponent, antagonist. —**Ant. 1–3.** friend.

foehn (fān; *Ger.* fœn), *n.* a warm, dry wind descending a mountain, as on the north side of the Alps. Also, **föhn.** [< G *Föhn* < OHG *phōnno* < VL **faōnius* < L *Favōn(ius)*]

foe·man (fō′mən), *n., pl.* **-men.** *Literary.* an enemy in war. [ME *foman*, OE *fāhman*]

foe·ta·tion (fē tā′shən), *n.* fetation.

foe·ti·cide (fē′ti sīd′), *n.* feticide. —**foe′ti·cid′al,** *adj.*

foet·id (fet′id, fē′tid), *adj.* fetid.

foe·tor (fē′tər), *n.* fetor.

foe·tus (fē′təs), *n., pl.* **-tus·es.** fetus. —**foe′tal,** *adj.*

fog[1] (fog, fôg), *n., v.,* **fogged, fog·ging.** —*n.* **1.** a cloudlike mass or layer of minute water droplets or ice crystals near the surface of the earth, appreciably reducing visibility. Cf. **mist, smog. 2.** a state of mental confusion or obscurity; daze; vagueness. **3.** *Photog.* a hazy effect on a negative or positive, caused by light, improper handling, or by the use of excessively old film. **4.** *Phys. Chem.* a mixture consisting of liquid particles dispersed in a gaseous medium. —*v.t.* **5.** to coat or envelop with or as with fog. **6.** *Photog.* to produce fog on (a negative or positive). **7.** to confuse or obscure: *The debate did little else but fog the issue.* **8.** to bewilder or perplex: *to fog the mind.* —*v.i.* **9.** to become enveloped or obscured with or as with fog. **10.** *Photog.* (of a negative or positive) to become affected by fog. [back formation from FOGGY. See FOG[2]] —**fog′less,** *adj.* —**Syn. 1.** See **cloud. 8.** befuddle, muddle, mystify.

fog[2] (fog, fôg), *n.* **1.** a second growth of grass, as after mowing. **2.** long grass left standing in fields during the winter. [ME *fogge, fog* < Scand; cf. Norw *fogg* long grass on damp ground, obs. E *foggy* marshy]

fog′ bank′, a stratum of fog as seen from a distance.

fog·bound (fog′bound′, fôg′-), *adj.* *Naut.* unable to navigate because of heavy fog.

fog·bow (fog′bō′, fôg′-), *n.* a bow, arc, or circle of white or yellowish hue seen in or against a bank of fog. Also called **mistbow, seadog, white rainbow.** [FOG[1] + (RAIN)-BOW]

fog·dog (fog′dôg′, -dog′, fôg′-), *n.* a bright spot sometimes seen in a fog bank.

fo·gey (fō′gē), *n., pl.* **-geys.** fogy.

fog·gage (fog′ij, fô′gij), *n.* *Chiefly Scot.* fog[2]. [< legal L *fogāg(ium)*]

Fog·gia (fôd′jä), *n.* a city in SE Italy. 117,485 (1961).

fog·gy (fog′ē, fô′gē), *adj.,* **-gi·er, -gi·est. 1.** thick with or having much fog; misty: *a foggy valley; a foggy spring day.* **2.** resembling fog; dim; obscure. **3.** confused or unclear; vague: *foggy thinking.* **4.** *Photog.* affected by fog. [FOG[2] + -Y[1]; orig. meaning marshy, thick, murky] —**fog′gi·ly,** *adv.* —**fog′gi·ness,** *n.*

fog·horn (fog′hôrn′, fôg′-), *n.* a deep, loud horn for sounding warning signals to ships in foggy weather.

fog′ light′, an automobile headlight whose beam is of a color that can penetrate fog.

fo·gy (fō′gē), *n., pl.* **-gies.** an excessively conservative or old-fashioned person, esp. one who is dull (usually prec. by *old*): *a faculty of old fogies.* Also, **fogey.** [?] —**fo′gy·ish,** *adj.* —**fo′gy·ism,** *n.*

föhn (fān; *Ger.* fœn), *n.* foehn.

foi·ble (foi′bəl), *n.* **1.** a minor weakness or failing of character; slight flaw or defect. **2.** the weaker part of a sword blade, between the middle and the point (opposed to *forte*). [< F, obs. form of *faible* FEEBLE] —**Syn. 1.** frailty, quirk, crotchet, eccentricity, peculiarity. See **fault.** —**Ant. 1.** strength.

foie gras (fwä grä′; *Fr.* fwä gʀä′), the liver of specially fattened geese or ducks, used as a table delicacy, esp. in the form of a paste (**pâté de foie gras**). [< F: lit., fat liver]

foil[1] (foil), *v.t.* **1.** to prevent the success of (an enterprise, plan, etc.); frustrate; balk: *Loyal troops foiled the revolt.* **2.** to keep (a person) from succeeding in an enterprise, plan, etc. —*n.* **3.** *Archaic.* a defeat; check; repulse. [ME *foile(n)*, aberrant adaptation of OF *fuler* to trample, FULL[2]] —**foil′a·ble,** *adj.* —**Syn. 1.** thwart; impede, hamper.

foil[2] (foil), *n.* **1.** metal in the form of very thin sheets: *aluminum foil.* **2.** the metallic backing applied to glass to form a mirror. **3.** a thin layer of metal placed under a gem in a closed setting to improve its color or brilliancy. **4.** a person or thing that makes another seem better by contrast: *The straight man was an able foil to the comic.* **5.** *Archit.* an arc or a rounded space between cusps, as in the tracery of a window or other ornamentation. **6.** an airfoil or hydrofoil. —*v.t.* **7.** to cover or back with foil. **8.** to set off by contrast. [ME *foille, foil* < OF *fuelle, fueille, foille* (< L *folia* leaves), *fuel, fueil, foil* (< L *folium* leaf, blade)]

foil[3] (foil), *n.* *Fencing.* **1.** a flexible four-sided rapier having a blunt point. **2. foils,** the art or practice of fencing with this weapon. [?]

foils·man (foilz′mən), *n., pl.* **-men.** *Fencing.* a person who fences with a foil.

foin (foin), *Archaic.* —*n.* **1.** a thrust with a weapon. —*v.i.* **2.** to thrust with a weapon; lunge. [ME (v.), appar. < OF *foine* fish spear < L *fuscina*]

foi·son (foi′zən), *n.* *Archaic.* **1.** abundance; plenty. **2.** abundant harvest. [ME *foisoun* < MF *foison* < L *fūsiōn-* (s. of *fūsiō*) an outpouring. See FUSION]

foist (foist), *v.t.* **1.** to force upon or impose fraudulently or unjustifiably (usually fol. by *on* or *upon*): *to foist inferior merchandise on a customer.* **2.** to bring, put, or introduce surreptitiously or fraudulently (usually fol. by *in* or *into*): *to foist subversive ideas into a book.* [< D (dial.) *vuist(en)* (to) take in the hand, MD *vūsten* < *vūst* fist]

Fo·kine (fō kēn′; *Fr.* fô kēn′; *Russ.* fô′kin), *n.* **Mi·chel** (mi shel′), 1880–1942, Russian choreographer and ballet dancer, in the U.S. after 1925.

Fok·ker (fok′ər; *Du.* fôk′əʀ), *n.* **An·tho·ny Her·man Ge·rard** (än tō′nē heʀ′män кнā′ʀäʀt), 1890–1939, Dutch airplane designer and builder.

fol., 1. folio. **2.** followed. **3.** following.

fol·a·cin (fol′ə sin), *n.* *Biochem.* See **folic acid.** [FOL(IC) AC(ID) + -IN[2]]

fold[1] (fōld), *v.t.* **1.** to bend (cloth, paper, etc.) over upon itself. **2.** to bring into a compact form by bending and laying parts together (often fol. by *up*): *Fold your napkin.* **3.** to bring (the arms, hands, etc.) together in an intertwined or crossed manner; clasp; cross: *He folded his arms on his chest.* **4.** to bend or wind (usually fol. by *about, round,* etc.): *to fold one's arms about a person's neck.* **5.** to bring (the wings) close to the body, as a bird on alighting. **6.** to enclose; wrap; envelop: *to fold something in paper.* **7.** to clasp or embrace; enfold: *to fold someone in one's arms.* **8.** *Cookery.* to mix in or add, as beaten egg whites to a batter, by gently turning one part over another with a spatula, spoon, or the like (usually fol. by *in*): *Gently fold in the eggs.* **9.** *Cards.* to place (one's cards) face down so as to withdraw from the play. —*v.i.* **10.** to be folded or be capable of folding: *The doors fold back.* **11.** *Cards.* to place one's cards face down so as to withdraw from the play. **12.** to end or close, esp. through lack of patronage: *The show will fold Saturday.* **13. fold up,** *Informal.* **a.** to break down; collapse: *He folded up when the prosecutor discredited his story.* **b.** to fail, esp. to go out of business. —*n.* **14.** a part that is folded; pleat; layer: *to wrap something in folds of cloth.* **15.** a crease made by folding: *He cut the paper along the fold.* **16.** *Geol.* a portion of strata that is folded or bent, as an anticline or syncline, or that connects two horizontal or parallel portions of strata of different levels (as a monocline). **17.** the act of folding or doubling over. **18.** *Anat.* a margin or ridge formed by the folding of a membrane or other flat body part; plica. [ME *folde(n),* OE *faldan;* r. OE *fealdan,* c. G *falten*] —**fold′a·ble,** *adj.*

fold[2] (fōld), *n.* **1.** an enclosure for sheep or, occasionally, other domestic animals. **2.** the sheep or other animals contained in it. **3.** a flock of sheep. **4.** a church or its members. **5.** a group sharing common beliefs, values, etc. —*v.t.* **6.** to confine (sheep or other domestic animals) in a fold. [ME *fold, fald,* OE *fald, falod;* akin to OS *faled* pen, enclosure, MLG *vālt* pen, enclosure, manure heap, MD *vaelt, vaelde*]

-fold, a native English suffix meaning "of so many parts," or denoting multiplication by the number indicated by the stem or word to which the suffix is attached: *twofold; manifold.* [ME; OE *-fald;* r. OE *-feald,* c. G *-falt,* Goth *-falps;* akin to Gk *-paltos* (as in *dípaltos* double), L *-plex*]

fold·a·way (fōld′ə wā′), *adj.* designed to be folded out of the way when not in use: *a foldaway bed.*

fold·boat (fōld′bōt′), *n.* faltboat.

fold·er (fōl′dər), *n.* **1.** a person or thing that folds. **2.** a printed sheet, as a circular or timetable, folded into a number of usually pagelike sections. **3.** a folded sheet of light cardboard used to cover or hold papers, letters, etc.

fol·de·rol (fol′də rol′), *n.* falderal.

fold′ing door′, a door that is opened by folding, having hinged sections that can be set flat against one another.

fo·li·a (fō′lē ə), *n.* pl of **folium.**

fo·li·a·ceous (fō′lē ā′shəs), *adj.* **1.** of, like, or of the nature of a plant leaf; leaflike. **2.** consisting of leaflike plates or laminae. [< L *foliāceus*] —**fo′li·a′ceous·ness,** *n.*

fo·li·age (fō′lē ij), *n.* **1.** the leaves of a plant, collectively; leafage. **2.** leaves in general. [ME *foilage* < MF *fueillage, foillage* < *feuille* leaf; influenced by L *folium* FOLIUM. See FOIL[2], -AGE] —**fo′li·aged,** *adj.*

fo·li·ar (fō′lē ər), *adj.* of, pertaining to, or having the nature of a leaf or leaves. [< NL *foliār(is)*]

fo·li·ate (*adj.* fō′lē it, -āt′; *v.* fō′lē āt′), *adj., v.,* **-at·ed, -at·ing.** —*adj.* **1.** covered with or having leaves. **2.** like a leaf, as in shape. **3.** Also, **foliated.** *Archit.* **a.** ornamented with or composed of foils: *foliate tracery.* **b.** ornamented with representations of foliage: *a foliate capital.* —*v.i.* **4.** to put forth leaves. **5.** to split into thin leaflike layers or laminae. —*v.t.* **6.** to shape like a leaf or leaves. **7.** to decorate with foils or foliage. **8.** to form into thin sheets. **9.** to spread over with a thin metallic backing. **10.** to number leaves, as distinguished from pages, of (a book). [< L *foliāt(us)* leafy]

fo·li·at·ed (fō′lē ā′tid), *adj.* **1.** shaped like a leaf or leaves: *foliated ornaments.* **2.** *Crystall.* consisting of thin and separable laminae. **3.** *Archit.* foliate (def. 3).

fo·li·a·tion (fō′lē ā′shən), *n.* **1.** the act or process of forming leaves. **2.** the state of being in leaf. **3.** *Bot.* **a.** the arrangement of leaves within a bud. **b.** the arrangement of leaves on a plant. **4.** leaves or foliage. **5.** *Print.* the act of foliating a book. **6.** *Archit.* **a.** ornamentation with foils. **b.** ornamentation with representations of foliage.

fo′lic ac′id (fō′lik, fol′ik), *Biochem.* a synthetic form of one of the B-complex vitamins, used in treating anemia. Also called **folacin.** [L *foli(um)* FOLIUM + -IC]

fo·lie à deux (fo lē′ ə do͞o′; *Fr.* fô lē A dœ′), *pl.* **fo·lies à deux** (fo lēz′ ə do͞o′; *Fr.* fô lē ZA dœ′). *Psychiatry.* the sharing of delusional ideas by two people who are closely associated. [< F]

fo·li·o (fō′lē ō′), *n., pl.* **-li·os,** *adj., v.,* **-li·oed, -li·o·ing.** —*n.* **1.** a sheet of paper folded once to make two leaves (four pages) of a book. **2.** a volume having pages of the largest size, esp. one more than 30 centimeters in height. **3.** a leaf of a manuscript or book numbered only on the front side. **4.** *Print.* **a.** (in a book) the number of each page. **b.** (in a newspaper) the number of each page together with the date and the name of the newspaper. **5.** *Bookkeeping.* a page of an account book or a left-hand page and a right-hand page facing each other and having the same serial number. **6.** *Law.* a certain number of words, in the U.S. generally 100, taken as a unit for computing the length of a document. —*adj.* **7.** pertaining to or having the format of a folio: *a folio volume.* —*v.t.* **8.** to number each leaf or page of. [< L *foliō* (orig. in phrase *in foliō* in a leaf, sheet), abl. of *folium* FOLIUM]

fo·li·o·late (fō′lē ə lāt′), *adj.* *Bot.* pertaining to or consisting of leaflets (often used in combination, as *bifoliolate*). [< LL **foliolāt(us)* = *foliol(um)* (dim. of *folium* leaf) + *-ātus* -ATE[1]]

fo·li·ose (fō′lē ōs′), *adj.* *Bot.* leafy. Also, **fo·li·ous** (fō′lē əs). [< L *foliōs(us)*]

-folious, an adjectival suffix meaning "having leaves (of a specified number or type)": *unifolious.* [comb. form repr. L *foliōsus* FOLIOSE]

Y X O

Folium (of Descartes)

fo·li·um (fō′lē əm), *n., pl.* **-li·a** (-lē ə). **1.** a thin, leaflike stratum or layer; a lamella. **2.** *Geom.* a loop; part of a curve terminated at both ends by the same node. [< L: lit., a leaf]

folk (fōk), *n.* **1.** Usually, **folks.** (*construed as pl.*) people in general. **2.** Often, **folks.** (*construed as pl.*) people of a specified class or group: *town folk; poor folks.* **3.** (*construed as pl.*) people as the carriers of culture, esp. as representing a society's mores. **4. folks,** *Informal.* **a.** members of one's family; relatives. **b.** one's parents. **5.** *Archaic.* a people or tribe. —*adj.* **6.** originating among the common people: *folk belief.* **7.** having unknown origins and reflecting the traditional forms of a society: *folk dance; folk music.* [ME; OE *folc;* c. OS, OIcel *folk,* OHG *folk* (G *Volk*)] —**folk′·ish,** *adj.* —**folk′ish·ness,** *n.*

folk′ dance′, **1.** a dance which originated among, and has been transmitted through, the common people. **2.** a piece of music for such a dance.

Folke·stone (fōk′stən), *n.* a seaport in E Kent, in SE England, on the Strait of Dover. 44,129 (1961).

folk′ etymol′ogy, modification of a linguistic form according to a falsely assumed etymology, as *Welsh rarebit* from *Welsh rabbit.*

folk·lore (fōk′lōr′, -lôr′), *n.* **1.** the traditional beliefs, legends, customs, etc., of a people; lore of a people. **2.** the study of such lore. —**folk′lor′ic,** *adj.* —**folk′lor′ist,** *n.* —**folk′lor·is′tic,** *adj.*

folk′ med′icine, the traditional medicine, consisting typically of home-made remedies, usually herbal in nature, and often based on superstition.

folk·moot (fōk′mo͞ot′), *n.* (formerly, in England) a general assembly of the people of a shire, town, etc. Also, **folk·mote, folk·mot** (fōk′mōt′). [ME; OE *folcmōt* folk meeting]

folk′ mu′sic, **1.** music, usually of simple character and anonymous authorship, handed down by oral tradition and characteristic chiefly of rural communities. **2.** (not in technical use) music by known composers that has become part of the folk tradition of a country or region.

folk-rock (fōk′rok′), *n.* a style of music combining characteristics of rock-'n'-roll and folk music, often protest songs to a rock-'n'-roll beat.

folk′ sing′er, a singer who specializes in folk songs, usually providing his own accompaniment on a guitar.

folk′ song′, **1.** a song originating among the people of a country or area, passed by oral tradition from one singer or generation to the next and often existing in several versions. **2.** a song of similar character written by a known composer.

folk·sy (fōk′sē), *adj.,* **-si·er, -si·est.** sociable; neighborly; casual; familiar; unceremonious: *The Senator affected a folksy style.* —**folk′si·ness,** *n.*

folk′ tale′, a tale of anonymous origin and forming part of the oral tradition of a people. Also called **folk′ sto′ry.**

Follicle of milkweed

folk·ways (fōk′wāz′), *n.pl.* *Sociol.* the traditional patterns of life common to a people.

foll., following.

fol·li·cle (fol′i kəl), *n.* **1.** *Bot.* a dry, one-celled seed vessel consisting of a single carpel and dehiscent only by the ventral suture, as the fruit of milkweed. **2.** *Anat.* a small cavity, sac, or gland. [< L *follicul(us)* small bag, shell, pod, dim. of *follis* bag, bellows; see -CLE] —**fol·lic·u·lar** (fə lik′yə lər), **fol·lic·u·late** (fə lik′yə lit, -lāt′), **fol·lic′u·lat′ed,** *adj.*

fol′li·cle-stim·u·lat·ing hor′mone (fol′ə kəl stim′yə lā′ting), *Biochem.* See **FSH.**

fol·lis (fol′is), *n., pl.* **fol·les** (fol′ēz). **1.** a unit in the ancient Roman money of account. **2.** a silver-plated copper coin of ancient Rome, first issued by Diocletian. **3.** a copper coin of the Eastern Roman Empire, A.D. c500. [< L: lit., bag, bellows]

fol·low (fol′ō), *v.t.* **1.** to come after in sequence, order of time, etc.; succeed. **2.** to go or come after; move behind in the same direction: *Drive ahead, and I'll follow you.* **3.** to accept as a guide or leader; accept the authority of. **4.** to conform to, comply with, or act in accordance with; obey: *to follow orders or advice.* **5.** to imitate or copy; use as an exemplar: *She followed the fashions slavishly.* **6.** to move forward along (a road, path, etc.). **7.** to come after as a result or consequence; result from: *Reprisals often follow victory.* **8.** to go after or along with (a person) as companion. **9.** to go in pursuit of: *to follow an enemy.* **10.** to try for or attain to: *to follow an ideal.* **11.** to engage in or be concerned with as a pursuit: *He followed the sea as his true calling.* **12.** to watch the movements, progress, or course of: *to follow a bird in flight.* **13.** to watch the development of or keep up with: *to follow the news.* **14.** to keep up with and understand (an argument, story, etc.): *Do you follow me?* —*v.i.* **15.** to come next after something else in sequence, order of time, etc. **16.** to happen or occur after something else; come next as an event: *After the defeat great disorders followed.* **17.** to attend or serve. **18.** to go or come after a person or thing in motion: *Go on ahead, and I'll follow.* **19.** to result as an effect; occur as a consequence: *It follows then that he must be innocent.* **20. follow out,** to carry to a conclusion; execute: *They followed out their orders to the letter.* **21. follow suit.** See **suit** (def. 9). **22. follow through, a.** to carry out fully, as a stroke of a club in golf, a racket in tennis, etc. **b.** to proceed in an endeavor and pursue it to completion. **23. follow up, a.** to pursue closely and tenaciously. **b.** to increase the effect of by further action. **c.** to pursue to a solution or conclusion. —*n.* **24.** the act of following. [ME *folwe(n),* OE *folgian;* c. OS *folgon,* OHG *folgēn, folgōn* (G *folgen*)] —**fol′low·a·ble,** *adj.* —**Syn. 3.** obey. **4.** heed, observe. **8.** accompany, attend. **9.** pursue, chase; trail, track, trace. **19.** arise, proceed. FOLLOW, ENSUE, RESULT, SUCCEED imply coming after something else, in a natural sequence. FOLLOW is the general word: *A detailed account follows.* ENSUE implies a logical sequence, what might be expected normally to come after a given act, cause, etc., and indicates some duration: *When the power lines were cut, a paralysis of transportation ensued.* RESULT emphasizes the connection between a cause and its effect: *The accident resulted in injuries to those involved.* SUCCEED implies coming after in time, particularly coming into a title, office, etc.: *Formerly the oldest son succeeded to his father's title.* —**Ant. 1.** precede. **2, 3.** lead. **4.** disregard.

fol·low·er (fol′ō ər), *n.* **1.** a person or thing that follows. **2.** a person who follows another in regard to his ideas or belief; disciple or adherent. **3.** a person who imitates, copies, or takes as an exemplar: *He was little more than a follower of current modes.* **4.** an attendant, servant, or retainer. **5.** *Mach.* a part receiving motion from or following the movements of another part, esp. a cam. [ME *folwer,* OE *folgere*]

fol·low·ing (fol′ō ing), *n.* **1.** a body of followers, attendants, adherents, etc. **2.** the body of admirers, attendants, patrons, etc., of someone or something: *That television show has a large following.* **3. the following,** something that comes immediately after, as pages, lines, etc.: *See the following for an explanation.* —*adj.* **4.** that follows or moves in the same direction: *a following wind.* **5.** that comes after or next in order or time; ensuing: *the following day.* [ME *folwing*]

fol·low-through (fol′ō thro͞o′, -thro͞o′), *n.* **1.** the completion of a motion, as in the stroke of a tennis racket. **2.** the execution of a plan, project, scheme, or the like.

fol·low-up (fol′ō up′), *n.* **1.** the act of following up. **2.** a letter or circular sent to a person to increase the effectiveness of a previous one, as in advertising. —*adj.* **3.** of or pertaining to a follow-up or to following up: *follow-up care in treating mental illness.*

fol·ly (fol′ē), *n., pl.* **-lies** for 2-5. **1.** the state or quality of being foolish. **2.** a foolish action, practice, idea, etc.; absurdity: *the folly of performing without a rehearsal.* **3.** a costly and foolish undertaking, as an unwise investment. **4. follies,** a theatrical revue. **5.** *Obs.* wickedness; wantonness. [ME *folie* < OF < *fol, fou* foolish, mad. See FOOL[1]]

Fol·som (fōl′səm), *adj.* of or pertaining to a prehistoric people who inhabited an extensive part of the North American continent, distinguished chiefly by their characteristic flint blades. [after *Folsom,* N.M., one of the settlements]

fo·ment (fō ment′), *v.t.* **1.** to instigate or foster (discord, rebellion, etc.); promote the growth or development of: *to foment trouble.* **2.** to apply warm water or medicated liquid, cloths dipped in such liquid, or the like, to (the surface of the body). [ME *foment(en)* <LL *fōmentāre* < L *fōment(um)* warm application, poultice, contr. of **fōvimentum* = *fōv(ēre)* (to) keep warm + *-mentum* -MENT] —**fo·ment′er,** *n.* —**Syn. 1.** incite, provoke, arouse, inflame, stir up.

fo·men·ta·tion (fō′men tā′shən), *n.* **1.** instigation; encouragement of discord, rebellion, etc. **2.** the application of warm liquid, ointments, etc., to the surface of the body. **3.** the liquid, ointments, etc., so applied. [< LL *fōmentātiōn-* (s. of *fōmentātiō*) = *fōmentāt(us)* (ptp. of *fōmentāre* to FOMENT) + *-iōn-* -ION]

fond[1] (fond), *adj.* **1.** having a liking for (usually fol. by of): *to be fond of animals; fond of sweets.* **2.** loving; affectionate: *to give someone a fond look.* **3.** excessively tender; overindulgent; doting: *a fond parent.* **4.** cherished with strong or unreasoning feeling: *to nourish fond hopes of becoming president.* **5.** *Chiefly Dial.* foolish or silly. **6.** *Archaic.* foolishly credulous or trusting. —*v.t. Obs.* **7.** to pamper. **8.** to love. **9.** to fondle. **10.** to make foolish. —*v.i. Obs.* **11.** to display affection. **12.** to be foolish. [ME *fond, fonned* (ptp. of *fonnen* to be foolish) < *fon, fonne* a fool]

fond[2] (fond; *Fr.* fôN), *n., pl.* **fonds** (fondz; *Fr.* fôN). **1.** a background or groundwork, esp. of lace. **2.** *Obs.* fund; stock. [< F; see FUND]

fon·dant (fon′dənt; *Fr.* fôN däN′), *n.* **1.** a thick, creamy sugar paste, the basis of many candies. **2.** a candy made of this paste. [< F: lit., melting; see FOUND[3]]

Fond du Lac (fon′ də lak′, jōō lak′), a city in E Wisconsin, on Lake Winnebago. 35,515 (1970).

fon·dle (fon′dəl), *v.,* **-dled, -dling.** —*v.t.* **1.** to handle or touch lovingly, affectionately, or tenderly; caress: *to fondle a precious object; to fondle a child.* **2.** *Obs.* to treat with fond indulgence. —*v.i.* **3.** to show fondness, as by manner, words, or caresses. [FOND[1] (V.) + -LE] —**fon′dler,** *n.*

fond·ly (fond′lē), *adv.* **1.** in a fond manner; lovingly or affectionately. **2.** with complacent credulity: *They fondly believed the war would come to a favorable end.* [ME]

fond·ness (fond′nis), *n.* **1.** the state or quality of being fond. **2.** tenderness or affection. **3.** doting affection. **4.** a liking or weakness for something: *a fondness for sweets.* **5.** *Archaic.* complacent credulity. [ME]

fon·due (fon dōō′, fon′dōō; *Fr.* fôN dY′), *n., pl.* **-dues** (-dōōz′, -dōōz; *Fr.* -dY′). *Cookery.* a saucelike dish of Swiss origin, made with melted cheese and seasonings, together with dry white wine and sometimes eggs and butter, usually flavored with kirsch: served as a hot dip for pieces of bread. [< F, fem. of *fondu,* ptp. of *fondre* to melt, FOUND[3]]

fons et o·ri·go (fons′ et ō rē′gō; *Eng.* fonz et ō rī′gō), *Latin.* source and origin.

font[1] (font), *n.* **1.** a receptacle for the water used in baptism. **2.** a receptacle for holy water; stoup. **3.** the reservoir for oil in a lamp. **4.** *Archaic.* a fountain. **5.** *Archaic.* a source. [ME; OE *font, fant* < L *font-* (s. of *fons*) baptismal font, spring, fountain] —**font′al,** *adj.*

Font[1] (def. 1)

font[2] (font), *n. Print.* a complete assortment of type of one style and size. Also, *Brit.,* **fount.** [< MF *fonte* < VL **funditus* a pouring, molding, casting, L, ptp. of *fundere.* See FOUND[3]]

Fon·taine·bleau (fon′tin blō′; *Fr.* fôN ten blō′), *n.* a town in N France, SE of Paris: famous palace, long a residence of French kings. 19,595.

fon·ta·nel (fon′tənel′), *n. Anat.* one of the spaces, covered by a membrane, between the bones of the fetal or young skull. Also, **fon′ta·nelle′.** [ME *fontinel* < MF *fontanele* little spring, dim. of *fontaine* FOUNTAIN]

Fon·teyn (fon tān′), *n.* **Dame Mar·got** (mär′gō), (*Margaret Hookham*), born 1919, English ballerina.

fon·ti·na (fon tē′nə), *n.* a type of Italian cheese, semisoft to firm, made of ewe's milk. [< It]

Foo·chow (fōō′chou′; *Chin.* fōō′jō′), *n.* a seaport in and the capital of Fukien, in SE China, opposite Taiwan. 900,000. Also called **Minhow.**

food (fōōd), *n.* **1.** any nourishing substance that is eaten or otherwise taken into the body to sustain life, provide energy, promote growth, etc. **2.** more or less solid nourishment, as distinguished from liquids. **3.** a particular kind of solid nourishment: *a breakfast food.* **4.** whatever supplies nourishment to organisms: *a plant food.* **5.** anything serving for consumption or use: *food for thought.* [ME *fode,* OE *fōda;* cf. OE *fēdan,* Goth *fōdjan* to FEED; cf. FODDER, FOSTER] —**food′less,** *adj.* —**food′less·ness,** *n.*
—**Syn. 1.** nutriment, bread, sustenance, victuals; meat, viands; diet, menu. FOOD, FARE, PROVISIONS, RATION(S) all refer to nutriment. FOOD is the general word: *Breakfast foods are popular. Many animals prefer grass as food.* FARE refers to the whole range of foods that may nourish a person or animal: *an extensive bill of fare; The fare of some animals is limited in range.* PROVISIONS is applied to a store or stock of necessary things, esp. food, prepared beforehand: *provisions for a journey.* RATION implies an allotment or allowance of provisions: *a daily ration for each man of a company.* RATIONS often means food in general: *to be on short rations.*

food′ bank′, a neighborhood center where donated food is stored and distributed, usually to needy people ineligible for public assistance.

food′ chain′, *Ecol.* a series of organisms interrelated in their feeding habits, each being fed upon by a larger one that in turn feeds a still larger one.

food′ fish′, any fish used for food by man.

food-gath·er·ing (fōōd′gath′ər ing), *adj.* (of a primitive people) procuring food by hunting or fishing or the gathering of seeds, berries, or roots, rather than by agricultural means.

food′ poi′soning, an acute gastrointestinal condition characterized by headache, fever, chills, abdominal and muscular pain, nausea, diarrhea, and prostration, caused by foods that are naturally toxic, by vegetable foods that are chemically contaminated, or by bacteria or their toxins. Cf. **ptomaine.**

food′ proc′essor, a high-speed electric kitchen appliance that can be fitted with various attachments for slicing, chopping, grinding, or grating food, kneading dough, etc.

food′ stamp′, *U.S.* any of the coupons sold under a federal program to eligible needy persons at a price lower than their face value, redeemable at face value only for food at designated grocery stores. Also called **food′ cou′pon.**

food·stuff (fōōd′stuf′), *n.* a substance used or capable of being used as nutriment.

foo·fa·raw (fōō′fə rô′), *n. Informal.* **1.** a fuss or disturbance about very little. **2.** an excessive amount of decoration. [?]

fool[1] (fōōl), *n.* **1.** a silly or stupid person; one who lacks sense. **2.** a professional jester, formerly kept by a person of rank for amusement. **3.** a person who has been imposed on by others and made to appear silly or stupid: *to make a fool of someone.* **4.** an ardent enthusiast who cannot resist an opportunity to indulge his enthusiasm (usually prec. by a present participle): *He's just a dancing fool.* **5. be nobody's fool,** to be wise or shrewd. —*v.t.* **6.** to trick, deceive, or impose on: *They tried to fool him.* —*v.i.* **7.** to act like a fool; joke; play. **8.** to jest; pretend; make believe: *I was only fooling.* **9. fool around, a.** to putter aimlessly; waste time. **b.** to trifle; philander. **10. fool with,** to handle or play with idly or carelessly: *to be hurt while fooling with a loaded gun; to fool with someone's affections.* [ME *fol, fool* < OF *fol* < L *foll(is)* bellows, bag] —**Syn. 1.** simpleton, dolt, dunce, blockhead, numskull, ignoramus, dunderhead, ninny, nincompoop, booby, saphead, sap. **2.** zany, clown. **6.** delude, hoodwink, cheat, gull, hoax, cozen, dupe.

fool[2] (fōōl), *n. British Cookery.* a dish made of fruit, scalded or stewed, crushed and mixed with cream or the like: *gooseberry fool.* [prob. special use of FOOL[1]]

fool·er·y (fōō′lə rē), *n., pl.* **-er·ies.** **1.** foolish behavior. **2.** a foolish action, performance, or thing.

fool·fish (fōōl′fish′), *n., pl.* (*esp. collectively*) **-fish,** (*esp. referring to two or more kinds or species*) **-fish·es.** filefish (def. 1).

fool·har·dy (fōōl′här′dē), *adj.,* **-di·er, -di·est.** bold without judgment; foolishly rash or venturesome; reckless. [ME *folhardy* < OF *fol hardi*] —**fool′har′di·ly,** *adv.* —**fool′har′di·ness,** *n.* —**Syn.** incautious, audacious, daring.

fool·ish (fōō′lish), *adj.* **1.** lacking forethought or caution. **2.** resulting from or showing a lack of sense; unwise: *a foolish action.* **3.** trifling; paltry. [ME *folish, foolish*] —**fool′ish·ly,** *adv.* —**fool′ish·ness,** *n.*
—**Syn. 1.** senseless, vacant, vapid, simple, witless. FOOLISH, FATUOUS, SILLY, INANE, STUPID, ASININE imply weakness of intellect and lack of judgment. FOOLISH implies lack of common sense or good judgment or, sometimes, weakness of mind: *a foolish decision; The child seems foolish.* FATUOUS implies being not only foolish, dull, and vacant in mind, but complacent and highly self-satisfied as well: *fatuous and self-important; fatuous answers.* SILLY denotes extreme and conspicuous foolishness; it may also refer to pointlessness of jokes, remarks, etc.: *silly and senseless behavior; a perfectly silly statement.* INANE applies to silliness that is notably lacking in content, sense, or point: *inane questions that leave one no reply.* STUPID implies natural slowness or dullness of intellect, or, sometimes, a benumbed or dazed state of mind; it is also used to mean foolish or silly: *well-meaning but stupid; rendered stupid by a blow; It is stupid to do such a thing.* ASININE originally meant like an ass; it applies to witlessly stupid conversation or conduct and suggests a lack of social grace or perception: *He failed to notice the reaction to his asinine remarks.* —**Ant. 1, 2.** wise, intelligent.

fool·proof (fōōl′prōōf′), *adj.* **1.** involving no risk or harm, even when tampered with. **2.** never-failing: *a foolproof method.*

fools·cap (fōōlz′kap′), *n.* **1.** *Chiefly Brit.* a size of drawing or printing paper, $13\frac{1}{2} \times 17$ inches. *Abbr.:* cap., fcp. **2.** Also called **fools′cap octa′vo.** a size of book, about $4\frac{1}{4} \times 6\frac{3}{4}$ inches, untrimmed. **3.** Also called **fools′cap quar′to.** *Chiefly Brit.* a size of book, about $6\frac{3}{4} \times 8\frac{1}{2}$ inches untrimmed. [so called from the watermark of a fool's cap formerly used on such paper]

fool's′ cap′, **1.** a traditional jester's cap or hood, often multicolored and usually having several drooping peaks from which bells are hung. **2.** See **dunce cap.**

fool's′ er′rand, an absurd or useless errand.

fool's′ gold′, iron or copper pyrites, sometimes mistaken for gold.

fool's′ par′adise, enjoyment based on false beliefs or hopes; a state of illusory happiness.

fool's-pars·ley (fōōlz′pärs′lē), *n.* an Old World fetid, poisonous, umbelliferous, herb, *Aethusa Cynapium,* resembling parsley.

foot (fŏŏt), *n., pl.* **feet** for 1–3, 7, 8, 11, 13, 16; **foots** for 14, 15; *v.* —*n.* **1.** (in vertebrates) the terminal part of the leg, below the ankle joint, on which the body stands and moves. **2.** (in invertebrates) any part similar in position or function. **3.** a unit of length derived from the length of the human foot. In English-speaking countries it is divided into 12 inches and equal to 30.48 centimeters. **4.** infantry. **5.** walking or running motion; pace: *swift of foot.* **6.** quality or character of movement or motion; tread; step. **7.** any part or thing resembling a foot, as in function, placement, shape, etc. **8.** the part of a stocking, sock, etc., covering the foot. **9.** the lowest part, or bottom, as of a hill, ladder, page, etc. **10.** the part of anything opposite the top or head: *the foot of a bed; the foot of a column.* **11.** *Print.* the part of the type body that forms the sides of the groove, at the base. **12.** the last, as of a series. **13.** *Pros.* a group of stressed and unstressed syllables constituting a metrical unit of a verse. **14.** Usually, **foots.** sediment or dregs. **15.** **foots,** *Theat.* footlights. **16.** *Naut.* the lower edge of a sail. **17.** **fall** or **land on one's feet,** to be successful in spite of unfavorable circumstances. **18.** **feet first, a.** with one's feet going before: *We plunged into the river feet first.* **b.** dead: *The only way you'll get out of there is feet first.* **19.** **get off on the right** or **wrong foot,** to begin favorably or unfavorably. **20.** **on foot,** by walking or running, rather than by riding. **21.** **put one's best foot forward,** to attempt to make as good an impression as possible. **22.** **put one's foot down,** to take a firm stand; be decisive or determined. **23.** **put one's foot in it** or **into it,** *Informal.* to make an embarrassing blunder. Also, **put one's foot in one's mouth.** **24.** **set foot on** or **in,** to go on or into; enter (used in negative constructions): *Never set foot on our property again!* —*v.i.* **25.** to walk; go on foot (often fol. by *it*): *We'll have to foot it.* **26.** to move the feet rhythmically, as in dance (often fol. by *it*). **27.** (of vessels) to move forward; cover distance. —*v.t.* **28.** to walk or dance on. **29.** to perform (a dance). **30.** to traverse on or as if on foot. **31.** to make or attach a foot to: *to foot a stocking.* **32.** *Informal.* to pay or settle, as a bill. **33.** *Archaic.* to establish. **34.** *Obs.* to set foot on. **35.** *Obs.* to kick, esp. to kick away. **36.** **foot up,** to total, or add up, as an account or bill. [ME; OE *fōt;* c. G *Fuss;* akin to L *pēs,* Gk *poûs*]

-foot, a combining form of **foot** used with numerals to form compound adjectives: *ten-foot; two-foot.*

foot·age (fŏŏt′ij), *n.* **1.** length or extent in feet: *the footage of lumber.* **2.** a motion-picture scene or scenes: *newsreel footage; jungle footage.*

foot′-and-mouth′ disease′ (fŏŏt′ᵊn mouth′), *Vet. Pathol.* an acute, contagious disease of cattle, and other hoofed animals, characterized by vesicular eruptions in the mouth and about the hoofs, teats, and udder. Also called **hoof-and-mouth disease.**

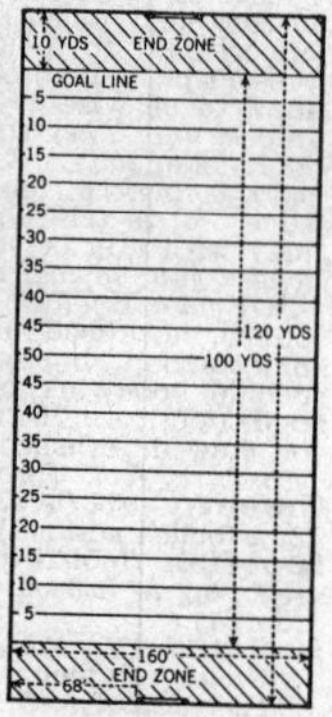

foot·ball (fŏŏt′bôl′), *n.* **1.** *U.S.* **a.** a game in which two opposing teams of 11 players each defend goals at opposite ends of a field, points being scored chiefly by carrying the ball across the opponent's goal line and by place-kicking or drop-kicking the ball over the crossbar between the opponent's goal posts. Cf. **conversion** (def. 10), **field goal** (def. 1), **safety** (def. 4), **touchdown. b.** the ball used in this game, an inflated oval with a bladder contained in a casing usually made of leather. **2.** *Brit.* Rugby (def. 2). **3.** *Brit.* soccer. **4.** any person, subject, or thing treated roughly, casually, etc.: *They're making a political football out of the tax reform bill before it even comes up for a vote.* [late ME *fut ball*]

Football field (Intercollegiate)

foot·board (fŏŏt′bōrd′, -bôrd′), *n.* **1.** a board or small platform on which to support the foot or feet. **2.** an upright piece across the foot of a bedstead. **3.** a treadle.

foot·boy (fŏŏt′boi′), *n.* a boy in livery employed as a servant; page.

foot·bridge (fŏŏt′brij′), *n.* a bridge intended for pedestrians only. [ME *fotbrigge*]

foot-can·dle (fŏŏt′kan′dᵊl), *n.* *Optics.* a unit of illuminance or illumination, equivalent to the illumination produced by a source of one candle at a distance of one foot and equal to one lumen incident per square foot. *Abbr.:* ft-c Also, **foot′ can′dle.**

foot·cloth (fŏŏt′klôth′, -kloth′), *n., pl.* **-cloths** (-klôthz′, -klothz′, -klôths′, -kloths′). **1.** a carpet or rug. **2.** a richly ornamented caparison for a horse, hanging to the ground.

foot·ed (fŏŏt′id), *adj.* having a foot or feet (often used in combination): *a four-footed animal.* [late ME]

foot·er (fŏŏt′ər), *n.* **1.** a person who walks; walker; pedestrian. **2.** *Brit. Informal.* **a.** Rugby (def. 2). **b.** soccer.

foot·fall (fŏŏt′fôl′), *n.* **1.** a footstep. **2.** the sound of a footstep.

foot·gear (fŏŏt′gēr′), *n.* covering for the feet, as shoes or boots.

foot·hill (fŏŏt′hil′), *n.* a low hill at the base of a mountain or mountain range.

foot·hold (fŏŏt′hōld′), *n.* **1.** a hold or support for the feet; a place where a person may stand or tread securely. **2.** a secure position, esp. a firm basis for further progress or development.

foot·ing (fŏŏt′ing), *n.* **1.** a secure and established position; foothold. **2.** the basis or foundation on which anything is established. **3.** a place or support for the feet. **4.** the act of a person who moves on foot, as in walking or dancing. **5.** a firm placing of the feet; stability: *He regained his footing.* **6.** *Building Trades, Civ. Eng.* the part of a foundation bearing directly upon the earth. **7.** position or status assigned to a person, group, etc., in estimation or treatment. **8.** mutual standing; reciprocal relation: *to be on a friendly footing with someone.* **9.** entrance into a new position or relationship: *to gain a footing in society.* **10.** the act of adding a foot to something, as to a stocking. **11.** that which is added as a foot. **12.** the act of adding up a column of figures. **13.** the total of such a column. [ME]

foot-lam·bert (fŏŏt′lam′bərt), *n.* *Optics.* a unit of luminance or photometric brightness, equal to the luminance of a surface emitting a luminous flux of one lumen per square foot, the luminance of a perfectly reflecting surface receiving an illumination of one foot-candle. *Abbr.:* ft-L

foot·le (fŏŏt′ᵊl), *v.,* **-led, -ling,** *n.* —*v.i.* **1.** to act or talk in a foolish or silly way. —*n.* **2.** nonsense; foolishness; silliness. [?; cf. FOOTY]

foot·less (fŏŏt′lis), *adj.* **1.** lacking a foot or feet. **2.** having no support or basis; unsubstantial. **3.** *Informal.* awkward, helpless, or inefficient. [ME] —**foot′less·ly,** *adv.* —**foot′less·ness,** *n.*

foot·light (fŏŏt′līt′), *n.* **1.** Usually, **footlights.** Also called **foots.** *Theat.* the lights at the front of a stage that are nearly on a level with the feet of the performers. **2.** **the footlights,** the acting profession; the stage.

foot·ling (fŏŏt′ling), *adj.* *Informal.* foolish; silly; trifling.

foot·lock·er (fŏŏt′lok′ər), *n.* a small trunk, esp. for containing the personal effects of a soldier and kept at the foot of his bed.

foot-loose (fŏŏt′lōōs′), *adj.* free to go or travel about; not confined by responsibilities.

foot·man (fŏŏt′mən), *n., pl.* **-men. 1.** a liveried servant who attends the door or carriage, waits on table, etc. **2.** *Rare.* an infantryman. [ME *fotman*]

foot·mark (fŏŏt′märk′), *n.* a footprint.

foot·note (fŏŏt′nōt′), *n., v.,* **-not·ed, -not·ing.** —*n.* **1.** an explanatory comment or reference note at the bottom of a page, keyed to a specific part of the text on the page. **2.** a minor or tangential comment added to a main statement. —*v.t.* **3.** to add footnotes to (a text); annotate.

foot·pace (fŏŏt′pās′), *n.* **1.** a walking pace. **2.** a raised portion of a floor; platform.

foot·pad (fŏŏt′pad′), *n.* a highwayman or robber who goes on foot.

foot·path (fŏŏt′path′, -päth′), *n., pl.* **-paths** (-pathz′, -päthz′, -paths′, -päths′). **1.** a path for pedestrians. **2.** *Brit.* footway (def. 2).

foot-pound (fŏŏt′pound′), *n.* *Physics.* a foot-pound-second unit of work or energy, equal to the work done by a force of one pound when its point of application moves through a distance of one foot in the direction of the force. *Abbr.:* ft-lb

foot-pound·al (fŏŏt′poun′dᵊl), *n.* *Physics.* a foot-pound-second unit of work or energy equal to the work done by a force of one poundal when its point of application moves through a distance of one foot in the direction of the force. *Abbr.:* ft-pdl

foot-pound-sec·ond (fŏŏt′pound′sek′ənd), *adj.* of or pertaining to the system of units in which the foot, pound, and second are the principal units of length, mass, and time. *Abbr.:* fps, f.p.s.

foot·print (fŏŏt′print′), *n.* **1.** a mark left by the shod or unshod foot, as in earth, sand, etc. **2.** an impression of the sole of a person's foot, esp. one taken for purposes of identification.

foot·rest (fŏŏt′rest′), *n.* a support for a person's feet.

foot·rope (fŏŏt′rōp′), *n.* *Naut.* **1.** the portion of the boltrope to which the lower edge of a sail is sewn. **2.** a rope suspended a few feet beneath a yard, bowsprit, jib boom, or spanker boom to give a footing for men handling sails.

foot′ rot′, **1.** *Bot.* a disease of plants, esp. the genus *Citrus,* affecting the base of the stem or trunk. **2.** *Vet. Pathol.* an infection of sheep, causing inflammatory changes in the area of the hoofs and lameness. Also called **fouls.**

foot·scrap·er (fŏŏt′skrā′pər), *n.* a metal bar, set in a small frame and attached to a doorstep, used in cleaning the bottoms of the shoes before entering a house.

foot·sie (fŏŏt′sē), *n.* **1.** *Informal.* the act of flirting or sharing a surreptitious intimacy. **2.** **play footsie with, a.** to flirt with, esp. by clandestinely touching someone's foot or leg; be furtively intimate with. **b.** to curry favor with, esp. by surreptitious means. [childish dim. of FOOT]

foot′ sol′dier, an infantryman.

foot·sore (fŏŏt′sōr′, -sôr′), *adj.* having sore or tender feet, as from much walking. —**foot′sore′ness,** *n.*

foot·stalk (fŏŏt′stôk′), *n.* *Bot., Zool.* a pedicel; peduncle.

foot·stall (fŏŏt′stôl′), *n.* **1.** the stirrup of a woman's sidesaddle. **2.** *Archit.* a pedestal, plinth, or base, as of a statue, column, or pier.

foot·step (fŏŏt′step′), *n.* **1.** the setting down of a foot, or the sound so produced; footfall; tread. **2.** the distance covered by a step in walking; pace. **3.** a footprint. **4.** a step by which to ascend or descend. **5.** **follow in someone's footsteps,** to succeed or imitate another person. [ME *foote steppe*]

foot·stone (fŏŏt′stōn′), *n.* a stone placed at the foot of a grave.

foot·stool (fŏŏt′stōōl′), *n.* a low stool upon which to rest one's feet while seated.

foot-ton (fŏŏt′tun′), *n.* *Physics.* a unit of work or energy equal to the energy expended in raising one ton a distance of one foot.

foot·way (fŏŏt′wā′), *n.* **1.** a way or path for pedestrians. **2.** Also called **footpath.** *Brit.* a sidewalk. [ME *fotewey*]

foot·wear (fŏŏt′wâr′), *n.* articles to be worn on the feet, as shoes or slippers.

foot·work (fŏŏt′wûrk′), *n.* **1.** the use of the feet, as in tennis or boxing. **2.** travel by foot from one place to another, as in fulfilling an assignment; legwork. **3.** the act or process of maneuvering, esp. in a skillful manner: *It took a bit of fancy footwork to avoid the issue.*

foot·worn (fŏŏt′wōrn′, -wôrn′), *adj.* **1.** worn away by footsteps: *a footworn pavement.* **2.** footsore.

foo·ty (fōō′tē), *adj.,* **-ti·er, -ti·est.** *Chiefly Dial.* poor; worthless; paltry. [var. of *foughty* musty, OE *fūht* moist, damp (c. G *feucht*); see -Y¹]

foo·zle (fōō′zəl), *v.,* **-zled, -zling,** *n.* —*v.t., v.i.* **1.** to bungle; play clumsily: *to foozle a stroke in golf; to foozle on the last hole.* —*n.* **2.** the act of foozling, esp. of making a bad stroke in golf. [? < dial. G *fuseln* to work badly, clumsily, hurriedly]

fop (fop), *n.* a man who is excessively vain and concerned about his manners and appearance. [ME *foppe, fop;* akin to FOB²]

fop·per·y (fop′ə rē), *n., pl.* **-per·ies. 1.** the clothes, manners, actions, etc., of a fop. **2.** something foppish.

fop·pish (fop′ish), *adj.* resembling or befitting a fop; excessively refined and fastidious in taste and manner. —**fop′pish·ly,** *adv.* —**fop′pish·ness,** *n.*

for (fôr; *unstressed* fər), *prep.* **1.** with the object or purpose of: *to run for exercise.* **2.** intended to belong to, or be used in connection with: *equipment for the army; a closet for dishes.* **3.** suiting the purposes or needs of: *medicine for the aged.* **4.** in order to obtain, gain, or acquire: *a suit for alimony; to work for wages.* **5.** (used to express a wish): *O, for a cold drink!* **6.** sensitive or responsive to: *an eye for beauty; an ear for music.* **7.** directed to; centered or focused upon: *a longing for something; a taste for fancy clothes.* **8.** in consideration of, or in return for: *three for a dollar; to be thanked for one's efforts.* **9.** appropriate or adapted to: *a subject for speculation; clothes for winter.* **10.** with regard or respect to: *pressed for time; too warm for April.* **11.** during the continuance of: *for a long time.* **12.** in favor of; on the side of: *to be for honest government.* **13.** in place of; instead of: *a substitute for butter.* **14.** in the interest of, or on behalf of: *to act for a client.* **15.** in exchange for; as an offset to: *blow for blow; money for goods.* **16.** in punishment of: *payment for the crime.* **17.** in honor of: *to give a dinner for a person.* **18.** with the purpose of reaching: *to start for London.* **19.** contributive to: *for the advantage of everybody.* **20.** in order to save: *to flee for one's life.* **21.** in order to become: *to go for a soldier.* **22.** in assignment or attribution to: *an appointment for the afternoon; That's for you to decide.* **23.** such as to allow of or to require: *too many for separate mention.* **24.** such as results in: *his reason for going.* **25.** in effect on the interests or circumstances of: *bad for one's health.* **26.** in proportion or with reference to: *He is tall for his age.* **27.** in the character of; as being: *to know a thing for a fact.* **28.** by reason of; because of: *to shout for joy; a city famed for its beauty.* **29.** in spite of: *He's a decent guy for all that.* **30.** to the extent or amount of: *to walk for a mile.* **31.** (used to introduce an infinitive phrase equivalent to a construction with a relative clause): *It's time for me to go.* **32.** **for it,** *Brit.* See **in** (def. 20). —*conj.* **33.** seeing that; since. **34.** because. [ME, OE; c. OS *for;* akin to FORE[1], L *per* through, Gk *prō* before, ahead]

for-, a prefix meaning "away," "off," "to the uttermost," "extremely," "wrongly," or imparting a negative or privative force, occurring in verbs and nouns formed from verbs of Old or Middle English origin, many of which are now obsolete or archaic: *forbid; forbear; forswear; forbearance.* [ME, OE; cf. G *ver-,* Gk *peri-,* L *per-*]

for., **1.** foreign. **2.** forester. **3.** forestry.

F.O.R., free on rails. Also, **f.o.r.**

for·age (fôr′ij, for′-), *n., v.,* **-aged, -ag·ing.** —*n.* **1.** food for horses or cattle; fodder; provender. **2.** the seeking or obtaining of such food. **3.** the act of searching for provisions of any kind. **4.** a raid. —*v.i.* **5.** to wander or go in search of supplies. **6.** to search about; rummage: *He went foraging in the attic for old mementos.* **7.** to make a raid. —*v.t.* **8.** to collect forage from; strip of supplies; plunder: *to forage the countryside.* **9.** to supply with forage. **10.** to obtain by foraging. [ME < OF *fourrage* < *fuerre* FODDER (< Gmc)] —**for′ag·er,** *n.* —**Syn. 1.** See **feed.**

For·a·ker (fôr′ə kər, for′-), *n.* **Mount,** a mountain in central Alaska, in the Alaska Range, near Mt. McKinley. 17,280 ft.

for·am (fôr′əm), *n.* a foraminifer. [by shortening]

fo·ra·men (fō rā′mən, fō-, fə-), *n., pl.* **-ram·i·na** (-ram′ə nə). an opening, orifice, or short passage, as in a bone or in the integument of the ovule of a plant. [< L: hole, opening = *forā(re)* (to) bore, pierce + *-men* resultative n. suffix] —**fo·ram·i·nal** (fə ram′ə nəl), *adj.*

fora′men mag′num (mag′nəm), the large hole in the occipital bone forming the passage from the cranial cavity to the spinal canal. [< NL: lit., great hole]

for·a·min·i·fer (fôr′ə min′ə fər, for′-), *n.* any chiefly marine rhizopod of the order *Foraminifera,* typically having a calcareous shell perforated by small holes or pores. [< L *forāmin-* (s. of *forāmen*) FORAMEN + -I- + -FER] —**fo·ram·i·nif·er·al** (fō ram′ə nif′ər əl, fô-, fə-), **fo·ram′i·nif′er·ous,** *adj.*

for·as·much (fôr′əz much′, fər-), *conj.* in view of the fact that; seeing that; since. [ME]

for·ay (fôr′ā, for′ā), *n.* **1.** a quick raid, usually for the purpose of taking plunder. **2.** a quick, sudden attack. —*v.i.* **3.** to make a raid; forage; pillage. —*v.t.* **4.** to ravage in search of plunder. [ME *forraie(n),* back formation from *forreier* < OF < *forrier* forager. See FORAGE, -ER[1]] —**for′ay·er,** *n.*

forb (fôrb), *n.* any herb that is not a grass or grasslike. [< Gk *phorbē* food, fodder < *phérbein* to feed; akin to OE *beorgan, birgan* to taste, eat, OIcel *bergja* to taste]

for·bade (fər bad′, -bād′, fôr-), *v.* a pt. of **forbid.** Also, **for·bad′.**

for·bear[1] (fôr bâr′), *v.,* **-bore, -borne, -bear·ing.** —*v.t.* **1.** to refrain or abstain from; desist from. **2.** to keep back; withhold. **3.** to endure. —*v.i.* **4.** to refrain; hold back. **5.** to be patient or self-controlled when subject to annoyance or provocation. [ME *forbere(n),* OE *forberan*] —**for·bear′er,** *n.* —**for·bear′ing·ly,** *adv.* —**Syn. 1.** forgo, renounce.

for·bear[2] (fôr′bâr′), *n.* forebear.

for·bear·ance (fôr bâr′əns), *n.* **1.** the act of forbearing or refraining. **2.** forbearing conduct or quality; patient endurance; leniency. **3.** an abstaining from the enforcement of a right. —**Syn. 1.** abstinence. **2.** tolerance, toleration, sufferance.

Forbes-Rob·ert·son (fôrbz′rob′ərt sən), *n.* **Sir Johnston,** 1853–1937, English actor and theatrical manager.

for·bid (fər bid′, fôr-), *v.t.,* **-bade** or **-bad, -bid·den** or **-bid, -bid·ding. 1.** to command (a person) not to do something, have something, etc., or not to enter some place: *to forbid him entry to the house.* **2.** to prohibit (something); place an interdiction against: *to forbid the use of lipstick; to forbid smoking.* **3.** to hinder or prevent; make impossible: *the steepness of the slope forbade ascent.* **4.** to exclude; bar: *Burlesque is forbidden in many cities.* [ME *forbede(n),* OE *forbēodan*] —**for·bid′der,** *n.* —**Syn. 1, 2.** interdict. FORBID, INHIBIT, PROHIBIT, TABOO indicate a command to refrain from some action. FORBID, a common and familiar word, usually denotes a direct or personal command of this sort: *I forbid you to go. It was useless to forbid children to play in the park.* INHIBIT implies a checking or hindering of impulses by the mind, sometimes involuntarily: *to inhibit one's desires; His responsiveness was inhibited by extreme shyness.* PROHIBIT, a formal or legal word, means usually to forbid by official edict, enactment, or the like: *to prohibit the sale of liquor.* TABOO, primarily associated with primitive superstition, means to prohibit by common disapproval and by social custom: *to taboo a subject in polite conversation.* **3.** preclude, stop, obviate, deter. —**Ant. 1.** permit.

for·bid·dance (fər bid′əns, fôr-), *n.* **1.** the act of forbidding. **2.** the state of being forbidden.

for·bid·den (fər bid′ən, fôr-), *v.* **1.** a pp. of **forbid.** —*adj.* **2.** not allowed; prohibited.

Forbid′den Cit′y, a walled section of Peking containing the imperial palace and other buildings of the former Chinese Empire.

forbid′den fruit′, **1.** the fruit of the tree of knowledge of good and evil, tasted by Adam and Eve against God's prohibition. Gen. 2:17; 3:3. **2.** any unlawful pleasure, esp. illicit sexual indulgence.

for·bid·ding (fər bid′ing, fôr-), *adj.* **1.** grim; unfriendly; hostile; sinister: *a forbidding countenance.* **2.** dangerous; threatening: *forbidding clouds.* —**for·bid′ding·ly,** *adv.* —**for·bid′ding·ness,** *n.*

for·bore (fôr bōr′, -bôr′), *v.* pt. of **forbear[1].**

for·borne (fôr bōrn′, -bôrn′), *v.* pp. of **forbear[1].**

for·by (fôʀ bī′), *prep., adv.* *Chiefly Scot.* **1.** close by; near. **2.** besides. Also, **for·bye′.** [ME]

force (fōrs, fôrs), *n., v.,* **forced, forc·ing.** —*n.* **1.** strength; energy; power. **2.** efficacious power; power to influence, affect, or control: *the force of circumstances; a force for law and order.* **3.** physical power or strength possessed by a living being: *He shoved with all his force.* **4.** strength or power exerted upon an object; physical coercion; violence: *to use force to open the window; to use force on a person.* **5.** *Law.* unlawful violence threatened or committed against persons or property. **6.** persuasive power; power to convince: *the force of his arguments.* **7.** mental or moral strength: *the force of one's mind.* **8.** might, as of a ruler or realm; strength for war. **9.** Often, **forces.** a large body of armed men; army. **10.** any body of persons combined for joint action: *a police force; an office force.* **11.** intensity or strength of effect: *the force of her acting; the force of his writing.* **12.** *Physics.* **a.** an influence on a body or system, producing or tending to produce a change in movement or in shape or other effects. **b.** the intensity of such an influence. *Symbol:* F, f **13.** binding power, as of an agreement. **14.** value; significance; meaning. **15.** **in force, a.** in operation; effective. **b.** in large numbers; at full strength. —*v.t.* **16.** to compel, constrain, or oblige (oneself or someone) to do something: *to force a suspect to confess.* **17.** to drive or propel against resistance: *They forced air into his lungs.* **18.** to bring about or effect by force; bring about of necessity or as a necessary result: *to force a passage; The strength of his position forced his opponent to resign.* **19.** to put or impose (something or someone) forcibly on or upon a person: *to force something on someone's attention.* **20.** to compel by force; overcome the resistance of: *to force acceptance of something.* **21.** to obtain or draw forth by or as if by force; extort: *to force a confession.* **22.** to overpower; enter or take by force: *They forced the town after a long siege.* **23.** to break open (a door, lock, etc.). **24.** to cause (plants, fruits, etc.) to grow or mature at an increased rate by artificial means. **25.** to press, urge, or exert (an animal, person, etc.) to violent effort or to the utmost. **26.** to use force upon. **27.** *Baseball.* to advance or put out a runner on a force play. **28.** *Cards.* **a.** to compel (a player) to trump by leading a suit of which he has no cards. **b.** to compel a player to play (a particular card). **c.** to compel (a player) to play so as to make known the strength of the hand. —*v.i.* **29.** to make one's way by force. [ME < MF < VL _*fortia_ < L *fortis* strong] —**force′a·ble,** *adj.* —**force′less,** *adj.* —**forc′er,** *n.* —**forc′ing·ly,** *adv.* —**Syn. 1.** vigor. See **strength. 6.** efficacy, effectiveness. **16.** coerce. **17.** impel. **22.** overcome; violate, ravish, rape. —**Ant. 1.** weakness. **6.** impotence.

forced (fōrst, fôrst), *adj.* **1.** enforced or compulsory: *forced labor.* **2.** strained, unnatural, or affected: *a forced smile.* **3.** subjected to force. **4.** emergency: *a forced landing.* —**forc·ed·ly** (fōr′sid lē, fôr′-), *adv.* —**forc′ed·ness,** *n.*

force de frappe (fôʀs də fʀäp′), *French.* France's nuclear power or capability, esp. as an independent military deterrent.

forced′ march′, *Mil.* any march that is longer than troops are accustomed to and maintained at a faster pace than usual.

force′ feed′, lubrication under pressure, as from a pump, used esp. in internal-combustion engines.

force-feed (fōrs′fēd′, fôrs′-), *v.t.,* **-fed, -feed·ing. 1.** to compel or force to eat or take food into the body. **2.** to compel to absorb or accept, as propaganda.

force·ful (fōrs′fəl, fôrs′-), *adj.* **1.** full of force; powerful; vigorous; effective: *a forceful plea for peace.* **2.** acting or driven with force. —**force′ful·ly,** *adv.* —**force′ful·ness,** *n.*

force ma·jeure (*Fr.* fôʀs ma zhœʀ′), *pl.* **forces ma·jeures** (*Fr.* fôʀs ma zhœʀ′). *Law.* an unexpected and disruptive event that may operate to excuse a party from a contract. [< F: lit., superior force]

force·meat (fōrs′mēt′, fôrs′-), *n.* *Cookery.* a mixture of finely chopped and seasoned foods, usually containing egg white, meat or fish, etc., used as a stuffing or served alone. Also, **farcemeat.** [*force,* var. of FARCE + MEAT]

force-out (fōrs′out′, fôrs′-), *n.* *Baseball.* a put-out of a base runner on a force play.

force′ play′, *Baseball.* a situation in which a player is forced to advance to a base or to home plate, either as a result of having batted a fair ball or in order to make room for another base runner.

for·ceps (fôr′səps, -seps), *n., pl.* **-ceps, -ci·pes** (-sə pēz′). an instrument, as pincers or tongs, for seizing and holding objects, esp. in surgical operations. [< L: pair of tongs, pincers, fire tongs = *for-* (s. of *formus*) warm, hot + *-cep-* (s. of *capere* to take) + *-s* nom. sing. suffix]

force′ pump′, a pump that delivers a liquid under pressure. Cf. **lift pump.**

for·ci·ble (fōr′sə bəl, fôr′-), *adj.* **1.** effected by force: *forcible entry into a house.* **2.** having force; producing a powerful effect; effective. **3.** convincing, as reasoning: *a forcible theory.* **4.** characterized by the use of force or violence. [ME < MF] —**for′ci·ble·ness, for′ci·bil′i·ty,** *n.* —**for′ci·bly,** *adv.*

ford (fōrd, fôrd), *n.* **1.** a place where a river or other body of water is shallow enough to be crossed by wading. —*v.t.* **2.** to cross (a river, stream, etc.) by a ford. [ME, OE; c. OFris *forda,* G *Furt;* akin to OIcel *fjörthr,* FARE, PORT[1]] —**ford′a·ble,** *adj.* —**ford′less,** *adj.*

Ford (fōrd, fôrd), *n.* **1. Ford Mad·ox** (mad′əks), (pen name of *Ford Madox Hueffer*), 1873–1939, English novelist. **2. Gerald R.,** born 1913, 38th president of the U.S. 1974–76. **3. Henry,** 1863–1947, U.S. automobile manufacturer. **4. John,** 1586?–c1640, English playwright.

for·do (fôr do͞o′), *v.t.,* **-did, -done, -do·ing.** *Archaic.* **1.** to do away with; kill; destroy. **2.** to ruin; undo. Also, **foredo.** [ME *fordo(n),* OE *fordōn* (see FORE-, DO[1]); c. D *verdoen,* OHG *fartuon*]

for·done (fôr dun′), *adj.* *Archaic.* exhausted with fatigue. Also, **foredone.** [ptp. of FORDO]

fore[1] (fōr, fôr), *adj.* **1.** situated at or toward the front, as compared with something else. **2.** first in place, time, order, rank, etc.; forward; earlier. **3.** *Naut.* **a.** of or pertaining to a foremast. **b.** situated at or toward the bow of a vessel; forward. —*adv.* **4.** *Naut.* at or toward the bow. **5.** *Archaic.* before. **6.** *Dial.* forward. **7. fore and aft,** *Naut.* in, at, or to both ends of a ship. —*n.* **8.** the forepart of anything; front. **9. the fore,** *Naut.* the foremast. **10. to the fore, a.** into a conspicuous place or position; to the front. **b.** at hand; ready; available. —*prep., conj.* **11.** Also **'fore.** *Dial.* before. [special use of FORE-, detached from words like *forepart, forefather,* etc.]

fore[2] (fōr, fôr), *interj.* *Golf.* (used as a cry of warning to persons on a course who are in danger of being struck by the ball.) [prob. aph. var. of BEFORE]

fore-, a native English prefix meaning "before" (in space, time, condition, etc.), "front," "superior," etc.: *forehead; forecast; foretell; foreman.* [comb. form repr. ME, OE *for(e)*]

fore-and-aft (fōr′ənd aft′, -äft′, fôr′-), *Naut.* —*adj.* **1.** located along or parallel to a line from the stem to the stern. —*adv.* **2.** fore[1] (def. 7).

fore′-and-aft′ rig′, *Naut.* a rig in which the principal sails are fore-and-aft. —**fore′-and-aft′-rigged′,** *adj.*

fore′-and-aft′ sail′, *Naut.* any of various sails, as jib-headed sails or gaff sails, that do not set on yards and whose normal position, when not trimmed, is in a fore-and-aft direction amidships.

fore·arm[1] (fōr′ärm′, fôr′-), *n.* **1.** the part of the arm or upper limb between the elbow and the wrist. **2.** the corresponding part of the foreleg in certain quadrupeds. [FORE- + ARM[1]]

fore·arm[2] (fōr ärm′, fôr-), *v.t.* to arm beforehand. [FORE- + ARM[2]]

fore·bear (fōr′bâr′, fôr′-), *n.* Usually, **forebears.** ancestors; forefathers. Also, **forbear.** [ME (Scot) = *fore-* FORE- + *-bear* being, var. of *beer;* see BE, -ER[1]]

fore·bode (fōr bōd′, fôr-), *v.,* **-bod·ed, -bod·ing.** —*v.t.* **1.** to foretell or predict; be an omen of; indicate beforehand: *clouds that forebode a storm.* **2.** to have a strong inner certainty of (a future misfortune, evil, catastrophe, etc.); have a presentiment of. —*v.i.* **3.** to prophesy. **4.** to have a presentment. —**fore·bod′er,** *n.* —**Syn. 1.** foreshadow, presage, forecast, augur, portend.

fore·bod·ing (fōr bō′diṅg, fôr-), *n.* **1.** a strong inner certainty of a future misfortune; presentiment. **2.** a portent. —*adj.* **3.** that forebodes, esp. evil. [ME *forbodyng* (n.)] —**fore·bod′ing·ly,** *adv.* —**fore·bod′ing·ness,** *n.*

fore·bod·y (fōr′bod′ē, fôr′-), *n., pl.* **-bod·ies.** *Naut.* the part of a ship's hull forward of the middle body.

fore·brain (fōr′brān′, fôr′-), *n.* *Anat.* **1.** the prosencephalon, being the anterior of the three primary divisions of the brain in the embryo of a vertebrate or the part of the adult brain derived from this tissue, including the diencephalon and telencephalon. **2.** the telencephalon.

fore·cast (fōr′kast′, -käst′, fôr′-), *v.,* **-cast** or **-cast·ed, -cast·ing,** *n.* —*v.t.* **1.** to form an opinion beforehand; predict. **2.** to make a prediction of: *to forecast the weather.* **3.** to serve as a forecast of; foreshadow. **4.** to contrive or plan beforehand; prearrange. —*v.i.* **5.** to conjecture beforehand; make a forecast. **6.** to plan or arrange beforehand. —*n.* **7.** a conjecture as to something in the future. **8.** a prediction, esp. as to the weather. **9.** *Rare.* the act, practice, or faculty of forecasting. **10.** *Archaic.* foresight in planning. [ME *fore cast*] —**fore′cast′er,** *n.* —**Syn. 1.** foretell, anticipate. See **predict. 5, 7.** guess, estimate.

F, Forecastle (def. 1)

fore·cas·tle (fōk′səl, fōr′kas′əl, -kä′səl, fôr′-), *n.* *Naut.* **1.** a superstructure at or immediately aft of the bow of a vessel, used as a shelter for stores, machinery, etc., or as quarters for seamen. **2.** any seamen's quarters located in the forward part of a vessel, as a deckhouse. **3.** the forward part of the weather deck of a vessel, esp. the part forward of the foremast. Also, **fo'c's'le, fo'c'sle.** [ME *forcastel*]

fore′castle deck′, *Naut.* a partial weather deck on top of a forecastle superstructure; topgallant forecastle.

fore·close (fōr klōz′, fôr-), *v.,* **-closed, -clos·ing.** —*v.t.* **1.** *Law.* **a.** to deprive (a mortgagor or pledgor) of the right to redeem his property, esp. on failure to make payment on a mortgage when due, ownership of property then passing to mortgagee. **b.** to take away the right to redeem (a mortgage or pledge). **2.** to shut out; exclude; bar. **3.** to hinder or prevent. **4.** to establish an exclusive claim to. **5.** to close, settle, or answer beforehand. —*v.i.* **6.** to foreclose a mortgage or pledge. [ME *foreclose(n)* < OF *forclos,* ptp. of *forclore* to exclude = *for-* out + *clore* to shut (< L *claudere*)] —**fore·clos′a·ble,** *adj.*

fore·clo·sure (fōr klō′zhər, fôr-), *n.* *Law.* the act of foreclosing a mortgage or pledge.

fore·course (fōr′kōrs′, fôr′kôrs′), *n.* the lowermost sail on a square-rigged foremast; a square foresail. See diag. at **ship.**

fore·court (fōr′kōrt′, fôr′kôrt′), *n.* **1.** a courtyard before an entrance to a building or group of buildings. **2.** *Tennis.* the part of either half of a tennis court that lies between the net and the line that marks the in-bounds limit of a service. Cf. **backcourt** (def. 2).

fore·deck (fōr′dek′, fôr′-), *n.* *Naut.* the fore part of a weather deck, esp. between a bridge house or superstructure and a forecastle superstructure.

fore·do (fōr do͞o′, fôr-), *v.t.,* **-did, -done, -do·ing.** fordo.

fore·done (fōr dun′, fôr-), *adj.* fordone.

fore·doom (*v.* fōr do͞om′, fôr-; *n.* fōr′do͞om′, fôr′-), *v.t.* **1.** to doom beforehand. —*n.* **2.** *Archaic.* a doom ordained beforehand.

fore·fa·ther (fōr′fä′t͟hər, fôr′-), *n.* an ancestor. [ME *forefader*] —**fore′fa′ther·ly,** *adj.*

fore·feel (*v.* fōr fēl′, fôr-; *n.* fōr′fēl′, fôr′-), *v.,* **-felt, -feel·ing,** *n.* —*v.t.* **1.** to feel or perceive beforehand; have a presentiment of. —*n.* **2.** a feeling beforehand.

fore·fend (fōr fend′, fôr-), *v.t.* forfend.

fore·fin·ger (fōr′fiṅg′gər, fôr′-), *n.* the finger next to the thumb. Also called **index finger.** [late ME *forefyngure*]

fore·foot (fōr′fo͝ot′, fôr′-), *n., pl.* **-feet. 1.** *Zool.* one of the front feet of a quadruped, an insect, etc. **2.** *Naut.* the point at which the stem of a hull joins the keel; the forward end of a keel. [late ME *forfot, forefote*]

fore·front (fōr′frunt′, fôr′-), *n.* the foremost part or place. [late ME *forfrount, forefrount*]

fore·gath·er (fōr gat͟h′ər, fôr-), *v.i.* forgather.

fore·go[1] (fōr gō′, fôr-), *v.t., v.i.* **-went, -gone, -go·ing.** to go before; precede. [ME *forgon, forgan,* OE *foregān*] —**fore·go′er,** *n.*

fore·go[2] (fōr gō′, fôr-), *v.t.,* **-went, -gone, -go·ing.** forgo. —**fore·go′er,** *n.*

fore·go·ing (fōr gō′iṅg, fôr-), *adj.* going before; preceding. [late ME] —**Syn.** precedent, previous, prior, earlier, former.

fore·gone (fōr gôn′, -gon′, fôr-; fōr′gôn′, -gon′, fôr′-), *adj.* that has gone before; previous; past.

fore′gone′ conclu′sion, an inevitable result.

fore·ground (fōr′ground′, fôr′-), *n.* the ground or parts situated, or represented as situated, in the front; the nearer portion of a scene (opposed to *background*).

fore·gut (fōr′gut′, fôr′-), *n.* *Embryol., Zool.* the upper part of the embryonic alimentary canal from which the pharynx, esophagus, stomach, and part of the duodenum develop. Cf. **hindgut, midgut.**

fore·hand (fōr′hand′, fôr′-), *adj.* **1.** (in tennis, squash, etc.) of, pertaining to, or noting a stroke made from the same side of the body as that of the hand holding the racket, paddle, etc. Cf. **backhand** (def. 5). **2.** being in front or ahead. **3.** foremost or leading. **4.** done beforehand; given or made in advance, as a payment. —*n.* **5.** (in tennis squash, etc.) a forehand stroke. **6.** the part of a horse that is in front of the rider. **7.** *Archaic.* a superior or advantageous position. —*adv.* **8.** (in tennis, squash, etc.) done or struck with a forehand stroke.

fore·hand·ed (fōr′han′did, fôr′-), *adj.* **1.** forehand (def. 1). **2.** capable of dealing or coping with unexpected problems. **3.** providing for the future; prudent; thrifty. **4.** in easy circumstances; well-to-do. —*adv.* **5.** forehand (def. 8). —**fore′hand′ed·ly,** *adv.* —**fore′hand′ed·ness,** *n.*

fore·head (fôr′id, for′-; fōr′hed′, fôr′-), *n.* **1.** the part of the face above the eyes; brow. **2.** the fore or front part of anything. [ME *forehe(v)ed,* OE *forhēafod*]

for·eign (fôr′in, for′-), *adj.* **1.** of, pertaining to, or derived from another country or nation; not native. **2.** of or pertaining to contact or dealings with other countries; connected with foreign affairs: *foreign policy.* **3.** external to one's own country or nation: *a foreign country.* **4.** carried on abroad, or with other countries: *foreign trade.* **5.** belonging to or coming from another district, province, etc. **6.** *Law.* **a.** within or pertaining to the laws of another nation (opposed to *domestic*). **b.** within or pertaining to another jurisdiction, as another state or district. **7.** belonging to or proceeding from other persons or things: *a statement supported by foreign testimony.* **8.** not belonging to the place or body where found: *a speck of foreign matter.* **9.** alien in character; irrelevant or inappropriate. **10.** strange or unfamiliar. [ME *forein* < OF *forain, forein* < VL **forān(us)* < L *forās* outside] —**for′eign·ly,** *adv.* —**for′eign·ness,** *n.* —**Syn. 1, 3.** alien. **4.** international. **9.** extraneous, outside.

for′eign affairs′, international relations; activities of a nation arising from its dealings with other nations.

for′eign aid′, government assistance, usually on a large scale, from a great power to a war-devastated or underdeveloped nation, consisting of economic, technical, or military aid, given primarily in the form of monetary or material grants or financial loans, for purposes of relief and rehabilitation, for economic stabilization, or for mutual defense. Also called **aid.** —**for′eign-aid′,** *adj.*

for′eign bill′, a bill of exchange drawn on a payer in one country by a maker in another.

for·eign-born (fôr′in bôrn′, for′-), *adj.* born in a country other than that in which one resides.

for·eign·er (fôr′ə nər, for′-), *n.* a person not native to or naturalized in a given country. [ME *foreiner*] —**Syn.** See **stranger.**

for′eign exchange′, 1. commercial paper drawn on a person or corporation in a foreign nation. **2.** the process of balancing accounts in commercial transactions between businessmen of different nations.

for·eign·ism (fôr′ə niz′əm, for′-), *n.* a foreign custom, mannerism, speech pattern, etc.

For′eign Le′gion, a former military body in the French army that consisted of men of all nationalities assigned to military operations and duties outside of France.

for′eign min′ister, (in countries other than the U.S.) the cabinet minister who conducts and supervises foreign

and diplomatic relations with other states. Also called, *esp. Brit.,* **foreign secretary.** Cf. **secretary of state** (def. 1). —**for′eign min′istry.**
for′eign of′fice, (in countries other than the U.S.) the department of a government that handles foreign affairs.
for′eign sec′retary, *Chiefly Brit.* See **foreign minister.**
for′eign serv′ice, a division of the U.S. Department of State or of a foreign office that maintains diplomatic and consular posts and personnel in other countries. Also, **For′eign Serv′ice.**
fore·judge (fōr juj′, fôr-), *v.t.,* **-judged, -judg·ing.** forjudge.
fore·know (fōr nō′, fôr-), *v.t.,* **-knew, -known, -know·ing.** to know beforehand. [late ME *foreknowe(n)*] —**fore·know′a·ble,** *adj.* —**fore·know′er,** *n.* —**fore·know′ing·ly,** *adv.*
fore·knowl·edge (fōr′nol′ij, fôr′-, fōr nol′ij, fôr-), *n.* knowledge of a thing before it exists or happens; prescience.
fore·la·dy (fōr′lā′dē, fôr′-), *n., pl.* **-dies.** a forewoman.
fore·land (fōr′land′, fôr′-), *n.* **1.** a cape or promontory. **2.** land or territory lying in front. [ME *forlonde*]
fore·leg (fōr′leg′, fôr′-), *n.* one of the front legs of a quadruped, an insect, etc. [late ME *forlegge*]
fore·limb (fōr′lim′, fôr′-), *n.* a front limb of a quadruped.
fore·lock (fōr′lok′, fôr′-), *n.* **1.** the lock of hair that grows from the fore part of the head. **2.** (of a horse) a tuft of hair above or on the forehead.
fore·man (fōr′mən, fôr′-), *n., pl.* **-men. 1.** a man in charge of a particular department, group of workmen, etc., as in a factory. **2.** the chairman and spokesman of a jury. [ME *forman* leader] —**fore′man·ship′,** *n.*
fore·mast (fōr′mast′, -mäst′, fôr′-; *Naut.* fōr′məst, fôr′-), *n. Naut.* the mast nearest the bow in all vessels having two or more masts.
fore·most (fōr′mōst′, -məst, fôr′-), *adj., adv.* first in place, order, rank, etc. [FORE¹ + -MOST; r. ME, OE *formest* = *form(a)* first, var. of *fruma* (cf. L *prīmus*) + *-est* -EST¹] —**Syn.** primary, prime, chief, principal, paramount.
fore·name (fōr′nām′, fôr′-), *n.* a name that precedes the family name or surname; given name.
fore·named (fōr′nāmd′, fôr′-), *adj.* named before; mentioned before in the same writing or discourse; aforementioned.
fore·noon (fōr′no͞on′, fôr′-; fōr′no͞on′, fôr′-), *n.* **1.** the period of daylight before noon. —*adj.* **2.** of or pertaining to the forenoon.
fo·ren·sic (fə ren′sik), *adj.* **1.** pertaining to, connected with, or used in courts of law or public discussion and debate. **2.** adapted or suited to argumentation; rhetorical. —*n.* **3. forensics,** (*construed as sing. or pl.*) the art or study of argumentation and formal debate. [< L *forēns(is)* of, belonging to the forum, public. See FORUM, -ESE, -IC] —**fo·ren·si·cal·i·ty** (fə ren′si kal′i tē), *n.* —**fo·ren′si·cal·ly,** *adv.*
foren′sic med′icine, the application of medical knowledge to questions of civil and criminal law, esp. in court proceedings.
fore·or·dain (fōr′ôr dān′, fôr′-), *v.t.* **1.** to ordain or appoint beforehand. **2.** to predestine; predetermine. [late ME *forordein(en)*] —**fore·or·di·na·tion** (fōr′ôr dᵊnā′shən, fôr′-), *n.* —**fore′or·dain′ment,** *n.*
fore·part (fōr′pärt′, fôr′-), *n.* the fore, front, or early part. [ME *forpart*]
fore·passed (fōr past′, -päst′, fôr-), *adj.* already in the past; bygone. Also, **fore·past′.**
fore·paw (fōr′pô′, fôr′-), *n.* the paw of a foreleg.
fore·peak (fōr′pēk′, fôr′-), *n. Naut.* the extreme forward part of the interior of a hull.
fore·play (fōr′plā′, fôr′-), *n.* sexual stimulation intended as a prelude to sexual intercourse.
fore·quar·ter (fōr′kwôr′tər, fôr′-), *n.* the forward end of half of a carcass, as of beef or lamb.
fore·reach (fōr rēch′, fôr-), *v.i.* **1.** to gain, as one ship on another. **2.** to maintain headway, as when coming about or drifting after taking in sail or stopping engines. —*v.t.* **3.** to gain upon; overhaul and pass.
fore·run (fōr run′, fôr-), *v.t.,* **-ran, -run, -run·ning. 1.** to run in front of; come before; precede. **2.** to be the precursor or harbinger of; prefigure. **3.** to anticipate or foretell. **4.** *Archaic.* to forestall. **5.** *Obs.* to outrun or outstrip. [OE *forarn* to run on in front]
fore·run·ner (fōr′run′ər, fôr′-, fōr run′ər, fôr-), *n.* **1.** predecessor; ancestor; forebear; precursor. **2.** an omen, sign, or symptom of something to follow; portent: *a forerunner of summer.* **3.** a person who goes or is sent in advance to announce the coming of someone or something that follows; herald; harbinger. [ME *forrenner*]
fore·said (fōr′sed′, fôr′-), *adj.* aforementioned; aforesaid. [ME *forsaid,* OE *foresǣd*]
fore·sail (fōr′sāl′, fôr′-; *Naut.* fōr′səl, fôr′-), *n. Naut.* **1.** the lowermost sail on a foremast. See diag. at **ship. 2.** the staysail or jib, set immediately forward of the mainmast of a sloop, cutter, knockabout, yawl, ketch, or dandy.
fore·see (fōr sē′, fôr-), *v.,* **-saw, -seen, -see·ing.** —*v.t.* **1.** to have prescience of; foreknow. **2.** to see beforehand. —*v.i.* **3.** to exercise foresight. [ME; OE *foresēon*] —**fore·see′a·bil′i·ty,** *n.* —**fore·see′a·ble,** *adj.* —**fore·se′er,** *n.* —**Syn. 1.** divine, discern. See **predict.**
fore·shad·ow (fōr shad′ō, fôr-), *v.t.* to show or indicate beforehand; prefigure. —**fore·shad′ow·er,** *n.*
fore·shank (fōr′shangk′, fôr′-), *n.* See under **shank** (def. 4).
fore·sheet (fōr′shēt′, fôr′-), *n. Naut.* **1.** the sheet of a headsail. **2. foresheets,** (*construed as pl.*) the space, in an open boat, in front of the foremost rower's seat. Also called **headsheet.**
fore·shore (fōr′shōr′, fôr′shôr′), *n.* **1.** the ground between the water's edge and cultivated land; land along the edge of a body of water. **2.** the part of the shore between the high-water and low-water marks.
fore·short·en (fōr shôr′tᵊn, fôr-), *v.t.* **1.** *Fine Arts.* to reduce or distort (a represented object) in order to convey the illusion of three-dimensional space. **2.** to abridge, reduce, or contract; make shorter.
fore·show (fōr shō′, fôr-), *v.t.,* **-showed, -shown, -show·ing.** to show beforehand; foretell; foreshadow. [ME *forescewe(n),* OE *forescēawian*]
fore·side (fōr′sīd′, fôr′-), *n.* **1.** the front side or part. **2.** the upper side. **3.** *U.S.* a stretch of land along the edge of the sea. [ME]
fore·sight (fōr′sīt′, fôr′-), *n.* **1.** care or provision for the future; provident care; prudence. **2.** the act or power of foreseeing; prevision; prescience. **3.** the act of looking forward. **4.** knowledge or insight gained by or as by looking forward; a view of the future. **5.** *Survey.* **a.** a sight or reading taken on a forward point. **b.** (in leveling) a rod reading on a point the elevation of which is to be determined. [ME *forsight*] —**fore′sight′ed,** *adj.* —**fore′sight′ed·ly,** *adv.* —**fore′sight′ed·ness,** *n.* —**Syn. 1.** See **prudence. 4.** fore knowledge.
fore·skin (fōr′skin′, fôr′-), *n.* the prepuce of the penis.
fore·speak (fōr spēk′, fôr-), *v.t.,* **-spoke** or (*Archaic*) **-spake; -spo·ken** or (*Archaic*) **-spoke; -speak·ing. 1.** to predict; foretell. **2.** to speak for, or claim, in advance. [ME *forespeke(n)*]
fore·spent (fōr spent′, fôr-), *adj. Archaic.* forspent.
for·est (fôr′ist, for′-), *n.* **1.** a large tract of land covered with trees and underbrush; extensive wooded area. **2.** the trees alone: *to cut down a forest.* **3.** *Eng. Law.* a tract of wooded grounds and pastures, generally belonging to the sovereign and set apart for game. **4.** a large number of things; a thick cluster. —*v.t.* **5.** to cover with trees; convert into a forest. [ME < OF < ML *forest(is)* an unenclosed wood (as opposed to a park) < L *foris* outside. See FOREIGN] —**for′est·al, fo·res·tial** (fə res′chəl), *adj.* —**for′est·less,** *adj.* —**for′est·like′,** *adj.*
—**Syn. 1.** FOREST, GROVE, WOOD(S) refer to an area covered with trees. A FOREST is an extensive area, preserving some or all of its primitive wildness and usually having game or wild animals in it: *the Black Forest; a tropical rain forest.* A GROVE is a group or cluster of trees, usually not very large in area and often cleared of underbrush. It may be wild or tended or cultivated: *a shady grove; a grove of pines; an orange grove; a walnut grove.* WOODS (a WOOD) resembles a forest but is a smaller tract of land, less wild in character, and generally closer to civilization: *lost in the woods; a wood covering several acres.*
fore·stall (fōr stôl′, fôr-), *v.t.* **1.** to prevent, hinder, or thwart by action in advance. **2.** to deal with or realize beforehand. **3.** to prevent sales at (a fair, market, etc.) by buying up, diverting, or manipulating the prices of goods. [ME *forstalle,* OE *foresteall* intervention (to defeat justice), waylaying] —**fore·stall′er,** *n.* —**fore·stall′ment, fore·stal′ment,** *n.* —**Syn. 1.** preclude, obviate, anticipate.
for·est·a·tion (fôr′i stā′shən, for′-), *n.* the planting of forests.
fore·stay (fōr′stā′, fôr′-), *n. Naut.* a stay leading aft and upward from the stem or knightheads to support the mast; the lowermost stay of a foremast. [ME *forstay*]
fore·stay·sail (fōr′stā′sāl′, fôr′-; *Naut.* fōr′stā′səl, fôr′-), *n. Naut.* a triangular sail set on a forestay; the innermost headsail of a vessel.
for·est·er (fôr′i stər, for′-), *n.* **1.** a person who is expert in forestry. **2.** an officer having charge of a forest. **3.** *Zool.* an animal of the forest. **4.** a large, gray kangaroo, *Macropus canguru.* **5.** any of several moths of the family *Agaristidae,* typically black with two yellowish or whitish spots on each wing. [ME < OF *forestier*]
For·est·er (fôr′i stər, for′-), *n.* **C(ecil) S(cott),** 1899–1966, English novelist and journalist.
For′est Hills′, a residential area in New York City, on W Long Island, in SE New York: tennis tournaments.
for′est ran′ger, an officer supervising the care of a forest, esp. a public forest.
for·est·ry (fôr′i strē, for′-), *n.* **1.** the science of planting and taking care of forests. **2.** forest land. [< MF *foresterie*]
fore·taste (*n.* fōr′tāst′, fôr′-; *v.* fōr tāst′, fôr-), *n., v.,* **-tast·ed, -tast·ing.** —*n.* **1.** a slight and partial experience, or awareness of something to come in the future; anticipation. —*v.t.* **2.** to have some taste, experience, knowledge, etc., of (something) beforehand. [ME *fortaste*]
fore·tell (fōr tel′, fôr-), *v.,* **-told, -tell·ing.** —*v.t.* **1.** to tell of beforehand; predict or prophesy. **2.** (of things) to foreshadow. —*v.i.* **3.** to utter a prediction or a prophecy. [ME *fortell*] —**fore·tell′er,** *n.* —**Syn. 1.** forecast, augur. **2.** presage, forebode.
fore·thought (fōr′thôt′, fôr′-), *n.* **1.** thoughtful provision beforehand; provident care; prudence. **2.** a thinking of something beforehand; previous consideration; anticipation. [ME *for-thoght*] —**Syn. 1.** See **prudence.**
fore·thought·ful (fōr thôt′fəl, fôr-), *adj.* full of or having forethought; provident. —**fore·thought′ful·ly,** *adv.* —**fore·thought′ful·ness,** *n.*
fore·time (fōr′tīm′, fôr′-), *n.* former or past time; the past.
fore·to·ken (*n.* fōr′tō′kən, fôr′-; *v.* fōr tō′kən, fôr-), *n.* **1.** a sign or token of a future event; a forewarning. —*v.t.* **2.** to foreshadow. [ME *fortokne,* OE *foretācn*]
fore·top (fōr′top′, fôr′-; *for 1 also Naut.* fōr′təp, fôr′-), *n.* **1.** *Naut.* a platform at the head of a fore lower mast. **2.** the forelock of an animal, esp. a horse. **3.** *Obs.* a human forelock, or a lock of hair on the front of a wig. [ME *fortop*]
fore-top·gal·lant (fōr′top gal′ənt, fôr′-; *Naut.* fōr′tə-gal′ənt, fôr′-), *adj. Naut.* noting a sail, yard, rigging, etc., belonging to a fore-topgallant mast.
fore′-top·gal′lant mast′, *Naut.* the spar or section of a spar forming the topgallant portion of a foremast.
fore-top·mast (fōr′top′mast′, -mäst′, fôr′-; *Naut.* fōr′-top′məst, fôr′-), *n. Naut.* the spar or section of a pole mast serving as the topmast of a foremast.
fore-top·sail (fōr′top′sāl′, fôr′-; *Naut.* fōr′top′səl, fôr′-), *n. Naut.* a topsail set on a foremast.
for·ev·er (fôr ev′ər, fər-), *adv.* **1.** eternally; without ever ending. **2.** continually; incessantly. **3. forever and a day,** eternally. [orig. phrase *for ever*]
for·ev·er·more (fôr ev′ər mōr′, -môr′, fər-), *adv.* for ever hereafter.

fore·warn (fōr wôrn′, fôr-), *v.t.* to warn beforehand. [ME *forwarn(en)*] —**fore·warn′er,** *n.* —**Syn. 1.** caution.

fore·went (fōr went′, fôr-), *v.* pt. of **forego.**

fore·wing (fōr′wing′, fôr′-), *n.* either of the anterior wings of an insect having four wings.

fore·wom·an (fōr′wo͝om′ən, fôr′-), *n., pl.* **-wom·en. 1.** a woman in charge of a particular department, group of workers, etc., as in a factory. **2.** the chairlady of a jury.

fore·word (fōr′wûrd′, -wərd, fôr′-), *n.* a preface or introductory statement in a book, magazine article, etc. Cf. **afterword.** —**Syn.** See **introduction.**

fore·worn (fōr wōrn′, fôr wôrn′), *adj. Archaic.* forworn.

fore·yard (fōr′yärd′, fôr′-), *n. Naut.* a yard on the lower mast of a square-rigged foremast, used to support the foresail.

For·far (fôr′fər, -fär), *n.* **1.** a town in and the county seat of Angus, in E Scotland. 10,252 (1961). **2.** former name of **Angus.**

for·feit (fôr′fit), *n.* **1.** a fine; penalty. **2.** the act of forfeiting; forfeiture. **3.** something to which the right is lost as a result of committing a crime or misdeed, neglecting a duty, violating a contract, etc. **4.** an article deposited in a game because of a mistake and redeemable by a fine or penalty. —*v.t.* **5.** to lose as a forfeit. **6.** to lose, or become liable to lose, in consequence of crime, fault, breach of engagement, etc. —*adj.* **7.** lost by forfeiture. [ME *forfet* < OF (ptp. of *forfaire* to commit crime, to lose possession or right through a criminal act) < ML *foris factum* penalty, ptp. of *foris facere* to transgress = *foris* outside, wrongly + *facere* to make, do] —**for′feit·a·ble,** *adj.* —**for′feit·er,** *n.*

for·fei·ture (fôr′fi chər), *n.* **1.** the act of forfeiting. **2.** something forfeited; fine. [ME *forfeiture, forfeture* < OF]

for·fend (fôr fend′), *v.t.* **1.** to defend, secure, or protect. **2.** *Archaic.* to fend off, avert, or prevent. Also, **forefend.** [ME *forfend(en)*]

for·gat (fər gat′), *v. Archaic.* a pt. of **forget.**

for·gath·er (fôr gath′ər), *v.i.* **1.** to gather together; convene; assemble. **2.** to encounter or meet, esp. by accident. **3.** to associate or fraternize. Also, **foregather.**

for·gave (fər gāv′), *v.* pt. of **forgive.**

forge[1] (fōrj, fôrj), *n., v.,* **forged, forg·ing.** —*n.* **1.** the special fireplace, hearth, or furnace in which metal is heated before shaping. **2.** the workshop of a blacksmith; smithy. —*v.t.* **3.** to form by heating and hammering; beat into shape. **4.** to form or make in any way. **5.** to invent (a fictitious story, a lie, etc.). **6.** to imitate (handwriting, a signature, etc.) fraudulently; fabricate a forgery. —*v.i.* **7.** to commit forgery. **8.** to work at a forge. [ME *forge(n)* < MF *forg(ier)* < L *fabricāre* FABRICATE] —**forge′a·ble,** *adj.* —**forg′er,** *n.*

forge[2] (fōrj, fôrj), *v.i.,* **forged, forg·ing. 1.** to move ahead or progress slowly, with difficulty, or by mere momentum (usually fol. by *ahead*). **2.** to move ahead with increased speed or effectiveness (usually fol. by *ahead*): *to forge ahead with one's work.* [?]

for·ger·y (fōr′jə rē, fôr′-), *n., pl.* **-ger·ies. 1.** *Law.* the false making or alteration of a writing by which the legal rights or obligations of another person are apparently affected. **2.** the production of a spurious work that is claimed to be genuine. **3.** something produced by forgery. **4.** the act of fabricating or producing falsely.

for·get (fər get′), *v.,* **-got** or (*Archaic*) **-gat; -got·ten** or **-got; -get·ting.** —*v.t.* **1.** to cease or fail to remember; be unable to recall. **2.** to omit or neglect unintentionally (usually fol. by an infinitive): *I forgot to shut the window.* **3.** to leave behind unintentionally; neglect to take: *to forget one's keys.* **4.** to omit mentioning; leave unnoticed. **5.** to fail to think of; take no note of. **6.** to neglect willfully; disregard or slight. —*v.i.* **7.** to cease or omit to think of something. **8. forget oneself,** to say or do something improper or unbefitting one's rank, position, or character. [FOR- + GET; r. ME *foryete(n)*, OE *forg(i)etan;* c. OS *fargetan*, OHG *firgezzan*] —**for·get′ta·ble,** *adj.* —**for·get′ter,** *n.*

for·get·ful (fər get′fəl), *adj.* **1.** apt to forget; that forgets: *a forgetful person.* **2.** heedless or neglectful (often fol. by *of*): *to be forgetful of others.* **3.** *Archaic.* causing to forget. [ME] —**for·get′ful·ly,** *adv.* —**for·get′ful·ness,** *n.*

for·ge·tive (fōr′ji tiv, fôr′-), *adj. Archaic.* inventive.

for·get-me-not (fər get′mē not′), *n.* **1.** a small, Old World, boraginaceous plant, *Myosotis palustris,* having a light-blue flower commonly regarded as an emblem of constancy and friendship. **2.** any of several other plants of the genus *Myosotis.* [trans. of MF *ne m'oubliez mye*]

forg·ing (fōr′jing, fôr′-), *n.* **1.** the act or an instance of forging. **2.** something that is forged; a piece of forged work in metal. [ME]

for·give (fər giv′), *v.,* **-gave, -giv·en, -giv·ing.** —*v.t.* **1.** to grant free pardon for or remission of (an offense, debt, etc.); absolve. **2.** to give up all claim on account of; remit (a debt, obligation, etc.). **3.** to grant free pardon to (a person). **4.** to cease to feel resentment against. —*v.i.* **5.** to pardon an offense or an offender. [FOR- + GIVE; r. ME *foryive(n)*, OE *forgiefan*] —**for·giv′a·ble,** *adj.* —**for·giv′er,** *n.* —**Syn. 1.** See **excuse. 3.** absolve. —**Ant. 1, 3.** blame.

for·give·ness (fər giv′nis), *n.* **1.** the act of forgiving. **2.** the state of being forgiven. **3.** disposition or willingness to forgive. [ME *forgifenesse*, OE *forgifennys*]

for·giv·ing (fər giv′ing), *adj.* that forgives; disposed to forgive; indicating forgiveness. —**for·giv′ing·ly,** *adv.* —**for·giv′ing·ness,** *n.*

for·go (fôr gō′), *v.t.,* **-went, -gone, -go·ing. 1.** to abstain or refrain from; do without; give up, renounce, or resign. **2.** *Archaic.* to neglect or overlook. **3.** *Archaic.* to quit or leave. Also, **forego.** [ME *forgo(n)*, OE *forgān*] —**for·go′er,** *n.*

for·got (fər got′), *v.* a pt. and pp. of **forget.**

for·got·ten (fər got′ən), *v.* a pp. of **forget.**

for·int (fôr′int), *n.* a monetary unit of Hungary, equal to 100 fillér. *Abbr.:* F., Ft. [< Hung < It *fiorino.* See FLORIN]

for·judge (fôr juj′), *v.t.,* **-judged, -judg·ing.** *Law.* to exclude, expel, dispossess, or deprive by a judgment. [ME *forjuge(n)* < OF *forjugie(r)* = *for-* out + *jugier* to JUDGE] —**for·judg′ment,** *n.*

fork (fôrk), *n.* **1.** an instrument having two or more prongs or tines, for holding, lifting, etc., esp. an implement for handling food. **2.** See **tuning fork. 3.** a division into branches. **4.** the point or part at which a thing, as a river or a road, divides into branches. **5.** any of such branches. **6.** *Chiefly U.S.* a principal tributary of a river. **7.** *Obs.* the barbed head of an arrow. —*v.t.* **8.** to pierce, raise, pitch, dig, etc., with a fork. **9.** to make into the form of a fork. **10.** *Chess.* to maneuver so as to place (two opponent's pieces) under simultaneous attack by the same piece. —*v.i.* **11.** to divide into branches. **12. fork over** or **out** or **up,** *Informal.* to hand over; deliver; pay. [ME *forke*, OE *forca* < L *furca* fork, gallows, yoke] —**fork′less,** *adj.* —**fork′like′,** *adj.*

forked (fôrkt, fôr′kid), *adj.* **1.** having a fork or forklike branches. **2.** zigzag, as lightning. **3.** expressing duality, insincerity, or untruthfulness. [ME] —**fork·ed·ly** (fôr′kid lē), *adv.* —**fork′ed·ness,** *n.*

forked′ tongue′, falsehood, duplicity, or deceit: *to speak with a forked tongue.* [perh. modeled on AmerInd idiom]

fork·lift (fôrk′lift′), *n.* **1.** Also called **fork′lift truck′, fork′ truck′,** a small vehicle with a power-operated pronged platform at the front that can be slid under heavy loads and then raised, for moving and stacking materials in warehouses, shipping depots, etc. —*v.t.* **2.** to move or stack by forklift.

For·lì (fōr lē′), *n.* a city in N Italy, SE of Bologna. 91,146 (1961).

for·lorn (fôr lôrn′), *adj.* **1.** desolate or dreary; unhappy or miserable, as in feeling, condition, or appearance. **2.** abandoned, deserted, or forsaken (sometimes fol. by *of*): *a city forlorn of life.* **3.** hopeless; despairing. **4.** bereft; destitute. [ME *foreloren* (ptp. of *forlesen* to lose completely), OE *forloren* (ptp. of *forlēosan*); c. OHG *firliosan* (G *verlieren*), Goth *fraliusan.* See FOR-, LORN] —**for·lorn′ly,** *adv.* —**for·lorn′ness,** *n.* —**Syn. 1.** pitiful, pitiable, helpless, woebegone. **2.** alone. See **desolate.** —**Ant. 1.** happy.

forlorn′ hope′, 1. a vain hope; an undertaking almost certain to fail. **2.** a perilous or desperate enterprise. **3.** *Obs.* a group of soldiers assigned to perform some unusually perilous service. [< D, folk-etym. alter. of *verloren hoop*, lit., lost troop]

form (fôrm), *n.* **1.** external appearance of a clearly defined area, as distinguished from color or material; configuration. **2.** the shape of a thing or person. **3.** a body, esp. that of a human being. **4.** a dummy used for fitting or displaying clothing. **5.** something that gives or determines shape; a mold. **6.** a particular condition, character, or mode in which something appears: *water in the form of ice.* **7.** the manner or style of arranging and coordinating parts for a pleasing or effective result. **8.** *Fine Arts.* **a.** the organization, placement, or relationship of basic elements so as to produce a coherent image; the formal structure of a work of art. **b.** three-dimensional quality or volume, as of a represented object or anatomical part. **c.** an object, person, or part of the human body or the appearance of any of these, esp. as seen in nature. **9.** any assemblage of things of a similar kind constituting a component of a group, especially of a zoological group. **10.** due or proper shape; orderly arrangement of parts; good order. **11.** *Philos.* **a.** the structure, pattern, organization, or essential nature of anything. **b.** structure or pattern as distinguished from matter. **c.** (*cap.*) *Platonism.* idea (def. 7c). **d.** *Aristotelianism.* that which places a thing in its particular species or kind. **12.** *Logic.* the abstract relations of terms in a proposition, and of propositions to one another. **13.** a set, prescribed, or customary order or method of doing something. **14.** a set order of words, as for use in religious ritual or in a legal document. **15.** a document with blank spaces to be filled in with particulars before it is executed. **16.** a typical document to be used as a guide in framing others for like cases. **17.** a conventional method of procedure or behavior. **18.** a formality or ceremony, often with implication of absence of real meaning. **19.** procedure according to a set order or method. **20.** formality; ceremony; conformity to the usages of society. **21.** procedure or conduct, as judged by social standards: *Such behavior is very bad form.* **22.** manner or method of performing something; technique. **23.** physical condition or fitness, as for performing: *a tennis player in peak form.* **24.** *Gram.* **a.** See **linguistic form. b.** a particular shape of word as it occurs in a specific context: in *I'm*, *'m* is a form of *am*, and *goes* is a form of *go.* **25.** *Building Trades.* a temporary mold for giving a desired shape to poured concrete, rammed earth, etc. **26.** a grade or class of pupils in a British secondary school. **27.** a grade or class in certain U.S. private schools. **28.** *Brit.* a bench or long seat. **29.** *Print.* an assemblage of types, leads, etc., secured in a chase to print from.
—*v.t.* **30.** to construct or frame. **31.** to make or produce. **32.** to serve to make up; serve as; compose; constitute. **33.** to place in order; arrange; organize. **34.** to frame (ideas, opinions, etc.) in the mind. **35.** to contract (habits, friendships, etc.). **36.** to give form or shape to; shape; fashion. **37.** to give a particular form or shape to; fashion in a particular manner. **38.** to mold by discipline or instructions. **39.** *Gram.* to stand in relation to (a particular derivative or other form) by virtue of the absence or presence of an affix or other grammatical element or change: "*Man*" *forms its plural by the change of -a- to -e-.* **40.** *Mil.* to draw up in lines or in formation.
—*v.i.* **41.** to take or assume form. **42.** to be formed or produced. **43.** to take a particular form or arrangement. [ME *forme* < OF < L *forma* form, figure, model, mold, sort, ML: seat] —**form′a·ble,** *adj.*
—**Syn. 1.** mold, appearance, cast, cut. FORM, FIGURE, SHAPE, OUTLINE refer to an appearance that can be recognized. FORM, FIGURE, and SHAPE are often used to mean an area clearly defined by contour without regard to other identifying qualities, as color or material. FORM often includes a sense of mass or volume. SHAPE usually refers to a flat area of definite outline; even when used with reference to the human body it connotes a silhouette of a particular character. OUTLINE refers to the line that delimits a form, figure, or shape: *the outline of a hill.* **5.** model, pattern, jig. **9.** sort, kind, order, type. **13.** ceremony, ritual, formality, convention. **15.** blank. **18, 19.** system, mode, practice, formula. **30.** model, fabricate, mold, forge, cast, outline.

-form, a suffix of Latin origin meaning "having the form of": *cruciform.* [< L *-formis*]

for·mal[1] (fôr′məl), *adj.* **1.** being in accordance with the usual requirements, customs, etc.; conventional. **2.** marked

by form or ceremony: *a formal occasion.* **3.** observant of conventional requirements of behavior, procedure, etc., as persons; ceremonious. **4.** excessively ceremonious. **5.** being a matter of form only; perfunctory. **6.** made or done in accordance with procedures that ensure validity: *a formal authorization.* **7.** of, pertaining to, or emphasizing the constituent elements in a work of art perceived separately from its subject matter: *the formal structure of a poem.* **8.** being in accordance with prescribed or customary forms: *a formal siege.* **9.** acquired in school; academic: *formal training in sociology.* **10.** symmetrical or highly organized: *a formal garden.* **11.** characterized by a usage of language that conforms to traditional standards of correctness, as in expository writing. **12.** *Philos.* pertaining to form. **13.** *Logic.* See **formal logic. 14.** pertaining to the form, shape, or mode of a thing, esp. as distinguished from the substance. **15.** being such merely in appearance or name; nominal. **16.** *Math.* **a.** (of a proof) in strict logical form with a justification for every step. **b.** (of a calculation) correct in form; made with strict justification for every step. **—n. 17.** a social event, as a dance or ball, that requires evening dress. **18.** See **evening dress. —adv. 19.** *Informal.* in formal attire. [ME *formal, formel* < L *formāl(is)*] **—for′mal·ness,** *n.*
—Syn. 2. FORMAL, ACADEMIC, CONVENTIONAL may have either favorable or unfavorable implications. FORMAL may mean in proper form, or may imply excessive emphasis on empty form. In the favorable sense, ACADEMIC applies to scholars or higher institutions of learning; it may, however, imply slavish conformance to mere rules, or to belief in impractical theories. CONVENTIONAL, in a favorable sense, applies to desirable conformity with accepted conventions or customs; but it more often is applied to arbitrary, forced, or meaningless conformity. **3.** conforming, conventional. **4.** stiff, prim, punctilious. **6.** official.

for·mal² (fôr′mal), *n. Chem.* methylal. [< FORMALDEHYDE]

form·al·de·hyde (fôr mal′də hīd′, fər-), *n. Chem.* a colorless, toxic, water-soluble gas, HCHO, having a suffocating odor, used chiefly in aqueous solution, as a disinfectant and preservative, and in the manufacture of various resins and plastics. Cf. **formalin.** [FORM(IC) + ALDEHYDE; modeled on G *Formaldehyd*]

for·ma·lin (fôr′mə lin), *n. Chem.* a clear, colorless, aqueous solution of 40 percent formaldehyde. Also called **formol.** [formerly trademark]

for·mal·ise (fôr′mə līz′), *v.t., v.i.,* **-ised, -is·ing.** *Chiefly Brit.* formalize. **—for′mal·i·sa′tion,** *n.* **—for′mal·is′er,** *n.*

for·mal·ism (fôr′mə liz′əm), *n.* strict adherence to, or observance of, prescribed or traditional forms. **—for′mal·ist,** *n.* **—for′mal·is′tic,** *adj.* **—for′mal·is′ti·cal·ly,** *adv.*

for·mal·i·ty (fôr mal′i tē), *n., pl.* **-ties. 1.** condition or quality of being formal; accordance with required or traditional rules, procedures, etc.; conventionality. **2.** rigorously methodical character. **3.** excessive adherence to established rules, procedures, etc.; rigidity. **4.** observance of form or ceremony. **5.** marked or excessive ceremoniousness. **6.** an established order or method of proceeding: *the formalities of judicial process.* **7.** a formal act or observance. **8.** something done merely for form's sake; a requirement of custom or etiquette. [< L *formālitās*] **—Syn. 7.** rite, ritual, ceremony.

for·mal·ize (fôr′mə līz′), *v.,* **-ized, -iz·ing. —v.t. 1.** to make formal, esp. for the sake of official or authorized acceptance. **2.** to give a definite form or shape to. **—v.i. 3.** to be formal; act with formality. Also, *esp. Brit.,* **formalise. —for′mal·i·za′tion,** *n.* **—for′mal·iz′er,** *n.*

for′mal log′ic, the branch of logic concerned exclusively with the principles of deductive reasoning and with the form rather than the content of propositions.

for·mal·ly (fôr′mə lē), *adv.* **1.** in a formal manner. **2.** as regards form; in form.

for·mant (fôr′mənt), *n. Acoustic Phonetics.* one of the regions of concentration of energy, prominent on a sound spectrogram, that collectively constitute the frequency spectrum of a speech sound. [< L *formant-* (s. of *formāns*), prp. of *formāre* to FORM; see -ANT]

for·mat (fôr′mat), *n.* **1.** the shape and size of a book as determined by the number of times the original sheet has been folded to form the leaves. Cf. **duodecimo, folio** (def. 2), **octavo, quarto. 2.** the general physical appearance of a publication, created by the type face, binding, quality of paper, etc. **3.** the organization, plan, style, or type of something: *a complicated format.* **4.** *Computer Technol.* the organization or disposition of symbols on a magnetic tape, punch card, or the like, in accordance with the input requirements of a computer, card-sort machine, etc. [< F < L (*liber*) *formāt(us)* (a book) formed (in a certain way)]

for·mate (fôr′māt), *n. Chem.* a salt or ester of formic acid. [FORM(IC) + -ATE²]

for·ma·tion (fôr mā′shən), *n.* **1.** the act or process of forming. **2.** the state of being formed. **3.** the manner in which a thing is formed; disposition of parts; formal structure or arrangement. **4.** *Mil.* a particular disposition of troops, as in columns, squares, etc. **5.** something formed. **6.** *Geol.* **a.** a body of rocks classed as a unit for geologic mapping. **b.** the process of depositing rock or mineral of a particular composition or origin. [ME *formacioun* < L *formātiōn-* (s. of *formātiō*) = *formāt(us)* (see FORM, -ATE¹) + *-iōn-* -ION] **—for·ma′tion·al,** *adj.*

form·a·tive (fôr′mə tiv), *adj.* **1.** giving form or shape; forming; shaping; fashioning; molding. **2.** pertaining to formation or development. **3.** *Biol.* **a.** capable of developing new cells or tissue by cell division and differentiation. **b.** concerned with the formation of an embryo, organ, or the like. **4.** *Gram.* pertaining to a formative. **—n. 5.** *Gram.* a derivational affix, particularly one that determines the part of speech of the derived word, as *-ness,* in *loudness, hardness,* etc. [< MF *formatif*] **—form′a·tive·ly,** *adv.* **—form′a·tive·ness,** *n.*

form′ class′, *Gram.* a class of words or forms in a given language that have one or more grammatical features in common.

for·mée (fôr mā′), *adj.* paty. [< F, fem. ptp. of *former* to FORM]

for·mer¹ (fôr′mər), *adj.* **1.** preceding in time; prior or earlier. **2.** past, long past, or ancient. **3.** preceding in order; being the first of two. **4.** being the first mentioned of two (distinguished from *latter*). **5.** having once, or previously, been; erstwhile. [ME = *forme* (OE *forma* first) + *-er* -ER⁴. Cf. FOREMOST] **—Syn. 3.** foregoing, antecedent. **5.** past, ex-.

form·er² (fôr′mər), *n.* a person or thing that forms or serves to form. [ME *fourmer*]

for·mer·ly (fôr′mər lē), *adv.* **1.** in time past; in an earlier period or age; previously. **2.** *Obs.* in time just past; just now.

form·fit·ting (fôrm′fit′ing), *adj.* designed to fit snugly; close-fitting: *a formfitting blouse.*

form′ ge′nus, *Biol.* an artificial taxonomic category including species grouped together on the basis of morphological resemblance.

for·mic (fôr′mik), *adj.* **1.** of or pertaining to ants. **2.** *Chem.* of or derived from formic acid. [irreg. < L *formīca* ant. Cf. F *formique*]

For·mi·ca (fôr mī′kə), *n. Trademark.* a thermosetting plastic, used as a chemical-proof and heat-proof covering for tables, wall-panels, etc.

for′mic ac′id, *Chem., Pharm.* an irritating, fuming liquid, HCOOH, used in dyeing and tanning and as a counterirritant and astringent.

for·mi·car·i·um (fôr′mə kâr′ē əm), *n., pl.* **-car·i·a** (-kâr′ē ə). formicary.

for·mi·car·y (fôr′mə ker′ē), *n., pl.* **-car·ies.** an ant nest. [< ML *formīcāri(um)* ant hill, n. use of neut. of **formīcāri(us)* of, pertaining to, ants. See FORMIC, -ARY]

for·mi·da·ble (fôr′mi də bəl), *adj.* **1.** feared or dreaded, esp. in encounters or dealings. **2.** of discouraging or awesome strength, size, difficulty, etc.; intimidating. **3.** arousing feelings of awe or admiration because of grandeur, strength, etc. **4.** vastly superior; great; exceptional. **5.** of great strength; forceful; powerful. [< F < L *formīdābil(is)* causing fear = *formīd-* (s. of *formīdāre* to fear) + *-ābilis* -ABLE] **—for′mi·da·ble·ness, for′mi·da·bil′i·ty,** *n.* **—for′mi·da·bly,** *adv.* **—Syn. 1.** dreadful, threatening, menacing, fearful.

form·less (fôrm′lis), *adj.* lacking a definite or regular form or shape; shapeless. **—form′less·ly,** *adv.* **—form′less·ness,** *n.*

form′ let′ter, a printed or typed letter that can be sent to any number of persons, occasionally personalized by inserting the name of each recipient in the salutation.

for·mol (fôr′môl, -mōl), *n. Chem.* formalin. [formerly trademark]

For·mo·sa (fôr mō′sə), *n.* Taiwan.

Formo′sa Strait′, an arm of the Pacific between China and Taiwan, connecting the East and South China seas. Also called **Taiwan Strait.**

For·mo·sus (fôr mō′səs), *n.* A.D. c816–896, Italian ecclesiastic: pope 891–896.

for·mu·la (fôr′myə lə), *n., pl.* **-las, -lae** (-lē′), *adj.* **—n. 1.** a set form of words for indicating procedure to be followed, or for prescribed use on some ceremonial occasion. **2.** any fixed or conventional method for doing something. **3.** *Math.* a rule or principle frequently expressed in algebraic symbols. **4.** *Chem.* an expression of the constituents of a compound by symbols and figures. Cf. **empirical formula, molecular formula, structural formula. 5.** a recipe or prescription. **6.** a mixture of milk and other ingredients for feeding a baby. **7.** a formal statement of religious doctrine. **—adj. 8.** Also, **for·mu·la·ic** (fôr′myə lā′ik). made or executed according to a formula; composed of formulas; being or constituting a formula. [< L: small pattern, form, rule, method. See FORM, -ULE] **—for′mu·la′i·cal·ly,** *adv.*

for·mu·lar·ise (fôr′myə lə rīz′), *v.t.,* **-ised, -is·ing.** *Chiefly Brit.* formularize. **—for′mu·lar·i·sa′tion,** *n.* **—for′mu·lar·is′er,** *n.*

for·mu·lar·ize (fôr′myə lə rīz′), *v.t.,* **-ized, -iz·ing.** formulate. [FORMULAR(Y) + -IZE] **—for′mu·lar·i·za′tion,** *n.* **—for′mu·lar·iz′er,** *n.*

for·mu·lar·y (fôr′myə ler′ē), *n., pl.* **-lar·ies,** *adj.* **—n. 1.** a collection or system of formulas. **2.** a set form of words; formula. **3.** *Pharm.* a book listing pharmaceutical substances and formulas for making medicinal preparations. **4.** *Eccles.* a book containing prescribed forms used in the service of a church. **—adj. 5.** of or pertaining to a formula or formulas. **6.** of the nature of a formula. [< MF *formulaire*]

for·mu·late (fôr′myə lāt′), *v.t.,* **-lat·ed, -lat·ing. 1.** to express in precise form; state definitely or systematically. **2.** to devise or develop, as a method, system, etc. **3.** to reduce to or express in a formula. **—for·mu·la·ble** (fôr′myə lə bəl), *adj.* **—for′mu·la′tion,** *n.* **—for′mu·la′tor,** *n.*

for·mu·lise (fôr′myə līz′), *v.t.,* **-lised, -lis·ing.** *Chiefly Brit.* formulize. **—for′mu·li·sa′tion,** *n.* **—for′mu·lis′er,** *n.*

for·mu·lism (fôr′myə liz′əm), *n.* **1.** adherence to or reliance on formulas. **2.** a system of formulas. **—for′mu·list,** *n.* **—for′mu·lis′tic,** *adj.*

for·mu·lize (fôr′myə līz′), *v.t.,* **-lized, -liz·ing.** formulate. Also, *esp. Brit.,* **formulise. —for′mu·li·za′tion,** *n.* **—for′mu·liz′er,** *n.*

for′myl group′, *Chem., Biochem.* the univalent group, O–CH–, derived from formic acid. Also, **for′myl rad′ical.** [FORM(IC) + -YL] **—for·myl** (fôr′mil), *adj.*

for·ni·cate¹ (fôr′nə kāt′), *v.i.,* **-cat·ed, -cat·ing.** to commit fornication. [< LL *fornicāt(us)* (ptp. of *fornicārī*) = L *fornic-* (s. of *fornix*) arch, vault, basement, brothel + *-ātus* -ATE¹] **—for′ni·ca′tor,** *n.*

for·ni·cate² (fôr′nə kit, -kāt′), *adj. Biol.* arched or vaulted in form. Also, **for′ni·cat′ed.** [< L *fornicāt(us)* = *fornic-* (see FORNICATE¹) + *-ātus* -ATE¹]

for·ni·ca·tion (fôr′nə kā′shən), *n.* **1.** voluntary sexual intercourse between two unmarried persons or two persons not married to each other. **2.** *Bible.* **a.** adultery. **b.** idolatry. [ME *fornicacioun* < LL *fornicātiōn-* (s. of *fornicātiō*)] **—for·ni·ca·to·ry** (fôr′nə kə tôr′ē, -tōr′ē), *adj.*

for·nix (fôr′niks), *n., pl.* **-ni·ces** (-ni sēz′). *Anat.* any of various arched or vaulted structures, as an arching fibrous formation in the brain. [< L: vault, arch] **—for′ni·cal,** *adj.*

For·rest (fôr′ist, for′-), *n.* **1. Edwin,** 1806–72, U.S. actor. **2. Nathan Bedford,** 1821–77, Confederate cavalry general in the U.S. Civil War.

for·sake (fôr sāk′), *v.t.*, **-sook, -sak·en, -sak·ing. 1.** to quit or leave entirely; desert. **2.** to give up or renounce (a habit, way of life, etc.). [ME *forsake(n)* (to) deny, reject, OE *forsacan* = *for-* FOR- + *sacan* to dispute] **—for·sak′er,** *n.* **—Syn. 1.** See **desert**[2]. **2.** forswear, relinquish, forgo.

for·sa·ken (fôr sā′kən), *v.* **1.** pp. of **forsake.** **—***adj.* **2.** deserted; abandoned; forlorn: *an old, forsaken farmhouse.* **—for·sak′en·ly,** *adv.* **—for·sak′en·ness,** *n.*

for·sook (fôr so͝ok′), *v.* a pt. of **forsake.**

for·sooth (fôr so͞oth′), *adv.* *Archaic.* in truth; in fact; indeed. [ME *forsothe,* OE *forsōth*]

for·spent (fôr spent′), *adj.* *Archaic.* exhausted. Also, **forespent.** [ptp. of ME *forspend(en),* OE *forspendan*]

For·ster (fôr′stər), *n.* **E(dward) M(organ),** 1879–1970, English novelist.

for·ster·ite (fôr′stə rīt′), *n.* *Mineral.* the magnesium end member, Mg_2SiO_4, of the olivine group. [named after J. R. *Forster* (1729–98), German naturalist; see -ITE[1]]

for·swear (fôr swâr′), *v.*, **-swore, -sworn, -swear·ing.** **—***v.t.* **1.** to reject or renounce upon oath or with protestations: *to forswear an injurious habit.* **2.** to deny vehemently or upon oath. **3.** to perjure (oneself). **—***v.i.* **4.** to swear falsely; commit perjury. [ME *forswere(n),* OE *forswerian*]

for·sworn (fôr swōrn′, -swôrn′), *v.* **1.** pp. of **forswear.** **—***adj.* **2.** perjured. **—for·sworn′ness,** *n.*

for·syth·i·a (fôr sith′ē ə, -sī′thē ə, fər-), *n.* any oleaceous shrub of the genus *Forsythia,* species of which are much cultivated for their showy yellow flowers. [named after William *Forsyth* (1737–1804), English horticulturist; see -IA]

fort (fōrt, fôrt), *n.* **1.** a strong or fortified place occupied by troops and usually surrounded by walls, ditches, and other defensive works; fortress. **2.** (in North America) a trading post. [< MF, n. use of adj. *fort* strong < L *fort(is)*]

fort., 1. fortification. **2.** fortified.

For·ta·le·za (fôr′tᵊlā′zə; *Port.* fôʀ′tə le′zə), *n.* a seaport in NE Brazil. 520,175. Also called **Ceará.**

for·ta·lice (fôr′tᵊlis), *n.* **1.** a small fort; an outwork. **2.** *Obs.* a fortress. [ME < ML *fortalitia, fortalitium.* See FORTRESS; cf. OF *fortalece*]

For·tas (fôr′təs), *n.* **Abe,** 1910–82, U.S. lawyer, government official, and jurist: associate justice of the U.S. Supreme Court 1965–69.

Fort′ Ben′ning (ben′ing), a town in W Georgia. 27,495 (1970).

Fort′ Bragg′, a town in S North Carolina. 46,995 (1970).

Fort′ Col′lins, a city in N Colorado. 43,337 (1970).

Fort′ Dear′born, a former U.S. fort on the site of Chicago, 1803–37.

Fort-de-France (fôʀ də fʀäɴs′), *n.* a seaport in and the capital of Martinique, in the French West Indies. 97,000 (est. 1970).

Fort′ Dix′, a town in central New Jersey. 26,290 (1970).

Fort′ Dodge′, a city in central Iowa, on the Des Moines River. 31,263 (1970).

Fort′ Don′elson, a Confederate fort in NW Tennessee, on the Cumberland River: captured by Union forces in 1862.

Fort′ Duquesne′, a French fort that stood on the site of Pittsburgh, Pennsylvania: captured in 1758 by the British in the French and Indian War.

forte[1] (fōrt, fôrt), *n.* **1.** a strong point, as of a person; that in which one excels. **2.** the stronger part of a sword blade, between the middle and the hilt (opposed to *foible*). [earlier *fort;* see FORT]

for·te[2] (fôr′tā; *It.* fôʀ′te), *Music.* **—***adj.* **1.** (a direction) loud; with force (opposed to *piano*). **—***adv.* **2.** (a direction) loudly. **—***n.* **3.** a passage that is loud and forcible, or is intended to be so. [< It < L *fortis* strong]

for·te-pi·a·no (fôr′tā pē ä′nō; *It.* fôʀ′te pyä′nô), *adj., adv.* *Music.* loud and immediately soft.

forth (fōrth, fôrth), *adv.* **1.** forward; onward or outward in place or space. **2.** onward in time, in order, or in a series: *from that day forth.* **3.** out, as from concealment or inaction; into view or consideration. **4.** away, as from a place or country; abroad: *to journey forth.* **—***prep.* **5.** *Archaic.* out of; forth from. [ME, OE; c. G *fort;* akin to FURTHER]

Forth (fōrth, fôrth), *n.* **1.** a river in S Scotland, flowing E into the Firth of Forth. 66 mi. long. **2. Firth of,** an arm of the North Sea, in SE Scotland: the estuary of the Forth River. 48 mi. long.

forth·com·ing (fōrth′kum′ing, fôrth′-), *adj.* **1.** coming forth, or about to come forth; about to appear; approaching in time. **2.** ready or available when needed or expected. **—***n.* **3.** a coming forth; appearance. **—forth′com′ing·ness,** *n.*

Fort′ Hen′ry, a Confederate fort in NW Tennessee, on the Tennessee River: captured by Union forces in 1862.

Fort′ Hood′, a town in central Texas, near Waco. 32,597 (1970).

forth·right (*adj., n.* fōrth′rīt′, fôrth′-; *adv.* fōrth′rīt′, fōrth′-, fōrth′rīt′, fôrth′-), *adj.* **1.** going straight to the point; outspoken. **2.** proceeding in a straight course; direct; straightforward. **—***adv.* Also, **forth′right′ly. 3.** straight or directly forward; in a direct or straightforward manner: *He told us forthright just what his objections were.* **4.** straightway; at once; immediately. **—***n.* **5.** *Archaic.* a straight course or path. [ME; OE *forthrihte*] **—forth′right′ness,** *n.*

forth·with (fōrth′with′, -with′, fôrth′-), *adv.* immediately; at once; without delay. [ME]

for·ti·eth (fôr′tē ith), *adj.* **1.** next after the thirty-ninth; being the ordinal number for 40. **2.** being one of 40 equal parts. **—***n.* **3.** a fortieth part, esp. of one (1/40). **4.** the fortieth member of a series. [ME *fourtithe,* OE *fēowertigotha*]

for·ti·fi·ca·tion (fôr′tə fə kā′shən), *n.* **1.** act of fortifying or strengthening. **2.** something that fortifies or protects. **3.** the art or science of building defensive military works. **4.** Often, **fortifications.** military works constructed for the purpose of strengthening a position; a fort. **5.** strengthening, as by the addition of or by intensification with another ingredient: *the fortification of wine with alcohol.* [late ME < LL *fortificātiōn-* (s. of *fortificātiō*) = *fortificāt(us)* fortified (see FORTIFY, -ATE[1]) + *-iōn-* -ION] **—Syn. 4.** fortress, citadel.

for′tified wine′, a wine, as port, sherry, or the like, to which brandy has been added to arrest fermentation or to increase the alcoholic content to between 16 and 23 percent.

for·ti·fy (fôr′tə fī′), *v.*, **-fied, -fy·ing.** **—***v.t.* **1.** to strengthen against attack; surround with defenses; provide with defensive military works; protect with fortifications. **2.** to furnish with a means of resisting force or standing strain, wear, etc. **3.** to make strong; impart strength or vigor to, as the body. **4.** to increase the effectiveness of (something), as by additional ingredients. **5.** to strengthen mentally or morally. **6.** to confirm or corroborate. **7.** to add alcohol to (wines or the like). **—***v.i.* **8.** to set up defensive works; erect fortifications. [ME *fortifie(n)* < MF *fortifie(r)* < LL *fortificāre*] **—for′ti·fi′a·ble,** *adj.* **—for′ti·fi′er,** *n.* **—for′ti·fy′ing·ly,** *adv.*

for·tis (fôr′tis), *adj., n., pl.* **-tes** (-tēz). *Phonet.* **—***adj.* **1.** pronounced with considerable muscular tension and breath pressure, resulting in a strong fricative or explosive sound: *p* and *t* are fortis as compared with *b* and *d* which are lenis. Cf. **lenis** (def. 1). **—***n.* **2.** a fortis consonant. [< L: strong, powerful, firm]

for·tis·si·mo (fôr tis′ə mō′; *It.* fôʀ tēs′sē mô′), *Music.* **—***adj.* **1.** (a direction) very loud. **—***adv.* **2.** (a direction) very loudly. [< It; superl. of FORTE[2]]

for·ti·tude (fôr′ti to͞od′, -tyo͞od′), *n.* patient courage under affliction, privation, or temptation; moral strength or endurance. [< L *fortitūdō* strength, firmness, courage] **—Syn.** See **patience.**

for·ti·tu·di·nous (fôr′ti to͞od′ᵊnəs, -tyo͞od′-), *adj.* having fortitude; marked by bravery or courage. [< L *fortitūdin-* (s. of *fortitūdō*) FORTITUDE + -OUS]

Fort′ Jef′ferson, a national monument in Dry Tortugas, Florida: a federal prison 1863–73; now a marine museum.

Fort′ Kear′ney, a former fort in S Nebraska, near Kearney: an important post on the Oregon Trail.

Fort′ Knox′, 1. a military reservation in N Kentucky, SSW of Louisville: location of U.S. federal gold depository. **2.** a town in N Kentucky, near this reservation. 37,608 (1970).

Fort-La·my (*Fr.* fôʀ lȧ mē′), *n.* former name of **N'Djamena.**

Fort′ Lar′amie, a former U.S. fort in SE Wyoming: important post on the Oregon Trail.

Fort′ Lau′der·dale (lô′dər dāl′), a city in SE Florida: seashore resort. 139,590 (1970).

Fort′ Lee′, a city in NE New Jersey. 30,631 (1970).

Fort′ Leon′ard Wood′, a town in central Missouri. 33,799 (1970).

Fort′ Lew′is, a town in W Washington, SW of Tacoma. 38,054 (1970).

Fort′ McHen′ry, a fort in N Maryland, at the entrance to Baltimore harbor: during its bombardment by the British in 1814, Francis Scott Key wrote *The Star-Spangled Banner.*

Fort′ Mims′, a stockade in SW Alabama, near the junction of the Alabama and Tombigbee rivers: Indian massacre, 1813.

Fort′ Moul′trie (mo͞ol′trē), a fort in the harbor of Charleston, South Carolina: defended against the British in the American Revolution; played an important role in the bombardment of Fort Sumter and in Confederate defense during the Civil War.

Fort′ My′ers, a city on the W coast of Florida. 27,351 (1970).

fort·night (fôrt′nīt′, -nit), *n.* the space of fourteen nights and days; two weeks. [ME *fourtenight,* contr. of OE *fēowertēne niht*]

fort·night·ly (fôrt′nīt′lē), *adj., adv., n., pl.* **-lies.** **—***adj.* **1.** occurring or appearing once a fortnight. **—***adv.* **2.** once a fortnight. **—***n.* **3.** a periodical issued every two weeks.

Fort′ Or′ange, a former Dutch fort on the site of Albany, New York.

Fort′ Pick′ens, a fort in NW Florida, at the entrance to Pensacola Bay: occupied by Union forces throughout the Civil War.

Fort′ Pierce′, a city on the E coast of Florida. 29,721 (1970).

Fort′ Pulas′ki, a fort in E Georgia, at the mouth of the Savannah River: captured by Union forces in 1862; now a national monument.

FORTRAN (fôr′tran), *n.* *Computer Technol.* a coding system using mathematical notation for programming scientific problems to be solved by a computer. [*for(mula) tran(slation)*]

for·tress (fôr′tris), *n.* **1.** a large fortified place; a fort or group of forts, often including a town. **2.** any place of security. **—***v.t.* **3.** to furnish with or defend by a fortress. [ME *forteresse* < OF < VL **fortaricia* (cf. ML *fortalitia*) = L *fort(is)* strong + *-ar-* of uncertain value + *-icia* -ICE]

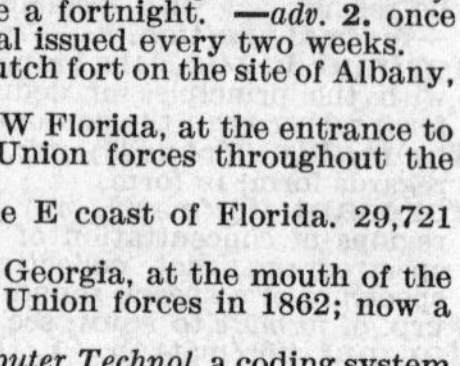

Fort′ Smith′, a city in W Arkansas, on the Arkansas River. 62,802 (1970).

Fort′ Sum′ter, a fort in SE South Carolina, in the harbor of Charleston: its bombardment by the Confederates opened the Civil War on April 12, 1861.

for·tu·i·tism (fôr to͞o′i tiz′əm, -tyo͞o′-), *n.* *Philos.* the doctrine or belief that adaptations in nature come about by chance, not by design. **—for·tu′i·tist,** *n., adj.*

for·tu·i·tous (fôr to͞o′i təs, -tyo͞o′-), *adj.* **1.** happening or produced by chance; accidental: *a fortuitous encounter.* **2.** lucky; fortunate: *a series of fortuitous circumstances that advanced her career.* [< L *fortuit(us),* irreg. < *forte* by chance (abl. of *fors* chance) + -OUS] **—for·tu′i·tous·ly,** *adv.* **—for·tu′i·tous·ness,** *n.* **—Syn. 1.** incidental. See **accidental.**

for·tu·i·ty (fôr to͞o′i tē, -tyo͞o′-), *n., pl.* **-ties** for 2, 3. **1.** the state or fact of being fortuitous; fortuitous character. **2.** accident or chance. **3.** an accidental occurrence.

For·tu·na (fôr to͞o′nə, -tyo͞o′-), *n.* the ancient Roman goddess of Fortune, identified with the Greek goddess Tyche.

for·tu·nate (fôr′chə nit), *adj.* **1.** having good fortune; receiving good from uncertain or unexpected sources; lucky. **2.** bringing or indicating good fortune; resulting favorably.

[ME *fortunat* < L *fortūnāt(us)* made prosperous or happy (ptp. of *fortūnāre*)] **—for′tu·nate·ly,** *adv.* **—for′tu·nate·ness,** *n.*
—Syn. 1. advantageous, successful, prosperous. FORTUNATE, HAPPY, LUCKY refer to persons who enjoy, or events that produce, good fortune. FORTUNATE implies that the success is obtained by the operation of favorable circumstances more than by direct effort; it is usually applied to grave or large matters (esp. those happening in the ordinary course of things): *fortunate in one's choice of a wife; a fortunate investment.* HAPPY emphasizes a pleasant ending or something which happens by chance at just the right moment: *By a happy accident I received the package on time.* LUCKY is applied to situations of minor import that turn out well by chance: *lucky at cards; my lucky day.* **2.** propitious, favorable.

for·tune (fôr′chən), *n., v.,* **-tuned, -tun·ing.** **—***n.* **1.** position in life as determined by wealth. **2.** amount or stock of wealth. **3.** great wealth; ample stock of wealth. **4.** chance; luck. **5.** Often, **fortunes.** something that happens or is to happen to a person in his life or in some particular incident. **6.** lot; destiny. **7.** (*cap.*) chance personified, commonly regarded as a goddess distributing arbitrarily or capriciously the lots of life. **8.** good luck; success; prosperity. **9.** *Archaic.* a woman of wealth; an heiress. **10. tell someone's fortune,** to profess to inform someone of future events in his own life; foretell. **—***v.t.* **11.** *Archaic.* to endow (someone or something) with a fortune. **—***v.i.* **12.** *Archaic.* to chance or happen; come by chance. [ME < OF < L *fortūna* chance, luck, fortune < *fort-* (s. of *fors*) chance] **—for′tune·less,** *adj.*

for′tune cook′ie, a thin wafer folded several times, containing a fortune or maxim on a slip of paper.

for′tune hunt′er, a person who hopes to gain wealth, esp. through marriage. **—for′tune-hunt′ing,** *adj., n.*

for·tune·tell·er (fôr′chən tel′ər), *n.* a person who professes to predict the future.

Fort′ Wayne′, a city in NE Indiana. 178,021 (1970).

Fort′ Wil′liam, a port in S Ontario, in S Canada, on Lake Superior. 45,214 (1961).

Fort′ Worth′, a city in N Texas. 393,476 (1970).

for·ty (fôr′tē), *n., pl.* **-ties,** *adj.* **—***n.* **1.** a cardinal number, ten times four. **2.** a symbol for this number, as 40 or XL or XXXX. **3.** a set of this many persons or things. **4. forties,** the numbers, years, degrees, or the like, between 40 and 49, as in referring to numbered streets, indicating the years of a lifetime or of a century, or degrees of temperature. **—***adj.* **5.** amounting to 40 in number. [ME *fourti,* OE *fēowertig* (c. OFris *fiuwertich,* OHG *fiorzug,* G *vierzig*)]

.45 (fôr′tē fīv′), *n., pl.* **.45s, .45's,** *adj.* **—***n.* **1.** a pistol or revolver cartridge having a diameter of .45 inch. **2.** a pistol or revolver using such a cartridge. **—***adj.* **3.** of, pertaining to, or using such a cartridge. **4.** of or pertaining to a pistol or revolver using such a cartridge.

for·ty-nin·er (fôr′tē nī′nər), *n.* a person who went to California in 1849 during the gold rush.

for′ty winks′, *Informal.* a short nap.

fo·rum (fōr′əm, fôr′əm), *n., pl.* **fo·rums, fo·ra** (fōr′ə, fôr′ə). **1.** the market place or public square of an ancient Roman city, the center of judicial and business affairs and a place of assembly for the people. **2.** a court or tribunal. **3.** an assembly for the discussion of questions of public interest. **4.** an outlet for discussion of matters of interest to a given group, as a periodical publication or a radio show. **5. the Forum,** the forum in the ancient city of Rome. [< L: an outside space, market place, public place, akin to *foris, foras* outside, *foris, fores* door]

for·ward (fôr′wərd), *adv.* Also, **forwards. 1.** toward or at a place, point, or time in advance; onward; ahead: *to move forward.* **2.** toward the front. **3.** out; forth; into view or consideration: *to come forward; to bring forward.* **4.** toward the bow or front of a vessel or aircraft. **5.** ahead (def. 5). **—***adj.* **6.** directed toward a point in advance; moving ahead; onward: *a forward motion.* **7.** being in a condition of advancement; well-advanced. **8.** ready, prompt, or eager. **9.** presumptuous, impertinent, or bold. **10.** situated in the front or forepart. **11.** lying ahead or to the front: *Take the forward path.* **12.** of or pertaining to the future: *forward buying.* **13.** radical or extreme, as persons or opinions. **—***n.* **14.** *Sports.* **a.** a player stationed in advance of others on his team. **b.** *Football.* a lineman. **c.** *Basketball.* either of two players stationed in the forecourt. **—***v.t.* **15.** to send forward; transmit, esp. to a new address: *to forward a letter.* **16.** to advance or help onward; hasten; promote. **17.** *Bookbinding.* to prepare (a book) for the finisher. Cf. **forwarding** (def. 1). [ME; OE *for(e)weard*] **—for′ward·ly,** *adv.*
—Syn. 1. FORWARD, ONWARD both indicate a direction toward the front or a movement in a frontward direction. FORWARD applies to any movement toward what is or is conceived to be the front or a goal: *to face forward; to move forward in the aisles.* ONWARD applies to any movement in continuance of a course: *to march onward toward a goal.* **9.** assuming, impudent. See **bold. 12.** early, preliminary, future, premature. **13.** progressive. **16.** further, foster. **—Ant. 6.** backward.

for·ward·er (fôr′wər dər), *n.* **1.** a person who forwards or sends forward. **2.** See **freight forwarder.**

for·ward·ing (fôr′wər diŋ), *n.* **1.** *Bookbinding.* a stage in which sections of a book are stitched, fitted with a back, pasted, etc., before being placed in the completed cover. **2.** *Engraving.* the process of starting a copper plate by etching and finishing with a graver.

for′warding a′gent. See **freight forwarder.**

for·ward-look·ing (fôr′wərd lo͝ok′iŋ), *adj.* planned with a view to the future; progressive.

for·ward·ness (fôr′wərd nis), *n.* **1.** overreadiness to push oneself forward; presumption; boldness; lack of due modesty. **2.** cheerful readiness; promptness; eagerness. **3.** condition of being forward or in advance.

for′ward pass′, *Football.* a pass in which the ball is thrown toward the opponent's goal.

for·wards (fôr′wərdz), *adv.* forward.

for·went (fôr went′), *v.* pt. of **forgo.**

for·why (fôr hwī′, -wī′), *Archaic.* **—***adv.* **1.** why; wherefore. **—***conj.* **2.** because. [ME; OE *for hwī*]

for·worn (fôr wōrn′, -wôrn′), *adj.* *Archaic.* worn-out; exhausted. Also, **foreworn.** [ptp. of obs. *forwear,* ME *forwere(n)*]

for·zan·do (fôrt sän′dō; *It.* fôr tsän′dô), *adj., adv.* *Music.* sforzando.

F.O.S., 1. free on station. **2.** free on steamer. Also, **f.o.s.**

Fos·dick (foz′dik), *n.* **Harry Emerson,** 1878–1969, U.S. preacher and author.

Fosh·an (fush′än′), *n.* Nanhai.

fos·sa (fos′ə), *n., pl.* **fos·sae** (fos′ē). *Anat.* a pit, cavity, or depression, as in a bone. [< L: ditch, trench, fosse, short for *fossa (terra)* dug or dug out (earth), n. use of fem. of *fossus,* ptp. of *fodere* to dig]

fosse (fos, fôs), *n.* **1.** a moat or defensive ditch in a fortification, usually filled with water. **2.** any ditch, trench, or canal. Also, **foss.** [ME < MF < L *fossa* FOSSA]

fos·sette (fo set′, fô-), *n.* a small hollow or depression, as in a bivalve shell; a dimple. [< F: dimple, small cavity]

fos·sick (fos′ik), *Australian.* **—***v.i.* **1.** to search for any object by which to make gain: *to fossick for clients.* **—***v.t.* **2.** to hunt; seek; ferret out. [cf. dial. *fossick* troublesome person, *fussick* to bustle about, appar. FUSS + *-ick,* var. of -OCK] **—fos′sick·er,** *n.*

fos·sil (fos′əl), *n.* **1.** any remains, impression, or trace of an animal or plant of a former geological age, as a skeleton, footprint, etc. **2.** *Informal.* an outdated or old-fashioned person or thing. **3.** *Obs.* anything dug out of the earth. **—***adj.* **4.** of the nature of a fossil: *fossil insects.* **5.** dug out of the earth; obtained by digging: *fossil fuel.* **6.** belonging to a past epoch or discarded system; fossilized; antiquated: *a fossil approach to teaching.* [< L *fossil(is)* dug up (cf. *fodere* to dig); r. earlier *fossile* < F] **—fos′sil·like′,** *adj.*

fos′sil fu′el, a naturally occurring fuel, as petroleum, coal, or natural gas, formed from the remains of prehistoric organisms.

fos·sil·if·er·ous (fos′ə lif′ər əs), *adj.* bearing or containing fossils, as rocks or strata.

fos·sil·ise (fos′ə līz′), *v.t., v.i.,* **-ised, -is·ing.** *Chiefly Brit.* fossilize. **—fos′sil·is′a·ble,** *adj.* **—fos′sil·i·sa′tion,** *n.*

fos·sil·ize (fos′ə līz′), *v.,* **-ized, -iz·ing.** **—***v.t.* **1.** *Geol.* to convert into a fossil; replace organic with mineral substances in the remains of an organism. **2.** to change as if into mere lifeless remains or traces of the past. **3.** to make rigidly antiquated, as persons, ideas, etc. **—***v.i.* **4.** to become a fossil or fossillike. **—fos′sil·iz′a·ble,** *adj.* **—fos′sil·i·za′tion,** *n.*

fos·so·ri·al (fo sōr′ē əl, -sôr′-), *adj.* *Zool.* **1.** digging or burrowing. **2.** adapted for digging, as the hands, feet, and skeleton of moles, armadillos, and aardvarks. [< ML *fossōri(us)* adapted to digging (L *fossor* digger (see FOSSA, -OR[2]) + *-ius* adj. suffix) + -AL[1]]

fos·ter (fô′stər, fos′tər), *v.t.* **1.** to promote the growth or development of; further; encourage. **2.** to bring up or rear, as a foster child. **3.** to care for or cherish. **4.** *Brit.* to place (a child) in a foster home. **5.** *Obs.* to feed or nourish. **—***adj.* **6.** giving or receiving parental care though not kin by blood or related legally: *They brought up a foster daughter.* [ME; OE *fōstor* nourishment, *fōstrian* to nourish; c. OIcel *fōstr;* akin to FOOD] **—fos′ter·er,** *n.* **—fos′ter·ing·ly,** *adv.*
—Syn. 1. forward, advance; foment. **2.** sustain, support, maintain. **3.** See **cherish. —Ant. 1.** discourage.

Fos·ter (fô′stər, fos′tər), *n.* **1. Stephen (Collins),** 1826–1864, U.S. song writer. **2. William Z(eb·u·lon)** (zeb′yə lən), 1881–1961, U.S. labor organizer: leader in the Communist party.

fos·ter·age (fô′stər ij, fos′tər-), *n.* **1.** the act of fostering or rearing another's child as one's own. **2.** the condition of being a foster child. **3.** the act or an instance of promoting or encouraging.

fos′ter child′, a child raised by someone not its own mother or father. [ME *fostercild*]

fos′ter fa′ther, a man who takes the place of a father in raising a child. [ME *foster fader,* OE *fōstorfæder*]

fos′ter home′, a household in which a child is raised by someone other than its own mother or father.

fos·ter·ling (fô′stər liŋ, fos′tər-), *n.* See **foster child.** [ME *fosterling,* OE *fōstorling*]

fos′ter moth′er, 1. a woman who takes the place of the mother in raising a child. **2.** a nurse. [ME *foster moder,* OE *fōstormōdor*]

fos′ter par′ent, a foster father or foster mother.

Foth·er·in·ghay (foth′ə riŋ gā′), *n.* a village in NE Northhamptonshire, in E England, near Peterborough: Mary, Queen of Scots, imprisoned here and executed 1587.

fou (fo͞o), *adj.* *Scot.* drunk. [ME (Scot) *fow* FULL]

Fou·cault (fo͞o kō′), *n.* **Jean Ber·nard Lé·on** (zhäN ber nar′ lā ôN′), 1819–68, French physicist.

Fouc·quet (*Fr.* fo͞o ke′), *n.* Fouquet.

fou·droy·ant (fo͞o droi′ənt; *Fr.* fo͞o drwa yäN′), *adj.* striking as with lightning; sudden and overwhelming in effect; stunning; dazzling. [< F, prp. of *foudroyer* to strike with lightning < *foudre* lightning < L *fulgur*]

fought (fôt), *v.* pt. and pp. of **fight.**

fought·en (fôt′ən), *adj.* *Archaic.* that has been the scene of fighting: *a foughten field.* [archaic ptp. of FIGHT]

foul (foul), *adj.* **1.** grossly offensive to the senses; disgustingly loathsome; noisome: *a foul smell.* **2.** charged with or characterized by offensive or noisome matter: *foul air.* **3.** filthy or dirty, as places, receptacles, clothes, etc. **4.** muddy, as a road. **5.** clogged or obstructed with foreign matter: *a foul gas jet.* **6.** unfavorable or stormy, as weather. **7.** contrary, as the wind. **8.** grossly offensive in a moral sense. **9.** abominable, wicked, or vile, as deeds, crime, slander, etc. **10.** scurrilous, profane, or obscene, as language. **11.** contrary to the rules or established usages, as of a sport or game; unfair. **12.** *Baseball.* pertaining to a foul ball or a foul line. **13.** obstructed, jammed, or entangled: *a foul anchor.* **14.** abounding in errors or in marks of correction, as a printer's proof, manuscript, or the like. **15.** *Naut.* impeding or unfavorable to navigation. **16.** *Dial.* not fair; ugly or unattractive. **17.** *Obs.* disfigured. **—***adv.* **18.** in a foul manner; vilely; unfairly. **19.** *Baseball.* into foul territory; so as to be foul. **20. fall foul or afoul of, a.** to collide with, as ships. **b.** to come into conflict with;

quarrel. **c.** to make an attack; assault. **21. run foul of,** to come into collision or controversy with.
—*n.* **22.** something that is foul. **23.** a collision or entanglement. **24.** a violation of the rules of a sport or game. **25.** *Baseball.* See **foul ball.**
—*v.t.* **26.** to make foul; defile; soil. **27.** to clog or obstruct, as a chimney or the bore of a gun. **28.** to collide with. **29.** to cause to become entangled or caught, as a rope. **30.** to defile; dishonor; disgrace. **31.** *Naut.* (of barnacles, seaweed, etc.) to cling to a hull so as to encumber it. **32.** *Baseball.* to hit (a pitch) foul.
—*v.i.* **33.** to become foul. **34.** *Naut.* to come into collision, as two boats. **35.** to become entangled or clogged: *The rope fouled.* **36.** *Sports.* to make a foul play; give a foul blow. **37.** *Baseball.* to hit a foul ball. **38. foul out, a.** *Baseball.* to be put out by hitting a foul ball caught on the fly by a player on the opposing team. **b.** *Basketball.* to be compelled to withdraw from a game for having exceeded the allowed number of fouls. **39. foul up,** *Slang.* to cause confusion or disorder; bungle; spoil. [ME *ful, foul,* OE *fūl;* c. Goth *ful(s),* Icel *ful(l),* OHG *fūl;* akin to L *pūs* pus, *pūtēre* to stink, Gk *pýon* pus] —**foul′ly,** *adv.*
—**Syn. 1.** repulsive, repellent. **2.** fetid, putrid, stinking. **3.** unclean, polluted, sullied, soiled, impure. See **dirty. 7.** adverse. **9.** base, shameful, infamous. **10.** smutty, vulgar.

fou·lard (fo͞o lärd′, fə-), *n.* a soft, lightweight silk, rayon, or cotton of plain or twill weave with printed design, for neckties, trimmings, etc. [< F < ?]

foul′ ball′, *Baseball.* **1.** a batted ball that rolls, settles, or passes outside the foul lines of the infield. **2.** a fly ball to the outfield that lands in foul territory. **3.** *Slang.* an incompetent, unlucky, or eccentric person.

fouled-up (fould′up′), *adj.* *Informal.* confused; chaotic; disorganized.

foul′ line′, 1. *Baseball.* either of the two lines connecting home plate with first and third base respectively, or their continuations to the end of the outfield. **2.** Also called **free throw line.** *Basketball.* a line on the court 15 feet from the backboard, from which foul shots are made. **3.** *Bowling.* a line that marks the limit for a fair delivery of the ball.

foul·mouthed (foul′mouthd′, -moutht′), *adj.* using obscene, profane, or scurrilous language.

foul·ness (foul′nis), *n.* **1.** the state or quality of being foul. **2.** something that is foul; foul matter; filth. **3.** wickedness. [ME; OE *fūlnes*]

foul′ play′, 1. any treacherous or unfair dealing, esp. one that involves murder. **2.** unfair conduct in a game.

fouls (foulz), *n.* (*construed as sing.*) *Vet. Pathol.* See **foot rot.**

foul′ shot′, *Basketball.* a throw from the foul line, given a player after a foul has been called against an opponent. Also called **free throw.**

foul′ tip′, *Baseball.* a pitched ball that glances off the bat and is legally caught by the catcher.

foul-up (foul′up′), *n.* *Informal.* confusion or disorder caused by inefficiency, stupidity, mechanical failure, etc.

found[1] (found), *v.* **1.** pt. and pp. of **find.** —*adj.* **2.** equipped, outfitted, or furnished: *He bought a new boat, fully found.* **3.** *Brit.* provided or furnished without additional charge, as to a tenant; included within the price, rent, etc., paid (often used postpositively): *Room to let, laundry found.* —*n.* **4.** *Brit.* something that is provided or furnished without charge, esp. meals given a domestic: *Maid wanted, good salary and found.*

found[2] (found), *v.t.* **1.** to set up or establish on a firm basis or for enduring existence: *to found a dynasty.* **2.** to lay the lowest part of, fix, or build (a structure) on a firm base or ground: *a house founded on solid rock.* **3.** to base or ground (usually fol. by *on* or *upon*): *a story founded on fact.* **4.** to provide a basis or ground for. —*v.i.* **5.** to be founded or based (usually fol. by *on* or *upon*). **6.** to base one's opinion (usually fol. by *on* or *upon*). [ME *found(en)* < OF *fond(er)* < L *fundāre* < *fund(us)* bottom, foundation]

found[3] (found), *v.t.* **1.** to melt and pour (metal, glass, etc.) into a mold. **2.** to form or make (an article) of molten material in a mold; cast. [ME *fond(en)* < MF *fondre* to melt, cast < L *fundere* to pour, melt, cast]

foun·da·tion (foun dā′shən), *n.* **1.** that on which something is founded. **2.** the basis or groundwork of anything: *the moral foundation of society.* **3.** the natural or prepared ground or base on which some structure rests. **4.** the lowest division of a building, wall, or the like, usually of masonry and partly or wholly below the surface of the ground. **5.** the act of founding, setting up, establishing, etc. **6.** the state of being founded. **7.** a donation or legacy for the support of an institution; an endowment. **8.** an endowed institution. **9.** a cosmetic, as a cream or liquid, used as a base for facial make-up. **10.** See **foundation garment. 11.** *Solitaire.* a card of given denomination on which other cards are to be added according to denomination or suit. [ME *foundacioun* < L *fundātiōn-* (s. of *fundātiō*) = *fundāt(us)* (ptp. of *fundāre* to FOUND[2]) + *-iōn-* -ION] —**foun·da′tion·al,** *adj.* —**foun·da′tion·al·ly,** *adv.* —**foun·da′tion·ar′y,** *adj.*
—**Syn. 3.** See **base**[1]. **3, 4.** footing. **5, 6.** establishment.

Founda′tion Day′, a legal holiday in Australia, the first Monday after January 25, to commemorate the landing of the British in 1788.

founda′tion gar′ment, a woman's undergarment, for supporting or shaping the body; corset. Also called **foundation.**

found·er[1] (foun′dər), *n.* a person who founds or establishes. [ME; see FOUND[2], -ER[1]]

found·er[2] (foun′dər), *v.i.* **1.** (of a ship, boat, etc.) to fill with water and sink. **2.** to fall or sink down, as buildings, ground, etc. **3.** to become wrecked; fail utterly. **4.** to stumble, break down, or go lame, as a horse. **5.** to become ill from overeating. **6.** *Vet. Pathol.* (of a horse) to suffer from laminitis. —*v.t.* **7.** to cause to founder. **8.** *Vet. Pathol.* to cause (a horse) to break down, go lame, or suffer from laminitis. [ME *foundre(n)* < MF *fondr(er)* (to) plunge to the bottom, submerge < L *fund(us)* bottom. See FOUND[2]]

found·er[3] (foun′dər), *n.* a person who founds or casts metal, glass, etc. [ME; see FOUND[3], -ER[1]]

foun·der·ous (foun′dər əs), *adj.* miry; swampy.

foun′ders' shares′, *Finance.* *Chiefly Brit.* shares of stock given to the organizers or original subscribers of a corporation.

Found′ing Fa′thers, *U.S.* **1.** the delegates to the Constitutional Convention in Philadelphia in 1787. **2.** (*l.c.*) any group of founders.

found·ling (found′ling), *n.* an infant found abandoned; a child without a parent or guardian. [ME *found(e)ling*]

found·ry (foun′drē), *n., pl.* **-ries. 1.** an establishment for producing castings in molten metal. **2.** the act or process of founding metal. **3.** the category of metal objects made by founding; castings. **4.** *Obs.* the casting of metals. [< F *fonderie*]

found′ry proof′, *Print.* a proof pulled for a final checking before printing plates are made.

found′ry type′, *Print.* type cast in individual characters for setting by hand.

fount[1] (fount), *n.* **1.** a spring of water; fountain. **2.** a source or origin. [short for FOUNTAIN]

fount[2] (fount, font), *n.* *Print. Brit.* font[2].

foun·tain (foun′tᵊn), *n.* **1.** a spring or source of water; the source or head of a stream. **2.** the source or origin of anything. **3.** a jet or stream of water (or other liquid) made by mechanical means to spout or rise from an opening or structure, as to afford water for use, or to cool the air, or to serve for ornament. **4.** a structure for discharging such a jet or a number of jets. **5.** See **soda fountain. 6.** a reservoir for a liquid to be supplied gradually or continuously, as in a fountain pen. [late ME *fontayne* < OF *fontaine* < LL *fontāna,* n. use of fem. of L *fontānus* of a spring = *font-* (s. of *fons* spring) + *-ānus* -AN] —**foun′tained,** *adj.* —**foun′tain·less,** *adj.* —**foun′tain·like′,** *adj.*

foun·tain·head (foun′tᵊn hed′), *n.* **1.** a fountain or spring from which a stream flows; the head or source of a stream. **2.** a chief source of anything.

Foun′tain of Youth′, a mythical spring, believed to cure illness and renew youth, sought in the Bahamas and Florida by Ponce de León, Narváez, DeSoto, and others.

foun′tain pen′, a pen with a reservoir that provides a continuous supply of ink to the point.

Foun′tain Val′ley, a city in SW California. 31,886 (1970).

Fou·qué (fo͞o kā′), *n.* **Frie·drich Hein·rich Karl, Baron de la Motte-** (frē′drikh hīn′rikh kärl, də lä mōt′-), 1777–1843, German romanticist: poet and novelist.

Fou·quet (*Fr.* fo͞o ke′), *n.* **1. Jean** or **Je·han** (zhäN), c1420–c80, French painter. **2. Ni·co·las** (nē kō lä′), (*Marquis de Belle-Isle*), 1615–80, French statesman. Also, **Foucquet.**

Fou·quier-Tin·ville (fo͞o kyā taN vēl′), *n.* **An·toine Quen·tin** (äN twaN′ käN taN′), 1747?–95, French revolutionist: prosecutor during the Reign of Terror.

four (fōr, fôr), *n.* **1.** a cardinal number, three plus one. **2.** a symbol of this number, 4 or IV or IIII. **3.** a set of this many persons or things. **4.** a playing card, die face, or half of a domino face with four pips. —*adj.* **5.** amounting to four in number. [ME *four, fower,* OE *fēower;* c. OHG *fior* (G *vier*), Goth *fidwor;* akin to L *quattuor,* Gk *téttares*]

4-A (fōr′ā′, fôr′-), *n.* **1.** a U.S. Selective Service classification designating a registrant who has had a specified amount of prior active service. **2.** a person so classified. Also, **IV-A.**

4-B (fōr′bē′, fôr′-), *n.* **1.** a U.S. Selective Service classification designating an official deferred by law. **2.** a person so classified. Also, **IV-B.**

four·bag·ger (fōr′bag′ər, fôr′-), *n.* *Baseball Slang.* See **home run.**

4-C (fōr′sē′, fôr′-), *n.* **1.** a U.S. Selective Service classification designating an alien not currently liable for military service. **2.** a person so classified. Also, **IV-C.**

four·chette (fo͝or shet′), *n.* **1.** *Anat.* the fold of skin that forms the posterior margin of the vulva. **2.** *Zool.* the frog of an animal's foot. [< F, dim. of *fourche* FORK]

four-cy·cle (fōr′sī′kəl, fôr′-), *adj.* noting or pertaining to an internal-combustion engine in which a complete cycle in each cylinder requires four strokes, one to draw in air or an air-fuel mixture, one to compress it, one to ignite it and do work, and one to scavenge the cylinder.

4-D (fōr′dē′, fôr′-), *n.* **1.** a U.S. Selective Service classification designating a minister of religion. **2.** a person so classified. Also, **IV-D.**

four-di·men·sion·al (fōr′di men′shə nᵊl, fôr′-), *adj.* *Math.* of a space having points, or a set having elements, that require four coordinates for their unique determination.

4-F (fōr′ef′, fôr′-), *n.* **1.** a U.S. Selective Service classification designating a person considered physically, psychologically, or morally unfit for military duty. **2.** a person so classified. Also, **IV-F.**

four′ flush′, *Poker.* a hand having four cards of one suit and one card of a different suit; an imperfect flush.

four-flush (fōr′flush′, fôr′-), *v.i.* **1.** *Poker.* to bluff on the basis of a four flush. **2.** *Informal.* to bluff.

four·flush·er (fōr′flush′ər, fôr′-), *n.* *Informal.* a person who makes pretensions that he cannot or does not bear out.

four·fold (fōr′fōld′, fôr′-), *adj.* **1.** comprising four parts or members. **2.** four times as great or as much. —*adv.* **3.** in fourfold measure. [ME *foure fald,* OE *fēowerfealdum*]

four-foot·ed (fōr′fo͝ot′id, fôr′-), *adj.* having four feet. [ME]

four′-four′ time′ (fōr′fōr′, fôr′fôr′). See **common time.**

four′ free′doms, freedom of speech and worship and freedom from want and fear: stated as U.S. goals by President Roosevelt, January 6, 1941.

four·gon (fo͝or gôN′), *n., pl.* **-gons** (-gôN′). *French.* a long covered wagon for carrying baggage, goods, military supplies, etc.; a van or tumbril.

four-hand·ed (fōr′han′did, fôr′-), *adj.* **1.** involving four hands or players, as a card game. **2.** written for four hands, as a piece of music for the piano. **3.** having four hands, or four feet adapted for use as hands; quadrumanous.

Four′-H′ Club′ (fōr′āch′, fôr′-), an organization sponsored by the U.S. Department of Agriculture, established chiefly to instruct young people of rural communities in modern farming methods. Also, **4-H Club.** [so called from the aim of the organization to improve head, heart, hands, and health] —**4-H,** *adj.* —**4-H′er,** *n.*

Four′ Hun′dred, *U.S.* the exclusive social set of a city or area. Also, **400.**

Fou·rier (fŏŏr′ē ā′, -ē ər; *Fr.* fo͞o ʀyā′), *n.* **1. Fran·çois Ma·rie Charles** (fʀäɴ swȧ′ mȧ ʀē′ s͟haʀl), 1772–1837, French socialist and writer. **2. Jean Bap·tiste Jo·seph** (zhäɴ bȧ tēst′ zhô zef′), 1768–1830, French mathematician and physicist.

Fou′rier anal′ysis, *Physics, Math.* the expression of any periodic function as a sum of sine and cosine functions. Cf. **Fourier series.** [named after J. B. J. Fourier]

Fou·ri·er·ism (fŏŏr′ē ə riz′əm), *n.* the utopian social system proposed by François Marie Charles Fourier, under which society was to be organized into phalanxes. [< F *fouriérisme;* see -ism] —**Fou′ri·er·ist, Fou·ri·er·ite** (fŏŏr′ē ə rīt′), *n.* —**Fou′ri·er·is′tic,** *adj.*

Fou′rier se′ries, *Math.* an infinite series that involves linear combinations of sines and cosines and approximates a given function on a specified domain.

four-in-hand (fōr′in hand′, fôr′-), *n.* **1.** a long necktie to be tied in a slipknot with the ends left hanging. **2.** a vehicle drawn by four horses and driven by one person. **3.** a team of four horses. —*adj.* **4.** of a four-in-hand.

four′-let·ter word′ (fōr′let′ər, fôr′-), any of a number of short words that are considered to be offensive or vulgar.

Four·nier (fŏŏr′nē ā′, fŏŏr′nē ā′; *Fr.* fo͞oʀ nyā′), *n.* **(Hen·ri) A·lain-** (äɴ ʀē′ ȧ laɴ′-), 1886–1914, French novelist.

four-o'clock (fōr′ə klok′, fôr′-), *n.* **1.** a common nyctaginaceous garden plant, *Mirabilis Jalapa,* having red, white, yellow, or variegated flowers that open in the late afternoon. **2.** a similar red-flowered plant, *M. laevis,* common in California.

four·pence (fōr′pəns, fôr′-), *n.* *Brit.* **1.** a sum of money of the value of four English pennies. **2.** a former silver coin of this value.

four·pen·ny (fōr′pen′ē, -pə nē, fôr′-), *adj.* *Carpentry.* **1.** noting a nail $1^1/_2$ inches long. **2.** noting certain fine nails $1^3/_8$ inches long. *Abbr.:* 4d

four·plex (fōr′pleks′), *adj., n.* quadplex.

four·post·er (fōr′pō′stər, fôr′-), *n.* a bed with four corner posts, as for supporting curtains, a canopy, etc.

four·ra·gère (fŏŏr′ə zhâr′; *Fr.* fo͞o ʀȧ zheʀ′), *n., pl.* **-gères** (-zhârz′; *Fr.* -zheʀ′). (in French and U.S. military use) **1.** an ornament of cord worn on the shoulder. **2.** such a cord awarded as an honorary decoration, as to members of a regiment or other unit that has received a requisite number of citations. [< F]

four·score (fōr′skōr′, fôr′skôr′), *adj.* four times twenty; eighty. [ME]

four·some (fōr′səm, fôr′-), *n.* **1.** *Golf.* **a.** a match between two pairs of players, each of whom plays his own ball. **b.** a match between two pairs of players, in which each pair plays one ball and partners stroke alternately. **2.** a company or set of four; two couples; a quartet. —*adj.* **3.** consisting of four persons, things, etc.; performed by or requiring four persons.

four·square (fōr′skwâr′, fôr′-), *adj.* **1.** consisting of four corners and four right angles; square. **2.** firm; steady; unswerving. **3.** forthright; frank; blunt. —*adv.* **4.** without equivocation; frankly; forthrightly. —*n.* **5.** a square. [ME *fouresquare*]

four·teen (fōr′tēn′, fôr′-), *n.* **1.** a cardinal number, ten plus four. **2.** a symbol for this number, as 14 or XIV. **3.** a set of this many persons or things. —*adj.* **4.** amounting to 14 in number. [ME *fourtene,* OE *fēowertēne*]

Four′teen Points′, The, a statement of the war aims of the Allies, made by President Wilson on January 8, 1918.

four·teenth (fōr′tēnth′, fôr′-), *adj.* **1.** next after the thirteenth; being the ordinal number for 14. **2.** being one of 14 equal parts. —*n.* **3.** a fourteenth part, esp. of one ($^1/_{14}$). **4.** the fourteenth member of a series. [ME *fourtenthe,* OE *fēowertēotha*]

fourth (fōrth, fôrth), *adj.* **1.** next after the third; being the ordinal number for four. **2.** being one of four equal parts. —*n.* **3.** a fourth part, esp. of one ($^1/_4$). **4.** the fourth member of a series. **5.** *Music.* **a.** a tone on the fourth degree from a given tone (counted as the first). **b.** the interval between such tones. **c.** the harmonic combination of such tones. **6.** (*cap.*) Independence Day; the Fourth of July (usually prec. by *the*). —*adv.* **7.** in the fourth place; fourthly. [ME *fourthe,* OE *fēowertha*]

fourth′ class′, (in the U.S. postal system) the class of mail consisting of merchandise exceeding 16 ounces and all other matter 8 ounces or over that is not sealed.

fourth-class (fōrth′klas′, -kläs′, fôrth′-), *adj.* **1.** of, pertaining to, or designated as a class next below third, as for mailing, shipping, etc. —*adv.* **2.** as fourth-class matter; by fourth-class mail.

fourth′ dimen′sion, the dimension of time, required in addition to three spatial dimensions, to locate a point in space-time. —**fourth′-di·men′sion·al,** *adj.*

fourth′ estate′, (*often caps.*) **1.** a group other than the usual powers, as the three estates of France, that wields influence in the politics of a country. **2.** the journalistic profession or its members; the press.

Fourth′ Interna′tional, a loose federation of small groups of radical socialists formed in 1936 under the leadership of Leon Trotsky and hostile to the Soviet Union. Cf. **international** (def. 5).

fourth·ly (fōrth′lē, fôrth′-), *adv.* in the fourth place; fourth.

Fourth′ of July′. See **Independence Day.**

Fourth′ Repub′lic, the republic established in France, 1946–58.

four-way (fōr′wā′, fôr′-), *adj.* **1.** providing access or passage in four directions. **2.** made up of four participants.

four-wheel (fōr′hwēl′, -wēl′, fôr′-), *adj.* **1.** having four wheels. **2.** functioning on or by four wheels: *a jeep with four-wheel drive.* Also, **four′-wheeled′.**

fo·ve·a (fō′vē ə), *n., pl.* **-ve·ae** (-vē ē′). *Biol.* a small pit or depression in a bone or other structure. [< L: small pit] —**fo′ve·al,** *adj.*

fo′vea cen·tra′lis (sen trā′lis), *Anat.* a small pit or depression at the back of the retina, forming the point of sharpest vision. [< NL: central fovea]

fo·ve·ate (fō′vē it, -āt′), *adj.* *Biol.* having foveae; pitted. Also, **fo′ve·at′ed.**

fo·ve·o·la (fō vē′ə lə), *n., pl.* **-lae** (-lē′). *Biol.* a small fovea; a very small pit or depression. [< NL; dim. of fovea] —**fo·ve′o·lar,** *adj.*

fo·ve·o·late (fō′vē ə lit, -lāt′), *adj.* *Biol.* having foveolae, or very small pits. Also, **fo′ve·o·lat′ed.**

fowl (foul), *n., pl.* **fowls,** (*esp. collectively*) **fowl,** *v.* —*n.* **1.** the domestic or barnyard hen or rooster; a chicken. Cf. **domestic fowl. 2.** any of several other usually gallinaceous birds as the duck, turkey, or pheasant. **3.** (in market and household use) a full-grown domestic fowl for food purposes. **4.** the flesh or meat of a domestic fowl. **5.** any bird (used chiefly in combination): *waterfowl.* —*v.i.* **6.** to hunt or take wild fowl. [ME *foul,* OE *fugol, fugel;* c. OS *fugal,* Goth *fugl(s),* OHG *fogal* (G *Vogel*)]

fowl′ chol′era, *Vet. Pathol.* a specific, acute, diarrheal disease of fowls, esp. chickens, caused by a bacterium, *Pasteurella multocida.*

fowl·er (fou′lər), *n.* a hunter of birds. [ME *foweler,* OE *fughelere*]

Fow·ler (fou′lər), *n.* **1. Henry H(am·ill)** (ham′əl), born 1908, U.S. lawyer and government official: Secretary of the Treasury 1965–68. **2. Henry Watson,** 1858–1933, English lexicographer.

Fow·liang (fo͞o′lyäng′, fō′-), *n.* a city in NE Kiangsi, in E China: known for manufacture of fine porcelain. 87,000 (1948). Formerly, **Kingtehchen.**

fowl·ing (fou′ling), *n.* the practice or sport of shooting or snaring birds. [ME *foulynge*]

fowl′ing piece′, a shotgun for shooting wild fowl.

fowl′ pox′, *Vet. Pathol.* a virus disease of chickens and other birds characterized by warty excrescences on the comb and wattles, and often by diphtherialike changes in the mucous membranes of the head. Also, **fowl′pox′.**

fox (foks), *n., pl.* **fox·es,** (*esp. collectively*) **fox,** *v.* —*n.* **1.** any of several carnivores of the dog family, esp. those of the genus *Vulpes,* smaller than wolves, having a pointed muzzle, erect ears, and a long, bushy tail. **2.** the fur of this animal. **3.** a cunning or crafty person. **4.** *Naut.* a length of small stuff made by hand by twisting a yarn against its lay or by twisting two or more yarns together. **5.** (*cap.*) a member of a tribe of North American Algonquian Indians merged with the Sac tribe. **6.** (*cap.*) the Algonquian language of the Fox, Sac, and Kickapoo Indians. —*v.t.* **7.** *Informal.* to deceive or trick. **8.** to repair or make (a shoe) with leather or other material applied so as to cover or form part of the upper front. **9.** *Obs.* to intoxicate or befuddle. —*v.i.* **10.** to act cunningly or craftily. **11.** (of book leaves, prints, etc.) to become stained or spotted a yellowish brown, as by age. [ME, OE; c. OS *vohs,* MLG *vos,* OHG *fuhs* (G *Fuchs*). See vixen] —**fox′like′,** *adj.*

Red fox, *Vulpes fulva* (16 in. high at shoulder; total length 4 ft.; tail 1½ ft.)

Fox (foks), *n.* **1. Charles James,** 1749–1806, British orator and statesman. **2. George,** 1624–91, English religious leader and writer: founder of the Society of Friends. **3. John.** See **Foxe, John. 4. Sir William,** 1812–1893, New Zealand statesman, born in England: prime minister 1856, 1861–1862, 1869–72, 1873.

Foxe (foks), *n.* **John,** 1516–87, English martyrologist.

fox-fire (foks′fīər′), *n.* *U.S.* **1.** organic luminescence, esp. from certain fungi on decaying wood. **2.** any of various fungi causing luminescence in decaying wood.

fox·glove (foks′gluv′), *n.* any scrophulariaceous plant of the genus *Digitalis,* esp. *D. purpurea,* of Europe, having drooping, tubular, purple or white flowers, and leaves that are used as digitalis in medicine. [ME *foxes glove,* OE *foxes glōfa*]

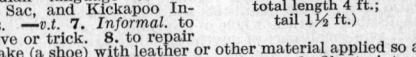

Foxglove, *Digitalis purpurea*

fox′ grape′, **1.** a grape, *Vitus Labrusca,* of the northern U.S., from which numerous cultivated varieties have been developed. **2.** the usually purplish-black, tart or sweet, musky fruit of this vine.

fox·hole (foks′hōl′), *n.* a small pit, usually for one or two men, used for cover in a battle area.

fox·hound (foks′hound′), *n.* one of any of several breeds of medium-sized hounds trained to hunt foxes and having a black-and-tan, black, tan, and white, or tan-and-white coat.

fox′ hunt′ing, a sport in which mounted hunters follow hounds in pursuit of a fox. —**fox′ hunt′er.**

Foxhound (23 in. high at shoulder)

fox·ing (fok′sing), *n.* **1.** material used to cover the upper portion of a shoe. **2.** discoloration, as of book leaves.

fox′ squir′rel, any of several North American arboreal squirrels varying in color and remarkable for large size.

fox·tail (foks′tāl′), *n.* **1.** the tail of a fox. **2.** any of various grasses having soft spikes of flowers. [ME]

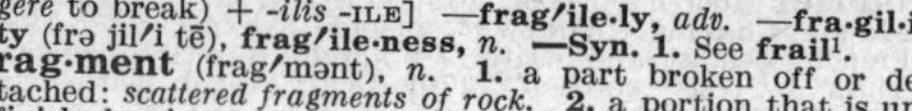

fox′ ter′rier, one of either of two English breeds of small terriers having either a long, wiry coat or a short, flat coat, formerly used for driving foxes from their holes.

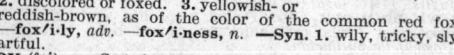

fox′ trot′, **1.** a social dance, in quadruple meter, performed by couples, characterized by various combinations of short, quick steps. **2.** a pace, as of a horse, consisting of a series of short steps, as in slackening from a trot to a walk.

Fox terrier (15 in. high at shoulder)

fox-trot (foks′trot′), *v.i.*, **-trot·ted, trot·ting.** to dance a fox trot.

fox·y (fok′sē), *adj.*, **fox·i·er, fox·i·est.** **1.** foxlike; cunning or crafty; clever. **2.** discolored or foxed. **3.** yellowish- or reddish-brown, as of the color of the common red fox. —**fox′i·ly,** *adv.* —**fox′i·ness,** *n.* —**Syn. 1.** wily, tricky, sly, artful.

foy (foi), *n. Scot.* **1.** a feast, gift, etc., given by or to a person about to start on a journey. **2.** a feast held on some special occasion, as at the end of the harvest. [< D *fooi*, *foye, voye*, ? < F *voie* way, journey]

foy·er (foi′ər, foi′ā; *Fr.* FWA yā′), *n.*, *pl.* **-ers** (-ərz, -āz; *Fr.* -yā′). **1.** the lobby of a theater or hotel. **2.** a vestibule or entrance hall in a house. [< F: fireplace, hearth (orig. a room to which theater audiences went for warmth between the acts) < VL **focār(ium)* < L *foc(us)* hearth; see -ARY]

fo·zy (fō′zē, foz′ē), *adj.*, **-zi·er, -zi·est.** *Chiefly Scot.* (of a vegetable or fruit) overripe. [cf. D *voos* spongy, LG *fussig*] —**fo′zi·ness,** *n.*

Fp, *Music.* forte-piano.

fp., **1.** fireplug. **2.** foot-pound. **3.** freezing point.

FPC, Federal Power Commission.

fpm, feet per minute. Also, **ft/min**

FPO, **1.** field post office. **2.** fleet post office.

fps, **1.** feet per second. **2.** foot-pound-second.

FR, freight release.

Fr, *Chem.* francium.

Fr., **1.** Father. **2.** *pl.* **Fr., Frs.** franc. **3.** frater. **4.** French. **5.** Friar. **6.** Friday.

fr., **1.** fragment. **2.** *pl.* **fr., frs.** franc. **3.** from.

Fra (frä), *n. Rom. Cath. Ch.* a title of address for a friar or brother. [< It, shortened form of *frate* brother, monk]

fra·cas (frā′kəs; *Brit.* frak′ä), *n.* a disorderly noise, disturbance, or fight; uproar. [< F < It *fracass(o)* < *fracassare* to smash = *fra-* (< L *infrā* among) completely + *cassare* to break; see CASSATION, QUASH[2]]

frac·tion (frak′shən), *n.* **1.** *Math.* **a.** a number usually expressed in the form *a/b*, where *a* is any real number and *b* is any real number different from 0, equal to the quotient of *a* divided by *b*; the ratio between any two numbers. **b.** a ratio of algebraic quantities similarly expressed. **2.** a part as distinct from the whole of anything; a portion or section. **3.** a very small part of anything; minute portion. **4.** a very small amount; a little bit. **5.** a piece broken off; fragment or bit. **6.** the act of breaking. —*v.t.* **7.** to divide or break into fractions. [ME *fraccioun* < LL *frāctiōn-* (s. of *frāctiō*) a breaking (in pieces) = L *frāct(us)* (ptp. of *frangere* to break) + *-iōn-* -ION]

frac·tion·al (frak′shə nəl), *adj.* **1.** pertaining to fractions; comprising a part or the parts of a unit; constituting a fraction. **2.** comparatively small; inconsiderable or insignificant. **3.** *Chem.* of or noting a process, as distillation, crystallization, or oxidation, by which the component substances of a mixture are separated according to differences in certain of their properties, as boiling point, critical temperature, solubility, etc. Also, **frac·tion·ar·y** (frak′shə ner′ē). —**frac′tion·al·ly,** *adv.*

frac·tion·ate (frak′shə nāt′), *v.t.*, **-at·ed, -at·ing.** **1.** to separate or divide into component parts, fragments, divisions, etc. **2.** to separate (a mixture) into its ingredients or into portions having different properties, as by distillation or crystallization. **3.** to obtain by such a process. —**frac′tion·a′tion,** *n.*

frac·tion·ise (frak′shə nīz′), *v.t., v.i.*, **-ised, -is·ing.** *Chiefly Brit.* fractionize. —**frac′tion·i·sa′tion,** *n.*

frac·tion·ize (frak′shə nīz′), *v.t., v.i.*, **-ized, -iz·ing.** to divide into fractions. —**frac′tion·i·za′tion,** *n.*

frac·tious (frak′shəs), *adj.* **1.** peevish, irritable, or quarrelsome. **2.** refractory or unruly. [FRACTI(ON) + -OUS] —**frac′tious·ly,** *adv.* —**frac′tious·ness,** *n.* —**Syn. 1.** testy, petulant, snappish, touchy. **2.** stubborn, difficult. **Ant. 1.** temperate. **2.** tractable.

frac·ture (frak′chər), *n.*, *v.*, **-tured, -tur·ing.** —*n.* **1.** the breaking of a bone, cartilage, or the like, or the resulting condition. Cf. **comminuted fracture, compound fracture, greenstick fracture, simple fracture.** **2.** the characteristic manner of breaking: *a material of unpredictable fracture.* **3.** the characteristic appearance of a broken surface, as of a mineral. **4.** the act of breaking. **5.** the state of being broken. **6.** a break, breach, or split. —*v.t.* **7.** to break or crack. **8.** to cause or to suffer a fracture in (a bone, etc.). —*v.i.* **9.** to become fractured; break. [late ME < MF < L *frāctūra* a breach, cleft, fracture = *frāct(us)* (ptp. of *frangere* to break) + *-ūra* -URE] —**frac′tur·a·ble,** *adj.* —**frac′tur·al,** *adj.*

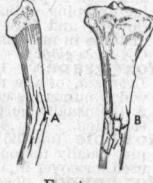

Fractures
A, Greenstick
B, Comminuted

frae (frā), *prep., adv. Scot.* from. [ME (north) *fra, frae* < ON *frā* FROM]

frae·num (frē′nəm), *n.*, *pl.* **-na** (-nə). frenum.

Fra Fi·lip·po Lip·pi (frä fi lip′ō lip′ē; *It.* FRä fē lēp′pô lēp′pē). See **Lippi, Fra Filippo.**

frag (frag), *v.t.*, **fragged, frag·ging.** *U.S. Army & Marine Corps Slang.* to injure or assault (esp. one's unpopular or overzealous superior) with a fragmentation grenade. [by shortening] —**frag′ging,** *n.*

frag·ile (fraj′əl; *Brit.* fraj′īl), *adj.* **1.** easily broken or damaged; delicate; frail. **2.** lacking in substance or force; flimsy: *a fragile excuse.* [< L *fragil(is)* = *frag-* (s. of *frangere* to break) + *-ilis* -ILE] —**frag′ile·ly,** *adv.* —**fra·gil·i·ty** (frə jil′i tē), **frag′ile·ness,** *n.* —**Syn. 1.** See **frail**[1].

frag·ment (frag′mənt), *n.* **1.** a part broken off or detached: *scattered fragments of rock.* **2.** a portion that is unfinished or incomplete: *fragments of a poem.* **3.** an odd piece, bit, or scrap. —*v.i.* **4.** to disintegrate; collapse or break into fragments. —*v.t.* **5.** to divide or break (something) into pieces or fragments. [ME < L *fragment(um)* a broken piece, remnant = *frag-* (s. of *frangere* to break) + *-mentum* -MENT]

frag·men·tal (frag men′təl), *adj.* **1.** fragmentary. **2.** *Geol.* clastic. —**frag·men′tal·ly,** *adv.*

frag·men·tar·y (frag′mən ter′ē), *adj.* consisting of or reduced to fragments; broken or incomplete. —**frag′men·tar′i·ly,** *adv.* —**frag′men·tar′i·ness,** *n.*

frag·men·ta·tion (frag′mən tā′shən), *n.* **1.** act or process of fragmenting. **2.** the state of being fragmented. **3.** the disintegration, collapse, or breakdown of norms of thought, behavior, or social relationship. —*adj.* **4.** designed to break, or equipped with a casing that shatters, into fragments on exploding: *fragmentation bombs; fragmentation grenades.*

frag·ment·ed (frag′mən tid), *adj.* **1.** reduced to fragments. **2.** disorganized or disunified: *a fragmented personality.*

frag·ment·ise (frag′mən tīz′), *v.t.*, **-ised, -is·ing.** *Chiefly Brit.* fragmentize. —**frag′ment·i·sa′tion,** *n.*

frag·ment·ize (frag′mən tīz′), *v.t.*, **-ized, -iz·ing.** to fragment. —**frag′ment·i·za′tion,** *n.*

Fra·go·nard (FRA gô NAR′), *n.* **Jean Ho·no·ré** (zhäN ô nô-RĀ′), 1732–1806, French painter.

fra·grance (frā′grəns), *n.* **1.** quality of being fragrant. **2.** a sweet or pleasing scent. [< MF < LL *frāgrantia*]

fra·gran·cy (frā′grən sē), *n.*, *pl.* **-cies.** fragrance.

fra·grant (frā′grənt), *adj.* **1.** having a pleasant odor; sweet-smelling. **2.** delightful: *fragrant memories.* [< L *frāgrant-* (s. of *frāgrāns*), prp. of *frāgrāre* to smell sweet] —**fra′grant·ly,** *adv.* —**fra′grant·ness,** *n.* —**Syn. 1.** odorous, aromatic. —**Ant. 1.** malodorous, noisome.

frail[1] (frāl), *adj.* **1.** weak; not robust; in delicate health. **2.** easily broken or destroyed; fragile. **3.** morally weak; easily tempted. [ME *frail(e), frel(e)* < OF < L *fragil(is)* FRAGILE] —**frail′ly,** *adv.* —**frail′ness,** *n.* —**Syn. 1, 2.** feeble; breakable, frangible. FRAIL, BRITTLE, FRAGILE imply a delicacy or weakness of substance or construction. FRAIL applies particularly to health, and immaterial things: *a frail constitution; frail hopes.* BRITTLE implies a hard material that snaps or breaks to pieces easily: *brittle as glass.* FRAGILE implies that the object must be handled carefully to avoid breakage or damage: *fragile bric-a-brac.* —**Ant. 1, 2.** sturdy.

frail[2] (frāl), *n.* a basket made of rushes, used esp. for dried fruits. [ME *frayel, fraelle* < OF *frayel* < ?]

frail·ty (frāl′tē), *n.*, *pl.* **-ties** for 3. **1.** the quality or state of being frail. **2.** moral weakness; liability to yield to temptation. **3.** a fault resulting from moral weakness. [ME *frailte, frelete* < OF *frailete* < L *fragilitāt-* (s. of *fragilitās*)] —**Syn. 1.** delicacy, weakness, fragility. **2.** susceptibility, suggestibility. **3.** flaw, defect.

fraise (frāz), *n. Fort.* a defense consisting of pointed stakes projecting from the ramparts in a horizontal or an inclined position. [< F < *fraise(r)* (to) frizzle, curl < Pr *frezar* << Gmc; cf. OE *frīs* curled]

Frak·tur (FRäk to͞or′), *n. Print.* German text, a style of type. [< G < L *fractūra* a breaking, FRACTURE; from the elaborate curls that break the continuity of line in a word]

fram·be·sia (fram bē′zhə), *n. Pathol.* yaws. Also, **fram·boe′sia.** [< NL, Latinization of F *framboise* raspberry]

frame (frām), *n.*, *v.*, **framed, fram·ing.** —*n.* **1.** an open border or case for enclosing a picture, mirror, etc. **2.** a rigid structure formed of relatively slender pieces, used as a major support in building or engineering works, machinery, furniture, etc. **3.** a body, esp. a human body, with reference to its size or build: *a man of unusually large frame.* **4.** a structure for admitting or enclosing something: *a window frame.* **5.** lines to enclose or set off printed matter in a newspaper, magazine, or the like; a box. **6.** Usually, **frames.** the framework for a pair of eyeglasses. **7.** any of various machines operating on or within a framework. **8.** any of various machines or parts of machines used in textile production. **9.** a particular state, as of the mind. **10.** form or structure; system; order. **11.** *Naut.* any of a number of transverse, riblike members for supporting and stiffening the shell of each side of a hull. **12.** *Baseball Slang.* an inning. **13.** *Bowling.* one of the 10 divisions of a game. **14.** *Pool.* rack[1] (def. 2). **15.** *Motion Pictures.* one of the successive small pictures on a strip of film. **16.** *Computer Technol.* a unit of computer equipment. —*v.t.* **17.** to form or make, as by fitting and uniting parts together; construct. **18.** to contrive, devise, or compose, as a plan, law, poem, etc. **19.** to conceive or imagine, as an idea. **20.** to give utterance to. **21.** to shape or adapt to a particular purpose: *to frame a reading list for ninth graders.* **22.** *Informal.* to contrive or prearrange fraudulently or falsely, as in a scheme, race, etc. **23.** *Informal.* to incriminate (an innocent person). **24.** to provide with or put into a frame, as a picture. **25.** *Obs.* to direct, as one's steps. —*v.i.* **26.** *Archaic.* to betake oneself; resort. **27.** *Archaic.* to prepare, attempt, give promise, or manage to do something. [ME *frame(n)*, OE *framian* to avail, profit; c. OIcel *frama* to further, OHG *(gi)framōn* to do] —**fram′a·ble, frame′a·ble,** *adj.* —**frame′less,** *adj.* —**fram′er,** *n.*

frame′ house′, *U.S.* a house constructed with a skeleton frame of timber, as the ordinary wooden house.

frame′ of ref′erence, *pl.* **frames of reference.** a conceptual structure to which data, ideas, etc., are related.

frame-up (frām′up′), *n. Informal.* a fraudulent incrimination of an innocent person.

frame·work (frām′wûrk′), *n.* **1.** a frame or structure composed of parts fitted and joined together. **2.** a skeletal structure designed to support or enclose something. **3.** frames collectively. **4.** work done in, on, or with a frame.

fram·ing (frā′ming), *n.* **1.** the act, process, or manner of constructing anything. **2.** the act of providing with a frame. **3.** framework; a frame or a system of frames. [late ME]

Fram·ing·ham (frā′ming ham′), *n.* a town in E Massachusetts. 64,048 (1970).

franc (frangk; *Fr.* FRäN), *n.*, *pl.* **francs** (frangks; *Fr.* FRäN). **1.** an aluminum or nickel coin and monetary unit of France, equal to 100 centimes. *Abbr.:* F., f., Fr., fr. **2.** any of the monetary units of various other nations and territories, as Belgium, Liechtenstein, Luxembourg, Martinique, Senegal, Switzerland, and Tahiti, equal to 100 centimes. **3.** the fractional currency unit of Morocco, the 100th part of the dirham. [ME *frank* < OF *franc,* so called because the coin was first inscribed with name of the king as *Rēx Francōrum* King of the Franks]

France (frans, fräns; *Fr.* fräns), *n.* **1. A·na·tole** (a na-tôl′), (pen name of *Jacques Anatole François Thibault*), 1844–1924, French novelist and essayist. **2.** a republic in W Europe. 53,000,000; 212,736 sq. mi. *Cap.:* Paris.

Fran·ces·ca (fran ches′kə, frän-; *It.* frän che′skä), *n.* **Pie·ro del·la** (pē âr′ō del′ə; *It.* pye′rô del′lä), (*Piero dei Franceschi*), c1420–92, Italian painter.

Franche-Com·té (fränsh kôn tā′), *n.* a former province in E France: once a part of Burgundy.

fran·chise (fran′chīz), *n., v.,* **-chised, -chis·ing.** —*n.* **1.** the right to vote. **2.** a privilege of a public nature conferred on an individual or body of individuals by a governmental grant. **3.** the right granted by a company to a dealer, retailer, or the like, to sell a product or service in a specified territory. **4.** the territory to which such right is restricted. **5.** a contract granted by a national or regional chain allowing one the exclusive right to operate one of their outlets within a specified area, based upon payment of an initial fee or a percentage of gross sales, usually with the parent company furnishing equipment, supplies, merchandising, and advertising. **6.** a privilege arising from the grant of a sovereign or government. **7.** *Archaic.* a legal immunity from a particular burden, exaction, etc. **8.** *Obs.* freedom, esp. from imprisonment, servitude, or moral restraint. —*v.t.* **9.** to grant (an individual, a company, etc.) a franchise. **10.** enfranchise. [ME < OF < *franc* free. See FRANK¹] —**fran·chise·ment** (fran′chiz mənt), *n.*

fran·chis·ee (fran′chī zē′), *n.* a person or group to whom a franchise is granted.

Fran·cis I (fran′sis), **1.** 1494–1547, king of France 1515–1547. **2.** 1768–1835, first emperor of Austria 1804–35; as Francis II, last emperor of Holy Roman Empire 1792–1806.

Francis II. See **Francis I** (def. 2).

Fran·cis·can (fran sis′kən), *adj.* **1.** of or pertaining to St. Francis of Assisi or the Franciscans. —*n.* **2.** a member of the mendicant order founded by St. Francis in the 13th century. [< ML *Francisc(us)* St. Francis + -AN]

Fran′cis Fer′dinand, 1863–1914, archduke of Austria whose assassination precipitated the outbreak of World War I (nephew of Francis Joseph I). German, **Franz Ferdinand.**

Fran′cis Jo′seph I, 1830–1916, emperor of Austria 1848–1916; king of Hungary 1867–1916. German, **Franz Josef.**

Fran′cis of Assi′si, Saint (*Giovanni Francesco Bernardone*), 1182?–1226, Italian friar: founder of the Franciscan order.

Fran′cis of Pau′la (pou′lä), **Saint,** 1416–1507, Italian monk: founder of order of Minims.

Fran′cis of Sales′ (sālz; *Fr.* sal), **Saint,** 1567–1622, French ecclesiastic and writer: bishop of Geneva 1602–22.

Fran′cis Xa′vier, Saint. See **Xavier, Saint Francis.**

fran·ci·um (fran′sē əm), *n. Chem.* a radioactive element of the alkali metal group. *Symbol:* Fr; *at. no.:* 87. [named after FRANCE where first identified; see -IUM]

Franck (frängk; *Fr.* fränk), *n.* **Cé·sar (Au·guste)** (sā-zar′ ō gyst′), 1822–90, French composer, born in Belgium.

Fran·co (frang′kō; *Sp.* fräng′kô), *n.* **Fran·cis·co** (fran-sis′kō; *Sp.* frän thēs′kô), (*Francisco Paulino Hermenegildo Teódulo Franco-Bahamonde*) ("*El Caudillo*"), 1892–1975, Spanish military leader and dictator: chief of state 1939–1947; regent of the kingdom of Spain 1947–75. —**Fran′-co·ism,** *n.* —**Fran′co·ist,** *n.*

Franco-, a combining form of **French** or **France:** *Francophile; Franco-Prussian.*

fran·co·lin (frang′kə lin), *n.* any of numerous Old World gallinaceous birds of the genus *Francolinus* and allied genera. [< F < It *francolino* < ?]

Fran·co·ni·a (frang kō′nē ə, -nyə, fran-), *n.* a medieval duchy in Germany, largely in the valley of the Main River.

Fran·co·ni·an (frang kō′nē ən, -nyən, fran-), *n.* **1.** a West Germanic language, consisting of Frankish and the dialects descended from Frankish. —*adj.* **2.** of, pertaining to, or characteristic of Franconia or Franconian.

Fran·co·phile (frang′kə fīl′), *adj.* **1.** friendly to or having a strong liking for France or the French. —*n.* **2.** a person who is friendly to or has a strong liking for France or the French. Also, **Fran·co·phil** (frang′kə fil). —**Fran·co·phil·i·a** (frang′kə fil′ē ə, -fēl′yə), *n.*

Fran·co·phobe (frang′kə fōb′), *adj.* **1.** fearing or hating France. —*n.* **2.** a person who fears or hates France. —**Fran′-co·pho′bi·a,** *n.*

Fran·co-Pro·ven·çal (frang′kō prō′vən säl′), *n.* a Romance dialect group of W Switzerland and neighboring parts of France: closely related to both Provençal and French.

Fran′co-Prus′sian War′ (frang′kō prush′ən), the war between France and Prussia, 1870–71.

fran·gi·ble (fran′jə bəl), *adj.* capable of being broken; breakable. [ME < OF << L *frangere* to break; see -IBLE] —**fran′gi·bil′i·ty, fran′gi·ble·ness,** *n.* —**Syn.** fragile, frail.

fran·gi·pane (fran′jə pān′), *n.* **1.** a pastry filled with cream, almonds, and sugar. **2.** frangipani. [< F; said to be named after *Frangipani* the inventor]

fran·gi·pan·i (fran′jə pan′ē, -pä′nē), *n., pl.* **-pan·is, -pan·i.** **1.** a perfume prepared from or imitating the odor of the flower of an apocynaceous tree or shrub, *Plumeria rubra,* of tropical America. **2.** the plant itself. [see FRANGIPANE]

Fran·glais (frän glā′), *n.* (*sometimes l.c.*) *French.* English words and expressions, esp. of American origin, that have become current in French. [b. F *français* and *anglais*]

frank¹ (frangk), *adj.* **1.** open or unreserved in speech; candid or outspoken; sincere. **2.** without inhibition or subterfuge; direct; undisguised: *a frank appeal to base motives.* **3.** *Archaic.* liberal or generous. **4.** *Obs.* free. —*n.* **5.** a signature or mark affixed by special privilege to a letter, package, or the like, to ensure free transmission. **6.** the privilege of franking letters, packages, etc. **7.** a franked letter, package, etc. —*v.t.* **8.** to mark (a letter, package, etc.) for free transmission; send free of charge. **9.** to convey (a person) free of charge. **10.** to enable to pass or go freely: *to frank a visitor through customs.* [ME < OF *franc* < LL *franc(us)* free, orig. FRANK] —**frank′er,** *n.*
—**Syn. 1.** free, bold, uninhibited. FRANK, CANDID, OPEN, OUTSPOKEN imply a freedom and boldness in speaking. FRANK is applied to a person unreserved in expressing the truth and his real opinions and sentiments: *a frank analysis of a personal problem.* CANDID suggests that a person is sincere and truthful or impartial and fair in judgment, sometimes unpleasantly so: *a candid expression of opinion.* OPEN implies a lack of reserve or of concealment: *open antagonism.* OUTSPOKEN applies to a person who expresses himself freely, even when this is inappropriate: *an outspoken criticism.*

frank² (frangk), *n. Informal.* frankfurter. [by shortening]

Frank (frangk), *n.* **1.** a member of a group of ancient Germanic peoples dwelling in the regions of the Rhine, one division of whom, the Salians, conquered Gaul about A.D. 500. **2.** (in the Levant) any native or inhabitant of western Europe. [ME *Franke,* OE *Franca* (c. OHG *Franko*)]

Frank·en·stein (frang′kən stīn′), *n.* **1.** a person who creates a destructive agency that he cannot control or that brings about his own ruin. **2.** Also called **Frank′enstein mon′ster.** the destructive agency itself. [after Baron *Frankenstein,* creator of a monster in *Frankenstein,* novel (1818) by Mary Shelley]

Frank·fort (frangk′fərt), *n.* **1.** a city in and the capital of Kentucky, in the N part. 21,902 (1970). **2.** See **Frankfort on the Main.**

Frank′fort on the Main′ (mān), a city in central West Germany, on the Main River. 631,000. Also called **Frankfort.** German, **Frank·furt am Main** (frängk′fŏŏrt äm mīn′), **Frank′furt.**

Frank′fort on the O′der (ō′dər), a city in E East Germany, on the Oder River. 62,000. German, **Frank·furt an der O·der** (frängk′fŏŏrt än dər ō′dər), **Frank′furt.**

frank·furt·er (frangk′fər tər), *n.* a small, smoked sausage, usually of beef and pork. Also, **frank′fort·er, frank′-fort, frank′furt.** [< G: Frankfort sausage]

Frank·furt·er (frangk′fər tər), *n.* **Felix,** 1882–1965, U.S. jurist born in Austria: associate justice of the U.S. Supreme Court 1939–62.

frank·in·cense (frang′kin sens′), *n.* an aromatic gum resin from various Asian and African trees of the genus *Boswellia,* esp. *B. Carteri,* used chiefly for burning as incense, in perfumery, and in pharmaceutical and fumigating preparations. Also called **olibanum.** [ME *fraunk encense*]

Frank·ish (frang′kish), *adj.* **1.** of or pertaining to the Franks. —*n.* **2.** the West Germanic language of the ancient Franks; Old Franconian. Cf. **Frank** (def. 1).

frank·lin (frangk′lin), *n. Eng. Hist.* (in the 14th and 15th centuries) a freeholder who was not of noble birth. [ME *fra(u)nkelin* < AF *fraunclein* (see FRANK¹, -LING¹)]

Frank·lin (frangk′lin), *n.* **1. Benjamin,** 1706–90, American statesman, diplomat, author, scientist, and inventor. **2. Sir John,** 1786–1847, English Arctic explorer. **3.** a district in extreme N Canada, in the Northwest Territories, including the Boothia and Melville peninsulas, Baffin Island, and other Arctic islands. 549,253 sq. mi.

frank·lin·ite (frangk′li-nīt′), *n.* a mineral of the spinel group, an oxide of zinc, manganese, and iron: an ore of zinc. [named after *Franklin,* New Jersey, where it is found; see -ITE¹]

Frank′lin Square′, a town on W Long Island, in SE New York. 32,156 (1970).

Frank′lin stove′, a cast-iron stove having the general form of a fireplace with enclosed top, bottom, sides, and back. [named after Benjamin FRANKLIN, who designed it]

Franklin stove

frank·ly (frangk′lē), *adv.* in a frank manner; freely; openly; unreservedly; candidly; plainly.

frank·ness (frangk′nis), *n.* plainness of speech; candor; openness.

frank·pledge (frangk′-plej′), *n. Old Eng. Law.* **1.** a system of dividing a community into tithings or groups of 10 men, each member of which was responsible for the conduct of the other members. **2.** a member of a tithing. **3.** the tithing itself. [ME *fra(u)nkplegge* < AF *fraunc-plege*]

fran·tic (fran′tik), *adj.* **1.** wild with excitement, passion, fear, pain, etc.; frenzied. **2.** *Archaic.* insane; mad. [ME *frantik, frenetik* < OF *frenetique* < L *phrenēticus* delirious < Gk *phrenētikós*] —**fran′ti·cal·ly, fran′tic·ly,** *adv.* —**fran′tic·ness,** *n.*

Franz Fer·di·nand (franz fûr′dᵊnand′; *Ger.* fränts fer′di nänt′). See **Francis Ferdinand.**

Franz Jo·sef (franz jō′səf; *Ger.* fränts yō′zef). See **Francis Joseph I.**

Franz′ Jo′sef Land′ (land; *Ger.* länt), an archipelago in the Arctic Ocean, E of Spitzbergen: belongs to the Soviet Union. Also called **Fridtjof Nansen Land.**

frap (frap), *v.t.,* **frapped, frap·ping.** *Naut.* to bind or wrap tightly with ropes or chains. [ME *frap(p)e(n)* < OF *frape(r)* (to) strike, beat, prob. < Gmc (cf. OIcel *hrapa* to hurl)]

frap·pé (fra pā′; *Fr.* fra pā′), *n., pl.* **-pés** (-pāz′; *Fr.* -pā′), *adj.* —*n.* **1.** *U.S.* a fruit juice mixture frozen to a mush. **2.** a liqueur poured over cracked or shaved ice. **3.** Also,

frappe (frap). See **milk shake.** —*adj.* **4.** chilled; iced. [< F: iced, beaten, ptp. of *frapper* to ice, strike]

Fra·ser (frā′zər), *n.* **1. John Malcolm,** born 1930, Australian political leader: prime minister 1975–83. **2.** a river in SW Canada, flowing S through British Columbia to the Pacific. 695 mi. long.

frat (frat), *n. Slang.* fraternity (def. 1). [by shortening]

fra·ter[1] (frā′tər), *n.* a brother, as in a religious or fraternal order; comrade. [< L: BROTHER]

fra·ter[2] (frā′tər), *n. Obs. Eccl. Hist.* the refectory of a religious house. [ME *frater, freitour* < OF *fraitur,* short for *refreitor* < LL *rēfectōr(ium)* REFECTORY]

fra·ter·nal (frə tûr′nəl), *adj.* **1.** of or befitting a brother or brothers; brotherly. **2.** of or being a society of men in brotherly union, as for mutual aid: *fraternal order.* [< L *frātern(us)* (*frāter* brother + *-nus* adj. suffix) + -AL[1]] —**fra·ter′nal·ism,** *n.* —**fra·ter′nal·ly,** *adv.*

frater′nal twin′, one of a pair of twins, not necessarily resembling one another, that develop from two fertilized ova. Cf. **identical twin.**

fra·ter·ni·ty (frə tûr′ni tē), *n., pl.* **-ties. 1.** *U.S.* a local or national organization of male students, primarily for social purposes, with secret initiation and rites and a name composed of two or three letters of the Greek alphabet. **2.** a group of persons associated by or as by ties of brotherhood. **3.** any group of persons having common purposes, interests, etc.: *the medical fraternity.* **4.** an organization of laymen for religious or charitable purposes. **5.** the quality of being brotherly; brotherhood: *liberty, equality, and fraternity.* **6.** the relation between brothers. [ME *fraternite* < L *frāternitās*]

frat·er·nize (frat′ər nīz′), *v.,* **-nized, -niz·ing.** —*v.i.* **1.** to associate in a fraternal way. **2.** to associate cordially or intimately with enemy troops, natives of a conquered country, etc. —*v.t.* **3.** *Rare.* to bring into fraternal association or sympathy. Also, *esp. Brit.,* **frat′er·nise′.** [< F *fraterniser* < ML *frāternizāre*] —**frat′er·ni·za′tion,** *n.* —**frat′er·niz′er,** *n.*

frat·ri·cide (fra′tri sīd′, frā′-), *n.* **1.** a person who kills his brother. **2.** the act of killing one's brother. [ME < MF < L *frātricīd(a)* (def. 1) = *frātri-* (s. of *frāter*) brother + *-cīda* a killer; LL *frātricīdium* (def. 2) < *frātricīda,* as above; see -CIDE] —**frat′ri·cid′al,** *adj.*

Frau (frou; *Eng.* frou), *n., pl.* **Frau·en** (frou′ən), *Eng.* **Fraus** (frouz). *German.* a married woman; wife; lady (often used as a term of address).

fraud (frôd), *n.* **1.** deceit, trickery, or breach of confidence, used to gain some unfair or dishonest advantage. **2.** a particular instance of such deceit or trickery: *mail fraud.* **3.** any deception or trickery. **4.** a deceitful person; impostor. [ME *fraude* < OF < L *fraud-* (s. of *fraus*) deceit, injury]

fraud·u·lent (frô′jə lənt), *adj.* **1.** given to or using fraud. **2.** characterized by or involving fraud. [ME < L *fraudulent-(us)*] —**fraud′u·len·cy,** *n.* —**fraud′u·lent·ly,** *adv.*

fraught (frôt), *adj.* **1.** involving; full of; accompanied by (usually fol. by *with*): *an undertaking fraught with danger.* **2.** *Archaic.* filled or laden (with): *ships fraught with precious wares.* —*n.* **3.** *Scot.* a load; cargo; freight (of a ship). [ME < MD or MLG *vracht* freight money, FREIGHT]

Fräu·lein (froi′līn; *Eng.* froi′līn *or, often,* frô′-, frou′-), *n., pl.* **Fräu·lein,** *Eng.* **Fräu·leins.** *German.* an unmarried woman; a young lady (often used as a term of address).

Fraun·ho·fer (froun′hō′fər, frou′ən hof′ər; *for 1 also Ger.* froun′hō′fər), *n.* **Jo·seph von** (jō′zəf von, -səf; *Ger.* yō′-zef fən), 1787–1826, German optician and physicist.

Fraun′hofer lines′, the dark lines of the solar spectrum. [named after J. VON FRAUNHOFER]

frax·i·nel·la (frak′sə nel′ə), *n.* dittany (def. 3). [< NL, dim. of L *frāxinus* ash tree]

fray[1] (frā), *n.* **1.** a noisy quarrel; fight, skirmish, or battle. **2.** *Archaic.* fright. —*v.t.* **3.** *Archaic.* to frighten. —*v.i.* **4.** *Archaic.* to fight. [ME *frai;* aph. var. of AFFRAY]

fray[2] (frā), *v.t.* **1.** to wear (cloth, rope, etc.) to loose, raveled threads or fibers at the edge or end; cause to ravel out. **2.** to wear by rubbing (sometimes fol. by *through*). **3.** to cause strain on (something); upset; discompose: *The argument frayed their nerves.* **4.** to rub. —*v.i.* **5.** to become frayed; ravel out. —*n.* **6.** a frayed part, as in cloth. [ME *fraie(n)* < OF *fray(er), frei(ier)* (to) rub < L *fricāre.* See FRICTION]

Fra·zer (frā′zər), *n.* **Sir James George,** 1854–1941, Scottish anthropologist and author.

fraz·zle (fraz′əl), *v.,* **-zled, -zling,** *n. Informal.* —*v.i., v.t.* **1.** to fray; wear to threads or shreds. **2.** to weary; tire out. —*n.* **3.** the state of being frazzled. **4.** a remnant; shred. [b. FRAY[2] and *fazzle,* ME *fasel(in)* (to) unravel, c. G *faseln*]

FRB, 1. Federal Reserve Bank. **2.** Federal Reserve Board.

freak[1] (frēk), *n.* **1.** a sudden and apparently causeless change or turn of events, the mind, etc.: *That kind of sudden storm is a freak.* **2.** any abnormal product or curiously unusual object; anomaly; aberration. **3.** a person or animal on exhibition as some strange deviation from nature; monster. **4.** *Slang.* **a.** a person who has withdrawn from normal, rational behavior and activities to pursue one interest or obsession: *a drug freak; a baseball freak.* **b.** a hippie. **5.** *Archaic.* capriciousness; whimsicality. —*adj.* **6.** unusual; odd; irregular. —*v.i., v.t.* **7.** *Slang.* to become or make uninhibited, excited, or deranged, esp. while under the influence of a drug. **8. freak out,** *Slang.* **a.** to react with wild excitement, as when under the influence of a hallucinogenic drug. **b.** to lose one's sanity, composure, or mental stability. [? akin to OE *frīcian* to dance]

freak[2] (frēk), *v.t.* **1.** to fleck, streak, or variegate, as with color. —*n.* **2.** a fleck or streak of color. [? v. use of FREAK[1]]

freak·ish (frē′kish), *adj.* **1.** given to or full of freaks; whimsical; capricious. **2.** resembling a freak; queer. —**freak′ish·ly,** *adv.* —**freak′ish·ness,** *n.*

freak-out (frēk′out′), *n. Slang.* a period or event characterized by wild excitement or loss of sanity. Also, **freak′out′.**

freak·y (frē′kē), *adj.,* **freak·i·er, freak·i·est.** freakish. —**freak′i·ly,** *adv.* —**freak′i·ness,** *n.*

freck·le (frek′əl), *n., v.,* **-led, -ling.** —*n.* **1.** a small, brownish spot on the skin, usually caused by exposure to sunlight. **2.** any small spot or discoloration. —*v.t.* **3.** to cover with freckles; produce freckles on. —*v.i.* **4.** to become freckled. [b. obs. *frecken* freckle (ME *frekne* < Scand; cf. Icel *freknur,* pl.) and SPECKLE (n.)]

freck·ly (frek′lē), *adj.,* **-li·er, -li·est.** full of freckles.

Frederick I, 1. ("*Frederick Barbarossa*") 1123?–90, emperor of the Holy Roman Empire 1152–90. **2.** 1194–1250, king of Sicily 1198–1212: as Frederick II, king of Germany and emperor of the Holy Roman Empire 1215–50. **3.** 1657–1713, king of Prussia 1701–13 (son of Frederick William).

Frederick II, 1. See **Frederick I** (def. 2). **2.** ("*Frederick the Great*") 1712–86, king of Prussia 1740–86 (son of Frederick William I).

Frederick III, 1. (*Frederick of Austria*) 1286?–1330, king of Germany 1314–26; rival king of Louis IV. **2.** 1415–93, emperor of the Holy Roman Empire and as Frederick IV king of Germany. **3.** ("*the Wise*") 1463–1525, elector of Saxony 1486–1525: protector of Martin Luther.

Fred′erick Bar·ba·ros′sa (bär′bə ros′ə). See **Frederick I** (def. 1).

Fred·er·icks·burg (fred′riks bûrg′), *n.* a city in NE Virginia, on the Rappahannock River: scene of a Confederate victory 1862. 14,450 (1970).

Fred′erick the Great′. See **Frederick II** (def. 2).

Fred′erick Wil′liam, ("*the Great Elector*") 1620–88, elector of Brandenburg who increased the power and importance of Prussia.

Frederick William I, 1688–1740, king of Prussia 1713–1740.

Frederick William II, 1744-97, king of Prussia 1786–97.

Frederick William III, 1770–1840, king of Prussia 1797–1840.

Frederick William IV, 1795–1861, king of Prussia 1840–61 (brother of William I of Prussia).

Fred·er·ic·ton (fred′ər ik tən), *n.* a city in and the capital of New Brunswick, in SE Canada. 19,683 (1961).

Fre·de·rik IX (frε′thə rεk), 1899–1972, king of Denmark 1947–72 (son of Christian X).

Fre·de·riks·berg (frε′thə rεks barkh′), *n.* a city in E Denmark: a part of Copenhagen. 114,285 (1960).

free (frē), *adj.,* **fre·er, fre·est,** *adv., v.,* **freed, free·ing.** —*adj.* **1.** enjoying personal rights or liberty, as one not in slavery: *a land of free men.* **2.** pertaining to or reserved for those who enjoy personal liberty: *They were thankful to be living on free soil.* **3.** existing under, characterized by, or possessing civil and political liberties. **4.** enjoying political independence. **5.** exempt from external authority, interference, restriction, etc.; independent; unfettered. **6.** able to do something at will; at liberty. **7.** not subject to special regulations, restrictions, duties, etc. **8.** not literal, as a translation, adaptation, or the like. **9.** not subject to rules, set forms, etc. **10.** clear of obstructions or obstacles, as a road or corridor. **11.** not occupied or in use. **12.** exempt or released from something specified that controls, restrains, burdens, etc. (usually fol. by *from* or *of*): *free from worry; free of taxes.* **13.** having immunity or being safe (usually fol. by *from*): *free from criticism.* **14.** uncombined chemically: *free oxygen.* **15.** that may be used by or is open to all: *a free market.* **16.** engaged in by all present; general: *a free fight.* **17.** unimpeded, as motion or movement. **18.** loose; not held fast; unattached. **19.** not joined to or in contact with something else. **20.** acting without self-restraint or reserve. **21.** frank and open; unconstrained or familiar. **22.** unrestrained by decency; loose or licentious. **23.** ready in giving; liberal; lavish. **24.** given readily or in profusion; unstinted. **25.** given without consideration of a return, as a gift. **26.** provided without, or not subject to, a charge or payment: *free schools.* **27.** at liberty to enter and enjoy at will. **28.** easily worked, as stone, land, etc. **29.** *Naut.* (of a wind) nearly on the quarter, so that a sailing vessel may sail free. **30.** *Phonet.* (of a vowel) situated in an open syllable (opposed to *checked*). **31.** traveling without power; under no force except that of gravity or inertia: *free flight.* **32. free and clear,** *Law.* without any encumbrance, as a lien or mortgage. **33. free and easy, a.** unrestrained; casual; informal. **b.** excessively casual; presumptuous. **34. set free,** to release; liberate. —*adv.* **35.** in a free manner; freely. **36.** without cost or charge. **37.** *Naut.* away from the wind so that the vessel need not be close-hauled: *running free.* —*v.t.* **38.** to make free; set at liberty. **39.** to exempt or deliver (usually fol. by *from*): *to free one from want.* **40.** to relieve or rid (usually fol. by *of*): *to free oneself of a burden.* **41.** to disengage; clear (usually fol. by *from* or *of*): *to free a desk of clutter.* [ME *fre,* OE *frēo;* c. Goth *frei(s),* OHG *frī* (G *frei*), D *vrij.* Skt *priyá-* dear] —**free′ness,** *n.* —**Syn. 38.** See **release.**

free′ along′side ship′. See **F.A.S.** Also called **free′ along′side ves′sel.**

free-as·so·ci·ate (frē′ə sō′shē āt′, -sē-), *v.t.,* **-at·ed, -at·ing.** to engage in free association.

free′ associa′tion, *Psychoanal.* the uncensored expression of the ideas, impressions, etc., passing through the mind of the analysand, used to facilitate access to the unconscious processes.

free·base (frē′bās′), *v.,* **-based, -bas·ing,** *n. Slang.* —*v.t., v.i.* **1.** to purify (cocaine) by dissolving in ether, sodium hydroxide, etc., and filtering off the precipitate. —*n.* **2.** the refined substance so produced.

free·bie (frē′bē), *n. Slang.* something given without charge or cost, as a theater ticket or pass. Also, **free′bee.**

free·board (frē′bôrd′, -bōrd′), *n. Naut.* **1.** (on a cargo vessel) the distance between the uppermost deck considered fully watertight and the official load line. **2.** the portion of the side of a hull that is above the water. [FREE + BOARD]

free·boot (frē′bo͞ot′), *v.i.* to act as a freebooter. [back formation from FREEBOOTER]

free·boot·er (frē′bo͞o′tər), *n.* a person who goes about in search of plunder; a pirate or buccaneer. [Anglicization of D *vrijbuiter*]

free·boot·y (frē′bo͞o′tē), *n. Obs.* plunder; loot; spoil. [FREEBOOT(ER + BOOT)Y]

free·born (frē′bôrn′), *adj.* **1.** born free, rather than in slavery, bondage, or vassalage. **2.** pertaining to or befitting persons born free. [ME *freborn, freeborn*]

free′ cit′y, a city having an independent government and forming a sovereign state by itself.

free′ coin′age, the unrestricted coinage of bullion, silver, etc., into money for any person bringing it to the mint, either with or without charge for minting.

freed·man (frēd′mən), *n., pl.* **-men.** a man who has been freed from slavery.

free·dom (frē′dəm), *n.* **1.** the state of being at liberty rather than in confinement or under physical restraint. **2.** exemption from external control, interference, regulation, etc. **3.** power of determining one's or its own action. **4.** *Philos.* the power to make one's own choices or decisions without constraint from within or without; autonomy; self-determination. **5.** civil liberty, as opposed to subjection to an arbitrary or despotic government. **6.** political or national independence. **7.** a particular privilege enjoyed, as by a city or corporation: *freedom to levy taxes.* **8.** personal liberty, as opposed to slavery. **9.** absence of or release from ties, obligations, etc. **10.** exemption or immunity from the presence of anything specified (usually fol. by *from*). **11.** ease or facility of movement or action. **12.** frankness of manner or speech. **13.** absence of ceremony or reserve. **14.** a liberty taken. **15.** the right of enjoying all the privileges or special rights of citizenship, membership, etc. **16.** the right to frequent, enjoy, or use at will. [ME *fredom,* OE *frēodōm*]
—**Syn. 1.** FREEDOM, INDEPENDENCE, LIBERTY refer to an absence of undue restrictions and an opportunity to exercise one's rights and powers. FREEDOM emphasizes the opportunity given for the exercise of one's rights, powers, desires, or the like: *freedom of speech or conscience; freedom of movement.* INDEPENDENCE implies not only lack of restrictions but also the ability to stand alone, unsustained by anything else: *Independence of thought promotes invention.* LIBERTY, though most often interchanged with FREEDOM, is also used to imply undue exercise of freedom: *He took liberties with the text.*

free′dom of speech′, the right of people to express their opinions publicly without governmental interference, subject to the laws against libel, incitement to violence or rebellion, etc. Also called **free speech.**

free′dom of the press′, the right to publish newspapers, magazines, and other printed matter without governmental restriction and subject only to the laws of libel, obscenity, sedition, etc.

free′dom of the seas′, *Internat. Law.* the doctrine that ships of neutral countries may sail anywhere on the high seas without interference by warring powers.

freed·wom·an (frēd′wo͝om′ən), *n., pl.* **-wom·en.** a woman who has been freed from slavery.

free′ en′terprise, **1.** an economic and political doctrine holding that a capitalist economy can regulate itself in a freely competitive market through the relationship of supply and demand with a minimum of governmental intervention and control. **2.** the practice of free enterprise in an economy.

free′ fall′, **1.** the fall of a body such that the only force acting upon it is that of gravity. **2.** the part of a parachute jump that precedes the opening of the parachute.

free′-fire′ zone′ (frē′fīər′), *Mil.* an area in which anyone or anything in sight can be indiscriminately shot or bombed.

free-for-all (frē′fər ôl′), *n.* a fight, argument, contest, etc., open to everyone and usually without rules.

free′ form′, **1.** *Linguistics.* a linguistic form that can occur by itself, as *fire, book, run,* etc. Cf. **bound form. 2.** a shape having an irregular contour, chiefly used in nonrepresentational art and industrial design.

free-form (frē′fôrm′), *adj.* **1.** characterized by free form: *a free-form bowl; free-form sculpture.* **2.** not organized or planned in a conventional way: *a free-form conglomerate; a free-form excursion.* **3.** spontaneous; impulsive: *free-form management.*

free′ gold′, **1.** *U.S.* treasury gold, including the legal reserve, not restricted to the redemption of gold certificates. **2.** *Mining.* gold found in a pure state in nature, as in placer mining.

free′ hand′, unrestricted freedom or authority: *They gave the decorator a free hand in doing their house.*

free·hand (frē′hand′), *adj., adv.* by hand without guiding instruments or other aids: *a freehand map.*

free-hand·ed (frē′han′did), *adj.* **1.** open-handed; generous; liberal. **2.** freehand. —*adv.* **3.** freehand. —**free′-hand′ed·ly,** *adv.* —**free′-hand′ed·ness,** *n.*

free-heart·ed (frē′här′tid), *adj.* spontaneous; frank; generous. [ME *free herted*]

free·hold (frē′hōld′), *n. Law.* **1.** a form of tenure by which an estate is held in fee simple, fee tail, or for life. **2.** an estate in land, inherited or held for life. [ME *frehold* (see FREE, HOLD[1]); trans. of AF *franc tenement*]

Free·hold (frē′hōld′), *n.* a town in E New Jersey: battle of Monmouth courthouse 1778. 10,545 (1970). Formerly, **Monmouth.**

free·hold·er (frē′hōl′dər), *n.* the owner of a freehold. [ME *freholder* (see FREE, HOLDER); trans. of AF *fraunc tenaunt* (see FRANK[1], TENANT)]

free′ lance′, **1.** a person who works as a writer, designer, etc., but not on a regular salary basis for any one employer. **2.** a person who contends in a cause without personal allegiance. **3.** a mercenary of the Middle Ages, usually a knight.

free-lance (frē′lans′, -läns′), *v.,* **-lanced, -lanc·ing,** *adj., adv.* —*v.i.* **1.** to act or work as a free lance. —*adj.* **2.** of or pertaining to a free lance or his work —*adv.* **3.** in the manner of a free lance: *She works free-lance.* —**free′-lanc′er,** *n.*

free′ list′, *Commerce U.S.* a list of duty-free goods.

free′ liv′er, a person who follows a way of life in which he freely indulges his appetites, desires, etc.

free-liv·ing (frē′liv′ing), *adj.* **1.** following a way of life in which one freely indulges his appetites, desires, etc. **2.** *Biol.* noting an organism that is neither parasitic, symbiotic, nor sessile.

free·load (frē′lōd′), *v.i. Informal.* to take advantage of others for free food, entertainment, etc. —**free′load′er,** *n.* —**free′load′ing,** *n.*

free′ love′, the doctrine or practice of having sexual relations without legal marriage or any continuing obligation.

free′ lunch′, food formerly provided without charge in some bars and saloons to attract customers.

free·ly (frē′lē), *adv.* in a free manner. [ME *freliche,* OE *frēolīce*]

free·man (frē′mən), *n., pl.* **-men. 1.** a man who is free; a man who enjoys personal, civil, or political liberty. **2.** a person who is entitled to citizenship, franchise, etc. [ME *freman,* OE *frēoman*]

free·mar·tin (frē′mär′tən), *n.* a usually sterile female calf that is born as a twin with a male. [?]

Free·ma·son (frē′mā′sən, frē′mā′-), *n.* **1.** a member of a widely distributed secret order having for its object mutual assistance and the promotion of brotherly love among its members. **2.** (*l.c.*) *Hist.* a member of a medieval society composed of skilled stoneworkers. [ME *fremason*] —**free·ma·son·ic** (frē′mə son′ik), *adj.*

free·ma·son·ry (frē′mā′sən rē), *n.* **1.** fellowship; instinctive sympathy: *the freemasonry of thinkers.* **2.** (*cap.*) the principles, practices, etc., of Freemasons. [ME *fremasonry*]

free′ on board′. See **f.o.b.**

free′ port′, **1.** a port open under equal conditions to all traders. **2.** a port not included in customs territory.

Free·port (frē′pōrt′, -pôrt′), *n.* **1.** a village on SW Long Island, in SE New York. 40,374 (1970). **2.** a city in NW Illinois. 27,736 (1970).

fre·er[1] (frē′ər), *n.* a person or thing that frees. [FREE + -ER[1]]

fre·er[2] (frē′ər), *adj.* comparative of **free.**

free′ rad′ical, *Chem.* an atom or compound in which there is an unpaired electron, as H· or ·CH_3; a group or radical.

free′ school′, a school organized as an alternative to the traditional public or private school, usually following a highly flexible approach to the curriculum and teaching methods.

free·si·a (frē′zhē ə, -zē ə, -zhə), *n.* any iridaceous plant of the genus *Freesia,* having fragrant tubular flowers. [< NL; named after E. M. *Fries* (1794–1878), Swedish botanist]

free′ sil′ver, *Econ.* the free coinage of silver, esp. at a fixed ratio with gold. —**free′-sil′ver,** *adj.*

free′ soil′, a region where slavery is forbidden, esp. such a U.S. territory before the Civil War.

Free-Soil (frē′soil′), *adj. U.S. Hist.* pertaining to or characteristic of the Free Soil party. —**Free′-Soil′er,** *n.*

Free′ Soil′ par′ty, *U.S.* a former political party (1848–56) that opposed the extension of slavery in the Territories.

free′ speech′. See **freedom of speech.**

free-spo·ken (frē′spō′kən), *adj.* given to speaking freely or without reserve; outspoken. —**free′-spo′ken·ly,** *adv.* —**free′-spo′ken·ness,** *n.*

free·stand·ing (frē′stan′ding), *adj.* (of sculpture, architectural elements, etc.) unattached to a supporting unit or background. Also, **free′-stand′ing.**

Free′ State′, **1.** *U.S.* (before the Civil War) a state prohibiting slavery. **2.** See **Irish Free State.**

free·stone (frē′stōn′), *n.* **1.** any stone, as sandstone, that cuts well in all directions without splitting. **2.** a freestone fruit, esp. a peach or plum. —*adj.* **3.** having a stone from which the pulp is easily separated, as certain peaches and plums. [ME *freston* (see FREE, STONE); trans. of OF *franche piere;* see FRANK[1]]

Free′stone State′ (frē′stōn′), Connecticut (used as a nickname).

free·style (frē′stīl′), *n. Swimming.* a race in which the stroke to be used is not specified, the competitors being free to use any stroke they choose.

free-swim·ming (frē′swim′ing), *adj. Zool.* (of aquatic animals) not fixed or attached; able to swim about.

free·think·er (frē′thing′kər), *n.* a person who forms his opinions independently of authority or tradition, esp. in religious matters. —**free′think′ing,** *adj., n.*

free′ thought′, thought unrestrained by deference to authority, esp. in matters of religion.

free′ throw′, *Basketball.* See **foul shot.**

free′ throw′ line′, *Basketball.* See **foul line** (def. 2).

Free·town (frē′toun′), *n.* a seaport in and the capital of Sierra Leone, in W Africa. 214,000.

free′ trade′, **1.** trade between different countries, free from governmental restrictions or duties. **2.** international trade free from protective duties. **3.** the system, principles, or maintenance of such trade. **4.** *Obs.* smuggling. —**free′-trade′,** *adj.*

free·trad·er (frē′trā′dər), *n.* **1.** a person who advocates free trade. **2.** *Obs.* a smuggler. Also, **free′ trad′er.**

free′ univer′sity, a school run informally by and for college students, organized to offer courses and approaches not usually offered at the established universities.

free′ verse′, *Pros.* verse without a fixed metrical pattern.

free·way (frē′wā′), *n.* an express highway, usually having traffic routed on and off by means of cloverleaves.

free·wheel (frē′hwēl′, -wēl′), *n.* **1.** an overrunning clutch device that automatically disengages the drive shaft whenever it tends to rotate more rapidly than the shaft driving it. **2.** a form of rear bicycle wheel that has a device freeing it from the driving mechanism, as when the pedals are stopped in coasting. —*v.i.* **3.** (of a vehicle or its operator) to coast with the wheels disengaged from the driving mechanism. **4.** to move, function, or be used freely, independently, unconcernedly, or the like.

free·wheel·ing (frē′hwē′ling, -wē′-), *adj.* **1.** operating in the manner of a freewheel. **2.** *Informal.* **a.** (of a person) moving about independently or irresponsibly. **b.** (of words, remarks, actions, etc.) unrestrained; irresponsible.

free′ will′, **1.** free choice; voluntary decision. **2.** *Philos.* the doctrine that human action expresses personal choice and is not solely determined by physical or divine forces.

free·will (frē′wil′), *adj.* **1.** made or done freely or of one's own accord; voluntary. **2.** of or pertaining to the doctrine of the freedom of the will. [ME *fre wil.* See FREE, WILL[2]]

free′ world′, the nations not under communist or totalitarian control, domination, or influence.

freeze (frēz), *v.,* **froze, fro·zen, freez·ing,** *n.* —*v.i.* **1.** to become hardened into ice or into a solid body by loss of heat; change from a liquid to a solid state because of cold temperatures. **2.** to become hard or rigid because of loss of heat, as objects containing moisture: *The washing froze on the line.* **3.** to become obstructed by the formation of ice, as pipes. **4.** to become fixed to something by or as by the action of frost. **5.** to be of the degree of cold at which water freezes. **6.** to have the sensation of or suffer the effects of intense cold. **7.** to die of frost or cold. **8.** to be chilled with fear, shock, etc. **9.** to stop suddenly; halt: *Fear made him freeze in his tracks.* **10.** to become immobilized through fear, shock, etc.: *When he got in front of the audience he froze.* —*v.t.* **11.** to harden into ice or into a solid body by loss of heat. **12.** to form ice on the surface of (a river, pond, etc.). **13.** to obstruct or close (a pipe or the like) by the formation of ice. **14.** to fix fast with ice. **15.** to harden or stiffen by cold, as objects containing moisture. **16.** to subject (something) to freezing temperature, as in a freezer. **17.** to cause to suffer the effects of intense cold. **18.** to kill by frost or cold. **19.** to dampen the enthusiasm of. **20.** to cause (a person or animal) to become fixed through fright, alarm, shock, etc.; chill with fear. **21.** *Finance Informal.* to render impossible of liquidation or collection. **22.** to fix (rents, prices, etc.) at a specific amount. **23.** *Surg.* to render part of the body insensitive to pain or slower in its function. **24. freeze on** or **onto,** *Informal.* to adhere closely to; hold on; seize. **25. freeze out,** *U.S. Informal.* to exclude or compel to withdraw from some position of influence or advantage by cold treatment or severe competition. **26. freeze over,** to coat or become coated with ice. —*n.* **27.** the act of freezing. **28.** state of being frozen. **29.** *Meteorol.* a widespread occurrence of temperatures below 32°F lasting several days. **30.** a frost. **31.** a legislative action to control prices, rents, etc. [ME *frese(n),* OE *frēosan;* c. MLG *vrēsen*] —**freez′a·ble,** *adj.*

freeze-dry (frēz′drī′), *v.t.,* **-dried, -dry·ing.** to subject to freeze-drying.

freeze-dry·ing (frēz′drī′ing), *n.* a process for drying heat-sensitive substances, as food, blood plasma, antibiotics, and the like, by freezing the substance and then subliming the ice or other frozen solvent in a high vacuum and at a low temperature.

freeze′ frame′, *Motion Pictures, TV.* an optical effect or technique in which a single frame of film is reprinted in a continuous series so as to give the illusion that the action has been frozen, as in a photograph. —**freeze′-frame′,** *adj.*

freez·er (frē′zər), *n.* **1.** a person or thing that freezes or chills. **2.** a machine containing cold brine, ice, etc., for making ice cream, sherbet, or the like. **3.** a refrigerator or cabinet that holds its contents at or below 32°F.

freez·ing (frē′zing), *adj.* **1.** (of temperatures) approaching, at, or below the freezing mark. **2.** extremely or uncomfortably cold. **3.** beginning to freeze; partially frozen. —**freez′ing·ly,** *adv.*

freez′ing point′, *Physical Chem.* the temperature at which a liquid freezes: *The freezing point of water is 32°F, 0°C.*

free′ zone′, a free port area.

Frei·burg (frī′bo͝ork′), *n.* **1.** a city in SW Baden-Württemberg, in SW West Germany. 174,000. **2.** German name of **Fribourg.**

freight (frāt), *n.* **1.** the ordinary conveyance or means of transport of goods provided by common carriers (distinguished from *express*). **2.** the charges, fee, or compensation paid for such transportation. **3.** *U.S. and Canada.* cargo or lading carried for pay either by water, land, or air. **4.** (esp. in Britain) the cargo, or any part of the cargo, of a vessel. **5.** *Chiefly Brit.* transportation of goods by water. —*v.t.* **6.** to load; burden: *a story heavily freighted with private meaning.* **7.** to load with goods or merchandise for transportation. **8.** to transport as freight; send by freight. [ME *freyght* < MD or MLG *vrecht*]—**freight′less,** *adj.*

freight·age (frā′tij), *n.* **1.** the transportation of goods. **2.** the price for this. **3.** freight, cargo, or lading.

freight′ car′, *Railroads.* any car for carrying freight.

freight·er (frā′tər), *n.* **1.** a vessel used mainly for carrying cargo. **2.** a person whose occupation it is to receive and forward freight. **3.** a person for whom freight is transported; a shipper.

freight′ for′warder, a person or firm that arranges to pick up or deliver goods on instructions of a shipper or a consignee from or to a point by various necessary conveyances and common carriers. Also called **forwarder, forwarding agent.**

freight′ ton′, ton^1 (def. 2).

Fre·ling·huy·sen (frē′ling hī′zən), *n.* **Frederick Theodore,** 1817–85, U.S. statesman.

Fre·man·tle (frē′man′tᵊl), *n.* a seaport in SW Australia, near Perth. 25,990.

fremd (fʀemd, fʀāmd), *adj. Scot.* **1.** foreign; strange. **2.** unfriendly. [ME *frem(e)d,* OE *frem(e)de*]

frem·i·tus (frem′i təs), *n., pl.* **-tus.** *Pathol.* palpable vibration, as of the walls of the chest. [< L: a roaring, murmuring, n. use of ptp. of *fremere*]

Fre·mont (frē′mont), *n.* a city in W California, near San Francisco Bay. 100,869 (1970).

Fré·mont (frē′mont), *n.* **John Charles,** 1813–90, U.S. general and explorer.

French (french), *n.* **1. Daniel Chester,** 1850–1931, U.S. sculptor. **2. Sir John Den·ton Pink·stone** (den′tᵊn pingk′stōn, -stən), **1st Earl of Ypres,** 1852–1925, English field marshal in World War I.

French (french), *adj.* **1.** of, pertaining to, or characteristic of France, its inhabitants, or their language, culture, etc. —*n.* **2.** the people of France and their direct descendants. **3.** a Romance language of the analytic type, spoken in France, parts of Belgium and Switzerland, and in areas colonized after 1500 by France. *Abbr.:* F, F. —*v.t.* **4.** (*often l.c.*) to cut (snap beans) into slivers or thin strips before cooking. [ME *Frensh, French,* OE *Frenc(i)sc*]

French′ Acad′emy, an association of 40 scholars and men of letters, established in 1635 by Cardinal Richelieu and devoted chiefly to preserving the purity of the French language and establishing standards of proper usage.

French′ and In′dian War′, the war between France and England on the North American continent 1754–60.

French′ bread′, a yeast-raised bread of dough containing water, having a thick, well-browned crust, and made in long, slender, tapered loaves.

French′ bull′dog, one of a French breed of small, bat-eared dogs having a large, square head, a short tail, and a short, sleek coat.

French′ Cameroons′, Cameroun (def. 2).

French′ Cana′dian, **1.** a descendant of the early French colonists of Canada. **2.** the language of the French Canadians.

French′ chalk′, a talc for removing grease spots and for marking lines on fabrics.

French′ chop′, a rib chop, usually of lamb, with the meat trimmed from the end of the bone.

French′ Commu′nity, a federation of France, its overseas departments and territories, and former French territories that chose to maintain association after becoming independent republics: formed 1958.

French′ Con′go, former name of the People's Republic of the Congo.

French′ cuff′, a sleeve cuff folded back and fastened with a cuff link. Cf. **barrel cuff.**

French′ curve′, a flat drafting instrument consisting of several scroll-like curves enabling a draftsman to draw curves of varying radii.

French curve and line drawn through three points

French′ door′, a door having glass panes throughout its length.

French′ dress′ing, (*often l.c.*) salad dressing prepared from oil, vinegar, and seasonings.

French′ en′dive, a variety of chicory used for salads.

French′ Equato′rial Af′rica, a former federation of French territories in central Africa, including Chad, Gabon, Middle Congo, and Ubangi-Shari.

French′ fried′ pota′toes, thin strips of potatoes, deep-fried. Also called **French′ fries′;** *Brit.* **chips.**

French-fry (french′frī′), *v.t.,* **-fried, -fry·ing.** to fry in deep fat: *to French-fry onion rings.*

French′ Gui·an′a (gē an′ə, gē ä′nə), an overseas department of France, on the NE coast of South America: formerly a French colony. 49,200; 35,135 sq. mi. *Cap.:* Cayenne. —**French′ Gui·a·nese′, French′ Gui·an′an.**

French′ Guin′ea, former name of **Guinea.**

French′ heel′, a high, curved heel, used on women's shoes. —**French′-heeled′,** *adj.*

French′ horn′, a musical brass wind instrument with a long, coiled tube, having a conical bore and a flaring bell. See illus. at **horn.**

French·i·fy (fren′chə fī′), *v.t.,* **-fied, -fy·ing.** *Informal.* (*often l.c.*) to make (something or someone) resemble the French, as in manners, customs, dress, etc. —**French′i·fi·ca′tion,** *n.*

French′ In′dia, the five small former French territories in India, including Chandernagor, Karikal, Pondicherry, Yanaon, and Mahé.

French′ In′dochi′na, an area in SE Asia, formerly a French colonial federation including Cochin-China, the protectorates of Annam, Cambodia, Tonkin, and Laos, and the leased territory of Kwangchowan: now comprising the independent states of Vietnam, Cambodia, and Laos.

French′ kiss′. See **soul kiss.**

French′ leave′, a departure without ceremony, permission, or notice.

French·man (french′mən), *n., pl.* **-men. 1.** a native or inhabitant of the French nation, esp. a male. **2.** a French ship. [ME *Frenshman,* OE *Frencisc man*]

French′ Moroc′co. See under **Morocco** (def. 1).

French′ Ocean′ia, former name of **French Polynesia.**

French′ pas′try, fine, rich, or fancy pastry, esp. made from puff paste and filled with cream or fruit.

French′ Polyne′sia, a French overseas territory in the S Pacific, including the Society Islands, Marquesas Islands, and other island groups. 119,168; 1544 sq. mi. *Cap.:* Papeete. Formerly, **French Oceania.**

French′ Revolu′tion, *Fr. Hist.* the revolution that began in 1789, overthrew the Bourbon monarchy, and ended with Napoleon's seizure of power in 1799.

French′ Revolu′tionary cal′endar. See **Revolutionary calendar.**

French′ seam′, *Sewing.* a seam sewn on both sides of the cloth.

French′ Soma′liland, former name of **Djibouti** (def.1).

French′ Sudan′, former name of **Mali.**

French′ tel′ephone, a telephone with the receiver and transmitter at the ends of a handle; handset.

French′ toast′, bread dipped in a batter of egg and milk and sautéed until brown.

French′ Un′ion, a former association of France and its overseas territories, colonies, and protectorates as constituted in 1946: superseded by the French Community in 1958.

French′ West′ Af′rica, a former French federation in W Africa, including Dahomey, French Guinea, French Sudan, Ivory Coast, Mauritania, Niger, Senegal, and Upper Volta.

French′ West′ In′dies, the French islands in the Caribbean, including Martinique and Guadaloupe and its dependencies: administered as two overseas departments. 676,900; 1114 sq. mi.

French′ win′dow, a window extending to the floor, closed by French doors.

French·wom·an (french′wo͝om′ən), *n., pl.* **-wom·en.** a female native or inhabitant of France.

French·y (fren′chē), *adj.,* **French·i·er, French·i·est.** characteristic or suggestive of the French. [FRENCH + -Y^1] —**French′i·ly,** *adv.* —**French′i·ness,** *n.*

French·y (fren′chē), *n., pl.* **French·ies.** *Slang.* a Frenchman. [FRENCH + -Y^2]

Fre·neau (fri nō′), *n.* **Philip,** 1752–1832, U.S. poet and editor.

fre·net·ic (frə net′ik), *adj.* frantic; frenzied. Also, **fre·net′i·cal, phrenetic, phrenetical.** [ME; see FRANTIC] —**fre·net′i·cally,** *adv.*

fre·num (frē′nəm), *n., pl.* **-na** (-nə). *Anat., Zool.* a fold of membrane that checks or restrains the motion of a part, as the fold on the underside of the tongue. Also, **fraenum.** [< NL, L *frēnum, fræ̆num* bridle]

fren·zied (fren′zēd), *adj.* wildly excited or enthusiastic; frantic. Also, **phrensied.** —**fren′zied·ly,** *adv.*

fren·zy (fren′zē), *n., pl.* **-zies,** *v.,* **-zied, -zy·ing.** —*n.* **1.** violent mental agitation; wild excitement or enthusiasm. **2.** a fit or spell of violent mental excitement; a paroxysm characteristic of or resulting from a mania. —*v.t.* **3.** to drive to frenzy; make frantic. Also, **phrensy.** [ME *frenesie* < OF < LL *phrenēsis* < LGk, r. Gk *phrenîtis*] —**fren′zi·ly,** *adv.* —**Syn. 2.** madness, insanity, lunacy; rage, fury, raving. —**Ant. 1.** calm. **2.** sanity.

Fre·on (frē′on), *n. Chem., Trademark.* any of a class of fluorinated hydrocarbons used chiefly as a refrigerant, as the gas dichlorodifluoromethane.

freq., **1.** frequent. **2.** frequentative. **3.** frequently.

fre·quen·cy (frē′kwən sē), *n., pl.* **-cies. 1.** Also, **fre′-quence.** state or fact of being frequent; frequent occurrence. **2.** rate of recurrence. **3.** *Physics.* **a.** the number of periods or regularly occurring events of any given kind in unit time, usually in one second. **b.** the number of cycles or completed alternations per unit time of a wave or oscillation. *Symbol:* f **4.** *Math.* the number of times a value recurs in a unit change of the independent variable of a given function. **5.** *Statistics.* the number of items occurring in a given category. Cf. **relative frequency** (def. 2). [< L *frequentia* assembly, multitude, crowd]

fre′quency distribu′tion, *Statistics.* the correspondence of a set of frequencies with the set of categories, intervals, or values into which a population is classified.

fre′quency modula′tion, *Electronics, Radio.* See **FM.**

fre·quent (*adj.* frē′kwənt; *v.* fri kwent′, frē′kwənt), *adj.* **1.** happening or occurring at short intervals: *to make frequent trips to a place.* **2.** constant, habitual, or regular: *a frequent guest.* **3.** located at short distances apart: *a coast with frequent lighthouses.* —*v.t.* **4.** to visit often; go often to; be often in: *to frequent the art galleries.* [late ME < L *frequent-* (s. of *frequēns*) crowded; *frequentāre* (v.) < *frequēns*] —**fre-quent′a·ble,** *adj.* —**fre·quent′er,** *n.* —**fre′quent·ness,** *n.*

fre·quen·ta·tion (frē′kwən tā′shən), *n.* the practice of frequenting. [< F *fréquentation* < L *frequentātiōn-* (s. of *frequentātiō*)]

fre·quen·ta·tive (fri kwen′tə tiv), *Gram.* —*adj.* **1.** noting or pertaining to a verb aspect expressing repetition of an action. —*n.* **2.** the frequentative aspect. **3.** a verb in the frequentative aspect, as *wrestle* from *wrest.* [< L *frequentātīv(us)* denoting repetition of an act]

fre·quent·ly (frē′kwənt lē), *adv.* often; many times; at short intervals. —**Syn. 1.** repeatedly. See **often.**

frère (frer), *n., pl.* **frères** (frer). *French.* **1.** brother; fellow member of an organization. **2.** friar; monk.

fres·co (fres′kō), *n., pl.* **-coes, -cos,** *v.,* **-coed, -co·ing.** —*n.* **1.** Also called **true fresco.** the art or technique of painting on a moist, plaster surface with colors ground in water or a limewater mixture. Cf. **fresco secco. 2.** a picture or design so painted. —*v.t.* **3.** to paint in fresco. [< It: cool, FRESH (< Gmc)] —**fres′co·er,** *n.*

Fres·co·bal·di (fres kō bäl′dē), *n.* **Gi·ro·la·mo** (jē rô′lä-mô), 1583–1643, Italian organist and composer.

fres′co sec′co, the technique of painting in water colors on dry plaster. Also called **dry fresco.** Cf. **fresco** (def. 1). [< It: lit., dry fresco]

fresh (fresh), *adj.* **1.** newly made or obtained: *fresh footprints; fresh lettuce.* **2.** newly arrived; just come: *fresh from school.* **3.** new; not previously known, met with, etc.; novel: *to seek fresh experiences.* **4.** additional or further: *fresh supplies.* **5.** not salt, as water. **6.** unimpaired; not deteriorated: *Is the milk still fresh?* **7.** not frozen or canned; not preserved by pickling, salting, drying, etc. **8.** not fatigued; brisk; vigorous. **9.** not faded, worn, obliterated, etc. **10.** looking youthful and healthy. **11.** pure, cool, or refreshing, as air. **12.** *Meteorol.* (of wind) moderately strong or brisk. **13.** inexperienced; green; callow: *fresh recruits.* **14.** *Informal.* forward or presumptuous. **15.** (of a cow) having recently given birth to a calf. —*n.* **16.** the fresh part or time. **17.** a freshet. —*v.t., v.i.* **18.** to make or become fresh. —*adv.* **19.** newly; recently; just now: *He is fresh out of ideas.* [ME; OE *fersc;* c. OFris *fersk,* OHG *frisc* (G *frisch*), ON *fersk(r)*] —**fresh′ly,** *adv.* —**fresh′ness,** *n.* —**Syn. 1.** recent. See **new. 11.** sweet, unadulterated. **13.** untrained, raw, uncultivated, unskilled. —**Ant. 1.** old. **6.** stale, contaminated.

fresh′ breeze′, *Meteorol.* (on the Beaufort scale) a wind of 19–24 miles per hour.

fresh·en (fresh′ən), *v.t.* **1.** to make fresh; refresh, revive, or renew: *We need a good rain to freshen the flowers.* **2.** to remove saltiness from. —*v.i.* **3.** to become or grow fresh. **4.** to make oneself fresh, as by washing, changing clothes, etc. (usually fol. by *up*): *to freshen up after a long trip.* **5.** to give birth, as a cow. **6.** to commence giving milk, as a cow. —**fresh′en·er,** *n.*

fresh·et (fresh′it), *n.* **1.** a sudden rise in the level of a stream, or a flood, due to heavy rains or the rapid melting of snow and ice. **2.** a fresh-water stream flowing into the sea. [dim. of FRESH used as n.]

fresh′ gale′, *Meteorol.* (on the Beaufort scale) a wind of 39–46 miles per hour. Cf. **gale**[1] (def. 2).

fresh·man (fresh′mən), *n., pl.* **-men,** *adj.* —*n.* **1.** a student in the first year of the course at a university, college, or school. **2.** a novice. —*adj.* **3.** of, pertaining to, or characteristic of a freshman. **4.** lacking seniority or experience: *freshman senator.* **5.** required of or suitable for freshmen: *freshman courses.* **6.** initial; first: *This is my freshman year with the company.*

fresh′ wa′ter, **1.** water that does not contain a large amount of salt. **2.** inland water, as ponds, lakes, streams, etc., that is not salt.

fresh-wa·ter (fresh′wô′tər, -wot′ər), *adj.* **1.** of or living in water that is fresh or not salt: *fresh-water fish.* **2.** accustomed to fresh water only. **3.** *Obs.* untrained or unskilled.

fres·nel (frā nel′, frə-; *Fr.* frā nel′), *n.* a unit of frequency, equal to 10^{12} cycles per second. [named after A. J. *Fresnel* (1788–1827), French physicist]

Fres·no (frez′nō), *n.* a city in central California, SE of San Francisco. 165,972 (1970).

fret[1] (fret), *v.,* **fret·ted, fret·ting,** *n.* —*v.i.* **1.** to feel or express worry, annoyance, discontentment, or the like. **2.** to cause corrosion; gnaw into something: *acids that fret at the strongest metals.* **3.** to make a way by gnawing, corrosion, wearing away, etc.: *The river frets at its banks until a new channel is formed.* **4.** to become eaten, worn, or corroded (often fol. by *away*): *to fret away under constant wear.* **5.** to move in agitation or commotion, as water. —*v.t.* **6.** to torment; irritate, annoy, or vex. **7.** wear away or consume by gnawing, friction, rust, corrosives, etc. **8.** to form or make by wearing away a substance. **9.** to agitate (water). —*n.* **10.** an irritated state of mind; annoyance; vexation. **11.** erosion; corrosion; gnawing. **12.** a worn or eroded place. [ME *frete(n),* OE *fretan* to eat up, consume; c. OS *fretan,* Goth *fraitan,* OHG *frezzan* (G *fressen*] —**Syn. 6.** worry, harass, goad, tease. **7.** erode, corrode, abrade. **10.** agitation, worry, irritation.

Fret[2] (def. 2)

fret[2] (fret), *n., v.,* **fret·ted, fret·ting.** —*n.* **1.** an interlaced, angular design; fretwork. **2.** an angular design of bands within a border. —*v.t.* **3.** to ornament with a fret or fretwork. [ME *frette* < ?; cf. MF *frete* trellis-work, OE *fretwian,* var. of *frætwian* to adorn] —**fret′less,** *adj.*

fret[3] (fret), *n., v.,* **fret·ted, fret·ting.** —*n.* **1.** any of the ridges of wood, metal, or string, set across the finger board of a guitar or similar instrument, which help the fingers to stop the strings at the correct points. —*v.t.* **2.** to provide with frets. [?] —**fret′less,** *adj.*

fret·ful (fret′fəl), *adj.* disposed to fret; irritable or peevish. Also, **fret·some** (fret′ səm). —**fret′ful·ly,** *adv.* —**fret′-ful·ness,** *n.*

fret′ saw′, a long, narrow-bladed saw used to cut ornamental work from thin wood.

fret·ted (fret′id), *adj.* ornamented or provided with frets: *a fretted molding.*

fret·ty (fret′ē), *adj.,* **-ti·er, -ti·est.** fretful; peevish.

fret·work (fret′wûrk′), *n.* **1.** ornamental work consisting of interlacing parts. **2.** any pattern of dark and light resembling this.

Freud (froid; *Ger.* froit), *n.* **Sig·mund** (sig′mənd; *Ger.* zēk′mŏŏnt), 1856–1939, Austrian neurologist: founder of psychoanalysis.

Freud·i·an (froi′dē ən), *adj.* **1.** of, pertaining to, or characteristic of Sigmund Freud or his doctrines. —*n.* **2.** a person, esp. a psychoanalyst, who adheres to the basic doctrines of Freud. —**Freud′i·an·ism,** *n.*

Freud′ian slip′, an inadvertent mistake in speech or writing that is thought to reveal a person's unconscious motives, wishes, or attitudes.

Frey (frā), *n. Scand. Myth.* the god of peace, prosperity, and marriage: one of the Vanir. Also, **Freyr** (frār).

Frey·a (frā′ə, frā′ä), *n. Teutonic Myth.* the goddess of love, beauty, and fecundity, and leader of the Valkyries. Also **Frey·ja** (frā′yä).

F.R.G.S., Fellow of the Royal Geographical Society.

Fri., Friday.

fri·a·ble (frī′ə bəl), *adj.* easily crumbled or reduced to powder; crumbly: *friable rock.* [< L *friābil(is)* = *fri-* (s. of *friāre* to rub, crumble) + *-ābilis* -ABLE] —**fri′a·bil′i·ty, fri′a·ble·ness,** *n.*

fri·ar (frī′ər), *n. Rom. Cath. Ch.* a member of a religious order, esp. the mendicant orders of Franciscans and Dominicans. [ME *frier, frere* brother < OF *frere* < L *frāter* BROTHER] —**Syn. 1.** See **monk.**

Fri′ar Mi′nor, *pl.* **Friars Minor.** *Rom. Cath. Ch.* a friar belonging to the branch of the Franciscan order that follows literally the rule of St. Francis. Cf. **Capuchin** (def. 4), **Friar Minor Conventual.**

Fri′ar Mi′nor Conven′tual, *pl.* **Friars Minor Conventual.** *Rom. Cath. Ch.* a friar belonging to a branch of the Franciscan order that observes a modification of the rule of St. Francis. Cf. **Friar Minor.**

fri·ar·y (frī′ə rē), *n., pl.* **-ar·ies. 1.** a monastery of friars, esp. those of a mendicant order. **2.** a brotherhood of friars. [alter. of earlier *frary* friary, brotherhood (see FRIAR, -Y[3]); r. ME *fra(i)rie* < MF, alter. of ML *frātria*]

frib·ble (frib′əl), *v.,* **-bled, -bling,** *n., adj.* —*v.i.* **1.** to act in foolish or frivolous manner; trifle. —*v.t.* **2.** to waste foolishly (often fol. by *away*): *to fribble away the day.* —*n.* **3.** a trifler. **4.** anything trifling or frivolous. **5.** frivolousness. —*adj.* **6.** frivolous; trifling. [? alter. of FRIVOL] —**frib′-bler,** *n.*

Fri·bourg (*Fr.* frē bōōr′), *n.* a town in W Switzerland. 32,583 (1960). German, **Freiburg.**

fric·an·deau (frik′ən dō′, frik′ən dō′), *n., pl.* **-deaus, -deaux** (-dōz′, -dōz′). a loin of veal, larded and braised, or roasted. [< F, MF; appar. akin to FRICASSEE]

fric·as·see (frik′ə sē′), *n., v.,* **-seed, -see·ing.** —*n.* **1.** meat, esp. chicken or veal, browned lightly, stewed, and served in a white sauce made with its own stock. —*v.t.* **2.** to prepare as a fricassee. [< MF, n. use of fem. ptp. of *fricasser* to fricassee, cf. *frire* to FRY[1]]

fri·ca·tion (fri kā′shən), *n. Phonet.* an audible, constrained rush of air accompanying certain speech sounds, as fricatives, affricates, and initial stops. [< L *fricātiōn-* (s. of *fricātiō*) = *fricāt(us)* rubbed (ptp. of *fricāre;* see FRICTION) + *-iōn-* -ION]

fric·a·tive (frik′ə tiv), *Phonet.* —*adj.* **1.** (of a speech sound) produced with frication; spirantal; spirant. —*n.* **2.** Also called **spirant.** a fricative consonant.

fric·tion (frik′shən), *n.* **1.** surface resistance to relative motion, as of a body sliding or rolling. **2.** the rubbing of the surface of one body against that of another. **3.** dissension or conflict between persons, nations, etc. [< L *frictiōn-* (s. of *frictiō*) a rubbing = *frict(us)* (ptp. of *fricāre*) + *-iōn-* -ION] —**fric′tion·less,** *n.*

fric·tion·al (frik′shə nəl), *adj.* **1.** of, pertaining to, or of the nature of friction. **2.** moved, worked, or produced by friction. —**fric′tion·al·ly,** *adv.*

fric′tion lay′er. See **surface boundary layer.**

fric′tion match′, a kind of match tipped with a compound that ignites by friction.

fric′tion tape′, a cloth adhesive tape used esp. to insulate electrical conductors.

Fri·day (frī′dē, -dā), *n.* the sixth day of the week, following Thursday. [ME; OE *Frīgedæg* Freya's day = *Frīge* (gen. sing. of *Frēo*) + *dæg* day; *Frēo* is identical with OE adj. *frēo* free]

fridge (frij), *n.* *Chiefly Brit. Informal.* a refrigerator.

Frid·ley (frid′lē), *n.* a city in SE Minnesota, near Minneapolis. 29,233 (1970).

Fridt′jof Nan′sen Land′ (frit′yôf nän′sən, nan′-). See **Franz Josef Land.**

fried (frīd), *adj.* **1.** cooked in fat. —*v.* **2.** pt. and pp. of **fry**[1].

fried·cake (frīd′kāk′), *n.* a doughnut or other small cake cooked in deep fat.

friend (frend), *n.* **1.** a person attached to another by feelings of affection or personal regard. **2.** a patron or supporter: *a list of friends of the Boston Symphony.* **3.** a person who is on good terms with another; one not hostile: *to identify oneself as friend or foe.* **4.** a member of the same nation, party, etc. **5.** (*cap.*) a member of the Religious Society of Friends; Quaker. **6. make friends with,** to enter into friendly relations with; become a friend to. —*v.t.* **7.** *Rare.* to befriend. [ME *friend, frend,* OE *frēond* friend, lover, relative (c. OS *friund,* OHG *friunt* (G *Freund*), Goth *frijōnd(s)*), orig. prp. of *frēogan,* c. Goth *frijōn* to love] —**friend′less,** *adj.* —**friend′less·ness,** *n.* —**Syn. 1.** comrade, chum, confidant. See **acquaintance. 2.** backer. **4.** ally, associate, confrere, compatriot. —**Ant. 1, 4.** enemy, foe.

friend′ at court′, a friend in a position of influence or power who may advance one's interests, esp. a helpful person who is close to someone in authority.

friend·ly (frend′lē), *adj.,* **-li·er, -li·est,** *adv.* —*adj.* **1.** characteristic of or befitting a friend. **2.** like a friend; kind; helpful. **3.** favorably disposed; inclined to approve, help, or support. **4.** not hostile or at variance; amicable: *friendly natives.* —*adv.* **5.** Also, **friend′li·ly.** in a friendly manner; like a friend. [ME *frendly,* OE *frēondlīc*] —**friend′li·ness,** *n.* —**Syn. 1.** companionable, neighborly. **2.** kindly, amiable, cordial, genial. **3.** benevolent, helpful.

Friend′ly Is′lands, Tonga.

friend·ship (frend′ship), *n.* **1.** friendly feeling or disposition. **2.** the state of being a friend; association as friends. **3.** a friendly relation or intimacy. [ME; OE *frēondscipe*]

fri·er (frī′ər), *n.* fryer.

fries (frīz), *n.* **1.** pl. of **fry**[1]. —*v.* **2.** 3rd pers. sing. pres. indic. of **fry**[1].

Frie·sian (frē′zhən), *adj., n.* Frisian.

Fries·land (frēz′lənd; *Du.* frēs′länt′), *n.* a province in the N Netherlands. 487,061 (1962); 1431 sq. mi. *Cap.:* Leeuwarden.

frieze[1] (frēz), *n.* **1.** *Archit.* **a.** the part of a classical entablature between the architrave and the cornice. **b.** any decorative band bearing lettering, sculpture, etc. **2.** *Furniture.* skirt (def. 5b). [ME *frise, frese* < OF *frise* ? < ML *phrygium, frigium, frisium* embroidered cloth, embroidery, L *Phrygium,* neut. of *Phrygius* Phrygian]

frieze[2] (frēz), *n.* a heavy, napped woolen cloth for coats. [ME *frise* < OF; see FRIEZE[1]]

frig (frig), *v.t.,* **frigged, frig·ging.** *Slang (vulgar).* to have coitus with (a woman). [prob. special use of dial. *frig* to rub, late ME *friggen*]

frig′ate (frig′it), *n.* **1.** a fast naval vessel of the late 18th and early 19th centuries, generally having a lofty ship rig and heavily armed on one or two decks. **2.** a warship that is smaller and more maneuverable than a destroyer. **3.** *U.S.* a warship that is larger than a destroyer. [< F *frégate* < It *fregata*]

frig′ate bird′, any of several rapacious, totipalmate sea birds of the genus *Fregata,* noted for their powers of flight. Also called **man-o'-war bird.**

Frigg (frig), *n.* *Teutonic Myth.* the wife of Odin and goddess of the clouds, the sky, and conjugal love: one of the Aesir. Also, **Frig·ga** (frig′ə).

fright (frīt), *n.* **1.** sudden and extreme fear; a sudden terror. **2.** a person or thing of shocking, grotesque, or ridiculous appearance. —*v.t.* **3.** to frighten. [ME; OE *frytu, fyrhto;* akin to G *Furcht*] —**Syn. 1.** dismay, consternation, alarm. See **terror.** —**Ant. 1.** bravery.

fright·en (frīt′ən), *v.t.* **1.** to throw into a fright; terrify; scare. **2.** to set in motion by scaring; rout (usually fol. by *away, off,* etc.): *to frighten away pigeons.* —**fright′en·a·ble,** *adj.* —**fright′en·er,** *n.* —**fright′en·ing·ly,** *adv.*
—**Syn. 1.** shock, startle, dismay, intimidate. FRIGHTEN, ALARM, SCARE, TERRIFY, TERRORIZE, APPALL all mean to arouse fear. To FRIGHTEN is to shock with sudden, startling, but usually short-lived fear, esp. that arising from the apprehension of physical harm: *to frighten someone by a sudden noise.* To ALARM is to arouse the feelings through the realization of some imminent danger: *to alarm someone by a scream.* To SCARE is to frighten into a loss of poise or dignity: *to scare a child so that he cries.* To TERRIFY is to strike with violent, overwhelming, or paralyzing fear: *to terrify a city by lawless acts.* To TERRORIZE is to terrify in a general, continued, systematic manner, either wantonly or in order to gain control: *His marauding armies terrorized the countryside.* To APPALL is to overcome or confound by dread, dismay, shock, or horror: *The suffering caused by the earthquake appalled him.*

fright·ened (frīt′ənd), *adj.* **1.** thrown into a fright; afraid; scared. **2.** afraid; fearful (usually fol. by *of*): *to be frightened of the dark.* —**fright′ened·ly,** *adv.* —**Syn. 2.** See **afraid.**

fright·ful (frīt′fəl), *adj.* **1.** such as to cause fright; dreadful, terrible, or alarming: *a frightful explosion.* **2.** horrible, shocking, or revolting: *frightful damage.* **3.** *Informal.* unpleasant; disagreeable: *We had a frightful time.* **4.** *Informal.* very great: *a frightful amount of money.* [ME] —**fright′ful·ly,** *adv.* —**fright′ful·ness,** *n.* —**Syn. 1.** fearful, awful. **2.** hideous, horrid, ghastly; gruesome. —**Ant. 1, 2.** delightful.

frig·id (frij′id), *adj.* **1.** very cold in temperature: *a frigid climate.* **2.** without warmth of feeling; without ardor or enthusiasm: *a frigid reaction to the proposal.* **3.** stiff or formal: *a welcome that was polite but frigid.* **4.** (of a woman) **a.** indifferent or hostile to sexual intercourse. **b.** not able to have an orgasm in sexual intercourse. **5.** unemotional or unimaginative: *a correct, but frigid presentation.* [< L *frīgid(us)* = *frīg(us)* coldness (akin to Gk *rhīgos;* see RIGID) + *-idus* -ID[4]] —**fri·gid′i·ty, frig′id·ness,** *n.* —**frig′id·ly,** *adv.*

Frig·id·aire (frij′i dâr′), *n.* *Trademark.* an electric refrigerator.

frig·i·dar·i·um (frij′i dâr′ē əm), *n., pl.* **-dar·i·a** (-dâr′ē ə). (in an ancient Roman bath) a room having a bath of unheated water. [< L; see FRIGID, -ARIUM]

Frig′id Zone′, either of two regions, one between the Arctic Circle and the North Pole, or one between the Antarctic Circle and the South Pole.

frig·o·rif·ic (frig′ə rif′ik), *adj.* causing or producing cold. [< L *frīgorific(us)* cooling = *frīgor-* (s. of *frīgus* cold) + *-i-* -I- + *-ficus* -FIC]

Fri·go·ris (fri gōr′is, -gôr′-), *n.* **Mare.** See **Mare Frigoris.**

fri·jol (frē′hōl; *Sp.* frē hôl′), *n., pl.* **fri·jo·les** (frē′hōlz, frē hō′lēz; *Sp.* frē hô′les). any bean of the genus *Phaseolus,* esp. the kidney bean, used for food. [< Sp, earlier *fresol, fesol* << L *faseol(us), phaseolus,* dim. of *phasēlus* < Gk *phásēlos* a kind of bean]

fri·jo·le (frē hō′lē), *n.* frijol. [back formation from *frijoles,* pl. of FRIJOL]

frill (fril), *n.* **1.** a trimming, as a strip of cloth or lace, gathered at one edge and left loose at the other; a ruffle. **2.** something resembling such a trimming, as the fringe of hair on the chest of some dogs. **3.** affectation of manner, style, etc. **4.** something that is superfluous and bothersome. **5.** *Photog.* wrinkling or loosening of an emulsion, usually because of high temperature. —*v.t.* **6.** to trim or ornament with a frill or frills. **7.** to form into a frill. —*v.i.* **8.** *Photog.* (of an emulsion) to wrinkle. [? < Flem *frul* frill (of a collar), *frullen* to have frills] —**frill′er,** *n.* —**frill′y,** *adj.*

frill·ing (fril′ing), *n.* frilled edging.

Fri·maire (frē mer′), *n.* (in the French Revolutionary calendar) the third month of the year, extending from November 21 to December 20. [< F = *frim(as)* hoarfrost < OF *frim* (< Gmc; cf. OE *hrīm* RIME[2]) + *-aire* -ARY]

Friml (frim′əl), *n.* **Rudolf,** 1881–1972, U.S. composer and pianist, born in Austria.

fringe (frinj), *n., v.,* **fringed, fring·ing.** —*n.* **1.** a decorative border of short threads, cords, or the like. **2.** anything resembling or suggesting this: *a fringe of grass.* **3.** something regarded as a part of something else without being fully typical of, or essential to it: *the lunatic fringe of a political party.* **4.** *Optics.* one of the alternate light and dark bands produced by diffraction or interference. —*v.t.* **5.** to furnish with or as with a fringe. **6.** to serve as a fringe for, or to be arranged so as to suggest a fringe: *Guards fringed the building to protect it from the rioters.* [ME *frenge* < OF (F *frange*) < LL *frimbia* (L *fimbria*) border, fringe] —**fringe′less,** *adj.* —**fringe′like′,** *adj.*

fringe′ ar′ea, a region in which television reception is weak or distorted because of distance from the station, obstruction, etc.

fringe′ ben′efit, a benefit, as free insurance, received by an employee in addition to his regular pay.

fringed′ gen′tian, a gentian, *Gentiana crinita,* of eastern North America, having a blue, fringed corolla.

fringed′ or′chis, any of several American orchids of the genus *Habenaria,* having a cut, fringed lip.

fringe′ tree′, an oleaceous shrub or small tree, *Chionanthus virginicus,* of the southern U.S., bearing panicles of white flowers with long, narrow petals.

frin·gil·lid (frin jil′id), *adj.* **1.** Also, **frin·gil·line** (frin jil′īn, -in), belonging or pertaining to the family *Fringillidae,* comprising the finches and related birds. —*n.* **2.** a fringillid bird. [< NL *Fringillid(ae)* = L *fringill(a)* chaffinch + *-idae* -ID[2]]

frip·per·y (frip′ə rē), *n., pl.* **-per·ies. 1.** finery in dress, esp. when showy or gaudy. **2.** an article of such finery. **3.** empty display; ostentation. **4.** gewgaws; trifles. [< F *friperie,* OF *freperie* = *frepe* rag + *-erie* -ERY]

Fris, Frisian (def. 2). Also, **Fris.**

Fris·bee (friz′bē), *n.* *Trademark.* a thin plastic disk about nine inches across, sailed between players in an outdoor game.

Fris·co (fris′kō), *n.* *Informal.* San Francisco. [by shortening]

fri·sé (fri zā′), *n.* a rug or upholstery fabric having the pile in uncut loops or in a combination of cut and uncut loops. [< F: curly]

fri·sette (fri zet′), *n.* a fringe of curled or frizzed hair, esp. artificial, formerly worn on the forehead by women. Also, **frizette.** [< F: little curl < *fris(er)* (to) curl]

fri·seur (frē zœr′), *n., pl.* **-seurs** (-zœr′). *French.* a male hairdresser.

Fri·sian (frizh′ən, frē′zhən), *adj.* **1.** of or pertaining to Friesland, its inhabitants, or their language. —*n.* **2.** the Germanic language most closely related to English, spoken in Friesland and nearby islands. *Abbr.:* Fris, Fris. **3.** *Chiefly Brit.* Holstein (def. 1). Also, **Friesian.** [< L *Frīsiī* the people of a Germanic tribe + -AN]

Fri′sian Is′lands, a chain of islands in the North Sea, extending along the coasts of the Netherlands, West Germany, and Denmark.

frisk (frisk), *v.i.* **1.** to dance, leap, skip, or gambol, as in frolic. —*v.t.* **2.** to search (a person) for concealed weapons, contraband goods, etc., by feeling his clothing. **3.** *Slang.* to steal something from (someone) in this way. —*n.* **4.** a leap, skip, or caper. **5.** a frolic or gambol. [orig. adj. < OF *frisque* < Gmc; cf. G *frisch* lively, FRESH] —**frisk′er,** *n.* —**frisk′ing·ly,** *adv.*

fris·ket (fris′kit), *n.* **1.** a mask laid over an illustration to shield certain areas when using an airbrush. **2.** *Print.* (in a press) a mask of strong paper to prevent accidental soiling or printing by furniture or the chase. [< F *frisquette*]

frisk·y (fris′kē), *adj.,* **frisk·i·er, frisk·i·est.** lively; frolicsome; playful. —**frisk′i·ly,** *adv.* —**frisk′i·ness,** *n.*

frit (frit), *n., v.,* **frit·ted, frit·ting.** —*n.* **1.** *Ceram.* **a.** a fused or partially fused material used as a basis for glazes or enamels. **b.** the composition from which artificial soft porcelain is made. **2.** fused or calcined material prepared as part of the batch in glassmaking. —*v.t.* **3.** to fuse (materials) in making frit. Also, **fritt.** [< It *fritta,* fem. ptp. of *friggere* to fry < L *frīgere*]

frith (frith), *n.* firth.

frit·il·lar·y (frit′əler′ē), *n., pl.* **-lar·ies.** any of several orange-brown nymphalid butterflies, usually marked with black lines and dots and with silvery spots on the undersides of the wings. [< NL *fritillaria*]

frit·ter[1] (frit′ər), *v.t.* **1.** to disperse, squander, or waste little by little (usually fol. by *away*): *to fritter away an afternoon.* **2.** to break or tear into small pieces or shreds. **—***v.i.* **3.** to dwindle, shrink, degenerate, etc. (often fol. by *away*): *His fortune just frittered away.* **4.** to separate or break into fragments. **—***n.* **5.** a small piece, fragment, or shred. [alter. of earlier *fitter* < *fit* (OE *fitt*) a part] **—frit′ter·er,** *n.*

frit·ter[2] (frit′ər), *n.* a small cake of batter, sometimes containing fruit, clams, or some other ingredient, fried in deep fat or sautéed. [ME *friture, frytour* < OF *friture* << L *frict(us)* (ptp. of *frigere* to FRY[1]); see -URE]

Fri·u·li·an (frē ōō′lē ən), *n.* a Rhaeto-Romanic dialect spoken by about half a million people of the plains of extreme NE Italy. [*Friuli* region of Italy + -AN]

Fri·u·li-Ve·ne·zia Giu·lia (frē ōō′lē ve ne′tsyä jōō′-lyä), a region in NE Italy: formerly part of Venezia Giulia, most of which was ceded to Yugoslavia. 1,205,222 (1961); 2947 sq. mi.

friv·ol (friv′əl), *v.*, **-oled, -ol·ing** or (*esp. Brit.*) **-olled, -ol·ling.** *Informal.* **—***v.i.* **1.** to behave frivolously; trifle. **—***v.t.* **2.** to spend frivolously (usually fol. by *away*): *to frivol away one's time.* [back formation from FRIVOLOUS] **—friv′ol·er;** *esp. Brit.*, **friv′ol·ler,** *n.*

fri·vol·i·ty (fri vol′i tē), *n.*, *pl.* **-ties** for 2. **1.** the quality or state of being frivolous. **2.** a frivolous act or thing. [< F *frivolité*]

friv·o·lous (friv′ə ləs), *adj.* **1.** of little or no worth, or importance; not worthy of serious notice: *a frivolous suggestion.* **2.** characterized by lack of seriousness or sense: *frivolous conduct.* **3.** (of a person) given to trifling or undue levity. [ME < L *frīvol(us)* silly, trifling; see -OUS] **—friv′o·lous·ly,** *adv.* **—friv′o·lous·ness,** *n.* **—Syn. 1.** trifling, petty, paltry, trivial. **3.** silly, foolish. **—Ant. 1.** weighty. **3.** serious.

friz (friz), *v.*, **frizzed, friz·zing,** *n.*, *pl.* **friz·zes.** **—***v.t., v.i.* **1.** to form into small, crisp curls or little tufts. **—***n.* **2.** the state of being frizzed. **3.** something frizzed; frizzed hair. Also, **frizz.** [back formation from FRIZZLE[1]] **—friz′er,** *n.*

fri·zette (fri zet′), *n.* frisette.

frizz[1] (friz), *v.i., v.t.* frizzle[2]. **—frizz′er,** *n.*

frizz[2] (friz), *v.i., v.t., n.* friz. **—frizz′er,** *n.*

friz·zle[1] (friz′əl), *v.*, **-zled, -zling,** *n.* **—***v.t., v.i.* **1.** to friz. **—***n.* **2.** a short, crisp curl. [? cf. OE *fris* curled, OFris *frēsle* lock of hair] **—friz′zler,** *n.*

friz·zle[2] (friz′əl), *v.*, **-zled, -zling.** **—***v.i.* **1.** to make a sizzling or sputtering noise in frying or the like. **—***v.t.* **2.** to make (food) crisp by frying. [b. FRY[1] and FRIZZLE[1]]

friz·zly (friz′lē), *adj.*, **-zli·er, -zli·est.** frizzy.

friz·zy (friz′ē), *adj.*, **-zi·er, -zi·est.** formed into small, tight curls, as hair; frizzed. **—friz′zi·ly,** *adv.* **—friz′zi·ness,** *n.*

fro (frō), *adv.* **1.** *Obs.* from; back. **2. to and fro,** alternating from one place to another; back and forth. [ME *frō, frā* < Scand; cf. OIcel *frā;* akin to OE *fram* FROM]

Fro·bish·er (frō′bi shər, frob′i-), *n.* **Sir Martin,** 1535?–1594, English navigator and explorer.

frock (frok), *n.* **1.** a dress worn by a woman. **2.** a loose outer garment worn by peasants and workmen; smock. **3.** a coarse outer garment with large sleeves, worn by monks. **4.** See **frock coat.** **—***v.t.* **5.** to provide with, or clothe in, a frock. **6.** to invest with priestly or clerical office. [ME *froke* < OF *froc* << Gmc] **—frock′less,** *adj.*

frock′ coat′, a man's close-fitting coat, usually double-breasted, with skirts extending approximately to the knees.

froe (frō), *n.* *Chiefly U.S.* frow.

Froe·bel (frœ′bəl), *n.* **Frie·drich** (frē′drikh), 1782–1852, German educational reformer: founder of the kindergarten system. **—Froe·bel·i·an** (frə bē′lē ən, -bēl′yən, frā-), *adj.*

Frog[1], *Rana catesbeiana* (Length to 8 in.)

frog[1] (frog, frôg), *n.*, *v.*, **frogged, frog·ging.** **—***n.* **1.** any of numerous tailless amphibians of the order *Anura* that have long hind legs adapted for jumping, esp. the smooth-skinned species that live in a damp or aquatic habitat. **2.** a slight hoarseness caused by mucus on the vocal cords: *a frog in the throat.* **3.** (*cap.*) *Offensive.* a Frenchman. **4.** a small holder made of heavy material, placed in a bowl or vase to hold flower stems in position. **5.** a sheath suspended from a belt and supporting a scabbard. **—***v.i.* **6.** to catch or search for frogs. [ME *frogge,* OE *frogga, frocga;* cf. ME *frosh,* OIcel *frosk(r),* OHG *frosk* (G *Frosch*)] **—frog′like′,** *adj.*

frog[2] (frog, frôg), *n.* an ornamental fastening for the front of a coat, consisting of a button and a loop through which it passes. [? < Pg *froco* < L *floccus* FLOCK[2]]

Frog[2]

frog[3] (frog, frôg), *n.* *Zool.* a triangular mass of elastic, horny substance in the middle of the sole of the foot of a horse or related animal. [special use of FROG[1]]

frog·eye (frog′ī′, frôg′ī′), *n.*, *pl.* **-eyes** for 1. *Plant Pathol.* **1.** a small, diseased, whitish leaf spot with a narrow darker border, produced by certain fungi. **2.** a disease so characterized. **—frog′eyed′,** *adj.*

frog·hop·per (frog′hop′ər, frôg′-), *n.* any of numerous leaping, homopterous insects of the family *Cercopidae,* that in the immature stages live in a spittlelike secretion on plants. Also called **spittle insect, spittle bug.**

frog′ kick′, *Swimming.* a kick in which the legs are bent, extended outward, and then brought together forcefully.

frog·man (frog′man′, -mən, frôg′-), *n.*, *pl.* **-men** (-men′, -mən). a swimmer specially equipped for underwater demolition, salvage, scientific exploration, etc.

frog′ spit′, any of several filamentous, fresh-water green algae forming floating masses. Also, **frog′ spit′tle.**

Frois·sart (froi′särt; *Fr.* frwa sar′), *n.* **Jean** (zhäN), 1333?–c1400, French chronicler.

frol·ic (frol′ik), *n.*, *v.*, **-icked, -ick·ing,** *adj.* **—***n.* **1.** merry play; gay prank; gaiety; fun. **2.** a merrymaking or party. **—***v.i.* **3.** to gambol merrily; to play in a frisky, light-spirited manner; have fun; play merry pranks. **—***adj.* **4.** *Archaic.* gay; merry; full of fun. [< D *vrolijk* joyful (c. G *fröhlich*) = *vro* glad + *-lijk* -LIKE] **—frol′ick·er,** *n.* **—Syn. 3.** sport, romp.

frol·ic·some (frol′ik səm), *adj.* merrily playful; full of fun. **—frol′ic·some·ly,** *adv.* **—frol′ic·some·ness,** *n.*

from (frum, from; *unstressed* frəm), *prep.* **1.** (used to specify a starting point in spatial movement): *a train running west from New York City.* **2.** (used to specify a starting point in an expression of limits): *The number of stores will be increased from 25 to a total of 30.* **3.** (used to express removal or separation, as in space, time, order, etc.): *two miles from shore.* **4.** (used to express discrimination or distinction): *to be excluded from membership; to differ from one's father.* **5.** (used to indicate source or origin): *to come from the Midwest.* **6.** (used to indicate agent or instrumentality): *death from starvation.* **7.** (used to indicate cause or reason): *From the evidence, he must be guilty.* [ME; OE, var. of *fram* from (prep.), forward (adv.); c. Goth *fram,* Icel *frā* (see FRO), *fram* (adv.)]

fro·mage (frô mazh′), *n.* *French.* cheese.

fro·men·ty (frō′mən tē), *n.* *Brit. Dial.* frumenty.

Fromm (from), *n.* **Er·ich** (er′ik), 1900–80, U.S. psychoanalyst and author, born in Germany.

frond (frond), *n.* *Bot.* **1.** an often large, finely divided leaf, esp. as applied to the ferns and certain palms. **2.** a leaflike expansion not differentiated into stem and foliage, as in lichens. [< L *frond-* (s. of *frōns*) branch, bough, foliage] **—frond′ed,** *adj.*

Fronde (frôNd; *Eng.* frônd, frond), *n.* **1.** *Fr. Hist.* a series of unsuccessful rebellions (1648–53) against the administration of Cardinal Mazarin during the minority of Louis XIV. **2.** groups that waged the rebellions. [< F: lit., sling]

fron·des·cence (fron des′əns), *n.* **1.** the process or period of putting forth leaves, as a tree, plant, or the like. **2.** leafage; foliage. [< NL *frondēscentia* < L *frondēscent-* (s. of *frondēscēns*) becoming leafy (prp. of *frondēscere*), freq. of *frondēre* to have leaves] **—fron·des′cent,** *adj.*

frons (fronz), *n.*, *pl.* **fron·tes** (fron′tēz). the upper anterior portion of the head of an insect, above or behind the clypeus. [< L: forehead, FRONT]

front (frunt), *n.* **1.** the foremost part or surface of anything. **2.** the part or side of anything, as a house, that seems to look or to be directed forward. **3.** any side or face, as of a house. **4.** a place or position directly before anything, in front of a person, etc. **5.** *Mil.* **a.** the foremost line or part of an army. **b.** a line of battle. **c.** the place where combat operations are carried on. **6.** land facing a road, river, etc.; frontage. **7.** *Informal.* a distinguished person listed as an official of an organization, for the sake of prestige, and who is usually inactive **8.** *Informal.* someone or something that serves as a cover or disguise for another activity, esp. one of a disreputable nature; a blind. **9.** *Informal.* outward impression of rank, position, or wealth. **10.** bearing or demeanor in confronting anything: *a calm front.* **11.** haughtiness; self-importance. **12.** the forehead, or the entire face. **13.** a coalition or movement to achieve a particular end, usually political: *people's front.* **14.** something attached or worn at the breast, as a shirt front, dicky, or the like. **15.** *Meteorol.* an interface separating two dissimilar air masses. **16.** *Theat.* **a.** the auditorium. **b.** the business offices of a theater. **c.** the front of the stage; downstage. **17. in front,** in a forward place or position. **18. in front of, a.** ahead of. **b.** outside the entrance of. **c.** in the presence of. **19. out front, a.** outside the entrance. **b.** ahead of competitors. **c.** *Theat.* in the audience or auditorium. **—***adj.* **20.** of or pertaining to the front. **21.** situated in or at the front: *front yard; front seats.* **22.** *Phonet.* (of a speech sound) articulated with the tongue blade relatively far forward in the mouth, as the sounds of *lay.* **—***v.t.* **23.** to have the front toward; face. **24.** to meet face to face; confront. **25.** to face in opposition, hostility, or defiance. **26.** to furnish or supply a front to. **27.** to serve as a front to. **—***v.i.* **28.** to have or turn the front in some specified direction. **29.** to serve as a cover or disguise for another activity, esp. something of a disreputable nature. **—***interj.* **30.** (used to call or command someone to come, look, etc., to the front, as in an order to troops on parade or in calling a hotel bellboy to the front desk). [ME *frount, front* < L *front-* (s. of *frōns*) forehead, brow, front]

front·age (frun′tij), *n.* **1.** the front of a building or lot. **2.** the lineal extent of this front. **3.** the direction it faces. **4.** land abutting on a river, street, etc. **5.** the space lying between a building and the street, a body of water, etc.

fron·tal (frun′tᵊl), *adj.* **1.** of, in, or at the front: *a frontal attack.* **2.** *Anat.* of, pertaining to, or situated near the forehead or the frontal bone. **3.** *Meteorol.* of or pertaining to the division between dissimilar air masses. **—***n.* **4.** *Eccles.* a movable cover or hanging for the front of an altar. **5.** frontlet (def. 3). **6.** *Anat.* any of several parts in the frontal region, esp. the frontal bone. [< LL *frontāl(is)* (NL, in anatomy sense); r. ME *frountel* < OF *frontel*] **—fron′tal·ly,** *adv.*

fron′tal bone′, *Anat.* a broad membrane bone of the skull, forming the forehead and upper portion of each orbit.

fron′tal lobe′, *Anat.* the anterior part of each cerebral hemisphere, in front of the central sulcus.

front′ bench′, *Brit.* (in the House of Commons) either of two seats near the Speaker, occupied by the party leaders.

front′ burn′er, *Informal.* top priority (usually prec. by *on the*): *Welfare reform is on the front burner.* **—front′-burn′er,** *adj.*

Fron·te·nac (fron′tᵊnak′; *Fr.* frôNtᵊ nak′), *n.* **Louis de Bu·ade de** (lwē də by ad′ də), **Comte,** c1620–98, French governor of Canada 1672–82, 1689–98.

front′ foot′, *U.S.* a unit of frontage, one foot measured along the front of a lot.

fron·tier (frun tēr′), *n.* **1.** the part of a country that borders another country; boundary; border. **2.** *U.S.* land that forms the furthest extent of a country's settled or inhabited regions. **3.** Often, **frontiers.** the limit of knowledge or the most advanced achievement in a particular field. **—***adj.* **4.**

of, pertaining to, or characteristic of the frontier: *frontier justice; a frontier town.* [ME *frounter* < OF *frontier* = *front* (in the sense of opposite side; see FRONT) + *-ier* -IER] —**fron·tier′like′,** *adj.*

fron·tiers·man (frun tērz′mən), *n., pl.* **-men.** *Chiefly U.S.* a man who lives on the frontier.

fron·tis·piece (frun′tis pēs′, fron′-), *n.* an illustrated leaf preceding the title page of a book. [alter. (conformed to PIECE) of earlier *frontispice* < F < ML *frontispic(ium)* = L *fronti-* FRONT + *-spicium* (comb. form repr. *specere* to look at)]

front·less (frunt′lis), *adj.* *Archaic.* shameless; unblushing. —**front′less·ly,** *adv.* —**front′less·ness,** *n.*

front·let (frunt′lit), *n.* **1.** the forehead of an animal. **2.** *Ornith.* the forehead when marked by a different color or texture of the plumage. **3.** Also, **frontal.** a decorative band, ribbon, or the like, worn across the forehead. **4.** *Judaism.* the phylactery worn on the forehead. [ME < OF *frontelet* (def. 3), dim. of *frontel;* see FRONTAL]

front′ mat′ter, *Print. U.S.* all matter in a book that precedes the text proper. Cf. **back matter.**

fron·to·gen·e·sis (frun′tə jen′i sis), *n.* *Meteorol.* the formation or increase of a front or frontal zone. Cf. **frontolysis.**

fron·tol·y·sis (frun tol′i sis), *n.* *Meteorol.* the dissipation or decrease of a front or frontal zone. Cf. **frontogenesis.**

fron·ton (fron′ton, fron ton′), *n.* a building in which jai alai is played. [< Sp *frontón,* irreg. aug. of *frente* forehead, FRONT]

front-page (frunt′pāj′), *adj., v.,* **-paged, -pag·ing.** —*adj.* **1.** of consequence; worth putting on the first page of a newspaper. —*v.t.* **2.** to print on the front page, esp. of a newspaper.

Front′ Range′, a mountain range extending from central Colorado to S Wyoming: part of the Rocky Mountains. Highest peak, Grays Peak, 14,274 ft.

front′ run′ner, 1. *Sports.* an entrant in a race who breaks to the front immediately and establishes the pace for the field. **2.** one who leads in any competition.

front′ sight′, the sight on the muzzle of a gun.

front·ward (frunt′wərd), *adv.* in a direction toward the front. Also, **front′wards.**

frore (frōr, frôr), *adj.* *Archaic.* frozen; frosty. [ME *frore(n);* ptp. of FREEZE]

frosh (frosh), *n., pl.* **frosh.** *Informal.* a college freshman. [by alter. and shortening]

frost (frôst, frost), *n.* **1.** a degree or state of coldness sufficient to cause the freezing of water. **2.** Also called **hoarfrost.** a covering of minute ice needles, formed from the atmosphere at night upon the ground and exposed objects when they have cooled by radiation below the dew point, and when the dew point is below the freezing point. **3.** the act or process of freezing. **4.** coldness of manner or temperament. **5.** *Informal.* a complete failure; fiasco. **6. degree of frost,** *Brit.* the degree of temperature Fahrenheit below the freezing point: *10 degrees of frost is equivalent to 22°F.* —*v.t.* **7.** to cover with frost. **8.** to give a frostlike surface to (glass, metal, etc.). **9.** to ice (cookies, a cake, etc.). **10.** to kill or injure by frost. —*v.i.* **11.** to freeze or become covered with frost. **12.** (of varnish, paint, etc.) to dry with a film resembling frost. [ME, OE *frost, forst;* c. OS, OHG, OIcel, G *frost;* akin to FREEZE] —**frost′like′,** *adj.*

Frost (frôst, frost), *n.* **Robert (Lee),** 1874–1963, U.S. poet.

frost·bite (frôst′bīt′, frost′-), *n., v.,* **-bit, -bit·ten, -bit·ing.** —*n.* **1.** the inflamed, gangrenous effect of excessive exposure to extreme cold. —*v.t.* **2.** to injure by frost or extreme cold.

frost·bit·ten (frôst′bit′ən, frost′-), *adj.* **1.** injured by frost or extreme cold. —*v.* **2.** pp. of **frostbite.**

frost·ed (frô′stid, fros′tid), *adj.* **1.** covered with or having frost. **2.** frostbitten. **3.** coated with frosting or icing, as a cake. **4.** made frostlike in appearance, as certain translucent glass. **5.** quick-frozen.

frost·flow·er (frôst′flou′ər, frost′-), *n.* **1.** a liliaceous plant, *Milla biflora,* of the southwestern U.S. and Mexico. **2.** its waxy-white, starlike flower. **3.** any aster.

frost′ heave′, *Geol.* an uplift in soil caused by the freezing of internal moisture.

frost·ing (frô′sting, fros′ting), *n.* **1.** a sweet mixture, cooked or uncooked, for coating or filling cakes, cookies, and the like; icing. **2.** a lusterless finish, as of metal or glass. **3.** a material used for decorative work, as signs, displays, etc., made from coarse flakes of powdered glass.

frost·work (frôst′wûrk′, frost′-), *n.* **1.** the delicate tracery formed by frost, esp. on glass. **2.** similar ornamentation, as on metal or glass.

frost·y (frô′stē, fros′tē), *adj.,* **frost·i·er, frost·i·est. 1.** attended with or producing frost; freezing; very cold: *frosty weather.* **2.** consisting of or covered with a frost. **3.** lacking warmth of feeling. **4.** resembling frost; white or gray, as hair. **5.** of or characteristic of old age. [ME] —**frost′i·ly,** *adv.* —**frost′i·ness,** *n.* —**frost′less,** *adj.*

froth (frôth, froth), *n.* **1.** an aggregation of bubbles, as on a fermented or agitated liquid, at the mouth of a hard-driven horse, etc.; foam; spume. **2.** a foam of saliva or fluid resulting from disease. **3.** something unsubstantial or evanescent, as idle talk; trivial ideas. —*v.t.* **4.** to cover with froth. **5.** to cause to foam. **6.** to emit like froth. —*v.i.* **7.** to give out froth; foam. [ME *frothe,* ? < Scand; cf. Icel *frodha, fraudh* foam; akin to OE *āfrēothan* to foam]

froth·y (frô′thē, froth′ē), *adj.,* **froth·i·er, froth·i·est. 1.** of, like, or having froth; foamy. **2.** unsubstantial; trifling; shallow. —**froth′i·ly,** *adv.* —**froth′i·ness,** *n.*

frot·tage (frô täzh′), *n.* *Psychol.* the practice of getting sexual stimulation and satisfaction by rubbing against something, esp. another person. [< F = *frott(er)* (to) rub + *-age* -AGE]

frot·teur (frô tûr′), *n.* *Psychol.* a person who practices frottage. [< F = *frott(er)* (to) rub + *-eur;* see -OR[2]]

Froude (fro͞od), *n.* **James Anthony,** 1818–94, English historian.

frou·frou (fro͞o′fro͞o′), *n.* **1.** a rustling, as of silk. **2.** elaborate decoration, esp. on women's clothing. [< F; imit.]

frounce (frouns), *n., v.,* **frounced, frounc·ing.** —*n.* **1.** *Archaic.* affectation; empty show. —*v.t. Obs.* **2.** to curl the hair of. **3.** to pleat. —*v.i.* **4.** *Obs.* to frown. [ME *fro(u)nce(n)* (v.) < OF *fronc(ier)* < *fronc* a wrinkle, fold < Gmc; cf. Icel *hrukka,* WRINKLE[1], G *Runzel* wrinkle]

frouz·y (frou′zē), *adj.,* **frouz·i·er, frouz·i·est.** frowzy.

frow (frō), *n.* *U.S.* a cleaving tool having a wedge-shaped blade, with a handle set at right angles to it. Also, **froe.** [special use of FROW(ARD) (turned away from)]

fro·ward (frō′wərd, frō′ərd), *adj.* perverse or willfully contrary; refractory; not easily managed. [ME *froward, fraward.* See FRO-, -WARD] —**fro′ward·ly,** *adv.* —**fro′ward·ness,** *n.*

frown (froun), *v.i.* **1.** to contract the brow, as in displeasure or deep thought; scowl. **2.** to look displeased; have an angry look. **3.** to look disapprovingly (usually fol. by *on* or *upon*): *to frown upon a scheme.* —*v.t.* **4.** to express by a frown. **5.** to force or shame with a disapproving frown. —*n.* **6.** a frowning look; scowl. **7.** any expression or show of disapproval. [ME *froune(n)* < OF *froign(ier)* < *froigne* surly expression < Celt] —**frown′er,** *n.* —**frown′ing·ly,** *adv.* —**Syn. 1.** glower, lower, gloom.

frowst·y (frou′stē), *adj.* **frowst·i·er, frowst·i·est.** *Brit. Informal.* musty; ill-smelling. [? dial. var. of FROWZY] —**frowst′i·ly,** *adv.* —**frowst′i·ness,** *n.*

frowz·y (frou′zē), *adj.,* **frowz·i·er, frowz·i·est. 1.** dirty and untidy; slovenly. **2.** ill-smelling; musty. Also, **frouzy.** [?] —**frowz′i·ly,** *adv.* —**frowz′i·ness,** *n.*

froze (frōz), *v.* pt. of **freeze.**

fro·zen (frō′zən), *v.* **1.** pp. of **freeze.** —*adj.* **2.** congealed by cold; covered with ice, as a stream. **3.** frigid; very cold. **4.** injured or killed by frost or cold. **5.** obstructed by ice, as pipes. **6.** chilly or cold in manner; unfeeling. **7.** (of food) chilled or refrigerated: *frozen custard.* **8.** not readily turned into cash: *frozen assets.* —**fro′zen·ly,** *adv.* —**fro′zen·ness,** *n.*

fro′zen cus′tard, a smooth-textured frozen-food product of skim milk, sweetened and variously flavored, often served in an ice-cream cone. Also called **ice milk.**

FRS, Federal Reserve System.

Frs., Frisian.

frs., francs.

F.R.S., Fellow of the Royal Society.

frt., freight.

fruct-, var. of **fructi-** before a vowel: *fructose.*

fructi-, a learned borrowing from Latin meaning "fruit," used in the formation of compound words: *fructiferous.* Also, *esp. before a vowel,* **fruct-.** [< L, comb. form of *frūctus* FRUIT]

Fruc·ti·dor (fryk tē dôr′), *n.* (in the French Revolutionary calendar) the 12th month of the year, extending from August 18 to September 16. [< F < L *frūcti-* FRUCTI- + Gk *dōr(on)* gift]

fruc·tif·er·ous (fruk tif′ər əs, fro͝ok′-), *adj.* fruitbearing; producing fruit. [< L *frūctiferus*] —**fruc·tif′er·ous·ly,** *adv.*

fruc·ti·fi·ca·tion (fruk′tə fə kā′shən, fro͝ok′-), *n.* **1.** the act of fructifying; the fruiting of a plant. **2.** the fruit of a plant. **3.** the organs of fruiting. [< LL *frūctificātion-* (s. of *frūctificātiō*) a bearing of fruit = L *frūctificāt(us)* (ptp. of *frūctificāre;* see FRUCTIFY) + *-iōn-* -ION]

fruc·ti·fy (fruk′tə fī′, fro͝ok′-), *v.,* **-fied, -fy·ing.** —*v.i.* **1.** to bear fruit; become fruitful. —*v.t.* **2.** to make fruitful or productive; fertilize. [ME *fructifie(n)* < OF *fructifi(er)* < L *frūctificāre*] —**fruc′ti·fi′er,** *n.*

fruc·tose (fruk′tōs, fro͝ok′-), *n.* *Chem., Pharm.* a levorotatory ketose sugar, $C_6H_{12}O_6$, sweeter than sucrose, occurring in invert sugar, honey, and a great many fruits, used in foods and as an intravenous nutrient. Also called **levulos, fruit sugar.**

fruc·tu·ous (fruk′cho͞o əs), *adj.* productive; fertile; profitable. [ME < L *frūctuōs(us)* < *frūctu(s)* FRUIT; see -OUS] —**fruc′tu·ous·ly,** *adv.* —**fruc′tu·ous·ness,** *n.*

frug (fro͞og), *n., v.,* **frugged, frug·ging.** —*n.* **1.** a dance deriving from the twist. —*v.i.* **2.** to dance the frug. [?]

fru·gal (fro͞o′gəl), *adj.* **1.** economical in use or expenditure; prudently saving or sparing. **2.** entailing little expense; requiring few resources; meager; scanty. [< L *frūgāl(is)* economical = *frūg(ī)* (indeclinable adj., orig. dat. of *frūx* produce, fruit) + *-ālis* -AL[1]] —**fru·gal·i·ty** (fro͞o gal′i tē), **fru′gal·ness,** *n.* —**fru′gal·ly,** *adv.* —**Syn. 1.** thrifty, provident. See **economical.** —**Ant. 1.** lavish, wasteful.

fru·giv·o·rous (fro͞o jiv′ər əs), *adj.* fruit-eating, as certain bats. [< L *frūgī* (see FRUGAL) + -VOROUS]

fruit (fro͞ot), *n., pl.* **fruits,** (*esp. collectively*) **fruit,** *v.* —*n.* **1.** any product of vegetable growth useful to men or animals. **2.** *Bot.* **a.** the developed ovary of a seed plant with its contents and accessory parts, as the pea pod, nut, tomato, pineapple, etc. **b.** the edible part of a plant developed from a flower, with any accessory tissues, as the peach, mulberry, banana, etc. **c.** the spores and accessory organs of a cryptogam. **3.** anything produced or accruing; product, result, or effect; return or profit. **4.** *Slang.* a male homosexual. —*v.i., v.t.* **5.** to bear or cause to bear fruit: *The tree fruits in late summer. Pruning will sometimes fruit a tree.* [ME < OF < L *frūct(us)* enjoyment, proceeds, fruit (n. use of ptp. of *fruī* to enjoy)] —**fruit′like′,** *adj.*

fruit·age (fro͞o′tij), *n.* **1.** the bearing of fruit. **2.** fruits collectively. **3.** a crop of fruit. [< MF]

fruit·cake (fro͞ot′kāk′), *n.* a rich cake containing raisins, nuts, citron, etc.

fruit·ed (fro͞o′tid), *adj.* **1.** having or bearing fruit. **2.** with fruit added.

fruit·er (fro͞o′tər), *n.* **1.** a cargo vessel carrying fruit. **2.** a person who grows fruit. [late ME]

fruit·er·er (fro͞o′tər ər), *n.* *Chiefly Brit.* a dealer in fruit. [ME; extended form of FRUITER]

fruit′ fly′, any of numerous small dipterous insects of the family *Trypetidae,* whose larvae feed on fruit.

fruit·ful (fro͞ot′fəl), *adj.* **1.** abounding in fruit, as trees or other plants; bearing fruit abundantly. **2.** producing an abundant growth, as of fruit. **3.** productive of good results; profitable. [ME] —**fruit′ful·ly,** *adv.* —**fruit′ful·ness,** *n.* —**Syn. 2, 3.** See **productive.** —**Ant. 3.** barren.

fru·i·tion (fro͞o ish′ən), *n.* **1.** attainment of anything desired; realization of good results: *the fruition of one's labor.* **2.** enjoyment, as of something attained or realized. **3.** the state of bearing fruit. [ME *fruicioun* < LL *fruitiōn-* (s. of

fruitiō) enjoyment = L *fruit(us)* (var. of *frūctus;* see FRUIT) + *-iōn-* -ION] —**Syn. 1.** consummation, fulfillment.
fruit·less (fro͞ot′lis), *adj.* **1.** useless; unproductive; without results or success. **2.** without fruit; barren. [ME] —**fruit′less·ly,** *adv.* —**fruit′less·ness,** *n.* —**Syn. 1.** ineffective, unprofitable, bootless, futile, unavailing, idle. **2.** sterile, unfruitful. —**Ant. 1.** useful, profitable. **2.** fertile.
fruit′ sug′ar, *Chem.* fructose.
fruit′ tree′, a tree bearing edible fruit.
fruit·y (fro͞o′tē), *adj.,* **fruit·i·er, fruit·i·est. 1.** resembling fruit; having the taste or flavor of fruit. **2.** rich in flavor; pungent. **3.** excessively sweet or mellifluous; cloying; syrupy. **4.** *Slang.* insane; crazy. **5.** *Slang.* homosexual. —**fruit′i·ness,** *n.*
fru·men·ta·ceous (fro͞o′mən tā′shəs), *adj.* of the nature of or resembling wheat or other grain. [< LL *frūmentāceus* of corn or grain]
Fru·men·ti·us (fro͞o men′shē əs), *n.* **Saint,** A.D. c300–c380, founder of the Ethiopian Church.
fru·men·ty (fro͞o′mən tē), *n. Brit. Dial.* a dish of hulled wheat boiled in milk and seasoned with sugar, cinnamon, and raisins. Also, **fromenty.** [ME *frumentee* < OF = *frument* grain (< L *frūmentum*) + *-ee* -Y[3]]
frump (frump), *n.* a woman who is dowdy, drab, and unattractive. [?] —**frump′ish,** *adj.* —**frump′ish·ly,** *adv.* —**frump′ish·ness,** *n.*
frump·y (frum′pē), *adj.,* **frump·i·er, frump·i·est.** frumpish. —**frump′i·ly,** *adv.* —**frump′i·ness,** *n.*
Frun·ze (frōōn′ze), *n.* a city in and the capital of Kirghizia, in the SW Soviet Union in Asia. 355,000 (1965).
frus·trate (frus′trāt), *v.,* **-trat·ed, -trat·ing,** *adj.* —*v.t.* **1.** to make (plans, efforts, etc.) worthless or of no avail; defeat; baffle; nullify. **2.** to disappoint or thwart (a person). —*v.i.* **3.** to become frustrated. —*adj.* **4.** *Archaic.* frustrated. [ME *frustrate(n)* < L *frustrāt(us)* (ptp. of *frustrārī*) = *frustr(ā)* in vain + *-ātus* -ATE[1]] —**frus′trat·er,** *n.* —**frus·trative** (frus′trā tiv, -trə-), *adj.* —**Syn. 1.** balk, foil, check.
frus·trat·ed (frus′trā tid), *adj.* disappointed; thwarted: *a salesman who was a frustrated actor.*
frus·tra·tion (fru strā′shən), *n.* **1.** the act of frustrating. **2.** the state of being frustrated. **3.** an instance of being frustrated. [ME *frustracioun* < L *frustrātiōn-* (s. of *frustrātiō*) deception, disappointment]
frus·tule (frus′cho͞ol), *n. Bot.* the siliceous cell wall of a diatom. [< F < LL *frustul(um),* dim. of *frustum* FRUSTUM]
frus·tum (frus′təm), *n., pl.* **-tums, -ta** (-tə). *Geom.* **1.** the part of a conical solid left after cutting off a top portion with a plane parallel to the base. **2.** the part of a solid, as a cone or pyramid, between two usually parallel cutting planes. [< L: piece, bit; prob. akin to OIr *brúid* he breaks, OE *brȳsan* to crush]

F

F, Frustum of a cone

fru·tes·cent (fro͞o tes′ənt), *adj. Bot.* tending to be shrublike; shrubby. [< L *frut(ex)* shrub, bush + -ESCENT] —**fru·tes′cence,** *n.*
fru·ti·cose (fro͞o′tə kōs′), *adj. Bot.* having the form of a shrub; shrublike. [< L *fruticōs(us)* full of shrubs, bushy = *frutic-* (s. of *frutex*) shrub + *-ōsus* -OSE[1]]
fry[1] (frī), *v.,* **fried, fry·ing,** *n., pl.* **fries.** —*v.t.* **1.** to cook with fat, oil, etc., usually over direct heat. —*v.i.* **2.** to undergo cooking in fat. **3.** *Slang.* to die by electrocution, esp. in an electric chair. —*n.* **4.** a dish of something fried. **5.** an occasion at which the chief food is fried, frequently outdoors: *a fish fry.* [ME *frie(n)* < OF *fri(re)* < L *frīgere* to fry]
fry[2] (frī), *n., pl.* **fry. 1.** the young of fish. **2.** the young of various other animals, as frogs. [ME *frie, fry* seed, descendant, perh. < Scand; cf. Icel *frjō,* Sw *frö,* Goth *fraiw* seed]
Fry (frī), *n.* **Christopher,** born 1907, English playwright.
fry·er (frī′ər), *n.* **1.** a person or thing that fries. **2.** something, as a young chicken, for frying. Also, **frier.**
fry′ing pan′, a shallow, long-handled pan for frying food. Also, **fry-pan, fry·pan** (frī′pan′). Also called **skillet.**
f.s., foot-second.
FSH, *Biochem.* a hormone that regulates the development of the Graafian follicle in the female and stimulates the production of spermatozoa in the male. Also called **follicle-stimulating hormone.**
f-stop (ef′stop′), *n. Photog.* a camera lens aperture setting calibrated to an f number.
ft, foot; feet.
ft., **1.** (in prescriptions) **a.** let it be made. [< L *fīat*] **b.** let them be made. [< L *fīant*] **2.** foot; feet. **3.** fort.
FTC, *U.S. Govt.* Federal Trade Commission: a board charged with investigating and enjoining illegal practices in interstate trade.
ft-c, *Optics.* foot-candle.
fth., fathom. Also, **fthm.**
ft-L, *Optics.* foot-lambert; foot-lamberts.
ft-lb, *Physics.* foot-pound; foot-pounds.
ft-pdl, *Physics.* foot-poundal; foot-poundals.
ft/sec, feet per second.
ft/sec², feet per second per second. Also, **ft/s².**
fub (fub), *v.t.,* **fubbed, fub·bing.** fob[2].
fub·sy (fub′zē), *adj.,* **-si·er, -si·est.** *Brit. Dial.* short and stout. [obs. *fubs, fub* chubby person + -Y[1]]
fuch·sia (fyo͞o′shə), *n.* **1.** any onagraceous plant of the genus *Fuchsia,* which includes many varieties cultivated for their handsome drooping flowers. **2.** a herbaceous shrub, *Zauschneria californica,* having large crimson flowers. **3.** a bright, purplish-red color. —*adj.* **4.** of the color fuchsia: *a fuchsia dress.* [< NL; named after Leonhard *Fuchs* (1501–1566), German botanist; see -IA]
fuch·sin (fo͝ok′sin), *n.* a greenish coal-tar derivative that forms deep-red solutions: used chiefly as a dye. Also, **fuchsine** (fo͝ok′sin, -sēn). Also called **basic magenta, magenta.** [FUCHS(IA) + -IN[2]]
fuck (fuk), *Slang (usually vulgar).* —*v.t.* **1.** to have sexual intercourse with. **2.** to treat unfairly or harshly. **3.** to bungle or botch (usually fol. by *up*). —*v.i.* **4.** to have sexual intercourse. **5.** to meddle (usually fol. by *with*). —*interj.* **6.** damn (used as an expletive, often fol. by *you*). —*n.* **7.** an act or instance of sexual intercourse. **8.** a partner in sexual intercourse. [ME; orig. uncertain. Cf. G *ficken*] —**fuck′er,** *n.*
fuck·ing (fuk′ing), *Slang (usually vulgar).* —*adj.* **1.** damned (def. 2). —*adv.* **2.** damned.
fu·coid (fyo͞o′koid), *adj.* **1.** resembling or related to seaweeds of the genus *Fucus.* —*n.* **2.** a fucoid seaweed.
fu·cus (fyo͞o′kəs), *n., pl.* **-ci** (-sī), **-cus·es.** any olive-brown seaweed or alga of the genus *Fucus,* having branching fronds and often air bladders. [< L < Gk *phŷkos* orchil, red color, rock lichen, rouge]
fud·dle (fud′əl), *v.,* **-dled, -dling,** *n.* —*v.t.* **1.** to intoxicate. **2.** to muddle or confuse. —*v.i.* **3.** to tipple. —*n.* **4.** a confused state; muddle; jumble. [?]
fud·dy-dud·dy (fud′ē dud′ē, -dud′ē), *n., pl.* **-dud·dies,** *adj. Informal.* —*n.* **1.** a person who is stuffy, old-fashioned, and conservative. **2.** a person who is fussy or picayune about details; fussbudget. —*adj.* **3.** resisting change; ultra-conservative. **4.** fussy; picayune. [?]
fudge[1] (fuj), *n.* a candy made of sugar, butter, milk, chocolate, etc., often with nuts and other flavoring. [?]
fudge[2] (fuj), *n., v.,* **fudged, fudg·ing.** —*n.* **1.** *Usually Contemptuous.* nonsense or foolishness (often used interjectionally). —*v.i.* **2.** to talk nonsense. [?]
fudge[3] (fuj), *n., v.,* **fudged, fudg·ing.** —*n.* **1.** a small stereotype or a few lines of specially prepared type, bearing a newspaper bulletin, for replacing a detachable part of a page plate without the need to replate the entire page. **2.** the bulletin thus printed, often in color. **3.** a machine or attachment for printing such a bulletin. —*v.t.* **4.** to avoid coming to grips with (a subject, issue, etc.); evade; dodge. —*v.i.* **5.** to cheat or welsh. [var. of FADGE]
Fu·e·gi·an (fyo͞o ē′jē ən, fwā′jē-), *adj.* **1.** of or belonging to Tierra del Fuego or its indigenous Indians. —*n.* **2.** a native or inhabitant of Tierra del Fuego.
Fueh·rer (fyo͝or′ər), *n.* Führer.
fu·el (fyo͞o′əl), *n., v.,* **-eled, -el·ing** or (*esp. Brit.*) **-elled, -el·ling.** —*n.* **1.** combustible matter used to maintain fire, as coal, wood, oil, etc. **2.** something that gives nourishment or incentive. —*v.t.* **3.** to supply with fuel. —*v.i.* **4.** to obtain or replenish fuel. [ME *fuel(le), feuel* < OF *feuaile* < VL **focālia,* neut. pl. of **focālis* of the hearth, fuel. See FOCUS, -AL[1]] —**fu′el·er, fu′el·ler,** *n.*
fu′el cell′, **1.** a device that produces a continuous electric current directly from the oxidation of a fuel, as that of hydrogen by oxygen. **2.** a device in which the chemical energy of a fuel is converted into continuous electrical energy as a result of the reaction between the fuel and an oxidant.
fu′el injec′tion, the spraying of liquid fuel into the cylinders or combustion chambers of an engine.
fu′el injec′tor, a valve mechanism for fuel injection.
fu′el oil′, an oil used for fuel, esp. one used as a substitute for coal, as crude petroleum.
Fuer·tes (fyo͝or′tēz, -tēs, fyo͞o′ər-), *n.* **Louis Ag·as·siz** (ag′ə sē), 1874–1927, U.S. painter and naturalist.
fu·ga·cious (fyo͞o gā′shəs), *adj.* **1.** *Bot.* falling or fading early. **2.** fleeting; transitory. [< L *fugāci-* (s. of *fugāx*) apt to flee, fleet. See FUGITIVE, -I-, -OUS] —**fu·ga′cious·ly,** *adv.* —**fu·ga′cious·ness, fu·gac·i·ty** (fyo͞o gas′i tē), *n.*
fu·gal (fyo͞o′gəl), *adj. Music.* of or pertaining to a fugue, or composed in the style of a fugue. —**fu′gal·ly,** *adv.*
fu·ga·to (fo͞o gä′tō, fyo͞o-; *It.* fo͞o gä′tô), *n., pl.* **-tos** (-tōz). *Music.* a section of a composition that is in fugal style but does not constitute a real fugue. [< It]
-fuge, a noun suffix indicating something that puts to flight: *vermifuge.* [comb. form repr. L *-fugia* < *fug(āre)* (to) put to flight]
fu·gi·tive (fyo͞o′ji tiv), *n.* **1.** a person who is fleeing, as from prosecution, intolerable circumstances, etc.; a runaway. —*adj.* **2.** having taken flight or run away: *a fugitive slave.* **3.** fleeting; transitory. **4.** dealing with subjects of passing interest, as writings; ephemeral: *fugitive essays.* **5.** wandering, roving, or vagabond. **6.** *Fine Arts.* (of a color) not permanent. [< L *fugitīv(us)* fleeing = *fugit(us)* (ptp. of *fugere* to flee) + *-īvus* -IVE; r. ME *fugitif* < OF] —**fu′gi·tive·ly,** *adv.* —**fu′gi·tive·ness,** *n.* —**Syn. 3.** transient, passing. **4.** trivial, light. **5.** straying, roaming. —**Ant. 3, 6.** permanent. **4.** lasting.
fu·gle (fyo͞o′gəl), *v.i.,* **-gled, -gling.** *Informal.* to signal, or motion as if signaling. [back formation from FUGLEMAN]
fu·gle·man (fyo͞o′gəl mən), *n., pl.* **-men. 1.** (formerly) a soldier placed in front of a military company as a model or guide for others. **2.** a leader of a group, political party, etc.; a manager. [m. G *Flügelmann,* lit., flank man]
fugue (fyo͞og), *n.* **1.** *Music.* a polyphonic composition based upon one, two, or more themes, that are enunciated by several voices or parts in turn, and subjected to contrapuntal treatment. **2.** *Psychiatry.* a period during which a patient suffers from loss of memory, often begins a new life, and, upon recovery, remembers nothing of the amnesic period. [< F < It *fuga* < L: flight] —**fugue′like′,** *adj.*
Füh·rer (fʏ′rᴀʀ; *Eng.* fyo͝or′ər), *n. German.* **1.** leader. **2.** **der Führer** (deʀ), the leader, applied to Adolf Hitler. Also, **Fuehrer.**
Fu·ji (fo͞o′jē), *n.* a dormant volcano in central Japan, on Honshu island: highest mountain in Japan. 12,395 ft. Also called **Fu·ji·ya·ma** (fo͞o′jē yä′mə; *Jap.* fo͞o′jē yä′mä), **Fu·ji·san** (fo͞o′jē sän′).
Fu·kien (fo͞o′kyen′), *n.* a province in SE China, opposite Taiwan. 18,000,000 (1970); 45,845 sq. mi. *Cap.:* Foochow.
Fu·ku·da (fo͞o′ko͞o dä′), *n.* **Ta·ke·o** (tä ke′ô), born 1905, Japanese political leader: prime minister 1976–78.
Fu·ku·o·ka (fo͞o′ko͞o ō′kä), *n.* a city on N Kyushu, in SW Japan. 771,679 (est. 1964).
Ful (fo͝ol), *n., pl.* **Fuls,** (*esp. collectively*) **Ful** for 1. **1.** Fulani (def. 1). **2.** Fulani (def. 2).
-ful, a suffix meaning "full of," "characterized by" (*shameful; beautiful; careful; thoughtful*); "tending to," "able to" (*wakeful; harmful*); "as much as will fill" (*spoonful*). [ME, OE *-full, -ful,* repr. *full,* ¹*ful* FULL[1]]
Fu·la (fo͞o′lə, fo͝ol′ə), *n., pl.* **-las,** (*esp. collectively*) **-la.** Fulani.

Fu·lah (fōō′lä), *n., pl.* **-lahs,** (*esp. collectively*) **-lah.** Fulani (def. 1).

Fu·la·ni (fōō′lä nē, fōō lä′-), *n., pl.* **-nis,** (*esp. collectively*) **-ni** for 1. **1.** Also, **Fulah.** a member of a pastoral and nomadic people of mixed Negroid and Mediterranean stock, scattered through the Sudan from Senegal eastward. **2.** the language of the Fulani, a Niger-Congo language closely related to Wolof. Also, **Ful, Fula.**

Ful·bright (fŏŏl′brīt′), *n.* **1. J(ames) William,** born 1905, U.S. politician. **2.** *Informal.* a grant awarded under the provisions of the Fulbright Act.

Ful′bright Act′, an act of Congress (1946) by which funds derived chiefly from the sale of U.S. surplus property abroad are made available to U.S. citizens for study, research, etc., in foreign countries as well as to foreigners to engage in similar activities in the U.S. [named after J. W. FULBRIGHT]

ful·crum (fŏŏl′krəm, ful′-), *n., pl.* **-crums, -cra** (-krə). **1.** the support, or point of rest, on which a lever turns in moving a body. **2.** any prop or support. **3.** *Zool.* any of various structures in an animal serving as a hinge or support. [< L: bedpost = *fulc(īre)* (to) support + *-rum* neut. suffix]

ful·fil (fŏŏl fil′), *v.t.,* **-filled, -fil·ling.** fulfill.

ful·fill (fŏŏl fil′), *v.t.* **1.** to carry out, or bring to realization, as a prophecy, promise, etc. **2.** to perform or do, as duty; obey or follow, as commands. **3.** to satisfy (requirements, obligations, etc.). **4.** to bring to an end; finish or complete, as a period of time. **5.** to develop the full potential of (usually used reflexively). **6.** *Archaic.* to fill. [ME *fulfille(n)*, OE *fulfyllan*] —**ful·fill′er,** *n.* —**Syn. 1.** accomplish, achieve, realize. **2.** execute, discharge. **3.** meet, fill.

ful·fill·ment (fŏŏl fil′mənt), *n.* **1.** the act of fulfilling. **2.** the state or quality of being fulfilled; completion; realization. Also, **ful·fil′ment.**

ful·gent (ful′jənt), *adj.* shining brightly; dazzling; resplendent. Also, **ful·gid** (ful′jid). [ME < L *fulgent-* (s. of *fulgēns,* prp. of *fulgēre*) = *fulg-* flash + *-ent-* -ENT] —**ful′gent·ly,** *adv.* —**ful′gent·ness,** *n.*

ful·gu·rant (ful′gyər ənt), *adj.* flashing like lightning. [< L *fulgurant-* (s. of *fulgurāns*), prp. of *fulgurāre*]

ful·gu·rate (ful′gyə rāt′), *v.,* **-rat·ed, -rat·ing.** —*v.i.* **1.** to flash or dart like lightning. —*v.t.* **2.** *Med.* to destroy (esp. an abnormal growth) by electricity. [< L *fulgurāt(us)* (ptp. of *fulgurāre* to flash, glitter, lighten) = *fulgur-* (s. of *fulgor* lightning) + *-ātus* -ATE[1]] —**ful′gu·ra′tion,** *n.*

ful·gu·rat·ing (ful′gyə rā′ting), *adj. Med.* (of pains) sharp and piercing, like lightning.

ful·gu·rite (ful′gyə rīt′), *n.* a tubelike formation in sand or rock, caused by lightning. [< L *fulgur-* (see FULGURATE) + -ITE[1]]

ful·gu·rous (ful′gyər əs), *adj.* characteristic of or resembling lightning. [< L *fulgur-* (see FULGURATE) + -OUS]

fu·lig·i·nous (fyōō lij′ə nəs), *adj.* **1.** sooty; smoky. **2.** of the color of soot, as dark gray, dull brown, black, etc. [< L *fūlīginōs(us)* full of soot = *fūlīgin-* (s. of *fūlīgō*) soot + *-ōsus* -OUS] —**fu·lig′i·nous·ly,** *adv.* —**fu·lig′i·nous·ness,** *n.*

full[1] (fŏŏl), *adj.* **1.** filled; containing all that can be held; filled to utmost capacity: *a full cup.* **2.** complete; entire; maximum: *a full supply of food.* **3.** of the maximum size, amount, extent, volume, etc.: *a full load of five tons; to receive full pay.* **4.** (of garments, drapery, etc.) wide, ample, or having ample folds. **5.** abundant; well-supplied: *a cabinet full of medicine.* **6.** filled or rounded out, as in form: *a full bust.* **7.** engrossed; occupied (usually followed by *of*): *She was full of her own anxieties.* **8.** of the same parents: *full brothers.* **9.** *Music.* ample and complete in volume or richness of sound. **10.** (of wines) having considerable body. **11. full and by,** *Naut.* so as to be close-hauled: *sailing full and by.* —*adv.* **12.** exactly or directly: *The blow struck him full in the face.* **13.** very: *You know it full well.* **14.** *Archaic.* fully, completely, or entirely; quite; at least. —*v.t.* **15.** *Sewing.* to make full, as by gathering or pleating. —*v.i.* **16.** (of the moon) to become full. —*n.* **17.** the highest or fullest state, condition, or degree. **18. in full, a.** to or for the full or required amount. **b.** without abridgment. **19. to the full,** to the greatest extent; thoroughly. [ME, OE *full ful;* c. Goth *full(s),* OIcel *full(r),* OHG *fol(l)* (G *voll*), L *plēnus,* Gk *plērēs*] —**full′ness,** *n.* —**ful′ly,** *adv.*

full[2] (fŏŏl), *v.t.* **1.** to cleanse and thicken (cloth) by special processes in manufacture. —*v.i.* **2.** (of cloth) to become compacted or felted. [ME *fulle(n)*; back formation from FULLER[1]]

full·back (fŏŏl′bak′), *n. Football.* a running back who lines up behind the quarterback and is farthest from the line of scrimmage.

full′ blood′, relationship through both parents.

full-blood·ed (fŏŏl′blud′id), *adj.* **1.** of unmixed ancestry; thoroughbred. **2.** vigorous; virile; hearty. —**full′-blood′ed·ness,** *n.*

full-blown (fŏŏl′blōn′), *adj.* **1.** in full bloom: *a full-blown rose.* **2.** completely developed.

full-bod·ied (fŏŏl′bod′ēd), *adj.* of full strength, flavor, richness, etc.

full′ bri′dle, a bridle with a bridoon and a curb, each controlled by a separate pair of reins.

full-cut (fŏŏl′kut′), *adj. Jewelry.* (of a brilliant) cut with 58 facets, including the table and culet.

full′ dress′, **1.** a ceremonial style of dress. **2.** formal attire, usually consisting of black tailcoats and white bow ties for men, and floor-length dresses for women. —**full′-dress′,** *adj.*

full·er[1] (fŏŏl′ər), *n.* a person who fulls cloth. [ME; OE *fullere* < L *full(ō)* fuller; see -ER[1]]

full·er[2] (fŏŏl′ər), *n.* a half-round hammer used for grooving and spreading iron. [appar. FULL[1] in sense to make full, close, compact + -ER[1]]

Ful·ler (fŏŏl′ər), *n.* **1. R(ichard) Buck·min·ster** (buk′-min stər), 1895–1983, U.S. engineer, designer, and architect. **2. (Sarah) Margaret** (*Marchioness Ossoli*), 1810–50, U.S. author and literary critic. **3. Thomas,** 1608–61, English clergyman and historian.

ful′ler's earth′, an absorbent clay, used esp. for removing grease from fabrics, in fulling, as a filter, and as a dusting powder.

ful′ler's tea′sel, the teasel, *Dipsacus fullonum.*

Ful·ler·ton (fŏŏl′ər tən), *n.* a city in SW California, SE of Los Angeles. 85,987 (1970).

full-faced (fŏŏl′fāst′), *adj.* **1.** having a plump or round face. **2.** facing squarely toward the spectator or in a given direction. **3.** *Print.* (of type) boldface. —**full′face′,** *n., adv.*

full-fash·ioned (fŏŏl′fash′ənd), *adj.* knitted to conform to the shape of a body part, as of the foot or leg.

full-fledged (fŏŏl′flejd′), *adj.* **1.** fully developed. **2.** of full rank or standing.

full′ gain′er, *Diving.* a dive in which the diver takes off facing forward and performs a backward somersault, entering the water feet first.

full-grown (fŏŏl′grōn′), *adj.* fully grown; mature.

full′ house′, *Poker.* a hand consisting of three of a kind and a pair. Also called **full′ hand′.**

full-length (fŏŏl′lengkth′, -length′), *adj.* **1.** of customary length; not abridged or skimpy. **2.** having, showing, or accommodating the full length or height of the human body.

full′ moon′, the moon when the whole of its disk is illuminated, occurring when in opposition to the sun. See diag. at **moon.** [ME *ful moyne,* OE *fulles monan*]

full-mouthed (fŏŏl′mouthd′), *adj.* **1.** (of cattle, sheep, etc.) having a complete set of teeth. **2.** noisy; loud.

full′ nel′son. See under **nelson.**

full′ness of time′, the proper or destined time.

full′ rhyme′, *Pros.* rhyme in which the stressed vowels and all following consonants and vowels are identical, but the consonants preceding the rhyming vowels are different, as in *chain, brain; marry, tarry.* Also called **perfect rhyme.**

full-rigged (fŏŏl′rigd′), *adj.* **1.** *Naut.* (of a sailing vessel) rigged as a ship; square-rigged on all of three or more masts. **2.** having all equipment.

full′ sail′, **1.** all the sails of a vessel. **2.** with all sails set: *The ship was moving ahead full sail.* —**full′-sailed′,** *adj.*

full-scale (fŏŏl′skāl′), *adj.* **1.** having the exact size or proportions of the original. **2.** using all possible means, facilities, etc.; complete.

full′ speed′, **1.** the maximum speed. **2.** *Naut.* the speed normally maintained on a passage. **3.** at maximum speed: *to move full speed ahead.*

full′ stop′, period (def. 15).

full′ swing′, full capacity; greatest activity: *The meeting was in full swing when we arrived.*

full′ tilt′, at the full potential, speed, energy, etc.: *The factory is now going full tilt.*

full-time (fŏŏl′tīm′), *adj.* working or operating the customary number of hours in a given period: *a full-time housekeeper; full-time production.* Cf. **part-time.**

ful·mar (fŏŏl′mər), *n.* any of certain oceanic birds of the petrel family, esp. *Fulmarus glacialis,* a gull-like arctic species. [orig. Hebrides dial. < Scand; cf. Icel *fūll* foul + *mār* gull (with reference to its stench)]

ful·mi·nant (ful′mə nənt), *adj.* **1.** occurring suddenly and with great intensity or severity; fulminating. **2.** *Pathol.* occurring or progressing suddenly. [< L *fulminant-* (s. of *fulmināns*), prp. of *fulmināre*]

ful·mi·nate (ful′mə nāt′), *v.,* **-nat·ed, -nat·ing,** *n.* —*v.i.* **1.** to explode with a loud noise; detonate. **2.** to issue denunciations or the like (usually fol. by *against*): *to fulminate against sin.* —*v.t.* **3.** to cause to explode. **4.** to issue or pronounce with vehement denunciation, condemnation, or the like. —*n.* **5.** *Chem.* one of a group of unstable, explosive compounds derived from fulminic acid, esp. its mercury salt, which is a powerful detonating agent. [late ME *fulminate(n)* < L *fulmināt(us)* (ptp. of *fulmināre*)] —**ful′mi·na′tor,** *n.* **ful·mi·na·to·ry** (ful′mə nə tôr′ē, -tōr′ē), *adj.*

ful′minating com′pound, *Chem.* a fulminate.

ful′minating pow′der, *Chem.* a fulminate.

ful·mi·na·tion (ful′mə nā′shən), *n.* **1.** a violent denunciation or censure. **2.** violent explosion. [< L *fulminātiōn-* (s. of *fulminātiō*) a thundering, fuming]

ful·mine (ful′min), *v.i., v.t.,* **-mined, -min·ing.** *Archaic.* to fulminate. [< L *fulmin(āre)*]

ful·min·ic (ful min′ik), *adj.* highly explosive; unstable. [< L *fulmin-* (s. of *fulmen*) lightning, thunder + -IC]

fulmin′ic ac′id, *Chem.* an unstable acid, HONC, isomeric with cyanic acid, and known only in the form of its salts.

ful·mi·nous (ful′mə nəs), *adj.* of, pertaining to, or resembling thunder and lightning. [< L *fulmin(e)us* of, belonging to lightning. See FULMINIC, -OUS]

ful·ness (fŏŏl′nis), *n.* fullness.

ful·some (fŏŏl′səm, ful′-), *adj.* **1.** offensive to good taste, esp. as being excessive; gross. **2.** disgusting; sickening; repulsive. [ME *fulsom*] —**ful′some·ly,** *adv.* —**ful′some·ness,** *n.*

Ful·ton (fŏŏl′tən), *n.* **Robert,** 1765–1815, U.S. engineer and inventor.

ful·vous (ful′vəs), *adj.* tawny; dull yellowish-gray or yellowish-brown. [< L *fulvus*]

fumar′ic ac′id, *Chem.* a crystalline solid, HOOCCH=CHCOOH, isomeric with maleic acid, essential to animal and vegetable respiration: used in the making of synthetic resins and as a replacement for tartaric acid in beverages and baking powders. Also called **boletic acid.** [< NL *Fumār(ia)* name of genus (LL: fumitory; see -ARIA) + -IC] —**fu·mar·ic** (fyōō mar′ik), *adj.*

fu·ma·role (fyōō′mə rōl′), *n.* a hole, in or near a volcano, from which vapor rises. [< F *fumerolle* < LL *fūmāriōl(um),* dim. of L *fūmārium* smoke chamber] —**fu·ma·rol·ic** (fyōō′mə rol′ik), *adj.*

fum·ble (fum′bəl), *v.,* **-bled, -bling,** *n.* —*v.i.* **1.** to feel or grope about clumsily. **2.** *Sports.* to fumble the ball. —*v.t.* **3.** to make, handle, etc., clumsily or inefficiently. **4.** *Sports* to fail to hold or maintain hold (on a ball) after having touched it or carried it. —*n.* **5.** the act of fumbling. **6.** *Sports.* the act or an instance of fumbling the ball. [? < Scand; cf. Sw *fumla* to grope] —**fum′bler,** *n.* —**fum′bling·ly,** *adv.* —**fum′bling·ness,** *n.*

fume (fyōōm), *n., v.,* **fumed, fum·ing.** —*n.* **1.** Often, **fumes.** any smokelike or vaporous exhalation from matter or substances, esp. of an odorous or harmful nature: *noxious fumes of carbon monoxide.* **2.** an irritable or angry mood: *to be in a fume.* —*v.t.* **3.** to emit or exhale, as fumes, vapor, or the like. **4.** to treat with or expose to fumes. —*v.i.* **5.** to rise, or pass off, as fumes. **6.** to emit fumes. **7.** to show fretful irritation or anger. [ME < OF *fum* < L *fūm(us)* smoke, steam, fume] —**fume′less,** *adj.* —**fume′like′,** *adj.* —**fum′er,** *n.* —**fum′ing·ly,** *adv.* —**Syn. 2.** rage, fury. **7.** chafe, fret, rage.

fumed (fyo͞omd), *adj.* darkened or colored by exposure to ammonia fumes, as oak and other wood.

fu·mi·gant (fyo͞o′mi gənt), *n.* any volatile or volatilizable chemical compound used as a disinfectant or pesticide. [< L *fūmigant-* (s. of *fūmigāns*), prp. of *fūmigāre*]

fu·mi·gate (fyo͞o′mə gāt′), *v.t.*, **-gat·ed, -gat·ing.** to expose to smoke or fumes, as in disinfecting. [< L *fūmigāt(us)* (ptp. of *fūmigāre*) smoked, fumigated = *fūmig-* FUME + *-ātus* -ATE[1]] —**fu′mi·ga′tion,** *n.* —**fu·mi·ga·to·ry** (fyo͞o′mə gə tôr′ē, -tōr′ē, -gā′tə rē), *adj.*

fu·mi·ga·tor (fyo͞o′mə gā′tər), *n.* **1.** a person or thing that fumigates. **2.** a structure in which plants are fumigated to destroy insects.

fu·mi·to·ry (fyo͞o′mi tōr′ē, -tôr′ē), *n., pl.* **-ries.** any plant of the genus *Fumaria*, of the family *Fumariaceae*, esp. a delicate herb, *F. officinalis*, having finely dissected leaves and racemes of purplish flowers. [alter. of earlier *fumiterre*, ME *fumetere* < MF < ML *fumus terrae*, lit., smoke of the earth]

fu·mu·lus (fyo͞o′myə ləs), *n., pl.* **-lus.** (formerly) a thin, almost transparent veil of clouds; a layer of haze. [< NL]

fum·y (fyo͞o′mē), *adj.*, **fum·i·er, fum·i·est.** emitting or full of fumes; fumelike.

fun (fun), *n., v.*, **funned, fun·ning,** *adj.* —*n.* **1.** something that provides mirth or amusement; enjoyment; playfulness. **2.** for or **in fun,** as a joke; not seriously; playfully. **3. like fun,** *Informal.* certainly not; of doubtful truth. **4. make fun of,** to make the object of ridicule; deride: *The youngsters made fun of their teacher.* —*v.i., v.t.* **5.** *Informal.* to joke; kid. —*adj.* **6.** *Informal.* of or pertaining to fun, esp. to social fun. **7.** *Informal.* whimsical; flamboyant: *The fashions that she wears are definitely on the fun side.* [? dial. var. of obs. *fon* to befool. See FOND[1]] —**Syn. 1.** merriment, pleasure, gaiety, frolic, revel.

fu·nam·bu·list (fyo͞o nam′byə list), *n.* a tightrope walker. [< L *fūnambul(us)* ropedancer + -IST] —**fu·nam′bu·lism,** *n.*

Fun·chal (*Port.* fo͞on shäl′), *n.* a seaport in and the capital of the Madeira Islands, on SE Madeira: winter resort. 63,044 (1960).

func·tion (fungk′shən), *n.* **1.** the kind of action or activity proper to any person or thing; the purpose for which something is designed or exists; role. **2.** any ceremonious public or social gathering or occasion. **3.** a factor related to or dependent upon other factors. **4.** *Math.* Also called **map, mapping, transformation.** a relation between two sets in which one or more elements of the second set are assigned to each element of the first set; operator. **5.** *Geom.* **a.** a formula expressing a relation between the angles of a triangle and its sides, as sine, cosine, etc. **b.** See **hyperbolic function. 6.** *Gram.* the grammatical role a linguistic form has in a particular construction. —*v.i.* **7.** to perform a specified action or activity; act; serve; operate: *The battery doesn't function. In earlier English the present tense often functioned as a future.* [< L *functiōn-* (s. of *functiō*) a performance, execution = *funct(us)* (ptp. of *fungī*) performed, executed + *-iōn-* -ION] —**func′tion·less,** *adj.*

func·tion·al (fungk′shə nəl), *adj.* **1.** of or pertaining to a function or functions. **2.** having or serving a utilitarian purpose; capable of serving the purpose for which it was designed. **3.** Also, **func′tion·al·is′tic.** (of a building or furnishing) constructed or made according to the principles of functionalism. **4.** capable of operating or functioning: *When will the ventilating system be functional again?* **5.** pertaining to an algebraic operation. **6.** *Psychol.* without a known organic cause or structural change: *functional disorder.* Cf. **organic** (def. 5). —**func′tion·al·ly,** *adv.*

func′tional disease′, *Pathol.* a disease in which there is an abnormal change in the function of an organ, but no structural alteration in the tissues involved (opposed to *organic disease*).

func′tional group′, *Chem.* a group of atoms that causes the characteristic behavior of a class of compounds, as the hydroxyl group in alcohols.

func′tional illit′erate, a person whose ability to read or write is inadequate for the needs of his job, the demands of a situation, or the like.

func·tion·al·ism (fungk′shə nəliz′əm), *n.* **1.** (*usually cap.*) *Chiefly Archit., Furniture.* **a.** a design movement evolved in the early 20th century, advocating the design of buildings, furnishings, etc., as direct fulfillments of material requirements, as for shelter or repose. **b.** the doctrines and practices associated with this movement. **2.** any doctrine that emphasizes purpose, practical utility, or adaptiveness.

func·tion·al·ist (fungk′shə nəlist), *n.* **1.** a person who advocates, or works according to, the principles of functionalism. —*adj.* **2.** of or pertaining to functionalism.

func·tion·ar·y (fungk′shə ner′ē), *n., pl.* **-ar·ies.** a person who functions in a specified capacity, esp. in government service; an official.

func′tion word′, a word, as a pronoun or preposition, that is used in a language as a substitute for another or as a marker of syntactic relationship; a member of a small, closed form class whose membership is relatively fixed.

fund (fund), *n.* **1.** a stock of money or pecuniary resources, as for some purpose: *a retirement fund.* **2.** a store or stock of something immaterial or material. **3. funds,** money in hand; pecuniary resources. —*v.t.* **4.** to provide a fund to pay the interest or principal of (a debt). **5.** to convert (general outstanding debts) into a more or less permanent debt. **6.** to provide money for (a project or the like). [< L *fund(us)* bottom, estate; r. FOND[2] in most of its meanings]

fun·da·ment (fun′də mənt), *n.* **1.** the physical characteristics of a geographical region, as land forms, drainage, climate, soils, etc. **2.** the buttocks. **3.** *Obs.* a base. [< L *fundāment(um)* foundation; r. ME *fondement* < OF]

fun·da·men·tal (fun′də men′təl), *adj.* **1.** serving as, or being an essential part of, a foundation or basis; basic; underlying: *fundamental principles.* **2.** of, pertaining to, or affecting the foundation or basis: *a fundamental revision.* **3.** being an original or primary source: *a fundamental idea.* **4.** *Music.* (of a chord) having its root as its lowest note. —*n.* **5.** a basic principle, rule, law, or the like, that serves as the groundwork of a system; essential part. **6.** Also called **fun′damen′tal note′, fun′damen′tal tone′.** *Music.* **a.** the root of a chord. **b.** the generator of a series of harmonics. **7.** *Physics.* the component of lowest frequency in a composite wave. [ME < NL *fundāmentāl(is)* of, belonging to a foundation] —**fun·da·men·tal·i·ty** (fun′də mental′i tē), **fun′da·men′tal·ness,** *n.* —**fun′da·men′tal·ly,** *adv.* —**Syn. 1.** indispensable, essential, necessary. **3.** first. —**Ant. 1.** secondary, superfluous; last; least.

fun·da·men·tal·ism (fun′də men′təliz′əm), *n.* **1.** (*sometimes cap.*) a movement in American Protestantism that arose in the early part of the 20th century and that stresses the infallibility of the Bible in all matters of faith and doctrine, accepting it as a literal historical record. **2.** the beliefs held by those in this movement. —**fun′da·men′tal·ist,** *n., adj.*

fun′damen′tal u′nit, *Physics.* one of the units of mass, length, and time taken as a basis for a system of units.

fun·dus (fun′dəs), *n., pl.* **-di** (-dī). *Anat.* the base of an organ, or the part opposite to or remote from an aperture. [< L: lit., the bottom] —**fun′dic,** *adj.*

Fun·dy (fun′dē), *n.* **Bay of,** an inlet of the Atlantic in SE Canada, between New Brunswick and Nova Scotia, known for its high tides.

Fü·nen (fʏ′nən), *n.* German name of **Fyn.**

fu·ner·al (fyo͞o′nər əl), *n.* **1.** the ceremonies for a dead person prior to burial or cremation; obsequies. **2.** a funeral procession. —*adj.* **3.** of or pertaining to a funeral. [ME < ML *fūnerāl(ia)*, neut. pl. n. use of adj. *fūnerāl(is)* = L *fūn(us)* funeral, death + *-ālis* -AL[1]]

fu′neral direc′tor, a mortician; undertaker.

fu′neral home′, an establishment where the dead are prepared for burial or cremation, where the body may be viewed, and where funeral services are sometimes held. Also called **fu′neral par′lor, mortuary.**

fu·ner·ar·y (fyo͞o′nə rer′ē), *adj.* of or pertaining to a funeral or burial: *a funerary urn.* [< LL *fūnerāri(us)* of, relating to a FUNERAL; see -ARY]

fu·ne·re·al (fyo͞o nēr′ē əl), *adj.* **1.** of or pertaining to a funeral. **2.** mournful; gloomy; dismal. [< L *fūnere(us)* of, belonging to a FUNERAL + -AL[1]] —**fu·ne′re·al·ly,** *adv.*

fu·nest (fyo͞o nest′), *adj.* boding or causing evil or death; sinister; fatal; disastrous. [< F *funeste* < L *fūnest(us)* < *fūn(us)* funeral, death]

Fünf·kir·chen (fʏnf′kēr′кнən), *n.* German name of **Pécs.**

fun·gal (fung′gəl), *adj.* **1.** fungous. —*n.* **2.** a fungus. [< NL *fungāl(is)*]

fun·gi (fun′jī), *n.* a pl. of **fungus.**

fungi-, a combining form of **fungus:** *fungicide.*

fun·gi·ble (fun′jə bəl), *Law.* —*adj.* **1.** (esp. of goods) being of such nature or kind as to be freely exchangeable or replaceable for another of like nature or kind. —*n.* **2.** a fungible thing, as money or grain. [< ML *fungibil(is)* = L *fungī* to perform the office of + *-bilis* -BLE] —**fun′gi·bil′i·ty,** *n.*

fun·gi·cide (fun′ji sīd′), *n.* an agent used for destroying fungi. —**fun′gi·cid′al,** *adj.* —**fun′gi·cid′al·ly,** *adv.*

fun·gi·form (fun′jə fôrm′), *adj.* having the form of a fungus or mushroom.

fun·gi·stat (fun′ji stat′), *n.* a fungistatic agent or preparation.

fun·gi·stat·ic (fun′ji stat′ik), *adj.* (of a substance or preparation) inhibiting the growth of a fungus. —**fun′gi·stat′i·cal·ly,** *adv.*

fun·go (fung′gō), *n., pl.* **-goes.** *Baseball.* **1.** (in practice sessions) a ball tossed into the air by the batter himself and struck as it comes down. **2.** a batted ball, esp. a fly ball, hit in this manner. [?]

fun·goid (fung′goid), *adj.* **1.** resembling a fungus; of the nature of a fungus. —*n.* **2.** a growth having the characteristics of a fungus.

fun·gous (fung′gəs), *adj.* **1.** of, pertaining to, or caused by fungi; fungal. **2.** of the nature of or resembling a fungus. [ME < L *fungōs(us)* full of holes, spongy]

fun·gus (fung′gəs), *n., pl.* **fun·gi** (fun′jī), **fun·gus·es,** *adj.* —*n.* **1.** any of numerous thallophytes of the division *Fungi*, comprising the mushrooms, molds, mildews, rusts, smuts, etc., characterized chiefly by absence of chlorophyll and by subsisting upon dead or living organic matter. **2.** *Pathol.* a spongy, abnormal growth, as proud flesh formed in a wound. —*adj.* **3.** fungous. [< L; cf. Gk *spóngos, sphóngos* sponge] —**fun·gic** (fun′jik), *adj.* —**fun′gus·like′,** *adj.*

fun′ house′, (in an amusement park) a building having devices for surprising and amusing patrons.

fu·ni·cle (fyo͞o′ni kəl), *n.* *Bot.* the stalk of an ovule or seed. [< L *fūnicul(us)*]

fu·nic·u·lar (fyo͞o nik′yə lər), *adj.* **1.** of or pertaining to a rope or cord, or its tension. **2.** worked by a rope or the like. —*n.* **3.** See **funicular railway.** [< L *fūnicul(us)* (see FUNICULUS) + -AR[1]]

funic′ular rail′way, a short, very steep cable railway operating in such a way that the ascending and descending cars are counterbalanced.

fu·nic·u·late (fyo͞o nik′yə lit, -lāt′), *adj.* *Bot.* having a funicle.

fu·nic·u·lus (fyo͞o nik′yə ləs), *n., pl.* **-li** (-lī′). **1.** *Anat.* a conducting cord such as a nerve cord, umbilical cord, etc. **2.** *Bot.* a funicle. [< L: small rope, cord = *fūni(s)* rope, line + *-culus* -CULE]

funk (fungk), *Informal.* —*n.* **1.** cowering fear; fright or terror. **2.** a dejected mood. —*v.t.* **3.** to frighten. **4.** to shrink from; try to shirk. —*v.i.* **5.** to shrink or quail in fear. [? < early Flem *fonck* disturbance] —**funk′er,** *n.*

Funk (fungk), *n.* **Cas·i·mir** (kaz′i mēr′), 1884–1967, Polish biochemist: discoverer of vitamins.

fun·ki·a (fung′kē ə, fo͞ong′-), *n.* See **plantain lily.** [<

NL; named after C. H. *Funck* (d. 1839), German botanist; see -IA]

funk·y[1] (fuŋ′kē), *adj.*, **funk·i·er, funk·i·est. 1.** *Informal.* overcome with fear; terrified. **2.** depressed. [FUNK[1] + -Y[1]]

funk·y[2] (fuŋ′kē), *adj.*, **funk·i·er, funk·i·est.** *Slang.* **1.** evil-smelling; foul. **2. a.** earthy; down-to-earth. **b.** pleasantly unconventional or offbeat. **c.** excellent; fine. **d.** sexy or sensual. —**funk′i·ness,** *n.* [*funk* stench (akin to ONF *funkier* < LL **fūmicāre;* see FUME) + -Y[1]]

fun·nel (fun′əl), *n.*, *v.*, **-neled, -nel·ing** or (*esp. Brit.*) **-nelled, -nel·ling.** —*n.* **1.** a cone-shaped utensil with a tube at the apex, for conducting liquid or other substance through a small opening, as into a bottle, jug, or the like. **2.** a smokestack, esp. of a steamship or a locomotive. **3.** a flue, tube, or shaft, as for ventilation. —*v.t.* **4.** to concentrate, channel, or focus. [late ME *fonel,* < MF **founel* < OPr *fonilh* < LL **fundibul(um),* aph. var. of L *infundibulum* < *infund(ere)* (to) pour in] —**fun′nel·like′,** *adj.*

fun′nel cloud′, tuba (def. 2).

fun·ny (fun′ē), *adj.*, **-ni·er, -ni·est,** *n.*, *pl.* **-nies.** —*adj.* **1.** providing fun; amusing; comical: *a funny remark; a funny person.* **2.** attempting to amuse; facetious. **3.** warranting suspicion; deceitful; underhanded: *He won't stand for any funny stuff.* **4.** insolent; sassy. **5.** *Informal.* curious; strange; peculiar; odd: *Her speech has a funny twang.* —*n.* **6. funnies,** *U.S.* **a.** comic strips. **b.** Also called **funny paper.** the section of a newspaper containing comic strips, word games, etc. —**fun′ni·ly,** *adv.* —**fun′ni·ness,** *n.*
—**Syn. 1.** diverting, comic, farcical, absurd, ridiculous, incongruous, droll, witty, facetious, humorous. FUNNY, LAUGHABLE, LUDICROUS refer to that which excites laughter. FUNNY and LAUGHABLE are both applied to that which provokes laughter or deserves to be laughed at: *a funny story, scene, joke; a laughable incident, mistake.* That which is LUDICROUS excites laughter by its incongruity and foolish absurdity: *The monkey's attempts to imitate the woman were ludicrous.* —**Ant. 1.** solemn, sad, melancholy.

fun′ny bone′, the part of the elbow where the ulnar nerve passes by the internal condyle of the humerus, which when struck causes a peculiar, tingling sensation in the arm and hand; crazy bone.

fun′ny busi′ness, *Slang.* improper or unethical conduct, as deception, trickery, etc.

fun′ny mon′ey, *Slang.* **1.** counterfeit currency. **2.** money from undisclosed or questionable sources, esp. for political purposes. **3.** warrants, convertible securities, and the like issued by a company as a means for acquiring another company or companies.

fun′ny pa′per, funny (def. 6b).

fur (fûr), *n.*, *adj.*, *v.*, **furred, fur·ring.** —*n.* **1.** *Zool.* the fine, soft, thick, hairy coating of the skin of a mammal. **2.** such a coat, as of sable, ermine, or beaver, used for lining, trimming, or making garments. **3.** Often, **furs.** a garment made of fur. **4.** any coating resembling fur, as matter on the tongue. **5. make the fur fly, a.** to cause a scene or disturbance, esp. of a violent nature; make trouble. **b.** to do things quickly. —*adj.* **6.** of or pertaining to fur, animal skins, dressed pelts, etc. —*v.t.* **7.** to line, face, or trim, with fur, as a garment. **8.** *Building Trades.* to apply furring to (a wall, ceiling, etc.). **9.** to clothe (a person) with fur. **10.** to coat with foul or deposited matter. [ME *furre* < MF *fourr(er)* (to) line a garment, OF *forrer,* orig. to encase < *fuerre* sheath < Gmc; akin to OE *fōdder* case, sheath, Icel *fōthr,* Gk *pōma*] —**fur′less,** *adj.*

fur., furlong; furlongs.

fu·ran (fyŏŏr′an, fyŏŏ ran′), *n.* *Chem.* a liquid heterocyclic compound, C_4H_4O, used chiefly in organic synthesis. Also called **furfuran.** [aph. form of FURFURAN]

fur·be·low (fûr′bə lō′), *n.* **1.** a festooned flounce, as on a woman's gown. **2.** any bit of showy trimming or finery. —*v.t.* **3.** to ornament with or as with furbelows. [var. of FALBALA]

fur·bish (fûr′bish), *v.t.* to restore to freshness of appearance or condition. [ME *furbish(en)* < MF *forbiss-,* long s. of *forbir* to polish, clean < Gmc; cf. OHG *furban*] —**fur′bish·er,** *n.*

fur·cate (*adj.* fûr′kāt, -kit; *v.* fûr′kāt), *adj.*, *v.*, **-cat·ed, -cat·ing.** —*adj.* **1.** forked; branching. —*v.i.* **2.** to form a fork; divide into branches. [< ML *furcāt(us)* cloven. See FORK, -ATE[1]] —**fur·ca·tion** (fər kā′shən), *n.*

fur·cu·la (fûr′kyə lə), *n.*, *pl.* **-lae** (-lē′). **1.** *Ornith.* the forked clavicular bone of a bird; wishbone. **2.** *Entomol.* the ventral, forked appendage on the abdomen of a springtail used in springing. [< L: a forked prop] —**fur′cu·lar,** *adj.*

fur·cu·lum (fûr′kyə ləm), *n.*, *pl.* **-la** (-lə). furcula. [< NL]

fur·fur (fûr′fər), *n.*, *pl.* **fur·fur·es** (fûr′fyə rēz′). **1.** the formation of flakelike particles on the surface of the skin, as of dandruff. **2. furfures,** these particles. [< L: bran, scurf]

fur·fu·ra·ceous (fûr′fyə rā′shəs), *adj.* **1.** resembling bran; branlike. **2.** scaly; scurfy. [< LL *furfurāceus* = *furfur* bran, scurf + *-āceus* -ACEOUS] —**fur·fu·ra′ceous·ly,** *adv.*

fur·fur·al (fûr′fə ral′, -fyə), *n.* *Chem.* a liquid heterocyclic aldehyde, C_4H_3OCHO, obtained from bran, corncobs, etc.: used chiefly in the manufacture of plastics and as a solvent in the refining of lubricating oils. Also called **fur·fur·al·de·hyde** (fûr′fə ral′də hīd′, -fyə-). [< L *furfur* bran, scurf + -AL[3]]

fur·fur·an (fûr′fə ran′), *n.* *Chem.* furan. [< L *furfur* bran, scurf + -AN]

Fu·ri·ae (fyŏŏr′ē ē′), *n.pl.* *Rom. Myth.* the Furies. Also called **Dirae.**

fu·ri·bund (fyŏŏr′ə bund′), *adj.* furious; frenzied; raging. [< L *furibund(us)* raging, furious, angry = *furi-* FURY + *-bundus* adj. suffix]

fu·ri·ous (fyŏŏr′ē əs), *adj.* **1.** full of fury, violent passion, or rage. **2.** intensely violent, as wind, storms, etc. **3.** of unrestrained energy, speed, etc. [ME < L *furiōs(us)*] —**fu′ri·ous·ly,** *adv.* —**fu′ri·ous·ness,** *n.*

furl (fûrl), *v.t.* **1.** to gather into a compact roll and bind securely, as a sail against a spar or a flag against its staff. —*v.i.* **2.** to become furled. —*n.* **3.** the act of furling. **4.** something furled, as a roll. [< MF *ferler,* OF *ferlier* = *fer* firm (< L *fir(mus)*) + *lier* to bind (< L *ligāre*)] —**furl′a·ble,** *adj.* —**furl′er,** *n.*

fur·long (fûr′lôŋ, -loŋ), *n.* a unit of distance, equal to 220 yards or ⅛ mile. *Abbr.:* fur. [ME; OE *furlang* length of a furrow]

fur·lough (fûr′lō), —*n.* **1.** *Mil.* vacation granted to an enlisted man: in the U.S. Army, one month per year. **2.** a temporary or permanent dismissal of a railroad worker because of insufficient work for him or her to do; layoff. —*v.t.* **3.** to grant a furlough to. **4.** to lay off (a railroad worker). [var. of earlier *furloff* < D *verlof;* cf. G *Verlaub* leave, permission; current pronunciation by assoc. with *dough, though*]

fur·nace (fûr′nəs), *n.*, *v.*, **-naced, -nac·ing.** —*n.* **1.** a structure or apparatus in which heat may be generated, as for heating houses, smelting ores, or producing steam. **2.** a place characterized by intense heat. —*v.t.* **3.** *Metall.* to heat (a piece) in a furnace, as to soften it for bending. [ME *furneis, furnais* < OF *fornais, fournais* < L *fornac-* (s. of *fornax*) kiln, oven, akin to *formus* warm] —**fur′nace·like′,** *adj.*

fur·nish (fûr′nish), *v.t.* **1.** to provide or supply (often fol. by *with*): *to furnish one with needed time.* **2.** to fit out (a house, room, etc.) with necessary appliances, esp. furniture. [ME *furnissh(en)* < OF *furniss-,* long s. of *furnir* to accomplish, furnish < Gmc; cf. OHG *frumjan* to provide] —**fur′nish·er,** *n.*
—**Syn. 1, 2.** rig, outfit, deck out. FURNISH, APPOINT, EQUIP all refer to providing something necessary. FURNISH emphasizes the idea of providing necessary or customary services or appliances in living quarters: *to furnish board; a room meagerly furnished with a bed, desk, and a wooden chair.* APPOINT (now found only in WELL-APPOINTED) means to furnish completely with all requisites or accessories or in an elegant style: *a well-appointed house.* EQUIP means to supply with necessary materials or apparatus for some service, action, or undertaking; it emphasizes preparation: *to equip a vessel, a soldier.*

fur·nish·ing (fûr′ni shiŋ), *n.* **1.** that with which anything is furnished. **2. furnishings, a.** fittings, appliances, articles of furniture, etc., for a house or room. **b.** accessories of dress.

fur·ni·ture (fûr′ni chər), *n.* **1.** the movable articles, as tables, chairs, bedsteads, desks, cabinets, etc., required for use or ornament in a house, office, or the like. **2.** fittings, apparatus, or necessary accessories for something. **3.** *Print.* pieces of wood or metal for holding pages of type in place in a chase. [< F *fourniture* < *fourn(ir)* (to) FURNISH]

fu·ror (fyŏŏr′ôr), *n.* **1.** a general outburst of enthusiasm, excitement, controversy, or the like. **2.** a prevailing mania or craze. **3.** fury; rage; madness. Also, *esp. Brit.*, **fu′rore** (for defs. 1, 2). [< L: a raging; r. late ME *fureur* < MF]

furred (fûrd), *adj.* **1.** having fur. **2.** made with or of fur, as garments. **3.** clad in fur or furs, as a person. **4.** coated with matter, as the tongue. [ME]

fur·ri·er[1] (fûr′ē ər), *n.* a fur dealer or fur dresser. [ME *furrer* < AF (OF *forrer, fourrer* to line with fur; see FUR) + *-er* -ER[2]]

fur·ri·er[2] (fûr′ē ər), *adj.* comparative of **furry.**

fur·ri·er·y (fûr′ē ə rē), *n.*, *pl.* **-er·ies.** the business, trade, or craftsmanship of a furrier.

fur·ring (fûr′iŋ), *n.* **1.** the act of lining, trimming, or clothing with fur. **2.** the fur used. **3.** the formation of a coating of matter, as on the tongue. **4.** *Building Trades.* **a.** the attaching of strips of wood or the like (**fur′ring strips′**) to a wall or other surface, as to provide an even support for lath or to provide an air space between the wall and plasterwork. **b.** material used for this purpose. [ME]

fur·row (fûr′ō, fur′ō), *n.* **1.** a narrow groove made in the ground, esp. by a plow. **2.** a narrow, trenchlike depression in any surface: *the furrows of a wrinkled face.* —*v.t.* **3.** to make a furrow or furrows in. **4.** to make wrinkles in (the face). —*v.i.* **5.** to make a furrow or furrows; become furrowed. [ME *forwe, furgh,* OE *furh;* c. OFris *furch,* OHG *fur(u)h* (G *Furche*), L *porca* ridge between furrows] —**fur′row·er,** *n.* —**fur′row·less,** *adj.* —**fur′row·like′,** *adj.* —**fur′row·y,** *adj.*

fur·ry (fûr′ē), *adj.*, **fur·ri·er, fur·ri·est. 1.** consisting of or resembling fur. **2.** covered with fur; wearing fur. **3.** obstructed or coated as if with fur. —**fur′ri·ly,** *adv.* —**fur′ri·ness,** *n.*

fur′ seal′, any of several eared seals, as *Callorhinus alascanus,* having a plush underfur used in making coats, trimmings, etc.

Fürth (fʏʀt), *n.* a city in S West Germany, near Nuremberg. 98,300 (1963).

fur·ther (fûr′thər), *adv.*, *compar.* of **far** *with* **furthest** *as superl.* **1.** at or to a greater distance; farther. **2.** at or to a more advanced point; to a greater extent. **3.** in addition; moreover. —*adj.*, *compar.* of **far** *with* **furthest** *as superl.* **4.** more distant or remote; farther. **5.** more extended. **6.** additional; more. —*v.t.* **7.** to help forward (an undertaking, cause, etc.); advance. [ME *furthere,* OE *furthra;* c. G *vordere* more advanced] —**fur′ther·er,** *n.*

fur·ther·ance (fûr′thər əns), *n.* the act of furthering; promotion; advancement. [late ME *fortheraunce*]

fur·ther·more (fûr′thər mōr′, -môr′), *adv.* moreover; besides; in addition. [ME]

fur·ther·most (fûr′thər mōst′), *adj.* most distant. [ME]

fur·thest (fûr′thist), *adj.*, *adv.*, *superl.* of **far** *with* **further** *as compar.* farthest.

fur·tive (fûr′tiv), *adj.* **1.** taken, done, used, etc., by stealth; secret: *a furtive glance.* **2.** sly; shifty: *a furtive manner.* [< L *furtīv(us)* = *furt(um)* theft (cf. *fūr* thief) + *-īvus* -IVE] —**fur′tive·ly,** *adv.* —**fur′tive·ness,** *n.* —**Syn. 1.** surreptitious, covert. **2.** underhanded, cunning, foxy.

fu·run·cle (fyŏŏr′uŋ kəl), *n.* *Pathol.* boil[2]. [< L *fūruncul(us)* petty thief, boil = *fūr* thief (see FURTIVE) + **-unc(o)-* dim. suffix + *-ulus* -ULE] —**fu·run·cu·lar** (fyŏŏ ruŋ′kyə lər), **fu·run′cu·lous,** *adj.*

fu·ry (fyŏŏr′ē), *n.*, *pl.* **-ries. 1.** unrestrained or violent anger, rage, passion, or the like. **2.** violence; vehemence; fierceness. **3. Furies,** *Class. Myth.* female divinities: the daughters of Gaea who punished crimes at the instigation of the victims; known to the Greeks as the Erinyes or Eumenides and to the Romans as the Furiae or Dirae. Originally there were an indefinite number, but later only Alecto, Megaera, and Tisiphone. **4.** a fierce and violent person, esp. a woman. **5. like fury,** *Informal.* violently; intensely: *It rained like fury.* [ME < L *furia* rage = *fur(ere)* (to) be angry, rage + *-ia* -Y[3]] —**Syn. 1.** frenzy, ire. See **anger.**

furze (fûrz), *n.* any leguminous plant of the genus *Ulex*, esp. *U. europaeus*, a low, many-branched, spiny shrub having yellow flowers, common on waste lands in Europe. Also called, *esp. Brit.*, **gorse.** [ME *furse, firse*, OE *fyr(e)s;* akin to Russ *pyrei*, Gk *pȳrós* wheat Lith *pūrai* autumn-sown wheat]

furz·y (fûr′zē), *adj.*, **furz·i·er, furz·i·est.** *Brit.* **1.** of or pertaining to furze. **2.** overgrown with furze.

fu·sain (fyo͞o zān′, fyo͞o′zān; *Fr.* fʏ zaɴ′), *n., pl.* **-sains** (-zānz′, -zānz; *Fr.* -zaɴ′) for 2. **1.** a fine charcoal used in drawing, made from the wood of the spindle tree. **2.** a drawing made with this charcoal. [< F: spindle tree, charcoal made from its wood < VL **fūsāgīn-* (s. of **fūsāgō*) < L *fūsus* spindle]

Fu·san (fo͞o′sän′), *n.* a Japanese name of **Pusan.**

fus·cous (fus′kəs), *adj.* of brownish-gray or dusky color. [< L *fusc(us)* dark, tawny, dusky + -ous]

fuse[1] (fyo͞oz), *n., v.*, **fused, fus·ing.** —*n.* **1.** a tube, cord, or the like, filled or saturated with combustible matter, for igniting an explosive. **2.** fuze (def. 1). —*v.t.* **3.** fuze (def. 3). [< It *fuso* < L *fūsus* spindle] —**fuse′less,** *adj.*

fuse[2] (fyo͞oz), *v.*, **fused, fus·ing,** *n.* —*v.t.* **1.** to combine or blend by melting together; melt. **2.** to unite or blend into a whole, as if by melting together. —*v.i.* **3.** to become liquid under the action of heat; melt. **4.** to become united or blended as if by melting together. —*n.* **5.** *Elect.* a protective device containing a piece of metal that melts under heat produced by an excess current in a circuit, thereby breaking the circuit. [< L *fūs(us)* melted, poured, cast, ptp. of *fundere*] —**Syn. 1.** See **melt. 2, 4.** amalgamate, liquefy, dissolve, merge. **4.** coalesce. —**Ant. 1, 3.** solidify. **2, 4.** separate.

Fu·se (fo͞o′sā), *n.* a city on SW Honshu, in S Japan, SE of Osaka. 256,593 (est. 1964).

fu·see (fyo͞o zē′), *n.* **1.** a wooden match having a large head and ignited by friction. **2.** a red flare light, used on a railroad as a warning signal to approaching trains. **3.** *Horol.* a spirally grooved, conical pulley and chain arrangement for counteracting the diminishing power of the uncoiling mainspring. **4.** fuse[1] (def. 1). Also, **fuzee.** [< F *fusée* spindleful < OF *fus* spindle]

fu·se·lage (fyo͞o′sə läzh′, -lij, -zə-), *n.* *Aeron.* the complete central structure to which the wing, tail surfaces, and engines are attached on an airplane. [< F = *fusel(é)* spindle-shaped (< *fuseau* spindle; see fusee) + *-age* -age]

Fu·se·li (fyo͞o′zə lē), *n.* **(John) Henry** (*Johann Heinrich Füssli*), 1741–1825, English painter, illustrator, and essayist; born in Switzerland.

fu′sel oil′ (fyo͞o′zəl, -səl), a mixture consisting chiefly of amyl alcohols. [< G *Fusel* bad liquor]

Fu·shih (fo͞o′shē′), *n.* Yenan.

fu·si·bil·i·ty (fyo͞o′zə bil′i tē), *n.* **1.** the quality of being fusible, or convertible from a solid to a liquid state by heat. **2.** the degree to which a substance is fusible. [< F *fusibilité*]

fu·si·ble (fyo͞o′zə bəl), *adj.* capable of being fused or melted. [ME < ML *fūsibil(is)*] —**fu′si·ble·ness,** *n.* —**fu′si·bly,** *adv.*

fu′sible met′al, *Metall.* any of various alloys, as one of bismuth, lead, and tin, that melt at comparatively low temperatures, and hence can be used for making various safety devices. Also called **fu′sible al′loy.**

fu·si·form (fyo͞o′zə fôrm′), *adj.* spindle-shaped; rounded and tapering from the middle toward each end, as some roots. [< L *fūs(us)* spindle + -i- + -form]

fu·sil[1] (fyo͞o′zəl, -sil), *n.* a light flintlock musket. [< F: musket, OF *fuisil, foisil* steel for striking fire < VL **focīl(is)* < L *foc(us)* fire. See focus]

fu·sil[2] (fyo͞o′zəl, -sil), *adj.* **1.** formed by melting or casting; fused; founded. **2.** *Archaic.* capable of being melted; fusible. **3.** *Archaic.* melted; molten. Also, **fu·sile** (fyo͞o′zəl, -sil, -sīl). [ME < L *fūsil(is)* molten, fluid. See fuse[2], -ile]

fu·sil[3] (fyo͞o′zəl, -sil), *n.* *Heraldry.* a narrow, elongated lozenge. [< MF, OF *fu(i)sel* < VL **fūsell(us)*, dim. of L *fūsus* spindle]

fu·sil·ier (fyo͞o′zə lēr′), *n.* **1.** (*cap.*) a term used in the names of certain British regiments. **2.** (formerly) a soldier armed with a fusil. Also, **fu′si·leer′.** [< F]

fu·sil·lade (fyo͞o′sə lād′, -läd′, -zə-), *n., v.*, **-lad·ed, -lad·ing.** —*n.* **1.** a simultaneous or continuous discharge of firearms. **2.** a general outpouring of anything: *a fusillade of questions.* —*v.t.* **3.** to attack or shoot by a fusillade. [< F = *fusill(er)* (to) shoot (see fusil[1]) + *-ade* -ade[1]]

fu·sion (fyo͞o′zhən), *n.* **1.** the act or process of fusing. **2.** the state of being fused. **3.** something that is fused; the result of fusing: *A theatrical production is the fusion of many talents.* **4.** *Politics.* **a.** a coalition of parties or factions. **b.** (*cap.*) the political party resulting from such a coalition. **5.** Also called **nuclear fusion.** *Physics.* a thermonuclear reaction in which nuclei of light atoms join to form nuclei of heavier atoms, as the combination of deuterium atoms to form helium atoms. Cf. **fission** (def. 3). [< L *fūsiōn-* (s. of *fūsiō*) a pouring out, melting]

fu′sion bomb′. See **hydrogen bomb.**

fu·sion·ism (fyo͞o′zhə niz′əm), *n.* *Politics.* the principle, policy, or practice of fusion. —**fu′sion·ist,** *n., adj.*

fuss (fus), *n.* **1.** an excessive display of anxious attention or activity; needless or useless bustle. **2.** an argument or noisy dispute. **3.** a complaint or protest, esp. about something unimportant. —*v.i.* **4.** to make a fuss; make much ado about trifles. **5.** to complain. —*v.t.* **6.** to disturb, esp. with trifles; annoy; bother. [?] —**fuss′er,** *n.* —**Syn. 1.** pother, stir, commotion.

fuss·budg·et (fus′buj′it), *n.* a fussy or needlessly fault-finding person. Also called **fuss·pot** (fus′pot′). —**fuss′-budg′et·y,** *adj.*

fuss·y (fus′ē), *adj.*, **fuss·i·er, fuss·i·est.** **1.** excessively busy with trifles; anxious or particular about petty details. **2.** (of clothes, decoration, etc.) elaborately made, trimmed, or decorated. **3.** full of details, esp. in excess. —**fuss′i·ly,** *adv.* —**fuss′i·ness,** *n.*

fus·tian (fus′chən), *n.* **1.** a stout fabric of cotton and flax. **2.** a fabric of stout twilled cotton or of cotton and low-quality wool, with a short nap or pile. **3.** inflated or turgid language in writing or speaking; bombast; rant; claptrap. —*adj.* **4.** made of fustian. **5.** pompous or bombastic. **6.** worthless; cheap. [ME < OF *fustaigne* < ML *fustān(eum)* (< L *fūstis* cudgel), trans. of Gk *xýlinon* < *xýlon* wood]

fus·tic (fus′tik), *n.* **1.** the wood of a large, moraceous tree, *Chlorophora tinctoria*, of tropical America, yielding a light-yellow dye. **2.** the tree itself. **3.** the dye. **4.** any of several other dyewoods. Also called **old fustic** (for defs. 1–3). [ME *fustik* < MF *fustoc* < Ar *fustuq;* akin to Gk *pistákē* pistachio tree]

fus·ti·gate (fus′tə gāt′), *v.t.*, **-gat·ed, -gat·ing.** **1.** to cudgel; beat; punish severely. **2.** to criticize harshly. [< L *fūstīgāt(us)* cudgeled to death (ptp. of *fūstīgāre;* see -ate[1]) < *fūstis* cudgel] —**fus′ti·ga′tion,** *n.* —**fus′ti·ga′tor,** *n.* —**fus·ti·ga·to·ry** (fus′tə gə tōr′ē, -tôr′ē), *adj.*

fus·ty (fus′tē), *adj.*, **-ti·er, -ti·est.** **1.** moldy; musty; having a stale smell; stuffy. **2.** old-fashioned or out-of-date, as architecture, furnishings, etc. **3.** stubbornly conservative or old-fashioned; fogyish. [*fust* (n.) < OF: wine cask, log (< L *fūstis* cudgel) + -y[1]] —**fus′ti·ly,** *adv.* —**fus′ti·ness,** *n.*

fu·thark (fo͞o′thärk), *n.* the runic alphabet. Also, **fu·thorc, fu·thork** (fo͞o′thôrk). [so called from first six letters of OE and Scand runic alphabet: *f, u, th, a* (or *q*), *r, k* (modeled on alphabet)]

fu·tile (fyo͞ot′ᵊl, fyo͞o′til; *Brit.* fyo͞o′tīl), *adj.* **1.** incapable of producing any result; ineffective; useless; not successful. **2.** trifling; frivolous; unimportant. [< L *fūt(t)il(is)* that which flows easily, is vain, worthless = *fūt-* (akin to *fundere* to pour, melt) + *-ilis* -ile] —**fu′tile·ly,** *adv.* —**fu′tile·ness,** *n.* —**Syn. 1.** See **useless.**

fu·til·i·tar·i·an (fyo͞o til′i târ′ē ən), *adj.* **1.** believing that human hopes are vain, and human strivings unjustified. —*n.* **2.** a person who holds this belief. [humorous b. futile + (util)itarian] —**fu·til′i·tar′i·an·ism,** *n.*

fu·til·i·ty (fyo͞o til′i tē), *n., pl.* **-ties** for 2, 3. **1.** the quality of being futile; ineffectiveness; uselessness. **2.** a trifle or frivolity. **3.** a futile act or event. [< L *fūtilitāt-* (s. of *fūtilitās*)]

fut·tock (fut′ək), *n.* *Naut.* any of the timbers forming the lower, more curved portion of a frame in a wooden hull. [perh. alter. of *foothook*]

fu·ture (fyo͞o′chər), *n.* **1.** time that is to be or come hereafter. **2.** something that will exist or happen in future time. **3.** a future condition, esp. of success or failure. **4.** *Gram.* **a.** the future tense. **b.** a verb form in the future, as *He will come.* **5.** Usually, **futures.** speculative purchases or sales of commodities for future receipt or delivery. —*adj.* **6.** that is to be or come hereafter. **7.** pertaining to or connected with time to come. **8.** *Gram.* designating a tense or other verb formation that refers to events or states in time to come. [ME *futur* < L *futūr(us)* about to be (fut. participle of *esse* to be)] —**fu′ture·less,** *adj.* —**fu′tur·is′tic,** *adj.* —**fu′tur·is′ti·cal·ly,** *adv.*

fu′ture life′, afterlife (def. 1).

fu′ture per′fect, *Gram.* **1.** perfect with respect to a temporal point of reference in time to come; completed with respect to a time in the future, esp. when incomplete with respect to the present. **2.** noting or pertaining to a tense or other verb formation or construction with such reference. **3.** the future perfect tense. **4.** another verb formation or construction with future perfect meaning. **5.** a form in the future perfect, as *He will have come.*

fu′ture shock′, **1.** physical and psychological disturbance caused by the inability of people to cope with very rapid social and technological change. **2.** any overload of a person's or an organization's capacity for adaption or decision making. [coined by Alvin *Toffler* (b.1928), U.S. author]

Fu·tur·ism (fyo͞o′chə riz′əm), *n.* (*often l.c.*) a style of art, literature, music, etc., and a theory of art and life in which violence, power, speed, mechanization, and hostility to the past or to traditional forms of expression were advocated or portrayed. [< It *futurism(o)*] —**Fu′tur·ist,** *n.*

fu·tur·is·tic (fyo͞o′chə ris′tik), *adj.* **1.** of or pertaining to the future: *a futuristic advance in automation.* **2.** (*often cap.*) of or pertaining to Futurism. —**fu′tur·is′ti·cal·ly,** *adv.*

fu·tu·ri·ty (fyo͞o to͝or′i tē, -tyo͝or′-, -cho͝or′-), *n., pl.* **-ties.** **1.** future time. **2.** succeeding generations; posterity. **3.** the after life. **4.** a future state or condition; a future event, possibility, or prospect. **5.** the quality of being future.

fu·tu·rol·o·gy (fyo͞o′chə rol′ə jē), *n.* the study or practice of forecasting trends or developments in science, technology, political or social structure, etc.

Fu·zan (fo͞o′zän′), *n.* a Japanese name of **Pusan.**

fuze (fyo͞oz), *n., v.*, **fuzed, fuz·ing.** —*n.* **1.** a mechanical or electronic device to detonate an explosive charge. **2.** fuse[1] (def. 1). —*v.t.* **3.** Also, **fuse.** to attach a fuze or fuzes to (a bomb, mine, etc.). [var. of fuse[1]]

fu·zee (fyo͞o zē′), *n.* fusee.

fuzz (fuz), *n., pl.* **fuzz.** **1.** loose, light, fibrous, or fluffy matter. **2.** a mass or coating of such matter. **3.** *U.S. Slang.* a policeman or the police. [cf. D *voos* spongy]

fuzz·y (fuz′ē), *adj.*, **fuzz·i·er, fuzz·i·est.** **1.** of the nature of or resembling fuzz. **2.** covered with fuzz. **3.** indistinct; blurred. **4.** muddleheaded; incoherent, often as a result of intoxication. —**fuzz′i·ly,** *adv.* —**fuzz′i·ness,** *n.*

f.v., on the back of the page. [< L *foliō versō*]

fwd., forward.

-fy, a verbal suffix meaning "to make," "cause to be," "render" (*simplify; beautify*); "to become," "be made" (*liquefy*). The suffix was introduced into English in loan words from Old French (*deify*), but is also used in the formation of new words, usually on a Latin root (*reify*). [< MF *-fi(er)* << L *-ficāre* to do, make]

FY, fiscal year.

fyke (fīk), *n.* *U.S.* a bag-shaped fish trap. [< D *fuik*, MD *vūke;* c. OFris *fūcke*]

fyl·fot (fil′fot), *n.* a swastika. [? var. of *fill-foot* foot filler]

Fyn (fʏn), *n.* an island in S Denmark. 376,872 (1960); 1149 sq. mi. German, **Fünen.**

fytte (fit), *n.* fit[3].

Fyz·a·bad (fī′zä bäd′), *n.* a city in SE Uttar Pradesh, in N India. 83,717 (1961). Also, **Faizabad.**

F.Z.S., Fellow of the Zoological Society, London. Also, **F.Z.S.L.**

DEVELOPMENT OF MAJUSCULE						
NORTH SEMITIC	GREEK	ETR.	LATIN	MODERN		
				GOTHIC	ITALIC	ROMAN
SEE LETTER C			C	𝔊	*G*	G

DEVELOPMENT OF MINUSCULE					
ROMAN CURSIVE	ROMAN UNCIAL	CAROL. MIN.	MODERN		
			GOTHIC	ITALIC	ROMAN
ς	ɕ	g	𝔤	*g*	g

The seventh letter of the English alphabet developed from North Semitic *ghimel* and Greek *gamma* (see **C**). The Etruscans, having no meaningful distinction between the *g*-sound and the *k*-sound in their language, used this symbol for both. When the distinction again had to be made in Latin, the small stroke was added to the lower curve of the C. Thus, a new letter was created (G) and was given the position of the Semitic and Greek Z, which was dropped (see **Z**). The minuscule (g) is a scribal variant of the capital.

G, g (jē), *n., pl.* **G's** or **Gs, g's** or **gs.** **1.** the seventh letter of the English alphabet, a consonant. **2.** any spoken sound represented by the letter *G* or *g*, as in *get, German,* or *camouflage.* **3.** a written or printed representation of the letter *G* or *g.* **4.** a device, as a printer's type, for reproducing the letter *G* or *g.*

G, *pl.* **Gs** or **G's.** *Slang.* the sum of one thousand dollars. [abbr. for GRAND]

G, 1. German (def. 5). **2.** good.

G, 1. the seventh in order or in a series. **2.** *Music.* **a.** the fifth tone in the scale of C major or the seventh tone in the relative minor scale, A minor. **b.** a written or printed note representing this tone. **c.** a string, key, or pipe tuned to this tone. **d.** the tonality having G as the tonic note. **3.** *Elect.* conductance. **4.** a designation by the motion-picture industry for films regarded as acceptable for all age groups.

g, 1. good. **2.** gram; grams. **3.** *Physics.* gravity.

g, 1. See **acceleration of gravity. 2.** *Elect.* conductance.

G., 1. German. **2.** gourde; gourdes. **3.** (specific) gravity. **4.** Gulf.

g., 1. gauge. **2.** gender. **3.** general. **4.** generally. **5.** genitive. **6.** gold. **7.** grain; grains. **8.** *Metric System.* gram; grams. **9.** *Football.* guard. **10.** *Brit.* guinea.

Ga, *Chem.* gallium.

Ga., Georgia.

GA, Georgia (approved esp. for use with zip code).

G.A., 1. General Assembly. **2.** General Average.

g.a., general average. Also, **G/A**

gab[1] (gab), *v.,* **gabbed, gab·bing,** *n. Informal.* **—***v.i.* **1.** to talk idly; chatter. **—***n.* **2.** idle talk; chatter. [(n.) ME *gab(be)* < ON; c. Icel *gabb;* (v.) ME *gabbe(n)* < ON; c. Icel *gabba*] **—gab′ber,** *n.*

gab[2] (gab), *n. Mach.* a hook or fork that engages temporarily with a moving rod or lever. [prob. < Flem *gabbe* notch]

gab·ar·dine (gab′ər dēn′, gab′ər dēn′), *n.* **1.** Also, **gaberdine.** firm, woven fabric of worsted, cotton, or spun rayon, with a twill weave. **2.** gaberdine (def. 1). [var. of GABERDINE]

gab·ble (gab′əl), *v.,* **-bled, -bling,** *n.* **—***v.i.* **1.** to speak or converse rapidly and unintelligibly; jabber. **2.** (of hens, geese, etc.) to cackle. **—***v.t.* **3.** to utter rapidly and unintelligibly. **—***n.* **4.** rapid, unintelligible talk; meaningless sounds. [GAB[1] + -LE] **—gab′bler,** *n.*

gab·bro (gab′rō), *n., pl.* **-bros.** *Petrog.* a granular igneous rock composed chiefly of labradorite and augite. [< It; akin to L *glaber* smooth] **—gab·bro·ic,** (gə brō′ik), **gab′-bro·it′ic,** *adj.*

gab·by (gab′ē), *adj.* **-bi·er, -bi·est.** talkative; loquacious. [GAB[1] + -Y[1]]

ga·belle (gə bel′), *n. Fr. Hist.* a tax on salt, abolished in 1790. [< F < It *gabell(a)* < Ar *gabālah* tax, receipt] **—ga·belled′,** *adj.*

gab·er·dine (gab′ər dēn′, gab′ər dēn′), *n.* **1.** Also, **gabardine.** a long, loose coat or frock for men, worn in the Middle Ages, esp. by Jews. **2.** gabardine (def. 1). [< MF *gauvardine, gallevardine,* ? < MHG *wallevart* pilgrimage; cf. Sp *gabardina*]

Ga·be·ro·nes (gä′bə rō′nes, gab′ə-), *n.* former name of **Gaborone.**

Ga·bès (gä′bes), *n.* **Gulf of,** a gulf of the Mediterranean on the E coast of Tunisia.

gab·fest (gab′fest′), *n. U.S. Informal.* a gathering at which there is a great deal of conversation.

ga·bi·on (gā′bē ən), *n.* **1.** a cylinder of wickerwork filled with earth, used as a military defense. **2.** a cylinder filled with stones and sunk in water, used in laying the foundations of a dam or jetty. [< MF: rough, two-handled basket < It *gabbione,* aug. of *gabbia* cage < L *cavea* cavity, cage]

ga·ble (gā′bəl), *n. Archit.* **1.** the portion of the front or side of a building enclosed by the end of or masking the end of a pitched roof **2.** a decorative member suggesting a gable, used esp. in Gothic architecture. [ME < ON (cf. OIcel *gafl*), OF (< Gmc); cf. OE *gafol, geafel* a fork] **—ga′ble-like′,** *adj.*

Gable (def. 1)

ga·bled (gā′bəld), *adj.* built with a gable or gables.

ga′ble roof′, a roof sloping downward in two parts at an angle from a central ridge, so as to leave a gable at each end. See illus. at **roof. —ga′ble-roofed′,** *adj.*

Ga·bo (gä′bō, gā′-), *n.* **Naum** (noum) (*Naum Pevsner*), 1890–1977, U.S. sculptor, born in Russia (brother of Antoine Pevsner).

Ga·bon (gᴀ bôɴ′), *n.* **1.** Official name, **Gab′onese Repub′lic.** a republic in W Africa: formerly a part of French Equatorial Africa; an independent member of the French Community. 950,000; 102,290 sq. mi. *Cap.:* Libreville. **2.** an estuary in W Gabon. ab. 40 mi. long. Also, **Ga·bun** (gə-bo͞on′).

Gab·o·nese (gab′ə nēz′, -nēs′, gä′bə-), *adj., n., pl.* **-nese.** **—***adj.* **1.** of or pertaining to Gabon, its inhabitants, or their language. **—***n.* **2.** an inhabitant or native of Gabon.

Ga·bo·riau (gᴀ bô ʀyō′), *n.* **É·mile** (ā mēl′), 1835–73, French author of detective stories.

Ga·bo·ro·ne (hä′bə rōn, gä′bə rōn), *n.* a town in and the capital of Botswana, in the SE part. 28,000 (est. 1972). Formerly, **Gaberones.**

Ga·bri·el (gā′brē əl), *n.* one of the archangels, appearing usually as a divine messenger. Dan. 8:16, 9:21; Luke 1:19, 26. [< Heb: perh. meaning "God is strong"]

Ga·bri·el (gᴀ bʀē el′), *n.* **Jacques Ange** (zhäk äɴzh), 1698–1782, French architect.

gad[1] (gad), *v.,* **gad·ded, gad·ding,** *n.* **—***v.i.* **1.** to move restlessly or aimlessly from place to place. **—***n.* **2.** the act of gadding. [ME *gadd(en),* ? back formation from *gadeling* wanderer, or vagabond; see GATHER] **—gad′der,** *n.*

gad[2] (gad), *n., v.,* **gad·ded, gad·ding.** **—***n.* **1.** a goad for driving cattle. **2.** a pointed mining tool for breaking up rock, coal, etc. **—***v.t.* **3.** to break up or loosen with a mining gad. [ME < Scand; cf. Icel *gaddr* spike; c. Goth *gazds*]

Gad (gad), *n.* **1.** a son of Zilpah. Gen. 30:11. **2.** one of the twelve tribes of Israel, traditionally descended from him. **3.** a Hebrew prophet and chronicler of the court of David. II Sam. 24:11–19.

Gad (gad), *interj. Informal.* (a euphemistic form of *God,* used as a mild oath.) Also, **gad.**

gad·a·bout (gad′ə bout′), *n.* a person who moves restlessly or aimlessly about, esp. for curiosity or gossip.

gad·di (gud′ē), *n. Anglo-Indian.* **1.** a hassock. **2.** a throne. **3.** the status of a ruler. Also, **ga′di.** [< Hindi *gaddī*]

gad·fly (gad′flī′), *n., pl.* **-flies.** **1.** any of various flies, as a warble fly, that bite or annoy domestic animals. **2.** a person who repeatedly and persistently annoys others with schemes, requests, etc.

gadg·et (gaj′it), *n.* a mechanical contrivance or device; any ingenious article. [< ?; cf. F *gâchette* catch of a lock, sear of a gunlock] **—gadg·et·y** (gaj′i tē), *adj.*

gadg·e·teer (gaj′i tēr′), *n.* a person who invents or is particularly fond of using gadgets.

gadg·et·ry (gaj′i trē), *n.* mechanical or electronic contrivances; gadgets: *the gadgetry of the well-equipped modern kitchen.*

Ga·dhel·ic (gə del′ik), *adj., n.* Goidelic.

ga·did (gā′did), *adj.* **1.** belonging or pertaining to the cod family, *Gadidae.* **—***n.* **2.** a gadid fish. [< NL *gad(us)* cod (< Gk *gádos* a kind of fish) + -ID[2]]

Gad·ite (gad′īt), *n.* a member of the tribe of Gad.

ga·doid (gā′doid), *adj., n.* gadid. [< NL *gad(us)* (see GADID) + -OID]

gad·o·lin·ite (gad′ᵊli nīt′), *n.* a silicate ore from which the rare-earth metals gadolinium, holmium, and rhenium are extracted. [named after J. *Gadolin* (1760–1852), Finnish chemist; see -ITE[1]]

gad·o·lin·i·um (gad′ᵊlin′ē əm), *n. Chem.* a rare-earth metallic element. *Symbol:* Gd; *at. wt.:* 157.25; *at. no.:* 64. [named after J. *Gadolin;* see -IUM] **—gad′o·lin′ic,** *adj.*

ga·droon (gə dro͞on′), *n.* **1.** *Archit.* an elaborately carved or indented convex molding. **2.** a decorative series of curved, inverted flutings, as on silversmith's work. [< F *godron,* OF *goderon* < ?] **—ga·drooned′,** *adj.*

Gads·bod·i·kins (gadz′bod′ə kinz), *interj. Archaic.* (used as a mild oath.) Also, **Odsbodikins, Odsbodkins.** [GAD + -'S[1] + *bodikin* (BODY + -KIN) + -S[1]]

Gads·den (gadz′dən), *n.* **1.** **James,** 1788–1858, U.S. railroad promoter and diplomat. **2.** a city in NE Alabama. 53,928 (1970).

Gads′den Pur′chase, a tract of 45,535 square miles, now contained in New Mexico and Arizona, purchased for $10,000,000 from Mexico in 1853, the treaty being negotiated by James Gadsden.

NEVADA
UTAH
COLO.
CALIF.
ARIZONA
NEW MEXICO
Colorado R.
Gila River
Gadsden Purchase
MEXICO

Gads·woons (gadz′wo͞onz′), *interj. Archaic.* (used as a mild oath.) [dial. var. of *God's wounds;* see GAD]

gad·wall (gad′wôl′), *n., pl.* **-walls,** (*esp. collectively*) **-wall.** a grayish-brown wild duck, *Anas strepera,* found in temperate parts of the Northern Hemisphere. [?]

Gad·zooks (gad′zo͞oks′), *interj. Archaic.* (used as a mild oath.) Also, **Odzooks, Odzookers.** [prob. var. of *God's hooks* (nails; i.e., of the Cross); see GAD]

Gae·a (jē′ə), *n.* the ancient Greek goddess of the earth, mother of Uranus, Pontus, and the mountains; also mother, with Uranus, of the Titans, Cyclops, and Hecatonchires; mother of various other beings, including the Erinyes. Also, **Gaia, Ge.** [< Gk *gaia* earth]

Gaek·war (gīk′wär), *n.* the title of the ruler of the former Indian native state of Baroda. Also, **Gaikwar.** [< Marathi: lit., cowherd]

Gael (gāl), *n.* a Gaelic-speaking Celt. [< ScotGael *Gaidheal;* akin to OIr *Gaidel, Goidel*]

Gael, Gaelic (def. 1). Also, **Gael.**

Gael·ic (gā′lik), *n.* **1.** a Celtic language that includes the speech of ancient Ireland and the dialects that have developed from it, esp. those usually known as Irish, Manx, and Scots Gaelic. Gaelic constitutes the Goidelic subbranch of Celtic. *Abbr.:* Gael, Gael. —*adj.* **2.** of or in Gaelic. **3.** of or pertaining to the Gaels or their language. [GAEL + -IC (repr. ScotGael *Gaidhlig* < *Gaidheal* GAEL)]

gaff (gaf), *n.* **1.** an iron hook with a handle for landing large fish. **2.** a metal spur for a gamecock. **3.** the spur on a climbing iron, esp. as used by linemen. **4.** *Naut.* a spar rising aft from a mast to support the head of a quadrilateral fore-and-aft sail: formed either as a permanently fixed spar, or as one secured to the mast by hoops and hoisted with the sail. **5. stand the gaff,** *U.S. Slang.* to weather hardship or strain; endure patiently. —*v.t.* **6.** to hook or land (a fish) with a gaff. [< F *gaffe* < Pr *gaf* boat hook]

gaffe (gaf), *n.* a social blunder; faux pas. [< F *gaffe* GAFF]

gaf·fer (gaf′ər), *n.* **1.** an old fellow, esp. an elderly rustic. **2.** *Brit.* **a.** a foreman or overseer, esp. the boss of a gang of physical laborers. **b.** *Slang.* father. **3.** *Glassmaking.* a master glassblower responsible for shaping glassware. [contr. of GODFATHER]

gaff′ top′sail, *Naut.* a jib-headed fore-and-aft sail set above a gaff.

gag[1] (gag), *v.,* **gagged, gag·ging,** *n.* —*v.t.* **1.** to stop up the mouth of (a person) by putting something in it, thus preventing speech, shouts, etc. **2.** to restrain by force or authority from freedom of speech. **3.** to fasten open the jaws of, as in surgical operations. **4.** to cause to retch or choke. **5.** *Metalworking.* to straighten or bend (a bar, rail, etc.) with a gag. —*v.i.* **6.** to retch or choke. —*n.* **7.** something put into a person's mouth to prevent speech, shouting, etc. **8.** any violent or arbitrary suppression of freedom of speech. **9.** a surgical instrument for holding the jaws open. **10.** *Metalworking.* a shaped block of steel used with a press to straighten or bend a bar, rail, etc. [ME *gagg(en)* (to) suffocate; perh. imit. of the sound made in choking]

gag[2] (gag), *v.,* **gagged, gag·ging,** *n.* *Informal.* —*v.i.* **1.** to tell a joke or jokes. —*n.* **2.** a joke. **3.** any contrived piece of wordplay or horseplay. [? special use of GAG[1]; cf. Icel *gagg* yelp]

ga·ga (gä′gä′), *adj.* silly; foolish. [< F; imit.]

gage[1] (gāj), *n., v.,* **gaged, gag·ing.** —*n.* **1.** something, as a glove, thrown down in token of challenge to combat. **2.** a challenge. **3.** a pledge or pawn; security. —*v.t.* **4.** *Archaic.* to pledge, stake, or wager. [ME < MF < Gmc; see WAGE]

gage[2] (gāj), *n., v.t.,* **gaged, gag·ing.** *Chiefly Technical.* gauge. —**gag′er,** *n.*

gage[3] (gāj), *n.* any of several varieties of the plum, *Prunus domestica.* [shortened form of GREENGAGE]

Gage (gāj), *n.* **Thomas,** 1721–87, British general in America 1763–76.

gag·ger[1] (gag′ər), *n.* **1.** a person or thing that gags. **2.** an L-shaped rod for reinforcing sand in a foundry mold. [GAG[1] + -ER[1]]

gag·ger[2] (gag′ər), *n.* a person who writes or tells gags. [GAG[2] + -ER[1]]

gag·gle (gag′əl), *v.,* **-gled, -gling,** *n.* —*v.i.* **1.** to cackle. —*n.* **2.** a flock of geese. **3.** a cackle. [imit.]

gag·man (gag′man′), *n., pl.* **-men.** a person who writes comic material for public performers. Also called **gagster.**

gag′ rule′, any rule restricting discussion or debate of a given issue, esp. in a deliberative body.

gag·ster (gag′stər), *n.* **1.** gagman. **2.** *Slang.* one who invents jokes or humorous remarks; joker; comic.

gahn·ite (gä′nīt), *n.* a dark-green to black mineral of the spinel group, zinc aluminate, $ZnAl_2O_4$. [named after J. G. *Gahn* (1745–1818), Swedish chemist; see -ITE[1]]

Gai·a (gā′ə), *n.* *Gk. Myth.* Gaea.

gai·e·ty (gā′i tē), *n., pl.* **-ties.** **1.** the state of being gay or cheerful; gay spirits. **2.** Often, **gaieties,** merrymaking or festivity: *the gaieties of the New Year season.* **3.** showiness; finery: *gaiety of dress.* Also, **gayety.** [< F *gaieté.* See GAY, -TY[2]] —**Syn. 1.** merriment, jollity, joyousness. **3.** brilliance, glitter, gaudiness. —**Ant. 1.** sadness.

Gaik·war (gīk′wär), *n.* Gaekwar.

Gail·lard′ Cut′ (gil yärd′, gā′lärd), an artificial cutting in the Panama Canal Zone, NW of the city of Panama; excavated for the Panama Canal. 8 mi. long. Formerly, **Culebra Cut.** [named after Col. D. DuB. *Gaillard* (1859–1913), U.S. Army engineer]

gail·lar·di·a (gā lär′dē ə), *n.* any herb of the genus *Gaillardia,* comprising the blanket-flowers. [< NL, named after *Gaillard* de Charentonneau, 18th-century French amateur botanist; see -IA]

gai·ly (gā′lē), *adv.* **1.** with merriment; merrily; cheerfully. **2.** with showiness; showily. Also, **gayly.** [ME]

gain[1] (gān), *v.t.* **1.** to get (something desired), esp. as a result of one's efforts; acquire; obtain. **2.** to win; get in competition: *to gain the prize.* **3.** to acquire as an increase or addition: *to gain weight; to gain speed.* **4.** to reach by effort; arrive at: *to gain one's destination.* —*v.i.* **5.** to improve; make progress; advance: *to gain in health.* **6.** to get nearer, as in pursuit (usually fol. by *on* or *upon*): *Our race horse was gaining on the favorite.* **7.** to draw away from or farther ahead of one's fellow contestants in a race, one's pursuers, etc. —*n.* **8.** profit; advantage. **9. gains,** profits; winnings. **10.** an increase or advance. **11.** the act of gaining; acquisition. **12.** an increase in the volume of sound from a radio, phonograph, etc. [late ME (n.) < MF, contr. of OF *gaaing,* back formation from *gaaignier* to till, earn, win < Gmc; cf. OHG *weidanōn* to hunt, forage for food] —**gain′a·ble,** *adj.*
—**Syn. 1.** procure, get. GAIN, ATTAIN, EARN, WIN imply obtaining a reward or something advantageous. GAIN carries the least suggestion of method or of effort expended. ATTAIN emphasizes the reaching of a goal. EARN emphasizes the exertions and labor expended which deserve reward. WIN emphasizes attainment in spite of competition or opposition.

gain[2] (gān), *n.* *Carpentry.* **1.** a notch, dado, or mortise cut into a piece of wood, as to receive another piece or to house a flap of a hinge. **2.** tusk (def. 4). **3.** a short rabbet, for receiving a flap of a butt hinge. —*v.t.* **4.** to make a gain or gains in. **5.** to fasten or support by means of a gain. [? akin to obs. *gane,* OE (north) *gan(ian)* (to) yawn, open]

gain·er (gā′nər), *n.* **1.** a person or thing that gains. **2.** See **full gainer.**

Gaines (gānz), *n.* **Edmund Pendleton,** 1777–1849, U.S. general.

Gaines·ville (gānz′vil), *n.* a city in N Florida. 64,510 (1970).

gain·ful (gān′fəl), *adj.* profitable; lucrative: *gainful employment.* —**gain′ful·ly,** *adv.* —**gain′ful·ness,** *n.*

gain·less (gān′lis), *adj.* unprofitable; profitless; unavailing. —**gain′less·ness,** *n.*

gain·ly (gān′lē), *adj.* *Chiefly Dial.* agile; handsome. [*gain,* obs. adj. (see AGAIN) + -LY] —**gain′li·ness,** *n.*

gain·say (gān′sā′), *v.t.,* **-said, -say·ing.** **1.** to deny. **2.** to speak or act against. [ME *gainsaie(n).* See AGAIN, SAY] —**gain′say′er,** *n.* —**Syn. 2.** dispute, controvert, contradict.

Gains·bor·ough (gānz′bûr′ō, -bur′ō; *Brit.* gānz′bər ə), *n.* **Thomas,** 1727–88, English painter.

'gainst (genst *or, esp. Brit.,* gānst), *prep., conj.* against. Also, **gainst.**

Gai·ser·ic (gī′zə rik), *n.* Genseric.

gait (gāt), *n.* **1.** a manner of walking, stepping, or running. **2.** any of the manners in which a horse moves, as a walk, trot, canter, gallop, single-foot, etc. —*v.t.* **3.** to teach a specified gait or gaits to (a horse). [Scot, ME sp. var. of GATE[1] in various senses]

gait·ed (gā′tid), *adj.* having a specified gait (usually used in combination): *slow-gaited; heavy-gaited oxen.*

gait·er (gā′tər), *n.* **1.** a covering of cloth or leather for the ankle and instep and sometimes also the lower leg. Cf. **upper** (def. 7). **2.** a cloth or leather shoe with elastic insertions at the sides. [< F *guêtre,* MF *guiestre, guestre,* perh. < Frankish **wrist* ankle; see WRIST] —**gai′ter·less,** *adj.*

Ga·ius (gā′əs), *n.* **1.** Also, **Caius.** A.D. c110–c180, Roman jurist. **2.** Caius (def. 1).

gal (gal), *n.* *Informal.* a girl or woman. [orig. vulgar or dial. pronunciation of GIRL]

gal, gallon; gallons.

Gal., Galatians.

ga·la (gā′lə, gal′ə; *esp. Brit.* gä′lə), *adj.* **1.** festive; festal; showy: *His birthday parties were always gala occasions.* —*n.* **2.** a celebration; festive occasion; special entertainment. **3.** festal pomp or dress. [< F < It < OF; see GALLANT]

galact-, var. of **galacto-** before a vowel: *galactagogue.*

ga·lac·ta·gogue (gə lak′tə gôg′, -gog′), *adj.* **1.** increasing the amount of milk collected, either with or without increasing the amount secreted. —*n.* **2.** a galactagogue agent or medicine.

ga·lac·tic (gə lak′tik), *adj.* **1.** *Astron.* pertaining to a galaxy or to the Milky Way. **2.** *Physiol.* pertaining to or stimulating the secretion of milk. [< Gk *galaktik(ós)* milky. See GALACT-, -IC]

galac′tic noise′, *Radio, Astron.* a very wide range of noise signals originating in the Milky Way.

galacto-, a learned borrowing from Greek meaning "milk," used in the formation of compound words: *galactopoietic.* Also, *esp. before a vowel,* **galact-.** [< Gk *galakto-,* comb. form of *galakt-,* s. of *gála* milk]

gal·ac·tom·e·ter (gal′ək tom′i tər), *n.* a lactometer. —**gal′ac·tom′e·try,** *n.*

ga·lac·to·poi·et·ic (gə lak′tə poi et′ik), *adj.* **1.** increasing the secretion of milk. —*n.* **2.** a galactopoietic agent or medicine. —**ga·lac·to·poi·e·sis** (gə lak′tə poi ē′sis), *n.*

ga·lac·tose (gə lak′tōs), *n.* *Chem.* a hexose sugar, $C_6H_{12}O_6$, obtained in its dextrorotatory form from milk sugar and in its levorotatory form from mucilages.

Gal·a·had (gal′ə had′), *n.* **1. Sir,** *Arthurian Romance.* the noblest and purest knight of the Round Table, son of Lancelot and Elaine: gained the Holy Grail. **2.** a man characterized by uncompromising devotion to the highest ideals.

ga·lan′ty show′ (gə lan′tē), (in 19th-century England) a shadow play in pantomime. [? < It *galanti* (pl.) < MF *galant.* See GALLANT]

Ga·lá′pa·gos Is′lands (gə lä′pə gōs′; *Sp.* gä lä′pä gôs′), an archipelago on the equator in the Pacific, ab. 600 mi. W of and belonging to Ecuador: many unique species of animal life. 1817 (est. 1959); 3029 sq. mi.

Ga·la·ta (gä′lä tä), *n.* the chief commercial section of Istanbul, Turkey.

gal·a·te·a (gal′ə tē′ə), *n.* a strong cotton fabric, plain or striped, for clothing. [named after the 19th-century British man-of-war H.M.S. *Galatea;* the fabric was once used for children's sailor suits]

Gal·a·te·a (gal′ə tē′ə), *n.* *Class. Myth.* an ivory statue of a maiden, brought to life by the prayers of its sculptor, Pygmalion.

Ga·lați (gä läts′), *n.* a city and port in E Rumania, on the Danube. 112,465 (est. 1964). Also, **Ga·latz′.**

Ga·la·tia (gə lā′shə, -shē ə), *n.* an ancient country in central Asia Minor: later a Roman province. —**Ga·la′tian,** *adj., n.*

Ga·la·tians (gə lā′shənz), *n.* (*construed as sing.*) a book in the New Testament, written by St. Paul to the Christians in Galatia.

gal·a·vant (gal′ə vant′), *v.i.* gallivant.

ga·lax (gā′laks), *n.* an evergreen herb, *Galax aphylla,* of the southeastern U.S., having small white flowers. [< NL < Gk *gála* milk + L *-x* n. suffix]

gal·ax·y (gal′ək sē), *n., pl.* **-ax·ies.** **1.** *Astron.* **a.** a large system of stars held together by mutual gravitation and isolated from similar systems by vast regions of space. **b.**

(*usually cap.*) See **Milky Way.** **2.** any large and brilliant assemblage of persons or things. [ME *galaxie, galaxias* < ML *galaxia,* var. of L *galaxias* < Gk; see GALACT-]

Gal·ba (gal′bə), *n.* **Ser·vi·us Sul·pi·cius** (sûr′vē əs sul-pish′əs), 5? B.C.–A.D. 69, Roman emperor A.D. 68–69.

gal·ba·num (gal′bə nəm), *n.* a gum resin with a peculiar, disagreeable odor, obtained from certain Asian plants of the apiaceous genus *Ferula,* used in medicine and the arts. [ME < L; c. Gk *chalbánē,* Heb *chelbenāh*]

Gal·braith (gal′brāth), *n.* **John Kenneth,** born 1908, U.S. economist and diplomat, born in Canada.

Gal·cha (gal′chä), *n., pl.* **-chas,** (*esp. collectively*) **-cha.** a member of an Iranian people inhabiting the Pamirs. —**Gal′-chic,** *adj.*

gale[1] (gāl), *n.* **1.** a strong wind. **2.** a wind of 32–63 miles per hour. **3.** a noisy outburst: *a gale of laughter.* **4.** *Archaic.* a gentle breeze. [? < Dan *gal* furious or Norw *geil* (< G *geil* rank, exuberant); c. OE *gāl* gay, wanton]

gale[2] (gāl), *n.* See **sweet gale.** [ME *gail,* OE *gagel;* c. G *Gagel*]

Gale (gāl), *n.* **Zo·na** (zō′nə), 1874–1938, U.S. novelist and playwright.

ga·le·a (gā′lē ə), *n., pl.* **-le·ae** (-lē ē′). **1.** *Bot.* any part of the calyx or corolla in the form of a helmet, as the upper lip of the corolla of the monkshood. **2.** a type of bandage for the head. [< L: helmet]

ga·le·ate (gā′lē āt′), *adj.* *Bot.* having a galea. Also, **ga′le·at′ed.** [< L *galeāt(us)* covered with a helmet]

ga·le·i·form (gə lē′ə fôrm′), *adj.* helmet-shaped; resembling a galea. Also, **gal·e·ate** (gal′ē āte′). [GALE(A) + -I- + -FORM]

Ga·len (gā′lən), *n.* **1.** Latin, **Ga·le·nus** (gə lē′nəs). **Claudius,** A.D. c130–c200, Greek physician and writer on medicine. **2.** any physician.

ga·le·na (gə lē′nə), *n.* a common, heavy mineral, lead sulfide, PbS: the principal ore of lead. Also called **galenite.** [< L: lead ore]

ga·len·ic (gə lē′nik, -len′ik), *adj.* of, pertaining to, or containing galena.

Ga·len·ic (gā len′ik, gə-), *adj.* **1.** of or pertaining to Galen, his principles, or his methods. **2.** (*usually l.c.*) of or pertaining to galenicals.

ga·len·i·cal (gā len′i kəl, gə-), *n.* *Pharm.* **1.** an herb or other vegetable drug, distinguished from a mineral or chemical drug. **2.** a crude drug, tincture, or decoction, distinguished from a preparation that has been refined. —*adj.* **3.** galenic. **4.** Galenic.

Ga·len·ism (gā′lə niz′əm), *n.* the medical system or principles of Galen. —**Ga′len·ist,** *n.*

ga·le·nite (gə lē′nīt), *n.* galena. [< G *Galenit.* See GALENA, -ITE]

Gales·burg (gālz′bûrg), *n.* a city in NW Illinois. 36,290 (1970).

gal′ Fri′day. See **girl Friday.**

Ga·li·ci·a (gə lish′ē ə, -lish′ə; *for 2 also Sp.* gä lē′thyä), *n.* **1.** a former crown land of Austria, included in S Poland after World War I, and now partly in the Soviet Union. ab. 30,500 sq. mi. **2.** a maritime region in NW Spain: a former kingdom, and later a province. 11,256 sq. mi. —**Ga·li′cian,** *adj., n.*

Gal·i·le·an (gal′ə lē′ən), *adj.* **1.** of or pertaining to Galilee. —*n.* **2.** a native or inhabitant of Galilee. **3. the Galilean,** Jesus. [< L *Galilae(a)* GALILEE + -AN]

Gal·i·le·an (gal′ə lē′ən), *adj.* of or pertaining to Galileo, his theories, or his discoveries.

gal·i·lee (gal′ə lē′), *n.* a porch or vestibule, often on the ground floor of a tower, at the entrance of some English churches. [< ML *galilaea* porch of a church, L *Galilaea* GALILEE; perh. alluding to Galilee as an outlying portion of the Holy Land]

Gal·i·lee (gal′ə lē′), *n.* **1.** an ancient Roman province in what is now N Israel. **2.** a mountainous province in N Israel. **3. Sea of.** Also called **Lake Tiberias.** a lake in NE Israel through which the Jordan River flows. 14 mi. long; 682 ft. below sea level.

Gal·i·le·o (gal′ə lē′ō, -lā′ō; *It.* gä′lē le′ô), *n.* (*Galileo Galilei*) 1564–1642, Italian physicist and astronomer.

gal·i·ma·ti·as (gal′ə mā′shē əs, -mat′ē əs), *n.* confused or unintelligible talk; gibberish. [< F < ?; perh. a student coinage, ending in Gk *amathís* ignorance]

gal·in·gale (gal′in gāl′), *n.* any sedge of the genus *Cyperus,* esp. *C. longus,* of England, having aromatic roots. [ME < MF *galingal, garingal* < Ar *khalanjān*]

gal·i·ot (gal′ē ət), *n.* a small galley propelled by both sails and oars. Also, **galliot.** [ME *galiote* < MF < ML *galeota,* dim. of *galea* GALLEY]

gal·i·pot (gal′ə pot′), *n.* a type of turpentine exuded on the stems of certain species of pine. Also, **gallipot.** [< F *galipot, galipo,* ? < OF *garipot* a species of pine tree]

gall[1] (gôl), *n.* **1.** something bitter or severe. **2.** bitterness of spirit; rancor. **3.** bile, esp. that of the ox. **4.** impudence; effrontery. [ME; OE *galla;* r. OE *gealla;* c. G *Galle;* akin to L *fel,* Gk *cholē* gall, bile]

gall[2] (gôl), *v.t.* **1.** to make sore by rubbing; chafe severely. **2.** to vex; irritate: *Discourtesy galls me.* —*v.i.* **3.** to be or become chafed. —*n.* **4.** a sore on the skin, esp. of a horse, due to rubbing; excoriation. **5.** something vexing or irritating. **6.** a state of irritation. [ME *galle* (n.), *gallen* (v.) gall, sore < LL *galla* tumor, L: gallnut, oak apple]

gall[3] (gôl), *n.* any abnormal vegetable growth or excrescence on plants, caused by various agents, as insects, nematodes, fungi, bacteria, viruses, chemicals, and mechanical injuries. [ME *galle* < MF < L *galla* gallnut. See GALL[2]]

Gal·la (gal′ə), *n., pl.* **-las,** (*esp. collectively*) **-la.** **1.** a member of a nomadic, pastoral people of Ethiopia and Kenya. **2.** the language of the Galla, a Cushitic language of the Afro-Asian family.

gal·lant (*adj.* gal′ənt *for 1, 2;* gə lant′, -länt′, gal′ənt *for 3, 4; n.* gə lant′, -länt′, gal′ənt; *v.* gə lant′, -länt′), *adj.* **1.** brave, high-spirited, or chivalrous: *a gallant knight.* **2.** stately; grand; elegant. **3.** polite and attentive to women; courtly. **4.** amorous; amatory. —*n.* **5.** a brave, high-spirited, or chivalrous man. **6.** a gay and dashing man. **7.** a man particularly attentive to women. **8.** a suitor or lover. **9.** a paramour. —*v.t.* **10.** to court or act as a lover of (a woman). **11.** to escort (a woman). —*v.i.* **12.** to attend or pay court as a gallant. [ME *gala(u)nt* < OF *galant,* prp. of *galer* to amuse oneself, make merry, perh. < Gmc; cf. OHG *wallan,* OE *weallan* to seethe, rage] —**gal′lant·ly,** *adv.* —**gal′lant·ness,** *n.* —**Syn. 1.** valorous, heroic, bold, daring. See **brave. 3.** chivalrous, courteous. —**Ant. 1.** cowardly. **3.** impolite.

gal·lant·ry (gal′ən trē), *n., pl.* **-ries. 1.** dashing courage; heroic bravery. **2.** gallant or courtly attention to women. **3.** a gallant act, action, or speech. [< MF *galanterie*] —**Syn. 1.** bravery, valor, heroism. **2.** chivalry, courtliness.

Gal·la·tin (gal′ə tin), *n.* **Albert,** 1761–1849, U.S. statesman: Secretary of the Treasury 1801–13.

Gal·lau·det (gal′ə det′), *n.* **Thomas Hopkins,** 1787–1851, U.S. educator and writer.

gall′ blad′der, *Anat.* a vesicle, attached to the under surface of the right lobe of the liver, that stores and concentrates the bile.

Galle (gäl), *n.* a seaport in SW Ceylon. 64,942 (1963).

gal·le·ass (gal′ē as′), *n.* *Naut.* a fighting galley, lateen-rigged on three masts, used in the Mediterranean Sea from the 15th to the 18th centuries. [< OF *galleasse, galiace* < OIt *galeazza,* aug. of *galea* GALLEY]

Gal·le·gos (gä ye′gôs), *n.* **Ró·mu·lo** (rô′mo͞o lô′), 1884–1969, Venezuelan educator, statesman, and writer: president of Venezuela 1948.

gal·le·on (gal′ē ən, gal′yən), *n.* a large sailing vessel of the 15th to the 19th centuries used as a fighting or merchant ship, square-rigged on the foremast and mainmast and generally lateen-rigged on one or two after masts. [< Sp *galeón,* aug. of *galea* GALLEY]

Galleon

gal·ler·y (gal′ə rē, gal′rē), *n., pl.* **-ler·ies. 1.** a long covered area, narrow and open at one or both sides, used esp. as a walk or corridor. **2.** a long porch or portico; veranda. **3.** a long, relatively narrow room. **4.** a raised, balconylike platform or passageway running along the exterior wall of a building. **5.** a raised area, passageway in a theater, church, etc., to accommodate spectators, exhibits, etc. **6.** the uppermost of such areas in a theater, usually containing the cheapest seats. **7.** the general public, esp. when regarded as having popular or uncultivated tastes. **8.** any group of spectators or observers, as at a golf match, a Congressional session, etc. **9.** a room, series of rooms, or building devoted to the exhibition and often the sale of works of art. **10.** a collection of art for exhibition. **11.** a large room or building used for photography, target practice, or other special purposes. **12.** *Naut.* a projecting balcony or structure on the quarter or stern of a vessel. **13.** *Furniture.* an ornamental railing or cresting surrounding the top of a table, stand, desk, etc. **14.** *Mining.* a level or drift. **15.** a small tunnel in a dam, mine, or rock, for various purposes, as inspection or drainage. **16.** *Obs.* a passageway made by an animal. **17.** *Fort. Obs.* an underground or covered passage to another part of a fortified position. **18. play to the gallery,** to attempt to appeal to popular taste. [ME < OF *galerie* < ML *galeria* (? alter of *galīlea, galīlaea;* see GALILEE)] —**gal′ler·ied,** *adj.*

gal·ley (gal′ē), *n., pl.* **-leys. 1.** *Naut.* **a.** a seagoing vessel propelled mainly by oars, sometimes with the aid of sails. **b.** a long rowboat, as one used as a ship's boat by a warship

Galley (def. 1a)

or one used for dragging a seine. **c.** a kitchen aboard a vessel. **2.** *Print.* **a.** a long, narrow tray, usually of metal, for holding type that has been set. **b.** Also called **gal′ley**

proof′. a proof printed from type in a galley. **c.** a rough unit of measurement for type composition (about 22 inches). [ME *galei(e)* < OF *galee, galie,* ? < OPr *galea* < LGk *galéa, galaía*]

gal′ley slave′, **1.** a person condemned to work at an oar on a galley. **2.** an overworked person; drudge.

gall·fly (gôl′flī′), *n., pl.* **-flies.** any of various insects that deposit their eggs in plants, causing the formation of galls.

gall′ gnat′. See **gall midge.**

Gal·li·a (gal′ē ä), *n.* Latin name of **Gaul.**

gal·liard (gal′yərd), *n.* **1.** a spirited dance for two dancers in triple rhythm, common in the 16th and 17th centuries. —*adj.* **2.** *Archaic.* lively or gay. [ME *gaillard* < OF *gaillard, gaillart* < ?]

gal·lic¹ (gal′ik), *adj.* *Chem.* of or containing gallium, esp. in the trivalent state. [GALL(IUM) + -IC]

gal·lic² (gal′ik, gô′lik), *adj.* pertaining to or derived from plant galls: *gallic acid.* [GALL³ + -IC]

Gal·lic (gal′ik), *adj.* **1.** pertaining to the Gauls or Gaul. **2.** pertaining to the French or France. [< L *Gallic(us)* = *Gall(us)* a GAUL + *-icus* -IC]

gal′lic ac′id, *Chem.* a crystalline solid, $C_6H_2(OH)_3COOH$, used chiefly in tanning and in ink dyes. [< F *acide gallique*]

Gal·li·can (gal′ə kən), *adj.* **1.** Gallic; French. **2.** *Eccles.* **a.** of or pertaining to the Roman Catholic Church in France. **b.** of or pertaining to a school or party of French Roman Catholics, before 1870, advocating restricting papal authority. [< L *Gallicān(us)* belonging to Gallia, Gallican. See GALLIC, -AN]

Gal·li·can·ism (gal′ə kə niz′əm), *n.* the body of doctrines advocating restriction of papal authority. Cf. **ultramontanism.** [< F *gallicanisme*]

Gal·li·cise (gal′i sīz′), *v.t., v.i.,* **-cised, -cis·ing.** *Chiefly Brit.* Gallicize. —**Gal′li·ci·sa′tion,** *n.* —**Gal′li·cis′er,** *n.*

Gal·li·cism (gal′i siz′əm), *n.* **1.** a French linguistic peculiarity. **2.** a French idiom or expression used in another language, as *Je ne sais quoi* when used in English. Also, **gal′li·cism.** [< F *gallicisme.* See GALLIC, -ISM]

Gal·li·cize (gal′i sīz′), *v.t., v.i.,* **-cized, -ciz·ing.** to make or become French in language, character, etc. Also, **gal′li·cize′;** *esp. Brit.,* **Gallicise.** [< L *Gallic(us)* GALLIC + -IZE] —**Gal′li·ci·za′tion,** *n.* —**Gal′li·ciz′er,** *n.*

Gal·li-Cur·ci (gal′i kûr′chē; *It.* gäl′lē ko͞or′chē), *n.* **A·me·li·ta** (ä′me lē′tä), 1889–1964, Italian soprano in the U.S.

gal·li·gas·kins (gal′ə gas′kinz), *n.* (*construed as pl.*) **1.** loose hose or breeches worn in the 16th and 17th centuries. **2.** loose baggy trousers. **3.** *Chiefly Dial.* leather leggings or gaiters. [appar. alter. of F *garguesque,* metathetic var. of *greguesque* < It *grechesa,* abstracted from *alla grechesa* in the Greek manner]

gal·li·mau·fry (gal′ə mô′frē), *n., pl.* **-fries.** **1.** a hodgepodge; jumble; confused medley. **2.** a ragout or hash. [< MF *galimafree* < ?]

gal·li·na·cean (gal′ə nā′shən), *n.* a gallinaceous bird. [< NL *Gallīnāce(ae)* name of a group (fem. pl. of L *gallīnāceus* (adj.) GALLINACEOUS) + -AN]

gal·li·na·ceous (gal′ə nā′shəs), *adj.* **1.** pertaining to or resembling the domestic fowls. **2.** belonging or pertaining to the order *Galliformes,* comprising the grouse, pheasants, turkeys, partridges, domestic fowls, etc. [< L *gallīnāceus* pertaining to poultry < *gallīna* hen (*gall(us)* cock + *-ina* -INE¹); see -ACEOUS]

Ga·lli·nas (gä yē′näs), *n.* **Pun·ta** (po͞on′tä), a cape in NE Colombia: northernmost point of South America.

gall·ing (gô′ling), *adj.* that galls; chafing; irritating; exasperating. [GALL² + -ING²] —**gall′ing·ly,** *adv.*

gal·li·nip·per (gal′ə nip′ər), *n.* *Informal.* any of various insects that sting or bite, esp. a large American mosquito, *Psorophora ciliata.* [?]

gal·li·nule (gal′ə no͞ol′, -nyo͞ol′), *n.* any of several aquatic birds of the family *Rallidae,* having elongated, webless toes. [< NL *Gallīnul-* (s. of *Gallīnula*) name of the genus, LL: chicken, dim. of L *gallīna* hen (see GALLINACEOUS); see -ULE]

gal·li·ot (gal′ē ət), *n.* galiot.

Gal·lip′o·li Penin′sula (gə lip′ə lē), a peninsula in European Turkey, between the Dardanelles and the Gulf of Saros. 60 mi. long.

gal·li·pot¹ (gal′ə pot′), *n.* a small glazed pot used by apothecaries for medicines, confections, or the like. [ME *galy pott.* See GALLEY, POT¹]

gal·li·pot² (gal′ə pot′) *n.* galipot.

gal·li·um (gal′ē əm), *n.* *Chem.* a rare, steel-gray, trivalent metallic element used in high-temperature thermometers because of its high boiling point (1983°C) and low melting point (30°C). *Symbol:* Ga; *at. wt.:* 69.72; *at. no.:* 31; *sp. gr.:* 5.91 at 20°C. [< NL < L *gall(us)* cock (trans. of F *coq,* from *Lecoq* de Boisbaudran, 19th-century French chemist) + *-ium* -IUM]

gal·li·vant (gal′ə vant′), *v.i.* **1.** to gad about gaily or frivolously. **2.** to act as a gallant. Also, **galavant.** [? fanciful alter. of GALLANT] —**gal′li·vant′er,** *n.*

gal·li·wasp (gal′ə wosp′), *n.* any of several New World lizards of the genera *Celustus* and *Diploglossus,* esp. *C. occiduus,* of Jamaica, which grows to a length of 22 inches. [?]

gall′ midge′, any of several dipterous insects of the family *Cecidomyiidae,* the larvae of which form characteristic galls on plants. Also called **gall gnat.**

gall·nut (gôl′nut′), *n.* a nutlike gall on plants.

Gallo-, a combining form of **Gallic:** *Gallo-Romance.* [< L, comb. form of *Gallus* a Gaul]

gal·lon (gal′ən), *n.* a common unit of capacity in English-speaking countries, equal to four quarts, the U.S. standard gallon being equal to 231 cubic inches (3.7853 liters), and the British imperial gallon to 277.42 cubic inches (4.546 liters). *Abbr.:* gal [ME *galo(u)n, gallon* < ONF *galon* << ML *gallēta* jug, bucket]

gal·lon·age (gal′ə nij), *n.* **1.** the number of gallons of something used. **2.** the rate at which gallons of something are used.

gal·loon (gə lo͞on′), *n.* a braid or trimming of worsted, silk or rayon tinsel, gold or silver, etc. [< MF *galon,* OF *galonn(er)* (to) adorn one's head with ribbons < *gale* GALA] —**gal·looned′,** *adj.*

gal·loot (gə lo͞ot′) *n.* galoot.

gal·lop (gal′əp), *v.i.* **1.** to ride a horse at a gallop; ride at full speed. **2.** to run rapidly by leaps, as a horse; go at a gallop. **3.** to go fast, race, or hurry, as a person, time, etc. —*v.t.* **4.** to cause (a horse or other animal) to gallop. —*n.* **5.** a fast gait of the horse or other quadruped in which, in the course of each stride, all four feet are off the ground at once. **6.** a run or ride at this gait. **7.** a rapid rate of going, or a period of going rapidly. [ME *galop(en)* (v.) < OF *galop(er)* < ?] —**gal′lop·er,** *n.*

gal·lo·pade (gal′ə pād′), *n.* galop. Also, **galopade.** [< F *galopade.* See GALLOP, -ADE¹]

Gallo-Rom., Gallo-Romance.

Gal·lo-Ro·mance (gal′ō rō mans′), *n.* the vernacular language, a development from Latin, spoken in France from about A.D. 600–900.

gal·lous (gal′əs), *adj.* *Chem.* containing bivalent gallium.

Gal·lo·way (gal′ə wā′), *n.* **1.** a region in SW Scotland, comprising the counties of Wigtown and Kircudbright. **2.** one of a Scottish breed of beef cattle having a coat of curly, black hair. **3.** one of a Scottish breed of small, strong horses.

gal·lows (gal′ōz, -əz), *n., pl.* **-lows·es, -lows.** **1.** a wooden frame, consisting of a cross beam on two uprights, on which condemned persons are executed by hanging. **2.** a similar structure from which something is suspended. [ME *galwes,* OE *g(e)algan,* pl. of *g(e)alga* gallows; c. G *Galgen*]

gal′lows bird′, a person who deserves to be hanged.

gal′lows hu′mor, ghoulish or macabre humor.

gal′lows tree′, a gallows. Also, **gal′low tree′.** [ME *galwe tree,* OE *galgtrēow*]

gall·stone (gôl′stōn′), *n.* *Pathol.* a calculus, or stone, formed in the gall bladder or bile passages.

Gal′lup poll′, a representative sampling of public opinion concerning a certain issue. [after George Horace *Gallup* (1901–84), U.S. statistician]

gal·lus (gal′əs), *n., pl.* **-lus·es.** Often, **galluses.** *Chiefly Dial.* a pair of suspenders for trousers. [var. of GALLOWS]

gall′ wasp′, any of several hymenopterous insects of the family *Cynipidae,* the larvae of which form characteristic galls on plants.

Ga·lo·fa·lo (*It.* gä lô′fä lô), *n.* modern name of **Charybdis.** Also, **Garofalo.**

ga·loot (gə lo͞ot′), *n.* *Slang.* an awkward, silly person. Also, **galloot.** [?]

gal·op (gal′əp), *n.* **1.** a lively round dance in duple time. **2.** a piece of music for, or in the rhythm of, this dance. Also called **gallopade, gal′o·pade′.** [< F; see GALLOP]

ga·lore (gə lōr′, -lôr′), *adv.* **1.** in abundance; in plentiful amounts. —*n.* **2.** *Obs.* abundance. [< Ir *go leōr* (Gael *gu leōr,* *leōir*) = *go* to + *leōr* sufficiency (OIr *lour*); see LUCRE]

ga·losh (gə losh′), *n.* Usually, **galoshes.** a high overshoe. Also, **ga·loshe′, golosh.** [< F *galoche,* prob. < L *gallicula* Gallic (sandal)]

gals., gallons.

Gals·wor·thy (gôlz′wûr′thē, galz′-), *n.* **John,** 1867–1933, English novelist: Nobel prize 1932.

Gal·ton (gôl′tᵊn), *n.* **Sir Francis,** 1822–1911, English scientist and writer. —**Gal·to·ni·an** (gôl tō′nē ən), *adj.*

ga·lumph (gə lumf′), *v.i.* *Informal.* to move along heavily and clumsily. [phonesthemic invention of Lewis Carroll]

Gal·va·ni (gäl vä′nē), *n.* **Lu·i·gi** (lo͞o ē′jē), 1737–98, Italian physiologist whose experiments led to the discovery that electricity may result from chemical action.

gal·van·ic (gal van′ik), *adj.* **1.** pertaining to or produced by galvanism; producing or caused by an electric current. **2.** affecting or affected as if by galvanism; startling; shocking. [< F *galvanique,* named after Luigi GALVANI; see -IC] —**gal·van′i·cal·ly,** *adv.*

galvan′ic bat′tery, *Elect.* See **voltaic battery.**

galvan′ic cell′, *Elect.* an electrolytic cell capable of producing electric energy by electrochemical action.

galvan′ic pile′. See **voltaic pile.**

gal·va·nise (gal′və nīz′), *v.t.,* **-nised, -nis·ing.** *Chiefly Brit.* galvanize. —**gal′va·ni·sa′tion,** *n.* —**gal′va·nis′er,** *n.*

gal·va·nism (gal′və niz′əm), *n.* **1.** *Elect.* electricity, esp. as produced by chemical action. **2.** *Med.* the therapeutic application of electricity to the body. [< F *galvanisme.* See GALVANIC, -ISM]

gal·va·nize (gal′və nīz′), *v.t.,* **-nized, -niz·ing.** **1.** to stimulate by or as by a galvanic current. **2.** *Med.* to stimulate or treat (muscles or nerves) with induced alternating current. **3.** to startle into sudden activity. **4.** to coat (metal, esp. iron or steel) with zinc. Also, *esp. Brit.,* **galvanise.** [< F *galvanis(er).* See GALVANIC, -IZE] —**gal′va·ni·za′tion,** *n.* —**gal′va·niz′er,** *n.*

gal′vanized i′ron, iron that is coated with zinc to prevent rust.

galvano-, a combining form representing **galvanic, galvanism:** *galvanometer.*

gal·va·nom·e·ter (gal′və nom′i tər), *n.* an instrument for detecting the existence and determining the strength of small electric currents.

gal·va·nom·e·try (gal′və nom′i trē), *n.* the method or process of determining the strength of electric currents. —**gal·va·no·met·ric** (gal′və nō me′trik, gal van′ə-), **gal′va·no·met′ri·cal,** *adj.* —**gal′va·no·met′ri·cal·ly,** *adv.*

gal·va·no·scope (gal′və nə skōp′, gal van′ə-), *n.* an instrument for detecting the existence and determining the direction of an electric current.

gal·va·no·ther·my (gal′və nō thûr′mē, gal van′ō-), *n.* *Med.* the production of heat by electric current.

gal·va·not·ro·pism (gal′və no′trə piz′əm), *n.* the growth or movement of an organism or any of its parts toward or away from an electric current. —**gal·va·no·trop·ic** (gal′və nō trop′ik, gal van′ō-), *adj.*

Gal·ves·ton (gal′vi stən), *n.* a seaport in SE Texas, on an island at the mouth of Galveston Bay. 61,809 (1970).

Gal′veston Bay′, an inlet of the Gulf of Mexico.

Gal′veston plan′. See **commission plan.**

Gal·way (gôl′wā), *n.* **1.** a county in S Connaught, in W Republic of Ireland. 149,887 (1961); 2293 sq. mi. **2.** its county seat: a seaport in the W part. 22,028 (1961).

Gal·we·gian (gal wē′jən), *n.* a native or inhabitant of Galloway. [irreg. < ML *Galwedi(a)* GALLOWAY + -AN]

gal·yak (gal′yak), *n.* a sleek, flat fur made from lambskin or from the pelt of a young goat. Also, **gal′yac.** [< native name in the Uzbek S.S.R.]

gam[1] (gam), *n., v.,* **gammed, gam·ming.** —*n.* **1.** a herd or school of whales. **2.** *U.S. Dial.* a social meeting, visit, or the like, as between vessels at sea. —*v.i.* **3.** (of whales) to assemble into a herd or school. **4.** *Naut.* (of the officers and crews of two whaling vessels) to visit or converse with one another for social purposes. **5.** *U.S. Dial.* to participate in a gam or social visit. —*v.t.* **6.** to have a gam with. [? dial. var. of GAME[1]]

gam[2] (gam), *n. Slang.* a person's leg, esp. an attractive female leg. [prob. dial. var. of F *gambe* leg. See JAMB[1]]

gam-, var. of **gamo-** before a vowel.

Ga·ma (gam′ə; *Port.* gä′mə), *n.* **Vas·co da** (vas′kō də; *Port.* väsh′kŏŏ də), c1460–1524, Portuguese navigator.

ga′ma grass′ (gä′mə), an ornamental, reedlike grass, *Tripsacum dactyloides:* one of the tallest grasses in the U.S., growing from four to seven feet high. [var. of GRAMA GRASS]

Ga·ma·li·el (gə mā′lē əl, -māl′yəl), *n.* ("*the Elder*" or "*Gamaliel I*"), died A.D. 50?, the teacher of Paul (Acts 22:3); the grandson of Hillel.

gam·ba·do[1] (gam bā′dō), *n., pl.* **-dos, -does. 1.** either of a pair of large protective boots or gaiters fixed to a saddle instead of stirrups. **2.** any long gaiter or legging. [< It *gamb(a)* leg (see JAMB[1]) + *-ado* -ADE[1]]

gam·ba·do[2] (gam bā′dō), *n., pl.* **-dos, -does. 1.** a spring or leap by a horse. **2.** a caper or antic. Also, **gambade** (gam bād′, -bäd′). [m. F *gambade* a leap; see GAMBOL]

gam·be·son (gam′bi sən), *n. Armor.* a quilted garment worn above or below mail in the Middle Ages. [ME *ga(u)mbeson* military tunic < OF *gambison, gambeison,* prob. < Gmc]

Gam·bet·ta (gam bet′ə; *Fr.* gäɴ be tA′), *n.* **Lé·on** (lā ôɴ′), 1838–82, French statesman.

Gam·bi·a (gam′bē ə), *n.* **1.** a river in W Africa, flowing W to the Atlantic. 500 mi. long. **2. Republic of The,** a republic extending inland along both sides of this river: formerly a British crown colony and protectorate; gained independence 1965; member of the British Commonwealth of Nations. 525,000; 4003 sq. mi. *Cap.:* Banjul.

Gam′bier Is′lands (gam′bēr), a group of islands in French Polynesia, belonging to the Tuamotu Archipelago. ab. 2000; 12 sq. mi.

gam·bit (gam′bit), *n.* **1.** *Chess.* an opening in which the player seeks by sacrificing a pawn or piece to obtain some advantage. **2.** any maneuver by which one seeks to gain an advantage. [< F < Sp *gambit(o)* or It *gambett(o)* (akin to OF *gambet, jambet*). See JAMB[1], -ET]

gam·ble (gam′bəl), *v.,* **-bled, -bling,** *n.* —*v.i.* **1.** to play at any game of chance for stakes. **2.** to stake or risk money, or anything of value, on the outcome of something involving chance; bet; wager. —*v.t.* **3.** to lose or squander by betting (usually fol. by *away*): *He gambled all his hard-earned money away in one night.* **4.** to bet or stake (something of value): *I'll gamble my life on his honesty.* —*n.* **5.** any matter or thing involving risk or hazardous uncertainty. **6.** a venture in a game of chance for stakes, esp. for high stakes. [ME *gamenen* to play (OE *gamenian*), with substitution of -LE for *-en;* see GAME[1]] —**gam′bler,** *n.*

gam·boge (gam bōj′, -bo͞ozh′), *n.* **1.** Also, **cambogia.** a gum resin from various trees of the genus *Garcinia,* esp. *G. Hanburyi,* of Cambodia, Thailand, etc., used as a yellow pigment and as a cathartic. **2.** yellow or yellow orange. [< NL *gambog-* (s. of *gambogium*), var. of *cambog-,* after CAMBODIA] —**gam·bo′gi·an,** *adj.*

gam·bol (gam′bəl), *v.,* **-boled, -bol·ing** or (*esp. Brit.*) **-bolled, -bol·ling,** *n.* —*v.i.* **1.** to skip about, as in dancing or playing; frolic. —*n.* **2.** a skipping or frisking about; frolic. [earlier *gambold, gambald, gamba(u)de* < MF *gambade;* see GAMBADO[2]] —**Syn. 1.** spring, caper, frisk, romp.

gam·brel (gam′brəl), *n.* **1.** the hock of an animal, esp. of a horse. **2.** Also called **gam′brel stick′.** a wood or metal device for suspending a slaughtered animal. [< ONF *gamberel,* akin to F *jambier* legging, *jambe* leg]

gam′brel roof′, a gable roof, each side of which has a shallower slope above a steeper one. Cf. **mansard.** See illus. at **roof.** —**gam′brel-roofed′,** *adj.*

Gam·bri·nus (gam brī′nəs), *n.* a mythical Flemish king, the reputed inventor of beer.

gam·bu·sia (gam byo͞o′zhə, -zhē ə, -zē ə), *n. Ichthyol.* any of several livebearers of the genus *Gambusia* that feed on aquatic insect larvae and are used to control mosquitoes. [< NL, m. CubanSp *gambusino*]

game[1] (gām), *n., adj.,* **gam·er, gam·est,** *v.,* **gamed, gam·ing.** —*n.* **1.** an amusement or pastime: *children's games.* **2.** the material or equipment used in playing certain games: *a store selling toys and games.* **3.** a competitive activity involving skill, chance, or endurance on the part of two or more persons who play according to a set of rules, usually for their own amusement or for that of spectators. **4.** a single occasion of such an activity, or a definite portion of one: *the final game of the season.* **5.** the number of points required to win a game. **6.** a particular manner or style of playing a game. **7.** anything resembling a game, as in requiring skill, endurance, etc.: *the game of politics.* **8.** a trick or strategy: *to see through someone's game.* **9.** fun; sport of any kind; joke: *That's about enough of your games.* **10.** wild animals, including birds and fishes, such as are hunted or taken for sport or profit. **11.** the flesh of such wild animals or other game, used as food. **12.** any object of pursuit, attack, abuse, etc. **13.** fighting spirit; pluck. **14. make game of,** to make fun of; ridicule. **15. play the game,** *Informal.* **a.** to act or play in accordance with the rules. **b.** to act honorably or justly. —*adj.* **16.** pertaining to or composed of animals hunted or taken as game or to their flesh. **17.** having the fighting spirit of a gamecock; plucky: *a game sportsman.* **18.** *Informal.* having the required spirit or will (often fol. by *for* or an infinitive). —*v.i.* **19.** to play games of chance for stakes; gamble. —*v.t.* **20.** *Archaic.* to squander in gaming. [ME *game(n),* OE *gamen;* c. OHG *gaman* glee] —**game′like′,** *adj.* —**game′ly,** *adv.* —**game′ness,** *n.* —**Syn. 3.** sport, contest, competition. **8.** scheme.

game[2] (gām), *adj. Informal.* lame: *a game leg.* [?]

game′ bird′, any bird hunted chiefly for sport, as a quail.

game·cock (gām′kok′), *n.* a rooster of a fighting breed, or one bred and trained for fighting.

game′ fish′, an edible fish capable of affording sport to the angler in its capture.

game′ fowl′, a domestic fowl of a breed much used for fighting.

game·keep·er (gām′kē′pər), *n. Chiefly Brit.* a person employed, as on an estate or game preserve, to prevent poaching and provide for the conservation of game. —**game′keep′ing,** *n.*

gam·e·lan (gam′ə lan′, -lən), *n.* a type of orchestra characteristic of Southeast Asia, using bowed stringed instruments, flutes, and a great variety of percussion instruments, and performing music that is heterophonic and rhythmically highly complex. [< Javanese: percussion instrument]

game′ law′, a law enacted for the preservation of game.

game′ of chance′, a game in which the outcome is determined by chance rather than by skill, as roulette.

game′ plan′, *U.S.* a carefully thought-out strategy or course of action, as for obtaining an economic goal.

game′ room′, a room for recreation, esp. table games.

games·man·ship (gāmz′mən ship′), *n.* the skilled or expert use of methods that are dubious or seemingly improper but not strictly illegal, as in a sports contest.

games′ mas′ter, *Brit.* a physical-education teacher or athletic director in a school. Also, *referring to a woman,* **games′ mis′tress.**

game·some (gām′səm), *adj.* playful; frolicsome; gay. [ME] —**game′some·ly,** *adv.* —**game′some·ness,** *n.*

game·ster (gām′stər), *n.* a person who gambles habitually.

gamet-, var. of **gameto-** before a vowel: *gametangium.*

gam·e·tan·gi·um (gam′i tan′jē əm), *n., pl.* **-gi·a** (-jē ə). *Bot.* an organ or body producing gametes. [< NL; see GAMET-, ANGIO-, -IUM]

gam·ete (gam′ēt, gə mēt′), *n. Biol.* a mature sexual reproductive cell, as a sperm or egg, that unites with another cell to form a new organism. [< NL *gamet(a)* < Gk *gamet-* (s. of *gametḗ* wife, *gamétēs* husband) *gamein* to marry] —**ga·met·ic** (gə met′ik), *adj.*

game′ the′ory, a mathematical theory that deals with strategies for maximizing gains and minimizing losses within prescribed constraints: widely applied in the solution of decision-making problems. Also called **theory of games.**

gameto-, a combining form representing **gamete:** *gametophore.* Also, *esp. before a vowel,* **gamet-.**

ga·me·to·cyte (gə mē′tə sīt′), *n. Biol.* a cell that produces gametes.

gam·e·to·gen·e·sis (gam′i tō jen′i sis), *n. Biol.* the development of gametes. —**gam′e·to·gen′ic, gam·e·tog·e·nous** (gam′i toj′ə nəs), *adj.*

ga·me·to·phore (gə mē′tə fōr′, -fôr′), *n. Bot.* a part or structure producing gametes. —**ga·me·to·phor·ic** (gə mē′tə fôr′ik, -for′-), *adj.*

ga·me·to·phyte (gə mē′tə fīt′), *n. Bot.* the sexual form of a plant in the alternation of generations (opposed to *sporophyte*). —**gam·e·to·phyt·ic** (gam′i tə fit′ik), *adj.*

game′ war′den, an officer who enforces game laws on public lands.

gam·ic (gam′ik), *adj. Biol.* sexual (def. 3). [< Gk *gamik(ós)* bridal, of marriage. See GAM-, -IC]

gam·in (gam′in; *Fr.* GA maɴ′), *n., pl.* **gam·ins** (gam′inz; *Fr.* GA maɴ′). a neglected boy left to run about the streets; street urchin. [< F]

gam·ine (gam′ēn, -in, ga mēn′; *Fr.* GA mēn′), *n., pl.* **gam·ines** (gam′ēnz, -inz, ga mēnz′; *Fr.* GA mēn′). **1.** a tomboy; hoyden. **2.** a diminutive girl, esp. one who is pert, impudent, or playfully mischievous. [< F; fem. of GAMIN]

gam·ing (gā′ming), *n.* **1.** gambling. —*adj.* **2.** of or pertaining to gambling.

gam·ma (gam′ə), *n.* **1.** the third letter of the Greek alphabet (γ, Γ). **2.** the third of any series, as in mathematics, biology, etc. **3.** (*cap.*) *Astron.* a star that is usually the third brightest of a constellation: *The third brightest star in the Southern Cross is Gamma Crucis.* **4.** a unit of weight equal to one microgram. **5.** *Photog.* a measure of the degree of development of a negative or print. **6.** a unit of magnetic field strength equal to 10^{-5} gauss. —*adj.* **7.** of, pertaining to, or composed of gamma rays. [< Gk]

gam·ma·di·on (gə mā′dē ən), *n., pl.* **-di·a** (-dē ə). an ornamental figure consisting of combinations of the Greek capital gamma, esp. in the form of a swastika or a voided Greek cross. [< LGk: little gamma (sp. var. of *gammátion*). See GAMMA, -IDION]

gam′ma glob′ulin, *Biochem.* a protein component of blood plasma, containing antibodies effective against certain microorganisms, as those of measles, infectious hepatitis, and poliomyelitis.

gam′ma ray′, *Physics.* a high-frequency, highly energetic, penetrating radiation emitted from the nucleus of a radioactive atom.

gam·mer (gam′ər), *n. Brit.* an old woman. [contr. of GODMOTHER; cf. GAFFER]

gam·mon[1] (gam′ən), *Backgammon.* —*n.* **1.** a victory in which the winner throws off all his men before his opponent throws off any. —*v.t.* **2.** to win a gammon over. [? special use of ME *gamen* GAME[1]]

gam·mon[2] (gam′ən), *n.* **1.** a smoked or cured ham. **2.** the lower end of a side of bacon. [< OF *gambon* ham (F *jambon*) < *gambe;* see JAMB[1]]

gam·mon[3] (gam′ən), *Brit. Informal.* —*n.* **1.** deceitful nonsense; bosh. —*v.i.* **2.** to talk gammon. **3.** to make pretense. —*v.t.* **4.** to humbug. [perh. special use of GAMMON[1]] —**gam′mon·er,** *n.*

gam·mon[4] (gam′ən), *v.t. Naut.* to fasten (a bowsprit) to the stem of a ship. [? akin to GAMMON[2], alluding to the tying up of a ham]

gamo-, a learned borrowing from Greek meaning "united," used in the formation of compound words: *gamopetalous.* Also, *esp. before a vowel,* **gam-.** [comb. form repr. Gk *gámos* marriage]

gam·o·gen·e·sis (gam′ə jen′i sis), *n. Biol.* sexual reproduction. —**gam·o·ge·net·ic** (gam′ō jə net′ik), **gam′o·ge·net′i·cal,** *adj.* —**gam′o·ge·net′i·cal·ly,** *adv.*

gam·o·pet·al·ous (gam′ə pet′əl əs), *adj. Bot.* having the petals united. [< NL]

Gamopetalous flower

gam·o·phyl·lous (gam′ə fil′əs), *adj. Bot.* having leaves united by their edges.

gam·o·sep·al·ous (gam′ə sep′ə ləs), *adj. Bot.* having the sepals united.

-gamous, a combination of **gamo-** and **-ous** as final element of compound adjectives: *polygamous.* [comb. form repr. Gk *-gamos* marrying]

gamp (gamp), *n. Brit. Facetious.* an umbrella. [after the umbrella of Mrs. Sarah *Gamp* in Dickens' *Martin Chuzzlewit*]

gam·ut (gam′ət), *n.* **1.** the entire scale or range. **2.** *Music.* **a.** the whole series of recognized musical notes. **b.** the major scale. [< ML; contr. of *gamma ut* = *gamma,* used to represent the first or lowest tone (G) in the medieval scale + *ut* later *do*); the notes of the scale (*ut, re, mi, fa, sol, la, si*) being named from a Latin hymn to St. John: *Ut* queant laxis *re*sonare fibris. *Mi*ra gestorum *fa*muli tuorum, *Sol*ve polluti *la*bi reatum, *S*ancte *I*ohannes]

gam·y (gā′mē), *adj.,* **gam·i·er, gam·i·est. 1.** having the flavor of game, esp. game kept uncooked until slightly tainted. **2.** plucky; spirited. —**gam′i·ly,** *adv.* —**gam′i·ness,** *n.*

-gamy, a combination of **gamo-** and **-y**[3] as final element of compounds: *polygamy.* [comb. form repr. Gk *-gamia* act of marrying]

gan (gan), *v.* pt. of **gin**[3].

Gand (gäN), *n.* French name of **Ghent.**

gan·der (gan′dər), *n.* **1.** the male of the goose. Cf. **goose** (def. 2). **2.** *U.S. Slang.* a look; glance: *Take a gander.* [ME; OE *gan(d)ra;* c. MLG *ganre,* D *gander;* akin to GOOSE, G *Gans*]

Gan·der (gan′dər), a town in NE Newfoundland: site of international airport on great circle route between New York and N Europe. 5725 (1961).

Gan·dha·ra (gun där′ə), *n.* **1.** an ancient region in NW India and E Afghanistan. —*adj.* **2.** Also, **Gan·dha·ran** (gun där′ən). of or pertaining to Gandhara, its inhabitants, or its art.

Gan·dhi (gän′dē, gan′-), *n.* **1. In·di·ra** (in dēr′ə), 1917–84, Indian political leader: prime minister 1966–77 and 1980–84 (daughter of Jawaharlal Nehru). **2. Mo·han·das K(ar·am·chand)** (mō′hən däs′ kur′əm chund′), (*Mahatma Gandhi*), 1869–1948, Hindu religious leader, nationalist, and social reformer. **3. Ra·jiv** (rä′jēv), born 1944, Indian prime minister since 1984 (son of Indira Gandhi).

Gan·dhi·an (gän′dē ən, gan′-), *adj.* of or pertaining to Mohandas Gandhi or to Gandhiism.

Gan·dhi·ism (gän′dē iz′əm, gan′-), *n.* the political and social principles of Mohandas Gandhi, esp. his principles of noncooperation and passive resistance. Also, **Gan·dhism** (gän′diz əm, gan′-).

gan′dy danc′er (gan′dē), *Railroad Slang.* a person who maintains or lays track. [?]

Gand·zha (*Russ.* gänd′zhä), *n.* former name of **Kirovabad.**

ga·nef (gä′nəf), *n. Slang.* **1.** a thief or petty crook. **2.** a person who is unscrupulously opportunistic, esp. in pursuit of career, ambitions, or profit. Also, **ga′nev, ganof, gonif, gonoph.** [< Yiddish < Heb *gannābh*]

gang[1] (gang), *n.* **1.** a group or band: *A gang of swimmers appeared at the dock.* **2.** a group of persons who gather together for social reasons. **3.** a group of persons working together; squad; shift: *a gang of laborers.* **4.** a group of persons associated for some criminal or other antisocial purpose: *a gang of thieves.* **5.** a set of tools, oars, etc., arranged to work together or simultaneously. —*v.t., v.i.* **6.** to arrange in gangs; form into a gang. **7. gang up on,** *Informal.* (of a number of persons) to unite in opposition to (someone); combine against. [ME *gong(e), gang(en),* OE *gongan, gangan* to go; ME, OE *gang* a going; c. OHG *gangan* to go, *gang* a going] —**Syn. 1.** company, crew; party, clique, coterie. **3.** team.

gang[2] (gang), *n.* gangue.

gang·er (gang′ər), *n.* a foreman of a gang of laborers.

Gan·ges (gan′jēz), *n.* a river flowing SE from the Himalayas in N India into the Bay of Bengal: sacred to the Hindus. 1550 mi. long.

gang·land (gang′land′, -lənd), *n.* the criminal underworld.

gan·gli·a (gang′glē ə), *n.* pl. of **ganglion.**

gan·gli·ate (gang′glē āt′, -it), *adj.* having ganglia.

gan·gli·form (gang′glə fôrm′), *adj.* having the form of a ganglion.

gan·gling (gang′gling), *adj.* awkwardly tall and spindly; lank and loosely built. Also, **gangly.** [akin to obs. *gangrel* gangling person; cf. GANG[1]]

gan·gli·oid (gang′glē oid′), *adj.* resembling a ganglion.

gan·gli·on (gang′glē ən), *n., pl.* **-gli·a** (-glē ə), **-gli·ons. 1.** *Anat.* a gray mass of nerve tissue existing outside the brain and spinal cord. **2.** *Pathol.* a cyst or enlargement in connection with the sheath of a tendon, usually at the wrist. **3.** a center of intellectual or industrial force, activity, etc. [< LL: type of swelling < Gk: a tumor under the skin, on or near a tendon] —**gan′gli·al, gan′gli·ar,** *adj.*

gan·gli·on·ate (gang′glē ə nāt′, -nit), *adj.* gangliate. Also, **gan′gli·on·at′ed.**

gan·gli·on·ic (gang′glē on′ik), *adj. Anat.* of, pertaining to, or consisting of ganglia.

gan·gly (gang′glē), *adj.,* **-gli·er, -gli·est.** gangling.

gang·plank (gang′plangk′), *n.* a flat plank or portable bridgelike structure for use by persons boarding or leaving a vessel at a pier. Also called **gangway.**

gan·grene (gang′grēn, gang grēn′), *n., v.,* **-grened, -gren·ing.** *Pathol.* —*n.* **1.** the dying or death of soft tissue on part of the body, as from the interruption of circulation; mortification. —*v.t., v.i.* **2.** to affect or become affected with gangrene. [< MF, earlier *cancrene* < L *gangraena* < Gk *gángraina* an eating sore] —**gan·gre·nous** (gang′grə nəs), *adj.*

gang′ saw′, a saw having several parallel blades for making simultaneous cuts. —**gang′ saw′yer.**

gang·ster (gang′stər), *n.* a member of a gang of criminals.

Gang·tok (geng′tôk′), *n.* a city in and the capital of Sikkim, in the S part. 12,000 (1964).

gangue (gang), *n.* the stony or earthy minerals occurring with the metallic ore in a vein or deposit. Also, **gang.** Also called **matrix.** [< F < G *Gang;* see GANG[1]]

gang·way (*n.* gang′wā′; *interj.* gang′wā′), *n.* **1.** a passageway. **2.** *Naut.* **a.** an opening in the railing or bulwark of a vessel, as that into which a gangplank fits. **b.** gangplank. **c.** an area of the weather deck of a vessel, between the side and a deckhouse. **3.** *Brit.* **a.** an aisle in a theater, restaurant, etc. **b.** an aisle in the House of Commons separating the more influential members of the political parties from the younger, less influential members. **4.** a temporary path of planks, as at a building site. **5.** *Mining.* a main passage or level. **6.** Also called **logway.** the ramp up which logs are moved into a sawmill. —*interj.* **7.** clear the way! [OE *gangweg*]

gan·is·ter (gan′i stər), *n.* **1.** a highly refractory, siliceous rock used to line furnaces. **2.** a synthetic product similar to this rock, made by mixing ground quartz with a bonding material. [?]

gan·net (gan′it), *n.* any of several large, webfooted, pelagic birds of the family *Sulidae,* having a long, pointed bill and wings and a wedge-shaped tail. [ME; OE *ganot;* akin to D *gent* GANDER]

ga·nof (gä′nəf), *n.* ganef.

gan·oid (gan′oid), *adj.* **1.** belonging or pertaining to the *Ganoidei,* a group of fishes that are now mostly extinct, many species of which have hard, smooth scales. **2.** (of the scale of a fish) having a smooth, shiny surface of a hard, enamellike substance. —*n.* **3.** a ganoid fish. [< F *ganoïde* < Gk *gán(os)* brightness + F *-oïde* -OID]

gant·let[1] (gant′lit, gônt′-), *n.* **1.** *Railroads.* a track construction used in narrow places, in which two parallel tracks converge so that their inner rails cross, run parallel, and diverge again: thus each train remains on its own track at all times. **2.** gauntlet[2] (defs. 1–3). —*v.t.* **3.** *Railroads.* to form or lay down as a gantlet: *to gantlet tracks.* Also, **gauntlet** (for defs. 1, 3). [var. of archaic *gantlope* < Sw *gatlopp,* lit., lane run = *gat(a)* way, lane + *lopp* a running, course]

Gantlet (def. 1)

gant·let[2] (gant′lit, gônt′-), *n.* gauntlet[1]. —**gant′let·ed,** *adj.*

gant·line (gant′līn′), *n. Naut.* a rope rove through a single block hung from a mast, funnel, etc., as a means of hoisting workmen, tools, staging, flags, or the like. [var. of *girtline.* See GIRT[1], LINE[1]]

gan·try (gan′trē), *n., pl.* **-tries. 1.** a framework spanning a railroad track or tracks for displaying signals. **2.** any of various spanning frameworks, as a bridgelike portion of certain cranes. **3.** *Rocketry.* a frame consisting of scaffolds on various levels used to erect vertically launched missiles. Also, **gauntry.** [? < OF *gantier* wooden stand, frame, var. of *chantier* < ML *cantār(ius),* L *canthērius* < Gk *kanthḗlios* pack ass]

Ga·nym·e·da (gə nim′i də), *n. Class. Myth.* Hebe.

Gan·y·mede (gan′ə mēd′), *n.* **1.** Also, **Gan·y·me·des** (gan′ə mē′dēz). *Class. Myth.* a Trojan youth who was abducted and taken to Olympus, where he was made the cupbearer of the gods and became immortal. **2.** *Astron.* one of the satellites of Jupiter. **3.** (*usually l.c.*) a young waiter who serves liquors.

Ga·o (gä′ō, gou), *n.* a city in E Mali. 21,000.

GAO, General Accounting Office.

gaol (jāl), *n., v.t. Brit.* jail. —**gaol′er,** *n.*

gap (gap), *n., v.,* **gapped, gap·ping.** —*n.* **1.** a break or opening, as in a fence, wall, or the like; breach. **2.** an empty space or interval; hiatus. **3.** a wide divergence or difference; disparity. **4.** a deep ravine or cleft, as in a mountain. —*v.t.* **5.** to make a gap, opening, or breach in. [ME < Scand; cf. OIcel *gap* chasm]

gape (gāp, gap), *v.,* **gaped, gap·ing,** *n.* —*v.i.* **1.** to stare with open mouth, as in wonder. **2.** to open the mouth wide involuntarily, as the result of hunger, sleepiness, or absorbed attention. **3.** to open as a gap; split or become open wide. —*n.* **4.** a wide opening; gap; breach. **5.** the act of gaping. **6.** a stare, as in astonishment or with the mouth wide open. **7.** a yawn. **8.** *Zool.* the width of the open mouth. [ME < Scand; cf. OIcel *gapa* to open the mouth wide; cf. G *gaffen*] —**gap′er,** *n.* —**gap′ing·ly,** *adv.* —**Syn. 1.** See **gaze. 2, 3.** yawn.

gapes (gāps, gaps), *n.* (*construed as sing.*) **1.** *Vet. Pathol.* a disease of poultry and other birds, attended with frequent gaping, due to infestation of the trachea and bronchi with gapeworms. **2.** a fit of yawning. [special use of GAPE] —**gap′y,** *adj.*

gape·seed (gāp′sēd′, gap′-), *n. Brit. Dial.* something that is gaped at; anything unusual or strange.

gape·worm (gāp′wûrm′, gap′-), *n.* a nematode worm, *Syngamus trachea,* that causes gapes.

gap·o·sis (gap ō′sis), *n. Informal.* a noticeable gap or series of gaps between buttoned buttons or closed snaps on a garment when worn.

gap-toothed (gap′tōōtht′, tōōthd′), *adj.* having a gap between two teeth. Also, **gat-toothed.**

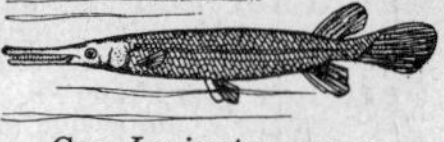

Gar, *Lepisosteus osseus* (Length to 5 ft.)

gar (gär), *n., pl.* (*esp. collectively*) **gar,** (*esp. referring to two or more kinds or species*) **gars. 1.** any of several predaceous, North American, fresh-water fishes of the genus *Lepisosteus,* covered with hard ganoid scales and having a long beak with large teeth. 2. needlefish (def. 1). [shortened form of GARFISH]

G.A.R., Grand Army of the Republic.

ga·rage (gə räzh′, -räj′ *or, esp. Brit.,* gar′ij, -äzh), *n., v.,* **-raged, -rag·ing.** —*n.* **1.** a building or place for sheltering, cleaning, or repairing motor vehicles. —*v.t.* **2.** to put or keep in a garage. [< F = *gar(er)* (to) shelter (< Gmc) + *-age* -AGE]

garage′ sale′, a sale of a family's used unwanted household goods, athletic equipment, bric-a-brac, etc., usually held in one's garage.

Gar·a·mond (gar′ə mond′), *n.* a printing type designed in 1540 by Claude Garamond, French type founder.

Gar′and ri′fle (gar′ənd, gə rand′). See **M-1.** [after John C. *Garand* (1888–1974), American who designed it]

garb (gärb), *n.* **1.** a fashion or mode of dress, esp. of a distinctive, uniform kind. **2.** wearing apparel; clothes. **3.** outward semblance or form. —*v.t.* **4.** to dress; clothe. [< MF *garbe* graceful outline < OIt *garb(o)* grace < Gmc; cf. OHG *garawen,* OE *gearwian* to prepare, adorn, and GEAR] —**garb′less,** *adj.* —**Syn. 1.** style, cut. **2.** clothing, dress, costume, attire, garments, raiment. **4.** attire, array.

gar·bage (gär′bij), *n.* **1.** discarded animal and vegetable matter from a kitchen; refuse. **2.** anything that is contemptibly worthless, inferior, or vile. **3.** *Slang.* worthless talk; lies; foolishness. [ME; prob. < AF *garbelage* removal of refuse]

gar′bage can′, a container for the disposal of waste matter, esp. kitchen refuse.

gar·ban·zo (gär ban′zō, -bän′-; *Sp.* gär vän′thô, -sô), *n., pl.* **-zos** (-zōz; *Sp.* -thôs, -sôs). chickpea (def. 1). [< Sp, alter. of OSp *arvanço;* perh. akin to L *ervum* (see ERVIL)]

gar·ble (gär′bəl), *v.,* **-bled, -bling,** *n.* —*v.t.* **1.** to make unfair or misleading selections from or arrangement of (fact, statements, writings, etc.); distort: *to garble a quotation.* **2.** to confuse innocently or ignorantly; jumble: *to garble instructions.* **3.** *Archaic.* to take out the best of. —*n.* **4.** the act or process of garbling. **5.** an instance of garbling; a garbled phrase, literary passage, etc. [late ME *garbel* < OIt *garbel(lare)* (to) sift < Ar *gharbala* < LL *cribellāre* < *cribel(lum)* sma l sieve] —**gar′bler,** *n.*

Gar·bo (gär′bō), *n.* **Greta** (*Greta Lovisa Gustafsson*), born 1906, U.S. actress, born in Sweden.

gar·board (gär′bōrd′, -bôrd′), *n. Naut.* a plank or plate forming part of the first strake (**gar′board strake′**) on each side of a keel. [< D *gaarboord*]

Gar·cí·a Lor·ca (gär thē′ä lôr′kä), **Fe·de·ri·co** (fe′the-rē′kô), 1899–1936, Spanish poet and dramatist.

Gar·cí·a Már·quez (gär sē′ä mär′kes), **Ga·bri·el** (gä′-vrē el′), born 1928, Colombian novelist and short-story writer: Nobel prize 1982.

Gar·cí·a Ro·bles (gär sē′ä rô′vles), **Al·fon·so** (äl fôn′-sô), born 1911, Mexican diplomat: Nobel peace prize 1982.

Gar·ci·la·so de la Ve·ga (gär′sē lä′sô the lä be′gä, gär′thē-), **1.** 1503?–36, Spanish poet. **2.** ("*el Inca*") 1539?–1616, Peruvian historian and author in Spain.

gar·çon (gar sôn′), *n., pl.* **-çons** (-sôn′). *French.* **1.** (usually in direct address) a waiter in a restaurant. **2.** a boy or a young unmarried man. **3.** a male employee or servant.

Gar·da (gär′də), *n.* **Lake,** a lake in N Italy: the largest lake in Italy. 35 mi. long; 143 sq. mi.

gar·dant (gär′dənt), *adj.* guardant.

gar·den (gär′dən), *n.* **1.** a plot of ground, usually near a house, where flowers, vegetables, or herbs are cultivated. **2.** a piece of ground or other space, commonly with ornamental plants, trees, etc., used as a park or other public area: *a public garden.* —*adj.* **3.** pertaining to or produced in a garden: *fresh garden vegetables.* **4.** garden-variety. —*v.i.* **5.** to lay out or cultivate a garden. —*v.t.* **6.** to cultivate as a garden. [ME *gardin* < ONF *gardin,* OF *jardin* < Gmc; cf. OHG *gartin-,* G *Garten,* YARD[2]] —**gar′den·less,** *adj.* —**gar′den·like′,** *adj.*

Gar·den (gär′dən), *n.* **Mary,** 1877–1967, Scottish soprano.

Gar·de·na (gär dē′nə), *n.* a city in SW California, near Los Angeles. 41,021 (1970).

gar′den apart′ment, 1. an apartment, usually on the ground floor, that adjoins a small private garden. **2.** an apartment in a complex of low buildings set in a landscaped area.

gar′den balm′, the lemon balm. See under **balm** (def. 5).

Gar′den Cit′y, 1. a city in SE Michigan, near Detroit. 41,864 (1970). **2.** a city on W Long Island, in SE New York. 25,373 (1970).

gar′den cress′, a peppergrass, *Lepidium sativum,* used as a salad vegetable.

gar·den·er (gärd′nər), *n.* **1.** a person who is employed to cultivate or care for a garden, lawn, etc. **2.** any person who gardens. [ME < ONF *gardinier* (OF *jardinier*)]

Gar′den Grove′, a city in SW California. 121,371 (1970).

gar·de·nia (gär dē′nyə, -nē ə), *n.* **1.** any evergreen, rubiaceous tree or shrub of the genus *Gardenia,* native to the warmer parts of the Eastern Hemisphere, cultivated for their fragrant, white flowers. **2.** the flower of any of these plants. [named after Dr. Alexander *Garden* (1730–1791), American physician; see -IA]

gar·den·ing (gärd′ning), *n.* **1.** the act of cultivating a garden. **2.** the work or art of a gardener.

Gar′den of E′den, Eden.

Gar′den State′, New Jersey (used as a nickname).

gar·den-va·ri·e·ty (gär′dən və rī′i tē), *adj.* common, usual, or ordinary: *He is just a garden-variety business executive.*

garde·robe (gärd′rōb′), *n. Archaic.* **1.** a wardrobe or its contents. **2.** a private room, as a bedchamber. [< F: lit., that (which) keeps clothing]

Gar·di·ner (gärd′nər, gär′di nər), *n.* **1. Samuel Raw·son** (rô′sən), 1829–1902, English historian. **2. Stephen,** 1483–1555, English statesman and ecclesiastic.

Gard·ner (gärd′nər), *n.* **Erle Stanley** (ûrl), 1889–1970, U.S. writer of detective stories.

Gar·eth (gar′ith), *n. Arthurian Romance.* nephew of King Arthur and a knight of the Round Table.

Gar·field (gär′fēld′), *n.* **1. James Abram,** 1831–81, 20th president of the United States, 1881. **2.** a city in NE New Jersey. 30,797 (1970).

Gar′field Heights′, a city in NE Ohio, near Cleveland. 41,417 (1970).

gar·fish (gär′fish′), *n., pl.* (*esp. collectively*) **-fish,** (*esp. referring to two or more kinds or species*) **-fish·es.** gar. (def. 1). [ME; cf. OE *gār* spear]

Gar·gan·tu·a (gär gan′cho͞o ə), *n.* any large, genial man with a large appetite for food and drink, after the amiable giant and king in Rabelais' satirical novels *Gargantua* (1534) and *Pantagruel* (1532). Cf. **Pantagruel.**

gar·gan·tu·an (gär gan′cho͞o ən), *adj.* gigantic; enormous; prodigious: *a gargantuan task.*

gar·get (gär′git), *n. Vet. Pathol.* inflammation of the udder of a cow; bovine mastitis. [ME *garget, gargat* throat < MF *gargate* throat; perh. orig. a disease of the throat] —**gar′get·y,** *adj.*

gar·gle (gär′gəl), *v.,* **-gled, -gling,** *n.* —*v.t.* **1.** to wash or rinse (the throat or mouth) with a liquid held in the throat and kept in motion by a stream of air from the lungs. **2.** to utter with a gargling sound. —*v.i.* **3.** to gargle the throat or mouth. —*n.* **4.** any liquid used for gargling. [< F *gargouill(er)* (to) gargle, rattle the throat < *gargouille* throat; perh. imit.] —**gar′gler,** *n.*

gar·goyle (gär′goil), *n.* **1.** a grotesquely carved figure of a human or animal. **2.** a spout, terminating in a grotesque representation of a human or animal figure with open mouth, projecting from the gutter of a building for throwing rain water clear of a building. [ME *gargulye* < OF *gargouille, gargoule,* appar. the same word as *gargouille* throat; see GARGLE] —**gar′goyled,** *adj.*

Gargoyle

gar·i·bal·di (gar′ə bôl′dē), *n.* a loose-fitting, long-sleeved blouse worn by women in the mid-19th century, resembling the red shirts of Garibaldi's soldiers.

Gar·i·bal·di (gar′ə bôl′dē; *It.* gä′rē bäl′dē), *n.* **Giu·sep·pe** (jə sep′ē; *It.* jo͞o zep′pe), 1807–82, Italian patriot and general. —**Gar′i·bal′di·an,** *adj., n.*

gar·ish (gâr′ish, gar′-), *adj.* **1.** crudely or tastelessly colorful, showy, or elaborate. **2.** excessively ornate. **3.** dressed in or ornamented with bright colors. **4.** excessively bright; glaring. [earlier *gaurish* = obs. *gaure* to stare (ME *gauren*) + -ISH[1]] —**gar′ish·ly,** *adv.* —**gar′ish·ness,** *n.* —**Syn. 1.** loud, tawdry. See **gaudy**[1]. **2.** overdecorated.

gar·land (gär′lənd), *n.* **1.** a wreath or festoon of flowers, leaves, or other material, worn for ornament or hung on something as a decoration. **2.** a representation of such a wreath or festoon. **3.** a collection of short literary pieces, as poems and ballads; literary miscellany. **4.** *Naut.* a band, collar, or grommet, as of rope. —*v.t.* **5.** to deck with a garland or garlands. [ME *ger(e)lande, garlande* < OF < ?]

Gar·land (gär′lənd), *n.* **1. Ham·lin** (ham′lin), 1860–1940, U.S. novelist, short-story writer, and poet. **2.** a city in NE Texas, near Dallas. 81,437 (1970).

gar·lic (gär′lik), *n.* **1.** a hardy liliaceous plant, *Allium sativum,* whose strong-scented, pungent bulb is used in cookery and medicine. **2.** any of various other plants of the genus *Allium.* **3.** the bulb of such a plant or the flesh of the bulb as used in any form for cooking, as a toe of such a bulb, a powdered quantity of it, etc. **4.** the flavor or smell of this bulb. —*adj.* **5.** cooked, flavored, or seasoned with garlic: *garlic bread; garlic salt.* **6.** of or pertaining to garlic. [ME *garlec,* OE *gārlēac* (*gār* spear (c. G *Ger*) + *lēac* LEEK)] —**gar′lick·y,** *adj.*

gar·ment (gär′mənt), *n.* **1.** any article of clothing. —*v.t.* **2.** to clothe or cover. [ME *garnement* < OF *garniment.* See GARNISH, -MENT]

Gar′ment Cen′ter, an area in the borough of Manhattan, in New York City, noted for the manufacture and wholesale distribution of women's clothing. Also called **Gar′ment Dis′trict.**

gar·ner (gär′nər), *v.t.* **1.** to gather or deposit in or as if in a granary or other storage facility. **2.** to get; acquire. **3.** to gather or collect; hoard. —*n.* **4.** a granary or grain bin. [ME *garner, gerner* < OF *gernier, grenier* < L *grānārium* GRANARY]

Gar·ner (gär′nər), *n.* **John Nance** (nans), 1868–1967, vice president of the U.S. 1933–41.

gar·net[1] (gär′nit), *n.* **1.** any of a group of hard, vitreous minerals, silicates of calcium, magnesium, iron, or manganese with aluminum or iron, varying in color: a deep-red transparent variety is used as a gem and as an abrasive. **2.** a deep red color. [ME *garnet, gernate* < OF *gernate, grenade* < L *grānāt(um)* granular; cf. POMEGRANATE] —**gar′net·like′,** *adj.*

gar·net[2] (gär′nit), *n. Naut.* a tackle having two single blocks; gun tackle. [< ?; cf. D *garnaat, karnaat*]

Gar·nett (gär′nit, gär net′), *n.* **Constance Black,** 1862–1946, English translator from Russian.

gar·ni·er·ite (gär′nē ə rīt′), *n.* a mineral, hydrous nickel magnesium silicate, an important ore of nickel. [named after Jules *Garnier* (d. 1904), French geologist; see -ITE[1]]

gar·nish (gär′nish), *v.t.* **1.** to provide or supply with something ornamental; adorn; decorate. **2.** to provide (a food) with something that adds flavor, decorative color, etc. **3.** *Law.* to garnishee. —*n.* **4.** something placed around or on a food or in a beverage for flavor or decoration. **5.** adornment or decoration. **6.** *Slang.* a fee demanded of a new worker or convict by his boss, warden, or fellow workers or prisoners. [ME *garnish(en)* < OF *garniss-* (extended s. of *garnir, guarnir* to furnish < Gmc); cf. WARN] —**Syn. 1.** embellish, ornament, beautify. **5.** ornament.

gar·nish·ee (gär′ni shē′), *v.,* **-nish·eed, -nish·ee·ing,** *n. Law.* —*v.t.* **1.** to attach (money or property) by garnishment. **2.** to serve (a person) with a garnishment. —*n.* **3.** a person served with a garnishment.

gar·nish·ment (gär′nish mənt), *n.* **1.** adornment or decoration. **2.** *Law.* **a.** a summons to appear in litigation pending between others. **b.** a warning served on a person, at the suit of a creditor plaintiff, to hold, subject to the court's direction, money or property of the defendant in his possession.

gar·ni·ture (gär′ni chər), *n.* something that garnishes; decoration; adornment. [< F = MF *garni(r)* (to) GARNISH + *-ture* n. suffix; see -URE]

Ga·ro·fa·lo (*It.* gä rô′fä lô), *n.* Galofalo.

Ga·ronne (gä rôn′), *n.* a river in SW France, flowing NW from the Pyrenees to the Gironde River. 350 mi. long.

ga·rotte (gə rot′, -rōt′), *n.*, *v.t.*, **-rot·ted, -rot·ting.** garrote. **—ga·rot′ter,** *n.*

gar·pike (gär′pīk′), *n.* gar. (def. 1). [formed after GARFISH]

gar·ret (gar′it), *n.* attic (def. 1). [ME *garite* watchtower < OF *garite, guerite* watch tower < *garir, guarir* to defend]

Gar·rick (gar′ik), *n.* **David,** 1717–79, English actor and theatrical manager.

gar·ri·son (gar′i sən), *n.* **1.** a body of troops stationed in a fortified place. **2.** the place where such troops are stationed. **3.** any military post, esp. a permanent one. **—***v.t.* **4.** to provide (a fort, town, etc.) with a garrison. **5.** to occupy (a fort, post, station, etc.) with troops. **6.** to put (troops) on duty in a fort, post, station, etc. [ME *garisoun* protection, stronghold < OF *garison, gareison* defense, provision < *gar(ir), guerir* to defend < Gmc]

Gar·ri·son (gar′i sən), *n.* **William Lloyd,** 1805–79, U.S. leader in the abolition movement.

gar′rison cap′. See **overseas cap.**

Gar′rison fin′ish, the finish of a race, esp. a horse race, in which the winner comes from behind to win at the last moment. [prob. named after Snapper *Garrison,* 19th-century American jockey who often won in this fashion]

gar·rote (gə rot′, -rōt′), *n.*, *v.*, **-rot·ed, -rot·ing.** **—***n.* **1.** a method of capital punishment of Spanish origin in which an iron collar is tightened around a condemned man's neck until death occurs by strangulation or by injury to the spinal column at the base of the brain. **2.** the collarlike instrument used for this method of execution. **3.** strangulation or throttling, esp. in the course of a robbery. **4.** an instrument, as a cord or wire with handles attached at the ends, for strangling a victim. **—***v.t.* **5.** to execute by the garrote. **6.** to strangle or throttle, esp. during a robbery. Also, **garotte.** [< Sp *garrote* or F *garrot* packing stick < ?] **—gar·rot′er,** *n.*

gar·ru·li·ty (gə rōō′li tē), *n.* the quality or state of being garrulous or talkative; loquacity. [< F *garrulité* < L *garrulitāt-*]

gar·ru·lous (gar′ə ləs, gar′yə-), *adj.* **1.** given to excessive chatter or talkativeness. **2.** wordy or diffuse: *a garrulous speech.* [< L *garrulus* = *garr(īre)* (to) chatter + *-ulus* -ULOUS] **—gar′ru·lous·ly,** *adv.* **—gar′ru·lous·ness,** *n.* **—Syn. 1.** prating, babbling. See **talkative. 2.** verbose.

gar·ter (gär′tər), *n.* **1.** Also called, *Brit.*, **sock suspender, suspender.** an elastic band worn around the leg or an elastic strap hanging from a girdle or other undergarment, for holding up a stocking or sock. **2.** a similar band worn to hold up a shirt sleeve. **3.** (*cap.*) *Brit.* **a.** the badge of the Order of the Garter. **b.** membership in the Order. **c.** the Order itself. **d.** a member of the Order. **—***v.t.* **4.** to fasten with a garter. [ME < ONF *gartier* < *garet* the bend of the knee < Celt; cf. Welsh *gar* shank, Breton *gâr* leg]

gar′ter belt′, an undergarment of cloth or elastic, with attached garters, worn by women to hold up stockings.

gar′ter snake′, any of numerous harmless snakes of the genus *Thamnophis,* common in North and Central America.

garth (gärth), *n.* **1.** an open courtyard enclosed by a cloister. **2.** *Archaic.* a yard or garden. [ME < Scand; cf. OIcel *gardh(r)* YARD[2]]

Gar·y (gâr′ē, gar′ē), *n.* **1. Elbert Henry,** 1846–1927, U.S. financier and lawyer. **2.** a port in NW Indiana, on Lake Michigan. 175,415 (1970).

gas (gas), *n.*, *pl.* **gas·es,** *v.*, **gassed, gas·sing.** **—***n.* **1.** *Physics.* a substance possessing perfect molecular mobility and the property of indefinite expansion, as opposed to a solid or liquid. **2.** any such fluid or mixture of fluids other than air. **3.** any such fluid used as an anesthetic. **4.** any such combustible fluid used as fuel. **5.** *U.S. Informal.* **a.** gasoline. **b.** the accelerator of an automobile or other vehicle. **6.** *Coal Mining.* an explosive mixture of firedamp with air. **7.** an aeriform fluid or a mistlike assemblage of fine particles suspended in air, used in warfare to asphyxiate, poison, or stupefy an enemy. **8.** *Slang.* empty talk. **9.** *Slang.* a person or thing that is very entertaining, pleasing, or successful. **—***v.t.* **10.** to supply with gas. **11.** to overcome, poison, or asphyxiate with gas or fumes. **12.** to treat or impregnate with gas. **—***v.i.* **13.** to give off gas, as a storage battery being charged. **14.** *Slang.* to indulge in idle, empty talk. **15. gas up,** to fill the gasoline tank of an automobile or truck. [coined by J. B. van Helmont (1577–1644), Flemish chemist; suggested by Gk *cháos* atmosphere] **—gas′less,** *adj.*

gas·bag (gas′bag′), *n.* **1.** a bag for holding gas, as in a dirigible. **2.** *Slang.* a talkative, boastful person; windbag.

gas′ black′, the soot of a natural-gas flame, used in paints; fine carbon.

gas′ blad′der. See **air bladder** (def. 2).

gas′ burn′er, **1.** the tip or nozzle of a gas fixture, from which the gas issues, as on a stove. **2.** a stove or the like that burns gas as a fuel.

gas′ cham′ber, a room used for the execution of prisoners by means of a poisonous gas.

Gas·cogne (gȧ skôn′yᵊ), *n.* French name of **Gascony.**

Gas·coigne (gas′koin), *n.* **George,** 1525?–77, English poet.

Gas·con (gas′kən), *n.* **1.** a native of Gascony, France, the inhabitants of which were noted for their boastfulness. **2.** (*l.c.*) a boaster or braggart. **—***adj.* **3.** pertaining to Gascony and its people. **4.** (*l.c.*) boastful. [ME *gascoun* < OF; akin to L *Vascōnēs* Basque]

gas·con·ade (gas′kə nād′), *n.*, *v.*, **-ad·ed, -ad·ing.** **—***n.* **1.** extravagant boasting; boastful talk. **—***v.i.* **2.** to boast extravagantly; bluster. [< F *gasconnade* < *gasconn(er)* (to) boast, chatter] **—gas′con·ad′er,** *n.*

Gas·co·ny (gas′kə nē), *n.* a former province in SW France. French, **Gascogne.**

gas·e·lier (gas′ə lēr′), *n.* gasolier.

gas′ en′gine, an internal-combustion engine driven by a mixture of air and gas.

gas·e·ous (gas′ē əs, gash′əs), *adj.* **1.** pertaining to or having the characteristics of gas. **2.** existing in the state of a gas; not solid or liquid. **—gas′e·ous·ness,** *n.*

gas′ fit′ter, a person who installs gas pipes and apparatus in buildings.

gas′ fit′ting, **1.** the work or business of a gas fitter. **2. gas fittings,** fittings for the use of illuminating gas.

gas′ fix′ture, a fixture attached to a ceiling or wall, for holding a gaslight.

gas′ guz′zler, *Informal.* an automobile having a high rate of gasoline consumption in relation to mileage. Also, **gas′-guz′zler. —gas′-guz′zling,** *adj.*

gash (gash), *n.* **1.** a long, deep wound or cut; slash. **—***v.t.* **2.** to make a long, deep cut in; slash. [alter. of ME *garsen* < OF *gars(er), jars(ier)* (F *gercer*) (to) scarify, wound < VL **charissāre* < Gk *charáss(ein)* (to) scratch, notch]

gas·hold·er (gas′hōl′dər), *n.* a container, esp. a cylindrical tank, for holding or storing gas.

gas·house (gas′hous′), *n.*, *pl.* **-hous·es** (-hou′ziz). gasworks.

gas·i·form (gas′ə fôrm′), *adj.* having the form of gas; gaseous.

gas·i·fy (gas′ə fī′), *v.t.*, *v.i.*, **-fied, -fy·ing.** to convert into or become a gas. **—gas′i·fi′a·ble,** *adj.* **—gas′i·fi·ca′tion,** *n.* **—gas′i·fi′er,** *n.*

gas′ jet′, **1.** a gas burner on a gas fixture. **2.** a flame of illuminating gas.

Gas·kell (gas′kəl), *n.* **Mrs.** (*Elizabeth Cleghorn Stevenson Gaskell*), 1810–65, English novelist.

gas·ket (gas′kit), *n.* **1.** a rubber, metal, or rope ring, for packing a piston or placing around a joint to make it watertight. **2.** *Naut.* a light line for securing a furled sail to a boom, gaff, or yard. [? < F *garcette* plait of rope]

gas·kin[1] (gas′kin), *n.* **1.** the part of the hind leg of a horse or other hoofed quadruped between the stifle and the hock. **2. gaskins,** *Obs.* hose or breeches. [perh. shortened form of GALLIGASKINS]

gas·kin[2] (gas′kin), *n.* a gasket. Also, **gas·king** (gas′king). [by alter.]

gas·light (gas′līt′), *n.* **1.** light produced by the combustion of illuminating gas. **2.** a gas burner or gas jet for producing such light.

gas·lit (gas′lit′), *adj.* **1.** having illumination provided by burning gas. **2.** characterized by the widespread use of the gaslight: *the gaslit era.*

gas′ log′, a gas burner in a fireplace, made to resemble a log.

gas′ main′, a large pipe for conducting and distributing gas to smaller pipes or ducts.

gas·man (gas′man′), *n.*, *pl.* **-men.** **1.** a man who reads gas meters to determine what charge is to be billed. **2.** See **gas fitter.**

gas′ man′tle, mantle (def. 4).

gas′ mask′, a masklike device that filters the air through charcoal and chemicals, for protecting the wearer against noxious gases and fumes, as in warfare or in certain industrial processes.

Gas mask

gas′ me′ter, an apparatus for measuring and recording the amount of gas produced or consumed, esp. such an apparatus metering the amount of household gas piped into a dwelling.

gas·o·gene (gas′ə jēn′), *n.* gazogene.

gas·o·hol (gas′ə hôl′, -hol′), *n.* a mixture of 90% unleaded gasoline and 10% anhydrous ethyl alcohol, used esp. as an automobile fuel. [GAS(OLINE + ALC)OHOL]

gas·o·lier (gas′ə lēr′), *n.* a chandelier furnished with gaslights. Also, **gaselier.** [GAS + -O- + (CHANDE)LIER]

gas·o·line (gas′ə lēn′, gas′ə lēn′), *n.* a volatile, flammable liquid mixture of hydrocarbons, obtained from petroleum, and used as fuel for internal-combustion engines, as a solvent, etc. Also, **gas′o·lene′.** [GAS + -OL[2] + -INE[2]] **—gas·o·lin·ic** (gas′ə lē′nik, -lin′ik), *adj.*

gas·om·e·ter (gas om′i tər), *n.* an apparatus for measuring and storing gas in a laboratory. [< F *gazomètre*]

gasp (gasp, gäsp), *n.* **1.** a sudden, short breath; a convulsive effort to breathe. **2.** a short, convulsive utterance. **—***v.i.* **3.** to catch the breath or struggle for breath with one's mouth open; breathe convulsively. **4.** to desire or crave (usually fol. by *for* or *after*). **—***v.t.* **5.** to utter with gasps (often fol. by *out, forth, away,* etc.): *She gasped out the words.* **6.** to breathe or emit with gasps (often fol. by *away*). [ME *gasp(en),* prob. OE **gāspen* = OIcel *geispa;* akin to GAPE] **—gasp′ing·ly,** *adv.* **—Syn. 3.** See **pant.**

Gas·pé′ Penin′sula (gas pā′; *Fr.* gȧ spā′), a peninsula in SE Canada, in Quebec province.

Gas·pe·ri (*It.* gäs′pe rē), *n.* **Al·ci·de De** (*It.* äl chē′de de). See **De Gasperi, Alcide.**

gas-plant (gas′plant′, -plänt′), *n.* dittany (def. 3).

gas′ range′, a cooking stove that uses gas as fuel.

gas·ser (gas′ər), *n.* **1.** a person or thing that gasses. **2.** a well yielding natural gas. **3.** *Slang.* something that is very funny, pleasing, or successful.

gas·sing (gas′ing), *n.* **1.** the act of a person or thing that gasses. **2.** an affecting, overcoming, or poisoning with gas or fumes. **3.** a process by which something is gassed, as in fumigation.

gas′ sta′tion. See **filling station.** Also called **service station.**

gas·sy (gas′ē), *adj.*, **-si·er, -si·est.** **1.** full of, containing, or resembling gas. **2.** flatulent. **—gas′si·ness,** *n.*

gas′ tank′, **1.** a tank for storing gas or gasoline. **2.** a tank containing the gasoline supply in a car, truck, or other gasoline-engine vehicle.

gas·ter·o·pod (gas′tər ə pod′), *n.*, *adj.* gastropod.

gas′ thermom′eter, a device for measuring temperature by observing the change in either pressure or volume of an enclosed gas.

gas·tight (gas′tīt′), *adj.* **1.** not penetrable by a gas. **2.** not admitting a given gas under a given pressure.

Gas·to·ni·a (ga stō′nē ə), *n.* a city in S North Carolina, W of Charlotte. 47,142 (1970).
gastr-, var. of **gastro-** before a vowel: *gastrectomy.*
gas·tral·gi·a (ga stral′jē ə, -jə), *n.* *Pathol.* **1.** neuralgia of the stomach. **2.** any stomach pain. —**gas·tral′gic,** *adj., n.*
gas·trec·to·my (ga strek′tə mē), *n., pl.* **-mies.** *Surg.* partial or total excision of the stomach.
gas·tric (gas′trik), *adj.* pertaining to the stomach.
gas′tric juice′, *Biochem.* the digestive fluid, containing pepsin and other enzymes, secreted by the glands of the stomach.
gas′tric ul′cer, *Pathol.* an erosion of the stomach's inner wall caused in part by the corrosive action of the gastric juice on the mucous membrane. Cf. **peptic ulcer.**
gas·trin (gas′trin), *n.* *Biochem.* a hormone that stimulates the secretion of gastric juice.
gas·tri·tis (ga strī′tis), *n.* *Pathol.* inflammation of the stomach, esp. of its mucous membrane. [< NL] —**gas·trit·ic** (ga strit′ik), *adj.*
gastro-, a learned borrowing from Greek meaning "stomach," used in the formation of compound words: *gastrology.* Also, *esp. before a vowel,* **gastr-.** [< Gk, comb. form of *gastḗr*]
gas·tro·en·ter·i·tis (gas′trō en′tə rī′tis), *n.* *Pathol.* inflammation of the stomach and intestines. —**gas·tro·en·ter·it·ic** (gas′trō en′tə rit′ik), *adj.*
gastroentero-, a combining form of **gastro-** and **entero-**: *gastroenterostomy.*
gas·tro·en·ter·ol·o·gy (gas′trō en′tə rol′ə jē), *n.* the study of the structure and diseases of digestive organs. —**gas′tro·en′te·rol′o·gist,** *n.*
gas·tro·en·ter·os·to·my (gas′trō en′tə ros′tə mē), *n., pl.* **-mies.** *Surg.* the making of a new passage between the stomach and the duodenum or esp. the jejunum.
gas·tro·in·tes·ti·nal (gas′trō in tes′tə nᵊl), *adj.* *Anat.* of, pertaining to, or affecting the stomach and intestines.
gas·trol·o·gy (ga strol′ə jē), *n.* the study of the structure, functions, and diseases of the stomach. —**gas·trol′o·gist,** *n.*
gas·tro·nome (gas′trə nōm′), *n.* a gourmet; epicure. Also, **gas·tron′o·mist.** [< F, back formation from *gastronomie* GASTRONOMY]
gas·tron·o·my (ga stron′ə mē), *n.* **1.** the art or science of good eating. **2.** a style or custom of cooking or eating. [< F *gastronomie* < Gk *gastronomía*] —**gas·tro·nom·ic** (gas′trə nom′ik), **gas′tro·nom′i·cal,** *adj.* —**gas′tro·nom′i·cal·ly,** *adv.*
gas·tro·pod (gas′trə pod′), *n.* **1.** any mollusk of the class *Gastropoda,* comprising the snails. —*adj.* **2.** Also, **gas·trop·o·dous** (ga strop′ə dəs). belonging or pertaining to the *Gastropoda.* Also, **gasteropod.** [< NL *Gast(e)ropod(a)* a class of mollusk(s)]
gas·tro·scope (gas′trə skōp′), *n.* *Med.* an instrument for inspecting the interior of the stomach. —**gas·tro·scop·ic** (gas′trə skop′ik), *adj.*
gas·tros·co·py (ga stros′kə pē), *n., pl.* **-pies.** *Med.* the examination with a gastroscope to detect disease.
gas·trot·o·my (ga strot′ə mē), *n., pl.* **-mies.** *Surg.* the operation of cutting into the stomach.
gas·tro·trich (gas′trə trik), *n.* any of the microscopic, multicellular animals of the class or phylum *Gastrotricha,* found in fresh or salt water. [< NL = *gastro-* GASTRO- + Gk *trich-* (s. of *thríx* hair)]
gas·tro·vas·cu·lar (gas′trō vas′kyə lər), *adj.* *Zool.* serving for digestion and circulation, as a cavity.
gas·tru·la (gas′trŏŏ lə), *n., pl.* **-las, -lae** (-lē′). *Embryol.* a metazoan embryo in an early state of germ-layer formation following the blastula stage, consisting of a cuplike body of two layers of cells enclosing a central cavity. [< NL] —**gas′tru·lar,** *adj.*
gas·tru·late (gas′trŏŏ lāt′), *v.i.,* **-lat·ed, -lat·ing.** *Embryol.* to undergo gastrulation.
gas·tru·la·tion (gas′trŏŏ lā′shən), *n.* *Embryol.* **1.** the formation of a gastrula. **2.** any process, as invagination, by which a blastula or other form of embryo is converted into a gastrula.
gas′ tube′, an electron tube whose envelope contains a highly rarefied gas.
gas·works (gas′wûrks′), *n., pl.* **-works.** (*construed as sing.*) a plant where heating and illuminating gas is manufactured and piped to homes and buildings. Also called **gashouse.**
gat¹ (gat), *v.* *Archaic.* pt. of **get.**
gat² (gat), *n.* *Slang.* a pistol or revolver. [abbr. of GATLING GUN]
gat³ (gat), *n.* a passage or channel that extends inland from a shore. [< Scand; cf. OIcel *gat* pathway]
gate¹ (gāt), *n., v.,* **gat·ed, gat·ing.** —*n.* **1.** a movable barrier closing an opening in a fence, wall, or other enclosure. **2.** an opening permitting passage through an enclosure. **3.** a tower, architectural setting, etc., for defending or adorning such an opening or for providing a monumental entrance to a street, park, etc. **4.** any means of access or entrance. **5.** a mountain pass. **6.** any movable barrier, as at a road or railroad crossing. **7.** a sliding barrier for regulating the passage of water, steam, or the like, as in a dam, pipe, etc.; valve. **8.** the total number of paid admissions at a public event. **9.** the total receipts from such admissions. **10.** *Foundry.* **a.** Also called **ingate.** a channel or opening in a mold through which molten metal is poured into the mold cavity. **b.** the waste metal left in such a channel after hardening. **11. get the gate,** *Slang.* to be rejected or dismissed. **12. give (someone) the gate,** *Slang.* **a.** to reject (a person), as one's fiancé, lover, friend, etc. **b.** to dismiss from one's employ. —*v.t.* **13.** (at British universities) to punish by restricting (a student) within the college gates. [ME *gat, gate,* OE *geat* (pl. *gatu*); c. LG, D *gat* hole, breach; cf. GATE²] —**gate′less,** *adj.* —**gate′like′,** *adj.*
gate² (gāt), *n.* **1.** *Archaic.* a path; way. **2.** *Dial.* habitual manner or way of acting. [ME < ON *gata* path; perh. akin to OE *geat* GATE¹; cf. GAT³]
gate-crash·er (gāt′krash′ər), *n.* a person who enters without an invitation or a ticket.
gate·fold (gāt′fōld′), *n.* *Print.* an outsize page of a book or periodical, folded so as not to extend beyond the edges.
gate·house (gāt′hous′), *n., pl.* **-hous·es** (-hou′ziz). **1.** a house at or over a gate, used as a keeper's quarters, fortification, etc. **2.** a house or structure at the gate of a dam, reservoir, etc., with equipment or controls for regulating the flow of water. [ME]
gate·keep·er (gāt′kē′pər), *n.* a person in charge of a gate, usually to supervise the traffic or flow through it.

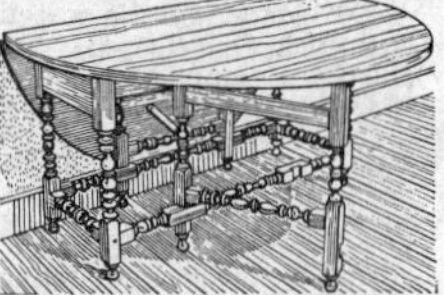
Gate-leg table (18th century)

gate′ leg′, *Furniture.* a leg attached to a hinged frame that can be swung out to support a drop leaf.
gate′-leg ta′ble (gāt′leg′), a table having drop leaves supported by gate legs. Also, **gate′-legged′ ta′ble.**
gate·man (gāt′mən, -man′), *n., pl.* **-men** (-mən, -men′). a gatekeeper.
gate·post (gāt′pōst′), *n.* the vertical post on which a gate is suspended by hinges, or the post against which the gate is closed.
Gates (gāts), *n.* **Horatio,** 1728–1806, American Revolutionary general, born in England.
Gates·head (gāts′hed′), *n.* a seaport in N Durham, in NE England, on the Tyne River opposite Newcastle. 103,232 (1961).
gate·way (gāt′wā′), *n.* **1.** a passage or entrance that may be closed by a gate. **2.** a structure for enclosing such an opening or entrance. **3.** any passage by or point at which a region may be entered: *New York soon became the gateway to America.*
Gath (gath), *n.* a Philistine city. I Sam. 6:17; Chron. 18:1.
gath·er (gath′ər), *v.t.* **1.** to bring together into one group, collection, or place. **2.** to learn or conclude from observation: *I gather that he is the real leader.* **3.** to pick or harvest (any crop or natural yield) from its place of growth. **4.** to pick up piece by piece: *Gather your toys from the floor.* **5.** to serve as a center of attention for; attract. **6.** to collect; make a collection of. **7.** to wrap or draw around or close to someone or something: *He gathered his scarf around his neck. She gathered the crying child in her arms.* **8.** to take by selection from among other things. **9.** to assemble or collect (one's energies or oneself), as for an effort (often fol. by *up*). **10.** to contract (the brow) into wrinkles. **11.** to draw (cloth) up on a thread in fine folds or puckers by means of even stitches. **12.** *Bookbinding.* to assemble (the printed sections of a book) in proper sequence for binding. **13.** to increase (speed, momentum, etc.), as a moving vehicle. **14.** *Naut.* to gain (way) from a dead stop or extremely slow speed. —*v.i.* **15.** to come together around a central point; assemble. **16.** to collect or accumulate: *Clouds gathered in the north.* **17.** to grow, as by accretion; increase. **18.** to become contracted into wrinkles, folds, creases, etc., as the brow or as cloth. **19.** to come to a head, as a sore in suppurating. **20. be gathered to one's fathers,** to die. —*n.* **21.** a drawing together; contraction. **22.** Often, **gathers.** a fold or pucker, as in gathered cloth. **23.** the act or an instance of gathering. **24.** an amount or number gathered, as during a harvest. [ME *gader(en),* OE *gaderian* < *geador* together, akin to *gæd* fellowship; cf. TOGETHER, GOOD] —**gath′er·a·ble,** *adj.* —**gath′er·er,** *n.*
—**Syn. 1.** accumulate, amass, hoard. GATHER, ASSEMBLE, COLLECT, MUSTER, MARSHAL imply bringing or drawing together. GATHER expresses the general idea usually with no implication of arrangement: *to gather sea shells.* ASSEMBLE is used of objects or facts brought together preparatory to arranging them: *to assemble data for a report.* COLLECT implies purposeful accumulation to form an ordered whole: *to collect evidence, stamps.* MUSTER, primarily a military term, suggests thoroughness in the process of collection: *to muster all one's resources.* MARSHAL, another term primarily military, suggests rigorously ordered, purposeful arrangement: *to marshal facts for effective presentation.* **2.** assume, understand. **3.** pluck, reap. —**Ant. 1, 15.** separate.
gath·er·ing (gath′ər ing), *n.* **1.** the act of a person or thing that gathers. **2.** something that is gathered together. **3.** an assembly or meeting. **4.** an assemblage of people; crowd. **5.** a collection, assemblage, or compilation of anything. **6.** a gather or a series of gathers in cloth. **7.** an inflamed and suppurating swelling. **8.** *Bookbinding.* a section in a book, usually a sheet cut into several leaves. [ME *gaderinge,* OE *gaderunge*] —**Syn. 3.** assemblage. **4.** congregation, company, throng. **7.** boil, abscess, carbuncle.
Gat′ling gun′ (gat′ling), an early type of machine gun having a revolving cluster of barrels, each barrel being automatically loaded and fired during every turn. [named after R. J. *Gatling* (1818–1903), American inventor]
GATT, General Agreement on Tariffs and Trade.
Gat·ti-Ca·saz·za (gät′tē kä zät′tsä), *n.* **Giu·lio** (jōōl′yô), 1869–1940, Italian opera impresario; in the U.S. 1908–35.
gat-toothed (gat′tōōtht′, -tōōthd′), *adj.* gap-toothed.
Ga·tun (gä tōōn′), *n.* **1.** a town in the N Canal Zone. 668 (1970). **2.** a large dam near this town.
Gatun′ Lake′, an artificial lake in the Canal Zone, part of the Panama Canal: created by the Gatun dam. 164 sq. mi.
gauche (gōsh), *adj.* lacking social grace; awkward; tactless. [< F: awkward, left, MF < *gauch(ir)* (to) turn, veer < Gmc] —**gauche′ness,** *n.*
gau·che·rie (gō′shə rē′; *Fr.* gōshᵊ rē′), *n., pl.* **-ries** (-rēz′; *Fr.* -rē′). **1.** lack of social grace; awkwardness; tactlessness. **2.** an act, movement, etc., that is gauche. [< F]
gau·cho (gou′chō; *Sp.* gou′chô), *n., pl.* **-chos** (-chōz; *Sp.* -chôs). a cowboy of the South American pampas. [< AmerSp < Arawak *cachu* comrade]
gaud (gôd), *n.* **1.** a showy ornament. **2.** Usually, **gauds.** showy display or ceremony. [ME, perh. < AF, n. use of *gaudir* to rejoice < L *gaudēre* to enjoy]
Gau·de·a·mus i·gi·tur (gou′dā ä′mŏŏs ig′i tōōr′), *Latin.* Let us therefore be joyful: title of a medieval German student song.
gaud·er·y (gô′də rē), *n., pl.* **-er·ies.** **1.** ostentatious show. **2.** finery; gawdy or showy things.

gaud·y[1] (gô′dē), *adj.*, **gaud·i·er, gaud·i·est.** **1.** brilliantly or excessively showy. **2.** showy without taste; flashy. **3.** ostentatiously ornamented; garish. [orig. attributive use of GAUDY[2] large bead of rosary, feast; later taken as < GAUD] —**gaud′i·ly,** *adv.* —**gaud′i·ness,** *n.*
—**Syn. 2.** loud; conspicuous, obvious. GAUDY, FLASHY, GARISH, SHOWY agree in the idea of conspicuousness and, often, bad taste. That which is GAUDY challenges the eye, as by brilliant colors or evident cost, and is not in good taste: *a gaudy hat.* FLASHY suggests insistent and vulgar display, in rather a sporty manner: *a flashy car.* GARISH suggests a glaring brightness or crude vividness of color and too much ornamentation: *garish decorations.* SHOWY applies to that which is strikingly conspicuous, but not necessarily offensive to good taste: *a garden of showy flowers; a showy dress.* —**Ant. 2.** modest, sober.

gaud·y[2] (gô′dē), *n.*, *pl.* **gaud·ies.** *Brit.* a festival or celebration, esp. an annual college dinner. [ME < L *gaudi(um)* joy, delight]

gauf·fer (gô′fər, gof′ər), *n.*, *v.t.* goffer.

gauge (gāj), *v.*, **gauged, gaug·ing,** *n.* —*v.t.* **1.** to appraise, estimate, or judge. **2.** to determine the exact dimensions, capacity, quantity, or force of; measure. **3.** to make conformable to a standard. **4.** to mark or measure off; delineate. **5.** to chip or rub (bricks or stones) to a uniform size or shape. —*n.* **6.** a standard of measure or measurement; dimension, size, or quantity. **7.** any device for measuring or testing something, esp. for measuring a dimension, quantity, or mechanical accuracy. **8.** a means of estimating or judging; criterion. **9.** extent; scope; capacity. **10.** *Ordn.* a unit of measure of the internal diameter of a shotgun barrel, determined by the number of spherical lead bullets of a diameter equal to that of the bore that are required to make one pound. **11.** *Railroads.* the distance between the inner edges of the heads of the rails in a track, usually 4 feet 8½ inches (**standard gauge**), but sometimes more (**broad gauge**) and sometimes less (**narrow gauge**). **12.** the distance between a pair of wheels on an axle. **13.** the thickness or diameter of various, usually thin, objects, as sheet metal or wire. **14.** the fineness of a knitted fabric as expressed in loops per every 1½ inch: *15-denier, 60-gauge stockings.* **15.** *Naut.* the position of one vessel as being to the windward or to the leeward of another on an approximately parallel course. Also, *esp. in technical use,* **gage.** [ME < ONF (F *jauge*) < Gmc] —**gauge′a·ble,** *adj.* —**gauge′a·bly,** *adv.*

gaug·er (gā′jər), *n.* **1.** a person or thing that gauges. **2.** a worker who checks the dimensions or quality of machined work. **3.** an exciseman, customs official, or the like. Also, *esp. in technical use,* **gager.** [ME < AF *gaugeour*]

Gau·guin (gō gaN′), *n.* **(Eu·gène Hen·ri) Paul** (œ zhen′ äN rē′ pôl), 1848–1903, French painter.

Gaul (gôl), *n.* **1.** an ancient region in W Europe, including the modern areas of N Italy, France, Belgium, and the S Netherlands: consisting of two main divisions, that part S of the Alps **(Cisalpine Gaul)** and that part N of the Alps **(Transalpine Gaul).** **2.** Latin, **Gallia.** a province of the ancient Roman Empire, including the territory corresponding to modern France, Belgium, the S Netherlands, Switzerland, N Italy, and the part of Germany W of the Rhine. **3.** an inhabitant of the ancient region of Gaul. **4.** an inhabitant of modern France.

Gau·lei·ter (gou′lī′tər), *n.* the chief official of a political district under Nazi control. [< G = *Gau* region + *Leiter* director]

Gaul·ish (gô′lish), *n.* **1.** the extinct Celtic language of ancient Gaul. —*adj.* **2.** of or pertaining to ancient Gaul, its inhabitants, or their language.

Gaull·ism (gō′liz əm, gô′-), *n.* **1.** a political movement in France led by Charles de Gaulle. **2.** the principles and policies of the Gaullists.

Gaull·ist (gō′list, gô′-), *n.* **1.** a supporter of the political principles of Charles de Gaulle. **2.** a Frenchman who supported the French resistance movement against the Nazi occupation in World War II. [< F *Gaulliste*]

gaul·the·ri·a (gôl thēr′ē ə), *n.* any aromatic, evergreen, ericaceous shrub of the genus *Gaultheria,* as the wintergreen. [< NL; named after Jean-François *Gaultier* (d. 1756), Canadian physician and botanist]

gaunt (gônt), *adj.* **1.** extremely thin and bony; haggard and drawn, as from great hunger, weariness, etc. **2.** bleak, desolate, or grim, as places or things. [ME, prob. < OF *gaunet, jaunet* yellowish < *gaune, jaune* yellow < L *galbin(us)* greenish-yellow] —**gaunt′ly,** *adv.* —**gaunt′ness,** *n.* —**Syn. 1.** lean, scrawny, angular, rawboned. See **thin.**

Gaunt (gônt, gänt), *n.* **John of.** See **John of Gaunt.**

gaunt·let[1] (gônt′lit, gänt′-), *n.* **1.** *Armor.* a glove, as of mail or plate, to protect the hand. **2.** a glove with an extended cuff for the wrist. **3. take up** or **throw down the gauntlet,** to accept (or extend) a challenge to fight. Also, **gantlet.** [ME *gantelet* < MF, dim. of *gant* glove < Gmc; c. OIcel *vǫttr*] —**gaunt′let·ed,** *adj.*

gaunt·let[2] (gônt′lit, gänt′-), *n.* Also, **gantlet** (for defs. 1–3). **1.** a former punishment, chiefly military, in which the offender was made to run between two rows of men who struck at him with switches or weapons as he passed. **2.** the two rows of men administering this punishment. **3.** trying conditions; ordeal. **4.** gantlet[1] (def. 1). —*v.t.* **5.** gantlet[1] (def. 3). [var. of GANTLET[1]]

gaun·try (gôn′trē), *n.*, *pl.* **-tries.** gantry.

gaur (gour, gou′ər), *n.*, *pl.* **gaurs,** (*esp. collectively*) **gaur.** a massive wild ox, *Bibos frontalis gaurus,* of southeastern Asia and the Malay Archipelago. [< Hindi < Skt *gaur(a)*]

gauss (gous), *n.*, *pl.* **gauss.** *Elect.* the centimeter-gram-second unit of magnetic induction, equal to the magnetic induction of a magnetic field in which one abcoulomb of charge, moving with a component of velocity perpendicular to the field and equal to one centimeter per second, is acted on by a force of one dyne; 1 maxwell per square centimeter or 10^{-4} weber per square meter. [named after K. F. GAUSS]

Gauss (gous), *n.* **Karl Frie·drich** (käRl frē′dRIKH), 1777–1855, German mathematician and astronomer. —**Gauss′-i·an,** *adj.*

Gauss′ian curve′, *Statistics.* See **normal curve.**

Gauss′ian distribu′tion, *Statistics.* See **normal distribution.**

gauss·me·ter (gous′mē′tər), *n.* a magnetometer calibrated in gauss.

Gau·ta·ma (gô′tə mə, gou′-), *n.* Buddha (def. 1). Also, **Gotama.** Also called **Gau′tama Bud′dha.**

Gau·tier (gō tyā′), *n.* **Thé·o·phile** (tā ô fēl′), 1811–72, French poet, novelist, and critic.

gauze (gôz), *n.* **1.** any thin transparent fabric made in a plain or leno weave. **2.** a surgical dressing of loosely woven cotton. **3.** any material made of an open, meshlike weave, as of wire. [< F *gaze* < ?]

gauz·y (gô′zē), *adj.*, **gauz·i·er, gauz·i·est.** like gauze; transparently thin and light. Also, **gauze′like′.** —**gauz′-i·ly,** *adv.* —**gauz′i·ness,** *n.*

ga·vage (gə väzh′; *Fr.* GA VAZH′), *n.* forced feeding, as of poultry or human beings, as by a flexible tube and a force pump. [< F = *gav(er)* (to) stuff (OF (dial.) *gave* gullet, throat) + *-age* -AGE]

gave (gāv), *v.* pt. of **give.**

gav·el[1] (gav′əl), *n.* a small mallet used by a judge, the presiding officer of a meeting, etc., for signaling for attention or order. [?]

gav·el[2] (gav′əl), *n.* feudal rent or tribute. [ME *govel,* OE *gafol,* akin to *giefan* to give; cf. GABELLE]

gav·el·kind (gav′əl kīnd′), *n.* *Eng. Law.* **1.** a customary system of land tenure, whose chief feature was equal division of land among the heirs of the holder. **2.** the land so held. [ME *gavelkinde, gavlikind*]

gav·e·lock (gav′ə lok′), *n.* *Brit. Dial.* a crowbar. [ME *gaveloc,* OE *gafeluc* < ?]

ga·vi·al (gā′vē əl), *n.* a large crocodilian, *Gavialis gangeticus,* of India and Pakistan. [< F < Hindi *ghariyāl*]

Gäv·le (yāv′le), *n.* a seaport in E Sweden. 59,686 (1965).

ga·votte (gə vot′), *n.* **1.** an old French dance in moderately quick quadruple meter. **2.** a piece of music for or in the rhythm of this dance, often forming one of the movements in the classical suite. Also, **ga·vot′.** [< F < Pr *gavot(o)* dance of the *Gavots* (name of Alpine mountaineers), fem. of *gavot* hillbilly < *gava* bird's crop (in allusion to the prevalence of goiter in those regions)]

G.A.W., guaranteed annual wage.

Ga·wain (gä′win, gô′-, gə wān′), *n.* *Arthurian Romance.* a knight of the Round Table: nephew of King Arthur.

gawk (gôk), *v.i.* **1.** to stare stupidly; gape. —*n.* **2.** an awkward, foolish person. [appar. repr. OE word meaning fool = *ga(gol)* foolish + *-oc* -OCK; used attributively in *gawk hand, gallock hand* left hand]

gawk·y (gô′kē), *adj.*, **gawk·i·er, gawk·i·est.** awkward; ungainly; clumsy. Also, **gawk·ish** (gô′kish). —**gawk′i·ly, gawk′ish·ly,** *adv.* —**gawk′i·ness, gawk′ish·ness,** *n.*

gay (gā), *adj.* **1.** having or showing a joyous mood. **2.** bright or showy: *gay colors.* **3.** given to or abounding in social or other pleasures: *a gay social season.* **4.** licentious; dissipated; wanton. **5.** *Slang.* homosexual. [ME *gai* < OF < Gmc; cf. OHG *gāhi* fast, sudden] —**gay′ness,** *n.*
—**Syn. 1.** joyous, cheerful, light-hearted; lively, frolicsome. GAY, JOLLY, JOYFUL, MERRY describe a happy or light-hearted mood. GAY suggests a lightness of heart or liveliness of mood that is openly manifested: *when hearts were young and gay.* JOLLY indicates a good-humored, natural, expansive gaiety of mood or disposition: *a jolly crowd at a party.* JOYFUL suggests gladness, happiness, rejoicing: *joyful over the good news.* MERRY is often interchangeable with gay: *a merry disposition; a merry party;* it suggests, even more than the latter, convivial animated enjoyment. —**Ant. 1.** unhappy, miserable.

Gay (gā), *n.* **John,** 1685–1732, English poet and dramatist.

Ga·ya (gä′yə gī′ə, gə yä′), *n.* a city in central Bihar, in NE India: Hindu center of pilgrimage. 151,100 (1961).

gay·e·ty (gā′i tē), *n.*, *pl.* **-ties.** gaiety.

Gay-Lus·sac (gā′lə sak′; *Fr.* gä ly sak′), *n.* **Jo·seph Lou·is** (jō′zəf lōō′ē, -səf; *Fr.* zhô zef′ lwē), 1778–1850, French chemist and physicist.

Gay-Lussac's′ law′, *Thermodynamics.* the principle that the density of an ideal gas at constant pressure varies inversely with the absolute temperature of the gas. Also called **Charles's law.** Cf. **Boyle's law.**

gay·ly (gā′lē), *adv.* gaily.

Ga·yo·mart (gä yō′märt), *n.* *Zoroastrianism.* the first Aryan and the sixth creation of Ahura Mazda. Also called **Ga′ya Mar′e·tan** (mar′i tan′).

Gay-Pay-Oo (gā′pā′ōō′; *Russ.* ge′pe′ōō′), *n.* See **G.P.U.**

gaz., **1.** gazette. **2.** gazetteer.

Ga·za (gä′zə, gaz′ə, gā′zə), *n.* a seaport adjacent to SW Israel, now under the administration of the United Arab Republic: ancient trade-route center. 37,820 (est. 1952).

Ga′za Strip′, a coastal area on the W Mediterranean, occupied by Israel 1967.

gaze (gāz), *v.*, **gazed, gaz·ing,** *n.* —*v.i.* **1.** to look steadily and intently, as with great interest, wonder, etc. —*n.* **2.** a steady or intent look. **3. at gaze,** *Heraldry.* (of a deer or deerlike animal) represented as seen from the side with the head looking toward the spectator: *a stag at gaze.* [ME *gase(n)* < ON; cf. Norw, Sw (dial.) *gasa* to gape, stare]
—**Syn. 1.** GAZE, STARE, GAPE suggest looking fixedly at something. To GAZE is to look steadily and intently, esp. at that which excites admiration, curiosity, or interest: *to gaze at scenery,* To STARE is to gaze with eyes wide open, as from surprise, wonder, stupidity, or impertinence: *to stare unbelievingly.* To GAPE is to stare with open-mouthed, often ignorant wonderment or curiosity: *to gape at a tall building.*

ga·ze·bo (gə zē′bō, -zā′-), *n.*, *pl.* **-bos, -boes.** a structure, as a pavilion or summer house, built on a site affording an enjoyable view. [?]

gaze·hound (gāz′hound′), *n.* a dog that hunts by sight rather than by scent.

ga·zelle (gə zel′), *n., pl.* **-zelles,** (*esp. collectively*) **-zelle.** any of various small antelopes of the genus *Gazella* and allied genera, noted for graceful movements and lustrous eyes. [< F; OF *gazel* < Ar *ghazāla*]

ga·zette (gə zet′), *n.* **1.** a newspaper (used chiefly in the names of newspapers): *The Phoenix Gazette.* **2.** *Chiefly Brit.* an official government journal containing lists of government appointments and promotions, bankruptcies, etc. [< F < It *gazzetta,* var. of Venetian *gazeta,* orig. a coin (the price of the paper), dim. of *gaza* magpie]

Gazelle, *Gazella subgutturosa* (2½ ft. high at shoulder; horns 14 in.; length 4 ft.)

gaz·et·teer (gaz′i tēr′), *n.* **1.** a geographical dictionary. **2.** *Archaic.* a journalist.

Ga·zi·an·tep (gä′zē än tep′), *n.* a city in S Turkey in Asia. 158,367 (1965). Formerly, **Aintab.**

gaz·o·gene (gaz′ə jēn′), *n.* an apparatus for impregnating a liquid with a gas, esp. carbon dioxide. Also, **gasogene.** [< F *gazogène*]

ga·zump (gə zəmp′), *Brit. Slang.* —*v.t., v.i.* **1.** to cheat (a house buyer) by raising the price, at the time a contract is to be signed, over the amount originally agreed upon. —*n.* **2.** an act or instance of gazumping. [orig. uncertain] —**ga·zump′er,** *n.* —**ga·zump′ing,** *n.*

G.B., Great Britain.

G.B.E., Knight Grand Cross of the British Empire or Dame Grand Cross of the British Empire.

GCA, *Aeron.* See **ground controlled approach.**

g-cal, See **gram calorie.** Also, **g-cal.**

G.C.B., Grand Cross of the Bath.

G.C.D., greatest common divisor. Also, **g.c.d.**

G.C.F., greatest common factor. Also, **g.c.f.**

G clef, *Music.* See **treble clef.**

G.C.M., greatest common measure. Also, **g.c.m.**

G.C.T., Greenwich Civil Time.

Gd, *Chem.* gadolinium.

gd., guard.

G.D., **1.** Grand Duchess. **2.** Grand Duke.

Gdańsk (gdänysk; *Eng.* gə dänsk′, -dansk′), *n.* Polish name of **Danzig.**

Gde., gourde; gourdes.

gds., goods.

Gdy·nia (gə din′ē ə; *Pol.* gdi′nyä), *n.* a seaport in N Poland, on the Bay of Danzig. 158,000 (est. 1963).

Ge (jē, gē), *n.* Gaea.

Ge, *Chem.* germanium.

ge·an·ti·cli·nal (jē′an ti klīn′ᵊl), *Geol.* —*adj.* **1.** of or pertaining to an anticlinal fold extending over a relatively large part of the earth's surface. —*n.* **2.** a geanticlinal fold. [< Gk *gê* earth + ANTICLINAL]

ge·an·ti·cline (jē an′ti klīn′), *n.* *Geol.* a geanticlinal fold. [< Gk *gê* earth + ANTICLINE]

gear (gēr), *n.* **1.** *Mach.* **a.** a moving part receiving or imparting force by means of teeth engaging with teeth or the like in a corresponding part. **b.** an assembly of such parts. **c.** the state of such parts engaging with each other: *out of gear.* **d.** a possible combination of such parts: *in low gear.* **e.** any of various mechanisms: *a steering gear.* **2.** implements, tools, or apparatus; paraphernalia: *fishing gear.* **3.** a harness, esp. of horses. **4.** *Naut.* **a.** the lines, tackles, etc., of a particular sail or spar. **b.** the tools, clothing, and other possessions of a sailor. **5.** portable items of personal property, including clothing. **6.** *Archaic.* armor or arms. —*v.t.* **7.** to provide with or connect by gearing. **8.** to provide with gear; supply; fit; harness. **9.** to prepare, adjust, or adapt to a particular situation, person, etc., in order to bring about satisfactory results. —*v.i.* **10.** to fit exactly, as one part of gearing into another; come into or be in gear. —*adj.* **11.** *Slang.* great; wonderful: *That's a real gear record!* [ME *gere* < ON; cf. OIcel *gervi, gørvi;* akin to OE *gearwe* equipment] —**gear′less,** *adj.*

gear·box (gēr′boks′), *n.* a transmission, as in an automobile. Also, **gear′ box′.**

gear·ing (gēr′ing), *n.* *Mach.* an assembly of gears for transmitting motion in a machine.

gear·shift (gēr′shift′), *n.* a lever or the like for engaging and disengaging gears for a power-transmission system, esp. in a motor vehicle. Also called, *Brit.,* **gear′ lev′er.**

gear·wheel (gēr′hwēl′, -wēl′), *n.* a wheel having teeth or cogs that engage with those of another wheel or part; cogwheel. Also, **gear′ wheel′.**

geb., born. [< G *geboren*]

geck·o (gek′ō), *n., pl.* **geck·os, geck·oes.** any of numerous harmless, typically nocturnal lizards of the family *Gekkonidae,* many of which have an adhesive pad at the tip of each digit and produce a loud call, found chiefly in the tropics. [< Malay *gēkoq;* imit.]

Ged·des (ged′ēz, -is), *n.* **1. Norman Bel** (bel), 1893–1958, U.S. industrial and stage designer and architect. **2. Sir Patrick,** 1854–1932, Scottish biologist, sociologist, and town planner.

gee[1] (jē), *interj., v.,* **geed, gee·ing.** —*interj.* **1.** (used as a word of command to a draft animal directing it to turn to the right.) **2. gee up,** (used as a word of command to a draft animal directing it to go faster.) —*v.i.* **3.** to turn to the right. —*v.t.* **4.** to turn (something) to the right. Cf. **haw**[3]. [?]

gee[2] (jē), *interj.* *Informal.* (used to express surprise, enthusiasm, or simple emphasis.) [euphemism for JESUS]

Gee·chee (gē′chē′), *n.* Gullah. (def. 2).

gee·gaw (jē′gô, gē′-), *n., adj.* gewgaw.

geek (gēk), *n.* *Slang.* **1.** a carnival performer who performs sensationally morbid or disgusting acts, as biting off the head of a live chicken. **2.** person; fellow. [prob. var. of Scot *geck* fool < LG]

Gee·long (ji lông′), *n.* a seaport in SE Australia, SW of Melbourne. 88,160 with suburbs (est. 1959).

Geel′vink Bay′ (*Du.* KHāl′vingk), a bay on the NW coast of New Guinea.

geese (gēs), *n.* a pl. of **goose.**

geest (gēst), *n.* *Geol.* an old alluvial deposit or group of old deposits. [< LG: dry or sandy soil]

Ge·ez (gē ez′, gā-), *n.* Ethiopic (def. 2). Also, **Ge′ez′.**

gee·zer (gē′zər), *n.* *Slang.* an odd or strange person. [var. of *guiser* (GUISE + -ER[1]), repr. dial. pronunciation]

ge·fil′te fish′ (gə fil′tə), *Jewish Cookery.* balls of boneless fish, esp. whitefish, carp, or pike, blended with eggs, matzo meal, and seasoning, simmered in a vegetable broth, and usually served chilled. Also, **ge·fill′te fish′, ge·ful′te fish′.** [< Yiddish < G *gefüllte Fische* stuffed fish]

ge·gen·schein (gā′gən shīn′), *n.* *Astron.* a faint, elliptical patch of light in the night sky: a reflection of sunlight by meteoric material in space. Also called **counterglow.** Cf. **zodiacal light.** [< G: counterglow]

Ge·hen·na (gi hen′ə), *n.* **1.** the valley of Hinnom, near Jerusalem, where propitiatory sacrifices were made to Moloch. II Kings 23:10. **2.** any place of extreme torment or suffering. [< LL < Gk *Géenna* < Heb *Gē-Hinnōm* hell, short for *gē ben Hinnōm,* lit., valley of the son of Hinnom]

geh·len·ite (gā′lə nīt′), *n.* a mineral, aluminum calcium silicate. [named after A. F. *Gehlen* (1775–1815), German chemist; see -ITE[1]]

Geh·rig (ger′ig), *n.* **Henry Louis** ("*Lou*"), 1903–41, U.S. baseball player.

Gei′ger count′er (gī′gər), an instrument for detecting ionizing radiations, consisting of a gas-filled tube in which electric-current pulses are produced when the gas is ionized by radiation, and of a device to register these pulses: used chiefly to measure radioactivity.

Gei·sel (gī′zəl), *n.* **Theodor Seuss** (so͞os), (pen name: *Dr. Seuss*), born 1904, U.S. author and illustrator of children's books.

gei·sha (gā′shə, gē′-), *n., pl.* **-sha, -shas.** a Japanese girl trained as a professional singer, dancer, and companion for men. [< Jap = *gei* art + *sha* person]

Geist (gīst), *n.* *German.* spirit; mind.

gel (jel), *n., v.,* **gelled, gel·ling.** —*n.* **1.** *Physical Chem.* a colloidal solution that has the consistency of a jelly, as a cold solution of gelatin in water (opposed to *sol*). —*v.i.* **2.** to form or become a gel. [back formation from GELATIN]

ge·län·de·sprung (gə len′də sprŏŏng′; *Ger.* gə len′də-shpRŏŏng′), *n.* *Skiing.* a jump, usually over an obstacle, in which the skier propels himself chiefly by the use of the poles. Also called **ge·län′de jump′** (gə len′də). [< G = *Gelände* countryside + *Sprung* jump]

Ge·la·si·us I (jə lā′shē əs, ′-zhē-, -zē-), **Saint,** died A.D. 496, pope 492–496.

Gelasius II, (*Giovanni de Gaeta*) died 1119, Italian ecclesiastic: pope 1118–19.

ge·lat·i·fi·ca·tion (jə lat′ə fə kā′shən), *n.* the process of gelatinizing.

gel·a·tin (jel′ə tin, -ə tᵊn), *n.* **1.** a nearly transparent glutinous substance, obtained by boiling animal tissue in water, forming the basis of jellies, glues, and the like. **2.** any similar substance, as vegetable gelatin. **3.** a preparation or product in which such a substance is the essential constituent. **4.** an edible jelly made of this substance. **5.** Also called **gel′atin slide′.** *Theat.* a thin sheet of translucent, colored gelatin for placing over stage lights, to obtain lighting effects. Also, **gel′a·tine.** [< F *gélatine* < ML *gelātin(a)* = L *gelāt(us)* frozen, thickened, ptp. of *gelāre* (*gel-* freeze + *-ātus* -ATE[1]) + *-ina* -IN[2]]

ge·lat·i·nate (jə lat′ᵊnāt′), *v.t., v.i.,* **-nat·ed, -nat·ing.** gelatinize. —**ge·lat′i·na′tion,** *n.*

ge·lat·i·nise (jə lat′ᵊnīz′, jel′ə tᵊnīz′), *v.t., v.i.,* **-nised, -nis·ing.** *Chiefly Brit.* gelatinize. —**ge·lat′i·ni·sa′tion,** *n.* —**ge·lat′i·nis′er,** *n.*

ge·lat·i·nize (jə lat′ᵊnīz′, jel′ə tᵊnīz′), *v.,* **-nized, -niz·ing.** —*v.t.* **1.** to make gelatinous. **2.** to coat with gelatin, as paper. —*v.i.* **3.** to become gelatinous. —**ge·lat′i·ni·za′tion,** *n.* —**ge·lat′i·niz′er,** *n.*

ge·lat·i·noid (jə lat′ᵊnoid′), *adj.* **1.** resembling gelatin; gelatinous. —*n.* **2.** a gelatinoid substance.

ge·lat·i·nous (jə lat′ᵊnəs), *adj.* **1.** having the nature of or resembling jelly, esp. in consistency. **2.** pertaining to, containing, or consisting of gelatin. —**ge·lat′i·nous·ly,** *adv.* —**ge·lat′i·nous·ness,** *n.*

ge·la·tion[1] (je lā′shən, jə-), *n.* solidification by cold; freezing. [< L *gelātiōn-* (s. of *gelātiō*). See GELATIN, -ION]

ge·la·tion[2] (je lā′shən, jə-), *n.* *Physical Chem.* the process of gelling. [GEL + -ATION]

geld[1] (geld), *v.t.,* **geld·ed** or **gelt, geld·ing.** to castrate (an animal, esp. a horse). [ME *geld(en)* < Scand; cf. OIcel *gelda*] —**geld′er,** *n.*

geld[2] (geld), *n.* *Early Eng. Hist.* a tax paid to the crown by landholders. [< ML *geld(um)* payment, tribute < Gmc; cf. OE *geld,* G *Geld*]

Gel·der·land (gel′dər land′; *Du.* KHel′dəR länt′), *n.* a province in the E Netherlands. 1,339,682 (1962); 1965 sq. mi. *Cap.:* Arnhem. Also called **Guelders.**

geld·ing (gel′ding), *n.* **1.** a castrated male horse. **2.** *Archaic.* a eunuch. [ME < Scand; cf. Icel *gelding(r)*]

ge·lech·i·id (jə lek′ē id), *n.* **1.** any of numerous small moths of the family *Gelechiidae,* including many crop pests. —*adj.* **2.** belonging or pertaining to the family *Gelechiidae.* [< NL *Gelechiid(ae)* = *Gelechi(a)* name of the genus (< Gk *gēlech(ḗs)* sleeping on earth) + *-idae* -ID[2]]

Ge·lée (zhə lā′), *n.* **Claude** (klōd). See **Lorraine, Claude.**

gel·id (jel′id), *adj.* very cold; icy. [< L *gelid(us)* = *gel(um)* frost, cold + *-idus* -ID[4]] —**ge·lid·i·ty** (jə lid′i tē), **gel′id·ness,** *n.* —**gel′id·ly,** *adv.*

gel·se·mi·um (jel sē′mē əm), *n., pl.* **-mi·ums, -mi·a** (-mē ə). *Pharm.* the dried rhizome and roots of yellow jasmine, formerly used as a sedative. [< NL < It *gelsom(ino)* jasmine; see -IUM]

Gel·sen·kir·chen (gel′zən kiR′KHən), *n.* a city in W West Germany, in the Ruhr valley. 380,600 (1963).

gelt[1] (gelt), *v.* a pt. and pp. of **geld**[1].

gelt[2] (gelt), *n. Slang.* money. [< Yiddish < MHG *geld* money; akin to YIELD]

gem (jem), *n., v.,* **gemmed, gem·ming,** *adj.* —*n.* **1.** a cut and polished precious stone or pearl fine enough for use in jewelry. **2.** something prized because of its beauty or worth. **3.** a person held in great esteem or affection. **4.** muffin (def. 1). **5.** *Print. Brit.* a 4-point type of a size between brilliant and diamond. —*v.t.* **6.** to adorn with or as with gems. —*adj.* **7.** *Jewelry.* noting perfection or very high quality: *a gem ruby.* [ME *gemme* < OF < L *gemma* bud, jewel] —**gem′like′,** *adj.*

Ge·ma·ra (gə mär′ə, -môr′ə; *Heb.* gə mä RÄ′), *n. Judaism.* **1.** the section of the Talmud consisting essentially of commentary on the Mishnah. **2.** the Talmud. —**Ge·ma′ric,** *adj.* —**Ge·ma′rist,** *n.*

gem·i·nate (*v.* jem′ə nāt′; *adj.* jem′ə nit, -nāt′), *v.,* **-nat·ed, -nat·ing,** *adj.* —*v.t., v.i.* **1.** to make or become doubled or paired. —*adj.* **2.** Also, **gem′i·nat′ed.** twin; combined or arranged in pairs; coupled. [< L *gemināt(us)* doubled (ptp. of *gemināre*) = *gemin-* double + *-ātus* -ATE[1]] —**gem′i·nate·ly,** *adv.*

gem·i·na·tion (jem′ə nā′shən), *n.* **1.** the act of geminating; a doubling or duplicating. **2.** *Phonet.* the doubling of a consonantal sound. **3.** *Rhet.* the immediate repetition of a word, phrase, etc., for rhetorical effect. [< L *geminātiōn-* (s. of *geminātiō*)]

Gem·i·ni (jem′ə nī′, -nē, jim′-), *n.pl., gen.* **Gem·i·no·rum** (jem′ə nôr′əm, -nōr′-, jim′-) for 1. **1.** *Astron.* the Twins, a zodiacal constellation between Taurus and Cancer containing the bright stars Castor and Pollux. **2.** *Astrol.* the third sign of the zodiac. See diag. at **zodiac. 3.** *U.S.* a two-man spacecraft for orbital rendezvous and docking. [< L *geminī,* pl. of *geminus*]

gem·ma (jem′ə), *n., pl.* **gem·mae** (jem′ē). **1.** *Bot.* a cell or cluster of cells, or a leaflike or budlike body, which separates from the parent plant and forms a new plant, as in mosses, liverworts, etc. **2.** *Zool., Bot.* a bud. [< L: bud, GEM] —**gem·ma·ceous** (je mā′shəs), *adj.*

gem·mate (jem′āt), *adj., v.,* **-mat·ed, -mat·ing.** *Bot., Zool.* —*adj.* **1.** having buds; increasing by budding. —*v.i.* **2.** to put forth buds; increase by budding. [< L *gemmāt(us)* budded, adorned with gems]

gem·ma·tion (je mā′shən), *n. Bot., Zool.* the process of reproduction by gemmae. [< F *gemmation*]

gem·mip·a·rous (je mip′ər əs), *adj.* producing or reproducing by buds or gemmae. [< NL *gemmiparus*] —**gem·mip′a·rous·ly,** *adv.*

gem·mu·la·tion (jem′yə lā′shən), *n. Biol.* the process of reproduction by gemmules.

gem·mule (jem′yo͞ol), *n.* **1.** *Bot.* gemma. **2.** *Zool.* an asexually produced mass of cells that will develop into an animal. **3.** *Biol.* one of the hypothetical living units considered by Darwin as the bearers of the hereditary attributes. [< F < L *gemmul(a)*]

gem·my (jem′ē), *adj.,* **-mi·er, -mi·est. 1.** having gems; set with gems. **2.** like a gem, esp. in being bright or sparkling. —**gem′mi·ly,** *adv.*

gem·ol·o·gy (je mol′ə jē), *n.* the science dealing with gemstones. Also, **gem·mol′o·gy.** —**gem·ol′o·gist, gem·mol′o·gist,** *n.*

ge·mot (gə mōt′), *n.* (in Anglo-Saxon England) a legislative or judicial assembly. Also, **ge·mote′.** [OE *gemōt* MOOT]

gems·bok (gemz′bok′), *n., pl.* **-boks,** (*esp. collectively*) **-bok.** a large antelope, *Oryx gazella,* of southern Africa, having long, straight horns and a long, tufted tail. [< SAfrD < G *Gemsbock* male chamois. See CHAMOIS, BUCK[1]]

Gemsbok
(4½ ft. high at shoulder; horns 3 to 4 ft.)

gems·buck (gemz′buk′), *n., pl.* **-bucks,** (*esp. collectively*) **-buck.** gemsbok.

gem·stone (jem′stōn′), *n.* a precious stone suitable for cutting and polishing for use as a gem or gems. [ME *gimstone,* OE *gimstān*]

ge·müt·lich (gə MYT′likH), *adj. German.* congenial; agreeable. Also, **ge·muet′lich.**

-gen, a learned borrowing from Greek meaning "production (of)," used in the formation of compound words: *endogen; hydrogen.* [< F *-gène* << Gk *-gen(ēs)* born, produced; akin to L *genus,* E KIN]

Gen., 1. *Mil.* General. **2.** Genesis. **3.** Geneva.

gen., 1. gender. **2.** general. **3.** genitive. **4.** genus.

ge·nappe′ yarn′, (jə nap′, zhə-), a worsted yarn that has been singed to remove protruding fibers, smoothed, and made lustrous. [after *Genappe,* Belgium, where orig. manufactured]

gen·darme (zhän′därm; *Fr.* zhäN DARM′), *n., pl.* **-darmes** (-därmz; *Fr.* -DARM′). **1.** a policeman in any of several European countries, esp. a French policeman. **2.** a soldier, esp. in France, serving as an armed policemen. [< F, back formation from *gens d'armes,* alter. of *gent d'armes* people at arms]

gen·dar·me·rie (zhän där′mə rē; *Fr.* zhäN DAR mə RĒ′), *n.* gendarmes collectively; a body of gendarmes. Also, **gen·darm′er·y.** [< F]

gen·der[1] (jen′dər), *n.* **1.** *Gram.* **a.** a set of classes of nouns, membership in a particular class being shown by the form of the noun itself or by the form or choice of words that modify, replace, or otherwise refer to the noun. The most familiar sets of genders are of three classes, as masculine, feminine, and neuter in Latin and German, or of two, as masculine and feminine in French and Spanish. **b.** one class of such a set. **c.** such classes or sets collectively or in general. **d.** membership of a word or grammatical form, or an inflectional form showing membership, in such a class. **2.** sex: *the feminine gender.* **3.** *Archaic.* kind, sort, or class. [ME < MF *gendre, genre* < L *gener-* (s. of *genus*) kind, sort]

gen·der[2] (jen′dər), *v.t., v.i. Archaic.* to engender. [ME *gendre(n), gender(en)* < MF *gendr(er)* < L *generāre* to beget < *gener-* GENDER[1]]

gen′der gap′, a significant difference between the attitudes of women and men toward specific political candidates or issues, esp. as reflected in public opinion polls.

gene (jēn), *n. Genetics.* the unit of heredity transmitted in the chromosome that, partially through interaction with other genes, controls the development of hereditary character. [< Gk *gene(á), gén(os)* race, stock, descent; c. L *genus, gener-*]

geneal., genealogy.

ge′nealog′ical tree′. See **family tree.**

ge·ne·al·o·gy (jē′nē ol′ə jē, -al′-, jen′ē-), *n., pl.* **-gies. 1.** a record or account of the ancestry and descent of a person, family, group, etc. **2.** the study of family ancestries and histories. **3.** descent from an original form or progenitor; lineage; ancestry. [ME *genealogie* < MF < LL *geneālogia* < Gk: pedigree = *geneá* race (see GENE) + *-logia* -LOGY] —**ge·ne·a·log·i·cal** (jē′nē ə loj′i kəl, jen′ē-), **ge′ne·a·log′ic,** *adj.* —**ge′ne·a·log′i·cal·ly,** *adv.* —**ge′ne·al′o·gist,** *n.*

gen·er·a (jen′ər ə), *n.* a pl. of **genus.**

gen·er·a·ble (jen′ər ə bəl), *adj.* capable of being generated or produced. [< L *generābil(is)* creative, productive]

gen·er·al (jen′ər əl), *adj.* **1.** of or pertaining to all persons or things belonging to a group or category: *a general meeting of the employees of a firm.* **2.** of, pertaining to, or true of such persons or things in the main, with possible exceptions: *the general will of the people.* **3.** not limited to one class, field, etc.; miscellaneous: *the general public.* **4.** dealing with all or the overall aspects of a subject without attempting to deal with specific aspects: *a general description.* **5.** not specific or definite. **6.** *Med.* (of anesthesia or an anesthetic) causing loss of consciousness and abolishing sensitivity to pain throughout the body. **7.** having extended command or superior or chief rank: *a general chairman.* —*n.* **8.** *Mil.* **a.** *U.S. Army and Air Force.* an officer ranking above a lieutenant general and below a general of the army or general of the air force. **b.** *U.S. Army.* an officer of any of the five highest ranks: a brigadier general, major general, lieutenant general, general, or general of the army. **c.** *U.S. Marine Corps.* an officer holding the highest rank in the corps. **d.** (in numerous foreign armies) an officer in the second or third highest rank, as one ranking immediately below a field marshal in the British army. **9.** *Eccles.* the chief official of a religious order. **10.** a statement or principle involving or applicable to the whole. **11.** *Archaic.* the general public. **12. in general, a.** with respect to the whole class referred to; as a whole. **b.** as a rule; usually. [ME < L *generāl(is).* See GENDER[1], -AL[1]]
—**Syn. 1, 2.** customary, prevailing, regular, ordinary. GENERAL, COMMON, UNIVERSAL agree in the idea of being nonexclusive and widespread. GENERAL means belonging to or prevailing throughout a whole class or body collectively, irrespective of individuals: *a general belief.* COMMON means shared by all, and belonging to one as much as another: *a common interest; common fund;* but use of this sense is frequently avoided because of ambiguity of sense. UNIVERSAL means found everywhere, and with no exceptions: *a universal longing.* —**Ant. 1.** special, limited.

Gen′eral Amer′ican Speech′, a pronunciation of American English showing few regional peculiarities.

Gen′eral Assem′bly, 1. the legislature in some states of the U.S. **2.** the main deliberative body of the United Nations, composed of delegations from member nations.

gen′eral confes′sion, confession of sins made in common by an entire congregation, esp. as part of a public prayer. **2.** a confession of sins committed over a long period.

Gen′eral Court′, 1. (in colonial New England) any of various local assemblies having both legislative and judicial powers. **2.** the state legislature of Massachusetts or New Hampshire.

gen·er·al·cy (jen′ər əl sē), *n.* the office or tenure of a general.

gen′eral deliv′ery, 1. a postal service delivering mail to a specific post office where it is held for collection by an addressee. **2.** Also called, *esp. Brit.,* **poste restante.** the postal department that handles such mail.

gen′eral dis′charge, *U.S. Mil.* **1.** a discharge from military service of a person who has served honorably but not met all the conditions for an honorable discharge. **2.** a certificate of such a discharge.

gen′eral elec′tion, 1. *U.S.* **a.** a final election of candidates for national, state, or local office, as opposed to a primary. **b.** a state or national election, as opposed to a local election. **2.** *Brit.* an election of members of the House of Commons that must be held within five years of the last election.

gen·er·al·ise (jen′ər ə līz′), *v.i., v.t.,* **-ised, -is·ing.** *Chiefly Brit.* generalize. —**gen′er·al·is′er,** *n.*

gen·er·al·is·si·mo (jen′ər ə lis′ə mō′), *n., pl.* **-mos.** (in certain foreign armies) the supreme commander of several armies acting together. [< It, superl. of *generale* GENERAL]

gen·er·al·ist (jen′ər ə list), *n.* a person whose knowledge, aptitudes, and skills are applied to a variety of different fields, as opposed to a specialist.

gen·er·al·i·ty (jen′ə ral′i tē), *n., pl.* **-ties. 1.** an indefinite, unspecific, or undetailed statement. **2.** a general principle, rule, or law. **3.** the greater part or majority. **4.** the state or quality of being general. [late ME *generalite* < L *generālitās*]

gen·er·al·i·za·tion (jen′ər ə li zā′shən *or, esp. Brit.,* -lī-), *n.* **1.** the act or process of generalizing. **2.** a general statement, idea, or principle. Also, *esp. Brit.,* **gen′er·al·i·sa′tion.**

gen·er·al·ize (jen′ər ə līz′), *v.,* **-ized, -iz·ing.** —*v.t.* **1.** to give a general rather than a specific or special character or form to. **2.** to infer (a general principle, trend, etc.) from facts, statistics, or the like. **3.** to infer or form (a principle, opinion, conclusion, etc.) from meager or insufficient facts, information, or the like. **4.** to make general; bring into general use or knowledge. —*v.i.* **5.** to form general notions. **6.** to deal, think, or speak in generalities. **7.** to make general inferences. Also, *esp. Brit.*, **generalise.** —**gen′er·al·iz′er,** *n.*

gen·er·al·ly (jen′ər ə lē), *adv.* **1.** with respect to the larger part; for the most part. **2.** usually; commonly. **3.** without reference to or disregarding particular persons, things, situations, etc., which may be an exception: *generally speaking.* [ME] —**Syn. 2.** See **often.**

gen′eral of′ficer, *Mil.* an officer ranking above colonel.

gen′eral of the air′ force′, the highest ranking officer in the U.S. Air Force.

gen′eral of the ar′my, the highest ranking officer in the U.S. Army. Cf. **fleet admiral.**

gen′eral or′ders, *Mil.* **1.** a set of permanent orders from a headquarters establishing policy for a command or announcing official acts. **2.** a set of permanent orders governing the duties and behavior of sentries on routine guard duty. Cf. **special order.**

gen′eral post′ of′fice, (in the U.S. postal system) the main post office of a city, county, etc., that also has branch post offices. *Abbr.:* GPO

gen′eral practi′tioner, a medical practitioner who does not limit his practice to a particular branch of medicine or to a specific class of diseases.

gen·er·al-pur·pose (jen′ər əl pûr′pəs), *adj.* useful in many ways; not limited in use or function.

gen′eral seman′tics, an educational discipline originated by Alfred Korzybski and concerned with the improvement of human behavior by means of a critical analysis of the function of words and nonverbal symbols.

gen·er·al·ship (jen′ər əl ship′), *n.* **1.** skill as commander of a large military force. **2.** management or tactics. **3.** the rank or functions of a general.

gen′eral staff′, *Mil.* a group of officers whose duty is to assist high commanders in planning and carrying out orders.

gen′eral store′, a store, usually in a rural area, that sells a wide variety of merchandise, as clothing, food, hardware, etc., but is not divided into departments.

gen′eral strike′, a mass strike in all or many trades and industries.

gen′eral the′ory of relativ′ity. See **relativity.**

gen·er·ate (jen′ə rāt′), *v.t.*, **-at·ed, -at·ing. 1.** to bring into existence; cause to be. **2.** to reproduce; procreate. **3.** to produce by a chemical process. **4.** to create by a vital or natural process. **5.** to create and distribute vitally and profusely: *A good diplomat generates good will.* **6.** *Math.* **a.** to trace (a figure) by the motion of another: *A point generates a line.* **b.** to act as base for all the elements of a given set: *The number 2 generates the set 2, 4, 8, 16.* [ME < L *generāt(us)*, ptp. of *generāre* to beget; see GENDER[2]]

gen·er·a·tion (jen′ə rā′shən), *n.* **1.** the entire body of individuals born and living at about the same time: *the postwar generation.* **2.** the term of years, accepted as the average period between the birth of parents and the birth of their offspring. **3.** a single step in natural descent, as of human beings, animals, or plants. **4.** a group of individuals, most of whom are the same approximate age, having similar ideas, problems, attitudes, etc. **5.** a group of individuals having equal status at the same time: *the generation of silent-screen stars.* **6.** the offspring of a certain parent or couple, considered as a step in natural descent. **7.** the act or process of generating; procreation. **8.** production by natural or artificial processes; evolution, as of heat or sound. **9.** *Biol.* a form or phase of a plant or animal with reference to its manner or reproduction. **10.** *Math.* the production of a geometrical figure by the motion of another figure. **11.** *Physics.* one of the successive sets of nuclei produced in a chain reaction. **12.** a stage of technological development or production distinct from but based upon another stage: *the third generation of rocket missiles.* —**gen′er·a′tion·al,** *adj.* —**gen′er·a′tion·al·ly,** *adv.* [ME *generacioun* < MF < L]

genera′tion gap′, the lack of communication between young people and their parents or between one generation and another, brought about by differences of tastes, values, outlook, etc.

gen·er·a·tive (jen′ə rā′tiv, -ər ə tiv), *adj.* **1.** pertaining to the production of offspring. **2.** capable of producing. [ME < LL *generātīv(us)*]

gen′erative gram′mar, *Linguistics.* **1.** any theory of grammar that considers language as consisting of an indefinitely large number of sentences all of which may be specified or generated by the application of a set of rules. **2.** a set of such rules.

gen·er·a·tor (jen′ə rā′tər), *n.* **1.** a person or thing that generates. **2.** a machine that converts one form of energy into another, esp. mechanical energy into electrical energy, as a dynamo. **3.** *Chem.* an apparatus for producing a gas or vapor. [< L]

gen·er·a·trix (jen′ə rā′triks), *n., pl.* **gen·er·a·tri·ces** (jen′ər ə trī′sēz). *Math.* an element generating a figure. [< L: she who brings forth]

ge·ner·ic (jə ner′ik), *adj.* **1.** of, pertaining to, or noting a genus, esp. in biology. **2.** of, applicable to, or referring to all the members of a genus, class, group, or kind; general. **3.** not protected by trademark registration. [< L *gener-* (see GENDER[1]) + -IC] —**ge·ner′i·cal·ly,** *adv.* —**Syn. 2.** common.

gen·er·os·i·ty (jen′ə ros′i tē), *n., pl.* **-ties. 1.** readiness or liberality in giving. **2.** freedom from meanness or smallness of mind or character. **3.** a generous act. **4.** largeness or fullness; amplitude. [ME *generosite* < L *generōsitāt-* (s. of *generōsitās*)] —**Syn. 1.** munificence, bountifulness.

gen·er·ous (jen′ər əs), *adj.* **1.** liberal in giving; munificent; unselfish. **2.** free from meanness or smallness of mind or character. **3.** large; abundant; ample. **4.** rich or strong in flavor: *a generous wine.* [ME < OF < L *generōs(us)* of noble birth. See GENDER[2], -OUS] —**gen′er·ous·ly,** *adv.* —**gen′er·ous·ness,** *n.* —**Syn. 1.** unstinting. **2.** noble. **3.** plentiful.

Gen·e·see (jen′i sē′), *n.* a river flowing N from N Pennsylvania through W New York into Lake Ontario. 144 mi.

gen·e·sis (jen′i sis), *n., pl.* **-ses** (-sēz′). an origin, creation, or beginning. [< L: birth < Gk: origin]

Gen·e·sis (jen′i sis), *n.* the first book of the Bible, dealing with the Creation and the Patriarchs.

-genesis, a combining form of **genesis:** *parthenogenesis.*

gene-splicing (jēn′splī′sing), *n. Biochem.* See **recombinant DNA.**

gen·et[1] (jen′it, ji net′), *n.* **1.** any small, Old World carnivore of the genus *Genetta,* esp. *G. genetta,* related to the civets but not having a scent pouch. **2.** the fur of such an animal. Also, **ge·nette′.** [ME < OF *genette* < Ar *jarnait*]

gen·et[2] (jen′it), *n.* jennet.

Ge·nêt (zhə nā′; *Fr.* zhə ne′), *n.* **1. Ed·mond Charles É·douard** (ed môN′ shARl ā dwAR′), ("*Citizen Genêt*"), 1763–1834, French minister to the U.S. in 1793. **2. Jean** (zhäN), 1910–86, French playwright and novelist.

ge·net·ic (jə net′ik), *adj.* **1.** *Biol.* pertaining or according to genetics. **2.** of, pertaining to, or produced by genes; genic. **3.** of, pertaining to, or influenced by geneses or origins. Also, **ge·net′i·cal.** [GENE(SIS) + -TIC] —**ge·net′i·cal·ly,** *adv.*

Genet[1], *Genetta genetta* (Total length 3 ft.; tail 18 in.)

-genetic, a suffix of adjectives corresponding to nouns with stems ending in **-genesis:** *parthenogenetic.*

genet′ic code′, *Biochem.* the order in which the four DNA bases are arranged in 64 different triplets to direct the order sequence of the 20 different amino acids in the proteins that determine inherited traits.

genet′ic engineer′ing, *Biochem.* the techniques by which genetic material can be altered by recombinant DNA so as to change or improve the hereditary properties of microorganisms, animals, plants, etc. —**genet′ic engineer′.**

ge·net·i·cist (jə net′i sist), *n.* a specialist in genetics.

ge·net·ics (jə net′iks), *n.* (*construed as sing.*) **1.** *Biol.* the science of heredity, dealing with resemblances and differences of related organisms resulting from the interaction of their genes and the environment. **2.** the genetic properties and phenomena of an organism.

ge·ne·va (jə nē′və), *n.* Hollands. [< D *genever* < OF *genevre* < L *jūniper(us)* JUNIPER]

Ge·ne·va (jə nē′və), *n.* **1.** a city in SW Switzerland, on the Lake of Geneva: seat of the League of Nations 1920–46. 171,900 (est. 1970). **2. Lake of.** Also called **Lake Leman.** a lake between SW Switzerland and France. 45 mi. long; 225 sq. mi. French, **Genève.**

Gene′va bands′, two white bands or pendent stripes worn at the throat in clerical dress. Also called **bands.**

Gene′va Conven′tion, *Mil.* an international agreement, first made in Geneva, Switzerland, in 1864 and followed by the U.S., Great Britain, and many other nations, establishing rules for the humane treatment of prisoners of war and of the sick, the wounded, and the dead in battle.

Gene′va cross′, a red Greek cross on a white background, displayed to distinguish ambulances, hospitals, and persons belonging to the Red Cross Society.

Gene′va gown′, a loose, large-sleeved, black preaching gown worn by Protestant clergymen.

Ge·ne·van (jə nē′vən), *adj.* **1.** of Geneva. **2.** Calvinistic. —*n.* **3.** a native or inhabitant of Geneva. **4.** a Calvinist.

Ge·nève (zhə nev′), *n.* French name of **Geneva.**

Gen·e·vese (jen′ə vēz′), *adj., n., pl.* **-vese.** Genevan.

Gen·e·vieve (jen′ə vēv′), *n.* **Saint,** A.D. 422–512, French nun: patron saint of Paris. Also, **Gene·viève** (*Fr.* zhən[ə] vyev′).

Gen·ghis Khan (jeng′gis kän′), 1162–1227, Mongol conqueror of much of Asia and of E Europe to the Dnieper River. Also, **Jenghis Khan, Jenghiz Khan.**

gen·ial[1] (jēn′yəl, jē′nē əl), *adj.* **1.** sympathetically cheerful; cordial. **2.** favorable for life, growth, or comfort; pleasantly warm; comfortably mild: *the genial climate of Hawaii.* **3.** *Rare.* characterized by genius. [< L *geniāl(is)* festive, jovial, pleasant. See GENIUS, -AL[1]] —**gen′ial·ly,** *adv.* —**gen′ial·ness,** *n.* —**Syn. 1.** friendly, pleasant, agreeable.

ge·ni·al[2] (jə nī′əl), *adj. Anat., Zool.* of or pertaining to the chin. [< Gk *génei(on)* chin < *gén(ys)* jaw (c. L *gena*) + -AL[1]]

ge·ni·al·i·ty (jē′nē al′i tē), *n.* the quality of being genial; sympathetic cheerfulness or kindliness. [< LL *geniālitās*]

gen·ic (jen′ik), *adj.* of or resembling a gene or genes.

-genic, an adjective suffix meaning "producing," "pertaining to a gene or genes," often corresponding to nouns with stems ending in **-gen** or **-geny:** *photogenic.*

ge·nic·u·late (jə nik′yə lit, -lāt′), *adj. Biol.* **1.** having kneelike joints or bends. **2.** bent at a joint like a knee. [< L *geniculāt(us)* knotted = *genicul(um)* (*gen(u)* knee + *-culum* -CULE) + *-ātus* -ATE[1]] —**ge·nic′u·late·ly,** *adv.*

ge·nic·u·la·tion (jə nik′yə lā′shən), *n.* **1.** the state of being geniculate. **2.** a geniculate formation. [< LL *geniculātiōn-* (s. of *geniculātiō*) a kneeling]

ge·nie (jē′nē), *n. Islamic Myth.* jinn. [< F *génie,* alter. (after L *geni(us)* GENIUS) of Ar *jinnī*]

ge·ni·i (jē′nē ī′), *n.* a pl. of **genius.**

gen·i·tal (jen′i t[ə]l), *adj.* **1.** of, pertaining to, or noting generation or the sexual organs. **2.** *Psychoanal.* **a.** of or pertaining to the final stage of psychosexual development, in which full gratification, as love or happiness, is found in the sexual partner. **b.** of or pertaining to the centering of sexual impulses and excitation on the genitalia. [ME < OF < L *genitālis* (< *genit(us),* ptp. of *gignere* to beget + -AL[1])]

gen·i·ta·lia (jen′i tā′lē ə, -tāl′yə), *n.pl. Anat.* the organs of reproduction, esp. the external organs. [< L] —**gen·i·tal·ic** (jen′i tal′ik), *adj.*

gen·i·tals (jen′i t[ə]lz), *n.pl.* genitalia.

gen·i·tive (jen′i tiv), *Gram.* —*adj.* **1.** noting a case that indicates a noun is a modifier of another noun, often to express possession, origin, characteristic, etc., as *John's* hat, *man's* fate, *week's* vacation. **2.** noting an affix or other element characteristic of this case, or a word containing such an element. —*n.* **3.** the genitive case. Cf. **possessive. 4.** a word in the genitive case. [ME < L *genetīv(us)* = *genit(us)* (ptp. of *gignere* to beget) + *-īvus* -IVE] —**gen·i·ti·val** (jen′i tī′vəl), *adj.* —**gen′i·ti′val·ly,** *adv.*

genito-, a combining form of **genital:** *genitourinary.*

gen·i·to·u·ri·nar·y (jen′i tō yŏŏr′ə ner′ē), *adj.* *Anat., Physiol.* of or pertaining to the genital and urinary organs; urogenital.

gen·i·ture (jen′i chər), *n.* *Obs.* birth; generation. [< L *genitūr-* (s. of *genitūra*)]

gen·ius (jēn′yəs), *n., pl.* **gen·ius·es** for 2, 3, 8, **gen·i·i** (jē′nē ī′) for 6, 7, 9. **1.** an exceptional natural capacity of intellect, esp. as shown in creative and original work in art, music, science, etc. **2.** a person having such capacity. **3.** a person having extraordinarily high intelligence, esp. one with an I.Q. of 140 or above. **4.** natural ability or capacity; strong inclination. **5.** distinctive character or spirit, as of a nation, period, language, etc. **6.** the guardian spirit of a place, institution, etc. **7.** either of two mutually opposed spirits, one good and the other evil, supposed to attend a person throughout his life. **8.** a person who strongly influences for good or ill the character, conduct, or destiny of a person, place, or thing. **9.** any demon or spirit, esp. a jinn. [< L: tutelary deity or genius of a person: cf. GENUS] **—Syn. 4.** gift, talent, aptitude, faculty.

ge·ni·us lo·ci (gen′i ŏŏs′ lō′kē; *Eng.* jē′nē əs lō′sī), *Latin.* **1.** guardian of a place. **2.** the peculiar character of a place with reference to the impression that it makes on the mind.

Genl., General.

gen·o·a (jen′ō ə), *n.* (*sometimes cap.*) *Naut.* a large jib for cruising and racing yachts, overlapping the mainsail. Also called **gen′oa jib′.** [after GENOA]

Gen·o·a (jen′ō ə), *n.* a seaport in NW Italy, S of Milan. 798,892. Italian, **Genova.**

gen·o·cide (jen′ə sīd′), *n.* the deliberate and systematic extermination of a national or racial group. [< Gk *géno(s)* race + -CIDE] **—gen′o·cid′al,** *adj.*

Gen·o·ese (jen′ō ēz′, -ēs′), *adj., n., pl.* **-ese.** **—***adj.* **1.** of, pertaining to, or characteristic of Genoa or its inhabitants. **—***n.* **2.** a native or inhabitant of Genoa. Also, **Genovese.**

gen·o·type (jen′ə tīp′), *n.* *Genetics.* **1.** the genetic constitution of an organism or group of organisms. **2.** a group or class sharing a specific genetic constitution. **3.** the sum total of genes transmitted from parent to offspring. Cf. **phenotype.** [< Gk *géno(s)* origin, race + -TYPE] **—gen·o·typ·ic** (jen′ə tip′ik), **gen′o·typ′i·cal,** *adj.*

-genous, a suffix of adjectives corresponding to nouns with stems in **-gen:** *erogenous.*

Ge·no·va (je′nô vä′), *n.* Italian name of **Genoa.**

Gen·o·vese (jen′ə vēz′, -vēs′), *adj., n., pl.* **-vese.** Genoese.

gen·re (zhän′rə; *Fr.* zhäN′Rᵊ), *n., pl.* **-res** (-rəz; *Fr.* -Rᵊ), *adj.* **—***n.* **1.** genus; kind; sort; style. **2.** a class or category of artistic endeavor having a particular form, content, technique, or the like. **3.** *Fine Arts.* **a.** paintings in which scenes of everyday life form the subject matter. **b.** a realistic style of painting using such subject matter. **—***adj.* **4.** *Fine Arts.* of or pertaining to genre. [< F: kind, sort; see GENDER[1]]

gen·ro (gen′rō′), *n.pl.* (*often cap.*) (formerly in Japan) a group of elder statesmen that advised the emperor. [< Jap: lit., old men]

gens (jenz), *n., pl.* **gen·tes** (jen′tēz). **1.** (in ancient Rome) a group of families constituting a clan and having a common name, the nomen. **2.** *Anthropol.* a group tracing common descent in the male line; clan. [< L: race, people. See GENUS]

Gen·san (gen′sän′), *n.* Japanese name of **Wönsan.**

gen·seng (jen′seng′), *n.* ginseng.

Gen·ser·ic (jen′sər ik, gen′-), *n.* A.D. c390–477, king of the Vandals, conqueror in northern Africa and Italy. Also, **Gaiseric.**

gent[1] (jent), *n.* **1.** *Informal.* gentleman. **2. gents,** *Slang.* See **men's room.** [by shortening]

gent[2] (jent), *adj.* *Obs.* elegant; graceful. [ME < OF < L *genit(us)* begotten, born. See GENITIVE]

Gent (KHent), *n.* Flemish name of **Ghent.**

Gent., gentleman; gentlemen. Also, **gent.**

gen·teel (jen tēl′), *adj.* **1.** belonging or suited to polite society. **2.** well-bred or refined; elegant; stylish. **3.** affectedly or pretentiously polite, delicate, etc. [< F *gentil;* see GENTLE] **—gen·teel′ly,** *adv.* **—gen·teel′ness,** *n.*

gen·teel·ism (jen tē′liz əm), *n.* a word or phrase used in place of another, supposedly less genteel, term.

gen·tian (jen′shən), *n.* **1.** any of several flowering plants of the genus *Gentiana,* esp. the fringed gentian of North America, or *G. lutea,* of Europe. **2.** any of various plants resembling the gentian. **3.** the root of *G. lutea,* or a preparation of it, used as a tonic. [ME *gencian* < L *gentiāna;* said to be named after *Gentius,* an Illyrian king]

gen·ti·a·na·ceous (jen′shē ə nā′shəs), *adj.* belonging to the *Gentianaceae,* or gentian family of plants. [< NL *Gentianace(ae)* + -OUS]

gen·tian·el·la (jen′shə nel′ə, -shē ə nel′-), *n.* any of several alpine gentians, esp. *Gentiana acaulis,* having showy blue flowers. [< NL, dim. of L *gentiāna* GENTIAN]

gen′tian vi′olet, a dye derived from rosaniline, used as a chemical indicator, as a fungicide and bactericide, and in the treatment of burns. Also called **crystal violet, methylrosaniline chloride.**

gen·til (zhäN tē′), *adj.* *French.* kind; gentle; noble.

gen·tile (jen′tīl), *adj.* **1.** of or pertaining to any people not Jewish. **2.** Christian, as distinguished from Jewish. **3.** *Mormonism.* neither Mormon nor Jewish. **4.** heathen or pagan. **5.** of or pertaining to a tribe, clan, people, nation, etc. **—***n.* **6.** a person who is not Jewish, esp. a Christian. **7.** (among Mormons) a non-Mormon. **8.** a heathen or pagan. Also, **Gen′tile.** [ME < L *gentīl(is).* See GENTLE]

gen·ti·lesse (jen′tᵊles′), *n.* *Archaic.* the quality of being gentle. [ME < MF *gentillesse.* See GENTEEL, -ESS]

gen·til·ism (jen′tᵊliz′əm), *n.* the quality of being a gentile, esp. the quality of being pagan; heathenism.

gen·til·i·ty (jen til′i tē), *n.* **1.** superior refinement or elegance. **2.** the condition of having gentle birth or of belonging to the gentry. **3.** persons of gentle birth; gentry. [ME < OF *gentilite* < L *gentīlitāt-* (s. of *gentīlitās*)]

gen·tle (jen′tᵊl), *adj.,* **-tler, -tlest,** *v.,* **-tled, -tling.** **—***adj.* **1.** kindly or amiable. **2.** mild; not severe, rough, or violent; moderate. **3.** gradual: *a gentle slope.* **4.** of good birth or family; wellborn. **5.** characteristic of good birth; honorable; respectable. **6.** easily handled or managed; tractable. **7.** soft or low: *a gentle sound.* **8.** polite; refined. **9.** entitled to a coat of arms; armigerous. **10.** *Archaic.* noble; chivalrous: *a gentle knight.* **—***v.t.* **11.** to tame; render tractable. **12.** to mollify; calm; pacify. **13.** to make gentle. **14.** to stroke; soothe by petting. **15.** *Obs.* to ennoble; dignify. [ME *gentle, gentil(e)* < OF *gentil* highborn, noble < L *gentīl(is)* belonging to the same family] **—gen′tle·ness,** *n.* **—gen′tly,** *adv.*
—Syn. 1. peaceful, soothing; humane, lenient, merciful. GENTLE, MEEK, MILD refer to an absence of bad temper or belligerence. GENTLE has reference esp. to disposition and behavior, and often suggests a deliberate or voluntary kindness or forbearance in dealing with others: *a gentle pat; gentle with children.* MEEK implies a submissive spirit, and may even indicate undue submission in the face of insult or injustice: *meek and even servile.* MILD suggests absence of harshness or severity, rather because of natural character or temperament than conscious choice: *a mild rebuke; a mild manner.* **2.** temperate. **4.** noble. **6.** manageable, docile.

gen′tle breeze′, *Meteorol.* (on the Beaufort scale) a wind of 8–12 miles per hour.

gen·tle·folk (jen′tᵊl fōk′), *n.* (*construed as pl.*) persons of good family and breeding. Also, **gen′tle·folks′.**

gen·tle·man (jen′tᵊl mən), *n., pl.* **-men.** **1.** a civilized, educated, sensitive, or well-mannered man. **2.** a polite term for any man. **3.** a male personal servant, esp. of a man of social position; valet. **4.** a male attendant upon a king, queen, or other royal person, who is himself of high birth or rank. **5.** a man of good breeding and social standing, as a noble. **6.** a man with an independent income who does not work for a living. **7.** a male member of the U.S. Congress. **8.** *Hist.* a man who is above the rank of yeoman. [ME]

gen·tle·man-at-arms (jen′tᵊl mən ət ärmz′), *n., pl.* **gen·tle·men-at-arms.** (in England) one of a guard of 40 gentlemen with their officers who attend the sovereign on state occasions.

gen·tle·man-com·mon·er (jen′tᵊl mən kom′ə nər), *n., pl.* **gen·tle·men-com·mon·ers.** (formerly) a member of a class of commoners enjoying special privileges at Oxford University.

gen·tle·man-farm·er (jen′tᵊl mən fär′mər), *n., pl.* **gen·tle·men-farm·ers.** a man whose income from other sources permits him to farm for pleasure rather than for profit.

gen·tle·man·ly (jen′tᵊl mən lē), *adj.* like, befitting, or characteristic of a gentleman. **—gen′tle·man·li·ness,** *n.*

gen′tleman's gen′tleman, a valet.

Gen′tleman Ush′er of the Black′ Rod′. See **Black Rod** (def. 1).

gen·tle·men (jen′tᵊl mən), *n.* pl. of **gentleman.**

gen′tlemen's agree′ment, **1.** an agreement that, although unenforceable at law, is binding as a matter of personal honor. **2.** an unwritten agreement by a socially prominent clique, private club, etc., to discriminate against or refuse to accept members of religious, racial, or national minority groups. Also, **gen′tleman's agree′ment.**

gen′tle sex′, women in general.

gen·tle·wom·an (jen′tᵊl wŏŏm′ən), *n., pl.* **-wom·en.** **1.** a woman of good family or breeding; a lady. **2.** a woman who attends a lady of rank. [ME] **—gen′tle·wom′an·ly,** *adj.*

Gen·too (jen′tōō), *n., pl.* **-toos,** *adj.* *Archaic.* **—***n.* **1.** a Hindu. **2.** any of the non-European languages of the Hindus, esp. Telugu. **—***adj.* **3.** of or relating to the Gentoos. [< Pg *gentio* GENTILE]

gen·tri·fi·ca·tion (jen′trə fi kā′shən), *n.* the buying and renovation of houses in deteriorated urban neighborhoods, esp. by middle-income professionals, thus improving property values but often displacing low-income families.

gen·try (jen′trē), *n.* **1.** wellborn and well-bred people. **2.** (in England) the class under the nobility. **3.** an aristocracy. **4.** nonnobles entitled to a coat of arms, esp. those owning large tracts of land. **5.** the state or condition of being a gentleman. [ME < OF *genterie.* See GENTILE]

gen·u·flect (jen′yŏŏ flekt′), *v.i.* **1.** to bend the knee or knees in reverence or worship. **2.** to express a servile attitude. [< ML *genūflect(ere)* (to) bend the knee = L *genu* knee + *flectere* to bend]

gen·u·flec·tion (jen′yŏŏ flek′shən), *n.* an act of bending the knee or knees in reverence or worship. Also, *esp. Brit.,* **gen′u·flex′ion.** [< ML *genūflexiōn-* (s. of *genūflexiō*)]

gen·u·ine (jen′yōō in), *adj.* **1.** possessing the purported character, quality, or origin; authentic. **2.** properly so called: *a genuine case of smallpox.* **3.** free from pretense, affectation, or hypocrisy; sincere. **4.** proceeding from the original stock; pure in breed. [< L *genuīn(us)* innate, natural = *genu-* (as in *ingenuus* native) + *-īnus* -INE[1]] **—gen′u·ine·ly,** *adv.* **—gen′u·ine·ness,** *n.*

ge·nus (jē′nəs), *n., pl.* **gen·e·ra** (jen′ər ə), **ge·nus·es.** **1.** a kind; sort; class. **2.** *Biol.* the usual major subdivision of a family or subfamily in the classification of plants and animals, usually consisting of more than one species. **3.** *Logic.* a class or group of individuals, or of species of individuals. [< L: race, stock, kind, gender; c. Gk *génos.* See GENS, GENDER[1]]

-geny, a learned borrowing from Greek meaning "origin," used in the formation of compound words: *phylogeny.* [< Gk *-geneia.* See -GEN, -Y[3]]

geo-, a learned borrowing from Greek meaning "the earth," used in the formation of compound words: *geochemistry.* [< Gk *geō-,* comb. form of *gê* earth]

ge·o·cen·tric (jē′ō sen′trik), *adj.* **1.** *Astron.* viewed or measured as from the center of the earth. **2.** having or representing the earth as a center: *a geocentric theory of the universe.* **3.** using the earth or earthly life as the only basis of evaluation. **—ge′o·cen′tri·cal·ly,** *adv.*

ge′ocen′tric par′allax. See under **parallax** (def. 2).

ge·o·chem·is·try (jē′ō kem′i strē), *n.* the science dealing with the chemical changes in and the composition of the earth's crust. **—ge·o·chem·i·cal** (jē′ō kem′i kəl), *adj.* **—ge′o·chem′ist,** *n.*

geod., **1.** geodesy. **2.** geodetic.

ge·ode (jē′ōd), *n.* **1.** *Geol.* a hollow concretionary or nodular stone often lined with crystals. **2.** the hollow or cavity of this. [< F *géode* < L *geōd(ēs)* < Gk *geṓdēs* earthlike. See GEO-, -ODE[1]] —**ge·od·ic** (jē od′ik), *adj.*

ge·o·des·ic (jē′ə des′ik, -dē′sik), *adj.* **1.** Also, **ge′o·des′i·cal.** pertaining to the geometry of curved surfaces, in which geodesic lines take the place of the straight lines of plane geometry. —*n.* **2.** See **geodesic line.** [< F *géodésique*]

ge′odes′ic dome′, a light, domelike structure developed to combine the structurally desirable properties of the tetrahedron and the sphere.

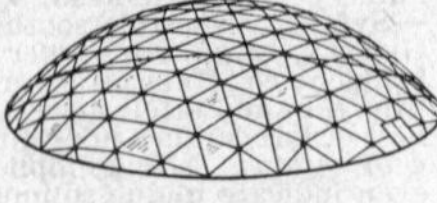

Geodesic dome

ge′odes′ic line′, *Math.* the shortest line lying on a given surface and connecting two given points.

ge·od·e·sy (jē od′i sē), *n.* the branch of applied mathematics that deals with the measurement of the shape and area of large tracts of country, the exact position of geographical points, and the curvature, shape, and dimensions of the earth. Also, **ge·o·det·ics** (jē′ə-det′iks). [< F *géodésie* < Gk *geōdaisía* = *geō-* GEO- + *dais-* (s. of *daíein* to divide) + *-ia* -Y[3]] —**ge·od′e·sist,** *n.*

ge·o·det·ic (jē′ə det′ik), *adj.* **1.** pertaining to geodesy. **2.** geodesic. Also, **ge′o·det′i·cal.** [irreg. from GEODESY; see -IC] —**ge′o·det′i·cal·ly,** *adv.*

ge′odet′ic sur′vey, a land area survey in which the curvature of the surface of the earth is taken into account.

ge·o·duck (gōō′ē duk), *n.* a very large edible clam, *Panope generosa,* of the NW coast of the U.S. [AmerInd: lit., dig deep]

ge·o·dy·nam·ics (jē′ō dī nam′iks), *n.* the science dealing with dynamic processes or forces within the earth. —**ge′o·dy·nam′ic,** *adj.*

Geof′frey of Mon′mouth, 1100?–1154, English chronicler.

geog., **1.** geographer. **2.** geographic; geographical. **3.** geography.

ge·og·no·sy (jē og′nə sē), *n.* the branch of geology that deals with the constituent parts of the earth, its atmosphere and water, its crust, and the condition of its interior. [< F *géognosie.* See GEO-, -GNOSIS] —**ge·og·nos·tic** (jē′og-nos′tik), *adj.*

ge·og·ra·pher (jē og′rə fər), *n.* a person who specializes in geographical research, delineation, and study. [< LL *geōgraph(us)* (< Gk *geōgráphos;* see GEO-, -GRAPH) + -ER[1]]

ge·o·graph·i·cal (jē′ə graf′i kəl), *adj.* **1.** of or pertaining to geography. **2.** of or pertaining to the natural features, population, industries, etc., of a region or regions. Also, **ge′o·graph′ic.** [< LL *geōgraphic(us)* (< Gk *geōgraphikós;* see GEO-, -GRAPH, -IC) + -AL[1]] —**ge′o·graph′i·cal·ly,** *adv.*

ge′ograph′ical mile′, mile (def. 2).

geograph′ic deter′minism, *Sociol.* a doctrine that regards geographical conditions as the determining or molding agency of group life.

ge·og·ra·phy (jē og′rə fē), *n., pl.* **-phies.** **1.** the science dealing with the areal differentiation of the earth's surface, as shown in the character, arrangement, and interrelations over the world of such elements as climate, elevation, soil, vegetation, population, land use, industries, national and political entities, and of the unit areas formed by the complex of these individual elements. **2.** the study of this science. **3.** a book dealing with this science or study. **4.** the topographical features of a region, usually of the earth, sometimes of the planets. [< L *geōgraphia* < Gk *geōgraphía*]

ge·oid (jē′oid), *n.* **1.** an imaginary surface that coincides with the mean sea level in the ocean and its extension through the continents. **2.** the geometric figure formed by this surface, an ellipsoid flattened at the poles. [< Gk *geoeid(ēs)* earthlike. See GEO-, -OID]

geol., **1.** geologic; geological. **2.** geologist. **3.** geology.

ge·o·log·ic (jē′ə loj′ik), *adj.* of or pertaining to geology. Also, **ge′o·log′i·cal.** —**ge′o·log′i·cal·ly,** *adv.*

ge′olog′ic time′, the succession of eras, periods, and epochs as considered in historical geology.

ge·ol·o·gise (jē ol′ə jīz′), *v.i., v.t.* **-gized, -giz·ing.** *Chiefly Brit.* geologize.

ge·ol·o·gist (jē ol′ə jist), *n.* a person who specializes in geologic research and study.

ge·ol·o·gize (jē ol′ə jīz′), *v.,* **-gized, -giz·ing.** —*v.i.* **1.** to study geology. —*v.t.* **2.** to examine geologically. Also, *esp. Brit.,* **geologise.**

ge·ol·o·gy (jē ol′ə jē), *n., pl.* **-gies.** **1.** the science that deals with the physical history of the earth, the rocks of which it is composed, and the physical changes which the earth has undergone or is undergoing. **2.** the study of this science. **3.** the geologic features and processes occurring in a given region on the earth or on a celestial body.

geom., **1.** geometric; geometrical. **2.** geometry.

ge·o·mag·net·ic (jē′ō mag net′ik), *adj.* of or pertaining to terrestrial magnetism. —**ge·o·mag·net·ism** (jē′ō mag′-ni tiz′əm), *n.*

ge·o·man·cy (jē′ə man′sē), *n.* divination by means of a figure made by a handful of earth thrown down at random or by figures or lines formed by a number of dots made at random. [ME < OF *geomancie* << LGk *geōmanteía*] —**ge′o·man′cer,** *n.* —**ge′o·man′tic,** *adj.*

ge·om·e·ter (jē om′i tər), *n.* geometrician. [ME < L *geōmetra* < Gk: land measurer; see GEOMETRY]

ge·o·met·ric (jē′ə me′trik), *adj.* **1.** of or pertaining to geometry or to the principles of geometry. **2.** resembling or employing the simple rectilinear or curvilinear lines or figures used in geometry. **3.** of or pertaining to painting, sculpture, or ornamentation of predominantly geometric characteristics. Also, **ge′o·met′ri·cal.** [< L *geōmetric(us)* < Gk *geōmétr(ēs)* geometer] —**ge′o·met′ri·cal·ly,** *adv.*

ge·om·e·tri·cian (jē om′i trish′ən, jē′ə mi-), *n.* a person skilled in geometry.

ge′omet′ric mean′, *Math.* the mean of n positive numbers obtained by taking the nth root of the product of the numbers: *The geometric mean of 6 and 24 is 12.*

geomet′ric progres′sion, *Math.* a sequence of terms in which the ratio between any two successive terms is the same, as the progression 1, 3, 9, 27, 81 or 144, 12, 1, $^1/_{12}$, $^1/_{144}$. Also called **geometric series.**

ge′omet′ric ra′tio, *Math.* the ratio of consecutive terms in a geometric progression.

ge′omet′ric se′ries, *Math.* **1.** an infinite series of the form, $c + cx + cx^2 + cx^3 + \ldots$, where c and x are real numbers. **2.** See **geometric progression.**

ge·om·e·trid (jē om′i trid), *adj.* **1.** belonging or pertaining to the family *Geometridae,* comprising slender-bodied, broad-winged moths, the larvae of which are called measuringworms. —*n.* **2.** a geometrid moth. [< NL *Geōmetrid(ae)* name of genus of moths. See GEOMETER, -ID[2]]

Geometrid
Fall cankerworm,
Alsophila pometaria
A, Larva; B, Adult male

ge·om·e·trise (jē om′i trīz′), *v.i., v.t.,* **-trised, -tris·ing.** *Chiefly Brit.* geometrize.

ge·om·e·trize (jē om′i trīz′), *v.,* **-trized, -triz·ing.** —*v.i.* **1.** to work by geometric methods. —*v.t.* **2.** to put into geometric form. [GEOMETR(Y) + -IZE]

ge·om·e·try (jē om′i trē), *n.* **1.** the branch of mathematics that deals with the deduction of the properties, measurement, and relationships of points, lines, angles, and figures in space from their defining conditions by means of certain assumed properties of space. **2.** any specific system of this that operates in accordance with a specific set of assumptions: *Euclidean geometry.* **3.** the study of this branch of mathematics. **4.** a book on this study, esp. a textbook. **5.** a design or arrangement of objects in simple rectilinear or curvilinear form. [ME < L *geōmetria* < Gk *geōmetría*]

ge·o·mor·phic (jē′ə môr′fik), *adj.* **1.** of or pertaining to the figure of the earth or the forms of its surface. **2.** resembling the earth in form.

ge·o·mor·phol·o·gy (jē′ə môr fol′ə jē), *n.* the study of the characteristics, origin, and development of land forms. —**ge·o·mor·pho·log·i·cal** (jē′ə môr′fə loj′i kəl), **ge′o-mor′pho·log′ic,** *adj.*

ge·oph·a·gy (jē of′ə jē), *n.* the practice of eating earthy matter, esp. clay or chalk. Also, **ge·o·pha·gia** (jē′ə fā′jə, -jē ə), **ge·oph′a·gism.** —**ge·oph′a·gist,** *n.* —**ge·oph·a·gous** (jē of′ə gəs), *adj.*

ge·o·phys·ics (jē′ō fiz′iks), *n.* (*construed as sing.*) the physics of the earth, including oceanography, seismology, volcanology, geomagnetism, etc. —**ge′o·phys′i·cal,** *adj.* —**ge′o·phys′i·cist,** *n.*

ge·o·phyte (jē′ə fīt′), *n.* *Bot.* a plant with underground buds. —**ge·o·phyt·ic** (jē′ə fit′ik), *adj.*

ge·o·pol·i·tics (jē′ō pol′i tiks), *n.* (*construed as sing.*) **1.** the study or the application of the influence of political and economic geography on the national power, foreign policy, etc., of a state. **2.** the combination of geographic and political factors influencing or delineating a country or region. **3.** a national policy based on the interrelation of politics and geography. [trans. of G *Geopolitik*] —**ge·o·po·lit·i·cal** (jē′ō pə lit′i kəl), *adj.* —**ge·o·pol·i·ti·cian** (jē′ō-pol′i tish′ən), *n.*

ge·o·pon·ic (jē′ə pon′ik), *adj.* of or pertaining to tillage or agriculture; agricultural. [< Gk *geōponik(ós)* pertaining to husbandry = *geōpón(os)* husbandman (*geō-* GEO- + *pon-*work, toil, cf. *pénesthai* to labor) + *-ikos* -IC]

ge·o·pon·ics (jē′ə pon′iks), *n.* (*construed as sing.*) the art or science of agriculture.

ge·o·po·ten·tial (jē′ō pə ten′shəl), *n.* *Physics.* the difference between the potential energy of a mass at a given altitude and the potential energy of an identical mass at sea level, equivalent to the energy required to move the mass from sea level to the given altitude.

George (jôrj), *n.* **1. David Lloyd.** See **Lloyd George, David.** **2. Henry,** 1839–97, U.S. economist: advocate of a single tax. **3. Saint,** died A.D. 303?, Christian martyr: patron saint of England. **4. Lake,** a lake in E New York. 36 mi. long.

George (jôrj), *n.* *Brit. Slang.* any coin bearing the image of St. George.

George I, **1.** 1660–1727, king of England 1714–27. **2.** 1845–1913, king of Greece 1863–1913.

George II, **1.** 1683–1760, king of England 1727–60 (son of George I). **2.** 1890–1947, king of Greece 1922–23, 1935–47.

George III, 1738–1820, king of England 1760–1820 (grandson of George II).

George IV, 1762–1830, king of England 1820–30 (son of George III).

George V, 1865–1936, king of England 1910–36 (son of Edward VII).

George VI, 1895–1952, king of England 1936–1952 (second son of George V; brother of Edward VIII).

Geor′ges Bank′ (jôr′jiz), a bank extending generally NE from Nantucket: fishing grounds. 150 mi. long.

George′ Town′, a seaport in and the capital of the state of Penang, in NW Malaysia. 234,903 (1957). Also, **George-town.** Also called **Penang.**

George·town (jôrj′toun′), *n.* **1.** See **George Town.** **2.** a seaport in and the capital of Guyana, at the mouth of the Essequibo. 182,000. **3.** a residential section in the District of Columbia.

Geor·gette (jôr jet′), *n.* a sheer silk or rayon crepe of dull texture. Also called **Georgette′ crepe′.**

Geor·gia (jôr′jə), *n.* **1.** a state in the SE United States. 4,589,575 (1970); 58,876 sq. mi. *Cap.:* Atlanta. *Abbr.:* Ga., GA **2.** Official name, **Geor′gian So′viet So′cialist Repub′lic.** Russian, **Gruziya.** a constituent republic of the Soviet Union in Caucasia, bordering on the Black Sea: an independent kingdom for ab. 2000 years. 4,500,000 (est. 1965); 26,872 sq. mi. *Cap.:* Tbilisi. **3. Strait of,** an inlet of the Pacific in SW Canada and NW U.S. between Vancouver Island and the mainland. 150 mi. long.

Geor·gian (jôr′jən), *adj.* **1.** of, pertaining to, or characteristic of the period of British history from the accession of

George I in 1714 to the death of George IV in 1830. **2.** of or pertaining to the reign of George V of England. **3.** of or pertaining to the state of Georgia in the U.S. **4.** of or pertaining to Georgia in the Soviet Union. —*n.* **5.** a person, esp. a writer, of either of the Georgian periods in England. **6.** the styles or character of either of the Georgian periods. **7.** a native or inhabitant of the state of Georgia in the U.S. **8.** a native or inhabitant of Georgia in the Soviet Union. **9.** the most important South Caucasian language, written in a distinctive script derived from the Aramaic alphabet.

Geor′gian Bay′, the NE part of Lake Huron, in Ontario, Canada. 6000 sq. mi.

Geor′gia pine′. See **longleaf pine.**

geor·gic (jôr′jik), *adj.* **1.** agricultural. —*n.* **2.** a poem on an agricultural theme; bucolic. [< L *geōrgic(us)* < Gk *geōrgikós* = *geōrg(ós)* husbandman (*gê* earth + *-ourgos* working, worker, akin to *érgon* work) + *-ikos* -IC]

ge·o·stat·ic (jē′ə stat′ik), *adj.* **1.** of or pertaining to pressure exerted by earth or a similar substance. **2.** (of a construction) resistant to such pressure.

ge·o·stroph·ic (jē′ə strō′fik), *adj.* of or pertaining to the balance between the Coriolis force and the horizontal pressure force in the atmosphere.

ge·o·syn·cli·nal (jē′ō sin klīn′əl), *Geol.* —*adj.* **1.** pertaining to a synclinal fold that involves a relatively large part of the earth's surface. —*n.* **2.** a geosyncline.

ge·o·syn·cline (jē′ō sin′klīn), *n.* *Geol.* a portion of the earth's crust subjected to downward warping during a large fraction of geologic time; a geosynclinal fold.

ge·o·tax·is (jē′ō tak′sis), *n.* *Biol.* oriented movement of a motile organism toward or away from a gravitational force. —**ge·o·tac·tic** (jē′ō tak′tik), *adj.*

ge·o·tec·ton·ic (jē′ō tek ton′ik), *adj.* of or pertaining to the structure of the earth's crust.

ge·o·ther·mal (jē′ō thûr′məl), *adj.* of or pertaining to the internal heat of the earth. Also, **ge′o·ther′mic.**

ge·o·trop·ic (jē′ō trop′ik), *adj.* *Biol.* of, pertaining to, or exhibiting geotropism. —**ge′o·trop′i·cal·ly,** *adv.*

ge·ot·ro·pism (jē o′trə piz′əm), *n.* *Biol.* oriented movement or growth with respect to the force of gravity.

Ger., **1.** German. **2.** Germany.

ger., **1.** gerund. **2.** gerundive.

Ge·ra (gā′rä), *n.* a city in S East Germany. 106,841 (1964).

ge·rah (gē′rə), *n.* a Hebrew weight and coin, equal to $^1/_{20}$ of a shekel. [< Heb < Akkadian *girū*]

ge·ra·ni·a·ceous (ji rā′nē ā′shəs), *adj.* belonging to the *Geraniaceae,* or geranium family of plants. [< NL *Geraniāce(ae)* (see GERANIUM, -ACEAE) + -OUS]

ge·ra·ni·um (ji rā′nē əm), *n.* **1.** any of several plants of the genus *Geranium,* comprising the crane's-bills. **2.** Also called **stork's-bill.** any of several plants of the allied genus *Pelargonium,* having showy flowers. **3.** a flower of this plant. [< L: the plant stork's-bill (sp. var. of *geranion*) < Gk *gerānion* crane's-bill, geranium < *géranos* crane; c. L *grūs*]

Ge·rard (zhā rär′), *n.* **É·tienne Mau·rice** (ā tyen′ mō rēs′), **Comte,** 1773–1852, French marshal.

ger·a·tol·o·gy (jer′ə tol′ə jē), *n.* the study of the decline of life, as in old age or in animals approaching extinction. [< Gk *gēra(s)* old age + connective *-t-* + -O- + -LOGY] —**ger·a·to·log·ic** (jer′ə tᵊloj′ik), *adj.*

ger·bil (jûr′bəl), *n.* any of numerous burrowing rodents of the genus *Gerbillus* and related genera, of Asia, Africa, and southern Russia. Also, **ger′bille.** [< F *gerbille* < NL *gerbill(us),* dim. of *gerbo* JERBOA]

ge·rent (jēr′ənt), *n.* *Rare.* a ruler or manager. [< L *gerent-* (s. of *gerēns,* prp. of *gerere*) bearing, conducting, managing = *ger-* bear + *-ent-* -ENT]

ger·e·nuk (ger′ə nŏŏk′, gə ren′ək), *n.* a reddish-brown antelope, *Litocranius walleri,* of eastern Africa, having a long, slender neck. [< Somali *garanug*]

ger·fal·con (jûr′fal′kən, -fôl′-, -fô′-), *n.* gyrfalcon.

ger·i·at·ric (jer′ē a′trik), *adj.* of or pertaining to geriatrics or aged persons. [< Gk *gēr(ōn)* old man + -IATRIC]

ger·i·at·rics (jer′ē a′triks), *n.* (*construed as sing.*) **1.** the medical science dealing with the diseases, debilities, and care of aged persons. **2.** the study of the physical process and problems of aging; gerontology. —**ger·i·a·tri·cian** (jer′ē ə trish′ən), **ger′i·at′rist,** *n.*

Gé·ri·cault (zhā rē kō′), *n.* **(Jean Louis An·dré) Thé·o·dore** (zhäN lwē äN drā′ tā ô dôr′), 1791–1824, French painter.

Ger·la·chov·ka (ger′lä khôf′kä), *n.* a mountain in E Czechoslovakia: highest peak of the Carpathian Mountains. 8737 ft.

germ (jûrm), *n.* **1.** a microorganism, esp. when disease-producing; microbe. **2.** something that serves as a source or initial stage for subsequent development. **3.** *Embryol.* **a.** a bud, offshoot, or seed. **b.** the rudiment of a living organism; an embryo in its early stages. **4.** *Biol.* the initial stage in development or evolution, as a germ cell or ancestral form. [< F *germe* < L *germen* seed]

ger·man (jûr′mən), *adj.* **1.** having the same father and mother, as a full brother or sister (usually used in combination): *a brother-german.* **2.** born of the brother or sister of one's father or mother, as a first cousin. (usually used in combination). **3.** *Archaic.* germane. [ME *germain* < OF < L *germān(us)* one who is of the same blood]

Ger·man (jûr′mən), *adj.* **1.** of or pertaining to Germany, its inhabitants, or their language. **2.** of or pertaining to the German-speaking inhabitants, tribes, or states of central Europe prior to 1871. —*n.* **3.** a native or inhabitant of Germany. **4.** a descendant of a native of Germany. **5.** Also called **High German.** a moderately inflecting Indo-European language that is based on a High German dialect, and is official in Germany, Austria, and Switzerland. *Abbr.:* G, G. **6.** *Linguistics.* any variety of West Germanic speech native to Germany, Austria, or Switzerland. [< L *Germān(us)* German; c. Gk *Germanoí* (pl.)]

Ger′man Bap′tist Breth′ren. See **Church of the Brethren.**

Ger′man cock′roach, a yellowish-brown cockroach, *Blatta germanica,* brought into the U.S. from Europe. Also called **Croton bug.** See illus. at **cockroach.**

Ger′man Democrat′ic Repub′lic, official name of **East Germany.**

ger·man·der (jər man′dər), *n.* **1.** any of several labiate herbs or shrubs of the genus *Teucrium,* as *T. Chamaedrys,* of Europe, and *T. canadense,* of America. **2.** Also called **german′der speed′well.** a speedwell, *Veronica Chamaedrys,* having blue flowers. [ME < ML *germandr(e)a* < LGk *chamandryá*]

ger·mane (jər mān′), *adj.* **1.** closely or significantly related; relevant; pertinent. **2.** *Obs.* closely akin. [var. of GERMAN] —**ger·mane′ly,** *adv.* —**ger·mane′ness,** *n.*

Ger′man East′ Af′rica, a former German territory in E Africa: the area now comprising Tanganyika and the independent republics of Rwanda and Burundi.

ger·man·ic (jər man′ik, -mān′-), *adj.* *Chem.* of or containing germanium, esp. in the tetravalent state.

Ger·man·ic (jər man′ik), *adj.* **1.** of or pertaining to the Teutons or their languages. **2.** German. **3.** of, pertaining to, or noting the Germanic branch of languages. —*n.* **4.** a branch of the Indo-European family of languages including German, Dutch, English, the Scandinavian languages, Afrikaans, Flemish, Frisian, and the extinct Gothic language. **5.** Also called **Primitive Germanic.** an ancient Indo-European language, the immediate linguistic ancestor of the Germanic languages. *Abbr.:* Gmc [< L *Germānic(us)*]

Ger·man′i·cus Cae′sar (jər man′ə kəs), 15 B.C.–A.D. 19, Roman general.

Ger·man·ise (jûr′mə nīz′), *v.t., v.i.,* **-ised, -is·ing.** *Chiefly Brit.* Germanize. —**Ger′man·i·sa′tion,** *n.*

Ger·man·ism (jûr′mə niz′əm), *n.* **1.** a usage, idiom, etc., that is characteristic of the German language. **2.** a manner, mode of thought, etc., that is characteristic of the German people. **3.** extreme partiality for or attachment to Germany, Germans, or German customs, manners, etc.

ger·ma·ni·um (jər mā′nē əm), *n.* *Chem.* a scarce, metallic element, normally tetravalent, used chiefly in transistors. *Symbol:* Ge; *at. wt.:* 72.59; *at. no.:* 32; *sp. gr.:* 5.36 at 20°C. [GERMAN(Y) + -IUM]

Ger·man·ize (jûr′mə nīz′), *v.t., v.i.,* **-ized, -iz·ing.** **1.** to make or become German in character, sentiment, etc. **2.** *Archaic.* to translate into German. Also, *esp. Brit.,* **Germanise.** —**Ger′man·i·za′tion,** *n.*

Ger′man mea′sles, *Pathol.* a contagious virus disease, usually milder than measles, characterized by fever, a sore throat, and a rash resembling that of scarlet fever. Also called **rubella.**

Germano-, a combining form of **German:** *Germanophile.*

Ger′man O′cean, former name of the **North Sea.**

Ger·man·o·phile (jər man′ə fīl′), *n.* a person who is friendly toward or admires Germany or German culture.

Ger·man·o·phobe (jər man′ə fōb′), *n.* a person who hates or fears Germany or German culture. —**Ger·man′o·pho′bi·a,** *n.*

ger·man·ous (jər man′əs, -mān′-), *adj.* *Chem.* containing bivalent germanium. [GERMAN(IUM) + -OUS]

Ger′man shep′herd, one of a breed of large shepherd dogs having a coat ranging in color from gray to brindled, black-and-tan, or black. Also called **Ger′man shep′herd dog′, Ger′man police′ dog′.**

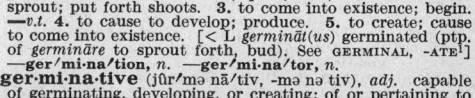

German shepherd (2 ft. high at shoulder)

Ger′man sil′ver, any of various alloys of copper, zinc, and nickel, usually white and used for utensils, drawing instruments, etc.; nickel silver.

Ger′man South′west Af′rica, former name of **South-West Africa.**

Ger·man·town (jûr′mən toun′), *n.* the NW part of Philadelphia, Pa.: American defeat by British 1777.

Ger·ma·ny (jûr′mə nē), *n.* **1.** a former country in central Europe, existing from 1871 to 1945 and having Berlin as its capital: now divided into East Germany and West Germany. **2.** the German-speaking states of central Europe prior to 1871. German, **Deutschland;** (formerly) **Deutsches Reich.** Cf. **East Germany, West Germany.**

germ′ cell′, *Biol.* the sexual reproductive cell at any stage from the primordial cell to the mature gamete.

ger·men (jûr′mən), *n., pl.* **-mens, -mi·na** (-mə nə). *Archaic.* a germ. [< L: offshoot, sprout, bud]

ger·mi·cide (jûr′mi sīd′), *n.* an agent for killing germs or microorganisms. —**ger′mi·cid′al,** *adj.*

ger·mi·nal (jûr′mə nᵊl), *adj.* **1.** of or pertaining to a germ or germs. **2.** of the nature of a germ or germ cell. **3.** being in the earliest stage of development: *germinal ideas.* [< NL *germināl(is)* = L *germin-* (s. of *germen* offshoot) + *-ālis* -AL[1]] —**ger′mi·nal·ly,** *adv.*

Ger·mi·nal (jûr′mə nᵊl; *Fr.* zher mē nal′), *n.* (in the French Revolutionary calendar) the seventh month of the year, extending from March 21 to April 19. [< F; special use of GERMINAL]

ger′minal disk′, *Embryol.* blastodisk.

ger′minal ves′icle, *Embryol. Obs.* the large, vesicular nucleus of an ovum before the polar bodies are formed.

ger·mi·nant (jûr′mə nənt), *adj.* germinating. [< L *germinant-* (s. of *germināns,* prp. of *germināre*). See GERMINAL, -ANT]

ger·mi·nate (jûr′mə nāt′), *v.,* **-nat·ed, -nat·ing.** —*v.i.* **1.** to begin to grow or develop. **2.** *Bot.* **a.** to develop into a plant or individual, as a seed, spore, bulb, or the like. **b.** to sprout; put forth shoots. **3.** to come into existence; begin. —*v.t.* **4.** to cause to develop; produce. **5.** to create; cause to come into existence. [< L *germināt(us)* germinated (ptp. of *germināre* to sprout forth, bud). See GERMINAL, -ATE[1]] —**ger′mi·na′tion,** *n.* —**ger′mi·na′tor,** *n.*

ger·mi·na·tive (jûr′mə nā′tiv, -mə nə tiv), *adj.* capable of germinating, developing, or creating; of or pertaining to germination.

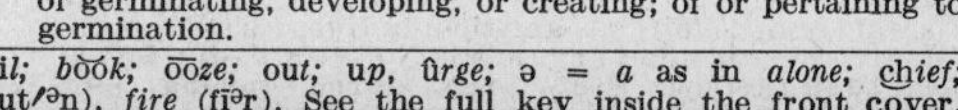

Ger·mis·ton (jûr′mi stən), *n.* a city in S Transvaal, in the NE Republic of South Africa. 148,102 (1960).

germ′ lay′er, one of the three primary embryonic cell layers. Cf. **ectoderm, entoderm, mesoderm.**

germ′ plasm′, the protoplasm of the germ cells containing the units of heredity, the chromosomes and genes.

germ′ the′ory, 1. *Pathol.* the theory that infection, diseases, etc., are due to the agency of germs or microorganisms. **2.** *Biol.* biogenesis.

ger·o·don·tics (jer′ə don′tiks), *n.* (*construed as sing.*) the branch of dentistry dealing with aging and aged persons. Also, **ger·o·don·tia** (jer′ə don′shə, -shē ə). Also called **ger·o·don·tol·o·gy** (jer′ō don tol′ə jē). [< Gk *gêr(as)* old age + -ODONT + -ICS] —**ger′o·don′tic,** *adj.*

Ge·ron·i·mo (jə ron′ə mō′), *n.* (*Goyathlay*) 1829–1909, American Apache Indian chief.

geronto-, a learned borrowing from Greek meaning "old age," used in the formation of compound words: *gerontology.* Also, *esp. before a vowel,* **geront-.** [< Gk, comb. form repr. *geront-,* s. of *gérōn* old man]

ger·on·toc·ra·cy (jer′ən tok′rə sē), *n., pl.* **-cies. 1.** government by a council of elders. **2.** a governing body consisting of old men.

ger·on·tol·o·gy (jer′ən tol′ə jē), *n.* the branch of science that deals with aging and the special problems of aged persons. —**ger′on·tol′o·gist,** *n.*

-gerous, a combining form meaning "bearing," "producing," used in the formation of compound words: *armigerous.* [< L *-ger* bearing + -OUS]

Ger·ry (ger′ē), *n.* **El·bridge** (el′brij), 1744–1814, U.S. politician: vice president 1813–14.

ger·ry·man·der (jer′i man′dər, ger′-), *U.S. Politics.* —*n.* **1.** the dividing of a state, county, etc., into election districts so as to give one political party a majority in many districts while concentrating the voting strength of the other party into as few districts as possible. —*v.t.* **2.** to subject (a state, county, etc.) to a gerrymander. [after Elbridge *Gerry* (governor of Massachusetts, whose party redistricted the state in 1812) + (*sala*)*mander,* from the fancied resemblance of the map of Essex County, Mass., to this animal, after the redistricting]

Gersh·win (gûrsh′win), *n.* **1. George,** 1898–1937, U.S. composer. **2.** his brother, **Ira,** 1896–1983, U.S. lyricist.

ger·und (jer′ənd), *n. Gram.* **1.** (in certain languages, as Latin) a form regularly derived from a verb and functioning as a noun, having in Latin all case forms but the nominative, as Latin *dicendī* gen., *dicendō,* dat., abl., etc., "saying." **2.** the English *-ing* form of a verb when functioning as a noun, as *writing* in *Writing is easy.* **3.** a form similar to the Latin gerund in meaning or function. [< LL *gerund(ium),* L *gerund(um)* that which is to be carried on (sp. var. of *gerendum,* neut. ger. of *gerere* to bear, carry on)] —**ge·run·di·al** (jə run′dē əl), *adj.*

ger·un·dive (jə run′div), *n.* **1.** (in Latin) the future passive participle, similar to the gerund in formation, as *dicendum* in *Haec dicendum est,* "This must be said." —*adj.* **2.** resembling a gerund. [< LL *gerundīv(us)*] —**ger·un·di·val** (jer′ən dī′vəl), *adj.* —**ge·run′dive·ly,** *adv.*

Ge·ry·on (jēr′ē ən, ger′ē-), *n. Class. Myth.* a monster who possessed a large herd of red cattle, the abduction of which was the 10th labor of Hercules.

Ge·sell (gə zel′), *n.* **Arnold Lucius,** 1880–1961, U.S. psychologist.

ges·so (jes′ō), *n.* **1.** gypsum or plaster of Paris prepared with glue for use as a surface for painting. **2.** a painting surface spread with this. [< It < L *gyps(um)* GYPSUM]

gest[1] (jest), *n. Archaic.* **1.** a metrical romance or history. **2.** a story or tale. **3.** a deed or exploit. [ME < OF *geste* action, exploit < L *gesta* exploits, neut. pl. ptp. of *gerere* to carry on, perform (war, etc.)]

gest[2] (jest), *n. Archaic.* **1.** deportment; conduct. **2.** gesture. [< F *geste* < L *gestus* gesture, bearing, ptp. of *gerere* to bear, deport (oneself)]

gest[3] (jest), *n. Obs.* any of the stages in a journey. [var. of *gist,* ME *giste* < OF; see GIST]

ge·stalt (gə shtält′), *n., pl.* **-stalts, -stal·ten** (-shtäl′-tən). (*sometimes cap.*) *Psychol.* **1.** a unified whole; a configuration, pattern, or organized field having specific properties that cannot be derived from the summation of its component parts. **2.** an instance or example of such a unified whole. [< G: figure, form, structure]

Gestalt′ psychol′ogy, (*sometimes l.c.*) the theory or doctrine that physiological or psychological phenomena do not occur through the summation of individual elements, as reflexes or sensations, but through gestalts functioning separately or interrelatedly. Also called **configurationism.**

Ge·sta·po (gə stä′pō; *Ger.* gə shtä′pō), *n.* the German state secret police during the Nazi regime. [< G *Ge(heime) Sta(ats)po(lizei)*]

ges·tate (jes′tāt), *v.,* **-tat·ed, -tat·ing.** —*v.t.* **1.** to carry in the womb during the period from conception to delivery. —*v.i.* **2.** to experience the process of gestating offspring. **3.** to develop slowly. [< L *gestāt(us)* carried (ptp. of *gestāre*) = *gest-* (s. of *gestus,* ptp. of *gerere* to carry) + *-ātus* -ATE[1]]

ges·ta·tion (je stā′shən), *n.* the state, process, or period of gestating. [< L *gestātiōn-* (s. of *gestātiō*)] —**ges·ta′tion·al, ges·ta·tive** (jes′tə tiv, je stā′-), *adj.*

ges·tic (jes′tik), *adj.* pertaining to bodily motions, esp. in dancing. Also, **ges′ti·cal.**

ges·tic·u·lar (je stik′yə lər), *adj.* pertaining to or characterized by gesticulation. [< LL *gesticul(us)* (see GESTICULATE) + -AR[1]]

ges·tic·u·late (je stik′yə lāt′), *v.,* **-lat·ed, -lat·ing.** —*v.i.* **1.** to make or use gestures, esp. in an animated or excited manner with or instead of speech. —*v.t.* **2.** to express by gesturing. [< L *gesticulāt(us)* (ptp. of *gesticulārī*) = LL (assumed in L) *gesticul(us)* gesture (see GEST[2], -CULE) + *-ātus* -ATE[1]] —**ges·tic′u·la′tor,** *n.*

ges·tic·u·la·tion (je stik′yə lā′shən), *n.* **1.** the act of gesticulating. **2.** an excited gesture. [< L *gesticulātiōn-* (s. of *gesticulātiō*)] —**ges·tic·u·la·tive** (je stik′yə lā′tiv, -lə tiv), **ges·tic·u·la·to·ry** (je stik′yə lə tōr′ē, -tôr′ē), *adj.*

ges·ture (jes′chər, jesh′-), *n., v.,* **-tured, -tur·ing.** —*n.* **1.** a movement of the body, head, arms, hands, or face that is expressive of an idea, opinion, emotion, etc. **2.** any action or proceeding intended for effect or as a formality; demonstration. —*v.i.* **3.** to make or use a gesture or gestures. —*v.t.* **4.** to express by a gesture or gestures. [ME < ML *gestūra* mode of action, manner, bearing] —**ges′tur·al,** *adj.* —**ges′tur·er,** *n.*

ge·sund·heit (gə zŏŏnt′hīt), *interj.* (used to wish good health, as a toast, or esp. to a person who has just sneezed.) [< G: lit., health-hood]

get (get), *v.,* **got** or (*Archaic*) **gat; got·ten** or **got; get·ting;** *n.* —*v.t.* **1.** to receive or come to have possession, use, or enjoyment of: *to get a birthday present; to get a pension.* **2.** to obtain or acquire, as for one's use or enjoyment: *to get oil by drilling; to get information.* **3.** to go after (something); fetch. **4.** to cause or cause to become, do, etc.: *to get one's hair cut; to get a fire to burn.* **5.** to communicate with over a distance; reach: *You can get me by telephone.* **6.** to hear: *I didn't get your last name.* **7.** to acquire a mental grasp or command of; learn or understand: *I don't get your meaning; to get a lesson.* **8.** to capture; seize. **9.** to receive as punishment: *to get 20 years in jail.* **10.** to influence or persuade: *We'll get him to go with us.* **11.** to prepare; make ready: *to get dinner.* **12.** (esp. of animals) to beget. **13.** to affect emotionally: *Her tears got me.* **14.** to take vengeance on. **15.** to suffer from or be subjected to or afflicted with: *He's got a bad cold.* **16.** *Slang.* to puzzle or irritate.
—*v.i.* **17.** to come to a specified place; arrive; reach: *What time do we get there?* **18.** to become or to cause oneself to become as specified; reach a certain condition: *to get tired; to get promoted.* **19.** to succeed in coming, going, or surviving (usually fol. by *away, in, into, out, over, through,* etc.): *I don't get into town very often.* **20.** to earn money; gain. **21.** *Informal.* to leave promptly; scram. **22.** to start or enter upon the action of (fol. by a present participle expressing action): *to get moving.* **23. get about, a.** to move about; be active. **b.** to become known; spread. **c.** to be socially active. Also, **get around. 24. get across,** to make or become understandable. **25. get ahead,** to be successful. **26. get ahead of,** to surpass; outdo. **27. get along, a.** to go away; leave. **b.** See **get** (def. 40). **28. get around, a.** to circumvent; outwit. **b.** to ingratiate oneself with (someone) through flattery or cajolery. **c.** to travel from place to place; circulate. **d.** See **get** (def. 23). **29. get at, a.** to reach; touch: *to stretch in order to get at a top shelf.* **b.** to hint at or imply; intimate: *What are you getting at?* **c.** to discover; determine: *to get at the root of a problem.* **30. get away, a.** to escape; flee. **b.** to start out; leave. **31. get away with,** to accomplish without detection or punishment. **32. get back, a.** to come back; return. **b.** to recover; regain. **c.** to be revenged. **33. get by, a.** to succeed in going past. **b.** to manage to exist, survive, etc., in spite of difficulties. **c.** to evade the notice of. **34. get down, a.** to bring or come down; descend. **b.** to concentrate; attend: *to get down to the matter at hand.* **c.** to depress; discourage; fatigue: *Nothing gets me down so much as a cold.* **d.** to swallow. **35. get even.** See **even**[1] (def. 21). **36. get going, a.** to begin; act. **b.** to make haste. **37. get in, a.** to go into a place; enter: *He forgot his key and couldn't get in.* **b.** to arrive: *They both got in on the same train.* **c.** to become associated. **38. get it,** *Informal.* **a.** to be punished or reprimanded. **b.** to understand something. **39. get off, a.** to escape the consequences of or punishment for one's actions. **b.** to help (someone) escape punishment: *A good lawyer might get you off.* **c.** to begin a journey; leave. **d.** to leave (a train, plane, etc.); dismount from (a horse); alight. **e.** to tell (a joke); express (an opinion). **f.** *Slang.* to have the effrontery: *Where does he get off telling me how to behave?* **40. get on, a.** to make progress; proceed; advance. **b.** to have sufficient means to manage, survive, or fare. **c.** to be on good terms; agree. **d.** to advance in age. **41. get out, a.** to leave (often fol. by *of*): *Get out of here!* **b.** to become publicly known. **c.** to withdraw or retire (often fol. by *of*). **d.** to produce or complete. **42. get over, a.** to recover from: *to get over an illness.* **b.** See **get** (def. 24). **43. get round.** See **get** (def. 28). **44. get there,** to reach one's goal; succeed. **45. get through, a.** to succeed, as in meeting or reaching (usually fol. by *to*): *The messenger wasn't able to get through to our cabin in the woods.* **b.** to complete; finish. **c.** to make oneself understood. **46. get to, a.** to get into communication with; contact. **b.** *Informal.* to make an impression on; affect. **47. get together, a.** to accumulate; gather. **b.** to congregate; meet: *The alumnae chapter gets together twice a year.* **c.** to come to an accord; agree: *They simply couldn't get together on matters of policy.* **48. get up, a.** to sit up or stand; arise. **b.** to rise from bed. **c.** to ascend or mount. **d.** to prepare; arrange; organize. **e.** to acquire a knowledge of. **f.** (to a horse) go! go ahead! go faster! **g.** *Informal.* to dress, as in a costume or disguise: *She got herself up as a peasant girl.* **h.** *Informal.* to produce in a specified style, as a book. **i.** to stimulate; rouse: *to get up one's courage.* **49. has** or **have got, a.** (used in place of "has" or "have," fol. by a direct object and often after a contraction or in a question): *She's got a new hat. Have you got the tickets?* **b.** (used in place of "has" or "have" to emphasize a statement or, esp. after a contraction, to indicate obligation or necessity): *I've got a car. He's got to get to a doctor right away.*
—*n.* **50.** the offspring, esp. of a male animal: *the get of a stallion.* **51.** a return of a ball, as in tennis, that would normally have resulted in a point for the opponent. [ME *get(en)* < Scand; cf. OIcel *geta;* c. OE *g(i)etan* (ME *yeten*), G *-gessen,* in *vergessen* to forget]
—**Syn. 1, 2.** GET, OBTAIN, ACQUIRE, PROCURE, SECURE imply gaining possession of something. GET may apply to coming into possession in any manner, and either voluntarily or not. OBTAIN suggests putting forth effort to gain possession, and ACQUIRE stresses the possessing after an effort. PROCURE suggests the method of obtaining as that of search or choice. SECURE suggests making possession sure and safe, after obtaining something by competition or the like. **2.** win, gain. **7.** apprehend, grasp. **10.** induce, dispose. **12.** engender. —**Ant. 1.** lose. —**Usage.** See **got.**

get·a·way (get′ə wā′), *n.* **1.** a getting away; an escape. **2.** the start of a race: *a fast getaway.*

Geth·sem·a·ne (geth sem′ə nē), *n.* **1.** a garden east of Jerusalem, near the brook of Kedron: scene of Jesus' agony and betrayal. Matt. 26:36. **2.** (*l.c.*) a scene or occasion of suffering.

get·ter (get′ər), *n.* **1.** a person or thing that gets. **2.** any substance introduced into a partial vacuum to combine chemically with the residual gas in order to increase the vacuum. [ME]

get-to·geth·er (get′tə geth′ər), *n.* an informal and usually small social gathering.

Get·tys·burg (get′iz bûrg′), *n.* a borough in S Pennsylvania: Confederate forces defeated in Civil War battle fought near here on July 1–3, 1863; national cemetery. 7275 (1970).

Get′tysburg Address′, the short speech made by President Lincoln on November 19, 1863, at the dedication of the national cemetery at Gettysburg.

get·up (get′up′), *n.* *Informal.* **1.** format; style. **2.** costume; outfit. Also, **get′-up′.**

get′ up′ and go′, energy, drive, and enthusiasm.

ge·um (jē′əm), *n.* any plant of the genus *Geum,* comprising the avens. [< NL: a plant genus, L: the herb bennet, avens]

GeV, See **gigaelectron volt.** Also, **Gev**

gew·gaw (gyo͞o′gô, go͞o′-), *n.* **1.** something gaudy and useless; bauble. —*adj.* **2.** showy, but without value. Also, **geegaw.** [gradational compound based on GAU(DY)[1]]

gey (gā), *adj.* *Scot.* considerable; tolerable. [var. of GAY]

gey·ser (gī′zər, -sər), *n.* a hot spring that intermittently sends up fountainlike jets of water and steam into the air. [< Icel *Geysir* gusher, name of a hot spring in Iceland < *geysa* to gush]

gey·ser·ite (gī′zə rīt′, -sə-), *n.* a variety of opaline silica deposited around geysers and hot springs.

Ge·zi·ra (jə zēr′ə), *n.* a region in central Sudan, S of Khartoum, between the Blue Nile and the White Nile: a former province. 54,880 sq. mi.

GG, gamma globulin.

GHA, *Navig.* Greenwich hour angle.

Gha·na (gä′nə, gan′ə), *n.* a republic in West Africa: member of the British Commonwealth of Nations since 1957. 8,559,313; 91,843 sq. mi. *Cap.:* Accra. —**Gha·na·ian, Gha·ni·an** (gä′nē ən, gan′ē-), *n., adj.*

ghar·ry (gar′ē), *n., pl.* **-ries.** a horse-drawn cab or carriage used in India. Also, **ghar′ri.** [< Hindi *gāṛī*]

ghast·ly (gast′lē, gäst′-), *adj.,* **-li·er, -li·est,** *adv.* —*adj.* **1.** shockingly frightful or dreadful; horrible. **2.** resembling a ghost, esp. in being very pale. **3.** terrible; very bad: *a ghastly error.* —*adv.* **4.** in a ghastly manner; horribly; terribly. **5.** with a deathlike quality. [ME *gastly,* OE *gāstlic* spiritual; see GHOSTLY] —**ghast′li·ness,** *n.* —**Syn. 1.** hideous, gruesome, dismal. **2.** pallid, cadaverous.

ghat (gôt), *n.* (in India) **1.** a passage or stairway descending to a river. **2.** a mountain pass. **3.** a mountain range or escarpment. Also, **ghaut.** [< Hindi *ghāṭ* < Skt *ghaṭṭa*]

Ghats (gôts), *n.* (*construed as sing.*) **1.** See **Eastern Ghats. 2.** See **Western Ghats.**

Ghaz·za·li (ga zä′lē), *n.* **Al-** (al), 1058–1111, Arab philosopher. Also, **Gha·za′li.** Also called **Al-Gazel.**

ghee (gē), *n.* (in the East Indies) a kind of liquid butter made from the milk of cows and buffaloes and clarified by boiling. [< Hindi *ghī;* akin to Skt *ghr* to sprinkle]

Ghent (gent), *n.* a port in NW Belgium, at the confluence of the Scheldt and Lys rivers: treaty 1814. 155,152 (est. 1964). French, **Gand.** Flemish, **Gent.**

gher·kin (gûr′kin), *n.* **1.** the small, immature fruit of a variety of cucumber, used in pickling. **2.** the small, spiny fruit of a cucurbitaceous vine, *Cucumis Anguria,* of the West Indies, the southern U.S., etc., used in pickling. **3.** the plant yielding this fruit. **4.** a pickle. [< D *gurken,* pl. of *gurk* (G *Gurke*) < Slav; cf. Pol *ogórek,* Czech *okurka* << Pers]

ghet·to (get′ō), *n., pl.* **-tos, -toes. 1.** a section of a city in which, in former times in most European countries, all Jews were required to live. **2.** a section predominantly inhabited by Jews. **3.** *U.S.* a section of a city, esp. a thickly populated slum area, inhabited predominantly by a minority group. [< It, perh. abbr. of *borghetto,* dim. of *borgo* settlement outside the city wall]

ghet·to·ize (get′ō īz′), *v.t.,* **-ized, -iz·ing.** to segregate in or as if in a ghetto. —**ghet′to·i·za′tion,** *n.*

Ghib·el·line (gib′ə lin, -lēn′), *n.* **1.** a member of the aristocratic party in medieval Italy and Germany that supported the claims of the German emperors against the papacy: politically opposed to the Guelphs. —*adj.* **2.** of or pertaining to the Ghibellines. [< It *Ghibellin(o)* < MHG **wībeling-* (G *Waiblingen*) a Hohenstaufen estate in Germany]

Ghi·ber·ti (gē ber′tē), *n.* **Lo·ren·zo** (lô ren′tsô), 1378–1455, Florentine sculptor, goldsmith, and painter.

Ghir·lan·da·io (gēr′län dä′yô), *n.* (*Domenico di Tommaso Curradi di Doffo Bigordi*) 1449–94, Italian painter. Also, **Ghir·lan·da·jo** (gēr′län dä′yô).

ghost (gōst), *n.* **1.** the soul of a dead person, a disembodied spirit imagined as wandering among or haunting living persons. **2.** a mere shadow or semblance; a trace. **3.** a remote possibility: *He hasn't a ghost of a chance.* **4.** (*sometimes cap.*) a spiritual being. **5.** the principle of life; soul; spirit. **6.** *Informal.* a ghost-writer. **7.** *Television.* a secondary image, appearing on a screen as a white shadow, caused by poor or double reception or by a defect in the receiver. **8. give up the ghost,** to die. —*v.t.* **9.** to ghostwrite (a book, speech, etc.). **10.** to haunt. —*v.i.* **11.** to go about or move like a ghost. **12.** to ghostwrite. [ME *goost,* OE *gāst;* c. G *Geist* spirit] —**ghost′like′,** *adj.*
—**Syn. 1.** apparition, phantom, phantasm, wraith, spook. GHOST, SPECTER, SPIRIT all refer to the disembodied soul of a person. A GHOST is the soul or spirit of a deceased person, which appears or otherwise makes its presence known to man: *the ghost of a drowned child.* A SPECTER is a ghost or apparition of more or less weird, unearthly, or terrifying aspect: *a frightening specter.* SPIRIT is often interchangeable with GHOST but may mean a supernatural being, usually with an indication of good or malign intent toward man: *the spirit of a friend; an evil spirit.*

ghost·ly (gōst′lē), *adj.,* **-li·er, -li·est. 1.** of, characteristic of, or resembling a ghost. **2.** *Literary.* spiritual. [ME; OE *gāstlīc*] —**ghost′li·ness,** *n.*

ghost′ town′, a town permanently abandoned by its inhabitants, esp. one that once was a boom town.

ghost·write (gōst′rīt′), *v.t., v.i.,* **-wrote, -writ·ten, writ·ing.** to write as a ghost writer. [back formation from GHOST WRITER]

ghost′ writ′er, a person who writes speeches, books, articles, etc., for another person who is named as or presumed to be the author. Also, **ghost′writ′er.**

ghoul (go͞ol), *n.* **1.** an evil demon, originally of Oriental legend, supposed to feed on human beings, rob graves, prey on corpses, etc. **2.** a grave robber. **3.** a person who revels in what is revolting. [< Ar *ghūl,* akin to *ghāla* to seize] —**ghoul′ish,** *adj.* —**ghoul′ish·ly,** *adv.* —**ghoul′ish·ness,** *n.*

G.H.Q., *Mil.* general headquarters. Also, **GHQ**

GHz, gigahertz.

GI (jē′ī′), *n., pl.* **GI's** or **GIs,** *adj., v.,* **GI'd, GI'ing.** *Informal.* —*n.* **1.** a member or former member of the U.S. Army, esp. an enlisted man. —*adj.* **2.** rigidly adhering to military regulations and practices: *a sergeant who was more GI than anyone.* **3.** of a standardized style or type issued by the U.S. Army: *GI shoes.* **4.** conforming to the regulations or practices of the U.S. Army: *a GI haircut.* **5.** of, pertaining to, or characteristic of a U.S. enlisted man. —*v.t.* **6.** to clean in preparation for inspection. Also, **G.I.** [orig. abbr. of *galvanized iron,* used in U.S. Army bookkeeping in entering articles (e.g., trash cans) made of it]

Gi, gilbert; gilberts.

gi., gill; gills.

G.I., **1.** galvanized iron. **2.** gastrointestinal. **3.** general issue. **4.** government issue. Also, **GI, g.i.**

Gia·co·met·ti (jä′kə met′ē; *It.* jä′kô met′tē), *n.* **Al·ber·to** (*It.* äl ber′tô), 1901–66, Swiss sculptor and painter.

gi·ant (jī′ənt), *n.* **1.** an imaginary being of human form but superhuman size, strength, etc. **2.** a person or thing of unusually great size, power, importance, etc. **3.** (*often cap.*) *Class. Myth.* any of the Gigantes. —*adj.* **4.** unusually large, great, or strong; gigantic. **5.** great or eminent above others. [ME *geant* < OF; r. OE *gigant* < L *gigant-* (s. of *gigās*) < Gk] —**gi′ant·like′,** *adj.*

gi·ant·ess (jī′ən tis), *n.* **1.** a female giant. **2.** any very large woman. [ME *geauntesse* < OF]

gi·ant·ism (jī′ən tiz′əm), *n.* **1.** *Pathol.* gigantism. **2.** the state or quality of being a giant.

gi′ant liz′ard. See **Komodo dragon.**

gi′ant pan′da, panda (def. 2).

Gi′ants' Cause′way, a large body of basalt, unusual in displaying perfect columnar jointing, on a promontory on the coast of Northern Ireland.

gi′ant star′, *Astron.* a star having a diameter of from 10 to 100 times that of the sun, as Arcturus or Aldebaran. Cf. **supergiant star.**

giaour (jour, jou′ər), *n.* an unbeliever; a non-Muslim, esp. a Christian. [< Turk *giaur* < Pers *gaur,* var. of *gabr*]

gib[1] (gib), *n., v.,* **gibbed, gib·bing.** —*n.* **1.** *Mach.* **a.** a thin, wedgelike strip of metal for controlling the area in which a moving part slides. **b.** a part, fastened by a cotter, for securing an assembly. **2.** (in carpentry or ironwork) a heavy metal strap for fastening two members together. —*v.t.* **3.** to fasten (parts) together by means of a gib. [?]

gib[2] (gib), *n.* a cat, esp. a male cat. [ME *gib(be),* short for *Gilbert* proper name]

Gib., Gibraltar.

gib·ber (jib′ər, gib′-), *v.i.* **1.** to speak inarticulately. **2.** to speak foolishly; chatter. —*n.* **3.** a gibbering utterance. [? freq. of *gib* (obs.) to caterwaul (see GIB[2]); sense and pronunciation influenced by assoc. with JABBER]

gib·be·rel′lic ac′id (jib′ə rel′ik), *Biochem.* a metabolite, $C_{18}H_{21}O_4COOH$, of the fungus *Gibberella fujikuroi,* a stimulator of plant growth. [GIBBERELL(IN) + -IC]

gib·ber·el·lin (jib′ə rel′in), *n.* any of a class of compounds, found in certain mold fungi, that regulates plant growth. [< NL *Gibberell(a)* genus name (dim. of L *gibber* hump) + -IN[2]]

gib·ber·ish (jib′ər ish, gib′-), *n.* **1.** meaningless or unintelligible talk or writing. **2.** talk or writing containing many obscure, pretentious, or technical words. [GIBBER + -ISH[1]]

gib·bet (jib′it), *n., v.,* **-bet·ed, -bet·ing.** —*n.* **1.** a gallows with a projecting arm at the top for suspending and displaying the bodies of criminals after hanging. —*v.t.* **2.** to put to death and display the body of on a gibbet. **3.** to hold up to public scorn. [ME < OF *gibet* (earlier, staff or cudgel), dim. of *gibe* staff, club; see GIBE[1]]

gib·bon (gib′ən), *n.* any of several small, slender, long-armed arboreal anthropoid apes of the genus *Hylobates,* of the East Indies and southern Asia. [< F, appar. from a dialect of India]

Gibbon, genus *Hylobates* (Height 2 ft.)

Gib·bon (gib′ən), *n.* **Edward,** 1737–1794, English historian.

Gib·bons (gib′ənz), *n.* **Orlando,** 1583–1625, English organist and composer.

gib·bos·i·ty (gi bos′i tē, ji-), *n.* **1.** the state of being gibbous. **2.** a protuberance or swelling. [ME < MF *gibbosite* < ML *gibbōsitāt-* (s. of *gibbōsitās*)]

gib·bous (gib′əs, jib′-), *adj.* *Astron.* (of a heavenly body) convex at both edges, as the moon when more than half full. Also, **gib·bose** (gib′ōs, jib′-). See diag. at **moon.** [ME < L *gibbōs(us)* humped = *gibb(a)* hump + *-ōsus* -OUS] —**gib′bous·ly, gib′bose·ly,** *adv.* —**gib′bous·ness, gib′bose·ness,** *n.*

Gibbs (gibz), *n.* **1. James,** 1682–1754, Scottish architect and author. **2. Josiah Willard,** 1839–1903, U.S. physicist.

gibbs·ite (gib′zīt), *n.* a mineral, hydrated aluminum oxide, $Al_2O_3 \cdot 3H_2O$, an important constituent of bauxite ore. [named after George *Gibbs* (d. 1833), American mineralogist; see -ITE[1]]

gibe[1] (jīb), *v.*, **gibed, gib·ing,** *n.* —*v.i.* **1.** to mock; jeer. —*v.t.* **2.** to taunt; deride; jeer. —*n.* **3.** a taunting or sarcastic remark. Also, **jibe.** [? < MF *gib(er)* (to) handle roughly, shake < *gibe* staff, billhook] —**gib′er,** *n.* —**gib′ing·ly,** *adv.* —**Syn. 2.** ridicule. **3.** scoff, jeer.

gibe[2] (jīb), *v.i., v.t.,* **gibed, gib·ing,** *n.* jibe[1].

Gib·e·on (gib′ē ən), *n.* a town in ancient Palestine, NW of Jerusalem. Josh. 9:3.

Gib·e·on·ite (gib′ē ə nīt′), *n.* one of the inhabitants of Gibeon, condemned by Joshua to be hewers of wood and drawers of water for the Israelites. Josh. 9.

GI Bill, *U.S. Informal.* any of various Congressional bills enacted to provide funds for college educations, home-buying loans, and other benefits for armed-services veterans. Also called **GI Bill of Rights.**

gib·let (jib′lit), *n.* Usually, **giblets.** the heart, liver, gizzard, neck, wing, leg ends, and the like, of a fowl, often cooked separately. [ME < OF *gibelet* a stew of game; cf. F *gibelotte* rabbit stew]

Gi·bral·tar (ji brôl′tər), *n.* **1.** a British crown colony comprising a fortress and seaport located on a narrow promontory near the S tip of Spain. 29,934; $1\frac{7}{8}$ sq. mi. **2. Rock of, a.** Ancient, **Calpe.** a long, precipitous mountain nearly coextensive with this colony: one of the Pillars of Hercules. 1396 ft. high; $2\frac{1}{2}$ mi. long. **b.** *Informal.* any person or thing whose strength and endurance can be relied on. **3. Strait of,** a strait between Europe and Africa at the Atlantic entrance to the Mediterranean. $8\frac{1}{2}$–23 mi. wide. **4.** any impregnable fortress or stronghold.

Gib·ran (ji brän′), *n.* **Kah·lil** (kä lēl′), 1883–1931, Lebanese mystic, author, and artist; in the U.S. after 1910.

Gib·son (gib′sən), *n.* **Charles Da·na** (dā′nə), 1867–1944, U.S. artist and illustrator.

Gib·son (gib′sən), *n.* a dry martini cocktail garnished with a pearl onion. [after the surname *Gibson*]

Gib′son Des′ert, a desert in W central Australia: scrub; salt marshes. ab. 85,000 sq. mi.

Gib′son Girl′, the idealized American girl of the 1890's as represented in the illustrations of Charles Dana Gibson.

gid (gid), *n.* *Vet. Pathol.* a disease of cattle and esp. of sheep in which the brain or spinal cord is infested with larvae of the dog tapeworm, *Multiceps multiceps,* producing staggers. Also called **sturdy.** Cf. **waterbrain.** [back formation from GIDDY]

gid·dy (gid′ē), *adj.*, **-di·er, -di·est,** *v.*, **-died, -dy·ing.** —*adj.* **1.** frivolous and light-hearted; impulsive; flighty. **2.** affected with vertigo; dizzy. **3.** attended with or causing dizziness: *a giddy climb.* —*v.t., v.i.* **4.** to make or become giddy. [ME *gidy,* OE *gidig* mad < *god* GOD; orig. sense of divine frenzy] —**gid′di·ly,** *adv.* —**gid′di·ness,** *n.* —**Syn. 1.** fickle, inconstant, vacillating. **2.** light-headed.

Gide (zhēd), *n.* **An·dré (Paul Guil·laume)** (äN drā′ pôl gē yōm′), 1869–1951, French novelist, essayist, poet, and critic: Nobel prize 1947.

Gid·e·on (gid′ē ən), *n.* a judge of Israel and conqueror of the Midianites. Judges 6–8.

Gid′e·ons Interna′tional (gid′ē ənz), **The.** an interdenominational society of laymen organized in 1899 to place Bibles in hotel rooms. Formerly, **Gid′eon Soci′ety.**

gie (gē), *v.i., v.t.*, **gied, gied** or **gien** (gēn), **gie·ing.** *Chiefly Scot.* to give.

Giel·gud (gil′go͝od, gēl′-), *n.* **Sir (Arthur) John,** born 1904, English actor.

Gie·se·king (gē′zə king, -sə-), *n.* **Wal·ter (Wil·helm)** (wôl′tər wil′helm; *Ger.* väl′tər vil′helm), 1895–1956, German pianist and composer.

gift (gift), *n.* **1.** something given voluntarily without charge; present. **2.** the act of giving. **3.** the power or right of giving. **4.** a special ability or capacity; talent. —*v.t.* **5.** to bestow gifts upon; endow with. [ME < Scand; cf. Icel *gift;* c. OE *gift* (ME *yift*) marriage gift; akin to GIVE] —**gift′less,** *adj.* —**Syn. 1.** donation, contribution, offering, benefaction, dowry. See **present**[2]. **4.** faculty, aptitude.

gift′ certif′icate, a certificate entitling the bearer to select merchandise of a specified cash value from a store without cost to him, usually presented as a gift.

gift·ed (gif′tid), *adj.* **1.** having a special talent or ability. **2.** having exceptionally high intelligence: *gifted children.* —**gift′ed·ly,** *adv.* —**gift′ed·ness,** *n.*

gift′ of gab′, *Informal.* an aptitude for speaking glibly, fluently, or persuasively.

gift′ of tongues′. See **speaking in tongues.**

gift-wrap (gift′rap′), *v.*, **-wrapped** or **-wrapt, -wrap·ping,** *n.* —*v.t.* **1.** to wrap (something) for presentation as a gift. —*n.* **2.** giftwrapping.

gift·wrap·ping (gift′rap′ing), *n.* decorative paper, ribbon, etc., for wrapping objects intended as gifts.

Gi·fu (gē′fo͞o′), *n.* a city on S Honshu, in central Japan. 409,000.

gig[1] (gig), *n., v.,* **gigged, gig·ging.** —*n.* **1.** *Naut.* a light boat rowed with four, six, or eight long oars. **2.** a light, two-wheeled, one-horse carriage. **3.** something that whirls. **4.** *Obs.* a toy for whirling or spinning; a top. —*v.i.* **5.** to ride in a gig. [ME *gigge, gig* flighty girl, ? < Scand; akin to Dan *gig* top; cf. Norw *giga* to shake about]

Gig[1] (def. 2)

gig[2] (gig), *n., v.,* **gigged, gig·ging.** —*n.* **1.** a device, commonly four hooks secured back to back, for dragging through a school of fish to hook them through the body. **2.** a spearlike device with a long, thick handle, used for spearing fish and frogs. —*v.t.* **3.** to catch or spear (a fish or frog) with a gig. **4.** to raise the nap on (a fabric). —*v.i.* **5.** to catch fish or frogs with a gig. [shortened from *fizgig* < Sp *fisga* harpoon]

gig[3] (gig), *n., v.,* **gigged, gig·ging.** *Slang.* —*n.* **1.** an official report of a minor infraction of regulations, as in school, the army, etc.; a demerit. **2.** a punishment for a minor infraction of rules. —*v.t.* **3.** to give a gig to or punish (someone) with a gig. [?]

giga-, a learned borrowing from Greek where it meant "giant," used with the meaning "billion" (10^9) in the formation of compound words: *gigameter.* [< Gk *gigā(s)* giant]

gi′ga·e·lec′tron volt′ (jī′gə i lek′tron, jig′ə-, jī′gə-, jig′ə-), one billion (10^9) electron volts. *Abbr.:* GeV, Gev

gi·ga·hertz (jī′gə hûrts′, jig′ə-), *n., pl.* **-hertz, -hertz·es.** one billion (10^9) cycles per second. *Abbr.:* GHz Also called **gi·ga·cy·cle** (jī′gə sī′kəl, jig′ə-).

gi·ga·me·ter (jī′gə mē′tər, jig′ə-), *n.* *Metric System.* a unit of distance equal to 1,000,000 kilometers or 621,370 miles. *Abbr.:* Gm

gi·gan·te·an (jī′gan tē′ən, jī gan′tē ən), *adj.* gigantic. [< L *gigante(us)* of giants (*gigant-* GIANT + *-eus* adj. suffix) + -AN]

Gi·gan·tes (ji gan′tēz), *n.pl.* *Class. Myth.* beings with the heads of men and the bodies of serpents, born to Gaea when she was impregnated with the blood of the mutilated Uranus: the Gigantes attacked the gods but were defeated with the help of Hercules. [< L < Gk (pl.): giants]

gi·gan·tesque (jī′gan tesk′), *adj.* of a gigantic size; of or suited to a giant. [< F < It *gigantesc(o)* = *gigant(e)* GIANT + *-esco* -ESQUE]

gi·gan·tic (jī gan′tik), *adj.* **1.** very large; huge. **2.** of, like, or befitting a giant. [< L *gigant-* GIANT + -IC] —**gi·gan′ti·cal·ly,** *adv.* —**gi·gan′tic·ness,** *n.*

—**Syn. 1.** enormous, immense. GIGANTIC, COLOSSAL, MAMMOTH are used of whatever is physically or metaphorically of great magnitude. GIGANTIC refers to the size of a giant, or to size or scope befitting a giant: *a gigantic stalk of corn.* COLOSSAL refers to the size of a colossus, to anything huge or vast as befitting a hero or god: *a colossal victory.* MAMMOTH refers to the size of the animal of that name and is used esp. of anything large and heavy: *a mammoth battleship.* —**Ant. 1.** tiny.

gi·gan·tism (jī gan′tiz əm, jī′gan tiz′əm), *n.* *Pathol.* abnormally great development in size or stature of the whole body or of parts of the body, most often due to dysfunction of the pituitary gland. [< L *gigant-* GIANT + -ISM]

gi·gan·to·ma·chi·a (jī gan′tə mā′kē ə), *n.* a war of giants, esp. the war of the giants of Greek mythology against the Olympian gods. [< LL < Gk; see GIANT, -O-, -MACHY]

gi·ga·watt (jī′gə wot′, jig′ə-), *n.* one billion (10^9) watts.

gig·gle (gig′əl), *v.*, **-gled, -gling,** *n.* —*v.i.* **1.** to laugh in a silly, undignified way, esp. with short, repeated gasps and titters. —*n.* **2.** a silly, spasmodic laugh; titter. [imit.; cf. D *gigelen,* G *gickeln*] —**gig′gler,** *n.* —**Syn.** snicker, snigger.

gig·gly (gig′lē), *adj.*, **-gli·er, -gli·est.** inclined to giggle.

gig·let (gig′lit), *n.* **1.** a giddy, playful girl. **2.** *Obs.* a lascivious woman. Also, **gig′lot.** [ME *gig(e)lot.* See GIG[1], -LET]

Gi·gli (jē′lyē), *n.* **Be·nia·mi·no** (be′nyä mē′nô), 1890–1957, Italian operatic tenor.

gig·o·lo (jig′ə lō′, zhig′-), *n., pl.* **-los. 1.** a man supported by a woman in return for his sexual attentions and companionship. **2.** a male professional escort or dancing partner. [< F, masc. of *gigole* female dancer < MF *gigu(er)* (to) dance. See JIG[2]]

gig·ot (jig′ət), *n.* **1.** a leg-of-mutton sleeve. **2.** a leg of lamb or mutton. [< MF, appar. dim. of *gigue* fiddle (< Gmc); in allusion to its shape]

gigue (zhēg), *n.* **1.** *Dance.* jig[2] (def. 1). **2.** *Music.* a jig, often forming the last movement in a classical suite. [< F < It *giga,* orig., a fiddle or lute < Gmc; cf. G *Geige*]

GI Joe, *Informal.* an enlisted soldier in the U.S. Army, esp. in WW II.

Gi·jon (gē hôn′; *Sp.* hē hôn′), *n.* a seaport in NW Spain, on the Bay of Biscay. 187,612.

Gi·la (hē′lə), *n.* a river flowing W from SW New Mexico across S Arizona to the Colorado River. 630 mi. long.

Gi′la mon′ster, a large, venomous lizard, *Heloderma suspectum,* of northwestern Mexico and the southwestern U.S., having the skin studded with yellow or orange and black beadlike tubercles. [after the GILA]

Gila monster
(Length to 20 in.)

gil·bert (gil′bərt), *n.* *Elect.* the centimeter-gram-second unit of magnetomotive force, equal to .7958 ampere turns. *Abbr.:* Gi [named after William *Gilbert* (1540–1603), English scientist]

Gil·bert (gil′bərt), *n.* **1. Cass,** 1859–1934, U.S. architect. **2. Sir Humphrey,** 1509?–83, English soldier, navigator, and colonizer in America. **3. Sir William Schwenck** (shwengk), 1836–1917, English dramatist and poet: collaborator with Sir Arthur Sullivan.

Gil′bert and El′lice Is′lands, a former British colony comprising the Gilbert Islands, the Ellice Islands, and other widely scattered islands in the central Pacific. 203 sq. mi. Cf. **Kiribati, Tuvalu.**

Gil′bert Is′lands, a group of islands in the central Pacific, on the equator: formerly part of the British colony of Gilbert and Ellice Islands; now part of Kiribati. 166 sq. mi.

gild[1] (gild), *v.t.*, **gild·ed** or **gilt, gild·ing. 1.** to coat with gold, gold leaf, or a gold-colored substance. **2.** to give a bright, pleasing, or specious aspect to. **3.** *Obs.* to make red, as with blood. [ME *gild(en),* OE *gyldan* < GOLD]

gild[2] (gild), *n.* guild.

gild·ed (gil′did), *adj.* **1.** covered or highlighted with gold or something of a golden color. **2.** having a pleasing, fine, or showy appearance that conceals something of little worth; superficially attractive. [ME; OE *gegyld*]

gild·er[1] (gil′dər), *n.* a person or thing that gilds. [GILD[1] + -ER[1]]

gil·der[2] (gil′dər), *n.* gulden (defs. 1, 2). [see GUILDER]

gild·hall (gild′hôl′), *n.* guildhall.

gild·ing (gil′ding), *n.* **1.** the application of gilt. **2.** the gold leaf or other material with which something is gilded. **3.** the golden surface produced. **4.** any deceptive coating or aspect used to give a pleasing, fine, or showy appearance. [late ME]

Gil·e·ad (gil′ē əd), *n.* **1.** an ancient district of Palestine, E of the Jordan River, in present Jordan. **2. Mount,** a mountain in NW Jordan. 3596 ft.
Gil·e·ad·ite (gil′ē ə dīt′), *n.* **1.** a member of a branch of the Israelite tribe descended from Manasseh. **2.** an inhabitant of ancient Gilead.
Giles (jīlz), *n.* **Saint,** 8th century A.D., Athenian hermit in France.
Gil·ga·mesh (gil′gə mesh′), *n.* a legendary Sumerian king, the hero of Sumerian and Babylonian epics.
gill[1] (gil), *n.* **1.** an aquatic respiratory organ for obtaining oxygen dissolved in the water, usually feathery, platelike, or filamentous. **2.** one of the radiating vertical plates on the underside of the cap of an agaric; lamella. —*v.t.* **3.** to catch (fish) by the gills in a gill net. **4.** to gut or clean (fish). [ME *gile* < Scand; cf. Sw *gäl,* Dan *gælle*] —**gill′-less,** *adj.* —**gill′-like′,** *adj.*
gill[2] (jil), *n.* a unit of liquid measure equal to ¼ pint. [ME *gille* < OF: vat, tub < LL *gillō* wine vessel, *gella* wine measure]
gill[3] (gil), *n.* *Brit. Dial.* a stream; brook; rivulet. [ME *gille* < ON *gil*]
gill[4] (jil), *n.* **1.** a girl; sweetheart. **2.** *Obs.* a wench. [ME; special use of short form of proper name *Gillian*]
Gil·lett (ji let′), *n.* **Frederick Huntington,** 1851–1935, U.S. political leader: Speaker of the House 1919–25.
Gil·lette (ji let′), *n.* **William (Hooker),** 1855–1937, U.S. actor and dramatist.
gill′ fun′gus (gil), an agaricaceous fungus; mushroom.
gil·lie (gil′ē), *n.* *Scot.* a sportsman's attendant, esp. a hunting or fishing guide. Also, **gilly.** [< Gael *gille* lad, servant]
gill′ net′ (gil), a net, suspended vertically in the water, whose meshes catch entering fish by the gills.
gil·ly[1] (gil′ē), *n., pl.* **-lies.** *Scot.* gillie.
gil·ly[2] (gil′ē), *n., pl.* **-lies,** *v.,* **-lied, -ly·ing.** —*n.* **1.** a truck or wagon, esp. one used to transport the equipment of a circus or carnival. —*v.t., v.i.* **2.** to carry or be carried on a gilly. [*gill* (dial.) < ? + -Y[2]]
gil·ly·flow·er (jil′ē flou′ər), *n.* **1.** any of various flowers, as the stock, *Matthiola incana.* **2.** *Archaic or Dial.* the clove pink. Also, **gil′li·flow′er.** [alter. (through influence of FLOWER) of ME *gilofre, geraflour* < OF *gilofre, girofle* < L *caryophyll(um)* < Gk *karyóphyllon* clove (*káryo(n)* nut + *phýllon* leaf)]
Gil·man (gil′mən), *n.* **Daniel Coit** (koit), 1831–1908, U.S. educator.
Gi·lo·lo (jī lō′lō, ji-), *n.* Halmahera.
Gi·lson (zhēl sôN′), *n.* **É·tienne Hen·ry** (ā tyen′ äN rē′), 1884–1978, French historian, esp. of medieval Christian philosophy.
Gil·son·ite (gil′sə nīt′), *n.* *Trademark.* an extremely pure asphalt valuable for the manufacture of paints and varnishes. Also called **uintaite, uintahite.**
gilt[1] (gilt), *v.* **1.** a pt. and pp. of **gild**[1]. —*adj.* **2.** gilded. **3.** gold in color; golden. —*n.* **4.** the gold or other material applied in gilding; gilding.
gilt[2] (gilt), *n.* a young female swine, esp. one that has not produced a litter. [ME *gilt(e)* < Scand; cf. OIcel *gylta, gilt(r)*]
gilt-edged (gilt′ejd′), *adj.* **1.** having the edge or edges gilded: *gilt-edged paper.* **2.** of the highest or best quality, kind, etc.: *gilt-edged securities.* Also, **gilt′-edge′.**
gim·bals (jim′bəlz, gim′-), *n.* (*construed as sing.*) Sometimes, **gimbal.** a contrivance, consisting of a ring or base on an axis, which permits an object, as a ship's compass, mounted in or on it to tilt freely in any direction, in effect, suspending the object so that it will remain horizontal even when its support is tipped. Also called **gim′bal ring′.** [alter. of GEMEL]
gim·crack (jim′krak′), *n.* **1.** a showy, useless trifle; gewgaw. —*adj.* **2.** showy but useless. [ME *gib(e)crake;* cf. ME *gibben* to waver (< OF *giber* to shake)]
gim·crack·er·y (jim′krak′ə rē), *n.* **1.** worthless or useless trifles, ornaments, etc. **2.** obvious or contrived effects, esp. in art, literature, etc.
gim·el (gim′əl; *Heb.* gē′mel), *n.* the third letter of the Hebrew alphabet. [< Heb *gīmel,* lit., camel]
gim·let (gim′lit), *n.* **1.** a small tool for boring holes, consisting of a shaft with a pointed screw at one end and a cross handle at the other. **2.** a cocktail made with gin or vodka and sweetened lime juice. —*v.t.* **3.** to pierce with or as with a gimlet. —*adj.* **4.** able to penetrate or bore through. [ME < OF *guimbelet* < Gmc; cf. MD *wimmel* WIMBLE]

Gimlet

gim·mal (gim′əl, jim′əl), *n.* any of various joints for transmitting motion between rotating parts, as in a timepiece. [alter. of GEMEL]
gim·mick (gim′ik), *n.* **1.** *U.S. Slang.* an ingenious or novel device, scheme, deception, or hidden disadvantage. **2.** *Informal.* a hidden mechanical device by which a magician works a trick or a gambler controls a game of chance. [?] —**gim′mick·y,** *adj.*
gim·mick·ry (gim′ik rē), *n.* **1.** the use or proliferation of gimmicks. **2.** an abundance of gimmicks.
gimp[1] (gimp), *n.* a flat trimming of silk, wool, or other cord. [appar. < D < ?]
gimp[2] (gimp), *n.* *Dial.* spirit, vigor, or ambition. [?]
gimp[3] (gimp), *n.* *Slang.* **1.** a limp. **2.** a cripple. [?]
gin[1] (jin), *n.* **1.** an alcoholic liquor made by distilling grain mash with juniper berries. **2.** a similar liquor made by redistilling spirits with flavoring agents. [shortened from GENEVA]
gin[2] (jin), *n., v.,* **ginned, gin·ning.** —*n.* **1.** See **cotton gin.** **2.** a trap or snare for game. **3.** a stationary prime mover having a drive shaft rotated by horizontal beams pulled by horses walking in a circle. —*v.t.* **4.** to clear (cotton) of seeds with a gin. **5.** to snare (game). [ME *gyn,* aph. var. of OF *engin* ENGINE] —**gin′ner,** *n.*
gin[3] (gin), *v.i., v.t.,* **gan, gun, gin·ning.** *Archaic.* to begin. [ME *ginne(n),* OE *ginnan,* aph. var. of *onginnan, beginnen* to BEGIN]
gin[4] (jin), *n.* *Cards.* a variety of rummy for two players, in which a player wins by matching all 10 cards or can end a game by laying down a hand containing 10 or fewer points in unmatched cards. Also called **gin rummy.** [? special use of GIN[1]]
gin′ block′ (jin), *Mach.* a block having a large sheave in an open metal frame, used esp. to support a cargo whip.
gin·ger (jin′jər), *n.* **1.** the pungent, spicy rhizome of any of the reedlike plants of the genus *Zingiber,* esp. of *Z. officinale,* used in cookery and medicine. **2.** any of these plants. **3.** a yellowish or reddish brown. **4.** *Informal.* piquancy; animation. —*adj.* **5.** flavored or made with ginger. [ME *ginger, gingivere* < OF *gingivre* < ML *gingiber* for L *zingiberi* < Gk *zingiberis*]
gin′ger ale′, a carbonated soft drink flavored with ginger extract.
gin′ger beer′, a soft drink similar to ginger ale but containing more ginger flavor.
gin·ger·bread (jin′jər bred′), *n.* **1.** a type of cake flavored with ginger and molasses. **2.** a rolled cooky similarly flavored, often cut in fanciful shapes, and sometimes frosted. **3.** elaborate, gaudy, or superfluous ornamentation. —*adj.* **4.** heavily, gaudily, and superfluously ornamented: *a gingerbread style of 19th-century architecture.* [ME *gingebreed* (influenced by *breed* bread), var. of *gingebrad, -brat* ginger paste < OF *gingembras, -brat* preserved ginger < ML **gingi(m)brāt(um)* medicinal preparation (neut. ptp.) < *gingiber* GINGER]
gin′gerbread tree′, a tree, *Parinarium macrophyllum,* of western Africa, bearing a large, edible, farinaceous fruit (**gin′gerbread plum′**).
gin′ger group′, *Chiefly Brit.* the most active group within an organization, as a political party.
gin·ger·ly (jin′jər lē), *adv.* **1.** warily. **2.** *Obs.* mincingly; daintily. —*adj.* **3.** cautious; wary. [perh. < MF *gensor, genzor* delicate, pretty, positive use of comp. of *gent* GENTLE] —**gin′ger·li·ness,** *n.*
gin′ger nut′, *Chiefly Brit.* a gingersnap.
gin·ger·snap (jin′jər snap′), *n.* a small, thin, brittle cooky flavored with ginger and molasses.
gin·ger·y (jin′jə rē), *adj.* **1.** gingerlike; pungent; spicy. **2.** of the color of ginger.
ging·ham (ging′əm), *n.* yarn-dyed, plain-weave cotton fabric, usually striped or checked. [< F *guingan* << Malay *ginggang,* lit., striped]
gin·gi·va (jin jī′və, jin′jə-), *n., pl.* **-gi·vae** (-jī′vē, -jə vē′). gum[2] (def. 1). [< L]
gin·gi·val (jin jī′vəl, jin′jə vəl), *adj.* **1.** of or pertaining to the gums. **2.** *Phonet.* alveolar.
gin·gi·vi·tis (jin′jə vī′tis), *n.* *Pathol.* inflammation of the gums. [< NL]
gink (gingk), *n.* *Slang.* a man, esp. one who is peculiar, insignificant, or unpleasant. [?]
gink·go (gingk′gō, jingk′-), *n., pl.* **-goes.** a large, ornamental, gymnospermous tree, *Ginkgo biloba,* native to China, having fan-shaped leaves, fleshy fruit, and edible nuts. Also, **ging′ko.** [< Jap *ginkyo* = *gin* silver + *kyo* apricot]
gin′ mill′ (jin), *Slang.* a bar or saloon, esp. a cheap or disreputable one.
Gin·nun·ga·gap (gin′o͝ong gä gäp′), *n.* *Scand. Myth.* a primordial void existing between Niflheim and Muspelheim.
gin′ rum′my, *Cards.* gin[4].
Gins·berg (ginz′bərg), **Allen,** born 1926, U.S. poet.
gin·seng (jin′seng), *n.* **1.** either of two araliaceous plants, *Panax Ginseng* (*Schinseng*), of China, Korea, etc., or *P. quinquefolium,* of North America, having an aromatic root. **2.** the root itself. **3.** a preparation made from it. Also, **genseng.** [< Chin (Mandarin) *jên shên* = *jên* man + *shên* of obscure meaning]
Gin·za (gin′zə), *n.* **the,** a street in Tokyo, Japan, famous for its nightclubs and bars.
Gior·gio·ne (jôr jô′ne; *Eng.* jôr jō′nē), *n.* (*Giorgione de Castelfranco, Giorgio Barbarelli*) 1478?–1511, Italian painter.
Gio·tto (jot′ō; *It.* jôt′tô), *n.* (*Giotto di Bondone*) 1266?–1337, Florentine painter, sculptor, and architect.
gip (jip), *v.t.,* **gipped, gip·ping,** *n.* *U.S. Slang.* gyp[1]. —**gip′per,** *n.*
gi·pon (ji pon′, jip′on), *n.* jupon.
gi·raffe (jə raf′ *or, esp. Brit.,* -räf′), *n.* **1.** a tall, long-necked, spotted ruminant, *Giraffa camelopardalis,* of Africa: the tallest living quadruped animal. **2.** (*cap.*) *Astron.* the constellation Camelopardalis. [< F *girafe* < Ar *zarāfah,* prob. of Afr orig.]

Giraffe
(Height 18 ft.)

gir·an·dole (jir′ən dōl′), *n.* **1.** a rotating and radiating firework. **2.** an ornate bracket for candelabra or the like. **3.** a pendant, as an earring, surrounded by smaller pendants or jewels. Also, **gi·ran·do·la** (ji ran′dᵊlə). [< F < It *girandol(a)* < *gir(are)* (to) turn in a circle < L *gӯrāre* < *gӯr(us)* a circle < Gk *gŷros*]
Gi·rard (jə rärd′), *n.* **Stephen,** 1750–1831, American merchant, banker, and philanthropist, born in France.
gir·a·sol (jir′ə sôl′, -sōl′, -sol′), *n.* **1.** an opal that reflects light in a bright luminous glow. **2.** See **Jerusalem artichoke.** —*adj.* **3.** (of a stone) translucent and bluish-white with reddish reflections under strong light; opalescent. Also, **gir·a·sole** (jir′ə sōl′), **girosol.** [< It = *gira(re)* (to) turn (see GIRANDOLE) + *sole* the sun]
Gi·raud (zhē rō′), *n.* **Hen·ri Ho·no·ré** (äN rē′ ô nô rā′) 1879–1949, French general.
Gi·rau·doux (zhēr′ō do͞o′; *Fr.* zhē rō do͞o′), *n.* **Jean** (zhäN), 1882–1944, French novelist, playwright, and diplomat.

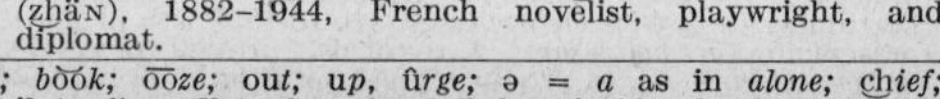

gird[1] (gûrd), *v.t.*, **gird·ed** or **girt, gird·ing.** **1.** to encircle or bind with a belt or band. **2.** to surround; hem in. **3.** to prepare (oneself) for action. **4.** to provide, equip, or invest, as with power, strength, etc. [ME *gird(en)*, OE *gyrdan;* c. G *gürten*]

gird[2] (gûrd), *v.i.* **1.** to gibe; jeer (usually fol. by *at*). —*v.t.* **2.** *Obs.* to gibe or jeer at; taunt. —*n.* **3.** *Archaic.* a gibe. [ME *gyrd* a stroke, blow, hence a cutting remark < *girden* to strike, smite < ?]

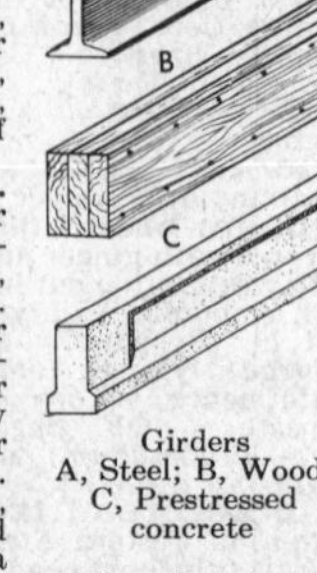

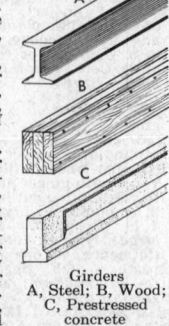

Girders
A, Steel; B, Wood; C, Prestressed concrete

gird·er (gûr′dər), *n.* **1.** a large beam, as of steel, reinforced concrete, or wood, for supporting masonry, joists, etc. **2.** a principal beam of wood, steel, etc., supporting the ends of joists.

gir·dle (gûr′dᵊl), *n.*, *v.*, **-dled, -dling.** —*n.* **1.** a supporting undergarment for the abdomen and hips, usually elasticized or boned. **2.** a belt, cord, sash, or the like, worn about the waist. **3.** anything that encircles, confines, or limits. **4.** *Jewelry.* the edge or narrow band between the upper and lower facets of a gem. **5.** *Anat.* the bony framework that unites the upper or lower extremities to the axial skeleton. **6.** a ring made about a tree trunk, branch, etc., by removing a band of bark. —*v.t.* **7.** to encircle with a belt; gird. **8.** to encompass; enclose; encircle. **9.** to move around (something or someone) in a circle. **10.** to cut away the bark in a ring around (a tree, branch, etc.). [ME; OE *gyrdel* < *girdan* to GIRD[1]] —**gir′dle·like′,** *adj.*

gir·dler (gûrd′lər), *n.* **1.** a person or thing that girdles. **2.** any of several insects, as a beetle, *Oncideres cingulata* **(twig girdler),** that cuts a groove around the bark of a twig, stem, etc. **3.** a person who makes girdles. [late ME; see GIRDLE, -ER[1]]

Gir·gen·ti (*It.* jēʀ jen′tē), *n.* former name of **Agrigento.**

girl (gûrl), *n.* **1.** a female child or young person. **2.** a young unmarried woman. **3.** a female servant or employee. **4.** a man's or boy's sweetheart. **5.** *Informal.* a woman. [ME *gurle, girle* child, young person, OE *gyrl-* (in *gyrlgyden* virgin goddess); cf. LG *göre* young person]

girl′ Fri′day, a female office worker with a wide variety of secretarial and clerical duties, esp. in a small office. Also, **gal Friday.** [modeled on MAN FRIDAY]

girl′ friend′, **1.** a female friend. **2.** a boy's or man's sweetheart.

girl′ guide′, a member of a British organization of girls **(Girl′ Guides′),** related to the Girl Scouts, founded by Lord Robert S. S. Baden-Powell and his sister Lady Agnes in 1910.

girl·hood (gûrl′ho͝od), *n.* **1.** the state or time of being a girl. **2.** girls collectively: *the nation's girlhood.*

girl·ie (gûr′lē), *adj.* **1.** featuring or depicting scantily clad young women: *a girlie magazine; a girlie show.* —*n.* **2.** a term of address for a girl or young woman. Also, **girl′y.**

girl·ish (gûr′lish), *adj.* of, like, or befitting a girl or girlhood. —**girl′ish·ly,** *adv.* —**girl′ish·ness,** *n.*

girl′ scout′, a member of an organization of girls **(Girl′ Scouts′)** founded in the U.S. in 1912 by Juliette Low to develop health, character, and homemaking ability.

gi·ro (jī′rō), *n.*, *pl.* **-ros.** autogiro. [by shortening]

Gi·ronde (jə rond′; *Fr.* zhē ʀôɴd′), *n.* an estuary in SW France, formed by the junction of the Garonne and Dordogne rivers. 45 mi. long.

Gi·ron·dist (jə ron′dist), *n.* **1.** *Fr. Hist.* a member of a political party of moderate republicans (1791–93) whose leaders were from the Gironde area. —*adj.* **2.** of or pertaining to the Girondists. [< F *Girondiste*] —**Gi·ron′dism,** *n.*

gir·o·sol (jir′ə sôl′, -sol′, -sol′), *n.* girasol.

girt[1] (gûrt), *v.* a pt. and pp. of **gird**[1].

girt[2] (gûrt), *v.t.* gird[1] (def. 1).

girt[3] (gûrt), *n.*, *v.t.* girth[1].

girt[4] (gûrt), *n.* *Carpentry.* **1.** a timber or plate connecting the corner posts of an exterior wooden frame, as a braced frame, at a floor above the ground floor. **2.** a heavy beam, as for supporting the ends of rafters. [alter. of GIRTH[1]]

girth[1] (gûrth), *n.* **1.** the measure around anything; circumference. **2.** a band that passes underneath a horse or other animal to hold a saddle in place. **3.** anything that encircles or girdles. —*v.t.* **4.** to bind or fasten with a girth. **5.** to girdle; encircle. Also, **girt.** [ME *girth, gerth* < Scand; cf. Icel *gjördh* girdle, hoop; akin to GIRD[1]]

girth[2] (gûrth), *n.* *Obs.* grith.

Gir·tin (gûr′tin), *n.* **Thomas,** 1775–1802, English painter.

Gis·borne (giz′bərn), *n.* a seaport on E North Island, in N New Zealand. 31,790.

Gis·card d'Es·taing (zhē skaʀ de staɴ′), **Va·lé·ry** (va lā ʀē′), born 1926, French politician: president 1974–81.

gis·mo (giz′mō), *n.*, *pl.* **-mos.** *Informal.* a gadget; a thing. Also, **gizmo.** [?]

Gis·sing (gis′ing), *n.* **George (Robert),** 1857–1903, English novelist.

gist (jist), *n.* **1.** the main or essential part of a matter: *What was the gist of his speech?* **2.** the ground of a legal action. [ME *giste* < OF *gist,* 3rd pers. pres. indic. of *gesir* to lie, *gesir en* to consist in, depend on < L *jacēre* to lie]

git (git), *v.* *Dial.* get.

git·tern (git′ərn), *n.* cittern. [ME *gitern(e)* < OF *guiterne.*]

Giu·ba (jo͞o′bä), *n.* Italian name of **Juba.**

Giu·ki (gyo͞o′kē), *n.* (in the *Volsunga Saga*) a king, the father of Gudrun and the husband of Grimhild. Also, **Gjuki.**

Giu·lio Ro·ma·no (jo͞ol′yô ʀô mä′nô), (*Giulio Pippi de' Giannuzzi*) 1492?–1546, Italian painter and architect.

give (giv), *v.*, **gave, giv·en, giv·ing,** *n.* —*v.t.* **1.** to present voluntarily; bestow: *to give a present.* **2.** to place in someone's care. **3.** to hand to someone: *Give me a match.* **4.** to pay or transfer possession to another in exchange for something: *What will you give for my car?* **5.** to grant (permission, opportunity, etc.): *Give me a chance.* **6.** to set forth or show; present: *He gave no reasons.* **7.** to furnish, provide, or proffer: *to give evidence.* **8.** to produce, yield, or afford. **9.** to make, do, or perform: *to give a lurch.* **10.** to put forth, emit, or utter; issue: *to give a cry.* **11.** to impart or communicate: *to give advice.* **12.** to deal or administer: *to give medicine.* **13.** to relinquish or sacrifice: *to give one's life for a cause.* **14.** to perform publicly: *to give a concert.* **15.** to cause; be responsible for (usually fol. by an infinitive): *They gave me to understand that you would be there.* **16.** to care about something to the extent of: *I don't give a hoot.* **17.** to present (someone) to an audience. **18.** to propose as the subject of a toast: *Ladies and gentlemen, I give you our country.* **19.** to provide as an entertainment: *to give a dinner.* **20.** to assign or allot, as a ration, name, etc. **21.** to attribute or ascribe: *to give the Devil his due.* **22.** to cause or occasion: *She gives me a pain in the neck.* **23.** to award by verdict or after consideration: *A decision was given for the defendant.* **24.** to inflict as a punishment; give a sentence of. **25.** to pledge or execute and deliver: *to give bond.* **26.** to concede or grant, as a point in an argument, a disputed score in a game, etc. —*v.i.* **27.** to make a gift or gifts; contribute. **28.** to afford a view or passage; open (usually fol. by *on, onto,* etc.): *The window gives on the sea.* **29.** to yield under force, pressure, etc. **30.** to collapse; break down; fail. **31.** *Informal.* to divulge information: *Okay now, give! What happened?* **32.** **give away, a.** to give as a present; bestow. **b.** to present (the bride) to the bridegroom in a marriage ceremony. **c.** to expose or betray (a person). **d.** to reveal (a secret): *That remark gives away his real opinion on the matter.* **33. give battle.** See **battle**[1] (def. 4). **34. give birth to.** See **birth** (def. 8). **35. give ground,** to yield before superior force, as of arms or of reasoning. **36. give in, a.** to acknowledge defeat; yield. **b.** to hand in; deliver. **37. give it to,** *Informal.* to reprimand or punish. **38. give of,** to devote or contribute generously of. **39. give off,** to put forth; emit, as odors. **40. give out, a.** to send out; emit. **b.** to make public; announce. **c.** to distribute; issue. **d.** to become exhausted. **e.** to become used up; fail: *The fuel gave out.* **41. give over, a.** to put into the care of; transfer. **b.** to put an end to; stop. **c.** to indulge in without restraint: *He gave himself over to tears.* **d.** to devote to a specified activity: *The day was given over to relaxing.* **42. give rise to.** See **rise** (def. 51). **43. give up, a.** to abandon hope; despair. **b.** to desist from: *to give up smoking.* **c.** to surrender; relinquish. **d.** to devote (oneself) entirely to: *The student gave himself up to studying.* —*n.* **44.** the quality or state of being resilient; springiness. [ME < Scand (cf. Dan *give*); r. ME *yeven, yiven,* OE *gefan, gi(e)fan;* c. D *geven,* G *geben,* Goth *giban*] —**give′a·ble,** *adj.* —**giv′er,** *n.*

—**Syn. 1.** offer, vouchsafe, furnish, provide, supply, donate, contribute. GIVE, CONFER, GRANT, PRESENT may mean that something concrete or abstract is bestowed on one person by another. GIVE is the general word: *to give someone a book, permission, etc.* CONFER usually means to give an honor or a favor; it implies courteous and gracious giving: *to confer a degree.* GRANT is limited to the idea of acceding to a request; it may apply to the bestowal of privileges, or the fulfillment of an expressed wish: *to grant a charter, a prayer, permission, etc.* PRESENT, a more formal word than give, usually implies a certain ceremony in the giving: *to present a citation to a regiment.* **26.** cede, yield. —**Ant. 1.** receive.

give-and-take (giv′ən tāk′), *n.* **1.** the practice of dealing by compromise or mutual concession; cooperation. **2.** good-humored exchange of talk, ideas, etc.

give·a·way (giv′ə wā′), *n.* **1.** a betrayal or disclosure, usually unintentional. **2.** a premium, as given to promote sales. **3.** an unscrupulous deal, esp. one which benefits some while defrauding others. **4.** a radio or television program on which prizes are given to contestants.

give·back (giv′bak′), *n.* (in union negotiations) a reduction in employee salary or benefits conceded by a union in exchange for other benefits or in recognition of depressed economic conditions.

giv·en (giv′ən), *v.* **1.** pp. of **give.** —*adj.* **2.** stated, fixed, or specified: *at a given time.* **3.** addicted or disposed (often fol. by *to*): *given to talking.* **4.** bestowed as a gift; conferred. **5.** assigned as a basis of calculation, reasoning, etc.: *Given A and B, C follows.* **6.** (on official documents) executed and delivered as of the date shown. —*n.* **7.** an established fact, condition, factor, etc.

giv′en name′, the name given to one, as contrasted with an inherited family name; first name.

Gi·za (gē′zə), *n.* **1.** a governorate in the United Arab Republic, SW of Cairo. 1,336,000 (1960). **2.** a city in and the capital of this governorate: the ancient Egyptian pyramids and the Sphinx are located nearby. 276,200 (est. 1962). Also, **Gi′zeh.**

giz·mo (giz′mō), *n.*, *pl.* **-mos.** gismo.

giz·zard (giz′ərd), *n.* **1.** the muscular portion of the stomach of birds, in which food is ground after leaving the proventriculus; ventriculus. **2.** *Informal.* the innards or viscera collectively, esp. the intestine and stomach. [ME *giser* < OF *giser, gezier* (F *gésier*) < VL **giger(ium);* cf. L *gigeria* cooked entrails of poultry]

Gjel·le·rup (gel′ə ro͞op), *n.* **Karl** (kärl), 1857–1919, Danish novelist: Nobel prize 1917.

Gju·ki (gyo͞o′kē), *n.* Giuki.

Gk, Greek (def. 4). Also, **Gk.**

Gl, *Chem.* glucinum.

gl., **1.** glass. **2.** gloss.

gla·bel·la (glə bel′ə), *n.*, *pl.* **-bel·lae** (-bel′ē). *Anat.* the flat area of bone between the eyebrows. [< NL, fem. of L *glabellus* smooth, hairless = *glab(er)* without hair, smooth + *-ella* dim. suffix] —**gla·bel′lar,** *adj.*

gla·brate (glā′brāt, -brit), *adj.* **1.** *Zool.* glabrous. **2.** *Bot.* becoming glabrous; somewhat glabrous. [< L *glabrāt(us)* made bare, deprived of hair (ptp. of *glabrāre*)]

gla·brous (glā′brəs), *adj.* *Zool., Bot.* smooth or bald; having a surface devoid of hair or pubescence. [< L *glabr-* (s. of *glaber*) smooth, hairless + -OUS] —**gla′brous·ness,** *n.*

gla·cé (gla sā′), *adj.*, *v.*, **-céed, -cé·ing.** —*adj.* **1.** frozen. **2.** frosted or iced, as cake. **3.** candied, as fruits. **4.** finished with a gloss, as kid or silk. —*v.t.* **5.** to make glacé; ice. [< F, ptp. of *glacer* to freeze < *glace* ice < L *glac(iēs)*]

gla·cial (glā′shəl), *adj.* **1.** of, pertaining to, or characterized by the presence of ice in extensive masses or glaciers. **2.** resulting from the action of ice or glaciers: *glacial terrain.* **3.** bitterly cold; frigid; icy. **4.** icily unsympathetic or immovable: *a glacial stare.* **5.** *Chem.* of, pertaining to, or tending to develop into icelike crystals. [< L *glaciāl(is)* icy. See GLACÉ, -AL[1]] —**gla′cial·ly,** *adv.*

gla′cial ace′tic ac′id, *Chem.* acetic acid of at least 99.5 percent concentration, solidifying at 16.7°C.

gla′cial ep′och, **1.** Also called **gla′cial pe′riod.** the geologically recent Pleistocene epoch, during which much of the northern hemisphere was covered by great ice sheets. **2.** any one of the Permian, Carboniferous, Cambrian, or Precambrian glaciations.

gla·ci·ate (glā′shē āt′, -sē-), *v.,* **-at·ed, -at·ing.** —*v.t.* **1.** to cover with ice or glaciers. **2.** to affect by glacial action. —*v.i.* **3.** to become frozen or covered with ice or glaciers. [< L *glaciāt(us)* made into ice (ptp. of *glaciāre*). See GLACÉ, -ATE[1]] —**gla′ci·a′tion,** *n.*

gla·cier (glā′shər), *n.* an extended mass of ice formed from snow falling and accumulating over the years and moving very slowly, either descending from high mountains, as in valley glaciers, or moving outward from centers of accumulation, as in continental glaciers. [< dial. F, OF *glace* < LL *glacia* (alter. of L *glaciēs* ice)] —**gla′ciered,** *adj.*

Gla′cier Na′tional Park′, a national park in NW Montana: glaciers; lakes; forest reserve. 1534 sq. mi.

gla·ci·ol·o·gy (glā′shē ol′ə jē, -sē-), *n.* the branch of geology that deals with the nature, distribution, and action of glaciers and with their effects on the earth's topography. [GLACI(ER) + -O- + -LOGY] —**gla·ci·o·log·i·cal** (glā′shē ə loj′i kəl, -sē-), **gla′ci·o·log′ic,** *adj.* —**gla′ci·ol′o·gist, gla·cial·ist** (glā′shə list), *n.*

gla·cis (glā′sis, glas′is), *n., pl.* **gla·cis** (glā′sēz, -siz, glas′ēz, -iz), **gla·cis·es.** **1.** a gentle slope. **2.** *Fort.* a bank of earth in front of a fortification. [< MF; akin to OF *glacier* to slip or slide. See GLANCE[1]]

Glack·ens (glak′ənz), *n.* **William James,** 1870–1938, U.S. painter and illustrator.

glad[1] (glad), *adj.,* **glad·der, glad·dest,** *v.,* **glad·ded, glad·ding.** —*adj.* **1.** feeling joy or pleasure; delighted; pleased. **2.** attended with or causing joy or pleasure: *a glad occasion.* **3.** characterized by or showing cheerfulness, joy, or pleasure, as looks, utterances, etc. —*v.t.* **4.** *Archaic.* to make glad. [ME; OE *glæd;* c. Icel *gladhr* bright, glad, D *glad,* G *glatt* smooth; akin to L *glaber* smooth] —**glad′ly,** *adv.* —**glad′ness,** *n.* —**Syn. 1.** elated, gratified. **3.** merry, joyous, joyful, cheerful, happy, cheery. —**Ant. 1–3.** sad.

glad[2] (glad), *n. Informal.* gladiolus (def. 1). [by shortening]

glad·den (glad′ən), *v.t.* **1.** to make glad. —*v.i.* **2.** *Obs.* to be glad. [ME] —**glad′den·er,** *n.* —**Syn. 1.** See **cheer.**

glade (glād), *n.* an open space in a forest. [akin to GLAD[1], in obs. sense "bright"] —**glade′like′,** *adj.*

glad′ eye′, *Informal.* a friendly or interested glance, esp. one intended to encourage attentions from someone of the opposite sex.

glad′ hand′, *Informal.* a hearty welcome or reception that is often effusive or hypocritical.

glad-hand (glad′hand′), *v.t. Informal.* **1.** to greet warmly. **2.** to greet in an insincerely effusive manner.

glad·i·ate (glad′ē it, -āt′, glā′dē-), *adj. Bot.* sword-shaped. [< L *gladi(us)* sword + -ATE[1]]

glad·i·a·tor (glad′ē ā′tər), *n.* **1.** (in ancient Rome) an armed person, often a slave or captive, who was compelled to fight for the entertainment of the spectators. **2.** a person who engages in a fight or controversy. **3.** a prizefighter. [< L *gladiātōr-* (s. of *gladiātor*) = *gladi(us)* sword + *-ātōr-* -ATOR] —**glad·i·a·to·ri·al** (glad′ē ə tōr′ē əl, -tôr′-), *adj.*

glad·i·o·la (glad′ē ō′lə), *n.* gladiolus (def. 1). [< L, neut. pl. treated as if fem. sing.] —**glad′i·o′lar,** *adj.*

glad·i·o·lus (glad′ē ō′ləs), *n., pl.* **-lus, -li** (-lī), **-lus·es** for 1; **-li** for 2. **1.** any iridaceous plant of the genus *Gladiolus,* native esp. to Africa, having erect, gladiate leaves and spikes of variously colored flowers. **2.** *Anat.* the middle and largest segment of the sternum. Cf. **manubrium** (def. 2a), **xiphisternum.** [< L: small sword, sword lily, dim. of *gladius* sword]

glad′ rags′, *Slang.* dressy clothes, esp. evening clothes.

glad·some (glad′səm), *adj.* **1.** giving joy; delightful. **2.** glad[1]. [ME] —**glad′some·ly,** *adv.* —**glad′some·ness,** *n.*

Glad·stone (glad′stōn′, -stən), *n.* **William Ew·art** (yōō′ərt), 1809–98, British statesman: prime minister four times between 1868 and 1894.

Glad·stone (glad′stōn′, -stən), *n.* **1.** a four-wheeled pleasure carriage with a calash top, two inside seats, and dickey seats. **2.** See **Gladstone bag.** [after William GLADSTONE]

Glad′stone bag′, a small rectangular suitcase hinged to open into two compartments of equal size. [after William GLADSTONE]

Glag·o·lit·ic (glag′ə lit′ik), *adj.* noting or written in an alphabet formerly used for Old Church Slavonic and other Slavic languages: replaced by Cyrillic. [< NL *glagolitic(us),* irreg. < Serbo-Croatian *glagolica* < OSlav *glagolŭ* word]

glaik·it (glā′kit), *adj. Scot. and North Eng.* **1.** foolish; senseless. **2.** (of women) giddy; flighty. Also, **glaik′et.** [ME < ?] —**glaik′it·ness, glaik′et·ness,** *n.*

glair (glâr), *n.* **1.** the white of an egg. **2.** a glaze or size made of egg white. **3.** any viscous substance like egg white. —*v.t.* **4.** to coat with glair. [ME *glaire* < OF: white of an egg < VL **clāria;* cf. L *clārus* clear]

glaire (glâr), *n., v.t.,* **glaired, glair·ing.** glair.

glair·y (glâr′ē), *adj.,* **glair·i·er, glair·i·est.** **1.** of the nature of glair; viscous. **2.** covered with glair. Also, **glair′e·ous.** —**glair′i·ness,** *n.*

glaive (glāv), *n. Archaic.* a sword or broadsword. [ME < OF *glaive, glai* < L *glad(ius)* sword] —**glaived,** *adj.*

Gla·mor·gan·shire (glə môr′gən shēr′, -shər), *n.* a county in SE Wales. 1,227,828 (1961); 816 sq. mi. *Co. seat:* Cardiff. Also called **Gla·mor′gan.**

glam·or·ize (glam′ə rīz′), *v.t.,* **-ized, -iz·ing.** **1.** to make glamorous. **2.** to glorify or romanticize. Also, **glamourize.** —**glam′or·i·za′tion,** *n.* —**glam′or·iz′er,** *n.*

glam·or·ous (glam′ər əs), *adj.* **1.** full of glamour; fascinatingly attractive and alluring. **2.** full of excitement and adventure. —**glam′or·ous·ly,** *adv.* —**glam′or·ous·ness,** *n.*

glam·our (glam′ər), *n.* **1.** alluring charm, fascination, and attractiveness. **2.** excitement and adventure: *the glamour of being an explorer.* **3.** magic or enchantment; witchery. Also, **glam′or.** [earlier *glammar,* dissimilated var. of GRAMMAR in sense of occult learning]

glam·our·ize (glam′ə rīz′), *v.t.,* **-ized, -iz·ing.** glamorize. —**glam′our·i·za′tion,** *n.* —**glam′our·iz′er,** *n.*

glance[1] (glans, gläns), *v.,* **glanced, glanc·ing,** *n.* —*v.i.* **1.** to look quickly or briefly. **2.** to gleam or flash. **3.** to strike a surface or object obliquely, esp. so as to bounce off at an angle (often fol. by *off*): *The arrow glanced off his shield.* **4.** to allude briefly to a subject in passing. —*v.t. Archaic.* **5.** to cast a glance or brief look at; catch a glimpse of. **6.** to cast or reflect, as a gleam. **7.** to throw or shoot (something) so that it glances off a surface or object. —*n.* **8.** a quick or brief look. **9.** a gleam or flash of light. **10.** a deflected movement or course; an oblique rebound. **11.** a passing reference or allusion; insinuation. **12.** *Cricket.* a stroke to deflect the ball. [late ME; nasalized var. (perh. influenced by obs. *glent;* see GLINT) of ME *glacen* to strike a glancing blow < OF *glac(i)er* to slip, slide < L *glaciāre* to freeze. See GLACÉ] —**glanc′ing·ly,** *adv.* —**Syn. 2.** glisten, scintillate. See **flash.**

glance[2] (glans, gläns), *n. Mining, Mineral.* any of various minerals having a luster that indicates a metallic nature. [< G *Glanz,* brightness, luster]

gland[1] (gland), *n.* **1.** *Anat.* **a.** a cell, group of cells, or organ producing a secretion. **b.** any of various organs or structures resembling the shape but not the function of true glands. **2.** *Bot.* a secreting organ or structure, esp. one on or near a surface. [ME < L *gland-* (s. of *glāns* acorn); cf. It *ghianda*] —**gland′less,** *adj.* —**gland′like′,** *adj.*

gland[2] (gland), *n. Mach.* **1.** a sleeve within a stuffing box, tightened against compressible packing to prevent leakage of fluid. **2.** See **stuffing box.** [?]

glan·dered (glan′dərd), *adj. Vet. Pathol.* affected with glanders. [GLANDER(S) + -ED[3]]

glan·ders (glan′dərz), *n.* (*construed as sing.*) *Vet. Pathol.* a contagious disease chiefly of horses and mules but communicable to man, caused by the microorganism *Actinobacillus mallei* and characterized by swellings beneath the jaw and a mucous discharge from the nostrils. Cf. **farcy.** [late ME < MF *glandre(s)* swollen glands < L *glandulae* swollen glands, lit., little acorns. See GLAND[1], -ULE] —**glan′der·ous,** *adj.*

glan·du·lar (glan′jə lər), *adj.* **1.** consisting of or bearing glands. **2.** of or pertaining to, or resembling a gland. Also, **glandulous.** [< L *glandul(a)* (see GLANDERS) + -AR[1]] —**glan′du·lar·ly,** *adv.*

glan′dular fe′ver, *Pathol.* See **infectious mononucleosis.**

glan·du·lous (glan′jə ləs), *adj.* glandular. [ME *glandelous* < L *glandulōs(us)* full of kernels. See GLANDERS, -OUS] —**glan′du·lous·ness,** *n.*

glans (glanz), *n., pl.* **glan·des** (glan′dēz). *Anat.* the head of the penis or of the clitoris. [< L: acorn, acorn-shaped ball; akin to Gk *bálanos*]

glare[1] (glâr), *n., v.,* **glared, glar·ing.** —*n.* **1.** a very harsh, bright, dazzling light. **2.** a fiercely or angrily piercing stare. **3.** dazzling or showy appearance; showiness. —*v.i.* **4.** to shine with a very harsh, dazzling light. **5.** to stare with a fiercely or angrily piercing look. **6.** *Archaic.* to appear conspicuous; stand out obtrusively. —*v.t.* **7.** to express with a glare. [ME *glare(n);* c. MD, MLG *glaren;* akin to GLASS (cf. OE *glæren* glassy)] —**glare′less,** *adj.* —**Syn. 1.** flare, glitter, flash. **4.** See **shine.**

glare[2] (glâr), *n.* a bright, smooth surface, as of ice. [special use of GLARE[1]]

glar·ing (glâr′ing), *adj.* **1.** dazzlingly or harshly bright. **2.** excessively showy or bright; garish. **3.** very conspicuous or obvious; flagrant: *glaring defects.* **4.** staring fiercely or angrily. [ME] —**glar′ing·ly,** *adv.* —**glar′ing·ness,** *n.* —**Syn. 2.** gaudy, flashy. **3.** prominent.

glar·y[1] (glâr′ē), *adj.,* **glar·i·er, glar·i·est.** harshly brilliant; glaring. [GLARE[1] + -Y[1]] —**glar′i·ness,** *n.*

glar·y[2] (glâr′ē), *adj.,* **glar·i·er, glar·i·est.** *U.S.* smooth and slippery, as ice. [GLARE[2] + -Y[1]]

Glas·gow (glas′gō, -kō *or, for 2,* glaz′-), *n.* **1. Ellen (Anderson Ghol·son)** (gōl′sən), 1874–1945, U.S. novelist. **2.** a seaport in SW Scotland, on the Clyde River: shipyards. 1,054,913 (1961).

Glas·pell (glas′pel), *n.* **Susan,** 1882–1948, U.S. novelist and dramatist.

Glas·phalt (glas′fôlt′, -falt′), *n. Trademark.* a road-paving material manufactured from crushed waste glass mixed with asphalt. [GLAS(S + AS)PHALT]

glass (glas, gläs), *n.* **1.** a hard, brittle, noncrystalline, more or less transparent substance produced by fusion, usually consisting of mutually dissolved silica and silicates that also contain soda and lime, as in the ordinary variety used for windows, bottles, etc. Cf. **crown glass, flint glass.** **2.** any artificial or natural substance having similar properties and composition, as fused borax, obsidian, or the like. **3.** something made of glass, as a window. **4.** a tumbler or other comparatively tall, handleless drinking container. **5.** a mirror. **6.** a lens, esp. one used as a magnifying glass. **7.** a barometer. **8. glasses,** eyeglass (def. 1). **9.** things made of glass, collectively; glassware. **10.** a glassful. —*adj.* **11.** made of glass: *a glass tray.* **12.** furnished with glass. —*v.t.* **13.** to fit with panes of glass. **14.** to cover with or encase in glass. **15.** *Literary.* to reflect. [ME *glas,* OE *glæs;* c. D, G *Glas*] —**glass′less,** *adj.* —**glass′like′,** *adj.*

glass′ blow′ing, the art or process of forming or shaping a mass of molten or heat-softened glass into ware by blowing air into it through a tube. —**glass′ blow′er.**

glass·ful (glas′fo͝ol, gläs′-), *n., pl.* **-fuls.** an amount contained by or sufficient to fill a glass or tumbler. [OE *glæs full*]

glass·house (glas′hous′, gläs′-), *n., pl.* **-hous·es** (-hou′ziz). **1.** a glassworks. **2.** *Chiefly Brit.* a greenhouse.

glass·ine (gla sēn′), *n.* a glazed, semitransparent paper used for book jackets, for packaging foods, etc.

glass′ liz′ard, any of several limbless lizards of the genus *Ophisaurus,* of the eastern U.S., having an extremely long and fragile tail.

glass·mak·ing (glas′mā′king, gläs′-), *n.* the art of making glass or glassware. —**glass′mak′er,** *n.*

glass·man (glas′mən, gläs′-), *n., pl.* **-men.** **1.** a person who makes or sells glass. **2.** a glazier.

glass′ snake′, **1.** (not used technically) a glass lizard. **2.** any of several lizards of Europe and Asia having an extremely fragile tail.

glass·ware (glas′wâr′, gläs′-), *n.* articles of glass, esp. glasses for a table setting.

glass′ wool′, spun glass similar to wool, used for insulation, filters, etc.

glass·work (glas′wûrk′, gläs′-), *n.* **1.** the manufacture of glass and glassware. **2.** the fitting of glass; glazing. **3.** articles of glass collectively; glassware. **—glass′work′er,** *n.*

glass·works (glas′wûrks′, gläs′-), *n., pl.* **-works.** (*usually construed as sing.*) a factory where glass is made.

glass·wort (glas′wûrt′, gläs′-), *n.* **1.** any of several chenopodiaceous herbs of the genus *Salicornia,* having succulent leafless stems, formerly used, when burned to ashes, as a source of soda for glassmaking. **2.** the saltwort, *Salsola kali.*

glass·y (glas′ē, glä′sē), *adj.,* **glass·i·er, glass·i·est.** **1.** resembling glass, as in transparency, smoothness, etc.: *a glassy sheet of water.* **2.** having an expressionless, dull stare: *glassy eyes.* **3.** of the nature of glass; vitreous. [ME *glasy*] **—glass′i·ly,** *adv.* **—glass′i·ness,** *n.*

glass·y-eyed (glas′ē īd′, glä′sē-), *adj.* having a dull or uncomprehending expression; staring fixedly.

Glas·we·gian (gla swē′jən, -jē ən), *adj.* **1.** of or characteristic of Glasgow or its inhabitants. **—***n.* **2.** a native or inhabitant of Glasgow. [GLAS(GOW) + *-wegian* (abstracted from GALWEGIAN)]

Glau′ber's salt′ (glou′bərz), *Chem., Pharm.* a colorless, crystalline sodium sulfate, used chiefly in textile dyeing and as a cathartic. Also, **Glau′ber salt′.** [named after J. R. *Glauber* (1604–68), German chemist]

Glau·ce (glô′sē), *n. Class. Myth.* Creüsa (def. 1).

glau·co·ma (glô kō′mə, glou-), *n. Ophthalm.* a disease of the eye characterized by increased pressure within the eyeball and progressive loss of vision. [< Gk *glaúkōma* opacity of the eye lens. See GLAUCOUS, -OMA] **—glau·co·ma·tous** (glô-kō′mə təs, -kom′ə-, glou-), *adj.*

glau·co·nite (glô′kə nīt′), *n.* a greenish micaceous mineral consisting essentially of a hydrous silicate of potassium, aluminum, and iron. [< Gk *glaukón,* neut. of *glaukós* (see GLAUCOUS) + -ITE[1]] **—glau·co·nit·ic** (glô′kə nit′ik), *adj.*

glau·cous (glô′kəs), *adj.* **1.** light bluish green or greenish blue. **2.** *Bot.* covered with a whitish bloom, as a plum. [< L *glaucus* silvery, gray, bluish-green < Gk *glaukós*] **—glau′cous·ly,** *adv.*

glaze (glāz), *v.,* **glazed, glaz·ing,** *n.* **—***v.t.* **1.** to furnish or fill with sheets of glass. **2.** to coat (a ceramic or the like), as by the application of a substance or by fusion of the body. **3.** to cover with a smooth, glossy surface or coating. **4.** *Fine Arts.* to cover (a painted surface or parts of it) with a thin layer of transparent color in order to modify the tone. **5.** to give a glassy surface to, as by polishing. **—***v.i.* **6.** to become glazed or glassy. **7.** (of a grinding wheel) to lose abrasive quality through wear. **—***n.* **8.** a smooth, glossy surface or coating. **9.** the substance for producing such a coating. **10.** *Ceram.* **a.** a vitreous layer or coating on a piece of pottery. **b.** the substance of which such a layer or coating is made. **11.** *Fine Arts.* a thin layer of transparent color spread over a painted surface. **12.** a smooth, lustrous surface on certain fabrics, produced by treating the material with a chemical and calendering. **13.** *Cookery.* a substance used to coat a food, esp. sugar or a paste. **14.** Also called **glaze′ ice′, silver frost, silver thaw, verglas;** *esp. Brit.,* **glazed′ frost′.** a thin coating of ice on land, trees, etc., caused by freezing rain. Cf. **rime**[2] (def. 1). [ME *glase(n)* < *glas* GLASS] **—glaz′er,** *n.*

gla·zier (glā′zhər), *n.* a person who fits windows or the like with glass or panes of glass. [ME *glas(i)er*]

gla·zier·y (glā′zhə rē), *n.* the work of a glazier; glasswork.

glaz·ing (glā′zing), *n.* **1.** the act of furnishing or fitting with glass; the business of a glazier. **2.** panes or sheets of glass set or made to be set in frames, as in windows, doors, or mirrors. **3.** the act of applying a glaze. **4.** a glazed surface. [ME]

Gla·zu·nov (glä zo͝o nôf′), *n.* **A·le·xan·der (Kon·stan·ti·no·vitch)** (ä′le ksän′dər kon stän tē′no vich), 1865–1936, Russian composer. Also, **Gla·zu·noff′.**

Gld., (in the Netherlands) gulden; guldens.

gleam (glēm), *n.* **1.** a flash or beam of light. **2.** a dim or subdued light. **3.** a brief or slight manifestation or occurrence; trace: *a gleam of hope.* **—***v.i.* **4.** to send forth a gleam or gleams. **5.** to appear suddenly and clearly like a flash of light. [ME *glem(e),* OE *glǣm;* c. OHG *gleimo* glowworm; akin to OS *glīmo* brightness. See GLIMMER, GLIMPSE] **—gleam′ing·ly,** *adv.* **—gleam′less,** *adj.*
—Syn. 1. GLEAM, GLIMMER, BEAM, RAY are terms for a stream of light. GLEAM denotes a not very brilliant, intermittent or nondirectional stream of light. GLIMMER indicates a nondirectional light that is feeble and unsteady: *a faint glimmer of moonlight.* BEAM usually means a directional, and therefore smaller, stream: *the beam from a searchlight.* RAY usually implies a still smaller amount of light than a beam, a single line of light: *a ray through a pinprick in a window shade.* **4.** shine, glimmer, flash, glitter, sparkle.

glean (glēn), *v.t.* **1.** to gather (grain or the like) after the reapers or regular gatherers. **2.** to gather, discover, or find out (facts) slowly and patiently. **—***v.i.* **3.** to collect or gather anything little by little or slowly. **4.** to gather what is left by reapers. [ME *glen(en)* < OF *glen(er);* c. OPr *glenar, grenar* < LL *glenāre* << Celt] **—glean′a·ble,** *adj.* **—glean′er,** *n.*

glean·ing (glē′ning), *n.* **1.** the act of a person or thing that gleans. **2.** Usually, **gleanings.** something that is gleaned. [ME *glenynge*]

glebe (glēb), *n.* **1.** *Archaic.* soil; field. **2.** Also called **glebe′ land′.** *Brit.* the cultivable land owned by a parish church or ecclesiastical benefice. [ME < L *glēba, glæba* clod of earth] **—glebe′less,** *adj.*

glede (glēd), *n. Brit. Dial.* the common European kite, *Milvus ictinus.* Also, **gled** (gled). [ME; OE *gli(o)da;* c. OIcel *gledha;* akin to GLIDE]

glee (glē), *n.* **1.** demonstrative joy; exultation. **2.** an unaccompanied part song for three or more voices. [ME; OE *glēo;* c. OIcel *glȳ,* akin to GLOW] **—Syn. 1.** jollity, hilarity, mirth, joviality. See **mirth.**

glee′ club′, a chorus organized for singing choral music.

gleed (glēd), *n. Dial.* a glowing coal. [ME *gleed(e),* OE *glēd;* c. G *Glut,* OIcel *glōdh;* akin to GLOW]

glee·ful (glē′fəl), *adj.* full of glee; merry; exultant. **—glee′ful·ly,** *adv.* **—glee′ful·ness,** *n.*

glee·man (glē′mən), *n., pl.* **-men.** *Archaic.* a strolling professional singer; minstrel. [ME; OE *gleōman*]

glee·some (glē′səm), *adj.* gleeful. **—glee′some·ly,** *adv.* **—glee′some·ness,** *n.*

gleet (glēt), *n.* **1.** *Pathol.* a thin, morbid discharge, as from a wound. **2.** Also called **nasal gleet.** *Vet. Pathol.* an inflammation of the air passages of the nose of a horse, producing a thick discharge. [ME *glete* < MF *glete,* OF *glette* < L *glitt(us)* sticky]

gleg (gleg), *adj. Scot. and North Eng.* quick or keen, esp. in sensory perception. [ME < Scand; cf. OIcel *gløggr;* c. Goth *glaggw(uba)* carefully; akin to GLOW] **—gleg′ly,** *adv.* **—gleg′ness,** *n.*

Glei·witz (glī′vits), *n.* German name of **Gliwice.**

glen (glen), *n.* a small, narrow, secluded valley. [< Gael *gle(a)nn;* c. Welsh *glynn*] **—glen′like′,** *adj.*

Glen′ Bur′nie (bûr′nē), a town in central Maryland, S of Baltimore. 38,608 (1970).

Glen′ Cove′, a city on NW Long Island, in SE New York. 25,770 (1970).

Glen·dale (glen′dāl′), *n.* **1.** a city in SW California, near Los Angeles. 132,752 (1970). **2.** a city in central Arizona, near Phoenix. 36,228 (1970).

Glen·do·ra (glen dōr′ə, -dôr′ə), *n.* a city in SW California, near Los Angeles. 31,349 (1970).

Glengarry

Glen·dow·er (glen dou′ər, glen′dou ər), *n.* **Owen,** 1359?–1416?, Welsh rebel against Henry IV of England.

glen·gar·ry (glen gar′ē), *n., pl.* **-ries.** a Scottish cap with straight sides, a crease along the top, and sometimes short ribbon streamers at the back. [after *Glengarry,* valley in Invernesshire, Scotland]

gle·noid (glē′noid), *adj. Anat.* **1.** shallow or slightly cupped, as the articular cavities of the scapula and the temporal bone. **2.** pertaining to such a cavity. [< Gk *glēnoeid(ēs)* = *glēn(ē)* pupil, eyeball + *-oeidēs* -OID]

Glen′ plaid′, **1.** a plaid pattern of muted colors or of black or gray and white, esp. one in which two dark and two light stripes alternate with four dark and four light stripes, both vertically and horizontally, forming a crossing pattern of irregular checks. **2.** having this pattern. [named after *Glen(urquhart),* a Scottish clan]

Glens′ Falls′, a city in E New York, on the Hudson River. 17,222 (1970).

Gles·sa·ri·ae (gle sâ′rē ē′), *n.pl. Class. Myth.* the Amber Islands.

gli·a·din (glī′ə din, -dᵊn), *n. Biochem.* **1.** a prolamin derived from the gluten of grain, used chiefly as a nutrient in high-protein diets. **2.** any prolamin. Also, **gli·a·dine** (glī′ə-dēn′, -din). [< It *gliadin(a)* < Gk *glía* glue; see -IN[2]]

glib (glib), *adj.,* **glib·ber, glib·best.** **1.** ready and fluent, often thoughtlessly or insincerely so: *a glib talker; glib conversation.* **2.** easy or unconstrained, as actions or manners. [cf. obs. *glibbery* slippery; c. D *glibberig*] **—glib′ly,** *adv.* **—glib′ness,** *n.* **—Syn. 1.** facile, smooth. See **fluent.**

glide (glīd), *v.,* **glid·ed, glid·ing,** *n.* **—***v.i.* **1.** to move smoothly and effortlessly, as a flying bird. **2.** to pass by gradual or unobservable change (often fol. by *along, away, by,* etc.). **3.** to move quietly or imperceptibly (usually fol. by *in, out, along,* etc.). **4.** *Aeron.* **a.** to descend at an easy angle, with less engine power than for level flight. **b.** to fly in a glider. **5.** *Music.* to pass from one note to another without a break. **—***v.t.* **6.** to cause to glide. **—***n.* **7.** a gliding movement, as in dancing. **8.** a dance marked by such gliding movements. **9.** *Music.* slur (def. 9a). **10.** *Phonet.* **a.** a semivowel. **b.** a transitional sound heard during the articulation linking two phonemically contiguous sounds, as the *y*-sound often heard between the *i* and *e* of *quiet.* **11.** a calm stretch of shallow, smoothly flowing water, as in a river. **12.** *Metall.* slip[1] (def. 41). [ME *glide(n),* OE *glīdan;* c. G *gleiten*] **—glid′ing·ly,** *adv.* **—Syn. 1.** See **slide.**

glid·er (glī′dər), *n.* **1.** a person or thing that glides. **2.** *Aeron.* a motorless, heavier-than-air craft for gliding from a higher to a lower level by the action of gravity or from a lower to a higher level by the action of upward air currents. **3.** a porch swing made of an upholstered seat suspended from a steel framework. [ME]

glim (glim), *n. Slang.* **1.** a light or lamp. **2.** an eye. **3.** *Scot.* a scrap; a little bit. [see GLIMPSE, GLIMMER]

glime (glīm), *n., v.,* **glimed, glim·ing.** *Brit. Dial.* **—***n.* **1.** a sly look or glance. **—***v.i.* **2.** to glance slyly. [< Scand]

glim·mer (glim′ər), *n.* **1.** a faint or unsteady light; gleam. **2.** a dim perception; inkling. **—***v.i.* **3.** to shine faintly or unsteadily; twinkle, shimmer, or flicker. **4.** to appear faintly or dimly. [ME *glimer(en)* (to) gleam; c. G *glimmern;* cf. OE *gleomu* splendor] **—Syn. 1.** See **gleam.**

glim·mer·ing (glim′ər ing), *n.* **1.** a faint or unsteady light; glimmer. **2.** a faint glimpse; inkling. **—***adj.* **3.** shining faintly or unsteadily; shimmering. [ME] **—glim′mer·ing·ly,** *adv.*

glimpse (glimps), *n., v.,* **glimpsed, glimps·ing.** **—***n.* **1.** a very brief, passing look, sight, or view. **2.** a momentary or slight appearance. **3.** a vague idea; inkling. **4.** *Archaic.* a gleam, as of light. **—***v.t.* **5.** to catch or take a glimpse of. **—***v.i.* **6.** to look briefly; glance (usually fol. by *at*). **7.** *Archaic.* to come into view; appear faintly. [ME *glimse(n);* c. MHG *glimsen* to glow; akin to GLIMMER] **—glimps′er,** *n.*

Glin·ka (gling′kə; *Russ.* glēn′kä), *n.* **Mi·kha·il I·va·no·vich** (mi кнä ēl′ i vä′no vich), 1803–57, Russian composer.

glint (glint), *n.* **1.** a gleam or glimmer; sparkle; flash. **2.** gleaming brightness; luster. **3.** a brief manifestation; inkling; trace. **—***v.i.* **4.** to gleam or flash. **5.** to move suddenly; dart. **—***v.t.* **6.** to cause to glint; reflect. [ME *glint,* var. of obs. *glent* < Scand; cf. Dan *glente,* Sw *glänta, glinta* to slip, shine] **—Syn. 4.** See **flash.**

glis·sade (gli säd′, -sād′), *n., v.,* **-sad·ed, -sad·ing.** **—***n.* **1.** a skillful glide over snow or ice in descending a mountain, as on skis or a toboggan. **2.** *Dance.* a sliding or gliding step. —*v.i.* **3.** to perform a glissade. [< F = *gliss(er)* (to) slip, slide + *-ade* -ADE[1]] —**glis·sad′er,** *n.*

glis·san·do (gli sän′dō), *adj., n., pl.* **-di** (-dē). *Music.* —*adj.* **1.** performed with a gliding effect by sliding one or more fingers rapidly over the keys of a piano or strings of a harp. —*n.* **2.** a glissando passage. **3.** (in string playing) a slice. [< F *gliss(er)* (to) slide + It *-ando* ger. ending]

glis·ten (glis′ən), *v.i.* **1.** to reflect a sparkling light or a faint intermittent glow; shine lustrously. —*n.* **2.** a glistening; sparkle. [ME *glis(t)en,* OE *glisnian* < *glisian* to GLITTER; see -EN[1]] —**glis′ten·ing·ly,** *adv.* —**Syn. 1.** glimmer, gleam, glitter. GLISTEN, SHIMMER, SPARKLE refer to different ways in which light is reflected from surfaces. GLISTEN refers to a lustrous light, as from something sleek or wet: *Wet fur glistens. Snow glistens in the sunlight.* SHIMMER refers to the play of light on a surface, as of water or silk: *Moonbeams shimmer on water. Silk shimmers in a bright light.* To SPARKLE is to give off sparks or to send forth small but brilliant gleams, sometimes by reflection: *A diamond sparkles with numerous points of light.*

glis·ter (glis′tər), *v.i.* **1.** *Archaic.* to glisten; glitter. —*n.* **2.** a glistening; glitter. [ME] —**glis′tering·ly,** *adv.*

glitch (glich), *n. Slang.* a minor defect or malfunction in a machine or plan. [< Yiddish *glitsh* a skid, slip < *glitshen* to slide, glide; c. dial. G *glitschen,* G *gleiten* GLIDE]

glit·ter (glit′ər), *v.i.* **1.** to reflect light with a brilliant luster; sparkle. **2.** to make a brilliant show. —*n.* **3.** a sparkling reflected light or luster. **4.** showy splendor. **5.** small glittering ornaments. [ME < Scand; cf. G *gleissen* to shine, glitter] —**glit′ter·ing·ly,** *adv.* —**glit′ter·y,** *adj.*

glitz (glits), *n. Slang.* ostentatious glitter or sophistication: *a cocktail lounge noted for its glitz.* [< G *glitz(ern)* to glitter; perh. via Yiddish]

glitz·y (glit′sē), *adj.,* **glitz·i·er, glitz·i·est.** *Slang.* pretentiously smart or elegant: *a glitzy gown designed for a movie premiere.* [< G *glitz(ern)* to glitter + -Y; perh. via Yiddish] —**glitz′i·ness,** *n.*

Gli·wi·ce (glē vē′tse), *n.* a city in SW Poland. 197,000. German, **Gleiwitz.**

gloam (glōm), *n. Archaic.* twilight; gloaming. [back formation from GLOAMING]

gloam·ing (glō′ming), *n. Literary.* twilight; dusk. [ME *gloming,* OE *glōmung;* appar. by assoc. with GLOW]

gloat (glōt), *v.i.* **1.** to look at or think about with great or excessive satisfaction: *The opposing team gloated over our bad luck.* —*n.* **2.** an act or feeling of gloating. [< Scand; cf. OIcel *glotta* to grin] —**gloat′er,** *n.* —**gloat′ing·ly,** *adv.*

glob (glob), *n.* **1.** a drop or globule. **2.** a usually rounded quantity or lump of some plastic or moldable substance: *a huge glob of whipped cream.* [perh. b. GLOBE and BLOB]

glob·al (glō′bəl), *adj.* **1.** pertaining to the whole world; world-wide; universal. **2.** comprehensive. **3.** globular, or globe-shaped. —**glo′bal·ly,** *adv.*

glo·bate (glō′bāt), *adj.* shaped like a globe. Also, **glo′bat·ed.** [< L *globāt(us)* made into a ball (ptp. of *globāre*)]

globe (glōb), *n., v.,* **globed, glob·ing.** —*n.* **1.** the planet earth (usually prec. by *the*). **2.** a planet or other celestial body. **3.** a sphere on which is depicted a map of the earth **(terrestrial globe)** or of the heavens **(celestial globe). 4.** a spherical body; sphere. **5.** anything more or less spherical, as a glass fishbowl. **6.** *Hist.* a golden ball borne as an emblem of sovereignty; orb. —*v.t.* **7.** to form into a globe. —*v.i.* **8.** to take the form of a globe. [< MF *globe* < L *glob(us)* round body, ball, sphere] —**Syn. 4.** See **ball**[1].

globe·fish (glōb′fish′), *n., pl.* (*esp. collectively*) **-fish,** (*esp. referring to two or more kinds or species*) **-fish·es.** puffer (def. 2).

globe·flow·er (glōb′flou′ər), *n.* **1.** a ranunculaceous plant, *Trollius europaeus,* of Europe, having pale-yellow, globelike flowers. **2.** a related American plant, *T. laxus.*

globe-trot·ter (glōb′trot′ər), *n.* a person who travels frequently to countries all over the world. Also, **globe′trot′ter.** —**globe′-trot′ting, globe′trot′ting,** *n., adj.*

glo·big·er·i·na (glō bij′ə rī′nə), *n., pl.* **-nas, -nae** (-nē). any marine foraminifer of the genus *Globigerina,* having a calcareous shell. [< NL = L *globi-* globe (comb. form of *globus*) + *-ger* carry (< *gerere* to carry) + *-ina* fem. n. suffix]

glo·bin (glō′bin), *n. Biochem.* the protein component of hemoglobin. [< L *glob(us)* globe, sphere + -IN[2]]

glo·boid (glō′boid), *adj.* **1.** approximately globular. —*n.* **2.** a globoid figure or body.

glo·bose (glō′bōs, glō bōs′), *adj.* globelike; globe-shaped. [< L *globōs(us)* round as a ball] —**glo′bose·ly,** *adv.* —**glo·bos·i·ty** (glō bos′i tē), **glo′bose·ness,** *n.*

glob·u·lar (glob′yə lər), *adj.* **1.** globe-shaped; spherical. **2.** composed of or having globules. **3.** world-wide; global. Also, **glob·u·lous.** —**glob·u·lar·i·ty** (glob′yə lar′i tē), **glob′u·lar·ness,** *n.* —**glob′u·lar·ly,** *adv.*

glob·ule (glob′yo͞ol), *n.* a small spherical body. [< L *globul(us)*]

glob·u·lin (glob′yə lin), *n. Biochem.* any of a group of proteins, as myosin, occurring in plant and animal tissue, insoluble in pure water but soluble in dilute salt water, and coagulable by heat.

glo·chid·i·ate (glō kid′ē it, -āt′), *adj. Bot., Zool.* barbed at the tip, as a hair or bristle. [GLOCHIDI(UM) + -ATE[1]]

glo·chid·i·um (glō kid′ē əm), *n., pl.* **-chid·i·a** (-kid′ē ə). **1.** *Bot.* a hair or bristle having a barbed tip. **2.** the larva of a fresh-water clam of the family *Unionidae,* that lives as a temporary parasite in the gills or on other external parts of fishes. [< NL < Gk **glōchídion* little arrow = *glōch(ís)* point of an arrow + *-idion* -IDION] —**glo·chid′i·al,** *adj.*

glock·en·spiel (glok′ən spēl′, -shpēl′), *n.* a musical instrument composed of a set of graduated steel bars mounted in a frame and struck with hammers, used esp. in bands. [< G = *Glocke* bell + *Spiel* play]

Glockenspiel

glom·er·ate (glom′ər it, -āt′), *adj.* compactly clustered. [< L *glomerāt(us)* wound or formed into a ball (ptp. of *glomerāre*). See GLOMERULUS, -ATE[1]]

glom·er·a·tion (glom′ə rā′shən), *n.* **1.** a glomerate condition; conglomeration. **2.** a glomerate mass.

glom·er·ule (glom′ə ro͞ol′), *n. Bot.* a cyme condensed into a headlike cluster. [< NL *glomerul(us)* GLOMERULUS]

glo·mer·u·lus (glō mer′yə ləs, -ə ləs, glə-), *n., pl.* **-li** (-lī′). *Anat.* a compact cluster of capillaries. [< NL = L *glomer-* (s. of *glomus* ball of yarn, clew) + *-ulus* -ULE] —**glo·mer′u·lar,** *adj.*

Glom·ma (glôm′mä), *n.* a river in E Norway, flowing S into the Skagerrak. 375 mi. long.

gloom (glo͞om), *n.* **1.** darkness; dimness. **2.** a state of melancholy or depression; low spirits. **3.** a despondent look or expression. —*v.i.* **4.** to appear or become dark, dim, or somber. **5.** to look dismal or dejected; frown. —*v.t.* **6.** to fill with gloom; make gloomy or sad; sadden. **7.** to make dark or somber. [ME *gloum(ben), glomen* to frown, ? OE **glūmian* (akin to early G *gläumen* to make turbid); see GLUM] —**gloom′ful,** *adj.* —**gloom′ful·ly,** *adv.* —**gloom′less,** *adj.* —**Syn. 1.** shadow, shade, obscurity. **2.** dejection, despondency, sadness. —**Ant. 1.** brightness. **2.** cheerfulness.

gloom·ing (glo͞o′ming), *n. Archaic.* gloaming.

gloom·y (glo͞o′mē), *adj.,* **gloom·i·er, gloom·i·est. 1.** dark or dim: *gloomy skies.* **2.** causing gloom; depressing: *a gloomy prospect.* **3.** filled with or showing gloom; melancholy. **4.** hopeless or despairing; pessimistic: *a gloomy view of the future.* —**gloom′i·ly,** *adv.* —**gloom′i·ness,** *n.* —**Syn. 1.** shadowy, dusky. **2.** dismal. **3.** dejected, downcast, downhearted, depressed, glum. —**Ant. 3.** happy.

Glo·ri·a (glōr′ē ə, glôr′-), *n.* **1.** *Liturgy.* **a.** See **Gloria in Excelsis Deo. b.** See **Gloria Patri. c.** the response *Gloria tibi, Domine* "Glory be to Thee, O Lord." **2.** (*l.c.*) a repetition of one of these. **3.** (*l.c.*) a musical setting for one of these. **4.** (*l.c.*) a halo, nimbus, or aureole. **5.** (*l.c.*) a fabric of silk, cotton, nylon, or wool for umbrellas, dresses, etc. [ME < L: glory, fame]

Glo·ri·a in Ex·cel·sis De·o (glōr′ē ə in ek sel′sis dā′ō, glôr′-), the hymn beginning, in Latin, *Gloria in Excelsis Deo* "Glory in the highest to God."

Glo·ri·a Pa·tri (glōr′ē ə pä′trē, glôr′-), the short hymn beginning, in Latin, *Gloria Patri.* "Glory be to the Father, and to the Son, and to the Holy Ghost. As it was in the beginning, is now, and ever shall be, world without end. Amen."

glo·ri·fi·ca·tion (glōr′ə fə kā′shən, glôr′-), *n.* **1.** the act of glorifying; exaltation to the glory of heaven. **2.** the state of being glorified. **3.** *Informal.* a glorified or more splendid form of something. [ME < LL *glōrificātiōn-* (s. of *glōrificātiō*)]

glo·ri·fy (glōr′ə fī′, glôr′-), *v.t.,* **-fied, -fy·ing. 1.** to magnify with praise; extol. **2.** to treat as more splendid, excellent, etc., than would normally be considered. **3.** to make glorious; invest with glory. **4.** to promote the glory of (God); ascribe glory and praise in adoration to (God). [ME < OF *glorifi(er)* < LL *glōrificāre*] —**glo′ri·fi′er,** *n.*

glo·ri·ole (glōr′ē ōl′, glôr′-), *n.* a halo, nimbus, or aureole. [< L *glōriola,* dim. of *glōria* GLORY]

glo·ri·ous (glōr′ē əs, glôr′-), *adj.* **1.** delightful; wonderful. **2.** conferring glory: *a glorious victory.* **3.** full of glory; entitled to great renown. **4.** brilliantly beautiful or magnificent; splendid: *the glorious heavens.* [ME < AF, OF *glorieus* < L *glōriōs(us)*] —**glo′ri·ous·ly,** *adv.* —**glo′ri·ous·ness,** *n.* —**Syn. 3.** renowned, illustrious, noted, celebrated. —**Ant. 3.** unknown.

Glo′rious Revolu′tion. See **English Revolution.**

glo·ry (glōr′ē, glôr′ē), *n., pl.* **-ries,** *v.,* **-ried, -ry·ing,** *interj.* —*n.* **1.** exalted praise, honor, or distinction bestowed by common consent. **2.** something that makes one honored or illustrious; an asset; an object of pride. **3.** adoring praise or worshipful thanksgiving: *Give glory to God.* **4.** resplendent beauty or magnificence: *the glory of autumn.* **5.** a state of absolute happiness; gratification, contentment, etc.: *to be in one's glory.* **6.** the splendor and bliss of heaven; heaven. **7.** a surrounding radiance of light represented about the head or the whole figure of a sacred person, as Christ, a saint, etc.; a halo, nimbus, or aureole. **8. go to glory,** to die. Also, **go to one's glory.** —*v.i.* **9.** to exult with triumph; rejoice proudly (usually fol. by *in*): *Their father gloried in their success.* **10.** *Obs.* to boast. —*interj.* **11.** Also, **glo′ry be′.** Glory be to God (used to express surprise, elation, wonder, etc.). [ME < OF *glorie* < L *glōria*] —**glo′ry·ing·ly,** *adv.* —**Syn. 1.** fame, eminence, renown, celebrity. —**Ant. 1.** disgrace, obloquy.

gloss[1] (glos, glôs), *n.* **1.** a superficial luster or shine: *the gloss of satin.* **2.** a false or deceptive appearance, show, etc. —*v.t.* **3.** to put a gloss upon. **4.** to give a speciously good appearance to (often fol. by *over*): *to gloss over flaws in the woodwork.* [< Scand; akin to D **gloos* a glowing, MHG *glosen* to glow, shine] —**gloss′er,** *n.* —**gloss′less,** *adj.* —**Syn. 1.** shine, glaze. See **polish. 2.** front, pretense.

gloss[2] (glos, glôs), *n.* **1.** an explanation, by means of a marginal or interlinear note or translation, of a technical or unusual expression in a manuscript text. **2.** an expanded interpretation of a text. **3.** a glossary. **4.** an artfully misleading interpretation. —*v.t.* **5.** to insert glosses on; annotate. **6.** to place (a word) in a gloss. **7.** to give a specious interpretation of; explain away (often fol. by *over* or *away*): *to gloss over a serious problem with a pat solution.* —*v.i.* **8.** to make glosses. [ME *glose* < LL *glosa, glōssa* difficult word needing explanation < Gk (Ionic) *glôssa* tongue, language] —**gloss′er,** *n.* —**gloss′ing·ly,** *adv.* —**Syn. 1.** comment, annotation. **2.** commentary, critique, exegesis, explication. **5.** explicate.

gloss-, var. of **glosso-** before a vowel: *glossectomy.*

gloss., glossary.

glos·sa (glos′ə, glô′sə), *n., pl.* **-sae** (-sē), **-sas. 1.** *Entomol.* one of a pair of median, sometimes fused lobes of the labium of an insect. **2.** *Anat.* the tongue. [< Gk; see GLOSS[2]]

Glos·sa (glô′sə), *n.* **Cape,** a promontory in SW Albania.

glos·sal (glos′əl, glô′səl), *adj.* of or pertaining to the tongue.

glos·sa·ry (glos′ə rē, glô′sə-), *n., pl.* **-ries.** a list of terms in a special subject, field, or area of usage, with accompanying definitions. [ME *glossarye* < L *glossāri(um)*] —**glos·sar·i·al** (glo sâr′ē əl, glô-), *adj.* —**glos′sa·rist,** *n.*

glos·sec·to·my (glo sek′tə mē, glô-), *n., pl.* **-mies.** *Surg.* the removal of all or a portion of the tongue.

glos·seme (glos′ēm, glô′sēm), *n. Linguistics.* the smallest meaningful unit of linguistic signaling, consisting of a morpheme and a tagmeme.

glos·si·tis (glo sī′tis, glô-), *n. Pathol.* inflammation of the tongue. —**glos·sit·ic** (glo sit′ik, glô-), *adj.*

glosso-, a learned borrowing from Greek meaning "tongue," "language," used in the formation of compound words: *glossology.* Also, *esp. before a vowel,* **gloss-.** [< Gk (Ionic), comb. form of *glôssa*]

glos·so·la·li·a (glos′ō lā′lē ə, glô′sō-), *n.* See **speaking in tongues.**

glos·sol·o·gy (glo sol′ə jē, glô-), *n. Archaic.* linguistics. —**glos·so·log·i·cal** (glos′ə loj′i kəl, glô′sə-), *adj.* —**glos·sol′o·gist,** *n.*

gloss·y (glos′ē, glô′sē), *adj.,* **gloss·i·er, gloss·i·est,** *n., pl.* **gloss·ies.** —*adj.* **1.** having a luster or shine; lustrous. **2.** having a false or deceptive appearance or air, esp. of experience or sophistication; specious. **3.** (of paper) having a shiny surface. Cf. **matte** (def. 1). —*n.* **4.** slick[1] (def. 8). **5.** a photograph printed on glossy paper. —**gloss′i·ly,** *adv.* —**gloss′i·ness,** *n.* —**Syn. 1.** shining, polished.

glost (glost, glôst), *n. Ceram.* glaze or glazed ware. [alter. of GLOSS[1]]

-glot, var. of **glotto-** as final element of a compound word: *polyglot.*

glot·tal (glot′əl), *adj.* **1.** of or pertaining to the glottis. **2.** *Phonet.* articulated at the glottis.

glot′tal stop′, *Phonet.* a plosive consonant whose occlusion and release are accomplished chiefly at the glottis.

glot·tic (glot′ik), *adj.* **1.** pertaining to the glottis; glottal. **2.** *Archaic.* linguistic. [< Gk *glōttik(ós)*]

glot·tis (glot′is), *n., pl.* **glot·tis·es, glot·ti·des** (glot′i dēz′). *Anat.* the opening at the upper part of the larynx, between the vocal cords. [< NL < Gk *glōttís,* var. of *glôtta* (Attic form of *glôssa* tongue)] —**glot·tid·e·an** (glo tid′ē ən), *adj.*

glotto-, a learned borrowing from Greek meaning "tongue," "language," used in the formation of compound words: *glottochronology.* Also, **-glot.** [< Gk (Attic) *glōtto-,* comb. form of *glôtta*]

glot·to·chro·nol·o·gy (glot′ō krə nol′ə jē, glot′ə-), *n. Linguistics.* the lexicostatistic study of the relations between two languages having a common origin in order to estimate the time of their divergence.

Glouces·ter (glos′tər, glô′stər), *n.* **1. Duke of.** See **Humphrey** (def. 1). **2.** a seaport in W Gloucestershire in SW England, on the Severn. 69,687 (1961). **3.** a seaport in NE Massachusetts. 27,941 (1970). **4.** Gloucestershire.

Glouces·ter·shire (glos′tər shēr′, -shər, glô′stər-), *n.* a county in SW England. 1,000,493 (1961); 1255 sq. mi. *Co. seat:* Gloucester. Also called **Gloucester.**

glove (gluv), *n., v.,* **gloved, glov·ing.** —*n.* **1.** a covering for the hand made with a separate sheath for each finger and for the thumb. **2.** See **boxing glove. 3.** See **baseball glove. 4.** gauntlet. **5. hand and glove.** See **hand** (def. 38). **6. handle with kid gloves.** See **kid gloves** (def. 2). **7. take up** or **throw down the glove.** See **gauntlet**[1] (def. 3). —*v.t.* **8.** to cover with or as if with a glove; provide with gloves. **9.** to serve as a glove for. [ME; OE *glōf;* c. OIcel *glōfi*] —**glove′less,** *adj.* —**glove′like′,** *adj.*

glove′ compart′ment, a compartment in the dashboard of an automobile for storing small items.

glov·er (gluv′ər), *n.* a maker or seller of gloves. [ME]

Glov·er (gluv′ər), *n.* **John,** 1732–97, American general.

glow (glō), *n.* **1.** a light emitted by or as by a substance heated to luminosity; incandescence. **2.** brightness of color, esp. ruddiness. **3.** a sensation or state of bodily heat. **4.** warmth of emotion or passion; ardor. —*v.i.* **5.** to emit bright light and heat without flame; become incandescent. **6.** to shine like something intensely heated. **7.** to exhibit a strong, bright color; be lustrously red or brilliant. **8.** to become or feel very warm or hot. **9.** to become filled with emotion: *to glow with pride.* [ME *glow(en),* OE *glōwan;* akin to G *glühen,* Icel *glōa*]

glow·er (glou′ər), *v.i.* **1.** to look or stare with sullen dislike, discontent, or anger. —*n.* **2.** a look of sullen dislike, discontent, or anger. [ME (Scot) *glowre(n)* (to) glower; akin to MLG *glūren* to be overcast, MD *gloeren* to leer] —**glow′er·ing·ly,** *adv.*

glow·fly (glō′flī′), *n., pl.* **-flies.** firefly.

glow·ing (glō′ing), *adj.* **1.** incandescent. **2.** rich and warm in coloring: *glowing colors.* **3.** showing the radiance of health, excitement, etc. **4.** warmly favorable or complimentary: *a glowing account of his valor.* [ME *glowynge*] —**glow′ing·ly,** *adv.*

glow·worm (glō′wûrm′), *n.* **1.** the wingless female or larva of the European beetle, *Lampyris noctiluca,* which emits a greenish light. **2.** any of the luminous larvae or wingless, grublike females of certain beetles of the family *Lampyridae.*

glox·in·i·a (glok sin′ē ə), *n.* any of several horticultural varieties of an herb of the genus *Sinningia,* esp. *S. speciosa.* [named after Benjamin *Gloxin,* 18th-century German physician and botanist; see -IA]

gloze[1] (glōz), *v.,* **glozed, gloz·ing,** *n.* —*v.t.* **1.** to explain away; extenuate; gloss over. **2.** to palliate with specious talk. —*v.i.* **3.** *Archaic.* to make glosses; comment. —*n.* **4.** *Archaic.* flattery or deceit. **5.** *Obs.* a specious show. [ME < OF *glose* < LL *glosa* GLOSS[2]] —**gloz′ing·ly,** *adv.*

gloze[2] (glōz), *v.t., v.i.,* **glozed, gloz·ing.** to shine; brighten; gleam. [akin to MHG *glosen* to glow; see GLOSS[1]]

glt., gilt.

gluc-, var. of **gluco-** before a vowel: *glucose.*

glu·ci·num (glōō sī′nəm), *n.* (esp. in France) *Chem.* beryllium. *Symbol:* Gl Also, **glu·cin·i·um** (glōō sin′ē əm). [< NL < Gk *glyk(ýs)* sweet (from the taste of some of the salts) + *-in-* -IN + L *-um* n. suffix] —**glu·cin·ic** (glōō sin′ik), *adj.*

Gluck (glŏŏk), *n.* **Chris·toph Wil·li·bald von** (kris′tôf vil′i bält fən), 1714–87, German operatic composer.

gluco-, var. of **glyco-:** *glucoprotein.* Also, *esp. before a vowel,* **gluc-.**

glu·co·pro·tein (glōō′kō prō′tēn, -tē in), *n. Biochem.* glycoprotein.

glu·cose (glōō′kōs), *n.* **1.** *Chem.* a sugar, $C_6H_{12}O_6$, having several optically different forms, the common or dextrorotatory form **(dextroglucose** or **d-glucose)** occurring in many fruits and in animal tissues, and having a sweetness about one half that of ordinary sugar. **2.** Also called **starch syrup.** a syrup containing dextrose, maltose, and dextrine. [< F] —**glu·cos·ic** (glōō kos′ik), *adj.*

glu·co·side (glōō′kə sīd′), *n. Chem.* any of an extensive group of compounds that yield glucose when treated with a dilute acid or decomposed by a ferment or enzyme. Cf. **glycoside.** —**glu′co·sid′al, glu·co·sid·ic** (glōō′kə sid′ik), *adj.*

glue (glōō), *n., v.,* **glued, glu·ing.** —*n.* **1.** an impure protein gelatin obtained by boiling skins, hoofs, and other animal substances in water and used as a strong adhesive. **2.** any of various solutions or preparations of this substance, used as an adhesive. **3.** any of various other solutions used as adhesives. —*v.t.* **4.** to join or attach firmly with or as with glue; make adhere closely. [ME *glū, gleu* < OF *glu* < L *glūt-* (s. of *glūs*); c. Gk *gloiós* gum, anything sticky] —**glue′like′,** *adj.* —**glu′er,** *n.*

glue′ sniff′ing, the inhaling of the fumes of certain kinds of glue, such as that used in making model airplanes, for effects of euphoria, hallucination, etc. —**glue′ sniff′er.**

glue·y (glōō′ē), *adj.,* **glu·i·er, glu·i·est. 1.** like glue; viscid. **2.** full of or smeared with glue. [ME] —**glu′ey·ness,** *n.*

glum (glum), *adj.,* **glum·mer, glum·mest.** sullenly or silently gloomy; dejected; morose. [var. of GLOOM] —**glum′ly,** *adv.* —**glum′ness,** *n.* —**Syn.** moody, sulky; despondent, melancholy.

glu·ma·ceous (glōō mā′shəs), *adj.* **1.** glumelike. **2.** consisting of or having glumes.

glume (glōōm), *n. Bot.* one of the characteristic bracts of the inflorescence of grasses, sedges, etc., esp. one of the pair of bracts at the base of a spikelet. [< L *glūm(a)* hull or husk (of corn); cf. *glūbere* to peel] —**glume′like′,** *adj.*

glu·on (glōō′on), *n.* an elementary particle that is conjectured to bind quarks together, thus forming most of the observable nuclear particles, such as protons, neutrons, pions, etc. [GLU(E) + ON]

glut (glut), *v.,* **glut·ted, glut·ting,** *n.* —*v.t.* **1.** to feed or fill to excess; cloy: *to glut the appetite.* **2.** to flood (the market) with a certain article or commodity so that the supply greatly exceeds the demand. **3.** to choke up: *to glut a channel.* —*v.i.* **4.** to eat to satiety or to excess. —*n.* **5.** an excessive supply or amount; surfeit. **6.** an act of glutting. **7.** the state of being glutted. [ME *glute,* back formation from *glutun* GLUTTON[1]] —**glut′ting·ly,** *adv.* —**Syn. 1.** surfeit, stuff, satiate. **4.** gorge, cram. **5.** surplus, excess, superabundance.

glu·tam′ic ac′id (glōō tam′ik), *Chem.* an amino acid, $HOOCCH_2CH_2CH(NH_2)COOH$, used chiefly in the form of its sodium salt as a seasoning. Also, **glu′ta·min′ic ac′id** (glōō′tə min′ik, glōō′-). [GLUT(EN) + AMIC ACID]

glu·ta·mine (glōō′tə mēn′, -min), *n. Chem.* an amino acid, $HOOCCH(NH_2)CH_2CH_2CONH_2$, related to glutamic acid. [GLUT(EN) + -AMINE]

glu·ta·thi·one (glōō′tə thī′ōn, -thī ōn′), *n. Biochem.* a peptide of glutamic acid, cysteine, and glycine, $C_{10}H_{17}N_3O_6S$, found in blood and in animal and plant tissues, and important in tissue oxidations and in the activation of some enzymes. [GLUT(AMIC ACID) + THI- + -ONE]

glu·te·al (glōō′tē əl, glōō tē′əl), *adj. Anat.* pertaining to buttock muscles or to the buttocks. [GLUTE(US) + -AL[1]]

glu·te·lin (glōōt′əlin), *n. Biochem.* any of a group of simple proteins of vegetable origin, esp. one from wheat. [? alter. of *glutenin.* See GLUTEN, -IN[2]]

glu·ten (glōōt′ən), *n.* the tough, viscid, nitrogenous substance remaining when flour is washed to remove the starch. [< L: glue] —**glu′te·nous,** *adj.*

glu·te·us (glōō′tē əs, glōō tē′-), *n., pl.* **-te·i** (-tē ī′, -tē′ī). *Anat.* any of several muscles of the buttocks, esp. the broad, thick, fleshy one nearest the surface **(gluteus maximus).** [< NL < Gk *gloutó(s)* the rump + L *-eus* adj. suffix]

glu′teus max′i·mus (mak′sə məs), *pl.* **glutei max·i·mi** (mak′sə mī′). See under **gluteus.** [< NL: largest gluteus]

glu·ti·nous (glōōt′ənəs), *adj.* gluey; viscid; sticky. [ME < L *glūtinōs(us)* gluey, sticky] —**glu′ti·nous·ly,** *adv.* —**glu′ti·nous·ness, glu·ti·nos·i·ty** (glōōt′ənos′i tē), *n.*

glut·ton[1] (glut′ən), *n.* **1.** a person who eats excessively. **2.** a person with a remarkably great desire or capacity for something: *He's a glutton for work.* [ME *glutun* < OF *glouton* < L *glutton-* (s. of *gluttō*), var. of *glūtō* akin to *glūtīre* to gulp down]

glut·ton[2] (glut′ən), *n.* the wolverine, *Gulo luscus,* of Europe. [trans. of G *Vielfrass* for Sw *fjällfräs,* lit., to much devour]

glut·ton·ize (glut′ənīz′), *v.,* **-ized, -iz·ing.** *Archaic.* —*v.i.* **1.** to eat like a glutton. —*v.t.* **2.** to feast gluttonously on.

glut·ton·ous (glut′ənəs), *adj.* **1.** tending to eat excessively; voracious. **2.** greedy; insatiable. [ME] —**glut′ton·ous·ly,** *adv.* —**glut′ton·ous·ness,** *n.*

glut·ton·y (glut′ənē), *n.* excessive eating and drinking. [ME *glotonie, glutonie* < OF *glotonie*]

glyc-, var. of **glyco-** before a vowel: *glycine.*

gly·cer′ic ac′id (gli ser′ik, glis′ər ik), *Chem.* a syrupy liquid, $CH_2OHCHOHCOOH$, obtained by oxidizing glycerol. [GLYCER(OL) + -IC]

glyc·er·ide (glis′ə rīd′, -ər id), *n. Chem.* any of a group of esters obtained from glycerol with a fatty acid: the principal constituent of adipose tissue. [GLYCER(IN) + -IDE]

glyc·er·in (glis′ər in), *n. Chem.* glycerol. Also, **glyc·er·ine** (glis′ər in, -ə rēn′, glis′ə rēn′). [< F *glycérine* = *glycer-* (s. of Gk *glykerós* sweet) + *-ine* -IN[2]]

glyc·er·in·ate[1] (glis′ər ə nāt′), *v.t.,* **-at·ed, -at·ing.** to impregnate with glycerin. [GLYCERIN + -ATE[1]]

glyc·er·in·ate[2] (glis′ər ə nāt′), *n. Chem.* any salt of glyceric acid. [GLYCERIN + -ATE[2]]

glyc·er·ol (glis′ə rōl′, -rôl′, -rol′), *n. Chem.* a syrupy liquid, $HOCH_2CHOHCH_2OH$, used in the preparation of food, cosmetics, medicine, etc. Also called **glycerin, glycerine.** [GLYCER(IN) + -OL[1]]

glyc′er·yl group′ (glis′ər il), *Chem.* the trivalent group, $-CH_2(CH-)CH_2-$, derived from glycerol. Also called **glyc′eryl rad′ical.** [GLYCER(IN) + -YL]

glyc′eryl tri·ni′trate (trī nī′trāt), *Chem.* nitroglycerin.
gly·cine (glī′sēn, glī sēn′), *n.* *Chem.* a crystalline solid, H_2NCH_2COOH, the simplest amino acid. [GLYC- + -INE[2]]
glyco-, a learned borrowing from Greek where it meant "sweet"; used as a combining form of **glucose** and of various substances, such as **glycerol, glycogen, glycol,** having initial *glyc-: glycoside.* Also, **gluc-, gluco-, glyc-.** [comb. form repr. Gk *glykýs* sweet]
gly·co·gen (glī′kə jən), *n.* *Biochem.* a polysaccharide, $(C_6H_{10}O_5)n$, molecularly similar to starch, constituting the principal carbohydrate storage material in animals and occurring also in fungi and yeasts. Also called **animal starch.** —**gly·co·gen·ic** (glī′kə jen′ik), *adj.*
gly·co·gen·e·sis (glī′kə jen′i sis), *n.* *Biochem.* the formation of glycogen from monosaccharides in the body, esp. glucose. —**gly·co·ge·net·ic** (gli′kō jə net′ik), *adj.*
gly·col (glī′kōl, -kôl, -kol), *n.* *Chem.* **1.** Also called **ethylene glycol.** a liquid, CH_2OHCH_2OH, used chiefly as an automobile antifreeze and as a solvent. **2.** any of a group of alcohols containing two hydroxyl groups. [GLYC(ERIN + ALCOH)OL] —**gly·col·ic, gly·col·lic** (glī kol′ik), *adj.*
glycol′ic ac′id, *Chem.* a powder, $CH_2OHCOOH$, used chiefly for textile printing and dyeing and in pesticides. Also, **glycol′lic ac′id.**
gly·co·lip·id (glī′kə lip′id), *n.* *Biochem.* any of the class of lipids comprising the cerebrosides and gangliosides, that upon hydrolysis yields galactose or a similar sugar, a fatty acid, and sphingosine. [GLYCO- + LIPID]
gly·co·pro·tein (glī′kō prō′tēn, -tē in), *n.* *Biochem.* any of a group of complex proteins containing a carbohydrate combined with a simple protein, as mucin. Also, **glucoprotein.** Also called **gly·co·pep·tide** (glī′kō pep′tīd).
gly·co·side (glī′kə sīd′), *n.* *Biochem.* any of the class of compounds that yield a sugar and a noncarbohydrate group upon hydrolysis. [*glycose,* var. of GLUCOSE + -IDE] —**gly·co·sid·ic** (glī′kə sid′ik), *adj.*
gly·cos·u·ri·a (glī′kōs yo͞o rē′ə), *n.* *Pathol.* excretion of glucose in the urine, as in diabetes. [*glycose,* var. of GLUCOSE + -URIA] —**gly′cos·ur′ic,** *adj.*
Glyn (glin), *n.* **Elinor,** 1864–1943, English writer.
gly·ox·a·line (glī ok′sə lēn′, -lin), *n.* *Chem.* imidazole. [GLYC(OL) + OXAL(IC) + -INE[2]]
glyph (glif), *n.* **1.** *Archit.* an ornamental channel or groove. **2.** a sculptured figure or relief carving. **3.** *Archaeol.* a pictograph or hieroglyph. [< Gk *glyph(ḗ)* carving < *glýph(ein)* (to) hollow out] —**glyph′ic,** *adj.*
gly·phog·ra·phy (gli fog′rə fē), *n.* *Print.* a method for making letterpress plates by engraving onto a waxed copper plate. —**glyph·o·graph** (glif′ə graf′, -gräf′), *n.* —**gly·phog′ra·pher,** *n.* —**glyph·o·graph·ic** (glif′ə graf′ik), *adj.*
glyp·tic (glip′tik), *adj.* **1.** of or pertaining to carving or engraving on gems or the like. —*n.* **2.** act or process of producing glyptic ornaments. [< Gk *glyptik(ós)* of engraving, of stone carving = *glypt(ós)* carved (< *glýphein* to engrave, hollow out) + *-ikos* -IC]
glyp·to·dont (glip′tə dont′), *n.* any edentate mammal, related to the armadillos, of the extinct genus *Glyptodon,* of the Pleistocene epoch, having the body, the top of the head, and the tail covered by a horny and bony armor. [< Gk *glypt(ós)* (see GLYPTIC) + -ODONT]

Glyptodont, genus *Glyptodon* (Length about 9 ft.)

glyp·tog·ra·phy (glip tog′rə fē), *n.* **1.** the description or study of engraved gems or other stones. **2.** Also called **glyp·tics** (glip′tiks). the art or process of engraving on gems or the like. [< Gk *glyptó(s)* carved + -GRAPHY] —**glyp·tog′ra·pher,** *n.* —**glyp·to·graph·ic** (glip′tə graf′ik), *adj.*
Gm, gigameter.
gm., *Metric System.* gram; grams.
G.M., **1.** General Manager. **2.** Grand Marshal. **3.** Grand Master.
G-man (jē′man′), *n.,* *pl.* **G-men.** an FBI agent. [prob. repr. *Government man*]
G.m.a.t., Greenwich mean astronomical time.
Gmc, Germanic (def. 5). Also, **Gmc.**
GMT, Greenwich Mean Time. Also, **G.M.T.**
G.N., Graduate Nurse.
gnar (när), *v.i.,* **gnarred, gnar·ring.** to snarl; growl. Also, **gnarr.** [imit; cf. OE *gnyrran,* G *knarren, knirren,* MD *gnerren, gnorren*]
gnarl[1] (närl), *n.* **1.** a knotty protuberance on a tree; knot. —*v.t.* **2.** to twist. [back formation from GNARLED]
gnarl[2] (närl), *v.i.* to growl; snarl. [var. of GNAR]
gnarled (närld), *adj.* **1.** (of trees) full of or covered with gnarls; bent; twisted. **2.** having a rugged, weather-beaten appearance. **3.** crabby; cantankerous. [var. of KNURLED]
gnarl·y (när′lē), *adj.,* **gnarl·i·er, gnarl·i·est.** gnarled. —**gnarl′i·ness,** *n.*
gnash (nash), *v.t.* **1.** to grind or strike (the teeth) together, esp. in rage or pain. **2.** to bite with grinding teeth. —*v.i.* **3.** to gnash the teeth. —*n.* **4.** an act of gnashing. [var. of obs. *gnast* < Scand; cf. OIcel *gnastan* gnashing of teeth] —**gnash′ing·ly,** *adv.*
gnat (nat), *n.* any of certain small flies, esp. the biting gnats or punkies of the family *Ceratopogonidae,* the midges of the family *Chironomidae,* and the buffalo gnats or black flies of the family *Simuliidae.* [ME; OE *gnæt(t)*; c. G (dial.) *Gnatze*] —**gnat′like′,** *adj.*
gnat·catch·er (nat′kach′ər), *n.* any of several small, American, insectivorous warblers of the genus *Polioptila,* of the family *Sylviidae.*
gnath·ic (nath′ik), *adj.* of or pertaining to the jaw. Also, **gnath′al.** [< Gk *gnáth(os)* jaw + -IC]

Gnat, *Simulium vittatum* (Length ¼ in.)

gna·thon·ic (na thon′ik), *adj.* sycophantic; fawning. [< L *gnathonic(us)* < *Gnathon-* (s. of *Gnatho*) name of a sycophantic character in the Roman comedy *Eunuchus* by Terence; see -IC] —**gna·thon′i·cal·ly,** *adv.*

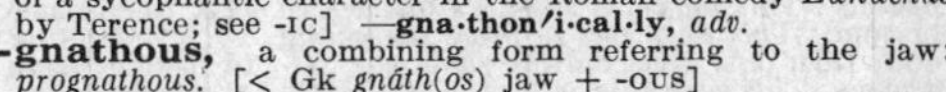

-gnathous, a combining form referring to the jaw: *prognathous.* [< Gk *gnáth(os)* jaw + -OUS]
gnaw (nô), *v.,* **gnawed, gnawed** or **gnawn, gnaw·ing.** —*v.t.* **1.** to wear away or remove by persistent biting. **2.** to form by gnawing. **3.** to erode; waste or wear away. **4.** to trouble or torment by constant annoyance; vex; plague. —*v.i.* **5.** to bite or chew on persistently. **6.** to cause erosion. **7.** to cause an effect resembling erosion: *Her mistake gnawed at her conscience.* [ME *gnaw(en),* OE *gnagen;* c. G *nagen,* OIcel *gnāga*] —**gnaw′a·ble,** *adj.* —**gnaw′er,** *n.*
gnaw·ing (nô′ing), *n.* **1.** the act of a person or thing that gnaws. **2.** Usually, **gnawings.** persistent, dull pains: *the gnawings of hunger.* [ME] —**gnaw′ing·ly,** *adv.*
gnawn (nôn), *v.* a pp. of **gnaw.**
gneiss (nīs), *n.* a metamorphic rock, generally made up of bands that differ in color and composition, some bands being rich in feldspar and quartz, others rich in hornblende or mica. [< G] —**gneiss′ic, gneiss′oid,** *adj.*
Gniez·no (gnyez′nô), *n.* a city in W central Poland, NE of Posen: first capital of the country; 14th-century cathedral. 45,000 (est. 1963). German, **Gnes·en** (gnā′zən).
gnome[1] (nōm), *n.* one of a legendary species of diminutive beings, usually described as shriveled little old men, that inhabit the interior of the earth and act as guardians of its treasures; troll. [< F < NL *gnom(us)* < ? Gk *gnṓmē* GNOME[2]] —**gnom′ish,** *adj.* —**Syn.** See **goblin, sylph.**
gnome[2] (nōm, nō′mē), *n.* a short, pithy expression of a general truth; aphorism. [< Gk: judgment, opinion, purpose]
gno·mic (nō′mik, nom′ik), *adj.* **1.** like or containing gnomes or aphorisms. **2.** of, pertaining to, or noting a writer of aphorisms, esp. any of certain Greek poets. Also, **gno′mi·cal.** [< Gk *gnōmik(ós)*] —**gno′mi·cal·ly,** *adv.*
gno·mist (nō′mist), *n.* a writer of aphorisms. [GNOME[2] + -IST]
gno·mol·o·gy (nō mol′ə jē), *n.* **1.** a collection or anthology of gnomes or aphoristic writing. **2.** gnomic or aphoristic writing. [< Gk *gnōmología*] —**gno·mo·log·ic** (nō′mə loj′ik), **gno′mo·log′i·cal,** *adj.* —**gno·mol′o·gist,** *n.*
gno·mon (nō′mon), *n.* **1.** an early astronomical instrument consisting of a vertical shaft, column, or the like, for determining the altitude of the sun or the latitude of a position by measuring the length of its shadow cast at noon. **2.** the raised part of a sundial that casts the shadow; a style. **3.** *Geom.* the part of a parallelogram that remains after a similar parallelogram has been taken away from one of its corners. [< L: pin of a sundial < Gk: one who knows, inspector]

EFGBCD, Gnomon (def. 3)

gno·mon·ic (nō mon′ik), *adj.* **1.** of or pertaining to a gnomon or to a sundial. **2.** of or pertaining to the measurement of time by a gnomon or a sundial. **3.** gnomic. Also, **gno·mon′i·cal.** [< L *gnōmonic(us)* < Gk *gnōmonikós*]
-gnomy, an element meaning "knowledge," occurring in loan words from Greek and used in combination with other elements of Greek origin: *physiognomy.* [< LL *-gnomia* < Gk]
gno·sis (nō′sis), *n.* knowledge of spiritual things; mystical knowledge. [< NL < Gk: a seeking to know = *gnō-* know + *-sis* -SIS]
-gnosis, a learned borrowing from Greek meaning "knowledge," used in the formation of compound words: *prognosis.* [< L < Gk: see GNOSIS]
Gnos·sus (nos′əs), *n.* Knossos. —**Gnos′si·an,** *adj.*
gnos·tic (nos′tik), *adj.* Also, **gnos′ti·cal.** **1.** pertaining to or having knowledge, esp. of spiritual things. **2.** (*cap.*) pertaining to or characteristic of the Gnostics. —*n.* **3.** (*cap.*) a member of any of certain heretical early Christian mystical sects that claimed that matter was evil and denied that Christ had a natural corporeal existence. [< LL *Gnostic(ī)* name of the sect < Gk *gnōstikós* pertaining to knowledge = *gnōst(ós)* known + *-ikos* -IC] —**gnos′ti·cal·ly,** *adv.* —**Gnos′ti·cism,** *n.*
-gnostic, a combination of **-gnosis** and **-ic,** used to form adjectives from stems ending in **-gnosis:** *prognostic.* [< ML *-gnosticus* < Gk *gnōstikós* GNOSTIC]
Gnos·ti·cise (nos′ti sīz′), *v.i., v.t.,* **-cised, -cis·ing.** *Chiefly Brit.* Gnosticize. Also, **gnos′ti·cise′.** —**Gnos′ti·cis′er,** *n.*
Gnos·ti·cize (nos′ti sīz′), *v.,* **-cized, -ciz·ing.** —*v.i.* **1.** to adopt or maintain Gnostic views. —*v.t.* **2.** to explain on Gnostic principles; give a Gnostic interpretation of or quality to. Also, **gnos′ti·cize′.** —**Gnos′ti·ciz′er,** *n.*
gno·thi se·au·ton (gnō′thi se ou ton′), *Greek.* know thyself.
GNP, See **gross national product.** Also, **G.N.P.**
gnu (no͞o, nyo͞o), *n., pl.* **gnus,** (*esp. collectively*) **gnu.** any of several African antelopes of the genus *Connochaetes,* having an oxlike head, curved horns, and a long tail. Also called **wildebeest.** [< Kaffir *nqu*]

Gnu, *Connochaetes taurinus* (4 ft. high at shoulder; total length 7 ft.; tail 1½ ft.)

go[1] (gō), *v.,* **went, gone, going,** *n., pl.* **goes,** *interj., adj.* —*v.i.* **1.** to move or proceed, esp. to or from something. **2.** to leave a place; depart. **3.** to keep or be in motion; function: *The engine's going now.* **4.** to become as specified: *to go mad.* **5.** to act as specified: *Go warily.* **6.** to act so as to come into a certain state or condition: *to go to sleep.* **7.** to be known: *to go by a false name.* **8.** to reach, extend, or give access to: *Where does this door go?* **9.** (of time) to pass; elapse. **10.** to be applied, allotted, transferred, etc., to a particular recipient or purpose: *My money goes for food and rent.* **11.** to be sold: *the house went for a song.* **12.** to be considered generally or usually: *This player is short, as pitchers go.* **13.** to conduce or tend: *This only goes to prove the point.* **14.** to result or end; turn out: *How did the game go?* **15.** to belong; have a place: *This book goes on the top shelf.* **16.** (of colors, styles, etc.) to harmonize; be compatible; be suited. **17.** to fit or extend around or into: *This belt won't go around my waist.* **18.** to be or become consumed, spent, finished, etc. **19.** to develop, progress, or proceed. **20.** to pass or circulate, as in transmission or communication: *The rumor has gone around.* **21.** to make a certain sound: *The gun goes bang.* **22.** to be phrased, written, or composed: *How does that song go?* **23.** to seek or have recourse; resort: *to go to court.* **24.** to become worn out or weakened. **25.** to die. **26.** to fail, break, or give way. **27.** to begin; come into action: *Go when you hear the bell.* **28.** to contribute in amount or quantity; be requisite: *Sixteen ounces go to the pound.* **29.** to be or be able to be divided into: *Three goes into fifteen five times.* **30.** to contribute to an end result. **31.** to be about, intending, or destined (usually used in the present tense, fol. by an infinitive): *He is going to write.* **32.** to be considered acceptable or true; succeed: *Anything goes.* **33.** to be authoritative; be the final word: *What I say goes!* **34.** to subject oneself: *Don't go to any trouble.* **35.** (used in the infinitive as an intensifier to indicate the idea of proceeding rapidly, impulsively, or desperately): *He decided to go borrow it.* —*v.t.* **36.** *Informal.* to endure or tolerate: *I can't go his preaching.* **37.** *Informal.* to afford, bet, or bid: *I'll go two dollars on number seven.* **38.** to share or participate in to the extent of: *to go halves.* **39.** to yield, weigh, or grow to: *These tomatoes will go half a pound each.* **40.** to assume the obligation or function of: *His father went bail for him.* **41. go about, a.** *Naut.* to change course by tacking or wearing. **b.** to occupy oneself with; perform. **42. go after,** to attempt to obtain; strive for. **43. go ahead,** to proceed without hesitation or delay. **44. go along,** to agree with; concur. **45. go and,** to be so thoughtless, unfortunate, or silly as to: *She had to go and lose her gloves.* **46. go around, a.** to be often in company. **b.** to be sufficient for all. **47. go at, a.** to assault; attack. **b.** to begin or proceed vigorously. **48. go by, a.** to pass: *Don't let this chance go by.* **b.** to be guided by. **49. go down, a.** to suffer defeat. **b.** to admit of being consumed: *This food goes down smoothly.* **c.** to be remembered in history or by posterity. **d.** *Brit.* to leave a university, permanently or at the end of a term. **e.** *Bridge.* to fall short of making one's contract. **50. go for, a.** to make an attempt at; try for: *He is going for the championship.* **b.** to assault. **c.** to favor; like. **d.** to sell at a certain price. **51. go in for,** to adopt as one's particular interest; to occupy oneself with; engage in. **52. go into, a.** to discuss or investigate. **b.** to undertake as one's study or work. **53. go in with,** to join in a partnership or union; combine with. **54. go off, a.** to explode; function abruptly: *The gun went off.* **b.** (of what has been expected or planned) to happen: *The interview went off very badly.* **55. go on, a.** to behave; act. **b.** to continue: *Go on working.* **c.** to talk effusively; chatter. **d.** to happen or take place: *What's going on here?* **e.** (used to express disbelief): *Go on, you're kidding me.* **f.** to appear onstage in a theatrical performance. **56. go out, a.** to come to an end, esp. to fade in popularity. **b.** to cease or fail to function: *The lights went out.* **c.** to participate in social activities. **d.** to take part in a strike. **e.** *Cards.* to achieve a point score equal to or above the score necessary to win the game. **57. go over, a.** to read; scan. **b.** to repeat; review. **c.** to be effective or successful. **d.** to examine. **58. go the whole hog,** to do something thoroughly or consistently. **59. go through, a.** to bear; experience. **b.** to examine or search carefully. **c.** to be successful or accepted, as a plan. **d.** to use up; spend completely. **60. go through with,** to persevere with to the end; to complete. **61. go to, a.** to attend, visit, or participate in: *Are you going to go to the party?* **b.** to be enrolled at; attend as a student: *He goes to Princeton.* **62. go to!** *Archaic.* **a.** you don't say! I don't believe you! **b.** let's do it! come on! **63. go together, a.** to be appropriate or harmonious. **b.** to keep company; date; court. **64. go to it,** *Informal.* to begin vigorously and at once. **65. go under, a.** to be overwhelmed or ruined; fail. **b.** (of a vessel) to founder. **66. go up, a.** to be in the process of construction, as a building. **b.** to increase in cost, value, etc. **c.** to forget, as an actor his lines. **d.** *Brit.* to go to a university at the beginning of a term. **67. go with,** *Informal.* to keep company with; court; date. Also, **go out with. 68. let go, a.** to release one's grasp or hold; free. **b.** to cease to employ; dismiss. **69. let oneself go,** to free oneself of inhibitions or restraint. **70. to go,** *Informal.* **a.** (of food) for consumption off the premises where sold: *coffee and doughnuts to go.* **b.** remaining: *two pages to go.* —*n.* **71.** the act of going. **72.** energy, spirit, or animation: *a man with a lot of go.* **73.** a try at something; attempt: *to have a go at winning the prize.* **74.** a successful accomplishment. **75.** *Brit. Informal.* the first or preliminary examination at Cambridge University for the degree of A.B. **76. from the word "go,"** from the very start. **77. no go,** *Informal.* futile; useless. **78. on the go,** very busy; active. —*interj.* **79.** (in calling the start of a race) start the race; leave the starting line: *On your mark! Get set! Go!* —*adj. U.S.* **80.** ready. **81.** functioning properly: *All systems are go.* [ME *go(n)*, OE *gān;* c. OHG *gēn, G gehen*] —**Syn. 1.** walk, run, ride, travel. —**Ant. 1.** stay.

go[2] (gō), *n.* a Japanese game played on a board having 361 intersections on which black and white stones are alternately placed, the object being to capture the opponent's stones and control the larger part of the board. Also called **I-go.** [< Jap]

G.O., **1.** general office. **2.** general order. Also, **g.o.**

go·a (gō′ə), *n.* a gazelle, *Procapra picticaudata*, of the Tibetan plateau. [< Tibetan *dgoba*]

Go·a (gō′ə), *n.* a former district in Portuguese India, on the Arabian Sea, ab. 250 mi. S of Bombay: annexed by India December 1961. 551,397 (1950); 1394 sq. mi. *Cap.:* Panjim.

goad (gōd), *n.* **1.** a stick with a pointed or electrically charged end, for driving cattle, oxen, etc.; prod. **2.** anything that pricks, wounds, or urges like such a stick; a stimulus. —*v.t.* **3.** to prick or drive with or as with a goad; prod; incite. [ME *gode*, OE *gād;* cf. Langobardic *gaida* spearhead] —**goad′like′,** *adj.* —**Syn. 3.** spur.

go-a·head (gō′ə hed′), *n.* **1.** permission or a signal to proceed: *They got the go-ahead on the construction work.* —*adj.* **2.** advancing directly and without pausing: *a frank, go-ahead manner of speaking.* **3.** enterprising: *a go-ahead Yankee peddler.* **4.** signifying permission to proceed.

goal (gōl), *n.* **1.** the result or achievement toward which effort is directed; aim; end. **2.** the terminal point in a race. **3.** a pole or other object by which such a point is marked. **4.** an area, basket, cage, etc., toward or into which players of various games attempt to throw, carry, kick, hit, or drive a ball, puck, etc., to score a point or points. **5.** the act of throwing, carrying, kicking hitting, or driving a ball, puck, etc., into such an area or object. **6.** the score made by this act. [ME *gol* boundary, limit; cf. OE *gǣlan* to hinder, impede] —**goal′less,** *adj.* —**Syn. 1.** purpose, object, objective, intention. **2.** finish.

goal·ie (gō′lē), *n.* a goalkeeper.

goal·keep·er (gōl′kē′pər), *n.* (in ice hockey, field hockey, lacrosse, soccer, etc.) a player whose chief duty is to prevent the ball or puck from crossing or entering the goal. —**goal′keep′ing,** *n.*

goal′ line′, *Sports.* the line that bounds a goal.

goal′ post′, a post supporting a crossbar and, with it, forming a goal on a playing field in certain sports, as football.

goal·tend·er (gōl′ten′dər), *n.* a goalkeeper.

goal·tend·ing (gōl′ten′diŋ), *n.* **1.** goalkeeping. **2.** *Basketball.* any of several illegal acts by a defensive player that prevents the ball from going through the basket.

Go′a pow′der, a brownish-yellow, odorless, crystalline powder, used as a source of chrysarobin. Also called **araroba.** [after GOA]

Goat, *Capra hircus* (2½ ft. high at shoulder; length 4½ ft.)

goat (gōt), *n.* **1.** any of numerous agile, hollow-horned ruminants of the genus *Capra*, of the family *Bovidae*, closely related to the sheep. **2.** any of various related animals, as the Rocky Mountain goat. **3.** (*cap.*) *Astron., Astrol.* the constellation or sign Capricorn. **4.** *Informal.* a scapegoat or victim. **5.** a licentious or lecherous man. **6. get one's goat,** *U.S. Informal.* to anger, annoy, or frustrate a person: *People who come to work late get my goat.* [ME *got*, OE *gāt;* c. G *Geiss*] —**goat′like′,** *adj.*

goat′ an′telope, **1.** a goatlike antelope of the genus *Naemorhedus.* **2.** any antelope of the tribe *Rupicaprini*, a subdivision of the sheep and goat family, including the chamois, goral, serow, and Rocky Mountain goat.

goat·ee (gō tē′), *n.* a man's beard trimmed to a tuft or point on the chin. [GOAT + -EE, from the resemblance to a goat's tufted chin] —**goat·eed′,** *adj.*

goat·fish (gōt′fish′), *n., pl.* **-fish·es,** (*esp. collectively*) **-fish.** any tropical and subtropical marine fish of the family *Mullidae*, having a pair of long barbels below the mouth.

goat′ god′, a deity with the legs and feet of a goat, as Pan or a satyr.

goat·herd (gōt′hûrd′), *n.* a person who tends goats. [ME; OE *gāthyrde*]

goat·ish (gō′tish), *adj.* **1.** of or like a goat. **2.** lustful; lecherous. —**goat′ish·ly,** *adv.* —**goat′ish·ness,** *n.*

goats·beard (gōts′bērd′), *n.* **1.** a composite plant, *Tragopogon pratensis.* **2.** a rosaceous herb, *Aruncus sylvester*, having long, slender spikes of small flowers.

goat·skin (gōt′skin′), *n.* **1.** the skin or hide of a goat. **2.** leather made from it. [ME]

goat·suck·er (gōt′suk′ər), *n.* **1.** a nocturnal, European bird, *Caprimulgus europaeus*, having a short bill and a wide mouth and feeding on insects captured in the air. **2.** any other nocturnal or crepuscular bird of the family *Caprimulgidae.* Also called **nightjar.** [so called because formerly believed to suck the milk of goats; trans. of L *caprimulgus*, itself trans. of Gk *aigothḗlas*]

gob[1] (gob), *n.,v.,* **gobbed, gob·bing.** —*n.* **1.** a mass or lump. **2. gobs,** *Informal.* a large quantity: *She must have gobs of money.* —*v.t.* **3.** *Mining.* to fill (an area of a mine or pit from which all the ore has been extracted) with waste material. [ME *gobbe*, var. of *gob(b)e(t)* GOBBET]

gob[2] (gob), *n.* *Informal.* a seaman in the U.S. Navy. [?]

go·bang (gō bäŋ′), *n.* a Japanese game played on a go board with players alternating and attempting to be first to place five counters in a row. Also, **go·ban** (gō bän′). Also called **go-moku.** [< Jap = *go* GO[2] + *bang*, var. of *ban* board]

Go·bat (*Fr.* gō bȧ′), *n.* **Al·bert** (*Fr.* al bėʀ′), 1843–1914, Swiss lawyer and statesman: Nobel peace prize 1902.

gob·bet (gob′it), *n.* **1.** a fragment or piece, esp. of raw flesh. **2.** a lump or mass. [ME *gobet* < OF: mouthful, dim. of *gobe*]

gob·ble[1] (gob′əl), *v.,* **-bled, -bling.** —*v.t.* **1.** to swallow or eat hastily or hungrily in large pieces; gulp. **2.** *Informal.* to seize upon eagerly (often fol. by *up*): *She gobbled up all the news I told her.* —*v.i.* **3.** to eat hastily. [prob. imit.; formed on GOB[1]] —**Syn. 1.** bolt, devour.

gob·ble[2] (gob′əl), *v.,* **-bled, -bling,** *n.* —*v.i.* **1.** to make the characteristic throaty cry of a male turkey. —*n.* **2.** the cry itself. [var. of GABBLE]

gob·ble·de·gook (gob′əl dē go͝ok′), *n.* language characterized by circumlocution and jargon: *the gobbledegook of government reports.* Also, **gob′ble·dy·gook′.** [fanciful formation from GOBBLE[2]]

gob·bler[1] (gob′lər), *n.* a male turkey. [GOBBLE[2] + -ER[1]]

gob·bler[2] (gob′lər), *n.* a person or thing that gobbles or consumes voraciously or quickly. [GOBBLE[1] + -ER[1]]

Gob·e·lin (gob′ə lin; *Fr.* gô blaN′), *adj.* **1.** made at the tapestry factory established in the 15th century by the Gobelins, a family of French dyers and weavers. **2.** resembling the tapestries made at the Gobelin factory.

go-be·tween (gō′bi twēn′), *n.* a person who acts as an intermediary between persons or groups.

Go·bi (gō′bē), *n.* a desert in E Asia, mostly in Mongolia. ab. 450,000 sq. mi. Chinese, **Shamo.** —**Go′bi·an,** *adj.*

gob·let (gob′lit), *n.* **1.** a drinking glass with a foot and stem. **2.** *Archaic.* a bowl-shaped drinking vessel. [ME *gobelet* < OF, dim. of *gobel* cup << Celt]

gob·lin (gob′lin), *n.* a grotesque sprite or elf that is mischievous or malicious toward people. [ME *gobelin* < MF < MHG *kobold*]

—**Syn.** GOBLIN, GNOME, GREMLIN refer to imaginary beings thought to be malevolent to man. GOBLINS are demons of any size, usually in human or animal forms, that are supposed to assail, afflict, and sometimes even torture human beings. GNOMES are small beings like ugly little old men, who live in the earth, guarding mines, treasures, etc. They terrify human beings by causing dreadful mishaps to occur. GREMLINS are invisible beings who were said by pilots in World War II to cause things to go wrong with airplanes.

go·bo·ny (gə bō′nē), *adj.* *Heraldry.* compony. Also, **go·bo·née** (gə bō′nā). [obs. *gobon* slice < ME *goboun* < AF **gobon* < OF *gobet* (see GOBBET) + -y as in *compony*]

go-by (gō′bī′), *n.* *Informal.* a going by without notice; an intentional passing by; snub: *to give one the go-by.*

go·by (gō′bē), *n., pl.* (*esp. collectively*) **-by,** (*esp. referring to two or more kinds or species*) **-bies.** any small marine or fresh-water fish of the family *Gobiidae,* often having the pelvic fins united to form a suctorial disk. [< L *gōbi(us)* gudgeon (sp. var. of *gōbio* or *cōbius*) < Gk *kōbiós* kind of fish, gudgeon] —**go′bi·oid′,** *adj.*

go-cart (gō′kärt′), *n.* **1.** a small carriage for young children to ride in; stroller. **2.** a small, wheeled framework in which children learn to walk; walker. **3.** a handcart. **4.** kart.

God (god), *n.* **1.** the Supreme Being, the creator and ruler of the universe. **2.** (*l.c.*) one of several deities, esp. a male deity, presiding over some portion of worldly affairs. **3.** *Christian Science.* the Supreme Being considered with reference to the sum of His attributes. **4.** (*l.c.*) any deified person or object. —*interj.* **5.** (used to express disappointment, disbelief, weariness, frustration, annoyance, or the like.) [ME, OE; c. D *god,* G *Gott,* Icel *godh,* Goth *guth*]

Go·da·va·ri (gō dä′və rē), *n.* a river flowing SE from W India to the Bay of Bengal. 900 mi. long.

God-aw·ful (god′ô′fəl), *adj.* *Informal.* (*sometimes l.c.*) extremely dreadful or shocking.

god·child (god′chīld′), *n., pl.* **-chil·dren.** a child for whom a godparent serves as sponsor, as at baptism. [ME]

god·damn (god′dam′), *interj.* *Informal.* **1.** (used as an exclamation of any strong feeling and often fol. by *it.*) —*n.* **2.** something of negligible value; damn: *not to give a good goddamn.* —*adj.* **3.** damned (def. 2). —*adv.* **4.** damned. Also, **god′dam′.**

god·damned (god′damd′), *adj., superl.,* **-damned·est, -damnd·est,** *adv.* *Informal.* —*adj.* **1.** damned (def. 2). **2.** (esp. in the superlative) difficult to deal with; extremely complicated or peculiar. —*adv.* **3.** damned. Also, **goddamn, god′dam′.**

God·dard (god′ərd), *n.* **Robert Hutch·ings** (huch′iŋz), 1882–1945, U.S. physicist: pioneer in rocketry.

god·daugh·ter (god′dô′tər), *n.* a female godchild. [ME; OE *goddohtor*]

god·dess (god′is), *n.* **1.** a female god or deity. **2.** a greatly admired or adored woman. [ME] —**god′dess·hood′,** *n.*

Go·de·froy de Bouil·lon (gôdə fʀwä′ də bōō yôɴ′), c1060–1100, French crusader.

Go·des·berg (gō′des bᴇʀk′), *n.* a city in W West Germany, SE of Bonn. 66,700 (1963). Official name, **Bad Godesberg.**

go-dev·il (gō′dev′əl), *n.* **1.** a dart dropped into a well to explode a charge of dynamite or nitroglycerin previously placed in a desired position. **2.** a sled used to drag or carry logs, stone, etc. **3.** a cultivator that rides on wooden runners and is used on listed furrows.

god·fa·ther (god′fä′thər), *n.* a man who serves as sponsor for a child, as at baptism. [ME *godfader,* OE *godfæder*]

God-fear·ing (god′fēr′iŋ), *adj.* **1.** deeply respectful or fearful of God. **2.** (*sometimes l.c.*) pious; devout; deeply religious.

god·for·sak·en (god′fər sā′kən, god′fər sā′-), *adj.* (*sometimes cap.*) **1.** desolate; remote; deserted: *She wants to move from that godforsaken place.* **2.** wretched; neglected; pitiable.

God·head (god′hed′), *n.* the essential being, nature, or condition of God. [ME]

god·hood (god′hŏŏd), *n.* divine character or condition; divinity. [ME; OE *godhād*]

Go·di·va (gə dī′və), *n.* ("*Lady Godiva*") died 1057, wife of Leofric. According to legend, she rode naked through the streets of Coventry, England, to win relief for the people from a burdensome tax.

god·less (god′lis), *adj.* **1.** having or acknowledging no god or deity; atheistic. **2.** wicked; evil; sinful. —**god′less·ly,** *adv.* —**god′less·ness,** *n.*

god·like (god′līk′), *adj.* like or befitting God or a god; divine. —**god′like′ness,** *n.*

god·ling (god′liŋ), *n.* a minor god, esp. one whose influence or authority is entirely local. [ME]

god·ly (god′lē), *adj.,* **-li·er, -li·est.** **1.** conforming to the laws and wishes of God; devout; pious. **2.** *Archaic.* coming from God; divine. [ME; OE *godlīc*] —**god′li·ness,** *n.*

god·moth·er (god′muth′ər), *n.* a woman who serves as a sponsor for a child, as at baptism. [ME; OE *godmōdor*]

Go·dol·phin (gō dol′fin, gə-), *n.* **Sidney, 1st Earl of,** 1645–1712, English statesman and financier.

go·down (gō doun′), *n.* (in India and other Oriental countries) a warehouse or other storage place. [< Malay *godong,* perh. < Telugu *giḍaŋgi,* Tamil *kiḍaŋgu,* akin to *kiḍu* to lie]

Go·doy Al·ca·ya·ga (*Sp.* gô thoi′ äl kä yä′gä), *n.* **Lu·ci·la** (*Sp.* lōō sē′lä), real name of Gabriela Mistral.

god·par·ent (god′pâr′ent, -par′-), *n.* a godfather or godmother.

God's′ a′cre, a cemetery or burial ground, esp. one adjacent to a church; churchyard. [trans. of G *Gottesacker*]

God's′ coun′try, **1.** an area supposedly favored by God, esp. a beautiful rural area. **2.** an isolated, rural region.

god·send (god′send′), *n.* an unexpected thing or event that is particularly welcome and timely, as if sent by God. [earlier *God's send,* var. (by infl. of to *send*) of *God's sond* or *sand,* OE *sond, sand* message, service]

god·ship (god′ship), *n.* the rank or condition of a god.

god·son (god′sun′), *n.* a male godchild. [ME; OE *godsunu*]

God·speed (god′spēd′), *n.* good fortune; success (used as a wish to a person starting on a journey, a new venture, etc.). [ME, in the phrase *God spede* may God prosper (you)]

Godt·haab (*Dan.* gôt′hôp′), *n.* a city in and the capital of Greenland, in the SW part. 4876 (1962).

Go·du·nov (god′ənôf′, gŏŏd′-; *Russ.* go dŏŏ nôf′), *n.* **Bo·ris Fe·do·ro·vich** (bo ʀᴇs′ fyô′do ʀô′vich), 1552–1605, regent of Russia 1584–98 and czar 1598–1605.

God·ward (god′wərd), *adv.* **1.** Also, **God′wards.** toward God. —*adj.* **2.** directed toward God. [ME]

God·win (god′win), *n.* **1.** Also, **God·wi·ne** (god′wi ne). **Earl of the West Saxons,** died 1053, English statesman (father of Harold II of England). **2. Mary Woll·stone·craft** (wŏŏl′stən kraft′, -kräft′), 1759–97, English writer. **3.** her husband, **William,** 1756–1836, English political philosopher, novelist, and essayist.

God·win Aus·ten (god′win ô′stin). See **K2.**

god·wit (god′wit), *n.* any of several large, New or Old World shore birds of the genus *Limosa,* having a long bill that curves upward slightly. [? alter. of *good wight*]

Goeb·bels (gœ′bəls), *n.* **Jo·seph Paul** (yō′zef poul), 1897–1945, Nazi German official: propaganda director.

go·er (gō′ər), *n.* **1.** a person or thing that goes. **2.** a person who attends frequently or habitually (usually used in combination): *churchgoer; moviegoer.* [ME]

Goe·ring (gœ′ʀiŋ), *n.* **Her·mann Wil·helm** (hᴇʀ′män vil′helm). See **Göring, Herman Wilhelm.**

goes (gōz), *v.* **1.** 3rd pers. sing. pres. indic. of **go.** —*n.* **2.** pl. of **go.**

Goes (gōōs; *Du.* ᴋʜōōs), *n.* **Hu·go van der** (hyōō′gō van dər; *Du.* hʏ′gō vän dəʀ), c1440–82, Flemish painter.

Goe·thals (gō′thəlz), *n.* **George Washington,** 1858–1928, U.S. major general and engineer: chief engineer of the Panama Canal 1907–14; governor of the Canal Zone 1914–16.

Goe·the (gûr′tə, *Ger.* gœ′tə), *n.* **Jo·hann Wolf·gang von** (yō′hän vôlf′gäŋ fən), 1749–1832, German poet, dramatist, and novelist. —**Goe·the·an, Goe·thi·an** (gûr′tē ən, gœ′-), *adj.*

goe·thite (gō′thīt, gœ′tīt), *n.* a very common mineral, iron hydroxide, FeO(OH), an ore of iron. Also, **göthite.** [named after GOETHE; see -ITE[1]]

gof·fer (gof′ər), *n.* **1.** an ornamental plaiting used for frills and borders. —*v.t.* **2.** to flute (a frill, ruffle, etc.), as with a heated iron. Also, **gauffer.** [< F *gaufre* honeycomb < MD *wāfel*]

Gog (gog), *n.* a chief prince of Meshech and Tubal who came from Magog. Ezek. 38–39.

Gog and Ma·gog (gog′ ən mā′gog), two nations to be led by Satan in a climactic battle at Armageddon against the kingdom of God. Rev. 20:8.

go-get·ter (gō′get′ər, -get′-), *n.* *U.S. Informal.* an enterprising, aggressive person. —**go′get′ting,** *adj.*

gog·gle (gog′əl), *n., v.,* **-gled, -gling,** *adj.* —*n.* **1. goggles,** large spectacles equipped with special lenses, protective rims, etc., to prevent injury to the eyes from strong wind, flying objects, blinding light, etc. **2.** a bulging or wide-open look of the eyes; stare. —*v.i.* **3.** to stare with bulging or wide-open eyes. **4.** (of the eyes) to bulge and be wide open in a stare. **5.** to roll the eyes. **6.** (of the eyes) to roll. —*v.t.* **7.** to roll (the eyes). —*adj.* **8.** (of the eyes) rolling, bulging, or staring. [ME *gogele(n)* (to) look aside; cf. AGOG]

gog·gle-eyed (gog′əl īd′), *adj.* **1.** having bulging, wide-open, or rolling eyes, esp. in astonishment or wonderment. —*adv.* **2.** with bulging, wide-open eyes.

Gogh (gō, gôᴋʜ; *Du.* ᴋʜôᴋʜ), *n.* **Vin·cent van** (vin′sənt van; *Du.* vin sent′ vän). See **Van Gogh, Vincent.**

gog·let (gog′lit), *n.* (esp. in India) a long-necked container, esp. for water, usually of porous earthenware so that its contents are cooled by evaporation. Also, **guglet, gurglet.** [< Pg *gorgoleta* (dim of *gorja* throat), r. F. *gargoulette* (dim. of *gargoule* throat); see GARGLE]

go·go (gō′gō), *n.* See **à gogo.**

go-go (gō′gō′), *adj.* *Informal.* **1. a.** full of energy, vitality, or daring: *the go-go generation.* **b.** stylish, modern, or up-to-date: *the go-go set.* **2. a.** seeking to gain in asset value by trading aggressively and often speculatively in stocks: *a go-go mutual fund.* **b.** marked by swift price upswings due to excessive speculation: *a go-go stock.* [redupl. of GO]

go′-go danc′er, an entertainer who performs the twist, frug, or other current popular dances, for the patrons of a discotheque, nightclub, etc.

Go·gol (gô′gəl; *Russ.* gô′gol), *n.* **Ni·ko·lai Va·si·lie·vich** (ni ko lī′ vä sē′lyə vich), 1809–52, Russian novelist, short-story writer, and playwright.

Goi·â·ni·a (goi ä′nē ə), *n.* a city in and the capital of Goiás, in central Brazil, SW of Brasília. 133,462 (1960).

Goi·ás (goi äs′), *n.* a state in central Brazil. 1,954,862 (1960); 247,826 sq. mi. *Cap.:* Goiânia.

Goi·del·ic (goi del′ik), *Linguistics.* —*adj.* **1.** of or belonging to Goidelic; Q-Celtic. —*n.* **2.** the subbranch of Celtic in which the Proto-Indo-European *kw*-sound remained a velar. Irish and Scots Gaelic belong to Goidelic. Cf. **Brythonic, P-Celtic.** Also, **Gadhelic.** [< OIr *Gōidil* a Gael + -IC]

go·ing (gō′iŋ), *n.* **1.** the act of leaving or departing; departure. **2.** the condition of surfaces, as those of roads, for walking or driving: *The going was bad.* **3.** progress; advancement: *good going toward the presidency.* **4.** Usually, **goings.** behavior; conduct; deportment. —*adj.* **5.** moving or working, as machinery. **6.** active, alive, or existing. **7.** continuing to operate or do business, esp. in a successful manner: *a going company.* **8.** current; prevalent; usual: *What is the going price of good farmland in Ohio?* **9.** leaving;

departing. **10. going on, a.** nearly; almost: *It's going on four o'clock.* **b.** happening: *What's going on here?* **c.** continuing; lasting: *That party has been going on all night.* [ME]

go·ing-o·ver (gō′ing ō′vər), *n., pl.* **go·ings-o·ver** (gō′ingz-ō′vər). **1.** an examination or investigation. **2.** a severe, thorough scolding. **3.** a sound thrashing; beating.

go′ings on′, *Informal.* **1.** conduct or behavior, esp. when open to criticism. **2.** happenings; events. Also, **go′ings-on′.**

go′ing train′, *Horol.* the gear train for moving the hands of a timepiece or giving some other visual indication of the time. Cf. **striking train.**

goi·ter (goi′tər), *n. Pathol.* an enlargement of the thyroid gland, on the front and sides of the neck. Also, **goi′tre.** [< F *goitre* << L *guttur* throat]

go-kart (gō′kärt′), *n.* kart.

Gol·con·da (gol kon′də), *n.* **1.** a ruined city in S India, near the modern city of Hyderabad. **2.** (*often l.c.*) a rich mine or other source of great wealth.

gold (gōld), *n.* **1.** a precious, yellow metallic element, highly malleable and ductile. *Symbol:* Au; *at. wt.:* 196.967; *at. no.:* 79; *sp. gr.:* 19.3 at 20°C. **2.** a quantity of gold coins: *to pay in gold.* **3.** See **gold standard. 4.** money; wealth; riches. **5.** something likened to this metal in brightness, preciousness, superiority, etc.: *a heart of gold.* **6.** a bright, metallic yellow color, sometimes tending toward brown. —*adj.* **7.** consisting of gold. **8.** pertaining to gold. **9.** like gold. **10.** of the color of gold. [ME, OE; c. G *Gold,* Goth *gulth*]

gol·darn (gol′därn′), *n., adj., adv. Informal.* goddamn (used as a euphemism in expressions of anger, disgust, surprise, etc.). Also, **goldurn.**

gol·darned (gol′därnd′), *adj., superl.* **-darned·est,** *adv. Informal.* goddamned (used as a euphemism in expressions of anger, disgust, surprise, etc.).

gold·beat·ing (gōld′bē′ting), *n.* the art or process of beating out gold into gold leaf. Also, **gold′ beat′ing.**

gold′ bee′tle, any of several beetles having a golden luster, as a chrysomelid, *Metriona bicolor,* that feeds on morning-glories and roses. Also called **goldbug** (gōld′bug′).

Gold·berg (gōld′bûrg), *n.* **Arthur Joseph,** born 1908, U.S. jurist and statesman: associate justice of the U.S. Supreme Court 1962–65; ambassador to the U.N. 1965–68.

gold-brick (gōld′brik′), *v.i. Slang.* to shirk; loaf.

gold·brick (gōld′brik′), *n. Slang.* a person, esp. a soldier, who loafs on his job. Also, **gold′brick′er.**

gold′ certif′icate. See under **certificate** (def. 4).

Gold′ Coast′, a former British territory in W Africa; now a part of Ghana.

gold′ dig′ger, 1. a person who seeks or digs for gold. **2.** *Informal.* a woman who associates with or marries a man chiefly for material gain.

gold′ dust′, gold in fine particles.

gold·en (gōl′dən), *adj.* **1.** of the color of gold; yellow; bright, metallic, or lustrous like gold: *her golden hair.* **2.** made or consisting of gold: *golden earrings.* **3.** exceptionally valuable, advantageous, or fine: *a golden opportunity.* **4.** having glowing vitality; radiant: *golden youth.* **5.** full of happiness, prosperity, or vigor: *golden hours, a golden era of exploration.* **6.** highly talented and favored; destined for success: *television's golden boy.* **7.** richly soft and smooth: *a golden voice.* **8.** indicating the 50th event of a series, as a wedding anniversary. [ME] —**gold′en·ly,** *adv.* —**gold′en·ness,** *n.*

gold′en age′, (*sometimes caps.*) **1.** *Class. Myth.* the first and best of the four ages of man; an era of peace and innocence. **2.** the most flourishing period in the history of a nation, literature, etc. **3.** the period in life after middle age, traditionally characterized by wisdom, contentment, and useful leisure. **4.** *Informal.* the age at which a person normally retires.

gold′en ag′er (ā′jər), *Informal.* an elderly person who has retired.

gold′en as′ter, any North American, asterlike, composite plant of the genus *Chrysopsis,* having bright, golden-yellow flowers, esp. *C. mariana,* of the eastern U.S.

gold′en ban′tam corn′, a variety of sweet corn.

Gold′en Bull′, an edict of Charles IV, emperor of the Holy Roman Empire, establishing the system of Electors, issued in 1356 and in force until 1806.

gold′en calf′, 1. a golden idol set up by Aaron. Ex. 32. **2.** either of the two similar idols set up by Jeroboam. I Kings 12:28, 29. **3.** money or material goods.

Gold′en Deli′cious, 1. an American variety of yellow apple. **2.** the tree bearing this fruit.

gold′en ea′gle, a large eagle, *Aquila chrysaëtos,* of the Northern Hemisphere, having golden-brown feathers on the back of the head and neck. See illus. at **raptorial.**

gold·en·eye (gōl′dən ī′), *n., pl.* **-eyes,** (*esp. collectively*) **-eye.** either of two diving ducks, *Brucephala clangula,* of Eurasia and North America, or *B. islandica,* of North America, having bright yellow eyes.

Gold′en Fleece′, *Class. Myth.* a fleece of pure gold kept at Colchis by King Aeëtes. It was stolen by Jason and the Argonauts with the help of Aeëtes's daughter, Medea.

Gold′en Gate′, a strait in W California, between San Francisco Bay and the Pacific. 2 mi. wide.

gold′en glow′, a tall coneflower, *Rudbeckia laciniata,* having yellow flowers.

gold′en goose′, a legendary goose that laid one golden egg a day and was killed by its impatient owner, who wanted all the gold immediately.

gold′en hand′shake, a special incentive, as generous severance pay, given to an older employee as an inducement to elect early retirement.

Gold′en Horde′, the army of Mongol Tartars that overran eastern Europe in the 13th century and controlled Russia until the 15th century.

Gold′en Horn′, an inlet of the Bosporus, in European Turkey: forms the inner part of Istanbul.

gold′en mean′, 1. the perfect moderate course; the happy medium. **2.** See **golden section.**

gold′en nem′atode, a yellowish nematode, *Heterodera rostochiensis,* that is parasitic on the roots of potatoes, tomatoes, and other solanaceous plants.

gold′en par′achute, an employment contract or agreement guaranteeing top executives of a company substantial severance pay and other financial benefits in the event of job loss caused by the company's being sold or merged.

gold′en retriev′er, one of an English breed of retrievers having a thick, flat or wavy, golden coat.

gold·en·rod (gōl′dən rod′), *n.* **1.** any composite plant of the genus *Solidago,* most species of which bear numerous small, yellow flowers. **2.** any of various related composite plants, as *Brachychaeta sphacelata.*

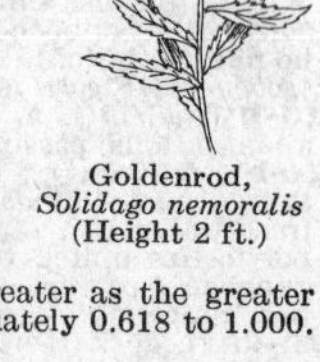

Goldenrod, *Solidago nemoralis* (Height 2 ft.)

gold′en rule′, a rule of ethical conduct, usually phrased "Do unto others as you would have them do unto you," or, as in Matt. 7:12, "Whatsoever ye would that men should do to you, do ye even so unto them."

gold·en·seal (gōl′dən sēl′), *n.* **1.** a ranunculaceous herb, *Hydrastis canadensis,* having a thick yellow rootstock. **2.** the rhizomes and roots of this plant, formerly much used in medicine.

gold′en sec′tion, *Fine Arts.* a ratio between two portions of a line, or the two dimensions of a plane figure, in which the lesser of the two is to the greater as the greater is to the sum of both: a ratio of approximately 0.618 to 1.000. Also called **golden mean.**

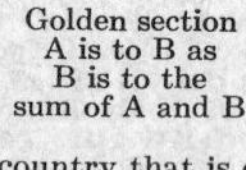

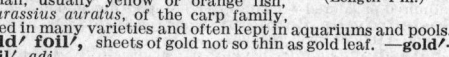

Golden section
A is to B as B is to the sum of A and B

Gold′en State′, California (used as a nickname).

gold′en wat′tle, a broad-leafed Australian acacia, *Acacia pycnantha,* having yellow flowers and yielding tanbark and a useful gum.

gold′en wed′ding, the 50th anniversary of a wedding.

gold′en years′, *Informal.* the years of retirement, normally after age 65.

gold′-ex·change′ stand′ard (gōld′iks chānj′), a monetary system in one country in which currency is maintained at a par with that of another country that is on the gold standard.

gold′ fe′ver, greed and excitement caused by a gold rush.

gold′ field′, an area or district where gold is mined.

gold-filled (gōld′fild′), *adj. Jewelry.* composed of a layer of gold backed with a base metal. Cf. **filled gold.**

gold·finch (gōld′finch′), *n.* **1.** a European fringilline songbird, *Carduelis carduelis,* having a crimson face and wings marked with yellow. **2.** any of certain related American finches of the genus *Spinus,* as *S. tristis,* the male of which has yellow body plumage in the summer. [ME; OE *goldfinc*]

gold·fish (gōld′fish′), *n., pl.,* (*esp. collectively*) **-fish,** (*esp. referring to two or more kinds or species*) **-fish·es.** a small, usually yellow or orange fish, *Carassius auratus,* of the carp family, bred in many varieties and often kept in aquariums and pools.

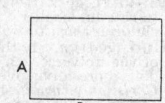

Goldfish (Length 4 in.)

gold′ foil′, sheets of gold not so thin as gold leaf. —**gold′-foil′,** *adj.*

Gol·ding (gōl′ding), *n.* **William,** born 1911, British novelist: Nobel prize 1983.

gold′ leaf′, gold in the form of very thin foil, as for gilding. —**gold′-leaf′,** *adj.*

gold′ mine′, 1. a mine yielding gold. **2.** *Informal.* a source of great wealth, profit, or any desirable thing.

gold·min·er (gōld′mī′nər), *n.* a person who mines gold or works in a gold mine.

gold′ note′, *U.S.* a bank note payable in gold coin.

gold-of-pleas·ure (gōld′əv plezh′ər), *n.* a brassicaceous herb, *Camelina sativa,* having small yellowish flowers.

Gol·do·ni (gol dō′nē; *It.* gôl dô′nē), *n.* **Car·lo** (kär′lô), 1707–93, Italian dramatist. —**Gol·do′ni·an,** *adj.*

gold′ plate′, 1. tableware or containers made of gold. **2.** a plating, esp. electroplating, of gold.

gold-plate (gōld′plāt′), *v.t.,* **-plat·ed, -plat·ing.** to coat (base metal) with gold, esp. by electroplating.

gold′ point′, the point at which it is equally expensive to buy, sell, export, import, or exchange gold in adjustment of foreign claims or counterclaims.

gold′ reserve′, 1. that part of the U.S. federal gold supply held by the Treasury in order to maintain the value of government promissory notes. **2.** the gold supply held by a country to maintain its monetary stability.

gold′ rush′, a large-scale, hasty emigration of people to a region where gold has been discovered, as to California in 1849.

Golds·bor·o (gōldz′bûr′ō, -bur′ō), *n.* a city in E North Carolina. 26,810 (1970).

gold·smith (gōld′smith′), *n.* **1.** a person who makes or sells articles of gold. **2.** (formerly) such a person also acting as a banker, moneylender, etc. [ME, OE]

Gold·smith (gōld′smith′), *n.* **Oliver,** 1730?–74, British poet, playwright, essayist, and novelist, born in Ireland.

gold′ stand′ard, a monetary system with gold of specified weight and fineness as the unit of value.

gold′ star′, a gold-colored star displayed, as on a service flag, to indicate that a member of one's family, organization, or the like, has been killed in war. —**gold′-star′,** *adj.*

gold·stone (gōld′stōn′), *n.* aventurine.

gold·thread (gōld′thred′), *n.* **1.** a white-flowered ranunculaceous herb, *Coptis trifolia,* having a slender, yellow root. **2.** the root itself, used in medicine.

Gold·wa·ter (gōld′wô′tər, -wot′ər), *n.* **Barry Morris,** born 1909, U.S. Republican candidate for President, 1964.

go·lem (gō′lem, -ləm), *n. Jewish Folklore.* a man-made figure constructed in the form of a human being and endowed with life. [< Yiddish *goylem* < Heb *gōlem* shapeless thing]

golf (golf, gôlf; *Brit. also* gof) *n.* **1.** a game in which each player uses a number of golf clubs to hit a small, white ball into a succession of holes, usually 9 or 18 in number, situated at various distances over a course having natural or artificial obstacles, the object being to get the ball into each hole in as few strokes as possible. **2.** a word used in communications to represent the letter *G*. **—***v.i.* **3.** to play golf. [ME, ? < Scot] **—golf′er,** *n.*

golf′ bag′, a bag, usually made of canvas, for carrying golf clubs and golf balls.

golf′ ball′, a small, white ball with a tough cover and a resilient core of rubber, used in playing golf.

golf′ club′, **1.** any of various long-handled clubs with wooden or metal heads, for hitting the ball in golf. Cf. **iron** (def. 6), **wood**[1] (def. 7). **2.** an organization of golf players.

golf′ course′, the ground or course, typically comprising 125 to 175 acres, over which golf is played. Also called **golf′ links′.**

Golfe du Li·on (gôlf dʏ lē ôɴ′), French name of the Gulf of Lions.

Gol′gi bod′y (gôl′jē), a netlike mass of material in the cytoplasm of animal cells, believed to function in cellular secretion. Also called **Gol′gi apparat′us.** [named after Camillo *Golgi* (1843?–1926), Italian physician and histologist]

Gol·go·tha (gol′gə thə, gol gä′-), *n.* **1.** Calvary (def. 1). **2.** a place of suffering or sacrifice. **3.** a place of burial. Also, **gol′go·tha** (for defs. 2, 3). [< L (Vulgate) < Gk < Aram *golgothā*, repr. Heb *gulgōleth* skull]

gol·iard (gōl′yərd), *n.* (*sometimes cap.*) one of a class of wandering scholar-poets in the 12th and 13th centuries, noted for their rioting, intemperance, and satirical Latin verse. [ME < OF *goliart, goliard* drunkard, glutton = *gole* throat (F *gueule*) + *-ard* -ARD] **—gol·iar·dic** (gōl yär′dik), *adj.* **—gol·iar′der·y,** *n.*

Go·li·ath (gə lī′əth), *n.* the giant warrior, champion of the Philistine army, whom David killed with a stone from a sling. I Sam. 17: 48–51.

gol·li·wogg (gol′ē wog′), *n.* (*sometimes cap.*) **1.** a grotesque black doll. **2.** a grotesque person. Also, **gol′li·wog′.** [after the name of a doll in an illustrated series of children's books by Bertha Upton (d. 1912), U.S. writer, and Florence Upton (d. 1922), illustrator]

gol·ly (gol′ē), *interj.* *Informal.* (used as a mild exclamation expressing surprise, wonder, puzzlement, or the like.) [euphemistic alter. of GOD]

go·losh (gə losh′), *n.* galosh.

Goltz (gôlts), *n.* **Baron Kol·mar von der** (kôl′mär fən dəʀ), 1843–1916, German field marshal and military historian.

gom·broon (gom bro͞on′), *n.* a type of Persian pottery ware. [after *Gombroon*, a town on the Persian Gulf]

Go·mel (gô′mel), *n.* a city in SE Byelorussia, in the W Soviet Union in Europe, on a tributary of the Dnieper. 208,000 (est. 1964).

gom·er·el (gom′ər əl), *n.* *Scot. and North Eng.* a fool. Also **gom′er·al, gom′er·il.** [obs. *gome* man (OE *guma;* c. Goth *guma,* L *homō*) + -REL]

Gó·mez (gō′mes), *n.* **Juan Vi·cen·te** (hwän bē sen′te), 1857?–1935, Venezuelan soldier and political leader: commander in chief and dictator of Venezuela 1908–35.

go·mo·ku (gō mō′ko͞o), *n.* gobang. [< Jap]

Go·mor·rah (gə môr′ə, -mor′ə), *n.* Also, *Douay Bible,* **Go·mor′rha.** an ancient city destroyed, with Sodom, because of its wickedness. Gen. 19:24, 25. **—Go·mor′re·an, Go·mor′rhe·an,** *adj.*

Gom·pers (gom′pərz), *n.* **Samuel,** 1850–1924, U.S. labor leader, born in England: president of the American Federation of Labor 1886–94, 1896–1924.

gom·pho·sis (gom fō′sis), *n., pl.* **-pho·ses** (-fō′sēz). *Anat.* an immovable articulation in which one bone or part is received in a cavity in another, as a tooth in its socket. [< NL < Gk *gomphō(ein)* (to) bolt together < *gómpho(s)* bolt, nail; see -OSIS]

Go·mul·ka (gə mo͝ol′kə), *n.* **Wla·dy·slaw** (vlä di′släf), 1905–82, Polish political leader: First Secretary of the Polish Communist party 1956–70.

go·mu·ti (gə mo͞o′tē), *n., pl.* **-tis.** **1.** Also called **gomu′ti palm′.** a sago palm, *Arenga pinnata*, of the East Indies, yielding palm sugar. **2.** a black, horsehairlike fiber obtained from this palm, used for making cords, ropes, cables, etc. [< Malay *gĕmuti*]

gon-, var. of **gono-** before a vowel: *gonidium.*

-gon, a suffix borrowed from Greek meaning "angled," "angular": *polygon; pentagon.* Cf. **gonio-.** [< Gk *-gōn(on),* neut. of *-gōnos*]

go·nad (gō′nad, gon′ad), *n.* *Anat.* a sex gland in which gametes are produced; an ovary or testis. [< NL *gonad-* (s. of *gonas*). See GON-, -AD[1]] **—go·nad′al,** *adj.*

go·nad·o·trop·ic (gō nad′ə trop′ik, gon′ə dō-), *adj.* *Biochem.* pertaining to substances, formed in the pituitary gland or the placenta, that affect the activity of the ovary or testis. Also, **go·nad·o·troph·ic** (gō nad′ə trof′ik, gon′ə dō-).

Go·na·ïves (*Fr.* gô nᴀ ēv′), *n.* a seaport in W Haiti. 14,000 (est. 1965).

Gon·court (gôɴ ko͞or′), *n.* **1. Ed·mond Louis An·toine Hu·ot de** (ed môɴ′ lwē äɴ twᴀɴ′ ʏ ō′ də), 1822–96, and his brother, **Jules Al·fred Huot de** (zhʏl ᴀl fʀed′), 1830–1870, French art critics, novelists, and historians: collaborators until the death of Jules. **2. Prix** (pʀē), an annual award of money made by a French literary society for the best prose work of the year.

Gond (gond), *n.* a member of an aboriginal people of Dravidian stock, in central India and the Deccan.

Gon·dar (gon′dər), *n.* a city in NW Ethiopia, N of Lake Tana: a former capital. 25,000 (est. 1962).

Gon·di (gon′dē), *n.* a Dravidian language, the language of the Gonds.

gon·do·la (gon′dᵊlə), *n.* **1.** a long, narrow, flat-bottomed boat, having a tall, ornamental stem and stern and sometimes a small cabin for passengers, rowed by a single oarsman, who stands at the stern, facing forward: used on the canals in Venice, Italy. **2.** *U.S.* **a.** a double-ended, sloop-rigged vessel of the 18th and 19th centuries. **b.** any of various barges or scows. **c.** *Railroads.* See **gondola car. 3.** the car of a dirigible. **4.** the basket or car suspended beneath a balloon. [< It (Venetian dial.); cf. It *dondolare* to rock, swing]

Gondola (Venetian)

gon′dola car′, *U.S.* an open railroad freight car with low sides, for transporting bulk freight and manufactured goods.

gon·do·lier (gon′dᵊlēr′), *n.* a man who rows or poles a gondola. [< It *gondoliere*]

Gond·wa·na (gond wä′nə), *n.* *Geol.* a hypothetical land mass in the Southern Hemisphere that separated near the end of the Paleozoic era to form South America, Africa, and Australia. Also called **Gond·wa′na·land′.** Cf. **Laurasia.**

gone (gôn, gon), *v.* **1.** pp. of **go. —***adj.* **2.** departed; left. **3.** lost or hopeless. **4.** ruined. **5.** that has passed away; dead. **6.** past. **7.** weak and faint: *a gone feeling.* **8.** used up. **9.** pregnant. **10.** *Slang.* outstanding; terrific (often prec. by *real*): *a real gone guy.* **11. far gone, a.** much advanced; deeply involved. **b.** nearly exhausted; almost worn out. **c.** dying. **12. gone on,** *Informal.* in love with.

gon·er (gô′nər, gon′ər), *n.* *Informal.* a person or thing that is dead, lost, or past recovery.

gon·fa·lon (gon′fə lən), *n.* **1.** a banner suspended from a crossbar, often with several streamers or tails. **2.** a standard, esp. one used by the medieval Italian republics. [< It *gonfalone* < Gmc]

gon·fa·lon·ier (gon′fə lə nēr′), *n.* **1.** the bearer of a gonfalon. **2.** a chief magistrate or other elected official in any of several medieval Italian republics. [< F < It *gonfaloniere*]

gong (gông, gong), *n.* **1.** a large bronze disk of Oriental origin that produces a vibrant, hollow tone when struck. **2.** a shallow bell sounded by a hammer operated electrically or mechanically. **3.** (in a clock or watch) a rod or wire, either straight or bent into a spiral, on which the time is struck. [< Malay; imit.] **—gong′like′,** *adj.*

Gón·go·ra y Ar·go·te (gông′gô ʀä′ ē äʀ gô′te), **Luis de** (lwēs′ de), 1561–1627, Spanish poet.

Gon·go·rism (gong′gə riz′əm, gông′-), *n.* imitation of the ornate and intricate style of Góngora y Argote. [< Sp *gongorism(o)*] **—Gon′go·rist,** *n.* **—Gon′go·ris′tic,** *adj.*

go·nid·i·um (gə nid′ē əm), *n., pl.* **nid·i·a** (-nid′ē ə). *Bot.* **1.** (in algae) any one-celled asexual reproductive body, as a tetraspore or zoospore. **2.** an algal cell, or a filament of an alga, growing within the thallus of a lichen. [< NL; see GON-, -IDIUM] **—go·nid′i·al, go·nid′ic,** *adj.* **—go·nid′i·oid′,** *adj.*

gonio-, a learned borrowing from Greek meaning "angle," used in the formation of compound words: *goniometer.* Cf. **-gon.** [< Gk, comb. form of *gōnía*]

go·ni·om·e·ter (gō′nē om′i tər), *n.* an instrument for measuring solid angles, as of crystals. **—go·ni·o·met·ric** (gō′nē ə me′trik), **go′ni·o·met′ri·cal,** *adj.* **—go′ni·o·met′ri·cal·ly,** *adv.* **—go′ni·om′e·try,** *n.*

go·ni·um (gō′nē əm), *n., pl.* **-ni·a** (-nē ə). *Biol.* the germ cell during the phase marked by mitosis. [< NL]

-gonium, a combining form of **gonium:** *archegonium.*

gon·na (gô′nə), *Eye Dialect.* going to: *Are ya gonna go or not?*

gono-, a learned borrowing from Greek meaning "sexual," "reproductive," used in the formation of compound words: *gonophore.* Also, *esp. before a vowel,* **gon-.** [< Gk, comb. form of *gónos, gonḗ* seed, generation, etc.; c. L *genus,* Skt *janas*]

gon·o·coc·cus (gon′ə kok′əs), *n., pl.* **-coc·ci** (-kok′sī). the bacterium *Neisseria gonorrhoeae*, causing gonorrhea. **—gon′o·coc′cal, gon·o·coc·cic** (gon′ə kok′sik), *adj.* **—gon′o·coc′coid,** *adj.*

gon·o·cyte (gon′ə sīt′), *n.* *Biol.* a germ cell, esp. during the maturation phase; oocyte; spermatocyte.

gon·oph (gon′əf), *n.* ganef.

gon·o·phore (gon′ə fōr′, -fôr′), *n.* **1.** *Zool.* an asexually produced bud in hydrozoans that gives rise to a medusa or its equivalent. **2.** *Bot.* a prolongation of the axis of a flower above the perianth, bearing the stamens and pistil. **—gon·o·phor·ic** (gon′ə fôr′ik, -for′-), **go·noph·o·rous** (gō nof′ər əs), *adj.*

gon·or·rhe·a (gon′ə rē′ə), *n.* *Pathol.* a venereal, purulent inflammation of the urethra or the vagina, caused by the gonococcus. Also, *esp. Brit.,* **gon′or·rhoe′a.** [< LL < Gk *gonórrhoia*] **—gon′or·rhe′al,** *esp. Brit.,* **gon′or·rhoe′al,** *adj.*

-gony, an element appearing in loan words from Greek, meaning "production," "genesis," "origination": *theogony; cosmogony.* [< L *-gonia* < Gk *-goneia.* See GON-, -Y[3]]

goo (go͞o), *n.* *Informal.* a thick or sticky substance: *Wash that goo off your hands.* [? short for BURGOO]

goo·ber (go͞o′bər), *n.* *U.S.* a peanut. Also called **goo′ber pea′.** [< Afr orig.; cf. Kimbundu *nguba* peanut]

good (go͝od), *adj.,* **bet·ter, best,** *n., interj., adv.* **—***adj.* **1.** morally excellent; virtuous; righteous: *a good man.* **2.** satisfactory in quality, quantity, or degree; excellent: *good food; good health; a good supply.* **3.** right; proper; fit: *It is good that you are here.* **4.** well-behaved: *a good child.* **5.** kind, beneficent, or friendly: *to do a good deed.* **6.** honorable or worthy: *a good name.* **7.** educated and refined: *She has a good background.* **8.** reliable; safe: *He's a good credit risk.* **9.** genuine; not counterfeit: *You can tell a good quarter by biting on it.* **10.** sound or valid: *good judgment.* **11.** healthful; beneficial: *Fresh fruit is good for you.* **12.** not spoiled or tainted; edible; palatable. **13.** agreeable; pleasant; genial: *Have a good time.* **14.** attractive: *She has a good figure.* **15.** (of the complexion) smooth; free from blemish. **16.** close; warm: *a good friend.* **17.** sufficient or ample: *a good supply.* **18.** fine; upstanding. **19.** advantageous; satisfactory for the purpose: *a good day for fishing.* **20.** competent or skillful; clever: *a good manager; good at arithmetic.* **21.** skillfully or expertly done: *a really good job; a good play.* **22.** comparatively new or of relatively fine quality: *Don't play in the woods, you're wearing good clothes.* **23.** best or most dressy: *He wore his good suit to the office today.* **24.** full: *a good day's journey away.* **25.** fairly great: *a good amount.* **26.** free from precipitation or cloudiness: *good weather.* **27.** *Horseracing.* (of the surface of a track) drying after a rain so as to be still slightly sticky. **28.** (of meat, esp. beef)

noting or pertaining to the specific grade below "choice," containing more lean muscle and less edible fat than "prime" or "choice." **29.** *Archaic.* an epithet for a ship, town, etc.: *the good ship Syrena.* **30. as good as.** See **as**[1] (def. 16). **31. good for, a.** certain to repay (money owed) because of integrity, financial stability, etc. **b.** the equivalent in value of: *Two thousand stamps are good for one coffeepot.* **c.** able to survive or continue functioning for (the length of time or the distance indicated): *These tires are good for another 10,000 miles.* **d.** valid or in effect for (the length of time indicated): *a license good for one year.* **e.** (used as an expression of approval): *Good for you!* **32. make good, a.** to make recompense for; repay. **b.** to implement an agreement; fulfill. **c.** to be successful. **d.** to substantiate; verify. **e.** to accomplish; execute: *The convicts made good their getaway.* —*n.* **33.** profit; worth; benefit: *We shall work for the common good.* **34.** excellence or merit; kindness: *to do good.* **35.** moral righteousness; virtue: *to be a power for good.* **36.** (esp. in the grading of U.S. beef) an official grade below that of "choice." **37. goods, a.** possessions. **b.** merchandise. **c.** *U.S. Informal.* what has been promised or is expected: *to deliver the goods.* **d.** *U.S. Informal.* the genuine article: *the real goods.* **e.** *U.S. Informal.* evidence of guilt, as stolen articles: *to catch someone with the goods.* **f.** *U.S.* cloth or textile material. **38. for good,** finally and permanently; forever: *to leave the country for good.* Also, **for good and all. 39. the good, a.** the ideal of goodness or morality. **b.** good things or persons collectively. **40. to the good, a.** generally advantageous: *That's all to the good, but what do I get out of it?* **b.** richer in profit or gain: *When he withdrew from the partnership, he was several thousand dollars to the good.* —*interj.* **41.** (used as an expression of approval or satisfaction.) —*adv.* **42.** *Informal.* well. **43. good and,** *Informal.* very; completely; exceedingly: *This soup is good and hot.* [ME; OE *gōd;* c. D *goed,* G *gut,* OIcel *gothr,* Goth *goths*]
—**Syn. 1.** pure, moral, conscientious, worthy, exemplary, upright. **2.** commendable, admirable. **4.** obedient, heedful. **5.** kindly, benevolent, humane, gracious. **17.** full, adequate. **19.** profitable, useful, serviceable, beneficial. **20.** efficient, proficient, capable, able, suited, suitable, expert, adroit. **37.** See **property.** —**Ant. 1–15, 18–21.** bad.
—**Usage. 42.** In the speech and writing of educated people, GOOD is rarely encountered as an adverb: *He did well* (not *good*) *on the test. She sees well* (not *good*) *with her new glasses.* Some confusion arises because WELL can be an adjective meaning "healthy": *He is a well man again.*

good′ afternoon′, a conventional expression used at meeting or parting in the afternoon.

good′ behav′ior, **1.** conduct conformable to law; orderly conduct: *The convict's sentence was reduced for good behavior.* **2.** proper fulfillment of the duties of an office, esp. a public office.

Good′ Book′, the Bible.

good-by (go͝od′bī′), *interj., n., pl.* **-bys.** —*interj.* **1.** farewell (a conventional expression used at parting). —*n.* **2.** a farewell. Also, **good′by′.** [contr. of *God be with you (ye)*]

good-bye (go͝od′bī′), *interj., n., pl.* **-byes.** good-by. Also, **good′bye′.**

good′ cheer′, **1.** cheerful spirits; courage: *to be of good cheer.* **2.** feasting and merrymaking: *to make good cheer.* **3.** good food and drink: *to be fond of good cheer.*

Good′ Con′duct Med′al, *U.S. Mil.* a medal awarded an enlisted man for meritorious behavior during his period of service.

good′ day′, a conventional expression used at meeting or parting during the daytime. [ME]

good′ egg′, *Slang.* an agreeable or trustworthy person.

good′ eve′ning, a conventional expression used at meeting or parting during the evening.

good′ faith′, accordance with standards of honesty, sincerity, etc. (usually prec. by *in*): *to act in good faith.*

good′ fel′low, a friendly and pleasant person.

good-fel·low·ship (go͝od′fel′ō ship′), *n.* a pleasant, convivial spirit; comradeship; geniality.

good-for-noth·ing (go͝od′fər nuth′ing, -nuth′-), *adj.* **1.** worthless. —*n.* **2.** a worthless person.

Good′ Fri′day, the Friday before Easter, commemorating the Crucifixion of Jesus. [ME]

good-heart·ed (go͝od′här′tid), *adj.* kind; considerate; benevolent. Also, **good′heart′ed.** —**good′-heart′ed·ly, good′heart′ed·ly,** *adv.* —**good′-heart′ed·ness, good′heart′ed·ness,** *n.*

Good′ Hope′, Cape of. See **Cape of Good Hope.**

good′ hu′mor, a cheerful or amiable mood.

good-hu·mored (go͝od′hyo͞o′mərd *or, often,* -yo͞o′-), *adj.* having or showing a pleasant, amiable mood: *a good-humored man; a good-humored remark.* —**good′-hu′mored·ly,** *adv.* —**good′-hu′mored·ness,** *n.*

good′ life′, **1.** a life lived according to the moral and religious laws of one's culture. **2.** a life abounding in material comforts and luxuries.

good-look·ing (go͝od′lo͝ok′ing), *adj.* of good or attractive appearance; handsome or beautiful.

good′ looks′, good or attractive personal appearance; handsomeness or beauty.

good·ly (go͝od′lē), *adj.,* **-li·er, -li·est. 1.** of a good quality: *a goodly gift.* **2.** of good or fine appearance. **3.** of good or substantial size, amount, etc.: *a goodly sum.* [ME; OE *gōdlic*] —**good′li·ness,** *n.*

good·man (go͝od′mən), *n., pl.* **-men.** *Archaic.* **1.** the master of a household; husband. **2.** a title of respect used for those below the rank of gentleman, esp. a farmer or yeoman. [ME]

Good·man (go͝od′mən), *n.* **Benjamin David** ("*Benny*"), 1909–86, U.S. jazz clarinetist and bandleader.

good′ morn′ing, a conventional expression used at meeting or parting during the morning.

good′ mor′row, *Archaic.* good morning. [ME *good morwe*]

good′ na′ture, cheerful or pleasant disposition.

good-na·tured (go͝od′nā′chərd), *adj.* having or showing a pleasant, cheerful disposition or mood: *a warm, good-natured person.* —**good′-na′tured·ly,** *adv.* —**good′-na′tured·ness,** *n.* —**Syn.** agreeable, cheerful, equable.

Good′ Neigh′bor Pol′icy, the policy of the U.S. in encouraging friendly relations and mutual defense by the nations of the Western Hemisphere: first presented by President Roosevelt in 1933.

good·ness (go͝od′nis), *n.* **1.** the state or quality of being good. **2.** moral excellence; virtue. **3.** kindly feeling; kindness; generosity. **4.** excellence of quality: *goodness of workmanship.* **5.** the best part of anything; essence; strength. **6.** a euphemism for God: *Thank goodness!* —*interj.* **7.** (used in expressions of surprise, alarm, etc.): *Goodness, you gave me a start!* [ME; OE *gōdnes*]
—**Syn. 2.** integrity, honesty, uprightness, probity. GOODNESS, MORALITY, VIRTUE refer to qualities of character or conduct that entitle the possessor to approval and esteem. GOODNESS is the simple word for the general quality recognized in character or conduct: *Many could tell of her goodness and kindness.* MORALITY implies conformity to the recognized standards of right conduct: *a citizen of the highest morality.* VIRTUE is a rather formal word, and usually suggests goodness that is consciously or steadily maintained, often in spite of temptations or evil influences: *unassailable virtue.* **4.** worth, value. —**Ant. 1.** badness, evil.

good′ night′, an expression of farewell used in parting at nighttime. [ME *good nyght*]

good-night (go͝od′nīt′), *n.* a farewell or leave-taking: *He said his good-nights before leaving the party.*

good′ of′fices, **1.** services rendered by a mediator in a dispute. **2.** influence, esp. with another in a position of power.

good-oh (go͝od′ō), *Brit. Informal.* —*interj.* **1.** good (used as an expression of approval, agreement, or admiration). —*adv.* **2.** all right. **3.** yes. Also, **good′-o.**

Good·rich (go͝od′rich), *n.* **Samuel Gris·wold** (griz′wəld, -wōld, -wôld), (pen name: *Peter Parley*), 1793–1860, U.S. author and publisher.

good′ Samar′itan, a person who gratuitously gives help or sympathy to someone in distress. Luke 10:30–37.

Good′ Shep′herd, Jesus Christ. John 10:11–14.

good-sized (go͝od′sīzd′), *adj.* of ample or large size; rather large for its kind.

good-tem·pered (go͝od′tem′pərd), *adj.* good-natured; amiable. —**good′-tem′pered·ly,** *adv.* —**good′-tem′pered·ness,** *n.*

good·wife (go͝od′wīf′), *n., pl.* **-wives** (-wīvz′). **1.** *Chiefly Scot.* the mistress of a household. **2.** *Archaic.* a title of respect for a woman. [ME]

good′ will′, **1.** friendly disposition; benevolence; kindness. **2.** cheerful acquiescence or consent. **3.** *Com.* an intangible, salable asset arising from the reputation of a business and its relations with its customers. Also, **good′will′.**

Good′win Sands′ (go͝od′win), a line of shoals at the N entrance to the Strait of Dover, off the SE coast of England. 10 mi. long.

good·y[1] (go͝od′ē), *n., pl.* **good·ies,** *interj. Informal.* —*n.* **1.** Usually, **goodies.** something very attractive or pleasing, esp. sweet food; candy. **2. goodies,** things that cause delight; choice specimens of anything: *A record collector played some goodies for me on his phonograph.* —*interj.* **3.** good (used to express childish delight). [GOOD + -Y[2]]

good·y[2] (go͝od′ē), *n., pl.* **good·ies.** *Archaic.* a polite term for a woman of humble social standing. [var. of GOODWIFE; cf. HUSSY]

Good·year (go͝od′yēr′), *n.* **Charles,** 1800–60, U.S. inventor: developer of the process of vulcanizing rubber.

good·y-good·y (go͝od′ē go͝od′ē), *adj., n., pl.* **-good·ies.** —*adj.* **1.** self-righteously good, often for sentimental reasons; affecting goodness. —*n.* **2.** a goody-goody person. [redupl. of *goody* (GOOD + -Y[1])]

goo·ey (go͞o′ē), *adj.,* **goo·i·er, goo·i·est.** *Informal.* **1.** like or covered with goo; sticky; viscid. **2.** extremely emotional or effusive.

goof (go͞of), *Slang.* —*n.* **1.** a foolish or stupid person. **2.** a mistake or blunder. —*v.i.* **3.** to blunder; make an error, misjudgment, etc. **4.** to kill time (often fol. by *off* or *around*): *We just goofed around till train time.* —*v.t.* **5.** to spoil or make a mess of (something); botch; bungle (often fol. by *up*): *You really goofed that up.* **6. goof off,** *Slang.* to waste time; evade work. [appar. var. of obs. *goff* dolt < MF *goffe* awkward, stupid]

goof-off (go͞of′ôf′, -of′), *n. Slang.* a person who habitually shirks responsibility.

goof·y (go͞o′fē), *adj.,* **goof·i·er, goof·i·est.** *Slang.* ridiculous; silly; wacky; nutty; *a goofy little hat; a fellow who is sort of goofy.* —**goof′i·ly,** *adv.* —**goof′i·ness,** *n.*

goo·gly (go͞o′glē), *n., pl.* **-glies.** *Cricket.* a bowled ball that swerves in one direction and breaks in the other. [?]

goo·gol (go͞o′gol, -gəl), *n.* a number that is equal to 1 followed by 100 zeros and expressed as 10^{100}. [fanciful coinage by Edward Kasner (1878–1955), American mathematician]

goo·gol·plex (go͞o′gol pleks′, -gəl-), *n.* a number that is equal to 1 followed by a googol of zeros, and expressed as $10^{10^{100}}$. [GOOGOL + *-plex* (as in *multiplex*); see -FOLD]

gook (go͝ok, go͞ok), *n. Informal.* **1.** dirt, grime, or sludge. **2.** a viscid liquid or sauce. **3.** *Disparaging.* an Oriental. [phonesthemic; GOO, MUCK]

goon (go͞on), *n.* **1.** *Slang.* a stupid person. **2.** *Informal.* a hired hoodlum or thug. [shortened from dial. *gooney,* var. of obs. *gony* a simpleton (< ?); influenced by the comic-strip characters so called in the series *Thimble Theatre* by E. C. Segar (1894–1938), American cartoonist]

goo′ney bird′ (go͞o′nē), *Slang.* any of several albatrosses. [prob. from dial. *gooney* idiot: see GOON]

goose (go͞os), *n., pl.* **geese** for 1–4, 6; **goos·es** for 5; *v.,* **goosed, goos·ing.** —*n.* **1.** any of numerous wild or domesticated, web-footed, swimming birds of the family *Anatidae,* esp. of the genera *Anser* and *Branta,* most of which are larger than ducks and have a longer neck and legs. **2.** the female of this bird. Cf. **gander. 3.** the flesh of a goose, used as food. **4.** a silly or foolish person; simpleton. **5.** a tailor's smoothing iron with a curved handle. **6. cook one's goose,** *Informal.* to ruin one's chances finally or irrevocably. —*v.t.* **7.** *Slang.* to poke (one)

Canada goose, *Branta canadensis* (Length to 3¾ ft.)

between the buttocks. [ME *gose, goos,* OE *gōs* (pl. *gēs*); c. G *Gans,* OIcel *gās,* L *anser* —**goose′like′,** *adj.*

goose′ bar′nacle. See under **barnacle.**

Goose′ Bay′, a town on the coast of Labrador, in Newfoundland: site of international airport on the great circle route between New York and N Europe. 3040 (1961).

goose·ber·ry (go͞os′ber′ē, -bə rē, go͞oz′-), *n., pl.* **-ries.** **1.** the small, edible, acid fruit of certain prickly shrubs of the genus *Ribes,* esp. *R. Grossularia.* **2.** the shrub itself.

goose′ egg′, *Slang.* a score or grade of zero.

goose′ flesh′, a rough condition of the skin, resembling that of a plucked goose, induced by cold or fear. Also, **goose′flesh′.** Also called **goose pimples, goose′ bumps′.**

goose·foot (go͞os′fo͝ot′), *n., pl.* **-foots.** **1.** any herb or shrub of the genus *Chenopodium,* having minute, green flowers. **2.** any chenopodiaceous plant.

goose·neck (go͞os′nek′), *n.* a curved object resembling the neck of a goose, as the flexible shaft of a type of desk lamp (**goose′neck lamp′**). —**goose′necked′,** *adj.*

goose′ pim′ples. See **goose flesh.** —**goose′-pim′ply,** *adj.*

goose′step′, a marching step of the German and other infantries, the legs being swung high and kept straight and stiff.

goose-step (go͞os′step′), *v.i.,* **-stepped, -step·ping.** to march in a goose step: *Troops goose-stepped past the reviewing stand.* —**goose′-step′per,** *n.*

G.O.P., Grand Old Party (an epithet of the Republican party since 1880).

go·pher[1] (gō′fər), *n.* **1.** any of several ground squirrels of the genus *Citellus,* of the prairie regions of North America. **2.** See **pocket gopher.** **3.** See **gopher snake.** **4.** (*cap.*) a native or inhabitant of Minnesota (the **Gopher State**) (used as a nickname). [? < F *gaufre* honeycomb, ref. to the animal's burrowing habit, prob. by folk etym. < AmerInd; cf. earlier *magofer*]

Pocket gopher, *Geomys bursarius* (Total length to 13 in.; tail to 4½ in.)

go·pher[2] (gō′fər), *n. Slang.* **1.** a zealously eager person, esp. a salesman. **2.** an errand boy, assistant, or the like, who is sent to fetch coffee, cigarettes, etc. [humorous sp. for *go fer* repr. *go for* or (as in def. 1) *go for broke*]

go′pher snake′, **1.** a bullsnake, *Pituophis catenifer,* of western North America, that invades burrows to prey on rodents. **2.** See **indigo snake.**

Go′pher State′, Minnesota (used as a nickname).

go′pher wood′, an unidentified wood used in building Noah's ark. Gen. 6:14. [< Heb *gōpher*]

go·pher·wood (gō′fər wo͝od′), *n.* yellowwood.

gor (gôr), *interj. Brit. Dial.* **1.** (used as a mild oath.) **2.** (used as an exclamation of surprise or disbelief.) [alter. of GOD]

go·ral (gôr′əl, gôr′-), *n.* a goat antelope, *Naemorhedus goral,* of the mountainous regions of southeastern Asia, having horns shorter than the distance between them at their bases. [? << Skt *gaura, gaur*]

Gor·ba·chev (gôr′bə chôf′, -chof′; *Russ.* gor bä chôf′), *n.* **Mi·kha·il S.** (mi kīl′, -kāl′; *Russ.* mi кнä ēl′), born 1931, Russian political leader: general secretary since 1985.

gor·bli·mey (gôr blī′mē), *interj. Brit. Slang.* blimey. Also, **gor·bli′my.** Cf. **gor.** [GOR + BLIMEY]

gor·di·a·cean (gôr′dē ā′shən), *n.* any worm of the phylum or class *Nematomorpha,* having a long, unsegmented body, as the hairworm. [< NL *Gordiacea* = *Gordius* genus of roundworms (after *Gordius;* see GORDIAN, GORDIAN KNOT) + *-acea* -ACEA + -AN]

Gor·di·an (gôr′dē ən), *adj.* **1.** pertaining to Gordius, ancient king of Phrygia, who tied a knot (the **Gor′dian knot′**) that, according to prophecy, was to be undone only by the person who was to rule Asia. It was cut, rather than untied, by Alexander the Great. **2. cut the Gordian knot,** to solve a problem quickly and boldly. [< L *Gordi(us)* (< Gk *Górdios* Gordius) + -AN]

Gor·don (gôr′dᵊn), *n.* **1. Charles George** ("*Chinese Gordon*"; "*Gordon Pasha*"), 1833–85, British general: administrator in China and Egypt. **2. Lord George,** 1751–93, English politician. **3. George Hamilton, 4th Earl of Aberdeen,** 1784–1860, British statesman, born in Scotland: prime minister 1852–55.

Gor′don set′ter, one of a Scottish breed of medium-sized setters having a black-and-tan coat. [after Alexander, 4th Duke of *Gordon* (1743–1827), Scottish sportsman partly responsible for developing the breed]

gore[1] (gōr, gôr), *n.* blood that is shed, esp. when clotted. [ME; OE *gor* dung, dirt; c. D *goor,* OHG *gor* filth]

gore[2] (gōr, gôr), *v.t.,* **gored, gor·ing.** (of an animal) to pierce with the horns or tusks. [ME *gore(n);* see GORE[3]]

gore[3] (gōr, gôr), *n., v.,* **gored, gor·ing.** —*n.* **1.** a triangular piece of material inserted in a garment, sail, etc. Cf. **gusset** (def. 1). **2.** one of the panels making up a skirt or other garment. **3.** a triangular tract of land, esp. one lying between larger divisions. —*v.t.* **4.** to make or furnish with a gore or gores. [ME; OE *gāra* corner (c. G *Gehre* gusset); cf. OE *gār* spear]

G

G, Gore[3]

Gor·gas (gôr′gəs), *n.* **William Crawford,** 1854–1920, U.S. physician and epidemiologist: chief sanitary officer of the Panama Canal 1904–13; surgeon general of the U.S. Army 1914–18.

gorge (gôrj), *n., v.,* **gorged, gorg·ing.** —*n.* **1.** a narrow cleft with steep, rocky walls, esp. one through which a stream runs. **2.** a small canyon. **3.** a gluttonous meal. **4.** something that is swallowed; contents of the stomach. **5.** a choking mass. **6.** *Fort.* the rear entrance or part of a bastion or similar outwork. See diag. under **bastion.** **7.** the throat; gullet. **8. make one's gorge rise,** to evoke strong disgust: *The cruelty of war made his gorge rise.* —*v.t.* **9.** to stuff with food (usually used reflexively or passively): *to gorge oneself; to be gorged.* **10.** to swallow, esp. greedily. **11.** to choke up (usually used passively). —*v.i.* **12.** to eat greedily. [ME < OF *gorg(er)* (v.) < *gorge* (n.) throat < VL **gurga, *gorga* < ?] —**gorge′a·ble,** *adj.* —**gorg·ed·ly** (gôr′jid lē), *adv.* —**gorg′er,** *n.* —**Syn. 1.** defile, ravine. **9.** glut, cram, fill. **10.** devour. **10, 12.** bolt, gulp, gobble.

gor·geous (gôr′jəs), *adj.* **1.** splendid or sumptuous in appearance, coloring, etc. **2.** extremely enjoyable: *I had a gorgeous time.* [ME *gorgeouse* < OF *gorgi(as)* fashionable, elegant (< ?); see -OUS] —**gor′geous·ly,** *adv.* —**gor′geous·ness,** *n.* —**Syn.** rich, superb, grand; brilliant, resplendent, glittering, dazzling. See **magnificent.** —**Ant.** poor, plain.

gor·get (gôr′jit), *n.* **1.** a piece of armor for the throat. See diag. under **armor.** **2.** a wimple of the Middle Ages, worn with the ends fastened in the hair. **3.** a patch on the throat of a bird or other animal, distinguished by its color, texture, etc. [ME < OF] —**gor′get·ed,** *adj.*

Gor·gi·as (gôr′jē əs), *n.* c483–c375 B.C., Greek philosopher.

Gor·gon (gôr′gən), *n.* **1.** *Class. Myth.* any of three sister monsters, Stheno, Euryale, and Medusa, commonly represented as having snakes for hair and eyes that turned anyone looking into them to stone. Medusa was beheaded by Perseus. **2.** (*l.c.*) a mean or repulsive woman. [< L *Gorgōn-* (s. of *Gorgō*) < Gk *Gorgṓ,* special use of *gorgós* fearful, terrible]

Gor·go·ni·an (gôr gō′nē ən), *adj.* of, pertaining to, or resembling a Gorgon.

Gor·go·ni·an (gôr gō′nē ən), *n.* **1.** any of numerous corals of the order *Gorgonacea,* having a usually branching, horny, or calcareous skeleton. —*adj.* **2.** belonging or pertaining to the Gorgonacea. [< NL *Gorgoni(a)* name of the genus (see GORGON, -IA) + -AN]

Gor·gon·zo·la (gôr′gən zō′lə), *n.* a strongly flavored, semisoft variety of Italian milk cheese veined with mold. Also called **Gor′gonzo′la cheese′.** [after *Gorgonzola,* Italy, where first produced]

go·ril·la (gə ril′ə), *n.* **1.** the largest of the anthropoid apes, *Gorilla gorilla,* terrestrial and herbivorous, of western equatorial Africa and the Kivu highlands. **2.** an ugly, brutish fellow. **3.** *Slang.* a hoodlum or thug, esp. one who threatens or inflicts violence. [< NL < Gk *gorílla(s)* (acc. pl.), prob. of Afr orig.] —**go·ril′li·an,** **go·ril·line** (gə ril′īn, -in), *adj.* —**go·ril′loid,** *adj.*

Gorilla (Standing height 6 ft.)

Gö·ring (gœ′riŋg), *n.* **Her·mann Wil·helm** (her′män vil′helm) 1893–1946, German field marshal and Nazi party leader. Also, **Goering.**

Go·ri·zia (gô rē′tsyä), *n.* a city in NE Italy, on the Isonzo River, N of Trieste. 136,989 (1961). German, **Görz.**

Gor·ki (gôr′kē), *n.* **1.** Also, **Gorky. Max·im** (mäk sēm′), (pen name of *Aleksvey Maksimovich Pyeshkov*), 1868–1936, Russian novelist, short-story writer, and dramatist. **2.** Formerly, **Nizhni Novgorod.** a city in the RSFSR, in the central Soviet Union in Europe, on the Volga River. 1,084,000 (1965).

Gor·ky (gôr′kē), *n.* **1. Ar·shile** (är′shēl), 1904–48, American painter, b. Armenia. **2. Maxim.** See **Gorki, Maxim.**

Gör·litz (gœr′lits), *n.* a city in SE East Germany, on the Neisse River, at the Polish boundary. 89,900 (est. 1960).

Gor·lov·ka (gor lôf′kä), *n.* a city in the SE Ukraine, in the SW Soviet Union in Europe. 309,000 (est. 1962).

gor·mand (gôr′mənd), *n.* gourmand. —**gor′mand·ism,** *n.*

gor·mand·ise (gôr′mən dīz′), *v.i., v.t.,* **-ised, -is·ing,** *n. Chiefly Brit.* gormandize. —**gor′mand·is′er,** *n.*

gor·mand·ize (gôr′mən dīz′), *v.,* **-ized, -iz·ing,** *n.* —*v.i., v.t.* **1.** to eat like a glutton. —*n.* **2.** *Rare.* epicurean selectivity in choosing one's food and drink. [< F *gourmandise* = MF *gourmand* GOURMAND + *-ise* n. suffix later taken as v. suffix -IZE] —**gor′mand·iz′er,** *n.*

gorp (gôrp), *n.* a mixture of nuts, dried fruits, chocolate, cereal, etc. eaten for high-energy nourishment, esp. by hikers. [?]

gorse (gôrs), *n. Chiefly Brit.* furze. [ME, OE *gors(t);* c. G *Gerste,* L *hordeum* barley] —**gors′y,** *adj.*

gor·y (gōr′ē, gôr′ē), *adj.,* **gor·i·er, gor·i·est,** **1.** covered or stained with gore; bloody. **2.** resembling gore. **3.** involving much bloodshed: *a gory battle.* **4.** unpleasant or disagreeable: *the gory details of a divorce.* [ME] —**gor′i·ly,** *adv.* —**gor′i·ness,** *n.*

Goshawk, *Accipiter gentilis* (Length 26 in.)

Görz (gœrts), *n.* German name of **Gorizia.**

gosh (gosh), *interj.* an exclamation or mild oath. [euphemistic alter. of GOD]

gos·hawk (gos′hôk′), *n.* any of several powerful, short-winged hawks formerly much used in falconry. [ME *goshauk,* OE *gōshafoc.* See GOOSE, HAWK[1]]

Go·shen (gō′shən), *n.* **1.** a pastoral region in Lower Egypt, occupied by the Israelites before the Exodus. Gen. 45:10. **2.** a land or place of comfort and plenty.

MEDITERRANEAN SEA
DELTA OF THE NILE
Goshen
Memphis
Nile River
SINAI PENINSULA

gos·ling (goz′liŋg), *n.* **1.** a young goose. **2.** a foolish, inexperienced person. [ME *goselyng,* var. (by recomposition) of *geslyng;* ? < Scand; cf. OIcel *gæslingr.* See GOOSE-, -LING[1]]

gos·pel (gos′pəl), *n.* **1.** the teachings of Jesus and the apostles; the Christian revelation. **2.** glad tidings, esp. concerning salvation and the kingdom of God. **3.** the story of Christ's life and teachings, esp. as contained in the first four books of the New Testament, namely Matthew, Mark, Luke, and John. **4.** (*usually cap.*) any of these four books. **5.** (*often cap.*) an extract from one of the four Gospels, forming part of a church service. **6.** something regarded as true and implicitly believed: *to take his report as gospel.* **7.** a doctrine regarded as of prime importance: *political gospel.* —*adj.* **8.** pertaining to or proclaiming the gospel or its teachings: *a gospel hymn; gospel singer; gospel preacher.* **9.** in accordance with the gospel; evangelical. [ME *go(d)spell,* OE *gōdspell* (see GOOD, SPELL[2]); trans. of Gk *eu-angélion*]

gos·pel·er (gos′pə lər), *n.* *Eccles.* one who reads or sings the Gospel in church. Also, *esp. Brit.,* **gos′pel·ler.** [ME; OE *gōdspellere*]

gos′pel truth′, an unquestionably true statement, fact, etc.

Gos·plan (gos plän′), *n.* the official Soviet Union planning organization in charge of industry, agriculture, education, and health. [< Russ *Gos(udarstvennaya) Plan(ovaya Komissiya)* State Planning Committee]

gos·po·din (gos po dēn′), *n., pl.* **-po·da** (-po dä′). *Russian.* a title of respect corresponding to *Mr.*

gos·sa·mer (gos′ə mər), *n.* **1.** a fine, filmy cobweb seen on grass or bushes or floating in the air in calm weather, esp. in autumn. **2.** a thread or a web of this substance. **3.** an extremely delicate variety of gauze. **4.** any thin, light fabric. —*adj.* **5.** Also, **gos·sa·mer·y** (gos′ə mə rē), **gos′sa·mered.** of or like gossamer; thin and light. [ME *gos(e)somer* (see GOOSE, SUMMER[1]); possibly first used as name for late, mild autumn, a time when goose was a favorite dish (cf. G *Gänsemonat* November), then transferred to the filmy matter also frequent at that time of year]

Gosse (gôs, gos), *n.* **Sir Edmund William,** 1849–1928, English poet, biographer, and critic.

gos·sip (gos′əp), *n., v.,* **-siped, -sip·ing.** —*n.* **1.** idle talk or rumor, esp. about the personal or private affairs of others. **2.** a casual conversation. **3.** Also, **gos′sip·per.** a person, esp. a woman, given to tattling or idle talk. **4.** *Chiefly Brit. Dial.* a godparent. **5.** *Archaic.* a friend, esp. a woman. —*v.i.* **6.** to talk idly, esp. about the affairs of others; go about tattling. [ME *gossib, godsib(be),* OE *godsibb,* orig. godparent. See GOD, SIB] —**gos′sip·ing·ly,** *adv.* —**gos′sip·y,** *adj.* —**Syn. 1.** hearsay, chitchat; scuttlebutt, rumor; dirt, scandal. **3.** chatterer, talker, rumormonger. **6.** chatter, prattle, prate.

gos·sip·mon·ger (gos′əp mung′gər, -mong′-), *n.* a person especially addicted to gossiping.

gos·sip·ry (gos′əp rē), *n.* **1.** the practice of gossiping; gossip. **2.** gossips considered collectively.

gos·sip·y (gos′ə pē), *adj.* **1.** given to or fond of gossip. **2.** full of gossip. —**gos′sip·i·ness,** *n.*

gos·soon (go sōōn′), *n.* *Irish Eng.* **1.** a boy; lad. **2.** a male servant. [alter. of F *garçon*]

got (got), *v.* a pt. and pp. of **get.**
—**Usage.** Some purists object to the form HAVE GOT. The construction *I've got the money* is criticized on the stylistic grounds of being tautological, since *I have the money* has basically the same meaning. Likewise, *You have got to be there on time* can be expressed as *You have to be there on time,* and critics see no rationale for the repetition of the idea of "must." However, English has many such intensive constructions and, while teachers and others may demand a more precise, elevated style in writing, there is nothing ungrammatical about these usages, esp. when used orally.

Go·ta·ma (gô′tə mə, gō′-), *n.* Buddha. Also, **Gautama.** Also called **Go′tama Bud′dha.**

Gö·te·borg (yœ′tə bôr′yᵊ), *n.* a seaport in SW Sweden, on the Kattegat. 416,220 (1965). Also, **Gothenburg.**

Goth (goth), *n.* **1.** a member of a Teutonic people who, in the 3rd to 5th centuries, invaded and settled in parts of the Roman Empire. **2.** a rude person; barbarian. [ME *Gothe* < LL *Gothī* (pl.); r. OE *Gotan* (pl.) (*Gota,* sing.); c. Goth *Gut-* (in *Gut-thiuda* Goth-people)]

Goth, Gothic (def. 7). Also, **Goth., goth.**

Go·tha (gō′tä), *n.* a city in S Thuringia, in SW East Germany. 56,300 (est. 1960).

Goth·am (goth′əm, gō′thəm *for 1;* got′əm, gō′thəm *for 2*), *n.* **1.** a nickname for the city of New York. **2.** an English village, proverbial for the foolishness of its inhabitants. [ME] —**Goth′am·ite′,** *n.*

Goth·en·burg (goth′ən bûrg′, got′ᵊn-), *n.* Göteborg.

Goth·ic (goth′ik), *adj.* **1.** noting or pertaining to a style of architecture, originating in the middle of the 12th century and continuing through the middle of the 16th century, characterized by the use of the pointed arch and the ribbed vault. **2.** pertaining to or designating the style of painting, sculpture, furniture, etc., produced between the 13th and 15th centuries, esp. in northern Europe, characterized by a tendency toward realism and interest in detail. **3.** (originally in derogatory use) noting all European art of this period. **4.** pertaining to the Middle Ages; barbarous; rude. **5.** noting or pertaining to a style of literature characterized by a gloomy setting, grotesque or violent events, and an atmosphere of degeneration and decay. —*n.* **6.** the arts and crafts of the Gothic period. **7.** the extinct Germanic language of the Goths, preserved esp. in the 4th-century translation of the Bible by Ulfilas. *Abbr.:* Goth, Goth., goth. **8.** *Brit.* See **black letter. 9.** (*l.c.*) *U.S.* a square-cut printing type, without serifs or hairlines. [< LL *Gothic(us)* of, pertaining to the Goths] —**Goth′i·cal·ly,** *adv.* —**Goth′ic·ness, Goth·ic·i·ty** (goth is′i tē), *n.*

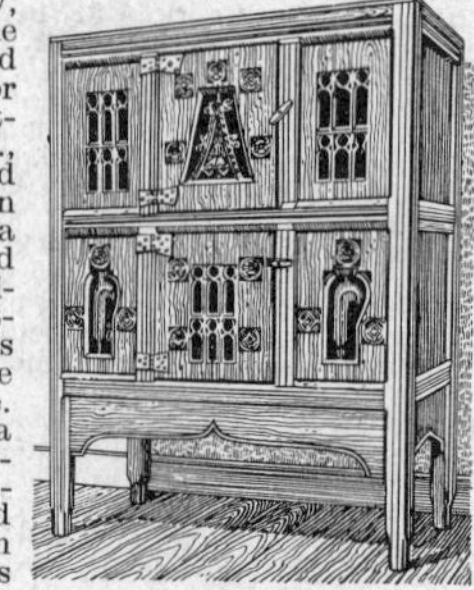

Gothic cupboard (16th century)

Goth′ic arch′, a pointed arch, esp. one having only two centers and equal radii.

Goth·i·cise (goth′i sīz′), *v.t.,* **-cised, -cis·ing.** *Chiefly Brit.* Gothicize. —**Goth′i·cis′er,** *n.*

Goth·i·cism (goth′i siz′əm), *n.* **1.** conformity or devotion to the Gothic style of architecture, sculpture, painting, etc. **2.** the principles and techniques of the Gothic style. **3.** adherence to aspects of Gothic culture. **4.** (*sometimes l.c.*) barbarism; rudeness.

Goth·i·cize (goth′i sīz′), *v.t.,* **-cized, -ciz·ing. 1.** to make Gothic, as in style. **2.** to make falsely or deceptively medieval. Also, *esp. Brit.,* **Gothicise.** —**Goth′i·ciz′er,** *n.*

Goth′ic nov′el, a style of fiction, esp. in the late 18th century and early 19th century, characterized by historical and picturesque settings, an atmosphere of mystery, gloom, and terror, supernatural or psychological plot elements, and violent and macabre events.

gö·thite (gō′tīt, gœ′-), *n.* *Mineral.* goethite.

Got·land (got′lənd; *Swed.* gôt′länd), *n.* an island in the Baltic, forming a province of Sweden. 54,323 (1960); 1212 sq. mi. *Cap.:* Visby. Also, **Gott′land.** —**Got′land·er, Gott′land·er,** *n.*

got·ten (got′ᵊn), *v.* a pp. of **get.**

Göt·ter·däm·mer·ung (*Ger.* gœt′ər dem′ə rōōng′), *n.* *German Myth.* the destruction of the gods and of all things in a final battle with evil powers: corresponds to the Scandinavian Ragnarok; Twilight of the Gods. [< G = *Götter,* pl. of *Gott* GOD + *Dämmerung* twilight]

Göt·tin·gen (gœt′ing ən), *n.* a city in central West Germany. 82,600 (1963).

Gott·lieb (got′lēb), *n.* **Adolph,** 1903–74, U.S. painter.

Gott mit uns (gôt′ mit ōōns′), *German.* God is with us; God be with us.

Gotts·chalk (gots′chôk), *n.* **Louis Mo·reau** (mō rō′, mô-), 1829–69, U.S. pianist and composer.

gouache (gwäsh, gōō äsh′; *Fr.* gwash), *n., pl.* **gouach·es** (gwä′shiz, gōō ä′shiz; *Fr.* gwash′) for 3. **1.** a technique of painting with opaque watercolors prepared with gum. **2.** an opaque color used in painting a gouache. **3.** a work executed in this medium or according to this technique. [< F < It *guazzo* place where there is water << L *aquātiō* < *aqua* water]

Gou·da (gou′də, gōō′-; *Du.* khou′dä), *n.* **1.** a city in the W Netherlands, NE of Rotterdam. 43,779 (1962). **2.** Also called **Gou′da cheese′.** a semisoft, cream-colored cheese made in Holland from whole or partly skimmed milk and usually coated with red wax.

Gou·dy (gou′dē), *n.* **Frederic William,** 1865–1947, U.S. designer of printing types.

gouge (gouj), *n., v.,* **gouged, goug·ing.** —*n.* **1.** a chisel having a partly cylindrical or V-section blade with the bevel on either the concave or the convex side. **2.** a groove or hole made by gouging. **3.** an extortion or swindle. —*v.t.* **4.** to scoop out or turn with, or as with, a gouge: *to gouge a channel.* **5.** to dig or force out with, or as with, a gouge. **6.** to extort from or swindle. [< F < LL *gu(l)bia;* cf. OPr *goja,* Sp *gubia*] —**goug′er,** *n.*

Gouges (Carpenter's)

gou·lash (gōō′läsh, -lash), *n.* a stew of beef, veal, vegetables, etc., with paprika or other seasoning. Also called **Hungarian goulash.** [< Hung *gulyas,* short for *gulyas hus* herdsman's meat]

Gould (gōōld), *n.* **Jay,** 1836–92, U.S. financier.

Gou·nod (gōō′nō; *Fr.* gōō nō′), *n.* **Charles Fran·çois** (chärlz fran swä′; *Fr.* sharl fräN swa′), 1818–93, French composer.

gou·ra·mi (gŏŏr′ə mē), *n., pl.* (*esp. collectively*) **-mi,** (*esp. referring to two or more kinds or species*) **-mis. 1.** a large, air-breathing, nest-building, fresh-water Asiatic fish, *Osphronemus goramy,* used for food. **2.** any of several small, air-breathing, nest-building Asiatic fishes of the genera *Trichogaster, Colisa,* and *Trichopsis,* often kept in aquariums. [< Malay *gurami*]

gourd (gōrd, gôrd, gŏŏrd), *n.* **1.** the fruit of any of various cucurbitaceous plants, esp. that of *Lagenaria Siceraria* **(bottle gourd),** whose dried shell is used for bottles and sometimes cultivated for ornament. **2.** a plant bearing such a fruit. **3.** a dried and excavated gourd shell used as a bottle, dipper, flask, etc. [ME *gourd(e), courde* < AF (OF *cöorde*) < L *cucurbita*] —**gourd′like′,** *adj.*

gourde (*Fr.* gōōrd; *Eng.* gŏŏrd), *n., pl.* **gourdes** (*Fr.* gōōrd; *Eng.* gŏŏrdz). a paper money and monetary unit of Haiti, equal to 100 centimes. *Abbr.:* G., Gde. [< F, n. use of fem. of *gourd* dull, slow, heavy < L *gurd(us)* dull, obtuse]

gour·mand (gŏŏr′mənd; *Fr.* gōōr mäN′), *n., pl.* **-mands** (-məndz; *Fr.* -mäN′). **1.** a person who is fond of good eating; gourmet; epicure. **2.** a glutton. Also, **gormand.** [ME *gourmaunt* < OF *gormant* a glutton] —**gour′mand·ism,** *n.*

gour·met (gŏŏr′mā; *Fr.* gōōr me′), *n., pl.* **-mets** (-māz; *Fr.* -me′). a connoisseur in the delicacies of the table; epicure. [< F; OF *gromet, grommes* valet (esp. of a wine merchant)]

Gour·mont (gōōr môN′), *n.* **Re·my de** (rə mē′ də), 1858–1915, French critic and novelist.

gout (gout), *n.* **1.** *Pathol.* a constitutional disease characterized by painful inflammation of the joints, chiefly those in the feet and hands, and esp. in the great toe. **2.** a drop, splash, or spot, as of blood. [ME *goute* < OF < L *gutta* a drop (of fluid); gout in the feet was formerly attributed to drops of a corrupted humor]

goût (gōō), *n.* *French.* taste; style; preference.

gout·y (gou′tē), *adj.,* **gout·i·er, gout·i·est. 1.** pertaining to or of the nature of gout. **2.** causing gout. **3.** diseased with or subject to gout. **4.** swollen as if from gout. [ME] —**gout′i·ness,** *n.*

Gov., governor.

gov., 1. governor. **2.** government.

gov·ern (guv′ərn), *v.t.* **1.** to rule by right of authority, as a sovereign does: *to govern a nation.* **2.** to exercise a directing or restraining influence over; guide: *the motives governing a decision.* **3.** to hold in check; control: *to govern one's temper.* **4.** to serve as or constitute a law for: *the principles governing a case.* **5.** *Gram.* to be regularly accompanied by or require the use of (a particular form). In *They helped us,* the verb *helped* governs the objective case of the pronoun *we*. **6.** to regulate the speed of (an engine) with a governor. **—*v.i.* 7.** to exercise the function of government. **8.** to have predominating influence. [ME *govern(en)* < OF *gouvern(er)* < L *gubernāre* to steer (a ship); c. Gk *kybernân* to steer] **—gov′ern·a·bil′i·ty, gov′ern·a·ble·ness,** *n.* **—gov′ern·a·ble,** *adj.* **—Syn. 1.** reign. See **rule. 2.** control, influence, check. **—Ant. 1.** obey.

gov·ern·ance (guv′ər nəns), *n.* **1.** government; exercise of authority; control. **2.** a method or system of government or management. [ME *governaunce* < OF < ML *gubernantia*]

gov·ern·ess (guv′ər nis), *n.* a woman who is employed to take charge of a child's upbringing, education, etc. [ME *govern(er)ess* < OF *gouverneresse,* fem. of *gouverneur* GOVERNOR; see -ESS]

gov·ern·ment (guv′ərn mənt, -ər mənt), *n.* **1.** the political direction and control exercised over the actions of the members, citizens, or inhabitants of communities, societies, and states; direction of the affairs of a state, community, etc. **2.** the form or system of rule by which a state, community, etc., is governed. **3.** the governing body of persons in a state, community, etc. **4.** (in some parliamentary systems, as that of the United Kingdom) **a.** the particular group of persons forming the cabinet at any given time: *The Prime Minister has formed a new government.* **b.** the parliament along with the cabinet. **5.** direction; control; rule: *the government of one's conduct.* **6.** a district governed; province. **7.** *Gram.* the established usage requiring that one word in a sentence should cause another to be of a particular form. [ME < OF *governement*] **—gov·ern·men·tal** (guv′ərn men′tᵊl), *adj.* **—gov′ern·men′tal·ly,** *adv.*

gov′ernment is′sue, (*often cap.*) issued or supplied by the government or one of its agencies.

gov·er·nor (guv′ər nər), *n.* **1.** the executive head of a state in the U.S. **2.** *Chiefly Brit.* a person charged with the direction or control of an institution, society, etc.: *the governors of a bank; the governor of a prison.* **3.** Also called, *Chiefly Brit.,* **governor-general.** the representative of the crown in a British colony or dependency. **4.** a ruler or chief magistrate appointed to govern a province, town, fort, or the like. **5.** *Mach.* **a.** a device for maintaining uniform speed regardless of changes of load as by regulating the supply of fuel or working fluid. **b.** a device for limiting maximum speed. **6.** *Brit. Informal.* **a.** one's father. **b.** one's employer. **c.** *Sometimes Facetious.* any man of superior rank or status. [ME *governour* < OF *governeor, gouverneur* < L *gubernātōr-* (s. of *gubernātor*). See GOVERN, -ATOR]

gov·er·nor·ate (guv′ər nər it, -nə rāt′), *n.* an administrative division of a country, esp. in the United Arab Republic.

gov′ernor gen′eral, *pl.* **governors general, governor generals. 1.** a governor who has under him subordinate or deputy governors. **2.** *Chiefly Brit.* governor (def. 3). Also, *esp. Brit.,* **gov′er·nor-gen′er·al. —gov′er·nor-gen′er·al·ship′,** *n.*

gov·er·nor·ship (guv′ər nər s̲h̲ip′), *n.* the duties, term in office, etc., of a governor.

Gov′ernors Is′land, an island in New York Bay at the S end of the East River. 2 sq. mi.

Govt., government. Also, **govt.**

gow·an (gou′ən), *n. Scot. and North Eng.* any of various yellow or white field flowers, esp. the English daisy. [? var. of obs. *gollan* < Scand; cf. Icel *gullinn* golden] **—gow′aned,** *adj.* **—gow′an·y,** *adj.*

Gow·er (gou′ər, gōr, gôr), *n.* **John,** 1325?–1408, English poet.

gowk (gouk, gōk), *n.* a fool or simpleton. [ME *goke* < Scand; cf. OIcel *gaukr;* c. OE *gēac,* G *Gauch*]

gown (goun), *n.* **1.** a woman's dress or robe; frock. **2.** a loose, flowing outer garment in any of various forms, worn by men and women as distinctive of office or profession. **3.** See **evening gown. 4.** the student and teaching body of a university, as contrasted with the townspeople. **—*v.t., v.i.* 5.** to dress in, or put on, a gown. [ME *goune* < OF < LL *gunn(a)* fur or leather garment < Celt]

gowns·man (gounz′mən), *n., pl.* **-men.** a man who wears a gown indicating his office, profession, or status.

goy (goi), *n., pl.* **goy·im** (goi′im), **goys.** *Often Disparaging.* a non-Jewish person; gentile. [< Yiddish < Heb *goi* people, non-Jews] **—goy′ish,** *adj.*

Go·ya (goi′ə; *Sp.* gô′yä), *n.* **Fran·cis·co de** (fran sis′kō də; *Sp.* fʀän t̲h̲ēs′kô t̲h̲e), (*Francisco José de Goya y Lucientes*), 1746–1828, Spanish painter.

G.P., 1. General Practitioner. **2.** Gloria Patri. **3.** Graduate in Pharmacy. **4.** Grand Prix.

gph, gallons per hour. Also, **g.p.h.**

gpm, gallons per minute. Also, **g.p.m.**

GPO, Government Printing Office.

G.P.O., See **general post office.**

G.P.U. (gā′pā′o͞o′, jē′pē′yo͞o′), the secret police of the U.S.S.R., 1922–35. Also called **Ogpu, Gay-Pay-Oo.** Cf. **Cheka, MVD, NKVD.** [*G(osudarstvennoe) P(oliticheskoe) U(pravlenie)*]

GQ, General Quarters.

gr, 1. grain; grains. **2.** gross (def. 10).

Gr., 1. Grecian. **2.** Greece. **3.** Greek.

gr., 1. grade. **2.** grain; grains. **3.** *Metric System.* gram; grams. **4.** grammar. **5.** great. **6.** gross (def. 10). **7.** group.

G.R., King George. [< L *Georgius Rēx*]

Graaf′i·an fol′licle (grä′fē ən, graf′-), (*sometimes l.c.*) one of the small vesicles containing a developing ovum in the ovary of a mammal. [named after Regnier de *Graaf* (d. 1673), Dutch anatomist; see -IAN]

grab (grab), *v.,* **grabbed, grab·bing,** *n.* **—*v.t.* 1.** to seize suddenly and eagerly; snatch; clutch. **2.** to take illegal possession of; seize forcibly or unscrupulously: *a vicious scheme to grab land.* **3.** *Slang.* to arouse interest or excitement in: *How does that grab you? This book just doesn't grab me at all.* **—*v.i.* 4.** to make a grasping or clutching motion (usually fol. by *at*). **5.** (of brakes, a clutch, etc.) to take hold suddenly or with a jolting motion. **—*n.* 6.** a sudden, eager grasp or snatch. **7.** seizure or acquisition by violent or unscrupulous means. **8.** something that is grabbed. **9.** a mechanical device for gripping objects. **10. up for grabs,** *Informal.* available to anyone willing to expend the energy to get it: *The Republican nomination for mayor was up for grabs.* [c. MD, MLG *grabben,* Sw *grabba*] **—grab′ber,** *n.* **—Syn. 1.** grasp, grip, catch.

grab·ble (grab′əl), *v.i.,* **-bled, -bling. 1.** to feel or search with the hands; grope. **2.** to sprawl; scramble. [GRAB + -LE; cf. D *grabbelen*] **—grab′bler,** *n.*

gra·ben (grä′bən), *n.* a portion of the earth's crust, bounded on at least two sides by faults, that has been moved downward in relation to adjacent portions. Cf. **horst.** [< G: ditch]

Grac·chus (grak′əs), *n.* **1. Ga·ius Sem·pro·ni·us** (gā′əs sem prō′nē əs), 153–121 B.C., and his brother, **Ti·be·ri·us Sempronius** (tī bēr′ē əs), 163–133 B.C., Roman tribunes and reformers. **2. the Grac·chi** (grak′ī), the brothers Gracchus.

grace (grās), *n., v.,* **graced, grac·ing. —*n.* 1.** elegance or beauty of form, manner, motion, or action. **2.** a pleasing or attractive quality or endowment. **3.** favor or good will. **4.** a manifestation of favor, esp. by a superior. **5.** mercy; clemency; pardon. **6.** favor shown in granting a delay or temporary immunity. **7.** *Theol.* **a.** the freely given, unmerited favor and love of God. **b.** the influence or spirit of God operating in man. **c.** a virtue or excellence of divine origin. **d.** the condition of being in God's favor or one of the elect. **8.** moral strength: *the grace to perform a duty.* **9.** a short prayer before or after a meal, in which a blessing is asked and thanks are given. **10.** (*usually cap.*) a formal title used in addressing or mentioning a duke, duchess, or archbishop, and formerly also a sovereign (usually prec. by *your, his,* etc.). **11. Graces,** *Class. Myth.* the goddesses of beauty, daughters of Zeus, usually three in number, personifying beauty, charm, and grace, and often associated with the arts and the muses. **12. in someone's good** or **bad graces,** regarded with favor or disfavor by someone. **—*v.t.* 13.** to lend or add grace to; adorn: *Many fine paintings graced the rooms of the house.* **14.** to favor or honor: *to grace an occasion with one's presence.* [ME < OF < L *grātia* favor, kindness, esteem < *grāt(us)* pleasing] **—Syn. 1.** gracefulness, comeliness. **4.** kindness, kindliness, condescension. **5.** leniency. **13.** embellish, beautify, deck, decorate, ornament. **—Ant. 1.** ugliness. **4.** animosity. **5.** harshness.

grace′ cup′, 1. a cup, as of wine, passed round at the end of the meal for the final health or toast. **2.** the drink.

grace·ful (grās′fəl), *adj.* characterized by elegance or beauty of form, manner, movement, or speech. [ME] **—grace′ful·ly,** *adv.* **—grace′ful·ness,** *n.*

grace·less (grās′lis), *adj.* **1.** lacking grace, elegance, or charm. **2.** without any sense of right or propriety. [ME] **—grace′less·ly,** *adv.* **—grace′less·ness,** *n.*

grace′ note′, *Music.* a note not essential to the harmony or melody, added as an embellishment, esp. an appoggiatura. See illus. at **acciaccatura.**

grac·ile (gras′il), *adj.* **1.** gracefully slender. **2.** slender; thin. [< L *gracil(is)* slender, slight, thin] **—gra·cil·i·ty** (gra sil′i tē, grə-), **grac′ile·ness,** *n.*

grac·i·lis (gras′ə lis), *n., pl.* **-les** (-lēz′). *Anat.* a muscle in the inner side of the thigh, the action of which assists in drawing the legs toward each other and in bending the knee. [< L: GRACILE]

gra·ci·o·so (grä′s̲h̲ē ō′sō, grä′sē-; *Sp.* gʀä t̲h̲yô′sô, -syô′-), *n., pl.* **-sos** (-sōz; *Sp.* -sôs). **1.** a character in Spanish comedy, resembling the English clown. **2.** a low comic character. [< Sp: amiable, gracious, spirited (n. use of adj.) < L *grātiōs(us)* GRACIOUS]

gra·cious (grā′s̲h̲əs), *adj.* **1.** disposed to show grace or favor; kind; benevolent; courteous. **2.** characterized by good taste, comfort, ease, or luxury: *gracious suburban living.* **3.** indulgent or beneficent in a pleasantly condescending way, esp. to inferiors. **4.** merciful or compassionate. **5.** *Obs.* fortunate or happy. **—*interj.* 6.** (used as an exclamation of surprise, relief, dismay, etc.) [ME *gracious* < OF < L *grātiōs(us)* amiable] **—gra′cious·ly,** *adv.* **—gra′cious·ness,** *n.* **—Syn. 1.** benign, friendly, polite. See **kind**[1]. **4.** tender, mild, gentle. **—Ant. 4.** cruel.

grack·le (grak′əl), *n.* **1.** any of several long-tailed American birds of the family *Icteridae,* esp. of the genera *Quiscalus* or *Cassidix,* having usually iridescent black plumage. **2.** any of several Old World birds of the family *Sturnidae,* esp. certain mynas. [< NL *Gracula* name of genus, special use of L *grāculus* jackdaw]

grad (grad), *n. Informal.* a graduate. [by shortening]

grad., 1. *Math.* gradient. **2.** graduate. **3.** graduated.

gra·date (grā′dāt), *v.,* **-dat·ed, -dat·ing. —*v.i.* 1.** to pass by insensible degrees, as one color into another. **—*v.t.* 2.** to cause to gradate. **3.** to arrange in grades. [back formation from GRADATION]

gra·da·tion (grā dā′s̲h̲ən), *n.* **1.** any process or change taking place through a series of stages, by degrees, or gradually. **2.** a stage, degree, or grade in such a series. **3.** the passing of one tint or shade of color to another, or one surface to another, by very small degrees, as in painting, sculpture, etc. **4.** the act of grading. **5.** ablaut. [< L *gradātiōn-* (s. of *gradātiō*)] **—gra·da′tion·al,** *adj.* **—gra·da′tion·al·ly,** *adv.*

grade (grād), *n., v.,* **grad·ed, grad·ing. —*n.* 1.** a degree in a scale, as of rank, advancement, quality, value, intensity, etc. **2.** a class of persons or things of the same relative rank, quality, etc. **3.** a step or stage in a course or process. **4.** a single division of a school classified according to the age or progress of the pupils. American public schools are commonly divided into twelve grades below college. **5.** the pupils in such a division. **6. grades,** elementary school (usually prec. by *the*). **7.** *U.S.* a number, letter, etc., indicating the relative quality of a student's work in a course, examination, or special assignment; mark. **8.** (of food) a classification or standard based on quality, size, etc.: *grade A eggs.* **9.** inclination with the horizontal of a road; slope. **10.** *Building Trades.* the ground level around a building. **11.** an animal resulting from a cross between a parent of common stock and one of a pure breed. **12. at grade, a.** on the same level. **b.** (of a stream bed) so adjusted to conditions of slope and the volume and speed of water that no gain or loss of sediment takes place. **13. make the grade,** to attain a specific goal; succeed. —*v.t.* **14.** to arrange in a series of grades; class; sort. **15.** to determine the grade of. **16.** to assign a grade to (a student's work); mark. **17.** to cause to pass by degrees, as from one color or shade to another. **18.** to reduce to a level or to practicable degrees of inclination: *to grade a road.* **19.** to cross (a nondescript animal or a low-grade one) with one of a pure breed. —*v.i.* **20.** to be graded. **21.** to be of a particular grade or quality. [< F: office < L *grad(us)* step, stage, degree < *grad(ī)* (to) go, step, walk]

-grade, an element occurring in loan words from Latin, where it meant "step": *retrograde.* [< L *-gradus,* comb. form repr. *gradus* step or *gradī* to walk. See GRADE]

grade′ cross′ing, an intersection of a railroad track and another track, a road, etc., at the same level.

grad·er (grā′dər), *n.* **1.** a person or thing that grades. **2.** a pupil of a specified grade at school: *a fourth grader.* **3.** *U.S.* a machine for grading ground.

grade′ school′, an elementary school.

gra·di·ent (grā′dē ənt), *n.* **1.** the degree of inclination, or the rate of ascent or descent, in a highway, railroad, etc. **2.** an inclined surface; grade; ramp. **3.** *Physics.* the rate of change with respect to distance of a variable quantity, as temperature or pressure, in the direction of maximum change. **4.** *Math.* a differential operator that, operating upon a function of several variables, results in a vector, the coordinates of which are the partial derivatives of the function. *Abbr.:* grad. *Symbol:* ∇ —*adj.* **5.** rising or descending by regular degrees of inclination. **6.** progressing by walking as an animal. **7.** of a type suitable for walking, as the feet of certain birds; gressorial. [< L *gradient-* (s. of *gradiēns*) walking, going (prp. of *gradī*) = *grad-* walk + *-i-* thematic vowel + *-ent-* -ENT]

gra·din (grā′din; *Fr.* GRA daN′), *n., pl.* **-dins** (-dinz; *Fr.* -daN′). one of a series of steps or seats raised one above another. Also, **gra·dine** (grə dēn′). [< F: step, ledge of altar < It *gradin(o),* dim. of *grado* GRADE]

grad·u·al (graj′o͞o əl), *adj.* **1.** taking place, changing, moving, etc., by degrees or little by little: *gradual improvement in health.* **2.** rising or descending at an even, moderate inclination: *a gradual slope.* —*n.* **3.** *Eccles.* (*often cap.*) **a.** an antiphon sung between the Epistle and the Gospel in the Eucharistic service. **b.** a book containing the words and music of the parts of the liturgy that are sung by the choir. [ME < ML *graduāl(is)* pertaining to steps, *graduāle* the part of the service sung as the choir stood on the altar steps] —**grad′u·al·ly,** *adv.* —**grad′u·al·ness,** *n.* —**Syn. 1.** See **slow.** —**Ant. 1.** sudden.

grad·u·al·ism (graj′o͞o ə liz′əm), *n.* **1.** the principle or policy of achieving some goal by gradual steps rather than by drastic change. **2.** *Philos.* a theory maintaining that two seemingly conflicting notions are not radically opposed, but are related by others partaking in varying degrees of the character of both. —**grad′u·al·ist,** *n., adj.* —**grad′u·al·is′tic,** *adj.*

grad·u·ate (*n., adj.* graj′o͞o it, -āt′; *v.* graj′o͞o āt′), *n., adj., v.,* **-at·ed, -at·ing.** —*n.* **1.** a person who has received a degree or diploma on completing a course of study, as in a university, college, or school. **2.** a student who holds the first or bachelor's degree and is studying for an advanced degree. **3.** a cylindrical or tapering graduated container, used for measuring. —*adj.* **4.** of, pertaining to, or involved in academic study beyond the first or bachelor's degree: *a graduate student.* **5.** graduated (def. 3). —*v.i.* **6.** to receive a degree or diploma on completing a course of study (often fol. by *from*): *to graduate from college.* **7.** to pass by degrees; change gradually. —*v.t.* **8.** to confer a degree upon, or to grant a diploma to, at the close of a course of study, as in a university, college, or school. **9.** to graduate from. **10.** to arrange in grades or gradations; establish gradation in. **11.** to divide into or mark with degrees or other divisions, as the scale of a thermometer. [< ML *graduāt(us)* (ptp. of *graduāre*) = *grād(us)* GRADE, step + *-u-* thematic vowel + *-ātus* -ATE[1]]

grad·u·a·ted (graj′o͞o ā′tid), *adj.* **1.** characterized by or arranged in degrees, esp. successively, as according to height, depth, difficulty, etc.: *a graduated series of lessons.* **2.** marked with divisions or units of measurement. **3.** (of a bird's tail) having the longest feathers in the center, the others being successively shorter. **4.** (of a tax) increasing along with the taxable base: *a graduated income tax.*

grad′uate nurse′, a person who has graduated from an accredited school of nursing. Also called **trained nurse.**

grad′uate school′, a school, usually a division of a college or university, offering courses leading to degrees more advanced than the bachelor's degree.

grad·u·a·tion (graj′o͞o ā′shən), *n.* **1.** the act of graduating. **2.** the state of being graduated. **3.** the ceremony of conferring degrees or diplomas, as at a college or school. **4.** marks or a mark on an instrument or a vessel for indicating degree, quantity, etc. [< ML *graduātiōn-* (s. of *graduātiō*)]

gra·dus (grā′dəs), *n., pl.* **-dus·es.** a dictionary of prosody, intended to aid students in the writing of Latin and Greek verse. [after *Gradus ad Parnassum* (a step to Parnassus), Latin title of a dictionary of prosody much used in English public schools during the 18th and 19th centuries]

Grae·ae (grē′ē), *n.pl. Class. Myth.* three old sea goddesses who had but one eye and one tooth among them and were the protectresses of the Gorgons, their sisters. Also, **Graiae.**

Grae·ci·a Mag·na (grē′shē ə mag′nə; *Lat.* GRĪ′ki ä′ mäg′nä). See **Magna Graecia.**

Grae·cise (grē′sīz), *v.t., v.i.,* **-cised, -cis·ing.** *Chiefly Brit.* Graecize.

Grae·cize (grē′sīz), *v.t., v.i.,* **-cized, -ciz·ing.** *Chiefly Brit.* Grecize. Also, **grae′cize.** —**Grae′cism,** *n.*

Graeco-, *Chiefly Brit.* var. of **Greco-.**

Graf (gräf), *n., pl.* **Graf·en** (grä′fən). *German.* a count: a title of nobility in Germany, Austria, and Sweden, equivalent in rank to an English earl.

graf·fi·to (grə fē′tō), *n., pl.* **-ti** (-tē). **1.** *Archaeol.* an ancient drawing or writing scratched on a wall or other surface. **2. graffiti,** words or phrases written on public sidewalks, on the walls of buildings, public rest rooms, or the like. [< It, dim. of *graffio* scratch (of a stylus) < L *graphi(um)* stylus; see GRAFT[1]]

graft[1] (graft, gräft), *n.* **1.** *Hort.* **a.** a bud, shoot, or scion of a plant inserted in a groove, slit, or the like in a stem or stock of another plant in which it continues to grow. **b.** the plant resulting from such an operation; the united stock and scion. **c.** the place where the scion is inserted. **2.** *Surg.* a portion of living tissue surgically transplanted from one part of an individual to another, or from one individual to another, with a view to its adhesion and growth. **3.** the act of grafting. —*v.t.* **4.** to insert (a graft) into a tree or other plant; insert a scion of (one plant) into another plant. **5.** to cause (a plant) to reproduce through grafting. **6.** *Surg.* to transplant (a portion of living tissue) as a graft. **7.** *Naut.* to cover (a rope) with a weaving of rope yarn. —*v.i.* **8.** to insert scions from one plant into another. **9.** to become grafted. [ME *graffe, craffe* < OF *graife, greffe, graffe* < LL *graph(ium)* (L: stylus) < Gk *grapheîon* < *gráph(ein)* (to) write; so called from the resemblance of the point of a (cleft) graft to a stylus] —**graft′er,** *n.*

A B C

Grafts
A, Splice;
B, Saddle; C, Cleft

graft[2] (graft, gräft), *n.* **1.** the acquisition of gain or advantage by dishonest, unfair, or sordid means, esp. through the abuse of one's position or influence in politics, business, etc. **2.** a particular instance, method, or means of thus acquiring gain. **3.** the gain or advantage acquired. —*v.t.* **4.** to obtain by graft. —*v.i.* **5.** to practice graft. [? special use of GRAFT[1]] —**graft′er,** *n.*

graft·age (graf′tij, gräf′-), *n. Hort.* the art or practice of grafting. [GRAFT[1] + -AGE]

gra·ham (grā′əm), *adj.* made of graham flour.

Gra·ham (grā′əm), *n.* **1. Martha,** born 1902?, U.S. dancer and choreographer. **2. Thomas,** 1805–69, Scottish chemist. **3. William Franklin** ("*Billy*"), born 1918, U.S. evangelist.

gra′ham crack′er, a semisweet cracker made chiefly of graham flour.

Gra·hame (grā′əm), *n.* **Kenneth,** 1852–1939, Scottish writer, esp. of children's stories.

gra′ham flour′, unbolted wheat flour, containing all of the wheat grain; whole-wheat flour. [named after S. *Graham* (1794–1851), American reformer in dietetics]

Gra′ham Land′, a part of the British Antarctic Territory, in the N section of the Antarctic Peninsula: formerly the British name for the entire peninsula.

Grai·ae (grā′ē, grī′ē), *n.pl.* Graeae.

Grail (grāl), *n.* (*sometimes l.c.*) a cup or chalice that in medieval legend was associated with unusual powers, esp. the regeneration of life and, later, Christian purity: became identified with the cup used at the Last Supper and given to Joseph of Arimathea. Also called **Holy Grail.** [ME *graiel, graile,* etc. < AF *grahel, grayel,* OF *gräel, grel* < ML *gradālis* platter ? < L *gradus* step (see GRADE) + *-ālis* -AL[1], as being orig. a stack of bowls or platters]

grain (grān), *n.* **1.** a small, hard seed, esp. the seed of one of the food plants, as wheat, corn, rye, oats, rice, and millet. **2.** the gathered seed of one of the food plants, esp. of cereal plants. **3.** the plants themselves taken collectively, whether standing or gathered. **4.** any small, hard particle, as of sand, gold, pepper, gunpowder, etc. **5.** the smallest unit of weight in most systems, originally determined by the weight of a plump grain of wheat. In the U.S. and British systems, as in avoirdupois, troy, and apothecaries' weights, the grain is identical. In an avoirdupois ounce there are 437.5 grains; in the troy and apothecaries' ounces there are 480 grains. **6.** the smallest possible amount of anything: *a grain of truth.* **7.** the arrangement or direction of fibers in wood, or the resulting pattern. **8.** the side of leather from which the hair has been removed. **9.** a granular pattern. **10.** the fibers or yarn in a piece of fabric as differentiated from the fabric itself. **11.** *Textiles.* the direction of threads in relation to the selvage of woven threads. **12.** the lamination or cleavage of stone, coal, etc. **13.** the size of constituent particles of any substance; texture: *sugar of fine grain.* **14.** a state of crystallization: *boiled to the grain.* **15. against the** or **one's grain,** in opposition to one's natural disposition. **16. with a grain of salt,** with reservations; critically. —*v.t.* **17.** to form into grains; granulate. **18.** to give a granular appearance to. **19.** to paint in imitation of the grain of wood, stone, etc. **20.** *Tanning.* **a.** to remove the hair from (skins). **b.** to soften and raise the grain of (leather). [ME *grain, grein* < OF *grain* < L *grān(um)* seed, grain] —**grain′er,** *n.*

grain′ al′cohol, alcohol (def. 1).

grain′ el′evator, elevator (def. 3).

grains′ of par′adise, the pungent, peppery seeds of a zingiberaceous plant, *Aframomum Melegueta* (*Granum-Paradisi*), of Africa, used to strengthen cordials and in veterinary medicine. Also called **guinea grains.**

grain′ sor′ghum, any of several varieties of sorghum, as durra or milo, having starchy seeds, grown for fodder in the U.S. and for the grain in the Orient.

grain·y (grā′nē), *adj.,* **grain·i·er, grain·i·est. 1.** resembling grain; granular. **2.** full of grains or grain. **3.** having a natural or simulated grain, as wood, wallpaper, etc. —**grain′i·ness,** *n.*

gral·la·to·ri·al (gral′ə tōr′ē əl, -tôr′-), *adj.* belonging or pertaining to the wading birds, as the snipes, cranes, storks, herons, etc. [< NL *grallātōri(us)* (L *grallātor* one who walks on stilts = *grall(ae)* stilts (cf. *gradus* GRADE) + *-ātor* -ATOR) + -AL[1]]

gram[1] (gram), *n.* a metric unit of mass, equal to 15.432 grains; one thousandth of a kilogram. *Abbr.:* g, g. Also, *esp. Brit.,* **gramme.** [< F *gramme* < LL *gramma* a small weight < Gk: something drawn, a small weight; see -GRAM[1]]

gram[2] (gram), *n.* **1.** (in the Orient) the chickpea, used as a food for man and cattle. **2.** any of various beans, as *Phaseolus aureus* and *P. Mungo,* cultivated in India for food. [< Pg *grão* < L *grān(um)* GRAIN]

Gram (gräm) *n.* (in the *Volsunga Saga*) the sword of Sigmund, broken by Odin, repaired by Regin, and used again by Sigurd in killing Fafnir. Cf. **Balmung.**

-gram[1], an element occurring in loan words from Greek, where it meant "something written," "drawing" (*diagram; epigram*); on this model, used in the formation of compound words (*oscillogram*). Cf. **-graph.** [< Gk *-gram(ma)*, comb. form of *grámma* something written or drawn; akin to CARVE]

-gram[2], a combining form of **gram**[1]: *kilogram.*

gram., 1. grammar. 2. grammarian. 3. grammatical.

gra′ma grass′ (grä′mə), any grass of the genus *Bouteloua*, of the western and southwestern U.S., as *B. gracilis* **(blue grama).** [< Sp *grama* < L *grāmina*, pl. of *grāmen* grass]

gram·a·rye (gram′ə rē), *n.* occult learning; magic. Also, **gram′a·ry.** [ME *gramary* < OF *gramaire*, lit., GRAMMAR]

gram′ at′om, *Chem.* the quantity of an element whose weight in grams is numerically equal to the atomic weight of the element. Also called **gram′-a·tom·ic weight′** (gram′ə tom′ik). Cf. **Avogadro's number.**

gram′ cal′orie, calorie (def. 1b). *Abbr.:* g-cal

gram′ equiv′alent, *Chem.* See under **equivalent weight.**

gra·mer·cy (grə mûr′sē), *interj.* **1.** *Archaic.* an exclamation expressing surprise or sudden strong feeling. —*n.* **2.** *Obs.* thanks. [ME *gramerci, grantmerci* < OF *grand merci* great thanks. See GRAND, MERCY]

gram·i·ci·din (gram′i sīd′ᵊn), *n.* *Pharm.* a crystalline, water-insoluble antibiotic used chiefly in treating local infections caused by Gram-positive organisms. Also called **gramicidin D.** [GRAM-(POSITIVE) + -I- + -CIDE + -IN[2]]

gra·min·e·ous (grə min′ē əs), *adj.* **1.** grasslike. **2.** pertaining or belonging to the *Gramineae* (or *Poaceae*), or grass family of plants. [< L *grāmineus* pertaining to grass = *grāmin-* (s. of *grāmen*) grass + *-eus* -EOUS] —**gra·min′e·ous·ness,** *n.*

gram·i·niv·o·rous (gram′ə niv′ər əs), *adj.* feeding on seeds or like food. [< L *grāmin-* (s. of *grāmen*) grass + -I- + -VOROUS]

gram·mar (gram′ər), *n.* **1.** the study of the formal features of a language, as the sounds, morphemes, words, or sentences. **2.** these features or constructions themselves: *English grammar.* **3.** a book dealing with these features. **4.** grammatical rules, esp. as criteria for evaluating speech or writing: *He knows his grammar.* **5.** knowledge or usage of the preferred or prescribed forms in speaking or writing: *She said his grammar was terrible.* **6.** the fundamental rules of any science, art, or subject. [ME *gramery* < OF *gramaire* < L *gramatica* < Gk *grammatikē* (*téchnē*) GRAMMATICAL (art); see -AR[2]] —**gram′mar·less,** *adj.*

gram·mar·i·an (grə mâr′ē ən), *n.* **1.** a specialist in the study of grammar. **2.** a person who has established standards of usage in a language. [ME *gramarien* < OF *gramairien*]

gram′mar school′, **1.** See **elementary school.** **2.** *Brit.* a secondary school corresponding to an American high school. **3.** (formerly) a secondary school in which Latin and Greek are among the principal subjects taught.

gram·mat·i·cal (grə mat′i kəl), *adj.* **1.** of or pertaining to grammar: *grammatical analysis.* **2.** conforming to standard usage: *grammatical speech.* [< L *grammatic(us)* (< Gk *grammatikós* knowing one's letters = *grammat-*, s. of *grámma* letter + *-ikos* -IC) + -AL[1]] —**gram·mat′i·cal·ly,** *adv.* —**gram·mat′i·cal·ness,** *n.*

grammat′ical gen′der, *Gram.* gender based on arbitrary assignment, without regard to the referent of a noun. Cf. **natural gender.**

grammat′ical mean′ing, the meaning of an inflectional morpheme or of some other syntactic device, as word order. Cf. **lexical meaning.**

gramme (gram), *n.* *Chiefly Brit.* gram[1].

gram′ mol′ecule, *Chem.* the quantity of a substance whose weight in grams is numerically equal to the molecular weight of the substance. Also called **gram′-molecular weight′.** Cf. **Avogadro's number.** —**gram-mo·lec·u·lar** (gram′mə lek′yə lər), **gram-mo·lar** (gram′mō′lər), *adj.*

Gram-neg·a·tive (gram′neg′ə tiv), *adj.* (*often l.c.*) (of bacteria) not retaining the violet dye when stained by Gram's method.

Gra·mont (GRA môN′), *n.* **Phi·li·bert de** (fē lē beR′ də), **Comte,** 1621–1707, French courtier, soldier, and adventurer.

Gram·o·phone (gram′ə fōn′), *n.* *Trademark.* a phonograph.

Gram·pi·ans, The (gram′pē ənz), (*construed as pl.*) a range of low mountains in central Scotland, separating the Highlands from the Lowlands. Highest peak, Ben Nevis, 4406 ft. Also called **Gram′pi·an Hills′.**

Gram-pos·i·tive (gram′poz′i tiv), *adj.* (*often l.c.*) (of bacteria) retaining the violet dye when stained by Gram's method.

gramps (gramps), *n.* *Informal.* grandfather. [alter. of *gramp*, short for GRANDPA]

gram·pus (gram′pəs), *n., pl.* **-pus·es.** **1.** a cetacean, *Grampus griseus*, of the dolphin family, widely distributed in northern seas. **2.** any of various related cetaceans, as the killer whale, *Orca orca.* [earlier *grampoys*, var. (by assimilation) of *graundepose* great fish = *graunde* GRAND + *pose, poys* < MF *pois, peis* < L *pisce-* (s. of *piscis*) fish; r. ME *gra(s)peis* < MF << L *crassus piscis* fat fish]

Grampus, *Grampus griseus* (Length 9 to 13 ft.)

Gram's′ meth′od (gramz), (*sometimes l.c.*) a method of staining and distinguishing bacteria that includes staining the fixed bacterial smears with gentian violet. Cf. **Gram-negative, Gram-positive.** [named after Hans C. J. *Gram* (1853–1938), Danish bacteriologist]

Gra·na·da (grə nä′də; *Sp.* grä nä′ᵺä), *n.* **1.** a medieval kingdom along the Mediterranean coast of S Spain. See map at **Castile.** **2.** a city in S Spain: the capital of this former kingdom and last stronghold of the Moors in Spain. 153,409 (est. 1960).

gran·a·dil·la (gran′ə dil′ə), *n.* **1.** the edible fruit of any of several species of passionflower, esp. *Passiflora edulis* and *P. quadrangularis.* **2.** any of the plants yielding these fruits. [< Sp, dim. of *granada* pomegranate]

Gra·na·dos (grä nä′ᵺōs), *n.* **En·ri·que** (en Rē′ke), 1867–1916, Spanish pianist and composer.

gra·na·ry (grā′nə rē, gran′ə-), *n., pl.* **-ries.** **1.** a storehouse or repository for grain, esp. after it has been threshed or husked. **2.** a region that produces great quantities of grain. [< L *grānāri(um)*. See GRAIN, -ARY]

Gran Ca·na·ria (gRän′ kä nä′Ryä), one of the Canary Islands, in the central part. 303,839 (1950); 650 sq. mi. *Cap.:* Las Palmas. Also, **Grand Canary.**

Gran Cha·co (gRän chä′kō), an extensive subtropical region in central South America, in Argentina, Bolivia, and Paraguay. 300,000 sq. mi. Cf. **Chaco.**

grand (grand), *adj., n., pl.* **grands** for 13, **grand** for 14. —*adj.* **1.** impressive or imposing in size, appearance, or general effect: *grand mountain scenery.* **2.** stately, majestic, or dignified; regal. **3.** highly ambitious or idealistic; lofty. **4.** magnificent; splendid. **5.** noble or revered: *a grand old man.* **6.** highest, or very high, in rank or official dignity: *a grand potentate.* **7.** main or principal; chief: *the grand staircase.* **8.** of great importance, distinction, or pretension: *grand personages.* **9.** complete or comprehensive: *a grand total.* **10.** pretending to grandeur; conceited. **11.** first-rate; very good; splendid: *a grand time.* **12.** *Music.* written on a large scale or for a large ensemble: *a grand fugue.* —*n.* **13.** a grand piano. **14.** *Informal.* a thousand dollars. [ME *gra(u)nd, gra(u)nt* < OF *grant, grand* < L *grand-* (s. of *grandis*) great, large, full-grown] —**grand′ly,** *adv.* —**grand′ness,** *n.* —**Syn. 2.** princely, royal, exalted. **4.** great; brilliant, superb, glorious. —**Ant. 1.** insignificant. **3.** base. **8.** minor.

grand-, a prefix used in genealogical terminology meaning "one generation more remote": *grandfather; grandnephew.* [special use of GRAND]

gran·dam (gran′dəm, -dam), *n.* **1.** a grandmother. **2.** an old woman. Also, **gran·dame** (gran′dām, -dəm). [ME *gra(u)ndame* < AF; see GRAND, DAME]

Grand′ Ar′my of the Repub′lic, an organization, founded in 1866, composed of men who served in the Union Army and Navy during the Civil War. The last member died in 1956.

grand·aunt (grand′ant′, -änt′), *n.* a great-aunt.

Grand′ Baha′ma, an island in the W Bahamas. 8230 (1963); 430 sq. mi.

Grand′ Banks′, an extensive shoal SE of Newfoundland: fishing grounds. 350 mi. long; 40,000 sq. mi. Also, **Grand′ Bank′.**

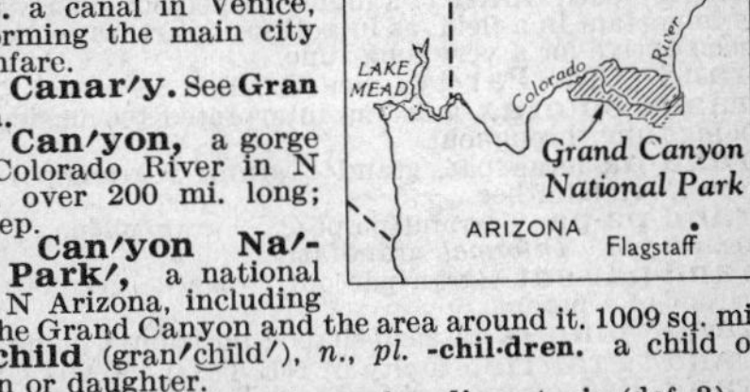

Grand′ Canal′, **1.** a canal in E China, extending S from Tientsin to Hangchow. 900 mi. long. **2.** a canal in Venice, Italy, forming the main city thoroughfare.

Grand′ Canar′y. See **Gran Canaria.**

Grand′ Can′yon, a gorge of the Colorado River in N Arizona. over 200 mi. long; 1 mi. deep.

Grand′ Can′yon Na′tional Park′, a national park in N Arizona, including part of the Grand Canyon and the area around it. 1009 sq. mi.

grand·child (gran′chīld′), *n., pl.* **-chil·dren.** a child of one's son or daughter.

grand′ climac′teric. See under **climacteric** (def. 3).

Grand′ Cou′lee (kōō′lē), **1.** a dry canyon in central Washington: cut by the Columbia River in the glacial period. 52 mi. long; over 400 ft. deep. **2.** Also called **Grand′ Cou′lee Dam′.** a dam on the Columbia River at the N end of this canyon: the largest concrete dam in the world. 550 ft. high.

grand·dad (gran′dad′), *n.* *Informal.* grandfather.

grand·dad·dy (gran′dad′ē), *n., pl.* **-dies.** *Informal.* grandfather.

grand·daugh·ter (gran′dô′tər), *n.* a daughter of one's son or daughter.

grand′ drag′on, a high-ranking official of the Ku Klux Klan.

grand′ duch′ess, **1.** the wife or widow of a grand duke. **2.** a woman who governs a grand duchy in her own right. **3.** a daughter of a czar or of a czar's son.

grand′ duch′y, a territory ruled by a grand duke or grand duchess.

Grand′ Duch′y of Mus′covy, Muscovy (def. 1). Also, **Grand′ Duch′y of Mos′cow.**

grand′ duke′, **1.** the sovereign of a grand duchy, ranking next below a king. **2.** a son or grandson of a czar. —**grand′-du′cal,** *adj.*

Gran·de (gran′dē, grän′dā; *Sp.* gRän′de; *Port.* gRäNN′də), *n.* **Rio.** See **Rio Grande.**

grande dame (gRäNd dAm′), *pl.* **grandes dames** (gRäNd dAm′). *French.* a great lady; a lady of dignified or aristocratic bearing.

gran·dee (gran dē′), *n.* a man of high social position or eminence, esp. a Spanish or Portuguese nobleman. [< Sp, Pg *grande*] —**gran·dee′ship,** *n.*

gran·deur (gran′jər, -jŏŏr), *n.* **1.** the quality or state of being impressive, awesome, or lofty; majesty; splendor. **2.** something that is grand. [< F, OF; see GRAND, -OR[1]]

Grand′ Falls′, a waterfall of the Hamilton River in Labrador. 200 ft. wide; 316 ft. high.

grand·fa·ther (gran′fä′ᵺər, grand′-), *n.* **1.** the father of one's father or mother. **2.** a forefather. [ME] —**grand′fa′ther·ly,** *adv.*

grand′father's clock′, a pendulum floor clock having a case as tall as, or taller than, a person; a tall-case clock. Also, **grand′father clock′.**

Grand′ Forks′, a town in E North Dakota. 39,008 (1970).

Grand Gui·gnol (*Fr.* grän gē nyôl′), a short drama stressing horror and sensationalism. [after *Le Grand Guignol,* small theater in Paris where such dramas were played]

gran·dil·o·quence (gran dil′ə kwəns), *n.* speech that is lofty or pompous in tone. [< L *grandiloqu(us)* speaking loftily (*grandi(s)* great + *-loquus* speaking) + -ENCE]

gran·dil·o·quent (gran dil′ə kwənt), *adj.* speaking or expressed in a lofty or pompous style. **—gran·dil′o·quent·ly,** *adv.* **—Syn.** inflated, rhetorical, pretentious.

grand′ inquis′itor, (*often cap.*) the presiding officer of a court of inquisition.

gran·di·ose (gran′dē ōs′), *adj.* **1.** grand in an imposing or impressive way. **2.** affectedly grand or stately; pompous. [< F < It *grandioso*] **—gran′di·ose′ly,** *adv.* **—gran·di·os·i·ty** (gran′dē os′i tē), *n.*

gran·di·o·so (gran′dē ō′sō), *adj., adv. Music.* majestic; broad. [< It: GRANDIOSE]

Grand′ Is′land, a city in S Nebraska. 31,269 (1970).

grand′ ju′ry, a jury, usually of 12 to 33 persons, designated to inquire into alleged violations of the law in order to ascertain whether the evidence is sufficient to warrant trial by a petty jury. [ME < AF *graund juree*]

Grand′ La′ma. See **Dalai Lama.**

grand′ lar′ceny, *Law.* larceny in which the value of the goods taken is above a certain amount. Cf. **petty larceny.**

grand·ma (gran′mä′, grand′-, gram′-, gram′mə), *n. Informal.* grandmother.

grand mal (gran′ mal′; *Fr.* grän mal′), *Pathol.* a form of epilepsy characterized by a sudden loss of consciousness, muscular spasms, and frothing at the mouth. Cf. **petit mal.** [< F: (the) great ailment, epilepsy]

grand·mam·ma (grand′mə mä′; gran′mä′mə, grand′-, gram′-), *n. Informal.* grandmother. Also, **grand′ma·ma′.**

Grand′ma Mo′ses. See **Moses, Anna Mary Robertson.**

Grand′ Ma·nan′ (mə nan′), a Canadian island at the entrance to the Bay of Fundy: a part of New Brunswick; summer resort. ab. 3000; 57 sq. mi.

grand′ march′, the opening ceremonies of a formal ball, in which guests promenade into or around the ballroom.

Grand′ Mas′ter, the head of a military order of knighthood, a lodge, fraternal order, or the like.

grand monde (grän mônd′), *French.* the fashionable world; the best society. [lit., great world]

grand·moth·er (gran′muth′ər, grand′-, gram′-), *n.* **1.** the mother of one's father or mother. **2.** an ancestress. [ME] **—grand′moth′er·ly,** *adv.*

Grand′ Muf′ti, 1. a Muslim religious leader. **2.** (formerly) the chief legal authority for Muslims in Jerusalem.

grand·neph·ew (gran′nef′yo͞o, -nev′yo͞o, grand′-), *n.* great-nephew.

grand·niece (gran′nēs′, grand′-), *n.* great-niece.

grand′ old′ man′, a highly respected, elderly man who is important in a field, as in politics or art, esp. one who has been active for a very long time.

Grand′ Old′ Par′ty. See **G.O.P.**

grand′ op′era, a drama interpreted by music, the text being sung throughout.

grand·pa (gran′pä′, grand′-, gram′-, gram′pə), *n. Informal.* grandfather.

grand·pa·pa (grand′pə pä′; gran′pä′pə, grand′-, gram′-), *n. Informal.* grandfather.

grand·par·ent (gran′pâr′ənt, -par′-, grand′-), *n.* a parent of a parent.

grand′ pian′o, a harp-shaped horizontal piano.

Grand′ Prai′rie, a city in NE Texas. 50,904 (1970).

Grand Pré (gran′ prā′; *Fr.* grän prā′), a village in central Nova Scotia, on Minas Basin: locale of Longfellow's *Evangeline.*

Grand Prix (grän prē′), *pl.* **Grand Prix** (grän prēz′), **Grands Prix** (grän prēz′), **Grand Prixes** (grän prēz′). any of a number of international automobile races over a long, arduous course, usually held annually between drivers of different countries driving automobiles of various manufacturers.

grand prix (grän prē′), *pl.* **grands prix** (grän prē′). *French.* grand prize; the highest award.

Grand′ Rap′ids, a city in SW Michigan: furniture factories. 197,649 (1970).

Grand′ Riv′er, 1. former name of the Colorado River above its junction with the Green River in SE Utah. **2.** a river in SW Michigan, flowing W to Lake Michigan. 260 mi. long. **3.** Hamilton (def. 6).

grand·sire (grand′sīər′), *n. Archaic.* a grandfather. [ME *graunt-sire* < AF]

grand′ slam′, 1. *Bridge.* the winning of all thirteen tricks of a deal. Cf. **little slam. 2.** *Baseball.* a home run hit with three men on base. **3.** *Sports.* the winning of all major championship contests in one season, as in golf or tennis. **4.** *Informal.* complete success.

grand·son (gran′sun′, grand′-), *n.* a son of one's son or daughter.

grand·stand (gran′stand′, grand′-), *n., v.,* **-stand·ed, -stand·ing,** *adj.* **—n. 1.** the part of a seating area of a stadium, racecourse, or the like, consisting of tiers with rows of individual seats. **2.** the people sitting in these seats. **—v.i. 3.** to conduct oneself or perform showily or ostentatiously in an attempt to impress onlookers: *He doesn't hesitate to grandstand if it makes his point.* **—adj. 4.** situated in or as in a grandstand: *grandstand seats.* **5.** having a vantage point resembling that of a grandstand: *a grandstand view of the parade.* **6.** *Informal.* intended to impress an onlooker or onlookers: *a grandstand play for applause.* **—grand′stand′er,** *n.*

Grand′ Te′ton Na′tional Park′ (tē′ton), a national park in NW Wyoming, including a portion of the Teton Range. 148 sq. mi.

grand′ tour′, an extended tour of Europe, formerly regarded as a necessary part of the education of wealthy or aristocratic young Britons and Americans.

grand·un·cle (grand′ung′kəl), *n.* a great-uncle.

grand′ vizier′, the chief officer of state of various Muslim countries, as in the former Ottoman Empire.

grange (grānj), *n.* **1.** a farm. **2.** *Chiefly Brit.* a country dwelling house with its various farm buildings; dwelling of a yeoman or gentleman farmer. **3.** an outlying farmhouse with barns, sheds, etc., belonging to a feudal manor or a religious establishment, where crops and tithes in kind were stored. **4.** (*cap.*) *U.S.* a lodge or local branch of the Patrons of Husbandry, an association for promoting the interests of agriculture. **5. the Grange,** the association itself. [ME *gra(u)nge* barn < AF < LL **grānica* (occurs in ML) = L *grān(um)* GRAIN + *-ica,* fem. of *-icus* -IC]

grang·er (grān′jər), *n.* **1.** a farmer. **2.** (*cap.*) *U.S.* a member of a Grange. [ME *gra(u)nger* farm-bailiff < AF; OF *grangier*]

grang·er·ise (grān′jə rīz′), *v.t.,* **-ised, -is·ing.** *Chiefly Brit.* grangerize. **—grang′er·is′er,** *n.*

grang·er·ize (grān′jə rīz′), *v.t.,* **-ized, -iz·ing. 1.** to augment the illustrative content of (a book) by inserting additional prints, drawings, engravings, etc., not included in the original volume. **2.** to mutilate (books) in order to get illustrative material for such a purpose. [after James *Granger* (1723–1776), English clergyman whose *Biographical History of England* (1769) was arranged for such illustration; see -IZE] **—grang′er·ism,** *n.* **—grang′er·iz′er,** *n.*

Gra·ni·cus (grə nī′kəs), *n.* a river in NW Turkey, flowing N to the Sea of Marmara: battle 334 B.C. 45 mi. long.

gran·ite (gran′it), *n.* **1.** a granular igneous rock composed chiefly of feldspars and quartz, usually with one or more other minerals. **2.** anything compared to this rock in great hardness, firmness, or durability. [< It *granit(o)* grainy. See GRAIN, -ITE[1]] **—gra·nit·ic** (grə nit′ik), *adj.* **—gran′ite·like′,** *adj.*

Gran′ite Cit′y, a city in SW Illinois, near St. Louis, Missouri. 40,440 (1970).

Gran′ite State′, New Hampshire (used as a nickname).

gran·it·ite (gran′i tīt′), *n.* a granite rich in biotite.

gra·niv·o·rous (gra niv′ər əs), *adj.* feeding on grain and seeds. [< NL *grānivorus.* See GRAIN, -I-, -VOROUS] **—gran·i·vore** (gran′ə vōr′, -vôr′), *n.*

gran·ny (gran′ē), *n., pl.* **-nies,** *adj.* **—n. 1.** *Informal.* a grandmother. **2.** an old woman. **3.** a fussy person. **4.** *Southern U.S.* a nurse or midwife. **5.** See **granny knot. —adj. 6.** of, pertaining to, or like a grandmother or old woman. **7.** of a style befitting a grandmother; old-fashioned: *to wear granny glasses; a long granny skirt.* Also, **gran′nie.** [nursery abbr. for GRANDMOTHER; cf. NANNY]

gran′ny knot′, an incorrect version of a square knot in which the bights cross each other in the wrong direction next to the end, so as purposely to produce a knot that will jam. Also, **gran′ny's knot′.** See illus. at **knot.** [so called in contempt]

gra·no·la (grə nō′lə), *n.* a breakfast food consisting of a dry mixture of cereals, nuts, dried fruit, etc., usually served in milk. [< L *gran(um)* grain + arbitrary suffix]

gran·o·phyre (gran′ə fīər′), *n.* a fine-grained or porphyritic granitic rock with a micrographic intergrowth of the minerals of the groundmass. [GRAN(ITE) + -O- + -PHYRE] **—gran·o·phy·ric** (gran′ə fir′ik), *adj.*

grant (grant, gränt), *v.t.* **1.** to bestow or confer, esp. by a formal act: *to grant a charter.* **2.** to give or accord: *to grant permission.* **3.** to agree or accede to: *to grant a request.* **4.** to admit or concede; accept for the sake of argument: *I grant that point.* **5.** to transfer or convey, esp. by deed or writing: *to grant property.* **—n. 6.** something granted, as a privilege or right, a sum of money, or a tract of land. **7.** the act of granting. **8.** *Law.* a transfer of property. **9.** a geographical unit in Vermont, Maine, and New Hampshire, originally a grant of land to a person or group of people. [ME *gra(u)nt(en)* < OF *graunt(er),* var. of *creanter* < VL **credentare* < L *crēdent-* (s. of *crēdēns,* prp. of *crēdere* to believe) + *-āre* inf. suffix] **—grant′a·ble,** *adj.* **—grant′er,** *n.* **—Syn. 1.** award, vouchsafe; give. **2.** See **give. 6, 7.** concession. **—Ant. 1, 2.** receive; take.

Grant (grant), *n.* **Ulysses S(imp·son)** (simp′sən), 1822–85, Union general in the Civil War: 18th president of the U.S. 1869–77.

Gran·ta (gran′tə), *n.* Cam.

gran·tee (gran tē′, grän-), *n. Law.* a person to whom a grant is made. [ME]

Granth (grunt), *n.* the sacred scripture of the Sikhs, original text compiled 1604. Also called **Grant′ Sa′hib** (grunt). [< Hindi < Skt *grantha* a tying together, book]

grant-in-aid (grant′in ād′), *n., pl.* **grants-in-aid. 1.** a subsidy furnished by a central government to a local one to help finance a public project. **2.** something similar to such a subsidy or grant, esp. financial assistance given to an individual or institution for educational purposes.

gran·tor (gran′tər, grän′-, gran tôr′, grän-), *n. Law.* a person who makes a grant. [< AF]

Gran Tu·ris·mo O·mo·lo·ga·to (grän to͝o riz′mō ə-mō′lə gä′tō; *It.* grän′ to͞o rēz′mô ô mô′lô gä′tô), (of an automobile) certified as conforming to the specifications for a class of standard automobiles **(Gran′ Turis′mo)** qualified to engage in various types of competitions. *Abbr.:* GTO [< It: approved (as) Gran Turismo]

gran·u·lar (gran′yə lər), *adj.* **1.** of the nature of granules. **2.** composed of or bearing granules or grains. **3.** showing a granulated structure. **—gran·u·lar·i·ty** (gran′yə lar′i tē), *n.* **—gran′u·lar·ly,** *adv.*

gran·u·late (gran′yə lāt′), *v.,* **-lat·ed, -lat·ing. —v.t. 1.** to form into granules or grains. **2.** to raise in granules; make rough on the surface. **—v.i. 3.** to become granular. **4.** *Pathol.* to form granulation tissue. **—gran′u·lat′er, gran′u·la′tor,** *n.* **—gran·u·la·tive** (gran′yə lā′tiv, -lə tiv), *adj.*

gran′ulated sug′ar, a coarsely ground white sugar, widely used as a sweetener.

gran·u·la·tion (gran′yə lā′shən), *n.* **1.** the act or process of granulating. **2.** a granulated condition. **3.** any of the grains of a granulated surface. **4.** *Pathol.* **a.** the formation of granulation tissue, esp. in healing. **b.** See **granulation tissue. 5.** *Astron.* one of the small, short-lived features of the sun's surface which in the aggregate give it a mottled appearance when viewed with a telescope.

granula′tion tis′sue, *Pathol.* tissue formed in ulcers and in early wound healing and repair, composed largely of newly growing capillaries and so called from its irregular surface in open wounds; proud flesh.

gran·ule (gran′yo͞ol), *n.* **1.** a little grain. **2.** a small particle; pellet. **3.** a corpuscle; sporule. [< LL *grānul(um)* small grain. See GRAIN, -ULE]

gran·u·lite (gran′yə līt′), *n.* *Petrog.* a metamorphic rock composed of granular minerals of uniform size, as quartz, feldspar, or pyroxene, and showing a definite banding. —**gran·u·lit·ic** (gran′yə lit′ik), *adj.*

gran·u·lo·cyte (gran′yə lō sīt′), *n.* *Anat.* a leukocyte, the cytoplasm of which contains granules. —**gran·u·lo·cyt·ic** (gran′yə lō sit′ik), *adj.*

gran·u·lo·ma (gran′yə lō′mə), *n., pl.* **-mas, -ma·ta** (-mə-tə). *Pathol.* an inflammatory tumor or growth composed of granulation tissue. —**gran·u·lom·a·tous** (gran′yə lom′ə-təs), *adj.*

gran·u·lose (gran′yə lōs′), *adj.* granular.

Gran·ville (gran′vil), *n.* **Earl of.** See **Carteret, John.**

Gran·ville-Bar·ker (gran′vil bär′kər), *n.* **Harley,** 1877–1946, English dramatist, actor, and critic.

grape (grāp), *n.* **1.** the edible, pulpy, smooth-skinned berry or fruit that grows in clusters on vines of the genus *Vitis,* and from which wine is made. **2.** any vine bearing this fruit. **3.** a dull, dark, purplish-red color. **4.** grapeshot. **5. the grape,** wine. [ME < OF, var. of *crape* cluster of fruit or flowers, orig. hook < Gmc; cf. G *Krapf* hook and GRAPPLE, GRAPNEL]

grape·fruit (grāp′fro͞ot′), *n.* **1.** Also called **pomelo.** a large, roundish, yellow-skinned, edible citrus fruit having a juicy, acid, pale yellow or pink pulp. **2.** the tropical or semi-tropical, rutaceous tree, *Citrus paradisi,* yielding it. [GRAPE + FRUIT, appar. from the resemblance of its clusters to those of grapes]

grape′ hy′acinth, any liliaceous plant of the genus *Muscari,* as *M. botryoides,* having globular, blue flowers resembling tiny grapes.

grape·shot (grāp′shot′), *n.* a cluster of small cast-iron balls formerly used as a charge for cannon.

grape′ sug′ar, dextrose.

grape·vine (grāp′vīn′), *n.* **1.** a vine that bears grapes. **2.** Also called **grape′vine tel′egraph.** a person-to-person method of relaying secret reports that cannot be obtained through regular channels.

graph (graf, gräf), *n.* **1.** a diagram representing a system of connections or interrelations among two or more things by a number of distinctive dots, lines, bars, etc. **2.** *Math.* **a.** a series of points, discrete or continuous, as in forming a curve or surface, each of which represents a value of a given function. **b.** a network of lines connecting points. **3.** a written symbol for an idea, a sound, or a linguistic expression. —*v.t.* **4.** to draw (a curve) as representing a given function. **5.** to represent by means of a graph. [short for *graphic formula;* see GRAPHIC] —**Syn. 1.** See **map.**

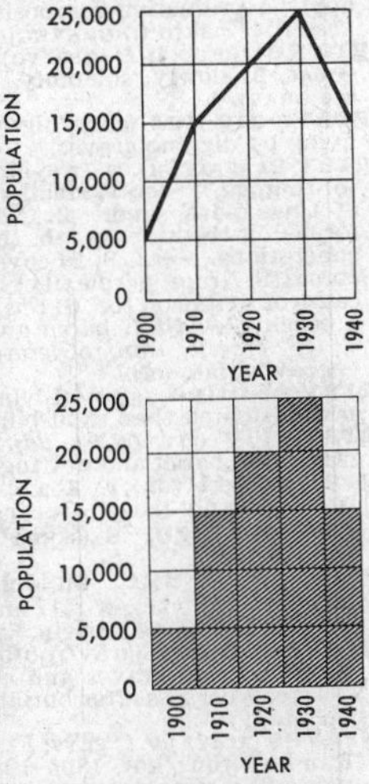

Graphs
Line graph (above)
Bar graph (below)

graph-, var. of **grapho-** before a vowel: *grapheme.*

-graph, an element, borrowed from Greek, meaning "drawn," "written" (*monograph; lithograph*); specialized in meaning to indicate the instrument rather than the written product of the instrument (*telegraph; phonograph*). [< Gk *-graph(os)* (something) drawn or written, one who draws or writes. See GRAPHO-]

graph·eme (graf′ēm), *n.* *Linguistics.* **1.** a minimal unit of a writing system. **2.** a unit of a writing system consisting of all the written symbols or sequences of written symbols that are used to represent a single phoneme. —**gra·phem′i·cal·ly,** *adv.*

gra·phe·mics (gra fē′miks), *n.* (*construed as sing.*) *Linguistics.* the study of writing systems and of their relation to speech.

-grapher, a combination of **-graph** and **-er**[1], used to form agent nouns to stems in **-graph:** *telegrapher.*

graph·ic (graf′ik), *adj.* **1.** giving a clear and effective picture; vivid: *a graphic account of an accident.* **2.** pertaining to the use of diagrams, graphs, mathematical curves, or the like; diagrammatic. **3.** of, pertaining to, or expressed by writing: *graphic symbols.* **4.** written, inscribed, or drawn. **5.** *Geol.* (of a rock) having a texture formed by the intergrowth of certain minerals so as to resemble written characters. **6.** *Math.* pertaining to the determination of values, solution of problems, etc., by direct measurement on diagrams instead of by ordinary calculations. **7.** of or pertaining to the graphic arts. Also, **graph′i·cal.** [< L *graphic(us)* of painting or drawing < Gk *graphikós* able to draw or paint = *gráph(ein)* (to) draw, write + *-ikos* -IC] —**graph′i·cal·ly, graph′ic·ly,** *adv.* —**Syn. 1.** striking, telling; detailed.

-graphic, a combination of **-graph** and **-ic,** used to form adjectives to stems in **-graph:** *telegraphic.*

graph′ic ac′cent, *Gram.* any mark written above a letter, esp. one indicating stress in pronunciation, as in Spanish *rápido.*

graph′ic arts′, **1.** Also called **graphics.** the arts or techniques, as engraving, etching, drypoint, woodcut, lithography, and other methods, by which copies of an original design are printed from a plate, block, or the like. **2.** the arts of drawing, painting, and printmaking.

graph·ics (graf′iks), *n.* **1.** (*construed as sing.*) the art of drawing, esp. as used in mathematics, engineering, etc. **2.** (*construed as pl.*) **a.** reproductions, as of drawings, photographs, or maps, used in magazines, books, etc. **b.** See **graphic arts** (def. 1). **3.** (*construed as sing.*) the science of calculating by diagrams. [see GRAPHIC, -ICS]

graph·ite (graf′īt), *n.* a very common mineral, soft native carbon, occurring in black to dark-gray masses, used for pencil leads, as a lubricant, and for making crucibles and electrodes; plumbago; black lead. [orig. < G *Graphit.* See GRAPH-, -ITE[1]] —**gra·phit·ic** (grə fit′ik), *adj.*

graph·i·tize (graf′i tīz′), *v.t.,* **-tized, -tiz·ing.** **1.** to convert into graphite. **2.** to cover (the surface of an object) with graphite. —**graph′i·ti·za′tion,** *n.*

grapho-, a learned borrowing from Greek meaning "writing," used in the formation of compound words: *graphology.* Also, *esp. before a vowel,* **graph-.** Cf. **-graph, -grapher, -graphic, -graphy.** [< Gk, comb. form of *graphḗ;* akin to CARVE]

graph·ol·o·gy (gra fol′ə jē), *n.* the study of handwriting, esp. as regarded as an expression of the writer's character. —**graph·o·log·ic** (graf′ə loj′ik), **graph′o·log′i·cal,** *adj.* —**graph·ol′o·gist,** *n.*

graph′ pa′per, paper having a pattern of straight or curved lines, for plotting graphs and curves.

-graphy, a combining form denoting some process or form of drawing, writing, representing, recording, describing, etc., or an art or science concerned with such a process: *biography; choreography; geography; orthography; photography.* [< Gk *-graphia.* See -GRAPH, -Y[3]]

grap·nel (grap′nᵊl), *n.* **1.** a device consisting essentially of one or more hooks or clamps for grasping or holding something; grapple; grappling iron. **2.** a small anchor with three or more flukes. Also called **grap·lin, grap·line** (grap′lin). [ME *grapnel(l),* dim. of OF *grapin,* dim. of *grape* hook, GRAPE]

Grapnel (def. 2)

grap·pa (gräp′pä), *n.* an unaged brandy, originally from Italy, distilled from the pomace of a wine press. [< It: grape stalk < Gmc; see GRAPE]

grap·ple (grap′əl), *n., v.,* **-pled, -pling.** —*n.* **1.** a hook or an iron instrument by which one thing, as a ship, fastens onto another; grapnel. **2.** a seizing or gripping. **3.** a hand-to-hand fight, as in wrestling. —*v.t.* **4.** to seize, hold, or fasten with or as with a grapple. **5.** to take close hold of; grab tightly. —*v.i.* **6.** to hold or make fast to something, as with a grapple. **7.** to use a grapple. **8.** to seize another, or each other, in a firm grip, as in wrestling; clinch. **9.** to engage in a struggle or close encounter (usually fol. by *with*): *He was grappling with a boy twice his size.* **10.** to struggle, contend, or cope (usually fol. by *with*): *to grapple with a problem.* [appar. freq. of OE *græppian* to seize; associated with GRAPNEL] —**grap′pler,** *n.*

grap·pling (grap′ling), *n.* **1.** any device by which something is seized and held. **2.** grapnel.

grap′pling i′ron, a grapnel. Also called **grap′pling hook′.**

grap·y (grā′pē), *adj.,* **grap·i·er, grap·i·est.** **1.** of, like, or composed of grapes. **2.** tasting of grapes or grape juice: *a grapy wine.*

Gras·mere (gras′mēr, gräs′-), *n.* **1.** a lake in Westmoreland, in NW England. 1 mi. long. **2.** a village on this lake: Wordsworth's home 1790–1808.

grasp (grasp, gräsp), *v.t.* **1.** to seize and hold by or as by clasping with the fingers. **2.** to seize upon; hold firmly. **3.** to get hold of mentally; comprehend; understand. —*v.i.* **4.** to make an attempt to seize, or a motion of seizing, something (usually fol. by *at* or *for*): *a drowning man grasping at a rope.* —*n.* **5.** the act of grasping or gripping, as with the hands or arms. **6.** a hold or grip. **7.** one's arms or hands, in embracing or gripping: *He took her in his grasp.* **8.** one's power of seizing and holding; reach: *to have a thing within one's grasp.* **9.** hold, possession, or mastery: *to wrest power from the grasp of a usurper.* **10.** mental hold or capacity; power to understand; comprehension. [ME *grasp(en), graps(en);* c. LG *grapsen;* akin to OE *gegræppian* to seize (see GRAPPLE)] —**grasp′a·ble,** *adj.* —**grasp′er,** *n.* —**Syn. 1.** grip, clutch; grab. See **catch. 9.** clutches.

grasp·ing (gras′ping, gräs′-), *adj.* **1.** that grasps. **2.** greedy; avaricious. —**grasp′ing·ly,** *adv.* —**grasp′ing·ness,** *n.*

grass (gras, gräs), *n.* **1.** any plant of the family *Gramineae,* characterized by jointed stems, sheathing leaves, flower spikelets, and fruit consisting of a seedlike grain or caryopsis. **2.** herbage in general, or the plants on which grazing animals pasture or which are cut and dried as hay. **3.** the grass-covered ground. **4.** pasture: *Half the farm is grass.* **5.** **grasses,** stalks or sprays of grass: *filled with dried grasses.* **6.** the season of the new growth of grass. **7.** *Slang.* marijuana. **8. let the grass grow under one's feet,** to become slack in one's efforts; be indifferent to progress. —*v.t.* **9.** to cover with grass or turf. **10.** to feed (an animal or animals) with growing grass; pasture. **11.** to lay (something) on the grass, as for the purpose of bleaching. —*v.i.* **12.** to feed on growing grass; graze. **13.** to produce grass; become covered with grass. [ME *gras,* OE *græs;* c. D, G, Icel, Goth *gras;* akin to GROW, GREEN] —**grass′like′,** *adj.*

Grass (gras; *Ger.* gräs), *n.* **Gün·ter (Wil·helm)** (gʏn′tər vil′helm), born 1927, German writer.

Grasse (gräs), *n.* **1. Fran·çois Jo·seph Paul** (fräN swA′ zhô zef′ pôl), **Comte de** (*Marquis de Grasse-Tilly*), 1722–1788, French admiral. **2.** a city in S France, near the Mediterranean: tourist center; perfume industry. 27,226 (1962).

grass·hop·per (gras′hop′ər, gräs′-), *n.* any of numerous herbivorous, orthopterous insects, esp. of the families *Acrididae* and *Tettigoniidae,* having the hind legs adapted for leaping, some species being highly destructive to vegetation. [ME]

grass·land (gras′land′, gräs′-), *n.* an area in which the natural vegetation consists largely of perennial grasses, characteristic of subhumid and semiarid climates.

grass′ roots′, (*construed as sing. or pl.*) **1.** the common or ordinary people; the rank and file. **2.** the agricultural and rural areas of a country. **3.** the people inhabiting these areas, esp. as a political, social, or economic group. —**grass-roots** (gras′ro͞ots′, -ro͝ots′, gräs′-), *adj.*

grass′ snake′, **1.** a common, European colubrid snake, *Natrix natrix*, having a collar of bright orange or yellow. **2.** any of several small, slender, harmless colubrid snakes of North America.

grass′ tree′, any Australian, liliaceous plant of the genus *Xanthorrhoea*, having a stout, woody stem bearing a tuft of long grasslike leaves and a dense flower spike.

grass′ wid′ow, a woman who is separated, divorced, or lives apart from her husband. [the first element may perh. be used in the sense of "at grass"; cf. D *grasweduwe*, G *Strohwittwe*, lit., straw widow] —**grass′wid′ow·hood′,** *n.*

grass′ wid′ower, a man who is separated, divorced, or lives apart from his wife.

grass·y (gras′ē, grä′sē), *adj.*, **grass·i·er, grass·i·est.** **1.** covered with grass. **2.** of, like, or pertaining to grass. **3.** of the color of grass. —**grass′i·ness,** *n.*

grate[1] (grāt), *n.*, *v.*, **grat·ed, grat·ing.** —*n.* **1.** a frame of metal bars for holding burning fuel, as in a fireplace or furnace. **2.** a framework of parallel or crossed bars, used as a partition, guard, cover, or the like; grating. **3.** a fireplace. —*v.t.* **4.** to furnish with a grate or grates. [ME < ML *grāt(a)* a grating, var. of *crāta* < L *crāt-* (s. of *crātis*) wickerwork, hurdle; cf. CRATE]

grate[2] (grāt), *v.*, **grat·ed, grat·ing.** —*v.i.* **1.** to have an irritating or unpleasant effect on the feelings. **2.** to make a sound of, or as of, rough scraping; rasp. **3.** to sound harshly; jar: *to grate on the ear.* **4.** to scrape or rub with rough or noisy friction, as one thing on or against another. —*v.t.* **5.** to rub together with a harsh, jarring sound: *to grate the teeth.* **6.** to reduce to small particles by rubbing against a rough surface or a surface with many sharp-edged openings: *to grate a carrot.* **7.** *Archaic.* to wear down or away by rough friction. [ME *grate(n)* < OF *grat(er)* < Gmc; cf. G *kratzen* to scratch] —**grat′er,** *n.*

grate·ful (grāt′fəl), *adj.* **1.** warmly or deeply appreciative of kindness or benefits received; thankful: *I am grateful to you for your kindness.* **2.** expressing or actuated by gratitude: *a grateful letter.* **3.** pleasing to the mind or senses; agreeable or welcome; refreshing: *the grateful sound of rain.* [obs. *grate* pleasing (< L *grātus*) + -FUL] —**grate′ful·ly,** *adv.* —**grate′ful·ness,** *n.*
—**Syn. 1.** obliged, indebted. GRATEFUL, THANKFUL describe an appreciative attitude for what one has received. GRATEFUL indicates a warm or deep appreciation of personal kindness: *grateful for favors; grateful to one's neighbors for help.* THANKFUL indicates a disposition to express gratitude by giving thanks, as to a benefactor or to a merciful Providence; there is often a sense of deliverance as well as of appreciation: *thankful that one's life was spared; thankful for one's good fortune.* **3.** pleasant, gratifying, satisfying.

Gra·ti·an (grā′shē ən, -shən), *n.* (*Flavius Gratianus*) A.D. 359–383, Roman emperor 375–383.

grat·i·fi·ca·tion (grat′ə fə kā′shən), *n.* **1.** the state of being gratified; great satisfaction. **2.** something that gratifies; source of pleasure or satisfaction. **3.** the act of gratifying. **4.** *Archaic.* a reward, recompense, or gratuity. [< L *grātificātiōn-* (s. of *grātificātiō*)]

grat·i·fy (grat′ə fī′), *v.t.*, **-fied, -fy·ing.** **1.** to give pleasure to (a person or persons) by satisfying desires or humoring inclinations or feelings. **2.** to satisfy; indulge; humor, as one's desires or appetites. **3.** *Obs.* to reward; remunerate. [ME *gratifi(en)* < L *grātificāre*. See GRATEFUL, -I-, -FY] —**grat′i·fi′er,** *n.*

grat·i·fy·ing (grat′ə fī′ing), *adj.* that gratifies; pleasing; satisfying. —**grat′i·fy′ing·ly,** *adv.*

grat·in (grat′ən, grät′-; *Fr.* GRA TAN′), *n.* See **au gratin.** [< F, MF; see GRATE[2]]

grat·ing (grā′ting), *n.* **1.** a fixed frame of bars or the like covering an opening, for allowing passage only of light, air, etc. **2.** *Physics.* See **diffraction grating.**

grat·is (grat′is, grā′tis), *adv.* **1.** without charge or payment; freely: *to provide a service gratis.* —*adj.* **2.** free; gratuitous. [ME < L: freely, contr. of *grātiīs* with favors, graces (abl. pl. of *grātia* GRACE)]

grat·i·tude (grat′i to͞od′, -tyo͞od′), *n.* the quality or feeling of being grateful or thankful. [ME < ML *grātitūdin-* (s. of *grātitūdō*) thankfulness. See GRATEFUL, -TUDE]

Grat·tan (grat′ən), *n.* **Henry,** 1746–1820, Irish statesman and orator.

gra·tu·i·tous (grə to͞o′i təs, -tyo͞o′-), *adj.* **1.** given, bestowed, or obtained without charge or payment; free. **2.** being without apparent reason, cause, or justification: *a gratuitous insult.* **3.** *Law.* given without receiving any return value. [< L *grātuīt(us)* free, freely given, spontaneous (< *grātia* favor, grace) + -OUS] —**gra·tu′i·tous·ly,** *adv.* —**gra·tu′i·tous·ness,** *n.* —**Syn. 2.** groundless, unprovoked, unjustified.

gra·tu·i·ty (grə to͞o′i tē, -tyo͞o′-), *n.*, *pl.* **-ties.** **1.** a gift of money, over and above payment due for service; tip. **2.** something given without claim or demand. **3.** *Brit.* **a.** a bonus granted to war veterans by the government. **b.** a bonus given military personnel on discharge or retirement. [< MF *gratuite* = L *grātuīt(us)* free + MF *-te* -TY[2]]

grat·u·lant (grach′ə lənt), *adj.* expressing gratification; congratulatory. [< L *grātulant-* (s. of *grātulāns*)]

grat·u·late (grach′ə lāt′), *v.t.*, *v.i.*, **-lat·ed, -lat·ing.** *Archaic.* to congratulate. [< L *grātulātus* having expressed joy (ptp. of *grātulārī*) = *grātul-* express joy, congratulate, thank (< *grātus* pleasing) + *-ātus* -ATE[1]]

grat·u·la·tion (grach′ə lā′shən), *n.* *Archaic.* **1.** a feeling of joy. **2.** the expression of joy. [< L *grātulātiōn-* (s. of *grātulātiō*)]

grau·pel (grou′pəl), *n.* See **snow pellets.** [< G, dim. of *Graupe* hulled grain]

gra·va·men (grə vā′mən), *n.*, *pl.* **-vam·i·na** (-vam′ə nə). *Law.* **1.** the part of an accusation that weighs most heavily against the accused. **2.** a grievance. [< LL: trouble, physical inconvenience = L *gravā(re)* (to) load, weigh down (see GRAVE[2]) + *-men* n. suffix]

grave[1] (grāv), *n.* **1.** an excavation made in the earth to receive a dead body in burial. **2.** any place of interment; a tomb or sepulcher. **3.** any place that becomes the receptacle of what is dead, lost, or past: *the grave of dead reputations.* **4.** death: *O grave, where is thy victory?* [ME; OE *græf*; c. G *Grab*; see GRAVE[3]]

grave[2] (grāv; *for 3, 5 also* gräv), *adj.*, **grav·er, grav·est** for 1, 2, 4, *n.* —*adj.* **1.** dignified; sedate; serious; earnest; solemn: *a grave person; grave thoughts.* **2.** weighty, momentous, or important; serious; critical: *grave responsibilities; a grave situation.* **3.** *Gram.* **a.** unaccented. **b.** spoken on a low or falling pitch. **c.** noting or having a particular accent (ˋ) indicating originally a comparatively low pitch (as in French *père*), distinct syllabic value (as in English *belovèd*), etc. (opposed to *acute*). **4.** (of colors) dull; somber. —*n.* **5.** the grave accent. [< MF < L *grav(is)*; akin to Gk *barýs* heavy] —**grave′ly,** *adv.* —**grave′ness,** *n.*
—**Syn. 1.** staid, thoughtful. GRAVE, SOBER, SOLEMN refer to the condition of being serious in demeanor or appearance. GRAVE indicates a weighty dignity, or the character, demeanor, speech, etc., of a person conscious of heavy responsibilities or cares, or of threatening possibilities: *The jury looked grave while studying the evidence.* SOBER (from its original sense of freedom from intoxication, and hence temperate, staid, sedate) has come to indicate absence of levity, gaiety, or mirth, and thus to be akin to serious and grave: *a sober expression on one's face.* SOLEMN implies an impressive seriousness and earnestness: *The minister's voice was solemn.* —**Ant. 1.** frivolous, gay.

grave[3] (grāv), *v.t.*, **graved, grav·en** or **graved, grav·ing.** **1.** to incise or engrave. **2.** to impress deeply: *graven on the mind.* [ME *grave(n)*, OE *grafan*; c. G *graben*] —**grav′er,** *n.*

grave[4] (grāv), *v.t.*, **graved, grav·ing.** *Naut.* to clean and apply a protective composition of tar to (the bottom of a vessel). [? akin to GRAVEL]

gra·ve[5] (grä′vā; *It.* GRÄ′ve), *Music.* —*adj.* **1.** slow; solemn. —*adv.* **2.** slowly; solemnly. [< It *grave* < L *gravis* heavy; see GRAVE[2]]

grave·dig·ger (grāv′dig′ər), *n.* a person who earns his living by digging graves.

grav·el (grav′əl), *n.*, *v.*, **-eled, -el·ing** or (*esp. Brit.*) **-elled, -el·ling,** *adj.* —*n.* **1.** small stones and pebbles, or a mixture of these with sand. **2.** *Pathol.* **a.** multiple small calculi formed in the kidneys. **b.** the disease characterized by such concretions. —*v.t.* **3.** to cover with gravel. **4.** to bring to a standstill from perplexity; puzzle. **5.** *Informal.* to be a cause of irritation to. **6.** *Obs.* to run (a vessel) aground, as on a beach. —*adj.* **7.** harsh and grating: *a gravel voice.* [ME < OF *gravele*, dim. of *grave* sandy shore, perh. < Celt] —**grav′el·ish,** *adj.*

grav·el-blind (grav′əl blīnd′), *adj.* *Literary.* more blind or dim-sighted than sand-blind and less than stone-blind.

grav·el·ly (grav′ə lē), *adj.* **1.** of, like, or abounding in gravel. **2.** harsh and grating: *a gravelly voice.*

grav·en (grā′vən), *v.* **1.** a pp. of **grave**[3]. —*adj.* **2.** deeply impressed; firmly fixed. **3.** carved; sculptured: *a graven image.*

Gra·ven·ha·ge, 's (skhrä′vən hä′khə), Dutch name of The Hague.

grav′en im′age, an idol.

grav·er (grā′vər), *n.* **1.** any of various tools for chasing, engraving, etc., as a burin. **2.** an engraver. [ME]

grave·rob·ber (grāv′rob′ər), *n.* **1.** a person who steals valuables from graves and crypts. **2.** (formerly) a person who steals corpses after burial, esp. for dissection. —**grave′rob′bing,** *n.*

Graves (grāvz *for 1*; gräv; *Fr.* GRAV *for 2 and 3*), *n.* **1. Robert (Ran·ke)** (rang′kə), 1895–1985, English poet, novelist, and critic. **2.** a wine-growing district in Gironde department, in SW France. **3.** a dry, red or white table wine produced in this region.

Graves′′ disease′, *Pathol.* a disease characterized by an enlarged thyroid, a rapid pulse, and increased basal metabolism due to excessive thyroid secretion; exophthalmic goiter. [named after R. J. *Graves* (1796–1853), Irish physician]

Graves·end (grāvz′end′), *n.* a seaport in NW Kent, in SE England, on the Thames River. 51,388 (1961).

grave·stone (grāv′stōn′), *n.* a stone marking a grave. [ME]

Gra·vett·i·an (grə vet′ē ən), *adj.* of, pertaining to, or characteristic of an Upper Paleolithic culture of Europe. [after *la Gravette* on the Dordogne, France; see -IAN]

grave·yard (grāv′yärd′), *n.* cemetery; burial ground.

grave′yard shift′, *Slang.* **1.** a work shift usually beginning at midnight and continuing through the early morning hours. **2.** those who work this shift. Also called **grave′yard watch′.**

grav·id (grav′id), *adj.* pregnant. [< L *gravid(us)* = *grav(is)* burdened, loaded + *-idus* -ID[4]] —**gra·vid·i·ty** (grə vid′i tē), **grav′id·ness,** *n.* —**grav′id·ly,** *adv.*

gra·vim·e·ter (grə vim′i tər), *n.* **1.** an instrument for measuring the specific gravity of a solid or liquid. **2.** Also called **gravity meter.** an instrument for measuring the strength of a gravitational field. [< F *gravimètre*]

grav·i·met·ric (grav′ə me′trik), *adj.* of or pertaining to measurement by weight. Also, **grav′i·met′ri·cal.** [*gravi-* (comb. form of L *gravis* heavy) + -METRIC] —**grav′i·met′ri·cal·ly,** *adv.*

gravimet′ric anal′ysis, *Chem.* analysis of materials by weight methods. Cf. **volumetric analysis.**

gra·vim·e·try (grə vim′i trē), *n.* the measurement of weight, density, or the strength of a gravitational field. [*gravi-* (comb. form of L *gravis* heavy) + -METRY]

grav′ing dock′, *Naut.* an excavated shore dry dock for the repair and maintenance of vessels, having means by which the water in the dry dock can be pumped out after the vessel has entered.

grav·i·tate (grav′i tāt′), *v.i.*, **-tat·ed, -tat·ing.** **1.** to move or tend to move under the influence of gravitational force. **2.** to tend toward the lowest level; sink; fall. **3.** to have a natural tendency or be strongly attracted (usually fol. by *to* or *toward*): *Artists gravitate toward one another.* [< NL *gravitāt(us)* (ptp. of *gravitāre*). See GRAVITY, -ATE[1]]

grav·i·ta·tion (grav′i tā′shən), *n.* **1.** *Physics.* **a.** the force of mutual attraction between all bodies, proportional to the product of the masses of the bodies divided by the square of the distance between them. **b.** an act or process caused by this force. **2.** a sinking or falling. **3.** a movement toward something or someone: *the gravitation of people toward the suburbs.* [< NL *gravitātiōn-* (s. of *gravitātiō*)] —**grav′i·ta′tion·al,** *adj.* —**grav′i·ta′tion·al·ly,** *adv.*

grav′ita′tional field′, *Physics.* a region surrounding a mass of such size that gravitational effects caused by the mass can be detected.

grav·i·ta·tive (grav′i tā′tiv), *adj.* **1.** of or pertaining to gravitation. **2.** tending or causing to gravitate.

grav·i·ty (grav′i tē), *n., pl.* **-ties. 1.** the force of attraction by which terrestrial bodies tend to fall toward the center of the earth. **2.** heaviness or weight. **3.** gravitation in general. **4.** serious or dignified behavior; dignity; solemnity. **5.** serious or critical character: *He seemed to ignore the gravity of his illness.* **6.** lowness in pitch, as of sounds. [< L *gravitāt-* (s. of *gravitās*) heaviness]

grav′ity cell′, *Elect.* a cell containing two electrolytes that have different specific gravities.

grav′ity fault′, *Geol.* a fault along an inclined plane in which the upper side or hanging wall appears to have moved downward with respect to the lower side or footwall (opposed to *thrust fault*).

grav′ity me′ter, gravimeter (def. 2).

gra·vure (grə vyŏŏr′, grā′vyər), *n.* **1.** an intaglio process of photomechanical printing, such as photogravure or rotogravure. **2.** a plate or a print produced by gravure. **3.** the metal or wooden plate used in photogravure. [< F = *grav(er)* (to) engrave < Gmc (see GRAVE[3]) + *-ure* -URE]

gra·vy (grā′vē), *n., pl.* **-vies. 1.** a sauce of the fat and juices from cooked meat, often thickened and seasoned. **2.** *Slang.* **a.** money easily obtained or received unexpectedly. **b.** something advantageous or of worth that is received or obtained as a benefit beyond what is due or expected. [ME *gravé, gravey* < OF *graué,* perh. misreading of *grané* (cf. *grain* anything used in cookery) < L *grānāt(us)* full of grains. See GRAIN, -ATE[1]]

gra′vy boat′, a boat-shaped dish for serving gravy or sauce; sauceboat.

gra′vy train′, *Slang.* a position in which a person or group receives excessive and unjustified advantages with little or no effort.

gray (grā), *adj.* **1.** of a color between white and black; having a neutral hue. **2.** dark, dismal, or gloomy: *gray skies.* **3.** having gray hair. **4.** elderly; old. **5.** indeterminate and intermediate in character; neutral. —*n.* **6.** any achromatic color. **7.** something of this color. **8.** gray material or clothing: *to dress in gray.* **9.** an unbleached and undyed condition. **10.** a member of the Confederate army, or the army itself. Cf. **blue** (def. 5). —*v.t., v.i.* **11.** to make or become gray. Also, **grey.** [ME; OE *grǣg;* c. G *grau*] —**gray′ly,** *adv.* —**gray′ness,** *n.*

Gray (grā), *n.* **1. A·sa** (ā′sə), 1810–88, U.S. botanist. **2. Thomas,** 1716–71, English poet.

gray·back (grā′bak′), *n.* any of various animals, as a bird, the knot, *Tringa canutus,* and a whale, *Rhachianectes glaucus,* of the northern Pacific.

gray·beard (grā′bērd′), *n.* a man whose beard is gray; old man; sage. —**gray′beard′ed,** *adj.*

gray′ duck′, any of several ducks in which certain immature or female plumages are predominantly gray, as the gadwall, *Anas strepera,* and the pintail, *A. acuta.*

gray′ em′inence, a person who wields unofficial power, esp. through another person and often surreptitiously or selfishly. French, **éminence grise.**

gray·fish (grā′fish′), *n., pl.* **-fish·es,** (*esp. collectively*) **-fish.** a name used in marketing for any of several American sharks, esp. the dogfishes of the genus *Squalus.*

gray′ fox′, a fox, *Urocyon cinereoargenteus,* found from Central America through the southwestern and eastern U.S., having blackish-gray upper parts and rusty-yellowish feet, legs, and ears.

Gray′ Fri′ar, a Franciscan friar. [ME; so called from the traditional color of the habit]

gray′ gum′, any of several Australian eucalyptuses, as *Eucalyptus tereticornis,* having a gray bark.

gray·hound (grā′hound′), *n.* greyhound.

gray·ish (grā′ish), *adj.* having a tinge of gray; slightly gray.

Gray′ La′dy, a woman worker in the American Red Cross who serves as a volunteer aide in medical services.

gray·ling (grā′ling), *n.* **1.** any fresh-water fish of the genus *Thymallus,* related to the trouts, but having a longer, and higher, brilliantly colored dorsal fin. **2.** any of several grayish or brownish butterflies of the family *Satyridae.* [ME]

gray′ mat′ter, 1. *Anat.* nerve tissue, esp. of the brain and spinal cord, that contains fibers and nerve cells and is of a dark reddish-gray color. Cf. **white matter. 2.** *Informal.* one's brains or intellect.

Gray's′ Inn′. See under **Inns of Court** (def. 1).

gray′ squir′rel, a common, grayish squirrel, *Sciurus carolinensis,* of eastern North America. See illus. at **squirrel.**

gray·wacke (grā′wak′, -wak′ə), *n.* a grit or sandstone, usually dark, containing feldspar, fragments of rock such as slate or schist, various dark minerals, and interstitial clay. Also, **greywacke.** [partly trans., partly adapted from G *Grauwacke;* see WACKE]

gray·weth·er (grā′weth′ər), *n.* sarsen.

gray′ whale′, a grayish-black whalebone whale, *Eschrichtius glaucus,* of the North Pacific, growing to a length of 50 feet.

gray′ wolf′, a wolf, *Canis lupus,* formerly common in Eurasia and North America, having a usually grizzled, blackish or whitish coat.

Graz (grɑ̈ts), *n.* a city in SE Austria. 237,041 (1961).

graze[1] (grāz), *v.,* **grazed, graz·ing.** —*v.i.* **1.** to feed on growing herbage, as do cattle, sheep, etc. —*v.t.* **2.** to feed on (growing grass). **3.** to put cattle, sheep, etc., to feed on (grass, pasture land, etc.). **4.** to tend (cattle, sheep, etc.) while they are at pasture. [ME *grase(n),* OE *grasian* < *græs* GRASS]

graze[2] (grāz), *v.,* **grazed, graz·ing,** *n.* —*v.t.* **1.** to touch or rub lightly in passing. **2.** to scrape the skin from; abrade. —*v.i.* **3.** to touch or rub something lightly, or so as to produce slight abrasion, in passing. —*n.* **4.** a grazing; a touching or rubbing lightly in passing. **5.** a slight scratch in passing; abrasion. [? special use of GRAZE[1]; for the semantic shift, cf. F *effleurer* < *fleur* flower, in the same meaning] —**graz′er,** *n.* —**graz′ing·ly,** *adv.*

gra·zier (grā′zhər), *n.* *Chiefly Brit.* a person who grazes cattle for the market. [late ME *grasier.* See GRAZE[1], -ER[2]]

graz·ing (grā′zing), *n.* pasture land; a pasture. [ME]

Gr. Br., Great Britain. Also, **Gr. Brit.**

grease (*n.* grēs; *v.* grēs, grēz), *n., v.,* **greased, greas·ing.** —*n.* **1.** the melted or rendered fat of animals, esp. when in a soft state. **2.** fatty or oily matter in general; lubricant. **3.** Also called **grease′ wool′.** wool, as shorn, before being cleansed of oily matter. —*v.t.* **4.** to put grease on; lubricate. **5. grease someone's palm.** See palm[1] (def. 10). [ME *grese, grece, greice* < AF *grece, gresse,* OF *craisse* (F *graisse*) < VL **crassia* = L *crass(us)* fat, thick + *-ia* n. suffix]

grease·ball (grēs′bôl′), *n.* *Disparaging.* a person of Italian, Spanish, Greek, or Portuguese descent.

grease·bush (grēs′bŏŏsh′), *n.* greasewood.

grease′ cup′, oilcup.

grease′ gun′, a hand-operated pump for greasing bearings under pressure.

grease′ mon′key, *Slang.* a mechanic, esp. on an automobile or airplane.

grease′ paint′, an oily mixture of melted tallow or grease and a pigment, used by actors, clowns, etc. for making up their faces. Also, **grease′paint′.**

grease′ pen′cil, a pencil of pigment and compressed grease, encased in a spiral paper strip that may be partially unwound to expose a new point, used esp. for writing on glossy surfaces.

greas·er (grē′sər), *n.* **1.** a person or thing that greases. **2.** *Disparaging.* a Latin-American, esp. a Mexican.

grease·wood (grēs′wŏŏd′), *n.* **1.** a chenopodiaceous shrub, *Sarcobatus vermiculatus,* of the alkaline regions of the western U.S., containing a small amount of oil and used for fuel. **2.** any of various similar shrubs. Also called **grease-bush.**

greas·y (grē′sē, -zē), *adj.,* **greas·i·er, greas·i·est. 1.** smeared or soiled with grease. **2.** composed of or containing grease; oily: *greasy food.* **3.** greaselike in appearance or to the touch; slippery. —**greas′i·ly,** *adv.* —**greas′i·ness,** *n.*

greas′y spoon′, *Slang.* a cheap, run-down, and rather unsanitary restaurant, esp. one specializing in short-order fried foods.

great (grāt), *adj., adv., n., pl.* **greats,** (*esp. collectively*) **great.** —*adj.* **1.** unusually or comparatively large in size or dimensions; big. **2.** large in number; numerous. **3.** unusual or considerable in degree, power, intensity, etc.: *great pain.* **4.** notable; remarkable; exceptionally outstanding: *a great occasion.* **5.** distinguished; famous: *a great inventor.* **6.** important; highly significant or consequential: *a great era in history.* **7.** chief or principal: *his greatest novel.* **8.** of high rank, official position, or social standing: *a great noble.* **9.** of noble or lofty character: *great thoughts.* **10.** much in use or favor: *"Humor" was a great word with the old physiologists.* **11.** being such in an extreme degree: *great friends.* **12.** of extraordinary powers; having unusual merit; very admirable: *a great statesman.* **13.** of marked duration or length: *to wait a great while.* **14.** *Informal.* **a.** enthusiastic about some specified activity (usually fol. by *at, for,* or *on*): *He's great on reading poetry aloud.* **b.** first-rate; very good: *a great movie.* **15.** *Chiefly Dial.* pregnant: *great with child.* —*adv.* **16.** *Informal.* very well: *The project is going great.* —*n.* **17.** a person who has achieved importance or distinction in his field: *one of the theater's greats.* [ME *greet,* OE *grēat;* c. D *groot,* G *gross*] —**great′ness,** *n.*

—**Syn. 1.** immense, enormous, gigantic, huge, vast, grand. GREAT, BIG, LARGE refer to size, extent, and degree. In reference to the size and extent of concrete objects, BIG is the most general and most colloquial word, LARGE is somewhat more formal, and GREAT is highly formal and even poetic, suggesting also that the object is notable or imposing: *a big tree; a large tree; a great oak; a big field; a large field; great plains.* When the reference is to degree or a quality, GREAT is the usual word: *great beauty; great mistake; great surprise;* although BIG sometimes alternates with it in colloquial style: *a big mistake.* LARGE is not used in reference to degree, but may be used in a quantitative reference: *a large number* (*great number*). **4.** noteworthy. **5.** eminent, prominent, celebrated, illustrious, renowned. **6.** momentous, vital, critical. **7.** main, grand, leading. **9.** elevated, exalted.

great′ ant′eater. See **ant bear** (def. 1).

great′ ape′, any anthropoid ape, as a gorilla or chimpanzee.

great′ auk′, a large, flightless, extinct auk, *Pinguinus impennis,* formerly found in northern areas of the North Atlantic.

great-aunt (grāt′ant′, -änt′), *n.* an aunt of one's father or mother; grandaunt.

Great′ Austral′ian Bight′, a wide bay in S Australia.

Great′ Awak′ening, the series of religious revivals among Protestants in the American colonies, esp. in New England, lasting from about 1725 to 1770.

Great′ Bar′rier Reef′, a coral reef parallel to the coast of Queensland, in NE Australia. 1250 mi. long. Also called **Barrier Reef.**

Great′ Ba′sin, a region in the W United States having no drainage to the ocean: includes most of Nevada and parts of Utah, California, Oregon, and Idaho. 210,000 sq. mi.

Great′ Bear′, *Astron.* the constellation Ursa Major.

Great′ Bear′ Lake′, a lake in NW Canada, in the Northwest Territories. 12,000 sq. mi.

great′ blue′ her′on, a large, American heron, *Ardea herodias,* having bluish-gray plumage. See illus. at **heron.**

Great′ Brit′ain, an island of NW Europe, separated from the mainland by the English Channel and the North Sea: since 1707 the name has applied politically to England,

Scotland, and Wales. 46,417,600; 88,139 sq. mi. Cf. **United Kingdom.**

great′ cir′cle, 1. a circle on a sphere such that the plane containing the circle passes through the center of the sphere. Cf. **small circle.** 2. the line of shortest distance between two points on the surface of the earth. —**great′-cir′cle,** *adj.*

great·coat (grāt′kōt′), *n. Chiefly Brit.* a heavy overcoat. —**great′coat′ed,** *adj.*

great′ coun′cil, 1. (in Norman England) an assembly composed of the king's tenants in chief that served as the principal council of the realm and replaced the witenagemot. 2. (formerly in Italy) the municipal council in some towns or cities, as in Venice.

Great Dane
(32 in. high at shoulder)

great′ crest′ed grebe′, a large, Old World grebe, *Podiceps cristatus,* having black, earlike tufts of feathers projecting backward from the top of the head. See illus. at **grebe.**

Great′ Dane′, one of a breed of large, powerful, short-haired dogs ranging in color from fawn to brindle, blue, black, or white with black spots.

Great′ Depres′sion, the economic crisis and period of low business activity in the U.S. and other countries, roughly beginning with the stockmarket crash in October, 1929, and continuing through the 1930's.

Great′ Divide′, the continental divide of North America; the Rocky Mountains.

Great′ Divid′ing Range′, a mountain range extending along the E coast of Australia: vast watershed region. 100 to 200 mi. wide.

Great′ Dog′, *Astron.* the constellation Canis Major.

great·en (grāt′ən), *Chiefly Literary.* —*v.t.* 1. to make greater; enlarge; increase. —*v.i.* 2. to become greater.

Great·er (grā′tər), *adj.* designating a city and its suburbs: *Greater New York.*

Great′er Antil′les. See under **Antilles.**

Great′er Bai′ram. See under **Bairam.**

great′er multan′gular bone′. See under **multangulum.**

Great′er Sun′da Is′lands. See under **Sunda Islands.**

great′er yel′lowlegs. See under **yellowlegs.**

great′est com′mon divi′sor, the largest number that is a common divisor of a given set of numbers.

Great′ Falls′, a city in central Montana, on the Missouri River. 60,091 (1970).

great-grand·child (grāt′gran′chīld′), *n., pl.* **-chil·dren.** a grandchild of one's son or daughter.

great-grand·daugh·ter (grāt′gran′dô′tər), *n.* a granddaughter of one's son or daughter.

great-grand·fa·ther (grāt′gran′fä′thər, -grand′-), *n.* a grandfather of one's father or mother.

great-grand·moth·er (grāt′gran′muth′ər, -grand′-, -gram′-), *n.* a grandmother of one's father or mother.

great-grand·par·ent (grāt′gran′pâr′ənt, -par′-, -grand′-), *n.* a grandfather or grandmother of one's father or mother.

great-grand·son (grāt′gran′sun′, -grand′-), *n.* a grandson of one's son or daughter.

great′ guns′, 1. *Informal.* in a relentlessly energetic or successful manner: *His work is going great guns.* 2. (used as an expression of surprise, astonishment, etc.)

great-heart·ed (grāt′här′tid), *adj.* 1. having or showing a generous heart; magnanimous. 2. high-spirited; courageous; fearless. Also, **great′heart′ed.** [ME *grete hartyd*] —**great′-heart′ed·ly, great′heart′ed·ly,** *adv.* —**great′-heart′ed·ness, great′heart′ed·ness,** *n.*

great′ horned′ owl′, a large, rapacious, American owl, *Bubo virginianus,* having a prominent, earlike tuft of feathers on each side of the head. See illus. at **owl.**

Great′ Lakes′, a series of five lakes between the U.S. and Canada, comprising Lakes Erie, Huron, Michigan, Ontario, and Superior; connected with the Atlantic by the St. Lawrence River.

great′ lau′rel. See **great rhododendron.**

Great′ Leap′ For′ward, an economic plan of the People's Republic of China, implemented between 1958 and mid-1960, for accelerating its nationwide industrial production.

great·ly (grāt′lē), *adv.* 1. in or to a great degree; much. 2. in a great manner. [ME]

Great′ Mo′gul, the emperor of the former Mogul Empire in India founded in 1526 by Baber.

great-neph·ew (grāt′nef′yōō, -nev′yōō), *n.* a son of one's nephew or niece; grandnephew.

great-niece (grāt′nēs′), *n.* a daughter of one's nephew or niece; grandniece.

Great′ Ouse′, Ouse (def. 2).

great′ pas′tern bone′. See under **pastern** (def. 2).

Great′ Plague′, the bubonic plague occurring in London in 1665. Also, **great′ plague′.**

Great′ Plains′, a semiarid region E of the Rocky Mountains, in the U.S. and Canada.

Great′ Pow′er, a nation that has exceptional military and economic strength, and consequently plays a major, often decisive, role in international affairs. —**Great′-Pow′er, great′-pow′er,** *adj.*

great′ prim′er, *Print.* an 18-point type of a size larger than Columbian, formerly used for Bibles.

Great′ Pyr′enees, one of a breed of large dogs having a heavy, white coat, raised originally in the Pyrenees.

Great′ Rebel′lion. See **English Civil War.**

great′ rhododen′dron, a tall rhododendron, *Rhododendron maximum,* of the eastern U.S., having pink or white flowers. Also called **great laurel, great′ rose′bay.**

Great′ Rus′sian, 1. a member of the main stock of the Russian people, dwelling chiefly in the northern or central parts of the Soviet Union in Europe. 2. the Russian language, excluding Ukrainian and Byelorussian.

Great′ Salt′ Lake′, a shallow salt lake in NW Utah. 2300 sq. mi.; 80 mi. long; maximum depth 60 ft.

Great′ Sand′y Des′ert, 1. a desert in NW Australia. ab. 300 mi. long; 500 mi. wide; ab. 160,000 sq. mi. 2. See **Rub′ al Khali.**

Great′ San′hedrin, Sanhedrin (def. 1).

Great′ Schism′, a period of division in the Roman Catholic Church, 1378–1417, over papal succession.

Great′ Scott′, (used as a euphemistic interjection or oath, usually expressing surprise, amazement, or the like.)

great′ seal′, 1. the principal seal of a government or state. 2. (*caps.*) *Brit.* **a.** the Lord Chancellor, keeper of the principal seal of Great Britain. **b.** his office. [ME *grete Seel*]

great′ sku′a, *Brit.* skua (def. 1).

Great′ Slave′ Lake′, a lake in NW Canada, in the Northwest Territories. 11,172 sq. mi.

Great′ Smok′y Moun′tains, a range of the Appalachian Mountains in North Carolina and Tennessee; most of the range is included in Great Smoky Mountains National Park. 720 sq. mi. Highest peak, Clingman's Dome, 6642 ft. Also called **Smoky Mountains, Great′ Smok′ies.**

Great′ Soci′ety, the goal of the Democratic party under the leadership of President Lyndon B. Johnson, chiefly to enact domestic programs to improve education, provide medical care for the aged, and eliminate poverty. Cf. **Fair Deal, New Deal, New Frontier.**

Great′ Spir′it, the chief deity in the religion of many North American Indian tribes.

Great St. Bernard. See **St. Bernard, Great.**

great′ toe′, *Anat.* See **big toe.**

great-un·cle (grāt′ung′kəl), *n.* an uncle of one's father or mother; granduncle.

Great′ Victo′ria Des′ert, a desert in SW central Australia. 125,000 sq. mi. Also called **Victoria Desert.**

Great′ Vow′el Shift′, *Linguistics.* a series of changes in the quality of the long vowels between Middle and Modern English as a result of which all were raised, while the high vowels (ē) and (ōō), already at the upper limit, underwent breaking to become the diphthongs (ī) and (ou).

Eighth Century A.D.
GOBI DESERT
Great Wall of China
Hwang Ho
CHINA
Yangtze River
Wuhsien
YELLOW SEA

Great′ Wall′ of Chi′na, a system of walls constructed as a defense for China against the nomads of the regions that are now Mongolia and Manchuria: completed in the third century B.C., but later repeatedly modified and rebuilt. 2000 mi. long. Also called **Chinese Wall.**

Great′ War′. See **World War I.**

Great′ White′ Fa′ther, *Facetious.* 1. the president of the U.S. 2. a man who holds a position of great authority.

great′ white′ her′on, 1. a large white heron, *Ardea occidentalis,* of Florida and the Florida Keys. 2. a large white egret, *Casmerodius albus,* of southeastern Europe, tropical Africa, Asia, and America.

great′ white′ shark′, a large shark, *Carcharodon carcharias,* found in tropical and temperate seas: occasionally attacks man. Also called **man-eater.**

Great′ White′ Way′, the theater district along Broadway, near Times Square in New York City.

Great′ Yar′mouth (yär′məth), a seaport in E Norfolk, in E England. 52,860 (1961).

greave (grēv), *n. Armor.* a piece of plate armor for the leg between the knee and the ankle, usually composed of front and back pieces. Also called **jamb, jambeau.** [ME *greve(s)* (pl.) < OF < ?] —**greaved,** *adj.*

greaves (grēvz), *n.* (*construed as sing. or pl.*) crackling (def. 3). [< LG *grev(en)*; c. OHG *griubo,* G *Grieben*]

Great crested grebe,
Podiceps cristatus
(Length 19 in.)

grebe (grēb), *n.* any of several diving birds of the family *Podicepedidae,* related to the loons, but having lobate rather than webbed toes and a rudimentary tail. [< F *grèbe* < ?]

Gre·cian (grē′shən), *adj.* 1. Greek. —*n.* 2. a Greek. 3. an expert in the Greek language or literature. [< L *Gr(a)eci(a)* GREECE + -AN]

Gre·cise (grē′sīz), *v.t., v.i.,* **-cised, -cis·ing.** *Chiefly Brit.* Grecize.

Gre·cism (grē′siz əm), *n.* 1. the spirit of Greek thought, art, etc. 2. adoption or imitation of this. 3. an idiom or peculiarity of Greek. Also, *esp. Brit.,* **Graecism.** [< ML *Graecism(us)*]

Gre·cize (grē′sīz), *v.,* **-cized, -ciz·ing.** (*often l.c.*) —*v.t.* 1. to impart Greek characteristics to. 2. to translate into Greek. —*v.i.* 3. to conform to what is Greek; adopt Greek speech, customs, etc. Also, *esp. Brit.,* **Grecise, Graecize, Graecise.** [< L *graecizāre* (to) imitate the Greeks < Gk *graikízein* (to) adopt a Greek manner; see -IZE]

Gre·co (grek′ō; *Sp.* gre′kô), *n.* **El** (el). See **El Greco.**

Greco-, a combining form of **Greek.** Also, *esp. Brit.,* **Graeco-.** [< L *Graeco-,* comb. form of *Graecus* Greek]

Gre·co-Ro·man (grē′kō rō′mən, grek′ō-), *adj.* of or having both Greek and Roman characteristics: *the Greco-Roman influence.*

gree[1] (grē), *n. Chiefly Scot.* 1. superiority, mastery, or victory. 2. the prize for victory. [ME *gre* < OF < L *grad(us)* step, GRADE; cf. DEGREE]

gree[2] (grē), *n. Archaic.* 1. favor; good will. 2. satisfaction, as for an injury. [ME *gre* < OF *gre* (F *gré*) < L *grāt(um)* what is agreeable]

Greece (grēs), *n.* a republic in S Europe at the S end of the Balkan Peninsula. 9,000,000; 50,147 sq. mi. *Cap.:* Athens. Ancient Greek, **Hellas.** Modern Greek, **Ellas.**

greed (grēd), *n.* excessive, inordinate, or rapacious desire, esp. for wealth. [back formation from GREEDY] —**Syn.** avarice, cupidity, covetousness. GREED, GREEDINESS denote an excessive, extreme desire for something, often more than one's proper share. GREED means avid desire for gain or wealth and is uncomplimentary in implication: *His greed drove him to exploit his workers.* GREEDINESS suggests a craving for food; it may, however, be applied to all avid desires, and is not always uncomplimentary: *greediness for knowledge, fame.* —**Ant.** generosity.

greed·y (grē′dē), *adj.*, **greed·i·er, greed·i·est.** **1.** excessively or inordinately desirous of wealth, profit, etc.; avaricious. **2.** having a strong or great desire for food or drink. **3.** keenly desirous; eager (often fol. by *of* or *for*). [ME *gredy*, OE *grēdig;* r. OE *grædig;* c. OIcel *grāthugr*, Goth *gredags*] —**greed′i·ly,** *adv.* —**greed′i·ness,** *n.* —**Syn. 1.** grasping, rapacious, selfish. **2.** ravenous, voracious.

gree·gree (grē′grē), *n.* grigri.

Greek (grēk), *adj.* **1.** of or pertaining to Greece, the Greeks, or their language. **2.** pertaining to the Greek Orthodox Church. —*n.* **3.** a native of Greece. **4.** the language of the ancient Greeks and any of the languages that have developed from it, as Hellenistic Greek, Biblical Greek, the Koine, and Modern Greek. *Abbr.:* Gk, Gk. **5.** *Informal.* anything unintelligible, as a speech, handwriting, etc.: *It's Greek to me.* **6.** a member of the Greek Church. **7.** Hellenic (def. 2). **8.** a person who belongs to a Greek-letter fraternity or sorority. [ME; OE *Grēcas* (pl.) < L *Graecī* the Greeks (nom. pl. of *Graecus*) < Gk *Graikoí*, pl. of *Graikós* Greek]

Greek′ Cath′olic, **1.** a member of the Greek Orthodox Church. **2.** a Uniat belonging to a church observing the Greek rite.

Greek′ Church′. See **Greek Orthodox Church** (def. 1).

Greek′ cross′, a cross consisting of an upright crossed in the middle by a horizontal piece of the same length. See illus. at **cross.**

Greek′ fire′, an incendiary mixture of unknown composition, used in warfare in medieval times by Byzantine Greeks.

Greek′ Or′thodox Church′, **1.** that branch of the Orthodox Church constituting the national church of Greece. **2.** See **Orthodox Church** (def. 2).

Gree·ley (grē′lē), *n.* **1. Horace,** 1811–72, U.S. journalist and political leader. **2.** a city in N Colorado. 38,902 (1970).

Gree·ly (grē′lē), *n.* **Adolphus Washington,** 1844–1935, U.S. general and arctic explorer.

green (grēn), *adj.* **1.** of the color of growing foliage, between yellow and blue in the spectrum. **2.** covered with herbage or foliage; verdant: *green fields.* **3.** made of green vegetables: *a green salad.* **4.** full of life and vigor; young. **5.** unseasoned; not dried or cured: *green lumber.* **6.** not fully developed or perfected in growth or condition; unripe or not properly aged. **7.** immature in age or judgment; untrained or inexperienced. **8.** fresh, recent, or new: *a green wound.* **9.** having a sickly appearance; pale; wan: *green with envy.* **10.** freshly killed: *green meat.* **11.** not fired, as bricks or pottery. **12.** (of cement or mortar) freshly set and not completely hardened. —*n.* **13.** a color intermediate in the spectrum between yellow and blue, found in nature as the color of most grasses and leaves while growing. **14.** green coloring matter, as paint, dye, etc. **15.** green material or clothing. **16.** grassy land; a plot of grassy ground. **17.** *Sports.* **a.** an area of grassy land intended for games, as bowling or archery. **b.** Also called **putting green.** *Golf.* the area of closely cropped grass surrounding the hole. **18.** a piece of grassy ground constituting a town or village common. **19. greens, a.** fresh leaves or branches of trees, shrubs, etc., used for decoration; wreaths. **b.** the leaves and stems of plants, as spinach, lettuce, cabbage, etc., used for food. **c.** a blue-green uniform of the U.S. Army. —*v.t., v.i.* **20.** to make or become green. [ME, OE *grēne;* c. G *grün;* akin to GROW] —**green′ly,** *adv.*

Green (grēn), *n.* **1. John Richard,** 1837–83, English historian. **2. Paul Eliot,** 1894–1981, U.S. playwright, novelist, and teacher. **3. Thomas Hill,** 1836–82, English idealist philosopher. **4. William,** 1873–1952, U.S. labor leader.

green′ al′ga, any grass-green alga of the class *Chlorophyceae.*

Green·a·way (grēn′ə wā′), *n.* **Kate** (*Catherine*), 1846–1901, English illustrator.

green·back (grēn′bak′), *n.* a United States legal-tender note, usually printed in green on the back.

Green′back par′ty, *U.S. Hist.* a former political party organized in 1874, opposed to the retirement or reduction of greenbacks. —**Green′back′er,** *n.* —**Green′back′ism,** *n.*

Green′ Bay′, **1.** an arm of Lake Michigan, in NE Wisconsin. 120 mi. long. **2.** a port in E Wisconsin at the S end of this bay. 87,809 (1970).

Green′ Beret′, a member of the U.S. Army Special Forces.

green·bri·er (grēn′brī′ər), *n.* a climbing, liliaceous plant, *Smilax rotundifolia*, of the eastern U.S., having a prickly stem and thick leaves.

green′ corn′. See **sweet corn** (def. 2).

green′ drag′on. See under **dragon** (def. 5).

Greene (grēn), *n.* **1. Graham,** born 1904, English novelist. **2. Nathanael,** 1742–86, American Revolutionary general. **3. Robert,** 1558–92, English dramatist and poet.

green·er·y (grē′nə rē), *n.* green foliage or vegetation; verdure.

green-eyed (grēn′īd′), *adj.* *Informal.* jealous or envious.

Green·field (grēn′fēld′), *n.* a city in SE Wisconsin, near Milwaukee. 24,424 (1970).

green·finch (grēn′finch′), *n.* a European finch, *Chloris chloris*, having green and yellow plumage.

green·gage (grēn′gāj′), *n.* any of several varieties of light-green plums. [GREEN + *Gage*, after Sir William *Gage*, 18th-century English botanist]

green′ gland′, *Zool.* one of the pair of excretory organs in each side of the head region of decapod crustaceans, emptying at the base of the antennae.

green′ glass′, glass of low quality, colored green by impurities in the materials from which it is made.

green·gro·cer (grēn′grō′sər), *n.* *Chiefly Brit.* a retailer of fresh vegetables and fruit.

green·gro·cer·y (grēn′grō′sə rē), *n., pl.* **-cer·ies.** *Chiefly Brit.* **1.** a greengrocer's shop. **2.** the fruits and vegetables stocked and sold in such a shop.

green·heart (grēn′härt′), *n.* **1.** a South American, lauraceous tree, *Ocotea* (or *Nectandra*) *Rodiaei*, yielding a hard, durable wood often used for wharves and bridges and in shipbuilding, and whose bark yields bebeerine. **2.** any of certain other timber trees of tropical America. **3.** their valuable greenish wood.

green·horn (grēn′hôrn′), *n.* *Slang.* a raw, inexperienced person. [ME; see GREEN, HORN; orig. applied to cattle with green (i.e., young) horns]

green·house (grēn′hous′), *n., pl.* **-hous·es** (-hou′ziz). a building, usually chiefly of glass, in which the temperature is maintained within a desired range, used for cultivating tender plants.

green·ing (grē′ning), *n.* any variety of apple whose skin is green when ripe.

green·ish (grē′nish), *adj.* somewhat green; having a tinge of green. [ME]

green·keep·er (grēn′kē′pər), *n.* greenskeeper.

Green·land (grēn′lənd, -land′), *n.* a Danish overseas territory located NE of North America: the largest island in the world. 40,000 (est. 1969); ab. 840,000 sq. mi. (over 700,000 sq. mi. ice-capped). *Cap.:* Godthaab. —**Green′land·er,** *n.* —**Green·land·ic** (grēn lan′dik), *adj.*

Green′land Sea′, a part of the Arctic Ocean, NE of Greenland and N of Iceland.

green·let (grēn′lit), *n.* a vireo.

green′ light′, a green lamp, used as a traffic signal to mean "go."

green·ling (grēn′ling), *n.* any spiny-finned fish of the genus *Hexagrammos*, found about rocks and kelp in the North Pacific. [late ME]

green·mail (grēn′māl′), *n.* *Stock Exchange.* the buying up of a large block of a company's stock, esp. in order to force the company to buy back the stock at an inflated price to thwart a possible takeover. [GREEN (in sense "money") + (BLACK)MAIL] —**green′mail′er,** *n.*

green′ manure′, *Agric.* **1.** a crop of growing plants plowed under to enrich the soil. **2.** manure which has not undergone decay.

green′ mold′. See **blue mold** (def. 1).

green′ mon′key, a monkey, *Cercopithecus aethiops sabaeus*, of West Africa, with a greenish-gray back and yellow tail.

Green′ Moun′tain Boys′, the soldiers from Vermont in the American Revolution, originally organized by Ethan Allen in 1775 to oppose the territorial claims of New York.

Green′ Moun′tains, a mountain range in Vermont: a part of the Appalachian system. Highest peak, Mt. Mansfield, 4393 ft.

Green′ Moun′tain State′, Vermont (used as a nickname).

green·ness (grēn′nis), *n.* **1.** the quality or state of being green. **2.** green vegetation, grass, or the like; verdure or verdancy. **3.** lack of maturity or experience; youthfulness. **4.** naïveté, innocence, or gullibility. [ME, OE *grēnnes*]

Green·ock (grē′nək, gren′ək), *n.* a seaport in SW Scotland, on the Firth of Clyde. 74,578 (1961).

Green·ough (grē′nō), *n.* **Horatio,** 1805–52, U.S. sculptor.

green′ pep′per, **1.** the fruit of the bell or sweet pepper, *Capsicum frutescens grossum.* **2.** the mild, unripe fruit of any of the garden peppers, *Capsicum frutescens*, used as a green vegetable.

Green′ Riv′er, a river flowing S from W Wyoming through E Utah to the Colorado River. 730 mi. long.

green·sand (grēn′sand′), *n.* a sandstone containing much glauconite, which gives it a greenish hue.

Greens·bo·ro (grēnz′bûr′ō, -bur′ō), *n.* a city in N North Carolina. 144,076 (1970).

greens′ fee′, a fee for playing on a golf course.

green·shank (grēn′shangk′), *n.* an Old World shore bird, *Tringa nebularia*, having green legs.

green·sick·ness (grēn′sik′nis), *n.* *Pathol.* chlorosis (def. 2). —**green′sick′,** *adj.*

greens·keep·er (grēnz′kē′pər), *n.* a person charged with the maintenance of a golf course. Also, **greenkeeper.**

green′ soap′, a soap made chiefly from potassium hydroxide and linseed oil, used in treating skin diseases.

green′stick frac′ture (grēn′stik′), an incomplete fracture of a long bone, in which one side is broken and the other side is still intact. See illus. at **fracture.**

green·stone (grēn′stōn′), *n.* any of various altered basaltic rocks having a dark-green color caused by the presence of chlorite, epidote, etc.

green·sward (grēn′swôrd′), *n.* green, grassy turf.

green′ tea′, a tea subjected to a heating process without previous special withering and fermenting.

green′ thumb′, a conspicuous aptitude for gardening or for growing plants successfully.

green′ tur′tle, a sea turtle, *Chelonia mydas*, common in tropical and subtropical seas, the flesh of which is used for turtle soup.

Green·ville (grēn′vil), *n.* **1.** a city in NW South Carolina. 61,436 (1970). **2.** a city in W Mississippi, on the Mississippi River. 39,648 (1970). **3.** a city in E North Carolina. 29,063 (1970).

green′ vit′riol. See **ferrous sulfate.**

Green·wich (grin′ij, -ich, gren′- *for 1;* gren′ich, grin′-, grēn′wich *for 2*), *n.* **1.** a borough in SE London, England: located on the prime meridian from which geographic longitude is measured; formerly the site of the Royal Greenwich Observatory. 85,585 (1961). **2.** a town in SW Connecticut. 59,755 (1970).

Green′wich Time′, the time as measured on the prime meridian running through Greenwich, England: used in England and as a basis of calculation elsewhere. Also called **Green′wich Mean′ Time′, Green′wich Civ′il Time′.**

Green′wich Vil′lage (gren′ich, grin′-), a section of New York City, in lower Manhattan: frequented by artists, writers, and students.

green·wood (grēn′wŏŏd′), *n.* a wood or forest when green, as in summer. [ME]

greet (grēt), *v.t.* **1.** to address with some form of salutation; welcome. **2.** to meet or receive: *to greet a proposal with boos and hisses.* **3.** to manifest (itself) to: *Music greeted our ears.* **—***v.i.* **4.** *Obs.* to give salutations on meeting. [ME *gret(en),* OE *grētan;* c. G *grüssen*] **—greet′er,** *n.* **—Syn. 1.** hail, accost.

greet·ing (grē′ting), *n.* **1.** the act or words of one who greets. **2.** a friendly message from someone who is absent. **3. greetings,** an expression of friendly or respectful regard. [ME *greting*]

greet′ing card′, card[1] (def. 5).

greg·a·rine (greg′ə rīn′, -ər in), *n.* **1.** a type of sporozoan parasite of the subclass *Gregarinidea* that inhabits the digestive and other cavities of various invertebrates and produces cysts filled with spores. **—***adj.* **2.** having the characteristics of or pertaining to a gregarine or gregarines. Also, **greg·a·rin·i·an** (greg′ə rin′ē ən). [< NL *Gregarīn(a)* name of type. See GREGARIOUS, -INE[1]]

gre·gar·i·ous (gri gâr′ē əs), *adj.* **1.** fond of the company of others; sociable. **2.** living in flocks or herds, as animals. **3.** *Bot.* growing in open clusters; not matted together. **4.** pertaining to a flock or crowd. [< L *gregārius* belonging to a flock] **—gre·gar′i·ous·ly,** *adv.* **—gre·gar′i·ous·ness,** *n*

Gregg (greg), *n.* **John Robert,** 1864–1948, U.S. educator: inventor of a system of shorthand.

Gre·go·ri·an (gri gôr′ē ən, -gōr′-), *adj.* of or pertaining to any of the popes named Gregory, esp. Gregory I or Gregory XIII. [< NL *gregoriān(us)* of, pertaining to Pope Gregory = LL *Gregori(us)* + L *-ānus* -AN]

Grego′rian cal′endar, the reformed Julian calendar now in use, according to which the ordinary year consists of 365 days, and a leap year of 366 days occurs in every year whose number is exactly divisible by 4 except centenary years whose numbers are not exactly divisible by 400, as 1700, 1800, and 1900. [named after Pope GREGORY XIII]

Grego′rian chant′, **1.** the plainsong used in the ritual of the Roman Catholic Church. **2.** a melody in this style. [named after Pope GREGORY I]

Greg·o·ry (greg′ə rē), *n.* **1. Lady (Isabella) Augusta,** nee **Persse** (pûrs), 1852–1932, Irish dramatist. **2. Horace,** 1898–1982, U.S. poet and critic. **3. James,** 1638–75, Scottish mathematician.

Gregory I, Saint ("*Gregory the Great*"), A.D. c540–604, Italian ecclesiastic, promoter of Benedictine monasticism, reformer of church liturgy, and reputedly the founder of Gregorian chant: pope 590–604.

Gregory II, Saint, died A.D. 731, pope 715–731.

Gregory III, Saint, died A.D. 741, pope 731–741.

Gregory IV, died A.D. 844, pope 827–844.

Gregory V, (*Bruno of Carinthia*) died A.D. 999, German ecclesiastic: pope 996–999.

Gregory VI, (*Johannes Gratianus*) died 1048, German ecclesiastic: pope 1045–46.

Gregory VII, Saint (*Hildebrand*), c1020–85, Italian ecclesiastic: pope 1073–85.

Gregory VIII, (*Alberto de Mora* or *Alberto di Morra*) died 1187, Italian ecclesiastic: pope 1187.

Gregory IX, (*Ugolino di Segni* or *Ugolino of Anagni*) c1143–1241, Italian ecclesiastic: pope 1227–41.

Gregory X, (*Teobaldo Visconti*) c1210–76, Italian ecclesiastic: pope 1271–76.

Gregory XI, (*Pierre Roger de Beaufort*) 1330–78, French ecclesiastic: pope 1370–78.

Gregory XII, (*Angelo Correr, Corrario,* or *Corraro*) c1327–1417, Italian ecclesiastic: pope 1406–15.

Gregory XIII, (*Ugo Buoncompagni*) 1502–85, Italian ecclesiastic: pope 1572–85, educator and innovator of the modern calendar.

Gregory XIV, (*Niccolò Sfandrati*) 1535–91, Italian ecclesiastic: pope 1590–91.

Gregory XV, (*Alessandro Ludovisi*) 1554–1623, Italian ecclesiastic: pope 1621–23.

Gregory XVI, (*Bartolommeo Alberto Cappellari*) 1765–1846, Italian ecclesiastic: pope 1831–46.

Greg′ory of Naz·i·an′zus (naz′ē an′zəs), **Saint,** ("*the Theologian*"), A.D. 329–389, Christian bishop, theologian, and monastic in Asia Minor.

Greg′ory of Nys′sa (nis′ə), **Saint,** A.D. c330–395?, Christian bishop and theologian in Asia Minor (brother of Saint Basil).

Greg′ory of Tours′, Saint, A.D. 538?–594, Frankish bishop and historian.

grei·sen (grī′zən), *n.* a hydrothermally altered rock of granite texture composed chiefly of quartz and mica, common in the tin mines of Saxony. [< G]

grem·lin (grem′lin), *n.* a mischievous invisible being. [?]

Gre·na·da (gri nā′də), *n.* a republic in the Windward Islands, in the E West Indies, consisting of the island of Grenada and the S part of the Grenadines: formerly a British colony; independent since 1974. 107,779; 133 sq. mi. *Cap.:* St. George's. **—Gre·na·di·an** (gri nā′dē ən), *adj., n.*

gre·nade (gri nād′), *n.* **1.** a small explosive shell for throwing by hand or firing from a rifle. **2.** a glass missile for scattering chemicals, as tear gas or fire-extinguishing substances. [< F < Sp *granad(a)* pomegranate, special use of *granado* having grains < L *grānātus.* See GRAIN, -ATE[1]]

gren·a·dier (gren′ə dēr′), *n.* **1.** (in the British army) a member of the first regiment of household infantry **(Gren′adier Guards′).** **2.** (formerly) a specially selected foot soldier in certain elite units. **3.** (formerly) a soldier who threw grenades. **4.** Also called **rat-tail, rat tail.** any of several deep-sea fishes of the family *Macrouridae,* having an elongated, tapering tail. [< F]

gren·a·dine[1] (gren′ə dēn′, gren′ə dēn′), *n.* a thin fabric of leno weave in silk, nylon, rayon, or wool. [< F, ? after GRANADA, Spain]

gren·a·dine[2] (gren′ə dēn′, gren′ə dēn′), *n.* a syrup made from pomegranate juice. [< F, dim. of *grenade* pomegranate. See GRENADE, -INE[1]]

Gren·a·dines (gren′ə dēnz′, gren′ə dēnz′), *n.* (*construed as pl.*) a chain of about 600 British islands in the E West Indies in the Windward Islands.

Gren·fell (gren′fel), *n.* **Sir Wilfred Thom·a·son** (tom′ə-sən), 1865–1940, English physician and missionary in Labrador and Newfoundland.

Gre·no·ble (grə nō′bəl; *Fr.* grə nô′blə), *n.* a city in SE France. 169,740.

Gren·ville (gren′vil), *n.* **1. George,** 1712–70, British statesman: prime minister 1763–65. **2.** Also, **Greynville. Sir Richard,** 1541?–91, British naval commander. **3. William Wynd·ham** (win′dəm), **Baron,** 1759–1834, British statesman: prime minister 1806–07 (son of George Grenville).

Gresh·am (gresh′əm), *n.* **Sir Thomas,** 1519?–79, English merchant and financier.

Gresh′am's law′, *Econ.* the tendency of the inferior of two forms of currency to circulate more freely than, or to the exclusion of, the superior, because of the hoarding of the latter. [named after Sir Thomas GRESHAM]

gres·so·ri·al (gre sōr′ē əl, -sôr′-), *adj. Zool.* adapted for walking, as the feet of some birds. [< NL *gressōri(us)* ambulatory (L *gress(us)* walked, stepped]

Gret′na Green′, a village in S Scotland, near the English border, to which many English couples formerly eloped.

Greuze (grœz), *n.* **Jean Bap·tiste** (zhäN bä tēst′), 1725–1805, French painter.

Grev·ille (grev′il), *n.* **Fulke** (fo͝olk), **1st Baron Brooke,** 1554–1628, English poet and statesman.

grew (gro͞o), *v.* pt. of **grow.**

grew·some (gro͞o′səm), *adj.* gruesome. **—grew′some·ly,** *adv.* **—grew′some·ness,** *n.*

grey (grā), *adj., n., v.t., v.i.* gray. **—grey′ish,** *adj.* **—grey′ly,** *adv.* **—grey′ness,** *n.*

Grey (grā), *n.* **1. Charles, 2nd Earl,** 1764–1845, British statesman: prime minister 1830–34. **2. Sir George,** 1812–1898, British statesman and colonial administrator: prime minister of New Zealand 1877–79. **3. Lady Jane** (*Lady Jane Dudley*), 1537–54, descendant of Henry VII of England; executed under orders of Mary I to eliminate her as a rival for the throne. **4. Zane** (zān), 1875–1939, U.S. novelist.

grey·hen (grā′hen′), *n. Brit.* the female of the black grouse.

grey·hound (grā′hound′), *n.* one of a breed of tall, slender, short-haired dogs, noted for its swiftness. Also, **grayhound.** [ME *greihund, gre-, gri-,* OE *grīghund* < ON *greyhund(r)* (cf. OIcel *grey* bitch); see HOUND[1]]

Greyhound (28 in. high at shoulder)

Greyn·ville (grān′vil, gren′-), *n.* **Sir Richard.** See **Grenville, Sir Richard.**

grey·wacke (grā′wak′, -wak′ə), *n.* graywacke.

grib·ble (grib′əl), *n.* a small, marine isopod crustacean of the genus *Limnoria,* which destroys submerged timber by boring into it. [? akin to GRUB]

grid (grid), *n.* **1.** a grating of crossed bars; gridiron. **2.** *Elect.* **a.** a metallic framework in a storage cell or battery for conducting the electric current and supporting the active material. **b.** a system of electrical distribution serving a large area, esp. by means of high-tension lines. **3.** *Electronics.* an electrode in a vacuum tube, for controlling the flow of electrons between the other electrodes. **4.** *Survey.* a basic system of reference lines for a region, consisting of straight lines intersecting at right angles, computed by establishing a system of scale corrections for measured distances. **5.** a system of coordinates used in mapping or planning. **6.** *Football.* gridiron (def. 3). [short for GRIDIRON]

grid′ bi′as, *Electronics.* the potential difference applied between a grid and the cathode of a vacuum tube.

grid′ cir′cuit, *Electronics.* that part of a circuit which contains the cathode and the grid of a vacuum tube.

grid′ cur′rent, *Electronics.* the current that moves within the vacuum tube from the grid to the cathode.

grid·dle (grid′əl), *n., v.,* **-dled, -dling.** **—***n.* **1.** a frying pan with a handle and a slightly raised edge, for cooking pancakes, bacon, etc. **2.** any flat, heated surface, esp. on the top of a stove, for cooking food. **—***v.t.* **3.** to cook on a griddle. [ME *gridel, gredil* < OF *gridil, gredil;* see GRILL[1]]

grid·dle·cake (grid′əl kāk′), *n.* a thin cake of batter cooked on a griddle; flapjack; pancake.

gride (grīd), *v.,* **grid·ed, grid·ing,** *n.* **—***v.i.* **1.** to grate; grind; scrape harshly; make a grating sound. **—***v.t.* **2.** to pierce or cut. **—***n.* **3.** a griding or grating sound. [ME; metathetic var. of GIRD[2]]

grid·i·ron (grid′ī′ərn), *n.* **1.** a utensil consisting of parallel metal bars on which to broil meat or other food. **2.** any framework or network resembling a gridiron. **3.** a football field. [ME *gridirne, gridir(e), gridere,* var. of *gridel* GRIDDLE; variants in *-irne, -ire,* etc., by assoc. with *irne,* IRON]

grid·lock (grid′lok′), *n.* **1.** the total paralysis of vehicular traffic in all directions in an urban area because key intersections are blocked by traffic. **2.** (loosely) the blocking of an intersection by vehicular traffic entering the intersection but unable to pass through it. [GRID + LOCK[1]]

grid′ varia′tion, *Navig.* the angle, at any point on the surface of the earth, between the magnetic and true meridians passing through that point. Also called **grivation.**

grief (grēf), *n.* **1.** keen mental suffering or distress over affliction or loss; sharp sorrow; painful regret. **2.** a cause or occasion of keen distress or sorrow. **3. come to grief,** to suffer disappointment or misfortune; fail. [ME *gref, grief* < AF *gref.* See GRIEVE] **—Syn. 1.** misery. **—Ant. 1.** joy.

grief-strick·en (grēf′strik′ən), *adj.* overwhelmed by grief; afflicted; sorrowful.

Grieg (grēg; *Norw.* grig), *n.* **Ed·vard** (ed′värd; *Norw.* ed′värt), 1843–1907, Norwegian composer.

griev·ance (grē′vəns), *n.* **1.** a wrong considered as grounds for complaint. **2.** resentment or complaint, or the grounds for complaint, against an unjust act. **3.** *Obs.* the act of inflicting a wrong or causing suffering. [ME *grev-a(u)nce* < OF *grevance*]

griev·ant (grē′vənt), *n.* a person who submits a complaint for arbitration.

grieve (grēv), *v.,* **grieved, griev·ing.** **—***v.i.* **1.** to feel grief; sorrow. **—***v.t.* **2.** to distress mentally; cause to feel grief or sorrow. **3.** *Obs.* to oppress or wrong. [ME *grev(en), griev(en)* < OF *grev(er)* < L *gravāre* to burden <

grav(is) heavy, GRAVE[2]] —**griev′er,** *n.* —**griev′ing·ly,** *adv.* —**Syn. 1.** lament, weep. GRIEVE, MOURN imply showing suffering caused by sorrow. GRIEVE is the stronger word, implying deep mental suffering often endured alone and in silence: *to grieve over the death of a friend.* MOURN usually refers to manifesting sorrow outwardly: *to mourn publicly and wear black.* **2.** sadden, pain.

griev·ous (grē′vəs), *adj.* **1.** causing grief or sorrow. **2.** flagrant; atrocious. **3.** full of or expressing grief; sorrowful. **4.** burdensome or oppressive. **5.** causing great physical suffering. [ME *grevous* < OF *grevo(u)s*] —**griev′ous·ly,** *adv.* —**griev′ous·ness,** *n.* —**Syn. 1.** distressing, sad, sorrowful, regrettable. **2.** deplorable, heinous, outrageous.

griff (grif), griffin[2]. [by shortening]

griffe (grif), *n.* *Archit.* an ornament at the base of a column, projecting from the torus toward a corner of the plinth. [< F: claw < Gmc]

Griffin[1]

grif·fin[1] (grif′in), *n.* *Class. Myth.* a fabled monster, usually having the head and wings of an eagle and the body of a lion. Also, **griffon, gryphon.** [ME *griffoun* < MF *grifon* < L *grȳph(us)* < Gk *gryp-* (s. of *grȳps*) curled, curved, having a hooked nose]

grif·fin[2] (grif′in), *n.* (in India and the East) a newcomer, esp. a white person from a Western country. [?]

Grif·fith (grif′ith), *n.* **D(avid Lew·el·yn) W(ark)** (lo͞o-el′in wôrk), 1875–1948, U.S. motion-picture producer and director.

grif·fon[1] (grif′ən), *n.* **1.** any of several varieties of the Brussels griffon differing from each other in coloration or in the texture of the coat. **2.** Also called **wirehaired pointing griffon.** one of a Dutch breed of medium-sized dogs having a coarse, steel-gray or grayish-white coat with chestnut markings, used for pointing and retrieving birds. [< F; akin to GRIFFIN[1]]

grif·fon[2] (grif′ən), *n.* *Class. Myth.* griffin[1].

grift (grift), *Slang.* —*n.* **1.** the obtaining of money by swindles, frauds, etc. **2.** money obtained from such practices. —*v.t.* **3.** to obtain (money or other profit) by grift. [perh. alter. of GRAFT[2]]

grift·er (grif′tər), *n.* **1.** *Slang.* a swindler, dishonest gambler, or the like. **2.** a person who manages a side show at a circus, fair, etc., esp. a gambling attraction.

grig (grig), *n.* *Chiefly Dial.* **1.** a cricket or grasshopper. **2.** a lively person. [ME *grig, grege,* perh. < Scand; cf. Sw (dial.) *krik* a little creature, Norw *krek* a crawling creature]

Gri·gnard (grēn yärd′; *Fr.* GRĒ NYAR′), *n.* **(Fran·çois Au·guste) Vic·tor** (FRÄN SWA′ Ō GYST′ VĒK TÔR′), 1871–1935, French organic chemist: Nobel prize 1912.

gri·gri (grē′grē), *n., pl.* **-gris.** a charm, amulet, or fetish. Also, **greegree, gris-gris.** [of Afr orig.]

grill[1] (gril), *n.* **1.** a grated utensil for broiling meat, fish, vegetables, etc., over a fire. **2.** a dish of grilled meat, fish, etc. **3.** *Philately.* a group of small pyramidal marks, embossed or impressed in parallel rows on certain U.S. and Peruvian stamps of the late 19th century to prevent erasure of cancellation marks. —*v.t.* **4.** to broil on or as on a gridiron over a fire. **5.** to torment with heat. **6.** to mark with a series of parallel bars like those of a grill. **7.** *Informal.* to subject to severe and persistent questioning; interrogate. —*v.i.* **8.** to undergo broiling. [< F *gril* gridiron << L *crātīcula,* dim. of *crātis* wickerwork, hurdle. See GRILLE] —**grill′er,** *n.*

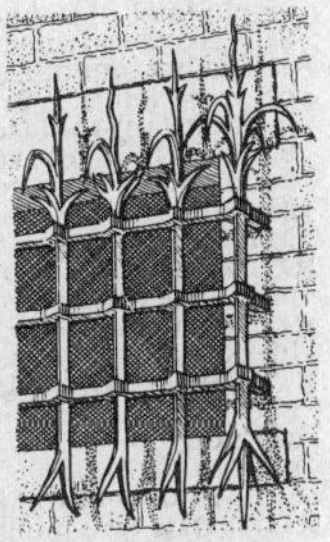

grill[2] (gril), *n.* grille.

gril·lade (gri lād′; *Fr.* GRĒ YAD′), *n., pl.* **gril·lades** (gri lādz′; *Fr.* GRĒ YAD′). a dish or serving of broiled or grilled meat. [< F: something grilled]

gril·lage (gril′ij), *n.* a framework of crossing beams used for spreading heavy loads over large areas. [< F]

grille (gril), *n.* **1.** a grating or openwork barrier, as for a gate, usually of metal and often of decorative design. **2.** an opening, usually covered by grillwork, for admitting air to cool the engine of an automobile or the like; radiator grille. **3.** any of various perforated screens, sheets, etc., used to cover something, as on a radio for protecting the amplifier. **4.** *Court Tennis.* a square-shaped winning opening on the hazard side of the court. Also, **grill.** [< F, OF < LL **graticula,* L *crātīcula* (cf. OPr *grazilha*), dim. of *crātis*] —**grilled,** *adj.*

Grille

Grill·par·zer (gril′pärt′sər), *n.* **Franz** (fränts), 1791–1872, Austrian poet and dramatist.

grill·work (gril′wûrk′), *n.* material formed so as to function as or have the appearance of a grill.

grilse (grils), *n., pl.* **grils·es,** (*esp. collectively*) **grilse.** a mature, undersized, male salmon returning to fresh water, to spawn for the first time. [ME *grills, grilles* (pl.) < ?]

grim (grim), *adj.,* **grim·mer, grim·mest. 1.** stern and admitting of no appeasement or compromise. **2.** having a sinister or ghastly character; repellent: *a grim joke.* **3.** having a harsh, surly, forbidding, or morbid air. **4.** fierce, savage, or cruel. [ME, OE; c. OS, OHG *grimm,* OIcel *grimmr*] —**grim′ly,** *adv.* —**grim′ness,** *n.* —**Syn. 1.** harsh, unyielding. **2.** frightful, horrible, horrid, grisly, gruesome. —**Ant. 1.** lenient. **3.** gentle.

grim·ace (grim′əs, gri mās′), *n., v.,* **-aced, -ac·ing.** —*n.* **1.** a facial expression, often ugly or contorted, that indicates disapproval, pain, etc. —*v.i.* **2.** to make grimaces. [< F << Frankish **grima* mask (cf. GRIME)] —**grim′ac·er,** *n.* —**grim′ac·ing·ly,** *adv.*

Gri·mal·di (gri mal′dē, -môl′-), *n.* **Joseph,** 1779–1837, English actor, mime, and clown.

gri·mal·kin (gri mal′kin, -môl′-), *n.* **1.** a cat. **2.** an old female cat. **3.** an ill-tempered old woman. [appar. alter. of GRAY + *malkin,* dim. of *Maud* proper name]

grime (grīm), *n., v.,* **grimed, grim·ing.** —*n.* **1.** dirt or foul matter, esp. lying upon or embedded in a surface. —*v.t.* **2.** to cover with dirt; soil. [appar. special use of OE *grīma* mask, to denote layer of dust; cf. Flem *grijm*]

Grimes′ Gold′en (grīmz), an edible yellow apple maturing in late autumn. [named after Thomas P. *Grimes* of West Virginia]

Grim·hild (grim′hild), *n.* (in the *Volsunga Saga*) a sorceress, the wife of Giuki and the mother of Gudrun and Gunnar. She gave Sigurd a potion to make him forget Brynhild so that he would marry Gudrun.

Grimm (grim), *n.* **Ja·kob Lud·wig Karl** (yä′kop lo͞ot′-viKH kärl, lo͞od′-), 1785–1863, and his brother **Wil·helm Karl** (vil′helm), 1786–1859, German philologists and folklorists.

Grimm's′ law′, *Linguistics.* the statement of the pattern of consonant correspondences presumed to represent changes from Proto-Indo-European to Germanic, according to which voiced aspirated stops became voiced obstruents, voiced unaspirated stops became unvoiced stops, and unvoiced stops became unvoiced fricatives: first formulated in 1820–22 by Jakob Grimm.

Grim′ Reap′er, reaper (def. 3).

Grims·by (grimz′bē), *n.* a seaport in NE Lincolnshire, in E England at the mouth of the Humber estuary. 96,665 (1961).

grim·y (grī′mē), *adj.,* **grim·i·er, grim·i·est.** covered with grime. —**grim′i·ly,** *adv.* —**grim′i·ness,** *n.*

grin[1] (grin), *v.,* **grinned, grin·ning,** *n.* —*v.i.* **1.** to smile broadly, esp. as an indication of pleasure, amusement, or the like. **2.** to draw back the lips so as to show the teeth, as a snarling dog or a person in pain. —*v.t.* **3.** to express by grinning. —*n.* **4.** the act of producing a broad smile, or the smile itself. **5.** the act of withdrawing the lips and showing the teeth. [ME *grinn(en), grenn(en),* OE *grennian;* c. OHG *grennan* to mutter] —**grin′ner,** *n.* —**grin′ning·ly,** *adv.*

grin[2] (grin), *n.* *Chiefly Scot.* a snare like a running noose. [ME *grin(e),* OE *grin, gryn*]

grind (grīnd), *v.,* **ground** or (*Rare*) **grind·ed; grind·ing;** *n.* —*v.t.* **1.** to wear, smooth, or sharpen by abrasion or friction; whet: *to grind a lens; to grind an ax.* **2.** to reduce to fine particles, as by pounding or crushing; pulverize. **3.** to oppress; torment; harass. **4.** to rub harshly or gratingly; grate together; grit: *to grind one's teeth.* **5.** to operate by turning a crank: *to grind a hand organ.* **6.** to produce by crushing or abrasion: *to grind flour.* —*v.i.* **7.** to reduce something to fine particles. **8.** to rub harshly; grate. **9.** to be or become ground. **10.** to be polished or sharpened by friction. **11.** *Informal.* to work or study laboriously (often fol. by *away*). **12.** (in a dance) to rotate the hips in a suggestive manner. Cf. **bump** (def. 9). —*n.* **13.** the act of grinding. **14.** a grinding sound. **15.** laborious, usually uninteresting work. **16.** *Slang.* an excessively diligent student. **17.** a dance movement in which the hips are rotated in a suggestive manner. Cf. **bump** (def. 17). [ME *grind(en),* OE *grindan;* akin to Goth *grinda-,* L *frendere*] —**grind′a·ble,** *adj.* —**grind′ing·ly,** *adv.* —**Syn. 2.** crush, powder. **4.** abrade.

grin·de·li·a (grin dē′lē ə, -dēl′yə), *n.* **1.** any of the coarse, yellow-flowered asteraceous herbs of the genus *Grindelia.* **2.** the dried leaves and tops of certain species of this plant, used in medicine. [named after D. H. *Grindel* (1777–1836), Russian scientist; see -IA]

grind·er (grīn′dər), *n.* **1.** a person or thing that grinds. **2.** a sharpener of tools. **3.** a molar tooth.

grind′ing wheel′, a wheel composed of abrasive material, used for grinding.

grind·stone (grīnd′stōn′), *n.* **1.** a rotating solid stone wheel used for sharpening, shaping, etc. **2.** a millstone.

grin·go (griŋ′gō), *n., pl.* **-gos.** *Disparaging.* (among Spanish-Americans) a foreigner, esp. one from the U.S. [< Sp: foreigner, perh. special use of *griego* a Greek]

grip (grip), *n., v.,* **gripped** or **gript, grip·ping.** —*n.* **1.** the act of grasping; a seizing and holding fast; firm grasp. **2.** the power of gripping. **3.** a grasp, hold, or control. **4.** a small suitcase. **5.** mental or intellectual hold: *to have a good grip on a problem.* **6.** a special mode of clasping hands: *Members of the club use the secret grip.* **7.** something which seizes and holds, as a clutching device on a cable car. **8.** a handle or hilt. **9.** a sudden, sharp pain; spasm of pain. **10.** grippe. **11.** *Slang. Theat., Motion Pictures, Television.* a stagehand. **12. come to grips with, a.** to encounter; meet; cope with. **b.** to deal with directly or firmly. —*v.t.* **13.** to grasp or seize firmly; hold fast. **14.** to take hold on; hold the interest of: *to grip the mind.* **15.** to attach by a grip or clutch. —*v.i.* **16.** to take firm hold; hold fast. **17.** to take hold on the mind. [ME, OE *gripe* grasp; c. G *Griff,* OE *gripa* handful; see GRIPE] —**grip′per,** *n.*

gripe (grīp), *v.,* **griped, grip·ing,** *n.* —*v.t.* **1.** to seize and hold firmly; grip; grasp; clutch. **2.** to distress or oppress. **3.** to produce pain in (the bowels) as if by constriction. **4.** *Informal.* to annoy or irritate: *His tone of voice gripes me.* —*v.i.* **5.** to grasp or clutch, as a miser. **6.** to suffer pain in the bowels. **7.** *Informal.* to complain naggingly or constantly; grumble. **8.** *Naut.* (of a sailing vessel) to tend to come into the wind. —*n.* **9.** the act of gripping, grasping, or clutching. **10.** a firm hold; clutch. **11.** a grasp; hold; control. **12.** that which grips or clutches; a claw or grip. **13.** *U.S. Informal.* complaint. **14.** a handle, hilt, etc. **15.** Usually, **gripes.** *Pathol.* an intermittent spasmodic pain in the bowels. [ME *grip(en),* OE *grīpan;* c. D *grijpen,* G *greifen;* see GRIP, GROPE] —**grip′er,** *n.* —**grip′ing·ly,** *adv.*

grip·ey (grī′pē), *adj.,* **grip·i·er, grip·i·est.** gripy.

grippe (grip), *n.* *Pathol.* influenza. [< F < *gripper* to seize suddenly < Gmc; akin to GRIP, GRIPE]

grip·ping (grip′iŋ), *adj.* holding the attention or interest; fascinating. —**grip′ping·ly,** *adv.* —**grip′ping·ness,** *n.*

grip·sack (grip′sak′), *n.* a traveling bag; grip.

gript (gript), *v.* a pp. and pt. of **grip.**

grip·y (grī′pē), *adj.,* **grip·i·er, grip·i·est.** resembling or causing gripes. Also, **gripey.**

Gri·qua (grē′kwə, grik′wə), *n.* a South African half-breed. [< SAfrD *Griekwa*]

Gris (grēs), *n.* **Juan** (hwän), (*José Vittoriano Gonzáles*), 1887–1927, Spanish painter in France.

gri·saille (gri zī′, -zāl′; *Fr.* grē zä′yᵊ), *n., pl.* **-sailles** (-zīz′, -zālz′; *Fr.* -zä′yᵊ) for 2. **1.** monochromatic painting in shades of gray. **2.** a work of art, as a painting or stained-glass window, executed in grisaille. [< F: painted in gray monotone = *gris* gray + *-aille* n. suffix]

gris·e·ous (gris′ē əs, griz′-), *adj.* gray; pearl-gray. [< ML *griseus* bluish-gray; see -EOUS]

gri·sette (gri zet′), *n.* a French working girl or salesgirl. [< F = *gris* gray + *-ette* -ETTE]

gris-gris (grē′grē′), *n., pl.* **gris-gris** (-grēz′). grigri.

gris·ly[1] (griz′lē), *adj.,* **-li·er, -li·est. 1.** causing a shudder or feeling of horror; gruesome. **2.** formidable; grim: *a grisly countenance.* [ME; OE *grislīc* horrible; c. OHG *grīsenlīh*] —**gris′li·ness,** *n.*

gris·ly[2] (gris′lē), *adj.,* **-li·er, -li·est.** *Obs.* gristly.

grist (grist), *n.* **1.** grain to be ground. **2.** ground grain; meal produced from grinding. **3.** a quantity of grain for grinding at one time; the amount of meal from one grinding. **4.** *Chiefly U.S. Dial.* a quantity or lot. **5. grist to** or **for one's mill,** something employed to one's profit or advantage. [ME, OE; akin to OE *grindan* to GRIND]

gris·tle (gris′əl), *n.* cartilage. [ME, OE; c. OFris, MLG *gristal;* akin to OE *grost* cartilage]

gris·tly (gris′lē), *adj.,* **-tli·er, -tli·est.** resembling or containing gristle; cartilaginous. [ME] —**gris·tli·ness** (gris′lē nis), *n.*

grist·mill (grist′mil′), *n.* a mill for grinding grain, esp. the customer's own grain.

Gris·wold (griz′wōld, -wəld), *n.* **Erwin Nathaniel,** born 1904, U.S. lawyer and educator: solicitor general, 1967–1973.

grit (grit), *n., v.,* **grit·ted, grit·ting.** —*n.* **1.** fine, abrasive particles, as those deposited as dust from the air or occurring as impurities in food. **2.** firmness of character; indomitable spirit; pluck. **3.** a coarse-grained siliceous rock, usually with sharp, angular grains. —*v.t.* **4.** to grate or grind: *to grit the teeth.* —*v.i.* **5.** to make a scratchy or slightly grating sound; grate. [ME *gret, griet, grit,* OE *grēot;* c. G *Griess,* OIcel *grjōt* pebble, boulder; see GRITS] —**Syn. 2.** resolution, fortitude.

grith (grith), *n.* *Chiefly Scot.* protection or asylum for a limited period of time. [ME, OE < Scand; cf. OIcel *grith* home; in pl.: peace, security]

grits (grits), *n.* (*construed as sing. or pl.*) **1.** grain hulled and coarsely ground. **2.** *Chiefly Southern U.S.* coarsely ground hominy. [ME *gryttes* (pl.), OE *gryt(t);* c. G *Grütze*]

grit·ty (grit′ē), *adj.,* **-ti·er, -ti·est. 1.** consisting of, containing, or resembling grit. **2.** resolute and courageous; plucky. —**grit′ti·ly,** *adv.* —**grit′ti·ness,** *n.*

gri·va·tion (gri vā′shən, grī-), *n.* See **grid variation.** [GRI(D) + V(ARI)ATION]

griv·et (griv′it), *n.* a small Abyssinian monkey, *Cercopithecus aethiops,* with a grayish back, gray tail, black face, and dark extremities. [?]

griz·zle[1] (griz′əl), *v., -zled, -zling, adj., n.* —*v.t., v.i.* **1.** to make or become gray or partly gray. —*adj.* **2.** gray; grayish; devoid of hue. —*n.* **3.** gray or partly gray hair. **4.** a gray wig. [ME *grisel* < OF < *gris* gray < Gmc; cf. G *greis* gray, hoary]

griz·zle[2] (griz′əl), *v.i.,* **-zled, -zling.** *Brit.* to complain; whimper; whine. [cf. MHG *grisgramen* to gnash one's teeth, G *Griesgram* sourpuss] —**griz′zler,** *n.*

griz·zled (griz′əld), *adj.* gray or partly gray.

griz·zly (griz′lē), *adj.* **-zli·er -zli·est,** *n., pl.* **-zlies.** —*adj.* **1.** somewhat gray; grayish. —*n.* **2.** See **grizzly bear.** [GRIZZLE[1] + -Y[1]]

griz′zly bear′, a large, ferocious bear, *Ursus horribilis,* of western North America, varying in color from grayish to brownish.

Grizzly bear (3 to 3½ ft. high at shoulder; length 6 to 8½ ft.)

gro., gross (def. 10).

groan (grōn), *n.* **1.** a low, mournful sound uttered in pain or grief. **2.** a deep, inarticulate sound uttered in derision, disapproval, etc. **3.** a deep grating or creaking sound due to a sudden or continued overburdening, as with a great weight. —*v.i.* **4.** to utter a deep, mournful sound expressive of pain or grief; moan. **5.** to make a deep, inarticulate sound expressive of derision, disapproval, etc. **6.** to make a sound resembling a groan; resound harshly: *The steps of the old house groaned under my weight.* **7.** to be overburdened or overloaded. —*v.t.* **8.** to utter or express with groans. [ME *gron(en),* OE *grānian;* c. G *greinen* to whine] —**groan′er,** *n.* —**groan′ing·ly,** *adv.*

groat (grōt), *n.* a silver coin of England, equal to four pennies, issued from 1279 to 1662. [ME *groot* < MD: lit., large (coin)]

groats (grōts), *n.* (*construed as sing. or pl.*) **1.** hulled grain, as wheat or oats, broken into fragments. **2.** hulled kernels of oats, buckwheat, or barley. [ME *grotes* (pl.), OE *grot* meal; akin to GRITS]

gro·cer (grō′sər), *n.* a dealer in general supplies for the table, as flour, sugar, coffee, etc., and in other articles of household use. [ME < OF *gross(i)er* wholesale merchant. See GROSS, -ER[2]]

gro·cer·y (grō′sə rē), *n., pl.* **-cer·ies. 1.** *U.S.* a grocer's store. **2.** Usually, **groceries.** food and other commodities sold by a grocer. **3.** the business of a grocer. [ME *grocerie* < OF *grosserie.* See GROSS, -ERY]

gro·cer·y·man (grō′sə rē mən, -man′), *n., pl.* **-men** (-mən, -men′). a grocer.

Groe·nen·dael (grōō′nən däl′, grō′-, grā′-, gren′ən-), *n.* a Belgian sheepdog having a long, black coat. [after the village in Belgium where it was bred]

Groe·te (*Du.* ᴋʜrōō′tə; *Eng.* grōt), *n.* **Ger·hard** (*Du.* ᴋʜā′rärt; *Eng.* gâr′härt). See **Groote, Gerhard.**

Gro·fé (grō′fā), *n.* **Fer·de** (fûr′dē), 1892–1972, U.S. composer.

grog (grog), *n.* **1.** a mixture of alcoholic liquor and water. **2.** strong drink. [from Old *Grog,* (alluding to his *grogram* cloak) the nickname of Edward Vernon (d. 1757), British admiral, who in 1740 ordered the alcoholic mixture to be served, instead of pure spirits, to sailors]

grog·gy (grog′ē), *adj.,* **-gi·er, -gi·est. 1.** staggering or dazed, as from exhaustion or blows. **2.** *Archaic.* drunk. —**grog′gi·ly,** *adv.* —**grog′gi·ness,** *n.*

grog·ram (grog′rəm), *n.* a coarse fabric of silk, of silk and mohair or wool, or of wool. [< MF *gros grain.* See GROSGRAIN]

grog·shop (grog′shop′), *n.* *Brit.* a saloon or barroom, esp. a cheap one.

groin (groin), *n.* **1.** *Anat.* the fold or hollow on either side of the body where the thigh joins the abdomen. **2.** *Archit.* the curved line or edge formed by the intersection of two vaults. See illus. at **vault**[1]. **3.** Also, **groyne.** a small jetty extending from a shore to prevent beach erosion. —*v.t.* **4.** *Archit.* to form with groins. [earlier *grine,* ME *grinde;* cf. OE *grynde* abyss, akin to *grund* bottom, GROUND[1]]

Gro·lier (grō′lē ər; *Fr.* grô lyā′), *adj.* *Bookbinding.* pertaining to a decorative design **(Gro′lier design′)** in bookbinding, consisting of bands interlaced in geometric forms. [named after J. GROLIER DE SERVIÈRES]

Gro·lier de Ser·vières (grô lyā′ də sᴇʀ vyeʀ′), **Jean** (zhäɴ), 1479–1565, French bibliophile.

grom·met (grom′it), *n.* **1.** *Mach.* **a.** any of various rings or eyelets of metal or the like. **b.** an insulated washer of rubber or plastic, inserted in a hole in a metal part to prevent grounding of a wire passing through the hole. **2.** *Naut.* **a.** a ring or strop of fiber or wire; becket. **b.** a ring having a thickness of three strands, made by forming a loop of a single strand, then laying the ends around the loop. **c.** a ring of fiber used as a seal or gasket, as under the head of a bolt. **3.** a washer or packing for sealing joints between sections of pipe. Also, **grummet.** [< obs. F *gromette* curb of bridle < ?]

grom·well (grom′wəl), *n.* any boraginaceous plant of the genus *Lithospermum,* having varicolored flowers and smooth, stony nutlets. [ME *gromil* < OF = *gro-* < ? + *mil* millet < L *milium*]

Gro·my·ko (grō mē′kō, grə-; *Russ.* gʀo mē′ko), *n.* **An·drei An·dre·ie·vich** (än dʀā′ än dre′yə vich), born 1909, Russian diplomat.

Gro·ning·en (grō′ning ən; *Du.* ᴋʜʀō′ning ən), *n.* a city in the NE Netherlands. 149,486 (est. 1962).

groom (grōōm, grŏŏm), *n.* **1.** a man or boy in charge of horses or a stable. **2.** a bridegroom. **3.** any of several officers of the English royal household. **4.** *Archaic.* a manservant. —*v.t.* **5.** to tend carefully as to person and dress; make neat or tidy. **6.** to tend (horses). **7.** to prepare (a person) for a position, election, etc. [ME *grom* boy, groom; appar. akin to GROW] —**groom′er,** *n.*

grooms·man (grōōmz′mən, grŏŏmz′-), *n., pl.* **-men.** a man who attends the bridegroom in a wedding ceremony.

Groot (*Du.* ᴋʜʀōt; *Eng.* grōt), *n.* **1. Huig** (*Du.* hoiᴋʜ) **de** (də) or **van** (vän). See **Grotius, Hugo. 2. Gerhard.** See **Groote, Gerhard.**

Groote (*Du.* ᴋʜʀō′tə; *Eng.* grōt), *n.* **Ger·hard** (*Du.* ᴋʜā′ʀäʀt; *Eng.* gâr′härt), (*Gerardus Magnus*) 1340–84, Dutch religious reformer, educator, and author. Also, **Groot, Groete.**

groove (grōōv), *n., v.,* **grooved, groov·ing.** —*n.* **1.** a long, narrow cut or indentation in a surface. **2.** the track or channel of a phonograph record for the needle or stylus. **3.** a fixed routine: *to get into a groove.* **4.** *Print.* the furrow at the bottom of a piece of type. **5.** *Slang.* an enjoyable time or experience. **6. in the groove,** *Slang.* in the popular fashion; up-to-date. —*v.t.* **7.** to cut a groove in; furrow. **8.** to fix in a groove. —*v.i.* **9.** *Slang.* **a.** to have a thoroughly good time. **b.** to get along well with someone; understand or appreciate someone fully. [ME *grofe, groof* mining shaft; c. MD *groeve,* D *groef,* G *Grube* pit, ditch; akin to GRAVE[1]]

grooved (grōōvd), *v.* **1.** pt. and pp. of **groove.** —*adj.* **2.** provided with a groove.

groov·y (grōō′vē), *adj.,* **groov·i·er, groov·i·est.** *Slang.* highly stimulating or attractive: *a groovy car.*

grope (grōp), *v.,* **groped, grop·ing.** —*v.i.* **1.** to feel about with the hands; feel one's way. **2.** to search blindly or uncertainly. —*v.t.* **3.** to seek by or as by feeling: *He groped his way up the stairs.* [ME *grop(ien),* OE *grāpian* < *grāp* grasp; akin to GRIPE, GRASP] —**grop′er,** *n.*

grop·ing (grō′ping), *adj.* **1.** moving or going about clumsily or hesitantly; stumbling. **2.** showing or reflecting a desire to understand, esp. something that proves puzzling. [ME] —**grop′ing·ly,** *adv.*

Gro·pi·us (grō′pē əs; *Ger.* gʀō′pē ŏŏs′), *n.* **Wal·ter** (wôl′tər; *Ger.* väl′tər), 1883–1969, German architect, in the U.S. after 1937.

Grop·per (grop′ər), *n.* **William,** 1897–1977, U.S. painter.

gros·beak (grōs′bēk′), *n.* any of various finches having a thick, conical bill. [< F *grosbec,* lit., large beak]

gro·schen (grō′shən), *n., pl.* **-schen. 1.** a zinc coin of Austria, the 100th part of a schilling. **2.** *Informal.* a German 10-pfennig piece made of nickel. **3.** any of the silver coins of various German regions first introduced in the 13th century. [< G; MHG *grosse, grosze* < L (*denarius*) *grossus* thick (coin); akin to GROAT]

gros·grain (grō′grān′), *n.* a heavy, corded ribbon or cloth of silk or rayon. [< MF *gros grain* large grain]

gross (grōs), *adj., n., pl.* **gross** for 10, **gross·es** for 11; *v.* —*adj.* **1.** without deductions (opposed to *net*): *gross profits.* **2.** unqualified; rank: *a gross scoundrel.* **3.** flagrant and extreme: *gross injustice.* **4.** indelicate, indecent, obscene, or vulgar: *gross remarks.* **5.** lacking in refinement, good manners, education, etc.; unrefined. **6.** large, big, or bulky. **7.** extremely or excessively fat. **8.** thick; dense; heavy: *gross vegetation.* **9.** of or concerning only the broadest or most general considerations, aspects, etc. —*n.* **10.** a group of 12 dozen, or 144, things. *Abbr.:* gr, gr., gro. **11.** income without deductions (opposed to *net*). **12.** *Obs.* the main body, bulk, or mass. —*v.t.* **13.** to make a gross profit of; earn a total of. [ME < OF *gros* large (as n., *grosse* twelve dozen) < LL *gross(us)* thick, coarse] —**Syn. 1.** aggregate. **6.** massive, great. —**Ant. 4.** decent. **6, 7.** delicate, small.

Gross (grōs), *n.* **Cha·im** (ᴋʜī′im), born 1904, U.S. sculptor and graphic artist, born in Austria.

gross′ na′tional prod′uct, the total monetary value

of all final goods and services produced in a country during one year. *Abbr.:* GNP Cf. **national income, net national product.**

gross′ prof′it, gross receipts less the immediate cost of production.

gross′ ton′, **1.** *Chiefly Brit.* a long ton. See under **ton**[1] (def. 1). **2.** *Naut.* Also called **gross′ reg′ister ton′.** See under **gross tonnage.**

gross′ ton′nage, *Naut.* the total volume of a vessel, expressed in units of 100 cubic feet **(gross ton),** with certain open structures, deckhouses, tanks, etc., exempted. Also called **gross′ reg′ister ton′nage.**

gros·su·lar·ite (gros′yə lə rit′), *n.* a mineral, calcium aluminum garnet, $Ca_3Al_2Si_3O_{12}$, occurring in gray-white to pinkish crystals. [< NL *grossulār(ia)* gooseberry (irreg. < F *groseille*) + -ITE[1]]

Gross·war·dein (gʀōs′väʀ dīn′), *n.* German name of **Oradea.**

gross′ weight′, total weight without deduction for tare, tret, or waste.

Gros·ve·nor (grōv′nər), *n.* **Gilbert Hov·ey,** (huv′ē), 1875–1966, U.S. geographer, writer, and editor.

grosz (gʀôsh), *n., pl.* **gro·szy** (gʀô′shē). an aluminum coin of Poland, the 100th part of a zloty. [< Pol < Czech *groš;* see GROSCHEN]

Grosz (grōs), *n.* **George,** 1893–1959, German painter and graphic artist, in the U.S. from 1932.

grot (grot), *n.* *Chiefly Literary.* a grotto. [< F *grotte* < It *grott(a);* see GROTTO]

Grote (grōt), *n.* **George,** 1794–1871, English historian.

Gro·tesk (grō tesk′), *n.* (in Europe) Gothic (def. 9). [var. of GROTESQUE]

gro·tesque (grō tesk′), *adj.* **1.** odd or unnatural in shape, appearance, or character; fantastically ugly or absurd; bizarre. **2.** fantastic in the shaping and combination of forms, as in decorative work combining incongruous human and animal figures with scrolls, foliage, etc. —*n.* **3.** any grotesque object, design, or thing. [< F < It *grottesco* (as n., *grottesca* grotesque decoration such as was appar. found in excavated dwellings). See GROTTO, -ESQUE] —**gro·tesque′ly,** *adv.* —**gro·tesque′ness,** *n.*

gro·tes·quer·y (grō tes′kə rē), *n., pl.* **-quer·ies. 1.** grotesque character. **2.** something grotesque. **3.** grotesque ornamental work. Also, **gro·tes′quer·ie.** [< F *grotesquerie*]

Gro·ti·us (grō′shē əs), *n.* **Hugo** (*Huig de Groot*), 1583–1645, Dutch jurist and statesman. —**Gro·tian** (grō′shən, -shē ən), *adj.* —**Gro′tian·ism,** *n.*

Gro·ton (grot′ən), *n.* a city in SE Connecticut. 38,244 (1970).

grot·to (grot′ō), *n., pl.* **-toes, -tos. 1.** a cave or cavern. **2.** an artificial cavernlike recess or structure. [< It *grotta* < VL **crypta* subterranean passage, chamber, CRYPT]

grouch (grouch), *Informal.* —*v.i.* **1.** to be sulky or morose; show discontent; complain. —*n.* **2.** a sulky or morose person. **3.** a sulky or morose mood. [var. of obs. *grutch* < OF *grouch(er)* (to) grumble. See *grudge*]

grouch·y (grou′chē), *adj.,* **grouch·i·er, grouch·i·est.** sullenly discontented; sulky; morose; ill-tempered. —**grouch′i·ly,** *adv.* —**grouch′i·ness,** *n.*

Grou·chy (gʀōō shē′), *n.* **Em·ma·nu·el** (e mA ny el′), **Marquis de,** 1766–1847, French general.

ground[1] (ground), *n.* **1.** the solid surface of the earth; firm or dry land. **2.** earth or soil. **3.** land having an indicated character: *rising ground.* **4.** Often, **grounds. a.** a tract of land appropriated to a special use: *picnic grounds.* **b.** the foundation or basis on which a belief or action rests; reason: *grounds for divorce.* **5.** subject for discussion; topic. **6.** rational or factual support for one's position or attitude, as in an argument or philosophical theory. **7.** the main surface or background in painting, decorative work, lace, etc. **8. grounds, a.** dregs or sediment: *coffee grounds.* **b.** the gardens, lawn, etc., surrounding and belonging to a building. **9.** *Elect.* a conducting connection between an electric circuit or equipment and the earth or some other conducting body. **10.** *Naut.* the bottom of a body of water. **11.** the earth's surface; land. **12.** *Carpentry.* **a.** a strip of wood to which woodwork can be attached, set flush with the plaster finish of a room. **b.** a strip of wood or length of corner bead used at an opening as a stop for plasterwork. **13. break ground, a.** to plow. **b.** to begin excavation for a construction project. **c.** to begin upon or take preparatory measures for an undertaking. **14. cover ground, a.** to pass or travel over a certain area. **b.** to make a certain amount of progress in (a piece of work, subject, etc.); deal with. **15. from the ground up, a.** gradually from the most elementary level to the highest level. **b.** extensively; thoroughly. **16. gain ground, a.** to make progress; advance. **b.** to gain approval or acceptance. **17. give ground,** to yield to force or forceful argument; retreat. **18. hold** or **stand one's ground,** to maintain one's position; be steadfast. **19. into the ground,** beyond a reasonable or necessary point (usually prec. by *run*). **20. lose ground, a.** to lose one's advantage; suffer a reverse. **b.** to wane in popularity or acceptance; begin to fail.
—*adj.* **21.** situated on or at, or adjacent to, the surface of the earth: *a ground attack.* **22.** pertaining to the ground. **23.** *Mil.* operating on land: *ground forces.*
—*v.t.* **24.** to lay or set on the ground. **25.** to place on a foundation; found; fix firmly; settle or establish. **26.** to instruct in elements or first principles. **27.** to furnish with a ground or background, as on decorative work. **28.** *Elect.* to establish a ground for (a circuit, device, etc.). **29.** *Naut.* to cause (a vessel) to run aground. **30.** *Aeron.* to restrict (an aircraft or the like) to the ground because of bad weather, the unsatisfactory condition of the aircraft, etc.
—*v.i.* **31.** to come to or strike the ground. **32.** *Baseball.* **a.** to hit a ground ball. **b.** to ground out. **33. ground out,** *Baseball.* to be put out at first base after hitting a ground ball to the infield. **34.** *Naut.* to run aground. [ME, OE *grund;* c. D *grond,* G *Grund*]

ground[2] (ground), *v.* **1.** a pt. and pp. of **grind.** —*adj.* **2.** reduced to fine particles or dust by grinding. **3.** having the surface abraded or roughened by or as by grinding.

ground′ bait′, chum[2].

ground′ ball′, *Baseball.* a batted ball that rolls or bounces along the ground. Also called **grounder.** Cf. **fly ball.**

ground′ cher′ry, 1. Also called **husk tomato.** any of several solanaceous herbs of the genus *Physalis,* bearing an edible berry enclosed in an enlarged calyx. **2.** any of several European dwarf cherries, esp. *Prunus fruticosa.* **3.** the fruit of any of these plants.

ground′ cloth′, 1. a covering, usually of canvas, for the floor of a stage. **2.** Also called **groundsheet.** a waterproof covering, usually of heavy canvas, spread on the ground as protection against moisture.

ground′ controlled′ approach′, *Aeron.* a system in which an observer interprets radar observations of the position of an aircraft and transmits continuous instructions to the pilot for its landing. *Abbr.:* GCA Also, **ground′ control′ approach′.**

ground′ cov′er, 1. the herbaceous plants and low shrubs in a forest, considered as a whole. **2.** any of several low, herbaceous plants used, esp. in shady places, for covering the ground in place of grass.

ground′ crew′, ground personnel connected with air operations, as maintenance technicians.

ground·er (groun′dər), *n.* *Baseball.* See **ground ball.**

ground′ fir′. See **ground pine** (def. 2).

ground′ floor′, 1. the floor of a building on or nearest to ground level. **2.** *Informal.* an advantageous position or opportunity in a business matter, as an offer to share in the founding of a promising enterprise.

ground′ glass′, 1. *Optics.* glass that has had its polished surface removed by fine grinding and that is used to diffuse light. **2.** glass that has been ground into fine particles, esp. for use as an abrasive.

ground′ hog′, woodchuck.

Ground′-hog Day′ (ground′hog′, -hôg′), February 2, the day on which, according to legend, the ground hog first emerges from hibernation. If he sees his shadow, there will be six more weeks of wintry weather. Also, **Ground′-hog's Day′.**

ground′ i′vy, a trailing, labiate herb, *Glecoma hederacea,* having blue flowers.

ground·keep·er (ground′kē′pər), *n.* a person who maintains or is responsible for the maintenance of a particular tract of land, as a park or sports field.

ground′ lay′er. See **surface boundary layer.**

ground·less (ground′lis), *adj.* without rational basis: *groundless fears.* [ME; OE *grundlēas*] —**ground′less·ly,** *adv.* —**ground′less·ness,** *n.*

ground′ lev′el, *Physics.* See **ground state.**

ground·ling (ground′ling), *n.* **1.** a plant or animal that lives on or close to the ground. **2.** any of various fishes that live at the bottom of the water. **3.** a person of crude or uncultivated tastes; an uncritical or uncultured person.

ground′ log′, *Naut.* a lead weight attached to a line, cast overboard in shoal water and allowed to pay out the line freely to show the speed of a vessel and the force of the current.

ground′ loop′, *Aeron.* a sharp horizontal loop performed, usually involuntarily, while touching the ground.

ground·mass (ground′mas′), *n.* the crystalline, granular, or glassy base or matrix of a porphyritic or other igneous rock, in which the more prominent crystals are embedded.

ground·nut (ground′nut′), *n.* **1.** any of various plants having edible underground portions, as the peanut, *Arachis hypogaea,* and the American, climbing, leguminous vine *Apios tuberosa,* having an edible, tuberous root. **2.** the edible tuber, pod, etc., of any of these plants.

ground′ owl′, *U.S. Dial.* the burrowing owl.

ground′ pine′, 1. a European, labiate herb, *Ajuga chamaepitys,* having a resinous odor. **2.** Also called **ground fir.** any of several species of club moss, esp. *Lycopodium obscurum* and *L. complanatum.*

ground′ pink′, 1. an annual herb, *Gilia dianthoides,* of southern California. **2.** See **moss pink.**

ground′ plan′, 1. the plan of a floor of a building. **2.** first or fundamental plan.

ground′ plum′, 1. a leguminous plant, *Astragalus caryocarpus,* of the prairie regions of North America. **2.** its plum-shaped fruit.

ground′ rule′, a basic or governing principle of conduct in any situation or field of endeavor.

ground·sel (ground′səl), *n.* *Chiefly Brit.* any asteraceous plant of the genus *Senecio,* as *S. vulgaris,* a weed having small, yellow flowers. [ME *grundeswilie,* etc., OE *grundeswelge, gundeswelge;* cf. OE *gund* pus, *swelgan* to swallow, absorb (from its use in medicine); the *-r* is by folk etym. from assoc. with GROUND[1]]

ground·sheet (ground′shēt′), *n.* See **ground cloth** (def. 2).

ground·speed (ground′spēd′), *n.* the speed of an aircraft with reference to the ground. Also, **ground′ speed′.**

ground′ squir′rel, any of several terrestrial rodents of the squirrel family, as of the genus *Citellus* and chipmunks of the genus *Tamias.*

ground′ state′, *Physics.* the state of least energy of a particle, as an atom, or of a system of particles. Also called **ground level.**

ground′ swell′, a broad, deep swell or rolling of the sea, due to a distant storm or gale.

ground′ wa′ter, the water beneath the surface of the ground, consisting largely of surface water that has seeped down: the source of water in springs and wells.

ground′ wave′, *Radio.* a radio wave propagated on or near the earth's surface and affected by the ground and the troposphere.

ground·work (ground′wûrk′), *n.* the foundation, base, or basis of an undertaking. —**Syn.** preparation, preliminaries.

ground′ ze′ro, the point on the surface of the earth or water directly below, directly above, or at which an atomic or hydrogen bomb explodes.

group (grōōp), *n.* **1.** any collection or assemblage of persons or things; cluster; aggregation. **2.** a number of persons or things ranged or considered together as being related in some way. **3.** Also called **radical.** *Chem.* two or more atoms specifically arranged, as the hydroxyl group, –OH. Cf. **free radical.** 4. *Linguistics.* a. (in the classification of related languages within a family) a category of a lower order than a subbranch and of a higher order than a subgroup. b. any grouping of languages, whether made on the basis of geography, genetic relationship, or something else. 5. *Geol.* a division of stratified rocks comprising two or more formations. 6. *Mil.* a. *U.S. Army.* a flexible administrative and tactical unit consisting of two or more battalions and a headquarters. b. *U.S. Air Force.* an administrative and operational unit subordinate to a wing, usually composed of two or more squadrons. 7. *Math.* an algebraic system that is closed under an associative operation, as multiplication or addition, and in which there is an identity element that, on operating on another element, leaves the second element unchanged, and in which each element has corresponding to it a unique element that, on operating on the first, results in the identity element. —*v.t.* 8. to place together in a group, as with others. 9. to form into a group or groups. —*v.i.* 10. to form a group. 11. to be part of a group. [< F *groupe* < It *gruppo* << Gmc]

group·er (gro͞o′pər), *n., pl.* (*esp. collectively*) **-er,** (*esp. referring to two or more kinds or species*), **-ers.** any of several serranoid sea basses, esp. of the genera *Epinephelus* and *Mycteroperca,* found in tropical and subtropical seas. [< Pg *garupa,* appar. repr. some South American name]

grou·pie (gro͞o′pē), *n. Slang.* a young girl devotee of rock-'n'-roll musicians, esp. one who follows them to make sexual conquests.

group′ insur′ance, life, accident, or health insurance available to a group of persons under a single contract.

group′ mar′riage, (among primitive peoples) a form of marriage in which a group of males is united with a group of females to form a single conjugal unit. Also called **communal marriage.**

group′ ther′apy, *Psychiatry.* psychotherapy in which a group of patients participate, usually under the leadership of a therapist, in a discussion of their problems in an attempt to solve them.

grouse[1] (grous), *n., pl.* **grouse, grous·es.** any of numerous gallinaceous birds of the family *Tetraonidae.* Cf. **black grouse, capercaillie, ruffed grouse.** [?]

Ruffed grouse, *Bonasa umbellus* (Length 18 in.)

grouse[2] (grous), *v.,* **groused, grous·ing,** *n. Informal.* —*v.i.* 1. to grumble; complain. —*n.* 2. a complaint. [?; see GROUCH] —**grous′er,** *n.*

grout (grout), *n.* 1. a thin, coarse mortar used for filling masonry joints, rock fissures, etc. 2. a finish coat of plaster for a ceiling or interior wall. 3. Usually, **grouts.** lees; grounds. 4. *Archaic.* a. coarse meal or porridge. b. **grouts,** groats. —*v.t.* 5. to fill or consolidate with grout. [OE *grūt;* see GRITS, GROATS, GRIT] —**grout′er,** *n.*

grout·y (grou′tē), *adj.,* **grout·i·er, grout·i·est.** *Dial.* sulky; surly; bad-tempered. [*grout* to grumble, sulk < ? (cf. GROUSE[2], GROUCH) + -Y[1]]

grove (grōv), *n.* 1. a small wood or forested area, usually with no undergrowth. 2. a small orchard or stand of fruit-bearing trees, esp. citrus trees. [ME; OE *grāf*] —**groved,** *adj.* —**grove′less,** *adj.*

grov·el (gruv′əl, grov′-), *v.i.,* **-eled, -el·ing** or (*esp. Brit.*) **-elled, -el·ling.** 1. to humble oneself or act in an abject manner. 2. to lie or move with the face downward and the body prostrate, as in abject humility, fear, etc. 3. to take pleasure in mean or base things. [back formation from obs. *groveling* (adv.) = obs. *grufe* face down (< Scand) + -LING[2], taken to be prp.] —**grov′el·er;** *esp. Brit.,* **grov′el·ler,** *n.* —**grov′el·ing·ly;** *esp. Brit.,* **grov′el·ling·ly,** *adv.*

grow (grō), *v.,* **grew, grown, grow·ing.** —*v.i.* 1. to increase by natural development, as any living organism or part by assimilation of nutriment. 2. to arise or issue as a natural development: *Our friendship grew from common interests.* 3. to increase gradually in size, amount, etc.; expand: *The influence of this group has grown over the last two decades.* 4. to become gradually attached or united by or as by growth: *The branches of the trees grew together.* 5. to come to be, or become, by degrees: *to grow old.* —*v.t.* 6. to cause to grow: *He grows corn.* 7. to allow to grow: *to grow a beard.* 8. to cover with a growth (used in the passive): *a field grown with corn.* 9. **grow into, a.** to become large enough for. b. to become mature or experienced enough for. 10. **grow on** or **upon, a.** to increase in influence or effect: *An uneasy feeling grew upon him.* b. to become fixed gradually in one's mind or affections: *a village by the sea that grows on one.* 11. **grow out of, a.** to become too large or mature for; outgrow. b. to originate in; develop from. 12. **grow up, a.** to be or become fully grown. b. to come into existence; arise. [ME *grow(en),* OE *grōwan;* c. D *groeien,* OHG *grouwan,* Icel *grōa*] —**grow′a·ble,** *adj.* —**Syn.** 1. develop, multiply, swell, enlarge, expand, extend. 2. originate. 3. wax. 6. raise. —**Ant.** 1. decrease. 3. wane.

grow·er (grō′ər), *n.* 1. a person who grows something. 2. a person or thing that grows in a certain way: *This plant is a quick grower.*

grow′ing pains′, 1. emotional difficulties experienced during adolescence and preadulthood. 2. cramps or pains experienced by children, esp. in the legs, apparently caused by excessive exertion, poor posture, or emotional difficulties. 3. difficulties attending any new project or any rapid development: *a city plagued with growing pains.*

growl (groul), *v.i.* 1. to utter a deep guttural sound of anger or hostility: *The dog growled.* 2. to murmur or complain angrily; grumble. 3. to rumble: *The thunder growled.* —*v.t.* 4. to express by growling: *to growl one's thanks.* —*n.* 5. the act or sound of growling. [ME *groule* to rumble (said of the bowels); c. G *grollen*] —**growl′ing·ly,** *adv.* —**Syn.** 2. See **complain.**

growl·er (grou′lər), *n.* 1. a person or thing that growls. 2. *Informal.* a pitcher, pail, or other container brought by a customer for beer. 3. an iceberg large enough to be a navigational hazard.

grown (grōn), *adj.* 1. advanced in growth: *a grown boy.* 2. arrived at full growth or maturity; adult: *a grown man.* —*v.* 3. pp. of **grow.**

grown-up (grōn′up′), *adj.* 1. having reached maturity. 2. of or for adults. —**grown′-up′ness,** *n.*

grown·up (grōn′up′), *n.* a mature, grown person; adult.

growth (grōth), *n.* 1. the act or process, or a manner of growing; development; gradual increase. 2. size or stage of development: *to reach one's full growth.* 3. completed development. 4. development from a simpler to a more complex stage. 5. development from another but related form or stage. 6. something that has grown or developed: *a growth of weeds.* 7. *Pathol.* an abnormal increase in a mass of tissue, as a tumor. 8. origin; source; production: *onions of English growth.* —*adj.* 9. of or denoting a business or equity security that moves or is likely to move ahead of its market year after year: *a growth industry; a growth stock.* [ME (north) *grouth;* c. Icel *grōthr*] —**Syn.** 1. expansion. —**Ant.** 1. decline, decrease.

groyne (groin), *n.* groin (def. 3).

Groz·ny (grôz′ni), *n.* a city in the S Soviet Union in Europe. 308,000 (est. 1964).

grub (grub), *n., v.,* **grubbed, grub·bing.** —*n.* 1. the thick-bodied, sluggish larva of several insects, as of a scarabaeid beetle. 2. a dull, plodding person; drudge. 3. *Informal.* food; victuals. —*v.t.* 4. to dig; clear of roots, stumps, etc. 5. to dig up by the roots; uproot (often fol. by *up* or *out*): *grubbing up tree stumps.* 6. *Slang.* to supply with food. 7. *Slang.* scrounge (def. 2). —*v.i.* 8. to dig; search by or as by digging. 9. to lead a laborious life; drudge. 10. to engage in laborious study. [ME *grubbe* (n.), *grubben* (v.); akin to OHG *grubilōn* to dig, G *grübeln* to rack (the brain), Icel *gryfia* hole, pit; see GRAVE[1], GROOVE] —**grub′ber,** *n.*

grub·by (grub′ē), *adj.,* **-bi·er, -bi·est.** 1. dirty; slovenly. 2. infested with grubs. 3. contemptible. —**grub′bi·ly,** *adv.* —**grub′bi·ness,** *n.*

grub·stake (grub′stāk′), *n., v.,* **-staked, -stak·ing.** —*n.* 1. provisions, outfit, etc., furnished to a prospector on condition that he share the profits of his discoveries. —*v.t.* 2. to furnish with a grubstake. —**grub′stak′er,** *n.*

Grub′ Street′, 1. a street in London, England: formerly inhabited by many impoverished minor writers and literary hacks; now called Milton Street. 2. petty and needy authors, or literary hacks, collectively.

grub·street (grub′strēt′), *adj.* 1. produced by a hack; poor in quality: *a grubstreet book.* —*n.* 2. See **Grub Street.**

grub·worm (grub′wûrm′), *n.* grub (def. 1).

grudge (gruj), *n., v.,* **grudged, grudg·ing.** —*n.* 1. a feeling of ill will or resentment. —*v.t.* 2. to give or permit with reluctance; begrudge. 3. to resent the good fortune of (another). —*v.i.* 4. to feel dissatisfaction or ill will. [ME *grudge(n), grugge(n),* var. of *gruchen* < OF *gro(u)c(h)ier* < Gmc; cf. MHG *grogezen* to complain, cry out] —**grudge′less,** *adj.* —**grudg′er,** *n.*

—**Syn.** 1. bitterness, rancor, malevolence, enmity, hatred. GRUDGE, MALICE, SPITE refer to ill will held against another or others. A GRUDGE is a feeling of resentment harbored because of some real or fancied wrong: *to hold a grudge because of jealousy; She has a grudge against him.* MALICE is the state of mind which delights in doing harm, or seeing harm done, to others, whether expressing itself in an attempt to injure or merely in sardonic humor: *malice in watching someone's embarrassment; to tell lies about someone out of malice.* SPITE is petty, and often sudden, resentment that manifests itself, usually in trifling retaliations: *to build a fence between properties out of spite.* 3. envy.

grudg·ing (gruj′ing), *adj.* displaying reluctance or unwillingness: *grudging acceptance of the victory of an opponent.* —**grudg′ing·ly,** *adv.*

gru·el (gro͞o′əl), *n.* a thin cereal of oatmeal boiled in water or milk. [ME < MF, OF = *gru-* (< Gmc; see GROUT) + *-el* dim. suffix]

gru·el·ing (gro͞o′ə ling, gro͞o′ling), *adj.* 1. exhausting; very tiring; arduously severe: *a grueling race.* —*n.* 2. any trying or exhausting procedure or experience. Also, *esp. Brit.,* **gru′el·ling.** [slang *gruel* punishment (n.), punish (v.) + -ING[2], -ING[1]]

grue·some (gro͞o′səm), *adj.* horribly repugnant; grisly. Also, **grewsome.** [obs. *grue* to shudder (c. G *grauen,* D *gruwen*) + -SOME[1]] —**grue′some·ly,** *adv.* —**grue′some·ness,** *n.* —**Syn.** shocking, horrid, horrendous.

gruff (gruf), *adj.* 1. low and harsh; hoarse: *a gruff voice.* 2. rough; surly: *a gruff manner.* [< MD *grof;* c. G *grob* rough, uncouth] —**gruff′ish,** *adj.* —**gruff′ly,** *adv.* —**gruff′ness,** *n.* —**Syn.** 2. brusque. —**Ant.** 2. courteous.

gruff·y (gruf′ē), *adj.,* **gruff·i·er, gruff·i·est.** gruff. —**gruff′i·ly,** *adv.* —**gruff′i·ness,** *n.*

grum·ble (grum′bəl), *v.,* **-bled, -bling,** *n.* —*v.i.* 1. to murmur or mutter in discontent. 2. to utter low, indistinct sounds; growl. 3. to rumble. —*v.t.* 4. to express or utter with murmuring or complaining. —*n.* 5. an expression of discontent; complaint. 6. **grumbles.** a grumbling, discontented mood. 7. a rumble. [? freq. of OE *grymman* to wail; cf. D *grommelen,* G *grummeln,* F *grommeler* (< Gmc)] —**grum′bler,** *n.* —**grum′bling·ly,** *adv.* —**grum′bly,** *adj.* —**Syn.** 1. See **complain.**

grum·met (grum′it), *n.* grommet.

gru·mous (gro͞o′məs), *adj.* having or resembling a clot of blood; clotted. [< L *grūm(us)* hillock + -OUS]

grump (grump), *n.* 1. a person characterized by constant complaining. 2. **grumps.** a depressed or sulky mood. —*v.i.* to complain or sulk. [dial. *grump* the sulks, surly remark]

grump·y (grum′pē), *adj.,* **grump·i·er, grump·i·est.** surly or ill-tempered. Also, **grump′ish.** —**grump′i·ly,** *adv.* —**grump′i·ness,** *n.*

Grun·dy (grun′dē), *n.* **Mrs.,** a narrow-minded person who is extremely critical of any breach of propriety. [after *Mrs. Grundy,* a character mentioned in the play *Speed the Plough* (1798) by Thomas Morton (1764?–1838), English playwright] —**Grun′dy·ism,** *n.* —**Grun′dy·ist, Grun′dy·ite′,** *n.*

grun·gy (grun′jē), *adj.* **-gi·er, -gi·est.** *Slang.* ugly, rundown, or dilapidated. [orig. uncertain]

grun·ion (grun′yən), *n.* a small, slender food fish, *Leuresthes tenuis,* of the silverside family, found in southern California. [prob. < Sp *gruñon* grunter < *gruñ(ir)* (to) grunt < L *grunnīre*]

grunt (grunt), *v.i.* **1.** to utter the deep, guttural sound characteristic of a hog. **2.** to utter a similar sound. **3.** to grumble. —*v.t.* **4.** to express with a grunt. —*n.* **5.** a sound of grunting. **6.** any food fish of the family *Pomadasyidae* (*Haemulidae*), found chiefly in tropical and subtropical seas, which emits grunting sounds. **7.** *U.S. Mil. Slang.* an infantryman. [ME *grunt(en)*, OE *grunnettan*, freq. of *grun(n)ian* to grunt; c. G *grunzen*, L *grunnīre*] —**grunt′ing·ly,** *adv.*

grunt·er (grun′tər), *n.* **1.** a hog. **2.** any animal or person that grunts. [late ME]

Gru·yère (gro͞o yâr′, gri-; *Fr.* gʀʏ yeʀ′), *n.* a firm, pale-yellow cheese, made of whole milk and having small holes. Also called **Gru·yère′ cheese′.** [after *Gruyère* district in Switzerland where the cheese is made]

Gru·zi·ya (gʀo͞o′zi yä), *n.* Russian name of **Georgia.**

gr. wt., gross weight.

gryph·on (grif′ən), *n.* *Class. Myth.* griffin[1].

GS, German silver.

G.S., **1.** general secretary. **2.** general staff. Also, **g.s.**

G.S.A., Girl Scouts of America.

G-string (jē′string′), *n.* **1.** a loincloth or breechcloth. **2.** a similar covering, usually decorated, worn by women entertainers, esp. in a striptease. [so called after the string tuned to G on several musical instruments]

G-suit (jē′so͞ot′), *n.* See **anti-G suit.** [*g(ravity) suit*]

gt., **1.** gilt. **2.** great. **3.** (in prescriptions) a drop. [< L *gutta*]

Gt. Br., Great Britain. Also, **Gt. Brit.**

g.t.c., **1.** good till canceled. **2.** good till countermanded. Also, **G.T.C.**

gtd., guaranteed.

GTO, See **Gran Turismo Omologato.**

gtt., (in prescriptions) drops. [< L *guttae*]

GU, Guam (approved esp. for use with zip code).

g.u., genitourinary. Also, **GU**

gua·ca·mo·le (gwä kə mō′lē; *Sp.* gwä kä mō′le), *n.* *Mexican Cookery.* a thick sauce or dip consisting of mashed avocado flavored with chopped onion, lemon juice, hot peppers, etc. [AmerSp < Nahuatl *ahuacamulli* (*ahuacatl* avocado + *mulli* sauce)]

gua·co (gwä′kō), *n., pl.* **-cos.** **1.** a climbing, asteraceous plant, *Mikania Guaco*, of tropical America. **2.** its medicinal leaves, or a substance obtained from them, used as an antidote for snake bites. **3.** a tropical American plant, *Aristolochia maxima*, also used for snake bites. [< AmerSp]

Gua·da·la·ja·ra (gwäd′əl ə här′ə; *Sp.* gwä′ᵺä lä hä′ʀä), *n.* a city in and the capital of Jalisco, in W Mexico. 1,048,351 (est. 1965).

Gua·dal·ca·nal (gwäd′əl kə nal′), *n.* the largest of the Solomon Islands, in the S Pacific: U.S. victory over the Japanese 1942–43. ab. 2500 sq. mi.

Gua·dal·qui·vir (gwä′ᵺäl kē vēʀ′), *n.* a river in S Spain, flowing W to the Gulf of Cádiz. 374 mi. long.

Gua·da·lupe Hi·dal·go (gwäd′əlo͞op′ hi däl′gō; *Sp.* gwä′ᵺä lo͞o′pe ē ᵺäl′gô), a city in the Federal District of Mexico: famous shrine; peace treaty 1848. 92,947 (1960). Official name, **Gustavo A. Madero.**

Gua′dalupe Moun′tains, a mountain range in S New Mexico and SW Texas, part of the Sacramento Mountains. Highest peak, Guadalupe Peak, 8751 ft.

Gua·de·loupe (gwäd′əlo͞op′), *n.* two islands separated by a channel in the Leeward Islands of the West Indies: with five dependencies they form an overseas department of France. 270,000 (est. 1960); 687 sq. mi. *Cap.:* Basse-Terre.

Gua·di·a·na (*Sp.* gwä ᵺyä′nä; *Port.* gwə dyä′nə), *n.* a river in SW Europe, flowing S from central Spain through SE Portugal to the Gulf of Cádiz. 515 mi. long.

guai·a·col (gwī′ə kōl′, -kôl′, -kol′), *n.* *Pharm.* a slightly yellowish, oily liquid, $CH_3OC_6H_4OH$, having an aromatic odor: used chiefly as an expectorant and local anesthetic. [GUAIAC(UM) + -OL[2]]

guai·a·cum (gwī′ə kəm), *n.* **1.** any of several tropical American, zygophyllaceous trees or shrubs of the genus *Guaiacum*, esp. *G. officinale* and *G. sanctum.* **2.** the hard, heavy wood of such a tree. Cf. **lignum vitae** (def. 1). **3.** a greenish-brown resin obtained from such a tree, used as a stimulant and tonic and as a remedy for rheumatism, cutaneous eruptions, etc. Also, **gui·ac** (gwī′ak) (for defs. 2, 3). [< NL < Sp *guayaco, guayacán* < Taino]

Guam (gwäm), *n.* an island, belonging to the U.S., in the N Pacific, E of the Philippines: the largest of the Marianas group; U.S. naval station. 84,996 (1970); 209 sq. mi. *Cap.:* Agaña. *Abbr.:* GU —**Gua·ma·ni·an** (gwä mā′nē ən), *n.*

guan (gwän), *n.* any of several large, gallinaceous birds of the family *Cracidae*, chiefly of Central and South America, related to the curassows. [< AmerSp]

Gua·na·ba·ra (gwä′nə bä′ʀə), *n.* a state in SE Brazil. 3,307,163 (1960); 452 sq. mi. *Cap.:* Rio de Janeiro.

gua·na·co (gwä nä′kō), *n., pl.* **-cos.** a wild South American ruminant, *Lama guanicoe*, of which the llama and alpaca are believed to be domesticated varieties: related to the camels. [< Sp < Quechuan *huanacu*]

Guanaco (3½ ft. high at shoulder; length to 5½ ft.)

Gua·na·jua·to (gwä′nä hwä′tô), *n.* **1.** a state in central Mexico. 1,735,490 (1960); 11,805 sq. mi. **2.** a city in and the capital of this state. 27,365 (1960).

guan·i·dine (gwan′i dēn′, -din, gwä′ni-), *n.* *Chem.* a water-soluble solid, $HN{=}C(NH_2)_2$, used in the manufacture of plastics, resins, and explosives. [GUAN(O) + -ID[3] + -INE]

gua·nine (gwä′nēn), *n.* *Chem., Biochem.* a solid, $C_5H_5N_5O$, used chiefly in biochemical research. [GUAN(O) + -INE[2]]

gua·no (gwä′nō), *n.* **1.** a natural manure composed chiefly of the excrement of sea birds, found esp. on islands near the Peruvian coast. **2.** any similar substance, as an artificial fertilizer made from fish. [< Sp: fertilizer, dung; AmerSp *huano* dung < Quechuan]

Guan·tá·na·mo (gwän tä′nə mō′; *Sp.* gwän tä′nä mô′), *n.* a city in SE Cuba: U.S. naval base. 124,685 (1960).

Guantá′namo Bay′, a bay on the SE coast of Cuba.

Gua·po·ré (*Port.* gwä po͝o ʀe′; *Sp.* gwä′pô ʀe′), *n.* **1.** a river forming part of the boundary between Brazil and Bolivia, flowing NW to the Mamoré River. 950 mi. long. **2.** former name of **Rondônia.**

guar., guaranteed.

gua·ra·ní (gwär′ə nē′, gwär′ə nē′), *n., pl.* **-ni, -nis.** a paper money and monetary unit of Paraguay, equal to 100 centimos. [< Sp, after GUARANÍ]

Gua·ra·ní (gwär′ə nē′), *n., pl.* **-nís, -níes,** (*esp. collectively*) **-ní.** **1.** a member of a central South American people of Tupian family and affiliation. **2.** a language belonging to the Tupi-Guaraní family of languages and spoken by the Guaraní Indians. Also, **Gua′ra·ni′.**

guar·an·tee (gar′ən tē′), *n., v.,* **-teed, -tee·ing.** —*n.* **1.** guaranty (def. 1). **2.** a promise or assurance, esp. one in writing, that something is of specified quality, content, benefit, etc., or that it will perform satisfactorily for a given length of time: *a money-back guarantee.* **3.** a person who gives a guarantee or guaranty; guarantor. **4.** one to whom a guarantee is made. **5.** guaranty (def. 2). **6.** something that has the force or effect of a guaranty: *Wealth is no guarantee of happiness.* —*v.t.* **7.** to secure, as by giving or taking security. **8.** to make oneself answerable for (something) in behalf of someone else. **9.** to undertake to ensure for another, as rights or possessions. **10.** to serve as a warrant or guaranty for. **11.** to engage (to do something). **12.** to promise (usually fol. by a clause as object): *I guarantee that I'll be there.* **13.** to engage to protect or indemnify: *to guarantee a person against loss.* [alter. of GUARANTY] —**Syn. 1.** surety, promise. **13.** insure.

guar′anteed in′come. See **negative income tax.** Also called **guar′anteed an′nual in′come.**

guar·an·tor (gar′ən tôr′, -tər), *n.* **1.** a person, group, system, etc., that guarantees: *the guarantor of world peace.* **2.** a person who makes or gives a guaranty, warrant, etc.

guar·an·ty (gar′ən tē′), *n., pl.* **-ties,** *v.,* **-tied, -ty·ing.** —*n.* **1.** a warrant, pledge, or formal assurance given as security that another's debt or obligation will be fulfilled. **2.** something that is taken or presented as security. **3.** the act of giving security. **4.** a person who acts as a guarantor. —*v.t.* **5.** guarantee. [< AF *guarantie.* See WARRANT, -Y[3]]

guard (gärd), *v.t.* **1.** to keep safe from harm or danger; protect; watch over. **2.** to keep under close watch in order to prevent escape, misconduct, etc. **3.** to keep under control as a matter of caution or prudence: *to guard one's temper.* **4.** to provide or equip with some safeguard or protective appliance, as to prevent loss, injury, etc. **5.** *Sports.* to position oneself so as to obstruct or impede the movement or progress of (an opponent on offense); cover. **6.** *Chess.* to protect (a piece or a square) by placing a piece in a supportive or defensive position relative to it. —*v.i.* **7.** to take precautions (usually fol. by *against*): *to guard against errors.* **8.** to give protection; keep watch; be watchful. —*n.* **9.** a person or group of persons that guards, protects, restrains, etc. **10.** a close watch, as over a prisoner or other person under restraint. **11.** a device, appliance, or attachment that prevents injury, loss, etc. **12.** something intended or serving to guard or protect; safeguard. **13.** a posture of defense or readiness, as in fencing, boxing, etc. **14.** *Football.* either of the linemen stationed between a tackle and the center. **15.** *Basketball.* either of the players stationed in the backcourt. **16.** *Chess.* a piece that supports or defends another. **17.** *Brit.* a railroad or streetcar conductor. **18. Guards,** the name of certain bodies of troops in the British army. **19. off one's guard,** unprepared for attack; unwary. Also, **off guard.** **20. on one's guard,** vigilant against attack; wary. Also, **on guard.** **21. stand guard,** to watch over; protect. [ME *garde* < OF *g(u)arde* (n.) < *g(u)arder* (v.) < Gmc; see WARD] —**guard′a·ble,** *adj.* —**guard′er,** *n.* —**guard′less,** *adj.* —**guard′like′,** *adj.* —**Syn. 1.** shield, safeguard; save. See **defend. 3.** watch. **9.** watchman, sentry, sentinel.

Guar·da·fui (gwär′də fwē′), *n.* **Cape,** a cape at the E extremity of Africa, in the Somali Republic.

guard·ant (gär′dənt), *adj.* *Heraldry.* (of an animal) depicted full-faced but with the body seen from the side: *a lion guardant.* Also, **gardant.** [< F *gardant*, prp. of *garder*]

guard′ cell′, *Bot.* either of two cells that flank the pore of a stoma and usually cause it to open and close.

guard′ du′ty, a military assignment involving watching over or protecting a person or place, or supervising military prisoners.

guard·ed (gär′did), *adj.* **1.** cautious; careful; prudent. **2.** protected, watched, or restrained. —**guard′ed·ly,** *adv.* —**guard′ed·ness,** *n.*

guard′ hair′, the long, usually stiff outer hair protecting the underfur in certain animals.

guard·house (gärd′hous′), *n., pl.* **-hous·es** (-hou′ziz). a building used for housing military personnel on guard duty or for the temporary detention of prisoners.

guard·i·an (gär′dē ən), *n.* **1.** a person who guards, protects, or preserves. **2.** *Law.* a person entrusted by law with the care of the person or property, or both, of another, as a minor. —*adj.* **3.** guarding; protecting: *a guardian deity.* [ME *gardein* < AF] —**guard′i·an·less,** *adj.* —**Syn. 1.** protector, defender.

guard′ian an′gel, **1.** an angel believed to protect a particular person, as from danger, error, etc. **2.** a person who looks after or concerns himself with the welfare of another.

guard·i·an·ship (gär′dē ən ship′), *n.* **1.** the position and responsibilities of a guardian, esp. toward a ward. **2.** care; responsibility; charge.

guard′ of hon′or, a guard specially designated for welcoming or escorting distinguished guests or for accompanying a casket in a military funeral. Also called **honor guard.**

guard·rail (gärd′rāl′), *n.* a protective railing, as along a road, stairway, etc.

guard′ ring′, a ring worn tightly over another ring to prevent the latter from slipping off the finger.

guard·room (gärd′ro͞om′, -ro͝om′), *n. Mil.* a room used by guards during the period they are on duty.

guards·man (gärdz′mən), *n., pl.* **-men.** **1.** a man who acts as a guard. **2.** *U.S.* a member of the National Guard. **3.** *Brit.* a member of any select body of troops traditionally organized to protect the person of the king.

Guar·ne·ri (gwär nâr′ē; *It.* gwäʀ ne′ʀē), *n.* **Giu·sep·pe An·to·nio** (jo͞o zep′pe än tô′nyô), 1683–1745, Italian violinmaker.

Guar·ne·ri·us (gwär nâr′ē əs), *n., pl.* **-us·es.** a violin made by Guarneri or by a member of his family.

Guat., Guatemala.

Gua·te·ma·la (gwä′tə mä′lə; *Sp.* gwä′te mä′lä), *n.* **1.** a republic in N Central America. 6,300,000; 42,042 sq. mi. **2.** Also called **Gua′tema′la Cit′y.** a city in and the capital of this republic. 717,322. —**Gua′te·ma′lan,** *adj., n.*

gua·va (gwä′və), *n.* **1.** any of various myrtaceous trees or shrubs of the genus *Psidium,* esp. *P. Guajava,* of tropical or subtropical America, having a berrylike fruit. **2.** the fruit, used for making jam, jelly, etc. [< Sp *guayaba* < Arawak]

Guay·a·quil (gwä′yä kēl′), *n.* **1.** a seaport in W Ecuador, on the Gulf of Guayaquil. 506,037 (est. 1963). **2. Gulf of,** an arm of the Pacific in SW Ecuador.

Guay·mas (gwī′mäs, gwä′ē-), *n.* a seaport in NW Mexico. 84,730.

Guay·na·bo (gwī nä′bō), *n.* a city in N Puerto Rico, S of San Juan. 55,310 (1970).

gua·yu·le (gwä yo͞o′lē; *Sp.* gwä yo͞o′le), *n., pl.* **-les** (-lēz; *Sp.* -les). **1.** a bushlike, composite plant, *Parthenium argentatum,* of the southwestern U.S. and Mexico, the tissues of which yield a form of rubber. **2.** the rubber obtained from this plant. [< AmerSp *guayule* < Nahuatl *cuauhuli* tree gum]

gu·ber·na·to·ri·al (go͞o′bər nə tôr′ē əl, -tôr′-, gyo͞o′-), *adj. Chiefly U.S.* of or pertaining to a state governor or the office of state governor. [< L *gubernātōr-* (s. of *gubernātor*) steersman, GOVERNOR + -IAL]

guck (guk, go͝ok), *n. Slang.* slime, oozy dirt, or any similar repulsive substance. [perh. b. GOO and MUCK]

gudg·eon[1] (guj′ən), *n.* **1.** a small, European, freshwater fish, *Gobio gobio,* of the minnow family, having a threadlike barbel at each corner of the mouth, used as bait. **2.** any of certain related fishes. **3.** a person who is easily duped or cheated. **4.** a bait or allurement. —*v.t.* **5.** to dupe; cheat. [ME *gogion* < OF *go(u)jon* < L *gōbiōn-* (s. of *gōbiō*), var. of *gōbius.* See GOBY]

gudg·eon[2] (guj′ən), *n.* **1.** *Mach.* a trunnion. **2.** a socket for the pintle of a hinge. [ME *gudyon* < OF *go(u)jon,* ? < LL *gu(l)bia* a chisel]

Gud·run (go͝od′ro͞on), *n.* (in *Volsunga Saga*) the daughter of the king of the Nibelungs. She married Sigurd and then, after his death, Atli, whom she killed: corresponds to Kriemhild in the *Nibelungenlied.* Also, **Guthrun.**

guel·der-rose (gel′dər rōz′), *n.* a variety of the cranberry tree, *Viburnum opulus roseum,* having white, sterile flowers borne in large, snowball-like clusters. [after GUELDERS]

Guel·ders (gel′dərz), *n.* Gelderland.

Guelph (gwelf), *n.* a member of the political party in medieval Italy and Germany that supported the sovereignty of the papacy against the German emperors: opposed to the Ghibellines. Also, **Guelf.** [< It *Guelfo* < MHG *Welf* name of founder of a princely German family] —**Guelph′ic, Guelf′ic,** *adj.* —**Guelph′ism, Guelf′ism,** *n.*

gue·non (gə nôɴ′, -non′), *n.* any of several long-tailed, African monkeys, esp. of the genus *Cercopithecus,* having a grizzled coat. [< F < ?]

guer·don (gûr′dᵊn), *Literary.* —*n.* **1.** a reward or recompense. —*v.t.* **2.** to give a guerdon to. [ME < OF, var. of *werdoun* < ML *widerdōn(um),* alter. (prob. by assoc. with L *dōnum* gift) of OHG *widarlōn* = *widar* again, back + *lōn* reward; c. OE *witherlēan*] —**guer′don·er,** *n.* —**guer′don·less,** *adj.*

Guer·ni·ca (gwâr′ni kə; *Sp.* geʀ nē′kä), *n.* Basque town in northern Spain: bombed and destroyed 1937 by German planes serving the insurgents in the Spanish civil war.

Guern·sey (gûrn′zē), *n., pl.* **-seys** for 2. **1. Isle of,** one of the Channel Islands, in the English Channel. With adjacent islands: 51,138; 24½ sq. mi. **2.** one of a breed of dairy cattle, raised originally on the Isle of Guernsey, producing rich, golden-colored milk.

Guer·re·ro (geʀ ʀe′ʀô), *n.* a state in S Mexico. 2,013,000; 24,885 sq. mi. *Cap.:* Chilpancingo.

guer·ril·la (gə ril′ə), *n.* **1.** a member of a small independent band of soldiers that harasses the enemy by surprise raids, attacks on communications, etc. —*adj.* **2.** pertaining to such fighters or their technique of warfare. Also, **gue·ril′la.** [< Sp: guerrilla band, dim. of *guerra* war < Gmc] —**guer·ril′la·ism, gue·ril′la·ism,** *n.*

guerril′la the′ater, the unannounced presentation of short plays on socio-political themes, such as war, justice, etc., to unsuspecting audiences, usually in the streets and other nontheater locations.

guess (ges), *v.t.* **1.** to arrive at or commit oneself to an opinion without sufficient evidence: *to guess a person's weight.* **2.** to estimate or conjecture about correctly: *to guess a riddle.* **3.** to think, believe, or suppose: *I guess you're right.* —*v.i.* **4.** to form an estimate or conjecture (often fol. by *at* or *about*): *We guessed at the height of the building.* **5.** to estimate or conjecture correctly. —*n.* **6.** an opinion that one reaches or to which one commits oneself on the basis of probability alone or in the absence of any evidence whatever. **7.** the act of forming such an opinion. [ME *gess(en),* prob. < Scand; cf. Sw, Dan *gisse;* c. MD *gessen.* See GET] —**guess′a·ble,** *adj.* —**guess′er,** *n.* —**guess′ing·ly,** *adv.*
—**Syn. 1.** hazard. **1, 2, 4.** GUESS, CONJECTURE, SURMISE imply attempting to form an opinion as to the probable. To GUESS is to risk an opinion regarding something one does not know about, or, wholly or partly by chance, to arrive at the correct answer to a question: *to guess the outcome of a game.* To CONJECTURE is to make inferences in the absence of sufficient evidence to establish certainty: *to conjecture the circumstances of the crime.* SURMISE implies making an intuitive conjecture that may or may not be correct: *to surmise the motives that led to a crime.* **6.** supposition. —**Ant. 3.** know.

guess·ti·mate (*v.* ges′tə māt′; *n.* ges′tə mit, -māt′), *v.,* **-mat·ed -mat·ing,** *n. Slang.* —*v.t.* **1.** to estimate without substantial facts or statistics. —*n.* **2.** an estimate arrived at by guesswork. [b. GUESS and ESTIMATE]

guess·work (ges′wûrk′), *n.* work or procedure based on the making of guesses or conjectures.

guest (gest), *n.* **1.** a person who receives hospitality at another person's home. **2.** a person who receives the hospitality of a club, a city, or the like. **3.** a person who patronizes a hotel, restaurant, etc. **4.** *Zool.* an inquiline. —*v.t.* **5.** to entertain as a guest. —*v.i.* **6.** *Informal.* to appear as a guest: *She is guesting on a television panel show.* [ME *gest* < Scand (cf. OIcel *gest(r)*); r. OE *g(i)est;* c. G *Gast,* Goth *gasts,* L *hostis*] —**guest′less,** *adj.* —**Syn. 1.** See **visitor.**

Guest (gest), *n.* **Edgar A(lbert),** 1881–1959, U.S. journalist and writer of verse, born in England.

guest·house (gest′hous′), *n., pl.* **-hous·es** (-hou′ziz). a building, separate from a main house or establishment, for the housing of guests.

guest′ of hon′or, **1.** a person in whose honor a dinner, party, etc., is given. **2.** a distinguished person invited to a dinner, meeting, etc., esp. on some unique occasion.

guest′ room′, a room for the lodging of guests.

guest-rope (gest′rōp′), *n. Naut.* **1.** a rope suspended from the side of a vessel or a boom as an object to which other vessels can moor, or to afford a hold for persons in such vessels. **2.** a line, in addition to the towrope, to steady a boat in tow. [*guest* < ? + ROPE]

Gue·va·ra (ge vä′ʀä), *n.* **Er·nes·to** (eʀ nes′tô), ("*Che*"), 1928–67, Cuban revolutionist, born in Argentina.

guff (guf), *n. Informal.* misleading or insolent talk. [? imit.]

guf·faw (gu fô′, gə-), *n.* **1.** a burst of loud laughter. —*v.i.* **2.** to laugh loudly and boisterously. [? imit.]

Gug·gen·heim (go͝og′ən hīm′, go͞o′gən-), *n.* **Daniel,** 1856–1930, U.S. industrialist and philanthropist.

gug·gle (gug′əl), *v.,* **-gled, -gling,** *n.* —*v.t., v.i.* **1.** to gurgle. —*n.* **2.** a guggling sound; gurgle. [imit.]

gug·let (gug′lit), *n.* goglet.

Gui., Guiana.

Gui·an·a (gē an′ə, -ä′nə; *Sp.* gyä′nä), *n.* **1.** a vast tropical region in NE South America, bounded by the Orinoco, Rio Negro, and Amazon rivers and the Atlantic. ab. 690,000 sq. mi. **2.** a coastal portion of this region, including Guyana, French Guiana, and Surinam. 1,004,000 (est. 1963); 175,275 sq. mi.

Gui·a·nese (gē′ə nēz′, -nēs′, gī′-), *adj., n., pl.* **-nese.** —*adj.* **1.** of or pertaining to the region of Guiana, its inhabitants, or their language. —*n.* **2.** an inhabitant or native of Guiana. Also, **Gui·an·an** (gē an′ən, -ä′nən).

guid·ance (gīd′ᵊns), *n.* **1.** the act or function of guiding; leadership; direction. **2.** advice or counseling service, esp. that provided for students. **3.** a program of supervised care or assistance, esp. therapeutic help in the treatment of minor emotional disturbances. **4.** something that guides. **5.** the process of controlling the flight of a missile or rocket by a built-in mechanism.

guide (gīd), *v.,* **guid·ed, guid·ing,** *n.* —*v.t.* **1.** to assist (a person) to travel through, or reach a destination in, an area in which he does not know the way. **2.** to accompany (a sightseer) to show him points of interest. **3.** to force (a person, object, or animal) to move in a certain path. **4.** to supply (a person) with advice or counsel. **5.** to supervise (someone's actions or affairs) in an advisory capacity. —*n.* **6.** a person who guides, esp. one hired to guide travelers, tourists, hunters, etc. **7.** a mark, tab, or the like, to catch the eye and thus provide quick reference. **8.** a guidebook. **9.** a guidepost. **10.** a contrivance for regulating progressive motion or action: *a sewing-machine guide.* **11.** a spirit believed to direct the utterances of a medium. **12.** *Mil.* a member of a group marching in formation who sets the pattern of movement or alignment for the rest. [ME *guide(n)* < OF *guid(er)* < Gmc; cf. OE *wītan* to look after] —**guid′a·ble,** *adj.* —**guide′less,** *adj.* —**guid′er,** *n.* —**guid′ing·ly,** *adv.*
—**Syn. 1.** pilot, steer, escort. GUIDE, CONDUCT, DIRECT, LEAD imply showing the way or pointing out or determining the course to be taken. GUIDE implies continuous presence or agency in showing or indicating a course: *to guide a traveler.* To CONDUCT is to precede or escort to a place, sometimes with a degree of ceremony: *to conduct a guest to his room.* To DIRECT is to give information for guidance, or instructions or orders for a course of procedure: *to direct someone to the station.* To LEAD is to bring onward in a course, guiding by contact or by going in advance; hence, figuratively, to influence or induce to some course of conduct: *to lead a procession; to lead astray.* **5.** regulate, manage, govern.

guide·book (gīd′bo͝ok′), *n.* a book of directions and information for travelers, tourists, etc.

guid′ed mis′sile, an aerial missile, as a rocket, steered by radio signals, clockwork controls, etc.

guide·line (gīd′līn′), *n.* **1.** a lightly marked line used as a guide, as in composing a drawing. **2.** a rope or cord that serves to guide one's steps, as over rocky terrain. **3.** any guide or indication of a future course of action.

guide·post (gīd′pōst′), *n.* **1.** a post mounted on the roadside or at an intersection, bearing directions. **2.** a guideline.

guide′ rail′, a track or rail designed to control the movement of an object, as a door or window.

guide′ rope′, **1.** *Aeron.* a long rope hung from a balloon and trailing along the ground, used to regulate its altitude. **2.** rope fastened to a hoisting or towing line, to guide the object being moved.

guide·way (gīd′wā′), *n.* a surface or overhead troughlike concrete track about six feet wide for specially designed rapid-transit vehicles on wheels or air cushions.

guide′ word′, catchword (def. 2).

Gui·do d'A·rez·zo (gwē′dô dä ʀet′tsô), (*Guido Aretinus*) ("*Fra Guittone*") c995–1049?, Italian monk and music theorist. —**Gui·do·ni·an** (gwi dō′nē ən), *adj.*

gui·don (gīd′ᵊn), *n. Mil.* **1.** a small flag or streamer carried for marking, signaling, or identification. **2.** the soldier carrying it. [< MF < It *guidone* = *guid(are)* (to) GUIDE + *-one* n. suffix]

Gui·enne (gwē yen′), *n.* a former province in SW France. Also, **Guyenne.** See map at **Burgundy.**

guild (gild), *n.* **1.** an organization of persons with related interests, goals, etc. **2.** any of various medieval associations, as of merchants or tradesmen, organized to maintain standards and to protect the interests of its members, and that sometimes constituted a local governing body. **3.** *Bot.* a group of plants, as parasites, having a similar habit of growth and nutrition. Also, **gild.** [ME *gild(e)* < Scand (cf. OIcel *gildi* guild, payment); r. OE *gegyld* guild; akin to G *Geld* money, Goth *-gild* tax]

guil·der (gil′dər), *n.* gulden (defs. 1, 2). Also, **gilder.** [earlier *guildren*, var. of ME *guldren*, both < D *gulden*]

guild·hall (gild′hôl′), *n.* the hall used by a guild or corporation for its assemblies; town hall. Also, **gildhall.** [ME]

guild·ship (gild′ship), *n.* **1.** guild (defs. 1, 2). **2.** the condition or standing of a guild member. [OE *gieldscipe*]

guilds·man (gildz′mən), *n., pl.* **-men.** a member of a guild.

guile (gīl), *n.* insidious cunning; duplicity; artful deception. [ME < OF < Gmc; akin to WILE] **—Syn.** trickery. See **deceit.**

guile·ful (gīl′fəl), *adj.* cunning; artfully deceptive; wily. [ME] **—guile′ful·ly,** *adv.* **—guile′ful·ness,** *n.*

guile·less (gīl′lis), *adj.* free from guile; sincere; straightforward. **—guile′less·ly,** *adv.* **—guile′less·ness,** *n.*

guil·le·mot (gil′ə mot′), *n.* **1.** any of several narrow-billed birds of the genus *Cepphus*, of northern seas. **2.** *Brit.* a murre of the genus *Uria.* [< MF, appar. dim. of *Guillaume* William]

guil·loche (gi lōsh′), *n.* **1.** an ornamental band or field with paired ribbons or lines flowing in interlaced curves around a series of circular voids. **2.** an ornamental and curvilinear motif of interlaced lines. [< F: graining tool < ?]

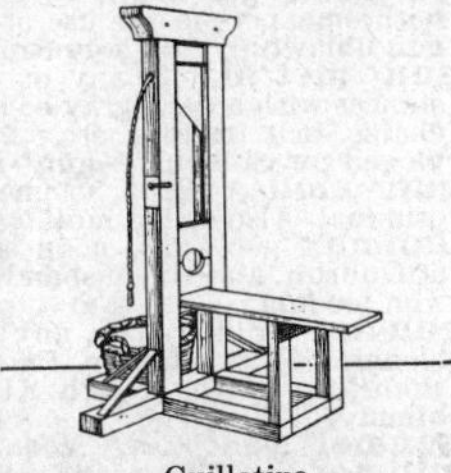

Guillotine

guil·lo·tine (*n.* gil′ə tēn′, gē′ə tēn′; *v.* gil′ə tēn′), *n., v.,* **-tined, -tin·ing.** **—***n.* **1.** a device for beheading persons by means of a heavy blade that is dropped between two posts that serve as guides. **2.** *Surg.* an instrument for cutting the tonsils. **3.** a machine with a vertical blade for cutting stacks of paper. **—***v.t.* **4.** to behead by the guillotine. [named after J. I. *Guillotin* (1738–1814), French physician who urged its use]

guilt (gilt), *n.* **1.** the fact or state of having committed an offense, crime, etc., esp. against moral or penal law; culpability. **2.** conduct involving the commission of such crimes, wrongs, etc.; criminality. **3.** a feeling of responsibility or remorse for some real or imagined offense, crime, etc. [ME *gilt*, OE *gylt* offense] **—Syn. 1.** guiltiness. **—Ant. 1.** innocence.

guilt·less (gilt′lis), *adj.* **1.** free from guilt; innocent. **2.** having no knowledge or experience (usually fol. by *of*): *guiltless of political life.* [ME; OE *gyltlēas*] **—guilt′less·ly,** *adv.* **—guilt′less·ness,** *n.* **—Syn.** See **innocent.**

guilt·y (gil′tē), *adj.,* **guilt·i·er, guilt·i·est.** **1.** having committed an offense, crime, etc., esp. against moral or penal law; culpable: *He is guilty of murder.* **2.** characterized by, connected with, or involving guilt: *guilty intent.* **3.** having or showing a sense of guilt: *a guilty conscience.* [ME; OE *gyltig*] **—guilt′i·ly,** *adv.* **—guilt′i·ness,** *n.*

guimpe (gimp, gamp), *n.* **1.** a chemisette worn with a low-cut dress. **2.** a wide, stiffly starched cloth for covering the neck and shoulders worn by nuns of certain orders. [earlier *gimp*; See GIMP[1]]

Guin., Guinea.

Guin·ea (gin′ē), *n.* **1.** a coastal region in W Africa, extending from the Gambia River to the Gabon estuary. **2.** Formerly, **French Guinea.** an independent republic in W Africa, on the Atlantic coast. 4,800,000; ab. 96,900 sq. mi. *Cap.:* Conakry. **3. Gulf of,** a part of the Atlantic Ocean that projects into the W coast of Africa and extends from the Ivory Coast to Gabon. **4.** (*l.c.*) a money of account of the United Kingdom, equal to 21 shillings (105 pence): formerly often used in quoting professional fees or expensive items. **5.** (*l.c.*) a gold coin of Great Britain issued from 1663 to 1813, valued in 1717 at 21 shillings. **6.** *Disparaging.* a person of Italian birth or descent. **—Guin′e·an,** *adj.*

Guin·ea-Bis·sau (gin′ē bi sou′), *n.* a republic on the W coast of Africa, between Guinea and Senegal: formerly a Portuguese overseas province; independence gained 1974. 600,000; 13,948 sq. mi. *Cap.:* Bissau. Formerly, **Portuguese Guinea.**

Guin′ea corn′, durra.

guin′ea fowl′, any of several African, gallinaceous birds of the family *Numididae*, esp. a common species, *Numida meleagris*, that has a bony casque on the head and dark gray plumage spotted with white and that is now domesticated and raised for its flesh and eggs.

Guinea fowl, *Numida meleagris* (Length 2 ft.)

guin′ea grains′. See **grains of paradise.**

guin′ea hen′, **1.** the female of the guinea fowl. **2.** any member of the guinea fowl family.

Guin′ea pep′per, the pods of a pepper, esp. of *Capsicum Frutescens longum*, from which cayenne is ground.

guin′ea pig′, **1.** a short-eared, tailless rodent of the genus *Cavia*, used in scientific experiments. **2.** *Informal.* the subject of any experiment.

Guinea pig, *Cavia porcellus* (Length 11 in.)

Guin′ea worm′, a long, slender, nematode worm, *Dracunculus medinensis*, of India and Africa, parasitic under the skin of man and animals.

Guin·e·vere (gwin′ə vēr′), *n. Arthurian Romance.* wife of King Arthur and mistress of Lancelot.

gui·pure (gi pyŏŏr′; *Fr.* gē pyʀ′), *n., pl.* **-pures** (-pyŏŏrz′; *Fr.* -pyʀ′). **1.** any of various heavy laces with the pattern connected by brides rather than by a net ground. **2.** any of various laces or trimmings formerly in use, made with cords or heavy threads, metal, etc. [< MF = *guip(er)* (to) cover or whip with silk, etc. (< Gmc)]

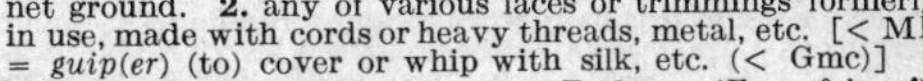

Guis·card (*Fr.* gē skar′), *n.* **Ro·bert** (*Fr.* rô bɛʀ′), (*Robert de Hauteville*), c1015–85, Norman conqueror in Italy.

guise (gīz), *n., v.,* **guised, guis·ing.** **—***n.* **1.** general external appearance; aspect; semblance: *an old principle in a new guise.* **2.** assumed appearance or mere semblance: *an enemy in friendly guise.* **3.** style of dress: *in the guise of a shepherdess.* **4.** *Archaic.* manner; mode. **—***v.t.* **5.** to dress; attire. [ME < OF < Gmc; see WISE[2]] **—Syn. 1.** form, shape. See **appearance.**

Guise (gēz), *n.* **1. Fran·çois de Lor·raine** (fʀäɴ swa′ də lô ʀen′), **2nd Duc de,** 1519–63, French general and statesman. **2.** his son, **Hen·ri I de Lorraine** (äɴ ʀē′), **Duc de,** 1550–88, French general and leader of opposition to the Huguenots.

Guitar

gui·tar (gi tär′), *n.* **1.** a stringed musical instrument with a long, fretted neck, a flat, somewhat violinlike body, and, typically, six strings, which are plucked with the fingers or with a plectrum. **2.** a similar instrument, sometimes having a solid body, with a pickup or pickups and a built-in cable for connecting the instrument to an amplifier. [< Sp *guitarr(a)* << Gk *kithára* cithara] **—gui·tar′like′,** *adj.*

gui·tar·fish (gi tär′fish′), *n., pl.* (*esp. collectively*) **-fish,** (*esp. referring to two or more kinds or species*) **-fish·es.** any of several sharklike rays of the family *Rhinobatidae*, found in warm seas, resembling a guitar in shape.

gui·tar·ist (gi tär′ist), *n.* a performer on the guitar.

guit·guit (gwit′gwit′), *n.* any of several tropical American honeycreepers. [imit.]

Gui·zot (gē zō′), *n.* **Fran·çois Pierre Guil·laume** (fʀäɴ swa′ pyeʀ gē yōm′), 1787–1874, French historian and statesman.

Gu·ja·rat (gŏŏj′ə rät′), *n.* a state in W India. 30,930,000; 72,138 sq. mi. *Cap.:* Ahmedabad. Also, **Gu′je·rat′.**

Gu·ja·ra·ti (gŏŏj′ə rä′tē), *n.* an Indic language of western India. [< Hindi < Skt *Gurjara* GUJARAT]

gu·lag (gōō′läg), *n.* **1.** a Soviet Union forced-labor camp. **2.** any prison or detention camp: *He survived the gulags of North Vietnam.* [< Russ *Gulag*, acronym for *G(lavnoye) U(pravleniye) Lag(erei)* Chief Administration of (Labor) Camps]

gulch (gulch), *n.* a deep, narrow ravine, esp. one marking the course of a stream or torrent. [prob. related to *gulch* throat, drunkard; see GULLY]

gul·den (gŏŏl′dᵊn), *n., pl.* **-dens, -den.** **1.** a silver coin and monetary unit of the Netherlands, equal to 100 cents; florin. *Abbr.:* Gld., f., fl. **2.** a former gold coin of the Netherlands; florin. **3.** the monetary unit of the Netherlands Antilles, equal to 100 cents. **4.** the Austrian florin. **5.** any of various gold coins formerly issued by German states. Also called **guilder** (for defs. 1, 2). [< D and G: lit., GOLDEN]

Gü·lek Bo·gaz (gʏ lek′ bō gäz′), Turkish name of the **Cilician Gates.**

gules (gyōōlz), *Heraldry.* **—***n.* **1.** the tincture, or color, red. **—***adj.* **2.** of the tincture, or color, red: *a lion gules.* [ME *goules* < OF *gueules* red fur neckpiece < *gole* throat < L *gula*]

gulf (gulf), *n.* **1.** a portion of an ocean or sea partly enclosed by land. **2.** a deep hollow; chasm or abyss. **3.** any wide separation, as in station, education, etc. **4.** something that engulfs or swallows up. **—***v.t.* **5.** to swallow like a gulf, or as in a gulf; engulf. [ME *go(u)lf* < OF *golfe* < It *golf(o)* < LGk *kólphos* < Gk *kólpos* bosom, lap, bay] **—gulf′like′,** *adj.* **—gulf′y,** *adj.*

Gulf·port (gulf′pōrt′, -pôrt′), *n.* a city in SE Mississippi, on the Gulf of Mexico. 40,791 (1970).

Gulf′ States′, the states of the U.S. bordering on the Gulf of Mexico: Florida, Alabama, Mississippi, Louisiana, and Texas.

Gulf′ Stream′, **1.** a warm ocean current flowing N from the Gulf of Mexico, along the E coast of the U.S., to an area off the SE coast of Newfoundland, where it merges with the North Atlantic Current. **2.** Also called **Gulf′ Stream′ sys′tem.** a major ocean-current system consisting of this current and the Florida and North Atlantic currents.

gulf·weed (gulf′wēd′), *n.* **1.** a coarse, olive-brown seaweed, *Sargassum bacciferum*, found in the Gulf Stream and tropical American seas, characterized by numerous berrylike air vessels. **2.** any seaweed of the same genus.

Gull[1], *Larus argentatus* (Length 26 in.; wingspread 4½ ft.)

gull[1] (gul), *n.* any of numerous long-winged, web-toed, aquatic birds of the family *Laridae*, having usually white plumage with a gray back and wings. [ME *gulle*, perh. < Welsh *gŵylan*, Cornish *guilan* (cf. F *goéland* < Breton *gwelan*)] **—gull′-like′,** *adj.*

gull[2] (gul), *v.t.* **1.** to deceive; trick; cheat. **—***n.* **2.** a person who is easily deceived or cheated; dupe. [? akin to obs. *gull* to swallow]

Gul·lah (gul′ə), *n.* **1.** a member of a black African people settled as slaves on the Sea Islands and the coastal regions of South Carolina, Georgia, and northeastern Florida. **2.** Also called **Geechee.** their English dialect. [from native name of African tribe or district; perh. Angolese]

gul·let (gul′it), *n.* **1.** the esophagus. **2.** the throat or pharynx. **3.** something like the esophagus. **4.** a channel for water. **5.** a gully or ravine. [ME *golet* < OF *goulet* << L *gula* throat; see -ET]

gul·ley (gul′ē), *n., pl.* **-leys.** gully (defs. 1, 2).

gul·li·ble (gul′ə bəl), *adj.* easily deceived or cheated. Also, **gul′la·ble.** **—gul′li·bil′i·ty, gul′la·bil′i·ty,** *n.* **—gul′li·bly, gul′la·bly,** *adv.*

gul·ly (gul′ē), *n., pl.* **-lies,** *v.,* **-lied, -ly·ing.** —*n.* **1.** a small valley or ravine originally worn away by running water and serving as a drainageway after prolonged heavy rains. **2.** a ditch or gutter. —*v.t.* **3.** to make gullies in. **4.** to form (channels) by the action of water. Also, **gulley** (for. defs. 1, 2). [appar. var. of GULLET, with -Y³ r. F *-et*]

gu·los·i·ty (gyo͞o los′i tē), *n.* gluttony; greediness. [ME < LL *gulōsitās* = L *gulōs(us)* (see GULLET, -OSE¹) + *-itās* -ITY]

gulp (gulp), *v.i.* **1.** to gasp or choke, as when taking large drafts of a liquid. —*v.t.* **2.** to swallow eagerly, or in large drafts or morsels (usually fol. by *down*): *to gulp down one's food.* **3.** to choke back as if by swallowing: *to gulp down a sob.* —*n.* **4.** the act of gulping. **5.** a mouthful. [ME *gulp(en)*; cf. D *gulpen,* Norw *glupa*] —**gulp′ing·ly,** *adv.* —**gulp′y,** *adj.*

gum¹ (gum), *n., v.,* **gummed, gum·ming.** —*n.* **1.** any of various viscid, amorphous exudations from plants, hardening on exposure to air and soluble in or forming a viscid mass with water. **2.** any of various similar exudations, as resin, glue, etc. **3.** a preparation of such a substance, as for use in the arts, bookbinding, etc. **4.** See **chewing gum. 5.** mucilage; glue. **6.** rubber¹ (def. 1). **7.** See **gum tree. 8.** *Philately.* the adhesive by which a postage stamp is affixed. Cf. **o.g.** —*v.t.* **9.** to smear, stiffen, or stick together with gum. **10.** to clog with or as with some gummy substance. —*v.i.* **11.** to exude or form gum. **12.** to become gummy; become clogged with some gummy substance. [ME *gomme* < OF << var. of L *gummi, cummi* < Gk *kómmi* < Egypt *kemai*] —**gum′less,** *adj.* —**gum′like′,** *adj.*

gum² (gum), *n., v.,* **gummed, gum·ming.** —*n.* **1.** Often, **gums.** the firm, fleshy tissue covering the alveolar parts of either jaw and enveloping the necks of the teeth. **2. beat one's gums,** *Slang.* to talk excessively or ineffectively. —*v.t.* **3.** to masticate (food) with the gums instead of teeth; mumble. [ME *gome,* OE *gōma* palate; akin to OIcel *gōmr,* G *Gaumen* palate]

gum³ (gum), *interj.* (used in mild oaths as a euphemism for God): *By gum!*

gum′ ammo′niac, a gum resin, obtained from the umbelliferous plant, *Dorema ammoniacum,* of Persia: used as an expectorant, as a counterirritant, and in the manufacture of porcelain cements. Also called **ammoniac, ammoniacum.**

gum′ ar′abic, a gummy exudation obtained from several species of acacia: used as mucilage, a food thickener, in inks, and in pharmaceuticals as an excipient for tablets. Also called **acacia, gum′ aca′cia.**

gum·bo (gum′bō), *n., pl.* **-bos,** *adj.* —*n.* **1.** the okra plant. **2.** its pods. **3.** a stew or thick soup, usually containing okra and chicken or seafood. **4.** soil that becomes sticky when wet. —*adj.* **5.** of, pertaining to, or resembling gumbo. [< LaF *gombo, gumbo* < Bantu *kingombo* = *ki-* prefix + *ngumbo* okra]

gum·boil (gum′boil′) *n. Pathol.* a small abscess on the gum.

gum·bo·til (gum′bə til), *n. Geol.* a sticky clay formed by the thorough weathering of glacial drift. [GUMBO + *til,* var. of TILL⁴]

gum·drop (gum′drop′), *n. U.S.* a small, soft or chewy candy made of gum arabic, gelatin, or the like, sweetened and flavored.

gum′ elas′tic, rubber¹ (def. 1).

gum′ el′emi, *Chem.* elemi.

gum·ma (gum′ə), *n., pl.* **gum·mas, gum·ma·ta** (gum′ə tə). *Pathol.* the rubbery, tumorlike lesion of tertiary syphilis. [< NL; see GUM¹] —**gum′ma·tous,** *adj.*

gum·mo·sis (gu mō′sis), *n. Bot.* a pathological condition in certain plants, characterized by the excessive formation of gum. [< NL]

gum·mous (gum′əs), *adj.* consisting of or resembling gum; gummy. [< L *gummōs(us)*]

gum·my (gum′ē), *adj.,* **-mi·er, -mi·est. 1.** of, resembling, or of the consistency of gum; viscid. **2.** covered with or clogged by gum or sticky matter. **3.** exuding gum. [ME] —**gum′mi·ness,** *n.*

gum′ plant′, any composite plant of the genus *Grindelia,* of the western U.S., covered with a viscid secretion.

gump·tion (gump′shən), *n. Informal.* **1.** initiative; aggressiveness; resourcefulness. **2.** courage; spunk; guts. [orig. Scot]

gum′ res′in, a plant exudation consisting of a mixture of gum and resin. —**gum′-res′i·nous,** *adj.*

gum·shoe (gum′sho͞o′), *n.* **1.** a rubber shoe; overshoe. **2.** sneaker. **3.** *U.S. Slang.* a policeman or detective.

gum′ tree′, **1.** any tree that exudes gum, as a eucalyptus, the sour gum, the sweet gum, etc. **2.** any of various other gum-yielding trees, as the sapodilla.

gum·wood (gum′wo͝od′), *n.* the wood of a gum tree, esp. the wood of the eucalyptus of Australia, or of a gum tree of the western U.S.

gun¹ (gun), *n., v.,* **gunned, gun·ning.** —*n.* **1.** a metallic tube, with its stock or carriage and attachments, from which missiles are shot by the force of an explosive; a piece of ordnance. **2.** any portable firearm, as a rifle, shotgun, revolver, etc. **3.** a long-barreled cannon having a relatively flat trajectory. **4.** any device for shooting something under pressure: *a paint gun.* **5.** *Brit.* a member of a shooting party. **6. give something the gun,** *Slang.* to put into motion or speed up. **7. jump the gun,** *Slang.* **a.** to begin a race before the starting signal. **b.** to begin (something) prematurely; act too hastily. **8. spike someone's guns,** to frustrate or prevent someone from accomplishing his plan. **9. stick to one's guns,** to maintain one's position in the face of opposition; stand firm. —*v.i.* **10.** to hunt with a gun. **11.** to shoot with a gun. —*v.t.* **12.** to shoot with a gun (often fol. by *down*): *to gun down a killer.* **13.** *Aeron. Slang.* to cause (an aircraft) to increase in speed very quickly. **14.** to feed gasoline to, suddenly and quickly: *to gun an engine.* **15. gun for, a.** to seek with intent to harm or kill. **b.** to seek; try earnestly to obtain. [ME *gunne, gonne,* appar. short for *Gunilda* (L), *gonnyld* (ME) name for engine of war; cf. Icel *Gunna,* short for *Gunnhildr* woman's name] —**gun′less,** *adj.*

gun² (gun), *v.* pp. of **gin**³.

gun., gunnery.

gun·boat (gun′bōt′), *n.* a small vessel of light draft carrying mounted guns.

gun′ car′riage, the structure on which a gun is mounted or moved and from which it is fired.

gun·cot·ton (gun′kot′ən), *n.* a highly explosive cellulose nitrate, made from cotton and used in making smokeless powder.

gun′ deck′, (formerly, on a warship) any deck, other than the weather deck, that has cannons from end to end.

gun′ dog′, a dog trained to hunt game by pointing.

gun·fight (gun′fīt′), *v.,* **-fought, -fight·ing,** *n.* —*v.i.* **1.** to fight with guns. —*n.* **2.** a battle between people in which the principal weapon is a gun.

gun·fight·er (gun′fī′tər), *n.* a person highly skilled in the use of a gun and a veteran of many gunfights, esp. one living during the frontier days of the West.

gun·fire (gun′fīᵊr′), *n.* **1.** the firing of a gun or guns. **2.** *Mil.* the tactical use of firearms, esp. cannon, as distinguished from other weapons, as bayonets or torpedoes, and from shock or charge tactics.

gun·flint (gun′flint′), *n.* the flint in a flintlock.

gung ho (guŋ′ hō′), *Informal.* wholeheartedly, often ingenuously, loyal and enthusiastic: *a gung ho military outfit.* [< Chin]

gunk (guŋk), *n. Informal.* repulsively greasy, sticky, or slimy matter. [prob. imit.]

gun·lock (gun′lok′), *n.* the mechanism of a firearm by which the charge is exploded.

gun·man (gun′mən), *n., pl.* **-men. 1.** *U.S.* a man armed with or expert in the use of a gun, esp. one ready to use a gun unlawfully. **2.** a gunsmith. —**gun′man·ship′,** *n.*

gun′ met′al, **1.** any of various alloys or metallic substances with a dark-gray or blackish color or finish, used for chains, belt buckles, etc. **2.** a bronze formerly much employed for cannon. —**gun′-met′al,** *adj.*

gun′ moll′, *Slang.* a female companion of a gun-carrying criminal. Also called **moll.**

Gun·nar (go͝on′när, go͝on′ər), *n. Scand. Myth.* the brother of Gudrun, and the husband of Brynhild, whom Sigurd had won for him.

gun·nel¹ (gun′əl), *n.* any of several elongated, bandlike blennies of the family *Pholidiidae* (*Pholidae*), esp. *Pholis gunnellus,* of the North Atlantic. Also called **bracketed blenny.** [?]

gun·nel² (gun′əl), *n. Naut.* gunwale.

gun·ner (gun′ər), *n.* **1.** a person who works a gun or cannon. **2.** *U.S. Army.* an occupational title in the artillery. **3.** *U.S. Navy.* one skilled in handling ammunition and gunnery equipment. **4.** *U.S. Marines.* a warrant officer who may be given any one of a number of assignments. **5.** *Brit.* **a.** *Mil.* a private in the artillery. **b.** *Informal.* any artilleryman. **6.** a person who hunts with a rifle or shotgun. [ME] —**gun′ner·ship′,** *n.*

gun·ner·y (gun′ə rē), *n.* **1.** the art and science of constructing and managing guns, esp. large guns. **2.** the act of firing guns. **3.** guns collectively.

gun·ny (gun′ē), *n., pl.* **-nies.** a strong, coarse material made commonly from jute, esp. for bagging; burlap. [< Hindi *gonī* < Skt: sack, perh. orig. of hide, cf. *gāus* an ox]

gun·ny·sack (gun′ē sak′), *n.* a sack made of gunny or burlap. Also called **gun·ny-bag** (gun′ē bag′).

gun·pa·per (gun′pā′pər), *n. Mil.* a type of paper treated with nitric acid so that it has a composition similar to that of guncotton.

gun·point (gun′point′), *n.* **1.** the point or aim of a gun. **2. at gunpoint,** under threat of being shot: *He obeyed only at gunpoint.*

gun·pow·der (gun′pou′dər), *n.* an explosive mixture of potassium nitrate, sulfur, and charcoal, formerly used in gunnery. [ME] —**gun′pow′der·y,** *adj.*

Gun′powder Plot′, an unsuccessful plot to kill King James I and the Lords and Commons by blowing up Parliament, November 5, 1605. Cf. **Guy Fawkes Day.**

gun′ room′, **1.** a room in which guns are kept. **2.** *Brit.* a room for the use of junior naval officers.

gun·run·ning (gun′run′iŋ), *n.* the smuggling of guns or other munitions into a country. —**gun′run′ner,** *n.*

gun·shot (gun′shot′), *n.* **1.** a bullet, projectile, or other shot fired from a gun. **2.** the range of a gun: *out of gunshot.* **3.** the shooting of a gun. —*adj.* **4.** made by a gunshot. [ME]

gun-shy (gun′shī′), *adj.* frightened by the shooting of a gun: *a gun-shy bird dog.*

gun·sling·er (gun′sliŋ′ər), *n. Slang.* gunfighter.

gun·smith (gun′smith′), *n.* a person who makes or repairs firearms. —**gun′smith′ing,** *n.*

gun·stock (gun′stok′), *n.* stock (def. 17). [ME]

gun′ tack′le, *Naut.* a tackle composed of a fall rove through two single blocks and secured to one of them. See diag. at **tackle.**

Gun·ter (gun′tər), *n.* **Edmund,** 1581–1626, English mathematician and astronomer: inventor of various measuring instruments and scales.

Gun′ter's chain′. See under **chain** (def. 8a). [named after Edmund GUNTER]

Gun·ther (go͝on′tər), *n.* (in the *Nibelungenlied*) a king of Burgundy, the husband of Brunhild and the brother of Kriemhild.

gun·wale (gun′əl), *n. Naut.* (loosely) the upper edge of the side or bulwark of a vessel. Also, **gunnel.** [GUN¹ + WALE¹; so-called because guns were set upon it]

gup·py (gup′ē), *n., pl.* **-pies.** a small, fresh-water topminnow, *Lebistes reticulatus,* often kept in aquariums. [after R.J.L. *Guppy* of Trinidad, who presented specimens to the British Museum]

gurge (gûrj), *n., v.,* **gurged, gurg·ing.** —*n.* **1.** a whirlpool. —*v.i.* **2.** to swirl like a whirlpool. [< L *gurge(s)* whirlpool]

gur·gi·ta·tion (gûr′ji tā′shən), *n.* a surging rise and fall; ebullient motion, as of water. [< LL *gurgitāt(us)* engulfed (ptp. of *gurgitāre* < L *gurgit-,* s. of *gurges* whirlpool; see -ATE¹) + -ION]

gur·gle (gûr′gəl), *v.,* **-gled, -gling,** *n.* —*v.i.* **1.** to flow in a broken, irregular, noisy current: *Water gurgles from a bottle.* **2.** to make a sound as of water doing this. —*v.t.* **3.** to utter or express with a gurgling sound. —*n.* **4.** act or noise of gurgling. [cf. D, MLG *gorgelen,* G *gurgeln* to gargle; akin to L *gurguliō* throat] —**gur′gling·ly,** *adv.*

gur·glet (gûr′glit), *n.* goglet.

Gur·kha (go͝or′kä; *Eng.* gûr′kə), *n., pl.* **-khas,** (*esp. collectively*) **-kha. 1.** a member of a Rajput people, Hindu in religion, living in Nepal. **2.** a soldier of this people serving in the British or Indian army.

gur·nard (gûr′nərd), *n., pl.* (*esp. collectively*) **-nard,** (*esp. referring to two or more kinds or species*) **-nards. 1.** any of several marine fishes of the family *Triglidae,* having a bony head armed with spines. **2.** See **flying gurnard.** [ME < OF *gornard,* prob. lit., grunter << L *grunnīre* to grunt]

gur·ney (gûr′nē), *n., pl.* **-neys.** a flat, padded table or stretcher with legs and wheels, for transporting patients, as to and from surgery.

gu·ru (go͞o′ro͞o, go͝o ro͞o′), *n.* **1.** *Hinduism.* a preceptor giving personal religious instruction. **2.** an intellectual or spiritual guide; wise leader. [< Hindi *gurū* < Skt *guru* venerable, weighty] **—gu′ru·ship′,** *n.*

gush (gush), *v.i.* **1.** to flow out or issue suddenly, copiously, or forcibly, as a fluid from confinement. **2.** to talk effusively. **3.** to have a sudden, copious, or forcible flow, as of blood, tears, etc. **—***v.t.* **4.** to emit suddenly, forcibly, or copiously. **—***n.* **5.** a sudden, copious, or forcible outflow. **6.** the fluid emitted. **7.** effusive language. [ME *goshe, gusche;* prob. phonesthemic in orig.; see GUST[1], RUSH[1]] **—gush′ing·ly,** *adv.* **—Syn. 1.** See **flow. 4.** spurt, spout.

gush·er (gush′ər), *n.* **1.** a flowing oil well, usually of large capacity. **2.** a person who gushes.

gush·y (gush′ē), *adj.,* **gush·i·er, gush·i·est.** given to or marked by effusive talk, behavior, etc. **—gush′i·ly,** *adv.* **—gush′i·ness,** *n.* **—Syn.** unrestrained, unreserved.

gus·set (gus′it), *n.* **1.** a small, triangular piece of material inserted into a shirt, shoe, etc., to improve the fit or for reinforcement. Cf. **gore**[3] (def. 1). **2.** a plate for uniting structural members at a joint, as in a steel frame or truss. [ME < OF *gousset* < *gousse* pod, husk]

gus·sy (gus′ē), *v.t.,* **-sied, -sy·ing.** *Slang.* **1.** to dress in one's best clothes (usually fol. by *up*). **2.** to decorate in a gimmicky, showy manner (usually fol. by *up*).

gust[1] (gust), *n.* **1.** a sudden, strong blast of wind. **2.** a sudden rush or burst of water, fire, etc. **3.** an outburst of passion. **—***v.i.* **4.** to blow or rush in gusts. [< Scand; cf. OIcel *gustr* a gust] **—gust′less,** *adj.*

gust[2] (gust), *n.* **1.** *Archaic.* flavor or taste. **2.** *Obs.* enjoyment or gratification. **—***v.t.* **3.** *Scot.* to taste; savor. [< L *gust(us)* a tasting (of food), eating a little < *gust(āre)* (to) taste] **—gust′a·ble,** *adj., n.*

gus·ta·tion (gu stā′shən), *n.* **1.** the act of tasting. **2.** the faculty of taste. [< L *gustātiōn-* (s. of *gustātiō*) = *gustāt(us)* (ptp. of *gustāre* to taste) + *-iōn-* -ION]

gus·ta·tive (gus′tə tiv), *adj.* gustatory. [< ML *gustātīv(us)*] **—gus′ta·tive·ness,** *n.*

gus·ta·to·ry (gus′tə tôr′ē, -tôr′ē), *adj.* of or pertaining to taste or tasting. [< L *gustāt(us)* (see GUSTATION) + -ORY[1]]

Gus·ta·vo A. Ma·de·ro (go͞os tä′vô ä′ mä the′rô), official name of **Guadalupe Hidalgo.**

Gus·ta·vus I (gu stā′vəs, -stä′-), (*Gustavus Vasa*) 1496–1560, king of Sweden 1523–60.

Gustavus II, (*Gustavus Adolphus*) ("*Lion of the North*") 1594–1632, king of Sweden 1611–32: national military hero (grandson of Gustavus I).

Gustavus III, 1746–92, king of Sweden 1771–92: economic and legal reformer.

Gustavus IV, (*Gustavus Adolphus*) 1778–1837, king of Sweden 1800, dethroned 1809 (son of Gustavus III).

Gustavus V, 1858–1950, king of Sweden 1907–50, advocator of Swedish neutrality during World Wars I and II. Also, **Gus·taf V, Gus·tav V** (gus′täv).

Gustavus VI, (*Gustaf Adolf*) 1882–1973, king of Sweden 1950–73 (son of Gustavus V). Also, **Gustav VI.**

gus·to (gus′tō), *n.* **1.** hearty or keen enjoyment, as in eating, drinking, etc., or in action or speech in general. **2.** individual taste, liking, or satisfaction. [< It < L *gust(us);* see GUST[2]]

gust·y[1] (gus′tē), *adj.,* **gust·i·er, gust·i·est. 1.** blowing or coming in gusts, as wind, rain, etc. **2.** affected or marked by gusts of wind, rain, etc.: *a gusty day.* **3.** occurring or characterized by sudden outbursts of sound, laughter, etc. **4.** full of meaningless, pretentious talk. **5.** vigorous; hearty. [GUST[1] + -Y[1]] **—gust′i·ly,** *adv.* **—gust′i·ness,** *n.*

gust·y[2] (gus′tē, go͞os′tē), *adj.,* **gust·i·er, gust·i·est.** *Chiefly Scot.* tasty; savory; appetizing. [GUST[2] + -Y[1]]

gut (gut), *n., v.,* **gut·ted, gut·ting,** *adj.* **—***n.* **1.** the alimentary canal, esp. between the pylorus and the anus, or some portion of it. **2. guts, a.** the bowels or entrails. **b.** *Slang.* courage; stamina; endurance. **3.** the substance forming the case of the intestine; intestinal tissue or fiber: *sheep's gut.* **4.** a preparation of the intestines of an animal, used for various purposes, as for violin strings, tennis rackets, or fishing lines. **5.** the silken substance taken from a silkworm killed when about to spin its cocoon, used in making snells for fishhooks. **6.** a narrow passage, as a channel of water or a defile between hills. **—***v.t.* **7.** to take out the guts or entrails of; disembowel. **8.** to plunder (a house, city, etc.) of contents. **9.** to destroy the interior of, as by fire. **—***adj.* **10.** *Informal.* **a.** basic or essential: *to discuss the gut issues.* **b.** based on instincts or emotions: *a gut reaction; gut decisions.* [ME *gut, guttes* (pl.), OE *guttas* (pl.), akin to *gēotan* to pour] **—gut′like′,** *adj.*

gut·buck·et (gut′buk′it), *n.* jazz played in the raucous and high-spirited style of barrelhouse.

gut′ course′, *Chiefly Northeastern U.S. Informal.* a college course requiring little effort; snap course.

Gu·ten·berg (go͞ot′ən bûrg′; *Ger.* go͞ot′ən berk′), *n.* **Jo·han·nes** (yō hän′əs), (*Johann Gensfleisch*), c1400–68, German printer: credited with invention of printing from movable type.

Gu′tenberg Bi′ble, an edition of the Vulgate printed at Mainz before 1456, ascribed to Gutenberg and others: probably the first large book printed with movable type.

Guth·rie (guth′rē), *n.* **Woodrow Wilson** ("*Woody*"), 1912–1967, U.S. composer and singer of folk songs.

Guth·run (go͝oth′ro͞on), *n.* Gudrun.

gut·less (gut′lis), *adj.* *Slang.* lacking courage, stamina, or endurance. **—gut′less·ness,** *n.*

guts·y (gut′sē), *adj.,* **guts·i·er, guts·i·est.** *Slang.* **1.** having a great deal of nerve or courage. **2.** forceful; lusty: *a gutsy style of singing.* [GUTS + -Y[1]] **—guts′i·ly,** *adv.* **—guts′i·ness,** *n.*

gut·ta (gut′ə), *n., pl.* **gut·tae** (gut′ē). **1.** a drop, or something resembling one. **2.** *Archit.* one of a series of pendent ornaments, generally in the form of a frustum of a cone. [< L: a drop]

gut·ta-per·cha (gut′ə pûr′chə), *n.* the milky juice of various Malaysian sapotaceous trees, esp. *Palaquium Gutta,* used in the arts, as a dental cement, and for insulating electric wires. [< Malay *gĕtah* gum, balsam + *pĕrcha* the tree producing the substance]

gut·tate (gut′āt), *adj.* *Biol.* resembling a drop; having droplike markings. Also, **gut′tat·ed.** [< L *guttāt(us)* speckled, spotted] **—gut·ta′tion,** *n.*

gut·ter (gut′ər), *n.* **1.** a channel at the side or in the middle of a road or street, for leading off surface water. **2.** any channel, trough, or the like, for carrying off fluid. **3.** a channel at the eaves or on the roof of a building, for carrying off rain water. **4.** a furrow or channel made by running water. **5.** *Bowling.* a sunken channel on each side of the alley. **6.** the state or abode of those who live in filth, immorality, crime, etc.: *the language of the gutter.* **7.** the margins between facing pages, as in a book. **—***v.i.* **8.** to flow in streams. **9.** (of a candle) to lose molten wax accumulated in a hollow space around the wick. **10.** (of a lamp or candle flame) to burn low or to be blown so as to be nearly extinguished. **11.** to form gutters, as water does. **—***v.t.* **12.** to make gutters in; channel. **13.** to furnish with a gutter or gutters: *to gutter a new house.* [ME *gutter, goter* < AF *goutier(e)* = *goutte* drop (see GOUT) + *-iere,* fem. of *-ier* -ER[2]] **—gut′ter·like′,** *adj.*

gut·ter·snipe (gut′ər snīp′), *n.* a person belonging to the lowest social group. **—gut′ter·snip′ish,** *adj.*

gut·tle (gut′əl), *v.i., v.t.,* **-tled, -tling.** to eat greedily; gormandize. [GUT + -LE; cf. GUZZLE] **—gut′tler,** *n.*

gut·tur·al (gut′ər əl), *adj.* **1.** of or pertaining to the throat. **2.** harsh; throaty. **3.** *Phonet.* pertaining to or characterized by a sound articulated in the back of the mouth, as the non-English velar fricative sound (kh) or its voiced counterpart, esp. French (r). **—***n.* **4.** a guttural sound. [< NL *gutturāl(is)* of the throat = L *guttur* gullet, throat + *-ālis* -AL[1]] **—gut′tur·al·ly,** *adv.* **—gut′tur·al·ness, gut′tur·al′i·ty, gut′tur·al·ism,** *n.*

gut·tur·al·ise (gut′ər ə līz′), *v.t., v.i.,* **-ised, -is·ing.** *Chiefly Brit.* gutturalize. **—gut′tur·al·i·sa′tion,** *n.*

gut·tur·al·ize (gut′ər ə līz′), *v.,* **-ized, -iz·ing. —***v.t.* **1.** to speak or pronounce (something) in a guttural manner. **2.** *Phonet.* to change into, pronounce as, or supplement with a guttural or gutturalized sound. **—***v.i.* **3.** to speak gutturally. **—gut′tur·al·i·za′tion,** *n.*

gut·ty (gut′ē), *adj.,* **-ti·er, -ti·est.** *Slang.* gutsy.

guy[1] (gī), *n., v.,* **guyed, guy·ing. —***n.* **1.** *Informal.* a fellow. **2.** (*often cap.*) *Brit.* a grotesque effigy of Guy Fawkes which is paraded and burned on Guy Fawkes Day. **3.** *Chiefly Brit. Slang.* a grotesquely dressed person. **4. give the guy to,** *Brit. Slang.* to give (someone) the slip. **—***v.t.* **5.** to ridicule. [after GUY FAWKES]

guy[2] (gī), *n., v.,* **guyed, guy·ing. —***n.* **1.** a rope, cable, or appliance used to guide, steady, or brace an object. **—***v.t.* **2.** to guide, steady, or secure with a guy or guys. [ME *gye* < OF *guie* a guide < *guie(r)* (to) GUIDE]

Gu·ya·na (gī an′ə, -än′ə), *n.* a republic on the NE coast of South America: a former British protectorate; independent 1966; member of British Commonwealth of Nations. 800,000; 82,978 sq. mi. *Cap.:* Georgetown. Formerly, **British Guiana.**

Guy·enne (gwē yen′), *n.* Guienne.

Guy′ Fawkes′ Day′ (gī′ fôks′), (in Britain) November 5, celebrating the anniversary of the capture of Guy Fawkes. Cf. **Gunpowder Plot.**

Guz·mán (go͞os män′), *n.* **Mar·tín Luis** (mär tēn′ lwēs), 1887–1976, Mexican novelist, journalist, and soldier.

guz·zle (guz′əl), *v.i., v.t.,* **-zled, -zling.** to drink or eat greedily, frequently, or plentifully. [?] **—guz′zler,** *n.*

g.v., gravimetric volume.

Gwa·li·or (gwä′lē ôr′), *n.* a city in N Madhya Pradesh, in central India. 406,755.

Gwyn (gwin), *n.* **Eleanor** ("*Nell*"), 1650–87, English actress: mistress of Charles II. Also, **Gwynne.**

gybe (jīb), *v.i., v.t.,* **gybed, gyb·ing,** *n.* *Naut.* jibe[1].

gym (jim), *n.* a gymnasium. [by shortening]

gym·kha·na (jim kä′nə), *n.* **1.** a field day held for equestrians, consisting of exhibitions of horsemanship and much pageantry. **2.** any sporting event, as a gymnastics exhibition, auto race, surfing contest, etc. **3.** a place where any such event is held. [m. Hindi *gendkhāna,* lit., ball-house (influenced by GYMNASTICS)]

gymn-, var. of **gymno-** before a vowel.

gym·na·si·a (jim nā′zē ə, -zhə), *n.* a pl. of **gymnasium.**

gym·na·si·ast[1] (jim nā′zē ast′), *n.* a gymnast. [GYMNASI(UM)[1] + *-ast,* akin to -IST]

gym·na·si·ast[2] (jim nā′zē ast′), *n.* a student in a gymnasium. [< G < NL *gymnasiast(a).* See GYMNASIUM[2], -IST]

gym·na·si·um[1] (jim nā′zē əm), *n., pl.* **-si·ums, -si·a** (-zē ə, -zhə). **1.** a building or room designed and equipped for physical education activities. **2.** a place where Greek youths met for exercise and discussion. [< L: public school for gymnastics < Gk *gymnásion* gymnastic school (< *gymnázein* to train, *gymnós* naked)] **—gym·na′si·al,** *adj.*

gym·na·si·um[2] (jim nā′zē əm; *Ger.* gim nä′zē o͝om′, gym-), *n.* (esp. in Germany) a classical school preparatory to the universities. [< G; special use of GYMNASIUM[1]]

gym·nast (jim′nast), *n.* a person trained and skilled in gymnastics, esp. a teacher of gymnastics. [< Gk *gymnast(ḗs)* trainer of athletes = *gymnáz(ein)* + *-tēs* agent suffix]

gym·nas·tic (jim nas′tik), *adj.* of or pertaining to physical exercises that develop strength and agility. Also, **gym·nas′ti·cal.** [< MF *gymnastique* < L *gymnastic(us)* < Gk *gymnastikós.* See GYMNAST, -IC] **—gym·nas′ti·cal·ly,** *adv.*

gym·nas·tics (jim nas′tiks), *n.* **1.** (*construed as pl.*) gymnastic exercises. **2.** (*construed as sing.*) the practice or art of gymnastic exercises. [see GYMNASTIC, -ICS]

gymno-, a learned borrowing from Greek meaning "naked," "bare," "exposed," used in the formation of compound words: *gymnosperm.* Also, *esp. before a vowel,* **gymn-.** [< Gk, comb. form of *gymnós*]

gym·nos·o·phist (jim nos′ə fist), *n.* one of a group of ascetic philosophers of the Jain sect in ancient India, characterized by refusal to wear clothes and the abandonment of caste marks. [< L *gymnosophist(ae)* Indian ascetic(s) < Gk *gymnosophistaí* naked philosophers] —**gym·nos′o·phy,** *n.*

gym·no·sperm (jim′nə spûrm′), *n.* *Bot.* a plant having its seeds exposed and not enclosed in an ovary; conifer. Cf. **angiosperm.** [< NL *gymnosperm(ae)* name of type] —**gym′no·sperm′ism,** *n.*

gym·no·sper·mous (jim′nə spûr′məs), *adj.* of or pertaining to a gymnosperm; having naked seeds. [< NL *gymnospermus* < Gk *gymnóspermos*]

gym′ shoe′, a canvas shoe with a rubber sole.

gym′ suit,′ any outfit prescribed for wear while participating in gymnastics or sports, usually a comfortable garment allowing freedom of movement.

gyn-, var. of **gyno-** before a vowel: *gynarchy.*

gyn·ae·ce·um[1] (jin′ə sē′əm, gī′nə-, jī′nə-), *n., pl.* **-ce·a** (-sē′ə). (among the ancient Greeks) the part of a dwelling used by women. [< L *gynaecēum* < Gk *gynaikeîon* = *gynaik-* (s. of *gynḗ*) woman + *-eion* n. suffix of place]

gyn·ae·ce·um[2] (jin′ə sē′əm, gī′nə-, jī′nə-), *n., pl.* **-ce·a** (-sē′ə). *Bot.* gynoecium.

gy·nan·dro·morph (ji nan′drə môrf′, gī-, jī-), *n.* *Biol.* an individual exhibiting morphological characters of both sexes. [< Gk *gýnandro(s)* (see GYNANDROUS) + -MORPH] —**gy·nan′dro·mor′phic, gy·nan′dro·mor′phous,** *adj.* —**gy·nan′dro·morph′ism, gy·nan′dro·mor′phy,** *n.*

gy·nan·drous (ji nan′drəs, gī-, jī-), *adj.* *Bot.* having the stamens borne on the pistil and united in a column, as in orchids. [< Gk *gýnandros* of doubtful sex]

gy·nan·dry (ji nan′drē, gī-, jī-), *n.* hermaphroditism. Also, **gy·nan′drism.** [< Gk *gýnandr(os)* (see GYNANDROUS) + -Y[3]]

gyn·ar·chy (jin′ər kē, gī′nər-, jī′nər-), *n., pl.* **-chies.** government by a woman or women. —**gy·narch·ic** (ji när′kik, gī-, jī-), *adj.*

gynec-, var. of **gyneco-** before a vowel: *gynecoid.*

gy·ne·cic (ji nē′sik, -nes′ik, gī-, jī-), *adj.* of or pertaining to women. [< Gk *gynaikik(ós)*]

gy·ne·ci·um (ji nē′sē əm, gī-, jī-), *n., pl.* **-ci·a** (-sē ə). gynoecium.

gyneco-, a learned borrowing from Greek meaning "female," used in the formation of compound words: *gynecology.* Also, **gynec-, gyn-, -gynous, -gyny.** [< Gk, comb. form repr. *gynaik-*, s. of *gynḗ* female, woman]

gyn·e·coc·ra·cy (jin′ə kok′rə sē, gī′nə-, jī′nə-), *n., pl.* **-cies.** gynarchy. [< Gk *gynaikokratía*] —**gy·ne·co·crat** (ji nē′kə krat′, gī-, jī-), *n.* —**gy·ne·co·crat·ic** (ji nē′kə-krat′ik, gī-, jī-; jin′ə-, gī′nə-, jī′nə-), *adj.*

gyn·e·coid (jin′ə koid′, gī′nə-, jī′nə-), *adj.* of or like a woman.

gynecol., 1. gynecological. 2. gynecology.

gy·ne·col·o·gist (gī′nə kol′ə jist, jin′ə-, jī′nə-), *n.* a physician specializing in gynecology.

gy·ne·col·o·gy (gī′nə kol′ə jē, jin′ə-, jī′nə-), *n.* the branch of medical science that deals with the care of women, esp. with reference to reproduction and the reproductive organs. —**gyn·e·co·log·ic** (jin′ə kə loj′ik, gī′nə-, jī′nə-), **gyn′e·co·log′i·cal,** *adj.*

gyn·i·at·rics (jin′ē a′triks, gī′nē-, jī′nē-), *n.* *Pathol.* the treatment of diseases peculiar to women. Also, **gyn′i·a′try.**

gyno-, a learned borrowing from Greek meaning "female," "woman," used in the formation of compound words: *gynophore.* Also, *esp. before a vowel,* **gyn-.** Cf. **gyneco-.** [< Gk, comb. form of *gynḗ*]

gy·noe·ci·um (ji nē′sē əm, gī-, jī-), *n., pl.* **-ci·a** (-sē ə). *Bot.* the pistil, or the pistils collectively, of a flower. Also, **gynaeceum, gynecium.** [< NL < Gk *gynaikeîon* = *gynaik-* GYNEC- + *-eion* suffix of place]

gyn·o·phore (jin′ə fōr′, -fôr′, gī′nə-, jī′nə-), *n.* *Bot.* the elongated pedicel or stalk bearing the pistil in some flowers. —**gyn′o·phor′ic,** *adj.*

-gynous, an adjective combining form referring to the female sex: *androgynous.* [< Gk *-gynos.* See GYNO-, -OUS]

-gyny, a combining form equivalent to a combination of **gyno-,** as final element of compounds, and **-y**[3], or **-gynous** and **-y**[3], used in the formation of abstract nouns: *androgyny.*

Győr (dyœr), *n.* a city in NW Hungary. 74,000 (est. 1962).

gyp[1] (jip), *v.,* **gypped, gyp·ping,** *n.* *Informal.* —*v.t.* **1.** to swindle; cheat; defraud or rob by some sharp practice. —*n.* **2.** a swindle. **3.** Also, **gyp′per.** a swindler or cheat. Also, **gip.** [back formation from GYPSY]

gyp[2] (jip), *n.* *Brit. Informal.* a male college servant, as at Cambridge. [perh. from GYPSY]

gyp·se·ous (jip′sē əs), *adj.* of or pertaining to gypsum. [< LL *gypseus.* See GYPSUM, -EOUS]

gyp·sif·er·ous (jip sif′ər əs), *adj.* containing gypsum. [GYP(SUM) + -I- + -FEROUS]

gyp·soph·i·la (jip sof′ə lə), *n.* any slender, graceful herb of the genus *Gypsophila,* of Mediterranean regions, allied to the pinks and having small, panicled flowers. [< NL < Gk *gýpso(s)* chalk + *phíla* fond of (neut. pl. of *phílos*)]

gyp·sum (jip′səm), *n.* a very common mineral, hydrated calcium sulfate, $CaSO_4 \cdot 2H_2O$, used to make plaster of Paris, as an ornamental material, as a fertilizer, etc. [< L: chalk < Gk *gýpsos* chalk, gypsum]

Gyp·sy (jip′sē), *n., pl.* **-sies,** *adj.* —*n.* **1.** a member of a nomadic, Caucasoid people of generally swarthy complexion, who migrated originally from India. **2.** Romany; the language of the Gypsies. **3.** (*l.c.*) a person who resembles or lives like a Gypsy. **4.** (*l.c.*) Also called **gypsy cab.** *U.S. Informal.* an unlicensed taxicab that is legally allowed to pick up passengers on call by telephone, but often illegally solicits business on the street. —*adj.* **5.** of or pertaining to the Gypsies. [back formation of *gipcyan,* aph. var. of EGYPTIAN, from a belief that Gypsies came originally from Egypt] —**gyp′sy·dom,** *n.* —**gyp′sy·esque′, gyp′sy·ish, gyp′sy·like′, gyp′se·ian,** *adj.* —**gyp′sy·hood′,** *n.* —**gyp′sy·ism,** *n.*

gyp′sy moth′, a moth, *Porthetria dispar,* introduced into the U.S. from Europe, the larvae of which feed on the foliage of trees.

gyr-, var. of **gyro-** before a vowel: *gyral.*

gy·ral (jī′rəl), *adj.* **1.** gyratory. **2.** *Anat.* of or pertaining to a gyrus. —**gy′ral·ly,** *adv.*

gy·rate (*v.* jī′rāt, jī rāt′; *adj.* jī′rāt), *v.,* **-rat·ed, -rat·ing,** *adj.* —*v.i.* **1.** to move in a circle or spiral, or around a fixed point; whirl. —*adj.* **2.** *Zool.* having convolutions. [< L *gȳrāt(us)* wheeled around, turned, rounded (ptp. of *gȳrāre*). See GYR-, -ATE[1]] —**gy′ra·tor,** *n.* —**gy·ra·to·ry** (jī′rə tōr′ē, -tôr′ē), *adj.*

gy·ra·tion (jī rā′shən), *n.* the act of gyrating; circular or spiral motion; revolution; rotation; whirling; spinning. [< LL *gȳrātiōn-* (s. of *gȳrātiō*)] —**gy·ra′tion·al,** *adj.*

gy·ra·to·ry (jī′rə tōr′ē, -tôr′ē), *adj.* moving in a circle or spiral; gyrating. [GYRAT(ION) + -ORY[1]]

gyre (jīᵊr), *n.* **1.** a ring or circle. **2.** a circular course or motion. [< L *gȳr(us)* < Gk *gŷros* ring, circle]

gyr·fal·con (jûr′fal′kən, -fôl′-, -fô′-), *n.* any of several large falcons of arctic and subarctic regions, as *Falco rusticolus candicans,* having white plumage with the upper parts barred and spotted with salty- or brownish-gray. Also, **gerfalcon.** [ME *gerfaucon,* etc. < MF, OF = *ger-* (? < OHG *giri* greedy) + *faucon* FALCON; cf. Icel *geirfalki*]

Gyrfalcon, *Falco rusticolus candicans* (Length 2 ft.)

gy·ro (jī′rō), *n., pl.* **-ros. 1.** gyrocompass. **2.** gyroscope. [independent use of GYRO-]

gyro-, a learned borrowing from Greek meaning "ring," "circle," "spiral," used in the formation of compound words: *gyromagnetic.* Also, *esp. before a vowel,* **gyr-.** [< Gk, comb. form of *gŷros* ring, circle]

gy·ro·com·pass (jī′rō kum′pəs), *n.* a navigational compass containing a gyroscope rotor, that registers the direction of true north along the surface of the earth. [GYRO(SCOPE) + COMPASS]

gy′ro hori′zon, *Aeron.* See **artificial horizon** (def. 3).

gy·roi·dal (jī roid′ᵊl), *adj.* having a spiral arrangement. [GYR- + -OID + -AL[1]] —**gy·roi′dal·ly,** *adv.*

gy·ro·mag·net·ic (jī′rō mag net′ik), *adj.* of or pertaining to the magnetic properties of a rotating charged particle.

gy·ro·pi·lot (jī′rə pī′lət), *n.* *Aeron.* See **automatic pilot.** [GYRO(SCOPE) + PILOT]

gy·ro·plane (jī′rə plān′), *n.* autogiro.

gy·ro·scope (jī′rə skōp′), *n.* an apparatus consisting of a rotating wheel so mounted that its axis can turn freely in certain or all directions, and capable of maintaining the same absolute direction in space in spite of movements of the mountings and surrounding parts. Also called **gyro.** [< F] —**gy·ro·scop·ic** (jī′rə skop′ik), *adj.* —**gy′ro·scop′i·cal·ly,** *adv.* —**gy′ro·scop′ics,** *n.*

Gyroscope

gy·rose (jī′rōs), *adj.* marked with wavy lines.

gy·ro·sta·bi·liz·er (jī′rə stā′bə lī′zər), *n.* a device for stabilizing a seagoing vessel by counteracting its rolling motion from side to side. Also called **gy′roscop′ic sta′bilizer.** [GYRO(SCOPE) + STABILIZER]

gy·ro·stat (jī′rə stat′), *n.* a modified gyroscope, consisting of a rotating wheel pivoted within a rigid case.

gy·ro·stat·ic (jī′rə stat′ik), *adj.* pertaining to the gyrostat or to gyrostatics. —**gy′ro·stat′i·cal·ly,** *adv.*

gy·ro·stat·ics (jī′rə stat′iks), *n.* (*construed as sing.*) *Mech.* the science that deals with the laws of rotating bodies.

gy·rus (jī′rəs), *n., pl.* **gy·ri** (jī′rī). *Anat.* a convolution, esp. of the brain. [< L; see GYRE]

gyve (jīv), *n., v.,* **gyved, gyv·ing.** —*n.* **1.** Usually, **gyves.** a shackle, esp. for the leg; fetter. —*v.t.* **2.** to shackle. [ME]

H

DEVELOPMENT OF MAJUSCULE									
NORTH SEMITIC	GREEK		ETR.	LATIN		MODERN		
						GOTHIC	ITALIC	ROMAN
𐤇	日	H	𐌇	日	H	𝕳	*H*	H

DEVELOPMENT OF MINUSCULE					
ROMAN CURSIVE	ROMAN UNCIAL	CAROL. MIN.	MODERN		
			GOTHIC	ITALIC	ROMAN
ɧ	h	h	𝔥	*h*	h

The eighth letter of the English alphabet is traceable to North Semitic origins. In that early alphabet its pronunciation was similar to that of Scottish *ch.* In Classical Greek, the symbol came to represent *eta* (written H). In English, this letter represents an aspirate sound, but in most Indo-European languages it has seldom been used in this way.

H, h (āch), *n., pl.* **H's** or **Hs, h's** or **hs. 1.** the eighth letter of the English alphabet, a consonant. **2.** any spoken sound represented by the letter *H* or *h*, as in *hot* or *behave.* **3.** something having the shape of an H. **4.** a written or printed representation of the letter *H* or *h.* **5.** a device, as a printer's type, for reproducing the letter *H* or *h.*

H, 1. hard. **2.** *Elect.* henry; henries. **3.** *Slang.* heroin.

H, 1. the eighth in order or in a series. **2.** *Chem.* hydrogen. **3.** *Physics.* **a.** enthalpy. **b.** horizontal component of the earth's magnetic field. **c.** intensity of a magnetic field.

H¹, *Chem.* protium. Also, **¹H, Hᵃ**

H², *Chem.* deuterium. Also, **²H, Hᵇ**

H³, *Chem.* tritium. Also, **³H, Hᶜ**

h, hard.

h, *Physics.* See **Planck's constant.**

h., 1. harbor. **2.** hard. **3.** hardness. **4.** heavy sea. **5.** height. **6.** hence. **7.** high. **8.** *Baseball.* hit; hits. **9.** horns. **10.** hour; hours. **11.** hundred. **12.** husband. Also, **H.**

ha (hä), *interj.* (used as an exclamation of surprise, suspicion, triumph, etc.) Also, **hah.** [ME; see HA-HA¹]

ha, *Metric System.* hectare; hectares.

h.a., in this year. [< L *hōc annō*]

haaf (häf), *n.* deep-sea fishing grounds off the Shetland and Orkney Islands. [< Scand; cf. Icel *haf* sea; c. OE *hæf*]

Haag (häkh), *n.* **Den** (den), a Dutch name of The Hague.

Haa·kon VII (hô′ko͝on), (*Prince Carl of Denmark*) 1872–1957, king of Norway 1905–57; in exile 1940–45.

Haar·lem (här′ləm), *n.* a city in the W Netherlands, W of Amsterdam. 171,009 (1962).

Hab., Habakkuk.

Ha·bak·kuk (hə bak′ək, hab′ə kuk′), *n.* **1.** a Minor Prophet of the 7th century B.C. **2.** a book of the Bible bearing his name. Also, *Douay Bible,* **Ha·bac′uc.**

Ha·ba·na (ä vä′nä), *n.* Spanish name of **Havana.**

ha·ba·ne·ra (hä′bə nâr′ə *or, often,* -nyâr′ə), *n.* **1.** a dance of Cuban origin. **2.** the music for this dance, having a slow duple meter and a rhythm similar to that of a tango. [< Sp (*danza*) *habanera* Havanan (dance)]

ha·be·as cor·pus (hā′bē əs kôr′pəs), *Law.* a writ requiring a person to be brought before a judge or court, esp. for investigation of a restraint of the person's liberty, used as a protection against illegal imprisonment. [late ME < L: lit., have the body (first words of writ) = *habeās* 2nd sing. pres. subj. (with impv. force) of *habēre* to have + *corpus* body]

Ha·ber (hä′bər; *Ger.* hä′bəʀ), *n.* **Fritz** (frits), 1868–1934, German chemist: Nobel prize 1918.

hab·er·dash·er (hab′ər dash′ər), *n.* **1.** *U.S.* a dealer in men's furnishings, as shirts, ties, etc. **2.** *Brit.* a dealer in small wares and notions. [ME *haberdasshere*]

hab·er·dash·er·y (hab′ər dash′ə rē), *n., pl.* **-er·ies. 1.** a haberdasher's shop. **2.** the goods sold there. [late ME *haberdasshrie*]

hab·er·geon (hab′ər jən), *n. Armor.* **1.** a mail garment similar to the hauberk but shorter. **2.** (loosely) a hauberk. Also, **haubergeon.** [ME *haubergeoun* < MF *haubergeon,* dim. of *hauberc* HAUBERK]

Ha′ber proc′ess, a process for synthesizing ammonia from gaseous nitrogen and hydrogen under high pressure and temperature in the presence of a catalyst. [named after Fritz HABER]

hab·ile (hab′il), *adj.* skillful; dexterous. [late ME *habyll* < L *habil(is)* ABLE]

ha·bil·i·ment (hə bil′ə mənt), *n.* **1. habiliments,** equipment; accouterments; furnishings. **2.** Usually, **habiliments.** clothes as worn in a particular profession, way of life, etc. [late ME *(h)abylement* < MF *habillement* = *habill(er),* *abill(ier)* (to) trim a log, hence, dress, prepare (< VL **adbiliare;* see A-⁵, BILLET²) + *-ment* -MENT]

ha·bil·i·tate (hə bil′i tāt′), *v.t.,* **-tat·ed, -tat·ing.** *Archaic.* to clothe or dress. [< LL *habilitāt(us)* made fit, equipped (ptp. of *habilitāre*). See ABILITY, -ATE¹] **—ha·bil′i·ta′tion,** *n.*

hab·it¹ (hab′it), *n.* **1.** customary practice or use. **2.** a particular practice, custom, or usage. **3.** compulsive need, inclination, or use; addiction. **4.** a dominant or regular disposition or tendency; prevailing character or quality. **5.** *Slang.* an addiction to narcotics, esp. to heroin. **6.** an acquired behavior pattern regularly followed until it has become almost involuntary. **7.** mental character or disposition: *a habit of mind.* **8.** characteristic bodily or physical condition. **9.** the characteristic form, aspect, mode of growth, etc., of an animal or plant: *a twining habit.* **10.** the characteristic crystalline form of a mineral. **11.** garb of a particular rank, profession, religious order, etc.: *monk's habit.* **—*v.t.* 12.** to clothe; array. [ME < L *habit(us)* state, style, practice = *habi-* (var. s. of *habēre* to have) + *-tus* verbal n. suffix; r. ME *abit* < OF] **—Syn. 1.** bent, wont. **2.** See **custom. 11.** dress.

hab·it² (hab′it), *v.t.* **1.** *Archaic.* to dwell in. **—*v.i.* 2.** *Obs.* to dwell. [ME *habit(en)* < L *habitā(re)* (to) inhabit; see HABITAT]

hab·it·a·ble (hab′i tə bəl), *adj.* capable of being inhabited. [ME < L *habitābil(is)* (see HABITAT, -BLE); r. ME *abitable* < MF] **—hab′it·a·bil′i·ty, hab′it·a·ble·ness,** *n.* **—hab′it·a·bly,** *adv.*

ha·bi·tan (*Fr.* A bē täɴ′), *n., pl.* **-tans** (-täɴ′). habitant².

hab·it·ant¹ (hab′i tᵊnt), *n.* an inhabitant. [< L *habitant-* (s. of *habitāns*), prp. of *habitāre* to inhabit]

ha·bi·tant² (hab′i tᵊnt; *Fr.* A bē täɴ′), *n., pl.* **ha·bi·tants** (hab′i tᵊnts; *Fr.* A bē täɴ′). a French settler in Canada or Louisiana, or a descendant of one, esp. a farmer. [< F, prp. of *habiter* < L *habitāre* to inhabit; see HABITAT]

hab·i·tat (hab′i tat′), *n.* **1.** the native environment of an animal or plant; the kind of place that is natural for the life and growth of an animal or plant. **2.** place of abode; habitation. **3.** a pressurized cylindrical chamber with compartments, used as undersea living quarters for aquanauts. [< L: it inhabits, 3rd sing. pres. ind. of *habitāre,* freq. of *habēre* to have, hold]

hab·i·ta·tion (hab′i tā′shən), *n.* **1.** a place of residence; dwelling; abode. **2.** the act of inhabiting; occupancy by inhabitants. **3.** a settlement or community. [< L *habitātiōn-* (s. of *habitātiō*) a dwelling = *habitāt(us)* inhabited (ptp. of *habitāre;* see HABITAT) + *-iōn-* -ION; r. ME *(h)abitacioun* < AF] **—hab′i·ta′tion·al,** *adj.* **—Syn. 1.** residence, domicile.

hab·it-form·ing (hab′it fôr′ming), *adj.* tending to become a habit, esp. when based upon physiological dependence.

ha·bit·u·al (hə bich′o͞o əl), *adj.* **1.** of the nature of a habit; fixed by or resulting from habit. **2.** being such by habit: *a habitual gossip.* **3.** commonly used, as by a particular person; customary: *She took her habitual place at the table.* [< ML *habituāl(is)* relating to dress, condition, or habit] **—ha·bit′u·al·ly,** *adv.* **—ha·bit′u·al·ness,** *n.* **—Syn. 2.** confirmed, inveterate. **3.** accustomed, regular. See **usual. —Ant. 2.** occasional. **3.** unaccustomed.

ha·bit·u·ate (hə bich′o͞o āt′), *v.t.,* **-at·ed, -at·ing. 1.** to accustom (a person, the mind, etc.) to something; make used to; acclimate: *Wealth habituated him to luxury.* **2.** *Archaic.* to frequent. [< LL *habituāt(us)* conditioned, constituted (ptp. of *habituāre*). See HABIT¹, -ATE¹] **—ha·bit′u·a′tion,** *n.* **—Syn. 1.** familiarize, acclimatize, train.

hab·i·tude (hab′i to͞od′, -tyo͞od′), *n.* **1.** customary condition or character. **2.** a habit or custom. **3.** *Obs.* familiar relationship. [late ME < MF < L *habitūd(ō)*] **—hab′i·tu′di·nal,** *adj.*

ha·bit·u·é (hə bich′o͞o ā′, -bich′o͞o ā′; *Fr.* A bē twā′), *n., pl.* **ha·bit·u·és** (hə bich′o͞o āz′, -bich′o͞o āz′; *Fr.* A bē twā′). a habitual frequenter of a place: *a habitué of bars and nightclubs.* [< F, n. use of masc. ptp. of *habituer* < LL *habituāre.* See HABITUATE]

Ha·bor (*Turk.* hä′bo͝oʀ), *n.* Khabur. Also, **Ha′bur.**

Habs·burg (haps′bûrg; *Ger.* häps′bo͝oʀk′), *n.* Hapsburg.

ha·ček (hä′chek), *n.* a mark (ˇ) placed over a consonant, as over *c* or *s* in Czech or *ğ* in Turkish, etc., to indicate that the sounds are palatalized, Czech *č* or *š* becoming (ch) or (sh) respectively, Turkish *ğ* becoming (y); or over a vowel, as over *e* in Czech, to indicate that the sound has a consonantal quality, *ě* becoming (ye). Also, **há′ček** [< Czech]

ha·chure (*n.* ha sho͝or′, hash′o͝or; *v.* ha sho͝or′), *n., v.,* **-chured, -chur·ing. —*n.* 1.** one of several parallel lines drawn on a map to indicate relief features, the width of the spacing between the lines, and the breadth of the lines indicating the slope. **2.** shading composed of such lines; hatching. **—*v.t.* 3.** to indicate or shade by hachures. [< F; see HATCH³, -URE]

ha·ci·en·da (hä′sē en′də; *Sp.* ä syen′dä), *n., pl.* **-das** (-dəz; *Sp.* -däs). (in Spanish America) **1.** a landed estate, esp. one used for farming or ranching. **2.** the main house on such an estate. **3.** a stock-raising, mining, or manufacturing establishment in the country. [< Sp < L *facienda* things to be done or made, neut. pl. of *faciendus,* fut. pass. participle of *facere* to DO¹, make]

Ha·ci·en·da Heights (hä′sē en′da hīts′), a town in SW California. 35,969 (1970).

hack¹ (hak), *v.t.* **1.** to cut, notch, slice, chop, or sever (something) with or as with heavy, irregular blows. **2.** to break up the surface of (the ground). **3.** to clear (a road, path, etc.) by cutting away vines, trees, brush, or the like: *They hacked a trail through the jungle.* **4.** to damage or injure by crude, harsh, or insensitive treatment; mutilate; mangle: *The editor hacked the story to bits.* **5.** to reduce or cut ruthlessly; trim: *The Senate hacked the budget almost in half before returning it to the House.* **6.** *Basketball.* to strike the arm of (an opposing ball handler). **7.** *Brit.* to kick or kick at the shins of (an opposing player) in Rugby football. **—*v.i.* 8.** to make rough cuts or notches; deal cutting blows. **9.** to cough harshly, usually in short and repeated spasms. **10.** *Brit.* to kick or kick at an opponent's shins in Rugby football. **—*n.* 11.** a cut, gash, or notch. **12.** a tool, as an ax, hoe, pick, etc., for hacking. **13.** an act or an instance of hacking; a cutting blow. **14.** a short, rasping cough. [ME *hacke(n),* OE *(tō)haccian* to hack to pieces; c. D *hakken,* G *hacken*] **—hack′er,** *n.* **—Syn. 1.** mangle, haggle. See **cut.**

hack² (hak), *n.* **1.** a person, as an artist or writer, who exploits, for money, his creative ability or training in the production of dull, unimaginative, and trite work; one who produces banal and mediocre work in the hope of gaining commercial success in the arts. **2.** a professional who renounces or surrenders individual independence, integrity, belief, etc., in return for money or other reward in the performance of a task normally thought of as involving a strong personal commitment: *a political hack.* **3.** a writer who works on the staff of a publisher at a dull or routine task; someone who works as a literary drudge. **4.** an old or worn-out horse; jade. **5.** *U.S.* a coach or carriage kept for hire; hackney. **6.** *Informal.* **a.** a taxi. **b.** Also, **hackie.** a cabdriver. **7.** *Brit.* **a.** a horse kept for common hire or adapted for general work, esp. ordinary riding. **b.** a saddle horse used for transportation, rather than for show, hunting, or the like. **—*v.t.* 8.** to make a hack of; let out for hire. **9.** to make trite or stale by frequent use. **—*v.i.* 10.** *Brit.* to ride on the road at an ordinary pace, as distinguished from cross-country or military riding. **11.** *Informal.* to drive a taxi. **—*adj.* 12.** hired; of a hired sort: *a hack writer; hack work.* **13.** hackneyed; trite; banal: *hack writing.* [short for HACKNEY]

hack[3] (hak), *n.* **1.** a rack for drying food, such as fish. **2.** a rack for holding fodder for livestock. **—*v.t.* 3.** to place (something) on a hack, as for drying, feeding, etc. [var. of HATCH[2]]

hack·a·more (hak′ə mōr′, -môr′), *n.* **1.** a simple looped bridle, by means of which controlling pressure is exerted on the nose of a horse, used chiefly in breaking colts. **2.** *Western U.S.* any of several forms of halter used esp. for breaking horses. [alter. (by folk etym.) of Sp *jáquima* headstall < Ar *shaqīmah*]

hack·ber·ry (hak′ber′ē, -bə rē), *n., pl.* **-ries. 1.** the small, edible, cherrylike fruit of any American, ulmaceous tree of the genus *Celtis.* **2.** a tree bearing this fruit. **3.** the wood of any of these trees. [var. of HAGBERRY]

hack·but (hak′but), *n.* harquebus. [earlier *hacquebuta* < MF, var. of *haquebusch* < MD *hakebusse,* lit., hook gun; see HARQUEBUS] **—hack·but·eer** (hak′bə tēr′), *n.*

Hack·en·sack (hak′ən sak′), *n.* a city in NE New Jersey, near New York City. 36,008 (1970).

hack·er (hak′ər), *n.* **1.** a person or thing that hacks. **2.** *Slang.* a person who engages in an activity without talent or skill. **3.** *Computer Technol. Slang.* **a.** a computer enthusiast. **b.** a microcomputer user who attempts to gain unauthorized access to proprietary computer systems.

hack′ ham′mer, an adzlike tool for dressing stone.

hack·ie (hak′ē), *n.* *Informal.* hack[2] (def. 6b).

hack′ing jack′et, *Chiefly Brit.* a riding jacket having a tight waist, flared skirt, slanted pockets with flaps, and slits or vents at the sides or back. Also called **hack′ing coat′.**

hack·le[1] (hak′əl), *n., v.,* **-led, -ling. —*n.* 1.** one of the long, slender feathers on the neck or saddle of certain birds, as the domestic rooster, much used in making artificial flies for anglers. **2.** the whole neck plumage of the domestic rooster or the like. **3. hackles, a.** the hair on the back of the neck of an animal. **b.** anger, esp. when aroused in a challenging or challenged manner: *with one's hackles up; to raise the hackles of someone.* **4.** *Angling.* **a.** the legs of an artificial fly made with feathers from the neck or saddle of a rooster or other such bird. **b.** See **hackle fly. 5.** a comb for dressing flax or hemp. **—*v.t.* 6.** *Angling.* to equip with a hackle. **7.** to comb, as flax or hemp. Also, **hatchel, heckle** (for defs. 5, 7). [ME *hakell;* see HECKLE] **—hack′ler,** *n.*

hack·le[2] (hak′əl), *v.t.,* **-led, -ling.** to cut roughly; hack; mangle. [HACK[1] + -LE; c. MD *hakkelen*]

hack′le fly′, *Angling.* an artificial fly made with hackles, usually without wings. Also called **hackle.**

hack·ly (hak′lē), *adj.* rough or jagged as if hacked: *a hackly fracture.*

hack·man (hak′mən, -man′), *n., pl.* **-men,** (-mən, -men′). *U.S.* the driver of a hack.

hack·ma·tack (hak′mə tak′), *n.* **1.** the tamarack, *Larix laricina.* **2.** the wood of this tree. [earlier *hakmantak* < Algonquian]

hack·ney (hak′nē), *n., pl.* **-neys,** *adj., v.* **—*n.* 1.** a horse used for ordinary riding or driving. **2.** a trotting horse used for drawing a light carriage or the like. **3.** (*cap.*) one of an English breed of horses having a high-stepping gait. **4.** a carriage or automobile for hire; cab. **—*adj.* 5.** let out, employed, or done for hire. **—*v.t.* 6.** *Archaic.* to make trite, common, or stale by frequent use. **7.** *Archaic.* to use as a hackney. [ME *hakeney,* special use of place-name *Hackney,* Middlesex, England] **—hack′ney·ism,** *n.*

hack′ney coach′, 1. a coach available for hire. **2.** a four-wheeled carriage having six seats and drawn by two horses.

hack·neyed (hak′nēd), *adj.* made commonplace or trite; stale; banal. **—Syn.** overdone, overused. See **commonplace.**

hack·saw (hak′sô′), *n.* a saw for cutting metal, consisting typically of a narrow, fine-toothed blade held in a frame. Also, **hack′ saw′.** See illus. at **saw**[1].

had (had), *v.* pt. and pp. of **have.**

Ha·das (had′əs, hä′dəs), *n.* **Moses,** 1900–66, U.S. classical scholar, teacher, and author.

Ha·das·sah (hə dä′sə, hä-), *n.* a benevolent organization of Jewish women founded in New York City in 1912 by Henrietta Szold. [after the Hebrew name (meaning "myrtle") of Queen Esther; see Esther 2:7]

Had·ding·ton (had′ing tən), *n.* former name of **East Lothian.**

had·dock (had′ək), *n., pl.* (*esp. collectively*) **-dock,** (*esp. referring to two or more kinds or species*) **-docks.** a food fish, *Melanogrammus aeglefinus,* of the cod family, found in the North Atlantic. [ME *haddok;* see -OCK]

hade (hād), *n., v.,* **had·ed had·ing.,** *Geol.* **—*n.* 1.** the angle between a fault plane and a vertical plane. **—*v.i.* 2.** to incline from a vertical position. [?]

Ha·des (hā′dēz), *n.* **1.** *Class. Myth.* **a.** the underworld inhabited by departed souls. **b.** the god ruling the underworld; Pluto. **2.** (in the Revised Version of the New Testament) the abode or state of the dead. **3.** (*often l.c.*) hell. **—Ha·de·an** (hā dē′ən, hā′dē ən), *adj.*

Ha·dhra·maut (hä′drä môt′), *n.* a coastal region in E Southern Yemen: unexcavated ruins. Also, **Ha′dra·maut′. —Ha·dhra·mau·tian** (hä′drə mô′shən), *adj., n.*

hadj (haj), *n., pl.* **hadj·es.** hajj.

hadj·i (haj′ē), *n., pl.* **hadj·is.** hajji.

had·n't (had′ənt), contraction of *had not.*

Ha·dri·an (hā′drē ən), *n.* (*Publius Aelius Hadrianus*) A.D. 76–138, Roman emperor 117–138. Also, **Adrian.**

Hadrian I, etc. See **Adrian I,** etc.

Ha′drian's Wall′, a wall of defense for the Roman province of Britain, constructed by Hadrian between Solway Firth and the mouth of the Tyne.

hadst (hadst), *v.* *Archaic.* a 2nd pers. sing. pt. indic. of **have.**

hae (hā, ha), *v.t., auxiliary verb. Scot.* have.

Haeck·el (hek′əl), *n.* **Ernst Hein·rich** (ernst hīn′rikh), 1834–1919, German biologist and philosopher. **—Haeck·e·li·an** (he kē′lē ən), *adj., n.* **—Haeck′el·ism,** *n.*

haem-, var. of **hem-:** *haemal.*

haema-, var. of **hema-:** *haemachrome.*

haem·a·chrome (hem′ə krōm′, hē′mə-), *n.* hemachrome.

hae·mal (hē′məl), *adj.* hemal.

haemat-, var. of **haemato-** before a vowel: *haematal.*

haem·a·tal (hem′ə tᵊl, hē′mə-), *adj.* hemal (def. 1).

hae·mat·ic (hi mat′ik), *adj., n.* hematic.

haem·a·tin (hem′ə tin, hē′mə-), *n.* hematin.

haemato-, var. of **hemato-:** *haematocryal.* Also, *esp. before a vowel,* **haemat-.**

haem·a·to·blast (hem′ə tō blast′, hē′mə-), *n.* hematoblast.

haem·a·toc·ry·al (hem′ə tok′rē əl, hem′ə tō krī′əl, hē′mə-), *adj.* hematocryal.

haem·a·to·cyte (hem′ə tō sīt′, hē′mə-), *n.* hemocyte.

haem·a·tog·e·nous (hem′ə toj′ə nəs, hē′mə-), *adj.* hematogenous.

haem·a·tol·o·gy (hem′ə tol′ə jē, hē′mə-), *n.* hematology.

haem·a·to·ma (hem′ə tō′mə, hē′mə-), *n., pl.* **-mas, -ma·ta** (-mə tə). hematoma.

haem·a·to·poi·e·sis (hem′ə tō poi ē′sis, hē′mə-), *n.* hematopoiesis.

haem·a·to·sis (hem′ə tō′sis, hē′mə-), *n.* hematosis.

haem·a·to·ther·mal (hem′ə tō thûr′məl, hē′mə-), *adj.* hematothermal.

hae·ma·tox·y·lin (hē′mə tok′sə lən, hem′ə-), *n.* hematoxylin. **—hae·ma·tox·yl·ic** (hē′mə tok sil′ik, hem′ə-), *adj.*

hae·ma·tox·y·lon (hē′mə tok′sə lon′, hem′ə-), *n.* **1.** the wood of the logwood. **2.** hematoxylin.

haem·a·to·zo·on (hem′ə tə zō′on, -ən, hē′mə-), *n., pl.* **-zo·a** (-zō′ə). hematozoon. Also, **haem′a·to·zo′ön.**

-haemia, var. of **-emia** after *p, t, k.*

hae·mic (hē′mik, hem′ik), *adj.* hemic.

hae·min (hē′min), *n.* hemin.

haemo-, var. of **hemo-:** *haemoglobin.* Also, *esp. before a vowel,* **haem-.**

hae·mo·blast (hē′mə blast′, hem′ə-), *n.* hematoblast.

hae·mo·cyte (hē′mə sīt′, hem′ə-), *n.* hemocyte.

hae·mo·glo·bin (hē′mə glō′bin, hem′ə-), *n.* hemoglobin. **—hae′mo·glo′bic, hae′mo·glo′bin·ous,** *adj.*

hae·mol·y·sin (hi mol′i sən, hē′mə lī′-, hem′ə-), *n.* hemolysin.

hae·mol·y·sis (hi mol′i sis), *n.* hemolysis. **—hae·mo·lyt·ic** (hē′mə lit′ik, hem′ə-), *adj.*

hae·mo·phil·i·a (hē′mə fil′ē ə, -fēl′yə, hem′ə-), *n.* hemophilia. **—hae′mo·phil,** *n.*

hae·mo·phil·i·ac (hē′mə fil′ē ak′, -fē′lē-, hem′ə-), *n.* hemophiliac.

hae·mo·phil·ic (hē′mə fil′ik, hem′ə-), *adj.* hemophilic.

haem·or·rhage (hem′ər ij, hem′rij), *n., v.,* **-rhaged, -rhag·ing.** hemorrhage. **—haem·or·rhag·ic** (hem′ə raj′ik), *adj.*

haem·or·rhoid (hem′ə roid′, hem′roid), *n.* hemorrhoid. **—haem′or·rhoi′dal,** *adj.*

hae·mo·sta·sis (hi mos′tə sis, hē′mə stā′sis, hem′ə-), *n.* *Med.* hemostasis. Also, **hae·mo·sta·sia** (hē′mə stā′zhə, -zhē ə, -zē ə, hem′ə-).

hae·mo·stat (hē′mə stat′, hem′ə-), *n.* hemostat.

hae·mo·stat·ic (hē′mə stat′ik, hem′ə-), *adj., n.* hemostatic.

Hae′mus Moun′tains (hē′məs), a mountain range in the first quadrant of the face of the moon forming the southeast border of Mare Serenitatis.

hae·res (hēr′ēz), *n., pl.* **hae·re·des** (hi rē′dēz). *Civil Law.* heres.

ha·fiz (hä′fiz), *n.* a title of respect for a Muslim who knows the Koran by heart. [< Ar *hāfiz* a guard, one who keeps (in memory)]

Ha·fiz (hä fiz′), *n.* (pen name of *Shams ud-din Mohammed*) c1320–89?, Persian poet.

haf·ni·um (haf′nē əm, häf′-), *n.* *Chem.* a metallic element having a valence of four, found in zirconium ores. *Symbol:* Hf; *at. wt.:* 178.49; *at. no.:* 72; *sp. gr.:* 12.1. [< NL *Hafn(ia)* Copenhagen + -IUM]

haft (haft, häft), *n.* **1.** a handle, esp. of a knife, sword, dagger, etc. **—*v.t.* 2.** to furnish with a haft or handle. [ME; OE *hæft* handle, lit., that which is taken, grasped; c. L *captus;* akin to G *Heft* handle] **—haft′er,** *n.*

Haf·ta·rah (häf tôr′ə; *Heb.* häf tä rä′), *n., pl.* **-ta·roth** (-tôr′ōt; *Heb.* -tä rôt′), **-ta·rahs.** *Judaism.* a portion of the Prophets that is chanted or read in the synagogue on the Sabbath and on holy days immediately following the Parashah. Also, **Haphtarah.** [< Heb: finish, ending]

hag[1] (hag), *n.* **1.** an ugly old woman, esp. a vicious or malicious one. **2.** a witch. **3.** a hagfish. [ME *hagge,* OE **hægge,* akin to *hægtes(se)* witch, *hagorūn* spell, G *Hexe* witch] **—hag′gish,** *adj.* **—hag′gish·ly,** *adv.* **—hag′gish·ness,** *n.*

hag[2] (hag, häg), *n.* *Brit. Dial.* **1.** a soft spot in a bog or marsh; quagmire. 2. a firm spot or island of firm ground in a bog or marsh. [ME: chasm < Scand; cf. Icel *högg* a cut, ravine]

Hag., Haggai.

Ha·gar (hā′gär, -gər), *n.* the mother of Ishmael. Gen. 16.

hag·ber·ry (hag′ber′ē, -bə rē), *n., pl.* **-ries.** the American hackberry. [< Scand; cf. Dan *hæggebær*]

hag·born (hag′bôrn′), *adj.* born of a hag or witch.

hag·but (hag′but), *n.* harquebus. [var. of HACKBUT]

Ha·gen (hä′gən), *n.* (in the *Nibelungenlied*) the killer of Siegfried, himself killed by Kriemhild, Siegfried's wife.

Ha·gers·town (hā′gərz toun′), *n.* a city in NW Maryland. 35,862 (1970).

hag·fish (hag′fish′), *n., pl.* (*esp. collectively*) **-fish,** (*esp. referring to two or more kinds or species*) **-fish·es.** any eellike, marine cyclostome of the order *Hyperotreta,* having undeveloped eyes, a barbel-rimmed, circular mouth, and horny teeth for boring into the flesh of fishes to feed on their interior parts.

Hagfish, *Myxine glutinosa* (Length 1½ ft.)

Hag·ga·da (hə gä′də; *Heb.* hä gä dä′), *n., pl.* **-doth** (-dōs, -dōt; *Heb.* -dôt′), **-dahs.** Haggadah (def. 1).

Hag·ga·dah (hə gä′də; *Heb.* hä gä dä′), *n., pl.* **-doth** (-dōs, -dōt; *Heb.* -dôt′), **-dahs.** 1. a book containing the liturgy for the Seder service. 2. Aggadah [< Heb: narrative, akin to *higgid* to tell] —**hag·gad·ic** (hə gad′ik, -gä′dik), **hag·gad′i·cal,** *adj.*

hag·ga·dist (hə gä′dist), *n.* 1. one of the writers of the Aggadah. 2. a person versed in the Aggadah. —**hag·ga·dist·ic** (hag′ə dis′tik), *adj.*

Hag·ga·i (hag′ē ī′, hag′ī), *n.* 1. a Minor Prophet of the 6th century B.C. 2. a book of the Bible bearing his name.

hag·gard (hag′ərd), *adj.* 1. having a gaunt, wasted, or exhausted appearance, as from suffering, exertion, anxiety, etc. 2. wild; wild-looking: *haggard eyes.* 3. *Falconry.* (esp. of a hawk caught after it has attained adult plumage) untamed. —*n.* 4. *Falconry.* a wild or untamed adult hawk. [orig., wild female hawk; see HAG[1], -ARD] —**hag′gard·ly,** *adv.* —**hag′gard·ness,** *n.* —**Syn.** 1. emaciated, drawn.

hag·gis (hag′is), *n. Chiefly Scot.* a dish made of the heart, liver, etc., of a sheep or calf, minced with suet and oatmeal, seasoned, and boiled in the stomach of the animal. [late ME *hageys* < AF **hageis* = *hag-* (root of *haguer* to chop, hash < MD *hacken* to HACK[1]) + *-eis* n. suffix used in cookery terms]

hag·gle (hag′əl), *v.,* **-gled, -gling,** *n.* —*v.i.* 1. to bargain in a petty, quibbling, and naggingly quarrelsome manner. 2. to wrangle, dispute, or cavil. —*v.t.* 3. to mangle in cutting; hack. 4. *Archaic.* to harass with wrangling or haggling. —*n.* 5. the act of haggling; a wrangle or dispute over terms. [ME *hagge* to cut, chop (< Scand) + -LE] —**hag′gler,** *n.*

hag·i·arch·y (hag′ē är′kē, hā′jē-), *n., pl.* **-arch·ies.** hagiocracy.

hagio-, a learned borrowing from Greek meaning "saint," "holy," used in the formation of compound words: *hagiography.* Also, *esp. before a vowel,* **hagi-.** [< Gk, comb. form of *hágios* holy, sacred]

hag·i·oc·ra·cy (hag′ē ok′rə sē, hā′jē-), *n., pl.* **-cies.** 1. government by a body of persons esteemed as holy. 2. a state so governed. Also, **hagiarchy.**

Hag·i·og·ra·pha (hag′ē og′rə fə, hā′jē-), *n.* (*construed as sing.*) the third of the three Jewish divisions of the Old Testament, usually comprising the Psalms, Proverbs, Job, Song of Solomon, Ruth, Lamentations, Ecclesiastes, Esther, Daniel, Ezra, Nehemiah, and Chronicles. Cf. **Law of Moses, Prophets.** [< LL < Gk: sacred writings = *hagio-* HAGIO- + *-grapha,* neut. pl. of *-graphos* -GRAPH]

hag·i·og·ra·pher (hag′ē og′rə fər, hā′jē-), *n.* 1. one of the writers of the Hagiographa. 2. a writer of lives of the saints. Also, **hag′i·og′ra·phist.** [< ML *hagiograph(us)* writer of sacred books (< Gk *hagiógraphos*) + -ER[1]]

hag·i·og·ra·phy (hag′ē og′rə fē, hā′jē-), *n., pl.* **-phies.** the writing and critical study of the lives of the saints. —**hag·i·o·graph·ic** (hag′ē ə graf′ik, hā′jē-), **hag′i·o·graph′i·cal,** *adj.*

hag·i·ol·a·try (hag′ē ol′ə trē, hā′jē-), *n.* the worship of saints. —**hag′i·ol′a·ter,** *n.* —**hag′i·ol′a·trous,** *adj.*

hag·i·ol·o·gy (hag′ē ol′ə jē, hā′jē-), *n., pl.* **-gies** for 2, 3. 1. the branch of literature dealing with the lives and legends of the saints. 2. a biography of a saint or saints. 3. a collection of these. —**hag·i·o·log·ic** (hag′ē ə loj′ik, hā′jē-), **hag′i·o·log′i·cal,** *adj.* —**hag′i·ol′o·gist,** *n.*

hag·rid·den (hag′rid′ən), *adj.* worried or tormented, as by a witch.

Hague, The (hāg), a city in the W Netherlands, near the North Sea: site of the government, royal residence, and of the International Court of Justice. 479,369. Dutch, **Den Haag, 's Gravenhage.**

Hague′ Tribu′nal, the court of arbitration for the peaceful settlement of international disputes, established at The Hague in 1899.

hah (hä), *interj.* ha.

ha-ha[1] (hä′hä′), *interj., n.* (used as an exclamation or representation of laughter, as in expressing amusement, derision, etc. Cf. **haw-haw.** [ME, OE; imit. orig.]

ha-ha[2] (hä′hä′), *n.* a barrier consisting of a trench or ditch. [< F *haha*]

Hah·ne·mann (hä′nə mən; *Ger.* hä′nə män′), *n.* **(Christian Fre·drich) Sam·u·el** (kris′chən frē′drik sam′yōō əl; *Ger.* kris′tē än frā′drikh zä′mōō el), 1755–1843, German physician: founder of homeopathy. —**Hah·ne·mann·i·an** (hä′nə man′ē ən, -mä′nē-), *adj.* —**Hah′ne·mann′ism,** *n.*

Hai·da (hī′də), *n., pl.* **-das,** (*esp. collectively*) **-da** for 1. 1. a member of an Indian people inhabiting the Queen Charlotte Islands in British Columbia and Prince of Wales Island in Alaska. 2. the language of the Haida people.

Hai·dar·a·bad (hī′dər ə bäd′, -bad′, hī′drə-), *n.* Hyderabad.

Hai·dar A·li (hī′dər ä′lē, ä lē′), 1722–82, Islamic prince and military leader of India: ruler of Mysore 1759–82. Also, **Hyder Ali.**

Hai·duk (hī′dŏŏk), *n.* 1. one of a class of mercenary soldiers in 16th-century Hungary. 2. a patriotic brigand in the Slav portions of the Balkan Peninsula. Also, **Heyduck, Heyduke, Heyduc, Heiduc, Heiduk.** [< Hung *hajdúk,* pl. of *hajdú* brigand]

Hai·fa (hī′fə), *n.* a seaport in NW Israel. 227,200.

Haig (hāg), *n.* 1. **Alexander,** born 1924, U.S. general and statesman: Secretary of State 1981–82. 2. **Douglas, 1st Earl,** 1861–1928, British field marshal: commander of British forces in France 1915–18.

haik (hīk, hāk), *n.* an oblong cloth used as an outer garment by the Arabs. [< Ar *ḥā'ik, ḥayk,* akin to *ḥāk* weave]

hai·ku (hī′kōō), *n., pl.* **-ku** for 2. 1. a major form of Japanese verse, written in 17 syllables, divided into 3 lines of 5, 7, and 5 syllables, and employing highly evocative allusions and comparisons. 2. a poem written in this form. [< Jap]

hail[1] (hāl), *v.t.* 1. to salute or greet; welcome. 2. to call out to in order to stop, attract attention, ask aid, etc.: *to hail a cab.* 3. to acclaim; approve enthusiastically: *The crowds hailed the conquerors.* —*v.i.* 4. to call out in order to greet, attract attention, etc. 5. **hail from,** to have as one's place of birth or residence. —*n.* 6. a shout or call to attract attention. 7. a salutation or greeting. 8. the act of hailing. —*interj.* 9. (used as a salutation, greeting, or acclamation.) [ME *haile,* earlier *heilen* < *hail* health < Scand; cf. Icel *heill;* c. OE *hǣl.* See WASSAIL] —**hail′er,** *n.*

hail[2] (hāl), *n.* 1. showery precipitation in the form of irregular pellets or balls of ice more than 1/3 inch in diameter, falling from a cumulonimbus cloud. 2. a shower or storm of such precipitation. 3. a shower of anything: *a hail of bullets.* —*v.i.* 4. to pour down hail (often used impersonally with *it* as subject): *It hailed the whole afternoon.* 5. to fall or shower as hail. —*v.t.* 6. to pour down on as or like hail: *The plane hailed leaflets on the city.* [ME; OE *hægl,* var. of *hagol;* c. G *Hagel,* Icel *hagl*]

Hai·le Se·las·sie (hī′lē sə las′ē, -lä′sē), (*Ras Taffari* or *Tafari*), 1891–1975, emperor of Ethiopia 1930–74: in exile 1936–41.

hail-fel·low (*n.* hāl′fel′ō; *adj.* hāl′fel′ō), *n.* 1. Also, **hail′ fel′low′, hail′-fel′low well′ met′.** a spiritedly sociable person; jolly companion. —*adj.* 2. sociable; genial.

Hail′ Mar′y. See **Ave Maria.** [ME, trans. of ML *Ave Maria*]

hail·stone (hāl′stōn′), *n.* a pellet of hail. [ME; OE *hagolstān*]

hail·storm (hāl′stôrm′), *n.* a storm with hail.

Hai·nan (hī′nän′), *n.* 1. an island in the South China Sea, separated from the mainland of S China by Hainan Strait: a part of Kwangtung province. 2,800,000; ab. 13,200 sq. mi. 2. **Strait,** a strait between this island and the S mainland of China. 50 mi. long; 15 mi. wide.

Hai·naut (e nō′), *n.* a medieval county in territory now in SW Belgium and N France.

hain't (hānt), *Dial.* ain't; have not; has not. [orig. contr. of *have not, has not* (with loss of consonant and compensatory lengthening of *a*): influenced in use by AIN'T]

Hai·phong (hī′fong′), *n.* a seaport near Hanoi in N Vietnam, on the Gulf of Tonkin. 1,190,900.

hair (hâr), *n.* 1. any of the numerous fine, usually cylindrical filaments growing from the skin of man and animals. 2. an aggregate of such filaments, as that covering the human head or forming the coat of most mammals. 3. a similar fine, filamentous outgrowth from the body of insects, spiders, etc.

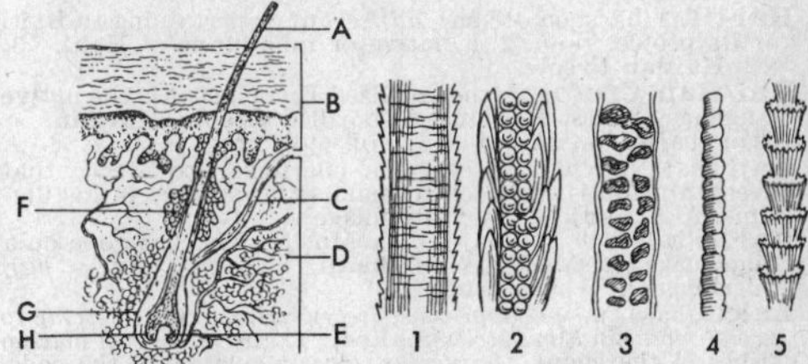

Hair
Cross section of skin containing: A, Hair; B, Epidermis; C, Muscle; D, Dermis; E, Papilla; F, Sebaceous glands; G, Follicle; H, Root. Longitudinal sections of hairs: 1, Man; 2, Sable; 3, Mouse. External view: 4, Mouse; 5, Indian bat

4. *Bot.* a filamentous outgrowth of the epidermis. 5. cloth made of hair from animals, as camel and alpaca. 6. a very small amount, degree, measure, magnitude, etc.; a fraction, as of time or space. 7. **get in someone's hair,** *Slang.* to annoy or bother someone. 8. **hair of the dog,** *Slang.* a drink of liquor, supposed to remedy a hangover. Also, **hair of the dog that bit one.** 9. **let one's hair down, a.** to relax; behave informally. **b.** to speak candidly or frankly; remove or reduce restraints. 10. **make one's hair stand on end,** to strike with horror; terrify. 11. **split hairs,** to make unnecessarily fine or petty distinctions. 12. **tear one's hair,** to manifest extreme anxiety, grief, or anger. Also, **tear one's hair out.** 13. **to a hair,** exactly; perfect to the smallest detail. 14. **without turning a hair,** showing no excitement or emotion; remaining calm. Also, **not turn a hair.** [ME *heer,* OE *hǣr* (c. D, G *haar,* Icel *hār*) + ME *haire* hair shirt < OF < OHG *hāria;* c. ME *here,* OE *hǣre,* Icel *hǣra*] —**hair′like′,** *adj.*

hair·brained (hâr′brānd′), *adj.* harebrained.

hair·breadth (hâr′bredth′, -bretth′), *n., adj.* hair's-breadth.

hair·brush (hâr′brush′), *n.* a brush for dressing the hair.

hair·cloth (hâr′klôth′, -kloth′), *n.* cloth of hair from the manes and tails of horses, woven with a cotton warp, and used for interlinings of clothes, upholstery, etc. Also called **cilice.**

hair·cut (hâr′kut′), *n.* **1.** the act or an instance of cutting the hair. **2.** the style in which the hair is cut and worn, esp. men's hair. —**hair′cut′ter,** *n.* —**hair′cut′ting,** *n., adj.*

hair·do (hâr′do͞o′), *n., pl.* **-dos.** **1.** the style in which a woman's hair is cut, arranged, and worn; coiffure. **2.** the hair itself, esp. when newly or elaborately arranged.

hair·dress·er (hâr′dres′ər), *n.* **1.** a person who arranges or cuts women's hair. **2.** *Chiefly Brit.* barber.

hair·dress·ing (hâr′dres′iŋ), *n.* **1.** the act or process of cutting, styling, or dressing hair. **2.** the vocation or occupation of a hairdresser. **3.** a hairdo; coiffure. **4.** a preparation applied to the hair for increased manageability.

hair′ fol′licle, *Anat.* a small cavity from which a hair develops.

hair·less (hâr′lis), *adj.* without hair; bald. —**hair′less·ness,** *n.*

hair·line (hâr′līn′), *n.* **1.** a very slender line. **2.** the lower edge of the hair, esp. along the upper forehead. **3.** worsted fabric woven with very fine lines or stripes. **4.** *Print.* **a.** a very thin line on the face of a type. **b.** a style of type consisting entirely of such lines.

hair′ net′, a cap of loose net, as of silk or human hair, for holding the hair in place.

hair·piece (hâr′pēs′), *n.* a toupee or any type of wig.

hair·pin (hâr′pin′), *n.* **1.** a slender U-shaped piece of wire, shell, etc., used by women to fasten up the hair or hold a headdress. —*adj.* **2.** (of a road, curve in a road, etc.) sharply curved, as in a U shape: *a hairpin turn.*

hair-rais·er (hâr′rā′zər), *n.* a story, experience, etc., that is terrifying or thrilling.

hair-rais·ing (hâr′rā′ziŋ), *adj.* terrifying.

hair's-breadth (hârz′bredth′, -bretth′), *n.* **1.** a very small space or distance: *We just missed the car by a hair's-breadth.* —*adj.* **2.** extremely narrow or close. Also, **hairs′breadth′, hairbreadth.**

hair′ shirt′, a garment of coarse haircloth, worn next to the skin as penance.

hair′ space′, *Print.* the thinnest metal divider used to separate words, symbols, etc.

hair·spray (hâr′sprā′), *n.* a cosmetic liquid in an aerosol container, for holding the hair in place.

hair·spring (hâr′spriŋ′), *n.* *Horol.* a fine, usually spiral, spring used for oscillating the balance of a timepiece. Also called **balance spring.**

hair·streak (hâr′strēk′), *n.* any of several small, dark butterflies of the family *Lycaenidae,* having hairlike tails on the hind wings.

hair′ trig′ger, a trigger that allows the firing mechanism of a firearm to be operated by very slight pressure.

hair-trig·ger (hâr′trig′ər), *adj.* easily activated or set off; put into operation by the slightest impulse.

hair·weav·ing (hâr′wē′viŋ), *n.* the attachment of matching hair to a base of nylon thread interwoven with a person's remaining hair, to cover a bald area. —**hair′-weav′er,** *n.*

hair·worm (hâr′wûrm′), *n.* any of a number of small, slender worms of the family *Trichostrongylidae,* parasitic in the alimentary canals of various animals.

hair·y (hâr′ē), *adj.,* **hair·i·er, hair·i·est.** **1.** covered with hair; having much hair. **2.** consisting of or resembling hair: *moss of a hairy texture.* **3.** *Informal.* difficult, frightening, or risky: *a hairy trip in a canoe down the rapids.* [ME *heeri*] —**hair′i·ness,** *n.*

Hai·ti (hā′tē), *n.* **1.** a republic in the West Indies occupying the W part of the island of Hispaniola. 5,000,000; 10,714 sq. mi. *Cap.:* Port-au-Prince. **2.** Also, **Hayti.** former name of **Hispaniola.**

Hai·tian (hā′shən, -tē ən), *adj.* **1.** of or pertaining to Haiti or its people. —*n.* **2.** a native or inhabitant of Haiti. **3.** See **Haitian Creole.**

Hai′tian Cre′ole, the creolized French that is the native language of most Haitians. Also called **Creole, Haitian.**

haj·i (haj′ē), *n., pl.* **haj·is.** hajji.

hajj (haj), *n., pl.* **hajj·es.** the pilgrimage to Mecca that every Muslim is supposed to make at least once in his lifetime. Also, **hadj.** [< Ar: pilgrimage]

haj·ji (haj′ē) *n., pl.* **haj·jis.** a Muslim who has gone on a pilgrimage to Mecca. Also, **hadji, haji.** [< Ar = *hajj* pilgrimage + *-i* agent suffix]

hake (hāk), *n., pl.* (*esp. collectively*) **hake,** (*esp. referring to two or more kinds or species*) **hakes.** **1.** any of several marine fishes of the genus *Merluccius,* closely related to the cods, esp. *M. bilinearis,* found off the New England coast. **2.** any of several related marine fishes, esp. of the genus *Urophycis.* [ME, special use of OE *haca* hook; cf. MLG *haken* kipper]

Ha·ken·kreuz (hä′kən kroits′), *n., pl.* **-kreu·ze** (-kroi′tsə). *Ger.* the Nazi swastika. [lit., hook cross]

ha·kim (hä kēm′), *n.* (esp. in Muslim countries) **1.** a wise or learned man. **2.** a physician. **3.** a ruler; governor; judge. Also, **ha·keem** (hä kēm′). [< Ar *ḥakīm* wise man]

Hak·luyt (hak′lit), *n.* **Richard,** 1552?–1616, English geographer and editor of explorers' narratives.

Ha·ko·da·te (hä′kô dä′te), *n.* a seaport on S Hokkaido, in N Japan. 250,457 (1964).

hal-, var. of **halo-** before a vowel: *halite.*

Ha·la·chah (hä lô′khə; *Heb.* hä lä khä′), *n.* Halakah. —**Ha·lach·ic** (hə lak′ik), *adj.*

Ha·la·kah (hä lô′khə; *Heb.* hä lä khä′), *n.* the entire body of Jewish law and tradition, comprising the laws of the Bible, the oral law as transcribed in the Talmud, and subsequent legal codes amending traditional precepts. [< Heb: rule to follow, lit., way] —**Ha·lak·ic** (hə lak′ik), *adj.*

ha·la·lah (hə lä′lə), *n., pl.* **ha·la·lah.** a money of account of Saudi Arabia, the 100th part of a riyal or the fifth part of a qursh. Also, **ha·la·la.** [< Ar]

ha·la·tion (hā lā′shən, ha-), *n.* *Photog.* a blurred effect at the edges of a light area on a photograph, caused by reflection of light through the emulsion from the surface of the film or plate. [HAL(O) + -ATION]

hal·berd (hal′bərd, hôl′-, hol′-; *formerly* hô′bərd), *n.* a shafted weapon with an axlike cutting blade, beak, and apical spike, used esp. in the 15th and 16th centuries. Also, **hal·bert** (hal′bərt, hôl′-, hol′-; *formerly* hô′bərt). [late ME < MF *hallebarde* < MLG *helmbarde* = *helm* handle (c. HELM[1]) + *barde* broadax (c. MHG *barte*)]

hal·berd·ier (hal′bər dēr′), *n.* a soldier, guard, or attendant armed with a halberd. [< MF *hallebardier*]

Halberd (Head)

hal·cy·on (hal′sē ən), *n.* **1.** a mythical bird, usually identified with the kingfisher, said to have the power of calming winds and waves at sea. **2.** any of various kingfishers, esp. of the genus *Halcyon.* **3.** (*cap.*) *Class. Myth.* Alcyone (def. 2). —*adj.* Also, **hal·cy·o·ni·an** (hal′sē ō′nē ən), **hal·cy·on·ic** (hal′sē on′ik). **4.** calm; peaceful; tranquil: *halcyon weather.* **5.** wealthy; prosperous. **6.** joyful; carefree: *halcyon days of youth.* **7.** of or pertaining to the halcyon or kingfisher. [< L < Gk *halkyṓn,* pseudo-etym. var. of *alkyṓn* kingfisher; r. ME *alceon, alicion* < L *alcyōn* < Gk]

hale[1] (hāl), *adj.,* **hal·er, hal·est.** **1.** free from disease or infirmity; robust; vigorous. **2.** *Scot. and North Eng.* free from defect or injury. [ME (north); OE *hāl* WHOLE] —**hale′ness,** *n.* —**Syn. 1.** sound, healthy. —**Ant. 1.** sickly.

hale[2] (hāl), *v.t.,* **haled, hal·ing.** **1.** to haul, pull, drag, or draw with force. **2.** to bring as by dragging: *to hale a man into court.* [ME *hale(n)* < MF *hale(r)* < Gmc; cf. D *halen* to pull, fetch; akin to OE *geholian* to get, G *holen* to fetch. See HAUL] —**hal′er,** *n.*

Hale (hāl), *n.* **1. Edward Everett,** 1822–1909, U.S. clergyman and author. **2. George El·ler·y** (el′ə rē), 1868–1938, U.S. astronomer. **3. Sir Matthew,** 1609–76, British jurist: Lord Chief Justice 1671–76. **4. Nathan,** 1755–76, American soldier hanged as a spy by the British during the American Revolution.

Ha·le·a·ka·la (hä′le ä′kä lä′), *n.* a dormant volcano in Hawaii, on the island of Maui. Crater, 19 sq. mi.; 2000 ft. deep; 10,032 ft. above sea level.

ha·ler (hä′lər), *n., pl.* **-lers, -le·ru** (-lə ro͞o′). **1.** heller[1] (def. 1). **2.** Also, **heller.** a minor coin of Czechoslovakia, the 100th part of a koruna. [< Czech < MHG *haller,* var. of *heller* HELLER[1]]

Ha·le·vi (hä lē′vī, -lā′vē), *n.* **Judah.** See **Judah ha-Levi.**

Ha·lé·vy (A lā vē′), *n.* **1. Fro·men·tal** (frô mäɴ tal′), (*Jacques François Fromental Élie Lévy*), 1790–1862, French composer, esp. of operas. **2.** his nephew, **Lu·do·vic** (ly dô-vēk′), 1834–1908, French novelist and playwright.

half (haf, häf), *n., pl.* **halves** (havz, hävz), *adj., adv.* —*n.* **1.** one of two equal or approximately equal parts, as of an object, unit of measure or time, etc. **2.** a half part, esp. of one (½). **3.** *Sports.* either of two equal periods of play. Cf. **quarter** (def. 10). **4.** one of two; a part of a pair. **5.** *Football.* a halfback. **6. not the half of,** a significant yet relatively minor part of something that remains to be described in full. Also, **not half of, not half.** —*adj.* **7.** being one of two equal or approximately equal parts: *a half quart.* **8.** being half or about half of anything in degree, amount, length, etc. **9.** partial or incomplete (usually in combination). —*adv.* **10.** semi- (used in combination). **11.** in or to the extent or measure of half. **12.** in part; partly; incompletely (usually in combination). **13.** to some extent: *half recovered.* **14. in half,** divided into halves. **15. not half, a.** not at all; not really. **b.** See **half** (def. 6). [ME; OE *h(e)alf;* c. G *Halb,* Icel *halfr,* Goth *halbs*]

half-ac·re (haf′ā′kər, häf′-), *n.* an area equal to 21,780 square feet or $^{1}/_{1280}$ square mile.

half-and-half (haf′ən haf′, häf′ən häf′), *adj.* **1.** half one thing and half another. —*adv.* **2.** in two equal parts. —*n.* **3.** a mixture of two things, esp. in equal or nearly equal proportions. **4.** milk and light cream combined in equal parts, esp. for table use. **5.** *Chiefly Brit.* a mixture of two malt liquors, esp. porter and ale.

half′ ar′mor, plate armor that leaves the legs exposed.

half-assed (haf′ast′, häf′äst′), *adj.* *Slang* (*vulgar*). **1.** haphazard; not fully planned. **2.** incompetent; lacking sufficient ability or knowledge. **3.** unrealistic.

half·back (haf′bak′, häf′-), *n.* **1.** *Football.* one of two backs who typically line up on each side of the fullback. **2.** (in soccer, Rugby, field hockey, etc.) a player stationed near the forward line to carry out chiefly offensive duties.

half-baked (haf′bākt′, häf′-), *adj.* **1.** insufficiently baked. **2.** insufficiently planned or prepared. **3.** unrealistic: *half-baked theorists.* **4.** *Informal.* eccentric; crazy.

half′ bind′ing, a type of book binding consisting of a leather binding on the spine and, sometimes, the corners, with paper or cloth sides. Also called **half leather.**

half′ blood′, the relation between persons having only one common parent.

half-blood (haf′blud′, häf′-), *n.* **1.** a half-breed. **2.** a person who has only one parent in common with another person, as a half sister or half brother. —**half′-blood′ed,** *adj.*

half′ boot′, a boot reaching about halfway to the knee.

half′-breadth′ plan′ (haf′bredth′, -bretth′, häf′-), *Naval Archit.* a diagrammatic plan of one half of the hull of a vessel divided lengthwise amidships. Cf. **body plan, sheer plan.**

half-breed (haf′brēd′, häf′-), *n.* **1.** the offspring of parents of different races, esp. of a white person and an American Indian. —*adj.* **2.** of or pertaining to the offspring of a white person and an American Indian.

half′-bril′liant cut′ (haf′bril′yənt, häf′-), *Jewelry.* See **single cut.**

half′ broth′er, brother (def. 2).

half′ buck′, *U.S. Slang.* a half dollar.

half-bush·el (haf′bo͝osh′əl, häf′-), *n.* a quantity of grain, vegetables, etc., equal to 2 pecks.

half′ ca′dence, *Music.* a cadence on the dominant.

half-caste (haf′kast′, häf′käst′), *n.* **1.** a person of mixed

half′-ac·quaint′ed, *adj.*
half′-ad·mir′ing, *adj.;* **-ly,** *adv.*
half′-ad·mit′ted, *adj.;* **-ly,** *adv.*
half′-a·fraid′, *adj.*
half′-a·live′, *adj.*
half′-A·mer′i·can·ized′, *adj.*
half′-An′gli·cized′, *adj.*
half′-an′gry, *adj.*
half′-a·shamed′, *adj.*
half′-a·sleep′, *adj.*
half′-a·wake′, *adj.*
half′-beg′ging, *adj.*
half′-be·gun′, *adj.*
half′-blind′, *adj.*
half′-bur′ied, *adj.*

race. **2.** a person of mixed European and Hindu or European and Muslim parentage. —*adj.* **3.** of or pertaining to a half-caste.

half′ cent′, a bronze coin of the U.S., equal to one-half cent, issued at various periods 1793–1857.

half′ cock′, the position of the hammer of a firearm when held halfway between the firing and retracted positions so that it will not operate.

half-cocked (haf′kokt′, häf′-), *adj.* **1.** (of a firearm) at the position of half cock. **2.** *U.S.* lacking mature consideration or enough preparation; ill-considered. **3. go off half-cocked,** to act or happen prematurely. Also, **go off at half cock.**

half′ crown′, a cupronickel coin of Great Britain equal to 2s. 6d.: use phased out in 1971.

half-cup (haf′kup′, häf′-), *n.* a volume equal to 4 fluid ounces or 8 tablespoons.

half′ dime′, a silver coin of the U.S., equal to five cents, issued 1794–1805 and 1829–73.

half′ dol′lar, a silver coin of the U.S., worth 50 cents, weighing 385.8 grains to the dollar, 0.900 fine.

half-doz·en (haf′duz′ən, häf′-), *n., pl.* **-doz·ens,** (*as after a numeral*) **-doz·en,** *adj.* —*n.* **1.** one half of a dozen; six. —*adj.* **2.** considering six as a unit; consisting of six.

half′ ea′gle, a gold coin of the U.S., discontinued in 1929, equal to five dollars.

half′ gain′er, *Fancy Diving.* a dive in which the diver takes off facing forward and performs a backward half-somersault, entering the water headfirst and facing the springboard.

half-gal·lon (haf′gal′ən, häf′-), *n.* **1.** a half of a gallon; equal to two quarts. —*adj.* **2.** holding or consisting of two quarts.

half-heart·ed (haf′här′tid, häf′-), *adj.* having or showing little enthusiasm. —**half′-heart′ed·ly,** *adv.* —**half′-heart′ed·ness,** *n.* —**Syn.** indifferent, perfunctory. —**Ant.** enthusiastic.

half′ hitch′, a knot or hitch made by forming a bight and passing the end of the rope around the standing part and through the bight. See illus. at **knot.**

half-hol·i·day (haf′hol′ə dā′, häf′-), *n.* a holiday limited to half a working day or half an academic day.

half-hour (haf′our′, -ou′ər, häf′-), *n.* **1.** a period of 30 minutes. **2.** the midpoint between the hours. —*adj.* **3.** of, pertaining to, or consisting of a half-hour.

half·hour·ly (haf′our′lē, -ou′ər-, häf′-), *adj.* **1.** half-hour (def. 3). **2.** occurring every half-hour. —*adv.* **3.** at half-hour intervals.

half-inch (haf′inch′, häf′-), *n.* a half of an inch; equal to $^1/_{24}$ foot.

half′ leath′er, *Bookbinding.* See **half binding.**

half-length (haf′lengkth′, -length′, häf′-), *n.* **1.** something that is only half a full length or height, esp. a portrait that shows only the upper half of the body. —*adj.* **2.** of half the complete length or height.

half-life (haf′līf′, häf′-), *n., pl.* **-lives.** *Physics.* the time required for one half the atoms of any given amount of a radioactive substance to disintegrate. Also, **half′ life′, half′life′.** Also called **half′-life pe′riod.**

half-light (haf′līt′, häf′-), *n.* light that is partially dimmed or obscured.

half-lined (haf′līnd′, häf′-), *adj.* partially or incompletely lined.

half-liter (haf′lē′tər, häf′-), *n.* a volume equal to 500 cubic centimeters.

half-mast (haf′mast′, häf′mäst′), *n.* **1.** a position approximately halfway between the top of a mast, staff, etc., and its base. —*v.t.* **2.** to place (a flag) at half-mast as a mark of respect for the dead or as a signal of distress.

half-mile (haf′mīl′, häf′-), *n.* **1.** a half of a mile. **2.** a race of half a mile. —*adj.* **3.** of or measuring half a mile. **4.** running half a mile.

half-moon (haf′mo͞on′, häf′-), *n.* **1.** the moon when, at either quadrature, half its disk is illuminated. **2.** the phase of the moon at this time. See diag. at **moon.**

half′ mourn′ing, 1. a mourning garb less somber than full mourning. **2.** the period during which it is worn.

half′ nel′son, *Wrestling.* See under **nelson.**

half′ note′, *Music.* a note equivalent in time value to one half of a semibreve. See illus. at **note.**

half-peck (haf′pek′, häf′-), *n.* a quantity of grain, vegetables, etc., equal to 4 quarts.

half·pen·ny (hā′pə nē, hāp′nē), *n., pl.* **half·pen·nies** for 1; **half·pence** (hā′pəns) for 3; *adj.* —*n.* **1.** a bronze coin of the United Kingdom, equal to half a penny: use phased out in 1971. **2.** Also called **new halfpenny.** a bronze coin of the United Kingdom, equal to half a new penny and equivalent to 1.2 old pence. **3.** the sum of half a penny. —*adj.* **4.** of the price or value of a halfpenny. [ME *halfpeny*]

half-pike (haf′pīk′, häf′-), *n.* **1.** spontoon. **2.** a short pike formerly used by seamen boarding enemy vessels.

half′ pint′, 1. a half of a pint; equal to 2 gills. **2.** *Informal.* a very short person. **3.** *Slang.* a person of little importance.

half-pound (haf′pound′, häf′-), *n.* a weight equal to 8 ounces avoirdupois, or 6 ounces troy or apothecaries' weight.

half-quire (haf′kwīər′, häf′-), *n.* 12 uniform sheets of paper.

half′ rest′, *Music.* a rest equal in value to a half note. See illus. at **rest**[1].

half′ rhyme′. See **slant rhyme.**

half-rod (haf′rod′, häf′-), *n.* **1.** a length equal to 2¾ yards or 8¼ feet. **2.** an area equal to 15⅛ square yards.

half-share (haf′shâr′, häf′-), *n.* **1.** a share, as in profits, equal to one half. **2.** a claim to half the income from a share of stock.

half′ shell′, either of the halves of a double-shelled creature, as of an oyster, clam, or other bivalve mollusk.

half′ sis′ter, sister (def. 2).

half′ size′, any size in women's garments designated by a fractional number from 12½ through 24½, designed for a short-waisted, full figure.

half-slip (haf′slip′, häf′-), *n.* a skirtlike undergarment.

half′ sole′, the part of the sole of a boot or shoe that extends from the shank to the end of the toe.

half-sole (haf′sōl′, häf′-), *v.t.,* **-soled, -sol·ing.** to repair or renew (a shoe) by putting on a new half sole.

half′ sov′ereign, a gold coin of the United Kingdom, discontinued in 1917, equal to 10 shillings.

half-staff (haf′staf′, häf′stäf′), *n.* half-mast.

half′ step′, 1. *Music.* semitone. **2.** *Mil.* a step 15 inches long in quick time and 18 inches long in double time.

half′ tide′, the state or time of the tide halfway between high water and low water.

half-tim·bered (haf′tim′bərd, häf′-), *adj.* (of a house or building) having the frame and principal supports of timber but with the interstices filled in with masonry, plaster, or the like. Also, **half′-tim′ber.**

half′ time′, *Sports.* the intermission or rest period between the two halves of a sports event. —**half′-time′,** *adj.*

half′ ti′tle, 1. Also called **bastard title.** the first printed page of certain books, appearing before the title page, and containing only the title of the book. **2.** the title of any subdivision of a book that immediately precedes that subdivision, when printed on a full page by itself.

half′ tone′, *Music.* semitone.

half·tone (haf′tōn′, häf′-), *n.* **1.** (in painting, drawing, graphics, photography, etc.) a value intermediate between light and dark. **2.** *Photoengraving.* **a.** a process in which gradation of tone is obtained by a system of minute dots. **b.** the metal plate made by photoengraving for reproduction by letterpress printing. **c.** a print from such a plate. Cf. **line cut.** —*adj.* **3.** pertaining to, using, used in, or produced by the halftone process.

half-track (haf′trak′, häf′-), *n.* a motor vehicle, esp. an armored vehicle, with rear driving wheels on caterpillar treads. —**half′-tracked′,** *adj.*

half-truth (haf′tro͞oth′, häf′-), *n., pl.* **-truths** (-tro͞o*th*z). a statement that is only partly true, esp. one intended to deceive, evade blame, or the like. —**half′-true′,** *adj.*

half·way (haf′wā′, häf′-), *adv.* **1.** to half the distance; to the midpoint: *The rope reaches only halfway.* **2.** almost; nearly; just about: *He halfway surrendered to their demands.* **3. meet halfway,** to compromise with or give in partially to. —*adj.* **4.** midway, as between two places or points. **5.** going to or covering only half or part of the full extent; partial. [ME *half wey*]

half′way house′, 1. an inn or stopping place approximately midway between two places on a road. **2.** any midway place or point. **3.** a special residence for former mental patients, drug addicts, prisoners, etc., during their adjustment back to normal life.

---

half′-cen′tu·ry, *n., pl.,* **-ries.**
half′-Chris′tian, *adj.*
half′-civ′il, *adj.;* **-ly,** *adv.*
half′-civ′il·ized′, *adj.*
half′-clad′, *adj.*
half′-closed′, *adj.*
half′-clothed′, *adj.*
half′-coax′ing, *adj.;* **-ly,** *adv.*
half′-com·plet′ed, *adj.*
half′-con·cealed′, *adj.*
half′-con·fessed′, *adj.*
half′-con′scious, *adj.;* **-ly,** *adv.*
half′-con·sumed′, *adj.*
half′-con·temp′tu·ous, *adj.;* **-ly,** *adv.*
half′-con·vinced′, *adj.*
half′-con·vinc′ing, *adj.;* **-ly,** *adv.*
half′-cooked′, *adj.*
half′-count′ed, *adj.*
half′-cov′ered, *adj.*
half′-crazed′, *adj.*
half′-cra′zy, *adj.*
half′-day′, *n.*
half′-dazed′, *adj.*
half′-daz′ed·ly, *adv.*
half′-dead′, *adj.*
half′-deaf′, *adj.*
half′-deaf′ened, *adj.*
half′-dec′ade, *n.*
half′-de·fi′ant, *adj.;* **-ly,** *adv.*
half′-de·ment′ed, *adj.*
half′-de·vel′oped, *adj.*
half′-di·gest′ed, *adj.*
half′-dis·posed′, *adj.*
half′-done′, *adj.*
half′-dressed′, *adj.*
half′-dried′, *adj.*
half′-drowned′, *adj.*
half′-drunk′, *adj.*
half′-drunk′en, *adj.*
half′-earn′est, *adj.;* **-ly,** *adv.*
half′-eat′en, *adj.*
half′-ed′u·cat′ee, *adj.*
half′-Eng′lish, *adj.*
half′-ex·pect′ant, *adj.;* **-ly,** *adv.*
half′-fam′ished, *adj.*
half′-fem′i·nine, *adj.*
half′-filled′, *adj.*
half′-fin′ished, *adj.*
half′-for·got′ten, *adj.*
half′-formed′, *adj.*
half′-ful·filled′, *adj.*
half′-full′, *adj.*
half′-grown′, *adj.*
half′-guil′ty, *adj.;* **-ti·ly,** *adv.*
half′-heard′, *adj.*
half′-hid′den, *adj.*
half′-hu′man, *adj.*
half′-in·clined′, *adj.*
half′-in·formed′, *adj.*
half′-in·stinc′tive, *adj.;* **-ly,** *adv.*
half′-in·tel′li·gi·ble, *adj.;* **-bly,** *adv.*
half′-in·tox′i·cat′ed, *adj.*
half′-jelled′, *adj.*
half′-jok′ing, *adj.;* **-ly,** *adv.*
half′-jus′ti·fied′, *adj.*
half′-learned′, *adj.*
half′-mad′, *adj.;* **-ly,** *adv.*
half′-meant′, *adj.*
half′-min′ute, *n.*
half′-na′ked, *adj.*
half′-nor′mal, *adj.;* **-ly,** *adv.*
half′-ob·lit′er·at′ed, *adj.*
half′-o′pen, *adj.*
half′-o′val, *n.*
half′-pet′ri·fied′, *adj.*
half′-play′ful, *adj.;* **-ly,** *adv.*
half′-pleased′, *adj.*
half′-pro·fessed′, *adj.*
half′-pro·test′ing, *adj.*
half′-proved′, *adj.*
half′-prov′en, *adj.*
half′-ques′tion·ing, *adj.;* **-ly,** *adv.*
half′-raw′, *adj.*
half′-rea′son·a·ble, *adj.;* **-bly,** *adv.*
half′-re·luc′tant, *adj.;* **-ly,** *adv.*
half′-re·mem′bered, *adj.*
half′-re·pent′ant, *adj.*
half′-right′, *adj., n.*
half′-rot′ted, *adj.*
half′-rot′ten, *adj.*
half′-rue′ful, *adj.;* **-ly,** *adv.*
half′-ru′ined, *adj.*
half′-sav′age, *adj.;* **-ly,** *adv.*
half′-sec′ond, *adj.*
half′-seen′, *adj.*
half′-sensed′, *adj.*
half′-se′ri·ous, *adj.;* **-ly,** *adv.*
half′-shut′, *adj.*
half′-spoon′ful, *adj.*
half′-starved′, *adj.*
half′-starv′ing, *adj.*
half′-stat′ed, *adj.*
half′-sub·merged′, *adj.*
half′-suc·cess′ful, *adj.;* **-ly,** *adv.*
half′-tast′ed, *adj.*
half′-term′, *n.*
half′-trained′, *adj.*
half′-un·der·stood′, *adj.*
half′-used′, *adj.*
half′-ver′i·fied′, *adj.*
half′-wild′, *adj.;* **-ly,** *adv.*
half′-wrong′, *adj.*

---

half-wit (haf′wit′, häf′-), *n.* **1.** a person who is feeble-minded. **2.** a person who is foolish or senseless. —**half′-wit′ted,** *adj.* —**half′-wit′ted·ly,** *adv.* —**half′-wit′ted·ness,** *n.*

hal·i·but (hal′ə bət, hol′-), *n., pl.* (*esp. collectively*) **-but,** (*esp. referring to two or more kinds or species*) **-buts. 1.** either of two large flatfishes, *Hippoglossus hippoglossus,* found in the North Atlantic, or *H. stenolepis,* found in the North Pacific, used for food. **2.** any of various other similar flatfishes. Also, **holibut.** [ME *halybutte* = *haly* (var. of HOLY) + *butte* flat fish (< MD); so called because eaten on holy days. Cf. D *heilbot*]

hal′i·but-liv·er oil′ (hal′ə bət liv′ər, hol′-), a fixed oil extracted from the liver of the halibut, *Hippoglossus hippoglossus:* used chiefly as a source of vitamins A and D.

Hal·i·car·nas·sus (hal′ə kär nas′əs), *n.* an ancient city of Caria, in SW Asia Minor. —**Hal′i·car·nas′si·an, Hal′i·car·nas′se·an,** *adj.*

hal·ide (hal′īd, -id, hā′līd, -lid), *Chem.* —*n.* **1.** a compound of two elements, one of which is a halogen. —*adj.* **2.** of, pertaining to, or characteristic of a halide. [HAL(OGEN) + -IDE]

hal·i·dom (hal′i dəm), *n.* a holy place, as a church or sanctuary. Also, **hal·i·dome** (hal′i dōm′). [ME; OE *hāligdōm.* See HOLY, -DOM]

Hal·i·fax (hal′ə faks′), *n.* **1. Earl of** (*Edward Frederick Lindley Wood*), 1881–1959, British statesman. **2.** a seaport in and the capital of Nova Scotia, in SE Canada. 92,511 (1961). **3.** a city in SW Yorkshire, in N England. 96,073 (1961).

hal·ite (hal′īt, hā′līt), *n.* a white or colorless mineral, sodium chloride, NaCl; rock salt.

hal·i·to·sis (hal′i tō′sis), *n.* bad breath. [< NL = L *halit(us)* vapor (see EXHALE, -ITE[2]) + *-ōsis* -OSIS]

hal·i·tus (hal′i təs), *n., pl.* **-tus·es.** *Archaic.* breath; exhalation; vapor. [< L = *hāl(āre)* (to) breathe, exhale + *-it-* -ITE[2] + *-us* n. suffix (4th decl.)] —**ha·lit·u·os·i·ty** (hə lich′o͞o-os′i tē), *n.* —**ha·lit·u·ous** (hə lich′o͞o əs), *adj.*

hall (hôl), *n.* **1.** a corridor or passageway in a building. **2.** the large entrance room of a house or building; vestibule; lobby. **3.** a large room or building for public gatherings; auditorium. **4.** a large building for residence, instruction, or other purposes at a college or university. **5.** (in English colleges) **a.** a large room in which the members and students dine. **b.** dinner in such a room. **6.** *Chiefly Brit.* a mansion or large residence, esp. one on a large estate. **7.** the chief room in a medieval castle or similar structure, used for eating, sleeping, and entertaining. **8.** the castle, house, or similar structure of a medieval chieftain or noble. [ME; OE *heall;* c. Icel *höll,* G *Halle;* akin to OE *helan* to cover, hide, L *cēlāre* to hide]

hal·lah (hä′lə, ᴋʜä′-; *Heb.* ᴋʜä lä′), *n., pl.* **hal·lahs,** *Heb.* **hal·loth** (ᴋʜä lōt′). challah.

Hal·lam (hal′əm), *n.* **1. Arthur Henry,** 1811–35, English poet and essayist. **2.** his father, **Henry,** 1777–1859, English historian.

Hal·le (häl′ə), *n.* a city in SW East Germany, NW of Leipzig. 274,402 (1964). Official name, **Hal·le an der Saa·le** (häl′ə än deʀ zäl′ə).

Hal·leck (hal′ik, -ək), *n.* **1. Fitz-Green** (fits′grēn′, fits-grēn′), 1790–1867, U.S. poet. **2. Henry Wa·ger** (wā′jər), 1815–72, Union general in the U.S. Civil War and writer on military subjects.

Hal·lel (hä lāl′), *n.* *Judaism.* a liturgical prayer consisting of all or part of Psalms 113–118. [< Heb: praise]

hal·le·lu·jah (hal′ə lo͞o′yə), *interj.* **1.** Praise ye the Lord! —*n.* **2.** an exclamation of "hallelujah!" **3.** a shout of joy, praise, or gratitude. Also, **hal′le·lu′iah.** [< Heb *hallēlūyāh* praise (ye) Jehovah]

Hal·ley (hal′ē), *n.* **Edmund** or **Edmond,** 1656–1742, English astronomer.

Hal′ley's Com′et, *Astron.* a comet regularly appearing over the earth every 75 or 76 years: appearances in the 20th century in 1910 and 1986. [named after Edmund HALLEY who first predicted its return]

hal·liard (hal′yərd), *n.* halyard.

hall·mark (hôl′märk′), *n.* **1.** an official mark or stamp indicating a standard of purity, used in marking gold and silver articles assayed by the Goldsmiths' Company of London; plate mark. **2.** any mark or special indication of genuineness, good quality, etc. **3.** any distinguishing feature or characteristic. —*v.t.* **4.** to stamp or imprint (something) with a hallmark. [after Goldsmiths' *Hall,* London, the seat of the Goldsmiths' Company; see MARK[1]] —**hall′mark′er,** *n.*

hal·lo (hə lō′), *interj., n., pl.* **-los,** *v.,* **-loed, -lo·ing.** —*interj.* **1.** (used to call or answer someone, or to incite dogs in hunting.) —*n.* **2.** the cry "hallo!" **3.** a shout of exultation. —*v.i.* **4.** to call with a loud voice; shout; cry, as after hunting dogs. —*v.t.* **5.** to incite or chase (something) with shouts and cries of "hallo!" **6.** to cry "hallo" to (someone). **7.** to shout (something). Also, **halloa, halloo, hallow, hollo, holloa, holloo.** [var. of HOLLO]

hal·loa (hə lō′, ha-), *interj., n., pl.* **-loas,** *v.i., v.t.,* **-loaed, -loa·ing.** hallo.

Hall′ of Fame′, 1. a national shrine commemorating the names of outstanding Americans, in New York City, at New York University. **2.** a room, building, etc., set aside to honor outstanding individuals in any sport, profession, or the like: *the Baseball Hall of Fame at Cooperstown, N.Y.*

hal·loo (hə lo͞o′), *interj., n., pl.* **-loos,** *v.i., v.t.,* **-looed, -loo·ing.** hallo.

hal·low[1] (hal′ō), *v.t.* **1.** to make holy; sanctify; consecrate. **2.** to honor as holy; venerate. [ME *hal(o)we(n),* OE *hālgian* (c. G *heiligen,* Icel *helga*) < *hālig* HOLY] —**hal′low·er,** *n.*

hal·low[2] (hə lō′), *interj., n., v.i., v.t.* hallo.

hal·lowed (hal′ōd; *in liturgical use often* hal′ō id), *adj.* regarded as holy or sacrosanct; venerated; sacred. —**hal′lowed·ness,** *n.* —**Syn.** See **holy.**

Hal·low·een (hal′ə wēn′, -ō ēn′, hol′-), *n.* the evening of October 31; the eve of All Saints' Day; Allhallows Eve. Also, **Hal′low·e′en′.** [(ALL)HALLOW(S) + E(V)EN[2]]

Hal·low·mas (hal′ō məs, -mas′), *n.* *Archaic.* the feast of Allhallows or All Saints' Day, on November 1.

Hall·statt·an (hôl stat′ən, häl shtät′ən), *adj.* of, pertaining to, or belonging to an early Iron Age culture in Europe, characterized by the use of bronze and the introduction of iron. Also, **Hall·stat·ti·an** (hôl stat′ē ən, häl-shtät′-), **Hall·statt** (hôl′stat, häl′shtät), **Hall·stad′tan, Hall′stadt′.** Cf. **La Tène** (def. 1). [named after *Hallstatt,* village in central Austria where remains were found; see -AN]

hall′ tree′, a hatrack or clothes tree. Also called **hat tree.**

hal·lu·ci·nate (hə lo͞o′sə nāt′), *v.,* **-nat·ed, -nat·ing.** —*v.i.* **1.** to have hallucinations. —*v.t.* **2.** to affect with hallucination. [< L *hallūcināt(us),* ptp. of *(h)allūcinārī* to wander in mind; see -ATE[1]] —**hal·lu′ci·na′tor,** *n.*

hal·lu·ci·na·tion (hə lo͞o′sə nā′shən), *n.* **1.** a sensory experience of something that does not exist outside the mind. **2.** the sensation caused by an hallucinatory condition or the object or scene experienced. **3.** (loosely) a false notion, belief, or impression; illusion; delusion. [< L *hallūcinātiōn-* (s. of *(h)allūcinātiō*) a wandering of the mind] —**hal·lu′ci·na′tion·al, hal·lu·ci·na·tive** (hə lo͞o′sə nā′tiv, -nə tiv), *adj.* —**Syn. 1.** phantasm, aberration. See **illusion.**

hal·lu·ci·na·to·ry (hə lo͞o′sə nə tōr′ē, -tôr′ē), *adj.* pertaining to or characterized by hallucination: *hallucinatory visions.*

hal·lu·cin·o·gen (hə lo͞o′sə nə jen′, hal′yə sin′ə-), *n.* a substance that produces hallucinations. [HALLUCIN(ATION) + -O- + -GEN] —**hal·lu·ci·no·gen·ic** (hə lo͞o′sə nō-jen′ik), *adj.*

hal·lu·ci·no·sis (hə lo͞o′sə nō′sis), *n.* *Psychiatry.* a psychosis or state characterized by hallucinations. [HALLUCIN(ATION) + -OSIS]

hal·lux (hal′əks), *n., pl.* **hal·lu·ces** (hal′yə sēz′). *Anat., Zool.* the first or innermost digit of the foot of man or of the hind foot of other air-breathing vertebrates; great toe. [< NL, alter. of LL *hallex* great toe]

hall·way (hôl′wā′), *n.* **1.** a corridor, as in a building. **2.** an entrance hall.

Hal·ma·he·ra (hal′mə hēr′ə), *n.* an island in NE Indonesia: the largest of the Moluccas. ab. 85,000; 6928 sq. mi. Also, **Hal′ma·hei′ra.** Also called **Gilolo, Jilolo.**

Halm·stad (hälm′städ′), *n.* a seaport in SW Sweden. 40,653 (1964).

ha·lo (hā′lō), *n., pl.* **-los, -loes,** *v.,* **-loed, -lo·ing.** —*n.* **1.** Also called **nimbus.** a conventional, geometric shape, usually in the form of a disk, circle, ring, or rayed structure, representing a radiant light around or above the head of a divine or sacred personage, an ancient or medieval monarch, etc. **2.** an atmosphere or quality of glory, majesty, sanctity, or the like. **3.** *Meteorol.* any of a variety of bright circles or arcs centered on the sun or moon, caused by the refraction or reflection of light by ice crystals suspended in the earth's atmosphere. —*v.t.* **4.** to surround with a halo. —*v.i.* **5.** *Rare.* to form a halo. [< L, acc. of *halōs* circle round sun or moon < Gk *hálōs* such a circle, disk, orig. threshing floor]

halo-, a learned borrowing from Greek meaning "salt," used in the formation of compound words (*halophyte*); sometimes specialized as a combining form of **halogen.** Also, *esp. before a vowel,* **hal-.** [< Gk, comb. form of *háls* salt]

hal·o·gen (hal′ə jən, hā′lə-), *n.* *Chem.* any of the nonmetallic elements fluorine, chlorine, iodine, bromine, and astatine. —**hal′o·gen·oid′,** *adj.* —**ha·log·e·nous** (ha loj′ə-nəs), *adj.*

hal·o·gen·ate (hal′ə jə nāt′, hā′lə-), *v.t.,* **-at·ed, -at·ing.** *Chem.* **1.** to treat or combine with a halogen. **2.** to introduce a halogen into (an organic compound). —**hal·o·gen·a·tion** (hal′ə je nā′shən, ha loj′ə-), *n.*

hal·oid (hal′oid, hā′loid), *adj.* *Chem.* resembling or derived from a halogen. Also, **hal·o·gen·oid** (hal′ə jə noid′, hā′lə-).

ha·lo·like (hā′lō līk′), *adj.* resembling a halo. Also, **ha′lo·esque′.**

hal·o·phyte (hal′ə fīt′), *n.* a plant that grows in salty or alkaline soil. —**hal·o·phyt·ic** (hal′ə fit′ik), *adj.* —**hal·o·phyt·ism** (hal′ə fī tiz′əm), *n.*

Hals (häls), *n.* **Frans** (fʀäns), 1581?–1666, Dutch painter.

Hal·sey (hôl′zē), *n.* **William Frederick** ("*Bull*"), 1882–1959, U.S. admiral.

Häl·sing·borg (hel′sing bôʀ′yə), *n.* a seaport in SW Sweden, opposite Helsingör. 78,582 (1964).

halt[1] (hôlt), *v.i.* **1.** to stop; cease moving, operating, etc., either permanently or temporarily. —*v.t.* **2.** to cause to halt; bring to a stop. —*n.* **3.** a temporary or permanent stop. —*interj.* **4.** (used as a command to stop and stand motionless, as to troops to stop marching or by a policeman to a fleeing suspect.) [from the phrase *make halt* for G *halt machen.* See HOLD[1]] —**Syn. 2.** See **stop.**

halt[2] (hôlt), *v.i.* **1.** to falter, as in speech, reasoning, etc.; be hesitant; stumble. **2.** to be in doubt; waver between alternatives; vacillate. **3.** *Archaic.* to be lame; walk lamely; limp. —*adj.* **4.** lame; limping. —*n.* **5.** *Archaic.* lameness; a limp. [ME; OE *healt;* c. OHG *halz,* Icel *haltr,* Goth *halts,* akin to L *clādēs* damage, loss] —**halt′ing·ly,** *adv.* —**halt′ing·ness,** *n.* —**halt′less,** *adj.*

hal·ter[1] (hôl′tər), *n.* **1.** a rope or strap with a noose or headstall for leading or restraining horses or cattle. **2.** a rope with a noose for hanging criminals; the hangman's noose. **3.** a woman's garment, worn above the waist and tied behind the neck and across the back, leaving the arms and back bare. —*v.t.* **4.** to put a halter on; restrain as by a halter. **5.** to hang (a person). [ME; OE *hælfter;* c. G *Halfter*] —**hal′ter·like′,** *adj.*

hal·ter[2] (hal′tər), *n., pl.* **hal·te·res** (hal tēr′ēz). one of a pair of slender, club-shaped appendages on the metathorax of a dipterous insect that serve to maintain its balance in flight. Also called **balancer.** [< NL, special use of L: jumping weight < Gk, akin to *hállesthai* to leap]

halt·er[3] (hôl′tər), *n.* a person who halts or brings to a stop. [HALT[1] + -ER[1]]

halt·er[4] (hôl′tər), *n.* a person who halts, falters, or hesitates. [HALT[2] + -ER[1]]

Hal′tom Cit′y (hôl′təm), a city in N Texas, near Fort Worth. 28,127 (1970).

ha·lutz (ᴋʜä lo͞ots′; *Eng.* hä lo͝ots′, ᴋʜä-), *n., pl.* **-lu·tzim** (-lo͞o tsēm′; *Eng.* -lo͞ot′sim). *Hebrew.* a person who emigrates to Israel to help develop the land. Also, **chalutz.** [lit., pioneer]

hal·vah (häl vä′, häl′vä), *n.* a sweet, candylike confection of Turkish origin, consisting chiefly of ground sesame seeds and honey. Also, **hal·va′.** [< Yiddish *halva* < Rumanian < Turk *helva* < Ar *halwa* sweet confection]

halve (hav, häv), *v.t.*, **halved, halv·ing. 1.** to divide into halves. **2.** to share equally. **3.** to reduce to half. **4.** *Golf.* to play (a hole, round, or match) in the same number of strokes as one's opponent. **5. halve together,** to join (two pieces of wood) by cutting from each, at the place of joining, a portion fitting to that left solid in the other. [ME *halve(n)* < HALF]

halves (havz, hävz), *n.* **1.** pl. of **half. 2. by halves, a.** incompletely. **b.** half-heartedly. **3. go halves,** to share equally; divide evenly.

hal·yard (hal′yərd), *n.* any of various lines or tackles for hoisting a spar, sail, flag, etc., into position for use. Also, **halliard.** Cf. **tye.** [ME *hal(ier)* rope to haul with (see HALE², -IER) + YARD¹]

ham¹ (ham), *n.* **1.** one of the rear quarters of a hog, esp. the heavy-muscled part, between hip and hock. **2.** the meat of this part. **3.** the part of the leg back of the knee. **4.** Often, **hams.** the back of the thigh, or the thigh and the buttock together. [ME *hamme,* OE *hamm* bend of the knee; c. OHG *hamma;* akin to Icel *höm* buttock, L *camur* crooked]

ham² (ham), *n., v.,* **hammed, ham·ming.** —*n.* **1.** *Theat. Slang.* **a.** an actor who overacts. **b.** overacting. **2.** *Informal.* an operator of an amateur radio station. —*v.i.* **3.** *Theat. Slang.* to act with exaggerated expression of emotion; overact. [short for *hamfatter,* after *The Hamfat Man,* a Negro minstrel song celebrating an awkward man]

Ham (ham), *n.* the second son of Noah. Gen. 10:1.

Ha·ma (hä′mä, hä mä′), *n.* a city in W Syria, on the Orontes River. 131,630 (est. 1964). Ancient, **Epiphania.** Biblical name, **Hamath.**

Ham·a·dan (ham′ə dan′; *Pers.* ha mə dän′), *n.* a city in W Iran. 114,610 (est. 1964). Ancient, **Ecbatana.**

ham·a·dry·ad (ham′ə drī′əd, -ad), *n., pl.* **-ads, -a·des** (-ə dēz′). **1.** *Class. Myth.* a dryad who is the spirit of a particular tree. **2.** See **king cobra.** [< L, s. of *Hamādryas* wood nymph < Gk = *háma* together with (c. SAME) + *dryás* DRYAD]

ha·mal (hə mäl′, hə môl′), *n.* **1.** (in the Middle East and Orient) a porter. **2.** (in India) a male house servant. Also, **hammal, hamaul.** [< Ar *ḥammāl* porter, carrier, akin to *hamala* to carry]

Ha·ma·ma·tsu (hä′mä mä′tso͝o), *n.* a city on S central Honshu, in central Japan. 372,912 (1964).

Ha·man (hā′mən), *n.* a powerful prince at the court of Ahasuerus, who was hanged upon exposure of his plan to destroy the Jews. Esther 3–6.

ha·mar·ti·a (hä′mär tē′ə), *n.* (in ancient Greek tragedy) error in judgment, esp. resulting from a defect in the character of a tragic hero; the tragic flaw. [< Gk: a fault = *hamart-* (base of *hamartánein* to err) + *-ia* -IA]

ha·mate (hā′māt), *Anat.* —*adj.* **1.** hook-shaped. **2.** having a hooklike process. —*n.* **3.** Also called **unciform.** a wedge-shaped bone of the carpus having a hooklike process projecting from the palmar surface. [< L *hāmāt(us)* hooked = *hām(us)* hook + *-ātus* -ATE¹]

Ha·math (hā′math), *n.* Biblical name of **Hama.**

ha·maul (hə môl′), *n.* hamal.

Ham·ble·to·ni·an (ham′bəl tō′nē ən), *n.* **1.** one of a superior strain of American trotting horses descended from the stallion *Hambletonian.* **2.** an annual harness race for three-year-old trotters, held at Du Quoin, Illinois.

Ham·burg (ham′bûrg; *Ger.* häm′bo͝ork), *n.* **1.** a state in N West Germany. 1,854,600 (1963); 288 sq. mi. **2.** a city in and the capital of this state, on the Elbe River: the largest seaport in continental Europe. 1,851,200 (1963).

ham·burg·er (ham′bûr′gər), *n.* **1.** Also called **Ham′burg steak′.** a patty of ground or chopped beef, seasoned, and fried or broiled. **2.** ground or chopped beef. **3.** a sandwich consisting of a cooked patty of ground or chopped beef between two halves of a roll or bun. Also, **ham′burg.** [short for *Hamburger steak;* see -ER¹]

Ham·den (ham′dən), *n.* a town in S Connecticut. 49,357 (1970).

hame (hām), *n.* either of two curved pieces lying upon the collar in the harness of an animal, to which the traces are fastened. [ME < MD; akin to OE *hamele* oarlock, Dan *hammel* splinter bar, Arm *samik* yoke pieces]

Ham·e·lin (ham′ə lin, ham′lin), *n.* a city in N West Germany, on the Weser River: scene of the legend of the Pied Piper of Hamelin. 49,500 (1963). German, **Ha·meln** (hä′məln).

hame′ tug′, a loop or short leather strap attaching a trace to a hame.

Ham·hung (häm′ho͝ong′), *n.* a city in central North Korea. 112,184 (1944).

Ha·mil·car Bar·ca (hə mil′kär bär′kə, ham′əl kär′), c270–228 B.C., Carthaginian general and statesman (father of Hannibal).

Ham·il·ton (ham′əl tən), *n.* **1. Alexander,** 1757–1804, American statesman and writer on government: the first Secretary of the Treasury, 1789–97. **2. Edith,** 1867–1963, U.S. classical scholar and writer. **3. Lady Emma** (*Amy,* or *Emily, Lyon*), 1765?–1815, mistress of Viscount Nelson. **4. Sir Ian Standish Mon·teith** (mon′tēth), 1853–1947, British general. **5. Sir William Row·an** (rō′ən), 1805–65, Irish mathematician and astronomer. **6.** Also called **Grand River.** a river flowing E through S Labrador into the Atlantic. 600 mi. long. **7. Mount,** a mountain of the Coast Range in California, near San Francisco: site of Lick Observatory. 4209 ft. **8.** a seaport in SE Ontario, in SE Canada, on Lake Ontario. 273,991 (1961). **9.** a city in SW Ohio. 67,865 (1970). **10.** a city on central North Island, in New Zealand. 57,800 (est. 1964). **11.** a city in S Scotland, SE of Glasgow. 41,928 (1961). **12.** a seaport in and the capital of Bermuda. 2,942 (1960).

Ham·il·to·ni·an (ham′əl tō′nē ən), *adj.* **1.** pertaining to or advocating Hamiltonianism. —*n.* **2.** a supporter of Alexander Hamilton or Hamiltonianism.

Ham·il·to·ni·an·ism (ham′əl tō′nē ə niz′əm), *n.* the political principles or doctrines associated with Alexander Hamilton, esp. those stressing a strong central government and protective tariffs. Cf. **federalism.**

Ham·ite (ham′īt), *n.* **1.** a descendant of Ham. Gen. 10:1, 6–20. **2.** a member of any of various peoples of northern and eastern Africa, as the ancient Egyptians and modern Berbers.

Ham·it·ic (ha mit′ik, hə-), *n.* **1.** the non-Semitic portion of the language family to which Semitic belongs. —*adj.* **2.** of or pertaining to the Hamites or Hamitic.

Ham·i·to-Se·mit·ic (ham′i tō sə mit′ik), *adj., n.* Afro-Asiatic. [comb. form of HAMITIC]

ham·let (ham′lit), *n.* **1.** a small village. **2.** *Brit.* a village without a church of its own, belonging to the parish of another village or town. [ME *hamelet* < MF = *hamel* (dim. of *ham* < Gmc; see HOME) + *-et* -ET] —**Syn. 1.** See **community.**

Ham·lin (ham′lin), *n.* **Hannibal,** 1809–91, U.S. political leader: vice president of the U.S. 1861–65.

ham·mal (hə mäl′, hə môl′), *n.* hamal.

Ham·mar·skjöld (hä′mər shōld′, -shəld, ham′ər-; *Sw.* häm′är shœld′), *n.* **Dag Hjal·mar** (däg yäl′mär), 1905–1961, Swedish statesman: Secretary General of the United Nations 1953–61: Nobel peace prize 1961.

ham·mer (ham′ər), *n.* **1.** a tool consisting of a solid head, usually of metal, set crosswise on a handle, used for driving nails, beating metals, etc. **2.** any of various instruments or devices resembling this in form, action, or use, as a mallet for playing the xylophone, a lever which rings against a doorbell or buzzer, etc. **3.** *Firearms.* the part of a lock that, by its fall or action, causes the discharge, as by exploding the percussion cap or striking the primer or firing pin; cock. **4.** one of the padded levers by which the strings of a piano are struck. **5.** *Track.* a metal ball, usually weighing 16 pounds, attached to a steel wire at the end of which is a grip, for throwing for distance in the hammer throw. **6.** *Anat.* malleus. **7. under the hammer,** for sale at public auction.
—*v.t.* **8.** to beat or drive (a nail, peg, etc.) with a hammer. **9.** to fasten by using hammer and nails; nail (often fol. by *down, up,* etc.): *to hammer up an announcement.* **10.** to assemble or build with a hammer and nails (often fol. by *together*): *He hammered together a picture frame.* **11.** to shape or ornament (metal or a metal object), by controlled and repeated blows of a hammer; beat out: *to hammer brass.* **12.** to form, construct, or make with or as if with a hammer; build by repeated, vigorous, or strenuous effort (often fol. by *out* or *together*): *to hammer out an agreement.* **13.** to pound or hit forcefully (often fol. by *out*): *to hammer out a tune on the piano.* **14.** to settle (a strong disagreement, argument, etc.); bring to an end, as by strenuous or repeated effort (usually fol. by *out*): *They hammered out their differences over a glass of beer.* **15.** to present (points in an argument, an idea, etc.) forcefully or compellingly; state strongly, aggressively, and effectively (often fol. by *home*): *to hammer home the need for action.* **16.** to impress (something) as by hammer blows: *hammer the rules into his head.*
—*v.i.* **17.** to strike blows with or as with a hammer. **18.** to make persistent or laborious attempts to finish or perfect something (sometimes fol. by *away*): *He hammered away at his speech for hours.* **19.** to reiterate; emphasize by repetition (often fol. by *away*): *The teacher hammered away at the multiplication tables.* [ME *hamer,* OE *hamor;* c. G *Hammer* hammer, Icel *hamarr* hammer, crag; orig. made of stone] —**ham′mer·er,** *n.* —**ham′mer·like′,** *adj.*

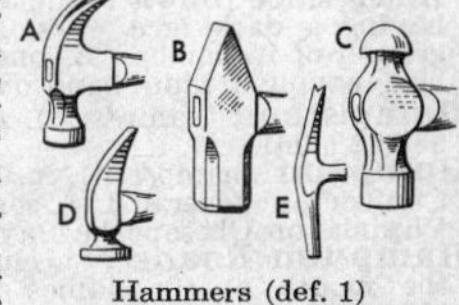

Hammers (def. 1)
A, Claw hammer; B, Engineer's hammer; C, Ball-peen hammer; D, Shoemaker's hammer; E, Carpetlayer's hammer

ham′mer and sick′le, the emblem of the Soviet Union, adopted in 1923 and consisting of an insignia of a hammer with its handle across the blade of a sickle and a star above.

ham′mer and tongs′, *Informal.* with great noise or vigor.

Ham·mer·fest (hä′mər fest′), *n.* a seaport in N Norway: the northernmost town in Europe. 5130 (1956).

ham·mer·head (ham′ər hed′), *n.* **1.** any shark of the genus *Sphyrna,* esp. *S. zygaena,* having the head expanded laterally so as to resemble a double-headed hammer. **2.** a brown, heronlike, African bird, *Scopus umbretta,* having the head so crested as to resemble a claw hammer. —**ham′mer·head′ed,** *adj.*

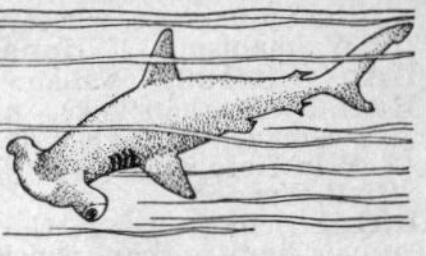
Hammerhead, *Sphyrna zygaena* (Length 15 ft.)

ham·mer·ing (ham′ər ing), *n.* **1.** the act, the process, or an instance of beating with or as with a hammer. **2.** design, texture, or pattern imparted by a hammer.

ham·mer·less (ham′ər lis), *adj.* (of a firearm) having the hammer concealed within the receiver.

ham·mer·lock (ham′ər lok′), *n.* *Wrestling.* a hold in which one arm of an opponent is twisted and forced upward behind his back.

Ham·mer·stein (ham′ər stīn′), *n.* **1. Oscar,** 1847?–1919, U.S. theatrical manager, born in Germany. **2.** his grandson, **Oscar II,** 1895–1960, U.S. lyricist and librettist.

ham′mer throw′, *Track.* a field event in which the hammer is thrown for distance. —**ham′mer throw′er.**

ham·mer·toe (ham′ər tō′), *n.* *Pathol.* **1.** a deformity of a toe in which there is a permanent angular flexion of the second and third joints. **2.** a toe having such a deformity.

Ham·mett (ham′it), *n.* **(Samuel) Da·shiell** (də shēl′, dash′ēl), 1894–1961, U.S. writer of detective stories.

ham·mock¹ (ham′ək), *n.* a kind of hanging bed or couch made of canvas, netted cord, or the like. [< Sp *hamac(a)* < Taino of Santo Domingo] —**ham′mock·like′,** *adj.*

ham·mock² (ham′ək), *n.* hummock (def. 1).

Ham·mond (ham′ənd), *n.* a city in NW Indiana, near Chicago. 107,888 (1970).

Ham·mu·ra·bi (hä′mŏŏ rä′bē, ham′ŏŏ-), *n.* 18th century B.C. or earlier, king of Babylonia. Also, **Ham·mu·ra·pi** (hä′mŏŏ rä′pē, ham′ŏŏ-). Cf. **Code of Hammurabi.**

ham·my (ham′ē), *adj.*, **-mi·er, -mi·est.** *Informal.* **1.** characteristic of one who overacts. **2.** overacted. **3.** exaggerated. —**ham′mi·ness,** *n.*

Hamp·den (hamp′dən, ham′dən), *n.* **John,** 1594–1643, British statesman who defended the rights of the House of Commons against Charles I.

ham·per[1] (ham′pər), *v.t.* **1.** to hold back; hinder; impede. **2.** to interfere with; curtail. —*n.* **3.** *Naut.* gear that, although necessary to the operations of a vessel, is sometimes in the way. [ME *hampre(n)*; akin to OE *hamm* enclosure, *hemm* HEM[1]] —**ham′pered·ness,** *n.* —**ham′per·er,** *n.* —**Syn. 1.** obstruct, encumber. See **prevent.** —**Ant. 1.** further.

ham·per[2] (ham′pər), *n.* a large basket or wickerwork receptacle, usually with a cover. [ME *hampere,* var. of *hanypere* HANAPER]

Hamp·shire (hamp′shēr, -shər), *n.* **1.** Also called **Hants.** a county in S England, including the administrative divisions of Southampton and the Isle of Wight. 1,336,084 (1961); 1650 sq. mi. *Co. seat:* Winchester. **2.** Also called **Hamp′shire Down′.** one of an English breed of sheep having a dark face, ears, and legs, noted for the rapid growth of its lambs. **3.** one of an English breed of black hogs having a white band over the shoulders and forelegs.

Hamp·stead (hamp′stid), *n.* a NW borough of London. 98,902 (1961).

Hamp·ton (hamp′tən), *n.* **1. Wade** (wād), 1818–1902, Confederate general: U.S. senator 1879–91. **2.** a city in SE Virginia, on Chesapeake Bay. 120,779 (1970).

Hamp′ton Roads′, a channel in SE Virginia between the mouth of the James River and Chesapeake Bay: battle between the *Monitor* and the *Merrimack* 1862.

ham·ster (ham′stər), *n.* **1.** any of several short-tailed, stout-bodied, burrowing rodents, as *Cricetus cricetus,* of Europe and Asia, having large cheek pouches. **2.** the fur of such an animal. [< G; cf. OHG *hamastro,* OS *hamstra* weevil]

Hamster, *Mesocricetus auratus* (Length 6 in.)

ham·string (ham′string′), *n., v.,* **-strung** or (*Rare*) **-stringed; -string·ing.** —*n.* **1.** (in man) any of the tendons which bound the ham, or hollow of the knee. **2.** (in quadrupeds) the great tendon at the back of the hock. —*v.t.* **3.** to disable by cutting the hamstring or hamstrings of. **4.** to render powerless or useless; thwart.

Ham·sun (häm′sŏŏn), *n.* **Knut** (knōōt), 1859–1952, Norwegian novelist: Nobel prize 1920.

Ham·tramck (ham tram′ik), *n.* a city in SE Michigan, completely surrounded by the city of Detroit. 27,245 (1970).

ham·u·lus (ham′yə ləs), *n., pl.* **-li** (-lī′). *Biol.* a small hook or hooklike process. [< L = *ham(us)* hook + *-ulus* -ULE] —**ham′u·lar, ham·u·late** (ham′yə lāt′), **ham·u·lose** (ham′yə lōs′), **ham′u·lous,** *adj.*

ham·za (häm′zä), *n.* the sign used in Arabic writing to represent the glottal stop, usually written above another letter: usually transliterated in English as an apostrophe. [< Ar *hamzah,* lit., a squeezing together]

Han (hän), *n.* **1.** a dynasty in China, 206 B.C.–A.D. 220, with an interregnum, A.D. 9–25: characterized by the revival of letters and the introduction of Buddhism. **2.** a river flowing from central China into the Yangtze at Wuhan. 900 mi. long.

Han·a·fi (han′ə fē), *n. Islam.* one of the four teachings of the Sunna sect, which allows for changes of law in accord with the times. Cf. **Hanbali, Maliki, Shafii.**

han·a·per (han′ə pər), *n.* a wicker receptacle for documents. [ME < AF (ML *hanaperium*), c. MF *hanapier* case to hold a drinking vessel = *hanap* (< Gmc) + *-ier* -ER[2]]

Han·ba·li (han′bə lē), *n. Islam.* one of the four teachings of the Sunna sect, whose tenets are suited to the movement of Wahhabism. Cf. **Hanafi, Maliki, Shafii.**

Han′ Cit′ies, Wuhan.

Han·cock (han′kok), *n.* **1. John,** 1737–93, American statesman: first signer of the Declaration of Independence. **2. Win·field Scott** (win′fēld′), 1824–86, Union general in the Civil War.

hand (hand), *n.* **1.** the terminal, prehensile part of the upper limb in man, consisting of the bones of the wrist or carpus, the metacarpus, fingers, and thumb. **2.** the corresponding part of the forelimb in any of the higher vertebrates. **3.** the terminal part of any limb when prehensile, as the hind foot of a monkey or the foot of a hawk. **4.** something resembling a hand in shape or function, as various types of pointers. **5.** index (def. 6). **6.** a person employed in manual labor or for general duties; worker; laborer: *a ranch hand.* **7.** a person who performs or is capable of performing a specific work, skill, or action. **8.** skill; workmanship; characteristic touch. **9.** a person with reference to ability or skill: *a poor hand at running a business.* **10.** one of a ship's crew; crewman: *All hands on deck!* **11.** Often, **hands.** possession or power; control, custody, or care. **12.** a position, esp. one of control, used for bargaining, negotiating, etc.: *an action to strengthen one's hand.* **13.** agency; instrumentality: *death by his own hand.* **14.** assistance; aid; active participation or cooperation in doing something: *Give me a hand.* **15.** side; direction. **16.** style of handwriting; penmanship. **17.** a person's signature. **18.** a round or outburst of applause for a performer. **19.** a pledge, as of marriage. **20.** a linear measure equal to four inches, used esp. in determining the height of horses. **21.** *Cards.* **a.** the cards dealt to or held by each player at one time. **b.** the person holding the cards. **c.** a single part of a game, in which all the cards dealt at one time are played. **22. hands,** *Manège.* skill at manipulating the reins of a horse. **23.** a bunch, cluster, or bundle of various leaves, fruit, etc., as a bundle of tobacco leaves tied together or a cluster of bananas. **24.** *Mach.* the deviation of a thread or tooth from the axial direction of a screw or gear, as seen from one end looking away toward the other. **25.** Also called **handle.** the properties of a fabric discernible through touch, as resilience or body: *the smooth hand of satin.* **26.** *Archaic.* a person considered as a source, as of information or of supply. **27. at first hand.** See **firsthand** (def. 1). **28. at hand, a.** within reach; nearby. **b.** near in time; soon. **c.** ready for use. **29. at the hand** or **hands of,** by the action of; through the agency of. **30. by hand,** by using the hands, as opposed to machines; manually. **31. change hands,** to pass from one owner to another; change possession. **32. come to hand, a.** to come within one's reach or notice. **b.** to be received; arrive. **33. eat out of one's hand,** to be at the beck and call of another; be very attentive or servile. **34. force one's hand,** to prompt a person to take immediate action or to reveal his intentions. **35. from hand to mouth,** improvidently; precariously; with nothing in reserve: *to live from hand to mouth.* **36. give someone one's hand on** or **upon something,** to give one's word; seal a bargain by or as by shaking hands. **37. hand and foot, a.** so as to hinder movement. **b.** slavishly; continually. **38. hand and glove,** very intimately associated; closely together. Also, **hand in glove. 39. hand in hand, a.** with one's hand enclasped in that of another person. **b.** closely associated; concurrently; conjointly: *Doctors and nurses work hand in hand to save lives.* **40. hand over fist,** *Informal.* speedily and in abundance; increasingly. **41. hands down, a.** effortlessly; easily. **b.** indisputably; incontestably. **42. hand to hand,** in close combat; at close quarters. **43. have a hand in,** to have a share in; participate in. **44. keep one's hand in,** to maintain interest in or some control of; remain proficient in; continue to practice. **45. on hand, a.** in one's possession; at one's disposal: *cash on hand.* **b.** about to occur; imminent. **c.** *U.S.* present. **46. show one's hand,** to disclose one's true intentions; reveal one's motives. **47. with a heavy hand, a.** with severity; oppressively. **b.** in a clumsy manner; awkwardly. **48. with a high hand,** in an arrogant or dictatorial manner; arbitrarily: *He ran the organization with a high hand.* —*v.t.* **49.** to deliver or pass with or as with the hand. **50.** to help, assist, guide, etc., with the hand: *He handed the elderly woman across the street.* **51.** *Naut.* **a.** to take in or furl (a sail). **b.** to haul on or otherwise handle. **52. hand down, a.** to deliver (the decision of a court). **b.** to transmit from one to another, esp. to bequeath to posterity. **53. hand it to,** *Informal.* to give just credit to; pay respect to. **54. hand on,** to transmit; pass on (to a successor, posterity, etc.): *The silver service was handed on to the eldest daughter.* **55. hand out,** to give or distribute; mete out. **56. hand over, a.** to deliver into the custody of another. **b.** to surrender control of. —*adj.* **57.** of, belonging to, using, or used by the hand. **58.** made by hand. **59.** carried in or worn on the hand. **60.** operated by hand; manual. [ME, OE; c. D, G *Hand,* Icel *hönd,* Goth *handus*] —**hand′like′,** *adj.*

Hand (hand), *n.* **Lear·ned** (lûr′nid), 1872–1961, U.S. jurist.

hand′ ax′. See **broad hatchet.**

hand·bag (hand′bag′), *n.* **1.** a bag or box, as of leather, commonly held in the hand and used by women for carrying money, toilet articles, etc. **2.** valise.

hand·ball (hand′bôl′), *n.* **1.** a game, similar to squash, played by two or four persons who strike a small ball against a wall or walls with the hand. **2.** the small, hard rubber ball used in this game. [late ME *handballe*] —**hand′ball′er,** *n.*

hand·bar·row (hand′bar′ō), *n.* **1.** a frame with handles at each end by which it is carried. **2.** a handcart. [late ME *handberwe*]

hand·bill (hand′bil′), *n.* a small printed bill or announcement, usually for distribution by hand.

hand·book (hand′bŏŏk′), *n.* a book of instruction, guidance, or information, as for an occupation, travel, or reference; manual. [OE *handbōc;* revived in 19th century as counterpart to G *Handbuch*]

hand·breadth (hand′bredth′, -bretth′), *n.* a unit of linear measure from 2½ to 4 inches. Also, **hand's-breadth.**

hand·car (hand′kär′), *n. U.S.* a small railroad car or platform on four wheels propelled by a mechanism worked by hand, used on some railroads for inspecting tracks and transporting workmen.

hand·cart (hand′kärt′), *n.* a small cart drawn or pushed by hand.

hand·clasp (hand′klasp′, -kläsp′), *n.* a clasping of hands by two or more people, as in greeting, parting, making a commitment, expressing affection, etc.

hand·craft (*n.* hand′kraft′, -kräft′; *v.* hand′kraft′, -kräft′), *n.* **1.** handicraft. —*v.t.* **2.** to make (something) by hand. [ME; OE *handcræft*]

hand·cuff (hand′kuf′), *n.* **1.** a ring-shaped metal device that can be locked around a prisoner's wrist, usually one of a pair connected by a short chain or linked bar; shackle. —*v.t.* **2.** to put handcuffs on.

hand·ed (han′did), *adj.* **1.** having a hand or hands. **2.** preferring or more adept at the use of a particular hand (usually used in combination): *left-handed.* **3.** manned; staffed (usually used in combination): *short-handed.*

hand·ed·ness (han′did nis), *n.* a tendency to use one hand more frequently than the other.

Han·del (han′dəl), *n.* **George Frederick** (*Georg Friedrich Händel*), 1685–1759, German composer in England after 1712.

hand·fast (hand′fast′, -fäst′), *n. Archaic.* a covenant, contract, or bargain completed by a handclasp, esp. a betrothal completed in this manner. [ME (ptp.), earlier *handfest* < Scand; cf. Icel *handfestr,* ptp. of *handfesta* to betroth with a joining of hands = *hand* HAND + *festa* to betroth, lit., make fast, FASTEN]

hand-feed (hand′fēd′), *v.t.,* **-fed, -feed·ing. 1.** *Agric.* to feed (animals) with apportioned amounts at regular intervals. Cf. **self-feed. 2.** to feed (an animal or person) by hand.

hand·ful (hand′fŏŏl′), *n., pl.* **-fuls. 1.** the quantity or amount that the hand can hold. **2.** a small amount or quantity. **3.** *Informal.* a person or thing that is as much as one can manage or control. [ME, OE]

hand′ glass′, 1. a small mirror with a handle. **2.** a magnifying glass for holding in the hand.

hand′ grenade′, a grenade or explosive shell that is thrown by hand and exploded usually by means of a fuze.

hand·grip (hand′grip′), *n.* **1.** mode of gripping, as of a handshake: *a firm handgrip; a friendly handgrip.* **2. handgrips,** hand-to-hand combat. **3.** a handle or similar part

of an object affording a grip by the hand, as for lifting. [ME; OE *handgripe*]
hand·gun (hand′gun′), *n.* any firearm that can be held and fired with one hand; a revolver or a pistol.
hand·hold (hand′hōld′), *n.* **1.** a grip with the hand or hands. **2.** something to grip or take hold of, as a support, handle, etc.
hand′ horn′, a forerunner of the modern French horn, developed during the mid-17th century.
hand·i·cap (han′dē kap′), *n., v.* **-capped, -cap·ping.** —*n.* **1.** a race or other contest in which certain disadvantages or advantages of weight, distance, time, etc., are placed upon competitors to equalize their chances of winning. **2.** the disadvantage or advantage itself. **3.** any disadvantage that makes success more difficult. **4.** a physical disability. —*v.t.* **5.** to place at a disadvantage; disable or burden: *He was handicapped by his age.* **6.** to subject to a disadvantageous handicap, as a competitor of recognized superiority. **7.** to assign handicaps to (competitors). **8.** *Sports.* **a.** to attempt to predict the winner of (a contest, esp. a horse race), as by comparing past performances of the contestants. **b.** to assign odds for or against (any particular contestant) winning a contest or series of contests. [orig. *hand i' cap* hand in cap, referring to a drawing before a horse race]
hand·i·capped (han′dē kapt′), *adj.* **1.** crippled or physically disabled. **2.** mentally deficient. **3.** (of a contestant) marked by, being under, or having a handicap: *a handicapped player.* —*n.* **4.** (*construed as pl.*) handicapped persons collectively (usually prec. by *the*).
hand·i·cap·per (han′dē kap′ər), *n.* *Horse Racing.* **1.** a race-track official or employee who assigns the weight a horse must carry in a race. **2.** a person who makes predictions on the outcome of horse races, as for a newspaper.
hand·i·craft (han′dē kraft′, -kräft′), *n.* **1.** manual skill. **2.** an art, craft, or trade requiring manual skill. **3.** the articles made by handicraft. Also, **handcraft.** [ME *hendi craft* dexterous skill] —**hand′i·craft′ship,** *n.*
hand·i·crafts·man (han′dē krafts′mən, -kräfts′-), *n., pl.* **-men.** a person skilled in a handicraft; craftsman.
hand·i·ly (han′di lē, -d^{ə}lē), *adv.* **1.** dexterously; easily. **2.** conveniently; accessibly.
hand·i·ness (han′dē nis), *n.* the state or quality of being handy.
hand·i·work (han′dē wûrk′), *n.* **1.** work done by hand. **2.** the work of a particular person. [ME *handiwerk,* OE *handgeweorc* var. of *handweorc* (c. G *Handwerk*). See HAND, Y-, WORK]
hand·ker·chief (hang′kər chif, -chēf′), *n.* **1.** a small piece of linen, silk, or other fabric, usually square, and used for personal or decorative purposes. **2.** a neckerchief.
hand-knit (hand′nit′), *v.,* **-knit·ted** or **-knit, -knit·ting,** *adj.* —*v.t.* **1.** to knit by hand. —*adj.* **2.** knitted by hand.
han·dle (han′d^{ə}l), *n., v.,* **-dled, -dling.** —*n.* **1.** a part of a thing made specifically to be grasped or held by the hand. **2.** anything resembling or serving as a handle. **3.** *Slang.* a person's name, esp. given name. **4.** the total amount wagered on an event, as in horse racing. **5.** hand (def. 25). **6. fly off the handle,** *Informal.* to become very agitated or angry. —*v.t.* **7.** to touch, pick up, carry, or feel with the hand or hands; use the hands on; take hold of. **8.** to manage, deal with, or be responsible for: *My wife handles the household accounts.* **9.** to use or employ, esp. in a particular manner; manipulate: *to handle color expertly in painting.* **10.** to manage, direct, train, or control: *to handle troops.* **11.** to deal with (a subject, theme, argument, etc.): *The poem handles the problem of instinct versus intellect in man.* **12.** to deal with or treat in a particular way: *to handle a person with tact.* **13.** to deal or trade in: *to handle dry goods.* —*v.i.* **14.** to behave or perform in a particular way when handled, directed, managed, etc.: *The troops handled well. The jet was handling poorly.* [(n.) ME *handel,* OE *hand(e)le;* (v.) ME *handelen,* OE *handlian,* c. G *handeln,* Icel *höndla.* See HAND, -LE] —**han′dle·a·ble,** *adj.* —**han′dle·less,** *adj.*
han·dle·bar (han′d^{ə}l bär′), *n.* Usually, **handlebars.** the curved steering bar of a bicycle, motorcycle, etc., placed in front of the rider and gripped by the hands.
han′dlebar moustache′, a man's moustache having long, curved ends that resemble handlebars.
han·dler (hand′lər), *n.* **1.** a person or thing that handles. **2.** *Boxing.* a person who assists in the training of a fighter or is his second during a fight. **3.** a person who exhibits a dog in a bench show or field trial. [ME]
han·dling (hand′ling), *n.* **1.** a touching, grasping, or using with the hands. **2.** the manner of treating or dealing with something; management; treatment. **3.** the manual or mechanical method or process by which something is moved, carried, transported, etc. —*adj.* **4.** of or pertaining to the process of moving, transporting, delivering, working with, etc.: *a 10 percent handling charge.* [ME; OE *handlung* (n.). See HANDLE, -ING[1], -ING[2]]
hand·loom (hand′lōōm′), *n.* a loom operated manually in contrast to a power loom.
hand·made (hand′mād′), *adj.* made by hand, rather than by machine.
hand·maid (hand′mād′), *n.* a female servant or attendant. Also, **hand′maid′en.** [ME]
hand-me-down (hand′mē doun′, han′-), *n.* **1.** an article of clothing handed down or acquired at second hand. **2.** anything cheap or inferior.
hand′ or′gan, a portable barrel organ played by means of a crank turned by hand.
hand·out (hand′out′), *n.* **1.** a portion of food or the like given to a needy person, as a beggar. **2.** *Journalism.* a press release. **3.** anything given away for nothing, as free samples of a product by an advertiser.
hand-pick (hand′pik′), *v.t.* **1.** to pick by hand. **2.** to select personally and with care.
hand·rail (hand′rāl′), *n.* a rail serving as a support or guard at the side of a stairway, platform, etc.
hand·saw (hand′sô′), *n.* any common saw with a handle at one end for manual operation with one hand. See illus. at **saw.**
hand's-breadth (handz′bredth′, -bretth′), *n.* handbreadth.
hand′ screw′, *Carpentry.* a clamp having two wooden jaws that are adjusted by two long screws. Also called **wood clamp.** See illus. at **clamp.**
hands-down (handz′doun′), *adj.* **1.** effortlessly achieved; easy: *a hands-down victory.* **2.** indubitable; certain: *a hands-down best seller.* —*adv.* **3.** easily; effortlessly: *He won the race hands-down.*
hand·sel (han′səl), *n., v.,* **-seled, -sel·ing** or (*esp. Brit.*) **-selled, -sel·ling.** —*n.* **1.** a gift or token for good luck or as an expression of good wishes, as at the beginning of the new year or when entering upon a new state, situation, or enterprise. **2.** the initial experience of anything; first encounter with or use of something taken as a token of what will follow; foretaste. —*v.t.* **3.** to give a handsel to. **4.** to inaugurate auspiciously. **5.** to use, try, or experience for the first time. Also, **hansel.** [ME *handselne* good-luck token, good-will gift, OE *handselen* manumission, lit., hand gift (see HAND, SELL[1]); c. Dan *handsel* earnest money]
hand·set (hand′set′), *n.* See **French telephone.**
hand·sewn (hand′sōn′), *adj.* sewn by hand.
hand·shake (hand′shāk′), *n.* a clasping and shaking of right hands by two individuals, as to symbolize greeting, congratulation, agreement, farewell, etc.
hands-off (handz′ôf′, -of′), *adj.* characterized by nonintervention, noninterference, etc.: *the new hands-off foreign policy.*
hand·some (han′səm), *adj.,* **-som·er, -som·est.** **1.** having an attractive, well-proportioned, and imposing appearance suggestive of health and strength; good-looking: *a handsome man; a handsome woman.* **2.** having pleasing proportions, relationships, or arrangements, as of shapes, forms, colors, etc.; attractive: *a handsome house.* **3.** considerable, ample, or liberal in amount: *a handsome fortune.* **4.** gracious; generous: *a handsome compliment.* **5.** dexterous; graceful: *a handsome speech.* [late ME *handsom* easy to handle (see HAND, -SOME[1]); c. D *handzaam* tractable] —**hand′some·ly,** *adv.* —**hand′some·ness,** *n.* —**Syn. 1.** See **beautiful. 3.** large, generous. —**Ant. 1.** ugly.
hand·spike (hand′spīk′), *n.* a bar used as a lever. [var. of *handspeck* < D, with assimilation to SPIKE[1]]
hand·spring (hand′spring′), *n.* an acrobatic feat in which a person starts from a standing position and turns the body forward or backward in a complete circle, landing first on the hands and then on the feet.
hand·stand (hand′stand′), *n.* the act or an instance of supporting the body in a vertical position by balancing on the palms of the hands.
hand-to-hand (hand′tə hand′), *adj.* close by one's adversary; at close quarters: *hand-to-hand combat.*
hand-to-mouth (hand′tə mouth′), *adj.* offering or providing the barest livelihood, sustenance, or support; precarious; unsettled: *a hand-to-mouth existence.*
hand′ truck′, truck[1] (def. 2).
hand·work (hand′wûrk′), *n.* work done by hand, as distinguished from that done by machine. [ME; OE *handweorc*]
hand·wo·ven (hand′wō′vən), *adj.* made on a handloom; handloomed.
hand·write (hand′rīt′), *v.t.,* **-wrote** or (*Archaic*) **-writ; -writ·ten** or (*Archaic*) **-writ; -writ·ing.** to write (something) by hand. [back formation from HANDWRITING]
hand·writ·ing (hand′rī′ting), *n.* **1.** writing done with the hand. **2.** a style or manner of writing by hand, esp. that which characterizes a particular person: *an eccentric handwriting.* **3.** *Obs.* a handwritten document; manuscript. **4. handwriting on the wall,** a premonition, portent, or clear indication, esp. of failure or disaster. Also, **writing on the wall.**
hand·y (han′dē), *adj.,* **hand·i·er, hand·i·est.** **1.** within easy reach; conveniently available; accessible: *The aspirin is handy.* **2.** convenient or useful: *a handy reference book.* **3.** skillful with the hands; deft; dexterous: *a handy person.*
Han·dy (han′dē), *n.* **W(illiam) C(hristopher),** 1873–1958, U.S. blues composer.
hand·y·man (han′dē man′), *n., pl.* **-men.** a man hired to do various small jobs.
Han·ford (han′fərd), *n.* a locality in SE Washington, on the Columbia River: site of an atomic energy plant **(Han′ford Works′).** Cf. **Richland.**
hang (hang), *v.,* **hung** or (*esp. for 4, 5, 11, 15*) **hanged; hang·ing;** *n.* —*v.t.* **1.** to fasten or attach (a thing) so that it is supported only from above or at a point near its own top; suspend. **2.** to attach or suspend so as to allow free movement: *to hang a pendulum.* **3.** to place in position or fasten, so as to allow easy or ready movement. **4.** to execute by suspending from a gallows, gibbet, yardarm, or the like, as a mode of capital punishment. **5.** to suspend by the neck until dead: *He hanged himself from a beam in the attic.* **6.** to furnish or decorate with something suspended: *to hang a room with pictures.* **7.** to fasten into position; fix at a proper angle: *to hang a scythe.* **8.** to fasten or attach (wallpaper, pictures, curtains, etc.) to a wall or the like. **9.** *Fine Arts.* **a.** to exhibit (a painting or paintings), as in a gallery. **b.** to put the paintings of (an art exhibition) on the wall of a gallery. **10.** to attach (a door, shutter, or the like) to its frame by means of hinges. **11.** (used in mild curses and emphatic expressions, often as a euphemism for *damn*): *I'll be hanged if I do. Hang it all!* **12.** to keep (a jury) from rendering a verdict, as one juror by refusing to agree with the others.
—*v.i.* **13.** to be suspended; dangle. **14.** to swing freely, as on a hinge. **15.** to be suspended by the neck, as from a gallows and suffer death in this way. **16.** to incline downward, jut out, or lean over or forward. **17.** to be conditioned or contingent; be dependent: *His future hangs on the outcome of their discussion.* **18.** to be doubtful or undecided; waiver; hesitate. **19.** to remain unfinished or undecided; be delayed. **20.** to linger, remain, or persist. **21.** to float or hover in the air. **22.** to remain in attention or consideration (often fol. by *on* or *upon*): *They hung on his every word.* **23.** *Fine Arts.* **a.** to be exhibited: *His works hang in most major museums.* **b.** to have one's works on display: *Rembrandt hangs in the Metropolitan Museum of Art.* **24.** to fail to agree, as a jury. **25.** to fit or drape in graceful lines: *That coat hangs well in back.* **26. hang around** or **about,** *Informal.* to spend time in a certain place; linger; loiter. **27. hang back,** to be reluctant to

proceed or move forward; hesitate. **28. hang fire.** See **fire** (def. 19). **29. hang in,** *Slang.* to keep up one's determination, courage, or good spirit in the face of adversity; persevere. Also, **hang in there. 30. hang in the balance,** to be in doubt or suspense. **31. hang on,** to hold fast; cling to; persevere. **32. hang one on,** *Slang.* **a.** to strike (someone) a blow; hit. **b.** to become extremely drunk. **33. hang out, a.** to lean or be suspended through an opening. **b.** *Slang.* to frequent a particular place, esp. in idling away one's free time. **34. hang together, a.** to be loyal to one another; remain united. **b.** to cling together; cohere. **c.** to be logical or consistent: *His story doesn't hang together.* **35. hang up, a.** to suspend by placing on a hook, peg, or hanger. **b.** to cause or encounter delay; hold back. **c.** to break a telephone connection by replacing the receiver on the hook.
—*n.* **36.** the way in which a thing hangs. **37.** *Informal.* the precise manner of doing, using, etc., something; knack: *to get the hang of a job.* **38.** *Informal.* meaning; thought; concept. **39.** the least degree of care, concern, etc. (used in mild curses and emphatic expressions as a euphemism for *damn*): *He doesn't give a hang about it.* [fusion of 3 verbs: (1) ME, OE *hōn* to hang, c. Goth *hāhan,* orig. **hanhan;* (2) ME *hang(i)en,* OE *hangian* to hang, c. G *hangen;* (3) ME *henge* < Scand; cf. Icel *hengja,* c. G *hängen* to hang]
—**Syn. 5.** HANG, LYNCH through a widespread misconception have been thought of as synonyms. They do have in common the meaning of "to put to death," but lynching is not always by hanging. HANG, in the sense of execute, is in accordance with a legal sentence, the method of execution being to suspend by the neck until dead. To LYNCH, however, implies the summary putting to death, by any method, of someone charged with a flagrant offense (though guilt may not have been proved). Lynching is done by private persons, usually a mob, without legal authority. **17.** depend, rely.

hang·ar (haŋ′ər), *n.* **1.** a shed or shelter. **2.** any enclosed structure used for housing airplanes or airships. [< F: shed, hangar; cf. ML *angārium* shed for shoeing horses < ?]

Hang·chow (haŋ′chou′; *Chin.* häŋ′jō′), *n.* a seaport in and the capital of Chekiang province, in E China, on Hangchow Bay. 1,100,000.

Hang′chow Bay′, a bay of the East China Sea.

hang·dog (haŋ′dôg′, -dog′), *adj.* **1.** browbeaten; defeated; intimidated; abject: *a hangdog look.* **2.** shamefaced; guilty. **3.** suitable to a degraded or contemptible person; furtive. —*n.* **4.** *Archaic.* a degraded, contemptible person.

hang·er (haŋ′ər), *n.* **1.** a shoulder-shaped frame with a hook at the top, usually of wire, wood, or plastic, for draping and hanging an article of clothing when not in use. **2.** a part of something by which it is hung, as a loop on a garment. **3.** a contrivance on which things are hung, as a hook. **4.** a person who hangs something.

hang·er-on (haŋ′ər on′, -ôn′), *n., pl.* **hang·ers-on.** a person who remains in a place or with a group, another person, etc., in the hope of gaining some personal end.

hang·fire (haŋ′fīᵊr′), *n.* a delay in the detonation of gunpowder or other ammunition, caused by some defect in the fuze.

hang′ glid′er, a kitelike glider consisting of a V-shaped wing underneath which the pilot is strapped: kept aloft by updrafts and guided by the pilot's shifting body weight.

hang′ glid′ing, the sport of launching oneself from a cliff or a steep incline and soaring through the air by means of a hang glider.

hang·ing (haŋ′iŋ), *n.* **1.** the act, an instance, or the form of capital punishment carried out by suspending one by the neck from a gallows, gibbet, or the like, until dead. **2.** Often, **hangings.** something that hangs or is hung on the walls of a room, as a drapery or tapestry. **3.** the act of a person or thing that hangs; suspension. —*adj.* **4.** punishable by, deserving, or causing death by hanging. **5.** suspended; pendent; overhanging. **6.** situated on a steep slope or at a height: *a hanging garden.* **7.** directed downward: *a hanging look.* **8.** made, holding, or suitable for a hanging object. [ME (n., adj.); OE *hangande* (adj.)]

Hang′ing Gar′dens of Bab′ylon, ornamental gardens planted on the terraces of the ziggurats of ancient Babylon. Cf. **Seven Wonders of the World.**

hang·man (haŋ′mən), *n., pl.* **-men.** a person who hangs persons condemned to death; public executioner. [ME]

hang′man's knot′, a slip noose for hanging a person.

hang·nail (haŋ′nāl′), *n.* a small piece of partly detached skin at the side or base of the fingernail. Also called **agnail.** [ME *angenayle* corn, OE *angnægl* = *ang-* + *nægl* callus, NAIL; modern *h-* by assoc. with HANG]

hang·out (haŋ′out′), *n.* *Informal.* a place where a person lives or frequently visits.

hang·o·ver (haŋ′ō′vər), *n.* **1.** the disagreeable physical aftereffects of drunkenness, usually felt several hours after cessation of drinking. **2.** something remaining behind from a former period or state of affairs.

hang-up (haŋ′up′), *n.* *Slang.* a preoccupation, fixation, or psychological block. Also, **hang′up′.**

hank (haŋk), *n.* **1.** a skein, as of thread or yarn. **2.** a definite length of thread or yarn: *A hank of cotton yarn measures 840 yards.* **3.** a coil, knot, or loop: *a hank of hair.* **4.** *Naut.* a ring, link, or shackle for securing the luff of a staysail or jib to its stay or the luff or head of a gaff sail to the mast or gaff. —*v.t.* **5.** *Naut.* to fasten (a sail) by means of hanks. [ME < Scand; cf. Icel *hönk* hank, coil, skein, clasp]

han·ker (haŋ′kər), *v.i.* to have a restless or incessant longing (often fol. by *after, for,* or an infinitive). [< Flem *hankere(n),* nasalized freq. of D *haken* to long, hanker] —**han′ker·er,** *n.*

han·ker·ing (haŋ′kər iŋ), *n.* a longing; craving. —**han′ker·ing·ly,** *adv.*

Han·kow (han′kou′; *Chin.* hän′kō′), *n.* a former city in E China: now part of Wuhan.

han·ky (haŋ′kē), *n., pl.* **-kies.** a handkerchief. Also, **han′kie.** [HAN(D)K(ERCHIEF) + -Y[2]]

han·ky-pan·ky (haŋ′kē paŋ′kē), *n.* *Informal.* **1.** unethical behavior; mischief; deceit. **2.** foolishness; playful talk or behavior. **3.** *Brit.* sleight of hand; magic. Also, **han′key-pan′key.** [rhyming compound modeled on HOCUS-POCUS]

Han·na (han′ə), *n.* **Marcus Alonzo** ("*Mark*"), 1837–1904, U.S. merchant and politician: senator 1897–1904.

Han·ni·bal (han′ə bəl), *n.* **1.** 247–183 B.C., Carthaginian general who crossed the Alps and invaded Italy (son of Hamilcar Barca). **2.** a port in NE Missouri, on the Mississippi: Mark Twain's boyhood home. 18,698 (1970).

Han·no (han′ō), *n.* Carthaginian statesman, fl. 3rd century B.C.: opponent of Hannibal.

Han·no·ver (hä nō′vər), *n.* German name of **Hanover.**

Ha·noi (ha noi′, hä′noi′), *n.* a city in and the capital of Vietnam, in the N part, on the Songka River. 1,443,500.

Ha·no·taux (A nô tō′), *n.* **(Al·bert Au·guste) Ga·bri·el** (Al bеr′ ō gyst′ gA brē el′), 1853–1944, French statesman and historian.

Han·o·ver (han′ō vər), *n.* **1.** a member of the royal family that ruled Great Britain under that name from 1714 to 1901. **2.** German, **Hannover.** a former province in N West Germany; now a district in Lower Saxony. 14,944 sq. mi. **3.** German, **Hannover.** a city in and the capital of Lower Saxony, in N West Germany. 549,100.

Han·o·ve·ri·an (han′ō vēr′ē ən), *adj.* **1.** of the house of Hanover. —*n.* **2.** a supporter of the house of Hanover.

Han·sa (han′sə, -zə), *n.* **1.** a company or guild of merchants in a medieval town. **2.** a fee paid to a guild by a new member. **3.** Also called **Han′sa town′, Hansetown.** a town that is a member of the Hanseatic League. **4.** See **Hanseatic League.** [< ML; r. ME *hans, hanze* < MLG *hanse;* c. OE *hōs,* OHG, Goth *hansa* company]

Han·sard (han′sərd), *n.* the official published reports of the debates and proceedings in the British Parliament. [named after Luke *Hansard* (1752–1828) and his descendants who compiled the reports until 1889]

Han·se·at·ic (han′sē at′ik), *adj.* **1.** of or pertaining to the Hanseatic League or to any of the towns belonging to it. —*n.* **2.** any of the towns belonging to the Hanseatic League. [< ML *Hanseāticus* = *hanse* (< MLG; see HANSA) + *-āt-* -ATE[1] + *-icus* -IC]

Han′seat′ic League′, a medieval league, principally of German towns, for the promotion and protection of trading privileges. Also called **Hansa.**

Centers of the Hanseatic League

han·sel (han′səl), *n., v.t.,* **-seled, -sel·ing** or (*esp. Brit.*) **-selled, -sel·ling.** handsel.

Han′sen's disease′, *Pathol.* leprosy. [named after G. H. *Hansen* (1841–1912), Norwegian physician and discoverer of leprosy-causing *Mycobacterium leprae*]

Hanse·town (hans′town′), *n.* Hansa (def. 3).

han·som (han′səm), *n.* a low-hung, two-wheeled, covered vehicle drawn by one horse, for two passengers, the driver being mounted on an elevated seat behind, and the reins running over the roof. Also called **han′som cab′.** [named after J. A. *Hansom* (1803–82), English architect who designed it]

Hansom

Han·son (han′sən), *n.* **Howard (Harold),** 1896–1981, U.S. composer and conductor.

hant (hant), *v.t., v.i., n.* *Dial.* haunt. Also, **ha'nt.**

Hants (hants), *n.* Hampshire (def. 1).

Ha·nuk·kah (hä′nə kə, -nŏŏ kä′, -kə; *Heb.* KHä nōō kä′), *n.* an eight-day Jewish festival starting on the 25th day of Kislev, commemorating the rededication of the Temple by the Maccabees following their victory over the Syrians and characterized chiefly by the lighting of the menorah on each night of the festival. Also, **Chanukah.** [< Heb: lit., a dedicating]

Han·u·man (hun′ŏŏ män′, hä′nŏŏ-; hun′ŏŏ män′, hä′nŏŏ-), *n.* *Hindu Myth.* a monkey chief who is a conspicuous figure in the *Ramayana.* [< Hindi *Hanumān* < Skt *hanuman,* lit., having (big) jaws < *hanu* jaw]

Han·yang (hän′yäŋ′), *n.* a former city in E China: now part of Wuhan.

hap[1] (hap), *n., v.,* **happed, hap·ping.** *Archaic.* —*n.* **1.** a person's luck or lot. **2.** an occurrence, happening, or accident. —*v.i.* **3.** to happen: *if it so hap.* [ME < Scand; cf. Icel *happ* luck, chance; akin to OE *gehæp* fit, convenient]

hap[2] (hap, ap), *v.t.,* **happed, hap·ping,** *n.* *Dial.* —*v.t.* **1.** to cover with or as with a fabric, esp. with a cloak or bedclothes. —*n.* **2.** a covering, esp. one of fabric for warmth. [ME *happe* to cover]

Hap (häp, KHäp), *n.* Apis.

hap·haz·ard (*adj., adv.* hap haz′ərd; *n.* hap′haz′ərd), *adj.* **1.** characterized by lack of order or planning; irregular; random; aimless. —*adv.* **2.** haphazardly. —*n.* **3.** mere chance; accident. —**hap·haz′ard·ness,** *n.*

hap·haz·ard·ly (hap haz′ərd lē), *adv.* at random; by chance; in a haphazard manner.

Haph·ta·rah (häf tôr′ə; *Heb.* häf tä Rä′), *n., pl.* **-ta·roth** (-tôr′ōt; *Heb.* -tä Rôt′), **-ta·rahs.** *Judaism.* Haftarah.

Ha·pi (hä′pē, ᴋʜä′pē), *n.* Apis.
hap·less (hap′lis), *adj.* luckless; unfortunate; unlucky. —**hap′less·ly,** *adv.* —**hap′less·ness,** *n.*
haplo-, a learned borrowing from Greek meaning "single," "simple," used in the formation of compound words: *haplology.* Also, *esp. before a vowel,* **hapl-.** [< Gk, comb. form of *haplóos* single, simple; akin to L *simplex*]
hap·loid (hap′loid), *adj.* Also, **hap·loi′dic. 1.** single; simple. **2.** *Biol.* pertaining to a single set of chromosomes. —*n.* **3.** *Biol.* an organism or cell having only one complete set of chromosomes, ordinarily half the normal diploid number.
hap·lol·o·gy (hap lol′ə jē), *n. Gram.* the syncope of a syllable within a word, as *syllabication* for *syllabification.* —**hap·lo·log·ic** (hap′lə loj′ik), *adj.*
hap·lo·pi·a (hap lō′pē ə), *n. Ophthalm.* normal vision (opposed to *diplopia*).
hap·lo·sis (hap lō′sis), *n. Biol.* the production of haploid chromosome groups during meiosis.
hap·ly (hap′lē), *adv.* perhaps; by chance. [ME *hapliche*]
hap·pen (hap′ən), *v.i.* **1.** to take place; come to pass; occur. **2.** to come to pass by chance; occur without apparent reason or design; chance. **3.** to have the fortune or lot (to do or be as specified): *I happened to see him on the street.* **4.** to befall, as to a person or thing. **5.** to meet or discover by chance (usually fol. by *on* or *upon*): *to happen on a clue to the mystery.* **6.** to be, come, go, etc., casually or by chance: *My friend happened along.* [ME *hap(pe)nen.* See HAP[1], -EN[1]]
—**Syn. 1.** betide. HAPPEN, CHANCE, OCCUR refer to the taking place of an event. HAPPEN, which originally denoted the taking place by hap or chance, is now the most general word for coming to pass: *When do you expect it to happen?* CHANCE suggests the fortuitousness of an event: *It chanced to rain that day.* OCCUR is often interchangeable with HAPPEN, but is more formal, and is usually more specific as to time and event: *His death occurred the following year.*
hap·pen·ing (hap′ə niṉg), *n.* **1.** an occurrence or event. **2.** a dramatic or similar performance consisting chiefly of a series of discontinuous events. **3.** any special event or gathering in which the audience is to perform a spontaneous creative part.
hap·pen·stance (hap′ən stans′), *n.* chance; accident.
hap·pi·ly (hap′ə lē), *adv.* **1.** in a happy manner; with pleasure. **2.** by good fortune; luckily; providentially. **3.** with skill; aptly; appropriately. [ME]
hap·pi·ness (hap′ē nis), *n.* **1.** the quality or state of being happy. **2.** good fortune; pleasure; contentment; joy. **3.** aptness or felicity, as of expression.
—**Syn. 1, 2.** contentedness, delight, enjoyment, satisfaction. HAPPINESS, BLISS, CONTENTMENT, FELICITY imply an active or passive state of pleasure or pleasurable satisfaction. HAPPINESS results from the possession or attainment of what one considers good: *the happiness of visiting one's family.* BLISS is unalloyed happiness or supreme delight: *the bliss of perfect companionship.* CONTENTMENT is a peaceful kind of happiness in which one rests without desires: *contentment in one's surroundings.* FELICITY is a formal word for happiness of an especially fortunate or intense kind: *to wish a young couple felicity in life.* —**Ant. 1, 2.** misery.
hap·py (hap′ē), *adj.,* **-pi·er, -pi·est. 1.** delighted, pleased, or glad, as over a particular thing. **2.** characterized by or indicative of pleasure, contentment, or joy: *a happy mood.* **3.** favored by fortune; fortunate or lucky: *a happy occurrence.* **4.** apt or felicitous, as actions, utterances, ideas, etc. **5.** obsessed by or quick to use the item indicated (usually used in combination): *a trigger-happy gangster.* [ME]
—**Syn. 1, 2.** joyful, cheerful, merry, contented, gay, blissful, satisfied. **3.** favorable, propitious. See **fortunate. 4.** appropriate, fitting, opportune. —**Ant. 1, 2.** sad.
hap·py-go-luck·y (hap′ē gō luk′ē), *adj.* **1.** trusting cheerfully to luck; happily unworried or unconcerned, esp. with reference to future events or practical matters; easygoing. —*adv.* **2.** *Archaic.* by mere chance; haphazardly.
hap′py hunt′ing ground′, the American Indian heaven for warriors and hunters.
Haps·burg (haps′bûrg; *Ger.* häps′bo͝ork′), *n.* a German princely family, prominent since the 11th century, that has furnished sovereigns to the Holy Roman Empire, Austria, Spain, etc. Also, **Habsburg.**
ha·ra-ki·ri (här′ə kēr′ē, har′ə-, har′ē-), *n.* **1.** ceremonial suicide by ripping open the abdomen with a dagger or knife: formerly practiced in Japan by members of the warrior class when disgraced or sentenced to death. **2.** suicide or any suicidal action; a self-destructive act: *political hara-kiri.* Also, **hari-kari.** [< Jap = *hara* belly + *kiri* cut]
ha·rangue (hə raṉg′), *n., v.,* **-rangued, -rangu·ing.** —*n.* **1.** a long, passionate, and vehement speech, esp. one delivered before a public gathering. **2.** any long, pompous speech or writing of a tediously hortatory or didactic nature; a sermonizing lecture. **3.** a scolding; verbal attack. —*v.t.* **4.** to address in a harangue. —*v.i.* **5.** to deliver a harangue. [< MF < ML *harenga* a meeting, speech made there < Gmc; cf. OHG, OS, OE *hring* RING[1]; r. late ME *arang* < MF *arenge*] —**ha·rangu′er,** *n.* —**Syn. 1.** See **speech.**
Ha·rar (här′ər), *n.* a city in E Ethiopia. 38,000 (est. 1962). Also, **Harrar.**
Ha·ra·re (hə rär′ā), *n.* a city in and the capital of Zimbabwe, in the NE part. 675,000. Formerly, **Salisbury.**
har·ass (har′əs, hə ras′), *v.t.* **1.** to trouble by repeated attacks, incursions, etc., as in war or hostilities; harry; raid. **2.** to disturb persistently; torment; pester; persecute. [< F *harass(er)* (to) tire out, wear down, based on OF *harer* to sic < OHG *harēn* to cry out] —**har′ass·er,** *n.* —**har′ass·ing·ly,** *adv.* —**har′ass·ment,** *n.* —**Syn. 2.** badger, vex, plague. See **worry.**
Har·bin (här′bin), *n.* a city in central Manchuria, in NE China. 1,552,000 (est. 1957). Also called **Pinkiang.**
har·bin·ger (här′bin jər), *n.* **1.** a person who goes before and makes known the approach of another; herald. **2.** anything that foreshadows a future event; omen; sign. **3.** a person sent in advance of troops, a royal train, etc., to provide or secure lodgings and other accommodations. —*v.t.* **4.** to act as harbinger to; herald the coming of. [late ME *herbenger,* nasalized var. of *herbegere* < MF, dissimilated var. of *herberg(i)ere* (nom.) host = *herberge* shelter (< Gmc; see HARBOR) + *-iere* -ER[2]]
har·bor (här′bər), *n.* **1.** a portion of a body of water along the shore deep enough for anchoring a ship, and so situated with respect to coastal features, whether natural or artificial, as to provide protection from winds, waves, and currents. **2.** such a body of water having docks or port facilities. **3.** any place of shelter or refuge. —*v.t.* **4.** to give shelter to; offer refuge to: *to harbor refugees.* **5.** to conceal; hide: *to harbor fugitives.* **6.** to keep or hold in the mind; maintain; entertain: *to harbor suspicion.* **7.** to house or contain. **8.** to shelter (a vessel), as in a harbor. —*v.i.* **9.** (of a vessel) to take shelter in a harbor. Also, *esp. Brit.,* **harbour.** [ME *herber(we), herberge,* OE *herebeorg* lodgings, quarters (*here* army + *(ge)beorg* refuge); c. G *Herberge*] —**har′bor·er,** *n.* —**har′bor·less,** *adj.* —**har′bor·side′,** *adv.*
—**Syn. 1.** HARBOR, HAVEN, PORT indicate a shelter for ships. A HARBOR may be naturally or artificially constructed or improved: *a fine harbor on the eastern coast.* A HAVEN is usually a natural harbor that can be utilized by ships as a place of safety; the word is common in poetic use: *a haven in time of storm; a haven of refuge.* A PORT is a HARBOR viewed esp. in its commercial relations, though it is frequently applied in the meaning of HARBOR or HAVEN also: *a thriving port; any port in a storm.* **3.** asylum, sanctuary, retreat. **4.** protect, lodge. **6.** See **cherish.**
har·bor·age (här′bər ij), *n.* **1.** shelter, esp. for vessels. **2.** a place of shelter; lodging. Also, *esp. Brit.,* **harbourage.**
har′bor mas′ter, an official who supervises operations in a harbor area and administers its rules.
har′bor seal′, a small, spotted seal, *Phoca vitulina,* of the Atlantic coasts of North America and Europe and the Pacific coast of northern North America.
har·bour (här′bər), *n., v.t., v.i. Chiefly Brit.* harbor.
hard (härd), *adj.* **1.** not soft; solid and firm to the touch. **2.** firmly formed; tight: *a hard knot.* **3.** difficult to do or accomplish; fatiguing; troublesome: *a hard task.* **4.** difficult or troublesome with respect to an action, situation, person, etc.: *hard to please.* **5.** difficult to deal with, manage, control, overcome, or understand: *a hard problem.* **6.** involving a great deal of effort, energy, or persistence: *hard labor; hard study.* **7.** performing or carrying on work with great effort, energy, or persistence: *a hard worker.* **8.** vigorous or violent in force; severe: *a hard rain; a hard fall.* **9.** bad; unendurable; unbearable: *hard luck.* **10.** oppressive; harsh; rough: *hard treatment.* **11.** austere; severe: *a hard winter.* **12.** harsh or severe in dealing with others: *a hard master.* **13.** difficult to explain away; undeniable: *hard facts.* **14.** harsh or unfriendly; resentful: *hard feelings.* **15.** of stern judgment or close examination; searching: *a hard look.* **16.** lacking delicacy or softness; sharp; harsh: *a hard face.* **17.** (of a photograph) contrasty. **18.** severe or rigorous in terms: *a hard bargain.* **19.** sternly realistic; dispassionate; unsentimental: *a hard view of life.* **20.** incorrigible; disreputable; tough: *a hard character.* **21.** *Chiefly Dial.* niggardly; stingy. **22.** (used to emphasize money as currency, distinguished from checks or other negotiable instruments): *hard cash.* **23.** (of money) supported by sufficient gold reserves: *hard currency.* **24.** (of alcoholic beverages) **a.** containing more than 22.5 percent alcohol by volume, as whiskey and brandy as opposed to beer and wine. **b.** strong; intoxicating: *hard cider.* **25.** (of water) containing mineral salts that interfere with the action of soap. **26.** (of bread and baked goods) **a.** having a firm, crisp crust or texture: *hard rolls.* **b.** stale or tough. **27.** (of a fabric) having relatively little nap; smooth. **28.** (of the landing of a space vehicle) destroying or damaging the vehicle or its contents: *a hard landing on the moon.* **29.** *Mil.* being underground and strongly protected from nuclear bombardment. **30.** *Phonet.* **a.** fortis. **b.** (of *c* and *g*) pronounced as (k) in *come* and (g) in *go,* rather than as in *cent, cello, suspicion, gem,* or *beige.* **c.** (of consonants in Slavic languages) not palatalized. Cf. **soft** (def. 18). **31. hard of hearing,** partly deaf. **32. hard up,** *Informal.* **a.** urgently in need of money. **b.** feeling a lack or need. —*adv.* **33.** with great exertion; with vigor or violence; strenuously: *to work hard.* **34.** earnestly, intently, or critically: *to look hard at a thing.* **35.** harshly or severely. **36.** so as to be solid, tight, or firm: *frozen hard.* **37.** with strong force or impact: *She tripped and came down hard on her back.* **38.** in a deeply affected manner; with genuine sorrow: *He took the news very hard.* **39.** closely; immediately; in immediate proximity: *War seemed hard at hand.* **40.** to an unreasonable or extreme degree; excessively; immoderately: *He's hitting the bottle pretty hard.* **41.** *Naut.* closely, fully or to the extreme limit: *hard aport.* **42. hard by,** in close proximity to; near. **43. hard put to it,** in great perplexity or difficulty; at a loss: *hard put to it to meet the deadline.* Also, **hard put.** [ME; OE *heard;* c. D *hard,* G *hart,* Icel *harthr,* Goth *hardus;* akin to Gk *kratýs* strong]
—**Syn. 1.** inflexible, rigid, unyielding. See **firm**[1]. **3.** toilsome, burdensome, wearisome, exhausting. HARD, DIFFICULT both describe something resistant to one's efforts or one's endurance. HARD is the general word: *hard times; It was hard to endure the severe weather.* DIFFICULT means not easy, and particularly denotes something that requires special effort or skill: *a difficult task.* **5.** complex, complicated, perplexing, puzzling, intricate, knotty, tough. **6.** arduous, onerous, laborious. **10.** severe, rigorous, cruel, merciless, unsparing. **12.** stern, austere, strict, exacting, obdurate, unpitying. HARD, CALLOUS, UNFEELING, UNSYMPATHETIC imply a lack of interest in, feeling for, or sympathy with others. HARD implies insensibility so that the plight of others makes no impression on one: *a hard taskmaster.* CALLOUS may mean the same or that one is himself insensitive to hurt as the result of continued repression and indifference: *a callous answer; callous to criticism.* UNFEELING implies an inability to feel with and for others: *an unfeeling and thoughtless remark.* UNSYMPATHETIC implies an indifference that precludes pity, compassion, or the like: *unsympathetic toward distress.* **13.** incontrovertible. **14.** unkind, unpleasant. —**Ant. 1.** soft. **3–6.** easy.
hard-and-fast (härd′ᵊn fast′, -fäst′), *adj.* strongly binding; not to be set aside or violated: *hard-and-fast rules.* —**hard′-and-fast′ness,** *n.*

hard·back (härd′bak′), *n., adj.* hardcover.

hard·ball (härd′bôl′), *Slang.* —*n.* **1.** baseball. **2. play hardball,** to take aggressive or ruthless action, as in business or politics. —*adj.* **3.** aggressive or ruthless: *hardball politics.* **4.** difficult; complicated: *hardball questions.*

hard-bit·ten (härd′bit′ᵊn), *adj.* conditioned by struggle; tough; stubborn.

hard·board (härd′bōrd′, -bôrd′), *n.* a material made from wood fibers compressed into sheets.

hard-boil (härd′boil′), *v.t.* to boil (an egg) until hard.

hard-boiled (härd′boild′), *adj.* **1.** boiled until hard, as an egg (distinguished from *soft-boiled*). **2.** tough; realistic; unsentimental: *a hard-boiled detective; a hard-boiled appraisal.*

hard·bound (härd′bound′), *adj.* (of a book) bound with a stiff cover; casebound. Cf. **paperback.**

hard′ can′dy, candy, often fruit-flavored, made by boiling together sugar and corn syrup.

hard′ ci′der. See under **cider.**

hard′ clam′, a quahog.

hard′ coal′, anthracite.

hard′ core′, 1. the permanent, dedicated, and completely faithful nucleus of a group or movement, as of a political party. **2.** an unyielding or intransigent element in a social or organizational structure; the part of a group that is difficult to deal with and resistant to change.

hard-core (härd′kôr′), *adj.* **1.** unswervingly committed; uncompromising; dedicated: *a hard-core segregationist.* **2.** pruriently explicit or detailed with little or no redeeming value: *hard-core pornography.* Cf. **soft-core. 3.** of those who suffer chronically because of inadequate skill, unequal opportunity, or depressed morale: *hard-core unemployment.*

hard·cov·er (härd′kuv′ər), *n.* **1.** a hardbound book. —*adj.* **2.** hardbound. **3.** noting or pertaining to hardcover books: *hardcover sales.* Cf. **paperback.** —**hard′cov′ered,** *adj.*

hard′ din′kum, *Australian Informal.* hard work.

hard′ drug′, any drug that is physiologically addictive and physically and psychologically harmful, such as heroin. Cf. **soft drug.**

Har·de·ca·nute (här′də kə no͞ot′, -nyo͞ot′), *n.* 1019?–42, king of Denmark 1035–42, king of England 1040–42 (son of Canute). Also, **Har′di·ca·nute′, Harthacnut.**

hard·en (här′dᵊn), *v.t.* **1.** to make hard or harder. **2.** to make pitiless or unfeeling: *to harden one's heart.* **3.** to make rigid or unyielding; reinforce; toughen. —*v.i.* **4.** to become hard or harder. **5.** to become pitiless or unfeeling. **6.** to become inured or unyielding; toughen. **7.** *Com.* (of a market, prices, etc.) **a.** to cease to fluctuate; firm. **b.** to rise higher. [ME] —**Syn. 1.** solidify, indurate; petrify.

Har·den·berg (här′dᵊn berk′), *n.* Novalis.

har·dened (här′dᵊnd), *adj.* **1.** made or become hard or harder. **2.** pitiless; unfeeling. **3.** confirmed; firmly established; unlikely to change: *a hardened criminal; a hardened attitude.* **4.** inured; toughened: *a hardened trooper.*

hard·en·er (här′dᵊnər), *n.* a substance that causes hardening, as a constituent of paint, epoxy cements, or the like.

hard·en·ing (här′dᵊning), *n.* **1.** a material that hardens another, as an alloy added to iron to make steel. **2.** the process of becoming hard or rigid.

hard-fist·ed (härd′fis′tid), *adj.* **1.** stingy; miserly; close-fisted. **2.** tough-minded; ruthless: *hard-fisted gangsters.* Also, **hard′fist′ed.** —**hard′-fist′ed·ness,** *n.*

hard′ goods′, durable merchandise, as automobiles, furniture, home appliances, etc. Cf. **soft goods.**

hard·hack (härd′hak′), *n.* a woolly-leaved, North American, rosaceous shrub, *Spiraea tomentosa,* having terminal panicles of rose-colored or white flowers.

hard-hand·ed (härd′han′did), *adj.* **1.** having hands hardened by toil. **2.** oppressive; cruel. Also, **hard′hand′ed.** —**hard′-hand′ed·ness, hard′hand′ed·ness,** *n.*

hard′ hat′, a protective helmet of metal or plastic, esp. as worn by construction workers.

hard-hat (härd′hat′), *n. Informal.* **1.** a construction worker, esp. a member of a construction workers' union. **2.** Also, **hard′ hat′, hard′hat′.** any working-class conservative, esp. one who dislikes modern liberals, long-haired students, etc.

hard·head (härd′hed′), *n.* **1.** a shrewd, practical person. **2.** a blockhead. **3.** a cyprinid fish, *Mylopharodon conocephalus,* found in the fresh waters of California. **4.** See **hardhead sponge.**

hard-head·ed (härd′hed′id), *adj.* **1.** not easily moved or deceived; practical; shrewd. **2.** obstinate; stubborn; willful. Also **hard′head′ed.** —**hard′-head′ed·ly, hard′head′ed·ly,** *adv.* —**hard′-head′ed·ness, hard′head′ed·ness,** *n.*

hard′head sponge′, any of several commercial sponges, as *Spongia officinalis dura,* of the West Indies and Central America, having a resilient, fibrous skeleton.

hard-heart·ed (härd′här′tid), *adj.* unfeeling; unmerciful; pitiless. Also, **hard′heart′ed.** [ME *hardherted*] —**hard′-heart′ed·ly, hard′heart′ed·ly,** *adv.* —**hard′-heart′ed·ness, hard′heart′ed·ness,** *n.*

har·di·hood (här′dē ho͝od′), *n.* **1.** hardy spirit or character; determination to survive; fortitude. **2.** strength; power; vigor. **3.** boldness or daring; courage.

har·di·ly (här′dᵊlē), *adv.* in a hardy manner. [ME]

har·di·ment (här′dē mənt), *n. Archaic.* hardihood. [ME]

har·di·ness (här′dē nis), *n.* **1.** the state or quality of being hardy; capacity for enduring hardship, privation, etc. **2.** courage; boldness; audacity. [ME]

Har·ding (här′ding), *n.* **Warren G(amaliel),** 1865–1923, 29th president of the U.S. 1921–23.

hard′ knocks′, *U.S. Informal.* adversity or hardships.

hard′ la′bor, compulsory labor imposed upon criminals in addition to imprisonment.

hard-line (härd′līn′), *adj.* adhering rigidly to a dogma, theory, or plan; uncompromising or unyielding: *a hard-line communist; hard-line union demands.*

hard-lin·er (härd′lī′nər), *n.* a person who adheres rigidly to a dogma, theory, or plan.

hard′ lines′, *Chiefly Brit. Slang.* tough luck; bad breaks.

hard·ly (härd′lē), *adv.* **1.** barely; almost not at all: *hardly any; hardly ever.* **2.** not quite: *That is hardly true.* **3.** with little likelihood: *He will hardly come now.* **4.** *Brit.* harshly or severely. **5.** *Rare.* hard. [ME; OE *heardlice*]

—**Syn. 1.** HARDLY, BARELY, SCARCELY imply a narrow margin by which performance was, is, or will be achieved. HARDLY, though often interchangeable with SCARCELY and BARELY, usually emphasizes the idea of the difficulty involved: *We could hardly endure the winter.* BARELY emphasizes the narrowness of the margin of safety, "only just and no more": *We barely succeeded.* SCARCELY implies a very narrow margin, below satisfactory performance: *He can scarcely read.*

—**Usage.** HARDLY, BARELY, and SCARCELY all have a negative connotation, and the use of any of them with a supplementary negative is considered nonstandard, as in *I can't hardly wait* for *I can hardly wait.*

hard′ ma′ple, *U.S.* the sugar maple, *Acer saccharum.*

hard·ness (härd′nis), *n.* **1.** the state or quality of being hard. **2.** a relative degree or extent of this quality. **3.** the quality in impure water that is imparted by the presence of dissolved salts, esp. calcium sulfate or bicarbonate. **4.** *Mineral.* the comparative capacity of a substance to scratch or be scratched by another. Cf. **Mohs scale. 5.** *Metall.* the measured resistance of a metal to indention, abrasion, deformation, or machining. [ME *hardnes,* OE *heardnes*]

hard-nosed (härd′nōzd′), *adj.* hard-headed or tough; unsentimentally practical: *a hard-nosed businessman.*

hard-of-hear·ing (härd′əv hēr′ing), *adj.* of, pertaining to, or having defective hearing.

hard-on (härd′on′, -ôn′), *n., pl.* **-ons.** *Slang (usually vulgar).* an erection of the penis.

hard′ pal′ate. See under **palate** (def. 1).

hard·pan (härd′pan′), *n. Chiefly U.S.* **1.** any layer of firm detrital matter, as of clay, underlying soft soil. **2.** hard, unbroken ground.

hard-pressed (härd′prest′), *adj.* heavily burdened or oppressed, as by overwork; harried.

hard′ rock′, the original form of rock-'n'-roll, basically dependent on a very loud, strong beat. Cf. **soft rock.**

hard′ rub′ber, rubber vulcanized with a large amount of sulfur, usually 25–35 percent, to render it inflexible.

hard′ sauce′, a creamed mixture of butter and confectioners' sugar, often with flavoring and cream.

hard·scrab·ble (härd′skrab′əl), *adj.* providing meagerly in return for much effort: *a hardscrabble existence.*

hard′ sell′, a forceful and insistent method of advertising or selling; high-pressure salesmanship (opposed to *soft sell*).

hard-set (härd′set′), *adj.* **1.** firmly or rigidly set; fixed: *a hard-set smile.* **2.** in a difficult or precarious position.

hard-shell (härd′shel′), *adj.* Also, **hard′-shelled′. 1.** having a firm, hard shell, as a crab in its normal state; not having recently molted. **2.** rigid or uncompromising. —*n.* **3.** See **hard-shell crab.**

hard′-shell clam′, quahog.

hard′-shell crab′, a crab, esp. an edible crab, that has not recently molted and therefore has a hard shell.

hard·ship (härd′ship), *n.* **1.** a condition that is difficult to endure; suffering; deprivation; oppression. **2.** an instance or cause of this; something hard to bear. [ME]

—**Syn. 1.** affliction, trouble. HARDSHIP, PRIVATION refer to a condition hard to endure. HARDSHIP applies to a circumstance in which excessive and painful effort of some kind is required, as enduring acute discomfort from cold, battling over rough terrain, and the like. PRIVATION has particular reference to lack of food, clothing, warmth, etc.

hard-spun (härd′spun′), *adj.* (of yarn) compactly twisted in spinning.

hard·tack (härd′tak′), *n.* a hard, saltless biscuit, formerly much used aboard ships and for army rations. Also called **pilot biscuit, pilot bread, ship biscuit, ship bread.**

hard·top (härd′top′), *n.* a style of car having a rigid metal top and no center posts between windows. Also called **hard′-top convert′ible.**

hard·ware (härd′wâr′), *n.* **1.** metalware, as tools, locks, hinges, cutlery, etc. **2.** the mechanical equipment necessary for conducting an activity. **3.** weapons and combat equipment. **4.** *Computer Technol.* any electronic or mechanical equipment used in association with data processing. Cf. **software.**

hard·wood (härd′wo͝od′), *n.* **1.** the hard, compact wood or timber of various trees, as the oak, cherry, maple, mahogany, etc. —*adj.* **2.** made or constructed of hardwood.

har·dy[1] (här′dē), *adj.,* **-di·er, -di·est. 1.** capable of enduring fatigue, hardship, exposure, etc.; sturdy; strong: *hardy animals.* **2.** (of plants) able to withstand the cold of winter in the open air. **3.** requiring great physical courage, vigor, or endurance: *the hardiest sports.* **4.** bold or daring; courageous: *hardy explorers.* **5.** unduly bold; presumptuous; foolhardy. [ME *hardi* < OF, ptp. of **hardir* to harden, make brave < Gmc; cf. Goth *-hardjan,* OE *hierdan,* etc.] —**Syn. 1.** vigorous, robust, hale, stout, sound. **4.** intrepid, resolute, brave.

har·dy[2] (här′dē), *n., pl.* **-dies.** a chisel or fuller with a square shank for insertion into a square hole **(har′dy hole′)** in a blacksmith's anvil. [HARD + -Y[2]]

Har·dy (här′dē), *n.* **Thomas,** 1840–1928, English novelist and poet.

hare (hâr), *n., pl.* **hares,** (*esp. collectively*) **hare. 1.** any of several rodentlike mammals of the genus *Lepus,* of the family *Leporidae,* having long ears, a divided upper lip, and long hind limbs adapted for leaping. **2.** any of the larger species of this genus, as distinguished from certain of the smaller ones known as rabbits. **3.** any of various similar animals of the same family. [ME; OE *hara;* c. Dan *hare;* akin to G *Hase* hare, OE *hasu* gray] —**hare′like′,** *adj.*

hare′ and hounds′, an outdoor game in which certain players, the hares, start off in advance on a long run, scattering small pieces of paper, called the scent, with the other players, the hounds, following the trail so marked in an effort to catch the hares before they reach a designated point.

hare·bell (hâr′bel′), *n.* **1.** a low, campanulaceous herb, *Campanula rotundifolia,* having blue, bell-shaped flowers. **2.** a liliaceous plant, *Scilla nonscripta,* having bell-shaped flowers. [ME]

hare·brained (hâr′brānd′), *adj.* giddy; reckless. Also, **hairbrained.** —**hare′brained′ness,** *n.*

Ha·re Krish·na (hä′re krish′nə), a religious sect based on Vedic scriptures, whose followers engage in joyful congregational chanting of God's name: founded in the U.S. in 1966. [from part of the chant]

hare·lip (hâr′lip′), *n.* **1.** a congenitally deformed lip, usually the upper one, in which there is a vertical fissure causing it to resemble the cleft lip of a hare. **2.** the deformity itself. —**hare′lipped′,** *adj.*

har·em (hâr′əm, har′-), *n.* **1.** that part of an Oriental palace or house reserved for the residence of women. **2.** the women in an Oriental household, including the mother, sisters, wives, concubines, daughters, entertainers, servants, etc. **3.** a group of female animals led by and mated to one male. [< Ar *ḥarīm,* lit., forbidden]

Har·gei·sa (här gā′sə), *n.* a city in NW Somali Republic. 45,000 (est. 1957).

Har·greaves (här′grēvz), *n.* **James,** died 1778, English weaver: reputed inventor of the spinning jenny.

Har·ia·na (hur yä′nə), *n.* Haryana.

har·i·cot (har′ə kō′), *n.* *Chiefly Brit.* **1.** any plant of the genus *Phaseolus,* esp. *P. vulgaris,* the kidney bean. **2.** the seed of any of these plants, eaten as a vegetable. [< F, ? << Nahuatl *ayacotl* bean; influenced by F *haricot* stew << Gmc]

ha·ri-ka·ri (här′ē kär′ē, har′ē kar′ē), *n.* hara-kiri.

hark (härk), *v.i.* **1.** to listen; harken (used chiefly in the imperative). —*v.t.* **2.** *Archaic.* to listen to; hear. **3. hark back, a.** (of hounds) to return along the course in order to regain a lost scent. **b.** to return to a previous subject or point; revert. —*n.* **4.** a hunter's shout to hounds, as to encourage them in following the scent. [ME *herk(i)e(n)*; c. OFris *herkia;* akin to MD *harken,* G *horchen.* See HARKEN, HEAR]

hark·en (här′kən), *v.i.* **1.** to listen; give heed or attend to what is said. —*v.t.* **2.** *Archaic.* to listen to; hear. Also, **hearken.** [ME *hercnen,* OE *he(o)rcnian*] —**hark′en·er,** *n.*

harl (härl), *n.* *Angling.* a herl. [ME *herle* < MLG: fiber]

Har·lan (här′lən), *n.* **John Marshall,** 1899–1971, U.S. jurist: associate justice of the U.S. Supreme Court 1955–71.

Har·lem (här′ləm), *n.* **1.** a section of New York City, in the NE part of Manhattan. **2.** a tidal river in New York City, between the boroughs of Manhattan and the Bronx, that, with Spuyten Duyvil Creek, connects the Hudson and East rivers. 8 mi. long.

har·le·quin (här′lə kwin, -kin), *n.* **1.** (*often cap.*) a comic character in commedia dell'arte and the harlequinade, usually masked, dressed in multicolored, diamond-patterned tights, and carrying a wooden sword or magic wand. **2.** a buffoon. **3.** any of various small, handsomely marked snakes. —*adj.* **4.** fancifully varied in color, decoration, etc. [< MF < ME **Herleching* (miswritten *herlething*) < ML *Herla rex* King Herla (mythical figure); modern meaning from It *arlecchino* < MF *harlequin* < ME, as above]

Harlequin

har·le·quin·ade (här′lə kwi nād′, -ki-), *n.* **1.** a pantomime, farce, or similar play in which Harlequin plays the principal part. **2.** buffoonery. [< F *arlequinade*]

Har·ley (här′lē), *n.* **Robert, 1st Earl of Oxford,** 1661–1724, British statesman.

Har′ley Street′, a street in London, England: noted for the doctors who have offices there.

Har·lin·gen (här′lin jin), *n.* a city in S Texas. 33,503 (1970).

har·lot (här′lət), *n.* **1.** a lewd or promiscuous woman. **2.** a prostitute; strumpet. —*adj.* **3.** pertaining to or like a harlot; low. [ME < OF *herlot* young idler or rogue]

har·lot·ry (här′lə trē), *n.* **1.** prostitution. **2.** harlots collectively. [ME *harlotrie*]

Har·low (här′lō), *n.* **1. Jean,** 1911–37, U.S. motion-picture actress. **2.** a town in W Essex, in SE England. 53,496 (1961).

harm (härm), *n.* **1.** injury; damage; hurt: *to do him bodily harm.* **2.** moral injury; evil; wrong. —*v.t.* **3.** to do or cause harm to; injure; damage; hurt: *to harm one's reputation.* [ME; OE *hearm;* c. G *Harm,* Icel *harmr*] —**harm′er,** *n.* —**Syn. 1, 2.** See **damage.** —**Ant. 1.** benefit. **3.** help.

har·mat·tan (här′mə tan′), *n.* a dry, parching land breeze, charged with dust, on the west coast of Africa. [< WAfr (Twi) *haramata*]

harm·ful (härm′fəl), *adj.* causing or capable of doing or causing harm; dangerous. [ME; OE *hearmful*] —**harm′ful·ly,** *adv.* —**harm′ful·ness,** *n.* —**Syn.** injurious, detrimental. —**Ant.** beneficial.

harm·less (härm′lis), *adj.* **1.** without the power or desire to do harm: *a harmless prank.* **2.** without injury; unhurt; unharmed. [ME *harmles*] —**harm′less·ly,** *adv.* —**harm′less·ness,** *n.*

har·mon·ic (här mon′ik), *adj.* **1.** pertaining to harmony, as distinguished from melody and rhythm. **2.** marked by harmony; in harmony; concordant; consonant. **3.** of, pertaining to, or noting a series of oscillations in which each oscillation has a frequency that is an integral multiple of the same basic frequency. **4.** *Math.* **a.** (of a set of values) related in a manner analogous to the frequencies of tones that are consonant. **b.** capable of being represented by sine and cosine functions. —*n.* **5.** *Music.* overtone (def. 1). **6.** *Physics.* a mode of vibration whose frequency is an integral multiple of the fundamental frequency. [< L *harmonic(us)* < Gk *harmonikós* musical, suitable] —**har·mon′i·cal·ly,** *adv.* —**har·mon′i·cal·ness,** *n.*

har·mon·i·ca (här mon′ə kə), *n.* a musical wind instrument consisting of a small rectangular case containing a set of metal reeds connected to a row of holes, over which the player places his mouth and exhales and inhales to produce the to.ˈes. Also called **mouth organ.** [n. use of fem. of L *harmonicus* HARMONIC]

Harmonica

harmon′ic anal′ysis, 1. *Math.* **a.** the calculation of Fourier series and integrals. **b.** the study of Fourier series and their generalization. **2.** *Acoustics.* the analysis of complex sounds into their component frequencies.

harmon′ic in′terval. See under **interval** (def. 5).

harmon′ic mean′, *Statistics.* the mean obtained by taking the reciprocal of the arithmetic mean of the reciprocals of a set of nonzero numbers.

harmon′ic mi′nor scale′. See **minor scale** (def. 1).

harmon′ic mo′tion, *Physics.* periodic motion consisting of one or more vibratory motions that are symmetric about a region of equilibrium, as the motion of a vibrating string of a musical instrument.

harmon′ic progres′sion, *Math.* a series of numbers the reciprocals of which are in arithmetic progression.

har·mon·ics (här mon′iks), *n.* *Music.* **1.** (*construed as sing.*) the science of musical sounds. **2.** (*construed as pl.*) the partials or overtones of a fundamental tone. Cf. **overtone** (def. 1).

harmon′ic se′ries, 1. *Math.* **a.** a series in which the reciprocals of the terms form an arithmetic progression. **b.** the divergent infinite series, $1 + \frac{1}{2} + \frac{1}{3} + \frac{1}{4} + \frac{1}{5} + \cdots$. **2.** *Acoustics.* the series of tones comprising the harmonics of a given fundamental tone.

har·mo·ni·ous (här mō′nē əs), *adj.* **1.** marked by agreement in feeling or action: *a harmonious group.* **2.** forming a pleasingly consistent whole; congruous: *harmonious colors.* **3.** agreeable to the ear; tuneful; melodious. [< Gk *harmónios* melodious, lit., fitting] —**har·mo′ni·ous·ly,** *adv.* —**har·mo′ni·ous·ness,** *n.* —**Syn. 1.** amicable, congenial; sympathetic. **2.** concordant, consistent. —**Ant. 1, 3.** discordant.

har·mo·nise (här′mə nīz′), *v.t., v.i.,* **-nised, -nis·ing.** *Chiefly Brit.* harmonize. —**har′mo·nis′a·ble,** *adj.* —**har′mo·ni·sa′tion,** *n.* —**har′mo·nis′er,** *n.*

har·mo·nist (här′mə nist), *n.* **1.** a person skilled in harmony. **2.** a person who makes a harmony, as of the Gospels.

har·mo·nis·tic (här′mə nis′tik), *adj.* **1.** pertaining to a harmonist or harmony. **2.** pertaining to the collation and harmonizing of parallel passages, as of the Gospels. —**har′mo·nis′ti·cal·ly,** *adv.*

har·mo·ni·um (här mō′nē əm), *n.* an organlike keyboard instrument with small metal reeds and a pair of bellows operated by the player's feet. [Latinization of Gk *harmónion,* neut. of *harmónios* HARMONIOUS]

har·mo·nize (här′mə nīz′), *v.,* **-nized, -niz·ing.** —*v.t.* **1.** to bring into harmony, accord, or agreement: *to harmonize one's views with the existing facts.* **2.** *Music.* to accompany with appropriate harmony. —*v.i.* **3.** to be in agreement in action, sense, or feeling. **4.** to sing in harmony. Also, *esp. Brit.,* **harmonise.** [late ME *armonise*] —**har′mo·niz′a·ble,** *adj.* —**har′mo·ni·za′tion,** *n.* —**har′mo·niz′er,** *n.* —**Syn. 1.** reconcile. **3.** agree, accord, correspond.

har·mo·ny (här′mə nē), *n., pl.* **-nies. 1.** agreement; accord; harmonious relations. **2.** a consistent, orderly, or pleasing arrangement of parts; congruity. **3.** *Music.* **a.** any simultaneous combination of tones. **b.** the simultaneous combination of tones, esp. when blended into chords pleasing to the ear; chordal structure, as distinguished from melody and rhythm. **c.** the science of the structure, relations, and practical combination of chords. **4.** an arrangement of the contents of the Gospels, either of all four or of the first three, designed to show their parallelism, mutual relations, and differences. [< L *harmoni(a)* < Gk: melody, lit., a joining (of sounds) = *harmó(s)* joint + *-ia* -Y³; r. ME *armonye* < MF] —**Syn. 1.** concord, unity, peace, amity, friendship. **2.** consonance, conformity, correspondence, consistency. See **symmetry. 3.** HARMONY, MELODY in music suggest a combination of sounds from voices or musical instruments. HARMONY is the blending of simultaneous sounds of different pitch, making chords: *harmony in part singing.* MELODY is the rhythmical combination of successive sounds of various pitch, making up the tune or air: *a tuneful melody.*

har·mo·tome (här′mə tōm′), *n.* a mineral of the zeolite family. [< F < Gk *harmó(s)* joint + *-tomos* -TOME]

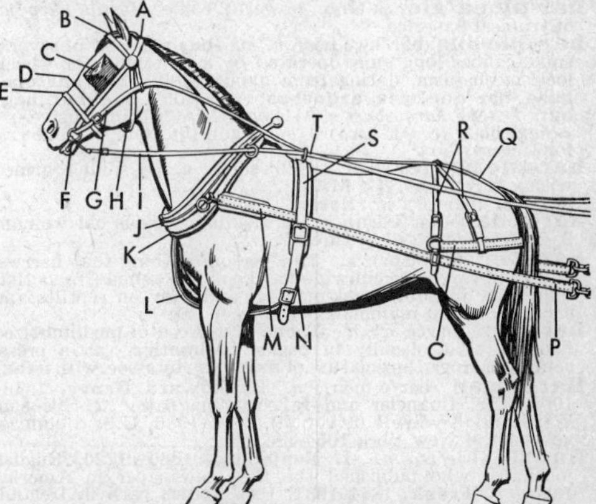

Harness of a horse
A, Crownpiece; B, Front; C, Blinker; D, Cheek strap; E, Noseband; F, Bit; G, Sidecheck; H, Throatlatch; I, Reins; J, Hame; K, Collar; L, Martingale; M, Hame tug; N, Bellyband; O, Breeching; P, Trace; Q, Crupper; R, Hip straps; S, Saddle; T, Terret

har·ness (här′nis), *n.* **1.** the combination of straps, bands, and other parts forming the working gear of a draft animal. Cf. **yoke¹** (def. 1). **2.** (on a loom) the frame containing heddles through which the warp is drawn. **3.** *Archaic.* armor for men or horses. **4. in harness, a.** engaged in one's usual routine of work. **b.** together as cooperating partners or equals. —*v.t.* **5.** to put a harness on (a horse, donkey, dog, etc.); attach by a harness, as to a vehicle. **6.** to bring under conditions for effective use; gain control over for a particular end: *to harness the energy of the sun.* **7.** *Archaic.* to array in armor or equipments of war. [ME *harneis, herneis* < OF: baggage, equipment, ? orig. army provisions < Gmc; cf. OE *here,* Icel *herr* army, OE, Icel *nest* provisions (for a journey)] —**har′ness·er,** *n.* —**har′ness·like′,** *adj.*

har′nessed an′telope, any of several antelopes of the genus *Tragelaphus,* having the body marked with white stripes and spots that resemble a harness.

har′ness hitch′, a hitch forming a loop around a rope, esp. one formed at the end of a bowline.

har′ness horse′, 1. a horse used for pulling vehicles. **2.** a horse used in harness racing.

har′ness race′, a trotting or pacing race for Standardbred horses harnessed to sulkies.

Har′ney Peak′ (här′nē), a mountain in SW South Dakota: the highest peak in the Black Hills. 7242 ft.

Harold I, ("*Harefoot*") died 1040, king of England 1035–40 (son of Canute).

Harold II, 1022?–66, king of England 1066: defeated by William the Conqueror at the Battle of Hastings.

Ha·roun-al-Ra·schid (hä ro͞on′äl-rä s̲h̲ēd′; *Arab.* hä ro͞on′är′rä s̲h̲ēd′), *n.* See **Harun al-Rashid.**

harp (härp), *n.* **1.** a musical instrument consisting of a triangular frame formed by a soundbox, a pillar, and a curved neck, and having strings that are stretched between the soundbox and the neck that are plucked with the fingers. **2.** anything resembling this instrument. —*v.i.* **3.** to play on a harp. —*v.t.* **4.** *Archaic.* to give voice or utterance to. **5. harp on** or **upon,** to dwell on persistently or tediously. [ME *harpe,* OE *hearpe;* c. D *harp,* G *Harfe,* Icel *harpa*] —**harp′er,** *n.*

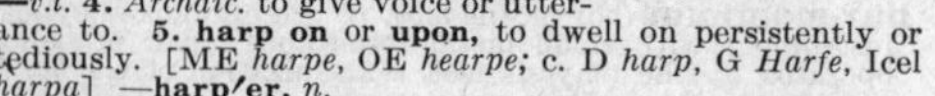

Harp

Har′pers Fer′ry (här′pərz), a town in NE West Virginia at the confluence of the Shenandoah and Potomac rivers: John Brown's raid 1859. 423 (1970). Also, **Har′per's Fer′ry.**

harp·ist (här′pist), *n.* a person who plays on the harp.

har·poon (här po͞on′), *n.* **1.** a barbed, spearlike missile attached to a rope, and thrown by hand or shot from a gun, used for killing and capturing whales and large fish. —*v.t.* **2.** to strike, catch, or kill with or as with a harpoon. [< D *harpoen* << OF *harpon* a clasp, brooch = *harp-* (< L *harpē* < Gk: hook) + *-on* dim. suffix; aspirate *h-* by assoc. with *harpe* HARP] —**har·poon′er,** *n.* —**har·poon′like′,** *adj.*

harpoon′ gun′, a small cannon for shooting harpoons.

harp·si·chord (härp′si kôrd′), *n.* a keyboard instrument, precursor of the piano, in which the strings are plucked by leather or quill points. [< NL *harpichord(ium)* (with intrusive *-s-*)] —**harp′si·chord′ist,** *n.*

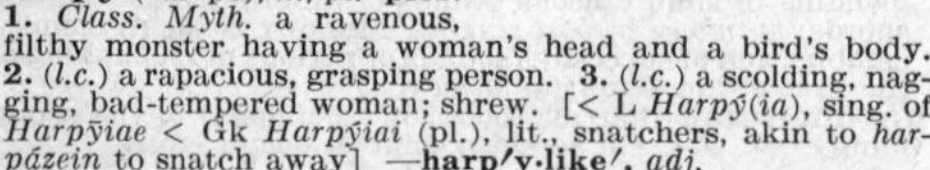

Harpsichord

Har·py (här′pē), *n., pl.* **-pies. 1.** *Class. Myth.* a ravenous, filthy monster having a woman's head and a bird's body. **2.** (*l.c.*) a rapacious, grasping person. **3.** (*l.c.*) a scolding, nagging, bad-tempered woman; shrew. [< L *Harpȳ(ia),* sing. of *Harpȳiae* < Gk *Harpȳiai* (pl.), lit., snatchers, akin to *harpázein* to snatch away] —**harp′y·like′,** *adj.*

har′py ea′gle, a large, powerful eagle, *Harpia harpyja,* of tropical America.

har·que·bus (här′kwə bəs), *n., pl.* **-bus·es.** any of several small-caliber long guns operated by a matchlock or wheel-lock mechanism, dating from about 1400. Also, **har′que·buse, har′que·buss, arquebus.** Also called **hackbut, hagbut.** [< MF *harquebuse* < MD *hakebusse* (with intrusive *-r-*) = *hake* hook (c. OE *haca*) + *busse* gun (lit., box) < LL *buxis* for L *buxus* BOX¹]

har·que·bus·ier (här′kwə bə sēr′), *n.* a soldier armed with a harquebus. [< MF]

Har·rar (här′ər), *n.* Harar.

har·ri·dan (har′i dⁿn), *n.* a scolding, vicious old woman; hag. [cf. F *haridelle* a jade]

har·ri·er¹ (har′ē ər), *n.* **1.** a person or thing that harries. **2.** any of several accipitrine hawks of the genus *Circus* that hunt over meadows and marshes and prey on reptiles and small birds and mammals. [HARRY + -ER¹]

har·ri·er² (har′ē ər), *n.* **1.** one of a breed of medium-sized hounds, used, usually in packs, in hunting. **2.** a cross-country runner. [special use of HARRIER¹, by assoc. with HARE]

Har·ri·man (har′ə mən), *n.* **1. Edward Henry,** 1848–1909, U.S. financier and railroad magnate. **2.** his son, **W(illiam) A·ve·rell** (ā′vər əl), 1891–1986, U.S. diplomat: governor of New York 1954–58.

Har·ris (har′is), *n.* **1. Benjamin,** c1660–c1720, English journalist who published the first newspaper in America 1690. **2. Frank,** 1854–1931, U.S. writer, born in Ireland. **3. Joel Chan·dler** (chan′dlər, c̲h̲än′-), 1848–1908, U.S. journalist, novelist, and short-story writer: creator of "Uncle Remus." **4. Roy,** 1898–1979, U.S. composer. **5. Thad·de·us William** (t̲h̲ad′ē əs), 1795–1856, U.S. entomologist: pioneer in applied entomology.

Har·ris·burg (har′is bûrg′), *n.* a city in and the capital of Pennsylvania, in the S part, on the Susquehanna River. 68,061 (1970).

Har·ri·son (har′i sən), *n.* **1. Benjamin,** 1833–1901, 23rd president of the U.S. 1889–93. **2. Peter,** 1716–75, English architect in the U.S. **3. William Henry,** 1773–1841, U.S. general: 9th president of the U.S. 1841 (grandfather of Benjamin Harrison).

Har′ris Tweed′, *Trademark.* a heavy, handwoven woolen fabric made in the Outer Hebrides.

har·row¹ (har′ō), *n.* **1.** an agricultural implement with spikelike teeth or upright disks, for leveling and breaking up clods in plowed land. —*v.t.* **2.** to draw a harrow over (land). **3.** to disturb keenly or painfully; distress the mind, feelings, etc., of. —*v.i.* **4.** to become broken up by harrowing, as soil. [ME *harwe;* akin to Icel *herfi* harrow, D *hark* rake, Gk *krōpion* sickle] —**har′row·er,** *n.* —**har′row·ing·ly,** *adv.*

har·row² (har′ō), *v.t.* *Archaic.* to ravish; violate; despoil. [ME *harwen, herwen,* OE *hergian* to HARRY]

Har·row (har′ō), *n.* a boarding school for boys, founded in 1571 at Harrow-on-the-Hill, England.

Har·row-on-the-Hill (har′ō on t̶h̶ə hil′, -ôn-), *n.* an urban district in SE England, near London. 208,963 (1961).

har·rumph (hə rumf′), *v.i.* to make a low, guttural sound, as in clearing the throat or in expression of disapproval. [imit.]

har·ry (har′ē), *v.,* **-ried, -ry·ing.** —*v.t.* **1.** to harass; annoy; torment. **2.** to ravage, as in war; devastate. —*v.i.* **3.** to make harrassing incursions. [ME *heri(en),* OE *her(g)ian* (< *here* army); c. G *(ver)heeren,* Icel *herja* to harry, lay waste] —**Syn. 1.** plague, trouble. **2.** plunder, rob, pillage.

harsh (härsh), *adj.* **1.** ungentle and unpleasant in action or effect: *harsh treatment.* **2.** grim or unpleasantly severe; stern; cruel; austere: *a harsh master.* **3.** physically uncomfortable; desolate; stark: *a harsh land.* **4.** unpleasant to the ear; grating; strident: *a harsh voice.* **5.** unpleasant or jarring to the senses. [ME *harsk* < Scand; cf. Dan *harsk* rancid; c. G *harsch* harsh; akin to G *herb* harsh] —**harsh′ly,** *adv.* —**harsh′ness,** *n.* —**Syn. 2.** hard, unfeeling, unkind, badtempered. See **stern¹. 4.** discordant, dissonant.

harsh·en (här′shən), *v.t., v.i.* to make or become harsh: *Avarice had harshened his features.*

hart (härt), *n., pl.* **harts,** (*esp. collectively*) **hart.** a male of the deer, commonly the red deer, *Cervus elaphus,* esp. after its fifth year. [ME *hert,* OE *heorot;* c. D *hert,* G *Hirsch,* Icel *hjörtr;* akin to L *cervus* stag, Gk *kéras* HORN]

Hart (härt), *n.* **1. Lo·renz** (lôr′ənts, lôr′-), 1895–1943, U.S. lyricist. **2. Moss** (môs, mos), 1904–61, U.S. playwright and librettist.

har·tal (här täl′), *n.* (in India) a closing of shops and stopping of work, esp. as a form of passive resistance. [< Hindi, var. of *haṭṭāl* = *haṭ* shop (Skt *haṭṭa*) + *tāl* locking (Skt *tālaka* lock, bolt)]

Harte (härt), *n.* **(Francis) Bret** (bret), 1839–1902, U.S. author, esp. of short stories.

har·te·beest (här′tə bēst′, härt′bēst′), *n., pl.* **-beests,** (*esp. collectively*) **-beest. 1.** any of several large, African antelopes of the genus *Alcelaphus,* having ringed horns that curve backward. **2.** any of several related African antelopes, as certain species of the genus *Damaliscus.* [< SAfrD; see HART, BEAST]

Hartebeest
Alcelaphus buselaphus
(4½ ft. high at shoulder; horns 1 ft.; length 6½ ft.)

Hart·ford (härt′fərd), *n.* a port in and the capital of Connecticut, in the central part, on the Connecticut River. 158,017 (1970).

Har·tha·cnut (här′t̶h̶ə kə no͞ot′, -nyo͞ot′), *n.* Hardecanute.

Hart·ley (härt′lē), *n.* **1. David,** 1705–57, English physician and philosopher. **2. Mars·den** (märz′dən), 1877–1943, U.S. painter.

harts·horn (härts′hôrn′), *n.* **1.** the antler of a hart, formerly used as a source of ammonia. **2.** *Old Chem., Pharm.* ammonium carbonate; sal volatile. [ME *hertis horn,* OE *heortes horn*]

har·um-scar·um (hâr′əm skâr′əm, har′əm skar′əm), *adj.* **1.** reckless; rash; irresponsible. **2.** disorganized; uncontrolled. —*adv.* **3.** recklessly; wildly. —*n.* **4.** a reckless person. **5.** *Archaic.* reckless or unpredictable behavior or action. [earlier *harum-starum* rhyming compound based on obs. *hare* to harass + STARE]

Ha·run al-Ra·shid (hä ro͞on′ äl rä s̲h̲ēd′; *Arab.* hä-ro͞on′ är′rä s̲h̲ēd′), A.D. 764?–809, caliph of Baghdad 786–809: one of the greatest Abbasides, he was made a legendary hero in the *Arabian Nights.* Also, **Haroun-al-Raschid, Ha·run ar-Ra·shid** (hä ro͞on′ är′rä s̲h̲ēd′; *Arab.* hä ro͞on′ är′rä s̲h̲ēd′).

ha·rus·pex (hə rus′peks, har′ə speks′), *n., pl.* **ha·rus·pi·ces** (hə rus′pi sēz′), (in ancient Rome) one of a class of minor priests who practiced divination, esp. from the entrails of animals killed in sacrifice. [< L = *haru* (akin to *hīra* gut; see CHORD¹) + *spec-* (s. of *specere* to look at) + *-s* nom. sing. ending]

Har·vard (här′vərd), *n.* **John,** 1607–38, English clergyman in U.S.: principal benefactor of Harvard College, now Harvard University.

Har′vard beets′, sliced or diced beets cooked in a mixture of sugar, cornstarch, vinegar, and water. [after HARVARD University]

har·vest (här′vist), *n.* **1.** Also, **har′vest·ing.** the gathering of crops. **2.** the season when ripened crops are gathered. **3.** a crop or yield of one growing season. **4.** a supply of anything gathered at maturity and stored: *a harvest of nuts.* **5.** the result or consequence of any act, process, or event: *a harvest of impressions.* —*v.t.* **6.** to gather (a crop or the like); reap. **7.** to gather the crop from: *to harvest the fields.* **8.** to gain, win, etc. (a prize, product, etc.). —*v.i.* **9.** to gather a crop; reap. [ME; OE *hærfest;* c. G *Herbst* autumn; akin to HARROW¹]

har·ves·ter (här′vi stər), *n.* **1.** a person who harvests. **2.** any of various farm machines for harvesting field crops.

har′vest home′, 1. the bringing home of the harvest. **2.** the time of gathering in the harvest. **3.** an English festival celebrated at the close of the harvest. **4.** a song sung as the harvest is brought home.

har·vest·man (här′vist mən), *n., pl.* **-men. 1.** a man engaged in harvesting. **2.** daddy-longlegs (def. 1).

har′vest moon′, the moon at and about the period of fullness nearest to the autumnal equinox.

Har·vey (här′vē), *n.* **1. William,** 1578–1657, English physician: discoverer of the circulation of the blood. **2.** a city in NE Illinois, near Chicago. 34,636 (1970).

Har·ya·na (hur yä′nə), *n.* a state in NW India, formed in 1966 from the S part of Punjab. 7,000,000 (est. 1966); 17,600 sq. mi. *Temporary Cap.* (shared with Punjab): Chandigarh. Also, **Hariana.**

Harz′ Moun′tains (härts), a range of low mountains in central Germany between the Elbe and Weser rivers. Highest peak, Brocken, 3745 ft.

has (haz), *v.* a 3rd pers. sing. pres. indic. of **have.**

Ha·sa (hä′sə), *n.* a region in E Saudi Arabia, on the Persian Gulf. Also, **El Hasa.**

has-been (haz′bin′), *n.* a person or thing that is no longer effective, successful, popular, etc.

Has·dru·bal (haz′dro͝o bəl, haz dro͞o′-), *n.* died 207 B.C., Carthaginian general (brother of Hannibal).

ha·sen·pfef·fer (hä′sən fef′ər), *n.* a stew of marinated rabbit meat. Also, **hassenpfeffer.** [< G: lit., hare's pepper]

hash[1] (hash), *n.* **1.** a dish of diced or chopped meat, as of leftover corned beef, potatoes, and sometimes vegetables sautéed in a frying pan or of meat, potatoes, and carrots cooked together in gravy. **2.** a mess, jumble, or muddle. **3. settle someone's hash,** *Informal.* to get rid of; subdue: *That remark sure settled her hash!* —*v.t.* **4.** to chop into small pieces; mince; make into hash. **5.** to muddle or mess up. **6. hash over,** *Slang.* to bring up again for consideration. [< F *hach(er)* (to) cut up < *hache* ax, HATCHET]

hash[2] (hash), *n.* *Slang.* hashish. [by shortening]

Hash·e·mite (hash′ə mīt′), *n.* **1.** a member of any Arab dynasty in the Middle East founded by Husein ibn-Ali or his descendants. —*adj.* **2.** of or pertaining to the Hashemites. Also, **Hash′i·mite′.** [*Hashim* great-grandfather of Muhammad + -ITE[1]]

Hash′e·mite King′dom of Jor′dan. See **Jordan.**

hash·head (hash′hed′), *n.* *Slang.* a hashish addict. [HASH(ISH) + HEAD]

hash′ house′, *Slang.* a cheap, short-order restaurant.

hash·ish (hash′ēsh, -ish), *n.* **1.** the flowering tops, leaves, etc., of Indian hemp, smoked, chewed, or drunk as a narcotic and intoxicant. **2.** any of certain narcotic preparations made from this plant. Also, **hash·eesh** (hä′shēsh). [< Ar *ḥashīsh,* lit., dry vegetation (e.g., hay)]

hash′ mark′, *Mil. Slang.* a service stripe.

Ha·sid (hä′sid, KHä′-; *Heb.* KHä sēd′), *n., pl.* **Ha·sid·im** (hä sid′im, KHä-; *Heb.* KHä sē dēm′). *Judaism.* **1.** a member of a sect, founded in Poland in the 18th century, characterized by emphasis on mysticism, prayer, religious zeal, and joy. **2.** an Assidean. Also, **Chasid.** [< Heb: pious (person)] —**Ha·sid·ic** (hə sid′ik), *adj.*

Has·mo·ne·an (haz′mə nē′ən), *n.* a member of a dynasty of Judean rulers and high priests 142–37 B.C. Also, **Has′mo·nae′an.** Cf. **Maccabees** (def. 1). [var. (with *h-* < Heb *kh-*) of *Asmonean* < LL *Asmōnae(us)* of *Hasmōn* (< Gk *Asmōnaios*) + -AN]

has·n't (haz′ənt), contraction of *has not.*

hasp (hasp, häsp), *n.* **1.** a clasp for a door, lid, etc., esp. one passing over a staple and fastened by a pin or padlock. —*v.t.* **2.** to fasten with or as with a hasp. [ME; OE *hæsp, hæpse;* c. G *Haspe* hasp; akin to Icel *hespa* skein, hasp]

Has·san II (hä′sən, ha san′), born 1929, king of Morocco since 1961.

has·sen·pfef·fer (hä′sən fef′ər), *n.* hasenpfeffer.

has·sle (has′əl), *n., v.,* **has·sled, has·sling.** *Informal.* —*n.* **1.** quarrel; squabble. —*v.t.* **2.** to badger; harass. —*v.i.* **3.** to dispute or quarrel. [var. of obs. *harsell* to irritate < MF *harcell(er)* < *herse* harrow; see HEARSE]

has·sock (has′ək), *n.* **1.** a thick firm cushion used as a footstool or for kneeling. **2.** a rank tuft of coarse grass or sedge, as in a bog. [ME; OE *hassuc* coarse grass]

hast (hast), *v.* *Archaic.* 2nd pers. sing. pres. indic. of **have.**

has·ta la vis·ta (äs′tä lä bēs′tä; *Eng.* hä′stə lə vē′stə), *Spanish.* until I see you; until we meet; so long; good-by.

has·ta ma·ña·na (äs′tä mä nyä′nä; *Eng.* hä′stə mən yä′nə), *Spanish.* until tomorrow; see you tomorrow.

has·tate (has′tāt), *adj.* *Bot.* (of a leaf) triangular or shaped like a spear point, with two spreading lobes at the base. [< L *hastāt(us)* armed with a spear = *hast(a)* spear + *-ātus* -ATE[1]] —**has′tate·ly,** *adv.*

Hastate leaf

haste (hāst), *n., v.,* **hast·ed, hast·ing.** —*n.* **1.** swiftness of motion; speed. **2.** urgent need of quick action; a hurry. **3.** unnecessarily quick action; thoughtless, rash, or undue speed: *Haste makes waste.* **4. make haste,** to act or go with speed; hurry. —*v.t., v.i.* **5.** *Chiefly Literary.* to hasten. [ME < OF < OFris *hāst;* akin to OE *hǣst* violence, ON *heifst* hatred, Goth *haifsts* struggle] —**haste′ful,** *adj.* —**haste′ful·ly,** *adv.* —**haste′less,** *adj.* —**haste′less·ness,** *n.* —**Syn. 1.** See **speed. 2.** flurry, bustle, ado, urgency. **3.** precipitancy.

has·ten (hā′sən), *v.i.* **1.** to move or act with haste; proceed with haste; hurry: *to hasten to a place.* —*v.t.* **2.** to cause to hasten; accelerate. —**has′ten·er,** *n.* —**Syn. 2.** expedite, quicken, speed.

Has·tings (hā′stingz), *n.* **1. Thomas,** 1860–1929, U.S. architect. **2. Warren,** 1732–1818, British statesman: first governor general of India 1773–85. **3.** a seaport in E Sussex, in SE England: William the Conqueror defeated the Saxons near here on Senlac Hill 1066. 66,346 (1961). **4.** a city in S Nebraska. 23,580 (1970).

hast·y (hā′stē), *adj.,* **hast·i·er, hast·i·est. 1.** moving or acting with haste; speedy; hurried. **2.** made or done with haste or speed: *a hasty visit.* **3.** unduly quick; precipitate; rash: *a hasty decision.* **4.** brief; fleeting; superficial: *a hasty glance.* **5.** easily excited to anger; irascible. [ME < MF *hasti,* back formation from *hastis* (pl.) = *hastif* (see HASTE, -IVE) + *-s* -S[3]] —**hast′i·ly,** *adv.* —**hast′i·ness,** *n.*

hast′y pud′ding, 1. *New England Cookery.* a pudding prepared with cornmeal and, usually, molasses. **2.** *Chiefly Brit.* a dish made of flour or oatmeal stirred into seasoned boiling water or milk and quickly cooked.

hat (hat), *n., v.,* **hat·ted, hat·ting.** —*n.* **1.** a shaped covering for the head, usually with a crown and brim. **2.** *Rom. Cath. Ch.* **a.** the distinctive head covering of a cardinal. **b.** the office or dignity of a cardinal. **3. hat in hand,** humbly; respectfully. **4. pass the hat,** *Informal.* to ask for contributions of money, as for charity. **5. take off one's hat to,** to express high regard for; praise: *I take off my hat to his courage.* **6. talk through one's hat,** *Informal.* to speak without knowing the facts. **7. throw** or **toss one's hat in the ring,** to declare one's candidacy for political office. **8. under one's hat,** *Informal.* confidential; secret. —*v.t.* **9.** to provide with a hat; put a hat on. [ME; OE *hætt;* c. Icel *höttr* hood; akin to L *cassis* helmet] —**hat′less,** *adj.* —**hat′less·ness,** *n.* —**hat′like′,** *adj.*

hat·a·ble (hā′tə bəl), *adj.* hateable.

Ha·ta·su (hə tä′so͞o), *n.* Hatshepsut.

hat·band (hat′band′), *n.* **1.** a band or ribbon placed around the crown of a hat, just above the brim. **2.** a black band worn similarly as a sign of mourning.

hat·box (hat′boks′), *n.* **1.** a case or box, usually drum-shaped, for a hat. **2.** a similarly shaped small suitcase for a woman.

hatch[1] (hach), *v.t.* **1.** to bring forth (young) from the egg. **2.** to cause young to emerge from (the egg), as by brooding or incubating. **3.** to bring forth or produce; contrive; plot. —*v.i.* **4.** to be hatched. **5.** to brood, as a hen. —*n.* **6.** the act of hatching. **7.** that which is hatched, as a brood. [ME *hacche(n);* akin to G *hecken* to hatch] —**hatch′a·bil′i·ty,** *n.* —**hatch′a·ble,** *adj.* —**hatch′er,** *n.*

hatch[2] (hach), *n.* **1.** *Naut.* **a.** an arrangement for covering and protecting a hatchway or other deck opening, generally consisting of a cover raised on a coaming. **b.** the cover itself: *Batten down the hatches!* **c.** hatchway (def. 1). **2.** an opening that serves as a doorway or window in the floor or roof of a building. **3.** the cover over such an opening. **4.** *Aeron.* (loosely) an opening or door in an aircraft. **5.** the lower half of a divided door, both parts of which can be opened separately. **6.** a bin or compartment built into a confined space, esp. a deep storage bin. [ME *hacche,* OE *hæcc* grating, hatch, half-gate; akin to D *hek* gate, railing]

hatch[3] (hach), *v.t.* **1.** to mark with lines, esp. closely set parallel lines, as for shading in drawing or engraving. —*n.* **2.** a shading line in drawing or engraving. [late ME *hache* < MF *hach(er)* (to) cut up < *hache* ax. See HATCHET]

hatch·back (hach′bak′), *n.* a style of automobile body whose rear deck lid and window lift open as a unit, with a back seat that can be folded down for additional cargo space. [HATCH[2] + BACK]

hat·check (hat′chek′), *adj.* **1.** of, pertaining to, or noting the checking of hats, coats, umbrellas, etc., into temporary safekeeping. **2.** used in checking hats, coats, etc.: *a hatcheck room.*

hatch·el (hach′əl), *n., v.,* **-eled, -el·ing** or (*esp. Brit.*) **-elled, -el·ling.** —*n.* **1.** hackle[1] (def. 5). —*v.t.* **2.** hackle[1] (def. 7).

hatch·er·y (hach′ə rē), *n., pl.* **-er·ies.** a place for hatching eggs of hens, fish, etc.

hatch·et (hach′it), *n.* **1.** a small, short-handled ax having the end of the head opposite the blade in the form of a hammer, made to be used with one hand. See illus. at **ax. 2.** a tomahawk. **3. bury the hatchet** or **tomahawk,** to become reconciled or reunited; make peace. [ME *hachet* < MF *hachette,* dim. (see -ET) of *hache* ax < Gmc **hapja* kind of knife; akin to Gk *kóptein* to cut] —**hatch′et·like′,** *adj.*

hatch′et face′, a thin face with sharp features. —**hatch′et-faced′,** *adj.*

hatch′et job′, *Informal.* a maliciously destructive critique or act.

hatch′et man′, *Informal.* **1.** a professional murderer. **2.** a writer or speaker who specializes in defamatory attacks, as on political candidates or public officials. **3.** a person whose job it is to execute unpleasant tasks for a superior, as criticizing or dismissing.

hatch·ing (hach′ing), *n.* a series of lines, generally parallel, used in shading or modeling, as in drawing.

hatch·ment (hach′mənt), *n.* *Chiefly Brit.* a square tablet, set diagonally, bearing the coat of arms of a deceased person. [var. (by syncopation and aspiration) of ACHIEVEMENT]

Hatchment

hatch·way (hach′wā′), *n.* **1.** Also called **hatch.** *Naut.* a covered opening in a deck, used as a means of passage for cargo, supplies, persons, machinery, etc. **2.** the opening of any trap door, as in a floor, ceiling, or roof.

hat′ dance′, a Mexican folk dance in which the man places his sombrero on the ground as an offer of love and the woman dances on the hat's brim and then places the hat on her head to indicate her acceptance of him.

hate (hāt), *v.,* **hat·ed, hat·ing,** *n.* —*v.t.* **1.** to dislike intensely or passionately; detest. **2.** to dislike; be unwilling: *I hate to do it.* —*v.i.* **3.** to feel intense dislike or extreme aversion or hostility. —*n.* **4.** intense dislike; extreme aversion or hostility. **5.** the object of extreme aversion or hostility. [ME *hat(i)e(n),* OE *hatian;* c. D *haten,* Icel *hata,* Goth *hatan,* G *hassen*] —**hat′er,** *n.*

—**Syn. 1.** loathe, execrate; despise. HATE, ABHOR, DETEST, ABOMINATE imply feeling intense dislike or aversion toward something. HATE, the simple and general word, suggests passionate dislike and a feeling of enmity: *to hate autocracy.* ABHOR expresses a deep-rooted horror and a sense of repugnance or complete rejection: *to abhor cruelty.* DETEST implies intense, even vehement, dislike and antipathy, besides a sense of disdain: *to detest arrogance.* ABOMINATE expresses a strong feeling of disgust and revulsion toward something thought of as unworthy, unlucky, or the like: *to abominate treachery.* **—Ant. 1.** love.

hate·a·ble (hā′tə bəl), *adj.* meriting hatred or loathing. Also, **hatable.**

hate·ful (hāt′fəl), *adj.* **1.** exciting hate or deserving to be hated: *hateful oppression.* **2.** unpleasant; dislikable; distasteful: *a hateful task.* **3.** full of or expressing hate; malignant; malevolent: *a hateful speech.* [ME] **—hate′ful·ly,** *adv.* **—hate′ful·ness,** *n.*
—Syn. 1. abominable, abhorrent, repugnant; loathsome. HATEFUL, OBNOXIOUS, ODIOUS, OFFENSIVE refer to that which causes strong dislike or annoyance. HATEFUL implies actually causing hatred or extremely strong dislike: *The sight of him is hateful to me.* OBNOXIOUS emphasizes causing annoyance or discomfort by objectionable qualities: *His piggish manners made him obnoxious.* ODIOUS emphasizes the disagreeable or displeasing: *an odious little man; odious servility.* OFFENSIVE emphasizes the distaste and resentment caused by something that may be either displeasing or insulting: *an offensive odor, remark.* **—Ant. 1.** likable, pleasant, agreeable.

hate·mon·ger (hāt′mung′gər, -mong′-), *n.* a person who kindles hatred, enmity, or prejudice in others. **—hate′mon′ger·ing,** *n.*

hate′ sheet′, a newspaper or other publication that consistently expresses biased hatred toward some race, nationality, religion, or other group.

hath (hath), *v. Archaic.* 3rd pers. sing. pres. indic. of **have.**

Hath·a·way (hath′ə wā′), *n.* **Anne,** 1557–1623, the wife of William Shakespeare.

Hath·or (hath′ôr, -ər), *n. Egyptian Religion.* the goddess of love and joy, often represented with the head, horns, or ears of a cow. **—Ha·thor·ic** (hə thôr′ik, -thor-), *adj.*

Ha·tik·vah (hä tēk′vä, -tik′vô, -və), *n.* the national anthem of Israel.

hat·pin (hat′pin′), *n.* a long pin for securing a woman's hat to her hair.

hat·rack (hat′rak′), *n.* a frame, stand, or post having knobs or hooks for hanging hats.

ha·tred (hā′trid), *n.* the feeling of a person who hates; intense dislike, aversion, or hostility. [ME] **—Syn.** animosity, detestation, loathing. **—Ant.** love.

Hat·shep·sut (hat shep′so͞ot), *n.* 1495–75 B.C., queen of Egypt. Also, **Hatasu, Hat·shep·set** (hat shep′set).

hat·ter (hat′ər), *n.* a maker or seller of hats. [ME]

Hat·ter·as (hat′ər əs), *n.* **Cape,** a promontory on an island off the E coast of North Carolina.

Hat·ties·burg (hat′ēz bûrg′), *n.* a city in SE Mississippi. 38,277 (1970).

hat′ tree′. See **hall tree.**

hau·ber·geon (hô′bər jən), *n. Armor.* habergeon.

hau·berk (hô′bûrk), *n. Armor.* a long defensive shirt, usually of mail, extending to the knees; byrnie. [ME < OF *hauberc,* earlier *halberc* < OHG *halsberc* = *hals* neck (see HAWSE) + *berc* protection (see HARBOR); c. OE *healsbeorg,* Icel *halsbjörg*]

haugh (häkн, häf), *n. Scot. and North Eng.* a stretch of alluvial land forming part of a river valley; bottom land. [ME *halche, hawgh,* OE *healh* corner, nook]

haugh·ty (hô′tē), *adj.,* **-ti·er, -ti·est. 1.** disdainfully proud; snobbish; arrogant. **2.** *Archaic.* exalted; lofty or noble. [obs. *haught* (sp. var. of late ME *haute* < MF << L *alt(us)* high, with *h-* < Gmc; cf. OHG *hoh* high) + -Y[1]] **—haugh′ti·ly,** *adv.* **—haugh′ti·ness,** *n.* **—Syn. 1.** lordly, disdainful, contemptuous. See **proud. —Ant. 1.** humble.

haul (hôl), *v.t.* **1.** to pull or draw with force; drag. **2.** to cart or transport; carry. **3.** to lower; cause to descend (often fol. by *down*): *to haul down the flag.* **4.** to arrest or bring before a magistrate or other authority (often fol. by *before, in, to, into,* etc.): *He was hauled before the judge.* **—***v.i.* **5.** to pull or tug. **6.** to go or come to a place, esp. with effort: *After a long drive they finally hauled into town at dusk.* **7.** to cart, transport, or move freight commercially. **8.** *Naut.* to sail, as in a particular direction. **9.** to draw or pull a vessel up on land, as for repairs or storage. **10.** *Naut.* (of the wind) to shift to a direction closer to the heading of a vessel (opposed to *veer*). **11. haul off,** *Informal.* to draw back the arm in order to strike; prepare to deal a blow: *He hauled off and socked the guy.* **—***n.* **12.** the act or an instance of hauling; a strong pull or tug. **13.** that which is hauled. **14.** a load hauled; quantity carried or transported. **15.** the distance or route over which anything is hauled. **16.** *Informal.* **a.** the act of taking or acquiring something. **b.** something that is taken or acquired. **17. long haul, a.** a relatively great period of time. **b.** a relatively great distance. **18. short haul, a.** a relatively short period of time. **b.** a relatively short distance. [earlier *hall,* var. of HALE[2]] **—haul′er,** *n.*

haul·age (hô′lij), *n.* **1.** the act or labor of hauling. **2.** a charge made by a railroad for hauling.

haulm (hôm), *n. Brit.* **1.** stems or stalks collectively, as of grain or of peas, beans, hops, etc., esp. as used for litter or thatching. **2.** a single stem or stalk. [ME *halm,* OE *healm;* c. D, G *halm,* Icel *halmr;* akin to L *culmus* stalk, Gk *kálamos* reed]

haunch (hônch, hänch), *n.* **1.** the hip. **2.** the fleshy part of the body about the hip. **3.** a hind quarter of an animal. **4.** the leg and loin of an animal, used for food. **5.** *Archit.* **a.** either side of an arch, extending from the vertex or crown to the impost. **b.** the part of a beam projecting below a floor or roof slab. [ME *haunche* < OF *hanche* < Gmc; cf. MD *hanke* haunch, G *Hanke* haunch] **—haunched,** *adj.*

haunt (hônt, hänt; *for 8 sometimes also* hant), *v.t.* **1.** to visit habitually or appear to frequent as a spirit or ghost: *to haunt a house; to haunt a person.* **2.** to recur persistently to the consciousness of; remain with: *Memories of love haunted him.* **3.** to visit frequently; go to often: *He haunted the art galleries.* **4.** to disturb or distress; cause to have anxiety: *His youthful escapades came back to haunt him.* **—***v.i.* **5.** to reappear continually as a spirit or ghost. **6.** to remain persistently; loiter; stay; linger. **—***n.* **7.** Often, **haunts.** a place frequently visited: *to return to one's old haunts.* **8.** *Chiefly Midland and Southern U.S.* a ghost. [ME *haunt(en)* < OF *hant(er)* < Gmc; cf. OE *hāmettan* to domicile < *hām* HOME] **—haunt′er,** *n.*

haunt·ed (hôn′tid), *adj.* **1.** inhabited or frequented by ghosts: *a haunted castle.* **2.** obsessed; preoccupied, as with an emotion, memory, or idea. [ME]

haunt·ing (hôn′ting), *adj.* remaining in the consciousness; not quickly forgotten: *haunting memories.* [ME] **—haunt′ing·ly,** *adv.*

Haupt·mann (houpt′män′), *n.* **Ger·hart** (geʀ′häʀt), 1862–1946, German dramatist, novelist, and poet.

Hau·sa (hou′sä), *n., pl.* **-sas,** (*esp. collectively*) **-sa. 1.** a member of a Negroid people of the Sudan and N Nigeria. **2.** the language of the Hausa people, an Afro-Asiatic language that is also widely used in Africa as a language of commerce. Also, **Haussa.**

haus·frau (hous′frou′), *n., pl.* **-fraus, -frau·en** (-frou′ən). a housewife. [< G = *Haus* HOUSE + *Frau* wife, woman]

Haus·sa (hou′sä), *n., pl.* **-sas,** (*esp. collectively*) **-sa.** Hausa.

Hauss·mann (hous′mən; *Fr.* ōs man′), *n.* **Georges Eu·gène** (zhôʀzh œ zhen′), **Baron,** 1809–91, French administrator and city planner.

haus·tel·late (hô stel′it, hô′stəlāt′), *adj. Zool.* having a haustellum.

haus·tel·lum (hô stel′əm), *n., pl.* **haus·tel·la** (hô stel′ə). (in certain crustaceans and insects) an organ or part of the proboscis adapted for sucking blood or plant juices. [< NL, dim. of L *haustrum* machine for drawing water = *haus-* (var. s. of *haurīre* to draw up) + *-trum* instrumental suffix]

haus·to·ri·um (hô stôr′ē əm, -stōr′-), *n., pl.* **haus·to·ri·a** (hô stôr′ē ə, -stōr′-). *Bot.* an intracellular feeding organ of a parasite that does not kill the host cells but lives with them. [< NL = L *haust(us)* drawn up, drained (ptp. of *haurīre*) + *-ōrium* -ORY[2]] **—haus·to′ri·al,** *adj.*

haut·boy (hō′boi, ō′boi), *n. Archaic.* oboe. [< MF *hautbois* = *haut* high (see HAUGHTY) + *bois* wood (see BUSH[1])] **—haut′boy·ist,** *n.*

haute cou·ture (ōt ko͞o tyʀ′), *French.* **1.** high fashion; the most fashionable and influential dressmaking and designing. **2.** the fashions created by the leading dressmakers.

haute cui·sine (ōt kwē zēn′), *French.* fine cooking; food preparation as an art.

hau·teur (hō tûr′; *Fr.* ō tœʀ′), *n.* haughty manner or spirit; haughtiness. [< F; see HAUGHTY, -OR[1]]

haut monde (ō mônd′), *French.* high society.

hav, *Trig.* haversine.

Ha·van·a (hə van′ə), *n.* **1.** Spanish, **Habana.** a seaport in and the capital of Cuba, on the NW coast. 1,800,000. **2.** a cigar made in Cuba or of Cuban tobacco.

have (hav; *unstressed* həv, əv), *v.* and *auxiliary v., pres. sing. 1st pers.* **have,** *2nd* **have** or (*Archaic*) **hast,** *3rd* **has** or (*Archaic*) **hath,** *pres. pl.* **have;** *past sing. 1st pers.* **had,** *2nd* **had** or (*Archaic*) **hadst** or **had·dest,** *3rd* **had,** *past pl.* **had;** *past part.* **had;** *pres. part.* **hav·ing,** *n.* **—***v.t.* **1.** to possess or own; hold for use; contain: *He has property. The book has an index.* **2.** to accept in some relation, as of kindred or relative position: *He wanted to marry her, but she wouldn't have him.* **3.** to get, receive, or take: *to have a part in a play; to have news.* **4.** to be under obligation with respect to (usually fol. by an infinitive): *I have ironing to finish, and then I have to go out.* **5.** to experience, undergo, or endure, as joy or pain: *Have a good time. He had a heart attack last year.* **6.** to hold in mind, sight, etc.: *to have doubts.* **7.** to cause to, as by command, invitation, etc.: *Have him come here at five.* **8.** to be related to or be in a certain relation to: *She has three cousins. He has a kind boss.* **9.** to show or exhibit in action or words: *She had the crust to refuse my invitation.* **10.** to be identified or distinguished by; possess the characteristic of: *This cloth has a silky texture.* **11.** to engage in or carry on: *to have a talk; to have a fight.* **12.** to partake of; eat or drink: *He had cake and coffee at noon.* **13.** to permit or allow: *I will not have it.* **14.** to assert, maintain, or represent as being: *Rumor has it that she's going to be married.* **15.** to know, understand, or be skilled in: *to have neither Latin nor Greek.* **16.** to beget or give birth to: *to have a baby.* **17.** to hold at a disadvantage: *He has you there.* **18.** *Slang.* **a.** to outwit, deceive, or cheat: *I've been had by that swindler.* **b.** to control or possess through bribery; bribe: *the attitude that any man can be had.* **19.** to gain possession of: *There are none to be had at that price.* **20.** to hold or put in a certain position or situation: *The problem had me stumped.* **21.** to exercise, display, or make use of: *Have pity on him.* **22.** to entertain; invite or cause to be present as a companion or guest: *We had Everett over for dinner.* **23.** to engage in sexual intercourse with.
—*v.i.* **24.** to be in possession of money and the accouterments of financial security: *There are some who have and some who have not.*
—*auxiliary verb.* **25.** (used with a past participle to form perfect tenses): *She has gone. It would have been an enjoyable party if he hadn't felt downcast.* **26. had better** or **best,** ought to. **27. had rather** or **sooner,** to prefer: *I'd much rather he went with you.* **28. have at,** to go at vigorously; attack. **29. have done,** to cease; finish. **30. have had it,** *Slang.* **a.** to be unable or unwilling to endure more: *I've been working like a fool, but now I've had it.* **b.** to suffer defeat; be finished; fail: *He was a great pitcher, but after this season he'll have had it.* **31. have it in for,** *Informal.* to wish harm to; hold a grudge against: *She has it in for me because I didn't invite her.* **32. have it out,** to come to an understanding or decision through discussion or combat. **33. have on, a.** to be clothed in; wear: *She had on a new dress.* **b.** to have arranged or planned: *What do you have on for Christmas?* **34. have to do with, a.** to have dealings or social relations with. **b.** to deal with; be concerned with: *The book has to do with Chicago politics.* **35. to have and to hold,** to possess legally; have permanent possession of.
—*n.* **36.** Usually, **haves.** a person, group, nation, etc., that has wealth, social position, etc. (contrasted with *have-nots*). [ME *have(n), habbe(n),* OE *habban;* c. G *haben,* Icel *hafa,* Goth *haban* to have; ? akin to HEAVE]
—Syn. 1. HAVE, HOLD, OCCUPY, OWN, POSSESS mean to be, in varying degrees, in possession of something. HAVE, being the most general word, admits of the widest range of application: *to have money, rights, discretion, a disease, a glimpse, an idea; to have a friend's umbrella.* To HOLD is to have in one's grasp or one's control, but not necessarily as one's own: *to hold stakes.* To OCCUPY is to hold and use, but

not necessarily by any right of ownership: *to occupy a chair, a house, a position.* To OWN is to have the full rights of property in a thing, that, however, another may be holding or enjoying: *to own a house that is rented to tenants.* POSSESS is a more formal equivalent for OWN and suggests control, and often occupation, of large holdings: *to possess vast territories.*

have·lock (hav′lok), *n.* a cap cover with a flap at the back to protect the neck from the sun, rain, etc. [named after Sir Henry *Havelock* (1795–1857), English general in India]

ha·ven (hā′vən), *n.* **1.** a harbor or port. **2.** any place of shelter and safety; refuge; asylum. **—*v.t.* 3.** to shelter, as in a haven. [ME; OE *hæfen;* c. D *haven,* G *Hafen,* Icel *höfn;* akin to OE *hæf,* Icel *haf* sea] **—Syn. 1.** See **harbor.**

have-not (hav′not′, -not′), *n.* Usually, **have-nots.** a person or group that is without wealth, social position, or other material benefits (contrasted with *have*).

have·n't (hav′ənt), contraction of *have not.*

hav·er[1] (hav′ər), *n. Brit. Dial.* oats. [ME < Scand; cf. Icel *hafrar* (pl.) oats; c. D *haver,* LG *hafer,* HG *Haber*]

ha·ver[2] (hā′vər), *v.i. Scot. and North Eng.* to talk foolishly. [?]

Hav·er·ford (hav′ər fərd), *n.* a township in SE Pennsylvania, near Philadelphia. 55,132 (1970).

Ha·ver·hill (hā′vər il, -vrəl), *n.* a city in NE Massachusetts, on the Merrimack River. 46,120 (1970).

hav·er·sack (hav′ər sak′), *n.* a single-strapped bag worn over one shoulder and used for carrying provisions. [earlier *havresack* < F *havresac* < G *Habersack* sack for oats]

Ha·ver′sian canal′ (hə vûr′zhən), (*sometimes l.c.*) a microscopic channel in bone, through which a blood vessel runs. [named after Clopton *Havers* (d. 1702), English anatomist; see -IAN]

hav·er·sine (hav′ər sīn′), *n. Trig.* one half the versed sine of a given angle or arc. *Abbr.:* hav [HA(LF) + VER(SED) + SINE[1]]

hav·oc (hav′ək), *n., v.,* **-ocked, -ock·ing.** **—*n.* 1.** devastation; ruinous damage. **2. cry havoc,** to warn of danger or disaster. **3. play havoc with, a.** to create confusion or disorder. **b.** to destroy; ruin. **—*v.t.* 4.** to work havoc upon; devastate. **—*v.i.* 5.** to work havoc. [late ME *havok* < AF (in phrase *crier havok* to cry havoc, i.e., utter the command *havoc!* as signal for pillaging), MF *havot* in same sense < Gmc; akin to HEAVE] **—hav′ock·er,** *n.* **—Syn. 1.** See **ruin.**

Ha·vre (hä′vrə, -vər), *n.* See **Le Havre.**

haw[1] (hô), *n.* the fruit of the Old World hawthorn, *Crataegus Oxyacantha,* or of other species of the same genus. [ME; OE *haga;* c. Icel *hagi* pasture, Dan *have* garden]

haw[2] (hô), *v.i.* **1.** to hesitate or falter in or as in speech: *He hemmed and hawed around but finally said what was on his mind.* **2.** to utter a sound representing a hesitation or pause in speech. **—*n.* 3.** a sound or pause of hesitation. [imit.]

haw[3] (hô), *interj.* **1.** (used as a word of command to a draft animal, usually directing it to turn to the left.) **—*v.t., v.i.* 2.** to turn or make a turn to the left. Cf. **gee**[1]. [appar. orig. the impv. *haw!* look! of ME *hawen,* OE *hāwian;* akin to L *cavēre* to beware]

haw[4] (hô), *n.* the nictitating membrane of a horse, dog, etc., formerly only when inflamed. [?]

Haw., Hawaii.

Ha·wai·i (hə wī′ē, -wä′-, -wä′yə), *n.* **1.** Formerly, **Sandwich Islands, Ter′ritory of Hawai′i.** a state of the United States comprised of the N Pacific islands of Hawaii, Kahoolawe, Kauai, Lanai, Maui, Molokai, Niihau, and Oahu. 769,913 (1970); 6424 sq. mi. *Cap.:* Honolulu. *Abbr.:* Haw., HI **2.** the largest island of Hawaii. 63,468 (1970); 4021 sq. mi.

Ha·wai·ian (hə wī′ən, -wä′yən), *adj.* **1.** of or pertaining to Hawaii or the Hawaiian Islands. **—*n.* 2.** a native or inhabitant of Hawaii or the Hawaiian Islands. **3.** the aboriginal language of Hawaii, a Polynesian language.

Hawai′ian Is′lands, a group of islands in the N Pacific; 2090 mi. SW of San Francisco: includes the eight islands comprising the state of Hawaii and volcanic, rock, and coral islets.

Hawai′i Na′tional Park′, a large national park that includes the active volcanoes Kilauea and Mauna Loa on the island of Hawaii and the extinct crater Haleakala on Maui. 343 sq. mi.

haw·finch (hô′finch′), *n.* a European grosbeak, *Coccothraustes coccothraustes.*

haw-haw (hô′hô′), *n.* **1.** (used to represent the sound of a loud, boisterous laugh.) **2.** a guffaw. [imit.; see HA-HA[1]]

hawk[1] (hôk), *n.* **1.** any of numerous diurnal birds of prey either of the family *Accipitridae,* as certain accipiters, or of the family *Falconidae,* as certain falcons, caracaras, etc. **2.** any of several similar, unrelated birds, as the nighthawk. **3.** *Informal.* a person who preys on others, as a sharper. **4.** Also called **war hawk.** *Informal.* a person, esp. one in public office, who advocates war or a belligerent national attitude. **—*v.i.* 5.** to fly, or hunt on the wing, like a hawk. **6.** to hunt with hawks or other birds of prey. [ME *hauk(e),* OE *hafoc;* c. OHG *habuh,* Icel *haukr* hawk, Pol *kobuz* hobby] **—hawk′like′,** *adj.*

Hawk (def. 1), *Buteo jamaicensis* (Length 2 ft.)

hawk[2] (hôk), *v.t.* **1.** to peddle or offer for sale by calling aloud or by going from door to door. **—*v.i.* 2.** to carry wares about for sale; peddle. [back formation from HAWKER[2]]

hawk[3] (hôk), *v.i.* **1.** to make an effort to raise phlegm from the throat; clear the throat noisily. **—*v.t.* 2.** to raise by hawking: *to hawk up phlegm.* **—*n.* 3.** a noisy effort to clear the throat. [imit.; see HAW[2]]

hawk[4] (hôk), *n.* a small, square board with a handle underneath it, used by plasterers and masons to hold plaster or mortar being applied; mortarboard. [? special use of HAWK[1]]

hawk·bill (hôk′bil′), *n.* See **hawksbill turtle.**

hawk·er[1] (hô′kər), *n.* a person who hunts with hawks or other birds of prey. [ME; OE *hafecere*]

hawk·er[2] (hô′kər), *n.* a person who offers goods for sale by shouting his wares in the street or going from door to door; peddler. [< MLG *haker* retail dealer; akin to MD *hac* in same sense]

Hawk·eye (hôk′ī′), *n., pl.* **-eyes.** a native or inhabitant of Iowa (the **Hawkeye State**) (used as a nickname). [back formation from HAWK-EYED]

hawk-eyed (hôk′īd′), *adj.* having very keen eyes.

Hawk′eye State′, Iowa (used as a nickname).

Haw·kins (hô′kinz), *n.* **Sir John,** 1532–95, English slave trader: commanded a squadron in the defeat of the Spanish Armada. Also, **Hawkyns.**

hawk·ish (hô′kish), *adj.* **1.** of, like, or suggesting a hawk. **2.** advocating war or a belligerently threatening diplomatic policy.

hawk′ moth′, any moth of the family *Sphingidae,* noted for very swift flight and the ability to hover while sipping nectar from flowers. Also called **sphinx moth.**

hawk·nose (hôk′nōz′), *n.* a nose curved like the beak of a hawk. [back formation from *hawk-nosed*] **—hawk′-nosed′,** *adj.*

hawks′bill tur′tle (hôks′bil′), a sea turtle, *Eretmochelys imbricata,* the source of tortoise shell. Also called **hawks′bill′, hawkbill, tortoise-shell turtle.**

hawk·shaw (hôk′shô′), *n.* a detective. [after *Hawkshaw,* a detective in the play *The Ticket of Leave Man* (1863) by Tom Taylor]

hawk·weed (hôk′wēd′), *n.* any composite herb of the genus *Hieracium,* having yellow, orange, or red flowers. [trans. of NL *hierācium* < Gk *hierākion* = *hierāk-* (s. of *hiērax* hawk) + *-ion* neut. suffix; see WEED[1]]

Haw·kyns (hô′kinz), *n.* **Sir John.** See **Hawkins, Sir John.**

hawse (hôz, hôs), *n. Naut.* **1.** the part of a bow where the hawseholes are located. **2.** a hawsehole or hawsepipe. **3.** the distance between the bow of an anchored vessel and the point on the surface of the water above the anchor. **4.** the relative position or arrangement of the port and starboard anchor cables when both are used to moor a vessel. [ME *hals,* OE *heals* bow of a ship, lit., neck; c. Icel *hals* in same senses, G *Hals* neck, throat]

hawse·hole (hôz′hōl′, hôs′-), *n. Naut.* a hole in the stem or bow of a vessel through which an anchor cable passes.

hawse·pipe (hôz′pīp′, hôs′-), *n. Naut.* an iron or steel pipe in the stem or bow of a vessel through which an anchor cable passes.

haw·ser (hô′zər, -sər), *n. Naut.* a heavy rope for mooring or towing. [ME *haucer* < AF *hauceour* = MF *hauci(er)* (to) hoist (< LL **altiāre* to raise < L *altus* high) + *-our* -OR[2], -ER[2]]

haw′ser bend′, a knot uniting the ends of two lines.

haw·thorn (hô′thôrn′), *n.* **1.** any of numerous rosaceous plants of the genus *Crataegus,* usually small trees with stiff thorns, certain species of which have white or pink blossoms and bright-colored fruits. **2.** a thorny, Old World shrub, *Crataegus oxyacantha.* [ME; OE *haguthorn*]

Haw·thorne (hô′thôrn′), *n.* **1. Nathaniel,** 1804–64, U.S. novelist and short-story writer. **2.** a city in California, SW of Los Angeles. 53,304 (1970).

hay (hā), *n.* **1.** grass, clover, alfalfa, etc., cut and dried for use as forage. **2.** grass mowed or intended for mowing. **3.** *Slang.* money. **4. hit the hay,** *Slang.* to go to bed. **5. make hay while the sun shines,** to seize an opportunity when it presents itself. Also, **make hay.** **—*v.t.* 6.** to convert (grass) into hay. **7.** to furnish (horses, cows, etc.) with hay. **—*v.i.* 8.** to cut grass, clover, or the like, and store for use as forage. [ME; OE *hēg;* c. G *Heu,* Icel *hey,*

hay·cock (hā′kok′), *n.* a small conical pile of hay stacked in a hayfield while the hay is awaiting removal to a barn. [late ME]

Hay·dn (hīd′ən), *n.* **Franz Jo·seph** (frants jō′zəf, -səf, franz; *Ger.* fʀänts yō′zef), 1732–1809, Austrian composer.

Hayes (hāz), *n.* **1. Carl·ton J(oseph) H(unt·ley)** (kärl′tən, hunt′lē), 1882–1964, U.S. historian, teacher, and diplomat. **2. Helen** (*Helen Hayes Brown MacArthur*), born 1900, U.S. actress. **3. Rutherford B(ir·chard)** (bûr′chərd), 1822–93, 19th president of the U.S. 1877–81.

hay′ fe′ver, *Pathol.* a catarrhal affection of the mucous membranes of the eyes and respiratory tract caused by an allergic response to the pollen of certain plants.

hay·fork (hā′fôrk′), *n.* **1.** a pitchfork. **2.** a machine for loading or unloading hay.

hay·loft (hā′lôft′, -loft′), *n.* a loft in a stable or barn for the storage of hay.

hay·mak·er (hā′mā′kər), *n.* **1.** *Informal.* a knockout punch. **2.** a person or a machine that cuts hay and spreads it to dry. [late ME *heymakere*] **—hay′mak′ing,** *adj., n.*

Hay·mar·ket (hā′mär′kit), *n.* **1.** a famous London market 1644–1830. **2.** a street in London, site of this market, known for its theaters.

Hay′market Square′, a square in Chicago: scene of a riot (**Hay′market Ri′ot**) in 1886 between police and labor unionists.

hay·mow (hā′mou′), *n.* **1.** a place in a barn where hay is stored. **2.** a mass of hay stored in a barn.

Haynes (hānz), *n.* **El·wood** (el′wo͝od′), 1857–1925, U.S. inventor.

hay·rack (hā′rak′), *n.* **1.** a rack for holding hay for feeding horses or cattle. **2.** a rack or framework mounted on a wagon, for use in carrying hay, straw, or the like.

hay·rick (hā′rik′), *n. Chiefly Brit.* haystack. [ME *heyrek*]

hay·ride (hā′rīd′), *n.* a pleasure ride or outing, usually at night, in an open truck or wagon partly filled with hay.

hay·seed (hā′sēd′), *n.* **1.** grass seed, esp. that shaken out of hay. **2.** small bits of the chaff, straw, etc., of hay. **3.** *Informal.* a yokel; hick.

hay·stack (hā′stak′), *n.* a stack of hay built up in the open air for preservation, and sometimes thatched or covered. Also called, *esp. Brit.,* **hayrick.**

Hay·ti (hā′tī), *n.* Haiti (def. 2).

Hay·ward (hā′wərd), *n.* a city in central California, SE of Oakland. 93,058 (1970).

hay·wire (hā′wīər′), *n.* **1.** wire used to bind bales of hay. **—*adj.* 2.** *Informal.* out of control or order.

ha·zan (ᴋʜä zän′; *Eng.* hä′zən, ᴋʜä′-), *n., pl.* **ha·za·nim** (ᴋʜä zä nēm′), *Eng.* **ha·zans.** *Hebrew.* a cantor of a synagogue. Also, **chazan.**

haz·ard (haz′ərd), *n.* **1.** danger; risk; peril. **2.** something causing danger, peril, risk, or difficulty: *the many hazards of the big city.* **3.** the absence or lack of predictability in an event; chance; uncertainty. **4.** an unexpected or unpredictable event; accident. **5.** *Golf.* a bunker, sand trap, or the like, constituting an obstacle. **6.** a game played with two dice, an earlier and more complicated form of craps. **7.** something risked or staked. **8.** *Court Tennis.* any of the winning openings. **9.** (in English billiards) a stroke by which the player pockets the object ball **(winning hazard)** or his own ball after contact with another ball **(losing hazard).** —*v.t.* **10.** to offer (a statement, conjecture, etc.) at the risk of criticism, disapproval, etc.; venture: *to hazard a guess.* **11.** to put to the risk of being lost; expose to risk; gamble: *In making the investment, he hazarded all his savings.* **12.** to take or run the risk of (a misfortune, penalty, etc.): *Thieves hazard arrest.* **13.** to venture upon (anything of doubtful issue). [ME *hasard* < OF; cf. Ar *az-zahr* the die] —**Syn. 1.** See **danger. 3.** accident, fortuity, fortuitousness.

haz·ard·ous (haz′ər dəs), *adj.* **1.** full of risk; perilous; risky. **2.** dependent on chance. —**haz′ard·ous·ly,** *adv.* —**haz′ard·ous·ness,** *n.*

haze[1] (hāz), *n.* **1.** an aggregation in the atmosphere of very fine, widely dispersed particles, giving the air an opalescent appearance that subdues colors. **2.** vagueness or obscurity, as of the mind, perception, etc. [n. use of ME *hase, OE *hasu*, var. of *haswa* ashen, dusky. See HAZY, HARE] —**Syn. 2.** See **cloud.**

haze (hāz), *v.t.,* **hazed, haz·ing.** to subject (freshmen, newcomers, etc.) to abusive or humiliating tricks and ridicule. [< MF *has(er)* (to) irritate, annoy] —**haz′er,** *n.*

ha·zel (hā′zəl), *n.* **1.** any betulaceous shrub or small tree of the genus *Corylus*, bearing edible nuts, as *C. Avellana*, of Europe, or *C. americana* and *C. cornuta*, of America. **2.** any of several other shrubs or trees, as an Australian, rhamnaceous shrub, *Pomaderris apetala.* **3.** the wood of any of these trees. **4.** light golden brown, as the color of a hazelnut. —*adj.* **5.** of or pertaining to the hazel. **6.** made of the wood of the hazel. **7.** having a light golden-brown color. [ME *hasel*, OE *hæs(e)l*; c. G *Hasel*, Icel *hasl*, L *corylus* hazel shrub]

ha·zel·nut (hā′zəl nut′), *n.* the nut of the hazel; filbert. [ME *haselnote*, OE *hæselhnutu*]

Ha·zle·ton (hā′zəl tən), *n.* a city in E Pennsylvania. 30,426 (1970).

Haz·litt (haz′lit), *n.* **William,** 1778–1830, English critic and essayist.

Ha·zor (hä zōr′, -zôr′), *n.* an ancient city in Israel, N of the Sea of Galilee: extensive excavations.

ha·zy (hā′zē), *adj.,* **-zi·er, -zi·est. 1.** characterized by the presence of haze; misty: *hazy weather.* **2.** lacking distinctness or clarity; vague. [earlier *hawsey*, metathetic var. of ME *haswy, OE *haswig* ashen, dusky] —**ha′zi·ly,** *adv.* —**ha′zi·ness,** *n.*

Hb, *Biochem.* hemoglobin.

h.b., *Football.* halfback.

H-beam (āch′bēm′), *n.* an I-beam having flanges the width of the web. Also called **H-bar** (āch′bär′). See illus. at **shape.**

H.B.M., His (or Her) Britannic Majesty.

H-bomb (āch′bom′), *n.* See **hydrogen bomb.**

H.C., House of Commons.

H.C.F., highest common factor. Also, **h.c.f.**

hd., **1.** hand. **2.** head.

hdkf., handkerchief.

HDL, *Biochem.* See **high-density lipoprotein.**

hdqrs., headquarters.

he[1] (hē; *unstressed* ē), *pron., nom.* **he,** *poss.* **his,** *obj.* **him;** *pl. nom.* **they,** *poss.* **their** or **theirs,** *obj.* **them;** *n., pl.* **hes.** —*pron.* **1.** the male being in question or last mentioned; that male. **2.** anyone; that person: *He who hesitates is lost.* —*n.* **3.** a man; any male person or animal: *hes and shes.* [ME, OE (masc. nom. sing.); c. D *hij*, OS *hē*, OHG *her* he, Ir *cē* this; see HIS, HIM, SHE, HER, IT]

he[2] (hā; *Heb.* hā), *n.* the fifth letter of the Hebrew alphabet. [< Heb]

HE, high explosive.

He, *Chem.* helium.

H.E., **1.** high explosive. **2.** His Eminence. **3.** His (or Her) Excellency.

head (hed), *n.* **1.** the upper part of the body in man, joined to the trunk by the neck, containing the brain, eyes, ears, nose, and mouth. **2.** the corresponding part of the body of an animal. **3.** the head considered as the center of the intellect; mind; brain: *She has a head for mathematics.* **4.** the position or place of leadership, greatest authority, or honor. **5.** a person to whom others are subordinate; director of an institution; leader or chief. **6.** a person considered with reference to his mind, disposition, attributes, status, etc.: *wise heads; crowned heads.* **7.** the part of anything that forms or is regarded as forming the top, summit, or upper end: *the head of a pin; the head of a page.* **8.** the foremost part or front end of anything or a forward projecting part: *the head of a procession; the head of a rock.* **9.** the part of a weapon, tool, etc., used for striking: *the head of a hammer.* **10.** a person or animal considered merely as one of a number, herd, or group: *ten head of cattle; a dinner at so much a head.* **11.** a culminating or critical point; crisis or climax: *to bring matters to a head.* **12.** the hair covering the head. **13.** froth or foam at the top of a liquid: *the head on beer.* **14.** *Bot.* **a.** any dense flower cluster or inflorescence. **b.** any other compact part of a plant, usually at the top of the stem, as that composed of leaves in the cabbage or lettuce. **15.** the maturated part of an abscess, boil, etc. **16.** a projecting point of a coast, esp. when high, as a cape, headland, or promontory. **17.** the obverse of a coin (opposed to *tail*). **18.** one of the chief parts or points of a written or oral discourse. **19.** something resembling a head in form or a representation of a head, as a piece of sculpture. **20.** the source of a river or stream. **21.** headline (def. 1). **22.** *Naut.* **a.** the forepart of a vessel; bow. **b.** the upper edge of a quadrilateral sail. **c.** the upper corner of a jib-headed sail. **d.** toilet; lavatory. **e.** crown (def. 19). **23.** *Gram.* the member of an endocentric construction that belongs to the same form class and may play the same grammatical role as the construction itself. **24.** the stretched membrane covering the end of a drum or similar musical instrument. **25.** *Coal Mining.* a level or road driven into the solid coal for proving or working a mine. **26.** *Mach.* any of various devices on machine tools for holding, moving, indexing, or changing tools or work, as the headstock or turret of a lathe. **27.** Also called **pressure head.** *Physics.* **a.** the vertical distance between two points in a fluid. **b.** the pressure differential resulting from this separation, expressed in terms of the vertical distance between the points. **c.** the pressure of a fluid expressed in terms of the height of a column of liquid yielding an equivalent pressure. **28.** the part or parts of a tape recorder that come into direct contact with the tape and serve to record, pick up, or erase electromagnetic impulses on it. **29. give one his head,** to permit a person to do as he likes. **30. go to one's head, a.** to make a person confused, dizzy, or drunk: *The brandy went to his head.* **b.** to make one conceited: *The adulation of the crowd went to his head.* **31. head and shoulders,** far better, more qualified, etc.; superior: *In intelligence, he was head and shoulders above the others.* **32. head over heels, a.** headlong, as in a somersault. **b.** intensely; completely: *head over heels in love.* **33. heads up!** *Informal.* be careful! watch out! **34. keep one's head,** to remain calm or poised, as in the midst of crisis or confusion. **35. keep one's head above water,** to remain financially solvent. **36. lose one's head,** to become uncontrolled or wildly excited. **37. not make head or tail of,** to be unable to understand or decipher: *They couldn't make head or tail of her explanation.* Also, **not make heads or tails of. 38. one's head off,** extremely; excessively: *She cries her head off at every sentimental scene.* **39. on one's head,** as one's responsibility or fault. **40. out of one's head or mind,** *Chiefly U.S.* **a.** insane; crazy. **b.** delirious; irrational. **41. over one's head, a.** to one having a prior claim or a superior position: *She went over her supervisor's head and spoke directly to a vice president.* **b.** beyond one's comprehension, ability, or resources: *The classical allusion went right over his head.* **c.** beyond one's financial resources or ability to pay: *He went in over his head in that poker game.* **42. turn one's head,** to cause one to become smug or conceited. —*adj.* **43.** first in rank or position; chief; leading; principal: *the head official.* **44.** of, pertaining to, or for the head (often used in combination): *headgear; headpiece.* **45.** situated at the top, front, or head of anything (often used in combination): *headline; headboard.* **46.** moving or coming from a direction in front of the head or prow of a vessel: *head sea.* —*v.t.* **47.** to go at the head of or in front of; lead; precede: *to head a list.* **48.** to outdo or excel; take the lead in or over. **49.** to be the head or chief of: *to head a department.* **50.** to direct the course of; turn the head or front of in a specified direction: *I'll head the boat for shore.* **51.** to go round the head of (a stream). **52.** to furnish or fit with a head. **53.** to take the head off; decapitate; behead. **54.** to poll (a tree). **55.** to get in front of in order to stop or turn aside, as stampeding livestock. **56.** headline (def. 4). —*v.i.* **57.** to move forward toward a point specified; direct one's course; go in a certain direction: *to head toward town.* **58.** to come or grow to a head; form a head: *Cabbage heads quickly.* **59. head off,** to go before in order to hinder the progress of; intercept: *The police headed off the fleeing driver.* [ME *he(v)ed*, OE *hēafod*; c. G *Haupt*, early Scand *haufuth*, Goth *haubith*; akin to OE *hafud-* (in *hafudland* headland), Icel *hofuth*, L *caput*] —**Syn. 5.** commander, director, chieftain, principal, superintendent, president, chairman. **43.** foremost, first, supreme. **49.** direct, command, govern. —**Ant. 1.** foot.

-head, a native English suffix meaning "state of being" (*godhead; maidenhead*), occurring in words now mostly archaic or obsolete, many being superseded by forms in **-hood.** [ME *-hede*, OE *-*hǣdu*, akin to *-hād* -HOOD]

head·ache (hed′āk′), *n.* **1.** a pain located in the head. **2.** *Informal.* anything or anyone annoying or bothersome. [ME; OE *hēafodece*]

head·ach·y (hed′ā′kē), *adj.* **1.** having a headache. **2.** accompanied by or causing headaches: *a headachy cold.*

head·band (hed′band′), *n.* **1.** a band worn around the head; fillet. **2.** *Print.* a band for decorative effect at the head of a chapter or of a page in a book. **3.** a band sewed or glued to the head or tail of the back of a book, or to both, for protection or decoration.

head·board (hed′bōrd′, -bôrd′), *n.* a board forming the head of anything, esp. of a bed.

head·cheese (hed′chēz′), *n.* a seasoned loaf made of the head meat of a calf or pig in its natural aspic.

head·dress (hed′dres′), *n.* a covering or decoration for the head: *a tribal headdress of feathers.*

head·er (hed′ər), *n.* **1.** a person or thing that removes or puts a head on something. **2.** a reaping machine that gathers only the heads of the grain. **3.** a chamber to which the ends of a number of tubes are connected so that water or steam may pass freely from one tube to the other. **4.** *Building Trades.* **a.** a brick or stone laid in a wall or the like so that its shorter ends are exposed or parallel to the surface. Cf. **stretcher** (def. 5). **b.** a framing member crossing and supporting the ends of joists, studs, or rafters so as to transfer their weight to parallel joists, studs, or rafters. **5.** *Informal.* a plunge or dive headfirst, as into water: *He stumbled and took a header into the ditch.* [late ME *heder*]

H S H

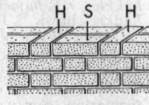

H, Header
S, Stretcher

head·first (hed′fûrst′), *adv.* **1.** with the head in front or bent forward: *He dived headfirst into the sea.* **2.** rashly; precipitately.

head′ gate′, **1.** a control gate at the upstream end of a canal or lock. **2.** a floodgate of a race, sluice, etc.

head·gear (hed′gēr′), *n.* **1.** any covering for the head, as a hat, cap, or bonnet. **2.** a protective covering for the head, as a helmet. 3. the parts of a harness around an animal's head.

head·hunt (hed′hunt′), *n.* 1. a headhunting expedition. —*v.i.* 2. to go headhunting. —**head′hunt′er,** *n.*

head·hunt·ing (hed′hun′ting), *n.* 1. (among certain primitive peoples) the practice of hunting down and decapitating victims and preserving their heads as trophies. 2. the recruitment of executives, technical experts, etc., in behalf of a client company. —*adj.* 3. of, pertaining to, or characteristic of headhunting.

head·ing (hed′ing), *n.* 1. something that serves as a head, top, or front. 2. a title or caption of a page, chapter, etc. 3. a section of the subject of a discourse. 4. (loosely) the compass direction toward which a traveler or vehicle is or should be moving; course. 5. *Aeron.* the angle between the axis from front to rear of an aircraft and some reference line, as magnetic north. [ME *hefding*]

head·land (hed′lənd), *n.* 1. a promontory extending into a large body of water. 2. a strip of unplowed land at the ends of furrows or near a fence or border. [ME *hedeland,* OE *hēafodland*]

head·less (hed′lis), *adj.* 1. without a head. 2. beheaded. 3. lacking a leader or chief. 4. foolish; stupid. [ME *he(ve)dles,* OE *hēafodlēas*] —**head′less·ness,** *n.*

head·light (hed′līt′), *n.* a light equipped with a reflector, on the front of a car, locomotive, etc.

head·line (hed′līn′), *n., v.,* **-lined, -lin·ing.** —*n.* Also called **head.** 1. a heading in a newspaper for any written material, sometimes for an illustration, to indicate subject matter. 2. the largest such heading on the front page, usually at the top. 3. the line at the top of a page, containing the title, pagination, etc. —*v.t.* 4. to furnish with a headline; head. 5. to mention or name in a headline. 6. to be the featured performer of (a show, nightclub, etc.). —*v.i.* 7. to be a featured performer.

head·lin·er (hed′lī′nər), *n.* *Theat. Slang.* a performer whose name appears at the head of a bill; star.

head·lock (hed′lok′), *n.* *Wrestling.* a hold in which a wrestler locks his arm around his opponent's head.

head·long (hed′lông′, -long′), *adv.* 1. with the head foremost; headfirst: *to plunge headlong into the water.* 2. without delay; hastily. 3. rashly; without deliberation. —*adj.* 4. undertaken quickly and suddenly; made precipitately; hasty: *a headlong retreat.* 5. rash; impetuous. 6. done or going with the head foremost. 7. *Archaic.* steep; precipitous. [late ME *hedlong,* alter. of ME *hedling*]

head′ louse′. See under **louse** (def. 1).

head·man (hed′mən, -man′), *n., pl.* **-men** (-mən, -men′). 1. a chief or leader. 2. headsman. [ME *he(ve)dman,* OE *hēafodman*]

head·mas·ter (hed′mas′tər, -mä′stər), *n.* 1. (in Britain) the principal of an elementary or secondary school. 2. (in the U.S.) a principal of a private school, esp. one for boys. —**head′mas′ter·ship′,** *n.*

head·mis·tress (hed′mis′tris), *n.* 1. (in Britain) the female principal of an elementary or secondary school. 2. (in the U.S.) a woman who is in charge of a private school, esp. one for girls. —**head′mis′tress·ship′,** *n.*

head·most (hed′mōst′ *or, esp. Brit.,* -məst), *adj.* foremost; most advanced.

head-on (hed′on′, -ôn′), *adj.* 1. (of two objects) meeting with the fronts or heads foremost: *a head-on collision.* 2. facing the direction of forward motion or alignment; frontal. 3. characterized by direct opposition: *a head-on confrontation.* —*adv.* 4. with the front or head foremost, esp. in a collision: *She walked head-on into the grocery boy.*

head·phone (hed′fōn′), *n.* Usually, **headphones.** a headset.

head·piece (hed′pēs′), *n.* 1. a piece of armor for the head; helmet. 2. any covering for the head. 3. a headset. 4. intellect; judgment. 5. *Print.* a decorative piece at the head of a page, chapter, etc.

head·pin (hed′pin′), *n.* *Bowling.* the pin standing nearest to the bowler when set up, at the head or front of the triangle; the number 1 pin.

head·quar·ter (hed′kwôr′tər), *v.t.* 1. to situate in headquarters. —*v.i.* 2. to establish one's headquarters. [back formation from HEADQUARTERS]

head·quar·ters (hed′kwôr′tərz), *n., pl.* **-ters.** (*construed as sing. or pl.*) 1. a center of operations, as of the police, a business, military commander, etc., from which orders are issued. 2. a military unit consisting of the commander, his staff, and other assistants.

head·race (hed′rās′), *n.* the race, flume, or channel leading to a water wheel or the like.

head·rest (hed′rest′), *n.* a rest or support of any kind for the head.

head·room (hed′ro͞om′, -ro͝om′), *n.* clear vertical space, as between the head and sill of a doorway. Also called **headway.**

heads (hedz), *adj.* (of a coin) with the obverse facing up: *On the first toss, the coin came up heads.*

head·sail (hed′sāl′; *Naut.* hed′səl), *n.* *Naut.* 1. any of various jibs or staysails set forward of the foremost mast of a vessel. 2. any sail set on a foremast, esp. on a vessel having three or more masts.

head·set (hed′set′), *n.* *Radio, Telephony.* a device consisting of one or two earphones with a headband for holding them over the ears and sometimes with a mouthpiece attached.

head·sheet (hed′shēt′), *n.* *Naut.* 1. foresheet (def. 1). 2. **headsheets,** foresheet (def. 2).

head·ship (hed′ship′), *n.* the position of head or chief; leadership; supremacy.

head′ shop′, *Slang.* a shop selling drug-culture paraphernalia, such as hashish pipes, incense, psychedelic posters, etc.

head′ shrink′er, *Slang.* a psychiatrist. Also called **shrink.**

heads·man (hedz′mən), *n., pl.* **-men.** a public executioner who beheads condemned persons. Also, **headman.**

head·spring (hed′spring′), *n.* 1. the fountainhead or source of a stream. 2. the source of anything. [late ME]

head·stall (hed′stôl′), *n.* the part of a bridle or halter that encompasses the head of an animal. [late ME *hedstall*]

head·stand (hed′stand′), *n.* the act or an instance of supporting the body in a vertical position by balancing on the head, usually with the aid of the hands.

head′ start′, an advantage given or acquired in any competition, as allowing one or more competitors in a race to start before the others.

head·stay (hed′stā′), *n.* (on a sailing vessel) a stay leading forward from the head of the foremost mast to the stem head or the end of the bowsprit.

head·stock (hed′stok′), *n.* the part of a machine containing or directly supporting the moving or working parts.

head·stone (hed′stōn′), *n.* a stone marker set at the head of a grave; gravestone.

head·stream (hed′strēm′), *n.* a stream that is the source or one of the sources of a river.

head·strong (hed′strông′, -strong′), *adj.* 1. determined to have one's own way; willful; obstinate: *a headstrong young man.* 2. proceeding from willfulness: *a headstrong course.* [ME *heedstronge*] —**head′strong′ly,** *adv.* —**head′strong′ness,** *n.* —**Syn.** 1. See **willful.**

heads-up (hedz′up′), *adj.* alert; quick to grasp a situation and take advantage of opportunities.

head·wait·er (hed′wā′tər), *n.* the man in charge of the waiters, busboys, etc., in an eating establishment.

head·wa·ters (hed′wô′tərz, -wot′ərz), *n.pl.* the upper tributaries of a river.

head·way[1] (hed′wā′), *n.* 1. movement forward or ahead; progress in space: *The ship was unable to make much headway in the storm.* 2. progress in general: *to make headway in a business career.* 3. *Railroads.* the time interval between two trains traveling in the same direction over the same track. [(A)HEAD + WAY]

head·way[2] (hed′wā′), *n.* headroom. [HEAD + WAY]

head·wind (hed′wind′), *n.* a wind opposed to the course of a vessel or aircraft. [(A)HEAD + WIND[1]]

head·work (hed′wûrk′), *n.* mental labor; thought.

head·y (hed′ē), *adj.,* **head·i·er, head·i·est.** 1. intoxicating: *a heady wine.* 2. exciting; exhilarating: *the heady news of victory.* 3. rashly impetuous. 4. violent; destructive. 5. clever; shrewd. [ME *hevedy, hedy*] —**head′i·ly,** *adv.* —**head′i·ness,** *n.*

heal (hēl), *v.t.* 1. to make whole or sound; restore to health; free from ailment. 2. to bring to an end or conclusion, as conflicts between people, groups, etc., to restore amity; settle; reconcile. 3. to free from evil; purify: *to heal the soul.* —*v.i.* 4. to effect a cure. 5. (of a wound, broken bone, etc.) to become whole or sound; mend; get well (often fol. by *up* or *over*). [ME *hele(n),* OE *hǣlan* (c. D *helen,* G *heilen,* Icel *heila,* Goth *hailjan*) < *hāl* HALE[1], WHOLE] —**heal′a·ble,** *adj.* —**heal′er,** *n.* —**Syn.** 1. See **cure.**

health (helth), *n.* 1. the general condition of the body or mind with reference to soundness and vigor: *good health.* 2. soundness of body or mind; freedom from disease or ailment: *to lose one's health.* 3. a toast to a person's health, happiness, etc. 4. vigor; vitality: *economic health.* [ME *helthe,* OE *hǣlth.* See HALE[1], WHOLE, -TH[1]]

health′ food′, any natural food believed to promote or sustain good health, as by containing vital nutrients, being organically grown without the use of pesticides, or having a low sodium or fat content.

health·ful (helth′fəl), *adj.* 1. conducive to health; wholesome or salutary: *a healthful diet.* 2. healthy: *to grow healthful after an illness.* [ME *helthful*] —**health′ful·ly,** *adv.* —**health′ful·ness,** *n.* —**Syn.** 2. See **healthy.**

health·y (hel′thē), *adj.,* **health·i·er, health·i·est.** 1. possessing or enjoying good health or a sound and vigorous mentality. 2. pertaining to or characteristic of good health, or a sound and vigorous mind: *a healthy appearance; healthy attitudes.* 3. conducive to health; healthful: *healthy recreations.* —**health′i·ly,** *adv.* —**health′i·ness,** *n.*

—**Syn.** 1. hale, hearty, well. HEALTHY, HEALTHFUL, SALUTARY, WHOLESOME refer to that which promotes health. HEALTHY, while applied esp. to what possesses health, is also used of what is conducive to health: *a healthy climate; not a healthy place to be.* HEALTHFUL is applied chiefly to what is conducive to health: *healthful diet or exercise.* SALUTARY is applied to that which is conducive to well-being generally, as well as beneficial in preserving or in restoring health: *salutary effects; to take salutary measures.* It is used also of what is morally beneficial: *to have a salutary fear of consequences.* WHOLESOME has connotations of attractive freshness and purity; it applies to what is good for one, physically, morally, or both: *wholesome food; wholesome advice.* —**Ant.** 1. sick.

heap (hēp), *n.* 1. a group of things lying one on another; pile: *a heap of stones.* 2. *Informal.* a great quantity or number; multitude: *a heap of people.* —*v.t.* 3. to gather, put, or cast in a heap; pile (often fol. by *up, on, together,* etc.). 4. to accumulate or amass (often fol. by *up* or *together*): *to heap up riches.* 5. to give, assign, or bestow in great quantity; load (often fol. by *on* or *upon*): *to heap work on someone.* 6. to load, supply, or fill abundantly: *to heap a plate with food.* —*v.i.* 7. to become heaped or piled, as sand, snow, etc.; rise in a heap or heaps (often fol. by *up*). [ME *heep,* OE *hēap;* c. D *hoop,* OHG *houf;* akin to G *Haufe*] —**Syn.** 1. mass.

hear (hēr), *v.,* **heard** (hûrd), **hear·ing.** —*v.t.* 1. to perceive by the ear. 2. to learn by the ear or by being told; be informed of: *to hear news.* 3. to listen to; give or pay attention to. 4. to be among the audience at or of (something): *to hear a recital.* 5. to give a formal, official, or judicial hearing to (something); consider officially, as a judge, sovereign, teacher, assembly, etc.: *to hear a case.* 6. to take or listen to the evidence or testimony of (someone): *to hear the defendant.* 7. to listen to with favor, assent, or compliance. —*v.i.* 8. to be capable of perceiving sound by the ear; have the faculty of perceiving sound vibrations. 9. to receive information by the ear or otherwise: *to hear from a friend.* 10. to listen with favor, assent, or compliance (often fol. by *of*): *I will not hear of your going.* 11. *Chiefly Brit.* to applaud or endorse a speaker (usually used imperatively in the phrase *Hear! Hear!*). [ME *here(n),* OE *hēran, hīeran;* c. D *horen,* G *hören,* Icel *heyra,* Goth *hausjan*] —**hear′a·ble,** *adj.* —**hear′er,** *n.* —**Syn.** 1, 2. attend. —**Ant.** 7. disregard.

hear·ing (hēr′ing), *n.* **1.** the faculty or sense by which sound is perceived. **2.** the act of perceiving sound. **3.** an opportunity to be heard: *to grant a hearing.* **4.** an instance or a session in which testimony and arguments are presented, esp. before an official, as a judge in a lawsuit. **5.** a preliminary examination of the basic evidence and charges by a magistrate to determine whether criminal procedures, a trial, etc., are justified. **6.** earshot. [ME]

hear′ing aid′, a compact amplifier worn to aid one's hearing.

heark·en (här′kən), *v.i., v.t.* harken. —**heark′en·er,** *n.*

Hearn (hûrn), *n.* **Laf·cad·i·o** (laf kad′ē ō′), (*Koizumi Yakumo*), 1850–1904, U.S. journalist, novelist, and essayist; born in Greece; Japanese citizen after 1894.

hear·say (hēr′sā′), *n.* unverified, unofficial information gained or acquired from another.

hear′say ev′idence, *Law.* testimony given by a witness based on what he has heard from another person.

hearse (hûrs), *n.* **1.** a vehicle for conveying a dead person to the place of burial. **2.** a triangular frame for holding candles, used at Tenebrae. **3.** a canopy erected over a tomb. [ME *herse* < MF *herce* a harrow, candle frame < L *hirpic-*, s. of *hirpex* harrow] —**hearse′like′,** *adj.*

Hearst (hûrst), *n.* **William Randolph,** 1863–1951, U.S. publisher and editor.

heart (härt), *n.* **1.** a hollow, muscular organ that by rhythmic contractions and relaxations keeps the blood in circulation throughout the body. **2.** the center of the total personality, esp. with reference to intuition, feeling, or emotion: *In your heart you know I'm an honest man.* **3.** the center of emotion. **4.** feeling; love; affection; capacity for sympathy: *to win a person's heart.* **5.** spirit, courage, or enthusiasm. **6.** the innermost or central part of anything: *Notre Dame stands in the very heart of Paris.* **7.** the vital or essential part; core: *the heart of the matter.* **8.** the breast or bosom: *to clasp a person to one's heart.* **9.** a person (used esp. in expressions of praise or affection): *dear heart.* **10.** a conventional figure representing a heart, with rounded sides meeting in a point at the bottom and curving inward to a cusp at the top. **11.** a red figure or pip of this shape on a playing card. **12.** a card of the suit bearing such figures. **13. hearts, a.** (*construed as sing. or pl.*) the suit so marked. **b.** (*construed as sing.*) a game in which the players try to avoid taking tricks containing this suit. **14. after one's own heart,** according to one's taste or preference. **15. at heart,** fundamentally; basically. **16. break one's heart,** to cause one great disappointment or sorrow, as to disappoint in love. **17. by heart,** by memory; word for word. **18. from the bottom of one's heart,** with complete sincerity. Also, **from the heart. 19. have a change of heart,** to reverse one's opinion or stand. **20. have a heart,** to be compassionate or merciful. **21. have at heart,** to have as an object, aim, or desire: *to have another's best interests at heart.* **22. have one's heart in one's mouth,** to be very anxious or fearful. **23. have one's heart in the right place,** to be fundamentally kind or generous. **24. heart and soul,** enthusiastically; fervently; completely. **25. not have the heart,** to lack the necessary courage or callousness to do something: *No one had the heart to tell him he was through as an actor.* **26. set one's heart on,** to wish for intensely; determine on: *She has set her heart on going to Europe after graduation.* Also, **have one's heart set on. 27. take to heart, a.** to think seriously about; concern oneself with. **b.** to be deeply affected by; grieve over. **28. to one's heart's content,** until one is satisfied; as much or as long as one pleases. **29. wear one's heart on one's sleeve,** to make one's intimate feelings or personal affairs known to all. **30. with all one's heart, a.** with earnestness or zeal. **b.** with willingness; cordially. —*v.t.* **31.** *Rare.* to fix in the heart: *to heart a warning.* **32.** *Archaic.* to encourage. [ME *herte,* OE *heorte;* c. D *hart,* G *Herz,* Icel *hjarta,* Goth *hairtō;* akin to L *cors,* Gk *kardía*]

Heart (human)
A, Superior vena cava; B, Right atrium; C, Right ventricle; D, Left ventricle; E, Left atrium; F, Pulmonary vein; G, Pulmonary artery; H, Aorta

Heart (def. 10)

heart·ache (härt′āk′), *n.* emotional distress; sorrow; grief; anguish. —**heart′ach′ing,** *adj.*

heart′ attack′, a sudden inability of the heart to function, usually due to an embolism or increased blood pressure; heart failure.

heart·beat (härt′bēt′), *n.* *Physiol.* a pulsation of the heart, including one complete systole and diastole.

heart′ block′, *Pathol.* a defect in the coordination of the heartbeat in which the atria and ventricles beat independently or the ventricles miss a beat completely.

heart·break (härt′brāk′), *n.* great sorrow, grief, or anguish.

heart·break·er (härt′brā′kər), *n.* a person, event, or thing causing heartbreak.

heart·break·ing (härt′brā′king), *adj.* causing intense anguish or sorrow. —**heart′break′ing·ly,** *adv.*

heart·bro·ken (härt′brō′kən), *adj.* crushed with sorrow or grief. —**heart′bro′ken·ly,** *adv.*

heart·burn (härt′bûrn′), *n.* **1.** Also called **brash, cardialgia, pyrosis, water brash.** *Pathol.* an uneasy burning sensation in the stomach, often extending toward the esophagus and sometimes associated with the eructation of an acid fluid. **2.** bitter jealousy; envy.

heart·ed (här′tid), *adj.* **1.** having a specified kind of heart (now used only in combination): *hard-hearted; sad-hearted.* **2.** *Archaic.* fixed or present in the heart. [ME *iherted.* See Y-, HEART, -ED[3]] —**heart′ed·ly,** *adv.* —**heart′ed·ness,** *n.*

heart·en (här′tᵊn), *v.t.* to give courage or confidence to; cheer. —**heart′en·er,** *n.* —**heart′en·ing·ly,** *adv.*

heart′ fail′ure, 1. a condition in which the heart ceases to function; death. **2.** *Pathol.* a condition in which the heart fails to pump blood adequately to either the systemic or the pulmonary arterial distribution.

heart·felt (härt′felt′), *adj.* deeply or sincerely felt; earnest; sincere: *heartfelt joy.*

hearth (härth), *n.* **1.** the floor of a fireplace, usually of stone, brick, etc., often extending a short distance into a room. **2.** the fireside; home: *the family hearth.* **3.** *Metall.* **a.** the lower part of a blast furnace, cupola, etc., in which the molten metal collects and from which it is tapped out. **b.** the part of an open hearth, reverberatory furnace, etc., upon which the charge is placed and melted down or refined. **4.** a brazier or chafing dish for burning charcoal. [ME *herth(e),* OE *he(o)rth;* c. G *Herd,* D *haard*] —**hearth′less,** *adj.* —**hearth′stead′,** *n.*

hearth·side (härth′sīd′), *n.* fireside (def. 1).

hearth·stone (härth′stōn′), *n.* **1.** a stone forming a hearth. **2.** hearth (def. 2). **3.** a soft stone or a preparation of powdered stone and clay, used to whiten or scour hearths, steps, floors, etc. [ME *hertston*]

heart·i·ly (här′tᵊlē), *adv.* **1.** in a hearty manner; cordially. **2.** sincerely; genuinely. **3.** without restraint; exuberantly: *They laughed heartily.* **4.** with a hearty appetite: *They ate heartily.* [ME *hertili*]

heart·land (härt′land′, -lənd), *n.* a central land area, relatively invulnerable to attack, capable of economic and political self-sufficiency.

heart·less (härt′lis), *adj.* **1.** unfeeling; cruel: *heartless words; a heartless person.* **2.** *Archaic.* lacking courage or enthusiasm; spiritless; disheartened. [ME *herteles,* OE *heortlēas*] —**heart′less·ly,** *adv.* —**heart′less·ness,** *n.*

heart′ mur′mur, *Med.* murmur (def. 3).

heart′ point′, *Heraldry.* See **fess point.**

heart·rend·ing (härt′ren′ding), *adj.* causing or expressing intense grief or anguish. —**heart′rend′ing·ly,** *adv.*

hearts′ and flow′ers, *Slang.* an expression or display of maudlin sentimentality.

hearts·ease (härts′ēz′), *n.* **1.** peace of mind. **2.** the pansy, or some other plant of the genus *Viola.* **3.** the lady's-thumb. Also, **heart's′-ease′.** [ME *hertes ese*]

heart·sick (härt′sik′), *adj.* sick at heart; extremely depressed or unhappy. —**heart′sick′en·ing,** *adj.* —**heart′sick′ness,** *n.*

heart·some (härt′səm), *adj.* *Chiefly Scot.* cheerful; spirited. —**heart′some·ly,** *adv.* —**heart′some·ness,** *n.*

heart·sore (härt′sōr′, -sôr′), *adj.* heartsick. [HEART + SORE; cf. OE *heortsārnes* grief]

heart-strick·en (härt′strik′ən), *adj.* deeply afflicted with grief, mental anguish, etc. Also, **heart-struck** (härt′struk′). —**heart′-strick′en·ly,** *adv.*

heart·strings (härt′stringz′), *n.pl.* the deepest feelings; the strongest affections: *to tug at one's heartstrings.*

heart·throb (härt′throb′), *n.* **1.** a rapid beat or pulsation of the heart. **2.** a passionate or sentimental emotion. **3.** sweetheart.

heart-to-heart (härt′tə härt′), *adj.* frank; sincere: *a heart-to-heart talk.*

heart·warm·ing (härt′wôr′ming), *adj.* **1.** tenderly moving: *a heartwarming experience.* **2.** gratifying; rewarding; satisfying: *a heartwarming response to his work.*

heart-whole (härt′hōl′), *adj.* **1.** courageous; dauntless; stout-hearted. **2.** having the heart untouched by love. **3.** wholehearted; sincere. —**heart′-whole′ness,** *n.*

heart·wood (härt′wŏŏd′), *n.* the hard central wood of the trunk of an exogenous tree; duramen.

heart·worm (härt′wûrm′), *n.* *Vet. Med.* a filarial worm, *Dirofilaria immitis,* that lives in the right ventricle and pulmonary artery of dogs.

heart·y (här′tē), *adj.,* **heart·i·er, heart·i·est,** *n., pl.* **heart·ies.** —*adj.* **1.** warm-hearted; affectionate; cordial; jovial: *a hearty welcome.* **2.** heartfelt, genuine; sincere: *hearty approval.* **3.** enthusiastic or zealous; vigorous: *hearty support.* **4.** exuberant; unrestrained: *hearty laughter.* **5.** violent; forceful: *a hearty push.* **6.** physically vigorous; strong and well: *hale and hearty.* **7.** substantial; abundant; nourishing: *a hearty meal.* **8.** enjoying or requiring abundant food: *a hearty appetite.* **9.** (of soil) fertile. —*n.* **10.** a brave or good fellow; shipmate; chum; buddy. **11.** a sailor. [ME *herti*] —**heart′i·ly,** *adv.* —**heart′i·ness,** *n.* —**Syn. 1.** warm, genial. **6.** healthy.

heat (hēt), *n.* **1.** the state of a body perceived as having or generating a relatively high degree of warmth. **2.** the condition or quality of being hot: *the heat of an oven.* **3.** the degree of hotness; temperature: *moderate heat.* **4.** the sensation of warmth or hotness: *unpleasant heat.* **5.** a bodily temperature higher than normal. **6.** added or external energy that causes a rise in temperature, expansion, evaporation, or other physical change. **7.** *Physics.* a nonmechanical energy transfer with reference to a temperature difference between a system and its surroundings or between two parts of the same system. *Symbol:* Q **8.** a hot condition of the atmosphere or physical environment; hot season or weather. **9.** a period of hot weather. **10.** a sharp, pungent flavor, as that produced by spices. **11.** warmth or intensity of feeling; vehemence; passion: *He spoke with much heat.* **12.** maximum intensity in an activity, condition, etc: *the heat of battle; the heat of passion.* **13.** *Sports.* **a.** a single course in or division of a race or other contest. **b.** a race or other contest in which competitors attempt to qualify for entry in the final race or contest. **14.** a single operation of heating, as of metal in a furnace, in the treating and melting of metals. **15.** an indication of high temperature, as by the condition or color of something. **16.** *Zool.* **a.** sexual excitement in animals, esp. females. **b.** the period or duration of such excitement: *to be in heat.* —*v.t.* **17.** to make hot or warm (often fol. by *up*). **18.** to excite emotionally; inflame or rouse with passion. —*v.i.* **19.** to become hot or warm (often fol. by *up*). **20.** to become excited emotionally. [ME *hete,* OE *hǣtu;* akin to G *Hitze;* see HOT] —**Syn. 2.** hotness, warmth. **11.** ardor, fervor, zeal. **18.** stir, excite, rouse. —**Ant. 1.** coolness. **18.** cool.

heat′ capac′ity, *Physics.* the heat required to raise the temperature of a substance one Celsius degree.

heat·ed (hē′tid), *adj.* **1.** warmed; made hot or hotter. **2.** excited; inflamed; vehement: *a heated discussion.* —**heat′ed·ly,** *adv.* —**heat′ed·ness,** *n.*

heat′ en′gine, an engine that transforms heat into mechanical energy.

heat·er (hē′tər), *n.* **1.** any of various apparatus for heating, esp. for heating water or room air. **2.** *Electronics.* the element of a vacuum tube that carries the current for heating a cathode.

heat′ exhaus′tion, a condition characterized by faintness, rapid pulse, nausea, vomiting, profuse sweating, a cold skin, and collapse, caused by prolonged exposure to high temperatures. Also called **heat prostration.**

heat′ gun′, a flameless device that produces a stream of extremely hot air, as for instant drying.

heath (hēth), *n.* **1.** *Brit.* a tract of open and uncultivated land; waste land overgrown with shrubs. **2.** any of various low, evergreen, ericaceous shrubs common on waste land, as the common heather, *Calluna vulgaris.* **3.** any plant of the genus *Erica,* or of the family *Ericaceae.* **4.** any of several similar but not ericaceous shrubs, as *Frankenia laevis.* [ME; OE *hǣth;* c. G *Heide,* Icel *heithr,* Goth *haithi;* akin to OWelsh *coit* forest] —**heath′like′,** *adj.*

Heath (hēth), *n.* **Edward (Richard George),** born 1916, British statesman: prime minister 1970–74.

heath′ as′ter, a weedy, North American aster, *Aster ericoides,* having small, white flower heads.

heath·ber·ry (hēth′ber′ē, -bə rē), *n., pl.* **-ries.** **1.** crowberry. **2.** any berry found on heaths, esp. the bilberry. [OE *hǣth berian*]

heath·bird (hēth′bûrd′), *n.* *Brit. Dial.* the black grouse.

heath′ cock′, *Brit. Dial.* the male of the black grouse.

hea·then (hē′thən), *n., pl.* **-thens, -then,** *adj.* —*n.* **1.** an unenlightened or barbaric idolater. **2.** an unconverted individual of a people that do not acknowledge the God of the Bible; pagan. **3.** (formerly) any person neither Christian nor Jewish, esp. a member of the Islamic faith or of a polytheistic religion. —*adj.* **4.** irreligious or unenlightened. **5.** of or pertaining to the heathen. [ME *hethen,* OE *hǣthen;* akin to G *Heide* (n.), *heidnisch* (adj.), Icel *heithingi* (n.), *heithinn* (adj.), Goth *heithnō* (n.)] —**hea′then·ness,** *n.*
—**Syn. 5.** heathenish, barbarous. HEATHEN, PAGAN are both applied to peoples who are not Christian, Jewish, or Muslim. HEATHEN is often distinctively applied to unenlightened or barbaric idolaters, esp. to primitive or ancient tribes: *heathen rites, idols.* PAGAN, though applied to any of the peoples not worshiping according to the three religions mentioned above, is most frequently used in speaking of the ancient Greeks and Romans: *a pagan poem; a pagan civilization.*

hea·then·dom (hē′thən dəm), *n.* **1.** heathenism; heathen customs. **2.** heathen lands or people. [ME; OE *hǣthendōm*]

hea·then·ise (hē′thə nīz′), *v.t., v.i.,* **-ised, -is·ing.** *Chiefly Brit.* heathenize.

hea·then·ish (hē′thə nish), *adj.* **1.** of or pertaining to the heathen: *heathenish practices of idolatry.* **2.** like or befitting the heathen; barbarous. [OE *hǣthenisc*]

hea·then·ism (hē′thə niz′əm), *n.* **1.** a belief or practice of heathens. **2.** pagan worship; idolatry. **3.** irreligion. **4.** barbaric morals or behavior.

hea·then·ize (hē′thə nīz′), *v.,* **-ized, -iz·ing.** —*v.t.* **1.** to make heathen or heathenish. —*v.i.* **2.** to become heathen or heathenish. Also, *esp. Brit.,* **heathenise.**

heath·er (heth′ər), *n.* any of various heaths, esp. *Calluna vulgaris,* of England and Scotland, having small, pinkish-purple flowers. [sp. var. of *hether,* earlier *hedder, hadder, hather,* ME *hathir;* akin to HEATH] —**heath′ered,** *adj.*

heath·er·y (heth′ə rē), *adj.* **1.** of or like heather. **2.** abounding in heather.

heath′ grass′, a European grass, *Sieglingia decumbens,* growing in spongy, wet, cold soils. Also called **heath′er grass′.**

heath′ hen′, **1.** an extinct, American, gallinaceous bird, *Tympanuchus cupido cupido,* closely related to the prairie chicken. **2.** *Brit. Dial.* the female of the black grouse.

heat′ing pad′, a flexible pad, covered with fabric, containing insulated electrical heating elements for applying heat, esp. to a part of the body.

heat′ light′ning, flashes of light near the horizon on summer evenings, reflections of more distant lightning.

heat′ of fu′sion, *Physics.* the heat required per unit mass of a given solid at its melting point for complete conversion of the solid to a liquid at the same temperature. Cf. **latent heat.**

heat′ of vaporiza′tion, *Physics.* the heat required per unit mass of a given liquid at its boiling point for complete conversion of the liquid to a gas at the same temperature. Cf. **latent heat.**

heat′ prostra′tion, *Med.* See **heat exhaustion.**

heat′ pump′, a device that, by means of a compressible refrigerant, transfers heat from one body, as the earth, air, water, etc., to another body, as a building, the process being reversible.

heat′ shield′, *Rocketry.* a coating or structure for protecting the nose cone or other vulnerable surfaces of a spacecraft from excessive heating during reentry.

heat·stroke (hēt′strōk′), *n.* collapse or fever caused by exposure to excessive heat.

heat′ wave′, **1.** an air mass of high temperature covering an extended area and moving relatively slowly. **2.** a period of excessively warm weather.

heaume (hōm), *n.* helm[2] (def. 1). [< MF; OF *helme* < Gmc; see HELM[2]]

heave (hēv), *v.,* **heaved** or (*esp. Naut.*) **hove; heav·ing;** *n.* —*v.t.* **1.** to raise or lift with effort or force; hoist: *to heave a heavy ax.* **2.** to throw, esp. to lift and throw with effort, force, or violence: *to heave a stone through a window.* **3.** *Naut.* to move into a certain position, situation, or direction: *to heave a vessel aback; to heave the capstan around.* **4.** to utter laboriously or painfully: *to heave a sigh.* **5.** to cause to rise and fall with or as with a swelling motion: *to heave one's chest in breathing heavily.* **6.** to vomit. **7.** *Geol.* to cause a horizontal displacement in (a stratum, vein, etc.). **8.** to haul or pull on (a rope, cable, line, etc.), as with the hands or a capstan: *Heave the anchor cable!* —*v.i.* **9.** to rise and fall in rhythmically alternate movements: *The ship heaved and rolled in the swelling sea.* **10.** to breathe with effort. **11.** to vomit; retch. **12.** to rise as if thrust up, as a hill; swell, surge, or billow. **13.** to pull or haul on a rope, cable, etc. **14.** to push, as on a capstan bar. **15.** *Naut.* **a.** to move in a certain direction or into a certain position or situation: *to heave about; to heave alongside.* **b.** (of a vessel) to rise and fall, as with a heavy beam sea. **16.** **heave down,** *Naut.* to careen (a vessel). **17.** **heave ho!** (an exclamation used by sailors, as when heaving the anchor up.) **18.** **heave to,** *Naut.* to stop the headway of (a vessel), esp. by bringing the head to the wind and trimming the sails so that they act against one another. —*n.* **19.** the act or effort of heaving. **20.** a throw, toss, or cast. **21.** *Geol.* the horizontal component of the apparent displacement resulting from a fault, measured in a vertical plane perpendicular to the strike. **22.** the rise and fall of the waves. **23.** **heaves,** (*construed as sing.*) Also called **broken wind.** *Vet. Pathol.* a disease of horses, similar to asthma in man, characterized by difficult breathing. [ME *heve(n),* var. (with *-v-* from pt. and ptp.) of *hebben,* OE *hebban;* c. G *heben,* Icel *hefja,* Goth *hafjan;* akin to L *capere* to take] —**Syn. 1.** See **raise.**

heave-ho (hēv′hō′), *n.* *Informal.* an act of rejection, dismissal, or forcible ejection, as of a lover, employee, or unruly patron.

heav·en (hev′ən), *n.* **1.** the abode of God, the angels, and the spirits of the righteous after death. **2.** (*cap.*) Often, **Heavens.** the celestial powers; God. **3.** a metonym for God (used in expressions of emphasis, surprise, etc.): *For heaven's sake!* **4.** **heavens,** (used interjectionally to express emphasis, surprise, etc.): *Heavens, what a cold room!* **5.** Usually, **heavens.** the sky, firmament, or expanse of space surrounding the earth. **6.** a place or state of supreme happiness: *a heaven on earth.* **7.** **move heaven and earth,** to do one's utmost to effect an end; make a supreme effort. [ME *heven,* OE *heofon;* c. MLG *heven;* akin to Icel *himinn,* Goth *himins,* G *Himmel*]

heav·en·ly (hev′ən lē), *adj.* **1.** of or pertaining to heaven or the heavens: *the heavenly bodies.* **2.** resembling or befitting heaven; beautiful: *a heavenly spot.* **3.** divine or celestial: *heavenly peace.* [ME *hevenly,* OE *heofonlīc.*] —**heav′en·li·ness,** *n.* —**Syn. 3.** sublime; blessed, beatific.

Heav′enly Cit′y. See **New Jerusalem.**

heav·en-sent (hev′ən sent′), *adj.* timely; opportune: *A heaven-sent rain revived the crops.*

heav·en·ward (hev′ən wərd), *adv.* **1.** Also, **heav′en·wards.** toward heaven. —*adj.* **2.** directed toward heaven.

heav·er (hē′vər), *n.* **1.** a person or thing that heaves. **2.** *Naut.* **a.** a lever inserted into a loop or between two parallel ropes and twisted in order to tauten a rope or ropes. **b.** a longshoreman handling a specified type of cargo (usually used in combination): *coal heaver.*

heav·i·er-than-air (hev′ē ər thən âr′), *adj.* *Aeron.* (of an aircraft) weighing more than the air that it displaces, hence having to obtain lift by aerodynamic means as an airplane.

heav·i·ly (hev′ə lē), *adv.* **1.** with a great weight or burden. **2.** in a manner suggestive of carrying a great weight; ponderously; lumberingly. **3.** in an oppressive manner: *Cares weigh heavily upon him.* **4.** severely; intensely: *to suffer heavily.* **5.** densely; thickly: *heavily wooded.* **6.** in large amounts or in great quantities: *It rained heavily on Tuesday.* **7.** without animation or vigor; in a dull manner. [ME *hevyly,* OE *hefiglīce*]

heav·i·ness (hev′ē nis), *n.* the state or quality of being heavy; weight; burden. [ME *hevinesse,* OE *hefignes*]

Heav′i·side lay′er (hev′ē sīd′). See **Kennelly-Heaviside layer.**

heav·y (hev′ē), *adj.,* **heav·i·er, heav·i·est,** *n., pl.* **heav·ies,** *adv.* —*adj.* **1.** of great weight; hard to lift or carry. **2.** of great amount, quantity, or size; extremely large; massive: *a heavy vote; a heavy snowfall.* **3.** of great force, turbulence, etc.: *a heavy sea.* **4.** of more than the usual or average weight: *a heavy person.* **5.** having much weight in proportion to bulk; being of high specific gravity: *a heavy metal.* **6.** of major import. **7.** deep; profound: *a heavy thinker.* **8.** *Mil.* **a.** thickly armed or equipped with guns of large size. **b.** (of guns) of the more powerful sizes: *heavy weapons.* **9.** hard to bear; burdensome; trying: *heavy taxes; a heavy task.* **10.** indulging to an unusually great degree: *a heavy drinker.* **11.** broad, thick, or coarse; not delicate: *heavy lines.* **12.** laden; fraught; charged: *words heavy with meaning.* **13.** depressed with trouble or sorrow: *a heavy heart.* **14.** without vivacity or interest; ponderous; dull: *a heavy style.* **15.** clumsy; slow in movement: *a heavy gait.* **16.** (of the sky) overcast or cloudy. **17.** (of baked goods, pancakes, etc.) exceptionally dense in substance; insufficiently raised or leavened: *heavy doughnuts.* **18.** (of food) not easily digested. **19.** pregnant; nearing childbirth: *heavy with child.* **20.** having a large capacity or output: *a heavy truck.* **21.** producing or refining basic materials, as steel or coal, used in manufacturing: *heavy industry.* **22.** *Chem.* of or pertaining to an isotope of greater than normal atomic weight, as heavy hydrogen or heavy oxygen, or to a compound containing such an element, as heavy water. **23.** *Slang.* very good; excellent. —*n.* **24.** *Theat.* **a.** a villainous part or character: *Iago is the heavy in* Othello. **b.** an actor who plays villainous parts or characters. **25.** *Mil.* a gun of great weight or large caliber. —*adv.* **26.** heavily. [ME *hevi,* OE *hefig* = *hef(e)* weight (akin to HEAVE) + *-ig* -Y[1]]
—**Syn. 1.** ponderous, massive, weighty. **5.** dense. **9.** onerous, oppressive, grievous, cumbersome; difficult, severe; hard, harsh. **12.** HEAVY, MOMENTOUS, WEIGHTY refer to anything having a considerable amount of figurative weight. HEAVY suggests the carrying of a figurative burden: *words heavy with menace.* MOMENTOUS emphasizes the idea of great and usually serious consequences: *a momentous occasion, statement.* WEIGHTY, seldom used literally, refers to something heavy with importance, often concerned with public affairs, that may require deliberation and careful judgment: *a weighty matter, problem.* **13.** serious, grave; gloomy, sad, mournful, melancholy, morose, dejected, despondent, down-

cast, downhearted. **14.** tedious, tiresome, wearisome, burdensome, boring. **15.** sluggish, lumbering. **16.** lowering, gloomy. **—Ant. 1–5, 8–11, 13, 17, 18, 20, 21.** light.

heav′y artil′lery, *Mil.* **1.** guns and howitzers of large caliber. **2.** *U.S.* guns and howitzers of 155-mm. caliber and larger. Cf. **light artillery** (def. 1), **medium artillery.**

heav′y bomb′er, *Mil.* a large plane capable of carrying heavy bomb loads for long distances, esp. at high altitudes. Cf. **light bomber, medium bomber.**

heav′y cream′, thick cream having a high percentage of butterfat.

heav′y cruis′er, a naval cruiser having eight-inch guns as its main armament. Cf. **light cruiser.**

heav·y-du·ty (hev′ē do͞o′tē, -dyo͞o′-), *adj.* made or designed to withstand great physical strain.

heav′y earth′, baryta.

heav·y-foot·ed (hev′ē fo͝ot′id), *adj.* clumsy or ponderous, as in movement or expressiveness.

heav·y-hand·ed (hev′ē han′did), *adj.* **1.** oppressive; harsh: *a heavy-handed master.* **2.** clumsy; graceless: *a heavy-handed treatment of the theme.* **—heav′y-hand′ed·ly,** *adv.* **—heav′y-hand′ed·ness,** *n.*

heav·y-heart·ed (hev′ē här′tid), *adj.* sorrowful; melancholy; dejected. **—heav′y-heart′ed·ly,** *adv.* **—heav′y-heart′ed·ness,** *n.*

heav′y hy′drogen, *Chem.* either of the heavy isotopes of hydrogen, esp. deuterium.

heav·y-lad·en (hev′ē lād′ən), *adj.* **1.** carrying a heavy load; heavily laden: *a heavy-laden cart.* **2.** very tired or troubled; burdened: *heavy-laden with cares.* [late ME *hevy ladyn*]

heav·y·set (hev′ē set′), *adj.* **1.** having a large body build. **2.** stout; stocky.

heav′y spar′, *Mineral.* barite.

heav′y wa′ter, *Chem.* water in which hydrogen atoms have been replaced by deuterium, used chiefly in research. *Symbol:* D_2O; *sp. gr.:* 1.1056 at 25°C.

heav·y·weight (hev′ē wāt′), *adj.* **1.** heavy in weight. **2.** of more than average weight or thickness: *a coat of heavyweight material.* **3.** noting or pertaining to a boxer, wrestler, etc., of the heaviest competitive class, esp. a professional boxer weighing over 175 pounds. **4.** of or pertaining to the weight class or division of such boxers: *a heavyweight bout.* **—***n.* **5.** a person of more than average weight. **6.** a heavyweight boxer or wrestler. **7.** *Informal.* **a.** a very influential person; one whose words carry much weight. **b.** a very intelligent person.

Heb, **1.** Hebrew (def. 2). **2.** Hebrews. Also, **Heb.**

Heb·bel (heb′əl), *n.* **(Chris·ti·an) Frie·drich** (kris′tē än′ frē′drikh), 1813–63, German lyric poet and playwright.

heb·do·mad (heb′də mad′), *n.* **1.** the number seven. **2.** a period of seven successive days; week. [< L *hebdomad-* < Gk (s. of *hebdomás* week) = *hébdom(os)* seventh (see HEPTA-) + *-ad-* -AD[1]]

heb·dom·a·dal (heb dom′ə dəl), *adj.* taking place, coming together, or published weekly: *hebdomadal journals.* Also, **heb·dom·a·dar·y** (heb dom′ə der′ē). [< LL *hebdomadāl(is)*] **—heb·dom′a·dal·ly,** *adv.*

He·be (hē′bē), *n.* *Class. Myth.* a goddess of youth and spring, the daughter of Zeus and Hera, and wife of Hercules: originally the cupbearer of the gods, but later replaced by Ganymede.

Hebe (hēb), *n.* *Disparaging.* a Jew. [short for HEBREW]

he·be·phre·ni·a (hē′bə frē′nē ə), *n.* *Psychiatry.* a form of schizophrenia usually developed before age 20, marked by incoherent behavior, emotional deterioration, delusions, and hallucinations. [< NL < Gk *hḗbē* youth; see -PHRENIA] **—he·be·phren·ic** (hē′bə fren′ik), *adj.*

Hé·bert (ā ber′), *n.* **Jacques Re·né** (zhäk rə nā′), ("*Père Duchesne*"), 1755–94, French journalist and revolutionary leader.

heb·e·tate (heb′i tāt′), *v.*, **-tat·ed, -tat·ing,** *adj.* **—***v.t.* **1.** to make dull or blunt, as the sensitivity, a faculty, etc. **—***v.i.* **2.** to become dull or blunt. **—***adj.* **3.** *Bot.* having a blunt, soft point, as awns. [< L *hebetāt(us)* made dull or blunt (ptp. of *hebetāre*) = *hebet-* (s. of *hebes*) blunt, dull + *-ātus* -ATE[1]] **—heb′e·ta′tion,** *n.* **—heb′e·ta′tive,** *adj.*

he·bet·ic (hi bet′ik), *adj.* *Physiol.* pertaining to or occurring in puberty. [< Gk *hēbētik(ós)* youthful = *hḗbē* youth + *-tikos* -TIC]

heb·e·tude (heb′i to͞od′, -tyo͞od′), *n.* the state of being dull or listless; lethargy: *moral hebetude.* [< LL *hebetūd(ō)* dullness, bluntness] **—heb′e·tu′di·nous,** *adj.*

Hebr., **1.** Hebrew. **2.** Hebrews.

He·bra·ic (hi brā′ik), *adj.* of, pertaining to, or characteristic of the Hebrews, their language, or their culture. Also, **Hebrew.** [< LL *Hebraic(us)* < Gk *Hebraïkós* (see HEBREW, -IC); r. OE *Ebrēisc*] **—He·bra′i·cal·ly,** *adv.*

He·bra·ise (hē′brā īz′, -brē-), *v.i., v.t.*, **-ised, -is·ing.** *Chiefly Brit.* Hebraize. **—He′bra·i·sa′tion,** *n.* **—He′bra·is′er,** *n.*

He·bra·ism (hē′brā iz′əm, -brē-), *n.* **1.** an expression or construction distinctive of the Hebrew language. **2.** the character, spirit, principles, or practices distinctive of the Hebrew people. [< LGk *Hebraïsm(ós).* See HEBRAIZE, -ISM]

He·bra·ist (hē′brā ist, -brē-), *n.* a specialist in the Hebrew language. [HEBRA(IZE) + -IST]

He·bra·is·tic (hē′brā is′tik, -brē-), *adj.* of or pertaining to Hebraists or characterized by Hebraism or Hebraisms.

He·bra·ize (hē′brā īz′, -brē-), *v.*, **-ized, -iz·ing.** **—***v.i.* **1.** to use expressions or constructions distinctive of the Hebrew language. **—***v.t.* **2.** to make conformable to the spirit, character, principles, or practices of the Hebrew people. Also, *esp. Brit.*, **Hebraise.** [< LGk *Hebraïz(ein)* (to) speak Hebrew, behave like a Jew] **—He′bra·i·za′tion,** *n.* **—He′bra·iz′er,** *n.*

He·brew (hē′bro͞o), *n.* **1.** a member of the Semitic peoples inhabiting ancient Palestine and claiming descent from Abraham, Isaac, and Jacob; Israelite. **2.** a Semitic language of the Afro-Asiatic family, the language of the ancient Hebrews, now the national language of Israel. *Abbr.:* Heb, Heb. **—***adj.* **3.** Hebraic. [ME *Hebreu*, var. (with *H-* < L) of *Ebreu* < OF < ML *Ebrē(us)* for L *Hebraeus* < LGk *Hebraîos* < Aram *Hebrai;* r. OE *Ebrēas* (pl.) < ML *Ebrēī*]

He′brew cal′endar. See **Jewish calendar.**

He·brews (hē′bro͞oz), *n.* (*construed as sing.*) a book of the New Testament.

Heb·ri·des (heb′ri dēz′), *n.* (*construed as pl.*) a group of islands **(Inner Hebrides** and **Outer Hebrides)** off the W coast of and belonging to Scotland. ab. 65,000; ab. 2900 sq. mi. Also called **Western Islands.** **—Heb′ri·de′an, He·brid′i·an,** *adj.*

He·bron (hē′brən), *n.* a city in W Jordan: occupied by Israel 1967. 38,348 (1968).

Hec·a·te (hek′ə tē; *in Shakespeare* hek′it), *n.* *Class. Myth.* a goddess of the earth and Hades, associated with sorcery, hounds, and crossroads, and identified with various other goddesses, esp. Artemis. Also, **Hekate.** [< L < Gk *hekátē*, n. use of fem. of *hékatos* far-shooting, said of Apollo as sun-god] **—Hec′a·te′an, Hec′a·tae′an,** *adj.*

hec·a·tomb (hek′ə tōm′, -to͞om′), *n.* **1.** (in ancient Greece and Rome) a public sacrifice of 100 oxen to the gods. **2.** any great slaughter. [< L *hecatombē* < Gk *hekatómbē* sacrifice of a hundred oxen = *hekatón* hundred + *-bē*, comb. form of *boûs* ox]

Hec·a·ton·chi·res (hek′ə ton kī′rēz) *n.pl.* *Class. Myth.* three giants, Briareus, Cottus, and Gyges, who were the sons of Uranus and Gaea and had 50 heads and 100 arms each: they were best known for having helped the gods in their struggle against the Titans. Also, **Hec′a·ton·chei′res.**

Hecht (hekt), *n.* **Ben,** 1894–1964, U.S. novelist and dramatist.

heck (hek), *interj.* *Informal.* (used as a mild expression of annoyance, rejection, disgust, etc.): *What the heck do you care?* [euphemistic alter. of HELL]

heck·le (hek′əl), *v.*, **-led, -ling,** *n.* **—***v.t.* **1.** to harass (a public speaker, performer, etc.) with impertinent questions, gibes, or the like. **2.** hackle[1] (def. 7). **—***n.* **3.** hackle[1] (def. 5). [late ME *hekele*, var. of *hechele;* akin to HACKLE[1], HATCHEL] **—heck′ler,** *n.*

hec·tare (hek′târ), *n.* *Metric System.* a unit of land measure equal to 100 ares or 10,000 square meters: equivalent to 2.471 acres. *Abbr.:* ha Also, **hektare.** [< F]

hec·tic (hek′tik), *adj.* **1.** characterized by intense agitation, feverish excitement, confused and rapid movement, etc.: *The period preceding the trip was hectic and exhausting.* **2.** marking a particular habit or condition of body, as the fever of phthisis **(hec′tic fe′ver)** when this is attended by flushed cheeks **(hec′tic flush′),** hot skin, and emaciation. **3.** pertaining to or affected with such fever; consumptive. [< LL *hectic(us)* < Gk *hektikós* habitual = *hekt-* (s. of *héxis*) state, condition + *-ikos* -IC; r. ME *etyk* < MF] **—hec′ti·cal·ly, hec′tic·ly,** *adv.* **—hec′tic·ness,** *n.*

hecto-, a learned borrowing from Greek meaning "hundred," used in the formation of compound words: *hectograph; hectogram.* Also, **hect-, hekt-, hekto-.** [< F, comb. form repr. Gk *hekatón* hundred]

hec·to·cot·y·lus (hek′tə kot′əl əs), *n.*, *pl.* **-y·li** (-əlī′). *Zool.* a modified arm of the male of certain cephalopods that is used to transfer sperm into the female. [< NL = *hecto-* HECTO- + *-cotylus* < Gk *kotýlē* cup]

hec·to·gram (hek′tə gram′), *n.* *Metric System.* a unit of 100 grams, equivalent to 3.527 ounces avoirdupois. *Abbr.:* hg Also, **hektogram;** *esp. Brit.*, **hec′to·gramme′.**

hec·to·graph (hek′tə graf′, -gräf′), *n.* **1.** a process for making copies of a letter, memorandum, etc., from a prepared gelatin surface to which the original writing has been transferred. **2.** the apparatus used. **—***v.t.* **3.** to copy with the hectograph. Also, **hektograph.** **—hec·to·graph·ic** (hek′tə graf′ik), *adj.* **—hec·tog·ra·phy** (hek tog′rə fē), *n.*

hec·to·li·ter (hek′tə lē′tər), *n.* *Metric System.* a unit of capacity of 100 liters, equivalent to 2.8378 U.S. bushels, or 26.418 U.S. gallons. *Abbr.:* hl Also, **hektoliter;** *esp. Brit.*, **hec′to·li′tre.** [< F *hectolitre*]

hec·to·me·ter (hek′tə mē′tər), *n.* *Metric System.* a unit of length equal to 100 meters, or 328.08 feet. *Abbr.:* hm Also, **hektometer;** *esp. Brit.*, **hec′to·me′tre.** [< F *hectomètre*]

Hec·tor (hek′tər), *n.* **1.** *Class. Myth.* the eldest son of Priam and husband of Andromache: the greatest Trojan hero in the Trojan War, killed by Achilles. **2.** (*l.c.*) a blustering, domineering fellow; a bully. **—***v.t.* **3.** (*l.c.*) to treat with insolence; bully. **—***v.i.* **4.** (*l.c.*) to act in a blustering, domineering way; be a bully. [< L < Gk *Héktōr*, special use of adj. *héktor* holding fast] **—Syn. 3.** persecute, badger, harass.

Hec·u·ba (hek′yo͞o bə), *n.* *Class. Myth.* the wife of Priam.

he'd (hēd; *unstressed* ēd), **1.** contraction of *he had.* **2.** contraction of *he would.*

hed·dle (hed′əl), *n.* one of the sets of vertical cords or wires in a loom, forming the principal part of the harness that guides the warp threads. [metathetic var. of *heald* < ME *helde* < OE *hefeld*]

he·der (khe′der; *Eng.* hā′dər, khā′-), *n.*, *pl.* **ha·da·rim** (khä dä rēm′), *Eng.* **he·ders.** *Hebrew.* (esp. in Europe) a Jewish school for teaching children Hebrew, Bible, and prayers. Also, **cheder.** [lit., room]

hedge (hej), *n.*, *v.*, **hedged, hedg·ing.** **—***n.* **1.** a row of bushes or small trees planted close together, esp. when forming a fence or boundary. **2.** any barrier or boundary: *a hedge of stones.* **3.** an act or means of preventing complete loss of a bet, an argument, an investment, or the like, with a partially counterbalancing or qualifying one. **—***v.t.* **4.** to enclose with or separate by a hedge (often fol. by *in, off, about,* etc.): *to hedge a garden.* **5.** to surround so as to protect or confine, as with a hedge (often fol. by *in, about,* etc.): *an island hedged in by water.* **6.** to protect with qualifications that allow for unstated contingencies or for withdrawal from commitment: *He hedged his program against attack and then presented it to the board.* **7.** to mitigate a possible loss by diversifying (one's bets, investments, etc.). **8.** to prevent or hinder free movement; obstruct. **—***v.i.* **9.** to avoid a rigid commitment by qualifying or modifying a position so as to permit withdrawal; allow for escape or retreat. **10.** to prevent complete loss of a bet by betting an additional amount or amounts against the original bet. **11.** *Finance.* to enter transactions that will protect against loss through a compensatory price movement. **12.** to hide as in a hedge; skulk. [ME, OE *hegge;* c. D *heg*, G *Hecke* hedge, Icel *heggr* bird cherry] **—hedge′less,** *adj.* **—hedg′er,** *n.*

hedge′ gar′lic, an erect, cruciferous herb, *Sisymbrium officinale,* having a garliclike odor.

hedge·hog (hej′hog′, -hôg′), *n.* **1.** any of several Old World, insectivorous mammals of the genus *Erinaceus,* esp. *E. europaeus,* having spiny hairs on the back and sides. **2.** *U.S.* the porcupine. [late ME *heyghoge*]

Hedgehog, *Erinaceus europaeus* (Length 9 in.)

hedge·hop (hej′hop′), *v.i.,* **-hopped, -hop·ping.** to fly an airplane at a very low altitude, as for spraying crops, low-level bombing in warfare, etc. —**hedge′hop′per,** *n.*

hedge′ hys′sop, **1.** any of several low, scrophulariaceous herbs of the genus *Gratiola,* as *G. officinalis,* of Europe. **2.** any of certain similar plants, as the skullcap, *Scutellaria minor.*

hedge·row (hej′rō′), *n.* a row of bushes or trees forming a hedge. [OE *heggerewe*]

hedge′ spar′row, a small European oscine bird, *Prunella modularis,* that frequents hedges.

He·djaz (hē jaz′; *Arab.* he zhäz′), *n.* Hejaz.

he·don·ic (hē don′ik), *adj.* **1.** of, characterizing, or pertaining to pleasure. **2.** pertaining to hedonism or hedonics. [< Gk *hēdonik(ós)* pleasurable = *hēdon(ḗ)* pleasure + *-ikos* -IC] —**he·don′i·cal·ly,** *adv.*

he·don·ics (hē don′iks), *n.* (*construed as sing.*) the branch of psychology that deals with pleasurable and unpleasurable states of consciousness. [see HEDONIC, -ICS]

he·don·ism (hēd′ᵊniz′əm), *n.* **1.** the doctrine that pleasure or happiness is the highest good. **2.** devotion to pleasure as a way of life. [< Gk *hēdon(ḗ)* pleasure + -ISM] —**he′don·ist,** *n., adj.* —**he′do·nis′tic,** *adj.* —**he′do·nis′ti·cal·ly,** *adv.*

-hedral, a suffix used to form adjectives corresponding to nouns with stems in **-hedron:** *polyhedral.*

-hedron, a learned borrowing from Greek meaning "face," used to denote geometrical solid figures having a certain form or number of faces: *tetrahedron.* [< Gk *-edron,* neut. of *-edros* having bases, -sided = *(h)édr(a)* seat, face of a geometrical form + *-os* adj. suffix]

hee·bie-jee·bies (hē′bē jē′bēz), *n.* (*construed as pl.*) *Slang.* a condition of extreme nervousness caused by fear, worry, strain, etc.; the jitters; the willies. [coined by W. De Beck (1890–1942), American comic-strip cartoonist]

heed (hēd), *v.t.* **1.** to give careful attention to. —*v.i.* **2.** to give attention; have regard. —*n.* **3.** careful attention; notice; observation. [ME *hede(n),* OE *hēdan;* c. G *hüten* to guard, protect; akin to HOOD[1]] —**heed′er,** *n.* —**heed′ful,** *adj.* —**heed′ful·ly,** *adv.* —**heed′ful·ness,** *n.* —**Syn. 1.** note, observe, consider, mark. **3.** consideration; caution, vigilance, watchfulness. —**Ant. 1.** disregard, ignore.

heed·less (hēd′lis), *adj.* careless; thoughtless; unmindful: *Heedless of the danger, he returned to the burning building to save his dog.* —**heed′less·ly,** *adv.* —**heed′less·ness,** *n.*

hee·haw (hē′hô′), *n.* **1.** the braying sound made by a donkey. **2.** rude laughter. —*v.i.* **3.** to bray. [imit. gradational compound; cf. SEESAW]

heel[1] (hēl), *n.* **1.** the back part of the foot in man, below and behind the ankle. **2.** an analogous part in other vertebrates. **3.** either hind foot or hoof of some animals, as the horse. **4.** the foot as a whole: *He was hung by the heels.* **5.** the part of a stocking, shoe, etc., covering the back part of the wearer's foot. **6.** a solid, raised base or support attached to the sole of a shoe or boot under the back part of the foot. **7.** something resembling the back part of the human foot in position, shape, etc.: *a heel of bread; the heel of a golf club.* **8.** the rear of the palm, adjacent to the wrist. **9.** the latter or concluding part of anything: *the heel of a session.* **10.** the lower end of any of various more or less vertical objects, as rafters, spars, or the sternposts of vessels. **11.** *Naut.* **a.** the after end of a keel. **b.** the inner end of a bowsprit or jib boom. **12. at one's heels,** close behind one. Also, **at heel. 13. cool one's heels,** to be kept waiting, esp. because of deliberate discourtesy. **14. down at the heels,** having a shabby, slipshod, or slovenly appearance. Also, **down at heel, down at the heel, out at heels, out at the heels. 15. kick up one's heels,** to have an entertaining time; frolic. **16. on** or **upon the heels of,** closely following; in quick succession of. **17. take to one's heels,** to run away; take flight. —*v.t.* **18.** to follow at the heels of; chase closely. **19.** to furnish with heels, as shoes. **20.** *Golf.* to strike (the ball) with the heel of the club. **21.** to arm (a gamecock) with spurs. —*v.i.* **22.** (of a dog) to follow at one's heels on command. **23.** to use the heels, as in dancing. [ME; OE *hēl(a);* c. D *hiel,* Icel *hǣll.* See HOCK[1]] —**heel′less,** *adj.*

heel[2] (hēl), *v.i.* **1.** to incline to one side; cant; tilt: *The ship heeled in going about.* —*v.t.* **2.** to cause to lean or cant. —*n.* **3.** a heeling movement; a cant. [earlier *heeld,* ME *helde(n),* OE *hieldan* to lean, slope; akin to OE *heald,* Icel *hallr* sloping]

heel[3] (hēl), *n.* *Informal.* a cad; a low character. [special use of HEEL[1]]

heel-and-toe (hēl′ən tō′), *adj.* noting a pace in which the heel of the front foot touches ground before the toes of the rear one leave it.

heeled (hēld), *adj.* **1.** provided with a heel or heels. **2.** provided with money; flush or wealthy. [HEEL[1] + -ED[3]]

heel·er (hē′lər), *n.* **1.** a person who heels shoes. **2.** See **ward heeler.**

heel·piece (hēl′pēs′), *n.* **1.** *Shoemaking.* a piece of leather, wood, etc., serving as the heel of a shoe or boot. **2.** an end piece of anything; a terminal part.

heel·post (hēl′pōst′), *n.* a post made to withstand strain, forming or fitted to the end of something, as the post on which a gate or door is hinged.

heel·tap (hēl′tap′), *n.* **1.** a lift for a shoe heel. **2.** a small portion of liquor left in a glass after drinking or in a bottle after decanting.

Heer·len (hâr′lən), *n.* a city in the SE Netherlands. 74,886 (1962).

heft (heft), *n.* **1.** weight; heaviness: *It was a rather flimsy chair, without much heft to it.* **2.** *Archaic.* the bulk or main part. —*v.t.* **3.** to try the weight of by lifting and balancing, as in the hand. **4.** to heave or lift. [HEAVE + *-t,* var. of -TH[1]] —**heft′er,** *n.*

heft·y (hef′tē), *adj.,* **heft·i·er, heft·i·est. 1.** heavy; weighty: *a hefty book.* **2.** big and strong; muscular: *a hefty fellow.* —**hef′ti·ly,** *adv.* —**hef′ti·ness,** *n.*

he·gar·i (hi gar′ē, -gâr′ē, heg′ə rē), *n.* a grain sorghum having chalky white seeds. [< Sudanese Ar, var. of Ar *hijārī* stonelike]

He·gel (hā′gəl), *n.* **Ge·org Wil·helm Frie·drich** (gā′ôʀk vil′helm fʀē′dʀiᴋʜ), 1770–1831, German philosopher.

He·ge·li·an (hā gā′lē ən, hi jē′-), *adj.* **1.** of, pertaining to, or characteristic of Hegel or his philosophical system. —*n.* **2.** a person who accepts or is an authority on the philosophical principles of Hegel.

Hege′lian dialec′tic, *Hegelianism.* an interpretive method, originally used to relate specific entities or events to the absolute idea, in which some assertible proposition **(thesis)** is necessarily opposed by an equally assertible and apparently contradictory proposition **(antithesis),** the mutual contradiction being reconciled on a higher level of truth by a third proposition **(synthesis).**

He·ge·li·an·ism (hā gā′lē ə niz′əm, hi jē′-), *n.* the philosophy of Hegel and his followers, characterized by the use of the Hegelian dialectic.

he·gem·o·ny (hi jem′ə nē, hej′ə mō′nē), *n., pl.* **-nies.** leadership or predominant influence, esp. when exercised by one state over others. [< Gk *hēgemonía* leadership, supremacy = *hēgemon-* (s. of *hēgemṓn*) leader + *-ia* -Y[3]] —**heg·e·mon·ic** (hej′ə mon′ik), **heg′e·mon′i·cal,** *adj.*

He·gi·ra (hi jī′rə, hej′ər ə), *n.* **1.** the flight of Muhammad from Mecca to Medina to escape persecution, A.D. 622: regarded as the beginning of the Muslim era. **2.** the Muslim era itself. **3.** (*l.c.*) any flight or journey to a desirable or congenial place. Also, **Hejira.** [< ML < Ar *hijrah* a flight]

he·gu·men (hi gyōō′men), *n.* *Eastern Ch.* the head of a monastery. Also, **he·gu·me·nos** (hi gyōō′mə nos′). [< ML *hēgūmen(us)* < Gk *hēgoúmenos* chief, lit., leading, prp. of *hēgeîsthai* to lead]

Hei·deg·ger (hī′deg ər, -di gər), *n.* **Martin,** 1889–1976, German philosopher and writer.

Hei·del·berg (hīd′ᵊl bûrg′; *Ger.* hīd′ᵊl beʀk′), *n.* a city in NW Baden-Württemberg, in SW West Germany: university, founded 1386. 126,500 (1963).

Hei′delberg man′, the primitive man of the early Middle Pleistocene age reconstructed from a human lower jaw found in 1907 near Heidelberg, Germany.

Hei·duc (hī′dŏŏk), *n.* Haiduk. Also, **Hei′duk.**

heif·er (hef′ər), *n.* a cow that has not produced a calf and is under three years of age. [ME *hayfre,* OE *hēa(h)f(o)re* = *hēah* high + *-fore,* akin to Gk *pôris* heifer]

Hei·fetz (hī′fits), *n.* **Ja·scha** (yä′shə), born 1901, U.S. violinist, born in Russia.

heigh (hā, hī), *interj.* (an exclamation used to call attention, give encouragement, etc.)

heigh-ho (hī′hō′, hā′-), *interj.* (an exclamation of surprise, exultation, melancholy, boredom, or weariness.)

height (hīt), *n.* **1.** extent or distance upward: *at a height of 500 feet; the height from the ground to the first floor.* **2.** the distance between the lowest and highest points of a person standing upright; stature. **3.** considerable or great altitude or elevation: *the height of the mountains.* **4.** Often, **heights. a.** a high place above a level; a hill or mountain: *They stood on the heights overlooking the valley.* **b.** the highest part; apex; summit: *to reach the heights in one's profession.* **5.** the highest point; utmost degree: *the height of pleasure.* **6.** *Archaic.* high degree of social status. [ME; OE *hīehtho*]
—**Syn. 2.** tallness. HEIGHT, ALTITUDE, ELEVATION refer to distance above a level. HEIGHT denotes extent upward (as from foot to head) as well as any measurable distance above a given level: *The tree grew to a height of ten feet. They looked down from a great height.* ALTITUDE usually refers to the distance, determined by instruments, above a given level, commonly mean sea level: *The airplane flew at an altitude of 30,000 feet.* ELEVATION implies a distance to which something has been raised or uplifted above a level: *a hill's elevation above sea level, the surrounding country.* **4.** prominence. **5.** peak, pinnacle; acme, zenith; culmination. —**Ant. 1.** depth.
—**Usage.** HEIGHT, and not HEIGHTH, is considered the standard English form for this word.

height·en (hīt′ᵊn), *v.t.* **1.** to increase the height of; make higher. **2.** to increase the degree or amount of; augment. **3.** to strengthen, deepen, or intensify: *to heighten one's appreciation.* **4.** to bring out the important features of, as in a drawing: *to heighten a picture with Chinese white.* —*v.i.* **5.** to become higher. **6.** to increase. **7.** to become brighter or more intense. —**height′en·er,** *n.*

heighth (hītth), *n.* *Dial.* height.

height′ of land′, divide (def. 17).

height-to-pa·per (hīt′tə pā′pər), *n.* *Print.* the standard height of type engravings, etc., from the foot to the face, in the U.S. 0.9186 of an inch.

Hei·jo (hā′jō′), *n.* Japanese name of **Pyongyang.**

heil (hīl), *interj.* *German.* hail! (used as a greeting, acclamation, etc.)

Heil·bronn (hīl′bʀôn), *n.* a city in N Baden-Württemberg, in SW West Germany. 92,400 (1963).

Hei·lung·kiang (hā′lŏŏng′gyäng′), *n.* a province of NE China, in NE Manchuria. 14,860,000 (est. 1957); 108,880 sq. mi. *Cap.:* Harbin.

Heim·dall (hām′däl′), *n.* *Scand. Myth.* the god of dawn and light, famous for his eyesight and hearing, destined to kill and to be killed by Loki. Also, **Heim′dal′, Heim·dallr** (hām′däl′ər).

Heim′lich maneu′ver (hīm′lik), an emergency procedure to aid a person choking on food or other objects, by an upper abdominal thrust that forces air from the lungs upward to dislodge the obstruction. [after H.J. *Heimlich* (b. 1920), U.S. physician who devised it]

Hei·ne (hī′nə), *n.* **Hein·rich** (hīn′ʀiᴋʜ), 1797–1856, German lyric and satiric poet, journalist, and critic.

hei·nie (hī′nē), *n.* *Disparaging.* a German, esp. a German soldier of World War I. [partly Anglicized var. of G *Heine,* familiar var. of *Heinrich* Henry; see -IE]

hei·nous (hā′nəs), *adj.* hateful; odious; abominable; totally reprehensible: *a heinous offense.* [ME *heynous* < MF *haineus* = *haine* hatred (< *haïr* to HATE < Gmc) + *-eus* -OUS] —**hei′nous·ly,** *adv.* —**hei′nous·ness,** *n.*

heir (âr), *n.* **1.** a person who inherits or is entitled to inherit the property, rank, title, position, etc., of another. **2.** *Law.* **a.** (in common law) a person who inherits all the property of a deceased person, as by descent, relationship, will, or legal process. **b.** *Civil Law.* a person who legally succeeds to the place of a deceased person and assumes his rights and obligations, as the liabilities for debts or the possessory rights to property. **3.** a person, society, etc., considered as inheriting the tradition, talent, etc., of a predecessor. —*v.t.* **4.** *Chiefly Dial.* to inherit; succeed to. [ME *eir, heir* < OF < L *hērēd-* (s. of *hērēs*); akin to Gk *chêros* bereaved] —**heir′less,** *adj.*

heir′ appar′ent, *pl.* **heirs apparent. 1.** an heir whose right is indefeasible, provided he survives the ancestor. **2.** a person whose succession to a position appears certain. [ME] —**heir′ appar′ency.**

heir′ at law′, *pl.* **heirs at law.** a person who inherits, or has a right of inheritance in, the real property of one who has died without leaving a valid will.

heir·dom (âr′dəm), *n.* heirship; inheritance.

heir·ess (âr′is), *n.* a female heir, esp. a woman who has inherited or will inherit considerable wealth.

heir·loom (âr′lo͞om′), *n.* **1.** any family possession transmitted from generation to generation. **2.** *Law.* a chattel that because of its close connection with the mansion house descends to the heir. [ME *heirlome*]

heir′ presump′tive, *pl.* **heirs presumptive.** a person who is expected to be an heir but whose expectations may be defeated by the birth of a nearer heir.

heir·ship (âr′ship), *n.* the position or rights of an heir; right of inheritance; inheritance. [ME]

heist (hīst), *U.S. Slang.* —*v.t.* **1.** to rob or steal, esp. by burglary. —*n.* **2.** a robbery, esp. a burglary. [alter. of HOIST] —**heist′er,** *n.*

He·jaz (hē jaz′; *Arab.* he zhäz′), *n.* a region in Saudi Arabia bordering on the Red Sea, formerly an independent kingdom: contains the Islamic holy cities of Medina and Mecca. ab. 1,500,000; ab. 150,000 sq. mi. Also, **Hedjaz.**

He·ji·ra (hi jī′rə, hej′ər ə), *n.* Hegira.

Hek·a·te (hek′ə tē; *in Shakespeare* hek′it), *n.* Hecate. —**Hek′a·te′an, Hek′a·tae′an,** *adj.*

hek·tare (hek′târ), *n.* hectare.

hekto-, var. of **hecto-:** *hektograph.* Also, *esp. before a vowel,* **hekt-.**

hek·to·gram (hek′tə gram′), *n.* hectogram.

hek·to·graph (hek′tə graf′, -gräf′), *n., v.t.* hectograph.

hek·to·li·ter (hek′tə lē′tər), *n.* hectoliter.

hek·to·me·ter (hek′tə mē′tər), *n.* hectometer.

Hel (hel), *n. Scand. Myth.* **1.** the goddess ruling Niflheim: a daughter of Loki. **2.** the home of the dead; Niflheim. Also, **Hel·a** (hel′ä).

held (held), *v.* pt. and a pp. of **hold.**

Hel·en (hel′ən), *n. Class. Myth.* the beautiful daughter of Zeus and Leda and wife of Menelaus. Her abduction by Paris was the cause of the Trojan War. Also called **Hel′en of Troy′.**

Hel·e·na (hel′ə nə), *n.* a city in and the capital of Montana, in the W part. 22,730 (1970).

Hel·go·land (hel′gō länt′), *n.* a German island in the North Sea. 148 (1953); $^1/_4$ sq. mi. Also, **Heligoland.**

heli-, var. of **helio-** before a vowel: *helianthus.*

he·li·a·cal (hi lī′ə kəl), *adj. Astron.* pertaining to or occurring near the sun, esp. applied to those risings and settings of a star most nearly coincident with those of the sun while yet visible. Also, **he·li·ac** (hē′lē ak′). [< LL *hēliac(us)* (< Gk *hēliakós*] —**he·li′a·cal·ly,** *adv.*

he·li·an·thus (hē′lē an′thəs), *n., pl.* **-thus·es.** any plant of the genus *Helianthus,* comprising the sunflowers. [< NL; see HELI-, -ANTHOUS] —**he·li·an·tha·ceous** (hē′lē ən thā′shəs), *adj.*

hel·i·borne (hel′ə bōrn′), *adj.* transported or carried out by helicopter; *heliborne troops; a heliborne assault.*

hel·i·cal (hel′i kəl), *adj.* pertaining to or having the form of a helix; spiral. —**hel′i·cal·ly,** *adv.*

hel′ical gear′, a cylindrical gear wheel the teeth of which follow the pitch surface in a helical manner.

Helical gears

hel·i·ces (hel′i sēz′), *n.* a pl. of **helix.**

helico-, a learned borrowing from Greek meaning "spiral"; used with this meaning and as a combining form of **helix** in the formation of compound words. Also, *esp. before a vowel,* **helic-.** [< Gk *heliko-,* comb. form of *hélix*]

hel·i·coid (hel′ə koid′, hē′lə-), *adj.* **1.** coiled or curving like a spiral. —*n.* **2.** *Geom.* a warped surface generated by a straight line moving so as to cut or touch a fixed helix. [< Gk *helikoeid(ēs)* of spiral form] —**hel′i·coi′dal,** *adj.* —**hel′i·coi′dal·ly,** *adv.*

hel·i·con (hel′ə kon′, -kən), *n.* a coiled tuba carried over the shoulder and used esp. in military bands. [prob. special use of HELICON, by assoc. with HELICO-]

Helicon

Hel·i·con (hel′ə kon′, -kən), *n.* a mountain in S central Greece. 5738 ft.: regarded by ancient Greeks as the abode of Apollo and the Muses.

hel·i·cop·ter (hel′ə kop′tər, hē′lə-), *n.* any of a class of engine-powered, heavier-than-air craft that are lifted and sustained in the air by rotating wings or blades turning on vertical axes. [< F *hélicoptère*]

Hel·i·go·land (hel′ə gō land′), *n.* Helgoland.

hel·i·lift (hel′ə lift′), *v.t.* **1.** to transport (personnel or matériel) by helicopter, esp. to an otherwise inaccessible area. —*n.* **2.** such a system of transportation.

helio-, a learned borrowing from Greek meaning "sun," used in the formation of compound words: *heliolatry.* Also, *esp. before a vowel,* **heli-.** [< Gk, comb. form of *hḗlios* SUN]

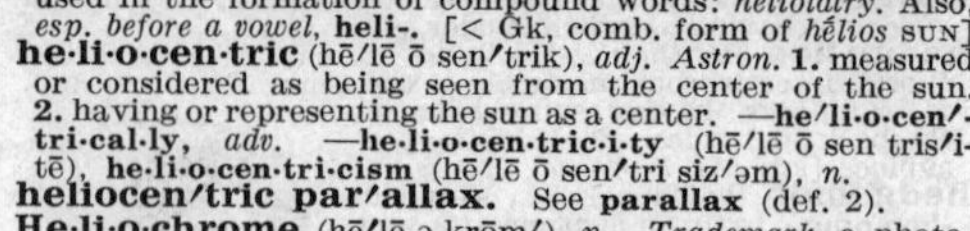

he·li·o·cen·tric (hē′lē ō sen′trik), *adj. Astron.* **1.** measured or considered as being seen from the center of the sun. **2.** having or representing the sun as a center. —**he′li·o·cen′tri·cal·ly,** *adv.* —**he·li·o·cen·tric·i·ty** (hē′lē ō sen tris′i tē), **he·li·o·cen·tri·cism** (hē′lē ō sen′tri siz′əm), *n.*

heliocen′tric par′allax. See **parallax** (def. 2).

He·li·o·chrome (hē′lē ə krōm′), *n. Trademark.* a photograph reproducing directly the natural colors of a subject. —**he′li·o·chro′mic,** *adj.* —**he′li·o·chro′my,** *n.*

He·li·o·gab·a·lus (hē′lē ə gab′ə ləs), *n.* (*Varius Avitus Bassianus*) ("*Marcus Aurelius Antoninus*") A.D. 204–222, Roman emperor 218–222. Also, **Elagabalus.**

he·li·o·gram (hē′lē ə gram′), *n.* a message sent by heliograph.

he·li·o·graph (hē′lē ə graf′, -gräf′), *n.* **1.** a device for signaling by means of a movable mirror that reflects beams of light. **2.** photoheliograph. **3.** *Meteorol.* an instrument for recording the duration and intensity of sunshine. —*v.t., v.i.* **4.** to communicate by heliograph. —**he·li·og·ra·pher** (hē′lē og′rə fər), *n.* —**he·li·o·graph·ic** (hē′lē ə graf′ik), **he′li·o·graph′i·cal,** *adj.* —**he′li·og′ra·phy,** *n.*

he·li·ol·a·try (hē′lē ol′ə trē), *n.* worship of the sun. —**he′li·ol′a·ter,** *n.* —**he′li·ol′a·trous,** *adj.*

he·li·om·e·ter (hē′lē om′i tər), *n.* a telescope with a divided, adjustable objective, formerly used to measure small angular distances, as those between celestial bodies. —**he·li·o·met·ric** (hē′lē ə me′trik), **he′li·o·met′ri·cal,** *adj.* —**he′li·o·met′ri·cal·ly,** *adv.*

He·li·op·o·lis (hē′lē op′ə lis), *n.* **1.** Biblical name, **On.** an ancient ruined city in N Arab Republic of Egypt, on the Nile delta. **2.** ancient Greek name of **Baalbek.**

He·li·os (hē′lē os′), *n.* the ancient Greek god of the sun, the son of Hyperion and Thia, and father of Phaëthon: represented as driving a chariot across the heavens; identified by the Romans with Sol; called Hyperion by Homer. Also, **He·li·us** (hē′lē əs).

he·li·o·scope (hē′lē ə skōp′), *n.* a telescope for viewing the sun, adapted to protect the eye of the viewer from the sun's glare. —**he·li·o·scop·ic** (hē′lē ə skop′ik), *adj.* —**he·li·os·co·py** (hē′lē os′kə pē), *n.*

he·li·o·stat (hē′lē ə stat′), *n.* an instrument containing a mirror moved by clockwork, for reflecting the sun's rays in a fixed direction. [< NL *heliostat(a)*] —**he′li·o·stat′ic,** *adj.*

he·li·o·tax·is (hē′lē ō tak′sis), *n. Biol.* movement of an organism toward or away from sunlight. —**he·li·o·tac·tic** (hē′lē ō tak′tik), *adj.*

he·li·o·ther·a·py (hē′lē ō ther′ə pē), *n.* treatment of disease by means of sunlight.

he·li·o·trope (hē′lē ə trōp′, hēl′yə- *or, esp. Brit.,* hel′yə-), *n.* **1.** *Bot.* any plant that turns toward the sun. **2.** any boraginaceous herb or shrub of the genus *Heliotropium,* esp. a garden species, *H. arborescens,* having small, fragrant, purple flowers. **3.** valerian (def. 2). **4.** a light tint of purple; reddish lavender. **5.** bloodstone.

he·li·o·trop·ic (hē′lē ə trop′ik, -trō′pik), *adj. Bot.* turning or growing toward the light. —**he′li·o·trop′i·cal·ly,** *adv.*

he·li·ot·ro·pism (hē′lē o′trə piz′əm), *n.* heliotropic tendency or growth.

he·li·o·zo·an (hē′lē ə zō′ən), *n.* **1.** a protozoan of the order *Heliozoa,* having a spherical body and radiating pseudopods. —*adj.* **2.** Also, **he·li·o·zo·ic** (hē′lē ə zō′ik). belonging or pertaining to the *Heliozoa.* [< NL *Hēliozo(a)* name of the group (see HELIO-, -ZOA) + -AN]

hel·i·pad (hel′ə pad′, hē′lə-), *n.* a takeoff and landing area for helicopters, usually without commercial facilities.

hel·i·port (hel′ə pōrt′, -pôrt′, hē′lə-), *n.* a landing place for helicopters, often the roof of a building.

he·li·um (hē′lē əm), *n. Chem.* an inert, gaseous element used as a substitute for flammable gases in lighter-than-air craft. *Symbol:* He; *at. wt.:* 4.0026; *at. no.:* 2; *density:* 0.1785 at 0°C and 760 mm pressure. [< NL; see HELIO-, -IUM]

he·lix (hē′liks), *n., pl.* **hel·i·ces** (hel′i sēz′), **he·lix·es. 1.** a spiral. **2.** *Geom.* the curve formed by a straight line drawn on a plane when that plane is wrapped round a cylindrical surface of any kind, esp. a right circular cylinder, as the curve of a screw. **3.** *Anat.* the curved fold forming most of the rim of the external ear. [< L: spiral, kind of ivy < Gk: anything twisted; cf. *helíssein* to turn, twist, roll]

hell (hel), *n.* **1.** the place or state of punishment of the wicked after death; the abode of evil and condemned spirits. **2.** any place or state of torment or misery: *She made his life a hell on earth.* **3.** anything that causes torment or misery, esp. severe verbal censure; a tongue-lashing. **4.** the abode of the dead; Sheol or Hades. **5.** a gambling house. **6.** a receptacle into which a tailor throws his scraps. **7.** Also called **hellbox.** *Print.* a box into which a printer throws discarded type. **8. be hell on,** *Slang.* **a.** to be unpleasant to or painful for: *She's hell on her servants.* **b.** to be harmful to: *These country roads are hell on tires.* **9. get** or **catch hell,** *Slang.* to suffer a scolding; receive a harsh reprimand: *He'll get hell for coming home late.* **10. hell of a,** *Slang.* **a.** very bad, disagreeable, or difficult: *a hell of a trip.* **b.** very; extremely; excessively (used as an intensive): *a hell of a long trip for an old car.* **11. raise hell,** *Slang.* **a.** to indulge in wild celebration. **b.** to create an uproar; object violently. —*interj.* **12.** (used to express surprise, irritation, disgust, etc.) [ME, OE *hel(l)*; c. OHG *hell(i)a* (G *Hölle*), Icel *hel,* Goth *halja*; akin to OE *helan* to cover, hide, and to HULL¹] —**Syn. 1.** inferno. —**Ant. 1, 2.** heaven, paradise.

he'll (hēl; *unstressed* ēl, hil, il), **1.** contraction of *he will.* **2.** contraction of *he shall.*

Hel·lad·ic (he lad′ik), *adj.* of or pertaining to the Bronze Age culture on the mainland of ancient Greece c2900–1100 B.C. [< L *Helladic(us)* < Gk *Helladikós* of, from Greece = *Hellad-* (s. of *Hellás*) Greece + *-ikos* -IC]

Hel·las (hel′əs), *n.* ancient Greek name of **Greece.**

hell·bend·er (hel′ben′dər), *n.* a large salamander, *Cryptobranchus alleganiensis,* found in rivers and streams of the eastern U.S., having a flat, stout body and broad head.

hell·bent (hel′bent′), *adj. Informal.* stubbornly or recklessly determined.

hell·box (hel′boks′), *n. Print.* hell (def. 7).

hell·broth (hel′brôth′, -broth′), *n.* a magical broth prepared for an infernal purpose.

hell·cat (hel′kat′), *n.* **1.** a bad-tempered, unmanageable woman; shrew. **2.** a sorceress or witch.

hell·div·er (hel′dī′vər), *n.* a grebe, esp. the pied-billed grebe.

Hel·le (hel′ē), *n. Class. Myth.* a maiden who, while fleeing from her stepmother Ino, fell into the Hellespont and was drowned.

hel·le·bore (hel′ə bōr′, -bôr′), *n.* **1.** any of several ranunculaceous herbs of the genus *Helleborus,* esp. *H. niger,* the Christmas rose. **2.** any of several coarse, melanthiaceous herbs of the genus *Veratrum,* as *V. album* and *V. viride.* **3.** the powdered root of American white hellebore, used to kill lice and caterpillars. [< Gk *hellébor(os);* r. earlier *ellebor(e),* ME *el(l)bre,* etc. < L *ellebor(us)*]

Hel·len (hel′ən), *n. Class. Myth.* a Thessalian king, son of Deucalion and Pyrrha and eponymous ancestor of the Hellenes.

Hel·lene (hel′ēn), *n.* a Greek. [< Gk *Héllēn;* see HELLEN]

Hel·len·ic (he len′ik, -lē′nik), *adj.* **1.** of, pertaining to, or characteristic of the ancient Greeks or their language, culture, thought, etc., esp. before the time of Alexander the Great. Cf. **Hellenistic** (def. 3). **—***n.* **2.** Also called **Greek.** a branch of Indo-European that comprises a variety of ancient, medieval, and modern dialects and languages, all of them called Greek. **3.** Katharevusa. [< Gk *Hellēnik(ós)* of, pertaining to the Greeks] **—Hel·len′i·cal·ly,** *adv.*

Hel·len·ise (hel′ə nīz′), *v.t., v.i.,* **-ised, -is·ing.** *Chiefly Brit.* Hellenize. **—Hel′len·i·sa′tion,** *n.* **—Hel′len·is′er,** *n.*

Hel·len·ism (hel′ə niz′əm), *n.* **1.** ancient Greek culture or ideals. **2.** the imitation or adoption of ancient Greek language, thought, customs, art, etc.: *the Hellenism of Alexandrian Jews.* **3.** the characteristics of Greek culture, esp. after the time of Alexander the Great; civilization of the Hellenistic period. [< Gk *Hellēnism(ós)* an imitation of or similarity to the Greeks]

Hel·len·ist (hel′ə nist), *n.* **1.** (in ancient Greece) a person who adopted Greek speech and customs. **2.** a specialist in ancient Greek civilization. [< Gk *Hellēnist(ḗs)*]

Hel·len·is·tic (hel′ə nis′tik), *adj.* **1.** pertaining to Hellenists. **2.** following or resembling Greek usage. **3.** of or pertaining to the Greeks or their language, culture, etc., after the time of Alexander the Great. **4.** of or pertaining to the architecture of Greece and Greek territories from the late 3rd century through the 1st century B.C., characterized by deviations of various sorts from the proportions and arrangements of the mature Greek orders. **5.** pertaining to or designating the style of the fine arts, from the end of the 4th to the 1st century B.C., that was developed in the area conquered by Alexander the Great. Cf. **archaic** (def. 3), **classical** (def. 2). **—Hel′len·is′ti·cal·ly,** *adv.*

Hel·len·ize (hel′ə nīz′), *v.,* **-ized, -iz·ing.** **—***v.t.* **1.** to make Greek in character. **—***v.i.* **2.** to adopt Greek ideas or customs. Also, *esp. Brit.,* **Hellenise.** [< Gk *Hellēníz(ein)* (to) imitate the Greeks, speak Greek] **—Hel′len·i·za′tion,** *n.* **—Hel′len·iz′er,** *n.*

hel·ler[1] (hel′ər), *n., pl.* **hel·ler. 1.** a former coin of various German states, usually equal to half a pfennig. **2.** a former bronze coin of Austria, the 100th part of a korona. **3.** haler (def. 2). [< G < MHG *haller, heller,* after *Hall* Swabian town where they were orig. minted; see -ER[1]]

hell·er[2] (hel′ər), *n. Slang.* a noisy, wild, troublesome person. [short for HELL-RAISER]

Hel·les (hel′is), *n.* **Cape,** a cape in European Turkey at the S end of Gallipoli Peninsula.

Hel·les·pont (hel′i spont′), *n.* ancient name of the **Dardanelles.**

hell·fire (hel′fīᵊr′), *n.* **1.** the fire of hell. **2.** punishment in hell. [ME]

hell·gram·mite (hel′grə mīt′), *n.* the aquatic larva of a dobsonfly, used as bait in fishing. [?]

hell·hole (hel′hōl′), *n.* **1.** a place totally lacking in comfort, cleanliness, order, etc. **2.** a place or establishment noted for its illegal or immoral practices. Also, **hell′ hole′.** [ME]

hell·hound (hel′hound′), *n.* **1.** a mythical watchdog of hell. **2.** a fiendish person. [ME, OE]

hel·lion (hel′yən), *n. Informal.* a disorderly, troublesome or rowdy person. [HELL + *-ion,* as in *scullion, (rap)scallion*]

hell·ish (hel′ish), *adj.* **1.** of, like, or suitable to hell; vile; horrible: *It was a hellish war.* **2.** miserable; abominable; execrable: *We had a hellish time getting through traffic.* **3.** wicked; devilish. **—hell′ish·ly,** *adv.* **—hell′ish·ness,** *n.*

Hell·man (hel′mən), *n.* **Lillian Florence,** 1905–84, U.S. playwright.

hel·lo (he lō′, hə-, hel′ō), *interj., n., pl.* **-los,** *v.,* **-loed, -lo·ing.** **—***interj.* **1.** (used to express a greeting, answer a telephone, or attract attention.) **2.** (an exclamation of surprise, wonder, elation, etc.) **—***n.* **3.** the call "hello" (used as an expression of greeting): *She gave me a warm hello.* **—***v.i.* **4.** to say "hello"; to cry or shout. Also, *esp. Brit.,* **hullo.** [var. of HALLO]

hell-rais·er (hel′rā′zər), *n. Slang.* a person or thing that raises hell, esp. habitually.

hell's′ bells′, (used interjectionally to indicate vexation or surprise.) [rhyming phrase]

hell·uv·a (hel′ə və), *adj., adv.* hell (def. 10).

hell′ week′, *Informal.* the week of hazing preceding initiation into a college fraternity.

helm[1] (helm), *n.* **1.** *Naut.* **a.** a wheel or tiller by which a ship is steered. **b.** the entire steering apparatus of a ship. **c.** the angle with the fore-and-aft line made by a rudder when turned: *15-degree helm.* **d.** an imaginary tiller regarded as extending forward of the rudderpost of a ship, formerly referred to in most steering orders given in terms of helm position instead of rudder position. **2.** the place or post of control. **—***v.t.* **3.** to steer; direct. [ME *helme,* OE *helma;* c. MHG *halme, helm* handle, OIcel *hjalm* rudder] **—helm′less,** *adj.*

helm[2] (helm), *n.* **1.** Also, **heaume.** a medieval helmet, typically formed as a single cylindrical piece with a flat or raised top, completely enclosing the head. **—***v.t.* **2.** to furnish or cover with a helmet. [ME, OE; c. D, G *helm;* akin to OE *helan* to cover]

Hel·mand (hel′mənd), *n.* a river in S Asia, flowing SW from E Afghanistan to a lake in E Iran. 650 mi. long.

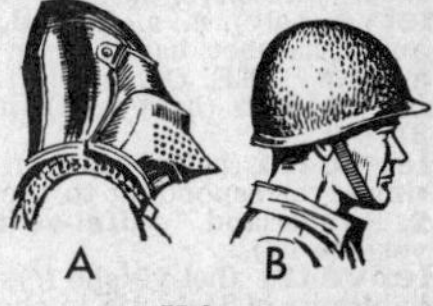

Helmets
A, Medieval; B, Modern

hel·met (hel′mit), *n.* **1.** any of various forms of protective head covering worn by soldiers, firemen, divers, cyclists, etc. **2.** armor for the head. **3.** anything resembling a helmet in form or position. [< MF *healmet, helmet,* dim. of *helme* HELM[2]] **—hel′met·ed,** *adj.* **—hel′met·like′,** *adj.*

Helm·holtz (helm′hōlts), *n.* **Her·mann Lud·wig Fer·di·nand von** (her′män lo͞ot′viᴋʜ fer′di nänt′ fən), 1821–94, German physiologist and physicist.

hel·minth (hel′minth), *n.* a worm, esp. a parasitic worm. [< Gk *helminth-* (s. of *hélmins*) a kind of worm] **—hel·min·thoid** (hel min′thoid, hel′min thoid′), *adj.*

hel·min·thi·a·sis (hel′min thī′ə sis), *n. Pathol.* a condition characterized by worms in the body. [< NL < Gk *helminthi(ân)* (to) suffer from worms (see HELMINTH) + *-asis* -ASIS]

hel·min·thic (hel min′thik), *adj.* **1.** of, pertaining to, or caused by worms or helminths. **2.** expelling intestinal worms; anthelminthic.

hel·min·thol·o·gy (hel′min thol′ə jē), *n.* the science of worms, esp. of parasitic worms. **—hel·min·tho·log·i·cal** (hel min′thə loj′i kəl), **hel·min′tho·log′ic,** *adj.* **—hel′min·thol′o·gist,** *n.*

helms·man (helmz′mən), *n., pl.* **-men.** a person who steers a ship; steersman.

Hé·lo·ïse (el′ō ēz′; *Fr.* ā lô ēz′), *n.* 1101?–1164, French abbess: pupil and wife of Pierre Abélard. Cf. **Abélard.**

Hel·ot (hel′ət, hē′lət), *n.* **1.** (in ancient Sparta) a member of a class of serfs owned by the state. **2.** (*l.c.*) a serf or slave; bondman. [< L *hēlōt(ēs)* (pl.) < Gk *heílōtes*] **—hel′ot·age,** *n.*

hel·ot·ism (hel′ə tiz′əm, hē′lə-), *n.* the state or quality of being a helot; serfdom.

hel·ot·ry (hel′ə trē, hē′lə-), *n.* **1.** serfdom; slavery. **2.** helots collectively.

help (help), *v.,* **helped** or (*esp. Dial.*) **holp; helped** or (*esp. Dial.*) **hol·pen; help·ing;** *n., interj.* **—***v.t.* **1.** to contribute strength or means to; render assistance to; cooperate effectively with; aid; assist: *He planned to help me with my work.* **2.** to save; rescue; succor: *Help me, I'm falling!* **3.** to refrain from; avoid (usually prec. by *can* or *cannot*): *He can't help doing it.* **4.** to relieve (someone) in need, sickness, pain, or distress. **5.** to remedy, stop, or prevent. **6.** to take or appropriate for oneself: *They helped themselves to the farmer's apples.* **—***v.i.* **7.** to give aid; be of service or advantage: *Every little bit helps.* **8. help out,** to assist in an effort; be of aid to: *Her relatives helped out when she became ill.* **9. so help me,** (used as a mild oath) I am speaking the truth; on my honor: *That's exactly what happened, so help me.* **—***n.* **10.** the act of helping; aid or assistance; relief or succor. **11.** a person or thing that helps: *She certainly is a help around the house.* **12.** a hired helper; employee. **13.** a body of such helpers. **14.** a means of remedying, stopping, or preventing: *The thing is done, and there is no help for it now.* **15.** *Dial.* helping (def. 2) **—***interj.* **16.** (used as an exclamation to call for assistance or to attract attention.) [ME *helpe(n),* OE *helpan;* c. G *helfen*] **—help′a·ble,** *adj.*

—Syn. 1. encourage, befriend; support, uphold, back, abet. HELP, AID, ASSIST, SUCCOR agree in the idea of furnishing another with something needed, esp. when the need comes at a particular time. HELP implies furnishing anything that furthers another's efforts or relieves his wants or necessities. AID and ASSIST, somewhat more formal, imply esp. a furthering or seconding of another's efforts. AID implies a more active helping; ASSIST implies less need and less help. To SUCCOR, still more formal and literary, is to give timely help and relief in difficulty or distress: *Succor him in his hour of need.* **4.** alleviate, cure, heal. **10.** support, backing. **—Ant. 4.** afflict. **8.** hinder.

—Usage. HELP BUT, in sentences like, *She's so beautiful you can't help but admire her,* has been condemned, esp. by British grammarians and purists. In American usage it can only be characterized as standard.

help·er (hel′pər), *n.* a person or thing that helps or gives assistance, support, etc. [ME] **—Syn.** aid, assistant; supporter, backer, auxiliary, ally.

help·ful (help′fəl), *adj.* giving or rendering aid or assistance; of service: *His comments were always helpful.* [ME] **—help′ful·ly,** *adv.* **—help′ful·ness,** *n.* **—Syn.** useful; beneficial, advantageous. **—Ant.** useless, inconvenient.

help·ing (hel′ping), *n.* **1.** the act of a person or thing that helps. **2.** a portion of food served to a person at one time. **—***adj.* **3.** giving aid, assistance, support, or the like. [ME]

help·less (help′lis), *adj.* **1.** unable to help oneself; weak or dependent: *a helpless invalid.* **2.** without help, aid, or succor. **3.** deprived of strength or power; powerless; incapacitated: *He was helpless with laughter.* **4.** bewildered; confused; perplexed: *He looked at her with a helpless expression on his face.* [ME] **—help′less·ly,** *adv.* **—help′less·ness,** *n.*

help·mate (help′māt′), *n.* **1.** a companion and helper. **2.** a wife or husband.

help·meet (help′mēt′), *n.* helpmate. [from the phrase *a help meet* (i.e., suitable to, like) *him*]

Hel·sing·ör (hel′sing œr′), *n.* a seaport on NE Zealand, in NE Denmark: the scene of Shakespeare's *Hamlet.* 30,211. Also called **Elsinore.**

Hel·sin·ki (hel′sing kē, hel sing′-), *n.* a seaport in and the capital of Finland, on the S coast. 496,872. Swedish, **Helsing·fors** (hel′sing fôrs′; *Sw.* hel′sing fôsh′).

hel·ter-skel·ter (hel′tər skel′tər), *adv.* **1.** in headlong and disorderly haste. **2.** in a haphazard manner; without regard for order: *His clothes were scattered helter-skelter about the room.* —*n.* **3.** tumultuous disorder; confusion. —*adj.* **4.** carelessly hurried; confused: *They ran in a mad, helter-skelter fashion for the door.* **5.** disorderly; haphazard. [imit.]

helve (helv), *n., v.,* **helved, helv·ing.** —*n.* **1.** the handle of an ax, hatchet, hammer, or the like. —*v.t.* **2.** to furnish with a helve. [ME, OE *h(i)elfe*]

Hel·vel·lyn (hel vel′in), *n.* a mountain in NW England. 3118 ft.

Hel·ve·tia (hel vē′shə), *n.* **1.** an Alpine region in Roman times, corresponding to the W and N parts of Switzerland. **2.** Switzerland. —**Hel·ve′tian,** *adj., n.* —**Hel·vet·ic** (hel-vet′ik), *adj.*

Hel·ve·ti·i (hel vē′shē ī′), *n., pl.* the ancient Celtic inhabitants of Helvetia in the time of Julius Caesar.

Hel·vé·tius (hel vē′shəs; *Fr.* el vā syys′), *n.* **Claude A·dri·en** (klōd ā′drē ən; *Fr.* klōd A drē äN′), 1715–71, French philosopher.

hem[1] (hem), *v.,* **hemmed, hem·ming,** *n.* —*v.t.* **1.** to enclose or confine (usually fol. by *in, around,* or *about*): *hemmed in by enemies.* **2.** to fold back and sew down the edge of (cloth, a garment, etc.). —*n.* **3.** the edge made by folding back the margin of cloth and sewing it down. **4.** the edge or border of a garment, drape, etc., esp. at the bottom. **5.** the edge, border, or margin of anything. [ME *hem(m),* OE *hem,* prob. akin to *hamm* enclosure] —**hem′mer,** *n.*

hem[2] (hem), *interj., n., v.,* **hemmed, hem·ming.** —*interj.* **1.** (an utterance resembling a slight clearing of the throat, used to attract attention, express doubt, etc.) —*n.* **2.** the utterance or sound of "hem." —*v.i.* **3.** to utter the sound "hem." **4.** to hesitate in speaking. **5. hem and haw,** to speak noncommittally; avoid giving a direct answer. [imit.]

hem-, var. of **hemo-** before a vowel: *hemal.* Also, **haem-.** Cf. **haemat-.**

hema-, var. of **hemo-:** *hemacytometer.* Also, **haema-.**

he·ma·chrome (hē′mə krōm′, hem′ə-), *n.* the red coloring matter of the blood. Also, **haemachrome.**

he·ma·cy·tom·e·ter (hē′mə sī tom′i tər, hem′ə-), *n. Med.* hemocytometer.

he·mal (hē′məl), *adj.* **1.** Also, **hem·a·tal** (hem′ə tᵊl, hē′mə-), **haematal.** of or pertaining to the blood or blood vessels. **2.** *Zool.* noting, pertaining to, or on the side of the body ventral to the spinal axis, containing the heart and principal blood vessels. Also, **haemal.**

he-man (hē′man′), *n., pl.* **-men.** a strong, tough, virile man.

hemat-, var. of **hemato-** before a vowel: *hematic.* Also, **haemat-.**

hem·a·te·in (hem′ə tē′in, hē′mə-), *n. Chem.* a reddish-brown solid, $C_{16}H_{12}O_6$, used chiefly as a stain in microscopy. [var. of HEMATIN]

he·mat·ic (hə mat′ik), *adj.* **1.** of or pertaining to blood; hemic. **2.** acting on the blood, as a medicine. —*n.* **3.** a hematic medicine. Also, **haematic.**

hem·a·tin (hem′ə tin, hē′mə-), *n.* **1.** *Biochem.* a pigment, $C_{34}H_{32}N_4O_4FeOH$, produced in the decomposition of hemoglobin. **2.** (loosely) hematein. Also, **haematin, hem·a·tine** (hem′ə tēn′, -tin, hē′mə-). [HEMAT- + -IN[2]]

hem·a·tin·ic (hem′ə tin′ik, hē′mə-), *n.* **1.** a medicine, as a compound of iron, that tends to increase the amount of hematin or hemoglobin in the blood. —*adj.* **2.** of or obtained from hematin. Also, **haematinic.**

hem·a·tite (hem′ə tīt′, hē′mə-), *n.* a very common mineral, iron oxide, Fe_2O_3, the principal ore of iron. [< L *haematīte(s)* bloodstone < Gk *haimatī́tēs (líthos)* bloodlike (stone). See HEMAT-, -ITE[1]] —**hem·a·tit·ic** (hem′ə tit′ik, hē′mə-), *adj.*

hemato-, a learned borrowing from Greek equivalent to **hemo-:** *hematocryal.* Also, **hemat-, haemat-, haemato-.** [< NL, comb. form repr. Gk *haimat-,* s. of *haîma* blood]

hem·a·to·blast (hem′ə tō blast′, hē′mə-), *n. Anat.* an immature blood cell, esp. a red blood cell. Also, **hemoblast, haematoblast, haemoblast.**

hem·a·to·crit (hem′ə tō krit, hē′mə-), *n.* **1.** a centrifuge for separating the cells of the blood from the plasma. **2.** Also called **hem′atocrit val′ue.** the ratio of the volume of cells to a given volume of blood so centrifuged, expressed as a percentage. [HEMATO- + *-crit* < Gk *krit(ḗs)* judge]

hem·a·toc·ry·al (hem′ə tok′rē əl, -tō krī′əl, hē′mə-), *adj.* cold-blooded, as a vertebrate. Also, **haematocryal.**

hem·a·to·cyte (hem′ə tō sīt′, hē′mə-), *n.* hemocyte.

hem·a·tog·e·nous (hem′ə toj′ə nəs, hē′mə-), *adj.* **1.** originating in the blood. **2.** blood-producing. **3.** distributed or spread by way of the bloodstream, as in metastases of tumors or in infections; blood-borne. Also, **haematogenous.**

hem·a·tol·o·gy (hem′ə tol′ə jē, hē′mə-), *n. Med.* the study of the nature, function, and diseases of the blood and of blood-forming organs. Also, **haematology.** —**hem·a·to·log·ic** (hem′ə tᵊloj′ik, hē′mə-), **hem′a·to·log′i·cal,** *adj.* —**hem′a·tol′o·gist,** *n.*

hem·a·to·ma (hem′ə tō′mə, hē′mə-), *n., pl.* **-mas, -ma·ta** (-mə tə). *Pathol.* a swelling filled with extravasated blood. Also, **haematoma.**

hem·a·to·poi·e·sis (hem′ə tō poi ē′sis, hē′mə-), *n.* the formation of blood. Also, **haematopoiesis.** [< NL *haematopoiēsis*] —**hem·a·to·poi·et·ic** (hem′ə tō poi et′ik, hē′mə-), *adj.*

hem·a·to·sis (hem′ə tō′sis, hē′mə-), *n.* **1.** hematopoiesis. **2.** *Physiol.* the conversion of venous into arterial blood; oxygenation in the lungs. Also, **haematosis.** [< NL *haematōsis*]

hem·a·to·ther·mal (hem′ə tō thûr′məl, hē′mə-), *adj.* warm-blooded; homoiothermal. Also, **haematothermal.**

he·ma·tox·y·lin (hē′mə tok′sə lin, hem′ə-), *n.* a colorless or pale-yellow compound, $C_{16}H_{14}O_6 \cdot 3H_2O$, used as a mordant dye and as an indicator. Also, **haematoxylin.** —**he·ma·tox·yl·ic** (hē′mə tok sil′ik, hem′ə-), *adj.*

hem·a·to·zo·on (hem′ə tə zō′on, -ən, hē′mə-), *n., pl.* **-zo·a** (-zō′ə). an animal parasite, usually a protozoan, living in the blood. Also, **haematozoon, hem′a·to·zo′ön, haematozoön.** —**hem′a·to·zo′al, hem′a·to·zo′ic,** *adj.*

he·ma·tu·ri·a (hē′mə tŏŏr′ē ə, -tyŏŏr′-, hem′ə-), *n. Pathol.* the presence of blood in the urine. —**he′ma·tu′ric,** *adj.*

heme (hēm), *n. Biochem.* a deep-red pigment, $C_{34}H_{32}N_4O_4Fe$, obtained from hemoglobin. [shortened form of HEMATIN]

Hem′el Hemp′stead (hem′əl), a town in W Hertfordshire, in SE England. 54,816 (1961).

hem·el·y·tron (he mel′i tron′), *n., pl.* **-tra** (-trə). *Entomol.* one of the forewings of a hemipterous insect, having a hard, thick basal portion and a thinner, membranous apex. Also, **hemielytron.** —**hem·el·y·tral** (he mel′i trəl), *adj.*

hem·er·a·lo·pi·a (hem′ər ə lō′pē ə), *n. Ophthalm.* **1.** Also called **day blindness.** a condition of the eyes in which sight is normal in the night or in a dim light but is abnormally poor or wholly absent in the day or in a bright light. **2.** nyctalopia. [< NL < Gk *hēmeralōp-* (s. of *hēmerálōps*) day blindness = *hēmér(a)* day + *al(aós)* blind + *-opia* -OPIA] —**hem·er·a·lop·ic** (hem′ər ə lop′ik), *adj.*

Hem·er·o·cal·lis (hem′ər ə kal′is), *n.* the genus comprising the day lilies. [< NL < Gk *hēmerokallís* = *hēméra* day + *kállos* beauty]

hemi-, a learned borrowing from Greek meaning "half," used in the formation of compound words: *hemimorphic.* [< Gk *hēmi-* half; c. L *sēmi-* SEMI-]

-hemia, var. of **-emia** after *p, t, k: leucocythemia.*

he·mic (hē′mik, hem′ik), *adj.* hematic. Also, **haemic.**

hem·i·cel·lu·lose (hem′i sel′yə lōs′), *n. Chem.* any of a group of gummy polysaccharides, intermediate in complexity between sugar and cellulose.

hem·i·chor·date (hem′i kôr′dāt), *Zool.* —*adj.* **1.** belonging or pertaining to the chordates of the subphylum *Hemichordata,* comprising small, widely distributed, marine animals, as the acorn worms. —*n.* **2.** a hemichordate animal.

hem·i·cy·cle (hem′i sī′kəl), *n.* **1.** a semicircle. **2.** a semicircular structure. [< F *hémicycle* < L *hēmicycl(ium)* < Gk *hēmikýklion*] —**hem·i·cy·clic** (hem′i sī′klik, -sik′lik), *adj.*

hem·i·dem·i·sem·i·qua·ver (hem′ē dem′ē sem′ē kwā′vər), *n. Music Chiefly Brit.* a sixty-fourth note. See illus. at **note.**

hem·i·el·y·tron (hem′ē el′i tron′), *n., pl.* **-tra** (-trə). *Entomol.* hemelytron. —**hem′i·el′y·tral,** *adj.*

he·mi·glo·bin (hē′mi glō′bin, hem′i-; hē′mi glō′bin, hem′i-), *n. Biochem.* methemoglobin.

hem·i·he·dral (hem′i hē′drəl), *adj.* (of a crystal) having only half the planes or faces required by the maximum symmetry of the system to which it belongs. —**hem′i·he′dral·ly,** *adv.*

hem·i·hy·drate (hem′i hī′drāt), *n. Chem.* a hydrate in which there are two molecules of the compound for each molecule of water. —**hem′i·hy′drat·ed,** *adj.*

hem·i·me·tab·o·lous (hem′ē mi tab′ə ləs), *adj. Entomol.* undergoing incomplete metamorphosis. Also, **hem·i·met·a·bol·ic** (hem′ē met′ə bol′ik). —**hem′i·me·tab′o·lism, hem′i·me·tab′o·ly,** *n.*

hem·i·mor·phic (hem′i môr′fik), *adj.* (of a crystal) having the two ends of an axis unlike in their planes or modifications; lacking a center of symmetry. —**hem′i·mor′phism, hem′i·mor′phy,** *n.*

hem·i·mor·phite (hem′i môr′fīt), *n.* a mineral, $Zn_4(OH)_2Si_2O_7 \cdot H_2O$; calamine. [HEMIMORPH(IC) + -ITE[1]]

he·min (hē′min), *n. Biochem.* the typical, reddish-brown crystals, of microscopic size, $C_{34}H_{32}N_4O_4FeCl$, resulting when a sodium chloride crystal, a drop of glacial acetic acid, and some blood are heated on a slide: used to indicate the presence of blood. Also, **haemin.**

Hem·ing·way (hem′ing wā′), *n.* **Ernest (Miller),** 1899–1961, U.S. novelist, short-story writer, and journalist: Nobel prize 1954.

hem·i·ple·gi·a (hem′i plē′jē ə, -jə), *n. Pathol.* paralysis of one side of the body, resulting from a disease of the brain or of the spinal cord. [< NL < MGk] —**hem·i·ple·gic** (hem′i-plē′jik, -plej′ik), *adj., n.*

He·mip·ter·a (hi mip′tər ə), *n.* the order comprising the hemipterous insects, esp. the true bugs. [< NL (neut. pl.)]

he·mip·ter·ous (hi mip′tər əs), *adj.* **1.** belonging or pertaining to the *Hemiptera,* an order of insects having forewings that are thickened and leathery at the base and membranous at the apex, comprising the true bugs. **2.** belonging or pertaining to the order *Hemiptera,* in some classifications comprising the heteropterous and homopterous insects. [< NL *Hemipter(a)* (neut. pl.) name of the order (see HEMI-, -PTER) + -OUS]

hem·i·sphere (hem′i sfēr′), *n.* **1.** half of the terrestrial globe or celestial sphere. **2.** a map or projection representing either half. **3.** the half of a sphere. **4.** *Anat.* either of the lateral halves of the cerebrum or cerebellum. [< L *hēmisphaer(ium)* < Gk *hēmisphaírion;* r. ME *emysperie* < OF *emispere*]

hem·i·spher·ic (hem′i sfer′ik), *adj.* **1.** of or pertaining to a hemisphere. **2.** having the form of a hemisphere. Also, **hem′i·spher′i·cal.** —**hem′i·spher′i·cal·ly,** *adv.*

hem·i·spher·oid (hem′i sfēr′oid), *n.* half of a spheroid. —**hem′i·spher·oi′dal,** *adj.*

hem·i·stitch (hem′i stik′), *n. Pros.* **1.** the exact or approximate half of a stitch, or poetic verse or line, esp. as divided by a caesura or the like. **2.** an incomplete line, or a line of less than the usual length. [< LL *hēmistich(ium)* < Gk *hēmistíchion* a half-verse] —**he·mis·ti·chal** (hə mis′ti kəl, hem′i stik′əl), *adj.*

hem·i·trope (hem′i trōp′), *Crystall.* —*n.* **1.** twin (def. 4). —*adj.* **2.** twin (def. 11). [< F] —**hem·i·trop·ic** (hem′i trop′ik), *adj.* —**hem′i·tro′pism, he·mit·ro·py** (hē mi′trə pē), *n.*

hem·i·zy·gote (hem′i zī′gōt, -zig′ōt), *n. Genetics.* an individual having only one of a given pair of genes. —**hem·i·zy·gous** (hem′i zī′gəs), *adj.*

hem·line (hem′līn′), *n.* **1.** the bottom edge of a coat, dress, skirt, etc. **2.** the level of this edge.

hem·lock (hem′lok′), *n.* **1.** *Chiefly Brit.* a poisonous, umbelliferous herb, *Conium maculatum,* having spotted stems, finely divided leaves, and small white flowers, used medicinally as a powerful sedative. **2.** a poisonous drink made from this herb. **3.** any of various other apiaceous herbs, esp. of the genus *Cicuta,* as the water hemlock. **4.** Also called **hem′lock spruce′.** any of several coniferous trees of the genus *Tsuga,* native to the U.S., characterized by its pyramidal manner of growth. Cf. **eastern hemlock, western hemlock.** **5.** the soft, light wood of a hemlock tree. [ME *hemlok, humlok,* OE *hymlic, hemlic;* ? akin to OE *hymele* hop plant]

hemo-, a learned borrowing from Greek meaning "blood," used in the formation of compound words: *hemocyte.* Also, **hem-, haem-, haemo-.** Cf. **hema-, haema-, haemat-,**

haemato-, hemat-, hemato-. [< NL, comb. form repr. Gk *haima* blood]

he·mo·blast (hē′mə blast′, hem′ə-), *n.* *Anat.* hematoblast.

he·mo·cyte (hē′mə sīt′, hem′ə-), *n.* a blood cell. Also, **hematocyte, haemocyte, haematocyte.**

he·mo·cy·tom·e·ter (hē′mō sī tom′i tər, hem′ō-), *n.* *Med.* an instrument for counting blood cells. Also, **hemacytometer.**

he·mo·di·a·lyz·er (hē′mō dī′ə lī′zər, hem′ō-), *n.* *Med.* See **kidney machine.**

he·mo·flag·el·late (hē′mə flaj′ə lāt′, hem′ə-), *n.* a flagellate that is parasitic in the blood.

he·mo·glo·bin (hē′mə glō′bin, hem′ə-; hē′mə glō′bin, hem′ə-), *n.* *Biochem.* the protein coloring matter of the red blood corpuscles, serving to convey oxygen to the tissues and occurring in reduced form **(reduced hemoglobin)** in venous blood and in combination with oxygen **(oxyhemoglobin)** in arterial blood. *Symbol:* Hb Also, **haemoglobin.** [shortening of *hematoglobulin*] —**he′mo·glo′bic, he′mo·glo′bin·ous,** *adj.*

he·mo·glo·bi·nu·ri·a (hē′mə glō′bi no͝or′ē ə, -nyo͝or′-, hem′ə-), *n.* *Pathol.* the presence of hemoglobin pigment in the urine. —**he′mo·glo′bi·nu′ric,** *adj.*

he·mol·y·sin (hi mol′i sin, hē′mə lī′-, hem′ə-), *n.* *Immunol.* a substance, as an antibody, that in cooperation with complement causes dissolution of erythrocytes. Also, **haemolysin.**

he·mol·y·sis (hi mol′i sis), *n.* *Immunol.* the breaking down of the erythrocytes with liberation of hemoglobin. Also, **haemolysis.** —**he·mo·lyt·ic** (hē′mə lit′ik, hem′ə-), *adj.*

he·mo·phile (hē′mə fīl′, hem′ə-), *n.* **1.** *Pathol.* hemophiliac. **2.** a hemophilic bacterium. —*adj.* **3.** hemophilic.

he·mo·phil·i·a (hē′mə fil′ē ə, -fēl′yə, hem′ə-), *n.* *Pathol.* an abnormal condition of males inherited through the mother, characterized by a tendency to bleed excessively: caused by inadequate coagulation of the blood. Also, **haemophilia.** [< NL] —**he·mo·phil·i·oid** (hē′mə fil′ē oid′, hem′ə-), *adj.*

he·mo·phil·i·ac (hē′mə fil′ē ak′, -fē′lē-, hem′ə-), *n.* *Pathol.* a person having hemophilia. Also, **haemophiliac, hemophile.**

he·mo·phil·ic (hē′mə fil′ik, hem′ə-), *adj.* **1.** *Pathol.* affected by hemophilia. **2.** *Biol.* (of bacteria) developing best in a culture containing blood, or in blood itself. Also, **haemophilic.**

hem·or·rhage (hem′ər ij, hem′rij), *n., v.,* **-rhaged, -rhag·ing.** —*n.* **1.** a discharge of blood, as from a ruptured blood vessel. —*v.i.* **2.** to bleed profusely. Also, **haemorrhage.** [< L *haemorrhag(ia)* < Gk *haimorrhagía*] —**hem·or·rhag·ic** (hem′ə raj′ik), *adj.*

hem·or·rhoid (hem′ə roid′, hem′roid), *n.* Usually, **hemorrhoids.** *Pathol.* a venous dilatation inside the anal sphincter of the rectum and beneath the mucous membrane, or outside the anal sphincter and beneath the surface of the skin. Also, **haemorrhoid.** Also called **pile.** [< L *haemorrhoida* < Gk *haimorroïda* (adj.) discharging blood] —**hem′or·rhoi′dal,** *adj.*

hem·or·rhoid·ec·to·my (hem′ə roi dek′tə mē), *n., pl.* **-mies.** *Surg.* an operation for removal of hemorrhoids.

he·mo·sid·er·in (hē′mō sid′ər in, hem′ō-), *n.* *Biochem.* a yellowish-brown pigment, derived chiefly from hemoglobin, and found in body tissue and phagocytes, esp. as the result of disorders in iron metabolism and the breakdown of red blood cells.

he·mos·ta·sis (hi mos′tə sis, hē′mə stā′sis, hem′ə-), *n.* *Med.* **1.** the stoppage of bleeding. **2.** the stoppage of the circulation of blood in a part of the body. **3.** stagnation of blood in a part. Also, **haemostasis, he·mo·sta·sia** (hē′mə-stā′zhə, -zhē ə, -zē ə, hem′ə-). [< NL]

he·mo·stat (hē′mə stat′, hem′ə-), *n.* *Med.* an instrument or agent used to compress or treat bleeding vessels in order to arrest hemorrhage. Also, **haemostat.** [shortened form of HEMOSTATIC]

he·mo·stat·ic (hē′mə stat′ik, hem′ə-), *adj.* *Med.* **1.** arresting hemorrhage, as a drug; styptic. —*n.* **2.** a hemostatic agent or substance. Also, **haemostatic.**

hemp (hemp), *n.* **1.** a tall, annual, moraceous herb, *Cannabis sativa,* native to Asia, but cultivated in many parts of the world. **2.** the tough fiber of this plant, used for making rope, coarse fabric, etc. **3.** an East Indian variety of the hemp *Cannabis sativa indica* (or *Cannabis indica*), yielding hashish, bhang, cannabin, etc. **4.** any of various plants resembling the hemp. **5.** any of various fibers similar to hemp. **6.** a narcotic preparation, as bhang, obtained from the Indian hemp. [ME; OE *henep, hænep;* c. G *Hanf,* Gk *kánnabis*] —**hemp′like′,** *adj.*

hemp′ ag′rimony, a European, composite herb, *Eupatorium cannabinum,* having dull purplish flowers.

hemp·en (hem′pən), *adj.* **1.** of or pertaining to hemp. **2.** made of hemp. **3.** resembling hemp. [ME *hempyn*]

hemp′ net′tle, **1.** a coarse, labiate weed, *Galeopsis Tetrahit,* resembling the hemp in appearance and having bristly hairs like the nettle. **2.** any other plant of the genus *Galeopsis.*

Hemp·stead (hemp′sted, hem′-), *n.* a village on W Long Island, in SE New York. 39,411 (1970).

hemp·y (hem′pē), *adj.* *Scot.* mischievous; often in trouble for mischief. [HEMP + -Y[1]; so called because a person often in trouble was thought fit to be hanged]

hem·stitch (hem′stich′), *v.t.* **1.** to hem along a line from which threads have been drawn out, stitching the cross threads into a series of little groups. —*n.* **2.** the stitch used or the needlework done in hemstitching.

hen (hen), *n.* **1.** the female of the domestic fowl. **2.** the female of any bird, esp. of a gallinaceous bird. **3.** *Informal.* a woman, esp. a busybody or gossip. [ME; OE *hen(n)* (cf. OE *hana* cock); c. G *Henne;* akin to L *canere* to sing] —**hen′like′,** *adj.*

hen·bane (hen′bān′), *n.* an Old World, solanaceous herb, *Hyoscyamus niger,* having sticky, hairy foliage of a disagreeable odor, and possessing narcotic and poisonous properties esp. destructive to domestic fowls. [ME]

hence (hens), *adv.* **1.** as an inference from this fact; for this reason; therefore. **2.** from this time; from now: *They will leave a month hence.* **3.** *Rare.* **a.** henceforth; from this time on. **b.** of this moment or the present. **4.** *Archaic.* **a.** from this place; from here; away. **b.** from this world or from the living. **5.** *Obs.* from this source or origin. —*interj.* **6.** *Obs.* depart (usually used imperatively). [ME *hens, hennes* = *henne* (OE *heonan*) + *-es* -s[1]]

hence·forth (hens′fōrth′, -fôrth′; hens′fōrth′, -fôrth′), *adv.* from now on; from this point forward. Also, **hence·for·ward** (hens′fōr′wərd, -fôr′-; hens′fōr′wərd; -fôr′-). [ME]

hench·man (hench′mən), *n., pl.* **-men.** **1.** an unscrupulous supporter or adherent of a political figure or cause, esp. one motivated by the hope of personal gain: *Hitler and his henchmen.* **2.** a trusted attendant, supporter, or follower. **3.** an associate in crime. **4.** *Obs.* a squire or page. [ME *henchman, hensh-, henks-, hengest-,* OE *hengest* stallion (c. G *Hengst*) + *man* MAN[1]]

hendeca-, a learned borrowing from Greek meaning "eleven," used in the formation of compound words: *hendecasyllable.* [comb. form repr. Gk *héndeka* eleven = *hen-* one (neut. of *heís*) + *déka* TEN]

hen·dec·a·gon (hen dek′ə gon′), *n.* a polygon having 11 angles and 11 sides.

hen·dec·a·he·dron (hen dek′ə hē′drən, hen′dek-), *n., pl.* **-drons, -dra** (-drə). a solid figure having 11 faces.

hen·dec·a·syl·la·ble (hen dek′ə sil′ə bəl, hen′dek ə-sil′-), *n.* a word or line of verse of 11 syllables. [< L *hendecasyllab(us)* < Gk *hendekasýllab(os)*] —**hen·dec·a·syl·lab·ic** (hen dek′ə si lab′ik), *adj., n.*

hen·di·a·dys (hen dī′ə dis), *n.* *Rhet.* a figure in which a complex idea is expressed by two words connected by a copulative conjunction: "to look with eyes and envy" instead of "with envious eyes." [< ML; alter. of Gk phrase *hèn dià dyoîn* one through two, one by means of two]

Hen·don (hen′dən), *n.* a city in Middlesex, in SE England, NW of London. 151,500 (1961).

Hen·dricks (hen′driks), *n.* **Thomas Andrews,** 1819–1885, vice president of the U.S. 1885.

hen·e·quen (hen′ə kin), *n.* the fiber of an agave, *Agave fourcroydes,* of Yucatan, used for making ropes, coarse fabrics, etc. Also, **hen′e·quin, hen′i·quen.** [< AmerSp *henequén* < native name]

Heng·e·lo (heng′ə lō′), *n.* a city in the E Netherlands. 58,197 (1960).

Hen·gist (heng′gist, hen′jist), *n.* died A.D. 488? chief of the Jutes: with his brother Horsa led the Teutonic invasion of southern Britain c440. Also, **Hen′gest.**

hen·house (hen′hous′), *n., pl.* **-hous·es** (-hou′ziz). a shelter for poultry.

Hen·ley (hen′lē), *n.* **1. William Ernest,** 1849–1903, English poet, critic and editor. **2.** Henley-on-Thames.

Henley-on-Thames (hen′lē on temz′, -ôn-), *n.* a city in SE Oxfordshire, in S England: annual rowing regatta. 9131 (1961). Also called **Henley.**

hen·na (hen′ə), *n., v.,* **-naed, -na·ing.** **1.** a shrub or small tree, *Lawsonia inermis,* of Asia and the Levant. **2.** a reddish-orange dye or cosmetic made from the leaves of this plant, used esp. as a hair tint. **3.** a color midway between red-brown and orange-brown. —*v.t.* **4.** to tint or dye with henna. [< Ar *hinnā'*]

Hen·ne·pin (hen′ə pin; *Fr.* en paN′), *n.* **Louis** (lwē), 1640?–1701?, Belgian Roman Catholic missionary and explorer in America.

hen·ner·y (hen′ə rē), *n., pl.* **-ner·ies.** a place where fowls are kept.

hen·o·the·ism (hen′ə thē iz′əm), *n.* the worship of a particular god without disbelieving in the existence of others. [< Gk *heno-,* comb. form of *hén* one (neut. of *heís*) + THEISM] —**hen′o·the′ist,** *n.* —**hen′o·the·is′tic,** *adj.*

hen·peck (hen′pek′), *v.t.* to nag, scold, or regularly find fault with (one's husband) in an effort to dominate. [back formation from *henpecked*]

hen·ry (hen′rē), *n., pl.* **-ries, -rys.** *Elect.* the meter-kilogram-second unit of inductance, equal to the inductance of a circuit in which an electromotive force of one volt is produced by a current in the circuit that varies at the rate of one ampere per second. *Abbr.:* H [named after Joseph HENRY]

Hen·ry (hen′rē), *n.* **1. Joseph,** 1797–1878, U.S. physicist. **2. O.** See **O. Henry.** **3. Patrick,** 1736–99, American patriot, orator, and statesman. **4. Cape,** a cape in SE Virginia at the mouth of the Chesapeake Bay. **5. Fort.** See **Fort Henry.**

Henry I, **1.** ("*Beauclerc*") 1068–1135, king of England 1100–35 (son of William the Conqueror). **2.** 1008–60, king of France 1031–60.

Henry II, **1.** ("*Curtmantle*") 1133–89, king of England 1154–89: first king of the Plantagenet line (grandson of Henry I of England). **2.** 1519–59, king of France 1547–59 (son of Francis I).

Henry III, **1.** 1207–72, king of England 1216–72 (son of John, king of England). **2.** 1551–89, king of France 1574–1589 (son of Henry II of France).

Henry IV, **1.** 1050–1106, Holy Roman Emperor and King of the Germans 1056–1106. **2.** (*Bolingbroke*) ("*Henry of Lancaster*") 1367–1413, king of England 1399–1413 (son of John of Gaunt). **3.** ("*Henry of Navarre*"; "*Henry the Great*") 1553–1610, king of France 1589–1610: first of the French Bourbon kings.

Henry V, 1387–1422, king of England 1413–22 (son of Henry IV, king of England).

Henry VI, 1421–71, king of England 1422–61, 1470–71 (son of Henry V).

Henry VII, (*Henry Tudor*) 1457–1509, king of England 1485–1509: first king of the house of Tudor.

Henry VIII, ("*Defender of the Faith*") 1491–1547, king of England 1509–47 (son of Henry VII).

Hen′ry of Por′tugal, ("*the Navigator*") 1394–1460, prince of Portugal: sponsor of geographic explorations.

Hens·lowe (henz′lō), *n.* **Philip,** died 1616, English theater manager.
hent (hent), *v.,* **hent, hent·ing,** *n.* —*v.t.* **1.** *Archaic.* to grasp; apprehend. —*n.* **2.** *Obs.* intent; purpose. [ME *hent(en),* OE *hentan*]
hep[1] (hep), *adj. Slang.* hip[4].
hep[2] (hut, hup, hep), *interj.* one (used in counting cadence while marching). [?]
hep·a·rin (hep′ə rin), *n.* **1.** *Biochem.* a mucopolysaccharide acid occurring in various tissues, esp. the liver. **2.** *Pharm.* a commercial form of this substance that when injected into the blood prevents coagulation: used chiefly in the treatment of thrombosis. [< Gk *hêpar* the liver + -IN[2]] —**hep′a·rin·oid′,** *adj.*
hep·a·rin·ize (hep′ər ə nīz′), *v.t.,* **-ized, -iz·ing.** *Biochem.* to treat blood or plasma with heparin so as to prevent clotting. —**hep′a·rin·i·za′tion,** *n.*
hepat-, var. of **hepato-** before a vowel.
he·pat·ic (hi pat′ik), *adj.* **1.** of or pertaining to the liver. **2.** acting on the liver, as a medicine. **3.** liver-colored; dark reddish-brown. **4.** *Bot.* belonging or pertaining to the liverworts. —*n.* **5.** a medicine acting on the liver. **6.** a liverwort. [< L *hēpatic(us)* < Gk *hēpatik(ós)*]
he·pat·i·ca (hi pat′i kə), *n.* any ranunculaceous herb of the genus *Hepatica,* having delicate purplish, pink, or white flowers. [< ML: liverwort, n. use of fem. of L *hēpaticus* HEPATIC]
hep·a·ti·tis (hep′ə tī′tis), *n. Pathol.* inflammation of the liver. [< Gk]
hepato-, a learned borrowing from Greek meaning "liver," used in the formation of compound words. Also, *esp. before a vowel,* **hepat-.** [comb. form repr. Gk *hēpat-,* s. of *hêpar* liver]
hep·cat (hep′kat′), *n. Jazz Slang.* an enthusiast for jazz, esp. swing.
He·phaes·tus (hi fes′təs), *n.* the ancient Greek god of fire, metalworking, and handicrafts, identified by the Romans with Vulcan. Also, **He·phais·tos** (hi fī′stəs).
Heph·zi·bah (hef′zi bə), *n.* **1.** the wife of Hezekiah and the mother of Manasseh. II Kings 21:1. **2.** a name applied to Jerusalem, possibly as denoting its prophesied restoration to the Jews after the Captivity. Isa. 62:4. Cf. **Beulah.**

Hepplewhite chair

Hep·ple·white (hep′əl hwīt′, -wīt′), *n.* **1. George,** died 1786, English furniture designer and cabinetmaker. —*adj.* **2.** noting the style prevailing in English furniture c1780–c95, as illustrated in designs published by the firm of George Hepplewhite in 1788, reflecting Adam and Louis XVI influences.
hepta-, a learned borrowing from Greek meaning "seven," used in the formation of compound words: *heptahedron.* [< Gk, comb. form of *heptá* seven; c. L *septem*]
hep·ta·chlor (hep′tə klōr′, -klôr′), *n. Chem.* a waxy, water-insoluble solid, $C_{10}H_5Cl_7$, used as an insecticide.
hep·ta·chord (hep′tə kôrd′), *n.* **1.** a musical scale of seven notes. **2.** an ancient Greek stringed instrument. [< Gk *heptáchord(os)*]
hep·tad (hep′tad), *n.* **1.** the number seven. **2.** a group of seven. **3.** *Chem.* an element, atom, or group having a valence of seven. [< Gk *heptad-* (s. of *heptás*)]
hep·ta·gon (hep′tə gon′), *n.* a polygon having seven angles and seven sides. [< Gk *heptágōn(os)* seven-cornered]

Heptagon (Regular)

hep·tag·o·nal (hep tag′ə nəl), *adj.* having seven sides or angles.
hep·ta·he·dron (hep′tə hē′drən), *n., pl.* **-drons, -dra** (-drə). a solid figure having seven faces. —**hep′ta·he′dral, hep′ta·he′dri·cal,** *adj.*
hep·ta·hy·drate (hep′tə hī′drāt), *n. Chem.* a hydrate that contains seven molecules of water, as magnesium sulfate, $MgSO_4 \cdot 7H_2O$. —**hep′ta·hy′drat·ed,** *adj.*
hep·tam·er·ous (hep tam′ər əs), *adj.* **1.** consisting of or divided into seven parts. **2.** *Bot.* (of flowers) having seven members in each whorl.
hep·tam·e·ter (hep tam′i tər), *n. Pros.* a verse of seven metrical feet. [< ML *heptametr(um)* < Gk *heptámetron* a verse of seven feet] —**hep·ta·met·ri·cal** (hep′tə me′tri kəl), *adj.*
hep·tane (hep′tān), *n. Chem.* any of nine isomeric hydrocarbons, C_7H_{16}, of the alkane series, some of which are obtained from petroleum: used in fuels, as solvents, and as chemical intermediates.
hep·tan·gu·lar (hep taŋ′gyə lər), *adj.* having seven angles.
hep·tar·chy (hep′tär kē), *n., pl.* **-chies.** (*often cap.*) the seven principal concurrent early English kingdoms. —**hep′tarch,** *n.* —**hep·tar′chic, hep·tar′chi·cal, hep·tar′chal,** *adj.*
hep·ta·stich (hep′tə stik′), *n. Pros.* a strophe, stanza, or poem of seven lines or verses.
hep·ta·syl·la·ble (hep′tə sil′ə bəl), *n.* a word or line of seven syllables. —**hep·ta·syl·lab·ic** (hep′tə si lab′ik), *adj.*
Hep·ta·teuch (hep′tə to͞ok′, -tyo͞ok′), *n.* the first seven books of the Old Testament. [< LL *Heptateuch(os)* < LGk = Gk *hepta-* HEPTA- + *teûchos* a book]
hep·ta·va·lent (hep′tə vā′lənt), *adj. Chem.* septivalent.
her (hûr; *unstressed* hər, ər), *pron.* **1.** the objective case of **she,** both as direct and indirect object: *We saw her this morning. Give it to her.* **2.** the possessive case of **she** (used as an attributive adjective): *Her coat is the one on the chair. I'm sorry about her leaving. Did you mind her doing that?* Cf. **hers. 3.** the dative case of **she:** *I gave her the book.* [ME *her(e),* OE *hire,* gen. and dat. of *hēo* she (fem. of *hē* HE[1])] —**Usage.** See **me.**
her., **1.** heraldic. **2.** heraldry.
He·ra (hēr′ə), *n.* the ancient Greek queen of heaven, a daughter of Cronus and Rhea and the wife and sister of Zeus, identified by the Romans with Juno. Also, **Here.**
Her·a·cle·a (her′ə klē′ə), *n.* an ancient city in S Italy, near the Gulf of Taranto: Roman defeat 280 B.C.
Her·a·cles (her′ə klēz′), *n.* Hercules (def. 1). Also, **Her′a·kles′.** [< Gk *Hēraklês,* lit., having the glory of Hera = *Hḗra* HERA + *kléos* glory, fame] —**Her′a·cle′an, Her′a·kle′an,** *adj.*
Her·a·clid (her′ə klid), *n., pl.* **Her·a·cli·dae** (her′ə klī′dē). a person claiming descent from Hercules, esp. one of the Dorian aristocracy of Sparta. Also, **Heraklid.** —**Her·a·cli·dan** (her′ə klīd′ən), *adj.*
Her·a·cli·tus (her′ə klī′təs), *n.* ("*the Obscure*") c540–c470 B.C., Greek philosopher. —**Her·a·cli·te·an** (her′ə klī′tē ən, -klī tē′-), **Her·a·clit·ic** (her′ə klit′ik), *adj., n.* —**Her·a·cli′te·an·ism,** *n.*
Her·a·cli·us (her′ə klī′əs, hi rak′lē əs), *n.* A.D. 575?–641, Byzantine emperor 610–641.
He·ra·klei·on (ē rä′klē ôn), *n.* Greek name of **Candia.**
Her·a·klid (her′ə klid), *n., pl.* **Her·a·kli·dae** (her′ə klī′dē). Heraclid. —**Her·a·kli·dan** (her′ə klīd′ən), *adj.*
her·ald (her′əld), *n.* **1.** (formerly) a royal or official messenger, esp. one representing a monarch in an ambassadorial capacity during wartime. **2.** any messenger. **3.** a person or thing that precedes or comes before; forerunner; harbinger: *The returning swallows are heralds of spring.* **4.** a person or thing that proclaims or announces: *A good newspaper should be a herald of truth.* **5.** (in the Middle Ages) an officer who arranged tournaments, announced challenges, marshaled combatants, etc. —*v.t.* **6.** to give tidings of; announce; proclaim: *a publicity campaign to herald a new film.* **7.** to usher in. [ME *herauld* < OF *heraut, hirauz* < Frankish **heriwald* army chief]
he·ral·dic (he ral′dik), *adj.* of, pertaining to, or characteristic of heraldry or heralds: *heraldic history; a heraldic device.* —**he·ral′di·cal·ly,** *adv.*
her·ald·ry (her′əl drē), *n., pl.* **-ries. 1.** the science of armorial bearings. **2.** the art of blazoning armorial bearings, of settling the rights of persons to bear arms or to use certain bearings, of tracing and recording genealogies, of recording honors, and of deciding questions of precedence. **3.** the office or duty of a herald. **4.** a coat of arms; armorial bearings. **5.** heraldic symbolism. **6.** heraldic pomp or ceremony. —**her′ald·ist,** *n.*
Her′alds′ Col′lege, a royal corporation in England, instituted in 1483, occupied chiefly with armorial bearings, genealogies, honors, and precedence. Also called **College of Arms.**
He·rat (he rät′), *n.* a city in NW Afghanistan. 100,000 (est. 1964).
herb (ûrb, hûrb), *n.* **1.** a flowering plant whose stem above ground does not become woody. **2.** such a plant when valued for its medicinal properties, flavor, scent, or the like. **3.** *Archaic.* herbage. [ME *herbe* < OF *erbe, herbe* < L *herb(a)*] —**herb′less,** *adj.* —**herb′like′,** *adj.*
her·ba·ceous (hûr bā′shəs, ûr-), *adj.* **1.** of, pertaining to, or characteristic of an herb; herblike. **2.** (of plants or plant parts) not woody. **3.** (of flowers, sepals, etc.) having the texture, color, etc., of an ordinary foliage leaf. [< L *herbāce(us)* grassy, like grass] —**her·ba′ceous·ly,** *adv.*
herb·age (ûr′bij, hûr′-), *n.* **1.** nonwoody vegetation. **2.** the succulent parts, as leaves, of herbaceous plants. **3.** *Brit.* vegetation grazed by animals; pasturage. [< F]
herb·al (hûr′bəl, ûr′-), *adj.* **1.** of, pertaining to, or consisting of herbs. —*n.* **2.** a treatise on herbs or plants. **3.** a herbarium. [< ML *herbāl(is)* of, belonging to grass or herbs]
herb·al·ist (hûr′bə list, ûr′-), *n.* **1.** a person who collects or deals in herbs, esp. medicinal herbs. **2.** See **herb doctor. 3.** (formerly) a botanist.
her·bar·i·um (hûr bâr′ē əm), *n., pl.* **-bar·i·ums, -bar·i·a** (-bâr′ē ə). **1.** a collection of dried plants systematically arranged. **2.** a room or building in which such a collection is kept. [< LL] —**her·bar′i·al,** *adj.*
Her·bart (heʀ′bärt), *n.* **Jo·hann Frie·drich** (yō′hän frē′drikh), 1776–1841, German philosopher and educator.
herb′ ben′net, a perennial, European, rosaceous herb, *Geum urbanum,* having yellow flowers and an aromatic, tonic, and astringent root.
herb′ doc′tor, a person who heals by the use of herbs. Also called **herbalist.**
Her·bert (hûr′bərt), *n.* **1. George,** 1593–1633, English clergyman and poet. **2. Victor,** 1859–1924, U.S. composer and orchestra conductor, born in Ireland.
herb·i·cide (ûr′bi sīd′, hûr′-), *n.* a substance or preparation for killing plants, esp. weeds. —**her′bi·cid′al,** *adj.*
her·bi·vore (hûr′bə vōr′, -vôr′), *n.* a herbivorous animal, esp. any member of the former group *Herbivora,* comprising the hoofed mammals. [< NL *herbivor(a)* (neut. pl.)]
her·biv·o·rous (hûr biv′ər əs), *adj.* feeding on plants. [< NL *herbivor(us)*] —**her·bi·vor·i·ty** (hûr′bə vôr′i tē, -vor′-), *n.*
herb′ Par′is, *pl.* **herbs Paris.** a European, liliaceous herb, *Paris quadrifolia,* formerly used in medicine. [< ML *herba paris* < ?]
herb′ Rob′ert, *pl.* **herbs Robert.** a wild geranium, *Geranium robertianum,* having reddish-purple flowers. [< ML *herba Roberti* Robert's herb < ?]
herb·y (ûr′bē, hûr′bē), *adj.,* **herb·i·er, herb·i·est. 1.** abounding in herbs or grass. **2.** of, pertaining to, or characteristic of an herb or herbs in taste or appearance.
Her·ce·go·vi·na (heʀ′tse gô′vi nä), *n.* Serbo-Croatian name of **Herzegovina.**
Her·cu·la·ne·um (hûr′kyə lā′nē əm), *n.* an ancient city in SW Italy, on the Bay of Naples: buried along with Pompeii by the eruption of Mount Vesuvius in A.D. 79; partially excavated. —**Her′cu·la′ne·an,** *adj.*
her·cu·le·an (hûr′kyə lē′ən, hûr kyo͞o′lē ən), *adj.* **1.** requiring the strength of a Hercules; very hard to perform: *Digging the tunnel was a herculean task.* **2.** having enormous strength, courage, or size. **3.** (*cap.*) of or pertaining to Hercules. [< L *Hercule(us)* of, belonging to HERCULES + -AN]
Her·cu·les (hûr′kyə lēz′), *n., gen.* **-cu·lis** (-kyə lis) for 2. **1.** Also, **Heracles, Herakles.** *Class. Myth.* a celebrated hero, the son of Zeus and Alcmene, possessing exceptional strength. Cf. **labors of Hercules. 2.** *Astron.* a northern constellation, between Lyra and Corona Borealis. [< L]
Her·cu·les′-club (hûr′kyə lēz klub′), *n.* **1.** a prickly,

rutaceous tree, *Zanthoxylum Clava-Herculis*, having a medicinal bark and berries. **2.** Also called **angelica tree.** a prickly, araliaceous shrub, *Aralia spinosa*, having a medicinal bark and root.

Her′cules′ Pil′lars. See **Pillars of Hercules.**

herd[1] (hûrd), *n.* **1.** a number of animals kept, feeding, or traveling together; drove; flock. **2.** *Informal.* a large group of people; crowd; mob: *a herd of autograph seekers.* **3. the herd,** *Disparaging.* the common people; the masses. **—*v.i.*** **4.** to unite or go in a herd; to assemble or associate as a herd. **—*v.t.*** **5.** to form into or as if into a herd: *He herded everyone together to sing folk songs.* [ME; OE *heord;* c. Goth *hairda,* G *Herde*] **—Syn. 1.** See **flock**[1].

herd[2] (hûrd), *n.* **1.** a herdsman (usually used in combination): *a goatherd.* **—*v.t.*** **2.** to tend, drive, or lead (cattle, sheep, etc.). **3.** to conduct or drive (a group of people) to a destination: *The teacher herded the children into the classroom.* [ME *herd(e), hirde,* OE *hierde;* c. Goth *hairdeis,* G *Hirt(e);* all < E root of HERD[1]]

herd·er (hûr′dər), *n.* a person in charge of a herd of cattle or a flock of sheep; herdsman.

Her·der (heʀ′dəʀ), *n.* **Jo·hann Gott·fried von** (yō′hän gôt′fʀēt fən), 1744–1803, German philosopher and poet.

he·rdic (hûr′dik), *n.* a low-hung carriage with two or four wheels, having the entrance at the back and the seats at the sides. [named after P. *Herdic,* 19th-century American, the inventor]

herd′ in′stinct, the impulse or tendency toward clustering or acting in a group, esp. the presumed instinct toward or need for gregariousness and conformity.

herd·man (hûrd′mən), *n., pl.* **-men.** *Obs.* herdsman (def. 1). [ME *hird-man,* OE *hyrdemann*]

herds·man (hûrdz′mən), *n., pl.* **-men. 1.** a herder. **2.** (*cap.*) *Astron.* the constellation Boötes. [alter. of earlier HERDMAN]

here (hēr), *adv.* **1.** in this place; in this spot or locality (opposed to *there*): *Put the pen here.* **2.** to or toward this place; hither: *Come here.* **3.** at this point; at this juncture: *Here the speaker paused.* **4.** (used to call attention to some person or thing present, or to what the speaker has, offers, brings, or discovers): *Here is your paycheck. My friend here knows the circumstances.* **5.** present (used to answer roll call). **6.** in the present life or existence (often fol. by *below*): *Man wants but little here below.* **7.** under consideration, in this instance or case: *The matter here is of grave concern.* **8. here and now,** at the present moment; without delay; immediately. **9. here and there, a.** in this place and in that; at various times or places. **b.** hither and thither. **10. here goes!** *Informal.* (expressing one's resolution in beginning a bold or unpleasant action) here I go. **11. here's to,** (a formula in offering a toast) hail to; salutations to: *Here's to a long and happy life!* **12. neither here nor there,** without relevance or importance; immaterial. **—*n.*** **13.** this place: *It's only a short distance from here.* **14.** this world; this life; the present. **—*interj.*** **15.** (often used to command attention, give comfort, etc.) now; all right: *Here, let me try it. Here, don't cry.* [ME; OE *hēr;* c. G *hier,* OIcel, Goth *hēr*]

—Usage. It is generally considered nonstandard to place HERE, for emphasis, in an adjectival position between a demonstrative adjective and a noun, as in *This here book is the one you're looking for.*

He·re (hēr′ē), *n.* Hera.

here-, a word element meaning "this (place)," "this (time)," etc., used in combination with certain adverbs and prepositions: *hereafter.* [ME *her-,* OE *hēr-;* special use of HERE]

here·a·bout (hēr′ə bout′), *adv.* about this place; in this neighborhood. Also, **here′a·bouts′.** [ME]

here·af·ter (hēr af′tər, -äf′-), *adv.* **1.** after this in time or order; at some future time; from now on. **2.** in the world to come. **—*n.*** **3.** a life or existence after death; the future beyond mortal existence. **4.** time to come; the future. [ME; OE *hērǣfter*]

here·at (hēr at′), *adv.* **1.** at this time; when this happened. **2.** because of this. [ME *here at*]

here·by (hēr bī′, hēr′bī′), *adv.* **1.** by this, or the present, declaration, document, etc.; by means of this; as a result of this: *I hereby resign my office.* **2.** *Obs.* nearby. [ME *here by*]

he·re·des (hi rē′dēz), *n.* pl. of **heres.**

he·red·i·ta·ble (hə red′i tə bəl), *adj.* heritable. [< MF < LL *hērēdit(āre)* (to) inherit < L *hērēd-* (s. of *hērēs*) HEIR; see -ABLE] **—he·red′i·ta·bil′i·ty,** *n.* **—he·red′i·ta·bly,** *adv.*

her·e·dit·a·ment (her′i dit′ə mənt), *n.* *Law.* any inheritable estate or interest in property. [< ML *hērēditāment(um)* < LL *hērēditā(re)*]

he·red·i·tar·y (hə red′i ter′ē), *adj.* **1.** passing, or capable of passing, genetically from parents to offspring: *hereditary traits.* **2.** of or pertaining to inheritance or heredity: *a hereditary title.* **3.** existing by reason of feeling, opinions, or prejudices held by predecessors: *a hereditary enemy.* **4.** *Law.* **a.** transmitted or transmissible in the line of descent by force of law. **b.** holding title, rights, etc., by inheritance. [< L *hērēditāri(us)* relating to inheritance] **—he·red·i·tar·i·ly** (hi red′i târ′ə lē, -red′i ter′-), *adv.* **—he·red′i·tar′i·ness,** *n.*

he·red·i·ty (hə red′i tē), *n., pl.* **-ties.** *Biol.* **1.** the transmission of genetic characters from parents to offspring, dependent upon the segregation and recombination of genes during meiosis and fertilization. **2.** the genetic characters so transmitted. [< MF *heredite* < L *hērēditāt-* (s. of *hērēditās*) inheritance = *hērēd-* (s. of *hērēs*) HEIR + *-itāt-* -ITY]

Her·e·ford (hûr′fərd, her′ə- *for 1;* her′ə fərd *for 2, 3*), *n.* **1.** one of an English breed of red beef cattle having a white face and white body markings. **2.** a city in and the county seat of Herefordshire, in W England: cathedral. 40,431 (1961). **3.** Herefordshire.

Her·e·ford·shire (her′ə fərd shēr′, -shər), *n.* a county in W England. 130,919 (1961); 842 sq. mi. *Co. seat:* Hereford. Also called **Hereford.**

here·in (hēr in′), *adv.* **1.** in or into this place. **2.** in this fact, circumstance, etc.; in view of this. [ME; OE *hērinne*]

here·in·af·ter (hēr′in af′tər, -äf′-), *adv.* afterward in this document, statement, etc.

here·in·be·fore (hēr′in bi fōr′, -fôr′), *adv.* before in this document, statement, etc.

here·in·to (hēr in′tōō), *adv.* **1.** into this place. **2.** into this matter or affair.

here·of (hēr uv′, -ov′), *adv.* **1.** of this: *upon the receipt hereof.* **2.** concerning this: *more hereof later.* [ME *her of,* OE *hereof*]

here·on (hēr on′, -ôn′), *adv.* hereupon. [ME *her on,* OE *heron*]

he·res (hēr′ēz), *n., pl.* **he·re·des** (hi rē′dēz). *Civil Law.* an heir. Also, **haeres.** [< L: HEIR]

here's (hērz), contraction of *here is.*

he·re·si·arch (hə rē′zē ärk′, -sē-, her′ə-), *n.* a leader in heresy. [< LL *haeresiarch(a)* < Gk *hairesiárch(ēs)*]

her·e·sy (her′i sē), *n., pl.* **-sies. 1.** religious opinion or doctrine at variance with the orthodox or accepted doctrine. **2.** the maintaining of such an opinion or doctrine. **3.** *Rom. Cath. Ch.* the willful and persistent rejection of any article of faith by a baptized member of the church. **4.** any belief or theory that is strongly at variance with established beliefs, mores, etc. [ME *heresie* < OF *eresie* < L *haeresis:* school of thought, sect < Gk *hairesis,* lit., act of choosing, cf. *haireîn* to choose]

her·e·tic (*n.* her′i tik; *adj.* her′i tik, hə ret′ik), *n.* **1.** a professed believer who maintains religious opinions contrary to those of his church. **2.** *Rom. Cath. Ch.* a baptized Roman Catholic who willfully and persistently rejects any article of faith. **3.** anyone who does not conform with an established attitude, doctrine, or principle. **—*adj.*** **4.** heretical. [ME *heretik* < MF *heretique* < eccl. L *haeretic(us)* < Gk *hairetikós* able to choose (LGk: heretical) < *hairet(ós)* that may be taken (verbal adj. of *haireîn*)]

he·ret·i·cal (hə ret′i kəl), *adj.* of, pertaining to, or characteristic of heretics or heresy. [< ML *haereticāl(is)*] **—he·ret′i·cal·ly,** *adv.* **—he·ret′i·cal·ness,** *n.*

here·to (hēr tōō′), *adv.* to this matter, document, subject, etc.; regarding this point: *attached hereto; agreeable hereto.* Also, **here·un·to** (hēr un′tōō, hēr′un tōō′). [ME *herto*]

here·to·fore (hēr′tə fōr′, -fôr′), *adv.* before this time. [ME *heretoforn* = *here-* HERE- + *toforn,* OE *tōforan* (*tō* TO + *foran* before; see FORE[1])]

here·un·der (hēr un′dər), *adv.* **1.** under or below this; subsequent to this. **2.** under authority of this. [ME]

here·up·on (hēr′ə pon′, -pôn′), *adv.* **1.** upon or on this. **2.** immediately following this. [ME *herupon*]

here·with (hēr with′, -wiŧħ′), *adv.* **1.** along with this. **2.** by means of this; hereby. [ME *herwith,* OE *hērwith*]

Her·ges·hei·mer (hûr′gəs hī′mər), *n.* **Joseph,** 1880–1954, U.S. novelist.

her·i·ot (her′ē ət), *n.* *Eng. Law.* a feudal service or tribute due to the lord on the death of a tenant. [ME *heriot, heriet,* OE *heregeate, -geatu, -geatwa* war gear = *here* army + *geatwa* equipment; c. OIcel *gǫtvar* (pl.)]

her·it·a·ble (her′i tə bəl), *adj.* **1.** capable of being inherited; inheritable; hereditary. **2.** capable of inheriting. [ME < MF = *herit(er)* (to) inherit + *-able* -ABLE] **—her′it·a·bil′i·ty,** *n.* **—her′it·a·bly,** *adv.*

her·it·age (her′i tij), *n.* **1.** something that comes or belongs to a person by reason of birth; an inherited portion. **2.** something reserved for one: *the heritage of the righteous.* **3.** *Law.* any property, esp. land, that devolves by right of inheritance. [ME < MF = *herit(er)* (to) inherit + *-age* -AGE; see HEIR] **—Syn. 1.** patrimony, estate. **3.** estate.

her·i·tor (her′i tər), *n.* inheritor. Also, *referring to a woman,* **her·i·tress** (her′i tris). [alter. of ME *heriter* < MF *heritier* < L *hērēditār(ius)* HEREDITARY]

Herm (Upper part of a double herm)

Her·ki·mer (hûr′kə mər), *n.* **Nicholas,** 1728–77, American Revolutionary general.

herl (hûrl), *n.* **1.** a barb, or the barbs, of a feather, used esp. in dressing anglers' flies. **2.** an artificial fly so dressed. [ME; c. MLG *herle, harle,* LG *harl* fiber, hair of flax or hemp. See HARL]

herm (hûrm), *n.* a monument consisting of a four-sided shaft, tapering inward from top to bottom and bearing a head or bust; terminal figure. [< L *herm(a)* < Gk *hermês* statue of Hermes]

her·ma (hûr′mə), *n., pl.* **-mae** (-mē), **-mai** (-mī). herm. **—her·mae·an** (hər mē′ən), *adj.*

her·maph·ro·dite (hûr maf′rə dīt′), *n.* **1.** an individual in which reproductive organs of both sexes are present. **2.** *Biol.* an animal, as an earthworm, or plant having normally both the male and female organs of generation. **3.** a person or thing in which two opposite qualities are combined. **—*adj.*** **4.** of, pertaining to, or characteristic of a hermaphrodite. **5.** combining two opposite qualities. **6.** *Bot.* monoclinous. [< L *hermaphrodīt(us)* < Gk *hermaphróditos* hemaphrodite (so called from the son of Hermes and Aphrodite, HERMAPHRODITUS)] **—her·maph·ro·dit·ic** (hər maf′rə dit′ik), **her·maph′ro·dit′i·cal,** *adj.* **—her·maph′ro·dit′i·cal·ly,** *adv.* **—her·maph·ro·dit·ism,** (hûr maf′rə dī tiz′əm), *n.*

hermaph′rodite brig′, *Naut.* a two-masted sailing vessel, square-rigged on the foremast and fore-and-aft-rigged on the mainmast. Also called **brigantine.**

Hermaphrodite brig

Her·maph·ro·di·tus (hûr maf′rə dī′təs), *n.* *Class. Myth.* a son of Hermes and Aphrodite who became joined with a nymph **(Salmacis)** into a single bisexual person.

her·me·neu·tic (hûr′mə nōō′tik, -nyōō′-), *adj.* of or pertaining to hermeneutics; interpretative; explanatory. Also, **her′me·neu′ti·cal.** [< Gk *hermēneutik(ós)* of, skilled in, interpreting = *hermēneú(ein)* (to) make clear, interpret (*hermēneús* an interpreter < *Hermês* HERMES) + *-tikos* -TIC] —**her′me·neu′ti·cal·ly,** *adv.*

her·me·neu·tics (hûr′mə no͞o′tiks, -nyo͞o′-), *n.* (*construed as sing.*) the science of interpretation, esp. of the Scriptures. [*hermeneutic* < Gk *hermēneutik(ós)* of, skilled in, interpreting = *hermēneú(ein)* (to) make clear, interpret (*hermēneús* interpreter < *Hermês* HERMES) + *-tikos* -TIC; see -ICS]

Her·mes (hûr′mēz), *n.* the ancient Greek herald and messenger of the gods and the god of roads, commerce, invention, cunning, and theft: identified by the Romans with Mercury.

Her′mes Trismegis′tus, a name variously ascribed by Neoplatonists and others to an ancient Egyptian priest or to the Egyptian god Thoth, to some extent identified with the Grecian Hermes: various mystical, religious, philosophical, astrological, and alchemical writings were ascribed to him. [< ML < Gk: Hermes thrice greatest]

her·met·ic (hûr met′ik), *adj.* **1.** made airtight by fusion or sealing. **2.** of, pertaining to, or characteristic of occult science, esp. alchemy. **3.** (*usually cap.*) of or pertaining to Hermes Trismegistus or the writings ascribed to him. Also, **her·met′i·cal.** [< ML *hermētic(us)* of, pertaining to Hermes Trismegistus. See HERMES, -TIC]

her·met·i·cal·ly (hûr met′ik lē), *adv.* so as to be airtight: *hermetically sealed.*

Her·met·i·cism (hûr met′i siz′əm), *n.* (*sometimes l.c.*). **1.** the body of ideas set forth in hermetic writings. **2.** adherence to the ideas expressed in hermetic writings. Also, **Her′me·tism.** —**Her′me·tist,** *n.*

Her·mi·o·ne (hûr mī′ə nē′), *n.* *Class. Myth.* the daughter of Menelaus and Helen and the wife of Orestes.

her·mit (hûr′mit), *n.* **1.** a person who has withdrawn to a solitary place for a life of religious seclusion. **2.** any person living in seclusion; recluse. **3.** a spiced molasses cookie. **4.** *Obs.* a beadsman. [ME *ermite, hermite, heremite* < OF < LL *erēmīta* < Gk *erēmī́tēs* living in a desert = *erēm(ía)* desert (< *erêmos* desolate) + *-itēs* -ITE[1]] —**her·mit′ic, her·mit′i·cal, her′mit·ish,** *adj.* —**her·mit′i·cal·ly,** *adv.* —**her′mit·like′,** *adj.* —**her′mit·ry,** *n.*

her·mit·age (hûr′mi tij), *n.* **1.** the habitation of a hermit. **2.** any secluded place of residence or habitation; retreat. **3.** (*cap.*) a palace in Leningrad: built by Catherine II; now used as an art museum. [ME < OF]

her′mit crab′, any of numerous decapod crustaceans of the genera *Pagurus, Eupagurus,* etc., which protect their soft uncovered abdomen by occupying the castoff shell of a univalve mollusk.

her′mit thrush′, a North American thrush, *Hylocichla guttata,* noted for its beautiful song.

Her·mon (hûr′mən), *n.* **Mount,** a mountain in SW Syria, 9232 ft.

Her·mo·si·llo (ER′mô sē′yô), *n.* a city in and the capital of Sonoro, in NW Mexico. 143,215 (est. 1965).

hern (hûrn), *n.* *Archaic.* heron.

Hern·don (hûrn′dən), *n.* **William Henry,** 1818–91, U.S. law partner and biographer of Abraham Lincoln.

Herne (hûrn), *n.* a city in W West Germany, in the Ruhr region. 111,200 (1963).

her·ni·a (hûr′nē ə), *n., pl.* **-ni·as, -ni·ae** (-nē ē′). *Pathol.* the protrusion of an organ or tissue through an opening in its surrounding walls, esp. in the abdominal region. [< L: a rupture] —**her′ni·al,** *adj.* —**her·ni·at·ed** (hûr′nē ā′tid), *adj.*

hernio-, a combining form of **hernia:** *herniotomy.*

her·ni·o·plas·ty (hûr′nē ə plas′tē), *n., pl.* **-ties.** *Surg.* an operation for the cure of a hernia.

her·ni·or·rha·phy (hûr′nē ôr′ə fē, -or′-), *n., pl.* **-phies.** *Surg.* correction of a hernia by a suturing procedure.

her·ni·ot·o·my (hûr′nē ot′ə mē), *n., pl.* **-mies.** *Surg.* correction of a hernia by a cutting procedure.

he·ro (hēr′ō), *n., pl.* **-roes;** for 3 also **-ros. 1.** a man of distinguished courage or ability, admired for his brave deeds and noble qualities. **2.** a man who is regarded as having heroic qualities and is considered a model or ideal. **3.** See **hero sandwich. 4.** a small loaf of Italian bread. **5.** the principal male character in a story, play, film, etc. **6.** *Class. Myth.* **a.** a being of godlike prowess and beneficence who often came to be honored as a divinity. **b.** (in the Homeric period) a warrior-chieftain of special strength, courage, or ability. **c.** (in later antiquity) an immortal being; demigod. [back formation from ME *heroes* (pl.) < L *hērōs* < Gk]

He·ro (hēr′ō), *n.* **1.** *Class. Myth.* a priestess of Aphrodite who drowned herself after her lover Leander drowned while swimming the Hellespont to visit her. **2.** Also, **Heron.** (*Hero of Alexandria*) fl. c1st century A.D., Greek scientist.

Her·od (her′əd), *n.* ("*the Great*") 73?–4 B.C., king of Judea 37–4.

Her′od A·grip′pa (ə grip′ə), (*Julius Agrippa*) c10 B.C.–A.D. 44, king of Judea 41–44 (grandson of Herod the Great).

Her′od An′ti·pas (an′ti pas′), died after A.D. 39, ruler of Galilee, A.D. 4–39: ordered the execution of John the Baptist and participated in the trial of Jesus.

He·ro·di·an (hi rō′dē ən), *adj.* **1.** of or pertaining to Herod the Great, his family, or its partisans. —*n.* **2.** a partisan of the house of Herod.

He·ro·di·as (hə rō′dē əs), *n.* the second wife of Herod Antipas and the mother of Salome: she told Salome to ask Herod for the head of John the Baptist.

He·rod·o·tus (hi rod′ə təs), *n.* ("*Father of History*") 484?–425? B.C., Greek historian.

he·ro·ic (hi rō′ik), *adj* Also, **he·ro′i·cal. 1.** of, pertaining to, or characteristic of a hero or heroes. **2.** suitable to the character of a hero in size or concept; daring; noble: *a heroic ambition.* **3.** having or displaying the character or attributes of a hero; extraordinarily bold, altruistic, determined, etc.: *a heroic explorer.* **4.** dealing with or describing the deeds, attributes, etc., of heroes, as in literature. **5.** used in heroic poetry. Cf. **heroic verse. 6.** resembling heroic poetry in language or style; grandiloquent. **7.** (of style or language) lofty; extravagant; grand. **8.** being larger than life-size: *a statue of heroic proportions.* —*n.* **9.** Usually, **heroics.** See **heroic verse. 10. heroics,** extravagant language, sentiment, or behavior. [< L *hērōic(us)* < Gk *hērōikós*] —**he·ro′i·cal·ly,** *adv.* —**he·ro′i·cal·ness, he·ro′ic·ness,** *n.* —**Syn. 2, 3.** valiant, gallant, brave. **6.** epic. —**Ant. 1–3.** cowardly.

hero′ic age′, 1. one of the five ages of man when, according to Hesiod, gods and demigods performed heroic and glorious deeds. **2.** any period in the history of a nation, esp. in ancient Greece and Rome, when heroes of legend lived.

hero′ic cou′plet, *Pros.* a stanza consisting of two rhyming lines in iambic pentameter, esp. one forming a rhetorical unit and written in an elevated style, as, *Know then thyself, presume not God to scan / The proper study of Mankind is Man.*

hero′ic verse′, a form of verse adapted to the treatment of heroic or exalted themes: in classical poetry, dactylic hexameter; in English and German, iambic pentameter; and in French, the Alexandrine.

her·o·in (her′ō in), *n.* *Pharm.* an addictive, narcotic powder, $C_{17}H_{17}NO(C_2H_3O_2)_2$, derived from morphine, formerly used as a sedative: manufacture or importation is now prohibited by federal law in the U.S. [formerly trademark]

her·o·ine (her′ō in), *n.* **1.** a woman of heroic character; female hero. **2.** the principal female character in a story, play, film, etc. [< L *hērōīnē* < Gk, fem. of *hḗrōs*]

her·o·ism (her′ō iz′əm), *n.* **1.** the qualities or attributes of a hero or heroine. **2.** heroic conduct; courageous action. —**Syn. 1.** valor, bravery, courage. —**Ant. 1.** cowardice.

her·on (her′ən), *n.* any of numerous long-legged, long-necked, usually long-billed birds of the family *Ardeidae,* comprising the true herons, egrets, night herons, bitterns, etc. [ME *heiro(u)n, hero(u)n* < MF *hairon* (F *héron*) < Gmc; cf. OHG *heigir*]

Great blue heron, *Ardea herodias* (Height 4 to 5 ft.; length 4¼ ft.)

He·ron (hēr′on), *n.* Hero (def. 2).

her·on·ry (her′ən rē), *n., pl.* **-ries.** a place where a colony of herons breeds.

her·on's-bill (her′ənz bil′), *n.* any geraniaceous herb of the genus *Erodium,* having pink, purple, white, or yellow flowers and long, slender fruit. Also called **stork's-bill.**

he′ro sand′wich, a large sandwich, consisting of a small loaf of Italian bread filled with meats, cheeses, onions, etc. Also called **poor boy, submarine.**

he′ro wor′ship, 1. a profound reverence for great men. **2.** extravagant admiration for a personal hero.

he·ro-wor·ship (hēr′ō wûr′ship), *v.t.,* **-shiped, -ship·ing** or (*esp. Brit.*) **-shipped, -ship·ping.** to feel or express hero worship for. —**he′ro-wor′ship·er,** *esp. Brit.,* **he′ro-wor′ship·per,** *n.*

herp., herpetology. Also, **herpet.**

her·pes (hûr′pēz), *n.* *Pathol.* any of certain inflammations of the skin or mucous membrane, characterized by clusters of vesicles that tend to spread. [< NL: cutaneous eruption < Gk: lit., a creeping, cf. *hérpein* to creep, spread] —**her·pet·ic** (hər pet′ik), *adj.*

her′pes sim′plex (sim′pleks), *Pathol.* an acute infection caused by a virus, characterized by the formation of groups of vesicles on the skin or mucous membrane. [< NL: lit., simple herpes]

her′pes zos′ter (zos′tər), *Pathol.* shingles. [< NL: lit., belt herpes]

her·pe·tol·o·gy (hûr′pi tol′ə jē), *n.* the branch of zoology dealing with reptiles and amphibians. [< Gk *herpetó(n)* a creeping thing (cf. *hérpein* to creep) + -LOGY] —**her·pe·to·log·ic** (hûr′pi tᵊloj′ik), **her′pe·to·log′i·cal,** *adj.* —**her′pe·to·log′i·cal·ly,** *adv.* —**her′pe·tol′o·gist,** *n.*

Herr (heʀ), *n., pl.* **Her·ren** (heʀ′ən). the conventional German title of respect and term of address for a man, corresponding to *Mr.* or in direct address to *sir.* [< G]

Her·ren·volk (heʀ′ən fôlk′), *n., pl.* **-völ·ker** (-fœl′kəʀ). *German.* See **master race.**

Her·rick (her′ik), *n.* **Robert,** 1591–1674, English poet.

her·ring (her′ing), *n., pl.* (*esp. collectively*) **-ring,** (*esp. referring to two or more kinds or species*) **-rings. 1.** an important food fish, *Clupea harengus,* found in enormous shoals in the North Atlantic. **2.** a similar fish, *Clupea pallasii,* of the North Pacific. **3.** any fish of the family *Clupeidae,* including these species and the shads, sardines, etc. [ME *hering,* OE *hǣring;* c. G *Häring*] —**her′ring·like′,** *adj.*

her·ring·bone (her′ing bōn′), *n.* **1.** a pattern consisting of adjoining vertical rows of slanting lines, any two contiguous lines forming either a V or an inverted V, used in masonry, textiles, embroidery, etc. **2.** *Skiing.* a method of going up a slope in which a skier sets the skis in a form resembling a V. —*adj.* **3.** having or resembling herringbone: *herringbone tweed.*

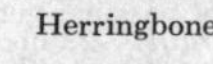
Herringbone

her′ringbone gear′, a helical gear having V-shaped teeth.

her′ring gull′, a common, large gull, *Larus argentatus,* of the Northern Hemisphere.

Her·ri·ot (e ʀyō′), *n.* **Édouard** (ā dwaʀ′), 1872–1957, French statesman, political leader, and author.

hers (hûrz), *pron.* **1.** a form of the possessive case of **she** used as a predicate adjective: *The red umbrella is hers. Are you a friend of hers?* **2.** that or those belonging to her: *Hers are the yellow ones.* [ME *hirs.* See HER, 's[1]]

Herringbone gears

Her·schel (hûr′shəl, her′-), *n.* **1. Sir John Frederick William,** 1792–1871, English astronomer. **2.** his father, **Sir William** (*Friedrich Wilhelm Herschel*), 1738–1822, English astronomer, born in Germany.

her·self (hər self′), *pron.* **1.** an emphatic appositive of *her* or *she: She herself wrote the letter.* **2.** a reflexive form of *her: She supports herself.* **3.** (used as the object of a preposition or as the direct or indirect object of a verb): *She gave herself a facial massage. He asked her for a picture of herself.* **4.** her normal or customary self: *After a few weeks of rest, she will be herself again.* [ME *hire-selfe,* OE *hire-self*] —**Usage.** See **myself.**

Her·sey (hûr′sē, -zē), *n.* **John (Richard),** born 1914, U.S. journalist, novelist, and educator.

Her·shey (hûr′shē), *n.* **Lewis Blaine,** 1893–1978, U.S. general and government official: director of Selective Service System 1941–70.

Her·ter (hûr′tər), *n.* **Christian Archibald,** 1895–1966, U.S. politician: Secretary of State 1959–61.

Hert·ford (här′fərd, härt′fərd), *n.* **1.** a city in and the county seat of Hertfordshire, in SE England. 15,734 (1961). **2.** Hertfordshire.

Hert·ford·shire (här′fərd shēr′, -shər, härt′-), *n.* a county in SE England. 832,088 (1961); 632 sq. mi. *Co. seat:* Hertford. Also called **Hertford, Herts** (härts, hûrts).

Her·to·gen·bosch, 's (*Du.* seʀ′tō ᴋʜən bôs′). See **'s Hertogenbosch.**

hertz (hûrtz), *n., pl.* **hertz, hertz·es.** a unit of frequency, equal to one cycle per second. *Abbr.:* Hz [named after H. R. Hertz]

Hertz (hûrts; *Ger.* heʀts), *n.* **Hein·rich Ru·dolph** (hīn′ʀiᴋʜ ʀōō′dôlf), 1857–94, German physicist. —**Hertz·i·an** (heʀt′sē ən), *adj.*

Her·tzog (*Du.* heʀ′tsôᴋʜ), *n.* **James Barry Mun·nik** (mœn′ək), South African statesman and general: prime minister 1924–39.

Her·ze·go·vi·na (her′tsə gō vē′nə), *n.* a former Turkish province in S Europe: a part of Austria-Hungary 1878–1914; now part of Bosnia and Herzegovina, a republic of Yugoslavia. Serbo-Croatian, **Hercegovina.** —**Her′ze·go·vi′ni·an,** *adj., n.*

Her·zl (heʀ′tsəl), *n.* **The·o·dor** (tā′ô dōʀ′), 1860–1904, writer and journalist in Austria, born in Hungary: founder of the political Zionist movement.

Her·zog (*Fr.* eʀ zôg′), *n.* **É·mile Sa·lo·mon Wil·helm** (*Fr.* ā mēl′ sᴀ lô môɴ vē lelm′). See **Maurois, André.**

he's (hēz; *unstressed* ēz), **1.** contraction of *he is.* **2.** contraction of *he has.*

Hesh·van (hesh′vən, ᴋʜesh′-; *Heb.* ᴋʜesh vän′), *n.* the second month of the Jewish calendar. Also, **Cheshvan.** Also called **Marheshvan, Marcheshvan.** Cf. **Jewish calendar.** [< Heb *(mar)heshwān*]

He·si·od (hē′sē əd, hes′ē-), *n.* fl. 8th century B.C., Greek poet. —**He·si·od·ic** (hē′sē od′ik, hes′ē-), *adj.*

He·si·o·ne (hi sī′ə nē′), *n.* *Class. Myth.* daughter of Laomedon: rescued from a sea monster by Hercules.

hes·i·tan·cy (hez′i tᵊn sē), *n., pl.* **-cies.** hesitation; indecision or disinclination. Also, **hes′i·tance.** [< LL *haesitantia* (L: a stammering)]

hes·i·tant (hez′i tᵊnt), *adj.* **1.** hesitating; undecided or disinclined. **2.** lacking readiness of speech. [< L *haesitant-* (s. of *haesitāns,* prp. of *haesitāre*) stammering, hesitating = *haes(us)* stuck, held fast (ptp. of *haerēre*) + *-it-* intensive and freq. suffix + *-ant-* -ANT] —**hes′i·tant·ly,** *adv.*

hes·i·tate (hez′i tāt′), *v.i.,* **-tat·ed, -tat·ing.** **1.** to be reluctant or wait to act because of fear, indecision, or disinclination: *She hesitated to take the job.* **2.** to have scruples or doubts; be unwilling: *He hesitated to break the law.* **3.** to pause. **4.** to falter in speech; stammer. [< L *haesitāt(us)* stuck fast, held in place, ptp. of *haesitāre*] —**hes′i·tat′er, hes′i·ta′tor,** *n.* —**hes′i·tat′ing·ly,** *adv.*

hes·i·ta·tion (hez′i tā′shən), *n.* **1.** the act of hesitating; a delay due to uncertainty of mind or fear: *His hesitation cost him the championship.* **2.** a state of doubt or uncertainty. **3.** a halting or faltering in speech. [< L *haesitātiōn-* (s. of *haesitātiō*) a stammering, hesitating] —**Syn. 1.** hesitancy, indecision, irresolution, vacillation. **3.** stammer.

hes′ita′tion waltz′, a waltz based on a step that consists of a pause and a glide.

hes·i·ta·tive (hez′i tā′tiv), *adj.* characterized by hesitation; hesitating. —**hes′i·ta′tive·ly,** *adv.*

Hes·pe·ri·an (he spēr′ē ən), *adj.* **1.** western; occidental. **2.** of or pertaining to the Hesperides. —*n.* **3.** a native or inhabitant of a western land. [< L *Hesperi(us)* of, toward the West (< Gk *hespérios* western < *hésperos* evening) + -AN]

Hes·per·i·des (he sper′i dēz′), *n.* *Class. Myth.* **1.** (*construed as pl.*) the nymphs who, with the dragon Ladon, guarded the golden apples which were the wedding gift of Gaea to Hera. **2.** (*construed as sing.*) the garden where the golden apples were grown. **3.** (*construed as pl.*) See **Islands of the Blessed.** —**Hes·per·id·i·an** (hes′pə rid′ē ən), *adj.*

hes·per·i·din (he sper′i din), *n.* *Biochem.* a bioflavinoid glycoside, $C_{28}H_{34}O_{15}$, occurring in most citrus fruits, esp. in the spongy envelope of oranges and lemons. [< NL]

Hes·per·us (hes′pər əs), *n.* an evening star, esp. Venus. [< L < Gk *hésperos* evening, western]

Hess (hes), *n.* **1. Dame Myra,** 1890–1965, English pianist. **2. (Wal·ther Rich·ard) Ru·dolf** (väl′təʀ ʀiᴋʜ′ärt ʀōō′dôlf), born 1894, German leader in the Nazi party.

Hes·se (hes′ə *for 1;* hes *for 2*), *n.* **1. Her·mann** (heʀ′män), 1877–1962, German novelist and poet: Nobel prize 1946. **2.** German, **Hes·sen** (hes′ən). a state in E West Germany 4,973,000 (1963); 8150 sq. mi. *Cap.:* Wiesbaden.

Hesse-Nas·sau (hes′nas′ô), *n.* a former state in W Germany, now part of Hesse. German, **Hes·sen-Nassau** (hes′ən näs′ou).

Hes·sian (hesh′ən), *adj.* **1.** of or pertaining to Hesse or its inhabitants. —*n.* **2.** a native or inhabitant of Hesse. **3.** a Hessian mercenary used by England during the American Revolution. **4.** a hireling or ruffian.

Hes′sian boots′, knee-high tasseled boots, fashionable in England during the early 19th century.

Hes′sian fly′, a small dipterous insect, *Phytophaga destructor,* the larvae of which feed on the stems of wheat and other grasses.

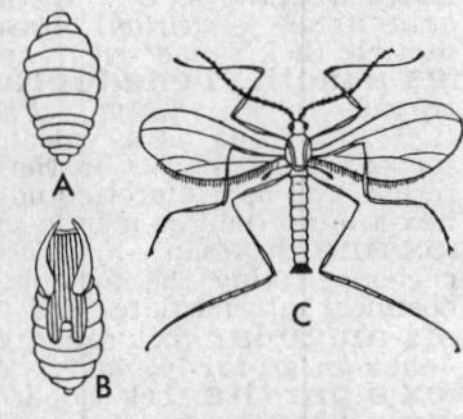

Hessian fly
A, Larva; B, Pupa;
C, Adult (male)

hes·so·nite (hes′ə nīt′), *n.* *Mineral.* See **cinnamon stone.** [var. of ESSONITE]

hest (hest), *n.* *Archaic.* behest. [ME *hest(e),* OE *hǣs,* akin to *hātan* to bid]

Hes·ti·a (hes′tē ə), *n.* ancient Greek goddess of the hearth, identified by the Romans with Vesta.

Hes·ton and I·sle·worth (hes′tən; ī′zəl wûrth′), a city in SE England, near London. 102,897 (1961).

Hes·y·chast (hes′ə kast′), *n.* one of a sect of mystics that originated in the 14th century among the monks on Mount Athos, Greece. [< ML *hesychast(a)* < Gk *hēsychast(ḗs)* a recluse = *hēsych(ázein)* (to) be quiet, be still (< *hēsych(os)* quiet, still) + *-a-* thematic vowel + *-tēs* suffix of agency] —**Hes′y·chast′ic,** *adj.*

he·tae·ra (hi tēr′ə), *n., pl.* **-tae·rae** (-tēr′ē). **1.** a female paramour or concubine, esp. in ancient Greece. **2.** any woman who uses her charm to gain wealth or social position. Also, **hetaira.** [< Gk *hetaíra*] —**he·tae′ric,** *adj.*

he·tae·rism (hi tēr′iz əm), *n.* concubinage. Also, **he·tai·rism** (hi tīᵊr′iz əm).

he·tai·ra (hi tīᵊr′ə), *n., pl.* **-tai·rai** (-tī′rī). hetaera.

het·er·o (het′ə rō′), *adj.* *Chem.* of or pertaining to an atom other than carbon, particularly in a cyclic compound. [independent use of HETERO-]

hetero-, a learned borrowing from Greek meaning "different," "other," used in the formation of compound words: *heterocyclic.* Also, *esp. before a vowel,* **heter-.** [comb. form of Gk *héteros* the other of two, other, different]

het·er·o·cer·cal (het′ər ə sûr′kəl), *adj.* *Ichthyol.* **1.** having an unequally divided tail or caudal fin, the spinal column usually running into a much larger upper lobe. **2.** noting such a tail or caudal fin. [HETERO- + Gk *kérk(os)* a tail + -AL[1]]

Heterocercal tail

het·er·o·chro·mat·ic (het′ər ə krō-mat′ik, -ō krə-), *adj.* **1.** of, having, or pertaining to more than one color. **2.** having a pattern of mixed colors. **3.** *Genetics.* of or pertaining to heterochromatin. Also, **het·er·o·chrome** (het′ər ə krōm′). —**het·er·o·chro·ma·tism** (het′ər ə krō′mə tiz′əm), *n.*

het·er·o·chro·ma·tin (het′ər ə krō′mə tin), *n.* *Genetics.* the dense, highly stainable part of a chromosome. Cf. **euchromatin.**

het·er·o·chro·mo·some (het′ər ə krō′mə sōm′), *n.* *Genetics.* See **sex chromosome.**

het·er·o·chro·mous (het′ər ə krō′məs), *adj.* of different colors.

het·er·och·tho·nous (het′ə rok′thə nəs), *adj.* not indigenous; foreign (opposed to *autochthonous*): *heterochthonous flora and fauna.* [HETERO- + Gk *chthṓn* the earth, land, country + -OUS]

het·er·o·clite (het′ər ə klīt′), *adj.* Also, **het·er·o·clit·ic** (het′ər ə klit′ik), **het′er·o·clit′i·cal.** **1.** irregular or abnormal; anomalous. **2.** *Gram.* irregular in inflection; having inflected forms belonging to more than one class of stems. —*n.* **3.** a person or thing that deviates from the ordinary rule or form. **4.** *Gram.* a heteroclite word. [< MF < LL *heteroclit(us)* < Gk *heteróklitos* = *hetero-* HETERO- + *-klitos,* verbal adj. of *klínein* to bend, inflect]

het·er·o·cy·clic (het′ər ə sī′klik, -sik′lik), *adj.* *Chem.* **1.** of or pertaining to the branch of chemistry dealing with cyclic compounds in which at least one of the ring members is not a carbon atom. **2.** noting such compounds, as ethylene oxide, $H_2C(O)CH_2$. —**het·er·o·cy·cle** (het′ər ə sī′kəl), *n.*

het·er·o·dac·ty·lous (het′ə rō dak′tᵊləs), *adj.* *Ornith.* having the first and fourth toes directed backward, and the second and third forward, as in trogons. Also, **het′er·o·dac′tyl.** [HETERO- + Gk *-daktylos;* see DACTYL-, -OUS]

het·er·o·dox (het′ər ə doks′), *adj.* **1.** not in accordance with established doctrines, esp. in theology. **2.** holding unorthodox doctrines or opinions. [< Gk *heteródox(os)* of another opinion = *hetero-* HETERO- + *dóx(a)* an opinion (cf. *dokeîn* to think, suppose) + *-os* adj. suffix]

het·er·o·dox·y (het′ər ə dok′sē), *n., pl.* **-dox·ies.** **1.** a heterodox state or quality. **2.** a heterodox opinion, view, etc. [< Gk *heterodoxía*]

het·er·o·dyne (het′ər ə dīn′), *adj., v.,* **-dyned, -dyn·ing.** *Radio.* —*adj.* **1.** noting or pertaining to a method of changing the frequency of an incoming radio signal by adding it to a signal generated within the receiver to produce fluctuations or beats of a frequency equal to the difference between the two signals. —*v.i.* **2.** to produce a heterodyne effect. —*v.t.* **3.** to mix (a frequency) with a different frequency so as to achieve a heterodyne effect.

het·er·oe·cism (het′ə rē′siz əm), *n.* *Biol.* the development of different stages of a parasitic species on different host plants, as in fungi. [HETER- + Gk *oik(ía)* a house + -ISM] —**het′er·oe′cious,** *adj.*

het·er·o·gam·ete (het′ər ə gam′ēt, -ə rō gə mēt′), *n.* *Biol.* either of a pair of conjugating gametes differing in form, size, structure, or sex. Cf. **isogamete.**

het·er·og·a·mous (het′ə rog′ə məs), *adj.* **1.** *Biol.* having unlike gametes, or reproducing by the union of such gametes (opposed to *isogamous*). **2.** *Bot.* having flowers or florets of two sexually different kinds (opposed to *homogamous*). —**het′er·og′a·my,** *n.*

het·er·o·ge·ne·i·ty (het′ə rō jə nē′i tē), *n.* the quality or state of being heterogeneous; composition from dissimilar parts; disparateness. [< ML *heterogeneitās*]

het·er·o·ge·ne·ous (het′ər ə jē′nē əs, -jēn′yəs), *adj.* **1.** different in kind; unlike; incongruous. **2.** composed of parts of different kinds; having widely dissimilar elements or constituents; not homogeneous. [< ML *heterogene(us)* < Gk *heterogenḗs*] —**het′er·o·ge′ne·ous·ly,** *adv.* —**het′er·o·ge′ne·ous·ness,** *n.*

het·er·o·gen·e·sis (het′ər ə jen′i sis), *n.* *Biol.* **1.** Also, **het·er·og·e·ny** (het′ə roj′ə nē). alternation of generations, esp. the alternation of parthenogenetic and sexual generations. **2.** abiogenesis. —**het·er·o·ge·net·ic** (het′ə rō jə net′ik), **het′er·o·gen′ic,** *adj.* —**het′er·o·ge·net′i·cal·ly,** *adv.*

het·er·og·e·nous (het′ə roj′ə nəs), *adj. Biol., Pathol.* having its source or origin outside the organism; having a foreign origin.

het·er·og·o·nous (het′ə rog′ə nəs), *adj.* **1.** *Bot.* of or pertaining to monoclinous flowers of two or more kinds occurring in different individuals of the same species, the kinds differing in the relative length of stamens and pistils (opposed to *homogonous*). **2.** heterogynous. **3.** of, pertaining to, or characterized by heterogony. Also, **het·er·o·gon·ic** (het′ər ə gon′ik). [HETERO- + Gk *gón(os)* race, descent, birth + -OUS] —**het′er·og′o·nous·ly,** *adv.*

het·er·og·o·ny (het′ə rog′ə nē), *n. Biol.* **1.** the alternation of dioecious and hermaphroditic individuals in successive generations, as in certain nematodes. **2.** the alternation of parthenogenetic and sexual generations.

het·er·og·ra·phy (het′ə rog′rə fē), *n.* **1.** spelling different from that in current use. **2.** the use of the same letter or combination of letters to represent different sounds, as, in English, the use of *s* in *sit* and *easy.* —**het·er·o·graph·ic** (het′ər ə graf′ik), **het′er·o·graph′i·cal,** *adj.*

het·er·og·y·nous (het′ə roj′ə nəs), *adj. Zool.* having females of two different kinds, one sexual and the other abortive or neuter, as ants.

het·er·ol·o·gous (het′ə rol′ə gəs), *adj. Biol.* of different origin; pertaining to heterology.

het·er·ol·o·gy (het′ə rol′ə jē), *n.* **1.** *Biol.* the lack of correspondence of apparently similar organic structures as the result of unlike origins of constituent parts. **2.** *Pathol.* abnormality; structural difference from a normal standard.

het·er·ol·y·sis (het′ə rol′i sis), *n. Biochem.* dissolution of the cells of one organism by the lysins of another. —**het·er·o·lyt·ic** (het′ər ə lit′ik), *adj.*

het·er·om·er·ous (het′ə rom′ər əs), *adj.* having or consisting of parts that differ in quality, number of elements, or the like.

het·er·o·mor·phic (het′ər ə môr′fik), *adj.* **1.** *Biol.* dissimilar in shape, structure, or magnitude. **2.** *Entomol.* undergoing complete metamorphosis; assuming varying forms. —**het′er·o·mor′phism,** *n.*

het·er·on·o·mous (het′ə ron′ə məs), *adj.* **1.** subject to or involving different laws. **2.** pertaining to or characterized by heteronomy. **3.** *Biol.* subject to different laws of growth or specialization. —**het′er·on′o·mous·ly,** *adv.*

het·er·on·o·my (het′ə ron′ə mē), *n.* the condition of being under the rule or domination of another.

het·er·o·nym (het′ər ə nim′), *n.* a word having a different sound and meaning from another, but the same spelling, as *lead* (to conduct) and *lead* (a metal). [< LGk *heterṓnym(os).* See HETERO-, -ONYM]

het·er·on·y·mous (het′ə ron′ə məs), *adj.* **1.** of, pertaining to, or characteristic of a heteronym. **2.** having different names, as a pair of correlatives. *Father* and *son* are heteronymous designations. [< LGk *heterṓnymos* having a different name] —**het′er·on′y·mous·ly,** *adv.*

Het·er·o·ou·si·an (het′ər ō o͞o′sē ən, -ou′sē ən), *Eccles.* —*n.* **1.** a person who believes the Father and the Son to be unlike in substance or essence; an Arian. —*adj.* **2.** of or pertaining to the Heteroousians or their doctrine. Also, **Het′er·o·ü′si·an.** [< LGk *heteroousi(os)* (Gk *hetero-* HETERO- + *ousí(a)* nature, essence) + -AN]

het·er·o·phyl·lous (het′ər ə fil′əs), *adj. Bot.* having different kinds of leaves on the same plant. —**het′er·o·phyl′ly,** *n.*

het·er·o·plas·ty (het′ər ə plas′tē), *n. Surg.* the repair of lesions with tissue from another individual or species. —**het′er·o·plas′tic,** *adj.*

het·er·o·po·lar (het′ər ə pō′lər), *adj. Chem.* polar (def. 3). —**het·er·o·po·lar·i·ty** (het′ər ō pō lar′i tē), *n.*

het·er·op·ter·ous (het′ə rop′tər əs), *adj.* belonging or pertaining to the *Heteroptera,* in some classifications a suborder of hemipterous insects comprising the true bugs. [< NL *Heteropter(a)* name of the class]

het·er·o·sex·u·al (het′ər ə sek′sho͞o əl), *adj.* **1.** *Biol.* pertaining to the opposite sex or to both sexes. **2.** of, pertaining to, or exhibiting heterosexuality. —*n.* **3.** a heterosexual person.

het·er·o·sex·u·al·i·ty (het′ər ə sek′sho͞o al′i tē), *n.* sexual feeling or behavior directed toward a person or persons of the opposite sex.

het·er·o·sis (het′ə rō′sis), *n. Genetics.* (in hybrids) the increase over the parents in growth, size, fecundity, function, yield, or other characters. Also called **hybrid vigor.** [< LGk: an alteration. See HETERO-, -SIS]

het·er·os·po·ry (het′ə ros′pə rē), *n. Bot.* the production of both microspores and megaspores. —**het·er·os·por·ous** (het′ə ros′pər əs, het′ər ə spōr′əs, -spôr′-), *adj.*

het·er·o·tax·is (het′ər ə tak′sis), *n.* abnormal or irregular arrangement, as of parts of the body, geological strata, etc. Also, **het·er·o·tax·i·a** (het′ər ə tak′sē ə), **het′er·o·tax′y.** —**het·er·o·tac·tic** (het′ər ə tak′tik), **het′er·o·tac′tous, het′er·o·tax′ic,** *adj.*

het·er·o·tel·ic (het′ər ə tel′ik, -tē′lik), *adj.* (of an entity or event) having the purpose of its existence or occurrence outside of or apart from itself.

het·er·o·to·pi·a (het′ər ə tō′pē ə), *n. Pathol.* the formation of tissue in a part where its presence is abnormal. Also, **het·er·ot·o·py** (het′ə rot′ə pē). [< NL] —**het·er·o·top·ic** (het′ər ə top′ik), **het·er·ot·o·pous** (het′ə rot′ə pəs), *adj.*

het·er·o·troph (het′ər ə trof′), *n.* a microorganism requiring a complex organic compound, as glucose, for its source of energy. Cf. **autotroph.**

het·er·o·troph·ic (het′ər ə trof′ik), *adj. Biol.* capable of utilizing only organic materials as a source of food, as most animals and some plants.

het·er·o·typ·ic (het′ər ə tip′ik), *adj. Biol.* **1.** of or pertaining to the first or reductional division in meiosis. **2.** of or pertaining to a genus consisting of not truly related species. Also, **het′er·o·typ′i·cal.** Cf. **homeotypic.** [HETERO- + *typic* (see TYPICAL)]

het·er·o·zy·go·sis (het′ər ō zī gō′sis), *n. Biol.* the state of being a heterozygote. —**het·er·o·zy·gos·i·ty** (het′ə rō zī gos′i tē), *n.*

het·er·o·zy·gote (het′ər ə zī′gōt, -zig′ōt), *n. Genetics.* a hybrid containing genes for two unlike characteristics, and therefore not breeding true to type. —**het·er·o·zy·got·ic** (het′ə rō zī got′ik), *adj.*

het·er·o·zy·gous (het′ər ə zī′gəs), *adj. Biol.* **1.** having dissimilar pairs of genes for any hereditary characteristic. **2.** of or pertaining to a heterozygote. [HETERO- + Gk *zygṓs* < *zygó(n)* yolk; see -OUS]

heth (hes, KHes; *Heb.* KHet), *n.* **1.** the eighth letter of the Hebrew alphabet. **2.** the consonant sound represented by this letter. Also, **cheth.** [< Heb]

het·man (het′mən), *n., pl.* **-mans.** a Cossack chief. [< Pol < G *Hauptmann* headman]

het·man·ate (het′mə nāt′), *n.* the authority, rule, or domain of a hetman. Also called **het′man·ship′.**

heu·ris·tic (hyo͝o ris′tik), *adj.* **1.** serving to indicate or point out; stimulating interest as a means of furthering investigation. **2.** (of a teaching method) encouraging the student to discover for himself. —*n.* **3.** a heuristic method or argument. [< NL *heuristic(us)* = Gk *heur(ískein)* (to) find out, discover + L *-isticus* -ISTIC] —**heu·ris′ti·cal·ly,** *adv.*

He·ve·sy (he′ve shē), *n.* **Ge·org von** (ge ôRg′ vôn), 1885–1966, Hungarian chemist: Nobel prize 1943.

hew (hyo͞o), *v.,* **hewed, hewed** or **hewn, hew·ing.** —*v.t.* **1.** to strike forcibly with an ax, sword, or other cutting instrument; chop; hack. **2.** to make, shape, smooth, etc., with cutting blows: *to hew a statue from marble.* **3.** to sever (a part) from a whole by means of cutting blows (usually fol. by *from, away,* etc.): *to hew branches from the tree.* **4.** to cut down; fell: *trees hewn down by the storm.* —*v.i.* **5.** to strike with cutting blows; cut. **6.** to uphold, follow closely, or conform to (usually fol. by *to*): *to hew to the party line.* [ME *hew(en)* OE *hēawan;* c. G *hauen*] —**hew′a·ble,** *adj.* —**hew′er,** *n.* —**Syn. 1.** See **cut.**

HEW, (formerly) Department of Health, Education, and Welfare.

hew′ers of wood′ and draw′ers of wa′ter, performers of menial tasks. Josh. 9:21.

hewn (hyo͞on), *adj.* **1.** felled and roughly shaped by hewing. **2.** given a rough surface. [ME *hewen;* ptp. of HEW]

hex (heks), *v.t.* **1.** to bewitch; practice witchcraft on. —*n.* **2.** a spell or charm, usually associated with witchcraft. **3.** a witch. [< G *Hexe* witch; see HAG[1]] —**hex′er,** *n.*

hexa-, a learned borrowing from Greek meaning "six," used in the formation of compound words: *hexapartite.* Also, *esp. before a vowel,* **hex-.** [comb. form repr. Gk *héx* SIX]

hex·a·chlo·ro·phene (hek′sə klōr′ə fēn′, -klôr′-), *n. Chem.* a crystalline powder, $(C_6HCl_3OH)_2CH_2$, used as an antibacterial agent chiefly in toothpastes and soaps.

hex·a·chord (hek′sə kôrd′), *n. Music.* a diatonic series of six tones having, in medieval music, a half step between the third and fourth tones and whole steps between the others. [< LGk *hexáchord(os)* having six strings]

hex·ad (hek′sad), *n.* **1.** the number six. **2.** a group or series of six. [< LL *hexad-* (s. of *hexas*) < Gk: unit of six] —**hex·ad′ic,** *adj.*

hex·a·eth′yl tetraphos′phate (hek′sə eth′əl), *Chem.* a poisonous liquid, $(C_2H_5O)_6P_4O_7$, used as an insecticide. Also called **HETP.**

hex·a·gon (hek′sə gon′, -gən), *n.* a polygon having six angles and six sides. [< Gk *hexágōn(on)*]

120°

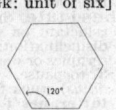

Hexagon (Regular)

hex·ag·o·nal (hek sag′ə nəl), *adj.* **1.** of, pertaining to, or having the form of a hexagon. **2.** having a hexagon as a base or cross section: *a hexagonal prism.* **3.** divided into hexagons, as a surface. **4.** *Crystall.* noting or pertaining to a system of crystallization in which three equal axes intersect at angles of 60° on one plane, and the fourth axis, of a different length, intersects them perpendicularly. Cf. **system** (def. 11). —**hex·ag′o·nal·ly,** *adv.*

hex·a·gram (hek′sə gram′), *n.* **1.** a six-pointed starlike figure formed of two equilateral triangles placed concentrically with each side of a triangle parallel to a side of the other and on opposite sides of the center. **2.** *Geom.* a figure of six lines —**hex′a·gram′moid,** *adj., n.*

Hexagram

hex·a·he·dron (hek′sə hē′drən), *n., pl.* **-drons, -dra** (-drə). a solid figure having six faces. [< Gk *hexáedron*] —**hex′a·he′dral,** *adj.*

hex·a·hy·drate (hek′sə hī′drāt), *n. Chem.* a hydrate that contains six molecules of water, as magnesium chloride, $MgCl_2 \cdot 6H_2O$. —**hex′a·hy′drat·ed,** *adj.*

hex·am·er·ous (hek sam′ər əs), *adj.* **1.** consisting of or divided into six parts. **2.** *Zool.* having a radially symmetrical arrangement of organs in six groups. **3.** *Bot.* having six members in each whorl. Also, **hex·am′er·al.** —**hex·am′er·ism,** *n.*

hex·am·e·ter (hek sam′i tər), *Pros.* —*n.* **1.** a dactylic line of six feet, as in Greek and Latin epic poetry, in which the first four feet are dactyls or spondees, the fifth is ordinarily a dactyl, and the last is a trochee or spondee, with a caesura usually following the long syllable in the third foot. **2.** any line of verse in six feet. —*adj.* **3.** consisting of six metrical feet. [< L < Gk *hexámetr(os)* of six measures = *hexa-* HEXA- + *métr(on)* measure + *-os* adj. suffix] —**hex·a·met·ric** (hek′sə me′trik), **hex·am′e·tral,** *adj.*

hex·a·meth·yl·ene·tet·ra·mine (hek′sə meth′ə lēn te′trə mēn′), *n. Chem., Pharm.* a crystalline powder, $(CH_2)_6N_4$, used as a vulcanization accelerator, as an absorbent in gas masks, in the manufacture of explosives and resins, and as a diuretic and urinary antiseptic. Also called **hex·a·mine** (hek′sə mēn′), **methenamine.**

hex·ane (hek′sān), *n. Chem.* any of five isomeric hydrocarbons having the formula C_6H_{14}, used as solvents and chemical intermediates and in fuels.

hex·an·gu·lar (hek sang′gyə lər), *adj.* having six angles. —**hex·an′gu·lar·ly,** *adv.*

hex·a·par·tite (hek′sə pär′tīt), *adj.* sexpartite.

hex·a·pla (hek′sə plə), *n.* (*often cap.*) an edition of a book, esp. the Old Testament, containing six versions or texts in parallel columns, esp. the one compiled by Origen. [< Gk *Hexaplâ* (title of Origen's edition), neut. pl. of *hexaploûs, -plóos* sixfold] —**hex′a·plar, hex·a·plar·ic** (hek′sə plar′ik), **hex·a·plar·i·an** (hek′sə plâr′ē ən), *adj.*

hex·a·pod (hek′sə pod′), *n.* **1.** an insect; a member of the class *Insecta* (formerly *Hexapoda*). —*adj.* **2.** having six feet. [< Gk *hexapod-* (s. of *hexápous*) six-footed] —**hex·ap·o·dous** (hek sap′ə dəs), *adj.*

hex·ap·o·dy (hek sap′ə dē), *n., pl.* **-dies.** *Pros.* a measure consisting of six feet. [< Gk *hexapod-* (see HEXAPOD) + -Y[3]] —**hex·a·pod·ic** (hek′sə pod′ik), *adj.*

hex·a·stich (hek′sə stik′), *n.* *Pros.* a strophe, stanza, or poem consisting of six lines. Also, **hexastichon.** [< Gk *hexástich(on)*, neut. of *hexástichos* of six lines] —**hex·a·stich·ic** (hek′sə stik′ik), *adj.*

hex·as·ti·chon (hek sas′tə kon′), *n., pl.* **-cha** (-kə). hexastich.

hex·a·style (hek′sə stīl′), *adj.* *Archit.* **1.** having six columns. **2.** (of a classical temple or similar building) having six columns on one or both fronts. Also, **hex′a·sty′lar.** [< L *hexastyl(os)* = Gk *hexa-* HEXA- + *stŷlos* pillar]

hex·a·syl·la·ble (hek′sə sil′ə bəl), *n.* a word or line of verse of six syllables. —**hex·a·syl·lab·ic** (hek′sə si lab′ik), *adj.*

Hex·a·teuch (hek′sə to͞ok′, -tyo͞ok′), *n.* the first six books of the Old Testament. [HEXA- + (PENTA)TEUCH]

hex·os·a·mine (hek sos′ə mēn′), *n.* *Biochem.* any hexose derivative in which a hydroxyl group is replaced by an amino group.

hex·ose (hek′sōs), *n.* *Chem.* any of the class of sugars, including glucose and fructose, containing six atoms of carbon.

hex′ sign′, a magical symbol of usually stylized design for protection against evil spirits.

hex′yl group′, *Chem.* any of five univalent, isomeric groups having the formula C_6H_{13}–. Also called **hex′yl rad′ical.** —**hex·yl** (hek′sil), *adj.*

hex·yl·res·or·cin·ol (hek′sil rə zôr′sə nōl′, -nôl′, -nol′), *n.* *Pharm.* needle-shaped crystals, $CH_3(CH_2)_5C_6H_3(OH)_2$, used chiefly as an antiseptic and for the expulsion of intestinal worms.

hey (hā), *interj.* (used as an exclamation to call attention or to express pleasure, surprise, bewilderment, etc.)

hey·day[1] (hā′dā′), *n.* **1.** the stage or period of greatest vigor, strength, success, etc.; prime: *the heyday of the robber baron.* **2.** *Rare.* high spirits. Also, **hey′dey.** [var. of HIGH DAY, appar. by confusion with archaic *heyday* (exclamation)]

hey·day[2] (hā′dā), *interj.* *Archaic.* (used as an exclamation of cheerfulness, surprise, wonder, etc.) [rhyming compound based on HEY[1]; r. *heyda* < G *hei da* hey there]

Hey·duck (hī′do͝ok), *n.* Haiduk. Also, **Hey′duke, Hey′duc.**

hey′ rube′, **1.** a fight between townspeople and the members of a circus or carnival. **2.** come help (used as a call to carnival or circus people in a fight with townspeople).

Hey·se (hī′zə), *n.* **Paul (Jo·hann von)** (poul yō′hän fən), 1830–1914, German playwright and writer: Nobel prize 1910.

Hey·ward (hā′wərd), *n.* **Du·Bose** (də bōz′), 1885–1940, U.S. playwright, novelist, and poet.

Hey·wood (hā′wo͝od), *n.* **1. John,** 1497?–1580?, English dramatist and epigrammatist. **2. Thomas,** 1573?–1641, English dramatist, poet, and actor.

Hez·e·ki·ah (hez′ə kī′ə), *n.* a king of Judah of the 7th and 8th centuries B.C. II Kings 18. [< Heb *ḥizqīyāh* God strengthens = *ḥizeq* strengthen + *yāh* God]

HF, See **high frequency.**

Hf, *Chem.* hafnium.

hf., half.

hf. bd., half-bound.

hf. cf., half-calf.

hf. mor., half-morocco.

HG, **1.** High German (def. 1). **2.** *Brit.* Home Guard.

Hg, *Chem.* mercury. [< L *hydrargyrum*]

hg, hectogram; hectograms.

H.G., **1.** High German. **2.** His (or Her) Grace.

hgt., height.

H.H., **1.** His (or Her) Highness. **2.** His Holiness.

hhd, hogshead; hogsheads.

H-hour (āch′our′, -ou′ər), *n.* the time set for the beginning of a military attack.

hi (hī), *interj.* hello (used as an exclamation of greeting). [late ME *hy*, perh. var. of *hei* HEY]

HI, Hawaii (approved esp. for use with zip code).

H.I., Hawaiian Islands.

Hi·a·le·ah (hī′ə lē′ə), *n.* a city in SE Florida, near Miami: race track. 102,452 (1970).

hi·a·tus (hī ā′təs), *n., pl.* **-tus·es, -tus.** **1.** a break or interruption in the continuity of a work, series, action, etc.; a missing part; gap. **2.** *Gram., Pros.* the coming together, with or without break or slight pause and without contraction, of two vowel sounds in successive words or syllables, as in *see easily.* [< L: an opening, a gap, n. use of ptp. of *hiāre* to gape, open]

hi·ba·chi (hē bä′chē), *n.* a small Japanese charcoal stove. [< Jap]

Hib·bing (hib′ing), *n.* a city in NE Minnesota: iron mining. 16,104 (1970).

hi·ber·nac·u·lum (hī′bər nak′yə ləm), *n., pl.* **-la** (-lə). **1.** a protective case or covering, esp. for winter, as of an animal or a plant bud. **2.** winter quarters, as of a hibernating animal. Also, **hi·ber·nac·le** (hī′bər nak′əl). [< L: winter residence]

hi·ber·nal (hī bûr′nᵊl), *adj.* of or pertaining to winter; wintry. [< L *hībernāl(is)* = *hībern(us)* wintry + *-ālis* -AL[1]; see HIEMAL]

hi·ber·nate (hī′bər nāt′), *v.i.,* **-nat·ed, -nat·ing.** **1.** to spend the winter in close quarters in a dormant condition, as certain animals. **2.** to withdraw or be in seclusion; retire. [< L *hībernāt(us)* (ptp. of *hībernāre* to spend the winter) = *hibernā-* (v. s.) + *-tus* ptp. suffix] —**hi′ber·na′tion,** *n.* —**hi′ber·na′tor,** *n.*

Hi·ber·ni·a (hī bûr′nē ə), *n.* *Literary.* Ireland.

Hi·ber·ni·an (hī bûr′nē ən), *adj.* **1.** of, pertaining to, or characteristic of Ireland or its inhabitants; Irish. —*n.* **2.** a native of Ireland.

Hi·ber·ni·cism (hī bûr′ni siz′əm), *n.* **1.** an idiom peculiar to Irish English. **2.** an Irish characteristic. Also, **Hi·ber·ni·an·ism** (hī bûr′nē ə niz′əm). [< ML *Hibernic(us)* Hibernian]

hi·bis·cus (hī bis′kəs, hi-), *n., pl.* **-cus·es.** any malvaceous herb, shrub, or tree of the genus *Hibiscus*, certain species of which have large, showy flowers. [< NL, L < Gk *hibiskos* mallow]

hic (hik), *interj.* (an onomatopoeic word used to imitate or represent a hiccup.)

hic·cup (hik′up, -əp), *n., v.,* **-cuped** or **-cupped, -cup·ing** or **-cup·ping.** —*n.* **1.** a quick, involuntary inspiration suddenly checked by closure of the glottis, producing a short, relatively sharp sound. **2.** Usually, **hiccups.** the condition of having such spasms: *She got the hiccups just as she began to speak.* —*v.i.* **3.** to make the sound of a hiccup: *The motor hiccuped as it started.* **4.** to have the hiccups. Also, **hic·cough** (hik′up, -əp). [alter. of *hickock* = HIC + -OCK; akin to LG *hick* hiccup]

hic ja·cet (hēk′ yä′ket; *Eng.* hik jā′set), *Latin.* here lies (often used to begin epitaphs on tombstones).

hick (hik), *n.* *Informal.* an unsophisticated, boorish, and provincial person; rube. [after *Hick*, familiar form of *Richard*]

hick·ey (hik′ē), *n., pl.* **-eys.** **1.** any device or gadget whose name is not known or is momentarily forgotten. **2.** *Elect.* a fitting used to mount a lighting fixture in an outlet box or on a pipe or stud. **3.** *Slang.* **a.** a pimple. **b.** a mark from a passionate kiss. [orig. U.S.; perh. from surname *Hickey*]

Hick·ok (hik′ok), *n.* **James Butler** ("*Wild Bill*"), 1837–1876, U.S. frontiersman.

hick·o·ry (hik′ə rē, hik′rē), *n., pl.* **-ries.** **1.** any of several North American, juglandaceous trees of the genus *Carya*, certain species of which bear edible nuts or yield a valuable wood. Cf. **pecan, shagbark.** **2.** a switch, stick, etc., of this wood. [earlier *pohickery*; akin to Algonquian *pawcohiccora* mush made of hickory nut kernels]

Hicks·ville (hiks′vil), *n.* a town on W Long Island, in SE New York. 49,820 (1970).

hid (hid), *v.* pt. and a pp. of **hide.**

hi·dal·go (hi dal′gō; *Sp.* ē thäl′gô), *n., pl.* **-gos** (-gōz; *Sp.* -gôs). **1.** a man of the lower nobility in Spain. **2.** a man of landed property or special prestige in Spanish America. [< Sp, contr. of *hi(jo) dalgo*, OSp *fijo dalgo* a noble, a person with property, a son with something < L *filius* son + *dē* with (lit., from) + *aliquō* something] —**hi·dal′go·ism, hi·dal′gism,** *n.*

Hi·dal·go (hi dal′gō; *Sp.* ē thäl′gô), *n.* a state in central Mexico. 994,598 (1960); 8057 sq. mi. *Cap.:* Pachuca.

Hi·dal·go y Cos·til·la (ē thäl′gô ē kôs tē′yä), **Mi·guel** (mē gel′), 1753–1811, Mexican priest, patriot, and revolutionist.

Hi·dat·sa (hē dät′sä), *n., pl.* **-sas,** (*esp. collectively*) **-sa** for 1. **1.** a member of a Siouan people dwelling on the Missouri River. **2.** the Siouan language of the Hidatsa tribe.

hid·den (hid′ᵊn), *adj.* concealed; obscure; covert: *hidden meaning; hidden hostility.* —**hid′den·ly,** *adv.* —**hid′den·ness,** *n.* —**Syn. 1.** secret; veiled; occult.

hide[1] (hīd), *v.,* **hid, hid·den** or **hid, hid·ing,** *n.* —*v.t.* **1.** to conceal from sight; prevent from being seen or discovered. **2.** to obstruct the view of; cover up: *The sun was hidden by the clouds.* **3.** to conceal from knowledge or exposure; keep secret: *to hide one's feelings.* —*v.i.* **4.** to conceal oneself; lie concealed: *He hid in the closet.* **5. hide out,** to go into or remain in hiding: *After breaking out of jail, he hid out in a deserted farmhouse.* [ME *hide(n)*, OE *hȳdan*; c. OFris *hūda*, Gk *keúthein* to conceal] —**hid′a·ble,** *adj.* —**hid′er,** *n.* —**Syn. 1.** mask, cloak, shroud, disguise. HIDE, CONCEAL, SECRETE mean to put out of sight or in a secret place. HIDE is the general word: *to hide one's money or purpose; A dog hides a bone.* CONCEAL is somewhat more formal: *A rock concealed them from view.* SECRETE means to put away carefully, in order to keep secret: *The spy secreted the stolen microfilms.* **3.** disguise, dissemble, suppress. —**Ant. 1.** reveal, display.

hide[2] (hīd), *n., v.,* **hid·ed, hid·ing.** —*n.* **1.** the pelt of one of the larger animals (cow, horse, buffalo, etc.), raw or dressed. **2.** *Informal.* the skin of a human being: *Get out of here or I'll tan your hide!* —*v.t.* **3.** *Informal.* to administer a beating to; thrash. [ME; OE *hȳd*; c. D *huid*, Icel *húth*, Dan, Sw *hud*, OHG *hūt* (G *Haut*), L *cutis* skin; see CUTICLE] —**hide′less,** *adj.* —**Syn. 1.** See **skin.**

A B C D E F C

Hide
A, Head;
B, Shoulder;
C, Shank; D, Bend;
E, Belly; F, Butt

hide[3] (hīd), *n.* *Old Eng. Law.* a unit of land measurement varying from 60 to 120 acres or more depending upon local usage. [ME; OE *hīd(e)*, *hīg(i)d* portion of land, family = *hīg(an)* household (c. L *civis* citizen, Gk *keîmai* to lie, abide) + *-id* pertaining to; see CITY]

hide-and-seek (hīd′ᵊn sēk′), *n.* a children's game in which one player gives the other players a chance to hide and then attempts to find them. Also called **hide-and-go-seek** (hīd′ᵊn gō sēk′).

hide·a·way (hīd′ə wā′), *n.* **1.** a place to which one can retreat; refuge. —*adj.* **2.** hidden; concealed: *a hideaway bed.*

hide·bound (hīd′bound′), *adj.* **1.** narrow and rigid in opinion: *a hidebound pedant.* **2.** confined to the past; extremely conservative. **3.** (of a horse, cow, etc.) having the back and ribs bound tightly by the hide. —**hide′bound′ness,** *n.*

hid·e·ous (hid′ē əs), *adj.* **1.** horrible or frightful to the senses; repulsive; very ugly: *a hideous monster.* **2.** shocking or revolting to the moral sense: *a hideous crime.* **3.** distressingly large: *the hideous expense of moving.* [ME *hid(ous)* (< OF *hisdos* = *hisde* horror, fright + *-os* -OUS) + -EOUS] —**hid′e·ous·ly,** *adv.* —**hid′e·ous·ness, hid·e·os·i·ty** (hid′ē os′i tē), *n.* —**Syn. 1, 2.** grisly, dreadful, appalling, ghastly. —**Ant. 1.** attractive, pleasing.

hide·out (hīd′out′), *n.* a safe place for hiding, esp. from the law. Also, **hide′-out′.**

hid·ing[1] (hī′ding), *n.* **1.** the act of concealing. **2.** the state of being concealed; concealment: *to remain in hiding.* **3.** a place or means of concealment. [ME]

hid·ing[2] (hī′ding), *n. Informal.* a flogging or thrashing.

hi·dro·sis (hi drō′sis, hī-), *n. Pathol.* excessive perspiration due to drugs, disease, or the like. [< NL, special use of Gk *hīdrōsis* sweating = *hidrō(s)* sweat + *-sis* -SIS] —**hi·drot·ic** (hi drot′ik, hī-), *adj.*

hie (hī), *v.,* **hied, hie·ing** or **hy·ing.** —*v.i.* **1.** to hasten; speed; go in haste. —*v.t.* **2.** to hasten (oneself). [ME *hie(n), hye(n),* OE *hīgian* to strive; c. D *hijgen* to pant, Gk *kī(ein)* (to) go; L *ci(ēre)* (to) cause to go]

hi·e·mal (hī′ə məl), *adj.* of or pertaining to winter; wintry. [< L *hiemāl(is)* pertaining to winter = *hiem(s)* winter (akin to Gk *chiṓn* snow, *cheimṓn* winter, Skt *hima* cold, frost, snow) + *-ālis* -AL[1]; see HIBERNAL]

hier-, var. of **hiero-** before a vowel: *hierarchy.*

hi·er·a·co·sphinx (hī′ə rā′kə sfingks′), *n., pl.* **-sphinx·es, -sphin·ges** (-sfin′jēz). (in ancient Egyptian art) a hawk-headed sphinx. [< Gk *hierāko-* (comb. form of *hiérax* hawk) + SPHINX]

hi·er·arch (hī′ə rärk′, hī′rärk), *n.* **1.** a person who rules or has authority in sacred things; high priest. **2.** a person having high position or considerable authority. **3.** one of a body of officials or minor priests in certain ancient Greek temples. [< ML *hierarch(a)* < Gk *hierárchēs* steward of sacred rites] —**hi′er·ar′chal,** *adj.*

hi·er·ar·chi·cal (hī′ə rär′ki kəl, hī rär′-), *adj.* of, belonging to, or characteristic of a hierarchy. Also, **hi′er·ar′chic.** —**hi′er·ar′chi·cal·ly,** *adv.*

hi·er·ar·chy (hī′ə rär′kē, hī′rär-), *n., pl.* **-chies.** **1.** any system of persons or things ranked one above another. **2.** government by ecclesiastical rulers. **3.** the power or dominion of a hierarch. **4.** government by an elite group. **5.** an organized body of ecclesiastical officials in successive ranks or orders. **6.** one of the three divisions of the angels, each made up of three orders, conceived as constituting a graded body. **7.** angels collectively. [< ML *hierarchi(a)* < LGk: rule or power of the high priest (see HIER-, -ARCHY); r. ME *gerarchie* < MF *ierarchie* < ML *ierarchia,* var. of *hierarchia*] —**hi′er·ar′chism,** *n.* —**hi′er·ar′chist,** *n.*

hi·er·at·ic (hī′ə rat′ik, hī rat′-), *adj.* **1.** Also, **hi′er·at′i·cal.** of or pertaining to priests or the priesthood; priestly. **2.** noting or pertaining to a form of ancient Egyptian writing consisting of abridged forms of hieroglyphics, used by the priests in keeping records. **3.** noting or pertaining to certain styles in art whose types or methods are fixed by or as if by religious tradition. [< L *hierātic(us)* < Gk *hierātikós* pertaining to the priesthood, priestly = *hier-* HIER- + *-ā-* v. suffix + *-tikos* -TIC] —**hi′er·at′i·cal·ly,** *adv.*

hiero-, a learned borrowing from Greek meaning "sacred," "priestly," used in the formation of compound words: *hierocracy.* Also, *esp. before a vowel,* **hier-.** [< Gk *hierό(s)* holy, sacred]

hi·er·oc·ra·cy (hī′ə rok′rə sē, hī rok′-), *n., pl.* **-cies.** rule or government by priests or ecclesiastics. —**hi·er·o·crat·ic** (hī′ər ə krat′ik, hī′rə-), **hi′er·o·crat′i·cal,** *adj.*

hi·er·o·dule (hī′ər ə do͞ol′, -dyo͞ol′, hī′rə-), *n.* (in ancient Greece) a temple slave. [< Gk *hieródoul(os)* temple slave = *hierό(n)* temple + *doûlos* slave] —**hi′er·o·du′lic,** *adj.*

hi·er·o·glyph·ic (hī′ər ə glif′ik, hī′rə-), *adj.* Also, **hi′er·o·glyph′i·cal.** **1.** designating or pertaining to a pictographic script, particularly that of the ancient Egyptians, in which many of the symbols are conventionalized pictures of the things represented by the words for which the symbols stand. **2.** inscribed with hieroglyphic symbols. **3.** hard to decipher; hard to read. —*n.* **4.** Also, **hi′er·o·glyph′.** a hieroglyphic symbol. **5.** Usually, **hieroglyphics.** hieroglyphic writing. **6.** a figure or symbol with a hidden meaning. **7. hieroglyphics,** writing, figures, characters, etc., difficult to decipher. [< LL *hieroglyphic(us)* < Gk *hieroglyphikós* pertaining to sacred writing] —**hi′er·o·glyph′i·cal·ly,** *adv.*

Hieroglyphics

hi·er·ol·o·gy (hī′ə rol′ə jē, hī rol′-), *n.* **1.** literature or learning regarding sacred things. **2.** hagiological literature or learning.

Hi·er·on·y·mus (hī′ə ron′ə məs), *n.* **Eu·se·bi·us** (yo͞o sē′bē əs). See **Jerome, Saint.**

hi·er·o·phant (hī′ər ə fant′, hī′rə-, hī er′ə-), *n.* **1.** (in ancient Greece) a high priest, esp. of the Eleusinia. **2.** any interpreter of sacred mysteries or esoteric principles. [< LL *hierophant(a)* < Gk *hierophántēs* = *hiero-* HIERO- + *phántēs,* prp. of *phaínein* to show, make known] —**hi′er·o·phan′tic,** *adj.* —**hi′er·o·phan′ti·cal·ly,** *adv.*

hi·fa·lu·tin (hī′fə lo͞ot′ən), *adj.* highfalutin. Also, **hi′fa·lu′tin′.**

hi-fi (hī′fī′), *n.* **1.** See **high fidelity. 2.** a radio receiver, phonograph, or other sound-reproducing apparatus possessing high fidelity. —*adj.* **3.** of, pertaining to, or characteristic of such apparatus; high-fidelity. [short form]

Hig·gin·son (hig′in sən), *n.* **Thomas Wentworth Stor·row** (stor′ō), 1823–1911, U.S. clergyman and author.

hig·gle (hig′əl), *v.i.,* **-gled, -gling.** to bargain, esp. in a petty way; haggle. [appar. var. of HAGGLE]

hig·gle·dy-pig·gle·dy (hig′əl dē pig′əl dē), *adv.* **1.** in a jumbled confusion. —*adj.* **2.** confused; jumbled. [rhyming compound < ?]

hig·gler (hig′lər), *n.* a huckster or peddler.

high (hī), *adj.* **1.** having a considerable reach or extent upward; lofty; tall. **2.** having a specified extent upward. **3.** situated above the ground or some base; elevated. **4.** intensified; greater than usual; exceeding the common degree or measure; strong or intense: *high speed; high color.* **5.** expensive, costly, or dear: *high prices; high rents.* **6.** exalted in rank, station, etc.; of exalted character or quality. **7.** *Music.* **a.** acute in pitch. **b.** a little sharp, or above the desired pitch. **8.** produced by relatively rapid vibrations; shrill. **9.** extending to or from an elevation: *a high dive.* **10.** great in quantity, as number, degree, or force. **11.** chief; principal; main. **12.** of great consequence; important; grave; serious. **13.** lofty; haughty; arrogant. **14.** advanced to the utmost extent or to the culmination: *high tide.* **15.** elated; merry or hilarious. **16.** rich, extravagant, or luxurious: *high living.* **17.** *Informal.* intoxicated with alcohol or drugs. **18.** remote: *high latitude.* **19.** extreme in opinion or doctrine, esp. religious or political. **20.** designating or pertaining to highland or inland regions. **21.** having considerable energy or potential power. **22.** *Auto.* of, pertaining to, or operating at the gear transmission ratio at which the speed of the engine crankshaft and of the drive shaft most closely correspond. **23.** *Phonet.* (of a vowel) articulated with the upper surface of the tongue relatively close to some portion of the palate, as the vowels of *eat* and *boot.* Cf. **close** (def. 50), **low**[1] (def. 31). **24.** (of meat, esp. game) tending toward a desirable or undesirable amount of decomposition; slightly tainted. **25.** *Baseball.* (of a pitched ball) crossing the plate at a level above the batter's shoulders. **26.** *Cards.* **a.** having greater value than other denominations or suits. **b.** able to take a trick; being a winning card. —*adv.* **27.** at or to a high point, place, or level. **28.** in or to a high rank or estimate: *He aims high in his political ambitions.* **29.** at or to a high amount or price. **30.** in or to a high degree. **31.** luxuriously; richly; extravagantly. **32.** *Naut.* as close to the wind as is possible while making headway with sails full. **33. fly high,** to be full of hope or elation. **34. high and dry, a.** (of a ship) grounded so as to be entirely above water at low tide. **b.** deserted; stranded. **35. high and low,** in every possible place; everywhere. —*n.* **36.** *Auto.* high gear. **37.** *Informal.* See **high school.** **38.** *Meteorol.* a pressure system characterized by relatively high pressure at its center. Cf. **anticyclone, low**[1] (def. 45). **39. on high, a.** at or to a height; above. **b.** in heaven. [ME *heigh,* var. of *hegh, hey, heh,* OE *hēah, hēh;* c. D *hoog,* Icel *hār,* Sw *hög,* G *hoch* (OHG *hoh*), Goth *hauhs,* Lith *kaũkas* swelling, *kaukarà* hill]
—**Syn. 1.** HIGH, LOFTY, TALL refer to something that has considerable height. HIGH is a general term, and denotes either extension upward or position at a considerable height: *six feet high; a high shelf.* LOFTY denotes imposing or even inspiring height: *lofty crags.* TALL is applied either to something that is high in proportion to its breadth, or to anything higher than the average of its kind: *a tall tree, building.* **6.** elevated, eminent, distinguished. —**Ant. 1.** low.

high·ball (hī′bôl′), *n.* **1.** a drink of whiskey or other liquor diluted with water, soda, or ginger ale. **2.** *Railroads.* **a.** a signal to start a train, given with the hand or with a lamp. **b.** a signal for a train to move at full speed. —*v.i.* **3.** *Slang.* (of a train) to move at full speed. —*v.t.* **4.** to signal to (the engineer of a train) to proceed. [orig. game of chance, railway signal, later taken as a missile, shot of drink, to make the drinker high]

high′ bar′, *Gymnastics.* See **horizontal bar.**

high′ beam′, an automobile headlight beam providing long-range illumination of a road. Cf. **low beam.**

high·bind·er (hī′bīn′dər), *n.* **1.** a swindler; confidence man; cheat. **2.** a member of a secret Chinese band or society employed in U.S. cities in blackmail, assassination, etc. **3.** a ruffian or rowdy.

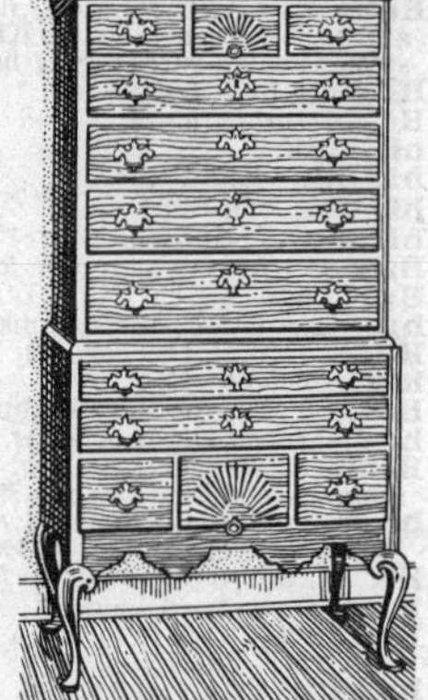
Highboy (18th century)

high′ blood′ pres′sure, elevation of the arterial blood pressure or a condition resulting from it; hypertension.

high·born (hī′bôrn′), *adj.* of high rank by birth. [ME]

high·boy (hī′boi′), *n. U.S. Furniture.* a tall chest of drawers on legs. [alter. of TALLBOY]

high·bred (hī′bred′), *adj.* **1.** of superior breed. **2.** characteristic of superior breeding.

high·brow (hī′brou′), *n.* **1.** a person of superior intellectual interests and tastes. **2.** *Disparaging.* a person with excessive intellectual or cultural pretensions; an intellectual snob. —*adj.* **3.** Also, **high′browed′.** of, pertaining to, or characteristic of a highbrow. —**high′brow′ism,** *n.*

high·chair (hī′châr′), *n.* a chair having very long legs, and usually a removable tray for use by a young child during meals.

High′ Church′, pertaining or belonging to a party in the Anglican Church emphasizing church authority and jurisdiction and upholding the historical forms of worship. Cf. **Broad Church, Low Church.** [abstracted from *High Churchman*] —**High′ Church′man.**

high-class (hī′klas′, -kläs′), *adj.* of a type superior in quality or degree: *a high-class hotel; high-class entertainment.*

high-col·ored (hī′kul′ərd), *adj.* **1.** deep in color; vivid. **2.** flushed or red; florid.

high′ com′edy, *Theat.* comedy dealing with polite society, characterized by sophisticated, witty dialogue and an intricate plot. Cf. **low comedy.** —**high′ come′dian.**

high′ command′, **1.** the leadership or highest authority of a military command or other organization. **2.** the highest headquarters of a military force.

high′ commis′sioner, **1.** an ambassadorial representative of one sovereign member of the British Commonwealth of Nations in the country of another. **2.** the head of government in a mandate, protectorate, possession, or the like.

High′ Court′ of Jus′tice. See under **Supreme Court of Judicature.**

high′ day′, **1.** a holy or festal day. **2.** heyday. [ME *heye dai* feast day]

high′-den′si·ty lipopro′tein (hī′den′si tē), *Biochem.* a blood constituent involved in the transport of cholesterol and associated with a decreased risk of atherosclerosis and heart disease. *Abbr.:* HDL Cf. **low-density lipoprotein.**

high′er ap′sis. See under **apsis.**

high′er crit′icism, the study of the Bible having as its object the establishment of such facts as authorship and date of composition, as well as provision of a basis for exegesis. Cf. **lower criticism.**

high′er educa′tion, education beyond high school, specifically that provided by colleges, graduate schools, and professional schools.

high′er mathemat′ics, the advanced areas of mathematics, customarily considered as embracing all beyond ordinary arithmetic, geometry, algebra, and trigonometry.

high·er-up (hī′ər up′), *n. Informal.* a person in a position of major authority in an organization.

high′ explo′sive, a class of explosive, as TNT, in which the reaction is so rapid as to be practically instantaneous. —**high′-ex·plo′sive,** *adj.*

high·fa·lu·tin (hī′fə lo͞ot′ən), *adj. Informal.* pompous; haughty; pretentious. Also, **high′fa·lu′tin′, hifalutin, hifalutin′, high·fa·lu·ting** (hī′fə lo͞o′tiṉg). [HIGH + *falutin* (perh. orig. *flutin*), var. of FLUTING]

high′ fidel′ity, *Electronics.* sound reproduction over the full range of audible frequencies with very little distortion of the original signal. —**high′-fi·del′i·ty,** *adj.*

high-flown (hī′flōn′), *adj.* **1.** extravagant in aims, pretensions, etc. **2.** pretentiously lofty; bombastic.

high′ fre′quency, the range of frequencies in the radio spectrum between 3 and 30 megacycles per second. —**high′-fre′quen·cy,** *adj.*

High′ Ger′man, **1.** the group of West Germanic languages that in A.D. c400–c500 underwent the second consonant shift described by Grimm's Law. The group includes German, Yiddish, Bavarian, Alemannic, and most of the dialects of central Germany. **2.** German (def. 4).

high-grade (hī′grād′), *adj.* **1.** of excellent or superior quality. **2.** (of ore) yielding a relatively large amount of the metal for which it is mined.

high-hand·ed (hī′han′did), *adj.* overbearing; arbitrary. Also, **high′hand′ed.** —**high′-hand′ed·ly, high′hand′ed·ly,** *adv.* —**high′-hand′ed·ness, high′hand′ed·ness,** *n.*

high′ hat′. See **top hat.**

high-hat (hī′hat′), *v.,* **-hat·ted, -hat·ting,** *adj. Informal.* —*v.t.* **1.** to snub or treat condescendingly. —*adj.* **2.** snobbish; disdainful; haughty. —**high′-hat′ter,** *n.*

High′ Ho′ly Day′, *Judaism.* Rosh Hashanah or Yom Kippur. Also, **High′ Hol′iday.**

high′ horse′, a haughty attitude or manner.

high′ hur′dles, *Track.* See under **hurdle** (def. 2).

high·jack (hī′jak′), *v.t., v.i.* hijack. —**high′jack′er,** *n.*

high′ jinks′, *Slang.* boisterous celebration or merrymaking; unrestrained fun. Also, **hijinks.**

high′ jump′, *Track.* a field event in which athletes compete in jumping for height over a crossbar. —**high′ jump′er.**

high-keyed (hī′kēd′), *adj.* **1.** high-strung; nervous. **2.** (of a painting) having bright or chiefly pure colors.

high·land (hī′lənd), *n.* **1.** an elevated region; a plateau. **2. highlands,** a mountainous region or elevated part of a country. —*adj.* **3.** of, pertaining to, or characteristic of highlands. [ME; OE *hēahlond*]

High·land·er (hī′lən dər), *n.* **1.** a Gael inhabiting the Highlands. **2.** (*l.c.*) an inhabitant of any highland region.

High′land fling′, fling (def. 9).

High′land Park′, **1.** a city in SE Michigan, within the city limits of Detroit. 35,444 (1970). **2.** a city in NE Illinois, on Lake Michigan. 32,263 (1970).

High·lands (hī′ləndz), *n.* (*construed as pl.*) a mountainous region in N Scotland, N of the Grampians.

high-lev·el (hī′lev′əl), *adj.* **1.** undertaken by or composed of members having a high status: *a high-level meeting.* **2.** having high status: *high-level personnel.* **3.** undertaken at or from a high altitude.

high·light (hī′līt′), *v.,* **-light·ed, -light·ing,** *n.* —*v.t.* **1.** to emphasize or make prominent. **2.** to create highlights in (a photograph, painting, etc.). —*n.* **3.** Also, **high′ light′.** an important, conspicuous, memorable, or enjoyable event, scene, part, or the like. **4.** *Art.* the point of most intense light on a represented form.

high-low (hī′lō′), *n.* a game of poker in which both high and low hands are eligible to win.

high-low-jack (hī′lō′jak′), *n.* See **all fours** (def. 2).

high·ly (hī′lē), *adv.* **1.** in or to a high degree: *highly amusing; highly seasoned food.* **2.** with high appreciation or praise: *to speak highly of a person.* **3.** at or to a high price: *a highly paid consultant.* [ME *heihliche,* OE *hēalīce*]

High′ Mass′, *Rom. Cath. Ch.* a sung Mass celebrated according to the complete rite, usually with music and incense, and at which the celebrant is attended by a deacon and subdeacon. Cf. **Low Mass.** [ME; OE *hēah-mæsse*]

high-mind·ed (hī′mīn′did), *adj.* **1.** having or showing high, exalted principles or feelings. **2.** *Rare.* proud or arrogant. —**high′-mind′ed·ly,** *adv.* —**high′-mind′ed·ness,** *n.*

high-muck-a-muck (hī′muk′ə muk′, -muk′ə muk′), *n. Slang.* an important or high-ranking person, esp. one who is pompous or conceited. Also, **high′-muck′e·ty-muck′** (-muk′ə tē-). [< Chinook jargon *hiu muckamuck,* lit., plenty food]

high-necked (hī′nekt′), *adj.* (of a garment) high at the neck.

high·ness (hī′nis), *n.* **1.** quality or state of being high; loftiness; dignity. **2.** (*cap.*) a title of honor given to members of a royal family (usually prec. by *His, Her, Your,* etc.). [ME *heyenes,* OE *hēanes*]

high′ noon′, **1.** the exact moment of noon. **2.** the high point of a stage or period; peak; pinnacle. [ME *non heye*]

high-oc·tane (hī′ok′tān), *adj.* noting a gasoline with a relatively high octane number.

high-pitched (hī′picht′), *adj.* **1.** *Music.* played or sung at a high pitch. **2.** emotionally intense. **3.** (of a roof) having an almost perpendicular slope; steep. **4.** lofty or ambitious in tone or character.

High′ Point′, a city in central North Carolina. 63,259.

high-pres·sure (hī′presh′ər), *adj., v.,* **-sured, -sur·ing.** —*adj.* **1.** having or involving a pressure above the normal. **2.** vigorous; persistent; aggressive: *high-pressure salesmanship.* —*v.t.* **3.** to employ aggressively forceful and unrelenting sales tactics on (a prospective customer).

high′ priest′, **1.** a chief priest. **2.** a person in a high position of power or influence; leader; arbiter. **3.** *Judaism.* (from Aaronic times to the 1st century A.D.) the priest ranking above all others in the priestly hierarchy and the only one permitted to enter the holy of holies. [ME *heiye prest*] —**high′ priest′hood.**

high′ relief′, *Fine Arts.* sculptured relief in which volumes are strongly projected from the background. See illus. at **relief**[2].

High′ Ren′aissance, a style of art developed in Italy in the late 15th and early 16th centuries. Cf. **Early Renaissance.**

high-rise (hī′rīz′), *adj.* **1.** (of a building) having a comparatively large number of stories and equipped with elevators: *a high-rise apartment house.* **2.** of, pertaining to, or characteristic of high-rise buildings. **3.** (of a bicycle) of a small-wheeled model with higher-than-normal handlebars and a banana-shaped seat, usually for boys or girls. —*n.* **4.** Also, **high′ rise′, high-riser.** a high-rise apartment or office building.

high-ris·er (hī′rī′zər), *n.* **1.** a bed composed of two units, with a bottom section that may be pulled out and raised to make a double bed. **2.** a high-rise bicycle.

high·road (hī′rōd′), *n.* **1.** a main road; highway. **2.** an easy or certain course.

high′ school′, **1.** a school following the ordinary grammar school and consisting of grades 9 through 12. **2.** either of two schools, one **(junior high school)** corresponding to the upper grades or grade of the ordinary grammar school together with one or more years of the ordinary high school, and another **(senior high school)** corresponding to the remainder of the ordinary high school. —**high′-school′,** *adj.*

high′ sea′, **1.** the sea or ocean beyond the three-mile limit or territorial waters of a country. **2.** Usually, **high seas. a.** the open, unenclosed waters of any sea or ocean. **b.** *Law.* the area within which transactions are subject to court of admiralty jurisdiction. [ME; OE *hēah-sæ*] —**high′-sea′,** *adj.*

high′ sign′, *Slang.* a gesture, glance, etc., used as a warning or signal.

high′ soci′ety, society (def. 9).

high-sound·ing (hī′soun′diṉg), *adj.* having an impressive or pretentious sound: *high-sounding titles.*

high-speed (hī′spēd′), *adj.* fit to operate or operating at a high speed.

high-spir·it·ed (hī′spir′i tid), *adj.* characterized by energetic enthusiasm, elation, vivacity, etc.; boldly courageous; mettlesome. —**high′-spir′it·ed·ly,** *adv.* —**high′-spir′it·ed·ness,** *n.*

high-strung (hī′struṉg′), *adj.* highly tense or nervous.

hight (hīt), *adj.* **1.** *Archaic.* called or named. —*v.t.* **2.** *Scot. Archaic.* to order; command. [ME; OE *heht,* reduplicated preterit of *hātan* to name, call, promise, command; c. G *heissen* to call, be called, mean; akin to BEHEST]

high·tail (hī′tāl′), *v.i. Informal.* **1.** to go away or leave rapidly, esp. in escaping from something or someone. **2. hightail it,** hurry; rush; scamper.

High′ Ta′tra. See **Tatra Mountains.**

high′ tea′, *Brit.* a late afternoon or early evening tea, usually consisting of meat, salad, fruit, cake, and tea.

high-tech (hī′tek′), *n.* **1.** See **high technology. 2.** a style of design in which industrial fixtures, as metal shelving, sprinkler systems, etc., are incorporated into the decor. —*adj.* **3.** of or pertaining to high-tech or high technology.

high′ technol′ogy, any technology requiring the most sophisticated scientific equipment and advanced engineering techniques, as microelectronics, data processing, genetic engineering, or telecommunications. —**high′-tech·nol′o·gy,** *adj.*

high-ten·sion (hī′ten′shən), *adj. Elect.* subjected to or capable of operating under relatively high voltage.

high-test (hī′test′), *adj.* (of gasoline) boiling at a relatively low temperature.

high′ tide′, **1.** the tide at its highest level of elevation. **2.** the time of high water. **3.** a culminating point. [ME]

high′ time′, the time just before it is too late; the appropriate time or past the appropriate time.

high-toned (hī′tōnd′), *adj.* **1.** having high principles; dignified. **2.** marked by dignified, well-bred character. **3.** affectedly stylish or genteel. Also, **high′-tone′.**

high′ trea′son, treason against the sovereign or state.

high-up (hī′up′), *adj., n., pl.* **-ups.** —*adj.* **1.** holding a high position or rank. —*n.* **2.** a person holding a high position or rank; higher-up.

high′ wa′ter, **1.** water at its greatest elevation, as in a river. **2.** See **high tide.**

high′-wa′ter mark′ (hī′wô′tər, -wot′ər), **1.** a mark showing the highest level reached by a body of water. **2.** the highest point of anything; the apex.

high·way (hī′wā′), *n.* **1.** a main road, esp. one between towns or cities. **2.** any public passage, either a road or waterway. **3.** any main or ordinary route, track, or course. [ME *heyewei,* OE *heiweg*]

high·way·man (hī′wā′mən), *n., pl.* **-men.** a holdup man, esp. one on horseback, who robs travelers along a public road.

high′ wire′, a tightrope stretched very high above the ground.

hi·jack (hī′jak′), *v.t.* **1.** to steal (something) in transit. —*v.i.* **2.** to engage in such stealing. Also, **highjack.** [back formation from *hijacker* HIGH(WAYMAN) + *jacker,* appar. JACK[1] to hunt by night + -ER[1])] —**hi′jack′er,** *n.*

hi·jinks (hī′jiṉgks′), *n.* (*construed as pl.*) See **high jinks.**

hike (hīk), *v.,* **hiked, hik·ing,** *n.* —*v.i.* **1.** to walk or march a great distance, esp. through rural areas, for pleasure, for military training, or the like. **2.** to move up or rise, as out of place or position (often fol. by *up*): *My shirt hikes up if I don't wear a belt.* **3.** to hold oneself outboard on the windward side of a heeling sailboat to reduce the amount of heel. —*v.t.* **4.** to move, draw, or raise with a jerk (often fol. by *up*): *to hike up one's socks.* **5.** to increase, often sharply and unexpectedly. —*n.* **6.** a long walk or march for pleasure, for military training, or the like. **7.** an increase or rise. [perh. dial. var. of HITCH] —**hik′er,** *n.*

hi·lar·i·ous (hi lâr′ē əs, -lar′-, hī-), *adj.* **1.** boisterously gay. **2.** cheerful; merry. **3.** funny; arousing merriment. [< L *hilari(s)* cheerful (c. Gk *hilarós* GLAD[1]) + -OUS] —**hi·lar′i·ous·ly,** *adv.* —**hi·lar′i·ous·ness,** *n.*

hi·lar·i·ty (hi lar′i tē, -lâr′-, hī-), *n.* **1.** boisterous gaiety. **2.** cheerfulness; mirthfulness. [earlier *hilaritie* < L *hilaritās.* See HILARIOUS, -TY[2]] —**Syn. 1.** See **mirth.**

Hi·lar·i·us (hi lâr′ē əs), *n.* **Saint,** died A.D. 468, pope 461–468. Also, **Hil·a·rus** (hil′ar əs).

Hil′a·ry of Poitiers′ (hil′ə rē), **Saint,** A.D. c300–368, French bishop and theologian. French, **Hi·laire de Poi·tiers** (ē lεʀ′ də pwa tyā′).

Hil·bert (hil′bərt; *Ger.* hil′bəʀt), *n.* **Da·vid** (dā′vid; *Ger.* dä′vit), 1862–1943, German mathematician.

Hil·de·brand (hil′də brand′), *n.* See **Gregory VII, Saint.** —**Hil′de·bran′di·an,** *adj., n.* —**Hil·de·brand·ine** (hil′də bran′din, -dīn), *adj.*

Hil·des·heim (hil′des hīm′), *n.* a city in N West Germany. 98,800 (1963).

hil·ding (hil′diñg), *Archaic.* —*n.* **1.** a base, contemptible person. —*adj.* **2.** base; contemptible. [ME; OE *hylding* = *hyld(an)* (to) bend, incline + *-ing* -ING[1], -ING[2]]

hill (hil), *n.* **1.** a natural elevation of the earth's surface, smaller than a mountain. **2.** an incline, esp. in a road. **3.** an artificial heap, pile, or mound. **4.** a small mound of earth raised about a cultivated plant or a cluster of such plants. **5.** the plant or plants so surrounded. **6. go over the hill,** *Slang.* **a.** to break out of prison. **b.** to absent oneself without leave from one's military unit. **7. over the hill,** past the peak of effectiveness or power. —*v.t.* **8.** to surround with hills. **9.** to form into a hill or heap. [ME; OE *hyll;* c. MD *hille,* L *coll(is)* hill, *cul(men)* top, peak, *cel(sus)* lofty, very high, Goth *hallus* rock, Lith *kal(nas)* mountain, Gk *kol(ōnós)* hill, *kol(ophṓn)* summit] —**hill′er,** *n.* —**Syn. 1.** eminence, prominence; mound, knoll, hillock; foothill.

Hill (hil), *n.* **1. Ambrose Pow·ell** (pou′əl), 1825–61, Confederate general in the U.S. Civil War. **2. James Jerome,** 1838–1916, U.S. railroad builder and financier, born in Canada.

Hil·la·ry (hil′ə rē), *n.* **Sir Edmund P.,** born 1919, New Zealand mountain climber who scaled Mt. Everest 1953.

hill·bil·ly (hil′bil′ē), *n., pl.* **-lies,** *adj.* —*n.* **1.** *Often Disparaging.* a person from a backwoods area, esp. from the mountains of the southern U.S. —*adj.* **2.** of or pertaining to a hillbilly. [HILL + *Billy,* for *William*]

hill′billy mu′sic, country-and-western music, esp. in a commercialized form.

Hil·lel (hil′āl, hil′əl; *Heb.* hē lāl′), *n.* ("*ha-Zaken*") c60 B.C.–A.D. 9?, Palestinian rabbi, president of the Sanhedrin and interpreter of Biblical law: first to formulate definite hermeneutic principles.

Hil′lel Founda′tion, *U.S.* a national organization fostering programs to enrich the religious, cultural, and social life of Jewish college students.

Hill·man (hil′mən), *n.* **Sidney,** 1887–1946, U.S. labor leader, born in Lithuania.

hill′ my′na, any of several Asian birds of the genus *Gracula,* of the starling family *Sturnidae,* esp. *G. religiosa,* that has glossy black plumage and yellow neck wattles, and that is easily tamed and taught to mimic speech.

hil·loa (hi lō′), *interj., n., pl.* **-loas,** *v.i., v.t.,* **-loaed, -loa·ing.** hallo.

hill·ock (hil′ək), *n.* a little hill. [ME *hilloc*] —**hill′ocked, hill′ock·y,** *adj.*

hill·side (hil′sīd′), *n.* the side or slope of a hill. [ME]

hill·top (hil′top′), *n.* the top or summit of a hill.

hill·y (hil′ē), *adj.,* **hill·i·er, hill·i·est. 1.** full of hills; having many hills. **2.** resembling a hill; elevated; steep. [ME; OE *hyllīc*] —**hill′i·ness,** *n.*

Hill·yer (hil′yər), *n.* **Robert (Sil·li·man)** (sil′i mən), 1895–1961, U.S. poet and critic.

Hi·lo (hē′lō), *n.* a seaport on E Hawaii island, in SE Hawaii. 26,353 (1970).

hilt (hilt), *n.* **1.** the handle of a sword or dagger. **2.** the handle of any weapon or tool. **3. to the hilt,** to the maximum extent or degree; completely; fully. —*v.t.* **4.** to furnish with a hilt. [ME, OE *hilt(e);* c. MD *hilt(e),* Icel *hjalt,* OHG *helza* sword hilt] —**hilt′less,** *adj.*

hi·lum (hī′ləm), *n.* **1.** *Bot.* **a.** the mark or scar on a seed produced by separation from its funicle or placenta. **b.** the nucleus of a granule of starch. **2.** *Anat.* the region at which the vessels, nerves, etc., enter or emerge from a part. [< NL < L: little thing, trifle; see NIHIL, NIL]

Hil·ver·sum (hil′vər səm), *n.* a city in the central Netherlands. 98,998 (1959).

him (him; *unstressed* im), *pron.* the objective case of **he,** both as direct and as indirect object: *I'll see him tomorrow. Give him the message.* [ME, OE, dat. of *hē* HE[1]]

H.I.M., His (or Her) Imperial Majesty.

Hi·ma·chal Pra·desh (hi mä′chəl prə dāsh′), a union territory in N India. 1,351,144 (1961); 10,904 sq. mi. *Cap.:* Simla.

Him·a·la·yas (him′ə lā′əz, hi mäl′yəz), *n.* **the,** a mountain range extending about 1500 mi. along the border between India and Tibet. Highest peak, Mt. Everest, 29,028 ft. Also called **the Him′a·la′ya, Him′ala′ya Moun′tains.** —**Him′a·la′yan,** *adj.*

hi·mat·i·on (hi mat′ē on′), *n., pl.* **-mat·i·a** (-mat′ē ə). *Gk. Antiq.* a garment consisting of a rectangular piece of cloth thrown over the left shoulder and wrapped about the body. [< Gk, dim. of *h(e)imat-* (s. of *heima*) dress, garment]

Hi·me·ji (hē′me jē′), *n.* a city on SW Honshu, in S Japan, W of Kobe. 361,179 (1964).

Himm·ler (him′lər; *Ger.* him′ləʀ), *n.* **Hein·rich** (hīn′rikh), 1900–45, German Nazi leader and chief of the secret police.

him·self (him self′; *medially often* im self′), *pron.* **1.** an emphatic appositive of **him** or **he:** *He himself spoke to the men.* **2.** a reflexive form of **him:** *He cut himself.* **3.** (used in absolute constructions): *Himself the soul of honor, he included many rascals among his intimates.* **4.** *Nonstandard.* (used in comparisons after *as* or *than*): *His wife is as stingy as himself.* **5.** *Nonstandard.* (used as the object of a preposition or as the direct or indirect object of a verb): *The old car only had room for himself and three others.* **6.** his normal or customary self. **7.** *Irish Eng.* a man of importance, esp. the master of the house. [ME *him selven,* OE *him selfum,* dat. sing. of *hē self*] —**Usage.** See **myself.**

Him·yar·ite (him′yə rīt′), *n.* **1.** one of an ancient people of southern Arabia speaking a Semitic language. **2.** a descendant of these people. —*adj.* **3.** Himyaritic. [< Ar *Himyar* (name of a tribe and an old dynasty of Yemen) + -ITE[1]]

Him·yar·it·ic (him′yə rit′ik), *adj.* **1.** of or pertaining to the Himyarites and to the remains of their civilization. —*n.* **2.** a Semitic language anciently spoken in southern Arabia: extinct by 1100.

hin (hin), *n.* an ancient Hebrew unit of liquid measure equal to about one and one half gallons. [< L (Vulgate) < Gk (Septuagint) < Heb *hīn* < Egypt *hnw*]

Hi·na·ya·na (hē′nə yä′nə), *n.* the earlier of the two great schools of Buddhism, still prevalent in Ceylon, Burma, Thailand, and Cambodia, emphasizing personal salvation through one's own efforts. Also called **Theravada.** Cf. **Mahayana.** [< Skt = *hīna* left behind (i.e., poorer) + *yāma* vehicle (lit., movement)] —**Hi′na·ya′nist,** *n.*

hind[1] (hīnd), *adj.* situated in the rear or at the back; posterior. [ME *hinde* (adv.), OE *hindan* from behind, at the back; c. G *hinten;* see BEHIND, HINDER[2]] —**Syn.** See **back**[1].

hind[2] (hīnd), *n., pl.* **hinds,** (*esp. collectively*) **hind. 1.** *Zool.* the female of the deer, chiefly the red deer, esp. in and after the third year. **2.** any of several speckled serranid fishes of the genus *Epinephelus,* found in the warmer waters of the western Atlantic Ocean. [ME, OE; c. D *hinde,* Icel, Dan, Sw *hind,* OHG *hinta* (G, LG *Hinde*)]

hind[3] (hīnd), *n. Archaic.* **1.** a peasant or rustic. **2.** a farm laborer. [ME *hine* (sing.), *hīne* (pl.), OE *hīne* < *hī(g)na,* gen. pl. of *hīgan* members of a household, domestics]

Hind, Hindustani (def. 1).

Hind., 1. Hindustan. 2. Hindustani.

hind·brain (hīnd′brān′), *n. Anat.* **1.** the rhombencephalon, being the posterior of the three primary divisions of the brain and including the cerebellum, pons, and medulla oblongata. **2.** the metencephalon.

Hin·de·mith (hin′də mith; *Ger.* hin′də mit), *n.* **Paul** (pôl; *Ger.* poul), 1895–1963, German composer.

Hin·den·burg (hin′dən bûrg′; *Ger.* hin′dən bŏŏʀk′), *n.* **1. Paul von** (pôl von; *Ger.* poul fən), (*Paul von Beneckendorff und von Hindenburg*), 1847–1934, German field marshal; 2nd president of Germany 1925–34. **2.** German name of **Zabrze.**

Hin′denburg line′, a line of fortifications established by the German army in World War I, near the French-Belgian border. [named after P. von HINDENBURG]

hin·der[1] (hin′dər), *v.t.* **1.** to cause delay, interruption, or difficulty in; check; retard; hamper. **2.** to prevent from doing, acting, or happening; stop. —*v.i.* **3.** to be an obstacle or impediment. [ME *hindre(n),* OE *hindrian* to hold back < *hinder* HINDER[2]; c. G *hindern*] —**hin′der·er,** *n.* —**hin′der·ing·ly,** *adv.* —**Syn. 1.** impede, encumber, obstruct. **2.** block, thwart. See **prevent.** —**Ant. 1.** encourage. **2.** aid.

hind·er[2] (hīn′dər), *adj.* situated at the rear or back; posterior: *the hinder part of the ship.* [ME; OE *hinder* (adv.) behind; c. G *hinter* (prep.) behind]

hind·er·most (hīn′dər mōst′ *or, esp. Brit.,* -məst), *adj. Obs.* hindmost.

hind·gut (hīnd′gut′), *n. Embryol., Zool.* the lower part of the embryonic alimentary canal from which the colon and rectum develop. Cf. **foregut, midgut.**

Hin·di (hin′dē), *n.* **1.** the most widely spoken of the modern Indic vernaculars, esp. its best-known variety, Western Hindi. **2.** a literary language derived from Hindustani, used by Hindus. [< Hindi, Urdu = *Hind* INDIA + *-ī* suffix of appurtenance; r. *Hinduee* < Pers *Hinduī*]

hind·most (hīnd′mōst′ *or, esp. Brit.,* -məst), *adj.* farthest behind; nearest the rear; last.

Hin·doo (hin′dōō), *n., pl.* **-doos,** *adj.* Hindu.

Hin·doo·ism (hin′dōō iz′əm), *n.* Hinduism.

Hin·doo·sta·ni (hin′dŏŏ stä′nē, -stan′ē), *n., adj.* Hindustani. Also, **Hin·do·sta·ni** (hin′dō stä′nē, -stan′ē).

hind·quar·ter (hīnd′kwôr′tər), *n.* **1.** the posterior end of a halved carcass of beef, lamb, etc., sectioned usually between the twelfth and thirteenth ribs. **2. hindquarters,** the rear part of an animal.

hin·drance (hin′drəns), *n.* **1.** an impeding, stopping, preventing, or the like. **2.** the state of being hindered. **3.** a means or cause of hindering. [late ME *hinderaunce*] —**Syn. 3.** impediment, obstruction. See **obstacle.**

hind′ shank′. See under **shank** (def. 4).

hind·sight (hīnd′sīt′), *n.* recognition of the nature and requirements of a situation, event, etc., after its occurrence.

Hin·du (hin′dōō), *n.* **1.** a person who adheres to Hinduism. **2.** a native or inhabitant of Hindustan or India. —*adj.* **3.** of or pertaining to the people of Hindustan or India. **4.** of or pertaining to Hindus or Hinduism. Also, **Hindoo.** [< Pers *Hindū* Indian (adj., n.) = *Hind* INDIA + *-ū* adj. suffix]

Hin·du·ism (hin′dōō iz′əm), *n.* the common religion of India, based upon the religion of the original Aryan settlers as expounded and evolved in the Vedas, the Upanishads, the Bhagavad-Gita, etc. Also, **Hindooism.**

Hin′du Kush′, a mountain range in S Asia, mostly in NE Afghanistan, extending W from the Himalayas. Highest peak, Tirach Mir, 25,420 ft. Also called **Hin′du Kush′ Moun′tains.**

Hin·du·stan (hin′dŏŏ stän′, stan′), *n.* **1.** Persian name of India, esp. the part N of the Deccan. **2.** the predominantly Hindu areas of India, as contrasted with the predominantly Muslim areas of Pakistan. Cf. **India.**

Hin·du·sta·ni (hin′dŏŏ stä′nē, -stan′ē), *n.* **1.** a language and lingua franca of northern India based on a dialect of Western Hindi spoken around Delhi. *Abbr.:* Hind, Hind. Cf. **Hindi** (def. 2), **Urdu.** —*adj.* **2.** of or pertaining to Hindustan, its people, or their languages. Also, **Hindoostani, Hindostani.** [< Hindi, Urdu < Pers = *Hindūstān* (*Hindū* HINDU + *stān* country) + *-ī* suffix of appurtenance]

Hines (hīnz), *n.* **Earl** ("*Fatha*"), 1905–83, U.S. jazz pianist.

hinge (hinj), *n., v.,* **hinged, hing·ing.** —*n.* **1.** a joint device or flexible piece on which a door, gate, shutter, lid, or other attached part turns, swings, or moves. **2.** a natural anatomical joint at which motion occurs around a transverse axis, as that of the knee or a bivalve shell. **3.** that on which something is based or depends; principle; central rule. **4.** Also called **mount.** *Philately.* a gummed sticker for affixing a stamp to a page of an album, so folded as to form a hinge, allowing the stamp to be raised to reveal the text beneath. —*v.i.* **5.** to depend or turn on, or as on, a hinge (usually followed by *on* or *upon*): *Everything hinges on his decision.* —*v.t.* **6.** to furnish with or attach by a hinge or hinges. **7.** to attach as if by a hinge. **8.** to cause to depend; condition. [ME *henges* (pl.) OE **hencg* (sing.); c. LG *heng(e),* MD *henge* hinge; akin to HANG] —**hinge′less,** *adj.* —**hinge′-like′,** *adj.* —**hing′er,** *n.*

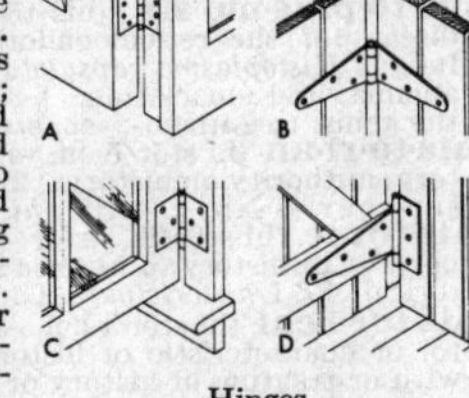

Hinges
A, Butt hinge; B, Strap-hinge; C, Flap hinge; D, Cross-garnet

hin·ny (hin′ē), *n., pl.* **-nies.** the offspring of a female donkey and a stallion. Cf. **mule**[1] (defs. 1, 2). [obs. *hinne* (< L *hinnus* hinny) + -Y[2]]

hint (hint), *n.* **1.** an indirect or covert suggestion or implication; an intimation or clue. **2.** a very slight or hardly noticeable amount. **3.** *Obs.* an occasion or opportunity. —*v.t.* **4.** to give a hint of. —*v.i.* **5.** to make indirect suggestion or allusion. [var. of *hent* (n.), ME *hentne, hinten* to seize, OE *hentan,* perh. syncopated var. of **hendettan* = *hend(an)* (to) handle (see HAND) + *-ettan* v. suffix] —**hint′er,** *n.* —**hint′ing·ly,** *adv.*
—**Syn. 1.** allusion, insinuation, innuendo; inkling. **4.** imply. HINT, INTIMATE, INSINUATE denote the conveying of an idea to the mind indirectly or without full or explicit statement. To HINT is to convey an idea covertly or indirectly, but intelligibly: *to hint that one would like a certain present; to hint that bits of gossip might be true.* To INTIMATE is to give a barely perceptible hint, often with the purpose of influencing action: *to intimate that something may be possible.* To INSINUATE is to hint artfully, often at what one would not dare to say directly: *to insinuate something against someone's reputation.* —**Ant. 4.** express, declare.

hin·ter·land (hin′tər land′), *n.* **1.** an inland area supplying goods to a port. **2.** the land lying behind a coastal district. **3.** Often, **hinterlands.** the remote or less developed parts of a country; back country. [< G: lit., hinder land, i.e., land behind]

Hior·dis (hyôr′dis), *n.* (in the *Volsunga Saga*) the second wife of Sigmund and the mother of Sigurd.

hip[1] (hip), *n., adj., v.,* **hipped, hip·ping.** —*n.* **1.** the projecting part of each side of the body formed by the side of the pelvis and the upper part of the femur and the flesh covering them; haunch. **2.** See **hip joint. 3.** *Archit.* the inclined projecting angle formed by the junction of a sloping side and a sloping end, or of two adjacent sloping sides, of a roof. **4. on** or **upon the hip,** *Archaic.* at a disadvantage. **5. smite hip and thigh,** to attack unmercifully; overcome. Judg. 15:8. —*adj.* **6.** (esp. of a garment) extending to the hips; hiplength. —*v.t.* **7.** to injure or dislocate the hip of (an animal). [ME *hipe, hupe,* OE *hype;* c. OHG *huf* (G *Hüf(te)* hip), Goth *hups* hip, loin; cf. Gk *kýbos* cube, the hollow above the hips, L *cubitus* elbow] —**hip′less,** *adj.* —**hip′like′,** *adj.*

hip[2] (hip), *n.* the ripe fruit of a rose, esp. of a wild rose. [ME *hepe,* OE *hēope* hip, briar; c. OHG *hiufo* bramble]

hip[3] (hip), *interj.* (used as a cheer or in signaling for cheers): *Hip, hip hurrah!* [?]

hip[4] (hip), *adj.,* **hip·per, hip·pest.** *Slang.* familiar with the latest ideas, styles, etc.; informed; knowledgeable. [?]

hip·bone (hip′bōn′), *n.* See **innominate bone.**

hip′ boot′, a hip-high boot, usually of rubber.

hip·hug·gers (hip′hug′ərz), *n.* (*construed as pl.*) slacks that are belted or fastened at the hips rather than at the waist.

hip′ joint′, a ball-and-socket joint between the head of the femur and the innominate bone.

hip·length (hip′lengkth′, -length′), *adj.* reaching to or covering the hips, as clothing.

hipp-, var. of **hippo-** before a vowel.

hip·parch (hip′ärk), *n.* a cavalry commander in ancient Greece. [< Gk *hípparch(os)* = *hipp-* HIPP- + *-archos* -ARCH]

Hip·par·chus (hi pär′kəs), *n.* **1.** died 514 B.C., tyrant of Athens 527–514. **2.** c190–c125 B.C., Greek astronomer. **3.** a walled plain in the fourth quadrant of the face of the moon. ab. 100 mi. in diam.

hipped[1] (hipt), *adj.* **1.** having hips. **2.** having hips as specified (usually used in combination): *broad-hipped; narrow-hipped.* **3.** (esp. of livestock) having the hip injured or dislocated. **4.** *Archit.* formed with a hip or hips, as a roof. [HIP[1] + -ED[3]]

hipped[2] (hipt), *adj.* *Informal.* greatly interested or preoccupied; obsessed (usually fol. by *on*): *He's hipped on golf.* [archaic *hip* altered shortening of HYPOCHONDRIA + -ED[3]]

Hip·pi·as (hip′ē əs), *n.* fl. 6th century B.C., tyrant of Athens (brother of Hipparchus, son of Pisistratus).

hip·pie (hip′ē), *n.* a person, esp. of the late 1960's, who rejects established institutions and values and seeks spontaneity, direct personal relations expressing love, and expanded consciousness, most obviously expressed by wearing nonconventional costumes ornamented with flowers, beads, and bells, and by taking psychedelic drugs. Also, **hippy.** [HIP[4] + -IE]

hip·po (hip′ō), *n., pl.* **-pos.** *Informal.* hippopotamus. [by shortening]

Hip·po (hip′ō), *n.* See **Hippo Regius.**

hippo-, an element appearing in loan words from Greek, where it meant "horse" (*hippodrome*); on this model, used in the formation of compound words. Also, *esp. before a vowel,* **hipp-.** [< Gk *híppo(s)* horse; c. L *equus,* OIr *ech,* OE *eoh,* Skt *aśvas*]

hip·po·cam·pus (hip′ə kam′pəs), *n., pl.* **-pi** (-pī). *Anat.* an enfolding of cerebral cortex into the lateral fissure of a cerebral hemisphere having the shape in cross section of a sea horse. [< L < Gk *hippókampos* = *hippo-* HIPPO- + *kámpos* sea monster] —**hip′po·cam′pal,** *adj.*

hip·po·cras (hip′ə kras′), *n.* an old medicinal cordial made of wine mixed with spices. [ME *ypocras,* appar. short for *ypocras wyn* (trans. of ML *vīnum hippocraticum;* so called because clarified by filtering through a strainer named after Hippocrates); ME *Ypocras* < ML *Hippocrās,* alter. of L *Hippocratēs* HIPPOCRATES, on model of words like *cīvitās* (nom.), *cīvitātis* (gen.)]

Hip·poc·ra·tes (hi pok′rə tēz′), *n.* ("*Father of Medicine*") c460–c360 B.C., Greek physician. —**Hip·po·crat·ic** (hip′ə krat′ik), **Hip′po·crat′i·cal,** *adj.*

Hip′pocrat′ic oath′, an oath embodying the duties and obligations of physicians, usually taken by those about to begin the practice of medicine.

Hip·po·crene (hip′ə krēn′, hip′ə krē′nē), *n.* a spring on Mount Helicon sacred to the Muses and regarded as a source of poetic inspiration. —**Hip′po·cre′ni·an,** *adj.*

hip·po·drome (hip′ə drōm′), *n.* **1.** an arena or structure for equestrian and other spectacles. **2.** (in ancient Greece and Rome) a course or circus for horse races and chariot races. [< L *hippodrom(os)* < Gk]

hip·po·griff (hip′ə grif′), *n.* a fabulous creature resembling a griffin but having the body and hind parts of a horse. Also, **hip′po·gryph′.** [earlier *hippogryph,* Latinized < It *ippogrifo*]

Hip·pol·y·te (hi pol′i tē′), *n.* *Class. Myth.* a queen of the Amazons, variously said to have been killed by Hercules or to have been conquered and married by Theseus. Also, **Hip·po·ly·ta** (hi pol′i tə).

Hip·pol·y·tus (hi pol′i təs), *n.* *Class. Myth.* the son of Theseus who was falsely accused by his stepmother, Phaedra, of raping her after he had rejected her advances and was killed by Poseidon. —**Hip·pol′y·tan,** *adj.*

Hip·pom·e·don (hi pom′i don′), *n.* *Class. Myth.* one of the Seven against Thebes.

Hip·pom·e·nes (hi pom′ə nēz′), *n.* *Class. Myth.* the successful suitor of Atalanta.

hip·po·pot·a·mus (hip′ə pot′ə məs), *n., pl.* **-mus·es, -mi** (-mī′). a large herbivorous mammal, *Hippopotamus amphibius,* having a thick hairless body, short legs, and a large head and muzzle, found in and near the rivers, lakes, etc., of Africa, and able to remain under water for a considerable time. [< L < Gk *hippopótamos* the river horse (of Egypt) = *híppo(s)* HIPPO- + *potamós* river] —**hip·po·po·tam·ic** (hip′ə pə tam′ik), **hip·po·po·ta·mi·an** (hip′ə pə tā′mē ən), *adj.*

Hippopotamus
(4½ ft. high at shoulder; length 13 ft.)

Hip·po Re·gi·us (hip′ō rē′jē əs), a seaport of ancient Numidia: St. Augustine was bishop here 395–430 A.D. Also called **Hippo.**

Hip·po Za·ry·tus (hip′ō zə rī′təs), ancient name of **Bizerte.**

-hippus, var. of **hippo-** as final element of compounds: *eohippus.* [< L < Gk *-hippos*]

hip·py[1] (hip′ē), *adj.,* **-pi·er, -pi·est.** having big hips: *a hippy girl.* [HIP[1] + -Y[1]]

hip·py[2] (hip′ē), *n., pl.* **-pies.** hippie. [HIP[4] + -Y[1]]

hip′ roof′, *Archit.* a roof with sloping ends and sides; a hipped roof. See illus. at **roof.** —**hip′-roofed′,** *adj.*

hip·shot (hip′shot′), *adj.* **1.** having the hip dislocated. **2.** lame; awkward.

hip·ster (hip′stər), *n.* *Slang.* **1.** a person who is hip. **2.** a person, esp. during the 1950's, characterized by a particularly strong sense of alienation from most social intercourse and endeavor.

hi·ra·ga·na (hēr′ə gä′nə), *n.* the cursive and more widely used of the two Japanese syllabaries. Cf. **katakana.** [< Jap = *hira* extended, flat, broad + *kana* syllabary, spelling; see KATAKANA]

Hi·ram (hī′rəm), *n.* a king of Tyre in the 10th century B.C. I Kings 5.

Hi·ra·nu·ma (hē rä′nōō mä′), *n.* **Baron Ki·i·chi·ro** (kē ē′chē rō′), 1867?–1952, Japanese statesman.

hir·cine (hûr′sīn, -sin), *adj.* **1.** of, pertaining to, or resembling a goat. **2.** having a goatish odor. **3.** lustful. [< L *hircīn(us)* of a goat = *hirc(us)* goat + *-īnus* -INE[1]]

hire (hīər), *v.,* **hired, hir·ing,** *n.* —*v.t.* **1.** to engage the services of for wages or other payment. **2.** to engage the temporary use of at a set price. **3.** to grant the temporary use of, or the services of, for a compensation (often fol. by *out*): *We hired ourselves out as baby-sitters. They hire out glassware for parties.* **4.** to pay for the desired action or conduct of. **5. hire on,** to obtain employment. **6. hire out,** to offer or exchange one's services for payment. —*n.* **7.** the price or compensation paid for the temporary use of something, as for services or labor; pay. **8.** the act of hiring. **9.** the state or condition of being hired. **10. for hire,** available for use or service in exchange for payment. [ME (n.); OE *hȳr;* c. D *huur,* LG *hüre* (whence D *hyre,* Sw *hyra,* G *Heuer*), OFris *hēre,* ME *hire(n),* OE *hȳrian* (v.); c. D *huren,* LG *hüren,* OFris *hēra*] —**hir′a·ble, hire′a·ble,** *adj.* —**hir′er,** *n.*
—**Syn. 1.** employ. **2, 3.** let, lease. HIRE, CHARTER, RENT refer to paying money for the use of something. HIRE is a general word, most commonly applied to paying money for labor or services, but is also used in reference to paying for the temporary use of automobiles (usually with a chauffeur), halls, etc.: *to hire a gardener, a delivery truck, a hall for a convention.* CHARTER formerly meant to pay for the use

of a vessel, but is now applied with increasing frequency to leasing any conveyance for the use of a group: *to charter a boat.* RENT is used in the latter sense, also, but is usually applied to paying a set sum once or at regular intervals for the use of a dwelling, personal effects, an automobile that one drives oneself, etc.: *to rent a car, a building.*

hire·ling (hīər′liṉg), *n.* **1.** a person who works for payment, esp. one who works only for the sake of payment. **2.** a venal or mercenary person. **—*adj.* 3.** serving for hire. **4.** venal; mercenary. [OE *hȳrling*]

hire′-pur′chase sys′tem (hīər′pûr′chəs), *Brit.* a system of paying for a commodity in regular installments while using it. Also called **hire′-pur′chase.**

Hi·ro·hi·to (hēr′ō hē′tō; *Jap.* hē′Rô hē′tô), *n.* ("*Showa*") born 1901, emperor of Japan since 1926.

Hi·ro·shi·ge (hēr′ō shē′gā; *Jap.* hē′Rô shē′ge), *n.* **An·do** (än′dô′), ("*Tokube*"), 1797–1858, Japanese painter.

Hi·ro·shi·ma (hēr′ō shē′mə, hi rō′shi mə; *Jap.* hē′Rô-shē′mä), *n.* a seaport on SW Honshu, in SW Japan: first military use of atomic bomb August 6, 1945. 492,127 (1964).

hir·ple (hûr′pəl, hir′-), *v.*, **-pled, -pling,** *n.* *Brit. Dial.* **—*v.i.* 1.** to walk lamely; hobble. **—*n.* 2.** a crawling or limping gait. [late ME (Scot) < ?]

hir·sute (hûr′so͞ot, hûr so͞ot′), *adj.* **1.** hairy; shaggy. **2.** *Bot., Zool.* covered with long, stiff hairs. **3.** of, pertaining to, or characteristic of hair. [< L *hirsūt(us)* rough, shaggy, bristly; akin to HORRID] **—hir′sute·ness,** *n.*

hir·u·din (hir′yə din, hir′ə-, hi ro͞od′ən), *n.* a powder, used as an anticoagulant. [formerly trademark]

hi·ru·di·noid (hi ro͞od′ənoid′), *adj.* of, pertaining to, or resembling a leech. [< L *hirudin-* (s. of *hirudō*) leech + -OID]

hi·run·dine (hi run′din, -dīn), *adj.* of, pertaining to, or resembling the swallow. [< LL *hirundine(us)* of a swallow = *hirundin-* (s. of *hirundō*) swallow + *-eus* -EOUS]

his (hiz; *unstressed* iz), *pron.* **1.** the possessive form of **he** (used as an attributive or predicative adjective): *His hat is the brown one. Do you mind his speaking first? This book is his.* **2.** that or those belonging to him: *His was the cleverest remark of all. I borrowed a tie of his.* [ME, OE, gen. of *hē* HE[1]] **—Usage.** See **me.**

his'n (hiz′ən), *pron.* *Nonstandard.* his. Also, **hisn.** [ME *hysene*]

His·pa·ni·a (hi spā′nē ə, -spän′yə), *n.* *Literary.* Spain.

His·pan·ic (hi span′ik), *adj.* **1.** Spanish. **2.** Latin American. **—*n.* 3.** an American citizen or resident of Spanish descent. [< L *hispānic(us).* See HISPANIA, -IC]

His·pan·i·cize (hi span′i sīz′), *v.t.*, **-cized, -ciz·ing.** (*sometimes l.c.*) **1.** to make Spanish in character, custom, or style. **2.** to bring under Spanish domination or influence. Also, *Brit.*, **His·pan′i·cise′.** **—His·pan′i·ci·za′tion,** *n.*

His·pan·io·la (his′pən yō′lə; *Sp.* ēs′pän yô′lä), *n.* an island in the West Indies, comprising the republic of Haiti and the Dominican Republic. 7,572,700 (est. 1965); 29,843 sq. mi. Formerly, **Haiti, Hayti.**

his·pa·nism (his′pə niz′əm), *n.* (*often cap.*) a word, phrase, feature, etc., characteristic of or associated with Spain. [< Sp *hispanism(o)* = *hispan(o)* Spanish (< L *Hispānus*) + *-ismo* -ISM]

His·pa·no (hi spa′nō, hi spä′nō), *n., pl.* **-nos.** Hispanic.

his·pid (his′pid), *adj.* *Bot., Zool.* rough with stiff hairs, bristles, or minute spines. [< L *hispid(us)* rough, shaggy] **—his·pid′i·ty,** *n.*

his·pid·u·lous (hi spij′ə ləs), *adj.* *Bot., Zool.* covered with stiff, short hairs.

hiss (his), *v.i.* **1.** to make or emit a sharp sound like that of the letter *s* when prolonged. **2.** to express disapproval or contempt by making this sound. **—*v.t.* 3.** to express disapproval of by hissing. **4.** to silence or drive away by hissing. **—*n.* 5.** a hissing sound, esp. one made in disapproval. [unexplained var. of dial. *hish,* ME *hisshe(n)* (to) hiss, OE *hyscan* to jeer at, rail < *husc* jeering; c. OS, OHG *hosc*] **—hiss′er,** *n.* **—hiss′ing·ly,** *adv.*

Hiss (his), *n.* **Alger,** born 1904, U.S. public official; accused of espionage 1948 and imprisoned for perjury 1950–54.

his·self (hi self′, hiz-), *pron.* *Nonstandard.* himself. [ME]

hist (st; *spelling pron.* hist), *interj.* (a sibilant exclamation used to attract attention, command silence, etc.)

hist-, var. of **histo-** before a vowel: *histidine.*

hist., **1.** histology. **2.** historian. **3.** historical. **4.** history.

His·ta·drut (his tä dro͞ot′), *n.* a labor federation in Israel, founded in 1920.

his·tam·i·nase (hi stam′ə nās′), *n.* *Biochem.* an enzyme that catalyzes the decomposition of histamine, used in treating allergies.

his·ta·mine (his′tə mēn′, -min), *n.* *Biochem.* **1.** an amine compound, $C_5H_9N_3$, released in allergic reactions: it dilates blood vessels, stimulates gastric secretions, and causes contraction of the uterus. **2.** *Pharm.* a commercial form of this compound, obtained from histidine. Also, **his·ta·min** (his′tə-min). Cf. **antihistamine.** [HIST(IDINE) + -AMINE] **—his·ta·min·ic** (his′tə min′ik), *adj.*

his·ti·dine (his′ti dēn′, -din), *n.* *Biochem.* a basic amino acid, $C_3H_3N_2CH_2CH(NH_2)COOH$, converted by putrefactive organisms into histamine. Also, **his·ti·din** (his′ti din). [HIST- + -ID[3] + -INE[2]]

his·ti·o·cyte (his′tē ə sīt′), *n.* *Anat.* a macrophage. [< Gk *histío(n),* dim. of *histós* web + -CYTE] **—his·ti·o·cyt·ic** (his′tē ə sit′ik), *adj.*

histo-, a learned borrowing from Greek meaning "tissue," used in the formation of compound words: *histology.* Also, *esp. before a vowel,* **hist-.** [< Gk, comb. form of *histós* web (of a loom), tissue]

his·to·gen·e·sis (his′tə jen′i sis), *n.* *Biol.* the origin and development of tissues. **—his·to·ge·net·ic** (his′tə jə net′ik), *adj.* **—his′to·ge·net′i·cal·ly,** *adv.*

his·to·gram (his′tə gram′), *n.* *Statistics.* a graph of a frequency distribution in which rectangles with bases on the horizontal axis are given widths equal to the class intervals and heights equal to the corresponding frequencies. [HISTO(RY) + -GRAM]

his·tol·o·gist (hi stol′ə jist), *n.* a specialist in histology.

his·tol·o·gy (hi stol′ə jē), *n.* **1.** the branch of biology dealing with the study of tissues. **2.** the structure, esp. the microscopic structure, of organic tissues. **—his·to·log·i·cal** (his′tᵊloj′i kəl), **his′to·log′ic,** *adj.* **—his′to·log′i·cal·ly,** *adv.*

his·tol·y·sis (hi stol′i sis), *n.* *Biol.* disintegration or dissolution of organic tissues. **—his·to·lyt·ic** (his′tᵊlit′ik), *adj.*

his·tone (his′tōn), *n.* *Biochem.* any of a class of protein substances, as globin, having marked basic properties.

his·to·plas·mo·sis (his′tō plaz mō′sis), *n.* *Pathol.* a disease of the reticuloendothelial system, caused by the fungus *Histoplasma capsulatum* and characterized by fever, anemia, and emaciation. [< NL = *Histoplasm(a)* name of the genus (see HISTO-, -PLASM) + *-ōsis* -OSIS]

his·to·ri·an (hi stôr′ē ən, -stôr′-), *n.* **1.** an expert in history; authority on history. **2.** a writer of history; chronicler. [HISTORY + -AN; r. earlier *historien* < MF]

his·tor·ic (hi stôr′ik, -stor′-), *adj.* **1.** well-known or important in history: *a historic spot; historic occasions.* **2.** historical. [< L *historic(us)* < Gk *historikós* historical, scientific]

his·tor·i·cal (hi stôr′i kəl, -stor′-), *adj.* **1.** of, pertaining to, or characteristic of history or past events. **2.** dealing with or treating of history or past events. **3.** based on history or on documented material from the past: *a historical pageant at Versailles.* **4.** of, pertaining to, or of the nature of history, as opposed to legend or fiction or as distinguished from religious belief. **5.** narrated or mentioned in history; belonging to the past. **6.** historic (def. 1). **7.** noting or pertaining to analysis based on a comparison among several periods of development of a phenomenon, as in language, economics, etc. [< L *historic(us)* HISTORIC + -AL[1]] **—his·tor′i·cal·ly,** *adv.* **—his·tor′i·cal·ness,** *n.*

histor′ical linguis′tics. See **diachronic linguistics.**

histor′ical mate′rialism, (in Marxism) the body of theory, in dialectical materialism, dealing with historical process and social causation. Cf. **economic determinism.**

histor′ical meth′od, the development of general principles by the study of historical facts.

histor′ical nov′el, a narrative in novel form, characterized chiefly by an imaginative reconstruction of historical events and personages.

histor′ical pres′ent, *Gram.* the present tense used in narrating a past event.

histor′ical school′, **1.** a school of economists who maintained that the factors making up an economy are variable and develop out of social institutions. **2.** *Law.* the school of jurists who maintain that law is not to be regarded so much as resulting from commands of sovereigns as from historical and social circumstances.

his·tor·i·cism (hi stôr′i siz′əm, -stor′-), *n.* **1.** a theory that history is determined by immutable laws and not by human agency. **2.** a theory that all cultural phenomena are historically determined and that historians must study each period without imposing any personal or absolute value system. **3.** a profound or excessive respect for historical institutions, as laws or traditions. **4.** a search for laws of historical evolution that would explain and predict historical phenomena. **—his·tor′i·cist,** *n., adj.*

his·to·ric·i·ty (his′tə ris′i tē), *n.* historical authenticity. [prob. < F *historicité*]

his·to·ried (his′tə rēd), *adj.* containing history; storied; historical.

his·to·ri·og·ra·pher (hi stôr′ē og′rə fər, -stôr′-), *n.* **1.** a historian. **2.** an official historian, as of a court, institution, society, etc. [< L *historiograph(us)* (< Gk *historiográphos;* see HISTORY, -O-, -GRAPH) + -ER[1]] **—his·to′ri·og′ra·pher·ship′,** *n.*

his·to·ri·og·ra·phy (hi stôr′ē og′rə fē, -stôr′-), *n., pl.* **-phies.** **1.** the body of literature dealing with historical matters; histories collectively. **2.** the body of techniques, theories, and principles of historical research and presentation; methods of historical scholarship. **3.** the narrative presentation of history based on a critical examination, evaluation, and selection of material from primary and secondary sources and subject to scholarly criteria. **4.** an official history. [< MF *historiographie* < Gk *historiographía*] **—his·to·ri·o·graph·ic** (hi stôr′ē ə graf′ik, -stôr′-), **—his·to′ri·o·graph′i·cal,** *adj.* **—his·to′ri·o·graph′i·cal·ly,** *adv.*

his·to·ry (his′tə rē, his′trē), *n., pl.* **-ries.** **1.** the branch of knowledge dealing with past events. **2.** a continuous, systematic narrative of past events as relating to a particular people, country, period, person, etc., usually written in chronological order. **3.** the aggregate of past events. **4.** the record of past events, esp. in connection with the human race. **5.** a past that is full of important, unusual, or interesting events. **6.** acts, ideas, or events that will or can shape the course of the future. **7.** a systematic account of any set of natural phenomena, without reference to time. **8.** a drama representing historical events. [ME *historie* < L *historia* < Gk *historía* learning or knowing by inquiry, history] **—Syn. 2.** chronicle; annals. See **narrative.**

his·tri·on·ic (his′trē on′ik), *adj.* **1.** of or pertaining to actors or acting. **2.** artificial or affected in behavior or speech. Also, **his′tri·on′i·cal.** [< LL *histrionic(us)* of actors = *histriōn-* (s. of *histriō*) actor + *-icus* -IC] **—his′tri·on′i·cal·ly,** *adv.*

his·tri·on·ics (his′trē on′iks), *n.* (*construed as sing. or pl.*) **1.** dramatic representation; theatricals; acting. **2.** artificial behavior or speech done for effect, as insincere assumption of an emotion. [see HISTRIONIC, -ICS]

hit (hit), *v.*, **hit, hit·ting,** *n.* **—*v.t.* 1.** to deal a blow or stroke: *Hit the nail with the hammer.* **2.** to come against with an impact or collision, as a missile, a flying fragment, a falling body, or the like: *The wheel hit the curb.* **3.** to reach with a missile, a weapon, a blow, or the like, as one throwing, shooting, or striking. **4.** to succeed in striking. **5.** *Baseball.* **a.** to make (a base hit). **b.** bat[1] (def. 12). **6.** to drive or propel by a stroke: *to hit a ball onto the green.* **7.** to have a marked effect or influence on; affect severely. **8.** to assail effectively and sharply (often fol. by *out*): *The speech hits out at warmongering.* **9.** to request or demand of: *He hit me for a loan.* **10.** to reach or attain (a specified level or amount): *The new train can hit 100 mph.* **11.** to appear in; be published in or released to: *When will this report hit the papers?* **12.** to land on or arrive in: *When does Harry hit town?* **13.** to give (someone) another playing card, drink, portion, etc. **14.** to light upon; meet with; find: *to* *hit the right answer.* **15.** to agree with; suit exactly. **16.** to guess correctly: *You've hit it!* **17.** to succeed in representing or producing exactly. **18.** *Informal.* to begin to travel on: *Let's hit the road.* **—*v.i.*** **19.** to strike with a missile, a weapon, or the like; deal a blow or blows. **20.** (of an internal-combustion engine) to ignite a mixture of air and fuel as intended. **21.** to come into collision. **22.** to come or light (usually fol. by *upon* or *on*): *to hit on a new way.* **23. hit it off,** *Informal.* to be congenial or compatible; get along; agree. **24. hit the bottle.** See **bottle** (def. 4). **—*n.*** **25.** an impact or collision, as of one thing against another. **26.** a stroke that reaches an object; blow. **27.** *Baseball.* See **base hit. 28.** *Backgammon.* **a.** a game won by a player after his opponent has thrown off one or more men from the board. **b.** any winning game. **29.** a successful stroke, performance, or production; success: *The play is a hit.* **30.** *Slang.* a rendezvous for an illicit purpose, as the sale of narcotics. **31. hit or miss,** without concern for correctness or detail; haphazardly. [ME *hitte(n),* OE *hittan* < Scand; cf. Icel *hitta* to come upon (by chance), meet with] —**hit′less,** *adj.* —**hit′ter,** *n.* —**Syn. 1.** See **strike, beat. 27, 29.** See **blow**[1].

hit-and-run (hit′ᵊn run′), *adj.* **1.** guilty of leaving the scene of an accident caused by a vehicle driven by oneself: *a hit-and-run driver.* **2.** resulting from such action or conduct. **3.** *Baseball.* pertaining to or noting a play in which a base runner begins to run to the next base as the pitcher delivers the ball to the batter, who must try to hit it in order to protect the runner.

hitch (hich), *v.t.* **1.** to fasten or tie, esp. temporarily, by means of a hook, rope, strap, etc.; tether. **2.** to harness (an animal) to a vehicle. **3.** to raise with jerks (usually fol. by *up*); hike up: *to hitch up one's trousers.* **4.** to move or draw (something) with a jerk. **5.** to get (a ride) from someone going the same way; thumb. **6.** *Slang.* to bind by marriage vows; unite in marriage; marry. **7.** to catch, as on a projection. **—*v.i.*** **8.** to stick, as when caught. **9.** to fasten oneself or itself to something. **10.** to move roughly or jerkily. **11.** to hobble or limp. **—*n.*** **12.** the act or fact of fastening, as to something, esp. temporarily. **13.** any of various readily undone knots or loops made in a rope to attach it to something, esp. temporarily. Cf. **bend**[1] (def. 17). **14.** *Mil. Slang.* a period of military service. **15.** an unexpected halt, delay, or obstruction: *a hitch in our plans for the picnic.* **16.** a hitching movement; jerk or pull. **17.** a hitching gait; a hobble or limp. **18.** a fastening that joins a movable tool to the mechanism that pulls it. [late ME *hytche(n)* < ?] —**hitch′er,** *n.* —**Syn. 1.** attach, connect, hook. **2.** yoke.

hitch·hike (hich′hīk′), *v.i.,* **-hiked, -hik·ing.** to travel by getting free automobile rides and sometimes by walking between rides. —**hitch′hik′er,** *n.*

hitch′ing post′, a post to which horses, mules, etc., are tied.

hith·er (hith′ər), *adv.* **1.** to or toward this place. **2. hither and thither,** in various quarters; here and there. **3. hither and yon,** from here to over there, esp. to a farther place; in or to a great many places. **—*adj.*** **4.** being on this or the closer side; nearer: *the hither side of the meadow.* [ME, OE *hider;* c. Icel *hethra,* L *citer* on this side]

hith·er·most (hith′ər mōst′ *or, esp. Brit.,* -məst), *adj.* nearest in this direction.

hith·er·to (hith′ər to͞o′), *adv.* **1.** up to this time; until now: *a fact hitherto unknown.* **2.** *Archaic.* to here. [ME *hiderto*]

hith·er·ward (hith′ər wərd), *adv.* hither. Also, **hith′er·wards.** [ME, OE *hiderward*]

Hit·ler (hit′lər), *n.* **Ad·olf** (ad′olf, ā′dolf; *Ger.* ä′dôlf), (*Adolf Schicklgruber*) ("*der Führer*"), 1889–1945, Nazi dictator of Germany, born in Austria: chancellor 1933–45; dictator 1934–45.

Hit·ler·ism (hit′lə riz′əm), *n.* the Nazism as developed by Hitler.

hit-or-miss (hit′ər mis′), *adj.* careless; haphazard.

Hit·tite (hit′īt), *n.* **1.** a member of an ancient people who established a powerful empire in Asia Minor and Syria, dominant from about 1900 to 1200 B.C. **2.** an extinct language of the Anatolian branch of Indo-European, preserved in cuneiform inscriptions of the second millennium B.C. Hittite was formerly regarded by some specialists as descended from a sister language of Proto-Indo-European. **—*adj.*** **3.** of, pertaining to, or belonging to the Hittites or their language. [< Heb *Ḥitt(īm)* (cf. Hittite *Khatti*) + -ITE[1]]

Hittite, Uriah the. See **Uriah the Hittite.**

HIV, human immunodeficiency virus: a retrovirus that invades and damages cells of the immune system and is the cause of AIDS.

hive (hīv), *n., v.,* **hived, hiv·ing.** **—*n.*** **1.** an artificial shelter for honeybees; beehive. **2.** the bees inhabiting a hive. **3.** something resembling a beehive in structure or use. **4.** a place swarming with busy occupants: *a hive of industry.* **5.** a swarming or teeming multitude. **—*v.t.*** **6.** to gather into or cause to enter a hive. **7.** to shelter as in a hive. **8.** to store up in a hive. **9.** to store or lay away for future use or enjoyment. **—*v.i.*** **10.** to enter a hive, as bees. **11.** to live together in or as in a hive. [ME; OE *hȳf;* akin to Icel *hūfr* ship's hull, L *cūpa* vat]

Hive (def. 1) showing removable combs

hives (hīvz), *n.* (*construed as sing. or pl.*) *Pathol.* any of various eruptive conditions of the skin, as the wheals of urticaria. [Scot < ?]

H.J., here lies. [< L *hīc jacet*]

hl, *Metric System.* hectoliter; hectoliters.

H.L., House of Lords.

hm, *Metric System.* hectometer; hectometers.

h'm (hmm), *interj.* (used typically to express thoughtful absorption, hesitation, doubt, or perplexity.)

H.M., His (or Her) Majesty.

HMO, health maintenance organization.

H.M.S., **1.** His (or Her) Majesty's Service. **2.** His (or Her) Majesty's Ship.

ho (hō), *interj.* **1.** (used as an exclamation of surprise, delight, exultation, etc.) **2.** (used as a call to attract attention, sometimes specially used after a word denoting a destination): *Westward ho! Land ho!* [ME]

Ho, *Chem.* holmium.

ho·ac·tzin (hō ak′tsin, wäk′-), *n.* hoatzin.

hoa·gy (hō′gē), *n., pl.* **-gies.** *Chiefly Northeastern U.S.* See **hero sandwich.** Also, **hoa′gie.** [?]

Hoang·ho (hwäng′hō′; *Chin.* hwäng′hu′), *n.* See **Hwang Ho.**

hoar (hōr, hôr), *n.* **1.** a hoary coating or appearance. **2.** hoarfrost. **3.** *Rare.* hoariness. **—*adj.*** **4.** *Rare.* hoary. [ME *hor,* OE *hār;* c. Icel *hārr* gray with age, OFris *hēr* gray, OHG *hēr* old (G *hehr* august, sublime)]

hoard (hōrd, hôrd), *n.* **1.** a supply or accumulation that is hidden or carefully guarded for preservation, future use, etc. **—*v.t.*** **2.** to accumulate for preservation, future use, etc., in a hidden or carefully guarded place. **—*v.i.*** **3.** to accumulate money, food, or the like, in a hidden or carefully guarded place for preservation, future use, etc. [ME *hord(e),* OE *hord;* c. Icel *hodd,* OHG *hort*] —**hoard′er,** *n.*

hoard·ing[1] (hōr′ding, hôr′-), *n.* **1.** the act of a person who hoards. **2. hoardings,** things that are hoarded. [HOARD + -ING[1]]

hoard·ing[2] (hōr′ding, hôr′-), *n.* *Brit.* a billboard. [obs. *hoard* (<< OF *hourd(e)* palisade made of hurdles < Gmc; cf. G *Hürde* hurdle) + -ING[1]]

Hoare (hōr, hôr), *n.* **Sir Samuel John Gur·ney** (gûr′nē), **1st Viscount Tem·ple·wood** (tem′pəl wo͝od′), 1880–1959, British statesman.

hoar·frost (hōr′frôst′, -frost′, hôr′-), *n.* frost (def. 2). [ME *hor-forst*]

hoar·hound (hōr′hound′, hôr′-), *n.* horehound.

hoarse (hōrs, hôrs), *adj.,* **hoars·er, hoars·est.** **1.** having a vocal tone characterized by weakness of intensity and excessive breathiness; husky. **2.** having a raucous voice. **3.** making a harsh, low sound. [late ME *hors* < Scand; cf. Icel *hāss* (var. of **hārs*); r. ME *hoos,* OE *hās,* c. OHG *heis,* OS *hēs*] —**hoarse′ly,** *adv.* —**hoarse′ness,** *n.*

hoars·en (hōr′sən, hôr′-), *v.t., v.i.* to make or become hoarse.

hoar·y (hōr′ē, hôr′ē), *adj.,* **hoar·i·er, hoar·i·est.** **1.** gray or white with age. **2.** ancient or venerable. **3.** gray or white. —**hoar′i·ly,** *adv.* —**hoar′i·ness,** *n.*

ho·at·zin (hō at′sin, wät′-), *n.* a crested, South American bird, *Opisthocomus hoazin,* the young of which have a claw on the second and third fingers of the wing. Also, **hoactzin.** [< AmerSp < Nahuatl *uatzin* pheasant]

hoax (hōks), *n.* **1.** a humorous or mischievous deception, esp. a practical joke. **2.** something intended to deceive or defraud. **—*v.t.*** **3.** to deceive by a hoax. [HOC(U)S] —**hoax′er,** *n.*

hob[1] (hob), *n.* **1.** a projection or shelf at the back or side of a fireplace, used for keeping food warm. **2.** a rounded peg or pin used as a target in quoits and similar games. **3.** a game in which such a peg is used. **4.** *Mach.* a milling cutter for gear and sprocket teeth, splines, threads, etc., having helically arranged teeth and fed across the work as the work is rotated. [var. of obs. *hub* hob (in a fireplace); ? same as HUB]

hob[2] (hob), *n.* **1.** a hobgoblin or elf. **2. play hob with,** *Informal.* to do mischief or harm to. **3. raise hob with,** *Informal.* to cause a destructive commotion in; disrupt completely. [ME, special use of *Hob,* for *Robert* or *Robin,* man's name] —**hob′like′,** *adj.*

Ho·bart (hō′bərt *or, for 1, 2* -bärt), *n.* **1. Gar·ret Augustus** (gar′it), 1844–99, U.S. lawyer and politician: vice president of the U.S. 1897–99. **2.** a seaport on and the capital of Tasmania, SE of Australia. 144,900 (1968).

Hob·be·ma (hob′ə mə; *Du.* hô′bə mä), *n.* **Mein·dert** (mīn′dərt), 1638–1709, Dutch painter.

Hobbes (hobz), *n.* **Thomas,** 1588–1679, English philosopher and author. —**Hobbes′i·an,** *n., adj.*

Hob·bism (hob′iz əm), *n.* the doctrines of Hobbes, esp. the doctrine of absolute submission to a royal sovereign in order to avoid the anarchic disorder resulting from uncontrolled competition among individual interests. —**Hob′bist,** *n.*

hob·ble (hob′əl), *v.,* **-bled, -bling,** *n.* **—*v.i.*** **1.** to walk lamely; limp. **2.** to proceed irregularly and haltingly. **—*v.t.*** **3.** to cause to limp. **4.** to fasten together the legs of (a horse, mule, etc.) by short lengths of rope to prevent free motion. **5.** to impede; hamper the progress of. **—*n.*** **6.** the act of hobbling; an uneven, halting gait; a limp. **7.** a rope, strap, etc., used to hobble an animal. **8.** *Archaic.* an awkward or difficult situation. [ME *hobele(n),* appar. akin to *hob* protuberance, uneven ground, and to D *hobbelen,* HG *hoppeln* to jolt] —**hob′bler,** *n.* —**hob′bling·ly,** *adv.*

hob·ble·bush (hob′əl bo͝osh′), *n.* a North American, caprifoliaceous shrub, *Viburnum alnifolium,* having white flowers and berrylike fruit. [HOBBLE + BUSH[1]; so called from the fact that it obstructs the way with its branches]

hob·ble·de·hoy (hob′əl dē hoi′), *n.* an awkward, clumsy youth. [var. of *hoberdyhoy,* alliterative compound = *hoberd* (var. of *Roberd* Robert) + -Y[2] + *-hoy* for BOY (*b* > *h* for alliteration's sake)]

hob′ble skirt′, a woman's skirt that is very narrow at the bottom.

Hobbs (hobz), *n.* a city in SE New Mexico. 26,025 (1970).

hob·by[1] (hob′ē), *n., pl.* **-bies.** **1.** an activity or interest pursued for pleasure or relaxation and not as a main occupation. **2.** a child's hobbyhorse. **3.** *Archaic.* a small horse. [ME *hoby(n),* prob. for *Robin,* or *Robert,* used as horse's name, as in DOBBIN] —**hob′by·less,** *adj.*

hob·by[2] (hob′ē), *n., pl.* **-bies.** a small Old World falcon, *Falco subbuteo,* formerly flown at such small game as larks. [late ME *hoby* < MF *hobet* = *hobe* falcon (? akin to OF *hober* to move) + *-et* -ET]

hob·by-horse (hob′ē hôrs′), *n.* a stick with a horse's head, or a rocking horse, ridden by children.

hob·by·ist (hob′ē ist), *n.* a person who pursues a hobby or hobbies.

hob·gob·lin (hob′gob′lin), *n.* **1.** anything causing superstitious fear; a bogy. **2.** a mischievous goblin.

hob·nail (hob′nāl′), *n.* a large-headed nail for protecting the soles of heavy boots and shoes.

hob·nailed (hob′nāld′), *adj.* furnished with hobnails.
hob·nob (hob′nob′), *v.i.*, **-nobbed, -nob·bing. 1.** to associate on very friendly terms. **2.** to drink together. [from the phrase *hab or nab* have or have not, OE *hab(ban)* (to) have + *nab(ban)* not to have (*n(e)* not + *hab(ban)* (to) have)]
ho·bo (hō′bō), *n., pl.* **-bos, -boes. 1.** a tramp or vagrant. **2.** a migratory worker. [? rhyming compound based on BEAU, used sarcastically as greeting; see HO, HEY] **—ho′bo·ism,** *n.*
Ho·bo·ken (hō′bō kən), *n.* a seaport in NE New Jersey, opposite New York City. 45,380 (1970).
Hob·son (hob′sən), *n.* **Richmond Pear·son** (pēr′sən), 1870–1937, U.S. naval officer and politician.
Hob′son's choice′ (hob′sənz), the choice of taking either that which is offered or nothing; the absence of a real choice. [after Thomas *Hobson* (1544–1631), of Cambridge, England, who rented horses and gave his customer only one choice, that of the horse nearest the stable door]
Hoc·cleve (hok′lēv), *n.* **Thomas,** 1370–1450, English poet.
hoc est (hōk est; *Eng.* hok est), *Latin.* this is.
Hoch·hei·mer (hok′hī′mər; *Ger.* hōkн′hī′məʀ), *n.* a Rhine wine of West Germany.
Ho Chi Minh (hō′ chē′ min′), 1890?–1969, North Vietnamese political leader: president of North Vietnam 1954–69.
Ho′ Chi′ Minh′ City′, official name of **Saigon.**
hock[1] (hok), *n.* **1.** the joint in the hind leg of a horse, cow, etc., above the fetlock joint, corresponding anatomically to the ankle in man. **2.** a corresponding joint in a fowl. **—***v.t.* **3.** to hamstring. [var. of dial. *hough,* ME *ho(u)gh,* appar. back formation from ME *hokschyn,* etc., OE *hōhsinu* hock (lit., heel) sinew; see HEEL[1]]
hock[2] (hok), *n.* *Chiefly Brit.* any white Rhine wine. [short for obs. *Hockamore* HOCHHEIMER]
hock[3] (hok), *v.t., n.* *Informal.* pawn[1] (defs. 1, 3, 6). [< D *hok* hovel, prison, debt] **—hock′er,** *n.*
hock·ey (hok′ē), *n.* **1.** See **ice hockey. 2.** See **field hockey.** [earlier *hockie,* perh. = *hock-* HOOK + *-ie* -IE]
hock′ey stick′, the long stick, hooked at the striking end, used in field hockey or ice hockey.
Hock·ing (hok′ing), *n.* **William Ernest,** 1873–1966, U.S. philosopher.
hock·shop (hok′shop′), *n.* *Informal.* a pawnshop.
ho·cus (hō′kəs), *v.t.,* **-cused, -cus·ing** or (*esp. Brit.*) **-cussed, -cus·sing. 1.** to play a trick on; hoax; cheat. **2.** to stupefy with drugged liquor. **3.** to drug (liquor). [short for HOCUS-POCUS]
ho·cus-po·cus (hō′kəs pō′kəs), *n., v.,* **-cused, -cus·ing** or (*esp. Brit.*) **-cussed, -cus·sing. —***n.* **1.** a meaningless formula used in conjuring or incantation. **2.** a juggler's trick; sleight of hand. **3.** trickery; deception. **4.** unnecessarily mysterious or elaborate activity or talk. **—***v.t.* **5.** to play tricks on or with. **—***v.i.* **6.** to perform tricks; practice trickery. [sham-Latin rhyming formula used by jugglers]
hod (hod), *n.* **1.** a portable trough for carrying mortar, bricks, etc., fixed crosswise on top of a pole and carried on the shoulder **2.** a coal scuttle. [< MD *hodde* basket]
hod′ car′rier, a mason's assistant whose work is to carry hods of materials to the mason.
hod·den (hod′ən), *n.* *Scot.* coarse woolen cloth, as handloomed by a country weaver. Also, **hod′din.** [?]
Ho·dei·da (hōō dā′dä), *n.* the chief seaport in the Yemen Arab Republic, on the Red Sea. 100,000.
Hodg·en·ville (hoj′ən vil′), *n.* a town in central Kentucky: birthplace of Abraham Lincoln. 2562 (1970).
hodge·podge (hoj′poj′), *n.* a heterogeneous mixture; jumble. [var. of HOTCHPOTCH]
Hodg′kin's disease′, a disease characterized by progressive chronic inflammation and enlargement of the lymph nodes. [named after Thomas *Hodgkin* (1798–1866), London physician who described it]
ho·dom·e·ter (hō dom′i tər), *n.* odometer.
hoe (hō), *n., v.,* **hoed, hoe·ing. —***n.* **1.** a long-handled implement having a thin, flat blade usually set transversely, used to break up the surface of the ground, destroy weeds, etc. **2.** any of various implements of similar form, as for mixing plaster or mortar. **—***v.t.* **3.** to dig, scrape, weed, cultivate, etc., with a hoe. **—***v.i.* **4.** to use a hoe. [ME *howe* < OF *houe* < Gmc; cf. MD *houwe,* OHG *houwa* mattock; akin to HEW] **—ho′er,** *n.* **—hoe′like′,** *adj.*
Hoe (hō), *n.* **1. Richard,** 1812–86, U.S. inventor and manufacturer of printing-press equipment. **2.** his father **Robert,** 1784–1833, U.S. manufacturer of printing presses.
hoe·cake (hō′kāk′), *n.* *Southern U.S.* a cake made with corn meal, originally baked on a hoe.
hoe·down (hō′doun′), *n.* **1.** a community party typically featuring square-dancing. **2.** the hillbilly or country music typical of a hoedown.
Hoek van Hol·land (hōōk vän hôl′änt), Dutch name of **Hook of Holland.**
Ho·fei (hu′fā′), *n.* a city in and the capital of Anhwei province, in SE China. 400,000.
Ho·fer (hō′fər), *n.* **An·dre·as** (än drā′əs), 1767–1810, Tyrolese patriot.
Hof·fa (hof′ə), *n.* **James Rid·dle** (rid′əl), 1913–75?, U.S. labor leader: president of the International Brotherhood of Teamsters 1957–71.
Hoff·man (hof′mən; *Ger.* hôf′män′), *n.* **1. Au·gust Wil·helm von** (ou′gōōst vil′helm fən), 1818–92, German chemist. **2. E(rnst) T(he·o·dor) A(ma·de·us) (Wil·helm)** (ᴇʀnst tā′ō dōʀ ä′mä dā′ōōs vil′helm), 1776–1822, German author, composer, and illustrator. **3. Mal·vi·na** (mal vī′nə), 1887–1966, U.S. sculptor.
Hof·mann (hof′mən; *Ger.* hôf′män′), *n.* **Hans** (hanz; *Ger.* häns), 1880–1966, U.S. painter, born in Germany.
Hof·manns·thal (hôf′mäns täl′), *n.* **Hu·go von** (hōō′gō fən), 1874–1929, Austrian poet, playwright, and librettist.
Ho·fuf (hōō fōōf′), *n.* a city in E Saudi Arabia. 100,000. Also, **Hufuf.**
hog (hôg, hog), *n., v.,* **hogged, hog·ging. —***n.* **1.** an omnivorous nonruminant mammal of the family *Suidae,* suborder *Artiodactyla,* and order *Ungulata;* pig, sow, or boar; swine. **2.** a domesticated swine weighing more than 120 pounds, raised for market. **3.** *Informal.* a selfish, gluttonous, or filthy person. **4.** *Brit. Dial.* **a.** a sheep about one year old that has not been shorn. **b.** the wool shorn from such a sheep. **c.** any of several other domestic animals, as a bullock, that is one year old. **5. go the whole hog,** *Informal.* to carry to the utmost extent; do completely and unreservedly. Also, **go whole hog. 6. live** or **eat high off the hog,** *Informal.* to be in prosperous circumstances. **—***v.t.* **7.** *Slang.* to appropriate selfishly; take more than one's share of. **8.** to arch (the back) upward like that of a hog. **9.** roach[3] (def. 2). **—***v.i.* **10.** *Naut.* (of a hull) to droop at both ends in the manner of a hog's back, or have less than the proper amount of sheer because of structural weakness; arch. Cf. **sag** (def. 6a). [ME; OE *hogg,* perh. < Celt; cf. Welsh *hwch* swine] **—hog′ger,** *n.* **—hog′like′,** *adj.*

Hog (Domestic)

ho·gan (hō′gôn, -gən), *n.* a Navaho Indian dwelling constructed of earth and branches and covered with mud or sod. [< Navaho]
Ho·garth (hō′gärth), *n.* **William,** 1697–1764, English painter and engraver. **—Ho·garth′i·an,** *adj.*
hog·back (hôg′bak′, hog′-), *n.* *Geol.* a long, sharply crested ridge, generally formed of steeply inclined strata that are especially resistant to erosion.
hog′ chol′era, *Vet. Pathol.* a highly contagious, usually fatal, virus disease of swine characterized by high fever and lethargy.
hog·fish (hôg′fish′, hog′-), *n., pl.* (*esp. collectively*) **-fish,** (*esp. referring to two or more kinds or species*) **-fish·es. 1.** a large wrasse, *Lachnolaimus maximus,* of the western Atlantic Ocean, used for food. **2.** any of various other fishes having a fancied resemblance to a hog, as the pigfish. [trans. of ML *porcopiscis* PORPOISE]
Hogg (hog), *n.* **James** ("*the Ettrick Shepherd*"), 1770–1835, Scottish poet.
hog·gish (hô′gish, hog′ish), *adj.* **1.** like or befitting a hog. **2.** selfish; gluttonous. **—hog′gish·ly,** *adv.* **—hog′gish·ness,** *n.*
hog·ma·nay (hog′mə nā′), *n.* *Scot. and North Eng.* **1.** the last day of the year, December 31; New Year's Eve. Also, **hog′me·nay′, hog′ma·ne′.** [?]
hog′nose snake′ (hôg′nōz′, hog′-), any of several harmless, North American snakes of the genus *Heterodon,* having an upturned snout.
hog·nut (hôg′nut′, hog′-), *n.* the nut of the brown hickory, *Carya glabra.*
hog′ pea′nut, a twining, fabaceous plant, *Amphicarpa bracteata,* bearing pods that ripen in or on the ground.
hogs·head (hôgz′hed′, hogz′-), *n.* **1.** a large cask, esp. one containing from 63 to 140 gallons. **2.** any of various units of liquid measure, esp. one equivalent to 63 gallons. *Abbr.:* hhd [ME *hoggeshed,* lit., hog's head; unexplained]
hog·tie (hôg′tī′, hog′-), *v.t.,* **-tied, -ty·ing. 1.** to tie an animal with all four feet together. **2.** *Informal.* to hamper or thwart: *Repeated delays hogtied the investigation.*
Hogue (*Fr.* ôg), *n.* **La** (lᴀ). See **La Hogue.**
hog·wash (hôg′wosh′, -wôsh′, hog′-), *n.* **1.** refuse given to hogs; swill. **2.** any worthless stuff. **3.** meaningless or insincere talk, writing, etc.
hog-wild (hôg′wīld′, hog′-), *adj.* *Informal.* wildly or intemperately enthusiastic or excited.
Ho·hen·lin·den (hō′ən lin′dən), *n.* a village in S West Germany, in Bavaria, near Munich: French victory over the Austrians 1800.
Ho·hen·lo·he (hō′ən lō′ə), *n.* a member of a German princely family, fl. 12th to 19th centuries.
Ho·hen·stau·fen (hō′ən shtou′fən), *n.* a member of the royal family that ruled in Germany from 1138 to 1208 and from 1215 to 1254, and in Sicily from 1194 to 1266.
Ho·hen·zol·lern (hō′ən zol′ərn; *Ger.* hō′ən tsôl′əʀn), *n.* a member of the royal family that ruled in Rumania from 1866 to 1947, in Prussia from 1701 to 1918, and in the German Empire from 1871 to 1918.
ho-hum (hō′hum′), *interj.* **1.** (an exclamation expressing drowsiness, boredom, or weariness.) **—***adj.* **2.** dull, boring, or uninteresting; so-so: *a ho-hum performance.* [imit.]
hoi·den (hoid′ən), *n., adj.* hoyden **—hoi′den·ish,** *adj.*
hoi pol·loi (hoi′ pə loi′), the common people; the masses (often preceded by *the*). [< Gk: the many]
hoist (hoist), *v.t.* **1.** to raise or lift, esp. by some mechanical appliance. **—***n.* **2.** an apparatus for hoisting, as an elevator. **3.** *Chiefly Brit.* a freight elevator. **4.** the act of hoisting; a lift. **5.** *Naut.* **a.** the vertical dimension amidships of any square sail that is hoisted with a yard. Cf. **drop** (def. 20). **b.** the distance between the hoisted and the lowered position of such a yard. **c.** the dimension of a fore-and-aft sail along the luff. **d.** a number of flags raised together as a signal. **6.** (on a flag) **a.** the vertical dimension as flown from a vertical staff. **b.** the edge running next to the staff. Cf. **fly** (def. 29). [later var. of archaic *hoise* (late ME *hysse,* orig. sailors' cry; see HUZZA), with *-t* as in AGAINST, etc.] **—hoist′er,** *n.* **—Syn. 1.** elevate. See **raise. —Ant. 1.** lower.
hoi·ty-toi·ty (hoi′tē toi′tē), *adj.* **1.** assuming airs; haughty. **2.** *Chiefly Brit.* giddy; flighty. **—***n.* **3.** a display of pretentiousness; haughtiness. **4.** *Obs.* giddy behavior. [rhyming compound based on obs. *hoit* to romp, riot]
ho·key (hō′kē), *adj.* *Slang.* faked; false; contrived. [irreg. HOK(UM) + -Y[1]]
ho·key-po·key (hō′kē pō′kē), *n.* **1.** hocus-pocus; trickery. **2.** ice cream sold by street vendors. [var. of HOCUS-POCUS]
Ho·kiang (hō′kyäng′; *Chin.* hu′gyäng′), *n.* a former province in Manchuria, in NE China.
Hok·kai·do (hôk′kī dô′; *Eng.* ho kī′dō), *n.* a large island in N Japan. 5,184,287; 30,303 sq. mi. Formerly, **Yezo.**
hok·ku (hô′kōō, hok′ōō), *n., pl.* **-ku.** *Pros.* **1.** the opening verse of a linked verse series. **2.** haiku. [< Jap = *hok* opening, first + *ku* hemistich]
Ho·ko Gun·to (hô′kô gōōn′tô), Japanese name of the **Pescadores.** Also called **Ho·ko·to** (hô′kô tô′).
ho·kum (hō′kəm), *n.* *Informal.* **1.** nonsense; bunk. **2.** sentimental, pathetic, or comic matter of an elementary or stereotyped kind introduced into a play, novel, etc. **3.** false

or irrelevant material introduced into a speech, essay, etc., for spurious appeal. [HO(CUS-POCUS + BUN)KUM]

Ho·ku·sai (hō′ko͝o sī′, hō′ko͝o sī′; *Jap.* hô′ko͞o sī′), *n.* **Ka·tsu·shi·ka** (kä′tso͞o shē′kä), 1760–1849, Japanese painter and illustrator.

Hol·arc·tic (hol ärk′tik, -är′tik, hōl-), *adj. Zoogeog.* belonging or pertaining to a geographical division comprising the Nearctic and Palearctic regions. [HOL(O)- + ARCTIC]

Hol·bein (hōl′bīn; *Ger.* hôl′bīn), *n.* **1. Hans** (häns), ("*the elder*"), 1465?–1524, German painter. **2.** his son, **Hans** ("*the younger*"), 1497?–1543, German painter who worked chiefly in England.

hold[1] (hōld), *v.*, **held; held** or (*Archaic*) **hold·en; hold·ing;** *n.* —*v.t.* **1.** to have or keep in the hand; grasp. **2.** to set aside; reserve or retain: *to hold merchandise until called for.* **3.** to bear, sustain, or support, as with the hands or arms, or by any other means. **4.** to keep in a specified state, relation, etc.: *He held them spellbound.* **5.** to detain. **6.** to engage in; preside over; carry on; observe or celebrate: *to hold a meeting.* **7.** to keep back from action; hinder; restrain. **8.** to have the ownership or use of; keep as one's own; occupy: *to hold political office.* **9.** to contain or be capable of containing: *This bottle holds a quart.* **10.** to have or keep in the mind; think or believe: *We hold this belief.* **11.** to regard or consider: *I hold you responsible.* **12.** to decide legally. **13.** to consider of a certain value; rate: *We held her best of all the applicants.* **14.** to keep forcibly, as against an adversary. **15.** to point, aim, or direct: *He held a gun on the prisoner.* —*v.i.* **16.** to remain or continue in a specified state, relation, etc.: *to hold still.* **17.** to remain fast; adhere; cling. **18.** to keep or maintain a grasp on something. **19.** to maintain one's position against opposition. **20.** to agree or side (usually fol. by *with*): *to hold with new methods.* **21.** to hold property by some tenure; derive title (usually fol. by *by*, *from*, *in*, or *of*). **22.** to remain attached, faithful, or steadfast (usually fol. by *to*): *to hold to one's purpose.* **23.** to remain valid; be in force: *The rule does not hold.* **24.** to refrain or forbear (usually used imperatively). **25. hold back, a.** to restrain or check. **b.** to retain possession of; keep back. **c.** to refrain from revealing; withhold. **d.** to refrain from participating or engaging in some activity. **26. hold down, a.** to restrain; check: *Hold down that noise!* **b.** to continue to hold and manage well, as a job. **27. hold forth, a.** to extend or offer; propose. **b.** to talk at great length; harangue. **28. hold in, a.** to restrain; check; curb. **b.** to contain (oneself): *He held himself in for fear of saying something he would regret.* **29. hold off, a.** to keep at a distance; resist; repel. **b.** to postpone action; defer: *to hold off applying for a passport.* **30. hold on, a.** to keep a firm grip on. **b.** to keep going; continue. **c.** to maintain, as one's opinion or position. **d.** *Informal.* to stop; halt (usually used imperatively): *Hold on now! That isn't what I meant at all.* **31. hold one's own.** See **own** (def. 4). **32. hold one's peace.** See **peace** (def. 10). **33. hold one's tongue.** See **tongue** (def. 19). **34. hold out, a.** to present; offer. **b.** to stretch forth; extend. **c.** to continue to exist; last. **d.** to refuse to yield or submit. **e.** *Slang.* to withhold something expected or due: *to hold out important information.* **35. hold over, a.** to keep for future consideration or action; postpone. **b.** to remain in possession or in office beyond the regular term. **c.** to remain beyond the arranged period. **d.** *Music.* to prolong (a tone) from one measure to the next. **36. hold up, a.** to offer; give: *She held up his father as an example to follow.* **b.** to present to notice; expose: *to hold someone up to ridicule.* **c.** to hinder; delay. **d.** *U.S. Informal.* to stop by force in order to rob. **e.** to support; uphold. **f.** to stop; halt. **g.** to maintain one's position or condition; endure. **37. hold water.** See **water** (def. 14). **38. hold with, a.** to be in agreement with; concur with. **b.** to approve of; condone. —*n.* **39.** the act of holding fast by a grasp of the hand or by some other physical means; grasp; grip: *Take hold. Get hold of the rope.* **40.** something to hold a thing by, as a handle; something to grasp, esp. for support. **41.** a thing that holds fast or supports something else. **42.** an order reserving something: *to put a hold on a library book.* **43.** a controlling force or dominating influence: *to have a hold on a person.* **44.** *Music.* fermata. **45.** a pause or delay, as in a continuing series: *a hold in the movements of a dance.* **46.** a prison or prison cell. **47.** a receptacle for something: *a basket used as a hold for letters.* **48.** *Archaic.* a fortified place; stronghold. [ME *hold(en)*, OE *h(e)aldan;* c. OFris, Icel *halda*, OS, Goth *haldan*, G *halten* (OHG *haltan*)] —**hold′a·ble,** *adj.* —**Syn. 8.** possess, own. See **have. 9.** See **contain. 10.** embrace, espouse. **11.** deem, judge. **16.** persist, last, endure. **17.** stick.

hold[2] (hōld), *n. Naut.* **1.** the entire cargo space in the hull of a vessel, esp. between the lowermost deck and the bottom. **2.** any individual compartment of such cargo spaces, closed by bulkheads and having its own hatchway. [var. of HOLE; c. D *hol* hole, hold]

hold·back (hōld′bak′), *n.* **1.** an iron or strap on the shaft of a horse-drawn vehicle, enabling the horse to hold back or to back the vehicle. **2.** a device for restraining or checking. **3.** a stop or delay. **4.** a withholding: *the holdback of a day's pay.*

hold-down (hōld′doun′), *n.* **1.** restraint or limitation, as on military spending. **2.** a device used to hold an object in position.

hold·en (hōl′dᵊn), *v. Archaic.* a pp. of **hold.**

hold·er (hōl′dər), *n.* **1.** any device for holding: *a toothbrush holder.* **2.** a person who has the ownership, possession, or use of something; owner; tenant. **3.** *Law.* a person who has the legal right to enforce a negotiable instrument. [ME *haldere*] —**hold′er·ship′,** *n.*

hold·fast (hōld′fast′, -fäst′), *n.* **1.** any device used to hold a thing in place; a catch, hook, clamp, etc. **2.** *Bot.* any of several rootlike or suckerlike organs or parts serving for attachment.

hold·ing (hōl′ding), *n.* **1.** the act of a person or thing that holds. **2.** a section of land leased or otherwise tenanted. **3.** a company owned by a holding company. **4.** Often, **holdings.** property, esp. stocks, bonds, and real estate. [ME *holdung*]

hold′ing com′pany, *Finance.* a company controlling one or more other companies by virtue of stock ownership.

hold′ing pat′tern, a traffic pattern for planes in the air near the airport while waiting to be cleared for landing.

hold·out (hōld′out′), *n.* **1.** the act of holding out. **2.** an instance of this. **3.** something held out. **4.** a person who delays signing a contract in hopes of gaining more favorable terms. **5.** a person who declines to participate in a group activity or undertaking.

hold·o·ver (hōld′ō′vər), *n.* **1.** a person or thing remaining from a former period. **2.** a movie, play, or the like, whose engagement is continued beyond the planned closing date.

hold·up (hōld′up′), *n.* **1.** *U.S.* a forcible stopping and robbing of a person. **2.** a stop or delay in the progress of something. **3.** an instance of being charged excessively.

hole (hōl), *n., v.,* **holed, hol·ing.** —*n.* **1.** an opening through something; an aperture. **2.** a hollow place in a solid body or mass; a cavity: *a hole in the ground.* **3.** the excavated habitation of an animal; burrow. **4.** a small, dingy, or shabby abode. **5.** a place of solitary confinement; dungeon. **6.** an embarrassing position or predicament: *to find oneself in a hole.* **7.** *U.S.* a cove or small harbor. **8.** a fault or flaw: *They found serious holes in his reasoning.* **9.** a deep, still place in a stream: *a swimming hole.* **10.** *Sports.* **a.** a small cavity, into which a marble, ball, or the like is to be played. **b.** a score made by so playing. **11.** *Golf.* **a.** the cup in a green into which the ball is to be played. **b.** a part of a golf course from a tee to the hole corresponding to it, including fairway, rough, and hazards. **12.** *Electronics.* a mobile vacancy in the electronic structure of a semiconductor that acts as a positive charge carrier. **13. in the hole, a.** in debt; in straitened circumstances. **b.** *Stud Poker.* being the card or one of the cards dealt face down in the first round: *a king in the hole.* —*v.t.* **14.** to make a hole or holes in. **15.** to put or drive into a hole. **16.** *Golf.* to hit (the ball) into a hole. **17.** to bore (a tunnel, passage, etc.). —*v.i.* **18.** to make a hole or holes. **19. hole out,** *Golf.* to strike the ball into a hole. **20. hole up, a.** to go into a hole; retire for the winter, as a hibernating animal. **b.** *Slang.* to hide, as from pursuers, the police, etc. [ME; OE *hol* hole, cave, orig. neut. of *hol* (adj.) hollow; c. G *hohl* hollow] —**hole′less,** *adj.* —**hole′y,** *adj.* —**Syn. 1, 2.** pit, hollow, concavity. **3.** den, cave; lair. **4.** hovel, shack.

hole′ card′, *Stud Poker.* the card dealt face down in the first round of a deal.

hole′ in one′, *Golf.* ace (def. 5).

Hol·guín (ôl gēn′), *n.* a city in NE Cuba. 57,573 (1960).

hol·i·but (hol′ə bət), *n., pl.* (*esp. collectively*) **-but,** (*esp. referring to two or more kinds or species*) **-buts.** halibut.

hol·i·day (hol′i dā′), *n.* **1.** a day fixed by law or custom on which ordinary business is suspended in commemoration of some event or person. **2.** any day of exemption from labor. **3.** a religious feast day; holy day. **4.** Sometimes, **holidays.** *Chiefly Brit.* a period of cessation from work or one of recreation; vacation. **5.** any of several usually commemorative holy days observed in Judaism; holy day. —*adj.* **6.** of or pertaining to a festival; festive; joyous: *a holiday mood.* **7.** suitable for a holiday: *holiday attire.* —*v.i.* **8.** *Chiefly Brit.* to vacation. [ME; OE *hāligdæg*]

ho·li·er-than-thou (hō′lē ər thən thou′), *adj.* sanctimonious; self-righteous.

ho·li·ly (hō′lə lē), *adv.* in a pious, devout, or sacred manner.

ho·li·ness (hō′lē nis), *n.* **1.** the quality or state of being holy; sanctity. **2.** (*cap.*) a title of the pope (usually prec. by *His* or *Your*). [ME *holynesse*, OE *hālignes*]

Hol·ins·hed (hol′inz hed′, hol′in shed′), *n.* **Raphael,** died c1580, English chronicler. Also, **Hollingshead.**

ho·lism (hō′liz əm), *n. Philos.* the theory that whole entities, as fundamental and determining components of reality, have an existence other than as the mere sum of their parts. [HOL(O)- + -ISM] —**ho′list,** *n.* —**ho·lis′tic,** *adj.* —**ho·lis′ti·cal·ly,** *adv.*

Hol·land (hol′ənd), *n.* **1.** the Netherlands. **2.** a medieval county and province on the North Sea, corresponding to the modern North and South Holland provinces of the Netherlands. **3.** a city in W Michigan. 26,337 (1970). **4.** *Textiles.* a cotton cloth treated to produce an opaque finish, as for window shades.

hol′lan·daise sauce′ (hol′ən dāz′, hol′ən dāz′), a rich sauce for vegetables, fish, etc., made with egg yolks, butter, lemon juice, and seasonings. [< F *sauce hollandaise* Dutch sauce]

Hol·land·er (hol′ən dər), *n.* a native of the Netherlands; Dutchman.

Hol·lan·di·a (ho lan′dē ə), *n.* former name of **Kotabaru.**

Hol·lands (hol′əndz), *n.* (*construed as sing.*) a type of gin in which the juniper is mixed in the mash. Also called **Hol′land gin′.** [< D *hollands(ch) genever* Dutch gin. See GENEVA]

hol·ler (hol′ər), *Informal.* —*v.i.* **1.** to cry aloud; shout. —*v.t.* **2.** to shout (something): *to holler insults.* —*n.* **3.** a loud cry to attract attention, call for help, etc. [var. of HOLLO]

Hol′ler·ith code′ (hol′ə rith), *Computer Technol.* a system for coding data into punch cards by assigning combinations of punch cards to letters, numerals, and special signs. [after Herman *Hollerith* (1860–1929), U.S. inventor]

Hol·lings·head (hol′ingz hed′), *n.* Holinshed.

hol·lo (hol′ō, hə lō′), *interj., n., pl.* **-los,** *v.i., v.t.,* **-loed, -lo·ing.** hallo. [var. of *holla* < MF *hola* = *ho* ahoy + *la* there]

hol·loa (hol′ō, hə lō′), *interj., n., pl.* **-loas,** *v.i., v.t.,* **-loaed, -loa·ing.** hallo.

hol·loo (hol′o͞o, hə lo͞o′), *interj., n., pl.* **-loos,** *v.i., v.t.,* **-looed, -loo·ing.** hallo.

hol·low (hol′ō), *adj.* **1.** having a space or cavity inside; not solid; empty. **2.** having a depression or concavity. **3.** sunken, as the cheeks or eyes. **4.** (of sound) not resonant; dull, muffled, or deep: *a hollow voice.* **5.** without worth; meaningless: *a hollow victory.* **6.** insincere or false. **7.** hungry; having an empty feeling. —*n.* **8.** an empty space within anything; a hole, depression, or cavity. **9.** a valley. —*v.t.* **10.** to make hollow (often fol. by out): *to hollow out a log.* **11.** to form by making something hollow (often fol. by *out*): *boats hollowed out of logs.* —*v.i.* **12.** to become hollow. —*adv.* **13.** in a hollow manner: *The accusations rang hollow.* **14. beat all hollow,** *Informal.* to outdo completely. Also, **beat hollow.** [ME *holw(e)*, *hol(o)w*, OE *holh* a hollow place; akin to HOLE] —**hol′low·ly,** *adv.* —**hol′low·ness,** *n.*

hol·low-eyed (hol′ō īd′), *adj.* having sunken eyes.

hol·low·ware (hol′ō wâr′), *n.* silver dishes having some depth (distinguished from *flatware*).

hol·ly (hol′ē), *n., pl.* **-lies.** **1.** any of several trees or shrubs of the genus *Ilex*, as *I. opaca* (**Amer′ican hol′ly**), the state tree of Delaware, or *I. aquifolium* (**Eng′lish hol′ly**), having glossy, spiny-toothed leaves, small, whitish flowers, and red berries. **2.** the foliage and berries, used for decoration, esp. at Christmas. [ME *holi(e)*, *holyn*, OE *hole(g)n;* c. Welsh *celyn*, Ir *cuillean;* akin to D, G *hulst*, F *houx* (< G)]

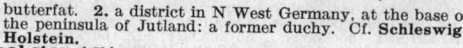

Holly, *Ilex opaca*

hol·ly·hock (hol′ē hok′, -hôk′), *n.* **1.** a tall, malvaceous plant, *Althea rosea*, having showy flowers of various colors. **2.** the flower itself. See illus. at **monadelphous.** [ME *holihoc* = *holi* HOLY + *hoc* mallow, OE *hocc*]

hol′ly oak′. See **holm oak.**

Hol·ly·wood (hol′ē wŏŏd′), *n.* **1.** the NW part of Los Angeles, California: motion-picture studios. **2.** a city in SE Florida, near Miami. 106,873 (1970).

holm[1] (hōm), *n.* *Brit. Dial.* **1.** a low, flat tract of land beside a river or stream. **2.** a small island, esp. one in a river or lake. [ME; OE *holm;* c. Icel *holm* islet, Dan *holm*, Sw *holme* a small island, G *Holm* hill, island, L *columen, culmen* hill]

holm[2] (hōm), *n.* See **holm oak.** [ME, by dissimilation from *holn*, OE *holen* HOLLY]

Hol·man-Hunt (hōl′mən hunt′), *n.* See **Hunt.**

Holmes (hōmz, hōlmz), *n.* **1. John Haynes** (hānz), 1879–1964, U.S. clergyman. **2. Oliver Wen·dell** (wen′dᵊl), 1809–1894, U.S. writer and physician. **3.** his son, **Oliver Wendell,** 1841–1935, U.S. jurist: associate justice of the U.S. Supreme Court 1902–32.

hol·mi·um (hōl′mē əm), *n.* *Chem.* a rare-earth element. *Symbol:* Ho; *at. wt.:* 164.930; *at. no.:* 67. [< NL; named after (STOCK)HOLM, Sweden; see -IUM] —**hol′mic,** *adj.*

holm′ oak′, an evergreen oak, *Quercus ilex*, of southern Europe, having foliage resembling that of the holly.

holo-, a learned borrowing from Greek meaning "whole," "entire," used in the formation of compound words: *holohedral.* [< Gk, comb. form of *hólos*]

hol·o·blas·tic (hol′ə blas′tik, hō′lə-), *adj.* *Embryol.* (of certain eggs) undergoing total cleavage. Cf. **meroblastic.** [*holoblast* (HOLO- + -BLAST) + -IC] —**ho′lo·blas′ti·cal·ly,** *adv.*

hol·o·caust (hol′ə kôst′, hō′lə-), *n.* **1.** devastation, esp. by fire. **2.** a sacrifice completely consumed by fire; burnt offering. **3. the Holocaust,** the systematic mass extermination of European Jews in Nazi concentration camps prior to and during World War II. [ME < LL *holocaust(um)* (Vulgate) < Gk *holókauston* (Septuagint), neut. of *holókaustos* burnt whole. See HOLO-, CAUSTIC] —**hol′o·caus′tic,** *adj.*

Hol·o·cene (hol′ə sēn′, hō′lə-), *Geol.* —*adj.* **1.** recent (def. 3). —*n.* **2.** recent (def. 4).

hol·o·crine (hol′ə krin, -krīn′, hō′lə-), *adj.* **1.** (of a gland) producing a secretion formed by the disintegration of the glandular cells. **2.** (of a secretion) produced by such a gland. [HOLO- + *-crine* < Gk *krī́n(ein)* (to) separate]

Hol·o·fer·nes (hol′ə fûr′nēz, hō′lə-), *n.* (in the Book of Judith) a general of Nebuchadnezzar killed by Judith.

ho·lo·gram (hō′lə gram, hol′ə-), *n.* a true three-dimensional photograph recorded on film by a reflected laser beam of a subject illuminated by a portion of the same laser beam. [HOLO- + -GRAM[1]]

hol·o·graph (hol′ə graf′, -gräf′, hō′lə-), *adj.* **1.** Also, **hol·o·graph·ic** (hol′ə graf′ik), **hol′o·graph′i·cal.** wholly written by the person in whose name it appears. —*n.* **2.** a holograph writing. [< LL *holograph(us)* < LGk *hológraphos*]

ho·log·ra·phy (hə log′rə fē), *n.* the process or technique of making holograms. [HOLO- + -GRAPHY] —**hol·o·graph·ic** (hol′ə graf′ik), *adj.*

hol·o·he·dral (hol′ə hē′drəl, hō′lə-), *adj.* (of a crystal) having all the planes or faces required by maximum symmetry. —**hol′o·he′dry, hol′o·he′drism,** *n.*

hol·o·me·tab·o·lous (hol′ə mi tab′ə ləs), *adj.* *Entomol.* undergoing complete metamorphosis. Also, **hol·o·met·a·bol·ic** (hol′ə met′ə bol′ik). [HOLO- + Gk *metabólos;* see METABOLISM, -OUS] —**hol′o·me·tab′o·lism, hol′o·me·tab′o·ly,** *n.*

hol·o·mor·phic (hol′ə môr′fik), *adj.* *Math.* analytic (def. 5). —**hol′o·mor′phism, hol′o·mor′phy,** *n.*

hol·o·phote (hol′ə fōt′, hō′lə-), *n.* *Rare.* an apparatus for directing the light from a lighthouse lamp.

hol·o·phras·tic (hol′ə fras′tik, hō′lə-), *adj.* using a single word that functions as a phrase or sentence, as the imperative, *Go!* [HOLO- + *-phrastic;* see PERIPHRASTIC]

hol·o·phyt·ic (hol′ə fit′ik, hō′lə-), *adj.* (of a plant) obtaining food by synthesizing inorganic substances; autotrophic. [HOLO- + *-phytic;* see -PHYTE, -IC] —**hol·o·phyte** (hol′ə fīt′), *n.*

hol·o·thu·ri·an (hol′ə thŏŏr′ē ən, hō′lə-), *n.* **1.** any echinoderm of the class *Holothuroidea*, comprising the sea cucumbers. —*adj.* **2.** belonging or pertaining to the *Holothuroidea.* Also, **hol·o·thu·ri·oid** (hol′ə thŏŏr′ē oid′). [< NL *Holothūri(a)* genus name (pl. of L *holothūrium* < Gk *holothoúrion* kind of zoophyte = *holo-* HOLO- + *-thourion* < ?) + -AN]

hol·o·type (hol′ə tīp′, hō′lə-), *n.* *Biol.* the type specimen used in the original description of a species. —**hol·o·typ·ic** (hol′ə tip′ik), *adj.*

hol·o·zo·ic (hol′ə zō′ik, hō′lə-), *adj.* *Biol.* feeding on solid food particles in the manner of most animals, as protozoans. [HOLO- + *-zoic* < Gk *zōik(ós)* of animals = *zō(ê)* life + *-ikos* -IC]

holp (hōlp), *v.* a pt. of **help.**

hol·pen (hōl′pən), *v.* *Dial.* a pp. of **help.**

Holst (hōlst), *n.* **Gus·tav Theodore** (gŏŏs′täv), 1874–1934, English composer.

Holstein (4 ft. high at shoulder)

Hol·stein (hōl′stīn; *for 1 also* hōl′stēn; *for 2 also Ger.* hōl′shtīn′), *n.* **1.** Also called **Hol·stein-Frie·sian** (hōl′stīn frē′zhən, -stēn-). one of a breed of black-and-white dairy cattle, raised originally in North Holland and Friesland, yielding large quantities of milk that has a low content of butterfat. **2.** a district in N West Germany, at the base of the peninsula of Jutland: a former duchy. Cf. **Schleswig-Holstein.**

hol·ster (hōl′stər), *n.* a leather case for a pistol, attached to a belt at the hip or over the shoulder or to a saddle. [var. of *hulster* < Sw *hölster* (> D *holster*); c. Icel *hulstr* sheath; akin to OE *heolstor* to cover, *helan* to cover, hide] —**hol′stered,** *adj.*

holt (hōlt), *n.* *Archaic.* **1.** a wood or grove. **2.** a wooded hill. [ME *holte*, OE *holt;* c. D *hout*, Icel *holt*, G *Holz* wood; akin to Gk *kládos* twig, OIr *caill* wood]

Holt (hōlt), *n.* **Harold Edward,** 1908–67, Australian political leader: prime minister 1966–67.

ho·lus-bo·lus (hō′ləs bō′ləs), *adv.* *Informal.* all at once; altogether. [sham-Latin compound based on *whole bolus*]

ho·ly (hō′lē), *adj.*, **-li·er, -li·est,** *n., pl.* **-lies.** —*adj.* **1.** specially recognized as or declared sacred by religious use or authority; consecrated: *holy ground.* **2.** dedicated or devoted to the service of God, the church, or religion. **3.** saintly; godly; pious; devout: *a holy life.* **4.** of religious purity, exaltation, etc.: *a holy love.* **5.** entitled to worship or profound religious reverence: *a holy relic.* **6.** religious: *holy rites.* **7.** inspiring fear, awe, etc. **8. holy terror,** a difficult or obstreperous person. —*n.* **9.** a place of worship; a sacred place. **10.** holy things or persons collectively. [ME *holi*, OE *hālig*, var. of *hāleg* (see WHOLE, -Y[1]); c. D, G *heilig*, Icel *heilagr*]
—**Syn. 1.** blessed. HOLY, SACRED, CONSECRATED, HALLOWED imply possession of a sanctity which is the object of religious veneration. HOLY refers to the divine, that which has its sanctity directly from God or is connected with Him: *Remember the Sabbath day to keep it holy.* That which is SACRED, while sometimes accepted as entitled to religious veneration, may have its sanctity from human authority: *a sacred oath.* That which is CONSECRATED is specially or formally dedicated to some religious use: *a life consecrated to service.* That which is HALLOWED has been made holy by being worshiped: *a hallowed shrine.* **4.** spiritual, pure.

Ho′ly Alli′ance, a league formed (1815) by the major sovereigns of continental Europe, which professed Christian brotherhood but actually sought to suppress democratic institutions.

Ho′ly Ark′, *Judaism.* a cabinet in a synagogue containing the scrolls of the Torah.

Ho′ly Bi′ble, Bible (def. 1).

ho′ly bread′, **1.** bread used in a Eucharistic service, both before and after consecration. **2.** *Eastern Ch.* eulogia (def. 1). **3.** *Gk. Orth. Ch.* antidoron (def. 1). [ME *holibrede*]

Ho′ly Cit′y, (*sometimes l.c.*) **1.** a city regarded as particularly sacred by the adherents of a religious faith. **2.** heaven. **3.** Jerusalem.

Ho′ly Commun′ion, communion (def. 6).

Ho′ly Cross′, Mountain of the, a peak in central Colorado, in the Sawatch Range. 13,996 ft.

ho′ly day′, a consecrated day or religious festival, esp. one other than Sunday. [see HOLIDAY]

ho′ly day′ of obliga′tion, **1.** a day on which Roman Catholics are required to attend Mass and abstain from certain kinds of work. **2.** a day on which Episcopalians are expected to take communion.

Ho′ly Fa′ther, *Rom. Cath. Ch.* a title of the pope.

Ho′ly Ghost′, the third person of the Trinity. Also called **Holy Spirit.**

Ho′ly Grail′, Grail.

Hol·y·head (hol′ē hed′), *n.* **1.** Also called **Ho′ly Is′land.** an island off the W coast of Anglesey, in NW Wales. **2.** a seaport on this island.

Ho′ly In′nocents' Day′, December 28, a day of religious observance commemorating the slaughter of the children of Bethlehem by Herod's order.

Ho′ly Land′, Palestine (def. 1).

ho′ly mack′erel, *Slang.* (used as an exclamation to express surprise or wonder.)

ho′ly Mo′ses, *Slang.* (used as an exclamation to express surprise or wonder.)

Ho·ly·oake (hō′lē ōk′), *n.* **Keith Jack·a** (jak′ə), born 1904, New Zealand agricultural and political leader: prime minister 1957 and 1960–72.

Ho′ly Of′fice, *Rom. Cath. Ch.* a congregation founded in 1542 in connection with the Inquisition; now entrusted with matters pertaining to faith and morals.

ho′ly of ho′lies, **1.** a place of special sacredness. **2.** the innermost chamber of the Biblical tabernacle and the Temple in Jerusalem, in which the ark of the covenant was kept. [trans. of LL *sanctum sanctōrum* (Vulgate), trans. of Gk *tò hágion tôn hagíōn*, itself trans. of Heb *qōdesh haqqodāshīm*]

Hol·yoke (hōl′yōk, hō′lē ōk′), *n.* a city in SW Massachusetts, on the Connecticut River. 50,112 (1970).

ho′ly or′ders, **1.** the rite of ordination. **2.** the rank or status of an ordained Christian minister. **3.** the degrees of the Christian ministry.

Ho′ly Roll′er, *Disparaging and Offensive.* a member of a Pentecostal sect noted for ecstatic religiosity. —**Ho′ly Roll′er·ism.**

Ho′ly Ro′man Em′pire, a Germanic empire of central European states considered as beginning with either Charlemagne in 800 or Otto the Great in 962 and lasting until 1806.

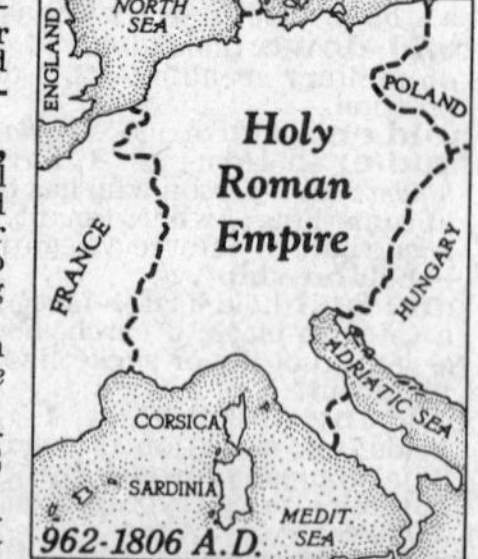

Ho′ly Rood′, the cross on which Jesus died. [ME *holie rode*, OE *halige rod*]

Ho′ly Sat′urday, the Saturday in Holy Week. [ME *holi Saterday*]

Ho′ly Scrip′ture, Scripture (def. 1). Also, **Ho′ly Scrip′tures.**

Ho′ly See′, **1.** *Rom. Cath Ch.* the see of Rome; the office or jurisdiction of the pope. **2.** the papal court.

Ho′ly Sep′ulcher, the sepulcher of Jesus.
Ho′ly Spir′it, 1. the spirit of God. 2. See **Holy Ghost.**
ho·ly·stone (hō′lē stōn′), *n., v.,* **-stoned, -ston·ing.** —*n.* 1. a block of soft sandstone used in scrubbing the decks of a vessel. —*v.t.* 2. to scrub with a holystone. [HOLY + STONE; perh. orig. jocular or profane]
ho′ly syn′od, *Eastern Ch.* the governing council of an autocephalous church, composed of bishops and presided over by the patriarch or some other prelate.
Ho′ly Thurs′day, 1. See **Ascension Day.** 2. the Thursday in Holy Week; Maundy Thursday. [ME *halewe-thoresday,* OE *halgan thunresdæg*]
ho·ly·tide (hō′lē tīd′), *n. Archaic.* a time of religious observances. [ME *holi tid,* OE *hālig tīd*]
ho′ly wa′ter, water blessed by a priest. [ME *haliwater,* OE *hāligwæter*]
Ho′ly Week′, the week preceding Easter Sunday. [trans. of It *settimana santa*]
Ho′ly Writ′, the Scriptures. [ME *holi writ,* OE *hālige writu* (pl.)]
Ho′ly Year′, *Rom. Cath. Ch.* a jubilee year.
hom·age (hom′ij, om′-), *n.* 1. respect or reverence. 2. the formal public acknowledgment by which a feudal tenant or vassal declared his fealty to his lord. 3. the relation thus established of a vassal to his lord. 4. something done or given in consideration of vassalage. [ME *(h)omage* < OF = *(h)ome* man (< L *homin-,* s. of *homo;* see HOMO) + *-age* -AGE] —**Syn.** 1. deference, obeisance; honor, tribute. 3. fidelity.
hom·ag·er (hom′ə jər, om′-), *n.* a feudal vassal. [late ME *omager* < AF]
hom·a·lo·graph·ic (hom′ə lō graf′ik), *adj.* homolographic. [< Gk *homalό(s)* even, regular + GRAPHIC]
hom·bre (hom′bər), *n. Cards.* omber.
hom·bre (ôm′bre; *Eng.* om′brā, -brē), *n., pl.* **-bres** (-bres; *Eng.* -brāz, -brēz). *Spanish.* man.
hom·burg (hom′bûrg), *n.* a felt hat with a soft crown dented lengthwise and a slightly rolled brim. [after *Homburg,* Germany, first site of its manufacture]
home (hōm), *n., adj., adv., v.,* **homed, hom·ing.** —*n.* 1. a house, apartment, or other place of residence. 2. the place in which one's domestic affections are centered. 3. an institution for the homeless, sick, etc.: *a nursing home.* 4. the dwelling place or retreat of an animal. 5. the native place or region of a thing. 6. any place of residence or refuge. 7. a person's native place or country. 8. (in games) the destination or goal. 9. *Baseball.* See **home plate.** 10. *Lacrosse.* one of three attack positions nearest the opposing goal. 11. **at home, a.** in one's own house or place of residence. **b.** in one's own town or country. **c.** prepared or willing to receive social visits. **d.** in a situation familiar to one; at ease. **e.** well-informed; proficient. **f.** (of a game) played in one's home town or on one's own grounds. —*adj.* 12. of, pertaining to, or connected with one's home or country; domestic. 13. *Sports.* **a.** local: *the home team.* **b.** played in a team's home town: *a home game.* —*adv.* 14. to, toward, or at home. 15. deep; to the heart; effectively and completely. 16. to the mark or point aimed at: *Her arguments hit home.* 17. *Naut.* **a.** into the position desired, perfectly or to the greatest possible extent: *sails sheeted home.* **b.** in the proper stowed position: *The anchor is home.* **c.** toward its vessel: *to bring the anchor home.* 18. **bring home to,** to make evident to; clarify or emphasize for: *The irrevocability of her decision was brought home to her.* 19. **home free,** *Slang.* safe, secure, settled, etc.: *The tax cut is hardly home free.* 20. **write home about,** *Informal.* to comment or remark on especially. —*v.i.* 21. to go or return home. 22. (of guided missiles, aircraft, etc.) to proceed, esp. under control of an automatic aiming mechanism, toward a specified target (often fol. by *in on*): *to home in on an enemy plane.* 23. to have a home where specified; reside. —*v.t.* 24. to bring or send home. 25. to provide with a home. 26. to direct, esp. under control of an automatic aiming device, toward an airport, target, etc. [ME *hom,* OE *hām* dwelling, home; c. D *heim,* Icel *heimr,* Dan *hjem,* Sw *hem,* G *Heim* home, Goth *haims* village] —**Syn.** 1. abode, dwelling, habitation; domicile, residence. See **house.** 2. hearth, fireside. 3. asylum.
home′ base′, *Baseball.* See **home plate.**
home·bod·y (hōm′bod′ē), *n., pl.* **-bod·ies.** a person whose pleasures and activities center around the home.
home·bred (hōm′bred′), *adj.* 1. bred at home; native; indigenous; domestic. 2. unpolished; unsophisticated.
home-brew (hōm′brōō′), *n.* beer or any alcoholic beverage made at home. —**home′-brewed′,** *adj.*
home·com·ing (hōm′kum′ing), *n.* 1. a return to one's home; arrival at home. 2. an annual event held by a college or university for visiting alumni. [ME *homcomyng;* r. ME *hamcume,* OE *hāmcyme* = *hām* HOME + *cyme* arrival]
home′ econom′ics, 1. the art and science of home management. 2. a college curriculum, usually including studies in nutrition, the purchase, preparation, and service of food, interior design, clothing and textiles, child development, family relationships, and household economics. —**home′ econ′omist.**
home′ fries′, slices of boiled potatoes, fried in butter or shortening. Also called **home′ fried′ pota′toes.**
home′ front′, the civilian sector of a nation at war.
home-grown (hōm′grōn′), *adj.* 1. (esp. of fruits or vegetables) produced or grown at home or in the region for local consumption: *home-grown tomatoes.* 2. native or indigenous to the region, country, etc.: *a home-grown school of painting.*
home′ guard′, a volunteer territorial force used for meeting local military and police emergencies.
home·land (hōm′land′), *n.* a person's native land.
home·less (hōm′lis), *adj.* 1. without a home: *a homeless child.* 2. *Rare.* affording no home: *the homeless sea.* [OE *hāmlēas*] —**home′less·ly,** *adv.* —**home′less·ness,** *n.*
home·like (hōm′līk′), *adj.* like or suggestive of home; familiar; comfortable.
home·ly (hōm′lē), *adj.,* **-li·er, -li·est.** 1. not beautiful; unattractive. 2. not having elegance or refinement. 3. plain; unpretentious. 4. commonly seen or known. 5. very friendly. [ME *homly*] —**home′li·ness,** *n.*
—**Syn.** 1–3. SIMPLE, HOMELY (HOMEY), PLAIN imply absence of adornment or embellishment. That which is SIMPLE is not elaborate or complex: *a simple kind of dress.* In the United States, HOMELY usually suggests absence of natural beauty: *an unattractive child almost homely enough to be called ugly.* In England, the word suggests a wholesome simplicity without artificial refinement or elegance; since it characterizes that which is comfortable and attractive, it is equivalent to HOMEY: *a homely cottage.* HOMEY emphasizes comfort and simple attractiveness and conveys a sense of intimate security: *a homey interior, arrangement, atmosphere.* That which is PLAIN has little or no adornment: *expensive but plain clothing.*
home·made (hōm′mād′), *adj.* 1. made at home, locally, in the present location, etc.: *All our pastry is homemade.* 2. made by oneself; amateurish.
home·mak·er (hōm′mā′kər), *n.* a person who manages a home, as a housewife or housekeeper.
home·mak·ing (hōm′mā′king), *n.* 1. the establishment or direction of a home; duties of a homemaker. —*adj.* 2. of or pertaining to the management of a home.
homeo-, a learned borrowing from Greek meaning "similar," used in the formation of compound words: *homeostatic.* Also, **homoeo-, homoio-.** [< Gk *homoio-,* comb. form of *hómoios* similar, like]
Home′ Of′fice, 1. the governmental department in Great Britain dealing with domestic matters. 2. (*l.c.*) the main office of a company.
ho·me·o·morph (hō′mē ə môrf′), *n.* any of the minerals characterized by a particular kind of homeomorphism.
ho·me·o·mor·phism (hō′mē ə môr′fiz əm), *n.* similarity in crystalline form but not necessarily in chemical composition. Also, **homoeomorphism.** —**ho′me·o·mor′phic, ho′me·o·mor′phous,** *adj.*
ho·me·op·a·thist (hō′mē op′ə thist), *n.* a person who practices or favors homeopathy. Also, **homoeopathist, ho·me·o·path** (hō′mē ə path′), **homoeopath.**
ho·me·op·a·thy (hō′mē op′ə thē), *n.* the method of treating disease by drugs, given in minute doses, that would produce in a healthy person symptoms similar to those of the disease (opposed to *allopathy*). Also, **homoeopathy.** —**ho·me·o·path·ic** (hō′mē ə path′ik), *adj.* —**ho′me·o·path′i·cal·ly,** *adv.*
ho·me·o·sta·sis (hō′mē ə stā′sis), *n.* the tendency of a system, esp. the physiological system of higher animals, to maintain internal stability, owing to the coordinated response of its parts to any disruptive situation or stimulus. —**ho·me·o·stat·ic** (hō′mē ə stat′ik), *adj.* —**ho′me·o·stat′i·cal·ly,** *adv.*
ho·me·o·typ·ic (hō′mē ə tip′ik), *adj. Biol.* of or pertaining to the second or equational division in meiosis. Also, **ho′me·o·typ′i·cal.** Cf. **heterotypic.**
home·own·er (hōm′ō′nər), *n.* a person who owns a house.
home′ plate′, *Baseball.* the base at which the batter stands and which a base runner must reach safely in order to score a run. Also called **home, the plate, home base.**
hom·er[1] (hō′mər), *Informal.* —*n.* 1. *Baseball.* See **home run.** —*v.i.* 2. *Baseball.* to hit a home run. [HOME + -ER[1]]
ho·mer[2] (hō′mər), *n.* a Hebrew unit of capacity equal to 10 baths in liquid measure or 10 ephahs in dry measure. Also called **kor.** [< Heb *homer,* lit., heap]
Ho·mer (hō′mər), *n.* 1. 8th century B.C., Greek epic poet: reputed author of the *Iliad* and *Odyssey.* 2. **Winslow,** 1836–1910, U.S. painter and illustrator.
home′ range′, *Ecol.* the area in which an animal normally lives.
Ho·mer·ic (hō mer′ik), *adj.* 1. of, pertaining to, or suggestive of Homer or his poetry. 2. heroic; imposing. [< L *Homēric(us)* < Gk *Homērikós*] —**Ho·mer′i·cal·ly,** *adv.*
Homer′ic laugh′ter, loud, hearty laughter, as of the gods.
home·room (hōm′rōōm′, -rŏŏm′), *n.* a school classroom in which students in the same grade meet at certain times under the supervision of a teacher. Also, **home′ room′.**
home′ rule′, self-government in local matters by a city, province, state, colony, or the like.
home′ run′, *Baseball.* a hit that enables a batter, without the aid of a fielding error, to score a run by making a nonstop circuit of the bases.
Home′ Sec′retary, *Brit.* the secretary of state for the Home Office.
home·sick (hōm′sik′), *adj.* longing for home. —**home′-sick′ness,** *n.*
home·spun (hōm′spun′), *adj.* 1. spun or made at home: *homespun cloth.* 2. made of such cloth: *homespun clothing.* 3. plain; unpolished; simple; rustic: *homespun humor.* —*n.* 4. a plain-weave cloth made at home, or of homespun yarn. 5. any cloth of similar appearance.
home·stead (hōm′sted, -stid), *n.* 1. *U.S.* a dwelling with its land and buildings, protected by a homestead law. 2. any dwelling with its land and buildings. —*v.t.* 3. to settle on (land), esp. under a homestead law. —*v.i.* 4. to settle on a property, esp. under a homestead law. [OE *hāmstede*]
Home′stead Act′, an act of Congress (1862) that made public lands in the West available to settlers without payment.
home·stead·er (hōm′sted′ər), *n.* 1. the owner or holder of a homestead. 2. *U.S.* a settler under the Homestead Act.
home′stead law′, 1. any law exempting homesteads from seizure or sale for debt. 2. any law making public lands available to settlers for purchase.
home·stretch (hōm′strech′), *n.* the straight part of a race track from the last turn to the finish line.
home·town (hōm′toun′), *n.* 1. the town or city in which a person lives or was born, or from which a person comes. —*adj.* 2. of or pertaining to a person's native town or city.
home·ward (hōm′wərd), *adv.* 1. Also, **home′wards.** toward home. —*adj.* 2. directed toward home. [ME *homward,* OE *hāmweard*]
home·work (hōm′wûrk′), *n.* 1. schoolwork assigned to be done outside the classroom. 2. any work done at home, esp. piecework.

home·y (hō′mē), *adj.*, **hom·i·er, hom·i·est.** comfortably informal and inviting; cozy; homelike. Also, **homy.** —**home′y·ness, hom′i·ness,** *n.* —**Syn.** See **homely.**

hom·i·ci·dal (hom′i sīd′əl), *adj.* **1.** of or pertaining to homicide. **2.** having a tendency to commit homicide. —**hom′i·ci′dal·ly,** *adv.*

hom·i·cide (hom′i sīd′), *n.* **1.** the killing of one human being by another. **2.** a person who kills another; murderer. [ME < MF < L *homicīd(ium)* a killing, *homicīd(a)* killer = *homi-* (comb. form of *homo* man) + *-cīdium, -cīda* -CIDE]

hom·i·let·ic (hom′ə let′ik), *adj.* **1.** of or pertaining to preaching or to homilies. **2.** of the nature of a homily. **3.** of or pertaining to homiletics. Also, **hom′i·let′i·cal.** [< Gk *homīlētik(ós)* affable = *homīlē-* (var. s. of *homīléein* to converse with; see HOMILY) + *-tikos* -TIC] —**hom′i·let′i·cal·ly,** *adv.*

hom·i·let·ics (hom′ə let′iks), *n.* (*construed as sing.*) the art of writing and preaching sermons.

hom·i·ly (hom′ə lē), *n., pl.* **-lies. 1.** a religious discourse addressed to a congregation; sermon. **2.** an admonitory or moralizing discourse. [< eccl. L *homīli(a)* < Gk: assembly, sermon = *homīl(os)* crowd (*hom(oû)* together + *īl(ē)* crowd) + *-ia* -Y[3]; r. ME *omelie* < MF < L, as above]

hom·ing (hō′miŋ), *adj.* **1.** returning home. **2.** guiding or directing homeward or to a destination. [HOME + -ING[2]]

hom′ing pi′geon, any pigeon used to carry messages and equipped by training and breeding to fly home.

hom·i·nid (hom′ə nid), *n.* *Anthropol.* a member of the *Hominidae,* the family of man and his ancestors. Also, **ho·min·i·an** (hō min′ē ən). [< NL *Hominid(ae)* = L *homin-* (s. of *homo*) man + *-idae* -ID[2]]

hom·i·nine (hom′ə nīn′), *adj.* resembling or characteristic of man. [< L *homin-* (s. of *homo*) man + -INE[1]]

hom·i·noid (hom′ə noid′), *n.* a member of the *Hominoidea,* a superfamily including the great apes and man. [< L *homin-* (s. of *homo*) man + -OID]

hom·i·ny (hom′ə nē), *n.* whole or ground hulled corn from which the bran and germ have been removed. [< Algonquian (New England or Va.); cf. *tackhummin* to grind corn = *ahäm* he beats + *min* berry, fruit]

hom′iny grits′, finely ground hominy.

hom·mock (hom′ək), *n.* hummock (def. 3).

Ho·mo (hō′mō), *n.* the primate genus that includes modern man, *Homo sapiens,* and a number of related extinct species, as the Neanderthal man. [< L: man, OL *hemō* the earthly one; akin to L *humus* earth, soil, *hūmānus* HUMAN, OE *guma* man, Gk *chamaí* on the ground]

homo-, an element appearing in loan words from Greek, where it meant "same" (*homology*); on this model, used in the formation of compound words (*homocercal*). [< Gk, comb. form of *homós* one and the same; akin to Skt *sama-*; see SAME]

ho·mo·cen·tric (hō′mə sen′trik, hom′ə-), *adj.* having a common center; concentric. Also, **ho′mo·cen′tri·cal.** —**ho′mo·cen′tri·cal·ly,** *adv.*

Homocercal tail

ho·mo·cer·cal (hō′mə sûr′kəl, hom′ə-), *adj.* *Ichthyol.* **1.** having an equally divided tail or caudal fin, the spinal column ending at or near the middle of the base of the tail. **2.** noting such a tail or caudal fin. [HOMO- + *cerc-* (< Gk *kérk(os)* tail) + -AL[1]] —**ho·mo·cer·cy** (hō′mə sûr′sē, hom′ə-), **ho·mo·cer·cal·i·ty** (hō′mə sər kal′i tē, hom′ə-), *n.*

ho·mo·chro·mat·ic (hō′mə krō mat′ik, -krə-, hom′ə-), *adj.* of or pertaining to one hue; monochromatic. Cf. **heterochromatic.** —**ho·mo·chro·ma·tism** (hō′mə krō′mə tiz′əm, hom′ə-), *n.*

ho·mo·cy·clic (hō′mə sī′klik, -sik′lik, hom′ə-), *adj.* *Chem.* of or noting a cyclic compound having atoms of only one element, usually carbon, in the ring.

homoeo-, var. of **homeo-:** *homoeopathy.*

ho·moe·o·mor·phism (hō′mē ə môr′fiz əm), *n.* homeomorphism. —**ho′moe·o·mor′phic, ho′moe·o·mor′phous,** *adj.*

ho·moe·op·a·thist (hō′mē op′ə thist), *n.* homeopathist. Also, **ho·moe·o·path** (hō′mē ə path′).

ho·moe·op·a·thy (ho′mē op′ə thē), *n.* homeopathy. —**ho·moe·o·path·ic** (hō′mē ə path′ik), *adj.* —**ho′moe·o·path′i·cal·ly,** *adv.*

ho·mo·e·rot·i·cism (hō′mō i rot′i siz′əm), *n.* *Psychoanal.* a tendency to be sexually aroused by a member of the same sex. Also, **ho·mo·er·o·tism** (hō′mō er′ə tiz′əm). —**ho·mo·e·rot·ic** (hō′mō i rot′ik), *adj.*

ho·mog·a·mous (hō mog′ə məs), *adj.* *Bot.* **1.** having flowers or florets that do not differ sexually (opposed to *heterogamous*). **2.** having the stamens and pistils maturing simultaneously (opposed to *dichogamous*). [< Gk *homógamos* married to sisters, or to the same woman]

ho·mog·a·my (hō mog′ə mē), *n.* **1.** *Bot.* the state of being homogamous. **2.** interbreeding of individuals having like characteristics.

ho·mo·ge·ne·i·ty (hō′mə jə nē′i tē, hom′ə-), *n.* the state or quality of being homogeneous. Also, **ho·mo·ge·ne·ous·ness** (hō′mə jē′nē əs nis, -jēn′yəs-, hom′ə-). [< ML *homogeneitās.* See HOMOGENEOUS, -ITY]

ho·mo·ge·ne·ous (hō′mə jē′nē əs, -jēn′yəs, hom′ə-), *adj.* **1.** composed of parts all of the same kind; not heterogeneous. **2.** of the same kind or nature; essentially alike. **3.** *Math.* **a.** having a common property throughout: *a homogeneous solid figure.* **b.** having all terms of the same degree: *a homogeneous equation.* **c.** remaining unchanged when each variable is replaced by the same specified number times the variable: *a homogeneous function.* **d.** (of an equation) formed by equating a homogeneous function to zero. [< ML *homogeneus* = *homogene-* (s. of Gk *homogenḗs* of the same kind; see HOMO-, GENE) + *-us* -OUS] —**ho′mo·ge′ne·ous·ly,** *adv.*

ho·mog·e·nize (hə moj′ə nīz′, hō-), *v.t.*, **-nized, -niz·ing. 1.** to form by blending unlike elements; make homogeneous; emulsify. **2.** to break up the fat globules in (milk or cream) in order to distribute them throughout. [HOMOGEN(EOUS) + -IZE] —**ho·mog′e·ni·za′tion,** *n.* —**ho·mog′e·niz′er,** *n.*

ho·mog·e·nous (hə moj′ə nəs, hō-), *adj.* **1.** *Biol.* corresponding in structure because of a common origin. **2.** homogeneous.

ho·mog·e·ny (hə moj′ə nē, hō-), *n.* *Biol.* correspondence in form or structure, owing to a common origin. [< Gk *homogéneia* community of origin]

ho·mog·o·nous (hə mog′ə nəs, hō-), *adj.* *Bot.* pertaining to monoclinous flowers that do not differ in the relative length of stamens and pistils (opposed to *heterogonous*). [HOMO- + *-gonous* < Gk *-gonos* generating; see -GONY] —**ho·mog′o·nous·ly,** *adv.*

ho·mog·o·ny (hə mog′ə nē, hō-), *n.* *Bot.* the state of being homogonous.

ho·mo·graft (hō′mə graft′, -gräft′, hom′ə-), *n.* *Surg.* a tissue or organ transplanted by grafting from one to another member of the same species. Cf. **autograft.**

hom·o·graph (hom′ə graf′, -gräf′), *n.* a word of the same written form as another but of different origin and meaning, whether pronounced the same way or not, as *homer*[1] "home run," and *homer*[2] "unit of measure." —**hom·o·graph·ic** (hom′ə graf′ik), *adj.*

homoio-, var. of **homeo-:** *homoiothermal.*

ho·moi·o·therm (hō moi′ə thûrm′), *n.* *Zool.* a homoiothermal animal. [back formation from HOMOIOTHERMAL]

ho·moi·o·ther·mal (hō moi′ə thûr′məl), *adj.* *Zool.* warm-blooded (def. 1). Also, **ho·moi′o·ther′mic, ho·moi′o·ther′mous.**

Ho·moi·ou·si·an (hō′moi o͞o′sē ən, -ou′-), *n.* **1.** a member of a 4th-century A.D. church party which maintained that the essence of the Son is similar to, but not the same as, that of the Father. —*adj.* **2.** relating to the Homoiousians or their belief. [< LGk *homoioúsi(os)* of like substance (Gk *homoi-* HOMOIO- + *ousí(a)* substance, essence + *-os* adj. suffix) + -AN] —**Ho′moi·ou′si·an·ism,** *n.*

ho·mol·o·gate (hə mol′ə gāt′, hō-), *v.t.*, **-gat·ed, -gat·ing.** to approve; ratify. [< ML *homologāt(us)* (ptp. of *homologāre* < Gk *homologeîn* to agree to, allow); see -ATE[1]] —**ho·mol′o·ga′tion,** *n.*

ho·mo·log·i·cal (hō′mə loj′i kəl), *adj.* homologous. Also, **ho′mo·log′ic.** —**ho′mo·log′i·cal·ly,** *adv.*

ho·mol·o·gise (hə mol′ə jīz′, hō-), *v.t., v.i.*, **-gised, -gis·ing.** *Chiefly Brit.* homologize. —**ho·mol′o·gis′er,** *n.*

ho·mol·o·gize (hə mol′ə jīz′, hō-), *v.*, **-gized, -giz·ing.** —*v.t.* **1.** to make or show to be homologous. —*v.i.* **2.** to be homologous; correspond. —**ho·mol′o·giz′er,** *n.*

ho·mol·o·gous (hə mol′ə gəs, hō-), *adj.* **1.** having the same or a similar relation; corresponding, as in relative position, structure, etc. **2.** *Biol.* corresponding in structure and in origin, but not necessarily in function: *The wing of a bird and the foreleg of a horse are homologous.* **3.** *Chem.* of the same chemical type, but differing by a fixed increment in certain constituents. [< ML *homologus* < Gk *homólogos* agreeing]

homol′ogous chro′mosomes, *Biol.* pairs of similar chromosomes, one of maternal, the other of paternal origin, that carry the Mendelian pairs of alleles or genes.

ho·mol·o·graph·ic (hō mol′ə graf′ik), *adj.* representing parts with like proportions. Also, **homalographic.** [var. of HOMALOGRAPHIC]

hom·o·logue (hom′ə lôg′, -log′), *n.* **1.** something homologous. **2.** *Biol.* a homologous organ or part. [< Gk *homólog(on),* neut. of *homólogos* HOMOLOGOUS]

ho·mol·o·gy (hə mol′ə jē, hō-), *n., pl.* **-gies. 1.** the state of being homologous, as in relation or correspondence. **2.** *Biol.* **a.** a fundamental similarity due to community of descent. **b.** a structural similarity of two segments of one animal based on a common developmental origin. **3.** *Chem.* the similarity of organic compounds of a series in which each member differs from its adjacent compounds by a fixed increment, as by CH_2. **4.** *Math.* a classification of figures according to certain geometric properties. [< Gk *homologí(a)* agreement]

ho·mol′o·sine projec′tion (hə mol′ə sin, -sīn′, hō-), *Cartog.* an equal-area projection of the world, distorting ocean areas in order to minimize the distortion of the continents. [irreg. HOMOLO(GRAPHIC) + SINE[1]]

ho·mo·mor·phism (hō′mə môr′fiz əm, hom′ə-), *n.* **1.** *Biol.* correspondence in form or external appearance but not in type of structure and in origin. **2.** *Bot.* possession of perfect flowers of only one kind. **3.** *Zool.* resemblance between the young and the adult. Also, **ho′mo·mor′phy.** [*homomorph* (see HOMO-, -MORPH) + -ISM] —**ho′mo·mor′phous,** *adj.*

hom·o·nym (hom′ə nim), *n.* **1.** a word the same as another in sound and spelling but different in meaning, as *chase,* to pursue, and *chase,* to ornament metal. **2.** homophone (def. 1). **3.** a homograph. **4.** a namesake. **5.** *Biol.* a name given to a species or genus that has been used at an earlier date for a different species or genus and is therefore rejected. [< L *homōnym(um)* < Gk *homṓnymon,* neut. of *homṓnymos* HOMONYMOUS] —**hom′o·nym′ic,** *adj.* —**hom′o·nym′i·ty,** *n.*

ho·mon·y·mous (hə mon′ə məs, hō-), *adj.* of the nature of homonyms; having the same name. [< L *homōnymus* < Gk *homṓnymos* of the same name. See HOMO-, -ONYM] —**ho·mon′y·mous·ly,** *adv.*

ho·mon·y·my (hə mon′ə mē, hō-), *n.* homonymous state. [< LL *homōnymia* < Gk]

Ho·mo·ou·si·an (hō′mō o͞o′sē ən, -ou′-, hom′ō-), *Eccles.* —*n.* **1.** a member of a 4th-century A.D. church party which maintained that the essence of the Father and the Son is the same. —*adj.* **2.** of or pertaining to the Homoousians or their doctrine. Also, **Ho′mo·ū′si·an.** [< LGk *homooúsi(os)* of the same substance (Gk *hom(o)-* HOMO- + *ousí(a)* substance, essence + *-os* adj. suffix) + -AN] —**Ho′mo·ou′si·an·ism,** *n.*

ho·mo·phile (hō′mə fīl′), *n.* **1.** a homosexual person. —*adj.* **2.** advocating the civil rights and welfare of homophiles: *a homophile organization.*

hom·o·phone (hom′ə fōn′, hō′mə-), *n.* **1.** *Phonet.* a word pronounced the same as, but differing in meaning from another, whether spelled the same way or not, as *heir* and *air.* **2.** a written element that represents the same spoken unit as another, as *ks,* a homophone of *x* in English. [back formation from HOMOPHONOUS]

hom·o·phon·ic (hom′ə fon′ik, hō′mə-), *adj.* **1.** having the same sound. **2.** *Music.* having one part or melody predominating. [< Gk *homóphōn(os)* (see HOMOPHONOUS) + -IC] —**hom′o·phon′i·cal·ly,** *adv.*

ho·moph·o·nous (hə mof′ə nəs), *adj.* identical in pronunciation. [< Gk *homóphōnos* of the same sound]

ho·moph·o·ny (hə mof′ə nē), *n.* **1.** the quality or state of being homophonic. **2.** homophonic music. [< Gk *homophōnía* unison]

ho·mo·po·lar (hō′mə pō′lər, hom′ə-), *adj.* *Chem.* of uniform polarity; not separated or changed into ions. —**ho·mo·po·lar·i·ty** (hō′mə pō lar′i tē, hom′ə-), *n.*

Ho·mop·ter·a (hō mop′tər ə), *n.* the order comprising the homopterous insects. [< NL (neut. pl.); see HOMOPTEROUS]

ho·mop·ter·ous (hə mop′tər əs, hō-), *adj.* belonging or pertaining to the *Homoptera*, an order of insects closely related to the hemipterous insects (in some classifications a suborder of *Hemiptera*) but having membranous forewings and hind wings, comprising the aphids, cicadas, etc. [< Gk *homópteros.* See HOMO-, -PTEROUS]

ho·mor·gan·ic (hō′môr gan′ik, hom′ôr-), *adj.* *Phonet.* (of two or more speech sounds) articulated by using the same speech organ or organs, as *p*, *b*, and *m*, which are homorganic with respect to being labial but not with respect to being velar. Cf. **homotypical.**

Ho·mo sa·pi·ens (hō′mō sā′pē ənz), **1.** (*italics*) modern man, the single surviving species of the genus *Homo* and of the primate family *Hominidae*, to which it belongs. **2.** mankind. [< NL: man, the wise]

ho·mo·sex·u·al (hō′mə sek′shōō əl, -mō-), *adj.* **1.** of, pertaining to, or exhibiting homosexuality. —*n.* **2.** a homosexual person.

ho·mo·sex·u·al·i·ty (hō′mə sek′shōō al′i tē, -mō-), *n.* sexual desire or behavior directed toward a person or persons of one's own sex.

ho·mos·po·rous (hə mos′pər əs, hō′mə spōr′əs, -spôr′-), *adj.* *Bot.* having spores of one kind only.

ho·mos·po·ry (hə mos′pə rē, hō-), *n.* the production of a single kind of spore, neither microspore nor megaspore.

ho·mo·tax·is (hō′mə tak′sis, hom′ə-), *n.* a similarity of arrangement, as of geological strata that have the same relative position but are not necessarily contemporaneous. —**ho′mo·tax′ic, ho·mo·tax·i·al** (hō′mə tak′sē əl, hom′ə-), *adj.* —**ho′mo·tax′i·al·ly,** *adv.*

ho·mo·thal·lic (hō′mə thal′ik, hom′ə-), *adj.* *Bot.* **1.** having all mycelia alike, the opposite sexual functions being performed by different cells of a single mycelium. **2.** monoecious. [HOMO- + THALL(US) + -IC] —**ho′mo·thal′lism,** *n.*

ho·mo·typ·i·cal (hō′mə tip′i kəl, hom′ə-), *adj.* *Phonet.* (of two or more speech sounds) articulated in a like manner but not with the same speech organ or organs, as the consonants of *pie* and *tie.* Cf. **homorganic.**

ho·mo·zy·go·sis (hō′mə zī gō′sis, -zi-, hom′ə-), *n.* *Biol.* the state of being a homozygote. [HOMO- + NL *zygōsis* < Gk]

ho·mo·zy·gote (hō′mə zī′gōt, -zig′ōt, hom′ə-), *n.* *Biol.* an organism with identical pairs of genes with respect to any given pair of heredity characters, and therefore breeding true to those characteristics.

ho·mo·zy·gous (hō′mə zī′gəs, hom′ə-), *adj.* *Biol.* **1.** having identical pairs of genes for any given pair of hereditary characteristics. **2.** of or pertaining to a homozygote. [HOMO- + Gk *-zygos*; see ZYGO-, -OUS]

Homs (hôms), *n.* a city in W Syria. 175,303 (est. 1963).

ho·mun·cu·lus (hō mung′kyə ləs), *n., pl.* **-li** (-lī′). **1.** a diminutive human; midget. **2.** (formerly) a fully formed, miniature human body believed to be contained in the spermatozoon. [< L = *homun-* (var. of *homin-*, s. of *homo* man) + *-culus* -CULE] —**ho·mun′cu·lar,** *adj.*

hom·y (hō′mē), *adj.,* **hom·i·er, hom·i·est.** homey.

Hon., Honorable.

hon., **1.** honorably. **2.** *Chiefly Brit.* honorary.

Ho·nan (hō′nan′; *Chin.* hœ′nän′), *n.* **1.** a province in E China. 50,320,000; 64,479 sq. mi. *Cap.:* Kaifeng. **2.** (*usually l.c.*) *Textiles.* a pongee fabric made from the filaments of the wild silkworm.

hon·cho (hon′chō′), *n., pl.* **-chos.** *U.S. Informal.* a chief or boss. [<Jap: alter. of *han* squad + *cho* leader]

Hond., Honduras.

Hon·do (*Jap.* hôn′dô), *n.* Honshu.

Hon·du·ras (hon dŏŏr′əs, -dyŏŏr′-), *n.* **1.** a republic in NE Central America. 3,036,004; 43,277 sq. mi. *Cap.:* Tegucigalpa. **2.** See **British Honduras.** —**Hon·du′ran, Hon·du·ra·ne·an, Hon·du·ra·ni·an** (hon′də rā′nē ən), *adj., n.*

hone[1] (hōn), *n., v.,* **honed, hon·ing.** —*n.* **1.** a whetstone of fine, compact texture for sharpening razors. **2.** a precision tool with a mechanically rotated abrasive tip, for enlarging holes. —*v.t.* **3.** to sharpen on or as on a hone: *to hone a razor.* **4.** to enlarge or finish (a hole) with a hone. [ME; OE *hān* stone, rock; c. Icel *hein* hone; akin to CONE]

hone[2] (hōn), *v.i.,* **honed, hon·ing.** *Dial.* **1.** to moan and groan. **2.** to yearn; long: *to hone for the simple life.* [< AF **hone(r)* = OF *hogner* to grumble, growl < Gmc; cf. OS *hōnian* to abuse, revile]

Ho·neg·ger (hon′ə gər, hō′neg′ər; *Fr.* ô ne GER′), *n.* **Ar·thur** (är′thər; *Fr.* AR TŎŎR′), 1892–1955, Swiss composer, born in France.

hon·est (on′ist), *adj.* **1.** honorable in principles, intentions, and actions; upright. **2.** showing uprightness and fairness: *honest dealings.* **3.** gained fairly: *honest wealth.* **4.** sincere; frank: *an honest face.* **5.** genuine or unadulterated: *honest weights.* **6.** respectable; having a good reputation: *an honest name.* **7.** truthful or creditable. **8.** humble, plain, or unadorned. **9.** *Archaic.* chaste or virtuous. [ME *honeste* < MF < L *honest(us)* honorable = *hones-* (var. s. of *honōs*) HONOR + *-tus* adj. suffix] —**hon′est·ness,** *n.* —**Syn. 1.** just. **2.** fair. **4.** straight forward, candid. —**Ant. 1.** corrupt.

hon′est bro′ker, *Informal.* an impartial intermediary or arbitrator.

hon′est in′jun (in′jən), *Informal.* honestly; truly. Also, **hon′est In′jun.**

hon·est·ly (on′ist lē), *adv.* **1.** in an honest manner. **2.** with honesty. —*interj.* **3.** (used to express mild dismay, disbelief, etc.): *Honestly, you are the limit!* [ME]

hon·es·ty (on′i stē), *n., pl.* **-ties. 1.** the quality or fact of being honest; uprightness, probity, or integrity. **2.** truthfulness, sincerity, or frankness. **3.** freedom from deceit or fraud. **4.** *Bot.* a cruciferous herb, *Lunaria annua*, having purple flowers and semitransparent, satiny pods. **5.** *Obs.* chastity. [ME *honeste* < MF < L *honestās*] —**Syn. 1.** fairness, justice; rectitude. See **honor. 2.** candor, veracity.

hone·wort (hōn′wûrt′), *n.* any of several umbelliferous herbs of the genus *Cryptotaenia*, esp. *C. canadensis*, having white flowers. [*hone* (< ?) + WORT[2]]

hon·ey (hun′ē), *n., pl.* **hon·eys,** *adj., v.,* **hon·eyed** or **hon·ied, hon·ey·ing.** —*n.* **1.** a sweet, viscid fluid produced by bees from the nectar collected from flowers, and stored in their nests or hives as food. **2.** the nectar of flowers. **3.** any of various similarly sweet, viscid products produced by insects or in other ways. **4.** something sweet, delicious, or delightful: *the honey of flattery.* **5.** (*often cap.*) darling; sweetheart (used as a term of endearment for a loved one). **6.** *Informal.* something of esp. high quality, degree of excellence, etc.: *That car is a honey.* —*adj.* **7.** of or pertaining to honey; like honey; sweet. **8.** containing honey or flavored or sweetened with honey. —*v.t.* **9.** *Informal.* to talk flatteringly or endearingly to (often used with *up*). **10.** to sweeten or flavor with or as with honey. —*v.i.* **11.** *Informal.* (often fol. by *up*) to use flattery, endearing terms, etc. [ME *hony*, OE *hunig*; c. D, G *honig*, Icel *hunang*; akin to Gk *knēkós* pale yellow, tawny] —**hon′ey·ful,** *adj.* —**hon′ey·less,** *adj.* —**hon′ey·like′,** *adj.*

hon·ey·bee (hun′ē bē′), *n.* a bee that collects and stores honey, esp. *Apis mellifera.*

hon·ey·bunch (hun′ē bunch′), *n.* sweetheart; honey (often cap. and used as a term of endearment). Also, **hon·ey·bun** (hun′ē-bun′).

hon·ey·comb (hun′ē kōm′), *n.* **1.** a structure of rows of hexagonal wax cells, formed by bees in their hive for the storage of honey, pollen, and their eggs. **2.** a piece of this containing honey and chewed as a sweet. **3.** anything whose appearance suggests such a structure. **4.** the reticulum of a ruminant. —*adj.* **5.** having the structure or appearance of a honeycomb. —*v.t.* **6.** to cause to be full of holes; pierce with many holes or cavities. **7.** to penetrate in all parts: *a city honeycombed with vice.* [ME *huny-comb*, OE *hunigcamb*]

Honeycomb

hon′eycomb tripe′, a part of the inner lining of the stomach of the steer, calf, hog, or sheep, resembling a honeycomb in appearance and considered a table delicacy.

hon·ey·dew (hun′ē dōō′, -dyōō′), *n.* **1.** the sweet material that exudes from the leaves of certain plants in hot weather. **2.** a sugary material secreted by aphids, leafhoppers, etc. **3.** See **honeydew melon.** —**hon′ey·dewed′,** *adj.*

hon′eydew mel′on, a sweet-flavored, white-fleshed muskmelon having a smooth, pale-green rind.

hon′ey eat′er, any of numerous oscine birds of the family *Meliphagidae*, chiefly of Australasia, having a bill and tongue adapted for extracting the nectar from flowers.

hon·eyed (hun′ēd), *adj.* **1.** dulcet or mellifluous: *honeyed tones.* **2.** flattering or ingratiating: *honeyed words.* **3.** containing, consisting of, or resembling honey: *honeyed drinks.* Also, **honied.** [ME *honyede*] —**hon′eyed·ly,** *adv.* —**hon′eyed·ness,** *n.*

hon′ey guide′, any of several small, usually dull-colored birds of the family *Indicatoridae*, of Africa and southern Asia, certain species of which are noted for their ability to find the nests of honeybees, to which they are followed by men or animals.

hon′ey lo′cust, a thorny, North American tree, *Gleditsia triacanthos*, having small, compound leaves and pods with a sweet pulp.

hon′ey mesquite′, a thorny shrub, *Prosopis juliflora*, of the West Indies.

hon·ey·moon (hun′ē mōōn′), *n.* **1.** a vacation or trip taken by a newly married couple. **2.** the month or so following a marriage. **3.** any new relationship characterized by an initial period of harmony: *The honeymoon between Congress and the President was over.* —*v.i.* **4.** to spend one's honeymoon (usually fol. by *in* or *at*). —**hon′ey·moon′er,** *n.*

hon′eymoon bridge′, *Cards.* any of several varieties of bridge for two players.

hon·ey·suck·er (hun′ē suk′ər), *n.* a bird that feeds on the nectar of flowers.

hon·ey·suck·le (hun′ē suk′əl), *n.* **1.** any upright or climbing, caprifoliaceous shrub of the genus *Lonicera*, certain species of which are cultivated for their fragrant white, yellow, or red tubular flowers. **2.** any of various other fragrant or ornamental plants. [ME *honiesoukel* = *honisouke* (OE *hunisūce*; see HONEY, SUCK) + *-el* -LE] —**hon′ey·suck′led,** *adj.*

hon′eysuckle or′nament, anthemion.

hon·ey-sweet (hun′ē swēt′), *adj.* sweet as honey. [ME *hony sweete*, OE *hunig swēte*]

hong (hông), *n.* **1.** (in China) a group of rooms or buildings forming a warehouse, factory, etc. **2.** one of the factories under foreign ownership formerly maintained at Canton. [< Chin (Cantonese) *hong* row, rank = Mandarin *hang*]

Hong Kong (hông′ kông′), **1.** a British crown colony comprising the island of Hong Kong (32 sq. mi.), nearby islands, and the adjacent mainland bordering SE China. 3,692,000 (est. 1964); 398 sq. mi. *Cap.:* Victoria. **2.** Victoria (def. 4). Also, **Hong′kong′.**

hon·ied (hun′ēd), *adj.* honeyed.

ho·ni soit qui mal y pense (ô nē SWA′ kē MAL ē PÄNS′), *French.* shamed be the one who thinks evil of it: motto of the Order of the Garter.

honk (hôngk, hongk), *n.* **1.** the cry of a goose. **2.** any similar sound. **3.** the sound of an automobile horn. —*v.i.* **4.** to emit a honk. **5.** to cause an automobile horn to emit a honk. —*v.t.* **6.** to cause (an automobile horn) to emit a honk. [imit.] —**honk′er,** *n.*

hon·ky (hông′kē), *n., pl.* **hon·kies.** *Disparaging.* a white man: used esp. by blacks. Also, **hon′key, hon′kie, hunky.** [orig. uncert.]

honk·y-tonk (hông′kē tôngk′, hông′kē tôngk′), *Informal.* —*n.* **1.** a cheap, noisy, and garish nightclub or dance hall. —*adj.* **2.** of, pertaining to, or characteristic of a honky-tonk. **3.** characterized by or having a large number of honky-tonks. **4.** *Music.* noting a style of ragtime piano-playing typically performed on a piano whose strings have been muffled and given a tinny sound. [rhyming compound (with euphonic *-y-*) based on HONK]

Hon·o·lu·lu (hon′ə lo͞o′lo͞o), *n.* a seaport in and the capital of Hawaii, on S Oahu. 324,871 (1970).

hon·or (on′ər), *n.* **1.** high public esteem; fame; glory: *to earn a position of honor.* **2.** honesty or integrity in one's beliefs and actions: *a man of honor.* **3.** a source of credit or distinction: *to be an honor to one's family.* **4.** high respect, as for worth, merit, or rank: *to be held in honor.* **5.** such respect manifested: *to be received with honor.* **6.** the privilege of being associated with or receiving a favor from a respected person, group, etc.: *to have the honor of serving on a prize jury.* **7.** Usually, **honors.** evidence, as a decoration, scroll, or title, of high rank, dignity, or distinction: *political honors.* **8.** (*usually cap.*) a deferential title, esp. for judges and mayors (prec. by *his, your,* etc.). **9. honors, a.** special rank or distinction conferred by a university, college, or school upon an outstanding student. **b.** an advanced course of study for superior students. **10.** chastity or purity in a woman. **11.** Also called **hon′or card′.** *Cards.* **a.** *Bridge.* any of the five highest trump cards, as an ace, king queen, jack, or ten in the trump suit, or any of the four aces in a no-trump contract. **b.** *Whist.* any of the four highest trump cards, as an ace, king, queen, or jack in the trump suit. **12.** *Golf.* the privilege of teeing off before the other player or side, given after the first hole to the player who or side that won the previous hole. **13. be on** or **upon one's honor,** to accept and acknowledge personal responsibility for one's actions. **14. do honor to, a.** to show respect to. **b.** to be a credit to. **15. do the honors,** to serve or preside as host, as in introducing people, carving or serving at table, etc. —*v.t.* **16.** to hold in honor or high respect; revere. **17.** to confer honor or distinction upon. **18.** to show a courteous regard for: *to honor an invitation.* **19.** *Com.* to accept or pay (a draft, check, etc.). **20.** to accept as valid and conform to the request or demands of (an official document). **21.** (in square dancing) to meet or salute with a bow. —*adj.* **22.** of, pertaining to, or noting honor. Also, *esp. Brit.,* **honour.** [ME *(h)on(o)ur* < AF (OF *onor,* etc.) < L *honōr-* (s. of *honor,* earlier *honōs*)] —**hon′or·er,** *n.* —**hon′or·less,** *adj.*
—**Syn. 1.** distinction. **2.** probity, uprightness. HONOR, HONESTY, INTEGRITY, SINCERITY refer to the highest moral principles and the absence of deceit or fraud. HONOR denotes a fine sense of, and a strict conformity to, what is considered morally right or due: *a high sense of honor; on one's honor.* HONESTY denotes the presence of probity and particularly the absence of deceit or fraud, esp. in business dealings: *uncompromising honesty and trustworthiness.* INTEGRITY indicates a soundness of moral principle which no power or influence can impair: *a man of unquestioned integrity and dependability.* SINCERITY implies absence of dissimulation or deceit, and a strong adherence to truth: *His sincerity was evident in every word.* **4.** deference, homage; reverence, veneration. HONOR, DISTINCTION refer to the regard in which one is held by his fellows. HONOR suggests a combination of liking and respect: *His townsmen held him in great honor.* DISTINCTION suggests particular honor because of qualities or accomplishments: *He achieved distinction as a violinist at an early age.* **16.** esteem, venerate.

hon·or·a·ble (on′ər ə bəl), *adj.* **1.** in accordance with or characterized by principles of honor; upright. **2.** of high rank, dignity, or distinction. **3.** (*cap.*) entitling to honor or distinction: a title prefixed to the names of the younger children of British peers, from earls to barons, and to certain government officials. *Abbr.:* Hon. **4.** worthy of honor and high respect; estimable; creditable. **5.** bringing honor or credit; consistent with honor: *an honorable discharge.* Also, *esp. Brit.,* **honourable.** [ME *hono(u)rable* < AF (MF *honorable*) < L *honōrābil(is)*] —**hon′or·a·ble·ness,** *n.* —**hon′or·a·bly,** *adv.* —**Syn. 1.** honest, noble, just. —**Ant. 1.** ignoble.

hon′orable dis′charge, *U.S. Mil.* **1.** a discharge from military service of a person who has fulfilled his obligations efficiently, honorably, and faithfully. **2.** a certificate of such a discharge.

hon·or·and (on′ə rand′), *n.* the recipient of an honorary degree. [< L *honōrand(us),* ger. of *honōrāre* to HONOR]

hon·o·rar·i·um (on′ə râr′ē əm), *n., pl.* **-rar·i·ums, -rar·i·a** (-râr′ē ə). **1.** a reward, in recognition of acts or professional services for which custom or propriety forbids a price to be set. **2.** a fee for services rendered by a professional person. [< L: fee paid on taking office, n. use of neut. of *honōrārius* HONORARY]

hon·or·ar·y (on′ə rer′ē), *adj.* **1.** given for honor only, without the usual duties, privileges, emoluments, etc.: *an honorary degree.* **2.** holding a title or position conferred for honor only: *an honorary president.* **3.** (of an obligation) depending on one's honor for fulfillment. **4.** conferring or commemorating honor or distinction. **5.** given, made, or serving as a token of honor. [< L *honōrāri(us)* of honor]

hon·or·ee (on′ə rē′), *n.* a person who receives an honor, award, or recognition.

hon′or guard′. See **guard of honor.**

hon·or·if·ic (on′ə rif′ik), *adj.* **1.** Also, **hon′or·if′i·cal.** doing or conferring honor. **2.** conveying honor, as a title or a grammatical form used in speaking to or about a superior, elder, etc. —*n.* **3.** a title or term of respect. [< L *honōrific(us)* honor-making] —**hon′or·if′i·cal·ly,** *adv.*

Ho·no·ri·us (hō nōr′ē əs, -nôr′-), *n.* **Fla·vi·us** (flā′vē əs), A.D. 384–423, Roman emperor of the West 395–423.

Honorius I, died A.D. 638. Italian ecclesiastic: pope 625–638.

Honorius II, (*Lamberto Scannabecchi*) died 1130, Italian ecclesiastic: pope 1124–30.

Honorius III, (*Cencio Savelli*) died 1227, Italian ecclesiastic: pope 1216–27.

Honorius IV, (*Giacomo Savelli*) 1210–87, Italian ecclesiastic: pope 1285–87.

hon′or roll′, 1. a list of elementary- or secondary-school pupils who have earned grades above a specific average during a semester or school year. Cf. **dean's list. 2.** a roster of names, usually in a memorial or other public place, of local citizens who have served or have died in the armed services.

hon′ors course′, a course in a university or college consisting largely of independent research terminating in a dissertation or a comprehensive examination, and earning for the student who passes it a degree with distinction.

hon′ors of war′, *Mil.* privileges granted to a capitulating force, as of marching out of their camp or entrenchments with all their arms and with colors flying.

hon′or sys′tem, a system whereby the students at a school, the inmates in a prison, etc., are put upon their honor to observe certain rules.

hon·our (on′ər), *n., v.t., adj. Chiefly Brit.* honor. —**hon′our·er,** *n.* —**hon′our·less,** *adj.*

hon·our·a·ble (on′ər ə bəl), *adj. Chiefly Brit.* honorable. —**hon′our·a·ble·ness,** *n.* —**hon′our·a·bly,** *adv.*

Hon·shu (hôn′sho͞o), *n.* an island in central Japan: chief island of the country. 71,343,511 (1960); 88,851 sq. mi. Also called **Hondo.**

hooch[1] (ho͞och), *n. Slang.* **1.** alcoholic liquor. **2.** liquor distilled and distributed illicitly. Also, **hootch.** [short for *Hoochinoo,* alter. of *Hutsnuwu,* name of Alaskan Indian tribe that made liquor]

hooch[2] (ho͞och), *n. U.S. Slang.* hootch[2]. Also, **hooch·ie** (ho͞o′chē).

Hooch (ho͞och; *Du.* hōkh), *n.* **Pie·ter de** (pē′tər də; *Du.* pē′tər də), 1629?–88?, Dutch painter. Also, **Hoogh.**

hood[1] (ho͝od), *n.* **1.** a soft or flexible covering for the head and neck, often attached to a coat, cloak, etc. **2.** something resembling or suggesting such a covering, esp. in shape, as certain petals or sepals. **3.** *U.S.* the part of an automobile body covering the engine. **4.** *Falconry.* a cover for the entire head of a hawk. **5.** an ornamental ruffle or fold on the back of the shoulders of an academic gown, jurist's robe, etc. **6.** a crest or band of color on the head of certain birds and animals. —*v.t.* **7.** to furnish or cover with a hood. [ME *hode,* OE *hōd;* c. OFris *hōde,* D *hoed,* G *Hut* hat] —**hood′less,** *adj.* —**hood′like′,** *adj.*

hood[2] (ho͝od, ho͞od), *n. Slang.* hoodlum. [by shortening]

Hood (ho͝od), *n.* **1. John Bell,** 1831–79, Confederate general in the U.S. Civil War. **2. Robin.** See **Robin Hood. 3. Thomas,** 1799–1845, English poet. **4. Mount,** a volcanic peak in N Oregon, in the Cascade Range. 11,253 ft.

-hood, a native English suffix denoting state, condition, character, nature, etc., or a body of persons of a particular character or class, formerly used in the formation of nouns: *childhood; likelihood; knighthood; priesthood.* [ME *-hode, -hod,* OE *-hād* (c. G *-heit*), special use of *hād* condition, state, order, quality, rank]

hood·ed (ho͝od′id), *adj.* **1.** having, or covered with, a hood. **2.** hood-shaped. **3.** *Zool.* having a hoodlike formation, crest, or the like. **4.** *Bot.* cucullate. [late ME *hodid*] —**hood′ed·ness,** *n.*

hood′ed seal′, bladdernose.

hood·lum (ho͞od′ləm, ho͝od′-), *n.* **1.** a gangster; racketeer. **2.** a thug. **3.** a teen-age tough. [? < dial. Bavarian *hodalum* a ragged beggar or rogue]

hoo·doo (ho͞o′do͞o), *n., pl.* **-doos,** *v.,* **-dooed, -doo·ing.** —*n.* **1.** bad luck. **2.** a person or thing that brings bad luck. **3.** *Geol.* a pillar of rock, usually of fantastic shape, left by erosion. **4.** voodoo. —*v.t.* **5.** to cause bad luck to. [appar. var. of VOODOO]

hood·wink (ho͝od′wingk′), *v.t.* **1.** to deceive or trick. **2.** *Archaic.* to blindfold. **3.** *Obs.* to cover or hide. —**hood′wink′er,** *n.*

hoo·ey (ho͞o′ē), *Informal.* —*interj.* **1.** (used to express disapproval or disbelief): *Hooey! You know that's not true.* —*n.* **2.** nonsense, hokum; bunkum. [?]

hoof (ho͝of, ho͞of), *n., pl.* **hoofs** or **hooves** for 1, 2, 4; **hoof** for 3, 5; *v.* —*n.* **1.** the horny covering protecting the ends of the digits or encasing the foot in certain animals, as the ox, horse, etc. **2.** the entire foot of a horse, donkey, etc. **3.** *Dial.* a hoofed animal, esp. one of a herd. **4.** *Informal.* the human foot. **5. on the hoof,** (of livestock) not butchered; live. —*v.t.* **6.** *Slang.* to walk (often fol. by *it*): *Let's hoof it to the supermarket.* —*v.i.* **7.** *Slang.* to dance, esp. to tap-dance. [ME; OE *hōf;* c. OFris *hōf,* D *hoef,* G *Huf,* Icel *hōfr,* Skt *saphás*] —**hoof′less,** *adj.* —**hoof′like′,** *adj.*

hoof′-and-mouth′ disease′ (ho͝of′ən mouth′, ho͞of′-). See **foot-and-mouth disease.**

hoof·beat (ho͝of′bēt′, ho͞of′-), *n.* the sound made by an animal's hoof in walking, running, etc.

hoof·bound (ho͝of′bound′, ho͞of′-), *adj. Vet. Pathol.* (of horses) having the heels of the hoofs dry and contracted, causing lameness.

hoofed (ho͝oft, ho͞oft), *adj.* having hoofs; ungulate.

hoof·er (ho͝of′ər, ho͞o′fər), *n. Slang.* a professional dancer, esp. a tap-dancer.

hoof·print (ho͝of′print′, ho͞of′-), *n.* the impression made by an animal's hoof.

Hoogh (*Du.* hōkh), *n.* See **Hooch.**

Hoogh·ly (ho͞og′lē), *n.* a river in NE India, in W Bengal: the westernmost channel by which the Ganges enters the Bay of Bengal. 120 mi. long. Also, **Hugli.**

hook (ho͝ok), *n.* **1.** a curved or angular piece of metal or other hard substance for catching, pulling, holding, or suspending something. **2.** a fishhook. **3.** something that catches; snare; trap. **4.** something having a sharp curve, bend, or angle at one end, as a mark, symbol, etc. **5.** a sharp curve or angle in the length or course of anything. **6.** a curved spit of land. **7.** a recurved and pointed organ or appendage of an animal or plant. **8.** *Sports.* **a.** the path described by a ball, as in baseball, bowling, or golf, that curves in a direction opposite to the throwing hand or to the side of the ball from which it was struck. **b.** a ball describing such a path. **9.** *Boxing.* a short, circular punch delivered with the elbow bent. **10.** Also called **pennant.** *Music.* a stroke or line attached to the stem of eighth notes, sixteenth notes, etc. **11. hooks,** *Slang.* hands or fingers. **12. by hook or by crook,** by any means. Also, **by hook or crook. 13. hook, line, and sinker,** *Informal.* entirely; completely: *He fell for the story—hook, line, and sinker.* **14. off the hook,** *Slang.* out of trouble; released from some difficulty or obligation. **15. on one's own hook,** *Informal.* on one's own initiative or responsibility; independently. **16. on the hook,** *Slang.* **a.** obliged; committed; involved. **b.** subjected to a delaying tactic; waiting. —*v.t.* **17.** to seize, fasten, suspend from, pierce, or catch hold of and draw with or as with a hook. **18.** to catch (fish) with a fishhook. **19.** *Slang.* to steal or seize by stealth. **20.** *Informal.* to catch or trick by artifice. **21.** (of a bull or other horned animal) to catch on the horns or attack with the horns. **22.** to catch hold of and draw (loops of yarn) through cloth with or as with a hook. **23.** to make (a rug, garment, etc.) in this fashion. **24.** *Sports.* to hit or throw (a ball) so that a hook results. **25.** *Boxing.* to deliver a hook with. **26.** to make hook-shaped; crook. **—***v.i.* **27.** to become attached or fastened by or as by a hook. **28.** to curve or bend like a hook. **29.** *Sports.* **a.** (of a player) to hook the ball. **b.** (of a ball) to describe a hook in course. **30. hook up, a.** to fasten with a hook or hooks. **b.** to assemble, as a mechanical apparatus, and connect to a source of power. [ME *hoke,* OE *hōc;* c. D *hoek* hook, angle, corner; akin to G *Haken,* Icel *haki*] **—hook′less,** *adj.* **—hook′like′,** *adj.*

hook·ah (ho͝ok′ə), *n.* a tobacco pipe with a long, flexible tube by which the smoke is drawn through a jar of water and thus cooled. Also, **hook′a.** Also called **narghile.** [< Ar *huqqah* box, vase, pipe for smoking]

Hookah

hook′ and eye′, a two-piece fastening, usually of metal, consisting of a hook attached to one part that catches onto a loop or small bar attached to the part with which it is to close.

hook′ and lad′der, a fire engine with a semitrailer fitted with long, extensible ladders and other equipment. Also called **hook′-and-lad′der truck′.**

Hooke (ho͝ok), *n.* **Robert,** 1635–1703, English philosopher, microscopist, and physicist.

hooked (ho͝okt), *adj.* **1.** bent like a hook; hook-shaped. **2.** having a hook or hooks. **3.** made with a hook or by hooking. **4.** *Slang.* **a.** addicted to narcotic drugs. **b.** addicted to or obsessed with anything. [ME *hoked,* OE *hōkede*] **—hook·ed·ness** (ho͝ok′id nis), *n.*

hooked′ rug′, *U.S.* a rug made by drawing loops of yarn or cloth through a foundation of burlap or the like.

hook·er[1] (ho͝ok′ər), *n.* *Naut. Slang.* any old-fashioned or clumsy vessel. [< D *hoeker*]

hook·er[2] (ho͝ok′ər), *n.* *Slang.* **1.** prostitute. **2.** a large drink of liquor. [HOOK + -ER[1]]

Hook·er (ho͝ok′ər), *n.* **1. Joseph,** 1814–79, Union general in the U.S. Civil War. **2. Richard,** 1554?–1600, English author and clergyman. **3. Thomas,** 1586?–1647, English Puritan clergyman: one of the founders of the colony of Connecticut.

Hooke's′ law′, *Physics.* the law that the stress on a solid substance is directly proportional to the strain applied, provided the stress is less than the elastic limit of the substance. [named after Robert HOOKE who formulated it]

hook·ey (ho͝ok′ē), *n.* hooky[2].

hook·nose (ho͝ok′nōz′), *n.* an aquiline nose. **—hook′-nosed′,** *adj.*

Hook′ of Hol′land, a cape and the harbor it forms in the SW Netherlands. Dutch, **Hoek van Holland.**

hook·up (ho͝ok′up′), *n.* **1.** *Electronics.* **a.** a diagram showing the connection of the different elements in one assembly or device. **b.** the elements as set up for operation. **2.** any combination of related parts; a connection. **3.** a network, as of radio or television stations. **4.** an alliance between groups, individuals, etc.

hook·worm (ho͝ok′wûrm′), *n.* **1.** any of certain blood-sucking nematode worms, as *Ancylostoma duodenale* and *Necator americanus,* parasitic in the intestine of man and animals. **2.** Also called **hook′worm disease′.** *Pathol.* a disease caused by hookworms, characterized by severe anemia. **—hook′worm′y,** *adj.*

hook·y[1] (ho͝ok′ē), *adj.,* **hook·i·er, hook·i·est. 1.** full of hooks. **2.** hook-shaped.

hook·y[2] (ho͝ok′ē), *n.* *U.S. Informal.* unjustifiable absence from school (usually used in the phrase *play hooky*). Also, **hookey.** [? alter. of phrase *hook it* escape, make off (turned into noun by dropping the *-t*)]

hoo·li·gan (ho͞o′lə gən), *n.* a ruffian or hoodlum. [var. of *Houlihan,* Irish surname which came to be associated with rowdies] **—hoo′li·gan·ism,** *n.*

hoop (ho͞op, ho͝op), *n.* **1.** a circular band or ring of metal, wood, or other stiff material. **2.** such a band for holding together the staves of a cask, tub, etc. **3.** a large ring of iron, wood, plastic, etc., used as a plaything for a child. **4.** a circular or ringlike object, part, figure, etc. **5.** that part of a ring which surrounds the finger. **6.** *Croquet.* a wicket. **7.** a circular band of stiff material used to expand and display a woman's skirt. **—***v.t.* **8.** to bind or fasten with or as with a hoop or hoops. **9.** to encircle; surround. [ME *hop(e),* late OE *hōp;* c. D *hoep*] **—hoop′less,** *adj.* **—hoop′like′,** *adj.*

hoop·er (ho͞o′pər, ho͝op′ər), *n.* a person who makes or puts hoops on barrels, tubs, etc.; a cooper.

hoop·la (ho͞op′lä), *n.* *Informal.* **1.** bustling excitement or activity; commotion. **2.** speech or writing intended to mislead or to obscure an issue. [*hoop,* var. of WHOOP + LA[2]]

hoo·poe (ho͞o′po͞o), *n.* any of several Old World birds of the family *Upupidae,* esp. *Upupa epops,* of Europe, having an erectile, fanlike crest. [var. of obs. *hoopoop* (imit.); c. LG *huppup;* cf. L *upupa*]

Hoopoe, *Upupa epops* (Length 11 in.)

hoop′ skirt′, a woman's skirt made to bell out by a framework of flexible hoops.

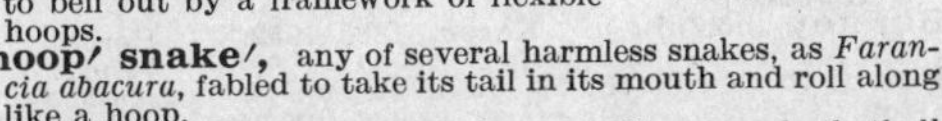

hoop′ snake′, any of several harmless snakes, as *Farancia abacura,* fabled to take its tail in its mouth and roll along like a hoop.

hoop·ster (ho͞op′stər, ho͝op′-), *n.* *Slang.* a basketball player.

hoo·rah (ho͝o rä′), *interj., v.i., v.t., n.* hurrah. Also, **hoo·ray** (ho͝o rā′).

hoose·gow (ho͞os′gou), *n.* *Slang.* a jail. Also, **hoos′gow.** [< MexSp *jusga(d)o* jail (Sp: court of justice, orig. ptp. of *juzgar* to judge) < L *jūdicātum* = *jūdic-* (s. of *jūdex*) JUDGE + *-ātum* -ATE[1]]

Hoo·sier (ho͞o′zhər), *n.* a native or inhabitant of Indiana (the **Hoosier State**) (used as a nickname). [?]

Hoo′sier State′, Indiana (used as a nickname).

hoot[1] (ho͞ot), *v.i.* **1.** to cry out or shout, esp. in disapproval or derision. **2.** to utter the cry characteristic of an owl. **3.** to utter a similar sound. **—***v.t.* **4.** to assail with shouts of disapproval or derision. **5.** to drive out, off, or away by hooting. **6.** to express in hoots: *to hoot one's displeasure.* **—***n.* **7.** the cry of an owl. **8.** any similar sound, as an inarticulate shout. **9.** a cry or shout, esp. of disapproval or derision. **10.** *Informal.* the least bit of concern, interest, or thought; trifle: *I don't give a hoot.* [ME *hote(n), hute(n), houte(n)* < ?] **—hoot′er,** *n.*

hoot[2] (ho͞ot), *interj.* *Scot. and North Eng.* (used as an expression of impatience, objection, or dislike.) [?]

hootch[1] (ho͞och), *n.* *Slang.* hooch[1].

hootch[2] (ho͞och), *n.* *U.S. Slang.* **1.** an Asian shack or hut. **2.** any dwelling or house. Also, **hooch, hoochie.** [m. Jap *uchi* house, home]

hootch·y-kootch·y (ho͞o′chē ko͞o′chē), *n., pl.* **-kootch·ies.** a sinuous, quasi-Oriental dance performed by a woman and characterized chiefly by gyrating and shaking of the body. Also, **hoot′chie-koot′chie, hoot′chy-kootch′.** [perh. alter. of HULA-HULA]

hoot·en·an·ny (ho͞ot′ənan′ē), *n., pl.* **-nies. 1.** *U.S.* a social gathering or informal concert featuring folk singing and, sometimes, dancing. **2.** *Chiefly Dial.* a thingumbob. [?]

Hoo·ton (ho͞ot′ən), *n.* **Ear·nest Albert** (ûr′nist), 1887–1954, U.S. anthropologist and writer.

Hoo·ver (ho͞o′vər), *n.* **1. Herbert (Clark),** 1874–1964, 31st president of the U.S. 1929–33. **2. J(ohn) Edgar,** 1895–1972, U.S. government official: director of the FBI 1924–72.

Hoo′ver Dam′, official name of **Boulder Dam.**

hooves (ho͝ovz, ho͞ovz), *n.* a pl. of **hoof.**

hop[1] (hop), *v.,* **hopped, hop·ping,** *n.* **—***v.i.* **1.** to make a short, bouncing leap; move by leaping with all feet off the ground. **2.** to spring or leap on one foot. **3.** to make a flight or any short, quick trip: *He hopped up to Boston for the day.* **—***v.t.* **4.** to jump over; clear with a hop: *to hop a fence.* **5.** *Informal.* to board or get onto a vehicle: *to hop a train; to hop a plane.* **—***n.* **6.** an act of hopping; short leap. **7.** a leap on one foot. **8.** *Informal.* **a.** a flight of an airplane. **b.** a short trip. **9.** *Informal.* a dance or dancing party. **10.** a bounce or rebound of a ball. [ME *hoppe(n),* OE *hoppian;* c. G *hopfen,* Icel *hoppa*]

hop[2] (hop), *n., v.,* **hopped, hop·ping. —***n.* **1.** any twining, dioecious plant of the genus *Humulus,* the male flowers of which grow in panicled racemes and the female in conelike forms. **2. hops,** the dried ripe cones of the female flowers of this plant, used in brewing, medicine, etc. **3.** *Slang.* opium. **—***v.t.* **4.** to treat or flavor with hops. **5. hop up,** *Slang.* **a.** to excite; make enthusiastic. **b.** to add to the power of. [late ME *hoppe* < MD *hoppe* (D *hop*); c. G *Hopfen* (OHG *hopfe*)]

hop′ clo′ver, a trefoil, *Trifolium procumbens,* having withered, yellow flowers that resemble the strobiles of a hop, naturalized from Europe.

hope (hōp), *n., v.,* **hoped, hop·ing. —***n.* **1.** the feeling that what is desired is also possible, or that events may turn out for the best. **2.** a particular instance of this feeling: *the hope of winning.* **3.** grounds for this feeling in a particular instance: *There is little or no hope of his recovery.* **4.** a person in whom or thing in which expectations are centered: *The drug was the patient's last hope.* **—***v.t.* **5.** to look forward to with desire and reasonable confidence. **6.** to believe, desire, or trust: *I hope that my work will be satisfactory.* **—***v.i.* **7.** to feel that something desired may happen: *We hope for an early spring.* **8.** *Archaic.* to place trust; rely. **9. hope against hope,** to continue to hope, although the situation does not warrant it. [(n.) ME; OE *hopa;* c. D *hoop,* G *Hoffe;* (v.) ME *hopen,* OE *hopian*] **—hop′er,** *n.*

hope′ chest′, a chest or the like in which a young woman collects clothing, linens, and other articles toward furnishing a home of her own in anticipation of marriage.

hope·ful (hōp′fəl), *adj.* **1.** full of hope; expressing hope: *hopeful words.* **2.** exciting hope; promising advantage or success: *a hopeful prospect.* **—***n.* **3.** a promising or aspiring young person. **—hope′ful·ness,** *n.* **—Syn. 1.** expectant; sanguine, optimistic, confident.

hope·ful·ly (hōp′fə lē), *adv.* **1.** in a hopeful manner: *We worked hopefully toward success.* **2.** it is hoped; if all goes well: *Hopefully, we'll win.*

Ho·peh (hō′pā′; *Chin.* hu′bā′), *n.* a province in NE China. 44,720,000 (est. 1957); 81,479 sq. mi. *Cap.:* Peking. Also, **Ho′pei′.** Formerly, **Chihli.**

hope·less (hōp′lis), *adj.* **1.** providing no hope; beyond hope; desperate: *a hopeless case of cancer.* **2.** without hope; despairing: *hopeless grief.* **—hope′less·ly,** *adv.* **—hope′less·ness,** *n.* **—Syn. 1.** irremediable, incurable. **2.** forlorn, disconsolate, dejected. HOPELESS, DESPAIRING, DESPONDENT, DESPERATE all describe an absence of hope. HOPELESS is used of a feeling of futility and passive abandonment of oneself to fate: *Hopeless and grim, he still clung to the cliff.* DESPAIRING refers to the loss of hope in regard to a particular situation whether important or trivial; it suggests an intellectual judgment concerning probabilities: *despairing of victory; despairing of finding his gloves.* DESPONDENT always suggests melancholy and depression; it refers to an emotional state rather than to an intellectual judgment: *despondent over ill health.* DESPERATE conveys a suggestion of recklessness resulting from loss of hope; it may apply either to feelings or situations: *a desperate remedy; As the time grew shorter, he became desperate.*

hop·head (hop′hed′), *n.* *U.S. Slang.* a drug addict.

Ho·pi (hō′pē), *n., pl.* **-pis,** (*esp. collectively*) **-pi. 1.** a member of a Shoshonean Pueblo Indian people of northern Arizona. **2.** a Uto-Aztecan language, the language of the Hopi Indians. [< Hopi *hópitu* peaceful ones]

Hop·kins (hop′kinz), *n.* **1. Gerard Man·ley** (man′lē),

1844–89, English poet. **2. Harry Lloyd,** 1890–1946, U.S. government administrator and social worker. **3. Johns,** 1795–1873, U.S. financier and philanthropist. **4. Mark,** 1802–87, U.S. clergyman and educator.

Hop·kin·son (hop′kin sən), *n.* **Francis,** 1737–91, American statesman and satirist.

hop·lite (hop′līt), *n.* a heavily armed foot soldier of ancient Greece. [< Gk *hoplī́t(ēs)* = *hópl(on)* piece of armor, particularly the large shield + *-itēs* -ITE[1]]

hopped-up (hopt′ up′), *adj.* *U.S. Slang.* **1.** excited; enthusiastic; overexuberant. **2.** having added power: *a hopped-up jalopy.* **3.** drugged; doped.

hop·per (hop′ər), *n.* **1.** a person or thing that hops. **2.** any of various jumping insects, as grasshoppers, leafhoppers, etc. **3.** a funnel-shaped chamber or bin in which loose material, as grain, coal, etc., is stored temporarily, being filled through the top and later dispensed through the bottom. **4.** *Railroads.* See **hopper car.** [ME]

Hop·per (hop′ər), *n.* **Edward,** 1882–1967, U.S. painter and etcher.

hop′per car′, *Railroads.* a freight car capable of quickly discharging bulk cargo through its bottom.

hop·ping (hop′ing), *adj.* **1.** working energetically; busy. **2.** going from one place to another of a similar specified type: *restaurant-hopping.* **3. hopping mad,** furious; enraged.

hop·ple (hop′əl), *v.t.*, **-pled, -pling.** to hobble; tether. [? HOP[1] + -LE]

hop·sack·ing (hop′sak′ing), *n.* **1.** bagging made chiefly of hemp and jute. **2.** a coarse fabric of cotton, wool, etc., similar to burlap, used for apparel.

hop·scotch (hop′skoch′), *n.* a children's game in which a player tosses a small stone into one of several numbered sections of a diagram marked on the pavement or ground and then hops on one foot from section to section, picking up the stone on his return.

hop′, step′, and jump′, *Track.* a jumping event for distance involving three coordinated movements: a leap on one foot from a take-off point, a stride, and a jump.

hop·toad (hop′tōd′), *n.* *U.S. Dial.* a toad.

hor., 1. horizon. 2. horizontal. 3. horology.

ho·ra (hōr′ə, hôr′ə), *n.* a traditional Rumanian and Israeli round dance. [< ModHeb *hōrāh* < Rum *horă* < Turk *hora*]

Hor·ace (hôr′is, hor′-), *n.* (*Quintus Horatius Flaccus*) 65–8 B.C., Roman poet and satirist.

Ho·rae (hōr′ē, hôr′ē), *n.pl.* *Class. Myth.* goddesses of the seasons, of growth and decay, and sometimes of social order. [< L: lit., hours]

ho·ral (hōr′əl, hôr′-), *adj.* of or pertaining to an hour or hours; hourly. [< LL *hōrāl(is).* See HOUR, -AL[1]]

ho·ra·ry (hōr′ə rē, hôr′-), *adj.* *Archaic.* **1.** pertaining to an hour; indicating the hours: *the horary circle.* **2.** occurring every hour; hourly. [< ML *hōrāri(us).* See HOUR, -ARY]

Ho·ra·tian (hə rā′shən, hō-, hô-), *adj.* **1.** of or pertaining to Horace. **2.** *Pros.* **a.** of, pertaining to, or resembling the poetic style or diction of Horace. **b.** of, pertaining to, or noting a Horatian ode. [< L *Horātiān(us)*]

Hora′tian ode′, *Pros.* an ode consisting of several stanzas all of the same form. Also called **Sapphic ode.** Cf. **Pindaric ode.**

Ho·ra·ti·i (hə rā′shē ī′, hō-, hô-), *n.pl.* *Rom. Legend.* three brothers who fought as champions of Rome against three other brothers (the **Curiatii**), who were the champions of Alba Longa, to determine which city should rule the other.

Ho·ra·tius (hə rā′shəs, hō-, hô-), *n.* (*Publius Horatius Cocles*) *Rom. Legend.* a hero celebrated for his defense of the bridge over the Tiber against the Etruscans.

horde (hōrd, hôrd), *n.*, *v.*, **hord·ed, hord·ing.** —*n.* **1.** a large group, multitude, number, etc.; a mass or crowd. **2.** a tribe or troop of Asian nomads. **3.** any nomadic group. —*v.i.* **4.** to gather in a horde. [earlier *hord(a)* < Pol *horda* < Mongolian *orda, ordu* camp (see URDU); *-e* perh. < F, G *horde,* but may have been added to mark length of *o,* as in BORNE[1], etc.] —**Syn. 1.** mob, herd, throng.

hor·de·in (hôr′dē in), *n.* *Biochem.* a prolamin found in barley grain. [< F *hordéine* < L *horde(um)* barley + F *-ine* -IN[2]]

Ho·reb (hōr′eb, hôr′-), *n.* *Bible.* a mountain sometimes identified with Mount Sinai.

Hore-Be·li·sha (hōr′bə lē′shə, hôr′-), *n.* **Leslie,** 1893–1957, British politician.

hore·hound (hōr′hound′, hôr′-), *n.* **1.** a perennial, Old World herb, *Marrubium vulgare,* containing a bitter, medicinal juice. **2.** any of various plants of the mint family. **3.** a brittle candy or lozenge flavored with horehound extract. Also, **hoarhound.** [ME *horehune,* OE *hārhūne* = *hār* gray, HOAR + *hūne* horehound]

ho·ri·zon (hə rī′zən), *n.* **1.** the line or circle that forms the apparent boundary between earth and sky. **2.** *Astron.* **a.** the small circle of the celestial sphere whose plane is tangent to the earth at the position of a given observer, or the plane of such a circle **(sensible horizon). b.** the great circle of the celestial sphere whose plane passes through the center of the earth and is parallel to the sensible horizon of a given position, or the plane of such a circle **(celestial horizon). 3.** the limit or range of perception, knowledge, or the like. **4.** *Geol.* a plane in rock strata representing the deposit of a particular period and characterized by special features, as the occurrence of distinctive fossil species. **5.** any of the series of distinctive layers found in a vertical cross section of any well-developed soil. [< L < Gk *horī́zōn* (*kýklos*) bounding (circle) = *horī́z(ein)* (to) bound, limit + *-ōn* prp. suffix (nom. sing.); r. ME *orizonte* < MF < L *horizont-,* s. of *horīzōn*] —**ho·ri′zon·less,** *adj.*

hor·i·zon·tal (hôr′i zon′tᵊl, hor′-), *adj.* **1.** at right angles to the vertical; parallel to level ground. **2.** reclining: *a horizontal position.* **3.** near, on, or parallel to the horizon. **4.** of or pertaining to the horizon. **5.** measured or contained in a plane parallel to the horizon: *a horizontal distance.* **6.** within the same social or occupational level; of similar status. [< L *horīzont-* (s. of *horīzōn* HORIZON) + -AL[1]] —**hor′i·zon′tal·ly,** *adv.*

hor′izon′tal bar′, *Gymnastics.* **1.** a bar fixed in a position parallel to the floor or ground, for use in chinning and other exercises. **2.** an event in gymnastic competitions, judged on strength and grace while performing specific movements on such a bar. Also called **high bar.**

horizon′tal mobil′ity, *Sociol.* movement from one position to another within the same social level, as changing jobs without altering occupational status, or moving between social groups having the same social status. Cf. **vertical mobility.**

Hor·mis·das (hôr miz′dəs), *n.* **Saint,** died A.D. 523, pope 514–523.

hor·mone (hôr′mōn), *n.* **1.** *Biochem.* any of various internally secreted compounds, as insulin or thyroxine, formed in endocrine organs, that affect the functions of specifically receptive organs or tissues when carried to them by the body fluids. **2.** a synthetic substance used in medicine to act like such a compound when introduced into the body. [< Gk *hormôn* (prp. of *hormáein* to set in motion, excite, stimulate) = *horm(ḗ)* impetus, impulse + *-ōn* prp. suffix] —**hor·mo′nal,** *adj.*

Hor·muz (hôr′muz), *n.* **Strait of,** a strait between Iran and the United Arab Emirates, connecting the Persian Gulf and the Gulf of Oman. Also, **Ormuz.**

horn (hôrn), *n.* **1.** one of the bony, often curved and pointed, hollow, paired growths on the upper part of the head of certain ungulate mammals. **2.** either of the pair of solid, deciduous, usually branched, bony growths, or antlers, on the head of a deer. **3.** a similar growth, sometimes of hair, as the median horn or horns on the snout of the rhinoceros, or the tusk of the narwhal. **4.** a process projecting from the head of an animal and suggestive of such a growth, as a feeler, tentacle, or crest. **5.** the bony substance of which such animal growths are composed. **6.** any similar substance, as that forming tortoise shells, hoofs, nails, corns, etc. **7.** an article made of the material of an animal horn or like substance, as a thimble, a spoon, or a shoehorn. **8.** any projection or extremity resembling the horn of an animal. **9.** something resembling or suggesting an animal horn: *a drinking horn.* **10.** a part resembling an animal horn attributed to deities, demons, etc.: *the devil's horn.* **11.** Usually, **horns.** the imaginary projections on a cuckold's brow. **12.** *Music.* **a.** a wind instrument, originally formed from the hollow horn of an animal but now usually made of brass or other metal or plastic. **b.** See **French horn. 13.** something used as or resembling such a wind instrument. **14.** *Slang.* a trumpet. **15.** an instrument for sounding a warning signal: *automobile horn.* **16.** *Aeron.* any of certain short, armlike levers on the control surfaces of an airplane. **17.** *Radio.* **a.** a tube of varying cross section used in some loudspeakers to couple the diaphragm to the sound-transmitting space. **b.** *Slang.* a loudspeaker. **18.** the high protuberant part at the front and top of certain saddles; a pommel, esp. a high one. **19.** one of the curved extremities of a crescent, esp. of the crescent moon. **20.** a pyramidal mountain peak, esp. one having concave faces. **21.** a symbol of power, as in the Bible: *a horn of salvation.* **22.** each of the alternatives of a dilemma. **23.** *Geol.* a mountain peak formed by the intersection of three or more glacial cinques. **24. blow one's own horn,** to publicize or boast about one's abilities or achievements. **25. lock horns,** to conflict; disagree. **26. take the bull by the horns.** See **bull**[1], (def. 9). —*v.t.* **27.** to butt or gore with the horns. **28. horn in,** *U.S. Slang.* to intrude or interrupt. —*adj.* **29.** made of horn. [ME *horn(e),* OE *horn;* c. D *horen,* Icel, Dan, Sw *horn,* G *Horn,* Goth *haurn,* L *cornu,* IrGael *côrn,* Welsh *corn;* akin to Gk *kéras* horn] —**horn′less,** *adj.* —**horn′less·ness,** *n.* —**horn′like′,** *adj.*

Horn (def. 12)
French horn

Horn (hôrn), *n.* **Cape.** See **Cape Horn.**

horn·beam (hôrn′bēm′), *n.* any betulaceous shrub or tree of the genus *Carpinus,* yielding a hard, heavy wood.

horn·bill (hôrn′bil′), *n.* any of several large birds of the family *Bucerotidae,* of the Old World tropics, characterized by a large bill surmounted by a horny protuberance.

horn·blende (hôrn′blend′), *n.* any of the common black or greenish aluminous varieties of amphibole. [< G] —**horn·blen′dic,** *adj.*

horn·book (hôrn′bŏŏk′), *n.* **1.** a leaf or page containing the alphabet, a table of numbers, a prayer, etc., covered with a sheet of transparent horn and fixed in a frame with a handle, formerly used in teaching children to read. **2.** a primer or book or rudiments.

horned (hôrnd), *adj.* **1.** having horns (often used in combination): *a horned beast; blunt-horned.* **2.** having a crescent-shaped part or form. [ME] —**horn·ed·ness** (hôr′nid nis), *n.*

Horned lizard,
genus *Phrynosoma*
(Length to 4½ in.)

horned′ liz′ard, any of several insectivorous lizards of the genus *Phrynosoma,* of western North America, having hornlike spines on the head and a flattened body covered with spiny scales. Also called **horned′ toad′.**

horned′ pout′, a bullhead, esp. the brown bullhead.

horned′ vi′per, a highly venomous viper, *Cerastes cornutus,* of northern Africa and Arabia, having a scaly process resembling a horn just above each eye.

hor·net (hôr′nit), *n.* any of several large, stinging social wasps of the family *Vespidae.* [ME *harnete,* OE *hyrnet(u);* c. OHG *hornaz* (G *Horniss*)]

Hornet,
Vespula maculata
(Length 1 in.)

Hor·ney (hôr′nī), *n.* **Karen,** 1885–1952, U.S. psychiatrist and author.

hor·ni·to (hôr nē′tō; *Sp.* ôR nē′tô), *n., pl.* **-tos** (-tōz; *Sp.* -tôs). *Geol.* a low, oven-shaped mound, such as is common in the volcanic districts of South America, usually emitting hot smoke and vapors from its sides and summit. [< Sp, dim. of *horno* oven < L *furnus, fornus*]

horn-mad (hôrn′mad′), *adj.* **1.** enraged enough to gore with the horns, as a bull. **2.** intensely angry; furious.

horn′ of plen′ty, cornucopia. [trans. of LL *cornūcōpia.* See CORNUCOPIA]

horn·pipe (hôrn′pīp′), *n.* **1.** an English folk clarinet having one ox horn concealing the reed and another forming the bell. **2.** a lively jiglike dance, originally to music played on a hornpipe, performed usually by one person, and traditionally a favorite of sailors.

horn-rimmed (hôrn′rimd′), *adj.* having the frames or rims made of horn, tortoise shell, or plastic that simulates either of these: *horn-rimmed glasses.*

Horns·by (hôrnz′bē), *n.* **Rogers,** 1896–1963, U.S. baseball player and manager.

horn′ sil′ver, cerargyrite. [trans. of G *Hornsilber*]

horn·stone (hôrn′stōn′), *n.* **1.** a variety of quartz resembling flint. **2.** an argillaceous rock baked and partly recrystallized by the heat of an igneous intrusion. [trans. of G *Hornstein*]

horn·swog·gle (hôrn′swog′əl), *v.t.*, **-gled, -gling.** *Slang.* to swindle, cheat, or hoax. [?]

horn·tail (hôrn′tāl′), *n.* any of various wasplike insects of the family *Siricidae*, the females of which have a hornlike ovipositor.

horn·worm (hôrn′wûrm′), *n.* the larva of any of several hawk moths, having a hornlike process at the rear of the abdomen.

horn·wort (hôrn′wûrt′), *n.* any aquatic herb of the genus *Ceratophyllum*, found in ponds and slow streams.

horn·y (hôr′nē), *adj.*, **horn·i·er, horn·i·est. 1.** hornlike through hardening; callous: *horny hands.* **2.** consisting of a horn or a hornlike substance; corneous. **3.** having a horn or horns or hornlike projections. **4.** *Slang.* lustful. [ME] —**horn′i·ly,** *adv.* —**horn′i·ness,** *n.*

horol., horology.

hor·o·loge (hôr′ə lōj′, -loj′, hor′-), *n.* any instrument for indicating the time, esp. a sundial or an early form of the clock. [late ME < L *hōrologium* < Gk *hōrológion* = *hōro-lóg(os)* time teller (*hōro-*, comb. form of *hṓra* HOUR + *-log-* (see LOGOS) + *-os* adj. suffix) + *-ion* dim. suffix; r. ME *orloge* < MF < L, as above]

hor·o·log·ic (hôr′ə loj′ik, hor′-), *adj.* **1.** of or pertaining to horology. **2.** of or pertaining to horologes. Also, **hor′o·log′i·cal.** [< LL *hōrologic(us)* < Gk *hōrologikós*]

ho·rol·o·gist (hō rol′ə jist, hō-), *n.* **1.** an expert in horology. **2.** a person who makes clocks or watches. Also, **ho·rol′o·ger.**

ho·rol·o·gy (hō rol′ə jē, hô-), *n.* the art or science of making timepieces or of measuring time. [< Gk *hōro-* (comb. form of *hṓra* HOUR) + -LOGY]

hor·o·scope (hôr′ə skōp′, hor′-), *n.* **1.** a diagram of the heavens, showing the relative position of planets and the signs of the zodiac, for use in calculating births, foretelling events in a person's life, etc. **2.** a prediction of future events or advice for future behavior based on such a diagram. [ME, OE *horoscop(us)* < L < Gk *hōroskópos* = *hōro-* (comb. form of *hṓra* HOUR) + *skópos* -SCOPE] —**hor·o·scop·ic** (hôr′ə skop′ik, -skō′pik, hor′ə-), *adj.* —**ho·ros·co·py** (hō-ros′kə pē, hō-), *n.*

Hor·o·witz (hôr′ə wits, hor′-; *Russ.* hô′RO vits), *n.* **Vladi·mir** (vlad′i mēr′; *Russ.* vlä dē′miR), born 1904, Russian pianist in the U.S.

hor·ren·dous (hô ren′dəs, ho-), *adj.* dreadful; horrible: *a horrendous crime.* [< L *horrendus* (ger. of *horrēre* to bristle, shudder) dreadful, to be feared = *horr-* (akin to HIRSUTE) + *-endus* fut. pass. participial suffix] —**hor·ren′dous·ly,** *adv.*

hor·rent (hôr′ənt, hor′-), *adj.* bristling; standing erect like bristles. [< L *horrent-* (s. of *horrēns*), prp. of *horrēre.* See HORRENDOUS, -ENT]

hor·ri·ble (hôr′ə bəl, hor′-), *adj.* **1.** causing or tending to cause horror; dreadful: *a horrible sight.* **2.** extremely unpleasant; deplorable; disgusting: *horrible living conditions.* [ME *(h)orrible* < OF < L *horribil(is).* See HORRENDOUS, -IBLE] —**hor′ri·ble·ness,** *n.* —**hor′ri·bly,** *adv.* —**Syn. 1.** appalling, frightful; hideous, horrid, horrendous.

hor·rid (hôr′id, hor′-), *adj.* **1.** such as to cause horror; dreadful; abominable. **2.** extremely unpleasant or disagreeable: *horrid weather.* [< L *horrid(us)* bristling, rough. See HORRENDOUS, -ID[4]] —**hor′rid·ly,** *adv.* —**hor′rid·ness,** *n.*

hor·rif·ic (hô rif′ik, ho-), *adj.* causing horror. [< L *horrific(us).* See HORRENDOUS, -I-, -FIC] —**hor·rif′i·cal·ly,** *adv.*

hor·ri·fy (hôr′ə fī′, hor′-), *v.t.*, **-fied, -fy·ing.** to cause to feel horror; affect with horror. [< L *horrifi(cāre)* (to) cause horror. See HORRENDOUS, -I-, -FY] —**hor′ri·fy′ing·ly,** *adv.* —**Syn.** frighten, terrify; revolt, repel, appall.

hor·rip·i·late (hô rip′ə lāt′, ho-), *v.t.*, **-lat·ed, -lat·ing.** to produce horripilation on. [< L *horripilāt(us)* (ptp. of *horripilāre* to bristle with hairs)]

hor·rip·i·la·tion (hô rip′ə lā′shən, ho-), *n.* a bristling of the hair on the skin from cold, fear, etc.; goose flesh. [< LL *horripilātiōn-* (s. of *horripilātiō*)]

hor·ror (hôr′ər, hor′-), *n.* **1.** an overwhelming and painful feeling caused by something frightfully shocking, terrifying, or revolting; a shuddering fear: *to shrink back from a corpse in horror.* **2.** anything that causes such a feeling: *the horrors of war.* **3.** such a feeling as a quality or condition: *to have known the horror of slow starvation.* **4.** a strong aversion; abhorrence: *to have a horror of emotional outbursts.* **5.** *Informal.* something considered to be bad or in poor taste: *That hat is a horror.* **6.** *Obs.* a bristling. —*interj.* **7. horrors,** (used as a mild expression of dismay, surprise, disappointment, etc.) [< L = *horr-* (see HORRENDOUS) + *-or* -OR[1]; r. ME *orrour* < AF < L *horrōr-*, s. of *horror*] —**Syn. 1.** dread, dismay. See **terror. 4.** loathing, antipathy, detestation, hatred. —**Ant. 1.** serenity. **4.** attraction.

hor·ror-struck (hôr′ər struk′, hor′-), *adj.* stricken with horror; aghast. Also, **hor·ror-strick·en** (hôr′ər strik′ən, hor′-).

Hor·sa (hôr′sə), *n.* died A.D. 455, Jutish chief (brother of Hengist).

hors de com·bat (ôR də kôN bA′), *French.* out of the fight; disabled; no longer able to fight.

hors d'oeu·vre (ôr dûrv′; *Fr.* ôR dœ′vRə), *pl.* **hors d'oeuvre, hors d'oeuvres** (ôr dûrvz′; *Fr.* ôR dœ′vRə). an appetizer, often served on crackers or small pieces of toast. [< F: lit., out of (the) work, i.e., the main course]

horse (hôrs), *n.*, *pl.* **hors·es,** (*esp. collectively*) **horse,** *v.*, **horsed, hors·ing,** *adj.* —*n.* **1.** a large, solid-hoofed, herbivorous quadruped, *Equus caballus*, domesticated since prehistoric times, bred in a number of varieties, and used for carrying or pulling loads, for riding, etc. **2.** a fully mature male animal of this type; stallion. **3.** any animal of the family *Equidae*, including the ass, donkey, etc. **4.** soldiers serving on horseback; cavalry: *a thousand horse.* **5.** something on which a person rides, sits, or exercises, as if astride the back of such an animal: *a rocking horse.* **6.** *Gymnastics.* a cylindrical, leather-covered block mounted horizontally on one or two posts, for use chiefly in vaulting. **7.** a frame, block, etc., with legs, on which something is mounted or supported. **8.** *Slang.* heroin. **9.** *Mining.* a mass of rock enclosed within a lode or vein. **10.** *Chess Informal.* a knight. **11. from the horse's mouth,** *Slang.* on good authority; from a trustworthy source. **12. hold one's horses,** to check one's impulsiveness; be calm. **13. horse of another color,** something entirely different. Also, **horse of a different color. 14. look a gift horse in the mouth,** to be critical of a gift. —*v.t.* **15.** to provide with a horse or horses. **16.** to set on horseback. —*v.i.* **17.** to mount or go on a horse. **18.** (of a mare) to be in heat. **19. horse around,** *Slang.* to fool around; indulge in horseplay. —*adj.* **20.** of, for, or pertaining to a horse or horses: *the horse family.* **21.** drawn or powered by a horse or horses. **22.** mounted or serving on horses: *horse troops.* [ME, OE *hors*; c. Icel *hross*, D *ros*, G *Ross* (MHG *ros*, OHG *hros*)] —**horse′like′,** *adj.*

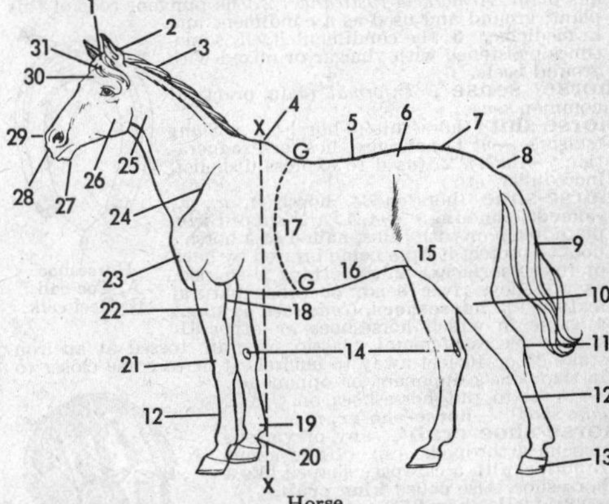

Horse
1, Poll; 2, Ear; 3, Mane; 4, Withers; 5, Back; 6, Loin; 7, Croup; 8, Dock; 9, Tail; 10, Gaskin; 11, Hock; 12, Cannon or shank; 13, Hoof; 14, Chestnut; 15, Stifle; 16, Belly; 17, Ribs; 18, Elbow; 19, Fetlock; 20, Pastern; 21, Knee; 22, Forearm; 23, Chest; 24, Shoulder; 25, Neck; 26, Cheek; 27, Chin; 28, Muzzle; 29, Nostril; 30, Forehead; 31, Forelock; GG, Girth; XX, Height

horse·back (hôrs′bak′), *n.* **1.** the back of a horse. **2.** *U.S.* a low, natural ridge of sand, gravel, or rock. Cf. **hogback.** —*adv.* **3.** on horseback: *to ride horseback.* [ME *horsbak*]

horse·car (hôrs′kär′), *n.* **1.** *U.S.* (formerly) a streetcar drawn by a horse or horses. **2.** a railroad car or a truck fitted with stalls for the transportation of horses.

horse′ chest′nut, 1. the shiny, brown, nutlike seed of a tree of the genus *Aesculus*, esp. *A. Hippocastanum.* **2.** any such tree having large, digitate leaves and upright clusters of showy white, red, or yellow flowers. [trans. of obs. bot. L *castanea equina*; so named from its use in treating respiratory diseases of horses]

horse-faced (hôrs′fāst′), *adj.* having a large face with lantern jaws and large teeth.

horse·feath·ers (hôrs′feth′ərz), *Slang.* —*n.* **1.** (*construed as sing. or pl.*) something not worth considering. —*interj.* **2.** rubbish; nonsense (used to express contemptuous rejection).

horse·flesh (hôrs′flesh′), *n.* **1.** the flesh of a horse. **2.** horses collectively, esp. for riding, racing, etc. [late ME]

horse·fly (hôrs′flī′), *n.* any of several bloodsucking, usually large flies of the family *Tabanidae*, esp. of the genus *Tabanus*, which are serious pests of horses, cattle, etc. Also called **horse′ fly′.** [ME *horsfleeye*]

Horse′ Guards′, 1. a body of cavalry serving as a guard. **2.** a cavalry brigade from the household troops of the British monarch.

horse·hair (hôrs′hâr′), *n.* **1.** a hair or the hair of a horse, esp. from the mane or tail. **2.** a sturdy, glossy fabric woven of this hair. [ME *hors here*]

Horse′head Neb′ula (hôrs′hed′), a dark nebula in the constellation Orion, composed of opaque cosmic dust and resembling the head of a horse.

horse·hide (hôrs′hīd′), *n.* **1.** the hide of a horse. **2.** leather made from this. **3.** *Slang.* a baseball.

horse′ lat′itudes, *Naut.* the latitudes, approximately 30° N and S, forming the edges of the trade-wind belt, characterized by high atmospheric pressure with calms and light variable winds. [either from the climate being fatal to horses on board, or from sailors working off the dead horse (advanced pay) by that point in the voyage]

horse·laugh (hôrs′laf′, -läf′), *n.* a loud, coarse laugh, esp. of derision.

horse·leech (hôrs′lēch′), *n.* a large leech, as *Haemopsis* *marmoratis,* which infests the mouth and nasal passages of horses while they are drinking. [late ME *horsleych*]

horse′less car′riage (hôrs′lis), *Archaic.* an automobile.

horse′ mack′erel, 1. See **bluefin tuna.** 2. See **jack mackerel.**

horse·man (hôrs′mən), *n., pl.* **-men.** 1. a man who rides on horseback. 2. a man skilled in riding horses. 3. a man who owns, breeds, trains, or tends horses. [ME *horsman*]

horse·man·ship (hôrs′mən ship′), *n.* 1. the art, ability skill, or manner of a horseman. 2. equitation.

horse′ marine′, 1. (formerly) a marine mounted on horseback or a cavalryman doing duty on shipboard. 2. a person out of his element.

horse·mint (hôrs′mint′), *n.* any of various menthaceous plants, esp. the erect, odorous herb, *Monarda punctata,* of America. [ME *horsminte*]

horse′ net′tle, a prickly, North American, solanaceous weed, *Solanum carolinense.*

horse′ op′era, *U.S. Slang.* a film, television play, etc., dealing with the Wild West.

horse′ pis′tol, a large pistol formerly carried by horsemen.

horse·play (hôrs′plā′), *n.* rough or boisterous play or pranks.

horse·play·er (hôrs′plā′ər), *n.* a habitual bettor on horse races.

horse·pow·er (hôrs′pou′ər), *n.* a foot-pound-second unit of power, equivalent to 550 foot-pounds per second.

horse·pow·er-hour (hôrs′pou′ər our′, -ou′ər), *n.* a unit of energy or work, equal to the work done by a mechanism with a power output of one horsepower over a period of one hour.

horse·rad·ish (hôrs′rad′ish), *n.* 1. a cultivated, cruciferous plant, *Armoracia rusticana.* 2. the pungent root of this plant, ground and used as a condiment and in medicine. 3. the condiment itself, sometimes moistened with vinegar or mixed with ground beets.

horse′ sense′, *Informal.* plain, practical common sense.

horse·shit (hôrs′shit′, hôrsh′-), *Slang (vulgar).* —*n.* 1. nonsense, lies, or exaggeration. —*interj.* 2. (used to express disbelief, incredulity, etc.)

horse·shoe (hôrs′shōō′, hôrsh′-), *n., v.,* **-shoed, -shoe·ing.** —*n.* 1. a U-shaped iron plate, plain or with calks, nailed to a horse's hoof to protect it from being injured by hard or rough surfaces. 2. something U-shaped, as a valley, river bend, or other natural feature. 3. **horseshoes,** (*construed as sing.*) a game in which horseshoes or other U-shaped pieces of metal, plastic, etc., are tossed at an iron stake 30 or 40 feet away to encircle it or to come closer to it than one's opponent or opponents. —*v.t.* 4. to put horseshoes on. [ME *hors shoo*] —**horse′sho′er,** *n.*

A

B

Horseshoe
A, Toe calk
B, Heel calk

horse′shoe crab′, any of various marine arthropods, esp. of the genus *Limulus,* with a carapace shaped like a horseshoe. Also called **king crab.**

horse·tail (hôrs′tāl′), *n.* 1. any perennial, herbaceous, pteridophytic plant of the genus *Equisetum,* having hollow, jointed stems. 2. a horse's tail formerly used as a Turkish military standard or as an ensign of a pasha, the number of tails increasing with the rank. [ME *horse tayle*]

horse′ trade′, *U.S. Informal.* a shrewdly conducted exchange, as of favors, objects, etc., usually resulting from or accompanied by very close bargaining.

Horseshoe crab,
Limulus polyphemus
(Length 2 ft.)

horse-trade (hôrs′trād′), *v.i.,* **-trad·ed, -trad·ing.** *U.S. Informal.* to bargain or trade shrewdly.

horse′ trad′er, 1. *U.S. Informal.* a person who is shrewd and clever at bargaining. 2. a person who trades in horses.

horse·weed (hôrs′wēd′), *n.* 1. an asteraceous weed, *Erigeron canadense.* 2. any of various other plants, as the wild lettuce, *Lactuca canadensis.*

horse·whip (hôrs′hwip′, -wip′), *n., v.,* **-whipped, -whip·ping.** —*n.* 1. a whip for controlling horses. —*v.t.* 2. to beat with a horsewhip. —**horse′whip′per,** *n.*

horse·wom·an (hôrs′wo͝om′ən), *n., pl.* **-wom·en.** 1. a woman who rides on horseback. 2. a woman skilled in riding horses.

hors·ey (hôr′sē), *adj.,* **hors·i·er, hors·i·est.** horsy.

horst (hôrst), *n.* a portion of the earth's crust, bounded on at least two sides by faults, that has been moved upward in relation to adjacent portions. Cf. **graben.** [< G: thicket]

hors·y (hôr′sē), *adj.,* **hors·i·er, hors·i·est.** 1. of, pertaining to, or characteristic of a horse or horses. 2. dealing with horses or sports involving them: *the horsy set in local society.* —**hors′i·ly,** *adv.* —**hors′i·ness,** *n.*

hort., 1. horticultural. 2. horticulture.

hor·ta·tive (hôr′tə tiv), *adj.* hortatory. [< L *hortātīv(us)* = *hortāt(us)* (*hor-* want, desire (c. YEARN) + *-t-* v. suffix + *-ātus* -ATE[1]) + *-īvus* -IVE] —**hor′ta·tive·ly,** *adv.*

hor·ta·to·ry (hôr′tə tôr′ē, -tōr′ē), *adj.* urging to some course of conduct or action; exhorting; encouraging: *a hortatory speech.* [< LL *hortātōri(us)* encouraging. See HORTATIVE, -ORY[1]]

Hor·tense′ de Beauharnais′ (*Fr.* ôR tāNs′). See **Beauharnais, Eugénie Hortense de.**

hor·ti·cul·ture (hôr′tə kul′chər), *n.* 1. the cultivation of flowers, fruits, vegetables, or ornamental plants. 2. the science and art of cultivating such plants. [< L *hort(us)* garden + (AGR)ICULTURE] —**hor′ti·cul′tur·al,** *adj.* —**hor′ti·cul′tur·ist,** *n.*

hor·tus sic·cus (hôr′təs sik′əs), a collection of dried plants; herbarium. [< L *hortus* GARDEN + *siccus* dry]

Ho·rus (hōr′əs, hôr′-), *n.* *Egyptian Religion.* a solar deity, regarded as either the son or the brother of Isis and Osiris, and usually represented as a falcon or as a man with the head of a falcon. [< LL < Gk *Hōros* < Egypt *Hur* hawk]

Hos., Hosea

ho·san·na (hō zan′ə), *interj., n., pl.* **-nas,** *v.,* **-naed, -na·ing.** —*interj.* 1. (an exclamation in praise of God or Christ.) —*n.* 2. a cry of "hosanna." 3. a shout of praise or adoration; an acclamation. —*v.t.* 4. to praise, applaud, etc. [< LL < Gk < Heb *hōsh(i) 'āh nnā* save, we pray; r. ME, OE *osanna* < LL]

hose (hōz), *n., pl.* **hose** for 1, 3; **hos·es** for 2, 4; (*Archaic*) **hos·en;** *v.,* **hosed, hos·ing.** —*n.* 1. (*construed as pl.*) an article of clothing for the feet and lower legs; stockings. 2. a flexible tube for conveying a liquid, as water, to a desired point: *a fire hose.* 3. (of men's attire in former time) **a.** an article of clothing for the leg, extending from about the knee to the ankle and worn with knee breeches. **b.** (*construed as pl.*) knee breeches. **c.** (*construed as pl.*) tights, as were worn with, and usually attached to, a doublet. 4. *Brit. Dial.* a sheath, or sheathing part, as that enclosing a kernel of grain. —*v.t.* 5. to water, wash, spray, or drench by means of a hose. [ME, OE; c. D *hoos,* Icel *hosa,* G *Hose*]

Ho·se·a (hō zē′ə, -zā′ə), *n.* 1. a Minor Prophet of the 8th century B.C. 2. a book of the Bible bearing his name. [< Heb *Hōshēa'* salvation, help]

ho·sier (hō′zhər), *n.* a person who makes or deals in hose or goods knitted or woven like hose. [late ME *hosiare, etc.*]

ho·sier·y (hō′zhə rē), *n.* 1. hose or stockings of any kind. 2. the business of a hosier.

hosp., hospital.

hos·pice (hos′pis), *n.* a house of shelter or rest for pilgrims, strangers, etc., esp. one kept by a religious order. [< F < L *hospit(ium)* hospitable reception, entertainment = *hospit-* (s. of *hospes*) host, guest, stranger + *-ium* -Y[3]]

hos·pi·ta·ble (hos′pi tə bəl, ho spit′ə bəl), *adj.* 1. receiving or treating guests or strangers warmly and generously: *a hospitable family.* 2. characterized by or betokening warmth and generosity toward guests or strangers: *a hospitable smile.* 3. favorably receptive or open (usually fol. by *to*): *to be hospitable to new ideas.* [< ML *hospitā-* (s. of *hospitāre* to receive as guest; cf. L *hospitārī* to be a guest) + -BLE] —**hos′pi·ta·ble·ness,** *n.* —**hos′pi·ta·bly,** *adv.*

hos·pi·tal (hos′pi tᵊl), *n.* 1. an institution in which sick or injured persons are given medical or surgical treatment. 2. a similar establishment for the care of animals. 3. *Brit.* an institution supported by charity or taxes for the care of the needy, as an orphanage or old people's home. [ME *hospitale* < ML (neut.), n. use of L *hospitālis* hospitable = *hospit-* (see HOSPICE) + *-ālis* -AL[1]]
—**Syn. 1.** retreat, clinic. HOSPITAL, ASYLUM, SANATORIUM, SANITARIUM are names of institutions for persons needing care. A HOSPITAL is an institution in which sick or injured persons are given medical or surgical treatment, therapy, etc.: *to be in a hospital recuperating from an operation.* An ASYLUM is an institution (usually owned by the state) for the care of particularly afflicted or dependent persons: *an asylum for the deaf, insane, blind; an orphan asylum.* The terms SANATORIUM and SANITARIUM are sometimes used interchangeably. However, the former, stressing curative and healing measures, often means a health resort for persons needing mainly rest and recuperation in pleasant surroundings: *Nature therapy and raw foods are specialties of this sanatorium.* SANITARIUM stresses hygienic conditions, and usually has patients needing special treatment: *the sanitarium for tubercular patients.*

hos′pital bed′, a bed having a mattress base in three jointed sections so that the head, foot, or middle may be raised, allowing a patient to lie in various positions.

Hos·pi·tal·er (hos′pi tᵊlər), *n.* 1. a member of the religious and military order **(Knights Hospitalers** or **Knights of St. John of Jerusalem)** originating about the time of the first Crusade (1096–99) and taking its name from a hospital at Jerusalem. 2. (*l.c.*) a person, esp. a member of a religious order, devoted to the care of the sick or needy in hospitals. Also, **Hos′pi·tal·ler.** [HOSPITAL + -ER[1]; r. ME *hospitalier* < MF < ML *hospitālārius;* see -IER]

Hos·pi·ta·let (ôs′pē tä let′), *n.* a city in NE Spain, near Barcelona. 122,813 (1960).

hos·pi·tal·i·ty (hos′pi tal′i tē), *n., pl.* **-ties.** 1. the friendly reception and treatment of guests or strangers. 2. the quality or disposition of receiving and treating guests and strangers in a warm, friendly, generous way. [ME *hospitalite* < MF < L *hospitālitās.* See HOSPITAL, -TY[2]]

hos·pi·tal·i·za·tion (hos′pi tᵊli zā′shən *or, esp. Brit.,* -tᵊlī-), *n.* 1. the act of hospitalizing. 2. the state of being hospitalized. 3. the period during which a person is hospitalized.

hos·pi·tal·ize (hos′pi tᵊlīz′), *v.t.,* **-ized, -iz·ing.** to place in a hospital for medical or surgical treatment.

hos·pi·tal·man (hos′pi tᵊl mən), *n., pl.* **-men.** *U.S. Navy.* an enlisted man working as a hospital assistant; corpsman.

host[1] (hōst), *n.* 1. a person who receives or entertains guests in his own home or elsewhere. 2. a master of ceremonies or moderator for a television or radio program. 3. the landlord of an inn. 4. a living animal or plant from which a parasite obtains nutrition. —*v.t.* 5. to be or act as host at. [ME *(h)oste* < MF < L *hospit-* (s. of *hospes*) host, guest, stranger, prob. contr. of *hostipit-* = *hosti-* (see HOST[2]) + *-pit-,* var. of *-pot-* mastery (see POTENT[1])]

host[2] (hōst), *n.* 1. a multitude or great number of persons or things: *a host of details.* 2. *Archaic.* an army. [ME *(h)oste* < OF < L *host-* (s. of *hostis*) enemy, host]

Host (hōst), *n.* *Eccles.* the consecrated wafer of the Eucharist. [ME *hoste* < LL *hostia* Eucharistic wafer (L: victim, sacrifice); r. ME *oyst* < MF *oiste* < LL, as above]

hos·tage (hos′tij), *n.* 1. a person given or held as security for the performance of certain actions, promises, etc., by another. 2. *Rare.* a security or pledge. [ME < OF = *h-* (? < *host;* see HOST[2]) + *ostage* << VL **obsidāticum* state of being a hostage = L *obsid-* (s. of *obses*) hostage (see OB-, SIT) + *-āticum* -AGE]

hos·tel (hos′tᵊl), *n.* 1. Also called **youth hostel.** a supervised lodging place for young people traveling by bicycle or hiking. 2. an inn. —*v.i., v.t.* 3. to travel, lodging each night at a hostel. [ME *(h)ostel* < OF < LL *hospitāle* guest room. See HOSPITAL]

hos·tel·er (hos′tᵊlər), *n.* 1. a person who operates a hostel. 2. a person who stays at a hostel or goes hosteling. [ME; see HOSTEL, -ER[2]; akin to OF *hostelier*]

hos·tel·ry (hos′tᵊl rē), *n., pl.* **-ries.** a hostel or inn. [ME *hostelrye,* var. of *hostelerie* < MF]

host·ess (hō′stis), *n.* **1.** a female host; a woman who serves in the capacity of a host. **2.** a woman employed to assist patrons, as at a restaurant. **3.** See **taxi dancer.** —*v.t.* **4.** to be or act as hostess at. [ME (*h*)*ostesse* < OF]

hos·tile (hos′tᵊl *or, esp. Brit.*, -tīl), *adj.* **1.** opposed in feeling, action, or character; antagonistic: *hostile criticism.* **2.** of, pertaining to, or characteristic of an enemy: *a hostile nation.* **3.** not friendly; inhospitable. [< L *hostīl*(*is*). See HOST², -ILE] —**hos′tile·ly,** *adv.* —**Syn. 1.** adverse, averse.

hos·til·i·ty (ho stil′i tē), *n., pl.* **-ties. 1.** a hostile state, condition, or attitude; enmity; antagonism. **2.** a hostile act. **3.** opposition or resistance to an idea, plan, project, etc. **4. hostilities, a.** acts of warfare. **b.** war. [< L *hostīlitās*] —**Syn. 1.** animosity, animus, hatred.

hos·tler (hos′lər, os′lər), *n.* a person who takes care of horses, esp. at an inn. Also, **ostler.** [var. of HOSTELER]

hot (hot), *adj.,* **hot·ter, hot·test,** *adv., v.,* **hot·ted, hot·ting.** —*adj.* **1.** having or communicating heat; having a high temperature: *hot coffee.* **2.** having or causing a sensation of great bodily heat; attended with or producing such a sensation. **3.** creating a burning sensation; peppery or pungent: *hot mustard.* **4.** having or showing intense or violent feeling; ardent or fervent; vehement; excited: *hot temper.* **5.** lustful; lascivious. **6.** violent, furious, or intense: *the hottest battle of the war.* **7.** strong or fresh, as a scent or trail. **8.** absolutely new; fresh: *hot from the press.* **9.** *Slang.* following very closely; close: *to be hot on the trail of a thief.* **10.** (in children's games) extremely close to the object of search or the correct answer. **11.** (of colors) extremely intense. **12.** currently popular; in demand; marketable: *the hottest singer of the year.* **13.** *Slang.* extremely lucky: *a hot crap shooter.* **14.** *Slang.* funny; absurd: *That's a hot one!* **15.** *Slang.* extremely exciting or interesting; sensational or scandalous: *a hot news story.* **16.** *Jazz.* (of music) emotionally intense, propulsive, and marked by aggressive attack and warm, full tone. **17.** *Slang.* **a.** stolen recently or otherwise illegal and dangerous to possess. **b.** dangerous. **18.** in the mood to perform exceedingly well, or rapidly: *Finish writing that story while you're still hot.* **19.** actively conducting an electric current or containing a high voltage: *a hot wire.* **20.** of, pertaining to, or noting radioactivity. **21.** *Metalworking.* noting any process involving plastic deformation of a metal at a temperature high enough to permit recrystallization due to the strain: *hot working.* **22. make it hot for,** *Informal.* to make something unpleasant for; cause trouble for. —*adv.* **23.** in a hot manner; hotly. **24.** *Metalworking.* at a temperature high enough to permit recrystallization: *The wire was drawn hot.* —*v.t., v.i.* **25.** *Chiefly Brit. Informal.* to heat; warm (usually fol. by *up*). [ME *ho*(*o*)*t,* OE *hāt;* c. D *heet,* Icel *heitr,* Sw *het,* Dan *hed,* G *heiss*] —**hot′ly,** *adv.* —**hot′ness,** *n.* —**Syn. 1.** heated; fiery, burning, scorching; scalding, boiling; torrid, sultry. **3.** biting, piquant, sharp, spicy. **4.** fervid; fiery, passionate.

hot′ air′, *Slang.* empty, exaggerated, or pretentious talk or writing.

hot·bed (hot′bed′), *n.* **1.** a bottomless, boxlike, usually glass-covered structure and the bed of earth it covers, heated by fermenting manure, for growing plants out of season. **2.** a place or environment favoring the rapid growth or spread of something, esp. something bad: *A slum is often a hotbed of vice.*

hot-blood·ed (hot′blud′id), *adj.* **1.** excitable; impetuous. **2.** ardent; passionate. **3.** (of livestock) of superior or pure breeding. **4.** (of horses) being a Thoroughbred or having Arab blood. —**hot′-blood′ed·ness,** *n.*

hot·box (hot′boks′), *n. Railroads.* a journal box overheated by excessive friction of an axle as a result of inadequate lubrication or the presence of foreign matter.

hot′ cake′, 1. griddlecake; pancake. **2. sell** or **go like hot cakes,** to be disposed of very quickly and effortlessly: *That new recording sold like hot cakes.*

hotch·pot (hoch′pot′), *n. Law.* the bringing together of shares or properties in order to divide them equally. [ME *hochepot* < AF (legal), lit., shake pot = *hoche*(*r*) (to) shake (< Gmc) + *pot* POT¹]

hotch·potch (hoch′poch′), *n.* **1.** a thick soup or stew of vegetables or meat, often thickened with barley. **2.** *Brit.* hodgepodge. **3.** *Law.* a hotchpot. [ME *hoche poche;* rhyming var. of HOTCHPOT]

hot′ cross′ bun′, a bun with a cross of frosting on it, eaten chiefly during Lent.

hot′ dog′, *U.S. Informal.* **1.** a frankfurter. **2.** a sandwich consisting of a frankfurter in a split roll, usually eaten with mustard, relish, or the like.

ho·tel (hō tel′), *n.* **1.** a commercial establishment offering lodging to transients, and often having restaurants, public rooms, shops, etc., that are available to the general public. **2.** a word used in communications to represent the letter *H.* [< F *hôtel,* OF *hostel* HOSTEL] —**Syn. 1.** hostelry, hostel, guesthouse, motel. HOTEL, HOUSE, INN, TAVERN refer to establishments for the lodging or entertainment of travelers and others. HOTEL is the common word, suggesting a more or less commodious establishment with up-to-date appointments, although this is not necessarily true: *the best hotel in the city; a cheap hotel near the docks.* The word HOUSE is often used in the name of a particular hotel, the connotation being luxury: *the Parker House; the Palmer House.* INN suggests a place of homelike comfort and old-time appearance or ways; it is used for quaint or archaic effect in the names of some public houses and hotels in the U.S.: *the Pickwick Inn; the Wayside Inn.* A TAVERN is a house where liquors are sold for drinking on the premises; until recently it was archaic or dialectal in the U.S., but has been revived to substitute for *saloon,* which had unfavorable connotations: *Taverns are required to close by two o'clock in the morning.* The word has also been used in the sense of INN, esp. in New England, since Colonial days.

hô·tel de ville (ō tel′ də vēl′), *pl.* **hô·tels de ville** (ō tel′ də vēl′). *French.* a city hall. [lit., mansion of the city]

hô·tel Dieu (ō tel dyœ′), *pl.* **hô·tels Dieu** (ō tel dyœ′). *French.* a hospital. [lit., mansion of God]

ho·tel·ier (ō tel yā′), *n.* a manager or owner of a hotel. [< F]

hot·foot (hot′fo͝ot′), *n., pl.* **-foots,** *v., adv.* —*n.* **1.** a practical joke in which a match, inserted surreptitiously between the sole and upper of the victim's shoe, is lit and allowed to burn down. —*v.i.* **2.** to go in great haste (often fol. by *it*): *to hotfoot it over to a neighbor's house.* —*adv.* **3.** with great speed in going; in haste. [ME *hot fot*]

hot·head (hot′hed′), *n.* a hotheaded person.

hot·head·ed (hot′hed′id), *adj.* **1.** hot or fiery in spirit or temper; impetuous; rash. **2.** easily angered; quick to take offense. —**hot′head′ed·ly,** *adv.* —**hot′head′ed·ness,** *n.*

hot·house (hot′hous′), *n., pl.* **-hous·es** (-hou′ziz). an artificially heated greenhouse for the cultivation of tender plants.

Ho·tien (hō′tyen′), *n.* Khotan (def. 2).

hot′ line′, 1. a direct-line teletype between the chiefs of state of the Soviet Union and the U.S., for use during international emergencies. **2.** Also, **hot′line′.** any direct communications system, usually telephone, established for instant contact, information, counseling, etc.

hot′ pep′per, 1. any of variously shaped pungent peppers of the genus *Capsicum,* containing large amounts of capsaicin and usually having thin walls. **2.** a plant bearing such a pepper.

hot′ plate′, 1. a portable appliance for cooking, usually having an electric heating coil. **2.** a plate for keeping food warm.

hot′ pota′to, 1. *Informal.* a situation or issue which is difficult, unpleasant, or risky to deal with. **2.** *Brit. Informal.* a baked potato.

hot′ pursuit′, the act of chasing a criminal or enemy closely, esp. across a border.

hot′ rod′, *U.S. Slang.* a car, esp. an old one, whose engine has been altered or replaced for increased speed, and whose chassis and body are often radically modified.

hot′ rod′der, *U.S. Slang.* **1.** a driver or builder of hot rods. **2.** a fast and reckless driver.

hot-roll (hot′rōl′, -rōl′), *v.t. Metalworking.* to roll (metal) at a temperature high enough to permit recrystallization.

hot′ seat′, *Slang.* See **electric chair.**

hot·shot (hot′shot′), *Slang.* —*adj.* **1.** highly successful and aggressive. **2.** displaying skill flamboyantly. **3.** moving, going, or operating without a stop; fast: *a hotshot express.* —*n.* **4.** Also, **hot′ shot′.** a hotshot person or thing.

hot′ spring′, a thermal mineral spring having waters warmer than 98°F.

Hot′ Springs′, a city in central Arkansas: adjoining a national park (**Hot′ Springs′ Na′tional Park′**) noted for its thermal mineral springs. 35,631 (1970).

hot·spur (hot′spûr′), *n.* an impetuous person. [after Sir Henry PERCY, to whom it was applied as a nickname]

hot′ stuff′, *Slang.* **1.** a person or thing of exceptional interest or merit. **2.** a person who is erotically stimulating or is easily aroused sexually. **3.** something unconventional, sensational, or daring: *This movie is hot stuff.*

Hot·ten·tot (hot′ᵊn tot′), *n.* **1.** a member of a people of southern Africa. **2.** the speech of the Hottentots, consisting of two languages that belong to the Khoisan family of languages. —*adj.* **3.** of, pertaining to, or characteristic of the Hottentots or their language. [< SAfrD]

Hot′tentot's bread′, 1. elephant's-foot. **2.** the edible rhizome of this plant.

hot′ tub′, a large circular wooden tub, accommodating several persons, that is filled with hot aerated water and often equipped with a thermostat and whirlpool: used for recreation or physical therapy and often placed out of doors, as on a porch. —**hot′-tub′ber,** *n.* —**hot′-tub′bing,** *n.*

hot′ war′, open military conflict; armed conflict between nations. Cf. **cold war.**

hot′ wa′ter, *Informal.* trouble; a predicament.

hou·dah (hou′də), *n.* howdah.

Hou·dan (ho͞o′dan), *n.* one of a French breed of chickens having mottled black-and-white plumage. [after *Houdan,* village near Paris where these hens were bred]

Hou·don (o͞o dôN′), *n.* **Jean An·toine** (zhäN äN twAN′), 1741–1828, French sculptor.

Hou·ma (ho͞o′mə), *n.* a city in S Louisiana. 30,922 (1970).

hound¹ (hound), *n.* **1.** one of any of several breeds of dogs trained to pursue game either by sight or by scent, esp. one with a long face and large drooping ears. **2.** any dog. **3.** *Informal.* a mean, despicable fellow. **4.** *Informal.* an addict or devotee: *an autograph hound.* **5. follow the hounds,** *Fox Hunting.* to participate in a hunt, esp. as a member of the field. **6. ride to hounds,** *Fox Hunting.* to participate in a hunt, whether as a member of the field or of the hunt staff. —*v.t.* **7.** to hunt or track with hounds, or as a hound does; pursue. **8.** to pursue or harass without respite. **9.** to incite (a hound) to pursuit or attack; urge on. **10.** *Informal.* to incite or urge (a person) to do something. [ME *h*(*o*)*und,* OE *hund;* c. D *hond,* Icel *hundr,* Dan, Sw *hund,* G *Hund,* Goth *hunds;* akin to L *canis,* Gk *kýōn* (gen. *kynós*), Skt *śvā́n* (gen. *śúnas*), OIr *cú* (gen. *con*); Welsh *ci* (pl. *cwn*), Tocharian *kū*] —**hound′er,** *n.* —**Syn. 7.** dog, follow, chase, trail. **8.** pester, annoy, persecute, bully.

hound² (hound), *n.* **1.** *Naut.* either of a pair of fore-and-aft members at the lower end of the head of a mast, for supporting the trestletrees, that support an upper mast at its heel. **2.** a horizontal bar or brace, usually one of a pair, for strengthening the running gear of a horse-drawn wagon or the like. [ME *hūn* < Scand; cf. Icel *húnn* knob at the masthead]

hound′ dog′, *Southern U.S. Dial.* hound¹ (def. 1).

hound's-tongue (houndz′tung′), *n.* **1.** a boraginaceous weed, *Cynoglossum officinale,* having prickly nutlets and tonguelike leaves. **2.** any other plant of the genus *Cynoglossum.* [ME; OE *hundestunge,* trans. of L *cynoglōssos* < Gk *kynóglōssos, -on,* lit., dog-tongued object]

hound's′ tooth′, a pattern of broken or jagged checks, often used on fabrics. Also called **hound's′-tooth check′.** —**hound's′-tooth′,** *adj.*

Hound's tooth

hour (our, ou′ər), *n.* **1.** a period of time equal to $^{1}/_{24}$th of a mean solar or civil day and equivalent to 60 minutes: *He slept* *for an hour.* **2.** any specific one of these 24 periods, usually reckoned in two series of 12, one series from midnight to noon and the second from noon to midnight, but sometimes reckoned in one series of 24, from midnight to midnight: *He slept for the hour between 2 and 3* A.M. *The hour for the bombardment was between 1300 and 1400.* **3.** any specific time of day; the time indicated by a timepiece: *What is the hour?* **4.** a particular or appointed time: *What hour do you open?* **5.** a customary or usual time: *dinner hour.* **6.** the present time: *the man of the hour.* **7. hours, a.** time spent in an office, factory, or the like, or for work, study, etc.: *The doctor's hours were from 10 to 4.* **b.** customary time of going to bed and getting up: *to keep late hours.* **c.** (in the Christian church) the seven stated times of the day for prayer and devotion. **d.** the offices or services prescribed for these times. **e.** a book containing them. **8.** distance normally covered in an hour's traveling: *We live about an hour from the city.* **9.** *Astron.* **a.** a unit of measure of right ascension, etc., representing 15°, or the 24th part of a great circle. **b.** See **sidereal hour. 10.** *Educ.* **a.** a single period of class instruction, usually from 40 to 55 minutes. **b.** Also called **credit hour.** one unit of academic credit, usually representing attendance at one scheduled period of instruction per week throughout a semester, quarter, or term. **11. the Hours,** *Class. Myth.* the Horae. **12. one's hour, a.** Also, **one's last hour.** the instant of death. **b.** any crucial moment. **—***adj.* **13.** of, pertaining to, or noting an hour. [ME *(h)oure* < AF; OF *(h)ore* < L *hōra* < Gk: time, season]

hour′ an′gle, *Astron.* the angle, measured westward through 360°, between the celestial meridian of an observer and the hour circle of a celestial body.

hour′ cir′cle, a great circle on the celestial sphere passing through the celestial poles and containing a point on the celestial sphere, as a star or the vernal equinox.

hour·glass (our′glas′, -gläs′, ou′ər-), *n.* **1.** an instrument for measuring time, consisting of two bulbs of glass joined by a narrow passage through which a quantity of sand or mercury runs in just an hour. **—***adj.* **2.** having a notably slim or narrow waist, midsection, or joining segment: *She has an hourglass figure.*

Hourglass

hour′ hand′, the hand that indicates the hours on a clock or watch.

hou·ri (ho͝or′ē, hour′ē), *n., pl.* **-ris.** one of the beautiful virgins provided in Paradise for all faithful Muslims. [< F < Pers *hūrī* < Ar *hūrīyah* gazelle-eyed (woman), lit., black-eyed like a gazelle]

hour·ly (our′lē, ou′ər-), *adj.* **1.** of, pertaining to, occurring, or done each successive hour. **2.** frequent; continual. **—***adv.* **3.** every hour; hour by hour. **4.** at each hour or during every hour. **5.** frequently; continually. [late ME]

Hou·sa·ton·ic (ho͞o′sə ton′ik), *n.* a river flowing S from NW Massachusetts through SW Connecticut to Long Island Sound near Stratford, Connecticut. 148 mi. long.

house (*n., adj.* hous; *v.* houz), *n., pl.* **hous·es** (hou′ziz), *v.,* **housed, hous·ing,** *adj.* **—***n.* **1.** a building in which people live; residence for human beings. **2.** a household. **3.** (*often cap.*) a family, including ancestors and descendants: *the great houses of France; the House of Hapsburg.* **4.** a building for any purpose: *a house of worship.* **5.** a theater, concert hall, or auditorium. **6.** the audience of a theater or the like. **7.** a place of shelter for an animal, bird, etc. **8.** the building in which a legislative or official deliberative body meets. **9.** (*cap.*) the body itself, esp. of a bicameral legislature: *the Houses of Parliament.* **10.** a quorum of such a body. **11.** (*often cap.*) a commercial establishment; business firm. **12.** a gambling casino. **13.** the management of a commercial establishment or of a gambling casino: *rules of the house.* **14.** an advisory or deliberative group, esp. in church or college affairs. **15.** a residential hall in a college or school; dormitory. **16.** the members or residents of any such residential hall. **17.** *Informal.* a brothel; whorehouse. **18.** *Naut.* any enclosed shelter above the weather deck of a vessel: *a bridge house.* **19.** *Astrol.* **a.** the sign of the zodiac in which a planet is felt to exert its greatest influence. **b.** one of the 12 divisions of the celestial sphere. **20. bring down the house,** *Informal.* to call forth vigorous applause from an audience. **21. clean house,** to eliminate forcibly all undesirable elements: *The new mayor cleaned house.* **22. on the house,** as a gift from the management; free.
—*v.t.* **23.** to put or receive into a house, dwelling, or living quarters. **24.** to give shelter to; harbor; lodge. **25.** to provide with a place to work, study, or the like. **26.** to provide storage space for; be a receptacle for or repository of: *The library houses 600,000 books.* **27.** to remove from exposure; put in a safe place. **28.** *Carpentry.* **a.** to fit the end or edge of (a board or the like) into a gain, dado, or mortise. **b.** to form (a joint) between two pieces of wood by fitting the end or edge of one into a dado of the other.
—*v.i.* **29.** to take shelter; dwell.
—*adj.* **30.** of, pertaining to, or noting a house. **31.** for or suitable for a house: *house paint.* [ME *h(o)us,* OE *hūs*]
—Syn. 1. domicile. HOUSE, DWELLING, RESIDENCE, HOME are terms applied to a place to live in. HOUSE is the general term for a structure to be lived in. DWELLING is now chiefly poetic, or used in legal or technical contexts, as in a lease or in the phrase *multiple dwelling.* RESIDENCE is characteristic of formal usage and often implies size and elegance of structure and surroundings. HOME has recently become practically equivalent to HOUSE, but still retains some of its older connotations of family ties and domestic comfort.

House (hous), *n.* **Edward Man·dell** (man′dᵊl), ("*Colonel House*"), 1858–1938, U.S. diplomat.

house′ a′gent, *Brit.* a real-estate agent.

house′ arrest′, confinement of an arrested person to his residence or to a public institution, as a hospital, instead of in a jail.

house·boat (hous′bōt′), *n.* a flat-bottomed, bargelike boat fitted for use as a floating dwelling but not suited to rough water.

house·boy (hous′boi′), *n.* houseman.

house·break (hous′brāk′), *v.t.,* **-broke, -brok·en, -break·ing.** to train (a pet) to avoid excreting indoors or to excrete in a specific place.

house·break·er (hous′brā′kər), *n.* **1.** a person who breaks into and enters a house with felonious intent. **2.** *Brit.* **a.** a wrecking company that or worker who demolishes houses and buildings. **b.** a person who buys doors, paneled walls, etc., from standing houses, to sell as antiques. **—house′break′ing,** *n.*

house·bro·ken (hous′brō′kən), *adj.* (of a pet) trained to avoid excreting inside the house or in improper places.

house·carl (hous′kärl′), *n.* a member of the household troops or bodyguard of a Danish or early English king or noble. [late OE *hūscarl* < Dan *hūskarl.* See HOUSE, CARL]

house·clean (hous′klēn′), *v.t.* **1.** to subject (a house, room, etc.) to housecleaning. **—***v.i.* **2.** to engage in housecleaning. [back formation from HOUSECLEANING] **—house′clean′er,** *n.*

house·clean·ing (hous′klē′ning), *n.* **1.** the act of cleaning a house, room, etc., and its furnishings, esp. the act of cleaning thoroughly and completely. **2.** the act of improving or reforming by weeding out excess or corrupt personnel or of revising methods of operation.

house·coat (hous′kōt′), *n.* a woman's long, tailored, one-piece, dresslike garment for casual wear about the house.

house′ detec′tive, an employee of a department store, hotel, etc., engaged to prevent thefts, violations of regulations, or other forms of misconduct on the part of patrons.

house′ doc′tor. See **house physician.**

house·dress (hous′dres′), *n.* a relatively simple and inexpensive dress suitable for housework.

house·fa·ther (hous′fä′thər), *n.* a man responsible for a group of young people, as students, living in a dormitory, hostel, etc. [HOUSE + FATHER; cf. L *paterfamilias*]

house·fly (hous′flī′), *n., pl.* **-flies.** a common dipterous insect, *Musca domestica,* found in nearly all parts of the world.

Housefly, *Musca domestica* (Length ¼ in.)

house·ful (hous′fo͝ol), *n., pl.* **-fuls.** the quantity that a house will hold.

house·hold (hous′hōld′, -ōld′), *n.* **1.** the people of a house collectively; a family including its servants. **—***adj.* **2.** of or pertaining to a household. **3.** for use in maintaining a home, esp. for use in cooking, cleaning, laundering, repairing, etc., in the home. **4.** common or usual; ordinary. [ME *houshold*]

house′hold art′, any of the skills necessary to the efficient running of a household, as cooking or keeping a family budget.

house′hold cav′alry, (in Britain) cavalry units forming part of the ceremonial guard of the monarch.

house′hold effects′, privately owned goods, consisting chiefly of furniture, appliances, etc., for keeping house. Also called **house′hold goods′.** Cf. **personal effects.**

house·hold·er (hous′hōl′dər, -ōl′-), *n.* **1.** a person who holds title to or occupies a house. **2.** the head of a family. [ME *housholdere*] **—house′hold′er·ship′,** *n.*

house′hold troops′, troops guarding or attending a sovereign or his residence.

house′hold word′, a well-known word, phrase, etc. Also called **house′hold name′.**

house·hus·band (hous′huz′bənd), *n.* a man who is married to a working woman and who stays home to manage their household.

house·keep (hous′kēp′), *v.i.,* **-kept, -keep·ing.** to keep or maintain a house. [back formation from HOUSEKEEPING and HOUSEKEEPER]

house·keeper (hous′kē′pər), *n.* a person, sometimes hired, who does or directs the domestic work and planning necessary for a home. [late ME *howskepare*]

house·keep·ing (hous′kē′ping), *n.* **1.** the maintenance of a house or domestic establishment. **2.** the management of household affairs. **3.** the management, care, and servicing of property and equipment of an industrial or commercial building or organization.

hou·sel (hou′zəl), *n., v.,* **-seled, -sel·ing** or (*esp. Brit.*) **-selled, -sel·ling.** *Archaic.* **—***n.* **1.** the Eucharist. **—***v.t.* **2.** to administer the Eucharist to. [ME; OE *hūsl* the Eucharist, prob. orig. offering; c. Icel *hūsl,* Goth *hunsl* sacrifice, offering]

house·leek (hous′lēk′), *n.* **1.** an Old World, crassulaceous herb, *Sempervivum tectorum,* found growing on the roofs and walls of houses. **2.** any other plant of the genus *Sempervivum.* [late ME *howsleke*]

house·less (hous′lis), *adj.* **1.** without a house or houses. **2.** homeless. [ME *housles*] **—house′less·ness,** *n.*

house·lights (hous′līts′), *n.pl.* the lamps providing illumination of the seating area of a theater.

house·line (hous′līn′), *n.* *Naut.* small stuff of three yarns of tarred hemp laid left-handed, used esp. for seizings.

house·maid (hous′mād′), *n.* a female servant employed in general domestic work in a home.

house′maid's knee′, *Pathol.* inflammation of the bursa over the anterior region of the kneepan.

house·man (hous′man′, -mən), *n., pl.* **-men** (-men′, -mən). a male servant who performs general duties in a home, hotel, etc.

house·moth·er (hous′muth′ər), *n.* a woman in charge of a residence, esp. for children, students, or young women, who acts as hostess, chaperon, and occasionally as housekeeper.

house′ mouse′, a brownish-gray, Old World mouse, *Mus musculus,* now common in the U.S. in or near houses.

House′ of Bur′gesses, the assembly of representatives in Colonial Virginia.

house′ of cards′, a structure or plan that is insubstantial and subject to imminent collapse.

House′ of Com′mons, the elective, lower house of the British Parliament.

house′ of correc′tion, a place for the confinement and reform of persons convicted of minor offenses and not regarded as confirmed criminals.

House′ of Del′egates, the lower house of the General Assembly in Virginia, West Virginia, and Maryland.

house′ of deten′tion, a place maintained by the civil authorities for persons charged with a crime, and sometimes for witnesses, awaiting trial.

house′ of God′, a building devoted to religious worship;

a church, temple, chapel, etc. Also called **house′ of wor′ship, house′ of prayer′** (prâr).
house′ of ill′ repute′, a house of prostitution. Also called **house′ of ill′ fame′.**
House′ of Lords′, the nonelective, upper house of the British Parliament, comprising the lords spiritual and lords temporal.
House′ of Represen′tatives, the lower legislative branch in many national and state bicameral governing bodies, as in the United States, Mexico, Japan, etc.
house′ or′gan, a periodical issued by a business or other establishment for its employees and customers.
house·par·ent (hous′pâr′ənt, -par′-), *n.* **1.** one of a married couple responsible for a group of young people, as students, living in a dormitory, hostel, etc., sometimes acting solely as an advisor, but often serving as host or hostess, chaperon, housekeeper, etc. **2.** a housemother or housefather.
house′ par′ty, the entertainment of guests for one or more nights at one's home, a fraternity or sorority house, etc.
house·phone (hous′fōn′), *n.* a telephone, as in a hotel, that does not have a direct line to an exchange and whose calls are routed through the building's switchboard.
house′ physi′cian, a resident physician in a hospital, hotel, or other public institution. Also called **house doctor.**
house-rais·ing (hous′rā′zing), *n.* a gathering of persons in a rural community to help one of its members build a house.
house·room (hous′ro͞om′, -ro͝om′), *n.* lodging or accommodation in a house.
house′ seat′, one of the theater seats reserved for special guests or friends of the producer, performers, etc.
house-sit (hous′sit′), *v.i.,* **-sat, -sit·ting.** to occupy and look after a house, apartment, etc., during the owner's or tenant's extended absence, often in return for free rent or a small fee. [by anal. with BABY-SIT] —**house′-sit′ter,** *n.*
house′ slip′per, a slipper worn in the house or indoors, usually having a back and heel.
house′ spar′row, a small weaverbird, *Passer domesticus,* of Europe, introduced into America.
house·top (hous′top′), *n.* **1.** the top or roof of a house. **2. from the housetops,** publicly; generally: *Shout it from the housetops.*
house′ trail′er, a large trailer that has been fitted for use as a mobile home.
House′ Un-Amer′ican Activ′ities Commit′tee, an investigative committee of the U.S. House of Representatives. Originally created in 1938, with Representative Martin Dies as chairman, to inquire into subversive activities in the U.S., it was established permanently in 1945 as the Committee on Un-American Activities, and in 1969 renamed the Committee on Internal Security. *Abbr.:* HUAC.
house·wares (hous′wârz′), *n.pl.* articles of household equipment, as kitchen utensils, glassware, etc.
house·warm·ing (hous′wôr′ming), *n.* a party to celebrate a person's or family's occupancy of a new house.
house·wife (hous′wīf′ *or, usually,* huz′if *for 2*), *n., pl.* **-wives** (-wīvz′ *or, usually* -ifs *for 2*). **1.** the woman in charge of a household, esp. a wife who does all or most of the cleaning and cooking in her own household and who holds no other job. **2.** *Chiefly Brit.* a sewing box; a small case or box for needles, thread, etc. [ME *hus(e)wif*]
house·wife·ly (hous′wīf′lē), *adj.* of, like, or befitting a housewife. —**house′wife′li·ness,** *n.*
house·wif·er·y (hous′wī′fə rē, -wīf′rē), *n.* the function or work of a housewife; housekeeping. [late ME *huswyfery*]
house·work (hous′wûrk′), *n.* the work of cleaning, cooking, etc., to be done in housekeeping.
house·wreck·er (hous′rek′ər), *n.* wrecker (def. 4).
house′ wren′, a common American wren, *Troglodytes aedon,* that nests around houses. See illus. at **wren.**
hous·ing[1] (hou′zing), *n.* **1.** any shelter, lodging, or dwelling place. **2.** houses collectively. **3.** the act of a person who houses or puts under shelter. **4.** the providing of houses for a group or community: *the housing of an influx of laborers.* **5.** anything that covers or protects. **6.** *Mach.* a fully enclosed case and support for a mechanism. **7.** *Carpentry.* the space made in one piece of wood, or the like, for the insertion of another. **8.** *Naut.* **a.** the portion of a mast below the deck. **b.** the portion of a bowsprit abaft the forward part of the stem of a vessel. [ME *husing.* See HOUSE, -ING[1]]
hous·ing[2] (hou′zing), *n.* **1.** a covering of cloth for the back and flanks of a horse or other animal, for protection or ornament. **2.** Usually, **housings.** a caparison; trappings. [late ME *husynge* = ME *hous* cloth cover (? < OF *houce* or special use of HOUSE) + *-ynge* -ING[1]]
hous′ing proj′ect, project (def. 4).
Hous·man (hous′mən), *n.* **A(lfred) E(dward),** 1859–1936, English poet and classical scholar.
Hous·ton (hyo͞o′stən), *n.* **1. Sam(uel),** 1793–1863, U.S. soldier and political leader: president of the Republic of Texas 1836–38. **2.** a city in SE Texas: a port on a ship canal, ab. 50 mi. from the Gulf of Mexico. 1,232,802 (1970).
hous·to·ni·a (ho͞o stō′nē ə), *n.* any North American, rubiaceous herb of the genus *Houstonia,* as *H. caerulea,* the common bluet or innocence. [named after Dr. W. *Houston* (d. 1733), British botanist; see -IA]
Hou·yhn·hnm (ho͞o in′əm, hwin′əm, win′-), *n.* one of a race of horses, in Swift's *Gulliver's Travels* (1726), endowed with reason, who rule the Yahoos. [appar. alter. of WHINNY]
hove (hōv), *v.* pt. and pp. of **heave.**
hov·el (huv′əl, hov′-), *n., v.,* **-eled, -el·ing** or (*esp. Brit.*) **-elled, -el·ling.** —*n.* **1.** a small, mean dwelling house; a wretched hut. **2.** any dirty, disorganized dwelling. **3.** an open shed, as for sheltering cattle, tools, etc. —*v.t.* **4.** to shelter or lodge as in a hovel. [late ME *hovell* < ?]
hov·er (huv′ər, hov′-), *v.i.* **1.** to hang fluttering or suspended in the air: *The helicopter hovered over the building.* **2.** to keep lingering about; wait near at hand. **3.** to remain in an uncertain or irresolute state; waver: *to hover between life and death.* —*n.* **4.** the act or state of hovering. [ME *hoveren,* freq. of *hoven* to hover < ?] —**hov′er·er** *n.* —**hov′er·ing·ly,** *adv.* —**Syn. 1.** See **fly**[1].
Hov·er·craft (huv′ər kraft′, -kräft′), *n.* *Trademark.* a vehicle that can travel rapidly over water, marshland, or smooth terrain, while hovering several feet above the surface on a cushion of air provided by large fans blowing downward from the chassis.
hov′ering ac′cent, *Pros.* indeterminacy as to which of two consecutive syllables in a line of verse bears the metrical stress, as in any of the first three feet of *Slow, slow, / fresh fount, / keep time / with my / salt tears.*
how[1] (hou), *adv.* **1.** in what way or manner?; by what means?: *How did it happen?* **2.** to what extent, degree, etc.?: *How damaged is the car?* **3.** in what state or condition?: *How are you?* **4.** for what reason?; why?: *How can you talk such nonsense?* **5.** to what effect?; with what meaning?: *How is one to interpret his action?* **6.** what?: *How do you mean? If they don't have vanilla, how about chocolate?* **7.** (used as an intensifier): *How seldom I go there!* **8.** by what title or name?: *How does one address the president?* **9. and how!** *Informal.* certainly! you bet!: *Am I happy? And how!* **10. how come?** *Informal.* how is it that? why? *How come you never visit us anymore?* **11. how so?** how does it happen to be so? why?: *You haven't any desire to go? How so?* —*conj.* **12.** the manner or way in which: *He couldn't figure out how to solve the problem.* **13.** about the manner, condition, or way in which: *I don't care how you leave your desk when you go. Be careful how you act.* **14.** in whatever manner or way; however: *You can travel how you please.* —*n.* **15.** a question concerning the way or manner in which something is done, achieved, etc.: *a child's unending whys and hows.* **16.** a way or manner of doing something: *to consider all the hows and wherefores.* [ME *how, hu,* OE *hu;* c. OFris *hū, ho,* D *hoe;* akin to G *wie* (OHG *hweo*), Goth *hwaiwa*]
how[2] (hou), *interj.* *Facetious.* (used as a greeting in imitation of American Indian speech.) [< Siouan]
How·ard (hou′ərd), *n.* **1. Catherine,** c1520–42, fifth wife of Henry VIII. **2. Henry.** See **Surrey, Henry Howard, Earl of. 3. Roy Wilson,** 1883–1964, U.S. editor and newspaper publisher. **4. Sidney (Coe)** (kō), 1891–1939, U.S. playwright and short-story writer.
how·be·it (hou bē′it), *adv.* **1.** nevertheless. —*conj.* **2.** although. [ME *how be it* however it may be; parallel to ALBEIT]
how·dah (hou′də), *n.* (in the East Indies) a seat, commonly with a railing and a canopy, placed on the back of an elephant. Also, **houdah.** [< Hindi *haudah* < Ar *haudaj*]
how·die (hou′dē, ou′-; hō′dē, ō′dē), *n.* *Scot. and North Eng. Slang.* a midwife. Also, **howdy.** [?]
how′ do you do′, (a conventional expression used in greeting a person or upon being introduced.)
how-do-you-do (hou′də yə do͞o′), *n.* *Informal.* an awkward or unpleasant event or situation. Also, **how-de-do** (hou′dē do͞o′).
how·dy[1] (hou′dē), *n., pl.* **-dies,** *interj.* *Chiefly Dial.* hello; how do you do (an expression of greeting). [from the phrase *how d(o) ye?*]
how·dy[2] (hou′dē), *n., pl.* **-dies.** *Scot. and North Eng. Slang.* howdie.
Howe (hou), *n.* **1. Elias,** 1819–67, U.S. inventor of the sewing machine. **2. Julia Ward,** 1819–1910, U.S. writer and reformer. **3. William, 5th Viscount,** 1729–1814, British general in the American Revolutionary War.
how·e'er (hou âr′), *adv., conj.* *Literary.* however.
How·ells (hou′əlz), *n.* **William Dean,** 1837–1920, U.S. author, critic, and editor.
how·ev·er (hou ev′ər), *adv.* **1.** nevertheless; yet; on the other hand; in spite of that: *We have not yet won; however, we shall try again.* **2.** to whatever extent or degree; no matter how: *However much you spend, I will reimburse you.* **3.** how?; how under the circumstances?: *However did you manage?* —*conj.* **4.** in whatever way, manner, or state: *Arrange your hours however you like.* [ME *hou-ever*] —**Syn. 1.** See **but**[1].
how·itz·er (hou′it sər), *n.* *Ordn.* a cannon having a comparatively short barrel, used esp. for firing shells at a high angle of elevation, as for reaching a target behind cover, in a trench, etc. [earlier *hauwitzer* < D *houvietser* < G *Haubitze* (MHG *haufnitz* < Czech *houfnice* slingshot) + *-er* -ER[1]]
howl (houl), *v.i.* **1.** to utter a loud, prolonged, mournful cry, as that of a dog or wolf. **2.** to utter a similar cry in distress, pain, rage, etc.; wail. **3.** to make a sound like an animal howling: *The wind howls through the trees.* **4.** *Informal.* to laugh loudly. —*v.t.* **5.** to utter with howls. **6.** to drive or force by howls (often fol. by *down*): *to howl down the opposition.* —*n.* **7.** the cry of a dog, wolf, etc. **8.** a cry or wail, as of pain, rage, protest, etc. **9.** a sound like wailing: *the howl of the wind.* **10.** a loud, scornful laugh or yell. **11.** something that causes a laugh or a scornful yell, as a joke or funny or embarrassing situation. [ME *hul(en), houle;* c. D *huilen,* G *heulen,* LG *hülen,* Dan *hyle;* with loss of *h,* Icel *ȳla*]
How′land Is′land (hou′lənd), an island in the central Pacific, near the equator: U.S. aerological station and airfield. 1 sq. mi.
howl·er (hou′lər), *n.* **1.** a person or thing that howls. **2.** Also called **howl′ing mon′key.** any of the large, prehensile-tailed tropical American monkeys of the genus *Alouatta,* the males of which make a howling noise. **3.** *Informal.* a humorous or embarrassing blunder.
howl·ing (hou′ling), *adj.* **1.** producing or uttering a howling noise. **2.** *Informal.* very great; tremendous: *a howling success.* —**howl′ing·ly,** *adv.*
How·rah (hou′rä), *n.* a city in E India, on the Hooghly River opposite Calcutta. 512,600 (1961).
how·so·ev·er (hou′sō ev′ər), *adv.* **1.** to whatsoever extent or degree. **2.** in whatsoever manner. [ME]
how-to (hou′to͞o′), *adj.* giving basic instructions to the layman on the methods for doing or making something as a hobby or for practical use, as in carpentry, furniture building, or a similar craft: *a how-to book.* [by shortening]
hoy[1] (hoi), *n.* *Naut.* **1.** a heavy barge used in harbors. **2.** a small vessel of the 17th and 18th centuries, used for fishing and coastal trading. [late ME *hoy(e)* < MD *hoei*]
hoy[2] (hoi), *interj.* **1.** (used as an exclamation to attract attention.) —*n.* **2.** a shout or hail. [ME; var. of HEY]
hoy·den (hoid′ən), *n.* **1.** a boisterous, ill-bred girl; a tomboy. —*adj.* **2.** boisterous; rude. Also, **hoiden.** [? < MD *heyden* boor; c. HEATHEN] —**hoy′den·ish,** *adj.* —**hoy′den·ish·ness,** *n.* —**hoy′den·ism,** *n.*

Hoyle (hoil), *n.* **1. Edmond,** 1672–1769, English authority and writer on card games. **2. according to Hoyle,** according to the rules or authority; correctly.
hp, horsepower. Also, **HP**
H.P., 1. *Elect.* high power. 2. high pressure. 3. horsepower. Also, **h.p.**
H.Q., headquarters. Also, **h.q., HQ.**
Hr., Herr.
hr., hour; hours. Also, **h.**
H.R., 1. King Henry. [< L *Hēnricus Rex*] 2. House of Representatives.
Hra·dec Krá·lo·vé (hrä′dets krä′lô ve), Czech name of **Königgrätz.**
Hr·dlič·ka (hûrd′lich kə; *Czech.* hr′dlich kä), *n.* **A·leš** (ä′lesh), 1869–1943, U.S. anthropologist, born in Czechoslovakia.
Hreid·mar (hrād′mär), *n.* (in the *Volsunga Saga*) the father of Fafnir, Otter, and Regin: he demanded wergild from the gods for killing Otter, and was killed by Fafnir when he got it.
H.R.H., His (or Her) Royal Highness.
H.R.I.P., here rests in peace. [< L *hīc requiescit in pāce*]
Hrolf (hrolf), *n.* Rollo.
Hroz·ny (hrôz′nē), *n.* **Frie·drich** (*Ger.* frē′drikh) or **Be·dřich** (*Czech.* be′drzhikh), 1879–1952, Czech archaeologist and orientalist.
hrs., hours.
Hr·vat·ska (khr′vät skä), *n.* Serbo-Croatian name of **Croatia.**
H.S., 1. High School. 2. *Brit.* Home Secretary.
h.s., 1. in this sense. [< L *hōc sēnsū*] 2. (in prescriptions) at bedtime. [< L *hōrā somnī* at the hour of sleep]
H.S.H., His (or Her) Serene Highness.
Hsing·an (shing′än′), *n.* a former province in Manchuria, in NE China.
Hsin·hua (shin′hwä′), *n.* the official press agency of the People's Republic of China. [< Chin = *hsin* new + *hua* China]
Hsi·ning (shē′ning′), *n.* Sining.
Hsin·king (shin′jing′), *n.* Changchun.
H.S.M., His (or Her) Serene Majesty.
Hsüan T'ung (shy än′ tōōng′). See **Pu-yi, Henry.**
ht., height.
Hts., Heights (used in place names).
HUAC (hyōō′ak), *n.* House Un-American Activities Committee.
Hua Kuo-feng (hwä′ kwō′fung′), born 1920?, Chinese communist leader: chairman of the Chinese Communist party 1976–81.
Huam·bo (*Port.* wäm′bô), *n.* former name of **Nova Lisboa.**
Huan·ca·yo (wän kä′yô), *n.* a city in central Peru. 46,014 (1961).
Huang Ti (hwäng′ dē′), the legendary first emperor of China. Also called **Yellow Emperor.**
hua·ra·che (wə rä′chē; *Sp.* wä rä′che), *n., pl.* **-ches** (-chēz; *Sp.* -ches). a Mexican sandal having the upper woven of leather strips. [< MexSp]
Huás·car (wäs′kär), *n.* 1495?–1533, Inca prince of Peru (half brother of Atahualpa; son of Huayna Capac).
Huas·ca·rán (wäs′kä rän′), *n.* a mountain in W Peru, in the Andes. 22,205 ft.
Huay·na Ca·pac (wī′nä kä′päk), c1450–1527?, Inca ruler of Peru 1493?–1527? (father of Atahualpa and Huascar). Also, **Huai′na Ca′pac.**
hub (hub), *n.* **1.** the central part of a wheel, propeller, fan, etc., into which spokes are inserted. **2.** the part in central position around which all else revolves; a center of activity: *the hub of the universe.* **3. the Hub,** Boston, Massachusetts (used as a nickname). **4.** *Coining.* a design of hardened steel in relief, used as a punch in making a die. [? var. of hob¹]
hub·ba hub·ba (hub′ə hub′ə), *Slang.* (an exclamation of approval or enthusiasm, used esp. by G.I.'s of World War II as a shout in appreciation of a pretty girl.) [?]
Hub·bard (hub′ərd), *n.* **Elbert Green,** 1856–1915, U.S. author, editor, and printer.
Hub′bard squash′, **1.** a variety of winter squash having a green or yellow skin and yellow flesh. **2.** the plant bearing this fruit. [after the surname *Hubbard*]
hub·ble-bub·ble (hub′əl bub′əl), *n.* **1.** a form of the hookah; water pipe. **2.** a bubbling sound. **3.** an uproar; turmoil. [rhyming compound based on bubble]
hub·bub (hub′ub), *n.* **1.** a loud, confused noise, as of many voices. **2.** tumult; uproar. [appar. of Ir orig.; akin to ScotGael cry *ubub!* (redupl. of *ub!*) expressing aversion or contempt] **—Syn. 1.** See **noise. 2.** disorder, confusion.
hub·by (hub′ē), *n., pl.* **-bies.** *Informal.* husband. [by shortening; see -y²]
hu·bris (hyōō′bris, hōō′-), *n.* excessive pride or self-confidence; arrogance. Also, **hybris.** [< Gk: insolence] **—hu·bris′tic,** *adj.*
huck·a·back (huk′ə bak′), *n.* toweling of linen or cotton, of a distinctive absorbent weave. Also called **huck.** [?]
huck·le·ber·ry (huk′əl ber′ē), *n., pl.* **-ries,** *adj.* **—n. 1.** the dark-blue or black, edible berry of any of various ericaceous shrubs of the genus *Gaylussacia.* **2.** the shrub itself. **3.** blueberry (def. 1). **—adj. 4.** made with or containing huckleberries: *huckleberry pie.* [dial. var. of hurtleberry]
huck·le·bone (huk′əl bōn′), *n.* **1.** See **innominate bone. 2.** talus¹. [*huckle* hip, haunch (cf. ME *hokebone,* perh. akin to MD *hoken,* ON *hūka* to squat; see -le) + bone¹]
huck·ster (huk′stər), *n.* **1.** a retailer of small articles, esp. a peddler of fruits and vegetables. **2.** a cheaply mercenary person. **3.** *Informal.* **a.** a persuasive and aggressive salesman. **b.** a person who prepares advertising, esp. for radio and television. **—v.t., v.i. 4.** to deal, as in small articles, or to make petty bargains: *to huckster fresh corn; to huckster for a living.* [early ME *huccstere* (? c. MD *hokester*) = *hucc-* haggle, bargain (c. dial. G *hucken* to huckster) + *-stere* -ster] **—huck′ster·ism,** *n.*
HUD (hud), *n.* Department of Housing and Urban Development.
Hud·ders·field (hud′ərz fēld′), *n.* a town in SW Yorkshire, in N England. 130,307 (1961).
hud·dle (hud′ᵊl), *v.,* **-dled, -dling,** *n.* **—v.t. 1.** to heap or crowd together closely. **2.** to draw (oneself) closely together; nestle (often fol. by *up*). **3.** *Chiefly Brit.* to do hastily and carelessly. **4.** to put on (clothes) with careless haste. **—v.i. 5.** to gather or crowd together in a close mass. **6.** *Football.* to get together in a huddle. **7.** to confer or consult; meet to discuss. **8.** to crouch, curl up, or draw oneself together. **—n. 9.** a closely gathered group, mass, or heap; bunch. **10.** confusion or disorder. **11.** a conference, or consultation, esp. a private one. **12.** *Football.* a gathering of the team behind the line of scrimmage for instructions, signals, etc. [*hud-* (weak grade of root found in hide¹) + -le; r. ME *hoder* = *hod-* (c. *hud-*) + *-er* -er⁶] **—hud′dler,** *n.* **—hud′dling·ly,** *adv.*
Hu·di·bras·tic (hyōō′də bras′tik), *adj.* **1.** of, pertaining to, or resembling the style of Samuel Butler's *Hudibras* (published 1663–78), a mock-heroic poem in tetrameter couplets. **2.** of a playful, burlesque style. **—n. 3.** a Hudibrastic couplet or stanza. **—Hu′di·bras′ti·cal·ly,** *adv.*
Hud·son (hud′sən), *n.* **1. Henry,** died 1611?, English navigator and explorer. **2. William Henry,** 1841–1922, English naturalist and author. **3.** a river in E New York, flowing S to New York Bay. 306 mi. long.
Hud′son Bay′, a large inland sea in N Canada. 850 mi. long; 600 mi. wide; 400,000 sq. mi.
Hud′son Riv′er School′, *Fine Arts.* a group of American painters of the mid-19th century whose works are characterized by a highly romantic treatment of landscape.
Hud′son's Bay′ Com′pany, a company chartered in England in 1670 to carry on fur trading with the Indians in North America.
Hud′son seal′, muskrat fur sheared and dyed to simulate seal.
Hud′son Strait′, a strait connecting Hudson Bay and the Atlantic. 450 mi. long; 100 mi. wide.
hue¹ (hyōō), *n.* **1.** the property of light by which the color of an object is classified as red, blue, green, or yellow in reference to the spectrum. **2.** a gradation or variety of a color; tint: *pale hues.* **3.** color: *all the hues of the rainbow.* **4.** *Obs.* form or appearance. **5.** *Obs.* complexion. [ME *hewe,* OE *hīw* form, appearance, color; c. Icel *hȳ* bird's down, Sw *hy* skin, complexion, Goth *hiwi* form, appearance] **—hue′less,** *adj.* **—hue′less·ness,** *n.*
hue² (hyōō), *n.* outcry, as of pursuers; clamor. [ME *hu(e)* < MF: a hoot, outcry (> *huer* to hoot, cry out)]
Hué (hwā), *n.* a seaport in central Vietnam: former capital of Annam. 103,900 (est. 1963).
hue′ and cry′, **1.** *Early Eng. Law.* the pursuit of a felon or an offender with loud outcries to give an alarm. **2.** any public clamor, protest, or alarm. [< AF *hu et cri.* See hue², cry]
hued (hyōōd), *adj.* having the hue or color as specified (usually used in combination): *many-hued; golden-hued.* [ME *hewed,* OE *(ge)hīwod*]
Huel·va (wel′vä), *n.* a seaport in SW Spain, near the Gulf of Cádiz. 77,231 (est. 1963).
Huer·ta (wâr′tə; *Sp.* wer′tä), *n.* **Vic·to·ria·no** (bēk′tô ryä′nô), 1854–1916, Mexican general: provisional president of Mexico 1913–14.
huff (huf), *n.* **1.** a mood of sulking anger; a fit of resentment: *to leave in a huff.* **—v.t. 2.** to give offense to; make angry. **3.** to treat with arrogance or contempt; hector or bully. **—v.i. 4.** to take offense; speak indignantly. **5.** to puff or blow; breathe heavily. **6.** *Archaic.* to swell with pride or arrogance; swagger or bluster. [imit.; see puff]
huff·ish (huf′ish), *adj.* **1.** peevish; irritable. **2.** *Archaic.* insolent; bullying. **—huff′ish·ly,** *adv.* **—huff′ish·ness,** *n.*
huff·y (huf′ē), *adj.,* **huff·i·er, huff·i·est. 1.** easily offended or touchy. **2.** offended; sulky: *a huffy mood.* **—huff′i·ly,** *adv.* **—huff′i·ness,** *n.*
Hu·fuf (hōō fōōf′), *n.* Hofuf.
hug (hug), *v.,* **hugged, hug·ging,** *n.* **—v.t. 1.** to clasp tightly in the arms, esp. with affection; embrace. **2.** to cling firmly or fondly to; cherish: *to hug an opinion.* **3.** to keep close to: *to hug the shore.* **—v.i. 4.** to cling together; lie close. **—n. 5.** a tight clasp with the arms; embrace. [? < Scand; cf. Icel *hugga* to soothe, console; akin to OE *hogian* to care for] **—hug′ga·ble,** *adj.* **—hug′ger,** *n.* **—hug′ging·ly,** *adv.*
huge (hyōōj *or, often,* yōōj), *adj.,* **hug·er, hug·est.** extraordinarily large in bulk, extent, character, etc. [ME *huge, hoge* < OF *ahuge, ahoge* enormous = *a-* a-⁵ + *hoge* height < Gmc; cf. Icel *haugr* hill] **—huge′ly,** *adv.* **—huge′ness,** *n.*
—Syn. mammoth, gigantic, colossal; vast; stupendous. Huge, enormous, tremendous, immense imply great magnitude. Huge, when used of concrete objects, usually adds the idea of massiveness, bulkiness, or even shapelessness: *a huge mass of rock.* Enormous, literally out of the norm, applies to what exceeds in extent, magnitude, or degree, a norm or standard: *an enormous iceberg.* Tremendous, in informal use, applies to anything so huge as to be astonishing or to inspire awe: *a tremendous amount of equipment.* Immense, literally not measurable, is particularly applicable to what is exceedingly great, without reference to a standard: *immense buildings.* All are used figuratively: *a huge success; enormous curiosity; tremendous effort; immense joy.* **—Ant.** small, tiny.
hug·ger-mug·ger (hug′ər mug′ər), *n.* **1.** secrecy; concealment. **2.** disorder or confusion; muddle. **—adj. 3.** secret or clandestine. **4.** disorderly or confused. **—v.t. 5.** to keep secret or concealed; hush up. **—v.i. 6.** to act secretly; take secret counsel. [earlier *hucker-mucker,* rhyming compound based on *mucker,* ME *mokere* to hoard]
Hug·gins (hug′inz), *n.* **Charles Bren·ton** (bren′tᵊn), born 1901, U.S. physician and medical researcher, born in Canada: Nobel prize 1966.
Hugh Ca·pet (hyōō kā′pit, kap′it, ka pā′). See **Capet, Hugh.**
Hughes (hyōōz), *n.* **1. Charles Evans,** 1862–1948, U.S. jurist and statesman: Chief Justice of the U.S. 1930–41. **2. (John) Lang·ston** (lang′stən), 1902–1967, U.S. novelist and poet. **3. Rupert,** 1872–1956, U.S. novelist and biographer. **4. Thomas,** 1822–96, English novelist, reformer, and jurist.
Hug·li (hōōg′lē), *n.* Hooghly.
Hu·go (hyōō′gō; *Fr.* y gō′), *n.* **Vic·tor (Ma·rie, Viscount)** (vik′tər mə rē′; *Fr.* vēk tôr′ ma rē′), 1802–85, French poet, novelist, and dramatist.
Hu·gue·not (hyōō′gə not′), *n.* a member of the Reformed or Calvinistic communion of France in the 16th and 17th

centuries; a French Protestant. [< F, perh. b. *Hugues* (name of a political leader in Geneva) and *eidgenot,* back formation from *eidgenots,* Swiss var. of G *Eidgenoss* confederate, lit., oath comrade] —**Hu′gue·not′ic,** *adj.* —**Hu′gue·not·ism,** *n.*

huh (hu), *interj.* (used as an exclamation of surprise, bewilderment, disbelief, contempt, or the like.)

huic (hīk), *interj. Fox Hunting.* (used as a cry by the huntsman to encourage the hounds.) Also called **yoicks.**

Hui·la (wē′lä), *n.* **Mount,** a volcano in central Colombia. 18,700 ft.

hu′la hoop′, a tube-shaped plastic hoop for rotating about the body, used for physical exercise or in children's play.

hu·la-hu·la (ho͞o′lə ho͞o′lə), *n.* a sinuous Hawaiian native dance with intricate arm movements that tell a story in pantomime. Also called **hu′la.** [< Hawaiian]

hu′la skirt′, a skirt made of long stems of grass bound to a waistband, worn typically by a Hawaiian hula dancer.

hulk (hulk), *n.* **1.** the body of an old or dismantled ship. **2.** a vessel specially built to serve as a storehouse, prison, etc., and not for sea service. **3.** *Disparaging.* a clumsy-looking or unwieldy ship or boat. **4.** a bulky or unwieldy person, object, or mass. **5.** the shell of a wrecked, burned-out, or abandoned vehicle, building, or the like. —*v.i.* **6.** to loom in bulky form; appear as a large, massive bulk. **7.** *Brit. Dial.* to lounge, slouch, or move in a heavy, loutish manner. [ME *hulke,* OE *hulc;* ? < ML *hulcus* < Gk *holkás* trading vessel, orig. towed ship, akin to *hélkein* to drag]

hulk·ing (hul′king), *adj.* bulky; heavy and clumsy.

hulk·y (hul′kē), *adj.,* **hulk·i·er, hulk·i·est.** hulking.

hull[1] (hul), *n.* **1.** the husk, shell, or outer covering of a seed or fruit, as of a nut. **2.** the calyx of certain fruits, as the strawberry and raspberry. **3.** any covering or envelope. —*v.t.* **4.** to remove the hull of. [ME; OE *hulu* husk, pod; akin to OE *helan* to cover, hide, L *celāre* to hide, Gk *kalýptein* to cover up. See HALL, HELL, HOLE] —**hull′er,** *n.*

hull[2] (hul), *n.* **1.** *Naut.* the hollow, lowermost portion of a vessel, floating partially immersed in the water and supporting the remainder of the vessel. **2.** *Aeron.* **a.** the boatlike fuselage of a flying boat on which the plane lands or takes off. **b.** the cigar-shaped arrangement of girders enclosing the gasbag of a rigid dirigible. —*v.t.* **3.** to pierce (the hull of a vessel), esp. below the water line. [special use of HULL[1]] —**hull′-less,** *adj.*

Hull (hul), *n.* **1. Cor·dell** (kôr′del, kôr del′), 1871–1955, U.S. statesman: Secretary of State 1933–44; Nobel peace prize 1945. **2. William,** 1753–1825, U.S. general. **3.** Official name, **Kingston-upon-Hull.** a seaport in SE Yorkshire, in E England, on the Humber River. 303,268 (1961). **4.** a city in SE Canada, on the Ottawa River opposite Ottawa. 56,929 (1961).

hul·la·ba·loo (hul′ə bə lo͞o′), *n., pl.* **-loos.** a clamorous noise or disturbance; uproar. [appar. var. of *haloobaloo,* rhyming compound based on Scot *baloo* lullaby]

hul·lo (hə lō′), *interj., n., pl.* **-los,** *v.i., v.t.,* **-loed, -lo·ing. 1.** hallo. **2.** *Chiefly Brit.* hello.

hul·loa (hu lō′, hul′ō), *interj., n., pl.* **-loas,** *v.i.,* **-loaed, -loa·ing.** *Chiefly Brit.* hello.

hum (hum), *v.,* **hummed, hum·ming,** *n., interj.* —*v.i.* **1.** to make a low, continuous, droning sound. **2.** to give forth an indistinct sound of mingled voices or noises. **3.** to utter an indistinct sound in hesitation, embarrassment, dissatisfaction, etc.; hem. **4.** to sing with closed lips, without articulating words. **5.** to be in a state of busy activity: *The household hummed.* —*v.t.* **6.** to sound, sing, or utter by humming: *to hum a tune.* **7.** to bring, put, etc., by humming: *to hum a child to sleep.* —*n.* **8.** the act or sound of humming; an inarticulate or indistinct murmur; hem. —*interj.* **9.** (an inarticulate sound uttered in contemplation, hesitation, dissatisfaction, doubt, etc.) [ME *humme(n);* c. G *hummen* to hum; imit.] —**hum′mer,** *n.*

hu·man (hyo͞o′mən *or, often,* yo͞o′-), *adj.* **1.** of, pertaining to, or characteristic of mankind. **2.** consisting of people or men: *the human race.* **3.** of or pertaining to the social aspect or character of man: *human affairs.* **4.** sympathetic; humane: *human understanding.* —*n.* **5.** a human being. [< L *hūmān(us)* = *hūm-* (see HOMO) + *-ānus* -AN; r. ME *humain* < MF] —**hu′man·like′,** *adj.* —**hu′man·ness,** *n.*

hu·mane (hyo͞o mān′ *or, often,* yo͞o-), *adj.* **1.** characterized by tenderness, compassion, and sympathy for men and animals. **2.** of or pertaining to humanistic studies. [var. of HUMAN; cf. GERMANE, GERMAN] —**hu·mane′ly,** *adv.* —**hu·mane′ness,** *n.* —**Syn. 1.** gentle, sympathetic; benevolent.

humane′ soci′ety, *(often caps.)* an organization devoted to promoting humane ideals, esp. with reference to the treatment of animals.

hu·man·ise (hyo͞o′mə nīz′ *or, often,* yo͞o′-), *v.t., v.i.,* **-ised, -is·ing.** *Chiefly Brit.* humanize. —**hu′man·i·sa′tion,** *n.*

hu·man·ism (hyo͞o′mə niz′əm *or, often,* yo͞o′-), *n.* **1.** any system or mode of thought or action in which human interests, values, and dignity are taken to be of primary importance, as in moral judgments. **2.** devotion to or study of the humanities. **3.** *(sometimes cap.)* the studies, principles, or culture of the Humanists.

hu·man·ist (hyo͞o′mə nist *or, often,* yo͞o′-), *n.* **1.** a student of human nature or affairs. **2.** a person having a strong interest in or concern for human welfare, values, and dignity. **3.** a person devoted to or versed in the humanities. **4.** a classical scholar. **5.** *(sometimes cap.)* one of the scholars of the Renaissance who pursued and disseminated the study and understanding of the cultures of ancient Rome and Greece. **6.** *(sometimes cap.)* a person who follows a form of scientific or philosophical humanism. [< It *umanist(a)*] —**hu′man·is′tic,** *adj.* —**hu′man·is′ti·cal·ly,** *adv.*

hu·man·i·tar·i·an (hyo͞o man′i târ′ē ən *or, often,* yo͞o-), *adj.* **1.** having concern for or helping to improve the welfare of mankind. **2.** of or pertaining to ethical or theological humanitarianism. —*n.* **3.** a person actively engaged in promoting human welfare, as a philanthropist. **4.** a person who professes ethical or theological humanitarianism.

hu·man·i·tar·i·an·ism (hyo͞o man′i târ′ē ə niz′əm *or, often,* yo͞o-), *n.* **1.** humanitarian principles or practices. **2.** *Ethics.* **a.** the doctrine that man's obligations are concerned wholly with the welfare of the human race. **b.** the doctrine that mankind may become perfect without divine aid. —**hu·man′i·tar′i·an·ist,** *n.*

hu·man·i·ty (hyo͞o man′i tē *or, often,* yo͞o-), *n., pl.* **-ties. 1.** the human race; mankind. **2.** the condition of being human; human nature. **3.** the quality of being humane; kindness; benevolence. **4. the humanities, a.** the study of classical Latin and Greek language and literature. **b.** literature, philosophy, art, etc., as distinguished from the sciences. [ME *humanite* < L *hūmānitās*]

hu·man·ize (hyo͞o′mə nīz′ *or, often,* yo͞o′-), *v.,* **-ized, -iz·ing.** —*v.t.* **1.** to make humane, kind, or gentle. **2.** to make human. —*v.i.* **3.** to become human or humane. Also, *esp. Brit.,* **humanise.** —**hu′man·i·za′tion,** *n.* —**hu′man·iz′er,** *n.*

hu·man·kind (hyo͞o′mən kīnd′, -kīnd′ *or, often,* yo͞o′-), *n.* human beings collectively. [from the phrase *human kind;* modeled on *mankind*]

hu·man·ly (hyo͞o′mən lē *or, often,* yo͞o′-), *adv.* **1.** in a human manner. **2.** by human means. **3.** within the limits of human knowledge and capability.

hu′man na′ture, 1. the psychological and social qualities that characterize mankind. **2.** *Sociol.* the character of human conduct, generally regarded as produced by living in primary groups.

hu·man·oid (hyo͞o′ mə noid′), *adj.* **1.** having human characteristics or form. —*n.* **2.** a humanoid being: *to search for humanoids in outer space.* [HUMAN + -OID]

hu·ma·num est er·ra·re (o͞o mä′no͞om est er rä′re; *Eng.* hyo͞o mā′nəm est e râr′ē), *Latin.* to err is human.

Hum·ber (hum′bər), *n.* an estuary of the Ouse and Trent rivers in E England. 37 mi. long.

Hum·bert I (hum′bərt), *(Umberto)* 1844–1900, king of Italy 1878–1900.

hum·ble (hum′bəl, um′-), *adj.,* **-bler, -blest,** *v.,* **-bled, -bling.** —*adj.* **1.** not proud or arrogant; modest. **2.** having a feeling of insignificance, inferiority, subservience, etc. **3.** low in rank, importance, size, etc. **4.** courteously respectful. —*v.t.* **5.** to lower in condition, importance, or dignity; abase. **6.** to destroy the independence, power, or will of. **7.** to make meek. [ME *(h)umble* < OF < L *humil(is)* lowly, insignificant, on the ground. See HUMUS, -ILE] —**hum′ble·ness,** *n.* —**hum′bler,** *n.* —**hum′bling·ly,** *adv.* —**hum′bly,** *adv.*
—**Syn. 1.** unpretentious. **2.** submissive; meek. **3.** plain, common, poor. **4.** polite. **5.** mortify, shame. **6.** subdue, break. HUMBLE, DEGRADE, HUMILIATE suggest lowering or causing to seem lower. To HUMBLE is to bring down the pride of another or to reduce him to a state of abasement: *to humble an arrogant enemy.* To DEGRADE is to demote in rank or standing, or to reduce to a low level in condition, manners, or morals: *to degrade an officer; to degrade one's dependents.* To HUMILIATE is to make others feel or appear inadequate or unworthy, esp. in some public setting: *to humiliate a sensitive person.* —**Ant. 1, 2.** proud. **3.** noble, exalted. **4.** insolent.

hum·ble·bee (hum′bəl bē′), *n. Chiefly Brit.* bumblebee. [late ME *humbul-be;* akin to D *hommel* drone, G *Hummelbiene* kind of wild bee, MLG *homelbe;* prob. akin to HUM]

hum′ble pie′, 1. *Obs.* a pie made of the numbles of deer or the like. **2. eat humble pie,** to be forced to apologize humbly; suffer humiliation. [earlier *an umble pie,* erroneous for *a numble pie;* see NUMBLES]

Hum·boldt (hum′bōlt; *Ger.* ho͝om′bôlt), *n.* **1. Frie·drich Hein·rich A·lex·an·der** (frē′drikh hīn′rikh ä′lek sän′dər), **Baron von** (fən), 1769–1859, German naturalist, writer, and statesman. **2.** his brother, **(Karl) Wil·helm** (kärl vil′helm), **Baron von,** 1767–1835, German philologist and diplomat.

Hum′boldt Cur′rent. See **Peru Current.**

hum·bug (hum′bug′), *n., v.,* **-bugged, -bug·ging,** *interj.* —*n.* **1.** a deluding trick; hoax, fraud, or deception. **2.** the quality of falseness or deception. **3.** a person who is not what he claims or pretends to be; impostor. **4.** something devoid of sense or meaning; nonsense. —*v.t.* **5.** to delude or deceive. —*v.i.* **6.** to practice humbug. —*interj.* **7.** nonsense! [?] —**hum′bug′ger,** *n.* —**Syn. 1.** pretense, sham. **3.** pretender, charlatan, swindler, quack. **5.** cheat, swindle, trick.

hum·ding·er (hum′ding′ər), *n. Slang.* a person or thing of remarkable excellence or effect. [HUM + DING + -ER[1]; from the fact that a missile *hums* through the air and *dings* when it strikes the mark]

hum·drum (hum′drum′), *adj.* **1.** lacking variety; dull; tedious. —*n.* **2.** humdrum character or routine; monotony. **3.** monotonous or tedious talk. **4.** a dull, boring person. [earlier *humtrum,* rhyming compound based on HUM] —**hum′drum′ness,** *n.*

Hume (hyo͞om), *n.* **David,** 1711–76, Scottish philosopher and historian. —**Hum′ism,** *n.*

hu·mec·tant (hyo͞o mek′tənt), *n.* **1.** a substance that absorbs or helps another substance retain moisture, as glycerol. —*adj.* **2.** moistening; diluting. **3.** of or pertaining to a humectant or humectants. [< L *hūmectant-* (s. of *hūmectāns,* prp. of *humectāre* to moisten) = *(h)ūmect(us)* moist, damp + *-ant-* -ANT]

hu·mer·al (hyo͞o′mər əl), *adj.* **1.** *Anat., Zool.* of or pertaining to the humerus or brachium. **2.** of or pertaining to the shoulder. [< L *(h)umer(us)* HUMERUS + -AL[1]]

hu·mer·us (hyo͞o′mər əs), *n., pl.* **-mer·i** (-mə rī′). *Anat., Zool.* **1.** the long bone in the arm of man extending from the shoulder to the elbow. **2.** brachium. **3.** a corresponding bone, structure, or region in the forelimbs of other animals or in the wings of birds or insects. [< L *(h)umerus* shoulder; c. Gk *ômos,* Goth *ams,* Skt *ámsas*]

hu·mic (hyo͞o′mik), *adj. Chem.* of or noting a substance, as an acid, obtained from humus. [< L *hum(us)* mould + -IC]

hu·mid (hyo͞o′mid *or, often,* yo͞o′-), *adj.* moist or damp with liquid or vapor: *humid air.* [< L *(h)ūmid(us)* = *(h)ūm(ēre)* (to) be moist + *-idus* -ID[4]] —**hu′mid·ly,** *adv.* —**hu′mid·ness,** *n.*

hu·mid·i·fi·er (hyo͞o mid′ə fī′ər *or, often,* yo͞o-), *n.* **1.** a device for increasing the amount of water vapor in the air of a room or building. **2.** any device for regulating the amount of water vapor in a specific container or area.

hu·mid·i·fy (hyo͞o mid′ə fī′ *or, often,* yo͞o-), *v.t.,* **-fied, -fy·ing.** to make humid. —**hu·mid′i·fi·ca′tion,** *n.*

hu·mid·i·ty (hyo͞o mid′i tē *or, often,* yo͞o-), *n.* **1.** humid condition; dampness. **2.** See **relative humidity.** [late ME *humydite* < L *(h)ūmiditās*]

hu·mi·dor (hyo͞o′mi dôr′), *n.* a container or storage room for cigars or other preparations of tobacco, fitted with means for keeping the tobacco suitably moist.

hu·mil·i·ate (hyo͞o mil′ē āt′ *or, often,* yo͞o-), *v.t.,* **-at·ed, -at·ing.** to lower the pride or self-respect of; cause a painful loss of dignity to; mortify; embarrass. [< LL *humiliāt(us)* (ptp. of *humiliāre* to humble). See HUMBLE, -ATE[1]] **—hu·mil′i·at′ing·ly,** *adv.* **—hu·mil′i·a′tor,** *n.* **—hu·mil·i·a·to·ry** (hyo͞o mil′ē ə tôr′ē, -tōr′ē *or, often,* yo͞o-), **hu·mil·i·a·tive** (hyo͞o mil′ē ā′tiv, -ē ə tiv *or, often,* yo͞o-), *adj.* **—Syn.** disgrace, shame; degrade, debase. See **humble.**

hu·mil·i·a·tion (hyo͞o mil′ē ā′shən *or, often,* yo͞o-), *n.* **1.** the act of humiliating. **2.** the state or feeling of being humiliated; mortification. [ME < LL *humiliātiōn-* (s. of *humiliātiō*)] **—Syn. 2.** degradation, dishonor. See **shame.**

hu·mil·i·ty (hyo͞o mil′i tē *or, often,* yo͞o-), *n.* the quality or condition of being humble; modest sense of one's own importance, rank, etc. [ME *humilite* < L *humilitās.* See HUMBLE, -TY[2]] **—Syn.** lowliness, meekness, submissiveness. **—Ant.** pride.

hum·ming (hum′ing), *adj.* **1.** making a droning sound; buzzing. **2.** very busy; briskly active: *a humming commercial center.* **—hum′ming·ly,** *adv.*

Hummingbird, *Archilochus colubris* (Length 3½ in.)

hum·ming·bird (hum′ing bûrd′), *n.* any of numerous very small, American birds of the family *Trochilidae,* characterized by the brilliant, iridescent plumage of the male, a slender bill, and narrow wings, the rapid beating of which produces a humming sound.

hum·mock (hum′ək), *n.* **1.** Also, **hammock.** an elevated, well-drained tract of land rising above the general level of a marshy region. **2.** a knoll or hillock. **3.** Also, **hommock.** a ridge in an ice field. [*humm-* (akin to HUMP) + -OCK] **—hum′mock·y,** *adj.*

hu·mon·gous (hyo͞o mung′gəs, -mong′- *or, often,* yo͞o-). *adj. Slang.* extraordinarily large. [perh. HU(GE) + MON(STROUS) + G(REAT) + (ENORM)OUS]

hu·mor (hyo͞o′mər *or, often,* yo͞o′-), *n.* **1.** a comic quality causing amusement: *the humor of a situation.* **2.** the faculty of perceiving, appreciating, or expressing what is amusing or comical. **3.** comical writing or talk in general. **4. humors,** amusing or comical features: *humors of the occasion.* **5.** mental disposition or temperament. **6.** a temporary mood or frame of mind: *He's in a bad humor today.* **7.** a capricious or freakish inclination; whim or caprice; odd trait. **8.** *Biol.* any animal or plant fluid, whether natural or morbid, such as the blood or lymph. **9.** *Old Physiol.* one of the four elemental fluids of the body, blood, phlegm, black bile, and yellow bile, regarded as determining, by their relative proportions, a person's physical and mental constitution. **10. out of humor,** displeased; dissatisfied; cross. **—***v.t.* **11.** to comply with the humor or mood of; indulge. **12.** to adapt or accommodate oneself to. Also, *esp. Brit.,* **humour.** [ME *(h)umour* < AF < L *(h)ūmōr-* (s. of *(h)ūmor*) moisture, fluid = *(h)ūm(ēre)* (to) be wet + *-or* -OR[1]] **—hu′mor·ful,** *adj.* **—hu′mor·less,** *adj.* **—hu′mor·less·ness,** *n.*
—Syn. 2. HUMOR, WIT are contrasting terms that agree in referring to an ability to perceive and express a sense of the clever or amusing. HUMOR consists principally in the recognition and expression of incongruities or peculiarities present in a situation or character. It is frequently used to illustrate some fundamental absurdity in human nature or conduct, and is generally thought of as more kindly than wit: *a genial and mellow type of humor; his biting wit.* WIT is a purely intellectual manifestation of cleverness and quickness of apprehension in discovering analogies between things really unlike, and expressing them in brief, diverting, and often sharp observations or remarks. **7.** fancy, vagary.

hu·mor·al (hyo͞o′mər əl *or, often,* yo͞o′-), *adj. Biol., Physiol.* of, pertaining to, or proceeding from a fluid of the body. [< ML *hūmōrāl(is)*]

hu·mor·esque (hyo͞o′mə resk′ *or, often,* yo͞o′-), *n.* a musical composition of humorous or capricious character. [modeled on G *Humoreske*] **—hu′mor·esque′ly,** *adv.*

hu·mor·ist (hyo͞o′mər ist *or, often,* yo͞o′-), *n.* **1.** a person who is skillful in the use of humor, as in writing, acting, etc. **2.** a person with an active sense of humor. [< F *humoriste*] **—hu′mor·is′tic, hu′mor·is′ti·cal,** *adj.*

hu·mor·ous[1] (hyo͞o′mər əs *or, often,* yo͞o′-), *adj.* **1.** characterized by humor; funny; comic: *the humorous side of life.* **2.** having or showing a sense of humor; droll; facetious. [HUMOR + -OUS] **—hu′mor·ous·ly,** *adv.* **—hu′mor·ous·ness,** *n.*
—Syn. 1. ludicrous, laughable. **2.** jocose, jocular, comic, comical. HUMOROUS, WITTY, FACETIOUS, WAGGISH imply that which arises from cleverness or a sense of fun. HUMOROUS implies a genuine sense of fun and the comic, impersonal or gently personal: *a humorous version of an incident; a humorous view of life.* WITTY implies quickness to perceive the amusing, striking, or unusual and to express it cleverly and entertainingly; it sometimes becomes rather sharp and unkind, particularly in quick repartee of a personal nature: *a witty companion; to be witty at someone else's expense.* FACETIOUS suggests a desire or attempt to be jocular or witty, often unsuccessful, inappropriate, or trifling: *a facetious treatment of a serious subject.* WAGGISH suggests the spirit of sly mischief and roguery of the constant joker with no harm intended: *a waggish fellow.*

hu·mor·ous[2] (hyo͞o′mər əs *or, often,* yo͞o′-), *adj.* **1.** *Old Physiol.* pertaining or due to the bodily humors. **2.** *Archaic.* moist; wet. [< LL *(h)ūmōrōsus*]

hu·mour (hyo͞o′mər), *n., v.t., Chiefly Brit.* humor. **—hu′mour·ful,** *adj.* **—hu′mour·less,** *adj.*

hump (hump), *n.* **1.** a rounded protuberance, esp. a fleshy protuberance on the back, as that due to abnormal curvature of the spine in man, or that normally present in certain animals such as the camel and bison. **2.** a low, rounded rise of ground; hummock. **3. the Hump,** (in World War II) the Himalayas. **4. over the hump,** past the most difficult, time-consuming, or dangerous part or period. **—***v.t.* **5.** to raise (the back) in a hump; hunch. **6.** *Informal.* to exert (oneself) in a great effort. **7.** *Slang (vulgar).* to copulate with (a female). **8.** *Australian Slang.* **a.** to place or bear on the back or shoulder. **b.** to carry. **—***v.i.* **9.** to rise in a hump. **10.** *Informal.* to exert oneself; hustle or hurry. [prob. abstracted from HUMPBACKED] **—hump′less,** *adj.*

hump·back (hump′bak′), *n.* **1.** a back that is humped. **2.** hunchback. **3.** a whale of the genus *Megaptera,* having a humplike back. [appar. back formation from HUMPBACKED]

hump·backed (hump′bakt′), *adj.* having a hump on the back. [b. *huckbacked* (*huck* haunch + BACKED) and *crump-backed* (OE *crump* crooked + BACKED)]

Hum·per·dinck (ho͝om′pər dingk′), *n.* **En·gel·bert** (eng′əl bert′), 1854–1921, German composer.

humph (humf), *interj.* (an expression resembling a snort, used to indicate disbelief, contempt, etc.).

Hum·phrey (hum′frē), *n.* **1.** (*Duke of Gloucester*) 1391–1447, English soldier and statesman (youngest son of Henry IV). **2. Hubert H(oratio),** 1911–78, U.S. political leader: vice president 1965–69.

hump·y (hum′pē), *adj.,* **hump·i·er, hump·i·est. 1.** full of humps. **2.** resembling a hump. **—hump′i·ness,** *n.*

hu·mus (hyo͞o′məs *or, often,* yo͞o′-), *n.* the dark organic material in soils, produced by the decomposition of vegetable or animal matter and essential to the fertility of the earth. [< L: earth, ground] **—hu′mus·like′,** *adj.*

Hun (hun), *n.* **1.** a member of a nomadic and warlike Asian people who controlled large parts of eastern and central Europe under Attila in the 5th century A.D. **2.** (*often l.c.*) a barbarous, destructive person. **3.** *Disparaging.* **a.** a German soldier in World War I or II. **b.** a German. [OE *Hūnas* (pl.); from a native name] **—Hun′like′,** *adj.*

Hu·nan (ho͞o′nän′), *n.* a province in S China. 37,810,000; 81,274 sq. mi. *Cap.:* Changsha.

hunch (hunch), *v.t.* **1.** to thrust out or up in a hump; arch: *to hunch one's back.* **2.** to shove, push, or jostle. **—***v.i.* **3.** to thrust oneself forward jerkily; lunge forward. **4.** to stand, sit, or walk in a bent posture. **—***n.* **5.** a hump. **6.** *Informal.* a premonition or suspicion. **7.** a push or shove. **8.** a lump or thick piece. [appar. var. of obs. *hinch* to push < ?]

hunch·back (hunch′bak′), *n.* a humpbacked person.

hunch·backed (hunch′bakt′), *adj.* humpbacked. [b. *huckbacked* and *bunchbacked*]

hund., **1.** hundred. **2.** hundreds.

hun·dred (hun′drid), *n., pl.* **-dreds,** (*as after a numeral*) **-dred,** *adj.* **—***n.* **1.** a cardinal number, ten times ten. **2.** a symbol for this number, as 100 or C. **3.** a set of this many persons or things: *a hundred of the men.* **4.** *Informal.* a one hundred dollar bill. **5.** (formerly) an administrative division of an English county. **6.** a similar division in present-day Delaware. **7. hundreds,** the numbers, degrees, or the like, between 100 and 199, or between 100 and 999, as in referring to numbered streets, an amount of money, or degrees of temperature. **8.** Also called **hun′dred's place′.** *Math.* **a.** (in a mixed number) the position of the third digit to the left of the decimal point. **b.** (in a whole number) the position of the third digit from the right. **—***adj.* **9.** amounting to one hundred in number. [ME, OE (c. OFris *hunderd,* OS *hunderod,* Icel *hundrath,* D *honderd,* G *hundert*) = *hund* 100 (c. Goth *hund;* akin to L *cent(um),* Gk *(he)kat(ón),* Avestan *sat(em),* Skt *śatám,* OSlav *seto,* Russ *sto*) + *-red* tale, count, akin to Goth *rathjan* to reckon]

hun·dred·fold (hun′drid fōld′), *adj.* **1.** comprising a hundred parts or members. **2.** a hundred times as great or as much. **—***adv.* **3.** in a hundredfold measure. [ME *hundredfald*]

hun·dredth (hun′dridth, -dritth), *adj.* **1.** next after the ninety-ninth; being the ordinal number for 100. **2.** being one of 100 equal parts. **—***n.* **3.** a hundredth part, esp. of one (1/100). **4.** the hundredth member of a series. **5.** Also called **hun′dredth's place′.** *Math.* (in decimal notation) the position of the second digit to the right of the decimal point. [ME *hundreth*]

hun·dred·weight (hun′drid wāt′), *n., pl.* **-weights,** (*as after a numeral*) **-weight.** a unit of avoirdupois weight commonly equivalent to 100 pounds in the U.S. and 112 pounds in England. *Abbr.:* cwt

Hun′dred Years′′ War′, the series of wars between England and France 1337–1453.

Hun·e·ker (hun′ə kər), *n.* **James (Gib·bons)** (gib′ənz), 1860–1921, U.S. music critic and writer.

hung (hung), *v.* **1.** pt. and pp. of **hang. 2. hung over,** *Slang.* suffering the effects of a hangover. **3. hung up,** *Slang.* **a.** detained on account of a difficulty. **b.** *Baseball.* (of a base runner) trapped between bases and in danger of being tagged out. **4. hung up on, a.** *Slang.* to be obsessively interested in. **b.** to be infatuated with.

Hung, Hungarian (def. 3).

Hung., **1.** Hungarian (def. 3). **2.** Hungary.

Hun·gar·i·an (hung gâr′ē ən), *adj.* **1.** of, pertaining to, or characteristic of Hungary, its people, or their language. **—***n.* **2.** a native or inhabitant of Hungary. Cf. **Magyar. 3.** Also called **Magyar.** the Uralic language of Hungary. *Abbr.:* Hung, Hung.

Hungar′ian gou′lash, goulash.

Hun·ga·ry (hung′gə rē), *n.* a republic in central Europe. 10,672,000; 35,926 sq. mi. *Cap.:* Budapest. Hungarian, **Magyarország.**

hun·ger (hung′gər), *n.* **1.** a compelling need or desire for food. **2.** the painful sensation or state of weakness caused by need of food: *to collapse from hunger.* **3.** a strong or compelling desire or craving: *hunger for power.* **—***v.i.* **4.** to feel hunger; be hungry. **5.** to have a strong desire. **—***v.t.* **6.** to subject to hunger; starve. [ME, OE *hungor;* c. G *Hunger*] **—hun′ger·less,** *adj.*

hun′ger strike′, a deliberate refusal to eat, undertaken in protest against imprisonment, objectionable conditions, etc. **—hun′ger strik′er.**

Hung·nam (ho͝ong′näm′), *n.* a seaport in W North Korea. 150,000.

hun·gry (hung′grē), *adj.,* **-gri·er, -gri·est. 1.** having a desire or need for food; feeling hunger. **2.** indicating, characteristic of, or characterized by hunger: *a lean and hungry look.* **3.** strongly or eagerly desirous. **4.** lacking needful or desirable elements; not fertile; poor. **5.** marked

by a scarcity of food: *hungry times.* [ME, OE *hungrig*] —**hun′gri·ly, hun′ger·ing·ly,** *adv.* —**hun′gri·ness,** *n.*
—**Syn. 1.** ravenous, starving. HUNGRY, FAMISHED, STARVED describe a condition resulting from a lack of food. HUNGRY is a general word, expressing various degrees of eagerness or craving for food: *hungry between meals; desperately hungry after a long fast.* FAMISHED denotes the condition of a person reduced to actual suffering from want of food but sometimes is used lightly or in an exaggerated statement: *famished after being lost in a wilderness; simply famished (hungry).* STARVED denotes a condition resulting from long-continued lack or insufficiency of food, and implies enfeeblement, emaciation, or death (originally death from any cause, but now death from lack of food): *He looks thin and starved. Thousands had starved (to death).* It is also used exaggeratingly: *I only had a sandwich for lunch, so I'm starved (hungry).* —**Ant. 1.** sated, satiated, surfeited.

Hung′tow Is′land (hŏŏng′tō′), an island off the SE coast of Taiwan. 8 mi. long.

hung-up (hung′up′), *adj. Slang.* **1.** beset with serious psychological problems. **2.** worried; anxious; concerned.

hunk (hungk), *n. Informal.* a large piece or lump; chunk. [< Flem *hunke*]

hun·ker (hung′kər). *Scot.* —*v.i.* **1.** to squat on one's heels (often fol. by *down*). —*n.* **2. hunkers,** buttocks. **3. on one's hunkers,** squatting on one's heels. [appar. *hunk* (? nasalized var. of *huck* haunch; akin to Icel *hūka* to crouch) + -ER[6]]

hunks (hungks), *n.* (*construed as sing. or pl.*) **1.** a crabbed, disagreeable person. **2.** a covetous, sordid man; miser. [?]

hunk·y (hung′kē), *n., pl.* **hunk·ies.** *U.S. Disparaging.* **1.** (*sometimes cap.*) an unskilled or semiskilled workman of foreign birth, esp. a Hungarian. **2.** honky. [? HUN(GARIAN) + (DON)KEY]

hunk·y-do·ry (hung′kē dōr′ē, -dôr′ē), *adj. U.S. Slang.* about as well as one could wish or expect; fine; O.K. Also, **hunk′y.** [?]

Hun·nish (hun′ish), *adj.* **1.** of or pertaining to the Huns. **2.** (*sometimes l.c.*) barbarous; destructive. —**Hun′nish·ness,** *n.*

hunt (hunt), *v.t.* **1.** to chase or search for (game or other wild animals) for the purpose of catching or killing. **2.** to pursue with force, hostility, etc. (often fol. by *down*): *to hunt down a dangerous criminal.* **3.** to search for; seek; endeavor to obtain or find (often fol. by *up* or *out*): *I'll hunt up another tennis racket.* **4.** to search (a place) thoroughly. **5.** to scour (an area) in pursuit of game. **6.** to use or direct (a horse, hound, etc.) in chasing game. **7.** *Change Ringing.* to alter the place of (a bell) in a hunt. —*v.i.* **8.** to engage in the pursuit of game. **9.** to make a search or quest. **10.** *Change Ringing.* to alter the place of a bell in its set according to certain rules. —*n.* **11.** an act of hunting game or other wild animals. **12.** a search; a seeking or endeavor to find. **13.** a pursuit. **14.** an association of huntsmen. **15.** an area hunted over. **16.** *Change Ringing.* a regularly varying order of permutations in the ringing of a group of from five to twelve bells. [ME *hunte(n),* OE *huntian* < *hunta* hunter, akin to *hentan* to pursue] —**hunt′a·ble,** *adj.* —**hunt′ed·ly,** *adv.* —**Syn. 1, 2.** pursue, track.

Hunt (hunt), *n.* **1. (James Henry) Leigh** (lē), 1784–1859, English essayist, poet, and editor. **2. Richard Morris,** 1828–95, U.S. architect. **3. (William) Hol·man** (hōl′mən), 1827–1910, English painter.

hunt·er (hun′tər), *n.* **1.** a person who hunts game or other wild animals. **2.** a person who searches for or seeks something: *a treasure hunter.* **3.** a horse specially trained for use on a hunt. **4.** a dog trained to hunt game. **5.** (*cap.*) *Astron.* the constellation Orion. [ME *huntere*]

hunt·ing (hun′ting), *n.* **1.** the act of a person or thing that hunts. **2.** *Elect.* the periodic oscillating of a rotating electromechanical system about a mean space position, as in a synchronous motor. —*adj.* **3.** of, for, engaged in, or used while hunting: *a hunting cap.* [ME *huntung,* OE (n.)]

hunt′ing box′, *Chiefly Brit.* a lodge or house near or in a hunting area for use during the hunting season.

Hun·ting·don·shire (hun′ting dən shēr′, -shər), *n.* a county in E England. 79,879 (1961); 366 sq. mi. *Co. seat:* Huntingdon. Also called **Hun′ting·don, Hunts** (hunts).

hunt′ing horn′, *Music.* the earliest form of the modern horn, consisting of a conical tube coiled in a circle for carrying over the shoulder, and having a flaring bell and a mouthpiece like that of a trumpet.

hunt′ing knife′, a large, sharp knife used to skin and cut up game.

Hun·ting·ton (hun′ting tən), *n.* **1. Samuel,** 1731–96, U.S. statesman: governor of Connecticut 1786–96. **2.** a city in W West Virginia, on the Ohio River. 74,315 (1970).

Hun′tington Beach′, a city in SW California, SE of Los Angeles. 115,960 (1970).

Hun′tington Park′, a city in SW California, near Los Angeles. 33,744 (1970).

Hun′tington Sta′tion, a town on W Long Island, in SE New York. 28,817 (1970).

hunt·ress (hun′tris), *n.* **1.** a woman who hunts. **2.** a mare used as a hunting horse. [ME *hunteresse*]

hunts·man (hunts′mən), *n., pl.* **-men. 1.** the member of a hunt staff who manages the hounds during the hunt. **2.** a hunter.

hunt's-up (hunts′up′), *n.* (formerly) a call played on a hunting horn to awaken the hunters. [from phrase (*the*) *hunt is up*]

Hunts·ville (hunts′vil), *n.* a city in N Alabama: rocket and missile center. 137,802 (1970).

Hu·nya·di (hŏŏ′nyo dē), *n.* **Já·nos** (yä′nôsh), 1387?–1456, Hungarian soldier and national hero. Also, **Hu′nya·dy.**

Hu·peh (hōō′pā′; *Chin.* hōō′bā′), *n.* a province in central China. 30,790,000 (est. 1957); 72,394 sq. mi. *Cap.:* Wuchang. Also, **Hu′pei′.**

hur·dle (hûr′dəl), *n., v.,* **-dled, -dling.** —*n.* **1.** a portable barrier over which a contestant must leap in certain running races. **2. hurdles,** (*construed as sing.*) a race in which contestants must leap such barriers, which are either 3 feet 6 inches **(high hurdles)** or 2 feet 6 inches **(low hurdles)** in height. **3.** a barrier, as a hedge or low wall, over which horses must jump in certain types of turf races, as a steeplechase. **4.** a difficult problem to be overcome; obstacle. **5.** *Chiefly Brit.* a movable rectangular frame of interlaced twigs, crossed bars, or the like, as for a temporary fence. **6.** a frame or sledge on which criminals were formerly drawn to the place of execution. —*v.t.* **7.** to leap over (a hurdle, barrier, fence, etc.), as in a race. **8.** to master (a difficulty, problem, etc.); overcome. **9.** to construct with hurdles; enclose with hurdles. —*v.i.* **10.** to leap over a hurdle or other barrier. [ME *hirdel, hurdel,* OE *hyrdel* = *hȳrd-* (c. G *Hürde* hurdle; akin to L *crātis* hurdle, wickerwork, Gk *kýrtos* basket, cage, Skt *kṛt* spin) + *-el* -LE] —**hur′dler,** *n.*

Hurdy-gurdy (def. 2)

hur·dy-gur·dy (hûr′dē gûr′dē, -gûr′-), *n., pl.* **-gur·dies. 1.** a barrel organ or similar instrument played by turning a crank. **2.** a lute- or guitar-shaped stringed musical instrument sounded by the revolution, against the strings, of a rosined wheel turned by a crank. [var. of Scot *hirdy-girdy* uproar, influenced by HURLY-BURLY] —**hur′dy-gur′dist, hur′dy-gur′dy·ist,** *n.*

hurl (hûrl), *v.t.* **1.** to throw or fling with great force. **2.** to throw or cast down. **3.** to utter with vehemence. —*v.i.* **4.** to throw a missile. **5.** *Baseball.* to pitch a ball. —*n.* **6.** a forcible or violent throw; fling. [ME *hurle* = *hur-* (? akin to HURRY) + *-le* -LE; akin to LG *hurreln* to toss, Fris *hurreln* to roar (said of the wind), dial. G *hurlen* to roll, rumble (said of thunder)] —**hurl′er,** *n.* —**Syn. 1.** cast, pitch.

hurl·ing (hûr′ling), *n.* **1.** the act of throwing or casting, esp. with great force or strength. **2.** a traditionally Irish game resembling field hockey.

hurl·y (hûr′lē), *n., pl.* **hurl·ies.** commotion; hurly-burly.

hurl·y-burl·y (hûr′lē bûr′lē, -bûr′-), *n., pl.* **-burl·ies,** *adj.* —*n.* **1.** commotion; uproar; tumult. —*adj.* **2.** full of commotion; tumultuous. [alter. of *hurling (and) burling,* phrase based on HURLING in its (now obs.) sense of uproar]

Hu·ron (hyŏŏr′ən, -on), *n.* **1.** a member of an Indian tribe of the Iroquoian family, living west of Lake Huron. **2.** the Iroquoian language of the Huron Indians. **3. Lake,** a lake between the U.S. and Canada: second largest of the Great Lakes. 23,010 sq. mi.

hur·rah (hə rä′, -rô′), *interj.* **1.** (used as an exclamation of joy, exultation, appreciation, encouragement, or the like.) —*v.i.* **2.** to shout "hurrah." —*v.t.* **3.** to cheer with "hurrahs." —*n.* **4.** an exclamation of "hurrah." **5.** hubbub; commotion; fanfare. Also, **hur·ray** (hə rā′), **hoorah, hooray.** [< G *hurra;* r. HUZZAH]

hur·ri·cane (hûr′ə kān′, hur′- *or, esp. Brit.,* -kən), *n.* **1.** a violent, tropical, cyclonic storm of the western North Atlantic, having wind speeds of or in excess of 73 miles per hour. **2.** anything suggesting a violent storm. [< Sp *huracán* < Taino *hurakán*]

hur′ricane deck′, a covered deck at the top of a passenger steamer, esp. a river boat.

hur·ri·cane-force wind (hûr′ə kān′fōrs′ wind′, -fôrs′, hur′- *or, esp. Brit.,* -kən-), a wind, not necessarily a hurricane, of Beaufort scale numbers 12–17, or having a speed of at least 73 miles per hour: the strongest of the winds.

hur′ricane lamp′, a candlestick or kerosene or oil lantern protected against draughts by a glass chimney.

hur·ried (hûr′ēd, hur′-), *adj.* **1.** moving or working rapidly, esp. forced or required to hurry. **2.** characterized by or done with hurry; hasty. —**hur′ried·ly,** *adv.* —**hur′ried·ness,** *n.*

hur·ry (hûr′ē, hur′ē), *v.,* **-ried, -ry·ing,** *n., pl.* **-ries.** —*v.i.* **1.** to move, proceed, or act with haste (often fol. by *up*): *Hurry, or we'll be late. Hurry up, it's starting to rain.* —*v.t.* **2.** to drive, carry, or cause to move or perform with speed. **3.** to hasten; urge forward: *to hurry a lazy horse; to hurry mail delivery.* **4.** to impel or perform with undue haste: *to hurry someone into a decision; to hurry a ceremony.* —*n.* **5.** a state of urgency or eagerness. **6.** hurried movement or action; haste. [ME *horye(n),* perh. of imit. orig.; c. L *currere* to run (see also CURRENT, SCURRY, HURL)] —**hur′ry·ing·ly,** *adv.* —**Syn. 1–5.** See **rush**[1]. **2.** hasten. **6.** expedition, dispatch; speed, quickness, celerity. —**Ant. 3.** delay, slow.

hur·ry-scur·ry (hûr′ē skûr′ē, hur′ē skur′ē), *n., adv., adj., v.,* **-scur·ried, -scur·ry·ing.** —*n.* **1.** headlong, disorderly haste; hurry and confusion. —*adv.* **2.** with hurrying and scurrying; confusedly. —*adj.* **3.** characterized by headlong, disorderly flight or haste. —*v.i.* **4.** to go hurry-scurry.

hur·ry-skur·ry (hûr′ē skûr′ē, hur′ē skur′ē), *n., adv., adj., v.i.,* **-skur·ried, -skur·ry·ing.** hurry-scurry.

Hurst (hûrst), *n.* a city in N Texas, near Fort Worth. 27,215 (1970).

hurt (hûrt), *v.,* **hurt, hurt·ing,** *n., adj.* —*v.t.* **1.** to cause bodily injury to; injure. **2.** to cause bodily pain to or in: *The wound still hurts him.* **3.** to damage or injure; affect adversely; harm: *to hurt one's reputation.* **4.** to cause mental pain to; offend or grieve: *She hurt his feelings.* —*v.i.* **5.** to feel or suffer bodily or mental pain: *My finger still hurts.* **6.** to cause injury, damage, or pain. —*n.* **7.** a blow that inflicts a wound; cause of injury. **8.** injury, damage, or pain. **9.** the cause of mental pain or offense, as an insult. —*adj.* **10.** physically injured. **11.** offended; suffering, as in mind: *hurt pride.* **12.** damaged: *hurt merchandise.* [ME *hurte(n)* (to) strike, hit < OF *hurte(r)* (cf. F *heurter*) ? < Gmc **hurt-* to butt; cf. MHG *hurt* an impact, Icel *hrūtr* ram] —**hurt′er,** *n.* —**Syn. 3.** mar, impair. **4.** afflict, wound. **5.** ache. **7.** See **injury. 9.** cut, slight.

hurt·ful (hûrt′fəl), *adj.* causing hurt or injury; injurious; harmful. —**hurt′ful·ly,** *adv.* —**hurt′ful·ness,** *n.*

hur·tle (hûr′təl), *v.,* **-tled, -tling,** *n.* —*v.i.* **1.** to rush violently; move with great speed: *The car hurtled down the highway.* **2.** to rush noisily or resoundingly. **3.** *Rare.* to strike together or against something; collide. —*v.t.* **4.** to drive violently; fling; dash. **5.** *Rare.* to collide with. —*n.* **6.** clash; collision. [ME = *hurt(en)* (see HURT) + *-le* -LE]

hur·tle·ber·ry (hûr′tᵊl ber′ē), *n., pl.* **-ries.** whortleberry.
Hus (hus; *Ger., Czech.* ho͝os), *n.* **Jan** (jan; *Ger., Czech.* yän). See **Huss, John.**
hus·band (huz′bənd), *n.* **1.** a married man, esp. considered in relation to his wife. **2.** a prudent or frugal manager. **3.** *Archaic.* a manager. **—*v.t.*** **4.** to manage, esp. with prudent economy. **5.** to use frugally; conserve: *to husband one's resources.* **6.** *Archaic.* **a.** to be or become a husband to. **b.** to find a husband for. **7.** *Archaic.* to till. [ME *husband(e),* OE *hūsbonda* master of the house < Scand; cf. Icel *hūsbōndi* = *hūs* HOUSE + *bōndi* (*bō-,* var. of *bū-* dwell (see BOOR) + *-ndi* prp. suffix] **—hus′band·er,** *n.* **—hus′band·less,** *adj.*
hus·band·man (huz′bənd mən), *n., pl.* **-men.** a farmer. [ME *husbondeman*]
hus·band·ry (huz′bən drē), *n.* **1.** the cultivation and production of crops and animals; agriculture; farming. **2.** the science of raising crops or food animals. **3.** careful or thrifty management. **4.** the management of domestic affairs or of resources generally. [ME *housebondrie*]
Hu·sein ibn-A·li (ho͞o sīn′ ib′ən ä′lē, -ä lē′, ho͞o sān′), 1856–1931, 1st king of Hejaz 1916–24.
hush (hush), *interj.* **1.** (used as a command to be silent or quiet.) **—*v.i.*** **2.** to become or be silent or quiet. **—*v.t.*** **3.** to make silent; silence. **4.** to suppress mention of; keep concealed (often fol. by *up*): *to hush up a scandal.* **5.** to calm, quiet, or allay: *to hush someone's fears.* **—*n.*** **6.** silence or quiet, esp. after noise. **—*adj.*** **7.** *Archaic.* silent; quiet. [appar. back formation from *husht* WHIST[1] (ME *huissht*), the *-t* being taken for ptp. suffix] **—hush·ed·ly** (hush′id lē, husht′lē), *adv.* **—hush′ful,** *adj.* **—hush′ful·ly,** *adv.*
hush-hush (hush′hush′), *adj.* *Informal.* highly secret or confidential: *a hush-hush report.* [redupl. based on HUSH]
Hu Shih (ho͞o′ shœ′), 1891–1962, Chinese scholar and diplomat.
hush′ mon′ey, a bribe to keep someone silent about something, as a scandal, incriminating fact, etc.
hush′ pup′py, *Chiefly Southern U.S.* a small, deep-fried, cornmeal cake. [so called from the fact that it was fed to dogs]
husk (husk), *n.* **1.** the dry external covering of certain fruits or seeds, esp. of an ear of corn. **2.** the enveloping or outer part of anything, esp. when dry or worthless. **—*v.t.*** **3.** to remove the husk from. [ME *huske* = *hus-* (akin to OE *hosu* pod, husk) + *-ke,* weak var. of -OCK] **—husk′er,** *n.* **—husk′like′,** *adj.*
husk′ing bee′, *U.S.* a gathering of farm families to husk corn, usually as part of a celebration or party. Also called **husk′ing.**
husk′ toma′to. See **ground cherry** (def. 1).
husk·y[1] (hus′kē), *adj.,* **husk·i·er, husk·i·est. 1.** burly; big and strong. **2.** (of the voice) having a semi-whispered vocal tone; somewhat hoarse. **3.** like, covered with, or full of husks. [HUSK + -Y[1]] **—husk′i·ly,** *adv.* **—husk′i·ness,** *n.*
husk·y[2] (hus′kē), *n., pl.* **husk·ies.** *Informal.* a big, strong person. [HUSK + -Y[2]]
husk·y[3] (hus′kē), *n., pl.* **husk·ies,** *adj.* (*sometimes cap.*) **—*n.*** **1.** See **Eskimo dog. 2.** *Chiefly Canadian.* **a.** an Eskimo. **b.** any Eskimo-Aleut language or dialect. **—*adj.*** **3.** *Chiefly Canadian.* Eskimo. [? var. of ESKI(MO)]
Huss (hus; *Ger., Czech.* ho͝os), *n.* **John,** 1369?–1415, Czech religious reformer and martyr. Also, **Hus. —Huss′ism,** *n.*
hus·sar (ho͞o zär′), *n.* **1.** (originally) one of a body of Hungarian light cavalry formed during the 15th century. **2.** one of a class of similar troops, usually with striking or flamboyant uniforms, in European armies. [< Hung *huszár,* orig. freebooter < Old Serbian *husar,* var. of *kursar* < It *corsaro* CORSAIR]
Hus·sein I (ho͞o sān′), born 1935, king of Jordan since 1953.
Hus·serl (ho͝os′ərl), *n.* **Ed·mund (Gus·tav Al·brecht)** (et′mo͝ont go͝os′täf äl′brekht), 1859–1938, German philosopher, born in Austria: founder of phenomenology.
Huss·ite (hus′īt), *n.* **1.** a member of the religious reformist and nationalistic movement initiated by John Huss in Bohemia in the late 14th century. **—*adj.*** **2.** of or pertaining to John Huss or the Hussites. **—Huss′it·ism,** *n.*
hus·sy (hus′ē, huz′ē), *n., pl.* **-sies. 1.** a bold or lewd woman. **2.** a mischievous or ill-behaved girl. [earlier *hussive* HOUSEWIFE]
hus·tings (hus′tingz), *n.* (*construed as sing. or pl.*) **1.** (before 1872) a temporary platform on which candidates for the British Parliament stood to electioneer. **2.** *Chiefly Brit.* **a.** any electioneering platform. **b.** election proceedings. **3.** Also called **hus′tings court′.** a local court in certain parts of Virginia. [ME, OE < ODan *hūs-thing* house meeting]
hus·tle (hus′əl), *v.,* **-tled, -tling,** *n.* **—*v.i.*** **1.** to proceed or work rapidly or energetically. **2.** to push or force one's way; jostle or shove. **3.** *Informal.* to be aggressive, esp. in business or other financial dealings. **4.** *Slang.* **a.** to earn one's living by illicit or unethical means. **b.** (of a prostitute) to solicit clients. **—*v.t.*** **5.** to jostle, push, or shove roughly. **6.** to force to leave, esp. roughly or hurriedly: *They hustled him out of the bar.* **7.** to urge, prod, or speed: *He hustled the suspect away.* **8.** *Informal.* to pressure or coerce (a person) to buy or do something. **9.** *Informal.* to sell (something) by high-pressure tactics: *to hustle souvenirs.* **10.** *Slang.* to obtain (money or the like) by aggressive or illicit means. **—*n.*** **11.** energetic activity, as in work. **12.** discourteous shoving or jostling. **13.** a fast, lively, popular ballroom dance evolving from Latin American, swing, rock, and disco dance styles, with a strong basic rhythm and simple step pattern augmented by strenuous turns, breaks, etc. [< D *hussel(en),* var. of *hutselen* = *huts(en)* (to) shake, jog + *-el-* -LE]
hus·tler (hus′lər), *n.* **1.** *Informal.* an enterprising person determined to succeed; go-getter. **2.** *Slang.* a person who employs fraudulent or unscrupulous methods to obtain money; swindler. **3.** *Slang.* a prostitute; streetwalker.
hut (hut), *n., v.,* **hut·ted, hut·ting. —*n.*** **1.** a small or humble dwelling, esp. one made of logs, grass, etc. **2.** a simple roofed shelter, often with one or two sides left open. **3.** *Mil.* a wooden or metal structure for the temporary housing of troops. **—*v.t.*** **4.** to furnish with a hut as temporary housing; billet. **—*v.i.*** **5.** to lodge or take shelter in a hut. [< F *hutte* < MHG *hütte,* OHG *hutt(e)a* < WGmc **hudjā;* akin to HIDE[1]] **—hut′like′,** *adj.* **—Syn. 1.** See **cottage.**
hutch (huch), *n.* **1.** a pen or enclosed coop for small animals: *a rabbit hutch.* **2.** a hut, cabin, or a small shack; shanty. **3.** a chest, bin, etc., for storage. **4.** a chestlike cabinet having doors or drawers and sometimes open shelves. **5.** a baker's kneading trough. **—*v.t.*** **6.** *Rare.* to put away in or as in a hutch; hoard. [ME *hucche,* var. of *whucce,* OE *hwicce* chest]
Hutch·ins (huch′inz), *n.* **Robert Maynard,** 1899–1977, U.S. educator.
Hutch·in·son (huch′in sən), *n.* **1. Anne Mar·bur·y** (mär′bə rē), 1591–1643, American religious liberal, born in England: banished from Massachusetts 1637. **2. Thomas,** 1711–80, American colonial administrator: royal governor of Massachusetts 1769–74; in exile after 1774. **3.** a city in central Kansas, on the Arkansas River. 36,885 (1970).
hut·ment (hut′mənt), *n.* an encampment of huts.
Hux·ley (huks′lē), *n.* **1. Al·dous (Leonard)** (ôl′dəs), 1894–1963, English novelist, essayist, and critic. **2. Sir Julian Sor·ell** (sor′əl), 1887–1975, English biologist and writer (brother of Aldous). **3. Thomas Henry,** 1825–95, English biologist and writer (grandfather of Aldous and Julian).
Huy·gens (hī′gənz, hoi′-; *Du.* hoi′gens), *n.* **Chris·tian** (kris′chən; *Du.* kris′tē än′), 1629–95, Dutch mathematician, physicist, and astronomer. Also, **Huy′ghens.**
Huys·mans (wēs mäns′), *n.* **Jo·ris Karl** (zhō rēs′ kärl), (pen name of *Charles Marie Georges Huysmans*), 1848–1907, French novelist.
huz·zah (hə zä′), *interj.* **1.** (used as an exclamation of joy, applause, appreciation, etc.) hurrah! **—*n.*** **2.** the exclamation "huzzah." **—*v.i.*** **3.** to shout "huzzah." **—*v.t.*** **4.** to salute with huzzahs: *Crowds huzzahed the triumphant hero.* [var. of earlier *hussa, hissa* sailors' cry; see HOISE]
H.V., high voltage. Also, **h.v.**
hwan (hwän, wän), *n., pl.* **hwan.** the former paper money and monetary unit of South Korea. [< Korean]
Hwang Hai (hwäng′ hī′), Chinese name of the **Yellow Sea.**
Hwang Ho (hwäng′ hō′; *Chin.* hwäng′ hu′), a river flowing from W China into the Gulf of Pohai. 2800 mi. long. Also, **Hoangho.** Also called **Yellow River.**
hy·a·cinth (hī′ə sinth), *n.* **1.** any bulbous, liliaceous plant of the genus *Hyacinthus,* esp. *H. orientalis,* cultivated for its spikes of fragrant, white or colored, bell-shaped flowers. **2.** the flower or a bulb of such a plant. **3.** a plant fabled to have sprung from the blood of Hyacinthus and variously identified as iris, gladiolus, larkspur, etc. **4.** a reddish-orange zircon. **5.** a gem of the ancients, held to be the amethyst or sapphire. Also called **jacinth** (for defs. 4, 5). [< L *hyacinth(us)* < Gk *hyákinthos* blue larkspur, also, a gem of blue color; r. JACINTH] **—hy·a·cin·thine** (hī′ə-sin′thin, thīn), *adj.*

Hyacinth, *Hyacinthus orientalis*

Hy·a·cin·thus (hī′ə sin′thəs), *n.* *Class. Myth.* a beautiful youth loved by Apollo, who accidentally killed him with a discus: from his blood sprang a flower whose petals are marked with the letters AI AI (alas!).
Hy·a·des (hī′ə dēz′), *n.pl.* **1.** *Astron.* a group of stars in the constellation Taurus, supposed by the ancients to indicate the approach of rain when they rose with the sun. **2.** *Class. Myth.* a group of nymphs who nurtured the infant Dionysus and were placed among the stars as a reward. Also, **Hy·ads** (hī′adz). [< L < Gk = *hý(ein)* (to) rain + *-ades,* pl. of *-as* -AD[1]]
hy·ae·na (hī ē′nə), *n.* hyena. **—hy·ae′nic,** *adj.*
hyal-, var. of **hyalo-** before a vowel: *hyalite.*
hy·a·line (*n.* hī′ə lēn′, -lin; *adj.* hī′ə lin, -līn′), *n.* **1.** Also, **hy·a·lin** (hī′ə lin). *Biochem.* a horny substance found in hydatid cysts, closely resembling chitin. **2.** something glassy or transparent. **—*adj.*** **3.** glassy, crystalline, or transparent. **4.** of or pertaining to glass. **5.** amorphous; not crystalline. [< LL *hyalin(us)* < Gk *hyálinos* of glass]
hy′aline cart′ilage, *Anat.* the typical, translucent form of cartilage, containing little fibrous tissue.
hy′aline mem′brane disease′, *Pathol.* a frequently fatal disease of the lungs, occurring in the newborn, esp. premature infant, and characterized by a fibrinous membrane lining the air sacs, and associated with rapid, difficult respiration.
hy·a·lite (hī′ə līt′), *n.* a colorless variety of opal.
hyalo-, a learned borrowing from Greek meaning "glass," used in the formation of compound words: *hyaloplasm.* Also, *esp. before a vowel,* **hyal-.** [< Gk, comb. form of *hýalos* glass]
hy·a·loid (hī′ə loid′), *n.* **1.** See **hyaloid membrane. —*adj.*** **2.** glassy; hyaline. [< Gk *hyaloeid(ēs)* like glass]
hy′aloid mem′brane, *Anat.* the delicate, pellucid, and nearly structureless membrane enclosing the vitreous humor of the eye.
hy·al·o·plasm (hī al′ə plaz′əm, hī′ə lō-), *n.* *Biol.* the clear portion of the protoplasm of a cell, as distinguished from the granular and reticular portions. **—hy·al′o·plas′mic,** *adj.*
hy′aluron′ic ac′id, *Biochem.* a mucopolysaccharide found in all tissue, and serving as a viscous agent in the ground substance of tissues and as a lubricant in joints. [HYAL- + Gk *oûron* urine + -IC] **—hy·a·lu·ron·ic** (hī′ə-lo͞o ron′ik), *adj.*
hy·a·lu·ron·i·dase (hī′ə lo͞o ron′i dās′, -dāz′), *n.* **1.** *Biochem.* a mucolytic enzyme that decreases the viscosity of the intercellular matrix by breaking down hyaluronic acid. **2.** *Pharm.* a commercial form of this substance, used chiefly to promote the diffusion of intradermally injected drugs. [HYAL- + Gk *oûron* urine + -ID[3] + -ASE]
hy·brid (hī′brid), *n.* **1.** the offspring of two animals or plants of different races, breeds, varieties, species, or genera. **2.** a person or group of persons produced by the interaction or crossbreeding of two unlike cultures, traditions, etc. **3.** anything derived from heterogeneous sources. **—*adj.*** **4.** bred from two distinct races, breeds, varieties, species, or genera. **5.** composite; formed or composed of heterogeneous elements. **6.** composed of elements originally drawn from different languages, as a word. [< L *hybrid(a),* var. of *hibrida* offspring of a tame sow and wild boar, mongrel] **—hy′brid·ism,** *n.*
—Syn. 4. HYBRID, MONGREL refer to animals or plants of mixed origin. HYBRID is the scientific term: *hybrid corn; a hybrid variety of sheep.* MONGREL, used originally of dogs, is

now extended to other animals and to plants; it is usually depreciatory, denoting mixed, nondescript, or degenerate breed or character: *a mongrel pup.* **—Ant. 4.** purebred, thoroughbred.

hy·brid·ise (hī′bri dīz′), *v.t., v.i.,* **-ised, -is·ing.** *Chiefly Brit.* hybridize. **—hy′brid·is′a·ble,** *adj.* **—hy′brid·i·sa′tion,** *n.* **—hy′brid·is′er,** *n.*

hy·brid·ize (hī′bri dīz′), *v.,* **-ized, -iz·ing.** **—***v.t.* **1.** to cause to produce hybrids; cross. **2.** to form in a hybrid manner. **—***v.i.* **3.** to produce hybrids. **—hy′brid·iz′a·ble,** *adj.* **—hy′brid·i·za′tion,** *n.* **—hy′brid·iz′er,** *n.*

hy′brid perpet′ual, a cultivated, continuously blooming rose noted for its vigorous growth.

hy′brid vig′or, heterosis.

hy·bris (hī′bris), *n.* hubris. **—hy·bris′tic,** *adj.*

hyd., 1. hydraulics. **2.** hydrostatics.

hy·da·tid (hī′də tid), *Pathol.* **—***n.* **1.** a cyst with watery contents that is produced in man and animals by a tapeworm in the larval state. **2.** the encysted larva of a tapeworm; cysticercus. **—***adj.* **3.** Also, **hy′da·tid′i·nous** containing or affected by hydatids. [< Gk *hydatid-* (s. of *hydatís*) watery vesicle]

Hyde (hīd), *n.* **1. Douglas,** 1860–1949, Irish author and statesman: president of Eire 1938–45. **2. Edward.** See **Clarendon, Edward Hyde.**

Hyde′ Park′, 1. a public park in London, England. **2.** a village in SE New York, on the Hudson: site of the estate and burial place of Franklin D. Roosevelt. 2805 (1970).

Hy·der·a·bad (hī′dər ə bäd′, -bad′, hī′drə-), *n.* **1.** a former state in S India: now part of Andhra Pradesh. **2.** a city in and the capital of Andhra Pradesh, in the W part. 1,251,100 (1961). **3.** a city in SE Pakistan, on the Indus River. 434,000 (est. 1961). Also, **Haidarabad.**

Hy·der A·li (hī′dər ä′lē, ä lē′). See **Haidar Ali.**

hyd′no·car′pic ac′id (hid′nō kär′pik, hid′-), *Pharm.* a white, crystalline acid, $C_5H_7(CH_2)_{10}COOH$, used in the treatment of leprosy. [< Gk *hýdno(n)* truffle + *karp(ós)* fruit + -IC]

hydr-¹, var. of **hydro-¹** before a vowel: *hydrant.*

hydr-², var. of **hydro-²** before a vowel: *hydride.*

hy·dra (hī′drə), *n., pl.* **-dras, -drae** (-drē) for 1–3, *gen.* **-drae** (-drē) for 4. **1.** (*often cap.*) *Class. Myth.* a water or marsh serpent with nine heads, each of which, if cut off, grew back as two; Hercules killed this serpent by cauterizing the necks as he cut off the heads. **2.** a persistent or many-sided problem that presents new obstacles as soon as one aspect is solved. **3.** *Zool.* any freshwater polyp of the genus *Hydra.* **4.** (*cap.*) *Astron.* a southern constellation, the longest of all constellations. [< L < Gk: water serpent (r. ME *ydre* < MF); see OTTER]

Hydra (def. 3), genus *Hydra* (Length to ½ in.)

hy·dra-head·ed (hī′drə hed′id), *adj.* **1.** having many branches, divisions, authorities, facets, etc. **2.** containing many problems, difficulties, or obstacles.

hy·dran·gea (hī drān′jə, -jē ə, -dran′-), *n.* **1.** any shrub of the genus *Hydrangea,* species of which are cultivated for their large, showy, white, pink, or blue flower clusters. **2.** a flower cluster of this shrub. [< NL < Gk *hydr-* HYDR-¹ + *angeîa,* pl. of *angeîon* vessel; so called from cup-shaped seed capsule]

hy·drant (hī′drənt), *n.* **1.** an upright pipe with an outlet, usually in the street, for drawing water from a main or pipe; fireplug. **2.** a water faucet. [HYDR-¹ + -ANT]

hy·dranth (hī′dranth), *n.* *Zool.* the terminal part of a hydroid polyp that bears the mouth and tentacles and contains the stomach region. [HYDR(A) + Gk *ánth(os)* flower]

hy·drar·gy·rum (hī drär′jər əm), *n.* *Chem.* mercury. [< NL = L *hydrargyr(us)* (< Gk *hydrárgyros* mercury = *hydr-* HYDR-¹ + *árgyros* silver) + *-um,* on model of *aurum,* etc.; see -IUM] **—hy·drar·gyr·ic** (hī′drär jir′ik), *adj.*

hy·dras·tine (hī dras′tēn, -tin), *n.* *Pharm.* an alkaloid, $C_{21}H_{21}NO_6$, used as a stomachic and to inhibit uterine bleeding. [HYDRAST(IS) + -INE²]

hy·dras·ti·nine (hī dras′tə nēn′, -nin), *n.* *Pharm.* a poisonous alkaloid, $C_{11}H_{13}NO_3$, used to inhibit uterine bleeding.

hy·dras·tis (hī dras′tis), *n.* goldenseal (def. 2). [< NL < Gk *hydr-* HYDR-¹ + *-astis* < ?]

hy·drate (hī′drāt), *n., v.,* **-drat·ed, -drat·ing.** *Chem.* **—***n.* **1.** any of a class of compounds containing chemically combined water. **—***v.t., v.i.* **2.** to combine chemically with water. **—hy·dra′tion,** *n.* **—hy′dra·tor,** *n.*

hy′drated alu′mina, *Chem.* See **aluminum hydroxide.**

hy′drated lime′. See **slaked lime.**

hydraul. hydraulics.

hy·drau·lic (hī drô′lik, -drol′ik), *adj.* **1.** operated by or employing water or other liquids in motion. **2.** operated by water or other liquids under pressure. **3.** of or pertaining to hydraulics. **4.** hardening under water, as a cement. [< L *hydraulic(us)* < Gk *hydraulikós* of a water organ = *hýdraul(os)* water organ (*hydr-* HYDR-¹ + *aulós* pipe) + *-ikos* -IC] **—hy·drau′li·cal·ly,** *adv.*

hydrau′lic brake′, a brake operated by fluid pressures in cylinders and connecting tubular lines.

hydrau′lic flu′id, a fluid, usually of low viscosity, as oil, used in a hydraulic system.

hydrau′lic lift′, an elevator operated by fluid pressure, esp. one used for raising automobiles in service stations and garages.

hydrau′lic min′ing, placer mining using an artificially created stream of water.

hydrau′lic press′, a machine permitting a small force applied to a small piston to produce, through fluid pressure, a large force on a large piston.

hydrau′lic ram′, a device by which the energy of descending water is utilized to raise a part of the water to a height greater than that of the source.

hy·drau·lics (hī drô′liks, -drol′iks), *n.* (*construed as sing.*) the science that deals with the laws governing water or other liquids in motion and their applications in engineering; practical or applied hydrodynamics. [see HYDRAULIC, -ICS]

hy·dra·zine (hī′drə zēn′, -zin), *n.* *Chem.* **1.** a fuming liquid, H_2NNH_2, used chiefly as a reducing agent and a jet-propulsion fuel. **2.** a class of substances derived by replacing one or more hydrogen atoms in hydrazine by an organic group. [HYDR-² + AZO- + -INE²]

hy′drazo′ic ac′id, *Chem.* a colorless, very explosive, poisonous liquid, HN_3, having a penetrating odor and irritating to the eyes and mucous membranes. **—hy·dra·zo·ic** (hī′drə zō′ik), *adj.*

hy·dri·a (hī′drē ə), *n., pl.* **-dri·ae** (-drē ē′). *Gk. and Rom. Antiq.* a water jar having a short neck and large body with two horizontal handles immediately below the shoulder and a vertical handle extending from the shoulder to immediately below the lip. [< L < Gk: water pot = *hydr-* HYDR-¹ + *-ia* -IA; r. ME *ydre* < OF < L]

Hydria

hy·dric (hī′drik), *adj.* of, pertaining, or adapted to a wet or moist environment.

hy·dride (hī′drīd, -drid), *n.* *Chem.* a binary compound formed by hydrogen and another, usually more electropositive, element or group, as sodium hydride, NaH, or methyl hydride, CH_4.

hy′driod′ic ac′id, *Chem.* a corrosive liquid, HI, an aqueous solution of hydrogen iodide. [HYDR-² + IODIC] **—hy·dri·od·ic** (hī′drē od′ik), *adj.*

hy·dro (hī′drō), *Chiefly Canadian.* **—***adj.* **1.** hydroelectric. **—***n.* **2.** hydroelectric power. **3.** a hydroelectric power plant. [by shortening; see HYDRO-¹]

hydro-¹, a learned borrowing from Greek meaning "water," used in the formation of compound words: *hydroplane; hydrogen.* Also, *esp. before a vowel,* **hydr-.** [< Gk, comb. form of *hýdōr* water]

hydro-², *Chem.* a combining form of **hydrogen,** often indicating a combination of hydrogen with some negative element or radical: *hydrobromic.* Also, *esp. before a vowel,* **hydr-.**

hy·dro·bomb (hī′drə bom′), *n.* an aerial torpedo propelled by a rocket engine after entering the water.

hy′drobro′mic ac′id, *Chem.* a corrosive liquid, HBr, an aqueous solution of hydrogen bromide. **—hy·dro·bro·mic** (hī′drə brō′mik), *adj.*

hy·dro·car·bon (hī′drə kär′bən), *n.* *Chem.* any of a class of compounds containing only hydrogen and carbon, as an alkane, methane, CH_4, an alkene, ethylene, $CH_2{=}CH_2$, an alkyne, acetylene, $CH{\equiv}CH$, or an aromatic compound, benzene, C_6H_6. **—hy·dro·car·bo·na·ceous** (hī′drə kär′bə nā′shəs), *adj.*

hy·dro·cele (hī′drə sēl′), *n.* *Pathol.* an accumulation of serous fluid, usually about the testis. [< L < Gk *hydrokḗlē*]

hy·dro·cel·lu·lose (hī′drə sel′yə lōs′), *n.* *Chem.* a gelatinous substance obtained by the hydrolysis of cellulose, used chiefly in the manufacture of paper and rayon.

hy·dro·ceph·a·lus (hī′drə sef′ə ləs), *n.* *Pathol.* an accumulation of serous fluid within the cranium, esp. in infancy, often causing great enlargement of the head. Also, **hy·dro·ceph·a·ly** (hī′drə sef′ə lē). [< LL *hydrocephalus* (*morbus*) water-headed (sickness), trans. of Gk *tò hydroképhalon* (*páthos*)] **—hy·dro·ce·phal·ic** (hī′drō sə fal′ik), **hy′dro·ceph′a·lous,** *adj.*

hy′drochlo′ric ac′id, *Chem.* a corrosive and fuming liquid, HCl, used chiefly in chemical and industrial processes. **—hy·dro·chlo·ric** (hī′drə klōr′ik, -klôr′-), *adj.*

hy·dro·chlo·ride (hī′drə klōr′īd, -id, -klôr′-), *n.* *Chem.* a salt, esp. of an alkaloid, formed by the direct union of hydrochloric acid with an organic base.

hydrocinnam′oyl group′, *Chem.* the univalent group, $C_6H_5CH_2CH_2CO$–. Also called **hydrocinnam′oyl rad′ical.** [HYDRO-² + CINNAMO(N) + -YL] **—hy·dro·cin·nam·o·yl** (hī′drō si nam′ō il), *adj.*

hydrocinnam′yl group′, *Chem.* the univalent group, $C_6H_5CH_2CH_2CH_2$–. Also called **hydrocinnam′yl rad′ical.** HYDRO-² + CINNAM(ON) + -YL] **—hy·dro·cin·nam·yl** (hī′drō si nam′il, -drə sin′ə mil), *adj.*

hy·dro·cor·ti·sone (hī′drə kôr′ti sōn′, -zōn′), *n.* **1.** *Biochem.* a steroid hormone, $C_{21}H_{30}O_5$, of the adrenal cortex, active in carbohydrate and protein metabolism. **2.** *Pharm.* a commercial form of this compound, used chiefly in the form of its acetate in the treatment of arthritis and certain skin conditions. Also called **Compound F, cortisol.**

hy′drocyan′ic ac′id, *Chem.* a highly poisonous liquid HCN, an aqueous solution of hydrogen cyanide. Also called **prussic acid.** **—hy·dro·cy·an·ic** (hī′drō sī an′ik), *adj.*

hy·dro·dy·nam·ic (hī′drō dī nam′ik, -di-), *adj.* **1.** pertaining to forces in or motions of fluids. **2.** of or pertaining to hydrodynamics. **—hy′dro·dy·nam′i·cal·ly,** *adv.*

hy·dro·dy·nam·ics (hī′drō dī nam′iks, -di-), *n.* (*construed as sing.*) **1.** Also called **hydromechanics.** the science of the mechanics of fluids, including hydrostatics and hydrokinetics. **2.** hydrokinetics. [see HYDRODYNAMIC, -ICS]

hy·dro·e·lec·tric (hī′drō i lek′trik), *adj.* pertaining to the generation and distribution of electric energy derived from the energy of falling water or any other hydraulic source. **—hy·dro·e·lec·tric·i·ty** (hī′drō i lek tris′i tē, -ē′lek-), *n.*

hy′drofluor′ic ac′id, *Chem.* a colorless, fuming, corrosive liquid, HF, an aqueous solution of hydrogen fluoride, used chiefly for etching glass. **—hy·dro·flu·or·ic** (hī′drō flōō ōr′ik, -ôr′-), *adj.*

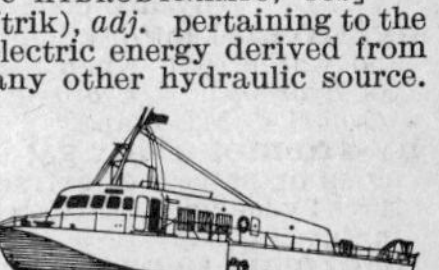

Hydrofoil (def. 3)

hy·dro·foil (hī′drə foil′), *n.* **1.** *Naval Archit.* a surface form creating a thrust against water in a direction perpendicular to the plane approximated by the surface. **2.** *Naut.* a winglike member having this form, designed to lift the hull of a moving vessel. **3.** a vessel equipped with hydrofoils.

hy·dro·gen (hī′drə jən), *n.* *Chem.* a colorless, odorless, flammable gas that combines chemically with oxygen to form water: the lightest of the known elements. *Symbol:* H; *at. wt.:* 1.00797; *at. no.:* 1; *weight of one liter at 760 mm pressure and 0°C:* .08987 g. [< F *hydrogène*]

hy·dro·gen·ate (hī′drə jə nāt′, hī droj′ə-), *v.t.*, **-at·ed, -at·ing.** *Chem.* to combine or treat with hydrogen, esp. to add hydrogen to the molecule of (an unsaturated organic compound). Also, **hydrogenize.** —**hy′dro·gen·a′tion,** *n.*

hy′drogen bomb′, a bomb, more powerful than an atomic bomb, that derives its explosive energy from the thermonuclear fusion reaction of hydrogen isotopes. Also called **H-bomb, fusion bomb, thermonuclear bomb.**

hy′drogen bro′mide, *Chem.* a colorless gas, HBr, having a pungent odor: the anhydride of hydrobromic acid.

hy′drogen chlo′ride, *Chem.* a colorless gas, HCl, having a pungent odor: the anhydride of hydrochloric acid.

hy′drogen cy′anide, *Chem.* a colorless, poisonous gas, HCN, having a bitter, almondlike odor: the anhydride of hydrocyanic acid.

hy′drogen flu′oride, *Chem.* a colorless corrosive gas, HF, the anhydride of hydrofluoric acid, used chiefly as a catalyst and in the fluorination of hydrocarbons.

hy′drogen i′odide, *Chem.* a colorless gas, HI, having a suffocating odor: the anhydride of hydriodic acid.

hy′drogen i′on, *Chem.* ionized hydrogen of the form H^+, found in aqueous solutions of all acids.

hy·dro·gen·ise (hī′drə jə nīz′, hī droj′ə-), *v.t.*, **-ised, -is·ing.** *Chiefly Brit.* hydrogenize. —**hy′dro·gen·i·sa′tion,** *n.*

hy·dro·gen·ize (hī′drə jə nīz′, hī droj′ə-), *v.t.*, **-ized, -iz·ing.** hydrogenate. —**hy′dro·gen·i·za′tion,** *n.*

hy·dro·gen·ol·y·sis (hī′drō ji nol′i sis), *n., pl.* **-ses** (-sēz′). *Chem.* decomposition resulting from the interaction of a compound and hydrogen.

hy·drog·e·nous (hī droj′ə nəs), *adj.* of or containing hydrogen.

hy′drogen perox′ide, an unstable liquid, H_2O_2, the aqueous solution of which is used as an antiseptic and a bleaching agent.

hy′drogen sul′fide, *Chem.* a flammable, cumulatively poisonous gas, H_2S, having the odor of rotten eggs: used chiefly in the manufacture of chemicals and in metallurgy.

hy·dro·graph (hī′drə graf′, -gräf′), *n.* a graph of the water level or rate of flow of a body of water as a function of time, showing the seasonal change.

hy·drog·ra·phy (hī drog′rə fē), *n.* the science of the measurement, description, and mapping of the surface waters of the earth, with special reference to their use for navigation. —**hy·drog′ra·pher,** *n.* —**hy·dro·graph·ic** (hī′drə graf′ik), **hy′dro·graph′i·cal,** *adj.* —**hy′dro·graph′i·cal·ly,** *adv.*

hy·droid (hī′droid), *adj.* **1.** noting or pertaining to that form of hydrozoan which is asexual and grows into branching colonies by budding. —*n.* **2.** the phase of a hydrozoan coelenterate that consists of polyp forms usually growing as an attached colony.

hy·dro·ki·net·ic (hī′drō ki net′ik, -kī-), *adj.* **1.** pertaining to the motion of fluids. **2.** of or pertaining to hydrokinetics. Also, **hy′dro·ki·net′i·cal.**

hy·dro·ki·net·ics (hī′drō ki net′iks, -kī-), *n.* (*construed as sing.*) the branch of hydrodynamics that deals with the laws governing liquids or gases in motion. Also called **hydrodynamics.** [see HYDROKINETIC, -ICS]

hy·drol·o·gy (hī drol′ə jē), *n.* the science that deals with the occurrence, circulation, distribution, and properties of the water of the earth and the earth's atmosphere. —**hy·dro·log·ic** (hī′drə loj′ik), **hy′dro·log′i·cal,** *adj.* —**hy′dro·log′i·cal·ly,** *adv.* —**hy·drol′o·gist,** *n.*

hy·drol·y·sate (hī drol′i sāt′), *n.* *Chem.* any compound formed by hydrolysis. [HYDROLYS(IS) + -ATE[2]]

hy·dro·lyse (hī′drə līz′), *v.t., v.i.*, **-lysed, -lys·ing.** *Chiefly Brit.* hydrolyze. —**hy′dro·lys′a·ble,** *adj.* —**hy′dro·ly·sa′tion,** *n.* —**hy′dro·lys′er,** *n.*

hy·drol·y·sis (hī drol′i sis), *n., pl.* **-ses** (-sēz′). *Chem.* decomposition in which a compound is split into other compounds by taking up the elements of water.

hy·dro·lyte (hī′drə līt′), *n.* *Chem.* a substance subjected to hydrolysis.

hy·dro·lyt·ic (hī′drə lit′ik), *adj.* producing, noting, or resulting in hydrolysis.

hy·dro·lyze (hī′drə līz′), *v.t., v.i.*, **-lyzed, -lyz·ing.** to subject or be subjected to hydrolysis. Also, *esp. Brit.*, **hydrolyse.** [HYDROL(YSIS) + -IZE] —**hy′dro·lyz′a·ble,** *adj.* —**hy′dro·ly·za′tion,** *n.* —**hy′dro·lyz′er,** *n.*

hy·dro·mag·net·ics (hī′drō mag net′iks), *n.* (*construed as sing.*) magnetohydrodynamics.

hy·dro·man·cy (hī′drə man′sē), *n.* divination by means of signs observed in water. [earlier *hydromantie, -cie* < L *hydromantīa* < Gk *hydromanteía* divination by water; r. ME *ydromancye* < MF *ydromancie* < L] —**hy′dro·manc′er,** *n.* —**hy′dro·man′tic,** *adj.*

hy·dro·me·chan·ics (hī′drō mə kan′iks), *n.* (*construed as sing.*) hydrodynamics (def. 1). —**hy′dro·me·chan′i·cal,** *adj.*

hy·dro·me·du·sa (hī′drō mi do͞o′sə, -zə, -dyo͞o′-), *n., pl.* **-sae** (-sē). the medusa form of a hydrozoan coelenterate. [< NL] —**hy′dro·me·du′san,** *adj.*

hy·dro·mel (hī′drə mel′), *n.* a liquor consisting of honey and water that, when fermented, becomes mead. [< L < Gk *hydrómeli* = *hydro-* HYDRO-[1] + *méli* honey; r. late ME *ydromel* < ML (var.)]

hy·dro·met·al·lur·gy (hī′drə met′əlûr′jē), *n.* the technique or process of extracting metals at ordinary temperatures by leaching ore with liquid solvents. —**hy′dro·met′al·lur′gi·cal,** *adj.*

hy·dro·me·te·or (hī′drə mē′tē ər), *n.* *Meteorol.* the state or effect of liquid water or ice in the atmosphere, as rain, ice crystals, hail, fog, and clouds. —**hy′dro·me′te·or·o·log′i·cal,** *adj.* —**hy′dro·me′te·or·ol′o·gy,** *n.*

hy·drom·e·ter (hī drom′i tər), *n.* an instrument for determining the specific gravity of a liquid, consisting of a sealed cylinder and weighted bulb, that, when placed in a liquid, indicates its specific gravity by a comparison of the surface of the liquid with the graduations on the emerging stem. —**hy·dro·met·ric** (hī′drə me′trik), **hy′dro·met′ri·cal,** *adj.* —**hy·drom′e·try,** *n.*

hy·drop·a·thy (hī drop′ə thē), *n.* the curing of disease by the internal and external use of water. Cf. **hydrotherapy.** —**hy·dro·path·ic** (hī′drə path′ik), **hy′dro·path′i·cal,** *adj.* —**hy·drop′a·thist, hy′dro·path′,** *n.*

hy·dro·phane (hī′drə fān′), *n.* a partly translucent variety of opal that becomes more translucent or transparent when immersed in water. —**hy·droph·a·nous** (hī drof′ə nəs), *adj.*

hy·dro·phil·ic (hī′drə fil′ik), *adj.* *Chem.* having a strong affinity for water.

hy·droph·i·lous (hī drof′ə ləs), *adj.* *Bot.* **1.** pollinated by the agency of water. **2.** hydrophytic. [< NL *hydrophilus*] —**hy·droph′i·ly,** *n.*

hy·dro·phobe (hī′drə fōb′), *n.* *Chem.* a hydrophobic substance.

hy·dro·pho·bi·a (hī′drə fō′bē ə), *n.* *Pathol.* **1.** rabies. **2.** an abnormal or unnatural dread of water. [< LL < Gk: horror of water. See HYDRO-[1], -PHOBIA]

hy·dro·pho·bic (hī′drə fō′bik), *adj.* **1.** *Pathol.* of or pertaining to hydrophobia. **2.** *Chem.* having little or no affinity for water. —**hy·dro·pho·bic·i·ty** (hī′drə fō bis′i tē), *n.*

hy·dro·phone (hī′drə fōn′), *n.* **1.** an instrument used to detect the flow of water through a pipe. **2.** a device for locating sources of sound under water, as for detecting submarines by the noise of their engines. **3.** *Med.* an instrument used in auscultation, whereby sounds are intensified through a column of water.

hy·dro·phyte (hī′drə fīt′), *n.* a plant growing in water or very moist ground. —**hy·dro·phyt·ic** (hī′drə fit′ik), *adj.* —**hy′dro·phyt′ism,** *n.*

hy·drop·ic (hī drop′ik), *adj.* dropsical. Also, **hy·drop′i·cal.** [< L *hydrōpic(us)* < Gk *hydrōpikós* = *hydrōp-* (s. of *hýdrōps*) dropsy (*hydr-* HYDR-[1] + *-ōp* appearance, lit., eye, face, appar. by confusion with *ópsis* appearance) + *-ikos* -IC; r. ME *ydropike* < OF < L] —**hy·drop′i·cal·ly,** *adv.*

hy·dro·plane (hī′drə plān′), *n., v.*, **-planed, -plan·ing.** —*n.* **1.** a light, high-powered boat, esp. one with hydrofoils or a stepped bottom, designed to plane at very high speeds. **2.** an airplane with floats or with a boatlike underpart enabling it to land on and take off from water. **3.** an attachment to an airplane enabling it to glide on the water. **4.** a horizontal rudder for submerging or elevating a submarine. —*v.i.* **5.** to skim over water like a hydroplane. **6.** to travel in a hydroplane.

hy·dro·pon·ics (hī′drə pon′iks), *n.* (*construed as sing.*) the cultivation of plants by placing the roots in liquid nutrient solutions rather than in soil. [HYDRO-[1] + (GEO)PONICS] —**hy′dro·pon′ic,** *adj.* —**hy′dro·pon′i·cal·ly,** *adv.* —**hy·drop·o·nist** (hī drop′ə nist), *n.*

hy·dro·pow·er (hī′drə pou′ər), *n.* hydroelectric power.

hy·dro·qui·none (hī′drō kwi nōn′, -drə kwin′ōn), *n.* *Chem.* a crystalline compound, $C_6H_4(OH)_2$, formed by the reduction of quinone: used chiefly in photography and to inhibit autoxidation reactions. Also called **hy·dro·quin·ol** (hī′drə kwin′ōl, -ôl, -ol), **quinol.**

hydros., hydrostatics.

hy·dro·scope (hī′drə skōp′), *n.* an optical device for viewing objects below the surface of water. —**hy·dro·scop·ic** (hī′drə skop′ik), **hy′dro·scop′i·cal,** *adj.*

hy·dro·sol (hī′drə sol′), *n.* *Physical Chem.* a colloidal suspension in water. [HYDRO-[1] + SOL(UTION)]

hy·dro·some (hī′drə sōm′), *n.* *Zool.* the entire body of a compound hydrozoan. [*hydro-* (comb. form repr. HYDRA) + -SOME[3]]

hy·dro·sphere (hī′drə sfēr′), *n.* the water on or surrounding the surface of the globe, including the water of the oceans and the water in the atmosphere.

hy·dro·stat (hī′drə stat′), *n.* an electrical device for detecting the presence of water, as from overflow or leakage.

hy·dro·stat·ics (hī′drə stat′iks), *n.* (*construed as sing.*) the branch of hydrodynamics that deals with the statics of fluids, usually confined to the equilibrium and pressure of liquids. [HYDRO-[1] + STAT(IC) + -ICS] —**hy′dro·stat′ic, hy′dro·stat′i·cal,** *adj.* —**hy′dro·stat′i·cal·ly,** *adv.*

hy·dro·sul·fate (hī′drə sul′fāt), *n.* *Chem.* a salt formed by the direct union of sulfuric acid with an organic base, esp. an alkaloid, and usually more soluble than the base. Also, **hy′dro·sul′phate.**

hy·dro·sul·fide (hī′drə sul′fīd, -fid), *n.* *Chem.* a compound containing the univalent group, –HS. Also, **hy′dro·sul′phide.**

hy·dro·sul·fite (hī′drə sul′fīt), *n.* *Chem.* hyposulfite (def. 1). Also, **hy′dro·sul′phite.** [HYDROSULF(UROUS) + -ITE[1]]

hy·dro·tax·is (hī′drə tak′sis), *n.* *Biol.* oriented movement toward or away from water. —**hy·dro·tac·tic** (hī′drə-tak′tik), *adj.*

hy·dro·ther·a·peu·tics (hī′drō ther′ə pyo͞o′tiks), *n.* (*construed as sing.*) hydrotherapy. —**hy′dro·ther′a·peu′tic,** *adj.*

hy·dro·ther·a·py (hī′drə ther′ə pē), *n.* *Med.* the treatment of disease by the scientific application of water both internally and externally. Cf. **hydropathy.** —**hy′dro·ther′a·pist,** *n.*

hy·dro·ther·mal (hī′drə thûr′məl), *adj.* *Geol.* noting or pertaining to the action of hot, aqueous solutions or gases within or on the surface of the earth. —**hy′dro·ther′mal·ly,** *adv.*

hy·dro·tho·rax (hī′drə thōr′aks, -thôr′-), *n.* *Pathol.* the presence of serous fluid in one or both pleural cavities. —**hy·dro·tho·rac·ic** (hī′drō thə ras′ik), *adj.*

hy·dro·trop·ic (hī′drə trop′ik), *adj.* **1.** *Bot.* turning or tending toward or away from moisture. **2.** taking a particular direction with reference to moisture.

hy·drot·ro·pism (hī dro′trə piz′əm), *n.* *Biol.* **1.** oriented growth or movement in response to water. **2.** hydrotropic tendency or growth.

hy·drous (hī′drəs), *adj.* **1.** containing water. **2.** *Chem.* containing water or its elements in some kind of union, as in hydrates or hydroxides.

hy·drox·ide (hī drok′sīd, -sid), *n.* *Chem.* a compound containing the hydroxyl group.

hy·drox·y (hī drok′sē), *adj.* *Chem.* hydroxyl. [HYDR-[2] + OXY(GEN)]

hydrox′y ac′id, *Chem.* an organic acid containing both a carboxyl and a hydroxyl group.

hy·drox·yl (hī drok′sil), *adj.* *Chem.* containing the hydroxyl group. Also, **hydroxy.** —**hy′drox·yl′ic,** *adj.*

hy·drox·yl·a·mine (hī drok′sil ə mēn′, -am′in), *n.* *Chem.* an unstable compound, NH_2OH, used as a reducing agent, analytical reagent, and chemical intermediate.

hydrox′yl group′, *Chem.* the univalent group, –OH. Also called **hydrox′yl rad′ical.**

Hy·dro·zo·a (hī′drə zō′ə), *n.* the class comprising the hydrozoans. [< NL; see HYDROZOAN]

hy·dro·zo·an (hī′drə zō′ən), *adj.* **1.** belonging or pertaining to the *Hydrozoa.* —*n.* **2.** any coelenterate of the class *Hydrozoa,* comprising solitary or colonial polyps and free-swimming medusae. [< NL *Hydrozo(a)* (see HYDRA, -O-, -ZOA) + -AN]

hy·e·na (hī ē′nə), *n.* any nocturnal carnivore of the family *Hyaenidae,* feeding chiefly on carrion. Also, **hyaena.** Cf. **spotted hyena.** [< ML *hyēna* < L *hyaena* < Gk *hýaina* = *hu-* (s. of *hȳs*) hog + *-aina* fem. suffix; r. ME *hyane, hyene* < MF *hiene* < L] —**hy·e′nic, hy·e·nine** (hī ē′nīn, -nin), *adj.* —**hy·e′noid,** *adj.*

Spotted hyena, *Crocuta crocuta* (3 ft. high at shoulder; total length 5½ ft.; tail 1 ft.)

hy·e·tal (hī′i tᵊl), *adj.* of or pertaining to rain or rainfall. [< Gk *hyet(ós)* rain + -AL¹]

hyeto-, a learned borrowing from Greek meaning "rain," used in the formation of compound words: *hyetology.* Also, *esp. before a vowel,* **hyet-.** [comb. form repr. Gk *hyetós* rain]

hy·et·o·graph (hī et′ə graf′, -gräf′, hī′i tə-), *n.* a map or chart showing the average rainfall for the localities represented. [< Gk *hyetó(s)* rain + -GRAPH]

hy·e·tog·ra·phy (hī′i tog′rə fē), *n.* the study of the annual and geographical distribution of rainfall. [< Gk *hyetó(s)* rain + -GRAPHY] —**hy·e·to·graph·ic** (hī′i tə graf′ik), **hy′e·to·graph′i·cal,** *adj.* —**hy′e·to·graph′i·cal·ly,** *adv.*

hy·e·tol·o·gy (hī′i tol′ə jē), *n. Rare.* the branch of meteorology dealing with precipitation. —**hy·e·to·log·i·cal** (hī′i tᵊloj′i kəl), *adj.* —**hy′e·tol′o·gist,** *n.*

Hy·ge·ia (hī jē′ə), *n. Class. Myth.* the ancient Greek goddess of health; the daughter of Asclepius. [< Gk, late var. of *Hygíeia,* personification of *hygíeia* health = *hygiḗ(s)* healthy + *-ia* -IA] —**Hy·ge′ian,** *adj.*

hy·giene (hī′jēn, -jē ēn′), *n.* **1.** Also, **hygienics.** the science that deals with the preservation of health. **2.** a condition or practice conducive to the preservation of health, as cleanliness. [< medical L *hygiēnē* (var. of *hygiēna, hygieina*) < Gk *hygieinḗ (téchnē)* healthful (art), fem. of *hygieinós* healthful = *hygiḗ(s)* healthy + *-inos* -INE¹] —**hy·gi·en·ic** (hī′jē en′ik, hī jē′nik), **hy′gi·en′i·cal,** *adj.* —**hy′gi·en′i·cal·ly,** *adv.*

hy·gi·en·ics (hī′jē en′iks, hī jē′niks), *n.* (*construed as sing.*) hygiene (def. 1).

hy·gien·ist (hī jē′nist, -jen′ist, hī′jē nist, hī′jē en′ist), *n.* an expert in hygiene. Also, **hy·ge·ist, hy·gie·ist** (hī′jē ist).

Hy·gi·nus (hi jī′nəs), *n.* **Saint,** died A.D. 140, pope 136–140.

hygro-, a learned borrowing from Greek meaning "wet," "moist," "moisture," used in the formation of compound words: *hygrometer.* [< Gk, comb. form of *hygrós* wet, moist]

hy·gro·graph (hī′grə graf′, -gräf′), *n.* a self-recording hygrometer.

hy·grom·e·ter (hī grom′i tər), *n.* any instrument for measuring the water-vapor content of the atmosphere.

hy·gro·met·ric (hī′grə me′trik), *adj.* of or pertaining to the hygrometer or hygrometry. —**hy′gro·met′ri·cal·ly,** *adv.*

hy·grom·e·try (hī grom′i trē), *n.* the branch of physics dealing with measurement of the humidity of air and gases.

hy·gro·scope (hī′grə skōp′), *n.* an instrument that indicates the approximate humidity of the air.

hy·gro·scop·ic (hī′grə skop′ik), *adj.* absorbing or attracting moisture from the air. —**hy′gro·scop′i·cal·ly,** *adv.* —**hy·gro·sco·pic·i·ty** (hī′grə skō pis′i tē), *n.*

hy·ing (hī′ing), *v.* pp. of **hie.**

Hyk·sos (hik′sōs, -sos), *n.* a nomadic people who conquered and ruled ancient Egypt between the 13th and 18th dynasties, c1700–1580 B.C.: believed to have been a Semitic people that originally migrated into Egypt from Asia. [< Gk *Hyksṓs* < Egypt *ḥḳ′š′sw* leader of nomads]

hy·la (hī′lə), *n.* a tree frog of the genus *Hyla.* [< NL < Gk *hýlē* forest]

hylo-, a learned borrowing from Greek meaning "wood," "matter," used in compound words: *hylophagous; hylotheism.* [< Gk, comb. form of *hýlē* wood, matter]

hy·loph·a·gous (hī lof′ə gəs), *adj.* xylophagous (def. 1). [< Gk *hylophágos*]

hy·lo·the·ism (hī′lə thē′iz əm), *n.* any philosophical doctrine identifying a god or gods with matter. —**hy′lo·the′ist,** *n., adj.* —**hy′lo·the·is′tic,** *adj.*

hy·lo·zo·ism (hī′lə zō′iz əm), *n. Philos.* the doctrine that matter is inseparable from life, which is a property of matter. [HYLO- + *zo-* (s. of Gk *zōḗ*) life + -ISM] —**hy′lo·zo′ic,** *adj.* —**hy′lo·zo′ist,** *n.* —**hy′lo·zo·is′tic,** *adj.* —**hy′lo·zo·is′ti·cal·ly,** *adv.*

hy·men (hī′mən), *n. Anat.* a fold of mucous membrane partially closing the external orifice of the vagina in a virgin. [< Gk: skin, membrane, the virginal membrane]

Hy·men (hī′mən), *n. Class. Myth.* the god of marriage, represented as a handsome youth bearing a torch. Also called **Hy·me·nae·us** (hī′mə nē′əs).

hy·me·ne·al (hī′mə nē′əl), *adj.* **1.** of or pertaining to marriage. —*n.* **2.** a marriage song. [< L *hymenae(us)* (< Gk *hyménaios* wedding song = *Hymḗn* HYMEN + *-aios* pertaining to) + -AL¹]

hy·me·ni·um (hī mē′nē əm), *n., pl.* **-ni·a** (-nē ə). *Bot.* the sporogenous layer in a fungus, composed of asci or basidia often interspersed with various sterile structures, as paraphyses. [< NL; see HYMENO-, -IUM] —**hy·me′ni·al,** *adj.*

hymeno-, an element appearing in loan words from Greek, where it meant "membrane:" *hymenopteron.* [< Gk, comb. form of *hymḗn* membrane, hymen]

Hy·me·nop·ter·a (hī′mə nop′tər ə), *n.* the order comprising the hymenopterous insects. [< NL < Gk (neut. pl.). See HYMENOPTEROUS]

hy·me·nop·ter·an (hī′mə nop′tər ən), *adj.* **1.** hymenopterous. —*n.* **2.** hymenopteron.

hy·me·nop·ter·on (hī′mə nop′tər ən), *n., pl.* **-ter·a** (-tər ə). a hymenopterous insect. Also, **hy′me·nop′ter.** [< Gk, neut. sing. of *hymenópteros* HYMENOPTEROUS]

hy·me·nop·ter·ous (hī′mə nop′tər əs), *adj.* belonging or pertaining to the *Hymenoptera,* an order of insects having, when winged, four membranous wings, and comprising the wasps, bees, ants, ichneumon flies, sawflies, etc. [< Gk *hymenópteros*]

Hy·met·tus (hī met′əs), *n.* a mountain in SE Greece, near Athens. 3370 ft. —**Hy·met′ti·an, Hy·met′tic,** *adj.*

hymn (him), *n.* **1.** a song or ode in praise or honor of God, a deity, a nation, etc. **2.** something resembling this, as a song, speech, or book in praise of someone or something. —*v.t.* **3.** to praise or celebrate in a hymn. —*v.i.* **4.** to sing hymns. [< L *hymn(us)* < Gk *hýmnos* song in praise of gods or heroes; r. ME *ymne* (< OF) and OE *ymn,* etc. (< LL *ymnus*)] —**hymn′less,** *adj.* —**hymn′like′,** *adj.*

hym·nal (him′nᵊl), *n.* **1.** Also called **hymn′book′.** a book of hymns. —*adj.* **2.** of or pertaining to hymns. [< ML *hymnāl(e),* n. use of neut. of *hymnālis* (adj.)]

hym′nal stan′za. See **common measure** (def. 2).

hym·nist (him′nist), *n.* a composer of hymns. Also, **hym·no·dist** (him′nə dist).

hym·no·dy (him′nə dē), *n.* **1.** the singing or the composition of hymns or sacred songs. **2.** hymns collectively. [< ML *hymnōdi(a)* < Gk *hymnōidía* chanting of a hymn = *hýmn(os)* HYMN + *ōidía* singing (see ODE, -IA)] —**hym·nod·i·cal** (him nod′i kəl), *adj.*

hym·nol·o·gy (him nol′ə jē), *n.* **1.** the study of hymns, their history, classification, etc. **2.** the composition of hymns. **3.** hymns collectively. —**hym·no·log·ic** (him′nᵊloj′ik), **hym′no·log′i·cal,** *adj.* —**hym·nol′o·gist,** *n.*

hy·oid (hī′oid), *Anat., Zool.* —*adj.* **1.** Also, **hy·oi′dal, hy·oi′de·an.** noting or pertaining to a U-shaped bone at the root of the tongue in man, or a corresponding bone or collection of bones in animals. —*n.* **2.** the hyoid bone. [< medical L *hyoïd(es)* < Gk *hyoeídēs* shaped like the letter hypsilon (i.e., UPSILON) = *hy-* (< letter name *hŷ,* var. of *ŷ*) + *-oeidēs* -OID]

hy·os·cine (hī′ə sēn′, -sin), *n. Pharm.* scopolamine. [HYOSC(YAMUS) + -INE²]

hy·os·cy·a·mine (hī′ə sī′ə mēn′, -min), *n. Pharm.* a poisonous alkaloid, $C_{17}H_{23}NO_3$, used as a sedative, analgesic, mydriatic, and antispasmodic. [HYOSCYAM(US) + -INE²]

hy·os·cy·a·mus (hī′ə sī′ə məs), *n.* the dried leaves of the henbane herb *Hyoscyamus niger,* containing the alkaloids hyoscyamine and scopolamine: used as an antispasmodic and sedative. [< NL < Gk *hyoskýamos* = *hyô(s)* (gen. of *hŷs* hog) + *kýamos* bean]

hyp-, var. of **hypo-** before a vowel: *hypabyssal.*

hyp., **1.** hypotenuse. **2.** hypothesis. **3.** hypothetical.

hyp·a·byss·al (hip′ə bis′əl), *adj. Geol.* **1.** intermediate in texture between coarse-grained igneous rocks and fine-grained lava. **2.** noting any of various minor intrusions, as dikes and sills, intermediate in position between deeply situated plutonic bodies and superficial lava.

hy·pae·thral (hi pē′thrəl, hī-), *adj.* hypethral.

Hyp·a·nis (hip′ə nis), *n.* ancient name of the **Kuban.**

hy·pan·thi·um (hi pan′thē əm, hī-), *n., pl.* **-thi·a** (-thē ə). *Bot.* a cup-shaped or tubular body, formed by the enlargement of the receptacle of a flower, bearing the sepals, petals, and stamens on its rim. [< NL = *hyp-* HYP- + *anthium* < Gk *ánthion,* dim. of *ánthos* flower] —**hy·pan′thi·al,** *adj.*

Hy·pa·tia (hī pā′shə, -pat′ē ə), *n.* A.D. c370–415, Greek philosopher renowned for her beauty.

hype (hīp), *n., v.,* **hyped, hyp·ing.** *Slang.* —*v.t.* **1.** to stimulate, excite, or agitate (usually fol. by *up*). **2.** to intensify (advertising, promotion, or publicity) by ingenious or questionable claims, methods, etc. (usually fol. by *up*). —*n.* **3.** an ingenious or questionable claim, method, etc., used in advertising, promotion, or publicity to intensify the effect. **4.** a swindle, deception, or trick. **5.** a drug addict, esp. one who uses a hypodermic needle. [by shortening of HYPODERMIC]

hyper-, an element appearing in loan words from Greek, where it meant "over," usually implying excess or exaggeration (*hyperbole*); on this model used, esp. as opposed to **hypo-,** in the formation of compound words (*hyperthyroid*). Cf. **super-.** [< Gk, repr. *hypér* over, above; c. L *super*]

hy·per·a·cid·i·ty (hī′pər ə sid′i tē), *n.* excessive acidity, as of the gastric juice. —**hy·per·ac·id** (hī′pər as′id), *adj.*

hy·per·ac·tive (hī′pər ak′tiv), *adj.* unusually or excessively active: *the child's hyperactive imagination.* —**hy·per·ac·tion** (hī′pər ak′shən), *n.* —**hy′per·ac·tiv′i·ty,** *n.*

hy·per·a·cu·sis (hī′pər ə kyōō′sis, -kōō′-), *n. Pathol.* excessive acuteness of the sense of hearing. Also, **hy·per·a·cou·sia** (hī′pər ə kōō′zhə, -zhē ə, -zē ə), **hy·per·a·cu·sia** (hī′pər ə kyōō′zhə, -zhē ə, -zē ə, -kōō-). [HYPER- + Gk *ákousis* hearing (*akoú(ein)* to hear + *-sis* -SIS)]

hy·per·ae·mi·a (hī′pər ē′mē ə), *n. Pathol.* hyperemia. —**hy′per·ae′mic,** *adj.*

hy·per·aes·the·sia (hī′pər is thē′zhə, -zhē ə, -zē ə), *n. Pathol.* hyperesthesia. —**hy·per·aes·thet·ic** (hī′pər is thet′ik), *adj.*

hy·per·bar·ic (hī′pər bar′ik), *adj.* of, pertaining to, utilizing, or supplied with oxygen at higher pressure than normal, for therapeutic purposes: *hyperbaric treatment.*

hy·per·bo·la (hī pûr′bə lə), *n. Geom.* the set of points in a plane whose distances to two fixed points in the plane have a constant difference; a curve consisting of two distinct and similar branches, formed by the intersection of a plane with a right circular cone when the plane makes a greater angle with the base than does the generator of the cone. Equation: $x^2/a^2 - y^2/b^2 = 1$. See diag. at **conic section.** [< Gk *hyperbolḗ* the geometrical term, lit., excess. See HYPERBOLE]

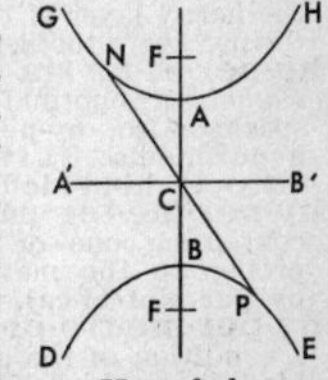

Hyperbola DBE, GAH, Opposite branches of a hyperbola; F, Focus; C, Center; AB, Transverse axis; A′B′, Conjugate axis; NCP, Diameter

hy·per·bo·le (hī pûr′bə lē), *n.* *Rhet.* **1.** obvious and intentional exaggeration. **2.** an extravagant statement or figure of speech not intended to be taken literally, as "to wait an eternity." Cf. **litotes.** [< Gk: excess, exaggeration, throwing beyond = *hyper-* HYPER- + *bolḗ* throw]

hy·per·bol·ic (hī′pər bol′ik), *adj.* **1.** having the nature of hyperbole; exaggerated. **2.** using hyperbole; exaggerating. **3.** *Math.* **a.** of or pertaining to a hyperbola. **b.** derived from a hyperbola, as a hyperbolic function. Also, **hy′per·bol′i·cal.** —**hy′per·bol′i·cal·ly,** *adv.*

hy′perbol′ic func′tion, *Math.* a function of an angle expressed as a relationship between the distances from a point on a hyperbola to the origin and to the coordinate axes, as hyperbolic sine, hyperbolic cosine, etc.: often expressed as combinations of exponential functions.

hy·per·bo·lism (hī pûr′bə liz′əm), *n.* the use of hyperbole.

hy·per·bo·lize (hī pûr′bə līz′), *v.,* **-lized, -liz·ing.** —*v.i.* **1.** to use hyperbole; exaggerate. —*v.t.* **2.** to represent or express with hyperbole or exaggeration.

hy·per·bo·loid (hī pûr′bə loid′), *n.* *Math.* a quadric surface having a finite center and some of its plane sections hyperbolas. $\frac{x^2}{a^2} + \frac{y^2}{b^2} - \frac{z^2}{c^2} = 1.$ —**hy·per′bo·loi′dal,** *adj.*

Hyperboloids A, Two-sheet hyperboloid; B, One-sheet hyperboloid

Hy·per·bo·re·an (hī′pər bôr′ē ən, -bôr′-, -bə rē′-), *n.* **1.** *Class. Myth.* one of a people supposed to live in a land of perpetual sunshine and abundance beyond the north wind. —*adj.* **2.** of or pertaining to the Hyperboreans. **3.** (*sometimes l.c.*) arctic; frigid. [< L *hyperbore(us)* (< Gk *hyperbóreos* beyond the north wind, northern, polar; see HYPER-, BOREAS) + -AN]

hy·per·cap·ni·a (hī′pər kap′nē ə), *n.* *Med.* the presence of an excessive amount of carbon dioxide in the blood. Also called **hy·per·car·bi·a** (hī′pər kär′bē ə). [HYPER- + Gk *kapn(ós)* smoke + -IA]

hy·per·cat·a·lec·tic (hī′pər kat′ᵊlek′tik), *adj.* *Pros.* (of a line of verse) containing an additional syllable after the last dipody or foot. Cf. **acatalectic, catalectic.**

hy·per·cor·rect (hī′pər kə rekt′), *adj.* overly correct; excessively fastidious; fussy. —**hy′per·cor·rect′ness,** *n.*

hy·per·cor·rec·tion (hī′pər kə rek′shən), *n.* *Linguistics.* a pronunciation or grammatical form or usage that results from an effort to replace incorrect or seemingly incorrect forms with correct ones, as *between you and I, Whom does she think she is?,* etc.

hy·per·crit·ic (hī′pər krit′ik), *n.* a person who is excessively or captiously critical. [< NL *hypercritic(us)*] —**hy′per·crit′i·cal,** *adj.* —**hy′per·crit′i·cal·ly,** *adv.* —**hy′per·crit′i·cism,** *n.*

hy·per·du·li·a (hī′pər dōō lē′ə, -dyōō-), *n.* *Rom. Cath. Theol.* the veneration offered to the Virgin Mary as the most exalted of creatures. Cf. **dulia, latria.** [< ML] —**hy·per·du·lic** (hī′pər dōō′lik, -dyōō′-), **hy′per·du′li·cal,** *adj.*

hy·per·e·mi·a (hī′pər ē′mē ə), *n.* *Pathol.* an abnormally large amount of blood in any part of the body. Also, **hyperaemia.** —**hy′per·e′mic,** *adj.*

hy·per·es·the·sia (hī′pər is thē′zhə, -zhē ə, -zē ə), *n.* *Pathol.* an abnormally acute sense of pain, heat, cold, or touch. Also, **hyperaesthesia.** Cf. **hypesthesia.** —**hy·per·es·thet·ic** (hī′pər is thet′ik), *adj.*

hy·per·eu·tec·toid (hī′pər yōō tek′toid), *adj.* *Metall.* **1.** (of an alloy) having more of the alloying element than the eutectoid element. **2.** (of steel) having more carbon than the 0.8 percent of eutectoid steel.

hy·per·ex·ten·sion (hī′pər ik sten′shən), *n.* *Physiol.* **1.** the extension of a part of the body beyond normal limits. **2.** the state of being so extended.

hy·per·func·tion (hī′pər fungk′shən), *n.* abnormally increased function, esp. of glands (opposed to *hypofunction*).

hy·per·gly·ce·mi·a (hī′pər glī sē′mē ə), *n.* *Med.* an abnormally high level of glucose in the blood. Also, **hy′per·gly·cae′mi·a.** [< NL] —**hy′per·gly·ce′mic, hy′per·gly·cae′mic,** *adj.*

hy·per·gol (hī′pər gōl′, -gôl′, -gol′), *n.* any hypergolic agent. [HYP(ER-) + ERG + -OL²]

hy·per·gol·ic (hī′pər gô′lik, -gol′ik, -gō′lik), *adj.* (esp. of rocket-fuel propellant constituents) igniting spontaneously upon contact with a complementary substance.

Hy·pe·ri·on (hī pēr′ē ən), *n.* **1.** *Class. Myth.* a Titan, the father of Helios, Selene, and Eos: later identified with Apollo. **2.** *Homeric Legend.* Helios. [< L < Gk]

hy·per·ir·ri·ta·bil·i·ty (hī′pər ir′i tə bil′i tē), *n.* extreme irritability. —**hy′per·ir′ri·ta·ble,** *adj.*

hy·per·ker·a·to·sis (hī′pər ker′ə tō′sis), *n.* *Pathol.* **1.** proliferation of the cells of the cornea. **2.** a thickening of the horny layer of the skin. [< NL] —**hy·per·ker·a·tot·ic** (hī′pər ker′ə tot′ik), *adj.*

hy·per·ki·ne·sia (hī′pər ki nē′zhə, -zhē ə, -zē ə, -kī-), *n.* *Pathol.* an abnormal amount of uncontrolled muscular action; spasm. Also, **hy·per·ki·ne·sis** (hī′pər ki nē′sis, -kī-). Cf. **hypokinesia.** [HYPER- + Gk *kī́nēs(is)* movement + -IA] —**hy·per·ki·net·ic** (hī′pər ki net′ik, -kī-), *adj.*

hy·per·me·ter (hī pûr′mi tər), *n.* *Pros.* a verse or line containing one or more additional syllables after those proper to the meter. —**hy·per·met·ric** (hī′pər me′trik), **hy′per·met′ri·cal,** *adj.*

hy·per·me·tro·pi·a (hī′pər mə trō′pē ə), *n.* *Ophthalm.* a condition of the eye in which parallel rays are focused behind the retina, distant objects being seen more distinctly than near ones; far-sightedness (opposed to *myopia*). Also called **hyperopia.** [< Gk *hypérmetr(os)* beyond measure, excessive (see HYPER-, METER²) + -OPIA] —**hy·per·me·trop·ic** (hī′pər mə trop′ik), *adj.* —**hy·per·met·ro·py** (hī′pər me′trə pē), *n.*

Hy·perm·nes·tra (hī′pərm nes′trə), *n.* *Class. Myth.* the only one of the Danaides who did not kill her husband.

hy·per·mo·til·i·ty (hī′pər mō til′i tē), *n.* excessive motility of the stomach or intestine (opposed to *hypomotility*).

hy·per·on (hī′pə ron′), *n.* *Physics.* any of several elementary particles having a mass between that of a neutron and a deuteron. [HYPER- + *-on,* as in *proton, neutron*]

hy·per·o·pi·a (hī′pə rō′pē ə), *n.* *Ophthalm.* hypermetropia. —**hy·per·op·ic** (hī′pə rop′ik), *adj.*

hy·per·os·to·sis (hī′pər o stō′sis), *n.* *Pathol.* **1.** an increase or protuberance of bony tissue. **2.** an overgrowth of bone. —**hy·per·os·tot·ic** (hī′pər o stot′ik), *adj.*

hy·per·ox·ide (hī′pər ok′sīd, -sid), *n.* *Chem.* superoxide.

hy·per·phys·i·cal (hī′pər fiz′i kəl), *adj.* above or beyond the physical; immaterial; supernatural. —**hy′per·phys′i·cal·ly,** *adv.*

hy·per·pi·tu·i·ta·rism (hī′pər pi tōō′i tə riz′əm, -tyōō′-), *n.* *Pathol.* **1.** overactivity of the pituitary gland. **2.** a resultant condition of this, as giantism or acromegaly.

hy·per·pla·sia (hī′pər plā′zhə, -zhē ə, -zē ə), *n.* **1.** *Pathol., Bot.* abnormal multiplication of cells. **2.** *Pathol.* enlargement of a part due to an abnormal numerical increase of its cells. —**hy·per·plas·tic** (hī′pər plas′tik), *adj.*

hy·per·ploid (hī′pər ploid′), *Biol.* —*adj.* **1.** having a chromosome number that is greater than but not a multiple of the diploid number. —*n.* **2.** a hyperploid cell or organism. —**hy′per·ploid′y,** *n.*

hy·perp·ne·a (hī′pərp nē′ə, hī′pər nē′ə), *n.* *Pathol.* abnormally energetic or labored respiration. Also, **hy′perp·noe′a.** [< NL = *hyper-* HYPER- + *pnēa,* var. of *pnoea* < Gk *pnoiḗ* breathing]

hy·per·py·rex·i·a (hī′pər pī rek′sē ə), *n.* *Pathol.* an abnormally high fever. —**hy·per·py·ret·ic** (hī′pər pī ret′ik), **hy′per·py·rex′i·al,** *adj.*

hy·per·se·cre·tion (hī′pər si krē′shən), *n.* an excessive secretion (opposed to *hyposecretion*).

hy·per·sen·si·tive (hī′pər sen′si tiv), *adj.* **1.** excessively sensitive: *to be hypersensitive to criticism.* **2.** *Pathol.* allergic to a substance to which a normal individual does not react.

hy·per·sen·si·tize (hī′pər sen′si tīz′), *v.t.,* **-tized, -tiz·ing.** *Photog.* to treat (a film or emulsion) so as to increase its speed. Also, *esp. Brit.,* **hy′per·sen′si·tise′.** [HYPERSENSIT(IVE) + -IZE] —**hy′per·sen′si·ti·za′tion,** *n.*

hy·per·son·ic (hī′pər son′ik), *adj.* noting or pertaining to speed at least five times that of sound in the same medium.

hy·per·so·phis·ti·cat·ed (hī′pər sə fis′tə kā′tid), *adj.* extremely or overly sophisticated.

hy·per·space (hī′pər spās′, hī′pər spās′), *n.* *Math.* a Euclidean space of dimension greater than three. —**hy·per·spa·tial** (hī′pər spā′shəl), *adj.*

hy·per·sthene (hī′pər sthēn′), *n.* *Mineral.* an orthorhombic pyroxene, iron magnesium silicate, containing more than 14 percent ferrous oxide. [HYPER- + Gk *sthén(os)* strength, might; r. *hyperstene* < F *hyperstène*] —**hy·per·sthen·ic** (hī′pər sthen′ik), *adj.*

hy·per·ten·sion (hī′pər ten′shən), *n.* **1.** excessive or extreme tension. **2.** *Pathol.* **a.** elevation of the blood pressure, esp. the diastolic pressure. **b.** an arterial disease characterized by this condition.

hy·per·ten·sive (hī′pər ten′siv), *Pathol.* —*adj.* **1.** characterized by or causing high blood pressure. —*n.* **2.** a person who has high blood pressure.

hy·per·ther·mi·a (hī′pər thûr′mē ə), *n.* *Med.* **1.** abnormally high fever. **2.** treatment of disease by the induction of fever, as by the injection of foreign protein or the application of heat. Also, **hy·per·ther·my** (hī′pər thûr′mē). [< NL]

hy·per·thy·roid (hī′pər thī′roid), *adj.* **1.** of, pertaining to, or having hyperthyroidism. **2.** characterized by extreme intensity, emotionalism, or lack of restraint.

hy·per·thy·roid·ism (hī′pər thī′roi diz′əm), *n.* *Pathol.* **1.** overactivity of the thyroid gland. **2.** a condition resulting from this, characterized by increased metabolism and exophthalmos.

hy·per·ton·ic (hī′pər ton′ik), *adj.* **1.** *Physiol.* (of tissue) having a greater than normal tone. **2.** *Physical Chem.* noting a solution of higher osmotic pressure than another solution with which it is compared (opposed to *hypotonic*). Cf. **isotonic** (def. 1). —**hy·per·to·nic·i·ty** (hī′pər tō nis′i tē), *n.*

hy·per·tro·phy (hī pûr′trə fē), *n., pl.* **-phies,** *v.,* **-phied, -phy·ing.** —*n.* **1.** *Pathol., Bot.* abnormal enlargement of a part or organ; excessive growth. **2.** excessive growth or accumulation of any kind. —*v.t., v.i.* **3.** to affect with or undergo hypertrophy. —**hy·per·troph·ic** (hī′pər trof′ik), *adj.*

hy·per·ven·ti·la·tion (hī′pər ven′tᵊlā′shən), *n.* *Med.* excessively rapid and deep breathing, resulting esp. in the decrease of carbon dioxide in the blood.

hy·per·vi·ta·mi·no·sis (hī′pər vī′tə mi nō′sis), *n.* *Med.* an abnormal condition caused by an excessive intake of vitamins.

hyp·es·the·sia (hip′is thē′zhə, -zhē ə, -zē ə), *n.* *Pathol.* an abnormally weak sense of pain, heat, cold, or touch. Cf. **hyperesthesia.** —**hyp·es·the·sic** (hip′is thē′sik), *adj.*

hy·pe·thral (hi pē′thrəl, hī-), *adj.* (of a classical building) wholly or partly open to the sky. Also, **hypaethral.** [< L *hypaethr(us)* (< Gk *hýpaithros* open to the sky = *hyp-* HYP- + *aíthros* clear sky) + -AL¹]

hy·pha (hī′fə), *n., pl.* **-phae** (-fē). *Bot.* (in fungi) one of the threadlike elements of the mycelium. [< NL < Gk *hyphḗ* web] —**hy′phal,** *adj.*

hy·phen (hī′fən), *n.* **1.** a short line (-) used to connect the parts of a compound word or the parts of a word divided for any purpose. —*v.t.* **2.** hyphenate. [< LL < Gk: together (adv.) < *hyph' hén* (prep. phrase) = *hypó* under + *hén,* neut. of *heîs* one]

hy·phen·ate (*v.* hī′fə nāt′; *adj.* hī′fə nit, -nāt′), *v.,* **-at·ed, -at·ing,** *adj.* —*v.t.* **1.** to join by a hyphen. **2.** to write with a hyphen. —*adj.* **3.** of or pertaining to something of distinct form or origin that has been joined; connected by a hyphen. —**hy′phen·a′tion,** *n.*

hypno-, a learned borrowing from Greek meaning "sleep," "hypnosis," used in the formation of compound words: *hypnotherapy.* Also, *esp. before a vowel,* **hypn-.** [< Gk *hýpno(s)* sleep; see HYPNOS]

hyp·no·a·nal·y·sis (hip′nō ə nal′i sis), *n.* *Psychoanal.* a method of psychoanalysis in which a patient is put into hypnosis in an attempt to secure analytic data, free associations, and early emotional reactions from him. —**hyp·no·an·a·lyt·ic** (hip′nō an′ᵊlit′ik), *adj.*

hyp·no·graph (hip′nə graf′, -gräf′), *n.* an instrument that measures activities of the human body during sleep.

hyp·noi·dal (hip noid′ᵊl), *adj.* *Psychol.* characterizing a state that resembles mild hypnosis but that is usually induced by other than hypnotic means. Also, **hyp′noid.**

hyp·nol·o·gy (hip nol′ə jē), *n.* the science dealing with the phenomena of sleep. —**hyp·no·log·ic** (hip′nəloj′ik), **hyp′no·log′i·cal,** *adj.* —**hyp·nol′o·gist,** *n.*

Hyp·nos (hip′nos), *n. Class. Myth.* the god of sleep, brother of Thanatos and often regarded as a son of Erebus and Nyx: identified by the Romans with Somnus. Also, **Hypnus.** [< Gk: sleep; c. OE *swefn,* L *somnus*]

hyp·no·sis (hip nō′sis), *n., pl.* **-ses** (-sēz). **1.** an artificially induced state resembling sleep, characterized by heightened susceptibility to suggestion. **2.** hypnotism (defs. 1, 2).

hyp·no·ther·a·py (hip′nō ther′ə pē), *n.* treatment of disease by means of hypnotism.

hyp·not·ic (hip not′ik), *adj.* **1.** of or pertaining to hypnosis or hypnotism. **2.** inducing or like that which induces hypnosis. **3.** susceptible to hypnotism, as a person. **4.** under the influence of hypnosis; hypnotized. **5.** inducing sleep. —*n.* **6.** an agent or drug that produces sleep; sedative. **7.** a person who is susceptible to hypnosis. **8.** a person under the influence of hypnotism. [< medical L *hypnōtic(us)* < Gk *hypnōtikós* sleep-inducing, narcotic = *hypnō-* (var. s. of *hypnōein* to put to sleep) + *-tikos* -TIC] —**hyp·not′i·cal·ly,** *adv.*

hyp·no·tise (hip′nə tīz′), *v.t., v.i.,* **-tised, -tis·ing.** *Chiefly Brit.* hypnotize. —**hyp′no·tis′a·bil′i·ty,** *n.* —**hyp′no·tis′a·ble,** *adj.* —**hyp′no·ti·sa′tion,** *n.*

hyp·no·tism (hip′nə tiz′əm), *n.* **1.** the science dealing with the induction of hypnosis. **2.** the act of hypnotizing. **3.** hypnosis (def. 1). [HYPNOT(IC) + -ISM]

hyp·no·tist (hip′nə tist), *n.* a person who hypnotizes. [HYPNOT(IC) + -IST]

hyp·no·tize (hip′nə tīz′), *v.,* **-tized, -tiz·ing.** —*v.t.* **1.** to put in the hypnotic state. **2.** to influence, control, or direct completely, as if by hypnotic suggestion. —*v.i.* **3.** to practice hypnosis; put or be able to put others into a hypnotic state. Also, *esp. Brit.,* **hypnotise.** [HYPNOT(IC) + -IZE] —**hyp′no·tiz′a·bil′i·ty,** *n.* —**hyp′no·tiz′a·ble,** *adj.* —**hyp′no·ti·za′tion,** *n.*

Hyp·nus (hip′nəs), *n. Class. Myth.* Hypnos.

hy·po[1] (hī′pō), *n.* See **sodium thiosulfate.** [short for HYPOSULFITE]

hy·po[2] (hī′pō), *n., pl.* **-pos,** *v.,* **-poed, -po·ing.** *Informal.* —*n.* **1.** a hypodermic syringe or injection. —*v.t.* **2.** to administer a hypodermic injection to. **3.** to stimulate as by administering a hypodermic injection. [HYPO(DERMIC)]

hypo-, an element appearing in loan words from Greek, where it meant "under" (*hypostasis*); on this model used, esp. as opposed to **hyper-,** in the formation of compound words (*hypothyroidism*). Also, *esp. before a vowel,* **hyp-.** [< Gk, comb. form of *hypó* under (prep.), below (adv.); c. L *sub;* see SUB-]

hy·po·a·cid·i·ty (hī′pō ə sid′i tē), *n.* acidity in a lesser degree than is usual or normal, as of the gastric juice. —**hy·po·ac·id** (hī′pō as′id), *adj.*

hy·po·blast (hī′pə blast′), *n. Embryol.* **1.** the entoderm. **2.** the cells entering into the inner layer of a young gastrula, capable of becoming entoderm and, to a certain extent, mesoderm. —**hy′po·blas′tic,** *adj.*

hy·po·caust (hī′pə kôst′, hip′ə-), *n.* a hollow space or system of flues in the floor or walls of an ancient Roman building or room that received and distributed the heat from a furnace. [< L *hypocaust(um)* < Gk *hypókauston* room heated from below = *hypo-* HYPO- + *kaustón,* neut. of *kaustós* heated, burned, verbal adj.; see CAUSTIC]

hy·po·chlor·hy·dri·a (hī′pə klōr hī′drē ə, -klôr-), *n. Pathol.* an abnormally small amount of hydrochloric acid in the gastric secretions.

hy·po·chlor·ite (hī′pə klōr′īt, -klôr′-), *n. Chem.* a salt or ester of hypochlorous acid. [HYPO- + CHLORITE[2]]

hy′po·chlor′ous ac′id (hī′pə klōr′əs, -klôr′-), *Chem.* an acid, HOCl, known only in solution and in the form of its salts, whose solutions have strong bleaching properties.

hy·po·chon·dri·a (hī′pə kon′drē ə), *n.* **1.** Also, **hypochondriasis.** *Psychiatry.* an abnormal condition characterized by a depressed emotional state and imaginary ill health, referable to the physical condition of the body or one of its parts. **2.** excessive worry or talk about one's health. [< LL < Gk, neut. pl. of *hypochóndrios* pertaining to the upper abdomen (supposed seat of melancholy) = *hypo-* HYPO- + *chóndr(os)* ensiform cartilage + *-ios* adj. suffix]

hy·po·chon·dri·ac (hī′pə kon′drē ak′), *adj.* **1.** Also, **hy·po·chon·dri·a·cal** (hī′pō kon drī′ə kəl). pertaining to or suffering from hypochondria: *hypochondriac depression.* **2.** produced by hypochondria. **3.** of or pertaining to the hypochondrium. —*n.* **4.** a person suffering from or subject to hypochondria. **5.** a person who worries or talks excessively about his health. [< medical L *hypochondriac(us)* < Gk *hypochondriakós* affected in the upper abdomen] —**hy′po·chon·dri′a·cal·ly,** *adv.*

hy·po·chon·dri·a·sis (hī′pō kən drī′ə sis), *n. Psychiatry.* hypochondria (def. 1).

hy·po·chon·dri·um (hī′pə kon′drē əm), *n., pl.* **-dri·a** (-drē ə). *Anat., Zool.* **1.** either of two regions of the abdomen of man, situated on each side of the epigastrium and above the lumbar regions. **2.** a corresponding region in certain other vertebrates. [< NL < Gk *hypochóndrion* abdomen. See HYPOCHONDRIA, -IUM]

hy·poc·o·rism (hī pok′ə riz′əm, hi-), *n.* **1.** a pet name. **2.** the practice of using a pet name. **3.** the use of forms of speech imitative of baby talk, esp. by an adult. [< Gk *hypokórism(a)* pet name. See HYPOCORISTIC, -ISM]

hy·po·co·ris·tic (hī′pō kō ris′tik, -kô-, hip′ə-), *adj.* endearing, as a pet name, diminutive, or euphemism. [< Gk *hypokoristik(ós)* diminutive = *hypokor(ízesthai)* (to) play the child, call by endearing names (*hypo-* HYPO- + *kor-* child, cf. *kórē* girl, *kóros* boy) + *-istikos* -ISTIC] —**hy′po·co·ris′ti·cal·ly,** *adv.*

hy·po·cot·yl (hī′pə kot′əl), *n. Bot.* (in the embryo of a plant) that part of the stem below cotyledons. See diag. under **cotyledon.** [HYPO- + COTYL(EDON)] —**hy′po·cot′y·lous,** *adj.*

hy·poc·ri·sy (hi pok′rə sē), *n., pl.* **-sies.** a semblance of having desirable or publicly approved attitudes, beliefs, principles, etc., that one does not actually possess. [ME *ipocrisie* < OF < LL *hypocrisis* < Gk *hypókrisis* play acting = *hypokrí(nesthai)* (to) play a part, explain (see HYPO-, CRITIC) + *-sis* -SIS; *h-* (reintroduced in 16th century) < L and Gk] —**Syn.** See **deceit.**

hyp·o·crite (hip′ə krit), *n.* a person who pretends to have desirable or publicly approved attitudes, beliefs, principles, etc., he does not actually possess. [ME *ipocrite* < OF < LL *hypocrit(a)* < Gk *hypokritḗs* stage actor, hence one who pretends to be what he is not = *hypokrí(nesthai)* (see HYPOCRISY) + *-tēs* agent suffix] —**hyp′o·crit′i·cal,** *adj.* —**hyp′o·crit′i·cal·ly,** *adv.* —**Syn.** deceiver, pretender, pharisee.

hy·po·cy·cloid (hī′pə sī′kloid), *n. Geom.* a curve generated by the motion of a point on the circumference of a circle that rolls internally, without slipping, on a given circle. —**hy′po·cy·cloi′dal,** *adj.*

H, Hypocycloid; P, Point tracing hypocycloid within fixed circle

hy·po·derm (hī′pə dûrm′), *n.* **1.** *Zool.* the epidermis of an arthropod. **2.** *Bot.* hypodermis. —**hy′po·der′mal,** *adj.*

hy·po·der·mic (hī′pə dûr′mik), *adj.* **1.** characterized by the introduction of medical remedies under the skin: *hypodermic injection.* **2.** introduced under the skin: *a hypodermic medication.* **3.** pertaining to parts under the skin. **4.** stimulating; causing greater energy, awareness, etc. —*n.* **5.** a hypodermic remedy. **6.** a hypodermic injection. **7.** See **hypodermic syringe.** —**hy′po·der′mi·cal·ly,** *adv.*

hypoder′mic nee′dle, a hollow needle used to inject solutions subcutaneously.

hypoder′mic syringe′, a small glass piston or barrel syringe having a detachable, hollow needle for use in injecting solutions subcutaneously.

Hypodermic syringe

hy·po·der·mis (hī′pə dûr′mis), *n.* **1.** *Zool.* the surface epithelium of an invertebrate when covered over by the noncellular secretion that it produces. **2.** *Bot.* a tissue or layer of cells beneath the epidermis. [HYPO- + (EPI)DERMIS]

hy·po·eu·tec·toid (hī′pō yo͞o tek′toid), *adj. Metall.* (of steel) having less carbon than the 0.8 percent of eutectoid steel.

hy·po·func·tion (hī′pō fungk′shən), *n.* abnormally diminished function, esp. of glands or other organs (opposed to *hyperfunction*).

hy·po·gas·tric (hī′pə gas′trik), *adj.* of, pertaining to, or situated in the hypogastrium. [< medical L *hypogastric(us).* See HYPOGASTRIUM, -IC]

hy·po·gas·tri·um (hī′pə gas′trē əm), *n., pl.* **-tri·a** (-trē ə). *Anat.* the lower and median part of the abdomen. [< medical L < Gk *hypogástrion* = *hypo-* HYPO- + *gastríon,* dim. of *gastḗr* paunch]

hy·po·ge·al (hī′pə jē′əl), *adj.* underground; subterranean. [< L *hypogē(us)* HYPOGEOUS + -AL[1]]

hy·po·gene (hī′pə jēn′, hip′ə-), *adj. Geol.* **1.** formed beneath the earth's surface, as granite (opposed to *epigene*). **2.** formed by ascending waters, as mineral or ore deposits. [HYPO- + *-gene,* var. of -GEN] —**hy·po·gen·ic** (hī′pə jen′ik, hip′ə-), *adj.*

hy·pog·e·nous (hī poj′ə nəs, hi-), *adj. Bot.* growing beneath, or on the undersurface, as fungi on leaves.

hy·po·ge·ous (hī′pə jē′əs, hip′ə-), *adj.* **1.** underground; subterranean. **2.** *Bot.* growing or remaining underground. [< L *hypogēus* < Gk *hypógeios* = *hypo-* HYPO- + *gê* earth + *-ios* adj. suffix]

hy·po·ge·um (hī′pə jē′əm, hip′ə-), *n., pl.* **-ge·a** (-jē′ə). **1.** *Anc. Archit.* the underground part of a building, as a vault. **2.** an underground burial chamber; a subterranean tomb. [< L *hypogēum* < Gk *hypógeion* underground chamber (neut. of *hypógeios* underground) = *hypo-* HYPO- + *gê* earth + *-ion* neut. adj. suffix]

hy·po·glos·sal (hī′pə glos′əl, -glô′səl), *Anat.* —*adj.* **1.** situated under the tongue. —*n.* **2.** See **hypoglossal nerve.** [HYPO- + Gk *glôss(a)* tongue + -AL[1]]

hy′poglos′sal nerve′, *Anat.* either one of the twelfth pair of cranial nerves, consisting of motor fibers that innervate the muscles of the tongue.

hy·po·gly·ce·mi·a (hī′pō glī sē′mē ə), *n. Pathol.* an abnormally low level of glucose in the blood. —**hy′po·gly·ce′mic,** *adj.*

hy·pog·na·thous (hī pog′nə thəs), *adj.* **1.** *Zool.* (of birds and insects) having the lower jaw or mandible longer than the upper. **2.** *Anthropol.* having the lower jaw longer and more projecting than the upper. —**hy·pog′na·thism,** *n.*

hy·pog·y·nous (hī poj′ə nəs, hi-), *adj. Bot.* **1.** situated on the receptacle beneath the pistil, as stamens, sepals, etc. **2.** having stamens, sepals, etc., so arranged. —**hy·pog′y·ny,** *n.*

hy′poid gear′ (hī′poid), *Mach.* a gear resembling a bevel gear in form but designed to mesh with a similar gear in such a way that their axes would not intersect, one axis crossing over the other in approximately a right angle. [HYP(ERBOL)OID]

hy·po·ki·ne·si·a (hī′pō ki nē′zhə, -zhē ə, -zē ə, -kī-), *n. Pathol.* an abnormally diminished motor function or mobility, esp. through lack of physical exercise. Also, **hy·po·ki·ne·sis** (hī′pō ki nē′sis, -kī-). Cf. **hyperkinesia.** [HYPO- + Gk *kinēs(is)* movement + -IA] —**hy·po·ki·net·ic** (hī′pō ki net′ik, -kī-), *adj.*

hy·po·ma·ni·a (hī′pə mā′nē ə, -mān′yə), *n. Psychiatry.* a mania of low intensity. —**hy·po·man·ic** (hī′pə man′ik), *adj., n.*

hy·po·mo·til·i·ty (hī′pə mō til′i tē), *n.* abnormally slow motility of the stomach or intestine (opposed to *hypermotility*).

hy·po·nas·ty (hī′pə nas′tē), *n. Bot.* increased growth along the lower surface of an organ or part, causing it to bend upward. —**hy′po·nas′tic,** *adj.* —**hy′po·nas′ti·cal·ly,** *adv.*

hy′poni′trous ac′id, *Chem.* an unstable, crystalline acid, $H_2N_2O_2$. —**hy·po·ni·trous** (hī′pə nī′trəs), *adj.*

hy·po·noi·a (hī′pə noi′ə), *n.* dulled mental activity; diminished function of thought. Also, **hy·po·ne·a** (hī′pə nē′ə). Also called **hypopsychosis.**

hy·po·phar·ynx (hī′pə far′iŋgks), *n., pl.* **-pha·ryn·ges** (-fə rin′jēz), **-phar·ynx·es.** (in an insect) a tonguelike lobe on the floor of the mouth.

hy·po·phos·phate (hī′pə fos′fāt), *n. Chem.* a salt or ester of hypophosphoric acid.

hy·po·phos·phite (hī′pə fos′fīt), *n. Chem.* a salt of hypophosphorus acid, as sodium hypophosphite, NaH_2PO_2.

hy′pophosphor′ic ac′id, *Chem.* a tetrabasic acid, $H_4P_2C_6$. —**hy·po·phos·phor·ic** (hī′pə fos fôr′ik, -for′-), *adj.*

hy′pophos′phorous ac′id, *Chem.* a monobasic acid, H_3PO_2, used as a reducing agent. —**hy·po·phos·phor·ous** (hī′pə fos′fər əs, -fos fôr′əs, -fôr′-), *adj.*

hy·poph·y·ge (hī pof′i jē, hi-), *n.* apophyge (def. 1).

hy·poph·y·sec·to·my (hī pof′i sek′tə mē, hi-), *n., pl.* **-mies.** *Surg.* excision of the pituitary gland. [HYPOPHYS(IS) + -ECTOMY]

hy·poph·y·sis (hī pof′i sis, hi-), *n., pl.* **-ses** (-sēz′). *Anat.* See **pituitary gland.** [< Gk: outgrowth (from below) = *hypophý(ein)* (to) grow beneath (*hypo-* HYPO- + *phy-* grow, c. BE) + *-sis* -SIS] —**hy·po·phys·e·al** (hī′pə-fiz′ē əl, hip′ə-, hī pof′i sē′əl, hi-), **hy·po·phys·i·al** (hī′pə-fiz′ē əl, hip′ə-), *adj.*

hy·po·pi·tu·i·ta·rism (hī′pō pi to͞o′i tə riz′əm, -tyo͞o′-), *n. Pathol.* **1.** abnormally diminished activity of the pituitary gland, esp. of the anterior lobe. **2.** the condition produced by this, characterized by obesity, retention of adolescent traits, sterility, and, in extreme cases, dwarfism.

hy·po·pla·si·a (hī′pə plā′zhə, -zhē ə, -zē ə), *n.* **1.** *Pathol., Bot.* abnormal deficiency of cells or structural elements. **2.** *Pathol.* an underdeveloped condition in which an organ or structure remains immature or subnormal in size. Also, **hy·po·plas·ty** (hī′pō plas′tē). —**hy′po·plas′tic,** *adj.*

hy·po·ploid (hī′pə ploid′), *Biol.* —*adj.* **1.** having a chromosome number that is less than the diploid number. —*n.* **2.** a hypoploid cell or organism. —**hy′po·ploid′y,** *n.*

hy·pop·ne·a (hī pop′nē ə, hi-), *n. Med.* abnormally shallow breathing. [< NL = *hypo-* HYPO- + *pnēa*, var. of *pnoea* < Gk *pnoē* breathing]

hy·po·psy·cho·sis (hī′pō sī kō′sis), *n.* hyponoia.

hy·po·py·on (hī pō′pē on′, hi-), *n. Ophthalm.* an effusion of pus into the anterior chamber of the eye. [HYPO- + Gk *pýon* pus, discharge from a sore]

hy·po·se·cre·tion (hī′pō si krē′shən), *n.* a diminished secretion (opposed to *hypersecretion*).

hy·po·spray (hī′pō sprā′), *n.* an instrument, similar to a hypodermic syringe but using no needle, for forcing extremely fine jets of a medicated solution through the unbroken skin.

hy·pos·ta·sis (hī pos′tə sis, hi-), *n., pl.* **-ses** (-sēz′). **1.** *Metaphys.* **a.** something that stands under and supports; foundation. **b.** the underlying or essential part of anything, as distinguished from attributes; substance, essence, or essential principle. **2.** *Theol.* **a.** one of the three real and distinct subsistences in the one substance of God. **b.** a person of the Trinity. **c.** the one personality of Christ uniting the human and the divine. **3.** *Med.* **a.** the accumulation of blood or its solid components in parts of an organ or body due to poor circulation. **b.** such sedimentation, as in a test tube. [< LL < Gk: that which settles at the bottom, substance, nature, essence]

hy·pos·ta·sise (hī pos′tə sīz′, hi-), *v.t.,* **-sised, -sis·ing.** *Chiefly Brit.* hypostasize.

hy·pos·ta·size (hī pos′tə sīz′, hi-), *v.t.,* **-sized, -siz·ing.** hypostatize.

hy·po·stat·ic (hī′pə stat′ik), *adj.* **1.** of or pertaining to a hypostasis; fundamental. **2.** *Theol.* pertaining to or constituting a distinct personal being or subsistence. **3.** *Genetics.* (of nonallelic genes) recessive. Also, **hy′po·stat′i·cal.** [< Gk *hypostatik(ós)* pertaining to substance = *hypostat(ós)* placed under, giving support (*hypo-* HYPO- + *sta-* STAND + *-tos* verbal adj. suffix) + *-ikos* -IC] —**hy′po·stat′i·cal·ly,** *adv.*

hy·pos·ta·tise (hī pos′tə tīz′, hi-), *v.t.,* **-tised, -tis·ing.** *Chiefly Brit.* hypostatize. —**hy·pos′ta·ti·sa′tion,** *n.*

hy·pos·ta·tize (hī pos′tə tīz′, hi-), *v.t.,* **-tized, -tiz·ing.** to treat or regard (a concept, idea, etc.) as a distinct substance or reality. [< Gk *hypostat(ós)* (see HYPOSTATIC) + -IZE] —**hy·pos′ta·ti·za′tion,** *n.*

hy·pos·the·ni·a (hī′pos thē′nē ə), *n. Pathol.* abnormal lack of strength; weakness. —**hy·pos·then·ic** (hī′pos then′-ik), *adj.*

hy·po·style (hī′pə stīl′, hip′ə-), *Archit.* —*adj.* **1.** having many columns carrying the roof or ceiling: *a hypostyle hall.* —*n.* **2.** a hypostyle structure. [< Gk *hypóstȳl(os)* resting on pillars = *hypo-* HYPO- + *stŷlos* pillar]

hy·po·sul·fite (hī′pə sul′fīt), *n. Chem.* **1.** Also, **hydrosulfite.** a salt of hyposulfurous acid. **2.** See **sodium thiosulfate.** Also, **hy′po·sul′phite.**

hy′posulfur′ous ac′id, *Chem.* an acid, $H_2S_2O_4$, known only in solution or in the form of its salts. —**hy·po·sul·fur·ous** (hī′pə sul fyo͝or′əs, -sul′fər əs), *adj.*

hy·po·tax·is (hī′pə tak′sis), *n. Gram.* dependent relation or construction, as of clauses; syntactic subordination. [< Gk: subjection] —**hy·po·tac·tic** (hī′pə tak′tik, hip′ə-), *adj.*

hy·po·ten·sion (hī′pə ten′shən), *n. Pathol.* **1.** decreased or lowered blood pressure. **2.** a disease or condition characterized by this symptom.

hy·po·ten·sive (hī′pō ten′siv), *Pathol.* —*adj.* **1.** characterized by or causing low blood pressure, as shock. —*n.* **2.** a hypotensive person or agent. [HYPOTENS(ION) + -IVE]

hy·pot·e·nuse (hī pot′ənno͞os′, -nyo͞os′), *n. Geom.* the side of a right triangle opposite the right angle. Also, **hypothenuse.** [earlier *hypotenusa* < L < Gk *hypoteínousa (grammḗ)* subtending (line) (fem. prp. of *hypoteínein* to subtend) = *hypo-* HYPO- + *tein-* stretch + *-ousa* fem. prp. suffix]

Hypotenuse

90°

Hypotenuse of a right triangle

hypoth., **1.** hypothesis. **2.** hypothetical.

hy·po·thal·a·mus (hī′pə thal′ə məs), *n., pl.* **-mi** (-mī′). *Anat.* the portion of the diencephalon forming the floor of the median ventricle of the brain. [< NL] —**hy·po·tha·lam·ic** (hī′pō thə lam′ik, hip′ō-), *adj.*

hy·poth·ec (hī poth′ik, hi-), *n. Roman and Civil Law.* **1.** a mortgage or security held by a creditor on the property of his debtor without possession of it. **2.** (in some modern legal systems) a security interest created in immovable property. [earlier *hypotheca* < LL < Gk *hypothḗkē* deposit, pledge, mortgage (akin to *hypotithénai* to deposit as pledge). See HYPO-, THECA]

hy·poth·e·car·y (hī poth′ə ker′ē, hi-), *adj.* **1.** of or pertaining to a hypothec. **2.** created or secured by a hypothec.

hy·poth·e·cate[1] (hī poth′ə kāt′, hi-), *v.t.,* **-cat·ed, -cat·ing.** to pledge as security without delivering over. [< ML *hypothēcāt(us)*, ptp. of *hypothecāre*] —**hy·poth′e·ca′tion,** *n.* —**hy·poth′e·ca′tor,** *n.*

hy·poth·e·cate[2] (hī poth′ə kāt′, hi-), *v.i., v.t.,* **-cat·ed, -cat·ing.** hypothesize. [< Gk *hypothḗk(ē)* suggestion, counsel (akin to *hypotithénai* to assume, suppose) + -ATE[1]] —**hy·poth′e·cat′er,** *n.*

hy·poth·e·nuse (hī poth′ə no͞os′, -nyo͞os′), *n.* hypotenuse.

hy·po·ther·mal (hī′pə thûr′məl), *adj.* **1.** lukewarm. **2.** characterized by subnormal body temperature.

hy·po·ther·mi·a (hī′pə thûr′mē ə), *n. Med.* the artificial reduction of body temperature to slow metabolic processes, usually for facilitating heart surgery.

hy·poth·e·sis (hī poth′i sis, hi-), *n., pl.* **-ses** (-sēz′). **1.** a proposition or set of propositions set forth as an explanation for the occurrence of some specified group of phenomena, either asserted merely as a provisional conjecture to guide investigation **(working hypothesis)** or accepted as highly probable in the light of established facts. **2.** a proposition assumed as a premise in an argument. **3.** the antecedent of a conditional proposition. **4.** a mere assumption or guess. [< Gk: basis, supposition] —**hy·poth′e·sist,** *n.* —**Syn. 1.** See **theory.**

hy·poth·e·sise (hī poth′i sīz′, hi-), *v.i., v.t.,* **-sised, -sis·ing.** *Chiefly Brit.* hypothesize. —**hy·poth′e·sis′er,** *n.*

hy·poth·e·size (hī poth′i sīz′, hi-), *v.,* **-sized, -siz·ing.** —*v.i.* **1.** to form a hypothesis. —*v.t.* **2.** to assume by hypothesis. Also, **hypothecate.** —**hy·poth′e·siz′er,** *n.*

hy·po·thet·i·cal (hī′pə thet′i kəl), *adj.* **1.** assumed by hypothesis; supposed: *a hypothetical case.* **2.** of, pertaining to, involving, or characterized by hypothesis: *hypothetical reasoning.* **3.** presumed to exist: *a hypothetical acid known only from its salts.* **4.** *Logic.* **a.** (of a proposition) highly conjectural; not well supported by available evidence. **b.** (of a proposition or syllogism) conditional. Also, **hy′po·thet′ic.** [< Gk *hypothetik(ós)* supposed (*hypo-* HYPO- + *the-* put (unreduplicated s. of *tithénai* to put) + *-tikos* -TIC) + -AL[1]] —**hy′po·thet′i·cal·ly,** *adv.*

hypothet′ical imper′ative, *Kantianism.* a statement formulating the action necessary to attain a desired end.

hy·po·thy·roid·ism (hī′pə thī′roi diz′əm), *n. Pathol.* **1.** deficient activity of the thyroid gland. **2.** the condition produced by a deficiency of thyroid secretion, resulting in goiter, myxedema, and, in children, cretinism. —**hy′po-thy′roid,** *adj.*

hy·po·ton·ic (hī′pə ton′ik), *adj.* **1.** *Physiol.* (of tissue) having less than the normal tone. **2.** *Physical Chem.* noting a solution of lower osmotic pressure than another solution with which it is compared (opposed to *hypertonic*). Cf. **isotonic** (def. 1). —**hy·po·to·nic·i·ty** (hī′pō tō nis′i tē), *n.*

hy·po·xan·thine (hī′pə zan′thēn, -thin), *n. Chem.* an alkaloidal purine derivative, $C_5H_4N_4O$, used chiefly in biochemical research. —**hy′po·xan′thic,** *adj.*

hy·pox·i·a (hī pok′sē ə), *n. Pathol.* a deficiency in the amount of oxygen that reaches the tissues of the body. [HYP- + OX(Y)- + -IA] —**hy·pox·ic** (hī pok′sik), *adj.*

hypso-, a learned borrowing from Greek meaning "height," "altitude," used in the formation of compound words: *hypsometer.* Also, **hypsi-.** [< Gk, comb. form of *hýpsos* height]

hyp·sog·ra·phy (hip sog′rə fē), *n.* **1.** a branch of geography that deals with the measurement and mapping of the topography of the earth above sea level. **2.** topographical relief, esp. as represented on a map. —**hyp·so·graph·ic** (hip′sə graf′ik), **hyp′so·graph′i·cal,** *adj.*

hyp·som·e·ter (hip som′i tər), *n.* a device for determining the elevation above sea level or the reliability of a thermometer from the boiling point of liquids.

hyp·som·e·try (hip som′i trē), *n.* measurement of elevations or altitudes. —**hyp·so·met·ric** (hip′sə me′trik), **hyp′-so·met′ri·cal,** *adj.* —**hyp′so·met′ri·cal·ly,** *adv.*

hy·ra·coid (hī′rə koid′), *adj.* belonging or pertaining to the order *Hyracoidea*, comprising the hyraxes. [< NL *Hyracoid(ea)* = *hyrac-* (s. of *hyrax*) HYRAX + *-oidea* -OID] —**hy·ra·coi·di·an** (hī′rə koi′dē ən), *adj., n.*

hy·rax (hī′raks), *n., pl.* **hy·rax·es, hy·ra·ces** (hī′rə sēz′). any of numerous small mammals of the order *Hyracoidea*, of Africa and the Mediterranean region, having short legs, ears, and tail, and hooflike nails on the toes. [< NL < Gk: shrewmouse]

Hyr·ca·ni·a (hər kā′nē ə), *n.* an ancient province of the Persian empire, SE of the Caspian Sea. —**Hyr·ca′ni·an,** *adj.*

hy·son (hī′sən), *n.* a Chinese green tea dried and prepared from twisted leaves, esp. of the early crop **(young hyson).** [< Chin (Cantonese) *hei-ch'un* blooming spring, c. Mandarin *hsi-ch'un*]

hys·sop (his′əp), *n.* **1.** an aromatic, labiate herb, *Hyssopus officinalis*, having blue flowers. **2.** *Bible.* a plant, perhaps the origan, whose twigs were used in ceremonial sprinkling. [< L *hyssōp(us)* < Gk *hýssōpos* < Sem (cf. Heb *ēzōv*); r. ME, OE *ysope* < LL *ysōpus*]

hyster-, var. of **hystero-** before a vowel: *hysterectomy.*

hys·ter·ec·to·my (his′tə rek′tə mē), *n., pl.* **-mies.** *Surg.* excision of the uterus.

hys·ter·e·sis (his′tə rē′sis), *n. Physics.* **1.** the time lag exhibited by a body in reacting to changes in the forces, esp. magnetic forces, affecting it. **2.** the phenomenon exhibited by a system in which the reaction of the system to changes is dependent upon its past reactions to change. [< Gk: deficiency, state of being behind or late, whence inferior = *hýster(os)* behind + *-ēsis* state of, result of] —**hys·ter·et·ic** (his′tə ret′ik), **hys·ter·e·si·al** (his′tə rē′sē əl), *adj.* —**hys′-ter·et′i·cal·ly,** *adv.*

hys·te·ri·a (hi stēr′ē ə, -ster′-), *n.* **1.** an uncontrollable outburst of emotion or fear, often characterized by irrationality, laughter, weeping, etc. **2.** a psychoneurotic disorder characterized by violent emotional outbreaks, disturbances of sensory and motor functions, and various abnormal effects due to autosuggestion. [HYSTER(IC) + -IA]

hys·ter·ic (hi ster′ik), *n.* **1.** Usually, **hysterics.** a fit of uncontrollable laughter or weeping; hysteria. **2.** a person subject to hysteria. **—*adj.* 3.** hysterical. [< L *hysteric(us)* < Gk *hysterikós* of the womb]

hys·ter·i·cal (hi ster′i kəl), *adj.* **1.** of, pertaining to, or characterized by hysteria. **2.** irrational from fear, emotion, or an emotional shock. **3.** suffering from or subject to hysteria. **4.** causing unrestrained laughter; very funny. [< L *hysteric(us)* HYSTERIC + -AL[1]] **—hys·ter′i·cal·ly,** *adv.*

hystero-, a learned borrowing from Greek meaning "uterus," used in the formation of compound words: *hysterotomy.* Also, *esp. before a vowel,* **hyster-.** [< Gk, comb. form of *hystéra*]

hys·ter·o·gen·ic (his′tər ə jen′ik), *adj. Med.* inducing hysteria. [HYSTER(IA) + -O- + -GENIC] **—hys·ter·og·e·ny** (his′tə roj′ə nē), *n.*

hys·ter·oid (his′tə roid′), *adj.* resembling hysteria. Also, **hys′ter·oi′dal.** [HYSTER(IA) + -OID]

hys·ter·on prot·er·on (his′tə ron′ prot′ə ron′), **1.** *Logic.* a fallacious proof that begs the question at issue by assuming as a premise the conclusion to be proved. **2.** *Rhet.* a figure of speech in which the logical order of two elements in discourse is reversed, as in "bred and born" for "born and bred." [< LL < Gk *hýsteron* (neut. of *hýsteros*) latter + *próteron* (neut. of *próteros*) former]

hys·ter·ot·o·my (his′tə rot′ə mē), *n., pl.* **-mies.** *Surg.* the operation of cutting into the uterus, as in Caesarean section.

hys·tri·co·mor·phic (his′trə kō môr′fik), *adj.* belonging or pertaining to the *Hystricomorpha,* the suborder of rodents that includes the porcupine, chinchilla, agouti, coypu, guinea pig, etc. [< L *hystric-* (s. of *hystrix* porcupine < Gk) + -O- + -MORPHIC] **—hys·tric·o·morph** (hi strik′ə môrf′), *n.*

Hythe (hīth), *n.* a town in E Kent, in SE England: one of the Cinque Ports. 10,990 (est. 1965).

Hz, hertz.

I

DEVELOPMENT OF MAJUSCULE								
NORTH SEMITIC	GREEK		ETR.	LATIN		MODERN		
						GOTHIC	ITALIC	ROMAN
𐤉	⌈	I	I	I	I	𝔍	*I*	I

DEVELOPMENT OF MINUSCULE					
ROMAN CURSIVE	ROMAN UNCIAL	CAROL. MIN.	MODERN		
			GOTHIC	ITALIC	ROMAN
I	I	i	i	*i*	i

The ninth letter of the English alphabet developed from North Semitic consonant *yodh* (y) which became the Greek vowel *iota* (ι). Originally, it was much like a Z in form, acquiring its present shape in Greek. The minuscule (i) was first written with a dot in early Medieval Latin to distinguish it from the *n* (written ıı), the *m* (written ııı), and other letters written with similar vertical strokes.

I, i (ī), *n., pl.* **I's** or **Is, i's** or **is. 1.** the ninth letter of the English alphabet, a vowel. **2.** any spoken sound represented by the letter *I* or *i*, as in *nice, big,* or *ski.* **3.** something having the shape of an I. **4.** a written or printed representation of the letter *I* or *i.* **5.** a device, as a printer's type, for reproducing the letter *I* or *i.*

I (ī), *pron., nom.* **I,** *poss.* **my** or **mine,** *obj.* **me;** *pl. nom.* **we,** *poss.* **our** or **ours,** *obj.* **us;** *n., pl.* **I's.** —*pron.* **1.** the nominative singular pronoun, used by a speaker in referring to himself. —*n.* **2.** (used to denote the narrator of a literary work written in the first person singular.) **3.** *Metaphys.* the ego. [ME *ik, ich, i;* OE *ic, ih;* c. G *ich,* Icel *ek,* L *ego,* Gk *egṓ,* Skt *ahám*]

I, 1. the ninth in order or in a series. **2.** (*sometimes l.c.*) the Roman numeral for 1. Cf. **Roman numerals. 3.** *Chem.* iodine.

i, *Math.* the imaginary number $\sqrt{-1}$.

i-, var. of **y-.**

-i-, the typical ending of the first element of compounds of Latin words, as **-o-** is of Greek words, but often used in English with a first element of any origin, if the second element is of Latin origin: *cuneiform; Frenchify.*

I., 1. Independent. **2.** Island; Islands. **3.** Isle; Isles.

i., 1. imperator. **2.** incisor. **3.** interest. **4.** intransitive. **5.** island. **6.** isle; isles.

I-131, *Chem.* See **iodine 131.** Also, **I 131.**

-ia, a noun suffix having restricted application in various fields, as in names of diseases (*malaria; anemia*), place names (*Italia; Rumania*), names of Roman feasts (*Lupercalia*), Latin or Latinizing plurals (*Amphibia; insignia; Reptilia*), and in other loan words from Latin (*militia*). [< NL, L, Gk = *-i-* (formative or connective) or *-ī-* (Gk *-ei-*) + *-a,* fem. sing. or neut. pl. n. or adj. ending]

Ia., Iowa.

IA, Iowa (approved esp. for use with zip code).

IAEA, International Atomic Energy Agency.

-ial, an adjective suffix appearing in loan words from Latin: *filial; imperial.* [< L *-iāl(is)* (m. and f.), *-iāle* (neut.) adj. suffix. See -I-, -AL[1]]

i·amb (ī′am, ī′amb), *n. Pros.* a foot of two syllables, a short followed by a long in quantitative meter, or an unstressed followed by a stressed in accentual meter, as in *Come live / with me / and be / my love.* [short for IAMBUS]

i·am·bic (ī am′bik), *adj.* **1.** *Pros.* **a.** pertaining to the iamb. **b.** consisting of or employing an iamb or iambs. **2.** *Gk. Lit.* noting or pertaining to satirical poetry written in iambs. —*n.* **3.** *Pros.* **a.** an iamb. **b.** Usually, **iambics.** a verse or poem consisting of iambs. **4.** *Gk. Lit.* a satirical poem in this meter. [< L *iambic(us)* < Gk *iambikós.* See IAMBUS, -IC] —**i·am′bi·cal·ly,** *adv.*

i·am·bus (ī am′bəs), *n., pl.* **-bi** (-bī), **-bus·es.** iamb. [< L < Gk *íambos*]

-ian, var. of **-an:** *amphibian; humanitarian.* [< L *-iān(us).* See -I-, -AN]

-iana. See **-an, -ana.** [< L, neut. pl. of *-iānus* -IAN]

I·ap·e·tus (ī ap′ i təs), *n.* **1.** *Class. Myth.* a Titan, son of Uranus and Gaea and father of Atlas, Epimetheus, and Prometheus. **2.** *Astron.* one of the nine satellites of Saturn.

Iaşi (yäsh, yä′shē), *n.* Rumanian name of **Jassy.**

-iasis, a noun suffix occurring in loan words from Greek: *psoriasis.* Cf. **-asis.** [< Gk = *-iā-* (abstracted from verbs with stems so ending) + *-sis* -SIS]

IATA, International Air Transport Association.

i·at·ric (ī a′trik, ē a′-), *adj.* of or pertaining to a physician or medicine. Also, **i·at′ri·cal.** [< Gk *iātrik(ós)* of healing]

-iatrics, a combination of **-iatry** and **-ics:** *pediatrics.*

iatro-, a learned borrowing from Greek meaning "healer," "medicine," "healing," used in the formation of compound words: *iatrogenic.* [< Gk, comb. form of *iātrós* healer = *iâ(sthai)* (to) heal + *-tros* n. suffix]

i·at·ro·gen·ic (ī a′trə jen′ik, ē a′-), *adj.* (of a neurosis or physical disorder) caused by the diagnosis, manner, or treatment of a physician or surgeon. —**i·at·ro·ge·nic·i·ty** (ī a′trō jə nis′i tē, ē a′-), *n.*

-iatry, a learned borrowing from Greek meaning "medical care," used in the formation of compound words: *psychiatry.* [< Gk *iātreía* healing. See IATRO-, -Y[3]]

ib., ibidem.

I·ba·dan (ē bä′dän, ē bäd′ən), *n.* a city in SW Nigeria. 627,379 (1963).

I·bá·ñez (ē vän′yeth), *n.* **Vi·cen·te Blas·co** (bē then′te bläs′kō). See **Blasco Ibáñez, Vicente.**

I-beam (ī′bēm′), *n.* a roller or extruded metal beam or shape having a cross section resembling a capital I. See illus. at **shape.**

I·be·ri·a (ī bēr′ē ə), *n.* **1.** Also called **Ibe′rian Penin′sula.** a peninsula in SW Europe, comprising Spain and Portugal. **2.** an ancient region S of the Caucasus in the S Soviet Union; modern Georgia.

I·be·ri·an (ī bēr′ē ən), *adj.* **1.** of or pertaining to Iberia in SW Europe, its inhabitants, or their language. **2.** *Ethnol.* noting or pertaining to a dark, dolichocephalic people inhabiting parts of southern Europe and northern Africa. **3.** of or pertaining to ancient Iberia in the Caucasus or its inhabitants. —*n.* **4.** one of the ancient inhabitants of Iberia in Europe, supposed ancestors of the Basques. **5.** the language of the ancient Iberians of SW Europe, not known to be related to any other language. **6.** one of the ancient inhabitants of Iberia in Asia.

I·bert (ē bеʀ′), *n.* **Jacques (Fran·çois An·toine)** (zhäk fʀäɴ swa′ äɴ twaɴ′), 1890–1962, French composer.

I·ber·ville, d' (dē beʀ vēl′), *n.* **Pierre le Moyne** (pyeʀ lə mwaɴ′), **Sieur,** 1661–1706, French naval officer, born in Canada: founder of the first French settlement in Louisiana 1699.

i·bex (ī′beks), *n., pl.* **i·bex·es, ib·i·ces** (ib′i sēz′, ī′bi-), (*esp. collectively*) **i·bex.** any of several wild goats of the genus *Capra,* found in mountainous regions of Asia, North Africa, and Europe, having long, recurved horns. [< L]

Ibex, genus *Capra* (About 3 ft. high at shoulder; horns to 3 ft.; length 4½ ft.)

ibid. (ib′id), *n.* ibidem.

i·bi·dem (i bē′dem; *Eng.* ib′i dəm, i bī′dəm), *adv. Latin.* in the same book, chapter, page, etc. [lit., in the same place]

-ibility, var. of **-ability:** *extensibility; frangibility; reducibility.* [< L *-ibilitāt-* = *-ibili(s)* -IBLE + *-tāt-* -TY[2]]

i·bis (ī′bis), *n., pl.* **i·bis·es** (ī′bi siz), (*esp. collectively*) **i·bis.** any of several large wading birds of the family *Threskiornithidae,* related to the herons and storks, and characterized by a long, thin, downward-curved bill. [ME < L < Gk < Egypt *hbj* (vowels not written)]

Ibis, *Threskiornis aethiopica* (Length 2½ ft.)

I·bi·za (ē vē′thä), *n.* Spanish name of **Iviza.**

-ible, var. of **-able,** occurring in words borrowed from Latin (*credible; horrible; visible*), or modeled on the Latin type (*reducible*). [< L *-ibil(is)* or *-ībil(is).* See -I-, -BLE]

Ib·lis (ib′lēs), *n. Islamic Myth.* Eblis.

-ibly, var. of **-ably:** *credibly.* [-IBLE + -Y[1]]

ibn-, a prefix occurring in Arabic personal names: *ibn-Saud.* [< Ar: son (of)]

ibn-Rushd (ib′ən rŏŏsht′), *n.* Arabic name of **Averroës.**

ibn-Sa·ud (ib′ən sä ōōd′), *n.* **Ab·dul-A·ziz** (äb dŏŏl′ä zēz′), 1880–1953, king of Saudi Arabia 1932–53.

ibn-Si·na (ib′ən sē′nä), *n.* Arabic name of **Avicenna.**

ibn-Zohr (ib′ən zōōʀ′), *n.* Arabic name of **Avenzoar.**

I·bo (ē′bō), *n., pl.* **I·bos,** (*esp. collectively*) **I·bo. 1.** a member of a Negro people of the lower Niger in Nigeria. **2.** the language of the Ibo, a Kwa language.

Ib·ra·him Pa·sha (ib′rä hēm′ pä′shä), 1789–1848, Egyptian general: governor of Syria 1833–40 (son of Mehemet Ali).

Ib·sen (ib′sən; *Norw.* ip′sən), *n.* **Hen·rik** (hen′rik; *Norw.* hen′ʀik), 1828–1906, Norwegian dramatist and poet.

-ic, 1. a suffix forming adjectives from nouns or stems not used as words themselves (*poetic; metallic; Homeric*), found extensively in adjective nouns of a similar type (*public; magic*), and in nouns the adjectives of which end in **-ical** (*music; critic*). **2.** *Chem.* a suffix, specialized in opposition to **-ous,** used to show the higher of two valences: *ferric chloride.* [ME *-ic, -ik* < L *-ic(us)* -Y[1]; in many words repr. the cognate Gk *-ikos* (directly or through L); in some words r. *-ique* < F < L *-ic(us)*]

I.C., Jesus Christ. [< L *Iesus Christus*]

IC, See **integrated circuit.**

ICA, International Cooperation Administration.

I·ça (ē′sä), *n.* Portuguese name of **Putumayo.**

ICAAAA (*called* ī′sē′fôr′ā′, -fôr′ā′), Intercollegiate Association of Amateur Athletes of America.

-ical, a combination of **-ic** and **-al[1],** used in forming adjectives from nouns (*rhetorical*), providing synonyms to words ending in **-ic** (*poetical*), and providing an adjective with additional meanings to those in the **-ic** form (*economical*). [ME < L *-icāl(is).* See -IC, -AL[1]]

-ically, a suffix used to form adverbs from adjectives ending in **-ic** (*terrifically*) and **-ical** (*poetically; magically*).

ICAO, International Civil Aviation Organization.

I·car·i·a (i kâr′ē ə, ī kâr′-; *Gk.* ē′kä ʀē′ä), *n.* a Greek island in the Aegean Sea: a part of the Southern Sporades group. 11,913 (1951); 99 sq. mi. Also, **Ikaria.**

I·car·i·an (i kâr′ē ən, ī kâr′-), *adj.* **1.** of or like Icarus. **2.** of or pertaining to Icaria or its inhabitants. —*n.* **3.** an inhabitant of Icaria.

Icar′ian Sea′, part of the Aegean Sea, between Turkey and the Greek island of Patmos.

Ic·a·rus (ik′ər əs, ī′kər-), *n. Class. Myth.* a youth who, with his father, Daedalus, attempted to escape from Crete with wings of wax and feathers. Daedalus was successful but Icarus flew so high that the sun melted his wings and he plunged to his death in the sea.

ICBM, See **intercontinental ballistic missile.** Also, **I.C.B.M.**

I.C.C., See **Interstate Commerce Commission.** Also, **ICC**

ice (īs), *n., v.,* **iced, ic·ing,** *adj.* —*n.* **1.** the solid form of water, produced by freezing; frozen water. **2.** the frozen surface of a body of water. **3.** any substance resembling this: *camphor ice.* **4.** *U.S.* a frozen dessert made of sweetened water and fruit juice. **5.** *Brit.* See **ice cream. 6.** icing, as on a cake. **7.** *Slang.* money paid by a businessman for protection, special favors, etc. **8. break the ice, a.** to succeed initially. **b.** to overcome reserve, awkwardness, or formality between people. **9. cut no ice,** *U.S. Informal.* to fail to make a favorable impression. **10. on thin ice,** in a risky or delicate situation. —*v.t.* **11.** to cover with ice. **12.** to change into ice; freeze. **13.** to cool with or as with ice. **14.** to cover (cakes, buns, etc.) with icing; frost. —*v.i.* **15.** to freeze. **16.** to be coated with ice (often fol. by *up*): *The windshield has iced up.* —*adj.* **17.** of or made of ice: *ice shavings.* **18.** for or holding ice: *an ice chest.* **19.** on or done on the ice: *ice yachting.* [ME, OE *īs;* c. G *Eis,* Icel *īss*] —**ice′less,** *adj.* —**ice′like′,** *adj.*

-ice, a suffix of nouns, indicating state or quality, appearing in loan words from French: *notice.* [ME *-ice, -ise* < OF < L *-iti(us), -iti(a), -iti(um)* abstract n. suffix]

Ice., **1.** Iceland. **2.** Icelandic.

ice′ age′, *Geol.* the glacial epoch.

ice′ bag′, a bag for holding ice, applied to the head or another part of the body to be cooled. Also called **ice pack.**

ice·berg (īs′bûrg), *n.* a large floating mass of ice, detached from a glacier and carried out to sea. [half Anglicization, half adoption of D *ijsberg* ice mountain; c. G *Eisberg,* Sw *isberg*]

ice′berg let′tuce, a variety of lettuce having a cabbagelike head of crisp leaves.

ice·boat (īs′bōt′), *n.* **1.** a vehicle for rapid movement on ice, usually consisting of a T-shaped frame on runners driven by sails. **2.** a boat for breaking through ice; icebreaker.

ice·bound (īs′bound′), *adj.* **1.** held fast or hemmed in by ice; frozen in: *an icebound ship.* **2.** obstructed or shut off by ice: *an icebound harbor.*

ice·box (īs′boks′), *n.* **1.** an insulated cabinet or chest with a partition for ice, used for preserving or cooling food, beverages, etc. **2.** a refrigerator.

ice·break·er (īs′brā′kər), *n.* **1.** a vessel especially built for forcing navigable passages through ice. **2.** a tool or machine for chopping ice into small pieces. **3.** anything that relieves the tension, formality, etc., of a social situation.

Iceboat (def. 1)

ice·cap (īs′kap′), *n.* a cap of ice over an area, sloping in all directions from the center.

ice′ cave′, a cave containing ice all or most of the year.

ice-cold (īs′kōld′), *adj.* **1.** cold as ice: *her ice-cold feet.* **2.** unemotional; passionless. [OE *is-calde*]

ice′ cream′, **1.** a frozen food made of cream, sweetened and variously flavored. **2.** (in commercial use) a food made in imitation of this, and containing milk, egg whites, custard, cornstarch, etc.

ice′-cream cone′ (īs′krēm′), **1.** a thin, crisp, conical wafer for holding one or more scoops of ice cream. **2.** a confection consisting of one or more scoops of ice cream in such a cone.

ice′ crys′tals, *Meteorol.* precipitation consisting of small, slowly falling crystals of ice. Also called **ice needles, snow mist.**

ice′ cube′, a small cube of ice made in a mold, as in the freezing compartment of a refrigerator.

iced (īst), *adj.* **1.** covered with ice. **2.** cooled with ice: *iced tea.* **3.** *Cookery.* covered with icing.

ice·fall (īs′fôl′), *n.* **1.** a jumbled mass of ice in a glacier. **2.** a mass of ice overhanging a precipice. **3.** a falling of ice from a glacier, iceberg, etc.

ice′ field′, a large sheet of floating ice, larger than an ice floe.

ice′ floe′, **1.** a large flat mass of floating ice. **2.** floe (def. 1).

ice′ foot′, (in polar regions) a belt of ice frozen to the shore.

ice′ hock′ey, a game played on ice between two teams, each having six players, who wear skates and compete in scoring goals by shooting the puck into each other's cage with hockey sticks.

ice·house (īs′hous′), *n., pl.* **-hous·es** (-hou′ziz). a building for storing ice.

Icel, Icelandic (def. 2).

Icel., **1.** Iceland. **2.** Icelandic.

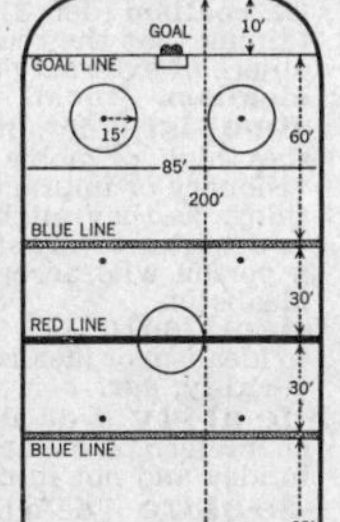

Ice hockey rink (Professional)

Ice·land (īs′lənd), *n.* a large island in the N Atlantic between Greenland and Scandinavia: formerly a Danish possession; an independent republic since 1944. 219,033; 39,698 sq. mi. *Cap.:* Reykjavik. —**Ice·land·er** (īs′lan′dər, -lən dər), *n.*

Ice·lan·dic (īs lan′dik), *adj.* **1.** of or pertaining to Iceland, its inhabitants, or their language. —*n.* **2.** the language of Iceland, a North Germanic language. *Abbr.:* Icel, Icel., Ice.

Ice′land moss′, an edible lichen, *Cetraria islandica,* of arctic regions, containing a starchlike substance used in medicine.

Ice′land spar′, a transparent variety of calcite that is double-refracting and is used as a polarizer.

ice·man (īs′man′), *n., pl.* **-men.** a man engaged in gathering, storing, selling, or delivering ice.

ice′ milk′, **1.** a kind of ice cream made of skimmed milk. **2.** See **frozen custard.**

ice′ nee′dle, *Meteorol.* **1.** a long, thin crystal of ice. **2. ice needles.** See **ice crystals.**

I·ce·ni (ī sē′nī), *n.* (*construed as sing. or pl.*) an ancient Celtic tribe of eastern England, whose queen was Boadicea. —**I·ce·nic** (ī sē′nik), *adj.*

ice′ pack′, **1.** See **pack ice. 2.** See **ice bag.**

ice′ pick′, a pick or other tool for chipping ice.

ice′ plant′, an Old World figwort, *Mesembryanthemum crystallinum,* having leaves covered with glistening vesicles. Cf. **fig marigold.**

ice′ point′, the temperature at which a mixture of ice and air-saturated water at a pressure of one atmosphere is in equilibrium, represented by 0°C and 32°F. Cf. **steam point.**

ice′ sheet′, **1.** a broad, thick sheet of ice covering an extensive area for a long period of time. **2.** a glacier covering a large fraction of a continent.

ice′ skate′, **1.** a shoe fitted with a metal blade, for skating on ice. **2.** skate[1] (def. 3).

ice-skate (īs′skāt′), *v.i.,* **-skat·ed, -skat·ing.** to skate on ice.

ice′ tongs′, **1.** tongs for handling a large block of ice. **2.** a small pair of tongs for serving ice cubes.

ice′ wa′ter, **1.** melted ice. **2.** ice-cold water.

I·chang (ē′chäng′), *n.* a port in SW Hupeh, in central China, on the Yangtze River. 110,000 (est. 1960).

ich dien (iᴋʜ dēn′), *German.* I serve: motto of the Prince of Wales.

I Ching (ē′ jing′), an ancient Chinese book of divination.

I·chi·no·mi·ya (ē′chē nô′mē yä′), *n.* a city on central Honshu, in central Japan. 193,579 (1964).

ich·neu·mon (ik nōō′mən, -nyōō′-), *n.* a slender, carnivorous mammal, *Herpestes ichneumon,* of Egypt, resembling a weasel. [< L < Gk: lit., tracker = *ichneú(ein)* (to) track (*íchnos* a track, footstep) + *-mōn* agent suffix]

ichneu′mon fly′, any of numerous hymenopterous insects of the family *Ichneumonidae.*

ich·nol·o·gy (ik nol′ə jē), *n.* the branch of paleontology dealing with fossil footprints. [< Gk *íchno(s)* track, footstep + -LOGY] —**ich·no·log·i·cal** (ik′nᵊloj′i kəl), *adj.*

i·chor[1] (ī′kôr, ī′kər), *n. Class. Myth.* an ethereal fluid supposed to flow in the veins of the gods. [< Gk]

i·chor[2] (ī′kôr, ī′kər), *n. Pathol.* an acrid, watery discharge, as from an ulcer or wound. [< LL: sanies < Gk: ICHOR[1]] —**i·chor·ous** (ī′kər əs), *adj.*

ichth., ichthyology.

ich·tham·mol (ik tham′ōl, -ôl, -ol; ik′thə mōl′, -môl′, -mol′), *n. Pharm.* a viscous substance, obtained by the destructive distillation of bituminous schists, used chiefly as an antiseptic and analgesic. [ICHTH(YO)- (from *ichthyosulfonate*) + AMM(ONIUM) + -OL[1]]

ich·thy·ic (ik′thē ik), *adj.* piscine. [< Gk *ichthyik(ós)* fishy]

ichthyo-, a learned borrowing from Greek meaning "fish," used in the formation of compound words: *ichthyology.* Also, *esp. before a vowel,* **ichthy-.** [< Gk, comb. form of *ichthýs*]

ich·thy·oid (ik′thē oid′), *adj.* **1.** Also, **ich′thy·oi′dal.** fishlike. —*n.* **2.** any fishlike vertebrate. [< Gk *ichthyoeid(ḗs)*]

Ich·thy·ol (ik′thē ōl′, -ôl′, -ol′), *n. Pharm., Trademark.* ichthammol.

ichthyol., ichthyology.

ich·thy·o·lite (ik′thē ə līt′), *n.* a fossil fish. —**ich·thy·o·lit·ic** (ik′thē ə lit′ik), *adj.*

ich·thy·ol·o·gy (ik′thē ol′ə jē), *n.* the branch of zoology dealing with fishes. —**ich·thy·o·log·ic** (ik′thē ə loj′ik), **ich′thy·o·log′i·cal,** *adj.* —**ich′thy·o·log′i·cal·ly,** *adv.* —**ich′thy·ol′o·gist,** *n.*

ich·thy·oph·a·gy (ik′thē of′ə jē), *n.* the practice of eating or subsisting on fish. —**ich·thy·oph·a·gous** (ik′thē of′ə gəs), *adj.* —**ich′thy·oph′a·gist,** *n.*

Ich·thy·or·nis (ik′thē ôr′nis), *n.* an extinct genus of toothed birds having vertebrae resembling those of fishes. [< NL; see ICHTHY-, ORNITHO-]

ich·thy·o·saur·us (ik′thē ə sôr′əs), *n., pl.* **-us·es.** any fishlike marine reptile of the extinct order *Ichthyosauria,* ranging from 4 to 40 feet in length. Also, **ich·thy·o·saur** (ik′thē ə sôr′). [< NL]

Ichthyosaurus, *Stenopterygius quadriscissus*

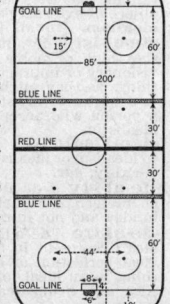

ich·thy·o·sis (ik′thē ō′sis), *n. Pathol.* a congenital skin disease in which the epidermis continuously flakes off in large scales or plates. Also called **fishskin disease.** [< NL] —**ich·thy·ot·ic** (ik′thē ot′ik), *adj.*

-ician, a combination of **-ic** and **-ian,** used to form agent nouns to stems in **-ic:** *musician; geometrician.* [-IC + -IAN; r. ME *-icien* < OF < L *-ic(a)* + *-iānus*]

i·ci·cle (ī′si kəl), *n.* a pendent, tapering mass of ice formed by the freezing of dripping water. [ME *isikel,* OE *īsgicel* = *īs* ICE + *gicel* icicle; akin to Icel *jökul* mass of ice, glacier] —**i′ci·cled,** *adj.*

i·ci·ly (ī′sə lē), *adv.* in an icy manner.

i·ci·ness (ī′sē nis), *n.* the state of being icy or very cold.

ic·ing (ī′sing), *n.* **1.** a preparation, as of confectioner's sugar, butter, vanilla extract, etc., for covering cakes, cookies, etc.; frosting. **2.** *Meteorol.* a coating of ice on a solid object. Cf. **glaze** (def. 14), **rime**[2] (def. 1).

i·ci on parle fran·çais (ē sē′ ôɴ PARL FRÄN se′), *French.* French is spoken here. [lit., here one speaks French]

ick·er (ik′ər), *n. Scot.* the fruit-bearing spike of any cereal plant, esp. an ear of corn. [OE *æhher, eher* (Northumbrian dial.), var. of *ēar* ear of grain; see EAR[2]]

ick·y (ik′ē), *adj.*, **ick·i·er, ick·i·est.** *Slang.* **1.** repulsive, distasteful, or disgusting, esp. because of appearance or texture. **2.** excessively sweet or sentimental. **3.** sticky or viscid; gooey. [*ick* (<?) + -Y[1]]

i·con (ī′kon), *n.* **1.** a picture, image, or other representation. **2.** *Eastern Ch.* a representation in painting, enamel, etc., of some sacred personage, as Christ or a saint or angel, itself venerated as sacred. **3.** *Logic.* a sign or representation that stands for its object by virtue of a resemblance or analogy to it. Also, **eikon, ikon** (for defs. 1, 2). [< L < Gk *eikṓn* likeness, image, figure] —**i·con′ic, i·con′i·cal,** *adj.* —**Syn. 2.** See **image.**

I·co·ni·um (ī kō′nē əm), *n.* ancient name of **Konya.**

icono-, a learned borrowing from Greek meaning "image," "likeness," used in the formation of compound words: *iconology.* Also, *esp. before a vowel,* **icon-.** [< L < Gk *eikono-,* comb. form of *eikṓn* ICON]

i·con·o·clasm (ī kon′ə klaz′əm), *n.* the action, doctrines, or spirit of iconoclasts. [ICONOCL(AST) + *-asm* on model of pairs like *enthusiast: enthusiasm*]

i·con·o·clast (ī kon′ə klast′), *n.* **1.** a person who attacks cherished beliefs, traditional institutions, etc., as being based on error or superstition. **2.** a breaker or destroyer of images, esp. those set up for religious veneration. [< ML *īconoclast(ēs)* < MGk *eikonoklástēs* = Gk *eikono-* ICONO- + *-klastēs* breaker = *klas-* (var. s. of *klân* to break) + *-tēs* agent n. suffix] —**i·con′o·clas′tic,** *adj.* —**i·con′o·clas′ti·cal·ly,** *adv.*

i·con·o·graph·ic (ī kon′ə graf′ik), *adj.* of or pertaining to iconography. Also, **i·con′o·graph′i·cal.**

i·co·nog·ra·phy (ī′kə nog′rə fē), *n., pl.* **-phies. 1.** symbolic representation, esp. of conventional meanings by means of an image or images. **2.** subject matter in the visual arts, esp. with reference to the conventions regarding the treatment of a subject in artistic representation. **3.** the study or analysis of subject matter and its meaning in the visual arts; iconology. [< ML *īconographia* < Gk *eikonographía*] —**i·con·o·graph** (ī kon′ə graf′, -gräf′), *n.* —**i′co·nog′ra·pher,** *n.*

i·co·nol·a·try (ī′kə nol′ə trē), *n.* the worship or adoration of icons. —**i′co·nol′a·ter,** *n.* —**i′co·nol′a·trous,** *adj.*

i·co·nol·o·gy (ī′kə nol′ə jē), *n.* **1.** the historical analysis and interpretive study of symbols or images and their contextual significance; iconography. **2.** the study of icons or symbolic representations. —**i·con·o·log·i·cal** (ī kon′ᵊloj′i kəl, ī′kə nᵊloj′-), *adj.* —**i′co·nol′o·gist,** *n.*

I·con·o·scope (ī kon′ə skōp′), *n. Trademark.* a television camera tube in which a beam of high-velocity electrons scans a photoemissive mosaic. Cf. **orthicon.**

i·co·nos·ta·sis (ī′kə nos′tə sis), *n., pl.* **-ses** (-sēz′). *Eastern Ch.* a partition or screen on which icons are placed, separating the sanctuary from the main part of the church. Also, **i·con·o·stas** (ī kon′ə-stas′). [< eccl. L < eccl. Gk *eikonóstasis,* m. LGk *eikonostásion* shrine = *eikono-* ICONO- + *sta-* (root of *histánai* to stand) + *-sion* dim. suffix]

i·co·sa·he·dron (ī kō′sə hē′drən, ī-kos′ə-), *n., pl.* **-drons, -dra** (-drə). a solid figure having twenty faces. [< Gk *eikosáedron* = *eikosa-* (var. of *eikosi-,* comb. form of *eíkosi* twenty) + *-edron* -HEDRON] —**i·co′sa·he′dral,** *adj.*

Icosahedron (Regular)

-ics, a suffix of nouns, originally plural as denoting things pertaining to a particular subject, but now mostly used as singular as denoting the body of matters, facts, knowledge, principles, etc., pertaining to a subject, and hence a science or art: *ethics; physics; politics; tactics.* [pl. of -IC, repr. L *-ica* (< Gk *-ika,* neut. pl. of *-ikos*), as in *rhētorica* (pl.) rhetoric book]

ICSH, 1. *Biochem.* interstitial-cell-stimulating hormone: a hormone that, in the female, regulates the development of the corpus luteum and, in the male, stimulates the interstitial cells of the testis to produce testosterone. **2.** *Pharm.* a commercial form of this substance.

ic·ter·us (ik′tər əs), *n. Pathol.* jaundice (def. 1). [< L < Gk *íkteros* jaundice, a yellow bird said to cure jaundice when seen] —**ic·ter·ic** (ik ter′ik), **ic·ter′i·cal,** *adj.*

ic·tus (ik′təs), *n., pl.* **-tus·es, -tus.** *Pros.* rhythmical or metrical stress. [< L: a stroke, n. use of ptp. of *icere*] —**ic′tic,** *adj.*

ICU, *Med.* intensive-care unit.

i·cy (ī′sē), *adj.,* **i·ci·er, i·ci·est. 1.** made of, full of, or covered with ice. **2.** resembling ice. **3.** cold: *icy wind.* **4.** slippery: *an icy road.* **5.** without warmth of feeling; frigid: *an icy stare.* [ME *isy,* OE *īsig*]

id (id), *n. Psychoanal.* the part of the psyche that is the source of instinctive energy. Its impulses are modified by the ego and the superego: the source of the libido. [special use of L *id* it, as a trans. of G *Es* primal urge]

ID, 1. Idaho (approved esp. for use with zip code). **2.** identification. **3.** inside diameter.

I'd (īd), contraction of *I would, I should,* or *I had.*

-id[1], **1.** a noun suffix meaning "daughter of" (*Nereid*); used also to form names of meteors appearing to radiate in showers from particular constellations or comets (*Andromedid*). **2.** a suffix used in naming epics: *Aeneid.* [< L *-id-,* s. of *-is* fem. suffix of source or origin < Gk]

-id[2], a suffix of nouns and adjectives indicating members of a zoological family (*cichlid*), or some other group or division (*acarid; arachnid*). [back formation from NL *-idae* -IDAE and from NL *-ida* -IDA]

-id[3], var. of **-ide:** *parotid.*

-id[4], a quasi suffix common in adjectives, esp. of states that appeal to the senses: *torrid; acid.* [< L *-id(us)* adj. suffix, often with the meaning "full of"]

Id., Idaho.

id., idem.

I.D., 1. identification. **2.** *Mil.* Infantry Division. **3.** Intelligence Department.

i.d., inside diameter.

I·da (ī′də), *n.* **1. Mount,** a mountain in NW Asia Minor, SE of ancient Troy. 5810 ft. **2.** Modern, **Mount Psiloriti.** the highest mountain in Crete. 8058 ft.

-ida, *Zool.* a suffix of the names of orders and classes: *Arachnida.* [< NL (neut. pl. of L) *-idēs* offspring of < Gk]

Ida., Idaho.

-idae, *Zool.* a suffix of the names of families: *Canidae.* [< NL, L < Gk *-idai,* pl. of *-idēs* offspring of]

I·da·ho (ī′də hō′), *n.* a state in the NW United States. 713,008 (1970); 83,557 sq. mi. *Cap.:* Boise. *Abbr.:* Id., Ida., ID —**I·da·ho·an** (ī′də hō′ən, ī′də hō′-), *adj., n.*

I′daho Falls′, a city in E Idaho. 35,776 (1970).

I.D. card. See **identity card.** Also, **ID card.**

-ide, a suffix used in the names of chemical compounds: *bromide.* Also, **-id.** [abstracted from OXIDE]

i·de·a (ī dē′ə, ī dēᵊ′), *n.* **1.** any conception existing in the mind as a result of mental understanding, awareness, or activity. **2.** a thought, conception, or notion: *That is an excellent idea.* **3.** an impression: *Give me a general idea of what you want.* **4.** an opinion, view, or belief. **5.** a plan of action; an intention: *the idea of becoming an engineer.* **6.** a groundless supposition; fantasy. **7.** *Philos.* **a.** a concept developed by the mind. **b.** a conception of what is desirable or ought to be; ideal. **c.** (*cap.*) *Platonism.* an archetype or pattern of which the individual objects in any natural class are imperfect copies and from which they derive their being. **8.** *Obs.* a likeness. **9.** *Obs.* a mental image. [< LL < Gk: pattern = *ide-* (s. of *ideîn* to see) + *-a* n. ending; r. late ME *idee* < MF < LL, as above; akin to WIT[1]]

—**Syn. 1.** IDEA, THOUGHT, CONCEPTION, NOTION refer to a product of mental activity. IDEA, although it may refer to thoughts of any degree of seriousness, is commonly preferred for mental concepts considered important or elaborate: *We pondered the idea of the fourth dimension. The idea of his arrival frightened me.* THOUGHT, which reflects its primary emphasis on the mental process, may denote any concept except the more weighty and elaborate ones: *I welcomed his thoughts on the subject. A thought came to him.* CONCEPTION suggests a thought that seems complete, individual, recent, or somewhat intricate: *The architect's conception delighted them.* NOTION suggests a fleeting, vague, or imperfect thought: *a bare notion of how to proceed.*

i·de·a·is·tic (ī dē′ə is′tik, ī′dē ə-, ī′dē is′-), *adj.* of ideas, esp. in their abstract or symbolic character.

i·de·al (ī dē′əl, ī dēl′), *n.* **1.** a conception of something in its perfection. **2.** a standard of perfection or excellence. **3.** a person or thing regarded as embodying such a conception or conforming to such a standard, and taken as a model for imitation. **4.** an ultimate object or aim of endeavor, esp. one of high or noble character: *He refuses to compromise any of his ideals.* **5.** something that exists only in the imagination. —*adj.* **6.** conceived as constituting a standard of perfection or excellence: *ideal beauty.* **7.** regarded as perfect of its kind: *an ideal spot for a home.* **8.** existing only in the imagination; not real or practical; visionary: *an ideal future.* **9.** advantageous; excellent; best: *It would be ideal if she could stay.* **10.** based upon an ideal or ideals: *the ideal theory of numbers.* **11.** *Philos.* **a.** existing as an archetype or Platonic Idea. **b.** pertaining to or of the nature of idealism. [< LL *ideāl(is)*]

—**Syn. 1, 2.** epitome. IDEAL, EXAMPLE, MODEL refer to something considered as a standard to strive toward or something considered worthy of imitation. An IDEAL is a concept or standard of perfection, existing merely as an image in the mind, or based upon a person or upon conduct: *Sir Philip Sidney was considered the ideal in gentlemanly conduct.* An EXAMPLE is a person or his conduct or achievements regarded as worthy of being followed or imitated in a general way; or sometimes, as properly to be avoided: *an example of courage; a bad example to one's children.* A MODEL is primarily a physical shape to be closely copied, but is also a pattern for exact imitation in conduct or character: *They took their leader as a model.* **4.** intention, objective. **6.** perfect, consummate, complete. **8.** impractical, imaginary.

i·de·al·ise (ī dē′ə līz′), *v.t., v.i.,* **-ised, -is·ing.** *Chiefly Brit.* idealize. —**i·de′al·i·sa′tion,** *n.* —**i·de′al·is′er,** *n.*

i·de·al·ism (ī dē′ə liz′əm), *n.* **1.** the cherishing or pursuit of high or noble principles, purposes, goals, etc. **2.** the practice of idealizing. **3.** something idealized; an ideal representation. **4.** *Fine Arts.* treatment of subject matter or form in a work of art according to a standard of perfection. Cf. **realism** (def. 3). **5.** *Philos.* any system or theory maintaining that the real is of the nature of thought or that the object of external perception consists of ideas. Cf. **absolute idealism.** [IDEAL + -ISM, prob. modeled on G *Idealismus*]

i·de·al·ist (ī dē′ə list) *n.* **1.** a person who cherishes or pursues high or noble principles, purposes, goals, etc. **2.** a visionary or impractical person. **3.** a person who represents things as they might or should be rather than as they are. **4.** a writer or artist who treats subjects imaginatively. **5.** a person who accepts the doctrines of idealism. —*adj.* **6.** idealistic.

i·de·al·is·tic (ī dē′ə lis′tik, ī′dē ə-), *adj.* of or pertaining to idealism or idealists. Also, **i·de′al·is′ti·cal.** —**i·de′al·is′ti·cal·ly,** *adv.*

i·de·al·i·ty (ī′dē al′i tē), *n., pl.* **-ties. 1.** ideal quality or character. **2.** capacity to idealize. **3.** *Philos.* existence only in idea and not in reality.

i·de·al·ize (ī dē′ə līz′), *v.,* **-ized, -iz·ing.** —*v.t.* **1.** to make ideal; represent in an ideal form or character; exalt to an ideal perfection or excellence. —*v.i.* **2.** to represent something in an ideal form; imagine or form an ideal or ideals. Also, *esp. Brit.,* **idealise.** —**i·de′al·i·za′tion,** *n.* —**i·de′al·iz′er,** *n.*

i·de·al·ly (ī dē′ə lē), *adv.* **1.** in accordance with an ideal; perfectly. **2.** in idea, thought, or imagination. **3.** in theory or principle.

i·de·ate (ī′dē āt′, ī dē′āt), *v.,* **-at·ed, -at·ing.** —*v.t.* **1.** to form in idea, thought, or imagination. —*v.i.* **2.** to form ideas; think. [IDE(A) + -ATE[1]] —**i·de·a·tive** (ī dē′ə tiv, ī′dē ā′-), *adj.*

i·de·a·tion (ī′dē ā′shən), *n.* the process of forming ideas or images.

i·de·a·tion·al (ī′dē ā′shə nᵊl), *adj.* of, pertaining to, or involving ideas, concepts, or projected happenings. —**i′de·a′tion·al·ly,** *adv.*

i·dée fixe (ē dā fēks′), *pl.* **i·dées fixes** (ē dā fēks′). *French.* **1.** See **fixed idea** (def. 1). **2.** Also called **fixed idea.** *Music.* a recurring motif in a musical composition, esp. in those of Berlioz. Cf. **leitmotif.**

i·dem (ī′dem, id′em), *pron., adj. Latin.* the same as previously given or mentioned.

i·den·tic (ī den′tik, i den′-), *adj.* **1.** identical. **2.** *Diplomacy.* (of action, notes, etc.) identical in form, as when two or more states deal with another state. [< ML *identic(us)* the same. See IDENTITY, -IC]

i·den·ti·cal (ī den′ti kəl, i den′-), *adj.* **1.** exactly the same; being the very same: *The manager gave us the identical cottage each summer.* **2.** similar or alike in every way: *He replaced the broken dish with an identical one.* [< ML *identic(us)*] —**i·den′ti·cal·ly,** *adv.* —**i·den′ti·cal·ness,** *n.*

iden′tical rhyme′, *Pros.* **1.** rhyme created by the repetition of a word. **2.** See **rime riche.**

iden′tical twin′, one of a pair of twins of the same sex, usually resembling one another closely, that develop from a single fertilized ovum. Cf. **fraternal twin.**

i·den·ti·fi·ca·tion (ī den′tə fə kā′shən, i den′-), *n.* **1.** the act of identifying. **2.** the state of being identified. **3.** something that identifies one: *He carries identification with him at all times.* **4.** *Sociol.* acceptance as one's own of the values and interests of a social group. **5.** *Psychol.* a process by which a person ascribes to himself the qualities or characteristics of another person.

i·den·ti·fy (ī den′tə fī′, i den′-), *v.,* **-fied, -fy·ing.** —*v.t.* **1.** to recognize or establish as being a particular person or thing; verify the identity of: *to identify handwriting.* **2.** to make, represent to be, or regard or treat as the same or identical. **3.** to associate in feeling, interest, action, etc. (usually fol. by *with*): *He preferred not to identify himself with that group.* **4.** *Biol.* to determine to what group (a given specimen) belongs. **5.** *Psychol.* to associate (one or oneself) with another person or a group of persons by identification. **6.** to serve as a means of identification for: *His gruff voice identified him.* —*v.i.* **7.** to put oneself in the place of another or others: *to identify with the hero of a novel.* [< ML *identific(āre).* See IDENTITY, -FY] —**i·den′ti·fi′a·ble,** *adj.* —**i·den′ti·fi′a·ble·ness,** *n.* —**i·den′ti·fi′er,** *n.*

i·den·ti·ty (ī den′ti tē, i den′-), *n., pl.* **-ties.** **1.** the state or fact of remaining the same one or ones, as under varying aspects or conditions: *The identity of the fingerprints on the gun proved that he was the killer.* **2.** the condition of being oneself or itself, and not another: *He doubted his own identity.* **3.** condition or character as to who a person or what a thing is: *a case of mistaken identity.* **4.** state or fact of being the same one. **5.** exact likeness in nature or qualities: *an identity of interests.* **6.** an instance or point of sameness or likeness: *to mistake resemblances for identities.* [< LL *identitās* = L *identi(dem)* repeatedly (*idem* same + *-ti-* < ?) + *-tās* -TY[2]]

iden′tity card′, a card, usually of an official nature, for identifying the bearer, giving his name, address, and other personal data. Also called **ID card, I.D. card.**

iden′tity cri′sis, a variably intense period of psychosocial distress, normative in adolescence but often prolonged into adulthood, when a person is struggling more or less consciously for a clear sense of unified self and role in society. [coined by Erik H. *Erikson* (b. 1902), U.S. psychoanalyst]

ideo-, a learned borrowing from Greek meaning "idea," used in the formation of compound words: *ideology.* [< Gk *ideō-* (s. of *idéa*) IDEA + -o-]

id·e·o·gram (id′ē ə gram′, ī′dē-), *n.* **1.** a written symbol that represents an idea or object directly rather than a particular word or speech sound. **2.** a written symbol that represents a morpheme or any of several morphemes, as 7, =, &.

id·e·o·graph (id′ē ə graf′, -gräf′, ī′dē-), *n.* an ideogram. —**id·e·o·graph·ic** (id′ē ə graf′ik, ī′dē-), **id′e·o·graph′i·cal,** *adj.* —**id′e·o·graph′i·cal·ly,** *adv.*

id·e·og·ra·phy (id′ē og′rə fē, ī′dē-), *n.* the use of ideograms.

i·de·o·log·ic (ī′dē ə loj′ik, id′ē-), *adj.* **1.** of or pertaining to ideology. **2.** speculative; visionary. Also, **i′de·o·log′i·cal.** —**i′de·o·log′i·cal·ly,** *adv.*

i·de·ol·o·gist (ī′dē ol′ə jist, id′ē-), *n.* **1.** an expert in ideology. **2.** a person who deals with systems of ideas. **3.** a person who advocates a particular ideology. **4.** a visionary. Also, **i·de·o·logue** (ī′dē ə lôg′, -log′, id′ē-, ī dē′-).

i·de·ol·o·gy (ī′dē ol′ə jē, id′ē-), *n., pl.* **-gies.** **1.** the body of doctrine, myth, symbol, etc., of a social movement, institution, class, or large group. **2.** such a body of doctrine, myth, etc., with reference to some political and cultural plan, along with the devices for putting it into operation: *fascist ideology.* **3.** *Philos.* **a.** the study of the nature and origin of ideas. **b.** a system that derives ideas exclusively from sensation. **4.** visionary or impractical theorizing.

i·de·o·mo·tor (ī′dē ə mō′tər, id′ē ə-), *adj. Psychol.* of or pertaining to motor activity caused by an idea. Cf. **sensorimotor** (def. 1). —**i′de·o·mo′tion,** *n.*

ides (īdz), *n.* (*construed as sing. or pl.*) (in the ancient Roman calendar) the 15th day of March, May, July, or October, and the 13th day of the other months. [ME < MF < L *īdūs* (fem. pl.) < ?]

id est (id est′), *Latin.* See **i.e.**

-idia, pl. of **-idion** or **-idium.**

idio-, a learned borrowing from Greek meaning "proper to one," "peculiar," used in the formation of compound words: *idiomorphic.* [< Gk *ídios* own, personal]

id·i·o·blast (id′ē ə blast′), *n. Bot.* a cell that differs greatly from the surrounding cells or tissue. —**id′i·o·blas′tic,** *adj.*

id·i·o·cy (id′ē ə sē), *n., pl.* **-cies** for 2. **1.** the condition of being an idiot; extreme degree of mental deficiency. **2.** utterly senseless or foolish behavior; a foolish act, statement, etc. [late ME; see IDIOT, -CY]

id·i·o·graph (id′ē ə graf′, -gräf′), *n.* a mark or signature characteristic of a particular person, organization, etc.; trademark. Cf. **logotype** (def. 2). [< LGk *idiógraph(on),* n. use of neut. of Gk *idiógraphos* self-written]

id·i·o·graph·ic (id′ē ə graf′ik), *adj.* of or involving the study or explication of individual cases or events.

id·i·o·lect (id′ē ə lekt′), *n. Linguistics.* a person's individual speech pattern. Cf. **dialect** (def. 1).

id·i·om (id′ē əm), *n.* **1.** an expression whose meaning cannot be derived from its constituent elements, as *kick the bucket* in the sense of "to die." **2.** a language, dialect, or style of speaking peculiar to a people. **3.** a construction or expression peculiar to a language. **4.** a distinct style or character, as in music or art: *the idiom of Bach.* [< L *idiōm(a)* < Gk = *idiō-* (var. of *idio-* IDIO-) + *-ma* n. suffix]

id·i·o·mat·ic (id′ē ə mat′ik), *adj.* **1.** peculiar to or characteristic of a particular idiom: *idiomatic French.* **2.** having a distinct style or character, esp. in the arts: *idiomatic writing; an idiomatic composer.* Also, **id′i·o·mat′i·cal.** [< LGk *idiōmatik(ós)* = *idiōmat-* (s. of *idíōma*) IDIOM + *-ikos* -IC] —**id′i·o·mat′i·cal·ly,** *adv.* —**id′i·o·mat′i·cal·ness,** *n.*

id·i·o·mor·phic (id′ē ə môr′fik), *adj.* having its own characteristic form. [< Gk *idiómorph(os)* having an individual form (see IDIO-, -MORPHOUS) + -IC] —**id′i·o·mor′phi·cal·ly,** *adv.* —**id′i·o·mor′phism,** *n.*

-idion, a diminutive suffix occurring in loan words from Greek: *enchiridion.* Cf. **-idium.** [< Gk]

id·i·o·path·ic (id′ē ə path′ik), *adj. Pathol.* of unknown cause, as a disease.

id·i·op·a·thy (id′ē op′ə thē), *n., pl.* **-thies.** *Pathol.* a disease not preceded or occasioned by any other. [< NL *idiopathīa* < Gk *idiopátheia* a feeling peculiar to one's self]

id·i·o·phone (id′ē ə fōn′), *n.* a musical instrument that is made from a solid, naturally sonorous material, as a gong or a glass harmonica. [< G *Idiophon*] —**id·i·o·phon·ic** (id′ē ə fon′ik), *adj.*

id·i·o·plasm (id′ē ə plaz′əm), *n. Biol.* See **germ plasm.** —**id′i·o·plas′mic, id·i·o·plas·mat·ic** (id′ē ō plaz mat′ik), *adj.*

id·i·o·syn·cra·sy (id′ē ə siŋ′krə sē, -sin′-), *n., pl.* **-sies.** **1.** a characteristic, habit, mannerism, or the like, that is peculiar to an individual. **2.** the physical constitution peculiar to an individual. **3.** a peculiarity of the physical or the mental constitution, esp. susceptibility toward drugs, food, etc. Cf. **allergy** (def. 1). [< Gk *idiosynkrāsía* = *idio-* IDIO- + *-synkrāsia* = *syn-* SYN- + *krâs(is)* a blending + *-ia* -Y[3]] —**id·i·o·syn·crat·ic** (id′ē ō sin krat′ik), *adj.* —**id′i·o·syn·crat′i·cal·ly,** *adv.* —**Syn. 1.** peculiarity, quirk.

id·i·ot (id′ē ət), *n.* **1.** an utterly foolish or senseless person. **2.** a person hopelessly deficient, esp. from birth, in the ordinary mental powers; one lacking the capacity to develop beyond the mental age of three or four years. [ME < L *idiōt(a)* < Gk *idiṓtēs* private person, ignoramus = *idiō-* (lengthened var. of *idio-* IDIO-) + *-tēs* agent n. suffix] —**Syn. 1.** fool, half-wit; imbecile; dolt, dunce, numskull.

id·i·ot·ic (id′ē ot′ik), *adj.* of, pertaining to, or characteristic of an idiot; senselessly foolish. Also, **id′i·ot′i·cal.** [< LL *idiōtic(us)* < Gk *idiōtikós* private, ignorant] —**id′i·ot′i·cal·ly,** *adv.* —**id′i·ot′i·cal·ness,** *n.* —**Syn.** stupid.

id·i·ot·ism (id′ē ə tiz′əm), *n.* **1.** idiotic conduct or action. **2.** idiocy.

id′iot light′, *Auto.* a small warning light on the instrument panel that turns on automatically when there are deficiencies or malfunctions in the battery, oil supply, or the like.

-idium, a diminutive suffix, corresponding to **-idion,** used in zoological, biological, botanical, anatomical, and chemical terms: *peridium.* [< L < Gk *-idion* -IDION]

i·dle (īd′^{ə}l), *adj.,* **i·dler, i·dlest,** *v.,* **i·dled, i·dling.** —*adj.* **1.** not working or active; unemployed: *idle workmen.* **2.** not filled with activity: *idle hours.* **3.** not in use or operation: *idle machinery.* **4.** habitually doing nothing or avoiding work; lazy. **5.** of no real worth, importance, or significance: *idle talk.* **6.** having no basis or reason; groundless: *idle fears.* **7.** frivolous; vain: *idle pleasures.* **8.** futile; ineffective: *idle threats.* **9.** useless: *idle rage.* **10.** *Mach.* noting a gear, wheel, or pulley serving only as a means of transmitting power from another idle part or a power source to a mechanism being driven. —*v.i.* **11.** to pass time in idleness. **12.** to move, loiter, or saunter idly: *to idle along the avenue.* **13.** (of a machine or mechanism) to operate without doing useful work, usually at minimum speed. —*v.t.* **14.** to pass (time) in idleness (often fol. by *away*): *to idle away the afternoon.* **15.** to cause to be idle: *The strike idled many workers.* [ME, OE *īdel;* c. G *eitel*] —**i′dle·ness,** *n.* —**i′dly,** *adv.* —**Syn. 1, 4.** sluggish. IDLE, INDOLENT, LAZY, SLOTHFUL apply to a person who is not active. To be IDLE is to be inactive or not working at a job. The word is sometimes derogatory, but not always, since a person may be relaxing temporarily or may be idle through necessity: *pleasantly idle on a vacation; to be idle because one is unemployed or because supplies are lacking.* The INDOLENT person is naturally disposed to avoid exertion: *indolent and slow in movement; an indolent and contented fisherman.* The LAZY person is averse to exertion or work, and esp. to continued application; the word is usually derogatory: *too lazy to earn a living.* SLOTHFUL denotes a reprehensible unwillingness to do such work as is demanded of man: *so slothful as to be a burden on others.* **5.** worthless, trivial. **7.** wasteful. **12.** See **loiter. 14.** waste.

i′dle gear′, a gear placed between a driving and a driven gear to transmit motion between them. Also called **i′dler gear′.**

i′dle pul′ley, *Mach.* a pulley made to press or rest on a belt in order to tighten or guide it. Also, **i′dler pul′ley.**

i·dler (īd′lər), *n.* **1.** a person who idles. **2.** *Mach.* a gear or wheel that transmits motion between other gears or wheels.

I

I, Idle wheel

i·dlesse (īd′les), *n. Chiefly Literary.* idleness. [IDLE + *-esse,* as in *finesse*]

i′dle wheel′, *Mach.* a wheel for transmitting power and motion between a driving and a driven part, either by friction or by means of teeth.

i·do·crase (ī′də krās′, id′ə-), *n. Mineral.* vesuvianite. [< F < Gk *eîdo(s)* form + *krâs(is)* mixture]

i·dol (īd′^{ə}l), *n.* **1.** an image, as a statue or other material object, worshiped as a deity. **2.** *Bible.* a deity other than God. **3.** any person or thing devotedly or excessively admired: *His political idol was Roosevelt.* **4.** a mere image or semblance of something, as a phantom. **5.** a figment of the mind; fantasy. **6.** a false conception or notion; fallacy. [ME < LL *īdōl(um)* < Gk *eídōlon* image, idol < *eîdo(s)* shape] —**Syn. 1.** See **image. 3.** favorite, darling, pet.

i·dol·a·ter (ī dol′ə tər), *n.* **1.** a worshiper of idols. **2.** a person who is a devoted or excessive admirer; hero worshiper; devotee. Also, *referring to a woman,* **i·dol·a·tress** (ī dol′ə tris). [ME *idolatrer* = *idolatr(ie)* IDOLATRY + *-er* -ER[2]; *-rer* > *-er* by dissimilation]

i·dol·a·trise (ī dol′ə trīz′), *v.t., v.i.,* **-trised, -tris·ing.** *Chiefly Brit.* idolatrize. —**i·dol′a·tris′er,** *n.*

i·dol·a·trize (ī dol′ə trīz′), *v.,* **-trized, -triz·ing.** —*v.t.* **1.** to idolize. —*v.i.* **2.** to worship idols. [IDOLATR(Y) + -IZE] —**i·dol′a·triz′er,** *n.*

i·dol·a·trous (ī dol′ə trəs), *adj.* **1.** of or pertaining to idolatry. **2.** worshiping idols. **3.** blindly adoring. —**i·dol′a·trous·ly,** *adv.* —**i·dol′a·trous·ness,** *n.*

i·dol·a·try (ī dol′ə trē), *n., pl.* **-tries. 1.** the religious worship of idols. **2.** excessive or blind adoration, reverence, devotion, etc. [ME *idolatrie* < ML *īdōlatria,* LL *īdōlolatrīa* (by syncope) < New Testament Gk *eidōlolatreía*]

i·dol·ise (īd′ᵊlīz′), *v.t., v.i.,* **-ised, -is·ing.** *Chiefly Brit.* idolize. —**i′dol·i·sa′tion,** *n.* —**i′dol·is′er,** *n.*

i·dol·ize (īd′ᵊlīz′), *v.,* **-ized, -iz·ing.** —*v.t.* **1.** to regard with blind adoration, devotion, etc. —*v.i.* **2.** to practice religious idolatry. —**i′dol·i·za′tion,** *n.* —**i′dol·iz′er,** *n.*

I·dom·e·neus (ī dom′ə no͞os′, -nyo͞os′), *n. Class. Myth.* a Cretan king, one of the leaders of the Greeks in the Trojan War.

i·do·ne·ous (ī dō′nē əs), *adj. Archaic.* fit; suitable. [< L *idōneus*] —**i·do·ne·i·ty** (īd′ᵊnē′i tē), **i·do′ne·ous·ness,** *n.*

IDP, See **integrated data processing.**

Id·u·mae·a (id′yo͞o mē′ə), *n.* Greek name of **Edom.** Also, **Id′u·me′a.** —**Id′u·mae′an, Id′u·me′an,** *adj., n.*

I·dun (ē′tho͞on), *n. Scand. Myth.* the goddess of spring and the wife of Bragi. She kept the apples by which the Aesir were rejuvenated. Also, **I·dun·a** (ē′tho͞on ə), **Ithunn, Ithun.**

i·dyll (īd′ᵊl), *n.* **1.** a poem or prose composition describing pastoral scenes or events or any charmingly simple episode, appealing incident, or the like. **2.** a long narrative poem on a major theme. **3.** material suitable for an idyll. **4.** an episode or scene of idyllic charm. **5.** *Music.* a composition, usually instrumental, of a pastoral or sentimental character. Also, **i′dyl.** [< L *īdyl(lium)* < Gk *eidýllion* short pastoral poem, dim. of *eídos* form]

i·dyl·lic (ī dil′ik), *adj.* **1.** suitable for or suggestive of an idyll; charmingly simple or poetic. **2.** of, pertaining to, or characteristic of an idyll. —**i·dyl′li·cal·ly,** *adv.*

i·dyl·list (īd′ᵊlist), *n.* a writer of idylls. Also, **i′dyl·ist.**

IE, Indo-European (def. 1).

-ie, var. of **-y**[2], used as a hypocoristic suffix of nouns: *dearie; laddie; Willie.*

I.E., 1. Indo-European. **2.** Industrial Engineer.

i.e., that is. [< L *id est*]

-iensis, var. of **-ensis.** [< L; see -I-, -ESE]

Ie·per (ē′pər), *n.* Flemish name of **Ypres.**

-ier, var. of **-eer:** *brigadier; halberdier.* [unstressed: ME *-ier(e),* var. of *-yer(e)* = OE *-i-* v. stem ending + *-ere* -ER[1] (in some words < OF *-ier* < L *-ārius* -ARY); stressed: var. of -EER]

I·e·ya·su (ē′ye yä′so͞o), *n.* Iyeyasu.

if (if), *conj.* **1.** in case; granting or supposing that; on condition that: *Sing if you want to. Stay home if it rains. I'll go if he goes.* **2.** even though: *an enthusiastic if small audience.* **3.** whether: *He asked if I knew Spanish.* **4.** (used to introduce an exclamatory phrase): *If only Dad could see me now! If he isn't the laziest guy on earth!* —*n.* **5.** a supposition; uncertain possibility: *The future is full of ifs.* **6.** a condition, requirement, or stipulation: *There are too many ifs in his agreement.* [ME, var. of *yif,* OE *gif, gef;* akin to Icel *ef* if, Goth *ibai* whether, OHG *iba* condition, stipulation]
—**Syn. 1, 2.** IF, PROVIDED, PROVIDING imply a condition on which something depends. IF is general. It may be used to indicate suppositions or hypothetical conditions (often involving doubt or uncertainty): *If you like, we can go straight home. If I had known, I wouldn't have gone.* IF may mean "even though": *If I am wrong, you are not right.* It may mean "whenever": *If I do not understand, I ask questions.* PROVIDED always indicates some stipulation: *I will subscribe ten dollars provided that you do, too. Provided he goes, we can go along.* PROVIDING means just in case some certain thing should happen: *Providing he should come, we must have extra supplies ready.*
—**Usage.** IF meaning WHETHER, as in *I haven't decided if I'll go,* is sometimes criticized, but the usage has been established in standard English for a long time.

IF, See **intermediate frequency.** Also, **if**

IFC, International Finance Corporation.

if·fy (if′ē), *adj. Informal.* full of unresolved points or questions: *an iffy problem.*

If·ni (ēf′nē), *n.* a small enclave in SW Morocco: a former Spanish overseas province. 741 sq. mi. *Cap.:* Sidi Ifni.

I.F.S., Irish Free State.

-ify, var. of **-fy** after a consonant: *intensify.* [ME *-ifie(n)* < MF *-ifi(er)* < L *-ificāre*]

I.G., 1. Indo-Germanic. **2.** Inspector General.

ig·loo (ig′lo͞o), *n., pl.* **-loos.** an Eskimo house or hut usually built of blocks of hard snow and shaped like a dome. Also, **ig′lu.** [< Eskimo *ig(d)lu* house]

ign., 1. ignition. **2.** unknown. [< L *ignōtus*]

Ig·na·tius (ig nā′shəs), *n.* **1. Saint** (*Ignatius Theophorus*), A.D. c40–107?, bishop of Antioch and Apostolic Father. **2. Saint** (*Nicetas*), A.D. 799?–878, patriarch of Constantinople 846–858, 867–878.

Igna′tius of Loyo′la, Saint. See **Loyola, Saint Ignatius.**

ig·ne·ous (ig′nē əs), *adj.* **1.** *Geol.* produced under intense heat, as rocks of volcanic origin. **2.** of, pertaining to, or characteristic of fire. [< L *igneus* = *ign(is)* fire + *-eus* -EOUS]

ig·nes·cent (ig nes′ənt), *adj. Rare.* **1.** emitting sparks of fire, as certain stones when struck with steel. **2.** bursting into flame. [< L *ignescent-* (s. of *ignescēns* catching fire, prp. of *ignescere*) = *ign(is)* fire + *-escent-* -ESCENT]

ig·nis fat·u·us (ig′nis fach′o͞o əs), *pl.* **ig·nes fat·u·i** (ig′nēz fach′o͞o ī′). **1.** Also called **will-o'-the-wisp.** a flitting phosphorescent light seen chiefly over marshy ground, and supposed to be due to spontaneous combustion of gas from decomposed organic matter. **2.** something deluding or misleading. [< ML: lit., foolish fire]

ig·nite (ig nīt′), *v.,* **-nit·ed, -nit·ing.** —*v.t.* **1.** to set on fire; kindle. **2.** *Chem.* to heat intensely; roast. —*v.i.* **3.** to catch fire; begin to burn. [< L *ignīt(us)* ignited, set on fire (ptp. of *ignīre*) = *ign(is)* fire + *-ītus* -ITE[2]] —**ig·nit′a·ble, ig·nit′i·ble,** *adj.* —**ig·nit′a·bil′i·ty, ig·nit′i·bil′i·ty,** *n.* —**Syn. 1.** See **kindle.**

ig·nit·er (ig nī′tər), *n.* **1.** a person or thing that ignites. **2.** *Electronics.* the carborundum rod used to initiate the discharge in an ignitron.

ig·ni·tion (ig nish′ən), *n.* **1.** the act or fact of igniting. **2.** the state of being ignited. **3.** (in an internal-combustion engine) the process that ignites the fuel in the cylinder. **4.** a means or device for igniting. [< ML *ignitiōn-* (s. of *ignitiō*) a setting on fire]

ig·ni·tron (ig nī′tron, ig′ni tron′), *n. Electronics.* a heavy-duty rectifier tube containing a pool of mercury. [IGNI(TER + ELEC)TRON]

ig·no·ble (ig nō′bəl), *adj.* **1.** of low character, aims, etc.; mean; base. **2.** of low grade or quality; inferior. **3.** not noble; of humble birth or station. [late ME < L *ignōbil(is)* unknown, inglorious = *i-* (var. of *in-* IN-[3]) + OL *gnōbilis* NOBLE] —**ig′no·bil′i·ty, ig·no′ble·ness,** *n.* —**ig·no′bly,** *adv.* —**Syn. 1.** dishonorable, contemptible. **3.** lowly, obscure. —**Ant. 1.** honorable. **2.** superior.

ig·no·min·i·ous (ig′nə min′ē əs), *adj.* **1.** marked by or attended with ignominy; humiliating: *an ignominious retreat.* **2.** bearing or deserving ignominy; contemptible. [late ME < L *ignōminiōs(us).* See IGNOMINY, -OUS] —**ig′no·min′i·ous·ly,** *adv.* —**ig′no·min′i·ous·ness,** *n.* —**Syn. 2.** ignoble.

ig·no·min·y (ig′nə min′ē), *n., pl.* **-min·ies** for 2. **1.** disgrace; dishonor; public contempt. **2.** shameful or dishonorable quality or conduct or an instance of this. [< L *ignōminia* = *ig-* (for *in-* IN-[3], abstracted, by folk etym., from *ignōbilis* IGNOBLE) + *nōmin-* (s. of *nōmen*) NAME + *-ia* -Y[3]] —**Syn. 1.** disrepute, shame. See **disgrace.** —**Ant. 1.** credit.

ig·no·ra·mus (ig′nə rā′məs, -ram′əs), *n., pl.* **-mus·es.** an ignorant person. [< legal L: we ignore (1st pers. pl. pres. indic. of *ignōrāre* to be ignorant of, IGNORE); hence name of an ignorant lawyer in the play *Ignoramus* (1615) by G. Ruggle, whence current sense]

ig·no·rance (ig′nər əns), *n.* the state or fact of being ignorant; lack of knowledge, learning, information, etc. [ME *ignora(u)nce* < L *ignōrantia*]

ig·no·rant (ig′nər ənt), *adj.* **1.** lacking in knowledge or training; unlearned. **2.** lacking knowledge about a particular subject or fact. **3.** uninformed; unaware: *They left him ignorant of their plans.* **4.** showing lack of knowledge: *an ignorant statement.* [ME *ignora(u)nt* < L *ignōrant-* (s. of *ignōrāns*) prp. of *ignōrāre*] —**ig′no·rant·ly,** *adv.*
—**Syn. 1.** uninstructed, untutored, untaught. IGNORANT, ILLITERATE, UNEDUCATED mean lacking in knowledge or in training. IGNORANT may mean knowing little or nothing, or it may mean uninformed about a particular subject: *An ignorant person can be dangerous. I confess I'm ignorant of mathematics.* ILLITERATE originally meant lacking a knowledge of literature or similar learning, but is specifically applied to a person unable to read or write: *necessary training for illiterate soldiers.* UNEDUCATED refers esp. to lack of schooling or to lack of access to a body of knowledge equivalent to that learned in schools: *uneducated but highly intelligent.* **2.** unenlightened. —**Ant. 1.** literate.

ig·nore (ig nōr′, -nôr′), *v.t.,* **-nored, -nor·ing. 1.** to refrain from noticing or recognizing: *to ignore another's remarks.* **2.** *Law.* (of a grand jury) to reject (a bill of indictment), as on the grounds of insufficient evidence. [< L *ignōr(āre)* (to) not know, disregard = *ignōr-* (var. of *ignār-,* s. of *ignārus* ignorant of, unknown = *i-* IN-[3] + *gnār-* KNOW) + *-ā-* thematic vowel + *-re* inf. ending] —**ig·nor′a·ble,** *adj.* —**ig·nor′er,** *n.* —**Syn. 1.** overlook; slight, disregard, neglect.

I-go (ē′gō′), *n.* go[2]. [< Jap < Chin *wei ch'i* a kind of chess = *wei* surround + *ch'i* chessman]

Ig·o·rot (ig′ə rōt′, ē′gə-), *n., pl.* **-rots,** (*esp. collectively*) **-rot.** a member of a people of the Malay stock in northern Luzon in the Philippines, comprising various tribes, some noted as headhunters.

Iguana,
Iguana iguana
(Length to 6 ft.)

i·gua·na (i gwä′nə), *n.* any lizard of the genus *Iguana,* esp. the edible, arboreal *I. iguana,* of tropical America, that grows to a length of more than five feet. [< Sp < Arawak *iwana*]

i·guan·o·don (i gwä′nə don′, i-gwan′ə-), *n.* a herbivorous, early Cretaceous dinosaur of the genus *Iguanodon* that grew to a length of 15 to 30 feet and walked erect. [< NL; see IGUANA, -ODONT]

I·guas·sú (ē′gwä so͞o′), *n.* a river in S Brazil, flowing W to the Paraná River. 380 mi. long.

I′guassú′ Falls′, a waterfall on the Iguassú River, on the boundary between Brazil and Argentina. 210 ft. high. Also called **Victoria Falls.**

I.G.Y., See **International Geophysical Year.**

IHD, See **International Hydrological Decade.**

IHS, 1. Jesus. [< LL < Gk *ΙΗΣ,* short for *ΙΗΣΟΥΣ* Jesus] **2.** Jesus Savior of Men. [< L *Iēsus Hominum Salvātor*]

Ijs·sel (ī′səl), *n.* a river in the central Netherlands, flowing N to Ijssel Lake: a branch of the Rhine River. 70 mi. long. Also, **Ij** (ī). Dutch, **IJs′sel, IJ.**

Ijs′sel Lake′, a lake in the NW Netherlands: created by diking of the Zuider Zee. 465 sq. mi. Dutch, **IJs·sel·meer** (ī′səl mār′).

I·ka·ri·a (i kâr′ē ə, ī kâr′-; *Gk.* ē′kä rē′ä), *n.* Icaria.

i·ke·ba·na (ē′ke bä′nä), *n. Japanese.* the art of arranging flowers, esp. for decorative use in the home.

Ikh·na·ton (ik nät′ᵊn), *n.* See **Amenhotep IV.**

i·kon (ī′kon), *n.* icon (defs. 1, 2).

il-[1], var. of **in-**[2] (by assimilation) before *l: illation.*

il-[2], var. of **in-**[3] (by assimilation) before *l: illogical.*

-il, var. of **-ile:** *civil.*

IL, Illinois (approved esp. for use with zip code).

ILA, 1. International Law Association. **2.** International Longshoremen's Association. Also, **I.L.A.**

i·lang-i·lang (ē′läng ē′läng), *n.* ylang-ylang.

ile-, var. of **ileo-** before a vowel: *ileac.*

-ile, a suffix of adjectives expressing capability, susceptibility, liability, aptitude, etc.: *agile; docile; ductile; fragile; prehensile; volatile.* Also, **-il.** [< L *-ilis, -īlis*]

il·e·ac[1] (il′ē ak′), *adj.* of or pertaining to the ileum. [ILE- + -AC, on model of *iliac*]

il·e·ac[2] (il′ē ak′), *adj. Pathol.* of or pertaining to ileus. [ILE(US) + -AC, on model of *iliac*]

Île de France (ēl də fräns′), a former province in N France, including Paris and the region around it. See map at **Picardy.**

Île du Dia·ble (ēl dy dyaᴬ′blᵊ), French name of **Devil's Island.**

il·e·i·tis (il′ē ī′tis), *n. Pathol.* inflammation of the ileum.

ileo-, a combining form of **ileum:** *ileostomy.* Also, *esp. before a vowel,* **ile-.** [< NL]

il·e·os·to·my (il′ē os′tə mē), *n., pl.* **-mies.** *Surg.* the formation of an artificial opening into the ileum, usually of a permanent or semipermanent nature.

Îles Co·mores (ēl kō môr′), French name of **Comoro Islands.**

Îles du Sa·lut (ēl dy sa ly′), French name of **Safety Islands.**

Il·e·tin (il′i tin), *n. Pharm., Trademark.* insulin (def. 2).

il·e·um (il′ē əm), *n.* **1.** *Anat.* the third and lowest division of the small intestine, extending from the jejunum to the cecum. **2.** *Entomol.* the anterior portion of the hindgut of an insect. [< NL, LL *īleum,* var. of L *īle* gut; by transfer, loin, flank (usually in pl.: *īlia*)]

il·e·us (il′ē əs), *n. Pathol.* intestinal obstruction characterized by abdominal pain and vomiting. [< L: colic < Gk *eileós* = *eile-* (s. of *eílein* to roll) + *-os* n. suffix]

i·lex[1] (ī′leks), *n.* See **holm oak.** [ME < L]

i·lex[2] (ī′leks), *n.* **1.** any tree or shrub of the genus *Ilex.* **2.** a holly. [< NL, L]

Il·ford (il′fərd), *n.* a city in SW Essex, in SE England, near London. 178,210 (1961).

I.L.G.W.U., International Ladies' Garment Workers' Union. Also, **ILGWU**

Il·i·a (il′ē ə), *n. Rom. Legend.* the mother of Romulus and Remus.

il·i·ac (il′ē ak′), *adj.* of, pertaining to, or situated near the ilium. [ILI(UM) + -AC]

il′iac ar′tery, *Anat.* either of two large arteries that conduct blood to the pelvis and the legs, the outer branch of which becomes the femoral artery while the inner branch conducts blood to the gluteal region.

Il·i·ad (il′ē əd), *n.* **1.** (*italics*) a Greek epic poem describing the siege of Troy, ascribed to Homer. **2.** (*sometimes l.c.*) any similar poem; long narrative. **3.** (*often l.c.*) a long series of woes, trials, etc. [< L *Īliad-* (s. of *Īlias*) < Gk. See ILION, -AD[1]] —**Il·i·ad·ic** (il′ē ad′ik), *adj.*

Il·i·on (il′ī ən), *n.* Greek name of ancient **Troy.**

-ility, a compound suffix used to form abstract nouns from adjectives with stems in **-(i)le, -le:** *agility; civility; ability.* [< F *-ilité* < L *-ilitās*]

il·i·um (il′ē əm), *n., pl.* **il·i·a** (il′ē ə). *Anat.* the broad, upper portion of either innominate bone. [< NL, special use of LL var. of L *īle.* See ILEUM]

Il·i·um (il′ē əm), *n.* Latin name of ancient **Troy.**

ilk[1] (ilk), *n.* **1.** family, class, or kind: *he and all his ilk.* **2. of that ilk, a.** (in Scotland) of the same family name or place: *Ross of that ilk,* i.e., *Ross of Ross.* **b.** of the same. —*adj.* **3.** *Obs.* same. [ME *ilke,* OE *ilca* (pron.) the same class or kind = demonstrative *i* (c. Goth *is* he, L *is* that) + a form of LIKE[1]]

ilk[2] (ilk), *pron. Chiefly Scot.* each. [ME *ilk,* north var. of *ilch,* OE *ylc* (pron.) EACH]

ill (il), *adj.,* **worse, worst,** *n., adv.* —*adj.* **1.** of unsound physical or mental health; unwell; sick. **2.** evil; wicked; bad: *of ill repute.* **3.** objectionable; unsatisfactory; poor; faulty: *ill manners.* **4.** hostile; unkindly: *ill feeling.* **5.** unfavorable; adverse: *ill fortune.* **6.** of inferior worth or ability; unskillful; inexpert: *an ill example of scholarship.* **7. ill at ease,** uncomfortable; nervous. —*n.* **8.** evil. **9.** harm; injury. **10.** a disease; ailment. **11.** trouble; misfortune. **12.** *Archaic.* wickedness or sin. —*adv.* **13.** wickedly. **14.** unsatisfactorily; poorly: *It ill befits a man to betray old friends.* **15.** in a hostile manner. **16.** unfavorably; unfortunately. **17.** with displeasure or offense. **18.** faultily; improperly. **19.** with difficulty or inconvenience; scarcely: *an expense we can ill afford.* [ME *ill(e)* < Scand; cf. Icel *illr* ill, bad] —**il′ly,** *adv.* —**Syn. 1.** unhealthy, ailing, diseased, afflicted. ILL, SICK mean being in bad health, not being well. ILL is the more formal word. In the U.S. the two words are used practically interchangeably except that SICK is used when the word modifies the following noun or is used as a collective noun: *to be very sick (ill) of a fever; to look sick (ill); a sick person; a home for the sick.* There are certain phrases, also, in which SICK is used: *sick at heart; sick for home; It makes me sick.* In England, SICK is not interchangeable with ILL, but usually has the connotation of nausea; SICK, however, is used before nouns, as a collective and in set phrases, just as in the U.S.: *to be ill; to feel ill; a sick man.* **2.** wrong, iniquitous. See **bad**[1]. **8.** mischief. **9.** hurt, pain, misery. **10.** illness, affliction. **11.** calamity. **12.** depravity. **14.** badly. —**Ant. 1.** well, healthy. **2–6.** good.

I'll (īl), contraction of *I will* or *I shall.*

Ill., Illinois.

ill., **1.** illustrated. **2.** illustration. **3.** illustrator. **4.** most illustrious. [< L *illustrissimus*]

ill-ad·vised (il′əd vīzd′), *adj.* acting or done without due consideration; imprudent: *an ill-advised remark.* —**ill-ad·vis·ed·ly** (il′əd vī′zid lē), *adv.*

I·llam·pu (*Sp.* ē yäm′po͞o), *n.* a peak of Mount Sorata. Cf. **Sorata.**

ill-at-ease (il′ət ēz′), *adj.* uncomfortable; uneasy.

il·la·tion (i lā′shən), *n.* **1.** the act of inferring. **2.** an inference or conclusion. [< LL *illātiōn-* (s. of *illātiō*) a carrying in = L *illāt(us)* brought in, ptp. of *inferre* (*il-* -IL[1] + *lātus* brought, var. of earlier **tlātus;* see TOLERATE) + *-iōn-* -ION]

il·la·tive (il′ə tiv, i lā′tiv), *adj.* **1.** of, pertaining to, or expressing illation; inferential: *an illative word such as "therefore."* **2.** *Gram.* noting a case, as in Finnish, whose distinctive function is to indicate place into or toward which. —*n.* **3.** *Gram.* the illative case. [< LL *illātīv(us)*]

il·laud·a·ble (i lô′də bəl), *adj.* unworthy of praise; not laudable. [< LL *illaudābil(is)*] —**il·laud′a·bly,** *adv.*

ill-be·ing (il′bē′ing), *n.* the state or condition of lacking health, solvency, etc. [modeled on WELL-BEING]

ill-bod·ing (il′bō′ding), *adj.* foreboding evil; inauspicious; unlucky: *ill-boding stars.*

ill-bred (il′bred′), *adj.* showing lack of proper breeding; unmannerly; rude.

ill-con·sid·ered (il′kən sid′ərd), *adj.* done without thorough consideration; ill-suited; unwise.

ill-dis·posed (il′di spōzd′), *adj.* **1.** unfriendly, hostile, or unsympathetic, as toward another person, an idea, etc. **2.** having an objectionable disposition. [ME] —**ill-dis·pos·ed·ness** (il′di spō′zid nis, -spōzd′-), *n.*

il·le·gal (i lē′gəl), *adj.* not legal; contrary to existing statutes, regulations, etc.; unauthorized (distinguished from *nonlegal*). [< ML *illēgāl(is)*] —**il·le′gal·ly,** *adv.* —**Syn.** unlawful; illegitimate; illicit; unlicensed.

il·le·gal·ise (i lē′gə līz′), *v.t.,* **-ised, -is·ing.** *Chiefly Brit.* illegalize. —**il·le′gal·i·sa′tion,** *n.*

il·le·gal·i·ty (il′ē gal′i tē), *n., pl.* **-ties.** **1.** an illegal condition or quality; unlawfulness. **2.** an illegal act. [< ML *illēgālitās*]

il·le·gal·ize (i lē′gə līz′), *v.t.,* **-ized, -iz·ing.** to make illegal. Also, *esp. Brit.,* **illegalise.** —**il·le′gal·i·za′tion,** *n.*

il·leg·i·ble (i lej′ə bəl), *adj.* not legible; impossible or hard to read or decipher. —**il·leg′i·bil′i·ty, il·leg′i·ble·ness,** *n.* —**il·leg′i·bly,** *adv.*

il·le·git·i·ma·cy (il′i jit′ə mə sē), *n., pl.* **-cies.** the state or quality of being illegitimate.

il·le·git·i·mate (*adj., n.* il′i jit′ə mit; *v.* il′i jit′ə māt′), *adj., v.,* **-mat·ed, -mat·ing,** *n.* —*adj.* **1.** not legitimate; unlawful; illegal: *an illegitimate action.* **2.** (of a person) born out of wedlock. **3.** irregular; not in good usage. **4.** *Logic.* not in accordance with the principles of valid inference. —*v.t.* **5.** to declare illegitimate. —*n.* **6.** a person recognized or looked upon as illegitimate; bastard. —**il′le·git′i·mate·ly,** *adv.* —**il′le·git′i·mate·ness,** *n.* —**il′le·git′i·ma′tion,** *n.*

il·le·git·i·ma·tise (il′i jit′ə mə tīz′), *v.t.,* **-tised, -tis·ing.** *Chiefly Brit.* illegitimatize.

il·le·git·i·ma·tize (il′i jit′ə mə tīz′), *v.t.,* **-tized, -tiz·ing.** to make illegitimate; bastardize.

ill′ fame′, bad repute or name.

ill-fat·ed (il′fā′tid), *adj.* **1.** destined, as though by fate, to an unhappy or unfortunate end: *an ill-fated voyage.* **2.** bringing bad fortune.

ill-fa·vored (il′fā′vərd), *adj.* **1.** unpleasant in appearance; ugly: *an ill-favored child.* **2.** offensive; unpleasant; objectionable: *ill-favored remarks.* Also, *esp. Brit.,* **ill′-fa′voured.**

ill-found·ed (il′foun′did), *adj.* based on weak evidence, illogical reasoning, or the like.

ill-got·ten (il′got′ᵊn), *adj.* acquired by evil or improper means: *ill-gotten gains.*

ill′ hu′mor, a disagreeable or surly mood. —**ill′-hu′mored;** *esp. Brit.,* **ill′-hu′moured,** *adj.*

il·lib·er·al (i lib′ər əl, i lib′rəl), *adj.* **1.** narrow-minded; bigoted. **2.** *Chiefly Literary.* without culture; unscholarly; vulgar. **3.** *Rare.* not generous in giving; niggardly; stingy. [< L *illīberāl(is)*] —**il·lib′er·al′i·ty, il·lib′er·al·ness, il·lib′er·al·ism,** *n.* —**il·lib′er·al·ly,** *adv.*

il·lic·it (i lis′it), *adj.* not permitted or authorized; unlicensed; unlawful. [< L *illicit(us)*] —**il·lic′it·ly,** *adv.* —**il·lic′it·ness,** *n.*

I·lli·ma·ni (ē′yē mä′nē), *n.* a mountain in W Bolivia, in the Andes, near La Paz. 21,188 ft.

il·lim·it·a·ble (i lim′i tə bəl), *adj.* not limitable; limitless; boundless. —**il·lim′it·a·bil′i·ty, il·lim′it·a·ble·ness,** *n.* —**il·lim′it·a·bly,** *adv.*

Il·li·nois (il′ə noi′, -noiz′), *n.* **1.** a state in the midwestern United States. 11,113,976 (1970); 56,400 sq. mi. *Cap.:* Springfield. *Abbr.:* Ill., IL **2.** a river flowing SW from NE Illinois to the Mississippi River: connected by a canal with Lake Michigan. 273 mi. long. —**Il·li·nois·an** (il′ə noi′ən, -zən), **Il·li·noi·an** (il′ə noi′ən), **Il·li·nois·i·an** (il′ə noi′zē ən, -zhən), *n., adj.*

Il·li·nois (il′ə noi′, -noiz′), *n., pl.* **-nois** (-noi′, -noiz′). **1.** a member of a confederacy of North American Indians of Algonquian stock, formerly occupying Illinois and adjoining regions westward. **2.** the Algonquian language of the Illinois and Miami Indians. [< F < Algonquian; akin to Shawnee *hileni,* Fox *ineniwa* man (*n* < *l* by assimilation)]

il·liq·uid (i lik′wid), *adj.* not readily convertible into cash.

il·lit·er·a·cy (i lit′ər ə sē), *n., pl.* **-cies** for 3. **1.** the lack of ability to read and write. **2.** the state of being illiterate; lack of education. **3.** a mistake in writing or speaking considered to be characteristic of an illiterate person; solecism.

il·lit·er·ate (i lit′ər it), *adj.* **1.** unable to read and write. **2.** lacking education. **3.** showing lack of culture, esp. in language and literature. **4.** displaying a marked lack of knowledge in a particular field: *He is musically illiterate.* —*n.* **5.** an illiterate person. [< L *illīterāt(us)* unlettered] —**il·lit′er·ate·ly,** *adv.* —**il·lit′er·ate·ness,** *n.* —**Syn. 1.** See **ignorant.**

ill-judged (il′jujd′), *adj.* injudicious; unwise.

ill-man·nered (il′man′ərd), *adj.* having bad manners; impolite; discourteous; rude. [ME] —**Syn.** coarse, uncouth, unpolished, crude; uncivil.

ill-na·tured (il′nā′chərd), *adj.* having or showing an unkindly or unpleasant disposition. —**ill′-na′tured·ly,** *adv.* —**ill′-na′tured·ness,** *n.* —**Syn.** cranky, petulant, sulky, sour, crusty, bitter. See **cross.** —**Ant.** kindly, amiable.

ill·ness (il′nis), *n.* **1.** the state of being ill; indisposition; sickness. **2.** *Obs.* wickedness.

il·log·ic (i loj′ik), *n.* the state or quality of being illogical; illogicality.

il·log·i·cal (i loj′i kəl), *adj.* not logical; contrary to or disregardful of the rules of logic; unreasoning. —**il·log′i·cal·ness,** *n.* —**il·log′i·cal·ly,** *adv.*

il·log·i·cal·i·ty (i loj′i kal′i tē), *n., pl.* **-ties** for 2. **1.** illogic. **2.** an instance of illogic.

ill-o·mened (il′ō′mənd), *adj.* having or attended by bad omens; ill-starred.

ill-sort·ed (il′sôr′tid), *adj.* poorly arranged; badly matched.

ill-spent (il′spent′), *adj.* misspent; wasted.

ill-starred (il′stärd′), *adj.* under the influence of an evil star; ill-fated; unlucky.

ill-suit·ed (il′so͞o′tid), *adj.* not suitable; inappropriate.

ill′ tem′per, bad or irritable disposition. —**ill′-tem′pered,** *adj.* —**ill′-tem′pered·ly,** *adv.*

ill-timed (il′tīmd′), *adj.* badly timed; inopportune.

ill-treat (il′trēt′), *v.t.* to treat badly; maltreat. —**ill′-treat′ment,** *n.*

il·lume (i lo͞om′), *v.t.*, **-lumed, -lum·ing.** *Archaic.* to illuminate. [short for ILLUMINE]

il·lu·mi·nance (i lo͞o′mə nəns), *n. Optics.* illumination (def. 5).

il·lu·mi·nant (i lo͞o′mə nənt), *n.* an illuminating agent or material. [< L *illūminant-* (s. of *illūmināns*) lighting up, prp. of *illūmināre*]

il·lu·mi·nate (*v.* i lo͞o′mə nāt′; *adj., n.* i lo͞o′mə nit, -nāt′), *v.*, **-nat·ed, -nat·ing,** *adj., n.* —*v.t.* **1.** to supply with light; light up. **2.** to throw light on (a subject); make lucid or clear. **3.** *Chiefly Brit.* to decorate with lights, as in celebration. **4.** to enlighten, as with knowledge. **5.** to make radiant or illustrious: *A smile illuminated her face. His leadership illuminated the epoch.* **6.** to decorate (a letter, page, manuscript, etc.) with color, gold, or the like. —*v.i.* **7.** to display lights, as in celebration. **8.** to become illuminated. —*adj.* **9.** *Archaic.* illuminated. **10.** *Obs.* enlightened. —*n.* **11.** *Archaic.* a person who is or affects to be specially enlightened. [< L *illūmināt(us)* lighted up (ptp. of *illūmināre*)] —**il·lu′mi·na·ble,** *adj.* —**il·lu′mi·nat′ing·ly,** *adv.* —**il·lu′mi·na′tive,** *adj.* —**il·lu′mi·na′tor,** *n.*

il·lu·mi·na·ti (i lo͞o′mə nä′tī, -nä′tē), *n.pl., sing.* **-to** (-tō). **1.** persons possessing or claiming to possess superior enlightenment. **2.** (*cap.*) a name given to different religious societies or sects because of their claim to enlightenment. [< L. pl. of *illūminātus* enlightened; see ILLUMINATE]

il·lu·mi·nat·ing (i lo͞o′mə nā′ting), *adj.* **1.** giving or casting light. **2.** informing or making clear; enlightening.

il·lu·mi·na·tion (i lo͞o′mə nā′shən), *n.* **1.** the act of illuminating. **2.** the fact or condition of being illuminated. **3.** *Chiefly Brit.* a decoration of lights, usually colored lights. **4.** intellectual or spiritual enlightenment. **5.** Also called **illuminance.** *Optics.* the intensity of light falling at a given place on a lighted surface; the luminous flux incident per unit area, expressed in lumens per unit of area. **6.** a supply of light. **7.** decoration, as of a letter, page, or manuscript, with a painted design in color, gold, etc. **8.** a design used in such decoration. [ME < eccl. L *illūminātiōn-* (s. of *illūminātiō*) spiritual enlightenment] —**il·lu′mi·na′tion·al,** *adj.*

il·lu·mi·na·tor (i lo͞o′mə nā′tər), *n.* **1.** a person or thing that illuminates. **2.** a device for illuminating, as a light source with lens or a mirror for concentrating light. **3.** a person who paints manuscripts, books, etc., with designs in color, gold, or the like. [late ME < LL]

il·lu·mine (i lo͞o′min), *v.t., v.i.*, **-mined, -min·ing.** to illuminate. [ME < L *illūmin(āre)* (to) light up = *il-* IL-[1] + *lūmin-* (s. of *lūmen*) light + *-āre* inf. suffix]

il·lu·mi·nism (i lo͞o′mə niz′əm), *n.* the doctrines or claims of Illuminati. —**il·lu′mi·nist,** *n.*

illus., 1. illustrated. **2.** illustration.

ill-use (*v.* il′yo͞oz′; *n.* il′yo͞os′), *v.*, **-used, -us·ing,** *n.* —*v.t.* **1.** to treat badly, unjustly, cruelly, etc. —*n.* **2.** Also, **ill′-us′age.** bad, unjust, or cruel treatment.

il·lu·sion (i lo͞o′zhən), *n.* **1.** something that deceives by producing a false impression. **2.** the state or condition of being deceived; misapprehension. **3.** an instance of being deceived. **4.** *Psychol.* a perception that represents what is perceived in an unreal way. **5.** a very thin, delicate tulle of silk or nylon having a cobwebbed appearance, for trimmings, veilings, and the like. **6.** *Obs.* the act of deceiving; deception. [ME < L *illūsiōn-* (s. of *illūsiō*) irony, mocking = *illūs(us)* mocked, ridiculed (ptp. of *illūdere* = *il-* IL-[1] + *lūd-* play (see LUDICROUS) + *-tus* ptp. suffix) + *-iōn-* -ION] —**il·lu′sioned,** *adj.*

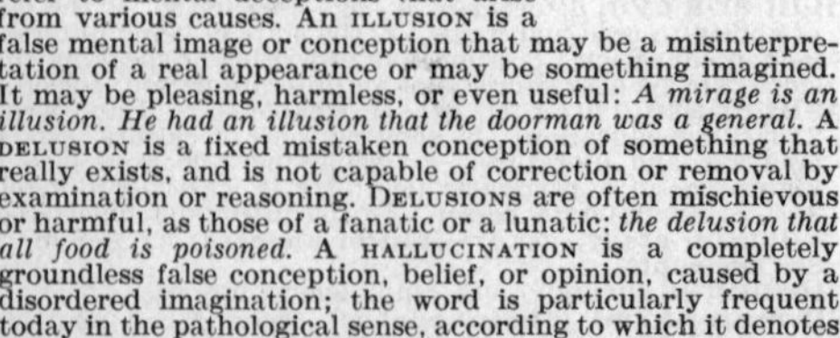

Optical illusion
Line AB equals
line BC

—**Syn. 1.** aberration, fantasy, chimera. ILLUSION, DELUSION, HALLUCINATION refer to mental deceptions that arise from various causes. An ILLUSION is a false mental image or conception that may be a misinterpretation of a real appearance or may be something imagined. It may be pleasing, harmless, or even useful: *A mirage is an illusion. He had an illusion that the doorman was a general.* A DELUSION is a fixed mistaken conception of something that really exists, and is not capable of correction or removal by examination or reasoning. DELUSIONS are often mischievous or harmful, as those of a fanatic or a lunatic: *the delusion that all food is poisoned.* A HALLUCINATION is a completely groundless false conception, belief, or opinion, caused by a disordered imagination; the word is particularly frequent today in the pathological sense, according to which it denotes hearing or seeing something that does not exist: *hallucinations caused by nervous disorders.*

il·lu·sion·ar·y (i lo͞o′zhə ner′ē), *adj.* of, pertaining to, or characterized by illusions: *anticipated sales that were largely illusionary.* Also, **il·lu′sion·al.**

il·lu·sion·ism (i lo͞o′zhə niz′əm), *n.* **1.** *Philos.* a theory or doctrine that the material world is an illusion. **2.** a technique of using pictorial methods in order to deceive the eye. Cf. **trompe l'oeil.** —**il·lu′sion·is′tic,** *adj.*

il·lu·sion·ist (i lo͞o′zhə nist), *n.* **1.** a conjurer or magician who creates illusions, as by sleight of hand. **2.** an adherent of illusionism.

il·lu·so·ry (i lo͞o′sə rē, -zə-), *adj.* **1.** causing illusion; deceptive. **2.** of the nature of an illusion; unreal. Also, **il·lu·sive** (i lo͞o′siv). [< LL *illūsōri(us)* = *illūsōr-* (s. of *illūsor*) mocker, deceiver (see ILLUSION, -OR[2]) + *-ius* adj. suffix; see -ORY[1]] —**il·lu′so·ri·ly, il·lu′sive·ly,** *adv.* —**il·lu′so·ri·ness, il·lu′sive·ness,** *n.* —**Syn. 1.** misleading, fallacious, specious, false. **2.** imaginary; visionary, fancied.

illust., 1. illustrated. **2.** illustration.

il·lus·trate (il′ə strāt′, i lus′trāt), *v.*, **-trat·ed, -trat·ing.** —*v.t.* **1.** to make clear or intelligible, as by examples; exemplify. **2.** to furnish (a book, magazine, etc.) with drawings or pictorial representations intended for elucidation or adornment. **3.** *Archaic.* to enlighten. —*v.i.* **4.** to clarify with examples. [< L *illustrāt(us)* made bright or clear, honored (ptp. of *illustrāre*)] —**il′lus·trat′a·ble,** *adj.*

il·lus·trat·ed (il′ə strā′tid), *adj.* **1.** containing pictorial illustrations. —*n.* **2.** *Brit.* a magazine or newspaper regularly containing many photographs or drawings.

il·lus·tra·tion (il′ə strā′shən), *n.* **1.** something that illustrates, as a picture in a book or magazine. **2.** a comparison or an example intended for explanation or corroboration. **3.** elucidation. **4.** *Rare.* illustriousness; distinction. [ME < eccl. L *illustrātiōn-* (s. of *illustrātiō*) spiritual enlightenment] —**il′lus·tra′tion·al,** *adj.* —**Syn. 2.** explication. See **case**[1].

il·lus·tra·tive (i lus′trə tiv, il′ə strā′tiv), *adj.* serving to illustrate: *illustrative examples.* —**il·lus′tra·tive·ly,** *adv.*

il·lus·tra·tor (il′ə strā′tər, i lus′trā tər), *n.* **1.** an artist who makes illustrations. **2.** a person or thing that illustrates. [< LL]

il·lus·tri·ous (i lus′trē əs), *adj.* **1.** highly distinguished; renowned; famous. **2.** glorious, as deeds. **3.** *Obs.* luminous; bright. [< L *illustri(s)* bright, clear, famous = *illustr(āre)* (to) ILLUSTRATE + *-i(s)* adj. suffix + -OUS] —**il·lus′tri·ous·ly,** *adv.* —**il·lus′tri·ous·ness,** *n.* —**Syn. 1.** celebrated, eminent, famed.

il·lu·vi·al (i lo͞o′vē əl, i lo͞ov′yəl), *adj.* of or pertaining to illuviation or illuvium. [< L *illuvi(ēs)* mud, flood, lit., what washes or is washed in (*il-* IL-[1] + *-luvi-* wash + *-ēs* n. suffix) + -AL[1]]

il·lu·vi·ate (i lo͞o′vē āt′), *v.i.*, **-at·ed, -at·ing. 1.** to undergo illuviation. **2.** to produce illuviation. [< L *illuvi(ēs)* mud (see ILLUVIAL) + -ATE[1]]

il·lu·vi·a·tion (i lo͞o′vē ā′shən), *n.* the accumulation in one layer of soil of materials that have been leached out of another layer.

il·lu·vi·um (i lo͞o′vē əm), *n., pl.* **-vi·ums, -vi·a** (-vē ə). the material accumulated through illuviation. [< NL; see IL-[1], ALLUVIUM]

ill′ will′, hostile feeling; antipathy; enmity. [ME] —**Syn.** hostility, animosity. —**Ant.** benevolence.

ill-wish·er (il′wish′ər), *n.* a person who wishes misfortune to another.

Il·lyr·i·a (i lēr′ē ə), *n.* an ancient country along the E coast of the Adriatic.

Il·lyr·i·an (i lēr′ē ən), *adj.* **1.** of or pertaining to Illyria. —*n.* **2.** a native or inhabitant of Illyria. **3.** the extinct language of the Illyrians, an Indo-European language.

il·men·ite (il′mə nīt′), *n.* a very common black mineral, iron titanate, $FeTiO_3$, occurring in crystals but more commonly massive. [named after *Ilmen,* mountain range in Urals, Russia; see -ITE[1]]

ILO, See **International Labor Organization.** Also, **I.L.O.**

I·lo·ca·no (ē′lō kä′nō), *n., pl.* **-nos,** (*esp. collectively*) **-no. 1.** a member of a people of Luzon in the Philippines. **2.** the Malayo-Polynesian, Indonesian language of the Ilocano. Also, **Ilokano.** [< Sp = *iloc-* (< Tagalog *ilog* river) + *-ano* -AN]

I·lo·i·lo (ē′lō ē′lō), *n.* a seaport on S Panay, in the central Philippines. 137,476 (est. 1960).

I·lo·ka·no (ē′lō kä′nō), *n., pl.* **-nos,** (*esp. collectively*) **-no.** Ilocano.

I.L.W.U., International Longshoremen's and Warehousemen's Union.

I'm (īm), contraction of *I am.*

im-[1], var. of **in-**[2] before *b, m, p: imbrute; immingle; impassion.*

im-[2], var. of **in-**[3] before *b, m, p: imbalance; immoral; imperishable.*

im-[3], var. of **in-**[1] before *b, m, p: imbed; immure; impose.*

-im, a plural ending occurring in loan words from Hebrew: *cherubim.*

I.M., Isle of Man.

im·age (im′ij), *n., v.*, **-aged, -ag·ing.** —*n.* **1.** a physical likeness or representation of a person, animal, or thing, photographed, painted, sculptured, or otherwise produced. **2.** an optical counterpart or appearance of an object, such as is produced by reflection from a mirror. **3.** a mental representation; idea; conception. **4.** form; appearance; semblance: *God created man in his own image.* **5.** counterpart; copy: *That child is the image of his mother.* **6.** a symbol; emblem. **7.** a type; embodiment: *He was the image of frustration.* **8.** a description of something in speech or writing. **9.** an idol or representation of a deity. **10.** *Rhet.* a figure of speech, esp. a metaphor or a simile. **11.** *Archaic.* an illusion or apparition. —*v.t.* **12.** to picture or represent in the mind; imagine; conceive. **13.** to make an image of; portray in sculpture, painting, etc. **14.** to set forth in speech or writing; describe. **15.** to reflect the likeness of; mirror. **16.** to project (photographs, film, etc.) on a surface: *Familiar scenes were imaged on the screen.* **17.** to symbolize; typify. **18.** to resemble. [ME < OF, var. of *imagene* (appar. taken as base + suffix by folk etym.) < L *imāgin-,* s. of *imāgō* a copy, likeness; see IMITATE]

—**Syn. 1, 9.** IMAGE, ICON, IDOL refer to material representations of persons or things. An IMAGE is a representation as in a statue or effigy, and is sometimes regarded as an object of worship: *to set up an image of Apollo; an image of a saint.* An ICON, in the Greek or Orthodox Eastern Church, is a representation of Christ, an angel, or a saint, in painting, relief, mosaic, or the like: *At least two icons are found in each church.* Small icons are also carried by the peasants; these are folded tablets of wood or metal, with representations of sacred subjects: *An icon is honored by offerings of incense and lights.* An IDOL is an image, statue, or the like, representing a deity and worshiped as such: *a wooden idol; The heathen worship idols.* It may be used figuratively: *to make an idol of wealth.* **2.** likeness, figure, representation. **3.** notion. **5.** facsimile. —**Ant. 5.** original.

im·age·ry (im′ij rē, im′ij ə rē), *n., pl.* **-ries. 1.** mental images collectively, esp. those produced by the action of imagination. **2.** pictorial images. **3.** the use of rhetorical images. **4.** figurative description or illustration; rhetorical images collectively. [ME *imagerie* < MF]

im·ag·i·na·ble (i maj′ə nə bəl), *adj.* capable of being imagined or conceived. [ME < LL *imāginābil(is)*] —**im·ag′i·na·ble·ness,** *n.* —**im·ag′i·na·bly,** *adv.*

im·ag·i·nal (i maj′ə nᵊl), *adj.* *Entomol.* of or pertaining to an imago. [< LL *imāginal(is)* = *imāgin-* (s. of *imāgō*) IMAGE + *-ālis* -AL[1]]

im·ag·i·nar·y (i maj′ə ner′ē), *adj., n., pl.* **-ries.** —*adj.* **1.** existing only in the imagination; not real. —*n.* **2.** *Math.* See **imaginary number.** [ME < L *imāginārī(us)*] —**Syn. 1.** fanciful, visionary, chimerical, illusory. —**Ant. 1.** real.

imag′inary num′ber, *Math.* **1.** the imaginary part of a complex number, as *bi* in the expression $a + bi$ where *a* and *b* are real numbers and i^2 is defined as −1. **2.** Also called **pure imaginary number.** a complex number having its real part equal to zero. Also called **imaginary.**

im·ag·i·na·tion (i maj′ə nā′shən), *n.* **1.** the act of imagining. **2.** the faculty of imagining. **3.** *Psychol.* the power of reproducing images stored in the memory under the suggestion of associated images or of recombining former experiences to create new images. **4.** the faculty of producing ideal creations consistent with reality, as in literature, as distinct from the power of creating illustrative or decorative imagery. **5.** a mental conception or creation, often a baseless or fanciful one. **6.** ability to meet and resolve difficulties; resourcefulness. [ME < L *imāginātiōn-* (s. of *imāginātiō*) fancy = *imāgināt(us)* imagined (ptp. of *imāginārī* to IMAGINE; see -ATE[1]) + *-iōn-* -ION] —**Syn. 4.** See **fancy.**

im·ag·i·na·tive (i maj′ə nə tiv, -nā′tiv), *adj.* **1.** characterized by or bearing evidence of imagination. **2.** of, pertaining to, or concerned with imagination. **3.** given to imagining. **4.** having exceptional powers of imagination. **5.** lacking truth; fanciful. [ME < ML *imāginātīvus;* r. ME *imaginatif* < MF] —**im·ag′i·na·tive·ly,** *adv.* —**im·ag′i·na·tive·ness,** *n.*

im·ag·ine (i maj′in), *v.,* **-ined, -in·ing.** —*v.t.* **1.** to form a mental image of (something not actually present to the senses). **2.** to believe, suppose, or conjecture. **3.** *Archaic.* to plan, scheme, or plot. —*v.i.* **4.** to form mental images of things not present to the senses; use the imagination. **5.** to suppose, conjecture, or assume. [ME *imagine(n)* < *imāgin(ārī)* = *imāgin-* (s. of *imāgō*) IMAGE + *-ārī* inf. suffix] —**im·ag′in·er,** *n.*

—**Syn. 1.** image, picture. IMAGINE, CONCEIVE, CONCEIVE OF refer to bringing something before the mind. To IMAGINE is, literally, to form a mental image of something: *to imagine yourself in London.* To CONCEIVE is to relate ideas or feelings to one another in a pattern: *How has the author conceived the first act of his play?* To CONCEIVE OF is to comprehend through the intellect something not perceived through the senses: *Wilson conceived of a world free from war.*

im·ag·ism (im′ə jiz′əm), *n.* *Literature.* a style of poetry that employs free verse, precise imagery, and the patterns and rhythms of common speech, esp. as developed by a group of English and American poets between 1900 and 1917. —**im′ag·ist,** *n., adj.* —**im′ag·is′tic,** *adj.* —**im′ag·is′ti·cal·ly,** *adv.*

i·ma·go (i mā′gō), *n., pl.* **im·a·goes, i·ma·gi·nes** (i maj′ə nēz′). **1.** *Entomol.* an adult insect. **2.** *Psychoanal.* an idealized concept of a loved one, formed in childhood and retained unchanged in adult life. [< NL, L; see IMAGE]

i·mam (i mäm′), *n.* *Islam.* **1.** the officiating priest of a mosque. **2.** the title for a Muslim religious leader or chief. **3.** one of a succession of seven or twelve religious leaders, believed to be divinely inspired, of the Shiites. **4.** (formerly) any of the hereditary rulers of Yemen. Also, **i·maum** (i mäm′, i môm′). [< Ar *imām* leader, guide]

i·mam·ate (i mä′māt), *n.* **1.** the office of an imam. **2.** the region or territory governed by an imam.

I·mam·ite (i mä′mīt), *n.* *Islam.* a member of the principal sect of Shiah, believing in a succession of 12 divinely inspired imams, beginning with Ali and ending with Muhammad al-Muntazar.

i·ma·ret (i mä′ret), *n.* (in Turkey) a hospice for pilgrims, travelers, etc. [< Turk < Ar *'imārah* building]

im·bal·ance (im bal′əns), *n.* **1.** the state or condition of lacking balance. **2.** faulty muscular or glandular coordination.

im·balm (im bäm′), *v.t.* *Obs.* embalm. —**im·balm′er,** *n.*

im·bark (im bärk′), *v.t., v.i.* *Obs.* embark. —**im′bar·ka′tion, im·bark′ment,** *n.*

im·be·cile (im′bi sil, -səl *or, esp. Brit.,* -sēl′), *n.* **1.** a person of defective mentality, above the level of idiocy; one lacking the capacity to develop beyond a mental age of seven or eight years. —*adj.* **2.** mentally feeble. **3.** silly; absurd. [earlier *imbecill* < L *imbēcill(us)* weak; *-ile* r. *-ill* by confusion with suffix -ILE] —**im·be·cil·ic** (im′bi sil′ik), *adj.*

im·be·cil·i·ty (im′bi sil′i tē), *n., pl.* **-ties. 1.** feebleness of mind; mentality somewhat above that of idiocy. **2.** silliness; absurdity. **3.** an instance of this. [earlier *imbecillity* < L *imbēcillitās*]

im·bed (im bed′), *v.t.,* **-bed·ded, -bed·ding.** embed.

im·bibe (im bīb′), *v.,* **-bibed, -bib·ing.** —*v.t.* **1.** to consume (liquids) by drinking; drink. **2.** to absorb or soak up. **3.** to take or receive into the mind. —*v.i.* **4.** to drink; absorb liquid or moisture. **5.** *Obs.* to soak or saturate; imbue. [< L *imbibe(re)* (to) drink in = *im-* IM-[1] + *bibere* to drink; r. ME *enbiben* < MF *embib(er)* < L, as above] —**im·bib′er,** *n.* —**im·bi·bi·tion** (im′bi bish′ən), *n.*

im·bit·ter (im bit′ər), *v.t.* embitter. —**im·bit′ter·er,** *n.* —**im·bit′ter·ment,** *n.*

im·bod·y (im bod′ē), *v.t.,* **-bod·ied, -bod·y·ing.** embody. —**im·bod′i·ment,** *n.*

im·bold·en (im bōl′dᵊn), *v.t.* embolden.

im·bos·om (im bo͝oz′əm, -bo͞o′zəm), *v.t.* embosom.

im·bow·er (im bou′ər), *v.t., v.i.* embower.

Imbricate
A, Flower bud
B, Scale of cone

im·bri·cate (*adj.* im′brə kit, -kāt′; *v.* im′brə kāt′), *adj., v.,* **-cat·ed, -cat·ing.** —*adj.* **1.** overlapping in sequence, as tiles or shingles on a roof. **2.** of, pertaining to, or resembling overlapping tiles, as decoration, drawings, etc. **3.** *Biol.* overlapping like tiles, as scales, leaves, etc. **4.** characterized by or as by overlapping shingles. —*v.t., v.i.* **5.** to overlap, as tiles or shingles. [< LL *imbricāt(us)* tiled, shaped like a convex gutter tile (ptp. of *imbricāre*) = *imbric-* (s. of *imbrex* gutter tile) + *-ātus* -ATE[1]] —**im′bri·cate·ly,** *adv.*

im·bri·ca·tion (im′brə kā′shən), *n.* **1.** an overlapping, as of tiles or shingles. **2.** a decoration or pattern resembling this.

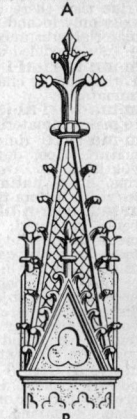

A, Imbrication of roof tiles; B, Ornamental imbrication on pinnacle

Im·bri·um (im′brē əm), *n.* **Mare.** See **Mare Imbrium.**

im·bro·glio (im brōl′yō), *n., pl.* **-glios. 1.** a confused state of affairs; a complicated or difficult situation. **2.** a misunderstanding, disagreement, etc., of a complicated or bitter nature. **3.** a confused heap. [< It < *imbrogli(are)* (to) EMBROIL]

im·brue (im bro͞o′), *v.t.,* **-brued, -bru·ing. 1.** to drench in or with something that stains, esp. blood; stain with blood. **2.** to impregnate or imbue. Also, **embrue.** [ME *enbrewe(n)* < MF *embreuv(er)* (to) cause to drink in, soak, drench < VL **imbiberāre;* see IMBIBE]

im·brute (im bro͞ot′), *v.t., v.i.,* **-brut·ed, -brut·ing.** to degrade or sink to the level of a brute. Also, **embrute.**

im·bue (im byo͞o′), *v.t.,* **-bued, -bu·ing. 1.** to impregnate or inspire, as with feelings, opinions, etc. **2.** to saturate or impregnate with moisture, color, etc. **3.** to imbrue. [< L *imbue(re)* (to) wet, steep, soak] —**im·bue′ment,** *n.* —**Syn. 1.** charge, infect, fire. **2.** permeate, infuse, tincture, soak.

IMF, International Monetary Fund. Also, **I.M.F.**

im·id·az·ole (im′id az′ōl, -id ə zōl′), *n.* *Chem.* a heterocyclic compound, $C_3H_4N_2$, used chiefly in organic synthesis. Also called **glyoxaline.**

im·ide (im′īd, im′id), *n.* *Chem.* a compound derived from ammonia by replacement of two hydrogen atoms by acidic groups, characterized by the =NH group. [alter. of AMIDE] —**im·id·ic** (i mid′ik), *adj.*

im′ido group′, *Chem.* **1.** the bivalent group, =NH, linked to one or two acid groups. **2.** (erroneously) imino. Also called **im′ido rad′ical.** [independent use of *imido-*, comb. form of IMIDE] —**im·i·do** (im′i dō′), *adj.*

i·mine (i mēn′, im′in), *n.* *Chem.* a compound containing the =NH group united with a nonacid group. [alter. of AMINE]

im′ino group′, *Chem.* the bivalent group, =NH, not linked to any acid group. Also called **im′ino rad′ical.** Cf. **imido group.** [independent use of *imino-*, comb. form of IMINE] —**i·mi·no** (im′ə nō′), *adj.*

imit., **1.** imitation. **2.** imitative.

im·i·ta·ble (im′i tə bəl), *adj.* capable of being imitated. [< L *imitābil(is).* See IMITATE, -BLE] —**im′i·ta·bil′i·ty, im′i·ta·ble·ness,** *n.*

im·i·tate (im′i tāt′), *v.t.,* **-tat·ed, -tat·ing. 1.** to follow or endeavor to follow in action or manner. **2.** to copy; mimic; counterfeit. **3.** to make a copy of; reproduce closely. **4.** to have or assume the appearance of; simulate. [< L *imitāt(us)* copied, ptp. of *imitārī;* akin to *imāgō* IMAGE] —**im′i·ta′tor,** *n.*

—**Syn. 2.** ape, mock, impersonate; simulate. **3.** IMITATE, COPY, DUPLICATE, REPRODUCE all mean to follow or try to follow an example or pattern. IMITATE is the general word for the idea: *to imitate someone's handwriting, behavior.* To COPY is to make a fairly exact imitation of an original creation: *to copy a sentence, a dress, a picture.* To DUPLICATE is to produce something that exactly resembles or corresponds to something else; both may be originals: *to duplicate the terms of two contracts.* To REPRODUCE is to make a likeness or reconstruction of an original: *to reproduce a 16th-century theater.*

im·i·ta·tion (im′i tā′shən), *n.* **1.** a result or product of imitating. **2.** the act of imitating. **3.** *Biol.* close external resemblance of an organism to some other organism or to objects in its environment. **4.** *Psychol.* the performance of an act whose stimulus is the observation of the act performed by another person. **5.** a counterfeit; copy. **6.** a literary composition that imitates the manner or subject of another author or work. **7.** *Art.* **a.** (in Aristotelian aesthetics) the representation of an object or an action as it ought to be. **b.** the representation of actuality in art or literature. **8.** *Music.* the repetition of a melodic phrase at a different pitch or key from the original or in a different voice part. —*adj.* **9.** designed to imitate a genuine or superior article or thing. [< L *imitātiōn-* (s. of *imitātiō*)] —**im′i·ta′tion·al,** *adj.*

im·i·ta·tive (im′i tā′tiv), *adj.* **1.** imitating; copying; given to imitation. **2.** of, pertaining to, or characterized by imitation. **3.** *Biol.* mimetic. **4.** made in imitation of something; counterfeit. **5.** onomatopoeic. [< LL *imitātīv(us)*] —**im′i·ta′tive·ly,** *adv.* —**im′i·ta′tive·ness,** *n.*

im·mac·u·late (i mak′yə lit), *adj.* **1.** free from spot or stain; spotlessly clean: *an immaculate tablecloth.* **2.** free from moral blemish or impurity; pure; undefiled. **3.** free from fault or flaw; free from errors, as a text. **4.** *Biol.* having no spots or colored marks; unicolor. [ME *immaculat* < L *immaculāt(us)* unspotted] —**im·mac′u·la·cy, im·mac′u·late·ness,** *n.* —**im·mac′u·late·ly,** *adv.*

Immac′ulate Concep′tion, *Rom. Cath. Ch.* the dogma

that the Virgin Mary was conceived without the stain of original sin.

im·ma·nent (im′ə nənt), *adj.* **1.** remaining within; indwelling; inherent. **2.** *Philos.* (of a mental act) taking place within the mind of the subject and having no effect outside of it. Cf. **transeunt. 3.** *Theol.* (of the Deity) indwelling the universe, time, etc. Cf. **transcendent** (def. 3) • [< LL *immanent-* (s. of *immanēns*) staying in (prp. of *immanēre*) = *im-* IM-¹ + *man-* stay + *-ent-* -ENT; see REMAIN] —**im′ma·nence, im′ma·nen·cy,** *n.* —**im′ma·nent·ly,** *adv.*

Im·man·u·el (i man′yo͞o əl), *n.* the name of the Messiah as prophesied by Isaiah, often represented in Christian exegesis as being Jesus Christ. Isa. 7:14. Also, **Emmanuel.** [< Heb *'immānū'el* God with us]

im·ma·te·ri·al (im′ə tēr′ē əl), *adj.* **1.** of no essential consequence; unimportant. **2.** not material; incorporeal; spiritual. [ME < ML *immāteriāl(is)*] —**im′ma·te′ri·al·ly,** *adv.* —**im′ma·te′ri·al·ness,** *n.*

im·ma·te·ri·al·ise (im′ə tēr′ē ə līz′), *v.t.,* **-ised, -is·ing.** *Chiefly Brit.* immaterialize.

im·ma·te·ri·al·ism (im′ə tēr′ē ə liz′əm), *n.* **1.** the doctrine that there is no material world, but that all things exist only in and for minds. **2.** the doctrine that only immaterial substances or spiritual beings exist. [IMMATERIAL + -ISM, modeled on *materialism*] —**im′ma·te′ri·al·ist,** *n.*

im·ma·te·ri·al·i·ty (im′ə tēr′ē al′i tē), *n., pl.* **-ties** for 2. **1.** the state or character of being immaterial. **2.** something immaterial.

im·ma·te·ri·al·ize (im′ə tēr′ē ə līz′), *v.t.,* **-ized, -iz·ing.** to make immaterial. Also, *esp. Brit.,* **immaterialise.**

im·ma·ture (im′ə to͝or′, -tyo͝or′, -cho͝or′), *adj.* **1.** not mature, ripe, developed, perfected, etc. **2.** *Phys. Geog.* youthful. **3.** *Archaic.* premature. [< L *immātūr(us)* unripe, hence untimely] —**im′ma·ture′ly,** *adv.* —**im′ma·tu′ri·ty, im′ma·ture′ness,** *n.*

im·meas·ur·a·ble (i mezh′ər ə bəl), *adj.* incapable of being measured; limitless. [late ME *inmesurable*] —**im·meas′ur·a·bil′i·ty, im·meas′ur·a·ble·ness,** *n.* —**im·meas′ur·a·bly,** *adv.*

im·me·di·a·cy (i mē′dē ə sē), *n.* **1.** the state, condition, or quality of being immediate. **2.** *Philos.* **a.** immediate presence of an object of knowledge to the mind, without any distortions, inferences, or interpretations, and without involvement of any intermediate agencies. **b.** the direct content of the mind as distinguished from representation or cognition. [IMMEDIA(TE) + -CY]

im·me·di·ate (i mē′dē it), *adj.* **1.** occurring or accomplished without delay; instant. **2.** of or pertaining to the present time or moment. **3.** following without a lapse of time. **4.** having no object or space intervening; nearest or next. **5.** without intervening medium or agent; direct. **6.** having a direct bearing. **7.** *Philos.* directly intuited. [< ML *immediāt(us)*] —**im·me′di·ate·ness,** *n.* —**Syn. 1.** instantaneous. **4.** close.

imme′diate constit′uent, *Gram.* one of the usually two largest constituents of a construction: The immediate constituents of *He ate his dinner* are *he* and *ate his dinner;* of *ate his dinner* are *ate* and *his dinner.* Cf. **ultimate constituent.**

im·me·di·ate·ly (i mē′dē it lē), *adv.* **1.** without lapse of time; without delay; instantly; at once. **2.** without intervening medium or agent; concerning or affecting directly. **3.** with no object or space intervening. **4.** closely: *immediately in the vicinity.* —*conj.* **5.** *Chiefly Brit.* immediately that; the moment that; as soon as. [late ME]
—**Syn. 1.** instantaneously, forthwith. IMMEDIATELY, INSTANTLY, DIRECTLY, PRESENTLY were originally close synonyms denoting complete absence of delay or of any lapse of time. INSTANTLY is the only one retaining the meaning of action or occurrence on the instant: *He replied instantly to the accusation.* It is never used with the future tense (which must suggest a slight delay). IMMEDIATELY may have the same force: *He immediately got up;* more often, a slight delay: *The game will begin immediately.* DIRECTLY is equivalent to soon or in a little while: *You go ahead, we'll be there directly.* PRESENTLY, which once meant at once, changed to mean soon or in a little while: *You go ahead, I'll be there presently.* The expressions that have supplanted them are *right away* and *at once* (which is still usually equivalent to immediately): *He will come right away. I want to see him at once.* —**Ant. 1.** later.

im·med·i·ca·ble (i med′ə kə bəl), *adj.* incurable. [< L *immedicābil(is)* incurable] —**im·med′i·ca·ble·ness,** *n.* —**im·med′i·ca·bly,** *adv.*

Im′mel·mann turn′ (im′əl män′, -mən), a maneuver in which an airplane makes a half loop, then resumes its normal, level position by making a half roll: used to gain altitude while turning to fly in the opposite direction. Also called **Im′mel·mann′.** [named after Max *Immelmann* (1890–1916), German aviator in World War I]

im·me·mo·ri·al (im′ə mōr′ē əl, -môr′-), *adj.* extending back beyond memory, record, or knowledge: *from time immemorial.* [< ML *immemoriāl(is)*] —**im′me·mo′ri·al·ly,** *adv.*

im·mense (i mens′), *adj.* **1.** vast; very great; extensive. **2.** immeasurable; boundless. **3.** *Informal.* very good; fine; splendid. [late ME < L *immens(us)* = *im-* IM-² + *mensus* measured (ptp. of *mētīrī*)] —**im·mense′ly,** *adv.* —**im·mense′ness,** *n.* —**Syn. 1.** See **huge.**

im·men·si·ty (i men′si tē), *n., pl.* **-ties** for 3. **1.** vastness; hugeness; enormous extent. **2.** the state or condition of being immense; boundless extent; infinity. **3.** a vast expanse; an immense quantity. [late ME < L *immensitās*]

im·men·su·ra·ble (i men′sho͝o rə bəl, -sər ə-), *adj.* immeasurable. [< LL *immensurābil(is)*] —**im·men′su·ra·bil′i·ty, im·men′su·ra·ble·ness,** *n.*

im·merge (i mûrj′), *v.,* **-merged, -merg·ing.** —*v.i.* **1.** to plunge, as into a fluid. —*v.t.* **2.** *Rare.* to immerse. [< L *immerge(re)* (to) dip, plunge, sink] —**im·mer′gence,** *n.*

im·merse (i mûrs′), *v.t.,* **-mersed, -mers·ing. 1.** to plunge into or place under a liquid; dip; sink. **2.** to baptize by immersion. **3.** to embed; bury. **4.** to involve deeply; absorb. [< L *immers(us)* dipped, plunged into, ptp. of *immergere* to IMMERGE] —**im·mers′i·ble,** *adj.* —**Syn. 1.** immerge, duck, douse. See **dip. 4.** engage. —**Ant. 3.** disinter.

im·mersed (i mûrst′), *adj.* **1.** plunged or sunk in or as in a liquid. **2.** *Biol.* somewhat or wholly sunk in the surrounding parts, as an organ. **3.** *Bot.* growing under water. **4.** *Rare.* baptized.

im·mer·sion (i mûr′zhən, -shən), *n.* **1.** the act of immersing. **2.** the state of being immersed. **3.** baptism in which the whole body of the person is submerged in the water. **4.** the state of being deeply engaged; absorption. **5.** Also called **ingress.** *Astron.* the entrance of a heavenly body into an eclipse by another body, an occultation, or a transit. Cf. **emersion** (def. 1). [late ME < LL *immersiōn-* (s. of *immersiō*) a dipping in]

im·mer·sion·ism (i mûr′zhə niz′əm, -shə-), *n.* **1.** the doctrine that immersion is essential to Christian baptism. **2.** baptism by immersion. —**im·mer′sion·ist,** *n.*

im·mesh (i mesh′), *v.t.* enmesh.

im·me·thod·i·cal (im′ə thod′i kəl), *adj.* not methodical; without method. —**im′me·thod′i·cal·ly,** *adv.*

im·mi·grant (im′ə grənt), *n.* **1.** a person who migrates to a country for permanent residence. **2.** a plant or animal found living in a new habitat. —*adj.* **3.** of or pertaining to immigrants and immigration. **4.** immigrating. [< L *immigrant-* (s. of *immigrāns*) moving into, prp. of *immigrāre*]

im·mi·grate (im′ə grāt′), *v.,* **-grat·ed, -grat·ing.** —*v.i.* **1.** to come to a country of which one is not a native, for the purpose of permanent residence. **2.** to pass or come into a new place or habitat, as plants, animals, etc. —*v.t.* **3.** to introduce as settlers. [< L *immigrāt(us)* removed, gone into (ptp. of *immigrāre*)] —**im′mi·gra′tor,** *n.* —**Syn. 1.** See **migrate.**

im·mi·gra·tion (im′ə grā′shən), *n.* **1.** the act of immigrating. **2.** a group or number of immigrants. —**im′mi·gra′tion·al, im·mi·gra·to·ry** (im′ə grə tōr′ē, -tôr′ē), *adj.*

im·mi·nence (im′ə nəns), *n.* **1.** Also, **im′mi·nen·cy.** the state or condition of being imminent or impending. **2.** something that is imminent, esp. impending evil or danger. [< LL *imminentia*]

im·mi·nent (im′ə nənt), *adj.* **1.** likely to occur at any moment; impending. **2.** threateningly or menacingly near or at hand. **3.** *Rare.* projecting or leaning forward; overhanging. [< L *imminent-* (s. of *imminēns*) overhanging (prp. of *imminēre*) = *im-* IM-¹ + *min-* overhang + *-ent-* -ENT] —**im′mi·nent·ly,** *adv.* —**im′mi·nent·ness,** *n.*
—**Syn. 1, 2.** IMMINENT, IMPENDING, THREATENING apply to something that is likely to occur, usually something that menaces or portends misfortune or disaster. IMMINENT is applied usually to danger or evil that hangs, as it were, over one's head, ready to fall at any moment: *Because of recent heavy rains, a flood is imminent.* IMPENDING is similarly used but with less suggestion of immediateness: *A reform has been impending for some time.* THREATENING is applied loosely to something that indicates coming evil, or conveys some ominous or unfavorable suggestion: *threatening weather; a threatening frown.* —**Ant. 1, 2.** distant, remote.

im·min·gle (i ming′gəl), *v.t., v.i.,* **-gled, -gling.** to mingle in; intermingle.

im·mis·ci·ble (i mis′ə bəl), *adj.* not miscible; incapable of being mixed. —**im·mis′ci·bil′i·ty,** *n.* —**im·mis′ci·bly,** *adv.*

im·mit·i·ga·ble (i mit′ə gə bəl), *adj.* not mitigable; not to be mitigated. [< LL *immītigābil(is)* that cannot be softened] —**im·mit′i·ga·bly,** *adv.*

im·mix (i miks′), *v.t.* to mix in; mingle. [back formation from ME *immixt(e)* mixed in < L *immixt(us)* blended (ptp. of *immiscēre*)]

im·mix·ture (i miks′chər), *n.* **1.** the act of immixing. **2.** the state of being immixed; involvement. [< L *immixt(us)* blended (see IMMIX) + -URE; see MIXTURE]

im·mo·bile (i mō′bil, -bēl), *adj.* **1.** not mobile; immovable. **2.** incapable of moving or being moved; motionless. [ME *inmobile* < L *immōbil(is)*]

im·mo·bi·lise (i mō′bə līz′), *v.t.,* **-lised, -lis·ing.** *Chiefly Brit.* immobilize. —**im·mo′bi·li·sa′tion,** *n.*

im·mo·bil·i·ty (im′ō bil′i tē), *n.* the quality or condition of being immobile or irremovable. [late ME < LL *immōbilitās*]

im·mo·bi·lize (i mō′bə līz′), *v.t.,* **-lized, -liz·ing. 1.** to make immobile; fix so as to be or become immovable. **2.** *Finance.* **a.** to establish a monetary reserve by withdrawing (specie) from circulation. **b.** to create fixed capital in place of (circulating capital). **3.** to deprive of the capacity for mobilization. Also, *esp. Brit.,* **immobilise.** [IMMOBILE + -IZE; see MOBILIZE and cf. F *immobiliser*] —**im·mo′bi·li·za′tion,** *n.*

im·mod·er·ate (i mod′ər it), *adj.* **1.** not moderate; exceeding just or reasonable limits; excessive; extreme. **2.** *Obs.* intemperate. **3.** *Obs.* without bounds. [< L *immoderāt(us)*] —**im·mod′er·ate·ly,** *adv.* —**im·mod′er·ate·ness,** *n.* —**Syn. 1.** exorbitant, unreasonable; extravagant. —**Ant. 1.** reasonable.

im·mod·er·a·tion (i mod′ə rā′shən), *n.* a lack of moderation. Also, **im·mod·er·a·cy** (i mod′ər ə sē). [< L *immoderātiōn-* (s. of *immoderātiō*). See IM-², MODERATION]

im·mod·est (i mod′ist), *adj.* **1.** not modest in conduct, utterance, etc.; indecent; shameless. **2.** not modest in assertion or pretension; forward; impudent. [< L *immodest(us)* unrestrained, immoderate] —**im·mod′est·ly,** *adv.* —**im·mod′es·ty,** *n.*

im·mo·late (im′ə lāt′), *v.t.,* **-lat·ed, -lat·ing. 1.** to sacrifice. **2.** to kill as a sacrificial victim, as by fire; offer in sacrifice. [< L *immolāt(us)* sprinkled with holy grits, sacrificed (ptp. of *immolāre*) = *im-* IM-¹ + *mol(a)* grits (orig. millstone; see MILL¹) + *-ātus* -ATE¹] —**im′mo·la′tor,** *n.*

im·mo·la·tion (im′ə lā′shən), *n.* **1.** the act of immolating. **2.** the state of being immolated. **3.** a sacrifice. [< L *immolātiōn-* (s. of *immolātiō*) a sprinkling with holy grits in the sacrificial ceremony, hence, a sacrifice. See IMMOLATE, -ION]

im·mor·al (i môr′əl, i mor′-), *adj.* not moral; not conforming to the patterns of conduct usually accepted or established as consistent with principles of personal and social ethics. —**im·mor′al·ly,** *adv.*
—**Syn.** wicked, licentious, profligate. IMMORAL, ABANDONED, DEPRAVED describe a person who makes no attempt to curb self-indulgence. IMMORAL, referring to conduct, applies to a person who acts contrary to or does not obey or conform to standards of morality; it may also mean licentious and dissipated. ABANDONED, referring to condition, applies to one hopelessly sunk in wickedness and unrestrained appe-

tites. DEPRAVED, referring to character, applies to a person who voluntarily seeks evil and viciousness. IMMORAL, AMORAL NONMORAL, and UNMORAL are sometimes confused with one another. IMMORAL means not moral and connotes evil or licentious behavior. AMORAL, NONMORAL and UNMORAL, virtually synonymous, although the first is by far the most common form, mean utterly lacking in morals (either good or bad), neither moral nor immoral.

im·mor·al·ise (i môr′ə līz′, i mor′-), *v.t.*, **-ised, -is·ing.** *Chiefly Brit.* immoralize.

im·mor·al·ist (i môr′ə list, i mor′-), *n.* a person who advocates or practices immorality.

im·mo·ral·i·ty (im′ə ral′i tē, im′ô-), *n., pl.* **-ties. 1.** immoral quality, character, or conduct; wickedness; evilness. **2.** sexual misconduct; unchastity or lewdness. **3.** an immoral act.

im·mor·al·ize (i môr′ə līz′, i mor′-), *v.t.*, **-ized, -iz·ing.** to make or cause to be immoral. Also, *esp. Brit.*, **immoralise.**

im·mor·tal (i môr′t[ə]l), *adj.* **1.** not mortal; not liable or subject to death. **2.** remembered or celebrated through all time. **3.** not liable to perish or decay; imperishable; everlasting. **4.** perpetual; lasting; constant. **5.** of or pertaining to immortal beings or immortality. —*n.* **6.** an immortal being. **7.** a person, esp. an author, of enduring fame. **8. the Immortals,** the 40 members of the French Academy. **9.** (*often cap.*) any of the gods of classical mythology. [ME < L *immortāl(is)*] —**im·mor′tal·ly,** *adv.*

im·mor·tal·ise (i môr′t[ə]līz′), *v.t.*, **-ised, -is·ing.** *Chiefly Brit.* immortalize. —**im·mor′tal·i·sa′tion,** *n.* —**im·mor′tal·is′er,** *n.*

im·mor·tal·i·ty (im′ôr tal′i tē), *n.* **1.** immortal condition or quality; unending life. **2.** enduring fame. [ME *immortalite* < L *immortālitās*]

im·mor·tal·ize (i môr′t[ə]līz′), *v.t.*, **-ized, -iz·ing. 1.** to make immortal; endow with immortality. **2.** to bestow unending fame upon; perpetuate. Also, *esp. Brit.*, **immortalise.** —**im·mor′tal·i·za′tion,** *n.* —**im·mor′tal·iz′er,** *n.*

im·mor·telle (im′ôr tel′), *n.* an everlasting plant or flower, esp. *Xeranthemum annuum.* [< F, n. use of fem. of *immortel* IMMORTAL]

im·mo·tile (i mōt′[ə]l), *adj.* not able to move; not motile.

im·mov·a·ble (i mōō′və bəl), *adj.* **1.** incapable of being moved; fixed; stationary. **2.** not moving; motionless. **3.** not subject to change; unalterable. **4.** incapable of being affected with feeling; emotionless. **5.** incapable of being moved from one's purpose, opinion, etc.; steadfast; unyielding. **6.** not changing from one date to another in different years: *an immovable holiday.* **7.** *Law.* (of property) real, as distinguished from personal. —*n.* **8.** something immovable. **9. immovables,** *Law.* immovable property. Also, **im·move′a·ble.** [ME] —**im·mov′a·bil′i·ty, im·mov′a·ble·ness,** *n.* —**im·mov′a·bly,** *adv.*

im·mune (i myōōn′), *adj.* **1.** protected from a disease or the like, as by inoculation. **2.** exempt. —*n.* **3.** a person who is immune. [ME < L *immūn(is)* exempt = *im-* IM-[2] + *mūn(us)* office, duty, tax + *-is* adj. suffix]

immune′ se′rum, *Med.* a serum containing naturally or artificially produced antibodies, obtained from human or animal sources.

im·mu·nise (im′yə nīz′, i myōō′nīz), *v.t.*, **-nised, -nis·ing.** *Chiefly Brit.* immunize. —**im′mu·ni·sa′tion,** *n.* —**im′mu·nis′er,** *n.*

im·mu·ni·ty (i myōō′ni tē), *n., pl.* **-ties. 1.** the state of being immune from or insusceptible to a particular disease or the like. **2.** exemption from any natural or usual liability. **3.** exemption from obligation, service, duty, or liability to taxation, jurisdiction, etc. [ME *immunite* < L *immūnitās*] —**Syn. 2.** See **exemption. 3.** license, liberty, prerogative. —**Ant. 1.** susceptibility. **2.** proneness. **3.** liability.

im·mu·nize (im′yə nīz′, i myōō′nīz), *v.t.*, **-nized, -niz·ing.** to make immune. Also, *esp. Brit.*, **immunise.** —**im′mu·ni·za′tion,** *n.* —**im′mu·niz′er,** *n.*

immuno-, a combining form of **immune** or **immunity:** *immunology.*

im·mu·no·ge·net·ics (im′yə nō jə net′iks, i myōō′nō-), *n.* (*construed as sing.*) **1.** the branch of immunology dealing with the study of immunity in relation to genetic makeup. **2.** the study of genetic relationships among animals by comparison of immunological reactions. —**im′mu·no·ge·net′ic, im′mu·no·ge·net′i·cal,** *adj.*

im·mu·no·gen·ic (im′yə nō jen′ik, i myōō′nə-), *adj.* producing immunity. —**im′mu·no·gen′i·cal·ly,** *adv.*

immunol., immunology.

im·mu·nol·o·gy (im′yə nol′ə jē), *n.* the branch of medicine dealing with immunity from disease and the production of such immunity. —**im·mu·no·log·ic** (i myōō′n[ə]loj′ik), **im·mu′no·log′i·cal,** *adj.* —**im·mu′no·log′i·cal·ly,** *adv.* —**im′mu·nol′o·gist,** *n.*

im·mure (i myŏŏr′), *v.t.*, **-mured, -mur·ing. 1.** to enclose within walls. **2.** to shut in; confine; imprison. **3.** to build into or entomb in a wall. [< ML *immūr(āre)* = L *im-* IM-[1] + *mūr(us)* wall + *-āre* inf. suffix] —**im·mure′ment,** *n.*

im·mu·ta·ble (i myōō′tə bəl), *adj.* not mutable; unchangeable; unalterable; changeless. [ME < L *immūtābil(is)*] —**im·mu′ta·bil′i·ty, im·mu′ta·ble·ness,** *n.* —**im·mu′ta·bly,** *adv.*

imp (imp), *n.* **1.** a little devil or demon; an evil spirit. **2.** a mischievous child. **3.** *Archaic.* a scion or offshoot of a plant or tree. **4.** *Archaic.* an offspring. [ME *impe,* OE *impa* or *impe* a shoot, graft > *impian* to graft; c. G *Impfen*]

Imp., 1. Emperor. [< L *Imperātor*] **2.** Empress. [< L *Imperātrix*]

imp., 1. imperative. **2.** imperfect. **3.** imperial. **4.** impersonal. **5.** implement. **6.** import. **7.** important. **8.** imported. **9.** importer. **10.** imprimatur. **11.** in the first place. [< L *imprīmīs*] **12.** imprint. **13.** improper. **14.** improved. **15.** improvement.

im·pact (*n.* im′pakt; *v.* im pakt′), *n.* **1.** the striking of one body against another. **2.** the force of such a striking. **3.** an impinging: *the impact of light on the eye.* **4.** influence; effect: *the impact of Hegel on modern philosophy.* —*v.t.* **5.** to drive or press closely or firmly into something; pack in. **6.** to fill up; congest; throng. **7.** to collide with; strike forcefully. —*v.i.* **8.** to have impact or make contact forcefully. [back formation from IMPACTED]

im·pact·ed (im pak′tid), *adj.* **1.** wedged in. **2.** *Dentistry.* noting a tooth so confined in its socket as to be incapable of normal eruption. **3.** driven together; tightly packed. **4.** densely crowded; overcrowded. [obs. *impact* adj. (< L *impact(us)* driven in, pinned to (ptp. of *impingere*) = *im-* IM-[1] + *pag-,* ptp. s. of *pangere* to drive in + *-tus* ptp. suffix) + -ED[2]]

im·pac·tion (im pak′shən), *n.* **1.** the act of impacting. **2.** the state of being impacted; close fixation. **3.** *Dentistry.* the condition in which a tooth is impacted. [< LL *impactiōn-* (s. of *impactiō*)]

im·pair (im pâr′), *v.t.* **1.** to make or cause to become worse; diminish in value, excellence, etc.; weaken or damage. —*v.i.* **2.** *Obs.* to grow or become worse, lessen. —*n.* **3.** *Archaic.* impairment. [ME *empair(en), empeir(en)* (to) make worse < MF *empeir(er)* = *em-* -IM[1] + *peirer* < LL *pējōrāre* = L *pējor* worse + *-āre* inf. suffix] —**im·pair′a·ble,** *adj.* —**im·pair′er,** *n.* —**im·pair′ment,** *n.*

im·pal·a (im pal′ə, -pä′lə), *n., pl.* **-pal·as,** (*esp. collectively*) **-pal·a.** an African antelope, *Aepyceros melampus,* the male of which has ringed, lyre-shaped horns: noted for its leaping ability. [< Zulu]

Impala (2½ ft. high at shoulder; horns 2 ft.; total length 5½ ft.; tail 1 ft.)

im·pale (im pāl′), *v.t.*, **-paled, -pal·ing. 1.** to fix upon a sharpened stake or the like. **2.** to pierce with a sharpened stake thrust up through the body, as for torture or punishment. **3.** to make helpless as if pierced through with a stake. Also, **empale.** [< ML *impāl(āre).* See IM-[1], PALE[2]] —**im·pal′er,** *n.* —**im·pale′ment,** *n.*

im·pal·pa·ble (im pal′pə bəl), *adj.* **1.** not palpable; intangible. **2.** incapable of being readily grasped by the mind. **3.** (of powder) so fine that when rubbed between the fingers no grit is felt. —**im·pal′pa·bil′i·ty,** *n.* —**im·pal′pa·bly,** *adv.*

im·pa·na·tion (im′pə nā′shən), *n.* *Theol.* the doctrine that the body and blood of Christ are in the bread and wine after consecration. [< ML *impanātiōn-* (s. of *impanātiō*) = *impanāt(us)* embodied in bread (L *im-* IM-[1] + *pan(is)* bread + *-ātus* -ATE[1]) + *-iōn-* -ION]

im·pan·el (im pan′[ə]l), *v.t.*, **-eled, -el·ing** or (*esp. Brit.*) **-elled, -el·ling. 1.** to enter on a panel or list for jury duty. **2.** to select (a jury) from the panel. Also, **empanel.** [late ME *empanel* < AF *empanell(er)*] —**im·pan′el·ment,** *n.*

im·par·a·dise (im par′ə dīs′), *v.t.*, **-dised, -dis·ing.** to put in or as in paradise; make supremely happy.

im·par·i·ty (im par′i tē), *n., pl.* **-ties.** lack of parity or equality; disparity, difference, or inequality. [< LL *imparitās*]

im·park (im pärk′), *v.t.* **1.** to shut up, as in a park. **2.** to enclose as a park. [ME *imparke(n)* < AF *empark(er)*] —**im′par·ka′tion,** *n.*

im·part (im pärt′), *v.t.* **1.** to make known; tell; relate. **2.** to give; bestow; transmit. **3.** to grant a part or share of. [late ME < L *impart(īre)* (to) share] —**im·part′a·ble,** *adj.* —**im′par·ta′tion, im·part′ment,** *n.* —**im·part′er,** *n.* —**Syn. 1.** disclose, reveal, divulge. **2.** grant, cede, confer. —**Ant. 1.** conceal.

im·par·tial (im pär′shəl), *adj.* not partial or biased. —**im·par·ti·al·i·ty** (im pär′shē al′i tē), **im·par′tial·ness,** *n.* —**im·par′tial·ly,** *adv.* —**Syn.** unbiased, unprejudiced. See **fair**[1].

im·part·i·ble (im pär′tə bəl), *adj.* not partible; indivisible. [ME < LL *impartībil(is)* indivisible] —**im·part′i·bil′i·ty,** *n.* —**im·part′i·bly,** *adv.*

im·pass·a·ble (im pas′ə bəl, -pä′sə-), *adj.* **1.** not passable; not allowing passage over, through, along, etc. **2.** unable to be surmounted. **3.** (of currency) unable to be circulated. —**im·pass′a·bil′i·ty, im·pass′a·ble·ness,** *n.* —**im·pass′a·bly,** *adv.*

im·passe (im′pas, im pas′), *n., pl.* **-pass·es** (-pas iz, -pas′iz). **1.** a position from which there is no escape; deadlock. **2.** a road or way that has no outlet. [< F]

im·pas·si·ble (im pas′ə bəl), *adj.* **1.** incapable of suffering pain. **2.** incapable of suffering harm. **3.** incapable of emotion; impassive. [ME < LL *impassībil(is).* See IM-[2], PASSIBLE] —**im·pas′si·bil′i·ty, im·pas′si·ble·ness,** *n.* —**im·pas′si·bly,** *adv.*

im·pas·sion (im pash′ən), *v.t.* to fill, or affect strongly, with passion; inflame; excite. [< It *impassion(are)*]

im·pas·sion·ate[1] (im pash′ə nit), *adj.* filled with passion; impassioned. [IMPASSION + -ATE[1]] —**im·pas′sion·ate·ly,** *adv.*

im·pas·sion·ate[2] (im pash′ə nit), *adj.* *Archaic.* free from passion; dispassionate. [IM-[2] + PASSIONATE] —**im·pas′sion·ate·ly,** *adv.*

im·pas·sioned (im pash′ənd), *adj.* filled with passion; passionate; ardent. —**im·pas′sioned·ly,** *adv.* —**Syn.** emotional, vehement, fervent, fiery. —**Ant.** apathetic.

im·pas·sive (im pas′iv), *adj.* **1.** without emotion; apathetic; unmoved. **2.** calm; serene. **3.** unconscious; insensible. **4.** not subject to suffering. —**im·pas′sive·ly,** *adv.* —**im·pas′sive·ness, im·pas·siv·i·ty** (im′pa siv′i tē), *n.* —**Syn. 1.** emotionless, indifferent, unperturbed. **2.** tranquil, unruffled, composed. **4.** unaffected; unflinching.

im·paste (im pāst′), *v.t.*, **-past·ed, -past·ing. 1.** to cover with or enclose in a paste. **2.** to form into a paste. **3.** to lay on thickly, as paste. [< It *impast(are).* See IM-[1], PASTE] —**im·pas·ta·tion** (im′pa stā′shən), *n.*

im·pas·to (im pä′stō, -pas′tō), *n.* *Painting.* **1.** the laying on of paint thickly. **2.** the paint so laid on. [< It; see IMPASTE]

im·pa·tience (im pā′shəns), *n.* **1.** lack of patience. **2.** eager desire for relief or change; restlessness. **3.** intolerance of anything that thwarts or hinders. [ME *impacience* < L *impatientia*]

im·pa·ti·ens (im pā′shē enz′), *n., pl.* **-ti·ens.** any annual, balsaminaceous plant of the genus *Impatiens*, having irregular flowers in which the calyx and corolla are not clearly distinguishable. [< NL, L: IMPATIENT]

im·pa·tient (im pā′shənt), *adj.* **1.** not patient. **2.** indicating lack of patience. **3.** restless in desire or expectation. [ME *impacient* < L *impatient-* (s. of *impatiēns*) not putting up with] —**im·pa′tient·ly,** *adv.* —**Syn. 1.** uneasy, unquiet. **1, 2.** irritable, testy; curt, brusque, abrupt. **3.** hasty, impetuous. —**Ant. 1.** calm.

im·pav·id (im pav′id), *adj. Rare.* fearless. [< L *impavid(us)* fearless, undaunted] —**im·pav′id·ly,** *adv.*

im·pawn (im pôn′), *v.t. Rare.* to put in pawn; pledge.

im·peach (im pēch′), *v.t.* **1.** to accuse (a public official) before an appropriate tribunal of misconduct in office. **2.** to challenge the credibility of. **3.** to bring an accusation against. **4.** to call in question; cast an imputation upon. [ME *empeche(n)* < AF *empech(er)* < LL *impedicāre* to fetter, trap = L *im-* IM-[1] + *pedic(a)* a fetter (see PEDI-[1], -IC) + *-āre* inf. suffix] —**im·peach′er,** *n.*

im·peach·a·ble (im pē′chə bəl), *adj.* **1.** liable to be impeached. **2.** making one subject to impeachment. —**im·peach′a·bil′i·ty,** *n.*

im·peach·ment (im pēch′mənt), *n.* **1.** the impeaching of a public official before an appropriate tribunal. **2.** *U.S.* (in Congress or a state legislature) the presentation of formal charges against a public official by the lower house, trial to be before the upper house. **3.** demonstration that a witness is less worthy of belief. **4.** the act of impeaching. **5.** the state of being impeached. [ME *empechement* < AF]

im·pearl (im pûrl′), *v.t.* **1.** to form into drops resembling pearls. **2.** to make pearllike or pearly. **3.** *Chiefly Literary.* to adorn with pearls or pearllike drops. [IM-[1] + PEARL[1]; cf. F *emperler*]

im·pec·ca·ble (im pek′ə bəl), *adj.* **1.** faultless; irreproachable: *impeccable manners.* **2.** not liable to sin; exempt from the possibility of doing wrong. —*n.* **3.** *Rare.* an impeccable person. [< L *impeccābil(is)* faultless, sinless] —**im·pec′ca·bil′i·ty,** *n.* —**im·pec′ca·bly,** *adv.*

im·pec·cant (im pek′ənt), *adj.* not sinning; sinless. —**im·pec′cance, im·pec′can·cy,** *n.*

im·pe·cu·ni·ous (im′pə kyōō′nē əs), *adj.* having no money. [IM-[2] + *pecunious* wealthy (late ME) < L *pecūniōs(us)* = *pecūni(a)* wealth + *-ōsus* -OUS] —**im′pe·cu′ni·ous·ly,** *adv.* —**im′pe·cu′ni·ous·ness,** *n.* —**Syn.** destitute.

im·ped·ance (im pēd′ᵊns), *n.* **1.** *Elect.* the total opposition to alternating current by an electric circuit, equal to the square root of the sum of the squares of the resistance and reactance of the circuit and usually expressed in ohms. *Symbol:* Z **2.** *Physics.* the ratio of the force on a system undergoing simple harmonic motion to the velocity of the particles in the system.

im·pede (im pēd′), *v.t.,* **-ped·ed, -ped·ing.** to retard in movement or progress by means of obstacles or hindrances; obstruct; hinder. [< L *impedi-* (s. of *impedīre* to entangle, lit., to snare the feet)] —**im·ped′er,** *n.* —**Syn.** slow, delay, check, stop, block, thwart. See **prevent.** —**Ant.** advance, encourage; aid, help.

im·pe·di·ent (im pē′dē ənt), *adj.* **1.** impeding; hindering. —*n.* **2.** something that impedes; hindrance. [< L *impedient-* (s. of *impediēns*) entangling, prp. of *impedīre*]

im·ped·i·ment (im ped′ə mənt), *n.* **1.** an obstruction, hindrance, or obstacle. **2.** some physical defect that impedes ready speech; a speech disorder. **3.** *Chiefly Eccles. Law.* a bar, usually of blood or affinity, to marriage. [ME < L *impedīment(um)*] —**im·ped·i·men·tal** (im ped′ə men′təl), **im·ped′i·men′ta·ry,** *adj.* —**Syn. 1.** bar, encumbrance, check. See **obstacle.** —**Ant. 1.** help, encouragement.

im·ped·i·men·ta (im ped′ə men′tə), *n.pl.* baggage or other encumbrances that impede one's progress, esp. supplies carried with an army. [< L, pl. of *impedīmentum* IMPEDIMENT]

im·ped·i·tive (im ped′i tiv), *adj.* tending to impede; obstructive. [obs. *impedite* to hinder (< L *impedīt(us)*, ptp. of *impedīre* to IMPEDE; see -ITE[2]) + -IVE]

im·pel (im pel′), *v.t.,* **-pelled, -pel·ling.** **1.** to drive or urge forward; incite or constrain to action. **2.** to drive or cause to move onward; propel; impart motion to. [late ME *impell* < L *impell(ere)* (to) strike against (something), start (it) moving = *im-* IM-[1] + *pellere* to strike, move (something)]

im·pel·lent (im pel′ənt), *adj.* **1.** impelling. —*n.* **2.** something that impels; an impelling agency or force. [< L *impellent-* (s. of *impellēns*) setting in motion, prp. of *impellere*]

im·pel·ler (im pel′ər), *n.* **1.** a person or thing that impels. **2.** a rotor for transmitting motion, as in a centrifugal pump, blower, turbine, fluid coupling, etc.

im·pend (im pend′), *v.i.* **1.** to be imminent or near at hand. **2.** to be a threat or menace. **3.** *Rare.* to hang or be suspended; overhang (usually fol. by *over*). [< L *impend(ere)* (to) hang over, threaten]

im·pend·ent (im pen′dənt), *adj.* impending. [< L *impendent-* (s. of *impendēns*) overhanging, prp. of *impendere*] —**im·pend′ence, im·pend′en·cy,** *n.*

im·pend·ing (im pen′ding), *adj.* **1.** about to happen; imminent. **2.** imminently threatening or menacing. **3.** *Rare.* overhanging. —**Syn. 1.** See **imminent.**

im·pen·e·tra·bil·i·ty (im pen′i trə bil′i tē, im′pen-), *n.* **1.** the state or quality of being impenetrable. **2.** *Physics.* that property of matter by virtue of which two bodies cannot occupy the same space simultaneously.

im·pen·e·tra·ble (im pen′i trə bəl), *adj.* **1.** not penetrable; unable to be penetrated, pierced, entered, etc. **2.** inaccessible to ideas, influences, etc. **3.** incapable of being comprehended; unfathomable. **4.** *Physics.* possessing impenetrability. [late ME *impenetrabel* < L *impenetrābil(is)*] —**im·pen′e·tra·ble·ness,** *n.* —**im·pen′e·tra·bly,** *adv.*

im·pen·i·tent (im pen′i tᵊnt), *adj.* not penitent; obdurate. [< LL *impaenitent-* (s. of *impaenitēns*)] —**im·pen′i·tence, im·pen′i·ten·cy, im·pen′i·tent·ness,** *n.* —**im·pen′i·tent·ly,** *adv.*

imper., imperative.

im·per·a·ti·val (im per′ə tī′vəl), *adj.* of, pertaining to, or characteristic of the grammatical imperative. —**im·per′a·ti′val·ly,** *adv.*

im·per·a·tive (im per′ə tiv), *adj.* **1.** not to be avoided or evaded. **2.** of the nature of or expressing a command; commanding. **3.** *Gram.* noting or pertaining to the mood of the verb used in commands, requests, etc. Cf. **indicative** (def. 2), **subjunctive** (def. 1). —*n.* **4.** a command. **5.** a fact that compels attention or action; obligation; need. **6.** *Gram.* **a.** the imperative mood. **b.** a verb in this mood. **7.** an obligatory statement, principle, or the like. [< LL *imperātīv(us)*] —**im·per′a·tive·ly,** *adv.* —**im·per′a·tive·ness,** *n.* —**Syn. 1.** inescapable; indispensable, necessary, essential.

im·pe·ra·tor (im′pə rā′tər), *n.* **1.** an absolute or supreme ruler. **2.** (in Imperial Rome) emperor. **3.** (in Republican Rome) a temporary title accorded a victorious general. [< L; see EMPEROR] —**im·per·a·to·ri·al** (im per′ə tōr′ē əl, -tôr′-) *adj.* —**im·per′a·to′ri·al·ly,** *adv.* —**im′pe·ra′tor·ship′,** *n.*

im·per·cep·ti·ble (im′pər sep′tə bəl), *adj.* **1.** very slight, gradual, or subtle. **2.** not perceptible; not perceived by or affecting the senses. —*n.* **3.** something not capable of being perceived by the senses. [< ML *imperceptibil(is)*] —**im′per·cep′ti·bil′i·ty, im′per·cep′ti·ble·ness,** *n.* —**im′per·cep′ti·bly,** *adv.*

im·per·cep·tion (im′pər sep′shən), *n.* lack of perception.

im·per·cep·tive (im′pər sep′tiv), *adj.* not perceptive; lacking perception. —**im′per·cep·tiv′i·ty, im′per·cep′tive·ness,** *n.*

imperf., imperfect.

im·per·fect (im pûr′fikt), *adj.* **1.** of, pertaining to, or characterized by defects. **2.** not perfect; lacking completeness: *imperfect knowledge.* **3.** *Bot.* (of a flower) diclinous. **4.** *Gram.* designating a tense or other verb formation noting incompleted action or state, esp. with reference to the past. **5.** *Law.* being without legal effect. **6.** *Music.* of or relating to the interval of a major or minor third or sixth. Cf. **perfect** (def. 12a). —*n. Gram.* **7.** the imperfect tense. **8.** any verb formation or construction with imperfect meaning. **9.** a verb form in the imperfect tense. [< L *imperfect(us)* unfinished (see IM-[2], PERFECT); r. ME *imparfit* < MF *imparfait* < L, as above] —**im·per′fect·ly,** *adv.* —**im·per′fect·ness,** *n.* —**Syn. 1.** defective, faulty. **2.** incomplete, underdeveloped; immature. —**Ant. 2.** complete, developed.

im·per·fect·i·ble (im′pər fek′tə bəl), *adj.* that cannot be perfected. —**im′per·fect′i·bil′i·ty,** *n.*

im·per·fec·tion (im′pər fek′shən), *n.* **1.** a flaw or defect. **2.** the quality or condition of being imperfect. [ME *imperfeccio(u)n* < LL *imperfectiōn-* (s. of *imperfectiō*) incompleteness]

im·per·fec·tive (im′pər fek′tiv), *Gram.* —*adj.* **1.** noting an aspect of the verb, as in Russian, that indicates incompleteness of the action or state at a temporal point of reference. —*n.* **2.** the imperfective aspect. **3.** a verb in this aspect.

imper′fect rhyme′, *Pros.* See **slant rhyme.**

im·per·fo·rate (im pûr′fər it, -fə rāt′), *adj.* **1.** Also, **im·per′fo·rat′ed.** not perforate; having no perforation. **2.** *Philately.* (of a number of stamps joined together) lacking the perforations usually separating individual stamps. —*n.* **3.** an imperforate stamp. —**im·per′fo·ra′tion,** *n.*

Im·pe·ria (ēm pe′ʀyä), *n.* a seaport in NW Italy. 35,180 (1961).

im·pe·ri·al[1] (im pēr′ē əl), *adj.* **1.** of or pertaining to an empire. **2.** of or pertaining to an emperor or empress. **3.** characterizing the rule or authority of a sovereign state over its dependencies. **4.** of the nature or rank of an emperor or supreme ruler. **5.** of a commanding quality, manner, aspect, etc. **6.** domineering; imperious. **7.** of or befitting an emperor or empress. **8.** of special size or quality. **9.** (of weights and measures) conforming to the standards legally established in Great Britain. —*n.* **10.** a size of printing or drawing paper, 22 × 30 inches in England, 23 × 33 inches in America. **11.** the top of a carriage, esp. of a diligence. **12.** an emperor or empress. **13.** any of various articles of exceptional size or quality. [ME < LL *imperiāl(is)* (see IMPERIUM, -AL[1]); r. ME *emperial* < MF] —**im·pe′ri·al·ly,** *adv.* —**im·pe′ri·al·ness,** *n.*

im·pe·ri·al[2] (im pēr′ē əl), *n.* a small, pointed beard beneath the lower lip. [< F *impériale*, n. use of fem. of *impérial* IMPERIAL[1]]

Imperial[2]

im·pe·ri·al[3] (im pēr′ē əl), *n.* an imperial Russian gold coin originally worth 10 rubles and from 1897–1917 worth 15 rubles. [< Russ << ML *imperiālis* a coin, n. use of LL *imperiālis* IMPERIAL[1]]

Impe′rial bush′el. See under **bushel**[1] (def. 1).

impe′rial gal′lon, a British gallon equivalent to 1[1]/5 U.S. gallons, or 277.42 cubic inches.

Impe′rial Hol′iday, (*sometimes l.c.*) a day of traditional significance to the entire British Commonwealth, as the Queen's Birthday, Victoria Day, etc., but which is not a legal holiday.

im·pe·ri·al·ism (im pēr′ē ə liz′əm), *n.* **1.** the policy of extending the rule or authority of an empire or nation over foreign countries, or of acquiring and holding colonies and dependencies. **2.** advocacy of imperial interests. **3.** imperial government. **4.** an imperial system of government. —**im·pe′ri·al·ist,** *n., adj.* —**im·pe′ri·al·is′tic,** *adj.* —**im·pe′ri·al·is′ti·cal·ly,** *adv.*

impe′rial moth′, a yellow moth, *Eacles imperialis*, having dotted wings each with a diagonal band of pinkish-brown or purple, the hairy larvae of which feed on the leaves of hickory, oak, etc.

Impe′rial Val′ley, an irrigated agricultural region in SE California, adjacent to Mexico, formerly a part of the Colorado Desert: it is largely below sea level and contains the Salton Sink.

im·per·il (im per′əl), *v.t.,* **-iled, -il·ing** or (*esp. Brit.*) **-illed, -il·ling.** to put in peril; endanger. —**im·per′il·ment,** *n.*

im·pe·ri·ous (im pēr′ē əs), *adj.* **1.** domineering; dictatorial; overbearing: *an imperious manner; an imperious person.* **2.** urgent; imperative: *imperious need.* [< L *imperiōs(us)* commanding, tyrannical. See IMPERIUM, -OUS] —**im·pe′ri·ous·ly,** *adv.* —**im·pe′ri·ous·ness,** *n.* —**Syn. 1.** tyrannical, despotic. **2.** necessary. —**Ant. 1.** submissive. **2.** unnecessary.

im·per·ish·a·ble (im per′i shə bəl), *adj.* not perishable; indestructible; enduring. **—im·per′ish·a·bil′i·ty, im·per′ish·a·ble·ness,** *n.* **—im·per′ish·a·bly,** *adv.*

im·pe·ri·um (im pēr′ē əm), *n., pl.* **-pe·ri·a** (-pēr′ē ə). **1.** command; supreme power. **2.** area of dominion; sphere of control or monopoly; empire. **3.** *Law.* the right to command the force of the state in order to enforce the law. [< L: command (i.e., thing commanded), empire = *imper(āre)* (to) rule (see EMPEROR) + *-ium* neut. suffix]

im·per·ma·nent (im pûr′mə nənt), *adj.* not permanent; transitory. **—im·per′ma·nence, im·per′ma·nen·cy,** *n.* **—im·per′ma·nent·ly,** *adv.*

im·per·me·a·ble (im pûr′mē ə bəl), *adj.* **1.** not permeable; impassable. **2.** (of substances) not permitting the passage of a fluid through the pores, interstices, etc. [< LL *impermeābil(is)*] **—im·per′me·a·bil′i·ty, im·per′me·a·ble·ness,** *n.* **—im·per′me·a·bly,** *adv.*

im·per·mis·si·ble (im′pər mis′ə bəl), *adj.* not permissible; unallowable. **—im′per·mis′si·bil′i·ty,** *n.*

impers., impersonal.

im·per·son·al (im pûr′sə n^{ə}l), *adj.* **1.** not personal; without personal reference or connection. **2.** having no personality or human traits: *an impersonal deity.* **3.** *Gram.* **a.** (of a verb) having only third person singular forms and either accompanied by an empty subject word, as in *It is raining,* or not having an expressed subject. **b.** (of a pronoun or pronominal reference) indefinite. **—***n.* **4.** *Gram.* an impersonal verb or pronoun. [< LL *impersōnāl(is)*] **—im·per′son·al·ly,** *adv.*

im·per·son·al·ise (im pûr′sə n^{ə}līz′), *v.t.,* **-ised, -is·ing.** *Chiefly Brit.* impersonalize. **—im·per′son·al·i·sa′tion,** *n.*

im·per·son·al·i·ty (im pûr′sə nal′i tē), *n., pl.* **-ties** for 6. **1.** absence of human character or of the traits associated with the human character. **2.** lack of emotional involvement. **3.** absence or reduction of concern for individual needs or desires: *the impersonality of an institution.* **4.** lack of a personal agent or of a known personal agent: *the impersonality of folk art.* **5.** the quality of not being concerned with particular persons: *the impersonality and universality of his interests.* **6.** something that is impersonal.

im·per·son·al·ize (im pûr′sə n^{ə}līz′), *v.t.,* **-ized, -iz·ing.** to make impersonal. Also, *esp. Brit.,* **impersonalise. —im·per′son·al·i·za′tion,** *n.*

im·per·son·ate (*v.* im pûr′sə nāt′; *adj.* im pûr′sə nit, -nāt′), *v.,* **-at·ed, -at·ing,** *adj.* **—***v.t.* **1.** to assume the character of; pretend to be. **2.** to personate, esp. on the stage. **3.** *Rare.* to represent in personal or bodily form; personify; typify. **—***adj.* **4.** embodied in a person; invested with personality. **—im·per′son·a′tion,** *n.* **—im·per′son·a′tor,** *n.*

im·per·ti·nence (im pûr′t^{ə}nəns), *n.* **1.** unmannerly intrusion or presumption; insolence. **2.** irrelevance, inappropriateness, or absurdity. **3.** an impertinent person, act, statement, etc. [IMPERTIN(ENCY) + -ENCE]

im·per·ti·nen·cy (im pûr′t^{ə}nən sē), *n., pl.* **-cies.** impertinence. [< ML *impertinentia.* See IMPERTINENT, -ENCY]

im·per·ti·nent (im pûr′t^{ə}nənt), *adj.* **1.** intrusive or presumptuous; rude; uncivil. **2.** not pertinent; irrelevant. [ME < LL *impertinent-* (s. of *impertinēns*) not belonging] **—im·per′ti·nent·ly,** *adv.* **—im·per′ti·nent·ness,** *n.*
—Syn. 1. fresh, bold, insulting, saucy, pert, brazen. IMPERTINENT, IMPUDENT, INSOLENT refer to bold, rude, and arrogant behavior. IMPERTINENT, from its primary meaning of not pertinent and hence inappropriate or out of place, has come to imply often an unseemly intrusion into what does not concern one, or a presumptuous rudeness toward one entitled to deference or respect: *an impertinent interruption, question, manner toward a teacher.* IMPUDENT suggests a bold and shameless impertinence: *an impudent speech, young rascal.* INSOLENT suggests insulting or arrogantly contemptuous behavior: *unbearably insolent toward those in authority.*

im·per·turb·a·ble (im′pər tûr′bə bəl), *adj.* incapable of being perturbed or agitated; not easily excited; calm. [< LL *imperturbābil(is)*] **—im′per·turb′a·bil′i·ty, im′per·turb′a·ble·ness,** *n.* **—im′per·turb′a·bly,** *adv.* **—Syn.** composed, collected, impassive, cool, unmoved.

im·per·tur·ba·tion (im′pər tər bā′shən), *n.* freedom from perturbation; tranquillity; calmness. [< LL *imperturbātiōn-* (s. of *imperturbātiō*)]

im·per·vi·ous (im pûr′vē əs), *adj.* **1.** not permitting penetration or passage; impenetrable. **2.** incapable of being injured or impaired. **3.** incapable of being influenced or affected. Also, **im·per′vi·a·ble.** [< L *impervius*] **—im·per′vi·ous·ly,** *adv.* **—im·per′vi·ous·ness,** *n.*

im·pe·ti·go (im′pi tī′gō), *n.* *Pathol.* a contagious skin disease, esp. of children, marked by a superficial pustular eruption, particularly on the face. [< L = *impet(ere)* (to) make for, attack (see IMPETUS) + *-īgō,* as in *vertīgō* VERTIGO] **—im·pe·tig·i·nous** (im′pi tij′ə nəs), *adj.*

im·pe·trate (im′pi trāt′), *v.t.,* **-trat·ed, -trat·ing. 1.** to obtain by entreaty. **2.** to entreat; ask for urgently. [< L *impetrāt(us)* got by asking (ptp. of *impetrāre*) = *im-* IM-^{1} + *petr-* (var. of *patr-,* root of *patrāre* to father, hence, to bring about, cause < *pater* father) + *-ātus* -ATE^1] **—im′pe·tra′tion,** *n.*

im·pet·u·os·i·ty (im pech′o͞o os′i tē, im′pe cho͞o-), *n., pl.* **-ties** for 2. **1.** the quality or condition of being impetuous. **2.** an impetuous action.

im·pet·u·ous (im pech′o͞o əs), *adj.* **1.** of, pertaining to, or characterized by sudden or rash energy, action, emotion, etc.; impulsive. **2.** having great impetus; moving with great force; violent. [ME < LL *impetuōs(us).* See IMPETUS, -OUS] **—im·pet′u·ous·ly,** *adv.* **—im·pet′u·ous·ness,** *n.*
—Syn. 1. eager, violent. IMPETUOUS, IMPULSIVE both refer to persons who are hasty and precipitate in action, or to actions not preceded by thought. IMPETUOUS suggests eagerness, violence, rashness: *impetuous desire; impetuous words.* IMPULSIVE emphasizes spontaneity and lack of reflection: *an impulsive act of generosity.* **—Ant. 1.** planned, careful.

im·pe·tus (im′pi təs), *n., pl.* **-tus·es. 1.** moving force; impulse; stimulus. **2.** the force with which a moving body tends to maintain its velocity and overcome resistance; energy of motion. [< L: an attack, lit., a rushing into = *impet(ere)* (to) attack (*im-* IM-^{1} + *petere* to make for) + *-us* n. suffix (4th decl.)]

impf., imperfect.

imp. gal., imperial gallon.

Imp·hal (imp′hul), *n.* a city in and the capital of Manipur territory, in NE India. 102,862 (1951).

im·pi·e·ty (im pī′i tē), *n., pl.* **-ties** for 3. **1.** lack of piety; lack of reverence for God or sacred things; ungodliness. **2.** lack of dutifulness or respect. **3.** an impious act, practice, etc. [ME *impietie* < L *impietās* = *impi(us)* IMPIOUS + *-etās,* var. of *-itās* -ITY]

im·pig·no·rate (im pig′nə rāt′), *v.t.,* **-rat·ed, -rat·ing.** to put up or give as security; pledge; mortgage. [< ML *impignorāt(us)* pledged (ptp. of *impignorāre*) = L *im-* IM-^{1} + *pignor-* (s. of *pignus*) a pledge + *-ātus* -ATE^1] **—im·pig′no·ra′tion,** *n.*

im·pinge (im pinj′), *v.,* **-pinged, -ping·ing. —***v.i.* **1.** to strike; dash; collide (usually fol. by *on, upon,* or *against*): *rays of light impinging on the eye.* **2.** to encroach; infringe (usually fol. by *on* or *upon*): *to impinge upon another's rights.* **3.** to make an impression; have an effect (usually fol. by *on* or *upon*): *to impinge upon the imagination.* [< ML *impinge(re)* (to) strike against, drive at = L *im-* IM-^{1} + *-pingere,* var. of *pangere* to fasten, drive in, fix] **—im·ping′er,** *n.* **—im·pinge′ment,** *n.*

im·pi·ous (im′pē əs), *adj.* **1.** not pious; irreligious; ungodly. **2.** disrespectful. [< L *impius*] **—im′pi·ous·ly,** *adv.* **—im′pi·ous·ness,** *n.*

imp·ish (im′pish), *adj.* of, pertaining to, or characteristic of an imp; mischievous. **—imp′ish·ly,** *adv.* **—imp′ish·ness,** *n.*

im·plac·a·ble (im plak′ə bəl, -plā′kə-), *adj.* not placable; not to be appeased or pacified; inexorable. [late ME < L *implācābil(is)*] **—im·plac′a·bil′i·ty, im·plac′a·ble·ness,** *n.* **—im·plac′a·bly,** *adv.* **—Syn.** unappeasable, unbending. See **inflexible.**

im·pla·cen·tal (im′plə sen′t^{ə}l), *adj.* **1.** *Zool.* having no placenta, as a monotreme or marsupial. **—***n.* **2.** an implacental mammal. Also, **im·pla·cen·tate** (im′plə sen′tāt).

im·plant (*v.* im plant′, -plänt′; *n.* im′plant′, -plänt′), *v.t.* **1.** to instill; imbue; inculcate. **2.** to plant in something; infix. **3.** *Rare.* to plant. **—***n.* **4.** *Med.* **a.** a tissue implanted into the body by grafting. **b.** a small tube containing a radioactive substance, as radium, surgically implanted in tissue for the treatment of tumors, cancer, etc. **—im·plant′er,** *n.*

im·plan·ta·tion (im′plan tā′shən), *n.* **1.** the act of implanting. **2.** the state of being implanted. **3.** *Med.* the application of solid medicine underneath the skin.

im·plau·si·bil·i·ty (im plô′zə bil′i tē), *n., pl.* **-ties** for 2. **1.** the quality or condition of being implausible. **2.** something that is implausible.

im·plau·si·ble (im plô′zə bəl), *adj.* not plausible; not having the appearance of truth or credibility. **—im·plau′si·bly,** *adv.*

im·plead (im plēd′), *v.t.* **1.** to sue in a court of law. **2.** *Rare.* to accuse; impeach. **3.** *Archaic.* to plead (a suit). [ME *emplede(n)* < AF *empleder(er)*] **—im·plead′a·ble,** *adj.*

im·plead·er (im plē′dər), *n.* *Law.* a procedural method by which an original party to an action may bring in a third party and make a claim against him in connection with the claim made against the original party. Also called **third party procedure.**

im·ple·ment (*n.* im′plə mənt; *v.* im′plə ment′), *n.* **1.** an instrument; tool, utensil. **2.** an article of equipment, as household furniture, clothing, or the like. **3.** a means; agent. **—***v.t.* **4.** to fulfill; perform; carry out. **5.** to put into effect according to or by means of a definite plan or procedure. **6.** to fill out or supplement. **7.** to provide with implements. [late ME < LL *implēment(um)* a filling up = L *implē(re)* (to) fill up (*im-* IM-^{1} + *-plēre* to fill) + *-mentum* -MENT] **—im′ple·men′tal,** *adj.* **—im′ple·men·ta′tion,** *n.* **—im′ple·ment′er, im′ple·men′tor,** *n.* **—Syn. 1.** See **tool.**

im·ple·tion (im plē′shən), *n.* *Rare.* **1.** the act of filling. **2.** the state of being filled. [< LL *implētiōn-* (s. of *implētiō*) = L *implēt(us)* filled up (ptp. of *implēre;* see IMPLEMENT) + *-iōn-* -ION]

im·pli·cate (im′plə kāt′), *v.t.,* **-cat·ed, -cat·ing. 1.** to involve as being concerned in a matter, affair, condition, etc. **2.** to imply as a necessary circumstance, or as something to be inferred or understood. **3.** to connect or relate to intimately; affect as a consequence. **4.** *Rare.* to fold or twist together; intertwine; interlace. [< L *implicāt(us)* interwoven (ptp. of *implicāre*) = *im-* IM-^{1} + *plic(āre)* (to) fold + *-ātus* -ATE^1] **—Syn. 1.** See **involve.**

im·pli·ca·tion (im′plə kā′shən) *n.* **1.** something implied or suggested as naturally to be inferred or understood. **2.** the act of implying. **3.** the state of being implied. **4.** *Logic.* the relation that holds between two propositions, or classes of propositions, in virtue of which one is logically deducible from the other. **5.** the act of implicating. **6.** the state of being implicated. **7.** Usually, **implications.** relationships of a close or intimate nature; involvements. [ME *implicacio(u)n* < L *implicātiōn-* (s. of *implicātiō*) an interweaving] **—im′pli·ca′tion·al,** *adj.*

im·pli·ca·tive (im′plə kā′tiv, im plik′ə tiv), *adj.* tending to implicate or imply; characterized by or involving implication. Also, **im·pli·ca·to·ry** (im′plə kə tôr′ē, -tōr′ē), *adj.* **—im′pli·ca′tive·ly,** *adv.*

im·plic·it (im plis′it), *adj.* **1.** implied, rather than expressly stated. **2.** potentially contained (usually fol. by *in*): *to bring out the drama implicit in the occasion.* **3.** unquestioning; unreserved; absolute. [< L *implicit(us),* var. ptp. of *implicāre.* See IMPLICATE, -ITE^2] **—im·plic′it·ly,** *adv.* **—im·plic′it·ness, im·plic′i·ty,** *n.*

im·plied (im plīd′), *adj.* involved, indicated, or suggested by implying; tacitly understood: *an implied compliment.*

im·plode (im plōd′), *v.,* **-plod·ed, -plod·ing. —***v.i.* **1.** to burst inward (opposed to *explode*). **—***v.t.* **2.** *Phonet.* to pronounce by implosion. [IM-^{1} + (EX)PLODE]

im·plore (im plōr′, -plôr′), *v.,* **-plored, -plor·ing. —***v.t.* **1.** to call upon in urgent or piteous supplication, as for aid or mercy; beseech; entreat. **2.** to make urgent supplication for (aid, mercy, pardon, etc.). **—v.i. 3.** to make urgent or piteous supplication. [< L *implōr(āre)* = *im-* IM-[1] + *plōrāre* to lament] **—im·plor′er,** *n.* **—im·plor′ing·ly,** *adv.* **—Syn. 1, 2.** beg. **2.** crave, solicit. **—Ant. 2.** spurn, reject.

im·plo·sion (im plō′zhən), *n.* **1.** the act of imploding; a bursting inward. **2.** *Phonet.* **a.** the occlusive phase of stop consonants. **b.** the nasal release of a stop consonant, heard in the common pronunciation of *eaten, sudden,* or *mitten,* in which the vowel of the final syllable is greatly reduced. **c.** the ingressive release of a suction stop. Cf. **plosion.** [IM-[1] + (EX)PLOSION]

im·plo·sive (im plō′siv), *Phonet.* **—adj. 1.** characterized by a partial vacuum behind the point of closure. **—n. 2.** an implosive stop. [IM-[1] + (EX)PLOSIVE] **—im·plo′sive·ly,** *adv.*

im·ply (im plī′), *v.t.,* **-plied, -ply·ing. 1.** to indicate or suggest without express statement, as something to be inferred. **2.** to involve or require as a necessary condition: *Speech implies a speaker.* **3.** to indicate by a hint or a sign: *Blushing implies shyness.* **4.** *Obs.* to enfold. [ME *emplie(n)* < MF *empli(er)* < L *implicāre;* see IMPLICATE] **—im·pli·ed·ly** (im plī′id le, -plīd′-), *adv.* **—Syn. 1.** assume. **—Usage.** See **infer.**

im·pol·i·cy (im pol′i sē), *n., pl.* **-cies** for 2. **1.** condition or quality of being injudicious; bad policy; inexpediency. **2.** an impolitic or injudicious act.

im·po·lite (im′pə līt′), *adj.* not polite or courteous; uncivil; rude. [< L *impolīt(us)* rough, unpolished] **—im′po·lite′ly,** *adv.* **—im′po·lite′ness,** *n.* **—Syn.** discourteous, disrespectful; insolent; boorish, ill-mannered, rough.

im·pol·i·tic (im pol′i tik), *adj.* inexpedient; injudicious. **—im·pol′i·tic·ly,** *adv.* **—im·pol′i·tic·ness,** *n.*

im·pon·der·a·ble (im pon′dər ə bəl), *adj.* **1.** not ponderable; that cannot be precisely determined, measured, or evaluated. **—n. 2.** an imponderable thing, force, agency, etc. [< ML *imponderābil(is)*] **—im·pon′der·a·bil′i·ty, im·pon′der·a·ble·ness,** *n.* **—im·pon′der·a·bly,** *adv.*

im·port (*v.* im pōrt′, -pôrt′; *n.* im′pōrt, -pôrt), *v.t.* **1.** to bring in (merchandise) from a foreign country for sale, use, etc. **2.** to bring or introduce from one use, connection, or relation into another. **3.** to convey as meaning or information, as by statements or actions. **4.** to involve as a necessary circumstance; imply. **5.** *Rare.* to be of consequence or importance to; concern. **—v.i. 6.** to be of consequence or importance; matter. **—n. 7.** something imported from abroad; an imported commodity or article. **8.** the act of importing or bringing in; importation, as of goods from abroad. **9.** meaning; implication; purport. **10.** consequence or importance. [ME *importe(n)* < L *import(āre)*] **—im·port′a·bil′i·ty,** *n.* **—im·port′a·ble,** *adj.* **—im·port′er,** *n.* **—Syn. 3.** mean, signify. **9.** significance, sense.

im·por·tance (im pôr′tᵊns), *n.* **1.** the quality or state of being important. **2.** important position or standing; personal or social consequence. **3.** consequential air or manner. **4.** *Obs.* an important matter. **5.** *Obs.* importunity. **6.** *Obs.* import or meaning. [< ML *importantia*]
—Syn. 1. moment, weight, concern. IMPORTANCE, CONSEQUENCE, SIGNIFICANCE refer to a quality, character, or standing such as to entitle to attention or consideration. IMPORTANCE, referring originally to the bringing or involving of noteworthy results, is the general term. CONSEQUENCE, though of the same general sense, is a weaker word, less suggestive of seriousness, dignity, or extensiveness: *The weather is a matter of consequence to the tourist, but of real importance to the farmer.* SIGNIFICANCE emphasizes the relation of the important matter to other things or people: *of great significance for economic thought.*

im·por·tant (im pôr′tᵊnt), *adj.* **1.** of much significance or consequence. **2.** mattering much (usually fol. by *to*): *details important to a fair decision.* **3.** of more than ordinary title to consideration or notice. **4.** prominent or large. **5.** of considerable influence, authority, social consequence, or distinction. **6.** pompous. **7.** *Obs.* importunate. [< ML *important-* (s. of *importāns*) weighing, of weight, prp. of *importāre*] **—im·por′tant·ly,** *adv.*

im·por·ta·tion (im′pōr tā′shən, -pôr-), *n.* **1.** the act of importing. **2.** something imported.

im·por·tu·nate (im pôr′chə nit), *adj.* **1.** urgent or persistent in solicitation. **2.** pertinacious, as solicitations or demands. **3.** troublesome; annoying. [late ME; perh. IMPORTUNE (adj.) + -ATE[1]] **—im·por′tu·nate·ly,** *adv.* **—im·por′tu·nate·ness,** *n.*

im·por·tune (im′pôr tōōn′, -tyōōn′, im pôr′chən), *v.,* **-tuned, -tun·ing,** *adj.* **—v.t. 1.** to beset with solicitations; demand with urgency or persistence. **2.** to make improper advances toward (a person). **3.** to beg for (something) urgently or persistently. **4.** *Obs.* to annoy. **5.** *Obs.* to press; impel. **—v.i. 6.** to make urgent or persistent solicitations. **7.** to make improper advances toward another person. **—adj. 8.** importunate. [ME (adj.) < L *importūn(us)* unsuitable, troublesome, assertive; see IM-[2], OPPORTUNE] **—im′por·tune′ly,** *adv.* **—im′por·tun′er,** *n.* **—Syn. 1, 3.** beseech, entreat, implore. **6.** plead.

im·por·tu·ni·ty (im′pôr tōō′ni tē, -tyōō′-), *n., pl.* **-ties** for 2. **1.** the state or quality of being importunate; persistence in solicitation. **2. importunities,** importunate solicitations or demands. [late ME *importunite* < L *importūnitās*]

im·pose (im pōz′), *v.,* **-posed, -pos·ing. —v.t. 1.** to lay on or set as something to be borne, endured, obeyed, fulfilled, paid, etc. **2.** to put or set by or as by authority. **3.** to obtrude or thrust (oneself, one's company, etc.) upon others. **4.** to pass or palm off fraudulently or deceptively. **5.** *Print.* to lay (type pages, plates, etc.) in proper order on an imposing stone or the like and secure in a chase for printing. **6.** to lay on or inflict, as a penalty. **7.** *Archaic.* to put or place on something, or in a particular place. **8.** *Obs.* to lay on (the hands) ceremonially, as in confirmation or ordination. **—v.i. 9.** to make an impression on the mind. **10.** to obtrude oneself or one's requirements, as upon others. **11.** to presume, as upon patience or good nature. **12. impose on** or **upon, a.** to thrust oneself offensively upon others; intrude. **b.** to take unfair advantage of; misuse (influence, friendship, etc.). **c.** to defraud; cheat, deceive. [late ME < MF *impos(er)* = *im-* IM-[1] + *poser* to POSE[1]; see also POSE[2]] **—im·pos′er,** *n.*

im·pos·ing (im pō′zing), *adj.* very impressive; making an impression on the mind, as by great size, stately appearance, etc. **—im·pos′ing·ly,** *adv.* **—im·pos′ing·ness,** *n.* **—Syn.** dignified, majestic, lofty, grand, august.

im·po·si·tion (im′pə zish′ən), *n.* **1.** the laying on of something as a burden, obligation, etc. **2.** something imposed, as a burden, duty, etc.; an unusual or extraordinarily burdensome requirement or task. **3.** the act of imposing by or as by authority. **4.** the act or an instance of imposing upon a person, as by exploiting his good nature. **5.** the act or an instance of imposing fraudulently on others; imposture. **6.** the ceremonial laying on of hands as in confirmation or ordination. **7.** *Print.* the arrangement of page plates in proper order on a press for printing a signature. **8.** the act of putting, placing, or laying on. [ME *imposicio(u)n* < LL *impositiōn-* (s. of *impositiō*) = L *imposit(us)* placed on, imposed, ptp. of *impōnere* (*im-* IM-[1] + *posi-,* perf. s. of *pōnere* to put, + *-tus* ptp. suffix) + *-iōn-* -ION]

im·pos·si·bil·i·ty (im pos′ə bil′i tē, im′pos-), *n., pl.* **-ties** for 2. **1.** condition or quality of being impossible. **2.** something impossible. [ME *impossibilite* < LL *impossibilitās*]

im·pos·si·ble (im pos′ə bəl), *adj.* **1.** not possible; unable to be, exist, happen, etc. **2.** unable to be done, performed, effected, etc. **3.** incapable of being true, as a rumor. **4.** not to be done, endured, etc., with any degree of reason or propriety. **5.** utterly impracticable. **6.** hopelessly unsuitable, difficult, undesirable, or objectionable. [ME < L *impossibil(is)*] **—im·pos′si·ble·ness,** *n.*

im·pos·si·bly (im pos′ə blē), *adv.* **1.** in an impossible manner. **2.** to an extent that produces hardship or prevents a solution. **3.** to an extreme or excessive degree.

im·post[1] (im′pōst), *n.* **1.** a tax; tribute; duty. **2.** a customs duty. **3.** *Horse Racing.* the weight assigned to a horse in a race. [< ML *impost(us)* tax, n. use of L *impostus,* var. of *impositus* imposed; see IMPOSITION] **—im′post·er,** *n.*

im·post[2] (im′pōst), *n.* *Archit.* **1.** the point of springing of an arch; spring. **2.** an architectural feature immediately beneath this point. [< F *imposte* < It *impost(a)* < fem. of L *impostus* (ptp.); see IMPOST[1]]

im·pos·tor (im pos′tər), *n.* **1.** a person who imposes fraudulently upon others. **2.** a person who practices deception under an assumed character or name. Also, **im·post′er.** [< LL] **—Syn. 1.** deceiver, cheat, charlatan. **2.** pretender.

im·pos·tume (im pos′chōōm, -tōōm, -tyōōm), *n.* *Archaic.* an abscess. Also, **im·pos·thume** (im pos′thōōm). [< MF *empostume,* var. of *apostume* < ML *apostūma,* var. of LL *apostēma* abscess < Gk: lit., separation (of pus) = *apostê(nai)* (to) separate (*apo-* APO- + *stē* STAND + *-nai* inf. suffix) + *-ma* n. suffix; r. ME *emposteme* < MF]

im·pos·ture (im pos′chər), *n.* **1.** the action or practice of imposing fraudulently upon others. **2.** deception practiced under an assumed character or name, as by an impostor. **3.** an instance or piece of fraudulent imposition. [< LL *impostūr(a).* See IMPOST[1], -URE] **—im·pos·trous** (im pos′trəs), **im·pos′tur·ous** *adj.* **—Syn. 3.** fraud, hoax, swindle.

im·po·tence (im′pə tᵊns), *n.* **1.** the condition or quality of being impotent; weakness. **2.** complete failure or serious impairment of sexual power, esp. in the male. **3.** *Obs.* lack of self-restraint. Also, **im′po·ten·cy, im′po·tent·ness.** [ME, var. (see -ENCE) of *impotencie* < L *impotentia* want of self-control]

im·po·tent (im′pə tᵊnt), *adj.* **1.** not potent; lacking power or ability. **2.** utterly unable (to do something). **3.** without force or effectiveness. **4.** lacking bodily strength, or physically helpless. **5.** (esp. of a male) wholly or seriously lacking in sexual power. **6.** *Obs.* without restraint. [ME < L *impotent-* (s. of *impotēns*) without power over oneself or others] **—im′po·tent·ly,** *adv.*

im·pound (im pound′), *v.t.* **1.** to shut up in a pound, as a stray animal. **2.** to confine within an enclosure or within limits. **3.** to seize, take, or appropriate summarily. **4.** to seize and retain in custody of the law, as a document for evidence. **—im·pound′er,** *n.* **—im·pound′ment,** *n.*

im·pov·er·ish (im pov′ər ish, -pov′rish), *v.t.* **1.** to reduce to poverty. **2.** to make poor in quality, productiveness, etc.; exhaust the strength or richness of. [late ME *empoveris(en)* < MF *empovriss-* (long s. of *empovrir*). See EM-[1], POOR, -ISH[2]] **—im·pov′er·ish·er,** *n.* **—im·pov′er·ish·ment,** *n.* **—Syn. 2.** deplete, drain; weaken, enervate, fatigue, cripple. **—Ant. 1, 2.** enrich.

im·pov·er·ished (im pov′ər isht, -pov′risht), *adj.* **1.** reduced to poverty. **2.** deprived of strength, vitality, etc. **3.** (of a country or region) having few trees, flowers, birds, wild animals, etc. **—Syn. 1.** See **poor.**

im·pow·er (im pou′ər), *v.t.* *Obs.* empower.

im·prac·ti·ca·ble (im prak′tə kə bəl), *adj.* **1.** not practicable, as a plan. **2.** unsuitable for practical use. **3.** (of ground, places, etc.) impassable. **4.** *Rare.* (of persons) hard to deal with because of stubbornness, stupidity, etc. **—im·prac′ti·ca·bil′i·ty, im·prac′ti·ca·ble·ness,** *n.* **—im·prac′ti·ca·bly,** *adv.*

im·prac·ti·cal (im prak′tə kəl), *adj.* not practical. **—im·prac′ti·cal′i·ty, im·prac′ti·cal·ness,** *n.*

im·pre·cate (im′prə kāt′), *v.t.,* **-cat·ed, -cat·ing.** to call down or invoke (evil or curses), as upon a person. [< L *imprecāt(us)* invoked, prayed to (ptp. of *imprecārī*). See IM-[1], PRAY, -ATE[1]] **—im′pre·ca′tor,** *n.* **—im·pre·ca·to·ry** (im′prə kə tōr′ē, -tôr′ē), *adj.* **—Syn.** curse, execrate, denunciate. **—Ant.** bless.

im·pre·ca·tion (im′prə kā′shən), *n.* **1.** the act of imprecating; cursing. **2.** a curse; malediction. [< L *imprecātiōn-* (s. of *imprecātiō*)]

im·pre·cise (im′pri sīs′), *adj.* not precise; not exact; vague or ill-defined. **—im′pre·cise′ly,** *adv.* **—im′pre·cise′ness,** *n.*

im·pre·ci·sion (im′pri sizh′ən), *n.* **1.** the condition or quality of being imprecise or inaccurate. **2.** an instance of vagueness or inaccuracy.

im·preg·na·ble[1] (im preg′nə bəl), *adj.* **1.** strong enough to resist or withstand attack: *an impregnable fortress.* **2.** not to be overcome, as an argument. [ME *imprenable* < MF] **—im·preg′na·bil′i·ty, im·preg′na·ble·ness,** *n.* **—im·preg′na·bly,** *adv.* **—Syn. 1.** invulnerable. **1, 2.** See **invincible. 2.** unassailable. **—Ant. 1.** vulnerable.

im·preg·na·ble[2] (im preg′nə bəl), *adj.* susceptible of impregnation, as an egg. [IMPREGN(ATE) + -ABLE]

im·preg·nate (*v.* im preg′nāt, im′preg-; *adj.* im preg′nit, -nāt), *v.*, **-nat·ed, -nat·ing,** *adj.* —*v.t.* **1.** to make pregnant; get with child or young. **2.** to fertilize. **3.** to cause to be infused or permeated throughout, as with a substance; saturate. **4.** to furnish with some actuating or modifying element infused or introduced; imbue, infect; tincture: *advice impregnated with wisdom.* —*adj.* **5.** impregnated. [< LL *impraegnāt(us)* impregnated, made pregnant (ptp. of *impraegnāre*). See IM-[1], PREGNANT, -ATE[1]] —**im′preg·na′tion,** *n.* —**im·preg′na·tor,** *n.* —**Syn. 3.** permeate, infuse, penetrate.

im·pre·sa (im prā′zə; *It.* ēm prē′zä), *n., pl.* **-sas,** *It.* **-se** (-ze). *Obs.* **1.** a device or emblem. **2.** a motto. Also, **imprese** (im prēz′). [< It: lit., undertaking, n. use of fem. of *impreso,* ptp. of *imprendere* to undertake; see EMPRISE]

im·pre·sa·ri·o (im′pri sär′ē ō′, -sâr′-; *It.* ēm′pre sä′ryô), *n., pl.* **-sa·ri·os,** *It.* **-sa·ri** (-sä′rē). **1.** a person who organizes or manages public entertainments. **2.** any manager, director, or the like. [< It; see IMPRESA, -ARY]

im·pre·scrip·ti·ble (im′pri skrip′tə bəl), *adj.* *Law.* not subject to prescription. [< ML *imprēscriptibil(is)*] —**im′pre·scrip′ti·bil′i·ty,** *n.* —**im′pre·scrip′ti·bly,** *adv.*

im·press[1] (*v.* im pres′; *n.* im′pres), *v.*, **-pressed** or (*Archaic*) **-prest; -press·ing;** *n.* —*v.t.* **1.** to affect deeply or strongly in mind or feelings; influence in opinion. **2.** to fix deeply or firmly on the mind or memory. **3.** to urge, as something to be remembered or done. **4.** to press (a thing) into or on something. **5.** to impose a particular characteristic or quality upon (something). **6.** to produce (a mark, figure, etc.) by pressure; stamp; imprint. **7.** to apply with pressure so as to leave a mark. **8.** to subject to or mark by pressure with something. **9.** to furnish with a mark, figure, etc., by or as by stamping. **10.** *Elect.* to produce (a voltage) or cause (a voltage) to appear or be produced on a conductor, circuit, etc. —*v.i.* **11.** to create a favorable impression. —*n.* **12.** the act of impressing. **13.** a mark made by or as by pressure; stamp; imprint. **14.** a distinctive character or effect imparted. [ME *impresse(n)* < L *impress(us)* pressed into or upon, impressed (ptp. of *imprimere*). See IM-[1], PRESS[1]] —**im·press′er,** *n.* —**Syn. 1.** move, sway.

im·press[2] (*v.* im pres′; *n.* im′pres), *v.*, **-pressed** or (*Archaic*) **-prest; -press·ing;** *n.* —*v.t.* **1.** to press or force into public service, as seamen. **2.** to seize or take for public use. —*n.* **3.** impressment. [IM-[1] + PRESS[2]]

im·press·i·ble (im pres′ə bəl), *adj.* impressionable. —**im·press′i·bil′i·ty,** *n.* —**im·press′i·bly,** *adv.*

im·pres·sion (im presh′ən), *n.* **1.** a strong effect produced on the intellect, feelings, or conscience, etc. **2.** the first and immediate effect of an experience or perception upon the mind. **3.** the effect produced by an agency or influence. **4.** a notion, remembrance, belief, etc., often of a vague or indistinct nature. **5.** a mark, indentation, figure, etc., produced by pressure. **6.** *Chiefly Print.* **a.** the process or result of printing from type, plates, etc. **b.** a printed copy from type, a plate, an engraved block, etc. **c.** one of a number of printings made at different times from the same set of type, without alteration (distinguished from *edition*). **d.** the total number of copies of a book, pamphlet, etc., printed at one time from one setting of type or from one set of plates. **7.** *Dentistry.* a mold taken of teeth and the surrounding tissues. **8.** *Metalworking.* a portion of a die having in reverse the intended form of an object to be forged. **9.** an image in the mind caused by something external to it. **10.** the act of impressing. **11.** the state of being impressed. **12.** an imitation of recognizable traits of famous persons, as by an entertainer. [ME *impressio(u)n* < L *impressiōn-* (s. of *impressiō*)] —**im·pres′sion·al,** *adj.* —**im·pres′sion·al·ly,** *adv.*

im·pres·sion·a·ble (im presh′ə nə bəl, -presh′nə-), *adj.* easily impressed or influenced; impressible. [IMPRESSION + -ABLE; cf. F *impressionnable*] —**im·pres′sion·a·bly,** *adv.* —**im·pres′sion·a·bil′i·ty, im·pres′sion·a·ble·ness,** *n.*

im·pres·sion·ism (im presh′ə niz′əm), *n.* **1.** *Fine Arts.* (*usually cap.*) a style of painting developed in the last third of the 19th century, characterized by short brush strokes of bright colors used to recreate the impression of light on objects. **2.** a theory and practice in literature that emphasizes immediate aspects of objects or actions without exhaustive examination. **3.** a late 19th-century and early 20th-century style of musical composition in which free use of harmonies and rhythms and unusual tonal colors are used to evoke moods and impressions. [IMPRESSION + -ISM; cf. G *Impressionismus,* F *impressionnisme*]

im·pres·sion·ist (im presh′ə nist), *n.* **1.** *Fine Arts.* (*usually cap.*) a person who adheres to the theories, methods, and practices of impressionism in painting. **2.** an adherent or practitioner of literary impressionism. **3.** an entertainer, esp. one who imitates the mannerisms of famous personalities. —*adj.* **4.** *Fine Arts.* (*usually cap.*) of, pertaining to, or characteristic of impressionism. [< F *impressionniste*] —**im·pres′sion·is′tic,** *adj.*

im·pres·sive (im pres′iv), *adj.* having the ability to impress the mind; imposing; awesome. —**im·pres′sive·ly,** *adv.* —**im·pres′sive·ness,** *n.*

im·press·ment (im pres′mənt), *n.* the act of impressing men, property, etc.

im·pres·sure (im presh′ər), *n.* *Archaic.* impression. [IMPRESS[1] + -URE, modeled on *pressure*]

im·prest (im prest′), *v.* *Archaic.* pt. and pp. of **impress.**

im·pri·ma·tur (im′pri mä′tər, -mā′-, -prī-), *n.* **1.** an official license to print or publish a book, pamphlet, etc., esp. a license issued by a censor of the Roman Catholic Church. Cf. **nihil obstat. 2.** license; sanction; approval. [< NL: let it be printed, L: let it be made by pressing upon (something); see IMPRESS[1]]

im·pri·ma·tu·ra (im prē′mə to͝or′ə), *n.* *Painting.* a tinted or glazed priming; underpainting. [< It *imprimitura* = *imprimit(o)* impressed (ptp. of *imprimere;* see IMPRESS[1]) + *-ura* -URE]

im·pri·mis (im prī′mis), *adv.* in the first place. [late ME < L, contr. of phrase *in prīmīs* among the first, in the first place]

im·print (*n.* im′print; *v.* im print′), *n.* **1.** a mark made by pressure; a figure impressed or printed on something. **2.** any impression or impressed effect. **3.** *Bibliog.* the publisher's name, usually accompanied by the place and date of publication, printed on the title page or elsewhere in a book. **4.** the printer's name and address as indicated on any printed matter. —*v.t.* **5.** to impress (a quality, character, distinguishing mark, etc.). **6.** to produce (a mark) on something by pressure. **7.** to fix firmly on the mind, memory, etc. **8.** to make an imprint upon. [IM-[1] + PRINT; r. ME *empreynte(n)* < MF *empreint(er)* < *empreinte,* fem. ptp. of *empreindre* < L *imprimere* to IMPRESS[1]] —**im·print′er,** *n.*

im·pris·on (im priz′ən), *v.t.* **1.** to put into or confine in a prison; detain in custody. **2.** to hold in restraint. [ME *enprisone(n)* < OF *enprison(er)*] —**im·pris′on·er,** *n.*

im·pris·on·ment (im priz′ən mənt), *n.* **1.** the act of imprisoning. **2.** the state of being imprisoned. **3.** forcible restraint of a person against his will. [ME *enprisonment* << OF *emprisonnement*]

im·prob·a·bil·i·ty (im prob′ə bil′i tē, im′prob-), *n., pl.* **-ties** for 2. **1.** the quality or condition of being improbable. **2.** something improbable or unlikely.

im·prob·a·ble (im prob′ə bəl), *adj.* not probable; unlikely to be true or to happen. [< L *improbābil(is)*] —**im·prob′a·bly,** *adv.* —**im·prob′a·ble·ness,** *n.*

im·pro·bi·ty (im prō′bi tē, -prob′i tē), *n.* lack of moral principles; dishonesty; wickedness. [ME *improbite* < L *improbitās*]

im·promp·tu (im promp′to͞o, -tyo͞o), *adj.* **1.** made or done without previous preparation. **2.** suddenly or hastily prepared, made, etc. **3.** improvised; having the character of an improvisation. —*adv.* **4.** without preparation. —*n.* **5.** an impromptu speech, musical composition, performance, etc. **6.** a short piece for piano, common in the 19th century, having a seemingly improvisatory character. [< F < L *in promptū* in readiness; see PROMPT] —**Syn. 1.** See **extemporaneous.**

im·prop·er (im prop′ər), *adj.* **1.** not proper; not strictly belonging, applicable, correct, etc.; erroneous. **2.** not in accordance with propriety of behavior, manners, etc. **3.** unsuitable or inappropriate, as for the purpose or occasion. **4.** abnormal or irregular. [< L *impropr(ius)*] —**im·prop′er·ly,** *adv.* —**im·prop′er·ness,** *n.*

—**Syn. 1–3.** inapplicable, unsuited, unfit. **2.** indecorous. IMPROPER, INDECENT, UNBECOMING, UNSEEMLY are applied to that which is unfitting or not in accordance with propriety. IMPROPER has a wide range, being applied to whatever is not suitable or fitting, and often specifically to what does not conform to the standards of conventional morality: *improper diet; improper behavior in church; improper language.* INDECENT, a strong word, is applied to what is offensively contrary to standards of propriety and esp. of modesty: *indecent behavior, literature.* UNBECOMING is applied to what is especially unfitting in the person concerned: *conduct unbecoming an officer.* UNSEEMLY is applied to whatever is unfitting or improper under the circumstances: *unseemly mirth.* —**Ant. 1, 3.** fitting, suitable. **2.** modest.

improp′er frac′tion, a fraction having the numerator greater than the denominator.

im·pro·pri·ate (*adj.* im prō′prē it, -āt′; *v.* im prō′prē āt′), *adj., v.*, **-at·ed, -at·ing.** —*adj.* **1.** *Eng. Eccles. Law.* devolved into the hands of a layman. **2.** *Obs.* appropriated to private use. —*v.t.* **3.** *Eng. Eccles. Law.* to place (ecclesiastical property) in the hands of lay persons. **4.** *Obs.* to appropriate. [< ML *impropriāt(us)* made one's own (ptp. of *impropriāre*). See IM-[1], APPROPRIATE] —**im·pro′pri·a′tion,** *n.*

im·pro·pri·e·ty (im′prə prī′i tē), *n., pl.* **-ties** for 4, 5. **1.** the quality or condition of being improper; incorrectness. **2.** inappropriateness; unsuitableness. **3.** unseemliness; indecorousness. **4.** an erroneous or unsuitable expression, act, etc. **5.** an improper use of a word. [< LL *improprietās*]

im·prove (im pro͞ov′), *v.*, **-proved, -prov·ing.** —*v.t.* **1.** to bring into a more desirable or excellent condition. **2.** to make (land) more useful, profitable, or valuable by enclosure, cultivation, etc. **3.** to increase the value of (real property) by betterments, as the construction of buildings. **4.** to make good use of; turn to account. —*v.i.* **5.** to increase in value, excellence, etc.; become better. **6. improve on** or **upon,** to make improvements, as by revision, addition, or emendation. [< AF *emprou(er)* (to) turn (something) into profit < phrase *en prou* into profit = *en* (see EN-[1]) + *prou* < LL *prōde* useful, back formation from L *prōdesse* to be useful; see PROUD] —**im·prov′a·ble,** *adj.* —**im·prov′a·bil′i·ty, im·prov′a·ble·ness,** *n.* —**im·prov′er,** *n.*

—**Syn. 1.** amend, emend. IMPROVE, AMELIORATE, BETTER imply bringing to a more desirable state. IMPROVE usually implies remedying a lack or a felt need: *to improve a process, oneself (as by gaining more knowledge).* AMELIORATE, a formal word, implies reforming oppressive, unjust, or difficult conditions: *to ameliorate working conditions.* TO BETTER is to improve something that is adequate but could be more satisfactory: *to better a situation oneself (gain a higher salary).* **5.** mend, gain. —**Ant. 1, 5.** worsen.

im·prove·ment (im pro͞ov′mənt), *n.* **1.** the act of improving. **2.** the state of being improved. **3.** a change or addition by which a thing is improved. **4.** some thing or person that represents an advance on another in excellence or achievement. **5.** a bringing into a more valuable or desirable condition, as of land or real property; a making or becoming better; betterment. **6.** something done or added to real property which increases its value. **7.** profitable use, as of a period of time. [< AF *emprouement* something profitable (especially exploitation of land)]

im·prov·i·dent (im prov′i dənt), *adj.* not provident; lacking foresight; incautious; unwary. **2.** neglecting to provide for future needs. —**im·prov′i·dence,** *n.* —**im·prov′i·dent·ly,** *adv.* —**Syn. 1.** thoughtless, careless, imprudent. **2.** unthrifty; wasteful, prodigal. —**Ant. 1.** prudent. **2.** economical.

im·prov·i·sa·tion (im prov′i zā′shən, im′prə vi-, *or, esp. Brit.,* im′prə vī-), *n.* **1.** the act of improvising. **2.** something improvised. —**im·prov′i·sa′tion·al,** *adj.*

im·prov·i·sa·tor (im prov′i zā′tər, im′prə vi-), *n.* a person who improvises. [IMPROVISE + -ATOR; cf. It *improvvisatore*]

im·pro·vi·sa·to·ry (im′prə vī′zə tōr′ē, -tôr′ē, -viz′i-), *adj.* of, pertaining to, or characteristic of an improvisation or improvisator. [IMPROVISATOR + -Y[1]; see -ORY[1]] Also, **im·prov·i·sa·to·ri·al** (im prov′i zə tōr′ē əl, -tôr′-).

im·pro·vise (im′prə vīz′), *v.*, **-vised, -vis·ing.** —*v.t.* **1.** to perform or provide without previous preparation; extemporize. **2.** to compose (verse, music, etc.) on the spur of the moment. **3.** to recite, sing, etc., extemporaneously. —*v.i.* **4.** to compose, utter, or execute anything extemporaneously. [back formation from *improviso* improvised < It *improvviso* < L *imprōvīsō* suddenly. See IM-[2], PROVISO] —**im′pro·vis′er,** *n.*

im·pru·dent (im prōōd′ənt), *adj.* not prudent; lacking discretion. [ME < L *imprūdent-* (s. of *imprūdēns*) unforeseeing, rash] —**im·pru′dence,** *n.* —**im·pru′dent·ly,** *adv.*

im·pu·dence (im′pyə dəns), *n.* **1.** the quality or condition of being impudent; effrontery; insolence. **2.** impudent conduct or language. **3.** *Obs.* lack of modesty; shamelessness. Also, **im′pu·den·cy.** [ME < L *impudentia* shamelessness] —**Syn. 1, 2.** impertinence, rudeness; brazenness, gall.

im·pu·dent (im′pyə dənt), *adj.* **1.** of, pertaining to, or characterized by boldness, impertinence, or effrontery. **2.** *Obs.* shameless or brazenly immodest. [ME < L *impudent-* (s. of *impudēns*) shameless. See IM-[2], PUDENCY, -ENT] —**im′pu·dent·ly,** *adv.* —**im′pu·dent·ness,** *n.* —**Syn. 1.** insulting, rude; saucy, pert, presumptuous, fresh; brazen. See **impertinent.** —**Ant. 1.** courteous.

im·pu·dic·i·ty (im′pyŏŏ dis′i tē), *n.* immodesty. [< MF *impudicite* < ML **impudīcitās* (r. L *impudīcitia*) < L *impudīc(us)* immodest (*im-* IM-[2] + *pudīcus*) + *-itās* -ITY]

im·pugn (im pyōōn′), *v.t.* **1.** to assail by words or arguments, as statements, motives, veracity, etc.; call in question; challenge as false. **2.** *Obs.* to assail (a person) physically. [ME *impugne(n)* < MF *impugn(er)* < L *impugnāre* to attack = *im-* IM-[1] + *pugnāre* to fight < *pugn(a)* a battle; see PUGNACIOUS] —**im·pugn′a·ble,** *adj.* —**im·pugn′er,** *n.* —**Syn. 1.** attack, malign, criticize, censure.

im·pu·is·sant (im pyōō′i sənt, im′pyōō is′ənt, im pwis′ənt), *adj.* impotent; feeble; weak. [< MF] —**im·pu′is·sance,** *n.*

im·pulse (im′puls), *n.* **1.** the influence of a particular feeling, mental state, etc.: *to act under a generous impulse.* **2.** sudden, involuntary inclination prompting to action. **3.** an instance of this. **4.** an impelling action or force, driving onward or inducing motion. **5.** the effect of an impelling force; motion induced; impetus given. **6.** *Physiol.* a progressive wave of excitation over a nerve or muscle fiber, having either a stimulating or inhibitory effect. **7.** *Mech.* the product of the average force acting upon a body and the time during which it acts. **8.** *Elect.* a single, usually sudden, flow of current in one direction. [< L *impuls(us)* pressure, impulse, n. use of *impulsus* pushed on, ptp. of *impellere* to IMPEL]

im′pulse buy′ing, the purchasing of consumer goods on impulse rather than by plan or from need.

im·pul·sion (im pul′shən), *n.* **1.** the act of impelling, driving onward, or pushing. **2.** the resulting state or effect; impulse; impetus. **3.** the inciting influence of some feeling or motive; mental impulse. **4.** a constraining or inciting action exerted on the mind or conduct: *divine impulsion.* [ME < L *impulsiōn-* (s. of *impulsiō*) incitement]

im·pul·sive (im pul′siv), *adj.* **1.** actuated or swayed by emotional or involuntary impulses. **2.** having the power or effect of impelling; characterized by impulsion. **3.** inciting to action. **4.** *Mech.* (of forces) acting momentarily; not continuous. [ME < ML *impulsīv(us)*] —**im·pul′sive·ly,** *adv.* —**im·pul′sive·ness,** *n.* —**Syn. 1.** rash, quick, hasty. See **impetuous.**

im·pu·ni·ty (im pyōō′ni tē), *n.* exemption from punishment; immunity from detrimental effects, as of an action. [< L *impūnitās* = *im-* IM-[2] + *pūnitās* punishment (*pūn-* (s. of *pūnīre* to punish) + *-itās* -ITY)]

im·pure (im pyŏŏr′), *adj.* **1.** not pure; mixed with extraneous matter, esp. of an inferior or contaminating nature. **2.** modified by admixture, as color. **3.** mixed or combined with something else. **4.** ceremonially unclean, as things, animals, etc. **5.** not morally pure or proper; unchaste or obscene. **6.** marked by foreign and unsuitable or objectionable elements or characteristics. [< L *impūr(us)*] —**im·pure′ly,** *adv.* —**im·pure′ness,** *n.*

im·pu·ri·ty (im pyŏŏr′i tē), *n., pl.* **-ties** for 2. **1.** the quality or state of being impure. **2.** Often, **impurities.** something that is or makes impure. [late ME *impurite* < L *impūritās*]

im·put·a·ble (im pyōō′tə bəl), *adj.* able to be imputed; attributable. [< ML *imputābil(is)*] —**im·put′a·bil′i·ty,** *n.* —**im·put′a·bly,** *adv.*

im·pu·ta·tion (im′pyŏŏ tā′shən), *n.* **1.** the act of imputing. **2.** an attribution, esp. of fault, crime, etc.; accusation. [< LL *imputātiōn-* (s. of *imputātiō*) = L *imputāt(us)* ascribed (ptp. of *imputāre* to IMPUTE) + *-iōn-* -ION]

im·pute (im pyōōt′), *v.t.*, **-put·ed, -put·ing.** **1.** to attribute (something discreditable), as to a person. **2.** to attribute or ascribe. **3.** *Law.* to charge, as with some misdemeanor. **4.** *Theol.* to attribute to a person or persons (righteousness, guilt, etc.) vicariously; ascribe as derived from another. **5.** *Obs.* to charge (a person) with fault. [ME *impute(n)* < L *imput(āre)* = *im-* IM-[1] + *put(āre)* (to) reckon; see PUTATIVE] —**im·put·a·tive** (im pyōō′tə tiv), *adj.* —**im·put′a·tive·ly,** *adv.* —**Syn. 2.** See **attribute.**

im·pu·tres·ci·ble (im′pyōō tres′ə bəl), *adj.* not liable to decomposition or putrefaction; incorruptible. [< LL *imputrescibil(is)*] —**im′pu·tres′ci·bil′i·ty,** *n.*

impv., imperative.

in (in), *prep., adv., adj., n., v.,* **inned, in·ning.** —*prep.* **1.** (used to indicate inclusion within space, a place, or limits): *walking in the park.* **2.** (used to indicate inclusion within something immaterial): *in politics; in the autumn.* **3.** (used to indicate inclusion within or occurrence during a period or limit of time): *in ancient times; a task done in ten minutes.* **4.** (used to indicate limitation or qualification, as of situation, condition, relation, manner, action, etc.): *to speak in a whisper; to be similar in appearance.* **5.** (used to indicate means): *sketched in ink; spoken in French.* **6.** (used to indicate motion or direction from outside to a point within) into: *Let's go in the house.* **7.** (used to indicate transition from one state to another): *to break in half.* **8.** (used to indicate object or purpose): *speaking in honor of the event.* **9. in that,** because; inasmuch as. —*adv.* **10.** in or into some place, position, state, relation, etc. **11.** on the inside; within. **12.** in one's house or office. **13.** in office or power. **14.** in possession or occupancy. **15.** having the turn to play, as in a game. **16.** on good terms; in favor: *He's in with his boss.* **17.** in vogue; in style: *Turbans are in this year.* **18.** in season. **19. be in for,** to be bound to undergo something, esp. a disagreeable experience: *We are in for a long speech.* **20. in for it,** *Slang.* about to suffer unpleasant consequences, esp. of one's own actions or omissions. Also, *Brit.,* **for it. 21. in with,** on friendly terms with; familiar with: *They are in with the junior executive set.* —*adj.* **22.** located or situated within; inner; internal: *the in part of a mechanism.* **23.** *Informal.* fashionable: *the in place to dine.* **24.** *Informal.* comprehensible only to a special or presumably ultrasophisticated group: *an in joke.* **25.** incoming; inbound: *to have mail for the in basket.* **26.** plentiful; available: *Summer squash is in now.* **27.** being in power, authority, control, etc.: *the in party.* —*n.* **28.** Usually, **ins.** persons in office or political power. **29.** a member of the political party in power: *The election made him an in.* **30.** pull or influence: *He's got an in with influential people.* **31.** (in tennis, squash, handball, etc.) a return or service that lands within the in-bounds limits of a court or section of a court (opposed to *out*). —*v.t. Dial.* **32.** to take in (a crop); harvest. **33.** to enclose. [ME, OE; c. G, D, Goth *in,* Icel *í,* L *in,* Gk *en*]

In, *Chem.* indium.

IN, Indiana (approved esp. for use with zip code).

in-[1], a prefix representing English *in* (*income, indwelling, inland,* etc.) but used also as a verb-formative with transitive, intensive, or sometimes little apparent force (*intrust; inweave,* etc.). It often assumes the same phases as **in-**[2], as **en-, em-, im-**[3]. [ME, OE; see IN]

in-[2], a prefix of Latin origin meaning primarily "in," but used also as a verb-formative with the same force as **in-**[1] (*incarcerate; incantation*). Also, **il-, im-, ir-.** Cf. **em-**[1], **en-**[1]. [< L, comb. form of *in* (prep.); c. IN]

in-[3], a prefix of Latin origin, corresponding to English *un-*, having a negative or privative force, freely used as an English formative, esp. of adjectives and their derivatives and of nouns (*inattention; indefensible; inexpensive; inorganic; invariable*). It assumes the same phonetic phases as **in-**[2] (*impartial; immeasurable; illiterate; irregular,* etc.). In French, it became *en-* and thus occurs unfelt in such words as *enemy* (French *ennemi,* Latin *inimicus,* lit., not friendly). Also, **il-, im-, ir-.** [< L; akin to AN-[1], A-[6], UN-[1]]
—**Syn.** The prefixes IN- and UN- may both have, among other uses, a negative force. IN- is the form derived from Latin, and is therefore used in learned words or in words derived from Latin or (rarely) Greek: *inaccessible, inaccuracy, inadequate,* etc. UN- is the native form going back to Old English, used in words of native origin, and sometimes used in combination with words of other origins if these words are in common use: *unloving, unmanly, unfeeling, unnecessary, unsafe.* Occasionally the prefix UN- is used with a frequently used word in a common meaning, as in *unsanitary* (not clean), and IN- with the same word in a more technical sense: *insanitary* (likely to cause disease). In England the prefix IN- is more commonly used than in the United States.

-in[1], a formal element, occurring in adjectives of Greek and Latin origin, meaning "pertaining to," and (in nouns thence derived) also imitated in English (*coffin; cousin,* etc.); occurring unfelt in abstract nouns formed as nouns in Latin (*ruin*). [ME *-in, -ine* < OF < L *-inus, -ina, -inum* < Gk *-inos, -inē, -inon*]

-in[2], a noun suffix used in a special manner in chemical and mineralogical nomenclature (*glycerin; acetin,* etc.). In spelling, usage wavers between *-in* and *-ine.* In chemistry a certain distinction of use is attempted, basic substances having the termination *-ine* rather than *-in* (*aconitine; aniline,* etc.), and *-in* being restricted to certain neutral compounds, glycerides, glucosides, and proteids (*albumin; palmitin,* etc.), but this distinction is not always observed. [< NL *-ina.* See -INE[2]]

-in[3], a combining form of **in** freely attached to verbs in order to create compound nouns that refer to various organized social, political, or cultural activities: *be-in; design-in; kneel-in; lecture-in; scrub-in; study-in; sweep-in.* [by analogy with SIT-IN]

in., inch; inches.

in·a·bil·i·ty (in′ə bil′i tē), *n.* lack of ability; lack of power, capacity, or means. [ME *inabilite* < ML *inhabilitās*] —**Syn.** incapability, incompetence. See **disability.**

in ab·sen·tia (in ab sen′shə, -shē ə, -tē ə), *Latin.* in absence.

in·ac·ces·si·ble (in′ək ses′ə bəl), *adj.* not accessible; inapproachable. [< LL *inaccessibil(is)*] —**in′ac·ces′si·bil′i·ty,** *n.* —**in′ac·ces′si·ble·ness,** *n.* —**in′ac·ces′si·bly,** *adv.*

in·ac·cu·ra·cy (in ak′yər ə sē), *n., pl.* **-cies** for 2. **1.** the quality or state of being inaccurate. **2.** something that is inaccurate; error. —**Syn. 1.** incorrectness, erroneousness, inexactness. **2.** mistake, blunder, slip, inexactitude.

in·ac·cu·rate (in ak′yər it), *adj.* not accurate; not exact; incorrect or untrue. —**in·ac′cu·rate·ly,** *adv.* —**in·ac′cu·rate·ness,** *n.* —**Syn.** inexact, loose; erroneous, wrong.

In·a·chus (in′ə kəs), *n. Class. Myth.* a river god, the first king of Argos and father of Io.

in·ac·tion (in ak′shən), *n.* absence of action; idleness.

in·ac·ti·vate (in ak′tə vāt′), *v.t.*, **-vat·ed, -vat·ing.** **1.** to make inactive. **2.** *Immunol.* to stop the activity of (certain biological substances). —**in·ac′ti·va′tion,** *n.*

in·ac·tive (in ak′tiv), *adj.* **1.** not active; inert. **2.** sedentary or passive. **3.** sluggish; indolent. **4.** *Mil.* not on active duty or status. **5.** *Physical Chem.* noting a compound that does not rotate the plane of vibration of polarized light. —**in·ac′tive·ly,** *adv.* —**in′ac·tiv′i·ty, in·ac′tive·ness,** *n.* —**Syn. 1.** unmoving, immobile, inoperative. **3.** lazy, idle, slothful. —**Ant. 1–3.** lively.

in·a·dapt·a·ble (in′ə dap′tə bəl), *adj.* not adaptable; incapable of being adapted. —**in′a·dapt′a·bil′i·ty,** *n.*

in·ad·e·quate (in ad′ə kwit), *adj.* not adequate; insufficient. —**in·ad′e·qua·cy, in·ad′e·quate·ness,** *n.*

—**in·ad′e·quate·ly,** *adv.* —**Syn.** incompetent; incomplete. —**Ant.** sufficient.

in·ad·mis·si·ble (in′əd mis′ə bəl), *adj.* not admissible; not allowable. —**in′ad·mis′si·bil′i·ty,** *n.* —**in′ad·mis′si·bly,** *adv.*

in·ad·vert·ence (in′əd vûr′t^{ə}ns), *n.* **1.** the quality or condition of being inadvertent; heedlessness. **2.** the act or effect of inattention; an oversight. [< ML *inadvertentia.* See INADVERTENCY]

in·ad·vert·en·cy (in′əd vûr′t^{ə}n sē), *n., pl.* **-cies.** inadvertence. [< ML *inadvertentia* = L *in-* IN-^{3} + *advert-* turn to (see ADVERT) + *-entia* -ENCY]

in·ad·vert·ent (in′əd vûr′t^{ə}nt), *adj.* **1.** not attentive. **2.** of, pertaining to, or characterized by lack of attention. **3.** unintentional. [abstracted from INADVERTENCE, INADVERTENCY] —**in′ad·vert′ent·ly,** *adv.* —**Syn. 1.** inattentive. **2.** thoughtless, careless, negligent.

in·ad·vis·a·ble (in′əd vī′zə bəl), *adj.* not advisable; unwise. —**in′ad·vis′a·bil′i·ty, in′ad·vis′a·ble·ness,** *n.* —**in′ad·vis′a·bly,** *adv.*

in ae·ter·num (in ī ter′no͝om; *Eng.* in ē tûr′nəm), *Latin.* forever.

in·al·ien·a·ble (in āl′yə nə bəl, -ā′lē ə-), *adj.* not alienable; not transferable to another or capable of being repudiated: *inalienable rights.* —**in·al′ien·a·bil′i·ty, in·al′ien·a·ble·ness,** *n.* —**in·al′ien·a·bly,** *adv.*

in·al·ter·a·ble (in ôl′tər ə bəl), *adj.* unalterable. —**in·al′ter·a·bil′i·ty, in·al′ter·a·ble·ness,** *n.* —**in·al′ter·a·bly,** *adv.*

in·am·o·ra·ta (in am′ə rä′tə, in′am-), *n., pl.* **-tas. 1.** a female lover. **2.** a woman who is loved. [< It *innamorata;* fem. of INNAMORATO]

in·am·o·ra·to (in am′ə rä′tō, in′am-), *n., pl.* **-tos. 1.** a male lover. **2.** a man who is loved. [< It *innamorato,* masc. ptp. of *innamorare* to inflame with love. See ENAMOR]

in-and-in (in′ənd in′), *adv.* repeatedly within the same family, strain, etc.: *to breed stock in-and-in.*

in·ane (i nān′), *adj.* **1.** lacking sense or ideas; silly: *inane questions.* **2.** empty; void. —*n. Rare.* **3.** something that is empty or void, as infinite space. [< L *inān(is)*] —**in·ane′ly,** *adv.* —**Syn. 1.** pointless. See **foolish.**

in·an·i·mate (in an′ə mit), *adj.* **1.** not animate; lifeless. **2.** spiritless; dull. [< LL *inanimāt(us)*] —**in·an′i·mate·ly,** *adv.* —**in·an′i·mate·ness,** *n.* —**Syn. 1.** inorganic, inert, dead. **2.** inactive, dormant, torpid.

in·a·ni·tion (in′ə nish′ən), *n.* **1.** exhaustion or depletion from lack of nourishment; starvation. **2.** lack of mental or moral vigor; emptiness: *the inanition of a decadent society.* [ME < LL *inānitiōn-* (s. of *inānitiō*). See INANE, -ITION]

in·an·i·ty (i nan′i tē), *n., pl.* **-ties** for 2. **1.** lack of sense or ideas; silliness. **2.** something inane, as a remark, opinion, etc. **3.** emptiness; lack of depth or meaning. [< L *inānitās.* See INANE, -ITY]

I·nan·na (ē nä′nä), *n.* the Sumerian goddess of love and war, who reigns over heaven: identified with the Assyrian and Babylonian Ishtar.

in·ap·peas·a·ble (in′ə pē′zə bəl), *adj.* not appeasable; not to be appeased.

in·ap·pe·tence (in ap′i təns), *n.* lack of appetite. Also, **in·ap′pe·ten·cy.** —**in·ap′pe·tent,** *adj.*

in·ap·pli·ca·ble (in ap′lə kə bəl), *adj.* not applicable; unsuitable. —**in·ap′pli·ca·bil′i·ty, in·ap′pli·ca·ble·ness,** *n.* —**in·ap′pli·ca·bly,** *adv.*

in·ap·po·site (in ap′ə zit), *adj.* not apposite; not pertinent. —**in·ap′po·site·ly,** *adv.* —**in·ap′po·site·ness,** *n.*

in·ap·pre·ci·a·ble (in′ə prē′shē ə bəl, -shə bəl), *adj.* imperceptible; insignificant: *an inappreciable difference.* —**in′ap·pre′ci·a·bly,** *adv.*

in·ap·pre·ci·a·tive (in′ə prē′shē ā′tiv, -shə tiv), *adj.* not appreciative; lacking in appreciation. —**in′ap·pre′ci·a′tive·ly,** *adv.* —**in′ap·pre′ci·a′tive·ness,** *n.*

in·ap·pre·hen·si·ble (in′ap ri hen′sə bəl), *adj.* not to be grasped by the senses or intellect. —**in′ap·pre·hen′sion,** *n.*

in·ap·pre·hen·sive (in′ap ri hen′siv), *adj.* **1.** not apprehensive (often fol. by *of*): *to be inapprehensive of danger.* **2.** without apprehension: *inapprehensive pupils.* —**in′ap·pre·hen′sive·ly,** *adv.* —**in′ap·pre·hen′sive·ness,** *n.*

in·ap·proach·a·ble (in′ə prō′chə bəl), *adj.* **1.** not approachable. **2.** without rival. —**in′ap·proach′a·bil′i·ty,** *n.* —**in′ap·proach′a·bly,** *adv.*

in·ap·pro·pri·ate (in′ə prō′prē it), *adj.* not appropriate; not proper or suitable. —**in′ap·pro′pri·ate·ly,** *adv.* —**in′ap·pro′pri·ate·ness,** *n.*

in·apt (in apt′), *adj.* **1.** not apt or fitting. **2.** without aptitude. —**in·apt′ly,** *adv.* —**in·apt′ness,** *n.* —**Syn. 1.** unsuited, unsuitable, inappropriate. **2.** incapable, clumsy. —**Ant. 1.** appropriate. **2.** capable.

in·ap·ti·tude (in ap′ti to͞od′, -tyo͞od′), *n.* **1.** lack of aptitude; unfitness. **2.** unskillfulness.

in·arch (in ärch′), *v.t. Hort.* to graft by uniting a growing branch to a stock without separating the branch from its parent stock.

in·ar·gu·a·ble (in är′gyo͞o ə bəl), *adj.* not arguable: *an inarguable fact.* —**in·ar′gu·a·bly,** *adv.*

in·ar·tic·u·late (in′är tik′yə lit), *adj.* **1.** not uttered or emitted with expressive or intelligible modulations: *He could utter only inarticulate sounds.* **2.** unable to use articulate speech: *inarticulate with rage.* **3.** lacking the ability to express oneself in clear and effective speech. **4.** *Anat., Zool.* not jointed; having no articulation or joint. [< LL *inarticulāt(us)*] —**in′ar·tic′u·late·ly,** *adv.* —**in′ar·tic′u·late·ness,** *n.*

in·ar·tis·tic (in′är tis′tik), *adj.* **1.** not artistic; unaesthetic. **2.** lacking an artistic sense or appreciation. Also, **in′ar·tis′ti·cal.** —**in′ar·tis′ti·cal·ly,** *adv.*

in·as·much′ as′ (in′əz much′), **1.** in view of the fact that; seeing that; since. **2.** insofar as; to such a degree as. [ME *in as much(e) as*] —**Syn. 1.** See **because.**

in·at·ten·tion (in′ə ten′shən), *n.* **1.** lack of attention. **2.** an act of neglect.

in·at·ten·tive (in′ə ten′tiv), *adj.* not attentive. —**in′at·ten′tive·ly,** *adv.* —**in′at·ten′tive·ness,** *n.* —**Syn.** heedless, neglectful, oblivious, unmindful.

in·au·di·ble (in ô′də bəl), *adj.* incapable of being heard. —**in·au′di·bil′i·ty, in·au′di·ble·ness,** *n.* —**in·au′di·bly,** *adv.*

in·au·gu·ral (in ô′gyər əl, -gər əl), *adj.* **1.** of or pertaining to an inauguration. **2.** marking the beginning of a new venture, series, etc. —*n.* **3.** an address, as of a president, at the beginning of a term of office. **4.** an inaugural ceremony. [obs. *inaugure* (< L *inaugur(āre)* (to) INAUGURATE) + -AL^1]

in·au·gu·rate (in ô′gyə rāt′, -gə-), *v.t.,* **-rat·ed, -rat·ing. 1.** to begin formally; initiate; commence. **2.** to induct into office with formal ceremonies; install. **3.** to introduce into public use by some formal ceremony. [< L *inaugurāt(us)* formally installed (ptp. of *inaugurāre,* lit., to take auguries). See IN-^{2}, AUGUR, -ATE^1] —**in·au′gu·ra′tion,** *n.* —**in·au′gu·ra′tor,** *n.*

Inaugura′tion Day′, the day on which the President of the United States is inaugurated, being the January 20 following his election.

in·aus·pi·cious (in′ô spish′əs), *adj.* not auspicious; boding ill; unfavorable. —**in′aus·pi′cious·ly,** *adv.* —**in′aus·pi′cious·ness,** *n.*

in·be·ing (in′bē′ing), *n.* **1.** the condition of existing in something else; inherence; immanence. **2.** inward nature. [IN (adv.) + BEING]

in-be·tween (in′bi twēn′), *n.* **1.** Also, **in′be·tween′er.** a person or thing that is between two extremes, two contrasting conditions, etc.: *yeses, noes, and in-betweens.* —*adj.* **2.** being between one thing, condition, etc., and another: *a coat for in-between weather.*

in·board (in′bōrd′, -bôrd′), *adj.* **1.** located inside a hull or aircraft. **2.** located nearer the center, as of an airplane: *the inboard end of a wing.* **3.** (of a motorboat) having the motor inboard. —*adv.* **4.** inside or toward the center of a hull or aircraft. Cf. **outboard** (def. 4). [orig. phrase *in board*]

in·born (in′bôrn′), *adj.* innate. [OE *inboren* native] —**Syn.** inbred, inherent. —**Ant.** acquired, learned.

in·bound (in′bound′), *adj.* inward bound: *inbound ships.*

in·breathe (in′brēth′, in brēth′), *v.t.,* **-breathed, -breath·ing. 1.** to breathe in; inhale. **2.** to inspire; infuse with.

in·bred (in′bred′), *adj.* **1.** innate; native. **2.** resulting from or involved in inbreeding. [ptp. of INBREED] —**Syn. 1.** inborn.

in·breed (in′brēd′, in brēd′), *v.t.,* **-bred, -breed·ing. 1.** to breed (animals) in-and-in. **2.** *Rare.* to breed within; engender. [IN-^{1} + BREED]

in·breed·ing (in′brē′ding), *n. Biol.* the mating of related individuals or self-fertilized plants, esp. in order to produce desired characteristics.

Inc., incorporated.

inc., **1.** engraved. [< L *incīsus*] **2.** inclosure. **3.** included. **4.** including. **5.** inclusive. **6.** income. **7.** incorporated. **8.** increase. **9.** incumbent.

In·ca (ing′kə), *n.* **1.** a member of any of the dominant groups of South American Indian peoples who established an empire in Peru (c. A.D. 1400) prior to the Spanish conquest. **2.** a ruler or member of the royal family in the Incan empire. [< Sp < Quechua *inka* male of the blood royal] —**In·ca·ic** (ing kā′ik, in-), *adj.* —**In′can,** *n., adj.*

in·cal·cu·la·ble (in kal′kyə lə bəl), *adj.* **1.** unable to be calculated; beyond calculation. **2.** incapable of being forecast or predicted. **3.** uncertain; unsure. —**in·cal′cu·la·bil′i·ty, in·cal′cu·la·ble·ness,** *n.* —**in·cal′cu·la·bly,** *adv.*

in·ca·les·cent (in′kə les′ənt), *adj.* increasing in heat or ardor. [< L *incalescent-* (s. of *incalescēns*) glowing, prp. of *incalescere*] —**in′ca·les′cence,** *n.*

in·can·desce (in′kən des′), *v.i., v.t.,* **-desced, -desc·ing.** to glow or cause to glow with heat. [back formation from INCANDESCENT]

in·can·des·cence (in′kən des′əns), *n.* **1.** the emission of visible light by a body, caused by its high temperature. Cf. **luminescence. 2.** the light produced by such an emission. [INCANDESC(ENT) + -ENCE]

in·can·des·cent (in′kən des′ənt), *adj.* **1.** (of light) produced by incandescence. **2.** glowing or white with heat. **3.** intensely bright; brilliant. **4.** brilliant; extraordinarily lucid: *incandescent wit.* **5.** aglow with ardor, purpose, etc. [< L *incandescent-* (s. of *incandescēns*), prp. of *incandescere* to glow. See IN-^{2}, CANDESCENT] —**in′can·des′cent·ly,** *adv.*

in′candes′cent lamp′, a lamp, as the electric light bulb, that emits light due to the glowing of a heated material, as a filament.

in·can·ta·tion (in′kan tā′shən), *n.* **1.** the chanting or uttering of words purporting to have magical power. **2.** the formula employed; a spell or charm. **3.** magical ceremonies. **4.** magic; sorcery. **5.** repetitious wordiness; obfuscation. [ME < LL *incantātiōn-* (s. of *incantātiō*) = *incantāt(us)* enchanted (ptp. of *incantāre;* see ENCHANT, -ATE^1) + *-iōn-* -ION] —**in′can·ta′tion·al,** *adj.* —**in·can·ta·to·ry** (in kan′tə tōr′ē, -tôr′ē), *adj.*

in·ca·pa·ble (in kā′pə bəl), *adj.* **1.** not capable. **2.** not having a necessary capacity or power of performance. **3.** without ordinary capability or ability; incompetent. **4. incapable of, a.** not having the capacity or power for (a specified act or function). **b.** not susceptible or admitting to: *These materials are incapable of exact measurement.* **c.** legally unqualified for. —*n.* **5.** a thoroughly incompetent person, esp. one of defective mentality. [< ML *incapābil(is)*] —**in·ca′pa·bil′i·ty,** *n.* —**in·ca′pa·bly,** *adv.*

—**Syn. 1.** INCAPABLE, INCOMPETENT, INEFFICIENT are applied to a person or thing that is lacking in ability, preparation, or power for whatever is to be done. INCAPABLE usually means inherently lacking in ability or power: *incapable of appreciating music; a bridge incapable of carrying heavy loads.* INCOMPETENT, generally used only of persons, means unfit or unqualified for a particular task: *incompetent as an administrator.* INEFFICIENT means wasteful in the use of effort or power: *an inefficient manager; inefficient methods.* **2.** impotent. —**Ant. 1.** able.

in·ca·pac·i·tate (in′kə pas′i tāt′), *v.t.,* **-tat·ed, -tat·ing. 1.** to deprive of capacity; make incapable or unfit; disqualify. **2.** *Law.* to deprive of the legal power to act in a specified way or ways. —**in′ca·pac′i·ta′tion,** *n.*

in·ca·pac·i·ty (in′kə pas′i tē), *n.* **1.** lack of capacity; incapability. **2.** lack of the legal power to act in a specified way or ways. [< ML *incapācitās*]

in·car·cer·ate (*v.* in kär′sə rāt′; *adj.* in kär′sər it, -sə-rāt′), *v.*, **-at·ed, -at·ing,** *adj.* —*v.t.* **1.** to imprison; confine. **2.** to enclose; constrict closely. —*adj.* **3.** imprisoned. [< ML *incarcerāt(us)* imprisoned (ptp. of *incarcerāre*) = *in-* IN-[2] + *carcer* prison + *-ātus* -ATE[1]] —**in·car′cer·a′tion,** *n.*

in·car·na·dine (in kär′nə dīn′, -din, -dēn′), *adj., n., v.,* **-dined, -din·ing.** —*adj.* **1.** flesh-colored; pale pink. **2.** blood-red; crimson. —*n.* **3.** an incarnadine color. —*v.t.* **4.** to make incarnadine. [< MF, fem. of *incarnadin* flesh-colored < It *incarnatino*. See INCARNATE, -INE[1], CARNATION]

in·car·nate (*adj.* in kär′nit, -nāt; *v.* in kär′nāt), *adj., v.,* **-nat·ed, -nat·ing.** —*adj.* **1.** invested with a bodily, esp. a human, form: *a devil incarnate.* **2.** personified or typified, as a quality or idea: *chivalry incarnate.* **3.** flesh-colored or crimson. —*v.t.* **4.** to put into or represent in a concrete form, as an idea. **5.** to be the embodiment or type of. **6.** to invest with a bodily, esp. a human, form. [late ME *incarnat* < LL *incarnāt(us)* made flesh (ptp. of *incarnāre*). See IN-[2], CARNAL, -ATE[1]]

in·car·na·tion (in′kär nā′shən), *n.* **1.** an incarnate being or form. **2.** a being embodying a deity or spirit. **3.** assumption of human form or nature. **4. the Incarnation,** (*sometimes l.c.*) *Theol.* the doctrine that the second person of the Trinity assumed human form in the person of Jesus Christ and is completely both God and man. **5.** a person or thing regarded as embodying some quality, idea, or the like. **6.** the act of incarnating. **7.** the state of being incarnated. [ME *incarnacion* < eccl. L *incarnātiōn-* (s. of *incarnātiō*)]

in·case (in kās′), *v.t.,* **-cased, -cas·ing.** encase. —**in·case′ment,** *n.*

in·cau·tion (in kô′shən), *n.* lack of caution; heedlessness; carelessness.

in·cau·tious (in kô′shəs), *adj.* not cautious; careless; heedless. [IN-[3] + CAUTIOUS; cf. L *incautus* unwary] —**in·cau′tious·ly,** *adv.* —**in·cau′tious·ness,** *n.*

in·cen·di·a·rism (in sen′dē ə riz′əm), *n.* **1.** the act or practice of an arsonist; malicious burning. **2.** inflammatory behavior; agitation.

in·cen·di·ar·y (in sen′dē er′ē), *adj., n., pl.* **-ar·ies.** —*adj.* **1.** of, pertaining to, or using bombs, shells, etc., that ignite upon bursting. **2.** of or pertaining to the criminal burning of property. **3.** tending to arouse strife, sedition, etc.; inflammatory. **4.** tending to inflame the senses —*n.* **5.** a person who maliciously sets fire to buildings or other property. **6.** *Mil.* a shell, bomb, etc., containing a substance that burns with an intense heat. **7.** a person who stirs up strife; an agitator. [< L *incendiāri(us)* = *incendi(um)* a fire (< *incendere* to kindle) + *-ārius* -ARY]

in·cense[1] (in′sens), *n., v.,* **-censed, -cens·ing.** —*n.* **1.** an aromatic gum or other substance producing a sweet odor when burned. **2.** the perfume or smoke of such a substance. **3.** any pleasant perfume or fragrance. **4.** homage or adulation. —*v.t.* **5.** to perfume with incense. **6.** to burn incense for. —*v.i.* **7.** to burn or offer incense. [ME < eccl. L *incens(um)*, lit., something kindled, neut. of *incensus* (ptp. of *incendere* to set on fire) = *in-* IN-[2] + *cend-* (var. of *cand-;* see CANDENT) + *-tus* ptp. suffix; r. ME *ansens, ensenz* < OF]

in·cense[2] (in sens′), *v.t.,* **-censed, -cens·ing.** to inflame with wrath; make angry; enrage. [late ME < L *incens(us)* kindled, fired (see INCENSE[1]); r. ME *encensen* < AF < L, as above] —**in·cense′ment,** *n.* —**Syn.** anger, provoke.

in·cen·tive (in sen′tiv), *n.* **1.** something that incites to action. —*adj.* **2.** inciting, as to action; stimulating; provocative. [ME < LL *incentīv(us)* provocative, L: setting the tune = *incent(us)* (unrecorded ptp. of *incinere* to sing) + *-īvus* -IVE] —**in·cen′tive·ly,** *adv.* —**Syn. 1.** stimulus, spur, incitement, encouragement. See **motive.**

in·cept (in sept′), *v.i.* **1.** *Brit.* to complete the taking of a master's or doctor's degree in a university, esp. Cambridge. —*v.t.* **2.** to take in; intussuscept. [< L *incept(us)* begun, undertaken (ptp. of *incipere*) = *in-* IN-[2] + *cep-* (var. of *cap-* take; see CAPTIVE) + *-tus* ptp. suffix] —**in·cep′tor,** *n.*

in·cep·tion (in sep′shən), *n.* **1.** beginning; start. **2.** *Brit.* **a.** the act of earning a university degree, usually a master's or doctor's degree, esp. at Cambridge University. **b.** the graduation ceremony; commencement. [late ME < L *inceptiōn-* (s. of *inceptiō*)] —**Syn. 1.** origin, outset.

in·cep·tive (in sep′tiv), *adj.* **1.** *Gram.* (of a derived verb, or of an aspect in verb inflection) expressing the beginning of the action indicated by the basic verb, as Latin verbs in *-sco,* which generally have inceptive force, as *calescō* "become or begin to be hot" from *caleō* "be hot." **2.** beginning; initial. —*n. Gram.* **3.** the inceptive aspect. **4.** a verb in this aspect. [< LL *inceptīv(us)*] —**in·cep′tive·ly,** *adv.* —**Syn. 1.** inchoative.

in·cer·ti·tude (in sûr′ti to͞od′, -tyo͞od′), *n.* **1.** uncertainty; doubtfulness. **2.** insecurity. [< LL *incertitūd(ō)*]

in·ces·sant (in ses′ənt), *adj.* continuing without interruption: *an incessant noise.* [late ME < LL *incessant-* = L *in-* IN-[3] + *cessant-* (s. of *cessāns*), prp. of *cessāre* to stop work; see CEASE, -ANT] —**in·ces′sant·ly,** *adv.* —**Syn.** ceaseless, unceasing, constant, continual.

in·cest (in′sest), *n.* sexual intercourse, cohabitation, or marriage between persons so closely related that marriage is legally or ritually forbidden. [ME < L *incest(us)* = *incest-* (s. of *incestus* impure; see IN-[3], CHASTE) + *-us* n. suffix (4th decl.)]

in·ces·tu·ous (in ses′cho͞o əs), *adj.* **1.** involving incest. **2.** guilty of incest. [< LL *incestuōs(us)*] —**in·ces′tu·ous·ly,** *adv.* —**in·ces′tu·ous·ness,** *n.*

inch[1] (inch), *n.* **1.** a unit of length, 1/12 foot, equivalent to 2.54 centimeters. **2.** a very small amount, distance, or degree: *He wouldn't budge an inch.* **3. by inches, a.** Also, **by an inch.** narrowly; by a narrow margin: *escaped by inches.* **b.** Also, **inch by inch.** by small degrees or stages; gradually. **4. every inch,** in every respect; completely. **5. within an inch of,** nearly; close to. —*v.t., v.i.* **6.** to move by inches or small degrees. [ME; OE *ynce* < L *uncia* twelfth part, inch, ounce. See OUNCE[1]]

inch[2] (inch), *n. Scot.* an island, esp. a small island near the seacoast. [ME < Gael *innse,* gen. of *innis* island]

inch·meal (inch′mēl′), *adv.* by inches; inch by inch; little by little. [INCH[1] + -MEAL]

in·cho·ate (in kō′it), *adj.* **1.** just begun; incipient. **2.** rudimentary; imperfect; incomplete. **3.** not organized. [< L *inchoāt(us),* var. of *incohātus* begun (ptp. of *incohāre*) = *in-* IN-[2] + *coh(um)* yokestrap + *-ātus* -ATE[1]] —**in·cho′ate·ly,** *adv.* —**in·cho′ate·ness,** *n.*

in·cho·a·tion (in′kō ā′shən), *n.* a beginning; origin. [< LL *inchoātiōn-* (s. of *inchoātiō*)]

in·cho·a·tive (in kō′ə tiv), *adj.* **1.** *Gram.* inceptive. **2.** *Archaic.* inchoate. —*n.* **3.** *Gram.* an inceptive. [< LL *inchoātīv(um)* (*verbum*) inceptive (verb)]

In·chon (in′chon′), *n.,* a seaport in W South Korea. 401,473 (1960). Also called **Chemulpo.** Japanese, **Jinsen.**

inch-pound (inch′pound′), *n.* one-twelfth of a foot-pound. *Abbr.:* in-lb

inch·worm (inch′wûrm′), *n.* measuringworm.

in·ci·dence (in′si dəns), *n.* **1.** the rate or range of occurrence or influence of something, esp. of something unwanted. **2.** a falling upon or befalling; occurrence. **3.** *Optics, Physics.* **a.** the striking of a ray of light, beam of electrons, etc., on a surface, or the direction of striking. **b.** See **angle of incidence** (def. 1). **4.** the fact or the manner of being incident. **5.** *Geom.* partial coincidence of two figures, as of a line and a plane containing it. [ME < LL *incidentia.* See INCIDENT, -ENCE]

in·ci·dent (in′si dənt), *n.* **1.** an occurrence or event. **2.** a distinct piece of action, or an episode, as in a story or play. **3.** something that occurs casually in connection with something else. **4.** something appertaining or attaching to something else. **5.** an occurrence of seemingly minor importance, esp. involving nations or factions, that can lead to serious consequences: *border incident.* **6.** an embarrassing occurrence, esp. of a social nature. —*adj.* **7.** likely or apt to happen. **8.** naturally appertaining. **9.** conjoined or attaching, esp. as subordinate to something; incidental. **10.** falling or striking on something, as light rays. [ME < ML *incident-* (s. of *incidēns* a happening, n. use of prp. of L *incidere* to befall) = L *in-* IN-[2] + *-cid-* (var. of *cad-* fall) + *-ent* -ENT] —**Syn. 1.** See **event.**

in·ci·den·tal (in′si den′tᵊl), *adj.* **1.** happening or likely to happen in fortuitous or subordinate conjunction with something else. **2.** likely to happen or naturally appertaining. **3.** incurred casually and in addition to the regular amount. —*n.* **4.** something incidental, as a circumstance. **5. incidentals,** minor expenses. —**in′ci·den′tal·ness,** *n.* —**Syn. 1.** casual, chance. —**Ant. 1.** fundamental.

in·ci·den·tal·ly (in′si den′tᵊlē), *adv.* **1.** in an incidental manner. **2.** apart or aside from the main subject of attention, discussion, etc.; by the way.

in·cin·er·ate (in sin′ə rāt′), *v.t.,* **-at·ed, -at·ing.** to burn or reduce to ashes. [< ML *incinerāt(us)* (ptp. of *incinerāre*). See IN-[2], CINERARIA, -ATE[1]] —**in·cin′er·a′tion,** *n.*

in·cin·er·a·tor (in sin′ə rā′tər), *n.* a furnace or apparatus for incinerating, as one for burning refuse.

in·cip·i·ent (in sip′ē ənt), *adj.* beginning to exist or appear; initial. [< L *incipient-* (s. of *incipiēns,* prp. of *incipere* to take in hand, begin) = *in-* IN-[2] + *-cipi-* (var. of *capi-* take) + *-ent-* -ENT] —**in·cip′i·ence, in·cip′i·en·cy,** *n.* —**in·cip′i·ent·ly,** *adv.*

in·ci·pit (in′si pit, in kip′it; *Lat.* ing′ki pit), *n.* the introductory words or opening phrase of a text, or the opening notes or phrase of a musical composition. [< L: (here) begins, 3rd sing. pres. indic. of *incipere*]

in·cise (in sīz′), *v.t.,* **-cised, -cis·ing. 1.** to cut into; cut marks, figures, etc., upon. **2.** to make (marks, figures, etc.) by cutting; engrave; carve. [< L *incīs(us)* carved, cut into (ptp. of *incīdere*) = *in-* IN-[2] + *cīd-* cut + *-tus* ptp. suffix]

in·cised (in sīzd′), *adj.* **1.** cut into: *the incised gums.* **2.** made by cutting: *an incised pattern.* **3.** *Med.* (of a wound) made or cut cleanly. **4.** (of a leaf) sharply, deeply, and somewhat irregularly notched.

in·ci·sion (in sizh′ən), *n.* **1.** a cut, gash, or notch. **2.** the act of incising. **3.** a cutting into, esp. for surgical purposes. **4.** incisiveness; keenness. [ME < L *incīsiōn-* (s. of *incīsiō*)]

in·ci·sive (in sī′siv), *adj.* **1.** penetrating; cutting: *an incisive edge; an incisive tone of voice.* **2.** sharp; keen; acute: *an incisive wit.* **3.** of or pertaining to the incisors: *the incisive teeth.* [< ML *incīsīv(us)*] —**in·ci′sive·ly,** *adv.* —**in·ci′sive·ness,** *n.* —**Syn. 2.** acid; sardonic.

in·ci·sor (in sī′zər), *n. Dentistry.* one of the four anterior teeth in each jaw, used for cutting. [< NL: lit., cutter]

in·ci·so·ry (in sī′zə rē), *adj.* adapted for cutting, as the incisor teeth.

in·cite (in sīt′), *v.t.,* **-cit·ed, -cit·ing.** to urge on; stimulate or prompt to action. [late ME < L *incitāre*] —**in·ci·ta·tion** (in′sī tā′shən, -si-), *n.* —**in·cit′er,** *n.* —**Syn.** encourage; instigate, provoke, goad, spur, arouse, exhort; fire; induce. —**Ant.** discourage.

in·cite·ment (in sīt′mənt), *n.* **1.** the act of inciting. **2.** the state of being incited. **3.** something that incites; motive; incentive. [< L *incitāment(um)*]

in·ci·vil·i·ty (in′sə vil′i tē), *n., pl.* **-ties** for 2. **1.** the quality or condition of being uncivil; uncivil behavior or treatment. **2.** an uncivil act. [< LL *incīvīlitās*] —**in·civ·il** (in siv′əl), *adj.*

incl., **1.** inclosure. **2.** including. **3.** inclusive.

in·clem·ent (in klem′ənt), *adj.* **1.** (of the weather, the elements, etc.) severe or harsh; stormy. **2.** not kind or merciful. [< L *inclēment-* (s. of *inclēmens*)] —**in·clem′en·cy, in·clem′ent·ness,** *n.* —**in·clem′ent·ly,** *adv.*

in·clin·a·ble (in klī′nə bəl), *adj.* **1.** having a certain mental bent or tendency; inclined. **2.** favorable: *to be inclinable to a plea.* **3.** capable of being inclined.

in·cli·na·tion (in′klə nā′shən), *n.* **1.** a set or bent, esp. of the mind or will; a liking or preference. **2.** something to which a person is inclined. **3.** the act of inclining. **4.** the state of being inclined. **5.** a tendency toward a certain condition, action, etc.: *the door's inclination to stick.* **6.** deviation or amount of deviation from the horizontal or vertical. **7.** an inclined surface. **8.** *Math.* **a.** the angle between two lines or two planes. **b.** the angle formed by the x-axis and a given line. **9.** *Astron.* **a.** the angle between the orbital plane of a planet and another given plane, usually the ecliptic. **b.** the angle between the equatorial and orbital planes of a planet. [late ME < L *inclīnātiōn-* (s. of *inclīnātiō*) = *inclīnāt(us)* ptp. (see INCLINE, -ATE[1]) + *-iōn-* -ION] —**in′cli·na′tion·al,** *adj.* —**Syn. 1.** tendency; propensity, proclivity, predilection, penchant. **6, 7.** slope, slant, grade.

in·cline (*v.* in klīn′; *n.* in′klīn, in klīn′), *v.*, **-clined, -clin·ing,** *n.* —*v.i.* **1.** to have a mental tendency, preference, etc.; be disposed. **2.** to deviate from the vertical or horizontal; slant. **3.** to tend in a physical quality or degree. **4.** to tend in character or in course of action. **5.** to lean; bend. —*v.t.* **6.** to dispose (a person) in mind, habit, etc. (usually fol. by *to*): *His attitude did not incline me to help him.* **7.** to bow or bend (the head, body, etc.). **8.** to cause to lean or bend in a particular direction. —*n.* **9.** an inclined surface; a slope. **10.** *Railroads.* **a.** Also called **inclined plane, in′cline plane′.** a cable railway the gradient of which is approximately 45°. **b.** any railway or portion of a railway the gradient of which is too steep for ordinary locomotive adhesion alone to be effective. [late ME < L *inclīn(āre)* = *in-* IN-[2] + *clīnāre* to bend (see LEAN[1]); r. ME *enclyne(n)* < MF] —**in·clin′er,** *n.* —**Syn. 1.** tend, lean. **2.** lean, slope, rise, fall, pitch. **3, 4.** verge, veer.

in·clined (in klīnd′), *adj.* **1.** disposed; of a mind (usually fol. by *to*): *He was inclined to stay.* **2.** having a physical tendency; leaning. **3.** deviating in direction from the horizontal or vertical; sloping. **4.** in a direction making an angle with anything else. [ME *enclyned*]

inclined′ plane′, **1.** a plane surface forming an acute angle with a horizontal plane. **2.** incline (def. 10a).

in·clin·ing (in klī′niṅg), *n.* **1.** inclination; disposition. **2.** *Archaic.* a following or party. [ME *enclinynge*]

in·cli·nom·e·ter (in′klə nom′i tər), *n.* **1.** *Aeron.* an instrument for measuring the angle an aircraft makes with the horizontal. **2.** an instrument for determining the inclination or dip of the earth's magnetic force.

in·close (in klōz′), *v.t.*, **-closed, -clos·ing.** enclose. —**in·clos′er,** *n.*

in·clo·sure (in klō′zhər), *n.* enclosure.

in·clude (in klo͞od′), *v.t.*, **-clud·ed, -clud·ing. 1.** to contain, as a whole does parts or any part or element: *to include impurities.* **2.** to place in an aggregate, class, category, or the like. **3.** to contain as a subordinate element; involve as a factor. **4.** to take in or consider as a part or member of: *That item is included in the bill. He was included in the party.* [ME < L *inclūde(re)* (to) shut in = *in-* IN-[2] + *-clūdere,* var. of *claudere* to shut] —**in·clud′a·ble, in·clud′i·ble,** *adj.* —**Syn. 1.** embody. INCLUDE, COMPREHEND, COMPRISE, EMBRACE imply containing parts of a whole. To INCLUDE is to contain as a part or member, or among the parts and members, of a whole: *The list includes many new names.* To COMPREHEND is to have within the limits, scope, or range of references, as either a part or the whole number of items: *The plan comprehends several projects.* To COMPRISE is to consist of, as the various parts serving to make up the whole: *This genus comprises 50 species.* EMBRACE emphasizes the extent or assortment of that which is comprised: *The report embraces a great variety of subjects.* —**Ant. 1.** exclude, preclude.

in·clud·ed (in klo͞o′did), *adj.* **1.** contained in; embraced by; covered by. **2.** *Bot.* not projecting beyond the mouth of the corolla, as stamens or a style. **3.** *Archaic.* enclosed. —**in·clud′ed·ness,** *n.*

in·clu·sion (in klo͞o′zhən), *n.* **1.** the act of including. **2.** the state of being included. **3.** something that is included. **4.** *Biol.* a body suspended in the cytoplasm, as a granule. **5.** *Mineral.* a solid body or a body of gas or liquid enclosed within the mass of a mineral. **6.** *Logic, Math.* the relationship between sets when all the members of one are also members of another. [< L *inclūsiōn-* (s. of *inclūsiō*) a shutting in = *inclūs(us)* confined (ptp. of *inclūdere;* see INCLUDE) + *-iōn-* -ION]

inclu′sion bod′y, *Pathol.* a particle that takes a characteristic stain, found in a virus-infected cell.

in·clu·sive (in klo͞o′siv), *adj.* **1.** including the stated limit or extremes: *from six to ten inclusive.* **2.** including a great deal or everything concerned; comprehensive: *an inclusive fee.* **3. inclusive of,** including; embracing: *Europe, inclusive of the British Isles.* [< ML *inclusīv(us)*] —**in·clu′sive·ly,** *adv.* —**in·clu′sive·ness,** *n.*

in·co·er·ci·ble (in′kō ûr′sə bəl), *adj.* **1.** not coercible. **2.** *Physics.* (of a gas) incapable of being reduced to a liquid form by pressure.

in·cog·i·tant (in koj′i tᵊnt), *adj.* **1.** thoughtless; inconsiderate. **2.** not having the faculty of thought. [< L *incōgitant-* = *in-* IN-[3] + *cōgitant-* (s. of *cōgitāns*), prp. of *cōgitāre* to think; see COGITATE, -ANT]

in·cog·ni·to (in kog′ni tō′, in′kog nē′-), *adj., adv., n., pl.* **-tos** for 3, 5. —*adj.* **1.** having one's identity concealed, as under an assumed name, esp. to avoid notice. —*adv.* **2.** with the real identity concealed: *to travel incognito.* —*n.* **3.** a person who is incognito. **4.** the state of being incognito. **5.** the disguise or character assumed by an incognito. Also, *referring to a woman,* **in·cog·ni·ta** (in kog′ni tə, in′kog nē′-). [< It < L *incognitus* unknown = *in-* IN-[3] + *cognitus* known; see COGNITION]

in·cog·ni·zant (in kog′ni zənt), *adj.* not cognizant; without knowledge; unaware (usually fol. by *of*). —**in·cog′ni·zance,** *n.*

in·co·her·ence (in′kō hēr′əns), *n.* **1.** the quality or state of being incoherent. **2.** something incoherent, as a statement or article.

in·co·her·en·cy (in′kō hēr′ən sē), *n., pl.* **-cies.** incoherence.

in·co·her·ent (in′kō hēr′ənt), *adj.* **1.** without logical connection; disjointed; rambling. **2.** characterized by such thought or language, as a person. **3.** without physical cohesion; loose: *incoherent dust.* **4.** without unity or harmony of elements or parts. **5.** different or incompatible by nature, as things. —**in′co·her′ent·ly,** *adv.*

in·com·bus·ti·ble (in′kəm bus′tə bəl), *adj.* **1.** not combustible; incapable of being burned. —*n.* **2.** an incombustible substance. [late ME < ML *incombustibil(is)*] —**in′com·bus′ti·bil′i·ty, in′com·bus′ti·ble·ness,** *n.* —**in′com·bus′ti·bly,** *adv.*

in·come (in′kum), *n.* **1.** the monetary or equivalent returns that come in periodically, esp. annually, from property, business, labor, etc.; revenue; receipts. **2.** something that comes in as an addition, esp. by chance. **3.** *Archaic.* a coming in. [ME: lit., that which has come in, n. use of *incomen* (ptp. of *income* to come in), OE *incumen*] —**Syn. 1.** earnings, salary, wages, annuity, interest. —**Ant. 1.** outgo, expenditure.

in′come account′, **1.** an account maintained for a particular item of revenue or income. **2.** Also called **profit and loss account.** a summary account for income and expenditures, used in closing the general ledger at the end of the year.

in·com·er (in′kum′ər), *n.* **1.** a person who comes in. **2.** *Chiefly Brit.* an immigrant. **3.** an intruder. **4.** a successor.

in′come tax′, a tax levied on individual and corporate incomes.

in·com·ing (in′kum′iṅg), *adj.* **1.** coming in: *the incoming tide.* **2.** succeeding, as an officeholder: *the incoming mayor.* **3.** accruing, as profit. **4.** entering, beginning, etc. —*n.* **5.** the act of coming in; arrival; advent. **6.** Usually, **incomings.** funds received; revenue. [ME (n.). See IN, COMING]

in·com·men·su·ra·ble (in′kə men′shər ə bəl, -sər ə-), *adj.* **1.** not commensurable; having no common measure or standard of comparison. **2.** utterly disproportionate. **3.** *Math.* (of two or more quantities) having no common measure. —*n.* **4.** something that is incommensurable. **5.** *Math.* one of two or more incommensurable quantities. [< LL *incommensūrābil(is)*] —**in′com·men′su·ra·bil′i·ty, in′com·men′su·ra·ble·ness,** *n.* —**in′com·men′su·ra·bly,** *adv.*

in·com·men·su·rate (in′kə men′shər it, -sər it), *adj.* **1.** disproportionate; inadequate. **2.** incommensurable. —**in′com·men′su·rate·ly,** *adv.* —**in′com·men′su·rate·ness,** *n.*

in·com·mode (in′kə mōd′), *v.t.*, **-mod·ed, -mod·ing. 1.** to inconvenience or discomfort; discommode. **2.** to impede; hinder. [< L *incommod(āre)* < *incommod(us)* inconvenient. See IN-[3], COMMODE] —**Syn. 1.** disturb, trouble. **2.** delay, obstruct. —**Ant. 1.** help. **2.** expedite.

in·com·mo·di·ous (in′ kə mō′dē əs), *adj.* inconvenient, as not affording sufficient space or room; uncomfortable. —**in′com·mo′di·ous·ly,** *adv.* —**in′com·mo′di·ous·ness,** *n.*

in·com·mod·i·ty (in′kə mod′i tē), *n., pl.* **-ties** for 1. **1.** something inconvenient; a disadvantage or inconvenience. **2.** *Obs.* the quality or state of being inconvenient. [ME < L *incommoditās*]

in·com·mu·ni·ca·ble (in′kə myo͞o′nə kə bəl), *adj.* **1.** that cannot be communicated or shared. **2.** incommunicative. [< LL *incommūnicābil(is)*] —**in′com·mu′ni·ca·bil′i·ty, in′com·mu′ni·ca·ble·ness,** *n.* —**in′com·mu′ni·ca·bly,** *adv.*

in·com·mu·ni·ca·do (in′kə myo͞o′nə kä′dō), *adj.* (esp. of a prisoner) deprived of communication with others. [< Sp *incomunicado.* See IN-[3], COMMUNICATE]

in·com·mu·ni·ca·tive (in′kə myo͞o′nə kā′tiv, -kə tiv), *adj.* not communicative; reserved; uncommunicative. —**in′com·mu′ni·ca′tive·ly,** *adv.* —**in′com·mu′ni·ca′tive·ness,** *n.*

in·com·mut·a·ble (in′kə myo͞o′tə bəl), *adj.* **1.** not exchangeable. **2.** unchangeable; unalterable. [< L *incommūtābil(is)*] —**in′com·mut′a·bil′i·ty, in′com·mut′a·ble·ness,** *n.* —**in′com·mut′a·bly,** *adv.*

in·com·pact (in′kəm pakt′), *adj.* not compact; loose. —**in′com·pact′ly,** *adv.* —**in′com·pact′ness,** *n.*

in·com·pa·ra·ble (in kom′pər ə bəl, -prə bəl), *adj.* **1.** matchless or unequaled: *incomparable beauty.* **2.** not validly comparable, as two or more unlike objects; incommensurable. [ME < L *incomparābil(is)*] —**in·com′pa·ra·bil′i·ty, in·com′pa·ra·ble·ness,** *n.* —**in·com′pa·ra·bly,** *adv.*

in·com·pat·i·ble (in′kəm pat′ə bəl), *adj.* **1.** not compatible; incapable of existing together in harmony: *two persons who were utterly incompatible.* **2.** contrary or opposed in character; discordant: *incompatible colors.* **3.** that cannot coexist or be conjoined. **4.** *Logic.* (of two or more propositions) unable to be true simultaneously. **5.** (of positions, ranks, etc.) unable to be held simultaneously by one person. **6.** *Med.* of or pertaining to biological substances that interfere with one another physiologically. **7.** *Pharm., Med.* of or pertaining to drugs that interfere with one another chemically. —*n.* **8.** Usually, **incompatibles.** incompatible persons, things, etc. [< ML *incompatibil(is)*] —**in′com·pat′i·bil′i·ty, in′com·pat′i·ble·ness,** *n.* —**in′com·pat′i·bly,** *adv.* —**Syn. 1.** unsuitable, unsuited. See **inconsistent. 1, 2.** unharmonious. **2.** contradictory.

in·com·pe·tence (in kom′pi təns), *n.* **1.** the quality or condition of being incompetent; lack of ability. **2.** *Law.* lack of ability or legal qualification to perform a specified act or acts or to be held legally responsible for such action. Also, **in·com′pe·ten·cy.** [var. (with -ENCE for -ENCY) of earlier *incompetency*]

in·com·pe·tent (in kom′pi tənt), *adj.* **1.** not competent; lacking qualification or ability. **2.** characterized by or showing incompetence. **3.** *Law.* not legally qualified. —*n.* **4.** an incompetent person. **5.** *Law.* **a.** being unable or legally unqualified to perform a specified act or acts or to be held legally responsible for such action. **b.** inadmissible, as evidence. [< LL *incompetent-* (s. of *incompetēns*) unequal to] —**in·com′pe·tent·ly,** *adv.* —**Syn. 1.** unqualified, inadequate, unfit. See **incapable.** —**Ant. 1.** able, qualified.

in·com·plete (in′kəm plēt′), *adj.* **1.** not complete; lacking some part. **2.** *Football.* (of a forward pass) not having been completed; not caught by a receiver. [ME < LL *incomplēt(us)*] —**in′com·plete′ly,** *adv.* —**in′com·ple′tion, in′com·plete′ness,** *n.*

in·com·pli·ant (in′kəm plī′ənt), *adj.* **1.** not compliant; unyielding. **2.** not pliant. —**in′com·pli′ance, in′com·pli′an·cy,** *n.* —**in′com·pli′ant·ly,** *adv.*

in·com·pre·hen·si·ble (in′kom pri hen′sə bəl, in kom′-), *adj.* **1.** not comprehensible or intelligible; unable to be understood. **2.** *Archaic.* limitless. [ME < L *incomprehensibil(is)*] —**in′com·pre·hen′si·bil′i·ty, in′com·pre·hen′si·ble·ness,** *n.* —**in′com·pre·hen′si·bly,** *adv.*

in·com·pre·hen·sive (in′kom pri hen′siv, in kom′-), *adj.* **1.** not comprehensive. **2.** not comprehending readily. —**in′com·pre·hen′sive·ly,** *adv.* —**in′com·pre·hen′sive·ness,** *n.*

in·com·press·i·ble (in′kəm pres′ə bəl), *adj.* not compressible. —**in′com·press′i·bil′i·ty,** *n.* —**in′com·press′i·bly,** *adv.*

in·com·put·a·ble (in′kəm pyo͞o′tə bəl), *adj.* incapable of being computed; incalculable. —**in′com·put′a·bly,** *adv.*

in·con·ceiv·a·ble (in′kən sē′və bəl), *adj.* not conceivable; unimaginable; unthinkable; incredible: *inconceivable brutality; inconceivable splendor.* —**in′con·ceiv′a·bil′i·ty, in′con·ceiv′a·ble·ness,** *n.* —**in′con·ceiv′a·bly,** *adv.*

in·con·clu·sive (in′kən klo͞o′siv), *adj.* **1.** not conclusive; indefinite; not resolving fully all doubts or questions. **2.** without final results. —**in′con·clu′sive·ly,** *adv.* —**in′con·clu′sive·ness,** *n.*

in·con·den·sa·ble (in′kən den′sə bəl), *adj.* not condensable; incapable of being condensed. Also, **in′con·den′si·ble.** —**in′con·den′sa·bil′i·ty, in′con·den′si·bil′i·ty,** *n.*

in·con·dite (in kon′dit, -dīt), *adj.* **1.** ill-constructed; unpolished: *incondite prose.* **2.** crude; rough; unmannerly. [< L *incondit(us)* disordered = *in-* IN-[3] + *conditus* built, composed, ptp. of *condere* (*con-* CON- + *-di-* put, set + *-tus* ptp. suffix)]

in·con·form·i·ty (in′kən fôr′mi tē), *n.* lack of conformity; failure or refusal to conform; nonconformity.

in·con·gru·ent (in kong′gro͞o ənt), *adj.* not congruent; incongruous. [< L *incongruent-* (s. of *incongruēns*) inconsistent] —**in·con′gru·ence,** *n.* —**in·con′gru·ent·ly,** *adv.*

in·con·gru·i·ty (in′kong gro͞o′i tē), *n., pl.* **-ties** for 2. **1.** the quality or condition of being incongruous. **2.** something incongruous. [< LL *incongruitās*]

in·con·gru·ous (in kong′gro͞o əs), *adj.* **1.** out of keeping or place; inappropriate; unbecoming. **2.** not harmonious in character; inconsonant; lacking harmony of parts. **3.** inconsistent. [< L *incongruus* inconsistent] —**in·con′gru·ous·ly,** *adv.* —**in·con′gru·ous·ness,** *n.* —**Syn. 1.** discrepant, unsuitable, ridiculous. **2.** inharmonious, discordant. **3.** contradictory. See **inconsistent.** —**Ant. 1.** appropriate. **2.** consonant. **3.** consistent.

in·con·sec·u·tive (in′kən sek′yə tiv), *adj.* not consecutive. —**in′con·sec′u·tive·ly,** *adj.* —**in′con·sec′u·tive·ness,** *n.*

in·con·se·quent (in kon′sə kwent′), *adj.* **1.** characterized by lack of proper sequence in thought, speech, or action. **2.** not following from the premises. **3.** characterized by lack of logical sequence; illogical; inconsecutive. **4.** irrelevant. **5.** not in keeping with the general character or design; inconsistent. **6.** without consequence; trivial. [< LL *inconsequent-* (s. of *inconsequēns*) not following] —**in·con′se·quence′, in·con′se·quent′ness,** *n.* —**in·con′se·quent′ly,** *adv.*

in·con·se·quen·ti·a (in′kon sə kwen′shē ə, in kon′-), *n. pl.* inconsequential details; trivia. [< LL, neut. pl. of *inconsequēns*]

in·con·se·quen·tial (in′kon sə kwen′shəl, in kon′-), *adj.* **1.** of no consequence; trivial. **2.** illogical; irrelevant. —**in′con·se·quen′ti·al′i·ty,** *n.* —**in′con·se·quen′tial·ly,** *adv.*

in·con·sid·er·a·ble (in′kən sid′ər ə bəl), *adj.* **1.** small, as in value, amount, etc. **2.** not worthy of consideration or notice; trivial. —**in′con·sid′er·a·ble·ness,** *n.* —**in′con·sid′er·a·bly,** *adv.*

in·con·sid·er·ate (in′kən sid′ər it), *adj.* **1.** without due regard for the rights or feelings of others. **2.** acting without consideration; thoughtless. **3.** rash; ill-considered. [late ME < L *inconsīderāt(us)*] —**in′con·sid′er·ate·ly,** *adv.* —**in′con·sid′er·ate·ness, in′con·sid′er·a′tion,** *n.*

in·con·sist·en·cy (in′kən sis′tən sē), *n., pl.* **-cies** for 2. **1.** the quality or condition of being inconsistent. **2.** something inconsistent. Also, **in′con·sist′ence.**

in·con·sist·ent (in′kən sis′tənt), *adj.* **1.** lacking in harmony between the different parts or elements; self-contradictory. **2.** lacking agreement, as one thing with another or two or more things in relation to each other; at variance. **3.** not consistent in principles, conduct, etc. **4.** acting at variance with professed principles. —**in′con·sist′ent·ly,** *adv.*
—**Syn. 1.** incoherent. **2.** discrepant, disagreeing, irreconcilable. INCONSISTENT, INCOMPATIBLE, INCONGRUOUS refer to things which are out of keeping with each other. Something that is INCONSISTENT involves variance, discrepancy, or even contradiction, esp. from the point of view of truth, reason, or logic: *His actions are inconsistent with his statements.* INCOMPATIBLE implies incapability of close association or harmonious relationship, as from differences of nature, character, temperament, and the like: *actions incompatible with honesty of purpose; qualities which make two people incompatible.* Something that is INCONGRUOUS is inappropriate or out of keeping, often to the point of being ridiculous or absurd: *Incongruous characters or situations frequently provide a basis for comedy.* —**Ant. 1.** harmonious.

in·con·sol·a·ble (in′kən sō′lə bəl), *adj.* not consolable: *inconsolable grief.* [< L *inconsōlābil(is)*] —**in′con·sol′a·bil′i·ty, in′con·sol′a·ble·ness,** *n.* —**in′con·sol′a·bly,** *adv.*

in·con·so·nant (in kon′sə nənt), *adj.* not consonant or in accord. —**in·con′so·nance,** *n.* —**in·con′so·nant·ly,** *adv.*

in·con·spic·u·ous (in′kən spik′yo͞o əs), *adj.* not conspicuous, noticeable, or prominent. [< L *inconspicuus*] —**in′con·spic′u·ous·ly,** *adv.* —**in′con·spic′u·ous·ness,** *n.*

in·con·stant (in kon′stənt), *adj.* not constant; changeable; fickle; variable. [ME < L *inconstant-* (s. of *inconstāns*) changeable] —**in·con′stan·cy,** *n.* —**in·con′stant·ly,** *adv.* —**Syn.** capricious, vacillating, unstable. —**Ant.** steady.

in·con·sum·a·ble (in′kən so͞o′mə bəl), *adj.* not consumable; incapable of being consumed. —**in′con·sum′a·bly,** *adv.*

in·con·test·a·ble (in′kən tes′tə bəl), *adj.* not contestable; incontrovertible: *incontestable proof.* —**in′con·test′a·bil′i·ty, in′con·test′a·ble·ness,** *n.* —**in′con·test′a·bly,** *adv.*

in·con·ti·nent[1] (in kon′tᵊnənt), *adj.* **1.** *Pathol.* unable to restrain natural discharges or evacuations. **2.** unable to contain or retain (usually fol. by *of*): *incontinent of temper.* **3.** unceasing or unrestrained: *an incontinent flow of talk.* **4.** lacking in moderation or control, esp. in seeking sexual gratification. [ME < L *incontinent-* (s. of *incontinēns*)] —**in·con′ti·nence, in·con′ti·nen·cy,** *n.* —**in·con′ti·nent·ly,** *adv.*

in·con·ti·nent[2] (in kon′tᵊnənt), *adv. Archaic.* immediately; at once; straightway. Also, **in·con′ti·nent·ly.** [ME < MF < LL *in continentī* (*tempore*) in continuous (time), i.e., without pause. See CONTINENT]

in·con·trol·la·ble (in′kən trō′lə bəl), *adj.* not controllable; uncontrollable. —**in′con·trol′la·bly,** *adv.*

in·con·tro·vert·i·ble (in′kon trə vûr′tə bəl, in kon′-), *adj.* not controvertible; indisputable: *absolute and incontrovertible truth.* —**in′con·tro·vert′i·bil′i·ty, in′con·tro·vert′i·ble·ness,** *n.* —**in′con·tro·vert′i·bly,** *adv.* —**Syn.** incontestable, undeniable, unquestionable.

in·con·ven·ience (in′kən vēn′yəns), *n., v.,* **-ienced, -ienc·ing.** —*n.* **1.** the quality or state of being inconvenient. **2.** an inconvenient circumstance or thing; something that causes discomfort, trouble, etc. —*v.t.* **3.** to put to inconvenience; incommode. [ME < LL *inconvenientia*]

in·con·ven·ien·cy (in′kən vēn′yən sē), *n., pl.* **-cies.** inconvenience.

in·con·ven·ient (in′kən vēn′yənt), *adj.* arranged or happening in such a way as to be awkward, inopportune, etc. [ME < L *inconvenient-* (s. of *inconveniēns*)] —**in′con·ven′ient·ly,** *adv.* —**Syn.** untimely; annoying.

in·con·vert·i·ble (in′kən vûr′tə bəl), *adj.* **1.** (of paper money) not convertible into specie. **2.** not interchangeable. [< LL *inconvertibil(is)* not alterable] —**in′con·vert′i·bil′i·ty, in′con·vert′i·ble·ness,** *n.* —**in′con·vert′i·bly,** *adv.*

in·con·vin·ci·ble (in′kən vin′sə bəl), *adj.* incapable of being convinced. —**in′con·vin′ci·bil′i·ty,** *n.* —**in′con·vin′ci·bly,** *adv.*

in·co·or·di·nate (in′kō ôr′dᵊnit), *adj.* not coordinate; not coordinated. Also, **in′co-or′di·nate, in′co·ör′di·nate.**

in·co·or·di·na·tion (in′kō ôr′dᵊnā′shən), *n.* lack of coordination. Also, **in′co-or′di·na′tion, in′co·ör′di·na′tion.**

incor., incorporated. Also, **incorp.**

in·cor·po·ra·ble (in kôr′pər ə bəl), *adj.* able to be incorporated. [< LL *incorpor(āre)* (to) embody + -ABLE]

in·cor·po·rate[1] (*v.* in kôr′pə rāt′; *adj.* in kôr′pə rit, -prit), *v.,* **-rat·ed, -rat·ing,** *adj.* —*v.t.* **1.** to form into a corporation. **2.** to form into a society or organization. **3.** to put or introduce into a body or mass as an integral part or parts. **4.** to take in or include as a part or parts, as the body or a mass does. **5.** to form or combine into one body or uniform substance, as ingredients. **6.** to embody. —*v.i.* **7.** to unite or combine so as to form one body. **8.** to form a corporation. —*adj.* **9.** incorporated, as a company. **10.** combined into one body, mass, or substance. **11.** *Archaic.* embodied. [ME < LL *incorporāt(us)* embodied. See IN-[2], CORPORATE] —**in·cor′po·ra′tive,** *adj.*

in·cor·po·rate[2] (in kôr′pər it, -prit), *adj. Rare.* not embodied; incorporeal. [< LL *incorporāt(us)* not embodied]

in·cor·po·rat·ed (in kôr′pə rā′tid), *adj.* **1.** formed or constituted as a corporation. **2.** combined in one body; made part of. —**in·cor′po·rat′ed·ness,** *n.*

incor′porated bar′, *Law.* See **integrated bar.**

in·cor·po·ra·tion (in kôr′pə rā′shən), *n.* **1.** the act of forming a corporation. **2.** the act of incorporating. **3.** the state of being incorporated. [ME *incorporacion* < LL *incorporātiōn-* (s. of *incorporātiō*)]

in·cor·po·ra·tor (in kôr′pə rā′tər), *n.* **1.** one of the signers of the articles or certificate of incorporation. **2.** one of the persons to whom the charter is granted in a corporation. **3.** a person who incorporates.

in·cor·po·re·al (in′kôr pōr′ē əl, -pôr′-), *adj.* **1.** not corporeal or material; insubstantial. **2.** of or pertaining to nonmaterial beings. **3.** *Law.* without material existence but existing in contemplation of law, as a franchise. [< LL *incorpore(us)* + -AL[1]] —**in′cor·po′re·al′i·ty,** *n.* —**in′cor·po′re·al·ly,** *adv.*

in·cor·po·re·i·ty (in′kôr pə rē′i tē), *n.* **1.** the quality or state of being incorporeal; incorporeality. **2.** something incorporeal, as a right, trait, etc. [< ML *incorporeitās*]

in·cor·rect (in′kə rekt′), *adj.* **1.** not correct as to fact; inaccurate. **2.** improper or unbecoming. **3.** not correct in form, use, or manner: *an incorrect copy.* [ME < L *incorrect(us)* not corrected] —**in′cor·rect′ly,** *adv.* —**in′cor·rect′ness,** *n.* —**Syn. 1.** erroneous; untrue, wrong. **2.** unsuitable, inappropriate. **3.** faulty.

in·cor·ri·gi·ble (in kôr′i jə bəl, -kor′-), *adj.* **1.** not corrigible; bad beyond reform: *an incorrigible liar.* **2.** impervious to punishment: *an incorrigible child.* **3.** firmly fixed; not easily changed: *an incorrigible habit.* **4.** not easily swayed or influenced: *an incorrigible optimist.* —*n.* **5.** an incorrigible person. [ME < L *incorrigibil(is)*] —**in·cor′ri·gi·bil′i·ty, in·cor′ri·gi·ble·ness,** *n.* —**in·cor′ri·gi·bly,** *adv.*

in·cor·rupt (in′kə rupt′), *adj.* **1.** not corrupt; morally upright. **2.** incorruptible. **3.** without errors or alterations. **4.** *Obs.* free from decay. Also, **in′cor·rupt′ed.** [ME < L *incorrupt(us)* unspoiled] —**in′cor·rupt′ly,** *adv.* —**in′cor·rupt′ness,** *n.*

in·cor·rupt·i·ble (in′kə rup′tə bəl), *adj.* **1.** not corruptible; incapable of corruption. **2.** that cannot be perverted or bribed. **3.** that will not dissolve, disintegrate, decay, etc.: *an incorruptible metal.* [ME < LL *incorruptibil(is)*] —**in′cor·rupt′i·bil′i·ty, in′cor·rupt′i·ble·ness,** *n.* —**in′cor·rupt′i·bly,** *adv.*

incr., **1.** increased. **2.** increasing.

in·cras·sate (*v.* in kras′āt; *adj.* in kras′it, -āt), *v.,* **-sat·ed, -sat·ing,** *adj.* —*v.t.* **1.** *Pharm.* to make (a liquid) thicker. **2.** *Obs.* to thicken. —*v.i.* **3.** *Obs.* to become thick or thicker. —*adj.* **4.** Also, **in·cras′sat·ed.** *Bot., Entomol.* thickened. [< LL *incrassāt(us)* made thick or stout (ptp. of *incrassāre*)] —**in′cras·sa′tion,** *n.*

in·crease (*v.* in krēs′; *n.* in′krēs), *v.,* **-creased, -creas·ing,** *n.* —*v.t.* **1.** to make greater in any respect; augment; add to. **2.** to make more numerous. —*v.i.* **3.** to become greater or more numerous. **4.** to multiply by propagation. **5.** to wax, as the moon. —*n.* **6.** growth or augmentation in numbers. **7.** the act or process of increasing. **8.** the amount by which something is increased. **9.** the result of increasing. **10.** produce of the earth. **11.** product; profit; interest. **12.** *Obs.* **a.** multiplication by propagation; production of offspring. **b.** offspring; progeny. [ME *increse,* var. of *encrese(n)* < AF *encres-* < MF *encreiss-,* s. of *encreistre* < L *incrēscere.* See IN-[2], CRESCENT] —**in·creas′a·ble,** *adj.* —**in·creas·ed·ly** (in krē′sid lē), **in·creas′ing·ly,** *adv.* —**in·creas′er,** *n.*
—**Syn. 1.** expand, extend, prolong. INCREASE, AUGMENT, ENLARGE may all mean to make larger. To INCREASE means to make greater, as in quantity, extent, degree: *to increase someone's salary; to increase the velocity; to increase the (degree of) concentration.* ENLARGE means to make greater in size, extent, or range: *to enlarge a building, a business, one's conceptions.* AUGMENT, a more formal word, means to make greater esp. by addition from the outside: *to augment one's*

income (by doing extra work). 3. expand, grow, develop. 6. enlargement, expansion. —**Ant.** 1, 3. decrease.

in·cre·ate (in′krē āt′, in′krē āt′), *adj.* (of divine beings) existing without having been created. [ME *increat* < LL *increāt(us)* not made] —**in′cre·ate′ly,** *adv.*

in·cred·i·ble (in kred′ə bəl), *adj.* 1. so extraordinary as to seem impossible: *incredible speed.* 2. not credible; unbelievable: *The plot of the book is incredible.* [ME < L *incrēdibil(is)*] —**in·cred′i·bil′i·ty, in·cred′i·ble·ness,** *n.* —**in·cred′i·bly,** *adv.*

in·cre·du·li·ty (in′kri do͞o′li tē, -dyo͞o′-), *n.* the quality or state of being incredulous; refusal of belief. [ME *incredulite* < L *incrēdulitās*] —**Syn.** disbelief, skepticism, doubt. —**Ant.** faith, belief.

in·cred·u·lous (in krej′ə ləs), *adj.* 1. not credulous; skeptical; unbelieving. 2. indicating unbelief: *an incredulous smile.* [< L *incrēdulus*] —**in·cred′u·lous·ly,** *adv.* —**in·cred′u·lous·ness,** *n.*

in·cre·ment (in′krə mənt, ing′-), *n.* 1. an addition or increase. 2. profit; gain. 3. act or process of increasing; growth. 4. *Math.* a. a change, positive, negative, or zero, in an independent variable. b. the increase of a function due to an increase in the independent variable. [ME < L *incrēmentum* an increase. See INCREASE, -MENT] —**in·cre·men·tal** (in′krə men′t^{ə}l, ing′-), *adj.*

in·cres·cent (in kres′ənt), *adj.* increasing or waxing, as the moon. [< L *incrēscent-* (s. of *incrēscēns*) growing, prp. of *incrēscere*) to INCREASE] —**in·cres′cence,** *n.*

in·cre·tion (in krē′shən), *n.* *Physiol.* 1. a substance, as an autacoid, secreted internally. 2. the process of such secretion. [IN-[2] + (SE)CRETION] —**in·cre′tion·ar′y, in·cre·to·ry** (in′kri tōr′ē, -tôr′ē), *adj.*

in·crim·i·nate (in krim′ə nāt′), *v.t.*, **-nat·ed, -nat·ing.** 1. to charge with a crime or fault. 2. to involve in an accusation; implicate. 3. to charge with responsibility for a bad situation, effect, etc. [< LL *incrīmināt(us)* accused of a crime (ptp. of *incrīmināre*)] —**in·crim′i·na′tion,** *n.* —**in·crim′i·na′tor,** *n.* —**in·crim·i·na·to·ry** (in krim′ə nə tōr′ē, -tôr′ē), *adj.*

in·crust (in krust′), *v.t.* 1. to cover or line with a crust or hard coating. 2. to form into a crust. 3. to deposit as a crust. 4. to inlay or embellish, as with jewels. —*v.i.* 5. to form a crust. Also, **encrust.** [< L *incrustāre*] —**in·crust′ant,** *adj., n.*

in·crus·ta·tion (in′kru stā′shən), *n.* 1. an incrusting or being incrusted. 2. a crust, hard coating, or scale. 3. the inlaying or addition of ornamentation on or to a surface or an object. 4. the ornamentation itself. Also, **encrustation.** [< LL *incrustātiōn-* (s. of *incrustātiō*)]

in·cu·bate (in′kyə bāt′, ing′-), *v.*, **-bat·ed, -bat·ing.** —*v.t.* 1. to sit upon (eggs) for the purpose of hatching. 2. to hatch (eggs) in this manner or by artificial heat. 3. to maintain at a favorable temperature and in other conditions promoting development, as premature babies or cultures of microorganisms. 4. to produce as if by hatching; give form to. —*v.i.* 5. to sit upon eggs. 6. to undergo incubation. 7. to develop; grow; take form. [< L *incubāt(us)* sat upon, hatched (ptp. of *incubāre*). See IN-[2], COVEY, -ATE[1]] —**in′cu·ba′tive,** *adj.*

in·cu·ba·tion (in′kyə bā′shən, ing′-), *n.* 1. the act or process of incubating. 2. the state of being incubated. [< L *incubātiōn-* (s. of *incubātiō*)] —**in′cu·ba′tion·al,** *adj.*

incuba′tion pe′riod, *Pathol.* the period between infection and the appearance of signs of a disease.

in·cu·ba·tor (in′kyə bā′tər, ing′-), *n.* 1. an apparatus for hatching eggs. 2. an apparatus in which prematurely born infants are kept in favorable conditions for growth. 3. an apparatus in which microorganisms are cultivated. 4. a person or thing that incubates. [< LL: lit., one who lies]

in·cu·bus (in′kyə bəs, ing′-), *n., pl.* **-bi** (-bī′), **-bus·es.** 1. a demon supposed to descend upon sleeping persons, esp. one in male form fabled to have sexual intercourse with women in their sleep. Cf. **succubus** (def. 1). 2. something that oppresses one like a nightmare. 3. a nightmare. [ME < LL: nightmare = L *incub(āre)* (to) lie upon (see INCUBATE) + *-us* n. suffix]

in·cu·des (in kyo͞o′dēz), *n.* a pl. of **incus.**

in·cul·cate (in kul′kāt, in′kul kāt′), *v.t.*, **-cat·ed, -cat·ing.** 1. to impress by repeated statement or admonition; teach persistently and earnestly (usually fol. by *upon* or *in*): *to inculcate virtue in the young.* 2. to cause or influence (someone) to accept an idea or feeling (usually fol. by *with*): *Socrates inculcated his pupils with the love of truth.* [< L *inculcāt(us)* stamped or trodden in (ptp. of *inculcāre*) = *in-* IN-[2] + *culc-* (var. of *calc-*, s. of *calx* heel) + *-ātus* -ATE[1]] —**in′cul·ca′tion,** *n.* —**in·cul′ca·tor,** *n.* —**Syn.** 1. instill, infix, implant, ingrain.

in·cul·pa·ble (in kul′pə bəl), *adj.* not culpable; blameless; guiltless. [late ME < LL *inculpābil(is)*] —**in·cul′pa·bil′i·ty, in·cul′pa·ble·ness,** *n.* —**in·cul′pa·bly,** *adv.*

in·cul·pate (in kul′pāt, in′kul pāt′), *v.t.*, **-pat·ed, -pat·ing.** 1. to charge with fault; blame; accuse. 2. to involve in a charge; incriminate. [< ML *inculpāt(us)* blamed (ptp. of *inculpāre*)] —**in′cul·pa′tion,** *n.* —**in·cul·pa·to·ry** (in kul′pə tōr′ē, -tôr′ē), *adj.* —**Ant.** 1, 2. exonerate.

in·cult (in kult′), *adj.* *Archaic.* 1. uncultivated; untilled. 2. wild; rude; unrefined. [< L *incult(us)*]

in·cum·ben·cy (in kum′bən sē), *n., pl.* **-cies** for 2–5. 1. the quality or state of being incumbent. 2. something that is incumbent. 3. the position or term of an incumbent. 4. a duty or obligation. 5. *Rare.* an incumbent weight, mass, or load.

in·cum·bent (in kum′bənt), *adj.* 1. holding an indicated position, role, office, etc.: *the incumbent senator.* 2. obligatory (often fol. by *on* or *upon*): *a duty incumbent upon me.* 3. resting, lying, leaning, or pressing on something. —*n.* 4. the holder of an office. 5. *Brit.* a person who holds an ecclesiastical benefice. [ME (n.) < L *incumbent-* (s. of *incumbēns* lying or leaning on, prp. of *incumbere*) = *in-* IN-[2] + *cumb-* (nasalized var. of *cub-* sit, lie; see INCUBUS) + *-ent-* -ENT] —**in·cum′bent·ly,** *adv.*

in·cum·ber (in kum′bər), *v.t.* encumber.

in·cum·brance (in kum′brəns), *n.* encumbrance.

in·cu·nab·u·la (in′kyo͝o nab′yə lə), *n.pl., sing.* **-lum** (-ləm). 1. extant copies of books produced before 1500. 2. the earliest stages of anything. [< L: swaddling clothes, hence, beginnings = *in-* IN-[2] + *cūnābula* (neut. pl.) cradle (*cūnā-* (s. of *cūnae*, fem. pl.) cradle + *-bula* dim. suffix)] —**in′cu·nab′u·lar,** *adj.*

in·cur (in kûr′), *v.t.*, **-curred, -cur·ring.** 1. to run or fall into (some consequence, usually undesirable or injurious). 2. to bring upon oneself: *to incur someone's displeasure.* [ME < L *incurr(ere)* (to) run into, come upon. See IN-[2], CURRENT] —**in·cur′ra·ble,** *adj.*

in·cur·a·ble (in kyo͝or′ə bəl), *adj.* 1. not curable. —*n.* 2. a person suffering from an incurable disease. [ME < LL *incūrābili(s)*] —**in·cur′a·bil′i·ty, in·cur′a·ble·ness,** *n.* —**in·cur′a·bly,** *adv.*

in·cu·ri·ous (in kyo͝or′ē əs), *adj.* not curious; not inquisitive or observant; indifferent. [< L *incūriōs(us)*] —**in·cu·ri·os·i·ty** (in′kyo͝or ē os′i tē), **in·cu′ri·ous·ness,** *n.* —**in·cu′ri·ous·ly,** *adv.* —**Syn.** uninterested, unconcerned.

in·cur·rence (in kûr′əns, -kur′-), *n.* the act of incurring, bringing on, or subjecting oneself to something. [INCURR(ENT) + -ENCE]

in·cur·rent (in kûr′ənt, -kur′-), *adj.* carrying or relating to an inward current. [< L *incurrent-* (s. of *incurrēns*), prp. of *incurrere*]

in·cur·sion (in kûr′zhən, -shən), *n.* 1. a hostile, usually sudden, entrance into or invasion of a place; raid. 2. a harmful inroad. 3. a running in: *the incursion of the sea water.* [ME < L *incursiōn-* (s. of *incursiō*) raid = *incurs(us)* (ptp. of *incurrere* to INCUR) + *-iōn-* -ION; see EXCURSION]

in·cur·sive (in kûr′siv), *adj.* making incursions. [INCURS(ION) + -IVE]

in·cur·vate (*adj.* in′kûr vāt′, in kûr′vit; *v.* in′kûr vāt′, in kûr′vāt), *adj., v.,* **-vat·ed, -vat·ing.** —*adj.* 1. curved, esp. inward. —*v.t.* 2. to make curved; turn from a straight line or course; curve, esp. inward. [< L *incurvāt(us)*, ptp. of *incurvāre*] —**in·cur·va·ture** (in kûr′və chər), **in′cur·va′tion,** *n.*

in·curve[1] (in kûrv′), *v.i., v.t.* **-curved, -curv·ing,** to curve inward. [IN-[1] + CURVE]

in·curve[2] (in′kûrv′), *n.* *Baseball.* a pitch that breaks toward a batter. Cf. **outcurve.** [IN + CURVE]

in·cus (ing′kəs), *n., pl.* **in·cu·des** (in kyo͞o′dēz) for 1; **in·cus** for 2. 1. *Anat.* the middle one of a chain of three small bones in the middle ear of man and other mammals; anvil. Cf. **malleus, stapes.** 2. Also called **anvil, anvil cloud, anvil top.** the spreading, anvil-shaped, upper portion of a mature cumulonimbus; thunderhead. [< NL, L: anvil = *incūd-* (s. of *incūdere* to hammer, beat upon) + *-s* nom. sing. ending; see INCUSE] —**in·cu·date** (ing′kyə dāt′, -dit, in′-), **in·cu·dal** (ing′kyə d^{ə}l, in′-), *adj.*

in·cuse (in kyo͞oz′, -kyo͞os′), *adj., n., v.,* **-cused, -cus·ing.** —*adj.* 1. hammered or stamped in, as a figure on a coin. —*n.* 2. an incuse figure or impression. —*v.t.* 3. to stamp or hammer in, as a design or figure in a coin. [< L *incūs(us)* forged with a hammer (ptp. of *incūdere*) = *in-* IN-[2] + *cūd-* beat + *-tus* ptp. suffix]

Ind (ind), *n.* 1. *Literary.* India. 2. *Obs.* the Indies.

ind-, var. of **indo-** before a vowel: *indamine.*

Ind., 1. India. 2. Indian. 3. Indiana. 4. Indies.

ind., 1. independent. 2. index. 3. indicated. 4. indigo. 5. indirect. 6. industrial. 7. industry.

I.N.D., in the name of God. [< L *in nōmine Deī*]

in·da·ba (in dä′bä), *n.* a conference or consultation between or with South African natives. [< Zulu]

in·da·gate (in′də gāt′), *v.t.*, **-gat·ed, -gat·ing.** *Archaic.* to investigate. [< L *indāgāt(us)* tracked down (ptp. of *indāgāre*) = *ind(u)* in + *-āg-* (var. s. of *agere* to drive) + *-ātus* -ATE[1]] —**in′da·ga′tion,** *n.* —**in′da·ga′tor,** *n.*

in·da·mine (in′də mēn′, -min), *n.* *Chem.* any of a series of basic organic compounds derived from $H_2NC_6H_4N=C_6H_4=NH$, which form bluish and greenish salts, used in the manufacture of dyes.

in·debt·ed (in det′id), *adj.* 1. being bound or obligated to repay a monetary loan. 2. being under obligation to someone for favors or kindness received. [ME *endetted* < OF *endet(e)*, ptp. of *endeter*]

in·debt·ed·ness (in det′id nis), *n.* 1. the state of being indebted. 2. an amount owed. 3. debts collectively.

in·de·cen·cy (in dē′sən sē), *n., pl.* **-cies** for 4. 1. the quality or condition of being indecent. 2. impropriety; immodesty. 3. obscenity; indelicacy. 4. an indecent act, remark, etc. [< L *indecentia*]

in·de·cent (in dē′sənt), *adj.* 1. offending against recognized standards of propriety or good taste; vulgar. 2. not decent; unbecoming or unseemly: *indecent haste.* [ME < L *indecent-* (s. of *indecēns*) unseemly] —**in·de′cent·ly,** *adv.* —**Syn.** 1. indelicate, coarse, obscene, lewd. See **improper.** 2. inappropriate. —**Ant.** 2. appropriate; becoming.

in·de·cid·u·ous (in′di sij′o͞o əs), *adj.* *Bot.* 1. not deciduous, as leaves. 2. (of trees) evergreen.

in·de·ci·pher·a·ble (in′di sī′fər ə bəl), *adj.* not decipherable. —**in′de·ci′pher·a·bil′i·ty, in′de·ci′pher·a·ble·ness,** *n.* —**in′de·ci′pher·a·bly,** *adv.*

in·de·ci·sion (in′di sizh′ən), *n.* inability to decide.

in·de·ci·sive (in′di sī′siv), *adj.* 1. not decisive or conclusive: *a severe but indecisive battle.* 2. (of a person) characterized by indecision. 3. lacking definition; indistinct. —**in′de·ci′sive·ly,** *adv.* —**in′de·ci′sive·ness,** *n.*

in·de·clin·a·ble (in′di klī′nə bəl), *adj.* *Gram.* not declined; without inflections. [ME < L *indēclīnābil(is)* unchangeable] —**in′de·clin′a·ble·ness,** *n.* —**in′de·clin′a·bly,** *adv.*

in·dec·o·rous (in dek′ər əs, in′di kōr′əs, -kôr′-), *adj.* not decorous; violating propriety; improper or unseemly. [< L *indecōrus*] —**in·dec′o·rous·ly,** *adv.* —**in·dec′o·rous·ness,** *n.* —**Syn.** indecent. —**Ant.** seemly.

in·de·co·rum (in′di kōr′əm, -kôr′-), *n.* 1. indecorous behavior or character. 2. something indecorous. [< L, neut. of *indecōrus* INDECOROUS]

in·deed (in dēd′), *adv.* 1. in fact; in reality; in truth; truly. —*interj.* 2. (used as an expression of surprise, in-

credulity, irony, etc.): *Indeed! I can scarcely believe it.* [ME; orig. phrase *in deed*]
indef., indefinite.
in·de·fat·i·ga·ble (in′di fat′ə gə bəl), *adj.* incapable of being tired out. [< L *indēfatīgābil(is)* untiring = IN-³ + *dēfatīgā(re)* (to) tire out + -BLE] —**in′de·fat′i·ga·bil′i·ty, in′de·fat′i·ga·ble·ness,** *n.* —**in′de·fat′i·ga·bly,** *adv.*
in·de·fea·si·ble (in′di fē′zə bəl), *adj.* not defeasible; not to be annulled or made void; not forfeitable. —**in′de·fea′si·bil′i·ty, in′de·fea′si·ble·ness,** *n.* —**in′de·fea′si·bly,** *adv.*
in·de·fect·i·ble (in′di fek′tə bəl), *adj.* **1.** not liable to defect or failure; unfailing. **2.** not liable to imperfection; faultless. —**in′de·fect′i·bil′i·ty,** *n.* —**in′de·fect′i·bly,** *adv.*
in·de·fen·si·ble (in′di fen′sə bəl), *adj.* **1.** not justifiable; inexcusable. **2.** incapable of being defended against attack. **3.** incapable of being defended against criticism or denial. —**in′de·fen′si·bil′i·ty, in′de·fen′si·ble·ness,** *n.* —**in′de·fen′si·bly,** *adv.*
in·de·fin·a·ble (in′di fī′nə bəl), *adj.* not definable; not readily identified, described, analyzed, or determined. —**in′de·fin′a·ble·ness,** *n.* —**in′de·fin′a·bly,** *adv.*
in·def·i·nite (in def′ə nit), *adj.* **1.** not definite; without fixed limit. **2.** not clearly defined or determined. **3.** *Gram.* **a.** See **indefinite article. b.** See **indefinite pronoun. 4.** *Bot.* **a.** very numerous or not easily counted, as stamens. **b.** (of an inflorescence) indeterminate. [< L *indēfīnīt(us)*] —**in·def′i·nite·ly,** *adv.* —**in·def′i·nite·ness,** *n.*
indef′inite ar′ticle, *Gram.* an article, as English *a, an,* that denotes class membership of the noun it modifies without particularizing it. Cf. **definite article.**
indef′inite in′tegral, *Math.* a representation, usually in symbolic form, of any function whose derivative is a given function. Cf. **definite integral.**
indef′inite pro′noun, *Gram.* a pronoun, as English *some, any, somebody,* that leaves unspecified the identity of its referent.
in·de·his·cent (in′di his′ənt), *adj.* *Bot.* not dehiscent; not opening at maturity. —**in′de·his′cence,** *n.*
in·del·i·ble (in del′ə bəl), *adj.* **1.** incapable of being deleted or obliterated: *an indelible impression.* **2.** making indelible marks. [< ML *indēlibil(is)*; r. earlier *indeleble* < L *indēlēbil(is)* indestructible] —**in·del′i·bil′i·ty, in·del′i·ble·ness,** *n.* —**in·del′i·bly,** *adv.*
in·del·i·ca·cy (in del′ə kə sē), *n., pl.* **-cies** for 2. **1.** the quality or condition of being indelicate. **2.** something indelicate, as language or behavior.
in·del·i·cate (in del′ə kit), *adj.* **1.** not delicate; lacking delicacy; rough. **2.** offensive to a sense of propriety, modesty, or decency. —**in·del′i·cate·ly,** *adv.* —**in·del′i·cate·ness,** *n.* —**Syn. 2.** indecorous, untactful, gauche, rude.
in·dem·ni·fi·ca·tion (in dem′nə fə kā′shən), *n.* **1.** the act of indemnifying. **2.** the state of being indemnified. **3.** something that serves to indemnify; compensation.
in·dem·ni·fy (in dem′nə fī′), *v.t.,* **-fied, -fy·ing. 1.** to compensate for damage or loss sustained, expense incurred, etc. **2.** to give security against (future damage or liability). [< L *indemni(s)* without loss (see INDEMNITY) + -FY] —**in·dem′ni·fi′er,** *n.* —**Syn. 1.** recompense, reimburse, repay.
in·dem·ni·tee (in dem′ni tē′), *n.* a person, company, etc., that receives indemnity.
in·dem·ni·tor (in dem′ni tər), *n.* a person, company, etc., that gives indemnity.
in·dem·ni·ty (in dem′ni tē), *n., pl.* **-ties. 1.** protection or security against damage or loss. **2.** compensation for damage or loss. **3.** something paid as such compensation. **4.** protection, as by insurance, from liabilities or penalties incurred. [late ME *indem(p)nite* < legal L *indemnitās* = L *indemni(s)* without loss (*in-* IN-³ + *demn-*, var. of *damn-* (s. of *damnum* loss) + *-is* adj. suffix) + *-tās* -TY²]
in·de·mon·stra·ble (in′di mon′strə bəl, in dem′ən-), *adj.* incapable of being demonstrated or proved. —**in′de·mon′stra·bly,** *adv.*
in·dene (in′dēn), *n.* *Chem.* a colorless, liquid hydrocarbon, C_9H_8, obtained from coal tar by fractional distillation.
in·dent[1] (*v.* in dent′; *n.* in′dent, in dent′), *v.t.* **1.** to form deep recesses in: *The sea indents the coast.* **2.** to set in or back from the margin, as the first line of a paragraph. **3.** to sever (a document drawn up in duplicate) along an irregular line as a means of identification. **4.** to cut or tear the edge of (copies of a document) in an irregular way. **5.** to make toothlike notches in; notch. **6.** to indenture, as an apprentice. **7.** *Brit.* to draw an order upon. **8.** *Chiefly Brit.* to order, as commodities. —*v.i.* **9.** to form a recess. **10.** *Chiefly Brit.* to make out an order or requisition in duplicate. **11.** *Brit. Mil.* to make a requisition. **12.** *Obs.* **a.** to draw upon a person or thing for something. **b.** to enter into an agreement by indenture; make a compact. —*n.* **13.** an indentation. **14.** an indention. **15.** an indenture. **16.** *U.S. Hist.* a certificate issued by the government at the close of the American Revolution for the principal or interest due on the public debt. **17.** *Brit.* an official requisition for stores. [ME; back formation from *indented* < ML *indentāt(us)*] —**in·dent′er, in·den′tor,** *n.*
in·dent[2] (*v.* indent′; *n.* in′dent, in dent′), *v.t.* **1.** to dent; press in so as to form a dent. **2.** to make a dent in. —*n.* **3.** a dent. [ME; see IN-², DENT¹]
in·den·ta·tion (in′den tā′shən), *n.* **1.** a cut, notch, or deep recess. **2.** a series of incisions or notches: *the indentation of a maple leaf.* **3.** a notching or being notched. **4.** an indention. [INDENT¹ + -ATION]
in·den·tion (in den′shən), *n.* **1.** the act of indenting. **2.** the state of being indented. **3.** an indentation. **4.** the indenting of a line or lines in writing or printing. **5.** the blank space left by indenting. [INDENT¹ + -ION]
in·den·ture (in den′chər), *n., v.,* **-tured, -tur·ing.** —*n.* **1.** a deed or agreement executed in two or more copies with edges correspondingly indented as a means of identification. **2.** any deed, written contract, or sealed agreement. **3.** a contract by which a person, as an apprentice, is bound to service. **4.** any official or formal list, certificate, etc., authenticated for use as a voucher or the like. **5.** the formal agreement between a group of bondholders and the debtor as to the terms of the debt. **6.** indentation. —*v.t.* **7.** to bind by indenture, as an apprentice. [ME < ML *indentūra.* See INDENT¹, -URE] —**in·den′ture·ship′,** *n.*
inden′tured serv′ant, *Amer. Hist.* a person who came to America and was placed under contract to work for another over a period of time, usually seven years, esp. during the 17th to 19th centuries.
in·de·pend·ence (in′di pen′dəns), *n.* **1.** Also, **independency.** state or quality of being independent. **2.** freedom from subjection, or from the influence of others. **3.** exemption from external control or support. [INDEPEND(ENT) + -ENCE]
In·de·pend·ence (in′di pen′dəns), *n.* a city in W Missouri: starting point of the Santa Fe and Oregon trails. 111,630 (1970).
Independ′ence Day′, *U.S.* July 4, a holiday commemorating the adoption of the Declaration of Independence on July 4, 1776. Also called **Fourth of July.**
in·de·pend·en·cy (in′di pen′dən sē), *n., pl.* **-cies. 1.** independence (def. 1). **2.** an independent territory. **3.** (*cap.*) *Eccles.* **a.** the principle that a congregation or church is autonomous and equalitarian, free from external ecclesiastical control. **b.** the polity based on this principle.
in·de·pend·ent (in′di pen′dənt), *adj.* **1.** not influenced or controlled by others in matters of opinion, conduct, etc. **2.** not subject to another's authority or jurisdiction. **3.** not guided by others: *independent research.* **4.** not depending or contingent upon something else for existence, operation, etc. **5.** not relying on another or others for aid or support. **6.** declining others' aid or support. **7.** possessing sufficient financial resources to be free of another's control or the need to work. **8.** providing financial support sufficient to enable one to be free of the need to work: *independent means.* **9.** self-confident; unconstrained. **10.** free from party commitments in politics. **11.** *Math.* (of a quantity or function) not depending upon another for value. **12.** *Gram.* capable of standing syntactically as a complete sentence. Cf. **dependent** (def. 4), **main**[1] (def. 4). **13.** (*cap.*) *Eccles.* of or pertaining to the Independents. **14. independent of,** irrespective of; regardless of. —*n.* **15.** an independent person. **16.** *Politics.* **a.** a person who votes for candidates without regard to the endorsement of any political party. **b.** a voter who is not registered as a member of any political party. **17.** (*cap.*) *Eccles.* an adherent of Independency. **18.** *Brit.* a Congregationalist. —**in′de·pend′ent·ly,** *adv.*
in′depend′ent var′iable, *Math.* a variable in a functional relation whose value determines the value or values of other variables, as x in the relation, $y = 3x^2$. Cf. **dependent variable.**
in-depth (in′depth′), *adj.* **1.** extensive, thorough, or profound. **2.** well-balanced or fully-developed.
in·de·scrib·a·ble (in′di skrī′bə bəl), *adj.* not describable. —**in′de·scrib′a·bil′i·ty, in′de·scrib′a·ble·ness,** *n.* —**in′de·scrib′a·bly,** *adv.*
in·de·struct·i·ble (in′di struk′tə bəl), *adj.* not destructible; that cannot be destroyed. [LL *indēstructibilis*] —**in′de·struct′i·bil′i·ty, in′de·struct′i·ble·ness,** *n.* —**in′de·struct′i·bly,** *adv.*
in·de·ter·mi·na·ble (in′di tûr′mə nə bəl), *adj.* **1.** not determinable; incapable of being ascertained. **2.** incapable of being decided or settled. [< LL *indēterminābil(is)*] —**in′de·ter′mi·na·ble·ness,** *n.* —**in′de·ter′mi·na·bly,** *adv.*
in·de·ter·mi·na·cy (in′di tûr′mə nə sē), *n.* the condition or quality of being indeterminate; indetermination.
indeter′minacy prin′ciple, *Physics.* See **uncertainty principle.**
in·de·ter·mi·nate (in′di tûr′mə nit), *adj.* **1.** not fixed in extent; indefinite; uncertain. **2.** not clear; vague. **3.** not established. **4.** not settled or decided. **5.** *Math.* **a.** (of a quantity) undefined, as *0/0.* **b.** (of an equation) able to be satisfied by more than one value for each unknown. **6.** *Bot.* (of an inflorescence) having the axis or axes not ending in a flower or bud, thus allowing further elongation. **7.** *Engineering.* unable to be analyzed completely by means of the principles of statics. [ME < LL *indēterminīt(us)*] —**in′de·ter′mi·nate·ly,** *adv.* —**in′de·ter′mi·nate·ness,** *n.*
in·de·ter·mi·na·tion (in′di tûr′mə nā′shən), *n.* **1.** the condition or quality of being indeterminate. **2.** an unsettled state, as of the mind.
in·de·ter·min·ism (in′di tûr′mə niz′əm), *n.* *Philos.* **1.** the doctrine that human actions are not entirely governed by external conditions but retain a certain freedom and spontaneity as a result of freedom of the will. **2.** the view that natural phenomena are not uniquely determined and cannot be precisely predicted by the laws of physics. —**in′de·ter′min·ist,** *n., adj.* —**in′de·ter′min·is′tic,** *adj.*
in·dex (in′deks), *n., pl.* **-dex·es, -di·ces** (-di sēz′), *v.* —*n.* **1.** (in a nonfiction book, a dissertation, etc.) an alphabetical listing of names, places, and topics along with the numbers of the pages on which they are mentioned or discussed. **2.** any sequential arrangement of material. **3.** a sign, token, or indication: *a true index of his character.* **4.** a pointer or indicator in a scientific instrument. **5.** a piece of wood, metal, or the like, serving as a pointer or indicator. **6.** Also called **fist, hand.** *Print.* a sign (☞) used to point out a particular note, paragraph, etc. **7.** the index finger; forefinger. **8.** a number or formula expressing some property, ratio, etc., of something indicated: *index of growth.* **9.** *Algebra.* **a.** an exponent. **b.** the integer n in a radical $\sqrt[n]{\ }$ defining the nth root. **c.** a subscript or superscript indicating the position of an object in a series of similar objects, as the subscripts 1, 2, and 3 in the series x_1, x_2, x_3. **10.** (*cap.*) *Rom. Cath. Ch.* See **Index Librorum Prohibitorum. 11.** (*usually cap.*) any list of forbidden or otherwise restricted material deemed morally or politically harmful by authorities: *an Index of books relating to Communism.* —*v.t.* **12.** to provide with an index, as a book. **13.** to enter in an index, as a word. **14.** to serve to indicate. **15.** to place (a book) on an official list as politically or morally harmful. **16.** to adjust (wages, taxes, etc.) according to changes in the cost of living or some other economic indicator, esp. to offset inflation. [ME < L: informer, pointer] —**in′dex·er,** *n.*
in·dex·a·tion (in′dek sā′shən), *n.* the automatic adjustment of wages, taxes, pension benefits, interest rates, or any other payments or charges to compensate for or keep pace with inflation, fluctuations in the cost of living, or some other economic indicator.
in′dex fin′ger, forefinger.

In·dex Li·bro·rum Pro·hib·i·to·rum (in′deks lī brōr′əm prō hib i tōr′əm, -tôr′-, -brôr′-), *pl.* **In·di·ces Li·bro·rum Pro·hib·i·to·rum** (in′di sēz′ lī brōr′əm prō hib′i tōr′əm, -tôr′-, -brôr′-). *Rom. Cath. Ch.* a list of books that Roman Catholics were formerly forbidden by Church authority to read without special permission, or that were not to be read unless expurgated or changed. [< NL: index of prohibited books]

in′dex num′ber, *Statistics.* a quantity whose variation over a period of time measures the change in some phenomenon.

in′dex of refrac′tion, *Optics.* a number indicating the speed of light in a given medium, usually as the ratio of the speed of light in a vacuum, or in air, to that in the given medium. *Symbol:* n Also called **refractive index.**

In·di·a (in′dē ə), *n.* a republic in S Asia: comprises most of former British India and the semi-independent Indian States and Agencies; became a dominion in 1947; became fully independent on January 26, 1950, with membership in the British Commonwealth of Nations. 634,700,000; 1,246,880 sq. mi. *Cap.:* New Delhi. Hindi, **Bharat.** [OE < L < Gk = *Ind(ós)* the Indus river (< OPers *Hindu,* lit., the river; c. Skt *sindhu*) + *-ia* -IA]

In′dia drug′get, drugget (def. 1).

In′dia ink′, (*sometimes l.c.*) **1.** a black pigment consisting of lampblack mixed with glue or size. **2.** an ink made from this.

In·di·an (in′dē ən), *n.* **1.** Also called **American Indian.** a member of the aboriginal peoples of North and South America, usually excluding the Eskimos and generally regarded as a subdivision of the Mongoloid race. **2.** *Informal.* any of the indigenous languages of the American Indians. **3.** a member of any of the peoples native to India or the East Indies. **4.** *U.S. Slang.* a member of the rank and file of an organization: *All chiefs and no Indians can't run a committee.* —*adj.* **5.** of, pertaining to, or characteristic of the American Indians or their languages. **6.** of, pertaining to, or characteristic of India or the East Indies. **7.** *Zoogeog.* oriental (def. 2). **8.** *Phytogeog.* belonging or pertaining to a geographical division comprising India south of the Himalayas, and Pakistan and Ceylon. [ME < ML *Indiān(us)*]

In·di·an·a (in′dē an′ə), *n.* a state in the central United States: a part of the Midwest. 5,193,669 (1970); 36,291 sq. mi. *Cap.:* Indianapolis. *Abbr.:* Ind., IN —**In·di·an·i·an** (in′dē an′ē ən), *adj., n.*

In′dian a′gent, an official representing the U.S. government in dealing with an Indian tribe or tribes.

In·di·an·ap·o·lis (in′dē ə nap′ə lis), *n.* a city in and the capital of Indiana, in the central part. 744,743 (1970).

In′dian bread′, **1.** See **corn bread.** **2.** tuckahoe.

In′dian club′, a metal or wooden club shaped like a large bottle, used singly or in pairs for exercising the arms.

In′dian corn′, corn[1] (def. 1).

In′dian Des′ert. See **Thar Desert.**

In′dian file′, in single file, as of persons walking.

In′dian giv′er, *Informal.* a person who takes back a gift that he has given. —**In′dian giv′ing.**

In′dian hemp′, **1.** a dogbane, *Apocynum cannabinum,* of North America, the root of which has laxative and emetic properties. **2.** hemp (def. 1).

In′dian lic′orice, a woody, East Indian, fabaceous shrub, *Abrus precatorius,* having a root used as a substitute for licorice.

In′dian mal′low, **1.** a malvaceous plant, *Abutilon Theophrasti,* having yellow flowers and velvety leaves, introduced into America from southern Asia. **2.** any of certain related species.

In′dian mil′let, durra.

In′dian mul′berry, a small tree, *Morinda citrifolia,* found from India to Australia, having shiny leaves, white flowers, and fleshy, yellowish fruit, yielding red and yellow dyes; al.

In′dian Mu′tiny. See **Sepoy Rebellion.**

In′dian O′cean, an ocean S of Asia, E of Africa, and W of Australia. 28,357,000 sq. mi.

In′dian paint′brush, any of several showy, scrophulariaceous herbs of the genus *Castilleja,* as *C. linariaefolia,* of the southwestern U.S.: the state flower of Wyoming.

In′dian pipe′, a leafless, saprophytic plant, *Monotropa uniflora,* of North America and Asia, having a solitary flower and resembling a tobacco pipe.

In′dian pud′ding, a sweet baked pudding made of corn meal, molasses, milk, and spices.

In′dian red′, earth of a yellowish-red color, found esp. in the Persian Gulf, that serves as a pigment and as a polish for gold and silver objects.

In′dian rice′, the wild rice plant.

In′dian silk′. See **India silk.**

In′dian States′ and A′gencies, the former semi-dependent states and agencies in India and Pakistan: became independent states of, or otherwise affiliated with, the republics of India and Pakistan 1947. Also called **Native States.**

In′dian sum′mer, a period of mild, dry weather occurring in the U.S. and Canada in late autumn or early winter.

In′dian Ter′ritory, a former territory of the United States: now in E Oklahoma. ab. 31,000 sq. mi.

In′dian wres′tling, **1.** a form of wrestling in which two opponents, lying side by side on their backs and facing in opposite directions, lock corresponding legs and each attempts to force the other's leg down until one opponent is unable to remain lying flat on his back. **2.** a form of wrestling in which two opponents clasp each other's right or left hands and, placing the corresponding feet side by side, attempt to unbalance each other. **3.** a form of wrestling in which two opponents, usually facing one another across a table, rest their right or left elbows on the table and, placing their corresponding forearms upward and parallel, grip each other's hand, the object being to force the opponent's hand down so that it touches the table.

In′dia pa′per, **1.** a fine, thin, but opaque paper made in the Orient, used chiefly in the production of thin-paper editions and for impressions of engravings. **2.** See **Bible paper.**

In′dia print′, a plain-weave cotton characterized by brilliantly colored motifs resembling those designed in India, rendered by the block-print method.

In′dia rub′ber, **1.** rubber[1] (def. 1). **2.** a rubber eraser. **3.** *Archaic.* a rubber overshoe. Also, **in′dia rub′ber.**

In′dia silk′, a soft, lightweight fabric in plain weave. Also, **Indian silk.**

In·dic (in′dik), *adj.* **1.** of or pertaining to India; Indian. **2.** *Linguistics.* of or belonging to a subbranch of Indo-Iranian that includes Sanskrit, Hindi, Urdu, Bengali, and many other Indo-European languages of India, Ceylon, and Pakistan; Indo-Aryan. [< L *Indic(us)* of India < Gk *Indikós.* See INDIA, -IC]

indic., **1.** indicating. **2.** indicative. **3.** indicator.

in·di·can (in′də kən), *n.* **1.** *Chem.* a glucoside, $C_{14}H_{17}NO_6$, from which indigo is obtained. **2.** *Biochem.* indoxyl potassium sulfate, $C_8H_6O_4SK$, a component of urine. [< L *indic(um)* INDIGO + -AN]

in·di·cant (in′də kənt), *n.* **1.** something that indicates. —*adj.* **2.** *Obs.* serving to indicate; indicative. [< L *indicant-* (s. of *indicāns*) pointing, prp. of *indicāre.* See INDICATE, -ANT]

in·di·cate (in′də kāt′), *v.t.,* **-cat·ed, -cat·ing.** **1.** to be a sign of; betoken; imply: *His hesitation indicates unwillingness.* **2.** to point out or point to; direct attention to: *to indicate a place on a map.* **3.** to show; make known: *The thermometer indicates air temperature.* **4.** to state or express, esp. briefly or in a general way. [< L *indicāt(us)* pointed out or at (ptp. of *indicāre*). See INDEX, -ATE[1]] —**in′di·cat′a·ble,** *adj.* —**in·dic·a·to·ry** (in dik′ə tōr′ē, -tôr′ē, in′də kə-), *adj.*

in·di·ca·tion (in′də kā′shən), *n.* **1.** anything serving to indicate or point out, as a sign, token, etc. **2.** act of indicating. **3.** the degree marked by an instrument. [< L *indicātiōn-* (s. of *indicātiō*)]

in·dic·a·tive (in dik′ə tiv), *adj.* **1.** indicating; pointing out; suggestive (usually fol. by *of*): *behavior indicative of mental disorder.* **2.** *Gram.* noting or pertaining to the mood of the verb used for ordinary objective statements, questions, etc., as the verb *plays* in *John plays football.* Cf. **imperative** (def. 3), **subjunctive** (def. 1). —*n. Gram.* **3.** the indicative mood. **4.** a verb in the indicative. [< LL *indicātīv(us)*] —**in·dic′a·tive·ly,** *adv.*

in·di·ca·tor (in′də kā′tər), *n.* **1.** a person or thing that indicates. **2.** a pointing or directing device, as a pointer on an instrument. **3.** an instrument that indicates the condition of a machine or the like. **4.** an instrument for measuring and recording variations of pressure in the cylinder of an engine. **5.** *Chem.* **a.** a substance that indicates the presence, and sometimes the concentration, of a certain constituent. **b.** a substance often used in a titration to indicate the point at which the reaction is complete. **6.** *Ecol.* a plant or animal that indicates, by its presence in a given area, the existence of certain environmental conditions. [< LL]

in·di·ces (in′di sēz′), *n.* a pl. of **index.**

in·di·ci·a (in dish′ē ə), *n., pl.* **-ci·a, -ci·as.** **1.** an envelope marking substituted for a stamp or a regular cancellation on each item in a large shipment of mail. **2.** Also called **indicium.** an indication; token; evidence. [< L, pl. of *indicium* INDICIUM]

in·di·ci·um (in dish′ē əm), *n., pl.* **-di·ci·a** (-dish′ē ə), **-di·ci·ums.** indicia (def. 2). [< L = *indici-* (s. of *index*) INDEX + *-um* neut. sing. ending]

in·dict (in dīt′), *v.t.* **1.** to charge with an offense or crime; accuse of wrongdoing. **2.** (of a grand jury) to bring a formal accusation against. [var. sp. (< ML) of INDITE] —**in·dict′a·ble,** *adj.* —**in·dict′a·bly,** *adv.* —**in·dict′er, in·dic′tor,** *n.* —**Syn. 2.** arraign. —**Ant. 2.** acquit.

in·dic·tion (in dik′shən), *n.* the recurring fiscal period of 15 years in the Roman Empire, long used for dating ordinary events. Also called **cycle of indiction.** [ME *indiccio(u)n* < L *indictiōn-* (s. of *indictiō*) announcement. See INDITE, -ION] —**in·dic′tion·al,** *adj.*

in·dict·ment (in dīt′mənt), *n.* **1.** the act of indicting. **2.** *Law.* a formal accusation presented by a grand jury and usually required for the prosecution of felonies and other serious crimes. **3.** any charge or accusation. **4.** the state of being indicted. [INDICT + -MENT; r. ME *enditement* < AF]

In·dienne (an′dē en′; *Fr.* AN dyen′), *adj.* (of food) prepared or seasoned in East Indian style, as with curry. [< F, fem. of *indien* INDIAN]

In·dies (in′dēz), *n.,* **the.** **1.** (*construed as pl.*) See **West Indies** (def. 1). **2.** (*construed as sing.*) a region in and near S and SE Asia; India, Indochina, and the East Indies. **3.** (*construed as pl.*) See **East Indies** (def. 2).

in·dif·fer·ence (in dif′ər əns, -dif′rəns), *n.* **1.** lack of interest or concern. **2.** unimportance: *a matter of indifference.* **3.** the quality or condition of being indifferent. **4.** mediocre quality; mediocrity. [late ME; var. of INDIFFERENCY < L] —**Syn. 1.** INDIFFERENCE, UNCONCERN, APATHY, INSENSIBILITY all imply lack of feeling. INDIFFERENCE denotes an absence of feeling or interest; UNCONCERN, an absence of concern or solicitude, a calm or cool indifference in the face of what might be expected to cause uneasiness or apprehension; APATHY, a profound intellectual and emotional indifference suggestive of faculties either naturally sluggish or dulled by emotional disturbance, mental illness, or prolonged sickness; INSENSIBILITY, an absence of capacity for feeling or of susceptibility to emotional influences. —**Ant. 1.** eagerness, responsiveness.

in·dif·fer·en·cy (in dif′ər ən sē), *n. Archaic.* indifference. [late ME < L *indifferentia.* See INDIFFERENT, -ENCY]

in·dif·fer·ent (in dif′ər ənt, -dif′rənt), *adj.* **1.** without interest or concern; not caring; apathetic. **2.** having no bias or preference; impartial. **3.** neutral in character or quality. **4.** not particularly good: *an indifferent performance.* **5.** of only moderate amount, extent, etc. **6.** immaterial or unimportant. **7.** not essential or obligatory, as an observance. **8.** neutral in chemical, electric, or magnetic quality. **9.** *Biol.* not differentiated or specialized, as cells or tissues. —*n.* **10.** a person who is indifferent, esp. in matters of religion or politics. [ME < L (adj.) *indifferent-* (s. of *indifferēns*)] —**in·dif′fer·ent·ly,** *adv.*

in·dif·fer·ent·ism (in dif′ər ən tiz′əm, -dif′rən-), *n.* **1.** systematic indifference. **2.** the principle or opinion that differences of religious belief are unimportant. [< F *indifférentisme*] —**in·dif′fer·ent·ist,** *n.*

in·di·gence (in′di jəns), *n.* an indigent state; poverty. [ME < L *indigentia* need. See INDIGENT, -ENCE] —**Syn.** privation, need, want, penury. —**Ant.** wealth.

in·di·gene (in′di jēn′), *n.* a person or thing that is indigenous or native. Also, **in·di·gen** (in′di jən). [< MF < L *indigen(a)* a native. See INDIGENOUS]

in·dig·e·nous (in dij′ə nəs), *adj.* **1.** originating in and characterizing a particular region or country; native (usually fol. by *to*): *the plants indigenous to Canada.* **2.** innate; inherent; natural (usually fol. by *to*): *feelings indigenous to human beings.* [< L *indigenus* native = *indigen(a)* inborn (person), native (*indi-* in + *-gena* born) + *-us* -OUS] —**in·dig′e·nous·ly,** *adv.* —**in·dig′e·nous·ness, in·di·gen·i·ty** (in′di jen′i tē), *n.* —**Syn. 1.** autochthonous, aboriginal, natural. —**Ant. 1.** foreign, alien.

in·di·gent (in′di jənt), *adj.* **1.** lacking the necessities of life because of poverty; needy; poor; impoverished. **2.** *Archaic.* deficient; destitute (usually fol. by *of*). —*n.* **3.** a person who is indigent. [ME < L *indigent-* (s. of *indigēns* needing, needy, prp. of *indigēre*) = *ind-* in + *-ig-* (var. of *eg-* want) + *-ent-* -ENT] —**in′di·gent·ly,** *adv.*

in·di·gest·ed (in′di jes′tid, -dī-), *adj.* *Rare.* **1.** without arrangement or order. **2.** unformed or shapeless. **3.** not digested; undigested. **4.** not duly considered.

in·di·gest·i·ble (in′di jes′tə bəl, -dī-), *adj.* not digestible; not easily digested. [< LL *indīgestibil(is)*] —**in′di·gest′i·bil′i·ty, in′di·gest′i·ble·ness,** *n.* —**in′di·gest′i·bly,** *adv.*

in·di·ges·tion (in′di jes′chən, -dī-, -jesh′-), *n.* **1.** incapability of or difficulty in digesting food; dyspepsia. **2.** an instance or case of this. [late ME < LL *indīgestiōn-* (s. of *indīgestiō*)] —**in′di·ges′tive,** *adj.*

in·dign (in dīn′), *adj.* **1.** *Chiefly Literary.* undeserved. **2.** *Archaic.* unworthy. **3.** *Obs.* unbecoming or disgraceful. [late ME *indigne* < MF < L *indign(us)* = *in-* IN-[3] + *dignus* worthy; see DIGNITY] —**in·dign′ly,** *adv.*

in·dig·nant (in dig′nənt), *adj.* feeling, characterized by, or expressing indignation. [< L *indignant-* (s. of *indignāns*), prp. of *indignārī* to deem unworthy, take offense] —**in·dig′nant·ly,** *adv.*

in·dig·na·tion (in′dig nā′shən), *n.* strong displeasure at something deemed unworthy, unjust, or base; righteous anger. [ME *indignacio(u)n* < L *indignātiōn-* (s. of *indignātiō*) = *indignāt(us)* made indignant (ptp. of *indignārī*; see INDIGNANT) + *-iōn-* -ION] —**Syn.** exasperation, wrath, ire. See **anger.**

in·dig·ni·ty (in dig′ni tē), *n., pl.* **-ties. 1.** an injury to one's dignity; humiliating affront or injury. **2.** *Obs.* **a.** unworthiness. **b.** disgrace or disgraceful action. [< L *indignitās* unworthiness] —**Syn. 1.** outrage. See **insult.**

in·di·go (in′də gō′), *n., pl.* **-gos, -goes,** *adj.* —*n.* **1.** a blue dye obtained from various plants, esp. of the genus *Indigofera.* **2.** See **indigo blue** (def. 2). **3.** any leguminous plant of the genus *Indigofera.* **4.** deep violet blue. —*adj.* **5.** Also called **indigo-blue, in·di·got·ic** (in′də got′ik). of the color indigo. [< Sp or Pg, var. of *índico* < L *indicum* < Gk *indikón,* n. use of neut. of *Indikós* INDIC]

in′digo blue′, 1. the color indigo. **2.** Also called **indigo, indigotin.** a dark-blue powder, $C_{16}H_{10}N_2O_2$, contained in the dye indigo. —**in′di·go-blue′,** *adj.*

in′digo bunt′ing, a North American bunting, *Passerina cyanea,* the male of which is indigo.

in′digo snake′, a large, deep blue or brown, colubrid snake, *Drymarchon corais,* that preys on small mammals. Also called **gopher snake.**

in·dig·o·tin (in dig′ə tin, in′də gōt′ən), *n.* See **indigo blue** (def. 2). [INDIGO + hiatus-filling *-t-* + -IN[2]]

in·di·rect (in′də rekt′, -dī-), *adj.* **1.** deviating from a straight line, as a path. **2.** not resulting directly or immediately, as effects or consequences. **3.** not direct in action or procedure. **4.** devious; not straightforward. **5.** not descending in a direct line of succession, as a title or inheritance. **6.** not direct in application, force, etc.: *indirect evidence.* **7.** of, pertaining to, or characteristic of indirect discourse: *an indirect quote.* [ME < ML *indīrect(us)*] —**in′di·rect′ly,** *adv.* —**in′di·rect′ness,** *n.*

in′direct dis′course, discourse consisting of a version of a speaker's words, transformed for grammatical inclusion in a larger sentence, as in *He said he was hungry.* Cf. **direct discourse.**

in·di·rec·tion (in′də rek′shən, -dī-), *n.* **1.** indirect action or procedure. **2.** a roundabout course or method. **3.** a lack of direction or goal; aimlessness. **4.** deceitful or crooked dealing. [INDIRECT + -ION, modeled on *direction*]

in′direct light′ing, reflected or diffused light used esp. in interiors.

in′direct ob′ject, a word or group of words representing the person or thing with reference to which the action of verbs is performed, in English generally coming between the verb and the direct object. *The boy* is the indirect object of the verb *gave* in *He gave the boy a book.*

in′direct tax′, a tax levied indirectly, though ultimately, on one group of persons by taxing another which passes on the expense to the first, as a tax levied on commodities before they reach the consumer but being paid ultimately by the consumer as part of their market price.

in·dis·cern·i·ble (in′di sûr′nə bəl, -zûr′-), *adj.* not discernible; imperceptible. —**in′dis·cern′i·bly,** *adv.*

in·dis·ci·pline (in dis′ə plin), *n.* **1.** lack of discipline. **2.** an instance of this.

in·dis·cov·er·a·ble (in′di skuv′ər ə bəl), *adj.* not discoverable; undiscoverable.

in·dis·creet (in′di skrēt′), *adj.* not discreet; lacking prudence or sound judgment: *an indiscreet confidence.* [ME *indiscret* < LL *indiscrēt(us),* L: undivided; see INDISCRETE] —**in′dis·creet′ly,** *adv.* —**in′dis·creet′ness,** *n.*

in·dis·crete (in′di skrēt′, in dis′krēt), *adj.* not discrete; not divided into parts. [< L *indiscrēt(us)* undivided]

in·dis·cre·tion (in′di skresh′ən), *n.* **1.** lack of discretion. **2.** an indiscreet act or step. [ME < LL *indiscrētiōn-* (s. of *indiscrētiō*)] —**in′dis·cre′tion·ar′y,** *adj.*

in·dis·crim·i·nate (in′di skrim′ə nit), *adj.* **1.** not discriminating; choosing at random. **2.** not discriminate; haphazard. **3.** not kept apart or divided; thrown together; jumbled. —**in′dis·crim′i·nate·ly,** *adv.* —**in′dis·crim′i·nate·ness,** *n.* —**in·dis·crim·i·na·tion** (in′di skrim′ə nā′shən), *n.* —**in′dis·crim′i·na′tive,** *adj.* —**Syn. 3.** mixed.

in·dis·crim·i·nat·ing (in′di skrim′ə nā′ting), *adj.* not discriminating. —**in′dis·crim′i·nat′ing·ly,** *adv.*

in·dis·pen·sa·ble (in′di spen′sə bəl), *adj.* **1.** not dispensable; absolutely necessary or essential; needed. **2.** incapable of being disregarded or neglected. —*n.* **3.** a person or thing that is indispensable. [< ML *indispensābil(is)* not subject to dispensation] —**in′dis·pen′sa·bil′i·ty, in′dis·pen′sa·ble·ness,** *n.* —**in′dis·pen′sa·bly,** *adv.* —**Syn. 1.** See **necessary.** —**Ant. 1–3.** unessential.

in·dis·pose (in′di spōz′), *v.t.,* **-posed, -pos·ing. 1.** to make unfit; disqualify. **2.** to make ill, esp. slightly. **3.** to disincline; render averse or unwilling. [back formation from INDISPOSED]

in·dis·posed (in′di spōzd′), *adj.* **1.** sick or ill, esp. slightly: *to be indisposed with a cold.* **2.** disinclined or unwilling: *indisposed to help.* [ME: out of order, not suitable] —**in·dis·pos·ed·ness** (in′di spō′zid nis, -spōzd′-), *n.* —**Syn. 1.** unwell. See **sick**[1]. **2.** reluctant, averse, loath.

in·dis·po·si·tion (in′dis pə zish′ən), *n.* **1.** the state of being indisposed; a slight illness. **2.** disinclination; unwillingness. [late ME]

in·dis·put·a·ble (in′di spyōō′tə bəl, in dis′pyə-), *adj.* not disputable or deniable. [< LL *indisputābil(is)*] —**in′dis·put′a·bil′i·ty, in′dis·put′a·ble·ness,** *n.* —**in′dis·put′a·bly,** *adv.* —**Syn.** incontestable, undeniable, unquestionable. —**Ant.** questionable; uncertain.

in·dis·sol·u·ble (in′di sol′yə bəl), *adj.* **1.** not dissoluble; incapable of being dissolved, decomposed, undone, or destroyed. **2.** firm or stable. **3.** perpetually binding or obligatory. [< L *indissolūbil(is)*] —**in′dis·sol′u·bil′i·ty, in′dis·sol′u·ble·ness,** *n.* —**in′dis·sol′u·bly,** *adv.*

in·dis·tinct (in′di stingkt′), *adj.* **1.** not distinct; not clearly marked or defined. **2.** not clearly distinguishable or perceptible. **3.** not able to distinguish clearly: *indistinct vision.* [ME < L *indistinct(us)*] —**in′dis·tinct′ly,** *adv.* —**in′dis·tinct′ness,** *n.*

in·dis·tinc·tive (in′di stingk′tiv), *adj.* **1.** without distinctive characteristics. **2.** incapable of distinguishing. —**in′dis·tinc′tive·ly,** *adv.* —**in′dis·tinc′tive·ness,** *n.*

in·dis·tin·guish·a·ble (in′di sting′gwi shə bəl), *adj.* **1.** not distinguishable. **2.** indiscernible; imperceptible. —**in′dis·tin′guish·a·ble·ness, in′dis·tin′guish·a·bil′i·ty,** *n.* —**in′dis·tin′guish·a·bly,** *adv.*

in·dite (in dīt′), *v.t.,* **-dit·ed, -dit·ing.** to compose or write, as a speech or poem. [ME *endite(n)* < OF *endit(er)* < VL **indictāre* < L *indictus* announced, hence, worded (ptp. of *indīcere*). See IN-[2], DICTUM] —**in·dite′ment,** *n.* —**in·dit′er,** *n.*

in·di·um (in′dē əm), *n.* *Chem.* a rare metallic element, socalled from the two indigo-blue lines in its spectrum. *Symbol:* In; *at. wt.:* 114.82; *at. no.:* 49; *sp. gr.:* 7.3 at 20°C. [< NL; see INDIGO, -IUM]

in·di·vert·i·ble (in′də vûr′tə bəl, -dī-), *adj.* not divertible; not to be turned aside. —**in′di·vert′i·bly,** *adv.*

individ., individual. Also, **indiv.**

in·di·vid·u·al (in′də vij′ōō əl), *adj.* **1.** particular; separate, esp. from similar things. **2.** existing as a distinct, indivisible entity; single. **3.** of, pertaining to, or characteristic of a particular person or thing: *individual tastes.* **4.** intended for the use of one person only: *individual portions.* **5.** characterized by unique or unusual qualities: *a highly individual style.* —*n.* **6.** a single human being, as distinguished from a group. **7.** a person. **8.** a distinct, indivisible entity. **9.** *Biol.* **a.** a single or simple organism capable of independent existence. **b.** a member of a compound organism or colony. [ME < ML *indīviduāl(is)* = L *indīvidu(us)* indivisible (see IN-[3], DIVIDE) + *-ālis* -AL[1]] —**Syn. 7.** See **person.**

in·di·vid·u·al·ise (in′də vij′ōō ə līz′), *v.t.,* **-ised, -is·ing.** *Chiefly Brit.* individualize. —**in′di·vid′u·al·i·sa′tion,** *n.* —**in′di·vid′u·al·is′er,** *n.*

in·di·vid·u·al·ism (in′də vij′ōō ə liz′əm), *n.* **1.** a social theory advocating the liberty, rights, or independent action of the individual. **2.** the principle or habit of independent thought or action. **3.** the pursuit of individual rather than common or collective interests; egoism. **4.** *Philos.* **a.** the doctrine that only individual things are real. **b.** the doctrine or belief that all actions are determined by or take place for the benefit of the individual, not the mass of men.

in·di·vid·u·al·ist (in′də vij′ōō ə list), *n.* **1.** a person who is characterized by great independence or individuality in thought or action. **2.** an advocate of individualism. —**in′di·vid′u·a·lis′tic,** *adj.* —**in′di·vid′u·al·is′ti·cal·ly,** *adv.*

in·di·vid·u·al·i·ty (in′də vij′ōō al′i tē), *n., pl.* **-ties. 1.** the particular character, or aggregate of qualities, that distinguishes one person or thing from others. **2.** the state or quality of being individual; existence as a distinct individual. **3.** *Archaic.* the state or quality of being indivisible or inseparable. —**Syn. 1.** See **character.**

in·di·vid·u·al·ize (in′də vij′ōō ə līz′), *v.t.,* **-ized, -iz·ing. 1.** to make individual or distinctive; give an individual or distinctive character to. **2.** to mention, indicate, or consider individually; specify; particularize. Also, *esp. Brit.,* **individualise.** —**in′di·vid′u·al·i·za′tion,** *n.* —**in′di·vid′u·al·iz′er,** *n.*

in·di·vid·u·al·ly (in′də vij′ōō ə lē), *adv.* **1.** in an individual or personally unique manner. **2.** one at a time; separately. **3.** personally: *Each of us is individually responsible.*

in·di·vid·u·ate (in′də vij′ōō āt′), *v.t.,* **-at·ed, -at·ing. 1.** to form into an individual or distinct entity. **2.** to give an individual or distinctive character to. [< ML *indīviduāt(us)* made individual, ptp. of *indīviduāre.* See INDIVIDUAL, -ATE[1]] —**in′di·vid′u·a′tor,** *n.*

in·di·vid·u·a·tion (in′də vij′ōō ā′shən), *n.* **1.** the act of individuating. **2.** the state of being individuated; individual existence; individuality. **3.** *Philos.* the development of the individual from the general.

in·di·vis·i·ble (in′də viz′ə bəl), *adj.* **1.** not divisible; not separable into parts. —*n.* **2.** something indivisible. [ME < LL *indīvīsibil(is)*] —**in′di·vis′i·bil′i·ty, in′di·vis′i·ble·ness,** *n.* —**in′di·vis′i·bly,** *adv.*

indo-, a combining form of **indigo:** *indophenol.* Also, *esp. before a vowel,* **ind-.**

Indo-, a combining form of **India:** *Indo-European.* [< L < Gk; comb. form of L *Indus,* Gk *Indós*]

In·do-Ar·y·an (in′dō âr′ē ən, -yən, -ar′-; -är′yən), *n.* **1.** a member of a people of India who are Indo-European in speech and Caucasoid in physical characteristics. —*adj.* **2.** of, pertaining to, or characteristic of the Indo-Aryans.

In·do·chi·na (in′dō chī′nə), *n.* a peninsula in SE Asia, between the Bay of Bengal and the South China Sea, comprising Vietnam, Cambodia, Laos, Thailand, Malaya, and Burma. Also called **Farther India.** Cf. **French Indochina.**

In·do-Chi·nese (in′dō chī nēz′, -nēs′), *adj., n., pl.* **-nese.** Sino-Tibetan (no longer current).

in·doc·ile (in dos′il), *adj.* not docile; not amenable to teaching or training. [< L *indocil(is)*] —**in·do·cil·i·ty** (in′dō sil′i tē), *n.*

in·doc·tri·nate (in dok′trə nāt′), *v.t.,* **-nat·ed, -nat·ing. 1.** to instruct in a doctrine, principle, ideology, etc. **2.** to teach or inculcate. **3.** to imbue (a person) with learning. [IN-² + ML *doctrīnāt(us)* taught, ptp. of *doctrīnāre*] —**in·doc′tri·na′tion,** *n.* —**in·doc′tri·na′tor,** *n.*

In·do-Eu·ro·pe·an (in′dō yŏŏr′ə pē′ən), *n.* **1.** a family of languages characterized by inflection, grammatical number, and, typically, gender and ablaut, and by basic vocabularies that have many correspondences, jointly in sound and in meaning, and including many politically or culturally important languages, esp. those of the Germanic, Italic, Hellenic, Slavic, and Indo-Iranian branches. *Abbr.:* IE, I.E. Cf. **family** (def. 11), **number** (def. 11). **2.** Also called **Proto-Indo-European.** the prehistoric parent language of this family. **3.** a member of any of the peoples speaking an Indo-European language. —*adj.* **4.** of or belonging to Indo-European. **5.** speaking an Indo-European language.

In·do-Ger·man·ic (in′dō jər man′ik), *adj., n.* (no longer current) Indo-European.

In·do-Hit·tite (in′dō hit′īt), *n.* a language family in which Proto-Anatolian and Proto-Indo-European are considered coordinate. Cf. **Hittite** (def. 2).

In·do-I·ra·ni·an (in′dō i rā′nē ən), *n.* **1.** a branch of the Indo-European family of languages, including Persian, Pashto, Avestan, Kurdish, and the Indo-European languages of the Indian subcontinent. —*adj.* **2.** of or belonging to Indo-Iranian.

in·dole (in′dōl), *n. Chem.* a colorless to yellowish solid, C_8H_7N, having a low melting point and a fecal odor, found in the oil of jasmine and clove and as a putrefaction product from animals' intestines: used in perfumery and as a reagent.

in′dole·a·ce′tic ac′id (in′dōl ə sē′tik, -set′ik, in′-), *Biochem.* a plant hormone, $C_8H_6NCH_2COOH$, used for stimulating growth and root formation in plant cutting.

in′dole·bu·tyr′ic ac′id (in′dōl byōō tir′ik, in′-), *Biochem.* a plant hormone, $C_8H_6N(CH_2)_3COOH$, similar to indoleacetic acid and used for the same purposes.

in·do·lence (in′dᵊləns), *n.* the quality or state of being indolent. [< L *indolentia* freedom from pain = *in-* IN-³ + *dolentia* pain < *dolent-* (see INDOLENT); see -ENCE]

in·do·lent (in′dᵊlənt), *adj.* **1.** having or showing a disposition to avoid exertion; lazy; slothful. **2.** *Pathol.* causing little or no pain. [< L *indolent-* (s. of *indolēns*) = *in-* IN-³ + *dolent-* (s. of *dolēns*) painful, prp. of *dolēre*] —**in′do·lent·ly,** *adv.* —**Syn. 1.** slow, inactive, sluggish, torpid. See **idle.**

in·dom·i·ta·ble (in dom′i tə bəl), *adj.* unable to be subdued or overcome, as persons, pride, or courage. [< LL *indomitābil(is)* = L *indomit(us)* untamed (*in-* IN-³ + *domitus,* ptp. of *domāre*) + *-ābilis* -ABLE] —**in·dom′i·ta·bil′i·ty, in·dom′i·ta·ble·ness,** *n.* —**in·dom′i·ta·bly,** *adv.* —**Syn.** unconquerable, unyielding.

In·do·ne·sia (in′də nē′zhə, -shə, -zē ə, -dō-), *n.* **1.** See **East Indies** (def. 2). **2. Republic of.** Formerly, **Netherlands East Indies, Dutch East Indies.** Former official name (1949), **United States of Indonesia.** a republic in the Malay Archipelago, consisting of Sumatra, Java, Celebes, Kalimantan, and about 3000 small islands: received independence from the Netherlands in 1949. 132,000,000; ab. 580,000 sq. mi. *Cap.:* Djakarta. [INDO- + Gk *nēs(os)* island + -IA]

In·do·ne·sian (in′də nē′zhən, -shən, -zē ən, -dō-), *n.* **1.** Also called **Malaysian.** a member of the ethnic group consisting of the natives of Indonesia, the Filipinos, and the Malays of Malaya. **2.** a member of a light-colored race supposed to have been dominant in the Malay Archipelago before the Malays. **3.** Official name, **Bahasa Indonesia.** an amalgam of several Indonesian languages that is based mostly on Malay and is used as the official language of the Republic of Indonesia. **4.** the westernmost subfamily of Malayo-Polynesian languages, including those of Formosa, the Philippines, the Malagasy Republic, and Indonesia, as well as Malay. —*adj.* **5.** of or pertaining to the Malay Archipelago. **6.** of or pertaining to Indonesia, the Indonesians, or their languages.

Indone′sian Ti′mor, Timor (def. 2).

in·door (in′dōr′, -dôr′), *adj.* occurring, used, etc., in a house or building, rather than out of doors. [aph. var. of *within-door,* orig. phrase *within* (*the*) *door,* i.e., inside the house]

in·doors (in dōrz′, -dôrz′), *adv.* in or into a house or building: *Stay indoors. He ran indoors.*

In·do-Pa·cif·ic (in′dō pə sif′ik), *adj.* of or pertaining to the areas of the Indian and Pacific oceans off the coast of SE Asia.

in·do·phe·nol (in′dō fē′nōl, -nôl, -nol), *n. Chem.* **1.** the para form of $HOC_6H_4N{=}C_6H_4{=}O$, a quinonimine derivative that is the parent substance of the blue and green indophenol dyes. **2.** any derivative of this compound. **3.** any of various related dyes.

In·dore (in dôr′), *n.* **1.** a former state in central India: now part of Madhya Pradesh. **2.** a city in W Madhya Pradesh, in central India. 394,900 (1961).

in·dorse (in dôrs′), *v.t.,* **-dorsed, -dors·ing.** endorse. —**in·dors′a·ble,** *adj.* —**in·dor·see** (in′dôr sē′, in dôr′sē), *n.* —**in·dors′er, in·dor′sor,** *n.*

in·dorse·ment (in dôrs′mənt), *n.* endorsement.

in·dox·yl (in dok′sil), *n. Chem.* a crystalline compound, C_8H_7NO, readily oxidized to furnish indigo. [IND- + (HY-DR)OXYL]

In·dra (in′drə), *n. Hinduism.* the chief of the Vedic gods, the god of rain and thunder.

Indra

in·draft (in′draft′, -dräft′), *n.* an inward flow or current, as of air or water. Also, *esp. Brit.,* **in′draught′.**

in·drawn (in′drôn′), *adj.* **1.** reserved; introspective. **2.** made with the breath drawn in.

in·dri (in′drē), *n., pl.* **-dris.** a short-tailed lemur, *Indri indri,* of Madagascar, about two feet in length. [< F < Malagasy *indry* look! wrongly taken as animal's name]

in·du·bi·ta·ble (in dōō′bi tə bəl, -dyōō′-), *adj.* not to be doubted; unquestionable; certain. [< L *indubitābil(is)*] —**in·du′bi·ta·bil′i·ty, in·du′bi·ta·ble·ness,** *n.* —**in·du′bi·ta·bly,** *adv.*

induc., induction.

in·duce (in dōōs′, -dyōōs′), *v.t.,* **-duced, -duc·ing. 1.** to influence or persuade, as to some action, state of mind, etc.: *Induce him to stay.* **2.** to bring about or cause: *sleep induced by drugs.* **3.** *Physics.* to produce (magnetism, charge, emf, or electric current) by induction. **4.** *Logic.* to assert or establish (a proposition) on the basis of observations of particular facts. [ME < L *indūce(re)* (to) lead or bring in, introduce = *in-* IN-² + *dūcere* to lead] —**in·duc′er,** *n.* —**in·duc′i·ble,** *adj.* —**Syn. 1.** actuate, prompt, incite, urge, spur. See **persuade.** —**Ant. 1.** dissuade.

induced′ drag′, *Aeron.* the drag force generated in the production of lift.

in·duce·ment (in dōōs′mənt, -dyōōs′), *n.* **1.** the act of inducing. **2.** something that induces, motivates, or persuades; an incentive. —**Syn. 2.** stimulus, spur, incitement; attraction, lure. See **motive.**

in·duct (in dukt′), *v.t.* **1.** to install in an office, benefice, position, etc., esp. with formal ceremonies. **2.** to introduce, esp. to something requiring special knowledge or experience; initiate (usually fol. by *to* or *into*): *They inducted him into the mystic rites of the order.* **3.** *U.S.* to enlist (a draftee) into military service; draft. **4.** to bring in as a member or participant; admit: *to induct one into a new profession.* [ME < L *induct(us)* led or brought in, introduced, ptp. of *indūcere* to INDUCE]

in·duct·ance (in duk′təns), *n. Elect.* **1.** the property of a circuit or a pair of circuits by which a change in current induces an electromotive force. **2.** inductor; coil.

in·duc·tee (in′duk tē′), *n.* a person inducted into military service.

in·duc·tile (in duk′til), *adj.* not ductile; not pliable or yielding. —**in′duc·til′i·ty,** *n.*

in·duc·tion (in duk′shən), *n.* **1.** *Elect., Magnetism.* the process by which a body having electric or magnetic properties produces magnetism, an electric charge, or an electromotive force in a neighboring body without contact. **2.** *Logic.* **a.** any form of reasoning in which the conclusion, though supported by the premises, does not follow from them necessarily. **b.** the process of estimating the validity of observations of part of a class of facts as evidence for a proposition about the whole class. **c.** a conclusion reached by this process. **3.** a presentation or bringing forward, as of facts, evidence, etc. **4.** the act of inducing. **5.** *Embryol.* the process by which an organizer influences the differentiation of another part. **6.** the act of inducting; introduction; initiation. **7.** formal installation in an office, benefice, or the like. **8.** *U.S.* the act or process of enlisting a draftee into military service. **9.** *Archaic.* a preface. [ME *induccio(u)n* < L *inductiōn-* (s. of *inductiō*)] —**in·duc′tion·less,** *adj.*

induc′tion coil′, *Elect.* a transformer for producing a high alternating voltage from a low-voltage direct-current source. Also called **spark coil.**

in·duc·tive (in duk′tiv), *adj.* **1.** of, pertaining to, operating by, or involving electrical or magnetic induction. **2.** of, pertaining to, or employing logical induction. **3.** *Embryol.* eliciting the action of an organizer. **4.** serving to induce; leading or influencing. **5.** introductory. [< LL *inductīv(us)*] —**in·duc′tive·ly,** *adv.* —**in·duc′tive·ness,** *n.* —**Syn. 2.** See **deductive.**

induc′tive reac′tance, *Elect.* the opposition of inductance to alternating current, equal to the product of the angular frequency of the current times the self-inductance. *Symbol:* X_L Cf. **capacitive reactance.**

in·duc·tor (in duk′tər), *n.* **1.** *Elect.* a device that introduces inductance into an electric circuit; coil. **2.** a person who inducts, as into office. [< L: one who rouses]

in·due (in dōō′, -dyōō′), *v.t.,* **-dued, -du·ing.** endue.

in·dulge (in dulj′), *v.,* **-dulged, -dulg·ing.** —*v.i.* **1.** to yield to an inclination or desire; indulge oneself. —*v.t.* **2.** to yield to or gratify (desires, feelings, etc.). **3.** to yield to the wishes or whims of (oneself or another). [< L *indulgē(re)* (to) be long-suffering, forbearing, too kind = *in-* IN-² + *-dulgēre;* akin to Gk *dolichós* long] —**in·dulg′er,** *n.* —**in·dulg′ing·ly,** *adv.* —**Syn. 3.** pamper. —**Ant. 3.** refuse.

in·dul·gence (in dul′jəns), *n., v.,* **-genced, -genc·ing.** —*n.* **1.** the act or practice of indulging; humoring. **2.** tolerance; forbearance. **3.** something granted or taken in gratification of desire. **4.** *Rom. Cath. Ch.* a partial remission of the temporal punishment that is still due for sin after absolution. Cf. **plenary indulgence. 5.** *Eng. and Scot. Hist.* (in the reigns of Charles II and James II) a royal dispensation granting Protestant dissenters and Roman Catholics a certain amount of religious freedom. **6.** *Com.* an extension, through favor, of time for payment or performance. —*v.t.* **7.** *Rom. Cath. Ch.* to provide with an indulgence. [ME < L *indulgentia*]

in·dul·gen·cy (in dul′jən sē), *n., pl.* **-cies.** indulgence. [< L *indulgentia*]

in·dul·gent (in dul′jənt), *adj.* characterized by or showing indulgence; benignly permissive. [< L *indulgent-* (s. of *in-*

dulgēns), prp. of *indulgēre* to INDULGE; see -ENT] —**in·dul′gent·ly,** *adv.*

in·du·line (in′dyə lēn′, -lin, in′dᵊlēn′), *n.* any of a large class of dyes yielding colors similar to indigo. [IND- + -ULE + -INE²]

in·dult (in dult′), *n. Rom. Cath. Ch.* a faculty granted by the pope to bishops and others permitting them to deviate from the common law of the church. [late ME < eccl. L *indult(um),* n. use of neut. of *indultus,* ptp. of *indulgēre* to INDULGE]

in·du·pli·cate (in dōō′plə kit, -kāt′, -dyōō′-), *adj. Bot.* folded or rolled inward: said of the calyx or corolla in flower buds, or of leaves in vernation. Also, **in·du′pli·ca′tive.** —**in·du′pli·ca′tion,** *n.*

in·du·rate (*v.* in′dŏŏ rāt′, -dyŏŏ-; *adj.* in′dŏŏ rit, -dyŏŏ-; in dŏŏr′it, -dyŏŏr′-), *v.,* **-rat·ed, -rat·ing,** *adj.* —*v.t.* **1.** to make hard; harden, as rock, tissue, etc. **2.** to make callous, stubborn, or unfeeling. **3.** to inure; accustom. **4.** to make enduring; confirm; establish. —*v.i.* **5.** to become hard; harden. **6.** to become established or confirmed. —*adj.* **7.** hardened; callous; inured. [ME *indurat* < L *indūrāt(us)* hardened (ptp. of *indūrāre*)]

in·du·ra·tion (in′dŏŏ rā′shən, -dyŏŏ-), *n.* **1.** the act or state of indurating. **2.** the state of being indurated. **3.** *Geol.* **a.** consolidation of sediments to produce sedimentary rocks. **b.** hardening of rocks by heat, pressure, cementation, etc. **4.** *Pathol.* **a.** a hardening of an area of the body as a reaction to inflammation, hyperemia, or neoplastic infiltration. **b.** an area or part of the body that has undergone such a reaction. [ME < LL *indūrātiōn-* (s. of *indūrātiō*) a hardening] —**in′du·ra′tive,** *adj.*

In·dus (in′dəs), *n.* a river in S Asia, flowing from W Tibet through Kashmir and Pakistan to the Arabian Sea. 1900 mi. long.

indus., **1.** industrial. **2.** industry.

In′dus civiliza′tion. See **Indus valley civilization.**

in·du·si·um (in dōō′zē əm, -zhē əm, -dyōō′-), *n., pl.* **-si·a** (-zē ə, -zhē ə). **1.** *Bot.* a membranous overgrowth covering the sori in ferns. **2.** *Anat., Zool.* **a.** an enveloping layer or membrane. **b.** a thin layer of gray matter on the corpus callosum. [< NL, L: kind of tunic < *indu(ere)* (to) don] —**in·du′si·al,** *adj.*

in·dus·tri·al (in dus′trē əl), *adj.* **1.** of, pertaining to, of the nature of, or resulting from industry. **2.** having many and highly developed industries. **3.** engaged in an industry or industries. **4.** of or pertaining to the workers in industries. **5.** fashioned for use in industry. —*n.* **6.** an employee in some industry, esp. a manufacturing industry. **7.** a company engaged in industrial enterprises. **8.** an industrial product. **9. industrials,** stocks and bonds of industrial companies. —**in·dus′tri·al·ly,** *adv.*

indus′trial arts′, the methods of using tools and machinery, as taught in secondary and technical schools.

indus′trial design′, the art that deals with the design of manufactured objects. —**indus′trial design′er.**

in·dus·tri·al·ise (in dus′trē ə līz′), *v.t.,* **-ised, -is·ing.** *Chiefly Brit.* industrialize. —**in·dus′tri·al·i·sa′tion,** *n.*

in·dus·tri·al·ism (in dus′trē ə liz′əm), *n.* an economic organization of society built largely on mechanized industry.

in·dus·tri·al·ist (in dus′trē ə list), *n.* **1.** a person who owns or manages an industrial enterprise. —*adj.* **2.** of, pertaining to, or characterized by industrialism.

in·dus·tri·al·ize (in dus′trē ə līz′), *v.,* **-ized, -iz·ing.** —*v.t.* **1.** to introduce industry into (an area) on a large scale. —*v.i.* **2.** to undergo industrialization. Also, *esp. Brit.,* **industrialise.** —**in·dus′tri·al·i·za′tion,** *n.*

indus′trial park′, an area of land developed in an orderly, planned way with transportation, utilities, etc., and leased or sold to various industrial firms.

indus′trial psychol′ogy, the application of psychological principles and techniques to business and industrial problems, as in the selection of personnel, development of training programs, etc.

indus′trial rela′tions, **1.** the dealings or relations of an industrial concern with its employees, with labor in general, and with the public. **2.** the administration of such relations, esp. to maintain good will for an industrial concern.

indus′trial revolu′tion, the complex of social and economic changes resulting from the mechanization of productive processes that began in England about 1760.

indus′trial school′, **1.** a school for teaching one or more branches of industry. **2.** a school for educating neglected children and training them to some form of industry.

indus′trial un′ion, a labor union composed of workers in various trades and crafts within an industry. Cf. **craft union.**

Indus′trial Work′ers of the World′, an international industrial labor union that was organized in Chicago in 1905 and disintegrated after 1920. *Abbr.:* I.W.W., IWW

in·dus·tri·ous (in dus′trē əs), *adj.* **1.** hard-working; diligent. **2.** *Obs.* skillful. [< L *industrius,* OL *indostruus,* of disputed origin] —**in·dus′tri·ous·ly,** *adv.* —**in·dus′tri·ous·ness,** *n.* —**Syn. 1.** assiduous, sedulous, energetic. See **busy.** —**Ant. 1.** lazy, indolent.

in·dus·try (in′də strē), *n., pl.* **-tries** for 1, 2. **1.** the aggregate of manufacturing or technically productive enterprises in a particular field, often named after its principal product. **2.** any general business field. **3.** trade or manufacture in general. **4.** owners and managers collectively. **5.** systematic work or labor. **6.** assiduous activity at any work or task; diligence. [ME *industrie* < L *industria,* n. use of fem. of *industrius* INDUSTRIOUS] —**Syn. 6.** effort, attention, devotion.

In′dus val′ley civiliza′tion, an ancient civilization that flourished in the Indus River valley from about 2500–1500 B.C. Also called **Indus civilization.**

in·dwell (in dwel′), *v.,* **-dwelt, -dwell·ing.** —*v.t.* **1.** to inhabit. **2.** to possess (a person), as a principle, motivating force, etc. —*v.i.* **3.** to dwell. **4.** to abide within, as a guiding force. [ME *indwelle(n)*] —**in′dwell′er,** *n.*

In·dy, d′ (daN dē′), **Vin·cent** (vaN säN′), 1851–1931, French composer.

-ine¹, a suffix of adjectives of Greek or Latin origin, meaning "of or pertaining to," "of the nature of," "made of," "like": *asinine; crystalline; equine; marine.* Cf. **-in¹.** [< L *-īnus, -inus* < Gk *-inos*]

-ine², **1.** a suffix, of no assignable meaning, appearing in nouns of Greek, Latin, or French origin: *doctrine; famine; routine.* **2.** a noun suffix used particularly in chemical terms (*bromine; chlorine*), and esp. in names of basic substances (*amine; aniline; caffeine; quinine; quinoline*). Cf. **-in².** **3.** a suffix of feminine nouns (*heroine*), given names (*Clementine*), and titles (*landgravine*). [< F < L *-ina,* orig. fem. of *-inus;* also repr. Gk *-inē* fem. n. suffix]

in·earth (in ûrth′), *v.t. Archaic.* to bury; inter.

in·e·bri·ant (in ē′brē ənt, i nē′-), *adj.* **1.** inebriating; intoxicating. —*n.* **2.** an intoxicant. [< L *inēbriant-* (s. of *inēbrians,* prp. of *inēbriāre* to make drunk) = *in-* IN-² + *ēbri(us)* drunk + *-ant-* -ANT]

in·e·bri·ate (*v.* in ē′brē āt′, i nē′-; *n., adj.* in ē′brē it, i nē′-), *v.,* **-at·ed, -at·ing,** *n., adj.* —*v.t.* **1.** to make drunk; intoxicate. **2.** to intoxicate mentally or emotionally; exhilarate. —*n.* **3.** an intoxicated person. **4.** a habitual drunkard. —*adj.* **5.** Also, **in·e′bri·at′ed.** drunk; intoxicated. [< L *inēbriāt(us)* made drunk (ptp. of *inēbriāre*)] —**in·e′bri·a′tion,** *n.* —**Syn. 4.** See **drunkard.**

in·e·bri·e·ty (in′i brī′i tē), *n.* drunkenness; intoxication. [IN-² + *ebriety* < L *ēbrietās* = *ēbri(us)* drunk + *-etās, -itās* var. of -ITY]

in·ed·i·ble (in ed′ə bəl), *adj.* not edible; unfit to be eaten. —**in·ed′i·bil′i·ty,** *n.*

in·ed·i·ta (in ed′i tə), *n.pl.* unpublished literary works: *the late author's inedita.* [< L, neut. pl. of *inēditus* not made known = *in-* IN-³ + *ēditus* (ptp. of *ēdere* to publish, lit., put or give out); see EDITION]

in·ed·it·ed (in ed′i tid), *adj.* **1.** unpublished. **2.** not edited; published without alterations.

in·ed·u·ca·ble (in ej′ŏŏ kə bəl, -ed′yŏŏ-), *adj.* incapable of being educated, esp. because of some condition, as mental retardation or emotional disturbance, that prevents benefiting from instruction. —**in·ed′u·ca·bil′i·ty,** *n.*

in·ef·fa·ble (in ef′ə bəl), *adj.* **1.** incapable of being expressed or described; inexpressible; unspeakable. **2.** not to be spoken; unutterable. [late ME < L *ineffābil(is)*] —**in·ef′fa·bil′i·ty, in·ef′fa·ble·ness,** *n.* —**in·ef′fa·bly,** *adv.*

in·ef·face·a·ble (in′i fā′sə bəl), *adj.* not effaceable; indelible. —**in′ef·face′a·bil′i·ty,** *n.* —**in′ef·face′a·bly,** *adv.*

in·ef·fec·tive (in′i fek′tiv), *adj.* **1.** not effective; not producing results; ineffectual. **2.** inefficient or incompetent; incapable. —**in′ef·fec′tive·ly,** *adv.* —**in′ef·fec′tive·ness,** *n.*

in·ef·fec·tu·al (in′i fek′chōō əl), *adj.* **1.** not effectual; without satisfactory or decisive effect: *an ineffectual remedy.* **2.** unavailing; futile: *ineffectual efforts.* [ME] —**in′ef·fec′tu·al′i·ty, in′ef·fec′tu·al·ness,** *n.* —**in′ef·fec′tu·al·ly,** *adv.* —**Syn. 2.** ineffective, fruitless. See **useless.**

in·ef·fi·ca·cious (in′ef ə kā′shəs), *adj.* not efficacious; unable to produce the desired effect. —**in′ef·fi·ca′cious·ly,** *adv.* —**in′ef·fi·ca′cious·ness, in·ef·fi·cac·i·ty** (in′ef ə kas′i tē), *n.*

in·ef·fi·ca·cy (in ef′ə kə sē), *n.* lack of power or capacity to produce the desired effect. [< LL *inefficācia*]

in·ef·fi·cien·cy (in′i fish′ən sē), *n., pl.* **-cies** for 2. **1.** the quality or condition of being inefficient; lack of efficiency. **2.** an instance of inefficiency.

in·ef·fi·cient (in′i fish′ənt), *adj.* not efficient; unable to effect or achieve the desired result with reasonable economy of means. —**in′ef·fi′cient·ly,** *adv.* —**Syn.** See **incapable.**

in·e·las·tic (in′i las′tik), *adj.* not elastic; lacking flexibility or resilience; unyielding. —**in·e·las·tic·i·ty** (in′i la-stis′i tē), *n.* —**Syn.** inflexible; rigid, uncompromising.

in·el·e·gance (in el′ə gəns), *n.* **1.** the quality or state of being inelegant; lack of elegance. **2.** something that is inelegant. [INELEG(ANT) + -ANCE]

in·el·e·gan·cy (in el′ə gən sē), *n., pl.* **-cies.** inelegance.

in·el·e·gant (in el′ə gənt), *adj.* not elegant; lacking in refinement, gracefulness, or good taste. [< L *inēlegant-* (s. of *inēlegāns*)] —**in·el′e·gant·ly,** *adv.*

in·el·i·gi·ble (in el′i jə bəl), *adj.* **1.** not eligible. **2.** legally disqualified to hold an office, perform a civic function, receive a privilege, or the like. —*n.* **3.** a person who is ineligible as a suitor, team member, etc. —**in·el′i·gi·bil′i·ty, in·el′i·gi·ble·ness,** *n.*

in·el·o·quent (in el′ə kwənt), *adj.* not eloquent. —**in·el′o·quence,** *n.* —**in·el′o·quent·ly,** *adv.* [< LL *inēloquēns*]

in·e·luc·ta·ble (in′i luk′tə bəl), *adj.* incapable of being evaded; inescapable. [< L *inēluctābil(is)* = *in-* IN-³ + *ēluctā(rī)* (to) surmount (*ē-* E- + *luctārī* to wrestle) + *-bilis* -BLE] —**in′e·luc′ta·bil′i·ty,** *n.* —**in′e·luc′ta·bly,** *adv.*

in·e·lud·i·ble (in′i lōō′də bəl), *adj.* inescapable. —**in′e·lud′i·bly,** *adv.*

in·ept (in ept′, i nept′), *adj.* **1.** not apt; without skill or aptitude, esp. for a particular task. **2.** inappropriate; out of place. **3.** absurd or foolish. [< L *inept(us)* = *in-* IN-³ + *-eptus,* var. of *aptus* APT] —**in·ept·i·tude** (in ep′ti tōōd′, -tyōōd′, i nep′-), *n.* —**in·ept′ly,** *adv.* —**in·ept′ness,** *n.* —**Syn. 1.** unfitting, unsuited. **3.** pointless, inane.

in·e·qual·i·ty (in′i kwol′i tē), *n., pl.* **-ties.** **1.** the condition of being unequal, as in size, status, or natural endowments; lack of equality; disparity. **2.** injustice; partiality. **3.** unevenness, as of surface. **4.** an instance of unevenness. **5.** variableness, as of climate or temperament. **6.** *Astron.* **a.** any component part of the departure from uniformity in astronomical phenomena, esp. in orbital motion. **b.** the amount of such a departure. **7.** *Math.* an expression or proposition that two quantities are unequal, indicated by the symbol <, when the quantity preceding the symbol is less than that following, or >, when the quantity preceding the symbol is greater than that following. [late ME < L *inaequālitās*]

in·eq·ui·ta·ble (in ek′wi tə bəl), *adj.* not equitable; unjust or unfair. —**in·eq′ui·ta·ble·ness,** *n.* —**in·eq′ui·ta·bly,** *adv.*

in·eq·ui·ty (in ek′wi tē), *n., pl.* **-ties** for 2. **1.** lack of equity; unfairness. **2.** an unfair circumstance or proceeding.

in·e·rad·i·ca·ble (in′i rad′ə kə bəl), *adj.* not eradicable; not capable of being eradicated. —**in′e·rad′i·ca·ble·ness,** *n.* —**in′e·rad′i·ca·bly,** *adv.*

in·e·ras·a·ble (in′i rā′sə bəl), *adj.* not erasable; incapable of being erased or effaced. —**in′e·ras′a·ble·ness,** *n.* —**in′e·ras′a·bly,** *adv.*

in·er·ra·ble (in er′ə bəl, -ûr′-), *adj.* incapable of erring; infallible. [< LL *inerrābil(is)* unerring] —**in·er′ra·bil′i·ty, in·er′ra·ble·ness,** *n.* —**in·er′ra·bly,** *adv.*

in·er·rant (in er′ənt, -ûr′-), *adj.* free from error. [< L *inerrant-* (s. of *inerrāns*) = *in-* IN-^{3} + *errant-* (s. of *errāns* wandering, prp. of *errāre*)] —**in·er′ran·cy,** *n.* —**in·er′rant·ly,** *adv.*

in·ert (in ûrt′, i nûrt′), *adj.* **1.** having no inherent power of action, motion, or resistance (opposed to *active*): *inert matter.* **2.** *Chem.* having little or no ability to react, as nitrogen which occurs uncombined in the atmosphere. **3.** *Pharm.* having no pharmacological action, as the excipient of a pill. **4.** inactive or sluggish by habit or nature. [< L *inert-* (s. of *iners*) unskillful = *in-* IN-^{3} + *-ert-*, var. of *art-* (s. of *ars*) skill; see ART^1] —**in·ert′ly,** *adv.* —**in·ert′ness,** *n.* —**Syn. 1.** unmoving, motionless.

in·er·tia (in ûr′shə, i nûr′-), *n.* **1.** inert condition; inactivity; sluggishness. **2.** *Physics.* the property of matter by which it retains its state of rest or its velocity along a straight line so long as it is not acted upon by an external force. [< L: lack of skill, slothfulness] —**in·er′tial,** *adj.*

iner′tial guid′ance, *Rocketry.* guidance of a missile solely by instruments within it that determine its course on the basis of the directions and magnitudes of acceleration that the missile undergoes in flight. Also called **iner′tial naviga′tion.**

iner′tial sys′tem, *Physics.* a frame of reference in which a body remains at rest or moves with constant linear velocity unless acted upon by forces. Also called **iner′tial ref′erence frame′.** Cf. **law of motion.**

in·es·cap·a·ble (in′e skā′pə bəl), *adj.* incapable of being escaped, ignored, or avoided. —**in′es·cap′a·bly,** *adv.*

in es·se (in es′e; *Eng.* in es′ē), *Latin.* in being; in actuality; actually existing (contrasted with *in posse*).

in·es·sen·tial (in′i sen′shəl), *adj.* **1.** not essential; not necessary; nonessential. **2.** without essence; insubstantial. —*n.* **3.** something that is not essential. —**in′es·sen′ti·al′i·ty,** *n.*

in·es·ti·ma·ble (in es′tə mə bəl), *adj.* incapable of being estimated; too great to be estimated. [ME < L *inaestimābil(is)*] —**in·es′ti·ma·bil′i·ty, in·es′ti·ma·ble·ness,** *n.* —**in·es′ti·ma·bly,** *adv.*

in·ev·i·ta·ble (in ev′i tə bəl), *adj.* **1.** unable to be avoided, evaded, or escaped; certain; necessary. —*n.* **2.** something that is unavoidable. [ME < L *inēvītābil(is)*] —**in·ev′i·ta·bil′i·ty, in·ev′i·ta·ble·ness,** *n.* —**in·ev′i·ta·bly,** *adv.*

in·ex·act (in′ig zakt′), *adj.* not exact; not strictly accurate. —**in·ex·act·i·tude** (in′ig zak′ti to͞od′, -tyo͞od′), *n.* —**in′ex·act′ly,** *adv.* —**in′ex·act′ness,** *n.*

in·ex·cus·a·ble (in′ik skyo͞o′zə bəl), *adj.* not excusable; incapable of being justified. [ME < L *inexcūsābil(is)*] —**in′ex·cus′a·bil′i·ty, in′ex·cus′a·ble·ness,** *n.* —**in′ex·cus′a·bly,** *adv.*

in·ex·er·tion (in′ig zûr′shən), *n.* lack of exertion; inaction.

in·ex·haust·i·ble (in′ig zôs′tə bəl), *adj.* **1.** not exhaustible; incapable of being used up: *an inexhaustible supply.* **2.** unfailing; tireless: *an inexhaustible runner.* [< L *inexhaust(us)* not exhausted + -IBLE] —**in′ex·haust′i·bil′i·ty, in′ex·haust′i·ble·ness,** *n.* —**in′ex·haust′i·bly,** *adv.*

in·ex·ist·ent (in′ig zis′tənt), *adj.* not existent; having no existence. [< LL *inexistent-* (s. of *inexistēns*) not existing] —**in′ex·ist′ence, in′ex·ist′en·cy,** *n.*

in·ex·o·ra·ble (in ek′sər ə bəl), *adj.* **1.** unyielding; unalterable. **2.** not to be persuaded, moved, or affected by prayers or entreaties; unrelenting; merciless. [< L *inexōrābil(is)*] —**in·ex′o·ra·bil′i·ty, in·ex′o·ra·ble·ness,** *n.* —**in·ex′o·ra·bly,** *adv.* —**Syn. 2.** relentless, unrelenting, implacable. See **inflexible.** —**Ant. 2.** flexible; merciful.

in·ex·pe·di·ent (in′ik spē′dē ənt), *adj.* not expedient; not suitable, judicious, or advisable. —**in′ex·pe′di·ence, in′ex·pe′di·en·cy,** *n.* —**in′ex·pe′di·ent·ly,** *adv.*

in·ex·pen·sive (in′ik spen′siv), *adj.* not expensive; not high in price; costing little. —**in′ex·pen′sive·ly,** *adv.* —**in′ex·pen′sive·ness,** *n.* —**Syn.** See **cheap.** —**Ant.** costly.

in·ex·pe·ri·ence (in′ik spēr′ē əns), *n.* lack of experience, or of knowledge or skill gained from experience. [< LL *inexperientia*]

in·ex·pe·ri·enced (in′ik spēr′ē ənst), *adj.* not experienced; without knowledge or skill gained from experience. —**Syn.** untrained, unskilled; green, naïve.

in·ex·pert (in eks′pûrt, in′ik spûrt′), *adj.* not expert; unskilled. [late ME < L *inexpert(us)*] —**in·ex′pert·ly,** *adv.* —**in·ex′pert·ness,** *n.*

in·ex·pi·a·ble (in eks′pē ə bəl), *adj.* **1.** not to be expiated; not allowing for expiation or atonement: *an inexpiable crime.* **2.** not to be appeased by expiation; implacable: *inexpiable hate.* [< L *inexpiābil(is)*] —**in·ex′pi·a·ble·ness,** *n.* —**in·ex′pi·a·bly,** *adv.*

in·ex·pi·ate (in eks′pē āt′), *adj.* not expiated or atoned for. [< LL *inexpiāt(us)* = L *in-* IN-^{3} + *expiātus;* see EXPIATE]

in·ex·plain·a·ble (in′ik splā′nə bəl), *adj.* not explainable; incapable of being explained; inexplicable.

in·ex·pli·ca·ble (in eks′plə kə bəl *or, esp. Brit.,* in′ik-splik′ə bəl), *adj.* not explicable; incapable of being explained. [ME < L *inexplicābil(is)*] —**in·ex′pli·ca·bil′i·ty, in·ex′pli·ca·ble·ness,** *n.* —**in·ex′pli·ca·bly,** *adv.*

in·ex·plic·it (in′ik splis′it), *adj.* not explicit or clear; not clearly stated. [< L *inexplicit(us)* not straightforward] —**in′ex·plic′it·ly,** *adv.* —**in′ex·plic′it·ness,** *n.*

in·ex·press·i·ble (in′ik spres′ə bəl), *adj.* not expressible; incapable of being uttered or represented in words. —**in′ex·press′i·bil′i·ty, in′ex·press′i·ble·ness,** *n.* —**in′ex·press′i·bly,** *adv.*

in·ex·pres·sive (in′ik spres′iv), *adj.* **1.** not expressive; lacking in expression. **2.** *Obs.* inexpressible. —**in′ex·pres′sive·ly,** *adv.* —**in′ex·pres′sive·ness,** *n.*

in·ex·pug·na·ble (in′ik spug′nə bəl), *adj.* incapable of being taken by force; unconquerable. [< L *inexpugnābil(is)* = *in-* IN-^{3} + *expugnābilis* (*expugnā(re)* (to) take by storm (*ex-* EX-^{1} + *pugnāre* to fight) + *-bilis* -BLE)] —**in′ex·pug′na·bil′i·ty, in′ex·pug′na·ble·ness,** *n.* —**in′ex·pug′na·bly,** *adv.*

in·ex·pung·i·ble (in′ik spun′jə bəl), *adj.* not capable of being expunged, erased, or obliterated. —**in′ex·pung′i·bil′i·ty,** *n.*

in·ex·ten·si·ble (in′ik sten′sə bəl), *adj.* not extensible; incapable of being extended or stretched. —**in′ex·ten′si·bil′i·ty,** *n.*

in ex·ten·so (in eks ten′sō; *Eng.* in ik sten′sō), *Latin.* at full length.

in·ex·tin·guish·a·ble (in′ik sting′gwi shə bəl), *adj.* not extinguishable; not to be extinguished, quenched, suppressed, or brought to an end. —**in′ex·tin′guish·a·bly,** *adv.*

in·ex·tir·pa·ble (in′ik stûr′pə bəl), *adj.* incapable of being extirpated; not removable or eradicable: *an inextirpable disease.* [< L *inex(s)tirpābil(is).* See IN-^{3}, EXTIRPATE, -BLE] —**in′ex·tir′pa·ble·ness,** *n.*

in ex·tre·mis (in eks tre′mēs; *Eng.* in ik strē′mis), *Latin.* **1.** in extremity. **2.** near death. [lit., on the outer edges, i.e. at the uttermost limit]

in·ex·tri·ca·ble (in eks′trə kə bəl), *adj.* **1.** from which one cannot extricate oneself: *an inextricable maze.* **2.** incapable of being disentangled, undone, or loosed. **3.** hopelessly intricate, involved, or perplexing: *inextricable confusion.* [ME < L *inextrīcābil(is)*] —**in·ex′tri·ca·bil′i·ty, in·ex′tri·ca·ble·ness,** *n.* —**in·ex′tri·ca·bly,** *adv.*

Inf., **1.** infantry. **2.** infuse. [< L *infunde*]

inf., **1.** infantry. **2.** inferior. **3.** infinitive. **4.** infinity. **5.** information. **6.** below; after. [< L *infrā*] **7.** (in prescriptions) infuse. [< L *infunde*]

in·fal·li·ble (in fal′ə bəl), *adj.* **1.** not fallible; exempt from liability to error, as persons, their judgment, pronouncements, etc. **2.** absolutely trustworthy or sure: *an infallible rule.* **3.** unfailing in effectiveness or operation; certain: *an infallible remedy.* **4.** *Rom. Cath. Ch.* immune from fallacy or error in expounding matters of faith or morals. —*n.* **5.** an infallible person or thing. [ME < ML *infallibil(is)*] —**in·fal′li·bil′i·ty, in·fal′li·ble·ness,** *n.* —**in·fal′li·bly,** *adv.* —**Syn. 2, 3.** See **reliable.**

in·fa·mous (in′fə məs), *adj.* **1.** having an extremely bad reputation. **2.** deserving of or causing an evil reputation; detestable; shamefully bad. **3.** *Law.* **a.** deprived of certain rights as a citizen, as a consequence of conviction of certain offenses. **b.** of or pertaining to offenses involving such deprivation. [ME < L *infām(is)* (see INFAMY) + -OUS] —**in′fa·mous·ly,** *adv.* —**in′fa·mous·ness,** *n.* —**Syn. 1.** disreputable, notorious. **2.** disgraceful, scandalous; nefarious, wicked, heinous, villainous.

in·fa·my (in′fə mē), *n., pl.* **-mies** for 3. **1.** evil reputation, public reproach, or strong condemnation as the result of a shameful, criminal, or outrageous act. **2.** infamous character or conduct. **3.** an infamous act or circumstance. **4.** *Law.* loss of rights, incurred by conviction of an infamous offense. [late ME *infamye* < L *infāmia* = *infām(is)* ill-famed (*in-* IN-^{3} + *fām(a)* FAME + *-is* adj. suffix) + *-ia* -Y^3] —**Syn. 1.** disrepute, obloquy, odium, opprobrium, shame. See **disgrace.** —**Ant. 1.** credit, honor.

in·fan·cy (in′fən sē), *n., pl.* **-cies.** **1.** the state or period of being an infant; babyhood; early childhood. **2.** the corresponding period in the existence of anything: *Space science is still in its infancy.* **3.** infants collectively. **4.** *Law.* the period of life to the age of majority; minority. [< L *infantia*]

in·fant (in′fənt), *n.* **1.** a child during the earliest period of its life, esp. before able to walk; baby. **2.** *Law.* a person who has not attained the age of 21 years; a minor. **3.** a beginner, as in experience or learning; novice. **4.** *Rare.* anything in the first stage of existence or progress. —*adj.* **5.** of or pertaining to infants or infancy. **6.** being in infancy. [< L *infant-* (s. of *infāns*) not speaking = *in-* IN-^{3} + *-fāns,* prp. of *fārī* to speak; r. ME *enfaunt* < AF]

in·fan·ta (in fan′tə), *n.* **1.** a daughter of the king of Spain or of Portugal. **2.** an infante's wife. [< Sp or Pg; fem. of INFANTE]

in·fan·te (in fan′tā), *n.* any son of the king of Spain or of Portugal who is not heir to the throne. [< Sp or Pg; see INFANT]

in·fan·ti·cide (in fan′ti sīd′), *n.* **1.** the act of killing an infant. **2.** a person who kills an infant. [(def. 1) < LL *infanticīd(ium);* (def. 2) < LL *infanticīd(a)*] —**in·fan′ti·cid′al,** *adj.*

in·fan·tile (in′fən tīl′, -til), *adj.* **1.** characteristic of or befitting an infant; babyish. **2.** of or pertaining to infants or infancy. **3.** being in the earliest stage of development. [< LL *infantil(is)*] —**in·fan·til·i·ty** (in′fən til′i tē), *n.* —**Syn. 1.** puerile, immature. See **childish.** —**Ant. 1.** adult.

in′fantile paral′ysis, *Pathol.* poliomyelitis.

in·fan·til·ism (in′fən tᵊliz′əm, -tī liz′-, in fan′tᵊliz′əm), *n.* **1.** the persistence in an adult of markedly childish anatomical, physiological, or psychological characteristics. **2.** an infantile act, trait, etc., esp. in an adult.

in·fan·try (in′fən trē), *n., pl.* **-tries.** **1.** soldiers or military units that fight on foot, with bayonets, rifles, machine guns, grenades, mortars, etc. **2.** a branch of an army composed of such soldiers. [< It *infanteria* = *infante* boy, foot soldier (see INFANT) + *-ria* -RY]

in·fan·try·man (in′fən trē mən), *n., pl.* **-men.** a soldier of the infantry.

in·farct (in färkt′), *n.* *Pathol.* a localized area of tissue that is dying or dead, having been deprived of its blood supply because of an obstruction by embolism or thrombosis. [< NL, L *infarct(us)* stuffed in. See IN-^{2}, FARCE] —**in·farct′ed,** *adj.*

in·farc·tion (in färk′shən), *n.* *Pathol.* **1.** the formation of an infarct. **2.** an infarct.

in·fat·u·ate (*v.* in fach′o͞o āt′; *adj.,* in fach′o͞o it, -āt′), *v.,* **-at·ed, -at·ing,** *adj.* —*v.t.* **1.** to inspire or possess with a foolish or unreasoning passion, as of love. **2.** to make foolish or fatuous. —*adj.* **3.** infatuated. [< L *infatuāt(us),* ptp. of *infatuāre.* See IN-^{2}, FATUOUS, -ATE^1]

in·fat·u·at·ed (in fach′o͞o ā′tid), *adj.* characterized by foolish or irrational love or desire; blindly in love. —**in·fat′u·at′ed·ly,** *adv.* —**Syn.** fond, doting, overaffectionate.

in·fat·u·a·tion (in fach′o͞o ā′shən), *n.* **1.** the state of being infatuated; foolish or all-absorbing passion. **2.** the object of a person's infatuation. [< LL *infatuātiōn-* (s. of *infatuātiō*)]

in·fea·si·ble (in fē′zə bəl), *adj.* not feasible; impracticable. —**in·fea′si·bil′i·ty, in·fea′si·ble·ness,** *n.*

in·fect (in fekt′), *v.t.* **1.** to affect or contaminate (a person, wound, etc.) with disease-producing germs. **2.** to affect with disease. **3.** to taint or contaminate with harmful substances. **4.** to corrupt or affect morally. **5.** to affect so as to influence feeling or action. —*v.i.* **6.** to become infected. [ME *in-*

fecte(n) < L *infect(us)* worked in, stained, tainted (ptp. of *inficere*) = *in-* IN-[2] + *fec-* (var. of *fac-* make) + *-tus* ptp. suffix] —**in·fec′tor, in·fect′er,** *n.*

in·fec·tion (in fek′shən), *n.* **1.** the act or fact of infecting. **2.** the state of being infected. **3.** an infecting with germs of disease, as through the medium of infected insects, air, water, clothing, etc. **4.** an infecting agency or influence. **5.** an infectious disease. **6.** corruption of another's opinions, beliefs, etc. [ME *infeccio(u)n* < LL *infectiōn-* (s. of *infectiō*) a dyeing]

in·fec·tious (in fek′shəs), *adj.* **1.** communicable by infection, as from one person to another or from one part of the body to another. **2.** causing or communicating infection. **3.** tending to affect others. Also, **infective.** [INFECT(ION) + -IOUS] —**in·fec′tious·ly,** *adv.* —**in·fec′tious·ness,** *n.* —**Syn. 3.** catching. See **contagious.**

infec′tious mononucleo′sis, *Pathol.* an acute, infectious form of mononucleosis characterized by sudden fever, a benign swelling of lymph nodes, and an increase in the blood stream of leucocytes having only one nucleus. Also called **glandular fever.**

in·fec·tive (in fek′tiv), *adj.* infectious. [ME < ML *infectīv(us)*] —**in·fec′tive·ness, in′fec·tiv′i·ty,** *n.*

in·fe·cund (in fē′kənd, -fek′ənd), *adj.* not fecund; unfruitful; barren. [ME *infecounde* < L *infēcund(us)*] —**in·fe·cun·di·ty** (in′fi kun′di tē), *n.*

in·fe·lic·i·tous (in′fə lis′i təs), *adj.* not felicitous; inapt; inappropriate: *an infelicitous remark.*

in·fe·lic·i·ty (in′fə lis′i tē), *n., pl.* **-ties** for 3, 5. **1.** the quality or state of being unhappy; unhappiness. **2.** misfortune; bad luck. **3.** an unfortunate circumstance. **4.** inaptness or inappropriateness, as of action or expression. **5.** something infelicitous. [ME *infelicite* < L *infēlīcitās*]

in·feoff (in fef′, -fēf′), *v.t. Obs.* enfeoff. —**in·feoff′ment,** *n.*

in·fer (in fûr′), *v.,* **-ferred, -fer·ring.** —*v.t.* **1.** to derive by reasoning; conclude or judge from premises or evidence. **2.** (of facts, circumstances, statements, etc.) to indicate or involve as a conclusion; lead to. **3.** *Informal.* to hint; imply; suggest. **4.** to guess; speculate; surmise. —*v.i.* **5.** to draw a conclusion, as by reasoning. [< L *inferre* = *in-* IN-[2] + *ferre* to bring, carry, BEAR[1]] —**in·fer′a·ble, in·fer′i·ble, in·fer′ri·ble,** *adj.* —**in·fer′a·bly,** *adv.* —**in·fer′rer,** *n.*

—**Usage.** INFER and IMPLY have quite distinct meanings: *One infers from what another has implied.* The use of one of these words for the other is regarded as a solecism by educated persons.

in·fer·ence (in′fər əns, -frəns), *n.* **1.** the act or process of inferring. **2.** something that is inferred. **3.** *Logic.* the process of deriving from assumed premises either the strict logical conclusion or one that is to some degree probable. [< ML *inferentia*]

in·fer·en·tial (in′fə ren′shəl), *adj.* of, pertaining to, by, or derivable by inference. [< ML *inferenti(a)* INFERENCE + -AL[1]] —**in′fer·en′tial·ly,** *adv.*

in·fe·ri·or (in fēr′ē ər), *adj.* **1.** low or lower in station, rank, degree, or grade. **2.** low or lower in position; close or closer to the bottom. **3.** of little or less importance, value, or excellence. **4.** *Bot.* **a.** situated below some other organ. **b.** (of a calyx) inserted below the ovary. **c.** (of an ovary) having a superior calyx. **5.** *Anat., Zool.* (of an organ or part) situated beneath another. **6.** *Astron.* **a.** (of a planet) having an orbit within that of the earth: applied to the planets Mercury and Venus. **b.** (of a conjunction of an inferior planet) taking place between the sun and the earth. **c.** lying below the horizon. **7.** *Print.* written or printed low on a line of text, as the "2" in H_2O; subscript. Cf. **superior** (def. 10). —*n.* **8.** one inferior to another or others, as in rank or merit. **9.** Also called **subscript.** *Print.* a letter, number, or symbol written or printed low on a line of text. (Cf. **superior** (def. 13). [ME < L = *infer(us)* below + *-ior* comp. suffix] —**in·fe·ri·or·i·ty** (in fēr′ē ôr′i tē, -or′-), *n.* —**in·fe′ri·or·ly,** *adv.*

inferior′ity com′plex, 1. *Psychiatry.* intense feeling of inferiority, producing a personality characterized either by extreme reticence or, as a result of overcompensation, by extreme aggressiveness. **2.** lack of self-esteem; feeling of inadequacy; lack of self-confidence.

in·fer·nal (in fûr′nəl), *adj.* **1.** *Class. Myth.* of or pertaining to the underworld. **2.** of, inhabiting, or befitting hell. **3.** hellish; fiendish; diabolical: *an infernal plot.* **4.** *Informal.* outrageous: *an infernal nuisance.* [ME < LL *infernāl(is)* = L *infern(a)* the lower regions (neut. pl. of *infernus* hellish; see INFERIOR) + *-ālis* -AL[1]] —**in′fer·nal′i·ty,** *n.* —**in·fer′nal·ly,** *adv.*

infer′nal machine′, a concealed or disguised explosive device intended to destroy life or property.

in·fer·no (in fûr′nō), *n., pl.* **-nos. 1.** hell; the infernal regions. **2.** a place or region that resembles hell. [< It < L *infernus* hellish]

in·fer·tile (in fûr′təl *or, esp. Brit.,* -tīl), *adj.* not fertile; unproductive; sterile; barren. [< L *infertil(is)*] —**in·fer′tile·ly,** *adv.* —**in·fer·til·i·ty** (in′fər til′i tē), **in·fer′tile·ness,** *n.*

in·fest (in fest′), *v.t.* **1.** to haunt or overrun in a troublesome manner, as predatory bands, destructive animals, or vermin do. **2.** to be numerous in, as anything troublesome. [late ME < L *infest(āre)* (to) assail, molest < *infest(us)* hostile] —**in′fes·ta′tion,** *n.* —**in·fest′er,** *n.*

in·feu·da·tion (in′fyōō dā′shən), *n. Eng. Law.* **1.** the grant of an estate in fee. **2.** the relation of lord and vassal established by the grant and acceptance of such an estate. [< ML *infeudātiōn-* (s. of *infeudātiō*)]

in·fi·del (in′fi dəl), *n.* **1.** a person who has no religious faith; unbeliever. **2.** *Relig.* **a.** a person who does not accept a particular faith, esp. Christianity. **b.** (in Muslim use) a person who does not accept the Islamic faith; a kaffir. —*adj.* **3.** without religious faith. **4.** due to or manifesting unbelief: *infidel ideas.* **5.** not accepting a particular faith, esp. Christianity or Islam; heathen. **6.** of, pertaining to, or characteristic of unbelievers or infidels. [late ME < ML *infidēl(is)* a Moslem, L: unfaithful. See IN-[3], FEAL] —**Syn. 2.** See **atheist.**

in·fi·del·i·ty (in′fi del′i tē), *n., pl.* **-ties. 1.** unfaithfulness; disloyalty. **2.** adultery. **3.** an instance of disloyalty or adultery. **4.** lack of religious faith, esp. Christian faith. **5.** a breach of trust; disloyalty. [ME < L *infidēlitās*]

in·field (in′fēld′), *n. Baseball.* **1.** the diamond. **2.** the positions played by the first baseman, second baseman, third baseman, and shortstop, taken collectively. **3.** the infielders considered as a group (contrasted with *outfield*).

in·field·er (in′fēl′dər), *n. Baseball.* any of the players stationed in the infield.

in·fight·ing (in′fī′ting), *n.* **1.** fighting at close range. **2.** fighting between rival organizations, members of a group, etc., that is kept secret from outsiders. **3.** free-for-all fighting. —**in′fight′er,** *n.*

in·fil·trate (in fil′trāt, in′fil trāt′), *v.,* **-trat·ed, -trat·ing,** *n.* —*v.t.* **1.** to filter into or through; permeate. **2.** to go into by, or as by, filtering. **3.** to cause to infiltrate. —*v.i.* **4.** to pass into or through a substance, place, etc., by or as by filtering. —*n.* **5.** something that infiltrates. —**in·fil·tra·tive** (in′fil trā′tiv, in fil′trə-), *adj.* —**in·fil·tra·tor** (in′fil trā′tər, in fil′trā-), *n.*

in·fil·tra·tion (in′fil trā′shən), *n.* **1.** the act or process of infiltrating. **2.** the state of being infiltrated. **3.** something that infiltrates; an infiltrate. **4.** *Mil.* a method of attack in which small groups of soldiers or individual soldiers penetrate into the enemy's line in order to assemble behind the enemy position.

infin., infinitive.

in·fi·nite (in′fə nit), *adj.* **1.** immeasurably, indefinitely, or exceedingly great: *a discovery of infinite importance; infinite sums of money.* **2.** unbounded or unlimited; perfect: *God's infinite mercy.* **3.** endless or innumerable; inexhaustible. **4.** *Math.* not finite. —*n.* **5.** something that is infinite. **6.** the boundless regions of space. **7. the Infinite** or **the Infinite Being,** God. [ME < L *infīnīt(us)* boundless] —**in′fi·nite·ly,** *adv.* —**in′fi·nite·ness,** *n.*

in′finite prod′uct, *Math.* a sequence of numbers in which an infinite number of terms are multiplied together.

in′finite re′gress, *Philos.* causal or logical relationship of terms in a series without the possibility of a term initiating the series.

in′finite se′ries, *Math.* a sequence of numbers in which an infinite number of terms are added successively in a given pattern.

in·fin·i·tes·i·mal (in′fin i tes′ə məl), *adj.* **1.** indefinitely or exceedingly small; minute: *infinitesimal vessels in the circulatory system.* **2.** immeasurably small; less than an assignable quantity: *to an infinitesimal degree.* **3.** of, pertaining to, or involving infinitesimals. —*n.* **4.** an infinitesimal quantity. **5.** *Math.* a variable having zero as a limit. [< NL *infīnītēsim(us)* (*infīnīt(us)* INFINITE + *-ēsimus,* var. of *-ensimus* ordinal suffix) + -AL[1]] —**in′fin·i·tes′i·mal·ly,** *adv.*

in′finites′imal cal′culus, the differential calculus and the integral calculus, considered together.

in·fin·i·tive (in fin′i tiv), *Gram.* —*n.* **1.** a verb form found in many languages that functions as a noun or is used with auxiliary verbs, and that names the action or state without specifying the subject. **2.** (in English) the simple or basic form of the verb, as *come, take, eat, be,* used after auxiliary verbs, as in *I didn't come, He must be,* or this simple form preceded by a function word, as *to* in *I want to eat.* —*adj.* **3.** consisting of or containing an infinitive: *an infinitive construction.* [late ME < LL *infīnītīv(us)* indefinite = *in-* IN-[3] + *fīnītīvus* definite; see FINITE, -IVE] —**in·fin·i·ti·val** (in′fi ni tī′vəl), *adj.* —**in′fin·i·ti′val·ly, in·fin′i·tive·ly,** *adv.*

infin′itive clause′, *Gram.* a clause containing an infinitive as its main or only verb form, as *to do* in *What to do?* and *to speak* in *so young to speak so clearly.* Also called **infin′itive phrase′.**

in·fin·i·tize (in fin′i tīz′), *v.t.,* **-tized, -tiz·ing.** to cause to become infinite.

in·fin·i·tude (in fin′i tōōd′, -tyōōd′), *n.* **1.** infinity: *divine infinitude.* **2.** an infinite extent, amount, or number. [INFINI(TE) + -TUDE]

in·fin·i·ty (in fin′i tē), *n., pl.* **-ties. 1.** the quality or state of being infinite. **2.** something that is infinite. **3.** infinite space, time, or quantity. **4.** an infinite extent, amount, or number. **5.** an indefinitely great amount or number. **6.** *Math.* **a.** the assumed limit of a sequence, series, etc., that increases without bound, indicated by the sign ∞. **b.** infinite distance, or an infinitely distant part of space. [ME *infinite* < L *infīnītās*]

in·firm (in fûrm′), *adj.* **1.** feeble or weak in body or health, often because of age. **2.** unsteadfast, faltering, or irresolute, as persons, the mind, etc.: *infirm of purpose.* **3.** not firm, solid, or strong. **4.** unsound or invalid, as an argument, a property title, etc. —*v.t.* **5.** *Archaic.* to invalidate. [ME *infirme* < L *infirm(us)*] —**in·firm′ly,** *adv.* —**in·firm′ness,** *n.* —**Syn. 1, 3, 4.** weak. **2.** wavering, vacillating, indecisive. **3.** tottering, shaky, unsteady. —**Ant. 1, 2, 3.** strong.

in·fir·mar·i·an (in′fər mâr′ē ən), *n.* (in a religious house) a person who nurses the sick. [INFIRMARY + -AN]

in·fir·ma·ry (in fûr′mə rē), *n., pl.* **-ries. 1.** a place for the care of the infirm, sick, or injured; hospital. **2.** a dispensary. [late ME < ML *infirmāria*]

in·fir·mi·ty (in fûr′mi tē), *n., pl.* **-ties** for 1, 3. **1.** a physical weakness or ailment: *the infirmities of age.* **2.** the quality or state of being infirm; lack of strength. **3.** a moral weakness or failing. [ME *infirmite* < L *infirmitās*]

in·fix (*v.* in fiks′, in′fiks′; *n.* in′fiks′), *v.t.* **1.** to fix, fasten, or drive in. **2.** to implant. **3.** to infix in the mind or memory, as a fact or idea; impress. **4.** *Gram.* to add as an infix. —*v.i.* **5.** *Gram.* (of a linguistic form) to admit an infix. —*n.* **6.** *Gram.* an affix inserted within the body of the element to which it is added, as Latin *m* in *accumbō* "I lie down," as compared with *accubuī* "I lay down." [< L *infix(us)* fastened in, ptp. of *infīgere*] —**in·fix·ion** (in fik′shən), *n.* —**Syn. 3.** inculcate, instill.

in fla·gran·te de·lic·to (in flä grän′te de lik′tō; *Eng.* in flə gran′tē di lik′tō), *Latin.* in the very act of committing the offense. [lit., in blazing crime, i.e., in the heat of the evil deed]

in·flame (in flām′), *v.,* **-flamed, -flam·ing.** —*v.t.* **1.** to set aflame or afire; set on fire. **2.** to redden with or as with flames. **3.** to kindle or excite (passions, desires, etc.). **4.** to arouse to a high degree of passion, or feeling. **5.** (of an emotion, as rage) to cause to redden or grow heated. **6.** to cause inflammation in. **7.** to raise (the blood, bodily tissue, etc.) to a morbid or feverish heat. —*v.i.* **8.** to burst into flame;

take fire. 9. to be kindled, as passion. 10. to become hot with passion, as the heart. 11. to become excessively affected with inflammation. Also, enflame. [IN-[2] + FLAME; r. ME *enflamme(n)* < MF *enflamm(er)* < L *inflammāre* to kindle] —**in·flam′er,** *n.* —**Syn. 1.** fire. See **kindle. 3.** incite, stimulate. —**Ant. 3.** cool, soothe.

in·flam·ma·ble (in flam′ə bəl), *adj.* **1.** capable of being set on fire; combustible; flammable. **2.** easily aroused to passion or anger; excitable; irascible. —*n.* **3.** something inflammable. [< ML *inflammābil(is)*] —**in·flam′ma·bil′i·ty, in·flam′ma·ble·ness,** *n.* —**in·flam′ma·bly,** *adv.*

in·flam·ma·tion (in′flə mā′shən), *n.* **1.** the act or fact of inflaming. **2.** the state of being inflamed. **3.** *Pathol.* redness, swelling, pain, tenderness, heat, and disturbed function of an area of the body, esp. as a reaction of tissues to injurious agents. [< L *inflammātiōn-* (s. of *inflammātiō*) = *inflammāt(us)* (ptp. of *inflammāre;* see INFLAME) + *-iōn-* -ION]

in·flam·ma·to·ry (in flam′ə tōr′ē, -tôr′ē), *adj.* **1.** tending to arouse anger, hostility, passion, etc. **2.** *Pathol.* pertaining to or attended with inflammation. [< L *inflammāt(us)* (see INFLAMMATION) + -ORY[1]] —**in·flam·ma·to·ri·ly** (in flam′ə-tōr′ə lē, -tôr′-, -flam′ə tōr′-, -tôr′-), *adv.*

in·flate (in flāt′), *v.,* **-flat·ed, -flat·ing.** —*v.t.* **1.** to distend; swell or puff out; dilate. **2.** to distend with gas. **3.** to puff up with pride, satisfaction, etc. **4.** to elate. **5.** to expand (currency, prices, etc.) unduly. —*v.i.* **6.** to become inflated. [< L *inflāt(us)* blown into (ptp. of *inflāre*) = *in-* IN-[2] + *flā-* blow + *-tus* ptp. suffix] —**in·flat′a·ble,** *adj.* —**in·flat′er, in·fla′tor,** *n.* —**Syn. 1.** enlarge. See **expand.** —**Ant. 1.** deflate; shrink.

in·flat·ed (in flā′tid), *adj.* **1.** distended with air or gas; swollen. **2.** puffed up, as with pride. **3.** turgid or bombastic, as language. **4.** unduly increased in level. **5.** unduly expanded in volume, as currency. **6.** *Bot.* hollow or swelled out with air. —**in·flat′ed·ly,** *adv.* —**in·flat′ed·ness,** *n.*

in·fla·tion (in flā′shən), *n.* **1.** undue expansion or increase of the currency of a country, esp. by the issuing of paper money not redeemable in specie. **2.** a substantial rise of prices caused by an undue expansion in paper money or bank credit. **3.** the act of inflating. **4.** the state of being inflated. [ME *inflacio(u)n* < L *inflātiōn-* (s. of *inflātiō*)]

in·fla·tion·ar·y (in flā′shə ner′ē), *adj.* of, pertaining to, or causing inflation.

in·fla·tion·ist (in flā′shə nist), *n.* an advocate of inflation through expansion of currency or bank deposits. —**in·fla′tion·ism,** *n.*

in·flect (in flekt′), *v.t.* **1.** to bend; turn from a direct line or course. **2.** to modulate (the voice). **3.** *Gram.* **a.** to change the form of (a word) by inflection. **b.** to recite the inflections of (a word) in a fixed order. —*v.i.* **4.** *Gram.* to be characterized by inflection. [ME *inflecte(n)* < L *inflect(ere)* (to) bend in = *in-* IN-[2] + *flectere* to bend, curve] —**in·flect′ed·ness,** *n.* —**in·flec′tive,** *adj.* —**in·flec′tor,** *n.*

in·flec·tion (in flek′shən), *n.* **1.** modulation of the voice; change in pitch or tone of voice. **2.** Also, **flection.** *Gram.* **a.** the process or device of adding affixes to or changing the form of a base word to express syntactic function without changing its form class. **b.** the paradigm of a word. **c.** a single pattern of a paradigm: *noun inflection; verb inflection.* **d.** the change in the shape of a word, generally by affixation, indicating a change of meaning or syntactic relationship. **e.** the affix added to produce this change, as the *-s* in *dogs* or the *-ed* in *played.* **f.** the systematic description of such processes in a given language, as in *serves* from *serve, sings* from *sing,* and *harder* from *hard* (contrasted with *derivation*). **3.** a bend or angle. **4.** *Math.* a change of curvature from convex to concave or vice versa. Also, *esp. Brit.,* **inflexion.** [var. sp. of *inflexion* < L *inflexiōn-* (s. of *inflexiō*) a bending] —**in·flec′tion·less,** *adj.*

in·flec·tion·al (in flek′shə nᵊl), *adj.* of, pertaining to, characterized by, or used in inflection: *an inflectional ending; an inflectional language.* —**in·flec′tion·al·ly,** *adv.*

inflec′tion point′, *Math.* a point of inflection on a curve.

in·flexed (in flekst′), *adj.* *Bot., Zool.* inflected; bent or folded downward or inward. [< L *inflex(us)* bent in (ptp. of *inflectere*) + -ED[2]]

in·flex·i·ble (in flek′sə bəl), *adj.* **1.** not flexible; incapable of or resistant to being bent; rigid: *an inflexible rod.* **2.** of an unyielding temper, purpose, will, etc.; immovable: *an inflexible will to succeed.* **3.** not permitting change or variation; unalterable: *arbitrary and inflexible laws.* [< L *inflexibil(is)* that cannot be bent] —**in·flex′i·bil′i·ty, in·flex′i·ble·ness,** *n.* —**in·flex′i·bly,** *adv.*

—**Syn. 1.** unbendable, stiff. **2.** rigorous, stern, unrelenting, unremitting, stubborn, obstinate, intractable, obdurate, unbending, adamant. INFLEXIBLE, RELENTLESS, IMPLACABLE, INEXORABLE imply having the quality of not being turned from a purpose. INFLEXIBLE means unbending, adhering undeviatingly to a set plan, purpose, or the like: *inflexible in interpretation of rules.* RELENTLESS suggests so pitiless and unremitting a pursuit of purpose as to convey a sense of inevitableness: *as relentless as the passing of time.* IMPLACABLE means incapable of being placated or appeased: *implacable in wrath.* INEXORABLE means unmoved by prayer or entreaty: *inexorable in demanding payment.* **3.** undeviating. —**Ant. 2.** amenable.

in·flex·ion (in flek′shən), *n.* *Chiefly Brit.* inflection. —**in·flex′ion·al,** *adj.* —**in·flex′ion·al·ly,** *adv.* —**in·flex′ion·less,** *adj.*

in·flict (in flikt′), *v.t.* **1.** to lay on: *to inflict a dozen lashes.* **2.** to afflict, as with suffering or punishment. **3.** to impose (anything unwelcome). [< L *inflict(us)* struck or dashed against (ptp. of *inflīgere*) = *in-* IN-[2] + *flig-* (var. s. of *flīgere* to beat down) + *-tus* ptp. suffix] —**in·flict′er, in·flic′tor,** *n.* —**in·flic′tive,** *adj.*

in·flic·tion (in flik′shən), *n.* **1.** the act of inflicting. **2.** something inflicted, as punishment, suffering, etc. [< LL *inflictiōn-* (s. of *inflictiō*)]

in-flight (in′flīt′), *adj.* done, served, or shown during an air voyage: *an in-flight movie.* Also, **in′flight′.**

in·flo·res·cence (in′flō res′əns, -flô-, -flə-), *n.* **1.** a flowering or blossoming. **2.** *Bot.* **a.** the arrangement of flowers on the axis. **b.** the flowering part of a plant. **c.** a flower cluster. **d.** flowers collectively. **e.** a single flower. [< NL *inflōrescentia* < LL *inflōrescent-* (s. of *inflōrescēns* blooming, prp. of *inflōrescere*)] —**in′flo·res′cent,** *adj.*

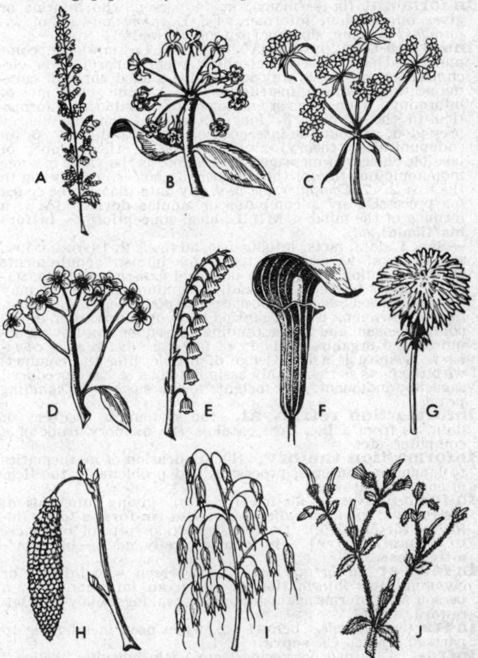

Inflorescence

A, Spike of heather, *Calluna vulgaris;* B, Simple umbel of milkweed, *Asclepias syriaca;* C, Compound umbel of water parsnip, *Sium cicutaefolium;* D, Corymb of red chokeberry, *Aronia arbutifolia;* E, Raceme of lily of the valley, *Convallaria majalis;* F, Spadix of jack-in-the-pulpit, *Arisaema triphyllum;* G, Head (anthodium) of dandelion, *Taraxacum officinale;* H, Male ament of birch, genus *Betula;* I, Panicle of oats, *Avena sativa;* J, Cyme of chickweed, genus *Cerastium*

in·flow (in′flō′), *n.* something that flows in; influx.

in·flu·ence (in′flo͞o əns), *n., v.,* **-enced, -enc·ing.** —*n.* **1.** the capacity or power to produce effects on others by intangible or indirect means. **2.** the action or process of producing effects on others by intangible or indirect means. **3.** a person or thing that exerts influence. **4.** *Astrol.* the supposed radiation of an ethereal fluid from the stars, regarded as affecting human destiny. —*v.t.* **5.** to exercise influence on; affect; sway. **6.** to move or impel (a person), as to some action. [ME < ML *influentia* stellar emanation. See INFLUENT, -ENCE] —**in′flu·ence·a·ble,** *adj.* —**in′flu·enc·er,** *n.* —**Syn. 2.** sway, rule. See **authority. 5.** impress, bias, direct, control. **6.** induce, persuade.

in·flu·ent (in′flo͞o ənt), *adj.* **1.** flowing in. —*n.* **2.** a tributary. **3.** *Ecol.* a plant or animal that has an important effect on the biotic balance in a community. [ME < L *influent-* (s. of *influēns*)]

in·flu·en·tial (in′flo͞o en′shəl), *adj.* having or exerting influence. [< ML *influenti(a)* stellar emanation (see INFLUENCE) + -AL[1]] —**in′flu·en′tial·ly,** *adv.*

in·flu·en·za (in′flo͞o en′zə), *n.* **1.** *Pathol.* an acute, extremely contagious, virus disease, characterized by general prostration, occurring in several forms, usually with nasal catarrh and bronchial inflammation. **2.** *Vet. Pathol.* an acute, contagious virus disease occurring in horses and swine, characterized by fever, depression, and catarrhal inflammations. Also called **flu.** [< It < ML *influentia* INFLUENCE]

in·flux (in′fluks′), *n.* **1.** act of flowing in. **2.** an inflow (opposed to *outflux*): *an influx of tourists.* **3.** the place or point at which one stream flows into another or into the sea. **4.** the mouth of a stream. [< LL *influx(us)* influence of the stars, L: flowed in, ptp. of *influere*]

in·fold (in fōld′), *v.t.* enfold. —**in·fold′er,** *n.* —**in·fold′ment,** *n.*

in·form[1] (in fôrm′), *v.t.* **1.** to impart knowledge or information to: *He informed them of his arrival.* **2.** to supply (oneself) with knowledge, as of a subject. **3.** to pervade or permeate, with resulting effect on the character: *A love of nature informed his writing.* **4.** to animate or inspire. **5.** *Obs.* to train or instruct. —*v.i.* **6.** to give information; supply knowledge or enlightenment. **7.** to furnish incriminating evidence to a prosecuting officer. [ME *informe(n)* < L *inform(āre)* (to) form, shape (see IN-[2], FORM); r. ME *enfourme(n)* < MF *enfourm(er)*] —**in·form′a·ble,** *adj.* —**in·form′ed·ly,** *adv.* —**in·form′ing·ly,** *adv.* —**Syn. 1.** apprise; notify, advise, tell. —**Ant. 1.** conceal.

in·form[2] (in fôrm′), *adj.* *Obs.* without form; formless. [< L *inform(is)* formless, deformed. See IN-[3], -FORM]

in·for·mal (in fôr′məl), *adj.* **1.** without formality or ceremony; casual. **2.** not according to prescribed, official, or customary forms; irregular; unofficial. **3.** suitable to or characteristic of casual or familiar speech or writing. —**in·for′mal·ly,** *adv.* —**Syn. 1.** natural, easy. **3.** See **colloquial.**

in·for·mal·i·ty (in′fôr mal′i tē), *n., pl.* **-ties** for 2. **1.** the state of being informal; absence of formality. **2.** an informal act.

in·form·ant (in fôr′mənt), *n.* a person who informs or gives information; informer. [< L *informant-* (s. of *informāns*) forming, shaping (prp. of *informāre*)]

in·for·ma·tion (in′fər mā′shən), *n.* **1.** knowledge communicated or received concerning a particular fact or circumstance; news. **2.** any knowledge gained through communication, research, instruction, etc. **3.** the act or fact of informing. **4.** an office or employee for distributing information to the public. **5.** *Law.* an official criminal charge presented, without the interposition of a grand jury. **6.** (in communication theory) an indication of the number of possible choices of messages, expressible as the value of some monotonic function of the number of choices, usually log to the base 2. **7.** *Computer Technol.* any data that can be coded for processing by a computer or similar device. [ME: a forming of the mind < ML, L: idea, conception] —**in′for·ma′tion·al,** *adj.*
—**Syn. 1.** data, facts, intelligence, advice. **2.** INFORMATION, KNOWLEDGE, WISDOM are terms for human acquirements through reading, study, and practical experience. INFORMATION applies to facts told, read, or communicated that may be unorganized and even unrelated: *to pick up useful information.* KNOWLEDGE is an organized body of information, or the comprehension and understanding consequent on having acquired and organized a body of facts: *a knowledge of chemistry.* WISDOM is a knowledge of people, life, and conduct, with the facts so thoroughly assimilated as to have produced sagacity, judgment, and insight: *to use wisdom in handling people.*

informa′tion retriev′al, the systematic recovery of data, as from a file, card catalog, the memory bank of a computer, etc.

informa′tion the′ory, the application of mathematics to language, concepts, processes, and problems in the field of communications.

in·form·a·tive (in fôr′mə tiv), *adj.* giving information; instructive: *an informative book.* Also, **in·form·a·to·ry** (in fôr′mə tôr′ē, -tōr′ē). [< L *informāt(us)* (ptp. of *informāre* to INFORM[1]) + -IVE] —**in·form′a·tive·ly,** *adv.* —**in·form′a·tive·ness,** *n.*

in·form·er (in fôr′mər), *n.* **1.** a person who informs or communicates information or news; an informant. **2.** a person who informs against another, esp. for money or other reward. [ME]

in·fra (in′frə), *adv.* below, esp. when used in referring to parts of a text. Cf. **supra.** [< L]

infra-, a learned borrowing from Latin meaning "below," used, with second elements of any origin, in the formation of compound words: *infrasonic; infrared.* [< L, repr. *infrā,* adv. or prep.]

in·fract (in frakt′), *v.t.* to break; violate; infringe. [< L *infract(us)* broken, bent, weakened (ptp. of *infringere*). See INFRINGE, FRACTURE] —**in·frac′tor,** *n.*

in·frac·tion (in frak′shən), *n.* breach; violation; infringement. [< L *infractiōn-* (s. of *infractiō*)]

in·fra dig (in′frə dig′), beneath one's dignity; undignified. [short for L *infrā dignitātem* beneath (one's) dignity]

in·fra·lap·sar·i·an·ism (in′frə lap sâr′ē ə niz′əm), *n. Theol.* the doctrine that God decreed the election of a chosen number for redemption after decreeing the Fall (opposed to *supralapsarianism*). [INFRA- + L *laps(us)* a fall (see LAPSE) + -ARIAN + -ISM] —**in′fra·lap·sar′i·an,** *adj., n.*

in·fran·gi·ble (in fran′jə bəl), *adj.* **1.** unbreakable. **2.** inviolable. [< LL *infrangibil(is)*] —**in·fran′gi·bil′i·ty, in·fran′gi·ble·ness,** *n.* —**in·fran′gi·bly,** *adv.*

in·fra·red (in′frə red′), *n.* **1.** the part of the invisible spectrum that is contiguous to the red end of the visible spectrum and that comprises electromagnetic radiations of wavelengths from 0.8 to 1000 microns. —*adj.* **2.** noting or pertaining to the infrared or its component rays: *infrared radiation.* Also, **in′fra-red′.** Cf. **ultraviolet.**

in·fra·son·ic (in′frə son′ik), *adj.* noting or pertaining to a sound wave with a frequency below the audio-frequency range.

in·fra·son·ics (in′frə son′iks), *n.* (*construed as sing.*) the branch of science that deals with infrasonic phenomena. [see INFRASONIC, -ICS]

in·fra·struc·ture (in′frə struk′chər), *n.* the basic, underlying framework or features of something, esp. of a technological kind, as the military installations, communication and transport facilities, etc., of a country or organization.

in·fre·quen·cy (in frē′kwən sē), *n.* the state of being infrequent. Also, **in·fre′quence.** [< L *infrequentia* fewness]

in·fre·quent (in frē′kwənt), *adj.* **1.** happening or occurring at long intervals or rarely. **2.** not constant, habitual, or regular. **3.** not plentiful or many. **4.** far apart in space. [< L *infrequent-* (s. of *infrequēns*)] —**in·fre′quent·ly,** *adv.*
—**Syn. 1, 3.** scarce, rare, uncommon.

in·fringe (in frinj′), *v.,* **-fringed, -fring·ing.** —*v.t.* **1.** to commit a breach or infraction of; violate or transgress. —*v.i.* **2.** to encroach or trespass (usually fol. by *on* or *upon*): *to infringe on someone's privacy.* [< L *infringe(re)* (to) break, weaken = *in-* IN-[2] + *-fringere,* var. of *frangere* to BREAK] —**in·fring′er,** *n.*
—**Syn. 1.** break, disobey. **2.** poach. See **trespass.** —**Ant. 1.** obey.

in·fringe·ment (in frinj′mənt), *n.* **1.** a breach or infraction, as of a law, right, or obligation; violation; transgression. **2.** the act of infringing.

Infundibuliform corolla of morning-glory flower, *Ipomoea purpurea*

in·fun·dib·u·li·form (in′fun dib′yə lə fôrm′), *adj. Bot.* funnel-shaped.

in·fun·dib·u·lum (in′fun dib′yə ləm), *n., pl.* **-la** (-lə). *Anat.* **1.** a funnel-shaped organ or part. **2.** a funnel-shaped extension of the cerebrum connecting the pituitary gland to the base of the brain. [< NL, L: funnel = *infundi-* (s. of *infundere* to pour into; see IN-[2], FOUND[3]) + *-bulum* instrumental suffix] —**in′fun·dib′u·lar, in·fun·dib·u·late** (in′fun dib′yə lāt′), *adj.*

in·fur·i·ate (*v.* in fyŏŏr′ē āt′; *adj.* in fyŏŏr′ē it), *v.,* **-at·ed, -at·ing,** *adj.* —*v.t.* **1.** to make furious; enrage. —*adj.* **2.** *Rare.* infuriated; enraged. [< ML *infuriāt(us)* maddened, enraged (ptp. of *infuriāre*)] —**in·fu′ri·ate·ly,** *adv.* —**in·fu′ri·a′tion,** *n.* —**Syn. 1.** anger.

in·fu·ri·at·ing·ly (in fyŏŏr′ē ā′ting lē), *adv.* to an irritating or exasperating degree.

in·fuse (in fyōōz′), *v.,* **-fused, -fus·ing.** —*v.t.* **1.** to introduce, as by pouring; cause to penetrate; instill (usually fol. by *into*): *to infuse loyalty into the new employees.* **2.** to imbue or inspire (usually fol. by *with*): *The new coach infused the team with enthusiasm.* **3.** to steep or soak (leaves, bark, roots, etc.) in a liquid so as to extract the soluble properties or ingredients. **4.** *Obs.* to pour in. —*v.i.* **5.** to undergo infusion; become infused. [ME < L *infūs(us)* poured in, ptp. of *infundere*] —**in·fus′er,** *n.* —**in·fu·sive** (in fyōō′siv), *adj.* —**Syn. 1.** ingrain; inculcate.

in·fu·si·ble[1] (in fyōō′zə bəl), *adj.* not fusible; incapable of being fused or melted. —**in·fu′si·bil′i·ty, in·fu′si·ble·ness,** *n.* [IN-[3] + FUSIBLE]

in·fu·si·ble[2] (in fyōō′zə bəl), *adj.* capable of being infused. [INFUSE + -IBLE]

in·fu·sion (in fyōō′zhən), *n.* **1.** the act or process of infusing. **2.** something that is infused. **3.** *Pharm.* **a.** the steeping or soaking of a crude drug in water. **b.** the liquid so prepared. **4.** *Med.* **a.** the introduction of a saline or other solution into a vein. **b.** the solution used. [late ME < L *infūsiōn-* (s. of *infūsiō*)]

in·fu·sion·ism (in fyōō′zhə niz′əm), *n. Theol.* the doctrine that the soul existed in a previous state and is infused into the body at conception or birth. —**in·fu′sion·ist,** *n.*

In·fu·so·ri·a (in′fyŏŏ sôr′ē ə, -sōr′-), *n.pl.* **1.** protozoans of the class *Ciliata* (or *Ciliophora*). **2.** *Obs.* any of various microscopic organisms found in infusions of decayed or decaying organic matter. [< NL, neut. pl. of *infūsōrius.* See INFUSE, -ORY[1]]

in·fu·so·ri·al (in′fyŏŏ sôr′ē əl, -sōr′-), *adj.* containing or consisting of infusorians: *infusorial earth.*

in·fu·so·ri·an (in′fyŏŏ sôr′ē ən, -sōr′-), *n.* **1.** any of the Infusoria. —*adj.* **2.** infusorial.

in fu·tu·ro (in fŏŏ tōō′rō; *Eng.* in fyŏŏ tŏŏr′ō, -tyŏŏr′ō), *Latin.* in the future.

-ing[1], a suffix of nouns formed from verbs, expressing the action of the verb or its result, product, material, etc. (*the art of building; a new building; cotton wadding*). It is also used to form nouns from other words than verbs (*offing; shirting*). Verbal nouns ending in *-ing* are often used attributively (*the printing trade*) and in composition (*drinking song*). In some compounds (*sewing machine*), the first element might reasonably be regarded as the participial adjective, **-ing**[2], the compound thus meaning "a machine that sews," but it is commonly taken as a verbal noun, the compound being explained as "a machine for sewing." Cf. **-ing**[2]. [ME; OE *-ing, -ung*]

-ing[2], a suffix forming the present participle of verbs, such participles being often used as participial adjectives: *warring factions.* Cf. **-ing**[1]. [ME *-ing, inge,* r. ME *-inde, ende,* OE *-ende*]

-ing[3], a native English suffix, meaning "one belonging to," "of the kind of," "one descended from," and sometimes having a diminutive force, formerly used in the formation of nouns: *farthing; shilling; bunting; gelding; whiting.* Cf. **-ling.** [ME, OE *-ing;* c. ON *-ingr, -ungr,* Goth *-ings*]

in·gate (in′gāt′), *n. Foundry.* gate[1] (def. 10a).

in·gath·er (in′gath′ər, in gath′ər), *v.t.* **1.** to gather or bring in, as a harvest. —*v.i.* **2.** to collect; assemble. —**in·gath′er·er,** *n.*

Inge (inj *for 1;* ing *for 2*), *n.* **1. William (Mot·ter)** (mot′ər), 1913–1973, U.S. playwright. **2. William Ralph,** 1860–1954, Anglican clergyman, scholar, and author: dean of St. Paul's 1911–34.

in·gem·i·nate (in jem′ə nāt′), *v.t.,* **-nat·ed, -nat·ing.** to repeat; reiterate. [< L *ingemināt(us)* redoubled, repeated (ptp. of *ingemināre*)] —**in·gem′i·na′tion,** *n.*

in·gen·er·ate[1] (in jen′ər it), *adj.* not generated; self-existent. [< LL *ingenerāt(us)* not begotten. See IN-[3], GENERATE]

in·gen·er·ate[2] (*v.* in jen′ə rāt′; *adj.* in jen′ər it), *v.,* **-at·ed, -at·ing,** *adj. Archaic.* —*v.t.* **1.** to engender; produce. —*adj.* **2.** inborn; innate. [< L *ingenerāt(us)* implanted. See IN-[2], GENERATE] —**in·gen′er·a′tion,** *n.*

in·gen·ious (in jēn′yəs), *adj.* **1.** characterized by cleverness or originality of invention or construction. **2.** cleverly inventive; resourceful. [ME < L *ingeniōs(us).* See ENGINE, -OUS] —**in·gen′ious·ly,** *adv.* —**in·gen′ious·ness,** *n.*
—**Syn. 2.** bright, gifted, able, resourceful; adroit. INGENIOUS, INGENUOUS are now distinct from each other and should not be confused or thought of as synonyms. INGENIOUS means clever, inventive, resourceful in contriving new explanations or methods, and the like: *an ingenious executive.* INGENUOUS means frank, candid, free from guile or deceit: *an ingenuous and sincere statement.* —**Ant. 2.** unskillful.

in·gé·nue (an′zhə nōō′, -nyōō′; *Fr.* AN zhā NY′), *n., pl.* **-nues** (-nōōz′, -nyōōz′; *Fr.* -NY′). **1.** the role of an ingenuous girl, esp. as represented on the stage. **2.** an actress who plays such a role or specializes in playing such roles. Also, **in′ge·nue′.** [< F, fem. of *ingénu* < L *ingenu(us)* native, inborn, etc.; see INGENUOUS]

in·ge·nu·i·ty (in′jə nōō′i tē, -nyōō′-), *n., pl.* **-ties** for 3. **1.** the quality of being ingenious; inventive talent. **2.** cleverness or skillfulness of conception or design, as of things, actions, etc. **3.** an ingenious contrivance. **4.** *Obs.* ingenuousness. [< L *ingenuitās* innate virtue, etc. (see INGENUOUS, -ITY); current senses by assoc. with INGENIOUS]

in·gen·u·ous (in jen′yōō əs), *adj.* **1.** free from reserve, restraint, or dissimulation. **2.** artless; innocent; naive. [< L *ingenuus* native, inborn, honorable, tender = *ingenu-* (perf. s. of *ingignere to implant = *in-* IN-[2] + *gignere* to beget) + *-us* -OUS] —**in·gen′u·ous·ly,** *adv.* —**in·gen′u·ous·ness,** *n.* —**Syn. 1.** candid. See **ingenious.**

In·ger·soll (ing′gər sôl′, -sol′, -səl), *n.* **Robert Green,** 1833–99, U.S. lawyer, political leader, orator, and lecturer.

in·gest (in jest′), *v.t.* to take into the body, as food or liquid (opposed to *egest*). [< L *ingest(us)* poured, thrown into, ptp. of *ingere.* See IN-[2], GEST] —**in·gest′i·ble,** *adj.* —**in·ges′tion,** *n.* —**in·ges′tive,** *adj.*

in·ges·ta (in jes′tə), *n.pl.* substances ingested. [< NL, neut. pl. of L *ingestus.* See INGEST]

in·ges·tant (in jes′tənt), *n.* **1.** something that is ingested. **2.** an allergen that is ingested rather than inhaled.

in·gle (ing′gəl), *n.* *Brit. Dial.* a fire burning in a hearth. [? < Gael *aingeal* cinder]

in·gle·nook (ing′gəl no͝ok′), *n.* *Chiefly Brit.* a corner by the fire; chimney corner. Also, **in′gle nook′.**

In·gle·wood (ing′gəl wo͝od′), *n.* a city in SW California, near Los Angeles. 89,985 (1970).

in·glo·ri·ous (in glōr′ē əs, -glôr′-), *adj.* **1.** shameful; disgraceful: *inglorious retreat.* **2.** *Archaic.* not famous. [< L *inglōrius*] —**in·glo′ri·ous·ly,** *adv.* —**in·glo′ri·ous·ness,** *n.*

In God′ We′ Trust′, **1.** a motto appearing on U.S. currency. **2.** motto of Florida.

in·go·ing (in′gō′ing), *adj.* going in; entering.

in·got (ing′gət), *n.* **1.** a mass of metal cast in a convenient form for shaping, remelting, or refining. —*v.t.* **2.** to make ingots of; shape into ingots. [ME: lit., (something) poured in = *in-* IN-[1] + *got* poured < OE *goten,* ptp. of *gēotan*]

in·graft (in graft′, -gräft′), *v.t.* engraft. —**in·graft′er,** *n.* —**in·graft′ment, in′graf·ta′tion,** *n.*

in·grain (*v.* in grān′; *adj., n.* in′grān′), *v.t.* **1.** to fix deeply and firmly, as in the nature or mind. —*adj.* **2.** ingrained; firmly fixed. **3.** (of carpets) made of yarn dyed before weaving and so woven as to show a different pattern on each side; reversible. **4.** dyed in grain, or through the fiber. **5.** dyed in the yarn, or in a raw state, before manufacture. —*n.* **6.** yarn, wool, etc., dyed before manufacture. **7.** an ingrain carpet. Also, **engrain** (for defs. 1, 2). [orig. phrase (*dyed*) *in grain* (i.e., with kermes)] —**Syn. 1.** infuse, imbue.

in·grained (in grānd′, in′grānd′), *adj.* **1.** firmly fixed; deep-rooted; inveterate: *ingrained superstition.* **2.** wrought into or through the grain or fiber. Also, **engrained.** —**in·grain·ed·ly** (in grā′nid lē, -grānd′-), *adv.* —**in·grain′ed·ness,** *n.*

in·grate (in′grāt), *n.* **1.** an ungrateful person. —*adj.* **2.** *Archaic.* ungrateful. [ME *ingrat* < L *ingrāt(us)* ungrateful. See IN-[3], GRATEFUL] —**in′grate·ly,** *adv.*

in·gra·ti·ate (in grā′shē āt′), *v.t.,* **-at·ed, -at·ing.** to establish (oneself) in the favor or good graces of others (usually fol. by *with*): *He ingratiated himself with the boss.* [? < It *ingraziato,* ptp. of *ingraziare* < phrase *in grazia* < L *in grātiam* into favor. See IN, GRACE, -ATE[1]] —**in·gra′ti·a′tion,** *n.*

in·gra·ti·at·ing (in grā′shē ā′ting), *adj.* **1.** charming; agreeable; pleasing. **2.** meant to gain favor. —**in·gra′ti·at′ing·ly,** *adv.*

in·gra·ti·a·to·ry (in grā′shē ə tōr′ē, -tôr′ē), *adj.* serving or intended to ingratiate.

in·grat·i·tude (in grat′i to͞od′, -tyo͞od′), *n.* the state of being ungrateful. [ME < ML *ingrātitūd(ō)*]

in·gre·di·ent (in grē′dē ənt), *n.* **1.** something that enters as an element into a mixture: *the ingredients of a cake.* **2.** a constituent element of anything: *the ingredients of political success.* [late ME < L *ingredient-* (s. of *ingrediēns* going into (prp. of *ingredī*) = *in-* IN-[2] + *-gredient-* going; see GRADIENT] —**Syn. 1.** See **element.** —**Ant.** whole.

In·gres (aN′grᵊ), *n.* **Jean Au·guste Do·mi·nique** (zhäN ō gyst′ dô mē nēk′), 1780–1867, French painter.

in·gress (in′gres), *n.* **1.** the act of going in or entering. **2.** the right to enter. **3.** a means or place of entering; entryway. **4.** *Astron.* immersion (def. 5). [< L *ingress(us)* a going in = *ingress-* (ptp. s. of *ingredī*) + *-us* n. suffix (4th decl.)] —**in·gres·sion** (in gresh′ən), *n.* —**in·gres′sive,** *adj.* —**in·gres′sive·ness,** *n.*

in·group (in′gro͞op′), *n.* *Sociol.* a group of people sharing similar interests, attitudes, etc., and considering those outside the group as inferior or alien. Cf. **outgroup.**

in·grow·ing (in′grō′ing), *adj.* **1.** growing into the flesh: *an ingrowing nail.* **2.** growing within or inward.

in·grown (in′grōn′), *adj.* **1.** having grown into the flesh: *an ingrown toenail.* **2.** grown within or inward.

in·growth (in′grōth′), *n.* **1.** growth inward. **2.** something formed by growth inward.

in·gui·nal (ing′gwə nᵊl), *adj.* of, pertaining to, or situated in the groin. [< L *inguināl(is)* of the groin = *inguin-* (s. of *inguen*) groin + *-ālis* -AL[1]]

in·gulf (in gulf′), *v.t.* engulf. —**in·gulf′ment,** *n.*

in·gur·gi·tate (in gûr′ji tāt′), *v.,* **-tat·ed, -tat·ing.** —*v.t.* **1.** to swallow greedily or in great quantity, as food. **2.** to engulf; swallow up. —*v.i.* **3.** to drink or eat greedily; guzzle; swill. [< L *ingurgitāt(us)* flooded, filled (ptp. of *ingurgitāre*) = *in-* IN-[2] + *gurgit-* (s. of *gurges*) whirlpool, flood + *-ātus* -ATE[1]] —**in·gur′gi·ta′tion,** *n.*

in·hab·it (in hab′it), *v.t.* **1.** to live or dwell in (a place), as persons or animals. **2.** to exist or be situated within; indwell: *Weird notions inhabit his mind.* —*v.i.* **3.** *Archaic.* to live or dwell, as in a place. [< L *inhabit(āre)* (see IN-[2], HABIT[2]); r. ME *enhabite* < MF *enhabite(r)*] —**in·hab′it·a·bil′i·ty,** *n.* —**in·hab′it·a·ble,** *adj.* —**in·hab′i·ta′tion,** *n.*

in·hab·it·an·cy (in hab′i tᵊn sē), *n., pl.* **-cies.** a place of residence; dwelling. Also, **in·hab′it·ance.**

in·hab·it·ant (in hab′i tᵊnt), *n.* a person or an animal that inhabits a place; permanent resident. Also, **in·hab′it·er.** [late ME < L *inhabitant-* (s. of *inhabitāns*) dwelling in]

in·hab·it·ed (in hab′i tid), *adj.* having inhabitants: *an inhabited island.*

in·hal·ant (in hā′lənt), *adj.* **1.** used for inhaling. —*n.* **2.** an apparatus or medicine used for inhaling.

in·ha·la·tor (in′hə lā′tər), *n.* an apparatus to help one inhale air, an anesthetic, medicinal vapors, etc.

in·hale (in hāl′), *v.,* **-haled, -hal·ing.** —*v.t.* **1.** to breathe in; draw in by breathing: *to inhale air.* —*v.i.* **2.** to breathe in, esp. tobacco smoke. [IN-[2] + (EX)HALE] —**in·ha·la·tion** (in′hə lā′shən), *n.*

in·hal·er (in hā′lər), *n.* **1.** an apparatus used in inhaling medicinal vapors, anesthetics, etc. **2.** a respirator. **3.** a person who inhales. **4.** snifter (def. 1).

In·ham·ba·ne (in′yəm bä′nə), *n.* a seaport in SE Mozambique. 68,654 (est. 1955).

in·har·mon·ic (in′här mon′ik), *adj.* not harmonic; dissonant. —**in·har·mo·ny** (in här′mə nē), *n.*

in·har·mo·ni·ous (in′här mō′nē əs), *adj.* **1.** not harmonious; discordant. **2.** not congenial; disagreeable. —**in′har·mo′ni·ous·ly,** *adv.* —**in′har·mo′ni·ous·ness,** *n.*

in·haul (in′hôl′), *n.* *Naut.* any of various lines for hauling a sail, spar, etc., inward or inboard in order to stow it after use. Also, **in′haul′er.**

in·here (in hēr′), *v.i.,* **-hered, -her·ing.** to exist permanently and inseparably in, as a quality, attribute, or element; belong intrinsically; be inherent. [< L *inhaer(ēre)* = *in-* IN-[2] + *haerēre* to stick]

in·her·ence (in hēr′əns, -her′-), *n.* the state or fact of inhering or being inherent. [< ML *inhaerentia.* See INHERENT, -ENCE]

in·her·en·cy (in hēr′ən sē, -her′-), *n., pl.* **-cies** for 2. **1.** inherence. **2.** something inherent. [< ML *inhaerentia.* See INHERENT, -ENCY]

in·her·ent (in hēr′ənt, -her′-), *adj.* existing in something as a permanent and inseparable element, quality, or attribute. [< L *inhaerent-* (s. of *inhaerēns*), prp. of *inhaerēre* to INHERE; see -ENT] —**in·her′ent·ly,** *adv.* —**Syn.** innate, native, inbred, ingrained.

in·her·it (in her′it), *v.t.* **1.** to take or receive (property, a right, a title, etc.) by succession or will, as an heir. **2.** to succeed (a person) as heir. **3.** to receive (anything), as by succession from predecessors. **4.** to receive (a genetic character) by the transmission of hereditary factors. **5.** to receive as one's portion. **6.** *Obs.* to make (one) heir (usually fol. by *of*). —*v.i.* **7.** to take or receive property or the like by virtue of being heir to it. **8.** to have succession as heir. **9.** to receive qualities, powers, duties, etc., as by inheritance. [ME *en(h)erit(i)e(n)* < MF *enherite(r)* < LL *inhērēditāre* to make heir. See IN-[2], HEREDITARY] —**in·her′it·a·bil′i·ty, in·her′it·a·ble·ness,** *n.* —**in·her′it·a·ble,** *adj.* —**in·her′it·a·bly,** *adv.*

in·her·it·ance (in her′i tᵊns), *n.* **1.** something that is or may be inherited; any property passing at the owner's death to the heir or those entitled to succeed. **2.** the genetic characters transmitted from parent to offspring. **3.** something, as a quality or characteristic, received from progenitors or predecessors. **4.** the act or fact of inheriting: *to receive property by inheritance.* **5.** birthright; heritage. **6.** *Obs.* right of possession; ownership. [ME *enheritance* < AF]

inher′itance tax′, a tax imposed on the right of heirs to receive a decedent's property.

in·her·it·ed (in her′i tid), *adj.* received by inheritance: *an inherited estate; inherited traits.*

in·her·i·tor (in her′i tər), *n.* a person who inherits; an heir. [ME *enheritour,* -er]

in·he·sion (in hē′zhən), *n.* the state or fact of inhering; inherence. [< LL *inhaesiōn-* (s. of *inhaesiō*) = L *inhaes(us)* stuck in (ptp. of *inhaerēre* to INHERE) + *-iōn-* -ION]

in·hib·it (in hib′it), *v.t.* **1.** to restrain, hinder, arrest, or check (an action, impulse, etc.). **2.** to prohibit; forbid. [late ME *inhibite* < L *inhibit(us)* held in (ptp. of *inhibēre*) = *in-* IN-[2] + *-hib-* (var. of *hab-* hold) + *-itus* -ITE[1]] —**in·hib′it·er,** *n.* —**in·hib·i·to·ry** (in hib′i tōr′ē, -tôr′ē), **in·hib′i·tive,** *adj.* —**Syn. 1.** repress, discourage. **2.** See **forbid.**

in·hi·bi·tion (in′i bish′ən, in′hi-), *n.* **1.** the act of inhibiting. **2.** the state of being inhibited. **3.** *Psychol.* the blocking or holding back of one psychological process by another. **4.** *Physiol.* **a.** a restraining, arresting, or checking of the action of an organ or cell. **b.** the reduction of a reflex or other activity as the result of an antagonistic stimulation. **c.** a state created at synapses making them less excitable by other sources of stimulation. [ME *inhibicio(u)n* < L *inhibitiōn-* (s. of *inhibitiō*)]

in·hib·i·tor (in hib′i tər), *n.* **1.** *Chem.* a substance that decreases the rate of or stops completely a chemical reaction. **2.** any impurity in a mineral that prevents luminescence. Cf. **activator** (def. 3). **3.** *Rocketry.* an inert antioxidant used with solid propellants to inhibit burning on certain surfaces. **4.** an inhibiter.

in hoc sig·no vin·ces (in hōk′ sig′nō wing′kās; *Eng.* in hok′ sig′nō vin′sēz), *Latin.* in this sign shalt thou conquer: motto used by Constantine the Great, from his vision, before battle, of a cross bearing these words.

in·hos·pi·ta·ble (in hos′pi tə bəl, in′ho spit′ə bəl), *adj.* **1.** not inclined to or characterized by hospitality, as persons, actions, etc. **2.** (of a region, climate, etc.) not offering shelter, favorable conditions, etc. [< MF] —**in·hos′pi·ta·ble·ness,** *n.* —**in·hos′pi·ta·bly,** *adv.*

in·hos·pi·tal·i·ty (in′hos pi tal′i tē, in hos′-), *n.* lack of hospitality; inhospitable attitude toward visitors, guests, etc. [< L *inhospitālitās*]

in-house (in′hous′), *adj., adv.* within, conducted within, or utilizing an organization's own staff or resources rather than external or nonstaff facilities: *in-house research; in-house proofreading.*

in·hu·man (in hyo͞o′mən *or, often,* -yo͞o′-), *adj.* **1.** lacking sympathy, pity, warmth, compassion, or the like; cruel; brutal. **2.** not human. [< L *inhūmān(us)*; r. late ME *inhumain* < MF] —**in·hu′man·ly,** *adv.* —**in·hu′man·ness,** *n.* —**Syn. 1.** unfeeling, callous, savage, brutish.

in·hu·mane (in′hyo͞o mān′ *or, often,* -yo͞o-), *adj.* not humane; lacking humanity or kindness. [var. of INHUMAN] —**in′hu·mane′·ly,** *adv.*

in·hu·man·i·ty (in′hyo͞o man′i tē *or, often,* -yo͞o-), *n., pl.* **-ties** for 2. **1.** the state or quality of being inhuman or inhumane; cruelty. **2.** an inhuman or inhumane act. [late ME *inhumanite* < L *inhūmānitās*]

in·hume (in hyo͞om′), *v.t.,* **-humed, -hum·ing.** to bury; inter. [< L *inhum(āre)* = *in-* IN-[2] + *humāre* to bury < *hum(us)* earth] —**in·hu·ma′tion,** *n.* —**in·hum′er,** *n.*

in·im·i·cal (i nim′i kəl), *adj.* **1.** unfriendly; hostile. **2.** adverse in tendency or effect; harmful. Also, **in·im′i·ca·ble.** [< L *inimīc(us)* ENEMY + -AL[1]] —**in·im′i·cal·ly,** *adv.* —**in·im′i·cal·ness, in·im′i·cal′i·ty,** *n.*

in·im·i·ta·ble (i nim′i tə bəl), *adj.* incapable of being imitated; surpassing imitation. [< L *inimitābil(is)*] —**in·im′i·ta·bil′i·ty, in·im′i·ta·ble·ness,** *n.* —**in·im′i·ta·bly,** *adv.*

in·iq·ui·tous (i nik′wi təs), *adj.* characterized by iniquity; wicked; sinful. —**in·iq′ui·tous·ly,** *adv.* —**in·iq′ui·tous·ness,** *n.* —**Syn.** nefarious, evil, base.

in·iq·ui·ty (i nik′wi tē), *n., pl.* **-ties. 1.** gross injustice; wickedness. **2.** a violation of right or duty; wicked act; sin. [ME < L *inīquitās* unevenness, unfairness = *inīqu(us)* uneven, unfair (*in-* IN-3 + *-īquus*, var. of *aequus* EQUI-) + *-itās* -ITY]

init., initial.

in·i·tial (i nish′əl), *adj., n., v.,* **-tialed, -tial·ing** or (*esp. Brit.*) **-tialled, -tial·ling.** —*adj.* **1.** of or pertaining to the beginning; first: *the initial step in a process.* —*n.* **2.** an initial letter, as of a word. **3.** the first letter of a proper name. **4.** a letter of extra size or an ornamental character used at the beginning of a chapter or other division of a book or the like. —*v.t.* **5.** to mark or sign with an initial or the initials of one's name, sometimes as a token of approval. [< L *initiāl(is)* = *initi(um)* beginning (*init(us)* begun (ptp. of *inīre* to go in, enter upon) = *in-* IN-2 + *-i-* go + *-tus* ptp. suffix + *-ium* n. suffix) + *-ālis* -AL1] —**in·i′tial·er;** *esp. Brit.*, **in·i′tial·ler,** *n.* —**in·i′tial·ly,** *adv.*

Ini′tial Teach′ing Al′phabet, an alphabet system of 44 letters representing the basic sounds of English, often used in teaching beginners to read. *Abbr.:* I.T.A.

in·i·ti·ate (*v.* i nish′ē āt′; *adj., n.* i nish′ē it, -āt′), *v.,* **-at·ed, -at·ing,** *adj., n.* —*v.t.* **1.** to begin, set going, or originate. **2.** to introduce into the knowledge of some art or subject. **3.** to admit with formal rites into secret knowledge, a society, etc. **4.** to propose (a measure) by initiative procedure: *to initiate a constitutional amendment.* —*adj.* **5.** initiated; begun. **6.** admitted into a society, club, etc., or into the knowledge of a subject. —*n.* **7.** a person who has been initiated. [< L *initiāt(us)* initiated (ptp. of *initiāre*). See INITIAL, -ATE1] —**in·i′ti·a′tor;** *referring to a woman,* **in·i′ti·a′tress,** *n.* —**Syn. 1.** commence; introduce, inaugurate. See **begin. 2.** teach, indoctrinate.

in·i·ti·a·tion (i nish′ē ā′shən), *n.* **1.** formal admission into a society, club, etc. **2.** the ceremonies of admission. **3.** the act of initiating. **4.** the fact of being initiated. [< L *initiātiōn-* (s. of *initiātiō*)]

in·i·ti·a·tive (i nish′ē ə tiv, i nish′ə-), *n.* **1.** an introductory act or step; leading action: *to take the initiative.* **2.** readiness and ability in initiating action; enterprise. **3.** one's personal, responsible decision: *to act on one's own initiative.* **4.** *Govt.* **a.** a procedure by which a specified number of voters may propose a statute, constitutional amendment, or ordinance. Cf. **referendum** (def. 1). **b.** the general right to present a new legislative bill. —*adj.* **5.** of or pertaining to initiation; serving to initiate. —**in·i′ti·a·tive·ly,** *adv.*

in·i·ti·a·to·ry (i nish′ē ə tôr′ē, -tōr′ē), *adj.* **1.** introductory; initial: *an initiatory step.* **2.** serving to initiate or admit into a society, club, etc. —**in·i·ti·a·to·ri·ly** (i nish′ē ə tôr′ə lē, -tōr′-; i nish′ē ə tôr′ə lē, -tōr′-), *adv.*

in·ject (in jekt′), *v.t.* **1.** to force (a fluid) into a passage, cavity, or tissue. **2.** to introduce (something new or different) into a thing. **3.** to introduce arbitrarily or inappropriately; intrude. **4.** to interject (a remark, suggestion, etc.), as into conversation. [< L *inject(us)* thrown in (ptp. of *in(j)icere*) = *in-* IN-2 + *-jec-* (var. of *jac-* throw) + *-tus* ptp. suffix] —**in·ject′a·ble,** *adj.* —**in·jec′tor,** *n.*

in·jec·tion (in jek′shən), *n.* **1.** the act of injecting. **2.** anything that is injected. **3.** a liquid injected into the body, esp. for medicinal purposes, as a hypodermic. [< L *injectiōn-* (s. of *injectiō*)]

in·ju·di·cious (in′jo͞o dish′əs), *adj.* not judicious; unwise; imprudent. —**in′ju·di′cious·ly,** *adv.* —**in′ju·di′cious·ness,** *n.*

In·jun (in′jən), *n. Dial.* an American Indian. [var. of INDIAN]

in·junc·tion (in jungk′shən), *n.* **1.** *Law.* a judicial process or order requiring the person or persons to whom it is directed to do or refrain from doing a particular act. **2.** the act or an instance of enjoining. **3.** a command; order; admonition. [< LL *injunctiōn-* (s. of *injunctiō*) = L *injunct(us)* joined to, brought upon (ptp. of *injungere;* see ENJOIN) + *-iōn-* -ION] —**in·junc′tive,** *adj.* —**in·junc′tive·ly,** *adv.*

in·jure (in′jər), *v.t.,* **-jured, -jur·ing. 1.** to do or cause harm of any kind to; damage; hurt; impair: *to injure one's hand.* **2.** to do wrong or injustice to: *to injure a friend's feelings.* [back formation from INJURY (formerly v.)] —**in′jur·a·ble,** *adj.* —**in′jur·er,** *n.* —**Syn. 1.** spoil, mar. **2.** maltreat, abuse. —**Ant. 1.** benefit.

in·jured (in′jərd), *adj.* **1.** wounded or harmed; damaged; hurt. **2.** offended; wronged: *an injured reputation.* **3.** showing or revealing a feeling of injury; offended; reproachful: *Her face wore an injured look.* —**in′jured·ly,** *adv.* —**in′jured·ness,** *n.*

in·ju·ri·ous (in jo͝or′ē əs), *adj.* **1.** harmful, hurtful, or detrimental, as in effect. **2.** insulting; abusive; offensive. [late ME < L *injūriōsus.* See INJURY, -OUS] —**in·ju′ri·ous·ly,** *adv.* —**in·ju′ri·ous·ness,** *n.* —**Syn. 1.** damaging, deleterious; destructive. **2.** derogatory, defamatory, slanderous, libelous. —**Ant. 1.** beneficial.

in·ju·ry (in′jə rē), *n., pl.* **-ju·ries. 1.** harm done or sustained. **2.** a particular form or instance of harm: *an injury to his pride.* **3.** wrong or injustice done or suffered. **4.** *Law.* any wrong or violation of the rights, property, reputation, etc., of another. **5.** *Obs.* injurious speech; calumny. [ME *injurie* < L *injūria,* n. use of fem. of *injūrius* injurious = *in-* IN-3 + *jūri-* (s. of *jūs* right, law) + *-us* -OUS]
—**Syn. 1.** damage, impairment, mischief. **1–3.** INJURY, HURT, WOUND refer to material or moral impairments or wrongs. INJURY, originally denoting a wrong done or suffered, is now used for any kind of evil, impairment, or loss, caused or sustained: *physical injury; injury to one's reputation.* HURT suggests esp. physical injury, often bodily injury attended with pain: *a bad hurt from a fall.* A WOUND is usually a physical hurt caused by cutting, shooting, etc., or an emotional hurt: *a serious wound in the shoulder; to inflict a wound by betraying someone's trust.* —**Ant. 1.** benefit.

in·jus·tice (in jus′tis), *n.* **1.** the quality or fact of being unjust; inequity. **2.** violation of the rights of others; unjust or unfair action or treatment. **3.** an unjust act; wrong; unfairness. [ME < MF < L *injustitia*] —**Syn. 2.** injury, wrong.

ink (ingk), *n.* **1.** a fluid or viscous substance used for writing or printing. **2.** a dark, protective fluid ejected by the cuttlefish and other cephalopods. —*v.t.* **3.** to mark, stain, or smear with ink. [ME *inke, enke* < MF *enque* < LL *enc(austum)* < Gk *énkauston* purple ink, n. use of neut. of *énkaustos* burnt in. See EN-2, CAUSTIC] —**ink′er,** *n.* —**ink′less,** *adj.* —**ink′like′,** *adj.*

ink·ber·ry (ingk′ber′ē, -bə rē), *n., pl.* **-ries. 1.** a shrub, *Ilex glabra,* having leathery, evergreen leaves and black berries. **2.** the pokeweed. **3.** the berry of either plant.

Ink·er·man (ing′kər män′), *n.* a town in S Crimea, in the SW Soviet Union in Europe: Russian defeat by the English and French 1854.

ink·horn (ingk′hôrn′), *n.* a small container of horn or other material, formerly used to hold writing ink.

in·kle (ing′kəl), *n.* **1.** a linen tape used for trimmings. **2.** the linen thread or yarn from which this tape is made. [?]

ink·ling (ingk′ling), *n.* **1.** a slight suggestion; hint; intimation. **2.** a vague idea or notion; slight understanding. [obs. *inkle* to hint (ME *incle*) + -ING1; akin to OE *inca* suspicion]

ink·stand (ingk′stand′), *n.* **1.** a small stand for holding ink, pens, etc. **2.** an inkwell.

Ink·ster (ingk′stər), *n.* a city in SE Michigan, near Detroit. 38,595 (1970).

ink·well (ingk′wel′), *n.* a container for ink. Also called, *esp. Brit.,* **ink·pot** (ingk′pot′).

ink·y (ing′kē), *adj.,* **ink·i·er, ink·i·est. 1.** black as ink: *inky shadows.* **2.** resembling ink. **3.** stained with ink: *inky fingers.* **4.** of or pertaining to ink. **5.** consisting of or containing ink. —**ink′i·ness,** *n.*

ink′y cap′, any mushroom of the genus *Coprinus,* esp. *C. atramentarius,* whose gills disintegrate into blackish liquid after the spores mature.

in·land (*adj.* in′lənd; *adv., n.* in′land′, -lənd), *adj.* **1.** pertaining to or situated in the interior part of a country or region. **2.** *Brit.* carried on within a country; domestic. —*adv.* **3.** in or toward the interior of a country. —*n.* **4.** the interior part of a country, away from the border. [ME, OE]

in·land·er (in′lən dər), *n.* a person living inland.

In′land Sea′, a sea in SW Japan, enclosed by the islands of Honshu, Shikoku, and Kyushu. 240 mi. long.

in-law (in′lô′), *n.* a relative by marriage. [back formation from MOTHER-IN-LAW and the like]

in·lay (*v.* in′lā′, in′lā′; *n.* in′lā′), *v.,* **-laid, -lay·ing,** *n.* —*v.t.* **1.** to decorate (an object) with veneers of fine materials set in its surface. **2.** to insert or apply (layers of fine materials) in the surface of an object. —*n.* **3.** a veneer of fine material inserted in something else, esp. for ornament. **4.** a design or decoration made by inlaying. **5.** *Dentistry.* a filling of metal, porcelain, or the like, that is first shaped to fit a cavity and then cemented into it. —**in′lay′er,** *n.*

in-lb, inch-pound.

in·let (*n.* in′let, -lit; *v.* in′let′, in let′), *n., v.,* **-let, -let·ting.** —*n.* **1.** an indentation of a shoreline, usually long and narrow. **2.** a narrow passage between islands. **3.** an entrance. **4.** something put in or inserted. —*v.t.* **5.** to put in; insert. [ME]

in·li·er (in′lī′ər), *n. Geol.* an outcrop of a formation completely surrounded by another of later date. [IN + (OUT)LIER]

in loc. cit., in the place cited. [< L *in locō citātō*]

in lo·co (in lō′kō), *Latin* in place; in the proper place.

in lo·co pa·ren·tis (in lō′kō pä ren′tēs; *Eng.* in lō′kō pə ren′tis), *Latin.* in the place of a parent; replacing a parent.

in·ly (in′lē), *adv. Chiefly Literary.* **1.** inwardly. **2.** intimately; deeply. [ME *inliche,* OE *inlīce*]

in·mate (in′māt′), *n.* **1.** a person who is confined in a hospital, prison, etc. **2.** *Archaic.* a person who dwells with another or others in the same house.

in me·di·as res (in me′di äs′ res′; *Eng.* in mē′dē as′ rēz′, in mā′dē äs′ rās′), *Latin.* in the middle of things: used esp. of a narrative that opens in the middle rather than at the chronological beginning.

in mem., in memoriam.

in me·mo·ri·am (in mə mōr′ē əm, -môr′-), in memory (of); to the memory (of); as a memorial (to). [< L]

in·mesh (in mesh′), *v.t.* enmesh.

in·most (in′mōst′ *or, esp. Brit.,* -məst), *adj.* **1.** situated farthest within: *the inmost recesses of the forest.* **2.** most intimate: *one's inmost thoughts.* [ME (see IN-1, -MOST); r. *inmest,* OE *innemest* = *inne-* within + *-mest* -most]

inn (in), *n.* **1.** a commercial establishment that provides lodging, food, etc., for the public, esp. travelers; small hotel: *a country inn.* **2.** a tavern. **3.** (*cap.*) *Brit.* **a.** any of several buildings used as a place of residence for students. Cf. **Inns of Court. b.** a legal society occupying such a building. [ME, OE *in(n)* house; akin to Icel *inni*] —**inn′less,** *adj.* —**Syn. 1.** hostelry. See **hotel.**

Inn (in), *n.* a river in central Europe, flowing from S Switzerland through Austria and Germany into the Danube. 320 mi. long.

in·nards (in′ərdz), *n.* (*construed as pl.*) *Informal.* **1.** the interior parts of an animal body; entrails; viscera. **2.** the internal parts of a mechanism or structure: *an engine's innards.* [var. of *inwards,* n. pl. use of INWARD]

in·nate (i nāt′, in′āt), *adj.* **1.** existing in one from birth; inborn; native: *innate talent.* **2.** inherent in the character of something: *an innate defect in the hypothesis.* **3.** arising from the intellect or the constitution of the mind, rather than learned through experience: *innate knowledge.* [< L *innāt(us)* inborn (ptp. of *innascī*). See IN-2, NATAL] —**in·nate′ly,** *adv.* —**in·nate′ness,** *n.* —**Syn. 1.** natural, congenital.

in·ner (in′ər), *adj.* **1.** situated farther within; interior. **2.** more intimate, private, or secret: *his inner circle of friends.* **3.** mental; spiritual: *the inner life.* **4.** not obvious; hidden; obscure: *an inner meaning.* [ME; OE *innera,* comp. of *inne* within] —**in′ner·ly,** *adv., adj.* —**in′ner·ness,** *n.*

in′ner bar′, *Eng. Law.* a body of the King's Counsel who sit and plead inside the dividing bar in the court, ranking above the junior counsel. Cf. **outer bar.**

in′ner cit′y, an older part of a city, densely populated and usually deteriorating, inhabited mainly by poor minority groups. Cf. **central city.**

in·ner-di·rect·ed (in′ər di rek′tid, -dī-), *adj.* guided by internalized values rather than external pressures. Cf. **other-directed.** —**in′ner-di·rec′tion,** *n.*

in′ner ear′. See **internal ear.**

In′ner Heb′rides. See under **Hebrides.**

In′ner Light′, (in Quakerism) the light of Christ in the soul of every man, considered as a guiding force.

in′ner man′, 1. one's spiritual or intellectual being. 2. the stomach or appetite: *a hearty meal to satisfy the inner man.*
In′ner Mongo′lia, Mongolia (def. 2).
in·ner·most (in′ər mōst′ *or, esp. Brit.,* -məst), *adj.* 1. farthest inward; inmost. —*n.* 2. innermost part.
in′ner prod′uct, *Math.* See **scalar product.**
in·ner·spring (in′ər spring′), *adj.* having a number of enclosed helical springs supporting padding: *an innerspring mattress.*
In′ner Tem′ple, 1. See under **Inns of Court** (def. 1). 2. See under **temple**[1] (def. 7).
in′ner tube′, a doughnut-shaped, flexible rubber tube inflated inside a tire to bear the weight of a vehicle.
in·ner·vate (i nûr′vāt, in′ər vāt′), *v.t.*, **-vat·ed, -vat·ing.** 1. to communicate nervous energy to. 2. to furnish with nerves.
in·ner·va·tion (in′ər vā′shən), *n.* 1. the act of innervating. 2. the state of being innervated. 3. *Anat.* the distribution of nerves to a part. —**in′ner·va′tion·al,** *adj.*
in·nerve (i nûrv′), *v.t.*, **-nerved, -nerv·ing.** to supply with nervous energy; invigorate; animate.
In·ness (in′is), *n.* **George,** 1825–94, and his son, **George,** 1854–1926, U.S. painters.
inn·hold·er (in′hōl′dər), *n.* innkeeper.
in·ning (in′ing), *n.* 1. *Baseball.* a division of a game during which each team has an opportunity to score until three outs have been made against it. 2. a similar opportunity to score in certain other games, as horseshoes. 3. an opportunity for activity; a turn. 4. **innings,** (*construed as sing.*) *Cricket.* a unit of play in which each team has a turn at bat. 5. **innings,** (*construed as sing.*) land reclaimed, esp. from the sea. 6. the act of reclaiming marshy or flooded land. [ME *inninge,* OE *innung* a getting in = *inn(ian)* (to) go in + *-ung* -ING[1]]
inn·keep·er (in′kē′pər), *n.* a person who owns or operates an inn. Also, **innholder.**
in·no·cence (in′ə səns), *n.* 1. the quality or state of being innocent; freedom from sin or moral wrong. 2. chastity or purity: *She has not lost her innocence.* 3. freedom from legal or specific wrong; guiltlessness. 4. simplicity; guilelessness; ingenuousness. 5. lack of knowledge or understanding; naïveté. 6. harmlessness; innocuousness. 7. an innocent person or thing. 8. Also, **innocent, innocents.** the North American bluet, *Houstonia caerulea.* 9. a scrophulariaceous herb, *Collinsia verna,* having a blue-and-white flower. 10. a related herb, *Collinsia bicolor,* of California. [ME < L *innocentia.* See INNOCENT, -ENCE]
in·no·cen·cy (in′ə sən sē), *n., pl.* **-cies.** innocence (defs. 1–6). [ME; var. of INNOCENCE]
in·no·cent (in′ə sənt), *adj.* 1. free from moral wrong; without sin; pure: *innocent children.* 2. free from legal or specific wrong; guiltless. 3. not involving evil intent or motive: *an innocent misrepresentation.* 4. not causing physical or moral injury; harmless: *innocent fun.* 5. devoid (usually fol. by *of*): *innocent of merit.* 6. having or appearing to have the simplicity or naïveté of an unworldly person. —*n.* 7. an innocent person. 8. a young child. 9. a guileless person. 10. a simpleton or idiot. 11. Usually, **innocents.** (*construed as sing.*) *U.S.* innocence (def. 8). [ME < L *innocent-* (s. of *innocēns*) harmless = *in-* IN-[3] + *nocēns* harmful, prp. of *nocēre* to harm; see -ENT] —**in′no·cent·ly,** *adv.*
—**Syn.** 1. sinless, virtuous; faultless, impeccable, spotless, immaculate. 2. INNOCENT, BLAMELESS, GUILTLESS imply freedom from the responsibility of having done wrong. INNOCENT may imply having done no wrong at any time, and having not even a knowledge of evil: *an innocent victim.* BLAMELESS denotes freedom from blame, esp. moral blame: *a blameless life.* GUILTLESS denotes freedom from guilt or responsibility for wrongdoing, usually in a particular instance: *guiltless of a crime.* 6. naïve, unsophisticated, artless, guileless. —**Ant.** 1, 2. guilty.
In·no·cent I (in′ə sənt), **Saint,** died A.D. 417, Italian ecclesiastic: pope 401–417.
Innocent II, (*Gregorio Papareschi*) died 1143, Italian ecclesiastic: pope 1130–43.
Innocent III, (*Giovanni Lotario de' Conti*) 1161?–1216, Italian ecclesiastic: pope 1198–1216.
Innocent IV, (*Sinbaldo de Fieschi*) c1180–1254, Italian ecclesiastic: pope 1243–54.
Innocent V, (*Pierre de Tarentaise*) c1225–76, French ecclesiastic: pope 1276.
Innocent VI, (*Étienne Aubert*) died 1362, French jurist and ecclesiastic: pope 1352–62.
Innocent VII, (*Cosimo de' Migliorati*) 1336–1406, Italian ecclesiastic: pope 1404–06.
Innocent VIII, (*Giovanni Battista Cibò*) 1432–92, Italian ecclesiastic: pope 1484–92.
Innocent IX, (*Giovanni Antonio Facchinetti*) 1519–91, Italian ecclesiastic: pope 1591.
Innocent X, (*Giambattista Pamfili*) 1574–1655, Italian ecclesiastic: pope 1644–55.
Innocent XI, (*Bendetto Odescalchi*) 1611–89, Italian ecclesiastic: pope 1676–89.
Innocent XII, (*Antonio Pignatelli*) 1615–1700, Italian ecclesiastic: pope 1691–1700.
Innocent XIII, (*Michelangelo Conti*) 1655–1724, Italian ecclesiastic: pope 1721–24.
in·noc·u·ous (i nok′yo͞o əs), *adj.* 1. not harmful or injurious; harmless: *an innocuous home remedy.* 2. not likely to irritate; inoffensive. 3. without power to interest or excite; pallid; insipid: *an innocuous novel.* [< L *innocuus*] —**in·noc′u·ous·ly,** *adv.* —**in·noc′u·ous·ness,** *n.*
in·nom·i·nate (i nom′ə nit), *adj.* having no name; nameless; anonymous. [< LL *innōminat(us)* unnamed]
innom′inate bone′, *Anat.* either of the two bones forming the sides of the pelvis, each consisting of three consolidated bones, the ilium, ischium, and pubis.
in·no·vate (in′ə vāt′), *v.*, **-vat·ed, -vat·ing.** —*v.i.* 1. to introduce something new; make changes (often fol. by *on* or *in*): *to innovate on another's creation.* —*v.t.* 2. to introduce (something new). 3. *Obs.* to alter. [< L *innovāt(us)* renewed, altered (ptp. of *innovāre*). See IN-[2], NOVATION] —**in′no·va′tive, in·no·va·to·ry** (in′ō və tōr′ē, -tôr′ē, -vā′tə rē), *adj.* —**in′no·va′tor,** *n.*
in·no·va·tion (in′ə vā′shən), *n.* 1. something new or different introduced. 2. the act of innovating; introduction of new things or methods. [< LL *innovātiōn-* (s. of *innovātiō*)] —**in′no·va′tion·al,** *adj.*
in·nox·ious (i nok′shəs), *adj.* harmless; innocuous. [< L *innoxius*] —**in·nox′ious·ly,** *adv.* —**in·nox′ious·ness,** *n.*
Inns·bruck (inz′bro͝ok; *Ger.* ins′brŏŏk), *n.* a city in W Austria, on the Inn river. 100,699 (1961).
Inns′ of Court′, 1. the four voluntary legal societies in England (**Lincoln's Inn,** the **Inner Temple,** the **Middle Temple,** and **Gray's Inn**) that have the exclusive privilege of calling candidates to the English bar. 2. the buildings owned and used by the Inns.
in·nu·en·do (in′yo͞o en′dō), *n., pl.* **-dos, -does.** 1. an indirect intimation about a person or thing, esp. of a derogatory nature. 2. *Law.* **a.** a parenthetic explanation or specification in a pleading. **b.** (in an action for slander or libel) the explanation and elucidation of the words alleged to be defamatory. [< L: a hint, lit., by signaling, abl. of *innuendum,* ger. of *innuere* to signal = *in-* IN-[2] + *nuere* to nod]
in·nu·mer·a·ble (i no͞o′mər ə bəl, -nyo͞o′-), *adj.* 1. very numerous. 2. incapable of being numbered or counted. Also, **in·nu′mer·ous.** [ME < L *innumerābil(is)* countless, innumerable. See IN-[3], NUMERAL, -BLE] —**in·nu′mer·a·ble·ness, in·nu′mer·a·bil′i·ty,** *n.* —**in·nu′mer·a·bly,** *adv.* —**Syn.** 1. See **many.** 2. numberless, countless.
in·nu·tri·tion (in′no͞o trish′ən, -nyo͞o-), *n.* lack of nutrition. —**in′nu·tri′tious,** *adj.*
in·ob·serv·ance (in′əb zûr′vəns), *n.* 1. lack of observance; inattention: *drowsy inobservance.* 2. nonobservance. [< L *inobservantia*] —**in′ob·serv′ant,** *adj.* —**in′ob·serv′ant·ly,** *adv.*
in·oc·u·la·ble (i nok′yə lə bəl), *adj.* capable of being inoculated. —**in·oc′u·la·bil′i·ty,** *n.*
in·oc·u·lant (i nok′yə lənt), *n.* inoculum.
in·oc·u·late (i nok′yə lāt′), *v.*, **-lat·ed, -lat·ing.** —*v.t.* 1. to implant (a disease) in a person or animal by the introduction of germs or virus, as through a puncture, in order to produce a mild form of the disease and thereby secure immunity. 2. to affect or treat (a person or animal) in this manner. 3. to introduce (microorganisms) into surroundings suited to their growth, esp. into the body. 4. to imbue (a person), as with ideas; indoctrinate. 5. *Metall.* to treat (molten metal) chemically to strengthen the microstructure. —*v.i.* 6. to perform inoculation. [ME < L *inoculāt(us)* implanted (ptp. of *inoculāre*) = *in-* IN-[2] + *-oculā-* (s. of *-oculāre* to graft < *oculus* eye, bud) + *-tus* ptp. suffix] —**in·oc·u·la·tive** (i nok′yə lā′tiv, -yə lə-), *adj.* —**in·oc′u·la′tor,** *n.*
in·oc·u·la·tion (i nok′yə lā′shən), *n.* 1. the act or process of inoculating. 2. an instance of this. [ME < L *inoculātiōn-* (s. of *inoculātiō*) an engrafting]
in·oc·u·lum (i nok′yə ləm), *n., pl.* **-la** (-lə). the substance used to make an inoculation. [< NL = *inocul(āre)* (to) INOCULATE + *-um* n. suffix]
in·of·fen·sive (in′ə fen′siv), *adj.* doing no harm; unoffending; unobjectionable. —**in′of·fen′sive·ly,** *adv.* —**in′of·fen′sive·ness,** *n.*
in·of·fi·cious (in′ə fish′əs), *adj.* 1. *Law.* being inconsistent with moral duty and natural affection: *an inofficious will.* 2. *Obs.* disinclined to fulfill obligations; disobliging. [< L *inofficiōs(us)*] —**in′of·fi′cious·ness, in·of·fi·ci·os·i·ty** (in′ə fish′ē os′i tē), *n.*
I·nö·nü (i nœ ny′), *n.* **Is·met** (is met′), (*Ismet Paşa*), 1884–1973, Turkish political leader: president 1938–50; prime minister 1923–24, 1925–37, 1961–65.
in·op·er·a·ble (in op′ər ə bəl), *adj.* 1. not operable. 2. not admitting of a surgical operation without undue risk. Cf. **operable** (def. 2).
in·op·er·a·tive (in op′ər ə tiv, -ə rā′tiv), *adj.* 1. not in operation. 2. without effect: *inoperative remedies.* —**in·op′er·a·tive·ness,** *n.*
in·op·por·tune (in op′ər to͞on′, -tyo͞on′), *adj.* not opportune; inappropriate; untimely or unseasonable: *an inopportune visit.* [< LL *inopportūn(us)*] —**in·op′por·tune′ly,** *adv.* —**in·op′por·tune′ness, in·op′por·tu′ni·ty,** *n.*
in·or·di·nate (in ôr′dənit), *adj.* 1. not within proper limits; immoderate; excessive. 2. unrestrained in conduct, feelings, etc.; intemperate: *an inordinate prankster.* 3. not regulated; irregular. [ME *inordinat* < L *inordināt(us)* disordered] —**in·or′di·nate·ly,** *adv.* —**in·or′di·nate·ness;** *Obs.,* **in·or·di·na·cy** (in ôr′dənə sē), *n.* —**Syn.** 1. immoderate, extreme, exorbitant, outrageous, unreasonable, disproportionate. —**Ant.** 1. reasonable.
inorg., inorganic.
in·or·gan·ic (in′ôr gan′ik), *adj.* 1. not having the structure or organization characteristic of living bodies. 2. not characterized by vital processes. 3. *Chem.* noting or pertaining to compounds that are not hydrocarbons or their derivatives. Cf. **organic** (def. 1). 4. not fundamental or related; extraneous. —**in′or·gan′i·cal·ly,** *adv.*
in′organ′ic chem′istry, the branch of chemistry dealing with inorganic substances.
in·os·cu·late (in os′kyə lāt′), *v.i., v.t.*, **-lat·ed, -lat·ing.** 1. to connect or join so as to become or make continuous, as fibers; blend. 2. to unite intimately. —**in·os′cu·la′tion,** *n.*
in·o·si·tol (i nō′si tōl′, -tôl′, -tol′), *n.* 1. *Biochem.* an essential growth factor for animal life, $C_6H_6(OH)_6$, widely distributed in plants and seeds and present in animal tissues, urine, and the vitamin B complex. 2. *Pharm.* the commercial form of this compound, used chiefly in the treatment of certain liver conditions. [*inosite* (Gk *in-,* s. of *is* fiber, sinew + -OSE[2] + -ITE[1]) + -OL[1]]
in·pa·tient (in′pā′shənt), *n.* a patient who is lodged and fed as well as treated in a hospital.
in per·pe·tu·um (in per pet′o͞o o͝om′; *Eng.* in pər pet′yo͞o əm, -pech′o͞o-), *Latin.* forever.
in per·so·nam (in pər sō′nam), *Law.* (of a legal proceeding) brought against a party or parties, rather than against property. Cf. **in rem.** [< L: lit., against the person]

in pet·to (ēn pet′tô; *Eng.* in pet′ō), *Italian.* (of cardinals whom the pope appoints but does not disclose in consistory) not disclosed. [lit., in (the) breast]

in pos·se (in pō′se; *Eng.* in pos′ē), *Latin.* in possibility; potentially (contrasted with *in esse*).

in·pour (in pōr′, -pôr′), *v.i., v.t.* to pour in.

in pro·pri·a per·so·na (in prō′prē ä′ per sō′nä; *Eng.* in prō′prē ə pər sō′nə), *Latin.* in one's own person.

in·put (in′po͝ot′), *n.* **1.** something that is put in. **2.** the power or energy supplied to a machine. **3.** the current or voltage applied to an electric or electronic circuit or device. Cf. **output** (def. 4). **4.** *Computer Technol.* **a.** information properly coded for feeding into a computer. **b.** the process of introducing data into the internal storage of a computer. **5.** the available data for solving a technical problem. **6.** *Scot.* a monetary contribution, as to charity. —*adj.* **7.** *Chiefly Computer Technol.* of or pertaining to information or equipment used for input: *an input device.* —*v.t.* **8.** *Computer Technol.* to enter (data) into a computer by means of a keyboard, tape, telecommunications line, etc. [IN-[1] + PUT, modeled on *output*]

in·quest (in′kwest), *n.* **1.** a legal or judicial inquiry, esp. before a jury. **2.** the body of men appointed to hold such an inquiry, esp. a coroner's jury. **3.** the decision or finding based on such inquiry. [ME < ML *inquēst(a)* = L *in-* IN-[2] + *quaesīta,* pl. (taken as sing.) of *quaesītum* question (see QUEST); r. ME *enqueste* < AF] —**Syn. 1.** hearing, inquisition.

in·qui·et (in kwī′ət), *v.t. Archaic.* to destroy the peace of; disturb; disquiet. [ME *inquiet(en)* < L *inquiēt(āre)*] —**in·qui′et·ly,** *adv.* —**in·qui′et·ness,** *n.*

in·qui·e·tude (in kwī′i to͞od′, -tyo͞od′), *n.* **1.** restlessness; uneasiness. **2. inquietudes,** disquieting thoughts. [late ME < LL *inquiētūdō*]

in·qui·line (in′kwə līn′, -lin), *n.* **1.** *Zool.* an animal living in the nest or burrow of another animal. —*adj.* **2.** of the nature of an inquiline. [< L *inquilīn(us)* tenant = *in-* IN-[2] + *-quil-* (var. of *col-*) + *-īnus* -INE[1]] —**in·qui·lin·i·ty** (in′kwə lin′i tē), *n.* —**in·qui·li·nous** (in′kwə lī′nəs), *adj.*

in·quire (in kwīər′), *v.,* **-quired, -quir·ing.** —*v.t.* **1.** to seek to learn by asking. **2.** *Obs.* to seek. **3.** *Obs.* to question (a person). —*v.i.* **4.** to seek information by questioning; ask: *to inquire about a person.* **5.** to make investigation (usually fol. by *into*): *to inquire into the incident.* **6. inquire after,** to ask about the welfare of. Also, **enquire.** [late ME < L *inquīre(re)* (to) seek for (see IN-[2], QUERY); r. ME *enquere(n)* < OF *enquerre*] —**in·quir′a·ble,** *adj.* —**in·quir′er,** *n.* —**Syn. 1, 4, 5.** investigate, examine, query. INQUIRE, ASK, QUESTION imply that a person (or persons) addresses another (or others) to obtain information. ASK is the general word: *to ask what time it is.* INQUIRE is more formal and always implies asking about something specific: *to inquire about a rumor.* To QUESTION implies repetition and persistence in asking; it often applies to legal examination or investigation: *to question the survivor of an accident.* —**Ant. 1.** tell.

in·quir·ing (in kwīər′ing), *adj.* **1.** seeking facts, information, or knowledge: *an inquiring mind.* **2.** curious; probing; inquisitive in seeking facts: *an inquiring reporter.* **3.** scrutinizing; questioning: *He looked at his father with inquiring eyes.* —**in·quir′ing·ly,** *adv.*

in·quir·y (in kwīər′ē, in′kwə rē), *n., pl.* **-quir·ies. 1.** a seeking for truth, information, or knowledge. **2.** an investigation, as into an incident. **3.** the act of inquiring or of seeking information by questioning; interrogation. **4.** a question; query. Also, **enquiry.** [INQUIRE + -Y[3]; r. late ME *enquery*] —**Syn. 1.** study, scrutiny, exploration. See **investigation.** —**Ant. 4.** answer, reply.

in·qui·si·tion (in′kwi zish′ən), *n.* **1.** an official investigation, esp. one of a political or religious nature, characterized by lack of regard for individual rights, prejudice on the part of the examiners, and recklessly cruel punishments. **2.** any harsh or prolonged questioning. **3.** the act of inquiring; inquiry; research. **4.** an investigation, or process of inquiry. **5.** a judicial or official inquiry. **6.** the document embodying the result of such inquiry. **7.** (*cap.*) *Rom. Cath. Ch.* **a.** a former special tribunal, engaged chiefly in combating and punishing heresy. Cf. **Holy Office. b.** See **Spanish Inquisition.** [ME *inquisicio(u)n* < legal L *inquīsītiōn-* (s. of *inquīsītiō*) = *inquīsīt(us)* sought for (ptp. of *inquīrere* to INQUIRE) + *-iōn-* -ION] —**in′qui·si′tion·al,** *adj.* —**Syn. 5.** inquest, hearing.

in·quis·i·tive (in kwiz′i tiv), *adj.* **1.** given to inquiry or research; eager for knowledge; curious: an *inquisitive mind.* **2.** unduly curious; prying. —*n.* **3.** an inquisitive person or persons. [< LL *inquīsītīv(us)* (see INQUISITION, -IVE); r. ME *inquisitif* < MF] —**in·quis′i·tive·ly,** *adv.* —**in·quis′i·tive·ness,** *n.* —**Syn. 2.** See **curious.**

in·quis·i·tor (in kwiz′i tər), *n.* **1.** a person who makes inquisition. **2.** a questioner, esp. an unduly curious one. **3.** a member of the Inquisition. Also, **in·qui·si·tion·ist** (in′kwi zish′ə nist). Also, *referring to a woman,* **in·quis·i·tress** (in kwiz′i tris). [< legal L; see INQUISITION, -OR[2]] —**in·quis·i·to·ri·al** (in kwiz′i tōr′ē əl, -tôr′-), *adj.* —**in·quis′i·to′ri·al·ly,** *adv.* —**in quis′i·to′ri·al·ness,** *n.*

in re (in rē′, rā′), in the matter of. [< L]

in rem (in rem′), *Law.* (of a legal proceeding) brought against property, rather than against a party or parties, as a tax judgment against real property. Cf. **in personam.** [< L: lit., against the thing]

in re·rum na·tu·ra (in rā′ro͝om nä to͞o′rä; *Eng.* in rēr′əm nə to͝or′ə, -tyo͝or′ə), *Latin.* in the nature of things.

I.N.R.I., Jesus of Nazareth, King of the Jews. [< L *Iēsus Nazarēnus, Rēx Iūdaeōrum*]

in·road (in′rōd′), *n.* **1.** a forcible or serious encroachment: *inroads on our savings.* **2.** a hostile raid or foray.

in·rush (in′rush′), *n.* a rushing in; influx. —**in′rush′ing,** *n., adj.*

ins., **1.** inches. **2.** *Chiefly Brit.* inscribed. **3.** inspector. **4.** insurance.

I.N.S., International News Service.

in·sal·i·vate (in sal′ə vāt′), *v.t.,* **-vat·ed, -vat·ing.** to mix with saliva, as food. —**in·sal′i·va′tion,** *n.*

in·sa·lu·bri·ous (in′sə lo͞o′brē əs), *adj.* unfavorable to health. [< L *insalūbri(s)* + -OUS] —**in′sa·lu′bri·ous·ly,** *adv.* —**in·sa·lu·bri·ty** (in′sə lo͞o′bri tē), *n.*

in·sane (in sān′), *adj.* **1.** not sane; not of sound mind; mentally deranged. **2.** characteristic of a person who is mentally deranged: *insane actions.* **3.** set apart for the care and confinement of mentally deranged persons: *insane asylum.* **4.** utterly senseless: *an insane attempt.* [< L *insān(us)*] —**in·sane′ly,** *adv.* —**in·sane′ness,** *n.* —**Syn. 1.** lunatic, crazed, crazy; maniacal. See **mad. 4.** foolish, irrational.

in·san·i·tar·y (in san′i ter′ē), *adj.* not sanitary; unclean; unhealthy; likely to cause disease. —**in·san′i·tar′i·ness, in·san·i·ta·tion** (in san′i tā′shən), *n.*

in·san·i·ty (in san′i tē), *n., pl.* **-ties. 1.** the condition of being insane; more or less permanent derangement of one or more psychical functions, due to disease of the mind. **2.** *Law.* such unsoundness of mind as affects legal responsibility or capacity. **3.** extreme folly; foolhardiness. [< L *insānitās*] —**Syn. 1.** dementia, lunacy, madness, craziness, mania.

in·sa·tia·ble (in sā′shə bəl, -shē ə-), *adj.* not satiable; incapable of being satisfied: *insatiable ambition.* [ME *insaciable* < L *insatiābil(is)*] —**in·sa′tia·bil′i·ty, in·sa′tia·ble·ness,** *n.* —**in·sa′tia·bly,** *adv.*

in·sa·ti·ate (in sā′shē it), *adj.* insatiable: *insatiate greed.* [< L *insatiāt(us)* not filled full] —**in·sa′ti·ate·ly,** *adv.* —**in·sa′ti·ate·ness, in·sa·ti·e·ty** (in′sə tī′i tē, in sā′shi tē, -sā′shē i-), *n.*

in·scribe (in skrīb′), *v.t.,* **-scribed, -scrib·ing. 1.** to write or engrave (words, characters, etc.). **2.** to mark (a surface) with words, characters, etc., esp. in a durable or conspicuous way. **3.** to address, autograph, or dedicate (a book, photograph, etc.) to someone. **4.** to enroll, as on an official list. **5.** *Brit.* **a.** to issue (a loan) in the form of shares with registered stockholders. **b.** to sell (stocks). **c.** to buy (stocks). **6.** *Geom.* to draw (one figure) within another figure so that the inner lies entirely within the boundary of the outer, touching it at as many points as possible. [< L *inscrībe(re)*] —**in·scrib′a·ble,** *adj.* —**in·scrib′a·ble·ness,** *n.* —**in·scrib′er,** *n.*

in·scrip·tion (in skrip′shən), *n.* **1.** something inscribed. **2.** a brief, usually informal, dedication, as in a book. **3.** the act of inscribing. **4.** *Brit.* **a.** an issue of securities or stocks. **b.** a block of shares in a stock, as bought or sold by one person. [ME *inscripcio(u)n* < L *inscriptiōn-* (s. of *inscriptiō*) = *inscript(us)* written on (ptp. of *inscrībere* to INSCRIBE) + *-iōn-* -ION] —**in·scrip′tion·al,** *adj.* —**in·scrip′tion·less,** *adj.* —**in·scrip′tive,** *adj.* —**in·scrip′tive·ly,** *adv.*

in·scroll (in skrōl′), *v.t.* enscroll.

in·scru·ta·ble (in skro͞o′tə bəl), *adj.* **1.** incapable of being searched into or scrutinized; impenetrable to investigation. **2.** not easily understood; mysterious; unfathomable: *an inscrutable smile.* [< LL *inscrūtābil(is)*] —**in·scru′ta·bil′i·ty, in·scru′ta·ble·ness,** *n.* —**in·scru′ta·bly,** *adv.* —**Syn. 1.** hidden, incomprehensible, undiscoverable, inexplicable.

in·sculp (in skulp′), *v.t. Archaic.* to carve in or on something; engrave. [ME *insculpe(n)* < L *insculp(ere)*]

in·sect (in′sekt), *n.* **1.** any animal of the class *Insecta,* comprising small, air-breathing arthropods having the body divided into three parts (head, thorax, and abdomen), and having three pairs of legs and usually two pairs of wings. **2.** (loosely) any small arthropod, such as a spider, tick, or centipede, having a superficial, general similarity to the *Insecta.* **3.** a contemptible person. —*adj.* **4.** of, pertaining to, like, or for an insect or insects: *insect life; insect bite; insect powder.* [< L *insect(um),* sing. of *insecta,* trans. of Gk *éntoma* insects, lit., (beings) notched, cut into; see ENTOMO-] —**in·sec′te·an, in·sec′tan, in·sec·ti·val** (in′sek tī′vəl, in sek′tə-), **in·sec′tile,** *adj.* —**in′sect·like′,** *adj.*

Insect (Grasshopper)
A, Compound eye; B, Simple eye; C, Antenna; D, Head; E, Thorax; F, Abdomen; G, Wings; H, Ovipositor; I, Spiracle; J, Femur; K, Ears; L, Legs; M, Palpus

in·sec·tar·i·um (in′sek târ′ē əm), *n., pl.* **-tar·i·ums, -tar·i·a** (-târ′ē ə). a place in which a collection of living insects is kept, as in a zoo. [< NL]

in·sec·tar·y (in′sek ter′ē), *n., pl.* **-tar·ies.** a laboratory for the study of live insects, their effects on plants, reaction to insecticides, etc. [var. of INSECTARIUM]

in·sec·ti·cide (in sek′ti sīd′), *n.* a substance or preparation used for killing insects. —**in·sec′ti·cid′al,** *adj.*

in·sec·ti·fuge (in sek′tə fyo͞oj′), *n.* an insect repellent.

in·sec·ti·vore (in sek′tə vōr′, -vôr′), *n.* **1.** an insectivorous animal or plant. **2.** any mammal of the order *Insectivora,* comprising the moles, shrews, and Old World hedgehogs. [back formation from INSECTIVOROUS]

in·sec·tiv·o·rous (in′sek tiv′ər əs), *adj.* adapted to feeding on insects, as shrews, moles, hedgehogs, etc. [< NL *insectivorus*]

in′sect wax′, *Chem.* See **Chinese wax.**

in·se·cure (in′si kyo͝or′), *adj.* **1.** exposed to danger; unsafe. **2.** not firm or safe: *insecure foundations.* **3.** subject to fear, doubt, etc.: *an insecure person.* [< ML *insēcūr(us)*] —**in′se·cure′ly,** *adv.* —**in′se·cure′ness,** *n.* —**Syn. 1.** unprotected, dangerous. **2.** unsure, risky.

in·se·cu·ri·ty (in′si kyo͝or′i tē), *n., pl.* **-ties. 1.** the quality or state of being insecure; instability. **2.** lack of assurance; self-doubt: *He is plagued by insecurity.* **3.** something insecure: *the insecurities of life.* [< ML *insēcūritās*]

in·sem·i·nate (in sem′ə nāt′), *v.t.,* **-nat·ed, -nat·ing. 1.** to sow; implant seed into. **2.** to inject semen into (the female reproductive tract); impregnate. **3.** to sow as seed in something; implant: *to inseminate a group with new ideas.* [< L *insēmināt(us)* sowed in (ptp. of *insēmināre*). See IN-[2], SEMINATION] —**in·sem′i·na′tion,** *n.*

in·sen·sate (in sen′sāt, -sit), *adj.* **1.** not endowed with sensation: *insensate stone.* **2.** without feeling or sensitivity. **3.** without sense, understanding, or judgment. [< LL *insensāt(us)* irrational] —**in·sen′sate·ly,** *adv.* —**in·sen′sate·ness,** *n.* —**Syn. 1.** inanimate, lifeless, inorganic. **2.** insensible. **3.** stupid, irrational, senseless, witless, dumb.

in·sen·si·bil·i·ty (in sen′sə bil′i tē), *n.* **1.** lack of physical sensibility; absence of feeling or sensation. **2.** lack of moral sensibility or susceptibility of emotion. [< LL *insensibilitās*] —**Syn. 1.** unconsciousness. **2.** See **indifference.**

in·sen·si·ble (in sen′sə bəl), *adj.* **1.** incapable of feeling or perceiving; deprived of sensation; unconscious. **2.** without or not subject to a particular feeling: *insensible to shame.* **3.** unconscious; unaware; inappreciative: *insensible of kindness.* **4.** not perceptible by the senses. **5.** unresponsive in feeling. [ME < L *insensibil(is)*] —**in·sen′si·bly,** *adv.* —**Syn. 5.** apathetic, indifferent, passionless, emotionless.

in·sen·si·tive (in sen′si tiv), *adj.* **1.** not sensitive: *an insensitive skin.* **2.** not susceptible to agencies or influences: *insensitive to light.* **3.** deficient in sensibility or acuteness of feeling: *an insensitive nature.* —**in·sen′si·tive·ly,** *adv.* —**in·sen′si·tive·ness, in·sen′si·tiv′i·ty,** *n.*

in·sen·ti·ent (in sen′shē ənt, -shənt), *adj.* not sentient; without sensation or feeling; inanimate. —**in·sen′ti·ence, in·sen′ti·en·cy,** *n.*

in·sep·a·ra·ble (in sep′ər ə bəl, -sep′rə-), *adj.* **1.** incapable of being separated, parted, or disjoined. —*n.* Usually, **inseparables. 2.** inseparable objects, qualities, etc. **3.** inseparable companions or friends. [ME < L *insēparābil(is)*] —**in·sep′a·ra·bil′i·ty, in·sep′a·ra·ble·ness,** *n.* —**in·sep′a·ra·bly,** *adv.*

in·sert (*v.* in sûrt′; *n.* in′sûrt), *v.t.* **1.** to put or set in. **2.** to introduce or cause to be introduced into the body of something: *to insert an ad in a newspaper.* —*n.* **3.** something inserted or to be inserted. **4.** an extra leaf, printed independently, for binding or tipping into a book or periodical. **5.** (in the postal service) a paper, circular, etc., placed within the folds of a newspaper or the leaves of a book, periodical, etc. [< L *insert(us)* inserted (ptp. of *inserere*) = *in-* IN-[2] + *ser-* (s. of *serere* to put together) + *-tus* ptp. suffix] —**insert′a·ble,** *adj.* —**in·sert′er,** *n.*

in·sert·ed (in sûr′tid), *adj.* **1.** *Bot.* (esp. of the parts of a flower) attached to or growing out of some part. **2.** *Anat.* having an insertion, as a muscle, tendon, or ligament; attached, as the end of a muscle that moves a bone.

in·ser·tion (in sûr′shən), *n.* **1.** the act of inserting. **2.** something inserted. **3.** *Bot., Zool.* **a.** the manner or place of attachment, as of an organ. **b.** attachment of a part or organ, with special reference to the site or manner of such attachment. **4.** lace, embroidery, etc., inserted between parts of other material. [< LL *insertiōn-* (s. of *insertiō*)] —**in·ser′tion·al,** *adj.*

in·ses·so·ri·al (in′sə sōr′ē əl, -sôr′-), *adj.* **1.** adapted for perching, as a bird's foot. **2.** habitually perching, as a bird. [< NL *Insessōr(ēs)* the perching birds (L: perchers = *insess(us)* perched on (ptp. of *insīdere* = *in-* IN-[2] + *sīdere* to settle, alight) + *-ōrēs*, pl. of *-or* -OR[2]) + -IAL]

in·set (*n.* in′set′; *v.* in set′), *n., v.,* **-set, -set·ting.** —*n.* **1.** something inserted; an insert. **2.** a smaller picture, map, etc., inserted within the border of a larger one. **3.** influx. **4.** the act of setting in. —*v.t.* **5.** to set in or insert, as an inset: *to inset a panel in a dress* **6.** to insert an inset in. —**in′set′ter,** *n.*

in·sheathe (in shēth′), *v.t.,* **-sheathed, -sheath·ing.** ensheathe. Also, **in·sheath** (in shēth′).

in·shore (in′shōr′, -shôr′), *adj.* **1.** carried on or lying close to the shore: *inshore fishing.* —*adv.* **2.** toward the shore.

in·shrine (in shrīn′), *v.t.,* **-shrined, -shrin·ing.** enshrine.

in·side (*prep.* in′sīd′, in′sīd′; *adv.* in′sīd′; *n.* in′sīd′; *adj.* in′sīd′, in′-), *prep.* **1.** on the inner side or part of; within. **2.** prior to the elapse of: *He promised to arrive inside an hour.* —*adv.* **3.** in or into the inner part: *to be inside; go inside.* **4.** indoors: *He plays inside on rainy days.* **5.** by true nature; basically: *Inside, she's really very shy.* **6. inside of,** within the space or period of: *Our car broke down again inside of a mile.* —*n.* **7.** the inner part; interior. **8.** the inner side or surface: *the inside of the hand.* **9.** Usually, **insides.** the inward parts of the body, esp. the stomach and intestines. **10.** a select circle of power, prestige, etc. **11.** inward nature, mind, feelings, etc. **12. inside out, a.** with the inner side reversed to face the outside. **b.** perfectly; completely: *He knew his trade inside out.* —*adj.* **13.** situated or being on or in the inside; interior; internal: *an inside seat.* **14.** indoor. **15.** private; confidential; restricted: *inside information.* **16.** *Baseball.* (of a pitched ball) passing between home plate and the batter.
—**Syn. 7.** INSIDE, INTERIOR both refer to the inner part or space within something. INSIDE is a common word, and is used with reference to things of any size, small or large: *the inside of a pocket.* INTERIOR, somewhat more formal, denotes the inner part or the space or the regions within; it usually suggests considerable size or extent, and sometimes a richness of decoration: *the interior of a country, of the earth; interior of a cathedral.* —**Ant. 7.** outside, exterior.

in′side job′, *Informal.* a crime committed by a person or persons closely associated with or, sometimes, in collusion with the victim.

in·sid·er (in′sī′dər), *n.* **1.** a member of a certain society, circle of friends, etc. **2.** a person who has some special advantage, knowledge, or influence.

in′side track′, 1. the inner or shorter track of a racecourse. **2.** *Informal.* an advantageous position; precedence; favor.

in·sid·i·ous (in sid′ē əs), *adj.* **1.** intended to entrap or beguile. **2.** stealthily treacherous or deceitful: *an insidious enemy.* **3.** operating or proceeding inconspicuously but with grave effect: *an insidious disease.* [< L *insidiōs(us)* deceitful = *insidi(ae)* (pl.) an ambush (< *insidēre* to sit in) + *-ōsus* -OUS] —**in·sid′i·ous·ly,** *adv.* —**in·sid′i·ous·ness,** *n.* —**Syn. 2.** artful, cunning, wily, crafty.

in·sight (in′sīt′), *n.* **1.** an instance of apprehending the true nature of a thing, esp. through intuitive understanding: *an insight into medieval life.* **2.** penetrating mental vision or discernment: *a man of great insight.* [ME] —**Syn. 2.** perception, intuition, understanding, grasp.

in·sight·ful (in′sīt′fəl), *adj.* characterized by or displaying insight: *an insightful new treatise.*

in·sig·ne (in sig′nē), *n.* **1.** sing. of **insignia. 2.** insignia.

in·sig·ni·a (in sig′nē ə), *n., formally a pl. of* **insigne,** *but usually used as a sing. with pl.* **-ni·a** *or* **-ni·as. 1.** a badge or distinguishing mark of office or honor. **2.** a distinguishing mark or sign of anything: *an insignia of mourning.* Also, **insigne.** [< L, pl. of *insigne* mark, badge, n. use of *insignis* distinguished (by a mark)]

in·sig·nif·i·cance (in′sig nif′ə kəns), *n.* the quality or condition of being insignificant; lack of importance or consequence.

in·sig·nif·i·can·cy (in′sig nif′ə kən sē), *n., pl.* **-cies** for **2. 1.** insignificance. **2.** an insignificant person or thing.

in·sig·nif·i·cant (in′sig nif′ə kənt), *adj.* **1.** unimportant, trifling, or petty, as things, matters, details, etc. **2.** too small to be important: *an insignificant sum.* **3.** without weight of character; contemptible: *an insignificant fellow.* **4.** without meaning; meaningless. —**in′sig·nif′i·cant·ly,** *adv.*

in·sin·cere (in′sin sēr′), *adj.* not sincere; not honest in the expression of actual feeling. [IN-[3] + SINCERE; cf. L *insincērus* tainted] —**in′sin·cere′ly,** *adv.*

in·sin·cer·i·ty (in′sin ser′i tē), *n., pl.* **-ties** for **2. 1.** the quality of being insincere; deceitfulness. **2.** an instance of this.

in·sin·u·ate (in sin′yo͞o āt′), *v.,* **-at·ed, -at·ing.** —*v.t.* **1.** to suggest or hint slyly, esp. something malicious: *He insinuated that she was lying.* **2.** to instill or infuse subtly or artfully, as into the mind: *to insinuate doubt.* **3.** to bring or introduce into a position by indirect or artful methods; ingratiate: *to insinuate oneself into favor.* —*v.i.* **4.** to make insinuations. [< L *insinuāt(us),* ptp. of *insinuāre.* See IN-[2], SINUOUS, -ATE[1]] —**in·sin·u·a·tive** (in sin′yo͞o ā′tiv, yo͞o-ə-), **in·sin·u·a·to·ry** (in sin′yo͞o ə tōr′ē, -tôr′ē), *adj.* —**in·sin′u·a′tive·ly,** *adv.* —**in·sin′u·a′tor,** *n.* —**Syn. 1.** See **hint. 2.** introduce, inject, inculcate.

in·sin·u·at·ing (in sin′yo͞o ā′ting), *adj.* **1.** tending to instill doubts, distrust, etc.; suggestive: *an insinuating letter.* **2.** gaining favor or winning confidence by artful means: *his insinuating charm.* —**in·sin′u·at′ing·ly,** *adv.*

in·sin·u·a·tion (in sin′yo͞o ā′shən), *n.* **1.** an indirect or covert suggestion or hint, esp. of a derogatory nature. **2.** the art or power of stealing into the affections and pleasing; ingratiation. **3.** *Archaic.* a slow winding, worming, or stealing in. **4.** *Obs.* an ingratiating act or speech. [< L *insinuātiōn-* (s. of *insinuātiō*)]

in·sip·id (in sip′id), *adj.* **1.** without distinctive, interesting, or attractive qualities: *an insipid tale.* **2.** without sufficient taste to be pleasing, as food or drink: *a rather insipid fruit.* [< L *insipid(us)* = *in-* IN-[3] + *-sipidus,* var. of *sapidus* SAPID] —**in′si·pid′i·ty, in·sip′id·ness,** *n.* —**in·sip′id·ly,** *adv.* —**Syn. 1.** uninteresting, pointless, vapid. **1, 2.** flat, dull. **2.** tasteless, bland.

in·sip·i·ence (in sip′ē əns), *n.* *Archaic.* lack of wisdom; foolishness. [late ME < L *insipientia* foolishness = *insipient-* (s. of *insipiēns*) foolish (*in-* IN-[3] + *-sipient-,* var. of *sapient-* SAPIENT) + *-ia;* see -ENCE] —**in·sip′i·ent,** *adj.* —**in·sip′i·ent·ly,** *adv.*

in·sist (in sist′), *v.i.* **1.** to be emphatic, firm, or resolute on some matter: *He insists on working late every night.* **2.** to lay emphasis in assertion. **3.** to dwell with earnestness or emphasis (usually fol. by *on* or *upon*): *to insist on a point.* —*v.t.* **4.** to assert or maintain firmly (usually fol. by a clause): *He insists that he is right.* **5.** to demand or persist in demanding (usually fol. by a clause): *I insist that you go.* [< L *insist(ere)* (to) stand still on, persist in = *in-* IN-[2] + *sistere* to stand, make stand, akin to *stare* to stand] —**insist′er,** *n.* —**in·sist′ing·ly,** *adv.*

in·sist·ence (in sis′təns), *n.* **1.** act or fact of insisting. **2.** quality of being insistent.

in·sist·en·cy (in sis′tən sē), *n., pl.* **-cies.** insistence.

in·sist·ent (in sis′tənt), *adj.* **1.** emphatic in dwelling upon or demanding something; persistent. **2.** compelling attention or notice: *an insistent tone.* [< L *insistent-* (s. of *insistēns*)] —**in·sist′ent·ly,** *adv.*

in si·tu (in sit′o͞o; *Eng.* in sī′to͞o, -tyo͞o), *Latin.* in its original place. [lit., in place]

in·snare (in snâr′), *v.t.,* **-snared, -snar·ing.** ensnare. —**in·snare′ment,** *n.* —**in·snar′er,** *n.*

in·so·bri·e·ty (in′sə brī′i tē), *n.* lack of sobriety; intemperance or immoderation; drunkenness.

in·so·far (in′sə fär′, -sō-), *adv.* to such an extent (usually fol. by *as*): *insofar as I am able.* [orig. phrase *in so far*]

in·so·late (in′sō lāt′), *v.t.,* **-lat·ed, -lat·ing.** to expose to the sun's rays; treat by exposure to the sun's rays. [< L *insōlāt(us)* placed in the sun, ptp. of *insōlāre.* See IN-[2], SOLI-[2], -ATE[1]]

in·so·la·tion (in′sō lā′shən), *n.* **1.** exposure to the sun's rays, esp. as a process of treatment. **2.** *Pathol.* sunstroke. **3.** *Meteorol.* solar radiation received on a given body or over a given area. [< L *insōlātiōn-* (s. of *insōlātiō*)]

in·sole (in′sōl′), *n.* **1.** the inner sole of a shoe or boot. **2.** a thickness of warm or waterproof material laid as an inner sole within a shoe.

in·so·lence (in′sə ləns), *n.* **1.** contemptuously rude or impertinent behavior or speech. **2.** the quality or condition of being insolent. [ME < L *insolentia.* See INSOLENT, -ENCE]

in·so·lent (in′sə lənt), *adj.* **1.** boldly rude or disrespectful; contemptuously impertinent; insulting. —*n.* **2.** an insolent person. [ME < L *insolent-* (s. of *insolēns*) departing from custom = *in-* IN-[3] + *sol-* (s. of *solēre* to be accustomed) + *-ent-* -ENT] —**in′so·lent·ly,** *adv.* —**Syn. 1.** brazen; contemptuous. See **impertinent.**

in·sol·u·ble (in sol′yə bəl), *adj.* **1.** incapable of being dissolved. **2.** incapable of being solved. [< L *insolūbil(is);* r. ME *insolible* < MF *insoluble*] —**in·sol′u·bil′i·ty, in·sol′u·ble·ness,** *n.* —**in·sol′u·bly,** *adv.*

in·solv·a·ble (in sol′və bəl), *adj.* incapable of being solved or explained; insoluble: *an insolvable problem.* —**in·solv′a·bil′i·ty,** *n.* —**in·solv′a·bly,** *adv.*

in·sol·ven·cy (in sol′vən sē), *n.* the condition of being insolvent; bankruptcy.

in·sol·vent (in sol′vənt), *Law.* —*adj.* **1.** not solvent; unable to satisfy creditors or discharge liabilities. **2.** pertaining to bankrupt persons or bankruptcy. —*n.* **3.** a person who is insolvent.

in·som·ni·a (in som′nē ə), *n.* inability to sleep, esp. when chronic; sleeplessness. [< L = *insomn(is)* sleepless (*in-* IN-[3] + *somn(us)* sleep + *-is* adj. suffix) + *-ia* -IA] —**in·som′ni·ous,** *adj.*

in·som·ni·ac (in som′nē ak′), *n.* **1.** a person who suffers from insomnia. —*adj.* **2.** having insomnia. **3.** of, pertaining to, or causing insomnia: *insomniac heat.*

in·so·much (in′sō much′), *adv.* **1.** to such an extent or degree; so (usually fol. by *that*). **2.** inasmuch (usually fol. by *as*). [orig. phrase *in so much*]

in·sou·ci·ance (in so͞o′sē əns; *Fr.* aN so͞o syäNs′), *n.* the quality of being insouciant; lack of care or concern; indifference. [< F; see INSOUCIANT, -ANCE]

in·sou·ci·ant (in so͞o′sē ənt; *Fr.* aN so͞o syäN′), *adj.* free from concern; without anxiety; carefree. [< F = *in-* IN-[3] + *souciant* worrying, prp. of *soucier* < L *sollicitāre* to disturb; see SOLICITOUS] —**in·sou′ci·ant·ly,** *adv.*

in·soul (in sōl′), *v.t.* ensoul.

in·spect (in spekt′), *v.t.* **1.** to look carefully at or over; view closely and critically: *to inspect every part.* **2.** to view or examine formally or officially: *to inspect troops.* [v. use of *inspect* inspection, examination (late ME) < L *inspect(us)*, n. use of ptp. of *inspicere* to look into, inspect. See IN-[2], SPECIES] —**in·spect′a·ble,** *adj.* —**in·spect′ing·ly,** *adv.*

in·spec·tion (in spek′shən), *n.* **1.** the act of inspecting or viewing, esp. carefully or critically. **2.** formal or official viewing or examination: *an inspection of the troops.* [ME *inspeccio(u)n* < L *inspectiōn-* (s. of *inspectiō*)] —**in·spec′tion·al,** *adj.* —**Syn. 2.** See **examination.**

in·spec·tive (in spek′tiv), *adj.* **1.** given to making inspection; watchful; attentive. **2.** of or pertaining to inspection. [< LL *inspectīv(us)*]

in·spec·tor (in spek′tər), *n.* **1.** an officer appointed to inspect. **2.** an officer of police, usually ranking next below a superintendent. **3.** a person who inspects. [< L] —**in·spec′to·ral, in·spec·to·ri·al** (in′spek tôr′ē əl, -tôr′-), *adj.* —**in·spec′tor·ship′,** *n.*

in·spec·tor·ate (in spek′tər it), *n.* **1.** the office or function of an inspector. **2.** a body of inspectors. **3.** a district under an inspector.

in·sphere (in sfēr′), *v.t.,* **-sphered, -spher·ing.** ensphere.

in·spi·ra·tion (in′spə rā′shən), *n.* **1.** an inspiring or animating action or influence. **2.** something inspired, as a thought. **3.** a result of inspired activity. **4.** a person or thing that inspires. **5.** *Theol.* a divine influence directly and immediately exerted upon the mind or soul of man. **6.** the drawing of air into the lungs; inhalation. **7.** the act of inspiring. **8.** the state of being inspired. [ME *inspiracio(u)n* < LL *inspīrātiōn-* (s. of *inspīrātiō*)] —**Syn. 1.** stimulus.

in·spi·ra·tion·al (in′spə rā′shə nᵊl), *adj.* **1.** imparting inspiration. **2.** under the influence of inspiration; inspired. **3.** of or pertaining to inspiration. —**in′spi·ra′tion·al·ly,** *adv.*

in·spir·a·to·ry (in spīᵊr′ə tôr′ē, -tōr′ē), *adj.* of or pertaining to inspiration, or inhalation. [< L *inspīrāt(us)* breathed upon or into (ptp. of *inspīrāre*; see INSPIRE, -ATE[1]) + -ORY[1]]

in·spire (in spīᵊr′), *v.,* **-spired, -spir·ing.** —*v.t.* **1.** to infuse an animating, quickening, or exalting influence into. **2.** to produce or arouse (a feeling, thought, etc.): *to inspire confidence.* **3.** to influence or impel: *opposition inspired him to a greater effort.* **4.** to animate, as an influence, feeling, thought, or the like does. **5.** to communicate or suggest by a divine or supernatural influence. **6.** to guide or control by divine influence. **7.** to give rise to, bring about, cause, etc.: *to inspire revolution.* **8.** to take (air, gases, etc.) into the lungs; inhale. **9.** *Archaic.* to infuse (breath, life, etc.) by breathing. **10.** *Archaic.* to breathe into or upon. —*v.i.* **11.** to give inspiration. **12.** to inhale. [ME *inspire(n)* < L *inspīr(āre)* (to) breathe upon or into = *in-* IN-[2] + *spīrāre* to breathe] —**in·spir′a·ble,** *adj.* —**in·spir·a·tive** (in spīᵊr′ə tiv, in′spə rā′tiv), *adj.* —**in·spir′er,** *n.* —**in·spir′ing·ly,** *adv.*

in·spired (in spīᵊrd′), *adj.* **1.** aroused, animated, or imbued with the spirit to do a certain thing, by or as by supernatural or divine influence: *an inspired poet.* **2.** resulting from such inspiration: *an inspired poem.* **3.** inhaled: *inspired air.* [late ME] —**in·spir·ed·ly** (in spī′rid lē, -spīᵊrd′-), *adv.*

in·spir·it (in spir′it), *v.t.* to infuse spirit or life into; enliven. —**in·spir′it·er,** *n.* —**in·spir′it·ing·ly,** *adv.* —**in·spir′it·ment,** *n.*

in·spis·sate (in spis′āt), *v.t., v.i.,* **-sat·ed, -sat·ing.** to thicken, as by evaporation; make or become dense. [< LL *inspissāt(us)* thickened (ptp. of *inspissāre*) = L *in-* IN-[2] + *spiss-* (base of *spissāre* to thicken < *spiss(us)* thick) + *-ātus* -ATE[1]] —**in′spis·sa′tion,** *n.* —**in′spis·sa′tor,** *n.*

inst., 1. instant (def. 3). **2.** instantaneous. **3.** (*usually cap.*) institute. **4.** (*usually cap.*) institution. **5.** instrumental.

in·sta·bil·i·ty (in′stə bil′i tē), *n.* the quality or state of being instable; lack of stability or firmness. [ME *instabilite* < L *instabilitās*]

in·sta·ble (in stā′bəl), *adj.* not stable; unstable. [late ME < L *instabil(is)*]

in·stal (in stôl′), *v.t.,* **-stalled, -stal·ling.** install.

in·stall (in stôl′), *v.t.* **1.** to place in position for service or use, as a heating system, etc. **2.** to establish in an office, position, or place: *to install a new assistant.* **3.** to induct into an office with ceremonies or formalities, as by seating in a stall or official seat. Also, **instal.** [late ME < ML *installāre*] —**in·stall′er,** *n.*

in·stal·la·tion (in′stə lā′shən), *n.* **1.** something installed, as a system of machinery or apparatus placed in position for use. **2.** the act of installing. **3.** the fact of being installed. **4.** *Mil.* any more or less permanent post, camp, base, or the like. [< ML *installātiōn-* (s. of *installātiō*)]

in·stall·ment[1] (in stôl′mənt), *n.* **1.** any of several parts into which a debt is divided for payment at successive fixed times. **2.** a single portion of something furnished or issued in parts at successive times: *a magazine serial in six installments.* Also, **in·stal′ment.** [IN-[2] + obs. *(e)stallment* = obs. *estall* to arrange payment on installment plan (? < AF) + -MENT]

in·stall·ment[2] (in stôl′mənt), *n.* **1.** the act of installing. **2.** the fact of being installed; installation. Also, **in·stal′ment.** [INSTALL + -MENT]

install′ment plan′, *Chiefly U.S.* a system for paying a debt by installments.

in·stance (in′stəns), *n., v.,* **-stanced, -stanc·ing.** —*n.* **1.** a case or example of anything: *fresh instances of oppression.* **2.** *Law.* prosecution of a case (used chiefly in the phrase *court of first instance*). **3.** *Archaic.* urgency. **4.** *Obs.* an impelling motive. **5. at the instance of,** at the urging or suggestion of. **6. for instance,** as an example; for example. —*v.t.* **7.** to cite as an instance or example. **8.** to exemplify by an instance. —*v.i.* **9.** *Archaic.* to cite an instance. [ME < L *instantia* presence, urgency (ML: case, example). See INSTANT, -ANCE] —**Syn. 1.** See **case**[1].

in·stan·cy (in′stən sē), *n.* **1.** the quality of being instant; urgency; pressing nature. **2.** immediateness. [< L *instantia.* See INSTANCE, -ANCY]

in·stant (in′stənt), *n.* **1.** an infinitesimal or very short space of time; a moment. **2.** a particular moment: *at the instant of contact.* **3.** the present or current month. *Abbr.:* inst. Cf. **proximo, ultimo.** —*adj.* **4.** succeeding without any interval of time; immediate: *instant relief.* **5.** pressing or urgent: *instant need.* **6.** (of a food) requiring only water, milk, etc., to prepare. **7.** *Archaic.* present, current. —*adv.* **8.** instantly. [late ME < L *instant-* (s. of *instāns*) present, urgent (prp. of *instāre*) = *in-* IN-[2] + *stā-* stand + *-ant-* -ANT]

in·stan·ta·ne·ous (in′stən tā′nē əs), *adj.* **1.** occurring or completed in an instant: *an instantaneous explosion.* **2.** existing at or pertaining to a particular instant. [< ML *instantāneus*] —**in′stan·ta′ne·ous·ly,** *adv.* —**in′stan·ta′ne·ous·ness, in·stan·ta·ne·i·ty** (in stan′tᵊnē′i tē, in′stan tə nē′-), *n.*

in′stanta′neous sound′ pres′sure, *Physics.* See **sound pressure** (def. 1).

in·stan·ter (in stan′tər), *adv.* instantly. [< legal L: urgently = *instant-* INSTANT + *-er* adv. suffix]

in·stan·ti·ate (in stan′shē āt′), *v.t.,* **-at·ed, -at·ing.** to provide an instance of or concrete evidence in support of (a theory, concept, claim, etc.). [< L *instantia* (in ML sense) INSTANCE + -ATE[1]]

in·stant·ly (in′stənt lē), *adv.* **1.** immediately; at once. **2.** *Archaic.* urgently. —*conj.* **3.** as soon as; directly. —**Syn. 1.** See **immediately.**

in′stant re′play, *Television.* an immediately repeated broadcast of a small segment of a recorded event, especially of a sports event, often in slow motion: *an instant replay of the finish of the race.*

in·star (in′stär), *n.* an insect in any one of its periods of postembryonic growth between molts. [< NL, L: image, likeness, lit., a stand-in]

in·state (in stāt′), *v.t.,* **-stat·ed, -stat·ing.** **1.** to put or place in a certain state or position, as in an office; install. **2.** *Obs.* to endow with something. —**in·state′ment,** *n.*

in sta·tu quo (in stä′to͞o kwō′; *Eng.* in stā′tyo͞o kwō′, stach′o͞o), *Latin.* in the state in which (anything was or is).

in·stau·ra·tion (in′stô rā′shən), *n.* **1.** renewal; restoration; renovation. **2.** *Obs.* an act of instituting or inaugurating something; establishment. [< L *instaurātiōn-* (s. of *instaurātiō*) a renewing, repeating. See IN-[2], STORE, -ATION] —**in′stau·ra·tor** (in′stô rā′tər), *n.*

in·stead (in sted′), *adv.* **1.** in preference; as a preferred or accepted alternative. **2.** as a replacement; in the place or stead of someone or something. **3. instead of,** in place of; in lieu of: *Use milk instead of cream in this recipe.* [ME; orig. phrase *in stead* in place]

in·step (in′step′), *n.* **1.** the arched upper surface of the human foot between the toes and the ankle. **2.** the part of a shoe, stocking, etc., covering the instep. **3.** the front of the hind leg of a horse, cow, etc., between the hock and the pastern joint; cannon. [appar. IN-[1] + STEP]

in·sti·gate (in′stə gāt′), *v.t.,* **-gat·ed, -gat·ing.** **1.** to provoke or incite to some action or course. **2.** to bring about by incitement; foment. [< L *instīgāt(us)* goaded on (ptp. of *instīgāre*). See IN-[2], STIGMA, -ATE[1]] —**in′sti·gat′ing·ly,** *adv.* —**in′sti·ga′tive,** *adj.* —**in′sti·ga′tor,** *n.*

in·sti·ga·tion (in′stə gā′shən), *n.* **1.** the act of instigating. **2.** an incentive. [ME < L *instīgātiōn-* (s. of *instīgātiō*)]

in·stil (in stil′), *v.t.,* **-stilled, -stil·ling.** instill. —**in·stil′ment,** *n.*

in·still (in stil′), *v.t.* **1.** to infuse slowly into the mind or feelings; insinuate: *to instill courtesy in a child.* **2.** to put in drop by drop. [< L *instill(āre)* = *in-* IN-[2] + *stillāre* to drip] —**in·still′er,** *n.* —**in·still′ment,** *n.* —**Syn. 1.** inculcate.

in·stil·la·tion (in′stə lā′shən), *n.* **1.** the act of instilling. **2.** something instilled. [< L *instillātiōn-* (s. of *instillātiō*) = *instillāt(us)* instilled (ptp. of *instillāre*) + *-iōn-* -ION]

in·stinct[1] (in′stiŋkt), *n.* **1.** *Psychol.* an inborn pattern of activity or tendency to action common to a given biological species. **2.** a natural or innate impulse, inclination, or aptitude. **3.** natural intuitive power. [late ME < L *instinct(us)* an impulse, instigation; see INSTINCT[2]]

in·stinct[2] (in stiŋkt′), *adj.* **1.** infused or filled with some animating principle (usually fol. by *with*): *instinct with life.* **2.** *Obs.* urged or animated by some inner force. [< L *instinct(us)* incited, instigated (ptp. of *instinguere*) = *in-* IN-[2] + *-stinctus*, as in *distinctus* DISTINCT]

in·stinc·tive (in stiŋk′tiv), *adj.* **1.** of, pertaining to, or of the nature of instinct. **2.** prompted by or resulting from instinct. Also, **in·stinc·tu·al** (in stiŋk′cho͞o əl). —**in·stinc′tive·ly, in·stinc′tu·al·ly,** *adv.* —**Syn. 2.** spontaneous.

in·sti·tute (in′sti to͞ot′, -tyo͞ot′), *v.,* **-tut·ed, -tut·ing,** *n.* —*v.t.* **1.** to set up; establish: *to institute a government.* **2.** to inaugurate; initiate; get under way. **3.** to establish in an office or position. **4.** *Eccles.* to invest with a spiritual charge, as of a parish. —*n.* **5.** a society or organization for carrying on a particular work, as of literary, scientific, or educational character. **6.** the building occupied by such a society. **7.** *Educ.* **a.** a college devoted to instruction in technical subjects. **b.** a unit within a university organized for advanced instruction and research in a relatively narrow field. **c.** a short instructional program in some specialized activity. **8.** something instituted or established, as a principle, law, custom, or organization. **9. institutes,** an elementary textbook of law designed for beginners. [ME < L *institūt(us)* placed, built, set up (ptp. of *instituere*) = *in-* IN-[2] + *-stitū-* (var. of *statū-*; see STATUS) + *-tus* ptp. suffix] —**in′sti·tu′tor, in′sti·tut′er,** *n.*

in·sti·tu·tion (in′sti to͞o′shən, -tyo͞o′-), *n.* **1.** an organization or establishment devoted to the promotion of a particular object, esp. one of a public, educational, or charitable character. **2.** the building devoted to such work. **3.** a place of confinement, as a prison, mental hospital, etc. **4.** *Sociol.* a well-established and structured pattern of behavior or of relationships that is accepted as a fundamental part of a culture, as marriage. **5.** any established law, custom, etc. **6.** any familiar practice or object. **7.** the act of instituting or setting up; establishment: *the institution of laws.* **8.** *Eccles.* **a.** the origination of a sacrament by Christ, esp. the Eucharist. **b.** the investment of a clergyman with a spiritual charge. [ME < L *institūtiōn-* (s. of *institūtiō*)]

in·sti·tu·tion·al (in′sti to͞o′shə nəl, -tyo͞o′-), *adj.* **1.** of, pertaining to, or established by institution. **2.** of or pertaining to organized societies or to the buildings devoted to their work. **3.** characterized by the blandness and uniformity attributed to large organizations that serve many people: *institutional food.* **4.** (of advertising) having as the primary object the establishment of good will and a favorable image rather than immediate sales. **5.** pertaining to institutes or principles, esp. of jurisprudence. —**in′sti·tu′tion·al·ly,** *adv.*

in·sti·tu·tion·al·ise (in′sti to͞o′shə nəlīz′, -tyo͞o′-), *v.t.*, **-ised, -is·ing.** *Chiefly Brit.* institutionalize. —**in′sti·tu′tion·al·i·sa′tion,** *n.*

in·sti·tu·tion·al·ism (in′sti to͞o′shə nəliz′əm, -tyo͞o′-), *n.* **1.** the system of institutions or organized societies devoted to public, charitable, or similar purposes. **2.** strong attachment to established institutions. —**in′sti·tu′tion·al·ist,** *n.*

in·sti·tu·tion·al·ize (in′sti to͞o′shə nəlīz′, -tyo͞o′-), *v.t.*, **-ized, -iz·ing.** **1.** to make institutional. **2.** to make into or treat as an institution. **3.** to place or confine in an institution, esp. one for the special care of mental illnesses, alcoholism, etc. Also, *esp. Brit.*, **institutionalise.** —**in′sti·tu′tion·al·i·za′tion,** *n.*

in·sti·tu·tion·ar·y (in′sti to͞o′shə ner′ē, -tyo͞o′-), *adj.* **1.** of or pertaining to an institution or institutions; institutional. **2.** of or pertaining to institution, esp. ecclesiastical institution.

in·sti·tu·tive (in′sti to͞o′tiv, -tyo͞o′-), *adj.* tending or intended to institute or establish. —**in′sti·tu′tive·ly,** *adv.*

instr., 1. instructor. **2.** instrument. **3.** instrumental.

in·struct (in strukt′), *v.t.* **1.** to furnish with knowledge, esp. by a systematic method; teach; train; educate. **2.** to furnish with information; inform; apprise. **3.** to direct or command; order. [late ME < L *instruct(us)* equipped, trained (ptp. of *instruere*). See IN-[2], STRUCTURE] —**in·struct′i·ble,** *adj.* —**Syn. 1.** tutor, coach; school. **2.** enlighten.

in·struc·tion (in struk′shən), *n.* **1.** the act or practice of instructing or teaching; education. **2.** the knowledge or information imparted. **3.** an item of such knowledge or information. **4.** Usually, **instructions.** orders or directions. **5.** *Computer Technol.* a character or set of characters that together with one or more operands defines an operation and, when taken as a unit, causes a computer to operate on the indicated quantities. [ME *instruccio(u)n* < L *instructiōn-* (s. of *instructiō*)] —**in·struc′tion·al,** *adj.* —**Syn. 1.** tutoring, coaching; training; schooling.

in·struc·tive (in struk′tiv), *adj.* serving to instruct or inform; conveying information. —**in·struc′tive·ly,** *adv.* —**in·struc′tive·ness,** *n.*

in·struc·tor (in struk′tər), *n.* **1.** a person who instructs; a teacher. **2.** a teacher in a college or university who ranks below an assistant professor. Also, *referring to a woman,* **in·struc′tress.** [late ME < L] —**in·struc·to·ri·al** (in′struk tôr′ē əl, -tōr′-), *adj.* —**in·struc′tor·ship′,** *n.* —**Syn. 1.** tutor, schoolmaster, preceptor, pedagogue.

in·stru·ment (in′strə mənt), *n.* **1.** a mechanical device or contrivance; tool; implement: *a surgeon's instruments.* **2.** a contrivance for producing musical sounds. **3.** any means of effecting something; agency: *an instrument of government.* **4.** a formal legal document, as a contract, deed, or grant. **5.** a person used by another for some private end. **6.** a device for measuring the present value of the quantity under observation. **7.** a mechanical or electronic measuring device, esp. one used in navigation. —*adj.* **8.** *Aeron.* relying only on the observation of instruments for navigation: *instrument landing.* —*v.t.* **9.** to equip with instruments. **10.** to orchestrate. [ME < L *instrūment(um)* equipment. See INSTRUCT, -MENT] —**Syn. 1.** See **tool.**

in·stru·men·tal (in′strə men′təl), *adj.* **1.** serving as an instrument or means; helpful; useful. **2.** of or pertaining to an instrument. **3.** performed on or written for a musical instrument or musical instruments. **4.** *Gram.* noting or pertaining to a case that indicates means or agency. —*n. Gram.* **5.** the instrumental case. **6.** a word in the instrumental case. [ME < ML *instrūmentāl(is)*]

in·stru·men·tal·ism (in′strə men′təliz′əm), *n. Philos.* the variety of pragmatism developed by John Dewey maintaining that the truth of an idea is determined by its success in the active solution of a problem, and that the value of ideas is determined by their function in human experience or progress.

in·stru·men·tal·ist (in′strə men′təlist), *n.* **1.** a person who performs on a musical instrument. **2.** an advocate of instrumentalism. —*adj.* **3.** of, pertaining to, or advocating instrumentalism.

in·stru·men·tal·i·ty (in′strə men tal′i tē), *n., pl.* **-ties** for 2, 3. **1.** the quality or state of being instrumental. **2.** the fact or function of serving some purpose. **3.** a means or agency.

in·stru·men·tal·ly (in′strə men′təlē), *adv.* **1.** by or with the use of an instrument. **2.** with or on an instrument, esp. a musical instrument.

in·stru·men·ta·tion (in′strə men tā′shən), *n.* **1.** the arranging of music for instruments, esp. for an orchestra. **2.** the list of instruments for which a composition is scored. **3.** the use of, or work done by, instruments. **4.** instrumental agency; instrumentality. **5.** the science of developing, manufacturing, and utilizing instruments, esp. those used in science and industry.

in′strument pan′el, a panel containing gauges, indicators, etc., as in an automobile or airplane.

in·sub·or·di·nate (in′sə bôr′dənit), *adj.* **1.** not submitting to authority; disobedient. **2.** not lower. —*n.* **3.** a person who is insubordinate. —**in′sub·or′di·nate·ly,** *adv.* —**in′sub·or′di·na′tion,** *n.*

in·sub·stan·tial (in′səb stan′shəl), *adj.* **1.** not substantial; slight. **2.** without reality; unreal. [< LL *insubstantiāl(is)*] —**in′sub·stan′ti·al′i·ty,** *n.* —**in′sub·stan′tial·ly,** *adv.*

in·suf·fer·a·ble (in suf′ər ə bəl), *adj.* not to be endured; intolerable; unbearable: *insufferable insolence.* —**in·suf′fer·a·ble·ness,** *n.* —**in·suf′fer·a·bly,** *adv.*

in·suf·fi·cien·cy (in′sə fish′ən sē), *n., pl.* **-cies** for 2. **1.** deficiency in amount, force, or fitness; inadequateness: *insufficiency of supplies.* **2.** an instance of this. Also, **in′suf·fi′cience.** [late ME < LL *insufficientia*]

in·suf·fi·cient (in′sə fish′ənt), *adj.* not sufficient; deficient in force, quality, or amount; inadequate. [ME < LL *insufficient-* (s. of *insufficiēns*)] —**in′suf·fi′cient·ly,** *adv.*

in·suf·flate (in suf′lāt, in′sə flāt′), *v.t.*, **-flat·ed, -flat·ing.** to blow or breathe (something) into or upon. [< LL *insufflāt(us)* blown into or upon] —**in′suf·fla′tion,** *n.* —**in′suf·fla′tor,** *n.*

in·su·lar (in′sə lər, ins′yə-), *adj.* **1.** of or pertaining to an island or islands: *insular possessions.* **2.** dwelling or situated on an island. **3.** forming an island: *insular rocks.* **4.** detached; standing alone; isolated. **5.** of, pertaining to, or characteristic of islanders. **6.** narrowly exclusive; illiberal: *insular attitudes.* **7.** *Anat.* pertaining to an island of cells or tissue, as the islets of Langerhans. —*n.* **8.** an inhabitant of an island; islander. [< LL *insulār(is).* See ISLE, -AR[1]] —**in′su·lar·ism, in·su·lar·i·ty** (in′sə lar′i tē, ins′yə-), *n.* —**in′su·lar·ly,** *adv.*

in·su·late (in′sə lāt′, ins′yə-), *v.t.*, **-lat·ed, -lat·ing.** **1.** to cover, surround, or separate with nonconducting material to prevent or reduce the transfer of electricity, heat, or sound. **2.** to place in an isolated situation or condition; segregate. [< LL *insulāt(us)* made into an island. See ISLE, -ATE[1]]

in·su·la·tion (in′sə lā′shən, ins′yə-), *n.* **1.** material used for insulating. **2.** the act of insulating. **3.** the state of being insulated.

in·su·la·tor (in′sə lā′tər, ins′yə-), *n.* **1.** *Elect.* a material of low conductivity, as glass or porcelain, used to isolate and support a charged conductor. **2.** a person or thing that insulates.

in·su·lin (in′sə lin, ins′yə-), *n.* **1.** *Biochem.* a hormone, produced by the islets of Langerhans of the pancreas, that regulates the metabolism of glucose and other carbohydrates. **2.** *Pharm.* any of several commercial preparations of this substance, used in the treatment of diabetes. [< NL *insul(a)* (L: island, with reference to the islets of the pancreas) + -IN[2]]

in′sulin shock′, *Pathol.* a state of collapse caused by a decrease in blood sugar resulting from the administration of excessive insulin. Also called **in′sulin reac′tion.**

In·sull (in′səl), *n.* **Samuel,** 1859–1938, U.S. public utilities magnate, born in England.

in·sult (*v.* in sult′; *n.* in′sult), *v.t.* **1.** to treat insolently or with contemptuous rudeness; affront. **2.** *Archaic.* to attack; assault. —*n.* **3.** an insolent or contemptuously rude action or speech; affront. **4.** something having the effect of an affront: *That book is an insult to one's intelligence.* **5.** *Med.* **a.** an injury or trauma. **b.** an agent that inflicts this. **6.** *Archaic.* an attack or assault. [< L *insult(āre)* (to) jump on, insult = *in-* IN-[2] + *-sultāre,* var. of *saltāre* to jump; see SALTANT] —**in·sult′er,** *n.* —**in·sult′ing·ly,** *adv.* —**Syn. 1.** offend, scorn, injure, abuse. **3.** offense, outrage. INSULT, INDIGNITY, AFFRONT, SLIGHT imply an act which injures another's honor, self-respect, etc. INSULT implies such insolence of speech or manner as deeply humiliates or wounds a person's feelings and arouses him to anger. INDIGNITY is esp. used of inconsiderate, contemptuous treatment toward a person entitled to respect. AFFRONT implies open disrespect or offense shown, as it were, to the face. SLIGHT may imply inadvertent indifference or disregard, which may also indicate ill-concealed contempt. —**Ant. 1, 3.** compliment.

in·sult·ing (in sul′ting), *adj.* tending to give or cause insult; characterized by rudeness, insolence, etc.

in·su·per·a·ble (in so͞o′pər ə bəl), *adj.* incapable of being passed over, overcome, or surmounted: *an insuperable barrier.* [ME < L *insuperābil(is)*] —**in·su′per·a·bil′i·ty, in·su′per·a·ble·ness,** *n.* —**in·su′per·a·bly,** *adv.*

in·sup·port·a·ble (in′sə pôr′tə bəl, -pōr′-), *adj.* **1.** not endurable; insufferable. **2.** incapable of support, as by evidence or collected facts: *an insupportable accusation.* [< LL *insupportābil(is)*] —**in′sup·port′a·ble·ness,** *n.* —**in′sup·port′a·bly,** *adv.*

in·sup·press·i·ble (in′sə pres′ə bəl), *adj.* incapable of being suppressed. —**in′sup·press′i·bly,** *adv.*

in·sur·a·ble (in sho͝or′ə bəl), *adj.* capable of being insured, as against risk of loss or harm; proper to be insured. —**in·sur′a·bil′i·ty,** *n.*

in·sur·ance (in sho͝or′əns), *n.* **1.** the act, system, or business of insuring property, life, one's person, etc., against loss or harm, in consideration of a payment proportionate to the risk involved. **2.** coverage by contract in which one party agrees to indemnify or reimburse another for any loss that occurs under the terms of the contract. **3.** the contract itself, set forth in a written or printed agreement or policy. **4.** the amount for which anything is insured. **5.** *Rare.* an insurance premium.

in·sur·ant (in sho͝or′ənt), *n. Rare.* a person who takes out an insurance policy.

in·sure (in sho͝or′), *v.*, **-sured, -sur·ing.** —*v.t.* **1.** to secure indemnity to or on, in case of loss, damage, or death. **2.** to issue or procure an insurance policy on or for. **3.** ensure (defs. 1–3). —*v.i.* **4.** to issue or procure an insurance policy. [var. of ENSURE] —**Syn. 1.** warrant. **3.** assure.

in·sured (in sho͝ord′), *n.* a person covered by an insurance policy.

in·sur·er (in sho͝or′ər), *n.* **1.** a person or company that contracts to indemnify another in the event of loss or damage. **2.** a person or thing that insures.

in·sur·gence (in sûr′jəns), *n.* an act of rebellion. [IN-SURG(ENT) + -ENCE]

in·sur·gen·cy (in sûr′jən sē), *n.* **1.** the state or condition of being insurgent. **2.** insurrection against an existing government, usually one's own, by a group not recognized as having the status of a belligerent. **3.** rebellion or revolt within a group, as by members against leaders.

in·sur·gent (in sûr′jənt), *n.* **1.** a person who engages in armed resistance to a government or to the execution of its laws; rebel. **2.** a member of a group, as a political party, who revolts against the policies of the group. **—***adj.* **3.** rising in revolt; rebellious. **4.** surging or rushing in: *insurgent waves.* [< L *insurgent-* (s. of *insurgēns*) rising up against, prp. of *insurgere*]

in·sur·mount·a·ble (in′sər moun′tə bəl), *adj.* incapable of being surmounted, passed over, or overcome: *an insurmountable obstacle.* **—in′sur·mount′a·bil′i·ty, in′sur·mount′a·ble·ness,** *n.* **—in′sur·mount′a·bly,** *adv.*

in·sur·rec·tion (in′sə rek′shən), *n.* the act or an instance of rising in open rebellion against an established government or authority. [late ME < LL *insurrectiōn-* (s. of *insurrectiō*) = *insurrect(us)* risen up against (ptp. of *insurgere;* see INSURGENT) + *-iōn-* -ION] **—in′sur·rec′tion·al,** *adj.* **—in′sur·rec′tion·ism,** *n.* **—in′sur·rec′tion·ist,** *n.* **—Syn.** insurgency, uprising; mutiny. See **revolt.**

in·sur·rec·tion·ar·y (in′sə rek′shə ner′ē), *adj., n., pl.* **-ar·ies.** **—***adj.* **1.** of, pertaining to, or of the nature of insurrection. **2.** given to or causing insurrection. **—***n.* **3.** a person who engages in insurrection; rebel; insurgent.

in·sus·cep·ti·ble (in′sə sep′tə bəl), *adj.* not susceptible; incapable of being influenced or affected (usually fol. by *of* or *to*): *insusceptible of flattery; insusceptible to infection.* **—in′sus·cep′ti·bil′i·ty,** *n.* **—in′sus·cep′ti·bly,** *adv.*

in·swathe (in swāth′), *v.t.,* **-swathed, -swath·ing.** *Rare.* enswathe. **—in·swathe′ment,** *n.*

in·swept (in′swept′), *adj.* tapering at the front or tip.

int., **1.** interest. **2.** interior. **3.** interjection. **4.** internal. **5.** international. **6.** intransitive.

in·tact (in takt′), *adj.* not altered, impaired, or diminished; remaining uninjured, sound, or whole. [late ME < L *intact(us)* untouched = *in-* IN-[3] + *tactus,* ptp. of *tangere* to touch] **—in·tact′ness,** *n.* **—Syn.** See **complete.**

in·tagl·io (in tal′yō, -täl′-; *It.* ēn tä′lyô), *n., pl.* **-tagl·ios,** *It.* **-ta·gli** (-tä′lyē). **1.** a gem, seal, piece of jewelry, or the like, having an incised or sunken design. **2.** incised carving, as opposed to carving in relief. **3.** an incised or countersunk die. **4.** a printmaking process in which the design, text, etc., is engraved into the surface of a plate, ink being transferred to paper from the grooves. **5.** an impression or printing from such a design, engraving, etc. [< It < *intagli(are)* (to) cut in, engrave = *in-* IN-[2] + *tagliare* to cut < LL *tāliāre;* see TALLY]

in·take (in′tāk′), *n.* **1.** the place at which a fluid is taken into a channel, pipe, etc. **2.** the act or an instance of taking in. **3.** something that is taken in. **4.** a quantity taken in: *the intake of oxygen.* **5.** a narrowing; contraction.

in·tan·gi·ble (in tan′jə bəl), *adj.* **1.** not tangible; incapable of being perceived by the sense of touch, as incorporeal or immaterial things. **2.** not definite or clear to the mind: *intangible arguments.* **—***n.* **3.** something intangible, esp. an intangible asset, as good will. [< ML *intangibil(is)*] **—in·tan′gi·bil′i·ty, in·tan′gi·ble·ness,** *n.* **—in·tan′gi·bly,** *adv.*

in·tar·si·a (in tär′sē ə), *n.* an art or technique of decorating a surface with inlaid patterns, esp. of wood mosaic, developed during the Renaissance. Also, **tarsia.** [m. (influenced by It *tarsia*) of It *intarsio* < *intarsiare* to inlay = *in-* IN-[2] + *tarsiare* < Ar *tarṣī‘* an inlay, incrustation]

in·te·ger (in′ti jər), *n.* **1.** one of the positive or negative numbers 1, 2, 3, 4, etc., or 0; a whole number, as distinguished from a fraction or a mixed number. **2.** a complete entity. [< L: untouched, hence, undivided, whole = *in-* IN-[3] + *-teg-* (var. of *tag-* root of *tangere* to touch) + *-er* adj. suffix]

in·te·ger vi·tae (in′te ger wē′tī; *Eng.* in′ti jər vī′tē), *Latin.* blameless in life; innocent. Horace, *Odes,* I.

in·te·gra·ble (in′tə grə bəl), *adj. Math.* capable of being integrated, as a mathematical function or differential equation. **—in′te·gra·bil′i·ty,** *n.*

in·te·gral (in′tə grəl), *adj.* **1.** of, pertaining to, or belonging as an essential part of the whole; constituent or component. **2.** made up of parts that together constitute a whole. **3.** entire; complete; whole. **4.** *Arith.* pertaining to or being an integer; not fractional. **5.** *Math.* pertaining to or involving integrals. **—***n.* **6.** an integral whole. **7.** *Math.* **a.** Also called **Riemann integral.** the numerical measure of the area bounded by the graph of a given function, below by the x-axis, and on the sides by ordinates drawn at the endpoints of a specified interval. **b.** a primitive. **c.** any of several analogous quantities. [< ML *integrāl(is).* See INTEGER, -AL[1]] **—in·te·gral·i·ty** (in′tə gral′i tē), *n.* **—in′te·gral·ly,** *adv.*

in′tegral cal′culus, the branch of mathematics that deals with integrals, esp. the methods of ascertaining indefinite integrals and applying them to the solution of differential equations and the determining of areas, volumes, and lengths.

in′tegral equa′tion, *Math.* an equation in which an integral involving a dependent variable appears.

in·te·grand (in′tə grand′), *n. Math.* the expression to be integrated. [< L *integrand(um),* n. use of neut. of *integrandus,* ger. of *integrāre* to INTEGRATE]

in·te·grant (in′tə grənt), *adj.* **1.** making up or being a part of a whole; constituent. **—***n.* **2.** an integrant part. [< L *integrant-* (s. of *integrāns*) making whole, prp. of *integrāre.* See INTEGER, -ANT]

in·te·grate (in′tə grāt′), *v.,* **-grat·ed, -grat·ing.** **—***v.t.* **1.** to bring together or incorporate (parts) into a whole. **2.** to make up, combine, or complete to produce a whole or a larger unit, as parts do. **3.** to indicate the total amount or the mean value of. **4.** *Math.* to find the integral of. **5.** *U.S.* **a.** to make the occupancy or use of (a school, restaurant, organization, etc.) available to persons of all races. **b.** to give or cause to give equal opportunity and consideration to (a racial, religious, or ethnic group or a member of such a group). **—***v.i. U.S.* **6.** (of a school, neighborhood, place of business, etc.) to become integrated. **7.** (of a racial, religious, or ethnic group) **a.** to become integrated. **b.** to meld with and become part of the dominant culture. [< L *integrāt(us)* made whole, restored (ptp. of *integrāre*). See INTEGER, -ATE[1]] **—in′te·gra′tive,** *adj.*

in·te·grat·ed (in′tə grā′tid), *adj.* **1.** having on a basis of equal membership individuals of different racial, religious, and ethnic groups: *an integrated school.* Cf. **segregated.** **2.** combining or coordinating separate elements so as to provide a harmonious, interrelated whole: *an integrated plot; an integrated personality.* **3.** organized or structured so that constituent units function cooperatively: *an integrated economy.*

in′tegrated bar′, *Law.* (in some states) a system of bar associations to which all lawyers are required to belong. Also called **incorporated bar.**

in′tegrated cir′cuit, *Electronics.* an interconnected group of circuit elements, as of resistors and transistors, on a single tiny chip of semiconductor material, each chip comprising a complete operable electronic circuit whose size is approximately a tenth of an inch square. *Abbr.:* IC

in′tegrated da′ta proc′essing, the processing of information by systematic techniques which reduce human intervention to a minimum and which employ a language common to all the machines in the system. *Abbr.:* IDP Cf. **automatic data processing.**

in·te·gra·tion (in′tə grā′shən), *n.* **1.** the act or an instance of combining into an integral whole. **2.** behavior in harmony with the environment. **3.** *Psychol.* the organization of the constituent elements of the personality into a coordinated, harmonious whole. **4.** *Math.* the operation of finding the integral of a function or equation, esp. solving a differential equation. **5.** *U.S.* the combination of educational and other public facilities, previously segregated by race, into one unified system. [INTEGRATE + -ION; cf. L *integrātiō* renewal]

in·te·gra·tion·ist (in′tə grā′shə nist), *n. U.S.* a person who works for or favors integration.

in·te·gra·tor (in′tə grā′tər), *n.* **1.** a person or thing that integrates. **2.** an instrument for performing numerical integrations.

in·teg·ri·ty (in teg′ri tē), *n.* **1.** adherence to moral and ethical principles; soundness of moral character; honesty. **2.** a sound, unimpaired, or perfect condition: *the integrity of a ship's hull.* [late ME *integrite* < L *integritās*] **—Syn. 1.** probity, virtue. See **honor.** **—Ant. 1.** dishonesty.

in·teg·u·ment (in teg′yə mənt), *n.* **1.** a natural covering, as a skin, shell, or rind. **2.** any covering, coating, or enclosure. [< L *integument(um)* a covering] **—in·teg′u·men′ta·ry,** *adj.* **—Syn. 1.** cortex, involucre, involucrum.

in·tel·lect (in′tᵊlekt′), *n.* **1.** the power or faculty of the mind by which one knows or understands, as distinguished from that by which one feels and that by which one wills; the faculty of thinking and acquiring knowledge. **2.** capacity for thinking and acquiring knowledge. **3.** a particular mind or intelligence, esp. of a high order. **4.** a person possessing a great capacity for thought and knowledge. [ME < L *intellect(us)* = *intellect-* (ptp. s. of *intellegere* to understand; see INTELLIGENT) + *-us* n. suffix] **—in′tel·lec′tive,** *adj.* **—in′tel·lec′tive·ly,** *adv.* **—Syn. 1.** brains. See **mind.**

in·tel·lec·tion (in′tᵊlek′shən), *n.* **1.** the exercise of the intellect. **2.** a particular act of the intellect. [late ME < ML *intellectiōn-* (s. of *intellectiō*)]

in·tel·lec·tu·al (in′tᵊlek′cho͞o əl), *adj.* **1.** appealing to or engaging the intellect: *intellectual pursuits.* **2.** of or pertaining to the intellect or its use: *intellectual powers.* **3.** possessing or showing a notable mental capacity: *an intellectual person.* **4.** guided or developed by or relying on the intellect rather than upon emotions or feelings. **—***n.* **5.** a person of superior intellect. **6.** a person who pursues things of interest to the intellect. **7.** an extremely rational person; one who relies on intellect rather than on emotions or feelings. **8.** a person professionally engaged in mental labor. **9.** **intellectuals, a.** *Archaic.* the mental faculties. **b.** *Obs.* things pertaining to the intellect. [ME < L *intellectuāl(is)*] **—in′tel·lec′tu·al′i·ty, in′tel·lec′tu·al·ness,** *n.* **—in′tel·lec′tu·al·ly,** *adv.* **—Syn. 1, 2.** mental. **3.** See **intelligent.**

in·tel·lec·tu·al·ise (in′tᵊlek′cho͞o ə līz′), *v.t., v.i.,* **-ised, -is·ing.** *Chiefly Brit.* intellectualize. **—in′tel·lec′tu·al·i·sa′tion,** *n.* **—in′tel·lec′tu·al·is′er,** *n.*

in·tel·lec·tu·al·ism (in′tᵊlek′cho͞o ə liz′əm), *n.* **1.** the exercise of the intellect. **2.** devotion to intellectual pursuits. **3.** excessive emphasis on abstract or intellectual matters, esp. with a lack of proper consideration for emotions. **—in′tel·lec′tu·al·ist,** *n.* **—in′tel·lec′tu·al·is′tic,** *adj.* **—in′tel·lec′tu·al·is′ti·cal·ly,** *adv.*

in·tel·lec·tu·al·ize (in′tᵊlek′cho͞o ə līz′), *v.,* **-ized, -iz·ing.** **—***v.t.* **1.** to seek or consider the rational content or form of. **2.** to ignore the emotional or psychological significance of (an action, feeling, dream, etc.) by an excessively intellectual or abstract explanation. **—***v.i.* **3.** to talk or write intellectually; reason; philosophize: *to intellectualize about world problems.* Also, *esp. Brit.,* **intellectualise.** **—in′tel·lec′tu·al·i·za′tion,** *n.* **—in′tel·lec′tu·al·iz′er,** *n.*

in·tel·li·gence (in tel′i jəns), *n.* **1.** capacity for reasoning, understanding, and for similar forms of mental activity. **2.** manifestation of such capacity: *He writes with intelligence and wit.* **3.** the faculty of understanding. **4.** knowledge of an event, circumstance, etc., received or imparted; news, information. **5.** the gathering or distribution of information, esp. secret information. **6.** *Gov.* **a.** information about an enemy or a potential enemy. **b.** the evaluated conclusions drawn from such information. **c.** an organization or agency employed in gathering such information: *military intelligence.* **7.** (*often cap.*) an intelligent being, esp. an incorporeal one. [ME < L *intelligentia.* See INTELLIGENT, -ENCE] **—in·tel′li·gen′tial,** *adj.* **—Syn. 1.** See **mind. 1, 2.** discernment, reason, penetration. **—Ant. 1, 2.** stupidity.

intel′ligence quo′tient, *Psychol.* mental age divided by chronological age, usually expressed as a multiple of 100. The intelligence quotient of a ten-year-old child whose mental age equals that of the average twelve-year-old is 1.2, or 120. *Abbr.:* IQ, I.Q. Cf. **achievement quotient.**

in·tel·li·genc·er (in tel′i jən sər), *n.* **1.** a person or thing that conveys information. **2.** an informer; spy.

intel′ligence test′, *Psychol.* any of various tests designed to measure the mental ability or capacity of an individual.

in·tel·li·gent (in tel′i jənt), *adj.* **1.** having good understanding or a high mental capacity; quick to comprehend, as persons or animals. **2.** displaying or characterized by quickness of understanding, sound thought, or good judgment: *an intelligent reply.* **3.** having the faculty of reasoning and understanding; possessing intelligence: *an intelligent being.* **4.** *Archaic.* having understanding or knowledge (usually fol. by *of*). [< L *intelligent-* (s. of *intelligēns,* prp. of *intelligere,*

var. of *intellegere* to understand, lit., choose between) = *intel-* (var. of *inter-* INTER-) + *-lig-* choose (var. of *leg-*, root of *legere*) + *-ent-* -ENT] —**in·tel′li·gent·ly,** *adv.*
—**Syn. 1.** bright. INTELLIGENT, INTELLECTUAL describe distinctive mental capacity. INTELLIGENT often suggests a natural quickness of understanding: *an intelligent reader.* INTELLECTUAL implies not only having a high degree of understanding, but also a capacity and taste for the higher forms of knowledge: *intellectual interests.* **2.** astute, alert, bright, smart. See **sharp.** —**Ant. 1, 2.** stupid.

in·tel·li·gent·si·a (in tel′i jent′sē ə, -gent′sē ə), *n.pl.* intellectuals considered as an artistic, social, or political elite. [< Russ < L *intelligentia* INTELLIGENCE]

in·tel·li·gi·bil·i·ty (in tel′i jə bil′i tē), *n.* the quality or condition of being intelligible.

in·tel·li·gi·ble (in tel′i jə bəl), *adj.* **1.** capable of being understood; comprehensible: *an intelligible response.* **2.** *Philos.* apprehensible by the mind only; conceptual. [ME < L *intelligibil(is).* See INTELLIGENT, -IBLE] —**in·tel′li·gi·ble·ness,** *n.* —**in·tel′li·gi·bly,** *adv.*

in·tem·er·ate (in tem′ər it), *adj.* *Rare.* inviolate; undefiled; unsullied; pure. [< L *intemerāt(us)* = *in-* IN-[3] + *temerā-* (s. of *temerāre* to darken, hence, sully) + *-tus* ptp. suffix] —**in·tem′er·ate·ly,** *adv.* —**in·tem′er·ate·ness,** *n.*

in·tem·per·ance (in tem′pər əns, -prəns), *n.* **1.** immoderate indulgence in alcoholic beverages. **2.** excessive indulgence of a natural appetite or passion. **3.** lack of moderation or due restraint, as in action or speech. **4.** an act or instance of any of these: *a long series of intemperances.* [ME < L *intemperantia*]

in·tem·per·ate (in tem′pər it, -prit), *adj.* **1.** given to or characterized by immoderate indulgence in intoxicating drink. **2.** immoderate as regards indulgence of appetite or passion. **3.** not temperate; unrestrained; unbridled. **4.** extreme in temperature, as climate. [ME < L *intemperāt(us)*] —**in·tem′per·ate·ly,** *adv.* —**in·tem′per·ate·ness,** *n.*

in·tend (in tend′), *v.t.* **1.** to have in mind as something to be done or brought about. **2.** to design or mean for a particular purpose, use, recipient, etc.: *a fund intended for emergency use only.* **3.** to design, express, or indicate. **4.** (of words, terms, statements, etc.) to signify. **5.** *Archaic.* to direct (the eyes, mind, etc.). —*v.i.* **6.** to have a purpose or design. **7.** *Obs.* to set out on one's course. [< L *intend(ere)* (to) stretch towards, aim at (see IN-[2], TEND[1]); r. ME *entenden* < OF *entend(re)*] —**in·tend′er,** *n.* —**Syn. 1.** plan, expect, purpose.

in·tend·ance (in ten′dəns), *n.* **1.** a department of the public service. **2.** superintendance. [< F; see INTENDANT, -ANCE]

in·tend·an·cy (in ten′dən sē), *n., pl.* **-cies. 1.** the office or function of an intendant. **2.** a body of intendants. **3.** Also, **intendency.** a district under the charge of an intendant.

in·tend·ant (in ten′dənt), *n.* a person who has the direction or management of some public business, the affairs of an establishment, etc., esp. a provincial administrator or a superintendent. [< F < L *intendent-* (s. of *intendēns*) attending to, prp. of *intendere*]

in·tend·ed (in ten′did), *adj.* **1.** intentional: *an intended snub.* **2.** prospective: *his intended wife.* —*n.* **3.** *Informal.* one's fiancé or fiancée. —**in·tend′ed·ly,** *adv.* —**in·tend′ed·ness,** *n.*

in·tend·en·cy (in ten′dən sē), *n., pl.* **-cies.** intendancy (def. 3).

in·tend·ment (in tend′mənt), *n.* **1.** *Law.* sense or meaning. **2.** *Obs.* intention; design; purpose. [INTEND + -MENT; r. ME *entendement* < MF < ML *intendiment(um)*]

in·ten·er·ate (in ten′ə rāt′), *v.t.,* **-at·ed, -at·ing.** *Archaic.* to make soft or tender; soften. [IN-[2] + L *tener* TENDER[1] + -ATE[1]] —**in·ten′er·a′tion,** *n.*

intens., intensive.

in·tense (in tens′), *adj.* **1.** existing or occurring in a high or extreme degree: *intense heat.* **2.** acute, strong, or vehement, as sensations, feelings, or emotions. **3.** of an extreme kind; very great, severe, etc.: *an intense gale.* **4.** having a characteristic quality in a high degree: *blindingly intense sunlight.* **5.** strenuous or earnest: *an intense life.* **6.** having or showing great strength, strong feeling, emotions, or tension, as a person, the face, etc. [ME < L *intens(us)* stretched out, ptp. of *intendere* to INTEND] —**in·tense′ly,** *adv.* —**in·tense′ness,** *n.*

in·ten·si·fy (in ten′sə fī′), *v.,* **-fied, -fy·ing.** —*v.t.* **1.** to make intense or more intense. **2.** to make more acute; strengthen or sharpen. **3.** *Photog.* to increase the density and contrast of (a negative). —*v.i.* **4.** to become intense or more intense. —**in·ten′si·fi·ca′tion,** *n.* —**in·ten′si·fi′er,** *n.*
—**Syn. 1.** deepen, quicken. **2.** concentrate. See **aggravate.**
—**Ant. 1.** alleviate, weaken.

in·ten·sion (in ten′shən), *n.* **1.** intensification; increase in degree. **2.** intensity; high degree. **3.** relative intensity; degree. **4.** exertion of the mind; determination. **5.** *Logic.* the set of attributes belonging to anything to which a given term is correctly applied; connotation; comprehension. Cf. **extension** (def. 9). [< L *intensiōn-* (s. of *intensiō*)] —**in·ten′sion·al,** *adj.* —**in·ten′sion·al·ly,** *adv.*

in·ten·si·ty (in ten′si tē), *n., pl.* **-ties. 1.** the quality or condition of being intense. **2.** energy, strength, concentration, vehemence, etc., as of activity, thought, or feeling: *He went at the job with great intensity.* **3.** a high or extreme degree, as of cold or heat. **4.** a high degree of emotional excitement; depth of feeling. **5.** *Speech.* the correlate of physical energy and the degree of loudness of a speech sound. **6.** *Physics.* magnitude, as of energy or a force per unit of area, volume, time, etc.

in·ten·sive (in ten′siv), *adj.* **1.** of, pertaining to, or characterized by intensity: *intensive questioning.* **2.** tending to intensify; intensifying. **3.** noting or pertaining to a system of agriculture concentrating on the cultivation of limited areas and on raising the crop yield per unit area (opposed to *extensive*). **4.** *Gram.* indicating increased emphasis or force. —*n.* **5.** something that intensifies. **6.** *Gram.* an intensive element or formation, as *-self* in *himself.* [late ME < ML *intensīv(us)*] —**in·ten′sive·ly,** *adv.* —**in·ten′sive·ness,** *n.*

in·tent[1] (in tent′), *n.* **1.** the act or fact of intending, as to do something: *criminal intent.* **2.** that which is intended; purpose; intention. **3.** *Law.* the state of a person's mind that directs his actions toward a specific object. **4.** meaning or significance. **5. to all intents and purposes,** for all practical purposes; practically speaking. [ME < LL *intent(us)* an aim, purpose, lit., a stretching out (n. use of L *intentus* IN-TENT[2]); r. ME *entent(e)* < OF] —**Syn. 1.** See **intention.**

in·tent[2] (in tent′), *adj.* **1.** firmly or steadfastly fixed or directed, as the eyes, mind, etc.: *intent concentration.* **2.** having the attention sharply fixed on something: *intent on one's job.* **3.** determined; having the mind or will fixed on some purpose or goal; *intent on revenge.* [< L *intent(us)* taut, intent, ptp. of *intendere* to INTEND] —**in·tent′ly,** *adv.* —**in·tent′ness,** *n.* —**Syn. 1, 2.** concentrated. **3.** resolute, set.

in·ten·tion (in ten′shən), *n.* **1.** the act or an instance of determining upon some action or result. **2.** the end or object intended; purpose. **3. intentions, a.** one's attitude toward the effect of one's actions or conduct: *a bungler with good intentions.* **b.** one's attitude with respect to marriage: *Are his intentions serious?* **4.** *Logic.* **a.** Also called **first intention, primary intention.** reference by signs, concepts, etc., to concrete things, their properties, classes, or the relationships among them. **b.** Also called **second intention, secondary intention.** reference to properties, classes, or the relationships among first intentions. **5.** *Surg., Med.* a manner or process of healing, as in the healing of a lesion or fracture without granulation or the healing of a wound by granulation after suppuration. **6.** *Archaic.* intentness. [ME *intencio(u)n* < L *intentiōn-* (s. of *intentiō*)]
—**Syn. 2.** goal. INTENTION, INTENT, PURPOSE all refer to a wish one means to carry out. INTENTION is the general word: *His intention is good.* INTENT is chiefly legal or poetical: *attack with intent to kill.* PURPOSE implies having a goal or a settled determination to achieve something: *Her strong sense of purpose is reflected in her studies.*

in·ten·tion·al (in ten′shə nᵊl), *adj.* **1.** done deliberately or on purpose: *an intentional insult.* **2.** of or pertaining to intention or purpose. **3.** *Philos.* **a.** pertaining to an appearance, phenomenon, or representation in the mind; phenomenal; representational. **b.** pertaining to the capacity of the mind to refer to an existent or nonexistent object. **c.** pointing beyond itself, as consciousness, a sign, etc. —**in·ten′tion·al′i·ty,** *n.* —**in·ten′tion·al·ly,** *adv.* —**Syn. 1.** planned, intended. See **deliberate.** —**Ant. 1.** accidental.

in·ten·tioned (in ten′shənd), *adj.* having specified intentions (usually used in combination): *a well-intentioned person.*

in·ter (in tûr′), *v.t.,* **-terred, -ter·ring. 1.** to deposit (a dead body) in a grave or tomb; bury. **2.** *Obs.* to put into the earth. [ME *entere(n)* < MF *enterr(er)* << L *in-* IN-[2] + *terra* earth]

inter-, a prefix occurring in loan words from Latin, where it meant "between," "among," "in the midst of," "mutually," "reciprocally," "together," "during" (*intercept; interest*); on this model, used in the formation of compound words (*intercom; interdepartmental*). [ME < L (in some words r. ME *entre-* < MF < L *inter-*), comb. form of *inter* (prep. and adv.); see INTERIOR]

inter., **1.** intermediate. **2.** interrogation. **3.** interrogative.

in·ter·act (in′tər akt′), *v.i.* to act one upon another. —**in′ter·ac′tive,** *adj.*

in·ter·ac·tion (in′tər ak′shən), *n.* reciprocal action or influence. —**in′ter·ac′tion·al,** *adj.*

in·ter a·li·a (in′teʀ ä′li ä′; *Eng.* in′tər ā′lē ə), *Latin.* among other things.

in·ter a·li·os (in′teʀ ä′li ōs′; *Eng.* in′tər ā′lē ōs′), *Latin.* among other persons.

in·ter-A·mer·i·can (in′tər ə mer′i kən), *adj.* of or pertaining to some or all of the countries of North and South America.

in·ter·bor·ough (in′tər bûr′ō, -bur′ō), *adj.* **1.** between boroughs. **2.** of, pertaining to, or located in two or more boroughs. —*n.* **3.** a subway, streetcar, bus, etc., or a transportation system, operating between boroughs.

in·ter·brain (in′tər brān′), *n.* the diencephalon.

in·ter·breed (in′tər brēd′), *v.,* **-bred, -breed·ing.** —*v.t.* **1.** to crossbreed. **2.** to cause to breed together. —*v.i.* **3.** to crossbreed. **4.** to breed or mate with a closely related individual.

in·ter·ca·lar·y (in tûr′kə ler′ē, in′tər kal′ə rē), *adj.* **1.** interpolated; interposed; intervening. **2.** inserted in the calendar, as an extra day or month. **3.** having such an inserted day, month, etc., as a particular year. [< L *intercalāri(us).* See INTERCALATE, -ARY] —**in·ter′ca·lar′i·ly,** *adv.*

in·ter·ca·late (in tûr′kə lāt′), *v.t.,* **-lat·ed, -lat·ing. 1.** to interpolate; interpose. **2.** to insert (an extra day, month, etc.) in the calendar. [< L *intercalāt(us)* inserted (ptp. of *intercalāre*) = *inter-* INTER- + *calā-* (s. of *calāre* to proclaim) + *-tus* ptp. suffix] —**in·ter′ca·la′tion,** *n.* —**in·ter′ca·la′tive,** *adj.* —**Syn. 1.** interject, introduce, insinuate.

in·ter·cede (in′tər sēd′), *v.i.,* **-ced·ed, -ced·ing. 1.** to plead or petition in behalf of one in difficulty or trouble: *to intercede with the governor for a condemned man.* **2.** to mediate; attempt to reconcile differences between two people or groups. [< L *intercēde(re)*] —**in′ter·ced′er,** *n.* —**Syn.** intervene.

in·ter·cel·lu·lar (in′tər sel′yə lər), *adj.* situated between or among cells or cellules.

in·ter·cept (*v.* in′tər sept′; *n.* in′tər sept′), *v.t.* **1.** to take, seize, or halt (someone or something on the way from one place to another); cut off from a destination: *to intercept a messenger.* **2.** to stop or check (passage, travel, etc.): *to intercept an escape.* **3.** to stop or interrupt the course, progress, or transmission of. **4.** *Math.* to mark off or include, as between two points or lines. **5.** *Sports.* to take possession of (a ball or puck) during an attempted pass by an opposing team. **6.** to intersect. **7.** *Obs.* to prevent the operation or effect of. **8.**

Intercept (def. 4) Arc of circle intercepted by line between points X and Y

in′ter·ac′a·dem′ic, *adj.*
in′ter·a·tom′ic, *adj.*
in′ter·bank′, *adj.*
in′ter·bel·lig′er·ent, *adj.*
in′ter·branch′, *adj.*
in′ter·cap′il·lary, *adj.*
in′ter·car′di·nal, *adj.*
in′ter·caste′, *adj.*

Obs. to cut off from access, sight, etc. —*n.* **9.** an interception. **10.** *Math.* **a.** an intercepted segment of a line. **b.** (in a coordinate system) the distance from the origin to the point at which a curve or line intersects an axis. [< L *intercept(us)* intercepted (ptp. of *intercipere*) = *inter-* INTER- + *-cep-* (var. of *cap-*, s. of *capere* to take) + *-tus* ptp. suffix] —**in′ter·cep′tive,** *adj.*

in·ter·cep·tion (in′tər sep′shən), *n.* **1.** the act or an instance of intercepting. **2.** the state or fact of being intercepted. **3.** *Mil.* the engaging of an enemy force in an attempt to prevent it from carrying out its mission. [< L *interceptiōn-* (s. of *interceptiō*)]

in·ter·cep·tor (in′tər sep′tər), *n.* **1.** a person or thing that intercepts. **2.** *Mil.* a fighter airplane with a high rate of climb and speed, used chiefly for the interception of enemy aircraft. Also, **in′ter·cept′er.** [< L]

in·ter·ces·sion (in′tər sesh′ən), *n.* **1.** the act or an instance of interceding. **2.** a prayer to God on behalf of another or others. [< L *intercessiōn-* (s. of *intercessiō*) = *intercess(us)* (ptp. of *intercēdere* to INTERCEDE) + *-iōn-* -ION] —**in′ter·ces′sion·al,** *adj.*

in·ter·ces·sor (in′tər ses′ər, in′tər ses′ər), *n.* a person who intercedes. [late ME < L; see INTERCESSION, -OR^2]

in·ter·ces·so·ry (in′tər ses′ə rē), *adj.* having the function of interceding: *an intercessory prayer.* [< ML *intercessōri(us)*]

in·ter·change (*v.* in′tər chānj′; *n.* in′tər chānj′), *v.*, **-changed, -chang·ing,** *n.* —*v.t.* **1.** to put each (of two things) in the place of the other. **2.** to cause (one thing) to change places with another; transpose. **3.** to give and receive (things) reciprocally; exchange. —*v.i.* **4.** to occur by turns or in succession; alternate. **5.** to change places, as two persons or things, or as one with another. —*n.* **6.** the act or an instance of interchanging; reciprocal exchange: *the interchange of commodities.* **7.** a highway junction consisting of a system of road levels such that vehicles may move from one road to another without crossing the stream of traffic. [INTER- + CHANGE; r. ME *entrechaunge(n)* < MF *entrechangi(er)*]

in·ter·change·a·ble (in′tər chān′jə bəl), *adj.* **1.** (of two things) capable of being put or used in the place of each other: *interchangeable words.* **2.** (of one thing) capable of replacing or changing places with something else: *an interchangeable part.* [r. late ME *entrechaungeable* < MF *entrechangeable*] —**in′ter·change′a·bil′i·ty, in′ter·change′a·ble·ness,** *n.* —**in′ter·change′a·bly,** *adv.*

in·ter·col·le·giate (in′tər kə lē′jit, -jē it), *adj.* taking place between or participating in activities between different colleges: *intercollegiate athletics.*

in·ter·co·lum·ni·a·tion (in′tər kə lum′nē ā′shən), *n.* *Archit.* **1.** the space between two adjacent columns, usually the clear space between the lower parts of the shafts. **2.** the system of spacing between columns. [< L *intercolumni(um)* space between columns (see INTER-, COLUMN) + -ATION] —**in′ter·co·lum′nar,** *adj.*

in·ter·com (in′tər kom′), *n.* *Informal.* an intercommunication system. [shortened form]

in·ter·com·mu·ni·cate (in′tər kə myōō′nə kāt′), *v.*, **-cat·ed, -cat·ing.** —*v.i.* **1.** to communicate mutually, as people. **2.** to afford passage from one to another, as rooms. —*v.t.* **3.** to exchange (messages or communications) with one another. [< ML *intercommūnicāt(us)* (ptp.)] —**in′ter·com·mu′ni·ca·bil′i·ty,** *n.* —**in′ter·com·mu′ni·ca·ble,** *adj.* —**in′ter·com·mu′ni·ca′tion,** *n.* —**in·ter·com·mu·ni·ca·tive** (in′tər kə myōō′nə kā′tiv, -kə tiv), *adj.* —**in′ter·com·mu′ni·ca′tor,** *n.*

in′tercommunica′tion sys′tem, a communication system within a building, ship, airplane, local area, etc., with a loudspeaker or receiver for listening and a microphone for speaking at each of two or more points.

in·ter·com·mun·ion (in′tər kə myōōn′yən), *n.* **1.** mutual communion, association, or relations. **2.** *Eccles.* a communion service among members of different denominations.

in·ter·con·ti·nen·tal (in′tər kon′t^{ə}nen′t^{ə}l), *adj.* **1.** of, pertaining to, or between continents: *intercontinental trade.* **2.** traveling or capable of traveling between continents.

in′tercontinen′tal ballis′tic mis′sile, a ballistic missile that has a range of at least 3500 nautical miles.

in·ter·cos·tal (in′tər kos′t^{ə}l, -kô′st^{ə}l), *adj.* **1.** pertaining to muscles, parts, or intervals between the ribs. **2.** situated between the ribs. —*n.* **3.** an intercostal muscle, member, or space. [< NL *intercostāl(is)*] —**in′ter·cos′tal·ly,** *adv.*

in·ter·course (in′tər kōrs′, -kôrs′), *n.* **1.** dealings or communication between individuals, groups, countries, etc. **2.** interchange of thoughts, feelings, etc. **3.** sexual relations or a sexual coupling, esp. coitus. [late ME *intercurse* < ML *intercurs(us)* communication, trading, L: a running between]

in·ter·crop (in′tər krop′), *v.*, **-cropped, -crop·ping.** *Agric.* —*v.i.* **1.** to grow one crop between the rows of another, as in an orchard, vineyard, or field. —*v.t.* **2.** to grow a crop between the rows of (another).

in·ter·cross (*v.* in′tər krôs′, -kros′; *n.* in′tər krôs′, -kros′), *v.t.* **1.** to cross (things), one with another. **2.** to cross (each other), as streets do; intersect. **3.** to interbreed. —*v.i.* **4.** to cross each other; intersect. **5.** to interbreed. —*n.* **6.** an instance of cross-fertilization.

in·ter·cur·rent (in′tər kûr′ənt, -kur′-), *adj.* intervening, as of time or events. [< L *intercurrent-* (s. of *intercurrēns*) running between, prp. of *intercurrere*] —**in′ter·cur′rence,** *n.* —**in′ter·cur′rent·ly,** *adv.*

in·ter·de·nom·i·na·tion·al (in′tər di nom′ə nā′shə n^{ə}l), *adj.* common to, involving, or occurring between different religious denominations. —**in′ter·de·nom′i·na′tion·al·ism,** *n.*

in·ter·den·tal (in′tər den′t^{ə}l), *adj.* **1.** situated between teeth. **2.** *Phonet.* articulated with the tip of the tongue between the upper and lower front teeth, as the fricatives (*th*) and (th) of *thy* and *thigh.* —**in′ter·den′tal·ly,** *adv.*

in·ter·de·part·men·tal (in′tər dē′pärt men′t^{ə}l, -di pärt-), *adj.* involving or characterized by exchange or cooperation between two or more departments, esp. of an educational institution. —**in′ter·de′part·men′tal·ly,** *adv.*

in·ter·de·pend·ent (in′tər di pen′dənt), *adj.* mutually dependent; dependent on each other: *interdependent influences.* —**in′ter·de·pend′ence, in′ter·de·pend′en·cy,** *n.* —**in′ter·de·pend′ent·ly,** *adv.*

in·ter·dict (*n.* in′tər dikt′; *v.* in′tər dikt′), *n.* **1.** *Civil Law.* any prohibitory act. **2.** *Rom. Cath. Ch.* a punishment by which the faithful are prohibited from participation in certain sacred acts. **3.** *Roman Law.* a general or special order of the Roman praetor forbidding or commanding an act. —*v.t.* **4.** to forbid; prohibit. **5.** *Eccles.* to cut off authoritatively from certain ecclesiastical functions and privileges. **6.** to impede by steady bombardment: *Constant air attacks interdicted the enemy's advance.* [< L *interdict(um)* prohibition, n. use of neut. of *interdictus* forbidden (ptp. of *interdīcere*) (see INTER-, DICTUM); r. ME *entredit* < OF] —**in′ter·dic′tor,** *n.*

in·ter·dic·tion (in′tər dik′shən), *n.* **1.** the act or an instance of interdicting. **2.** the state of being interdicted. **3.** an interdict. —**in′ter·dic′to·ry,** *adj.*

in·ter·dig·i·tate (in′tər dij′i tāt′), *v.i.*, *v.t.*, **-tat·ed, -tat·ing.** to interlock, as or like the fingers of both hands. —**in·ter·dig·i·ta·tion** (in′tər dij′i tā′shən), *n.*

in·ter·dis·ci·pli·nar·y (in′tər dis′ə plə ner′ē), *adj.* combining or involving two or more academic disciplines.

in·ter·est (in′tər ist, -trist), *n.* **1.** one's feelings or attitudes of concern, involvement, or curiosity, as aroused by something or someone. **2.** a person or thing that arouses such feelings or attitudes: *She is his current interest. His chief interest is chess.* **3.** the power to excite such feelings or attitudes: *questions of great interest.* **4.** a legal share, right, or title, as in ownership of property or a business. **5.** the enterprise, property, etc., in which one has such an interest. **6.** Often, **interests.** a body of persons exerting influence on and often financially involved in a given enterprise, industry, or sphere of activity. **7.** benefit; advantage: *Keep your own interests in mind.* **8.** regard for one's own advantage or profit; self-interest. **9.** *Finance.* **a.** a sum paid or charged for the use of money or for borrowing money. **b.** the rate percent per unit of time represented by such payment or charge. **10. in the interest** or **interests of,** to the advantage or advancement of; in behalf of: *in the interests of good government.* —*v.t.* **11.** to excite the attention or curiosity of: *Mystery stories interest him greatly.* **12.** to be of concern to (a person, nation, etc.); involve. **13.** to cause to take a personal concern or share; induce to participate: *to interest a person in an enterprise.* [ME < ML, L: it concerns, lit., it is between; r. ME *interesse* < ML, L: to concern, lit., to be between. See INTER-, ESSE]

in·ter·est·ed (in′tər i stid, -tri stid, -tə res′tid), *adj.* **1.** having an interest in something; concerned: *Interested members will meet at two.* **2.** participating; having an interest or share; having money involved. **3.** having the attention or curiosity engaged: *an interested spectator.* **4.** influenced by personal or selfish motives: *an interested witness.* —**in′ter·est·ed·ly,** *adv.* —**in′ter·est·ed·ness,** *n.*

in′terest group′, a group of people drawn or acting together because of a common interest, concern, or purpose.

in·ter·est·ing (in′tər i sting, -tri sting, -tə res′ting), *adj.* engaging or exciting and holding the attention or curiosity: *an interesting book.* —**in′ter·est·ing·ly,** *adv.* —**in′ter·est·ing·ness,** *n.* —**Syn.** absorbing. —**Ant.** dull.

in·ter·face (in′tər fās′), *n.*, *v.*, **-faced, -fac·ing.** —*n.* **1.** a surface regarded as the common boundary of two bodies or spaces. **2.** the facts, problems, considerations, theories, practices, etc., shared by two or more disciplines, procedures, or fields of study: *the interface of chemistry and physics.* **3.** a common boundary or interconnection between systems, equipment, concepts, or human beings. **4.** *Computer Technol.* **a.** equipment or programs designed to communicate information from one system of computing devices or programs to another. **b.** any arrangement for such communication. —*v.t.* **5.** to bring into an interface. —*v.i.* **6.** to be in an interface. **7.** to function as an interface. —**in′ter·fa′cial,** *adj.*

in′terfa′cial ten′sion, *Physical Chem.* the surface tension at the interface of two liquids.

in·ter·faith (in′tər fāth′), *adj.* of or operating or occurring between persons or groups belonging to different religions.

in·ter·fere (in′tər fēr′), *v.i.*, **-fered, -fer·ing.** **1.** to come into opposition, as one thing with another, esp. with the effect of hampering action or procedure (often fol. by *with*): *Constant distractions interfere with work.* **2.** to take part in the affairs of others; meddle (often fol. by *with* or *in*): *to interfere in another's life.* **3.** to strike one foot or leg against another in moving, as a horse. **4.** *Sports.* **a.** to obstruct the action of an opposing player in a way barred by the rules. **b.** *Football.* to run interference for a teammate carrying the ball. **5.** *Physics.* to cause interference. **6.** to clash; come in collision; be in opposition: *The claims of two nations may interfere.* [INTER- + *-fere* < L *fer(īre)* (to) strike; modeled on MF *s'entreferir*] —**in′ter·fer′er,** *n.* —**in′ter·fer′ing·ly,** *adv.*

in·ter·fer·ence (in′tər fēr′əns), *n.* **1.** the act, fact, or an instance of interfering. **2.** something that interferes. **3.** *Physics.* the process in which two or more light, sound, or electromagnetic waves combine to reinforce or cancel each other, the amplitude of the resulting wave being equal to the sum of the amplitudes of the combining waves. **4.** *Radio.* **a.** a jumbling of radio signals, caused by the reception of undesired ones. **b.** the signals or device producing the incoherence. **5.** the distorting or inhibiting effect of previously learned behavior on subsequent learning. **6.** *Football.* **a.** the act of one or more teammates running ahead of a ball-carrier to block prospective tacklers. **b.** such teammates collectively. **c.** the illegal prevention of a pass receiver from catching a pass. —**in·ter·fe·ren·tial** (in′tər fə ren′shəl), *adj.*

in·ter·fer·om·e·ter (in′tər fə rom′i tər), *n.* **1.** *Optics.* a device that separates a beam of light into two ray beams and brings the rays together to produce interference, used to measure wavelength, index of refraction, and astronomical distances. **2.** *Astron.* an instrument for measuring the angular separation of double stars of the diameter of giant stars by means of the interference phenomena of light emitted by these stars. —**in·ter·fer·o·met·ric** (in′tər fēr′ə me′trik), *adj.* —**in′ter·fer′o·met′ri·cal·ly,** *adv.* —**in′ter·fer·om′e·try,** *n.*

in′ter·cit′y, *adj.*
in′ter·clasp′, *v.t.*
in′ter·class′, *adj.*
in′ter·club′, *adj.*
in′ter·com′pa·ny, *adj.*
in′ter·con·nect′, *v.*
in′ter·con·nec′tion, *n.*
in′ter·con′so·nan′tal, *adj.*
in′ter·coun′ty, *adj.*
in′ter·dig′i·tal, *adj.*; **-ly,** *adv.*
in′ter·dis′trict, *adj.*
in′ter·fac′tion·al, *adj.*

in·ter·fer·on (in′tər fēr′on), *n. Biochem.* a protein substance produced by virus-invaded cells that prevents reproduction of the virus. [INTERFERE + *-on* arbitrary suffix]

in·ter·fer·tile (in′tər fûr′tᵊl), *adj. Bot., Zool.* able to interbreed. —**in′ter·fer·til′i·ty,** *n.*

in·ter·file (in′tər fīl′), *v.t.*, **-filed, -fil·ing.** to combine two or more similarly arranged sets of items, as cards, documents, etc., into a single arrangement.

in·ter·flu·ent (in′tər flo͞o′ənt), *adj.* flowing into one another; intermingling. [< L *interfluent-* (s. of *interfluēns*)]

in·ter·fluve (in′tər flo͞ov′), *n.* the land area separating adjacent stream valleys. [back formation from *interfluvial*. See INTER-, FLUVIAL] —**in′ter·flu′vi·al,** *adj.*

in·ter·fold (in′tər fōld′), *v.t.* to fold one within another.

in·ter·fra·ter·nal (in′tər frə tûr′nᵊl), *adj.* **1.** occurring between brothers. **2.** occurring between fraternities. —**in′ter·fra·ter′nal·ly,** *adv.*

in·ter·fuse (in′tər fyo͞oz′), *v.*, **-fused, -fus·ing.** —*v.t.* **1.** to pour or pass (something) between, into, or through; infuse. **2.** to intersperse, intermingle, or permeate with something. **3.** to blend or fuse, one with another. —*v.i.* **4.** to become blended or fused, one with another. [< L *interfūs(us)* poured between, ptp. of *interfundere*] —**in′ter·fu′sion,** *n.*

in·ter·ga·lac·tic (in′tər gə lak′tik), *adj.* of or existing or occurring in the space between galaxies.

in·ter·gla·cial (in′tər glā′shəl), *adj. Geol.* occurring or formed between times of glacial action.

in·ter·grade (*n.* in′tər grād′; *v.* in′tər grād′), *n.*, *v.*, **-grad·ed, -grad·ing.** —*n.* **1.** an intermediate grade, form, stage, etc. —*v.i.* **2.** to merge gradually, one into another, as different species through evolution. —**in′ter·gra·da′tion,** *n.* —**in′ter·gra·da′tion·al,** *adj.*

in·ter·group (in′tər gro͞op′), *adj. Sociol.* taking place or being between groups: *intergroup relationships.*

in·ter·growth (in′tər grōth′), *n.* growth or growing together, as of one thing with or into another.

in·ter·im (in′tər im), *n.* **1.** an intervening time; meantime: *in the interim.* —*adj.* **2.** belonging to or connected with an intervening period of time; temporary: *an interim order.* [< L: in the meantime]

in·te·ri·or (in tēr′ē ər), *adj.* **1.** being within; inside of anything; internal; further toward a center: *the interior rooms of a house.* **2.** of or pertaining to something within; inside: *an interior view of a house.* **3.** situated well inland from the coast or border: *the interior towns of a country.* **4.** of or pertaining to the inland. **5.** domestic: *the interior trade.* **6.** inner; private; secret: *the interior life of man.* —*n.* **7.** the internal part; inside. **8.** a pictorial representation of the inside of a room. **9.** the inland parts of a region, country, etc. **10.** the domestic affairs of a country: *the Department of the Interior.* **11.** the inner or inward nature or character of anything. [< L = *inter-* inward + *-ior* comp. suffix; see EXTERIOR] —**in·te·ri·or·i·ty** (in tēr′ē ôr′i tē, -or′-), *n.* —**in·te′ri·or·ly,** *adv.* —**Syn. 7.** See **inside.** —**Ant. 1, 7.** exterior.

B/B
A/A
A/A
B/B

A, Interior angle; B, Exterior angle

inte′rior an′gle, *Geom.* **1.** an angle formed between parallel lines by a third line that intersects them. **2.** an angle formed within a polygon by two adjacent sides.

inte′rior decora′tion, **1.** Also called **inte′rior design′.** the designing and furnishing of the interior of a house, apartment, office, etc., esp. as an art, business, or profession. **2.** materials used to decorate an interior, including furnishings, draperies, etc.

inte′rior dec′orator, a person whose occupation is planning the decoration, including the furnishings and draperies, of homes, offices, etc. Also called **inte′rior design′er.**

inte′rior mon′ologue, *Literature.* a form of stream-of-consciousness writing that represents the inner thoughts of a character.

interj., interjection.

in·ter·ja·cent (in′tər jā′sənt), *adj.* between or among others; intervening; intermediate. [< L *interjacent-* (s. of *interjacēns*) lying between, prp. of *interjacēre.* See INTER-, ADJACENT] —**in′ter·ja′cence,** *n.*

in·ter·ject (in′tər jekt′), *v.t.* **1.** to interpolate; interpose: *to interject a clarification of a previous statement.* **2.** *Obs.* to come between. [< L *interject(us)* thrown between (ptp. of *interjicere*) = *inter-* INTER- + *-jec-* (var. of *jac-*, s. of *jacere* to throw) + *-tus* ptp. suffix] —**in′ter·jec′tor,** *n.* —**Syn. 1.** introduce, insert.

in·ter·jec·tion (in′tər jek′shən), *n.* **1.** the act of putting between; insertion; interposition. **2.** the utterance of a word or phrase expressive of emotion; the uttering of an exclamation. **3.** something interjected, as a remark. **4.** *Gram.* a grammatically autonomous word or expression, esp. one conveying emotion, as *Hey! Good grief!* [ME *interjeccio(u)n* < L *interjectiōn-* (s. of *interjectiō*)] —**in′ter·jec′tion·al, in·ter·jec·tur·al** (in′tər jek′chər əl), **in·ter·jec·to·ry** (in′tər jek′tə rē), *adj.* —**in′ter·jec′tion·al·ly,** *adv.*

in·ter·knit (in′tər nit′), *v.t.*, **-knit·ted** or **-knit, -knit·ting.** to knit together, one with another; intertwine.

in·ter·lace (in′tər lās′), *v.*, **-laced, -lac·ing.** —*v.i.* **1.** to cross one another as if woven together; intertwine: *Their hands interlaced.* —*v.t.* **2.** to unite or dispose (threads, strips, parts, branches, etc.) so as to intercross one another, passing alternately over and under; intertwine. **3.** to mingle; blend. [INTER- + LACE; r. ME *entrelace(n)* < MF *entrelac(er)*] —**in·ter·lac·ed·ly** (in′tər lā′sid lē), *adv.* —**in′ter·lace′ment,** *n.*

Interlacing arcade

in′terlacing arcade′, an arcade, esp. a blind one, composed of arches (**in′terlacing arch′es**) so disposed and cut that each arch seems to intersect and be intersected by one or more other arches, giving an interlaced effect to the whole.

In·ter·la·ken (in′tər lä′kən, in′tər lä′kən), *n.* a town in central Switzerland: tourist center. 4738 (1960).

in·ter·lam·i·nate (in′tər lam′ə nāt′), *v.t.*, **-nat·ed, -nat·ing.** to interlay or lay between laminae; interstratify. —**in′ter·lam′i·na′tion,** *n.*

in·ter·lard (in′tər lärd′), *v.t.* **1.** to diversify by mixing in or interjecting something unique, striking, or contrasting (usually fol. by *with*): *to interlard one's speech with oaths.* **2.** (of things) to be intermixed in. **3.** *Obs.* to mix, as fat with lean. [INTER- + LARD; r. *enterlard* < MF *entrelard(er)*]

in·ter·lay (in′tər lā′), *v.t.*, **-laid, -lay·ing. 1.** to lay between; interpose. **2.** to diversify with something laid between or inserted: *to interlay silver with gold.*

in·ter·leaf (in′tər lēf′), *n.*, *pl.* **-leaves** (-lēvz′). an additional leaf, usually blank, inserted between the regular printed leaves of a book, as for a reader's notes.

in·ter·leave (in′tər lēv′), *v.t.*, **-leaved, -leav·ing. 1.** to provide blank leaves in (a book) for notes or written comments. **2.** to insert blank leaves between (the regular printed leaves).

in′ter·li′brar·y loan′ (in′tər lī′brer ē, -brə rē, -brē, in′-), **1.** a system by which one library obtains a publication for a reader by borrowing it from another library. **2.** a loan made by this system.

in·ter·line[1] (in′tər līn′), *v.t.*, **-lined, -lin·ing. 1.** to write or insert (words, phrases, etc.) between the lines of writing or print. **2.** to mark or inscribe (a document, book, etc.) between the lines. [ME < ML *interlīne(āre).* See INTER-, LINE[1]]

in·ter·line[2] (in′tər līn′), *v.t.*, **-lined, -lin·ing.** to provide with an interlining. [INTER- + LINE[2]] —**in′ter·lin′er,** *n.*

in·ter·lin·e·ar (in′tər lin′ē ər), *adj.* Also, **in′ter·lin′e·al. 1.** situated or inserted between lines, as of the lines of print in a book: *an interlinear translation.* **2.** having interpolated lines; interlined. **3.** having the same text in various languages set in alternate lines: *the interlinear Bible.* —*n.* **4.** a book, esp. a textbook, having interlinear matter, as a translation. [< ML *interlīneār(is)*] —**in′ter·lin′e·ar·ly, in′ter·lin′e·al·ly,** *adv.*

in·ter·lin·e·ate (in′tər lin′ē āt′), *v.t.*, **-at·ed, -at·ing.** interline[1]. [< ML *interlīneāt(us),* ptp. of *interlīneāre* to INTERLINE[1]; see -ATE[1]] —**in′ter·lin′e·a′tion,** *n.*

In·ter·lin·gua (in′tər ling′gwə), *n.* an artificial language for international communication, based primarily upon the Romance languages and intended mainly as a common language for scientists. [< It: lit., interlanguage]

in·ter·lin·ing[1] (in′tər lī′ning), *n.* an inner lining placed between the ordinary lining and the outer fabric of a garment. [INTERLINE[2] + -ING[1]]

in·ter·lin·ing[2] (in′tər lī′ning), *n.* anything written or inserted between lines of writing or print. [INTERLINE[1] + -ING[1]]

in·ter·link (in′tər lingk′), *v.t.* to link, one with another.

in·ter·lock (*v.* in′tər lok′; *n.* in′tər lok′), *v.i.* **1.** to engage or interlace, one with another: *The branches of the trees interlock to form a natural archway.* **2.** to fit into each other, as parts of machinery, so that all action is synchronized. —*v.t.* **3.** to lock, one with another. **4.** to fit (parts) together so that their action is coordinated. —*n.* **5.** the fact or condition of interlocking or of being interlocked. **6.** a device to insure that a mechanism will operate in proper sequence with another mechanism. —**in′ter·lock′er,** *n.*

in·ter·lo·cu·tion (in′tər lō kyo͞o′shən), *n.* conversation; dialogue. [< L *interlocūtiōn-* (s. of *interlocūtiō*) a speaking between. See INTERLOCUTOR, -ION]

in·ter·loc·u·tor (in′tər lok′yə tər), *n.* **1.** a person who takes part in a conversation or dialogue. **2.** *U.S.* the man in the middle of the line of performers in a minstrel troupe, who acts as the announcer and carries on humorous conversation with the end men. [< L *interlocūt(us)* spoken between (ptp. of *interloquī*) + -OR[2]]

in·ter·loc·u·to·ry (in′tər lok′yə tôr′ē, -tōr′ē), *adj.* **1.** of the nature of, pertaining to, or occurring in conversation: *interlocutory instruction.* **2.** interjected into the main course of speech. **3.** *Law.* **a.** pronounced during the course of an action, as a decision; not finally decisive: *an interlocutory decree.* **b.** pertaining to an intermediate decision. [< ML *interlocūtōri(us).* See INTERLOCUTOR, -ORY[1]] —**in′ter·loc′u·to′ri·ly,** *adv.*

in·ter·loc·u·tress (in′tər lok′yə tris), *n.* a female interlocutor. Also, **in′ter·loc′u·trice, interlocutrix.** [INTERLOCUT(O)R + -ESS]

in·ter·loc·u·trix (in′tər lok′yə triks), *n.*, *pl.* **-loc·u·tri·ces** (-lok′yə trī′sēz). interlocutress. [INTERLOCU(TOR) + -TRIX]

in·ter·lope (in′tər lōp′), *v.i.*, **-loped, -lop·ing. 1.** to intrude into some region or field of trade without a proper license. **2.** to thrust oneself into the affairs of others. [prob. back formation from INTERLOPER = INTER- + *-loper* (see LANDLOPER)] —**in′ter·lop′er,** *n.* —**Syn. 1.** trespass, poach, encroach.

in·ter·lude (in′tər lo͞od′), *n.* **1.** an intervening episode, period, space, etc. **2.** an early English farce or comedy. **3.** any intermediate performance or entertainment, as between the acts of a play. **4.** an instrumental passage or composition played between the parts of a song, church service, drama, etc. [ME < ML *interlūd(ium)* = L *inter-* INTER- + *lūd(us)* play + *-ium,* neut. of *-ius* -IOUS]

in·ter·lu·nar (in′tər lo͞o′nər), *adj.* pertaining to the moon's monthly period of invisibility between the old moon and the new.

in·ter·lu·na·tion (in′tər lo͞o nā′shən), *n.* the interlunar period.

in·ter·mar·riage (in′tər mar′ij), *n.* **1.** marriage or the state of marriage between a man and woman of different races, religions, or ethnic groups. **2.** marriage or the state of marriage between a man and woman within a specific group, as required by custom or law; endogamy.

in·ter·mar·ry (in′tər mar′ē), *v.i.*, **-ried, -ry·ing. 1.** to become connected by marriage, as two families, tribes, castes, or religions. **2.** to marry within one's family. **3.** to marry outside one's religion, ethnic group, etc.

in·ter·med·dle (in′tər med′ᵊl), *v.i.*, **-dled, -dling.** to take

in′ter·fi′brous, *adj.* **in′ter·gov′ern·men′tal,** *adj.* **in′ter·i·on′ic,** *adj.* **in′ter·li′brar·y,** *adj.*

part in a matter, esp. officiously; interfere; meddle. [INTER- + MEDDLE; r. ME *entremedle(n)* < AF *entremedl(er)*, OF *entremesler*] —**in′ter·med′dler,** *n.*

in·ter·me·di·ar·y (in′tər mē′dē er′ē), *adj., n., pl.* **-ar·ies.** —*adj.* **1.** being between; intermediate. **2.** acting between persons, parties, etc.; serving as an intermediate agent or agency: *an intermediary power.* —*n.* **3.** an intermediate agent or agency; a go-between or mediator. **4.** a medium or means. **5.** an intermediate form or stage. [< LL *intermedi(um)* (n.) + -ARY; see INTERMEDIATE[1]]

in·ter·me·di·ate[1] (in′tər mē′dē it), *adj.* **1.** being, situated, or acting between two points, stages, things, persons, etc.: *the intermediate stages of development.* **2.** of a size smaller than a full-sized standard automobile but larger than a compact automobile: *an intermediate car.* —*n.* **3.** something intermediate, as a form or class. **4.** a person who acts between others; intermediary; mediator. **5.** *Chem.* a derivative of the initial material formed before the desired product of a chemical process. **6.** an intermediate automobile. [< ML *intermediāt(us)* = L *intermedi(us)* intermediary (*inter-* INTER- + *medius* middle, in the middle) + *-ātus* -ATE[1]] —**in′ter·me′di·a·cy,** *n.* —**in′ter·me′di·ate·ly,** *adv.* —**in′ter·me′di·ate·ness,** *n.*

in·ter·me·di·ate[2] (in′tər mē′dē āt′), *v.i.,* **-at·ed, -at·ing.** to act as an intermediary; intervene; mediate. [< ML *intermediāt(us),* ptp. of *intermediāre.* See INTER-, MEDIATE] —**in′ter·me′di·a′tion,** *n.* —**in′ter·me′di·a′tor,** *n.* —**in·ter·me·di·a·to·ry** (in′tər mē′dē ə tōr′ē, -tôr′ē), *adj.*

in′terme′diate fre′quency, *Radio.* the middle frequency in a superheterodyne receiver, at which most of the amplification takes place. *Abbr.:* IF, if

interme′diate range′ ballis′tic mis′sile, a ballistic missile that has a range of 800 to 1500 nautical miles.

in·ter·ment (in tûr′mənt), *n.* the act or a ceremony of interring; burial. [INTER- + -MENT; r. ME *enter(e)ment* < MF *enterrement*]

in·ter·mez·zo (in′tər met′sō, -med′zō; *It.* ēn′ter med′dzô), *n., pl.* **-zos, -zi** (-sē, -zē; *It.* -dzē). **1.** a short dramatic, musical, or other entertainment of light character introduced between the acts of a drama or opera. **2.** a short musical composition between main divisions of an extended musical work. **3.** a short, independent musical composition. [< It < LL *intermed(ium)*; see INTERMEDIARY]

in·ter·mi·gra·tion (in′tər mī grā′shən), *n.* reciprocal migration; interchange of habitat by migrating groups.

in·ter·mi·na·ble (in tûr′mə nə bəl), *adj.* **1.** having no apparent limit or end; unending: *an interminable job.* **2.** monotonously or annoyingly protracted or continued: *her interminable chatter.* [ME < LL *interminābil(is)*] —**in·ter′mi·na·ble·ness, in·ter′mi·na·bil′i·ty,** *n.* —**in·ter′mi·na·bly,** *adv.*

in·ter·min·gle (in′tər miŋ′gəl), *v.t., v.i.,* **-gled, -gling.** to mingle together. [late ME]

in·ter·mis·sion (in′tər mish′ən), *n.* **1.** an interval between periods of action or activity: *They studied for hours without an intermission.* **2.** a short interval between the acts of a play or parts of a public performance. **3.** the act or fact of intermitting. **4.** the state of being intermitted. [late ME < L *intermissiōn-* (s. of *intermissiō*) interruption = *intermiss(us)* (ptp. of *intermittere* to INTERMIT) + *-iōn-* -ION]

in·ter·mis·sive (in′tər mis′iv), *adj.* **1.** of, pertaining to, or characterized by intermission. **2.** intermittent.

in·ter·mit (in′tər mit′), *v.,* **-mit·ted, -mit·ting.** —*v.t.* **1.** to discontinue temporarily; suspend. —*v.i.* **2.** to stop or pause at intervals; be intermittent. **3.** to cease, stop, or break off operations for a time. [< L *intermitt(ere)* (to) leave a space between, drop (for a while), leave off = *inter-* INTER- + *mittere* to send, let go] —**in′ter·mit′ter, in′ter·mit′tor,** *n.* —**in′ter·mit′ting·ly,** *adv.* —**Syn. 1, 3.** interrupt. **3.** desist.

in·ter·mit·tent (in′tər mit′ənt), *adj.* **1.** stopping or ceasing for a time; alternately ceasing and beginning again: *an intermittent pain.* **2.** (of streams, lakes, or springs) recurrent; showing water only part of the time. [< L *intermittent-* (s. of *intermittēns*) leaving off, prp. of *intermittere* to INTERMIT; see -ENT] —**in′ter·mit′tence, in′ter·mit′ten·cy,** *n.* —**in′ter·mit′tent·ly,** *adv.*

in·ter·mix (in′tər miks′), *v.t., v.i.* to intermingle. [back formation from *intermixt* (now *intermixed*) < L *intermixt(us)* mingled together, ptp. of *intermiscēre*] —**in′ter·mix′a·ble,** *adj.* —**in·ter·mix·ed·ly** (in′tər mik′sid lē, -mikst′lē), *adv.*

in·ter·mix·ture (in′tər miks′chər), *n.* **1.** the act of intermixing. **2.** a mass of ingredients mixed together. **3.** something added by intermixing.

in·ter·mod·al (in′tər mōd′əl), *adj.* providing, utilizing, or designed for a transportation system that combines several modes of carrier (surface, sea, and air) for a single shipment: *an intermodal service; intermodal containers.* —**in′ter·mod′al·ly,** *adv.*

in·ter·mu·ral (in′tər myŏŏr′əl), *adj.* of, pertaining to, or taking place between two or more institutions, cities, etc.: *an intermural track meet.* [< L *intermūrāl(is)* between walls]

in·tern[1] (*v.* in tûrn′; *n.* in′tûrn), *v.t.* **1.** to restrict to or confine within prescribed limits, as enemy aliens or combat troops who take refuge in a neutral country. **2.** to impound until the termination of a war, as a vessel of a belligerent. —*n.* **3.** an internee. [< F *intern(er)* << L *intern(us)* INTERN[3]]

in·tern[2] (in′tûrn), *n.* Also, **interne. 1.** a resident member of the medical staff of a hospital, commonly a recent medical-school graduate serving an apprenticeship under supervision. **2.** *Educ.* See **student teacher.** —*v.i.* **3.** to perform the duties of or be an intern. [< F *interne* < L *intern(us)* INTERN[3]] —**in′tern·ship′,** *n.*

in·tern[3] (in tûrn′), *adj. Archaic.* internal. [< L *intern(us)* inward = *in-* (see IN-[2]) + *-ternus* adj. suffix; see EXTERN]

in·ter·nal (in tûr′nəl), *adj.* **1.** situated or existing in the interior of something; interior. **2.** of, pertaining to, or noting the inside or inner part. **3.** *Pharm.* oral (def. 4). **4.** existing, occurring, or found within the limits or scope of something; intrinsic: *a theory having internal logic.* **5.** of or pertaining to the domestic affairs of a country: *internal politics.* **6.** existing solely within the individual mind: *internal malaise.* **7.** coming from, produced, or motivated by the psyche or inner recesses of the mind; subjective: *an internal response.* **8.** *Anat., Zool.* inner; not superficial; away from the surface or next to the axis of the body or of a part: *the internal carotid artery.* **9.** present or occurring within an organism or one of its parts: *an internal organ.* —*n.* **10.** Usually, **internals.** entrails; innards. **11.** an inner or intrinsic attribute. [< ML *internāl(is).* See INTERN[3], -AL[1]] —**in′ter·nal′i·ty, in·ter′nal·ness,** *n.* —**in·ter′nal·ly,** *adv.*

inter′nal au′ditory mea′tus, *Anat.* the canal extending through the petrous portion of the temporal bone, through which pass the facial nerve and the auditory nerve and artery.

in·ter′nal-com·bus′tion en′gine (in tûr′nəl kəm bus′chən), an engine in which the process of combustion takes place within the cylinder or cylinders.

inter′nal ear′, the inner portion of the ear, consisting of a bony labyrinth that is composed of a vestibule, semicircular canals, and a cochlea and that encloses a membranous labyrinth. Cf. **ear** (def. 1).

inter′nal gear′, a gear having teeth cut on an inner cylindrical surface.

in·ter·nal·ize (in tûr′nəlīz′), *v.t.,* **-ized, -iz·ing. 1.** to incorporate in oneself (the values, mores, etc., of another or of a group). **2.** to make subjective or give a subjective character to. —**in·ter′nal·i·za′tion,** *n.*

inter′nal med′icine, the branch of medicine dealing with the diagnosis and nonsurgical treatment of diseases.

inter′nal rev′enue, the revenue of a government from any domestic source, usually considered to be any source other than customs.

inter′nal rhyme′, *Pros.* **1.** a rhyme created by two or more words in the same line of verse. **2.** a rhyme created by words within two or more lines of a verse.

inter′nal stress′, (in metal or glass pieces, or the like) a stress existing within the material as a result of thermal changes, having been worked, or irregularity of molecular structure.

internat., international.

in·ter·na·tion·al (in′tər nash′ə nəl), *adj.* **1.** between or among nations; involving two or more nations. **2.** of or pertaining to two or more nations or their citizens: *a matter of international concern.* **3.** pertaining to the relations between nations: *international legislation.* **4.** having members or dealings in several nations. —*n.* **5.** (*cap.*) any of several international socialist or Communist organizations formed in the 19th and 20th centuries. **6.** (*sometimes cap.*) a labor union having locals in two or more countries. —**in′ter·na′tion·al′i·ty,** *n.* —**in′ter·na′tion·al·ly,** *adv.*

in′terna′tional air′ mile′, mile (def. 3).

Interna′tional Bank′ for Reconstruc′tion and Devel′opment, official name of the **World Bank.**

in′terna′tional can′dle, *Optics.* candela.

In′terna′tional Code′, a code used at sea by the navies of certain nations, using a series of flags representing digits from zero through nine.

Interna′tional Court′ of Jus′tice, official name of the **World Court.**

In′terna′tional Date′ Line′, a theoretical line following approximately the 180th meridian, the regions to the east of which are counted as being one day earlier in their calendar dates than the regions to the west.

In·ter·na·tio·nale (an ter na syô nal′), *n.* a revolutionary song, first sung in France in 1871 and since popular as a song of workers and communists. [< F, short for *chanson internationale* international song]

Interna′tional Geo·phys′ical Year′, the 18-month period from July 1, 1957 to Dec. 31, 1958, designated as a time of intensive geophysical exploration and sharing of knowledge by all countries. *Abbr.:* IGY

in·ter·na·tion·al·ise (in′tər nash′ə nəlīz′), *v.t.,* **-ised, -is·ing.** *Chiefly Brit.* internationalize.

in·ter·na·tion·al·ism (in′tər nash′ə nəliz′əm), *n.* **1.** the principle of cooperation among nations, for the promotion of their common good. **2.** international character, relations, cooperation, or control. **3.** (*cap.*) the principles or methods of a Communist or socialist International.

in·ter·na·tion·al·ist (in′tər nash′ə nəlist), *n.* **1.** an advocate of internationalism. **2.** a person versed in international law and relations. **3.** (*cap.*) a member or adherent of a Communist or socialist International.

in·ter·na·tion·al·ize (in′tər nash′ə nəlīz′), *v.t.,* **-ized, -iz·ing.** to make international; bring under international control. Also, *esp. Brit.,* **internationalise.** —**in′ter·na′tion·al·i·za′tion,** *n.*

In′terna′tional La′bor Organiza′tion, a specialized agency of the United Nations formed to improve working conditions throughout the world. *Abbr.:* ILO, I.L.O.

in′terna′tional law′, the body of rules that civilized nations recognize as binding them in their conduct toward one another.

In′terna′tional Mon′etary Fund′, an international organization that promotes the stabilization of the world's currencies and maintains a monetary pool from which member nations can draw: an agency of the United Nations.

interna′tional Morse′ code′, a form of Morse code used in international telegraphy. Also, **continental code.**

interna′tional nau′tical mile′, mile (def. 3).

in′ter·mesh′, *v.i.* **in′ter·me·tal′lic,** *adj.* **in′ter·mo·lec′u·lar,** *adj.* **in′ter·mus′cu·lar,** *adj.*

THE INTERNATIONAL PHONETIC ALPHABET

(Revised to 1951)

		Bi-labial	*Labio-dental*	*Dental and Alveolar*	*Retro-flex*	*Palato-alveolar*	*Alveolo-palatal*	*Palatal*	*Velar*	*Uvular*	*Pharyn-gal*	*Glottal*
CONSONANTS	*Plosive*	p b		t d	ʈ ɖ			c ɟ	k g	q ɢ		ʔ
	Nasal	m	ɱ	n	ɳ			ɲ	ŋ	ɴ		
	Lateral Fricative			ɬ ɮ								
	Lateral Non-fricative			l	ɭ			ʎ				
	Rolled			r						ʀ		
	Flapped			ɾ	ɽ					ʀ		
	Fricative	ɸ β	f v	θ ð s z ɹ	ʂ ʐ	ʃ ʒ	ɕ ʑ	ç ʝ	x ɣ	χ ʁ	ħ ʕ h ɦ	
	Frictionless Continuants and Semi-vowels	w ɥ	ʋ	ɹ				j (ɥ)	(w)	ʁ		

		Bi-labial	*Front*	*Central*	*Back*
VOWELS	*Close*	(y ʉ u)	i y	ɨ ʉ	ɯ u
	Half-close	(ø o)	e ø		ɤ o
				ə	
	Half-open	(œ ɔ)	ɛ œ		ʌ ɔ
			æ	ɐ	
	Open	(ɒ)		a	ɑ ɒ

(Secondary articulations are shown by symbols in brackets.)

Other Sounds.—Palatalized consonants: ƫ, ɖ, etc.; palatalized ʃ, ʒ: ʆ, ʓ. Velarized or pharyngalized consonants: ɫ, ɗ, ɀ, etc. Ejective consonants (with simultaneous glottal stop): p', t', etc. Implosive voiced consonants: ɓ, ɗ, etc. ɼ fricative trill. σ, ϱ (labialized θ, ð, or s, z). ʆ, ʓ (labialized ʃ, ʒ). ʇ, ʗ, ʖ (clicks, Zulu *c, q, x*). ɺ (a sound between r and l). ɴ Japanese syllabic nasal. ɧ (combination of x and ʃ). ʍ (voiceless w). ɩ, ʏ, ɷ (lowered varieties of i, y, u). ɜ (a variety of ə). ɵ (a vowel between ø and o).

Affricates are normally represented by groups of two consonants (ts, tʃ, dʒ, etc.), but, when necessary, ligatures are used (ʦ, ʧ, ʤ, etc.), or the marks ⁀ or ‿ (t͡s or t‿s, etc.). ⁀ ‿ also denote synchronic articulation (m͡ŋ = simultaneous m and ŋ). c, ɟ may occasionally be used in place of tʃ, dʒ, and ƻ, ƨ for ts, dz. Aspirated plosives: ph, th, etc. r-colored vowels: eɹ, aɹ, ɔɹ, etc., or eʴ, aʴ, ɔʴ, etc., or ᶒ, ᶏ, ᶗ, etc.; r-colored ə : əɹ or əʴ or ɹ or ᶕ or ɚ.

Length, Stress, Pitch.— ː (full length). ˑ (half length). ˈ (stress, placed at beginning of the stressed syllable). ˌ (secondary stress). ¯ (high level pitch); _ (low level); ˊ (high rising); ˏ (low rising); ˋ (high falling); ˎ (low falling); ^ (rise-fall); ˇ (fall-rise).

Modifiers.— ˜ nasality. ˳ breath (l̥ = breathed l). ˬ voice (s̬ = z). ʻ slight aspiration following p, t, etc. ̫ labialization (n̫ = labialized n). ̪ dental articulation (t̪ = dental t). ˙ palatalization (ż = ʓ). ̣ specially close vowel (ẹ = a very close e). ̨ specially open vowel (ę = a rather open e). ˔ tongue raised (e˔ or ẹ = ẹ). ˕ tongue lowered (e˕ or ę = ę). ˖ tongue advanced (u˖ or u̟ = an advanced u, t̟ = ṭ). - or ˗ tongue retracted (i- or i̠ = i˖, t̠ = alveolar t). ̹ lips more rounded. ̜ lips more spread. Central vowels: ï (= ɨ), ü (= ʉ), ë (= ə˖), ö (= ɵ), ɛ̈, ɔ̈. ̩ (e.g. n̩) syllabic consonant. ̆ consonantal vowel. ʃˢ variety of ʃ resembling s, etc.

Interna/tional Phonet/ic Al/phabet, the set of symbols devised by the International Phonetic Association to provide a consistent and universally understood system for transcribing the speech sounds of any language. *Abbr.:* IPA

In/terna/tional Style/, **1.** the general form of modern architecture developed in the 1920's and 1930's characterized by simple geometric forms, large untextured, often white, surfaces, large areas of glass, and general use of steel or reinforced concrete construction. **2.** a style of Gothic painting of the late 14th and early 15th centuries, characterized by elaborate, naturalistic detail and complex perspective effects.

in·terne (in/tûrn), *n.* intern². —**in/terne·ship/,** *n.*

in·ter·ne·cine (in/tər nē/sēn, -sīn, -nes/ēn, -īn), *adj.* **1.** mutually destructive. **2.** of or pertaining to conflict or struggle within a group: *an internecine feud among proxy holders.* **3.** characterized by great slaughter. Also, **in·ter·ne·cive** (in/ter nē/siv, -nes/iv). [< L *internecīn(us)* murderous = *internec(āre)* (to) kill out, exterminate (*inter-* INTER- + *necāre* to kill) + *-īnus* -INE¹]

in·tern·ee (in/tûr nē/), *n.* a person who is or has been interned, as a prisoner of war.

in·tern·ist (in/tûr nist, in tûr/nist), *n.* a physician who specializes in internal medicine, esp. as distinguished from a surgeon.

in·tern·ment (in tûrn/mənt), *n.* **1.** the act or an instance of interning. **2.** the state of being interned; confinement.

intern/ment camp/, a prison camp for the confinement of enemy aliens, prisoners of war, political prisoners, etc.

in·ter·node (in/tər nōd/), *n.* a part or space between two nodes, knots, or joints, as the portion of a plant stem between two nodes. [< L *internōd(ium)*] —**in/ter·nod/al,** *adj.*

in·ter nos (in/teʀ nōs/; *Eng.* in/tər nōs/), *Latin.* between ourselves.

in·ter·nun·cial (in/tər nun/shəl), *adj.* **1.** *Anat.* (of a nerve cell or a chain of nerve cells) linking the incoming and outgoing nerve fibers of the nervous system. **2.** of or pertaining to an internuncio.

in·ter·nun·ci·o (in/tər nun/shē ō/, -sē ō/), *n., pl.* **-ci·os.** a papal ambassador ranking next below a nuncio. [< It < L *internunti(us)*]

in·ter·o·cep·tive (in/tər ō sep/tiv), *adj. Physiol.* pertaining to interoceptors, the stimuli acting upon them, or the nerve impulses initiated by them.

in·ter·o·cep·tor (in/tər ō sep/tər), *n. Physiol.* a receptor responding to stimuli originating from within the body. [< NL *intero-* inside (comb. form of **interus,* parallel to L *exterus* outside) + *-ceptor,* comb. form of *captor;* see CAPTOR]

in·ter·oc·u·lar (in/tər ok/yə lər), *adj.* being, or situated, between the eyes.

in·ter·of·fice (in/tər ô/fis, -of/is), *adj.* functioning or communicating between the offices of a company or organization; within a company: *interoffice memo.*

in·ter·os·cu·late (in/tər os/kyə lāt/), *v.i.,* **-lat·ed, -lat·ing.** **1.** to interpenetrate; inosculate. **2.** to form a connecting link. —**in/ter·os/cu·la/tion,** *n.*

in·ter·pel·late (in/tər pel/āt, in tûr/pə lāt/), *v.t.,* **-lat·ed, -lat·ing.** to cause to undergo an interpellation. [< L *interpellāt(us)* interrupted (ptp. of *interpellāre*) = *inter-* INTER- + *-pellā-* speak + *-tus* ptp. suffix] —**in·ter·pel·la·tor** (in/tər pə lā/tər, in tûr/pə lā/-), **in·ter·pel·lant** (in/tər pel/ənt), *n.*

in·ter·pel·la·tion (in/tər pə lā/shən, in tûr/pə-), *n.* a procedure in some legislative bodies of asking a government official to explain an act or policy. [< L *interpellātiōn-* (s. of *interpellātiō*) interruption]

in·ter·pen·e·trate (in/tər pen/i trāt/), *v.,* **-trat·ed, -trat·ing.** —*v.t.* **1.** to penetrate thoroughly; permeate. **2.** to penetrate with (something else) mutually or reciprocally. —*v.i.* **3.** to penetrate between things or parts. **4.** to penetrate each other. —**in·ter·pen·e·tra·ble** (in/tər pen/i trə bəl), *adj.* —**in/ter·pen/e·trant,** *adj.* —**in/ter·pen/e·tra/tion,** *n.* —**in/ter·pen/e·tra/tive,** *adj.* —**in/ter·pen/e·tra/tive·ly,** *adv.*

in·ter·per·son·al (in/tər pûr/sə nəl), *adj.* **1.** existing or occurring between persons. **2.** of or pertaining to the relations between persons. —**in/ter·per/son·al·ly,** *adv.*

in·ter·phone (in/tər fōn/), *n.* an intercommunication system using telephones to connect offices, stations, etc., as in a building or ship. [formerly trademark]

in·ter·plan·e·tar·y (in/tər plan/i ter/ē), *adj.* being or occurring between planets or between a planet and the sun.

in·ter·play (*n.* in/tər plā/; *v.* in/tər plā/), *n.* **1.** reciprocal play, action, or influence. —*v.i.* **2.** to exert influence on each other.

in·ter·plead (in/tər plēd/), *v.i.,* **-plead·ed** or **-plead** or **-pled, -plead·ing.** *Law.* to litigate with each other in order to determine which of two parties is the rightful claimant against a third party. [INTER- + PLEAD; r. late ME *enterplede* < AF *enterpled(er)*]

in/ter·nu/cle·ar, *adj.* **in/ter·o·ce·an/ic,** *adj.* **in/ter·or/bi·tal,** *adj.;* **-ly,** *adv.* **in/ter·plait/,** *v.t.*

in·ter·plead·er[1] (in′tər plē′dər), *n.* *Law.* a judicial proceeding by which, when two parties make the same claim against a third party, the rightful claimant is determined. [var. of *enterpleder* < AF (inf. used as n.). See INTERPLEAD]

in·ter·plead·er[2] (in′tər plē′dər), *n.* *Law.* a party who interpleads. [INTERPLEAD + -ER[1]]

In·ter·pol (in′tər pōl′), *n.* an official international agency that coordinates the police activities of member nations. [*Inter*(*national Criminal*) *Pol*(*ice Organization*)]

in·ter·po·late (in tûr′pə lāt′), *v.*, **-lat·ed, -lat·ing.** —*v.t.* **1.** to alter (a text) by the insertion of new matter, esp. deceptively or without authorization. **2.** to insert (new or spurious matter) in this manner. **3.** to introduce (something additional or extraneous) between other things or parts; interject; interpose. **4.** *Math.* to insert, estimate, or find an intermediate term in (a sequence). —*v.i.* **5.** to make an interpolation. [< L *interpolāt*(*us*) furbished up, altered (ptp. of *interpolāre*) = *inter-* INTER- + *-polā-* furbish (akin to *polīre* to POLISH) + *-tus* ptp. suffix] —**in·ter′po·lat′er, in·ter′po·la′tor,** *n.* —**in·ter′po·la′tive,** *adj.*

in·ter·po·la·tion (in tûr′pə lā′shən), *n.* **1.** the act or process of interpolating. **2.** the state of being interpolated. **3.** something interpolated, as a passage introduced into a text. [< L *interpolātiōn-* (s. of *interpolātiō*)]

in·ter·pose (in′tər pōz′), *v.*, **-posed, -pos·ing.** —*v.t.* **1.** to place between; cause to intervene: *to interpose an opaque body between a light and the eye.* **2.** to bring (influence, action, etc.) to bear between parties, or on behalf of a party or person. **3.** to put in (a remark, question, etc.) in the midst of a conversation, discourse, or the like. —*v.i.* **4.** to come between other things; assume an intervening position or relation. **5.** to step in between parties at variance; mediate. **6.** to put in or make a remark by way of interruption. [< MF *interpose*(*r*)] —**in′ter·pos′a·ble,** *adj.* —**in′ter·pos′al,** *n.* —**in′ter·pos′er,** *n.* —**in′ter·pos′ing·ly,** *adv.* —**Syn. 1.** introduce. **3, 6.** interject. **5.** intervene, intercede.

in·ter·po·si·tion (in′tər pə zish′ən), *n.* **1.** the act or fact of interposing. **2.** the condition of being interposed. **3.** something interposed. **4.** *U.S.* the doctrine that an individual state may oppose any federal action that it believes encroaches on its sovereignty. [ME *interposicio*(*u*)*n* < L *interpositiōn-* (s. of *interpositiō*) = *interposit*(*us*) placed between (ptp. of *interpōnere*) + *-iōn-* -ION]

in·ter·pret (in tûr′prit), *v.t.* **1.** to set forth the meaning of; explain; explicate; elucidate: *to interpret a parable.* **2.** to construe, or understand in a particular way: *to interpret a reply as favorable.* **3.** to perform or render (a song, role in a play, etc.) according to one's understanding or sensitivity. **4.** to translate. **5.** *Computer Technol.* to translate (a stored program expressed in pseudo-code) into machine language and to perform the indicated operations as they are translated. —*v.i.* **6.** to translate what is said in a foreign language. **7.** to explain something. [ME *interprete*(*n*) < L *interpret*(*ārī*) = *interpret-* (s. of *interpres* explainer; see INTER-, PRICE) + *-ārī* inf. suffix] —**in·ter′pret·a·bil′i·ty, in·ter′pret·a·ble·ness,** *n.* —**in·ter′pret·a·ble,** *adj.* —**in·ter′pret·a·bly,** *adv.* —**in·ter′pret·er,** *n.* —**Syn. 1.** See **explain.**

in·ter·pre·ta·tion (in tûr′pri tā′shən), *n.* **1.** the act of interpreting; elucidation; explication. **2.** an elucidation or explanation, as of a creative work, political event, or the like. **3.** a conception of another's behavior: *a charitable interpretation of his tactlessness.* **4.** the rendering of music, a dramatic part, etc., so as to bring out the meaning, or to indicate one's particular conception of it. **5.** translation. [ME *interpretacio*(*u*)*n* < L *interpretātiōn-* (s. of *interpretātiō*)] —**in·ter′pre·ta′tion·al,** *adj.*

in·ter·pre·ta·tive (in tûr′pri tā′tiv), *adj.* **1.** serving to interpret; explanatory. **2.** deduced by interpretation. **3.** made because of interpretation: *an interpretative distortion of language.* **4.** of or pertaining to those arts that require an intermediary, such as a performer, for realization, as in music or theater. Also, **in·ter·pre·tive** (in tûr′pri tiv). [< L *interpretāt*(*us*) interpreted (ptp. of *interpretārī* to INTERPRET) + -IVE] —**in·ter′pre·ta′tive·ly, in·ter′pre·tive·ly,** *adv.*

inter′pretative dance′, a form of modern dance in which the dancer's movements explicitly or symbolically depict an emotion, a story, or an idea.

in·ter·ra·cial (in′tər rā′shəl), *adj.* **1.** involving members of different races. **2.** of, for, or among persons of different races: *interracial amity.*

in·ter·ra·di·al (in′tər rā′dē əl), *adj.* situated between the radii or rays: *the interradial petals in an echinoderm.* —**in′ter·ra′di·al·ly,** *adv.*

in·ter·reg·num (in′tər reg′nəm), *n., pl.* **-nums, -na** (-nə). **1.** an interval of time between the close of a sovereign's reign and the accession of his normal or legitimate successor. **2.** any period during which a state is without a permanent ruler. **3.** any pause or interruption in continuity. [< L; see INTER-, REIGN] —**in′ter·reg′nal,** *adj.*

in·ter·re·late (in′tər ri lāt′), *v.t., v.i.,* **-lat·ed, -lat·ing.** to bring or enter into reciprocal relation. [back formation from INTERRELATED]

in·ter·re·lat·ed (in′tər ri lā′tid), *adj.* reciprocally or mutually related: *an interrelated series of experiments.* —**in′ter·re·lat′ed·ly,** *adv.* —**in′ter·re·lat′ed·ness, in′ter·re·la′tion, in′ter·re·la′tion·ship′,** *n.*

in·ter·rex (in′tər reks′), *n., pl.* **in·ter·re·ges** (in′tər rē′jēz). a person who rules during an interregnum. [< L]

in·ter·ro·bang (in ter′ə bang′), *n.* a punctuation mark (‽) that is a combination of the question mark (?) and the exclamation point (!), indicating a mixture of query and interjection. Also, **in·ter′a·bang′.** [INTERRO(GATION) + BANG[1], printers' slang for an exclamation point]

interrog., **1.** interrogation. **2.** interrogative.

in·ter·ro·gate (in ter′ə gāt′), *v.t., v.i.,* **-gat·ed, -gat·ing.** to examine (a person) by questioning, esp. formally or officially: *to interrogate a suspect.* [late ME < L *interrogāt*(*us*) questioned, examined (ptp. of *interrogāre*). See INTER-, ROGATION] —**in·ter′ro·gat′ing·ly,** *adv.*

in·ter·ro·ga·tion (in ter′ə gā′shən), *n.* **1.** the act of interrogating; questioning. **2.** an instance of being interrogated: *He seemed shaken after his interrogation.* **3.** a question. **4.** a question mark. [ME *interrogacio*(*u*)*n* < L *interrogātiōn-* (s. of *interrogātiō*)] —**in·ter′ro·ga′tion·al,** *adj.*

interroga′tion point′. See **question mark** (def. 1). Also called **interroga′tion mark′.**

in·ter·rog·a·tive (in′tə rog′ə tiv), *adj.* **1.** of, pertaining to, or conveying a question. **2.** *Gram.* forming, constituting, or used in or to form a question. —*n.* **3.** *Gram.* an interrogative word, element, or construction, as *who?* and *what?* [< LL *interrogātīv*(*us*)] —**in′ter·rog′a·tive·ly,** *adv.*

in·ter·ro·ga·tor (in ter′ə gā′tər), *n.* **1.** a person who interrogates. **2.** *Radio.* a transmitter that emits a signal to trigger a transponder. [< LL]

in·ter·rog·a·to·ry (in′tə rog′ə tōr′ē, -tôr′ē), *adj., n., pl.* **-to·ries.** —*adj.* **1.** conveying a question; interrogative. —*n.* **2.** a question; inquiry. **3.** *Law.* a formal or written question. [< LL *interrogātōri*(*us*)] —**in·ter·rog·a·to·ri·ly** (in′tə rog′ə tōr′ə lē, -tôr′-, -rog′ə tōr′-, -tôr′-), *adv.*

in·ter·rupt (in′tə rupt′), *v.t.* **1.** to break off or cause to cease, as in the middle of something: *He interrupted his work to answer the bell.* **2.** to stop (a person) in the midst of doing or saying something, esp. by an interjected remark. —*v.i.* **3.** to interfere with action or speech, esp. by interjecting a remark: *Please don't interrupt.* [ME *interrupte*(*n*) < L *interrupt*(*us*) broken apart (ptp. of *interrumpere*). See INTER-, RUPTURE] —**in′ter·rupt′ed·ly,** *adv.* —**in′ter·rupt′ed·ness,** *n.* —**in′ter·rupt′i·ble,** *adj.* —**in′ter·rup′tive,** *adj.*
—**Syn. 1.** INTERRUPT, DISCONTINUE, SUSPEND imply breaking off something temporarily or permanently. INTERRUPT may have either meaning: *to interrupt a meeting.* TO DISCONTINUE is to stop or leave off, often permanently: *to discontinue a building program.* TO SUSPEND is to break off relations, operations, proceedings, privileges, etc., for a certain period of time, usually with the stipulation that they will be resumed at a stated time: *to suspend operations during a strike.* —**Ant. 1.** continue.

in·ter·rupt·er (in′tə rup′tər), *n.* **1.** a person or thing that interrupts. **2.** *Elect.* a device for interrupting or periodically opening and closing a circuit, as in a doorbell.

in·ter·rup·tion (in′tə rup′shən), *n.* **1.** the act or an instance of interrupting. **2.** the state of being interrupted. **3.** something that interrupts. **4.** cessation; intermission. [ME *interrupcio*(*u*)*n* < L *interruptiōn-* (s. of *interruptiō*)]

in·ter·scho·las·tic (in′tər skə las′tik), *adj.* between or among schools: *interscholastic athletics.*

in·ter se (in′teʀ se′; *Eng.* in′tər sē′), *Latin.* among themselves; between themselves.

in·ter·sect (in′tər sekt′), *v.t.* **1.** to cut or divide by passing through or across: *The highway intersects the town.* —*v.i.* **2.** to cross, as lines, wires, etc. **3.** *Geom.* to have one or more points in common: *intersecting lines.* [< L *intersect*(*us*) severed between (ptp. of *intersecāre*)]

in·ter·sec·tion (in′tər sek′shən, in′tər sek′-), *n.* **1.** a place where two or more roads meet, esp. when at least one is a major highway. **2.** any area or place of intersection. **3.** the act or fact of intersecting. **4.** *Math.* the set of elements which two or more sets have in common. *Symbol:* ∩ [< L *intersectiōn-* (s. of *intersectiō*)] —**in′ter·sec′tion·al,** *adj.*

in·ter·ses·sion (in′tər sesh′ən), *n.* a period between two academic terms or semesters.

in·ter·sex (in′tər seks′), *n.* *Biol.* an individual displaying sexual characteristics intermediate between male and female. [back formation from INTERSEXUAL]

in·ter·sex·u·al (in′tər sek′shōō əl), *adj.* **1.** existing between the sexes. **2.** *Biol.* pertaining to or having the characteristics of an intersex. —**in′ter·sex′u·al′i·ty, in′ter·sex′u·al·ism,** *n.* —**in′ter·sex′u·al·ly,** *adv.*

in·ter·space (*n.* in′tər spās′; *v.* in′tər spās′), *n., v.,* **-spaced, -spac·ing.** —*n.* **1.** an intervening space; interval. —*v.t.* **2.** to put a space between. **3.** to occupy or fill the space between. —**in·ter·spa·tial** (in′tər spā′shəl), *adj.* —**in′ter·spa′tial·ly,** *adv.*

in·ter·sperse (in′tər spûrs′), *v.t.,* **-spersed, -spers·ing.** **1.** to scatter here and there or place at intervals among other things: *to intersperse flowers among shrubs.* **2.** to diversify with something scattered or placed at intervals: *to intersperse the shrubs with flowers.* [< L *interspers*(*us*) strewn among (ptp. of **interspergere*) = *inter-* INTER- + *-spersus,* var. of *sparsus,* ptp. of *spargere* to scatter] —**in·ter·spers·ed·ly** (in′tər spûr′sid lē), *adv.* —**in·ter·sper·sion** (in′tər spûr′zhən *or, esp. Brit.,* -shən), **in′ter·sper′sal,** *n.*

in·ter·state (in′tər stāt′), *adj.* connecting or jointly involving states, esp. of the U.S.: *interstate commerce.*

In′terstate Com′merce Commis′sion, *U.S. Govt.* a board that supervises and regulates all carriers, except airplanes, engaged in interstate commerce. *Abbr.:* I.C.C., ICC

in·ter·stel·lar (in′tər stel′ər), *adj.* between or among the stars: *interstellar space.*

in·ter·stice (in tûr′stis), *n., pl.* **-stic·es** (-sti siz *or, often,* -sēz′). **1.** a small or narrow space or interval between things or parts: *The interstices between the slats of a fence.* **2.** an interval of time. [< LL *interstit*(*ium*) = *interstit-* (perf. s. of *intersistere* to stand or put between) + *-ium,* neut. of *-ius* -IOUS]

in·ter·sti·tial (in′tər stish′əl), *adj.* **1.** pertaining to, situated in, or forming interstices. **2.** *Anat.* situated between the cellular elements of a structure or part. [< LL *interstiti*(*um*) INTERSTICE + -AL[1]] —**in′ter·sti′tial·ly,** *adv.*

in·ter·sti′tial-cell′-stim′u·lat·ing hor′mone (in′tər stish′əl sel′stim′yə lā′ting), *Biochem.* See **ICSH.**

in·ter·strat·i·fy (in′tər strat′ə fī′), *v.,* **-fied, -fy·ing.** —*v.i.* **1.** to lie in interposed or alternate strata. —*v.t.* **2.** to interlay with or interpose between other strata. —**in′ter·strat′i·fi·ca′tion,** *n.*

in·ter·tex·ture (in′tər teks′chər), *n.* **1.** the act of interweaving. **2.** the condition of being interwoven. **3.** something formed by interweaving.

in·ter·tid·al (in′tər tīd′əl), *adj.* of or pertaining to the littoral region between low-water mark and high-water mark.

in·ter·trop·i·cal (in′tər trop′i kəl), *adj.* situated or occurring between the tropic of Cancer and the tropic of Capricorn.

in′ter·po′lar, *adj.*
in′ter·pro·fes′sion·al, *adj.*
in′ter·re′gion·al, *adj.*
in′ter·re·li′gious, *adj.*
in′ter·school′, *n.*
in′ter·si·de′re·al, *adj.*
in′ter·so·ci′e·tal, *adj.*
in′ter·tan′gle, *v.t.,* **-gled, -gling.**
in′ter·tan′gle·ment, *n.*
in′ter·ter′ri·to′ri·al, *adj.*
in′ter·trib′al, *adj.*

in·ter·twine (in′tər twīn′), *v.t., v.i.,* **-twined, -twin·ing.** to twine together. —**in′ter·twine′ment,** *n.* —**in′ter·twin′ing·ly,** *adv.*

In·ter·type (in′tər tīp′), *n. Trademark.* a typesetting machine similar to the Linotype.

in·ter·ur·ban (in′tər ûr′bən), *adj.* **1.** located in, of, or pertaining to two or more cities. —*n.* **2.** a train, bus, etc., or a transportation system operating between cities.

in·ter·val (in′tər vəl), *n.* **1.** an intervening period of time: *an interval of 50 years.* **2.** a space between things, points, limits, etc.; interspace: *an interval of 10 feet between posts.* **3.** *Brit.* an intermission, as between the acts of a play. **4.** *Math.* the totality of points on a line between two designated points or endpoints that may or may not be included. **5.** *Music.* the difference in pitch between two tones, as two sounded simultaneously (**harmonic interval**) or sounded successively (**melodic interval**). **6. at intervals,** at particular periods of time; now and then: *At intervals there were formal receptions at the governor's mansion.* [ME *intervall(e)* < L *intervall(um)* interval, lit., space between two palisades. See INTER-, WALL]

in·ter·vale (in′tər vāl′), *n. Chiefly New Eng.* a low-lying tract of land along a river. [var. of INTERVAL; by folk etym. taken as INTER- + VALE[1]]

in·ter·vene (in′tər vēn′), *v.i.,* **-vened, -ven·ing. 1.** to come between, as in action; intercede: *to intervene in a dispute.* **2.** to occur or be between two things. **3.** to occur between other events or periods: *Nothing interesting has intervened.* **4.** (of things) to occur incidentally so as to modify or hinder: *We enjoyed the picnic until a thunderstorm intervened.* **5.** to interfere, esp. with force or a threat of force: *to intervene in the affairs of another country.* **6.** *Law.* to interpose and become a party to a suit pending between other parties. [< L *interven(īre)* (to) come between = *inter-* INTER- + *venīre* to come] —**in′ter·ven′er, in′ter·ve′nor,** *n.* —**in′ter·ven′ient,** *adj.* —**Syn. 1.** interpose.

in·ter·ven·tion (in′tər ven′shən), *n.* **1.** the act or fact of intervening. **2.** interposition or interference of one state in the affairs of another: *intervention in the domestic policies of smaller nations.* [ME < LL *interventiōn-* (s. of *interventiō*) a coming between. See INTERVENE, -TION] —**in′ter·ven′tion·al,** *adj.*

in·ter·ven·tion·ist (in′tər ven′shə nist), *n.* **1.** a person who favors intervention, as in the affairs of another state. —*adj.* **2.** of or pertaining to intervention. —**in′ter·ven′tion·ism,** *n.*

in′terver′tebral disk′, *Anat.* the plate of fibrous cartilage between the bodies of adjacent vertebrae.

in·ter·view (in′tər vyōō′), *n.* **1.** a meeting for obtaining information by questioning a person or persons, as for a magazine article or a television broadcast. **2.** the report of such a meeting. **3.** a formal meeting in which a person or persons question, consult, or evaluate another or others: *to arrange a job interview.* —*v.t.* **4.** to have an interview with: *to interview the president.* [INTER- + VIEW; r. *enterview* < MF *entrevue,* n. use of fem. of *entrevu,* ptp. of *entrevoir* to glimpse] —**in′ter·view′er,** *n.*

in·ter vi·vos (in′tər vī′vōs), *Law.* (esp. of a gift or trust) taking effect during the lifetimes of the parties involved. [< L: lit., among (the) living]

in·ter·vo·cal·ic (in′tər vō kal′ik), *adj. Phonet.* (usually of a consonant) immediately following a vowel and preceding a vowel, as the *d* in *widow.* —**in′ter·vo·cal′i·cal·ly,** *adv.*

in·ter·volve (in′tər volv′), *v.t., v.i.,* **-volved, -volv·ing.** to roll, wind, or involve, one within another. [< L *inter-* INTER- + *volve(re)* (to) roll; see REVOLVE] —**in·ter·vo·lu·tion** (in′tər və lōō′shən), *n.*

in·ter·weave (*v.* in′tər wēv′; *n.* in′tər wēv′), *v.,* **-wove** or **-weaved; -wo·ven** or **-wove** or **-weaved; -weav·ing;** *n.* —*v.t.* **1.** to weave together, one with another, as threads or branches. **2.** to intermingle or combine as if by weaving: *to interweave truth with fiction.* —*v.i.* **3.** to become woven together, interlaced, or intermingled. —*n.* **4.** the act of interweaving. **5.** the fact of being interwoven; blend. —**in′ter·weav′er,** *n.*

in·ter·work (in′tər wûrk′), *v.,* **-worked** or **-wrought, -work·ing.** —*v.t.* **1.** to work or weave together; interweave. —*v.i.* **2.** to act upon each other; interact.

in·tes·ta·cy (in tes′tə sē), *n.* the state or fact of being intestate at death.

in·tes·tate (in tes′tāt, -tit), *adj.* **1.** (of a person) not having made a will: *He died intestate.* **2.** (of things) not disposed of by will: *His property remains intestate.* —*n.* **3.** a person who dies intestate. [ME < L *intestāt(us)*]

in·tes·ti·nal (in tes′tə nᵊl; *Brit.* in′tes tīn′ᵊl), *adj.* **1.** of or pertaining to the intestines. **2.** occurring, affecting, or found in the intestines. [< MF] —**in·tes′ti·nal·ly,** *adv.*

intes′tinal for′titude, *U.S.* resoluteness; guts.

in·tes·tine (in tes′tin), *n.* **1.** Usually, **intestines.** the lower part of the alimentary canal, extending from the pylorus to the anus. **2.** Also called **small intestine.** the narrow, longer part of the intestines, comprising the duodenum, jejunum, and ileum, that serves to digest and absorb nutrients. **3.** Also called **large intestine.** the broad, shorter part of the intestines, comprising the cecum, colon, and rectum, that absorbs water from and eliminates the residues of digestion. —*adj.* **4.** within a country; domestic; civil: *intestine strife.* [< L *intestīn(um),* n. use of neut. of *intestīnus* internal = *intes-* (var. of *intus* inside) + *-īnus* adj. suffix]

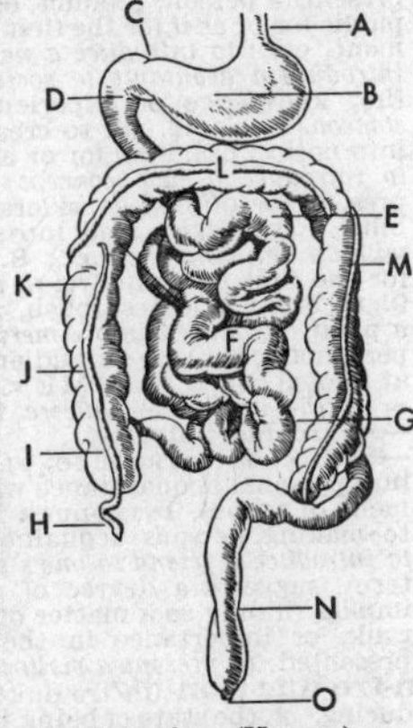

Intestines (Human)
A, End of esophagus; B, Stomach; C, Pylorus; D, Duodenum; E, Jejunum; F, Small intestine; G, Ileum; H, Vermiform appendix; I, Cecum; J, Large intestine; K, Ascending colon; L, Transverse colon; M, Descending colon; N, Rectum; O, Anus

in·thral (in thrôl′), *v.t.,* **-thralled, -thral·ling.** enthrall. —**in·thral′ment,** *n.*

in·thrall (in thrôl′), *v.t.* enthrall. —**in·thrall′ment,** *n.*

in·throne (in thrōn′), *v.t.,* **-throned, -thron·ing.** enthrone.

in·ti·ma (in′tə mə), *n., pl.* **-mae** (-mē′). *Anat.* the innermost membrane or lining of some organ or part, esp. that of an artery, vein, or lymphatic. [< NL, n. use of fem. of L *intimus,* var. of *intumus* inmost = *intu(s)* within + *-mus* superl. suffix] —**in′ti·mal,** *adj.*

in·ti·ma·cy (in′tə mə sē), *n., pl.* **-cies. 1.** the state of being intimate. **2.** a close, familiar, and usually affectionate or loving, personal relationship. **3.** a detailed knowledge or deep understanding of a place, subject, period of history, etc.: *His intimacy with Japan makes him a likely choice as ambassador.* **4.** an act or expression serving as a token of familiarity, affection, or the like: *The teacher allowed his pupils the intimacy of calling him by his first name.* **5.** a sexually familiar act; a sexual liberty. **6.** privacy, esp. an atmosphere of privacy suitable to the telling of a secret: *He refused to tell it to me except in the intimacy of his room.* [INTIMA(TE)[1] + -CY]

in·ti·mate[1] (in′tə mit), *adj.* **1.** associated in close personal relations: *an intimate friend.* **2.** characterized by or involving warm friendship or a personally close or familiar association or feeling: *an intimate gathering.* **3.** private; closely personal: *one's intimate affairs.* **4.** characterized by or suggesting privacy or intimacy; cozy: *an intimate little café.* **5.** engaged in sexual relations. **6.** (of an association, knowledge, understanding, etc.) arising from close personal connection or familiar experience. **7.** detailed; deep: *a more intimate analysis.* **8.** inmost; deep within. **9.** of, pertaining to, or characteristic of the inmost or essential nature; intrinsic: *the intimate structure of an organism.* —*n.* **10.** an intimate friend or associate, esp. a confidant. [< L *intim(us)* a close friend (n. use of adj., var. of *intumus* inmost = *intu(s)* within + *-mus* superl. suffix) + -ATE[1]] —**in′ti·mate·ly,** *adv.* —**in′ti·mate·ness,** *n.* —**Syn. 1.** dear. See **familiar. 3.** privy, secret. **7.** thorough. **10.** crony.

in·ti·mate[2] (in′tə māt′), *v.t.,* **-mat·ed, -mat·ing. 1.** to make known indirectly; suggest. **2.** *Archaic.* to make known, esp. formally; announce. [< LL *intimāt(us)* made known (ptp. of *intimāre*) = *intim(us)* inmost (see INTIMATE[1]) + *-ātus* -ATE[1]] —**in′ti·mat′er,** *n.* —**in′ti·ma′tion,** *n.* —**Syn. 1.** See **hint.**

in·time (aN tēm′), *adj. French.* intimate; cozy: *intime conversation; an* intime *little restaurant.*

in·tim·i·date (in tim′i dāt′), *v.t.,* **-dat·ed, -dat·ing. 1.** to make timid; inspire with fear. **2.** to overawe or cow, esp. with a forceful personality or superior display of fluency, fame, wealth, etc. **3.** to force into or deter from some action by inducing fear. [< ML *intimidāt(us)* made afraid (ptp. of *intimidāre*)] —**in·tim′i·da′tion,** *n.* —**in·tim′i·da′tor,** *n.* —**Syn. 1.** frighten, daunt. —**Ant. 1.** calm.

in·tinc·tion (in tiŋk′shən), *n.* (in a communion service) the act of steeping the bread or wafer in the wine in order to offer them conjointly. [< LL *intinctiōn-* (s. of *intinctiō*) a dipping in = *intinct(us)* (see IN-[2], TINT) + *-iōn-* -ION]

in·ti·tle (in tīt′ᵊl), *v.t.,* **-tled, -tling.** entitle.

in·tit·ule (in tit′yōōl), *v.t.,* **-uled, -ul·ing.** *Archaic.* to give a title to; entitle. [< LL *intitul(āre)* (see IN-[2], TITLE); r. late ME *entitule* < MF *entitul(er)*] —**in·tit′u·la′tion,** *n.*

in·to (in′tōō; *unstressed* in′tŏŏ, -tə), *prep.* **1.** to the inside of; in toward: *He walked into the room.* **2.** toward or in the direction of: *going into town; veered into the wind.* **3.** to a point of contact with; against: *backed into a parked car.* **4.** (used to indicate insertion or immersion in): *plugged into the socket.* **5.** (used to indicate entry, inclusion, or introduction in a place or condition): *received into the church; voted into membership.* **6.** to the state, condition, or form assumed or brought about: *went into shock; lapsed into disrepair; translated into another language.* **7.** to the occupation, action, possession, circumstance, or acceptance of: *went into banking; coerced into complying.* **8.** (used to indicate a continuing extent in time or space): *lasted into the night; a line of men far into the distance.* **9.** (used to indicate the division of one number by another number): *2 into 20 equals 10.* [ME, OE]

in·tol·er·a·ble (in tol′ər ə bəl), *adj.* **1.** not tolerable; unendurable; insufferable: *intolerable agony.* **2.** excessive or extreme. [ME < L *intolerābil(is)*] —**in·tol′er·a·bil′i·ty, in·tol′er·a·ble·ness,** *n.* —**in·tol′er·a·bly,** *adv.* —**Syn. 1.** unbearable. —**Ant. 1.** endurable.

in·tol·er·ance (in tol′ər əns), *n.* **1.** lack of toleration; unwillingness or inability to tolerate contrary opinions or beliefs, persons of different races or backgrounds, etc. **2.** incapacity or indisposition to bear or endure: *intolerance of heat.* **3.** sensitivity or allergy to a food, drug, etc. [< L *intolerantia.* See INTOLERANT, -ANCE]

in·tol·er·ant (in tol′ər ənt), *adj.* **1.** not tolerating beliefs, opinions, usages, manners, etc., different from one's own, as in political or religious matters; bigoted. **2.** unable or indisposed to tolerate or endure (usually fol. by *of*): *intolerant of excesses.* [< L *intolerant-* (s. of *intolerāns*) impatient] —**in·tol′er·ant·ly,** *adv.*

—**Syn. 1.** illiberal, narrow, prejudiced. INTOLERANT, BIGOTED, FANATICAL refer to strongly illiberal attitudes. INTOLERANT refers to an active refusal to allow others to be different from oneself or to have or put into practice beliefs different from one's own: *intolerant in politics; intolerant of other customs.* BIGOTED is to be so emotionally or subjectively attached to one's own belief as to be unthinkingly hostile to all others: *a bigoted person.* FANATICAL applies to unreasonable or extreme action in maintaining one's beliefs

in′ter·u′ni·ver′si·ty, *adj.* **in′ter·var′si·ty,** *adj.* **in′ter·ver′te·bral,** *adj.* **in′ter·wrought′,** *adj.*

and practices without necessary reference to others: *a fanatical religious sect.* **—Ant. 1.** liberal.

in·tomb (in to͞om′), *v.t.* entomb. **—in·tomb′ment,** *n.*

in·to·nate (in′tō nāt′, -tə-), *v.t.*, **-nat·ed, -nat·ing. 1.** to utter with a particular tone or modulation of voice. **2.** to intone; chant. [< ML *intonāt(us)* intoned, ptp. of *intonāre*]

in·to·na·tion (in′tō nā′shən, -tə-), *n.* **1.** the pattern or melody of pitch changes in connected speech, esp. the pitch pattern of a sentence. **2.** the act or manner of intonating. **3.** the manner of producing musical tones, specifically the relation in pitch of tones to their key or harmony. **4.** that which is intoned or chanted. **5.** the opening phrase in a Gregorian chant. [< ML *intonātiōn-* (s. of *intonātiō*)] **—in′to·na′tion·al,** *adj.*

in·tone (in tōn′), *v.*, **-toned, -ton·ing.** **—***v.t.* **1.** to utter with a particular tone or voice modulation. **2.** to give tone or variety of tone to; vocalize. **3.** to utter in a singing voice (the first tones of a section in a liturgical service). **4.** to recite or chant in monotone. **—***v.i.* **5.** to speak or recite in a singing voice, esp. in monotone; chant. **6.** *Music.* to produce a tone or a particular series of tones, as a scale, esp. with the voice. [< ML *inton(āre)*; r. late ME *entone* < MF *enton(er)*] **—in·to′ner,** *n.*

in·tor·sion (in tôr′shən), *n.* a twisting or winding about an axis or fixed point, as of the stem of a plant. [m. LL *intortiōn-* (s. of *intortiō*)]

in·tort (in tôrt′), *v.t.* to twist inward about an axis or fixed point; curl; wind: *intorted horns.* [< L *intort(us)* turned or twisted in, var. ptp. of *intorquēre*]

in to·to (in tō′tō), *Latin.* in all; in the whole; wholly.

in·town (in′toun′, in toun′), *adj.* being in the central or metropolitan area of a city: *an intown motel.*

in·tox·i·cant (in tok′sə kənt), *adj.* **1.** intoxicating or exhilarating. **—***n.* **2.** an intoxicating agent, as alcoholic liquor or certain drugs. [< ML *intoxicant-* (s. of *intoxicāns*) poisoning, prp. of *intoxicāre*]

in·tox·i·cate (*v.* in tok′sə kāt′; *adj.* in tok′sə kit, -kāt′), *v.*, **-cat·ed, -cat·ing,** *adj.* **—***v.t.* **1.** to affect temporarily with diminished control over the physical and mental powers, by means of alcoholic liquor, a drug, or other substance, esp. to stupefy or excite with liquor. **2.** to make enthusiastic; exhilarate: *The prospect of success intoxicates me.* **3.** *Pathol.* to poison. **—***v.i.* **4.** to cause or produce intoxication. **—***adj.* **5.** *Archaic.* intoxicated. [< ML *intoxicāt(us)* poisoned, ptp. of *intoxicāre*] **—in·tox·i·ca·ble** (in tok′sə kə bəl), *adj.* **—in·tox′i·cat′ed·ly,** *adv.* **—in·tox′i·cat′ing·ly,** *adv.*

in·tox·i·ca·tion (in tok′sə kā′shən), *n.* **1.** drunkenness. **2.** the act or an instance of intoxicating. **3.** overpowering excitement. [< ML *intoxicātiōn-* (s. of *intoxicātiō*) a poisoning]

intr., intransitive.

intra-, a learned borrowing from Latin meaning "within," used in the formation of compound words: *intramural.* Cf. **intro-.** [< LL, repr. L *intrā* (adv. and prep.); akin to INTERIOR, INTER-]

in·tra·cel·lu·lar (in′trə sel′yə lər), *adj.* within a cell or cells. **—in′tra·cel′lu·lar·ly,** *adv.*

In′tra·coast′al Wa′terway (in′trə kō′stəl, in′-), a mostly inland water route, extending 1550 mi. along the Atlantic coast from Boston to Florida Bay and 1116 mi. along the Gulf coast from Carrabelle, Florida to Brownsville, Texas.

in·trac·ta·ble (in trak′tə bəl), *adj.* **1.** not docile; stubborn; obstinate. **2.** (of things) hard to shape or work with. **3.** resisting treatment or cure: *an intractable malady.* [< L *intractābil(is)*] **—in·trac′ta·bil′i·ty, in·trac′ta·ble·ness,** *n.* **—in·trac′ta·bly,** *adv.* **—Syn. 1.** headstrong, obdurate, willful. **1, 2.** fractious, unyielding. **—Ant. 1.** amiable.

in·tra·cu·ta·ne·ous (in′trə kyo͞o tā′nē əs), *adj.* *Anat.* intradermal. **—in′tra·cu·ta′ne·ous·ly,** *adv.*

in·tra·der·mal (in′trə dûr′məl), *adj.* *Anat.* **1.** within the skin. **2.** going or done between the layers of the skin, as an injection. Also, **in′tra·der′mic.** [INTRA- + DERM(A) + -AL[1]] **—in′tra·der′mal·ly, in′tra·der′mi·cal·ly,** *adv.*

in·tra·dos (in′trə dos′, -dōs′, in trā′dos, -dōs), *n.*, *pl.* **-dos** (-dōz′, -dōz), **-doses.** *Archit.* the interior curve or surface of an arch or vault. Cf. **extrados.** [< F = *intra-* INTRA- + *dos* back; see DOSSER]

in·tra·mo·lec·u·lar (in′trə mə lek′yə lər, -mō-), *adj.* existing or occurring within the molecule or molecules.

in·tra·mu·ral (in′trə myo͝or′əl), *adj.* **1.** involving representatives of a single school: *intramural athletics.* **2.** within the walls, boundaries, or enclosing units, as of an institution. Cf. **extramural. 3.** *Anat.* situated or occurring within the substance of a wall, as of an organ.

in·tra·mus·cu·lar (in′trə mus′kyə lər), *adj.* located or occurring within a muscle. **—in′tra·mus′cu·lar·ly,** *adv.*

intrans., intransitive.

in·tran·si·gent (in tran′si jənt), *adj.* **1.** uncompromising or inflexible; irreconcilable. **—***n.* **2.** an intransigent person. Also, **in·tran′si·geant.** [< Sp *intransigent(e)* = *in-* IN-[3] + *transigente* compromising (prp. of *transigir*) < L *transigent-* (s. of *transigēns*, prp. of *transigere* to come to an agreement); see TRANSACT] **—in·tran′si·gence, in·tran′si·gen·cy, in·tran′si·geance, in·tran′si·gean·cy,** *n.* **—in·tran′si·gent·ly, in·tran′si·geant·ly,** *adv.*

in·tran·si·tive (in tran′si tiv), *adj.* **1.** noting or having the quality of an intransitive verb. **—***n.* **2.** See **intransitive verb.** [< L *intransitīv(us)*] **—in·tran′si·tive·ly,** *adv.* **—in·tran′si·tive·ness,** *n.*

intran′sitive verb′, a verb that indicates a complete action without being accompanied by a direct object, as *sit, lie,* etc., and, in English, that does not form a passive.

in·tra·pre·neur (in′trə prə nûr′, -no͝or′), *n.* an employee of a large corporation who is allowed to create new products, services, etc., without adhering to the usual company policies. [INTRA- + (ENTRE)PRENEUR] **—in′tra·pre·neur′ship,** *n.*

in·tra·state (in′trə stāt′), *adj.* existing or occurring within a state, esp. one of the states of the U.S.: *intrastate commerce.*

in·tra·tel·lu·ric (in′trə tə lo͝or′ik), *adj.* **1.** *Geol.* located in, taking place in, or resulting from action beneath the lithosphere. **2.** *Petrog.* noting or pertaining to crystallization of an eruptive rock previous to its extrusion on the surface.

in·tra·u·ter·ine (in′trə yo͞o′tər in, -tə rīn′), *adj.* located or occurring within the uterus.

intrau′terine device′. See **IUD.**

in·tra·ve·nous (in′trə vē′nəs), *adj.* **1.** within a vein or the veins. **2.** of, pertaining to, employed in, or administered by an injection into the vein: *intravenous feeding.* **—in·tra·ve′nous·ly,** *adv.*

in′trave′nous drip′, *Med.* drip (def. 9).

in·tra vi·res (in′trə vī′rēz), *Law.* within the legal power or authority of an individual or corporation (opposed to *ultra vires*). [< L: within the powers]

in·tra·vi·tal (in′trə vīt′əl), *adj.* *Biol.* occurring during life.

in·tra vi·tam (in′trə vī′tam), *Biol.* during life: *the staining of tissues intra vitam.* [< L]

in·treat (in trēt′), *v.t., v.i.* *Archaic.* entreat.

in·trench (in trench′), *v.t., v.i.* entrench. **—in·trench′er,** *n.* **—in·trench′ment,** *n.*

intrench′ing tool′, a small, collapsible spade used by a soldier in the field for digging foxholes and the like. Also, **entrenching tool.**

in·trep·id (in trep′id), *adj.* fearless or dauntless: *an intrepid explorer.* [< L *intrepid(us)* = *in-* IN-[3] + *trepidus* anxious] **—in′tre·pid′i·ty, in·trep′id·ness,** *n.* **—in·trep′id·ly,** *adv.* **—Syn.** brave, courageous, bold. **—Ant.** timid.

Int. Rev., Internal Revenue.

in·tri·ca·cy (in′trə kə sē), *n.*, *pl.* **-cies** for 2. **1.** intricate character or state. **2.** an intricate part, action, etc.

in·tri·cate (in′trə kit), *adj.* **1.** entangled or involved; having many interrelated parts or facets. **2.** complicated; hard to understand. [< L *intrīcāt(us)* entangled (ptp. of *intrīcāre*) = *in-* IN-[2] + *trīc(ae)* perplexities + *-ātus* -ATE[1]] **—in′tri·cate·ly,** *adv.* **—in′tri·cate·ness,** *n.*

in·tri·gant (in′trə gənt; *Fr.* aN trē gäN′), *n.*, *pl.* **-gants** (-gənts; *Fr.* -gäN′). a person who engages in intrigue or intrigues. Also, **in′tri·guant.** [< F < It *intrigante*, prp. of *intrigare* to INTRIGUE]

in·tri·gante (in′trə gant′, -gänt′; *Fr.* aN trē gäNt′), *n.*, *pl.* **-gantes** (-gants′, -gänts′; *Fr.* -gäNt′). a female intrigant. Also, **in′tri·guante′.** [< F; fem. of INTRIGANT]

in·trigue (*v.* in trēg′; *n.* in trēg′, in′trēg), *v.*, **-trigued, -tri·guing,** *n.* **—***v.t.* **1.** to arouse the curiosity or interest of by unusual, unique, new, or otherwise fascinating qualities. **2.** to accomplish or force by crafty plotting or underhand machinations. **3.** *Rare.* to puzzle; cause to ponder. **4.** *Obs.* to entangle. **5.** *Obs.* to trick or cheat. **6.** *Obs.* to plot for. **—***v.i.* **7.** to plot craftily or use underhand machinations. **8.** to carry on a clandestine or illicit love affair. **—***n.* **9.** the use of underhand machinations or deceitful stratagems. **10.** such a machination or stratagem or a series of them: *political intrigues.* **11.** a clandestine or illicit love affair. **12.** the series of complications forming the plot of a play. [< F *intrigue(r)* < It *intrigare* < L *intrīcāre* to entangle; see INTRICATE] **—in·tri′guer,** *n.* **—in·tri′guing·ly,** *adv.* **—Syn. 1.** interest, attract, fascinate.

in·trin·sic (in trin′sik, -zik), *adj.* **1.** belonging to a thing by its very nature: *intrinsic merit.* **2.** *Anat.* (of certain muscles, nerves, etc.) belonging to or lying within a given part. Also, **in·trin′si·cal.** [< ML *intrinsec(us)* inward (adj.), L (adv.) = *intrin-* (*int(e)r-*, as in *interior* + *-in* locative suffix) + *secus* beside, akin to *sequī* to follow] **—in·trin′si·cal·ly,** *adv.* **—Syn. 1.** innate, natural, true. **—Ant. 1.** extrinsic.

in·tro (in′trō), *n.*, *pl.* **-tros.** *U.S. Informal.* an introduction. [shortened form of INTRODUCTION]

intro-, a prefix, meaning "inwardly," "within," occurring in loan words from Latin (*introspection*); occasionally used in the formation of new words (*introversion*). Cf. **intra-.** [< L, repr. *intrō* (adv.) inwardly, within]

intro., **1.** introduction. **2.** introductory. Also, **introd.**

in·tro·duce (in′trə do͞os′, -dyo͞os′), *v.t.*, **-duced, -duc·ing. 1.** to present (a person or persons) to another or others so as to make acquainted. **2.** to make (two or more persons) acquainted with one another: *Will you introduce us?* **3.** to present (a person, product, etc.) to a group or to the general public for or as if for the first time by a formal act, announcement, etc.: *to introduce a new soap product to the public; to introduce a debutante to society.* **4.** to bring (a person) to first knowledge or experience of something: *to introduce someone to skiing.* **5.** to create, propose, advance, or bring into notice, use, etc., for or as if for the first time; institute: *to introduce a new concept in architectural design.* **6.** to present for official consideration or action, as a legislative bill. **7.** to begin; lead into; preface: *to introduce a speech with an amusing anecdote.* **8.** to put or place into something for the first time; insert: *to introduce a figure into a design.* **9.** to bring in or establish, as something foreign or alien: *a plant introduced into America.* **10.** to present (a speaker, performer, etc.) to an audience. **11.** to present (a person) at a royal court. [late ME < L *intrōdūce(re)* (to) lead inside = *intrō-* INTRO- + *dūcere* to lead] **—in′tro·duc′er,** *n.* **—in′tro·duc′i·ble,** *adj.*

—Syn. 1, 2. INTRODUCE, PRESENT mean to bring persons into personal acquaintance with each other, as by announcement of names. INTRODUCE is the ordinary term, referring to making persons acquainted who are ostensibly equals: *to introduce a friend to one's sister.* PRESENT, a more formal term, suggests a degree of ceremony in the process, and implies (if only as a matter of compliment) superior dignity, rank, or importance in the person to whom another is presented: *to present a visitor to the president.*

in·tro·duc·tion (in′trə duk′shən), *n.* **1.** the act of introducing. **2.** the state of being introduced. **3.** a formal presentation of one person to another or others. **4.** something introduced. **5.** a preliminary part, as of a book or musical composition, leading up to the main part. **6.** an elementary treatise: *an introduction to botany.* **7.** the act or an instance of inserting. [ME *introduccion* < L *intrōductiōn-* (s. of *intrōductiō*)]

—Syn. 5. INTRODUCTION, FOREWORD, PREFACE refer to material given at the front of a book to explain or introduce it to the reader. An INTRODUCTION is a formal preliminary statement or guide to the book: *His purpose is stated in the introduction.* A FOREWORD is often an informal statement made to the reader. It is the same as PREFACE, but FOREWORD is the native term.

in·tro·duc·to·ry (in′trə duk′tə rē), *adj.* serving to introduce; prefatory. Also, **in′tro·duc′tive.** [ME < LL *intrōductōri(us)* = L *intrōduct(us)* led inside (ptp. of *introducere*)

+ -ōrius -ORY[1]] —**in′tro·duc′to·ri·ly,** *adv.* —**in′tro·duc′to·ri·ness,** *n.* —**Syn.** See **preliminary.**

in·tro·it (in′trō it, -troit), *n.* **1.** *Rom. Cath. Ch.* a part of a psalm with antiphon recited at the beginning of the Mass by the priest. **2.** *Anglican Ch., Lutheran Ch.* a psalm or anthem sung as the celebrant of the Holy Communion enters the sanctuary. **3.** a choral response sung at the beginning of a religious service. [< eccl. L *introit(us)*, L: entrance, beginning = *introit-* (ptp. s. of *introīre* to go in) + *-us* n. suffix (4th decl.)]

in·tro·mit (in′trə mit′), *v.t.*, **-mit·ted, -mit·ting.** to send, put, or let in; introduce; admit. [ME *intromitte(n)* < L *intrōmitt(ere)* (to) send in = *intrō-* INTRO- + *mittere* to send] —**in·tro·mis·si·bil·i·ty** (in′trə mis′ə bil′i tē), *n.* —**in′tro·mis′si·ble,** *adj.* —**in·tro·mis·sion** (in′trə mish′ən), *n.* —**in′tro·mis′sive,** *adj.* —**in′tro·mit′tent,** *adj.* —**in′tro·mit′ter,** *n.*

in·trorse (in trôrs′), *adj.* *Bot.* turned or facing inward, as anthers that open toward the gynoecium. [< L *introrsus*, contr. of *intrōversus* toward the inside. See INTRO-, VERSUS] —**in·trorse′ly,** *adv.*

in·tro·spect (in′trə spekt′), *v.i.* **1.** to practice introspection; consider one's own internal state or feelings. —*v.t.* **2.** to look into or examine (one's own mind, feelings, etc.). [back formation from INTROSPECTION] —**in′tro·spec′tive,** *adj.* —**in′tro·spec′tive·ly,** *adv.* —**in′tro·spec′tive·ness,** *n.*

in·tro·spec·tion (in′trə spek′shən), *n.* **1.** the observation or examination of one's own mental and emotional state, mental processes, etc. **2.** the quality, tendency, or disposition to do this. [< L *intrōspect(us)* looked within (ptp. of *intrōspicere* = *intrō-* INTRO- + *-spicere*, var. of *specere* to look) + -ION] —**in′tro·spec′tion·al,** *adj.* —**in′tro·spec′tion·ist,** *n., adj.*

in·tro·ver·sion (in′trə vûr′zhən, -shən, in′trə vûr′-), *n.* *Psychol.* the direction of interest inward, as in preoccupation with one's own thoughts and feelings. Cf. **extraversion.** [< NL *intrōversiōn-* (s. of *intrōversiō*)] —**in·tro·ver·sive** (in′trə vûr′siv), **in·tro·ver·tive** (in′trə vûr′tiv), *adj.*

in·tro·vert (*n., adj.* in′trə vûrt′; *v.* in′trə vûrt′), *n.* **1.** *Psychol.* a person characterized by concern primarily with his own thoughts and feelings. **2.** *Informal.* a shy person. **3.** *Zool.* a part that is or can be introverted. —*adj.* **4.** *Psychol.* marked by introversion. —*v.t.* **5.** to turn inward: *to introvert one's anger.* **6.** *Psychol.* to direct (the mind, one's interest, etc.) inward or to things within the self. **7.** *Zool.* to insheathe a part of within another part; invaginate. [INTRO- + (IN)VERT]

in·trude (in tro͞od′), *v.*, **-trud·ed, -trud·ing.** —*v.t.* **1.** to thrust or bring in without reason, permission, or welcome. **2.** *Geol.* to thrust or force in. —*v.i.* **3.** to thrust oneself without invitation or welcome: *to intrude upon his privacy.* [< L *intrūde(re)* (to) push in = *in-* IN-[2] + *trūdere* to push] —**in·trud′er,** *n.* —**in·trud′ing·ly,** *adv.* —**Syn. 3.** interfere, interlope. See **trespass.**

in·tru·sion (in tro͞o′zhən), *n.* **1.** the act or an instance of intruding. **2.** the state of being intruded. **3.** *Law.* an illegal act of entering, seizing, or taking possession of another's property. **4.** *Geol.* **a.** the forcing of extraneous matter, as molten rock, into some other formation. **b.** the matter forced in. [ME < ML (legal) *intrūsiōn-* (s. of *intrūsiō*) = L *intrūs(us)* pushed in (ptp. of *intrūdere* to INTRUDE) + *-iōn-* -ION] —**in·tru′sion·al,** *adj.*

in·tru·sive (in tro͞o′siv), *adj.* **1.** intruding; thrusting in. **2.** characterized by or involving intrusion. **3.** tending or apt to intrude. **4.** *Geol.* **a.** (of rocks) having been forced between preexisting rocks or rock layers while in a molten or plastic condition. **b.** noting or pertaining to plutonic rocks. **5.** *Phonet.* excrescent (def. 2). [late ME; see INTRUSION, -IVE] —**in·tru′sive·ly,** *adv.* —**in·tru′sive·ness,** *n.* —**Syn. 3.** annoying, interfering, distracting.

in·trust (in trust′), *v.t.* entrust.

in·tu·bate (in′to͞o bāt′, -tyo͞o-), *v.t.*, **-bat·ed, -bat·ing.** *Med.* **1.** to insert a tube into (the larynx or the like). **2.** to treat by inserting a tube, as into the larynx. —**in′tu·ba′tion,** *n.*

in·tu·it (in to͞o′it, -tyo͞o′-; in′to͞o it, -tyo͞o-), *v.t., v.i.* to know or understand by intuition. [back formation from INTUITION] —**in·tu′it·a·ble,** *adj.*

in·tu·i·tion (in′to͞o ish′ən, -tyo͞o-), *n.* **1.** direct perception of truth, fact, etc., independent of any reasoning process; immediate apprehension. **2.** a fact, a truth, knowledge, etc., perceived in this way. **3.** a keen and quick insight. **4.** the quality or ability of having such direct perception or quick insight. [< LL *intuitiōn-* (s. of *intuitiō*) contemplation = L *intuit(us)* gazed at, contemplated (ptp. of *intuērī*) + *-iōn-* -ION] —**in′tu·i′tion·al,** *adj.* —**in′tu·i′tion·al·ly,** *adv.*

in·tu·i·tion·ism (in′to͞o ish′ə niz′əm, -tyo͞o-), *n.* **1.** *Ethics.* the doctrine that moral values and duties can be discerned directly. **2.** *Metaphys.* **a.** the doctrine that in perception external objects are given immediately, without the intervention of a representative idea. **b.** the doctrine that knowledge rests upon axiomatic truths discerned directly. Also, **in′tu·i′tion·al·ism.** —**in′tu·i′tion·ist, in′tu·i′tion·al·ist,** *n., adj.*

in·tu·i·tive (in to͞o′i tiv, -tyo͞o′-), *adj.* **1.** perceiving by intuition. **2.** perceived by, resulting from, or involving intuition: *intuitive knowledge.* **3.** having or possessing intuition: *an intuitive person.* **4.** capable of being perceived or known by intuition. [< ML *intuitīv(us)*. See INTUITION, -IVE] —**in·tu′i·tive·ly,** *adv.* —**in·tu′i·tive·ness,** *n.*

in·tu·mesce (in′to͝o mes′, -tyo͝o-), *v.i.*, **-mesced, -mesc·ing.** **1.** to swell up, as with heat; become tumid. **2.** to bubble up. [< L *intumesce(re)* (to) swell up = *in-* IN-[2] + *tumescere* = *tum(ēre)* (to) swell + *-escere* -ESCE]

in·tu·mes·cence (in′to͝o mes′əns, -tyo͝o-), *n.* **1.** a swelling up, as with congestion. **2.** the state of being swollen. **3.** a swollen mass. [< F; see INTUMESCE, -ENCE] —**in′tu·mes′cent,** *adj.*

in·tus·sus·cept (in′təs sə sept′), *v.t.* to take within, as one part of the intestine into an adjacent part; invaginate. [back formation from INTUSSUSCEPTION] —**in′tus·sus·cep′tive,** *adj.*

in·tus·sus·cep·tion (in′təs sə sep′shən), *n.* **1.** a taking within. **2.** *Biol.* growth of a cell wall by the deposition of new particles among the existing particles of the wall. Cf. **apposition** (def. 4). **3.** Also called **invagination.** *Pathol.* the slipping of one part within another, as of the intestine. [< L *intus* within + *susceptiōn-* (s. of *susceptiō*) an undertaking = *suscept(us)* taken up (ptp. of *suscipere;* see SUSCEPTIBLE) + *-iōn-* -ION]

in·twine (in twīn′), *v.t., v.i.*, **-twined, -twin·ing.** entwine.

in·twist (in twist′), *v.t.* entwist.

In·u·it (in′o͞o it, -yo͞o-), *n., pl.* **-its,** (*esp. collectively*) **-it** for 1. **1.** a member of the Eskimo peoples inhabiting northernmost North America from northern Alaska to eastern Canada and Greenland. **2.** the language of the Inuit. [< Inuit: people, pl. of *inuk* person]

in·u·lin (in′yə lin), *n.* *Chem.* a polysaccharide, $(C_6H_{10}O_5)_n$, used chiefly as an ingredient in diabetic bread and in testing kidney function. [< NL *Inul(a)* a genus of plants (L: elecampane) + -IN[2]]

in·unc·tion (in ungk′shən), *n.* **1.** the act of anointing. **2.** *Pharm.* an unguent. [late ME < L *inunctiōn-* (s. of *inunctiō*) = *inunct(us)* anointed (ptp. of *inungere*) + *-iōn-* -ION]

in·un·dant (in un′dənt), *adj.* *Literary.* flooding or overflowing. [< L *inundant-* (s. of *inundāns*) overflowing, prp. of *inundāre;* see INUNDATE]

in·un·date (in′ən dāt′, -un-, in un′dāt), *v.t.*, **-dat·ed, -dat·ing.** **1.** to flood; overspread with water; overflow. **2.** to overspread, as in or with a flood; deluge; overwhelm: *inundated with letters of protest.* [< L *inundāt(us)* flooded, inundated (ptp. of *inundāre*) = *in-* IN-[2] + *und(a)* wave + *-ātus* -ATE[1]] —**in′un·da′tion,** *n.* —**in′un·da′tor,** *n.* —**in·un·da·to·ry** (in un′də tôr′ē, -tōr′ē), *adj.* —**Syn. 2.** glut.

in·ur·bane (in′ûr bān′), *adj.* not urbane; lacking in courtesy, refinement, etc. —**in·ur·ban·i·ty** (in′ûr ban′i tē), *n.* —**in′ur·bane′ly,** *adv.*

in·ure (in yo͝or′, i no͝or′), *v.*, **-ured, -ur·ing.** —*v.t.* **1.** to toughen or harden by use; accustom; habituate (usually fol. by *to*): *to inure a person to hardship.* —*v.i.* **2.** to come into use; take or have effect. **3.** to become beneficial or advantageous. Also, **enure.** [v. use of phrase *in ure* < AF *en ure* in use, at work = *en* in + *ure* < L *opera*, pl. of *opus* work; r. late ME *enure* < AF *en ure*] —**in·ure′ment,** *n.*

in·urn (in ûrn′), *v.t.* **1.** to put into a funeral urn. **2.** to bury; inter. —**in·urn′ment,** *n.*

in·u·tile (in yo͞o′til), *adj.* useless; of no use or service. [late ME < L *inūtil(is)*] —**in·u′tile·ly,** *adv.*

in·u·til·i·ty (in′yo͞o til′i tē), *n., pl.* **-ties.** **1.** uselessness. **2.** a useless thing or person. [< L *inūtilitās*]

inv., **1.** invented. **2.** invention. **3.** inventor. **4.** invoice.

in va·cu·o (in wä′ko͝o ō′; *Eng.* in vak′yo͞o ō′), *Latin.* **1.** in a vacuum. **2.** in isolation.

in·vade (in vād′), *v.*, **-vad·ed, -vad·ing.** —*v.t.* **1.** to enter forcefully as an enemy, esp. an enemy army: *Germany invaded Czechoslovakia.* **2.** to enter like an enemy: *Locusts invaded the fields.* **3.** to enter as if to take possession: *to invade a neighbor's home.* **4.** to enter and affect injuriously or destructively, as disease: *viruses that invade the blood stream.* **5.** to intrude upon: *to invade one's privacy.* **6.** to encroach or infringe upon: *to invade one's rights.* **7.** to penetrate; spread into or over: *city dwellers invading the suburbs.* —*v.i.* **8.** to make an invasion. [< L *invāde(re)* = *in-* IN-[2] + *vādere* to go; see WADE] —**in·vad′a·ble,** *adj.* —**in·vad′er,** *n.* —**Syn. 1, 2.** penetrate, attack.

in·vag·i·nate (*v.* in vaj′ə nāt′; *adj.* in vaj′ə nit, -nāt′), *v.*, **-nat·ed, -nat·ing,** *adj.* —*v.t.* **1.** to insert or receive, as into a sheath; sheathe. **2.** to fold or draw (a tubular organ) back within itself; introvert. —*v.i.* **3.** to become invaginated; undergo invagination. **4.** to form a pocket by turning in. —*adj.* **5.** folded or turned back upon itself. **6.** sheathed. [< ML *invāgināt(us)* sheathed in, ptp. of *invāgināre*]

in·vag·i·na·tion (in vaj′ə nā′shən), *n.* **1.** the act or process of invaginating. **2.** *Embryol.* the inward movement of a portion of the wall of a blastula in the formation of a gastrula. **3.** *Pathol.* intussusception (def. 3).

in·va·lid[1] (in′və lid *or, esp. Brit.,* in′və lēd′), *n.* **1.** an infirm or sickly person, esp. one who is too sick, weak, or old to care for himself. —*adj.* **2.** unable to care for oneself due to sickness, age, or a disability: *his invalid sister.* **3.** of or for invalids: *invalid diets.* —*v.t.* **4.** to affect with disease; make an invalid: *He was invalided for life.* **5.** *Chiefly Brit.* to remove (military personnel) from active duty because of injury or illness. [< L *invalid(us)* weak. See IN-[3], VALID]

in·val·id[2] (in val′id), *adj.* **1.** not valid; without force or foundation; indefensible. **2.** deficient in substance or cogency; weak. **3.** void or without legal force, as a contract. [< ML *invalid(us)* not legally valid. See IN-[3], VALID] —**in·val′id·ly,** *adv.* —**in·val′id·ness,** *n.*

in·val·i·date (in val′i dāt′), *v.t.*, **-dat·ed, -dat·ing.** **1.** to render invalid. **2.** to deprive of legal force or efficacy. —**in·val′i·da′tion,** *n.* —**in·val′i·da′tor,** *n.*

in·va·lid·ism (in′və li diz′əm), *n.* prolonged ill health.

in·va·lid·i·ty[1] (in′və lid′i tē), *n.* lack of validity. [< ML *invaliditās*. See INVALID[2], -ITY]

in·va·lid·i·ty[2] (in′və lid′i tē), *n.* invalidism. [INVALID[1] + -ITY]

in·val·u·a·ble (in val′yo͞o ə bəl), *adj.* beyond calculable or appraisable value; of inestimable worth; priceless. [IN-[3] + VALUABLE capable of valuation (obs. sense)] —**in·val′u·a·ble·ness,** *n.* —**in·val′u·a·bly,** *adv.* —**Syn.** precious.

in·var·i·a·ble (in vâr′ē ə bəl), *adj.* **1.** not variable or capable of being varied; static. —*n.* **2.** that which is invariable; a constant. [late ME] —**in·var′i·a·bil′i·ty, in·var′i·a·ble·ness,** *n.* —**in·var′i·a·bly,** *adv.* —**Syn. 1.** unalterable, unchanging, changeless, unvarying, uniform.

in·var·i·ant (in vâr′ē ənt), *adj.* **1.** invariable. —*n.* **2.** *Math.* a quantity or expression that is constant throughout a certain range of conditions.

in·va·sion (in vā′zhən), *n.* **1.** the act or an instance of invading or entering as an enemy, esp. by an army. **2.** the entrance or advent of anything troublesome or harmful, as disease. **3.** infringement by intrusion: *invasion of privacy.* [< LL *invāsiōn-* (s. of *invāsiō*) = *invās(us)* invaded (ptp. of *invādere* to INVADE) + *-iōn-* -ION]

in·va·sive (in vā′siv), *adj.* **1.** characterized by or involving invasion; offensive. **2.** invading, or tending to invade; intrusive. [late ME < ML *invāsīv(us).* See INVASION, -IVE]

in·vect·ed (in vek′tid), *adj. Heraldry.* **1.** noting an edge of a charge, as an ordinary, consisting of a series of small convex curves. **2.** (of a charge, as an ordinary) having such an edge: *a chevron invected.* [< L *invect(us)* driven into (see INVECTIVE) + -ED[2]]

in·vec·tive (in vek′tiv), *n.* **1.** vehement denunciation, censure, or abuse; vituperation. **2.** an insulting or abusive word or expression. —*adj.* **3.** vituperative or denunciatory; censoriously abusive. [< LL *invectīv(us)* abusive = L *invect(us)* driven into, attacked (ptp. of *invehī* to INVEIGH) + *-īvus* -IVE] —**in·vec′tive·ly,** *adv.* —**in·vec′tive·ness,** *n.* —**Syn. 1.** See **abuse.**

in·veigh (in vā′), *v.i.* to protest strongly or attack vehemently with words; rail (usually fol. by *against*): *to inveigh against isolationism.* [ME *inveh* < L *inveh(ī)* (to) burst into, attack = *in-* IN-[2] + *vehī* to sail, ride, drive] —**in·veigh′er,** *n.*

in·vei·gle (in vē′gəl, -vā′gəl), *v.t.,* **-gled, -gling. 1.** to entice, lure, or ensnare by artful talk or inducements (usually fol. by *into*): *to inveigle a person into playing bridge.* **2.** to acquire, win, or obtain by such talk or inducements (usually fol. by *from* or *away*). [var. of *envegle* < AF *enveogl(er)* = *en-* EN-[1] + OF *(a)vogler* to blind < *avogle* blind < ML *abocul(us)* eyeless, adj. use of phrase *ab oculīs,* lit., from eyes; see AB-, OCULAR] —**in·vei′gle·ment,** *n.* —**in·vei′gler,** *n.* —**Syn. 1.** induce, beguile, persuade. **2.** enmesh.

in·vent (in vent′), *v.t.* **1.** to originate as a product of one's own device or contrivance: *to invent a machine.* **2.** to produce or create with the imagination: *to invent a story.* **3.** to make up or fabricate (something fictitious or false): *to invent excuses.* **4.** *Obs.* to come upon; find. [late ME *invente* < L *invent(us)* found (ptp. of *invenīre*) = *in-* IN-[2] + *ven-* come + *-tus* ptp. suffix] —**in·vent′i·ble, in·vent′a·ble,** *adj.* —**Syn. 1.** devise, contrive. See **discover. 3.** concoct.

in·ven·tion (in ven′shən), *n.* **1.** the act of inventing. **2.** *U.S. Patent Laws.* a new, useful process, machine, improvement, etc., that did not exist previously, and that is not obvious to persons artfully skilled in the field. **3.** anything invented or devised. **4.** the exercise of imaginative or creative power in literature, art, or music. **5.** the power or faculty of inventing, devising, or originating. **6.** something fabricated, as a false statement. **7.** *Music.* a short piece, contrapuntal in nature, generally based on one subject. **8.** *Rhet.* (traditionally) one of the five steps in speech preparation, the process of choosing ideas appropriate to the subject, audience, and occasion. **9.** *Archaic.* the act of finding. [ME *invencio(u)n* < L *inventiōn-* (s. of *inventiō*) a finding out] —**in·ven′tion·al,** *adj.* —**in·ven′tion·less,** *adj.*

in·ven·tive (in ven′tiv), *adj.* **1.** apt at inventing, devising, or contriving. **2.** having the function of inventing. **3.** pertaining to, involving, or showing invention. [INVENT + -IVE; r. late ME *inventif* < MF] —**in·ven′tive·ly,** *adv.* —**in·ven′tive·ness,** *n.*

in·ven·tor (in ven′tər), *n.* a person who invents, esp. one who devises some new process, appliance, machine, article, or improvement. [< L]

in·ven·to·ry (in′vən tôr′ē, -tōr′ē), *n., pl.* **-to·ries,** *v.,* **-to·ried, -to·ry·ing.** —*n.* **1.** a detailed, often descriptive, list of articles, giving the code number, quantity, and value of each; catalog. **2.** a formal list of the property of a person or estate. **3.** a complete listing of merchandise or stock on hand, raw materials, etc., made each year by a business concern. **4.** the objects or items represented on such a list, as a merchant's stock of goods. **5.** their aggregate value. **6.** a catalog of natural resources. **7.** a tally of one's personality traits, aptitudes, skills, etc., for use in counseling and guidance. **8.** the act of making a catalog or detailed listing. —*v.t.* **9.** to make an inventory of; enter in an inventory; catalog. **10.** to summarize: *a book that inventories the progress in chemistry.* —*v.i.* **11.** to have value as shown by an inventory: *stock that inventories at two million dollars.* [< ML *inventōri(um)* (see INVENT, -ORY[2]); r. LL *inventārium* = L *invent(us)* found + *-ārium* -ARY] —**in′ven·to′ri·a·ble,** *adj.* —**in′ven·to′ri·al,** *adj.* —**in′ven·to′ri·al·ly,** *adv.* —**Syn. 1.** roster, record, register, account. See **list**[1].

in·ve·rac·i·ty (in′və ras′i tē), *n., pl.* **-ties** for 2. **1.** untruthfulness or mendacity. **2.** an untruth; falsehood.

In·ver·car·gill (in′vər kär′gil), *n.* a city on S South Island, in New Zealand. 42,500 (est. 1964).

In·ver·ness (in′vər nes′), *n.* **1.** Also called **In·ver·ness-shire** (in′vər nes′shēr, -shər). a county in NW Scotland. 84,425 (1961); 4211 sq. mi. **2.** its county seat: a seaport. 30,266 (est. 1964). **3.** (*often l.c.*) an overcoat with a long, removable cape (**Inverness′ cape′**).

in·verse (in vûrs′, in′vûrs), *adj.* **1.** reversed in position, direction, or tendency: *inverse order.* **2.** *Math.* (of a proportion) containing terms of which an increase in one results in a decrease in another. A term is said to be in inverse proportion to another term if it increases (or decreases) as the other decreases (or increases). **3.** inverted; turned upside down. —*n.* **4.** an inverted state or condition. **5.** that which is inverse; the direct opposite. **6.** *Math.* See **inverse function.** [< L *invers(us),* lit., turned in, i.e., inside out or upside down, ptp. of *invertere.* See IN-[2], VERSUS]

in′verse feed′back, *Electronics.* See under **feedback** (def. 1).

in′verse func′tion, *Math.* the function that replaces another function when the dependent and independent variables of the first function are interchanged for an appropriate set of values of the dependent variable. In $y = \sin x$ and $x = \text{arc sin} y$, the inverse function of *sin* is *arc sine.*

in·verse·ly (in vûrs′lē), *adv.* **1.** in an inverse manner. **2.** *Math.* in inverse proportion.

in·ver·sion (in vûr′zhən, -shən), *n.* **1.** the act or an instance of inverting. **2.** the state of being inverted. **3.** anything that is inverted. **4.** *Rhet.* reversal of the usual or natural order of words; anastrophe. **5.** *Gram.* any change from a basic word order or syntactic sequence, as in the placement of a subject after an auxiliary verb in a question. **6.** *Anat.* the turning inward of a part, as the foot. **7.** *Chem.* **a.** a hydrolysis of certain carbohydrates, as cane sugar, which results in a reversal of direction of the rotatory power of the solution. **b.** a reaction in which a starting material of one optical configuration forms a product of the opposite configuration. **8.** *Music.* **a.** the process, or result, of transposing the tones of an interval or chord so that the original bass becomes an upper voice. **b.** (in counterpoint) the transposition of the upper voice part below the lower, and vice versa. **c.** presentation of a melody in contrary motion to its original form. **9.** *Psychiatry.* assumption of the sexual role of the opposite sex; homosexuality. **10.** *Phonet.* retroflexion (def. 3). **11.** *Meteorol.* a reversal in the normal temperature lapse rate, the temperature rising with increased elevation instead of falling. **12.** *Electricity.* a converting of direct current into alternating current. **13.** *Math.* the operation of forming the inverse of a point, curve, function, etc. [< L *inversiōn-* (s. of *inversiō*) a turning in] —**in·ver′sive,** *adj.*

in·vert (*v.* in vûrt′; *adj., n.* in′vûrt), *v.t.* **1.** to turn upside down. **2.** to reverse in position, direction, or relationship. **3.** to turn or change to the opposite or contrary, as in nature, bearing, or effect: *to invert a process.* **4.** to turn inward or back upon itself. **5.** to turn inside out. **6.** *Chem.* to subject to inversion. **7.** *Music.* to subject to musical inversion. **8.** *Phonet.* to articulate as a retroflex vowel. —*v.i.* **9.** *Chem.* to become inverted. —*adj.* **10.** *Chem.* subjected to inversion. —*n.* **11.** a person or thing that is inverted. **12.** *Psychiatry.* a homosexual. [< L *invert(ere)* (to) turn the wrong way round = *in-* IN-[2] + *vertere* to turn] —**in·vert′er,** *n.* —**in·vert′i·bil′i·ty,** *n.* —**in·vert′i·ble,** *adj.* —**Syn. 2.** See **reverse.**

in·vert·ase (in vûr′tās), *n. Biochem.* an enzyme, occurring in yeast and in the digestive juices of animals, that causes the inversion of cane sugar into invert sugar. Also called **sucrase.**

in·ver·te·brate (in vûr′tə brit, -brāt′), *adj.* **1.** *Zool.* **a.** not vertebrate; without a backbone. **b.** of or pertaining to creatures without a backbone. **2.** without strength of character. —*n.* **3.** an invertebrate animal. **4.** a person who lacks strength of character. [< NL *invertebrāt(us)*] —**in·ver·te·bra·cy** (in vûr′tə brə sē), **in·ver′te·brate·ness,** *n.*

invert′ed com′ma, *Brit.* See **quotation mark.** Also called **turned comma.**

in·ver·tor (in vûr′tər), *n. Elect.* a converter. [< NL]

in′vert sug′ar, a mixture of the dextrorotatory forms of glucose and fructose.

in·vest (in vest′), *v.t.* **1.** to put (money) to use, by purchase or expenditure, in something offering profitable returns, esp. interest or income. **2.** to spend: *to invest large sums in books.* **3.** to use, give, or devote (time, talent, etc.), as to achieve something: *He invested a lot of time in trying to help retarded children.* **4.** to furnish with power, authority, rank, etc. **5.** to settle or secure a power, right, etc., in the possession of; vest: *Feudalism invested the lords with absolute authority over their vassals.* **6.** to endow with a quality or characteristic: *to invest one's gestures with elegance.* **7.** to infuse or belong to, as a quality or characteristic does: *Goodness invests his every action.* **8.** to provide with the insignia of office. **9.** to install in an office or position. **10.** to clothe; attire; dress. **11.** to cover, surround, or envelop, as if with a garment, or like a garment: *Spring invests the trees with leaves.* **12.** to surround (a place) with military forces or works so as to prevent approach or escape; besiege. —*v.i.* **13.** to invest money. **14.** to make an investment. [late ME < ML *invest(īre)* (to) install, invest (money), surround, clothe in, L: to clothe in = *in-* IN-[2] + *vestīre* to clothe < *vest(is)* garment; see VEST] —**in·vest′a·ble, in·vest′i·ble,** *adj.* —**in·ves′tor,** *n.*

in·ves·ti·gate (in ves′tə gāt′), *v.,* **-gat·ed, -gat·ing.** —*v.t.* **1.** to search or inquire into systematically; search or examine into the particulars of; examine in detail. **2.** to examine the particulars of in an attempt to learn the facts about something hidden, unique, or complex, esp. in search of a motive, cause, or culprit: *to investigate a murder.* —*v.i.* **3.** to make inquiry, examination, or investigation. [< L *investīgāt(us)* tracked down, esp. with dogs, ptp. of *investīgāre.* See IN-[2], VESTIGE, -ATE[1]] —**in·ves·ti·ga·ble** (in ves′tə gə bəl), *adj.* —**in·ves′ti·ga′tive, in·ves·ti·ga·to·ry** (in ves′tə gə tôr′ē, -tōr′ē), *adj.* —**in·ves′ti·ga′tor,** *n.*

in·ves·ti·ga·tion (in ves′tə gā′shən), *n.* **1.** the act or process of investigating. **2.** the condition of being investigated. **3.** a searching inquiry for ascertaining facts. [ME *investigacio(u)n* < L *investīgātiōn-* (s. of *investīgātiō*)] —**in·ves′ti·ga′tion·al,** *adj.*

—**Syn. 1, 2.** scrutiny, exploration. INVESTIGATION, EXAMINATION, INQUIRY, RESEARCH express the idea of an active effort to find out something. An INVESTIGATION is a systematic, minute, and thorough attempt to learn the facts about something complex or hidden; it is often formal and official: *an investigation of a bank failure.* An EXAMINATION is an orderly attempt to obtain information about or to make a test of something, often something presented for observation: *a physical examination.* An INQUIRY is an investigation made by asking questions rather than by inspection or by study of available evidence: *an inquiry into a proposed bond issue.* RESEARCH is careful and sustained investigation, usually into a subject covering a wide range or into remote recesses of knowledge: *chemical research.*

in·ves·ti·tive (in ves′ti tiv), *adj.* **1.** of, pertaining to, or empowered to invest authority, rank, etc.: *an investitive act.* **2.** of or pertaining to investiture. [< ML *investīt(us)* (see INVESTITURE) + -IVE]

in·ves·ti·ture (in ves′ti chər), *n.* **1.** the act or process of investing, as with an office or position. **2.** the state of being invested, as with a garment, quality, etc. **3.** something that covers or adorns. **4.** (in feudal or ecclesiastical law) the formal bestowal of a possessory or prescriptive right, as a fief or benefice. **5.** *Archaic.* investment of money. [ME < ML *investītūra* = *investīt(us)* installed (ptp. of *investīre;* see INVEST) + *-ūra* -URE]

in·vest·ment (in vest′mənt), *n.* **1.** the investing of money or capital for profitable returns. **2.** a particular instance or mode of investing money. **3.** money or capital invested. **4.** a property or right in which a person invests. **5.** a devoting, using, or giving of time, talent, emotional energy, etc., as to achieve something. **6.** *Biol.* any covering, coating, outer layer, or integument. **7.** the act or fact of investing, as with a garment. **8.** the state of being invested, as with a garment. **9.** the act of investing with a quality, attribute, etc. **10.** investiture with an office, dignity, or right. **11.** *Mil.* a siege or encirclement. **12.** *Archaic.* a garment or vestment.

invest′ment bank′, a financial institution that deals chiefly in the underwriting and selling of security issues. —**invest′ment bank′er.** —**invest′ment bank′ing.**

invest′ment com′pany, a company that invests its funds in other companies and issues its own securities against these investments.

in·vet·er·ate (in vet′ər it), *adj.* **1.** confirmed in a habit, practice, feeling, or the like: *an inveterate gambler.* **2.** firmly established by long continuance, as a disease; chronic. [ME < L *inveterāt(us)* grown old, deep-rooted (ptp. of *inveterāre*) = *in-* IN-[2] + *veter-* (s. of *vetus*) old + *-ātus* -ATE[1]] —**in·vet·er·a·cy** (in vet′ər ə sē), *n.* —**in·vet′er·ate·ly,** *adv.* —**Syn. 1.** hardened. **2.** set, fixed, rooted.

in·vid·i·ous (in vid′ē əs), *adj.* **1.** causing or tending to cause animosity, resentment, or envious dislike: *an invidious honor.* **2.** offensively or unfairly discriminating; harmful; injurious: *invidious comparisons.* **3.** *Obs.* envious. [< L *invidiōs(us)* envious, envied, hateful = *invidi(a)* ENVY + *-ōsus* -OUS] —**in·vid′i·ous·ly,** *adv.* —**in·vid′i·ous·ness,** *n.*

in·vig·i·late (in vij′ə lāt′), *v.i.,* **-lat·ed, -lat·ing. 1.** *Brit.* to keep watch over students at an examination. **2.** *Obs.* to keep watch. [< L *invigilāt(us)* watched over (ptp. of *invigilāre*) = *in-* IN-[2] + *vigilā-* (s. of *vigilāre* to watch; see VIGIL) + *-tus* ptp. suffix] —**in·vig′i·la′tion,** *n.* —**in·vig′i·la′tor,** *n.*

in·vig·or·ate (in vig′ə rāt′), *v.t.,* **-at·ed, -at·ing.** to give vigor to; fill with life and energy: *to invigorate the body.* [IN-[2] + *vigorate;* see VIGOR, -ATE[1]] —**in·vig′or·at′ing·ly,** *adv.* —**in·vig′or·a′tion,** *n.* —**in·vig′or·a′tive,** *adj.* —**in·vig′or·a′tive·ly,** *adv.* —**in·vig′or·a′tor,** *n.* —**Syn.** vitalize, energize.

in·vin·ci·ble (in vin′sə bəl), *adj.* **1.** incapable of being conquered, defeated, or subdued: *an invincible opponent.* **2.** insuperable or insurmountable: *invincible difficulties.* [ME < LL *invincibil(is)*] —**in·vin′ci·bil′i·ty, in·vin′ci·ble·ness,** *n.* —**in·vin′ci·bly,** *adv.*
—**Syn. 1.** unyielding. INVINCIBLE, IMPREGNABLE suggest that which cannot be overcome or mastered. INVINCIBLE is applied to that which cannot be conquered in combat or war, or overcome or subdued in any manner: *an invincible army; invincible courage.* IMPREGNABLE is applied to a place or position that cannot be taken by assault or siege, and hence to whatever is proof against attack: *an impregnable fortress; impregnable honesty.* —**Ant. 1.** conquerable.

Invin′cible Arma′da, Armada (def. 1).

in vi·no ve·ri·tas (in wē′nō we′ri täs′; *Eng.* in vī′nō ver′i tas′, vē′nō), *Latin.* in wine there is truth.

in·vi·o·la·ble (in vī′ə lə bəl), *adj.* **1.** prohibiting violation; secure from destruction, violence, infringement, or desecration: *an inviolable sanctuary.* **2.** incapable of being violated; incorruptible; unassailable. [< L *inviolābil(is)*] —**in·vi′o·la·bil′i·ty, in·vi′o·la·ble·ness,** *n.* —**in·vi′o·la·bly,** *adv.*

in·vi·o·late (in vī′ə lit, -lāt′), *adj.* **1.** free from violation, injury, desecration, or outrage. **2.** undisturbed or untouched. **3.** unbroken: *that promise which remains inviolate.* **4.** not infringed. [< L *inviolāt(us)* unhurt, inviolable] —**in·vi·o·la·cy** (in vī′ə lə sē), **in·vi′o·late·ness,** *n.* —**in·vi′o·late·ly,** *adv.*

in·vis·i·ble (in viz′ə bəl), *adj.* **1.** not visible; imperceptible to the eye. **2.** not in sight; hidden: *an invisible seam.* **3.** not perceptible or discernible by the mind: *invisible differences.* **4.** of or pertaining to services, tourist travel or spendings, etc., not normally recorded in foreign-trade statistics: *invisible exports.* —*n.* **5.** an invisible thing or being. [ME < L *invīsibil(is)*] —**in·vis′i·bil′i·ty, in·vis′i·ble·ness,** *n.* —**in·vis′i·bly,** *adv.*

invis′ible ink′, a fluid for producing writing that is invisible until brought out by heat, chemicals, etc.; sympathetic ink.

in·vi·ta·tion (in′vi tā′shən), *n.* **1.** the act of inviting. **2.** the written or spoken form with which a person is invited. **3.** an attraction or incentive; allurement. [< L *invītātiōn-* (s. of *invītātiō*) = *invītāt(us)* invited (ptp. of *invītāre*) + *-iōn-* -ION] —**in′vi·ta′tion·al,** *adj.*

in·vi·ta·to·ry (in vī′tə tōr′ē, -tôr′ē), *adj.* serving to invite; conveying an invitation. [ME < LL *invītātōri(us)*]

in·vite (*v.* in vīt′; *n.* in′vīt), *v.,* **-vit·ed, -vit·ing,** *n.* —*v.t.* **1.** to ask or request the presence or participation of in a kindly, courteous, or complimentary way: *to invite friends to dinner.* **2.** to request politely or formally: *to invite donations.* **3.** to act so as to bring on or render probable: *to invite danger by fast driving.* **4.** to attract, allure, entice, or tempt. —*v.i.* **5.** to give invitation; offer attractions or allurements. —*n.* **6.** *Chiefly Dial.* an invitation. [< L *invīt(āre)* = *in-* IN-[2] + root *vī-* strive, hasten + *-t-* formative suffix + *-āre* inf. ending] —**in·vit′er,** *n.* —**Syn. 1.** bid. See **call. 2.** solicit. **4.** lure.

in·vit·ing (in vī′ting), *adj.* offering an invitation, esp. one of an attractive or tempting nature: *an inviting offer.* —**in·vit′ing·ly,** *adv.* —**in·vit′ing·ness,** *n.*

in vi·tro (in vē′trō), *Biol.* within an artificial environment, as a test tube: *the cultivation of tissues in vitro.* Cf. **in vivo.** [< L: lit., in glass]

in vi·vo (in vē′vō), *Biol.* within a living organism: *the cultivation of tissues in vivo.* Cf. **in vitro.** [< L: in something alive]

in·vo·cate (in′və kāt′), *v.t.,* **-cat·ed, -cat·ing.** *Archaic.* invoke. [< L *invocāt(us)* called upon (ptp. of *invocāre*) = *in-* IN-[2] + *vocā-* (s. of *vocāre* to call) + *-tus* ptp. suffix] —**in·voc·a·tive** (in vok′ə tiv, in′və kā′tiv), *adj.* —**in′vo·ca′tor,** *n.*

in·vo·ca·tion (in′və kā′shən), *n.* **1.** the act of invoking or calling upon a deity, spirit, etc., for aid, protection, inspiration, or the like; supplication. **2.** any petitioning or supplication. **3.** a form of prayer invoking God's presence, said esp. at the beginning of a public ceremony. **4.** an entreaty for aid and guidance, as from a Muse, at the beginning of an epic poem. **5.** an incantation. **6.** the act of appealing to something, as a concept, for support and justification in a particular circumstance. **7.** the enforcing or use of a legal or moral precept or right. [ME *invocacio(u)n* < L *invocātiōn-* (s. of *invocātiō*)] —**in′vo·ca′tion·al,** *adj.* —**in·voc·a·to·ry** (in vok′ə tōr′ē, -tôr′ē), *adj.*

in·voice (in′vois), *n., v.,* **-voiced, -voic·ing.** —*n.* **1.** a detailed list of goods sold or services provided, together with the charges and terms. —*v.t.* **2.** to present an invoice to. **3.** to present an invoice for. [var. of *invoyes,* pl. of obs. *invoy,* r. *envoy* < MF: message; see ENVOY[2]]

in·voke (in vōk′), *v.t.,* **-voked, -vok·ing. 1.** to call for with earnest desire; make supplication or pray for: *to invoke God's mercy.* **2.** to call on (a deity, Muse, etc.), as in prayer or supplication. **3.** to declare to be binding or in effect: *to invoke a veto.* **4.** to appeal to, as for confirmation. **5.** to petition for help or aid. **6.** to call forth or upon (a spirit) by incantation. **7.** to cause, call forth, or bring about. [late ME < L *invoc(āre)* = *in-* IN-[2] + *vocāre* to call, akin to *vox* VOICE] —**in·vo′ca·ble,** *adj.* —**in·vok′er,** *n.*

in·vo·lu·cel (in vol′yə sel′), *n.* *Bot.* a secondary involucre, as in a compound cluster of flowers. [< NL *involūcel-l(um);* dim. of INVOLUCRUM] —**in·vol·u·cel·ate** (in vol′yə sel′it), **in·vol·u·cel·at·ed** (in vol′yə sel′ā tid), *adj.*

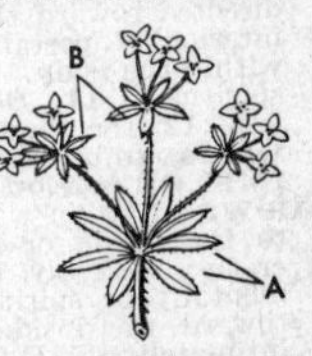

A, Involucre
B, Involucel

in·vo·lu·crate (in′və lo͞o′krit, -krāt), *adj.* having an involucre.

in·vo·lu·cre (in′və lo͞o′kər), *n.* **1.** *Bot.* a collection or rosette of bracts subtending a flower cluster, umbel, or the like. **2.** a covering, esp. a membranous one. [< MF < L; see INVOLUCRUM] —**in′vo·lu′cral,** *adj.*

in·vo·lu·crum (in′və lo͞o′krəm), *n., pl.* **-cra** (-krə). involucre. [< NL, L: a wrap, cover = *involū-* (ptp. s. of *involvere* to wrap, cover; see INVOLUTE) + *-crum* n. suffix]

in·vol·un·tar·y (in vol′ən ter′ē), *adj.* **1.** not voluntary; done or occurring without choice or against one's will. **2.** unintentional or unconscious: *an involuntary gesture.* **3.** *Physiol.* acting independently of, done, or occurring without volition: *involuntary muscles.* [< LL *involuntāri(us)*] —**in·vol·un·tar·i·ly** (in vol′ən ter′ə lē, -vol′ən târ′-), *adv.* —**in·vol·un·tar·i·ness** (in vol′ən ter′ē nis, -vol′ən târ′-), *n.* —**Syn. 1, 3.** See **automatic. 2.** instinctive. **3.** reflex, uncontrolled. —**Ant. 2.** intentional.

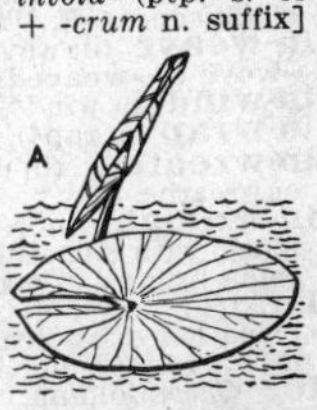

A, Involute leaves of white lotus, *Nymphaea lotus;* B, Transverse section

in·vo·lute (*adj., n.* in′və lo͞ot′; *v.* in′və lo͞ot′, in′və lo͞ot′), *adj., n., v.,* **-lut·ed, -lut·ing.** —*adj.* **1.** involved or intricate; complex. **2.** curled or curved inward or spirally. **3.** *Bot.* rolled inward from the edge, as a leaf. **4.** *Zool.* (of shells) having the whorls closely wound. —*n.* **5.** *Geom.* any curve of which a given curve is the evolute. —*v.i.* **6.** to roll or curl up; become involute. **7.** to return to a normal shape, size, or state. [< L *involūt(us)* rolled in or up (ptp. of *involvere*) = *in-* IN-[2] + *volūtus,* ptp. of *volvere* to roll] —**in′vo·lute′ly,** *adv.*

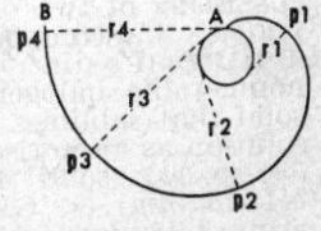

Involute produced by string r, unwinding about circle A. Locus of points p equals the involute

in·vo·lut·ed (in′və lo͞o′tid, in′və lo͞o′tid), *adj.* **1.** curving or curling inward. **2.** having an involved or complex nature. **3.** having resumed a normal size, shape, or condition.

in·vo·lu·tion (in′və lo͞o′shən), *n.* **1.** the act or an instance of involving or entangling; involvement. **2.** the state of being involved. **3.** something complicated. **4.** *Bot., Zool.* **a.** a rolling up or folding in upon itself. **b.** a part so formed. **5.** *Biol.* retrograde development; degeneration. **6.** *Physiol.* the regressive changes in the body occurring with old age. **7.** *Embryol.* the inward movement of cells around the blastopore in the formation of a gastrula. **8.** *Gram.* a complex construction in which the subject is separated from its predicate by intervening clauses or phrases. **9.** *Math.* **a.** a function that is its own inverse. **b.** (no longer in technical use) the raising of a quantity or expression to any given power. [< ML *involūtiōn-* (s. of *involūtiō*)]

in·volve (in volv′), *v.t.,* **-volved, -volv·ing. 1.** to include as a necessary circumstance, condition, or consequence; imply; entail. **2.** to affect; have a particular effect on. **3.** to include within itself or its scope. **4.** to bring into an intricate or complicated form or condition. **5.** to bring into difficulties (usually fol. by *with*): *a plot to involve one government in a war with another.* **6.** to cause to be troublesomely associated or concerned, as in something embarrassing or unfavorable: *Don't involve me in your quarrel!* **7.** to combine inextricably (usually fol. by *with*). **8.** to implicate, as in guilt or crime. **9.** to engage the interests or emotions or commitment of. **10.** to preoccupy or absorb fully (usually used passively or reflexively). **11.** to envelop or enfold, as if with a wrapping. **12.** *Archaic.* to roll, surround, or shroud, as in a wrapping. **13.** *Archaic.* to roll up on itself; coil. **14.** *Math. Obs.* to raise to a given power. [ME *involve(n)* < L *involv(ere)* (to) roll in or up = *in-* IN-[2] + *volvere* to roll] —**in·volve′ment,** *n.* —**in·volv′er,** *n.*
—**Syn. 1.** embrace, contain, comprehend, comprise. **5, 6, 8.** INVOLVE, ENTANGLE, IMPLICATE imply getting a person connected or bound up with something from which it is difficult for him to extricate himself. To INVOLVE is to bring more or less deeply into something, esp. of a complicated, embarrassing, or troublesome nature: *to involve someone in debt.* To ENTANGLE is to involve so deeply in a tangle as to confuse and make helpless: *to entangle oneself in a mass of contradictory statements.* To IMPLICATE is to connect a person with something discreditable or wrong: *implicated in a plot.* —**Ant. 6.** extricate.

in·volved (in volvd′), *adj.* **1.** intricate or complex. **2.** implicated or affected. **3.** concerned in an affair, esp. in a way likely to cause danger or unpleasantness. **4.** committed or engaged, as in a political cause. —**in·volv·ed·ly** (in vol′-vid lē, -volvd′-), *adv.* —**in·volv′ed·ness,** *n.* —**Syn. 1.** complicated, perplexing. —**Ant. 1.** simple.

invt., inventory. Also **invty.**

in·vul·ner·a·ble (in vul′nər ə bəl), *adj.* **1.** incapable of being wounded, hurt, or damaged. **2.** proof against or immune to attack. [< L *invulnerābil(is)*] —**in·vul′ner·a·bil′i·ty, in·vul′ner·a·ble·ness,** *n.* —**in·vul′ner·a·bly,** *adv.*

in·ward (in′wərd), *adv.* Also, **in′wards. 1.** toward the inside, interior, or center, as of a place, space, or body. **2.** into or toward the mind or soul: *He turned his thoughts inward.* **3.** *Obs.* on the inside or interior. **4.** *Obs.* mentally or spiritually: *inward pained.* —*adj.* **5.** proceeding or directed toward the inside or interior. **6.** situated within; interior. **7.** pertaining to the inside or inner part. **8.** located within the body. **9.** inland: *inward passage.* **10.** mental or spiritual. **11.** *Obs.* closely personal; intimate; familiar. —*n.* **12.** the inward or internal part; the inside. **13. in-wards,** *Informal.* the inward parts of the body; innards. [ME; OE *inweard*]

in·ward·ly (in′wərd lē), *adv.* **1.** in, on, or with reference to the inside or inner part; internally. **2.** privately; secretly: *Inwardly, he disliked his guest.* **3.** within the self; mentally or spiritually. **4.** in low tones; not aloud. **5.** toward the inside, interior, or center. **6.** *Obs.* closely; intimately. [ME *inwardli*, OE *inweardlīce*]

in·ward·ness (in′wərd nis), *n.* **1.** the state of being inward or internal. **2.** depth of thought or feeling; introspection. **3.** preoccupation with what concerns man's inner nature; spirituality. **4.** the fundamental or intrinsic character of something; essence. **5.** inner meaning or significance. **6.** *Obs.* intimacy; familiarity. [ME]

in·weave (in wēv′), *v.t.*, **-wove** or **-weaved; -wo·ven** or **-wove** or **-weaved; -weav·ing.** to weave in or together.

in·wind (in wīnd′), *v.t.*, **-wound, -wind·ing.** enwind.

in·wrap (in rap′), *v.t.*, **-wrapped, -wrap·ping.** enwrap.

in·wreathe (in rēth′), *v.t.*, **-wreathed, -wreath·ing.** enwreathe.

in·wrought (in rôt′), *adj.* **1.** worked in or closely combined with something. **2.** wrought or worked with something by way of decoration.

I·o (ī′ō), *n.* *Class. Myth.* the daughter of Inachus who, being loved by Zeus, was transformed at the wish of Hera into a white heifer.

Io, *Chem.* ionium.

Io., Iowa.

iod-, var. of **iodo-** before a vowel: *iodic.*

i·o·date (ī′ə dāt′), *n.*, *v.*, **-dat·ed, -dat·ing.** —*n.* **1.** *Chem.* a salt of iodic acid, as sodium iodate, $NaIO_3$. —*v.t.* **2.** to iodize. —**i′o·da′tion,** *n.*

i·od·ic (ī od′ik), *adj.* *Chem.* containing iodine, esp. in the pentavalent state.

iod′ic ac′id, *Chem.* a crystalline solid, HIO_3, used chiefly as a reagent in analytical chemistry.

i·o·dide (ī′ə dīd′, -did), *n.* *Chem* **1.** a salt of hydriotic acid consisting of two elements, one of which is iodine: *sodium iodide.* **2.** a compound containing iodine: *methyl iodide.*

i·o·dine (ī′ə dīn′, -din; *in Chem.* ī′ə dēn′), *n.* *Chem.* a nonmetallic halogen element, a grayish-black, crystalline solid that sublimes to a dense violet vapor: used in alcohol solution as an antiseptic. *Symbol:* I; *at. wt.*: 126.904; *at. no.:* 53; *sp. gr.:* (solid) 4.93 at 20°C. Also, **i·o·din** (ī′ə din). [< NL *iōd(um)* (< Gk *iōdēs*, orig. rust-colored, but by folk etym. taken as *ī(on)* violet + *-ōdēs* -ODE[1]) + -INE[2]]

iodine 131, *Chem.* a radioactive isotope of iodine having a mass number 131 and a halflife of 8.6 days, used in the diagnosis and treatment of disorders of the thyroid gland. Also called **I-131, I 131.**

i·o·dize (ī′ə dīz′), *v.t.*, **-dized, -diz·ing.** to treat, impregnate, or affect with iodine or an iodide. —**i′o·di·za′tion,** *n.* —**i′o·diz′er,** *n.*

iodo-, a combining form of **iodine:** *iodometry.* Also, *esp. before a vowel,* **iod-.**

i·o·do·form (ī ō′də fôrm′, ī od′ə-), *n.* *Chem.* a crystalline solid, CHI_3, analogous to chloroform, and having a penetrating odor: used chiefly as an antiseptic.

i·o·dom·e·try (ī′ə dom′i trē), *n.* *Chem.* a volumetric analytical procedure for determining iodine or materials that will liberate iodine or react with iodine. —**i·o·do·met·ric** (ī ō′də me′trik), *adj.* —**i′o·do·met′ri·cal·ly,** *adv.*

i·o·dop·sin (ī′ə dop′sin), *n.* a photosensitive violet pigment in the retina: important for daylight vision.

i·o·dous (ī ō′dəs, ī od′əs), *adj.* **1.** *Chem.* containing iodine, esp. in the trivalent state. **2.** pertaining to or resembling iodine.

i·o·lite (ī′ə līt′), *n.* cordierite. [< Gk *ío(n)* the violet + -LITE]

I′o moth′, a showy, yellow moth, *Automeris io*, of North America, having a prominent, pink and bluish eyespot on each hind wing. [named after Io]

i·on (ī′ən, ī′on), *n.* **1.** *Physics, Chem.* an electrically charged atom or group of atoms, as a cation, or positive ion, which is created by electron loss and is attracted to the cathode in electrolysis, or as an anion, or negative ion, which is created by an electron gain and is attracted to the anode. **2.** one of the electrically charged particles formed in a gas by an electric discharge or the like. [< Gk: going, neut. prp. of *iénai* to go]

-ion, a suffix, appearing in words of Latin origin, denoting action or condition, used in Latin and in English to form nouns from stems of Latin adjectives (*communion; union*), verbs (*legion; opinion*), and esp. past participles (*allusion; creation; fusion; notion; torsion*). Also, **-ation, -ition, -tion.** Cf. **-cion, -xion.** [< L *-iōn-* (s. of *-iō*) suffix forming nouns, esp. on ptp. stems; r. ME *-ioun* < AF < L *-iōn-*]

Ion., Ionic.

I·o·na (ī ō′nə), *n.* an island in the Hebrides, off the W coast of Scotland: center of early Celtic Christianity.

i′on cham′ber, *Physics.* See **ionization chamber.**

Io·nes·co (yə nes′kō, ē ə-), *n.* **Eu·gène** (*Fr.* œ zhen′; *Eng.* yōō jēn′, yōō′jēn), born 1912, French playwright, born in Rumania.

i′on exchange′, the process of reciprocal transfer of ions between a solution and a resin or other solid.

I·o·ni·a (ī ō′nē ə), *n.* an ancient region on the W coast of Asia Minor and on adjacent islands in the Aegean: colonized by the ancient Greeks.

I·o·ni·an (ī ō′nē ən), *adj.* **1.** of or pertaining to Ionia or its people. —*n.* **2.** an Ionian Greek. **3.** a member of one of the four main divisions of the prehistoric Greeks. Cf. **Achaean** (def. 5), **Aeolian** (def. 2), **Dorian** (def. 2).

Io′nian Is′lands, a group of Greek islands including Corfu, Levkas, Ithaca, Cephalonia, and Zante, off the W coast of Greece, and Cerigo, off the S coast.

Io′nian Sea′, an arm of the Mediterranean between S Italy, E Sicily, and Greece.

i·on·ic (ī on′ik), *adj.* **1.** of or pertaining to ions. **2.** pertaining to or occurring in the form of ions.

I·on·ic (ī on′ik), *adj.* **1.** *Archit.* noting or pertaining to one of the five classical orders that in ancient Greece consisted of a fluted column with a molded base and a capital composed of four volutes, and an entablature typically consisting of an architrave of three fascias, a richly ornamented frieze, and a cornice corbeled out on egg-and-dart and dentil moldings. Cf. **composite** (def. 3), **Corinthian** (def. 4), **Doric** (def. 2), **Tuscan** (def. 2). See illus. at **order. 2.** *Pros.* noting or employing a foot consisting either of two long followed by two short syllables or of two short followed by two long syllables. **3.** of or pertaining to Ionia or the Ionians. —*n.* **4.** *Pros.* an Ionic foot, verse, or meter. **5.** the dialect of ancient Greek spoken in Euboea, the Cyclades, and in parts of the mainland of Asia Minor. **6.** (*sometimes l.c.*) *Print.* a style of type. [< L *Iōnic(us)* < Gk *Iōnikós* of Ionia; see -IC]

ion′ic bond′, *Chem.* electrovalence (def. 2).

i·on·ise (ī′ə nīz′), *v.t.*, *v.i.*, **-ised, -is·ing.** *Chiefly Brit.* ionize. —**i′on·is′a·ble,** *adj.* —**i′on·i·sa′tion,** *n.*

i·o·ni·um (ī ō′nē əm), *n.* *Chem.* a naturally occurring radioactive isotope of thorium. *Symbol:* Io; *at. no.:* 90; *at. wt.:* 230. [NL; see ION, -IUM]

ioniza′tion cham′ber, *Physics.* an apparatus for detecting and analyzing ionizing radiation, consisting of a vessel filled with a gas and fitted with two electrodes such that the current between the electrodes is a function of the degree to which the gas is ionized; or the number of ions present. Also called **ion chamber.**

i·on·ize (ī′ə nīz′), *v.*, **-ized, -iz·ing.** —*v.t.* **1.** to separate or change into ions. **2.** to produce ions in. —*v.i.* **3.** to become changed into the form of ions, as by dissolving. Also, *esp. Brit.*, **ionise.** —**i′on·iz′a·ble,** *adj.* —**i′on·i·za′tion,** *n.*

i·on·o·mer (ī on′ə mər), *n.* *Chem.* any of a class of plastics that because of its ionic bonding is capable of conducting electric current. [ION + -O- + (POLY)MER]

i·on·o·sphere (ī on′ə sfēr′), *n.* the region of the earth's atmosphere between the stratosphere and the exosphere, consisting of several ionized layers and extending from about 50 to 250 miles above the surface of the earth. —**i·on·o·spher·ic** (ī on′ə sfer′ik), *adj.*

i′on propul′sion, *Rocketry.* a type of propulsion for vehicles in outer space, the exhaust consisting of positive ions and negative electrons repelled from the vehicle by electrostatic forces, resulting in a very high exhaust velocity.

I.O.O.F., Independent Order of Odd Fellows.

-ior, a suffix of comparatives in words of Latin origin: *superior; ulterior; junior.* [< L, masc. and fem. of comp. adjs.]

Iosh·kar-O·la (yosh kär′o lä′), *n.* a city in the RSFSR, in the central Soviet Union in Europe. 126,000 (est. 1964). Also, **Yoshkar-Ola.**

i·o·ta (ī ō′tə), *n.* **1.** a very small quantity; jot. **2.** the ninth letter of the Greek alphabet (I, ι). [< L < Gk < Sem; cf. Heb *yōdh*] —**Syn. 1.** bit, particle, atom, grain, mite.

i·o·ta·cism (ī ō′tə siz′əm), *n.* the conversion of other vowel sounds into that of iota, English (ē). [< LL *iōtacism(us)* < Gk *iōtakismós*. See IOTA, -AC, -ISM]

IOU, a written acknowledgment of a debt, esp. an informal one consisting only of the sum owed and the debtor's signature. Also, **I.O.U.** [repr. *I owe you*]

-ious, a combination of **-i-** and **-ous,** used to form adjectives; added to stems chiefly of Latin origin: *odious; religious; various.* Cf. **-eous.** [ME << L *-iōsus* (see -I-, -OSE[1]) and L *-ius* (masc. sing. ending of adjs., as in *varius*)]

I·o·wa (ī′ə wə; *sometimes* ī′ə wā′), *n.*, *pl.* **-was,** (*esp. collectively*) **-wa** for 3. **1.** a state in the central United States. 2,825,041 (1970); 56,290 sq. mi. *Cap.:* Des Moines. *Abbr.:* Ia., Io., IA **2.** a river flowing SE from N Iowa to the Mississippi River. 291 mi. long. **3.** a member of an American-Indian people of Oklahoma, Nebraska, and Kansas.

I′owa Cit′y, a city in SE Iowa. 46,850 (1970).

I·o·wan (ī′ə wən), *adj.* **1.** of or pertaining to Iowa. —*n.* **2.** a native or inhabitant of Iowa.

IPA, 1. See **International Phonetic Alphabet. 2.** International Phonetic Association. **3.** International Press Association. Also, **I.P.A.**

ip·e·cac (ip′ə kak′) **1.** either of two South American rubiaceous plants, *C phaelis Ipecacuanha* or *C. acuminata.* **2.** the dried roots of these plants, a drug used as an emetic, purgative, etc. Also, called **ip·e·cac·u·an·ha** (ip′ə kak′yōō-an′ə). [short for *ipecacuanha* < Pg < Tupi *ipekaaguéne* = *ipeh* low + *kaá* leaves + *guéne* vomit]

Iph·i·ge·ni·a (if′i jə nī′ə, -nē′ə), *n.* *Class. Myth.* the daughter of Agamemnon and Clytemnestra and sister of Orestes and Electra: when she was about to be sacrificed to ensure a wind to take the Greek ships to Troy, she was saved by Artemis, whose priestess she became.

ipm, inches per minute. Also, **i.p.m.**

I·poh (ē′pō), *n.* a city in central Perak, on the SW Malay peninsula, in Malaysia. 125,770 (1957).

ip·o·moe·a (ip′ə mē′ə, ī′pə-), *n.* **1.** any convolvulaceous plant of the genus *Ipomoea*, certain species of which are cultivated for their large, showy flowers. **2.** the dried root of the plant *Ipomoea orizabensis*, yielding a resin used as a cathartic. [< NL < Gk *ip-* (s. of *ips*) worm + *hómoia*, neut. pl. of *hómoios* like; see HOMEO-]

Ip·po·li·tov-I·va·nov (i po lē′tof i vä′nof), *n.* **Mi·kha·il Mi·khai·lo·vich** (mi кнä ēl′ mi кнī′lo vich), 1857–1935, Russian composer.

ips, inches per second. Also, **i.p.s.**

Ip·sam·bul (ip′sam bōōl′), *n.* See **Abu Simbel.**

ip·se dix·it (ip′se dik′sit; *Eng.* ip′sē dik′sit), *Latin.* **1.** he himself said it. **2.** an assertion without proof.

ip·sis·si·ma ver·ba (ip sis′si mä′ weʀ′bä; *Eng.* ip sis′ə mə vûr′bə), *Latin.* the very words; verbatim.

ip·so fac·to (ip′sō fak′tō), by the fact itself; by the very nature of the deed: *to be condemned ipso facto.* [< L]

ip·so ju·re (ip′sō yo͞o′ʀe; *Eng.* ip′sō jo͝or′ē), *Latin.* by the law itself; by operation of law.

Ip·sus (ip′səs), *n.* an ancient village in Phrygia: battle between the successors of Alexander the Great 301 B.C.

Ips·wich (ip′swich), *n.* a city in SE Suffolk, in E England. 117,325 (1961).

IQ, *Psychol.* See **intelligence quotient.** Also, **I.Q.**

i.q., the same as. [< L *idem quod*]

I·qui·que (ē kē′ke), *n.* a seaport in N Chile. 51,468 (1960).

I·qui·tos (ē kē′tôs), *n.* a city in NE Peru, on the upper Amazon. 55,695 (1961).

Ir, Irish (def. 4).

Ir, *Chem.* iridium.

ir-[1], var. of **in-**[2] (by assimilation) before *r: irradiate.*

ir-[2], var. of **in-**[3] (by assimilation) before *r: irreducible.*

Ir., **1.** Ireland. **2.** Irish.

I.R.A., **1.** Irish Republican Army. **2.** Investment Retirement Account.

i·ra·cund (ī′rə kund′), *adj.* *Archaic.* prone to anger; irascible. [< L *īrācund(us)* irascible = *īrā-* (see IRATE) + *-cundus* inclined to (adj. suffix)] —**i′ra·cun′di·ty,** *n.*

i·ra·de (*Turk.* i rä′de), *n.* a decree of a Muslim ruler. [< Turk < Ar *irādah* will, wish]

I·rak (i rak′; *Arab.* ē ʀäk′), *n.* Iraq.

I·ra·ki (i rak′ē; *Arab.* ē ʀä′kē), *n., pl.* **-kis,** *adj.* Iraqi.

I·ran (i ran′, ī ran′; *Pers.* ē ʀän′), *n.* a republic in SW Asia. 34,400,000; ab. 635,000 sq. mi. *Cap.:* Teheran. Formerly (until 1935), **Persia.**

Iran., Iranian.

I·ra·ni·an (i rā′nē ən, ī rā′-), *adj.* **1.** of or pertaining to Iran, its inhabitants, or their language. **2.** of or pertaining to the Iranian languages. —*n.* **3.** a subbranch of the Indo-European family of languages, including esp. Persian, Pashto, Avestan, and Kurdish. **4.** an inhabitant of Iran; Persian. Also, **I·ra·ni** (ī rā′nē) (for defs. 1, 4).

Ira′nian Plateau′, a plateau in SW Asia, mostly in Iran extending from the Tigris to the Indus rivers. 1,000,000 sq. mi.

I·raq (i rak′; *Arab.* ē ʀäk′), *n.* a republic in SW Asia, N of Saudi Arabia and W of Iran, centering in the Tigris-Euphrates basin of Mesopotamia. 11,505,000; 172,000 sq. mi. *Cap.:* Baghdad. Also, **Irak.**

I·ra·qi (i rak′ē; *Arab.* ē ʀä′kē), *n., pl.* **-qis,** *adj.* —*n.* **1.** a native of Iraq. **2.** Also called **Ira′qi Ar′abic.** the dialect of Arabic spoken in Iraq. —*adj.* **3.** of or pertaining to Iraq, its inhabitants, or their language. Also, **Iraki.** [< Ar *ʿIrāqī* = *ʿIrāq* IRAQ + *-ī* suffix of appurtenance]

i·ras·ci·ble (i ras′ə bəl, ī ras′-), *adj.* **1.** easily provoked to anger. **2.** characterized or produced by anger: *an irascible response.* [ME *irascibel* < LL *īrascibil(is)* = L *īrasc-* (s. of *īrascī* to grow angry; see IRE, -ESCE) + *-ibilis* -IBLE] —**i·ras′ci·bil′i·ty, i·ras′ci·ble·ness,** *n.* —**i·ras′ci·bly,** *adv.* —**Syn.** testy, touchy, irritable, choleric, short-tempered. —**Ant.** calm, even-tempered.

i·rate (ī′rāt, ī rāt′), *adj.* **1.** angry; enraged. **2.** arising from or characterized by anger: *an irate reply.* [< L *īrāt(us)* angered (ptp. of *īrascī*)] —**i·rate′ly,** *adv.* —**Syn. 1.** furious, provoked. —**Ant. 1.** calm.

Ir·bil (ir′bil), *n.* Erbil.

IRBM, See **intermediate range ballistic missile.** Also, **I.R.B.M.**

ire (īᵊr), *n.* anger; wrath. [ME < OF < L *īra* anger] —**ire′less,** *adj.* —**Syn.** fury, rage, choler, spleen.

Ire., Ireland.

ire·ful (īᵊr′fəl), *adj.* **1.** full of ire; wrathful: *an ireful look.* **2.** easily roused to anger; irascible. [ME] —**ire′ful·ly,** *adv.* —**ire′ful·ness,** *n.*

Ire·land (īᵊr′lənd), *n.* **1.** Also called **Emerald Isle.** Latin, **Hibernia.** a large western island of the British Isles, comprising Northern Ireland and the Republic of Ireland. 4,493,417; 32,375 sq. mi. **2. Republic of.** Formerly, **Irish Free State** (1922–37), **Eire** (1937–49). a republic occupying most of the island of Ireland: formerly associated with the British Commonwealth of Nations. 3,127,000; 27,137 sq. mi. *Cap.:* Dublin. —**Ire′land·er,** *n.*

I·re·ne (ī rē′nē), *n.* *Class. Myth.* one of the Horae, the personification of peace.

i·ren·ic (ī ren′ik, ī rē′nik), *adj.* tending to promote peace; peaceful. Also, **i·ren′i·cal.** [< Gk *eirēnik(ós)* = *eirḗn(ē)* peace + *-ikos* -IC] —**i·ren′i·cal·ly,** *adv.*

i·ren·ics (ī ren′iks, ī rē′niks), *n.* (*construed as sing.*) the branch of theology promoting conciliation among Christian churches. Cf. **polemics** (def. 2). [see IRENIC, -ICS]

IrGael, Irish Gaelic.

Ir·gun (ir go͞on′), *n.* a militant Zionist underground group, active chiefly during the period of British control of Palestine.

irid-, var. of **irido-** before a vowel: *iridectomy.*

ir·i·da·ceous (ir′i dā′shəs, ī′ri-), *adj.* **1.** belonging to the *Iridacea,* or iris family of plants, including certain flags, the crocus, and gladiolus. **2.** resembling or pertaining to plants of the genus *Iris.*

ir·i·dec·to·my (ir′i dek′tə mē, ī′ri-), *n., pl.* **-mies.** *Surg.* excision of part of the iris.

ir·i·des (ir′i dēz′, ī′ri-), *n.* a pl. of **iris.**

ir·i·des·cence (ir′i des′əns), *n.* an iridescent quality; a play of lustrous, changing colors.

ir·i·des·cent (ir′i des′ənt), *adj.* displaying a play of lustrous colors like those of the rainbow. —**ir′i·des′cent·ly,** *adv.*

i·rid·ic (i rid′ik, ī rid′-), *adj.* *Chem.* of or containing iridium, esp. in the tetravalent state.

i·rid·i·um (i rid′ē əm, ī rid′-), *n.* *Chem.* a precious metallic element resembling platinum: used in platinum alloys and for the points of gold pens. *Symbol:* Ir; *at. wt.:* 192.2; *at. no.:* 77; *sp. gr.:* 22.4 at 20°C. [< NL]

irido-, a combining form of Latin origin meaning "rainbow," "iridescent," "iris (of the eye)," "*Iris* (the genus)," "iridium," used in the formation of compound words: *iridosmine; iridotomy.* Also, *esp. before a vowel,* **irid-.** [comb. form repr. NL, L, Gk *īrid-* (s. of *îris*) rainbow, iris, etc.; see IRIS]

ir·i·do·cy·cli·tis (ir′i dō si klī′tis, ī′ri-), *n.* *Pathol.* inflammation of the iris and the ciliary body. [IRIDO- + *cyclitis;* see CYCL-, -ITIS]

ir·i·dos·mine (ir′i doz′min, -dos′-, ī′ri-), *n.* a native alloy of iridium and osmium, usually containing some rhodium, ruthenium, platinum; etc. Also, **ir·i·dos·mi·um** (ir′i doz′mē əm, -dos′-, ī′ri-). [IRID- + OSM(IUM) + -INE[2]]

Iris (Bearded)
Iris pallida

ir·i·dot·o·my (ir′i dot′ə mē, ī′ri-), *n., pl.* **-mies.** *Surg.* the formation of an artificial pupil by transverse division of fibers of the iris.

i·ris (ī′ris), *n., pl.* **i·ris·es, ir·i·des** (ir′i dēz′, ī′ri-). **1.** *Anat.* the contractile, circular diaphragm forming the colored portion of the eye and containing a circular opening, the pupil, in its center. **2.** *Bot.* any plant of the genus *Iris,* having showy flowers and sword-shaped leaves. **3.** a flower of this plant. **4.** (*cap.*) *Class. Myth.* a messenger of the gods, regarded as the goddess of the rainbow. **5.** a rainbow. **6.** iridescence. [ME < L: crystal < Gk: rainbow, goddess; in some senses < NL, L: flag, or NL < Gk: diaphragm of eye]

i′ris di′aphragm, *Optics, Photog.* an adjustable, composite diaphragm with a central aperture for size, used to regulate the amount of light admitted to a lens or optical system.

I·rish (ī′rish), *adj.* **1.** of, pertaining to, or characteristic of Ireland or its inhabitants. —*n.* **2.** the inhabitants of Ireland and their descendants elsewhere. **3.** the aboriginal Celtic-speaking people of Ireland. **4.** the Celtic language of Ireland in its historical or modern form. *Abbr.:* Ir, Ir. Cf. **Middle Irish, Old Irish. 5.** See **Irish English.** [ME; OE *Ir(as)* people of Ireland (c. Icel *Írar*); see -ISH[1]] —**I′rish·ly,** *adv.*

I′rish cof′fee, a beverage consisting of hot coffee and whiskey, sweetened and topped with whipped cream.

I′rish Eng′lish, **1.** the English dialects spoken in Ireland. **2.** the standard English of Ireland. Also called **Irish.**

I′rish Free′ State′, a former name of the Republic of Ireland. Gaelic, **Saorstat Eireann, Saorstat.**

I′rish Gael′ic, Gaelic as used in Ireland. *Abbr.:* IrGael

I·rish·ism (ī′ri shiz′əm), *n.* a custom, manner, practice, idiom, etc., characteristic of the Irish.

I·rish·man (ī′rish mən), *n., pl.* **-men. 1.** a man born in Ireland or of Irish ancestry. **2.** a native or inhabitant of Ireland.

I′rish moss′, a purplish-brown, cartilaginous seaweed, *Chondrus crispus,* of the Atlantic coasts of Europe and North America. Also called **carrageen, carragheen.**

I′rish Pale′, pale[2] (def. 6).

I′rish pota′to, potato (def. 1).

I′rish Repub′lican Ar′my, a secret Irish nationalist organization founded to gain Irish independence from Great Britain. *Abbr.:* I.R.A.

I′rish Sea′, a part of the Atlantic between Ireland and England.

I′rish set′ter, one of an Irish breed of setters having a golden-chestnut or mahogany-red coat.

Irish setter
(27 in. high at shoulder)

I′rish stew′, a stew usually made of mutton, lamb, or beef, with potatoes, onions, etc., and having thick gravy.

I′rish ter′rier, one of an Irish breed of terriers having a dense, wiry, reddish coat.

I′rish tweed′, a sturdy fabric of light warp and dark filling, used in men's suits and coats.

Irish terrier
(18 in. high at shoulder)

I′rish wa′ter span′iel, one of an Irish breed of large water spaniels having a thick, curly, liver-colored coat, a topknot of long curls, and a thin, tapering tail covered with short hair. See illus. at **water spaniel.**

I′rish whis′key, any whiskey made in Ireland, characteristically a product of barley.

I′rish wolf′hound, one of an Irish breed of large, tall dogs having a rough, wiry coat ranging in color from white to brindle to black.

i′ris shut′ter, a camera shutter having a group of overlapping blades that open and close at the center.

i·ri·tis (ī rī′tis), *n.* *Ophthalm.* inflammation of the iris of the eye. [IR(IS) + -ITIS] —**i·rit·ic** (ī rit′ik), *adj.*

irk (ûrk), *v.t.* to irritate, annoy, or exasperate. [ME *irk(en)* (to) grow tired, tire < Scand; cf. Icel *yrkja* to work, c. OE *wyrcan;* see WORK] —**Syn.** chafe, fret, bother; tire.

Irish wolfhound
(32 in. high at shoulder)

irk·some (ûrk′səm), *adj.* **1.** annoying or irritating; distressing; tiresome: *irksome restrictions.* **2.** *Obs.* causing weariness or disgust. —**irk′some·ly,** *adv.* —**irk′some·ness,** *n.*

Ir·kutsk (iʀ ko͞otsk′), *n.* a city in the S RSFSR, in the S Soviet Union in Asia, W of Lake Baikal. 543,000.

IRO, International Refugee Organization.

i·ron (ī′ərn), *n.* **1.** *Chem.* a ductile, malleable, silver-white metallic element, used in its crude or impure carbon-containing forms for making tools, implements, machinery, etc. *Symbol:* Fe; *at. wt.:* 55.847; *at. no.:* 26; *sp. gr.:* 7.86 at 20°C. Cf. **cast iron, pig iron, steel, wrought iron. 2.** something hard, strong, rigid, unyielding, or the like: *hearts of iron.* **3.** something made of iron. **4.** an iron appliance used, when heated, as by electric current, to press or smooth clothes, linens, etc. **5.** a branding iron. **6.** *Golf.* one of a series of nine metal-headed clubs having progressively sloped-back faces, used for driving or lofting the ball. Cf. **wood**[1] (def. 7). **7.** a harpoon. **8.** *Med.* a preparation of iron or containing iron, used chiefly in the treatment of anemia and as a styptic and astringent. **9. irons,** shackles or fetters. **10.** *Archaic.* a sword. **11. in irons, a.** *Naut.* (of a sailing vessel) unable to maneuver because of the position of the sails with relation to the direction of the wind. Cf. **stay**[3] (def. 2b). **b.** Also, **into irons.** in shackles or fetters. **12. irons in the fire,** matters with which a person is immediately concerned; undertakings; projects. **13. pump iron,** *Weight Lifting Informal.* to lift weights as an exercise or in competitive sports. **14. strike while the iron is hot,** to take immediate advantage of an opportunity. **—***adj.* **15.** of, containing, or made of iron. **16.** resembling iron in firmness, strength, color, etc. **17.** stern; harsh; cruel. **18.** inflexible; unrelenting; *an iron will.* **19.** strong; robust; healthy. **—***v.t.* **20.** to smooth or press with a heated iron, as clothes, linens, etc. **21.** to furnish, mount, or arm with iron. **22.** to shackle or fetter with irons. **—***v.i.* **23.** to iron clothes, linens, etc. **24. iron out,** *Informal.* to smooth out; clear up (difficulties, disagreements, etc.). [ME, OE *īren,* var. of *īsen* (c. G *Eisen*), *īsern* (c. Goth *eisarn*); akin to OIr *īarn*] —**i′ron·er,** *n.* —**i′ron·like′,** *adj.*

I′ron Age′, **1.** the period in the history of mankind, following the Stone Age and the Bronze Age, marked by the use of implements and weapons made of iron. **2.** (*l.c.*) *Class. Myth.* the present age, following the bronze age; the last and worst of the four ages of man, characterized by danger, corruption, and toil.

i·ron·bark (ī′ərn bärk′), *n.* any of various Australian eucalyptuses having a hard, solid bark, as *Eucalyptus resinifera,* a tall tree yielding a valuable timber and a gum.

i·ron·bound (ī′ərn bound′), *adj.* **1.** bound with iron. **2.** rock-bound; rugged. **3.** rigid; unyielding. [ME]

i·ron·clad (*adj.* ī′ərn klad′; *n.* ī′ərn klad′), *adj.* **1.** covered or cased with iron plates, as a vessel; armor-plated. **2.** very rigid or exacting; inflexible; unbreakable: *an ironclad contract.* **—***n.* **3.** a 19th-century warship having iron or steel armor plating with a heavy wooden backing.

I′ron Cross′, a Prussian and later a German military medal awarded in World War I as a service decoration and in World War II for outstanding courage.

i′ron cur′tain, a barrier to the exchange of information and ideas created by the hostility of one country toward another or others, esp. such a barrier between Soviet Russia or areas controlled by it and other countries. [used by Winston Churchill in 1946 to describe the line of demarcation between Western Europe and the Russian zone of influence]

I′ron Duke′. See **Wellington, 1st Duke of.**

i·rone (ī rōn′, ī′rōn), *n.* *Chem.* a liquid of isomeric, unsaturated ketones having the formula $C_{14}H_{22}O$, used in perfumery for its violet odor. [IR(IS) + -ONE]

i·ron·fist·ed (ī′ərn fis′tid), *adj.* ruthless and tyrannical.

I′ron Gate′, a gorge cut by the Danube through the Carpathian Mountains, between Yugoslavia and SW Rumania. 2 mi. long. Also, **I′ron Gates′.**

I′ron Guard′, a former Rumanian fascist party: eliminated after World War II.

i′ron hand′, strict or harsh control: *He governed the country with an iron hand.*

i·ron·hand·ed (ī′ərn han′did), *adj.* having or governing with an iron hand.

i′ron horse′, *Informal.* a locomotive.

i·ron·ic (ī ron′ik), *adj.* **1.** pertaining to, of the nature of, exhibiting, or characterized by irony or mockery: *an ironic compliment; an ironic smile.* **2.** using or prone to irony: *an ironic speaker.* Also, **i·ron′i·cal.** [< LL *īrōnic(us)* < Gk *eirōnikós*] —**i·ron′i·cal·ly,** *adv.* —**i·ron′i·cal·ness,** *n.*

i·ron·ing (ī′ər ning), *n.* **1.** the act or process of pressing clothes, linens, etc., with a heated iron. **2.** articles of clothing or the like that have been or are to be ironed.

i·ro·nist (ī′rə nist), *n.* a person who uses irony habitually, esp. a writer.

i·ro·nize (ī′rə nīz′, ī′ər-), *v.t.,* **-nized, -niz·ing.** to mix with nutritional iron. [IRON + -IZE]

i′ron lung′, a chamber, used esp. in the treatment of certain forms of poliomyelitis, that encloses the chest area and in which alternate pulsations of high and low pressure are used to effect normal lung movements, or to force air into and out of the lungs.

i′ron man′, *Slang.* a person who performs each given task or job tirelessly and with uniform efficiency.

i·ron·mon·ger (ī′ərn mung′gər, -mong′gər), *n.* *Chiefly Brit.* a dealer in hardware. [ME]

i′ron py′rites, **1.** pyrite; fool's gold. **2.** marcasite. **3.** pyrrhotite.

i′ron rust′, rust (def. 1).

i·ron·side (ī′ərn sīd′), *n.* **1.** a person with great power of endurance or resistance. **2.** (*cap.*) a nickname of Edmund II of England. **3.** (*cap.*) Usually, **Ironsides. a.** (*construed as sing.*). See **Cromwell, Oliver. b.** the soldiers serving under Cromwell. [ME]

i·ron·smith (ī′ərn smith′), *n.* a worker in iron; blacksmith. [ME *irensmith,* OE *īsensmith*]

i·ron·stone (ī′ərn stōn′), *n.* **1.** any iron-bearing mineral or rock with siliceous impurities. **2.** Also called **i′ronstone chi′na.** a hard white stoneware.

i·ron·ware (ī′ərn wâr′), *n.* articles of iron, as pots, kettles, and tools; hardware. [late ME]

i·ron·wood (ī′ərn wo͝od′), *n.* any of various trees yielding a hard, heavy wood, as the American hornbeam, *Carpinus caroliniana.*

i·ron·work (ī′ərn wûrk′), *n.* objects or parts of objects made of iron: *ornamental ironwork.* [late ME]

i·ron·work·er (ī′ərn wûr′kər), *n.* **1.** a worker in iron. **2.** a person employed in an ironworks. **3.** a person who works with structural steel.

i·ron·work·ing (ī′ərn wûr′king), *n.* the technique or practice of fashioning articles from iron.

i·ron·works (ī′ərn wûrks′), *n.* (*construed as sing. or pl.*) an establishment where iron is smelted or where it is cast or wrought.

i·ro·ny (ī′rə nē, ī′ər-), *n., pl.* **-nies. 1.** a figure of speech in which the words express a meaning that is often the direct opposite of the intended meaning. **2.** *Literature.* **a.** a technique of indicating, as through character or plot development, an intention or attitude opposite to that which is actually or ostensibly stated. **b.** (esp. in contemporary writing) a manner of organizing a work so as to give full expression to contradictory or complementary impulses, attitudes, etc., esp. as a means of indicating detachment from a subject, theme, or emotion. **3.** See **Socratic irony. 4.** See **dramatic irony. 5.** an outcome of events contrary to what was, or might have been, expected. **6.** the incongruity of this. **7.** an objectively sardonic style of speech or writing. **8.** an objectively or humorously sardonic utterance, disposition, quality, etc. [< L *īrōnīa* < Gk *eirōneía* = *eírōn* a dissembler + *-eia* -Y[3]]
—**Syn. 1, 2.** IRONY, SARCASM, SATIRE indicate mockery of something or someone. The essential feature of IRONY is the indirect presentation of a contradiction between an action or expression and the context in which it occurs. One thing is said and its opposite implied, as in the comment, "Beautiful weather, isn't it?" made when it is raining. Ironic literature exploits the paradoxical nature of reality or the contrast between an ideal and actual condition, set of circumstances, etc. In SARCASM ridicule or mockery is used harshly, often contemptuously, for destructive purposes. It may be used in an indirect manner, and have the form of irony, as in "What a fine musician you turned out to be!" or it may be used in the form of a direct statement, "You couldn't play one piece correctly if you had two assistants." The distinctive quality of SARCASM is present in the spoken word and manifested chiefly by vocal inflection, whereas SATIRE and IRONY, arising originally as literary and rhetorical forms, are exhibited in the organization or structuring of either language or literary material. SATIRE usually implies the use of irony or sarcasm for censorious or critical purposes and is often directed at public figures or institutions, conventional behavior, political situations, etc.

Ir·o·quoi·an (ir′ə kwoi′ən), *adj.* **1.** belonging to or constituting a linguistic family of the Iroquoian-Caddoan stock of North American Indians living in Canada and the eastern U.S. **2.** of, pertaining to, or characteristic of the Iroquois Indians.

Ir·o·quois (ir′ə kwoi′, -kwoiz′), *n., pl.* **-quois,** *adj.* **—***n.* **1.** a member of the Indian confederacy, the Five Nations, comprising the Mohawks, Oneidas, Onondagas, Cayugas, and Senecas, and, later, the Tuscaroras. **—***adj.* **2.** belonging or relating to the Iroquois or their tribes. [< F < Algonquian *irinakhoiw,* lit., real adders]

ir·ra·di·ance (i rā′dē əns), *n.* *Physics.* incident flux of radiant energy per unit area. Also, **irradiation.**

ir·ra·di·ant (i rā′dē ənt), *adj.* irradiating; radiant; shining. [< L *irradiant-* (s. of *irradiāns*) shining upon, prp. of *irradiāre*]

ir·ra·di·ate (*v.* i rā′dē āt′; *adj.* i rā′dē it, -āt′), *v.,* **-at·ed, -at·ing,** *adj.* **—***v.t.* **1.** to shed rays of light upon; illuminate. **2.** to illumine intellectually or spiritually. **3.** to brighten as with light. **4.** to radiate (light, illumination, etc.). **5.** to heat with radiant energy. **6.** to treat by exposure to radiation, as of ultraviolet light. **7.** to expose to radiation. **—***v.i.* **8.** *Archaic.* to emit rays; shine. **—***adj.* **9.** irradiated; bright. [< L *irradiāt(us)* illumined, ptp. of *irradiāre.* —**ir·ra′di·a′tive,** *adj.* —**ir·ra′di·a′tor,** *n.*

ir·ra·di·a·tion (i rā′dē ā′shən), *n.* **1.** the act of irradiating. **2.** the state of being irradiated. **3.** intellectual or spiritual enlightenment. **4.** a ray of light; beam. **5.** *Optics.* the apparent enlargement of an object when seen against a dark background. **6.** the use of x-rays or other radiations for the treatment of disease, the making of x-ray photographs, the manufacture of vitamin D, etc. **7.** exposure to x-rays or other radiation. **8.** irradiance. [< LL *irradiātiōn-* (s. of *irradiātiō*)]

ir·ra·tion·al (i rash′ə nəl), *adj.* **1.** without the faculty of, or not endowed with, reason. **2.** lacking sound judgment. **3.** utterly illogical: *irrational fear.* **4.** *Math.* **a.** (of a number) not capable of being expressed exactly as a ratio of two integers. **b.** (of a function) not capable of being expressed exactly as a ratio of two polynomials. **5.** *Algebra.* (of an equation) having an unknown under a radical sign or, alternately, with a fractional exponent. **6.** *Gk. and Lat. Pros.* **a.** of or pertaining to a substitution in the normal metrical pattern, esp. of a long syllable for a short one. **b.** noting a foot or meter containing such a substitution. **—***n.* **7.** *Math.* See **irrational number.** [late ME < L *irratiōnāl(is)*] —**ir·ra′tion·al·ly,** *adv.* —**ir·ra′tion·al·ness,** *n.*

ir·ra·tion·al·ism (i rash′ə nəliz′əm), *n.* **1.** irrationality in thought or action. **2.** a theory that nonrational forces govern the universe. —**ir·ra′tion·al·ist,** *adj., n.* —**ir·ra′tion·al·is′tic,** *adj.*

ir·ra·tion·al·i·ty (i rash′ə nal′i tē), *n., pl.* **-ties** for 2. **1.** the quality or condition of being irrational. **2.** an irrational, illogical, or absurd action, thought, etc.

irra′tional num′ber, *Math.* a number that cannot be exactly expressed as a ratio of two integers.

Ir·ra·wad·dy (ir′ə wod′ē, -wô′dē), *n.* a river flowing S through Burma to the Bay of Bengal. 1250 mi. long.

ir·re·claim·a·ble (ir′i klā′mə bəl), *adj.* not reclaimable; incapable of being reclaimed or reformed. —**ir′re·claim′a·bly,** *adv.*

ir·rec·on·cil·a·ble (i rek′ən sī′lə bəl, i rek′ən sī′-), *adj.* **1.** incapable of being brought into harmony or adjustment; incompatible. **2.** incapable of being made to acquiesce or compromise; implacably opposed: *irreconcilable enemies.* **—***n.* **3.** a person or thing that is irreconcilable. **4.** a person who remains firmly opposed to agreement or compromise. —**ir·rec′on·cil′a·bil′i·ty, ir·rec′on·cil′a·ble·ness,** *n.* —**ir·rec′on·cil′a·bly,** *adv.*

ir·re·cov·er·a·ble (ir′i kuv′ər ə bəl), *adj.* **1.** incapable of being recovered or regained. **2.** unable to be remedied or rectified; irretrievable. —**ir′re·cov′er·a·ble·ness,** *n.* —**ir′re·cov′er·a·bly,** *adv.*

ir·re·cu·sa·ble (ir′i kyōō′zə bəl), *adj.* not to be objected to or rejected. [< LL *irrecūsābil(is)*] —**ir′re·cu′sa·bly,** *adv.*

ir·re·deem·a·ble (ir i dē′mə bəl), *adj.* **1.** not redeemable; incapable of being bought back or paid off. **2.** inconvertible (def. 1). **3.** beyond redemption; irreclaimable. **4.** irreparable; hopeless. —**ir′re·deem′a·bil′i·ty, ir′re·deem′a·ble·ness,** *n.* —**ir′re·deem′a·bly,** *adv.*

ir·re·den·tist (ir′i den′tist), *n.* **1.** (*usually cap.*) a member of an Italian association that became prominent in 1878, advocating the redemption, or the incorporation into Italy, of certain neighboring regions (**Italia irredenta**) having a primarily Italian population. **2.** a member of a party in any country advocating the acquisition of some region included in another country. —*adj.* **3.** pertaining to or supporting such a party or its doctrine. [< It *irredentist(a)* = *(Italia) irredent(a)* (Italy) unredeemed (fem. of *irredento* = *ir-* IR-² + *redento* < L *redemptus*; see REDEMPTION) + *-ista* -IST] —**ir′re·den′tism,** *n.*

ir·re·duc·i·ble (ir′i dōō′sə bəl, -dyōō′-), *adj.* **1.** not reducible; incapable of being reduced, diminished, or simplified. **2.** incapable of being brought into a different condition or form. —**ir′re·duc′i·bil′i·ty, ir′re·duc′i·ble·ness,** *n.* —**ir′re·duc′i·bly,** *adv.*

ir·ref·ra·ga·ble (i ref′rə gə bəl), *adj.* not to be refuted; undeniable. [< LL *irrefragābil(is)* = L *ir-* IR-² + *refragā(rī)* (to) resist, oppose + *-bilis* -BLE] —**ir·ref′ra·ga·bil′i·ty, ir·ref′ra·ga·ble·ness,** *n.* —**ir·ref′ra·ga·bly,** *adv.*

ir·re·fran·gi·ble (ir′i fran′jə bəl), *adj.* **1.** not to be broken or violated; inviolable. **2.** incapable of being refracted. —**ir′re·fran′gi·bil′i·ty, ir′re·fran′gi·ble·ness,** *n.* —**ir′re·fran′gi·bly,** *adv.*

ir·ref·u·ta·ble (i ref′yə tə bəl, ir′i fyōō′tə bəl), *adj.* not refutable; incontrovertible. [< LL *irrefūtābil(is)*] —**ir·ref′u·ta·bil′i·ty, ir·ref′u·ta·ble·ness,** *n.* —**ir·ref′u·ta·bly,** *adv.*

irreg., 1. irregular. **2.** irregularly.

ir·re·gard·less (ir′i gärd′lis), *adj.* *Nonstandard.* regardless. [IR-² (prob. after *irrespective*) + REGARDLESS] —**Usage.** IRREGARDLESS is considered nonstandard because it is redundant: once the negative idea is expressed by the *-less* ending, it is poor style to add the negative *ir-* prefix to express the same idea. Nonetheless, it is occasionally used by some speakers, perhaps in an attempt to achieve greater emphasis.

ir·reg·u·lar (i reg′yə lər), *adj.* **1.** without symmetry, even shape, formal arrangement, etc.: *an irregular pattern.* **2.** not characterized by any fixed principle, method, continuity, or rate. **3.** not according to rule or to the accepted principle, method, etc. **4.** not conforming to established customs, etiquette, morality, etc. **5.** *Bot.* **a.** not uniform. **b.** (of a flower) having the members of some or all of its floral circles or whorls differing from one another in size or shape, or extent of union. **6.** *Gram.* not conforming to the prevalent pattern of inflection, construction, etc.: *The verbs "keep" and "see" are irregular in their inflections.* **7.** *Mil.* (of troops) not belonging to an organized group of the established forces. **8.** imperfect or failing to meet a specific standard of manufactured goods: *a sale of slightly irregular shirts.* —*n.* **9.** a person or thing that is irregular. **10.** a product or item that is imperfect or does not meet a specific standard of quality. **11.** *Mil.* a soldier not of a regular military force, as guerrilla or partisan. [< LL *irregulār(is)* (see IR-², REGULAR); r. ME *irreguler* < MF] —**ir·reg′u·lar·ly,** *adv.*

—**Syn. 1.** unsymmetrical, uneven. **2.** unmethodical, unsystematic; disorderly, capricious, erratic. **3.** anomalous, unusual. IRREGULAR, ABNORMAL, EXCEPTIONAL imply a deviation from the regular, the normal, the ordinary, or the usual. IRREGULAR, not according to rule, refers to any deviation, as in form, arrangement, action, and the like; it may imply such deviation as a mere fact, or as regrettable, or even censurable: *His conduct was highly irregular, but it was amusing.* ABNORMAL means a deviation from the common rule, often implying that this results in an aberrant or regrettably strange form or nature of a thing: *A two-headed calf is abnormal.* EXCEPTIONAL means out of the ordinary or unusual; it may refer merely to the rarity of occurrence, or to the superiority of quality: *an exceptional case; an exceptional mind.* Because of the stigma of ABNORMAL, EXCEPTIONAL is today frequently substituted for it in contexts where such a euphemism may be thought to be appropriate: *a school for exceptional children* (children who are abnormal in behavior, mental capacity, or the like).

ir·reg·u·lar·i·ty (i reg′yə lar′i tē), *n., pl.* **-ties** for 2, 3. **1.** the quality or state of being irregular. **2.** something irregular. **3.** a breach of rules, customs, etc. [ME *irregularite* < OF < ML *irregulāritās*]

ir·rel·a·tive (i rel′ə tiv), *adj.* **1.** not relative; without relation (usually fol. by *to*). **2.** not pertinent; irrelevant. —**ir·rel′a·tive·ly,** *adv.* —**ir·rel′a·tive·ness,** *n.*

ir·rel·e·vance (i rel′ə vəns), *n.* **1.** the quality or condition of being irrelevant. **2.** an irrelevant thing, act, etc.

ir·rel·e·van·cy (i rel′ə vən sē), *n., pl.* **-cies.** irrelevance.

ir·rel·e·vant (i rel′ə vənt), *adj.* not relevant; not applicable or pertinent. —**ir·rel′e·vant·ly,** *adv.*

ir·re·liev·a·ble (ir′i lē′və bəl), *adj.* not relievable; incapable of being relieved.

ir·re·li·gion (ir′i lij′ən), *n.* **1.** lack of religion. **2.** hostility to or disrespect toward religion; impiety. [< L *irreligiōn-* (s. of *irreligiō*)] —**ir′re·li′gion·ist,** *n.*

ir·re·li·gious (ir′i lij′əs), *adj.* **1.** not religious; not practicing a religion and feeling no religious impulses or emotions. **2.** showing or characterized by a lack of religion. **3.** showing disregard for or hostility to religion. [< L *irreligiōs(us)*] —**ir′re·li′gious·ly,** *adv.*

ir·rem·e·a·ble (i rem′ē ə bəl, i rē′mē-), *adj.* *Literary.* permitting no return; irreversible. [< L *irremeābil(is)* = *ir-* IR-² + *remeā(re)* (to) come back (*re-* RE- + *meāre* to go) + *-bilis* -BLE] —**ir·rem′e·a·bly,** *adv.*

ir·re·me·di·a·ble (ir′i mē′dē ə bəl), *adj.* not admitting of remedy, cure, or repair. [< L *irremediābil(is)*] —**ir′re·me′di·a·ble·ness,** *n.* —**ir′re·me′di·a·bly,** *adv.*

ir·re·mis·si·ble (ir′i mis′ə bəl), *adj.* **1.** not remissible; unpardonable, as a sin. **2.** unable to be remitted or postponed, as a duty. [ME < LL *irremissibil(is)*] —**ir′re·mis′si·bil′i·ty, ir′re·mis′si·ble·ness,** *n.* —**ir′re·mis′si·bly,** *adv.*

ir·re·mov·a·ble (ir′i mōō′və bəl), *adj.* not removable. —**ir′re·mov′a·bil′i·ty, ir′re·mov′a·ble·ness,** *n.* —**ir′re·mov′a·bly,** *adv.*

ir·rep·a·ra·ble (i rep′ər ə bəl), *adj.* not reparable; incapable of being rectified, remedied, or made good: *an irreparable mistake.* [ME < L *irreparābil(is)*] —**ir·rep′a·ra·bil′i·ty, ir·rep′a·ra·ble·ness,** *n.* —**ir·rep′a·ra·bly,** *adv.*

ir·re·peal·a·ble (ir′i pē′lə bəl), *adj.* incapable of being repealed or revoked. —**ir′re·peal′a·bil′i·ty, ir′re·peal′a·ble·ness,** *n.* —**ir′re·peal′a·bly,** *adv.*

ir·re·place·a·ble (ir′i plā′sə bəl), *adj.* incapable of being replaced; unique: *an irreplaceable antique.* —**ir′re·place′a·bly,** *adv.*

ir·re·press·i·ble (ir′i pres′ə bəl), *adj.* incapable of being repressed or restrained; uncontrollable: *an irrepressible urge to have a chocolate malt.* —**ir′re·press′i·bil′i·ty, ir′re·press′i·ble·ness,** *n.* —**ir′re·press′i·bly,** *adv.*

ir·re·proach·a·ble (ir′i prō′chə bəl), *adj.* not reproachable; free from blame. —**ir′re·proach′a·ble·ness, ir′re·proach′a·bil′i·ty,** *n.* —**ir′re·proach′a·bly,** *adv.*

ir·re·sist·i·ble (ir′i zis′tə bəl), *adj.* **1.** not resistible; incapable of being resisted or withstood: *an irresistible force.* **2.** extremely tempting or enticing, esp. tempting to own or possess: *She saw an irresistible hat in the store window.* [< ML *irresistibil(is)*] —**ir′re·sist′i·bil′i·ty, ir′re·sist′i·ble·ness,** *n.* —**ir′re·sist′i·bly,** *adv.*

ir·re·so·lu·ble (ir′i zol′yə bəl, i rez′əl yə bəl), *adj.* **1.** incapable of being solved or explained. **2.** *Archaic.* incapable of being relieved. [< L *irresolūbil(is)*] —**ir′re·sol′u·bil′i·ty,** *n.*

ir·res·o·lute (i rez′ə lōōt′), *adj.* not resolute; doubtful or undecided; vacillating. —**ir·res′o·lute′ly,** *adv.* —**ir·res′o·lute′ness,** *n.*

ir·res·o·lu·tion (i rez′ə lōō′shən), *n.* lack of resolution; vacillation.

ir·re·solv·a·ble (ir′i zol′və bəl), *adj.* not resolvable; incapable of being resolved; not analyzable or solvable. —**ir′re·solv′a·bil′i·ty, ir′re·solv′a·ble·ness,** *n.*

ir·re·spec·tive (ir′i spek′tiv), *adj.* without regard to; ignoring or discounting (usually fol. by *of*): *Irrespective of my wishes, I should go.* —**ir′re·spec′tive·ly,** *adv.*

ir·re·spon·si·ble (ir′i spon′sə bəl), *adj.* **1.** said, done, or characterized by a lack of a sense of responsibility. **2.** not capable of or qualified for responsibility. **3.** not responsible, answerable, or accountable to higher authority. —*n.* **4.** an irresponsible person. —**ir′re·spon′si·bil′i·ty, ir′re·spon′si·ble·ness,** *n.* —**ir′re·spon′si·bly,** *adv.*

ir·re·spon·sive (ir′i spon′siv), *adj.* not responsive; not responding or not responding readily. —**ir′re·spon′sive·ness,** *n.*

ir·re·ten·tive (ir′i ten′tiv), *adj.* not retentive; lacking power to retain, esp. mentally. —**ir′re·ten′tive·ness, ir′re·ten′tion,** *n.*

ir·re·trace·a·ble (ir′i trā′sə bəl), *adj.* not retraceable; unable to be retraced. —**ir′re·trace′a·bly,** *adv.*

ir·re·triev·a·ble (ir′i trē′və bəl), *adj.* not retrievable; irrecoverable; irreparable. —**ir′re·triev′a·bil′i·ty, ir′re·triev′a·ble·ness,** *n.* —**ir′re·triev′a·bly,** *adv.*

ir·rev·er·ence (i rev′ər əns), *n.* **1.** the quality of being irreverent; lack of reverence or respect. **2.** an irreverent act or statement. [ME < L *irreverentia*]

ir·rev·er·ent (i rev′ər ənt), *adj.* not reverent; lacking reverence or respect. [< L *irreverent-* (s. of *irreverēns*) disrespectful] —**ir·rev′er·ent·ly,** *adv.*

ir·re·vers·i·ble (ir′i vûr′sə bəl), *adj.* not reversible; incapable of being reversed or changed: *His decision is irreversible.* —**ir′re·vers′i·bil′i·ty, ir′re·vers′i·ble·ness,** *n.* —**ir′re·vers′i·bly,** *adv.*

ir·rev·o·ca·ble (i rev′ə kə bəl), *adj.* not to be revoked or recalled; unable to be repealed or annulled. [ME < L *irrevocābil(is)*] —**ir·rev′o·ca·bil′i·ty, ir·rev′o·ca·ble·ness,** *n.* —**ir·rev′o·ca·bly,** *adv.*

ir·ri·gate (ir′ə gāt′), *v.t.,* **-gat·ed, -gat·ing.** **1.** to supply (land) with water by artificial means, as by diverting streams, flooding, or spraying. **2.** *Med.* to supply or wash (an orifice, wound, etc.) with a spray or a flow of some liquid. **3.** to moisten; wet. [< L *irrigāt(us)* watered (ptp. of *irrigāre*) = *ir-* IR-¹ + *rigātus,* ptp. of *rigāre* to lead water] —**ir′ri·ga·ble,** *adj.* —**ir′ri·ga·bly,** *adv.* —**ir′ri·ga′tor,** *n.*

ir·ri·ga·tion (ir′ə gā′shən), *n.* **1.** the artificial application of water to land to assist in the production of crops. **2.** *Med.* the covering or washing out of anything with water or other liquid for the purpose of making or keeping it moist, as in local medical treatment. **3.** the state of being irrigated. [< L *irrigātiōn-* (s. of *irrigātiō*)] —**ir′ri·ga′tion·al,** *adj.*

ir·ri·ga·tive (ir′ə gā′tiv), *adj.* serving for or pertaining to irrigation.

ir·rig·u·ous (i rig′yōō əs), *adj.* *Archaic.* well-watered, as land. [< L *irriguus* = *ir-* IR-¹ + *riguus* watered, watering (*rig(āre)* (to) water + *-uus* -UOUS)]

ir·ri·ta·bil·i·ty (ir′i tə bil′i tē), *n.* **1.** the quality or state of being irritable. **2.** *Physiol., Biol.* the ability to be excited to a characteristic action or function by the application of some stimulus. [< L *irrītābilitās*]

ir·ri·ta·ble (ir′i tə bəl), *adj.* **1.** easily irritated; readily excited to impatience or anger. **2.** *Physiol., Biol.* displaying irritability. **3.** *Pathol.* susceptible to physical irritation; likely to shrink, become inflamed, etc., when stimulated: *an irritable wound.* [< L *irrītābil(is)*] —**ir′ri·ta·ble·ness,** *n.* —**ir′ri·ta·bly,** *adv.* —**Syn. 1.** testy, touchy, petulant.

ir·ri·tant (ir′i tᵊnt), *adj.* **1.** irritating; tending to cause irritation. —*n.* **2.** anything that irritates. **3.** *Physiol., Pathol.* a biological, chemical, or physical agent that stimulates a characteristic function or elicits a response, esp. an inflammatory response. [< L *irrītant-* (s. of *irrītāns*) irritating, prp. of *irrītāre*] —**ir′ri·tan·cy,** *n.*

ir·ri·tate (ir′i tāt′), *v.*, **-tat·ed, -tat·ing.** —*v.t.* **1.** to excite to impatience or anger. **2.** *Physiol., Biol.* to excite (a living system) to some characteristic action or function. **3.** *Pathol.* to bring (a body part) to an abnormally excited or sensitive condition. —*v.i.* **4.** to cause or induce impatience or anger. **5.** *Physiol., Pathol.* to cause or induce excitation, inflammation, etc. [< L *irrītāt(us)* aroused to anger (ptp. of *irrītāre*) = *ir-* IR-[1] + *-rītā-* arouse, excite (< ?) + *-tus* ptp. suffix] —**ir′ri·ta′tor,** *n.*
—**Syn. 1.** vex, chafe, gall; nettle, ruffle, pique. IRRITATE, EXASPERATE, PROVOKE mean to annoy or stir to anger. To IRRITATE is to excite to impatience or angry feeling, often of no great depth or duration: *to irritate by refusing to explain an action.* To EXASPERATE is to irritate to a point where self-control is threatened or lost: *to exasperate by continual delays.* To PROVOKE is to stir to a sudden, strong feeling of resentful anger: *to provoke an animal until it attacks.*

ir·ri·tat·ed (ir′i tā′tid), *adj.* **1.** annoyed. **2.** inflamed or made raw, as a part of the body. —**ir′ri·tat′ed·ly,** *adv.*

ir·ri·tat·ing (ir′i tā′ting), *adj.* causing irritation; provoking. —**ir′ri·tat′ing·ly,** *adv.*

ir·ri·ta·tion (ir′i tā′shən), *n.* **1.** the act or fact of irritating. **2.** the state of being irritated. **3.** *Physiol., Pathol.* **a.** the bringing of a bodily part or organ to an abnormally excited or sensitive condition. **b.** the condition itself. [< L *irrītātiōn-* (s. of *irrītātiō*)]

ir·ri·ta·tive (ir′i tā′tiv), *adj.* **1.** serving or tending to irritate. **2.** *Pathol.* characterized or produced by irritation of some body part: *an irritative fever.* —**ir′ri·ta′tive·ness,** *n.*

ir·rupt (i rupt′), *v.i.* **1.** to intrude suddenly or with force. **2.** to manifest violent activity or emotion, as a group of persons. **3.** (of animals) to increase suddenly in numbers through a lessening of the number of deaths. [< L *irrupt(us)*; see IRRUPTION]

ir·rup·tion (i rup′shən), *n.* **1.** a breaking or bursting in; a violent incursion or invasion. **2.** a sudden increase in an animal population. [< L *irruptiōn-* (s. of *irruptiō*) = *irrupt(us)* broken into (ptp. of *irrumpere;* see IR-[1], RUPTURE) + *-iōn-* -ION]

ir·rup·tive (i rup′tiv), *adj.* **1.** of, pertaining to, or characterized by irruption. **2.** irrupting or tending to irrupt. **3.** *Petrol.* intrusive. —**ir·rup′tive·ly,** *adv.*

IRS, Internal Revenue Service.

Ir·tish (ir tish′), *n.* a river flowing NW from the Altai Mountains in China through the W Soviet Union in Asia to the Ob River. ab. 1840 mi. long. Also, **Ir·tysh′.**

Ir·ving (ûr′ving), *n.* **1. Sir Henry** (*John Henry Brodribb*), 1838–1905, English actor. **2. Washington,** 1783–1859, U.S. essayist, story writer, and historian. **3.** a city in NE Texas, near Dallas. 97,260 (1970).

Ir·ving·ton (ûr′ving tən), *n.* a town in NE New Jersey, near Newark. 59,743 (1970).

is (iz), *v.* **1.** 3rd pers. sing. pres. indic. of **be. 2. as is.** See **as**[1] (def. 18). [ME, OE; c. D *is,* Icel *es, er;* akin to G, Goth *ist,* L *est,* Gk *estí,* Skt *asti*]

is-, var. of **iso-** before a vowel: *isallobar.*

Is., **1.** Isaiah. **2.** island. **3.** isle.

is., **1.** island. **2.** isle.

Isa., Isaiah.

I·saac (ī′zək), *n.* a son of Abraham and Sarah, and father of Jacob. Gen. 21:1–4.

Is·a·bel·la I (iz′ə bel′ə), (*"the Catholic"*) 1451–1504, wife of Ferdinand V: queen of Castile 1474–1504; joint ruler of Aragon 1479–1504.

Isabella II, 1830–1904, queen of Spain 1833–68.

is·a·go·ge (ī′sə gō′jē, ī′sə gō′jē), *n.* **1.** an introduction, esp. a scholarly introduction to a field of study or research. **2.** isagogics. [< L < Gk *eisagōgḗ* = *eisá(ein)* (to) introduce (*eis-* into + *ágein* to lead) + *-ōgē* n. suffix]

i·sa·gog·ic (ī′sə goj′ik), *adj.* **1.** introductory, esp. to the interpretation of the Bible. —*n.* **2.** isagogics. [< L *īsagōgic(us)* < Gk *eisagōgikós* = *eisagōg(ḗ)* introduction + *-ikos* -IC]

i·sa·gog·ics (ī′sə goj′iks), *n.* (*construed as sing.*) **1.** introductory studies. **2.** the branch of theology that is introductory to exegesis and the literary history of the Bible. Also, **isagogic, isagoge.** [see ISAGOGIC, -ICS]

I·sa·iah (ī zā′ə *or, esp. Brit.,* ī zī′ə), *n.* **1.** a Major Prophet of the 8th century B.C. **2.** a book of the Bible bearing his name. Also, *Douay Bible,* **I·sa·ias** (ī zā′əs, ī zī′əs). [< Heb *Yeshaʿ ʿyah,* lit., Jehovah's salvation]

is·al·lo·bar (ī sal′ə bär′), *n.* *Meteorol.* a line on a weather map connecting points having equal pressure changes.

I·sar (ē′zär), *n.* a river flowing NE from W Austria through S West Germany to the Danube River. 215 mi. long.

i·sa·rithm (ī′sə riŧħ′əm), *n.* isopleth. [IS- + *-arithm,* as in *logarithm*]

-isation, var. of **-ization.**

Is·car·i·ot (i skar′ē ət), *n.* the surname of Judas, the betrayer of Jesus. Mark 3:19; 14:10, 11. [< L *Iscariōta* < Gk *Iskariṓtēs* < Heb *īsh-qerīyōth* man of *Kerioth* a village in Palestine]

is·che·mi·a (i skē′mē ə), *n.* *Pathol.* local anemia produced by local obstacles to the arterial flow. Also, **is·chae′mi·a.** [< Gk *ísch(ein)* (to) suppress, check + -EMIA] —**is·che·mic, is·chae·mic** (i skē′mik, -skem′ik), *adj.*

Is·chia (ē′skyä), *n.* an Italian island in the Tyrrhenian Sea, W of Naples: earthquake 1883.

is·chi·um (is′kē əm), *n., pl.* **-chi·a** (-kē ə). *Anat.* **1.** the lower portion of either innominate bone. **2.** either of the bones on which the body rests when sitting. [< L < Gk *ischíon* hip joint]

-ise[1], var. of **-ize:** *organise.*

-ise[2], a noun suffix, occurring in loan words from French, indicating quality, condition, or function: *franchise; merchandise.* Cf. **-ice.** [ME < OF *-ise;* var. of -ICE]

I·sère (ē zâʀ′), *n.* a river in SE France, flowing from the Alps to the Rhone River. 150 mi. long.

I·seult (i so͞olt′), *n.* *Arthurian Romance.* **1.** the daughter of a king of Ireland and the wife of King Mark of Cornwall: she was the beloved of Tristram. **2.** daughter of the king of Brittany, and wife of Tristram. Also, **Yseult.** German, **Isolde.**

Is·fa·han (is′fə hän′), *n.* a city in central Iran: the capital of Persia from the 16th into the 18th century. 605,000. Also, **Ispahan.**

-ish[1], **1.** a suffix used to form adjectives from nouns, with the sense of "belonging to" (*British; Danish; English; Spanish*); "after the manner of," "having the characteristics of," "like" (*babyish; girlish; mulish*); "addicted to," "inclined or tending to" (*bookish; freakish*). **2.** a suffix used to form adjectives from other adjectives, with the sense of "somewhat," "rather" (*oldish; reddish; sweetish*). [ME; OE *-isc;* c. G *-isch,* Goth *-iska,* Gk *-iskos;* akin to -ESQUE]
—**Syn.** The suffixes -ISH, -LIKE, -LY agree in indicating that something resembles something else. One of the common meanings of -ISH is derogatory; that is, it indicates that something has the bad qualities of something else, or that it has qualities similar which are not suitable to it: *childish; mannish* (of a woman). The suffix -LIKE, in the formation of adjectives, is usually complimentary: *childlike innocence; godlike serenity.* The suffix -LY, when it means having the nature or character of, is distinctly complimentary: *kingly; manly; motherly.*

-ish[2], a suffix occurring in *i*-stem verbs borrowed from French: *ravish.* [< F *-iss-,* extended s. of verbs in *-ir* << L *-isc-,* in inceptive verbs]

Ish·er·wood (ish′ər wo͝od′), *n.* **Christopher (William Brad·shaw)** (brad′shô), 1904–86, U.S. novelist and playwright, born in England.

Ish·ma·el (ish′mē əl, -mā-), *n.* **1.** Also, *Douay Bible,* **Ismael.** the son of Abraham and Hagar: he and Hagar were cast out of Abraham's family by Sarah. Gen. 16:11, 12. **2.** an outcast. **3.** an Arab. [< Heb *Yishmāʿēl,* God will hear]

Ish·ma·el·ite (ish′mē ə līt′, -mā ə-, -mə-), *n.* **1.** a descendant of Ishmael. **2.** a wanderer or outcast. **3.** an Arab. —**Ish′ma·el·it′ish,** *adj.*

Ish·tar (ish′tär), *n.* the Assyrian and Babylonian goddess of love and war, identified with the Phoenician Astarte, the Semitic Ashtoreth, and the Sumerian Inanna. Also called **Mylitta.**

Is′i·dore of Seville′ (iz′i dōr′, -dôr′), **Saint** (*Isidorus Hispalensis*), A.D. c570–636, Spanish archbishop, historian, and encyclopedist. —**Is′i·do′ri·an, Is′i·do′re·an,** *adj.*

i·sin·glass (ī′zin glas′, -gläs′, ī′zing-), *n.* **1.** a pure, transparent or translucent form of gelatin, obtained from the air bladders of certain fish, esp. the sturgeon: used in glue and jellies and as a clarifying agent. **2.** mica. [< MD *huysenblase* (with *glass* for *blase* by folk etym.), lit., sturgeon bladder; c. G *Hausenblase*]

I·sis (ī′sis), *n.* *Egyptian Religion.* a goddess of fertility, the sister and wife of Osiris and mother of Horus, and usually represented as a woman with a cow's horns with the solar disk between them: later worshiped in the Greek and Roman empires. [< L < Gk < Egypt *Ese*] —**Is·i·ac** (is′ē ak′, iz′-, ī′sē-), **I·si·a·cal** (i sī′ə kəl, ī sī′-), *adj.*

Isis

Is·kan·der Bey (is kan′dər bā′), Turkish name of **Scanderbeg.**

Is·ken·de·run (is ken′də ro͞on′), *n.* **1.** Formerly, **Alexandretta.** a seaport in S Turkey, on the Gulf of Iskenderun 79,291. **2. Gulf of,** an inlet of the Mediterranean, off the S coast of Turkey. 45 mi. long; 28 mi. wide.

isl., **1.** island. **2.** isle. Also, **Isl.**

Is·lam (is′ləm, iz′-, is läm′), *n.* **1.** the religious faith of Muslims, as set forth in the Koran, which teaches that Allah is the only God and that Muhammad is his prophet. **2.** the whole body of Muslim believers, their civilization, and the countries in which theirs is the dominant religion. [< Ar: submission (to God) < *aslama* to surrender] —**Is·lam·ic** (is lam′ik, -läm′ik, iz-), **Is·lam·it·ic** (is′lə mit′ik, iz′-), *adj.*

Is·lam·a·bad (is läm′ä bäd′), *n.* the capital of Pakistan, in the N part, near Rawalpindi. 77,318.

Islam′ic Repub′lic of Maurita′nia, official name of **Mauritania.**

Is·lam·ise (is′lə mīz′, iz′-), *v.i., v.t.,* **-ised, -is·ing.** *Chiefly Brit.* Islamize. —**Is′lam·i·sa′tion,** *n.*

Is·lam·ism (is′lə miz′əm, iz′-), *n.* the religion or culture of Islam.

Is·lam·ite (is′lə mīt′, iz′-), *n.* a Muslim.

Is·lam·ize (is′lə mīz′, iz′-), *v.i., v.t.,* **-ized, -iz·ing.** to convert to or bring under the influence of Islam. Also, *esp. Brit.,* **Islamise.** —**Is′lam·i·za′tion,** *n.*

is·land (ī′lənd), *n.* **1.** a land area completely surrounded by water, and not large enough to be called a continent. **2.** a clump of woodland in a prairie. **3.** an isolated hill. **4.** something resembling an island, esp. in being isolated. **5.** *Anat.* a portion of tissue differing in structure from the surrounding tissue. **6.** (on an aircraft carrier) a structure above the flight deck containing command and control centers, antennas, etc. [ME *iland,* OE *ī(g)land,* var. of *īegland* = *īeg* island (c. Icel *ey*) + *land* LAND; sp. with *-s-* by assoc. with ISLE] —**is′land·less,** *adj.* —**is′land·like′,** *adj.*

is·land·er (ī′lən dər), *n.* a native or inhabitant of an island.

is′land of Lang′erhans. See **islet of Langerhans.**

Is′lands of the Blessed′, *Class. Myth.* islands in the ocean at the remotest western end of the world, to which the souls of heroes and good men were said to be transported after death. Also called **Hesperides.**

is′land u′niverse, an external galaxy.

isle (īl), *n.* **1.** a small island. **2.** any island. [ME *i(s)le* < OF < L *insula*] —**isle′less,** *adj.*

Isle′ of Ca′pri, *Literary.* Capri.

Isle′ of Man′. See **Man, Isle of.**

Isle′ of Pines′. See **Pines, Isle of.**

Isle′ of Wight′. See **Wight, Isle of.**

Isle′ Roy′ale (roi′əl), an island in Lake Superior: a part of Michigan; a national park. 208 sq. mi.

is·let (ī′lit), *n.* a very small island. [< MF *islette.* See ISLE, -ET]

is′let of Lang′erhans, *Anat.* any of several masses of endocrine cells in the pancreas that secrete insulin. Also, **island of Langerhans.** [named after P. *Langerhans* (1847–88), German anatomist, who first described them]

Is·ling·ton (iz′liŋ tən), *n.* a borough of N London, England. 228,833 (1961).

isls., islands.

ism (iz′əm), *n.* a distinctive doctrine, theory, system, or dogma. [abstracted from words so ending]

-ism, a suffix appearing in loan words from Greek, where it was used to form action nouns from verbs (*baptism*); on this model, used as a productive suffix in the formation of nouns denoting action or practice, state or condition, principles, doctrines, a usage or characteristic, etc. (*criticism; barbarism; Darwinism; witticism*). Cf. **-ist, -ize.** [< Gk *-ism(os), -ism(a)* n. suffixes, often directly, often through L *-ismus, -isma,* sometimes through F *-isme,* G *-ismus*]

Is·ma·el (is′mē əl, -mā-), *n.* *Douay Bible.* Ishmael (def. 1).

Is·ma·i·li (is′mä ē′lē), *n.* *Islam.* **1.** a sect of the Shiah, including in their number the Assassins and the Druses, having an esoteric philosophy. **2.** a member of the Ismaili sect. [< Ar: see ISMAILIAN]

Is·ma·i·li·a (is′mä i lē′yä), *n.* a city and seaport at the midpoint of the Suez Canal, in the NE United Arab Republic. 156,300 (est. 1962). Also, **Is′ma·i·li′ya.**

Is·ma·i·li·an (is′mä i lē′ən), *n.* *Islam.* Ismaili (def. 2). [after *Ismaili* follower of *Ismail* (d. A.D. 760), elder son of the imam Djafar, but disinherited by his father; see -AN]

Is·ma·il Pa·sha (is mä′ēl pä′shä), 1830–95, viceroy and khedive of Egypt 1863–79.

isn't (iz′ənt), contraction of *is not.*

iso-, **1.** a learned borrowing from Greek meaning "equal," used in the formation of compound words: *isochromatic.* **2.** *Chem.* a prefix added to the name of one compound to denote another isomeric with it. Also, *esp. before a vowel,* **is-.** [< Gk, comb. form of *ísos*]

i·so·ag·glu·ti·na·tion (ī′sō ə glo͞ot′ənā′shən), *n.* *Med.* the clumping of the red blood cells of a man or animal by a transfusion of the blood or serum of another individual of the same species. —**i·so·ag·glu·ti·na·tive** (ī′sō ə glo͞ot′ənā′tiv, -ənə-), *adj.*

i·so·ag·glu·ti·nin (ī′sō ə glo͞ot′ənin), *n.* an agglutinin which can effect isoagglutination.

i′so·am′yl ac′etate (ī′sō am′il, ī′sō-), *Chem.* a liquid, $CH_3COOCH_2CH_2CH(CH_3)_2$, used in flavorings, perfumery and as a solvent. Cf. **banana oil.**

i·so·bar (ī′sə bär′), *n.* **1.** *Meteorol.* a line drawn on a weather map or chart that connects points at which the barometric pressure is the same. **2.** Also, **i·so·bare** (ī′sə-bâr′). *Physics, Chem.* one of two or more atoms having equal atomic weights but different atomic numbers. Cf. **isotope.** [< Gk *isobar(ḗs)* of equal weight. See ISO-, BARO-] —**i′so·bar′ism,** *n.*

i·so·bar·ic (ī′sə bar′ik), *adj.* *Meteorol.* **1.** having or showing equal barometric pressure. **2.** of or pertaining to isobars.

i·so·bath (ī′sə bath′), *n.* **1.** a line drawn on a map connecting all points of equal depth below the surface of a body of water. **2.** a similar line indicating the depth below the surface of the earth of a particular geological stratum. [< Gk *isobath(ḗs)* of equal depth. See ISO-, BATHO-]

i·so·bath·ic (ī′sə bath′ik), *adj.* **1.** having the same depth. **2.** of or pertaining to an isobath.

i·so·bu·tane (ī′sə byo͞o′tān, -byo͞o tān′), *n.* *Chem.* a flammable gas, $(CH_3)_3CH$, used as a fuel, as a refrigerant, and in the manufacture of gasoline.

i·so·bu·tyl·ene (ī′sə byo͞ot′əlēn′), *n.* *Chem.* a very volatile liquid or flammable gas, $(CH_3)_2C{=}CH_2$, used chiefly in the manufacture of butyl rubber. Also, **i·so·bu·tene** (ī′sə-byo͞o′tēn).

i·so·car·pic (ī′sə kär′pik), *adj.* *Bot.* having carpels equal in number to the other floral parts.

i·so·cheim (ī′sə kīm′), *n.* *Climatology.* a line on a map connecting points that have the same mean winter temperature. Also, **i′so·chime′.** [ISO- + *-cheim* < Gk *cheima* winter cold] —**i′so·chei′mal, i·so·chei·me·nal** (ī′sə kī′mə nəl), **i′so·cheim′ic, i′so·chi′mal,** *adj.*

i·so·chro·mat·ic (ī′sə krō mat′ik, ī′sō krə-), *adj.* **1.** *Optics.* having the same color or tint. **2.** orthochromatic.

i·soch·ro·nal (ī sok′rə nəl), *adj.* **1.** equal or uniform in time. **2.** performed in equal intervals of time. **3.** characterized by motions or vibrations of equal duration. [< NL *isochron(us)* (< Gk *isóchronos* equal in age or time; see ISO-, CHRON-) + -AL¹] —**i·soch′ro·nal·ly,** *adv.*

i·soch·ro·nism (ī sok′rə niz′əm), *n.* an isochronal character or action.

i·soch·ro·nize (ī sok′rə nīz′), *v.t.,* **-nized, -niz·ing.** to make isochronal.

i·soch·ro·nous (ī sok′rə nəs), *adj.* isochronal. [< NL *isochronus* ISOCHRONAL] —**i·soch′ro·nous·ly,** *adv.*

i·soch·ro·ous (ī sok′rō əs), *adj.* having the same color throughout. Also, **i·soch′ro·öus.**

i·so·cli·nal (ī′sə klīn′əl, ī′sō-), *adj.* **1.** of or pertaining to equal direction of inclination; inclining or dipping in the same direction. **2.** noting or pertaining to an isoclinic line. **3.** *Geol.* noting or pertaining to a fold of strata which is of the nature of an isocline. —*n.* **4.** See **isoclinic line.** Also **i·so·clin·ic** (ī′sə klin′ik, ī′sō-). [ISO- + CLIN(O)- + -AL¹]

i·so·cline (ī′sə klīn′), *n.* *Geol.* a fold of strata so tightly compressed that the parts on each side dip in the same direction. [back formation from ISOCLINAL]

i′soclin′ic line′, an imaginary line connecting points on the earth's surface having equal magnetic dip. Also called **isoclinal, isoclinic.**

I·soc·ra·tes (ī sok′rə tēz′), *n.* 436–338 B.C., Athenian orator.

i·so·cy·a·nine (ī′sə sī′ə nēn′, -nin), *n.* *Chem.* a member of the group of cyanine dyes. Cf. **cyanine.**

i·so·di·a·met·ric (ī′sə dī′ə me′trik), *adj.* having equal diameters or axes.

i·so·di·mor·phism (ī′sō dī môr′fiz əm), *n.* *Crystall.* isomorphism between the forms of two dimorphous substances. —**i′so·di·mor′phous, i′so·di·mor′phic,** *adj.*

i·so·dy·nam·ic (ī′sō dī nam′ik, -di-), *adj.* **1.** pertaining to or characterized by equality of force, intensity, or the like. **2.** noting or pertaining to an imaginary line on the earth's surface connecting points of equal horizontal intensity of the earth's magnetic field. Also, **i′so·dy·nam′i·cal.**

i·so·e·lec·tron·ic (ī′sō i lek tron′ik, -ē′lek-), *adj.* *Physics. Chem.* noting or pertaining to atoms, radicals, or ions having either an equal number of electrons or an equal number of valence electrons.

i·so·gam·ete (ī′sə gam′ēt, ī′sō gə mēt′), *n.* *Biol.* one of a pair of conjugating gametes, exhibiting no differences in form, size, structure, or sex. Cf. **heterogamete.** —**i·so·ga·met·ic** (ī′sō gə met′ik), *adj.*

i·sog·a·mous (ī sog′ə məs), *adj.* *Biol.* having two similar gametes in which no differentiation can be distinguished, or reproducing by the union of such gametes (opposed to *heterogamous*).

i·sog·a·my (ī sog′ə mē), *n.* *Biol.* the fusion of two gametes of similar form, as in certain algae.

i·sog·e·nous (ī soj′ə nəs), *adj.* *Biol.* of the same or similar origin, as parts derived from the same or corresponding tissues of the embryo. —**i·sog′e·ny,** *n.*

i·so·ge·o·therm (ī′sə jē′ə thûrm′), *n.* an imaginary line on the earth's surface connecting points having the same mean temperature. —**i′so·ge′o·ther′mal, i′so·ge′o·ther′mic,** *adj.*

i·so·gloss (ī′sə glôs′, -glos′), *n.* (in the study of the geographical distribution of a dialect) a line on a map separating two localities which differ in a linguistic feature. [ISO- + Gk *glôss(a)* language; see GLOSS²] —**i′so·glos′sal,** *adj.*

i·so·gon (ī′sə gon′), *n.* a polygon having all angles equal.

i·sog·o·nal (ī sog′ə nəl), *adj.* **1.** equiangular; isogonic. —*n.* **2.** See **isogonal line.** [< Gk *isogṓn(ios)* equiangular (see ISO-, -GON) + -AL¹]

isog′onal line′, an imaginary line connecting all points of equal declination of the earth's magnetic field. Also called **i·so·gone** (ī′sə gōn′).

i·so·gon·ic (ī′sə gon′ik), *adj.* **1.** having or pertaining to equal angles. **2.** noting or pertaining to an isogonal line. —*n.* **3.** See **isogonal line.** [< Gk *isogṓn(ios)* having equal angles (see ISO-, -GON) + -IC]

i·so·gram (ī′sə gram′), *n.* *Meteorol., Geog.* a line representing equality with respect to a given variable, used to relate points on maps, charts, etc. Also called **isoline.**

i·so·graph (ī′sə graf′, -gräf′), *n.* (in the study of the geographical distribution of a dialect) a line drawn on a map to indicate areas having common linguistic characteristics. —**i·so·graph·ic** (ī′sə graf′ik), **i′so·graph′i·cal,** *adj.* —**i′so·graph′i·cal·ly,** *adv.*

i·so·hel (ī′sə hel′), *n.* *Meteorol.* a line on a weather map or chart connecting points that receive equal amounts of sunshine. [ISO- + Gk *hēl(ios)* sun]

i·so·hy·et (ī′sə hī′ət), *n.* *Meteorol.* a line drawn on a map connecting points having equal rainfall at a certain time. [ISO- + Gk *hyet(ós)* rain] —**i′so·hy′et·al,** *adj.*

i·so·la·ble (ī′sə lə bəl, is′ə-), *adj.* capable of being isolated. Also, **i·so·lat·a·ble** (ī′sə lā′tə bəl, is′ə-). —**i′so·la·bil′i·ty,** *n.*

i·so·late (*v.* ī′sə lāt′, is′ə-; *adj.* ī′sə lit, is′ə-), *v.,* **-lat·ed, -lat·ing,** *adj.* —*v.t.* **1.** to set or place apart; detach or separate so as to be alone. **2.** *Med.* to keep (an infected person) from contact with noninfected ones; quarantine. **3.** *Chem., Bacteriol.* to obtain (a substance or microorganism) in an uncombined or pure state. **4.** *Elect.* to insulate. —*adj.* **5.** isolated. [back formation from ISOLATED] —**i′so·la′tor,** *n.*

i·so·lat·ed (ī′sə lā′tid, is′ə-), *adj.* separated from other persons or things; alone; solitary. [< It *isolat(o)* (< L *insulātus;* see INSULATE) + -ED²]

i·so·la·tion (ī′sə lā′shən, is′ə-), *n.* **1.** the act or an instance of isolating. **2.** the state of being isolated. **3.** the complete separation from others of a person suffering from contagious or infectious disease; quarantine. **4.** the separation of a nation from other nations by isolationism. —**Syn. 2.** See **solitude.**

i·so·la·tion·ism (ī′sə lā′shə niz′əm, is′ə-), *n.* the policy or doctrine that peace and economic advancement can best be achieved by isolating one's country from alliances and commitments with other nations. —**i′so·la′tion·ist,** *n.*

I·solde (i sōld′, i sōl′də; *Ger.* ē zôl′də), *n.* Iseult.

i·so·leu·cine (ī′sə lo͞o′sēn, -sin), *n.* *Biochem.* an amino acid, $C_2H_5CH(CH_3)CH(NH_2)COOH$, occurring in casein, essential to the nutrition of man and animals.

i·so·line (ī′sə līn′), *n.* isogram.

i·sol·o·gous (ī sol′ə gəs), *adj.* *Chem.* (of two or more organic carbon compounds) similar chemically but differing from one another by other than nCH_2, as ethane, $H_3C\text{-}CH_3$, ethylene, $H_2C{=}CH_2$, and acetylene, $HC{\equiv}CH$. [ISO- + (HOMO)LOGOUS]

i·so·logue (ī′sə lôg′, -log′), *n.* *Chem.* one of two or more isologous compounds. Also, **i′so·log′.** [back formation from ISOLOGOUS, modeled after *homologue: homologous*]

i·so·mag·net·ic (ī′sō mag net′ik), *adj.* **1.** noting or pertaining to a line as on the earth's surface or a map, connecting places that have the same magnetic elements. —*n.* **2.** an isomagnetic line.

i·so·mer (ī′sə mər), *n.* **1.** *Chem.* a compound displaying isomerism with one or more other compounds. **2.** Also called **nuclear isomer.** *Physics.* a nuclide that exhibits isomerism with one or more other nuclides. [back formation from *isomeric.* See ISO-, -MERE, -IC]

i·som·er·ism (ī som′ə riz′əm), *n.* **1.** *Chem.* the relation of two or more compounds, radicals, or ions that are composed of the same kinds and numbers of atoms but differ from each other in structural arrangement (**structural isomerism**), as CH_3OCH_3 and CH_3CH_2OH, or in the arrangement of their atoms in space, and therefore in one or more properties. Cf. **stereoisomerism.** **2.** Also called **nuclear isomerism.** *Physics.* the relation of two or more nuclides that have the same atomic number and mass number but different energy levels and halflives. **3.** *Chem., Physics.* the phenomenon characterized by such a relation. **4.** the state or condition of being isomerous. —**i·so·mer·ic** (ī′sə mer′ik), *adj.*

i·som·er·ize (ī som′ə rīz′), *v.i., v.t.,* **-ized, -iz·ing.** *Chem.* to convert into an isomer. —**i·som′er·i·za′tion,** *n.*

i·som·er·ous (ī som′ər əs), *adj.* **1.** having an equal number of parts, markings, etc. **2.** *Bot.* (of a flower) having the same number of members in each whorl.

i·so·met·ric (ī′sə me′trik), *adj.* Also, **i′so·met′ri·cal.** **1.** of, pertaining to, or having equality of measure. **2.** *Crystall.* noting or pertaining to the system of crystallization characterized by three equal axes at right angles to one another. Cf. **system** (def. 11). **3.** *Pros.* made up of regular feet. **4.** *Drafting.* designating a method of projection **(i′somet′ric projec′tion)** in which a three-dimensional object is represented by a drawing **(i′somet′ric draw′ing)** having the horizontal edges of the object drawn usually at a 30° angle and all verticals projected perpendicularly from a horizontal base, all lines being drawn to scale. Cf. **axonometric, cabinet** (def. 17), **oblique** (def. 13). **5.** (of muscle action) occurring against resistance. **—***n.* **6.** an isometric drawing. **7. isometrics,** isometric exercises collectively. [< Gk *isometr(ía)* ISOMETRY + -IC] **—i′so·met′ri·cal·ly,** *adv.*

Isometric (def. 4)
A, Axonometric
B, Oblique
C, Cabinet

i′somet′ric ex′ercise, any of various exercises that pit one muscle or part of the body against another or against an immovable object in a strong but motionless pressing, flexing, contracting, etc.

i·so·me·tro·pi·a (ī′sō mə trō′pē ə), *n.* *Ophthalm.* equality of refraction in the two eyes of an individual. [< Gk *isómetr(os)* of equal measure (see ISO-, -METER) + -OPIA]

i·som·e·try (ī som′i trē), *n.* **1.** equality of measure. **2.** *Geog.* equality with respect to height above sea level. [< Gk *isometría*]

i·so·morph (ī′sə môrf′), *n.* **1.** an organism that is isomorphic with another or others. **2.** an isomorphous substance. [back formation from ISOMORPHOUS]

i·so·mor·phic (ī′sə môr′fik), *adj.* **1.** *Biol.* different in ancestry but having the same form or appearance. **2.** *Chem., Crystall.* isomorphous.

i·so·mor·phism (ī′sə môr′fiz əm), *n.* the state or property of being isomorphous or isomorphic.

i·so·mor·phous (ī′sə môr′fəs), *adj.* *Chem., Crystall.* **1.** (of a compound) capable of crystallizing in a form similar to that of another compound. **2.** (of an element) capable of crystallizing in a form similar to that of another element when combined with the same atom or group.

i·so·ni·a·zid (ī′sə nī′ə zid), *n.* *Pharm.* a solid, $C_5H_4NCONHNH_2$, used in the treatment of tuberculosis. [short for *isonicotinic acid hydrazide*]

i·son·o·my (ī son′ə mē), *n.* equality of political rights. [< Gk *isonomía*] **—i·so·nom·ic** (ī′sə nom′ik), **i·son′o·mous,** *adj.*

I·son·zo (ē zôn′tsô), *n.* a river flowing S from the Julian Alps in Yugoslavia to the Gulf of Trieste in Italy. 75 mi. long.

i·so·oc·tane (ī′sō ok′tān), *n.* *Chem.* the octane, $(CH_3)_3CCH_2CH(CH_3)_2$, used as one of the standards in establishing the octane number of a fuel. Cf. **octane number.**

i·so·pi·es·tic (ī′sō pī es′tik), *adj.* **1.** of or noting equal pressure; isobaric. **—***n.* **2.** isobar (def. 1). [ISO- + Gk *piest(ós)* compressible (verbal adj. of *piézein* to press) + -IC] **—i′so·pi·es′ti·cal·ly,** *adv.*

i·so·pleth (ī′sə pleth′), *n.* a line drawn on a map through all points having the same numerical value, as of a population figure, geographic measurement, etc. Also called **isarithm.** [< Gk *isoplēth(ḗs)* equal in number = *iso-* ISO- + *plêth(os)* a great number + *-ēs* adj. suffix]

i·so·pod (ī′sə pod′), *n.* **1.** any fresh-water, marine, or terrestrial crustacean of the order or suborder *Isopoda,* having seven pairs of legs, and having a body flattened dorsoventrally. **—***adj.* **2.** of, pertaining to, or characteristic of the *Isopoda.* [< NL *Isopod(a)* name of genus type. See ISO-, -POD] **—i·sop·o·dan** (ī sop′ə dən), *adj., n.* **—i·sop′o·dous,** *adj*

i·so·prene (ī′sə prēn′), *n.* *Chem.* a volatile liquid, $CH_2{=}C(CH_3)CH{=}CH_2$, used chiefly in the manufacture of synthetic rubber. [ISO- + *-pr-* (< ?) + -ENE; see TERPENE]

i′sopro′pyl al′cohol, *Chem.* a flammable liquid, $CH_3CHOHCH_3$, used chiefly in the manufacture of antifreeze and rubbing alcohol.

isopro′pyl group′, *Chem.* the univalent group, $(CH_3)_2CH-$, an isomer of the propyl group. Also called **isopro′pyl rad′ical.** **—is·o·pro·pyl** (ī′sə prō′pil), *adj.*

i·sos·ce·les (ī sos′ə lēz′), *adj.* (of a straight-sided plane figure) having two sides equal: *an isosceles triangle.* See diag. at **triangle.** [< LL < Gk *isoskelḗs* with equal legs = *iso-* ISO- + *skél(os)* leg + *-ēs* adj. suffix]

i·so·seis·mal (ī′sə sīz′məl), *adj.* **1.** Also, **i′so·seis′mic.** noting or pertaining to equal intensity of earthquake shock. **—***n.* **2.** Also called **isoseis′mal line′.** an imaginary line on the earth's surface connecting points characterized by equal intensity of earthquake shock.

i·sos·ta·sy (ī sos′tə sē), *n.* **1.** *Geol.* the equilibrium of the earth's crust, a condition in which the forces tending to elevate balance those tending to depress. **2.** the state in which pressures from every side are equal. [ISO- + *-stasy* < Gk *-stasia;* see STASIS, -Y[3]] **—i·so·stat·ic** (ī′sə stat′ik), *adj.*

i·so·ster·ic (ī′sə ster′ik), *adj.* *Chem.* having the same number of valence electrons in the same configuration but differing in the kinds and numbers of atoms.

i·so·there (ī′sə thēr′), *n.* *Climatology.* a line on a weather map connecting points that have the same mean summer temperature. [ISO- + Gk *there-,* var. s. of *théros* summer] **—i·soth·er·al** (ī soth′ər əl), *adj.*

i·so·therm (ī′sə thûrm′), *n.* **1.** *Meteorol.* a line on a weather map or chart connecting points having equal temperature. **2.** *Physics.* a curve on which every point represents the same temperature. [back formation from ISOTHERMAL]

i·so·ther·mal (ī′sə thûr′məl), *adj.* **1.** occurring at constant temperature. **2.** pertaining to an isotherm. **—***n.* **3.** *Meteorol.* an isotherm. [< F *isotherme*] **—i′so·ther′mal·ly,** *adv.*

isothiocy′ano group′, *Chem.* the univalent group, $-N{=}C{=}S$. Also called **isothiocy′ano rad′ical.** **—i·so·thi·o·cy·a·no** (ī′sə thī′ō sī′ə nō′), *adj.*

i·so·tone (ī′sə tōn′), *n.* *Physics.* one of two or more atoms having an equal number of neutrons but different atomic numbers.

i·so·ton·ic (ī′sə ton′ik), *adj.* **1.** *Physical Chem.* noting or pertaining to solutions characterized by equal osmotic pressure. Cf. **hypertonic** (def. 2), **hypotonic** (def. 2). **2.** *Physiol.* **a.** noting or pertaining to a solution containing the same salt concentration as mammalian blood. **b.** noting or pertaining to a contraction of a muscle when under constant tension. [< Gk *isóton(os)* having equal accent or tone (see ISO-, TONE) + -IC] **—i·so·to·nic·i·ty** (ī′sə tō nis′i tē), *n.*

i·so·tope (ī′sə tōp′), *n.* *Chem.* any of two or more forms of a chemical element, having the same number of protons in the nucleus, or the same atomic number, but having different numbers of neutrons in the nucleus, or different atomic weights. Isotopes of a single element possess almost identical chemical properties. [ISO- + Gk *tóp(os)* place] **—i·so·top·ic** (ī′sə top′ik), *adj.*

i·sot·o·py (ī sot′ə pē, ī′sə tō′pē), *n.* the quality or condition of being isotopic; isotopic character.

i·so·trop·ic (ī′sə trop′ik), *adj.* *Physics.* of equal physical properties along all axes. Cf. **anisotropic** (def. 1). Also, **i·sot·ro·pous** (ī so′trə pəs).

i·sot·ro·py (ī so′trə pē), *n.* the quality or condition of being isotropic; isotropic property.

i·so·type (ī′sə tīp′), *n.* **1.** a drawing, diagram, or other symbol that represents a specific quantity of or other fact about the thing depicted: *Every isotype of a house on that chart represents a million new houses.* **2.** a statistical graph, chart, diagram, etc., that employs such symbols. **—i·so·typ·ic** (ī′sə tip′ik), **i′so·typ′i·cal,** *adj.*

Is·pa·han (is′pə hän′), *n.* Isfahan.

Is·ra·el (iz′rē əl, -rā-), *n.* **1.** a republic in SW Asia, on the Mediterranean: formed as a Jewish state May 1948. 3,650,000; 7984 sq. mi. *Cap.:* Jerusalem. **2.** the people traditionally descended from Jacob; the Hebrew or Jewish people. **3.** a name given to Jacob after he had wrestled with the angel. Gen. 32: 28. **4.** (formerly) the northern kingdom of the Hebrews, including the 10 tribes. **5.** a group considered as God's chosen people. [ME, OE < L < Gk < Heb *Yisrāʼēl,* lit., wrestler with God]

Is′rael ben El·i·e·zer (ben el′ē ez′ər, -ā′zər). See **Baal Shem-Tov.**

Is·rae·li (iz rā′lē), *n., pl.* **-lis,** (*esp. collectively*) **-li,** *adj.* **—***n.* **1.** a native or inhabitant of modern Israel. **—***adj.* **2.** of or pertaining to modern Israel or its inhabitants. [< NHeb *Yisreʼēlī* = *Yisrāʼēl* ISRAEL + *-ī* suffix of appurtenance]

Is·ra·el·ite (iz′rē ə līt′, -rā-), *n.* **1.** a member of the Hebrew people who inhabited the ancient kingdom of Israel. **2.** one of a group considered as God's chosen people. **—***adj.* **3.** of or pertaining to ancient Israel or its people; Hebrew.

Is·ra·fil (iz′rə fēl′), *n.* *Islamic Myth.* the angel of music who will announce the end of the world. Also, **Is·ra·fel** (iz′rə fel′).

Is·sa·char (is′ə kär′), *n.* **1.** a son of Jacob and Leah. Gen. 30:18. **2.** one of the 12 tribes of Israel.

Is·sei (ēs′sā′), *n., pl.* **-sei.** **1.** a Japanese who emigrated to the U.S. after 1907 and was not eligible until 1952 for citizenship. **2.** any Japanese immigrant to the U.S. Also, **is′sei′.** Cf. **Kibei, Nisei, Sansei.** [< Jap = *is* first + *sei* generation]

is·su·a·ble (ish′o͞o ə bəl), *adj.* **1.** able to be issued or to issue. **2.** forthcoming; receivable. **3.** *Law.* admitting of issue being taken. **—is′su·a·bly,** *adv.*

is·su·ance (ish′o͞o əns), *n.* **1.** the act of issuing. **2.** issue.

is·su·ant (ish′o͞o ənt), *adj.* **1.** *Heraldry.* (of a beast) represented with the body erect and only the forepart visible: *a lion issuant.* **2.** *Rare.* emerging from a place.

is·sue (ish′o͞o *or, esp. Brit.,* is′yo͞o), *n., v.,* **-sued, -su·ing.** **—***n.* **1.** the act of sending out or putting forth; promulgation; distribution. **2.** something that is printed or published and distributed, esp. a given number of a periodical: *Have you seen the latest issue of the magazine?* **3.** that which is sent out or put forth in any form. **4.** a quantity sent out or put forth at one time: *a new issue of commemorative stamps.* **5.** the printing of copies of a work from the original setting of type with some slight changes: *the third issue of the poems.* **6.** a point in question or a matter that is in dispute. **7.** a point, matter, or dispute, the decision of which is of special or public importance. **8.** a point at which a matter is ready for decision. **9.** something proceeding from any source, as a product, effect, result, or consequence. **10.** the ultimate outcome of a proceeding, affair, etc. **11.** a distribution of food, equipment, or ammunition to military personnel. **12.** offspring; progeny: *to die without issue.* **13.** a going, coming, passing, or flowing out. **14.** a place or means of egress; outlet or exit. **15.** that which comes out, as an outflowing stream. **16.** *Pathol.* **a.** a discharge of blood, pus, or the like. **b.** an incision, ulcer, or the like, emitting such a discharge. **17.** *Law.* the yield or profit from land or other property. **18.** *Obs.* a proceeding or action. **19. at issue, a.** being disputed or under discussion. **b.** Also, **in issue.** being at opposite viewpoints. **20. take issue,** to disagree or dispute: *He took issue with me on my proposal.* **—***v.t.* **21.** to put into circulation. **22.** to mint, print, or publish for sale or distribution: *to issue a new book.* **23.** to distribute (food, clothing, etc.) to one or more officers or enlisted men or to a military unit. **24.** to send out; discharge; emit. **—***v.i.* **25.** to go, pass, or flow out; come forth; emerge: *to issue forth to battle.* **26.** to be sent, put forth, or distributed authoritatively or publicly. **27.** to be published, as a book. **28.** to originate or proceed from any source. **29.** to arise as a result or consequence; result. **30.** *Chiefly Law.* to proceed as offspring, or be born or descended. **31.** to result. **32.** *Archaic.* to have the specified outcome, result, etc. (often fol. by *in*). **33.** *Obs.* to end; terminate. [ME < MF: place or passage out, OF (*e*)*issue* < VL **exuta,* n. use of fem. of **exutus,* r. L *exitus* (ptp. of *exīre* to go out); see EXIT[1]] **—is′sue·less,** *adj.* **—is′su·er,** *n.*

—Syn. 2. copy, number, edition, printing. **10.** upshot, conclusion, end. **25.** See **emerge. 28.** flow, emanate, arise, spring. **29.** ensue. **—Ant. 25.** return.

Is·sus (is′əs), *n.* an ancient town, in Cilicia: victory of Alexander the Great over Darius III, 333 B.C.

Is·syk-Kul (is′ik ko͝ol′), *n.* a mountain lake in the SW Soviet Union in Asia. 2250 sq. mi.

-ist, a suffix of nouns, often accompanying verbs ending in *-ize* or nouns ending in *-ism,* denoting a person who practices or is concerned with something, or holds certain principles, doctrines, etc.: *apologist; dramatist; machinist; novelist; realist; socialist; Thomist.* Cf. **-ism, -istic, -ize.** [ME

-iste < L *-ista* < Gk *-istēs;* in some words, repr. F *-iste,* G *-ist,* It *-ista,* etc. << L < Gk, as above]

Is·tan·bul (is′tan bo͞ol′, -bo͝ol′, -tän-; is′tan bo͞ol′, -tän-; *Turk.* is täm′bo͝ol), *n.* a port in NW Turkey, on both the European and Asian banks of the Bosporus: built by Constantine I on the site of ancient Byzantium; capital of the Eastern Roman Empire and of the Ottoman Empire; capital removed to Ankara 1923. 1,750,642 (1965). Also, **Stambul, Stamboul.** Formerly (A.D. 330–1930), **Constantinople.**

Isth., isthmus. Also, **isth.**

isth·mi·an (is′mē ən), *adj.* **1.** of or pertaining to an isthmus. **2.** (*cap.*) of or pertaining to the Isthmus of Corinth or the Isthmus of Panama. —*n.* **3.** a native or inhabitant of an isthmus. [< L *isthmi(us)* (< Gk *isthmios* of a neck of land; see ISTHMUS) + -AN]

Isth′mian Games′, a festival of ancient Greece, held every two years on the Isthmus of Corinth.

isth·mus (is′məs), *n., pl.* **-mus·es, -mi** (-mī). **1.** a narrow strip of land, bordered on both sides by water, connecting two larger bodies of land. **2.** *Anat., Zool.* a connecting part, organ, or passage, esp. one that joins structures or cavities larger than itself. [< L < Gk *isthmós* neck (of land)] —**isth′moid,** *adj.*

-istic, a suffix of adjectives (and in the plural, of nouns from adjectives) formed from nouns in *-ist* and having reference to such nouns, or to associated nouns in *-ism* (*deistic; euphuistic; puristic*). In nouns, it usually has a plural form (*linguistics*). Cf. **-ist, -ic, -ics.** [< L *-istic(us)* < Gk *-istikos;* in some words, for *-istique* < F]

-istical, a combination of **-istic** and **-al**[1].

-istics, a combination of **-ist** and **-ics.**

is·tle (ist′lē), *n.* a fiber from any of several tropical American plants of the genera *Agave, Yucca,* and *Fourcroza,* used in making bagging, carpets, etc. Also, **ixtle.** [< MexSp *ixtle* < Nahuatl *ixtli*]

Is·tri·a (is′trē ə; *It.* ēs′trvä), *n.* a peninsula at the N end of the Adriatic, in NE Italy and NW Yugoslavia. —**Is′tri·an,** *adj., n.*

it (it), *pron., nom.* **it,** *poss.* **its** or (*Obs. or Dial.*) **it,** *obj.* **it;** *pl. nom.* **they,** *poss.* **their** or **theirs,** *obj.* **them;** *n.* —*pron.* **1.** (used to represent an inanimate thing understood, previously mentioned, or about to be mentioned): *It has whitewall tires and red upholstery. Although he didn't like it, I decided to see the movie anyway.* **2.** (used to represent a person or animal understood, previously mentioned, or about to be mentioned whose gender is unknown or disregarded): *Who was it? It was John.* **3.** (used to represent a group understood or previously stated): *It passed the bill over the governor's veto.* **4.** (used to represent a concept or abstract idea understood or previously stated): *It all started with Adam and Eve.* **5.** (used to represent an action or activity understood, previously mentioned, or about to be mentioned): *Since you don't like it, you don't have to go skiing.* **6.** (used as the impersonal subject of the verb *to be*): *It is six o'clock. It is foggy.* **7.** (used in statements expressing an action, condition, etc., without reference to an agent): *It rained last night. If it weren't for Edna, I wouldn't go.* **8.** (used in referring to something as the origin or cause of pain, pleasure, etc.): *Where does it hurt?* **9.** (used in referring to a source not specifically named or described): *It is said that love is blind.* **10.** (used as an anticipatory subject or object to make a sentence longer or more eloquent or to make or shift emphasis): *It is necessary that every man do his duty. It was then that he saw the gun.* —*n.* **11.** (in children's games) the player who is to perform some task, as in tag, the one who must catch the others. **12.** the general state of affairs or life in general: *How's it going with you?* **13. be with it,** *Slang.* **a.** to be attentive or alert. **b.** to be understanding or appreciative of something. **14. get with it,** *Slang.* to become active or interested. [ME, var. of ME, OE *hit,* neut. of HE[1]]

It, Italian (def. 3).

I.T.A., Initial Teaching Alphabet. Also, **i.t.a.**

it·a·col·u·mite (it′ə kol′yə mīt′), *n.* a sandstone noted for its flexibility when in thin slabs. [named after *Itacolumi,* mountain in Brazil; see -ITE[1]]

Ital., **1.** Italian. **2.** Italic. **3.** Italy. Also, **It.**

ital., italic; italics.

I·ta·lia (ē tä′lyä), *n.* Italian name of **Italy.**

Ita′lia ir·re·den′ta (*It.* ēR′Rē den′tä). See under **irredentist** (def. 1).

I·tal·ian (i tal′yən), *adj.* **1.** of or pertaining to Italy, its people, or their language. —*n.* **2.** a native or inhabitant of Italy, or a person of Italian descent. **3.** a Romance language, the language of Italy, official also in Switzerland. *Abbr.:* It [ME < L *Italiān(us)*] —**I·tal′ian·esque′,** *adj.*

I·tal·ian·ate (*adj.* i tal′yə nāt′, -nit; *v.* i tal′yə nāt′), *adj., v.,* **-at·ed, -at·ing.** —*adj.* **1.** Italianized; conforming to the Italian type or style or to Italian customs, manners, etc. —*v.t.* **2.** to Italianize. [< It *italianato*]

Ital′ian bread′, a crusty, yeast-raised bread, similar in appearance to French bread, but made without shortening and unsweetened.

Ital′ian East′ Af′rica, a former Italian territory in E Africa, formed in 1936 by the merging of Eritrea and Italian Somaliland with newly conquered Ethiopia: taken by the British Imperial forces 1941.

Ital′ian hand′, **1.** a medieval script considered a standard of fine handwriting. **2.** *Informal.* meddling or craftiness of a subtle nature.

I·tal·ian·ise (i tal′yə nīz′), *v.i., v.t.,* **-ised, -is·ing.** *Chiefly Brit.* Italianize. —**I·tal′ian·i·sa′tion,** *n.*

I·tal·ian·ism (i tal′yə niz′əm), *n.* **1.** an Italian practice, trait, or idiom. **2.** Italian quality or spirit.

I·tal·ian·ize (i tal′yə nīz′), *v.,* **-ized, -iz·ing.** —*v.i.* **1.** to become Italian in manner, character, etc. **2.** to speak Italian. —*v.t.* **3.** to make Italian, esp. in manner, character, etc. Also, *esp. Brit.,* **Italianise.** —**I·tal′ian·i·za′tion,** *n.*

Ital′ian Soma′liland, a former Italian colony and trust territory in E Africa: now part of the Somali Republic.

Ital′ian son′net. See **Petrarchan sonnet.**

i·tal·ic (i tal′ik, ī tal′-), *adj.* **1.** designating or pertaining to a style of printing types in which the letters usually slope to the right, used esp. for emphasis. **2.** (*cap.*) of or pertaining to Italy, esp. ancient Italy or its tribes. —*n.* **3.** Often, **italics.** italic type. **4.** (*cap.*) *Linguistics.* a branch of the Indo-European family of languages, including ancient Latin, Oscan, Umbrian, and modern Romance, and closely related to Celtic. [< L *Italic(us)* < Gk *Italikós*]

I·tal·i·cism (i tal′i siz′əm), *n.* Italianism, esp. an idiom or a characteristic of the Italian language.

i·tal·i·cize (i tal′i sīz′, ī tal′-), *v.,* **-cized, -ciz·ing.** —*v.t.* **1.** to print in italic type. **2.** to underscore (a word, sentence, or the like, in a manuscript) with a single line, as in indicating italics. —*v.i.* **3.** to use italics. —**i·tal′i·ci·za′tion,** *n.*

It·a·ly (it′əlē), *n.* a republic in S Europe, comprising a peninsula S of the Alps and Sicily, Sardinia, Elbe, and other smaller islands: a kingdom 1870–1946. 56,160,000; 116,294 sq. mi. *Cap.:* Rome. Italian, **Italia.**

I·tas·ca (ī tas′kə), *n.* **Lake,** a lake in N Minnesota: one of the sources of the Mississippi River.

itch (ich), *v.i.* **1.** to have or feel a peculiar tingling or uneasy irritation of the skin which causes a desire to scratch the part affected. **2.** to cause such a feeling: *This shirt itches.* **3.** to have a desire to do or to get something: *to itch after fame.* —*v.t.* **4.** to cause to have an itch: *His wool shirt always itches him.* **5.** to annoy; irritate. —*n.* **6.** the sensation of itching. **7.** an uneasy or restless desire or longing: *an itch for excitement.* **8.** a contagious disease caused by the itch mite, which burrows into the skin (usually prec. by *the*). Cf. **mange, scabies.** [ME *(y)icch(en),* OE *gicc(e)an;* akin to G *jucken,* D *jeuken*]

itch·ing (ich′ing), *adj.* **1.** of, pertaining to, or characterized by an irritating sensation of the skin. **2.** of, pertaining to, or having a longing or desire to do or to have something. **3.** characterized by a restless desire for action, adventure, etc.; marked by restlessness. **4.** characterized by a desire for money and material possessions; acquisitive; avaricious: *an itching palm.* —*n.* **5.** itch. [ME (n., adj.), OE (adj.)]

itch′ mite′, a parasitic mite, *Sarcoptes scabiei,* causing itch or scabies in man and a form of mange in animals.

itch·y (ich′ē), *adj.,* **itch·i·er, itch·i·est.** **1.** having or causing an itching sensation. **2.** characterized by itching. [OE *giccig*] —**itch′i·ness,** *n.*

-ite[1], a suffix of nouns denoting esp. persons associated with a place, tribe, leader, doctrine, system, etc. (*Campbellite; Israelite; laborite*); minerals and fossils (*ammonite; anthracite*); explosives (*cordite; dynamite*); chemical compounds, esp. salts of acids whose names end in *-ous* (*phosphite; sulfite*); pharmaceutical and commercial products (*vulcanite*); a member or component of a part of the body (*somite*). Cf. **-itis.** [ME < L *-ita* < Gk *-ītēs;* often directly < Gk; in some words repr. F *-ite,* G *-it,* etc., < L < Gk, as above]

-ite[2], a suffix forming adjectives and nouns from adjectives, and from some verbs: *composite; opposite; erudite; requisite.* [< L *-itus* or *-ītus* ptp. suffix]

i·tem (*n., v.* ī′təm; *adv.* ī′tem), *n.* **1.** a separate article or particular: *50 items on the list.* **2.** a separate piece of information or news, as a short paragraph in a newspaper. **3.** *Obs.* **a.** an admonition or warning. **b.** an intimation or hint. —*adv.* **4.** also; likewise (used esp. to introduce each article or statement in a list or series). —*v.t. Archaic.* **5.** to set down or enter as an item, or by or in items. **6.** to make a note or memorandum of. [< L: likewise] —**Syn. 1.** thing; entry.

i·tem·ize (ī′tə mīz′), *v.t.,* **-ized, -iz·ing.** to state by items; give the particulars of; list the individual units or parts of. —**i′tem·i·za′tion,** *n.* —**i′tem·iz′er,** *n.*

i·tem·ized (ī′tə mīzd′), *adj.* with each item separately listed with its own pertinent information: *an itemized bill.*

it·er·ance (it′ər əns), *n.* iteration. [ITER(ANT) + -ANCE]

it·er·ant (it′ər ənt), *adj.* characterized by repetition; repeating. [< L *iterant-* (s. of *iterāns*) repeating, prp. of *iterāre.* See ITERATE, -ANT]

it·er·ate (it′ə rāt′), *v.t.,* **-at·ed, -at·ing.** **1.** to utter again or repeatedly. **2.** to do (something) over again or repeatedly. [< L *iterāt(us)* repeated (ptp. of *iterāre*) *iter-* (s. of *iterum*) again + *-ātus* -ATE[1]] —**it′er·a′tion,** *n.* —**Syn. 1.** reiterate, repeat.

it·er·a·tive (it′ə rā′tiv, -ər ə tiv), *adj.* **1.** repeating; making repetition; repetitious. **2.** *Gram.* frequentative. [< LL *iterātīv(us)*] —**it′er·a′tive·ly,** *adv.* —**it′er·a′tive·ness,** *n.*

Ith·a·ca (ith′ə kə), *n.* **1.** one of the Ionian Islands, off the W coast of Greece: legendary home of Ulysses. 4156; 37 sq. mi. **2.** a city in S New York at the S end of Cayuga Lake. 26,226 (1970). —**Ith′a·can,** *adj.*

I·thunn (ē′tho͞on), *n.* Idun. Also, **I′thun.**

ith·y·phal·lic (ith′ə fal′ik), *adj.* **1.** of or pertaining to the phallus carried in ancient festivals of Bacchus. **2.** grossly indecent; obscene. **3.** *Class. Pros.* noting or pertaining to any of several meters employed in hymns sung in Bacchic processions. —*n.* **4.** a poem in ithyphallic meter. **5.** an indecent poem. [< LL *īthyphallic(us)* < Gk *īthyphallikós* = *īthý-phall(os)* erect phallus + *-ikos* -IC]

-itic, a combination of **-ite**[1] and **-ic,** used to form adjectives from nouns ending in **-ite:** *Semitic.* [< L *-itic(us)* < Gk *-itikos* (see -ITIS, -IC); in some words repr. F *-itique* < L, as above]

i·tin·er·an·cy (ī tin′ər ən sē, i tin′-), *n.* **1.** the act of traveling from place to place. **2.** a going around from place to place in the discharge of duty or the conducting of business. **3.** a body of itinerants, as ministers, judges, salesmen, etc. **4.** the state of being itinerant. **5.** the system of rotation governing the ministry of the Methodist Church. Also, **i·tin·er·a·cy** (ī tin′ər ə sē, i tin′-).

i·tin·er·ant (ī tin′ər ənt, i tin′-), *adj.* **1.** traveling from place to place, esp. on a circuit, as a minister, judge, or salesman. **2.** characterized by such traveling: *itinerant preaching.* **3.** working in one place for a short time and then moving on to work in another place, usually as a physical or outdoor laborer. —*n.* **4.** a person who travels from place to place, esp. for duty or business. **5.** a person who alternates between working and wandering. [< LL *itinerant-* (s. of *itinerāns*) journeying (prp. of *itinerārī* to journey) = *itiner-* (s. of *iter*) journey + *-ant-* -ANT] —**i·tin′er·ant·ly,** *adv.* —**Syn. 1, 3.** wandering, nomadic, migratory, roving, roaming. —**Ant. 1.** settled.

i·tin·er·ar·y (ī tin′ə rer′ē, i tin′-), *n., pl.* **-ar·ies,** *adj.* —*n.* **1.** a line of travel; route. **2.** a detailed plan for a journey, esp. a list of places to visit. **3.** an account of a journey; a record of travel. **4.** a guidebook for travelers. —*adj.* **5.** of or pertaining to travel or travel routes. **6.** *Obs.* itinerant. [late ME < LL *itinerāri(um),* n. use of neut. of *itinerārius* of a journey. See ITINERANT, -ARY]

i·tin·er·ate (ī tin′ə rāt′, i tin′-), *v.i.,* **-at·ed, -at·ing.** to go from place to place, esp. in a regular circuit, as a preacher or judge. [< LL *itinerāt(us)* traveled (ptp. of *itinerārī*). See ITINERANT, -ATE[1]] —**i·tin′er·a′tion,** *n.*

-ition, a compound suffix of nouns, being *-tion* with a preceding original or formative vowel, or, in other words, a combination of **-ite**[2] and **-ion:** *expedition; extradition.* [< L *-itiōn-* or *-ītiōn-,* s. of *-itiō* or *-ītiō.* See -ITE[2], -ION]

-itious, a compound suffix occurring in adjectives of Latin origin (*adventitious*) and with adjectives, formed in Latin or English, associated with nouns ending in *-ition* (*ambitious; expeditious*). Cf. **-ite**[2], **-ous.** [< L *-icius* or *-īcius* (as in *adventitious*); and < L *-itiōsus* or *-ītiōsus* (as in *ambitious*)]

-itis, a learned borrowing from Greek, used esp. in pathological terms to denote inflammation of an organ (*bronchitis; gastritis; neuritis*) and hence extended in meaning to include abnormal states or conditions, excesses, tendencies, obsessions, etc. (*telephonitis*). [< NL (or L) < Gk]

-itive, a suffix occurring in substantives of Latin origin: *definitive; fugitive.* [< L *-itīv(us)* or *-ītīv(us)*]

it'll (it′əl), a contraction of *it will* or *it shall.*

I·to (ē′tō′), *n.* **Prince Hi·ro·bu·mi** (hē′rō bo͞o′mē), 1841–1909, Japanese statesman.

-itol, *Chem.* a suffix used in names of alcohols containing more than one hydroxyl group: *inositol.* [-ITE[1] + -OL[1]]

its (its), *pron.* the possessive form of **it** (used as an attributive adjective): *The book has lost its jacket. I'm sorry about its being so late.* [IT + (HI)S] —**Usage.** See **me.**

it's (its), **1.** a contraction of *it is: It's starting to rain.* **2.** contraction of *it has: It's been a long time.*

it·self (it self′), *pron.* **1.** a reflexive form of **it:** *The battery recharges itself.* **2.** an emphatic appositive of **it, which, that, this,** or a noun: *The bowl itself is beautiful.* **3.** (used as the object of a preposition or as the direct or indirect object of a verb): *The chameleon's ability to change color is a protection for itself.* **4.** a normal or customary self. [ME; OE *hit self*] —**Usage.** See **myself.**

I.T.U., International Typographical Union.

I·túr·bi·de (ē to͞or′vē the), *n.* **A·gus·tín de** (ä′go͞os tēn′ de), 1783–1824, Mexican soldier and revolutionary: as Agustín I, emperor of Mexico 1822–23.

ITV, instructional television.

-ity, a suffix used to form abstract nouns expressing state or condition: *jollity; civility; Latinity.* [var. of earlier *-itie,* ME *-ite* < OF < L *-itāt-* (s. of *-itās*); in many words repr. L *-itās* directly]

IU, **1.** immunizing unit. **2.** international unit.

IUD, any small, variously shaped piece made esp. of polyethylene, for insertion in the uterus as a continuous contraceptive. Also called **intrauterine device, loop, coil.** [*i(ntra)-u(terine) d(evice)*]

I·u·lus (ī yo͞o′ləs), *n. Class. Myth.* Ascanius.

-ium, a suffix occurring in loan words from Latin (*tedium*); specialized in chemical terminology to form names of elements (*barium*). [< NL, L, neut. suffix]

i.v., **1.** increased value. **2.** initial velocity. **3.** intravenous. **4.** invoice value.

I·van III (ī′vən; *Russ.* i vän′), ("*Ivan the Great*") 1440–1505, grand duke of Muscovy 1462–1505.

Ivan IV, ("*Ivan the Terrible*") 1530–84, first czar of Russia 1547–84.

I·va·no·vo (i vä′no vo), *n.* a city in the W RSFSR, in the central Soviet Union in Europe, NE of Moscow. 380,000 (est. 1964). Formerly, **Iva′novo Voz·ne·sensk** (voz ne sensk′).

I've (īv), contraction of *I have.*

-ive, a suffix of adjectives (and nouns of adjectival origin) expressing tendency, disposition, function, connection, etc.: *active; corrective; destructive; detective; passive; sportive.* Cf. **-ative, -itive.** [< L *-īv(us)*; in some words, repr. F *-ive,* fem. of *-if*]

Ives (īvz), *n.* **1. Charles Edward,** 1874–1954, U.S. composer. **2. James Mer·ritt** (mer′it), 1824–95, U.S. lithographer. Cf. **Currier.**

i·vied (ī′vēd), *adj.* covered or overgrown with ivy: *ivied walls.*

I·vi·za (ē vē′sä), *n.* a Spanish island in the SW Balearic Islands, in the W Mediterranean Sea. Spanish, **Ibiza.**

I·vo·rien (ī vô′riən), *adj.* **1.** of or pertaining to Ivory Coast. —*n.* **2.** a native or inhabitant of Ivory Coast.

i·vo·ry (ī′və rē, ī′vrē), *n., pl.* **-ries,** *adj.* —*n.* **1.** the hard white substance, a variety of dentin, composing the main part of the tusks of the elephant, walrus, etc. **2.** this substance used to make carvings, billiard balls, etc. **3.** an article made of this or a similar substance, as a carving or a billiard ball. **4.** a tusk, as of an elephant. **5.** dentin of any kind. **6. ivories,** *Slang.* **a.** the keys of a piano. **b.** dice. **7.** Also called **vegetable ivory.** the hard endosperm of the ivory nut, used for ornamental purposes, for buttons, etc. **8.** a creamy or yellowish white. —*adj.* **9.** consisting or made of ivory. **10.** of the color ivory. [ME < OF *ivurie* < L *ebore(us)* (adj.) = *ebor-* (s. of *ebur*) ivory + *-eus* adj. suffix]

i′vo·ry-billed wood′pecker (ī′və rē bild′, ī′vrē-), a large, nearly extinct, black and white woodpecker, *Campephilus principalis,* of the southern U.S., having an ivory-colored bill.

i′vory black′, a fine black pigment made by calcining ivory.

I′vory Coast′, a republic in W Africa: formerly part of French West Africa. 7,200,000; 127,520 sq. mi. *Cap.:* Abidjan. —**I′vory Coast′er.**

i′vory nut′, **1.** the seed of a low, South American palm, *Phytelephas macrocarpa,* yielding vegetable ivory. **2.** a similar seed from other palms.

i′vory palm′, the palm bearing the common ivory nut.

i′vory tow′er, **1.** a place or situation remote from worldly or practical affairs: *His laboratory became an ivory tower where he could pursue his experiments in perfect contentment.* **2.** an attitude of aloofness from or disdain or disregard for worldly or practical affairs. —**i′vo·ry-tow′er·ish,** *adj.*

i·vy (ī′vē), *n., pl.* **i·vies.** **1.** Also called **English ivy.** a climbing vine, *Hedera helix,* having smooth, shiny, evergreen leaves, small, yellowish flowers, and black berries, grown as an ornamental. **2.** any of various other climbing or trailing plants. **3.** (*usually cap.*) See **Ivy League.** [ME; OE *īfig;* akin to G *Efeu*] —**i′vy·like′,** *adj.*

Ivy, *Hedera helix*

I′vy League′, **1.** a group of colleges and universities in the northeastern U.S., esp. Yale, Harvard, Princeton, Columbia, Dartmouth, Cornell, Pennsylvania, and Brown, having a reputation for high scholastic achievement and social prestige. **2.** characteristic of Ivy League colleges or their students and graduates: *an Ivy League education.* —**I′vy Lea′guer,** *n.*

i′vy vine′, a vinelike plant, *Ampelopsis cordata,* of the U.S., differing from the grapevine, esp. in having a corolla of wholly separate petals.

i.w., **1.** inside width. **2.** isotopic weight.

i·wis (i wis′), *adv. Obs.* certainly. Also, **ywis.** [ME, adv. use of neut. of OE *gewiss* (adj.) certain; c. D *gewis,* G *gewiss* certain, certainly; akin to WIT[2]]

I·wo (ē′wō), *n.* a city in SW Nigeria. 158,583 (1963).

I·wo Ji·ma (ē′wə jē′mə, ē′wō; *Jap.* ē′wô jē′mä), one of the Volcano Islands, in the N Pacific, S of Japan: captured by U.S. forces 1945; returned to Japan 1968.

I.W.W., See **Industrial Workers of the World.** Also, **IWW**

Ix·elles (ēk sel′), *n.* a city in central Belgium, near Brussels. 94,007 (est. 1964). Flemish, **Elsene.**

ix·i·a (ik′sē ə), *n.* any iridaceous plant of the genus *Ixia,* of southern Africa, having sword-shaped leaves and showy, ornamental flowers. [< NL < Gk: birdlime = *ix(ós)* mistletoe, birdlime (made with mistletoe berries) + *-ia* -IA]

Ix·i·on (ik sī′ən), *n. Class. Myth.* a king of the Lapithae who was punished by Zeus for his love for Hera by being bound on an eternally revolving wheel in Tartarus. —**Ix·i·o·ni·an** (ik′sē ō′nē ən), *adj.*

Ix·ta·ci·huatl (ēs′tä sē′wätəl), *n.* an extinct volcano in S central Mexico, SE of Mexico City. 17,342 ft. Also, **Ix·tac·ci·huatl** (ēs′täk sē′wätəl), **Iztaccihuatl.**

ix·tle (iks′tlē, ist′lē), *n.* istle.

I·yar (ē′yär; *Heb.* ē yär′), *n.* the eighth month of the Jewish calendar. Also, **Iy′yar.** Cf. **Jewish calendar.** [< Heb]

I·ye·ya·su (ē′ye yä′so͞o), *n.* **To·ku·ga·wa** (tô′ko͞o gä′wä), 1542–1616, Japanese general and statesman. Also, **Ieyasu.**

Iz·ard (iz′ərd), *n.* **Ralph,** 1742–1804, U.S. diplomat and statesman.

-ization, a combination of **-ize** and **-ation:** *civilization.*

-ize, a suffix of verbs having the sense, intransitively, of following some line of action, practice, policy, etc. (*Atticize; apologize; economize; theorize; tyrannize*), or of becoming as indicated (*crystallize; oxidize*); and transitively, of acting toward or upon, treating, or affecting in a particular way (*baptize; colonize; patronize; stigmatize*), or of making or rendering as indicated (*civilize; legalize; mobilize; realize*). Also, **-ise**[1]. Cf. **-ism, -ist.** [< LL *-iz(āre)* < Gk *-izein;* r. ME *-ise(n)* < OF *-ise(r)*]

I·zhevsk (i zhefsk′), *n.* a city in the E Soviet Union in Europe. 341,000 (est. 1964).

Iz·mir (iz′mēr), *n.* **1.** Formerly, **Smyrna.** a seaport in W Turkey on the Gulf of Izmir: important city of Asia Minor from ancient times. 417,413 (1965). **2. Gulf of.** Formerly, **Gulf of Smyrna.** arm of the Aegean Sea in W Turkey. 35 mi. long; 14 mi. wide.

Iz·tac·ci·huatl (ēs′täk sē′wätəl), *n.* Ixtaccihuatl.

Iz·ves·ti·a (iz ves′tē ə), *n.* the official newspaper of the Soviet government. Cf. **Pravda** [< Russ: lit., news]

iz·zard (iz′ərd), *n. Chiefly Dial.* the letter Z. [var. of ZED]

J

DEVELOPMENT OF MAJUSCULE						
NORTH SEMITIC	GREEK	ETR.	LATIN	MODERN		
				GOTHIC	ITALIC	ROMAN
SEE LETTER I				𝔍	*J*	J

DEVELOPMENT OF MINUSCULE					
ROMAN CURSIVE	ROMAN UNCIAL	CAROL. MIN.	MODERN		
			GOTHIC	ITALIC	ROMAN
SEE I	j	SEE I	𝔧	*j*	j

The tenth letter of the English alphabet developed as a variant form of I in Medieval Latin, and, except for the preference for the J as an initial letter, the two were used interchangeably, both serving to represent the vowel (i) and the consonant (y). Later, through specialization, it came to be distinguished as a separate sign, acquiring its present phonetic value under the influence of French.

J, j (jā), *n., pl.* **J's** or **Js, j's** or **js.** **1.** the 10th letter of the English alphabet, a consonant. **2.** any spoken sound represented by the letter *J* or *j*, as in *judge, major,* or *rajah.* **3.** a written or printed representation of the letter *J* or *j.* **4.** a device, as a printer's type, for reproducing the letter *J* or *j.*

J, *Physics.* joule. Also, **j**

J, the 10th in order or in a series, or, when *I* is omitted, the 9th.

j, *Math.* a vector on the *y*-axis, having length 1 unit.

J., **1.** Journal. **2.** Judge. **3.** Justice.

ja (yä), *adv. German.* yes.

Ja., January.

J.A., **1.** Joint Agent. **2.** Judge Advocate.

jab (jab), *v.,* **jabbed, jab·bing,** *n.* —*v.t., v.i.* **1.** to poke, or thrust smartly or sharply, as with the end or point of something. **2.** to punch, esp. with a short, quick blow. —*n.* **3.** a poke with the end or point of something; a smart or sharp thrust. **4.** a short, quick blow. Also, **job.** [var., orig. Scot, of JOB[2]] —**jab′bing·ly,** *adv.*

Jab·al·pur (jub′əl pôr′), *n.* a city in central Madhya Pradesh, in central India. 295,400 (1961). Also, **Jubbulpore.**

jab·ber (jab′ər), *v.i., v.t.* **1.** to speak rapidly, indistinctly, or nonsensically; chatter. —*n.* **2.** rapid, indistinct, or nonsensical talk; gibberish. [appar. imit.; cf. GIBBER, GAB[1]] —**jab′ber·er,** *n.* —**jab′ber·ing·ly,** *adv.*

Jab·ber·wock·y (jab′ər wok′ē), *n., pl.* **-wock·ies.** a parody of language consisting of meaningless syllables; nonsense; gibberish. Also, **jab′ber·wock′y, Jab·ber·wock, jab·ber·wock** (jab′ər wok′). [coined by Lewis Carroll in *Jabberwocky,* poem in *Through the Looking Glass*]

jab·i·ru (jab′ə ro͞o′), *n.* a large stork, *Jabiru mycteria,* of the warmer regions of America. [< Pg < Tupi-Guarani *jabirú*]

jab·o·ran·di (jab′ə ran′dē), *n., pl.* **-dis.** **1.** any of several South American, rutaceous shrubs of the genus *Pilocarpus.* **2.** the dried leaflets of certain of these plants, esp. *Pilocarpus jaborandi,* containing the alkaloid pilocarpine, which is used in medicine. [< Pg < Tupi-Guarani *yaborandí*]

ja·bot (zha bō′ *or, esp. Brit.,* zhab′ō), *n.* a falling ruffle, esp. of lace, worn at the neck by women. [< F: lit., bird's crop; akin to OF *gave* throat, bird's crop < ?]

jac·a·mar (jak′ə mär′), *n.* any tropical American bird of the family *Galbulidae,* having a long bill and usually metallic green plumage above. [< F < Tupi *jacamáciri*]

ja·ça·na (zhä′sə nä′), *n.* any of several tropical, ploverlike, aquatic birds of the family *Jacanidae,* most of them having extremely long toes and claws for walking on floating water plants. [< Pg *jaçanã* < Tupi-Guarani *jasanã*]

jac·a·ran·da (jak′ə ran′də), *n.* **1.** any tropical American, bignoniaceous tree of the genus *Jacaranda.* **2.** the fragrant, ornamental wood of any of these trees. **3.** any of various related or similar trees. **4.** their wood. [< Pg *jacarandá* < Tupi-Guarani *yacarandá*]

Ja·car·ta (jə kär′tə), *n.* Djakarta.

ja·cinth (jā′sinth, jas′inth), *n.* hyacinth (defs. 4, 5). [< ML *jacinth(us),* L *hyacinthus* HYACINTH; r. ME *jacin(c)t* < OF *jacin(c)te* < ML *jacin(c)t(us)*]

jack[1] (jak), *n.* **1.** any of various portable devices for lifting heavy objects short heights, using various mechanical, pneumatic, or hydraulic methods. **2.** Also called **knave.** *Cards.* a playing card bearing the picture of a servant or soldier. **3.** a device for turning a spit in roasting meat. **4.** *Games.* **a.** Also called **jackstone.** one of a set of small metal objects having six points, used in the game of jacks. **b. jacks.** Also called **jackstones.** (*construed as sing.*) a children's game in which these or similar objects are tossed and gathered in any of a number of prescribed ways, usually while bouncing a rubber ball. **5.** *Lawn Bowling.* a small, usually white bowl or ball used as a mark for the bowlers to aim at. **6.** a small flag flown at the bow of a vessel, usually symbolizing its nationality. **7.** a jackass. **8.** See **jack rabbit.** **9.** *Elect.* a connecting device in an electrical circuit designed for the insertion of a plug. **10.** (*cap.*) a sailor. **11.** *Slang.* money. **12.** a small wooden rod in the mechanism of a harpsichord, spinet, or virginal that rises when the key is depressed and causes the attached plectrum to strike the string. **13.** any of several carangid fishes, esp. of the genus *Caranx,* as *C. hippos,* of the western Atlantic Ocean. **14.** a lumberjack. **15.** *U.S.* applejack. **16.** *U.S.* jacklight. **17. every man jack,** everyone without exception. —*v.t.* **18.** to lift or move (something) with or as with a jack (usually fol. by *up*): *to jack a car up.* **19.** *Informal.* to increase, accelerate, or raise (prices, wages, speed, etc.). **20.** *U.S.* to seek (game or fish) with a jacklight. —*v.i.* **21.** *U.S.* to fish or hunt with the aid of a jacklight. —*adj.* **22.** *Carpentry.* having a height or length less than that of most of the others in a structure: *jack rafter; jack truss.* [ME *jakke, Jakke,* var. of *Jakken,* dissimilated var. of *Jankin* = *Jan* JOHN + *-kin* -KIN]

jack[2] (jak), *n.* **1.** a Polynesian, moraceous tree, *Artocarpus heterophyllus,* bearing a fruit resembling breadfruit. **2.** the fruit itself, which may weigh up to 70 pounds. [< Pg *jac(a)* < Malayalam *chakka*]

jack-, a combining form of **jack**[1]: *jackstay.*

jack-a-dan·dy (jak′ə dan′dē), *n., pl.* **-dies.** dandy (def. 1). [JACK- + *-a-* (< ?) + DANDY] —**jack′-a-dan′dy·ism,** *n.*

jack·al (jak′əl, -ôl), *n.* **1.** any of several wild dogs of the genus *Canis,* esp. *Canis aureus,* of Asia and Africa, which hunt in packs at night and which formerly were believed to hunt prey for the lion. **2.** a person who performs menial or degrading tasks for another. **3.** a person who performs dishonest or base deeds for his own or another's gain; villain; scoundrel; rogue. [< Turk *çakāl* < Pers *shag(h)āl;* c. Skt *sṛgāla*]

Jackal, *Canis aureus* (Total length 3 ft.; tail 1 ft.)

jack·a·napes (jak′ə nāps′), *n.* **1.** an impertinent, presumptuous young man; whippersnapper. **2.** an impudent, mischievous child. **3.** *Archaic.* an ape or monkey. [late ME *Jakken-apes,* lit., jack (i.e., man) of the ape, nickname of William de la Pole (1396–1450), Duke of Suffolk, whose badge was an ape's clog and chain]

jack·a·roo (jak′ə ro͞o′), *n., pl.* **-roos.** *Australian Informal.* jackeroo.

jack·ass (jak′as′), *n.* **1.** a male donkey. **2.** a fool, dolt, or blockhead; ass.

jack′ bean′, **1.** a bushy, leguminous plant, *Canavalia ensiformis,* of tropical regions, grown esp. for forage. **2.** the white seeds of this plant.

jack·boot (jak′bo͞ot′), *n.* a large leather boot reaching up over the knee.

jack·daw (jak′dô′), *n.* a glossy, black, European bird, *Corvus monedula,* of the crow family, that nests in towers, ruins, etc.

jack·e·roo (jak′ə ro͞o′), *n., pl.* **-roos.** *Australian Informal.* a novice on a sheep station or ranch. Also, **jackaroo.** [JACK- + (KANG)AROO]

jack·et (jak′it), *n.* **1.** a short coat, in any of various forms, usually opening down the front. **2.** something designed to be placed around the upper part of the body for a specific purpose other than clothing: *a cork jacket.* **3.** a protective outer covering. **4.** the skin of a potato, esp. when it has been cooked. **5.** See **book jacket.** **6.** the cover of a paperbound book. **7.** a paper or cardboard envelope for protecting a phonograph record. **8.** a metal casing, as the steel covering of a cannon. **9.** *U.S.* a folded paper or open envelope containing an official document. —*v.t.* **10.** to put a jacket on (someone or something). [late ME *jaket* < MF *ja(c)quet*]

Jack′ Frost′, frost or freezing cold personified.

jack·ham·mer (jak′ham′ər), *n.* a portable rock drill operated by compressed air.

jack-in-a-box (jak′in ə boks′), *n., pl.* **-box·es.** jack-in-the-box.

jack-in-the-box (jak′in *th*ə boks′), *n., pl.* **-box·es.** a toy consisting of a box from which, upon release of its lid, an enclosed figure springs up.

jack-in-the-pul·pit (jak′in *th*ə po͝ol′pit, pul′-), *n., pl.* **-pul·pits.** an araceous herb, *Arisaema atrorubens* (*A. triphyllum*), of North America, having an upright spadix arched over by a spathe.

Jack-in-the-pulpit

Jack′ Ketch′ (kech), *Brit. Slang.* a public executioner or hangman. [after *John Ketch* (1663?–86), English executioner noted for brutality]

jack·knife (jak′nīf′), *n., pl.* **-knives.** **1.** a large pocketknife. **2.** *Fancy Diving.* a dive during which the diver bends in midair to touch his toes and straightens out immediately before entering the water.

jack′ lad′der, *Naut.* See **Jacob's ladder** (def. 2).

jack·leg (jak′leg′), *adj. U.S. Slang.* **1.** unskilled; untrained for one's work. **2.** unscrupulous or without the accepted standards of one's profession. **3.** makeshift. [alter. of BLACKLEG; *jack* r. *black,* with which it rhymes]

jack·light (jak′līt′), *n.* a portable light for nighttime hunting or fishing.

jack′ mack′erel, a mackerellike food fish, *Trachurus symmetricus,* found along the Pacific coast of the U.S.

jack-of-all-trades (jak′əv ôl′trādz′), *n., pl.* **jacks-of-all-trades.** a man who is adept at many different trades or different kinds of work requiring manual skills.

jack-o'-lan·tern (jak′ə lan′tərn), *n.* **1.** a hollowed pumpkin with openings cut to represent human eyes, nose, and mouth and in which a candle or other light may be placed: traditionally made for display at Halloween. **2.** a commercially made lantern resembling this.

jack′ pine′, a pine, *Pinus Banksiana,* found on tracts of rocky, almost barren land in Canada and the northern U.S.

jack′ plane′, *Carpentry.* a plane for rough surfacing. See illus. at **plane**[2].

jack·pot (jak′pot′), *n.* **1.** *Poker.* a pot that accumulates until a player opens the betting with a pair of predetermined denomination, usually jacks or better. **2.** the chief prize or the cumulative stakes in any game. **3. hit the jackpot,** *Slang.* to achieve a sensational success; have sudden luck. Also, **jack′ pot′.** [?]

jack′ rab′bit, any of various large hares of western North America, having very long hind legs and long ears. [JACK(ASS) + RABBIT; so named from the size of its ears]

Jack rabbit, *Lepus townsendii* (Length 22 in.; ears 5 in.)

jack·screw (jak′skro͞o′), *n.* a jack consisting of a screw steadied by a threaded support and carrying a plate or other part bearing the load.

jack·shaft (jak′shaft′, -shäft′), *n.* *Mach.* **1.** Also called **countershaft.** a short shaft, connected by belting, gears, etc., that transmits motion from a motor or engine to a machine or machines that are driven from it. **2.** a shaft on which an idle wheel or fairlead turns.

jack·smelt (jak′smelt′), *n., pl.* **-smelts,** (*esp. collectively*) **-smelt.** a large silversides, *Atherinopsis californiensis,* found along the coast of California.

jack·snipe (jak′snīp′), *n., pl.* (*esp. collectively*) **-snipe,** (*esp. referring to two or more kinds or species*) **-snipes.** a small, short-billed snipe, *Limnocryptes minimus,* of Europe and Asia.

Jack·son (jak′sən), *n.* **1. Andrew** ("*Old Hickory*"), 1767–1845, U.S. general: 7th president of the U.S. 1829–37. **2. Helen Maria Hunt,** nee **Fiske,** 1830–85, U.S. novelist and poet. **3. Jesse (Louis),** born 1941, U.S. minister and civil-rights leader. **4. Robert Hough·wot** (hou′ət), 1892–1954, U.S. jurist: associate justice of the U.S. Supreme Court 1941–54. **5. Thomas Jonathan** ("*Stonewall Jackson*"), 1824–63, Confederate general in the U.S. Civil War. **6.** a city in and the capital of Mississippi, in the central part. 153,968 (1970). **7.** a city in S Michigan. 45,484 (1970). **8.** a city in W Tennessee. 39,996 (1970).

Jack′son Day′, January 8, a holiday commemorating Andrew Jackson's victory at the Battle of New Orleans in 1815: a legal holiday in Louisiana.

Jack·so·ni·an (jak sō′nē ən), *adj.* **1.** of or pertaining to Andrew Jackson or his ideas, political principles, etc. —*n.* **2.** a follower of Andrew Jackson or his ideas.

Jack·son·ville (jak′sən vil′), *n.* a seaport in NE Florida, on the St. John's River. 528,865 (1970).

jack′ staff′, a flagstaff at the bow of a vessel, on which a jack is flown.

jack·stay (jak′stā′), *n.* *Naut.* **1.** a rod or batten, following a yard, gaff, or boom, to which one edge of a sail is bent. **2.** a rail for guiding the movement of the hanks of a sail.

jack·stone (jak′stōn′), *n.* **1.** jack[1] (def. 4a). **2. jackstones,** (*construed as sing.*) jack[1] (def. 4b). [earlier *chackstone,* alter. of *checkstone* pebble < ?]

jack·straw (jak′strô′), *n.* **1.** a straw-stuffed figure of a man; scarecrow. **2.** an insignificant person. **3.** one of a group of strips of wood or similar objects, as straws or toothpicks, used in the game of jackstraws. **4. jackstraws,** (*construed as sing.*) a game in which players compete in picking up, one by one, as many jackstraws as possible without disturbing the heap. [after *Jack Straw,* name or nickname of one of the leaders of the rebellion headed by Wat Tyler in 1381 in England]

jack-tar (jak′tär′), *n.* a sailor. Also, **Jack′ Tar′.**

jack′ tow′el, a roller towel.

jack-up (jak′up′), *n.* *Informal.* an increase or rise.

Jack·y (jak′ē), *n., pl.* **Jack·ies. 1.** (*often l.c.*) a sailor. **2.** (*usually l.c.*) *Brit. Slang.* gin[1].

Ja·cob (jā′kəb), *n.* the second son of Isaac, the twin brother of Esau, and father of the 12 patriarchs. Gen. 25:24–34.

Ja·cob ben Ash·er (jā′kəb ben ash′ər), c1269–c1340, Hebrew commentator on the Bible and codifier of Jewish law.

Jac·o·be·an (jak′ə bē′ən), *adj.* **1.** of or pertaining to James I of England or to his period. **2.** noting or pertaining to the style of architecture and furnishings prevailing in England during the early 17th century. **3.** of or pertaining to the style of literature and drama produced during the early 17th century. —*n.* **4.** a writer, statesman, or other personage of the Jacobean period. [< NL *jacobae(us)* of *Jacobus* (Latinized form of *James*) + -AN]

Jacobean chair, c1620

Jac·o·bin (jak′ə bin), *n.* **1.** (in the French Revolution) a member of a radical political club that promoted the Reign of Terror, active chiefly from 1789 to 1794: so called from the Dominican convent in Paris, where they originally met. **2.** an extreme radical, esp. in politics. **3.** Dominican. [ME *Jacobin* < OF (*frere*) *jacobin* < ML (*frater*) *Jacobin(us).* See JACOB, -IN] —**Jac′o·bin′ic, Jac′o·bin′i·cal,** *adj.* —**Jac′o·bin′i·cal·ly,** *adv.*

Jac·o·bin·ism (jak′ə bi niz′əm), *n.* **1.** the political principles of the Jacobins. **2.** extreme radicalism, esp. in politics.

Jac·o·bite (jak′ə bīt′), *n.* a partisan, after 1688, of James II of England or of the Stuarts. [*Jacob-* (Latinized form of *James*) + -ITE[1]] —**Jac·o·bit·ic** (jak′ə bit′ik), *adj.* —**Jac′o·bit·ism,** *n.*

Ja′cob's lad′der, 1. a ladder seen by Jacob in a dream, reaching from the earth to heaven. Gen. 28:12. **2.** Also called **jack ladder.** *Naut.* a hanging ladder having ropes or chains supporting wooden or metal rungs or steps.

Ja·cob's-lad·der (jā′kəbz lad′ər), *n.* **1.** a garden plant, *Polemonium caeruleum,* whose leaves have a ladderlike arrangement. **2.** any of certain related plants.

ja·co·bus (jə kō′bəs), *n., pl.* **-bus·es.** a former gold coin of England issued by James I. [Latinized form of *James*]

jac·o·net (jak′ə net′), *n.* **1.** a lightweight cotton fabric for clothing and bandages. **2.** a cotton fabric much used as a lining for the spines of books. [< Urdu *jagannāthī,* after *Jagannāthpūrī* in Orissa, India, where cloth was first made]

jac·quard (jak′ärd, jə kärd′; *Fr.* zhA KAR′), *n.* (*often cap.*) fabric produced on a Jacquard loom. [named after J. M. *Jacquard.* See JACQUARD LOOM]

Jac′quard loom′, a loom for weaving elaborate designs, as for damasks or brocades. [named after J. M. *Jacquard* (1757–1834), French inventor]

Jac·que·rie (zhäkᵊ rē′), *n.* **1.** the revolt of the peasants of northern France against the nobles in 1358. **2.** (*l.c.*) any peasant revolt. [< F, MF: peasantry < *Jacques* (< LL *Jacōbus*) JACOB; see -RY]

Jacques Bon·homme (zhäk bô nôm′), any rebellious peasant who took part in the Jacquerie. [< F: lit., James goodfellow < *Jacques* (see JACQUERIE) + *bonhomme* (see BONHOMIE)]

jac·ta·tion (jak tā′shən), *n.* **1.** boasting; bragging. **2.** *Pathol.* a restless tossing of the body. [< L *jactātiōn-* (s. of *jactātiō*) bragging = *jactāt(us)* (ptp. of *jactāre,* freq. of *jacere* to throw) + *-iōn-* -ION]

jac·ti·ta·tion (jak′ti tā′shən), *n.* **1.** *Law.* a false boast or claim that causes harm to another. **2.** *Pathol.* jactation (def. 2). [< ML *jactitātiōn-* (s. of *jactitātiō*) tossing = L *jactitāt(us)* (ptp. of *jactitāre,* freq. of *jactāre* to throw about; see JACTATION) + *-iōn-* -ION]

jac·u·late (jak′yə lāt′), *v.t.,* **-lat·ed, -lat·ing.** to throw or hurl (a dart, javelin, etc.). [< L *jaculāt(us)* (ptp. of *jaculāre* to throw the javelin) = *jacul(um)* javelin (n. use of neut. of *jaculus* used for hurling = *jac-* hurl + *-ulus* adj. suffix) + *-ātus* -ATE[1]] —**jac′u·la′tion,** *n.*

jade[1] (jād), *n.* **1.** either of two minerals, jadeite or nephrite, sometimes green, highly esteemed as an ornamental stone for carvings, jewelry, etc. **2.** an object, as a carving, made from this material. **3.** Also called **jade′ green′.** green, varying from bluish green to yellowish green. [< F < It *giada* < obs. Sp (*piedra de*) *ijada* (stone of) flank < L *īlia* flank (see ILIUM) + *-ata* -ATE[1]; so called because supposed to cure nephritic colic]

jade[2] (jād), *n., v.,* **jad·ed, jad·ing.** —*n.* **1.** a worn-out, broken-down, worthless, or vicious horse. **2.** a worthless, vicious, or disreputable woman. —*v.t., v.i.* **3.** to make or become dull, worn-out, or weary, as from overwork or overuse. [?] —**jad′ish,** *adj.* —**Syn. 3.** exhaust; sate, satiate.

jad·ed (jā′did), *adj.* **1.** worn-out or wearied, as by overwork or overuse. **2.** dulled or satiated by overindulgence: *a jaded appetite.* **3.** dissipated: *a jaded woman.* —**jad′ed·ly,** *adv.* —**jad′ed·ness,** *n.*

jade·ite (jā′dīt), *n.* a mineral, essentially sodium aluminum silicate, $NaAlSi_2O_6$, occurring in tough masses, whitish to dark green: a form of jade.

Ja·dot·ville (*Fr.* zhä dō vēl′), *n.* a city in S Zaïre. 74,478 (est. 1958).

jae·ger (yā′gər; *for 1 also* jā′gər), *n.* **1.** any of several rapacious sea birds of the family *Stercorariidae* that pursue weaker birds in order to make them drop their prey. **2.** Also, **jager, jäger.** a hunter. [< G *Jäger* hunter = *jag(en)* (to) hunt + *-er* -ER[1]]

Ja·el (jā′əl), *n.* the woman who killed Sisera by hammering a tent pin through his head as he slept. Judges 4:17–22.

Ja·én (hä en′), *n.* a city in S Spain, NNW of Granada. 65,678 (est. 1963).

Jaf·fa (jaf′ə; *locally* yä′fä), *n.* a seaport in W Israel, part of Tel Aviv. Also called **Yafo.** Ancient, **Joppa.**

Jaff·na (jaf′nə), *n.* a seaport in N Ceylon. 94,248 (1963).

jag[1] (jag), *n., v.,* **jagged, jag·ging.** —*n.* **1.** a sharp projection on an edge or surface. —*v.t.* **2.** to cut or slash, esp. in points or pendants along the edge; form notches, teeth, or ragged points in. [late ME *jagge* (n.), *jaggen* (v.) < ?] —**jag′less,** *adj.*

jag[2] (jag), *n.* **1.** *Dial.* a load, as of hay or wood. **2.** *Slang.* a state of intoxication from liquor. **3.** *Informal.* a spree; binge: *an eating jag; a crying jag.* [perh. orig. load of broom or furze (OE *ceacga* broom, furze)]

J.A.G., Judge Advocate General.

Jag·an·nath (jug′ə nät′, -nôt′), *n.* **1.** *Hinduism.* a name of Krishna or Vishnu. **2.** Juggernaut (def. 2). Also, **Jag·an·na·tha** (jug′ə nät′hə), **Jag′ga·nath′.** [var. of JUGGERNAUT]

ja·ger (yā′gər), *n.* jaeger (def. 2). Also, **jä′ger.**

jag·ged (jag′id), *adj.* having ragged notches, points, or teeth; zigzag: *the jagged edge of a saw; a jagged wound.* —**jag′ged·ly,** *adv.* —**jag′ged·ness,** *n.*

jag·gy (jag′ē), *adj.,* **-gi·er, -gi·est.** jagged; notched.

jag·uar (jag′wär), *n.* a large, ferocious, spotted feline, *Panthera onca,* of tropical America. [< Pg < Tupi *jaguara*]

ja·gua·run·di (jä′gwə run′dē), *n., pl.* **-dis.** a short-legged, long-bodied, South American cat, *Felis eyra.* [< Pg < Tupi]

Jaguar (Total length 7 ft.; tail 2 ft.)

Ja·han·gir (yə hän′gēr), *n.* 1569–1627, 4th Mogul emperor in India 1605–27 (son of Akbar). Also, **Jehangir.**

Jahr·zeit (yär′tsīt, yôr′-), *n.* *Judaism.* Yahrzeit.

Jah·veh (yä′ve), *n.* Yahweh. Also, **Jah′ve, Jah·weh, Jah·we** (yä′we).

Jah·vism (yä′viz əm), *n.* Yahwism. Also, **Jah·wism** (yä′wiz əm).

Jah·vist (yä′vist), *n.* Yahwist. Also, **Jah·wist** (yä′wist). —**Jah·vis′tic, Jah·wis′tic,** *adj.*

jai a·lai (hī′ lī′, hī′ ə lī′, hī′ ə lī′), a game resembling handball, played on a three-walled court between two, four, or six players equipped with wicker, basketlike rackets. Cf. **fronton.** [< Sp < Basque = *jai* game + *alai* merry]

jail (jāl), *n.* **1.** a prison, esp. one for the detention of persons awaiting trial or convicted of minor offenses. —*v.t.* **2.** to take into or hold in lawful custody; imprison. Also, *Brit.*, **gaol.** [ME *jaile* < OF *jaiole* cage < VL **gaviola*, var. of **caveola*, dim. of L *cavea* CAVE]

jail·bait (jāl′bāt′), *n.* *U.S. Slang.* a girl with whom sexual intercourse is punishable as statutory rape because of her youth.

jail·bird (jāl′bûrd′), *n.* a person who is or has been confined in jail.

jail·break (jāl′brāk′), *n.* an escape from prison by forcible means.

jail·er (jā′lər), *n.* a person who is in charge of a jail, esp. a small jail. Also, **jail′or.** [ME *jayler, jaioler* < OF *jaiolier*]

jail·house (jāl′hous′), *n.*, *pl.* **-hous·es** (-hou′ziz). a building used as a jail.

Jain (jīn), *n.* **1.** an adherent of Jainism. —*adj.* **2.** of or pertaining to the Jains or Jainism. Also, **Jai·na** (jī′nə), **Jain′·ist.** [< Hindi: saint, lit., one who overcomes < Skt *jaina*]

Jain·ism (jī′niz əm), *n.* a dualistic, ascetic religion founded in the 6th century B.C. by a Hindu reformer as a revolt against the caste system and the vague world spirit of Hinduism.

Jai·pur (jī′pŏŏr), *n.* **1.** a former state in N India, now part of Rajasthan. **2.** a city in and the capital of Rajasthan, in N India. 403,400 (1961).

Ja·kar·ta (jə kär′tə), *n.* Djakarta.

jake (jāk), *adj.* *Slang.* satisfactory; O.K. [?]

jakes (jāks), *n.* (*usually construed as pl.*) *Chiefly Dial.* an outdoor privy; outhouse. [< F *Jacques*, proper name]

Ja·lal ud-din Ru·mi (jä läl′ ōōd dēn′ ʀōō′mē, ŏŏd-, ja-), 1207–73, Persian poet and mystic.

jal·ap (jal′əp), *n.* the dried root of any of several convolvulaceous plants, esp. *Ipomoea Purga* (*Exogonium Jalapa*), or the yellowish powder derived from it, used chiefly as a purgative. [< MF < Sp (*purga de*) *Jalapa* purgative from JALAPA] —**ja·lap·ic** (ja lap′ik), *adj.*

Ja·la·pa (hä lä′pä), *n.* a city in and the capital of Veracruz, in E Mexico. 66,509 (1960).

Ja·lis·co (hä lēs′kō), *n.* a state in W Mexico, 2,443,261 (1960); 31,152 sq. mi. *Cap.:* Guadalajara.

ja·lop·y (jə lop′ē), *n.*, *pl.* **-lop·ies.** *Informal.* an old, decrepit automobile. [?]

jal·ou·sie (jal′ə sē′ *or, esp. Brit.*, zhal′ŏŏ zē′), *n.* **1.** a type of blind or shutter made with horizontal slats fixed at an angle. **2.** a window made of glass slats of a similar nature. [< F; OF *gelosie* latticework, JEALOUSY]

jam[1] (jam), *v.*, **jammed, jam·ming,** *n.* —*v.t.* **1.** to press, squeeze, or wedge tightly between bodies or surfaces, so that motion or extrication is made difficult or impossible. **2.** to bruise or crush by squeezing: *He jammed his hand in the door.* **3.** to press, push, or thrust violently, as into a confined space or against some object: *She jammed her foot on the brake.* **4.** to fill or block up by crowding; pack or obstruct. **5.** to make (something) unworkable by causing parts to become stuck, blocked, caught, displaced, etc.: *to jam a lock.* **6.** *Radio.* **a.** to interfere with (radio signals or the like) by sending out others of approximately the same frequency. **b.** (of radio signals or the like) to interfere with (other signals). —*v.i.* **7.** to become stuck, wedged, fixed, blocked, etc.: *This door jams.* **8.** to press or push violently, as into a confined space or against one another: *They jammed into the elevator.* **9.** (of a machine, part, etc.) to become unworkable, as through the wedging or displacement of a part. —*n.* **10.** the act of jamming. **11.** the state of being jammed. **12.** a mass of objects, vehicles, etc., jammed together or otherwise unable to move except slowly: *a traffic jam.* **13.** *Informal.* a difficult or embarrassing situation; fix. Also, *Obs.*, **jamb** (for defs. 1–4, 7, 8). [appar. imit.; cf. CHAMP[1], DAM[1]] —**jam′mer,** *n.* —**Syn. 1.** crowd; ram, force.

jam[2] (jam), *n.* a preserve of whole fruit, slightly crushed, boiled with sugar. [? special use of JAM[1]]

Jam., Jamaica.

Ja·mai·ca (jə mā′kə), *n.* an island in the West Indies, S of Cuba: formerly a British colony; became independent in 1962 with dominion status in the British Commonwealth of Nations. 2,060,000; 4413 sq. mi. *Cap.:* Kingston. —**Ja·mai′can,** *adj.*, *n.*

Jamai′ca gin′ger, 1. ginger from Jamaica. **2.** a ginger extract used as a flavoring. **3.** powdered ginger root used for medicinal purposes.

Jamai′ca rum′, a heavy, pungent, slowly fermented rum made in Jamaica.

jamb[1] (jam), *n.* **1.** *Archit., Building Trades.* **a.** either of the sides of an opening. **b.** either of two stones, timbers, etc., forming the sidepieces for the frame of an opening. **2.** *Armor.* greave. Also, **jambe.** [ME *jambe* < MF: leg, jamb < LL *gamba* leg, var. of *camba* hock, fetlock < Gk *kámpē* joint, something jointed]

jamb[2] (jam), *v.t.*, *v.i.* *Obs.* jam[1] (defs. 1–4, 7, 8).

jam·ba·lay·a (jum′bə lī′ə), *n.* a Creole dish of rice, tomatoes, shrimp, herbs, etc. [< LaF < Pr *jambalaia*]

jam·beau (jam′bō), *n.*, *pl.* **-beaux** (-bōz). *Armor.* greave. [ME < AF = *jambe* leg (see JAMB[1]) + *-eau* < L *-ellus* n. suffix]

Jam·bi (jäm′bē), *n.* Djambi.

jam·bo·ree (jam′bə rē′), *n.* **1.** *Informal.* a carousal; any noisy merrymaking. **2.** a large gathering of members of the Boy Scouts, usually nationwide or international in scope (distinguished from *camporee*). [orig. uncert.]

James (jāmz), *n.* **1.** Also called **James′ the Great′.** one of the 12 apostles, the son of Zebedee and brother of the apostle John. Matt. 4:21. **2.** the person identified in Gal. 1:19 as the Lord's brother: probably the author of the Epistle of St. James. **3.** Also called **James′ the Less′.** ("*James the son of Alphaeus*") one of the 12 apostles. Matt. 10:3; Mark 3:18; Luke 6:15. **4.** one of the books of the New Testament. **5. Henry,** 1811–82, U.S. philosopher and author (father of Henry and William James). **6. Henry,** 1843–1916, U.S. novelist and critic in England (brother of William James). **7. Jesse (Wood·son)** (wŏŏd′sən), 1847–82, U.S. outlaw and legendary figure. **8. William,** 1842–1910, U.S. psychologist and philosopher (brother of Henry James).

James I, 1566–1625, king of England and Ireland 1603–1625; as James VI, king of Scotland 1567–1625 (son of Mary Stuart).

James II, 1633–1701, king of England, Ireland, and Scotland 1685–88 (son of Charles I of England).

James III. See **Stuart, James Francis Edward.**

James VI. See **James I.**

James′ Bay′, the S arm of Hudson Bay, in E Canada between Ontario and Quebec provinces. 300 mi. long; 160 mi. wide.

James′ Ed′ward. See **Stuart, James Francis Edward.**

James·i·an (jām′zē ən), *adj.* **1.** of, pertaining to, or characteristic of the novelist Henry James or his writings. **2.** of, pertaining to, or suggestive of William James or his philosophy. Also, **James′e·an.**

James′ Riv′er, 1. a river flowing E from the W part of Virginia to Chesapeake Bay. 340 mi. long. **2.** a river flowing S from central North Dakota through South Dakota to the Missouri River. 710 mi. long.

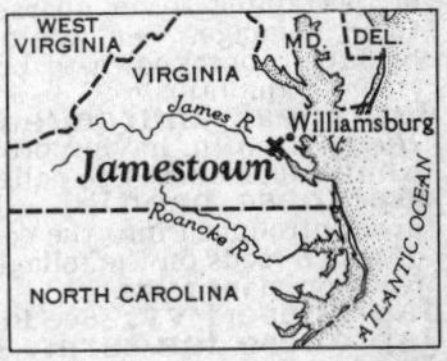

James·town (jāmz′toun′), *n.* **1.** a village in E Virginia: first permanent English settlement in North America 1607; restored 1957. **2.** a city in SW New York. 39,795 (1970).

Jam·mu and Kash·mir (jum′ōō; kash′mēr, kash mēr′), official name of **Kashmir.**

jam-packed (jam′pakt′), *adj.* filled or packed to the greatest possible extent.

jam′ ses′sion, *Jazz.* an impromptu meeting of a group of musicians at which they play for their own enjoyment. [? JAM[1], or ? shortening of JAMBOREE]

Jam·shed·pur (jam′shed pŏŏr′), *n.* a city in SE Bihar, in NE India. 303,500 (1961).

Jam·shid (jam shēd′), *n.* *Persian Myth.* the king of the peris who was given a human form as punishment for his boast of immortality and became a powerful and wonder-working Persian king. Also, **Jam·shyd′.**

jam-up (jam′up′), *n.* *Informal.* an act or instance of becoming blocked or unworkable because of congestion, obstruction, or malfunction: *mail jam-ups.*

Jan., January.

Ja·ná·ček (yä′nä chek′), *n.* **Le·oš** (le′ôsh), 1854–1928, Czech composer.

jane (jān), *n.* *Slang.* a girl or woman. [special use of the proper name]

Jane′ Doe′ (dō), a fictitious female person named in legal proceedings where the true name of the party in question is not known. [fem. of JOHN DOE]

Janes·ville (jānz′vil), *n.* a city in S Wisconsin. 46,426 (1970).

Ja·net (zhA ne′), *n.* **Pierre Ma·rie Fé·lix** (pyeʀ mA ʀē′ fā lēks′), 1859–1947, French psychologist and neurologist.

jan·gle (jang′gəl), *v.*, **-gled, -gling,** *n.* —*v.i.* **1.** to produce a harsh, discordant sound, as two small, thin pieces of metal hitting together. **2.** to speak angrily; wrangle. —*v.t.* **3.** to cause to make a harsh, discordant, usually metallic sound. **4.** to cause to become irritated or upset: *to jangle one's nerves.* —*n.* **5.** a harsh or discordant sound. **6.** an argument, dispute, or quarrel. [ME *jangle(n)* < OF *jangle(r)* < Gmc; cf. MD *jangelen* to haggle, whine] —**jan′gler,** *n.*

Ja·nic·u·lum (jə nik′yə ləm), *n.* a ridge near the Tiber in Rome, Italy. —**Ja·nic′u·lan,** *adj.*

jan·i·form (jan′ə fôrm′), *adj.* Janus-faced.

Jan·is·sar·y (jan′i ser′ē), *n.*, *pl.* **-sar·ies.** (*sometimes l.c.*) a member of a former elite military unit in the Ottoman Empire. Also, **Janizary.** [< F *janissaire* < It *gian(n)izzero* < Turk *yeniçeri* = *yeni* new + *çeri* soldiery, militia] —**Jan·is·sar·ian** (jan′i sâr′ē ən), *adj.*

jan·i·tor (jan′i tər), *n.* **1.** a person employed in an apartment house, office building, etc., to clean the public areas, remove garbage, and serve as a general handyman. **2.** a doorkeeper or porter. Also, *referring to a woman*, **jan′i·tress.** [< L: doorkeeper = *jāni-* (comb. form of *jānus* doorway, covered passage) + *-tor* -TOR] —**jan·i·to·ri·al** (jan′i tôr′ē əl, -tōr′-), *adj.*

Jan·i·zar·y (jan′i zer′ē), *n.*, *pl.* **-zar·ies.** (*sometimes l.c.*) Janissary. —**Jan·i·zar·i·an** (jan′i zâr′ē ən), *adj.*

Jan May·en (yän′ mī′en), a volcanic island in the Arctic Ocean between Greenland and Norway: a possession of Norway. 144 sq. mi.

Jan·sen (jan′sən; *Du.* yän′sən), *n.* **Cor·ne·lis Ot·to** (kôʀ-nā′lis ot′ō), (*Cornelius Jansenius*), 1585–1638, Dutch Roman Catholic theologian.

Jan·sen·ism (jan′sə niz′əm), *n.* the doctrinal system of Cornelis Jansen, denying free will and maintaining that human nature is corrupt and that Christ died for the elect and not for all men. [< F *jansénisme*] —**Jan′sen·ist,** *n.* —**Jan′sen·is′tic, Jan′sen·is′ti·cal,** *adj.*

Jan·u·ar·i·us (jan′yōō âr′ē əs), *n.* **Saint,** A.D. 272?–305?, Italian ecclesiastic and martyr: patron saint of Naples. Italian, **San Gennaro.**

Jan·u·ar·y (jan′yōō er′ē), *n.*, *pl.* **-ar·ies.** the first month of the year, containing 31 days. [< L *Jānuāri(us)*]

Ja·nus (jā′nəs), *n.* an ancient Roman god of doorways, of beginnings, and of the rising and setting of the sun, usually represented as having one head with two bearded faces back to back, looking in opposite directions. [< L, special use of *jānus* doorway, archway, arcade]

Ja·nus-faced (jā′nəs fāst′), *adj.* **1.** two-faced; deceitful. **2.** having contrasting aspects: *a Janus-faced foreign policy.*

Jap (jap), *n.* *Offensive.* a Japanese. [clipped form]

Jap, Japanese (def. 3). Also, **Jap.**

ja·pan (jə pan′), *n.*, *adj.*, *v.*, **-panned, -pan·ning.** —*n.* **1.** any of various hard, durable, black varnishes, originally from Japan, for coating wood, metal, or other surfaces. **2.** work varnished and figured in the Japanese manner. —*adj.*

3. of or pertaining to japan. —*v.t.* 4. to varnish with japan; lacquer. [special use of JAPAN] —**ja·pan′ner,** *n.*

Ja·pan (jə pan′), *n.* 1. a constitutional monarchy on a chain of islands off the E coast of Asia: main islands, Hokkaido, Honshu, Kyushu, and Shikoku. 113,000,000; 141,529 sq. mi. (1950). *Cap.:* Tokyo. Japanese, **Nihon, Nippon.** 2. **Sea of,** the part of the Pacific Ocean between Japan and Asia.

Japan., Japanese.

Japan′ clo′ver, a drought-resistant, perennial bush clover, *Lespedeza striata,* introduced to the southern Atlantic states from Asia, having numerous tiny trifoliate leaves valued for pasturage and hay.

Japan′ Cur′rent, a warm ocean current in the Pacific flowing N along the E coast of Taiwan, NE along the E coast of Japan, and continuing in an easterly direction into the open Pacific. Also called **Japan Stream, Kuroshio, Black Stream.**

Jap·a·nese (jap′ə nēz′, -nēs′), *adj., n., pl.* **-nese.** —*adj.* 1. of, pertaining to, or characteristic of Japan, its people, or their language. —*n.* 2. a native of Japan. 3. the language of Japan, not known to be related to any other language. *Abbr.:* Jap, Jap.

Jap′anese androm′eda, an Asian evergreen shrub, *Pieris japonica,* having broad, glossy leaves and clusters of whitish blossoms. Also called **andromeda.**

Jap′anese bee′tle, a scarabaeid beetle, *Popillia japonica,* introduced into the eastern U.S. from Japan, the adult of which feeds on the foliage of trees, and the larva of which feeds on plant roots.

Jap′anese i′vy. See **Boston ivy.**

Jap′anese lan′tern. See **Chinese lantern.**

Jap′anese persim′mon, 1. the soft, orange or reddish, edible fruit of an Asian tree, *Diospyros Kaki.* 2. the tree itself.

Jap′anese riv′er fe′ver, an infectious disease occurring chiefly in Japan and the East Indies, caused by the organism *Rickettsia tsutsugamushi,* transmitted by mites through biting.

Jap·a·nesque (jap′ə nesk′), *adj.* having a Japanese style.

Ja·pan·ism (jə pan′iz əm), *n.* 1. devotion to or preference for Japan and its institutions. 2. a custom, trait, or thing peculiar to Japan or its citizens. Also, **Japonism.** [< F *japonisme*]

Japan′ Stream′. See **Japan Current.**

Japan′ tea′, light, unfermented tea common to Japan.

Japan′ wax′, a pale-yellow, waxy, water-insoluble solid obtained from the fruit of certain sumacs, esp. *Rhus succedanea,* native to Japan and China: used chiefly in the manufacture of candles, furniture polishes, and floor waxes. Also called **Japan′ tal′low.**

jape (jāp), *v.,* **japed, jap·ing,** *n.* —*v.i.* 1. to jest; joke; gibe. —*v.t.* 2. to mock or make fun of. —*n.* 3. a joke; jest; quip. 4. a trick or practical joke played on someone. [ME *jape(n),* perh. < OF *jap(p)er* to bark] —**jap′er,** *n.* —**jap′er·y,** *n.* —**jap′ing·ly,** *adv.*

Ja·pheth (jā′fith), *n.* a son of Noah. Gen. 5:32. [< LL < Gk *Iápheth* < Heb *Yepheth* increase] —**Ja·phet·ic** (jə-fet′ik), *adj.*

ja·pon·i·ca (jə pon′ə kə), *n.* the camellia, *Camellia japonica.* [< NL = *Japon(ia)* JAPAN + *-ica,* fem. of *-icus* -IC]

Jap·o·nism (jap′ə niz′əm), *n.* Japanism.

Ja·pu·rá (*Port.* zhä′po͝o rä′), *n.* a river flowing E from the Andes in SW Colombia through NW Brazil to the Amazon. 1750 mi. long. Also, **Yapurá.**

Jaques-Dal·croze (*Fr.* zhäk′dal krōz′), *n.* **É·mile** (*Fr.* ā mēl′), 1865–1950, Swiss composer and teacher.

jar[1] (jär), *n.* 1. a broad-mouthed container, usually cylindrical and of glass or earthenware. 2. the quantity such a container can or does hold. [< MF *jarre* < OPr *jarra* < Ar *jarrah* earthen water vessel]

jar[2] (jär), *v.,* **jarred, jar·ring,** *n.* —*v.i.* 1. to produce a harsh, grating sound; sound discordantly. 2. to have a harshly unpleasant or perturbing effect on one's nerves, feelings, thoughts, etc. 3. to vibrate or shake. 4. to conflict, clash, or disagree. —*v.t.* 5. to cause to sound harshly or discordantly. 6. to cause to rattle or shake. 7. to have a sudden and unpleasant effect upon (the feelings, nerves, etc.). —*n.* 8. a harsh, grating sound. 9. a discordant sound or combination of sounds. 10. a jolt or shake; a vibrating movement, as from concussion. 11. a sudden, unpleasant effect upon the mind or feelings; shock. 12. a minor disagreement. [? OE *cearr(an)* (to) creak] —**jar′ring·ly,** *adv.*

jar[3] (jär), *n.* 1. *Archaic.* a turn or turning. 2. **on the jar,** partly opened; ajar. [var. of CHAR[3]; cf. AJAR[2]]

jar·di·niere (jär′dᵊnēr′, zhär′dᵊnyâr′), *n.* 1. an ornamental receptacle or stand for holding plants, flowers, etc. 2. various vegetables diced and boiled or glazed, each type usually separately, used for garnishing meat or poultry. Also, **jar′di·nière′.** [< F, fem. of *jardinier* gardener. See GARDEN, -ER[2]]

jar·gon[1] (jär′gən, -gon), *n.* 1. the language, esp. the vocabulary, peculiar to a particular trade, profession, or group: *medical jargon.* 2. unintelligible or meaningless talk or writing; gibberish. 3. pidgin. 4. speech or writing characterized by pretentious terminology and involved syntax. —*v.i.* 5. to utter or talk jargon or a jargon. [ME *jargoun* < MF *jargon;* akin to GARGLE] —**Syn.** 1. See **language.**

jar·gon[2] (jär′gon), *n.* a colorless to smoky gem variety of zircon. Also, **jar·goon** (jär go͞on′). [< F < It *giargone* << Pers *zargūn* gold-colored]

jar·gon·ise (jär′gə nīz′), *v.i., v.t.,* **-ised, -is·ing.** *Chiefly Brit.* jargonize. —**jar′gon·i·sa′tion,** *n.*

jar·gon·ize (jär′gə nīz′), *v.,* **-ized, -iz·ing.** —*v.i.* 1. to talk jargon or a jargon. —*v.t.* 2. to translate into jargon. —**jar′gon·i·za′tion,** *n.*

jarl (yärl), *n. Scand. Hist.* a chieftain; earl. [< ON; cf. Icel *jarl;* see EARL] —**jarl′dom,** *n.*

jar·o·site (jar′ə sīt′, jə rō′sīt), *n.* a yellowish or brownish mineral, $K_2Fe_6(SO_4)_4(OH)_{12}$, occurring in small crystals or large masses. [named after Barranco *Jaroso* (in Almería, Spain); see -ITE[1]]

jar·o·vize (yär′ə vīz′), *v.t.,* **-vized, -viz·ing.** to vernalize. [< Russ *yarov(oe)* spring grain (< *yara* spring; c. YEAR) + -IZE] —**jar′o·vi·za′tion,** *n.*

Jar·row (jar′ō), *n.* a seaport in NE Durham, in NE England, at the mouth of the Tyne River. 28,752 (1961).

Jas., *Bible.* James.

jas·mine (jaz′min, jas′-), *n.* 1. any of several oleaceous shrubs or vines of the genus *Jasminum,* having fragrant flowers. 2. any of several other plants having similar fragrant flowers, as the Carolina jessamine. 3. the fragrance itself. 4. a pale yellow. Also, **jessamine.** [< MF *jasmin,* var. of *jassemin* < Ar *yās(a)min* < Pers *yāsmīn*]

jas′mine tea′, tea scented with jasmine blossoms.

Ja·son (jā′sən), *n. Class. Myth.* a hero, the leader of the Argonauts, who, at the request of his uncle Pelias and with the help of Medea, retrieved the Golden Fleece from King Aeëtes of Colchis.

jas·per (jas′pər), *n.* 1. a compact, opaque, often highly colored, cryptocrystalline variety of quartz, often used in decorative carvings. 2. Also called **cameo ware, jas′perware′.** a fine, hard stoneware invented c1775 by Wedgwood, basically white but usually stained various colors by metallic oxides. [ME *jaspe, jaspre* < MF; OF *jaspe* < L *iaspis* < Gk < ?]

Jas′per Park′, a national park in the Canadian Rockies in W Alberta, in SW Canada.

Jas·pers (yäs′pərs), *n.* **Karl** (kärl), 1883–1969, German philosopher.

Jas·sy (yä′sē), *n.* a city in NE Rumania. 123,558 (est. 1964). Also, **Yassy.** Rumanian, **Iaşi.**

Jat (jät, jôt), *n.* a member of an Indo-Aryan people living mainly in northwestern India.

ja·to (jā′tō), *n., pl.* **-tos.** *Aeron.* a jet-assisted takeoff, esp. one using auxiliary rocket motors that are jettisoned after the takeoff. [*j(et) a(ssisted) t(ake)o(ff)*]

jauk (jäk, jôk), *v.i. Scot.* to dally; dawdle. [?]

jaun·dice (jôn′dis, jän′-), *n., v.,* **-diced, -dic·ing.** —*n.* 1. Also called **icterus.** *Pathol.* an abnormal body condition due to an increase of bile pigments in the blood, characterized by yellowness of the skin, of the whites of the eyes, etc., by lassitude, and by loss of appetite. 2. a state of feeling in which views are prejudiced or judgment is distorted. —*v.t.* 3. to distort or prejudice, as with envy, resentment, etc. [ME *jaundis* < OF *jaunisse* = *jaun(e)* yellow (< L *galbinus* pale green) + *-isse* -ICE]

jaunt (jônt, jänt), *v.i.* 1. to make a short journey, esp. for pleasure. —*n.* 2. such a journey. [?] —**jaunt′ing·ly,** *adv.*

jaunt′ing car′, a light, two-wheeled, one-horse cart, common in Ireland, having two seats set back to back and having a perch in front for the driver.

jaun·ty (jôn′tē, jän′-), *adj.,* **-ti·er, -ti·est.** 1. easy and sprightly in manner or bearing: *a jaunty step.* 2. smartly trim or effective, as clothing. [< F *gentil* noble, gentle, GENTEEL] —**jaun′ti·ly,** *adv.* —**jaun′ti·ness,** *n.*

Jau·rès (zhō res′), *n.* **Jean Lé·on** (zhäN lā ôN′), 1859–1914, French socialist and author.

Jav., Javanese.

Ja·va (jä′və), *n.* 1. the main island of Indonesia. 75,000,000 (est. 1970); 48,920 sq. mi. 2. the coffee bean or plant. 3. (*usually l.c.*) *Slang.* coffee, the beverage.

Ja′va man′, the hominid genus *Pithecanthropus.*

Jav·a·nese (jav′ə nēz′, -nēs′), *adj., n., pl.* **-nese.** —*adj.* 1. of or pertaining to the island of Java, its people, or their language. —*n.* 2. a member of the native Malayan race of Java, esp. of that branch of it in the central part of the island. 3. the language of central Java, of the Malayo-Polynesian family. [*Javan* (JAV(A) + -AN) + -ESE]

Ja·va·ry (zhä′vä rē′), *n.* a river in E South America, flowing NE from Peru to the upper Amazon, forming part of the boundary between Peru and Brazil. 650 mi. long. Also, **Ja′va·ri′.**

Ja′va Sea′, a sea between Java and Borneo.

Ja′va spar′row, a finchlike bird, *Padda oryzivora,* of the East Indies and Malaya, having gray plumage tinged with pink on the belly, often kept as a pet.

jave·lin (jav′lin, jav′ə lin), *n.* 1. a light spear, usually thrown by hand. 2. *Track.* **a.** a spearlike shaft about 8½ feet long, usually made of wood and tipped with steel. **b.** Also called **jave′lin throw′.** a field event in which the javelin is thrown for distance. —*v.t.* 3. to strike or pierce with or as with a javelin. [< MF *javeline* = *javel-* (? < Celt) + *-ine* -INE[2]]

Ja·vel′ wa′ter (zhə vel′), sodium hypochlorite, NaOCl, dissolved in water, used as a bleach, antiseptic, etc. Also, **Javelle′ wa′ter.** [trans. of F *eau de Javel,* after *Javel* former town, now in the city of Paris]

Jav·its (jav′its), *n.* **Jacob Kop·pel** (kō pel′), born 1904, U.S. senator from New York 1957–81.

jaw (jô), *n.* 1. either of two bones, the mandible or maxilla, forming the framework of the mouth. 2. the part of the face covering these bones, the mouth, or the mouth parts collectively: *His jaw is swollen.* 3. **jaws,** anything resembling a pair of jaws or evoking the concept of grasping and holding: *the jaws of a gorge; the jaws of death.* 4. *Mach.* **a.** one of two or more parts, as of a machine, that grasp or hold something: *the jaws of a vise.* **b.** any of two or more protruding parts for attaching to or meshing with similar parts. —*v.i.* 5. *Slang.* to talk; gossip. [ME *jowe* < OF *joue;* akin to It *gota* cheek] —**jaw′like′,** *adj.*

ja·wan (jə wän′), *n.* a common soldier of the army of India. [< Urdu *javān*]

jaw·bone (jô′bōn′), *n., v.,* **-boned, -bon·ing,** *adj.* —*n.* 1. a bone of either jaw; a maxilla or mandible. 2. the bone of the lower jaw; mandible. —*v.t.* 3. *Informal.* to attempt to convince or influence (a person, company, etc.) by moral persuasion instead of by using force or authority. —*adj.* 4. *Informal.* obtained by or resorting to such a practice: *jawbone controls.*

jaw·break·er (jô′brā′kər), *n.* 1. *Informal.* any word that is hard to pronounce. 2. a very hard, opaque ball of candy. 3. Also called **jaw′ crush′er.** a machine to break up ore, consisting of a fixed plate and a hinged jaw. —**jaw′-break′ing,** *adj.* —**jaw′break′ing·ly,** *adv.*

Jax·ar·tes (jak sär′tēz), *n.* ancient name of **Syr Darya.**

jay (jā), *n.* 1. any of several noisy, mischievous, corvine birds of the subfamily *Garrulinae,* as the common, crested *Garrulus glandarius,* of the Old World, having brownish plumage with blue, black, and white bars on the wings. 2.

Informal. a simple-minded or gullible person; simpleton. [ME < MF *jai* < LL *gāius, gāia*, special use of L *Gāius* man's name]

Jay (jā), *n.* **John,** 1745–1829, U.S. statesman and jurist: 1st Chief Justice of the U.S. 1789–95.

jay·bird (jā′bûrd′), *n.* jay.

Jay·cee (jā′sē′), *n.* a member of a civic group for young men (**United States Jaycees**) or of any one of the internationally affiliated groups of similar nature (**Junior Chamber International**). [pronunciation of *JC*, abbr. of its original title *United States Junior Chamber of Commerce*]

Jay·hawk·er (jā′hô′kər), *n.* **1.** a native or inhabitant of Kansas (the **Jayhawker State**) (used as a nickname). **2.** (*sometimes l.c.*) a plundering marauder, esp. one of the antislavery guerrillas in Kansas, Missouri, and other border states before and during the Civil War. [? *jay hawk* (a bird, but unattested) + -ER[1]]

Jay′hawker State′, Kansas (used as a nickname).

Jay's′ Trea′ty, *U.S. Hist.* the agreement in 1794 between England and the U.S. by which limited trade relations were established. [named after John JAY]

jay·vee (jā′vē′), *n.* *Sports Informal.* **1.** a player on the junior varsity. **2.** See **junior varsity.**

jay·walk (jā′wôk′), *v.i.* to cross a street at other than a regular crossing or to cross in a heedless manner, as against traffic lights. —**jay′walk′er,** *n.*

jazz (jaz), *n.* **1.** music based on Afro-American spirituals, blues, work songs, and the like, that evolved into increasingly complex styles marked by improvisation, propulsive rhythms, polyphonic ensemble playing, and a harmonic idiom ranging from simple diatonicism through chromaticism to atonality and tone clusters. **2.** a style of dance music, popular esp. in the 1920's, arranged for a large band and marked by some of the features of true jazz. **3.** *Slang.* liveliness; spirit. **4.** *Slang.* insincere, exaggerated, or pretentious talk. —*adj.* **5.** of, characteristic of, or noting jazz. —*v.t.* **6.** to play (music) in the manner of jazz. **7.** *Slang.* **a.** to put vigor or liveliness into (often fol. by *up*). **b.** to accelerate (often fol. by *up*). —*v.i.* **8.** to dance to jazz music. **9.** to play or perform jazz music. [?]

jazz·man (jaz′man′, -mən), *n., pl.* **-men** (-men′, -mən). an instrumentalist who plays jazz.

jazz·y (jaz′ē), *adj.,* **jazz·i·er, jazz·i·est.** *Slang.* **1.** pertaining to or suggestive of jazz music. **2.** wildly active or lively. —**jazz′i·ly,** *adv.* —**jazz′i·ness,** *n.*

J.C., 1. Jesus Christ. **2.** Julius Caesar. **3.** jurisconsult. [< L *juris consultus*]

J.C.D., 1. Doctor of Canon Law. [< L *Juris Canonici Doctor*] **2.** Doctor of Civil Law. [< L *Juris Civilis Doctor*]

JCI, Junior Chamber International.

J.C.S., Joint Chiefs of Staff. Also, **JCS**

jct., junction. Also, **jctn.**

JD, *Informal.* See **juvenile delinquent.**

J.D., 1. Doctor of Jurisprudence; Doctor of Law. [< L *Juris Doctor*] **2.** Doctor of Laws. [< L *Jurum Doctor*] **3.** *Informal.* See **juvenile delinquent.**

Je., June.

jeal·ous (jel′əs), *adj.* **1.** resentful and envious, as of someone's attainments or of a person because of his attainments, advantages, etc.: *jealous of his brother's wealth; jealous of his rich brother.* **2.** fearful of losing another's affection: *jealous of his wife.* **3.** troubled by suspicions or fears of rivalry, unfaithfulness, etc., as in love or aims: *a jealous husband.* **4.** solicitous or vigilant in maintaining or guarding something. **5.** *Bible.* intolerant of unfaithfulness or rivalry: *The Lord is a jealous God.* [ME *jelous, gelos* < OF *gelos* (F *jaloux*) < VL **zēlōs(us).* See ZEAL, -OSE[1]] —**jeal′ous·ly,** *adv.* —**jeal′ous·ness,** *n.*

jeal·ous·y (jel′ə sē), *n., pl.* **-ous·ies** for 4. **1.** jealous resentment against a rival, a person enjoying success or advantage, etc., or against another's success or advantage itself. **2.** mental uneasiness from suspicion or fear of rivalry, unfaithfulness, etc., as in love or aims. **3.** vigilance in maintaining or guarding something. **4.** a jealous feeling, disposition, state, or mood. [ME *gelusie, jelosie* < OF *gelosie*]

jean (jēn *or, esp. Brit.,* jān), *n.* **1.** Sometimes, **jeans.** a stout twilled cotton fabric. **2. jeans,** (*construed as pl.*) **a.** a garment, as overalls or trousers, made of this fabric. **b.** sturdy, low-waisted slacks with high patch pockets, cut and sewn in the style of work pants, esp. as worn by teen-agers of both sexes. Cf. **blue jeans, Levis. c.** *Slang.* trousers. [short for *jean fustian* Genoa fustian, late ME *Gene* GENOA + FUSTIAN]

Jeanne d'Arc (zhän dȧrk′). See **Joan of Arc.**

Jeans (jēnz), *n.* **Sir James (Hop·wood)** (hop′wŏŏd), 1877–1946, English astrophysicist and author.

Jeb·el ed Druz (jeb′əl ed drōōz′), a mountainous region in S Syria. ab. 2700 sq. mi. Also, **Jeb′el el Druz′, Jeb·el Druze** (jeb′əl drōōz′), **Djebel Druze.**

Jeb·el Mu·sa (jeb′əl mōō′sä), a mountain in NW Morocco, opposite Gibraltar: one of the Pillars of Hercules. 2775 ft.

Jed·burgh (jed′bûr ō, -bur ō, -bər ə), *n.* a border town in SE Scotland: ruins of a great abbey. 3679 (est. 1964).

Jed·da (jed′də), *n.* Jidda.

jee (jē), *interj., v.i., v.t.,* **jeed, jee·ing.** gee[1].

jeep (jēp), *n.* a small military motor vehicle having four-wheel drive. [? special use of *jeep*, name of fabulous animal in comic strip "Popeye," or alter. of G.P. (for General Purpose Vehicle), or both]

jee·pers (jē′pərz), *interj.* (used as a mild exclamation of surprise or emotion.) Also called **jee′pers cree′pers** (krē′pərz). [euphemism for *Jesus*]

jeer[1] (jēr), *v.i.* **1.** to speak or shout derisively; scoff or gibe rudely. —*v.t.* **2.** to shout derisively at; mock. —*n.* **3.** a jeering utterance; derisive or rude gibe. [< ?; cf. OE *cēir* clamor, akin to *cēgan* to call out] —**jeer′er,** *n.* —**jeer′ing·ly,** *adv.* —**Syn. 1.** sneer; jest. See **scoff. 2.** taunt, ridicule.

jeer[2] (jēr), *n.* Often, **jeers.** any of various combinations of tackles for raising or lowering heavy yards. [JEE + -ER[1]]

jeez (jēz), *interj.* (used as a mild expression of surprise, disappointment, astonishment, etc.) [euphemistic shortening of *Jesus*]

Jef·fers (jef′ərz), *n.* **(John) Robinson,** 1887–1962, U.S. poet.

Jef·fer·son (jef′ər sən), *n.* **1. Thomas,** 1743–1826, U.S. statesman, diplomat, and architect: 3rd president of the U.S. 1801–09. **2.** a town in NE Virginia, near Washington, D.C. 25,432 (1970).

Jef′ferson Cit′y, a city in and the capital of Missouri, in the central part, on the Missouri River. 32,407 (1970).

Jef′ferson Day′, April 13, Thomas Jefferson's birthday: a legal holiday in certain states.

Jef·fer·so·ni·an (jef′ər sō′nē ən), *adj.* **1.** pertaining to or advocating the political principles and doctrines of Thomas Jefferson. —*n.* **2.** a supporter of Thomas Jefferson or Jeffersonianism. —**Jef′fer·so′ni·an·ism,** *n.*

Jef·frey (jef′rē), *n.* **Francis** (*"Lord Jeffrey"*), 1773–1850, Scottish jurist, editor, and critic.

je·had (jē häd′), *n.* jihad.

Je·han·gir (yə hän′gēr), *n.* Jahangir.

Je·hol (jə hol′, rā′hō′; *Chin.* zhu′hu′, RU′-), *n.* **1.** a region and former province in NE China: divided among Hopeh, Liaoning, and Inner Mongolia in 1956. **2.** Chengteh.

Je·hosh·a·phat (ji hosh′ə fat′, -hos′-), *n.* a king of Judah who reigned in the 9th century B.C. I Kings 22:41–50.

Je·ho·vah (ji hō′və), *n.* **1.** a name of God in the Old Testament, an erroneous rendering of the ineffable name, JHVH, in the Hebrew Scriptures. **2.** (in modern Christian use) God. —**Je·ho·vic** (ji hō′vik), *adj.*

Jeho′vah's Wit′nesses, a Christian sect, founded in the U.S. in the late 19th century, that believes in the imminent end of the world and the establishment of a theocracy under God's rule.

Je·ho·vist (ji hō′vist), *n.* Yahwist. —**Je·ho′vism,** *n.* —**Je·ho·vis·tic** (jē′hō vis′tik), *adj.*

Je·hu (jē′hyōō), *n.* **1.** a king of Israel noted for his furious chariot attacks. II Kings 9. **2.** (*l.c.*) a fast driver.

je·june (ji jōōn′), *adj.* **1.** deficient or lacking in nutritive value: *a jejune diet.* **2.** without interest; dull; insipid. **3.** juvenile; immature; childish. [< L *jējūn(us)* empty, poor, mean] —**je·june′ly,** *adv.* —**je·june′ness, je·ju′ni·ty,** *n.*

je·ju·num (ji jōō′nəm), *n.* *Anat.* the middle portion of the small intestine, between the duodenum and the ileum. [< L *jējūnum*, n. use of neut. of *jējūnus* empty; so called because thought to be empty after death] —**je·ju′nal,** *adj.*

Je′kyll and Hyde′ (jē′kəl, jek′əl), a person marked by dual personality, one aspect of which is good and the other bad. [after the protagonist of R. L. Stevenson's novel (1886) *The Strange Case of Dr. Jekyll and Mr. Hyde*]

jell (jel), *v.i.* **1.** to congeal; become jellylike in consistency. **2.** to become clear, substantial, or definite; crystallize: *The plan began to jell.* —*n.* **3.** jelly. [back formation from JELLY]

Jel·li·coe (jel′ə kō′), *n.* **John Rush·worth** (rush′wûrth′), **1st Earl,** 1859–1935, British admiral.

jel·lied (jel′ēd), *adj.* **1.** congealed or brought to the consistency of jelly. **2.** containing or spread over with jelly or syrup.

jel·li·fy (jel′ə fī′), *v.,* **-fied, -fy·ing.** —*v.t.* **1.** to make into a jelly; reduce to a gelatinous state. —*v.i.* **2.** to turn into jelly; become gelatinous. —**jel′li·fi·ca′tion,** *n.*

Jell-O (jel′ō), *n.* *Trademark.* a dessert made from a mixture of gelatin, sugar, and fruit flavoring.

jel·ly (jel′ē), *n., pl.* **-lies,** *v.,* **-lied, -ly·ing.** —*n.* **1.** a food preparation of a soft, elastic consistency due to the presence of gelatin, pectin, etc., as fruit juice boiled down with sugar and used as a sweet spread for bread. **2.** anything of the consistency of jelly. —*v.t., v.i.* **3.** to bring or come to the consistency of jelly. [ME *gely* < OF *gelee* (frozen) jelly < ML **gelāta* frozen = L *gel-* freeze + *-āta* -ATE[1]] —**jel′ly·like′,** *adj.*

jel·ly·bean (jel′ē bēn′), *n.* a bean-shaped, usually brightly colored candy with a hard sugar coating and a firm gelatinous filling. Also, **jel′ly bean′.**

jel′ly dough′nut, a raised doughnut filled with jelly or jam.

jel·ly·fish (jel′ē fish′), *n., pl.* (*esp. collectively*) **-fish,** (*esp. referring to two or more kinds or species*) **-fish·es. 1.** any of various marine coelenterates of a soft, gelatinous structure, esp. one with an umbrellalike body and long, trailing tentacles; medusa. **2.** *Informal.* an indecisive or weak person.

Jellyfish, Class *Scyphozoa*

jel′ly roll′, a thin, rectangular layer of sponge cake spread with fruit jelly and rolled up.

Je·mappes (*Fr.* zhə mȧp′), *n.* a town in SW Belgium, near Mons: French victory over Austrians 1792. 12,766 (est. 1964).

jem·my (jem′ē), *v.,* **-mied, -my·ing,** *n., pl.* **-mies.** *Brit.* —*v.t.* **1.** jimmy. —*n.* **2.** jimmy. **3.** the baked head of a sheep. [special use of *Jemmy*, var. of **Jimmy**]

Je·na (yā′nä), *n.* a city in S East Germany: site of Napoleon's decisive defeat of the Prussians 1806. 83,073 (est. 1955).

je ne sais quoi (zhənᵊ se kwȧ′), *French.* an indefinable, elusive quality, esp. a pleasing one. [lit., I don't know what]

Jen·ghis Khan (jen′giz kän′, jeng′-). See **Genghis Khan.** Also, **Jen′ghiz Khan′.**

jên·min·piao (zhun′mēn′pyou′, RUN′-), *n., pl.* **jên·min·piao.** the monetary unit of the People's Republic of China. *Abbr.:* JMP Also, **jên·min·pi** (zhun′mēn′pē′, RUN′-). Also called **yuan.** [< Chin: people's banknote]

Jen·ner (jen′ər), *n.* **Edward,** 1749–1823, English physician: discoverer of smallpox vaccine.

jen·net (jen′it), *n.* **1.** a small Spanish horse. **2.** a female ass or donkey. Also, **genet.** [late ME < MF *genet* < Catalan, var. of *ginet* horse of the Zenete kind < Ar *zinētī*, dial. var. of *zanātī* pertaining to the Zenete tribe (of Moors) after *Zanātah* the Zenetes]

Jen·nings (jen′ingz), *n.* a city in E Missouri, near St. Louis. 19,379 (1970).

jen·ny (jen′ē), *n., pl.* **-nies. 1.** See **spinning jenny. 2.** the female of certain animals, esp. a female donkey or a female bird: *a jenny wren.* [special use of given name]

jeop·ard·ise (jep′ər dīz′), *v.t.,* **-ised, -is·ing.** *Chiefly Brit.* jeopardize.

jeop·ard·ize (jep′ər dīz′), *v.t.*, **-ized, -iz·ing.** to put in jeopardy; hazard; risk; imperil. Also, **jeop′ard.**

jeop·ard·ous (jep′ər dəs), *adj.* perilous; hazardous; risky. [late ME *jowpertous*] —**jeop′ard·ous·ly,** *adv.* —**Syn.** See **dangerous.**

jeop·ard·y (jep′ər dē), *n.* **1.** hazard or risk of or exposure to loss, harm, death, or injury; peril; danger: *For a moment his life was in jeopardy.* **2.** *Law.* the hazard of being found guilty, undergone by criminal defendants on trial. [ME *j(e)uparti*, etc. < AF, OF: lit., divided game or play, hence, uncertain chance, problem (in chess or love) = *j(e)u* play, game (< L *jocus* JOKE) + *parti*, ptp. of *partir* to divide; see PARTY] —**Syn. 1.** See **danger.**

Jeph·thah (jef′thə), *n.* a judge of Israel. Judges 11, 12. Also, *Douay Bible*, **Jeph·te** (jef′tə).

je·quir·i·ty (jə kwir′i tē), *n., pl.* **-ties. 1.** the Indian licorice, *Abrus precatorius.* **2.** Also called **jequir′ity beans′.** the seeds of this plant. [< Pg *jequiriti* < Tupi-Guarani *jekiriti*]

Jerboa, *Jaculus jaculus* (Total length 13 in.; tail 8 in.)

Jer., **1.** *Bible.* Jeremiah. **2.** Jersey.

Jer·ba (jer′bə), *n.* Djerba.

jer·bo·a (jər bō′ə), *n.* any of various mouselike rodents of North Africa and Asia, as of the genera *Jaculus, Dipus,* etc., with long hind legs used for jumping. [< NL < Ar *yarbū*ʽ]

je·reed (jə rēd′), *n.* a blunt wooden javelin used in games by horsemen in certain Muslim countries in the Middle East. Also, **jerid, jerreed, jerrid.** [< Ar *jarīd* rod, shaft]

jer·e·mi·ad (jer′ə mī′ad), *n.* a lamentation; mournful complaint. [JEREMI(AH) + -AD[1]]

Jer·e·mi·ah (jer′ə mī′ə), *n.* **1.** a Major Prophet of the 6th and 7th centuries B.C. **2.** a book of the Bible bearing his name. —**Jer′e·mi′an, Jer·e·mi·an·ic** (jer′ə mī an′ik), *adj.*

Je·rez (he reth′, -res′), *n.* a city in SW Spain: noted for its sherry. 130,900 (1960). Also called **Jerez′ de la Fron·te′ra** (the lä frôn te′rä). Formerly, **Xeres.**

Jer·i·cho (jer′ə kō′), *n.* an ancient city of Palestine, N of the Dead Sea.

je·rid (jə rēd′), *n.* jereed.

jerk[1] (jûrk), *n.* **1.** a quick, sharp pull, thrust, twist, throw, or the like; a sudden start. **2.** a spasmodic, usually involuntary, muscular movement, as the reflex action of pulling the hand away from a flame. **3.** any sudden, quick movement of the body, as in dodging something. **4.** *Slang.* a naïve, fatuous, or foolish person. **5.** (in weight lifting) the raising of a weight from shoulder height to above the head by straightening the arms. **6. the jerks,** *U.S.* paroxysms or violent spasmodic muscular movements, as from religious frenzy. —*v.t.* **7.** to pull, twist, move, thrust, or throw with a quick, suddenly arrested motion. **8.** to utter in a broken, spasmodic way. **9.** *Informal.* to prepare, dispense, and serve (soda) at a soda fountain. —*v.i.* **10.** to give a jerk or jerks. **11.** to move with a quick, sharp motion; move spasmodically. **12.** to talk in a broken, spasmodic way. **13.** *Informal.* to work as a soda jerk. **14. jerk off,** *Slang* (*usually vulgar*). to masturbate. [? dial. var. of *yerk* to draw stitches tight (shoemaker's term), thus making the shoe ready to wear, OE *gearc(ian)* (to) prepare, make ready] —**jerk′er,** *n.* —**jerk′ing·ly,** *adv.*

jerk[2] (jûrk), *v.t.* **1.** to preserve (venison or other meat) by cutting in strips and curing by drying in the sun. —*n.* **2.** jerky[2]. [back formation from JERKY[2]]

Jerkin

jer·kin (jûr′kin), *n.* a close-fitting, sleeveless jacket of the 16th and 17th centuries. [?]

jerk·wa·ter (jûrk′wô′tər, -wot′ər), *Informal.* —*n.* **1.** a train not running on the main line. —*adj.* **2.** ridiculously insignificant and out-of-the-way: *a jerkwater town.* [JERK[1] + WATER; so called from the jerking (i.e., drawing) of water to fill buckets for supplying a steam locomotive that has run short]

jerk·y[1] (jûr′kē), *adj.*, **jerk·i·er, jerk·i·est. 1.** characterized by jerks or sudden starts; spasmodic. **2.** *Slang.* silly; foolish; ridiculous. [JERK[1] + -Y[1]] —**jerk′i·ly,** *adv.* —**jerk′i·ness,** *n.*

jerk·y[2] (jûr′kē), *n.* meat, esp. venison, that has been jerked. Also, **jerk.** [popular alter. of CHARQUI]

Jer·o·bo·am (jer′ə bō′əm), *n.* **1.** the first king of the Biblical kingdom of Israel in N Palestine. **2.** (*l.c.*) a wine bottle having a capacity of about 4/5 of a gallon.

Je·rome (jə rōm′, jer′əm), *n.* **Saint** (*Eusebius Hieronymus*), A.D. c340–420, Christian ascetic and Biblical scholar: chief preparer of the Vulgate version of the Bible.

jer·reed (jə rēd′), *n.* jereed. Also, **jer·rid′.**

Jer·ry (jer′ē), *n., pl.* **-ries.** *Chiefly Brit. Informal.* **1.** a German. **2.** Germans collectively. [GER(MAN) + -Y[1]]

jer·ry-build (jer′ē bild′), *v.t.*, **-built, -build·ing. 1.** to build cheaply and flimsily. **2.** to contrive or develop in a haphazard, unsubstantial fashion, as a project, organization, etc. [back formation from *jerry-builder; jerry* in slang sense of chamber pot (short for JEROBOAM)] —**jer′ry-build′er,** *n.*

jer′ry can′, **1.** *Mil.* a narrow, flat-sided, five-gallon container for fluids, as fuel. **2.** *Brit.* a can with a capacity of 4½ imperial gallons. Also, **jer′ry·can′.** [*jerry*, short for JEROBOAM]

jer·sey (jûr′zē), *n., pl.* **-seys. 1.** a close-fitting, knitted sweater or shirt, worn by seamen, athletes, etc. **2.** a similar knitted garment of wool, silk, or the like, worn by women. **3.** (*cap.*) one of a breed of dairy cattle, raised originally on the island of Jersey, producing milk having a high content of butterfat. **4.** Also called **jer′sey cloth′.** a machine-knitted or machine-woven fabric of wool, nylon, rayon, silk, etc., used for garments. [after JERSEY] —**jer′seyed,** *adj.*

Jer·sey (jûr′zē), *n.* **1.** a British island in the English Channel: the largest of the Channel Islands. 79,342; 45 sq. mi. *Cap.:* St. Helier. **2.** See **New Jersey.** —**Jer′sey·an,** *n., adj.* —**Jer′sey·ite′,** *n.*

Jer′sey Cit′y, a seaport in NE New Jersey, opposite New York City. 260,545 (1970).

Je·ru·sa·lem (ji rōō′sə ləm), *n.* a city in and the capital of Israel, divided between Israel and Jordan in 1948 and unified by Israeli occupation in 1967: ancient holy city; the principal city of Palestine and a center of pilgrimage for Jews, Christians, and Muslims. 355,500.

Jeru′salem ar′tichoke, **1.** a sunflower, *Helianthus tuberosus*, having edible, tuberous, underground stems or rootstocks. **2.** the tuber itself. [popular alter. of It *girasole articiocco* edible sunflower. See GIRASOL, ARTICHOKE]

Jeru′salem cher′ry, an Old World, solanaceous plant, *Solanum Pseudo-Capsicum*, having white flowers and bearing round, scarlet or yellow fruits, cultivated as an ornamental.

Jeru′salem cross′, a cross whose four arms are each capped with a crossbar. See illus. at **cross.**

Jes·per·sen (yes′pər sən, jes′-), *n.* **(Jens) Ot·to (Har·ry)** (yens ot′ō här′ē), 1860–1943, Danish philologist.

jess (jes), *Falconry.* —*n.* **1.** a short strap fastened around the leg of a hawk and attached to the leash. —*v.t.* **2.** to put jesses on (a hawk). Also, *esp. Brit.*, **jesse.** [ME *ges* < OF *ges, gez, getz* (nom.) (*get* acc. > F *jet* JET[1]) << L *jact(us)* a throwing, n. use of *jactus*, ptp. of *jacere* to throw]

jes·sa·mine (jes′ə min), *n.* jasmine.

jesse (jes), *n., v.t.*, **jessed, jess·ing.** *Chiefly Brit.* jess.

Jes·se (jes′ē), *n.* the father of David. I Sam. 16.

Jes·sel·ton (jes′əl tən), *n.* former name of **Kota Kinabalu.**

jest (jest), *n.* **1.** a joke or witty remark; witticism. **2.** a bantering remark; a piece of good-natured ridicule. **3.** sport or fun: *to speak half in jest, half in earnest.* **4.** the object of laughter, sport, or mockery; laughingstock. **5.** *Obs.* an exploit. Cf. **gest**[1]. —*v.i.* **6.** to speak in a playful, humorous, or facetious way; joke. **7.** to speak or act in mere sport, rather than in earnest; trifle. **8.** to utter derisive speeches; gibe or scoff. —*v.t.* **9.** to deride or joke at; banter. [var. sp. of GEST[1]] —**jest′ful,** *adj.* —**Syn. 1.** quip. See **joke. 2.** jape, gibe. **4.** butt. **8.** jeer.

jest·er (jes′tər), *n.* **1.** a person who is given to witticisms, jokes, and pranks. **2.** a professional fool or clown, kept by a prince or noble, esp. during the Middle Ages. [ME *gester.* See GEST[1], -ER[1]]

jest·ing (jes′ting), *adj.* **1.** given to making jests; playful. **2.** fit for joking; unimportant; trivial: *This is no jesting matter.* —*n.* **3.** pleasantry; triviality. —**jest′ing·ly,** *adv.*

Je·su (jē′zōō, -sōō, jā′-, yā′-), *n. Literary.* Jesus. [< L, obl. (usually voc.) form of JESUS]

Jes·u·it (jezh′ōō it, jez′yōō-, jez′ōō-), *n.* **1.** a member of a Roman Catholic religious order **(Society of Jesus)** founded by Ignatius Loyola in 1534. **2.** (*usually l.c.*) *Offensive.* a crafty, intriguing, or equivocating person: so called in allusion to the methods ascribed to the order by its opponents. [< NL *Jēsuit(a).* See JESUS, -ITE[1]] —**Jes′u·it′ic, Jes′u·it′i·cal,** *adj.* —**Jes′u·it′i·cal·ly,** *adv.* —**Jes′u·it·ism, Jes′u·it·ry,** *n.*

Je·sus (jē′zəs), *n.* **1.** Also called **Jesus Christ, Je′sus of Naz′areth.** born 4? B.C., crucified A.D. 29?, the source of the Christian religion; the Savior. **2.** ("*the Son of Sirach*") the author of the Apocryphal book of Ecclesiasticus, who lived in the 3rd century B.C. **3.** *Christian Science.* the supreme example of God's nature expressed through man. —*interj.* **4.** (used as an oath or strong expression of disbelief, dismay, pain, etc.) [ME, OE < LL < Gk *Iēsous* < Heb *Yeshūaʽ*, syncopated var. of *Yehōshūaʽ* God is help]

Je′sus Christ′, **1.** Jesus (def. 1). **2.** Jesus (def. 4).

Je′sus freak′, a member of any of several youth groups originating in the early 1970's **(Je′sus peo′ple)** with a fundamentalist Christian background which emphasize intense personal devotion to and study of Jesus and his teachings.

jet[1] (jet), *n., v.*, **jet·ted, jet·ting,** *adj.* —*n.* **1.** a free or submerged stream of a liquid, gas, or small solid particles forcefully shooting forth from a nozzle, orifice, etc. **2.** something that issues in such a stream, as water or gas. **3.** a spout or nozzle for emitting liquid or gas: *a gas jet.* **4.** See **jet plane. 5.** See **jet engine.** —*v.t.* **6.** to shoot (something) forth in a stream; spout. —*v.i.* **7.** to be shot forth in a stream. **8.** to travel by or as by jet plane. —*adj.* **9.** of, pertaining to, associated with, or noting a jet, jet engine, or jet plane: *jet pilot; jet exhaust.* **10.** in the form of or producing a jet or jet propulsion: *jet nozzle; jet engine.* [< MF *jet(er)* (to) throw < VL **jectāre*, alter. of L *jactāre* = *jac-* throw + *t-* freq. suffix + *-āre* inf. suffix] —**jet′ting·ly,** *adv.*

jet[2] (jet), *n.* **1.** a compact black coal, susceptible of a high polish, used for making beads, jewelry, buttons, etc. **2.** a deep, glossy black. **3.** *Obs.* black marble. —*adj.* **4.** consisting or made of jet. **5.** of the color jet; black as jet. [ME *jet, get* < OF *jaiet* << L *gagāt(ēs)* < Gk (*líthos*) *gagátēs* (stone) of *Gágai*, town in Lycia; r. OE *gagāt-stān* jet stone]

jet-black (jet′blak′), *adj.* deep-black: *jet-black hair.*

je·té (zhə tā′), *n., pl.* **-tés** (-tāz′; *Fr.* -tā′). *Ballet.* a jump forward, backward, or to the side, from one foot to the other. [< F: lit., thrown, ptp. of *jeter* to throw; see JET[1]]

jet′ en′gine, an engine, esp. an aircraft engine, that produces forward motion by the rearward exhaust of a jet of fluid or heated air and gases. Also called **jet′ mo′tor.**

Jeth·ro (jeth′rō), *n.* the father-in-law of Moses. Ex. 3:1.

jet′ lag′, a temporary disruption of one's normal biological rhythms after long-distance travel by airplane through several time zones without sufficient rest en route. Also called **jet′ fatigue′.**

jet′ plane′, an airplane propelled by one or more jet engines.

jet·port (jet′pōrt′, -pôrt′), *n.* an airport for jet airplanes.

jet-pro·pelled (jet′prə peld′), *adj.* **1.** propelled by a jet engine or engines. **2.** having a force or speed suggesting something propelled by a jet engine; fast or powerful.

jet′ propul′sion, the propulsion of a body by its reaction to a force ejecting a gas or a liquid from it. —**jet′-pro·pul′sion,** *adj.*

jet·sam (jet′səm), *n.* goods cast overboard deliberately, as to lighten a vessel or improve its stability in an emergency, which sink where jettisoned or are washed ashore. Also, **jet′som.** Cf. **flotsam, lagan.** [alter. of *jetson*, syncopated var. of JETTISON]

jet′ set′, an ultrafashionable social set composed of people reputed to spend much of their leisure time in intercontinental jetting from resort to resort.

jet′ stream′, 1. strong, generally westerly winds concentrated in a relatively narrow and shallow stream in the upper troposphere. 2. the exhaust of a rocket engine.

jet·ti·son (jet′i sən, -zən), *n.* 1. the act of casting goods overboard to lighten a vessel or aircraft or to improve its stability in an emergency. 2. jetsam. —*v.t.* 3. to cast (goods) overboard in order to lighten a vessel or aircraft or to improve its stability in an emergency. 4. to throw off (an obstacle or burden). [ME *jetteson* < AF; OF *getaison* << L *jactātiōn-* (s. of *jactātiō*) JACTATION]

jet·ton (jet′ən), *n.* an inscribed counter or token. [< F *jeton* = *jet(er)* (to) throw, cast up (accounts), reckon (see JET[1]) + *-on* n. suffix]

jet·ty[1] (jet′ē), *n., pl.* **-ties.** 1. a pier or structure of stones, piles, or the like, projecting into the sea or other body of water to protect a harbor, deflect the current, etc. 2. a wharf or landing pier. 3. the piles or wooden structure protecting a pier. [ME *get(t)ey* < OF *jetee*, lit., something thrown out, a projection, n. use of *jetee*, fem. ptp. of *jeter* to throw; see JET[1]]

jet·ty[2] (jet′ē), *adj.* 1. made of jet. 2. resembling jet, esp. in color; of a deep, glossy black. [JET[2] + -Y[1]] —**jet′ti·ness,** *n.*

jet′ wash′, *Aeron.* the backwash caused by a jet engine.

jeu de mots (zhœdə mō′), *pl.* **jeux de mots** (zhœdə mō′). *French.* a pun. [lit., play of words]

jeu d'es·prit (zhœ des prē′), *pl.* **jeux d'es·prit** (zhœ des prē′). *French.* 1. a witticism. 2. a literary work showing keen wit or intelligence rather than profundity. [lit., play of spirit]

jeune fille (zhœn fē′yə), *pl.* **jeunes filles** (zhœn fē′yə). *French.* a young, unmarried girl.

jeu·nesse do·rée (zhœ nes′ dô rā′), *French.* wealthy, stylish, sophisticated young people. [lit., gilded youth]

Jev·ons (jev′ənz), *n.* **William Stanley,** 1835–82, English economist and logician.

Jew (jo͞o), *n.* 1. a person whose religion is Judaism. 2. one of a scattered group of people that traces its descent from the Biblical Hebrews or from postexilian adherents of Judaism; Israelite. 3. a subject of the ancient kingdom of Israel. —*v.t.* 4. (*l.c.*) *Offensive.* to bargain sharply with; beat down in price (often fol. by *down*). [ME *jewe, giu, gyu, ju* < OF *juiu, juieu, gyu* < LL *jūdē(us)*, L *jūdaeus* < Gk *ioudaîos* < Aram *yehūdāi*, c. Heb *yehūdī* Jew < *yehūdāh* JUDAH; r. OE *iūdēas* Jews < LL *jūdē(us)* + OE *-as* pl. ending]

Jew-bait·ing (jo͞o′bā′ting), *n.* active anti-Semitism. —**Jew′-bait′er,** *n.*

jew·el (jo͞o′əl), *n., v.,* **-eled, -el·ing** or (*esp. Brit.*) **-elled, -el·ling.** —*n.* 1. a cut and polished precious stone; gem. 2. a fashioned ornament for personal adornment, esp. of a precious metal set with gems. 3. a precious possession. 4. *Informal.* a person of great worth or rare excellence. 5. a durable bearing used in fine timepieces and other delicate instruments, made of natural or synthetic precious stone or other very hard material. —*v.t.* 6. to set or adorn with jewels. [ME *jouel, juel* < AF *jeul*, OF *jouel, joel* < VL **jocāle* plaything, n. use of neut. of **jocālis* (adj.) of play. See JOKE, -AL[1]] —**jew′el·like′,** *adj.*

jew′el case′, a box or small chest, often lined in a soft fabric and fitted with compartments, designed for holding jewelry. Also called **jew′el box′.**

jew·el·er (jo͞o′ə lər), *n.* a person who designs, makes, sells, or repairs jewelry, watches, etc. Also, *esp. Brit.,* **jew′el·ler.** [ME *jueler* < AF *jueler*, MF *juelier*]

jew′elers' put′ty. See **putty powder.**

jew′elers' rouge′, colcothar.

jew·el·ry (jo͞o′əl rē), *n.* 1. a number of articles of gold, silver, precious stones, etc., for personal adornment. 2. any ornament for personal adornment, as a necklace, cufflinks, etc. 3. jewels collectively. Also, *esp. Brit.,* **jew′el·ler·y.** [ME *juelrie* < OF *juelerie*]

jew·el·weed (jo͞o′əl wēd′), *n.* any of several plants of the genus *Impatiens,* esp. *I. biflora,* having orange-yellow flowers spotted with reddish brown, or *I. pallida,* having yellow flowers sometimes spotted with brownish red.

Jew·ess (jo͞o′is), *n.* *Often Offensive.* a Jewish girl or woman. [ME *jewesse*]

Jew·ett (jo͞o′it), *n.* **Sarah Orne** (ôrn), 1849–1909, U.S. short-story writer and novelist.

jew·fish (jo͞o′fish′), *n., pl.,* (*esp. collectively*) **-fish,** (*esp. referring to two or more kinds or species*) **-fish·es.** any of several very large fishes, esp. of the family *Serranidae,* as the giant sea bass and the groupers *Epinephelus itajara* and *E. nigritus,* of the tropical Atlantic Ocean. [?]

Jew·ish (jo͞o′ish), *adj.* 1. of, pertaining to, characteristic of, or noting the Jews. 2. *Informal.* Yiddish. —*n.* 3. *Informal.* Yiddish. [JEW + -ISH[1]; r. OE *iudēisc* < LL *jūdē(us)* Jew + OE *-isc* -ish] —**Jew′ish·ness,** *n.*

Jew′ish Auton′omous Re′gion, official name of **Birobizhan.**

Jew′ish cal′endar, the lunisolar calendar used by Jews, reckoned from 3761 B.C., the calendar year consisting of 353 days **(defective year)**, 354 days **(regular year)**, or 355 days **(perfect year** or **abundant year)** and containing 12 months: Tishri, Heshvan, Kislev, Tebet, Shebat, Adar, Nisan, Iyar, Sivan, Tammuz, Ab, and Elul, with the 29-day intercalary month of Adar Sheni added after Adar 7 times in every 19-year cycle. The Jewish ecclesiastical year begins with Nisan and the civil year begins with Tishri. Also called **Hebrew calendar.**

Jew·ish·ness (jo͞o′ish nis), *n.* the state or quality of being Jewish.

Jew·ry (jo͞o′rē), *n., pl.* **-ries.** 1. the Jewish people collectively. 2. *Archaic.* a district inhabited mainly by Jews; ghetto. 3. *Archaic.* Judea. [ME *jewerie* < AF *juerie* (OF *juierie*)]

jew's-harp (jo͞oz′härp′), *n.* a musical instrument consisting of a lyre-shaped metal frame containing a metal tongue, which is plucked while the frame is held between the teeth. Also, **jew's′-harp′.** [? jocular; earlier called *Jew's trump*]

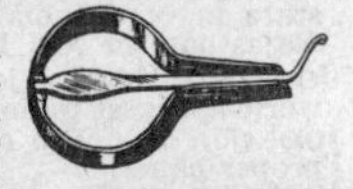
Jew's-harp

Jez·e·bel (jez′ə bel′, -bəl), *n.* 1. the wife of Ahab, king of Israel. I Kings 16:31. 2. a wicked, shameless woman.

Jez·re·el (jez′rē əl, jez rēl′), *n.* **Plain of,** a valley in N Israel, extending from the Mediterranean, near Mt. Carmel, to the Jordan River; scene of ancient battles. —**Jez′re·el·ite′,** *n.*

jg, junior grade. Also, **j.g.**

Jhan·si (jän′sē), *n.* a city in SW Uttar Pradesh, in central India. 140,200 (1961).

Jhe·lum (jā′ləm), *n.* a river flowing from S Kashmir into the Chenab River in Pakistan. 450 mi. long.

JHS, IHS (defs. 1, 2).

JHVH, YHVH. Also, **JHWH** [repr. Heb *J(a)hv(e)h* God]

jib[1] (jib), *Naut.* —*n.* 1. any of various triangular sails set forward of a forestaysail or fore-topmast staysail. Cf. **flying jib, inner jib, outer jib.** See diag. at **sail.** 2. the inner one of two such sails, set inward from a flying jib. —*adj.* 3. of or pertaining to a jib; *jib boom; jib clew.* [?]

jib[2] (jib), *v.i., v.t.,* **jibbed, jib·bing,** *n.* jibe[1]. Also, **jibb.**

jib[3] (jib), *v.,* **jibbed, jib·bing,** *n.* *Chiefly Brit.* —*v.i.* 1. to move restively sideways or backward instead of forward, as an animal in harness; balk. 2. to balk at doing something; procrastinate. —*n.* 3. a horse or other animal that jibs. [? special use of JIB[2]] —**jib′ber,** *n.*

jib[4] (jib), *n.* the projecting arm of a crane; the boom of a derrick. [appar. short for GIBBET]

jib′ boom′, *Naut.* a spar forming a continuation of a bowsprit. Also, **jib′boom′.**

jibe[1] (jīb), *v.,* **jibed, jib·ing,** *n.* *Naut.* —*v.i.* 1. to shift from one side to the other when running before the wind, as a fore-and-aft sail or its boom 2. to alter course so that a fore-and-aft sail shifts in this manner. —*v.t.* 3. to cause to jibe. —*n.* 4. act of jibing. Also, **gibe, gybe, jib.** [var. of *gybe* < D *gijbe(n)*]

jibe[2] (jīb), *v.t., v.i.,* **jibed, jib·ing,** *n.* gibe[1]. —**jib′er,** *n.* —**jib′ing·ly,** *adv.*

jibe[3] (jīb), *v.i.,* **jibed, jib·ing.** to be in accord with; agree: *The report does not jibe with the facts.* [?]

jib-head·ed (jib′hed′id), *adj.* *Naut.* 1. (of a sail) having a pointed head. 2. (of a rig) having all sails triangular, as a Marconi rig.

Ji·bu·ti (ji bo͞o′tē), *n.* Djibouti.

Jid·da (jid′də), *n.* the seaport of Mecca, in W Saudi Arabia, on the Red Sea. 147,859 (1963). Also, **Jedda.**

jif·fy (jif′ē), *n., pl.* **-fies.** *Informal.* a short time. [?]

jig[1] (jig), *n., v.,* **jigged, jig·ging.** —*n.* 1. *Mach.* a plate, box, or open frame for holding work and for guiding a machine tool to the work, used esp. for locating and spacing drilled holes; fixture. 2. *Angling.* any of several devices or lures, esp. a hook or gang of hooks weighted with metal and dressed with hair, feathers, etc., for jerking up and down or for drawing through the water to lure fish. 3. an apparatus for separating ore from other material by shaking in or treating with water. —*v.t.* 4. to treat, cut, produce, etc., with a jig. —*v.i.* 5. to use a jig. 6. to fish with a jig. [var. of GAUGE; cf. *jeg* templet]

jig[2] (jig), *n., v.,* **jigged, jig·ging.** —*n.* 1. a lively dance, usually in triple meter. 2. a piece of music for or in the rhythm of such a dance. 3. **in jig time,** with dispatch; rapidly: *We sorted the mail in jig time.* 4. **the jig is up,** *Slang.* it is hopeless; no chance remains. —*v.t.* 5. to dance (a jig or any lively dance). 6. to move with a jerky or bobbing motion. —*v.i.* 7. to dance a jig. 8. to move with a quick, jerky motion; hop; bob. [appar. var. of JOG[1]]

jig·ger[1] (jig′ər), *n.* 1. a person or thing that jigs. 2. *Naut.* a. the lowermost sail set on a jiggermast. b. jiggermast. c. a light tackle, as a gun tackle. 3. a jig for separating ore. 4. a jig for fishing. 5. *U.S.* a. a 1½-ounce measure used in cocktail recipes. b. a small whiskey glass holding 1½ ounces. —*adj.* 6. *Naut.* a. of or pertaining to a jiggermast. b. noting or pertaining to a sail, yard, boom, etc., or to any rigging belonging to a jigger lower mast or to some upper mast of a jiggermast. c. noting any stay running aft and upward to the head of a jigger lower mast or of some specified upper mast of a jiggermast: *jigger topmast stay.* [JIG[1] + -ER[1]]

jig·ger[2] (jig′ər), *n.* chigger.

jig·gered (jig′ərd), *adj.* *Informal.* confounded; blamed; damned. [? euphemistic alter. of *buggered;* see BUGGER]

jig·ger·mast (jig′ər məst), *n.* *Naut.* 1. a small mast set well aft in a yawl, ketch, or dandy; mizzenmast. 2. the fourth mast from forward in a vessel having five or more masts. Also, **jig′ger mast′.** Also called **jigger.**

jig·gers (jig′ərz), *interj.* *Slang.* watch out: *Jiggers, the cops!* [? *jigger,* as in JIGGERED + -S]

jig·gle (jig′əl), *v.,* **-gled, -gling,** *n.* —*v.t., v.i.* 1. to move up and down or to and fro with short, quick jerks. —*n.* 2. a jiggling movement. [JIG[2] + -LE] —**jig′gly,** *adj.*

jig′ saw′, a narrow saw, mounted vertically in a frame, for cutting curves or other difficult lines. [*jig,* var. of GIG[1]]

jig·saw (jig′sô′), *v.,* **-sawed, -sawed** or **-sawn, -saw·ing,** *adj., n.* —*v.t.* 1. to cut or form with a jig saw. —*adj.* 2. formed by or as by a jig saw: *jigsaw ornamentation.* —*n.* 3. See **jig saw.**

jig′saw puz′zle, a set of irregularly cut pieces of pasteboard, wood, or the like, that form a picture or design when fitted together.

ji·had (ji häd′), *n.* 1. a holy war undertaken as a sacred duty by Muslims. 2. any vigorous, often bitter crusade for an idea or principle. Also, **jehad.** [< Ar *jihād* struggle, strife]

jil·lion (jil′yən), *Informal.* —*n.* 1. a fanciful number suggesting a very large quantity. —*adj.* 2. of or noting such a quantity: *a jillion problems.* [*j-* (arbitrary letter) + *-illion,* as in *million*]

Ji·lo·lo (jī lō′lō), *n.* Halmahera.

jilt (jilt), *v.t.* 1. to reject or cast aside (a lover or sweetheart). —*n.* 2. a woman who jilts a lover. [*jilt* harlot, syncopated var. of dial. *jillet,* earlier *gillot* = *Gill* proper name + *-ot* (< F *-otte* as in *Charlotte*)] —**jilt′er,** *n.*

Jim Crow (jim′ krō′), a practice or policy of segregating or discriminating against Negroes. Also, **Jim′ Crow′ism.** [so called from the name of a song sung by Thomas Rice

(1808–60), in a Negro minstrel show] —**jim′-crow′, Jim′-Crow′,** *adj.*

jim-dan·dy (jim′dan′dē), *adj. Informal.* of superior quality; excellent: *a jim-dandy sports car.* [special use of *Jim* proper name + DANDY[1]]

Ji·mé·nez de Cis·ne·ros (hē me′neth de thēs ne′-rôs), **Fran·cis·co** (frän thēs′kō), 1436–1517, Spanish cardinal and statesman. Also called **Ximenes.**

Ji·mé·nez de Que·sa·da (hē me′neth de ke sä′thä, -me′nes), **Gon·za·lo** (gôn thä′lô, -sä′-), 1497?–1579, Spanish explorer and conqueror in South America.

jim·i·ny (jim′ə nē), *interj.* (used as a mild exclamation of surprise, emotion, or awe.) Also, **jim′mi·ny.** [obs. form of GEMINI, ? alter. of L *Jesu Domine* Lord Jesus!]

jim·jams (jim′jamz′), *n.* (*construed as pl.*) *Slang.* **1.** excessive nervousness; the jitters. **2.** See **delirium tremens.** [repetitive compound with gradation, based on JAM[1]]

jim·my (jim′ē), *n., pl.* **-mies,** *v.,* **-mied, -my·ing.** —*n.* **1.** a short crowbar. —*v.t.* **2.** to force open (a door, window, etc.) with a jimmy. Also, *Brit.,* **jemmy.**

jim′son weed′ (jim′sən), a coarse, rank-smelling weed, *Datura Stramonium,* having white or lavender flowers and poisonous leaves. Also, **Jim′son weed′.** [var. of *Jamestown weed,* after JAMESTOWN, Virginia]

jin (jin), *n., pl.* **jins,** (*esp. collectively*) **jin.** *Islamic Myth.* jinn.

jin·gle (jing′gəl), *v.,* **-gled, -gling,** *n.* —*v.i.* **1.** to make clinking or tinkling sounds, as metal objects, when struck together repeatedly. **2.** to move or proceed with such sounds: *The sleigh, decorated with bells, jingled along the snowy road.* **3.** to sound in a light, repetitious manner suggestive of this, as verse, sequence of words, piece of music, etc. **4.** to make rhymes. —*v.t.* **5.** to cause to jingle. —*n.* **6.** a tinkling or clinking sound. **7.** something that makes such a sound. **8.** a succession of like or repetitious sounds, as in music or verse. **9.** a piece of verse having such a succession of sounds. **10.** such a verse set to music. [ME *gyngle(n);* cf. D *jengelen*] —**jin′gler,** *n.* —**jin′gly,** *adj.*

jin·go (jing′gō), *n., pl.* **-goes,** *adj.* —*n.* **1.** a person who professes his patriotism loudly and excessively; chauvinist. **2. by jingo!** *Informal.* (used as an exclamation to emphasize the truth or importance of a foregoing statement, or to express astonishment, approval, etc.) —*adj.* **3.** of jingoes. **4.** characterized by jingoism. [orig. conjurer's call *hey jingo* appear! come forth! (opposed to *hey presto* hasten away!), taken into general use in the phrase *by Jingo,* euphemism for *by God;* chauvinistic sense from *by Jingo* in political song supporting use of British forces against Russia in 1878]

jin·go·ism (jing′gō iz′əm), *n.* the spirit, policy, or practice of jingoes; bellicose chauvinism. —**jin′go·ist,** *n., adj.* —**jin′go·is′tic,** *adj.* —**jin′go·is′ti·cal·ly,** *adv.*

jinn (jin), *n., pl.* **jinns,** (*esp. collectively*) **jinn.** *Islamic Myth.* any of a class of spirits, lower than the angels, capable of appearing in human and animal forms, and influencing mankind for good and evil. Also, **jin·ni** (ji nē′, jin′ē), **djin, djinn, djinni, jin.** [pl. of Ar *jinnī* demon]

jin·rik·i·sha (jin rik′shô, -shä), *n.* (in Japan, the Philippines, etc.) a small, two-wheeled passenger vehicle with a folding top, pulled by one man. Also, **jin·rick′sha, jin·rick′shaw, jin·rik′sha.** Also called **rickshaw, ricksha, rikisha, rikshaw.** [< Jap = *jin* man + *riki* power + *sha* vehicle]

Jin·sen (jin′sen′), *n.* Japanese name of **Inchon.**

jinx (jingks), *n.* **1.** a person, thing, or influence supposed to bring bad luck. —*v.t.* **2.** *Informal.* to bring bad luck to; place a jinx on. [< L *jynx* < Gk *iynx* wryneck (bird used in divination and magic)]

ji·pi·ja·pa (hē′pē hä′pä), *n.* **1.** a tropical American, palmlike plant, *Carludovica palmata.* **2.** a Panama hat made from the young leaves of this plant. [< AmerSp *jipijapa,* after *Jipijapa,* town in Ecuador]

jit·ney (jit′nē), *n., pl.* **-neys. 1.** a small passenger bus following a regular route at varying hours, originally charging each passenger five cents. **2.** *Slang.* a nickel. [?]

jit·ter (jit′ər), *n.* **1. jitters,** nervousness; a feeling of fright or uneasiness (usually prec. by *the*). —*v.i.* **2.** to behave nervously. [var. of *chitter* to shiver (ME *chiteren*), itself gradational var. of CHATTER]

jit·ter·bug (jit′ər bug′), *n., v.,* **-bugged, -bug·ging.** —*n.* **1.** a strenuous dance consisting of a few standardized steps augmented by twirls, splits, somersaults, etc., popular esp. in the early 1940's and performed to boogie-woogie and swing. **2.** a person who dances the jitterbug. —*v.i.* **3.** to dance the jitterbug.

jit·ter·y (jit′ə rē), *adj.* tense; strained; nervous; shaky.

jiu·ji·tsu (jōō ji′tsōō), *n.* jujitsu. Also, **jiu·ju′tsu.**

jive (jīv), *n., v.,* **jived, jiv·ing.** —*n.* **1.** swing music. **2.** *Slang.* the jargon of jazz and swing musicians and jazz, swing, and jitterbug devotees, esp. of the 1940's. **3.** *Slang.* unintelligible or deceptive talk. —*v.i.* **4.** to play jive. [?]

JJ., 1. Judges. **2.** Justices.

Jl., July.

JMP, jên-min-piao.

jna·na (jə nyä′nə, gə nyä′-, jnyä′-, gnyä′-), *n. Hinduism.* knowledge acquired through meditation and study as a means of reaching Brahman. Also called **Brahmajnana.** Cf. **bhakti** (def. 1), **karma** (def. 1). [< Skt *jñāna*]

jo (jō), *n., pl.* **joes.** *Scot.* beloved one; darling; sweetheart. [var. of JOY]

Jo·ab (jō′ab), *n.* a commander of David's army and the slayer of Abner and Absalom. II Sam. 3:27; 18:14.

jo·an·nes (jō an′ēz), *n., pl.* **-nes.** johannes.

Joan of Arc (jōn′ əv ärk′), **Saint** ("*the Maid of Orleans*"), 1412?–31, French heroine and martyr who raised the siege of Orléans. French, **Jeanne d'Arc.**

Jo·ão Pes·so·a (zhōō oun′ pe sô′ə), a seaport in NE Brazil. 137,788 (1960).

job[1] (job), *n., v.,* **jobbed, job·bing,** *adj.* —*n.* **1.** a piece of work done as part of the routine of one's occupation. **2.** anything one has to do; duty; responsibility: *It is your job to be on time.* **3.** a post of employment. **4.** an affair, matter, occurrence, or state of affairs: *to make the best of a bad job.* **5.** the unit or material being worked upon. **6.** the process of working. **7.** a public or official act or decision carried through for the sake of improper private gain. **8.** *U.S. Slang.* an automobile: *a sports job.* **9. on the job,** *Slang.* alert; observant. —*v.i.* **10.** to work at jobs or odd pieces of work; work by the piece. **11.** to do business as a jobber. **12.** to turn public business, planning, etc., improperly to private gain. —*v.t.* **13.** to buy in large quantities, as from wholesalers or manufacturers, and sell to dealers in smaller quantities. **14.** to assign or give (work, a contract for work, etc.) in separate portions, as among different contractors or workmen (often fol. by *out*): *to job out a contract.* **15.** to carry on (public or official business) for improper private gain. **16.** to swindle or trick (someone): *They jobbed him out of his property.* —*adj.* **17.** of or for a particular job or transaction. **18.** bought, sold, or handled together. [?] —**Syn. 3.** See **position.**

job[2] (job), *v.t., v.i.,* **jobbed, job·bing,** *n.* jab. [ME *jobbe(n)* < ?]

Job (jōb), *n.* **1.** the central figure in an Old Testament parable of the righteous sufferer. **2.** a book of the Bible bearing his name.

job′ ac′tion, *U.S.* any means used by organized employees to force a change in working conditions or in the employer's collective bargaining offer, such as a slowdown, strike, widespread absenteeism because of claimed illness, etc.

job′ bank′, *U.S.* a computerized data file for matching unemployed workers with appropriate job openings in a local or regional labor market, usually operated by government employment services.

job·ber (job′ər), *n.* **1.** a wholesale merchant, esp. one selling to retailers. **2.** a pieceworker. **3.** (formerly) a merchant who deals in special, odd, or job lots. **4.** a person who practices jobbery.

job·ber·y (job′ə rē), *n.* the conduct of public or official business for the sake of improper private gain.

job′ case′, *Print.* any of various cases for holding types, esp. one accommodating both upper-case and lower-case letters. Cf. **case**[2] (def. 8).

Job′ Corps′, *U.S.* an organization, under the auspices of the OEO, that operates rural conservation camps and urban training centers for poor youths.

job·less (job′lis), *adj.* **1.** without a job. **2.** noting or pertaining to persons without jobs. —*n.* **3.** (*construed as pl.*) unemployed persons collectively (usually prec. by *the*).

job′ lot′, 1. a large, often assorted quantity of goods sold or handled as a single transaction. **2.** a miscellaneous quantity; a quantity of odds and ends.

job′ print′er, a printer who does job work. —**job′ print′ing.**

job′ shop′, an employment agency that supplies engineers and other technical personnel on short-term temporary contracts. —**job′ shop′per.**

job′ work′, miscellaneous printing work, as distinguished from books, periodicals, etc.

Jo·cas·ta (jō kas′tə), *n. Class. Myth.* a queen of Thebes, the wife of Laius and the mother, later the wife, of Oedipus, by whom she bore Eteocles, Polynices, and Antigone: called Epicaste by Homer.

jock[1] (jok), *n. Informal.* **1.** jockey (def. 1). **2.** See **disk jockey.** [shortened form]

jock[2] (jok), *n.* **1.** a jockstrap. **2.** *Slang.* an athlete. [by shortening from JOCKSTRAP]

Jock (jok), *n. Scot. and Irish Eng.* an innocent lad; a country boy.

jock·ey (jok′ē), *n., pl.* **-eys,** *v.,* **-eyed, -ey·ing.** —*n.* **1.** a person who professionally rides horses in races. **2.** *Informal.* a person who pilots, operates, or guides the movement of something, as an airplane or automobile. —*v.t.* **3.** to ride (a horse) as a jockey. **4.** to move, bring, put, etc., by skillful maneuvering. **5.** to trick or cheat. **6.** to manipulate cleverly or trickily: *He jockeyed himself into office.* —*v.i.* **7.** to aim at an advantage by skillful maneuvering. **8.** to act trickily; seek an advantage by trickery. [*Jock,* proper name + -EY[2]]

jock′ey club′, an association for the regulating and promoting of thoroughbred horse racing.

jock·o (jok′ō), *n., pl.* **jock·os. 1.** a chimpanzee. **2.** any monkey. [< F, alter. of a word of a Bantu language (of Gabon) *ngeko*]

jock·strap (jok′strap′), *n.* an elastic supporter for the genitals, worn by men esp. while participating in athletics. Also called **athletic supporter.** [*jock* male organ (var. of JACK[1]) + STRAP]

jo·cose (jō kōs′), *adj.* given to or characterized by joking; jesting; humorous; playful. [< L *jocōs(us).* See JOKE, -OSE[1]] —**jo·cose′ly,** *adv.* —**jo·cose′ness,** *n.* —**Syn.** facetious, waggish, sportive, merry.

jo·cos·i·ty (jō kos′i tē), *n., pl.* **-ties. 1.** state or quality of being jocose. **2.** joking or jesting. **3.** a joke or jest.

joc·u·lar (jok′yə lər), *adj.* given to or characterized by joking or jesting; waggish; facetious. [< L *joculār(is)* = *jocul(us)* little joke (see JOKE, -ULE) + *-āris* -AR[1]] —**joc′u·lar·ly,** *adv.* —**Syn.** See **jovial.**

joc·u·lar·i·ty (jok′yə lar′i tē), *n., pl.* **-ties. 1.** the state or quality of being jocular. **2.** jocular speech or behavior. **3.** a jocular remark or act.

joc·und (jok′ənd, jō′kənd), *adj.* cheerful; merry; gay; blithe; glad. [ME *joc(o)und* < LL *jocund(us),* alter. of L *jūcundus* pleasant = *ju(vāre)* (to) please + *-cundus* adj. suffix] —**joc′und·ly,** *adv.* —**Syn.** joyous, joyful, jolly. See **jovial.**

jo·cun·di·ty (jō kun′di tē), *n., pl.* **-ties** for 2. **1.** the state or an instance of being jocund. **2.** a jocund remark or act.

jodh·pur (jod′pər, jōd′-), *n.* **1. jodhpurs,** (*construed as pl.*) riding breeches cut very full over the hips and tapering at the knees to become tight fitting from knees to ankles. **2.** Also called **jodh′pur shoe′, jodh′pur boot′.** an ankle-high shoe having a strap that buckles on the side. [after JODHPUR]

Jodh·pur (jōd′pōōr), *n.* **1.** Also called **Marwar.** a former state in NW India, now in Rajasthan. **2.** a city in W Rajasthan, in NW India. 224,800 (1961).

Jod′rell Bank′ (jod′rəl), a site in NE Cheshire, England: world's largest radio telescope.

joe[1] (jō), *n.* (*often cap.*) *Slang.* fellow; guy. [special use of proper name]

joe[2] (jō), *n. Slang.* coffee. [? alter. of JAVA]

Jo·el (jō′əl), *n.* **1.** a Minor Prophet of the postexilian period. **2.** a book of the Bible bearing his name.

joe-pye′ weed′ (jō′pī′), **1.** a tall, composite weed, *Eupatorium purpureum,* of North America, having clusters of pinkish or purple flowers. **2.** a related plant, *E. maculatum*, having similar flowers and stems that are often spotted with purple. Also, **Joe-Pye′ weed′.** [?]

jo·ey (jō′ē), *n., pl.* **-eys.** *Australian.* any young animal, esp. a kangaroo. [< native Austral]

Jof·fre (zhôf′Rᵊ), *n.* **Jo·seph Jacques Cé·saire** (zhō zef′ zhäk sā zeR′), 1852–1931, French general in World War I.

jog[1] (jog), *v.,* **jogged, jog·ging,** *n.* **—***v.t.* **1.** to move or shake with a push or jerk. **2.** to cause to function with a jolt for a moment or in a series of disconnected motions. **3.** to push slightly, as to arouse the attention; nudge. **4.** to stir or jolt into activity, as by a hint or reminder: *to jog a person's memory.* **5.** to cause (a horse) to go at a steady trot. **—***v.i.* **6.** to move with a jolt or jerk. **7.** to go or travel with a jolting pace or motion. **8.** to run or ride at a steady trot: *They jogged to the stable.* **9.** to run at a leisurely, slow pace, esp. as an outdoor exercise. **10.** to go in a desultory or humdrum fashion (usually fol. by *on* or *along*). **—***n.* **11.** a shake; slight push; nudge. **12.** a steady trot, as of a horse. **13.** the act of jogging. [b. dial. *jot* to jog and *shog* to shake, jog (late ME *shoggen*)] **—jog′ger,** *n.*

jog[2] (jog), *n.* **1.** an irregularity of line or surface. **2.** a bend or turn. **—***v.i.* **3.** to bend or turn. [var. of JAG[1]]

jog·gle (jog′əl), *v.,* **-gled, -gling,** *n.* **—***v.t.* **1.** to shake slightly; move to and fro, as by repeated jerks; jiggle. **2.** to join or fasten by fitting a projection into a recess. **3.** to fit or fasten with dowels. **—***v.i.* **4.** to have a jogging or jolting motion; shake. **—***n.* **5.** the act of joggling. **6.** a slight shake or jolt. **7.** a moving with jolts or jerks. **8.** a projection on one of two joining objects fitting into a corresponding recess in the other. **9.** *Carpentry.* an enlarged area, as of a post for supporting the foot of a strut, brace, etc.

Jog·ja·kar·ta (jōg′yä kär′tä), *n.* a city in central Java, in S Indonesia. 312,698 (1961). Also, **Jokjakarta.** Dutch, **Djokjakarta.**

jog′ trot′, a slow, regular, jolting pace, as of a horse.

Jo·han·an ben Zak·ka·i (jō han′ən ben zak′ā ī′), died A.D. c80, Palestinian rabbi: leading Pharisaic teacher and disciple of Hillel.

jo·han·nes (jō han′ēz), *n., pl.* **-nes.** a gold coin formerly used as currency in Portugal, first issued in the early 18th century. Also, **joannes.** [after the name *Joannes* (John V, of Portugal) on coin]

Jo·han·nes·burg (jō han′is bûrg′; *Du.* yō hän′əs bœRKH′), *n.* a city in S Transvaal, in the N Republic of South Africa. 595,083 (1960).

john (jon), *n. Slang.* toilet; bathroom. [special use of proper name]

John (jon), *n.* **1.** the apostle John, believed to be the author of the fourth Gospel, three Epistles, and the book of Revelation. **2.** See **John the Baptist. 3.** (*John Lackland*) 1167?–1216, king of England 1199–1216: signer of the Magna Charta 1215 (son of Henry II of England). **4. Augustus (Edwin),** 1878–1961, British painter and etcher. **5.** the fourth Gospel: the Gospel of St. John. **6.** any of the three Epistles of John: I, II, or III John. **7.** *Slang.* a prostitute's customer. [ME *Joh(a)n,* OE *Iōhannis* < ML *Iō(h)annēs* < Gk *Iōánnēs* < Heb *Yōḥānān* < *Yehōḥānān* God has been gracious]

John I, 1. Saint, died A.D. 526, Italian ecclesiastic: pope 523–526. **2.** ("*the Great*") 1357–1433, king of Portugal 1385–1433.

John II, (*Mercurius*) died A.D. 535, Italian ecclesiastic: pope 533–535.

John III, 1. (*Catelinus*) died A.D. 574, Italian ecclesiastic: pope 561–574. **2.** (*John Sobieski*) 1624–96, king of Poland 1674–96.

John IV, died A.D. 642, pope 640–642.

John V, died A.D. 686, pope 685–686.

John VI, died A.D. 705, Greek ecclesiastic: pope 701–705.

John VII, died A.D. 707, Greek ecclesiastic: pope 705–707.

John VIII, died A.D. 882, Italian ecclesiastic: pope 872–882.

John IX, died A.D. 900, Italian ecclesiastic: pope 898–900.

John X, died A.D. 929?, Italian ecclesiastic: pope 914–928.

John XI, died A.D. 936, Italian ecclesiastic: pope 931–936.

John XII, (*Octavian*) died A.D. 964, Italian ecclesiastic: pope 955–964.

John XIII, died A.D. 972, Italian ecclesiastic: pope 965–972.

John XIV, died A.D. 984, pope 983–984.

John XV, died A.D. 996, Italian ecclesiastic: pope 985–996.

John XVII, (*Sicco*) died 1003, pope 1003.

John XVIII, (*Fasanus*) died 1009, Italian ecclesiastic: pope 1003–09.

John XIX, died 1032, pope 1024–32.

John XXI, (*Petrus Hispanus*) died 1277, Portuguese ecclesiastic: pope 1276–77.

John XXII, (*Jacques Duèse*) c1244–1334, French ecclesiastic: pope 1316–34.

John XXIII, (*Angelo Giuseppe Roncalli*) 1881–1963, Italian ecclesiastic: pope 1958–63.

John′ Bar′leycorn, a humorous personification of barley as used in malt liquor, of malt liquor itself, or of any intoxicating liquor.

John′ Birch′ Soci′ety, an ultraconservative U.S. organization, founded chiefly to combat alleged Communist activities in the U.S. [named after *John Birch* (d. 1945), American USAF captain]

John′ Bull′, 1. the English people. **2.** the typical Englishman. [after *John Bull,* chief character in Arbuthnot's allegory *The History of John Bull* (1712)] **—John′ Bull′ish.**

John′ Doe′, 1. (in legal proceedings) a fictitious personage or one whose real name is not known. Cf. **Richard Roe. 2.** an anonymous, average man.

John′ Do′ry (dôr′ē, dōr′ē), any compressed marine fish of the family *Zeidae,* esp. *Zeus faber,* found in Europe, having long spines in the dorsal fin. [JOHN + DORY[2]; jocular, modeled on JOHN DOE]

John′ Han′cock, 1. See **Hancock, John. 2.** *Informal.* a person's signature. [after John HANCOCK, from the boldness and legibility of his signature on official documents]

John′ Hen′ry, *pl.* **John Henries.** *Informal.* a person's signature. [from the proper name]

john·ny·cake (jon′ē kāk′), *n. U.S.* a cake or bread made of corn meal and water or milk. Also, **john′ny cake′.** [? obs. *jonakin, jonikin* (appar. of AmerInd orig.) kind of griddlecake + CAKE]

John·ny-come-late·ly (jon′ē kum′lāt′lē), *n., pl.* **John·ny-come-late·lies, John·nies-come-late·ly.** a late arrival or participant; newcomer. Also, **John′nie-come-late′ly.**

John·ny-jump-up (jon′ē jump′up′), *n. U.S.* **1.** any of certain violets, esp. *Viola Kitaibeliana Rafinesquii.* **2.** a small form of the pansy, *Viola tricolor.* [so called from its rapid rate of growth]

John′ny-on-the-spot′, *n. Informal.* a person who is on hand to perform a duty, seize an opportunity, etc.

John′ny Reb′ (reb), *Informal.* **1.** *U.S. Hist.* a Confederate soldier. **2.** a native or inhabitant of the southern U.S.

John′ of Aus′tria, ("*Don John*") 1547?–78, Spanish general: victor at the battle of Lepanto.

John′ of Gaunt′ (gônt, gänt), (*Duke of Lancaster*) 1340–99, English soldier and statesman: 4th son of Edward III; founder of the royal house of Lancaster (father of Henry IV of England).

John′ of Ley′den (līd′ən), (*Jan Beuckelszoon* or *Bockhold*) 1509–36, Dutch Anabaptist.

John′ of Salis′bury, c1115–80, English prelate.

John′ of the Cross′, Saint (*Juan de Yepis y Álvarez*), 1542–91, Spanish mystic, writer, and theologian.

John′ o'Groat's′ House′ (ə grôts′, ə grōts′), a locality on the northern tip of Scotland, traditionally thought of as the northernmost point of Britain. Also called **John′ o'Groat's′.**

John Paul I, (*Albino Luciani*) 1912–78, Italian ecclesiastic: pope 1978.

John Paul II, (*Karol Wojtyla*) born 1920, Polish ecclesiastic: pope since 1978.

Johns (jonz), *n.* **Jasper,** born 1930, U.S. painter.

John·son (jon′sən), *n.* **1. Andrew,** 1808–75, 17th president of the U.S. 1865–69. **2. Jack** (*John Arthur*), 1878–1946, U.S. heavyweight prize fighter: world champion 1908–15. **3. James Weldon** (wel′dən), 1871–1938, U.S. poet and essayist. **4. Lyn·don Baines** (lin′dən bānz), 1908–73, 36th president of the U.S. 1963–69. **5. Philip C(ortelyou),** born 1906, U.S. architect and author. **6. Richard Men·tor** (men′tər, -tôr), 1780–1850, vice president of the U.S. 1837–1841. **7. Samuel** ("*Dr. Johnson*"), 1709–84, English lexicographer, critic, poet, and conversationalist. **8. Walter Perry** ("*Big Train*"), 1887–1946, U.S. baseball player. **9. Sir William,** 1715–74, British colonial administrator in America, born in Ireland.

John′son Cit′y, a city in NE Tennessee. 33,770 (1970).

John′son grass′, a perennial sorghum, *Sorghum halepense,* that spreads by creeping rhizomes, grown for fodder. [named after William *Johnson,* American agriculturist who first planted it in 1840]

John·ston (jon′stən, -sən), *n.* **1. Albert Sidney,** 1803–1862, Confederate general in U.S. Civil War. **2. Joseph Eggleston,** 1807–91, Confederate general in U.S. Civil War.

Johns·town (jonz′toun′), *n.* a city in SW Pennsylvania: disastrous flood 1889. 42,476 (1970).

John′ the Bap′tist, the forerunner and baptizer of Jesus. Matt. 3.

Jo·hore (jə hōr′, -hôr′), *n.* **1.** a state in Malaysia, on S Malay Peninsula. 1,064,814 (est. 1961); 7330 sq. mi. **2.** a city in and the capital of this state, in the S part. 672,590 (1957).

joie de vi·vre (zhwAdᵊ vē′vRᵊ), *French.* a delight in being alive. [lit., joy of living]

join (join), *v.t.* **1.** to bring or put together or in contact; connect. **2.** to come into contact or union with: *The brook joins the river.* **3.** to bring together in a particular relation or for a specific purpose, action, etc.; unite. **4.** to become a member of (a society, party, etc.): *to join a club.* **5.** to enlist in (one of the armed forces). **6.** to come into the company of; meet or accompany: *I'll join you later.* **7.** to participate with (someone) in some act or activity: *My wife joins me in thanking you for the gift.* **8.** to unite in marriage. **9.** to meet or engage in (battle, conflict, etc.): *The opposing armies joined battle.* **10.** to adjoin. **11.** to draw a curve or straight line between: *to join two points on a graph.* **—***v.i.* **12.** to come into or be in contact or connection. **13.** to become united, associated, or combined; associate or ally oneself (usually fol. by *with*): *Please join with us in our campaign.* **14.** to take part with others (often fol. by *in*): *Let's all join in.* **15.** to be contiguous or close; lie or come together; form a junction. **16.** to enlist in one of the armed forces (often fol. by *up*). **17.** to meet in battle or conflict: *Our cavalry joined with enemy troops and defeated them.* **—***n.* **18.** a joining. **19.** a place or line of joining; seam. [ME *joine(n)* < OF *joign-* (s. of *joindre* to join) < L *jung(ere)* (to) YOKE[1]] **—join′a·ble,** *adj.*

—Syn. 1. link, couple, fasten, attach; combine; associate. JOIN, CONNECT, UNITE all imply bringing two or more things together more or less closely. JOIN may refer to a connection or association of any degree of closeness, but often implies direct contact: *to join pieces of wood to form a corner.* CONNECT implies a joining as by a tie, link, wire, etc.: *to connect two batteries.* UNITE implies a close joining of two or more things, so as to form one: *to unite layers of veneer sheets to form plywood.* **10.** abut.

join·der (join′dər), *n.* **1.** the act of joining. **2.** *Law.* **a.** the joining of causes of action in a suit. **b.** the joining of parties in a suit. **c.** the acceptance by a party to an action of an issue tendered. [< F *joindre.* See JOIN, -ER]

join·er (joi′nər), *n.* **1.** a person or thing that joins. **2.** a carpenter, esp. one who constructs doors, window sashes, etc. **3.** a person who belongs to many clubs, associations, societies, etc. [JOIN + -ER[1]; r. ME *joinour* < AF *joignour*]

join·er·y (joi′nə rē), *n.* **1.** the craft or trade of a joiner. **2.** woodwork made by a joiner.

joint (joint), *n.* **1.** the place at which two things, or separate parts of one thing, are joined or united, either rigidly or in such a way as to admit of motion; juncture. **2.** *Anat., Zool.* **a.** the movable or fixed place or part where two bones or elements of a skeleton join. **b.** the form or structure of such a part, as a ball-and-socket, hinge, or other arrangement. **3.** *Biol.* **a.** a part, esp. of a plant, insect, etc., connected with another part by an articulation, node, or the like. **b.** a portion between two articulations, nodes, or the like. **4.** *Bot.* the part of a stem from which a branch or leaf grows; node. **5.** one of the large portions into which a section of meat is divided by a butcher, esp. for roasting. **6.** *Geol.* a fracture plane in rocks, generally at right angles to the bedding of sedimentary rocks and variously oriented in igneous and metamorphic rocks, commonly arranged in two or more sets of parallel intersecting systems. **7.** *Slang.* a dirty or disreputable place of public accommodation, esp. a cheap restaurant or night club. **8.** *Slang.* place; establishment. **9.** *Slang.* a marijuana cigarette. **10. out of joint, a.** dislocated, as a bone. **b.** in an unfavorable state; inauspicious: *The time is out of joint.* **c.** out of keeping; inappropriate. —*adj.* **11.** shared by or common to two or more: *a joint checking account.* **12.** sharing or acting in common. **13.** joined or associated, as in relation, interest, or action: *joint owners.* **14.** undertaken or produced by two or more in conjunction or in common. **15.** *Law.* joined together in obligation or ownership. **16.** *Parl. Proc.* of or pertaining to both branches of a bicameral legislature. **17.** pertaining to or noting diplomatic action in which two or more governments are formally united. —*v.t.* **18.** to unite by a joint or joints. **19.** to form or provide with a joint or joints. **20.** to cut (a fowl, piece of meat, etc.) at the joint; divide at a joint. **21.** *Carpentry.* to prepare (a board or the like) for fitting in a joint. **22.** to file the teeth of (a saw) to uniform height. —*v.i.* **23.** to fit together by or as by joints. [ME < OF *joint, jointe* < L *junct(um), juncta,* n. use of neut. and fem. of *junctus,* ptp. of *jungere* to JOIN]

joint′ bar′, a steel member for maintaining a rigid joint between two rail ends. See illus. at **fishplate.**

Joint′ Chiefs′ of Staff′, *U.S.* the Chiefs of Staff of the Army and the Air Force and the Chief of Naval Operations, together with a chairman selected from one of the branches of the armed forces, serving as the principal military advisory body to the President, the National Security Council, and the Secretary of Defense.

joint′ commit′tee, *Govt.* a committee appointed from both houses of a bicameral legislature.

joint·ed (join′tid), *adj.* **1.** having or provided with joints. **2.** formed with knots or nodes. —**joint′ed·ly,** *adv.* —**joint′ed·ness,** *n.*

joint·er (join′tər), *n.* **1.** a person or thing that joints. **2.** a tool or machine used in making joints. **3.** *Agric.* a device with a triangular head, used with a plow to bury trash.

joint·ly (joint′lē), *adv.* together; in common.

joint′ resolu′tion, a resolution adopted by both branches of a bicameral legislative assembly and requiring the signature of the chief executive to become law.

joint·ress (join′tris), *n. Law.* a woman on whom a jointure is settled. [JOINT(E)R + -ESS]

joint′-stock′ com′pany (joint′stok′), *U.S.* an association of individuals in a business enterprise with transferable shares of stock, much like a corporation except that stockholders are liable for the debts of the business.

join·ture (join′chər), *n. Law.* an estate or property settled on a woman in consideration of marriage, to be owned by her after her husband's death. [ME < OF < L *junctūr(a)*]

joint·weed (joint′wēd′), *n.* an American, polygonaceous herb, *Polygonella articulata,* having many-jointed, spikelike racemes of small, white or rose-colored flowers.

joint·worm (joint′wûrm′), *n.* the larva of any of several chalcid flies of the family *Eurytomidae,* esp. of the genus *Harmolita,* that feeds in the stems of grasses. Also called **strawworm.**

Join·ville (*Fr.* zhwaN vēl′), *n.* **Jean de** (zhäN də), 1224?–1317, French chronicler.

joist (joist), *n.* **1.** any of a number of small, parallel beams of timber, steel, reinforced concrete, etc., for supporting floors, ceilings, etc. —*v.t.* **2.** to furnish with or fix on joists. [ME *giste* < OF < VL *jacit(um) support, n. use of neut. of *jacitus,* ptp. of *jacēre* to lie]

A, Joist
B, Subfloor
C, Floorboards

joke (jōk), *n., v.,* **joked, jok·ing.** —*n.* **1.** something said or done to provoke laughter or amusement. **2.** something that is amusing or ridiculous; a thing, situation, or person laughed at rather than taken seriously. **3.** a matter for joking about; trifling matter: *The loss was no joke.* **4.** something that does not present the expected challenge; something very easy. **5.** See **practical joke.** —*v.i.* **6.** to speak or act in a playful or merry way. **7.** to say something in fun or sport, rather than in earnest: *He was only joking.* —*v.t.* **8.** to subject to jokes; make fun of. [< L *joc(us)* jest] —**jok′ing·ly,** *adv.* —**Syn. 1.** witticism, jape, prank, quip. JOKE, JEST refer to something said or done in sport, or to cause amusement. A JOKE is something said or done for the sake of exciting laughter; it may be raillery, a witty remark, or a prank or trick: *to tell a joke.* JEST, today a more formal word, nearly always refers to joking language and is more suggestive of scoffing or ridicule than is JOKE: *to speak in jest.*

jok·er (jō′kər), *n.* **1.** a person who jokes. **2.** one of two extra playing cards in a pack, usually imprinted with the figure of a jester, used in some games as the highest card or as a wild card. **3.** a seemingly minor, unsuspected clause or wording that is put into an agreement, legal document, etc., to change its effect. **4.** an unexpected or final fact, factor, or condition that changes or reverses a situation or result completely. **5.** any method, trick, or expedient for getting the better of another. **6.** *Informal.* a man; fellow; chap. **7.** Also, **joke·ster** (jōk′stər). a person who plays jokes or pranks; prankster. **8.** *Informal.* a wise guy; smart aleck.

Jok·ja·kar·ta (jok′yä kär′tä), *n.* Jogjakarta.

jole (jōl), *n.* jowl².

Jo·li·et (jō′lē et′, jō′lē et′; *for 1 also Fr.* zhô lye′), *n.* **1. Louis** (lwē), 1645–1700, French explorer of the Mississippi, born in Canada. **2.** a city in NE Illinois. 78,887 (1970).

Jo·liot-Cu·rie (zhô lyō′kʏ rē′), *n.* **1. I·rène** (ē ren′), (*Irène Curie*), 1897–1956, French nuclear physicist: Nobel prize for chemistry 1935 (daughter of Pierre and Marie Curie). **2.** her husband, **(Jean) Fré·dé·ric** (zhäN frā dā-rēk′), (*Jean Frédéric Joliot*), 1900–58, French nuclear physicist: Nobel prize for chemistry 1935.

Jo·li·vet (zhô lē ve′), *n.* **An·dré** (äN drā′), 1905–74, French composer.

jol·li·fi·ca·tion (jol′ə fə kā′shən), *n.* jolly merrymaking; jolly festivity.

jol·li·fy (jol′ə fī′), *v.t., v.i.,* **-fied, -fy·ing.** *Informal.* to make or become jolly or merry.

jol·li·ty (jol′i tē), *n., pl.* **-ties. 1.** jolly mood, condition, or activity; gaiety. **2. jollities,** jolly festivities. [ME *jolite* < OF; see JOLLY, -TY²] —**Syn. 1.** See **mirth.**

jol·ly (jol′ē), *adj.,* **-li·er, -li·est,** *v.,* **-lied, -ly·ing,** *adv., n., pl.* **-lies.** —*adj.* **1.** in good spirits; gay; merry. **2.** cheerfully festive or convivial. **3.** joyous; happy: *Christmas is a jolly season.* **4.** *Chiefly Brit. Informal.* delightful; charming. **5.** *Brit.* **a.** *Informal.* great; thorough. **b.** *Slang.* slightly drunk; tipsy. —*v.t.* **6.** *Informal.* to talk or act agreeably to (a person) in order to keep him in good humor, esp. in the hope of gaining something. —*adv.* **7.** *Brit. Informal.* extremely; very: *jolly well.* —*n.* **8.** Usually, **jollies.** *Slang.* fun or pleasurable excitement; kicks: *He got his jollies reading pornographic magazines.* [ME *joli, jolif* < OF *jolif, joli* gay = *jol-* (prob. < ON; cf. Icel *jōl* YULE) + *-if* -IVE] —**jol′li·ly,** *adv.* —**jol′li·ness,** *n.* —**Syn. 1–3.** glad, jovial, sportive, playful. See **gay.** —**Ant. 1–3.** gloomy, melancholy.

jol′ly boat′, *Naut.* a light boat carried at the stern of a sailing vessel. [*jolly* < Dan *jolle* YAWL¹]

Jol′ly Rog′er (roj′ər), a flag formerly flown by pirates, having the device of a white skull and crossbones on a black field. Also called **black flag.**

Jo·lo (hô lô′), *n.* **1.** an island in the SW Philippines: the main island of the Sulu Archipelago. 165,607; 345 sq. mi. **2.** a seaport on this island. 46,800.

jolt (jōlt), *v.t.* **1.** to jar, shake, or cause to move by or as by a sudden rough thrust; shake up roughly. **2.** to stun with a blow, esp. in boxing. **3.** to shock psychologically. **4.** to bring abruptly to a desired mental state. **5.** to interfere with or intrude upon, esp. in a rough or crude manner; interrupt disturbingly. —*v.i.* **6.** to move with a sharp jerk or a series of sharp jerks: *The car jolted to a halt.* —*n.* **7.** a jolting shock, movement, or blow. **8.** an emotional or psychological shock: *The news gave me quite a jolt.* **9.** that which causes such a shock. **10.** a sudden, unexpected rejection or defeat. **11.** a bracing dose of something: *a jolt of whiskey.* [b. *jot* to jolt and *joll* to bump, both now dial.] —**jolt′er,** *n.* —**jolt′ing·ly,** *adv.*

jolt·y (jōl′tē), *adj.,* **jolt·i·er, jolt·i·est.** full of jolts; bumpy. —**jolt′i·ness,** *n.*

Jo·nah (jō′nə), *n.* **1.** a Minor Prophet who was thrown overboard from his ship for an impiety and was swallowed by a large fish that after three days cast him up onto the shore unhurt. **2.** a book of the Bible bearing his name. —**Jo′nah·esque′,** *adj.*

Jo·nas (jō′nəs; *for 1 also Ger.* yō′näs), *n.* **1. Franz** (fränts), 1899–1974, Austrian political leader and public official: president 1965–74. **2.** Jonah.

Jon·a·than (jon′ə thən), *n.* **1.** a son of Saul and friend of David. I Sam. 18–20. **2.** *Archaic.* an American, esp. a New Englander.

Jon·a·than (jon′ə thən), *n. Hort.* a variety of red apple that matures in early autumn. [named after *Jonathan* Hasbrouck (d. 1846), American jurist]

Jones (jōnz), *n.* **1. An·son** (an′sən), 1798–1858, president of the Republic of Texas 1844–46. **2. Ca·sey** (kā′sē), (*John Luther Jones*), 1864–1900, U.S. locomotive engineer and folk hero. **3. Daniel,** 1881–1967, English phonetician. **4. Howard Mum·ford** (mum′fərd), 1892–1980, U.S. educator and critic. **5. In·i·go** (in′ə gō′), 1573–1652, English architect. **6. John Paul,** 1747–92, American naval commander in the Revolutionary War, born in Scotland. **7. Robert Tyre** (tīər), ("*Bobby*"), 1902–71, U.S. golfer.

Jones·bor·o (jōnz′bûr ō, -bur ō), *n.* a city in NE Arkansas. 27,050 (1970).

jon·gleur (jong′glər; *Fr.* zhôN glœr′), *n., pl.* **-gleurs** (-glərz; *Fr.* -glœr′). (in medieval France and Norman England) an itinerant minstrel who sang songs, often of his own composition, and told stories. [< F; MF *jougleur* (? by misreading, *ou* being read *on*), OF *jogleor* < L *joculātor* joker = *joculāt(us),* ptp. of *joculārī* to joke (*jocul-* (see JOCULAR) + *-ātus* -ATE¹) + *-or* -OR²]

Jön·kö·ping (yœn′chœ ping), *n.* a city in S Sweden. 52,576 (1965).

jon·quil (jong′kwil, jon′-), *n.* a narcissus, *Narcissus Jonquilla,* having long, narrow leaves and fragrant yellow or white flowers. [< F *jonquille* < Sp *junquillo,* dim. of *junco;* see JUNCO]

Jon·son (jon′sən), *n.* **Ben,** 1573?–1637, English dramatist and poet. —**Jon·so·ni·an** (jon sō′nē ən), *adj.*

Jop·lin (jop′lin), *n.* a city in SW Missouri. 39,256 (1970).

Jop·pa (jop′ə), *n.* ancient name of **Jaffa.**

Jor·dan (jôr′dən), *n.* **1.** Official name, **Hashemite Kingdom of Jordan.** a kingdom in SW Asia, consisting of the former Trans-Jordan and a part of Palestine: W part occupied by Israel 1967. 2,751,968; 37,264 sq. mi. *Cap.:* Amman. **2.** a river flowing from S Lebanon and SW Syria through the Sea of Galilee, then S between Israel and Jordan through W Jordan into the Dead Sea. 200 mi. long.

Jor′dan al′mond, 1. a large, hard-shelled, Spanish almond used esp. in confectionery. **2.** an almond with a hard, colored coating of sugar. [alter. of ME *jardyne almaund* garden almond = *jardyne* (see JARDINIERE) + *almaund* ALMOND]

jo·rum (jôr′əm, jōr′-), *n.* **1.** a large bowl or vessel for holding drink. **2.** the contents of such a vessel. **3.** any great quantity. [said to be named after *Joram,* who brought vessels of silver, gold, and brass to David (2 Samuel 8:10)]

Jo·seph (jō′zəf, -səf), *n.* **1.** the first son of Jacob and Rachel: sold into slavery by his brothers. Gen. 30:22–24; 37. **2.** the husband of Mary who was the mother of Jesus. Matt. 1:16–25. **3.** (*l.c.*) a woman's long cloak for riding.

Joseph II, 1741–90, emperor of the Holy Roman Empire 1765–90 (son of Francis I; brother of Leopold II and Marie Antoinette).

Jo·se·phine (jō′zə fēn′, -sə-), *n.* **Empress** (*Marie Joséphine Rose Tascher de la Pagerie*). See **Beauharnais, Joséphine de.**

Jo′seph of Ar·i·ma·thae′a (ar′ə mə thē′ə), a member of the Sanhedrin who placed the body of Jesus in the tomb. Matt. 27:57–60; Mark 15:43.

Jo·se·phus (jō sē′fəs), *n.* **Fla·vi·us** (flā′vē əs), (*Joseph ben Matthias*), A.D. 37?–c100, Jewish historian and general.

josh (josh), *Informal.* —*v.t., v.i.* **1.** to chaff; tease by bantering. —*n.* **2.** good-natured banter. [? b. JOKE and BOSH[1]] —**josh′er,** *n.*

Josh., Joshua.

Josh·u·a (josh′o͞o ə), *n.* **1.** the successor of Moses as leader of the Israelites. Deut. 31:14, 23; 34:9. **2.** a book of the Bible bearing his name.

Josh′ua tree′, a tree, *Yucca brevifolia,* growing in arid or desert regions of the southwestern U.S.

Jo·si·ah (jō sī′ə), *n.* a king of Judah, reigned 640?–609? B.C. II Kings 22. [<< Heb *Yōshīyāh* God upholds]

joss (jos), *n.* a Chinese house idol or cult image. [< pidgin E < Pg *deos* < L *deus* god]

joss′ house′, a Chinese temple for idol worship.

joss′ stick′, a slender stick of a dried, fragrant paste, burned by the Chinese as incense before a joss.

jos·tle (jos′əl), *v.,* **-tled, -tling,** *n.* —*v.t.* **1.** to bump, push, shove, or brush roughly or rudely against. **2.** to drive or force by, or as by, pushing or shoving: *The crowd jostled him into the subway.* **3.** to exist in close contact or proximity with. **4.** to contend with: *The candidates jostled each other to win the election.* **5.** to unsettle; disturb. —*v.i.* **6.** to bump or brush against someone or something; push; shove. **7.** to compete; contend. —*n.* **8.** a bump or brush against someone or something. Also, **justle.** [var. (in ME, var. sp.) of *justle.* See JOUST, -LE] —**jos′tler,** *n.*

jot (jot), *v.,* **jot·ted, jot·ting,** *n.* —*v.t.* **1.** to write or mark down quickly or briefly (usually fol. by *down*): *Jot down his license number.* —*n.* **2.** the least part of something; a little bit. [< L *jota* < Gk *iôta* IOTA]

jo·ta (hō′tə; *Sp.* hô′tä), *n., pl.* **-tas** (-təz; *Sp.* -täs). **1.** a Spanish dance in triple meter, performed by a couple and marked by complex rhythms executed with the heels and castanets. **2.** the music for this dance. [< Sp, prob. OSp *sota* dance < *sotar* to dance < L *saltāre*]

jot·ting (jot′ing), *n.* **1.** the act of a person who jots. **2.** a quickly written or brief note; memorandum. —**jot′ty,** *adj.*

Jo·tun (yô′to͝on), *n. Scand. Myth.* any of a race of giants frequently in conflict with the gods. Also, **Jo′tunn, Jö·tunn** (yœ′to͝on). [< Icel *jötunn* giant; c. OE *eoten;* akin to EAT]

Jo·tun·heim (yô′to͝on hām′), *n. Scand. Myth.* the outer world, or realm of giants; Utgard. Also, **Jo′tunn·heim′, Jö·tun·heim, Jö·tunn·heim** (yœ′to͝on hām′). [< Icel = *jötunn* giant + *heimr* world, HOME]

Jou·bert (zho͞o ber′), *n.* **Jo·seph** (zhô zef′), 1754–1824, French moralist and essayist.

joule (jo͞ol, joul), *n. Physics.* the meter-kilogram-second unit of work or energy, equal to the work done by a force of one newton when its point of application moves through a distance of one meter in the direction of the force: equivalent to 10^7 ergs and one watt-second. *Abbr.:* J, j [named after J. P. JOULE]

Joule (jo͞ol, joul), *n.* **James Prescott,** 1818–89, English physicist.

Joule's′ law′, *Physics.* **1.** the principle that the rate of production of heat by a constant direct current is directly proportional to the resistance of the circuit and to the square of the current. **2.** the principle that the internal energy of a given mass of an ideal gas is a function of its temperature alone. [named after J. P. JOULE]

jounce (jouns), *v.,* **jounced, jounc·ing,** *n.* —*v.t., v.i.* **1.** to move joltingly or roughly up and down; bounce. —*n.* **2.** a jolting fall or bounce. [late ME; appar. b. *joll* to bump (now obs.) and BOUNCE]

jour., **1.** journal. **2.** journeyman.

Jour·dan (zho͞or dän′), *n.* **Jean Bap·tiste** (zhän ba-tēst′), **Count,** 1762–1833, French marshal.

jour·nal (jûr′nəl), *n.* **1.** a daily record, as of occurrences or observations. **2.** a record, usually daily, of the proceedings and transactions of a legislative body, an organization, etc. **3.** a newspaper, esp. a daily one. **4.** a periodical or magazine, esp. one published for a learned society or profession. **5.** *Bookkeeping.* **a.** a daybook. **b.** (in the double-entry method) a book into which all transactions are entered from the daybook or blotter to facilitate posting into the ledger. **6.** *Naut.* a log or logbook. **7.** *Mach.* the portion of a shaft or axle contained by a plain bearing. [ME < OF: daily < L *diurnāl(is)* DIURNAL]

jour′nal box′, *Mach.* a box or housing for a journal and its bearing.

jour·nal·ese (jûr′nəlēz′, -nəlēs′), *n.* a manner of writing or speaking characterized by neologism, faulty or unusual syntax, etc., conceived of as typifying the journalistic style.

jour·nal·ise (jûr′nəlīz′), *v.i., v.t.,* **-ised, -is·ing.** *Chiefly Brit.* journalize. —**jour′nal·i·sa′tion,** *n.* —**jour′nal·is′er,** *n.*

jour·nal·ism (jûr′nəliz′əm), *n.* **1.** the occupation of reporting, writing, editing, photographing, or broadcasting news or of conducting any news organization as a business. **2.** press[1] (def. 26). **3.** a course of study preparing students for careers in reporting, writing, and editing for newspapers and magazines. [< F *journalisme*]

jour·nal·ist (jûr′nəlist), *n.* **1.** a person who practices the occupation of journalism. **2.** a person who keeps a diary.

jour·nal·is·tic (jûr′nəlis′tik), *adj.* of, pertaining to, or characteristic of journalists or journalism. —**jour′nal·is′ti·cal·ly,** *adv.*

jour·nal·ize (jûr′nəlīz′), *v.,* **-ized, -iz·ing.** —*v.t.* **1.** to enter or record in a journal. **2.** to tell or relate, as done in a journal. **3.** (in double-entry bookkeeping) to enter in a journal, preparatory to posting to the ledger. —*v.i.* **4.** to keep or make entries in a journal. Also, *esp. Brit.,* **journalise.** —**jour′nal·i·za′tion,** *n.* —**jour′nal·iz′er,** *n.*

jour·ney (jûr′nē), *n., pl.* **-neys,** *v.,* **-neyed, -ney·ing.** —*n.* **1.** travel from one place to another, usually taking a rather long time. **2.** a distance, course, or area traveled or suitable for traveling: *a desert journey.* **3.** a period of travel: *a week's journey.* **4.** passage or progress from one stage to another. —*v.i.* **5.** to make a journey; travel. [ME *journee day* < OF < VL **diurnāta* a day's time, day's work, etc. = L *diurn(us)* daily + *-āta* perfective suffix (fem.)] —**jour′ney·er,** *n.* —**Syn. 1.** excursion, tour. See **trip.**

jour·ney·man (jûr′nē mən), *n., pl.* **-men.** a person who has served his apprenticeship at a trade or handicraft and is certified to work at it for another. [JOURNEY a day's work (obs.) + MAN[1]]

joust (joust, just, jo͞ost), *n.* **1.** single combat in which two armored knights on horseback opposed each other with weapons of war, as the lance, sword, mace, etc. **2.** (in late medieval history) this type of combat fought in a highly formalized manner as part of a tournament. **3. jousts,** tournament. —*v.i.* **4.** to contend in a joust or tournament. Also, **just.** [ME *jouste* < OF *jouste, joste* < *joster, jouster* to tilt in the lists < VL **juxtāre* to approach, clash < L *juxtā* approaching, bordering] —**joust′er,** *n.*

Jove (jōv), *n.* **1.** Jupiter (def. 1). **2. by Jove!** (used as an exclamation to emphasize a previous remark or to express surprise, approval, etc.) [ME < L *Jov-* (obl. s. of *Juppiter* Jupiter), akin to *deus,* god; c. Gk *Zeús* (gen. *Diós*) Zeus]

jo·vi·al (jō′vē əl), *adj.* **1.** endowed with or characterized by a hearty, joyous humor or a spirit of good fellowship. **2.** (*cap.*) of or pertaining to the god Jove, or Jupiter. [< L *joviāl(is)* of Jupiter (the planet, supposed to exert a happy influence) = *jovi-* (see JOVIAN) + *-ālis* -AL[1]] —**jo′vi·al·ly,** *adv.* —**jo′vi·al·ness,** *n.*

—**Syn. 1.** merry, jolly, joyful, mirthful. JOVIAL, JOCULAR, JOCUND agree in referring to someone who is in a good humor. JOVIAL suggests a hearty, joyous humor. JOCULAR means humorous, facetious, and waggish. JOCUND, now a literary word, suggests a cheerful, light-hearted, and sprightly gaiety. —**Ant. 1.** gloomy.

jo·vi·al·i·ty (jō′vē al′i tē), *n.* the state or quality of being jovial; merriment; jollity. —**Syn.** See **mirth.**

Jo·vi·an (jō′vē ən), *adj.* **1.** of or pertaining to the Roman god Jupiter. **2.** of or pertaining to the planet Jupiter. [< L *Jovi-* (comb. form of *Juppiter*) + -AN]

Jow·ett (jou′it), *n.* **Benjamin,** 1817–93, English educator and Greek scholar.

jowl[1] (joul, jōl), *n.* **1.** a jaw, esp. the lower jaw. **2.** the cheek. [ME *chawl, chavell,* OE *ceafl* jaw; c. D *kevel,* G *Kiefer,* Icel *kjaptr*] —**jowled,** *adj.*

jowl[2] (joul, jōl), *n.* **1.** a fold of flesh hanging from the jaw, as of a fat person. **2.** the meat of the cheek of a hog. **3.** the dewlap of cattle. **4.** the wattle of fowls. Also, **jole.** [ME *cholle,* OE *ceole* throat; c. G *Kehle* throat]

jowl·y (jou′lē, jō′-), *adj.,* **jowl·i·er, jowl·i·est.** having prominent jowls.

joy (joi), *n.* **1.** the emotion of great delight or happiness caused by something good or satisfying; keen pleasure. **2.** a source or cause of keen pleasure or delight. **3.** the expression or display of glad feeling; festive gaiety. **4.** state of happiness or felicity. —*v.i.* **5.** to feel joy; be glad; rejoice. —*v.t.* **6.** *Obs.* to gladden. [ME *joy(e)* < OF *joie, joye* < LL *gaudia,* neut. pl. (taken as fem. sing.) of L *gaudium* joy = *gaud-* (base of *gaudēre* to be glad) + *-ium* n. suffix] —**Syn. 1.** rapture. **4.** bliss. See **pleasure.**

joy·ance (joi′əns), *n. Archaic.* joyous feeling; gladness.

Joyce (jois), *n.* **James (Augustine Aloysius),** 1882–1941, Irish novelist.

Joyc·e·an (joi′sē ən), *adj.* **1.** of, pertaining to, or characteristic of James Joyce or his work. —*n.* **2.** a student of the life and work of James Joyce.

joy·ful (joi′fəl), *adj.* **1.** full of joy, as a person, the heart, etc.; glad; delighted. **2.** showing or expressing joy, as looks, actions, speech, etc. **3.** causing or bringing joy, as an event, a sight, news, etc.; delightful. [ME] —**joy′ful·ly,** *adj.* —**joy′ful·ness,** *n.* —**Syn. 1.** joyous, happy, blithe; buoyant, elated, jubilant. See **gay.** —**Ant. 1.** melancholy.

joy·less (joi′lis), *adj.* **1.** without joy or gladness; unhappy. **2.** causing no joy. [ME *joyles*] —**joy′less·ly,** *adv.* —**joy′less·ness,** *n.* —**Syn. 1.** sad, cheerless, gloomy, dismal.

joy·ous (joi′əs), *adj.* joyful; happy; jubilant. [ME < AF; OF *joios,* etc.] —**joy′ous·ly,** *adv.* —**joy′ous·ness,** *n.*

joy′ ride′, *Informal.* a short ride in an automobile driven recklessly or without the owner's permission. —**joy′ rid′er.** —**joy′ rid′ing.**

joy-ride (joi′rīd′), *v.i.,* **-rode, -rid·den, -rid·ing.** *Informal.* to go on a joy ride.

joy′ stick′, *Aeron. Informal.* the control stick of an airplane. [appar. so called from the joy that controlling the plane gives]

J.P., Justice of the Peace.

Jr., **1.** Journal. **2.** Junior.

jr., junior.

J.S.D., Doctor of the Science of Law; Doctor of Juristic Science.

Ju., June.

Juan Car·los I (hwän kär′lôs), (*Juan Carlos Alfonso Victor María de Borbón y Borbón*), born 1938, king of Spain since 1975, born in Italy.

Ju·an de Fu·ca (jo͞o′ən di fyo͞o′kə, wän′; *Sp.* hwän′ de fo͞o′kä), a strait between Vancouver Island and NW Washington. 100 mi. long; 15–20 mi. wide. Also called **Ju′an de Fu′ca Strait′.**

Ju·an Fer·nán·dez (jo͞o′ən fər nan′dez, wän′; *Sp.* hwän′ fer nän′des), a group of three islands in the S Pacific, 400 mi. W of and belonging to Chile: Alexander Selkirk, the alleged prototype of Robinson Crusoe, was marooned here 1704.

Juá·rez (wär′ez; *Sp.* hwä′res), *n.* **1. Be·ni·to (Pa·blo)** (be nē′tô pä′vlô), 1806–72, president of Mexico 1858–72. **2. Ciudad.** See **Ciudad Juárez.**

ju·ba (jo͞o′bə), *n.* a lively dance accompanied by rhythmic hand clapping, developed by plantation slaves of the U.S. [?]

Ju·ba (jo͞o′bä), *n.* a river in E Africa, flowing S from S Ethiopia through the Somali Republic to the Indian Ocean. 1000 mi. long. Italian, **Giuba.**

Ju·bal (jo͞o′bəl), *n.* the progenitor of musicians and those who produce musical instruments. Gen 4:21.

Jub·bul·pore (jub′əl pôr′), *n.* Jabalpur.

ju·bi·lant (jo͞o′bə lənt), *adj.* **1.** showing great joy or triumph; rejoicing; exultant. **2.** expressing joy or exultation. [< L *jūbilant-* (s. of *jūbilāns*), prp. of *jūbilāre* to shout for joy; see -ANT] **—ju′bi·lance, ju′bi·lan·cy,** *n.* **—ju′bi·lant·ly,** *adv.*

ju·bi·late (jo͞o′bə lāt′), *v.i.,* **-lat·ed, -lat·ing. 1.** to show or feel great joy; rejoice; exult. **2.** to celebrate a jubilee or joyful occasion. [< L *jūbilāt(us)* (ptp. of *jūbilāre* to shout for joy); see -ATE[1]] **—ju·bi·la·to·ry** (jo͞o′bə lə tōr′ē, -tôr′ē), *adj.*

Ju·bi·la·te (jo͞o′bə lä′tē, -lā′tē), *n.* **1.** Also called **Ju′bi·la′te Sun′day.** the third Sunday after Easter: so called from the first word of the 65th Psalm in the Vulgate, which is used as the introit. **2.** a musical setting of this psalm. [< L: shout ye for joy]

ju·bi·la·tion (jo͞o′bə lā′shən), *n.* **1.** a feeling of joy or exultation. **2.** the act of rejoicing or jubilating; exultation. **3.** a joyful or festive celebration. [< L *jūbilātiōn-* (s. of *jūbilātiō*) a shouting for joy (see JUBILATE, -ION); r. ME *jubilacioun* < AF]

ju·bi·lee (jo͞o′bə lē′, jo͞o′bə lē′), *n.* **1.** the celebration of any of certain anniversaries, as the 25th **(silver jubilee),** 50th **(golden jubilee),** or 60th or 75th **(diamond jubilee). 2.** an anniversary marking the completion of 50 years of existence, activity, or the like, or its celebration. **3.** any season or occasion of rejoicing or festivity. **4.** rejoicing or jubilation. **5.** *Rom. Cath. Ch.* **a.** an appointed year or other period, ordinarily every 25 years. **b.** a special time of rejoicing, as declared by the pope, when a plenary indulgence is granted. **c.** Also called **ju′bilee indul′gence.** the plenary indulgence granted. **6.** Also, **Ju′bi·le′.** *Chiefly Biblical.* a yearlong period to be observed by Jews once every 50 years, during which Jewish slaves were to be freed, alienated lands restored to the original owner or his heir, the fields left untilled, and all agricultural labors suspended. Lev. 25. Cf. **sabbatical year** (def. 2). **—*adj.* 7.** flambé. [ME < MF *jubile* < eccl. L < *jūbilaeus* < eccl. Gk *iōbēlaîos* (with *ō* and *ē* > *u* and *i* by assimilation to L *jūbilāre* to shout for joy) < Heb *yōbhēl* ram's horn, jubilee]

Jud., **1.** Judges. **2.** Judith (Apocrypha).

jud., **1.** judge. **2.** judgment. **3.** judicial. **4.** judiciary.

Ju·dae·a (jo͞o dē′ə), *n.* Judea. **—Ju·dae′an,** *adj., n.*

Judaeo-, var. of **Judeo-.**

Ju·dah (jo͞o′də), *n.* **1.** the fourth son of Jacob and Leah. Gen. 29:35. **2.** one of the 12 tribes of Israel, traditionally descended from him. **3.** the Biblical kingdom of the Hebrews in S Palestine, including the tribes of Judah and Benjamin. Cf. **Ephraim** (def. 3). See map at **Philistia.**

Ju′dah ha-Le′vi (hä lē′vī), (*Judah ben Samuel Ha-levi*) 1085–1140, Spanish rabbi, physician, poet, and philosopher. Also, **Ju′dah Ha·le′vi.**

Ju·da·ic (jo͞o dā′ik), *adj.* **1.** of or pertaining to Judaism: *the Judaic idea of justice.* **2.** of or pertaining to the Jews; Jewish. [< L *jūdaic(us)* < Gk *ioudaikós*] **—Ju·da′i·cal·ly,** *adv.*

Ju·da·i·ca (jo͞o dā′i kə), *n.pl.* things Jewish, esp. when of a historical or literary nature, as books about Jewish life and customs. [< L, neut. pl. of *jūdaicus* JUDAIC]

Ju·da·ise (jo͞o′dē īz′, -dā-), *v.i., v.t.,* **-ised, -is·ing.** *Chiefly Brit.* Judaize. **—Ju′da·i·sa′tion,** *n.* **—Ju′da·is′er,** *n.*

Ju·da·ism (jo͞o′dē iz′əm, -dā-), *n.* **1.** the monotheistic religion of the Jews, based on the precepts of the Old Testament and the teachings and commentaries of the rabbis as found chiefly in the Talmud. Cf. **Conservative Jew, Orthodox Jew, Reform Jew. 2.** belief in and conformity to this religion, its practices, and ceremonies. **3.** this religion considered as forming the basis of the cultural and social identity of the Jews. **4.** Jews collectively. [< LL *jūdaism(us)* < Gk *ioudaismós*] **—Ju′da·ist,** *n.*

Ju·da·ize (jo͞o′dē īz′, -dā-), *v.,* **-ized, -iz·ing.** **—*v.i.* 1.** to conform to the spirit, character, principles, or practices of Judaism. **—*v.t.* 2.** to bring into conformity with Judaism. Also, *esp. Brit.,* **Judaise.** [< LL *jūdaiz(āre)* < Gk *ioudaḯzein*] **—Ju′da·i·za′tion,** *n.* **—Ju′da·iz′er,** *n.*

Ju·das (jo͞o′dəs), *n.* **1.** Judas Iscariot, the disciple who betrayed Jesus. Mark 3:19. **2.** a person treacherous enough to betray a friend; traitor. **3.** one of the 12 apostles (not Judas Iscariot). Luke 6:16; Acts 1:13; John 14:22. **4.** a brother of James (and possibly of Jesus). Matt. 13:55; Mark 6:3. **—*adj.* 5.** (of an animal) used as a decoy to lead other animals to slaughter. **—Ju′das·like′,** *adj.*

Ju′das Maccabae′us. See **Maccabaeus, Judas.**

Ju′das Priest′, (an exclamation of exasperation or disgust.) [euphemism for *Jesus Christ*]

Ju′das tree′, **1.** a Eurasian, purple-flowered, leguminous tree, *Cercis Siliquastrum,* supposed to be the kind upon which Judas hanged himself. **2.** any of various other trees of the same genus, as the redbud.

Jude (jo͞od), *n.* **1.** a book of the New Testament. **2.** the author of this book, sometimes identified with Judas, the brother of James.

Ju·de·a (jo͞o dē′ə), *n.* the S region of ancient Palestine: existed under Persian, Greek, and Roman rule; now absorbed by SW Israel and W Jordan. Also, **Judaea. —Ju·de′an,** *adj., n.*

Judeo-, a combining form meaning "Jewish," or referring to Judaism: *Judeo-Christian.* Also, **Judaeo-.**

Judg., Judges.

judge (juj), *n., v.,* **judged, judg·ing.** **—*n.* 1.** a public officer authorized to hear and determine causes in a court of law. **2.** a person appointed to decide in any competition or contest; authorized arbiter. **3.** one qualified to pass a critical judgment: *He is a good judge of horses.* **4.** (*often cap.*) an administrative head of Israel in the period between the death of Joshua and the accession to the throne by Saul. **—*v.t.* 5.** to pass legal judgment on; pass sentence on (a person). **6.** to hear evidence or legal arguments in (a case) in order to pass judgment; try. **7.** to form a judgment or opinion of or upon; decide upon critically: *You can't judge a book by its cover.* **8.** to decide or decree judicially or authoritatively. **9.** to infer, think, or hold as an opinion. **10.** to make a careful guess about; estimate: *We judged the distance to be about four miles.* **11.** (of the Hebrew judges) to govern. **—*v.i.* 12.** to act as a judge; pass judgment. **13.** to form an opinion or estimate. **14.** to make a mental judgment. [ME *jugge(n)* < AF *juge(r),* OF *jugier* < L *jūdicāre* to judge = *jūdic-* (s. of *jūdex*) a judge + *-āre* inf. suffix] **—judge′a·ble,** *adj.* **—judg′er,** *n.* **—judge′like′,** *adj.* **—judge′ship,** *n.* **—judg′ing·ly,** *adv.*

—Syn. 1. justice. **2.** arbitrator. JUDGE, REFEREE, UMPIRE refer to a person who is entrusted with decisions affecting others. JUDGE, in its legal and other uses, implies particularly that one has qualifications and authority for giving decisions in matters at issue: *a judge appointed to the Supreme Court.* A REFEREE usually examines and reports on the merits of a case as an aid to a court. An UMPIRE gives the final ruling when arbitrators of a case disagree. **3.** connoisseur, critic. **9.** determine; consider, regard. **12.** adjudge, adjudicate.

judge′ ad′vocate, *pl.* **judge advocates.** *Mil., Navy.* a staff officer designated as legal adviser to a commander and charged with the administration of military justice.

judge′ ad′vocate gen′eral, *pl.* **judge advocates general, judge advocate generals.** *Mil.* the chief legal officer of an army, navy, or air force.

Judg·es (juj′iz), *n.* (*construed as sing.*) a book of the Bible containing the history of Israel under the judges.

judg·ment (juj′mənt), *n.* **1.** the act or an instance of judging. **2.** *Law.* **a.** the judicial decision of a cause in court. **b.** the obligation, esp. a debt, arising from a judicial decision. **c.** the certificate embodying such a decision and issued against the obligor, esp. a debtor. **3.** the ability to judge, make a decision, or form an opinion objectively, authoritatively, and wisely, esp. in matters affecting action; good sense; discretion. **4.** demonstration or exercise of such ability or capacity. **5.** the forming of an opinion, estimate, notion, or conclusion, as from circumstances presented to the mind. **6.** the opinion formed. **7.** a misfortune regarded as inflicted by God. **8.** (*usually cap.*) Also called **Last Judgment.** the final trial of all mankind. Also, *esp. Brit.,* **judge′ment.** [ME *jug(g)ement* < OF *jugement.* See, JUDGE, -MENT] **—judg·men·tal;** *esp. Brit.,* **judge·men·tal** (juj men′tᵊl), *adj.*

—Syn. 1. determination. **2a.** verdict, decree. **3.** discrimination, discernment, sagacity, wisdom, prudence, taste.

Judg′ment Day′, the day of the Last Judgment; doomsday.

ju·di·ca·ble (jo͞o′də kə bəl), *adj.* capable of being or liable to be judged or tried. [< LL *jūdicābil(is).* See JUDGE, -ABLE]

ju·di·ca·tive (jo͞o′də kā′tiv), *adj.* having ability to judge; judging: *the judicative faculty.* [< ML *jūdicātīv(us).* See JUDGE, -ATIVE]

ju·di·ca·tor (jo͞o′də kā′tər), *n.* a person who acts as judge or sits in judgment. [< LL = L *jūdicāt(us)* (ptp. of *jūdicāre* to JUDGE; see -ATE[1]) + *-or* -OR[2]] **—ju·di·ca·to·ri·al** (jo͞o′də kə tōr′ē əl, -tôr′-), *adj.*

ju·di·ca·to·ry (jo͞o′də kə tōr′ē, -tôr′ē), *adj., n., pl.* **-to·ries.** **—*adj.* 1.** of or pertaining to judgment or the administration of justice; judiciary. **—*n.* 2.** a court of law and justice; tribunal; judiciary. **3.** the administration of justice. [< ML *jūdicātōr(ium)* law court. See JUDGE, -ATE[1], -ORY[2]]

ju·di·ca·ture (jo͞o′də kā′chər), *n.* **1.** the administration of justice, as by judges or courts. **2.** a body of judges. **3.** the power of administering justice by legal trial and determination. [< ML *jūdicātūr(a).* See JUDGE, -ATE[1], -URE]

ju·di·cial (jo͞o dish′əl), *adj.* **1.** pertaining to judgment in courts of justice or to the administration of justice: *judicial proceedings.* **2.** pertaining to courts of law or to judges: *judicial functions.* **3.** of or pertaining to a judge; proper to the character of a judge; judgelike: *judicial gravity.* **4.** inclined to make or give judgments; critical; discriminating: *a judicial mind.* **5.** decreed, sanctioned, or enforced by a court. **6.** giving or seeking judgment, as in a dispute or contest; determinative. **7.** inflicted by God as a judgment or punishment. [< L *jūdiciāl(is)* of the law courts = *jūdici(um)* judgment (see JUDGE) + *-ālis* -AL[1]] **—ju·di′cial·ly,** *adv.* **—Syn. 1, 2.** judicatory. **2.** forensic. **4.** See **judicious.**

judi′cial separa′tion, *Law.* a decree of separation of husband and wife that does not dissolve the marriage bond.

ju·di·ci·ar·y (jo͞o dish′ē er′ē, -dish′ə rē), *adj., n., pl.* **-ar·ies.** **—*adj.* 1.** pertaining to judgment in courts of justice or to courts or judges. **—*n.* 2.** the judicial branch of government. **3.** the system of courts of justice in a country. **4.** judges collectively. [orig. adj. < L *jūdiciāri(us)* of the law courts = *jūdici(um)* judgment (see JUDGE) + *-ārius* -ARY]

ju·di·cious (jo͞o dish′əs), *adj.* **1.** using or showing judgment as to action or practical expediency; discreet, prudent, or politic. **2.** having, exercising, or characterized by good judgment; wise, sensible, or well-advised: *a judicious selection.* [< L *jūdici(um)* judgment (see JUDGE) + -OUS] **—ju·di′cious·ly,** *adv.* **—ju·di′cious·ness,** *n.*

—Syn. 1. See **practical. 2.** reasonable, sound, sagacious. JUDICIOUS, JUDICIAL both refer to a balanced and wise judgment. JUDICIOUS implies the possession and use of discerning and discriminating judgment: *a judicious use of one's time.* JUDICIAL has connotations of judgments made in a courtroom, and refers to a fair and impartial kind of judgment: *cool and judicial in examining the facts.* **—Ant. 1.** imprudent. **2.** silly, unreasonable.

Ju·dith (jo͞o′dith), *n.* **1.** a devoutly religious woman of the ancient Jews who saved her town from conquest by entering the camp of the besieging Assyrian army and cutting off the head of its commander, Holofernes, while he slept. **2.** a book of the Apocrypha and Douay Bible bearing her name. [<< Heb *Yehūdīth* Judean woman]

ju·do (jo͞o′dō), *n.* **1.** a method of defending oneself or fighting without weapons, based on jujitsu but banning harmful throws and blows except in dangerous situations and stressing the sport element. **2.** the sport of fighting by this method. Cf. **jujitsu, karate.** **—*adj.* 3.** of or pertaining to this fighting method or sport. [< Jap = *jū* soft + *dō* art] **—ju′do·ist,** *n.*

ju·do·ka (jo͞o′dō kä′, jo͞o′dō kä′), *n., pl.* **-kas, -ka. 1.** a contestant in a judo match. **2.** a judo expert. [< Jap = *jūdō* JUDO + *-ka* n. suffix]

jug[1] (jug), *n., v.,* **jugged, jug·ging.** **—*n.* 1.** a container for liquid, usually made of pottery, metal, or glass, commonly having a handle, often a spout or lip, and sometimes a lid or cork. **2.** the contents of such a container; jugful. **3.** a deep vessel, usually of earthenware, with a handle and a narrow neck stopped by a cork. **4.** *Slang.* jail; prison. **—*v.t.*** **5.** to put into a jug. **6.** to stew (meat) in an earthenware jug. **7.** *Slang.* to commit to jail; imprison. [? special use of *Jug* hypocoristic var. of *Joan,* woman's name]

jug[2] (jug), *n., v.,* **jugged, jug·ging.** **—*n.*** **1.** a sound made by a bird, esp. a nightingale. **—*v.i.*** **2.** to make such a sound. [imit.]

ju·gal (jo͞o′gəl), *adj.* of or pertaining to the cheek or the cheekbone. [< L *jugāl(is)* = *jug(um)* YOKE[1] + *-ālis* -AL[1]]

ju′gal bone′, **1.** (in man) the cheekbone. **2.** a corresponding bone in animals.

ju·gate (jo͞o′gāt, -git), *adj.* **1.** *Bot.* having the leaflets in pairs, as a pinnate leaf. **2.** *Entomol.* having a jugum. [< L *jug(um)* YOKE[1] + -ATE[1]]

jug′ band′, a small musical combo usually consisting of homemade or makeshift instruments such as washboards, kazoos, and empty jugs of various sizes, played by blowing across the openings to produce bass sounds.

Ju·gend·stil (yo͞o′gənt shtēl′), *n.* (*sometimes l.c.*) *Fine Arts.* Art Nouveau as practiced in German-speaking countries. [< G = *Jugend* youth + *Stil* style]

jug·ful (jug′fo͝ol), *n., pl.* **-fuls.** the amount that a jug can hold.

jugged′ hare′, a stew made of wild rabbit, usually cooked in an earthenware or stone pot.

Jug·ger·naut (jug′ər nôt′), *n.* **1.** (*often l.c.*) any large, overpowering, destructive force or object, as a giant battleship, a powerful football team, etc. **2.** Also called **Jagannath.** an idol of Krishna, at Puri in Orissa, India, annually drawn on an enormous cart under whose wheels devotees are said to have thrown themselves to be crushed. [< Hindi *Jagannāth* < Skt *Jagannātha* lord of the world]

jug·gle (jug′əl), *v.,* **-gled, -gling,** *n.* **—*v.t.*** **1.** to keep (several objects, as balls, plates, tenpins, or knives) in continuous motion in the air simultaneously by tossing and catching. **2.** to hold, catch, carry, or balance precariously; almost drop and then catch hold again. **3.** to alter or manipulate in order to deceive, as by subterfuge or trickery. **—*v.i.*** **4.** to perform feats of manual or bodily dexterity, as tossing up and keeping in continuous motion a number of balls, plates, knives, etc. **5.** to use artifice or trickery. **—*n.*** **6.** the act or fact of juggling. [ME *jog(e)le(n)* < OF *jogle(r)* (to) serve as buffoon or jester < LL *joculāre* to joke (r. L *joculārī*) = L *jocul(us)* (see JOKE, -ULE) + *-āre* inf. suffix] **—jug′gling·ly,** *adv.*

jug·gler (jug′lər), *n.* **1.** a person who performs juggling feats, as with balls, knives, etc. **2.** a person who deceives by trickery; trickster. [ME *joglere* < OF *jogler* (nom.) < L *joculātor* joker = *joculāt(us),* ptp. of *joculārī* to joke + *-or* -OR[2]; r. OE *gēogelere* magician, c. G *Gaukler*]

ju·glan·da·ceous (jo͞o′glan dā′shəs), *adj.* belonging to the *Juglandaceae,* or walnut, family of trees. [< NL *Juglandāce(ae)* walnut family (L *jugland-,* s. of *juglans* walnut + *-āceae* -ACEAE) + -OUS]

Ju·go·slav (yo͞o′gō slāv′, -slav′), *n., adj.* Yugoslav. Also, **Ju′go·Slav′.** **—Ju′go·slav′ic,** *adj.*

Ju·go·sla·vi·a (yo͞o′gō slä′vē ə), *n.* Yugoslavia. **—Ju′go·sla′vi·an,** *adj., n.*

jug·u·lar (jug′yə lər, jo͞o′gyə-), *adj.* **1.** *Anat.* **a.** of or pertaining to the throat or neck. **b.** noting or pertaining to any of certain large veins of the neck that return blood from the head. **2.** (of a fish) having the pelvic fins at the throat, before the pectoral fins. **—*n.*** **3.** *Anat.* a jugular vein. [< LL *jugulār(is)* = L *jugul(um)* throat + *-āris* -AR[1]]

ju·gu·late (jo͞o′gyə lāt′), *v.t.,* **-lat·ed, -lat·ing.** to check or suppress (disease) by extreme measures. [< L *jugulāt(us)* (ptp. of *jugulāre* to cut the throat of) = *jugul(um)* throat (dim. of *jugum* YOKE[1]) + *-ātus* -ATE[1]] **—ju′gu·la′tion,** *n.*

ju·gum (jo͞o′gəm), *n.* *Entomol.* the posterior basal area or lobe in the forewing of certain insects. [< NL, L: YOKE[1]]

Ju·gur·tha (jo͞o gûr′thə), *n.* died 104 B.C., king of Numidia 113–104. **—Ju·gur·thine** (jo͞o gûr′thin, -thīn), *adj.*

jug′ wine′, an inexpensive wine sold in large bottles, esp. a bottle containing 1.5 liters (1.6 qts.) or more.

juice (jo͞os), *n., v.,* **juiced, juic·ing.** **—*n.*** **1.** the liquid part or contents of plant or animal substance. **2.** the natural fluids of an animal body. **3.** the natural fluid, fluid content, or liquid part that can be extracted from a plant or one of its parts, esp. of a fruit. **4.** essence, strength, or vitality. **5.** any extracted liquid. **6.** *U.S. Slang.* **a.** electricity or electric power. **b.** gasoline, fuel oil, etc., used to run an engine. **7. stew in one's own juice.** See **stew** (def. 4). **—*v.t.*** *Informal.* **8.** to extract juice from. **9. juice up,** to add more power, energy, excitement, or speed to. [ME *ju(i)s* < OF *jus* < L: broth, soup, sauce, juice] **—juice′less,** *adj.*

juic·er (jo͞o′sər), *n.* **1.** a kitchen appliance for extracting juice from fruits and vegetables. **2.** a stage electrician who works on the lighting of motion-picture, television, and theatrical sets.

juic·y (jo͞o′sē), *adj.,* **juic·i·er, juic·i·est.** **1.** full of juice; succulent. **2.** very interesting or colorful, esp. when slightly improper: *a juicy bit of gossip.* [ME *j(o)usy*] **—juic′i·ly,** *adv.* **—juic′i·ness,** *n.*

ju·ji·tsu (jo͞o ji′tso͞o), *n.* a method of defending oneself without weapons by using the strength and weight of an adversary to disable him. Also, **jiujitsu, jiujutsu, ju·ju·tsu** (jo͞o ju′tso͞o, -jo͝o′-). Cf. **judo, karate.** [< Jap = *jū* soft, + *jitsu* art]

ju·ju (jo͞o′jo͞o), *n.* **1.** a primitive fetish or magical amulet. **2.** the magical power attributed to such an object. [< Hausa *djudju* fetish] **—ju′ju·ism,** *n.* **—ju′ju·ist,** *n.*

ju·jube (jo͞o′jo͞ob), *n.* **1.** the edible, plumlike fruit of any of certain Old World trees of the genus *Zizyphus.* **2.** a fruit-flavored lozenge. [late ME < ML *jujub(a)* < L *zīzyph(um)* < Gk *zízyphon* jujube tree]

Ju·juy (ho͞o hwē′), *n.* a city in NW Argentina. 72,150 (1965).

juke·box (jo͞ok′boks′), *n.* a coin-operated phonograph, having a variety of records that can be selected by push button. Also called **juke.** [*juke* bawdy (shortened form of *juke house*) < Gullah + BOX[1]]

juke′ joint′, *U.S. Slang.* an establishment where patrons can eat, drink, and, usually, dance to music provided by a jukebox. [< Gullah *juke house* bawdyhouse; *joint* r. *house* for alliteration's sake]

Jukes (jo͞oks), *n.* the fictitious name of an actual New York family whose history over several generations showed a high incidence of disease, delinquency, and poverty. Cf. **Kallikak.**

Jul., July.

ju·lep (jo͞o′lip), *n.* **1.** a sweet drink, variously prepared and sometimes medicated. **2.** See **mint julep.** [ME < MF < Ar *julāb* < Pers *gulāb* = *gul* rose + *āb* water]

Jul·ian (jo͞ol′yən), *n.* (*Flavius Claudius Julianus*) ("*the Apostate*") A.D. 331–363, Roman emperor 361–363.

Jul·ian (jo͞ol′yən), *adj.* of, pertaining to, or characteristic of Julius Caesar. [< L *jūliān(us)* = *Jūli(us)* + *-ānus* -AN]

Ju·li·an·a (jo͞o′lē an′ə; *Du.* yʏ′lē ä′nä), *n.* (*Juliana Louise Emma Marie Wilhelmina*) born 1909, queen of the Netherlands 1948–80 (daughter of Wilhelmina I).

Jul′ian Alps′, a mountain range in NW Yugoslavia. Highest peak, Mt. Triglav, 9394 ft.

Jul′ian cal′endar, the calendar established by Julius Caesar in 46 B.C., fixing the length of the year at 365 days and at 366 days every fourth year. There are 12 months of 30 or 31 days, except for February (which has 28 days with the exception of every fourth year, or leap year, when it has 29 days). Cf. **Gregorian calendar.**

ju·li·enne (jo͞o′lē en′; *Fr.* zhʏ lyen′), *adj.* **1.** (of food, esp. vegetables) cut into thin strips or small, matchlike pieces. **—*n.*** **2.** a clear soup garnished, before serving, with julienne vegetables. [< F, special use of *Julienne* woman's name]

Ju·li·et (jo͞o′lē ət, jo͞o′lē et′; *esp. for 1* jo͞ol′yət), *n.* **1.** the heroine of Shakespeare's play *Romeo and Juliet.* **2.** (used in communications to represent the letter *J.*)

Ju′liet cap′, a skullcap, often set with pearls or other gems, worn by women for semiformal or bridal wear. [named after JULIET (def. 1)]

Jul·ius I (jo͞ol′yəs), **Saint,** died A.D. 352, Italian ecclesiastic: pope 337–352.

Julius II, (*Giuliano della Rovere*) 1443–1513, Italian ecclesiastic: pope 1503–13.

Julius III, (*Giammaria Ciocchi del Monte* or *Giovanni Maria del Monte*) 1487–1555, Italian ecclesiastic: pope 1550–55.

Jul·lun·dur (jul′ən dər), *n.* a city in central Punjab, in NW India. 222,600 (1961).

Ju·ly (jo͞o lī′, jə lī′), *n., pl.* **-lies.** the seventh month of the year, containing 31 days. [ME *julie* < AF < L *Jūlius* (CAESAR), after whom it was named; r. OE *Julius* < L; ME *ju(i)l* < OF]

Ju·ma·da (jo͝o mä′dä), *n.* either of two successive months of the Muslim year, the fifth (**Jumada I**) or the sixth (**Jumada II**). [< Ar]

jum·ble (jum′bəl), *v.,* **-bled, -bling,** *n.* **—*v.t.*** **1.** to mix in a confused mass; put or throw together without order. **2.** to confuse mentally; muddle. **—*v.i.*** **3.** to be mixed together in a disorderly heap or mass. **—*n.*** **4.** a mixed or disordered heap or mass. **5.** a state of confusion or disorder. [? b. dial. *joll* to bump and TUMBLE] **—jum′ble·ment,** *n.* **—jum′bler,** *n.* **—jum′bling·ly,** *adv.* **—Syn. 5.** muddle, hodgepodge; mess; chaos. **—Ant. 1.** separate. **5.** order.

jum·bo (jum′bō), *n., pl.* **-bos,** *adj.* **—*n.*** **1.** *Informal.* a very large person, animal, or thing. **—*adj.*** **2.** very large. [after *Jumbo,* name of large elephant in Barnum's show < Swahili *jumbe* chief]

Jum·na (jum′nə), *n.* a river in N India, flowing SE from the Himalayas to the Ganges at Allahabad. 860 mi. long.

jump (jump), *v.i.* **1.** to spring clear of the ground or other support by a sudden muscular effort; leap. **2.** to rise suddenly or quickly, as from a sitting position. **3.** to move or jerk suddenly, as from surprise or shock. **4.** to proceed hastily, as to a conclusion, without careful consideration of evidence. **5.** to act quickly, as to take advantage of an opportunity. **6.** to change or shift from one thing, state, etc., to another. **7.** to rise abruptly, as an amount or price. **8.** *Informal.* to obey quickly; hustle. **9.** *Checkers.* to move a man from one side of an opponent's man to a vacant square on the other, thus capturing it. **10.** *Bridge.* to make a jump bid. **—*v.t.*** **11.** to leap or spring over. **12.** to cause to leap: *to jump a horse.* **13.** to by-pass (something intermediate); skip. **14.** *Informal.* to flee or abscond from: *to jump town.* **15.** to board in haste; hop: *to jump a train.* **16.** to leave (the rails), as a train. **17.** to seize (the mining claim of another) unlawfully. **18.** *Checkers.* to capture (an opponent's man) by leaping over it to an unoccupied square. **19.** *Informal.* to attack without warning, as from ambush. **20.** *Bridge.* to raise (the bid) by more than necessary, esp. as a signal to one's partner. **21. jump bail.** See **bail**[1] (def. 5). **22. jump down someone's throat.** See **throat** (def. 9). **23. jump on** or **all over someone.** *Informal.* to rebuke; reprimand. **24. jump the gun.** See **gun**[1] (def. 7). **—*n.*** **25.** the act or an instance of jumping; leap. **26.** a space or obstacle that is cleared or to be cleared in a leap. **27.** a descent by parachute from an airplane. **28.** a sudden rise, as of an amount or price. **29.** an abrupt transition from one thing, state, etc., to another. **30.** *Sports.* any of several contests that feature a leap or jump. Cf. **broad jump, high jump. 31.** a sudden start as from nervous excitement. **32.** *Checkers.* the act of taking an opponent's man by leaping over it to an unoccupied square. **33.** *Informal.* **the jumps,** restlessness; nervousness; anxiety. **34. get** or **have the jump on,** *Informal.* to get or have a head start or an initial advantage over. **35.** *Informal.* **on the jump,** in a hurry; running about. **—*adj.*** **36.** *Jazz.* played at a bright tempo. **—*adv.*** **37.** *Obs.* exactly; precisely. [cf. Dan *gumpe* to jolt, *gimpe* to move up and down, Sw *gumpa,* LG *gumpen* to jump] **—jump′ing·ly,** *adv.*

—Syn. 1. JUMP, LEAP, VAULT imply propelling oneself by a muscular effort, either into the air or from one position or place to another. JUMP and LEAP are often used interchangeably, but JUMP indicates more particularly the springing movement of the feet in leaving the ground or support: *to jump up and down.* LEAP (which formerly also meant to run) indicates the passage, by a springing movement of the legs, from one point or position to another: *to leap across a brook.* VAULT implies leaping, esp. with the aid of the hands or some instrument, over or upon something: *to vault (over) a fence.* **25.** spring, bound; skip, hop, caper.

jump′ ball′, *Basketball.* a ball tossed into the air above and between two opposing players by the referee in putting the ball into play.

jump′ bid′, *Bridge.* a bid higher than necessary to reach the next bidding level, usually to indicate exceptional strength.

jump·er[1] (jum′pər), *n.* **1.** a person or thing that jumps. **2.** a boring tool or device worked with a jumping motion. **3.** *Elect.* a short length of conductor used to make a connection, usually temporary, between terminals of a circuit or to by-pass a circuit. **4.** a kind of sled. [JUMP + -ER[1]]

jump·er[2] (jum′pər), *n.* **1.** a one-piece, sleeveless dress, or a skirt with straps and a complete or partial bodice, usually worn over a blouse by women and children. **2.** *Brit.* a pullover sweater. **3. jumpers,** rompers. [obs. *jump* short coat (nasalized var. of JUPE) + -ER[1]]

jump′ing bean′, the seed of any of certain Mexican, euphorbiaceous plants of the genera *Sebastiania* and *Sapium*, that is inhabited by the larva of a small moth whose movements cause the seed to move about or jump.

jump′ing jack′, a toy consisting of a jointed figure that is made to jump, move, or dance by pulling a string or stick attached to it.

jump′ing-off′ place′ (jum′ping ôf′, -of′), **1.** the farthest limit of anything settled or civilized. **2.** a place for use as a starting point.

jump′ jet′, a jet airplane capable of taking off and landing vertically or on an extremely short runway or a flight deck. Cf. **STOL, VTOL.**

jump-off (jump′ôf′, -of′), *n.* **1.** the act of jumping off. **2.** a place for jumping off. **3.** a point or time of departure, as of a race or a military attack.

jump′ pass′, *Football, Basketball.* a pass in which a player leaps into the air and throws the ball to a teammate before returning to the ground.

jump′ rope′, **1.** a girl's game in which a rope is swung over and under the standing jumper, who must leap over it each time it reaches her feet. **2.** the rope used.

jump′ seat′, *Auto.* a movable or folding seat.

jump′ shot′, *Basketball.* a shot in which a player leaps into the air and shoots the ball at the basket at the highest point of his leap.

jump′ suit′, **1.** a one-piece paratrooper's uniform worn for jumping. **2.** an article of men's or women's lounging attire styled after this. Also, **jump′suit′.**

jump·y (jum′pē), *adj.*, **jump·i·er, jump·i·est. 1.** subject to or characterized by sudden starts or jumps. **2.** nervous or apprehensive. —**jump′i·ly,** *adv.* —**jump′i·ness,** *n.*

Jun., Junior.

Junc., Junction.

jun·ca·ceous (jung kā′shəs), *adj.* belonging or pertaining to the *Juncaceae*, or rush, family of plants. [< NL *juncāce(ae)* rush family (see JUNCO, -ACEAE) + -OUS]

jun·co (jung′kō), *n., pl.* **-cos.** any of several small North American finches of the genus *Junco*, as *J. hyemalis*, having slate-gray and white plumage. Also called **snowbird.** [< Sp: rush, bird found in rush beds < L *juncus* rush]

junc·tion (jungk′shən), *n.* **1.** the act of joining. **2.** the state of being joined; union. **3.** a place or point where things are joined together. **4.** a place or point where things meet or converge. **5.** a meeting place of roads, railroad lines, etc. **6.** something that serves to join other things. [< L *junctiōn-* (s. of *junctiō*) = *junct(us)*, ptp. of *jungere* to JOIN + *-iōn-* -ION] —**junc′tion·al,** *adj.*
—**Syn. 3.** union, linkage, coupling. **6.** connection. JUNCTION, JUNCTURE refer to a place, line, or point at which two or more things join. A JUNCTION is also a place where things come together: *the junction of two rivers.* A JUNCTURE is a line or point at which two bodies are joined, or a point of exigency or crisis in time: *the juncture of the head and neck; a critical juncture in a struggle.*

junc·ture (jungk′chər), *n.* **1.** a point of time, esp. one made critical or important by circumstances. **2.** a serious state of affairs; crisis. **3.** the line or point at which two bodies are joined; junction. **4.** the act of joining. **5.** the state of being joined. **6.** something by which two things are joined. **7.** *Gram.* a distinctive sound feature or modification of a sound feature marking the phonological boundary of a word, clause, or sentence. [< L *junctūr(a).* See JUNCTION, -URE] —**Syn. 1, 3.** See **junction.**

June (jo͞on), *n.* the sixth month of the year, containing 30 days. [ME *jun(e)*, OE *iuni(us)* < L *(mensis) Jūnius* after the clan name; r. ME *juyng* < OF *juin(g)* < L, as above]

Ju·neau (jo͞o′nō), *n.* a seaport in and the capital of Alaska, in the SE part. 6,050 (1970).

june·ber·ry (jo͞on′ber′ē, -bə rē), *n., pl.* **-ries.** the American serviceberry, *Amelanchier canadensis.*

June′ bug′, any of several large, brown scarabaeid beetles of the genus *Phyllophaga*, appearing in late spring and early summer.

June bug, *Phyllophaga fusca* (Length 1 in.)

June′ grass′. See **Kentucky bluegrass.**

Jung (yo͝ong), *n.* **Carl Gus·tav** (kärl go͝os′täf), 1875–1961, Swiss psychiatrist and psychologist. —**Jung′i·an,** *adj.*

Jung·frau (yo͝ong′frou′), *n.* a mountain in S Switzerland, in the Bernese Alps. 13,668 ft.

jun·gle (jung′gəl), *n.* **1.** wild land overgrown with dense vegetation, esp. tropical vegetation or a tropical rain forest. **2.** an area of such land. **3.** any confused mass or agglomeration of objects; jumble. **4.** a scene of violence or ruthless competition. **5.** *U.S. Slang.* a hobo camp. [< Hindi *jaṅgal* < Skt *jāṅgala* wilderness]

jun′gle fe′ver, *Pathol.* a severe variety of malarial fever occurring in tropical regions.

jun′gle fowl′, any of several East Indian, gallinaceous birds of the genus *Gallus*, as *G. gallus*, believed to be the ancestor of the domestic fowl.

jun·gly (jung′glē), *adj.* resembling a jungle.

jun·ior (jo͞on′yər), *adj.* **1.** younger (usually designating the younger of two men bearing the same full name, as a son named after his father; often written as *Jr.* or *jr.* following the name). Cf. **senior** (def. 1). **2.** of more recent appointment or admission, as to an office or status, usually with lower rank or standing. **3.** (in American universities, colleges, and schools) noting or pertaining to the class or year next below that of the senior. **4.** composed of younger members. —*n.* **5.** a person who is younger than another. **6.** a person who is newer or of lower rank in an office, class, profession, etc.; subordinate. **7.** a student who is in the class or year next below the senior. **8.** a garment size for short-waisted women. [< L: younger]

jun·ior·ate (jo͞on′yə rāt′), *n.* **1.** the two-year course of study for a Jesuit novice in preparation for the course in philosophy. **2.** a seminary for this course.

jun′ior col′lege, a collegiate institution offering courses only through the first one or two years of college instruction and granting a certificate of title instead of a degree.

jun′ior high′ school′. See under **high school** (def. 2).

jun·ior·i·ty (jo͞on yôr′i tē, -yor′-), *n.* the state or fact of being junior in age, rank, standing, etc.

Jun′ior League′, any local branch of a women's organization (**Associa′tion of the Jun′ior Leagues′ of Amer′ica, Inc.**), whose members engage in volunteer welfare work, civic affairs, etc. —**Jun′ior Lea′guer.**

jun′ior miss′, *Informal.* a girl in her early or middle teens.

jun′ior var′sity, *Sports.* a team that consists of players who failed to make the varsity.

ju·ni·per (jo͞o′nə pər), *n.* **1.** any evergreen, coniferous shrub or tree of the genus *Juniperus*, esp. *J. communis*, having cones that form purple berries used in flavoring gin and in medicine as a diuretic. **2.** a tree mentioned in the Old Testament, said to be the retem. [ME *junipere* < L *jūniper(us)*]

Jun·ius (jo͞on′yəs), *n.* the pen name of the unidentified author of a series of letters in a London newspaper (1769–72), attacking the king and his ministers' abuse of royal prerogative in denying John Wilkes his seat in Parliament.

junk[1] (jungk), *n.* **1.** old or discarded material or objects. **2.** anything regarded as worthless. **3.** old cable or cordage used untwisted to make gaskets, swabs, oakum, etc. —*v.t.* **4.** *Informal.* to discard as junk. —*adj.* **5.** cheap, unwanted, or trashy. [ME *jonke* < ?]

Junk[2]

junk[2] (jungk), *n.* a seagoing ship used in Chinese and adjacent waters, having square sails spread by battens, a high stern, and usually a flat bottom. [< Pg *junc(o)* a kind of sailboat < Javanese *joṅ*]

junk[3] (jungk), *n.* *Informal.* narcotics, esp. heroin. [? special use of JUNK[1]]

junk′ bond′, *Finance.* any corporate bond with a low rating and promising a high yield.

Jun·ker (yo͝ong′kər), *n.* a member of the East Prussian aristocracy, noted for its harsh, militaristic attitudes. [< G; OHG *junchērr(o)* = *junc* YOUNG + *hērro* HERR]

Jun·ker·dom (yo͝ong′kər dəm), *n.* **1.** the Junkers as a group. **2.** Also, **Jun′ker·ism** (*sometimes l.c.*) the militaristic, authoritarian spirit or character of the Junkers.

jun·ket (jung′kit), *n.* **1.** a sweet, custardlike food of flavored milk curded with rennet. **2.** a pleasure excursion. **3.** a trip, as by an official, made at public expense. —*v.i.* **4.** to feast, picnic, or go on a pleasure excursion. [ME *jonket* < OF (dial.) *jonquette* rush basket = *jonc* (< L *juncus* reed) + *-ette* -ETTE] —**jun′ket·er, jun·ke·teer** (jung′ki tēr′), *n.*

junk′ food′, food that is low in nutritional value and usually high in calories, as potato chips.

junk·ie (jung′kē), *n.* *Informal.* a drug addict, esp. one addicted to heroin.

junk′ mail′, *Informal.* unsolicited commercial mail.

junk·man (jungk′man′), *n., pl.* **-men.** a dealer in resalable junk.

junk·yard (jungk′yärd′), *n.* a yard for the collection, storage, and resale of junk.

Ju·no (jo͞o′nō), *n.* the ancient Roman queen of heaven, and the wife and sister of Jupiter: the protectress of women and marriage, identified with the Greek goddess Hera.

Ju·no·esque (jo͞o′nō esk′), *adj.* (of a woman) stately; regal.

Ju·not (zhʏ nō′), *n.* **An·doche** (äɴ dôsh′), (*Duc d'Abrantès*), 1771–1813, French marshal.

jun·ta (ho͝on′tə, ho͞on′-, jun′-, hun′-), *n.* **1.** a small group ruling a country, esp. immediately after a coup d'état and before a legally constituted government has been instituted. **2.** a council. **3.** a deliberative council, as in Spain. **4.** junto. [< Sp: a meeting, n. use of fem. of L *junctus* joined]

jun·to (jun′tō), *n., pl.* **-tos.** a self-appointed committee, esp. with political aims; cabal. [alter. of JUNTA]

Ju·pi·ter (jo͞o′pi tər), *n.* **1.** Also called **Jove.** the supreme deity of the ancient Romans: the god of the heavens and of weather, identified with the Greek god Zeus. **2.** *Astron.* the planet fifth in order from the sun, having a diameter of 88,640 miles, a mean distance from the sun of 483,000,000 miles, a period of revolution of 11.86 years, and 16 satellites: the largest planet in the solar system.

ju·pon (jo͞o′pon, jo͞o pon′; *Fr.* zhʏ pôɴ′), *n., pl.* **-pons** (-ponz, -ponz′; *Fr.* -pôɴ′). a close-fitting tunic, usually padded and bearing heraldic arms, worn over armor. Also, **gipon.** [ME *jopo(u)n* < MF *jupon*, aug. of *jupe* JUPE]

Ju·ra (jo͝or′ə), *n.* a department in E France. 225,682; 1952 sq. mi. *Cap.:* Lons-le-Saunier.

ju·ral (jo͝or′əl), *adj.* **1.** pertaining to law; legal. **2.** pertaining to rights and obligations. [< L *jur-* (s. of *jūs*) law + -AL[1]] —**ju′ral·ly,** *adv.*

Ju′ra Moun′tains (jo͝or′ə; *Fr.* zhʏ RA′), **1.** Also called **Jura.** a mountain range in W central Europe, between France and Switzerland, extending from the Rhine to the

Rhone. Highest peak, Crêt de la Neige, 5654 ft. **2.** a mountain range in the second quadrant of the face of the moon.

ju·rant (jo͝or′ənt), *Rare.* —*adj.* **1.** taking an oath; swearing. —*n.* **2.** a person who takes an oath. [< L *jūrant-* (s. of *jūrāns,* prp. of *jūrāre* to swear) = *jūr-* swear + *-ant-* -ANT]

Ju·ras·sic (jo͝o ras′ik), *Geol.* —*adj.* **1.** noting or pertaining to a period of the Mesozoic era, occurring from 135,000,000 to 180,000,000 years ago and characterized by the presence of dinosaurs and conifers. See table at **era.** —*n.* **2.** Also, **Jura.** the Jurassic period or system. [JUR(A) + *-assic,* suffix abstracted from TRIASSIC; cf. F *jurassique*]

ju·rat (jo͝or′at), *n.* **1.** *Law.* a certificate on an affidavit, showing by whom, when, and before whom it was sworn to. **2.** a sworn officer; magistrate. [< ML *jūrāt(us)* sworn man, n. use of L ptp. of *jūrāre* to swear; see -ATE[1]]

ju·ra·to·ry (jo͝or′ə tôr′ē, -tōr′ē), *adj.* pertaining to, constituting, or expressed in an oath. [< LL *jūrātōri(us)* sworn to]

Jur. D., Doctor of Jurisprudence; Doctor of Law. [< L *Juris Doctor*]

ju·rel (ho͞o rel′), *n.* any of several carangid food fishes, esp. of the genus *Caranx,* found in warm seas. [< Sp < Catalan *sorell,* prob. < L *saur(us)* < Gk *saûros* lizard]

ju·rid·i·cal (jo͝o rid′i kəl), *adj.* **1.** of or pertaining to the administration of justice. **2.** of or pertaining to law or jurisprudence; legal. Also **ju·rid′ic.** [< L *jūridic(us)* (*jūri-* comb. form of *jūs* law + *dic-,* root of *dicere* to say) + -AL[1]] —**ju·rid′i·cal·ly,** *adv.*

jurid′ical day′, a day on which a court can lawfully sit.

ju·ris·con·sult (jo͝or′is kon′sult, -kən sult′), *n.* *Roman and Civil Law.* a person authorized to give legal advice. *Abbr.:* J.C. [< L *jūris consultus* one skilled in the law. See JUS, CONSULT]

ju·ris·dic·tion (jo͝or′is dik′shən), *n.* **1.** the right, power, or authority to administer justice. **2.** authority; control. **3.** the extent or range of judicial or other authority. **4.** the territory over which the authority of a person, court, etc., is exercised. [ME < L *jūrisdictiōn-* (see JUS, DICTION); r. ME *jurediccioun* < OF *juredicion* < L, as above] —**ju′ris·dic′tive,** *adj.* —**ju′ris·dic′tion·al·ly,** *adv.*

jurisp., jurisprudence.

ju·ris·pru·dence (jo͝or′is pro͞od′ᵊns), *n.* **1.** the science or philosophy of law. **2.** a body or system of laws. **3.** a department of law. **4.** *Civil Law.* decisions of courts. [< L *jūris prūdentia* knowledge of the law. See JUS, PRUDENCE] —**ju·ris·pru·den·tial** (jo͝or′is pro͞o den′shəl), *adj.* —**ju′ris·pru·den′tial·ly,** *adv.*

ju·ris·pru·dent (jo͝or′is pro͞od′ᵊnt), *adj.* **1.** versed in jurisprudence. —*n.* **2.** a person versed in jurisprudence. [JURISPRUD(ENCE) + -ENT]

ju·rist (jo͝or′ist), *n.* **1.** a lawyer. **2.** a judge. **3.** a person versed in the law. **4.** a person who writes on the subject of law. [< F *juriste* < ML *jurist(a).* See JUS, -IST]

ju·ris·tic (jo͝o ris′tik), *adj.* of or pertaining to a jurist or to jurisprudence; juridical. Also, **ju·ris′ti·cal.** —**ju·ris′ti·cal·ly,** *adv.*

juris′tic act′, an act by an individual that changes, ends, or affects a legal right.

ju·ror (jo͝or′ər), *n.* **1.** one of a body of persons sworn to deliver a verdict in a case submitted to them; member of a jury. **2.** one of the panel from which a jury is selected. **3.** any of a group of persons who judge a competition. **4.** a person who has taken an oath or sworn allegiance. [ME *jurour* < AF (cf. OF *jureur*) = OF *jur(er)* (to) swear (< L *jurāre*) + *-our* -OR[2]]

Ju·ru·á (zho͞o′ro͞o ä′), *n.* a river in E and W South America, flowing NE from E Peru through W Brazil to the Amazon. 1200 mi. long.

ju·ry[1] (jo͝or′ē), *n., pl.* **-ries.** **1.** a body of persons sworn to render a verdict or true answer on a question or questions officially submitted to them. Cf. **grand jury, petty jury.** **2.** a body of persons chosen to adjudge prizes, awards, etc., as in a competition. [ME *jurie, juree* < OF *juree* oath, juridical inquiry, n. use of *juree,* fem. ptp. of *jurer* to swear]

ju·ry[2] (jo͝or′ē), *adj.* *Naut.* makeshift or temporary, as for an emergency. [?]

ju·ry·man (jo͝or′ē mən), *n., pl.* **-men.** a juror.

ju·ry-rig (jo͝or′ē rig′), *n., v.,* **-rigged, -rig·ging.** *Naut.* —*n.* **1.** a temporary rig to replace a permanent rig that has been disabled, lost overboard, etc. —*v.t.* **2.** to replace (a rudder, mast, etc.) with a jury-rig.

ju·ry·wom·an (jo͝or′ē wo͝om′ən), *n., pl.* **-wom·en.** a female juror.

jus (jus; *Lat.* yo͞os), *n., pl.* **ju·ra** (jo͝or′ə; *Lat.* yo͞o′RÄ). *Law.* **1.** a right. **2.** law as a system or in the abstract. [< L: law, right, gen. sing. *jūris,* nom. pl. *jūra,* comb. form *jūri-*]

jus ci·vi·le (jus′ si vī′lē), *Roman Law.* the civil law. [< L]

jus gen·ti·um (jus′ jen′shē əm), *Roman Law.* the law of nations. [< L]

jus na·tu·ra·le (jus′ nach′ə rā′lē, nat′yo͝o-), *Roman Law.* the law of nature. Also, **jus na·tu·rae** (jus nach′ə rē′, nat′yo͝o-). [< L]

jus san·gui·nis (jus′ sang′gwə nis), *Law.* the principle that the country of citizenship of a child is the same as that of his parents. Cf. **jus soli.** [< L: right of blood]

jus·sive (jus′iv), *Gram.* —*adj.* **1.** expressing a mild command. —*n.* **2.** a jussive form, mood, case, construction, or word. [< L *jūss(us)* (ptp. of *jubēre* to command) + -IVE]

jus so·li (jus sō′lī), *Law.* the principle that the country of citizenship of a child is that of his birth. Cf. **jus sanguinis.** [< L: right of soil (land)]

just[1] (just), *adj.* **1.** in accordance with or adhering to the principles of justice; fair. **2.** rational and informed: *a just appraisal.* **3.** in accordance with correct principles: *just proportions.* **4.** (esp. in Biblical use) righteous. —*adv.* **5.** within a brief preceding time: *The sun had just come out.* **6.** exactly or precisely. **7.** by a small amount; barely: *You've just missed seeing him.* **8.** merely: *just a tramp.* **9.** really; positively: *That's just splendid!* [ME < L *jūst(us)* righteous = *jūs* law, right + *-tus* adj. suffix] —**Syn. 1.** upright; equitable, impartial; legal; honorable. **2.** accurate; exact. —**Ant. 1.** biased. **2.** untrue.

just[2] (just), *n., v.i.* joust. —**just′er,** *n.*

jus·tice (jus′tis), *n.* **1.** the quality of conforming to principles of reason, to generally accepted standards of right and wrong, and to the stated terms of laws, rules, agreements, etc., in matters affecting persons who could be wronged or unduly favored. **2.** rightfulness or lawfulness, as of a claim: *to complain with justice.* **3.** the administering of deserved punishment or reward. **4.** the maintenance or administration of what is just according to law: *a court of justice.* **5.** decisions regarding the treatment of individuals or the disposition of cases, as in a court: *to administer justice.* **6.** a judge or magistrate. **7. bring to justice,** to cause to come before a court for trial or to receive punishment for one's misdeeds. **8. do justice, a.** to treat justly or fairly. **b.** to appreciate properly. [ME < OF < L *jūstitia.* See JUST[1], -ICE]

jus′tice of the peace′, a local public officer, usually having jurisdiction to try and determine minor civil and criminal cases, and having authority to administer oaths, solemnize marriages, etc.

jus·tice·ship (jus′tis ship′), *n.* the office of a justice.

jus·ti·ci·a·ble (ju stish′ē ə bəl), *adj.* *Law.* capable of being settled by law or by the action of a court. [< AF < ML *justitiābil(is)*] —**jus·ti′ci·a·bil′i·ty,** *n.*

jus·ti·ci·ar (ju stish′ē ər), *n.* **1.** a high judicial officer in medieval England. **2.** justiciary (def. 2). [ME < ML *justiciār(ius)* JUSTICIARY; see -AR[2]] —**jus·ti′ci·ar·ship′,** *n.*

jus·ti·ci·ar·y (ju stish′ē er′ē), *adj., n., pl.* **-ar·ies.** —*adj.* **1.** of or pertaining to the administration of justice. —*n.* **2.** the office or jurisdiction of a justiciar. **3.** justiciar (def. 1). [< ML *justiciāri(us).* See JUSTICE, -ARY]

jus·ti·fi·a·ble (jus′tə fī′ə bəl, jus′tə fī′-), *adj.* capable of being justified; defensible: *justifiable homicide.* [< MF; see JUSTIFY, -ABLE] —**jus′ti·fi′a·bil′i·ty, jus′ti·fi′a·ble·ness,** *n.* —**jus′ti·fi′a·bly,** *adv.*

jus·ti·fi·ca·tion (jus′tə fə kā′shən), *n.* **1.** a reason, fact, circumstance, or explanation that justifies or defends. **2.** the act or an instance of justifying. **3.** the state of being justified. **4.** Also called **justifica′tion by faith′.** *Theol.* the act of God whereby man is absolved of guilt for sin. **5.** *Print.* the spacing of words and letters within a line of type to make it meet both margins of a column. [ME < LL *justificātiōn-* (s. of *justificātiō*)]

jus·tif·i·ca·to·ry (ju stif′ə kə tôr′ē, -tōr′ē, jus′tə fə kā′tə rē), *adj.* serving to justify; providing justification. Also, **jus·ti·fi·ca·tive** (jus′tə fə kā′tiv). [< LL *justificāt(us)* (ptp. of *justificāre* to JUSTIFY; see -ATE[1]) + -ORY[1]]

jus·ti·fi·er (jus′tə fī′ər), *n.* a person or thing that justifies.

jus·ti·fy (jus′tə fī′), *v.,* **-fied, -fy·ing.** —*v.t.* **1.** to show (an act, claim, statement, etc.) to be just, right, or warranted: *Does the end justify the means?* **2.** to defend or uphold as blameless, just, or right. **3.** to absolve of guilt; acquit. **4.** *Print.* to make (a line of type) a desired length by spacing it, esp. so that full lines have even margins. —*v.i.* **5.** *Law.* **a.** to show a satisfactory reason or excuse for something done. **b.** to qualify as bail or surety. **6.** *Print.* (of a line of type) to fit exactly into a desired length. [ME *justifi(en)* < OF *justifie(r)* < L *justificāre* = *justi-* (comb. form of *justus* JUST[1]) + *-ficāre* -FY] —**jus′ti·fy′ing·ly,** *adv.* —**Syn. 2.** vindicate; exonerate; excuse. —**Ant. 2.** accuse, condemn, blame.

Jus·tin·i·an I (ju stin′ē ən), (*Flavius Anicius Justinianus*) ("*Justinian the Great*") A.D. 483–565, Byzantine emperor 527–565.

Justin′ian Code′, the body of Roman law that was codified and promulgated under Justinian I.

Jus·tin Mar·tyr (jus′tin mär′tər), **Saint,** A.D. c100–163?, early church historian and philosopher.

jus·ti·ti·a om·ni·bus (yo͞o stit′ē ä′ ōm′ni bo͝os′; *Eng.* ju stish′ē ə om′nə bəs), *Latin.* justice to all: motto of the District of Columbia.

jus·tle (jus′əl), *v.t., v.i.,* **-tled, -tling,** *n.* jostle.

just·ly (just′lē), *adv.* **1.** in a just manner; honestly; fairly. **2.** in conformity to fact or rule; accurately. **3.** deservedly; as deserved. [ME]

just·ness (just′nis), *n.* **1.** the quality or state of being just, fair, or right; lawfulness. **2.** conformity to fact or rule; correctness. [ME *justnesse*]

jut (jut), *v.,* **jut·ted, jut·ting,** *n.* —*v.i.* **1.** to extend beyond the main body or line; project; protrude (often fol. by *out*): *land jutting out into the bay.* —*n.* **2.** something that juts out. [var. of JET[1]] —**jut′ting·ly,** *adv.*

jute (jo͞ot), *n.* **1.** a strong, coarse fiber used for making burlap, gunny, cordage, etc., obtained from two East Indian tiliaceous plants, *Corchorus capsularis* and *C. olitorius.* **2.** either of these plants. **3.** any plant of the same genus. [< Bengali *jhuto* < Skt *jūta* braid (of hair)]

Jute (jo͞ot), *n.* a member of a continental Germanic tribe, probably from Jutland, that invaded Britain in the 5th century A.D. and settled in Kent. [OE (north) *Iuti,* later misread as *Juti,* whence modern form] —**Jut′ish,** *adj.*

Jut·land (jut′lənd), *n.* a peninsula comprising the continental portion of Denmark: naval battle between Britain and Germany 1916. 1,659,609 (1960); 11,441 sq. mi. Danish, **Jylland.** —**Jut′land·er,** *n.* —**Jut′land·ish,** *adj.*

Ju·ve·nal (jo͞o′və nᵊl), *n.* (*Decimus Junius Juvenalis*) A.D. c60–140, Roman poet. —**Ju·ve·na·li·an** (jo͞o′və nā′lē ən), *adj.*

ju·ve·nes·cent (jo͞o′və nes′ənt), *adj.* **1.** being or becoming youthful; young. **2.** having the power to make young or youthful. [< L *juvenēscent-* (s. of *juvenēscēns,* prp. of *juvenēscere* to become youthful). See JUVENILE, -ESCENT] —**ju′ve·nes′cence,** *n.*

ju·ve·nile (jo͞o′və nᵊl, -nil, -nīl′), *adj.* **1.** pertaining to, characteristic of, or suitable for young persons: *juvenile behavior; juvenile books.* **2.** young; youthful. **3.** immature; childish; infantile: *juvenile tantrums.* —*n.* **4.** a young person; youth. **5.** *Theat.* **a.** a youthful male role. **b.** an actor who plays such parts. **6.** *Ornith.* a young bird in the stage when it has fledged, if altricial, or has replaced down of hatching, if precocial. **7.** a book for children. [< L *juvenīlis* youthful = *juven(is)* youthful + *-īlis* -ILE] —**ju′ve·nile·ly,** *adv.* —**ju′ve·nile·ness,** *n.* —**Syn. 1.** See **young.**

ju′venile court′, a law court having jurisdiction over minors, generally those under 18 years.

ju′venile delin′quency, illegal or antisocial behavior

on the part of a minor, constituting a matter for action by the juvenile courts.

ju′venile delin′quent, a minor who cannot be controlled by parental authority and commits antisocial or criminal acts, as vandalism, violence, etc.

ju·ve·nil·i·a (jo͞o′və nil′ē ə, -nil′yə), *n.pl.* **1.** works, esp. writings, produced in youth. **2.** literary or artistic productions suitable or designed for the young. [< L, neut. pl. of *juvenilis* JUVENILE]

ju·ve·nil·i·ty (jo͞o′və nil′i tē), *n., pl.* **-ties. 1.** juvenile state, character, or manner. **2. juvenilities,** youthful qualities or acts.

juxta-, a learned borrowing from Latin meaning "beside," "near," used in the formation of compound words: *juxtaposition.* [< L *juxtā*]

jux·ta·pose (juk′stə pōz′), *v.t.,* **-posed, -pos·ing.** to place close together or side by side, esp. for comparison or contrast. [back formation from JUXTAPOSITION]

jux·ta·po·si·tion (juk′stə pə zish′ən), *n.* placing the act or fact of close together or side by side, as two or more objects, ideas, etc., for comparison or contrast. —**jux′ta·po·si′tion·al,** *adj.*

JV, junior varsity. Also, **J.V.**

J.W.V., Jewish War Veterans. Also, **JWV**

Jy., July.

Jyl·land (yyl′län), *n.* Danish name of **Jutland.**

DEVELOPMENT OF MAJUSCULE								
NORTH SEMITIC	GREEK		ETR.	LATIN		MODERN		
						GOTHIC	ITALIC	ROMAN
↓	ꓘ	K	ꓘ	ꓘ	K	𝕶	*K*	K

DEVELOPMENT OF MINUSCULE					
ROMAN CURSIVE	ROMAN UNCIAL	CAROL. MIN.	MODERN		
			GOTHIC	ITALIC	ROMAN
—	K	—	𝔨	*k*	k

The eleventh letter of the English alphabet corresponds to North Semitic *kaph* and Greek *kappa.* The Romans, adopting the alphabet from the Etruscans, at first had three symbols (C, K, and Q) for the *k*-sound. K fell into disuse. It did not appear in English until after the Norman conquest, when, under Norman-French influence, it came into use in place of C to distinguish the pronunciation of words of native origin: such words as *cyng* became *king; cene, keen; cyn, kin; cnif, knife;* and *cnotta, knot.* Under other influences, often through loan words, the symbol entered into more general use.

K, k (kā), *n., pl.* **K's** or **Ks, k's** or **ks.** **1.** the 11th letter of the English alphabet, a consonant. **2.** any spoken sound represented by the letter *K* or *k*, as in *keen, okra,* or *oink.* **3.** a written or printed representation of the letter *K* or *k.* **4.** a device, as a printer's type, for reproducing the letter *K* or *k.*

K, **1.** Kelvin. **2.** *Chess.* king. **3.** *Music.* K.V.

K, **1.** the 11th in order or in a series, or, when *I* is omitted, the 10th. **2.** *Chem.* potassium. [< NL *kalium*] **3.** *Computer Technol.* the number 1024 or 2^{10}. **4.** *Baseball.* strike-out; strike-outs.

k, *Math.* a vector on the *z*-axis, having length 1 unit.

K., **1.** kip; kips. **2.** Knight.

k., **1.** karat. **2.** kilogram; kilograms. **3.** *Chess.* king. **4.** knight. **5.** knot. **6.** kopeck.

K2, *n.* a mountain in N Kashmir, in the Karakoram range: second highest peak in the world. 28,250 ft. Also called **Godwin Austen, Dapsang.**

ka (kä), *n. Egyptian Religion.* a spiritual entity, an aspect of the individual, believed to live within the body during life and to survive it after death. [< Egypt]

Kaa·ba (kä′bə, kä′ə bə), *n.* a small, cubical building in the courtyard of the Great Mosque at Mecca containing a sacred black stone: the chief object of Muslim pilgrimages. Also, **Caaba.** [< Ar *ka'abah* a square building < *ka'b* cube]

Kaap·stad (käp′stät), *n.* Afrikaans name of **Cape Town.**

kab (kab), *n.* cab².

kab·a·la (kab′ə lə, kə bä′-), *n.* cabala. Also, **kab′ba·la.**

Ka·bar·di·an (kə bär′dē ən), *n.* an eastern Circassian language of the Kabardino-Balkar A.S.S.R.

Kab·ar·di′no-Bal·kar′ Auton′omous So′viet So′cialist Repub′lic (kab′ər dē′nō bôl kär′), an administrative division of the RSFSR, in the S Soviet Union in Europe. 507,000 (est. 1965); 4747 sq. mi.

ka·bob (kə bob′), *n.* Usually, **kabobs.** small pieces of meat, seasoned and broiled on a skewer. Also, **cabob, kebab, kebob, ka·bab′.** [< Ar, Hindi *kabāb* < Turk *kebab* roast meat. See SHISH KEBAB]

ka·bu·ki (kä bo͞o′kē, kə-, kä′bo͞o kē), *n.* popular drama of Japan, characterized by elaborate costuming, highly stylized acting, music, and dancing, and by the performance of both male and female roles by male actors. Cf. **No.** [< Jap = *kabu* singing and dancing + *ki* art, performance]

Ka·bul (kä′bo͝ol), *n.* **1.** a city in and the capital of Afghanistan, in the NE part. 377,715. **2.** a river flowing E from NE Afghanistan to the Indus River in Pakistan. 360 mi. long.

Ka·byle (kə bīl′), *n.* **1.** a member of a branch of the Berber race dwelling in Algeria and Tunisia. **2.** a Berber language spoken by the Kabyles. [< Ar *qabā'il*, pl. of *qabīlah* tribe]

ka·chi·na (kə chē′nə), *n.* any of various ancestral spirits deified by the Hopi Indians and impersonated in religious rituals by masked dancers. [< Hopi: supernatural]

Ka·dai (kä′dī), *n.* **1.** a group of languages related to the Thai group and spoken by a small population in southern China and northern Vietnam. **2.** a language family consisting of this group and the Thai group.

Ka·dar (kä′där), *n.* **Ja·nos** (yä′nōsh), born 1912, Hungarian political leader: premier 1956–58 and 1961–65; First Secretary of Hungarian Communist party since 1956. Hungarian, **Já·nos Ká·dár** (yä′nōsh kä′där).

Kad·dish (kä′dish; *Heb.* kä dēsh′), *n., pl.* **Kad·di·shim** (ka dish′im; *Heb.* kä dē shēm′). *Judaism.* **1.** a liturgical prayer, recited during each of the three daily services and on certain other occasions. **2.** the five-verse form of this prayer that is recited by mourners. [< Aram *qaddīsh* holy (one)]

ka·di (kä′dē, kā′dē), *n., pl.* **-dis.** cadi.

Ka·diak′ bear′ (kəd yak′, -yäk′). See **Kodiak bear.**

Ka·di·yev·ka (kä dē′yəf kä), *n.* a city in the E Ukraine, in the S Soviet Union in Europe. 192,000 (est. 1962).

Ka·du·na (kə do͞o′nə), *n.* a city in Nigeria. 149,910 (1963).

kaf·fee klatsch (kä′fā kläch′, klach′, -fē). See **coffee klatsch.**

Kaf·fir (kaf′ər, kä′fər), *n., pl.* **-firs,** (*esp. collectively*) **-fir.** **1.** a member of a Bantu-speaking South African Negroid race inhabiting parts of the Cape of Good Hope, Natal, etc. **2.** (*l.c.*) Kafir (def. 4). **3.** (*l.c.*) *Islam.* an infidel. [< Ar *kāfir* unbeliever, infidel, skeptic]

Kaf·frar·i·a (kə frâr′ē ə), *n.* a region in the S Republic of South Africa. —**Kaf·frar′i·an,** *adj., n.*

Kaf·ir (kaf′ər, kä′fər), *n., pl.* **-irs,** (*esp. collectively*) **-ir.** **1.** a member of an Indo-European people of Nuristan. **2.** (*l.c.*) *Islam.* Kaffir (def. 3). **3.** Kaffir (def. 1). **4.** (*l.c.*) Also, **kaffir, kaf′ir corn′.** a grain sorghum, *Sorghum vulgare caffrorum,* having stout, leafy stalks, introduced into the U.S. from southern Africa. [< Ar; see KAFFIR]

Ka·fi·ri·stan (kä′fi ri stän′), *n.* former name of **Nuristan.**

Kaf·ka (käf′kä, -kə), *n.* **Franz** (fränts), 1883–1924, Austrian novelist and writer of short stories, born in Prague.

Kaf·ka·esque (käf′kə esk′), *adj.* **1.** of, pertaining to, or characteristic of Franz Kafka. **2.** nightmarishly strange, mystifying, and bizarre.

kaf·tan (kaf′tən, käf tän′), *n.* caftan.

Ka·ga·wa (kä′gä wä′), *n.* **To·yo·hi·ko** (tô′yô hē′kô), 1888–1960, Japanese social reformer, religious leader, and writer.

Ka·ge·ra (kä gâr′ə), *n.* a river in equatorial Africa, flowing into Lake Victoria from the west: the most remote headstream of the Nile. 430 mi. long.

Ka·gi (kä′gē′), *n.* Japanese name of **Chiayi.**

Ka·go·shi·ma (kä′gô shē′mä), *n.* a seaport on S Kyushu, in SW Japan. 314,084 (1964).

Ka·hoo·la·we (kä′ho͞o lä′wē), *n.* an island in central Hawaii, S of Maui: uninhabited. 45 sq. mi.

ka·hu·na (kə ho͞o′nə), *n.* (in Hawaii) a native medicine man or priest. [< Hawaiian]

kai·ak (kī′ak), *n.* kayak.

Kai·e·teur (kī′ə to͝or′), *n.* a waterfall in central Guyana, on a tributary of the Essequibo River. 741 ft. high. Also, **Kaieteur′ Falls′.**

kaif (kīf), *n.* kef.

Kai·feng (kī′fung′), *n.* a city in and the capital of Honan, in E China. 330,000.

kail (kāl), *n.* kale.

Kai·lu·a (kī lo͞o′ä), *n.* a city on SE Oahu, in Hawaii. With Lanikai, 33,783 (1970).

kail·yard (kāl′yärd′), *n. Scot.* kaleyard.

Kain·gang (kīn′gang′), *n., pl.* **-gangs,** (*esp. collectively*) **-gang.** Caingang.

Kair·ouan (*Fr.* keʀ wäɴ′), *n.* a city in NE Tunisia: a holy city of Islam. 54,000. Also, **Kair·wan** (kīər wän′).

kai·ser (kī′zər), *n.* **1.** a German emperor: the title used from 1871–1918. **2.** (in the Holy Roman Empire) emperor. [< G << L *Caesar* emperor, special use of proper name (see CAESAR); r. ME (north) *caisere* (OE *cāsere*) and ME *keisere* (< Scand; cf. Icel *keisari*) << L *Caesar,* as above] —**kai′ser·dom, kai′ser·ism,** *n.*

Kai·ser (kī′zər), *n.* **Henry J(ohn),** 1882–1967, U.S. industrialist, wartime shipbuilder, and aluminum magnate.

Kai·sers·lau·tern (kī′zəʀs lou′təʀn), *n.* a city in S Rhineland-Palatinate, in SW West Germany. 86,900 (1963).

ka·ka (kä′kə), *n.* any of several New Zealand parrots of the genus *Nestor,* esp. *N. meridionalis,* having chiefly greenish and olive-brown plumage. [< Maori; ? imit. of the bird's cry]

ka·ka·po (kä′kä pō′), *n., pl.* **-pos** (-pōz′). a large, almost flightless, nocturnal parrot, *Strigops habroptilus,* of New Zealand. [< Maori: lit., night kaka]

ka·ke·mo·no (kä′ke mô′nô; *Eng.* kä′kə mō′nō), *n., pl.* **-no,** *Eng.* **-nos.** *Japanese.* a vertical hanging scroll containing either text or a painting. [lit., hanging object]

ka·ki (kä′kē), *n., pl.* **-kis.** **1.** the Japanese persimmon tree. **2.** the fruit of this tree. [< Jap]

kak·is·toc·ra·cy (kak′i stok′rə sē), *n., pl.* **-cies.** government by the worst men in the state. [< Gk *kākisto(s),* superl. of *kakós* bad + -CRACY]

kal., kalends.

Ka·la·ha·ri (kä′lä hä′rē), *n.* a desert region in SW Africa, largely in Botswana. 200,000 sq. mi.

ka·lam (kə läm′), *n.* *Islam.* **1.** a rationalistic school of theology asserting the existence of God as a prime mover and the freedom of the will. **2.** the word of Allah. [< Ar: word] —**Ka·lam′ist,** *n.*

Kal·a·ma·zoo (kal′ə mə zo͞o′), *n.* a city in SW Michigan. 85,555 (1970).

Ka·lat (kə lät′), *n.* a region in S Baluchistan, in SW Pakistan. Also, **Khelat.**

Kalb (kalb; *Ger.* kälp), *n.* **Jo·hann** (yō′hän), ("*Baron de Kalb*"), 1721–80, German general in the American Revolutionary Army.

kale (kāl), *n.* **1.** a cabbagelike plant, *Brassica oleracea acephala,* having curled or wrinkled leaves: used as a vegetable. **2.** *Scot.* cabbage. Also, **kail.** [ME *cale,* north var. of COLE]

ka·lei·do·scope (kə lī′də skōp′), *n.* an optical instrument in which bits of glass, beads, etc., held loosely at the end of a rotating tube, are shown in continually changing symmetrical forms by reflection in two or more mirrors set at angles to each other. [< Gk *kal(ós)* beautiful + *eîdo(s)* shape + -SCOPE]

ka·lei·do·scop·ic (kə lī′də skop′ik), *adj.* **1.** of, pertaining to, or created by a kaleidoscope. **2.** changing, complex, teeming, various, etc., in a manner suggesting the changing patterns of a kaleidoscope. —**ka·lei′do·scop′i·cal·ly,** *adv.*

Ka·le·mi (kə lä′mē), *n.* a city in E Zaïre, on Lake Tanganyika. 29,488 (est. 1958). Formerly, **Albertville.**
kal·ends (kal′əndz), *n.* (*usually construed as pl.*) calends.
Ka·le·va (kä′le və), *n.* a hero and progenitor of heroes in Finnish and Estonian folk epics.
Ka·le·va·la (kä′lə vä′lə; *Fin.* kä′le vä′lə), *n.* **1.** (*italics*) the national epic of Finland (1835, enlarged 1849), compiled and arranged by Elias Lönnrot from popular lays of the Middle Ages. **2.** the home or land of Kaleva; Finland. [< Finn = *kaleva* hero's + *-la* dwelling place]
kale·yard (kāl′yärd′), *n.* *Scot.* a kitchen garden. Also, **kailyard.**
kale′yard school′, a school of writers describing homely life in Scotland, with much use of Scottish dialect: in vogue toward the close of the 19th century.
Kal·gan (käl′gän′), *n.* former name of **Wanchüan.**
Kal·goor·lie (kal gŏŏr′lē), *n.* a city in SW Australia: gold-mining center. 9201, with suburbs 20,865.
Ka·li (kä′lē), *n.* *Hinduism.* a goddess personifying creation and destruction.
Ka·li·da·sa (kä′li dä′sə), *n.* fl. 5th century A.D., Hindu dramatist and poet. Also, **Kā′li·dā′sa.**
kal·if (kal′if, kā′lif, kä lēf′), *n.* caliph.
kal·i·fate (kal′ə fāt′, -fit), *n.* caliphate.
Ka·li·man·tan (kä′lē män′tän), *n.* Indonesian name of Borneo, esp. referring to the southern, or Indonesian, part.
Ka·li·nin (kä lē′nin), *n.* **1. Mi·kha·il Iva·no·vich** (mi KHä ēl′ i vä′no vich), 1875–1946, Russian revolutionary: president of the U.S.S.R. 1923–46. **2.** Formerly, **Tver.** a city in the W RSFSR, in the central Soviet Union in Europe, NW of Moscow, on the Volga. 408,000.
Ka·li·nin·grad (kä lē′nin gräd′), *n.* a seaport in the W RSFSR, in the W Soviet Union in Europe, on the Bay of Danzig. 359,000. German, **Königsberg.**
Kal·li·kak (kal′ə kak′), *n.* the fictitious name of an actual New Jersey family whose history over several generations showed a high incidence of disease, delinquency, and poverty. Cf. **Jukes.** [< Gk *kalli-* CALLI- + *kak-*; see CACO-]
Kal·mar (käl′mär), *n.* a seaport in Sweden, on Kalmar Sound. 52,385. —**Kal·mar·i·an** (kal mâr′ē ən), *adj.*
Kal′mar Sound′, a strait between SE Sweden and Öland Island. 85 mi. long; 14 mi. wide.
kal·mi·a (kal′mē ə), *n.* any North American, evergreen, ericaceous shrub of the genus *Kalmia,* having showy flowers, as the mountain laurel. [named after Peter *Kalm* (1715–79), Swedish botanist; see -IA]
Kal·muck (kal′muk), *n.* **1.** a member of any of a group of Buddhistic Mongol tribes of a region extending from western China to the valley of the lower Volga River. **2.** a Mongolian language used by the part of the Kalmuck people formerly in NW China, specifically in Ozungaria, and now NW of the Caspian Sea. Also, **Kal′muk.** [< Russ *kalmyk* < Tatar; akin to Turk *kalmak* abandon]
kal·pak (kal′pak), *n.* calpac.
kal·so·mine (kal′sə mīn′, -min), *n., v.t.,* **-mined, -min·ing.** calcimine.
Ka·lu·ga (kä lōō′gä), *n.* a city in the W RSFSR, in the central Soviet Union in Europe. 268,000.
Ka·ma (kä′mä), *n.* a river in the E Soviet Union in Europe, flowing from the central Ural Mountain region into the Volga River S of Kazan. 1200 mi. long.
Ka·ma (kä′mə), *n.* *Hindu Myth.* the god of erotic desire, sometimes seen as an aspect of the god whose other aspect is Mara, or death. [< Skt, special use of *kāma* love, lust]
kam·a·cite (kam′ə sīt′), *n.* a nickel-iron alloy found in meteorites. [< G (obs.) *Kamacit* < Gk *kamak-* (s. of *kámax*) pole + G *-it* -ITE[1]]
Ka·ma·ku·ra (kä′mä kōō′RÄ), *n.* a city on S Honshu, in central Japan: great bronze Buddha. 163,117.
ka·ma·la (kə mä′lə, kam′ə lə), *n.* a powder from the capsules of an East Indian, euphorbiaceous tree, *Malotus philippinensis,* used as a yellow dye and as an anthelmintic. [< Skt < Dravidian; cf. Kanarese *kōmale*]
Kam·chat·ka (kam chät′kə; *Russ.* käm chät′kä), *n.* a peninsula in the E Soviet Union in Asia, extending S between the Bering Sea and the Sea of Okhotsk. 750 mi. long; 104,200 sq. mi. —**Kam·chat′kan,** *adj., n.*
kame (kām), *n.* *Phys. Geog.* a ridge or mound of detrital material, esp. of stratified sand and gravel, left by a retreating ice sheet. [ME (north) *camb* comb, OE *camb*]
Ka·me·ha·me·ha I (kä mā′hä mā′hä, kə mā′ə mā′ə), ("*the Great*") 1737?–1819, king of the Hawaiian Islands 1810–19.
Kame′hame′ha Day′, June 11, observed in Hawaii as a holiday in celebration of the birth of Kamehameha I.
Ka·mensk-U·ral·ski (kä′mənsk ŏŏ RÄl′ski), *n.* a city in the W RSFSR, in the W Soviet Union in Asia, near the Urals. 189,000. Also, **Ka′mensk U·ral′skiy.**
Ka·mer·lingh On′nes (kä′mər liŋ ô′nəs), **Hei·ke** (hī′kə), 1853–1926, Dutch physicist: Nobel prize 1913.
Ka·me·run (kä′mə RŌŌn′), *n.* German name of **Cameroons.**
ka·mi·ka·ze (kä′mə kä′zē), *n.* **1.** (in World War II) a member of a corps in the Japanese air force, charged with the suicidal mission of crashing his aircraft, laden with explosives, into an enemy target, esp. a ship. **2.** the airplane used in such a mission. [< Jap = *kami* divine + *kaze* wind]
Ka·mi·na (kä mē′nä), *n.* a city in S Zaïre. 150,000.
Kam·pa·la (käm pä′lä), *n.* a city in and the capital of Uganda, in the central part. 331,900.
kam·pong (käm′pông, -poŋ, käm pông′, -poŋ′), *n.* a small village or community of houses in Malay-speaking lands. Also, **campong.** [< Malay]
Kam·pu·che·a (kam′pōō chē′ə), *n.* **Democratic,** official name of **Cambodia.** —**Kam′pu·che′an,** *adj., n.*
kam·seen (kam sēn′), *n.* khamsin. Also, **kam·sin** (kam′sin).
Kan., Kansas.
ka·na (kä′nä, -nə), *n.* the Japanese syllabic script, consisting of 71 (formerly 73) symbols and having two written varieties. Cf. **hiragana, katakana.** [< Jap: lit., pretended letters (so called because KANJI are considered real letters)]
Ka·nak·a (kə nak′ə, kan′ə kə), *n.* **1.** a native Hawaiian. **2.** a South Sea islander. [< Hawaiian: man]
ka·na·ma·ji·ri (kä′nə mä′jə rē; *Jap.* kä′nä mä′jē RĒ′), *n.* the standard script of modern Japanese. [< Jap: lit., kana mixture]
Ka·na·nur (kun′ə nŏŏr′), *n.* Cannanore.
Ka·na·ra (kə när′ə, kun′ər ə), *n.* a region in SW India, on the Deccan Plateau. ab. 60,000 sq. mi. Also, **Canara.**
Ka·na·rese (kä′nə rēz′, -rēs′), *adj., n., pl.* **-rese.** —*adj.* **1.** of or pertaining to Kanara, a part of the Maharashtra province in W India. —*n.* **2.** one of a Dravidian people of Kanara, in SW India. **3.** Kannada. Also, **Canarese.**
Ka·na·za·wa (kä′nä zä′wä), *n.* a seaport on W Honshu, in central Japan. 395,000.
Kan·chen·jun·ga (kän′chən jŏŏŋ′gə), *n.* a mountain in S Asia, on the boundary between NE India and Nepal, in the E Himalayas: third highest peak in the world. 28,146 ft. Also, **Kan·chan·jan·ga** (kän′chən jäŋ′gə), **Kinchinjunga.**
Kan·da·har (kun′də här′), *n.* a city in S Afghanistan. 115,000.
Kan·din·sky (kan din′skē; *Russ.* kän dēn′ski), *n.* **Was·si·ly** (vas′ə lē) or **Va·si·li** (vas′ə lē; *Russ.* vä sē′li), 1866–1944, Russian painter. Also, **Kan·din′ski.**
Kan·dy (kan′dē, kän′dē), *n.* a city in central Sri Lanka: famous Buddhist temples. 93,602.
Ka·ne·o·he (kä′nā ō′hā), *n.* a city in central Sri Lanka: famous Buddhist temples. 93,602.

Kangaroo, *Macropus giganteus* (Total length 7½ ft.; tail 3½ ft.)

kan·ga·roo (kaŋ′gə rōō′), *n., pl.* **-roos,** (*esp. collectively*) **-roo.** any herbivorous marsupial of the family *Macropodidae,* of Australia and adjacent islands, having a small head, short forelimbs, powerful hind legs used for leaping, and a long, thick tail serving as a support and balance. [? < native Austral]
kan′garoo court′, a self-appointed or irregular tribunal, usually disregarding or parodying existing principles of law, human rights, etc.
kangaroo′ rat′, **1.** any of various small jumping rodents of the family *Heteromyidae,* of Mexico and the western U.S., as those of the genus *Dipodomys.* **2.** an Australian rodent of the genus *Notomys,* found in arid areas.

Kangaroo rat, *Dipodomys phillipsii* (Total length 13 in.; tail 7 in.)

K'ang Hsi (käŋ′ shē′), (*Shêng-tsu*) 1654?–1722, Chinese emperor 1662–1722.
K'ang Tê (käŋ′ du′). See **Pu-yi, Henry.** Also, **Kang′ Teh′.**
kan·ji (kän′jē), *n., pl.* **-ji, -jis.** **1.** a system of Japanese writing using Chinese-derived characters. **2.** any one of these characters. [< Jap = *kan* Chinese + *ji* ideograph]
Kan·ka·kee (kaŋ′kə kē′), *n.* a city in NE Illinois. 30,944 (1970).
Kan·na·da (kä′nə də, kan′ə-), *n.* a Dravidian language used in most of Madras state in southern India. Also called **Kanarese.**
Kan·nap·o·lis (kə nap′ə lis), *n.* a city in W North Carolina. 36,293 (1970).
Ka·no (kä′nō), *n.* a city in N Nigeria. 300,000.
Kan·pur (kän′pŏŏr), *n.* Indian name of **Cawnpore.**
Kans., Kansas.
Kan·san (kan′zən), *adj.* **1.** of or pertaining to Kansas. —*n.* **2.** a native or inhabitant of Kansas. **3.** *Geol.* the second stage of the glaciation of North America during the Pleistocene.
Kan·sas (kan′zəs), *n.* **1.** a state in the central United States: a part of the Midwest. 2,249,071 (1970); 82,276 sq. mi. *Cap.:* Topeka. *Abbr.:* Kans., Kan., KS **2.** a river in NE Kansas, flowing E to the Missouri River. 169 mi. long.
Kan′sas Cit′y, **1.** a city in W Missouri at the confluence of the Kansas and Missouri rivers. 507,330 (1970). **2.** a city in NE Kansas, adjacent to Kansas City, Missouri. 168,213 (1970).
Kan′sas-Ne·bras′ka Act′ (kan′zəs nə bras′kə), *U.S. Hist.* the act of Congress in 1854 annulling the Missouri Compromise, providing for the organization of the territories of Kansas and Nebraska, and permitting these territories self-determination on the question of slavery.
Kan·su (kan′sōō′; *Chin.* gän′sōō′), *n.* a province in NW China. 18,000,000; 137,104 sq. mi. *Cap.:* Lanchow.
Kant (kant; *Ger.* känt), *n.* **Im·man·u·el** (i man′yōō əl; *Ger.* i mä′nōō el′), 1724–1804, German philosopher. —**Kant′i·an,** *adj., n.* —**Kant′i·an·ism,** *n.*
Kao·hsiung (gou′shyŏŏŋ′), *n.* a seaport on SW Taiwan. 1,000,000. Also called **Takao.**
Ka·o·lack (kä′ō lak, kou′lak), *n.* a city in W Senegal. 96,000. Also, **Ka′o·lak.**
ka·o·lin (kā′ə lin), *n.* a fine white clay used in the manufacture of porcelain. Also, **ka′o·line.** [< F < Chin *Kaoling* name of a mountain in China that yielded the first kaolin sent to Europe (*kao* high + *ling* hill)] —**ka′o·lin′ic,** *adj.*
ka·o·lin·ite (kā′ə lə nīt′), *n.* a very common mineral, hydrated aluminum disilicate, $Al_2Si_2O_5(OH)_4$, the commonest constituent of kaolin.
ka·on (kā′on), *n.* *Physics.* K-meson. [*ka* (name of letter *k*) + (MES)ON]
Kao Tsu (*Chin.* gou′ dzōō′). See **Chao K'uang-yin.**
Ka·pell·meis·ter (kä pel′mī′stər), *n., pl.* **-ter.** **1.** a choirmaster. **2.** a conductor of an orchestra or band. [< G: see CHAPEL, MASTER]
kaph (kuf, käf; *Heb.* käf), *n.* the 11th letter of the Hebrew alphabet. [< Heb: lit., palm of the hand]
Kap·lan (kap′lən), *n.* **Mor·de·cai Me·na·hem** (môr′də kī′ mə nä′hem), 1881–1983, U.S. religious leader and educator, born in Lithuania: founder of the Reconstruction movement in Judaism.
ka·pok (kā′pok, kap′ək), *n.* the silky down that invests the seeds of a silk-cotton tree (**ka′pok tree′**), *Ceiba pen-*

tandra, of the East Indies, Africa, and tropical America: used as a stuffing, and for acoustical insulation. [< Malay *kāpoq*]

ka′pok oil′, a yellowish-green oil expressed from the seeds of the kapok tree, used esp. in foods and in the manufacture of soap.

kap·pa (kap′ə), *n.* the 10th letter of the Greek alphabet (Κ, κ). [< Gk < Sem; see KAPH]

ka·put (kä po͝ot′, -po͞ot′, kə-), *adj. Slang.* ruined; done for; demolished. [< G: orig. trickless (in game of piquet) < F *(être) capot* (to be) without tricks, i.e., make zero score]

Ka·ra·chi (kə rä′chē), *n.* a seaport in S West Pakistan, near the Indus delta: former capital of Pakistan. 1,916,000 (est. 1961).

Ka·ra·gan·da (kä′rä gän′dä), *n.* a city in W Kazakstan in the SW Soviet Union in Asia. 477,000 (est. 1964).

Ka·ra·jan (kar′ə yən; *Ger.* kä′rä yän), *n.* **Her·bert von** (hûr′bərt von; *Ger.* heʀ′bəʀt fən), born 1908, Austrian conductor.

Ka·ra·ko·ram (kär′ə kōr′əm, -kôr′-), *n.* **1.** Also called **Mustagh.** a mountain range in NW India, in N Kashmir. Highest peak, K2, 28,250 ft. **2.** a pass traversing this range, on the route from NE Kashmir to Sinkiang province in China. 18,300 ft.

Ka·ra·ko·rum (kär′ə kōr′əm, -kôr′-), *n.* a ruined city in central Mongolian People's Republic: former capital of the Mongol Empire.

kar·a·kul (kar′ə kəl), *n.* **1.** one of an Asian breed of sheep the young of which have black fleece, the adults brown or gray fleece. **2.** caracul (def. 1). [orig. place name, widely used in Turkestan, esp. in naming lakes; cf. Turk *kara* black, *kul* lake]

Ka·ra Kum (kä rä′ ko͞om′), a desert in the SW Soviet Union in Asia, largely in Turkmenistan, S of the Aral Sea. ab. 110,000 sq. mi. Also, **Qara Qum.**

Ka′ra Sea′ (kär′ə), an arm of the Arctic Ocean between Novaya Zemlya and the N Soviet Union.

kar·at (kar′ət), *n.* a unit for measuring the fineness of gold, pure gold being 24 karats fine. *Abbr.:* k., kt. [sp. var. of CARAT]

ka·ra·te (kə rä′tē), *n.* **1.** a method of self-defense developed in Japan, in which a person strikes sensitive areas on an attacker's body with the hands, elbows, knees, or feet. **2.** a sport based on this form of combat. Cf. **judo, jujitsu.** [< Jap: lit., empty hands]

Kar·ba·la (kär′bə lə), *n.* Kerbela.

Ka·re·lia (kə rēl′yə; *Russ.* kä ʀe′li ä′), *n.* **1.** a region in the NW Soviet Union in Europe, comprising Lake Ladoga and Onega Lake and the adjoining area along the E border of Finland. **2.** See **Karelian Autonomous Soviet Socialist Republic.**

Ka·re·li·an (kə rē′lē ən, -rēl′yən), *adj.* **1.** of or pertaining to Karelia, its people, or their language. —*n.* **2.** the Uralic language of the Karelians, sometimes regarded as a dialect of Finnish.

Kare′lian Auton′omous So′viet So′cialist Repub′lic, an administrative division of the RSFSR, in the NW Soviet Union in Europe: formerly a constituent republic of the Soviet Union. 742,000; 69,720 sq. mi. *Cap.:* Petrozavodsk. Also called **Karelia.** Formerly, **Ka·re′lo-Fin′nish Auton′omous So′viet So′cialist Repub′lic** (kə-rē′lō fin′ish).

Kare′lian Isth′mus, a narrow strip of land between Lake Ladoga and the Gulf of Finland: part of the Soviet Union since 1945.

Ka·ren (kə ren′), *n., pl.* **-rens,** *(esp. collectively)* **-ren. 1.** a group of people of eastern and southern Burma. **2.** one of these people. **3.** the language of the Karen, a Sino-Tibetan language of the Tibeto-Burman branch.

Karl-Marx-Stadt (kärl′märks′shtät′), *n.* a city in S East Germany. 293,549 (1964). Formerly, **Chemnitz.**

Kar·lo·vy Va·ry (kär′lô vi vä′ri), Czech name of **Carlsbad.**

Karls·bad (kärls′bät′; *Eng.* kärlz′bad), *n.* German name of **Carlsbad.**

Karls·ruh·e (kärlz′ro͞o′ə), *n.* a city in SW West Germany: capital of the former state of Baden. 249,500 (1963).

Karl·stad (kärl′städ), *n.* a city in S Sweden. 47,416 (1965).

kar·ma (kär′mə), *n.* **1.** *Hinduism, Buddhism.* action, seen as bringing upon oneself inevitable results, good or bad, either in this life or in a reincarnation: in Hinduism one of the means of reaching Brahman. Cf. **bhakti** (def. 1), **jnana. 2.** *Theosophy.* the cosmic principle of rewards and punishments for the acts performed in a previous incarnation. **3.** fate; destiny. [< Skt: work, deed, fate (*kar-* do, make + *-ma* action of, result of)] —**kar′mic,** *adj.*

Kar·nak (kär′nak), *n.* a village in E Egypt, on the Nile: part of the ruins of ancient Thebes.

ka·ross (kə ros′), *n.* a mantle of animal skins worn by tribesmen in southern Africa. [< SAfrD *karos*, perh. < Hottentot]

Kar·roo (kə ro͞o′), *n., pl.* **-roos** for 2. **1.** a vast plateau in the S Republic of South Africa, in Cape of Good Hope province. 100,000 sq. mi.; 3000–4000 ft. above sea level. **2.** *(l.c.)* one of the arid tablelands of South Africa having red clay soil. [< SAfrD *karo* < Hottentot *garo* desert]

Kars (kärs), *n.* a city in NE Turkey. 41,236 (1965).

karst (kärst), *n. Geol.* an area of limestone formations characterized by sinks, ravines, and underground streams. [< G, special use of *Karst*, name of limestone plateau north of Trieste] —**karst′ic,** *adj.*

kart (kärt), *n.* a small, light, low-slung vehicle, consisting of wheels, a gasoline motor, a steering device, and a frame with a seat, for racing or recreation. Also called **go-cart, go-kart.** [var. of CART]

karyo-, a learned borrowing from Greek used, with the meaning "nucleus of a cell," in the formation of compound words: *karyotin.* Also, **caryo-.** [< Gk, comb. form of *káryon* nut, kernel]

kar·y·o·ki·ne·sis (kar′ē ō ki nē′sis, -kī-), *n. Biol.* **1.** mitosis. **2.** the series of active changes that take place in the nucleus of a living cell in the process of division. [KARYO- + Gk *kínēsis* motion (*kinē-*, verbid s. of *kīnein* to move + *-sis* -SIS)] —**kar·y·o·ki·net·ic** (kar′ē ō ki net′ik, -kī-), *adj.*

kar·y·o·lymph (kar′ē ə limf′), *n. Bot.* the transparent or translucent fluid in a nucleus.

kar·y·o·plasm (kar′ē ə plaz′əm), *n. Biol.* the substance of the nucleus of a cell. —**kar′y·o·plas′mic, kar·y·o·plas·mat·ic** (kar′ē ō plaz mat′ik), *adj.*

kar·y·o·some (kar′ē ə sōm′), *n. Biol.* **1.** any of several masses of chromatin in the reticulum of a cell nucleus. **2.** the nucleus of a cell. **3.** a chromosome.

kar·y·o·tin (kar′ē ō′tin), *n. Biol.* nuclear material; chromatin. [KARYO- + (CHROMA)TIN]

kar·y·o·type (kar′ē ə tīp′), *n. Genetics.* the sum total of the morphological characteristics of the chromosomes in a cell. —**kar·y·o·typ·ic** (kar′ē ə tip′ik), **kar′y·o·typ′i·cal,** *adj.*

Kas., Kansas.

Kas·a·vu·bu (kas′ə vo͞o′bo͞o, kä′sä-), *n.* **Joseph,** 1917?–1969, African political leader: president of the Republic of the Congo 1960–65.

Kas·bah (kaz′bə, -bä, käz′-), *n.* **1.** the older, native quarter in the city of Algiers. **2.** the old native quarter of most big cities in Arab N. African countries. Also, **Casbah.**

ka·sha (kä′shə), *n. Eastern European Cookery.* a cooked food prepared from hulled and crushed grain, esp. buckwheat; mush. [< Russ]

ka·sher (kä′shər), *adj., n., v.t.* kosher.

Kash·gar (käsh′gär′), *n.* a city in W Sinkiang, in extreme W China. 100,000. Also called **Shufu.**

kash·mir (kazh′mēr, kash′-), *n.* cashmere.

Kash·mir (kash′mēr, kash mēr′), *n.* a state in SW Asia, adjacent to India, Pakistan, Sinkiang, and Tibet: sovereignty in dispute between India and Pakistan since 1947. 5,220,000 live in the part occupied by India; 82,258 sq. mi. *Cap.:* Srinagar. Also, **Cashmere.** Official name, **Jammu and Kashmir.**

Kash·mir·i (kash mēr′ē), *n., pl.* **-mir·is,** *(esp. collectively)* **-mir·i. 1.** a native or inhabitant of Kashmir. **2.** the Indo-Iranian language of the Kashmiri. —**Kash·mir′i·an,** *adj., n.*

Kash′mir rug′, an Oriental handmade rug, woven flat without pile and having the patterns embroidered with colored yarns which entirely cover its surface.

kash·ruth (käsh ro͞ot′), *n. Hebrew.* the body of dietary laws prescribed for Jews. Also, **kash·rut′.** [lit., fitness]

Kas·sa (kosh′sho), *n.* Hungarian name of **Košice.**

Kas·sa·la (kä′sä lä′), *n.* a city in the E Sudan, near Eritrea. 49,000 (est. 1964).

Kas·sel (kä′səl), *n.* a city in E West Germany. 211,800 (1963). Also, **Cassel.**

Kas·tro (*Gk.* käs′trô), *n.* Mytilene (def. 2).

Ka·strop-Rau·xel (*Ger.* käs′trôp rouk′səl), *n.* Castrop-Rauxel.

kata-, var. of **cata-.** Also, **kat-, kath-.**

ka·tab·a·sis (kə tab′ə sis), *n., pl.* **-ses** (-sēz′). **1.** a march from the interior of a country to the coast, as that of the ten thousand Greeks after their defeat at Cunaxa. **2.** a retreat, esp. a military retreat. Cf. **anabasis.** [< Gk: a going down, descent = *kataba-* (s. of *katabaínein* to go down) + *-sis* -SIS. See KATA-, BASIS]

kat·a·bat·ic (kat′ə bat′ik), *adj. Meteorol.* (of a wind or air current) moving downward or down a slope. Cf. **anabatic.** [< Gk *katabatik(ós)* pertaining to going down = *kata-* KATA- + *ba-* (s. of *baínein* to go) + *-tikos* -TIC]

ka·tab·o·lism (kə tab′ə liz′əm), *n.* catabolism. —**kat·a·bol·ic** (kat′ə bol′ik), *adj.* —**kat′a·bol′i·cal·ly,** *adv.*

Ka·tah·din (kə tä′din), *n.* **Mount,** the highest peak in Maine, in the central part. 5273 ft.

ka·ta·ka·na (kä′tə kä′nə; *Jap.* kä′tä kä′nä), *n.* the more angular, less commonly used of the two Japanese syllabaries. Cf. **hiragana.** [< Jap = *kata* side, form, formal + *kana* syllabary; see HIRAGANA]

Ka·tan·ga (kə täng′gə, -tang′-), *n.* a province in SE Zaïre: mining area. 3,072,591; 191,878 sq. mi. *Cap.:* Lubumbashi. Official name, **Shaba.**

Kat·ang·ese (kat′äng gēz′, -gēs′, -ang-), *n., pl.* **-ese,** *adj.* —*n.* **1.** a native or inhabitant of Katanga. —*adj.* **2.** of or pertaining to Katanga or its people. Also, **Ka·tan·gan** (kə-täng′gən, -tang′-).

kat·a·pla·sia (kat′ə plā′zhə, -zhē ə, -zē ə), *n.* cataplasia.

Ka·tar (kot′or), *n.* Qatar.

kat·a·to·ni·a (kat′ə tō′nē ə, -tōn′yə), *n. Psychiatry.* catatonia. —**kat·a·ton·ic** (kat′ə ton′ik), *adj.*

Ka·tha·re·vu·sa (kä′thə rev′ə sä′, -sə, kath′ə-; *Gk.* kä′-thä ʀe′vo͞o sä), *n.* the puristic Modern Greek literary language (opposed to *demotic*). Also called **Hellenic.**

ka·thar·sis (kə thär′sis), *n.* catharsis. —**ka·thar·tic** (kə thär′tik), *adj.*

Ka·thi·a·war (kä′tē ä wär′), *n.* a peninsula on the W coast of India.

kath·ode (kath′ōd), *n.* cathode. —**ka·thod·ic** (kə thod′-ik), **kath·o·dal** (kath′ə d^{ə}l), *adj.*

kat·i·on (kat′ī′ən), *n. Phys. Chem.* cation.

Kat·mai (kat′mī), *n.* **1. Mount,** an active volcano in SW Alaska. 7500 ft. **2.** a national monument including Mt. Katmai and the Valley of Ten Thousand Smokes. 4215 sq. mi.

Kat·man·du (kät′män do͞o′), *n.* a city in and the capital of Nepal, in the E part. 150,000. Also, **Kath′man·du′.**

Ka·to·wi·ce (kä′tô vē′tse), *n.* a city in S Poland. 344,000. German, **Kat·to·witz** (kä′tō vits).

Kat·rine (ka′trin), *n.* **Loch,** a lake in central Scotland. 8 mi. long.

kat′su·ra tree′ (kät′sər ə), a Japanese tree, *Cercidiphyllum japonicum*, often cultivated as an ornamental in the U.S. [*katsura* < Jap]

Kat·te·gat (kat′ə gat′), *n.* a strait between Jutland and Sweden. 40–70 mi. wide. Also, **Cattegat.**

ka·ty·did (kā′tē did), *n.* any of several large, usually green, American longhorned grasshoppers, the males of which produce a characteristic song. [imit.]

Katydid, *Microcentrum rhombifolium* (Length 2 in.)

Katz·en·bach (kat′sən bak′), *n.*

Nicholas de·B(elle·ville) (də bel′vil), born 1922, U.S. lawyer and government official: Attorney-General 1964–66.
Ka·u·a·i (kä′o͞o ä′ē), *n.* an island in NW Hawaii. 29,761 (1970); 511 sq. mi.
Kauf·man (kôf′mən), *n.* **George S(imon),** 1889–1961, U.S. dramatist and journalist.
Kau·nas (kou′näs), *n.* a city in S central Lithuania, in the W Soviet Union, a former capital of Lithuania. 247,000 (est. 1962). Russian, **Kovno.**
Kau·ra·vas (kou′rə väz′), *n.* (*construed as pl.*) (in the Mahabharata) the cousins and enemies of the Pandavas.
kau·ri (kou′rē), *n., pl.* **-ris** for 1, 3. **1.** Also called **kau′ri pine′.** a tall, coniferous tree, *Agathis australis,* of New Zealand, yielding a valuable timber and a resin used in making varnishes. **2.** the wood of this tree. **3.** any of various other trees of the genus *Agathis.* [< Maori]
kau·ry (kou′rē), *n., pl.* **-ries.** kauri.
Kaut·sky (kout′skē), *n.* **Karl Jo·hann** (kärl′ yō′hän), 1854–1938, German socialist writer and editor.
ka·va (kä′və), *n.* **1.** a Polynesian, piperaceous shrub, *Piper methysticum,* the roots of which are used in making a beverage. **2.** the beverage. [< Polynesian (first recorded from Tonga Islands): lit., bitter]
Ka·val·la (kə val′ə; *Gk.* kä vä′lä), *n.* a seaport in E Greece. 44,517 (1961).
Ka·va·phis (kä vä′fēs), *n.* **Constantine.** See **Cavafy, Constantine.**
Ka·ver·i (kô′və rē), *n.* Cauvery.
Ka·wa·gu·chi (kä′wä go͞o′chē), *n.* a city on SE Honshu, in central Japan, N of Tokyo. 222,191 (1964).
Ka·wa·sa·ki (kä′wä sä′kē), *n.* a seaport on SE Honshu, in central Japan, SW of Tokyo. 789,303 (1964).
kay·ak (kī′ak), *n.* **1.** an Eskimo hunting craft with a skin cover on a light framework, made watertight by a flexible closure around the waist of the occupant. **2.** a small boat resembling this, made commercially, for use in sports. Also, **kaiak.** [< Eskimo]
kay·o (kā′ō′), *n., pl.* **kay·os,** *v.,* **kay·oed, kay·o·ing.** *Slang.* —*n.* **1.** a knockout in boxing. —*v.t.* **2.** to knock unconscious in a boxing match. [*kay* (letter *k*) + *o* (letter *o*), var. of *k.o.,* abbr. of *knockout*]
Kay·se·ri (kī′se rē′), *n.* a city in central Turkey. 126,913 (1965). Ancient, **Caesarea.**
Ka·zak (kə zäk′), *n.* a member of a Kirghiz people dwelling in central Asia, esp. in Kazakstan. Also, **Ka·zakh′.**
Ka·zak·stan (kä′zäk stän′), *n.* a constituent republic of the Soviet Union, NE of the Caspian Sea. 11,900,000 (est. 1965); 1,064,092 sq. mi. *Cap.:* Alma-Ata. Also, **Ka′zakh·stan′.** Official name, **Kazak′ So′viet So′cialist Repub′lic.**
Ka·zan (kə zan′, -zän′; *Russ.* kä zän′yᵊ), *n.* a city in the SE RSFSR, in the E Soviet Union in Europe, near the Volga River. 763,000 (1965). 643,000 (1959).
Ka·zant·za·kis (kaz′ən zak′is, kä′zən zä′kis; *Gk.* kä′zän dzä′kēs), *n.* **Ni·kos** (nē′kôs), 1883–1957, Greek poet and novelist.
Kaz·bek (käz bek′), *n.* **Mount,** an extinct volcano in the S Soviet Union, in the central Caucasus Mountains. 16,541 ft.
ka·zoo (kə zo͞o′), *n., pl.* **-zoos.** a musical toy consisting of an open tube having a hole in the side covered with parchment or membrane, against which the performer sings or hums. [appar. imit.]
KB, *Chess.* king's bishop.
kb, kilobar; kilobars.
K.B., **1.** King's Bench. **2.** Knight Bachelor.
K.B.E., Knight Commander of the British Empire.
KBP, *Chess.* king's bishop's pawn.
kc, **1.** kilocycle; kilocycles. **2.** kilocurie; kilocuries.
Kč., *pl.* **Kč., Kčs.** koruna. [< Czech *k(oruna) č(eskoslovenský)*]
K.C., **1.** King's Counsel. **2.** Knight Commander. **3.** Knights of Columbus.
kcal, *Physics.* kilocalorie; kilocalories.
K.C.B., Knight Commander of the Bath.
KD., (in Kuwait) dinar; dinars.
ke·a (kā′ə, kē′ə), *n.* a large, greenish New Zealand parrot, *Nestor notabilis.* [< Maori]
Ke·a (ke′ä), *n.* Keos.
Kean (kēn), *n.* **Edmund,** 1787–1833, English actor.
Kear·ny (kär′nē), *n.* **1. Philip,** 1814–62, U.S. general. **2.** a city in NE New Jersey, near Newark. 37,585 (1970).
Keats (kēts), *n.* **John,** 1795–1821, English poet.
ke·bab (kā′bob, kə bob′), *n.* kabob. Also, **ke·bob′.**
keb·lah (keb′lə), *n.* kiblah.
Ke·ble (kē′bəl), *n.* **John,** 1792–1866, English clergyman and poet.
Kech·ua (kech′wä, -wə), *n., pl.* **-uas,** (*esp. collectively*) **-ua.** Quechua.
Kech·uan (kech′wən), *adj., n., pl.* **-uans,** (*esp. collectively*) **-uan.** —*adj.* **1.** Quechuan. —*n.* **2.** Quechua.
keck (kek), *v.i.* **1.** to retch; be nauseated. **2.** to feel or show disgust or strong dislike. [? akin to CHOKE]
Kecs·ke·mét (kech′ke māt′), *n.* a city in central Hungary. 66,819 (1960).
Ke·dah (kā′dä), *n.* a state in Malaysia, on the SW Malay Peninsula. 783,993 (est. 1961); 3660 sq. mi. *Cap.:* Alor Star.
ked·dah (ked′ə), *n.* kheda.
kedge (kej), *v.,* **kedged, kedg·ing,** *n.* *Naut.* —*v.t.* **1.** to warp or pull (a vessel) along by hauling on its anchor cable. —*v.i.* **2.** (of a vessel) to move by being kedged. —*n.* **3.** Also called **kedge′ an′chor.** a small anchor used in kedging. [akin to ME *caggen* to fasten]
Ke·dron (kē′drən), *n.* a ravine in Jordan, E of Jerusalem. Also, **Kidron.**
ke·ef (kē ef′), *n.* kef (def. 2).
keek (kēk), *v.i.* *Scot. and North Eng.* to peep; look furtively. [ME *kike(n),* c. or < MD, MLG *kīken*]
keel[1] (kēl), *n.* **1.** *Naut.* **a.** a central fore-and-aft structural member in the bottom of a hull, extending from the stem to the sternpost. **b.** any of various barges or bargelike sailing vessels. **2.** a part corresponding to a ship's keel in some other structure, as in a dirigible. **3.** *Bot., Zool.* a longitudinal ridge, as on a leaf or bone; carina. **4.** *Chiefly Literary.* a ship or boat. **5. on an even keel,** in a state of balance or stability. —*v.t., v.i.* **6.** to turn or upset so as to bring the wrong side or part uppermost. **7. keel over,** to fall in or as in a faint, esp. without warning. [ME *kele* < Scand; cf. Icel *kjölr*] —**keel′less,** *adj.*
keel[2] (kēl), *n.* *Brit. Dial.* **1.** keelboat. **2.** a keelboat load of coal. **3.** a measure of coal equivalent to 21 tons and 4 hundredweight. [late ME *kele* < MD *kiel;* c. OE *cēol,* G *Kiel* ship]
keel[3] (kēl), *v.t.* *Archaic.* to cool, esp. by stirring. [ME *kele(n),* OE *celan;* akin to COOL]
keel[4] (kēl), *n.* a red ocher stain used for marking sheep, lumber, etc.; ruddle. [late ME *keyle* (north dial.); cf. Gael *cīl* (? < E)]
keel·boat (kēl′bōt′), *n.* *U.S.* a roughly built, shallow freight boat, formerly used on the Mississippi and its tributaries, having a keel to permit sailing into the wind.
keel·haul (kēl′hôl′), *v.t.* **1.** *Naut.* to haul (an offender) under the bottom of a vessel and up the other side as a punishment. **2.** to rebuke severely. Also, **keel·hale** (kēl′hāl). [< D *kielhal(en)*]
Kee′ling Is′lands (kē′ling). See **Cocos Islands.**
keel·son (kel′sən, kēl′-), *n.* *Naut.* any of various fore-and-aft structural members lying above or parallel to the keel in the bottom of a hull. Also, **kelson.** [< LG *kielswin,* lit., keel swine < Scand; cf. Sw *kjölsvin,* appar. dissimilated var. of *kjölsvill.* See KEEL[1], SILL]
Kee·lung (kē′lo͝ong′), *n.* a seaport on the N coast of Taiwan. 258,412 (est. 1963). Also, **Chilung.** Japanese, **Kiirun.**
keen[1] (kēn), *adj.* **1.** finely sharpened, so as to cut or pierce readily: *a keen edge.* **2.** sharp, piercing, or biting: *a keen wind; keen satire.* **3.** highly sensitive or perceptive: *keen hearing; a keen mind.* **4.** intense: *keen competition; keen ambition.* **5.** enthusiastic; ardent. **6.** *Slang.* great; wonderful; marvelous. [ME *kene,* OE *cēne;* c. G *kühn* bold, OIcel *koenn* wise, skillful; akin to CAN[1], KNOW[1]] —**keen′ly,** *adv.* —**keen′ness,** *n.* —**Syn. 1, 3.** See **sharp. 2.** cutting, bitter. **3.** penetrating, acute, discerning, quick. —**Ant. 1, 3.** dull.
keen[2] (kēn), *n.* **1.** a wailing lament for the dead. —*v.i.* **2.** to wail in lamentation for the dead. [< Ir *caoine* (n.), *caoin-* (v.; s. of *caoinim*) lament] —**keen′er,** *n.*
Keene (kēn), *n.* a city in SW New Hampshire. 20,467 (1970).
keep (kēp), *v.,* **kept, keep·ing,** *n.* —*v.t.* **1.** to commence or continue to hold as one's own: *If you like it, keep it.* **2.** to have the use of temporarily: *You may keep it all summer.* **3.** to have in a certain place until wanted: *You may keep your things in here.* **4.** to have under one's care or in one's charge: *Would you keep this until I return?* **5.** to have or maintain for continued enjoyment, use, or profit: *to keep a wine cellar; to keep cows; to keep a store.* **6.** to cause to remain in a good condition, or in a specified condition: *to keep meat; to keep a car badly.* **7.** to provide the livelihood of; support: *to keep a family.* **8.** to cause to stay, as in a certain place: *Keep that dog in the yard.* **9.** to maintain or cause to be or remain in a specified condition: *Keep that child quiet.* **10.** to prevent or restrain: *Keep that child from yelling.* **11.** to remain at, in, or on: *Keep your distance! Please keep your seats.* **12.** to associate with: *to keep bad company.* **13.** to protect, as from harm or injury: *May the Lord keep you!* **14.** to cause to be, or to continue to be, in effect; maintain: *to keep a lookout; to keep silence.* **15.** to show due or appropriate regard for in one's actions; observe: *to keep one's word, to keep the peace; to keep Christmas.* **16.** to provide financial support for, usually in return for sexual favors. —*v.i.* **17.** to remain or continue as specified: *to keep cool; to keep indoors.* **18.** to continue as heretofore: *Keep trying.* **19.** to remain free of deterioration: *Will this food keep?* **20.** to admit of postponement: *I have more to tell you, but it will keep.* **21.** to keep oneself as specified: *Keep off the grass.* **22. keep at,** to persist in a task: *It's a tough problem, but I'll keep at it.* **23. keep back, a.** to keep or refrain from advancing. **b.** to restrain: *to keep back tears.* **c.** to withhold, as a secret. **24. keep on,** to persist, as in an action. **25. keep tab** or **tabs on.** See **tab**[1] (def. 5). **26. keep time.** See **time** (def. 37). **27. keep to, a.** to adhere or conform to. **b.** to remain at or in: *to keep to one's bed.* **28. keep to oneself,** to remain aloof from others. **29. keep track of.** See **track** (def. 13). **30. keep up, a.** to persist in doing or performing: *Keep up the good work.* **b.** to maintain in good condition: *to keep up an estate.* **c.** to compete successfully: *to keep up with the Joneses.* **d.** to keep oneself informed: *to keep up on current events.* **31. keep your chin up.** See **chin** (def. 3). —*n.* **32.** sustenance; support: *to work for one's keep.* **33.** the most heavily fortified building of a medieval castle. **34. for keeps,** *Informal.* **a.** with the intention of keeping one's winnings. **b.** in earnest; with serious intent. [ME *kepe(n),* OE *cēpan* to observe, heed, watch, await, take; perh. akin to OE *gecōp* proper, fitting, *capian* to look, OIcel *kōpa* to stare] —**keep′a·ble,** *adj.*
—**Syn. 1, 2.** KEEP, RETAIN, RESERVE, WITHHOLD refer to having and holding in possession. KEEP (a common word) and RETAIN (a more formal word) agree in meaning to continue to have or hold, as opposed to losing, parting with, or giving up: *to keep a book for a week.* To RESERVE is to keep for some future use, occasion, or recipient, or to hold back for a time: *to reserve judgment.* To WITHHOLD is generally to hold back altogether: *to withhold help.* **6.** preserve. **8.** detain, hold, confine. **33.** donjon, dungeon, stronghold.
keep·er (kē′pər), *n.* **1.** a person or thing that keeps. **2.** a person who tends or guards (often used in combination): *a zookeeper.* **3.** a person who manages or owns a place of business (usually used in combination): *a motelkeeper.* **4.** a person responsible for the behavior of another: *to be one's brother's keeper.* **5.** a person in charge of an incompetent or of animals: *a lunatic and his keeper; a keeper of swine.* **6.** something that serves to hold in place, retain, etc., as on a door lock. **7.** See **guard ring.** [ME *keper*] —**Syn. 2.** guard, warden, jailer; custodian, guardian.
keep·ing (kē′ping), *n.* **1.** due or logical conformity with or of associated things, qualities, etc.: *actions in keeping with promises.* **2.** care or charge: *He has ten children in his keeping.* **3.** observance (often used in combination): *Sabbath-keeping.* **4.** maintenance; custody. **5.** reservation for future use. [ME *keping*] —**Syn. 1.** harmony. **2.** See **custody.**

keep·sake (kēp′sāk′), *n.* anything kept, or given to be kept, as a token of friendship or affection; remembrance.

kees·hond (kās′hond′), *n., pl.* **-honden** (-hon′dən). one of a Dutch breed of small dogs having thick, silver-gray hair tipped with black and a tail carried over the back. [< D, prob. special use of *Kees* (shortening of *Cornelius,* proper name) + *hond* dog; see HOUND[1]]

Keeshond (18 in. high at shoulder)

keet (kēt), *n.* the young of the guinea fowl. [imit.]

Kee·wa·tin (kē wä′tin), *n.* a district in the Northwest Territories, in N Canada. 228,160 sq. mi.

kef (kāf), *n.* (in the Middle East) **1.** a state of drowsy contentment, esp. from the use of a narcotic. **2.** Also, **keef.** a preparation of hemp leaves, used to produce this state by smoking. Also, **kaif, kief, kif.** [< Ar, var. of *kaif* well-being, pleasure]

Ke·fau·ver (kē′fô vər), *n.* **Es·tes** (es′tis), 1903–63, U.S. political leader: U.S. Senator 1949–63.

keg (keg), *n.* **1.** a small cask, usually having a capacity of from 5 to 10 gallons. **2.** a unit of weight, equal to 100 pounds, used for nails. [late ME *cag* < Scand; cf. Icel *kaggi*]

keg·ler (keg′lər), *n. Slang.* a participant in a bowling game. Also, **keg·el·er** (keg′ə lər, keg′lər). [< G = *Kegel* (nine)-pin + *-er* -ER[1]]

Kei·jo (kā′jō′; *Eng.* kā jō′), *n.* Japanese name of **Seoul.**

keir (kēr), *n.* kier.

keis·ter (kē′stər), *n. Slang.* the buttocks. [prob. < Yiddish < G *kiste* box, crate < OHG *kista* < L *cista* < Gk *kístē*]

Kei·tel (kīt′ᵊl), *n.* **Wil·helm** (vil′helm), 1882–1946, German marshal: chief of the Nazi supreme command 1938–45.

Ke′ku·lé's for′mula (kā′kə lāz′), *Chem.* the structural formula of benzene represented as a hexagonal ring with alternate single and double bonds between the carbon atoms. See diag. at **benzene ring.** [named after Friedrich August KEKULÉ VON STRADONITZ]

Ke·ku·lé von Stra·do·nitz (kā′kə lā′ fən shtʀä′dō-nits), **Frie·drich Au·gust** (fʀē′dʀiᴋʜ ou′go͝ost), 1829–96, German chemist.

Ke·lan·tan (kə län tän′), *n.* a state in Malaysia, on SE Malay Peninsula. 684,738; 5750 sq. mi. *Cap.:* Kota Bahru.

Kel·ler (kel′ər), *n.* **1. Gott·fried** (gôt′fʀēt), 1819–90, Swiss novelist. **2. Helen (Adams),** 1880–1968, U.S. lecturer, author, and educator: blind and deaf from infancy.

Kel·logg (kel′ôg, -og, -əg), *n.* **Frank Billings,** 1856–1937, U.S. statesman: Secretary of State 1925–29; Nobel peace prize 1929.

kel′ly green′ (kel′ē), a strong yellowish green. [special use of surname *Kelly,* taken as standing for stage Irishman]

ke·loid (kē′loid), *n. Pathol.* a fibrous tumor forming hard, irregular, clawlike excrescences upon the skin. Also, **cheloid.** [*kel(is)* keloid (< Gk: stain, spot) + -OID] —**ke·loi′dal,** *adj.*

kelp (kelp), *n.* **1.** any large, brown seaweed of the family *Laminariaceae.* **2.** the ash of such seaweeds. —*v.i.* **3.** to burn such seaweed for its ash. [? ME *culp* < ?]

kel·pie[1] (kel′pē), *n.* (in Scottish legends) a water spirit, usually having the form of a horse, reputed to cause drownings or to warn those in danger of drowning. [?]

kel·pie[2] (kel′pē), *n. Australian.* one of a breed of medium-sized dogs used for herding sheep. [after the name of one of these dogs]

kel·py (kel′pē), *n., pl.* **-pies.** kelpie[1].

kel·son (kel′sən), *n.* keelson.

Kelt (kelt), *n.* Celt. —**Kel′tic,** *n., adj.* —**Kel′ti·cal·ly,** *adv.*

Kel·vin (kel′vin), *n.* **1. William Thomson, 1st Baron,** 1824–1907, English physicist and mathematician. —*adj.* **2.** *Physics.* noting or pertaining to an absolute scale of temperature **(Kel′vin scale′)** in which the degree intervals are equal to those of the Celsius scale and in which 0° equals –273.16° Celsius. Cf. **absolute scale, Rankine** (def. 2).

Ke·mal A·ta·türk (ke mäl′ ä′tä tʏʀk′), (*Mustafa* or *Mustapha Kemal*) ("*Kemal Pasha*") 1881–1938, Turkish general: president of Turkey 1923–38. —**Ke·mal′ism,** *n.*

Kem·ble (kem′bəl), *n.* **1. Frances Anne** or **Fanny** (*Mrs. Butler*), 1809–93, English actress and author. **2.** her uncle, **John Philip,** 1757–1823, English actor.

Ke·me·ro·vo (ke′me ʀo vo), *n.* a city in the S RSFSR, in the S Soviet Union in Asia. 343,000 (est. 1964).

Kemp (kemp), *n.* **Jack F.,** born 1935, U.S. politician: congressman since 1970.

Kem·pis (kem′pis), *n.* **Thomas à,** 1379?–1471, German ecclesiastic and author.

ken (ken), *n., v.,* **kenned** or **kent, ken·ning.** —*n.* **1.** knowledge or understanding. **2.** range of sight or vision. —*v.t.* **3.** *Chiefly Scot.* **a.** to know of or about, or to be acquainted with (a person or thing). **b.** to understand or perceive (an idea or situation). **4.** *Archaic.* to see; descry; recognize. —*v.i. Brit. Dial.* **5.** to have knowledge of something. **6.** to understand. [ME *kenne(n)* (to) make known, see, know, OE *cennan* to make known, declare; c. Icel *kenna,* G *kennen;* akin to CAN[1]]

ke·naf (kə naf′), *n.* ambary. [< Pers]

Ken·dall (ken′dᵊl), *n.* a town in SE Florida, S of Miami. 35,497 (1970).

ken·do (ken dô′; *Eng.* ken′dō), *n.* a form of fencing with bamboo staves, wearing head guards and protective garments. [< Jap = *ken* sword + *dō* art]

Ken·il·worth (ken′ᵊl wûrth′), *n.* a town in central Warwickshire, in central England. 20,980 (1971).

Ken·more (ken′mōr′, -môr′), *n.* a city in NW New York, near Buffalo. 20,980 (1970).

Ken·ne·bec (ken′ə bek′), *n.* a river flowing S through W Maine to the Atlantic. 164 mi. long.

Ken·ne·dy (ken′i dē), *n.* **1. Edward Moore** ("Ted"), born 1932, U.S. politician: Senator since 1962. **2. John Fitzgerald,** 1917–63, 35th president of the U.S. 1961–63. **3. Joseph Patrick,** 1888–1969, U.S. financier and diplomat; chairman of Securities and Exchange Commission 1934–35 (father of John Fitzgerald, Robert Francis, and Edward Moore). **4. Robert Francis,** 1925–68, U.S. political leader and government official: Attorney General 1961–64; Senator from New York 1965–68. **5. Cape,** former name (1963–73) of Cape Canaveral.

ken·nel[1] (ken′ᵊl), *n., v.,* **-neled, -nel·ing** or (*esp. Brit.*) **-nelled, -nel·ling.** —*n.* **1.** a house for a dog or dogs. **2.** Often, **kennels.** an establishment where dogs are bred, raised, trained, or boarded. **3.** the lair of an animal, esp. a fox. —*v.t.* **4.** to put into or keep in a kennel. —*v.i.* **5.** to take shelter or lodge in a kennel. [ME *kenel* < AF **kenil* (F *chenil*) < VL **canīle* (L *can(is)* dog + *-īle* suffix of place)]

ken·nel[2] (ken′ᵊl), *n.* a gutter or open sewer. [var. of *cannel,* ME *canel* CHANNEL[1]]

ken′nel club′, an association of dog breeders, usually concerned only with certain breeds of dogs.

Ken′nel·ly-Heav′i·side lay′er (ken′ᵊlē hev′ē sīd′), (no longer in technical use) a radio-reflective layer on the ionosphere. [named after Arthur Edwin *Kennelly* (1861–1939), American electrical engineer and Oliver *Heaviside* (1850–1925), English physicist]

Ken·ner (ken′ər), *n.* a city in SE Louisiana, near New Orleans. 29,858 (1970).

Ken′ne·saw Moun′tain (ken′i sô′), a mountain in N Georgia, near Atlanta: battle 1864. 1809 ft.

ken·ning (ken′ing), *n.* a conventional phrase used for or in addition to the usual name of a person or thing, esp. in Icelandic and Anglo-Saxon verse, as "wave traveler" for "boat." [< Icel; see KEN, -ING[1]]

Ken·ny (ken′ē), *n.* **Elizabeth** ("*Sister Kenny*"), 1886–1952, Australian nurse: researcher in poliomyelitis therapy.

Ken′ny meth′od, *Med.* a method of treating poliomyelitis, in which hot, moist packs are applied to affected muscles and a regimen of exercises is prescribed. Also called **Ken′ny treat′ment.** [named after Elizabeth KENNY]

ke·no (kē′nō), *n.* a game of chance, adapted from lotto for gambling purposes. [< F *quine* five winning numbers (<< L *quīnī* five each) + (LOTT)O]

ke·no·gen·e·sis (kē′nō jen′i sis, ken′ō-), *n.* cenogenesis. —**ke·no·ge·net·ic** (kē′nō jə net′ik, ken′ō-), *adj.* —**ke′no·ge·net′i·cal·ly,** *adv.*

Ke·no·sha (ki nō′shə), *n.* a port in SE Wisconsin, on Lake Michigan. 78,805 (1970).

ke·no·sis (ki nō′sis), *n. Theol.* the acceptance by Christ of the limitations of human nature in becoming man, but without the impairment of His divinity. [< Gk: an emptying (*ken(oûn)* (to) empty out, drain + *-ōsis* -OSIS)] —**ke·not·ic** (ki not′ik), *adj.*

Ken·sing·ton (ken′zing tən), *n* a borough of W London, England. 170,891 (1961).

Kent (kent), *n.* **1. James,** 1763–1847, U.S. jurist. **2. Rock·well** (rok′wel′, -wəl) 1882–1971, U.S. illustrator, painter, and writer. **3. William,** 1685–1748, English painter architect, and landscape gardener. **4.** a county in SE England. 1,445,400; 1442 sq. mi. *Cap.:* Maidstone. **5.** an ancient English kingdom in SE Great Britain. See map at **Mercia. 6.** a city in NE Ohio. 28,183 (1970).

Kent·ish (ken′tish), *adj.* of or pertaining to Kent or its people. [ME *Kentissh,* OE *Centisc*]

kent·ledge (kent′lij), *n. Naut.* pig iron used as permanent ballast. [?]

Ken·tuck·y (kən tuk′ē), *n.* **1.** a state in the E central United States. 3,219,311 (1970); 40,395 sq. mi. *Cap.:* Frankfort. *Abbr.:* Ky., KY **2.** a river flowing NW from E Kentucky to the Ohio River. 259 mi. long. —**Ken·tuck′i·an,** *adj., n.*

Kentuck′y blue′grass, a grass, *Poa pratensis,* of the Mississippi valley, used for pasturage and hay.

Kentuck′y cof′fee tree′, a tall, North American tree, *Gymnocladus dioica,* whose brown seeds **(Kentuck′y cof′fee beans′)** were formerly used as a substitute for coffee beans.

Kentuck′y ri′fle, a muzzleloading flintlock rifle developed near Lancaster, Pa., in the early 18th century.

Ken·ya (kēn′yə, ken′-), *n.* **1.** a republic in E Africa: member of the British Commonwealth; formerly a British crown colony and protectorate. 13,500,000; 223,478 sq. mi. *Cap.:* Nairobi. **2. Mount,** an extinct volcano in central Kenya. 17,040 ft. —**Ken′yan,** *adj., n.*

Ken·yat·ta (ken yä′tə), *n.* **Jo·mo** (jō′mō), 1893?–1978, Kenyan political leader: president 1964–78.

Ke·o·kuk (kē′ə kuk′), *n.* a city in SE Iowa, on the Mississippi River: large power dam. 14,631 (1970).

Ke·os (ke′ôs), *n.* a Greek island in the Aegean, off the SE coast of the Greek mainland. 1666; 56 sq. mi. Also called **Kea, Zea.**

Ke·phal·le·ni·a (ke fä′lē nē′ä), *n.* Greek name of **Cephalonia.**

kep·i (kā′pē, kep′ē), *n., pl.* **kep·is.** a French military cap with a flat, circular top and a nearly horizontal visor. [< F *képi* < SwissG *Käppi* (*Kapp(e)* CAP[1] + *-i* dim. suffix)]

Kepi

Kep·ler (kep′lər), *n.* **Jo·hann** (yō′hän), 1571–1630, German astronomer. —**Kep·ler·i·an** (kep lēr′ē ən), *adj.*

kept (kept), *v.* pt. and pp. of **keep.**

Ker·ak (ker′äk, ke räk′), *n.* a town in W Jordan, near the S end of the Dead Sea: ancient citadel of the Moabites. 8184 (est. 1965). Ancient, **Kir Moab.**

Ke·ra·la (kā′rə lə), *n.* a state in SW India: formerly the regions of Travancore and Cochin. 16,903,715 (1961); 15,035 sq. mi. *Cap.:* Trivandrum.

kerat-, var. of **kerato-** before a vowel: *keratin.*

ker·a·tin (ker′ə tin), *n. Zool.* a scleroprotein, or albuminoid, substance, found in the dead outer corneal skin layer and in horn, hair, feathers, hoofs, nails, claws, bills, etc. Also, **ceratin.**

ker·a·tin·ize (ker′ə tᵊnīz′), *v.t., v.i.,* **-ized, -iz·ing.** to make or become keratinous. —**ker′a·tin·i·za′tion,** *n.*

ke·rat·i·nous (kə rat′ᵊnəs), *adj.* composed of or resembling keratin; horny.

ker·a·ti·tis (ker′ə tī′tis), *n. Pathol.* inflammation of the cornea.

kerato-, var. of **cerat-**: *keratogenous.* Also, *esp. before a vowel,* **kerat-.**

Ker·a·tode (ker′ə tōd), *n.* the horny substance forming the skeleton of certain sponges. [Gk *keratōd(es)* hornlike]

ker·a·tog·e·nous (ker′ə toj′ə nəs), *adj.* producing horn or a horny substance.

ker·a·toid (ker′ə toid′), *adj.* resembling horn; horny. [< Gk *keratoeid(ēs)* hornlike]

ker·a·to·ma (ker′ə tō′mə), *n., pl.* **-mas, -ma·ta** (-mə tə). *Pathol.* keratosis.

ker·a·to·plas·ty (ker′ə tō plas′tē), *n., pl.* **-ties.** plastic surgery performed upon the cornea, esp. a corneal transplantation. —**ker′a·to·plas′tic,** *adj.*

ker·a·to·sis (ker′ə tō′sis), *n., pl.* **-ses** (-sēz) for 2. *Pathol.* **1.** any skin disease characterized by a horny growth. **2.** any horny growth. Also, **ker·a·to·der·ma** (ker′ə tō dûr′mə), **keratoma.** —**ker′a·to′sic, ker·a·tot·ic** (ker′ə tot′ik), *adj.*

kerb (kûrb), *n., v.t. Brit.* curb (defs. 1, 10).

Ker·be·la (kûr′bə lə), *n.* a town in central Iraq: holy city of the Shiah sect. 60,804 (1957). Also, **Karbala.**

Kerch (kerch), *n.* **1.** a seaport in E Crimea, in the SW RSFSR, in the SW Soviet Union in Europe, on Kerch Strait. 114,000 (est. 1965). **2.** a strait in the SW Soviet Union in Europe, connecting the Sea of Azov and the Black Sea. 25 mi. long.

ker·chief (kûr′chif), *n.* a cloth worn as a head covering or scarf, esp. by women. [ME *kerchef,* syncopated var. of *keverchef* < OF *cuevrechef,* lit., cover (the) head. See COVER, CHIEF] —**ker′chiefed,** *adj.*

ker·choo (kər chōō′), *interj.* ahchoo.

Ke·ren·sky (ke ren′ski; *Russ.* ke′ren skē), *n.* **A·le·ksan·dr Fe·o·do·ro·vich** (ä′le ksän′dər fe ô′do rô′vich), 1881–1970, Russian revolutionary leader: premier 1917; in the U.S. after 1946. Also, **Ke·ren′skii.**

kerf (kûrf), *n.* **1.** a cut or incision made by a saw or the like in a piece of wood. **2.** the width of such a cut. —*v.t.* **3.** to make a kerf or kerfs in (a piece of wood). Also, **curf.** [ME *kerf, kirf,* OE *cyrf* a cutting (c. OFris *kerf*); akin to CARVE]

Ker·gue·len (kûr′gə len′), *n.* an archipelago in the S Indian Ocean: a possession of France. 2700 sq. mi. French, **Ker·gué·len** (ker gā len′).

Ker·ky·ra (ker′kē rä), *n.* Greek name of **Corfu.**

Ker·man (kər män′), *n.* a city in SE Iran. 62,175 (1956).

Ker·man·shah (kər′män shä′), *n.* **1.** a city in W Iran. 166,720 (est. 1963). **2.** Kirman.

ker·mes (kûr′mēz), *n.* **1.** a red dye formerly prepared from the dried bodies of the females of a scale insect, *Kermes ilices.* **2.** the small evergreen oak, *Quercus coccifera,* on which this insect is found. [earlier *chermez* < OIt *chermes* < Ar *qirmiz* < Pers; see CRIMSON]

ker·mis (kûr′mis), *n.* **1.** (in the Low Countries) an annual fair or festival. **2.** a similar entertainment, usually for charitable purposes. Also, **ker′mess, kirmess.** [< D, earlier *ker(c)misse* (*kerc* CHURCH + *misse* MASS); orig. a fair at the dedication of a church]

kern[1] (kûrn), *n. Archaic.* **1.** (in Ireland and the Scottish Highlands) a soldier. **2.** an Irish peasant, esp. a crude or boorish one. Also, **kerne.** [ME *kerne* < Ir *ceithern* band of foot soldiers]

kern[2] (kûrn), *Print.* —*n.* **1.** a part of the face of a type projecting beyond the body or shank as in certain italic letters. —*v.t.* **2.** to form or furnish with a kern, as a type or letter. [< F *carne* corner of type << L *cardin-* (s. of *cardō*) hinge]

Kern (kûrn), *n.* **Jerome (David),** 1885–1945, U.S. composer.

ker·nel (kûr′nəl), *n., v.,* **-neled, -nel·ing** or (*esp. Brit.*) **-nelled, -nel·ling.** —*n.* **1.** the softer, usually edible part contained in the shell of a nut or the stone of a fruit. **2.** the body of a seed within its husk or integuments. **3.** a whole seed grain, as of wheat or corn. **4.** the central part of anything; nucleus; core. —*v.t.* **5.** to enclose as a kernel. [ME *kirnel,* OE *cyrnel,* dim. of *corn* CORN[1]]

ker′nel sen′tence, a simple, active, declarative sentence containing no modifiers or connectives, which may be used in making more elaborate sentences. The sentence *Good tests are short* is made from two kernel sentences: (1) *Tests are short.* (2) *(The) tests are good.*

ker·o·sene (ker′ə sēn′, kar′-, ker′ə sēn′, kar′-), *n.* a mixture of liquid hydrocarbons obtained by distilling petroleum, bituminous shale, or the like: used chiefly as a fuel in lamps and as a solvent for cleaning. Also, **ker′o·sine′.** [irreg. < Gk *kērós* wax + -ENE]

Ker·ou·ac (ker′ōō ak′), *n.* **Jack** (*Jean Kerouac*), 1922–69, U.S. novelist.

ker·plunk (kər plungk′), *adv.* with or as with a muffled thud. [imit.]

ker·ry (ker′ē), *n., pl.* **-ries.** one of an Irish breed of small, black dairy cattle. [after KERRY, home of the breed]

Ker·ry (ker′ē), *n.* a county in W Munster province, in the SW Republic of Ireland. 116,458 (1961); 1815 sq. mi. *Co. seat:* Tralee.

Ker′ry blue′ ter′rier, one of an Irish breed of terriers having a soft, wavy, bluish-gray coat.

Kerry blue terrier (18½ in. high at shoulder)

ker·sey (kûr′zē), *n., pl.* **-seys.** **1.** a heavy overcoating of wool or wool and cotton, similar to beaver and melton. **2.** a coarse twilled woolen cloth with a cotton warp. [ME; ? after *Kersey,* in Suffolk, England]

ker·sey·mere (kûr′zi mēr′), *n.* a heavily fulled woolen cloth. [KERSEY + (CASSI)MERE]

Kes·sel·ring (kes′əl ring), *n.* **Al·bert** (al′bərt; *Ger.* äl′bert), 1885–1960, German field marshal in World War II.

kes·trel (kes′trəl), *n.* **1.** a common small falcon, *Falco tinnunculus,* of northern parts of the Eastern Hemisphere, notable for hovering in the air with its head to the wind. **2.** any of several related small, Old World falcons, as the sparrow hawk, *Falco sparverius.* [late ME *castrell* < MF *quercelle* (by metathesis), var. of *crecerelle,* of disputed orig.]

ket-, var. of **keto-** before a vowel: *ketene.*

ketch (kech), *n. Naut.* a sailing vessel rigged fore and aft on two masts, the larger, forward one being the main mast and the after one, stepped forward of the rudderpost, being the mizzen or jigger. Cf. **yawl**[1] (def. 2). [ME *cache,* appar. n. use of *cache* to CATCH]

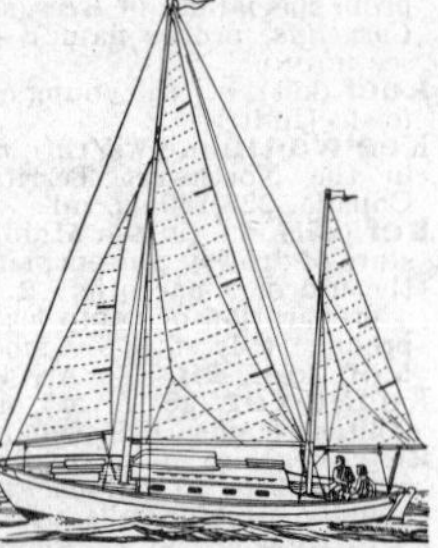
Ketch

Ketch·i·kan (kech′ə kan′), *n.* a seaport in SE Alaska. 6994 (1970).

ketch·up (kech′əp, kach′-), *n.* any of various tart sauces for meat, fish, etc.: *tomato ketchup; mushroom ketchup.* Also, **catchup, catsup.** [< Chin (Amoy dial.) *ke-tsiap* pickled-fish brine]

ke·tene (kē′tēn), *n. Chem.* **1.** a colorless, poisonous gas, $H_2C{=}C{=}O$, irritating to the lungs, used chiefly in the manufacture of commercial chemicals, as aspirin. **2.** a class of compounds having the type formulas $RHC{=}C{=}O$ and $R_2C{=}C{=}O$ where R is a radical.

ke·to (kē′tō), *adj. Chem.* of or derived from a ketone. [KETO(NE)]

keto-, a combining form of **ketone.** Also, *esp. before a vowel,* **ket-.**

ke′to-e′nol tautom′erism (kē′tō ē′nōl, -nôl, -nol), *Chem.* a type of tautomerism in which the individual tautomers are alternately a keto form and an enol.

ke′to form′, *Chem.* (in a keto-enol tautomeric substance) the form with the characteristics of a ketone.

ke·tone (kē′tōn), *n.* **1.** *Chem.* any of a class of organic compounds containing a carbonyl group, $>C{=}O$, attached to two organic groups, as CH_3COCH_3 or $CH_3COC_2H_5$. —*adj.* **2.** containing the ketone group. [< G *Keton,* aph. alter. of *Aceton* ACETONE] —**ke·ton·ic** (ki ton′ik), *adj.*

ke′tone bod′y, *Biochem.* any of three compounds, acetoacetic acid, beta-hydroxybutyric acid, or acetone, that are intermediate in the metabolism of fatty acids and are found in abnormal quantities in the blood and urine during certain pathological conditions, as diabetes mellitus.

ke′tone group′, *Chem.* the characteristic group occurring in ketones, consisting of the carbonyl group attached to two other organic groups. Also called **ke′tone rad′ical.**

ke·to·nu·ri·a (kē′tō nōōr′ē ə, -nyōōr′-), *n. Med.* the presence of ketone bodies in the urine.

ke·tose (kē′tōs), *n. Chem.* a monosaccharide that contains a ketone group.

ke·to·sis (ki tō′sis), *n. Pathol.* the accumulation of excessive ketones in the body, as in diabetic acidosis.

Ket·ter·ing (ket′ər ing), *n.* **1. Charles Franklin,** 1876–1958, U.S. engineer and inventor. **2.** a city in SW Ohio. 71,864 (1970).

ket·tle (ket′əl), *n.* **1.** a container in which to boil liquids, cook foods, etc.; pot. **2.** a teakettle. [ME *ketel* < Scand; cf. Icel *ketill;* c. OE *citel,* G *Kessel;* all < L *catill(us),* dim. of *catinus* pot]

ket·tle·drum (ket′əl drum′), *n.* a drum consisting of a hollow hemisphere of brass or copper over which is stretched a skin. Cf. **timpani.** —**ket′tle·drum′mer,** *n.*

Kettledrum

ket′tle of fish′, an awkward situation or state of affairs; muddle; mess.

Ke·tu·bim (ki tōō bēm′), *n. Hebrew.* the Hagiographa. Also, **Ke·tu·vim** (kə tōō vēm′). Cf. **Tanach.** [lit., writings]

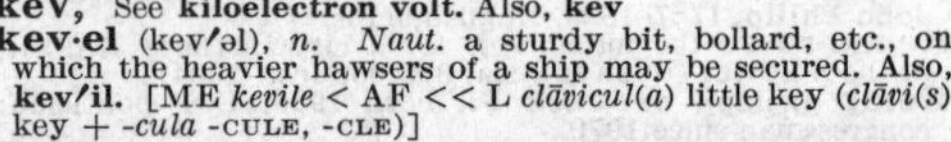

keV, See **kiloelectron volt.** Also, **kev**

kev·el (kev′əl), *n. Naut.* a sturdy bit, bollard, etc., on which the heavier hawsers of a ship may be secured. Also, **kev′il.** [ME *kevile* < AF << L *clāvicul(a)* little key (*clāvi(s)* key + *-cula* -CULE, -CLE)]

Kew (kyōō), *n.* a part of Richmond, in NE Surrey, in SE England: famous botanical gardens **(Kew′ Gar′dens).**

Kew·pie (kyōō′pē), *n. Trademark.* a small, plump doll, usually made of plaster or celluloid.

key[1] (kē), *n., pl.* **keys,** *adj., v.,* **keyed, key·ing.** —*n.* **1.** a metal instrument inserted into a lock to move its bolt. **2.** something that affords a means of access: *the key to happiness.* **3.** something that affords a means of clarifying a problem. **4.** a list of explanations, as of symbols or code words. **5.** a text that explains or gives useful information about another text. **6.** any of various mechanical devices for holding or locking an assembly. **7.** a device for turning a bolt or nut. **8.** one of a set of levers or parts pressed in operating a typewriter, calculating machine, etc. **9.** *Music.* **a.** (in a keyboard instrument) one of the levers that when depressed by the performer sets the playing mechanism in motion. **b.** (on a wind instrument) a metal lever that opens and closes a vent. **c.** the principal tonality of a composition: *a symphony in the key of C minor.* **10.** tone or pitch, as of voice. **11.** mood or characteristic style, as of expression or thought. **12.** *Elect.* **a.** a device for opening and closing electrical contacts. **b.** a hand-operated switching device ordinarily formed of concealed spring contacts with an exposed handle or push button, capable of switching one or more parts of a circuit. **13.** *Bot., Zool.* a systematic tabular classification of the significant characteristics of the members of a group of organisms to facilitate identification and comparison. **14.** *Masonry.* a keystone or vaulting boss. **15.** *Building Trades.* any grooving or roughness applied to a surface to improve its bond with another surface. **16.** *Masonry, Carpentry.* a wedge, as for tightening a joint or splitting a stone or timber. **17.** *Photog.* the dominant tonal value of a picture. **18.** *Painting.* the tonal value and intensity of a color or range of colors. **19.** *Bot.* a samara. —*adj.* **20.** chief; major; important; essential. —*v.t.* **21.** to regulate or adjust (actions, thoughts, speech, etc.) to a particular state or activity. **22.** *Painting.* **a.** to paint (a picture) in a given key. **b.** to adjust the colors in (a painting) to a particular hue. **23.** to fasten, secure, or adjust with a key. **24.** to provide with a key or keys. **25. key up, a.** to bring to a great intensity of feeling, energy, etc. **b.** to raise (a piece of masonry) by the insertion of a key. [ME *key(e), kay(e),* OE *cǣg, cǣge;* c. OFris *kei, kai*] —**key′less,** *adj.*

key[2] (kē), *n., pl.* **keys.** a reef or low island; cay. [< Sp *cay(o),* prob. < Arawak]

Key (kē), *n.* **Francis Scott,** 1780–1843, U.S. lawyer: author of *The Star-Spangled Banner.*

key·board (kē′bōrd′, -bôrd′), *n.* **1.** a row or set of keys on a piano, organ, or the like. **2.** a set of keys, usually arranged in tiers, for operating a typewriter, typesetting machine, computer terminal, or the like. —*v.t., v.i.* **3.** *Computer Technol.* to enter (information) into a computer by means of a keyboard. **4.** to set (text) in type, using a machine that is operated by a keyboard. —**key′board′er, key′board′ist,** *n.*

key′ club′, a private night club to which each member has a door key.

key′ fruit′, *Bot.* a samara.

key·hole (kē′hōl′), *n.* a hole in a lock for admitting its key, commonly a circle with a narrow part below it.

key′hole saw′, a compass saw for cutting keyholes, etc.

Keynes (kānz), *n.* **John May·nard** (mā′nərd, -närd), **1st Baron,** 1883–1946, English economist. —**Keynes′i·an,** *adj., n.* —**Keynes′i·an·ism,** *n.*

key·note (kē′nōt′), *n., v.,* **-not·ed, -not·ing.** —*n.* **1.** *Music.* the note or tone on which a key or system of tones is founded; the tonic. **2.** the main idea of a speech, program, thought, action, etc. —*v.t.* **3.** to make a keynote address at.

key′note address′, a speech, as at a political convention, that presents important issues, principles, policies, etc. Also called **key′note speech′.**

key·not·er (kē′nō′tər), *n.* a person who delivers a keynote address.

key·pad (kē′pad′), *n.* **1.** a separate section on some computer keyboards, grouping together numeric keys and those for mathematical or other special functions in an arrangement like that of a calculator. **2.** a panel similarly keyed and used in conjunction with a television set, electronic banking machine, or other electronic device.

key′ punch′, a machine, operated by a keyboard, for coding information by punching holes in cards in certain patterns.

key·punch (kē′punch′), *v.t.* to punch holes in with a key punch. —**key′punch′er,** *n.*

Key·ser·ling (kī′zər liŋ), *n.* **Her·mann A·le·xan·der** (her′män ä′le ksän′dər), **Count,** 1880–1946, German philosopher and writer.

key′ sig′nature, *Music.* (in notation) the group of sharps or flats placed after the clef to indicate the tonality of the music following.

key·stone (kē′stōn′), *n.* **1.** a voussoir at the summit of an arch. See diag. at **arch. 2.** something on which associated things depend. [KEY[1] + STONE]

Key′stone State′, Pennsylvania (used as a nickname).

key·stroke (kē′strōk′), *n.* one stroke of any key on a machine operated by a keyboard, as a typewriter, etc.

key·way (kē′wā′), *n.* **1.** Also called **key′ seat′.** *Mach.* a groove in a shaft, the hub of a wheel, etc., for receiving part of a key holding it to another part. **2.** a slot in a lock for receiving and guiding the key.

Key′ West′, 1. an island off S Florida, in the Gulf of Mexico. **2.** a seaport on this island: the southernmost city in the U.S.; naval base. 29,312 (1970).

key′ word′, a word that serves as a key, as to the meaning of another word, the composition of a cryptogram, etc.

kg, kilogram; kilograms.

kg., **1.** keg; kegs. **2.** kilogram; kilograms.

K.G., Knight of the Garter.

kg-m, *Physics.* kilogram-meter; kilogram-meters.

Kha·ba·rovsk (kнä bä′rofsk), *n.* **1.** an administrative division of the RSFSR in the E Soviet Union in Asia. 1,583,000; 965,400 sq. mi. **2.** a port in and the capital of this territory, on the Amur River. 536,000.

Kha·bur (*Arab.* kнä bōōr′), *n.* a river in W Asia, flowing S from SE Turkey through NE Syria to the Euphrates. 200 mi. long. Also, **Habor, Habur.**

Kha·cha·tu·ri·an (kä′chə tōōr′ē ən, kach′ə-; *Russ.* kнä′-chä tōō ryän′), *n.* **A·ram** (ä räm′), 1903–78, Russian composer, born in Armenia.

Khai′bar Pass′ (kī′bər). See **Khyber Pass.**

khak·i (kak′ē, kä′kē), *n., pl.* **khak·is,** *adj.* —*n.* **1.** dull yellowish brown. **2.** a stout twilled cotton uniform cloth of this color. **3.** a similar fabric of wool. **4. khakis, a.** pants made of khaki. **b.** a uniform made of khaki. —*adj.* **5.** made of khaki. [< Urdu < Pers: dusty]

khal·if (kal′if, kā′lif, kä lēf′), *n.* caliph. Also, **kha·li·fa** (kə lē′fə).

khal·i·fate (kal′ə fāt′, -fit), *n.* caliphate.

Khal·kha (kal′kə), *n.* an Altaic language, the official language of the Mongolian People's Republic.

Khal·ki·di·ke (kнäl′kə thē′kē), *n.* Greek name of **Chalcidice.**

Khal·kis (*Gk.* kнäl kēs′), *n.* Chalcis.

kham·sin (kam′sin, kam sēn′), *n.* **1.** a hot, dry southerly wind, that originates in the Sahara and blows in the Arab Republic of Egypt for about 50 days in the spring months. **2.** a dry heat wave. Also, **kamseen, kamsin.** [< Ar: lit., fifty]

khan[1] (kän, kan), *n.* **1.** (in the Middle Ages) ruler of the Tatar and Mongol tribes. **2.** a title of respect used in Iran, Afghanistan, Pakistan, India, and other countries of Asia. [late ME *Ca(a)n, Chan* << Turkic *Khān,* appar. contr. of *Khāgān* (Turk *kagan* ruler)]

khan[2] (kän, kan), *n.* an inn or caravansary. [< Ar < Pers]

khan·ate (kä′nāt, kan′āt), *n.* the area governed by a khan.

Kha·nia (kнä nyä′), *n.* Greek name of **Canea.**

Khar·kov (kär′kof, -kov; *Russ.* kнär′kof), *n.* a city in the E Ukraine, in S Soviet Union in Europe. 1,428,000.

Khar·toum (kär tōōm′), *n.* a city in and the capital of the Sudan, at the junction of the White and Blue Nile rivers. 400,000. Also, **Khar·tum′.**

Khay·yám (kī yäm′, -yam′), *n.* See **Omar Khayyám.**

khed·a (ked′ə), *n.* (in India) an enclosure constructed to ensnare wild elephants. Also, **keddah, khed′ah.** [< Hindi]

khe·dive (kə dēv′), *n.* the title of the Turkish viceroys in Egypt from 1867 to 1914. [< F *khédive* < Turk *hidiv* < Pers *khidīw* prince] —**khe·di′val, khe·di·vi·al** (kə dē′vē əl), *adj.*

Khe·lat (kə lät′), *n.* Kalat.

Kher·son (kнer sôn′), *n.* a port in the S Ukraine, in the SW Soviet Union in Europe, on the Dnieper River, near the Black Sea. 331,000.

Khi·os (kнē′ôs; *Eng.* kī′os), *n.* Greek name of **Chios.**

Khir·bet Qum·ran (kēr′bet kōōm′rän), an archaeological site in Jordan, near the NW coast of the Dead Sea: Dead Sea Scrolls found here. Also, **Khir′bet Qûm′ran.**

Khi·va (kнē′vä), *n.* a former Asian khanate along the Amu Darya River, S of the Aral Sea; now divided between the Uzbek and Turkman republics of the Soviet Union.

Khmer (kmer), *n.* **1.** a member of a people in Cambodia whose ancestors established an empire about the 5th century A.D. **2.** an Austroasiatic language that is the official language of Cambodia.

Khoi·san (koi′sän), *n.* a family of languages indigenous to southern Africa and including the languages of the Bushmen and the Hottentots.

Kho·mei·ni (kнō mā′nē, kнōō-), *n.* **Ru·hol·lah** (rōō hō′lə), born 1900?, Iranian Islamic leader: de facto head of state since 1979.

Kho·tan (kнō′tän′), *n.* **1.** an oasis in W China, in SW Sinkiang. **2.** Also, **Hotien.** the chief city in this oasis. 50,000.

Khru·shchev (krōōsh′chef, -chôf, krōōsh′-; *Russ.* kнrōō-shchôf′), *n.* **Ni·ki·ta S(er·gey·e·vich)** (ni kē′tə sər gā′ə-vich; *Russ.* ni kē′tä ser ge′-ye vich), 1894–1971, Russian political leader: premier of the U.S.S.R. 1958–64.

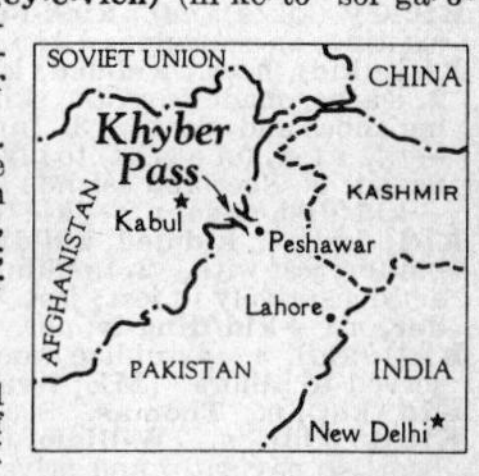

Khu·fu (kōō′fōō), *n.* Cheops.

Khy′ber Pass′ (kī′bər), the chief mountain pass between Pakistan and Afghanistan, W of Peshawar. 33 mi. long; 6825 ft. high. Also, **Khaibar Pass.**

kHz, *Physics.* kilohertz.

Ki., Kings.

ki·ang (kē äŋ′), *n.* a wild ass, *Equus hemionus kiang,* of Tibet and Mongolia. [< Tibetan *(r)kyaŋ*]

Kiang·si (kyäŋ′sē′; *Chin.* jyäŋ′sē′), *n.* a province in SE China. 28,000,000; 63,629 sq. mi. *Cap.:* Nanchang.

Kiang·su (kyäŋ′sōō′; *Chin.* jyäŋ′sōō′), *n.* a maritime province in E China. 55,000,000; 40,927 sq. mi. *Cap.:* Nanking.

Kiao·chow (kyou′chou′; *Chin.* jyou′jō′), *n.* **1.** a territory on the Shantung peninsula, in E China, around Kiaochow Bay: leased to Germany 1898–1914. ab. 200 sq. mi. Chief city, Tsingtao. **2. Bay,** an inlet of the Yellow Sea in E China, in Shantung province. 20 mi. long; 15 mi. wide.

kiaugh (kyäкн), *n.* *Scot.* trouble; worry. [? < Gael]

kib·ble (kib′əl), *v.,* **-bled, -bling,** *n.* —*v.t.* **1.** to grind or divide into coarse, relatively large particles. —*n.* **2.** grains or pellets resulting from a kibbling process. [?]

kib·butz (ki bōōts′, -bōōts′), *n., pl.* **-but·zim** (-bōōt sēm′). (in Israel) a settlement community, chiefly agricultural, organized under collectivist principles. [< ModHeb *qibbūs,* lit., gathering]

kib·butz·nik (ki bōōts′nik, -bōōts′-), *n.* a member of a kibbutz. [< Yiddish*kibutsnik* = *kibuts* KIBBUTZ + *-nik* suffix]

Ki·bei (kē′bā′), *n., pl.* **-bei.** a person of Japanese descent, born in the U.S. and educated in Japan (distinguished from *Nisei*). Also, **kibei.** Cf. **Issei, Sansei.** [< Jap]

kib·itz (kib′its), *v.i.* *Informal.* to act as a kibitzer. [< Yiddish *kibitzen* = G *kiebitzen* < *Kiebitz* busybody]

kib·itz·er (kib′it sər), *n.* *Informal.* **1.** a spectator, esp. at a card game, who gives unwanted advice to the players. **2.** any person who gives unsolicited advice or who meddles in the affairs of others. [< Yiddish]

kib·lah (kib′lä), *n.* *Islam.* **1.** the point toward which Muslims turn to pray, esp. the sacred stone in the Kaaba at Mecca. **2.** the direction of this from a given place. Also, **kib′la.** [< Ar *qiblah* something placed opposite]

ki·bosh (kī′bosh, ki bosh′), *n.* *Informal.* **put the kibosh on,** to render inactive or ineffective; squelch; check. [?]

kick (kik), *v.t.* **1.** to strike with a motion of the foot. **2.** to propel or force by or as by striking in such manner. **3.** *Football.* to score (a field goal or a conversion) by place-kicking or drop-kicking the ball. **4.** to strike in recoiling, as a gun. **5.** *Poker Slang.* raise (def. 18). —*v.i.* **6.** to make a rapid striking motion with the foot. **7.** to have a tendency to strike with the foot or feet. **8.** *Informal.* to resist, object, or complain. **9.** to recoil, as a gun when fired. **10.** to be active or vigorous: *alive and kicking.* **11. kick around,** *Slang.* **a.** to treat (someone) harshly or inconsiderately. **b.** to discuss (a proposal, project, etc.). **c.** to change one's residence or job frequently. **12. kick in,** *Slang.* to contribute one's share, esp. in money. **13. kick off, a.** *Football.* to begin play or begin play again by a kickoff. **b.** *Slang.* to die. **c.** *Informal.* to initiate. **14. kick out,** *Informal.* to dismiss or oust someone. **15. kick over,** *Informal.* (of an internal combustion engine) to begin ignition; turn over. **16. kick the bucket.** See **bucket** (def. 7). **17. kick the habit,** to get over an addiction, habit, etc. **18. kick up, a.** to drive or force upward by kicking. **b.** to make or cause (a disturbance, scene, etc.). **19. kick upstairs.** See **upstairs** (def. 4). —*n.* **20.** the act or an instance of kicking. **21.** a tendency or disposition to kick: *That horse has a mean kick.* **22.** potency: *That whiskey has quite a kick.* **23.** a recoil, as of a gun. **24.** *Informal.* an objection or complaint. **25.** vigor, energy, or vim.

26. *Slang.* **a.** thrill; pleasurable excitement. **b.** a strong but temporary interest, often an activity. **27.** *Football.* **a.** an instance of kicking the ball. **b.** any method of kicking the ball: *place kick.* **c.** a kicked ball. **d.** the distance such a ball travels. **e.** a turn at kicking the ball. **28.** *Glassmaking.* a solid-glass base or an indentation at the base of drinking glasses, bottles, etc. [ME *kike(n)*, ? < Scand] **—Syn. 1.** boot. **8.** grumble; protest.

Kick·a·poo (kik′ə po͞o′), *n.* a dialect of the Fox language.

kick·back (kik′bak′), *n. Informal.* a rebate on profits or wages given to the person who influenced a buyer, provided employment, etc.

kick·er (kik′ər), *n.* **1.** a person or thing that kicks. **2.** *Slang.* **a.** an advantageous point, detail, or circumstance, usually concealed or unnoticeable. **b.** a surprise change of course, as of events. **3.** *Draw Poker.* a card held with a pair or three of a kind in the hope of drawing a matching card. **4.** *Naut.* **a.** a small, low-powered outboard motor. **b.** an auxiliary engine on a sailing vessel. **5.** Also called **teaser.** *Print., Journ.* a short line of copy set in a distinctive type above a headline and intended to call attention to it. **6.** Also called **equity kicker.** *Informal.* a premium, such as a percentage of gross profit from rental, demanded by a mortgage lender in addition to the fixed interest rate.

kick·off (kik′ôf′, -of′), *n.* **1.** *Football.* a kick that begins play in the first or third period or resumes it after a touchdown or field goal. **2.** *Informal.* the initial stage of something. Also, **kick′-off′.**

kick·shaw (kik′shô′), *n.* **1.** a tidbit or delicacy. **2.** something showy but without value; trinket; trifle. [back formation from *kickshaws* < F *quelque chose* something]

kick·stand (kik′stand′), *n.* a device for supporting a bicycle or motorcycle when not in use, pivoted to the rear axle in such a way that it can be kicked down below the rear wheel.

kick′ turn′, *Skiing.* a turn from a stationary position involving the lifting of each ski to a point nearly perpendicular to the snow before setting it down in the direction to be turned.

kick·y (kik′ē), *adj.,* **kick·i·er, kick·i·est.** *Slang.* sprightly, exciting, or charming: *a kicky party dress.*

kid[1] (kid), *n., v.,* **kid·ded, kid·ding.** **—***n.* **1.** a young goat. **2.** leather made from the skin of a kid or goat, used in making shoes and gloves. **3.** *Informal.* a child or young person. **—***v.i., v.t.* **4.** (of a goat) to give birth to (young). [ME *kide* < Scand; cf. Shetland Islands *kidi* lamb, akin to Icel *kith* kid] **—kid′dish·ness,** *n.* **—kid′like′,** *adj.*

kid[2] (kid), *v.,* **kid·ded, kid·ding.** *Informal.* **—***v.t.* **1.** to tease; banter; jest with. **2.** to humbug or fool. **—***v.i.* **3.** to speak or act deceptively in jest; jest. [? special use of KID[1]] **—kid′der,** *n.* **—kid′ding·ly,** *adv.*

kid[3] (kid), *n.* a tublike wooden container in which food is served to sailors. [ME; ? var. of KIT[1]]

Kid (kid), *n.* **Thomas.** See **Kyd, Thomas.**

Kidd (kid), *n.* **William** ("*Captain Kidd*"), 1645?–1701, Scottish navigator and privateer: hanged for piracy.

Kid·der·min·ster (kid′ər min′stər), *n.* an ingrain carpet. [after town in Worcestershire, England, where first made]

kid′die car′ (kid′ē), a toy vehicle for a small child, having three wheels and pushed with the feet. Also, **kid′dy car′.**

kid·do (kid′ō), *n., pl.* **-dos, -does.** a form of familiar address, as to a close friend. [KID[1] + *-o* suffix of association]

Kid·dush (kē do͞osh′; *Eng.* kid′əsh), *n. Hebrew, Judaism.* a blessing, or prayer, recited over a cup of wine or over bread on the Sabbath or a festival. [< Heb *qiddūsh* sanctification]

kid·dy (kid′ē), *n., pl.* **-dies.** *Informal.* a child. Also, **kid′die.**

kid′ gloves′, **1.** gloves made of kid leather. **2. handle with kid gloves,** to treat with extreme tact or gentleness.

kid·nap (kid′nap), *v.t.,* **-napped** or **-naped, -nap·ping** or **-nap·ing.** to abduct (a person) by force or fraud, esp. for use as a hostage to extract ransom. [KID[1] + *nap,* var. of NAB] **—kid′nap·er;** *esp. Brit.,* **kid′nap·per,** *n.*

kid·ney (kid′nē), *n., pl.* **-neys.** **1.** *Anat.* either of a pair of bean-shaped, glandular organs in the back part of the abdominal cavity that excrete urine. **2.** a corresponding organ in other vertebrate animals, or an organ of like function in invertebrates. **3.** the meat of an animal's kidney used as food. **4.** constitution or temperament. **5.** kind, sort, or class. [ME *kidenei* = *kiden-* (of unknown meaning and orig.) + *-ei,* OE *ǣg* EGG[1]]

Human kidney (Section)
A, Adrenal gland; B, Cortex; C, Papilla; D, Pelvis; E, Ureter

kid′ney bean′, **1.** the common bean, *Phaseolus vulgaris.* **2.** its kidney-shaped seed.

kid′ney machine′, a mechanical device that operates outside of the body and substitutes for the kidney by removing waste products from the blood. Also called **hemodialyzer.**

kid′ney stone′, *Pathol.* a stone, or concretion, composed principally of oxalates and phosphates, abnormally grown in the kidney.

kid′ney vetch′, an Old World, leguminous herb, *Anthyllis Vulneraria,* formerly used as a remedy for kidney diseases. Also called **woundwort.**

Ki·dron (kē′drən), *n.* Kedron.

kid·skin (kid′skin′), *n.* **1.** leather made from the skin of a young goat; kid. **—***adj.* **2.** made of kidskin.

kief (kēf), *n.* kef.

Kief·fer (kē′fər), *n.* **1.** a large, brownish-red, hybrid variety of pear. **2.** the tree bearing this fruit. [named after Peter *Kieffer* (1812–90), American botanist]

Kiel (kēl), *n.* a seaport in N West Germany, at the Baltic end of the Kiel Canal. 260,900.

Kiel′ Canal′, a canal connecting the North and Baltic seas. 61 mi. long.

Kiel·ce (kyel′tse), *n.* a city in S Poland. 151,000.

Kien Lung (kyen′ lo͝ong′). See **Ch'ien Lung.**

kier (kēr), *n.* a large vat in which fibers, yarns, or fabrics are boiled, bleached, or dyed. Also, **keir.** [< Scand; cf. Icel *ker* tub]

Kier·ke·gaard (kēr′kə gärd′; *Dan.* kēr′kə gôr′), *n.* **Sö·ren Aa·bye** (sœ′rən ô′by), 1813–55, Danish philosopher and theologian. **—Kier·ke·gaard·i·an** (kēr′kə gär′dē ən, kēr′kə gär′-), *adj.*

kie·sel·guhr (kē′zəl go͝or′), *n.* See **diatomaceous earth.** [< G = *Kiesel* flint + *Gu(h)r* earthy deposit]

Ki·ev (kē′ef), *n.* a city in and the capital of the Ukraine in the SW Soviet Union in Europe, on the Dnieper River. 2,133,000. **—Ki·ev·an** (kē′ef ən, -ev ən), *adj.*

kif (kif), *n.* kef.

Ki·ga·li (kē gä′lē), *n.* a town in and the capital of Rwanda in the central part. 40,000.

Ki·i·run (kē′ē ro͞on′), *n.* Japanese name of **Keelung.**

kike (kīk), *n. Offensive.* a person of Jewish religion or descent. [appar. modeled on *hike* Italian, itself modeled on *mike* Irishman, short for *Michael*]

Ki·ku·yu (ki ko͞o′yo͞o), *n., pl.* **-yus,** (*esp. collectively*) **-yu.** **1.** a member of a Negroid people of Kenya. **2.** the language of the Kikuyu, a Bantu language.

kil., kilometer; kilometers.

Ki·lau·e·a (kē′lä o͞o ā′ä), *n.* a crater on Mauna Loa volcano, on SE Hawaii island. 2 mi. wide; 4040 ft. high.

Kil·dare (kil dâr′), *n.* a county in Leinster, in the E Republic of Ireland. 71,977; 654 sq. mi. *Co. seat:* Kildare.

kil·der·kin (kil′dər kin), *n.* **1.** a unit of capacity, usually equal to half a barrel or two firkins. **2.** an English unit of capacity, equal to 18 imperial gallons. [ME *kilderkyn,* dissimilated var. of *kinderkin* < MD = *kinder* (<< Ar *qinṭār* QUINTAL) + *-kin* -KIN]

Kil·i·man·ja·ro (kil′ə mən jär′ō), *n.* a volcanic mountain in N Tanzania: highest peak in Africa. 19,321 ft.

Kil·ken·ny (kil ken′ē), *n.* **1.** a county in Leinster, in the SE Republic of Ireland. 61,473; 796 sq. mi. **2.** its county seat. 10,292.

kill[1] (kil), *v.t.* **1.** to cause to die; deprive of life. **2.** to cause to be destroyed, discontinued, or discarded: *to kill someone's hopes; to kill a proposal.* **3.** to destroy or neutralize the active qualities or effectiveness of; deaden: *to kill an odor.* **4.** to cause to cease operating: *to kill an engine.* **5.** to while away (time) so as to avoid boredom or idleness. **6.** to overwhelm (a person), as with pain, pleasure, etc. **7.** *Tennis.* to hit (a ball) with such force that it is impossible to return. **—***v.i.* **8.** to inflict or cause death. **9.** to commit murder. **10.** to be killed: *an animal that kills easily.* **11.** to overcome completely; produce an irresistible effect: *dressed to kill.* **12. kill off,** to kill or destroy completely. **—***n.* **13.** the act of killing, esp. game. **14.** an animal or animals killed. [ME *cull(en), kill(en),* OE **cyllan;* c. dial. G *küllen* (Westphalian); akin to OE *-colla,* in *morgencolla* morning-killer] **—kill′er,** *n.* **—Syn. 1.** slaughter, massacre, butcher; hang, electrocute, behead, guillotine, strangle, garrote; assassinate. KILL, EXECUTE, MURDER all mean to deprive of life. KILL is the general word, with no implication of the manner, agent, or cause of killing or the nature of what is killed (whether human being, animal, or plant): *to kill a person.* EXECUTE is used with reference to the putting to death of a person in accordance with a legal sentence, no matter what the means are: *to execute a criminal.* MURDER is used of killing a human being unlawfully: *He murdered him for his money.*

kill[2] (kil), *n. U.S. Dial.* a channel; creek; stream; river. [< D *kil,* MD *kille* channel; akin to Icel *kīll* creek, inlet]

Kil·lar·ney (ki lär′nē), *n.* **Lakes of,** three lakes in the SW Republic of Ireland.

kill·deer (kil′dēr′), *n.* an American plover, *Charadrius vociferus,* having two black bands around the upper breast. Also, *U.S. Dial.,* **kill·dee** (kil′dē). [imit.]

Kil·leen (ki lēn′), *n.* a city in central Texas. 35,507 (1970).

kill′er bee′, a honeybee, *Apis mellifera adansonii,* native to Africa, that reacts aggressively and attacks in swarms when disturbed: accidentally released in Brazil and becoming established in the New World.

kill′er whale′, any of several predatory dolphins, esp. the black and white *Grampus orca,* found in all seas.

kil·lick (kil′ik), *n.* a small anchor or weight for mooring a boat, sometimes consisting of a stone secured by wood. [?]

kil·lic·kin·nic (kil′ə kə nik′), *n.* kinnikinnick.

Kil·lie·cran·kie (kil′ē krang′kē), *n.* a mountain pass in central Scotland, in the Grampians.

kil·li·fish (kil′ē fish′), *n., pl.,* (*esp. collectively*) **-fish,** (*esp. referring to two or more kinds or species*) **-fish·es.** **1.** any of several small, oviparous cyprinodont fishes, esp. of the genus *Fundulus,* found in salt, brackish, and fresh waters. **2.** any of several livebearers. [? KILL[2] + -I- + FISH]

kill·ing (kil′ing), *n.* **1.** the act of a person or thing that kills. **2.** the total game killed on a hunt. **3.** *Informal.* a stroke of extraordinary financial success: *He made a killing in the market.* **—***adj.* **4.** that kills. **5.** exhausting. **6.** *Informal.* irresistibly funny. [late ME] **—kill′ing·ly,** *adv.*

kill-joy (kil′joi′), *n.* a person or thing that spoils the joy or pleasure of others.

Kil·mar·nock (kil mär′nək), *n.* a city in SW Scotland, SW of Glasgow. 48,992.

Kil·mer (kil′mər), *n.* **(Alfred) Joyce,** 1886–1918, U.S. poet and journalist.

kiln (kil, kiln), *n.* **1.** a furnace or oven for burning, baking, or drying. **—***v.t.* **2.** to burn, bake, or treat in a kiln. [ME *kiln(e),* OE *cyl(e)n* < L *culīna* kitchen]

kiln-dry (kil′drī′, kiln′-), *v.t.,* **-dried, -dry·ing.** to dry in a kiln.

kil·o (kil′ō, kē′lō), *n., pl.* **kil·os.** **1.** kilogram. **2.** kilometer. **3.** (a word used in communications to represent the letter K.) [shortened form]

kilo-, a Greek prefix meaning "thousand," introduced from French in the nomenclature of the metric system (*kiloliter*); on this model, used in the formation of compound words in other scientific measurements (*kilowatt*). [< F, repr. Gk *chílioi* a thousand]

kil·o·bar (kil′ə bär′), *n.* a unit of pressure, equal to 14,500 pounds per square inch. *Abbr.:* kb

kil·o·bit (kil′ə bit′), *n. Computer Technol.* **1.** 1024 (2^{10}) bits. **2.** (loosely) one thousand bits.

kil·o·byte (kil′ə bīt′), *n. Computer Technol.* **1.** 1024 (2^{10}) bytes: abbreviated to "K" to describe memory capacity: *This computer memory is 64K.* **2.** (loosely) one thousand bytes.

kil·o·cal·o·rie (kil′ə kal′ə rē), *n. Physics.* calorie (def. 1a). *Abbr.:* kcal Also called **kil′ogram cal′orie.**

kil·o·cu·rie (kil′ə kyo͝or′ē, -kyo͝o rē′), *n.* a unit of radioactivity, equal to 1000 curies. *Abbr.:* kc

kil·o·cy·cle (kil′ə sī′kəl), *n.* a unit equal to 1000 cycles:

used esp. in radio as 1000 cycles per second for expressing the frequency of electromagnetic waves; largely replaced in technical usage by the equivalent term kilohertz. *Abbr.:* kc

kil′o·e·lec′tron volt′ (kil′ō i lek′tron), one thousand electron-volts. *Abbr.:* keV, kev

kil·o·grain (kil′ə grān′), *n.* one thousand grains.

kil·o·gram (kil′ə gram′), *n.* a unit of mass and weight, equal to 1000 grams, and equivalent to 2.2046 pounds avoirdupois. *Abbr.:* kg, kg. Also, *esp. Brit.,* **kil′o·gramme′.** [< F *kilogramme*]

kil·o·gram-force (kil′ə gram′fōrs′, -fôrs′), *n. Physics.* a meter-kilogram-second unit of force, equal to the force that produces an acceleration equal to the acceleration of gravity, when acting on a mass of one kilogram.

kil·o·gram-me·ter (kil′ə gram′mē′tər), *n. Physics.* a unit of work or energy, equal to the work done by a force of one kilogram when its point of application moves through a distance of one meter in the direction of the force; approximately 7.2300 foot-pounds. *Abbr.:* kg-m Also, *esp. Brit.,* **kil′o·gramme′-me′tre.**

kil·o·hertz (kil′ə hûrts′), *n. Physics.* a unit of frequency, equal to 1000 cycles per second. *Abbr.:* kHz

kil·o·li·ter (kil′ə lē′tər), *n. Metric System.* one thousand liters; a cubic meter. Also, *esp. Brit.* **kil′o·li′tre.** [< F *kilolitre*]

kilom., kilometer; kilometers.

ki·lom·e·ter (ki lom′i tər, kil′ə mē′-), *n. Metric System.* a unit of length, the common measure of distances equal to 1000 meters, and equivalent to 3280.8 feet or 0.621 mile. *Abbr.:* km, km. Also, *esp. Brit.,* **kil′o·me′tre.** [< F *kilomètre*] —**kil·o·met·ric** (kil′ə me′trik), **kil′o·met′ri·cal,** *adj.*

kil·o·mole (kil′ə mōl′), *n.* one thousand moles. *Abbr.:* kmole

kil·o-oer·sted (kil′ō ûr′sted), *n.* a unit of magnetic intensity, equal to 1000 oersteds. *Abbr.:* kOe

kil·o·par·sec (kil′ə pär′sec′), *n.* a unit of distance, equal to 1000 parsecs. *Abbr.:* kpc

kil·o·ton (kil′ə tun′), *n.* **1.** one thousand tons. **2.** an explosive force equal to that of 1000 tons of TNT.

kil·o·volt (kil′ə vōlt′), *n. Elect.* a unit of electromotive force, equal to 1000 volts. *Abbr.:* kV, kv

kil·o·volt-am·pere (kil′ə vōlt′am′pēr), *n.* an electrical unit, equal to 1000 volt-amperes. *Abbr.:* kVA, kva.

kil·o·watt (kil′ə wot′), *n. Elect.* a unit of power, equal to 1000 watts. *Abbr.:* kw.

kil·o·watt-hour (kil′ə wot′our′, -ou′ər), *n. Elect.* a unit of energy, equivalent to the energy transferred or expanded in one hour by one kilowatt of power; approximately 1.34 horsepower-hours. *Abbr.:* kWh, kwhr

Kil·pat·rick (kil pa′trik), *n.* **Hugh Jud·son** (jud′sən), 1836–81, Union general in the U.S. Civil War.

kilt (kilt), *n.* **1.** any short, pleated skirt, esp. a tartan wrap-around, as that worn by men in the Scottish Highlands. —*v.t.* **2.** to draw or tuck up, as the skirt, about oneself. **3.** to provide (a skirt) with kilt pleats. [ME *kylte,* ? < Scand; cf. Dan *kilte* to tuck up]

kilt·ed (kil′tid), *adj.* **1.** wearing a kilt. **2.** gathered in pleats; pleated.

kil·ter (kil′tər), *n. Informal.* good condition; order. [?]

kilt·ie (kil′tē), *n.* a person who wears a kilt, esp. a member of a regiment wearing the kilt as part of the dress uniform.

kilt·ing (kil′ting), *n.* an arrangement of kilt pleats.

Kim·ber·ley (kim′bər lē), *n.* a city in E Cape of Good Hope province, in the central Republic of South Africa: diamond mines. 77,180 with suburbs (1960).

Kim·bun·du (kim bŏŏn′dōō), *n.* a Bantu language of N Angola.

ki·mo·no (kə mō′nə, -nō), *n., pl.* **-nos. 1.** a loose, wide-sleeved robe, fastened at the waist with a wide sash. **2.** a woman's loose dressing gown. [< Jap: clothing, garb] —**ki·mo′noed,** *adj.*

kin (kin), *n.* **1.** a person's relatives collectively; kinfolk. **2.** family relationship or kinship. **3.** a group of persons descended from a common ancestor, or constituting a family, clan, tribe, or race. **4.** a relative or kinsman. **5.** someone or something of the same or similar kind. **6. of kin,** of the same family; related; akin. —*adj.* **7.** of the same family; related; akin. **8.** of the same kind or nature; having affinity. [ME; OE *cyn;* c. OS, OHG *kunni,* Icel *kyn,* Goth *kuni;* akin to L *genus,* Gk *génos,* Skt *jánas.* See GENDER]

-kin, a diminutive suffix of nouns: *lambkin.* [ME < MD, MLG *-ken;* c. G *-chen*]

Kin·a·ba·lu (kin′ə bə lōō′), *n.* a mountain in central Sabah: highest peak on the island of Borneo. 13,455 ft. Also, **Kin′a·bu·lu′.**

kin·aes·the·sia (kin′is thē′zhə), *n.* kinesthesia. Also, **kin′aes·the′sis.** —**kin·aes·thet·ic** (kin′is thet′ik), *adj.*

ki·nase (kī′nās, kin′ās), *n. Biochem.* a substance that causes a zymogen to change into an enzyme. [KIN(ETIC) + -ASE]

Kin·car·dine (kin kär′din), *n.* a county in E Scotland. 48,810 (1961); 379 sq. mi. *Co. seat:* Stonehaven. Also called **Kin·car·dine·shire** (kin kär′din shēr′, -shər).

Kin·chin·jun·ga (kin′chin jŏŏn′gä), *n.* Kanchenjunga.

kind[1] (kīnd), *adj.* **1.** of a good or benevolent nature or disposition, as a person: *a kind guardian.* **2.** having, showing, or proceeding from benevolence: *kind words.* **3.** *Archaic.* loving. [ME *kind(e)* natural, well-disposed, OE *(ge)cynde* natural. See KIND[2]]

—**Syn. 1.** benign, humane, gentle, tender, compassionate. KIND, GRACIOUS, KINDHEARTED, KINDLY imply a sympathetic attitude toward others, and a willingness to do good or give pleasure. KIND implies a deep-seated characteristic shown either habitually or on occasion by considerate behavior: *a kind father.* GRACIOUS often refers to kindness from a superior or older person to a subordinate, an inferior, a child, etc.: *a gracious monarch.* KINDHEARTED implies an emotionally sympathetic nature, sometimes easily imposed upon: *a kindhearted old woman.* KINDLY, a mild word, refers usually to general disposition, appearance, manner, etc.: *a kindly face.* —**Ant. 1.** cruel.

kind[2] (kīnd), *n.* **1.** a class or group of individual objects, people, animals, etc., of the same nature or character or classified together because they have traits in common; category. **2.** nature or character as determining likeness or difference between things: *a difference in degree rather than in kind.* **3.** a person or thing as being of a particular character or class. **4.** a more or less adequate or inadequate example of something; sort. **5.** *Archaic.* **a.** the nature, or natural disposition or character. **b.** manner; form. **6. in kind, a.** in something of the same kind or in the same way as that received or borne: *She will be repaid in kind for her rudeness.* **b.** in produce or commodities instead of money. **7. kind of,** *Informal.* to some extent; somewhat; rather. **8. of a kind,** of the same class, nature, character, etc. [ME *kinde,* OE *gecynd* nature, race, origin; c. Icel *kyndi,* OHG *kikunt,* L *gens, gentis.* See KIN] —**Syn. 1.** order, genus, species; race.

—**Usage 7.** KIND OF and SORT OF are frowned upon by teachers and others who are concerned with careful writing because both phrases characterize a vagueness in thinking and betoken a writer's or speaker's inadequacy in expression. If a person wishes to convey uncertainty or vagueness, he is better advised to use RATHER, QUITE, or even the relatively meaningless SOMEWHAT, any of which, before an adjective or adverb, yield the same sense but are less objectionable: *The movie was rather* (or *quite*) *good.* (Not, *kind of good.*) *He is feeling somewhat better today.* Before a noun or noun phrase, even SOMETHING LIKE is preferred to KIND OF, SORT OF: *The house is something like a castle,* or *The house resembles a castle.* (Not, *kind of* or *sort of like a castle.*)

kin·der·gar·ten (kin′dər gär′tən, -dən), *n.* a school for young children, usually five-year-olds. [< G: lit., children's garden = *Kinder* children (see KIND[2]) + *Garten* GARDEN]

kin·der·gart·ner (kin′dər gärt′nər, -gärd′-), *n.* a child who attends a kindergarten. Also, **kin′der·gar′ten·er.** [< G *Kindergärtner*]

kind·heart·ed (kīnd′här′tid), *adj.* having or showing kindness. —**kind′heart′ed·ness,** *n.* —**Syn.** See **kind**[1].

kin·dle[1] (kin′dəl), *v.,* **-dled, -dling.** —*v.t.* **1.** to start (a fire); cause (a flame, blaze, etc.) to begin burning. **2.** to set fire to or ignite (fuel or any combustible matter). **3.** to excite or animate, as emotions or actions originating in strong emotion. —*v.i.* **4.** to begin to burn, as combustible matter, a light, fire, or flame. **5.** to become roused, ardent, or inflamed. [ME *kindle(n)* < Scand; cf. OSw *quindla* to set fire to, Icel *kynda* to kindle]

—**Syn. 1–3.** fire, light. KINDLE, IGNITE, INFLAME imply setting something on fire. To KINDLE is esp. to cause something gradually to begin burning; it is often used figuratively: *to kindle someone's interest.* To IGNITE is to set something on fire with a sudden burst of flame: *to ignite dangerous hatreds.* INFLAME, a literary word meaning to set aflame, is now found chiefly in figurative uses, as referring to unnaturally hot, sore, or swollen conditions in the body, or to exciting the mind by strong emotion: *The wound was greatly inflamed.* **3.** arouse, awaken, bestir, incite, stimulate.

kin·dle[2] (kin′dəl), *v.,* **-dled, -dling,** *n.* —*v.t.* **1.** (of animals, esp. rabbits) to bear (young); produce (offspring). —*v.i.* **2.** (of animals, esp. rabbits) to give birth, as to a litter. —*n.* **3.** a litter of kittens, rabbits, etc. [ME, v. use of *kindle* young, offspring = *kind-* (OE *gecynd* offspring; see KIND[2]) + *-le* -LE]

kind·less (kīnd′lis), *adj.* **1.** lacking kindness; unkind. **2.** *Obs.* unnatural; inhuman. [ME] —**kind′less·ly,** *adv.*

kind·li·ness (kīnd′lē nis), *n.* **1.** the state or quality of being kindly; benevolence. **2.** a kindly deed. [late ME]

kin·dling (kind′ling), *n.* **1.** material that can be readily ignited, used in starting a fire. **2.** the act of a person who kindles. [ME]

kind·ly (kīnd′lē), *adj.,* **-li·er, -li·est,** *adv.* —*adj.* **1.** having, showing, or proceeding from a kind disposition. **2.** gentle or mild, as rule or laws. **3.** pleasant or beneficial: *a kindly soil.* —*adv.* **4.** in a kind manner. **5.** cordially or heartily: *We thank you kindly.* **6.** with liking; favorably: *to take kindly to an idea.* **7.** obligingly; please: *Would you kindly close the door?* [ME *kyndly,* OE *(ge)cyndelīc* natural] —**Syn. 1.** See **kind**[1].

kind·ness (kīnd′nis), *n.* **1.** the state or quality of being kind. **2.** a kind act. **3.** kind behavior. **4.** friendly feeling; liking. [ME *kindenes*] —**Syn. 1, 3.** benignity, benevolence, humanity, generosity, charity, sympathy.

kin·dred (kin′drid), *n.* **1.** a body of persons related to another; family, tribe, or race. **2.** a person's relatives collectively; kinfolk; kin. **3.** relationship by birth or descent, or sometimes by marriage; kinship. **4.** natural relationship; affinity. —*adj.* **5.** associated by origin, nature, qualities, etc. **6.** having the same belief, attitude, or feeling. **7.** related by birth or descent; having kinship. **8.** belonging to kin or relatives. [ME, var. (with epenthetic *d*) of *kinred(en).* See KIN, -RED] —**kin′dred·ly,** *adv.* —**kin′dred·ness,** **kin′dred·ship′,** *n.*

kine[1] (kīn), *n. Archaic.* pl. of **cow**[1]. [ME *kyn,* OE *cȳ* (nom., acc.), *cȳna* (gen.), pl. forms of *cū* cow[1]]

kin·e[2] (kin′ē), *n.* kinescope (def. 1). [shortened form]

kin·e·mat·ics (kin′ə mat′iks, kī′nə-), *n.* (*construed as sing.*) the branch of mechanics that deals with pure motion, without reference to the masses or forces involved in it. [< Gk *kīnēmat-* (s. of *kīnēma* movement; see CINEMA) + -ICS] —**kin′e·mat′ic, kin′e·mat′i·cal,** *adj.* —**kin′e·mat′i·cal·ly,** *adv.*

kin·e·mat·o·graph (kin′ə mat′ə graf′, -gräf′), *n.* cinematograph. —**kin·e·ma·tog·ra·pher** (kin′ə mə tog′rə fər), *n.* —**kin·e·mat·o·graph·ic** (kin′ə mat′ə graf′ik), **kin′e·mat′o·graph′i·cal,** *adj.* —**kin′e·mat′o·graph′i·cal·ly,** *adv.* —**kin′e·ma·tog′ra·phy,** *n.*

kin·e·scope (kin′i skōp′), *n., v.,* **-scoped, -scop·ing.** *Television.* —*n.* **1.** Also, **kine.** a cathode-ray tube with a fluorescent screen on which an image is reproduced by a directed beam of electrons. **2.** the motion-picture record of a television program. —*v.t.* **3.** to record (a program) on motion-picture film for later broadcasting. [formerly trademark]

ki·ne·sics (ki nē′siks, kī-), *n.* (*construed as sing.*) the study of body movements, gestures, postures, etc., as a means of communication; body language.

kin·es·the·sia (kin′is thē′zhə), *n.* the sensation of movement or strain in muscles, tendons, and joints; muscle sense. Also, **kinaesthesia, kin′es·the′sis.** [< Gk *kīn(ein)* (to) move, set in motion + ESTHESIA] —**kin·es·thet·ic** (kin′is-thet′ik), *adj.*

ki·net·ic (ki net′ik, kī-), *adj.* **1.** pertaining to motion. **2.** caused by motion. **3.** characterized by movement. [< Gk *kīnētik(ós)* moving = *kīnē-* (verbid s. of *kīnein* to move) + *-tikos* -TIC] —**ki·net′i·cal·ly,** *adv.*

kinet′ic en′ergy, *Physics.* the energy of a body or a system with respect to the motion of the body or of the particles in the system. Cf. **potential energy.**

ki·net·ics (ki net′iks, kī-), *n.* (*construed as sing.*) the branch of mechanics that deals with the actions of forces in producing or changing the motion of masses. [see KINETIC, -ICS]

kinet′ic the′ory of gas′es, *Physics.* a theory that the particles in a gas move freely and rapidly along straight lines but often collide, resulting in variations in their velocity and direction. Pressure is interpreted as arising from the impacts of these particles on the walls of a container, and other macroscopic variables are similarly treated.

kinet′ic the′ory of mat′ter, *Physics.* a theory that matter is composed of small particles, all in random motion.

kin·folk (kin′fōk′), *n.pl.* relatives or kindred. Also, **kin′-folks′, kinsfolk.**

king (king), *n.* **1.** a male sovereign or monarch; a man who holds by life tenure, and usually by hereditary right, the chief authority over a country and people. **2.** a person or thing preeminent in its class: *an oil king; the king of the beasts.* **3.** a playing card bearing a picture of a king. **4.** *Chess.* the piece of each color the checkmating of which is the object of the game of chess: moved one square at a time in any direction. **5.** *Checkers.* a man that has been moved entirely across the board and has been crowned, thus permitted to be moved in any direction. —*v.t.* **6.** to make a king of. —*v.i.* **7.** to reign as king. [ME, OE *cyng, cyni(n)g;* c. G *König,* D *koning,* Icel *konungr,* Sw *konung,* Dan *konge.* See KIN, -ING[1]] —**king′hood,** *n.* —**king′less,** *adj.* —**king′less·ness,** *n.* —**king′like′,** *adj.*

King (king), *n.* **1. Ernest Joseph,** 1878–1956, U.S. naval officer. **2. Martin Luther, Jr.,** 1929–68, U.S. minister and civil-rights leader: Nobel peace prize 1964. **3. Rufus,** 1755–1827, U.S. political leader and statesman. **4. William Lyon Mackenzie,** 1874–1950, Canadian statesman: prime minister 1921–26, 1926–30, 1935–48. **5. William Rufus De·Vane** (də vān′), 1786–1853, vice president of the U.S. 1853.

king·bird (king′bûrd′), *n.* any of several American tyrant flycatchers of the genus *Tyrannus,* having grayish-black plumage with a white-tipped tail.

king·bolt (king′bōlt′), *n.* **1.** a vertical bolt connecting the body of a horse-drawn vehicle with the fore axle, the body of a railroad car with a truck, etc. **2.** (in a roof truss) a metal rod serving as a king post. Also called **king rod.**

King′ Charles′ span′iel, a variety of the English toy spaniel having a black-and-tan coat. [named after *Charles* II of England from his liking for this variety]

king′ co′bra, a cobra, *Naja* (*Ophiophagus*) *hannah,* of southeastern Asia and the East Indies, that grows to a length of more than 15 feet: the largest of the venomous snakes. Also called **hamadryad.**

king′ crab′, 1. See **horseshoe crab. 2.** Also called **Alaskan crab.** a large, edible crab, *Paralithodes camtschatica,* found in the North Pacific, esp. along the coasts of Alaska and Japan.

king·craft (king′kraft′, -kräft′), *n.* the art of ruling as king; royal statesmanship.

king·cup (king′kup′), *n.* **1.** any of various common buttercups, as *Ranunculus bulbosus.* **2.** *Chiefly Brit.* the marsh marigold.

king·dom (king′dəm), *n.* **1.** a state or government having a king or queen as its head. **2.** anything conceived as constituting an independent entity: *the kingdom of thought.* **3.** a realm or province of nature, esp. one of the three great divisions of natural objects, the animal, vegetable, and mineral. **4.** the spiritual sovereignty of God or Christ. **5.** the domain over which this extends, whether in heaven or on earth. [ME; OE *cyningdōm*] —**king′dom·less,** *adj.* —**Syn. 2.** dominion, empire, domain.

king′dom come′, the next world; the condition or state of having died. [abstracted from the phrase *Thy kingdom come* in the Lord's Prayer]

King′dom Hall′, any meeting place of Jehovah's Witnesses for religious services.

king·fish (king′fish′), *n., pl.* (*esp. collectively*) **-fish,** (*esp. referring to two or more kinds or species*) **-fish·es. 1.** any of several marine food fishes of the drum family, esp. of the genus *Menticirrhus,* found off the E coast of the U.S. **2.** a marine food fish, *Genyonemus lineatus,* found off the California coast. **3.** See **king mackerel. 4.** a large game fish, *Seriola grandis,* found in Australia and New Zealand, closely related to the yellowtail.

king·fish·er (king′fish′ər), *n.* any of numerous fish- or insect-eating birds of the family *Alcedinidae* that have a large head and a long, stout bill and are usually crested and brilliantly colored. [KING + FISHER; r. *king's fisher,* late ME *kynggs fischare*]

Kingfisher, *Megaceryle alcyon* (Length 13 in.)

King′ George′'s War′, a war (1744–48) waged by England and its colonies against France, constituting the North American phase of the War of the Austrian Succession.

King′ James′ Ver′sion. See **Authorized Version.** Also called **King′ James′′ Bi′ble.**

king·let (king′lit), *n.* **1.** a king ruling over a small country or territory. **2.** any of several small, greenish, crested birds of the genus *Regulus.*

king·ly (king′lē), *adj.,* **-li·er, -li·est,** *adv.* —*adj.* **1.** having the rank of king. **2.** stately or splendid, as resembling, suggesting, or befitting a king; regal. **3.** pertaining or proper to a king or kings. —*adv.* **4.** in the manner of a king; regally. [ME] —**king′li·ness,** *n.*

—**Syn. 2, 3.** princely, sovereign, majestic, august, magnificent, exalted, grand. KINGLY, REGAL, ROYAL refer to something closely associated with a king, or suitable for one. What is KINGLY may either belong to a king, or be befitting, worthy of, or like a king: *a kingly presence, appearance, graciousness.* REGAL is esp. applied to the office of kingship or the outward manifestations of grandeur and majesty: *regal authority, bearing, splendor, munificence.* ROYAL is applied esp. to what pertains to or is associated with the person of a monarch: *the royal family, robes; a royal residence.* —**Ant. 2, 3.** lowly.

king′ mack′erel, a game fish, *Scomberomorus cavalla,* found in the western Atlantic Ocean.

king·mak·er (king′mā′kər), *n.* a person who has sufficient power and influence to choose a ruler or a candidate for public office.

king-of-arms (king′əv ärmz′), *n., pl.* **kings-of-arms.** a title of certain of the principal heralds of England and certain other kingdoms empowered by their sovereigns to grant armorial bearings. [late ME *king of armes*]

king′ of beasts′, the lion.

King′ of kings′, 1. Christ; Jesus. **2.** God; Jehovah. Also, **King′ of Kings′.**

king′ pen′guin, a large penguin, *Aptenodytes patagonicus,* found on islands bordering the Antarctic Circle.

King′ Phil′ip's War′, the war (1675–76) between New England colonists and a confederation of Indians under their leader, King Philip.

king·pin (king′pin′), *n.* **1.** *Bowling.* **a.** headpin. **b.** the pin at the center; the number five pin. **2.** *Informal.* the person of chief importance in a corporation, undertaking, etc. **3.** one of two pivots on which the front wheels of a car or other motor vehicle turn in steering.

king′ post′, a vertical suspension member depending from the apex of a triangular roof truss to support the feet of struts or the middle of a tie beam or rod. Also, **king′post′, king′-post′.**

A, King post; B, Tie beam; C, Strut; D, Principal rafter; E, Purlin; F, Common rafter

king′ rod′, kingbolt.

Kings (kingz), *n.* (*construed as sing.*) **1.** either of two books of the Bible, I Kings or II Kings, that contain the history of the kings of Israel and Judah. **2.** *Douay Bible.* one of the four books of the Old Testament, I, II, III, or IV Kings, corresponding to I and II Samuel and I and II Kings in the Authorized Version.

king′ salm′on. See **chinook salmon.**

King's′ Bench′, *Brit. Law.* a court, originally the principal court for criminal cases, gradually acquiring a civil jurisdiction concurrent with that of the Court of Common Pleas, and also possessing appellate jurisdiction over the Court of Common Pleas: now a division of the High Court of Justice. Also called, *when a queen is sovereign,* **Queen's Bench.**

King's′ Birth′day, an imperial holiday in Britain and most of the Commonwealth countries, celebrating the birthday of a reigning monarch, on either the birth date or an arbitrary date chosen by the monarch. Also called, *when a queen is sovereign,* **Queen's Birthday.**

king's′ col′our, *Brit.* **1.** a white ceremonial ensign with a royal cipher, flown on special occasions by the Royal Navy. **2.** the union jack as an emblem on the regimental colors of a British military unit. **3. king's colours,** a pair of silk flags with the royal cipher, announcing the monarch's presence. Also, **King's′ col′our, King's′ Col′our.** Also called, *when a queen is sovereign,* **queen's colour.**

King's′ Coun′sel, *Brit. Law.* **1.** a body of barristers who are appointed to be the Crown's counsel and are permitted to plead inside the bar in the court. **2.** a member of this body of barristers. Also called, *when a queen is sovereign,* **Queen's Counsel.**

king's′ Eng′lish, educated or correct English speech or usage, esp. of England. Also called, *when a queen is sovereign,* **queen's English.**

king's′ ev′idence, *Brit. Law.* evidence for the crown given by an accused person against his alleged accomplices. Also called, *when a queen is sovereign,* **queen's evidence.** Cf. **state's evidence.**

king's′ e′vil, scrofula: so called because it was supposed to be curable by the touch of the reigning sovereign. [ME *kynges evel*]

king's′ high′way, *Brit.* a highway built by the national government. Also, **King's′ high′way, King's′ High′way.** Also called, *when a queen is sovereign,* **queen's highway.**

king·ship (king′ship), *n.* **1.** the state, office, or dignity of a king. **2.** rule by a king; monarchy. **3.** aptitude for kingly duties. **4.** (*cap.*) a title used in referring to a king; Majesty (prec. by *his* or *your*). [ME *kingscip*]

king-size (king′sīz′), *adj.* **1.** larger than the usual size, as one of several sizes of cigarettes. **2.** (of a bed) extra large, usually at least 78 inches wide and 80 inches long. **3.** pertaining to or made for a king-size bed: *king-size sheets.* Also, **king′-sized′.**

Kings·ley (kingz′lē), *n.* **Charles,** 1819–75, English clergyman, novelist, and poet.

king·snake (king′snāk′), *n.* any of several New World constrictors of the genus *Lampropeltis,* that often feed on other snakes. Also, **king′ snake′.**

Kings·port (kingz′pōrt′, -pôrt′), *n.* a city in NE Tennessee. 31,938 (1970).

king's′ ran′som, an extremely large amount of money.

Kings·ton (kingz′tən, king′stən), *n.* **1.** a seaport in and the capital of Jamaica. 600,000. **2.** a city in SE New York, on the Hudson River. 25,544 (1970). **3.** a port in SE Ontario, in SE Canada, on Lake Ontario: Royal Military College of Canada. 56,032.

Kings·ton-up·on-Hull (kingz′tən ə pon′hul′, king′-stən-), *n.* official name of **Hull.**

Kings·town (kingz′toun′), *n.* a seaport on and the capital of St. Vincent. 29,000.

Kings·ville (kingz′vil), *n.* a city in S Texas. 28,915 (1970).

King·teh·chen (ging′du′jen′), *n.* former name of Fowliang.

King′ Wil′liam's War′, the war (1689–97) in which England and its American colonies and Indian allies opposed France and its Indian allies and which constituted the American phase of the War of the Grand Alliance.

kink (kingk), *n.* **1.** a twist or curl, as in a rope or hair, caused by its doubling or bending upon itself. **2.** a muscular stiffness or soreness, as in the neck or back. **3.** a flaw or imperfection likely to hinder the successful operation of something, as a machine or plan. **4.** a mental twist; notion; whim or crotchet. —*v.t., v.i.* **5.** to form or cause to form a kink or kinks. [< D: a twist in a rope; cf. Icel *kinka* to nod, *kikna* to bend the knee]

Kin·kaid (kin kād′), *n.* **Thomas Cas·sin** (kas′in), 1888–1972, U.S. admiral.

kin·ka·jou (king′kə jo͞o′), *n.* a brownish, arboreal mammal, *Potos flavus,* of Central and South America, having a prehensile tail, related to the raccoon and coati. [< F *quincajou* < Sp *quincajú* < Pg *kinkaju* < Tupi]

Kinkajou (Length 3 ft.)

kink·y (king′kē), *adj.,* **kink·i·er, kink·i·est. 1.** full of kinks; closely twisted. **2.** (of hair) closely or tightly curled. **3.** *Slang.* eccentric, bizarre, or quirky, esp. in sexual behavior. —**kink′·i·ly,** *adv.* —**kink′i·ness,** *n.*

kin·ni·kin·nick (kin′ə kə nik′), *n.* **1.** a mixture of bark, dried leaves, and sometimes tobacco, formerly smoked by the Indians and pioneers in the Ohio valley. **2.** any of various plants used in this mixture, as the bearberry, *Arctostaphylos Uva-ursi,* or the silky cornel, *Cornus Amomum.* Also, **kin′ni·kin·nic′, killickinnic.** [< Algonquian (Ojibwa): lit., that which is mixed]

ki·no (kē′nō), *n., pl.* **-nos.** (in Europe) a motion-picture theater; cinema. [< G (by shortening) *Kinematograph* < F *cinématographe* CINEMATOGRAPH]

Kin·ross (kin rôs′, -ros′), *n.* a county in E Scotland. 6704 (1961); 82 sq. mi. *Co. seat:* Kinross. Also called **Kinross-shire** (kin rôs′shēr, -shər, -ros′-).

Kin·sey (kin′zē), *n.* **Alfred Charles,** 1894–1956, U.S. zoologist: directed studies of human sexual behavior.

kins·folk (kinz′fōk′), *n.pl.* kinfolk. [late ME *kynsefolk* (see KIN, FOLK), modeled on *kinsman*]

Kin·sha·sa (kin′shä sä), *n.* a port in and the capital of Zaïre, in the W part, on the Zaïre River. 1,990,717. Formerly, **Léopoldville.**

kin·ship (kin′ship), *n.* **1.** the state or fact of being of kin; family relationship. **2.** relationship by nature, qualities, etc.; affinity. —**Syn. 1.** See **relationship. 2.** bearing.

kins·man (kinz′mən), *n., pl.* **-men. 1.** a blood relative, esp. a male. **2.** a relative by marriage. **3.** a person of the same race. [early ME *cunnes man, kynnes man*]

kins·wom·an (kinz′wo͝om′ən), *n., pl.* **-wom·en.** a female relative. [ME]

Kio·ga (kyō′gə), *n.* **Lake.** See **Kyoga, Lake.**

ki·osk (kē osk′, kī′osk), *n.* **1.** a kind of open pavilion or summerhouse common in Turkey and Iran. **2.** a similar structure used as a bandstand, as a newsstand, etc. [< F *kiosque* stand in a public park < Turk *köşk* villa < Pers *kūshk* garden pavilion]

Kio·to (kē ō′tō; *Jap.* kyô′tô), *n.* Kyoto.

Ki·o·wa (kī′ə wə), *n., pl.* **-was,** (*esp. collectively*) **-wa. 1.** a member of a Plains Indian people of the southwestern U.S. **2.** a Uto-Aztecan language that is most closely related to Tanoan and is the language of the Kiowa people.

kip[1] (kip), *n.* **1.** the hide of a young or small beast. **2.** a bundle or set of such hides. [ME *kipp* < MD, MLG *kip* pack (of hides); akin to Icel *kippa* bundle]

kip[2] (kip), *n.* a unit of weight equal to 1000 pounds. [KI(LO) + P(OUND)[2]]

kip[3] (kip), *n.* a paper money and monetary unit of Laos equal to 100 at. *Abbr.:* K. [< Thai]

Kip·ling (kip′ling), *n.* **(Joseph) Rud·yard** (rud′yərd), 1865–1936, English author: Nobel prize 1907.

Kip·nis (kip′nis; *Russ.* kip nēs′), *n.* **Al·ex·an·der** (al′ig zan′dər; *Russ.* ä′le ksän′dər), 1891–1978, Russian singer in the U.S.

kip·per (kip′ər), *n.* **1.** a kippered fish, esp. a herring. —*v.t.* **2.** to cure (herring, salmon, etc.) by cleaning, salting, etc., and drying in the air or in smoke. [ME *kypre,* OE *cypera* spawning salmon, appar. < *cyperen* copper-colored]

Kir·by-Smith (kûr′bē smith′), *n.* **Edmund,** 1824–93, Confederate general in the U.S. Civil War.

Kirch·hoff (kērkh′hôf), *n.* **Gus·tav Ro·bert** (go͝os′täf rō′bert), 1824–87, German physicist.

Kir·ghiz (kir gēz′), *n., pl.* **-ghiz, -ghiz·es. 1.** one of a people of Mongolian physical type and Turkic speech, dwelling chiefly in west central Asia. **2.** their language.

Kir·ghi·zia (kir gē′zhə), *n.* a constituent republic of the Soviet Union, in SW Asia, adjoining Sinkiang, China. 2,600,000 (est. 1965); ab. 77,800 sq. mi. *Cap.:* Frunze.

Kirghiz′ Steppe′, a steppe in the SW Soviet Union in Asia, in Kazakstan. Also called **the Steppes.**

Ki·ri·ba·ti (kēr′ē bä′tē, -bäs′), *n.* a republic in the central Pacific, on the equator, comprising several island groups: formerly part of the Gilbert and Ellice Islands; independent since 1979. 56,000; 263 sq. mi. *Cap.:* Tarawa.

Ki·rin (kē′rin′), *n.* **1.** a province in central Manchuria, in NE China. 23,000,000; 72,201 sq. mi. **2.** the capital of this province: a port on the Sungari River. 720,000.

kirk (kûrk; *Scot.* kirk), *n.* **1.** *Scot. and North Eng.* a church. **2. the Kirk,** (among the English) the Church of Scotland (Presbyterian), as distinguished from the Church of England or the Scottish Episcopal Church. [ME < Scand; cf. Icel *kirkja* CHURCH]

Kirk·cal·dy (kər kôl′dē, -kô′dē, -kä′-), *n.* a city in SE Fife, in E Scotland, on the Firth of Forth. 52,371 (1961).

Kirk·cud·bright (kər ko͞o′brē), *n.* a county in SW Scotland. 28,877 (1961); 896 sq. mi. *Co. seat:* Kirkcudbright.

kirk·man (kûrk′mən; *Scot.* kirk′mən), *n., pl.* **-men.** *Scot. and North Eng.* a member or follower of the Kirk.

Kirk·pat·rick (kûrk pa′trik), *n.* **Jeane J(ordan)** (jēn), born 1926, U.S. ambassador to the U.N. 1981–85.

Kir·kuk (kir ko͞ok′), *n.* a city in N Iraq. 176,794 (est. 1963).

Kirk·wall (kûrk′wôl′, -wəl), *n.* a town on Pomona, NE of Scotland: county seat of Orkney. 4618.

Kirk·wood (kûrk′wo͝od′), *n.* a city in E Missouri, near St. Louis. 31,769 (1970).

Kir·man (kir män′), *n.* a Persian rug marked by ornate flowing designs and light, muted colors. Also, **Kir·man·shah** (kir män′shä′), **Kermanshah.** [after KERMAN]

kir·mess (kûr′mis), *n.* kermis.

Kir Mo·ab (kûr mō′ab), ancient name of **Kerak.**

Ki·rov (kē′rof), *n.* a city in the E RSFSR, in the W Soviet Union in Europe. 292,000 (est. 1964). Formerly, **Vyatka.**

Ki·ro·va·bad (kē′ro vä bät′), *n.* a city in NW Azerbaijan, in the S Soviet Union in Europe. 126,000 (est. 1962). Formerly, **Elisavetpol, Gandzha.**

Ki·ro·vo·grad (kē′ro vo grät′), *n.* a city in the S central Ukraine, in the SW Soviet Union in Europe. 150,000 (est. 1964). Formerly, **Elisavetgrad, Zinovievsk.**

kirsch·was·ser (kērsh′vä′sər), *n.* a colorless, unaged brandy distilled from a fermented mash of cherries. Also called **kirsch.** [< G = *Kirsch(e)* CHERRY + *Wasser* WATER]

kir·tle (kûr′tᵊl), *n.* **1.** a woman's loose gown, worn in the Middle Ages. **2.** *Obs.* a man's tunic or coat. [ME *kirtel,* OE *cyrtel,* appar. = *cyrt(an)* (to) shorten (<< L *curtus* shortened) + *-el* -LE] —**kir′tled,** *adj.*

Ki·ru·na (kē′ry nä), *n.* a city in N Sweden: important iron-mining center. 28,226 (1965).

Ki·san·ga·ni (ki zäng′gä nē), *n.* a city in N Zaïre, on the Zaïre River. 400,000 (est. 1967). Formerly, **Stanleyville.**

Ki·se·levsk (ki se lyôfsk′), *n.* a city in the S RSFSR, in the Soviet Union in Asia. 142,000 (est. 1962).

Ki·shi·nev (ki shi nyôf′), *n.* a city in and the capital of Moldavia, in the central part, in the SW Soviet Union in Europe. 278,000 (est. 1965). Rumanian, **Chişinău.**

kish·ke (kish′kə), *n.* **1.** Also called **stuffed derma.** *Jewish Cookery.* a beef or fowl intestine stuffed with a mixture of flour, fat, onion, seasonings, etc., and roasted. **2. kishkes,** *Slang.* guts; belly; stomach: *to get kicked in the kishkes.* [< Yiddish < Slav; cf. Pol *kiszka* sausage]

Kis·lev (kis′ləv; *Heb.* kēs lāv′), *n.* the third month of the Jewish calendar. Cf. **Jewish calendar.** [< Heb]

kis·met (kiz′mit, kis′-), *n.* fate; destiny. Also, **kis·mat** (kiz′mət, kis′-). [< Turk < Pers *qismat* < Ar *qisma(t)* division, portion, lot, fate, akin to *qasama* to divide] —**kis·met·ic** (kiz met′ik, kis-), *adj.*

kiss (kis), *v.t.* **1.** to touch or press with the lips slightly pursed in token of greeting, affection, reverence, etc. **2.** *Billiards, Pool.* to make slight contact with or brush, as one ball with another. —*v.i.* **3.** to join lips, as in affection or love. **4.** *Billiards, Pool.* to carom gently off or touch another ball. —*n.* **5.** the act or an instance of kissing. **6.** *Billiards, Pool.* the slight touch of one ball by another. **7.** a cooky made of egg whites and confectioners' sugar. **8.** a piece of candy, often chocolate or toffeelike and sometimes containing nuts, coconut, etc. [ME *kiss(en),* OE *cyssan*]

kiss·a·ble (kis′ə bəl), *adj.* (of a person, esp. a woman) inviting kissing through being physically attractive. —**kiss′a·ble·ness,** *n.* —**kiss′a·bly,** *adv.*

kiss·er (kis′ər), *n.* **1.** a person or thing that kisses. **2.** *Slang.* **a.** the face. **b.** the mouth.

kiss′ing bug′, any of several assassin bugs that attack man, sometimes inflicting painful bites.

kiss′ing cous′in. See under **kissing kin.**

Kis·sin·ger (kis′ən jər), *n.* **Henry A(lfred),** born 1923, U.S. statesman, born in Germany: Secretary of State 1973–76; Nobel peace prize 1973.

kiss′ing kin′, any more or less distant kin familiar enough to be greeted with a kiss, as a cousin **(kissing cousin).**

kiss′ of death′, a fatal or destructive relationship, statement, or action.

kiss-off (kis′ôf′, -of′), *n.* *Slang.* dismissal.

kiss′ of peace′, *Eccles.* a ceremonial embrace given to signify Christian love and unity, esp. one given during forms of the Eucharistic service. Also called **pax.**

kist (kist), *n.* *Scot. and North Eng.* a coffer; a money chest. [ME *kiste* < Scand; cf. Icel *kista* CHEST]

Kist·na (kist′nə), *n.* a river in S India, flowing E from the Western Ghats to the Bay of Bengal. 800 mi. long.

Ki·su·mu (kē so͞o′mo͞o), *n.* a city in W Kenya. 36,000.

kit[1] (kit), *n., v.,* **kit·ted, kit·ting.** —*n.* **1.** a set of tools or supplies for performing certain kinds of jobs. **2.** a container for these. **3.** a set of materials or parts from which something can be assembled: *a model kit.* **4.** *Informal.* a set, lot, or collection of things or persons. **5. kit and caboodle** or **boodle,** *Informal.* the whole lot of certain persons or things (often prec. by *whole*). —*v.t.* **6.** *Chiefly Brit.* to outfit or equip. [ME *kyt, kitt* < MD *kitte* jug, tankard]

kit[2] (kit), *n.* a violin or rebec small enough to be carried in the pocket, used by dancing masters in the 17th and 18th centuries. Also called **sourdine.** [?]

kit[3] (kit), *n.* kitten. [shortened form]

kit′ bag′, a knapsack, as for a soldier.

kitch·en (kich′ən), *n.* **1.** a room or place equipped for cooking. **2.** the staff or equipment of this place. —*adj.* **3.** of, pertaining to, or used in a kitchen. **4.** *Informal.* (of language) of an inferior, mongrel, or pidginlike form: *kitchen French.* [ME *kichene,* OE *cycene* << L *coquīna* = *coqu(ere)* (to) COOK + *-īna* -INE[1]] —**kitch′en·less,** *adj.*

kitch′en cab′inet, 1. a cupboard built into a kitchen, or a chest of drawers for kitchen use. **2.** a group of unofficial advisers on whom a head of government appears to rely heavily.

kitch·en·er (kich′ə nər), *n.* **1.** a person employed in a kitchen. **2.** an elaborate kitchen stove. [late ME]

Kitch·e·ner (kich′ə nər), *n.* **1. Horatio Herbert** (*1st*

Earl Kitchener of Khartoum and of Broome), 1850–1916, English field marshal and statesman. **2.** a city in S Ontario, in SE Canada. 74,485 with suburbs (1961).

kitch·en·ette (kich′ə net′), *n.* a very small, compact kitchen. Also, **kitch′en·et′.**

kitch′en gar′den, a garden where vegetables, herbs, and fruit are grown for one's own use. —**kitch′en gar′dener.**

kitch′en match′, a wooden friction match with a large head, used esp. for igniting gas ovens or burners.

kitch′en mid′den, a mound consisting of shells of edible mollusks and other refuse, marking the site of a prehistoric human habitation. [trans. of Dan *kökkenmödding*]

kitch′en police′, *Mil.* **1.** duty as assistant to the cooks. *Abbr.:* K.P. **2.** soldiers detailed by roster or as punishment to assist in kitchen duties.

kitch·en·ware (kich′ən wâr′), *n.* cooking equipment or utensils.

kite (kīt), *n.*, *v.*, **kit·ed, kit·ing.** —*n.* **1.** a light frame covered with some thin material, to be flown in the wind at the end of a long string. **2.** any of several small birds of the hawk family *Accipitridae* having long, pointed wings: noted for their graceful flight. **3.** *Com.* a worthless or post-dated negotiable instrument used for raising money or sustaining credit. —*v.i.* **4.** *Com.* to obtain money or credit through kites. —*v.t.* **5.** *Com.* to employ as a kite. **6.** to increase the amount of (a check) falsely before cashing it. [ME *kyte,* OE *cȳta* kite, bittern; akin to G *Kauz* owl] —**kit′er,** *n.*

kith (kith), *n.* **1.** acquaintances, friends, neighbors, or the like. **2.** kindred. **3.** a group of people living in the same area and forming a culture with a common language, customs, economy, etc., usually endogamous. [ME; OE *cȳth,* earlier *cȳththu* kinship, knowledge = *cūth* known (see UNCOUTH) + *-thu* -TH[1]; akin to Goth *kunthi,* G *Kunde* knowledge]

kith′ and kin′, acquaintances and relatives.

kith·a·ra (kith′ər ə), *n.* a musical instrument of ancient Greece consisting of an elaborate wooden soundbox having two arms connected by a yoke to which the upper ends of the strings are attached. Also, **cithara.** [< L < Gk: lyre]

Kithara

kithe (kīth), *v.t., v.i.,* **kithed, kith·ing.** *Scot. and North Eng.* to make or become known by action; declare. Also, **kythe.** [ME *kithe(n),* OE *cȳthan* to make known < *cūth* known; see UNCOUTH]

kit·ling (kit′ling), *n.* *Brit. Dial.* the young of any animal, esp. a young cat; kitten; kit. [ME *kiteling* < Scand; cf. Icel *ketlingr.* See CAT, -LING[1]]

kitsch (kich), *n.* art or literature of little or no value, esp. when produced to satisfy popular taste. [< G < *Kitschen* to throw together (a work of art)]

kit·tel (kit′əl), *n.* *Yiddish.* a white ceremonial robe worn by Jews, esp. Orthodox Jews, on Yom Kippur.

kit·ten (kit′ən), *n.* **1.** a young cat. —*v.t.* **2.** to give birth to (kittens). —*v.i.* **3.** to bear kittens. [ME *kitoun,* appar. b. *kiteling* KITLING and MF *chitoun,* var. of *chaton* kitten]

kit·ten·ish (kit′ən ish), *adj.* artlessly playful like a kitten. —**kit′ten·ish·ly,** *adv.* —**kit′ten·ish·ness,** *n.*

kit·ti·wake (kit′ē wāk′), *n,* either of two gulls of the genus *Rissa,* having the hind toe very short or rudimentary. [imit.]

kit·tle (kit′əl), *v.,* **-tled, -tling,** *adj.,* **-tler, -tlest.** *Brit. Dial.* —*v.t.* **1.** to tickle or agitate. **2.** to excite or rouse (a person), esp. by flattery or strong words. —*adj.* **3.** ticklish; fidgety. [late ME *kytylle, ketil,* OE **cytelian* (whence *citelung* tickling); akin to Icel *kitla,* G *kitzeln* to tickle]

Kit·tredge (ki′trij), *n.* **George Ly·man** (lī′mən), 1860–1941, U.S. Shakespearean scholar, philologist, and educator.

kit·ty[1] (kit′ē), *n., pl.* **-ties.** **1.** a kitten. **2.** a pet name for a cat. [KIT[3] + -Y[2]]

kit·ty[2] (kit′ē), *n., pl.* **-ties.** **1.** a pool or reserve of money, usually collected from a number of persons or sources and designated for a particular purpose specified by the contributors. **2.** *Cards.* **a.** a pool into which each player in a game puts a certain amount of his winnings for some special purpose, as to pay for refreshments. **b.** the pot, or a special pot, for the collection of forfeits or payments for certain high hands. **c.** widow (def. 2). [KIT[1] + -Y[2]]

kit·ty-cor·nered (kit′ē kôr′nərd), *adj., adv.* *U.S. Informal.* cater-cornered. Also, **kit′ty-cor′ner.**

Kit′ty Hawk′, a village in NE North Carolina: Wright brothers' airplane flight 1903. Also, **Kit·ty·hawk** (kit′ē hôk′).

Ki·twe (kē′twā), *n.* a city in N Zambia. 155,800 (est. 1968).

Kiung·chow (kyōōng′chō′, -chou′; *Chin.* gyōōng′jō′), *n.* a seaport on S Hainan island, in S China. ab. 59,000. Also, **Kiung·shan** (kyōōng′shän′; *Chin.* gyōōng′shän′).

Kiu·shu (kyōō′shōō′), *n.* Kyushu.

ki·va (kē′və), *n.* a large chamber, often wholly or partly underground, in a Pueblo Indian village, used for religious ceremonies and other purposes. [< Hopi]

Ki·wa·nis (ki wä′nis), *n.* an organization founded in 1915 for the promulgation of higher ideals in business and professional life. [said to be < AmerInd: to make oneself known] —**Ki·wa′ni·an,** *n.*

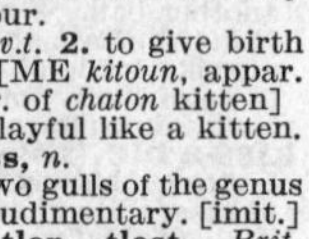

ki·wi (kē′wē), *n., pl.* **-wis.** **1.** any of several flightless, ratite birds of the genus *Apteryx,* of New Zealand, allied to the extinct moas. **2.** *Australian Informal.* a New Zealander. [< Maori]

Kiwi, *Apteryx australis* (Total length to 28 in.; bill 6 in.)

Ki·zil Ir·mak (ki zil′ ēr mäk′), *n.* a river rising in N central Turkey, E of Sivas, and flowing generally northward into the Black Sea. 600 mi. long.

Ki·zil Kum (ki zil′ kōōm′). See **Kyzyl Kum.**

Kjö·len (*Norw.* chœ′lən), *n.* a mountain range between Norway and Sweden. Highest peak, Mt. Kebnekaise, 7005 ft.

KKK, Ku Klux Klan. Also, **K.K.K.**

KKt, *Chess.* king's knight.

KKtP, *Chess.* king's knight's pawn.

kl., kiloliter. Also, **kl**

Kla·gen·furt (klä′gən fōōrt′), *n.* a city in and the capital of Carinthia, in S Austria. 67,782 (1961).

Klai·pe·da (klī′pe dä′), *n.* Lithuanian name of **Memel.**

Klam·ath (klam′əth), *n.* a river flowing from SW Oregon through NW California into the Pacific. 250 mi. long.

Klam·ath (klam′əth), *n., pl.* **-aths,** (*esp. collectively*) **-ath.** a member of an American Indian people belonging to the Lutuamian group and located in southern Oregon.

Klam′ath Lakes′, two lakes which drain into the Klamath River: one lake **(Upper Klamath Lake)** is in SW Oregon, and the other **(Lower Klamath Lake)** is in N California.

Klan (klan), *n.* **1.** See **Ku Klux Klan.** **2.** a chapter of the Ku Klux Klan. —**Klan′ism,** *n.*

Klans·man (klanz′mən), *n., pl.* **-men.** a member of the Ku Klux Klan.

Klau·sen·burg (klou′zən bōōrk′), *n.* German name of **Cluj.**

klav·ern (klav′ərn), *n.* **1.** a local branch of the Ku Klux Klan. **2.** a meeting place of the Ku Klux Klan. [KL(AN + C)AVERN]

klax·on (klak′sən), *n.* a loud electric horn for automobiles, trucks, etc. [formerly trademark]

klea·gle (klē′gəl), *n.* an official of the Ku Klux Klan. [KL(AN) + EAGLE]

Klé·ber (klā bɛʀ′), *n.* **Jean Bap·tiste** (zhäɴ bɑ tēst′), 1753–1800, French general.

Klebs′-Löf′fler bacil′lus (klebz′lef′lər; *Ger.* klāps′lœf′lәʀ), the bacterium, *Corynebacterium diphtheriae,* that causes diphtheria. [named after E. *Klebs* (1834–1913) and F. A. J. *Löffler* (1852–1915), German bacteriologists]

Klee (klā), *n.* **Paul** (poul), 1879–1940, Swiss painter and etcher.

Kleen·ex (klē′neks), *n.* *Trademark.* a soft, disposable paper tissue, for use esp. as a handkerchief.

kleig′ light′ (klēg). See **klieg light.**

Klein (klīn), *n.* **Fe·lix** (fē′liks; *Ger.* fā′liks), 1849–1925, German mathematician.

Klein′ bot′tle, *Geom.* a one-sided figure consisting of a tapered tube the narrow end of which is bent back, run through the side of the tube, and flared to join the wide end, thereby allowing any two points on the figure to be joined by an unbroken line. [named after F. KLEIN]

Kleist (klīst), *n.* **(Bernd) Hein·rich (Wil·helm) von** (bɛʀnt hīn′ʀiкн vil′helm fən), 1777–1811, German poet, dramatist, and story writer.

Klem·pe·rer (klem′pər ər), *n.* **Otto,** 1885–1973, German orchestra conductor and composer.

klepht (kleft), *n.* a Greek or Albanian brigand, exalted in the war of Greek independence as a patriotic robber; guerrilla. [< ModGk *klḗpht(ēs),* var. of Gk *kléptēs* thief, rogue] —**kleph′tic,** *adj.*

klep·to·ma·ni·a (klep′tə mā′nē ə, -mān′yə), *n.* *Psychol.* an irresistible impulse to steal, stemming from emotional disturbance. Also, **cleptomania.** [*klepto-* (repr. Gk *kléptēs* thief) + -MANIA]

klep·to·ma·ni·ac (klep′tə mā′nē ak′), *n.* *Psychol.* a person who has kleptomania. Also, **cleptomaniac.** [KLEPTOMANI(A) + -AC]

klieg′ light′ (klēg), a powerful floodlight with an arc-light source, used esp. in motion-picture studios. [named after J. H. *Kliegl* (1869–1959) and his brother Anton, German-born American inventors]

Klimt (klimt), *n.* **Gus·tav** (gōōs′täf), 1862-1918, Austrian painter.

klip·spring·er (klip′spring′ər), *n.* a small, active African antelope, *Oreotragus oreotragus,* of mountainous regions from the Cape of Good Hope to Ethiopia. [< SAfrD: lit., rock-springer]

Klon·dike (klon′dīk), *n.* **1.** a region of the Yukon territory in NW Canada: gold rush 1897–98. **2.** a river in this region, flowing into the Yukon. 90 mi. long. **3.** (*l.c.*) *Cards.* a variety of solitaire.

klong (klông, klong), *n.* (in Thailand) a canal: *the klongs of Bangkok.* [< Thai]

kloof (klōōf), *n.* (in Africa) a deep glen; ravine. [< SAfrD; akin to CLEAVE[2]]

Klop·stock (klôp′shtôk′), *n.* **Frie·drich Gott·lieb** (fʀē′dʀiкн gôt′lēp), 1724–1803, German poet.

klutz (kluts), *n.* *Slang.* **1.** a clumsy, awkward person. **2.** a stupid or foolish person; blockhead. [< G *Klotz,* lit., block of wood; akin to CLOT] —**klutz′y,** *adj.*

Klys·tron (klis′tron, klī′strən), *n.* *Trademark.* a specialized vacuum tube used for the generation and amplification of high-frequency currents.

km., *Metric System.* kilometer; kilometers. Also, **km**

k-me·son (kā′mē′son, -mes′on), *n.* *Physics.* a meson having a mass approximately half that of a proton, existing either with zero charge or with positive or negative charge equal in magnitude to that of an electron. Also, **K-me′son.** Also called **kaon.**

kmole, kilomole; kilomoles.

km/sec, kilometers per second.

kn, knot; knots.

kn., kronen.

knack (nak), *n.* a talent or aptitude: *He had a knack for saying the right thing when necessary.* [ME *knack* trick, perh. same word as *knak* sharp sounding blow, rap, cracking noise; imit.] —**Syn. 1.** aptness, facility, dexterity.

knack·er (nak′ər), *n.* *Brit.* **1.** a person who buys animal carcasses or useless livestock for a rendering works. **2.** a person who buys and dismembers old houses, ships, etc., to salvage usable parts, selling the rest as scrap. [*knack* (< Scand; cf. Icel *hnakkr* nape of the neck, saddle) + -ER[1]]

knack·wurst (nok′wûrst, -wōōrst), *n.* a short, thick, highly seasoned sausage. Also, **knockwurst.** [< G = *knacke(n)* (to) crack, break + *Wurst* sausage. Cf. KNACK]

knap[1] (nap), *n.* *Dial.* a crest or summit of a small hill. [ME; OE *cnæpp* top, summit; c. Icel *knappr* knob]

knap[2] (nap), *v.i., v.t.,* **knapped, knap·ping.** *Chiefly Brit. Dial.* **1.** to strike smartly; rap. **2.** to break off abruptly. **3.** to chip or become chipped, as a flint or stone. **4.** to bite suddenly or quickly. [late ME; c. D *knap* (n.), *knappen* (v.) crack; orig. imit.] —**knap′per,** *n.*

knap·sack (nap′sak′), *n.* a leather or canvas case for clothes and other supplies, carried on the back by soldiers, hikers, and the like. [< LG *knappsack,* lit., bitesack = *knapp* a bite (of food) + *sack* SACK[1]; cf. dial. E *knap* to snap up, eat greedily]

knap·weed (nap′wēd′), *n.* any composite plant of the genus *Centaurea,* esp. the perennial, weedy *C. nigra,* having rose-purple flowers set on a dark-colored, knoblike involucre. [late ME *knopwed.* See KNOP, WEED[1]]

knar (när), *n.* a knot on a tree or in wood. [ME *knarre;* c. D *knar,* LG *knarre*] —**knarred, knar′ry,** *adj.*

knave (nāv), *n.* **1.** an unprincipled or dishonest person. **2.** *Cards.* jack[1] (def. 2). **3.** *Archaic.* a male servant or man of humble position. [ME; OE *cnafa;* c. G *Knabe* boy; akin to Icel *knapi* page, boy]
—**Syn. 1.** blackguard, villain, scamp, scapegrace. KNAVE, RASCAL, ROGUE, SCOUNDREL are disparaging terms applied to persons considered base, dishonest, or worthless. KNAVE, which formerly meant merely a boy or servant, in modern use emphasizes baseness of nature and intention: *a swindling knave.* RASCAL suggests shrewdness and trickery in dishonesty: *a plausible rascal.* A ROGUE is a worthless fellow who sometimes preys extensively upon the community by fraud: *photographs of criminals in a rogues' gallery.* A SCOUNDREL is a blackguard and rogue of the worst sort: *a thorough scoundrel.* RASCAL and ROGUE are often used affectionately or humorously (*an entertaining rascal; a saucy rogue*), but KNAVE and SCOUNDREL are not. —**Ant. 1.** hero.

knav·er·y (nā′və rē), *n., pl.* **-er·ies** for 2. **1.** action or practice characteristic of a knave; trickery. **2.** a knavish act or practice.

knav·ish (nā′vish), *adj.* like or befitting a knave; dishonest. —**knav′ish·ly,** *adv.* —**knav′ish·ness,** *n.*

knead (nēd), *v.t.* **1.** to work (dough, clay, etc.) into a uniform mixture by pressing, folding, and stretching. **2.** to manipulate by similar movements, as the body in a massage. **3.** to make by kneading. [ME *knede(n),* OE *cnedan;* c. G *kneten,* D *kneden*] —**knead′er,** *n.*

knee (nē), *n., v.,* **kneed, knee·ing.** —*n.* **1.** *Anat.* the joint of the human leg that allows for movement between the femur and tibia and is protected by the patella. **2.** the part of the leg around this joint. **3.** the corresponding joint or region in the hind leg of a quadruped; stifle. **4.** a joint or region likened to this but not anatomically homologous with it, as the tarsal joint of a bird, the carpal joint in the forelimb of a horse, etc. **5.** the part of a garment covering the knee. **6.** something resembling a bent knee, esp. a rigid or braced angle between two framing members. —*v.t.* **7.** to strike or touch with the knee. —*v.i.* **8.** *Obs.* to genuflect; kneel. [ME *cneo,* OE *cnēo(w);* c. G, D *knie,* Icel *knē,* Goth *kniu,* L *genu,* Gk *gōny,* Skt *jānu* knee]

knee′ ac′tion, *Auto.* a form of suspension for the front wheels of a vehicle permitting each wheel to rise and fall independent of the other.

knee′ bend′, a physical exercise in which a person starts from an erect position, moves to a squatting position, and returns to the original position without using the hands to support the body.

knee′ breech′es, breeches (def. 1).

knee·cap (nē′kap′), *n.* the patella.

knee-deep (nē′dēp′), *adj.* **1.** so deep as to reach the knees: *knee-deep mud.* **2.** submerged or covered by something having such depth: *They were knee-deep in water.* **3.** embroiled; involved.

knee-high (nē′hī′), *adj.* as high as the knees.

knee·hole (nē′hōl′), *n.* a space for the knees, as under a desk.

knee′ jerk′, a reflex extension of the leg, resulting from a sharp tap on the patellar tendon.

knee-jerk (nē′jûrk′), *adj. Informal.* (used derogatively) responding in an automatic way without questioning: *a knee-jerk liberal.* Also, **knee′jerk′.**

kneel (nēl), *v.i.,* **knelt** or **kneeled, kneel·ing.** to fall or rest on the knees or a knee. [ME *knele(n),* OE *cnēowlian* (c. LG *knelen,* D *knielen*). See KNEE, -LE] —**kneel′er,** *n.*

knee·pad (nē′pad′), *n.* a pad to protect the knee.

knee·pan (nē′pan′), *n.* the kneecap or patella.

knell (nel), *n.* **1.** the sound made by a bell rung slowly for a death or a funeral. **2.** a sound or sign announcing the death of a person or the end, failure, etc., of something: *the knell of parting day.* **3.** any mournful sound. —*v.i.* **4.** to sound, as a bell, esp. a funeral bell. **5.** to give forth a mournful, ominous, or warning sound. —*v.t.* **6.** to proclaim or summon by or as by a bell. [(n.) ME *knel,* OE *cynll;* akin to D *knal* bang, G *Knall* explosion; (v.) ME *knell(en), knyllen,* OE *cynllan;* c. Icel *knylla* to beat, strike]

knelt (nelt), *v.* a pt. and pp. of **kneel.**

Knes·set (knes′et), *n.* the parliament of Israel. Also, **Knes·seth** (knes′et). [< Heb: lit., gathering]

knew (no͞o, nyo͞o), *v.* pt. of **know.**

Knick·er·bock·er (nik′ər bok′ər), *n.* **1.** a descendant of the Dutch settlers of New York. **2.** any New Yorker. [generalized from Diedrich *Knickerbocker,* fictitious author of Washington Irving's *History of New York*]

knick·ers (nik′ərz), *n.* (*construed as pl.*) loosely fitting short breeches gathered in at the knee. Also, **knick·er·bock·ers** (nik′ər bok′ərz). [shortened form of *knickerbockers*]

knick·knack (nik′nak′), *n.* **1.** a pleasing trifle; a trinket or gimcrack. **2.** a bit of bric-à-brac. Also, **nicknack.** [gradational compound based on KNACK in obs. sense of toy] —**knick′knacked′,** *adj.* —**knick′knack′y,** *adj.*

knife (nīf), *n., pl.* **knives** (nīvz), *v.,* **knifed, knif·ing.** —*n.* **1.** an instrument for cutting, consisting essentially of a thin, sharp-edged, metal blade fitted with a handle. **2.** a knifelike weapon; dagger; short sword. **3.** any blade for cutting, as in a tool or machine. **4. under the knife,** undergoing surgery; undergoing an operation. —*v.t.* **5.** to cut, stab, etc., with a knife. **6.** to attempt to defeat in an underhanded way. —*v.i.* **7.** to move or cleave through something with or as with a knife. [ME *knif,* OE *cnīf;* c. Icel *knīfr,* D *knijf,* G *Kneif*] —**knife′like′,** *adj.* —**knif′er,** *n.*

knife′ edge′, **1.** the cutting edge of a knife. **2.** anything very sharp. **3.** a wedge on the fine edge of which a scale beam, pendulum, or the like, oscillates.

knight (nīt), *n.* **1.** *Medieval Hist.* **a.** a mounted soldier serving under a feudal superior. **b.** a man, usually of noble birth, who after an apprenticeship as page and squire was raised to honorable military rank and bound to chivalrous conduct. **2.** any person of a rank similar to that of the medieval knight. **3.** a man upon whom a certain nonhereditary dignity, corresponding to that of the medieval knight, is conferred by a sovereign because of personal merit or for services rendered to the country. In the British Empire he holds the rank next below that of a baronet, and the title *Sir* is prefixed to the Christian name, as in *Sir John Smith.* **4.** *Chess.* a piece shaped like a horse's head, moved two squares vertically and one square horizontally or two squares horizontally and one vertically. **5.** a member of any order or association of men bearing the name of *Knights.* —*v.t.* **6.** to dub or create (a man) a knight. [ME; OE *cniht* boy, manservant; c. G, D *knecht* servant]

knight′ bach′elor, *pl.* **knights bachelors, knights bachelor.** bachelor (def. 3).

knight′ banneret′, *pl.* **knights bannerets.** banneret[1] (def. 2).

knight-er·rant (nīt′er′ənt), *n., pl.* **knights-er·rant.** *Hist.* a knight who traveled in search of adventures, to exhibit military skill, etc. [ME]

knight-er·rant·ry (nīt′er′ən trē), *n., pl.* **-er·rant·ries** for 2. **1.** the behavior, vocation, or character of a knight-errant or of knights-errant. **2.** quixotic conduct or action.

knight·head (nīt′hed′), *n. Naut.* either of a pair of upright members flanking and securing the bowsprit of a vessel at the bow, often used as mooring bitts.

knight·hood (nīt′ho͝od), *n.* **1.** the rank, dignity, or vocation of a knight. **2.** knightly character or qualities. **3.** the body of knights. [ME *knighthod,* OE *cnihthād*]

knight·ly (nīt′lē), *adj.* **1.** of or belonging to a knight: *knightly armor.* **2.** characteristic of a knight; noble and courageous: *knightly deeds.* **3.** composed of knights. —*adv.* **4.** in a manner befitting a knight. [ME; OE *cnihtlīc*] —**knight′li·ness,** *n.*

Knights′ Hos′pitalers. See under **Hospitaler** (def. 1).

Knights′ of Colum′bus, an international fraternal and benevolent organization of Roman Catholic men, founded in 1882.

Knights′ of La′bor, a workingmen's organization formed in 1869 to defend the interests of labor.

Knights′ of Mal′ta, the order of Hospitalers.

Knights′ of Pyth′ias, a fraternal order founded in Washington, D.C., in 1864.

Knights′ of St. John′ of Jeru′salem. See under **Hospitaler** (def. 1).

Knights′ of the Round′ Ta′ble, *Arthurian Romance.* the order of knights created by King Arthur.

Knights′ Tem′plars, **1.** a Masonic order in the U.S. claiming descent from the medieval order of Templars. **2.** a pl. of **Knight Templar.**

Knight′ Tem′plar, *pl.* **Knights Templars, Knights Templar.** Templar.

knish (knish), *n. Jewish Cookery.* a fried or baked turnover or roll of dough with a filling, as of meat, kasha, or potato. [< Yiddish < Pol *knysz;* c. Russ *knish* kind of cake]

knit (nit), *v.,* **knit·ted** or **knit, knit·ting.** —*v.t.* **1.** to make (a garment, fabric, etc.) by joining loops of yarn, either by hand with knitting needles or by machine. **2.** to join closely and firmly together, as members or parts. **3.** to contract into folds or wrinkles: *to knit the brow.* —*v.i.* **4.** to become closely and firmly joined together; grow together. **5.** to contract into folds or wrinkles, as the brow. [ME *knitte,* OE *cnytt(an)* (to) tie; c. G *knütten;* see KNOT[1]] —**knit′ta·ble,** *adj.* —**knit′ter,** *n.*

knit·ting (nit′ing), *n.* **1.** the act of a person or thing that knits. **2.** knitted work.

knit′ting nee′dle, a straight, slender rod tapered at one or both ends for use in knitting by hand.

knit·wear (nit′wâr′), *n.* clothing made of knitted fabric.

knives (nīvz), *n.* pl. of **knife.**

knob (nob), *n.* **1.** a projecting part, usually rounded, forming the handle of a door, drawer, or the like. **2.** a rounded lump or protuberance on the surface or at the end of something, as a knot on a tree trunk. **3.** a rounded hill or mountain. [ME *knobbe* < MLG] —**knobbed,** *adj.* —**knob′like′,** *adj.*

knob·by (nob′ē), *adj.,* **-bi·er, -bi·est.** **1.** full of rounded lumps or protuberances. **2.** like a lump or protuberance. —**knob′bi·ness,** *n.*

knob·ker·rie (nob′ker′ē), *n.* a short, heavy stick or club with a knob on one end, used by South African natives for striking and throwing. [< SAfrD *knopkiri* = *knop* KNOB + Hottentot *kiri, kirri* stick, club]

knock (nok), *v.i.* **1.** to strike a sounding blow, as in seeking admittance, calling attention, or giving a signal. **2.** to make a pounding or rattling noise: *The engine of our car is knocking badly.* **3.** *Informal.* to engage in trivial or carping criticism. **4.** to strike in collision; bump: *He knocked into a table.* —*v.t.* **5.** to give a sounding or forcible blow to; hit; strike; beat. **6.** to drive, force, or render by striking. **7.** to make by striking: *to knock a hole in the door.* **8.** to strike (a thing) against something else. **9.** *Informal.* to criticize, esp. in a carping manner. **10.** *Brit. Slang.* to astound; impress greatly. **11. knock around** or **about,** *Slang.* **a.** to wander aimlessly. **b.** to loiter; loaf. **c.** to mistreat (someone), esp. physically. **12. knock down, a.** to signify the sale of an article at auction by a blow of the hammer or mallet. **b.** *Com.* to take apart for facility in handling. **c.** *Slang.* to steal or embezzle (money). **d.** *Slang.* to receive, as a salary; earn. **e.** *Informal.* to lower the price of; reduce. **13. knock it off,** *Slang.* stop it (usually used to halt noise or a commotion, fight, or argument). **14. knock off,** *Slang.* **a.** to cease activity, esp. work. **b.** to dispose of; finish. **c.** to murder; kill. **d.** to get rid of; reduce. **e.** to disable or defeat. **15. knock (oneself) out,** to exert (oneself) to the limit; exhaust (oneself). **16. knock out, a.** to defeat (an opponent) in a boxing match by striking him a blow that makes him unable to rise within the specified time. **b.** to damage or destroy. **c.** to knock (a pitcher) out of the box. **17. knock out of the box,** *Baseball.* to cause a pitcher to be removed from the box because he has permitted too many hits. Also, **knock out. 18. knock over, a.** to strike (someone or something) down; fell. **b.** *Slang.* to rob: *He knocked over five banks.* **19. knock together,** to make or construct in a hurry or with little attention to detail. **20. knock up, a.** *Brit. Informal.* to wake up; rouse. **b.** *U.S. Slang.* to make pregnant. **—*n.* 21.** the act or sound of knocking. **22.** a rap, as at a door. **23.** a blow or thump. **24.** *Informal.* an adverse criticism. **25.** the noise resulting from incorrect functioning of some part of an internal-combustion engine. **26.** *Cricket.* an innings. [ME *knokke(n),* var. of *knoken,* OE *cnocian, cnucian;* c. Icel *knoka* to thump, knock] **—knock′less,** *adj.* **—Syn. 1.** See **strike.**

knock·a·bout (nok′ə bout′), *n.* **1.** *Naut.* any of various fore-and-aft-rigged sailing vessels having a single jib bent to a stay from the stemhead, no bowsprit being used: usually rigged as a sloop. **2.** something designed or suitable for rough or casual use, wear, etc. **—*adj.* 3.** suitable for rough use, as a garment. **4.** characterized by knocking about; rough; boisterous.

knock·down (nok′doun′), *adj.* **1.** capable of knocking something down; overwhelming: *a knockdown blow.* **2.** constructed in separate parts that can readily be taken apart for easy storage, shipping, etc. **—*n.* 3.** a knockdown object. **4.** the act of knocking down, esp. by a blow. **5.** something that fells or overwhelms. **6.** reduction or lowering, as in price or number.

knock·er (nok′ər), *n.* **1.** a person or thing that knocks. **2.** a hinged knob, bar, etc., on a door, for use in knocking. **3.** *Slang (vulgar).* a female breast. **4. on the knocker,** *Brit. Slang.* canvassing or selling door-to-door. [ME]

knock-knee (nok′nē′), *n.* **1.** inward curvature of the legs at the knees. **2. knock-knees,** knees having such curvature. **—knock′-kneed′,** *adj.*

knock·out (nok′out′), *n.* **1.** the act of knocking out. **2.** the state or fact of being knocked out. **3.** a knockout blow. **4.** *Informal.* a person or thing overwhelmingly successful or attractive. **—*adj.* 5.** successful in knocking out.

knock·wurst (nok′wûrst, -wŏŏrst), *n.* knackwurst.

knoll[1] (nōl), *n.* a small, rounded hill or eminence; hillock. [ME *cnol,* OE *cnoll;* c. Norw *knoll* hillock; akin to D *knol* turnip, Icel *knollur,* G *Knollen,* Dan *knold* tuber] **—knoll′y,** *adj.*

knoll[2] (nōl), *Archaic.* **—*v.t.* 1.** to ring or toll a bell for; announce by tolling. **2.** to ring or toll (a bell). **—*v.i.* 3.** to sound, as a bell; ring. **4.** to sound a knell. **—*n.* 5.** a stroke of a bell in ringing or tolling. [ME; var. of KNELL] **—knoll′er,** *n.*

knop (nop), *n.* a small knob or similar rounded protuberance. [ME; OE *cnop;* c. D *knop,* G *Knopf*]

Knos·sos (nos′əs, knos′-), *n.* a ruined city on N central Crete; capital of the ancient Minoan civilization. Also, **Cnossus, Gnossus. —Knos·si·an** (nos′ē ən), *adj.*

knot[1] (not), *n., v.,* **knot·ted, knot·ting. —*n.* 1.** an interlacing of a cord, rope, or the like, drawn tight into a knob or lump, for fastening two cords together or a cord to something else. **2.** a piece of ribbon or similar material tied or folded upon itself and used or worn as an ornament. **3.** a group or cluster of persons or things. **4.** *Anat., Zool.* a protuberance or swelling on or in a part or process, as in a muscle. **5.** *Bot.* a protuberance or excrescence on a stem, branch, or root, esp. a swollen node or joint in a stem. **6.** the hard, cross-grained mass of wood at the place where a branch joins the trunk of a tree. **7.** the part of this mass showing in a piece of lumber. **8.** any of various diseases of trees characterized by the formation of an excrescence, knob, or gnarl. **9.** *Naut.* **a.** a unit of speed equal to one nautical mile or about 1.15 statute miles per hour: *The cruising speed of this ship is 18 knots.* **b.** a unit of 47 feet 3 inches on a log line, marked off by knots. **c.** (loosely) a nautical mile. **10.** an intricate or difficult matter; complicated problem. **11.** a bond or tie. **—*v.t.* 12.** to tie in a knot or knots; form a knot or knots in. **13.** to secure or fasten by a knot. **14.** to form protuberances, bosses, or knobs in; make knotty. **—*v.i.* 15.** to become tied or tangled in a knot or knots. **16.** to form knots or joints. [ME *knot(te),* OE *cnotta;* c. D *knot,* G *knoten* to KNIT] **—knot′less,** *adj.* **—knot′like′,** *adj.* **—Syn. 3.** band, crew, gang, crowd. **4, 5.** lump, knob. **10.** puzzle, conundrum.

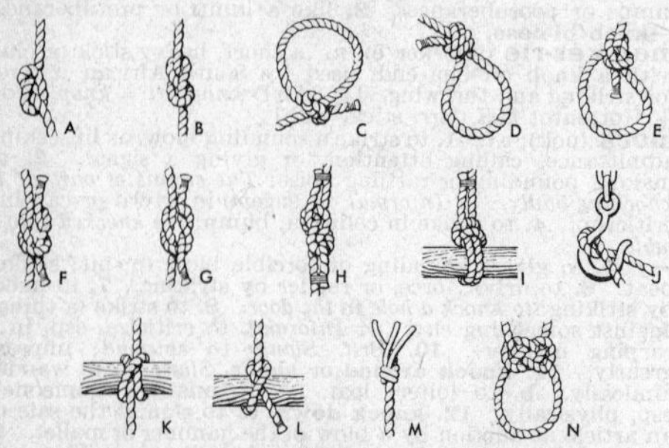

Knots
A, Overhand knot; B, Figure of eight; C, Slipknot; D, Loop knot; E, Bowline; F, Square knot; G, Granny knot; H, Carrick bend; I, Fisherman's bend; J, Blackwall hitch; K, Clove hitch; L, Half hitch; M, Matthew Walker; N, Prolonge knot

knot[2] (not), *n.* either of two large sandpipers, *Calidris canatus* or *C. tenuirostris,* that breed in the Arctic and winter in the Southern Hemisphere. [?]

knot·grass (not′gras′, -gräs′), *n.* **1.** a polygonaceous weed, *Polygonum aviculare,* having nodes in its stems. **2.** any of certain other species of this genus.

knot·hole (not′hōl′), *n.* a hole in a board or plank formed by the falling out of a knot or a portion of a knot.

knot·ted (not′id), *adj.* **1.** having knots; knotty. **2.** *Bot.* having many nodes or nodelike swellings; gnarled. **3.** *Zool.* having one or more swellings; nodose. [ME *cnotted*]

knot·ter (not′ər), *n.* a person or thing that ties or removes knots.

knot·ty (not′ē), *adj.,* **-ti·er, -ti·est. 1.** having knots; full of knots. **2.** involved, intricate, or difficult: *a knotty problem.* [late ME; early ME *cnotti*] **—knot′ti·ly,** *adv.* **—knot′ti·ness,** *n.* **—Syn. 2.** complex, complicated.

knot′ty rhat′any. See under **rhatany** (def. 1).

knot·weed (not′wēd′), *n.* any of several knotty-stemmed, polygonaceous plants of the genus, *Polygonum,* as *P. maritimum,* a glaucous herb of sandy soils.

know (nō), *v.,* **knew, known, know·ing,** *n.* **—*v.t.* 1.** to perceive or understand clearly and with certainty. **2.** to have fixed in the mind or memory: *to know a poem by heart.* **3.** to be cognizant or aware of; be acquainted with, as by sight, experience, or report: *to know the mayor.* **4.** to understand from experience or attainment (usually fol. by *how* before an infinitive): *to know how to make something.* **5.** to be able to distinguish, as one from another. **6.** *Archaic.* to have sexual intercourse with. **—*v.i.* 7.** to have knowledge, or clear and certain perception, as of fact or truth. **8.** to have information, as about something. **9. know the ropes,** *Informal.* to understand or be familiar with the particulars of a subject or business. **—*n.* 10. in the know,** *Informal.* having inside information. [ME *knowe(n), knawe(n),* OE *gecnāwan;* c. OHG *-cnāhan,* Icel *knā* to know how, can; akin to L *(g)nōvī* I know, Gk *gignṓskein,* etc. See GNOSTIC] **—know′er,** *n.* **—Syn. 1.** KNOW, COMPREHEND, UNDERSTAND imply being aware of meanings. To KNOW is to be aware of something as a fact or truth: *He knows the basic facts of the subject. I know that he agrees with me.* To COMPREHEND is to know something thoroughly and to perceive its relationships to certain other ideas, facts, etc. To UNDERSTAND is to be fully aware not only of the meaning of something but also its implications: *I could comprehend all he said, but did not understand that he was joking.*

know·a·ble (nō′ə bəl), *adj.* capable of being known. **—know′a·bil′i·ty,** *n.*

know-how (nō′hou′), *n.* knowledge of how to do something; faculty or skill for a particular activity.

know·ing (nō′ing), *adj.* **1.** shrewd, sharp, or astute. **2.** affecting or suggesting shrewd knowledge of secret or private information: *a knowing glance.* **3.** having knowledge or information; intelligent; wise. **4.** conscious; intentional; deliberate. [late ME *knawynge* (earlier *knowende, knawande*)] **—know′ing·ly,** *adv.* **—know′ing·ness,** *n.*

know-it-all (nō′it ôl′), *n.* *Informal.* a person who acts as though he alone knows everything.

knowl·edge (nol′ij), *n.* **1.** acquaintance with facts, truths, or principles, as from study or investigation; general erudition. **2.** familiarity or conversance, as with a particular subject or branch of learning. **3.** acquaintance or familiarity gained by sight, experience, or report: *a knowledge of human nature.* **4.** the fact or state of knowing; clear and certain perception of fact or truth. **5.** awareness, as of a fact or circumstance. **6.** that which is or may be known; information. **7.** the body of truths or facts accumulated by mankind in the course of time: *man's knowledge of the moon.* **8.** *Archaic.* sexual intercourse. [ME *knouleche,* OE *cnāwlǣc* acknowledgement = *cnāw(an)* (to) KNOW + *-lǣc,* akin to OE *lāc* play, c. Icel *(-)leikr*] **—Syn. 1.** enlightenment. See **information. 4.** understanding, discernment, comprehension, judgment, wisdom; **6.** lore, science.

knowl·edge·a·ble (nol′i jə bəl), *adj.* possessing knowledge or understanding; intelligent. Also, **knowl′edg·a·ble. —knowl′edge·a·ble·ness, knowl′edg·a·ble·ness,** *n.* **—knowl′edge·a·bly, knowl′edg·a·bly,** *adv.*

known (nōn), *v.* **1.** pp. of **know. —*n.* 2.** a known quantity.

know-noth·ing (nō′nuth′ing), *n.* **1.** an ignorant or totally uninformed person; ignoramus. **2.** an agnostic. **3.** *(caps.) U.S. Hist.* a member of a 19th-century political party opposed to foreigners and Catholics: so called because members professed ignorance of the party's activities. **—*adj.* 4.** grossly ignorant; totally uninformed. **5.** agnostic. **6.** of or pertaining to a political know-nothing. **—know′-noth′ing·ism,** *n.*

known′ quan′tity, *Math.* a quantity whose value is given: in algebra, frequently represented by a letter from the first part of the alphabet, as *a, b,* or *c.*

Knox (noks), *n.* **1. Henry,** 1750–1806, American Revolutionary general: 1st U.S. Secretary of War 1785–94. **2. John,** c1510–72, Scottish religious reformer and historian. **3. Phi·lan·der Chase** (fi lan′dər), 1853–1921, U.S. lawyer and politician: Secretary of State 1909–13. **4. (William) Frank(lin),** 1874–1944, U.S. publisher and government official. **5. Fort.** See **Fort Knox.**

Knox·ville (noks′vil), *n.* a city in E Tennessee, on the Tennessee River. 174,587 (1970).

KNP, *Chess.* king's knight's pawn.

Knt., Knight.

knuck·le (nuk′əl), *n., v.,* **-led, -ling. —*n.* 1.** a joint of a finger, esp. one of the joints at the roots of the fingers. **2.** the rounded prominence of such a joint when the finger is bent. **3.** a joint of meat, consisting of the parts about the carpal or tarsal joint of a quadruped. **4.** an angle or protrusion at the intersection of two members or surfaces, as in the timbers of a ship or in a roof. **5.** See **brass knuckles. 6.** a cylindrical projecting part on a hinge, through which an axis or pin passes; the joint of a hinge. **—*v.t.* 7.** *Marbles.* to shoot (a marble) from the thumb and forefinger. **8. knuckle down, a.** *Informal.* to apply oneself vigorously; become serious. **b.** Also, **knuckle under.** to submit, yield. [ME *knokel* (akin to D *kneukel,* G *Knöchel*), dim. of a word represented by D *knok,* G *Knochen* bone; see -LE] **—knuck′ly,** *adj.*

knuck′le ball′, *Baseball.* a slow pitch delivered by holding the ball between the thumb and the knuckles of the first joints of the first two or three fingers; giving the ball an erratic spin.

knuck·le·bone (nuk′əl bōn′), *n.* **1.** (in man) a bone forming a knuckle of a finger. **2.** (in quadrupeds) a bone homologous with a wrist, ankle, or finger bone of man, or its knobbed end.

knuck·le-dust·er (nuk′əl dus′tər), *n.* See **brass knuckles.**

knuck·le·head (nuk′əl hed′), *n. Informal.* a stupid, bumbling, inept person. —**knuck′le·head′ed,** *adj.*

knuck′le joint′, **1.** a joint forming a knuckle. **2.** *Mach.* a joint between two parts allowing movement in one plane only.

knuck·ler (nuk′lər), *n. Baseball Slang.* See **knuckle ball.**

knur (nûr), *n.* a knotty growth, as on a tree. [ME *knorre, knor;* c. MLG, MD, MHG *knorre*]

knurl (nûrl), *n.* **1.** a small ridge or bead, esp. one of a series, as on the edge of a thumbscrew to assist in obtaining a firm grip. **2.** a knur. —*v.t.* **3.** to make knurls or ridges on. Also, **nurl.** [var. of *knurle.* See KNUR, -LE]

knurled (nûrld), *adj.* **1.** having small ridges on the edge or surface; milled. **2.** having knurls or knots; gnarled.

knurl·y (nûr′lē), *adj.,* **knurl·i·er knurl·i·est.** having knurls or knots; gnarled.

Knut (kə nōōt′, -nyōōt′), *n.* Canute.

K.O., *pl.* **K.O.'s.** *Boxing.* knockout. Also, **k.o., KO**

ko·a·la (kō ä′lə), *n.* a sluggish, tailless, gray, furry, arboreal marsupial, *Phascolarctos cinereus,* of Australia. Also, **coala.** Also called **koa′la bear′.** [< native Austral]

Koalas (Length of adult 2½ ft.)

ko·an (kō′on), *n., pl.* **-ans, -an.** *Zen.* a nonsensical question to a student for which an answer is demanded, the stress of meditation on the question often being illuminating. Cf. **mondo.** [< Jap = *kō* public + *an* proposal, design]

Ko·ba·rid (*Serbo-Croatian.* kô′bä rēd′; *Eng.* kō′bə rēd′), *n.* a village in NW Yugoslavia, formerly in Italy: defeat of the Italians by the Germans and Austrians 1917. Italian, **Caporetto.**

Ko·be (kō′bē; *Jap.* kô′be′), *n.* a seaport on S Honshu, in S Japan. 1,195,152 (1964).

Kö·ben·havn (kœ′bən houn′), *n.* Danish name of **Copenhagen.**

Ko·blenz (kō′blents), *n.* Coblenz.

ko·bold (kō′bold, -bōld), *n.* (in German folklore) **1.** a kind of spirit or goblin, often mischievous, that haunts houses. **2.** a spirit that haunts mines or other underground places. [< G]

Koch (kōkh), *n.* **Ro·bert** (rō′bert), 1843–1910, German bacteriologist and physician: Nobel prize 1905.

Ko·chi (kō′chē; *Jap.* kô′chē′), *n.* a seaport on central Shikoku, in SW Japan. 224,900 (1964).

Ko·da·chrome (kō′də krōm′), *n. Trademark.* **1.** a color photograph. **2.** a process of color photography.

Ko·dak (kō′dak), *n. Trademark.* a portable camera introduced by George Eastman in 1888.

Ko·dá·ly (kō dī′, -dä′ē; *Hung.* kō′dä yə), *n.* **Zol·tán** (zôl′tän), 1882–1967, Hungarian composer.

Ko·di·ak (kō′dē ak′), *n.* **1.** an island in the N Pacific, near the base of the Alaska Peninsula. 100 mi. long. **2.** See **Kodiak bear.**

Ko′diak bear′, a large, brown bear, *Ursus middendorffi,* found along the coast of Alaska and British Columbia, that grows to a length of nine feet. Also, **Kadiak bear.**

Ko·dok (kō′dok), *n.* modern name of **Fashoda.**

kOe, kilo-oersted; kilo-oersteds.

Koest·ler (kest′lər; *Hung.* kœst′ler), *n.* **Ar·thur** (är′thər; *Hung.* or′tōōr), 1905–83, Hungarian novelist.

K. of C., Knights of Columbus.

Koff·ka (kôf′kä), *n.* **Kurt** (kōōrt), 1886–1941, German psychologist in the U.S.

K. of P., Knights of Pythias.

Ko·fu (kô′fōō), *n.* a city on S Honshu, in central Japan. 169,128 (1964).

Ko·hi·ma (kō′hē mä′), *n.* a town in and the capital of Nagaland, in E India. 7200 (1961).

Koh·i·noor (kō′ə nōōr′), *n.* an Indian diamond weighing 106 carats; now part of the British crown jewels. [< Pers: lit., mountain of light]

kohl (kōl), *n.* a powder, as finely powdered antimony sulfide, used in the East to darken the eyelids, eyebrows, etc. [< Ar *koḥl,* var. of *kuḥl.* See ALCOHOL]

Kohl (kōl), *n.* **Hel·mut** (hel′mōōt), born 1930, West German political leader: chancellor since 1982.

Köh·ler (kœ′lər), *n.* **Wolf·gang** (vôlf′gäng), 1887–1967, German psychologist.

kohl·ra·bi (kōl rä′bē, kōl′rä′-), *n., pl.* **-bies.** a brassicaceous plant, *Brassica oleracea gongylodes,* whose stem above ground swells into an edible bulblike formation. [< G < It *cavolrape* (pl. of *cavolrapa,* lit., stalk or cabbage turnip), with G *Kohl* cabbage for It *cavol-.* See COLE, RAPE[2]]

Kohlrabi

Ko·hou·tek (kō hou′tek, -hōō′-), *Astron.* a comet expected to be exceptionally bright but which was actually narrowly visible from earth as it passed around the sun in late 1973 and early 1974. [named after Lubos *Kohoutek* (b. 1935), Czech astronomer.

koi·ne (koi nā′), *n.* **the koine,** an amalgam of Greek dialects that replaced the classical Greek and flourished under the Roman Empire. [< Gk *koinḗ* (*diálektos*) common (dialect); see CENO-[2]]

Ko·kand (ko känt′), *n.* a city in NE Uzbekistan, in the SW Soviet Union in Asia: formerly the center of a powerful khanate. 117,000 (est. 1962).

Ko·ko·mo (kō′kə mō′), *n.* a city in central Indiana. 44,042 (1970).

Ko·ko Nor (kō′kō′ nôr′), **1.** a lake in W China, in Chinghai province. 23 sq. mi. **2.** Chinghai.

Ko·kosch·ka (kō kôsh′kä), *n.* **Os·kar** (ôs′kär), 1886–1980, Austrian painter and dramatist.

kok-sa·ghyz (kōk′sə gēz′), *n.* a dandelion, *Taraxacum kok-saghyz,* of central Asia, having fleshy roots that yield a rubberlike latex. [< Russ *kok-sagyz* < Turkic (Kazak) *kok-sagiz,* lit., root gum]

Ko·ku·ra (kô′kōō rä′), *n.* a seaport in N Kyushu, in SW Japan. 286,474 (1964).

ko·la (kō′lə), *n.* **1.** See **kola nut.** **2.** an extract prepared from it. **3.** the tree producing it. **4.** cola[1]. [appar. var. of Mandingo *kolo*]

Ko·la (kô′lä), *n.* a peninsula in the NW Soviet Union in Europe, between the White and Barents seas. Also called **Ko′la Penin′sula.**

ko′la nut′, a brownish seed, about the size of a chestnut, produced by a sterculiaceous tree, *Cola nitida,* of western tropical Africa, the West Indies, and Brazil, and containing both caffein and theobromine; formerly used in soft drinks.

Ko·lar′ Gold′ Fields′ (kō lär′), a city in SE Mysore, in S India: rich mining district. 146,811 (1961).

Kol·chak (kol chäk′), *n.* **A·le·ksan·dr Va·si·lye·vich** (ä le ksän′dər vä sē′lyə vich), 1874–1920, Russian counterrevolutionary and admiral.

Ko·li·ma (*Russ.* ko li mä′), *n.* Kolyma.

ko·lin·sky (kə lin′skē), *n., pl.* **-skies.** **1.** an Asian mink, *Mustela siberica,* having buff or tawny fur. **2.** the fur of such an animal. [< Russ *kolinski* pertaining to KOLA]

kol·khoz (kol khôz′), *n.* (in the U.S.S.R.) a collective farm. [< Russ = *kol*(*lektivnoe*) COLLECTIVE + *khoz*(*yaistvo*) household, farm]

Köln (kœln), *n.* German name of **Cologne.**

Kol Ni·dre (kôl nē drā′; *Eng.* kōl′ nid′rə, -rā, kôl′), *Judaism.* a liturgical prayer recited on the eve of Yom Kippur. [< Aram *kōl* all + *nidhrē* vows, promises]

Ko·lozs·vár (kô′lôzh vär′), *n.* Hungarian name of **Cluj.**

Kol·we·zi (kōl wez′ē), *n.* a city in S Zaïre. 47,772 (est. 1958).

Ko·ly·ma (ko li mä′), *n.* a river in the NE Soviet Union in Asia, flowing NE to the Arctic Ocean. 1000 mi. long. Also, **Kolima.**

Kolyma′ Range′, a mountain range in NE Siberia.

Ko·mi (kō′mē), *n.* Zyrian.

Ko′mi Auton′omous So′viet So′cialist Repub′lic, an administrative division of the RSFSR, in the NE Soviet Union in Europe. 804,000 (1959); 145,221 sq. mi. *Cap.:* Syktyvkar.

Kom·in·tern (kom′in tûrn′), *n.* Comintern.

Kom·mu·narsk (ko mōō närsk′), *n.* a city in the E Ukraine, in the Soviet Union. 110,000 (est. 1962).

Ko·mo′do drag′on (kə mō′dō), a monitor lizard, *Varanus komodoensis,* of certain Indonesian islands E of Java, that grows to a length of 10 feet: the largest lizard in the world. Also called **dragon lizard, giant lizard, Komo′do liz′ard.** [after *Komodo,* Indonesian island, its main habitat]

Kom·so·molsk (kom so môlsk′), *n.* a city in the E RSFSR, in the E Soviet Union in Asia, on the Amur River. 192,000 (est. 1962).

Ko·na·kri (*Fr.* kô na krē′), *n.* Conakry.

Kon·ia (kôn′yä), *n.* Konya.

Kö·nig·grätz (*Ger.* kœ′nikh grets′), *n.* a town in NW Czechoslovakia, on the Elbe River: Austrians defeated by Prussians in Battle of Sadowa 1866. 55,136 (1961). Czech, **Hradec Králové.**

Kö·nigs·berg (kœ′nikhs berk′; *Eng.* kōō′nigz bûrg′), *n.* German name of **Kaliningrad.**

Kö·nigs·hüt·te (kœ′nikhs hʏ′tə), *n.* German name of **Chorzów.**

ko·ni·ol·o·gy (kō′nē ol′ə jē), *n.* the study of atmospheric dust and other impurities suspended in the air, as germs, pollen, etc. Also, **coniology.** [< Gk *kóni*(*s*) dust + -o- + -LOGY]

Kon·stanz (kôn′stänts), *n.* German name of **Constance.**

Kon·ya (kôn′yä), *n.* a city in S Turkey, S of Ankara. 157,801 (1965). Also, **Konia.** Ancient, **Iconium.**

koo·doo (kōō′dōō), *n., pl.* **-doos.** kudu.

kook (kōōk), *n. Slang.* **1.** an unusual, peculiar, or foolish person. **2.** an insane person. [? alter. of CUCKOO]

kook·a·bur·ra (kŏŏk′ə bûr′ə), *n.* an Australian kingfisher, *Dacelo gigas,* having a loud, harsh cry that resembles laughter. Also called **laughing jackass.** [< native Austral]

kook·y (kōō′kē), *adj.,* **kook·i·er, kook·i·est.** *Slang.* of or pertaining to a kook. Also, **kook′ie.** —**kook′i·ness,** *n.*

koo·ra·jong (kŏŏr′ə jông′), *n.* kurrajong.

Koo·te·nay (kōōt′ənā′), *n.* a river flowing from SW Canada through NW Montana and N Idaho, swinging back into Canada to the Columbia River. 400 mi. long. Also, **Koo′te·nai′, Kutenai.**

Koo′tenay Lake′, a lake in W Canada, in S British Columbia. 64 mi. long.

kop (kop), *n.* (in South Africa) a hill. [< SAfrD: lit., head, hence high or top part. See COP[2]]

ko·peck (kō′pek), *n.* an aluminum-bronze coin of the Soviet Union, the 100th part of a ruble. Also, **ko′pek, copeck.** [< Russ *kopeika* = *kopyó* lance, spear + *-ka* dim. suffix; so called from bearing the figure of the Czar holding a lance]

Ko·peisk (ko pāsk′), *n.* a city in the SW RSFSR, in the W Soviet Union in Asia, near the Urals. 168,000 (est. 1962). Also, **Ko·peysk′.**

koph (kōf; *Heb.* kôf), *n.* the 19th letter of the Hebrew alphabet. [< Heb *qoph*] Also, **qoph.**

kop·je (kop′ē), *n.* (in South Africa) a small hill. [< SAfrD]

kop·pa (kop′ə), *n.* a letter ( ) of some early Greek alphabets, occurring between pi and rho and equivalent to Latin . It was later superseded by kappa except for its use as a numeral for 90. [< Gk < Sem; akin to Heb QOPH, KOPH]

kor (kōr, kôr), *n.* homer[2]. [< Heb]

Ko·ran (kō rän′, -ran′, kô-), *n.* the sacred text of Islam, believed to have been dictated to Muhammad by Gabriel and regarded by Muslims as the foundation of religion, law, culture, and politics. Also, **Quran.** [< Ar *qur'ān* book, reading, akin to *qara'a* to read, recite] —**Ko·ran·ic** (kō ran′ik, kō-), *adj.*

Kor·do·fan (kôr′dō fän′), *n.* a province in the central Sudan. 2,051,616 (est. 1961); ab. 147,000 sq. mi. *Cap.:* El Obeid.

Ko·re·a (kō rē′ə, kô-), *n.* **1.** Japanese, **Chosen.** a former country in E Asia, on a peninsula SE of Manchuria and between the Sea of Japan and the Yellow Sea: a kingdom prior to 1910; under Japanese rule 1910–45; now divided at 38° N into North Korea and South Korea. **2. Democratic People's Republic of,** official name of **North Korea. 3. Republic of,** official name of **South Korea.**

Ko·re·an (kō rē′ən, kô-), *adj.* **1.** of or pertaining to Korea, its inhabitants, or their language. **—*n.* 2.** a native of Korea. **3.** the language of Korea.

Kore′an War′, the war, 1950–53, between North Korea, aided by Communist China, and South Korea, aided by the U.S. and other United Nations members forming a United Nations armed force. Also called **Kore′an con′flict.**

Kore′a Strait′, a strait between Korea and Japan, connecting the Sea of Japan and the East China Sea. 120 mi. long.

Kort·rijk (kôrt′rīk), Flemish name of **Courtrai.**

ko·ru·na (kôr′ə nä′), *n., pl.* **ko·ru·ny** (kôr′ə nē), **ko·run** (kô′ro͞on), **ko·ru·nas.** an aluminum bronze coin and monetary unit of Czechoslovakia, equal to 100 halers. *Abbr.:* Kč. [< Czech < L *corōna* a crown, wreath; see CORONA]

Ko·rzyb·ski (kôr zip′skē; *Pol.* kô zhip′skē), *n.* **Alfred (Hab·dank Skar·bek)** (hab′dängk skär′bek; *Pol.* häp′-dängk skär′bek), 1879–1950, U.S. writer on general semantics, born in Poland.

kos (kōs), *n., pl.* **kos.** (in India) a unit of land distance of various lengths from 1 to 3 miles. [< Hindi << Skt *krośa*]

Kos (kos, kôs), *n.* one of the Greek Dodecanese Islands in the SE Aegean Sea, off the SW coast of Turkey. 18,197 (1962); 111 sq. mi. Also, **Cos.** Italian, **Coo.**

Kos·ci·us·ko (kos′ē us′kō; *for 1 also Pol.* kôsh cho͝osh′kô), *n.* **1. Thaddeus** (*Tadeusz Andrzej Bonawentura Kosciuszko*), 1746–1817, Polish patriot: general in the American Revolutionary army. **2. Mount,** the highest mountain in Australia, in SE New South Wales. 7316 ft.

ko·sher (kō′shər), *adj.* **1.** *Judaism.* **a.** fit or allowed to be eaten or used, according to the dietary or ceremonial laws: *kosher meat.* **b.** adhering to these laws: *a kosher restaurant.* **2.** *Informal.* **a.** genuine; authentic. **b.** proper; legitimate. **—*v.t.* 3.** *Judaism.* to make kosher. Also, **kasher.** [< Yiddish < Heb *kāshēr* right, fit]

Ko·shu (kō′sho͞o′), *n.* Japanese name of **Kwangju.**

Ko·ši·ce (kô′shi tse), *n.* a city in SE Slovakia, in SE Czechoslovakia. 93,864 (est. 1963). Hungarian, **Kassa.**

Kos·suth (kos′o͞oth; *Hung.* kô′sho͝ot), *n.* **1. Fer·enc** (fer′ents), 1841–1914, Hungarian statesman. **2.** his father, **La·jos** (lo′yôsh), 1802–94, Hungarian patriot, statesman, and writer.

Kos·ti (kôs′tē), *n.* a city in E Sudan, on the White Nile. 30,000 (est. 1964).

Ko·stro·ma (ko stro mä′), *n.* a city in the W RSFSR, in the central Soviet Union in Europe, NE of Moscow, on the Volga. 198,000 (est. 1964).

Ko·sy·gin (ko sē′gin), *n.* **A·lek·sei Ni·ko·la·ye·vich** (ä lek sā′ ni ko lä′yə vich), 1904–80, Russian politician: premier of the U.S.S.R. 1964–80.

Ko·ta·ba·ru (kō′tə bä′ro͞o), *n.* a city in and the capital of West Irian, on the NE coast, in Indonesia. 14,462 (est. 1961). Formerly, **Hollandia.**

Ko·ta Bha·ru (kō′tə bär′o͞o), a seaport in N Kelantan, in Malaysia, on the SE Malay Peninsula. 38,103 (1957). Also, **Ko′ta Bah′ru.**

Ko·ta Kin·a·ba·lu (ko′tə kin′ə bə lo͞o′), a seaport in and the capital of Sabah, in the NW part. 21,467 (1960). Formerly, **Jesselton.**

ko·to (kō′tō; *Jap.* kô′tô′), *n., pl.* **-tos,** *Jap.* **-to.** a Japanese musical instrument having numerous strings that are stretched over a convex wooden sounding board and are plucked with three plectra, worn on the right thumb, index finger, and middle finger. [< Jap]

ko·tow (kō′tou′, -tou′), *v.i., n.* kowtow. **—ko′tow′er,** *n.*

Kot·ze·bue (kôt′sə bo͞o′), *n.* **Au·gust Frie·drich Fer·di·nand von** (ou′go͝ost frē′drikh fer′di nänt′ fən), 1761–1819, German dramatist.

kou·mis (ko͞o′mis), *n.* kumiss. Also, **kou′miss, kou′myss.**

Kous·se·vitz·ky (ko͞o′sə vit′skē), *n.* **Serge** (sârzh), (*Sergei Alexandrovich Koussevitsky*), 1874–1951, Russian orchestra conductor in the U.S.

Kov·no (kôv′no), *n.* Russian name of **Kaunas.**

Kov·rov (kov rôf′), *n.* a city in the W RSFSR, in the central Soviet Union in Europe, ENE of Moscow. 105,000 (est. 1962).

Ko·weit (kō wāt′), *n.* Kuwait.

Kow·loon (kou′lo͞on′), *n.* **1.** a peninsula in SE China, opposite Hong Kong island: a part of the Hong Kong colony. 1,475,494 (1961); 3.75 sq. mi. **2.** a seaport on this peninsula.

kow·tow (kou′tou′, -tou′, kō′-), *v.i.* **1.** to touch the forehead to the ground while kneeling, as an act of worship, reverence, apology, etc., esp. in former Chinese custom. **2.** to act in an obsequious manner; show servile deference. **—*n.* 3.** the act of kowtowing. Also, **kotow.** [< Chin (Mandarin) *k'o-t'ou,* lit., knock (one's) head] **—kow′tow′er,** *n.*

Ko·zhi·kode (kō′zhi kōd′), *n.* Malayalam name of **Calicut.**

KP, *Chess.* king's pawn.

K.P., **1.** *Mil.* See **kitchen police. 2.** Knight of the Order of St. Patrick. **3.** Knights of Pythias.

kpc, kiloparsec; kiloparsecs.

KR, *Chess.* king's rook.

Kr, *Chem.* krypton.

Kr., **1.** (in Sweden) krona; kronor. **2.** (in Iceland) króna; krónur. **3.** (in Denmark and Norway) krone; kroner.

kr., **1.** kreutzer. **2.** krona; kronor. **3.** króna; krónur. **4.** krone; kroner.

Kra (krä), *n.* **Isthmus of,** the narrowest part of the Malay Peninsula, between the Bay of Bengal and the Gulf of Siam. 35 mi. wide.

kraal (kräl), *n.* **1.** a village of South African natives, usually surrounded by a stockade or the like and often having a central space for livestock. **2.** the kraal as a social unit. **3.** an enclosure for livestock in southern Africa. **—*v.t.* 4.** to shut up in a kraal, as cattle. Also, **craal.** [< SAfrD < Pg *curral* pen; see CORRAL]

Krae·pe·lin (kre′pə lēn′), *n.* **E·mil** (ā′mēl), 1856–1926, German psychiatrist.

Krafft-E·bing (kraft′eb′ing, kräft′-; *Ger.* kräft′ā′bing), *n.* **Rich·ard** (rich′ərd; *Ger.* rikh′ärt), **Baron von,** 1840–1902, German neurologist and writer on mental disease.

kraft (kraft, kräft), *n.* a strong, usually brown paper processed from wood pulp and used for bags and as wrapping paper. [< G: lit., strength]

kraft′ proc′ess. See **sulfate process.**

krait (krīt), *n.* any of several extremely venomous elapid snakes of the genus *Bungarus,* of southeastern Asia and the Malay Archipelago. [< Hindi *karait*]

Kra·ka·tau (krä′kə tou′), *n.* a small volcanic island in Indonesia, between Java and Sumatra: violent eruption 1883. Also, **Kra′ka·tao′, Kra·ka·to·a** (krä′kə tō′ə).

Kra·kau (krä′kou), *n.* German name of **Cracow.**

kra·ken (krä′kən), *n.* (*often cap.*) a legendary sea monster causing large whirlpools off the coast of Norway. [< Norw]

Kra·ków (krä′ko͝of), *n.* Polish name of **Cracow.**

Kra·ma·torsk (krä mä tôrsk′), *n.* a city in the E Ukraine, in the S Soviet Union in Europe. 126,000 (est. 1962).

Kras·no·dar (kräs′no där′), *n.* **1.** a territory of the RSFSR, in the S Soviet Union in Europe. 4,757,000; 34,200 sq. mi. **2.** Formerly, **Ekaterinodar.** a port in and the capital of this territory, on the Kuban River, near the Sea of Azov. 377,000 (est. 1964).

Kras·no·yarsk (kräs′no yärsk′), *n.* **1.** a territory of the RSFSR, in the central Soviet Union in Asia. 3,155,000; 827,507 sq. mi. **2.** a town in and the capital of this territory, on the Yenisei River. 542,000 (1965).

K ration, *U.S. Army.* an emergency field ration used in World War II. [K for Ancel *Keys* (b. 1904), American physiologist, who devised it]

Kraut (krout), *n.* (*often l.c.*) *Disparaging.* a German. [< G (*Sauer*)*kraut* pickled (sour) cabbage]

Krebs (kreps; *Eng.* krebz), *n.* **Hans A·dolf** (häns ä′dôlf; *Eng.* hanz ad′ôlf, ā′dôlf), born 1900, German biochemist in England: Nobel prize for medicine 1953.

Kre·feld (krā′feld; *Ger.* krā′felt′), *n.* a city in W North Rhine-Westphalia, in W West Germany, NW of Cologne. 216,900 (1963). Also, **Crefeld.**

Kreis·ler (krīs′lər), *n.* **Fritz** (fritz), 1875–1962, Austrian violinist and composer in the U.S.

Krem·lin (krem′lin), *n.* **1. the Kremlin, a.** the executive branch of the government of the Soviet Union. **b.** the citadel of Moscow, including within its walls the chief office of the Soviet government. **2.** (*l.c.*) the citadel of any Russian city or town. [earlier *Kremelin* < G (now obs.) < Russ *kreml'* fortress (< Tatar) + G *-in* fem. suffix; r. 17th-century *Kremelina,* Latinization of G *Kremelin*]

Krem·lin·ol·o·gy (krem′li nol′ə jē), *n.* the study of the government and policies of the Soviet Union. **—Krem·lin·ol·o·gist** (krem′li nol′ə jist), *n.*

kreut·zer (kroit′sər), *n.* **1.** any of various former minor coins issued by German states. **2.** a former copper coin of Austria, the 100th part of a florin. [< G *Kreuzer* = *Kreuz* CROSS (orig. the device on the coin) + *-er* -ER[1]]

Kreut·zer (kroit′sər; *Fr.* krœ tser′), *n.* **Ro·dolphe** (rô-dôlf′), 1766–1831, French violinist.

Kreym·borg (krām′bôrg), *n.* **Alfred,** 1883–1966, U.S. poet, playwright, and critic.

Krieg (krēkh; *Eng.* krēg), *n., pl.* **Krie·ge** (krē′gə), *Eng.* **Kreigs.** *German.* war.

krieg·spiel (krēg′spēl′), *n.* (*sometimes cap.*) a game using small figures and counters that represent troops, ships, etc., played on a map or miniature battle field, developed for teaching military tactics to officers. [< G *Kriegsspiel,* lit.: war's game. See KRIEG, 's[1], SPELL[3]]

Kriem·hild (krēm′hilt), *n.* (in the *Nibelungenlied*) the wife of Siegfried, whose death she avenges by killing Gunther and Hagen: corresponds to Gudrun in Scandinavian legends.

krill (kril), *n., pl.* **krill.** any of the small, pelagic, shrimplike crustaceans of the family *Euphausiidae,* used as food by certain whales. [< Norw *kril* young fry (of fish)]

krim·mer (krim′ər), *n.* a lambskin from the Crimean region, dressed as a fur. Also, **crimmer.** [< G = *Krim* CRIMEA + *-er* -ER[1]]

kris (krēs), *n.* creese.

Krish·na (krish′nə), *n.* *Hinduism.* an avatar of Vishnu and one of the most popular of Indian deities, who appears in the *Bhagavad-Gita* as the teacher of Arjuna. [< Skt: lit. black, dark]

Krish′na Men′on (men′ən), **Ven·ga·lil Krish·nan** (ven gä′lēl krish′nən), 1897–1974, Indian political leader: Minister of Defense 1957–62.

Kriss Krin·gle (kris′ kring′gəl). See **Santa Claus.** [< G *Christkindl* little Christ child = *Christ* CHRIST + *kind* child + *-l* -LE]

Kris·tian·sand (kris′chən sand′; *Norw.* kris′tyän sän′), *n.* a seaport in S Norway. 50,217 (est. 1965). Formerly, **Christiansand.**

Kri·voi Rog (kri voi′ rôg′), a city in the SE Ukraine in the SW Soviet Union in Europe. 448,000 (est. 1962).

Kroe·ber (krō′bər), *n.* **Alfred Louis,** 1876–1960, U.S. anthropologist.

Kró·lew·ska Hu·ta (*Pol.* kro͝o lef′skä ho͝o′tä), former name of **Chorzów.**

kro·na (krō′nə), *n., pl.* **-nor** (-nôr). a silver and copper coin and monetary unit of Sweden, equal to 100 öre. *Abbr.:* Kr., kr. [< Sw < ML *corōna;* see KRONA]

kró·na (krō′nə), *n., pl.* **kró·nur** (krō′nər). a copper coin and monetary unit of Iceland, equal to 100 aurar. *Abbr.:* Kr., kr. [< Icel < ML *corōna* gold coin (so called because it bore the imprint of a crown); see CROWN]

kro·ne[1] (krō′nə), *n., pl.* **-ner** (-nər). **1.** an aluminum bronze coin and monetary unit of Denmark, equal to 100 öre. *Abbr.:* Kr., kr. **2.** a cupronickel coin and monetary unit of Norway, equal to 100 öre. *Abbr.:* Kr., kr. [< Dan, Norw < MLG < ML *corōna;* see KRONA]

kro·ne[2] (krō′nə), *n., pl.* **-nen** (-nən). a former gold coin of Germany, equal to 10 marks. [< G; see KRONE[1]]

Kro·nos (krō′nos), *n.* Cronus.

Kron·stadt (kron shtät′ *for 1;* krōn′shtät *for 2*), *n.* **1.** a seaport in the NW RSFSR, in the NW Soviet Union in Europe, on an island in the Gulf of Finland, W of Leningrad: naval base. 175,264. **2.** German name of **Brașov.**

kroon (kro͞on), *n., pl.* **kroons, kroon·i** (kro͞o′nē). a former aluminum bronze coin and monetary unit of Estonia, equal to 100 marks or senti. [< Estonian *kron* < Sw *krona* KRONA]

Kro·pot·kin (krō pot′kin, krə-; *Russ.* KRO pôt′kin), *n.* **Prince Pë·ter A·le·kse·e·vich** (pyô′tər ä′le kse′yə vich), 1842–1921, Russian geographer, author, and anarchist.

KRP, *Chess.* king's rook's pawn.

Kru·ger (kro͞o′gər; *Du.* KRY′KHƏR), *n.* **Ste·pha·nus Jo·han·nes Paul·us** (ste fä′nœs yō hä′nəs pō′lœs), ("*Oom Paul*"), 1825–1904, South African statesman: president of the Transvaal 1883–1900.

Kru·ger·rand (kro͞o′gə rand′, -ränd′), *n.* (*sometimes l.c.*) a one-ounce gold coin of the Republic of South Africa, equal to 25 rand.

Kru·gers·dorp (kro͞o′gərz dôrp′; *Du.* KRY′KHƏRS dôRp′), *n.* a city in S Transvaal, in the NE Republic of South Africa, NW of Johannesburg. 91,202.

krul·ler (krul′ər), *n.* cruller.

Krupp (krup; *Ger.* kRo͝op), *n.* **Al·fred** (al′frid; *Ger.* äl′-fRāt), 1812–87, German manufacturer of armaments.

Krutch (kro͞och), *n.* **Joseph Wood,** 1893–1970, U.S. author, naturalist, teacher, and critic.

kryp·ton (krip′ton), *n.* *Chem.* an inert, monatomic gaseous element, present in very small amounts in the atmosphere: used in high-power, tungsten-filament light bulbs. *Symbol:* Kr; *at. wt.:* 83.80; *at. no.:* 36; *weight of one liter at 0°C and 760 mm pressure:* 3.708 g. [< Gk, neut. of *kryptós* hidden, secret; see CRYPT]

KS, Kansas (approved esp. for use with zip code).

Kshat·ri·ya (kshat′rē ə), *n.* a member of the Hindu royal and warrior caste above the Vaisyas and below the Brahmans. Cf. **Sudra.** [< Skt: lit., ruling, ruler]

Kt, *Chess.* knight.

Kt., Knight.

kt., **1.** karat. **2.** kiloton. **3.** knot.

K.T., **1.** Knight of the Order of the Thistle. **2.** Knights Templars.

Kt. Bach., knight bachelor.

Kua·la Lum·pur (kwä′lə lo͝om po͝or′), a city in and the capital of Malaysia, in the SW Malay Peninsula: also the capital of Selangor state. 500,000.

Kuang·chou (gwäng′jō′), *n.* Chinese name of **Canton.**

Ku·ban (ko͞o ban′; *Russ.* ko͝o bän′yᵊ), *n.* a river in the Soviet Union in Europe, flowing NW from the Caucasus Mountains to the Black and the Azov seas. 512 mi. long. Ancient, **Hypanis.**

Ku·ban·go (ko͝o bäng′gō), *n.* Okovanggo.

Ku·blai Khan (ko͞o′blī kän′), 1216–94, khan c1260–94: founder of the Mongol dynasty in China (grandson of Genghis Khan). Also, **Ku′bla Khan′** (ko͞o′blə), **Ku′bi·lai Khan′** (ko͞o′bi lī′).

ku·chen (ko͞o′KHən), *n.* a yeast-raised coffee cake, usually including fruit. [< G: cake]

Ku·ching (ko͞o′ching), *n.* a seaport in SW Sarawak, in E Malaysia: capital of the former colony of Sarawak. 50,579 (1960).

ku·dos (ko͞o′dōz, -dōs, -dos, kyo͞o′-), *n.* (*construed as sing.*) praise; glory. [irreg. transliteration of Gk *kŷdos*]

ku·du (ko͞o′do͞o), *n.* a large African antelope, *Strepsiceros strepsiceros,* the male of which has large corkscrewlike horns. Also, **koodoo.** [< Hottentot]

Kudu (5 ft. high at shoulder; horns 4 to 5 ft.; length 9 ft.)

Kuen·lun (ko͝on′lo͝on′), *n.* Kunlun.

Ku·fa (ko͞o′fə, -fa), *n.* a town in central Iraq: former seat of Abbassid caliphate; Muslim pilgrimage center. Also called **Al Kufa.**

Ku·fic (ko͞o′fik, kyo͞o′-), *adj.* **1.** of or pertaining to Kufa. **2.** noting or pertaining to the characters of the Arabic alphabet used in the writing of the original Koran. —*n.* **3.** the Kufic alphabet. Also, **Cufic.**

Kui·by·shev (kwē′bi shef′; *Russ.* ko͞o′i bi shef′), *n.* a port in the RSFSR, in the SE Soviet Union in Europe, on the Volga. 950,000 (est. 1965). Formerly, **Samara.**

Ku Klux·er (ko͞o′ kluk′sər, kyo͞o′), a member of a Ku Klux Klan. Also called **Ku′ Klux′ Klan′ner.**

Ku Klux Klan (ko͞o′ kluks′ klan′, kyo͞o′), **1.** a secret organization in the southern U.S., active for several years after the Civil War, which aimed to suppress the newly acquired rights of the Negroes. **2.** a secret organization inspired by the former, founded in Georgia, in 1915 and professing Americanism as its object. [*Ku Klux* (? < Gk *kýklos* circle, assembly) + *klan,* sp. var. of CLAN]

ku·lak (ko͝o läk′, ko͞o′läk), *n.* (in Russia) a comparatively wealthy peasant who employed hired labor. [< Russ: fist, tight-fisted person]

Kul·tur (*Ger.* ko͝ol to͞oR′), *n.* civilization; culture. [< G < L *cultūr(a)* CULTURE]

Kul·tur·kampf (*Ger.* ko͝ol to͞oR′ kämpf′), *n.* the conflict between the German imperial government and the Roman Catholic Church (1872–86), chiefly over the control of educational and ecclesiastical appointments. [< G: culture struggle]

Ku·lun (ko͞o′lo͞on′), *n.* Chinese name of **Ulan Bator.**

Ku·ma·mo·to (ko͞o′mə mō′tō; *Jap.* ko͞o′mä mô′tô), *n.* a city on W central Kyushu, in SW Japan. 405,488 (1964).

Ku·mas·i (ko͝o mä′sē), *n.* a city in and the capital of Ashanti district, in S Ghana. 230,449 (est. 1965).

ku·miss (ko͞o′mis), *n.* **1.** fermented mare's or camel's milk, used as a beverage by Asian nomads. **2.** a similar drink prepared from other milk, esp. that of the cow, and used for dietetic and medicinal purposes. Also, **koumis, koumiss, koumyss.** [< Russ *kumys* < Tatar *kumyz*]

küm·mel (kim′əl; *Ger.* KYM′əl) *n.* **1.** a colorless liqueur flavored with cumin, caraway seeds, etc. **2.** (*cap., italics*) *German.* caraway seed. [< G; OHG *kumil,* appar. dissimilated var. of *kumin* CUMIN]

kum·mer·bund (kum′ər bund′), *n.* cummerbund.

kum·quat (kum′kwot), *n.* **1.** a small, round or oblong citrus fruit having a sweet rind and acid pulp, used chiefly for preserves. **2.** any of several rutaceous shrubs of the genus *Fortunella,* native to China and cultivated in Japan, Florida, California, etc., bearing this fruit. Also, **cumquat.** [< Chin (Cantonese) *kam kwat* gold orange]

Kun (ko͝on), *n.* **Bé·la** (bā′lo), 1885–1937, Hungarian Communist leader.

kung fu (kung′ fo͞o′, gung′-), an ancient Chinese method of self-defense involving soft, fluid movements of hands and legs. [< Chin: lit., accomplished technique]

K'ung Fu-tzŭ (ko͝ong′ fo͞o′dzu′), Chinese name of **Confucius.** Also, **K'ung′ Fu′-tse′** (fo͞o′dzu′).

Ku·ni·yo·shi (ko͞o′nē yō′shē; *Jap.* ko͞o′nē yô′shē), *n.* **Ya·su·o** (yä so͞o′ô), 1893–1953, U.S. painter, born in Japan.

Kun·lun (ko͝on′lo͝on′), *n.* a mountain range in China, bordering on the N edge of the Tibetan plateau and extending W across central China: highest peak, 25,000 ft. Also, **Kuenlun.**

Kun·ming (ko͝on′ming′), *n.* a city in and the capital of Yünnan province, in SW China: an important transshipment point on the Burma Road in World War II. 1,100,000. Also called **Yünnan.**

kunz·ite (ko͝onts′īt), *n.* a transparent, lilac variety of spodumene, used as a gem. [named after G. F. *Kunz* (1856–1932), American expert in precious stones; see -ITE¹]

Kuo·min·tang (kwō′min′tang′, -täng′; *Chin.* gwô′min′-däng′), *n.* the main political party of China from 1928 to 1949, founded chiefly by Sun Yatsen in 1911 and later led by Chiang Kai-shek; main party of Republic of China (Taiwan) since 1949. [< Chin (Mandarin dial.): National People's Party = *kuo* nation + *min* people + *tang* party]

Kuo·pio (kwô′pyô), *n.* a city in central Finland. 51,051 (1965).

Ku·prin (ko͞o′prin; *Russ.* ko͝o pRēn′), *n.* **A·le·xan·der I·va·no·vich** (ä′le ksän′dər i vä′no vich), 1870–1938, Russian novelist and short-story writer.

Ku·ra (ko͝o rä′), *n.* a river flowing from NE Turkey, through the Georgian and Azerbaijan republics of the Soviet Union, SE to the Caspian Sea. 950 mi. long.

Kurd (kûrd; *Pers.* ko͞oRd), *n.* a member of an Islamic people speaking Kurdish and dwelling chiefly in Kurdistan. —**Kurd′ish,** *adj., n.*

Kurd·ish (kûr′dish, ko͝or′-), *adj.* **1.** of or pertaining to the Kurds or their language. **2.** of or pertaining to Kurdistan, its people, or their language. —*n.* **3.** the language of the Kurds, an Iranian language.

Kur·di·stan (kûr′di stan′; *Pers.* ko͞oR′di stän′), *n.* **1.** a mountain and plateau region in SE Turkey, NW Iran, and N Iraq: inhabited largely by Kurds. 74,000 sq. mi. **2.** any of several types of rug woven by the Kurds of Turkey or Iran.

Ku·re (ko͞o′Re′), *n.* a seaport on SW Honshu, in SW Japan. 225,722 (1964).

Kurg (ko͝org), *n.* Coorg.

Kur·gan (ko͝or gän′), *n.* a city in the S RSFSR, in the W Soviet Union in Asia, near the Ural Mountains. 191,000.

Ku′rile Is′lands (ko͝or′il, ko͝o rēl′), a chain of small islands off the NE coast of Asia, extending from N Japan to the S tip of Kamchatka: renounced by Japan in 1945; under Soviet administration since 1945. Also, **Ku′ril Is′lands.** Japanese, **Chishima.**

Kur·land (ko͝or′lənd), *n.* Courland.

Ku·ro·shi·o (ko͝o rō′shē ō′; *Jap.* ko͝o Rô′shē ô′), *n.* See **Japan Current.** [< Jap: black stream]

kur·ra·jong (kûr′ə jong′), *n.* a bottle tree, *Brachychiton populneum,* of Australia, having showy bell-shaped flowers. Also, **koorajong, currajong.** [< native Austral]

Kursk (ko͝orsk), *n.* a city in the W RSFSR, in the central Soviet Union in Europe. 240,000 (est. 1964).

kur·ta (kûr′tə), *n.* a long, collarless shirt worn by men in India. [< Hindi]

kur·to·sis (kûr tō′sis), *n.* *Statistics.* the degree of flatness or peakedness of a curve describing a frequency distribution. [< Gk *kýrtōsis* curvature = *kyrt(ós)* curved, arched + *-ōsis* -OSIS]

Ku·ta·i·si (ko͝o tä ē′si), *n.* a city in W Georgia, in the S Soviet Union in Europe. 141,000 (est. 1962). Also, **Ku·ta·is** (ko͝o tīs′; *Russ.* ko͝o tä ēs′).

Kutch (kuch), *n.* Cutch.

Ku·te·nai (ko͞ot′ᵊnā′, -ᵊnē′), *n.* Kootenay.

Ku·tu·zov (ko͝o to͞o′zof), *n.* **Mi·kha·il I·la·ri·o·no·vich** (mi KHä ēl′ i lä′Ri o nô′vich), **Prince of Smolensk,** 1745–1813, Russian field marshal and diplomat.

Ku·wait (ko͝o wāt′, -wīt′), *n.* **1.** a sovereign monarchy in NE Arabia, on the NW coast of the Persian Gulf: a former British protectorate. 1,100,000; ab. 8000 sq. mi. **2.** a seaport in and the capital of this monarchy. 800,000. Also, **Koweit.** —**Ku·wai·ti** (ko͝o wä′tē, -wī′-), *adj., n.*

Kuyp (*Du.* koip), *n.* **Ael·bert** (*Du.* äl′bəRt). See **Cuyp, Aelbert.**

Kuz·netsk′ Ba′sin (ko͞oz netsk′), an industrial region in the S Soviet Union in Asia: coal fields.

kV, *Elect.* kilovolt; kilovolts. Also, **kv**

K.V., *Music.* *Köchel-Verzeichnis,* the chronological listing of Mozart's works (used with a number to identify a specific work). Also, **K**

kVA, *Elect.* kilovolt-ampere; kilovolt-amperes. Also, **kva**

kvass (kväs, kwäs), *n.* a Russian beer made from barley, malt, and rye. Also, **quass.** [< Russ *kvas*],

kW, *Elect.* kilowatt. Also, **kw**

Kwa (kwä), *n.* a branch of the Niger-Congo subfamily of languages, including Ewe, Ibo, Yoruba, and other languages of coastal West Africa.

Kwa·ja·lein (kwä′jə lān′), *n.* an atoll in the Marshall Islands, in E Micronesia. ab. 65 mi. long. 3960 (1970).

Kwa·ki·u·tl (kwä′kē o͞ot′ᵊl), *n.* **1.** a member of an American Indian people of Vancouver Island and the adjacent British Columbian coast. **2.** the language of the Kwakiutl.

Kwang·chow (gwäng′jō′), *n.* Chinese name of **Canton.**

Kwang·cho·wan (kwäng′chō′wän′, kwang′-; *Chin.* gwäng′jō′wän′), *n.* a territory on the SW coast of Kwangtung province, in S China: leased to France 1898–1945. ab. 190 sq. mi.

Kwang·ju (gwäng′jo͞o′), *n.* a city in SW South Korea. 314,420 (1960). Japanese, **Koshu.**

Kwang·si-Chuang (kwäng′sē′chwäng′, kwang′-; *Chin.* gwäng′sē′jwäng′), *n.* an administrative division in S China. 19,390,000 (est. 1957); 85,096 sq. mi. *Cap.:* Nanning. Official name, **Kwang′si′-Chuang′ Auton′omous Re′gion.**

Kwang·tung (kwäng′to͝ong′, kwang′-; *Chin.* gwäng′-do͝ong′), *n.* a province in SE China. 37,960,000 (est. 1957); 89,344 sq. mi. *Cap.:* Canton.

Kwan·tung (kwän′to͝ong′, kwan′-; *Chin.* gwän′do͝ong′), *n.* a territory in NE China at the tip of Liaotung Peninsula, Manchuria: leased to Japan 1905–45; part of Shantung province.

kwash·i·or·kor (kwash′ē ôr′kôr, -kər, kwä′shē-), *n.* *Pathol.* a nutritional disease of infants and children, occurring chiefly in Africa, associated with a heavy corn diet and the resultant lack of protein, and characterized by edema, potbelly, and changes in skin pigmentation. [from native Ghanaian word]

Kwei·chow (kwā′chou′, -chō′; *Chin.* gwā′jō′), *n.* **1.** a province in S China. 16,890,000 (est. 1957); 67,181 sq. mi. *Cap.:* Kweiyang. **2.** Fengkieh.

Kwei·hwa·ting (gwā′hwä′ting′), *n.* former name of **Kweisui.**

Kwei·lin (kwā′lin′; *Chin.* gwā′lin′), *n.* a city in the Kwangsi-Chuwang region, in S China. 145,000 (est. 1957).

Kwei·sui (kwā′swā′; *Chin.* gwā′swā), *n.* a city in Inner Mongolia, in N China: formerly the capital of Suiyüan province. 140,000 (est. 1957). Formerly, **Kweihwating.**

Kwei·yang (kwā′yäng′, -yang′; *Chin.* gwā′yäng′), *n.* a city in and the capital of Kweichow province, in S China. 504,000 (est. 1957).

kWh, *Elect.* kilowatt-hour. Also, **kwhr, K.W.H.**

KY, Kentucky (approved esp. for use with zip code).

Ky., Kentucky.

ky·ack (kī′ak), *n.* a packsack that consists of two connected sacks and is hung on either side of a packsaddle. [?]

ky·a·nite (kī′ə nīt′), *n.* cyanite.

kyat (kyät, kē ät′), *n.* a cupronickel coin and monetary unit of Burma, equal to 100 pyas. [< Burmese]

Kyd (kid), *n.* **Thomas,** 1558–94, English dramatist, esp. of tragedies. Also, **Kid.**

ky·lix (kī′liks, kil′iks), *n., pl.* **ky·li·kes** (kī′lə kēz′, kil′ə-). *Gk. and Rom. Antiq.* a cup in the shape of a shallow bowl having two horizontal handles projecting from the sides, often set upon a stem terminating in a foot: used as a drinking vessel. Also, **cylix.** [< Gk: cup]

kymo-, var. of **cymo-:** *kymograph.*

ky·mo·graph (kī′mə graf′, -gräf′), *n.* **1.** an instrument for measuring and graphically recording variations in fluid pressure, as those of the human pulse. **2.** an instrument for measuring the angular oscillations of an airplane in flight, with respect to axes fixed in space. Also, **cymograph.** —**ky·mo·graph·ic** (kī′mə graf′ik), *adj.*

Kym·ric (kim′rik), *adj., n.* Cymric.

Kym·ry (kim′rē), *n.pl.* Cymry.

Kyn·e·wulf (kin′ə wo͝olf′), *n.* Cynewulf.

Kyo·ga (kyō′gə), *n.* **Lake,** a lake in central Uganda. ab. 1000 sq. mi. Also, **Kioga.**

Kyo·to (kē ō′tō; *Jap.* kyô′tô), *n.* a city on S Honshu, in central Japan: the capital of Japan A.D. 784–1868. 1,337,228 (1964). Also, **Kioto.**

ky·pho·sis (kī fō′sis), *n.* *Pathol.* a curvature of the spine, convex backward. [< Gk *kýphōsis* a hunched state; see -OSIS] —**ky·phot·ic** (kī fot′ik), *adj.*

Kyr·i·e e·le·i·son (kir′ē ā′ e lā′i sôn′, -son′, -sən; *Gk. Orth. Ch.* kē′RĒ e e le′i sôn), **1.** (*italics*) the brief petition "Lord, have mercy," used in various offices of the Greek Orthodox Church and of the Roman Catholic Church. **2.** Also called **Kyr′i·e′.** a musical setting for this. [ME *kyrieleyson* < LL *Kyrie, eleïson* < LGk *Kýrie, eléēson* Lord, have mercy]

kyte (kīt), *n.* *Scot. and North Eng.* the paunch; stomach; belly. [? < Scand; cf. Icel *kȳta* stomach of the blenny]

kythe (kīth), *v.t., v.i.,* **kythed, kyth·ing.** *Scot. and North Eng.* kithe.

Ky·the·ra (kē′thē RÄ), *n.* Greek name of **Cerigo.**

Kyu·shu (kē o͞o′sho͞o; *Jap.* kyo͞o′sho͞o), *n.* an island in SW Japan. 12,903,076 (1960); 15,750 sq. mi. Also, **Kiushu.**

Ky·zyl Kum (ki zil′ ko͞om′), a desert in S Asia, SE of the Aral Sea, in the Soviet Union in Asia. ab. 90,000 sq. mi. Also, **Kizil Kum, Qizil Qum.**

DEVELOPMENT OF MAJUSCULE								
NORTH SEMITIC	GREEK		ETR.	LATIN		MODERN		
						GOTHIC	ITALIC	ROMAN
ℓ	ᒣ	Λ	ᒍ	↾	L	𝔏	*L*	L

DEVELOPMENT OF MINUSCULE					
ROMAN CURSIVE	ROMAN UNCIAL	CAROL. MIN.	MODERN		
			GOTHIC	ITALIC	ROMAN
l	L	l	𝔩	*l*	l

The twelfth letter of the English alphabet derives from North Semitic *lamed,* with its shape exhibiting consistent development. It assumed its present form as a right angle (L) in Classical Latin. The minuscule (l) is a cursive variant of the capital.

L, l (el), *n., pl.* **L's** or **Ls, l's** or **ls.** **1.** the 12th letter of the English alphabet, a consonant. **2.** any spoken sound represented by the letter *L* or *l,* as in *let, dull,* or *cradle.* **3.** something having the shape of an L. **4.** a written or printed representation of the letter *L* or *l.* **5.** a device, as a printer's type, for reproducing the letter *L* or *l.*

L (el), *n., pl.* **L's** or **Ls.** *Informal.* an elevated railroad.

L (el), *n., pl.* **L's** or **Ls.** ell[1].

L, **1.** *Optics.* lambert; lamberts. **2.** large. **3.** Latin. **4.** left. **5.** length. **6.** *Brit.* pound; pounds. [< L *libra*] **7.** longitude. **8.** *Theat.* stage left.

L, **1.** the 12th in order or in a series, or, if *I* is omitted, the 11th. **2.** (*sometimes l.c.*) the Roman numeral for 50. Cf. **Roman numerals. 3.** *Elect.* inductance.

l, **1.** large. **2.** liter; liters. **3.** lumen.

L-, **1.** Also, **l-.** *Chem.* levo-. **2.** *U.S. Mil.* (in designations of light aircraft) liaison: *L-15.*

L., **1.** Lady. **2.** Lake. **3.** large. **4.** Latin. **5.** latitude. **6.** law. **7.** left. **8.** lempira; lempiras. **9.** leu; lei. **10.** lev; leva. **11.** book. [< L *liber*] **12.** Liberal. **13.** (in Italy) lira; lire. **14.** place. [< L *locus*] **15.** Lord. **16.** low. **17.** lumen. **18.** *Theat.* stage left.

l., **1.** large. **2.** latitude. **3.** law. **4.** leaf. **5.** league. **6.** left. **7.** length. **8.** *pl.* **ll.,** line. **9.** link. **10.** (in Italy) lira; lire. **11.** liter. **12.** lumen.

la[1] (lä), *n. Music.* **1.** the syllable used for the sixth tone of a diatonic scale. **2.** (in the fixed system of solmization) the tone A. Cf. **sol-fa** (def. 1). [see GAMUT]

la[2] (lô, lä), *interj.* (used as an exclamation of wonder, surprise, etc.): *La, sir, how you do go on!* [ME, OE; weak var. of OE *lā,* LO]

La, *Chem.* lanthanum.

La., Louisiana.

LA, Louisiana (approved esp. for use with zip code).

L.A., **1.** Latin America. **2.** Law Agent. **3.** Library Association. **4.** Local Agent. **5.** Los Angeles.

laa·ger (lä′gər), *South African.* —*n.* **1.** a camp or encampment, esp. within a circle of wagons. —*v.t., v.i.* **2.** to arrange or encamp in a laager. Also, **lager.** [< SAfrD, var. of *lager;* c. G *Lager* camp. See LAIR[1]]

Laa·land (lô′län), *n.* an island in SE Denmark, S of Zealand. 83,170 (1960); 495 sq. mi. Also, **Lolland.**

lab (lab), *n.* laboratory. [by shortening]

Lab., Labrador.

lab., **1.** labor. **2.** laboratory. **3.** laborer.

La·ban (lā′bən), *n.* the brother of Rebekah and the father-in-law of Jacob. Gen. 24:29; 29:16–30.

lab·a·rum (lab′ər əm), *n., pl.* **-a·ra** (-ər ə). **1.** an ecclesiastical standard or banner, as for carrying in procession. **2.** the military standard of Constantine the Great and later Christian emperors of Rome, bearing Christian symbols. [< LL < ?]

lab·da·num (lab′də nəm), *n.* a resinous juice that exudes from various rockroses of the genus *Cistus:* used in perfumery, fumigating substances, medicinal plasters, etc. Also, **ladanum.** [earlier *lapdanum* < ML, for L *lādanum* < Gk *lḗdanon,* akin to *lēdon* rockrose < Sem]

La·be (lä′be), *n.* Czech name of the **Elbe.**

lab·e·fac·tion (lab′ə fak′shən), *n.* a shaking or weakening; overthrow; downfall. [< LL *labefactiōn-* (s. of *labefactiō*) = *labefact(us)* (ptp. of *labefacere* to loosen) + *-iōn-* -ION]

la·bel (lā′bəl), *n., v.,* **-beled, -bel·ing** or (*esp. Brit.*) **-belled, -bel·ling.** —*n.* **1.** a slip of paper or other material bearing information, instructions, etc., concerning something to which it is attached. **2.** a descriptive word or phrase printed before a section of text, as a dictionary definition. **3.** an epithet or descriptive word. **4.** a short word or phrase descriptive of a person, group, political movement, or the like. **5.** *Archit.* a molding or dripstone over a door or window. **6.** a trademark, esp. of a manufacturer of phonograph records. **7.** *Heraldry.* a narrow horizontal strip with a number of downward extensions, usually placed in chief as the cadency mark of an eldest son. **8.** *Obs.* a strip or narrow piece of anything. —*v.t.* **9.** to affix a label to; mark with a label. **10.** to designate or describe by or as by a label: *The bottle was labeled poison.* **11.** to put in a certain class; classify. [ME < MF: ribbon, perh. < Gmc; see LAP[1]] —**la′bel·er;** *esp. Brit.,* **la′bel·ler,** *n.*

la·bel·lum (lə bel′əm), *n., pl.* **-bel·la** (-bel′ə). *Bot.* the division of the corolla of an orchidaceous plant that differs markedly in shape from the other divisions. [< L, dim. of *labrum* lip] —**la·bel′loid,** *adj.*

la·bi·a (lā′bē ə), *n.* pl. of **labium.**

la·bi·al (lā′bē əl), *adj.* **1.** of, pertaining to, or resembling a labium. **2.** *Music.* having the tones produced by the impact of a stream of air on a sharp liplike edge, as in a flute. **3.** of or pertaining to the lips. **4.** *Phonet.* involving lip articulation, as *p, v, m, w,* or a rounded vowel. —*n.* *Phonet.* **5.** any labial consonant, esp. a bilabial. **6.** any labial sound. [< ML *labiāl(is)*] —**la′bi·al′i·ty,** *n.* —**la′bi·al·ly,** *adv.*

la·bi·al·ise (lā′bē ə līz′), *v.t.,* **-ised, -is·ing.** *Chiefly Brit.* labialize. —**la′bi·al·i·sa′tion,** *n.*

la·bi·al·ize (lā′bē ə līz′), *v.t.,* **-ized, -iz·ing.** *Phonet.* to give a labial character to (a sound), for example, to round (a vowel). —**la′bi·al·i·za′tion,** *n.*

la·bi·a ma·jo·ra (lā′bē ə mə jōr′ə, -jôr′ə), *sing.* **la·bi·um ma·jus** (lā′bē əm mā′jəs). *Anat.* the outer folds of skin of the external female genitalia. [< NL: greater lips]

la·bi·a mi·no·ra (lā′bē ə mi nōr′ə, -nôr′ə), *sing.* **la·bi·um mi·nus** (lā′bē əm mī′nəs). *Anat.* the inner folds of skin of the external female genitalia. [< NL: lesser lips]

la·bi·ate (lā′bē āt′, -it), *adj.* **1.** having parts that are shaped or arranged like lips; lipped. **2.** *Bot.* **a.** belonging to the *Labiatae* (or *Menthaceae,* formerly *Lamiaceae*), the mint family of plants, most of which have bilabiate corollas. **b.** two-lipped; bilabiate: said of a gamopetalous corolla or gamosepalous calyx. —*n.* **3.** a labiate plant. [< NL *labiāt(us).* See LABIUM, -ATE[1]]

La·biche (LA bēsh′), *n.* **Eu·gène Ma·rin** (œ zhen′ MA RAN′), 1815–88, French dramatist.

la·bile (lā′bil *or, esp. Brit.,* -bīl), *adj.* apt to lapse or change; unstable. [late ME *labyl* < LL *lābil(is)* = L *lāb(ī)* (to) slip + *-ilis* -ILE] —**la·bil·i·ty** (lə bil′i tē), *n.*

labio-, a learned borrowing from Latin meaning "lip," used in the formation of compound words: *labiodental.* [comb. form repr. L *labium*]

la·bi·o·den·tal (lā′bē ō den′tᵊl), *Phonet.* —*adj.* **1.** articulated with the lower lip touching the upper front teeth, as *f* or *v.* —*n.* **2.** a labiodental speech sound.

la·bi·o·na·sal (lā′bē ō nā′zəl), *Phonet.* —*adj.* **1.** articulated with the lips and given resonance in the nasal cavity, as *m.* —*n.* **2.** a labionasal sound.

la·bi·o·ve·lar (lā′bē ō vē′lər), *Phonet.* —*adj.* **1.** pronounced with simultaneous bilabial and velar articulations, as *w.* —*n.* **2.** a labiovelar speech sound.

la·bi·um (lā′bē əm), *n., pl.* **-bi·a** (-bē ə). **1.** a lip or liplike part. **2.** *Anat.* **a.** a lip or lip-shaped structure or part. **b.** any of the folds of skin bordering the vulva. **3.** *Bot.* the lower lip of a bilabiate corolla. **4.** *Entomol.* the posterior, unpaired member of the mouth parts of an insect, formed by the united second maxillae. [< L: lip, akin to *lambere* to lick, LAP[3]. See LABRUM, LIP]

la·bor (lā′bər), *n.* **1.** productive activity, esp. for the sake of economic gain; work; toil. **2.** the body, class, or organizations of persons engaged in such activity, esp. as distinguished from management and capital. **3.** a job or task done or to be done: *the 12 labors of Hercules.* **4.** the pains and efforts of childbirth; travail. **5.** the period of these. —*v.i.* **6.** to perform labor; work; toil. **7.** to strive, as toward a goal (often fol. by *for*): *to labor for peace.* **8.** to act, behave, or function at a disadvantage (usually fol. by *under*): *to labor under a misapprehension.* **9.** to be in travail or childbirth. **10.** to roll or pitch heavily, as a ship. —*v.t.* **11.** to develop or dwell on excessive detail; elaborate: *Don't labor the point.* **12.** to burden or tire. **13.** *Archaic.* to work or till (soil or the like). —*adj.* **14.** of or pertaining to workers, their associations, or working conditions: *labor negotiations; labor reform.* Also, *esp. Brit.,* **labour.** [ME *labour* < MF < L *labōr-* (s. of *labor*) work] —**la′bor·ing·ly,** *adv.* —**Syn. 2.** working men, working class. **4.** parturition, delivery. **11.** overdo. —**Ant. 1.** idleness; leisure. **1, 6.** rest.

lab·o·ra·to·ry (lab′rə tōr′ē, -tôr′ē, lab′ər ə-; *Brit.* lə bor′ə tə rē, -ə trē), *n., pl.* **-ries,** *adj.* —*n.* **1.** a place for scientific experiments, tests, or demonstrations. **2.** time spent at such a place, esp. for educational purposes: *three hours of laboratory per week.* **3.** a place of manufacturing or processing under highly controlled conditions. **4.** a place or a session of experimental work, as in an art; workshop. —*adj.* **5.** of, pertaining to, or suitable for a laboratory. [< ML *labōrātōri(um)* workshop = L *labōrāt(us)* (ptp. of *labōrāre;* see LABOR, -ATE[1]) + *-ōrium* -ORY[2]]

la′bor camp′, **1.** a penal colony where inmates are forced to work. **2.** a camp for the shelter of migratory farm workers.

La′bor Day′, (in most states of the U.S.) a legal holiday, commonly the first Monday in September, in honor of labor. Cf. **Labour Day.**

la·bored (lā′bərd), *adj.* **1.** not easy; with difficulty; heavy: *labored breathing.* **2.** betraying effort; lacking spontaneity: *a labored prose style.* Also, *esp. Brit.,* **laboured.** —**la′bored·ly,** *adv.* —**la′bored·ness,** *n.* —**Syn. 2.** overdone, ornate, unnatural. See **elaborate.** —**Ant. 2.** plain, natural.

la·bor·er (lā′bər ər), *n.* **1.** a person engaged in physical work, esp. that requiring little skill. **2.** any person who labors. Also, *esp. Brit.,* **labourer.** [ME]

la·bor-in·ten·sive (lā′bər in ten′siv), *adj.* requiring or using a very large supply of labor relative to capital: *a labor-intensive industry.* Cf. **capital-intensive.**

la·bo·ri·ous (lə bōr′ē əs, -bôr′-), *adj.* **1.** requiring much labor, exertion, or perseverance. **2.** characterized by or requiring extreme care: *laborious research.* **3.** characterized by or exhibiting excessive effort; labored. **4.** given to or diligent in labor. [ME < L *labōriōs(us)*] —**la·bo′ri·ous·ly,** *adv.* —**la·bo′ri·ous·ness,** *n.* —**Syn. 1.** arduous, difficult, tiresome. **4.** hard-working, industrious.

la·bor·ite (lā′bə rīt′), *n.* a member of a group or political party promoting the interests of labor.

la′bor move′ment, organized labor, or its programs and policies.

la′bor of love′, a job or type of work done because of one's interest in the work itself.

la·bor om·ni·a vin·cit (lä′bôr ōm′nē ä′ wiṅ′kit; *Eng.* lā′bôr om′nē ə vin′sit), *Latin.* work conquers all: motto of Oklahoma.

la′bor pains′, the increasingly frequent and intense discomfort experienced by the mother prior to giving birth, caused by uterine contractions.

la′bor rela′tions, the relations between management and labor.

la·bor-sav·ing (lā′bər sā′viṅg), *adj.* made to reduce the work or number of workers required: *a labor-saving device.* Also, *esp. Brit.,* **labour-saving.**

la′bors of Her′cules, *Class. Myth.* the 12 extraordinary feats performed by Hercules for his cousin Eurystheus in order to gain immortality.

la′bor un′ion, an organization of employees for mutual aid and protection; trade union.

la·bour (lā′bər), *n., v.i., v.t., adj.* *Chiefly Brit.* labor. —**la′bour·ing·ly,** *adv.*

La′bour Day′, *Brit.* Labor Day, celebrated on May 1 in Britain and some parts of the Commonwealth, but on the first Monday in September in Canada, on the fourth Monday in October in New Zealand, and with varying dates in the different states of Australia.

la·boured (lā′bərd), *adj.* *Chiefly Brit.* labored. —**la′boured·ly,** *adv.* —**la′boured·ness,** *n.*

la·bour·er (lā′bər ər), *n.* *Chiefly Brit.* laborer.

la′bour exchange′, *Brit.* an employment agency.

La·bour·ite (lā′bə rīt′), *n.* a member or supporter of the Labour party. Also, **La′bour·ist.**

La′bour par′ty, a political party in Great Britain, formed in 1900 and characterized chiefly by the promotion of broad social reforms.

Lab·ra·dor (lab′rə dôr′), *n.* **1.** a peninsula in NE North America surrounded by Hudson Bay, the Atlantic, and the Gulf of St. Lawrence, containing the Canadian provinces of Newfoundland and Quebec. 510,000 sq. mi. **2.** the portion of Newfoundland in the E part of the peninsula. 13,534 (1961); ab. 120,000 sq. mi. **3.** See **Labrador retriever.** —**Lab′ra·dor′e·an, Lab′ra·dor′i·an,** *adj.*

Lab′rador Cur′rent, a cold ocean current flowing S along the Labrador coast through Davis Strait to the Grand Banks where it divides, the E branch joining the North Atlantic Current and the W branch flowing into the Gulf of St. Lawrence.

Lab′rador duck′, an extinct sea duck, *Camptorhynchus labradorius,* of northern North America, having black and white plumage.

lab·ra·dor·ite (lab′rə dô rīt′, lab′rə dôr′īt), *n.* a mineral of the plagioclase feldspar group, often characterized by a brilliant change of colors. [named after LABRADOR, where first discovered; see -ITE[1]] —**lab·ra·dor·it·ic** (lab′rə-dô rit′ik), *adj.*

Lab′rador retriev′er, one of a breed of retrievers having a short, thick, black or yellow coat, raised originally in Newfoundland. See illus. at **retriever.**

la·bret (lā′bret), *n.* an ornament worn in a pierced hole in the lip by some primitive peoples. [< L *labr(um)* lip + -ET]

la·brum (lā′brəm, lab′rəm), *n., pl.* **la·bra** (lā′brə, lab′rə). **1.** a lip or liplike part. **2.** *Zool.* **a.** the anterior, unpaired member of the mouth parts of an arthropod, projecting in front of the mouth. **b.** the outer margin of the aperture of a shell of a gastropod. **3.** *Anat.* a ring of cartilage about the edge of a joint surface of a bone. [< L: lip; akin to LABIUM]

La Bru·yère (lȧ brẏ yer′), **Jean de** (zhäN də), 1645–96, French moralist and author.

La·bu·an (lä′bo͞o än′), *n.* an island off the NW coast of Sabah, in Malaysia. 35 sq. mi.

la·bur·num (lə bûr′nəm), *n.* any of several small, leguminous trees of the genus *Laburnum,* having pendulous racemes of yellow flowers, esp. *L. anagyroides,* of Europe. [< NL, special use of L *laburnum* golden chain]

lab·y·rinth (lab′ə rinth), *n.* **1.** a devious arrangement of linear patterns forming a design. **2.** a system of passages or paths having such a design as a maze. **3.** anything that is bewildering by its complexity. **4.** (*cap.*) *Class. Myth.* a vast maze built in Crete by Daedalus, at the command of King Minos, to house the Minotaur. **5.** *Anat.* **a.** the internal ear, consisting of a bony portion **(bon′y lab′yrinth)** and a membranous portion **(mem′branous lab′yrinth).** **b.** the aggregate of air chambers in the ethmoid bone, between the eye and the upper part of the nose. [< L *labyrinth(us)* < Gk *labýrinthos;* r. ME *laborintus* < ML]

lab′yrinth fish′, any of several fresh-water fishes of the order *Labyrinthi,* found in southeastern Asia and Africa, having a labyrinthine structure above each gill chamber enabling them to breathe air while out of water.

lab·y·rin·thine (lab′ə rin′thin, -thēn), *adj.* **1.** of, pertaining to, or resembling a labyrinth. **2.** intricate; complicated; tortuous. Also, **lab·y·rin·thi·an** (lab′ə rin′thē ən), **lab′y·rin′thic.** —**lab′y·rin′thi·cal·ly,** *adv.*

lac[1] (lak), *n.* a resinous substance deposited on the twigs of various trees in southern Asia by the female of the lac insect: used in the manufacture of varnishes, sealing wax, etc., and in the production of a red coloring matter. Cf. **shellac** (defs. 1, 2). [< Hindi *lākh* < Skt *lākshā*]

lac[2] (läk), *n.* (in India) **1.** the sum of 100,000, esp. of rupees. **2.** an indefinitely large number. Also, **lakh.** [< Hindi *lākh* << Skt *lakshā*]

Lac′ca·dive Is′lands (lak′ə dīv′), a group of islands and coral reefs in the Arabian Sea, off the SW coast of India: a part of Madras province. 24,108 (1961); ab. 80 sq. mi.

lac·co·lith (lak′ə lith), *n.* *Geol.* a subterranean, lenticular mass of igneous rock formed from lava that has forced overlying strata upward. Also, **lac·co·lite** (lak′ə līt′). [< Gk *lákko(s)* pond + -LITH] —**lac′co·lith′ic, lac·co·lit·ic** (lak′ə lit′ik), *adj.*

lace (lās), *n., v.,* **laced, lac·ing.** —*n.* **1.** a netlike ornamental fabric of threads. **2.** a cord or string for holding or drawing together two flaps, being passed through holes in their edges. **3.** ornamental cord or braid. **4.** a small amount of liquor added to food or drink. —*v.t.* **5.** to fasten, draw together, etc., by or as by means of a lace. **6.** to pass (a cord, leather strip, etc.), as through holes. **7.** to compress the waist of (a person) by drawing tight the laces of a corset, or the like. **8.** to adorn or trim with lace. **9.** to interlace or intertwine. **10.** *Informal.* to lash, beat, or thrash. **11.** to mark or streak, as with color. **12.** to add a small amount of liquor to (food or drink). —*v.i.* **13.** to be fastened with a lace. **14.** to attack physically or verbally (usually fol. by *into*): *The teacher laced into his students for not studying.* [ME *las* < OF *laz, las* < L *laqueus* noose] —**lace′less,** *adj.* —**lace′like′,** *adj.*

Lac·e·dae·mon (las′i dē′mən), *n.* **1.** Sparta. **2.** the son of Zeus and Taygete and the legendary founder of the city of Sparta.

Lac·e·dae·mo·ni·an (las′i di mō′nē ən), *adj.* **1.** of or pertaining to ancient Sparta; Spartan. —*n.* **2.** a native or inhabitant of ancient Sparta; a Spartan.

lac·er·ate (*v.* las′ə rāt′; *adj.* las′ə rāt′, -ər it), *v.,* **-at·ed, -at·ing,** *adj.* —*v.t.* **1.** to tear roughly; mangle: *to lacerate the flesh.* **2.** to distress or torture mentally or emotionally. —*adj.* **3.** lacerated. [< L *lacerāt(us)* (ptp. of *lacerāre* to tear up) < *lacer* mangled; see -ATE[1]] —**lac·er·a·bil·i·ty** (las′ər ə-bil′i tē), *n.* —**lac′er·a·ble,** *adj.* —**lac·er·a·tive** (las′ə rā′-tiv, -ər ə tiv), *adj.* —**Syn. 1.** rend. See **maim.**

lac·er·at·ed (las′ə rā′tid), *adj.* **1.** mangled; jagged; torn. **2.** pained or distressed. **3.** *Bot., Zool.* having the edge variously cut as if torn into irregular segments, as a leaf.

lac·er·a·tion (las′ə rā′shən), *n.* **1.** act of lacerating. **2.** the result of lacerating; a rough, jagged tear. [< L *lacerātiōn-* (s. of *lacerātiō*)]

la·cer·tid (lə sûr′tid), *n.* **1.** any of numerous Old World lizards of the family *Lacertidae.* —*adj.* **2.** belonging or pertaining to the *Lacertidae* family of lizards. [< NL *Lacertid(ae).* See LACERTILIAN, -ID[2]]

lac·er·til·i·an (las′ər til′ē ən, -til′yən), *adj.* **1.** belonging or pertaining to the suborder *Lacertilia,* comprising the lizards. —*n.* **2.** a lacertilian reptile. Also, **la·cer·tian** (lə-sûr′shən, -shē ən). [< NL *Lacertili(a)* (L *lacert(a)* lizard + *-ilia,* neut. pl. of *-ilis* -ILE) + -AN]

lace·wing (lās′wiṅg′), *n.* any of several neuropterous insects of the family *Chrysopidae,* having delicate, lacelike wings, the larvae of which are predaceous on aphids.

lace·work (lās′wûrk′), *n.* lace (def. 1).

La·chaise (lə shez′; *Fr.* lȧ shez′), *n.* **Gas·ton** (gas′tən; *Fr.* gȧ stôN′), 1882–1935, U.S. sculptor, born in France.

lach·es (lach′iz), *n.* (*construed as sing.*) *Law.* (in equity) failure to do a thing at the proper time, esp. such delay as will bar a party from bringing a legal proceeding. [ME *lachesse* < AF, var. of MF *laschesse* < OF *lasche* slack (< Gmc); see -ICE]

Lach·e·sis (lach′i sis), *n.* *Class. Myth.* the Fate who determines the length of the thread of life. Cf. **Atropos, Clotho.** [< L < Gk, personification of *láchesis* destiny = *lache(in)* (to) happen by lot + *-sis* -SIS]

lach·ry·mal (lak′rə məl), *adj.* **1.** of or pertaining to tears; producing tears. **2.** characterized by tears; indicative of weeping. **3.** *Anat.* lacrimal (def. 2). —*n.* **4.** Also called **lach′rymal bone′.** *Anat.* See **lacrimal bone.** [< ML *lachrymāl(is),* var. of *lacrimālis* = L *lacrim(a)* tear (OL *dacruma;* akin to Gk *dákry)* + *-ālis* -AL[1]]

lach·ry·ma·tion (lak′rə mā′shən), *n.* the secretion of tears, esp. as a result of irritation or infection. Also, **lach′-ri·ma′tion.** [alter. of L *lacrimātiōn-* (s. of *lacrimātiō*)]

lach·ry·ma·tor (lak′rə mā′tər), *n.* *Chem.* a substance that causes the shedding of tears; tear gas. Also, **lacrimator.** [< ML *lacrimātor.* See LACHRYMATORY, -OR[2]]

lach·ry·ma·to·ry (lak′rə mə tôr′ē, -tōr′ē), *adj.* of, pertaining to, or causing the shedding of tears. Also, **lacrimatory.** [< ML *lachrymātōri(us)* = L *lacrimāt(us)* (ptp. of *lacrimāre* to weep; see LACHRYMAL) + *-ōrius* -ORY[1]]

lach·ry·mose (lak′rə mōs′), *adj.* **1.** given to or characterized by shedding tears; tearful. **2.** suggestive of or tending to cause tears; mournful. [< L lacrimōs(us). See LACHRYMAL, -OSE[1]] —**lach′ry·mose′ly,** *adv.* —**lach·ry·mos·i·ty** (lak′rə mos′i tē), *n.*

lac·ing (lā′siṅg), *n.* **1.** the act of a person or thing that laces. **2.** a lace used for fastening, as a shoe or corset lace. **3.** a trimming of lace or braid. **4.** a small amount of liquor added to food or drink. **5.** a beating or thrashing. [ME]

la·cin·i·ate (lə sin′ē āt′, -it), *adj.* *Bot., Zool.* cut into narrow, irregular lobes; slashed; jagged. [< NL *lacini(a)* (special use of L: lappet) + -ATE[1]]

Laciniate leaf

lack (lak), *n.* **1.** deficiency or absence of something wanted: *lack of money.* **2.** something wanted that is insufficient or absent. —*v.i.* **3.** to be wanting or deficient: *to be lacking in brains; not to lack for money.* **4.** to be missing from a total or minimum: *Three members are lacking for a quorum.* —*v.t.* **5.** to be wanting or deficient in. **6.** to be without (what would complete a total or minimum). [ME *lak;* c. MLG *lak,* MD *lac* deficiency; akin to Icel *lakr* deficient] —**Syn. 1.** dearth, scarcity, paucity, insufficiency. —**Ant. 1.** surplus.

lack·a·dai·si·cal (lak′ə dā′zi kəl), *adj.* **1.** without vigor or determination; listless. **2.** lazy; indolent. [*lackadais(y)* (var. of LACKADAY) + -ICAL] —**lack′a·dai′si·cal·ly,** *adv.* —**lack′a·dai′si·cal·ness,** *n.*

lack·a·day (lak′ə dā′), *interj.* *Archaic.* (used as an expression of regret, sorrow, or dismay.) [alter. of *alack the day*]

Lack·a·wan·na (lak′ə won′ə), *n.* a city in W New York, on Lake Erie, near Buffalo. 28,657 (1970).

lack·ey (lak′ē), *n., pl.* **-eys,** *v.,* **-eyed, -ey·ing.** —*n.* **1.** a footman or liveried manservant. **2.** a servile follower. —*v.t.* **3.** to attend as a lackey does. Also, **lacquey.** [< MF *laquais,* perh. < Catalan *lacayo, alacayo* < ?]

lack·lus·ter (lak′lus′tər), *adj.* **1.** lacking brilliance, radiance, liveliness, etc.; dull or vapid. —*n.* **2.** a lack of brilliance or vitality. Also, *esp. Brit.,* **lack′lus′tre.**

La·clos (lȧ klō′), *n.* **Pierre Am·broise Fran·çois Cho·der·los de** (pyer äN brwaz′ fräN swa′ shô der lō′ də), 1741–1803, French general and writer.

La·co·ni·a (lə kō′nē ə), *n.* an ancient country in the S part of Greece. *Cap.:* Sparta. —**La·co′ni·an,** *adj., n.*

la·con·ic (lə kon′ik), *adj.* using few words; expressing much in few words; concise: *a laconic style.* [< L *lacōnic(us)* < Gk *lakōnik(ós)* Laconian = *Lákōn* a Laconian + *-ikos* -IC]

—**la·con′i·cal·ly,** *adv.* —**Syn.** brief, pithy, terse; succinct.

la·con·i·cal (lə kon′i kəl), *adj. Archaic.* laconic. [< L *lacōnic(us)* (see LACONIC) + -AL[1]]

lac·o·nism (lak′ə niz′əm), *n.* **1.** laconic brevity. **2.** a laconic utterance. Also, **la·con·i·cism** (lə kon′i siz′əm). [< Gk *lakōnism(ós)*, n. answering to *lakōnízein* to favor or ape the Spartans. See LACONIC, -ISM]

La Co·ru·ña (lä′ kô ROO′nyä), a seaport in NW Spain. 169,750 (est. 1960). Also called **Coruña, Corunna.**

lac·quer (lak′ər), *n.* **1.** a protective coating consisting of a resin, cellulose ester, or both, dissolved in a volatile solvent, sometimes with pigment added. **2.** any of various resinous varnishes, esp. a resinous varnish obtained from a Japanese tree, *Rhus verniciflua*, used to produce a highly polished, lustrous surface on wood or the like. **3.** Also called **lac′quer ware′.** ware, esp. of wood, coated with such a varnish, and often inlaid. —*v.t.* **4.** to coat with lacquer. [earlier *leckar, laker* < OPg *lacre, lacar*, unexplained var. of *laca* < Ar *lakk* < Pers *lāk* LAC[1]] —**lac′quer·er,** *n.*

lac·quey (lak′ē), *n., pl.* **-queys,** *v.t.*, **-queyed, -quey·ing.** lackey.

lac·ri·mal (lak′rə məl), *adj.* **1.** lachrymal (defs. 1, 2). **2.** Also, **lachrymal.** *Anat.* of, pertaining to, or situated near the organs that secrete tears. —*n.* **3.** See **lacrimal bone.** [var. of LACHRYMAL]

lac′rimal bone′, *Anat.* a small, thin, membrane bone forming the front part of the inner wall of each orbit. Also called **lachrymal, lacrimal.**

lac·ri·ma·tor (lak′rə mā′tər), *n.* lachrymator.

lac·ri·ma·to·ry (lak′rə mə tôr′ē, -tōr′ē), *adj., n., pl.* **-ries.** lachrymatory.

La Crosse (lə krôs′, kros′), a city in W Wisconsin, on the Mississippi River. 51,153 (1970).

la·crosse (lə krôs′, -kros′), *n.* a game in which two 10-member teams attempt to send a small ball into each other's netted goal, each player being equipped with a stick **(crosse)** at the end of which is a netted pocket for catching, carrying, or throwing the ball. [< CanF: lit., the crook, CROSSE]

lact-, var. of **lacto-** before a vowel: *lactalbumin.*

lac·tal·bu·min (lak′təl byōō′min), *n. Biochem.* the simple protein of milk, resembling serum albumin, obtained from whey.

lac·tam (lak′tam), *n. Chem.* any of a group of cyclic amides characterized by the –NH–CO– group, derived from aminocarboxylic acids by the intramolecular elimination of water from the amino and carboxylic groups. [LACT(ONE) + AM(IDE)]

lac·tase (lak′tās), *n. Biochem.* an enzyme capable of hydrolyzing lactose into glucose and galactose.

lac·tate[1] (lak′tāt), *v.i.*, **-tat·ed, -tat·ing.** to produce milk. [< L *lactāt(us)*, ptp. of *lactāre* to suckle. See LACT-, -ATE[1]]

lac·tate[2] (lak′tāt), *n. Chem.* an ester or salt of lactic acid. [< L *lactāt(us)*, ptp. of *lactāre* to suckle. See LACT-, -ATE[1]]

lac·ta·tion (lak tā′shən), *n.* **1.** the secretion or formation of milk. **2.** the period of milk production. [< LL *lactātiōn-* (s. of *lactātiō*) a giving suck] —**lac·ta′tion·al,** *adj.* —**lac·ta′tion·al·ly,** *adv.*

lac·te·al (lak′tē əl), *adj.* **1.** pertaining to, consisting of, or resembling milk; milky. **2.** *Anat.* conveying or containing chyle. —*n.* **3.** *Anat.* any of the minute lymphatic vessels that convey chyle from the small intestine to the thoracic duct. [< L *lacte(us)* milky (see LACT-, -EOUS) + -AL[1]] —**lac′te·al·ly,** *adv.*

lac·te·ous (lak′tē əs), *adj. Archaic.* milky; of the color of milk. [< L *lacte(us)*. See LACTEAL, -OUS]

lac·tes·cent (lak tes′ənt), *adj.* **1.** becoming or being milky. **2.** secreting milk. **3.** *Bot., Entomol.* secreting or producing a milky juice, as certain plants. [< L *lactēscent-* (s. of *lactēscēns*) turning to milk, prp. of *lactēscere*. See LACT-, -ESCENT] —**lac·tes′cence, lac·tes′cen·cy,** *n.*

lac·tic (lak′tik), *adj.* of, pertaining to, or obtained from milk.

lac′tic ac′id, *Biochem.* a colorless or yellowish liquid, $CH_3CHOHCOOH$, found in sour milk, a waste product of muscle metabolism: used chiefly in food, medicine, and in dyeing and textile printing.

lac·tif·er·ous (lak tif′ər əs), *adj.* **1.** producing or secreting milk. **2.** conveying milk or a milky fluid: *lactiferous ducts.* [< L *lactifer* milk-bearing (see LACT-, -I-, -FER) + -OUS] —**lac·tif′er·ous·ness,** *n.*

lacto-, a learned borrowing from Latin meaning "milk," used in the formation of compound words (*lactometer*); specialized in chemical terminology to mean "lactate" or "lactic acid." Also, **lact-.** [comb. form repr. L *lact-* (s. of *lac*)]

lac·to·ba·cil·lus (lak′tō bə sil′əs), *n., pl.* **-cil·li** (-sil′ī). *Bacteriol.* any long, slender, rod-shaped, aerobic bacterium of the genus *Lactobacillus*, that produces large amounts of lactic acid in the fermentation of carbohydrates, esp. in milk. [< NL]

lac·to·fla·vin (lak′tō flā′vin, lak′tō flā′-), *n. Biochem.* riboflavin.

lac·to·gen·ic (lak′tə jen′ik), *adj.* stimulating lactation.

lac·tom·e·ter (lak tom′i tər), *n.* an instrument for determining the specific gravity of milk.

lac·tone (lak′tōn), *n. Chem.* any of a group of internal esters derived from hydroxy acids. —**lac·ton·ic** (lak ton′ik), *adj.*

lac·to·nize (lak′tō nīz′), *v.t., v.i.*, **-nized, -niz·ing.** to change into a lactone. —**lac′to·ni·za′tion,** *n.*

lac·to·pro·tein (lak′tō prō′tēn, -prō′tē in), *n.* any protein existing in milk.

lac·to·scope (lak′tə skōp′), *n.* an optical device for determining the amount of cream in milk.

lac·tose (lak′tōs), *n.* **1.** *Biochem.* a disaccharide, $C_{12}H_{22}O_{11} \cdot H_2O$, present in milk, that upon hydrolysis yields glucose and galactose. **2.** a white, crystalline, sweet, water-soluble commercial form of this compound, obtained from whey and used in infant feedings, in confections and other foods, in bacteriological media, and in pharmacy as a diluent and excipient. Also called **milk sugar, sugar of milk.**

La Cum·bre (*Sp.* lä kōōm′bre). See **Uspallata Pass.**

la·cu·na (lə kyōō′nə), *n., pl.* **-nae** (-nē), **-nas. 1.** a gap or missing part; hiatus. **2.** *Anat.* one of the numerous minute cavities in the substance of bone. **3.** *Bot.* an air space in the cellular tissue of plants. [< L: ditch, pit, hole, gap, deficiency, akin to *lacus* vat, lake. See LAGOON]

la·cu·nal (lə kyōōn′əl), *adj.* **1.** of or pertaining to a lacuna. **2.** having lacunae. Also, **lac·u·nar·y** (lak′yōō ner′ē, lə kyōō′nə rē).

la·cu·nar (lə kyōō′nər), *n., pl.* **la·cu·nars, lac·u·nar·i·a** (lak′yə nâr′ē ə), *adj.* —*n. Archit.* **1.** a coffered vault, ceiling, or soffit. **2.** coffer (def. 4). —*adj.* **3.** lacunal. [LACUN(A) + -AR[1]]

la·cu·nose (lə kyōō′nōs), *adj.* full of or having lacunae. [< L *lacūnōs(us)* full of holes or gaps] —**lac·u·nos·i·ty** (lak′yōō nos′i tē), *n.*

la·cus·trine (lə kus′trin), *adj.* **1.** of or pertaining to a lake. **2.** living or growing in lakes. **3.** formed at the bottom or along the shore of lakes, as geological strata. [< It *lacustr(e)* of lakes + -INE[1]]

lac·y (lā′sē), *adj.*, **lac·i·er, lac·i·est.** of or resembling lace; lacelike. —**lac′i·ly,** *adv.* —**lac′i·ness,** *n.*

lad (lad), *n.* **1.** a boy or youth. **2.** *Informal.* a familiar term of address for a man; chap. [ME *ladde*, OE *Ladda* (nickname) < ?]

lad·a·num (lad′ənəm), *n.* labdanum.

lad·der (lad′ər), *n.* **1.** a device for climbing, formed of a number of rungs or steps between uprights. **2.** something resembling such a device, esp. in having a series of levels, stages, ranks, etc. **3.** *Chiefly Brit.* a run in a stocking. —*v.t.* **4.** *Chiefly Brit.* to cause a run in (a stocking). —*v.i.* **5.** *Chiefly Brit.* to get a run, as in a stocking. [ME *laddre*, OE *hlǣder*; c. G *Leiter*, D *leer* (also *ladder* < Fris); akin to Goth *hleithra* tent; orig. something that slopes. See LEAN[1]]

lad′der back′, a chair back having a number of horizontal slats between uprights.

lad·die (lad′ē), *n. Chiefly Scot.* a young lad; boy.

lade (lād), *v.*, **lad·ed, lad·en** or **lad·ed, lad·ing.** —*v.t.* **1.** to load with or as with a cargo. **2.** to load oppressively; burden (used chiefly in the passive): *laden with debts.* **3.** to fill or cover abundantly (used chiefly in the passive): *trees laden with fruit.* **4.** to lift or transfer, as with a ladle. —*v.i.* **5.** to take on a load. **6.** to lade a liquid. [ME *lade(n)*, OE *hladan* to load, draw up (water); c. D *laden*, G *laden*, Icel *hlatha* to load. Cf. LADLE] —**lad′er,** *n.*

lad·en (lād′ən), *adj.* **1.** burdened. —*v.t.* **2.** to lade.

la-di-da (lä′dē dä′), *Informal.* —*adj.* **1.** affected; pretentious; foppish: *a la-di-da manner.* —*n.* **2.** behavior characterized by affected or exaggerated gentility. Also, **la′-de-da′.** [in derisive imitation of affected speech]

la·dies (lā′dēz), *n.* pl. of **lady.**

La′dies Aid′, a local organization of women who raise money for the church at which they worship.

La′dies Auxil′iary, an association whose members are usually the wives of members of an association with which it is affiliated.

La′dies, Day′, a special day on which women are invited to participate in a certain activity at a greatly reduced fee or at no cost: *Friday was Ladies' Day at the ball park.*

la·dies-in-wait·ing (lā′dēz in wā′ting), *n.* pl. of **lady-in-waiting.**

la′dies' man′, a man who is especially fond of the company of women and who strives especially to please them. Also, **lady's man.**

la′dies' room′, a public lavatory for women. Also called **powder room.**

La·din (lə dēn′), *n.* **1.** a Rhaeto-Romanic dialect of the southern Tyrol. **2.** a dialect of Romansh spoken in the Inn River valley of Grisons canton, Switzerland. **3.** a person who speaks Ladin. [< Romansh < L *Latīnus* LATIN]

lad·ing (lā′ding), *n.* **1.** the act of lading. **2.** freight or cargo.

La·di·no (lə dē′nō; *Sp.* lä thē′nô), *n., pl.* **-nos** (-nōz; *Sp.* -nôs) for 2. **1.** the Spanish dialect of the Sephardic Jews, written in the Hebrew script. **2.** (in Spanish America) a mestizo. [< Sp < L *Latīnus* LATIN. See LADIN]

Lad·is·laus (lad′is lôs′), *n.* **Saint,** c1040–95, king of Hungary 1077–95. Also, **Lad·is·las** (lad′is ləs, -läs′).

la·dle (lād′əl), *n., v.*, **-dled, -dling.** —*n.* **1.** a long-handled utensil with a cup-shaped bowl for dipping or conveying liquids. —*v.t.* **2.** to dip or convey with or as with a ladle. [ME *ladel*, OE *hlædel*. See LADE, -LE] —**la′dler,** *n.*

la·dle·ful (lād′əl fōōl′), *n., pl.* **-fuls.** the amount that fills a ladle. [late ME *ladelful*]

La·do·ga (lä′do gä′, -də-), *n.* **Lake,** a lake in the NW Soviet Union in Europe, NE of Leningrad: largest lake in Europe. 7000 sq. mi.

La·don (lād′ən), *n. Class. Myth.* a dragon with 100 heads who guarded the garden of the Hesperides and was killed by Hercules.

la·drone (lə drōn′), *n. Southwest U.S.* a thief. Also, **ladron′.** [< Sp *ladrón* < L *latrōn-* (s. of *latrō*) bandit]

La·drone′ Is′lands (lə drōn′), former name of **Mariana Islands.** Also called **La·drones** (lə drōnz′; *Sp.* läth rô′nes).

la·dy (lā′dē), *n., pl.* **-dies,** *adj.* —*n.* **1.** a woman of good family, social position, breeding, etc. **2.** a polite term for any woman. **3.** any woman; female: *a cleaning lady.* **4.** wife. **5.** (*cap.*) (in Great Britain) the proper title of any woman whose husband is higher in rank than baronet or knight, or who is the daughter of a nobleman not lower than an earl, although the title is given by courtesy also to the wives of baronets and knights. **6.** a woman who has proprietary rights or authority. Cf. **lord** (def. 4). **7.** (*cap.*) the Virgin Mary. **8.** a woman who is the object of the devotion of a knight. —*adj.* **9.** being a lady; female: *a lady judge.* [ME; earlier *lavedi*, OE *hlǣfdīge*, ? orig. meaning loaf-kneader = *hlāf* LOAF[1] + *dīge*, var. of *dǣge* kneader (see DOUGH); c. Icel *deigja* maid] —**la′dy·hood′,** *n.* —**la′dy·ish,** *adj.* —**Syn. 1.** See **woman.**

la·dy·bug (lā′dē bug′), *n.* any of numerous, often brightly colored beetles of the family *Coccinellidae*, feeding chiefly on aphids and other small insects, but including several forms that feed on plants. Also called **la′dy bee′tle, la′dy·bird′ bee′tle** (lā′dē bûrd′), **la′dy·bird′.**

Ladybug, *Hippodamia convergens* (Length ¼ in.)

La′dy chap′el, a chapel dedicated to the

Virgin Mary, attached to a church, and generally behind the high altar at the extremity of the apse.

La′dy Day′, 1. annunciation (def. 2). 2. *Brit.* the spring quarter day, when quarterly rents and accounts are due. Cf. **quarter day.** [ME (*oure*) *lady day*]

la·dy·fin·ger (lā′dē fiṅg′gər), *n.* a small, finger-shaped sponge cake.

La′dy in the Chair′, *Astron.* Cassiopeia.

la·dy-in-wait·ing (lā′dē in wā′tiṅg), *n., pl.* **la·dies-in-wait·ing.** a lady who is in attendance upon a queen or princess.

la·dy-kill·er (lā′dē kil′ər), *n. Informal.* a man who fascinates or is especially attractive to women, in fact or by reputation. —**la′dy-kill′ing,** *n., adj.*

la·dy·like (lā′dē līk′), *adj.* appropriate to a lady: *a ladylike appearance.* —**la′dy·like′ness,** *n.*

la·dy·love (lā′dē luv′), *n.* a sweetheart or mistress.

la′dy of the eve′ning, a prostitute. Also called **la′dy of pleas′ure.**

la′dy of the house′, the housewife or mistress of a house or apartment (usually prec. by *the*).

la·dy·ship (lā′dē ship′), *n.* 1. (*often cap.*) the form used in speaking of or to a woman having the title of *Lady* (usually prec. by *her* or *your*). 2. the rank of a lady. [ME]

la′dy's maid′, a maid who is a lady's personal attendant, as in dressing.

la′dy's man′. See **ladies' man.**

La·dy·smith (lā′dē smith′), *n.* a city in W Natal, in the E Republic of South Africa: besieged by Boers 1889–1900. 27,000.

la·dy's-slip·per (lā′dēz slip′ər), *n.* 1. any orchid of the genus *Cypripedium,* the flowers of which have a protruding labellum somewhat resembling a slipper. 2. any of several other related plants having similar flowers, as of the genera *Paphiopedilum, Phragmipedium,* and *Selenipedium.* Also, **la′dy-slip′per.**

Lady's-slipper, *Cypripedium reginae*

la·dy's-smock (lā′dēz smok′), *n.* a cruciferous plant, *Cardamine pratensis,* having white or purple flowers.

La·e (lä′ā, lā′ē), *n.* a seaport in E Papua New Guinea: major Japanese base in World War II. 38,707.

Laën·nec (lā nek′), *n.* **Re·né Thé·o·phile Hya·cinthe** (RƏ nā′ tā ô fēl′ YA SANT′), 1781–1826, French physician who invented the stethoscope.

La·er·tes (lā ûr′tēz), *n. Class. Myth.* the father of Odysseus.

Lae·tar′e Sun′day (lē târ′ē), the fourth Sunday of Lent when the introit begins with "*Laetare Jerusalem*" (Rejoice ye, Jerusalem).

la·e·trile (lā′ə tril′), *n.* a controversial drug prepared from the pits of apricots or peaches, claimed to cure cancer.

lae·vo (lē′vō), *adj.* levo.

laevo-, var. of **levo-.**

lae·vo·gy·rate (lē′vō jī′rāt), *adj.* levogyrate.

LaF, Louisiana French.

La Farge (lə färzh′, färj′), 1. **John,** 1835–1910, U.S. painter, stained-glass designer, and writer. 2. **Oliver Hazard Perry** (haz′ərd), ("*Oliver II*"), 1901–63, U.S. novelist and anthropologist.

La Fa·yette (laf′ē et′, lä′fē-, -fā-; *Fr.* LA FA yet′), **Ma·rie Ma·de·leine Pioche de la Vergne** (MA RĒ′ MADᵊ len′ pyôsh də LA VER′nyᵊ), **Comtesse de,** 1634–93, French novelist.

La·fa·yette (laf′ē et′, lä′fē-, -fā-; *for 1 also Fr.* LA FA yet′), *n.* 1. **Ma·rie Jo·seph Paul Yves Roch Gil·bert du Mo·tier** (MA RĒ′ zhô zef′ pôl ēv RôK zhēl ber′ DY mô tyā′), **Marquis de.** Also, **La Fayette.** 1757–1834, French soldier and statesman who served in the American Revolutionary Army. 2. a city in W Indiana, on the Wabash River. 44,955 (1970). 3. a city in S Louisiana. 68,908 (1970).

La·fitte (lä fēt′), *n.* **Jean** (zhäN), c1780–c1825, French privateer in the Americas. Also, **Laf·fite′.**

La Fol·lette (lə fol′it), **Robert Marion,** 1855–1925, U.S. political leader: U.S. Senator 1906–25.

La Fon·taine (LA fôN ten′; *Eng.* lä fon tān′, -ten′), **Jean de** (zhäN də), 1621–95, French poet and fabulist.

lag[1] (lag), *v.,* **lagged, lag·ging,** *n.* —*v.i.* 1. to fail to maintain a preestablished speed or pace. 2. to lose strength or intensity; flag: *Interest lagged as the meeting went on.* 3. *Marbles.* to throw one's shooting marble toward a line (**lag line**) on the ground in order to decide on the order of play. 4. *Billiards, Pool.* string (def. 13b). —*n.* 5. an instance of lagging. 6. a person or thing that lags. 7. *Mech.* the amount of retardation of some motion. 8. *Elect.* the retardation of one alternating quantity, as current, with respect to another related alternating quantity, as voltage, often expressed in degrees. 9. *Marbles, Billiards.* the act of lagging. [< Scand; cf. Norw *lagga* to go slowly] —**lag′ger,** *n.* —**Syn.** 1. loiter, linger.

lag[2] (lag), *v.,* **lagged, lag·ging,** *n. Slang.* —*v.t.* 1. to send to penal servitude; imprison. —*n.* 2. a convict or ex-convict. 3. a term of penal servitude. [?]

lag[3] (lag), *n., v.,* **lagged, lag·ging.** —*n.* 1. one of the staves or strips that form the periphery of a wooden drum, the casing of a steam cylinder, or the like. —*v.t.* 2. to cover with insulation, as a steam boiler, to prevent radiation of heat. [< Scand; cf. Sw *lagg* stave]

lag·an (lag′ən), *n. Law.* anything sunk in the sea, but attached to a buoy or the like so that it may be recovered. Also, **ligan.** [< ML *lagan*(*um*) right to own wreckage washed up from the sea, perh. < Gmc]

La·gash (lā′gash), *n.* an ancient Sumerian city between the Tigris and Euphrates rivers, at modern Telloh in SE Iraq.

Lag b'O·mer (läg bō′mər; *Heb.* läg bə ō′MER), a Jewish festival celebrated on the 18th day of Iyar, commemorating an unsuccessful revolt against the Romans in the 2nd century A.D. [< Heb = *lag* 33rd + *'omer* period from Passover (2nd day) to Shabuoth, special use of *'omer* OMER]

la·ger[1] (lä′gər, lô′-), *n.* a dry, light, carbonated beer aged in storage from six weeks to six months before use. Also called **la′ger beer′.** [short for *lager beer,* half adoption half trans. of G *Lagerbier.* See LAIR[1], BEER]

la·ger[2] (lä′gər), *n., v.t., v.i. South African.* laager.

La·ger·kvist (lä′gəR kvist′), *n.* **Pär** (paR), 1891–1974, Swedish novelist, poet, and essayist: Nobel prize 1951.

La·ger·löf (lä′gəR lœf′), *n.* **Sel·ma (Ot·ti·li·a·na Lo·vi·sa)** (sel′mä ôt′ti lē ä′nä lo͞o′vi sä′), 1858–1940, Swedish novelist and poet: Nobel prize 1909.

lag·gard (lag′ərd), *n.* 1. a person or thing that lags; lingerer; loiterer. —*adj.* 2. moving, developing, or responding slowly; sluggish; backward. —**lag′gard·ness,** *n.*

lag·gard·ly (lag′ərd lē), *adv.* 1. in the manner of a laggard. —*adj.* 2. of, pertaining to, characteristic of, or being a laggard.

lag·ging[1] (lag′iṅg), *n.* 1. the act of lagging behind. —*adj.* 2. lingering; loitering; slow and dragging: *lagging steps.* [LAG[1] + -ING[1]] —**lag′ging·ly,** *adv.*

lag·ging[2] (lag′iṅg), *n.* 1. the act of covering a boiler, engine, etc., with heat-insulating material. 2. the covering formed. 3. the material used. [LAG[3] + -ING[1]]

lag′ line′. See under **lag**[1] (def. 3).

-lagnia, a learned borrowing from Greek, where it meant "coition," used in the formation of compound words: *algolagnia.* [comb. form repr. Gk *lagneía* coition, lust]

la·gniappe (lan yap′, lan′yap), *n.* 1. *Chiefly Southern Louisiana and Southeast Texas.* something given with a purchase to a customer, for good measure. 2. a gratuity or tip. Also, **la·gnappe′.** [< LaF < AmerSp *la ñapa* the addition = *la* fem. definite article + *ñapa,* var. of *yapa* < Quechua]

lag·o·morph (lag′ə môrf′), *n.* any mammal of the order *Lagomorpha,* resembling the rodents but having two pairs of upper incisors, and comprising the hares, rabbits, and pikas. [< NL *Lagomorph*(*a*) name of the order = Gk *lagṓ*(*s*) hare + *morph*(*ḗ*) -MORPH + L *-a* neut. pl. suffix] —**lag′o·mor′phic, lag′o·mor′phous,** *adj.*

la·goon (lə go͞on′), *n.* 1. an area of shallow water separated from the sea by low banks, as in an atoll. 2. any small, pondlike body of water, esp. one communicating with a larger body of water. 3. a huge man-made pool for sanitary treatment of liquid sewage or industrial waste. Also, **lagune** (for 1, 2). [earlier *laguna* (sing.), *lagune* (pl.) < It < L *lacūna* ditch, pool, akin to *lacus* basin, lake] —**la·goon′al,** *adj.*

Lagoon′ Is′lands, former name of **Tuvalu.**

La·gos (lä′gōs, lā′gos), *n.* a seaport in and the capital of Nigeria, in the SW part. 1,060,848; 24 sq. mi.

La·grange (lə grānj′; *Fr.* LA GRÄNZH′), *n.* 1. **Jo·seph Louis** (zhô zef′ lwē), **Comte,** 1736–1813, French mathematician and astronomer. 2. a walled plain in the third quadrant of the face of the moon. ab. 100 mi. in diam.

lag′ screw′, a heavy wood screw having a square or hexagonal head driven by a wrench. Also called **coach screw.** See illus. at **screw.**

La Guar·di·a (lə gwär′dē ə), **Fi·o·rel·lo H(enry)** (fē′ə rel′ō), 1882–1947, U.S. lawyer and politician: mayor of New York City 1933–45.

la·gune (lə go͞on′), *n.* lagoon (defs. 1, 2).

La Ha·bra (lə hä′brə), a city in SW California, near Los Angeles. 41,350 (1970).

La Hogue (LA ôg′), a roadstead off the NW coast of France; defeat of French fleet by British and Dutch, 1692. Also, **La Houge** (LA o͞og′).

La·hore (lə hōr′, -hôr′), *n.* a city in NE Pakistan. 1,297,000 (est. 1961).

Lai·bach (lī′bäKH), *n.* German name of **Ljubljana.**

la·ic (lā′ik), *adj.* 1. Also, **la′i·cal.** lay; secular. —*n.* 2. layman. [< LL *lāic*(*us*) < Gk *lāikós* of the people = *lā*(*ós*) people + *-ikos* -IC] —**la′i·cal·ly,** *adv.*

la·i·cism (lā′i siz′əm), *n.* the nonclerical, or secular, control of political and social institutions in a society (distinguished from *clericalism*).

la·i·cize (lā′i sīz′), *v.t.,* **-cized, -ciz·ing.** to deprive of clerical character; secularize: *to laicize a school.* Also, *esp. Brit.,* **la·i·cise.** —**la′i·ci·za′tion,** *n.*

laid (lād), *v.* pt. and pp. of **lay**[1].

laid-back (lād′bak′), *adj. Slang.* 1. relaxed and unhurried: *laid-back music rhythms.* 2. feeling no social or moral pressure; carefree: *a laid-back way of living.*

laid′ deck′, *Shipbuilding.* a wooden deck having planking laid parallel to the sides of the hull so as to follow the curves toward the ends of the vessel.

laid′ pa′per, paper with fine parallel and cross lines produced in manufacturing. Cf. **wove paper.**

laigh (lāKH), *adj., adv. Scot.* low[1]. [ME *lawch.* See LOW[1]]

lain (lān), *v.* pp. of **lie**[2].

lair[1] (lâr), *n.* 1. a den or resting place of a wild animal. 2. a hideout or hideaway. 3. *Brit.* a place in which to lie or rest; a bed. [ME *leir,* OE *leger;* c. D, OHG *leger* bed, camp; akin to LIE[2]]

lair[2] (lâR), *v.i. Scot.* to sink or stick in mud or mire. [v. use of ME *lair* clay, mire < Scand; cf. Icel *leir* clay, LOAM]

laird (lârd; *Scot.* lāRd), *n. Scot.* a landed proprietor. [ME *laverd* (north) LORD] —**laird′ly,** *adj.* —**laird′ship,** *n.*

lais·sez faire (les′ā fâr′; *Fr.* le sā feR′), 1. the theory that government should intervene as little as possible in the direction of economic affairs. 2. the practice or doctrine of noninterference in the affairs of others. Also, **lais′ser faire′.** [< F: lit., allow to act] —**lais′sez-faire′, lais′ser-faire′,** *adj.*

lais·sez-pas·ser (le sā pä sā′), *n., pl.* **-ser.** *French.* permit; pass, esp. one issued in lieu of a passport. [lit., allow to pass]

la·i·ty (lā′i tē), *n.* 1. the body of religious worshipers, as distinguished from the clergy. 2. the people outside a particular profession, as distinguished from those belonging to it. [LAY[3] + -ITY]

La·ius (lā′əs, lā′ē əs), *n.* a king of Thebes, the husband of Jocasta and father of Oedipus: unwittingly killed by Oedipus.

La Jo·lla (lə hoi′yə), a resort area in San Diego, in S California.

lake[1] (lāk), *n.* 1. a body of fresh or salt water of considerable size, completely surrounded by land. 2. a body or pool of liquid suggesting this. [ME, OE *lacu* stream, pool, pond (c. G *Lache* pool, bog); r. early ME *lac* < OF < L *lac*(*us*)]

lake[2] (lāk), *n.* 1. any of various pigments prepared from animal, vegetable, or coal-tar coloring matters by chemical or other union with metallic compounds. 2. a red pigment prepared from lac or cochineal by combination with a metallic compound. [var. of LAC[1]]

Lake (lāk), *n.* **Simon,** 1866–1945, U.S. engineer and naval architect.

Lake′ Ar′al. See **Aral Sea.**

Lake′ Charles′, a city in SW Louisiana. 77,998 (1970).

Lake′ Dis′trict, a mountainous region in NW England containing many lakes. Also, **Lake′ Coun′try.**

lake′ dwell′er, an inhabitant of a lake dwelling.

lake′ dwell′ing, a dwelling, esp. of prehistoric times, built on piles over a lake.

lake·front (lāk′frunt′), *n.* the land along the edge of a lake. Also called **lakeshore.**

lake′ her′ring, a cisco or whitefish, esp. *Coregonus artedii,* of the Great Lakes.

Lake·land (lāk′lənd), *n.* a city in central Florida. 41,550 (1970).

Lake′land ter′rier, one of a breed of small, slender terriers, raised originally in NW England for hunting foxes.

Lake′ of the Woods′, a lake in S Canada and the N United States, between N Minnesota and Ontario and Manitoba provinces. 1485 sq. mi.

Lake′ Plac′id, a town in NE New York, in the Adirondack Mountains: resort. 2731 (1970).

Lake′ Po′ets, the poets Wordsworth, Coleridge, and Southey: so called from their residence in the Lake District.

lake·port (lāk′pōrt′, -pôrt′), *n.* a port city located on the shore of a lake, esp. one of the Great Lakes.

lak·er (lā′kər), *n.* **1.** a person closely associated with a lake, as a resident, visitor, or worker. **2.** a lake fish, esp. the lake trout. **3.** a vessel designed for navigating on lakes, esp. the Great Lakes.

Lakes′ Dis′trict, a town in W Washington. 48,195 (1970).

lake·shore (lāk′shōr′, -shôr′), *n.* lakefront.

Lake′ Success′, a town on Long Island, in SE New York: United Nations headquarters 1946–51. 3254 (1970).

lake′ trout′, a large, fork-tailed trout, *Salvelinus namaycush,* found in the lakes of Canada and the northern U.S., used for food.

Lake·wood (lāk′wŏŏd′), *n.* **1.** a city in SW California, near Los Angeles. 82,973 (1970). **2.** a city in NE Ohio, on Lake Erie, near Cleveland. 70,173 (1970). **3.** a city in central Colorado, near Denver. 92,787 (1970).

lakh (lak), *n.* lac[2].

lak·y (lā′kē), *adj.* of the color of a lake pigment.

la·la·pa·loo·za (lol′ə pə lo͞o′zə), *n.* lollapalooza. Also, **lal′la·pa·loo′za.**

-lalia, a combining form denoting a speech defect of a type specified by the preceding element: *echolalia.* [< NL, comb. form repr. Gk *laliá* talking, chatter = *lal(ein)* (to) chatter, babble + *-ia* -IA]

La Li·ne·a (lä lē′ne ä), a seaport in S Spain, near Gibraltar. 60,379 (1960).

lall (lal), *v.i.* *Phonet.* to make imperfect *l*- or *r*-sounds, or both. [imit.; see LALLATION]

Lal·lans (lal′ənz), *n.pl.* **1.** the Lowlands of Scotland. **2.** the inhabitants of the Scottish Lowlands. **3.** (*construed as sing.*) the literary form of the English dialect of the Scottish Lowlands. [var. of LOWLANDS]

lal·la·tion (la lā′shən), *n.* *Phonet.* a speech defect in which *l* is pronounced instead of *r,* or in which an *l* or *r*-sound is mispronounced. Cf. **lambdacism.** [< L *lallā(re)* (to) sing lullaby + -TION]

lal·ly·gag (lol′ē gag′), *v.i.,* **-gagged, -gag·ging.** *Informal.* to idle; loaf. Also, **lollygag.** [?]

La·lo (lᴀ lō′), *n.* **(Vic·tor An·toine) E·douard** (vēk tôʀ′ äɴ twaɴ′ ā dwaʀ′), 1832–92, French composer.

lam[1] (lam), *v.,* **lammed, lam·ming.** *Slang.* **—*v.t.*** **1.** to beat; thrash. **—*v.i.*** **2.** to beat; strike; thrash (usually fol. by *out* or *into*): *to lam out savagely against an invader.* [< Scand; cf. Icel *lamdi,* past tense of *lemja* to beat, akin to LAME[1]]

lam[2] (lam), *n., v.,* **lammed, lam·ming.** *Slang.* **—*n.*** **1. on the lam,** escaping, fleeing, or hiding, esp. from the police. **2. take it on the lam,** to flee or escape in great haste. **—*v.i.*** **3.** to run away quickly; escape; flee. [special use of LAM[1]]

Lam., Lamentations.

lam., laminated.

la·ma (lä′mə), *n.* a priest or monk in Lamaism. [< Tibetan *blama* (*b-* is silent)]

La·ma·ism (lä′mə iz′əm), *n.* the Buddhism of Tibet and Mongolia, a Mahayana form including non-Buddhist Indian elements. **—La′ma·ist,** *n.* **—La′ma·is′tic,** *adj.*

La Man·cha (lä män′chä), a plateau region in central Spain.

La·mar (lə mär′), *n.* **Lucius Quin·tus Cin·cin·nat·us** (kwin′təs sin′sə nat′əs, -nā′təs), 1825–93, U.S. politician and jurist: associate justice of the U.S. Supreme Court 1888–93.

La·marck (lə märk′; *Fr.* lᴀ mᴀʀk′), *n.* **Jean Bap·tiste Pierre An·toine de Mo·net de** (zhäɴ bᴀ tēst′ pyeʀ äɴ twäɴ′ də mô ne′ də), 1744–1829, French naturalist. **—La·marck′i·an,** *adj.*

La·marck·ism (lə mär′kiz əm), *n.* the Lamarckian theory that characteristics acquired by habit, use, disuse, or adaptations to changes in environment may be inherited.

La·mar·tine (lᴀ mᴀʀ tēn′), *n.* **Al·phonse Ma·rie Louis de Prat de** (ᴀl fôɴs′ mᴀ ʀē′ lwē də pʀᴀ də), 1790–1869, French poet, historian, and statesman.

la·ma·ser·y (lä′mə ser′ē), *n., pl.* **-ser·ies.** a monastery of lamas. [< F *lamaserie.* See LAMA, SERAI]

La·maze′ technique′ (lə mäz′, lä-), psychoprophylaxis. [named after Fernand *Lamaze* (1890–1957), French physician, its originator]

lamb (lam), *n.* **1.** a young sheep. **2.** the meat of a young sheep. **3.** an amiable or gentle person. **4.** a person who is easily cheated, esp. an inexperienced speculator. **5. the Lamb,** Christ. **—*v.i.*** **6.** to give birth to a lamb. [ME, OE; c. D *lam,* G *Lamm,* Icel, Goth *lamb;* akin to Gk *élaphos* deer. See also ELK] **—lamb′like′,** *adj.*

Lamb (lam), *n.* **1. Charles** (pen name: *Elia*), 1775–1834, English essayist and critic. **2. Mary (Ann),** 1764–1847, English author who wrote in collaboration with her brother Charles Lamb. **3. William, 2nd Viscount Melbourne,** 1779–1848, English statesman: prime minister 1834, 1835–41.

lam·baste (lam bāst′, -bast′), *v.t.,* **-bast·ed, -bast·ing.** *Informal.* **1.** to beat or whip severely. **2.** to reprimand or berate harshly; censure; excoriate. Also, **lam·bast′.** [appar. LAM[1] + BASTE[3]]

lamb·da (lam′də), *n.* the 11th letter of the Greek alphabet (Λ, λ). [< Gk < Sem; cf. LAMED]

lamb·da·cism (lam′də siz′əm), *n.* *Phonet.* excessive use of the sound *l.* Cf. **lallation.** [< LL *labdacism(us)* < Gk *labdakismós* = *labda, lambda* LAMBDA + connective *k* + *-ismos* -ISM]

lamb·doid (lam′doid), *adj.* having the shape of the Greek capital lambda. Also, **lamb·doi′dal.** [< NL *lambdoīd(ēs)* < Gk *lambdoeidḗs.* See LAMBDA, -OID]

lam·ben·cy (lam′bən sē), *n., pl.* **-cies.** **1.** the quality of being lambent. **2.** that which is lambent.

lam·bent (lam′bənt), *adj.* **1.** running or moving lightly over a surface: *lambent tongues of flame.* **2.** brilliantly playful: *lambent wit.* **3.** softly bright or radiant: *a lambent light.* [< L *lambent-* (s. of *lambēns*) lapping, prp. of *lambere* to lick, wash (said of water or fire); akin to LAP[2]; see -ENT] **—lam′bent·ly,** *adv.*

lam·bert (lam′bərt), *n.* *Optics.* the centimeter-gram-second unit of luminance or brightness, equivalent to .32 candle per square centimeter, and equal to the brightness of a perfectly-diffusing surface emitting or reflecting one lumen per square centimeter. *Abbr.:* L [named after J. H. *Lambert* (1728–77), German scientist and mathematician]

Lam·beth (lam′bith), *n.* a borough of S London, England. 223,162 (1961).

Lam′beth Pal′ace, the official residence of the archbishop of Canterbury, in S London.

Lam′beth walk′, a spirited ballroom dance popular, esp. in England, in the late 1930's.

lamb·kin (lam′kin), *n.* **1.** a little lamb. **2.** a young and innocent person, esp. a small child. [ME *lambkyn*]

Lamb′ of God′, Christ. [ME]

lam·bre·quin (lam′brə kin, lam′bər-), *n.* **1.** a woven fabric worn over a medieval helmet to protect it from heat and rust. **2.** a curtain or drapery covering the upper part of an opening, as a door or window, or suspended from a shelf. **3.** *Heraldry.* mantling. [< F, MF < MFlem **lamperkijn,* dim. of *lamper* kind of crepe, crepe veil (akin to LAP[1]); see -KIN]

lamb·skin (lam′skin′), *n.* **1.** the skin of a lamb, esp. when dressed with its wool, and used for clothing. **2.** leather made from such skin. **3.** parchment made from such skin. [ME]

lame[1] (lām), *adj.,* **lam·er, lam·est,** *v.,* **lamed, lam·ing.** **—*adj.*** **1.** crippled or physically disabled, esp. in the foot or leg. **2.** impaired or disabled through defect or injury: *His arm was lame.* **3.** weak; inadequate; clumsy: *a lame excuse.* **—*v.t.*** **4.** to make lame or defective. [ME; OE *lama;* c. D *lam,* G *lahm,* Icel *lami;* akin to Lith *lúomas*] **—lame′ly,** *adv.* **—lame′ness,** *n.*

lame[2] (lām; *Fr.* lᴀm), *n., pl.* **lames** (lāmz; *Fr.* lᴀm). *Armor.* any of a number of thin, overlapping plates composing a piece of plate armor, as a fauld, tasset, gauntlet, etc. [< MF < L *lāmina* a thin piece or plate]

la·mé (la mā′; *Fr.* lᴀ mā′), *n.* an ornamental fabric in which metallic threads are woven with silk, wool, rayon, or cotton. [< F = *lame* LAME[2] + *-é* < L *-ātus* -ATE[1]]

lame·brain (lām′brān′), *n.* *Slang.* a dunce; booby; fool; half-wit; dope.

la·med (lä′mid; *Heb.* lä′med), *n.* the 12th letter of the Hebrew alphabet. [< Heb]

lame′ duck′, *U.S. Informal.* an elected government official who is completing his term in office after an election in which he has failed to be reelected or who is ineligible for an additional term.

la·mel·la (lə mel′ə), *n., pl.* **-mel·lae** (-mel′ē), **-mel·las.** **1.** a thin plate, scale, membrane, or layer, as of bone, tissue, cell walls, etc. **2.** *Bot.* **a.** an erect scale or blade inserted at the junction of the claw and limb in some corollas and forming a part of their corona or crown. **b.** gill[1] (def. 2). **c.** (in mosses) a thin sheet of cells standing up along the midrib of a leaf. [< L, dim. of *lāmina* LAME[2]]

la·mel·lar (lə mel′ər, lam′ə lər), *adj.* **1.** referring to a lamella or lamellae. **2.** lamellate. **3.** noting a type of armor composed of small plates or lames laced together. **—la·mel′lar·ly,** *adv.*

lam·el·late (lam′ə lāt′, -lit; lə mel′āt, -it), *adj.* **1.** composed of or having lamellae. **2.** flat; platelike. Also, **lam′el·lat′ed, la·mel·lose** (lə mel′ōs, lam′ə lōs′). [< NL *lāmellāt(us)*] **—lam′el·late′ly,** *adv.* **—lam·el·los·i·ty** (lam′ə los′i tē), *n.*

la·mel·li·branch (lə mel′ə braŋk′), *n.* **1.** a mollusk of the class *Pelecypoda* (*Lamellibranchiata*); a pelecypod. **—*adj.*** **2.** pelecypod. Also, **la·mel·li·bran·chi·ate** (lə mel′ə braŋ′kē āt′, -it). [< NL *Lāmellibranch(ia).* See LAMELLA, -I-, -BRANCHIA]

la·mel·li·corn (lə mel′ə kôrn′), *Entomol.* **—*adj.*** **1.** having antennae with lamellate terminal segments, as beetles of the group *Lamellicornia,* including the scarabaeids and stag beetles. **2.** (of an antenna) having lamellate terminal segments. **—*n.*** **3.** a lamellicorn beetle. [< NL *lāmellicorn(is).* See LAMELLA, -I-, -CORN]

la·mel·li·form (lə mel′ə fôrm′), *adj.* shaped like a lamella; platelike; scalelike.

la·ment (lə ment′), *v.t.* **1.** to feel or express sorrow or regret for. **—*v.i.*** **2.** to feel, show, or express grief, sorrow, or regret; mourn deeply. **—*n.*** **3.** an expression of grief or sorrow. **4.** a formal expression of sorrow or mourning, esp. in verse or song; an elegy or dirge. [(n.) < L *lāment(um)* plaint; (v.) < L *lāment(ārī)* (< n.)] **—la·ment′er,** *n.* **—la·ment′ing·ly,** *adv.* **—Syn. 1.** bewail, bemoan. **2.** grieve, weep. **3.** lamentation, moan, wail. **4.** monody, threnody.

lam·en·ta·ble (lam′ən tə bəl, lə men′tə-), *adj.* that is to be lamented; regrettable; unfortunate; deplorable. [late ME < L *lāmentābil(is)*] **—lam′en·ta·ble·ness,** *n.* **—lam′en·ta·bly,** *adv.*

lam·en·ta·tion (lam′ən tā′shən), *n.* **1.** the act of lamenting or expressing grief. **2.** a lament. **3. Lamentations,** (*construed as sing.*) a book of the Bible, traditionally ascribed to Jeremiah. [< L *lāmentātiōn-* (s. of *lāmentātiō*) =

lāmentāt(us) (ptp. of *lāmentārī;* see LAMENT) + *-iōn-* -ION; r. ME *lamentacioun* < AF]

la·ment·ed (lə men′tid), *adj.* mourned for, as a person who is dead. —**la·ment′ed·ly,** *adv.*

La Me·sa (lä mā′sə), a city in SW California. 39,178 (1970).

la·mi·a (lā′mē ə), *n., pl.* **-mi·as, -mi·ae** (-mē ē′). **1.** *Class. Myth.* one of a class of monsters, commonly represented with the head and breast of a woman and the body of a serpent, said to allure youths and children in order to suck their blood. **2.** a vampire; a female demon. [ME < L < Gk: a female man-eater]

la·mi·a·ceous (lā′mē ā′shəs), *adj.* belonging to the *Labiatae* (or *Menthaceae,* formerly *Lamiaceae*) or mint family of plants. [< NL *Lāmi(um)* genus name (special use of L: dead nettle) + -ACEOUS]

lam·i·na (lam′ə nə), *n., pl.* **-nae** (-nē′), **-nas. 1.** a thin plate, scale, or layer. **2.** a layer or coat lying over another, as the plates of minerals, bones, etc. **3.** *Bot.* the blade or expanded portion of a leaf. [< L; see LAME[2]]

lam·i·nar (lam′ə nər), *adj.* composed of, or arranged in, laminae. Also, **lam·i·nar·y** (lam′ə ner′ē), **lam′i·nal.** [LAMIN(A) + -AR[1]]

lam·i·nate (*v.* lam′ə nāt′; *adj., n.* lam′ə nāt′, -nit), *v.,* **-nat·ed, -nat·ing,** *adj., n.* —*v.t.* **1.** to separate or split into thin layers. **2.** to form (metal) into a thin plate, as by beating or rolling. **3.** to construct by placing layer upon layer. **4.** to cover or overlay with laminae. —*v.i.* **5.** to split into thin layers. —*adj.* **6.** composed of or having a lamina or laminae. —*n.* **7.** a laminated product; lamination. [< NL *lāminät(us).* See LAMINA, -ATE[1]] —**lam′i·na·ble,** *adj.* —**lam′i·na′tor,** *n.*

lam·i·nat·ed (lam′ə nā′tid), *adj.* **1.** formed of or set in thin layers or laminae. **2.** made or constructed of a succession of layers: *laminated wood.*

lam·i·na·tion (lam′ə nā′shən), *n.* **1.** the act or process of laminating. **2.** the state of being laminated. **3.** laminated structure; arrangement in thin layers. **4.** a lamina.

lam·i·nose (lam′ə nōs′), *adj.* laminate; laminar. [LAMIN(A) + -OSE[1]]

La Mi·ra·da (lä′ mə rä′də), a city in SW California. 30,808 (1970).

Lam·mas (lam′əs), *n.* **1.** a former festival held in England on August 1, in which bread made from the first harvest of corn was blessed. **2.** a festival observed by Roman Catholics on August 1, in memory of St. Peter's imprisonment and his miraculous deliverance. Also called **Lam′mas Day′.** [ME *Lammesse,* OE *hlāmmæsse, hlāfmæsse.* See LOAF[1], -MAS]

Lam·mas·tide (lam′əs tīd′), *n.* the season of Lammas. [ME]

lam·mer·gei·er (lam′ər gī′ər), *n.* the largest European bird of prey, *Gypaëtus barbatus,* having a 9–10-foot wingspread, ranging in the mountains from southern Europe to China. Also, **lam′mer·gey′er, lam′mer·ge′ir.** [< G *Lämmergeier,* lit., lambs' vulture (from its preying on lambs) = *Lämmer,* pl. of *Lamm* LAMB + *Geier* vulture, c. D *gier*]

lamp (lamp), *n.* **1.** a device providing an isolated source of artificial light. **2.** See **incandescent lamp. 3.** See **fluorescent lamp. 4.** a device for providing radiant heat or rays of certain kinds: *infrared lamp.* **5.** *Archaic.* a celestial body that gives off light, as the moon or a star. **6.** *Archaic.* a torch. [ME *lampe* < OF < LL *lampada,* for L *lampas* (s. *lampad-*) < Gk *lámpē* torch, lamp, akin to *lampás* lamp]

lam·pas[1] (lam′pəs), *n.* *Vet. Pathol.* congestion of the mucous membrane of the hard palate of horses. Also, **lam·pers** (lam′pərz). [< MF: disease of horses, OF: disease (of men)]

lam·pas[2] (lam′pəs), *n.* an elaborately embellished fabric woven with a double warp and one or more fillings. [ME *lawmpas* < MFlem *lampers,* var. of *lamper* kind of crepe; see LAMBREQUIN]

lamp·black (lamp′blak′), *n.* a fine black pigment consisting of almost pure carbon, collected as soot from the smoke of burning oil, gas, etc.

Lam·pe·du·sa (läm′pe dōō′zä), *n.* an island in the Mediterranean, between Tunisia and Malta: belonging to Italy.

lam′per eel′ (lam′pər), lamprey.

lamp·light (lamp′līt′), *n.* the light shed by a lamp.

lamp·light·er (lamp′lī′tər), *n.* **1.** a person who lights street lamps, as before the use of electricity. **2.** a contrivance for lighting lamps.

lam·poon (lam pōōn′), *n.* **1.** a sharp, often virulent satire. —*v.t.* **2.** to mock or ridicule in a lampoon. [< F *lampon,* said to be n. use of *lampons* let us guzzle (from a drinking song), impv. of *lamper,* nasalized var. of *laper* to lap up < Gmc; see LAP[3]] —**lam·poon′er, lam·poon′ist,** *n.* —**lam·poon′er·y,** *n.* —**Syn. 1.** See **satire.**

lamp·post (lamp′pōst′), *n.* a post supporting a street lamp.

lam·prey (lam′prē), *n., pl.* **-preys.** any eellike, marine or fresh-water fish of the group *Hyperoartia,* having undeveloped eyes and a circular, suctorial mouth with horny teeth for boring into the flesh of other fishes to feed on their blood. Also called **lam′prey eel′, lamper eel.** [ME *lampreye* < AF **lampreie* (OF *lamproie*) < LL *lamprēda;* r. OE *lamprede* < ML *lampreda*]

Lamprey,
Petromyzon marinus
(Length 21 in.)

lamp·shade (lamp′shād′), *n.* a device, fitted over a lamp, for reflecting or partially cutting off its light.

lamp′ shell′, any of several brachiopods. [so called because its shape resembles that of an ancient oil lamp]

lam·py·rid (lam′pə rid), *n.* **1.** any of several insects of the family *Lampyridae,* comprising the fireflies. —*adj.* **2.** belonging or pertaining to the family *Lampyridae.* [< NL *Lampyrid(ae)* glowworm family = *Lampyr(is)* typical genus (< Gk: glowworm; see LAMP) + *-idae* -ID[2]]

La·na·i (lä nä′ē, lə nī′), *n.* an island in central Hawaii. 2204 (1970); 141 sq. mi.

la·na·i (lä nä′ē, lə nī′), *n., pl.* **-na·is.** *Hawaiian.* a veranda.

Lan·ark (lan′ərk), *n.* a county in S Scotland. 1,626,317 (1961); 898 sq. mi. *Co. seat:* Lanark. Also called **Lan·ark·shire** (lan′ərk shēr′, -shər).

la·nate (lā′nāt), *adj.* woolly; covered with something resembling wool. Also, **lanose.** [< L *lānāt(us)* woolly = *lān(a)* wool + *-ātus* -ATE[1]]

Lan·ca·shire (laŋ′kə shēr′, -shər), *n.* a county in NW England. 5,131,646 (1961); 1878 sq. mi. *Co. seat:* Lancaster. Also called **Lancaster.**

Lan·cas·ter (laŋ′kə stər; *for 3, 5, 6 also* laŋ′kas tər), *n.* **1.** the English royal family that reigned 1399–1461, descended from John of Gaunt (Duke of Lancaster), and which included Henry IV, Henry V, and Henry VI. Cf. **York** (def. 1). **2.** a member of this family. **3.** a city in SE Pennsylvania. 57,690 (1970). **4.** a city in and the county seat of Lancashire, in NW England. 48,887 (1961). **5.** a city in central Ohio. 32,911 (1970). **6.** a town in S California. 32,570 (1970).

Lan·cas·tri·an (laŋ kas′trē ən), *adj.* **1.** of or pertaining to the royal family of Lancaster. —*n.* **2.** an adherent or member of the house of Lancaster, esp. in the Wars of the Roses. **3.** a native or resident of Lancashire or Lancaster.

lance[1] (lans, läns), *n., v.,* **lanced, lanc·ing.** —*n.* **1.** a long, shafted weapon with a metal head, used by mounted soldiers in charging. **2.** a soldier armed with this weapon; lancer. **3.** an implement resembling the weapon, as a spear for killing a harpooned whale. **4.** a lancet. —*v.t.* **5.** to open with or as with a lancet. [ME *launce* < OF *lance* < L *lancea*] —**lance′like′,** *adj.*

lance[2] (lans, läns), *n.* See **sand lance.** [? special use of LANCE[1], from its shape]

lance′ cor′poral, 1. *U.S. Marine Corps.* an enlisted man ranking between private first class and corporal. **2.** *Brit. Mil.* **a.** a corporal of the lowest rank. **b.** (formerly) a private acting as corporal without increased pay. [earlier *lancepesade* < MF *lancepessade* lowest ranking grade of noncommissioned officer < It *lancia spezzata* superior soldier, lit., broken lance (from having shivered many lances, i.e., fought well in many battles)]

lance·let (lans′lit, läns′-), *n.* any small, fishlike, chordate animal of the subphylum *Cephalochordata,* having a notochord in the slender, elongated body pointed at each end.

Lan·ce·lot (lan′sə lət, -lot′, län′-), *n.* *Arthurian Romance.* the greatest of Arthur's knights and the lover of Queen Guinevere.

lan·ce·o·late (lan′sē ə lāt′, -lit), *adj.* **1.** shaped like the head of a lance. **2.** narrow, and tapering toward the apex or sometimes at the base, as a leaf. [< L *lanceolāt(us)* armed with a small lance = *lanceol(a)* small lance (*lance(a)* LANCE[1] + *-ola* dim. suffix) + *-ātus* -ATE[1]] —**lan′ce·o·late′ly,** *adv.*

lanc·er (lan′sər, län′-), *n.* a mounted soldier armed with a lance. [< MF *lancier*]

lance′ rest′, a support for a couched lance, fixed to the breastplate of a suit of armor.

lanc·ers (lan′sərz, län′-), *n.* (*construed as sing.*) a set of quadrilles danced in sequence. [pl. of LANCER]

Lanceolate leaf

lance′ ser′geant, *Brit. Mil.* **1.** a sergeant of the lowest rank. **2.** (formerly) a corporal appointed to act as sergeant, without increase in pay; an acting sergeant. [see LANCE CORPORAL]

lan·cet (lan′sit, län′-), *n.* a small surgical instrument, usually sharp-pointed and two-edged, for letting blood, opening abscesses, etc. [late ME *lancette* < MF]

lan′cet arch′, *Archit.* an arch having a head that is acutely pointed.

lan′cet win′dow, *Archit.* a high, narrow window terminating in a lancet arch.

lance·wood (lans′wŏŏd′, läns′-), *n.* **1.** the tough, elastic wood of any of various trees, as *Oxandra lanceolata,* of tropical America, used for carriage shafts, cabinetwork, etc. **2.** a tree that yields it.

Lan·chow (län′jō′), *n.* a city in and the capital of Kansu, in N China, on the Hwang Ho. 699,000 (est. 1957).

lan·ci·nate (lan′sə nāt′), *v.t.,* **-nat·ed, -nat·ing.** to stab or pierce. [< L *lancināt(us)* torn to pieces, ptp. of *lancināre,* akin to *lanius* butcher, *lacer* torn; see -ATE[1]] —**lan′ci·na′tion,** *n.*

land (land), *n.* **1.** the part of the earth's surface above water. **2.** an area or portion of this; ground: *arable land; to buy land in Florida; in England's green and pleasant land.* **3.** a nation or country. **4.** a realm or domain. **5.** a surface area left flush among grooves or hollows made by an industrial process. **6.** *Law.* **a.** any part of the earth's surface which can be owned as property, and everything annexed to it, whether by nature or by the hand of man. **b.** any legal interest held in land. **7.** *Econ.* natural resources as a factor of production. **8. the land, a.** the rural areas; the country. **b.** the occupation of farming: *Many workers left the land for jobs in town.* —*v.t.* **9.** to bring to or set on land. **10.** to bring into or cause to arrive in any place, position, or condition: *His behavior will land him in jail.* **11.** *Informal.* to catch, capture, or gain: *land a job.* **12.** *Angling.* to bring (a fish) to land, into a boat, etc. —*v.i.* **13.** to come to land or shore. **14.** to go or come ashore from a ship or boat. **15.** to alight upon or strike a surface from above. **16.** to come to rest or arrive in any place, position, or condition (sometimes fol. by *up*): *to land in trouble; to land up 40 miles from home.* [ME, OE; c. D, G, Icel, Goth *land;* akin to Ir *lann,* Welsh *llan* church (orig., enclosure), Breton *lann* heath. See LAWN[1]]

Land (land), *n.* **Edwin Herbert,** born 1909, U.S. inventor and businessman.

-land, a combining form of **land:** *hinterland; lowland.*

lan·dau (lan′dô, -dou), *n.* **1.** a four-wheeled, two-seated carriage with a two-part folding top. **2.** a sedanlike automobile with a collapsible top over the rear section. **3.** a fabriclike covering for the roof of an automobile. [after *Landau,* town in Germany where first made]

Landau

lan·dau·let (lan′dô let′), *n.* an automobile having a convertible top for the back seat, with the front seat either roofed or open. Also, **lan′dau·lette′.**

land′ bank′, a banking association that engages in the financing of transactions in real property, esp. in agricultural land.

land′ crab′, any of several crabs, esp. of the family *Gecarcinidae,* that live chiefly upon land, returning to the sea to breed.
land·ed (lan′did), *adj.* **1.** owning land: *a landed proprietor.* **2.** consisting of land: *landed property.* [ME; OE *(ge)landod*]
land·fall (land′fôl′), *n.* **1.** an approach to or sighting of land. **2.** the land sighted or reached. **3.** a landslide.
land′ grant′, a tract of land given by the government, as for colleges or railroads. —**land-grant** (land′grant′, -gränt′), *adj.*
land′-grant col′lege, *U.S.* a college or university **(land′-grant univer′sity)** entitled to support from the federal government under the provisions of the Morrill Acts.
land·grave (land′grāv′), *n.* **1.** (in medieval Germany) a nobleman with the rank of count. **2.** *(usually cap.)* the title of certain German princes. [< MLG; see GRAF, MARGRAVE, REEVE]
land·gra·vi·ate (land grā′vē it, -āt′), *n.* the office or territory of a landgrave. [< ML *landgraviāt(us).* See LANDGRAVE (ML *landgravius*), -ATE[1]]
land·gra·vine (land′grə vēn′), *n.* the wife of a landgrave. [< D *landgravin,* fem. of *landgraaf* LANDGRAVE]
land·hold·er (land′hōl′dər), *n.* a holder, owner, or occupant of land. [late ME] —**land′hold′ing,** *adj., n.*
land·ing (lan′ding), *n.* **1.** act of a person or thing that lands. **2.** a place where persons or goods are landed, as from a ship. **3.** *Archit.* **a.** the floor at the head or foot of a flight of stairs. **b.** a platform between flights of stairs.
land′ing craft′, *Navy.* any of various flat-bottomed vessels designed to move troops and equipment close to shore in amphibious operations.
land′ing field′, an area of land cleared for the landing and takeoff of aircraft.
land′ing flap′, a flap in the under surface of the trailing edge of an aircraft wing, capable of being moved downward to increase either lift or drag or both, as for landing.
land′ing gear′, the wheels, floats, etc., of an aircraft, upon which it moves on ground or water.
land′ing net′, *Angling.* a bag-shaped net with a handle, for scooping a hooked fish out of the water.
land′ing ship′, *Navy.* a ship designed for transporting troops and equipment in amphibious warfare, and making landings directly onto a beach.
land′ing strip′, **1.** a runway, esp. the part that an aircraft touches during landing or takeoff. **2.** a runway auxiliary to the regularly used runways of an airfield. **3.** a small runway serving as an airfield, esp. in remote or sparsely populated areas.
Lan·dis (lan′dis), *n.* **Ken·e·saw Mountain** (ken′i sô′), 1866–1944, U.S. jurist: first commissioner of baseball 1920–44.
land·la·dy (land′lā′dē), *n., pl.* **-dies.** a female landlord.
land·less (land′lis), *adj.* without landed property or ownership of land. [OE *landleas*] —**land′less·ness,** *n.*
land·locked (land′lokt′), *adj.* **1.** shut in completely, or almost completely, by land. **2.** not having access to the sea. **3.** living in waters shut off from the sea, as some fish.
land′locked salm′on, a variety of the Atlantic Ocean salmon, *Salmo salar,* confined to the fresh-water lakes of New England and adjacent areas of Canada.
land·lord (land′lôrd′), *n.* **1.** a person who owns land, buildings, apartments, etc., and leases them to others. **2.** the master of an inn, lodging house, etc. **3.** a landowner. [ME; OE *landhlāford*] —**land′lord′ly,** *adj.*
land·lub·ber (land′lub′ər), *n.* *Naut.* a landsman or raw seaman. —**land′lub′ber·ish,** *adj.* —**land′lub′ber·ly,** **land′lub′bing,** *adj.*
land·man (land′mən), *n., pl.* **-men.** landsman (def. 1). [ME; OE *landmann*]
land·mark (land′märk′), *n.* **1.** a prominent or conspicuous object on land that serves as a guide. **2.** a prominent or distinguishing feature, part, event, etc. **3.** something used to mark the boundary of land. [OE *landmearc*]
land′ mine′, *Mil.* an explosive charge concealed just under the surface of the ground.
Lan·do (län′dō), *n.* died A.D. 914, Italian ecclesiastic: pope 913–914.
land′ of′fice, a government office for the transaction of business relating to public lands.
land′-of·fice busi′ness (land′ô′fis, -of′is), *U.S. Informal.* a lively, booming, or very profitable business.
land′ of milk′ and hon′ey, **1.** a land of unusual fertility and abundance. **2.** the blessings of heaven. Also, **Land′ of Milk′ and Hon′ey.**
land′ of Nod′ (nod), the mythical land of sleep. [pun on *Land of Nod* (Gen. 4:16)]
Land′ of Prom′ise. See **Promised Land.**
Land′ of the Mid′night Sun′, **1.** any of those countries containing land within the Arctic Circle where there is a midnight sun in midsummer, esp. Norway, Sweden, or Finland. **2.** Lapland.
Land′ of the Ris′ing Sun′, *Informal.* Japan.
Lan·don (lan′dən), *n.* **Alf(red Moss·man)** (môs′mən, mos′-), born 1887, U.S. politician.
Lan·dor (lan′dər, -dôr), *n.* **Walter Savage,** 1775–1864, English poet and prose writer.
land·own·er (land′ō′nər), *n.* an owner or proprietor of land. —**land′own′er·ship′,** *n.* —**land′own′ing,** *n., adj.*
Lan·dow·ska (lan dôf′skə; *Pol.* län dôf′skä), *n.* **Wan·da** (won′də; *Pol.* vän′dä), 1879–1959, Polish harpsichordist, in the U.S. after 1940.
land-poor (land′pŏŏr′), *adj.* in need of ready money while owning much unremunerative land.
land′ reform′, any governmental program involving the redistribution of large holdings of agricultural land among the landless.
land·scape (land′skāp′), *n., v.,* **-scaped, -scap·ing.** —*n.* **1.** a section or portion of scenery, usually extensive, that may be seen from a single viewpoint. **2.** a picture representing such scenery. **3.** such pictures generally as a category of painting. —*v.t.* **4.** to improve the appearance of (an area of land, a highway, etc.), as with planting or by altering the contours of the ground. —*v.i.* **5.** to practice as a landscape architect or landscape gardener. [earlier *landscap, landskip* < MD *lantscap;* c. OE *landsceap, landscipe;* akin to G *Landschaft.* See LAND, -SHIP]
land′scape ar′chitecture, the art of arranging or modifying the features of a landscape, an urban area, etc., for aesthetic or practical reasons. —**land′scape ar′chitect.**
land′scape gar′dening, the art or trade of designing or rearranging large gardens, estates, etc. —**land′scape gar′dener.**
land·scap·ist (land′skā′pist), *n.* a person who paints landscapes.
Land·seer (land′sēr, -syər), *n.* **Sir Edwin Henry,** 1802–1873, English painter, esp. of animals.
Land's′ End′, the SW tip of England.
land·side (land′sīd′), *n.* the part of a plow consisting of a sidepiece opposite the moldboard, for guiding the plow and resisting the side pressure caused by the turning of the furrow.
lands·knecht (*Ger.* länts′kneKHt′), *n.* a European mercenary foot soldier of the 16th century, armed with a pike or halberd. Also, **lansquenet.** [< G; see LAND, KNIGHT]
land·slide (land′slīd′), *n., v.,* **-slid, -slid** or **-slid·den, -slid·ing.** —*n.* **1.** a fall or slide of soil, detritus, or rock, on or from a steep slope. **2.** the material that falls. **3.** an election in which a particular candidate or party receives an overwhelming mass or majority of votes. —*v.i.* **4.** to come down in or as in a landslide. **5.** to win an election by an overwhelming majority. Also called, *esp. Brit.,* **land·slip** (land′slip′) (for defs. 1, 2).
Lands·mål (länts′môl), *n.* *Norwegian.* Nynorsk. Formerly, **Lands′maal.**
lands·man (landz′mən), *n., pl.* **-men.** **1.** Also, **landman.** a person who lives or works on land. **2.** *Naut.* **a.** a sailor on his first voyage. **b.** an inexperienced seaman, rated below an ordinary seaman.
lands·man (länts′mən), *n., pl.* **lands·leit** (länts′līt′), *Eng.* **-men.** *Yiddish.* a person from the same town, geographical area, region, etc., as another; compatriot.
Land·stei·ner (land′stī′nər; *Ger.* länt′shtī′nəR), *n.* **Karl** (kärl; *Ger.* käRl), 1868–1943, Austrian pathologist in the U.S.: Nobel prize 1930.
land·ward (land′wərd), *adv.* **1.** Also, **land′wards.** toward the land or interior. —*adj.* **2.** lying, facing, or tending toward the land or inland. **3.** being in the direction of the land. [late ME]
lane[1] (lān), *n.* **1.** a narrow way or passage between hedges, fences, walls, or houses. **2.** any narrow or well-defined passage, track, channel, or course. **3.** a part of a highway wide enough to accommodate one vehicle. **4.** (in a running or swimming race) the marked-off space or path within which a competitor must remain during the course of a race. **5.** See **bowling alley** (def. 1). [ME, OE; c. D *laan* avenue, Icel *lön* row of houses, hayrick] —**Syn. 1.** alley. See **path.**
lane[2] (lān), *adj.* *Scot.* lone.
Lan·franc (lan′frangk), *n.* 1005?–89, Italian Roman Catholic prelate and scholar in England: archbishop of Canterbury 1070–89.
lang., language.
Lang·land (lang′lənd), *n.* **William,** 1332?–c1400, English poet. Also, **Langley.**
lang·lauf (läng′louf′), *n.* cross-country skiing. [< G: lit., long run. See LONG[1], LOPE, LEAP]
lang·läuf·er (läng′loi′fər), *n., pl.* **-läuf·er, -läuf·ers.** a participant in cross-country skiing. [< G]
Lang·ley (lang′lē), *n.* **1. Edmund of.** See **York, Edmund of Langley, 1st Duke of. 2. Samuel Pier·pont** (pēr′pont), 1834–1906, U.S. astronomer, physicist, and pioneer in aeronautics. **3. William.** See **Langland, William.**
Lan·go·bard (lang′gə bärd′), *n.* Lombard (def. 2). [< L *Langobardī* (pl.), Latinized form of Germanic tribal name; c. OE *Longbeardan*]
Lan·go·bar·dic (lang′gə bär′dik), *adj.* **1.** Lombard (def. 3). —*n.* **2.** a West Germanic language, the language of the ancient Lombards.
Lan·gre·o (läng grē′ō), *n.* a city in N Spain. 65,399 (1955).
lang·syne (lang′zīn′, -sīn′), *Scot.* —*adv.* **1.** long since; long ago. —*n.* **2.** time long past.
Lang·ton (lang′tən), *n.* **Stephen,** c1165–1228, English theologian, historian, and poet: archbishop of Canterbury.
Lang·try (lang′trē), *n.* **Lil·lie** (lil′ē), *(Emily Charlotte Le Breton)* (*"the Jersey Lily"*), 1852–1929, English actress.
lan·guage (lang′gwij), *n.* **1.** a body of words and systems for their use common to a people of the same community or nation, the same geographical area, or the same cultural tradition: *the two languages of Belgium; the French language.* **2.** communication by voice, using arbitrary, auditory symbols in conventional ways with conventional meanings. **3.** any set or system of such symbols as used in a more or less uniform fashion by a number of people, who are thus enabled to communicate intelligibly with one another. **4.** any system of formalized symbols, signs, gestures, or the like, used or conceived as a means of communication: *the language of mathematics; deaf-and-dumb language.* **5.** the means of communication used by animals: *the language of birds.* **6.** communication of meaning in any way: *the language of flowers; the language of art.* **7.** linguistics. **8.** the speech or phraseology peculiar to a class, profession, etc. **9.** a particular manner of verbal expression: *in his own language; flowery language; vile language.* **10.** diction or style of writing: *the language of poetry; the stilted language of official documents.* **11.** *Archaic.* faculty or power of speech. [ME < AF, var. sp. of *langage* < *langue* tongue. See LINGUA, -AGE] —**Syn. 2.** See **speech. 3, 8.** tongue; lingo. LANGUAGE, DIALECT, JARGON, VERNACULAR refer to patterns of vocabulary, syntax, and usage characteristic of communities of various sizes and types. LANGUAGE is applied to the general pattern of a people or race: *the English language.* DIALECT is applied to certain forms or varieties of a language, often those of provincial communities or special groups: *Scottish dialect.* A JARGON is a pattern used by a particular (usually occupational) group: *the jargon of the theater; the Chinook jargon.* A VERNACULAR is the authentic natural pattern of

speech, now usually on the informal level, used by persons indigenous to a certain community, large or small.

lan′guage arts′, the skills, including reading, composition, speech, spelling, dramatics, etc., taught in elementary and secondary schools to give students a thorough proficiency in using the English language.

lan′guage lab′orato′ry, a special room with sound-recording and -reproducing equipment on which students practice speaking foreign languages, usually with a teacher monitoring the program.

Langue·doc (läng dôk′), *n.* a former province in S France. *Cap.:* Toulouse. See map at **Burgundy.** —**Langue·do·cian** (lang dō′shən, lang′gwə dō′shən), *adj., n.*

langue d'oc (läng dôk′), the Romance language of medieval southern France. [< F: language of *oc,* yes << L *hoc (ille fecit)* this (he did)]

langue d'oïl (läng dô ēl′, dô′ē, doil), the Romance language of medieval northern France. [< F: language of *oïl,* yes << L *hoc ille (fecit)* this he (did)]

lan·guet (lang′gwet), *n.* any of various small tongue-shaped parts, processes, or projections. [late ME < MF *languete,* dim. of *langue* tongue; see -ET]

lan·guid (lang′gwid), *adj.* **1.** drooping or flagging from weakness or fatigue; faint. **2.** lacking in vigor or vitality; slack: *a languid manner.* **3.** lacking in spirit or interest; indifferent. [< L *languid(us)* faint. See LANGUISH, -ID[4]] —**lan′guid·ly,** *adv.* —**lan′guid·ness,** *n.* —**Syn. 1.** weak, feeble, weary, exhausted. **2.** listless, spiritless. **3.** sluggish.

lan·guish (lang′gwish), *v.i.* **1.** to be or become weak or feeble; droop; fade. **2.** to lose vigor and vitality. **3.** to undergo neglect. **4.** to pine with desire or longing. **5.** to assume an expression of tender sentimental melancholy. [ME < MF *languiss-,* long s. of *languir* << L *languēre* to languish; see -ISH[2]] —**lan′guish·er,** *n.*

lan·guish·ing (lang′gwi shing), *adj.* **1.** becoming languid, in any way. **2.** expressive of languor; indicating tender, sentimental melancholy: *a languishing sigh.* **3.** lingering: *a languishing death.* [ME] —**lan′guish·ing·ly,** *adv.*

lan·guor (lang′gər), *n.* **1.** physical weakness or faintness. **2.** lack of energy or vitality; sluggishness. [< L (see LANGUISH, -OR[1]); r. ME *langour* sickness, woe < OF]

lan·guor·ous (lang′gər əs), *adj.* **1.** characterized by languor; languid. **2.** inducing languor: *languorous fragrance.* [LANGUOR + -OUS; r. late ME *langorous* woeful] —**lan′guor·ous·ly,** *adv.*

lan·gur (lung gŏŏr′), *n.* any of several slender, long-tailed monkeys of the genus *Presbytis,* of Asia, feeding on leaves, fruits, and seeds. [< Hindi; akin to Skt *lāngūlin* having a tail]

lan·iard (lan′yərd), *n.* lanyard.

La·nier (lə nēr′), *n.* **Sidney,** 1842–81, U.S. poet and literary scholar.

La·ni·kai (lä′nē kī′), *n.* a town adjoining Kailua, on SE Oahu, in Hawaii. With Kailua, 33,783 (1970).

lank (langk), *adj.* **1.** (of hair) straight and limp; without spring or curl. **2.** (of plants) unduly long and slender. **3.** lean; gaunt; thin. [ME *lanc,* OE *hlanc;* akin to OHG *hlanca* loin, side. See FLANK] —**lank′ly,** *adv.* —**lank′ness,** *n.*

lank·y (lang′kē), *adj.,* **lank·i·er, lank·i·est.** ungracefully thin and rawboned; bony; gaunt: *a tall, lanky man.* —**lank′i·ly,** *adv.* —**lank′i·ness,** *n.*

lan·ner (lan′ər), *n.* **1.** a falcon, *Falco biarmicus,* of southern Europe, northern Africa, and southern Asia. **2.** *Falconry.* the female of this bird. [late ME *laner* < MF *lanier* kind of falcon, lit., wool weaver (< L *lānārius* = *lān(a)* wool + *-ārius* -ARY), a term of abuse in early Middle Ages, applied especially to sluggards, laggards, and cowards, and so to the lanner, slow in flight and thought to be cowardly]

lan·ner·et (lan′ə ret′), *n.* *Falconry.* the male lanner, which is smaller than the female. [late ME *lanret* < MF *laneret*]

lan·o·lin (lan′ᵊlin), *n.* a fatty substance, extracted from wool, used in ointments. Also, **lan·o·line** (lan′ᵊlin, -ᵊlēn′). Also called **wool fat.** [< L *lān(a)* wool + -OL[2] + -IN[2]] —**lan·o·lat·ed** (lan′ᵊlā′tid), *adj.*

la·nose (lā′nōs), *adj.* lanate. [< L *lānōs(us)*] —**la·nos·i·ty** (lā nos′i tē), *n.*

Lan·sing (lan′sing), *n.* **1.** a city in and capital of Michigan, in S part. 131,546 (1970). **2.** a city in NE Illinois, near Chicago. 25,805 (1970).

lans·que·net (lans′kə net′), *n.* landsknecht. [< F, m. G *Landsknecht*]

lan·ta·na (lan tā′nə, -tä′-), *n.* any of several chiefly tropical, verbenaceous plants of the genus *Lantana,* certain species of which, as *L. Camara,* are cultivated for their aromatic flowers. [< NL, special use of dial. It *lantana* wayfaring tree]

lan·tern (lan′tərn), *n.* **1.** a transparent or translucent case for enclosing a light and protecting it from the wind, rain, etc. **2.** the chamber at the top of a lighthouse, surrounding the light. **3.** See **magic lantern. 4.** *Archit.* **a.** a tall, more or less open construction admitting light to an enclosed area below. **b.** any light, decorative structure of relatively small size crowning a roof, dome, etc. [ME *lanterne* < L *lanterna* < Gk *lampt(ēr)* lamp, light + *-erna,* ? < Etruscan]

L

L, Lantern (def. 4b)

lan′tern fly′, any of several tropical, homopterous insects of the family *Fulgoridae,* formerly thought to be luminescent.

lan′tern jaw′, a long, thin jaw. [so called from the fancied resemblance of the face to the shape of a lantern] —**lan′tern-jawed′,** *adj.*

lan′tern slide′, a slide or transparency for a slide projector or magic lantern.

lan′tern wheel′, a wheel, used like a pinion, consisting essentially of two parallel disks or heads connected by a series of bars that engage with the teeth of another wheel. Also called **lan′tern pin′ion.**

lan·tha·nide (lan′thə nīd′, -nid), *n.* *Chem.* one of the rare-earth elements of atomic number 57–71, inclusive. [LANTHAN(UM) + -IDE]

lan·tha·num (lan′thə nəm), *n.* *Chem.* a rare-earth, trivalent, metallic element, allied to aluminum, found in certain rare minerals, as monazite. *Symbol:* La; *at. wt.:* 138.91; *at. no.:* 57; *sp. gr.:* 6.15 at 20°C. [< NL = *lanthan-* (< Gk *lanthán(ein)* (to) lurk unseen) + *-um,* var. o f*-ium* -IUM]

lant·horn (lant′hôrn′, lan′tərn), *n.* *Archaic.* lantern.

Lan·tsang (län′tsäng′), *n.* Chinese name of **Mekong.**

la·nu·gi·nose (lə nōō′jə nōs′, -nyōō′-), *adj.* **1.** covered with lanugo, or soft, downy hairs. **2.** of the nature of down; downy. Also, **la·nu·gi·nous** (lə nōō′jə nəs, -nyōō′-). [< L *lānūginōs(us)* downy, woolly = *lānūgin-* (s. of *lānūgo;* see LANUGO) + *-ōsus* -OSE[1]] —**la·nu·gi·nous·ness** (lə nōō′jə nəs nis, -nyōō′-), *n.*

la·nu·go (lə nōō′gō, -nyōō′-), *n., pl.* **-gos.** *Biol.* a coat of delicate, downy hairs, esp. that with which the human fetus or a newborn infant is covered. [< L: down < *lāna* wool]

lan·yard (lan′yərd), *n.* **1.** *Naut.* a short rope or wire rove through deadeyes to hold and tauten standing rigging. **2.** any of various small cords or ropes for securing or suspending small objects, as a whistle about the neck. **3.** *Mil.* a cord with a small hook at one end, used in firing certain kinds of cannon. **4.** *U.S. Mil.* **a.** a colored, single-strand cord worn around the left shoulder by a member of a military unit awarded a foreign decoration. **b.** a white cord worn around the right shoulder, as by a military policeman, and secured to the butt of a pistol. Also, **laniard.** [b. late ME *lanyer* (< MF *laniere,* OF *lasniere* thong = *lasne* noose + *-iere* -ER[2]) and YARD[1]]

Lao (lou), *n.* a language of Laos and northern Thailand that belongs to the Thai group of languages.

La·oag (lä wäg′), *n.* a seaport on NW Luzon, in the N Philippines. 22,218 (1948).

La·oc·o·on (lā ok′ō on′), *n.* *Class. Myth.* a priest of Apollo at Troy who warned the Trojans against the Trojan Horse, and who, with his two sons, was killed by serpents sent by Athena or Apollo. Also, **La·oc′o·ön′.**

La·od·i·ce·a (lā od′i sē′ə, lā′ə di sē′ə), *n.* ancient name of **Latakia.**

La·od·i·ce·an (lā od′i sē′ən, lā′ə di sē′ən), *adj.* **1.** lukewarm or indifferent, esp. in religion, as were the early Christians of Laodicea. —*n.* **2.** a person who is lukewarm or indifferent, esp. in religion.

Laoigh·is (lā′ish), *n.* a county in Leinster, in the central Republic of Ireland. 45,069 (1961); 623 sq. mi. *Co. seat:* Port Laoighise. Also called **Leix.**

La·om·e·don (lā om′i don′), *n.* *Class. Myth.* a king of Troy and the father of Priam.

La·os (lä′ōs, lā′os; *Fr.* lȧ ôs′), *n.* a kingdom in SE Asia: formerly part of French Indochina. 2,900,000; 91,500 sq. mi. *Caps.:* Vientiane *and* Luang Prabang. —**La·o·tian** (lā ō′shən), *n.*

Lao-tzu (lou′dzu′), *n.* (*Li Erh*) 6th century B.C., Chinese philosopher: reputed founder of Taoism. Also, **Lao-tse** (lou′dzu′).

lap[1] (lap), *n.* **1.** the front part of the human body from the waist to the knees when in a sitting position. **2.** the part of the clothing that covers this part of the body. **3.** a metaphorical area of responsibility, care, charge, or control: *The outcome is in the lap of the gods.* **4.** a hollow place, as a hollow among hills. [ME *lappe,* OE *læppa;* c. D *lap;* akin to G *lappen,* Icel *leppr* rag, patch]

lap[2] (lap), *v.,* **lapped, lap·ping,** *n.* —*v.t.* **1.** to fold over or about something; wrap; wind. **2.** to enwrap or enfold in something; wrap up; clothe. **3.** to lay (something) over another, or (two things) together in an overlapping arrangement. **4.** to get a lap or more ahead of (a competitor) in racing. **5.** to cut or polish with a lap. **6.** *Building Trades.* to join in a lap joint. —*v.i.* **7.** to fold or wind around something. **8.** to lie partly over or alongside of something else. **9.** to extend beyond a limit. —*n.* **10.** the act of lapping. **11.** the amount of material required to go around a thing once. **12.** a complete circuit of a course in racing or walking for exercise. **13.** an overlapping part. **14.** the extent or amount of overlapping. **15.** a rotating wheel or disk holding an abrasive or polishing powder on its surface, used for gems, cutlery, etc. [ME *lappe(n)* (to) fold, wrap; c. D *lappen* to patch, mend; akin to LAP[1]]

lap[3] (lap), *v.,* **lapped, lap·ping,** *n.* —*v.t.* **1.** to wash against (something) with a light, slapping or splashing sound, as water. **2.** to take in (liquid) with the tongue; lick in (often fol. by *up*). —*v.i.* **3.** to wash or move in small waves with a light slapping or splashing sound. **4.** to take up liquid with the tongue; lick up a liquid. —*n.* **5.** the act of lapping liquid. **6.** the sound of this. **7.** something lapped up, as liquid food for dogs. [ME *lappe,* unexplained var. of *lape,* OE *lap(ian);* c. MLG *lapen;* akin to Gk *láptein* to lick]

lap[4] (lap), *v.* *Dial.* pt. of **leap.**

laparo-, a learned borrowing from Greek, where it meant "flank," used in the formation of compound words to denote the abdominal wall: *laparotomy.* Also, *esp. before a vowel,* **lapar-.** [comb. form repr. Gk *lapárā* flank (lit., soft part), n. use of fem. of *laparós* soft]

lap·a·rot·o·my (lap′ə rot′ə mē), *n., pl.* **-mies.** *Surg.* **1.** incision into the loin. **2.** incision into the abdominal cavity through any point in the abdominal wall.

La Paz (lä päs′; *Eng.* lə päz′), **1.** a city in W Bolivia: seat of the government; Sucre is the nominal capital. 660,700; ab. 12,000 ft. above sea level. **2.** a city in SE Lower California, in NW Mexico. 46,000.

lap′ belt′, *Auto.* a safety belt or strap for fastening across the lap of the driver or passenger. Cf. **shoulder belt.**

lap·board (lap′bōrd′, -bôrd′), *n.* a thin, flat board to be held on the lap for use as a table or desk.

lap′ dissolve′, dissolve (def. 14).

lap′ dog′, a small pet dog. Also, **lap′dog′.**

la·pel (lə pel′), *n.* a part of a garment folded back on the breast, esp. a continuation of a coat collar. [dim. of LAP[1]; see -LE] —**la·pelled′,** *adj.*

lap·ful (lap′fo͝ol′), *n., pl.* **-fuls.** as much as the lap can hold.

lap·i·dar·y (lap′i der′ē), *n., pl.* **-dar·ies,** *adj.* —*n.* **1.** Also, **lap·i·dist** (lap′i dist). a workman who cuts, polishes, and engraves precious stones. **2.** the art of cutting, polishing, and engraving precious stones. **3.** Also, **la·pid·ar·ist** (lə pid′ər ist). an expert on or connoisseur of precious stones. —*adj.* **4.** of or pertaining to the cutting or engraving of precious stones. **5.** characterized by an exactitude and refinement suggestive of gem cutting. **6.** of, pertaining to, or suggestive of inscriptions on stone monuments. [ME *lapidarie* (n.) < L *lapidāri(us)* of stone (adj.) stonecutter (n.) = *lapid-* (s. of *lapis*) stone + *-ārius* -ARY]

la·pil·lus (lə pil′əs), *n., pl.* **-pil·li** (-pil′ī). a stony particle ejected from a volcano, esp. a round particle less than one inch in diameter. [< L: little stone, dim. of *lapis* stone]

lap·in (lap′in; *Fr.* LA PAN′), *n., pl.* **lap·ins** (lap′inz; *Fr.* LA PAN′). **1.** a rabbit. **2.** its fur. [< F, MF < ?]

la·pis (lā′pis, lap′is), *n., pl.* **lap·i·des** (lap′i dēz′). *Latin.* a stone: used in names of minerals, gems, etc.

lap·is laz·u·li (lap′is laz′o͝o lē, -lī′, laz′yo͝o-, lazh′o͝o-), **1.** a deep-blue mineral composed mainly of lazurite, used chiefly as a gem or as a pigment. **2.** a sky-blue color; azure. Also called **lap′is, lazuli.** [ME < ML = L *lapis* a stone + ML *lazulī*, gen. of *lazulum* lapis lazuli; see AZURE]

lap′ joint′, *Building Trades.* **1.** Also called **plain lap.** a joint in which the pieces overlap without any change in form. **2.** any of various joints in which an end or section of one member is partly cut away to be overlapped by an end or section of the other, often so that flush surfaces result. —**lap′-joint′ed,** *adj.*

La·place (LA PLAS′), *n.* **Pierre Si·mon** (pyeR sē môN′) **Marquis de,** 1749–1827, French astronomer and mathematician.

Lap·land (lap′land′), *n.* a region in N Norway, N Sweden, N Finland, and the Kola Peninsula of the NW Soviet Union in Europe: inhabited by Lapps.

La Pla·ta (lä plä′tä), **1.** a seaport in E Argentina. 406,000 (est. 1965). **2.** See **Plata, Rio de la.**

Lapp (lap), *n.* **1.** Also called **Lap·land·er** (lap′lan′dər, -lən-). a member of a Finnic people of northern Norway, Sweden, Finland, and adjacent regions. **2.** Also called **Lap′pish.** any of the languages of the Lapps, closely related to Finnish. [< Sw]

lap·pet (lap′it), *n.* **1.** a small lap, flap, or loosely hanging part, esp. of a garment or headdress. See illus. at **miter. 2.** a projecting, lobelike structure in certain invertebrate animals. **3.** *Ornith.* a wattle or other fleshy process on a bird's head. —**lap′pet·ed,** *adj.*

lap′ robe′, a fur robe, blanket, or the like, to cover the lap and legs of a person, esp. when riding in an automobile, carriage, etc.

lapse (laps), *n., v.,* **lapsed, laps·ing.** —*n.* **1.** an accidental or temporary decline from an expected or accepted condition or state. **2.** a slip or error, often of a trivial sort; failure. **3.** an interval or passage of time; an elapsed period. **4.** a moral fall, as from rectitude. **5.** a fall or decline to a lower grade, condition, or degree. **6.** *Law.* the termination of a right or privilege through neglect to exercise it. **7.** a falling into disuse. **8.** *Insurance.* discontinuance of coverage resulting from nonpayment of a premium; termination of a policy. **9.** *Meteorol.* See **lapse rate. 10.** the act of falling, slipping, sliding, etc., slowly or by degrees. **11.** *Archaic.* a gentle, downward flow, as of water. —*v.i.* **12.** to fall from a previous standard; fail to maintain a normative level. **13.** *Law.* to pass from one to another by lapse. **14.** *Insurance.* to cease being in force; terminate. **15.** to fall, slip, or sink; subside: *to lapse into silence.* **16.** to fall spiritually, as an apostate: *to lapse from grace.* **17.** to fall into disuse. **18.** to pass away, as time; elapse. [< L *lāps(us)* an error, slipping, failing < *lāpsus*, ptp. of *lābī* to slide, slip, fall, make mistakes] —**laps′a·ble, laps′i·ble,** *adj.*

lapse′ rate′, *Meteorol.* the rate of decrease of atmospheric temperature with increase of elevation.

lap·strake (lap′strāk′), *adj.* noting a hull having a shell each strake of which overlaps that below; clinker-built.

lap·sus lin·guae (läp′so͞os ling′gwī; *Eng.* lap′səs ling′gwē), *Latin.* a slip of the tongue.

Lap′tev Sea′ (läp′tef), an arm of the Arctic Ocean N of the Soviet Union in Asia, between Taimyr Peninsula and the New Siberian Islands. Also called **Nordenskjöld Sea.**

La Puen·te (lä pwen′tā), a city in SW California, E of Los Angeles. 31,092 (1970).

lap·wing (lap′wing′), *n.* **1.** a large, Old World plover, *Vanellus vanellus*, having a long, slender, upcurved crest, an erratic, flapping flight, and a shrill cry. **2.** any of several similar, related plovers. [ME, var. (by assoc. with WING) of *lapwinke*, OE *hlēapwince* plover]

lar (lär), *n., pl.* **lar·es** (lâr′ēz, lā′rēz), **lars** (lärz). *Rom. Religion.* any of the lares. [< L]

Lar·a·mie (lar′ə mē), *n.* **Fort.** See **Fort Laramie.**

lar·board (lär′bōrd′, -bôrd′; *Naut.* lär′bərd), *Naut. Obs.* —*n.* **1.** port² (def. 1). —*adj.* **2.** port² (defs. 2, 3). [ME *laddeborde* (? lit., loading side; see LADE, BOARD); later *larborde* (by analogy with *starboard*)]

lar·ce·nous (lär′sə nəs), *adj.* **1.** of, resembling, or characteristic of larceny. **2.** guilty of larceny. —**lar′ce·nous·ly,** *adv.*

lar·ce·ny (lär′sə nē), *n., pl.* **-nies.** *Law.* the wrongful taking and carrying away of the personal goods of another with intent to convert them to the taker's own use. Cf. **grand larceny, petty larceny.** [late ME < AF *larcin* theft (< L *latrōcin(ium)* robbery = *latrōcin(ārī)* (to) rob, orig. serve as mercenary soldier (< *latrō* hired soldier, robber) + *-ium* -IUM) + -Y³] —**lar′ce·nist, lar′ce·ner,** *n.*

larch (lärch), *n.* **1.** any coniferous tree of the genus *Larix*, yielding a tough durable wood. **2.** the wood of such a tree. [earlier *larche* < MHG << L *laric-* (s. of *larix*) larch]

lard (lärd), *n.* **1.** the rendered fat of hogs, esp. the internal fat of the abdomen. —*v.t.* **2.** to apply lard or grease to. **3.** to prepare or enrich (lean meat, chicken, etc.) with pork or fat, esp. with lardons. **4.** to intersperse with something for improvement or ornamentation. [ME (v.), late ME (n.) < MF *larder* (v.), *lard* (n.) < L *lār(i)dum* bacon fat]

lar·da·ceous (lär dā′shəs), *adj.* lardlike; fatty.

lar·der (lär′dər), *n.* a room or place where food is kept; pantry. [ME < AF (OF *lardier*)]

Lard·ner (lärd′nər), *n.* **Ring(gold Wil·mer)** (ring′gōld′ wil′mər), 1885–1933, U.S. short-story writer and journalist.

lar·don (lär′dᵊn), *n.* a strip of fat used in larding. Also, **lar·doon** (lär do͞on′). [late ME *lardun* < MF *lardon* piece of pork = *lard* LARD + *-on* n. suffix]

lard·y (lär′dē), *adj.,* **lard·i·er, lard·i·est. 1.** like or consisting of lard. **2.** fat or becoming fat.

La·re·do (lə rā′dō), *n.* a city in S Texas, on the Rio Grande. 69,024 (1970).

lar·es (lâr′ēz, lā′rēz), *n.pl., sing.* **lar** (lär). *Rom. Religion.* the spirits who, if propitiated, watched over the house or community to which they belonged. Cf. **penates.** [< L]

lar′es and pena′tes, 1. *Rom. Religion.* the benevolent spirits and gods of the household. **2.** the cherished possessions of a family or household.

large (lärj), *adj.,* **larg·er, larg·est,** *n., adv.* —*adj.* **1.** measuring or amounting to more than average size, quantity, etc.: *a large bed for a large man.* **2.** on a scale beyond the average: *a large buyer of antiques.* **3.** of considerable scope or range; broad: *a large variety of interests.* **4.** (of the scale of a map or model) representing the features of the original at considerable size. **5.** *Obs.* generous; bountiful; lavish. **6.** *Naut.* (of the wind) favorable. —*n.* **7.** *Obs.* generosity; bounty. **8. at large, a.** free from restraint or confinement; at liberty. **b.** to a considerable extent; at length. **c.** as a whole; in general. **d.** Also, **at-large.** representing the whole of a state, district, or body rather than one division or part of it. **9. in large,** on a large scale. Also, **in the large.** —*adv.* **10.** *Naut.* with the wind free or abaft the beam so that all sails draw fully. [ME < OF < L *larga*, fem. of *largus* ample, generous] —**large′ness,** *n.* —**Syn. 1.** huge, immense; vast. See **great.** —**Ant. 1.** small.

large-heart·ed (lärj′här′tid), *adj.* having or showing generosity. —**large′-heart′ed·ness,** *n.*

large′ intes′tine, intestine (def. 3).

large·ly (lärj′lē), *adv.* **1.** to a great extent; in great part; generally; chiefly. **2.** in great quantity; much. [ME]

large-mind·ed (lärj′mīn′did), *adj.* broad-minded. —**large′-mind′ed·ly,** *adv.* —**large′-mind′ed·ness,** *n.*

large·mouth bass (lärj′mouth′ bas′), a North American, fresh-water game fish, *Micropterus salmoides*, blackish-green above and lighter below, having the lower jaw extending beyond the eye. See illus. at **bass².**

large-scale (lärj′skāl′), *adj.* **1.** very extensive; of great scope. **2.** made to a large scale.

large′-scale′ in′tegra′tion. See **LSI.**

lar·gess (lär jes′, lär′jis), *n.* **1.** generous bestowal of gifts. **2.** the gift or gifts, as of money, so bestowed. **3.** *Obs.* generosity; liberality. Also, **lar·gesse′.** [ME *largesse* < OF; see LARGE, -ICE]

lar·ghet·to (lär get′ō), *adj., n., pl.* **-ghet·tos.** *Music.* —*adj.* **1.** somewhat slow; not so slow as largo. —*n.* **2.** a larghetto movement. [< It, dim. of *largo* LARGO]

larg·ish (lär′jish), *adj.* rather large.

lar·go (lär′gō), *adj., n., pl.* **-gos.** *Music.* —*adj.* **1.** slow; in a broad, dignified style. —*n.* **2.** a largo movement. [< It: see LARGE]

lar·i·at (lar′ē ət), *n.* **1.** a long, noosed rope used to catch horses, cattle, or other livestock; lasso. **2.** a rope used to picket grazing animals. [< Sp *la reata* the RIATA]

lar·ine (lar′in), *adj.* characteristic of or resembling a gull. [< NL *Larin(ae)* name of the subfamily = *Lar(us)* genus name (< Gk *lāros* a sea bird, a kind of gull) + *-inae* -INE¹]

La·ris·sa (lə ris′ə; *Gk.* lä′Rē sä), *n.* a city in E Thessaly, in E Greece. 55,733 (1961). Also, **La′ri·sa.**

lark¹ (lärk), *n.* **1.** any of numerous, chiefly Old World, oscine birds, of the family *Alaudidae*, characterized by an unusually long, straight hind claw, esp. the skylark, *Alauda arvensis.* **2.** any of various similar birds of other families, as the meadowlark or titlark. [ME *larke*, OE *lāwerce*; c. G *Lerche*, D *leeuwerik*, Icel *lǣvirki*]

lark² (lärk), *n.* **1.** a merry, carefree adventure; frolic. **2.** innocent or good-natured mischief; prank. —*v.i.* **3.** to have fun; frolic; romp. **4.** to behave mischievously; play pranks. [?] —**lark′er,** *n.* —**lark′ish·ness,** *n.* —**lark′some,** *adj.*

Larkspur, *Delphinium Ajacis*

lark·spur (lärk′spûr′), *n.* any plant of the genus *Delphinium*, characterized by the spur-shaped formation of the calyx and petals.

La Roche·fou·cauld (LA Rôsh fo͞o kō′), **Fran·çois** (fRäN swa′), **6th Duc de,** 1613–80, French moralist and composer of epigrams and maxims.

La Ro·chelle (LA Rô shel′), a seaport in W France: besieged while in Huguenot hands 1627–29. 68,445 (1962).

lar·ri·gan (lar′ə gən), *n.* *U.S. and Canada.* a knee-high boot with a moccasin foot. [?]

lar·ri·kin (lar′ə kin), *Australian Slang.* —*n.* **1.** a street rowdy; hoodlum. —*adj.* **2.** disorderly; rowdy. [?]

lar·rup (lar′əp), *v.t.,* **-ruped, -rup·ing.** *Dial.* to beat or thrash. [? < D *larpen* to thresh with flails] —**lar′rup·er,** *n.*

lar·um (lar′əm), *n.* alarum.

lar·va (lär′və), *n., pl.* **-vae** (-vē). **1.** *Entomol.* the immature, wingless, feeding stage of an insect that undergoes complete metamorphosis. See illus. at **metamorphosis. 2.** any animal in an analogous immature form. **3.** the young of any invertebrate animal. [< NL, special use of L: a ghost, specter, mask, skeleton; akin to LARES] —**lar·val** (lär′vəl), *adj.*

lar·vi·cide (lär′vi sīd′), *n.* an agent for killing larvae. —**lar′vi·cid′al,** *adj.*

la·ryn·ge·al (lə rin′jē əl, -jəl, lar′ən jē′əl), *adj.* of, pertaining to, or located in the larynx. Also, **la·ryn·gal** (lə ring′gəl). [< NL *larynge(us)* of, pertaining to the larynx (see LARYNG-, -EOUS) + -AL¹] —**la·ryn′ge·al·ly,** *adv.*

lar·yn·gi·tis (lar′ən jī′tis), *n.* *Pathol.* inflammation of the larynx. —**lar·yn·git·ic** (lar′ən jit′ik), *adj.*

laryngo-, a combining form of **larynx:** *laryngotomy.* Also, *esp. before a vowel,* **laryng-.** [comb. form repr. NL, Gk *lárynx* (s. *laryng-*) LARYNX; see -o-]

lar·yn·gol·o·gy (lar′ing gol′ə jē), *n.* the branch of medicine dealing with the larynx. —**la·ryn·go·log·i·cal** (lə ring′gə loj′i kəl), **la·ryn′go·log′ic,** *adj.* —**lar′yn·gol′o·gist,** *n.*

la·ryn·go·scope (lə ring′gə skōp′), *n. Med.* an apparatus for examining the larynx. —**la·ryn·go·scop·ic** (lə ring′gə skop′ik), **la·ryn′go·scop′i·cal,** *adj.* —**la·ryn′go·scop′i·cal·ly,** *adv.* —**la·ryn·gos·co·pist** (lar′ing gos′kə pist), *n.*

lar·ynx (lar′ingks), *n., pl.* **la·ryn·ges** (lə rin′jēz), **lar·ynx·es.** **1.** *Anat.* a muscular and cartilaginous structure lined with mucous membrane at the upper part of the trachea in man, in which the vocal cords are located. **2.** *Zool.* **a.** a similar vocal organ in other mammals. **b.** a corresponding structure in certain lower animals. [< NL < Gk: throat, gullet, larynx]

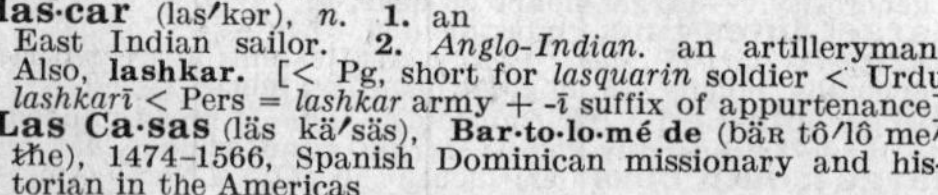

Human larynx (Section) A, Epiglottis; B, Hyoid bone; C, Thyroid cartilage; D, Esophagus; E, Cricoid cartilage; F, Trachea

la·sa·gne (lə zän′yə, lä-), *n.* **1.** *Italian Cookery.* large, flat, rectangular strips of pasta. **2.** a baked dish of this pasta, usually made with meat, cheese, and tomatoes. [< It, pl. of *lasagna,* appar. < L *lasanum* cooking pot < Gk *lásanon* trivet]

La Salle (lə sal′; *Fr.* LA SAL′), **(Re·né) Ro·bert Ca·ve·lier** (Rə nā′ Rô beR′ KA və lyā′), **Sieur de,** 1643–87, French explorer of North America.

las·car (las′kər), *n.* **1.** an East Indian sailor. **2.** *Anglo-Indian.* an artilleryman. Also, **lashkar.** [< Pg, short for *lasquarin* soldier < Urdu *lashkarī* < Pers = *lashkar* army + -*ī* suffix of appurtenance]

Las Ca·sas (läs kä′säs), **Bar·to·lo·mé de** (bäR tô′lô me′ the), 1474–1566, Spanish Dominican missionary and historian in the Americas

Las·caux′ Cave′ (lAs kō′), a cave in Lascaux, in SW France, containing Paleolithic wall drawings and paintings.

las·civ·i·ous (lə siv′ē əs), *adj.* **1.** inclined to lustfulness; wanton; lewd. **2.** arousing or inciting sexual desire. **3.** expressing lust or lewdness. [< L *lascīvi(a)* playfulness, wantonness (*lascīv(us)* playful, wanton + *-ia* -IA) + -OUS] —**las·civ′i·ous·ly,** *adv.* —**las·civ′i·ous·ness,** *n.*

Las Cru·ces (läs krōō′sis), a city in S New Mexico, on the Rio Grande. 37,857 (1970).

la·ser (lā′zər), *n.* a maser that amplifies radiation of frequencies within or near the range of visible light. [*l(ight) a(mplification by) s(timulated) e(mission of) r(adiation)*]

la′ser beam′, a beam of amplified light-frequency radiations, used in surgery, communications, industrial processes, etc.

lash[1] (lash), *n.* **1.** the flexible striking part of a whip. **2.** a swift stroke or blow, as with a whip. **3.** something that goads or pains in a manner compared to that of a whip. **4.** a swift dashing or sweeping movement. **5.** a violent beating or impact, as of waves or rain, against something. **6.** an eyelash. —*v.t.* **7.** to strike or beat, as with a whip. **8.** to beat violently or sharply against. **9.** to goad or drive by or as by strokes of a whip. **10.** to attack severely with words. **11.** to dash, fling, or switch suddenly and swiftly. —*v.i.* **12.** to strike vigorously at someone or something, as with a whip or one's fist. **13.** to attack or reprove someone with harsh words (often fol. by *out*): *The article lashed out at social injustice.* **14.** to move suddenly and swiftly; rush. [ME *lasshe,* perh. imit.] —**lash′er,** *n.* —**lash′ing·ly,** *adv.*

lash[2] (lash), *v.t.* to bind or fasten with a rope, cord, or the like. [late ME *lassch(yn)* < MD *lasschen* to patch, sew together, scarf (timber); akin to G *Lasche* flap, latchet] —**lash′er,** *n.* —**lash′ing·ly,** *adv.*

LASH (lash), *n.* an ocean-going freighter loaded with cargo-carrying barges that can be removed and sailed up inland waterways. [*l(ighter-)a(board-)sh(ip)*]

lashed (lasht), *adj.* having lashes or eyelashes.

lash·ing[1] (lash′ing), *n.* **1.** the act of a person or thing that lashes. **2.** a whipping with or as with a lash. **3.** a severe scolding; tongue-lashing. [LASH[1] + -ING[1]]

lash·ing[2] (lash′ing), *n.* **1.** a binding or fastening with a rope or the like. **2.** the rope or the like used. [LASH[2] + -ING[1]]

lash·kar (lash′kər), *n.* lascar.

Lash·kar (lush′kər), *n.* a part of Gwalior city in N India.

Las·ker (läs′kəR), *n.* **E·ma·nu·el** (ā mä′nōō el), 1868–1941, German chess player and mathematician.

Las Pal·mas (*Sp.* läs päl′mäs), a seaport on NE Gran Canaria, in the central Canary Islands. 193,984 (est. 1960).

La Spe·zia (lä spe′tsyä), a seaport in NW Italy, on the Ligurian Sea: naval base. 125,661 (1963).

lass (las), *n.* **1.** a girl or young woman, esp. one who is unmarried. **2.** a female sweetheart. [ME *lasse* < ?]

Las·sa (lä′sə, -sä), *n.* Lhasa.

Las·salle (lə sal′; *Ger.* lä säl′), *n.* **Fer·di·nand** (fûr′dᵊnand′; *Ger.* feR′di nänt′), 1825–64, German socialist and writer.

Las′sen Peak′ (las′ən), an active volcano in N California, in the S Cascade Range. 10,465 ft. Also called **Mount Lassen.**

las·sie (las′ē), *n.* a young girl; lass.

las·si·tude (las′i tōōd′, -tyōōd′), *n.* **1.** weariness of body or mind from strain, oppressive climate, etc.; languor. **2.** a condition of indolent indifference. [< L *lassitūdō* weariness = *lass(us)* weary + *-i-* -I- + *-tūdō* -TUDE]

las·so (las′ō, la sōō′), *n., pl.* **-sos, -soes,** *v.,* **-soed, -so·ing.** —*n.* **1.** a long rope or line of hide or other material with a running noose at one end, used for roping horses, cattle, etc.; lariat. —*v.t.* **2.** to catch with a lasso. [< Sp *lazo* < L *laqueus* bond; see LACE] —**las′so·er,** *n.*

last[1] (last, läst), *adj., a superl. of* **late** *with* **later** *as compar.* **1.** occurring or coming after all others, as in time, order, or place. **2.** the most recent; next before the present; latest: *last week.* **3.** being the only remaining. **4.** final: *in his last hours.* **5.** conclusive; definitive. **6.** utmost; extreme. **7.** coming after all others in one's expectations, consideration, etc. **8.** individual; single: *I want every last man here.* —*adv.* **9.** after all others. **10.** most recently: *He was alone when last seen.* **11.** in the end; in conclusion; lastly. —*n.* **12.** a person or thing that is last. **13.** a final appearance or mention: *We haven't heard the last of this.* **14.** the end or conclusion. **15. at last,** after a lengthy pause or delay. **16. at long last,** after much annoying or troublesome delay. **17. breathe one's last,** to die. [ME *last, latst,* syncopated var. of *latest,* OE *latest, lætest,* superl. of *læt,* LATE]
—**Syn. 1.** LAST, FINAL, ULTIMATE refer to what comes as an ending. That which is LAST comes or stands after all others in a stated series or succession; LAST may refer to objects or activities: *a seat in the last row.* That which is FINAL comes at the end, or serves to end or terminate, admitting of nothing further; FINAL is rarely used of objects: *to make a final attempt.* That which is ULTIMATE (literally, most remote) is the last that can be reached, as in progression or regression, experience, or a course of investigation: *ultimate truths.* —**Ant. 1, 2, 4, 7, 9, 11, 12, 14.** first.
—**Usage.** LAST is properly a superlative form of LATE, with LATER and, formerly, LATTER as comparatives. Therefore, English speakers who insist on precision maintain that LATTER should be used only to refer to the second of two items, with LAST being confined to the final item in a list of three or more. (LATER is not used in this sense in modern English.) *Of the two choices, I prefer the latter. John, George, and James were her sons, and she obviously favored the last.*

last[2] (last, läst), *v.i.* **1.** to go on or continue in time. **2.** to remain unexhausted; be enough: *Will our money last long?* **3.** to continue in force, vigor, effectiveness, etc. —*v.t.* **4.** to continue to survive for the duration of. [ME *last(en),* OE *lǣstan* to follow, (lit., go in the tracks of), perform, continue, last; c. G *laisten* to follow, Goth *laistjan.* See LAST[3]] —**last′er,** *n.* —**Syn. 1.** See **continue.**

last[3] (last, läst), *n.* **1.** a wooden or metal model of the human foot on which boots or shoes are shaped or repaired. **2. stick to one's last,** to keep to the work, field, etc., in which one is competent or skilled. —*v.t.* **3.** to shape on or fit to a last. [ME; OE *lǣste;* c. G *Leisten;* akin to OE *lāst,* Goth *laists* track] —**last′er,** *n.*

last[4] (last, läst), *n.* any of various large units of weight or capacity, varying in amount in different localities and for different commodities, often equivalent to 4000 pounds. [ME; OE *hlæst;* c. D *last* G *Last* load; akin to LADE]

last-ditch (last′dich′, läst′-), *adj.* constituting a final, desperate effort.

Las·tex (las′teks), *n. Trademark.* a yarn made from a core of rubber thread covered with fabric strands.

last·ing (las′ting, lä′sting), *adj.* **1.** that lasts; enduring; permanent; durable. —*n.* **2.** a strong, durable, closely woven fabric for shoe uppers, coverings on buttons, etc. [ME (adj.) (n. use for material is later)] —**last′ing·ly,** *adv.* —**last′ing·ness,** *n.*

Last′ Judg′ment, judgment (def. 8).

last·ly (last′lē, läst′-), *adv.* in conclusion; in the last place; finally. [ME *lestely*]

last′ mile′, the distance walked by a condemned man from his cell to the place of execution.

last′ name′, surname (def. 1).

last′ post′. See under **post**[2] (def. 7).

last′ quar′ter, *Astron.* the instant, approximately one week after a full moon, when half of the moon's disk is illuminated by the sun. See diag. at **moon.**

last′ rites′. See **extreme unction.**

last′ straw′, the last of a succession of irritations that strains one's patience to the limit. [after the proverb "It is the *last straw* that breaks the camel's back."]

Last′ Sup′per, the supper of Jesus and His disciples on the eve of His Crucifixion. Cf. **Lord's Supper** (def. 1).

last′ word′, **1.** the closing remark, as in an argument. **2.** a final or definitive work, statement, etc. **3.** *Informal.* the latest, most modern thing.

Las Ve·gas (läs vā′gəs), a city in SE Nevada. 125,787 (1970).

lat (lät), *n., pl.* **lats, la·ti** (lä′tē). a former silver coin of Latvia, equal to 100 santimi. [< Lettish *lats* = *Lat(vija)* Latvia + *-s* nom. sing. n. ending]

Lat., Latin.

lat., latitude.

Lat·a·ki·a (lat′ə kē′ə *or, esp. for 1,* lä′tä kē′ä), *n.* **1.** Ancient, **Laodicea.** a seaport in NW Syria. 72,378 (1962). **2.** a variety of Turkish tobacco.

latch (lach), *n.* **1.** a device for holding a door or the like closed, consisting basically of a bar falling or sliding into a catch, groove, hole, etc. —*v.t.* **2.** to close or fasten with a latch. —*v.i.* **3.** to close tightly so that the latch is secured. **4. latch onto,** *Informal.* **a.** to obtain; get. **b.** to acquire understanding of; comprehend. [ME *lacche(n),* OE *læccan* to take hold of, catch, seize; akin to Gk *lázesthai* to take]

latch·et (lach′it), *n. Archaic.* a strap or lace used to fasten a shoe. [ME *lachet* < MF, dial. var. of *lacet.* See LACE, -ET]

latch·key (lach′kē′), *n., pl.* **-keys.** a key for drawing back or releasing a latch, esp. on an outer door.

latch·string (lach′string′), *n.* a string passed through a hole in a door, for raising the latch from the outside.

late (lāt), *adj.,* **lat·er** or **lat·ter, lat·est** or **last,** *adv.* **lat·er, lat·est.** —*adj.* **1.** occurring after the usual or proper time. **2.** continued until after the usual time; protracted. **3.** coming toward the end of day or well into the night: *a late hour.* **4.** very recent: *a late bulletin.* **5.** immediately preceding the present one; former. **6.** recently deceased: *the late Mr. Phipps.* **7.** occurring at an advanced stage in life. **8.** belonging to an advanced period in history or development. **9. of late,** lately; recently. —*adv.* **10.** after the usual or proper time, or after delay. **11.** until after the usual time or hour. **12.** at or to an advanced time, period, or stage. **13.** recently but no longer; lately. [ME; OE *læt* slow, late; c. G *lass* slothful, Icel *latr,* Goth *lats,* L *lassus* tired] —**late′ness,** *n.*

late·com·er (lāt′kum′ər), *n.* a person who arrives late.

lat·ed (lā′tid), *adj. Literary.* belated.

la·teen (la tēn′, lə-), *adj.* pertaining to or having a lateen sail or sails. [< F (*voile*) *latine* Latin (sail)]

la·teen-rigged (la tēn′rigd′, lə-), *adj.* having lateen sails.

lateen′ sail′, a triangular sail set on a long sloping yard, used esp. on the Mediterranean Sea.

Lateen sail

Late′ Greek′, the Greek of the early Byzantine Empire and of patristic literature, from about A.D. 100 to 700. *Abbr.:* LGk

Late′ Lat′in, the Latin of the late Western Roman Empire and of patristic literature, from about A.D. 150 to 700. *Abbr.:* LL

late·ly (lāt′lē), *adv.* of late; recently; not long since. [ME]

la·ten·cy (lāt′ᵊn sē), *n.* **1.** the state of being latent. **2.** See **latent period.** [LAT(ENT) + -ENCY]

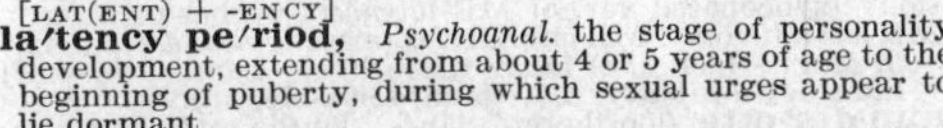

la′tency pe′riod, *Psychoanal.* the stage of personality development, extending from about 4 or 5 years of age to the beginning of puberty, during which sexual urges appear to lie dormant.

La Tène (*Fr.* LA ten′), **1.** *Archaeol.* designating the period or culture of the late Iron Age typified by the remains found at La Tène. Cf. **Hallstattan. 2.** a shallow area at the E end of the Lake of Neuchâtel, Switzerland.

la·tent (lāt′ᵊnt), *adj.* **1.** present or potential but not visible, apparent, or realized. **2.** *Bot.* (of buds that are not externally manifest) dormant or undeveloped. [< L *latent-* (s. of *latēns*) lying hidden, prp. of *latēre;* see -ENT] **—la′tent·ly,** *adv.* **—Syn. 1.** dormant, quiescent, veiled. LATENT, POTENTIAL refer to powers or possibilities existing but hidden or not yet actualized. LATENT emphasizes the hidden character or the dormancy of what is named: *latent qualities, defects, diseases.* That which is POTENTIAL exists in an as yet undeveloped state, but is thought of as capable of coming into full being or activity at some future time: *potential genius, tragedy.* POTENTIAL may be applied also to tangibles: *High-tension wires are a potential source of danger.* **—Ant. 1.** active.

la′tent heat′, *Physics.* heat absorbed or radiated during a change of phase at constant temperature and pressure. Cf. **heat of fusion, heat of vaporization.**

la′tent pe′riod, 1. *Pathol.* the period before the presence of a disease is manifested by symptoms. **2.** *Physiol.* the lag between stimulus and reaction. Also called **latency.**

lat·er (lā′tər), *adj., adv.* a comparative of **late.**

lat·er·al (lat′ər əl), *adj.* **1.** of or pertaining to the side; situated at, proceeding from, or directed to a side. **2.** *Phonet.* articulated so that the breath passes on either or both sides of the tongue, as *l.* **—***n.* **3.** a lateral part or extension. **4.** *Phonet.* a lateral speech sound. **5.** *Football.* See **lateral pass. —***v.i.* **6.** *Football.* to throw a lateral pass. [< L *laterāl(is)* of the side = *later-* (s. of *latus*) side + *-ālis* -AL[1]] **—lat′er·al·ly,** *adv.*

lat′eral chain′, *Chem.* See **side chain.**

lat′eral line′, the line, or system of lines, of sensory structures along the head and sides of fishes and amphibians, by which the animal is believed to detect water current and pressure changes and vibrations.

lat′eral pass′, *Football.* a pass thrown parallel to the goal line or backward from the position of the passer.

Lat·er·an (lat′ər ən), *n.* the church of St. John Lateran, the cathedral church of the city of Rome; the church of the pope as bishop of Rome.

lat·er·ite (lat′ə rīt′), *n. Geol.* **1.** a reddish ferruginous soil formed in tropical regions by the decomposition of the underlying rocks. **2.** a similar soil formed of materials deposited by water. **3.** any soil produced by the decomposition of the rocks beneath it. [< L *later* brick, tile + -ITE[1]] **—lat·er·it·ic** (lat′ə rit′ik), *adj.*

lat·est (lā′tist), *adj. a superl. of* **late** *with* **later** *as compar.* **1.** coming after all others; occurring last. **2.** most recent; current: *latest fashions.* **—***adv.* **3. at the latest,** not any later than (a specified time): *by 7 o'clock at the latest.* **—***n.* **4. the latest,** the most recent advance, development, etc.: *Have you heard the latest about the Joneses?* [late ME]

la·tex (lā′teks), *n., pl.* **lat·i·ces** (lat′i sēz′), **la·tex·es. 1.** a milky liquid in certain plants, as milkweeds, that coagulates on exposure to air. **2.** *Chem.* any emulsion in water of finely divided particles of synthetic rubber or plastic. [< NL, special use of L: something liquid]

lath (lath, läth), *n., pl.* **laths** (lathz, laths, läthz, läths), *v.* **—***n.* **1.** a thin, narrow strip of wood, used with others as a backing or support for plasterwork, roofing, etc. **2.** a number of such strips. **3.** wire mesh or the like used in place of wooden laths as a backing for plasterwork. **4.** a thin, narrow, flat piece of wood used for any purpose. **—***v.t.* **5.** to cover or line with laths. [ME *la(th)the;* r. ME *latt,* OE *lætt;* c. G *Latte,* D *lat*]

lathe (lāth), *n., v.,* **lathed, lath·ing. —***n.* **1.** a machine for use in working pieces of wood, metal, etc., by rotating them against a tool that shapes them. **—***v.t.* **2.** to cut, shape, or treat on a lathe. [late ME *lath* stand < Scand; cf. D *-lad* lathe, Icel *hlath* stack, c. OE *hlæd,* mound]

Lathe (wood-turning)
A, Headstock; B, Tool rest; C, Tailstock; D, Motor

lath·er[1] (lath′ər), *n.* **1.** foam or froth made by soap stirred or rubbed in water. **2.** foam or froth formed in profuse sweating, as on a horse. **3.** *Informal.* a state of excitement, agitation, or the like. **—***v.i.* **4.** to form a lather. **5.** to become covered with lather, as a horse. **—***v.t.* **6.** to apply lather to; cover with lather. [ME; OE *lēathor* soap; c. Icel *lauthr* (now *löthur*) foam] **—lath′er·er,** *n.* **—lath′er·y,** *adj.*

lath·er[2] (lath′ər, lä′thər), *n.* a workman who puts up laths. [LATH + -ER[1]]

lath·ing (lath′ing, lä′thing), *n.* **1.** the act or process of applying lath. **2.** a number of laths.

lath·y (lath′ē, lä′thē), *adj.,* **lath·i·er, lath·i·est.** lath-like; long and thin.

lat·i·ces (lat′i sēz′), *n.* a pl. of **latex.**

lat·i·fun·di·um (lat′ə fun′dē əm), *n., pl.* **-di·a** (-dē ə). *Rom. Hist.* a large estate. [< L = *lāt(us)* wide, broad + *-i-* -I- + *fund(us)* a piece of land, farm, estate + *-ium* -IUM]

Lat·i·mer (lat′ə mər), *n.* **Hugh,** c1470–1555, English Protestant Reformation bishop, reformer, and martyr.

Lat·in (lat′ᵊn, -in), *n.* **1.** an Italic language spoken in ancient Rome, fixed in the 2nd or 1st century B.C., and established as the official language of the Roman Empire. *Abbr.:* L **2.** any of the modifications of this language. **3.** a native or inhabitant of Latium: an ancient Roman. **4.** a member of any of the Latin peoples. **5.** *Rare.* a member of the Latin Church; a Roman Catholic. **—***adj.* **6.** denoting or pertaining to those peoples using languages derived from that of ancient Rome as Spanish, Portuguese, French, Italian, or Rumanian. **7.** of or pertaining to the Latin Church. **8.** of or pertaining to Latium or its inhabitants. [ME, OE < L *Latīn(us).* See LATIUM, -INE[1]]

Lat′in al′phabet, the alphabetical script derived from the Etruscan alphabet used from about the 7th century B.C. for the writing of Latin, and since adopted, with modifications and additions of letters such as *w,* by English, French, Turkish, and many other languages.

Lat′in Amer′ica, the part of the American continents south of the U.S. in which Romance languages are spoken. **—Lat′in-A·mer′i·can,** *n., adj.* **—Lat′in Amer′ican.**

Lat·in·ate (lat′ᵊnāt′), *adj.* of, like, pertaining to, or derived from Latin.

Lat′in Church′, the Roman Catholic Church.

Lat′in cross′, a vertical bar crossed near the top by a shorter horizontal bar. See illus. at **cross.**

La·tin·ic (lə tin′ik), *adj.* of or pertaining to the Latin language, peoples, or nations.

Lat·in·ise (lat′ᵊnīz′), *v.t., v.i.,* **-ised, -is·ing.** *Chiefly Brit.* Latinize. **—Lat′in·i·sa′tion,** *n.*

Lat·in·ism (lat′ᵊniz′əm), *n.* a mode of expression imitative of Latin. [< ML *latinism(us)*]

Lat·in·ist (lat′ᵊnist), *n.* a specialist in Latin. [< ML *latīnist(a)*]

La·tin·i·ty (lə tin′i tē), *n.* **1.** knowledge or use of the Latin language. **2.** Latin style or idiom. [< L *latīnitās* Latin style]

Lat·in·ize (lat′ᵊnīz′), *v.,* **-ized, -iz·ing. —***v.t.* **1.** to cause to conform to the customs, beliefs, etc., of the Latins or the Latin Church. **2.** to intermix with Latin elements. **3.** to translate into Latin. **—***v.i.* **4.** to use words and phrases from Latin. Also, *esp. Brit.,* **Latinise.** [< LL *latīnīz(āre)* (to) translate into Latin] **—Lat′in·i·za′tion,** *n.*

La·ti·no (la tē′nō), *n.* an American citizen or resident of Latin-American or Spanish-speaking descent.

Lat′in Quar′ter, the quarter of Paris on the south side of the Seine, frequented for centuries by students and artists.

Lat′in school′, a secondary school emphasizing instruction in Latin and Greek.

Lat′in square′, *Math.* a square array of numbers, letters, etc., in which each item appears exactly once in each row and column: used in statistical analysis.

lat·ish (lā′tish), *adj.* somewhat late.

lat·i·tude (lat′i to͞od′, -tyo͞od′), *n.* **1.** *Geog.* **a.** the angular distance north or south from the equator of a point on the earth's surface, measured on the meridian of the point. **b.** a place or region as marked by this distance. **2.** freedom from narrow restrictions; permitted freedom of action, opinion, etc. **3.** *Astron.* See **celestial latitude. 4.** *Photog.* the ability of an emulsion to record the brightness values of a subject in their true proportion to one another. [ME < L *lātitūdō* breadth = *lat(us)* broad + *-i-* -I- + *-tūdō* -TUDE] **—Syn. 2.** extent, liberty, indulgence. See **range.**

lat·i·tu·di·nal (lat′i to͞od′ᵊnᵊl, -tyo͞od′-), *adj.* of or pertaining to latitude. [< L *lātitūdin-* (s. of *lātitūdō*) LATITUDE + -AL[1]] **—lat′i·tu′di·nal·ly,** *adv.*

lat·i·tu·di·nar·i·an (lat′i to͞od′ᵊnâr′ē ən, -tyo͞od′-), *adj.* **1.** allowing or characterized by latitude in opinion or conduct, esp. in religious views. **—***n.* **2.** a person who is latitudinarian in opinion or conduct. **3.** *Anglican Ch.* one of the churchmen in the 17th century who favored the episcopal form of government and ritual but denied its divine origin and authority. [< L *lātitūdin-* (see LATITUDINAL) + -ARIAN] **—lat′i·tu′di·nar′i·an·ism,** *n.*

La·ti·um (lā′shē əm), *n.* a country in ancient Italy, SE of Rome.

La·to·na (lə tō′nə), *n.* the goddess Leto as identified in Roman mythology.

La Tor·tue (LA tôr ty′). French name of **Tortuga.**

La Trappe (LA TRAP′), an abbey in Normandy, France, at which the Trappist order was founded.

la·tri·a (lə trī′ə), *n. Rom. Cath. Theol.* the supreme worship that may be offered to God only. Cf. **dulia, hyperdulia.** [< LL < Gk *latreía* service, worship, akin to *látris* hired servant; see -IA]

la·trine (lə trēn′), *n.* a toilet or something used as a toilet, esp. in a military installation. [< F < L *lātrīna,* short for *lavātrīna* place for washing < *lavāre* to wash]

La·trobe (lə trōb′), *n.* **Benjamin Henry,** 1764–1820, U.S. architect and engineer, born in England.

-latry, an element occurring in loan words from Greek meaning "worship" (*idolatry*); on this model, used in the formation of compound words (*Mariolatry*). [< Gk *-latria.* See LATRIA, -Y[3]]

lat·ten (lat′ᵊn), *n.* **1.** a brasslike alloy commonly made in thin sheets. **2.** tin plate. **3.** any metal in thin sheets. [ME *lato(u)n* < MF *laton* copper-zinc alloy << Ar *lātūn* < Turkic; cf. Turk *altin* gold]

lat·ter (lat′ər), *adj.* **1.** being the second mentioned of two (distinguished from *former*). **2.** more advanced in time; later. **3.** near or comparatively near to the end: *the latter part of the century.* **4.** *Obs.* last; final. [ME *latt(e)re,* OE *lætra,* comp. of *læt* LATE] **—Usage.** See **last**[1].

lat·ter-day (lat′ər dā′), *adj.* **1.** of a later or following period. **2.** of the present period or time; modern.

Lat′ter-day Saint′, a Mormon.

lat·ter·ly (lat′ər lē), *adv.* **1.** lately. **2.** in a later time.

lat·ter·most (lat′ər mōst′, -məst), *adj.* latest; last.

lat·tice (lat′is), *n., v.,* **-ticed, -tic·ing.** —*n.* **1.** a structure of crossed wooden or metal strips usually arranged to form a diagonal pattern of open spaces. **2.** a window, gate, or the like, consisting of such a structure. **3.** *Physics.* the structure of fissionable and nonfissionable materials geometrically arranged within a nuclear reactor. **4.** Also called **crystal lattice, space lattice.** *Crystall.* an arrangement in space of isolated points in a regular pattern, showing the positions of atoms, molecules, or ions in the structure of a crystal. **5.** *Math.* a partially ordered set in which every subset containing exactly two elements has a greatest lower bound or intersection and a least upper bound or union. —*v.t.* **6.** to furnish with a lattice or latticework. **7.** to form into a lattice. [ME *latis* < MF *lattis* < *latte* lath < Gmc; see LATH]

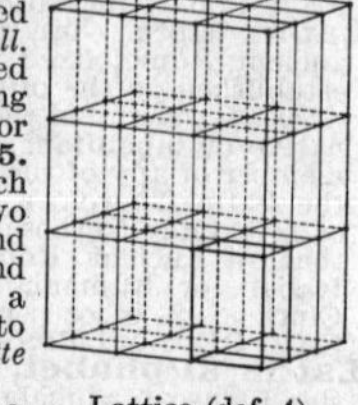
Lattice (def. 4)

lat·ticed (lat′ist), *adj.* **1.** having a lattice or latticework. **2.** *Biol.* clathrate.

lat′tice truss′, a truss having crisscrossed diagonals between chords.

lat·tice·work (lat′is wûrk′), *n.* **1.** work consisting of crossed strips usually arranged in a diagonal pattern of open spaces. **2.** a lattice.

lat·tic·ing (lat′i sing), *n.* **1.** the act or process of furnishing with or making latticework. **2.** latticework.

Lat·vi·a (lat′vē ə), *n.* a constituent republic of the Soviet Union in Europe, in the NW part, on the Baltic: an independent state 1918–40. 2,200,000 (est. 1965); 25,395 sq. mi. *Cap.:* Riga. Lettish, **Lat·vi·ja** (lät′vi yä′). Official name, **Lat′vian So′viet So′cialist Repub′lic.**

Lat·vi·an (lat′vē ən), *adj.* **1.** of or pertaining to Latvia, its inhabitants, or their language. —*n.* **2.** a native or inhabitant of Latvia. **3.** Lettish (def. 2).

lau·an (lo͞o′an′, lou′an′), *n.* **1.** any of several Philippine timber trees, as Philippine mahogany, of the genus *Shorea* and related genera that are pale to deep reddish-brown and of a soft texture. **2.** the wood of any of these trees, often used in plywood.

laud (lôd), *v.t.* **1.** to praise; extol. —*n.* **2. lauds,** (*construed as sing. or pl.*) *Eccles.* a canonical hour of praise, usually recited with matins. [(v.) ME *laude* < L *laudāre* to praise < *laus* (s. *laud-*) praise; (n.) ME *laudes* (pl.) eccl. L, special use of pl. of L *laus*] —**laud′er, lau·da·tor** (lô′dā tər), *n.*

Laud (lôd), *n.* **William,** 1573–1645, archbishop of Canterbury and opponent of Puritanism: executed for treason.

laud·a·ble (lô′də bəl), *adj.* praiseworthy or commendable. [late ME < L *laudābil(is)*] —**laud′a·bil′i·ty, laud′a·ble·ness,** *n.* —**laud′a·bly,** *adv.*

lau·da·num (lôd′ənəm, lôd′nəm), *n.* **1.** a tincture of opium. **2.** *Obs.* any preparation in which opium is the chief ingredient. [orig. ML var. of LADANUM; arbitrarily used by Paracelsus to name a remedy based on opium]

lau·da·tion (lô dā′shən), *n.* the act or an instance of lauding; tribute. [late ME *laudacion* < L *laudātiōn-* (s. of *laudātiō*) a praising = *laudāt(us)* praised (ptp. of *laudāre* to LAUD) + *-iōn-* -ION]

laud·a·to·ry (lô′də tōr′ē, -tôr′ē), *adj.* containing or expressing praise. Also, **laud′a·tive.** [< LL *laudātōri(us).* See LAUDATION, -ORY[1]] —**laud′a·to′ri·ly,** *adv.*

Lau·der (lô′dər), *n.* **Sir Harry (Mac·Len·nan)** (mə klen′ən), 1870–1950, Scottish balladeer and composer.

laugh (laf, läf), *v.i.* **1.** to express emotion, as mirth, pleasure, derision, or nervousness, with an audible, vocal expulsion of air from the lungs that can range from a loud burst of sound to a series of quiet chuckles. **2.** to experience mirth or derision. **3.** to produce a sound resembling human laughter, as a hyena. —*v.t.* **4.** to drive, put, bring, etc., by or with laughter (often fol. by *out, away,* etc.): *They laughed him out of town.* **5.** to express with laughter. **6. laugh at, a.** to make fun of; deride; ridicule. **b.** to show contempt or disbelief for. **7. laugh in** or **up one's sleeve.** See **sleeve** (def. 4). **8. laugh off,** to ridicule or dismiss as absurd. —*n.* **9.** the act or sound of laughing. **10. have the last laugh,** to prove ultimately successful after a seeming defeat. [ME *laughe(n),* OE *hlæhan* (Anglian); c. D, G *lachen,* Goth *hlahjan,* Icel *hlæja*] —**laugh′er,** *n.* —**Syn. 1.** chortle, cackle, guffaw, roar; giggle, titter.

laugh·a·ble (laf′ə bəl, lä′fə-), *adj.* such as to excite laughter; ludicrous; ridiculous. —**laugh′a·ble·ness,** *n.* —**laugh′a·bly,** *adv.* —**Syn.** See **funny.**

laugh·ing (laf′ing, lä′fing), *n.* **1.** laughter. —*adj.* **2.** that laughs or is given to laughter. **3.** laughable: *The mistake was no laughing matter.* [ME] —**laugh′ing·ly,** *adv.*

laugh′ing gas′. See **nitrous oxide.**

laugh′ing hye′na. See **spotted hyena.**

laugh′ing jack′ass, kookaburra. [so called because of its loud braying call]

laugh·ing·stock (laf′ing stok′, lä′fing-), *n.* an object of ridicule; butt of a joke or the like.

laugh·ter (laf′tər, läf′-), *n.* **1.** the action or sound of laughing. **2.** an experiencing of the emotion expressed by laughing. **3.** an expression or appearance of merriment or amusement, esp. mirth or derision. [ME; OE *hleahtor;* c. OHG *lahtar,* Icel *hlātr;* see LAUGH] —**laugh′ter·less,** *adj.*

launce (lans, läns), *n.* See **sand lance.** [var. of LANCE[2]]

Laun·ces·ton (lôn′ses′tən, län′-), *n.* a city on N Tasmania. 38,118, with suburbs 56,721 (est. 1961).

launch[1] (lônch, länch), *n.* **1.** a heavy open or half-decked boat propelled by oars or by an engine. **2.** a large utility boat carried by a warship. [< Sp *lancha* < Pg: pinnace < Malay *lanchāran* speedboat < *lanchār* speed, speedy]

launch[2] (lônch, länch), *v.t.* **1.** to set (a small vessel) in the water. **2.** to float (a newly constructed vessel) usually by allowing it to slide down inclined ways into the water. **3.** to cause or assist to start: *to launch a new business.* **4.** to put into action or effect: *to launch a project.* **5.** to throw; hurl. —*v.i.* **6.** to plunge boldly or directly into action, speech, etc. **7.** to start out or forth, as a vessel. —*n.* **8.** the act of launching. [late ME *launche* < AF *lanch(er)* < LL *lanceāre* to wield a lance; see LANCE[1]]

launch·er (lôn′chər, län′chər), *n.* **1.** a person or thing that launches. **2.** a structural device designed to support and hold a missile in position for firing.

launch′ pad′, *Rocketry.* a platform from which a rocket is launched. Also called **launch′ing pad′.**

laun·der (lôn′dər, län′-), *v.t.* **1.** to wash (clothes, linens, etc.). **2.** to wash and iron (clothes). **3.** *Slang.* to disguise the source of (money, esp. illegal campaign funds or profits from criminal activities), esp. by routing it abroad through a foreign bank. —*v.i.* **4.** to wash laundry. **5.** to undergo washing and ironing. —*n.* **6.** (in ore dressing) a passage carrying products of intermediate grade and residue in water suspension. [syncopated var. of ME *lavendere* washer of linen < MF *lavandier(e)* < ML *lavandārius* (masc.), *lavandāria* (fem.) = L *lavand-* (ger. s. of *lavāre* to wash) + *-ārius, -āria* -ER[2]] —**laun′der·a·bil′i·ty,** *n.* —**laun′der·a·ble,** *adj.*

laun·der·ette (lôn′də ret′, län′-, lôn′də ret′, län′-), *n.* Laundromat. [from *Launderette,* a trademark]

laun·dress (lôn′dris, län′-), *n.* a woman whose occupation is the washing and ironing of clothes, linens, etc. [obs. *launder* washer (see LAUNDER) + -ESS]

Laun·dro·mat (lôn′drə mat′, län′-), *n.* *Trademark.* a commercial laundry having coin-operated, automatic machines for the washing and drying of clothes, linens, etc.

laun·dry (lôn′drē, län′-), *n., pl.* **-dries. 1.** articles of clothes, linens, etc., to be washed. **2.** a room, business establishment, etc., where such articles are laundered. [ME *lavandrie* < MF *lavanderie.* See LAUNDER, -Y[3]]

laun′dry list′, *U.S. Informal.* a lengthy, usually indiscriminate, list of items.

laun·dry·man (lôn′drē man′, län′-), *n., pl.* **-men. 1.** a man who works in or operates a laundry. **2.** a man who collects and delivers laundry.

laun·dry·wom·an (lôn′drē wo͝om′ən, län′-), *n., pl.* **-wom·en.** laundress.

lau·ra·ceous (lô rā′shəs), *adj.* belonging to the *Lauraceae,* or laurel family of plants. [< NL *Laur(us)* genus name (special use of L: bay tree) + -ACEOUS]

Laur·a·sia (lô rā′zhə, -shə), *n.* *Geol.* a hypothetical land mass in the Northern Hemisphere near the end of the Paleozoic that separated to form North America and Eurasia. Cf. **Gondwana.** [b. LAURENTIAN (def. 2) and EURASIA]

lau·re·ate (lôr′ē it), *adj.* **1.** crowned or decked with laurel as a mark of honor. **2.** having or deserving high honor or special recognition in a field. —*n.* **3.** a person who has been honored in a particular field or with a particular award: *a Nobel laureate.* **4.** See **poet laureate.** [< L *laureāt(us)* crowned with laurel = *laure(us)* of laurel (see LAUREL, -EOUS) + *-ātus* -ATE[1]] —**lau′re·ate·ship′,** *n.* —**lau·re·a·tion** (lôr′ē ā′shən), *n.*

lau·rel (lôr′əl, lor′-), *n., v.,* **-reled, -rel·ing** or (*esp. Brit.*) **-relled, -rel·ling.** —*n.* **1.** a small, evergreen, lauraceous tree, *Laurus nobilis,* of Europe. **2.** any tree of the genus *Laurus.* **3.** any of various similar trees or shrubs, as the mountain laurel. **4.** the foliage of the laurel as an emblem of victory or distinction. **5.** a branch or wreath of laurel foliage. **6.** Usually, **laurels.** honor won, as for achievement in a field. **7. look to one's laurels,** to be alert to the possibility of being excelled: *New developments in the industry are forcing long-established firms to look to their laurels.* **8. rest on one's laurels,** to be content with one's present honors, achievements, etc. —*v.t.* **9.** to adorn or wreathe with laurel. **10.** to honor with marks of distinction. [dissimilated var. of ME *laurer,* earlier *lorer* < OF *lorier* bay tree = *lor* bay, laurel (< L *laurus*) + *-ier* -ER[2]]

Lau·ren·cin (lô räɴ saɴ′), *n.* **Ma·rie** (mȧ rē′), 1885–1956, French painter, lithographer, and stage designer.

Lau·ren·tian (lô ren′shən), *adj.* **1.** of or pertaining to the St. Lawrence River. **2.** *Geol.* noting or pertaining to the granite intrusions and orogeny in Canada around the Great Lakes during the Archeozoic. [< L *Laurenti(us)* Lawrence (orig. adj. = *Laurent(ēs)* men of *Lavinium* + *-ius* -IOUS) + -AN]

Lauren′tian Moun′tains, a range of low mountains in E Canada, between the St. Lawrence River and Hudson Bay. Also called **Lau·ren′tians.**

Lau′ren·tides Park′ (lôr′ən tīdz′, lor′-; *Fr.* lô räɴ-tēd′), a national park in SE Canada, in Quebec province between the St. Lawrence and Lake St. John.

lau′ryl al′cohol (lôr′il, lor′-), *Chem.* a crystalline solid or colorless liquid, $CH_3(CH_2)_{10}CH_2OH$, used chiefly in the manufacture of detergents. [< L *laur(us)* laurel + -YL]

Lau·sanne (lō zan′; *Fr.* lō zȧn′), *n.* a city in W Switzerland, on the Lake of Geneva. 135,800 (est. 1964).

laus De·o (lôs dē′ō, lous dā′ō), *Latin.* praise (be) to God.

Lau·trec (lō trek′), *n.* See **Toulouse-Lautrec, Henri.**

lav (lav), *n.* *Informal.* lavatory. [by shortening]

la·va (lä′və, lav′ə), *n.* **1.** the molten or fluid rock that issues from a volcano or volcanic vent. **2.** the substance formed when this solidifies, occurring in many varieties differing greatly in structure and constitution. [< It, orig. Neapolitan dial.: avalanche < L *lābēs* a sliding down, falling, akin to *lābī* to slide]

la·va·bo (lə vä′bō, -vā′-), *n., pl.* **-boes.** *Eccles.* **1.** the ritual washing of the celebrant's hands after the offertory in the Mass. **2.** the passage recited at this time. **3.** the small towel or the basin used. **4.** (in many medieval monasteries) a large stone washbasin. [< L: I shall wash]

lav·age (lə väzh′, lav′ij; *Fr.* lȧ vȧzh′), *n., pl.* **lav·a·ges** (lə vä′zhiz, lav′i jiz; *Fr.* lȧ vȧzh′). **1.** a washing. **2.** *Med.* **a.** cleansing by injection or the like. **b.** the washing out of the stomach; gastric lavage. [< F: lit., a washing = *lav(er)* (to) wash (< L *lavāre*) + *-age* -AGE]

La·val (lȧ vȧl′), *n.* **Pierre** (pyer), 1883–1945, French lawyer and politician: premier 1931–32, 1935–36; premier of the Vichy government 1942–44: executed for treason 1945.

la·va-la·va (lä′və lä′və), *n.* a Polynesian garment of printed cloth, worn as a loincloth or skirt. Also called **pareu.** [< Samoan: clothing]

lav·a·liere (lav′ə lēr′, lä′və-), *n.* an ornamental pendant, usually jeweled, worn on a chain around the neck. Also,

lav′a·lier′, la·val·lière (*Fr.* LA VA lyeʀ′). [after the Duchesse de *La Vallière* (1644–1710), mistress of Louis XIV]

La·va·ter (lä′vä tər, lä vä′tər), *n.* **Jo·hann Kas·par** (yō′hän käs′pär), 1741–1801, Swiss poet, theologian, and physiognomist.

la·va·tion (la vā′shən, lā-, lə-), *n.* the process of washing. [< L *lavātiōn-* (s. of *lavātiō*) a washing = *lavāt(us)* washed (ptp. of *lavāre;* see LAVE[1]) + *-iōn-* -ION] —**la·va′tion·al,** *adj.*

lav·a·to·ry (lav′ə tōr′ē, -tôr′ē), *n., pl.* **-ries. 1.** a room fitted with equipment for washing the hands and face and usually with toilet facilities. **2.** a bowl or basin with running water for purposes of washing or bathing. **3.** any place where washing is done. [ME *lavatorie* < LL *lavātōri(um)* washing place. See LAVATION, -ARY]

lave[1] (lāv), *v.,* **laved, lav·ing.** —*v.t.* **1.** to wash; bathe. **2.** to flow along, against, or past, as a river, sea, etc.; wash. **3.** *Literary.* to ladle; pour. —*v.i.* **4.** *Archaic.* to bathe. [ME *lave(n),* OE *lafian* to pour water on, wash, perh. < L *lavāre* to wash]

lave[2] (lāv), *n. Scot.* the remainder; the rest. [ME; OE *lāf;* c. OHG *leiba,* Icel *leif,* Goth *laiba;* akin to LEAVE[1]]

lav·en·der (lav′ən dər), *n.* **1.** pale bluish purple. **2.** any Old World, menthaceous herb or shrub of the genus *Lavandula,* esp. *L. officinalis,* having spikes of fragrant, pale purple flowers. **3.** the dried flowers or other parts of this plant placed among linen, clothes, etc., for scent or as a preservative. **4.** Also called **lav′ender wa′ter.** toilet water, shaving lotion, or the like, made with a solution of oil of lavender. [ME *lavendre* < AF < ML *lavendula,* var. of *livendula,* nasalized var. of **lividula* a plant livid in color. See LIVID, -ULE]

la·ver[1] (lā′vər), *n.* **1.** *Old Testament.* a large basin in the court of the Hebrew tabernacle and subsequently in the temple, used for ablutions. **2.** *Eccles.* the font or water of baptism. **3.** any spiritually cleansing agency. **4.** *Archaic.* a basin, bowl, or cistern to wash in. [ME *lavo(u)r* < MF *laveoir* < LL *lavātōr(ium)* LAVATORY]

la·ver[2] (lā′vər), *n.* any of several edible seaweeds, esp. of the genus *Porphyra.* [< NL, special use of L *laver* a plant]

La Vé·ren·drye (*Fr.* LA VĀ RÄN DRĒ′), **Pierre Gaul·tier de Va·renne** (*Fr.* pyeʀ gō tyā′ də VA ʀen′), **Sieur de,** 1685–1749, Canadian explorer of North America.

La·vin·i·a (lə vin′ē ə), *n. Rom. Legend.* the daughter of Latinus and second wife of Aeneas.

lav·ish (lav′ish), *adj.* **1.** using or giving in great amounts; prodigal (often fol. by *of*): *lavish of his time; lavish of affection.* **2.** expended, bestowed, or occurring in profusion; unlimited: *lavish spending.* —*v.t.* **3.** to expend or give in great amounts or without limit: *to lavish favors on a person.* [late ME *lavas* profusion (n.), profuse (adj.) < MF *lavasse* downpour of rain < *lav(er)* (to) wash < L *lavāre*] —**lav′ish·er,** *n.* —**lav′ish·ly,** *adv.* —**lav′ish·ment,** *n.* —**lav′ish·ness,** *n.* —**Syn. 1, 2.** unstinted, extravagant, excessive; generous, openhanded. LAVISH, PROFUSE refer to that which exists in abundance and is poured out copiously. LAVISH suggests (sometimes excessive) generosity and openhandedness: *lavish hospitality; much too lavish.* PROFUSE emphasizes abundance, but may suggest overemotionalism, exaggeration, or the like: *profuse thanks, compliments, apologies.* **3.** heap, pour; squander. —**Ant. 1, 2.** niggardly.

La·voi·sier (LA VWA zyā′), *n.* **An·toine Lau·rent** (äN-TWAN′ lō RÄN′), 1743–94, French scientist: pioneer in the field of chemistry.

law[1] (lô), *n.* **1.** the principles and regulations established by a government and applicable to a people, whether in the form of legislation or of custom and policies recognized and enforced by judicial decision. **2.** any written or positive rule or collection of rules prescribed under the authority of the state or nation, as by the people in its constitution. Cf. **bylaw. 3.** the controlling influence of such rules; the condition of society brought about by their observance: *maintaining law and order.* **4.** a system or collection of such rules. **5.** the department of knowledge concerned with these rules; jurisprudence: *to study law.* **6.** the body of such rules concerned with a particular subject or derived from a particular source: *commercial law.* **7.** an act of the supreme legislative body of a state or nation, as distinguished from the constitution. **8.** the principles applied in the courts of common law, as distinguished from equity. **9.** the profession that deals with law and legal procedure: *the practice of law.* **10.** legal action; litigation: *to go to law.* **11.** an agent or agency acting to enforce the law, esp. the police: *The law arrived at the scene immediately after the alarm went off.* **12.** any rule or injunction that must be obeyed: *Having a good breakfast was an absolute law in the household.* **13.** a rule or principle of proper conduct sanctioned by man's conscience, concepts of natural justice, or the will of a deity: *a moral law.* **14.** a rule or manner of behavior that is instinctive or spontaneous: *the law of self-preservation.* **15. a.** a statement of a relation or sequence of phenomena invariable under the same conditions. **b.** a mathematical rule. **16.** a principle based on the predictable consequences of an act, condition, etc.: *the law of supply and demand.* **17.** a rule, principle, or convention regarded as governing the structure or the relationship of an element in the structure of something, as of a language or work of art: *the laws of playwriting; the laws of grammar.* **18.** a commandment or a revelation from God. **19.** (*sometimes cap.*) a divinely appointed order or system. **20. the Law.** See **Law of Moses. 21.** the preceptive part of the Bible, esp. of the New Testament, in contradistinction to its promises: *the law of Christ.* **22. lay down the law, a.** to state one's views authoritatively. **b.** to give a command in an imperious manner. **23. take the law into one's own hands,** to administer justice as one sees fit without recourse to the usual legal processes. [ME *law, lagh,* OE *lagu* < Scand; cf. Icel *lag* layer, pl. *lög* law, lit., that which is laid down; akin to LAY[1], LIE[2]] —**law′like′,** *adj.*

law[2] (lô), *interj. Dial.* (used as an exclamation expressing astonishment.) [perh. var. of LORD or LA[2]]

Law (lô), *n.* **1. Andrew Bon·ar** (bon′ər), 1858–1923, English statesman, born in Canada: prime minister 1922–23. **2. John,** 1671–1729, Scottish financier.

law-a·bid·ing (lô′ə bī′ding), *adj.* abiding by or keeping the law; obedient to law: *law-abiding citizens.* —**law′-a·bid′ing·ness,** *n.*

law′ and or′der, strict control of crime and repression of violence, sometimes at the possible cost of civil rights. —**law′-and-or′der,** *adj.*

law·break·er (lô′brā′kər), *n.* a person who breaks or violates the law. [ME *lawbreker;* r. OE *lahbreca*] —**law′-break′ing,** *n., adj.*

Lawes (lôz), *n.* **Lewis E(dward),** 1883–1947, U.S. penologist.

law·ful (lô′fəl), *adj.* **1.** allowed or permitted by law; not contrary to law; legal. **2.** appointed or recognized by law; legally qualified: *a lawful king.* **3.** recognized or sanctioned by law; legitimate: *a lawful heir.* **4.** acting or living according to the law; law-abiding. [ME *laghful*] —**law′ful·ly,** *adv.* —**law′ful·ness,** *n.*

law·giv·er (lô′giv′ər), *n.* a person who promulgates a law or a code of laws. [ME *lawe givere*] —**law′giv′ing,** *n., adj.*

law·ing (lô′ing), *n. Scot.* a bill, esp. for food or drink in a tavern. [obs. Scot *law* bill (ME (dial.) *lagh* < ON *lag* price, tax, proper place) + -ING[1]]

law·less (lô′lis), *adj.* **1.** contrary to or without regard for the law: *lawless violence.* **2.** being without law; uncontrolled by a law; unbridled: *lawless passion.* **3.** illegal. [ME *laweles*] —**law′less·ly,** *adv.* —**law′less·ness,** *n.*

law·mak·er (lô′mā′kər), *n.* a person who makes or enacts law; legislator. [ME *lawe maker*] —**law′mak′ing,** *n., adj.*

law·man (lô′man′, -mən), *n., pl.* **-men** (-men′, -mən). an officer of the law, as a sheriff or policeman. [ME *laweman,* earlier *lageman,* OE *lahmann*]

Law·man (lô′mən), *n.* Layamon.

law′ mer′chant, the legal principles and rules dealing with commercial transactions.

lawn[1] (lôn, län), *n.* **1.** a stretch of grass-covered land, esp. one closely mowed, as near a house or in a park. **2.** *Archaic.* a glade. [ME *launde* < MF *lande* glade < Celt; cf. Breton *lann* heath. See LAND] —**lawn′y,** *adj.*

lawn[2] (lôn, län), *n.* a thin or sheer linen or cotton fabric, either plain or printed. [late ME *lawnd, laun,* perh. after LAON, where linen-making once flourished] —**lawn′y,** *adj.*

lawn′ bowl′ing, a game played with composition bowls or balls on a flat turf, the object being to roll one's ball as near as possible to a smaller white ball at the other end of the turf. Also called **bowls.** Cf. **jack**[1] (def. 5), **rink** (def. 5).

Lawn·dale (lôn′dāl′), *n.* a city in SW California, near Los Angeles. 24,825 (1970).

lawn′ mow′er, a machine for cutting grass.

lawn′ ten′nis, tennis, esp. when played on a grass court.

law′ of ac′tion and reac′tion, *Physics.* the third law of motion. See under **law of motion.**

law′ of av′erages, 1. a statistical principle formulated by Jakob Bernoulli to show a more or less predictable ratio between the number of random trials of an event and its occurrences. **2.** *Informal.* the principle that, in the long run, probability as naïvely conceived will operate and influence any one occurrence.

law′ of conserva′tion of en′ergy, *Physics.* See **conservation of energy.**

law′ of conserva′tion of mass′, *Physics.* See **conservation of mass.**

law′ of co′sines, *Math.* **1.** an equation stating that the square of one side of a plane triangle is equal to the sum of the squares of the other two sides, minus twice the product of these sides multiplied by the cosine of the angle between them. **2.** either of two analogous equations used in spherical trigonometry.

law′ of gravita′tion, *Physics.* **1.** the principle that all bodies and particles in the universe exert gravitational forces on one another. **2.** the quantitative statement that the gravitational force between any two bodies is directly proportional to the product of their masses and inversely proportional to the distance between them. Also called **law of universal gravitation.**

Law′ of Mo′ses, the Pentateuch, containing the Mosaic dispensations, or system of rules and ordinances. Cf. **Hagiographa, Prophets.**

law′ of mo′tion, *Physics.* any of three laws of classical mechanics, either the law that a body remains at rest or in motion with a constant velocity unless an external force acts on the body **(first law of motion),** the law that the sum of the forces acting on a body is equal to the product of the mass of the body and the acceleration produced by the forces, with motion in the direction of the resultant of the forces **(second law of motion),** or the law that for every force acting on a body, the body exerts a force having equal magnitude and the opposite direction along the same line of action as the original force **(third law of motion).** Also called **Newton's law of motion.**

law′ of sines′, *Math.* **1.** an equation stating that the ratio of a side of a plane triangle to the sine of the opposite angle is constant for any given triangle. **2.** an analogous equation used in spherical trigonometry.

law′ of the jun′gle, a mode of action in which the fittest survive, as animals in nature or as human beings not regulated by the laws of civilization, ethics, morals, or the like.

Law′ of the Medes′ and the Per′sians, unalterable law.

law′ of thermodynam′ics, any of three principles variously stated in equivalent forms, being the principle that the change of energy of a thermodynamic system is equal to the heat transferred minus the work done **(first law of thermodynamics),** the principle that no cyclic process is possible in which heat is absorbed from a reservoir at a single temperature and converted completely into mechanical work **(second law of thermodynamics),** and the principle that it is impossible to reduce the temperature of a system to absolute zero in a finite number of operations **(third law of thermodynamics).**

law′ of univer′sal gravita′tion. See **law of gravitation.**

Law·rence (lôr′əns, lor′-), *n.* **1. D(avid) H(erbert),** 1885–1930, English novelist. **2. Ernest O(rlando),** 1901–58,

act, āble, dâre, ärt; ebb, ēqual; if, īce; hot, ōver, ôrder; oil; bo͝ok; o͞oze; out; up, ûrge; ə = *a* as in *alone;* chief; sing; shoe; thin; that; zh as in *measure;* ə as in *button* (but′ən), *fire* (fīər). See the full key inside the front cover.

U.S. physicist: inventor of the cyclotron; Nobel prize 1939. **3. James,** 1781–1813, U.S. naval officer in the War of 1812. **4. Sir Thomas,** 1769–1830, English painter. **5. T(homas) E(dward)** (*T. E. Shaw*) ("*Lawrence of Arabia*"), 1888–1935, English archaeologist, soldier, and writer. **6.** a city in NE Massachusetts, on the Merrimack River. 66,915 (1970). **7.** a city in E Kansas, on the Kansas River. 45,698 (1970).

law·ren·ci·um (lô ren′sē əm, lo-), *n. Chem.* a synthetic, radioactive, metallic element. *Symbol:* Lw; *at. no.:* 103. [*Lawrence* Radiation Laboratory, Berkeley, California + -IUM]

law·suit (lô′so͞ot′), *n.* a suit at law; a prosecution of a claim in a court of law; an action.

Law·ton (lôt′ən), *n.* a city in SW Oklahoma. 74,470 (1970).

law·yer (lô′yər, loi′ər), *n.* **1.** a person whose profession is to conduct lawsuits for clients and to advise or act for them in other legal matters. **2.** a burbot: so called from the beardlike barbel. [ME *lawyere*] —**law′yer·like′,** *adj.*

lax (laks), *adj.* **1.** lacking in strictness or severity; careless or negligent: *lax morals.* **2.** not rigidly exact or precise; vague. **3.** loose or slack; not tense, rigid, or firm: *a lax cord.* **4.** open or not retentive, as the bowels. **5.** open or not compact; having a loosely cohering structure; porous: *lax texture.* **6.** *Phonet.* (of a vowel) articulated with relatively relaxed tongue muscles. Cf. **tense**[1] (def. 4). [late ME < L *lax(us)* loose, slack, wide] —**lax′ly,** *adv.* —**lax′ness,** *n.*

lax·a·tion (lak sā′shən), *n.* **1.** a loosening or relaxing. **2.** the state of being loosened or relaxed. **3.** a bowel movement. [ME *laxacion* < L *laxātiōn-* (s. of *laxātiō*) a loosening = *laxāt(us)* loosened (ptp. of *laxāre;* see LAX) + *-iōn-* -ION]

lax·a·tive (lak′sə tiv), *n.* **1.** a medicine or agent for relieving constipation. —*adj.* **2.** of, pertaining to, or constituting a laxative; purgative. **3.** *Archaic.* **a.** (of the bowels) subject to looseness. **b.** (of a disease) characterized by looseness of the bowels. [< ML *laxātīv(us)* loosening (see LAXATION, -IVE); r. ME *laxatif* < MF] —**lax′a·tive·ly,** *adv.* —**lax′a·tive·ness,** *n.*

lax·i·ty (lak′si tē), *n.* the state or quality of being lax; looseness. [< L *laxitās* wideness, openness]

Lax·ness (läks′nes), *n.* **Hall·dór Kil·jan** (häl′dōʀ kil′yän), born 1902, Icelandic writer: Nobel prize 1955.

lay[1] (lā), *v.,* **laid** or, for 8, **layed; lay·ing;** *n.* —*v.t.* **1.** to put or place in a horizontal position or a position of rest; set down: *to lay a book on a desk.* **2.** to beat down, as from an erect position; strike or throw to the ground: *One punch laid him low. The summer storm laid the grain flat.* **3.** to place before a person or bring to a person's notice or consideration: *He laid his case before the commission.* **4.** to present, bring forward, or prefer, as a claim, charge, etc. **5.** to impute, attribute, or ascribe: *to lay blame on someone.* **6.** to bury: *They laid him to rest.* **7.** to bring forth and deposit (an egg or eggs). **8.** to deposit as a wager; stake: *He layed $10 on the horse.* **9.** to bet (someone): *I'll lay you ten to one that he wins.* **10.** to place, set, or cause to be in a particular situation, state, or condition: *The failure of his crops laid him in debt.* **11.** to impose as a burden, duty, or penalty: *to lay an embargo on shipments of oil.* **12.** to set, place, or apply (often fol. by *to* or *on*). **13.** to set (a trap). **14.** to place or locate: *The scene is laid in France.* **15.** to dispose or place in proper position or in an orderly fashion: *to lay bricks.* **16.** to place in position on or along a surface or route: *to lay a pipeline; to lay a superhighway.* **17.** to place dinner service on (a table); set. **18.** to place on or over a surface, as paint; cover or spread with something. **19.** to devise or arrange, as a plan. **20.** to bring (a stick, lash, etc.) down, as on a person, in inflicting punishment. **21.** to smooth down or make even: *to lay the nap of cloth.* **22.** to form by twisting strands together, as a rope. **23.** to allay, quiet, or suppress: *to lay a person's doubts at rest.* **24.** to cause to subside: *laying the clouds of dust with a spray of water.* **25.** *Naut.* to move or turn into a certain position or direction. **26.** to aim (a cannon) in a specified direction at a specified elevation. **27.** to have sexual intercourse with.
—*v.i.* **28.** to lay eggs. **29.** to wager or bet. **30.** to deal or aim blows vigorously (usually fol. by *on, at, about,* etc.). **31.** to apply oneself vigorously. **32.** *Dial.* to plan or scheme (often fol. by *out*). **33.** *Naut.* to take up a specified position, direction, etc.: *to lay aloft; to lay close to the wind.* **34.** *Nonstandard.* lie[2]. **35. lay aside, a.** to abandon; reject: *They laid aside their childish pastimes.* **b.** to save for use at a later time; store. **36. lay away, a.** to reserve for later use; save. **b.** to hold (merchandise) pending final payment or request for delivery. **c.** to bury (someone). **37. lay by, a.** to put away for future use; store; save: *He had managed to lay by some money for college.* **b.** *Naut.* (of a sailing vessel) to come to a standstill; heave to; lay to. **38. lay down, a.** to give up; yield: *to lay down one's arms.* **b.** to stock; store. **c.** to assert firmly; state authoritatively; ordain or prescribe: *to lay down rigid rules.* **39. lay for,** *Slang.* to wait for in order to attack; lie in wait for. **40. lay in,** to store away for future use. **41. lay into,** *Slang.* to attack physically or verbally; assail. **42. lay it on,** *Informal.* to engage in exaggerated flattery or reproof. **43. lay low.** See **low**[1] (defs. 41, 42). **44. lay off, a.** to dismiss an employee, esp. temporarily because of slack business. **b.** *Slang.* to stop annoying or teasing; cease: *Lay off the complaining! Lay off me, will you?* **45. lay out, a.** to extend at length. **b.** to spread out in order; arrange; prepare. **c.** to ready (a corpse) for burial. **d.** *Informal.* to spend or contribute (money). **e.** *Slang.* to knock (someone) unconscious; strike down. **f.** to plan; plot; design: *to lay out a garden.* **g.** to make a layout of. **46. lay over, a.** to postpone until action may be taken: *The vote will have to be laid over until next week.* **b.** *U.S.* to make a stop, as during a trip. **47. lay siege to.** See **siege** (def. 7). **48. lay to, a.** *Naut.* to check the motion of (a ship). **b.** *Naut.* to put (a ship) in a dock or other place of safety. **c.** to put forth effort; apply oneself. **49. lay up, a.** to put away for future use; store up. **b.** to cause to be confined to bed or to be kept indoors; make ill; disable.
—*n.* **50.** the way or position in which a thing is laid or lies: *the lay of the south pasture.* **51.** *Ropemaking.* the quality of a fiber rope characterized by the degree of twist, the angles formed by the strands, and the fibers in the strands. **52.** a share of the profits or the catch of a whaling or fishing voyage, distributed to officers and crew. **53.** *Slang.* **a.** a partner in sexual intercourse. **b.** an instance of sexual intercourse. [ME *laye(n), legge(n),* OE *lecgan* (causative of *licgan* to LIE[2]); c. D *leggen,* G *legen,* Icel *legja,* Goth *lagjan*] —**Syn. 1.** See **put, lie**[2].

lay[2] (lā), *v.* pt. of **lie**[2].

lay[3] (lā), *adj.* **1.** belonging to, pertaining to, or performed by the people or laity, as distinguished from the clergy: *a lay sermon.* **2.** not belonging to a specified profession, esp. law or medicine. [ME < MF *lai* < eccl. L *lāic(us)* LAIC]

lay[4] (lā), *n.* **1.** a short narrative or other poem, esp. one to be sung. **2.** a song. [ME *lai* < OF prob. < Gmc; cf. OHG *leih* song, c. Goth *laiks* dance, OE *lāc,* Icel *leikr* play]

Lay·a·mon (lā′ə mən, lä′yə-), *n.* fl. c1200, English poet and chronicler. Also called **Lawman.**

lay′ an′alyst, a psychoanalyst who does not have a medical degree.

Layard (lârd, lā′ərd), *n.* **Sir Aus·ten Henry** (ô′stən), 1817–94, English archaeologist, writer, and diplomat.

lay′a·way plan′ (lā′ə wā′), a method of purchasing by which the purchaser reserves an article with a down payment and claims it only after paying the full balance.

lay′ broth′er, a man who has taken religious vows and habit but is employed by his order chiefly in manual labor.

lay-by (lā′bī′), *n.* **1.** *Brit.* a place beside a road or railroad track where vehicles may wait. **2.** *Naut.* a mooring place in a narrow river or canal, formed to one side so as to leave the channel free.

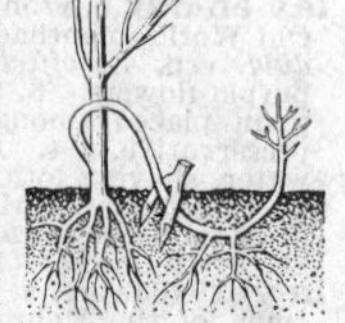
Layer (def. 4)

lay·er (lā′ər), *n.* **1.** a thickness of some material laid on or spread over a surface: *a layer of soot on the window sill; two layers of paint.* **2.** a bed; stratum: *alternating layers of basalt and sandstone.* **3.** a person or thing that lays. **4.** *Hort.* **a.** a shoot or twig that is induced to root while still attached to the living stock, as by bending and covering with soil. **b.** a plant so propagated. —*v.t.* **5.** to make a layer of. **6.** *Hort.* to propagate by layers. [ME *leyer, legger*]

lay′er cake′, a cake made in layers, with a cream, jelly, or other filling between them.

lay·ette (lā et′), *n.* an outfit of clothing, toilet articles, etc., for a newborn child. [< F; MF *laiete* small coffer = *laie* chest (< MD *laeye,* var. of *lade;* akin to LADE) + *-ete* -ETTE]

lay′ fig′ure, 1. a jointed model of the human body, usually of wood, from which artists work in the absence of a living model. **2.** a person of no importance, individuality, distinction, etc.; nonentity. [*lay,* abstracted from obs. *layman* < D *leeman,* lit., joint-man (*le(d)e-* joint, c. OE *lith* limb + *man* MAN[1])]

lay·man (lā′mən), *n., pl.* **-men.** a member of the laity; a person who is not a clergyman or who is not a member of a specified profession, esp. of law or medicine. [late ME]

lay·off (lā′ôf′, -of′), *n.* **1.** the act of laying off, as workers. **2.** an interval of enforced unemployment.

lay′ of the land′, the general state or condition of affairs under consideration. Also, *esp. Brit.,* **lie of the land.**

lay·out (lā′out′), *n.* **1.** a laying or spreading out. **2.** an arrangement or plan: *We objected to the layout of the house.* **3.** a plan or sketch, as of an advertisement or a page of a newspaper or magazine, indicating the arrangement and relationship of type, artwork, etc. **4.** *Informal.* a place, as of residence or business, and the things that go with it; setup: *a fancy layout with a swimming pool.* **5.** a collection or set of tools, implements, or the like. **6.** *Cards.* an arrangement of cards dealt according to a given pattern, as in solitaire.

lay·o·ver (lā′ō′vər), *n. U.S.* stopover.

lay′ read′er, *Anglican Ch.* a layman authorized by a bishop to conduct certain parts of a service.

lay′ sis′ter, a woman who has taken religious vows and habit but is employed by her order chiefly in manual labor.

lay-up (lā′up′), *n. Basketball.* a shot with one hand from a point close to the basket.

lay·wom·an (lā′wo͝om′ən), *n., pl.* **-wom·en.** a female member of the laity.

laz·ar (laz′ər; *more formally* lā′zər), *n.* a person infected with a loathsome disease, esp. a leper. [ME < ML *lazar(us)* leper, special use of LL *Lazarus* LAZARUS] —**laz′ar·like′,** *adj.*

laz·a·ret·to (laz′ə ret′ō), *n., pl.* **-tos. 1.** a hospital for those affected with contagious or loathsome diseases, as for lepers. **2.** a building or a ship set apart for quarantine purposes. **3.** *Naut.* a small storeroom within the hull of a vessel, esp. one at the extreme stern. Also, **laz·a·ret, laz·a·rette** (laz′ə ret′). [< It *lazareto* (Venetian dial.) = *l(azzaro)* LAZAR + *(N)azareto* popular name of a hospital maintained in Venice by the Church of Santa Maria di Nazaret]

Laz·a·rus (laz′ər əs), *n.* **1.** the diseased beggar in the parable of the rich man and the beggar. Luke 16:19–31. **2.** a brother of Mary and Martha whom Jesus raised from the dead. John 11:1–44; 12:1–18. **3. Emma,** 1849–87, U.S. poet. [< LL < Gk *Lázaros* < Heb *El'āzār* Eleazar (one God has helped)]

laze (lāz), *v.,* **lazed, laz·ing,** *n.* —*v.i.* **1.** to idle or lounge lazily. —*v.t.* **2.** to pass (time, life, etc.) lazily (usually fol. by *away*). —*n.* **3.** a period of ease or indolence: *a quiet laze in the hammock.* [back formation from LAZY]

laz·u·li (laz′o͝o lē, -lī′, laz′yo͝o-, lazh′o͝o-), *n.* See **lapis lazuli.**

laz·u·lite (laz′ə līt′, laz′yə-, lazh′ə-, lazh′yə-), *n.* an azure-blue mineral, hydrous magnesium iron aluminum phosphate, $(FeMg)Al_2P_2O_8(OH)_2$. [< ML *lāzul(um)* azure, LAPIS LAZULI + -ITE[1]] —**laz·u·lit·ic** (laz′yə lit′ik), *adj.*

laz·u·rite (laz′ə rīt′, laz′yə-, lazh′ə-), *n.* a mineral, sodium aluminum silicate and sulfide, $Na_5Al_3Si_3O_{12}S_3$, occurring in deep-blue crystals, used for ornamental purposes. [< ML *lāzur* AZURE + -ITE[1]]

la·zy (lā′zē), *adj.,* **la·zi·er, la·zi·est. 1.** having an aversion to work or effort; indolent. **2.** causing idleness or indolence: *a hot, lazy afternoon.* **3.** slow-moving; sluggish: *a lazy stream.* **4.** (of a livestock brand) placed on its side instead of upright. [?] —**la′zi·ly,** *adv.* —**la′zi·ness,** *n.* —**la′zy·ish,** *adj.* —**Syn. 1.** slothful. See **idle.** —**Ant. 1.** industrious.

la·zy·bones (lā′zē bōnz′), *n.* (*usually construed as sing.*) *Informal.* a lazy person.

la′zy Su′san, a large, revolving tray for food, condiments, etc., placed at the center of a dining table.

la′zy tongs′, extensible tongs for grasping objects at a distance, consisting of a series of pairs of crossing pieces, each pair pivoted together in the middle and connected with the next pair at the extremities.

lb., *pl.* **lbs., lb.** pound. [< L *libra,* pl. *librae*] Also, **lb**

L.B., **1.** landing barge. **2.** light bomber. **3.** Bachelor of Letters; Bachelor of Literature. [< L *Litterārum Baccalaureus; Līterārum Baccalaureus*] **4.** local board.

lb. ap., *Pharm.* pound apothecary's.

lb. av., pound avoirdupois.

lbf, *Physics.* pound-force.

lb. t., pound troy.

LC, landing craft.

L/C, See **letter of credit.** Also, **l/c**

L.C., **1.** See **letter of credit.** **2.** See **Library of Congress.**

l.c., **1.** left center. **2.** See **letter of credit.** **3.** in the place cited. [< L *locō citātō*] **4.** *Print.* lower case.

LCD, a method of displaying readings continuously on digital watches, calculators, etc., using a liquid-crystal film, sealed between glass plates, that changes its optical properties when a current is applied. [L(IQUID)-C(RYSTAL) D(ISPLAY)]

L.C.D., lowest common denominator. Also, **l.c.d.**

L.C.F., lowest common factor. Also, **l.c.f.**

L.C.L., *Com.* less than carload lot. Also, **l.c.l.**

L.C.M., least common multiple. Also, **l.c.m.**

LD, **1.** praise (be) to God. [< L *laus Deō*] **2.** lethal dose. **3.** long distance. **4.** Low Dutch.

Ld., **1.** limited. **2.** lord.

L.D., Low Dutch.

LDL, *Biochem.* See **low-density lipoprotein.**

L-dopa (el′ dō′pə, el′ dō′pä), *n.* a drug for reversing the crippling effects of Parkinson's disease. [*L-(3, 4) d(ihydr)-o(xy)p(henyl)a(lanine)*]

Ldp., **1.** ladyship. **2.** lordship.

L.D.S., **1.** Latter-day Saints. **2.** praise (be) to God forever. [< L *laus Deō semper*] **3.** Licentiate in Dental Surgery.

-le, **1.** a suffix of verbs having a frequentative force: *dazzle; twinkle.* **2.** a suffix of adjectives formed originally on verbal stems and having the sense of "apt to": *brittle.* **3.** a noun suffix having originally a diminutive meaning: *bramble.* **4.** a noun suffix indicating agent or instrument: *beadle; bridle; thimble.* [ME *-len,* OE *-lian* (v.); ME *-el,* OE *-ol* (adj.); ME *-el,* OE *-il* (dim.); ME *-el,* OE *-ol, -ul* (agent)]

lea[1] (lē, lā), *n.* **1.** a tract of open ground, esp. grassland; a meadow. **2.** land used for a few years for pasture or for growing hay, then plowed over and replaced by another crop. Also, **ley.** [ME *lege, lei,* OE *lēah;* c. OHG *lōh,* Flem *loo* (as in *Waterloo*), L *lūcus*]

lea[2] (lē), *n.* a measure of yarn of varying quantity, for wool usually 80 yards, for cotton and silk 120 yards, and for linen 300 yards. [? back formation from ME *lese,* var. of LEASH]

leach (lēch), *v.t.* **1.** to cause (water or other liquid) to percolate through something. **2.** to remove soluble constituents from (ashes, soil, etc.) by percolation. —*v.i.* **3.** (of ashes, soil, etc.) to undergo the action of percolating water. **4.** to percolate, as water. —*n.* **5.** a leaching. **6.** the material leached. **7.** a vessel for use in leaching. [unexplained var. of obs. *letch* to wet (> dial. *letch* bog), OE *leccan,* causative of LEAK] —**leach′a·ble,** *adj.* —**leach′er,** *n.*

leach·y (lē′chē), *adj.,* **leach·i·er, leach·i·est.** allowing water to percolate through, as sandy or rocky soil; porous.

Lea·cock (lē′kok), *n.* **Stephen (Butler),** 1869–1944, Canadian humorist and economist.

lead[1] (lēd), *v.,* **led, lead·ing,** *n., adj.* —*v.t.* **1.** to take or conduct on the way; go before or with to show the way: *to lead a group on a cross-country hike.* **2.** to conduct by holding and guiding: *to lead a horse by a rope.* **3.** to influence or induce; cause: *Subsequent events led him to reconsider his position.* **4.** to guide in direction, course, action, opinion, etc.; bring: *You can lead him around to your point of view if you are shrewd with him.* **5.** to conduct or bring (water, wire, etc.) in a particular course. **6.** (of a road, passage, etc.) to serve to bring (a person) to a place: *The first street on the left will lead you to Andrews Place.* **7.** to take or bring: *The prisoners were led in to the warden's office.* **8.** to command or direct (an army or other large organization): *He led the Allied forces during the war.* **9.** to go at the head of or in advance of (a procession, list, body, etc.); proceed first in: *The school band led the parade.* **10.** to be superior to; have the advantage over: *He leads his teammates in runs batted in.* **11.** to have top position or first place in: *Iowa leads the nation in corn production.* **12.** to have the directing or principal part in: *He led a peace movement in the late 1930's.* **13.** to act as leader of (an orchestra, band, etc.); conduct. **14.** to go through or pass (time, life, etc.): *to lead a full life.* **15.** *Cards.* to begin a round, game, etc., with (a card or suit specified). **16.** to aim and fire a missile ahead of (a moving target) in order to allow for the travel of the target while the missile is reaching it. —*v.i.* **17.** to act as a guide; show the way: *You lead, we'll follow.* **18.** to afford passage to a place: *That path leads directly to his house.* **19.** to go first; be in advance. **20.** to result in; tend toward (usually fol. by *to*): *The incident led to his resignation.* **21.** to take the directing or principal part. **22.** to take the offensive: *The contender led with a right to the body.* **23.** *Cards.* to make the first play. **24.** to be led or submit to being led: *A properly trained horse will lead easily.* **25.** *Baseball.* (of a base runner) to leave a base before the delivery of a pitch (often fol. by *away*). **26. lead off,** to take the initiative; begin. **27. lead (someone) on,** to induce to continue a course of action that will probably end unfavorably; mislead: *She led him on to think that she would eventually marry him.* **28. lead the way.** See **way** (def. 29). **29. lead up to, a.** to prepare the way for. **b.** to approach (a subject, disclosure, etc.) gradually or evasively. —*n.* **30.** the first or foremost place; position in advance of others: *He took the lead in the race.* **31.** the extent of such advance: *He had a lead of four lengths.* **32.** a person or thing that leads. **33.** a leash. **34.** a guide to or an indication of a road, course, method, etc., to follow. **35.** precedence; example; leadership: *They followed his lead in everything they did.* **36.** *Theat.* **a.** the principal part in a play. **b.** the person who plays it. **37.** *Cards.* **a.** the act or right of playing first, as in a round. **b.** the card, suit, etc., so played. **38.** *Journalism.* a short summary serving as an introduction to a news story, article, or other copy. **39.** *Elect.* an often flexible and insulated single conductor, as a wire, used in connections between pieces of electric apparatus. **40.** the act of taking the offensive. **41.** *Naut.* **a.** the direction of a rope, wire, or chain. **b.** Also called **leader.** any of various devices for guiding a running rope. **42.** *Mining.* **a.** a lode. **b.** an auriferous deposit in an old river bed. **43.** the act of aiming a missile ahead of a moving target. **44.** the distance ahead of a moving target that a missile must be aimed in order to score a direct hit. **45.** *Baseball.* an act or instance of leading. —*adj.* **46.** most important; first: *lead editorial.* [ME *lede(n),* OE *lǣdan* (causative of *līthan* to go, travel); c. D *leiden,* G *leiten,* Icel *leitha*] —**Syn. 1.** escort. See **guide.**

lead[2] (led), *n.* **1.** *Chem.* a heavy, comparatively soft, malleable, bluish-gray metal, sometimes found in its natural state but usually combined as a sulfide, esp. in galena. *Symbol:* Pb; *at. wt.:* 207.19; *at. no.:* 82; *sp. gr.:* 11.34 at 20°C. **2.** something made of this metal or of one of its alloys. **3.** a plummet or mass of lead suspended by a line, as for taking soundings. **4.** bullets collectively; shot. **5.** black lead or graphite. **6.** a small stick of graphite, as used in pencils. **7.** Also called **leading.** *Print.* a thin strip of type metal or brass less than type-high, used for increasing the space between lines of type. **8.** a grooved bar of lead or came in which sections of glass are set, as in stained-glass windows. **9.** See **white lead.** —*v.t.* **10.** to cover, line, weight, treat, or impregnate with lead or one of its compounds. **11.** *Print.* to insert leads between the lines of. **12.** to fix (window glass) in position with leads. —*adj.* **13.** made of or containing lead. [ME *lede,* OE *lēad;* c. D *lood,* G *Lot* plummet] —**lead′less,** *adj.* —**Syn. 3.** weight, plumb.

lead′ ac′etate (led), *Chem.* a poisonous solid, $Pb(C_2H_3O_2)_2 \cdot 3H_2O$, used chiefly as a mordant in dyeing and printing textiles and as a drier in paints and varnishes. Also called **sugar of lead.**

lead′ ar′senate (led), *Chem.* a highly poisonous powder, $PbHAsO_4$, used as an insecticide.

Lead·bel·ly (led′bel′ē), *n.* See **Ledbetter, Huddie.**

lead′ col′ic (led), *Pathol.* See **painter's colic.**

lead·ed (led′id), *adj.* (of gasoline) containing tetraethyl lead: on combustion it produces a toxic pollutant.

lead·en (led′ən), *adj.* **1.** heavy, or hard to lift or move. **2.** dull, spiritless, or gloomy. **3.** of a dull gray color. **4.** oppressive; heavy: *a leaden silence.* **5.** sluggish; listless: *He moved at a leaden pace.* **6.** of poor quality or little value. **7.** made or consisting of lead. —*v.t.* **8.** to make leaden or sluggish. [ME *leden,* OE *lēaden*] —**lead′en·ly,** *adv.*

lead·er (lē′dər), *n.* **1.** a person or thing that leads. **2.** a guiding or directing head, as of an army, political group, etc. **3.** *Music.* **a.** a conductor or director, as of an orchestra, band, or chorus. **b.** the principal player or singer in an organization or performance. **4.** *Angling.* **a.** a length of nylon, silkworm gut, wire, or the like, to which the lure or hook is attached. **b.** the net used to direct fish into a weir, pound, etc. **5.** blank film or tape at the beginning of a length of film or magnetic tape, used for threading a camera, tape recorder, etc. **6.** *Journalism Brit.* See **leading article** (def. 2). **7.** a featured article of trade, esp. one offered at a low price to attract customers. **8.** a pipe for conveying rain water downward, as from a roof; downspout. **9.** *Naut.* lead[1] (def. 41b). **10. leaders,** *Print.* a row of dots or a short line to lead the eye across a space. [ME *leder(e)*] —**lead′erless,** *adj.*

lead·er·ship (lē′dər ship′), *n.* **1.** the position or function of a leader: *He maintained his leadership of the party despite heavy opposition.* **2.** ability to lead: *He displayed leadership potential.* **3.** an act or instance of leading: *They prospered under his leadership.* **4.** the leaders of a group.

lead′ glass′ (led), glass containing lead oxide.

lead′ glaze′ (led), *Ceram.* a siliceous glaze containing lead oxide as a flux.

lead-in (lēd′in′), *n.* *Radio and Television.* the connection between an antenna and a transmitter or receiving set.

lead·ing[1] (lē′ding), *adj.* **1.** chief; principal; most or extremely important; foremost: *He was the leading tenor of his day.* **2.** coming in advance of others; first: *He rode in the leading car.* **3.** directing; guiding. —*n.* **4.** the act of a person or thing that leads. [ME (n.)]

lead·ing[2] (led′ing), *n.* **1.** a covering or framing of lead. **2.** *Print.* lead[2] (def. 7). [late ME]

lead′ing ar′ticle (lē′ding), *Journalism.* **1.** the most prominently featured article in a magazine. **2.** Also called **leader.** *Brit.* the principal editorial in a newspaper.

lead′ing edge′ (lē′ding), *Aeron.* the edge of an airfoil or propeller blade facing the direction of motion.

lead′ing la′dy (lē′ding), the actress who plays the principal female role, esp. in a motion picture or play.

lead′ing light′ (lē′ding), **1.** *Naut.* See **range light.** **2.** *Informal.* an important or influential person.

lead′ing man′ (lē′ding), the actor who plays the principal male role, esp. in a motion picture or play.

lead′ing ques′tion (lē′ding), a question so worded as to suggest the proper or desired answer.

lead′ing tone′ (lē′ding), *Music.* the seventh degree of the scale.

lead′ line′ (led), *Naut.* a line by which a lead is lowered into the water to take soundings. [ME *leede lyne*]

lead-off (lēd′ôf′, -of′), *adj.* leading off or beginning: *the lead-off item on the agenda.* [adj. use of v. phrase *lead off*]

lead·off (lēd′ôf′, -of′), *n.* **1.** an act that starts something; start; beginning. **2.** *Baseball.* Also called **lead′-off man′.** the player who is first in the batting order or who is first to bat in an inning. [n. use of v. phrase *lead off*]

lead′ pen′cil (led), a writing or drawing implement made of graphite in a wooden or metal holder.

lead′-pipe cinch′ (led′pīp′), *Slang.* **1.** an absolute certainty. **2.** something very easy to accomplish.

lead′ poi′soning (led), **1.** *Pathol.* **a.** an acute toxic condition produced by absorption of lead into the body through skin contact, ingestion, or inhalation and characterized by convulsions and coma, occurring chiefly in children from mouthing toys or furnishings coated with lead paint. **b.** Also called **plumbism, saturnism.** a chronic form of this condition, occurring chiefly in adults whose work involves contact with lead products. **2.** *Slang.* death or injury inflicted by a bullet or shot.

leads·man (ledz′mən), *n., pl.* **-men.** a seaman who sounds with a lead line.

lead′ tetraeth′yl (led), *Chem.* tetraethyllead.

lead′ time′ (lēd), the period of time between planning and completing the manufacture of a product.

lead·wort (led′wûrt′), *n.* any plumbaginaceous herb or shrub of the genus *Plumbago,* having spikes of blue, white, or red flowers.

lead·y (led′ē), *adj.,* **lead·i·er, lead·i·est.** like lead; leaden. [ME *leedy*]

leaf (lēf), *n., pl.* **leaves** (lēvz), *v.* —*n.* **1.** one of the expanded, usually green organs borne by the stem of a plant. **2.** any similar or corresponding lateral outgrowth of a stem. **3.** a petal: *a rose leaf.* **4.** leaves collectively; foliage. **5.** a unit generally comprising two printed pages of a book, one on each side, but also applied to blank or illustrated pages. **6.** a thin sheet of metal: *silver leaf.* **7.** a lamina or layer. **8.** a sliding, hinged, or detachable flat part, as of a door or table top. **9.** a single strip of metal in a leaf spring. **10. in leaf,** covered with foliage; having leaves. **11. turn over a new leaf,** to begin anew; make a fresh start: *Every New Year's we make resolutions to turn over a new leaf.* —*v.i.* **12.** to put forth leaves. **13.** to turn pages quickly (usually fol. by *through*): *to leaf through a book.* —*v.t.* **14.** to thumb or turn, as the pages of a book or magazine, in a casual or cursory inspection of the contents. [ME *leef,* OE *lēaf;* c. D *loof,* G *Laub,* Icel *lauf,* Goth *laufs*] —**leaf′like′,** *adj.*

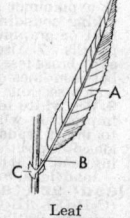

Leaf of willow, *Salix cordata*
A, Blade
B, Petiole
C, Stipule

leaf·age (lē′fij), *n.* foliage.

leaf′ bee′tle, any of numerous, often brightly colored beetles of the family *Chrysomelidae* that feed on the leaves of plants.

leaf′ blight′, *Plant Pathol.* a symptom or phase of many diseases of plants, characterized by necrotic spots or streaks on the leaves, accompanied by seed rot and seedling blight.

leaf′ blotch′, *Plant Pathol.* a symptom or phase of certain diseases of plants, characterized by necrotic discoloration of the leaves.

leaf′ bud′. See under **bud**[1] (def. 1a).

leaf′-cut·ting ant′ (lēf′kut′ing), any of several tropical American ants of the genus *Atta* that cut and chew bits of leaves and flowers into a mash, which they use to cultivate a fungus garden.

leaf′-cutting bee′, any of the bees of the family *Megachilidae* that cut circular pieces from leaves or flowers to line their nests.

leafed (lēft), *adj.* having leaves.

leaf′ fat′, a layer of fat, esp. that about the kidneys of a hog.

leaf·hop·per (lēf′hop′ər), *n.* any of numerous leaping homopterous insects of the family *Cicadellidae* that suck plant juices, many being serious crop pests.

leaf′ in′sect, any of several orthopterous insects of the family *Phasmatidae,* having a body that resembles a leaf in color and form. Also called **walking leaf.**

leaf′ lard′, lard prepared from the leaf fat of a hog.

leaf·less (lēf′lis), *adj.* without leaves. —**leaf′less·ness,** *n.*

leaf·let (lēf′lit), *n.* **1.** a small flat or folded sheet of printed matter, as for distribution. **2.** one of the separate blades or divisions of a compound leaf. **3.** a small leaflike part or structure. **4.** a small or young leaf.

leaf′ mus′tard. See under **mustard** (def. 2).

leaf′ roll′er, any of several insects, esp. moths of the family *Tortricidae,* the larvae of which form a nest by rolling and tying leaves with spun silk.

leaf′ rust′, *Plant Pathol.* a disease of cereals and other grasses, characterized by rust-colored pustules of spores on the affected leaf blades and sheaths: caused by any of several rust fungi of the genus *Puccinia.*

leaf′ scald′, *Plant Pathol.* a disease of plants, characterized by irregular, bleached areas on the leaves and defoliation: caused by any of several bacteria or fungi.

leaf′ spot′, *Plant Pathol.* a limited, often circular, discolored, diseased area on a leaf, usually including a central region of necrosis.

leaf′ spring′, *Mech.* a long, narrow, multiple spring composed of several layers of spring metal bracketed together. See illus. at **spring.**

leaf·stalk (lēf′stôk′), *n.* petiole (def. 1).

leaf·y (lē′fē), *adj.,* **leaf·i·er, leaf·i·est.** **1.** having large amounts of, covered with, or consisting of leaves or foliage: *the leafy woods.* **2.** leaflike; foliaceous.

league[1] (lēg), *n., v.,* **leagued, lea·guing.** —*n.* **1.** a covenant or compact made between persons, parties, states, etc., for the maintenance or promotion of common interests or for mutual assistance or service. **2.** the aggregation of persons, parties, states, etc., associated in such a covenant or compact; confederacy; coalition. **3.** an association of individuals having a common goal: *The League of Women Voters.* **4.** group; class; category: *He simply isn't in your league when it comes to brains.* **5.** a group of athletic teams organized to promote mutual interests and to compete chiefly among themselves: *a bowling league.* **6.** *Sports.* **a.** See **major league. b.** See **minor league. 7. in league,** having a compact or agreement, often for a harmful or wicked purpose; allied. —*v.t.* **8.** to unite in a league; combine. [earlier *leage* < It *lega,* back formation from *legare* < L *ligāre* to bind; r. late ME *ligg* < MF *ligue* < It *liga,* var. of *lega*] —**Syn. 1.** See **alliance.**

league[2] (lēg), *n.* **1.** a unit of distance, varying at different periods and in different countries, in English-speaking countries usually estimated roughly at three miles. **2.** a square league, as a unit of land measure. [ME *lege, leuge* < LL *leuga,* var. of *leuca* < Celt; r. OE *lēowa* < Celt]

League′ of Na′tions, an international organization to promote world peace and cooperation that was created by the Treaty of Versailles (1919): dissolved April 1946.

lea·guer[1] (lē′gər), *Archaic.* —*v.t.* **1.** to besiege. —*n.* **2.** a siege. [< D *leger* bed, camp. See LAIR[1], LAAGER]

lea·guer[2] (lē′gər), *n.* a member of a league. [LEAGUE[1] + -ER[1]]

Le·ah (lē′ə), *n.* the first wife of Jacob. Gen. 29:23–26.

Lea·hy (lā′hē), *n.* **William Daniel,** 1875–1959, U.S. admiral and diplomat.

leak (lēk), *n.* **1.** an unintended hole, crack, or the like, through which water, air, light, etc., enters or escapes: *a leak in a garden hose; a leak in a blackout curtain.* **2.** any means of unintended entrance, transmission, or escape. **3.** *Elect.* the loss of current from a conductor, usually resulting from poor insulation. **4.** the act or an instance of leaking. —*v.i.* **5.** to let water, air, light, etc., enter or escape, as through an unintended hole, crack, or the like: *The roof leaks.* **6.** to pass in or out in this manner, as water, air, light, etc.: *gas leaking from a pipe.* **7.** to transpire or become known undesignedly (usually fol. by *out*): *The news leaked out.* —*v.t.* **8.** to let (water, air, light, etc.) enter or escape: *This camera leaks light.* **9.** to allow to become known, as information given out covertly: *to leak the news of the ambassador's visit.* [ME *leke(n)* < Scand; cf. Icel *leka* to drip, leak; akin to D *lek,* obs. G *lech* leaky. See LEACH] —**leak′er,** *n.* —**leak′less,** *adj.*

leak·age (lē′kij), *n.* **1.** the act or an instance of leaking; leak. **2.** something that leaks in or out. **3.** the amount that leaks in or out.

Lea·key (lē′kē), *n.* **Louis Seymour Baz·ett** (baz′it), 1903–72, British archaeologist and anthropologist.

leak·y (lē′kē), *adj.,* **leak·i·er, leak·i·est.** **1.** allowing water, gas, etc., to leak in or out: *a leaky boat.* **2.** *Archaic.* unreliable: *a leaky memory.* —**leak′i·ness,** *n.*

leal (lēl), *adj. Scot.* loyal; true. [ME *leel* < OF < L *lēgālis* LEGAL; see LOYAL] —**leal′ly,** *adv.* —**le·al·ty** (lē′əl tē), *n.*

lean[1] (lēn), *v.,* **leaned** or (*esp. Brit.*) **leant; lean·ing;** *n.* —*v.i.* **1.** to incline or bend from a vertical position: *She leaned over the balustrade and shouted to the men downstairs.* **2.** to incline, as in a particular direction; slant: *The post leans to the left. The building leaned sharply before renovation.* **3.** to incline in feeling, opinion, action, etc.; tend: *to lean toward socialism.* **4.** to rest against or on something for support: *to lean against a wall.* **5.** to depend or rely: *to lean on empty promises.* —*v.t.* **6.** to incline or bend: *He leaned his head forward.* **7.** to cause to lean or rest; prop: *to lean a chair against the railing.* **8. lean over backward,** *Informal.* to go to great lengths, as to compensate for something: *He leans over backward to prove he's not prejudiced.* —*n.* **9.** the act or state of leaning; inclination. [ME *lene(n),* OE *hleonian, hlinian;* c. G *lehnen;* akin to L *clīnāre* to incline]

lean[2] (lēn), *adj.* **1.** (of persons or animals) without much flesh; not plump or fat; thin: *lean cattle.* **2.** (of meat) containing little or no fat. **3.** lacking in richness, fullness, or productivity; poor: *a lean diet; lean years.* **4.** (of paint) having more pigment than oil. Cf. **fat** (def. 5). —*n.* **5.** the part of flesh that consists of muscle rather than fat. **6.** the lean part of anything. [ME *lene,* OE *hlǣne*] —**lean′ly,** *adv.* —**lean′ness,** *n.* —**Syn. 1.** skinny, lank, lanky, emaciated. See **thin. 3.** sparse, barren. —**Ant. 1, 2.** fat.

Le·an·der (lē an′dər), *n. Class. Myth.* a youth who was the lover of Hero and was drowned while swimming the Hellespont.

lean·ing (lē′ning), *n.* inclination; tendency: *strong literary leanings.* [late ME *leninge,* OE *hlining*] —**Syn.** bent, propensity, proclivity.

Lean′ing Tow′er of Pi′sa, the, a round, marble campanile in Pisa, Italy, begun in 1174 and now 16½ feet out of the perpendicular in its height of 179 feet.

lean-to (lēn′to͞o′), *n., pl.* **-tos. 1.** a shack or shed supported at one side by trees or posts and having an inclined roof. **2.** a roof of a single pitch with the higher end abutting a wall or larger building. See illus. at **roof. 3.** a structure with such a roof.

leap (lēp), *v.,* **leaped** or **leapt, leap·ing,** *n.* —*v.i.* **1.** to spring through the air from one point or position to another; jump: *to leap over a ditch.* **2.** to move quickly and lightly: *to leap aside.* **3.** to pass, come, rise, etc., as if with a jump: *to leap to a conclusion.* —*v.t.* **4.** to jump over: *to leap a fence.* **5.** to pass over as if by a jump: *to leap the Atlantic in a jet.* **6.** to cause to leap. —*n.* **7.** a spring, jump, or bound; a light, springing movement. **8.** the amount of space cleared in a leap; distance jumped. **9.** a place leaped or to be leaped over or from. **10.** an abrupt transition: *a successful leap from piano class to concert hall.* **11.** a sudden and decisive increase: *a leap in the company's profits.* **12. by leaps and bounds,** very rapidly: *We are progressing by leaps and bounds.* [ME *lepe(n),* OE *hlēapan* to leap, run; c. G *laufen,* Icel *hlaupa,* Goth *hlaupan*] —**leap′er,** *n.* —**Syn. 1.** See **jump.**

leap·frog (lēp′frog′, -frôg′), *n., v.t.,* **-frogged, -frog·ging.** —*n.* **1.** a game in which players take turns leaping over another player who is bent over from the waist. —*v.t.* **2.** to jump over (a person or thing) in or as if in leapfrog. —**leap′frog′ger,** *n.*

leapt (lept, lēpt), *v.* a pt. and pp. of **leap.**

leap′ year′, **1.** (in the Gregorian calendar) a year that contains 366 days, with February 29 as an additional day added to offset the difference between the common year (365 days) and the astronomical year (365¼ days): occurring every fourth year, with the exception of centenary years not divisible by 400. **2.** a year containing an extra day in any calendar. Cf. **common year.** [ME *lepe yere*]

Lear (lēr), *n.* **Edward,** 1812–88, English writer of humorous verse and landscape painter.

learn (lûrn), *v.,* **learned** (lûrnd) or **learnt; learn·ing.** —*v.t.* **1.** to acquire knowledge of or skill in by study, instruction, or experience: *to learn French.* **2.** to become informed of or acquainted with; ascertain: *to learn the truth.* **3.** to memorize: *He learned the poem so he could recite it at the dinner.* **4.** to gain (a habit, mannerism, etc.) by experience, exposure to example, or the like; acquire: *He learned patience from his father.* **5.** *Nonstandard.* to instruct in; teach. —*v.i.* **6.** to acquire knowledge or skill: *to learn rapidly.* **7.** to become informed (usually fol. by *of*): *to learn of an accident.* [ME

lerne(n), OE *leornian* to learn, read, ponder, akin to *lesan* to glean; c. G *lernen* to learn, *lesen* to read] —**learn′a·ble,** *adj.* —**learn′er,** *n.*
—**Syn. 1.** LEARN, ASCERTAIN, DISCOVER imply adding to one's store of facts. To LEARN is to add to one's knowledge or information: *to learn a language.* To ASCERTAIN is to verify facts by inquiry or analysis: *to ascertain the truth about an event.* To DISCOVER is used with objective clauses as a synonym of LEARN in order to suggest that the new information acquired is surprising to the learner: *I discovered that he hadn't worked a day in his entire life.*

learn·ed (lûr′nid), *adj.* **1.** having much knowledge; scholarly: *a group of learned men.* **2.** connected or involved with the pursuit of knowledge, esp. of a scholarly nature: *a learned society; a learned journal.* **3.** of or showing learning: *He was learned in the ways of the world.* [ME *lerned*] —**learn′ed·ly,** *adv.* —**learn′ed·ness,** *n.*

learn′ed profes′sion, one of the three vocations of theology, law, and medicine, commonly held to require highly advanced learning, high principles, etc. Cf. **profession** (def. 1).

learn·ing (lûr′ning), *n.* **1.** knowledge acquired by systematic study in any field or fields of scholarly application. **2.** the act or process of acquiring knowledge or skill. **3.** *Psychol.* the modification of behavior through practice, training, or experience. [ME *lerning,* OE *leornung.* See LEARN, -ING[1]]
—**Syn. 1.** LEARNING, ERUDITION, LORE, SCHOLARSHIP refer to knowledge existing or acquired. LEARNING is knowledge acquired by systematic study, as of literature, history, or science: *a body of learning; fond of literary learning.* ERUDITION suggests a thorough, formal, and profound sort of knowledge obtained by extensive research; it is esp. applied to knowledge in fields other than those of mathematics and the physical sciences: *a man of vast erudition in languages.* LORE is accumulated knowledge in a particular field, esp. of a curious, anecdotal, or traditional nature; the word is now somewhat poetic: *nature lore; gypsy lore.* SCHOLARSHIP is the formalized learning that is taught in schools, esp. as actively employed by a person trying to master some field of knowledge or to extend its bounds: *high standards of scholarship in history.*

learnt (lûrnt), *v.* a pt. and pp. of **learn.**

lease (lēs), *n., v.,* **leased, leas·ing.** —*n.* **1.** a contract renting land, buildings, etc., to another; a contract or instrument conveying property to another for a specified period or for a period determinable at the will of either lessor or lessee in consideration of rent or other compensation. **2.** the property leased. **3.** the period of time for which a lease is made: *this lease is up in December.* **4. a new lease on life,** a chance to improve one's circumstances or to live more happily because of some good fortune. —*v.t.* **5.** to grant the temporary possession or use of (lands, tenements, etc.) to another, usually for compensation at a fixed rate; let: *She planned to lease her apartment to a friend.* **6.** to take or hold by lease: *He leased the farm from the old man.* —*v.i.* **7.** to grant a lease; let or rent: *to lease at a lower rental.* [late ME *les* < AF (OF *lais,* F *legs* legacy), back formation from *lesser* to lease, lit., let go (OF *laissier*) < L *laxāre* to release, let go. See LAX] —**leas′a·ble,** *adj.* —**leas′er,** *n.* —**Syn. 5, 6.** rent, charter, hire.

lease·hold (lēs′hōld′), *n.* **1.** a land interest acquired under a lease. —*adj.* **2.** held by lease.

lease·hold·er (lēs′hōl′dər), *n.* a tenant under a lease.

leash (lēsh), *n.* **1.** a thong or line for holding a dog or other animal in check; a lead. **2.** check; curb; restraint: *to keep one's temper in leash; a tight leash on one's subordinates.* **3.** *Hunting.* a brace and a half, as of foxes. —*v.t.* **4.** to secure or hold in or as in a leash; control: *to leash the energy of the atom.* **5.** to bind together by or as by a leash; connect; link; associate. [ME *lesh,* var. of *lece, lese* < OF *laisse.* See LEASE]

leas·ing (lē′zing), *n. Archaic.* lying; falsehood. [ME *lesing,* OE *lēasung* < *lēasian* to tell lies < *lēas* false. See -LESS, -ING[1]]

least (lēst), *adj., a superl. of* **little** *with* **less** *or* **lesser** *as compar.* **1.** smallest in size, amount, degree, etc.; slightest: *He walked the least distance of all.* **2.** lowest in consideration or importance. —*n.* **3.** something that is least; the least amount, quantity, degree, etc. **4. at least, a.** at the lowest estimate or figure: *The repairs will cost at least $100.* **b.** at any rate; in any case: *At least he has an alternative.* Also, **at the least.** —*adv.* **5.** *superl. of* **little** *with* **less** *as compar.* to the smallest extent, amount, or degree: *That's the least important of all. He talks least.* [ME *leest(e),* OE *lǣst,* superl. of *lǣs(sa)* LESS]

least′ com′mon denom′inator, *Math.* the smallest number that is a common denominator of a given set of fractions. Also called **lowest common denominator.**

least′ com′mon mul′tiple. See **lowest common multiple.**

least′ signif′icant dig′it, the digit farthest to the right in a number. *Abbr.:* LSD Cf. **most significant digit.**

least′ squares′, *Statistics.* a method of determining constants from observations by minimizing squares of residuals between observations and their theoretical expected values.

least·wise (lēst′wīz′), *adv. Informal.* at least; at any rate. Also, *Dial.,* **least·ways** (lēst′wāz′).

leath·er (leth′ər), *n.* **1.** the skin of an animal prepared for use by tanning or a similar process designed to preserve it against decay and to make it pliable or supple when dry. **2.** an article or appliance made of this material. —*adj.* **3.** pertaining to, made of, or resembling leather: *leather processing; leather upholstery.* —*v.t.* **4.** to cover or furnish with leather. [ME *lether,* OE *lether-* (in compounds); c. D, G *leder,* Icel *lethr,* Ir *leathar*]

leath′er·back tur′tle (leth′ər bak′), a large turtle, *Dermochelys coriacea,* having a leathery skin covering its shell, reaching a length of over eight feet and weighing over a thousand pounds: the largest living sea turtle. Also called **leath′er·back′.**

Leath·er·ette (leth′ə ret′), *n. Trademark.* material constructed of paper or cloth and finished to simulate the grain, color, and texture of leather, used in the manufacture of luggage, bookbindings, etc.

leath·ern (leth′ərn), *adj.* **1.** made of leather. **2.** resembling leather. [ME, OE *lether(e)n*]

leath·er·neck (leth′ər nek′), *n. Slang.* a U.S. marine. [from the leather-lined collar of original Marine uniform]

Leath·er·oid (leth′ə roid′), *n. Trademark.* an imitation leather product consisting of chemically treated and vulcanized paper or other vegetable fiber.

leath·er·wood (leth′ər wo͝od′), *n.* an American shrub, *Dirca palustris,* having a tough bark.

leath·er·y (leth′ə rē), *adj.* like leather; tough and flexible. —**leath′er·i·ness,** *n.*

leave[1] (lēv), *v.,* **left, leav·ing.** —*v.t.* **1.** to go away or depart from, as a place, a person, or a thing; quit: *to leave a room; to leave a job.* **2.** to let stay or be as specified: *to leave a door unlocked.* **3.** to let (a person or animal) remain in a position to do something without interference: *Leave the puppy alone. We left him to his work.* **4.** to stop or abandon: *He left drinking for nearly two years.* **5.** to let (a thing) remain for action or decision: *He left the details to his lawyer.* **6.** to disregard; neglect: *We will leave this for the moment and concentrate on the major problem.* **7.** to allow to remain in the same place, condition, etc.: *We left plenty of work.* **8.** to let remain or have remaining behind after going, disappearing, ceasing, etc.: *The wound left a scar.* **9.** to have remaining after death: *He leaves a widow.* **10.** to give for use after one's death or departure: *to leave money in a will.* **11.** to give in charge: *to leave a parcel with the porter.* **12.** to have as a remainder after subtraction: *2 from 4 leaves 2.* —*v.i.* **13.** to go away or depart; set out. **14. leave off,** to desist from; stop; abandon. **15. leave out,** to omit; exclude: *She left out an important detail in her account.* [ME *leve(n),* OE *lǣfan* (causative formation from root in *lāf* remainder); c. OHG *leiban* (cf. G *bleiben* to remain), Icel *leifa,* Goth *-laibjan*] —**leav′er,** *n.*
—**Syn. 1.** vacate; abandon, forsake; relinquish. **3.** See **let**[1]. **4.** forbear, cease, renounce. **10.** bequeath, will.

leave[2] (lēv), *n.* **1.** permission to do something: *to beg leave to go.* **2.** permission to be absent, as from duty: *to be on leave.* **3.** the time this permission lasts: *30 days' leave.* **4.** a parting; departure; farewell (often prec. by *take*): *He took his leave before the formal ceremonies began. He took leave o her after dinner.* Also called **leave′ of ab′sence** (for defs. 2, 3). [ME *leve,* OE *lēaf.* See FURLOUGH] —**Syn. 1–3.** liberty. **2, 3.** vacation, furlough.

leave[3] (lēv), *v.i.,* **leaved, leav·ing.** to put forth leaves; leaf. [ME *levi,* OE **lēafi(an)* < *lēaf* LEAF]

leaved (lēvd), *adj.* having leaves; leafed. [ME *leved*]

leav·en (lev′ən), *n.* **1.** a mass of fermenting dough reserved for producing fermentation in a new batch of dough. **2.** an agent or element that acts in or upon something to produce a gradual change or modification: *the leaven of wit in his writing.* —*v.t.* **3.** to produce bubbles of gas in (dough or batter) by means of any of a variety of leavening agents. **4.** to permeate with an altering or transforming influence. [ME *levain* < MF < VL **levāmen* leaven = L *levā(re)* (to) raise (see LEVEE[1]) + *-men* suffix of result. Cf. L *levāmen* alleviation < *levāre,* as above] —**leav′en·less,** *adj.* —**Syn. 4.** infect, lighten, enliven.

leav·en·ing (lev′ə ning), *n.* **1.** an agent used to produce fermentation in dough or batter; leaven. **2.** an additional element or quality that alters or modifies something.

Leav·en·worth (lev′ən wûrth′, -wərth), *n.* **1.** a city in NE Kansas. 25,147 (1970). **2.** a federal and military prison there.

leaves (lēvz), *n.* pl. of **leaf.**

leave-tak·ing (lēv′tā′king), *n.* a parting or good-by; departure: *His leave-taking was brief.* [ME]

leav·ing (lē′ving), *n.* **1.** something that is left; residue. **2. leavings,** remains; refuse. [ME *leving*]

Lea·vis (lē′vis), *n.* **F(rank) R(aymond),** 1895–1978, English critic and teacher.

leav·y (lē′vē), *adj.,* **leav·i·er, leav·i·est.** *Archaic.* leafy. [late ME *levy*]

Leb·a·nese (leb′ə nēz′, -nēs′), *adj., n., pl.* **-nese.** —*adj.* **1.** of or pertaining to Lebanon or its natives or inhabitants. —*n.* **2.** a native or inhabitant of Lebanon.

Leb·a·non (leb′ə nən), *n.* **1.** a republic at the E end of the Mediterranean, N of Israel. 2,780,000; 3927 sq. mi. *Cap.:* Beirut. **2.** a city in SE Pennsylvania. 28,572 (1970).

Leb′anon Moun′tains, a mountain range extending the length of Lebanon, in the central part. Highest peak, 10,049 ft.

Le·bens·raum (lā′bəns roum′, -bənz-), *n.* additional territory desired by a nation, as for the expansion of trade. [< G: space for living]

leb·ku·chen (lāb′ko͞o kən; *Ger.* lāp′ko͞o′KHən), *n., pl.* **-chen.** *German Cookery.* a hard or chewy cooky, usually flavored with honey and spices and containing nuts and citron. [< G; MHG *lebekuoche.* See LOAF[1], CAKE]

Le·brun (lə brœN′), *n.* **Charles** (sharl), 1619–90, French painter. Also, **LeBrun′.**

Lec·ce (let′che), *n.* a city in SE Italy: ancient Greek and Roman city; noted for its baroque architecture. 75,439 (1961).

lech (lech), *n., v.t., adj. Slang.* letch.

Le Châ′te·lier prin′ciple (lə shät′ᵊl yā′), *Physics.* the law that if a constraint is applied to a system in equilibrium, the system adjusts to a new equilibrium that tends to counteract the constraint. [named after H. L. *Le Châtelier* (1850–1936), French chemist]

le·cha·yim (lə KHä′yim, -KHä yēm′), *n. Hebrew.* lehayim.

lech·er (lech′ər), *n.* **1.** a man given to excessive sexual indulgence. —*v.i.* **2.** to engage in lechery. [ME *lech(o)ur* < OF *lecheor* glutton, libertine = *lech(ier)* (to) lick (< Gmc; cf. OHG *leccōn* to LICK) + *-eor* -OR[2]]

lech·er·ous (lech′ər əs), *adj.* **1.** given to or characterized by lechery: *a lecherous old man.* **2.** erotically suggestive; inciting to lust. [ME < MF *lechereus*] —**lech′er·ous·ly,** *adv.* —**lech′er·ous·ness,** *n.*

lech·er·y (lech′ə rē), *n., pl.* **-er·ies. 1.** excessive indulgence of sexual desire. **2.** a lecherous act. [ME *lecherie* < OF]

lec·i·thin (les′ə thin), *n.* **1.** *Biochem.* any of a group of yellow-brown fatty substances, occurring in animal and plant tissues and egg yolk, composed of units of choline, phosphoric acid, fatty acids, and glycerol. **2.** a commercial form of this substance, obtained chiefly from soybeans, corn, and egg yolk, used in candies, foods, cosmetics, and inks. [< Gk *lékith(os)* egg yolk + -IN[2]]

le·cith·i·nase (lə sith′ə nās′), *n. Biochem.* an enzyme that catalyzes the hydrolysis of lecithin.

Leck·y (lek′ē), *n.* **William Edward Hart·pole** (härt′pōl), 1838–1903, Irish essayist and historian.

Le·conte de Lisle (lə kôNt də lēl′), **Charles Ma·rie** (shARl MA RĒ′), 1818–94, French poet.

Le Cor·bu·sier (*Fr.* lə kôR BY zyā′), (*Charles Édouard Jeanneret*) 1887–1965, Swiss architect in France.

lect., **1.** lecture. **2.** lecturer.

lec·tern (lek′tərn), *n.* **1.** (in a church) a reading desk on which the Bible rests and from which the lessons are read during the service. **2.** a desk or stand with a slanted top, used to hold a book, manuscript, etc., at the proper height for a standing reader, lecturer, etc. [ME *lettorne* < MF *letrun,* var. of *letrin* < ML *lect(ō)rīn(um),* n. use of neut. of *lectōrīnus.* See LECTOR, -INE[1]]

lec·tion (lek′shən), *n.* **1.** a version of a passage in a particular copy or edition of a text; a variant reading. **2.** a portion of sacred writing read in a divine service; lesson. [< L *lectiōn-* (s. of *lectiō*) a reading = *lect(us)* chosen, read (ptp. of *legere;* c. Gk *légein* to speak) + *-iōn-* -ION]

lec·tion·ar·y (lek′shə ner′ē), *n., pl.* **-ar·ies.** a book or a list of lections for reading in a divine service. [< eccl. L *lectiōnāri(um)*]

lec·tor (lek′tər), *n.* **1.** a lecturer in a college or university. **2.** *Rom. Cath. Ch.* **a.** a member of the next to lowest-ranking of the minor orders. **b.** the order itself. Cf. **acolyte** (def. 2), **exorcist** (def. 2), **ostiary** (def. 1). [late ME < L: a reader] —**lec·tor·ate** (lek′tər it, -tə rāt′), **lec′tor·ship′,** *n.*

lec·ture (lek′chər), *n., v.,* **-tured, -tur·ing.** —*n.* **1.** a discourse read or delivered before an audience, esp. for instruction or to set forth some subject. **2.** a speech of warning or reproof as to conduct; a long, tedious reprimand. —*v.i.* **3.** to give a lecture or series of lectures. —*v.t.* **4.** to deliver a lecture to or before; instruct by lectures. **5.** to rebuke or reprimand at some length. [late ME < ML *lectūra* a reading. See LECTION, -URE] —**Syn. 1.** address, talk, speech. **4.** address.

lec·tur·er (lek′chər ər), *n.* **1.** a person who lectures. **2.** an academic rank given in American colleges to a temporary or part-time teacher.

lec·ture·ship (lek′chər ship′), *n.* the office of lecturer.

led (led), *v.* pt. and pp. of **lead**[1].

LED, a semiconductor diode that emits light when energized by a pulse of current: used in electronic equipment, and esp. for displaying readings on digital watches, calculators, etc. [L(IGHT)-E(MITTING) D(IODE)]

Le·da (lē′də), *n. Class. Myth.* the mother, by her husband Tyndareus, of Castor and Clytemnestra and, by Zeus in the form of a swan, of Pollux and Helen.

Led·bet·ter (led′bet ər), *n.* **Hud·die** (hud′ē), ("*Leadbelly*"), 1885?–1949, U.S. folk singer.

le·der·ho·sen (lā′dər hō′zən), *n.pl.* short leather pants as worn in Bavaria. [< G, pl. of *Lederhose* = *Leder* LEATHER + *Hose* trousers]

ledge (lej), *n.* **1.** any relatively narrow, projecting part, as a horizontal, shelflike projection on the façade of a building or a raised edge on a tray. **2.** a more or less flat shelf of rock protruding from a cliff or slope. **3.** a reef, ridge, or line of rocks in the sea or other body of water. **4.** *Mining.* **a.** an underground layer or mass of rock. **b.** a lode or vein. [ME *legge,* OE *lecg,* appar. the crossbar of a weapon, akin to *lecgan* to LAY[1]]

ledg·er (lej′ər), *n. Bookkeeping.* an account book of final entry, containing all the accounts. [ME *legger* book, prob. < *legg(en)* (to) LAY[1] + *-er* -ER[1]]

ledg′er line′, *Music.* a short line added when necessary above or below the staff to increase the range of the staff.

ledg·y (lej′ē), *adj.,* **ledg·i·er, ledg·i·est.** having ledges.

lee[1] (lē), *n.* **1.** shelter: *The lee of the rock gave us some protection against the storm.* **2.** the side or part that is sheltered or turned away from the wind. **3.** *Chiefly Naut.* the quarter or region toward which the wind blows. **4. under the lee,** *Naut.* to leeward. —*adj.* **5.** *Chiefly Naut.* pertaining to, situated in, or moving toward the quarter or region toward which the wind blows (opposed to *weather*). [ME; OE *hlēo(w)* shelter; c. Icel *hlȳ*]

lee[2] (lē), *n.* Usually, **lees.** the insoluble matter that settles from a liquid, esp. from wine; sediment; dregs. [ME *lie* < MF < ML *lia,* prob. < Celt; cf. Ir *lige* bed]

Lee (lē), *n.* **1. Ann,** 1736–84, British mystic: founder of Shaker sect in U.S. **2. Charles,** 1731–82, American Revolutionary general, born in England. **3. Francis Light·foot** (līt′fŏŏt′), 1734–97, American Revolutionary statesman (brother of Richard H. Lee). **4. Henry** ("*Light-Horse Harry*"), 1756–1818. American Revolutionary general (father of Robert E. Lee). **5. Kuan Yew** (kwän′ yōō′), born 1923, Singapore political leader: prime minister since 1959. **6. Richard Henry,** 1732–94, American Revolutionary statesman (brother of Francis L. Lee). **7. Robert E(dward),** 1807–70, U.S. soldier and educator: Confederate general in the American Civil War (son of Henry Lee). **8. Tsung-Dao** (dzŏŏng′dou′), born 1926, Chinese physicist, born in the U.S.: Nobel prize 1957.

lee·board (lē′bōrd′, -bôrd′), *n. Naut.* either of two broad, flat objects attached to the sides of a sailing vessel amidships, the one on the lee side being lowered into the water to prevent the vessel from making leeway. [late ME]

Leech, *Hirudo medicinalis* (Length 5 to 6 in.)

leech[1] (lēch), *n.* **1.** any bloodsucking or carnivorous aquatic or terrestrial worm of the class *Hirudinea,* certain fresh-water species of which were formerly much used in medicine for bloodletting. **2.** an instrument used for drawing blood. **3.** a person who clings to another for personal gain; parasite. —*v.t.* **4.** to cling to and feed upon or drain, as a leech. **5.** *Archaic.* to cure; heal. —*v.i.* **6.** to hang on to a person in the manner of a leech. [ME *leche,* OE *lǣce;* r. (by confusion with LEECH[2], def. 2) ME *liche,* OE *lȳce;* c. MD *lieke;* akin to OE *lūcan* to pull out, MHG *liechen* to pull] —**leech′like′,** *adj.*

leech[2] (lēch), *v.t.* **1.** to apply leeches to, so as to bleed. —*n.* **2.** *Archaic.* a physician. [ME *leche,* OE *lǣce;* c. OS *lāki,* OHG *lāchi,* Goth *lēkeis;* akin to Icel *læknir*]

leech[3] (lēch), *n. Naut.* **1.** either of the lateral edges of a square sail. **2.** the after edge of a fore-and-aft sail. [late ME *lek, leche, lyche;* akin to D *lijk* leech, Icel *līk* line for hauling up on a leech]

Leeds (lēdz), *n.* a city in central Yorkshire, in N England. 510,579 (1961).

leek (lēk), *n.* a liliaceous plant, *Allium Porrum,* allied to the onion, having a cylindrical bulb and leaves used in cookery. [ME; OE *lēac;* c. G *Lauch,* Icel *laukr*]

Leek, *Allium Porrum* (Height 2 ft. or more)

leer (lēr), *v.i.* **1.** to look with a sideways or oblique glance suggestive of lascivious interest or sly and malicious intention. —*n.* **2.** a lascivious or sly look. [perh. v. use of obs. *leer* cheek, ME *leor,* OE *hlēor;* c. Icel *hlȳr*] —**leer′ing·ly,** *adv.*

leer·y (lēr′ē), *adj.,* **leer·i·er, leer·i·est. 1.** wary, suspicious (usually fol. by *of*). **2.** *Archaic.* knowing; alert. —**leer′i·ly,** *adv.* —**leer′i·ness,** *n.*

lees (lēz), *n.* pl. of **lee**[2].

lee′ shore′, a shore toward which the wind blows.

lee′ tide′, a tidal current running in the direction toward which the wind is blowing. Also called **lee′ward tide′.**

Lee·u·war·den (lā′Y wäR′dən), *n.* a city in the N Netherlands. 85,386 (1962).

Lee·u·wen·hoek (lā′vən hŏŏk′; *Du.* lā′Y wən hŏŏk′), *n.* **An·ton van** (än′tôn vän), 1632–1723, Dutch naturalist and microscopist.

lee·ward (lē′wərd; *Naut.* lōō′ərd), *adj.* **1.** pertaining to, situated in, or moving toward the quarter toward which the wind blows (opposed to *windward*). —*n.* **2.** the lee side; the point or quarter toward which the wind blows. —*adv.* **3.** toward the lee. —**lee′ward·ly,** *adv.*

Lee′ward Is′lands (lē′wərd), **1.** a group of islands in the N Lesser Antilles of the West Indies, extending from Puerto Rico SE to Martinique. **2.** a former British colony in the E West Indies, consisting of Antigua, Barbuda, St. Kitts, Nevis, Anguilla, Montserrat, and the British Virgin Islands. 130,493 (1960); 413 sq. mi.

lee·way (lē′wā′), *n.* **1.** *Naut.* the amount or angle of the drift of a vessel to leeward from its heading. **2.** *Aeron.* the amount a plane is blown off its normal course by cross winds. **3.** extra time, space, materials, or the like, within which to operate: *With 10 minutes' leeway we can catch the train.* **4.** a degree of freedom of action or thought: *His instructions gave us plenty of leeway.*

left[1] (left), *adj.* **1.** of, pertaining to, or belonging to the side of a person or thing that is turned toward the west when the subject is facing north (opposed to *right*). **2.** of or belonging to the political left. —*n.* **3.** the left side or something that is on the left side. **4.** a left-hand turn: *Make a left at the next corner.* **5.** (*usually cap.*) *Govt.* **a.** the part of a legislative assembly, esp. in continental Europe, situated on the left side of the presiding officer: customarily assigned to the more radical and socialistic members. **b.** these members considered collectively. **6. the Left, a.** Also called **left wing.** the advocates of liberal reform or revolutionary change in the social, political, or economic order. **b.** the position held by these people. Cf. **right** (defs. 30a, b). **7.** *Boxing.* a blow delivered by the left hand. —*adv.* **8.** toward the left. [ME *left, lift, luft,* OE *left* idle, dial. var. of *lyft-* (in *lyftādl* palsy); c. D, LG *lucht;* akin to ME *libbe* (mod. dial. *lib*) to castrate, c. D, LG *lubben*]

left[2] (left), *v.* pt. and pp. of **leave**[1].

Left′ Bank′, a part of Paris, France, on the S bank of the Seine: frequented by artists, writers, and students.

left′ field′, **1.** *Baseball.* **a.** the area of the outfield to the left of center field, as viewed from home plate. **b.** the position of the player covering this area. **2. out in left field,** *Slang.* completely mistaken; wrong.

left′ field′er, *Baseball.* the player covering left field.

left-hand (left′hand′), *adj.* **1.** on or to the left. **2.** of, for, or with the left hand. [ME *left hande*]

left-hand·ed (left′han′did), *adj.* **1.** having the left hand more serviceable than the right; using the left hand: *a left-handed pitcher.* **2.** adapted to or performed by the left hand: *a left-handed punch; a left-handed tool.* **3.** situated on the side of the left hand. **4.** rotating counterclockwise. **5.** ambiguous or doubtful: *a left-handed compliment.* **6.** clumsy or awkward. **7.** of, pertaining to, or issuing from a morganatic marriage: so called from the custom, in morganatic marriage ceremonies, of having the bridegroom give his left hand to the bride. —*adv.* **8.** with the left hand: *He writes left-handed.* **9.** toward the left hand; in a counterclockwise direction. —**left′-hand′ed·ly,** *adv.* —**left′-hand′ed·ness,** *n.*

left-hand·er (left′han′dər, -han′-), *n.* a left-handed person.

left·ist (lef′tist), *n.* **1.** a member of the Left or a person sympathizing with its views. —*adj.* **2.** of, pertaining to, characteristic of, or advocated by the Left. Also, **Left′ist.** —**left′ism,** *n.*

left′-lug′gage of′fice (left′lug′ij), *Brit.* a checkroom for baggage.

left·o·ver (left′ō′vər), *n.* **1.** something left or remaining from a larger amount; remainder. **2.** a remnant of food, as from a meal. —*adj.* **3.** being left, as an unused portion or amount; remaining: *leftover meat loaf.*

left·ward (left′wərd), *adv.* **1.** Also, **left′wards.** toward or on the left. —*adj.* **2.** situated on the left. **3.** directed toward the left. [late ME] —**left′ward·ly,** *adv.*

left′ wing′, **1.** left (def. 6a). **2.** the part of a political or social organization maintaining a liberal or radical position. —**left′wing′,** *adj.* —**left′wing′er,** *n.*

left·y[1] (lef′tē), *n., pl.* **left·ies.** *Informal.* a left-handed person. [LEFT[1] + -Y[2]]

left·y[2] (lef′tē), *Informal.* —*adj.* **1.** left-handed. —*adv.* **2.** with the left hand; in a left-handed manner. [LEFT[1] + -Y[1]]

leg (leg), *n., v.,* **legged, leg·ging.** —*n.* **1.** one of the two lower limbs of a biped, as man, or one of the paired limbs of a quadruped, as a dog, that support and move the body. **2.** *Anat.* the lower limb of man from the knee to the ankle. **3.** something resembling or suggesting a leg in use, position, or appearance, as one of the supports for a table or chair. **4.** the part of a garment that covers the leg. **5.** one of the sides of a forked object, as of a compass or pair of dividers. **6.** one of the sides of a triangle other than the base or hypotenuse. **7.** one of the portions of any course: *the last leg of a trip.* **8.** *Naut.* one of the series of straight runs that make up the zigzag course of a sailing ship. **9.** *Sports.* one of the stretches or sections of a relay race. **10.** *Cricket.* **a.** the part of the field to the left of and behind a right-handed batsman as he faces the bowler. **b.** the fielder playing this part of the field. **c.** the position of this fielder. **11. not have a leg to stand on,** *Informal.* to lack a valid basis for one's argument or attitude. **12. on one's** or **its last legs,** just short of exhaustion, breakdown, failure, etc. **13. pull one's leg,** *Informal.* to make fun of; tease. **14. shake a leg,** *Slang.* to hurry up. **15. stretch one's legs,** to take a walk; get some needed exercise. —*v.t.* **16.** to move or propel (a boat) with the legs. **17. leg it,** *Informal.* to walk rapidly or run. [ME < Scand; cf. Icel *leggr*] —**leg′less,** *adj.* —**leg′like′,** *adj.*

leg., **1.** legal. **2.** legate. **3.** legato. **4.** legend. **5.** legislative. **6.** legislature.

leg·a·cy (leg′ə sē), *n., pl.* **-cies. 1.** *Law.* a gift of property, esp. personal property, as money, by will; a bequest. **2.** anything handed down from the past, as from an ancestor or predecessor: *our legacy from ancient Rome.* [ME *legacie* office of a deputy or legate < ML *lēgātia.* See LEGATE, -Y[3]] —**Syn.** inheritance.

le·gal (lē′gəl), *adj.* **1.** permitted by law; lawful: *Such acts are not legal.* **2.** of or pertaining to law; connected with the law or its administration: *the legal profession.* **3.** appointed, established, or authorized by law; deriving authority from law: *the legal owner.* **4.** recognized by law rather than by equity. **5.** of, pertaining to, or characteristic of the profession of law or of lawyers: *a legal mind.* —*n.* **6. legals,** authorized investments that may be made by fiduciaries, as savings banks or trustees. [< L *lēgāl(is)* of the law = *lēg-* (s. of *lēx*) law + *-ālis* -AL[1]] —**le′gal·ly,** *adv.*

le′gal aid′, free legal service to a person or persons unable to pay for it.

le′gal cap′, *U.S.* ruled writing paper, usually measuring 8 × 13½ inches, for use by lawyers.

le′gal hol′iday, *U.S.* a holiday established by law and limited as to the amount of work and official business that may be conducted.

le·gal·ise (lē′gə līz′), *v.t.,* **-ised, -is·ing.** *Chiefly Brit.* legalize. —**le′gal·i·sa′tion,** *n.*

le·gal·ism (lē′gə liz′əm), *n.* **1.** strict adherence to law, esp. to the letter rather than the spirit. **2.** *Theol.* the doctrine that salvation is gained through good works. —**le′gal·ist,** *n.* —**le′gal·is′tic,** *adj.* —**le′gal·is′ti·cal·ly,** *adv.*

le·gal·i·ty (lē gal′i tē), *n., pl.* **-ties. 1.** the state or quality of being in conformity with the law; lawfulness. **2.** adherence to law. **3.** a duty or obligation imposed by law. [late ME *legalite* < ML *lēgālitās*]

le·gal·ize (lē′gə līz′), *v.t.,* **-ized, -iz·ing.** to make legal; authorize. Also, *esp. Brit.,* **legalise.** —**le′gal·i·za′tion,** *n.*

Le Gal·lienne (lə gal′yən, gal yen′), **Eva,** born 1899, U.S. actress and producer, born in England.

le′gal reserve′, the amount of cash assets that a bank, insurance company, or the like, is required by law to set aside as reserves.

le′gal separa′tion. See **judicial separation.**

le·gal-size (lē′gəl sīz′), *adj.* **1.** (of paper) having a size measuring approximately 8½ × 13 inches. **2.** (of office supplies and equipment) made for holding legal-size sheets of paper: *legal-size file folders.* Cf. **letter-size.**

le′gal ten′der, currency that may be lawfully tendered or offered in payment of money debts and that may not be refused by creditors.

Le·gas·pi (lə gas′pē; *Sp.* le gäs′pē), *n.* a seaport on SE Luzon, in the Philippines. 98,410 (est. 1960).

leg·ate (leg′it), *n.* **1.** an ecclesiastic delegated by the pope as his representative. **2.** *Rom. Hist.* **a.** a commander of a legion. **b.** a provincial governor of senatorial rank appointed by the emperor. **3.** an envoy or emissary. [early ME *legat* < L *lēgāt(us)* deputy (orig. masc. ptp. of *lēgāre* to depute) = *lēg-* (s. of *lēx*) law + *-ātus* -ATE[1]] —**leg′ate·ship′,** *n.*

leg·a·tee (leg′ə tē′), *n.* a person to whom a legacy is bequeathed. [< L *lēgāt(us)* deputed, bequeathed + -EE]

leg·a·tine (leg′ə tin, -tīn′), *adj.* of, pertaining to, or authorized by a legate. [< ML *lēgātīn(us)*]

le·ga·tion (li gā′shən), *n.* **1.** a diplomatic minister and his staff in a foreign mission. **2.** the official headquarters of a minister in the diplomatic service. **3.** the office or position of a legate. [late ME *legacion* < L *lēgātiōn-* (s. of *lēgātiō*) embassy. See LEGATE, -ION] —**le·ga·tion·ar·y** (li gā′shə ner′ē), *adj.*

le·ga·to (lə gä′tō; *It.* le gä′tô), *adj. Music.* smooth and connected; without breaks between the successive tones. Cf. **staccato** (def. 1). [< It, ptp. of *legare* < L *ligāre* to bind]

le·ga·tor (li gā′tər, leg′ə tôr′), *n.* a person who bequeaths; testator. [< L; see LEGATE, -OR[2]] —**leg·a·to·ri·al** (leg′ə tōr′ē əl, -tôr′-), *adj.*

leg′ bye′, *Cricket.* a run or bye scored on a bowled ball that ricochets off any part of the batsman's body except the hand.

leg·end (lej′ənd), *n.* **1.** a nonhistorical or unverifiable story handed down by tradition from earlier times and popularly accepted as historical. **2.** the body of stories of this kind, esp. as they relate to a particular people, group, or clan: *a popular hero in American legend.* **3.** an inscription, esp. on a coat of arms, a monument, etc. **4.** a table on a map, chart, or the like, listing and explaining the symbols used. **5.** a collection of stories about an admirable person. **6.** a person who is the center of such stories. [ME *legende* collection of saints' lives < ML *legenda,* so called because appointed to be read on respective saints' days, lit., lesson to be read, n. use of fem. of L *legendus,* ger. of *legere* to read] —**Syn. 1.** LEGEND, FABLE, MYTH refer to fictitious stories, usually handed down by tradition (although some fables are modern). LEGEND, originally denoting a story concerning the life of a saint, is applied to any fictitious story, sometimes involving the supernatural and usually concerned with a real person, place, or other subject: *the legend of a haunted cave.* A FABLE is specifically a fictitious story (often with animals or inanimate things as speakers or actors) designed to teach a moral: *a fable about industrious bees.* A MYTH is one of a class of stories, usually concerning gods, semidivine heroes, etc., current since primitive times, the purpose of which is to attempt to explain some belief or natural phenomenon: *the Greek myth about Demeter.* —**Ant. 1.** fact.

leg·end·ar·y (lej′ən der′ē), *adj., n., pl.* **-ar·ies.** —*adj.* **1.** of, pertaining to, or of the nature of a legend or legends. **2.** celebrated or described in legend: *a legendary hero.* —*n.* **3.** a collection of legends. [< ML *legendāri(us)*] —**leg′end·ar′i·ly,** *adv.* —**Syn. 1.** heroic, supernatural, superhuman.

leg·end·ize (lej′ən dīz′), *v.t.,* **-ized, -iz·ing.** to make a legend of: *Devoted followers legendized his birth.*

Le·gen·dre (lə zhän′dər, -zhänd′; *Fr.* lə zhäN′drᵊ), *n.* **A·dri·en Ma·rie** (A drē aN′ MA rē′), 1752–1833, French mathematician.

leg·end·ry (lej′ən drē), *n.* legends collectively.

Lé·ger (lā zhā′), *n.* **Fer·nand** (feR näN′), 1881–1955, French artist.

leg·er·de·main (lej′ər də mān′), *n.* **1.** skill in or practice of feats of magic, jugglery, etc.; sleight of hand. **2.** trickery; deception. **3.** any artful trick. [earlier *leger de main* < MF: lit., light of hand; r. late ME *lygarde-de-mayne,* etc., alter. of MF form]

le·ges (lē′jēz; *Lat.* le′ges), *n.* pl. of **lex.**

leg·ged (leg′id, legd), *adj.* **1.** having a specified number or kind of legs (often used in combination): *two-legged; long-legged.* **2.** fitted with legs: *a legged desk.* [late ME]

leg·ging (leg′ing), *n.* a covering for the leg, as of leather or canvas. Also, **leg·gin** (leg′in). —**leg′ginged,** *adj.*

leg·gy (leg′ē), *adj.,* **-gi·er, -gi·est. 1.** having awkwardly long legs. **2.** having long, attractive legs. **3.** of or pertaining to legs. —**leg′gi·ness,** *n.*

Leg·horn (leg′hôrn′ *for 1–3;* leg′ərn, -hôrn′ *for 4*), *n.* **1.** Italian, **Livorno.** a seaport in W Italy on the Ligurian Sea. 159,973 (1961). **2.** (*l.c.*) a fine, smooth, plaited straw. **3.** (*l.c.*) a hat made of such straw, often having a broad, soft brim. **4.** one of a Mediterranean breed of chickens that are prolific layers of white-shelled eggs.

leg·i·bil·i·ty (lej′ə bil′i tē), *n.* the state or quality of being legible. Also, **leg′i·ble·ness.**

leg·i·ble (lej′ə bəl), *adj.* **1.** capable of being read or deciphered, esp. with ease, as writing or printing. **2.** easily discerned or distinguished. [< LL *legibil(is).* See LEGEND, -IBLE] —**leg′i·bly,** *adv.*

le·gion (lē′jən), *n.* **1.** (in ancient Rome) an infantry brigade usually combined with cavalry. **2.** a military or semimilitary unit. **3. the Legion, a.** See **American Legion. b.** See **Foreign Legion. 4.** any large body of armed men. **5.** any great host or multitude of persons or things. [< L *legiōn-* (s. of *legiō*) picked body of soldiers = *leg(ere)* (to) gather, choose, read, etc., + *-iōn-* -ION; r. ME *legi(o)un* < OF]

le·gion·ar·y (lē′jə ner′ē), *adj., n., pl.* **-ar·ies.** —*adj.* **1.** of, pertaining to, or belonging to a legion. **2.** constituting a legion or legions. —*n.* **3.** *Hist.* a soldier of a legion. **4.** *Brit.* a member of the British Legion. Cf. **legionnaire** (def. 1). **5.** legionnaire (def. 2). [< L *legiōnāri(us)*]

le·gion·naire (lē′jə nâr′), *n.* **1.** (*often cap.*) a member of the American Legion. **2.** a member of any legion; legionary. [< F; see LEGIONARY]

Le′gion of Hon′or, a French order of distinction instituted by Napoleon I in 1802. [trans. of F *Légion d'honneur*]

Le′gion of Mer′it, *Mil.* a decoration awarded to U.S. and foreign military personnel for exceptionally meritorious conduct in the performance of outstanding services to the United States.

Legis., Legislature.

leg·is·late (lej′is lāt′), *v.,* **-lat·ed, -lat·ing.** —*v.i.* **1.** to make or enact laws. —*v.t.* **2.** to create or control by or as by legislation: *attempts to legislate morality.* [back formation from LEGISLATION, LEGISLATOR]

leg·is·la·tion (lej′is lā′shən), *n.* **1.** the act of making or enacting laws. **2.** a law or a body of laws enacted. [< LL *lēgislātiōn-* (s. of *lēgislātiō*) = L phrase *lēgis lātiō* the bringing (i.e., proposing) of a law = *lēgis* (gen. of *lēx* law) + *lātiō* a bringing: see RELATION]

leg·is·la·tive (lej′is lā′tiv), *adj.* **1.** having the function of making laws. **2.** of or pertaining to the enactment of laws: *legislative proceedings.* **3.** pertaining to a legislature: *a legislative recess.* **4.** enacted or ordained by legislation or a legislature. —*n.* **5.** legislature. —**leg′is·la′tive·ly,** *adv.*

leg·is·la·tor (lej′is lā′tər), *n.* **1.** a person who gives or makes laws. **2.** a member of a legislative body. [< L phrase *lēgis lātor* a law's bringer (i.e., proposer) = *lēgis* (gen. of *lēx* law) + *lātor* bringer (*lāt(us),* ptp. of *ferre* to bring + *-or* -OR[2])] —**leg′is·la′tor·ship′,** *n.*

leg·is·la·to·ri·al (lej′is lə tōr′ē əl, -tôr′-), *adj.* of or pertaining to a legislator, legislature, or legislation; legislative.

leg·is·la·ture (lej′is lā′chər), *n.* **1.** a body of persons, usually elective, empowered to make, change, or repeal the laws of a country or state. **2.** *U.S.* the legislative branch of a state government.

le·gist (lē′jist), *n.* a person who is versed in law. [late ME < ML *lēgista.* See LEGAL, -IST]

le·git (lə jit′), *adj. Slang.* legitimate; truthful. [shortened form]

le·git·i·ma·cy (li jit′ə mə sē), *n.* the state or quality of being legitimate.

le·git·i·mate (*adj.* li jit′ə mit; *v.* li jit′ə māt′), *adj., v.,* **-mat·ed, -mat·ing.** —*adj.* **1.** according to law; lawful: *the property's legitimate owner.* **2.** in accordance with established rules, principles, or standards. **3.** born in wedlock. **4.**

in accordance with the laws of reasoning; logical: *a legitimate conclusion.* **5.** resting on or ruling by the principle of hereditary right: *a legitimate sovereign.* **6.** justified; genuine: *a legitimate complaint.* **7.** of the normal or regular type or kind. **8.** *Theat.* of or pertaining to professionally produced stage plays, as distinguished from burlesque, vaudeville, etc. —*v.t.* **9.** to make lawful or legal; pronounce or state as lawful: *to legitimate an accession to the throne.* **10.** to confer the status of legitimacy upon (a bastard). **11.** to show or declare to be legitimate or proper. **12.** to justify; sanction or authorize. [< ML *lēgitimāt(us)* made lawful (ptp. of *lēgitimāre*) = L *lēgitim(us)* lawful (*lēgi-*, s. of *lēx* law + *-timus*, var. of *-tumus* adj. suffix) + *-ātus* -ATE¹] —**le·git′i·mate·ly,** *adv.* —**le·git′i·mate·ness,** *n.* —**le·git′i·ma′tion,** *n.* —**Syn. 1.** legal, licit. **2.** sanctioned. **4.** valid. **9.** legalize. —**Ant. 1.** illegitimate.

le·git·i·ma·tise (li jit′ə mə tīz′), *v.t.,* **-tised, -tis·ing.** *Chiefly Brit.* legitimatize.

le·git·i·ma·tize (li jit′ə mə tīz′), *v.t.,* **-tized, -tiz·ing.** legitimate.

le·git·i·mise (li jit′ə mīz′), *v.t.,* **-mised, -mis·ing.** *Chiefly Brit.* legitimize. —**le·git′i·mi·sa′tion,** *n.*

le·git·i·mist (li jit′ə mist), *n.* **1.** a supporter of legitimate authority, esp. of a claim to a throne based on direct descent. —*adj.* **2.** Also, **le·git′i·mis′tic.** of, pertaining to, or supporting legitimate authority. [< L *lēgitim(us)* lawful (see LEGITIMATE) + -IST; modeled on F *légitimiste*] —**le·git′i·mism,** *n.*

le·git·i·mize (li jit′ə mīz′), *v.t.,* **-mized, -miz·ing.** legitimate. Also, *esp. Brit.,* **legitimise.** [< L *lēgitim(us)* (see LEGITIMATE) + -IZE] —**le·git′i·mi·za′tion,** *n.*

leg·man (leg′man′, -mən), *n., pl.* **-men** (-men′, -mən). **1.** a person employed to transact business outside an office. **2.** *Journalism.* a reporter who gathers information by visiting news sources.

Leg·ni·ca (leg nē′tsä), *n.* Polish name of **Liegnitz.**

leg-of-mut·ton (leg′ə mut′ən, -əv-), *adj.* having the triangular shape of a leg of mutton: *leg-of-mutton sleeves.* Also, **leg′-o′-mut′ton.**

leg·room (leg′ro͞om′, -ro͝om′), *n.* space sufficient for a person to keep his legs in a comfortable position.

leg·ume (leg′yo͞om, li gyo͞om′), *n.* **1.** any plant of the family *Leguminosae,* esp. those used for food or as a soil-improving crop. **2.** the pod or seed vessel of such a plant, usually divided into two parts. **3.** any table vegetable of the family *Leguminosae.* [< F *légume* vegetable < L *legūmen* plant with seed pods < *legere* to gather]

le·gu·mi·nous (li gyo͞o′mə nəs), *adj.* **1.** pertaining to, of the nature of, or bearing legumes. **2.** belonging or pertaining to the *Leguminosae,* a family comprising the legume-bearing plants. [< L *legūmin-* (s. of *legūmen;* see LEGUME) + -OUS]

leg·work (leg′wûrk′), *n. Informal.* work or research involving extensive walking or moving about, as gathering data.

Le·hár (lā′här; *Hung.* le′hän), *n.* **Franz** (fränts), 1870–1948, Hungarian composer of operettas.

Le Ha·vre (lə hä′vrə, -vər, häv′; *Fr.* lə ȧ′vrᵊ), a seaport in N France, at the mouth of the Seine. 184,133 (1962). Also called **Havre.**

le·ha·yim (lə ḵнä′yim), *n. Hebrew.* (a toast used by Jews in drinking to a person's health or well-being.) Also, **le-chayim.** [lit., to life]

Le·high (lē′hī), *n.* a river in E Pennsylvania, flowing SW and SE into the Delaware River. 103 mi. long.

Leh·man (lē′mən, lā′-), *n.* **Herbert H(enry),** 1878–1963, U.S. statesman: director of UNRRA 1943–46.

Leh·mann (lā′mən; *Ger.* lā′män), *n.* **1. Lil·li** (lil′ē), 1848–1929, German operatic soprano. **2. Lot·te** (lô′tə), 1888–1976, German operatic soprano in the U.S.

Lehm·bruck (läm′bro͝ok; *Eng.* lem′bro͝ok, läm′-), *n.* **Wil·helm** (vil′helm), 1881–1919, German sculptor.

le·hu·a (lā ho͞o′ä), *n.* **1.** a tree, *Metrosideros polymorpha,* of the Pacific islands, yielding a hard wood. **2.** the bright-red, corymbose flower of this tree: state flower of Hawaii. [< Hawaiian]

le·i¹ (lā′ē, lā), *n., pl.* **le·is.** (in the Hawaiian Islands) a wreath of flowers, leaves, etc. [< Hawaiian]

lei² (lā), *n.* pl. of **leu.**

Leib·niz (līb′nits; *Ger.* līp′nits), *n.* **Gott·fried Wil·helm von** (gôt′frēt vil′helm fən), 1646–1716, German philosopher, writer, and mathematician. Also, **Leib′nitz.** —**Leib·niz·i·an, Leib·nitz·i·an** (līb nit′sē ən), *adj., n.*

Leices·ter (les′tər), *n.* **1. 1st Earl of.** See **Dudley, Robert. 2.** a city in and the county seat of Leicestershire, in central England. 273,298 (1961). **3.** Leicestershire. **4.** one of an English breed of large sheep, noted for its coarse, long wool and large yield of mutton.

Leices·ter·shire (les′tər shēr′, -shər), *n.* a county in central England. 682,196 (1961); 832 sq. mi. *Co. seat:* Leicester. Also called **Leicester.**

Lei·den (līd′ən), *n.* a city in the W Netherlands. 96,440 (est. 1960). Also, **Leyden.**

Leigh·ton (lāt′ən), *n.* **Frederick** (*Baron Leighton of Stretton*), 1830–96, English painter and sculptor.

Leins·dorf (līnz′dôrf; *Ger.* līns′dôrf), *n.* **E·rich** (er′ik; *Ger.* ā′riḵн), born 1912, U.S. orchestra conductor, born in Austria.

Lein·ster (len′stər), *n.* a province in the E Republic of Ireland. 1,332,149 (1961); 7576 sq. mi.

Leip·zig (līp′sig, -sik; *Ger.* līp′tsiḵн), *n.* a city in S East Germany. 595,203 (1964). Also, **Leip·sic** (līp′sik).

leish·ma·ni·a (lēsh mā′nē ə), *n.* a protozoan of the genus *Leishmania,* occurring in vertebrates in nonflagellate form, and in invertebrates in flagellated form. [< NL, named after Gen. Sir W. B. *Leishman* (1865–1926), Scottish bacteriologist; see -IA] —**leish·ma′ni·al, leish·man·ic** (lēsh-man′ik), **leish·ma′ni·oid′,** *adj.*

leish·man·i·a·sis (lēsh′mə nī′ə sis, lish′-), *n. Pathol.* any infection caused by a protozoan of the genus *Leishmania.* Also, **leish·ma·ni·o·sis** (lēsh mā′nē ō′sis, -man′ē-, lish-). [LEISHMAN(IA) + -IASIS]

leis·ter (lē′stər), *n.* **1.** a spearlike implement having three or more prongs, used in fishing. —*v.t.* **2.** to spear (fish) with a leister. [< Scand; cf. Icel *ljōstr* salmon spear, akin to *ljōsta* to strike]

lei·sure (lē′zhər, lezh′ər), *n.* **1.** freedom from the demands of work or duty. **2.** free or unoccupied time. **3.** unhurried ease. **4. at leisure, a.** with free or unrestricted time. **b.** without haste; slowly. **c.** out of work; unemployed. **5. at one's leisure,** when one has free time. —*adj.* **6.** free or unoccupied: *leisure hours.* **7.** having leisure: *the leisure class.* [ME *leisir* < OF, n. use of inf. < L *licēre* to be permitted] —**lei′sure·less,** *adj.*

lei·sured (lē′zhərd, lezh′ərd), *adj.* **1.** having leisure: *the leisured classes.* **2.** leisurely; unhurried.

lei·sure·ly (lē′zhər lē, lezh′ər-), *adj.* **1.** acting, proceeding, or done without haste. **2.** showing or suggesting ample leisure. —*adv.* **3.** in a leisurely manner. [late ME *laiserly* (adv.)] —**lei′sure·li·ness,** *n.* —**Syn. 1.** See **slow.**

Leith (lēth), *n.* a seaport in SE Scotland, on the Firth of Forth: now part of Edinburgh.

leit·mo·tif (līt′mō tēf′), *n.* a motif or theme associated throughout a music drama with a particular person, situation, or idea. [< G: leading motif]

Leix (lāks), *n.* Laoighis.

lek (lek), *n.* a zinc coin and monetary unit of Albania, equal to 100 qintars. [< Albanian]

Lek (lek), *n.* a river in the central Netherlands, flowing W to the Meuse River; the N branch of the lower Rhine. 40 mi. long.

lek·y·thos (lek′ə thos′), *n., pl.* **-thoi** (-thoi′). *Gk. and Rom. Antiq.* an oil jar having an ellipsoidal body, narrow neck, flanged mouth, curved handle extending from below the lip to the shoulder, and a narrow base terminating in a foot: used chiefly for ointments. Also, **lecythus, lekythus.** Cf. **alabastron, aryballos, askos.** [< Gk]

Lekythos

Le·ly (lē′lē; *Du.* lā′lē), *n.* **Sir Pe·ter** (pē′tər; *Du.* pā′tər), (*Pieter van der Faes*), 1618–80, Dutch painter in England.

LEM, Lunar Excursion Module.

lem·an (lem′ən, lē′mən), *n. Archaic.* **1.** a sweetheart; beloved. **2.** a mistress. [ME *lemman,* earlier *leofman.* See LIEF, MAN¹]

Le·man (lē′mən), *n.* **Lake.** See **Geneva, Lake of.**

Le Mans (lə mäɴ′), a city in NW France: auto racing. 136,083 (1962).

Le·may (lə mā′), *n.* a town in E Missouri. 40,516 (1970).

Lem·berg (lem′berk; *Eng.* lem′bûrg), *n.* German name of **Lwów.**

Le·mes·sus (lə mes′əs), *n.* ancient name of **Limassol.**

lem·ma¹ (lem′ə), *n., pl.* **lem·mas, lem·ma·ta** (lem′ə tə). **1.** a subsidiary proposition introduced in proving some other proposition; a helping theorem. **2.** an argument, theme, or subject. **3.** the heading of a gloss, annotation, etc. [< L: theme, title, epigram < Gk: lit., premise, akin to *lambánein* to take (for granted), receive]

lem·ma² (lem′ə), *n., pl.* **lem·mas, lem·ma·ta** (lem′ə tə). *Bot.* a bract in a grass spikelet just below the pistil and stamens. [< Gk: shell, husk, akin to *lépein* to peel]

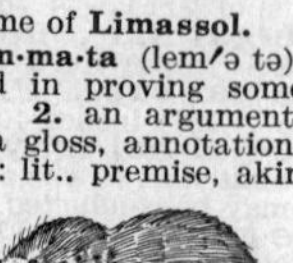

Lemming, *Lemmus trimucronatus* (Length to 6½ in.)

lem·ming (lem′ing), *n.* any of various small, mouselike rodents of the genera *Lemmus, Myopus,* and *Dicrostonyx,* of far northern regions, as *L. lemmus,* of Norway, Sweden, etc.: noted for periodic mass migrations, sometimes resulting in mass drownings. [< Norw; c. Icel *læmingi* lemming, *læmingr* loon; akin to Goth *laian* to revile, Icel *lá* to blame, L *lātrāre* to bark. See LAMENT]

lem·nis·cus (lem nis′kəs), *n., pl.* **-nis·ci** (-nis′ī, -nis′kē). *Anat.* a band of fibers, esp. of white nerve fibers in the brain. Also called **fillet.** [< NL, special use of L: pendent ribbon < Gk *lēmnískos* ribbon]

Lem·nos (lem′nos, -nōs; *Gk.* lēm′nôs), *n.* a Greek island in the NE Aegean. 24,016 (1951); 186 sq. mi. *Cap.:* Kastro. —**Lem·ni·an** (lem′nē ən), *adj., n.*

lem·on (lem′ən), *n.* **1.** the yellowish, acid fruit of a subtropical, rutaceous tree, *Citrus Limon.* **2.** the tree itself. **3.** clear, light yellow color. **4.** *Informal.* an inferior person or thing; dud. —*adj.* **5.** made of or with lemon, or having the color, taste, or odor of lemon. [< ML *lemōn(ium);* r. late ME *lymon* < ML *līmō* (s. *līmōn-*) << Ar *laymūn*] —**lem′on·ish,** *adj.* —**lem′on·like′, lem′on·y,** *adj.*

lem·on·ade (lem′ə nād′), *n.* a beverage consisting of lemon juice, sweetener, and water. [LEMON + -ADE¹, modeled on F *limonade* or Sp *limonada*]

lem′on balm′. See under **balm** (def. 5).

lem′on drop′, a lemon-flavored lozenge.

lem′on gera′nium, a garden geranium, *Pelargonium Limoneum,* having lemon-scented leaves.

lem′on squash′, *Brit.* lemon soda; a soft drink of lemon juice and soda water.

lem·pi·ra (lem pēr′ə), *n.* a paper money and monetary unit of Honduras, equal to 100 centavos. *Abbr.:* L. [< AmerSp, after *Lempira,* Indian chief]

le·mur (lē′mər), *n.* any of various small, arboreal, chiefly nocturnal mammals, esp. of the genus *Lemur,* allied to the monkeys, usually having a foxlike face and woolly fur, and found chiefly in Madagascar. [< NL, special use of L *lemurēs* (pl.) ghosts, specters]

lem·u·res (lem′yə rēz′; *Lat.* lem′o͝o-res′), *n.pl. Rom. Religion.* the ghosts of the dead of a family. [< L; see LEMUR]

Lemur, *Lemur catta* (Length 3½ ft.)

lem·u·roid (lem′yə roid′), *adj.* **1.** lemurlike; of the lemur kind. —*n.* **2.** a lemur. [< NL *Lemuroid(ea)*]

Le·na (lē′nə; *Russ.* le′nä), *n.* a river in the Soviet Union in Asia, flowing from Lake Baikal through the Yakutsk Republic into the Arctic Ocean. 2800 mi. long.

Len·a·pe (len′ə pē, lə nä′pē), *n., pl.* **-pes,** (*esp. collectively*) **-pe.** Delaware (defs. 4, 5). [< Algonquian (Delaware). lit., person]

Len·clos (läɴ klō′), *n.* **Anne** (än, ᴀɴ), (*Ninon de Lenclos*), 1620–1705?, French courtesan and wit.

lend (lend), *v.,* **lent, lend·ing.** —*v.t.* **1.** to give the temporary use of (money), often for a consideration. **2.** to grant the use of (something) with the understanding that it or its equivalent will be returned. **3.** to furnish or impart: *Distance lends enchantment to the view.* **4.** to give or contribute freely: *to lend one's aid to a cause.* **5.** to adapt (oneself or itself). —*v.i.* **6.** to make a loan or loans. [ME *lende* (orig. past tense), var. of *lene,* OE *lǣnan* (c. D *lenen,* G *leihen,* Icel *lāna*) < *lǣn* ʟᴏᴀɴ] —**lend′er,** *n.*

lend′ing li′brary, a small library maintained by a commercial establishment, as a drugstore, that lends books for a minimal daily fee. Also called **circulating library, rental library.**

lend-lease (lend′lēs′), *n., v.,* **-leased, -leas·ing.** —*n.* **1.** the matériel and services supplied by the U.S. to its allies during World War II under an act of Congress **(Lend′-Lease′ Act′)** passed in 1941. —*v.t.* **2.** to supply (matériel and services) as authorized by the Lend-Lease Act.

L'En·fant (läɴ fäɴ′), *n.* **Pierre Charles** (pyer s͟hᴀʀl), 1754–1825, U.S. engineer, architect, and soldier; born in France: designer of Washington, D.C.

length (leng̅kth, leng̅th), *n.* **1.** the linear extent of anything as measured from end to end. **2.** the measure of the greatest dimension of a plane or solid figure. **3.** extent from beginning to end of a series, enumeration, account, book, etc. **4.** extent in time; duration. **5.** a distance determined by the extent of something specified: *Hold the picture at arm's length.* **6.** a piece or portion of a certain extent: *a length of rope.* **7.** the quality or state of being long rather than short: *a journey remarkable for its length.* **8.** the extent to which a desired end is pursued: *He went to great lengths to get what he wanted.* **9.** a large extent or expanse of something. **10.** the measure from end to end of a horse, boat, etc., as a unit of distance in racing: *The horse won by two lengths.* **11.** *Pros., Phonet.* **a.** (of a vowel or syllable) quantity, whether long or short. **b.** the quality of vowels. **12.** *Bridge.* the possession of at least four cards in a given suit. **13. at length, a.** in or to the full extent; completely. **b.** after a time; finally. **14. go to any lengths,** to disregard any impediment to one's purpose. **15. keep at arm's length.** See **arm**[1] (def. 15). [ME *length(e),* OE *length(u);* c. D *lengte,* Icel *lengd.* See ʟᴏɴɢ[1], -ᴛʜ[1]] —**Syn. 1.** span, reach, measure.

length·en (leng̅k′t͟hən, leng̅′-), *v.t.* **1.** to make greater in length. —*v.i.* **2.** to become greater in length; grow long. —**length′en·er,** *n.*
—**Syn. 1.** elongate, draw out. ʟᴇɴɢᴛʜᴇɴ, ᴇxᴛᴇɴᴅ, ꜱᴛʀᴇᴛᴄʜ, ᴘʀᴏʟᴏɴɢ, ᴘʀᴏᴛʀᴀᴄᴛ agree in the idea of making longer. To ʟᴇɴɢᴛʜᴇɴ is to make longer, either in a material or an immaterial sense: *to lengthen a dress.* To ᴇxᴛᴇɴᴅ is to lengthen beyond some original point or so as to reach a certain point: *to extend a railroad line by a hundred miles.* To ꜱᴛʀᴇᴛᴄʜ is primarily to lengthen by drawing or tension: *to stretch a rubber band.* Both ᴘʀᴏʟᴏɴɢ and ᴘʀᴏᴛʀᴀᴄᴛ mean esp. to lengthen in time, and therefore apply to intangibles. To ᴘʀᴏʟᴏɴɢ is to continue beyond the desired, estimated, or allotted time: *to prolong an interview.* To ᴘʀᴏᴛʀᴀᴄᴛ is to draw out to undue length or to be slow in coming to a conclusion: *to protract a discussion.* —**Ant. 1.** shorten.

length·wise (leng̅kth′wīz′, leng̅th′-), *adv., adj.* in the direction of the length. Also, **length·ways** (leng̅kth′wāz′, leng̅th′-).

length·y (leng̅k′thē, leng̅′-), *adj.,* **length·i·er, length·i·est. 1.** very long. **2.** tediously verbose. —**length′i·ly,** *adv.* —**length′i·ness,** *n.*

le·ni·en·cy (lē′nē ən sē, lēn′yən-), *n.* the quality or state of being lenient. Also, **le′ni·ence.**

le·ni·ent (lē′nē ənt, lēn′yənt), *adj.* **1.** gently tolerant; permissive; indulgent. **2.** *Archaic.* softening, soothing, or alleviative. [< L *lēnient-* (s. of *lēniēns*) softening, alleviating, soothing, prp. of *lēnīre*] —**le′ni·ent·ly,** *adv.* —**Syn. 1.** easy, forbearing. —**Ant. 1.** harsh.

Len·in (len′in), *n.* **Vla·di·mir Il·yich** (vlad′ə mir′ il′yic͟h; *Russ.* vlä dē′miʀ il yēc͟h′), (*Vladimir Ilyich Ulyanov*) ("*N. Lenin*"), 1870–1924, Russian revolutionary leader: Soviet premier 1918–24.

Le·ni·na·kan (le′ni nä kän′), *n.* a city in NW Armenia, in the SW Soviet Union in Europe. 117,000 (est. 1962). Formerly, **Aleksandropol.**

Len·in·grad (len′in grad′; *Russ.* le′nin gʀät′), *n.* a seaport in the NW RSFSR, in the NW Soviet Union in Europe, on the Gulf of Finland, off the Baltic Sea: founded by Peter the Great 1703; capital of the Russian Empire 1712–1917. 3,636,000 (1965). Formerly, **St. Petersburg** (1703–1914); **Petrograd** (1914–24).

Len·in·ism (len′i niz′əm), *n.* the form of Communism taught by Lenin, with emphasis on the dictatorship of the proletariat.

Len·insk-Kuz·nets·ki (len′insk ko͝oz nets′ki), *n.* a city in the S RSFSR, in the W Soviet Union in Asia. 140,000 (est. 1962). Also, **Leninsk-Kuznetskiy.**

le·nis (lē′nis, lā′-), *adj., n., pl.* **le·nes** (lē′nēz, lā′-). *Phonet.* —*adj.* **1.** pronounced with relatively weak muscular tension and breath pressure, resulting in weak sound effect: *b, d,* and *t͟h* are lenis as compared with *p, t,* and *th,* which are fortis. Cf. **fortis** (def. 1). —*n.* **2.** a lenis consonant. [< L: soft, mild, gentle, calm]

len·i·tive (len′i tiv), *adj.* **1.** softening, soothing, or mitigating, as medicines or applications. **2.** mildly laxative. —*n.* **3.** a lenitive medicine or application; a mild laxative. **4.** *Archaic.* anything that softens or soothes. [< ML *lēnītīv(us)* = L *lēnīt(us)* softened (ptp. of *lēnīre;* see ʟᴇɴɪꜱ, -ɪᴛᴇ[2]) + *-īvus* -ɪᴠᴇ]

len·i·ty (len′i tē), *n., pl.* **-ties.** the quality or state of being mild or gentle. [< L *lēnitās.* See ʟᴇɴɪꜱ, -ᴛʏ[2]]

le·no (lē′nō), *n., pl.* **-nos. 1.** Also called **le′no weave′.** a mesh weave having paired warp yarns intertwined in a series of figure eights with filling yarn. **2.** any fabric in this weave. [? Anglicized var. of F *linon* lawn < *lin* ʟɪɴᴇɴ]

Le·nô·tre (lə nō′tʀᵊ), *n.* **An·dré** (äɴ dʀā′), 1613–1700, French architect and landscape designer.

Len·ox (len′əks), *n.* a town in W Massachusetts, in the Berkshire Hills: site of a former estate **(Tanglewood)** where music festivals are held each summer. 5804 (1970).

lens (lenz), *n., pl.* **lens·es. 1.** a piece of transparent substance, usually glass, having one or more curved surfaces used in changing the convergence of light rays, as for magnification or correcting defects of vision. **2.** a combination of such pieces. **3.** some analogous device, as for affecting sound waves, electromagnetic radiation, or streams of electrons. **4.** *Anat.* the crystalline body that focuses light rays in the eye. [< NL, special use of L: a lentil (from its shape); see ʟᴇɴᴛɪʟ]

lent (lent), *v.* pt. and pp. of **lend.**

Lent (lent), *n.* (in the Christian religion) an annual season of fasting and penitence beginning on Ash Wednesday and lasting 40 weekdays to Easter. [ME *lente(n),* OE *len(c)ten,* var. of *lengten* spring, Lent, lit., lengthening (of daylight hours); c. D *lente,* G *Lenz* spring]

-lent, an element occurring in adjectives borrowed from Latin, where it meant "full of": *pestilent.* [< L *-lent(us)*]

len·ta·men·te (len′tə men′tā; *It.* len′tä men′te), *adv. Music.* slowly. [< It = *lenta-* (see ʟᴇɴᴛᴏ) + *-mente* adv. suffix]

Lent·en (len′tᵊn), *adj.* **1.** of, pertaining to, or suitable for Lent. **2.** suggesting Lent, as in austerity. Also, **lent′en.** [ME; OE *lengten*]

len·tic (len′tik), *adj.* pertaining to or living in still water. [< L *lent(us)* slow, motionless + -ɪᴄ]

len·ti·cel (len′ti sel′), *n. Bot.* a body of cells formed on the periderm of a stem, appearing on the surface of the plant as a lens-shaped spot, and serving as a pore. [< NL *lenticell(a),* dim. of L *lenticula* little lentil = *lenti-* (s. of *lēns;* see ʟᴇɴꜱ) + *-cula* -ᴄᴜʟᴇ] —**len·ti·cel·late** (len′ti sel′it), *adj.*

len·tic·u·lar (len tik′yə lər), *adj.* **1.** of or pertaining to a lens. **2.** biconvex; convexo-convex. **3.** of the shape of a lentil seed. [< L *lenticulār(is)* lentil-like. See ʟᴇɴᴛɪᴄᴇʟ, -ᴀʀ[1]]

len·ti·go (len tī′gō), *n., pl.* **-tig·i·nes** (-tij′ə nēz′). *Med.* a freckle. [< L = *lentī-* (var. of *lenti-,* s. of *lēns* lentil) + *-gō* n. suffix]

len·til (len′til, -tᵊl), *n.* **1.** an annual, fabaceous plant, *Lens culinaris,* having flattened, biconvex seeds used as food. **2.** the seed itself. [ME < OF *lentille* < VL **lentīcula* for L *lenticula* little lentil. See ʟᴇɴᴛɪᴄᴇʟ]

len·tis·si·mo (len tis′ə mō′; *It.* len tēs′sē mô′), *Music.* —*adj.* **1.** very slow. —*adv.* **2.** very slowly. [< It, superl. of *lento* ʟᴇɴᴛᴏ]

len·to (len′tō; *It.* len′tô), *Music.* —*adj.* **1.** slow. —*adv.* **2.** slowly. [< It < L *lentus* slow]

len·toid (len′toid), *adj.* having the shape of a biconvex lens. [< L *lent-* (s. of *lēns*) lentil (see ʟᴇɴꜱ) + -ᴏɪᴅ]

Le·o (lē′ō), *n., gen.* **Le·o·nis** (lē ō′nis) for 1. **1.** *Astron.* the Lion, a zodiacal constellation between Virgo and Cancer, containing the bright star Regulus. **2.** *Astrol.* the fifth sign of the zodiac. See diag. at **zodiac.**

Le·o I (lē′ō; *It.* le′ô), **Saint** ("*Leo the Great*"), ᴀ.ᴅ. c390–461, Italian ecclesiastic: pope 440–461.

Leo II, Saint, died ᴀ.ᴅ. 683, Sicilian ecclesiastic: pope 682–683.

Leo III, 1. Saint, ᴀ.ᴅ. c750–816, Italian ecclesiastic: pope 795–816. **2.** ("*the Isaurian*") ᴀ.ᴅ. c680–741, Eastern Roman emperor 717–741.

Leo IV, Saint, died ᴀ.ᴅ. 855, Italian ecclesiastic: pope 847–855.

Leo V, fl. 10th century ᴀ.ᴅ., Italian ecclesiastic: pope 903.

Leo VI, pope ᴀ.ᴅ. 928.

Leo VII, died ᴀ.ᴅ. 939, Italian ecclesiastic: pope 936–939.

Leo VIII, died ᴀ.ᴅ. 965, Italian ecclesiastic: pope 963–965.

Leo IX, Saint (*Bruno*), 1002–54, German ecclesiastic: pope 1049–54.

Leo X, (*Giovanni de'Medici*) 1475–1521, Italian ecclesiastic: pope 1513–21 (son of Lorenzo de'Medici).

Leo XI, (*Alessandro de'Medici*) 1535–1605, Italian ecclesiastic: pope 1605.

Leo XII, (*Annibale Francesco della Genga*) 1760–1829, Italian ecclesiastic: pope 1823–29.

Leo XIII, (*Giovanni Vincenzo Pecci*) 1810–1903, Italian ecclesiastic: pope 1878–1903.

Leom·in·ster (lem′in stər), *n.* a city in N Massachusetts. 32,939 (1970).

Le·ón (le ôn′), *n.* **1.** a province in NW Spain: formerly a kingdom. 598,700 (est. 1960); 5936 sq. mi. **2.** the capital of this province. 71,697 (est. 1960). **3.** a city in W Guanajuato, in Mexico. 275,335 (est. 1965). **4.** a city in W Nicaragua: the former capital. 61,649 (1963). —**Le·on·ese** (lē′ə nēz′, -nēs′), *adj., n.*

Leon·ard (len′ərd), *n.* **William El·ler·y (Chan·ning)** (el′ə rē), 1876–1944, U.S. poet and teacher.

Le·o·nar·do da Vin·ci (lē′ə när′dō də vin′c͟hē; *It.* le′ô näʀ′dô dä vēn′c͟hē). See **Vinci, Leonardo da.**

Le·on·ca·val·lo (le ōn′kä väl′lô), *n.* **Rug·gie·ro** (ʀo͞od-je′ʀô), 1858–1919, Italian operatic composer and librettist.

le·one (lē ōn′), *n,* the monetary unit of Sierra Leone, equal to 100 cents. [< ꜱɪᴇʀʀᴀ ʟᴇᴏɴᴇ]

Le·o·nid (lē′ə nid), *n., pl.* **Le·o·nids, Le·on·i·des** (lē on′i-dēz′). *Astron.* any of a shower of meteors occurring around November 15 and appearing to radiate from a point in the constellation Leo. [back formation from NL *Leōnidēs* (pl.) = L *Leōn-* (s. of *Leō*) ʟᴇᴏ + *-idēs* -ɪᴅ[1]]

Le·on·i·das (lē on′i dəs), *n.* died 480 ʙ.ᴄ., Greek hero: king of Sparta 489?–480.

le·o·nine (lē′ə nīn′), *adj.* **1.** of or pertaining to the lion. **2.** resembling or suggestive of a lion. [ME *leonyn* < L *leōnīn(us)* lionlike. See ʟɪᴏɴ, -ɪɴᴇ[1]]

leop·ard (lep′ərd), *n.* **1.** a large, ferocious, spotted Asian or African carnivore, *Panthera pardus,* of the cat family, usually tawny with black markings. See illus. on next page. **2.** the fur or pelt of this animal. **3.** any of various related cats resembling this animal. **4.** *Heraldry.* a lion represented from the side as walking. **5.** *Numis.* **a.** a gold coin issued by Edward III, equal to half a florin, bearing the figure of a leopard. **b.** a silver coin issued by Henry V. [ME < LL *leōpard(us)* < LGk *leópardos,* syncopated var. of *leontópardos* = *leonto-* (s. of *léōn*) lion + *párdos* PARD[1]]

Leopard, *Panthera pardus* (About 2½ ft. high at shoulder; total length 7½ ft.; tail 3 ft.)

leop·ard·ess (lep′ər dis), *n.* a female leopard.

leop′ard frog′, a common green frog, *Rana pipiens,* of North America, having oval, white-edged, dark spots on the back.

Le·o·par·di (le′ô pär′dē), *n.* **Count Gia·co·mo** (jä′kô mô), 1798–1837, Italian poet.

Le·o·pold I (lē′ə pōld′), **1.** 1640–1705, king of Hungary 1655–1705; emperor of the Holy Roman Empire 1658–1705. **2.** 1790–1865, king of Belgium 1831–65.

Leopold II, 1. 1747–92, emperor of the Holy Roman Empire 1790–92 (son of Francis I; brother of Joseph II and Marie Antoinette). **2.** 1835–1909, king of Belgium 1865–1909 (son of Leopold I of Belgium).

Leopold III, 1901–83, king of Belgium 1934–51 (son of Albert I).

Lé·o·pold·ville (lē′ə pōld vil′, lā′-; *Fr.* lā ô pôld vēl′) *n.* former name of **Kinshasa.** Also, **Le·o·pold·ville** (lē′ə-pōld vil′, lā′-).

le·o·tard (lē′ə tärd′), *n.* a skin-tight, one-piece garment covering the torso and usually extending to the wrists and ankles, worn by acrobats, dancers, etc. Cf. **tights.** [named after J. *Léotard,* 19th-century French gymnast]

Le·pan·to (li pan′tō; *It.* le′pän tô), *n.* **1.** Greek, **Návpaktos.** a seaport in W Greece, on the Strait of Lepanto: Turkish naval defeat 1571. 8170. **2. Gulf of.** See **Corinth, Gulf of. 3. Strait of.** Also called **Rion Strait.** a strait between the Ionian Sea and the Gulf of Corinth. 1 mi. wide.

lep·er (lep′ər), *n.* a person affected with leprosy. [ME *lepre* leprosy < LL *lepra* < Gk, n. use of fem. of *leprós* scaly, akin to *lépos* scale, *lépein* to peel]

lepido-, a learned borrowing from Greek meaning "scale," used in the formation of compound words: *lepidopteron.* [< Gk, comb. form repr. *lepís* (s. *lepid-*) scale. See LEPER]

le·pid·o·lite (li pid′ᵊlīt′, lep′i dᵊlīt′), *n.* a mineral of the mica group, potassium lithium aluminum silicate, commonly occurring in lilac, rose-colored, or grayish-white scaly masses: an important ore of lithium.

lep·i·dop·ter·an (lep′i dop′tər ən), *adj.* **1.** lepidopterous. —*n.* **2.** a lepidopterous insect.

lep·i·dop·ter·ol·o·gy (lep′i dop′tə rol′ə jē), *n.* the branch of zoology dealing with butterflies and moths. —**lep·i·dop·te·ro·log·i·cal** (lep′i dop′tər ə loj′i kəl), *adj.* —**lep·i·dop·ter·ist** (lep′i dop′tər ist), *n.*

lep·i·dop·ter·on (lep′i dop′tər ən), *n., pl.* **-ter·a** (-tər ə). any lepidopterous insect. [< NL = *lepido-* LEPIDO- + Gk *pterón* wing]

lep·i·dop·ter·ous (lep′i dop′tər əs), *adj.* belonging or pertaining to the *Lepidoptera,* an order of insects comprising the butterflies, moths, and skippers, that in the adult state have four membranous wings more or less covered with small scales. Also, **lep′i·dop′ter·al.**

lep·i·do·si·ren (lep′i dō sī′rən), *n.* a lungfish, *Lepidosiren paradoxa,* found in the Amazon, having an eel-shaped body. [< NL; see LEPIDO-, SIREN]

lep·i·dote (lep′i dōt′), *adj. Bot.* covered with scurfy scales or scaly spots. [< NL *lepidōt(us)* < Gk *lepidōtós* scaly = *lepidō-* (verbid s. of *lepidoûn* to make scaly; see LEPIDO-) + *-tos* verbid suffix]

Lep·i·dus (lep′i dəs), *n.* **Marcus Ae·mil·i·us** (ē mil′ē əs), died 13 B.C., Roman politician: member of the second triumvirate.

Le·pon′tine Alps′ (li pon′tin), a central range of the Alps in S Switzerland and N Italy. Highest peak, Mt. Leone, 11,684 ft.

lep·o·rine (lep′ə rīn′, -rin), *adj. Zool.* of, pertaining to, or resembling a rabbit or hare. [< L *leporīn(us)* = *lepor-* (s. of *lepus*) hare + *-īnus* -INE[1]]

lep·re·chaun (lep′rə kôn′, -kon′), *n. Irish Folklore.* a pygmy, sprite, or goblin. [< Ir *leipreachān,* MIr *luchrupān,* OIr *luchorpān* = *lu* small + *corp* body (< L *corpus*) + *-ān* dim. suffix]

lep·ro·sar·i·um (lep′rə sâr′ē əm), *n., pl.* **-sar·i·a** (-sâr′ē ə). a hospital for the treatment of leprosy. [< ML; see LEPROUS, -ARY]

lep·rose (lep′rōs), *adj.* leprous.

lep·ro·sy (lep′rə sē), *n. Pathol.* a mildly infectious disease caused by an organism, *Mycobacterium leprae,* and variously characterized by ulcerations, loss of fingers and toes, anesthesia in certain nerve regions, etc. Also called **Hansen's disease.** [? < ML *leprōsi(a)* (recorded only as synonym for LEPROSARIUM) < Gk *léprōs(is)* leprosy + *-ia* -Y[3]]

lep·rous (lep′rəs), *adj.* **1.** *Pathol.* affected with leprosy. **2.** of or resembling leprosy. **3.** *Bot., Zool.* covered with scales. [ME *lepr(o)us* < LL *leprōs(us)*] —**lep′rous·ly,** *adv.* —**lep′rous·ness,** *n.*

Lep·si·us (lep′sē o͝os′), *n.* **Karl Rich·ard** (kärl rikн′-ärt), 1810–84, German philologist and Egyptologist.

-lepsy, a learned borrowing from Greek meaning "seizure," used in the formation of compound words: *epilepsy.* [comb. form repr. NL *-lēpsia* < Gk *-lēpsia* = *lēps(is)* a seizure (*lēp-* verbid s. of *lambánein* to seize + *-sis* -SIS) + *-ia* -Y[3]]

lepto-, a learned borrowing from Greek meaning "thin," "fine," "slight," used in the formation of compound words: *leptosome.* [< Gk *lepto-,* comb. form of *leptós* thin, slight, fine, lit., stripped = *lép(ein)* (to) strip + *-tos* adj. suffix]

lep·ton (lep′ton), *n., pl.* **-ta** (-tə). **1.** a money of account of modern Greece, the 100th part of a drachma. **2.** *Physics.* an elementary particle that is an electron, positron, neutrino, antineutrino, or mu meson. [< Gk *leptón* (*nómisma*) a small (coin), n. use of neut. of *leptós* small; see LEPTO-; def. 2: LEPTO- + -ON[1]]

lep·to·some (lep′tə sōm′), *n.* a person of asthenic build. —**lep′to·so′mic, lep·to·so·mat·ic** (lep′tō sə mat′ik), *adj.*

Lé·ri·da (le′rē ᵺä), *n.* a city in NE Spain. 66,847 (est. 1963).

Ler·mon·tov (ler′mon tôf′), *n.* **Mi·kha·il Yur·i·e·vich** (mi-кнä ēl′ yo͞or′yə vich), 1814–41, Russian poet and novelist.

Le Sage (lə säzн′), **A·lain Re·né** (a lan′ rə nā′), 1668–1747, French novelist and dramatist. Also, **Le·sage′.**

les·bi·an (lez′bē ən), *adj.* **1.** of, pertaining to, or characteristic of lesbianism. **2.** (*cap.*) of or pertaining to Lesbos. **3.** (*cap.*) erotic: so called from the reputed character of the ancient inhabitants of Lesbos and the tone of their poetry. —*n.* **4.** a female homosexual. **5.** (*cap.*) an inhabitant of Lesbos. [< L *Lesbi(us)* (< Gk *Lésbios* Lesbian = *Lésb(os)* LESBOS + *-ios* adj. suffix) + -AN]

les·bi·an·ism (lez′bē ə niz′əm), *n.* homosexual relations between women.

Les·bos (lez′bos, -bōs; *Gk.* lez′vôs), *n.* Mytilene (def. 1).

Les Cayes (lā kā′; *Fr.* lā ka′yᵊ), a seaport on the SW coast of Haiti. 14,000. Also called **Cayes.** Formerly, **Aux Cayes.**

lese′ maj′esty (lēz), **1.** *Law.* a crime or offense against the sovereign power in a state, esp. against the dignity of a ruler. **2.** an attack on any traditional custom, belief, etc. Also, **lèse′ maj′esty, lèse′ maj′esté.** [< F *lèse-majesté* < L *laesa mājestās,* lit., injured greatness. See LESION, MAJESTY]

Les Gueux (lā gœ′), a league of Dutch burghers and nobles formed in 1566 to oppose the Spanish Inquisition. [< F: lit., the beggars]

le·sion (lē′zhən), *n.* **1.** an injury; hurt; wound. **2.** *Pathol.* any localized, abnormal structural change in the body. [late ME < LL *laesiōn-* (s. of *laesiō*) injury (L: attack) = L *laes(us)* harmed (ptp. of *laedere*) + *-iōn-* -ION]

Le·so·tho (le sō′tђō, le so͞o′to͞o), *n.* a kingdom in S Africa: formerly a British protectorate; gained independence 1966; member of the British Commonwealth of Nations. 1,200,000; 11,716 sq. mi. *Cap.:* Maseru. Formerly, **Basutoland.**

les·pe·de·za (les′pi dē′zə), *n.* any leguminous shrub or herb of the genus *Lespedeza,* having trifoliolate leaves and lavender flowers, grown for forage, soil improvement, etc. [< NL, named after V. M. de *Zespedez* (misread as *Lespedez*), 18th-century Spanish governor of Florida]

less (les), *adv., a compar. of* **little** *with* **least** *as superl.* **1.** to a smaller extent, amount, or degree: *less exact.* **2.** most certainly not (often prec. by *much* or *still*): *He could barely pay for his own meal, much less for mine.* —*adj., a compar. of* **little** *with* **least** *as superl.* **3.** smaller in size, amount, degree, etc.; not so large, great, or much: *less speed.* **4.** lower in consideration, dignity, or importance: *no less a person than the manager.* —*n.* **5.** a smaller amount or quantity. —*prep.* **6.** minus; without: *a year less two days.* [ME; OE *lǣs(sa)*; c. OFris *lēs(sa).* See LEAST] —**Syn. 3.** See **small.** —**Usage. 3.** See **fewer.**

-less, an adjective suffix meaning "without" (*childless; peerless*), and in adjectives derived from verbs, indicating failure or inability to perform or be performed (*resistless; countless*). [ME *-les,* OE *-lēas,* special use of *lēas* free from, without, false; c. Icel *lauss,* G *los,* LOOSE]

les·see (le sē′), *n.* a person to whom a lease is granted. [late ME < AF. See LEASE, -EE] —**les·see′ship,** *n.*

less·en (les′ən), *v.i.* **1.** to become less. —*v.t.* **2.** to make less; reduce. **3.** *Archaic.* to represent as less; depreciate; disparage. [late ME; r. ME *lasnen* = *lasse* (var. of *lesse* LESS) + *-nen* -EN[1]] —**Syn. 1, 2.** decrease, diminish. —**Ant. 1, 2.** increase.

Les·seps (les′əps; *Fr.* le seps′), *n.* **Fer·di·nand Ma·rie, Vi·comte de** (fer dē nän′ ma rē′, vē kônt də), 1805–94, French engineer and diplomat: promoter of the Suez Canal.

less·er (les′ər), *adj., a compar. of* **little** *with* **least** *as superl.* **1.** less; smaller, as in size, amount, importance, etc.: *a lesser evil.* **2.** being the smaller or less important of two. [ME *lasser, lesser*]

Less′er Antil′les. See under **Antilles.**

Less′er Bai′ram. See under **Bairam.**

Less′er Bear′, *Astron.* the constellation Ursa Minor.

Less′er Dog′, *Astron.* the constellation Canis Minor.

less′er multan′gular bone. See under **multangulum.**

less′er pan′da, panda (def. 1).

Less′er Sanhed′rin, Sanhedrin (def. 2).

Less′er Sun′da Is′lands. See under **Sunda Islands.**

Les·sing (les′ing), *n.* **Gott·hold E·phra·im** (gôt′hôlt ā′frä im), 1729–81, German critic and dramatist.

les·son (les′ən), *n.* **1.** a part of a book or the like, as an exercise, a text, etc., assigned a pupil for study. **2.** a section into which a course of study is divided, esp. a single, continuous session of formal instruction in a subject. **3.** something to be learned or studied: *the lessons of the past.* **4.** a useful piece of practical wisdom acquired by experience or study: *lessons on how to travel light.* **5.** an instructive example: *His deportment was a lesson in good manners.* **6.** a reproof or punishment. **7.** a portion of the Scripture to be read at a divine service; lection; pericope. —*v.t.* **8.** to teach; give a lesson to. **9.** to admonish or reprove. [ME *lesso(u)n* < OF *leçon* < L *lectiōn-* (s. of *lectiō*) LECTION]

les·sor (les′ôr, le sôr′), *n.* a person who grants a lease. [late ME *lesso(u)r* < AF. See LEASE, -OR[2]]

lest (lest), *conj.* **1.** for fear that; so that (one) should not (used negatively to introduce a clause expressive of an action or occurrence requiring caution): *He kept notes lest faulty memory lead him astray.* **2.** that (used after words expressing fear, danger, etc.): *There was danger lest the plan become known.* [ME *leste,* late OE *the lǣste,* earlier *thȳ lǣs the* lest (lit., whereby less that; *the* is the relative particle)]

let[1] (let), *v.,* **let, let·ting.** —*v.t.* **1.** to allow or permit: *Let me do that for you.* **2.** to allow to pass, go, or come: *The maid let us into the house.* **3.** to grant the rental or hire of, as for occupancy. **4.** to contract (work) for performance: *to let work to a carpenter.* **5.** to cause or make: *to let one know the truth.* **6.** (used in the imperative as an auxiliary expressive of a request, command, warning, suggestion, etc.): *Let me see. Let them just try it!* —*v.i.* **7.** to be rented or leased: *The apartment lets for $100 per week.* **8. let alone.** See **alone** (def. 5). **9. let be,** to refrain from bothering; leave alone. **10. let down, a.** to disappoint; fail. **b.** to betray; desert. **c.** to slacken; abate. **d.** to lower, as hair or a hem. **11. let go.** See **go**[1] (def. 68). **12. let in, a.** to admit. **b.** to involve (a person) in without his knowledge or permission: *to let someone in for a loss.* **c.** Also, **let in on.** to share with; permit to participate in. **13. let off, a.** to release by exploding. **b.** to free or excuse, as from duty or responsibility. **c.** to allow to go with little or no punishment; pardon. **14. let on,** *Informal.* **a.** to reveal one's true feelings. **b.** to pretend. **15. let out, a.** to divulge; make known. **b.** to release from confinement, restraint, etc. **c.** to enlarge (a garment). **d.** to cut parallel diagonal slashes into (a pelt) and sew the slashed edges together for better appearance of the fur. **16. let someone have it.** *Informal.* to attack or assault, as by striking, shooting, or rebuking. **17. let up,** *Informal.* **a.** to slacken; abate. **b.** to stop. **18. let up on,** *Informal.* to be more lenient with. [ME *lete(n),* OE *lǣtan;* c. D *laten,* G *lassen,* Icel *lāta,* Goth *lētan;* akin to Gk *lēdein* to be weary, L *lassus* tired. See LATE] —**Syn. 1.** See **allow. 1, 5.** suffer, grant. LET, LEAVE, although not synonyms, are often confused. In the constructions in which the confusion arises, it should be noted that, although either verb can take a nominal object (*Let John leave home*), only LET can take the infinitive (with *to* not expressed): *let fly; let go.* In certain idiomatic expressions, the two verbs are used in parallel constructions, but the meanings differ widely: LET it out means "allow it to escape" (as the breath), but LEAVE it out means "omit it" (as a sentence). LET him alone means "allow him to be without interference" (don't bother him), and although purists insist that LEAVE him alone means "go away, so that he will be alone," the facts of usage show that this construction means "don't bother him" as frequently as it does "go away," if not more frequently.

let[2] (let), *n., v.,* **let·ted** or **let, let·ting.** —*n.* **1.** (in tennis, badminton, etc.) any play that is voided and must be replayed, esp. a service that hits the net and drops into the proper part of the opponent's court. —*v.t.* **2.** *Archaic.* to hinder; stand in the way of. [ME *lette(n),* OE *lettan* (< *læt* slow, tardy, LATE); c. Icel *letja* to hinder]

-let, a diminutive suffix attached to nouns: *ringlet; frontlet; bracelet.* [ME *-let, -lette* < MF *-elet* = *-el* (< L *-āle,* neut. of *-ālis* -AL[1] (see BRACELET); or < L *-ellus,* dim. suffix; see CHAPLET) + *-et* -ET]

letch (lech), *n. Slang.* **1.** a lecherous craving. **2.** a lecher. —*v.i.* **3.** to act like a lecher (often fol. by *for* or *after*). —*adj.* **4.** lecherous or lustful. Also, **lech.** [? alter. and back formation from LECHER]

let·down (let′doun′), *n.* **1.** a decrease in volume, force, etc. **2.** disillusionment or disappointment. **3.** depression; deflation. **4.** *Aeron.* the descent of an aircraft from a higher to a lower altitude preparatory to making an approach and landing, a target run, etc.

le·thal (lē′thəl), *adj.* **1.** of, pertaining to, or causing death; deadly; fatal: *a lethal weapon; a lethal dose.* **2.** made to cause death: *a lethal attack.* [< L *lēthāl(is)* var. of *lētālis* < *lēth(um)* var. of *lētum* death (*-h-* by confusion with Gk *lḗthē* oblivion); see -AL[1]] —**le·thal′i·ty,** *n.* —**le′thal·ly,** *adv.* —**Syn. 1.** See **fatal.**

le·thar·gic (lə thär′jik), *adj.* **1.** of, pertaining to, or affected with lethargy; drowsy; sluggish. **2.** producing lethargy. Also, **le·thar′gi·cal.** [< L *lēthargic(us)* < Gk *lēthargikós* drowsy (see LETHARGY, -IC); r. ME *litargik*] —**le·thar′gi·cal·ly,** *adv.*

lethar′gic encephali′tis, *Pathol.* See **sleeping sickness** (def. 2).

leth·ar·gy (leth′ər jē), *n., pl.* **-gies. 1.** the quality or state of being drowsy and dull; apathetic or sluggish inactivity. **2.** *Pathol.* an abnormal state of overpowering drowsiness or sleep. [< LL *lēthargīa* < Gk = *lētharg(os)* drowsy + *-ia* -Y[3] (see LETHE, -ALGIA); r. ME *litargie* < ML *lītargīa* < MGk (in which *ē* had the value *ī*)]

Leth·bridge (leth′brij′), *n.* a city in S Alberta, in SW Canada. 35,454 (1961).

Le·the (lē′thē), *n.* **1.** *Class. Myth.* a river in Hades whose water caused forgetfulness of the past in those who drank of it. **2.** forgetfulness; oblivion. [< L < Gk, special use of *lḗthē* forgetfulness, akin to *lanthánesthai* to forget] —**Le·the·an** (li thē′ən, lē′thē ən), *adj.*

le·thif·er·ous (li thif′ər əs), *adj. Archaic.* lethal. [< L *lēthifer* (*lethi-,* comb. form of *lēthum* death (see LETHAL) + *-fer* -FER) + -OUS]

Le·to (lē′tō), *n. Class. Myth.* the mother by Zeus of Apollo and Artemis.

let's (lets), contraction of *let us.*

Lett (let), *n.* **1.** one of a people living on or near the eastern coast of the Baltic Sea and being related to the Lithuanians. **2.** Lettish (def. 2).

Lett., Lettish.

let·ted (let′id), *v.* a pt. and pp. of **let**[2].

let·ter[1] (let′ər), *n.* **1.** a communication in writing or printing addressed to a person or a number of persons. **2.** one of the marks or signs conventionally used in writing and printing to represent speech sounds, alone or in combination; an alphabetic character. **3.** a piece of printing type bearing such a mark or character. **4.** a particular style of type. **5.** such types collectively. **6.** actual terms or wording, as distinct from implied meaning or intent (opposed to *spirit*): *the letter of the law.* **7. letters,** (*construed as sing. or pl.*) **a.** literature in general. **b.** the profession of literature: *a man of letters.* **c.** learning; knowledge, esp. of literature. **8.** an emblem consisting of the initial or monogram of a school, awarded to a student for outstanding performance, esp. in athletics. **9. to the letter, a.** with strict adherence to the actual wording or literal interpretation. **b.** to the last particular; precisely. —*v.t.* **10.** to mark or write with letters; inscribe. —*v.i.* **11.** to receive a letter in an interscholastic or intercollegiate activity, esp. a sport. [ME, var. of *lettre* < OF < L *littera* alphabetic character, in pl., epistle, literature] —**let′ter·er,** *n.* —**Syn. 7.** See **literature.**

let·ter[2] (let′ər), *n. Chiefly Brit.* a person who lets, esp. one who rents out property. [LET[1] + -ER[1]]

let′ter box′, **1.** *Brit.* mailbox. **2.** *U.S.* mailbox (def. 1).

let′ter car′rier, a mailman.

let·tered (let′ərd), *adj.* **1.** educated or learned. **2.** of, pertaining to, or characterized by learning or literary culture. **3.** marked with or as with letters. [ME]

let·ter·gram (let′ər gram′), *n.* a telegram sent at a reduced rate, as a day letter or night letter.

let·ter·head (let′ər hed′), *n.* **1.** a printed heading on stationery, esp. one giving a name and address. **2.** a sheet of paper with such a heading.

let·ter·ing (let′ər ing), *n.* **1.** the act or process of inscribing with or making letters. **2.** the letters themselves.

let·ter·man (let′ər man′, -mən), *n., pl.* **-men.** a person who has won a letter in an interscholastic or intercollegiate activity, esp. a sport.

let′ter of cred′it, **1.** an order issued by a banker allowing a person named to draw money to a specified amount from correspondents of the issuer. **2.** an instrument issued by a banker authorizing a person named to make drafts upon the issuer up to an amount specified.

let′ter of intent′, an agreement expressing the intention of one party to sign a contract with another and providing for compensation in case no such contract is signed.

let′ter of marque′, license granted by a state to a private citizen to capture the merchant ships of another nation. Also, **let′ters of marque′.** Also called **let′ter of marque′ and repris′al.**

let·ter-per·fect (let′ər pûr′fikt), *adj.* **1.** knowing one's part, lesson, etc., perfectly. **2.** verbatim; precise.

let·ter·press (let′ər pres′), *n.* matter printed from letters or type in relief, rather than from intaglio plates or planographically.

let·ter-size (let′ər sīz′), *adj.* **1.** (of paper) having a size measuring approximately 8½ × 11 inches. **2.** (of office supplies and equipment) made for holding letter-size sheets of paper: *letter-size filing cabinets.* Cf. **legal-size.**

let′ters of administra′tion, *Law.* an instrument issued by a court authorizing an administrator to administer the estate of a deceased person.

let′ters of cre′dence, credentials issued to a diplomat for presentation to a foreign country. Also called **let′ters creden′tial.**

let·ter·space (let′ər spās′), *v.t.,* **-spaced, -spac·ing.** *Print.* to space out (the letters of a word or line) for balance or emphasis.

let′ters pat′ent, *Law.* a written instrument issued by a government giving a person an exclusive right, as to property or a franchise.

let′ters testamen′tary, *Law.* an instrument issued by a court authorizing an executor to take control of and dispose of the estate of a deceased person.

let′ter stock′, *U.S.* stock unregistered with the Securities and Exchange Commission that cannot be publicly sold prior to its registration: so called because the buyer signs a letter that the purchase is for investment only for a certain period of time.

Let·tic (let′ik), *adj.* of or pertaining to the Letts or their language.

Let·tish (let′ish), *adj.* **1.** of or pertaining to the Letts or their language. —*n.* **2.** Also called **Latvian, Lett.** the Baltic language of Latvia.

let·tre de ca·chet (le′trə də kA shε′), *pl.* **let·tres de ca·chet** (le′trə də kA shε′). *French.* a letter under the seal of the sovereign, esp. one ordering imprisonment.

let·tuce (let′is), *n.* **1.** a leafy annual herb, *Lactuca sativa,* occurring in many varieties, used for salads. **2.** any species of *Lactuca.* **3.** *Slang.* paper money; cash. [ME *letuse,* appar. < OF *laitues,* pl. of *laitue* < L *lactūca* a lettuce, perh. orig. fem. of *lactūcus* milky (the *-ū-* of which is unexplained); see LACTIC]

let·up (let′up′), *n. Informal.* cessation; pause; relief.

le·u (le′o͞o), *n., pl.* **lei** (lā). a coin and monetary unit of Rumania, equal to 100 bani. *Abbr.:* L. Also, **ley.** [< Rumanian: lit., LION]

leuc-, var. of **leuco-** before a vowel: *leucemia.* Also, **leuk-.**

Leu·cas (lo͞o′kəs), *n.* Levkas.

leu·ce·mi·a (lo͞o sē′mē ə), *n. Pathol.* leukemia. —**leu·ce′mic,** *adj.*

leu·cine (lo͞o′sēn, -sin), *n. Chem.* an amino acid, $(CH_3)_2CHCH_2CH(NH_2)COOH$, essential in the nutrition of man and animals.

leu·cite (lo͞o′sīt), *n.* a whitish or grayish mineral, potassium aluminum silicate, $KAlSi_2O_6$, found in alkali volcanic rocks. [< G *Leukit*] —**leu·cit·ic** (lo͞o sit′ik), *adj.*

leuco-, a learned borrowing from Greek meaning "white," used in the formation of compound words: *leucoderma.* Also, **leuc-, leuk-, leuko-.** [< Gk *leuko-,* comb. form of *leukós* white; akin to L *lūx* LIGHT[1]]

leu′co base′ (lo͞o′kō), *Chem.* a noncolored or slightly colored compound that is produced by reducing a dye and is readily oxidized to regenerate the dye.

leu·co·crat·ic (lo͞o′kə krat′ik), *adj. Geol.* (of a rock) composed mainly of light-colored minerals.

leu·co·cyte (lo͞o′kə sīt′), *n.* leukocyte.

leu·co·cy·to·sis (lo͞o′kō sī tō′sis), *n. Physiol., Pathol.* leukocytosis. —**leu·co·cy·tot·ic** (lo͞o′kō sī tot′ik), *adj.*

leu·co·der·ma (lo͞o′kə dûr′mə), *n. Pathol.* vitiligo. Also, **leukoderma.** [< NL]

leu·co·ma (lo͞o kō′mə), *n. Pathol.* leukoma.

leu·co·ma·ine (lo͞o kō′mə ēn′, -in, lo͞o′kə mān′), *n. Biochem.* any of a class of poisonous nitrogenous substances normally produced in a living animal body through metabolism. [LEUCO- + (PTO)MAINE]

leu·co·pe·ni·a (lo͞o′kə pē′nē ə), *n. Med.* leukopenia.

leu·co·plast (lo͞o′kə plast′), *n. Bot.* one of the colorless bodies found within the protoplasm of vegetable cells, serving as points around which starch forms.

leu·co·poi·e·sis (lo͞o′kō poi ē′sis), *n.* leukopoiesis. —**leu·co·poi·et·ic** (lo͞o′kō poi et′ik), *adj.*

leu·cor·rhe·a (lo͞o′kə rē′ə), *n. Pathol.* leukorrhea. Also, **leu′cor·rhoe′a.** —**leu′cor·rhe′al, leu′cor·rhoe′al,** *adj.*

Leuc·tra (lo͞ok′trə), *n.* a town in ancient Greece, in Boeotia: Thebans defeated Spartans here 371 B.C.

leuk-, var. of **leuko-** before a vowel.

Leu·kas (lo͞o′kəs), *n.* Levkas.

leu·ke·mi·a (lo͞o kē′mē ə), *n. Pathol.* a usually fatal cancerous disease characterized by excessive production of white blood cells, and often accompanied by severe anemia. Also, **leu·kae′mi·a, leucemia.** [var. of NL *leuchaemia.* See LEUCO-, -HEMIA] —**leu·ke′mic, leu·kae′mic,** *adj.*

leuko-, var. of **leuco-.** Also, *esp. before a vowel,* **leuk-.**

leu·ko·cyte (lo͞o′kə sīt′), *n. Anat.* one of the white or colorless nucleate cells of the blood that are sometimes found in the tissues and help maintain immunity to infection and resistance against bacteria and other foreign particles. Also, **leucocyte.**

leu·ko·cy·to·sis (lo͞o′kō sī tō′sis), *n.* *Physiol., Pathol.* the presence of an increased number of leukocytes in the blood, esp. when temporary, as in infection, and not due to leukemia. Also, **leucocytosis.** [< NL] —**leu·ko·cy·tot·ic** (lo͞o′kə sī tot′ik), *adj.*

leu·ko·der·ma (lo͞o′kə dûr′mə), *n.* *Pathol.* vitiligo. Also, **leucoderma.** [< NL]

leu·ko·ma (lo͞o kō′mə), *n.* *Pathol.* a dense, white opacity of the cornea. Also, **leucoma.** [< NL *leucoma.* See LEUCO-, -OMA]

leu·ko·pe·ni·a (lo͞o′kə pē′nē ə), *n.* *Med.* a decrease in the number of leukocytes in the blood. Also, **leucopenia.** [< NL *leucopenia.* See LEUCO-, -PENIA] —**leu′ko·pe′nic,** *adj.*

leu·ko·poi·e·sis (lo͞o′kō poi ē′sis), *n.* the formation and development of leukocytes. Also, **leucopoiesis.** [< NL *leucopoiesis.* See LEUCO-, -POIESIS] —**leu·ko·poi·et·ic,** (lo͞o′kō poi et′ik), *adj.*

leu·kor·rhe·a (lo͞o′kə rē′ə), *n.* *Pathol.* a whitish discharge from the female genital organs. Also, **leu′kor·rhoe′a, leucorrhea, leucorrhoea.** [< NL *leucorrhea.* See LEUCO-, -RRHEA] —**leu′kor·rhe′al, leu′kor·rhoe′al,** *adj.*

lev (lef), *n., pl.* **lev·a** (lev′ə). a coin and monetary unit of Bulgaria, equal to 100 stotinki. *Abbr.:* L., LV. [< Bulg: lit., lion, OBulg *livŭ,* prob. < OHG *lewo* < L *lēo*]

lev-, var. of **levo-** before a vowel: *levulose.*

Lev., Leviticus.

Le·val·loi·si·an (lev′ə loi′zē ən, -zhən), *adj.* of, pertaining to, or characteristic of a distinctive Middle Paleolithic culture. Also, **Le·val·lois** (lə val′wä). [LEVALLOIS (-PERRET) + -IAN]

Le·val·lois-Per·ret (lə VAL WA′pe RE′), *n.* a suburb of Paris, in N France, on the Seine. 61,962 (1962).

Le·vant (li vant′), *n.* **1.** the lands bordering the E shores of the Mediterranean and Aegean seas, esp. Syria, Lebanon, and Israel. **2.** Also called **Levant′ moroc′co.** a superior grade of morocco having a large and prominent grain, originally made in the Levant. **3.** levanter. [late ME *levaunt* < MF *levant,* n. use (with reference to rising sun) of prp. of *lever* to raise (*se lever* to rise). See LEVER]

Levant′ dol′lar, a silver coin, either a Maria Theresa thaler or an imitation of one, formerly used for trade with Abyssinia, Eritrea, Aden, etc.

le·vant·er (li van′tər), *n.* a strong easterly wind that blows in the Mediterranean.

Le·van·tine (lev′ən tīn′, -tēn′, li van′tin, -tīn), *adj.* **1.** of or pertaining to the Levant. —*n.* **2.** a native of the Levant. —**Lev′an·tin′ism,** *n.*

Levant′ sto′rax. See under **storax** (def. 2).

Levant′ worm′seed. See under **wormseed** (def. 1).

le·va·tor (li vā′tər, -tôr), *n., pl.* **lev·a·to·res** (lev′ə tôr′ēz, -tôr′-). **1.** *Anat.* a muscle that raises a part of the body. **2.** *Surg.* an instrument used to raise a depressed part of the skull. [< NL, special use of ML: one who raises (levies) recruits or taxes = L *levāt(us)* raised (ptp. of *levāre*) + *-or* -OR[2]]

lev·ee[1] (lev′ē), *n., v.,* **lev·eed, lev·ee·ing.** —*n.* **1.** *Phys. Geog.* an embankment designed to prevent the flooding of a river. **2.** *Agric.* one of the small continuous ridges surrounding fields that are to be irrigated. **3.** *Hist.* a landing place for vessels; a quay. —*v.t.* **4.** to furnish with a levee. [< F *levee* < ML *levāta* embankment, n. use of fem. ptp. of L *levāre* to raise, orig. lighten, akin to *levis* light, not heavy]

lev·ee[2] (lev′ē, le vē′), *n.* **1.** (in Great Britain) a public court assembly, held in the early afternoon, at which men only are received. **2.** a reception, usually in someone's honor. **3.** *Hist.* a reception of visitors held on rising from bed, as formerly by a royal personage. [< F *levé,* var. sp. of *lever* rising (n. use of inf.) < L *levāre* to raise (oneself); see LEVEE[1]]

lev·el (lev′əl), *adj., n., v.,* **-eled, -el·ing** or (*esp. Brit.*) **-elled, -el·ling,** *adv.* —*adj.* **1.** having an even surface, with no part higher than another. **2.** being in a plane parallel to the plane of the horizon; horizontal. **3.** equal, as in quality or importance. **4.** even, equable, or uniform. **5.** filled to a height even with the rim of a container: *a level teaspoon of salt.* **6.** **a level head,** balanced, calm judgment. **7. one's level best,** *Informal.* one's very best; one's utmost. —*n.* **8.** a device used for determining or adjusting something to a horizontal surface. **9.** *Survey.* **a.** an instrument for observing levels, having a sighting device, usually telescopic, and capable of being made precisely horizontal. **b.** an observation made with this instrument. **10.** an imaginary line or surface everywhere at right angles to the plumb line. **11.** the horizontal line or plane in which anything is situated, with regard to its elevation. **12.** a horizontal position or condition. **13.** an extent of level land. **14.** a level or flat surface. **15.** a position with respect to a given or specified height: *The water rose to a level of 30 feet.* **16.** a position in a graded scale of values; status; rank. **17.** an extent, measure, or degree of achievement. **18. find one's** or **one's own level,** to attain the place or position merited by one's abilities or achievements. **19. on the level,** *Informal.* honest; sincere. —*v.t.* **20.** to make (a surface) level or even. **21.** to raise or lower to a particular level or position. **22.** to bring (something) to the level of the ground: *to level trees.* **23.** *Informal.* to knock down (a person). **24.** to make (two or more things) equal, as in status, condition, etc.: *to level social classes.* **25.** to make even or uniform, as coloring. **26.** to aim or point (a weapon, criticism, etc.) at a mark or objective. **27.** *Survey.* to find the relative elevation of different points in (land), as with a level. **28.** *Archaic.* to turn (one's eyes) in a particular direction. —*v.i.* **29.** to bring things or persons to a common level. **30.** to aim a weapon, criticism, etc., at a mark or objective. **31.** *Survey.* **a.** to take a level. **b.** to use a leveling instrument. **32.** *Aeron.* to fly parallel to the ground, usually just before landing (usually fol. by *off*). **33.** *Slang.* to tell the truth (often fol. by *with*): *Level with me about that trip to Chicago.* **34.** *Obs.* to direct the mind, purpose, etc., at something. —*adv.* **35.** *Obs.* in a level, direct, or even way or line. [ME, var. of *livel* (n.) < MF < VL **lībell(um),* r. L *lībella* plummet line, level, dim. of *lībra* balance, scales, water level, pound (12 oz.)] —**lev′el·ly,** *adv.* —**lev′el·ness,** *n.*

—**Syn. 1, 2.** flush. LEVEL, FLAT, EVEN, SMOOTH suggest a uniform surface without marked unevenness. That which is LEVEL is parallel to the horizon: *a level surface; A billiard table must be level.* FLAT is applied to any plane surface free from marked irregularities: *a flat roof.* With reference to land or country, FLAT connotes lowness or unattractiveness. That which is EVEN is free from irregularities, though not necessarily level or plane: *an even land surface with no hills.* SMOOTH suggests a high degree of evenness in any surface, esp. to the touch and sometimes to the sight: *as smooth as silk.* **20.** smooth, flatten. **22.** raze, demolish. —**Ant. 1.** uneven.

lev·el·er (lev′ə lər), *n.* a person or thing that levels. Also, *esp. Brit.,* **leveller.**

lev·el-head·ed (lev′əl hed′id), *adj.* having common sense and sound judgment. —**lev′el-head′ed·ness,** *n.*

lev′eling rod′, *Survey.* rod (def. 17).

lev·el·ler (lev′ə lər), *n.* **1.** *Chiefly Brit.* leveler. **2.** (*cap.*) *Eng. Hist.* a member of a group organized during the Civil War and composed chiefly of former Parliamentarians advocating universal suffrage, a written constitution, and religious tolerance.

Le·ven (lē′vən), *n.* **Loch,** a lake in E Scotland.

lev·er (lev′ər, lē′vər), *n.* **1.** a bar or rigid body used to lift weight and operating on the principle that force or power applied at one point to lift a resistive weight or force at a second point tends to rotate the bar in opposite directions about a fixed axis or fulcrum. **2.** *Mach.* any rigid bar, straight or bent, that oscillates about a pivot and acts with other parts in the manner of a lever. —*v.t.,* **3.** to move with or as with a lever. [ME *levere, levour* for **lever* < OF *levier* < *lev(er)* (to) lift (< L *levāre* to lighten, lift < *levis* light) + *-ier* -ER[2]] —**lev′er·like′,** *adj.*

Le·ver (lē′vər), *n.* **Charles James** (pen name: *Cornelius O'Dowd*). 1806–72, Irish novelist and essayist.

lev·er·age (lev′ər ij, lē′vər ij), *n.* **1.** the action of a lever. **2.** the mechanical advantage or power gained by using a lever. **3.** power to act or influence. **4.** the potential to increase financial gains as a percentage of an investment or equity by operating or financing largely on borrowed funds. —*v.t.* **5.** to provide (an investment or equity) with operating or financing leverage.

lev′er escape′ment, *Horol.* an escapement in which a pivoted lever, made to oscillate by the escape wheel, engages a balance staff and causes it to oscillate.

lev·er·et (lev′ər it), *n.* a young hare. [late ME < MF *levrete,* dim. of *levre* < L *lepor-,* s. of *lepus* hare; see -ET]

Le·ver·hulme (lē′vər hyo͞om′), *n.* **Viscount** (*William Hesketh Lever*), 1851–1925, English manufacturer.

Le·ver·rier (lə ve RYĀ′), *n.* **Ur·bain Jean Jo·seph** (YR-BAN′ zhäN zhô zef′), 1811–77, French astronomer.

Le·vi (lē′vī), *n.* **1.** a son of Jacob and Leah. Gen. 29:34. **2.** one of the 12 tribes of Israel, traditionally descended from him. **3.** a Levite.

lev·i·a·ble (lev′ē ə bəl), *adj.* **1.** that may be levied. **2.** liable or subject to a levy. [late ME *levyable*]

le·vi·a·than (li vī′ə thən), *n.* **1.** *Bible.* a sea monster, possibly the crocodile. **2.** any huge marine animal, as the whale. **3.** anything of immense size and power, as an ocean liner. [ME *levyathan* < LL *leviathan* << Heb *liwyāthān*]

lev·i·gate (lev′ə gāt′), *v.,* **-gat·ed, -gat·ing,** *adj.* —*v.t.* **1.** to rub, grind, or reduce to a fine powder with or without the addition of a liquid. **2.** *Chem.* to make a homogeneous mixture of, as gels. —*adj.* **3.** *Bot.* having a smooth, glossy surface; glabrous. [< L *lēvigāt(us)* smoothed (ptp. of *lēvigāre;* see -ATE[1]), akin to *lēvis* smooth] —**lev′i·ga′tion,** *n.* —**lev′i·ga′tor,** *n.*

lev·in (lev′in), *n.* *Archaic.* lightning. [ME *levene;* c. Goth *lauhmuni;* akin to L *lūmen* light]

Le·vine (lə vēn′), *n.* **Jack,** born 1915, U.S. painter.

lev·i·rate (lev′ər it, -ə rāt′, lē′vər it, -və rāt′), *n.* *Judaism.* the custom of marriage between a man and his brother's widow, required in Biblical times under certain circumstances. Deut. 25:5–10. [< L *lēvir* husband's brother (akin to Gk *daḗr,* Skt *dēvar,* OE *tācor*) + -ATE[1]] —**lev·i·rat·ic** (lev′ə-rat′ik, lē′və-), **lev′i·rat′i·cal,** *adj.*

Le·vis (lē′vīz), *n.* *Trademark.* close-fitting trousers made of heavy denim or denimlike material.

Levit., Leviticus.

lev·i·tate (lev′i tāt′), *v.,* **-tat·ed, -tat·ing.** —*v.i.* **1.** to rise or float in the air, esp. as a result of a supposed supernatural power that overcomes gravity. —*v.t.* **2.** to cause to rise or float in the air. [LEVIT(Y) + -ATE[1], modeled on *gravitate*] —**lev′i·ta′tion,** *n.* —**lev′i·ta′tor,** *n.*

Le·vite (lē′vīt), *n.* **1.** a member of the tribe of Levi. **2.** a descendant of Levi, esp. one appointed to assist the priests in the temple or tabernacle, and now having essentially honorific religious duties and prerogatives. [ME < LL *levīt(a)* < Gk *leuítēs* Levite = *Leuí* (< Heb *Lēvī* Levi, Levite) + *-tēs* suffix of appurtenance]

Le·vit·i·cal (li vit′i kəl), *adj.* **1.** of or pertaining to the Levites. **2.** of or pertaining to Leviticus or the law contained in Leviticus (**Levit′ical law′**). [< LL *Lēvitic(us)* (see LEVITICUS) + -AL[1]] —**Le·vit′i·cal·ly,** *adv.*

Le·vit·i·cus (li vit′ə kəs), *n.* the third book of the Bible, containing laws relating chiefly to Jewish ceremonial observance. [< LL *Lēviticus* (*liber*) Levitical (book) < Gk *Leuïtikós*]

Lev·it·town (lev′it toun′), *n.* a town on W Long Island, in SE New York. 65,440 (1970).

lev·i·ty (lev′i tē), *n., pl.* **-ties.** **1.** lightness of mind, character, or behavior. **2.** an instance or exhibition of this. **3.** fickleness. **4.** lightness in weight. [< L *levitās* lightness, frivolity = *levi(s)* light + *-tās* -TY[2]] —**Syn. 1, 2.** frivolity, flippancy, triviality, giddiness.

Lev·kas (lef käs′), *n.* an island in the Ionian group, off the W coast of Greece. 28,980 (1961); 114 sq. mi. Also, **Leucas, Leukas.** Italian, **Santa Maura.**

le·vo (lē′vō), *adj.* levorotatory. Also, **laevo.** [by shortening]

levo-, a combining form meaning "left," often used to denote a substance which rotates the plane of polarized light to the left: *levorotation.* Also, **laevo-, lev-.** [repr. L *laevus* left, on the left]

le·vo·gy·rate (lē′və jī′rāt), *adj.* *Optics, Chem.* levorotatory. Also, **laevogyrate, le·vo·gyre** (lē′vō jīər′).

le·vo·ro·ta·tion (lē′vō rō tā′shən), *n.* *Optics, Crystall.* a turning to the left of the plane of polarization.

le·vo·ro·ta·to·ry (lē′və rō′tə tōr′ē, -tôr′ē), *adj.* *Optics, Chem., Crystall.* turning to the left, as the rotation of the plane of polarization of light in certain crystals and compounds; levogyrate. Also, **le·vo·ro·ta·ry** (lē′vō rō′tə rē). Cf. **dextrorotatory.**

lev′u·lin′ic ac′id (lev′yə lin′ik, lev′-), *Chem.* a solid, $CH_3CO(CH_2)_2COOH$, used in the organic synthesis of nylon, plastics, etc. [LEVUL(OSE) + -IN[2] + -IC]

lev·u·lose (lev′yə lōs′), *n.* *Chem.* fructose.

lev·y (lev′ē), *n., pl.* **lev·ies,** *v.,* **lev·ied, lev·y·ing.** —*n.* **1.** a raising or collecting, as of money or troops, by authority or force. **2.** a person or thing that is collected in this manner. —*v.t.* **3.** to make a levy of; collect. **4.** to impose (a tax). **5.** to conscript or enlist (troops) for service. **6.** to start or make (war). —*v.i.* **7.** to make a levy. **8.** *Law.* to seize or attach property by judicial order. [late ME *levee* < MF, n. use of fem. ptp. of *lever* to raise. See LEVEE[1]] —**lev′i·er,** *n.*

lewd (lōōd), *adj.* **1.** inclined to, characterized by, or inciting to lust or lechery. **2.** obscene or indecent, as language or songs. **3.** *Obs.* **a.** low or vulgar. **b.** (of a person) base or vile. [ME *leud, lewed,* OE *lǣwde* lay, unlearned] —**lewd′ly,** *adv.* —**lewd′ness,** *n.*

Lew·es (lōō′is), *n.* **1. George Henry,** 1817–78, English writer and critic. **2.** a city in central Sussex, in SE England: battle 1264. 76,400.

lew·is (lōō′is), *n.* a device for lifting a dressed stone, consisting of a number of pieces fitting together to fill a dovetailed recess cut into the stone. Also called **lewisson.** [named after its inventor]

Lewis

Lew·is (lōō′is), *n.* **1. C(ecil) Day,** 1904–72, British poet: poet laureate after 1968. **2. C(live) S(ta·ples)** (stā′pəlz), (pen name: *Clive Hamilton*), 1898–1963, English novelist and essayist. **3. Gilbert Newton,** 1875–1946, U.S. chemist. **4. Isaac Newton,** 1858–1931, U.S. soldier and inventor. **5. John L(lewellyn),** 1880–1969, U.S. labor leader. **6. Matthew Gregory** ("*Monk Lewis*"), 1775–1809, English novelist, dramatist, and poet. **7. Mer·i·weth·er** (mer′i weth′ər), 1774–1809, U.S. explorer: leader of the Lewis and Clark expedition 1804–06. **8. (Percy) Wynd·ham** (win′dəm), 1884–1957, English novelist, essayist, and painter; born in the U.S. **9. Sinclair,** 1885–1951, U.S. novelist: Nobel prize 1930.

Lew′is ac′id, *Chem.* any substance capable of forming a covalent bond with a base by accepting a pair of electrons from it. [named after G. N. LEWIS]

Lew′is base′, *Chem.* any substance capable of forming a covalent bond with an acid by transferring a pair of electrons to it. [named after G. N. LEWIS]

Lew′is gun′, a light, air-cooled machine gun with a circular magazine, for operation by one man. Also called **Lew′is automat′ic, Lew′is machine′ gun′.** [named after I. N. LEWIS]

lew·is·ite (lōō′i sīt′), *n.* a chemical-warfare agent, $ClCH{=}CHAsCl_2$, characterized by its vesicant action. [named after Winford Lee *Lewis* (1878–1943), American chemist who developed it; see -ITE[1]]

lew·is·son (lōō′i sən), *n.* lewis.

Lew·is·ton (lōō′i stən), *n.* **1.** a city in SW Maine, on the Androscoggin River. 41,779 (1970). **2.** a city in W Idaho. 26,068 (1970).

Lew′is with Har′ris, the northernmost island of the Hebrides, in NW Scotland. 23,188; 825 sq. mi.

lex (leks), *n., pl.* **le·ges** (lē′jēz; *Lat.* le′ges). law[1]. [< L]

lex., **1.** lexical. **2.** lexicon.

lex·i·cal (lek′si kəl), *adj.* **1.** of or pertaining to the words or vocabulary of a language, esp. as contrasted with its grammatical and syntactical aspects. **2.** of, pertaining to, or of the nature of a lexicon. [LEXIC(ON) + -AL[1]] —**lex′i·cal′i·ty,** *n.* —**lex′i·cal·ly,** *adv.*

lex′ical mean′ing, the meaning of a base morpheme. Cf. **grammatical meaning.**

lexicog., **1.** lexicographer. **2.** lexicographical. **3.** lexicography.

lex·i·cog·ra·pher (lek′sə kog′rə fər), *n.* a writer or compiler of a dictionary. [< LGk *lexikográph(os)* (see LEXICON, -GRAPH) + -ER[1]]

lex·i·cog·ra·phy (lek′sə kog′rə fē), *n.* the writing or compiling of dictionaries. [LEXICO(N) + -GRAPHY] —**lex·i·co·graph·ic** (lek′sə kō graf′ik, -sə kə-), **lex′i·co·graph′i·cal,** *adj.* —**lex′i·co·graph′i·cal·ly,** *adv.*

lex·i·con (lek′sə kon′, -kən), *n., pl.* **lex·i·ca** (lek′sə kə), **lex·i·cons.** **1.** a wordbook or dictionary, esp. of Greek, Latin, or Hebrew. **2.** the vocabulary of a particular language, field, social class, person, etc. **3.** inventory or record: *unparalleled in the lexicon of human relations.* **4.** *Linguistics.* the total inventory of morphemes in a given language. [< ML < MGk, Gk *lexikón,* n. use of neut. of *lexikós* of words = *léx(is)* speech, word (akin to *légein* to speak) + *-ikos* -IC]

lex·i·co·sta·tis·tics (lek′sə kō stə tis′tiks), *n.* (*construed as sing.*) *Linguistics.* the statistical study of the vocabulary of a language or languages for historical purposes. Cf. **glottochronology.** [LEXICO(N) + STATISTICS] —**lex′i·co·sta·tis′tic, lex′i·co·sta·tis′ti·cal,** *adj.*

Lex·ing·ton (lek′sing tən), *n.* **1.** a town in E Massachusetts, NW of Boston: first battle of American Revolution fought here April 19, 1775. 31,886 (1970). **2.** a city in N Kentucky. 108,137 (1970).

lex lo·ci (leks lō′sī, -kē), *Law.* the law of a place. [< L]

lex non scrip·ta (leks non skrip′tə, nōn), *Law.* unwritten law; common law. [< L]

lex scrip·ta (leks skrip′tə), *Law.* written law; statute law. [< L]

lex ta·li·o·nis (leks tal′ē ō′nis), the principle or law that punishment should correspond in degree and kind to the offense, as an eye for an eye. Also called **talion.** [< L: law of talion]

ley[1] (lā, lē), *n.* lea[1].

ley[2] (lā), *n.* leu.

Ley·den (līd′ən), *n.* **1. Lu·cas van** (lōō′käs vän), (*Lucas Hugensz*), 1489?–1533, Dutch painter and engraver. **2.** Leiden.

Ley′den jar′, *Elect.* a device for storing electric charge, consisting essentially of a glass jar lined inside and outside, for about two thirds of its height, with tin foil. [so called because invented in Leiden]

Ley·te (lā′tē; *Sp.* lā′te), *n.* an island in the central Philippines. 1,146,000 (est. 1965); 3085 sq. mi.

Ley·ton (lāt′ən), *n.* a city in SE England, near London. 93,857 (1961).

LF, See **low frequency.**

lf., *Baseball.* left fielder.

l.f., **1.** *Baseball.* left field. **2.** *Printing.* Also, **lf** lightface.

LG, Low German (def. 1). Also, **L.G.**

lg., **1.** large. **2.** long.

l.g., *Football.* left guard.

L. Ger., **1.** Low German. **2.** Low Germanic.

LGk, Late Greek. Also, **LGk., L.Gk.**

lgth., length.

lg. tn., long ton.

l.h., left hand. Also, **L.H.**

Lha·sa (lä′sə, -sä, las′ə), *n.* a city in and the capital of Tibet, in the SE part: sacred city of Lamaism. 175,000; ab. 12,000 ft. above sea level. Also, **Lassa.**

l.h.b., *Football.* left halfback.

li (lē), *n., pl.* **li.** a Chinese unit of distance, equivalent to about one third of a mile. [< Chin]

Li, *Chem.* lithium.

L.I., Long Island.

li·a·bil·i·ty (lī′ə bil′i tē), *n., pl.* **-ties.** **1. liabilities, a.** moneys owed; debts or pecuniary obligations (opposed to *assets*). **b.** *Accounting.* liabilities as detailed on a balance sheet, esp. in relation to assets and capital. **2.** something disadvantageous. **3.** Also, **li′a·ble·ness.** the state or quality of being liable: *liability to disease.*

li·a·ble (lī′ə bəl), *adj.* **1.** subject, exposed, or open to something possible or likely. **2.** legally responsible. [< AF *li(er)* (to) bind (< L *ligāre*) + -ABLE] —**Syn. 1.** See **likely.**

li·ai·son (lē′ā zôn′, lē′ə zon′, -zən; lē ā′zən, -zon; *Fr.* lye zôɴ′), *n., pl.* **-sons** (-zônz′, -zonz′, -zənz, -zonz; *Fr.* -zôɴ′). **1.** *Mil.* the contact maintained between units to ensure concerted action. **2.** a similar connection or relation maintained between the units of any organization. **3.** an illicit, sexual relationship between a man and a woman. **4.** *Phonet.* the pronunciation, sometimes slightly changed, of an otherwise silent final consonant when the first sound of the next word is a vowel, as the pronunciation, in French, of the *s* in *les* in *les arbres* (lā zär′brᵊ) or the *d* in *grand* in *grand homme* (gräɴ tôm′). [< F, OF < L *ligātiōn-* (s. of *ligātiō*) a binding. See LIGATURE, -ION]

Lia·kou·ra (*Gk.* lyä′kōō rä), *n.* modern name of Mount Parnassus.

li·a·na (lē ä′nə, -an′ə), *n.* a climbing plant or vine. Also, **li·ane** (lē än′). [earlier *liannes* (pl.), appar. misspelling of F *lianes,* pl. of *liane*] —**li·a′noid,** *adj.*

liang (lyäng, lyang), *n., pl.* **liang, liangs.** a Chinese unit of weight, equal to 1/16 catty, and equivalent to about 1⅓ ounces. Also called **tael.** [< Chin]

Liao (lyou), *n.* a river in NE China, flowing through S Manchuria into the Gulf of Liaotung. 700 mi. long.

Liao·ning (lyou′ning′), *n.* a province in S Manchuria, in NE China. 29,500,000; 58,301 sq. mi. *Cap.:* Shenyang. Formerly, **Fengtien.**

Liao·peh (lyou′bā′), *n.* a former province in Manchuria, in NE China. 47,612 sq. mi.

Liao·tung (lyou′dōōng′), *n.* **1.** a peninsula in Manchuria, in NE China, extending S into the Yellow Sea. **2. Gulf of,** a gulf W of this peninsula.

Liao·yang (lyou′yäng′), *n.* a city in S Manchuria, in NE China, SW of Mukden. 250,000.

li·ar (lī′ər), *n.* a person who tells lies. [ME *lier,* OE *lēogere*]

li·ard (lē är′; *Fr.* lē aʀ′), *n., pl.* **li·ards** (lē ärz′; *Fr.* lē aʀ′). a former silver coin of France, the fourth part of a sol, issued from the 15th century to 1793. [named after G. *Liard,* 15th-century French minter]

Li·ard (lē′ärd, lē ärd′, -är′), *n.* a river in W Canada, flowing from S Yukon into the Mackenzie River. 550 mi. long.

Li·as (lī′əs), *n.* *Stratig.* the lowermost main part of the European Jurassic. [late ME *lyas* a kind of limestone < MF *liois,* prob. akin to *lie* dregs. See LEE[2]] —**Li·as·sic** (lī as′ik), *adj.*

lib (lib), *n.* *Informal.* liberation, esp. as a social reform: *women's lib; gay lib.* [by shortening] —**lib′ber,** *n.*

Lib., Liberal.

lib., **1.** book. [< L *liber*] **2.** librarian. **3.** library.

li·ba·tion (lī bā′shən), *n.* **1.** a pouring out of wine or other liquid in honor of a deity. **2.** the liquid poured out. **3.** *Often Facetious.* **a.** an intoxicating beverage, as wine. **b.** an act or instance of drinking such a beverage. [ME *libacio(u)n* < L *lībātiōn-* (s. of *lībātiō*) a drink offering = *lībāt(us)* poured (ptp. of *lībāre;* c. Gk *leíbein*) + *-iōn-* -ION] —**li·ba′tion·al, li·ba′tion·ar′y,** *adj.*

Li·bau (lē′bou), *n.* German name of **Liepāja.**

Li·ba·va (li bä′vä), *n.* Russian name of **Liepāja.**

Lib·by (lib′ē), *n.* **Willard Frank,** 1908–80, U.S. chemist.

li·bel (lī′bəl), *n., v.,* **-beled, -bel·ing** or (*esp. Brit.*) **-belled, -bel·ling.** —*n.* **1.** *Law.* **a.** defamation by written or printed words, pictures, or in any form other than by spoken words or gestures. **b.** the crime of publishing it. **2.** anything that is defamatory or that maliciously or damagingly misrepresents. —*v.t.* **3.** to publish a libel against. **4.** to misrepresent damagingly. [ME: little book, formal document, esp. plaintiff's statement < L *libell(us),* dim. of *liber* book]

li·bel·ant (lī′bə lənt), *n.* *Law.* a person who libels. Also, *esp. Brit.,* **li′bel·lant.**

li·bel·er (lī′bə lər), *n.* a person who libels; a person who publishes a libel assailing another. Also, *esp. Brit.,* **li′bel·ler.**

li·bel·ous (lī′bə ləs), *adj.* containing, constituting, or involving a libel; maliciously defamatory. Also, *esp. Brit.,* **li′bel·lous.** —**li′bel·ous·ly;** *esp. Brit.,* **li′bel·lous·ly,** *adv.*

li·ber[1] (lī′bər), *n.* *Bot.* phloem. [< L: bark]
li·ber[2] (lī′bər; *Lat.* li′beʀ), *n.*, *pl.* **li·bri** (lī′brī; *Lat.* li′bʀē), **li·bers.** a book of public records, as deeds, birth certificates, etc. [< L: book, orig. bark; see LIBER[1]]
lib·er·al (lib′ər əl, lib′rəl), *adj.* **1.** favorable to progress or reform, as in religious or political affairs. **2.** (*often cap.*) noting or pertaining to a political party advocating measures of progressive political reform. **3.** of or pertaining to representational forms of government rather than aristocracies and monarchies. **4.** of, pertaining to, based on, or advocating liberalism. **5.** favorable to or in accord with concepts of maximum individual freedom possible, esp. as guaranteed by law and secured by governmental protection of civil liberties. **6.** favoring or permitting freedom of action, esp. with respect to matters of personal belief or expression. **7.** free from prejudice or bigotry; tolerant. **8.** open-minded or tolerant, esp. free of or not bound by traditional or conventional ideas, values, etc. **9.** characterized by generosity and willingness to give in large amounts. **10.** given freely or abundantly. **11.** not strict or rigorous; free; not literal. **12.** of, pertaining to, or befitting a freeman. —*n.* **13.** a person of liberal principles or views. **14.** (*often cap.*) a member of a liberal party in politics, esp. of the Liberal party in Great Britain. [ME < L *līberāl(is)* of freedom, befitting the free = *līber* free + *-ālis* -AL[1]] —**lib′er·al·ly,** *adv.* —**lib′er·al·ness,** *n.* —**Syn. 1.** progressive. **7.** unprejudiced. **9.** generous, munificent. **10.** See **ample.** —**Ant. 1.** reactionary. **7.** intolerant.
lib′eral arts′, the course of instruction at a college granting an academic degree, comprising the arts, natural sciences, social sciences, and the humanities. [trans. of L *artēs līberālēs* work befitting a free man]
lib′eral educa′tion, an education based primarily on the liberal arts.
lib·er·al·ise (lib′ər ə līz′, lib′rə-), *v.t., v.i.,* **-ised, -is·ing.** *Chiefly Brit.* liberalize. —**lib′er·al·i·sa′tion,** *n.* —**lib′er·al·is′er,** *n.*
lib·er·al·ism (lib′ər ə liz′əm, lib′rə-), *n.* **1.** the quality or state of being liberal, as in behavior, attitude, etc. **2.** (*sometimes cap.*) the principles and practices of a liberal party in politics. **3.** a political or social philosophy advocating the freedom of the individual, and governmental guarantees of individual rights and civil liberties. **4.** a movement in modern Protestantism that emphasizes freedom from tradition and authority in matters of belief. —**lib′er·al·ist,** *n., adj.* —**lib′er·al·is′tic,** *adj.*
lib·er·al·i·ty (lib′ə ral′i tē), *n., pl.* **-ties. 1.** the quality or condition of being liberal in giving; generosity; bounty. **2.** a liberal gift. **3.** breadth of mind. **4.** broadness or fullness, as of proportions, physical attributes, etc. **5.** liberalism. [ME *liberalite* < L *līberālitās*]
lib·er·al·ize (lib′ər ə līz′, lib′rə-), *v.t., v.i.,* **-ized, -iz·ing.** to make or become liberal. Also, *esp. Brit.,* **liberalise.** —**lib′er·al·i·za′tion,** *n.* —**lib′er·al·iz′er,** *n.*
Lib′eral par′ty, 1. a political party in Great Britain, formed about 1830 and constituting one of the dominant British parties in the 19th century and early part of the 20th century. **2.** an American third party, formed in 1944 by labor-union members, intellectuals, and professional people and operating chiefly in New York State, that seeks to further liberal causes.
lib·er·ate (lib′ə rāt′), *v.t.,* **-at·ed, -at·ing. 1.** to set free, as from bondage; release. **2.** to disengage; set free from combination, as a gas. [< L *līberāt(us)* freed (ptp. of *līberāre*). See LIBERAL, -ATE[1]] —**lib′er·a′tion,** *n.* —**lib′er·a′tive, lib·er·a·to·ry** (lib′ər ə tōr′ē, -tôr′ē), *adj.* —**lib′er·a′tor,** *n.* —**Syn. 1.** deliver, loose. See **release.** —**Ant. 1.** imprison; enthrall.
Li·be·rec (li′be ʀets), *n.* a city in NW Czechoslovakia. 68,603 (1963). German, **Reichenberg.**
Li·be·ri·a (lī bēr′ē ə), *n.* a republic in W Africa: founded by freed American slaves 1822. 1,554,000; ab. 43,000 sq. mi. *Cap.:* Monrovia. —**Li·be′ri·an,** *adj., n.*
Li·be·ri·us (lī bēr′ē əs), *n.* died A.D. 366, pope 352–366.
lib·er·tar·i·an (lib′ər târ′ē ən), *n.* **1.** a person who advocates liberty, esp. with regard to thought or conduct. **2.** a person who maintains the doctrine of free will (distinguished from *necessitarian*). —*adj.* **3.** advocating liberty or conforming to principles of liberty. **4.** maintaining the doctrine of free will. —**lib′er·tar′i·an·ism,** *n.*
li·ber·té, é·ga·li·té, fra·ter·ni·té (lē beʀ tā′, ā gȧ lē-tā′, fʀȧ teʀ nē tā′), *French.* Liberty, Equality, Fraternity: motto of the French Revolution.
li·ber·ti·cide (li bûr′ti sīd′), *n.* **1.** destruction of liberty. **2.** a person who destroys liberty. —**li·ber′ti·cid′al,** *adj.*
lib·er·tin·age (lib′ər tē′nij, -tin ij), *n.* libertine conduct, esp. in sexual or religious matters.
lib·er·tine (lib′ər tēn′, -tin), *n.* **1.** a person who is morally or sexually unrestrained; profligate; rake. **2.** a person freed from slavery in ancient Rome. —*adj.* **3.** free of moral, esp. sexual, restraint; dissolute; licentious. **4.** *Archaic.* unrestrained; uncontrolled. [ME *libertyn* < L *lībertīn(us)* of a freedman (adj.), freedman (n.) = *lībert(us)* freedman (*lībert(ās)* LIBERTY + *-us* masc. n. suffix) + *-īnus* -INE[1]] —**Syn. 1.** roué, debauchee, lecher, sensualist. **3.** amoral, sensual, lascivious, lewd. —**Ant. 1.** prude.
lib·er·tin·ism (lib′ər tē niz′əm, -ti-), *n.* libertine practices or habits of life; disregard of authority or convention, esp. in sexual matters.
lib·er·ty (lib′ər tē), *n., pl.* **-ties. 1.** freedom from despotic government or rule. **2.** freedom from foreign rule; independence. **3.** freedom from bondage, captivity, or physical restraint. **4.** freedom from external control or interference, obligation, etc.; freedom to choose. **5.** Often, **liberties.** an act of impertinence, presumption, or excessive familiarity. **6.** See **shore leave. 7.** the freedom or right to be in or use a place. **8. at liberty, a.** free from captivity or restraint. **b.** unemployed; out of work. **c.** free to do or be as specified. [ME *liberte* < MF < L *lībertās.* See LIBERAL, -TY[2]] —**Syn. 3.** liberation. See **freedom. 7.** franchise, permission, license, privilege, immunity.
Lib′erty Bell′, the bell of Independence Hall in Philadelphia, rung on July 8, 1776 to proclaim the signing of the Declaration of Independence.
lib′erty cap′, a soft, conical cap given to a freed slave in ancient Rome at release from his servitude, used as a symbol of liberty, esp. since the 18th century. Cf. **Phrygian cap.**
Lib′erty Is′land, a small island in upper New York Bay: site of the Statue of Liberty. Formerly, **Bedloe's Island.**
Lib′erty ship′, a type of cargo ship built in large numbers by the U.S. during World War II, having a capacity of about 11,000 deadweight tons.
Li·bia (lē′byä), *n.* Italian name of **Libya.**
li·bid·i·nous (li bid′ᵊnəs), *adj.* **1.** of, pertaining to, or characteristic of the libido. **2.** full of lust; lustful; lewd. [late ME *lybydynous* < L *libīdinōs(us)* willful, lustful = *libīdin-* (s. of *libīdō*) LIBIDO + *-ōsus* -OUS] —**li·bid′i·nous·ly,** *adv.* —**li·bid′i·nous·ness,** *n.*
li·bi·do (li bē′dō, -bī′dō), *n.* **1.** *Psychoanal.* all of the instinctual energies and desires that are derived from the id. **2.** the sexual instinct. [< L: desire, lust, akin to *libēre* to like] —**li·bid·i·nal** (li bid′ᵊnᵊl), *adj.* —**li·bid′i·nal·ly,** *adv.*
li·bra[1] (lī′brə), *n., pl.* **-brae** (-brē). the ancient Roman pound (containing 5053 grains). [< L]
li·bra[2] (lē′brä), *n., pl.* **-bras.** sol[3] (def. 2). [< Sp < L]
Li·bra (lī′brə, lē′-), *n., gen.* **-brae** (-brē) for 1. **1.** *Astron.* the Balance, a zodiacal constellation. **2.** *Astrol.* the seventh sign of the zodiac. See diag. at **zodiac.** [< L: lit., pair of scales]
li·brar·i·an (lī brâr′ē ən), *n.* **1.** a person trained for and engaged in library service. **2.** an officer in charge of a library. **3.** a person who is in charge of any specialized body of literature. —**li·brar′i·an·ship′,** *n.*
li·brar·y (lī′brer′ē, -brə rē, -brē), *n., pl.* **-brar·ies. 1.** a place, as a room or building, containing books and other material for reading, study, or reference. **2.** a public body organizing and maintaining such an establishment. **3.** a commercial establishment lending books for a fixed charge; a rental library. **4.** a collection of manuscripts, publications, and other materials for reading, study, enjoyment, or reference. **5.** a series of books of similar character or alike in size, binding, etc., issued by a single publishing house. **6.** *Computer Technol.* a collection of standard programs, routines, and subroutines available for solving a variety of computer problems. [ME *libraire* < MF *librairie* < ML *librāria,* n. use of fem. of L *librārius* (adj.) of books. See LIBER[2], -ARY]
li′brary bind′ing, a tough, durable cloth binding for books.
li′brary card′, a card issued by a library entitling individuals to borrow its books.
Li′brary of Con′gress, the national library of the U.S. in Washington, D.C.
li′brary paste′, a white, thick, smooth paste.
li′brary sci′ence, the study of the organization and administration of a library and of its services.
li·brate (lī′brāt), *v.i.,* **-brat·ed, -brat·ing. 1.** to oscillate or move from side to side or between two points. **2.** to remain poised or balanced. [< L *lībrāt(us)* balanced, poised, ptp. of *lībrāre.* See LIBRA, -ATE[1]]
li·bra·tion (lī brā′shən), *n.* *Astron.* a real or apparent oscillatory motion, esp. of the moon. [< L *lībrātiōn-* (s. of *lībrātiō*) a balancing] —**li·bra′tion·al,** *adj.*
li·bra·to·ry (lī′brə tōr′ē, -tôr′ē), *adj.* oscillatory.
li·bret·tist (li bret′ist), *n.* the writer of a libretto. [< It *librettist(a)*]
li·bret·to (li bret′ō), *n., pl.* **-bret·tos, -bret·ti** (-bret′ē). **1.** the text of an opera or similar extended musical composition. **2.** a book or booklet containing such a text. [< It, dim of *libro* book. See LIBER[2], -ET]
Li·bre·ville (*Fr.* lē bre vēl′), *n.* a port in and the capital of Gabon, in the W part, on the Gulf of Guinea. 60,000.
li·bri (lī′brī; *Lat.* li′bʀē), *n.* pl. of **liber**[2].
li·bri·form (lī′brə fôrm′), *adj.* *Bot.* having the form of or resembling liber or phloem. [LIB(E)R[1] + -I- + -FORM]
Lib·y·a (lib′ē ə), *n.* **1.** *Anc. Geog.* the part of N Africa W of Egypt. **2.** Italian, **Libia.** a republic in N Africa between Tunisia and the Arab Republic of Egypt. 2,800,000; 679,400 sq. mi. *Capitals:* Tripoli *and* Benghazi.
Lib·y·an (lib′ē ən), *adj.* **1.** of or pertaining to Libya or its inhabitants. —*n.* **2.** a native or inhabitant of Libya. **3.** a Berber language of ancient Libya.
Lib′yan Des′ert, a desert in N Africa, in E Libya, W Arab Republic of Egypt, and NW Sudan, W of the Nile: part of the Sahara. ab. 650,000 sq. mi.
lice (līs), *n.* pl. of **louse.**
li·cence (lī′səns), *n., v.t.* **-cenced, -cenc·ing.** license. —**li′cence·a·ble,** *adj.*
li·cense (lī′səns), *n., v.,* **-censed, -cens·ing.** —*n.* **1.** formal permission from a constituted authority to do a specified thing, as to carry on some business, drive a car, etc. **2.** a certificate of such permission; an official permit. **3.** intentional deviation from rule, convention, or fact, as for the sake of literary or artistic effect. **4.** excessive or undue freedom or liberty, esp. licentiousness. **5.** the legal right to use a patent owned by another. —*v.t.* **6.** to issue or grant authoritative permission or license to or for. [ME *licence* < MF < ML *licentia* authorization, L: freedom = *licent-* (s. of *licēns,* prp. of *licēre* to be allowed) + *-ia* -IA; see -ENCE] —**li′cens·er;** *esp. Law,* **li′cen·sor,** *n.*
li·cen·see (lī′sən sē′), *n.* a person to whom a license is granted or issued. Also, **li′cen·cee′.**
li′cense plate′, a plate or tag, usually of metal, bearing evidence of official registration and permission, as for the use of an automobile, the keeping of a pet, etc.
li·cen·ti·ate (lī sen′shē it, -āt′), *n.* **1.** a person who has received a license, as from a university, to practice an art or profession. **2.** the holder of a university degree intermediate between that of bachelor and that of doctor, and granted by certain European universities. [< ML *licentiāt(us)* authorized (person), ptp. of *licentiāre.* See LICENSE, -ATE[1]] —**li·cen′ti·ate·ship′,** *n.* —**li·cen′ti·a′tion,** *n.*
li·cen·tious (lī sen′shəs), *adj.* **1.** sexually unrestrained; lewd. **2.** unrestrained by law or morality; lawless; immoral. **3.** going beyond customary or proper bounds or limits. [< L *licentiōs(us)* arbitrary. See LICENSE, -OUS] —**li·cen′tious·ly,** *adv.* —**li·cen′tious·ness,** *n.* —**Syn. 2.** abandoned, profligate. —**Ant. 2.** lawful.
li·chee (lē′chē′), *n.* litchi.
li·chen (lī′kən), *n.* **1.** any compound, thallophytic plant of the group *Lichenes* composed of a fungus in symbiotic

union with an alga, and having thallus growing in leaflike, crustlike, or branching forms on rocks, trees, etc. **2.** *Pathol.* any of various eruptive skin diseases. **—*v.t.*** **3.** to cover with or as with lichens. [< L < Gk *leichēn*] **—li′chen·like′,** *adj.* **—li′chen·oid′,** *adj.* **—li′chen·ous, li·chen·ose** (lī′kə nōs′), *adj.*

li·chen·ol·o·gy (lī′kə nol′ə jē), *n.* the branch of botany dealing with lichens. **—li·chen·o·log·ic** (lī′kə nəloj′ik), **li′chen·o·log′i·cal,** *adj.* **—li′chen·ol′o·gist,** *n.*

Lich·field (lich′fēld′), *n.* a town in SE Staffordshire, in central England, N of Birmingham: birthplace of Samuel Johnson. 87,700.

lich′ gate′ (lich), (esp. in England) a roofed gate to a churchyard under which a bier is set down during a funeral to await the coming of the clergyman. Also, **lych gate.** [ME *liche* body, OE *līc;* c. D *lijk,* Icel lík, Goth *leik.* See LIKE[1]]

li·chi (lē′chē), *n., pl.* **-chis.** litchi.

licht (likHt), *n., adj., v.t., v.i., adv.* *Scot.* light. **—licht′ly,** *adv.*

lic·it (lis′it), *adj.* legal; lawful; permitted. [< L *licit(us)* permitted (ptp. of *licēre*); r. late ME *licite* < MF; see -ITE[2]] **—lic′it·ly,** *adv.*

lick (lik), *v.t.* **1.** to pass the tongue over the surface of. **2.** to remove (glue, food, etc.) from a surface by licking (often fol. by *up, off, from,* etc.). **3.** (of waves, flames, etc.) to pass or play lightly over. **4.** *Informal.* **a.** to hit, esp. as a punishment; beat; thrash. **b.** to overcome, as in a fight; defeat. **c.** to outdo or surpass. **5. lick into shape,** *Informal.* to bring to completion or perfection, esp. through hard work. **6. lick someone's boots.** See **boot**[1] (def. 15). **—*n.*** **7.** a stroke of the tongue over something. **8.** the amount taken up by one stroke of the tongue. **9.** See **salt lick. 10.** *Informal.* **a.** a blow. **b.** a brief, brisk burst of activity or energy. **c.** a quick pace or clip; speed. **d.** a small amount: *a lick of work.* **11. lick and a promise,** *Informal.* a hasty and perfunctory doing of something. [ME *licke(n),* OE *liccian;* c. D *likk,* G *lecken;* akin to Goth *(bi)laigon,* L *lingere,* Gk *leíchein* to lick (up)] **—lick′er,** *n.*
—Syn. 10a. thwack, thump, rap, slap, cuff, buffet.

lick·er·ish (lik′ər ish), *adj.* *Archaic.* **1.** fond of and eager for choice food. **2.** greedy; longing. **3.** lustful; lecherous. Also, **liquorish.** [ME *liker(ous)* pleasing to the taste, lit., to a licker (see LICK, -ER[1]) + -ISH[1]] **—lick′er·ish·ly,** *adv.* **—lick′er·ish·ness,** *n.*

lick·e·ty-split (lik′i tē split′), *adv.* *Informal.* at great speed; rapidly. [? dial. *licket* rag (for wiping in haste, with one lick) + -Y[1] + SPLIT, as in *split second*]

lick·ing (lik′ing), *n.* **1.** *Informal.* **a.** a beating or thrashing. **b.** a reversal or disappointment; setback. **2.** the act of a person or thing that licks. [ME]

lick·spit·tle (lik′spit′əl), *n.* a contemptible, fawning person; a flatterer or toady. Also, **lick′spit′.**

lic·o·rice (lik′ə ris, -ər ish, lik′rish), *n.* **1.** a leguminous plant, *Glycyrrhiza glabra,* of Europe and Asia. **2.** the sweet-tasting, dried root of this plant or an extract made from it, used in medicine, confectionery, etc. **3.** any of various related or similar plants. **4.** a confection having a licorice flavor. Also, **liquorice.** [ME *lycorys* < AF < LL *liquirītia* for L *glycyrrhīza* < Gk *glykýrrhiza* sweetroot (plant). See GLYCO-, RHIZO-, -IA]

lic·tor (lik′tər), *n.* (in ancient Rome) a magistrate's attendant who carried the fasces in processions. [< L] **—lic·to·ri·an** (lik tōr′ē ən, -tôr′-), *adj.*

lid (lid), *n.* **1.** a movable piece, separate or hinged, for closing the opening, usually at the top, of a jar, trunk, etc.; a movable cover. **2.** an eyelid. **3.** (in mosses) **a.** the cover of the capsule; operculum. **b.** the upper section of a pyxidium. **4. blow the lid off,** *Slang.* to expose to public view, esp. to reveal something scandalous, illegal, etc. **5. flip one's lid,** *Slang.* **a.** to lose control; become hysterical. **b.** to go insane. [ME; OE *hlid;* c. D, G *lid,* Icel *hlith*] **—lid′ded,** *adj.*

Lid·del Hart (lid′əl härt′), **Basil Henry,** 1895–1970, English military authority and writer.

Li·di·ce (li′dyi tse; *Eng.* lē′də chā′, lid′i sē), *n.* a village in Czechoslovakia: destroyed by the Nazis in 1942 in revenge for the assassination of a high Nazi official.

lid·less (lid′lis), *adj.* **1.** (of objects) without a lid. **2.** (of eyes) without or as if without lids. **3.** vigilant.

Li·do (lē′dō; *It.* lē′dô), *n.* a chain of sandy islands in NE Italy, between the Lagoon of Venice and the Adriatic: resort.

lie[1] (lī), *n., v.,* **lied, ly·ing.** **—*n.*** **1.** a false statement made with deliberate intent to deceive; a falsehood. **2.** something intended or serving to convey a false impression; imposture. **3.** the charge or accusation of lying; a flat contradiction. **4. give the lie to, a.** to charge with lying; contradict. **b.** to prove or imply the falsity of; belie. **—*v.i.*** **5.** to speak falsely or utter untruth knowingly, as with intent to deceive. **6.** to express what is false, or convey a false impression. **—*v.t.*** **7.** to bring, take, put, etc., by lying (often used reflexively). **8. lie in one's throat** or **teeth,** to lie grossly or maliciously. [(n.) ME; OE *lyge;* c. G *Lüge,* Icel *lygi;* akin to Goth *liugn;* (v.) ME *lie(n),* OE *lēogan;* c. G *lügen,* Icel *ljūga,* Goth *liugan*]
—Syn. 1. prevarication, falsification. See **falsehood. 5.** prevaricate, fib. **—Ant. 1.** truth.

lie[2] (lī), *v.,* **lay, lain, ly·ing,** *n.* **—*v.i.*** **1.** to be in or get into a recumbent or prostrate position; recline (often fol. by *down*). **2.** to be buried in a particular spot. **3.** (of objects) to rest on a surface, esp. in a horizontal position. **4.** to be or remain in a position or state of inactivity, subjection, restraint, concealment, etc. **5.** to be found or located in a particular area, place, or situation: *The fault lies here.* **6.** to be placed or situated. **7.** to be stretched out or extended. **8.** to consist or be grounded (usually fol. by *in*): *The remedy lies in education.* **9.** to be in or have a specified direction. **10.** *Law.* to be sustainable or admissible, as an action or appeal. **11.** *Archaic.* to lodge; stay the night; sojourn. **12. lie by, a.** to pause for rest; stop activities, work, etc., temporarily. **b.** to lie unused. **13. lie down on the job,** *Informal.* to do less than one could or should do; shirk one's obligations. **14. lie in,** to be confined in childbed. **15. lie low.** See **low**[1] (def. 42). **16. lie over,** to be postponed for action at some future time. **17. lie to,** *Naut.* (of a ship) to lie comparatively stationary, usually with the head as near the wind as possible. **18. lie with, a.** to be the duty or function of: *The decision lies with him.* **b.** *Archaic.* to have sexual intercourse with. **19. take lying down,** *Informal.* to accept without objection or resistance: *I refuse to take that lying down!* **—*n.*** **20.** the manner of lying; the relative position or direction in which something lies. **21.** the haunt or covert of an animal. **22.** *Golf.* the position of the ball relative to how easy or how difficult it is to play. [ME *lie(n), liggen,* OE *licgan;* c. G *liegen,* D *liggen,* Icel *liggja,* Goth *ligan*]
—Syn. 1. LIE, LAY, often confused, are not synonyms. LIE, meaning to recline or rest, does not require an object. Its principal parts, too, are irregular, and are therefore distinctive. LAY with its forms *laid, have laid, laying,* etc., means to put or place. If "put" or "place" can be substituted in a contemplated sentence, the verb to use is LAY. Moreover, since one must always "put" or "place" *something,* the verb LAY is used only when there is a grammatical object to complete the sense. **20.** place, location, site. **—Ant. 1, 3.** stand.

Lie (lē), *n.* **Tryg·ve Halv·dan** (trig′və hälv′dän; *Nor.* tRYg′və hälv′dän), 1896–1968, Norwegian statesman: secretary-general of the United Nations 1946–53.

lieb·frau·milch (lēb′frou milk′, lēp′-; *Ger.* lēp′fRou-mĕlkH′), *n.* a white wine produced chiefly in the region of Hesse in West Germany. [< G, named after *Liebfrauenstift* convent of the Virgin, religious establishment in Worms, where the wine was first made; see MILK (G *Milch*)]

Lie·big (lē′bikH), *n.* **Jus·tus** (yo͝os′to͝os), **Baron von** (fən), 1803–73, German chemist.

Liech·ten·stein (lik′tən stīn′; *Ger.* likH′tən shtīn′), *n.* a small principality in central Europe between Austria and Switzerland. 25,000; 65 sq. mi. *Cap.:* Vaduz.

lied (lēd; *Ger.* lēt), *n., pl.* **lied·er** (lē′dər; *Ger.* lē′dəR). a German song, lyric, or ballad. [< G]

Lie·der·kranz (lē′dər kränts′, -krants′), *n.* **1.** *Trademark.* a strong, soft milk cheese with a creamy center. **2.** a German choral society or singing club, esp. of men. [< G: garland of songs]

lie′ detec′tor, an instrument for helping to determine the truth or falsity of a person's answers under questioning by recording impulses due to changes in certain body activities; polygraph.

lief (lēf), *adv.* **1.** gladly; willingly. **—*adj.*** *Archaic.* **2.** willing; desirous. **3.** dear; beloved; treasured. [ME *leef,* OE *lēof;* c. D *lief,* G *lieb,* Icel *ljufr,* Goth *liufs;* akin to LOVE] **—lief′ly,** *adv*

liege (lēj), *n.* **1.** a feudal lord entitled to allegiance and service. **2.** a feudal vassal or subject. **—*adj.*** **3.** owing allegiance and service to a feudal lord. **4.** pertaining to the relation between a feudal vassal and his lord. **5.** loyal; faithful: *the liege adherents of a cause.* [ME *li(e)ge* < OF << Gmc **lēt-* vassal + L *-icus* -IC; cf. ML *lētī* barbarians allowed to settle on Roman land (< Gmc; ? akin to LET[1]), *laeticus* for **lēticus* < *lēt(us)*]

Li·ège (lē āzh′; *Fr.* lyezh), *n.* **1.** a city in E Belgium, on the Meuse River. 155,898 (est. 1964). **2.** a province in E Belgium. 1,012,826 (est. 1964); 1521 sq. mi. *Cap.:* Liège. Also, **Li·ége** lē āzh′; *Fr.* lyāzh). Flemish, **Luik.**

liege·man (lēj′mən), *n., pl.* **-men. 1.** a vassal; subject. **2.** a faithful follower. [ME]

Lieg·nitz (lēg′nits), *n.* a city in SW Poland: formerly in Germany. 69,000 (est. 1963). Polish, **Legnica.**

lien (lēn, lē′ən), *n.* a legal right to hold property or to have it sold or applied for payment of a claim. [< MF << L *ligāmen* tie, bandage = *ligā(re)* (to) tie + *-men* n. suffix of result] **—lien′a·ble,** *adj.*

lie′ of the land′, *Chiefly Brit.* See **lay of the land.**

Lie·pā·ja (lye′pä yä), *n.* a seaport in W Latvia, in the W Soviet Union in Europe, on the Baltic. 104,000. German, **Libau.** Russian, **Libava.**

li·erne (lē ûrn′), *n.* *Archit.* an ornamental vaulting rib other than one springing from a pier or a ridge rib. [< F: lit., binding timber = *li(er)* (to) bind (< L *ligāre*) + *-erne* < ?]

Li·e·tu·va (lē′ə to͞o′vä), *n.* Lithuanian name of **Lithuania.**

lieu (lo͞o), *n.* **1.** *Archaic.* place; stead. **2. in lieu of,** instead of: *He gave us an IOU in lieu of cash.* [< MF; r. ME *liue* < OF *liu* < L *locus* place; see LOCUS]

Lieut., lieutenant.

lieu·ten·an·cy (lo͞o ten′ən sē; *in Brit. use, except in the navy,* lef ten′ən sē), *n., pl.* **-cies. 1.** the office, authority, or incumbency of a lieutenant. **2.** lieutenants collectively. [late ME *lieutenauncie.* See LIEUTENANT, -ANCY]

lieu·ten·ant (lo͞o ten′ənt; *in Brit. use, except in the navy,* lef ten′ənt), *n.* **1.** *Mil.* **a.** See **first lieutenant. b.** See **second lieutenant. 2.** *Navy.* a commissioned officer ranking between lieutenant junior grade and lieutenant commander. **3.** a person who holds an office, civil or military, in subordination to a superior for whom he acts. [ME < MF, n. use of adj. phrase *lieu tenant* place-holding. See LOCUM TENENS, LIEU, TENANT]

lieuten′ant colo′nel, *Mil.* a commissioned officer ranking next below a colonel and next above a major.

lieuten′ant comman′der, *Navy.* an officer next in rank below a commander and next above a lieutenant senior grade.

lieuten′ant gen′eral, *Mil.* an officer ranking next below a general and next above a major general.

lieuten′ant gov′ernor, 1. *U.S.* a state officer next in rank to the governor. **2.** *Brit.* a deputy governor.

lieuten′ant jun′ior grade′, *U.S. Navy.* a commissioned officer ranking above an ensign and below a lieutenant.

lieve (lēv), *adv.* *Dial.* lief.

life (līf), *n., pl.* **lives,** *adj.* **—*n.*** **1.** the condition that distinguishes animals and plants from inorganic objects and dead organisms, being manifested by growth through metabolism, reproduction, and the power of adaptation to environment through changes originating internally. **2.** the sum of the distinguishing phenomena of plants and animals, esp. metabolism, growth, reproduction, and adaptation to environment. **3.** the animate existence or term of animate existence of an individual: *to risk one's life.* **4.** a corresponding state, existence, or principle of existence conceived of as belonging to the soul. **5.** the general or universal condition of human existence: *Too bad, but life is like that.* **6.** any specified period of animate existence. **7.** the term of existence, activity, or effectiveness of something inanimate, as a machine, lease, play, etc. **8.** a living being: *several lives were lost.* **9.** living things collectively, whether animals or plants. **10.** a particular aspect of existence. **11.** the course of existence or sum of experiences and actions that constitute a person's existence. **12.** a biography. **13.** animation; liveliness. **14.** resilience; elasticity. **15.** that which makes or keeps something alive; the vivifying or quickening principle. **16.** a mode or manner of existence, as in the world of affairs, society, etc. **17.** the term or extent of authority, popularity, approval, etc. **18.** See **life sentence.** **19.** anything or anyone considered to be as precious as life: *She was his life. Baseball is his entire life.* **20.** a person or thing that enlivens. **21.** effervescence or sparkle, as of wines. **22.** pungency or strong, sharp flavor, as of substances when fresh or in good condition. **23.** nature or any of the forms of nature as the model or subject of a work of art: *drawn from life.* **24. as large as life,** actually; indeed. Also, **as big as life. 25. come to life, a.** to recover consciousness. **b.** to display animation and vigor. **c.** to appear lifelike. **26. for dear life,** with desperate energy or speed. Also, **for one's life. 27. for the life of one,** as hard as one tries; even with the utmost effort: *He can't understand it for the life of him.* **28. not on your life,** *Informal.* absolutely not; by no means. —*adj.* **29.** for or lasting a lifetime; lifelong. **30.** of or pertaining to animate existence. **31.** working from nature: *a life drawing.* [ME; OE *līf*; c. D *lijf*, G *Leib* body, Icel *līf* life, body; akin to LIVE[1]] —**life′ful,** *adj.*

life′ belt′, a beltlike life preserver.

life·blood (līf′blud′), *n.* **1.** the blood, considered as essential to maintain life. **2.** the element that vivifies or animates anything.

life·boat (līf′bōt′), *n.* **1.** a ship's boat, designed to be readily able to rescue and maintain persons from a sinking vessel. **2.** a similarly constructed boat used by shore-based rescue services.

life′ buoy′, a buoyant device for supporting a person fallen into the water until he can be recovered.

life′ cy′cle, *Biol.* the continuous sequence of changes undergone by an organism from one primary form to the development of the same form again.

life′ expect′ancy, the probable life span of an individual or class of persons determined statistically.

life-giv·ing (līf′giv′ing), *adj.* imparting, or having the ability to impart, life or vitality. —**life′-giv′er,** *n.*

life·guard (līf′gärd′), *n.* a person employed, as at a beach or pool, to protect bathers from drowning.

Life′ Guards′, (in Britain) a cavalry regiment forming part of the ceremonial guard of the monarch. Cf. **household cavalry.**

life′ his′tory, *Biol.* **1.** the series of living phenomena exhibited by an organism in the course of its development from inception to death. **2.** See **life cycle.**

life′ insur′ance, insurance providing for payment of a sum of money to a named beneficiary upon the death of the policyholder or, sometimes, to the policyholder should he reach a specified age.

life′ jack′et, a life preserver in the form of a sleeveless jacket. Also called **life vest;** *Brit.*, **air jacket.**

life·less (līf′lis), *adj.* **1.** not endowed with life; inanimate. **2.** destitute of living things. **3.** deprived of life; dead. **4.** without animation, liveliness, or spirit; dull; torpid. **5.** insensible, as one in a faint. [ME *lifles*, OE *līflēas*] —**life′less·ly,** *adv.* —**life′less·ness,** *n.* —**Syn. 1.** inorganic. **3.** defunct. See **dead. 4.** inactive, inert, sluggish.

life·like (līf′līk′), *adj.* resembling or simulating real life. —**life′like′ness,** *n.*

life′ line′, 1. a line, fired across a vessel in difficulty, by means of which a hawser for a breeches buoy may be hauled aboard. **2.** a line or rope for saving life, as one attached to a lifeboat. **3.** any of various lines running above the decks, spars, etc., of a vessel to give seamen something to grasp when there is danger of falling or being washed away. **4.** the line by which a diver is lowered and raised. **5.** any of several anchored lines used by swimmers for support. **6.** a route over which supplies must be sent to sustain an area or group of persons otherwise isolated.

life·long (līf′lông′, -long′), *adj.* lasting or continuing through life: *lifelong regret.*

life′ mask′, a cast of the face of a living person. Cf. **death mask.**

life′ net′, a strong net or the like held by firemen or others to catch persons jumping from a burning building.

life′ preserv′er, a buoyant or inflatable jacket, belt, or similar device for keeping a person afloat.

lif·er (lī′fər), *n.* *Slang.* a person sentenced to or serving a term of life imprisonment.

life′ raft′, a raft for use in emergencies, as when a ship must be abandoned.

life·sav·er (līf′sā′vər), *n.* **1.** a person who rescues another from danger of death, esp. from drowning. **2.** *Chiefly Brit.* a lifeguard. **3.** *Informal.* a person or thing that saves a person, as from a difficulty. —**life′sav′ing,** *adj.*, *n.*

life′ sen′tence, a sentence condemning a convicted felon to spend the rest of his life in prison. Cf. **death sentence.**

life-size (līf′sīz′), *adj.* of the natural size of an object in life; of the size of a living original: *a life-size statue.* Also, **life′-sized′.**

life′ span′, 1. the longest period over which the life of any plant or animal organism or species may extend, according to the available biological knowledge concerning it. **2.** the longevity of an individual.

life′ style′, a person's typical approach to living, including his moral attitudes, preferred entertainment, fads, fashions, etc. Also, **life·style** (līf′stīl′).

life′ ta′ble, *Insurance.* See **mortality table.**

life·time (līf′tīm′), *n.* **1.** the time that the life of someone or something continues; the term of a life. —*adj.* **2.** for the duration of a person's life. [ME *liftime*]

life′ vest′. See **life jacket.**

life·work (līf′wûrk′), *n.* the complete or principal work, labor, or task of a lifetime.

lift (lift), *v.t.* **1.** to move or bring (something) upward, as from the ground, to some higher position; hoist. **2.** to raise or direct upward: *to lift one's head.* **3.** to remove, rescind, or put an end to, esp. by an official act, as a ban, curfew, or blockade. **4.** to hold up or display on high. **5.** to raise in rank, condition, estimation, etc.; elevate or exalt. **6.** to make audible or louder, as the voice. **7.** *Informal.* to plagiarize. **8.** *Slang.* to steal, esp. from a store. **9.** airlift (def. 3). **10.** to remove (plants and tubers) from the ground, as after harvest or for transplanting. **11.** *U.S.* to pay off (a mortgage, promissory note, etc.). **12.** *Golf.* to pick up (the ball), as to move it from an unplayable lie. **13.** to perform a face lifting on. **14.** *Shipbuilding.* to transfer (measurements) from a drawing, model, etc., to a piece being built. —*v.i.* **15.** to go up; give to upward pressure. **16.** to pull or strain upward in the effort to lift something. **17.** to move upward or rise; rise and disperse, as clouds or fog. —*n.* **18.** the act of lifting or raising, or rising. **19.** the distance that anything rises or is raised. **20.** a lifting or raising force. **21.** the weight, load, or quantity lifted. **22.** an act or instance of helping to climb or mount. **23.** a ride in a vehicle, esp. one given to a pedestrian. **24.** a feeling of exaltation or uplift. **25.** a device or apparatus for lifting. **26.** *Skiing.* See **ski lift. 27.** *Chiefly Brit.* **a.** an elevator. **b.** any device used to lift or elevate, as a dumbwaiter or hoist. **28.** a rise or elevation of ground. **29.** *Aeron.* the component of the aerodynamic force exerted by the air on an airfoil, having a direction perpendicular to the direction of motion and causing an aircraft to stay aloft. **30.** one of the layers of leather forming the heel of a boot or shoe. **31.** a special arch support built or inserted into footwear. **32.** *Mining.* the slice or thickness of ore mined in one operation. **33.** airlift (defs. 1, 2). [ME *lifte(n)* < Scand; cf. Icel *lypta*, c. G *lüften*, lit., to take aloft; see LOFT] —**lift′a·ble,** *adj.* —**lift′er,** *n.* —**Syn. 1.** elevate. See **raise.** —**Ant. 1.** lower.

lift-off (lift′ôf′, -of′), *n.* *Rocketry, Aeron.* **1.** the action of a rocket in rising from its launching site under its own power or of an aircraft in becoming airborne. **2.** the instant when such action occurs. Also, **lift′off′.**

lift′ pump′, a pump in which a liquid is lifted rather than forced up from below. Cf. **force pump.**

lig·a·ment (lig′ə mənt), *n.* **1.** *Anat.* a band of tissue, usually white and fibrous, serving to connect bones, hold organs in place, etc. **2.** a tie or bond. [< ML *ligāment(um)* ligament, L: band = *ligā(re)* (to) tie + *-mentum* -MENT] —**lig·a·men·tous** (lig′ə men′təs), **lig·a·men·tal** (lig′ə men′tᵊl), **lig·a·men·ta·ry** (lig′ə men′tə rē), *adj.* —**lig′a·men′tous·ly,** *adv.*

li·gan (lī′gən), *n.* *Law.* lagan.

li·gate (lī′gāt), *v.t.*, **-gat·ed, -gat·ing.** to bind with or as with a ligature; tie up (a bleeding artery or the like). [< L *ligāt(us)* tied, bound (ptp. of *ligāre*); see -ATE[1]]

li·ga·tion (lī gā′shən), *n.* **1.** the act of ligating, esp. of surgically tying up a bleeding artery. **2.** anything that binds or ties up; ligature. [< LL *ligātiōn-* (s. of *ligātiō*)] —**lig·a·tive** (lig′ə tiv), *adj.*

lig·a·ture (lig′ə chər, -chŏŏr′), *n.*, *v.*, **-tured, -tur·ing.** —*n.* **1.** the act of binding or tying up. **2.** anything that serves for binding or tying up, as a band, bandage, or cord. **3.** *Print.*, *Writing.* a stroke or bar connecting two letters. **4.** *Print.* a character or type combining two or more letters, as fi, ffl. **5.** *Music.* **a.** slur. **b.** a group of notes connected by a slur. **c.** a metal band for securing the reed of a clarinet or saxophone to the mouthpiece. **6.** *Surg.* a thread or wire for constriction of blood vessels or for removing tumors by strangulation. —*v.t.* **7.** to bind with a ligature; tie up; ligate. [late ME < LL *ligātūra*]

light[1] (līt), *n.*, *adj.*, *v.*, **light·ed** or **lit, light·ing.** —*n.* **1.** something that makes things visible or affords illumination: *All colors depend on light.* **2.** *Physics.* **a.** electromagnetic radiation to which the organs of sight react, ranging in wavelength from about 4000 to 7700 angstrom units and is propagated at a speed of about 186,300 miles per second. **b.** a similar form of radiant energy that does not affect the retina, as ultraviolet or infrared rays. **3.** the sensation produced by stimulation of the organs of sight. **4.** an illuminating agent or source, as the sun, a lamp, or a beacon. **5.** the radiance or illumination from a particular source, as a candle or the sun. **6.** daybreak or dawn. **7.** daytime. **8.** a measure or supply of light; illumination. **9.** a particular light or illumination in which an object seen takes on a certain appearance. **10.** the aspect in which a thing appears or is regarded. **11.** a gleam or sparkle, as in the eyes. **12.** a means of igniting, as a spark or flame. **13.** the state of being visible, exposed to view, or revealed to public notice or knowledge; limelight. **14.** *Archit.* one compartment of a window or window sash. **15.** mental or spiritual illumination or enlightenment. **16. lights,** the information, ideas, or mental capacities possessed. **17.** a person who is an illuminating or shining example; luminary. **18.** a lighthouse. **19.** a traffic light. **20.** *Archaic.* the eyesight. **21. bring to light,** to discover or reveal. **22. come to light,** to be discovered; be revealed. **23. in a good** (or **bad**) **light,** under favorable (or unfavorable) circumstances. **24. in the light of,** taking into account; considering. **25. see the light, a.** to come into being. **b.** to be made public. **c.** to begin to accept or understand a point of view one formerly opposed. **26. shed** or **throw light on,** to clarify; clear up. —*adj.* **27.** having light or illumination; well-lighted. **28.** pale, whitish, or not deep or dark in color. **29.** (of coffee) containing a large amount of milk or cream. —*v.t.* **30.** to set burning, as a fire, cigarette, etc.; kindle; ignite. **31.** to turn or switch on (an electric light). **32.** to give light to; furnish with light or illumination. **33.** to make (an area or object) bright with or as with light (often fol. by *up*): *Hundreds of candles lighted up the ballroom.* **34.** to cause (the face, surroundings, etc.) to brighten, esp. with joy, animation, or the like (often fol. by *up*): *A smile lit up her face.* **35.** to guide or conduct with a light. —*v.i.* **36.** to take fire or become kindled. **37.** to ignite a cigar, cigarette, or pipe for purposes of smoking (usually fol. by *up*): *He lighted up before speaking.* **38.** to become bright, as with light or color (often fol. by *up*). **39.** to brighten with animation or joy, as the face or eyes (often fol. by *up*). [ME; OE *lēoht*; c. D, G *licht*, Goth *liuhath*; akin to Icel *ljōs*, L *lūx*, Gk *leukós*] —**light′ful,** *adj.* —**light′ful·ly,** *adv.*

light[2] (līt), *adj.* **1.** of little weight; not heavy. **2.** of little weight in proportion to bulk; of low specific gravity. **3.** of less than the usual or average weight. **4.** weighing less than the proper or standard amount. **5.** of small amount, force, intensity, etc. **6.** using or applying little or slight pressure or force. **7.** not distinct; faint. **8.** easy to endure, deal with, or perform; not difficult or burdensome. **9.** not very profound, serious, or heavy; amusing or entertaining. **10.** of little importance or consequence; trivial. **11.** (of food) easily digested. **12.** (esp. of wines) not heavy or strong. **13.** spongy or well-leavened, as bread. **14.** (of soil) containing much sand; porous or crumbly. **15.** slender or delicate in form or appearance. **16.** airy or buoyant in movement; nimble. **17.** characterized by good spirits, cheer, and gaiety. **18.** characterized by lack of proper seriousness; frivolous. **19.** sexually wanton; promiscuous; loose. **20.** easily swayed; changeable; volatile. **21.** dizzy; slightly delirious. **22.** *Mil.* lightly armed or equipped: *light infantry.* **23.** having little or no cargo, encumbrance, or the like; not burdened. **24.** adapted by small weight or slight build for small loads or swift movement. **25.** *Meteorol.* (of wind) having a speed up to seven miles per hour. Cf. **light air, light breeze. 26.** *Poker.* being in debt to the pot: *He's a dollar light.* **27. make light of,** to treat as unimportant or trivial. **—***adv.* **28.** lightly: *to travel light.* [ME; OE *lēoht, līht;* c. D *licht,* G *leicht,* Icel *lēttr,* Goth *leihts*] **—Ant. 1.** heavy.

light[3] (līt), *v.i.,* **light·ed** or **lit, light·ing. 1.** to get down or descend, as from a horse or a vehicle. **2.** to come to rest; fall or settle upon; land. **3.** to come by chance, happen, or hit (usually fol. by *on* or *upon*): *to light on a clue.* **4.** to fall, as a stroke, choice, etc., on a place or person. **5. light into,** *Informal.* to make a physical or verbal attack on. **6. light out,** *Slang.* to leave quickly. [ME *lihte(n),* OE *līhtan* to make light, relieve of a weight; see LIGHT[2]]

light′ air′, *Meteorol.* (on the Beaufort scale) a wind of 1–3 miles per hour.

light′ artil′lery, *U.S. Mil.* guns and howitzers of caliber up to and including 105 millimeters. Cf. **heavy artillery, medium artillery.**

light′ bomb′er, *U.S. Mil.* an airplane designed to carry light bomb loads relatively short distances, esp. one having a gross loaded weight of less than 100,000 pounds. Cf. **heavy bomber, medium bomber.**

light′ box′, a boxlike object having a uniformly lighted surface, as of ground glass, against which films or transparencies can be held for examination.

light′ breeze′, *Meteorol.* (on the Beaufort scale) a wind of 4–7 miles per hour.

light′ bulb′, an incandescent bulb.

light′ cream′, sweet cream with less butterfat than heavy cream.

light′ cruis′er, a naval cruiser having six-inch guns as its main armament. Cf. **heavy cruiser.**

light·en[1] (līt′ᵊn), *v.i.* **1.** to become lighter or less dark; brighten. **2.** to brighten or light up, as the eyes or features. **3.** *Rare.* to flash as or like lightning: *It thundered and lightened for hours.* **4.** *Archaic.* to shine, gleam, or be bright. **—***v.t.* **5.** to give light to; illuminate. **6.** to brighten (the eyes, features, etc.). **7.** to make lighter or less dark. **8.** *Obs.* enlighten. **9.** *Obs.* to flash or emit like lightning (usually fol. by *out, forth,* or *down*). [ME] **—light′en·er,** *n.*

light·en[2] (līt′ᵊn), *v.t.* **1.** to make lighter in weight. **2.** to lessen the load of or upon. **3.** to make less burdensome or oppressive; mitigate. **4.** to cheer or gladden. **—***v.i.* **5.** to become less severe, stringent, or harsh; ease up. **6.** to become less heavy, cumbersome, burdensome, oppressive, etc. **7.** to become less gloomy; perk up. [ME] **—Syn. 3.** ease, lessen, reduce. **—Ant. 3.** aggravate.

light·er[1] (lī′tər), *n.* **1.** a person or thing that lights or ignites. **2.** a mechanical device used in lighting cigars, cigarettes, or pipes for smoking. [LIGHT[1] + -ER[1]]

light·er[2] (lī′tər), *n.* **1.** a vessel, commonly an unpowered, flat-bottomed barge, used in lightening or unloading and in loading ships, or in transporting goods for short distances. **—***v.t.* **2.** to convey in or as in a lighter. [late ME < MD **lichter* (recorded in 16th century). See LIGHT[2], -ER[1]]

light·er·age (lī′tər ij), *n.* **1.** the use of lighters in loading and unloading ships and in transporting goods for short distances. **2.** a fee paid for lighter service. [late ME]

light·er-than-air (lī′tər *th*ən âr′), *adj.* *Aeron.* **1.** (of an aircraft) weighing less than the air it displaces, hence obtaining lift from aerostatic buoyancy. **2.** of or pertaining to lighter-than-air craft.

light·face (līt′fās′), *Print.* **—***n.* **1.** a type characterized by thin lines. **—***adj.* **2.** Also, **light′-faced′.** (of printed matter) set in lightface. Cf. **boldface.**

This is a sample of lightface.

light-fin·gered (līt′fiŋ′gərd), *adj.* having nimble fingers, esp. in picking pockets; inclined to pilfer or steal.

light-foot·ed (līt′fŏŏt′id), *adj.* stepping lightly or nimbly; light of foot; nimble. [late ME *lyght foted*] **—light′-foot′ed·ly,** *adv.* **—light′-foot′ed·ness,** *n.*

light-head·ed (līt′hed′id), *adj.* **1.** having or showing a frivolous or volatile disposition; thoughtless. **2.** giddy, dizzy, or delirious. **—light′-head′ed·ly,** *adv.* **—light′-head′ed·ness,** *n.*

light-heart·ed (līt′här′tid), *adj.* carefree; cheerful; gay; debonair. Also, **light′heart′ed.** [late ME *ligt-herted*] **—light′-heart′ed·ly, light′heart′ed·ly,** *adv.* **—light′-heart′ed·ness, light′heart′ed·ness,** *n.*

light′ heav′yweight, a boxer intermediate in weight between a middleweight and a heavyweight, esp. one weighing between 161 and 175 pounds.

light′ horse′, cavalry carrying light arms and equipment.

light-horse·man (līt′hôrs′mən), *n., pl.* **-men.** a light-armed cavalry soldier.

light·house (līt′hous′), *n., pl.* **-hous·es** (-hou′ziz). a tower or other structure displaying a light or lights for the guidance of mariners: either an aid to navigation or a warning of some hazard.

Lighthouse

light·ing (lī′tiŋ), *n.* **1.** the act of igniting or illuminating. **2.** the arrangement of lights to achieve particular effects. **3.** such an effect achieved by arrangement. **4.** the way light falls upon a face, object, etc., esp. in a picture. [ME *lightinge,* OE *lihting*]

light·ish[1] (lī′tish), *adj.* rather light in color. [LIGHT[1] + -ISH[1]]

light·ish[2] (lī′tish), *adj.* rather light in weight. [LIGHT[2] + -ISH[1]]

light·less (līt′lis), *adj.* **1.** without light or lights; receiving no light; dark. **2.** giving no light. [ME *lihtles,* OE *lēohtlēas*]

light·ly (līt′lē), *adv.* **1.** with little weight, force, intensity, etc. **2.** to a small amount or degree; slightly. **3.** easily; without trouble or effort. **4.** cheerfully; without complaining. **5.** frivolously; flippantly. **6.** without due consideration or reason (often used negatively): *an offer not to be refused lightly.* **7.** nimbly; quickly. **8.** with a lack of concern; indifferently. **9.** airily; buoyantly. [ME *lightli,* OE *lēohtlīce*]

light′ machine′ gun′, *Mil.* any air-cooled machine gun having a caliber not greater than .30 inch.

light′ meat′. See **white meat.**

light′ me′ter. See **exposure meter.**

light-mind·ed (līt′mīn′did), *adj.* having or showing a lack of serious purpose, attitude, etc.; frivolous; trifling. **—light′-mind′ed·ly,** *adv.* **—light′-mind′ed·ness,** *n.*

light·ness[1] (līt′nis), *n.* **1.** the state or quality of being light or illuminated. **2.** thin or pale coloration. [ME *lightnes,* OE *līhtnes*]

light·ness[2] (līt′nis), *n.* **1.** the state or quality of being light in weight. **2.** the quality of being agile, nimble, or graceful. **3.** lack of pressure or burdensomeness. **4.** gaiety of manner, speech, style, etc.; cheerfulness. **5.** lack of seriousness; levity in actions, thoughts, or speech. [ME *lightnesse*] **—Syn. 2.** agility, grace, nimbleness.

light·ning (līt′niŋ), *n., v.,* **light·ninged, light·ning,** *adj.* **—***n.* **1.** a luminous, electric discharge in the atmosphere caused by the electric-charge separation produced in cumulonimbus, or thunderstorm, clouds. **—***v.i.* **2.** to emit a flash or flashes of lightning (often used impersonally with *it* as subject): *It lightninged just as I was about to leave.* **—***adj.* **3.** of, pertaining to, or resembling lightning, esp. in regard to speed of movement. [ME, var. of *lightening.* See LIGHTEN[1], -ING[1]]

light′ning arrest′er, *Elect.* a device for preventing damage to radio, telephonic, or other electric equipment from lightning or other high-voltage currents.

light′ning bug′, firefly.

light′ning rod′, a rodlike conductor installed to divert lightning away from a structure by providing a direct path to the ground.

light′ op′era, operetta.

light′ quan′tum, *Physics.* photon (def. 1).

lights (līts), *n.pl.* the lungs, esp. of sheep, pigs, etc. [ME *lihte, lightes,* n. use of *liht* LIGHT[2]]

light·ship (līt′ship′), *n.* a ship anchored in a specific location and displaying a light or lights for the guidance of mariners.

light′ show′, a form of entertainment consisting of constantly changing patterns of light and color, usually accompanied by electronically amplified sounds.

light·some[1] (līt′səm), *adj.* **1.** light; buoyant or agile. **2.** cheerful; gay; light-hearted. **3.** frivolous; changeable. [late ME *lyghtesum* (c. MHG *lihtsam*)] **—light′some·ly,** *adv.* **—light′some·ness,** *n.*

light·some[2] (līt′səm), *adj.* **1.** emitting or reflecting light; luminous. **2.** well-lighted; illuminated. [late ME *lyghtesum*] **—light′some·ly,** *adv.* **—light′some·ness,** *n.*

light-struck (līt′struk′), *adj.* *Photog.* (of a film or the like) injured by accidental exposure to light.

light·weight (līt′wāt′), *adj.* **1.** light in weight. **2.** being lighter in weight, texture, etc., than another item or object of identical use, quality, or function. **3.** without seriousness of purpose; trivial or trifling. **4.** of or pertaining to a lightweight boxer. **—***n.* **5.** a person of less than average weight. **6.** *Informal.* a person of little influence, importance, or effect. **7.** a boxer or other contestant intermediate in weight between a featherweight and a welterweight, esp. a professional boxer weighing between 126 and 135 pounds.

light·wood (līt′wŏŏd′), *n.* *Southern U.S.* **1.** wood used in lighting a fire; kindling. **2.** resinous pine wood.

light-year (līt′yēr′, -yēr′), *n.* *Astron.* the distance traversed by light in one mean solar year, about 5,880,000,000,000 miles: used as a unit in measuring stellar distances. *Abbr.:* lt-yr

lig·ne·ous (lig′nē əs), *adj.* of the nature of or resembling wood; woody. [< L *ligneus* of wood. See LIGNI-, -EOUS]

ligni-, a learned borrowing from Latin meaning "wood," used in the formation of compound words: *ligniform.* Also, **ligno-.** [< L, comb. form repr. *lignum* wood]

lig·ni·form (lig′nə fôrm′), *adj.* having the form of wood; resembling wood, as a variety of asbestos.

lig·ni·fy (lig′nə fī′), *v.i., v.t.,* **-fied, -fy·ing.** to become or cause to become wood or woody. **—lig′ni·fi·ca′tion,** *n.*

lig·nin (lig′nin), *n.* *Bot.* an organic substance that, with cellulose, forms the chief part of woody tissue.

lig·nite (lig′nīt), *n.* an imperfectly formed coal, usually dark-brown and often having a woody texture; brown coal. **—lig·nit·ic** (lig nit′ik), *adj.*

lig·no·cel·lu·lose (lig′nō sel′yə lōs′), *n.* *Bot.* any of various compounds of lignin and cellulose comprising the essential part of woody cell walls. **—lig·no·cel·lu·los·ic** (lig′nō sel′yə los′ik), *adj.*

lig·num vi·tae (lig′nəm vī′tē), **1.** the hard, extremely heavy wood of either of two species of guaiacum, *Guaiacum officinale* or *G. sanctum,* used in making pulleys, rulers, etc., and formerly as a medicament. **2.** either tree. **3.** any of various other trees yielding a similar hard wood. [< NL, LL, name of the tree, lit., wood of life]

lig·ro·in (lig′rō in), *n.* a flammable mixture of hydrocarbons, obtained from petroleum by distillation and used as a solvent. Also, **lig′ro·ine.** [?]

lig·u·la (lig′yə lə), *n., pl.* **-lae** (-lē′), **-las.** **1.** *Bot., Zool.* a tonguelike or strap-shaped part or organ. **2.** *Bot.* ligule. [< NL, special use of L *li(n)gula* spoon, shoe strap = *ling(ere)* (to) lick up + *-ula* -ULE] —**lig′u·lar,** *adj.* —**lig′u·loid′,** *adj.*

lig·u·late (lig′yə lit, -lāt′), *adj.* **1.** having or forming a ligula. **2.** having the shape of a strap. Also, **lig·u·la·ted** (lig′yə lā′tid).

lig·ule (lig′yo͞ol), *n.* *Bot.* **1.** a thin, membranous outgrowth from the base of the blade of most grasses. **2.** a strap-shaped corolla, as in the ray flowers of the head of certain composite plants. [< L *ligul(a)*; see LIGULA]

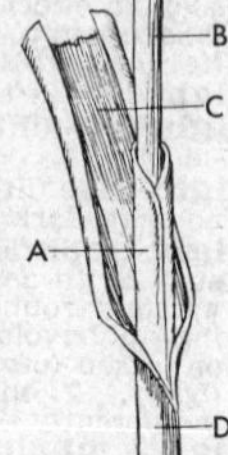

A, Ligule of a grass section; B, Stem; C, Leaf blade; D, Leaf sheath

lig·ure (lig′yo͝or), *n.* a precious stone, probably the jacinth. Ex. 28:19. [ME *ligury* < LL *ligūri(us)* < LGk *ligýrion* a kind of precious stone]

Li·gu·ri·a (li gyo͝or′ē ə), *n.* a region in NW Italy. 1,881,982; 2099 sq. mi. —**Li·gu′ri·an,** *adj., n.*

Ligu′rian Sea′, a part of the Mediterranean between Corsica and the NW coast of Italy.

lik·a·ble (lī′kə bəl), *adj.* readily or easily liked; pleasing. Also, **likeable.** —**lik′a·ble·ness, lik′a·bil′i·ty,** *n.*

like[1] (līk), *adj.,* (*Poetic*) **lik·er, lik·est,** *prep., adv., conj., n., v.,* **liked, lik·ing.** —*adj.* **1.** of the same form, appearance, kind, character, amount, etc. **2.** corresponding or agreeing in general or in some noticeable respect; similar; analogous. **3.** bearing resemblance. **4.** *Dial.* likely. **5.** *Dial.* about: *He was like to die!* —*prep.* **6.** similarly to; in the manner characteristic of. **7.** resembling (someone or something). **8.** characteristic of. **9.** as if there is promise of; indicative of. **10.** as if someone or something gives promise of being. **11.** disposed or inclined to (usually prec. by *feel*). **12.** similar or comparable to. **13.** (used correlatively to indicate similarity through relationship): *like father, like son.* **14.** (used to establish an intensifying, often facetious, comparison): *sleeping like a log; running like a bat out of hell.* **15.** *Nonstandard.* as; such as. **16. like anything,** *Informal.* very much; extremely; with great intensity. —*adv.* **17.** nearly; closely; approximately. **18.** *Informal.* likely or probably (usually fol. by *enough*): *like enough; like as not.* **19.** *Nonstandard.* **a.** as it were; in a way; somehow: *There was this old lady with her face all wrinkled like.* **b.** to a degree; more or less: *looking very tough like.* —*conj. Nonstandard.* **20.** in the same way as; just as; as: *It happened like you said it would.* **21.** as if: *He acted like he was afraid to go home.* —*n.* **22.** a like person or thing, or like persons or things; counterpart, match, or equal (usually prec. by a possessive adjective or *the*). **23.** kind; sort; type (usually prec. by a possessive adjective). **24. the like,** something of a similar nature. **25. the like** or **likes of,** someone or something like; the equal of. —*v.i.* **26. like to,** *Nonstandard.* came close to (doing something): *I like to died from laughing.* [ME; OE *gelīc*; c. D *gelijk*, G *gleich*, Icel *(g)līkr*, Goth *galeiks* like, lit., of the same body or form. See Y-, LICH GATE] —**lik′er,** *n.*
—**Usage. 20, 21.** The use of LIKE in place of AS is avoided by educated speakers and writers. *Do as I say, not as I do* does not admit of LIKE instead of AS. In an occasional idiomatic phrase, LIKE is less offensive when substituted for AS IF (*He raced down the street like mad*), but note that this is clearly colloquial.

like[2] (līk), *v.,* **liked, lik·ing,** *n.* —*v.t.* **1.** to take pleasure in; find agreeable or congenial to one's taste. **2.** to regard with favor, or have a kindly or friendly feeling for (a person, group, etc.). —*v.i.* **3.** to feel inclined; wish. **4.** *Archaic.* to suit the tastes or wishes; please. —*n.* **5.** Usually, **likes.** a favorable feeling; preference: *likes and dislikes.* [ME *like(n)*, OE *līcian*; c. D *lijken*, Icel *līka*; see LIKE[1]]

-like, a suffixal use of **like**[1] in the formation of adjectives (*childlike; lifelike*), sometimes hyphenated. —**Syn.** See **-ish**[1].

like·a·ble (lī′kə bəl), *adj.* likable. —**like′a·ble·ness, like′a·bil′i·ty,** *n.*

like·li·hood (līk′lē ho͝od′), *n.* **1.** the state of being likely or probable; probability. **2.** a probability or chance of something. **3.** *Archaic.* indication of a favorable end; promise. [ME *liklihood*]

like·ly (līk′lē), *adj.,* **-li·er, -li·est,** *adv.* —*adj.* **1.** probably or apparently destined (usually fol. by an infinitive). **2.** seeming like truth, fact, or certainty; reasonably to be believed or expected: *a likely story.* **3.** apparently suitable; seeming to fulfill requirements or expectations. **4.** showing promise of achievement or excellence; promising. —*adv.* **5.** probably. [ME < Scand; cf. Icel *līkligr*]
—**Syn. 1.** LIKELY, APT, LIABLE are not alike in indicating probability; though APT is used colloquially, and LIABLE, mistakenly, in this sense. LIKELY is the only one of these words which means "probable" or "to be expected": *It is likely to rain today.* APT refers to a natural bent or inclination; if something is natural and easy, it is often probable; hence APT comes to be associated with LIKELY and to be used informally as a substitute for it: *He is apt at drawing. He is apt to do well at drawing.* LIABLE should not be used to mean "probable." When used with an infinitive, it may remind one of LIKELY: *He is liable to be arrested.* But the true meaning, susceptibility to something unpleasant, or exposure to risk, becomes evident when it is used with a prepositional phrase: *He is liable to arrest. The machine is liable to error.* **3.** appropriate.

like-mind·ed (līk′mīn′did), *adj.* having a similar or identical opinion, purpose, etc. —**like′-mind′ed·ly,** *adv.* —**like′-mind′ed·ness,** *n.*

lik·en (lī′kən), *v.t.* to represent as like; compare: *to liken someone to a weasel.* [ME *liknen*. See LIKE[1], -EN[1]]

like·ness (līk′nis), *n.* **1.** a representation, picture, or image, esp. a portrait. **2.** the semblance or appearance of something; guise. **3.** the state or fact of being like. [ME *liknesse*, OE *līcnes*, var. of *gelīcnes*. See ALIKE, -NESS] —**Syn. 3.** resemblance, similitude.

like·wise (līk′wīz′), *adv.* **1.** moreover; in addition; also; too. **2.** in like manner; in the same way; similarly. [late ME; earlier *in like wise* in a like way]

lik·ing (lī′king), *n.* **1.** preference, inclination, or favor. **2.** pleasure or taste. **3.** the state or feeling of a person who likes. [ME; OE *līcung*] —**Syn. 1.** partiality, fondness. —**Ant. 1.** antipathy.

li·lac (lī′lək, -lok, -lak), *n.* **1.** any oleaceous shrub of the genus *Syringa*, as *S. vulgaris*, having large clusters of fragrant purple or white flowers: the state flower of New Hampshire. **2.** pale reddish purple. [< Sp < Ar *līlak* < Pers, assimilated var. of *nīlak* bluish = *nīl* blue, indigo (< Skt *nīla*) + *-ak* suffix of appurtenance]

li·la·ceous (lī lā′shəs), *adj.* of or approaching the color lilac.

lil·i·a·ceous (lil′ē ā′shəs), *adj.* **1.** of or like the lily. **2.** belonging to the *Liliaceae*, or lily family of plants. [< LL *līliāceus*]

lil·ied (lil′ēd), *adj.* **1.** abounding in lilies. **2.** *Archaic.* lilylike; white.

Lil·i·en·thal (lil′ē ən thôl′ *for 1;* lē′lē ən täl′ *for 2*), *n.* **1. David E(li),** 1899–1981, U.S. public administrator. **2. Ot·to** (ôt′ō), 1848–96, German aeronautical engineer and inventor.

Lil·ith (lil′ith), *n.* **1.** *Semitic Myth.* a female demon dwelling in deserted places and attacking children. **2.** *Jewish Folklore.* Adam's wife before Eve was created.

Li·li·u·o·ka·la·ni (lē lē′o͞o ō kä lä′nē), *n.* **Lydia Ka·me·ke·ha** (kä′me ke′hä), 1838–1917, last queen of the Hawaiian Islands 1891–93.

Lille (lēl), *n.* a city in N France. 177,218. Formerly, **Lisle.**

Lil·li·pu·tian (lil′i pyo͞o′shən), *adj.* **1.** extremely small; diminutive. —*n.* **2.** a very small person. **3.** a person who is narrow, petty, or has little influence. [after the tiny inhabitants of *Lilliput*, an imaginary country described in Swift's satire *Gulliver's Travels*, 1726]

Li·long·we (li lông′wā), *n.* a city in and the capital of Malawi, in the central part. 102,924.

lilt (lilt), *n.* **1.** rhythmic swing or cadence. **2.** a lilting song or tune. —*v.i., v.t.* **3.** to sing or play in a light, tripping, or rhythmic manner. [ME *lulte;* ? akin to D *lul* pipe]

lil·y (lil′ē), *n., pl.* **lil·ies,** *adj.* —*n.* **1.** any scaly-bulbed herb of the genus *Lilium*, having showy, funnel-shaped or bell-shaped flowers. **2.** the flower or the bulb of such a plant. **3.** any of various related or similar plants or their flowers, as the mariposa lily or the calla lily. **4.** fleur-de-lis, esp. as the symbol of France. —*adj.* **5.** white as a lily. **6.** delicately fair. [ME, OE *lilie* < L *līli(um)* < Gk *leírion*] —**lil′y·like′,** *adj.*

lil·y-liv·ered (lil′ē liv′ərd), *adj.* weak in courage; cowardly.

lil′y of the val′ley, *pl.* **lilies of the valley.** a stemless herb, *Convallaria majalis*, having a raceme of drooping, bell-shaped, fragrant, white flowers. [trans. of L (Vulgate) *lilium convallium*]

lil′y pad′, the large, floating leaf of a water lily.

lil·y-white (lil′ē hwīt′, -wīt′), *adj.* **1.** white as a lily. **2.** pure; untouched by corruption or imperfection; above reproach. **3.** designating or pertaining to any faction or group favoring the exclusion of Negroes. [ME *lylie-whyt*]

Li·ma (lē′mə; *Sp.* lē′mä *for 1;* lī′mə *for 2*), *n.* **1.** a city in and the capital of Peru, near the Pacific coast. 3,317,648. **2.** a city in NW Ohio. 53,734 (1970).

Li·ma (lē′mə), *n.* a word used in communications to represent the letter L.

li′ma bean′ (lī′mə), a bean, *Phaseolus limensis*, having a broad, flat, edible seed used for food. Also called **li′ma.** [after LIMA, Peru]

lim·a·cine (lim′ə sīn′, -sin, lī′mə-), *adj.* pertaining to or resembling a slug; sluglike. [< L *līmāc-* (s. of *līmāx*) slug, snail + -INE[1]]

Li·mas·sol (lim′ə sôl′), *n.* a seaport in S Cyprus: Phoenician ruins. 48,000. Also, **Limmasol.** Ancient, **Lemessus.**

limb[1] (lim), *n.* **1.** a part or member of an animal body distinct from the head and trunk, as a leg, arm, or wing. **2.** a large or main branch of a tree. **3.** a projecting part or member. **4.** a person or thing regarded as a part, member, or branch of something. **5. out on a limb,** *U.S. Informal.* in a dangerous or compromising situation; vulnerable. [ME, OE *lim*; akin to Icel *lim* foliage, *limr* limb, *līmi* rod, L *līmus* aslant, *līmen* threshold] —**limbed** (limd), *adj.* —**limb′less,** *adj.* —**Syn. 2.** See **branch.**

limb[2] (lim), *n.* **1.** *Astron.* the edge of the disk of the sun, a moon, or a planet. **2.** the graduated edge of a quadrant or similar instrument. **3.** *Bot.* **a.** the upper spreading part of a gamopetalous corolla. **b.** the expanded portion of a petal, sepal, or leaf. [< L *limb(us)*; see LIMBUS, LIMBO[1]]

lim·bate (lim′bāt), *adj.* *Bot., Zool.* bordered, as a flower in which one color is surrounded by an edging of another. [< LL *limbāt(us)* bordered, edged]

lim·ber[1] (lim′bər), *adj.* **1.** bending readily; flexible; pliant. **2.** characterized by ease in bending the body; supple; lithe. —*v.i.* **3.** to make oneself limber (usually fol. by *up*): *to limber up before the game.* —*v.t.* **4.** to make (something) limber (usually fol. by *up*): *to limber up one's wits before an exam.* [? akin to LIMB[1]] —**lim′ber·ly,** *adv.* —**lim′ber·ness,** *n.* —**Syn. 1.** pliable. See **flexible.** —**Ant. 1.** rigid, unbending. **1, 2.** stiff.

lim·ber[2] (lim′bər), *Mil.* —*n.* **1.** a two-wheeled vehicle, originally pulled by four or six horses, behind which is towed a field gun or caisson. —*v.t.* **2.** to attach the limber to (a gun) in preparation for moving away. —*v.i.* **3.** to attach a limber to a gun (usually fol. by *up*). [late ME *lymo(u)r* pole of a vehicle. See LIMB[1], -ER[1]]

lim·bo[1] (lim′bō), *n., pl.* **-bos.** **1.** (*often cap.*) *Theol.* a region on the border of hell or heaven, serving as the abode after death of unbaptized infants and of the righteous who died before the coming of Christ. **2.** a place or state of oblivion to which persons or things are regarded as being relegated when cast aside, forgotten, past, or out of date. **3.** a place or state of imprisonment or confinement. **4.** a state of being or place midway between two extremes. [ME, abstracted from ML phrase *in limbo* on hell's border (L: on the edge) = *in* on + *limbō*, abl. of *limbus* edge, border (L), place bordering on hell (ML)]

lim·bo[2] (lim′bō), *n., pl.* **-bos.** a dance of West Indian origin in which the dancer bends backward and moves with a shuffling step under a horizontal bar that is lowered after each successive pass. [? var. of LIMBER[2]; see BANJO]

Lim·bourg (*Fr.* laN bo͞or′), *n.* See under **Limburg.**

Lim·burg (lim′bûrg; *Du.* lim′bœrkh), *n.* a medieval duchy in W Europe: now divided into a province in the SE Netherlands (**Lim′burg**) and a province in NE Belgium (**Limbourg**).

Lim·burg·er (lim′bûr′gər), *n.* a variety of soft cheese of strong odor and flavor. Also called **Lim′burger cheese′, Lim′burg cheese′.** [after LIMBURG; see -ER[1]]

lim·bus (lim′bəs), *n., pl.* **-bi** (-bī). *Anat., Zool.* a border, edge, or limb. [< NL, L] —**lim′bic,** *adj.*

lime[1] (līm), *n., v.,* **limed, lim·ing.** —*n.* **1.** Also called **calcium oxide, quicklime.** a white or grayish-white solid, CaO, that when combined with water forms calcium hydroxide, obtained from calcium carbonate, limestone, or oyster shells: used chiefly in mortars, plasters, and cements, in bleaching powder, and in the manufacture of steel, paper, glass, and various chemicals of calcium. **2.** a calcium compound for improving crops grown in soils deficient in lime. **3.** birdlime. —*v.t.* **4.** to treat (soil) with lime or compounds of calcium. **5.** to smear (twigs, branches, etc.) with birdlime. **6.** to catch with or as with birdlime. **7.** to paint or cover (a surface) with a composition of lime and water; whitewash. [ME, OE *līm;* c. D *lijm,* G *Leim,* Icel *līm* glue, L *līmus* slime; akin to LOAM] —**lime′less,** *adj.*

lime[2] (līm), *n.* **1.** the small, greenish-yellow, acid fruit of a tropical tree, *Citrus aurantifolia,* allied to the lemon. **2.** the tree that bears this fruit. [< Sp *lima* < Ar *līmah, līm* citrus fruit]

lime[3] (līm), *n.* a linden. [unexplained var. of obs. *line, lind,* ME, OE *lind.* See LINDEN]

lime·ade (līm′ād′), *n.* a beverage consisting of lime juice, a sweetener, and plain or carbonated water.

Lime·house (līm′hous′), *n.* a district in the East End of London, England, notorious for its squalor.

lime′ hy′drate. See **slaked lime.**

lime·kiln (līm′kil′, -kiln′), *n.* a kiln or furnace for making lime by calcining limestone or shells. [ME *limkilne*]

lime·light (līm′līt′), *n.* **1.** *Theat.* (formerly) a spotlight unit for the stage, using a flame of mixed gases directed at a cylinder of lime and a special lens that concentrated the light in a strong beam. **2.** the light of public notice, interest, observation, or notoriety. —**lime′light′er,** *n.*

lime′ lin′iment, *Pharm.* See **carron oil.**

li·men (lī′mən), *n., pl.* **li·mens, lim·i·na** (lim′ə nə). *Psychol.* threshold (def. 4). [< L]

lim·er·ick (lim′ər ik), *n.* a kind of humorous verse of five lines, in which the first, second, and fifth lines rhyme with each other, and the third and fourth lines, which are shorter, form a rhymed couplet. [after LIMERICK: said to go back to social gatherings where the group sang "Will you come up to Limerick?" after each set of verses, extemporized in turn by the members of the party]

Lim·er·ick (lim′ər ik), *n.* **1.** a county in N Munster, in the SW Republic of Ireland. 83,298; 1037 sq. mi. **2.** its county seat: a seaport at the head of the Shannon estuary. 57,161.

lime·stone (līm′stōn′), *n.* any stone consisting wholly or mainly of calcium carbonate: some varieties suitable for burning into lime.

lime·sul·fur (līm′sul′fər), *n.* *Chem.* a mixture of lime and sulfur that has been boiled in water: used as an insecticide, fungicide, and sheep-dip. Also, **lime′sul′phur.**

lime·wa·ter (līm′wô′tər, -wot′ər), *n.* **1.** an aqueous solution of slaked lime, used in medicine, antacids, lotions, and to absorb carbon dioxide from the air. **2.** water containing naturally an unusual amount of calcium carbonate or calcium sulfate.

lim·ey (lī′mē), *n., pl.* **-eys,** *adj.* *Slang.* —*n.* **1.** a British sailor. **2.** an Englishman. —*adj.* **3.** British. [short for *lime-juicer* British sailor, so called because required by law to drink lime juice to ward off scurvy; see -Y[2]]

li·mic·o·line (lī mik′ə lin′, -lin), *adj.* shore-inhabiting; of or pertaining to numerous birds of the families *Charadriidae,* comprising the plovers, and *Scolopacidae,* comprising the sandpipers. [< LL *līmicol(a)* mud-dweller (see LIMICOLOUS) + -INE[1]]

li·mic·o·lous (lī mik′ə ləs), *adj.* dwelling in mud or muddy regions. [< LL *līmicol(a)* mud-dweller + -OUS; see LIME[1], -COLOUS]

lim·i·nal (lim′ə nəl, lī′mə-), *adj.* *Psychol.* of, pertaining to, or situated at the limen. [< L *līmin-* (s. of *līmen*) threshold + -AL[1]]

lim·it (lim′it), *n.* **1.** the final or furthest bound or point as to extent or continuance. **2.** a boundary or bound, as of a country or district. **3. limits,** the premises or region enclosed within boundaries. **4.** *Math.* **a.** a number such that the value of a given function remains arbitrarily close to this number when the independent variable is sufficiently close to a specified point or is sufficiently large. The limit of $1/x$ is zero as x approaches infinity. **b.** a number such that the absolute value of the difference between terms of a given sequence and the number approaches zero as the index of the terms increases to infinity. **c.** one of two numbers affixed to the integration symbol for a definite integral, indicating the interval or region over which the integration is taking place. **5.** *Games.* the maximum sum by which a bet may be raised at any one time. **6. the limit,** *Informal.* something or someone that exasperates, delights, etc., to an extreme or intolerable degree. —*v.t.* **7.** to restrict by or as by establishing limits. **8.** to confine or keep within limits. [ME *lymyt* < L *līmit-* (s. of *līmes*) boundary, path between fields] —**lim′it·a·ble,** *adj.* —**lim′it·a·ble·ness,** *n.* —**lim′it·er,** *n.* —**Syn. 2.** confine, frontier, border. **8.** restrain.

lim·i·tar·y (lim′i ter′ē), *adj.* **1.** of, pertaining to, or serving as a limit. **2.** *Archaic.* subject to limits; limited. [< L *līmitāri(s)* on the border]

lim·i·ta·tion (lim′i tā′shən), *n.* **1.** something that limits; a limit or bound; restriction. **2.** a restrictive weakness; lack of capacity: *to know one's limitations.* **3.** the act of limiting. **4.** the quality or state or being limited. **5.** *Law.* the assignment, as by statute, of a period of time within which an action must be brought. [ME *tymytacion* < L *līmitātiōn-* (s. of *līmitātiō*) a bounding = *līmitāt(us)* bounded (ptp. of *līmitāre;* see LIMIT, -ATE[1]) + *-iōn-* -ION]

lim·it·ed (lim′i tid), *adj.* **1.** confined within limits; restricted or circumscribed. **2.** restricted with reference to governing powers by limitations prescribed in laws and in a constitution. **3.** unable to think imaginatively or independently; lacking scope; narrow. **4.** *Chiefly Brit.* **a.** (of a business firm) owned by stockholders, each having a restricted liability for the company's debts. **b.** (*usually cap.*) incorporated; Inc. *Abbr.:* Ltd. **5.** (of railroad trains, buses, etc.) making only a limited number of stops en route. —*n.* **6.** *U.S.* a limited train, bus, etc. —**lim′it·ed·ly,** *adv.* —**lim′it·ed·ness,** *n.*

lim′ited edi′tion, an edition, as of a book or lithograph, limited to a specified number of copies.

lim′ited mon′archy, a monarchy that is limited by laws and a constitution. Also called **constitutional monarchy.**

lim·it·er (lim′i tər), *n.* **1.** someone or something that limits. **2.** *Electronics.* a device for limiting the amplitude of a frequency-modulated signal to a certain value in order to remove amplitude modulation. [LIMIT + -ER[1]; r. ME *limitour;* see -OR[2]]

lim·it·ing (lim′i ting), *adj.* **1.** serving to restrict or restrain; confining. **2.** *Gram.* of the nature of a limiting adjective or a restrictive clause.

lim′iting ad′jective, *Gram.* **1.** (in English and some other languages) one of a small group of adjectives that modify the nouns to which they are applied by restricting rather than describing or qualifying. *This, some,* and *certain* are limiting adjectives. **2.** an adjective, as *few* or *other,* that in English follows determiners and precedes descriptive adjectives: *a few red apples.*

lim·it·less (lim′it lis), *adj.* without limit; boundless. —**lim′it·less·ly,** *adv.* —**lim′it·less·ness,** *n.*

Lim·ma·sol (lim′ə sôl′), *n.* Limassol.

limn (lim), *v.t.* *Archaic.* **1.** to represent in drawing or painting. **2.** to portray in words; describe. [late ME *lymne,* var. of ME *lumine* to illuminate (manuscripts), aph. var. of *enlumine* < MF *enluminer* < L *inlūmināre* to embellish, lit., light up; see ILLUMINATE]

lim·ner (lim′nər), *n.* a painter, esp. a portrait painter. [ME *limnour.* See LIMN, -ER[1]]

lim·net·ic (lim net′ik), *adj.* pertaining to or living in the open water of a fresh-water pond or lake. [< Gk *limnēt(ēs)* marsh-dwelling (*límnē* pool, marsh + *-tēs* inhabiting) + -IC]

lim·nol·o·gy (lim nol′ə jē), *n.* the scientific study of bodies of fresh water, as lakes and ponds, with reference to their physical, biological, and other features. [*limno-* (comb. form repr. Gk *límnē* pool, marsh) + -LOGY] —**lim·no·log·i·cal** (lim′nəloj′i kəl), **lim′no·log′ic,** *adj.* —**lim′no·log′i·cal·ly,** *adv.* —**lim·nol′o·gist,** *n.*

lim·o (lim′ō), *n., pl.* **lim·os.** *Informal.* a limousine.

Li·moges (li mōzh′; *Fr.* lē môzh′), *n.* **1.** a city in S central France. 147,406. **2.** Also called **Limoges′ ware′.** a type of fine porcelain manufactured at Limoges.

lim·o·nene (lim′ə nēn′), *n.* *Chem.* a liquid terpene, $C_{10}H_{16}$, occurring in two optically different forms, the dextrorotatory form being present in the essential oils of lemon, orange, etc., and the levorotatory form in Douglas fir needle oil. [< NL *Limon(um)* lemon + -ENE]

li·mo·nite (lī′mə nīt′), *n.* an important iron ore, a hydrated ferric oxide. Also called **brown hematite.** [< Gk *leimṓn* meadow + -ITE[1]] —**li·mo·nit·ic** (lī′mə nit′ik), *adj.*

lim·ou·sine (lim′ə zēn′, lim′ə zēn′), *n.* **1.** any large, luxurious automobile. **2.** a large sedan or small bus, esp. one for transporting passengers to and from an airport, between train stations, etc. **3.** (formerly) an automobile having a permanently enclosed compartment for from three to five persons, the roof of which projects forward over the driver's seat in front. [< F, special use of *limousine* long cloak, so called because worn by shepherds of *Limousin,* former French province]

limp[1] (limp), *v.i.* **1.** to walk with a labored, jerky movement, as when lame. **2.** to proceed in a lame, faltering, or labored manner: *His writing limps from one cliché to another.* **3.** to progress with great difficulty; make little or no advance. —*n.* **4.** a lame movement or gait. [back formation from obs. *limphault,* OE *lempheallt* limping (see HALT[2]); akin to MHG *limpfen* to limp] —**limp′er,** *n.* —**limp′ing·ly,** *adv.*

limp[2] (limp), *adj.* **1.** lacking stiffness or firmness, as of substance or structure. **2.** lacking vitality; tired; fatigued. **3.** without proper firmness, force, etc., as of character. [? < Scand; cf. Icel *limpa* slackness, *limpilegur* soft, *limpíast* to become flabby] —**limp′ly,** *adv.* —**limp′ness,** *n.* —**Syn. 1.** flabby, flaccid, soft, loppy. **2, 3.** feeble, weak.

lim·pet (lim′pit), *n.* any of various marine gastropods with a low conical shell open beneath, found adhering to rocks, used for bait and sometimes for food. [ME *lempet,* OE *lempedu,* nasalized var. of **lepedu* < L *lepada,* acc. of *lepas* < Gk *lepás*]

lim·pid (lim′pid), *adj.* **1.** clear, transparent, or pellucid, as water or air. **2.** free from obscurity; lucid. **3.** completely calm; without distress or worry. [< L *limpid(us)* clear. See LYMPH, -ID[4]] —**lim·pid′i·ty, lim′pid·ness,** *n.* —**lim′pid·ly,** *adv.*

limp·kin (limp′kin), *n.* a large, loud-voiced, wading bird, *Aramus guarauna,* intermediate in size and character between the cranes and the rails, of the warmer regions of America. [LIMP[1] + -KIN; so called because of its jerky walk]

Lim·po·po (lim pō′pō), *n.* a river in S Africa, flowing from the N Republic of South Africa into the Indian Ocean. 1000 mi. long. Also called **Crocodile River.**

lim·u·loid (lim′yə loid′), *adj.* **1.** resembling or pertaining to a horseshoe crab, esp. of the genus *Limulus.* —*n.* **2.** See **horseshoe crab.**

lim·u·lus (lim′yə ləs), *n., pl.* **-li** (-lī′). a crab of the genus *Limulus;* a horseshoe crab. [< NL, name of the genus, special use of L, dim. of *līmus* sidelong; see -ULE]

lim·y (lī′mē), *adj.,* **lim·i·er, lim·i·est. 1.** consisting of, containing, or like lime. **2.** smeared with birdlime. —**lim′i·ness,** *n.*

lin (lin), *n.* linn.

lin., 1. lineal. 2. linear.

Lin·a·cre (lin′ə kər), *n.* **Thomas,** 1460?–1521, English humanist and physician.

lin·age (lī′nij), *n.* **1.** the number of printed lines, esp. agate lines, covered by a magazine article, newspaper advertisement, etc. **2.** the amount charged, paid, or received per printed line, as of a magazine article or short story. **3.** *Archaic.* alignment. Also, **lineage.**

Li·na·res (lē nä′res), *n.* a city in S Spain. 56,154 (1955).

linch·pin (linch′pin′), *n.* a pin inserted through the end of an axletree to secure a wheel. [unexplained alter. of ME *lynspin* = *lyns,* OE *lynis* axle-pin (c. G *Lünse*) + *pin* PIN]

Lin·coln (liŋ′kən), *n.* **1. Abraham,** 1809–65, 16th president of the U.S. 1861–65. **2. Benjamin,** 1733–1810, American Revolutionary general. **3.** a city in and the capital of Nebraska, in the SE part. 149,518 (1970). **4.** a city in and the county seat of Lincolnshire, in E central England. 77,065 (1961). **5.** Lincolnshire. **6.** one of an English breed of large mutton sheep, noted for its heavy fleece of coarse, long wool.

Lin·coln·esque (liŋ′kə nesk′), *adj.* like or characteristic of Abraham Lincoln.

Lin′coln green′, an olive-green color. [so called from the color of a fabric originally made in LINCOLN, England]

Lin·coln·i·an·a (liŋ kō′nē an′ə, -ä′nə, liŋ′kə-), *n.pl.* objects, writings, anecdotes, etc., pertaining to Abraham Lincoln.

Lin′coln Park′, a city in SE Michigan. 52,984 (1970).

Lin′coln's Birth′day, February 12, a legal holiday in many states of the U.S. in honor of the birth of Abraham Lincoln.

Lin·coln·shire (liŋ′kən shēr′, -shər), *n.* a county in E England. 743,383 (1961); 2663 sq. mi. *Co. seat:* Lincoln. Also called **Lincoln.**

Lin′coln's Inn′. See under **Inns of Court** (def. 1).

Lind (lind), *n.* **Jenny** (*Johanna Maria Lind Goldschmidt*) ("*The Swedish Nightingale*"), 1820–87, Swedish soprano.

lin·dane (lin′dān), *n.* *Chem.* a powder, $C_6H_6Cl_6$, used chiefly as an insecticide and weed-killer. [named after T. van der *Linden,* 20th-century Dutch chemist; see -ANE]

Lind·bergh (lind′bûrg, lin′-), *n.* **Charles A(ugustus),** 1902–74, U.S. aviator: made the first solo, nonstop, transatlantic flight 1927.

lin·den (lin′dən), *n.* **1.** any tree of the genus *Tilia,* as *T. americana* or *T. europaea,* having fragrant yellowish-white flowers and cordate leaves, grown as an ornamental or shade tree. **2.** the soft, light, white wood of any of these trees. [n. use of obs. ME, OE *linden* (adj.) of the lime tree. See LIME³, -EN²]

Lin·den (lin′dən), *n.* a city in NE New Jersey, near Newark. 41,409 (1970).

Lin·den·hurst (lin′dən hûrst′), *n.* a city on central Long Island, in SE New York. 28,359 (1970).

Lind·es·nes (lin′dis nes′), *n.* a cape at the S tip of Norway, on the North Sea. Also called **The Naze.**

Lind·ley (lind′lē, lin′-), *n.* **John,** 1799–1865, English botanist.

Lind·say (lind′zē, lin′-), *n.* **1. Howard,** 1889–1968, U.S. playwright, producer, and actor. **2. John V(liet)** (vlēt), born 1921, U.S. political leader: mayor of New York City 1966–73. **3. (Nicholas) Va·chel** (vā′chəl), 1879–1931, U.S. poet.

lin·dy (lin′dē), *n., pl.* **-dies.** an energetic jitterbug dance. Also called **lin′dy hop′.** [prob. from nickname of Charles A. LINDBERGH]

line¹ (līn), *n., v.,* **lined, lin·ing.** —*n.* **1.** a long mark of very slight breadth, made to divide an area, determine a direction, distribution, or limit, depict an object, etc. **2.** something occurring naturally or accidentally that resembles such a mark. **3.** such a mark imagined as lying on a surface or extending in space in order to understand the direction, distribution, limit, etc., of something. **4.** a number of persons or things situated along such an imaginary mark. **5.** *Math.* the path traced by a moving point having no breadth. **6.** a single row of letters or other characters on a page, inscription, etc. **7.** a series of words written, printed, or recited as one of the component units of a larger piece of writing, as a poem. **8.** Usually, **lines. a.** the spoken words of a dramatic performance. **b.** the spoken words or a speech given to an actor. **c.** a literary work, esp. a poem, or a portion of one. **9.** a brief written message. **10.** a precise mental limitation, as to what one will allow or approve. **11.** a course of action, belief, method, or explanation of these, as one formally adopted by a political group. **12.** a piece of discovered information (often fol. by *on*). **13.** a series of ancestors or of animals or plants of preceding generations. **14.** *Slang.* a form of conversation intended to persuade or impress. **15. lines, a.** the outer form or proportions of a ship, building, etc. **b.** a general form, as of an event or something that is made, which may be the basis of comparison, imitation, etc. **16. lines,** *Informal.* a certificate of marriage. **17. lines,** *Brit.* a person's lot or fortune: *hard lines.* **18.** a transportation company, or one of its routes. **19.** a person's occupation or business. **20.** a variety of related items for sale. **21.** a cord or rope, esp. a strong one used for fishing, hauling, hanging clothes, etc., or in rigging. **22.** a cord used in marking or taking measurements. **23.** *Elect.* **a.** a wire circuit connecting two or more pieces of electric apparatus, esp. the wire or wires connecting points or stations in a telegraph or telephone system, or the system itself. **b.** maxwell. **24.** *Fine Arts.* **a.** a mark made by a brush, pencil, etc., that defines the contour of a shape, form, hatching, etc. **b.** the edge of a shape. **c.** the linear aspect of a work of art considered as a formal element in its composition. **25. the line,** *Geog.* the equator. **26.** *Insurance.* **a.** a class or type of insurance: *casualty line.* **b.** the amount of insurance written for a particular risk. **27.** *Law.* the outline or boundary of a piece of real estate. **28.** *Journalism.* banner (def. 6). **29.** *Mil.* **a.** a defensive position or front. **b.** a series of fortifications. **c.** the combatant forces of an army or navy, or their officers. **d.** a formation of troops drawn up abreast (distinguished from *column*). **e.** a formation of ships, usually abreast. **f.** (formerly) an arrangement of troops or warships prepared for battle. **g.** (formerly) the regular forces of an army or navy. **30.** Usually, **lines.** *Mil.* a distribution of troops, sentries, etc., for the defense of a position or for an attack: *within the enemy's lines.* **31.** *Naut.* a pipe or hose: *a steam line.* **32.** *Football.* either of the two front rows of opposing players lined up opposite each other on the line of scrimmage: *a strong line.* **33.** *Textiles.* the longer and preferred flax or hemp fibers. Cf. **tow²** (def. 2). **34. draw the line,** to impose a limit on what is allowed or approved. **35. go up in one's lines,** *U.S. Theat.* to forget one's part. **36. hold the line,** to maintain the status quo, esp. in order to forestall unfavorable developments. **37. in line, a.** in alignment; straight. **b.** in conformity or agreement. **c.** in control (of one's conduct). **38. in line of duty,** in the performance of one's duty. Also, **in the line of duty. 39. into line, a.** into alignment. **b.** into agreement or conformity. **40. out of line, a.** not in a straight line. **b.** *Slang.* in disagreement with what is accepted or practiced. **c.** *Slang.* impertinent; presumptuous. **41. read between the lines,** to comprehend the unexpressed but implied meaning of something said or written. **42. toe the line, a.** to conform strictly to a rule, command, etc. **b.** to shoulder responsibilities; do one's duty. —*v.i.* **43.** to take a position in a line; range (often fol. by *up*). **44.** *Baseball.* **a.** to hit a line drive. **b.** to line out. —*v.t.* **45.** to bring into a line, or into line with others. **46.** to hire or induce to give assistance (usually fol. by *up*): *to line up a series of lecturers.* **47.** to mark with a line or lines. **48.** to sketch verbally or in writing; outline (often fol. by *out*): *We followed the plan he had lined out.* **49.** to arrange or form a closely set row or line along. **50.** to apply liner to (the eyes). **51.** *Archaic.* to measure or test with a line. **52. line out, a.** *Baseball.* to be put out by hitting a line drive caught on the fly by a player of the opposing team. **b.** to execute or perform: *He lined out a few old songs with great gusto.* [ME, OE: cord, rope, stroke, mark, row, guiding rule < L *līnea,* n. use of fem. of *līneus* flaxen. See LINE², -EOUS] —**lin′a·ble,line′a·ble,***adj.* —**line′less,***adj.* —**line′like′,***adj.*

line² (līn), *v.t.,* **lined, lin·ing. 1.** to cover the inner side of. **2.** to furnish or fill, as a pocket or purse with money. [ME *lyne(n)* < *line* flax, linen, OE *līn* < L *līn(um)* flax]

lin·e·age¹ (lin′ē ij), *n.* **1.** lineal descent from an ancestor; ancestry or extraction. **2.** the line of descendants of a particular ancestor; family; race. [LINE(AL) + -AGE; r. ME *linage* < AF; OF *lignage* < LL **lineāticum;* see LINE¹] —**Syn. 1.** pedigree, derivation. **2.** tribe, clan.

line·age² (lī′nij), *n.* linage.

lin·e·al (lin′ē əl), *adj.* **1.** being in the direct line, as a descendant, ancestor, etc., or in a direct line, as descent or succession. **2.** of or transmitted by lineal descent. **3.** linear. [late ME < LL *līneāl(is)*] —**lin′e·al·ly,** *adv.*

Linear leaf

lin·e·a·ment (lin′ē ə mənt), *n.* **1.** Often, **lineaments.** a feature or detail of a face, body, or figure, considered with respect to its outline or contour. **2.** Usually, **lineaments.** distinguishing features; distinctive characteristics. [< L *līneāment(um)* a stroke, pl., features = *līneā(re)* (to) draw a line (see LINE¹) + *-mentum* -MENT] —**lin·e·a·men·tal** (lin′ē-ə men′təl), *adj.* —**lin′e·a·men·ta′tion,** *n.*

lin·e·ar (lin′ē ər), *adj.* **1.** extended or arranged in a line: *a linear series.* **2.** involving measurement in one dimension only; pertaining to length. **3.** pertaining to or represented by lines: *linear dimensions.* **4.** consisting of or using lines: *linear design.* **5.** having the form of or resembling a line: *linear nebulae.* **6.** *Math.* **a.** consisting of, involving, or describable by terms of the first degree: *a linear equation.* **b.** having the same effect on a sum as on each of the summands: *a linear operation.* **7.** threadlike; narrow and elongated: *a linear leaf.* [< L *līneār(is)* of, belonging to lines] —**lin·e·ar·i·ty** (lin′ē ar′i tē), *adj.* —**lin′e·ar·ly,** *adv.*

Linear A, an ancient system of writing, not yet deciphered, found at Minoan sites.

lin′ear accel′erator, *Physics.* an accelerator in which particles are propelled in straight paths by the use of alternating electric voltages so timed that the particles receive increasing increments of energy.

Linear B, an ancient system of writing representing a very early form of Greek, found at Knossos and Pylos.

lin′ear equa′tion, *Math.* a first-order equation involving two variables: graphed as a straight line in the Cartesian coordinate system.

lin·e·ar·ise (lin′ē ə rīz′), *v.t.,* **-ised, -is·ing.** *Chiefly Brit.* linearize. —**lin′e·ar·i·sa′tion,** *n.*

lin·e·ar·ize (lin′ē ə rīz′), *v.t.,* **-ized, -iz·ing.** to make linear; give linear form to. —**lin′e·ar·i·za′tion,** *n.*

lin′ear meas′ure, 1. any system of measurement for measuring length. **2.** any unit of measurement used in linear measure, as the inch, foot, or meter.

lin′ear perspec′tive, a system for representing depth and volume on a flat surface by means of lines converging at a point or points on a horizon line. See diag. at **perspective.**

lin·e·ate (lin′ē it, -āt′), *adj.* marked with lines, esp. lengthwise, parallel lines; striped. Also, **lin′e·at′ed.** [< L *līneāt(us)* lined, made straight, ptp. of *līneāre.* See LINEAMENT, -ATE¹]

lin·e·a·tion (lin′ē ā′shən), *n.* **1.** the act of marking with or tracing by lines. **2.** a division into lines. **3.** an outline or delineation. **4.** an arrangement or group of lines. [ME *lyneacion* < LL *līneātion-* (s. of *līneātiō*)]

line·back·er (līn′bak′ər), *n.* *Football.* a player on defense who takes a position close behind the linemen.

line·breed·ing (līn′brē′diŋ), *n.* *Genetics.* a form of inbreeding directed toward keeping the offspring closely related to a superior ancestor.

line′ cut′, *Print.* an engraving consisting only of lines or areas that are solid black or white. Cf. **halftone** (def. 2).

line′ draw′ing, a drawing done exclusively in line, providing gradations in tone entirely through variations in width and density.

line′ drive′, *Baseball.* a batted ball that travels low, fast, and straight. Also called **liner.**

line′ engrav′ing, 1. a technique of engraving in which all effects are produced by variations in the width and density of lines incised with a burin. **2.** a metal plate so engraved. **3.** a print or picture made from it. —**line′ engrav′er.**

line′ gale′. See **equinoctial storm.**

line·man (līn′mən), *n., pl.* **-men. 1.** Also, **linesman.** a man who installs or repairs telephone, telegraph, or other wires. **2.** *Football.* one of the players in the line.

lin·en (lin′ən), *n.* **1.** fabric woven from flax yarns. **2.** Often, **linens.** clothing, bedding, etc., made of linen cloth or a more common substitute, as cotton. **3.** yarn made of flax fiber. **4.** thread made of flax yarns. **5. wash one's dirty linen in public,** to discuss in public one's personal scandals or domestic difficulties. **—***adj.* **6.** made of linen. [ME *lin(n)en* (n., adj.), OE *linnen, līnen* (adj.) made of flax. See LINE^2, -EN^1] **—lin′en·y,** *adj.*

lin′en clos′et, a closet for storing sheets, towels, table linen, etc.

lin′en drap′er, *Brit.* a dry-goods merchant.

lin′en pa′per, paper made from pure linen or from substitutes that produce a similar paper finish.

line′ of′ficer, *Mil.* an officer serving with combatant units or warships, as distinguished from a staff officer, supply officer, etc.

line′ of fire′, the straight horizontal line from the muzzle of a weapon in the direction of the axis of the bore, just prior to firing.

line′ of force′, *Physics.* an imaginary line or curve in a field of force, as an electric or a magnetic field, such that the direction of the line at any point corresponds to that exerted by the force in the field at that point. Also called **field line.**

line′ of sight′, 1. Also called **line′ of sight′ing.** an imaginary straight line running through the aligned sights of a firearm, surveying equipment, etc. **2.** *Astron.* an imaginary line from an observer to a celestial body, coincident with the path traveled by light rays received from the body. **3.** *Ophthalm.* See **line of vision. 4.** See **sight line.**

line′ of vi′sion, *Ophthalm.* a straight line that connects the fovea centralis of an eye with the point focused on.

lin·e·o·late (lin′ē ə lāt′), *adj.* *Zool., Bot.* marked with minute lines; finely lineate. Also, **lin′e·o·lat′ed.** [< L *līneol(a)* (dim. of *līnea* LINE^1) + -ATE^1]

lin·er^1 (lī′nər), *n.* **1.** one of a commercial line of steamships or airplanes. **2.** a person or thing that traces by or marks with lines. **3.** *Baseball.* See **line drive. 4.** a cosmetic, esp. a grease pencil or other preparation, used to outline or highlight the eyes. [LINE^1 + -ER^1]

lin·er^2 (lī′nər), *n.* **1.** a person who fits or provides linings. **2.** something serving as a lining. **3.** a stiff protective covering for a phonograph record. [LINE^2 + -ER^1]

lines·man (līnz′mən), *n., pl.* **-men. 1.** lineman (def. 1). **2.** *Sports.* **a.** an official, as in tennis and soccer, who assists the referee. **b.** *Football.* an official who marks the distances gained and lost and otherwise assists the referee and field judge.

lines′ plan′, *Naval Archit.* a set of scale drawings defining the hull form of a vessel, comprising a body plan, a half-breadth plan, and a sheer plan.

line′ squall′, (not in technical use) a squall advancing along a front that forms a more or less definite line.

line′ storm′. See **equinoctial storm.**

line-up (līn′up′), *n.* **1.** an orderly arrangement of persons or things in a queue or row. **2.** the persons or things themselves. **3.** a technique used in police investigation in which a victim or witness is asked to identify a suspect from a number of people standing in line. **4.** *Sports.* the list of the participating players in a game together with their positions. **5.** an organization of people, companies, etc., for some common purpose. Also, **line′up′.**

lin ft, linear foot; linear feet. Also, **lin. ft.**

ling^1 (ling), *n., pl.* (*esp. collectively*) **ling,** (*esp. referring to two or more kinds or species*) **lings. 1.** an elongated, marine, gadid food fish, *Molva molva,* found in Greenland and northern Europe. **2.** the burbot. **3.** any of various other elongated food fishes. [ME *ling, lenge;* c. D *leng;* akin to Icel *langa;* so called from its length. See LONG^1]

ling^2 (ling), *n.* the heather, *Calluna vulgaris.* [ME *lyng* < Scand; cf. Icel *lyng*]

-ling^1, a suffix of nouns, often pejorative, denoting a person or thing connected with a group, activity, or status (*hireling; underling*), and also used to form diminutives (*princeling; duckling*). [ME, OE; c. G *-ling,* Icel *-lingr,* Goth *-lings;* orig. *-l-* (OE *-la,* hypocoristic suffix) + *-ing* -ING^1]

-ling^2, an adverbial suffix expressing direction, position, state, etc.: *darkling; sideling.* [ME, OE; adv. use of gradational var. *lang* LONG^1]

ling., linguistics.

lin·ga (ling′gə), *n.* (in popular Hinduism) a phallus, symbol of Siva. Also, **lin·gam** (ling′gəm). Cf. **yoni.** [< Skt, s. of *lingam* mark, token, penis]

Lin·ga·yat (ling gä′yit), *n.* *Hinduism.* a member of the Lingayata cult. [< Kanarese *lingāyata;* see LINGA]

Lin·ga·ya·ta (ling gä′yə tə), *n.* *Hinduism.* a Saiva cult emphasizing devotion and faith. Also called **Vira Saiva.** [< Kanarese; akin to Skt *linga* LINGA]

Lin′ga·yén′ Gulf′ (ling′gä yen′), a gulf in the Philippines, on the NW coast of Luzon.

ling·cod (ling′kod′), *n., pl.* **-cods,** (*esp. collectively*) **-cod.** a large-mouthed game fish, *Ophiodon elongatus,* found in the North Pacific. Also, **ling′ cod′.**

lin·ger (ling′gər), *v.i.* **1.** to remain or stay on in a place, as if from reluctance to leave. **2.** to remain alive, as a person, or in use, as a custom, though with diminishing vitality. **3.** to dwell in contemplation, thought, or enjoyment. **4.** to be tardy in action; delay; dawdle. **5.** to walk slowly; saunter along. **—***v.t.* **6.** to pass (time) in a leisurely or a tedious manner (usually fol. by *away* or *out*): *We lingered away the summer at the beach.* **7.** *Archaic.* to drag out or protract. [ME *lenger* to dwell, remain (somewhere), freq. of *lengen,* OE *lengan* to delay, prolong, lit., lengthen. See LONG^1, -ER^6] **—lin′ger·er,** *n.* **—lin′ger·ing·ly,** *adv.* **—Syn. 1, 4.** tarry. **1, 5.** loiter.

lin·ge·rie (län′zhə rā′, lan′zhə rē′, -jə-; *Fr.* laNzh^ə rē′), *n.* **1.** undergarments, nightwear, or other intimate clothing worn by women. **2.** *Archaic.* linen goods in general. [< F = MF *linge* linen (< L *līneus* of flax; see LINE^1) + *-erie* -ERY]

lin·go (ling′gō), *n., pl.* **-goes.** *Informal.* **1.** language or speech, esp. if strange or foreign. **2.** the language or speech peculiar to a particular individual. [< Lingua Franca < It *lin(gua)* tongue (< L) + Pr *(len)go* tongue < L *lingua;* see LINGUA]

-lings, var. of **-ling^2.** [ME *-linges.* See -LING^2, -S^1]

lin·gua (ling′gwə), *n., pl.* **-guae** (-gwē). the tongue or a part like a tongue. [< L]

lin′gua fran′ca (frang′kə), *pl.* **lingua francas, lin·guae fran·cae** (ling′gwē fran′sē). **1.** any language widely used as a means of communication among speakers of other languages. **2.** (*caps.*) the Italian-Provençal jargon formerly widely used in eastern Mediterranean ports. [< It: lit., Frankish tongue]

lin′gua ge·ral′ (zhə räl′), (*often caps.*) a lingua franca based on Tupi and spoken in the Amazon basin of South America. [< Pg: general language]

lin·gual (ling′gwəl), *adj.* **1.** of or pertaining to the tongue or some tonguelike part. **2.** pertaining to languages. **3.** *Phonet.* articulated with the aid of the tongue, esp. the tip of the tongue, as *d, n, s,* or *r.* **—***n.* **4.** *Phonet.* a lingual sound. [< ML *linguāl(is).* See LINGUA, -AL^1] **—lin′gual·ly,** *adv.*

lin·gui·form (ling′gwə fôrm′), *adj.* tongue-shaped. [< L *lingu(a)* tongue + -I- + -FORM]

lin·gui·ni (ling gwē′nē), *n.* *Italian Cookery.* a type of pasta in long, slender, flat pieces. [< It, pl. of *linguino,* dim. of *lingua* tongue; see -INE^1]

lin·guist (ling′gwist), *n.* **1.** a person skilled in several languages; polyglot. **2.** a specialist in linguistics. [< L *lingu(a)* tongue + -IST]

lin·guis·tic (ling gwis′tik), *adj.* **1.** of or belonging to language: *linguistic change.* **2.** of or pertaining to linguistics. **—lin·guis′ti·cal·ly,** *adv.*

linguis′tic at′las. See **dialect atlas.**

linguis′tic form′, any meaningful unit of speech, as a sentence, phrase, or word.

linguis′tic geog′raphy. See **dialect geography. —linguis′tic geog′rapher.**

lin·guis·tics (ling gwis′tiks), *n.* (*construed as sing.*) the science of language, including phonetics, phonology, morphology, and syntax and often divided into historical linguistics and descriptive linguistics. Also called, *esp. Brit.,* **philology.** [see LINGUISTIC, -ICS]

linguis′tic stock′, 1. a parent language and all its derived dialects and languages. **2.** the people speaking any of these dialects or languages.

lin·gu·late (ling′gyə lāt′), *adj.* formed like a tongue; ligulate. Also, **lin′gu·lat′ed.** [< L *lingulāt(us)* tongue-shaped = *lingul(a)* (dim. of *lingua* tongue; see -ULE) + *-ātus* -ATE^1]

lin·i·ment (lin′ə mənt), *n.* a liquid preparation, usually oily and aromatic, for rubbing on or applying to the skin, as for sprains or bruises. [late ME *lynyment* < LL *linīmentum* ointment < *linī(re)* (var. of *linere* to smear) + *-mentum* -MENT]

li·nin (lī′nin), *n.* *Biol.* the substance forming the netlike structure that connects the chromatin granules in the nucleus of a cell. [< L *līn(um)* flax + -IN^2]

lin·ing^1 (lī′ning), *n.* **1.** a layer of material on the inner side of something. **2.** *Bookbinding.* the material used to strengthen the back of a book. **3.** the act or process of lining something. [late ME *lynyng.* See LINE^2, -ING^1]

lin·ing (lī′ning), *n.* **1.** the act or process of lining. **2.** the act of marking or ornamenting a surface with lines. **3.** a design or ornamentation composed of lines. [LINE^1 + -ING^1]

link^1 (lingk), *n.* **1.** any of the separate pieces that form a chain. **2.** anything serving to connect one part or thing with another; a bond or tie. **3.** a ring, loop, or the like: *a link of hair.* **4.** any of a number of connected sausages. **5.** a unit in a communications system, as a radio relay station. **6.** a cuff link. **7.** *Survey., Civ. Eng.* **a.** (in a surveyor's chain) a unit of length equal to 7.92 inches. **b.** one of 100 rods or loops of equal length forming a surveyor's or engineer's chain. **8.** *Chem.* bond^1 (def. 14). **9.** *Mach.* a rigid, movable piece or rod, connected with other parts by means of pivots or the like, for the purpose of transmitting motion. **—***v.t., v.i.* **10.** to join by or as by a link or links; unite. [late ME *link(e)* < ODan *lænkia* chain; c. Icel *hlekkr* link (pl., chain), OE *hlence* coat of chain mail, akin to G *Gelenk* joint] **—link′a·ble,** *adj.* **—link′y,** *adj.* **—Syn. 2.** connection. **10.** connect, fasten, bind.

link^2 (lingk), *n.* a torch, esp. of tow and pitch. [? special use of LINK^1; the torches so called may have been made of strands twisted together in chainlike form]

link·age (ling′kij), *n.* **1.** the act of linking. **2.** the state or manner of being linked. **3.** a system of links. **4.** *Genetics.* an association between two or more genes located on the same chromosome that tends to cause the characters determined by these genes to be inherited as an inseparable unit. **5.** *Mach.* an assembly of four or more rods for transmitting motion, usually in the same plane or in parallel planes. **6.** *Elect.* a quantity associated with the magnetic flux in a coil or circuit, equal to the product of the number of lines of magnetic flux times the number of turns in the coil or circuit.

link·boy (lingk′boi′), *n.* (formerly) a boy hired to carry a torch for a pedestrian on dark streets.

linked (lingkt), *adj.* *Genetics.* (of a gene) exhibiting linkage. [late ME]

linked′ rhyme′, *Pros.* a rhyme in which the end of one line together with the first sound of the next line forms a rhyme with the end of another line, as in *Some birds fly / Towards the night.*

linked′ verse′, *Pros.* a Japanese verse form in which stanzas of three lines alternating with stanzas of two lines are composed by two or more poets in alternation.

link′ing verb′, a copulative verb.

Lin·kö·ping (lēn′chœ′peng), *n.* a city in S Sweden. 70,691 (1965).

links (lingks), *n.pl.* See **golf course.** [ME *lynkys* slopes, OE *hlincas,* pl. of *hlinc* rising ground = *hlin(ian)* (to) LEAN^1 + *-k* suffix]

Link′ train′er, *Trademark.* a ground-training device used in instrument-flight training for pilots.

link·work (lingk′wûrk′), *n.* **1.** something composed of links, as a chain. **2.** a linkage.

Lin·lith·gow (lin lith′gō), *n.* former name of **West Lothian.**

linn (lin), *n. Chiefly Scot.* **1.** a cascade of water in a watercourse, esp. a waterfall or torrent of rushing water in a river or stream. **2.** a steep ravine or precipice. Also, **lin.** [OE *hlynn* torrent, lit., something noisy + ScotGael *linne* (Ir *linn,* Welsh *llyn*) pool]

Lin·nae·us (li nē′əs), *n.* **Car·o·lus** (kar′ə ləs), (*Carl von Linné*), 1707–78, Swedish botanist.

Lin·ne·an (li nē′ən), *adj.* of or pertaining to Linnaeus, to his binomial system of scientific nomenclature, or to his system of botanical classification. Also, **Lin·nae′an.**

lin·net (lin′it), *n.* a small, Old World, fringilline songbird, *Carduelis cannabina.* [OE *līnete,* short for *līnetwige* linnet; see LINTWHITE]

li·no·cut (lī′nə kut′), *n.* **1.** a cut made from a design carved into linoleum that has been mounted on a block of wood. **2.** a print made from such a cut. [LINO(LEUM) + CUT]

lin/o·le/ic ac/id (lin′ə lē′ik, li nō′lē ik), *Chem.* an unsaturated fatty acid, $C_{17}H_{31}COOH$, occurring as a glyceride in drying oils, as in linseed oil. Also, **li·no′lic ac′id** (lə nō′lik). [Gk *lín(on)* flax + OLEIC]

li·no·le·um (li nō′lē əm), *n.* a floor covering formed of burlap or canvas coated with linseed oil, powdered cork, and rosin. [< L *līn(um)* flax, linen + *oleum* oil]

lino′leum block′, a piece of soft cork linoleum, often mounted on a block of wood, incised or carved in relief and used in making prints.

Lin·o·type (lī′nə tīp′), *n., v.,* **-typed, -typ·ing.** —*n.* **1.** *Trademark.* a typesetting machine that casts solid lines of type from brass dies, or matrices, which are selected automatically by actuating a keyboard. —*v.t., v.i.* **2.** (*l.c.*) *Print.* to typeset on such a machine. —**lin′o·typ′er, lin′o·typ′ist,** *n.*

lin·sang (lin′sang), *n.* any of several catlike carnivores of the genera *Prionodon* (or *Linsang*), of the East Indies, or *Poina,* of Africa, having retractile claws and a long tail. [< Malay]

lin·seed (lin′sēd′), *n.* flaxseed. [ME *linsed,* OE *līnsǣd.* See LINE², SEED]

lin′seed oil′, a drying oil obtained by pressing flaxseed, used in making paints, printing inks, linoleum, etc.

lin·sey-wool·sey (lin′zē wo͝ol′zē), *n.* a coarse fabric woven from linen warp and coarse wool filling. Also called **lin′sey.** [ME *lynsy wolsye,* lit., linen cloth, wool cloth = *lyn* (see LINEN) + *-sy,* var. of *say* cloth (< OF *saie;* akin to ML *sagia* kind of weave, L *sagum* cloak) + *wol* WOOL + *-sye,* var. of *say*]

lin·stock (lin′stok′), *n.* a staff with one end forked to hold a match, formerly used in firing cannon. [earlier *lyntstock* < D *lontstok* match-stick, with LINT r. *lont*]

lint (lint), *n.* **1.** staple cotton fiber used to make yarn. **2.** minute shreds or ravelings of yarn; bits of thread. **3.** cotton waste produced by ginning. **4.** a soft material for dressing wounds, procured by scraping or otherwise treating linen cloth. [ME, var. of *linnet,* OE *līnet-* flax (or flax field) in *līnetwige* LINTWHITE] —**lint′less,** *adj.*

lin·tel (lin′tᵊl), *n.* a horizontal architectural member supporting the weight above an opening. Also, *Brit.,* **lin′tol.** [ME *lyntel* < MF *lintel,* assimilated var. of *linter < LL **līmitāris* of the boundary (taken as synonym of *līmināris* of the threshold). See LIMIT, -AR¹]

lint·white (lint′hwīt′, -wīt′), *n. Chiefly Scot.* the linnet, *Carduelis cannabina.* [*lint* (syncopated var. of LINNET) + WHITE; r. OE *līnetwige* linnet, lit., flax (or flax field) troublemaker, so called because the bird pecks out and eats flaxseed = *līnet-* (< ML *līnētum* flax-field) + *-wige,* fem. of *wiga* fighter]

lint·y (lin′tē), *adj.,* **lint·i·er, lint·i·est. 1.** full of or covered with lint. **2.** like lint: *linty bits on his coat.*

Li·nus (lī′nəs), *n.* **1.** *Class. Myth.* a musician and poet, the inventor of melody and rhythm. **2. Saint,** died A.D. 76?, pope 67?–76?

Lin·yu (lin′yo͞o′), *n.* a city in NE China, on the Gulf of Liaotung, at the E end of the Great Wall. 35,000 (est. 1957). Formerly, **Shanhaikwan.**

Lin Yu·tang (lin′ yo͞o′täng′), (*Lin Yu-t'ang*) 1895–1976, Chinese author and philologist in the U.S.

Linz (lints), *n.* a port in N Austria, on the Danube River. 196,206 (1961).

Lin·zer torte (lin′zər tôrt′), *pl.* **Lin·zer tortes.** (*sometimes l.c.*) a sweet pastry, often made with powdered nuts, having a filling of red jam and a lattice crust. [< G: lit., Linz torte]

Liod (lyôd), *n.* (in the *Volsunga Saga*) the wife of Volsung and mother of Sigmund and Signy.

li·on (lī′ən), *n.* **1.** a large, grayish-tan cat, *Panthera leo,* native in Africa and southern Asia, the male of which usually has a mane. **2.** any of various related large wildcats, as the cougar. **3.** a man of great strength, courage, etc. **4.** a person of note or celebrity who is much sought after. **5.** *Brit.* an object of interest or note. **6.** (*cap.*) *Astron., Astrol.* the constellation or sign of Leo. **7.** (*cap.*) a member of the International Association of Lions Clubs. **8.** any of various coins bearing the figure of a lion. [ME < OF, var. of *leon* < L *leōn-* (s. of *leō*) < Gk *léōn;* r. ME, OE *leo* < L]

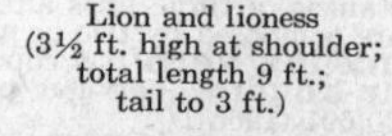

Lion and lioness (3½ ft. high at shoulder; total length 9 ft.; tail to 3 ft.)

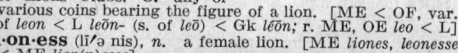

li·on·ess (lī′ə nis), *n.* a female lion. [ME *liones, leonesse* < MF *lion(n)esse*]

li·on·heart·ed (lī′ən här′tid), *adj.* courageous; brave. —**li′on·heart′ed·ly,** *adv.* —**li′on·heart′ed·ness,** *n.*

li·on·ise (lī′ə nīz′), *v.t., v.i.,* **-ised, -is·ing.** *Chiefly Brit.* lionize. —**li′on·i·sa′tion,** *n.* —**li′on·is′er,** *n.*

li·on·ize (lī′ə nīz′), *v.,* **-ized, -iz·ing.** —*v.t.* **1.** to treat (a person) as a celebrity. **2.** *Brit.* to visit or exhibit the objects of interest of (a place). —*v.i.* **3.** *Brit.* to visit the objects of interest of a place. **4.** to pursue celebrities or seek their company. —**li′on·i·za′tion,** *n.* —**li′on·iz′er,** *n.*

Li·ons (lī′ənz), *n.* **Gulf of,** a wide bay of the Mediterranean off the coast of S France. Also, **Gulf of the Lions.** French, **Golfe du Lion.**

li′on's share′, the largest share; an unreasonably large portion. [prob. after Aesop's fable in which the lion claimed all the spoils of a hunt]

lip (lip), *n., adj., v.,* **lipped, lip·ping.** —*n.* **1.** either of the two fleshy parts or folds forming the margins of the mouth and functioning in speech. **2.** Usually, **lips.** these parts regarded as the source of speech. **3.** *Slang.* impudent talk. **4.** a liplike part or structure, esp. of the body. **5.** *Bot.* either of the two parts into which the corolla or calyx of certain plants, esp. of the mint family, is divided. **6.** *Zool.* **a.** a labium. **b.** the outer or the inner margin of the aperture of a gastropod's shell. **7.** a projecting rim on a container or other hollow object: *the lip of a pitcher.* **8.** any edge or rim. **9.** the edge of an opening or cavity, as of a canyon or a wound. **10. button one's lip,** *Slang.* to keep silent. Also, **button up. 11. hang on the lips of,** to listen to attentively. **12. keep a stiff upper lip,** to face misfortune bravely. —*adj.* **13.** of or pertaining to the lips or a lip. **14.** pertaining to, characterized by, or made with the lips: *lip movements.* —*v.t.* **15.** *Golf.* to hit the ball over the rim of (the hole). **16.** *Archaic.* to kiss. [ME *lip(pe),* OE *lippa;* c. D *lip,* G *Lippe;* akin to Norw *lepe,* L *labium, labrum*] —**lip′less,** *adj.* —**lip′like′,** *adj.*

lip-, var. of **lipo-** before a vowel: *lipid.*

Lip′a·ri Is′lands (lip′ə rē; *It.* lē′pä rē), a group of volcanic islands N of Sicily, belonging to Italy. 11,799 (1951); 44 sq. mi.

li·pase (lī′pās, lip′ās), *n. Biochem.* any of a class of enzymes that break down fats, produced by the liver, pancreas, and other digestive organs or by certain plants.

Lip·chitz (lip′shits), *n.* **Jacques** (zhäk), 1891–1973, U.S. sculptor, born in Lithuania.

Li·petsk (lē′petsk), *n.* a city in the W RSFSR, in the central Soviet Union, SSE of Moscow. 218,000 (est. 1964).

li·pid (lī′pid, lip′id), *n. Biochem.* any of a group of organic compounds that are greasy to the touch, insoluble in water, and soluble in alcohol, ether, and other fat solvents. Lipids comprise the fats and other esters with analogous properties and constitute, with proteins and carbohydrates, the chief structural components of living cells. Also, **li·pide** (lī′pīd, -pid, lip′īd, -id), **lip·in** (lip′in), **lipoid.**

Li Po (lē′ pō′; *Chin.* lē′ bô′), A.D. 701?–762, Chinese poet of the Tang dynasty. Also called **Li Tai Po.**

lipo-, a learned borrowing from Greek meaning "fat," used in the formation of compound words: *lipolysis.* Also, *esp. before a vowel,* **lip-.** [< Gk *lípos*]

lip·oid (lip′oid, lī′poid), *adj.* **1.** Also, **lip·oi′dal.** fatty; resembling fat. —*n.* **2.** one of a group of fats or fatlike substances, as lecithins or waxes. **3.** lipid.

li·pol·y·sis (li pol′i sis), *n. Chem.* the hydrolysis of fats into fatty acids and glycerol, as by lipase. [< NL] —**lip·o·lit·ic** (lip′ə lit′ik), *adj.*

li·po·ma (li pō′mə), *n., pl.* **-mas, -ma·ta** (-mə tə). *Pathol.* a tumor consisting of fat tissue. [< NL] —**li·pom·a·tous** (li pom′ə təs), *adj.*

lip·o·phil·ic (lip′ə fil′ik), *adj. Physical Chem.* **1.** having a strong affinity for lipids. **2.** promoting the dissolvability or absorbability of lipids.

lip·o·pro·tein (lip′ə prō′tēn, -tē in, lī′pə-), *n. Biochem.* any of the class of proteins that contain a lipid combined with a simple protein.

lip·o·trop·ic (lip′ə trop′ik, -trō′pik, lī′pə-), *adj. Chem., Biochem.* having an affinity for lipids and thus preventing or correcting the excess accumulation of fat in the liver. —**li·pot·ro·pism** (li po′trə piz′əm), *n.*

Lip·pe (lip′ə), *n.* a former state in NW Germany: now part of North Rhine-Westphalia, in West Germany.

lipped (lipt), *adj.* **1.** having lips or a lip. **2.** *Bot.* labiate. [ME]

lip·pen (lip′ən), *Chiefly Scot.* —*v.t.* **1.** to trust (a person). **2.** to entrust (something) to a person. —*v.i.* **3.** to have confidence, faith, or trust. [early ME *lipn(i)en*]

lip·per (lip′ər), *n. Naut.* a slightly rough surface on a body of water. [n. use of dial. *lipper* to ripple. See LAP³, -ER⁶]

Lip·pi (lip′ē; *It.* lēp′pē), *n.* **1. Fi·lip·pi·no** (fil′ə pē′nō; *It.* fē′lēp pē′nô), 1457–1504, Italian painter. **2.** his father, **Fra Fi·lip·po** (frä fi lip′ō; *It.* frä fē lēp′pô) or **Fra Lip·po** (frä lip′ō; *It.* frä lēp′pô), 1406?–69, Italian painter.

Lip·pi·zan·er (lip′it sä′nər), *n.* one of a breed of compact, finely shaped, usually gray or white horses developed at the Austrian Imperial Stud and used generally in dressage exhibitions. Also, **Lip·piz·za·na** (lip′it sä′nə), **Lip′piz·zan′er.** [< G < *Lippiza,* near Trieste, where the stud was located]

Lipp·mann (lip′mən; *also Fr.* lēp män′), *n.* **Ga·bri·el** (ga brē el′), 1845–1921, French physicist: Nobel prize 1908.

Lip·pold (lip′ōld), *n.* **Richard,** born 1915, U.S. sculptor.

lip-read (lip′rēd′), *v.,* **-read** (-red′), **-read·ing.** —*v.t.* **1.** to comprehend (spoken words) by watching the movements of a speaker's lips. —*v.i.* **2.** to read lips. [back formation from LIP READING]

lip′ read′ing, the reading or understanding, as by a deaf person, of the movements of another's lips when forming words. —**lip′ read′er.**

lip′ serv′ice, insincere profession of devotion or good will: *He paid only lip service to the dictator.*

lip·stick (lip′stik′), *n.* a crayonlike oil-based cosmetic used in coloring the lips, usually in a tubular container.

Lip·ton (lip′tən), *n.* **Sir Thomas John·stone** (jon′stən, -sən), 1850–1931, Scottish merchant and yachtsman.

liq., 1. liquid. **2.** liquor. **3.** (in prescriptions) solution. [< L *liquor*]

li·quate (lī′kwāt), *v.t.,* **-quat·ed, -quat·ing.** *Metall.* to heat (an alloy or mixture) sufficiently to melt the more fusible matter and thus to separate it from the rest. [< L *liquāt(us)* liquefied, ptp. of *liquāre*] —**li·qua·tion** (lī kwā′shən, -zhən), *n.*

liq·ue·fac·tion (lik′wə fak′shən), *n.* **1.** the act or process of liquefying. **2.** the state of being liquefied. [< LL *liquefactiōn-* (s. of *liquefactiō*) a melting = L *liquefact(us)* melted (ptp. of *liquefacere;* see LIQUEFACIENT) + *-iōn-* -ION] —**liq′ue·fac′tive,** *adj.*

liq′uefied petro′leum gas′, a gas liquefied by compression, consisting of flammable hydrocarbons, as propane and butane, obtained as a by-product from the refining of petroleum or from natural gas: used chiefly as a fuel and in organic synthesis, esp. of synthetic rubber. Also called **bottled gas, LPG, LP gas.**

liq·ue·fy (lik′wə fī′), *v.t., v.i.,* **-fied, -fy·ing.** to make or become liquid. [late ME *lyquefye* < L *lique(facere).* See LIQUEFACIENT, -FY] —**liq′ue·fi′a·ble,** *adj.* —**liq′ue·fi′er,** *n.*

li·ques·cent (li kwes′ənt), *adj.* **1.** becoming liquid; melting. **2.** tending toward a liquid state. [< L *liquescent-* (s. of *liquescēns*) melting, prp. of *liquescere.* See LIQUID, -ESCENT] —**li·ques′cence,** *n.*

li·queur (li kûr′ *or, esp. Brit.,* -kyŏŏr′), *n.* any of a class of alcoholic liquors, usually strong, sweet, and highly flavored, as chartreuse or curaçao; cordial. [< F; see LIQUOR]

liq·uid (lik′wid), *adj.* **1.** composed of molecules that move freely among themselves but do not tend to separate like those of gases; neither gaseous nor solid. **2.** of, pertaining to, or consisting of, liquids. **3.** flowing like water. **4.** clear, transparent, or bright. **5.** (of sounds, tones, etc.) having an agreeable, flowing quality. **6.** (of movements, gestures, etc.) graceful; smooth; free and unconstricted. **7.** in cash or readily convertible into cash: *liquid assets.* **8.** *Phonet.* characterizing a frictionless speech sound pronounced with only partial obstruction of the breath stream and whose utterance can be prolonged as a vowel, esp. *l* and *r.* —*n.* **9.** a liquid substance. **10.** *Phonet.* either *r* or *l,* and sometimes *m, n, ng.* [ME *liquyd* < L *liquid(us)* = *liqu(ēre)* (to) be liquid + *-idus* -ID[4]] —**liq′uid·ly,** *adv.* —**liq′uid·ness,** *n.*
—**Syn.** LIQUID, FLUID agree in referring to that which is not solid. LIQUID commonly refers to substances such as water, oil, alcohol, and the like, that are neither solids nor gases: *Water ceases to be a liquid when it is frozen or turned to steam.* FLUID is applied to anything that flows, whether liquid or gaseous: *Pipes can carry fluids from place to place.*

liq′uid air′, a pale-blue, intensely cold liquid, obtained by the compression and cooling of air: used as a source of oxygen, nitrogen, and inert gases, and as a refrigerant.

liq·uid·am·bar (lik′wid am′bər), *n.* **1.** any tree of the genus *Liquidambar,* having maplelike, star-shaped leaves, and globose, spiny fruit. Cf. **sweet gum. 2.** the fragrant, yellowish, balsamic liquid exuded by this tree, used in medicine. Cf. **storax** (def. 2). [< NL; see LIQUID, AMBER]

liq·ui·date (lik′wi dāt′), *v.,* **-dat·ed, -dat·ing.** —*v.t.* **1.** to settle or pay (a debt). **2.** to reduce (accounts) to order. **3.** to determine the amount of (indebtedness or damages). **4.** to convert into cash. **5.** to get rid of, esp. by killing. **6.** to break up, abolish, or do away with: *to liquidate a partnership.* —*v.i.* **7.** to liquidate debts or accounts. [< LL *liquidāt(us)* made clear or liquid, ptp. of *liquidāre*]

liq·ui·da·tion (lik′wi dā′shən), *n.* **1.** the process of realizing upon assets and of discharging liabilities in concluding the affairs of a business, estate, etc. **2.** the process of converting securities or commodities into cash. **3.** the state of being liquidated.

liq·ui·da·tor (lik′wi dā′tər), *n.* **1.** a person who liquidates assets, esp. one authorized to do so by a court of law. **2.** an official appointed by a court to liquidate a business.

liq′uid crys′tal, a liquid having certain crystalline characteristics, esp. different optical properties in different directions.

liq′uid fire′, flaming petroleum or the like as employed against an enemy in warfare.

liq′uid glass′. See **sodium silicate.**

liq·uid·ise (lik′wi dīz′), *v.t.,* **-ised, -is·ing.** *Chiefly Brit.* liquidize.

li·quid·i·ty (li kwid′i tē), *n.* a liquid state or quality. [< L *liquiditās*]

liq·uid·ize (lik′wi dīz′), *v.t.,* **-ized, -iz·ing.** to make liquid; liquefy. Also, *esp. Brit.,* **liquidise.**

liq′uid meas′ure, the system of units of capacity ordinarily used in measuring liquid commodities, as milk or oil. 4 gills = 1 pint; 2 pints = 1 quart; 4 quarts = 1 gallon.

liq′uid ox′ygen, a liquid obtained by compressing oxygen and then cooling it below its boiling point: used chiefly as an oxidizer in liquid rocket propellants. Also called **lox.**

liq′uid petrola′tum. See **mineral oil.**

liq′uid sto′rax. See under **storax** (def. 2).

liq·uor (lik′ər *or, for 3,* lik′wôr), *n.* **1.** a distilled or spirituous beverage, as brandy or whiskey, as distinguished from a fermented beverage, as wine or beer. **2.** any liquid substance, as broth from cooked meats, vegetables, etc. **3.** a solution of a substance, esp. a concentrated one used in the industrial arts. [< L: a liquid, orig. liquidity (*liqu(ēre)* (to) be liquid + *-or* -OR[1]); r. ME *lic(o)ur* < OF < L *liquōrem,* acc. of *liquor*]

liq·uo·rice (lik′ə ris, -ə rish, lik′rish), *n.* licorice.

liq·uor·ish (lik′ə rish), *adj.* lickerish.

li·ra (lēr′ə; *It.* lē′rä), *n., pl.* **li·re** (lēr′ā; *It.* lē′re), **li·ras. 1.** an aluminum coin and monetary unit of Italy, equal to 100 centesimi. *Abbr.:* L., Lit. **2.** a coin and monetary unit of Turkey; Turkish pound. *Abbr.:* TL. [< It < OPr *lieura* < L *lībra* pound]

lir·i·o·den·dron (lir′ē ō den′drən), *n., pl.* **-drons, -dra** (-drə). any magnoliaceous tree of the genus *Liriodendron.* Cf. **tulip tree.** [< NL < Gk *leíro(n)* lily + *déndron* -DENDRON]

lir·i·pipe (lir′ē pīp′), *n.* **1.** the tail or pendent part at the back of a hood, as in medieval French costume. **2.** a scarf or tippet; hood. [< ML *liripip(ium)*]

Lis·bon (liz′bən), *n.* a seaport in and the capital of Portugal, in the SW part, on the Tagus estuary. 760,150. Portuguese, **Lis·bo·a** (lēzh bô′ə).

lisle (līl), *n.* **1.** Also called, **lisle′ thread′.** a fine, high-twisted and hard-twisted cotton thread, at least two-ply, used esp. for hosiery. —*adj.* **2.** made of lisle thread. [after *Lisle,* France, where first made]

Lisle (lēl), *n.* **1.** See **Leconte de Lisle. 2.** See **Rouget de Lisle. 3.** former name of **Lille.**

lisp (lisp), *n.* **1.** a speech defect consisting in pronouncing *s* and *z* like or nearly like the *th*-sounds of *thin* and *this,* respectively. **2.** the act, habit, or sound of lisping. —*v.t., v.i.* **3.** to pronounce or speak with a lisp. [ME *wlispen, lipsen,* OE *(ā)wlyspian;* akin to D *lisp(el)en,* G *lispeln,* Norw *leipsa*] —**lisp′er,** *n.* —**lisp′ing·ly,** *adv.*

lis pen·dens (lis pen′denz), *Law.* **1.** a pending suit listed on the court docket. **2.** the rule placing property involved in litigation under the court's jurisdiction. **3.** the principle that the filing of a suit constitutes notice of the claim asserted. [< L]

Lis′sa·jous fig′ure (lē′sə zhōō′, lē′sə zhōō′), *Physics.* the series of plane curves traced by an object executing two mutually perpendicular harmonic motions, forming a distinct pattern when the ratio of the frequencies of the motions is a ratio of small integers. [named after Jules A. *Lissajous* (1822–80), French physicist]

lis·some (lis′əm), *adj.* **1.** lithe, esp. of body; limber; supple. **2.** agile or active. Also, **lis′som.** [var. of LITHESOME] —**lis′some·ly, lis′som·ly,** *adv.* —**lis′some·ness, lis′som·ness,** *n.* —**Ant. 1.** rigid. **2.** clumsy.

list[1] (list), *n.* **1.** a series of names or other items written or printed together in a meaningful grouping or sequence so as to constitute a record. —*v.t.* **2.** to set down together in a list. **3.** to enter in a list with others. **4.** to register a security on a stock exchange so that it may be traded there. **5.** *Archaic.* enlist. —*v.i.* **6.** to be offered for sale, as in a catalog, at a specified price: *This radio lists at $34.98.* **7.** *Archaic.* enlist. [special use of LIST[2] (roll of names, perh. orig. of contestants in the LISTS); cf. F *liste* < It *lista* roll of names, earlier, band, strip (e.g., of paper), border < OHG (G *Leiste*)]
—**Syn. 1.** register. LIST, CATALOG, INVENTORY, ROLL, SCHEDULE imply a definite arrangement of items. LIST denotes a series of names, items, or figures arranged in a row or rows: *a list of groceries.* CATALOG adds the idea of alphabetical or other orderly arrangement, and, often, descriptive particulars and details: *a library catalog.* An INVENTORY is a detailed descriptive list of property, stock, goods, or the like, made for legal or business purposes: *a store inventory.* A ROLL is a list of names of members of some defined group often used to ascertain their presence or absence: *a class roll.* A SCHEDULE is a methodical (esp. official) list, often indicating the time or sequence of certain events: *a train schedule.* **2.** record, catalog. **3.** enroll.

list[2] (list), *n.* **1.** a border or bordering strip, usually of cloth. **2.** a selvage. **3.** selvages collectively. **4.** a strip of cloth or other material. **5.** a strip or band of any kind. **6.** a stripe of color. **7.** a division of the hair or beard. **8.** a ridge or furrow made by a lister. **9.** a strip of material, as bark or sapwood, to be trimmed from a board. —*adj.* **10.** made of selvages or strips of cloth. —*v.t.* **11.** to prepare (ground) for planting by making ridges and furrows. **12.** to cut away a narrow strip of wood from the edge of (a stave, plank, etc.). [ME *lista,* OE *līst* border; c. D *lijst,* G *Leiste* (OHG *līsta*)]

list[3] (list), *n.* **1.** a careening or leaning to one side, as of a ship. —*v.i.* **2.** (of a vessel) to incline to one side. —*v.t.* **3.** to cause (a vessel) to incline to one side. [?]

list[4] (list), *Archaic.* —*v.t.* **1.** to be pleasing to; please. **2.** to like or desire. —*v.i.* **3.** to like; wish; choose. [ME *liste(n), luste(n),* OE *(ge)lystan* to please; c. G *gelüsten,* Icel *lysta,* akin to Goth *lustōn* to desire. See LUST]

list[5] (list), *Archaic.* —*v.i.* **1.** to listen. —*v.t.* **2.** to listen to. [ME *liste(n),* OE *hlystan* to listen, hear; c. Sw *lysta;* akin to Icel *hlusta* to listen < *hlyst* hearing, akin to Icel *hlyst* meatus. See LISTEN]

list·ed (lis′tid), *adj.* **1.** (of a security) admitted to trading privileges on a stock exchange. **2.** represented in a telephone book, as a subscriber's name and telephone number.

lis·tel (lis′t[ə]l), *n.* *Archit.* a narrow fillet. [< F < It *listello,* dim. of *lista* band, LIST[2]]

lis·ten (lis′ən), *v.i.* **1.** to give attention for the purpose of hearing. **2.** to heed or pay attention to what is said; obey (often fol. by *to*): *I've told him repeatedly, but he doesn't listen.* **3.** to wait attentively for a specific sound (usually fol. by *for*): *to listen for the telephone.* **4. listen in,** to overhear a conversation or spoken communication; eavesdrop. —*v.t.* **5.** *Archaic.* to give ear to; hear. [ME *lis(t)ne(n),* OE *hlysnan;* c. MHG *lüsenen,* Sw *lyssna;* akin to LIST[5]] —**lis′ten·a·ble,** *adj.* —**lis′ten·er,** *n.*

lis′tening post′, **1.** *Mil.* a post or position, as in advance of a defensive line, established for the purpose of listening to detect the enemy's movements. **2.** any source of secret information.

list·er[1] (lis′tər), *n.* **1.** Also called **lis′ter plow′.** a plow with a double moldboard, used to prepare the ground for planting by producing furrows and ridges. **2.** Also called **lis′ter plant′er, list′er drill′.** a lister plow fitted with attachments for dropping and covering seeds. [LIST[2] + -ER[1]]

list·er[2] (lis′tər), *n.* a person who makes or compiles a list, esp. an appraiser, assessor, or the like. [LIST[1] + -ER[1]]

Lis·ter (lis′tər), *n.* **Joseph, 1st Baron Lister of Lyme Re·gis** (līm rē′jis), 1827–1912, English surgeon: founder of modern antiseptic surgery.

list·ing (lis′ting), *n.* **1.** the act of compiling a list. **2.** the fact of being included in a list. **3.** an entry on such a list. **4.** a list; record; catalog.

list·less (list′lis), *adj.* feeling or showing no inclination toward or interest in anything. [late ME *lystles*] —**list′less·ly,** *adv.* —**list′less·ness,** *n.*

list′ price′, *Com.* the price given by a wholesaler from which a trade discount is computed.

lists (lists), *n.* (*construed as sing. or pl.*) **1.** an enclosed arena for a tilting contest. **2.** the barriers enclosing this arena. **3.** any place or scene of combat, competition, controversy, etc. **4. enter the lists,** to involve oneself in a conflict or contest. [ME *listes,* pl. of *liste* LIST[2]]

Liszt (list), *n.* **Franz** (fränts), 1811–86, Hungarian composer and pianist. —**Liszt′i·an,** *adj.*

lit[1] (lit), *v.* a pt. and pp. of **light**[1].

lit[2] (lit), *v.* a pt. and pp. of **light**[3].

Lit., (in Italy) lira; lire.

lit., **1.** liter; liters. **2.** literal. **3.** literally. **4.** literary. **5.** literature.

Li Tai Po (*Chin.* lē′ tī′ bô′). See **Li Po.**

lit·a·ny (lit′ᵊnē), *n., pl.* **-nies.** **1.** a ceremonial or liturgical form of prayer consisting of a series of invocations or supplications with responses that are the same for a number in succession. **2.** **the Litany,** the supplication in this form in the Anglican *Book of Common Prayer.* **3.** a recitation or recital that resembles a litany. **4.** a prolonged or drearily monotonous account. [< LL *litanīa* < eccl. Gk *litaneía* litany, Gk: an entreating = *litan-* (s. of *litaínein,* var. of *litaneúein* to pray) + *-eia* -Y[3]; r. ME *letanie,* OE *letanīa* < ML]

Lit.B., Bachelor of Letters; Bachelor of Literature. [< L *Lit(t)erārum Baccalaureus*]

li·tchi (lē′chē), *n., pl.* **-tchis.** a Chinese, sapindaceous tree, *Litchi chinensis,* bearing a fruit consisting of a thin, brittle shell enclosing a sweet, jellylike pulp and a single seed. Also, **lichee, lichi.** [< Chin *li chih*]

li′tchi nut′, the brownish, dried litchi fruit.

Lit.D., Doctor of Letters; Doctor of Literature. [< L *Lit(t)erārum Doctor*]

lit de jus·tice (lē də zhʏs tēs′), *French.* **1.** (formerly) the sofa used by the king of France in formal sessions of the parliament. **2.** the session itself. [lit., bed of justice]

-lite, a word element used in the names of minerals or fossils: *aerolite; chrysolite.* Cf. **-lith.** [< F, simplified form of *-lithe* < Gk *líthos* stone; similarly G *-lit,* earlier *-lith*]

li·ter (lē′tər), *n.* *Metric System.* a unit of capacity redefined in 1964 by a reduction of 28 parts in a million to be exactly equal to one cubic decimeter. It is equivalent to 1.0567 U.S. liquid quarts. *Abbr.:* l, lit. Also, *esp. Brit.,* **litre.** [< F *litre,* back formation from *litron* an old measure of capacity < (with *-on* suffix) ML *litra* < Gk *lítra* pound]

lit·er·a·cy (lit′ər ə sē), *n.* the quality or state of being literate, esp. the ability to read and write.

lit′eracy test′, an examination to determine whether a person meets the literacy requirements for voting, serving in the armed forces, etc.; a test of one's ability to read and write.

lit·er·al (lit′ər əl), *adj.* **1.** following the words of the original as closely as possible: *a literal translation.* **2.** (of a person) tending to construe words in the strict sense or in an unimaginative way. **3.** in accordance with, involving, or being the primary or strict meaning of a word or words; not figurative or metaphorical. **4.** true to fact; not exaggerated: *a literal statement.* **5.** being actually such, without exaggeration or inaccuracy: *literal bankruptcy.* **6.** of or pertaining to the letters of the alphabet. **7.** of the nature of letters. **8.** expressed by letters. [ME < LL *litterāl(is).* See LETTER[1], -AL[1]] —**lit′er·al·ness,** *n.*

lit·er·al·ise (lit′ər ə līz′), *v.t.,* **-ised, -is·ing.** *Chiefly Brit.* literalize. —**lit′er·al·i·sa′tion,** *n.* —**lit′er·al·is′er,** *n.*

lit·er·al·ism (lit′ər ə liz′əm), *n.* **1.** adherence to the exact letter or the literal sense, as in translation or interpretation. **2.** a peculiarity of expression resulting from this. **3.** exact representation or portrayal, without idealization, as in art or literature. —**lit′er·al·ist,** *n.* —**lit′er·al·is′tic,** *adj.* —**lit′er·al·is′ti·cal·ly,** *adv.*

lit·er·al·i·ty (lit′ə ral′i tē), *n., pl.* **-ties.** **1.** the quality or state of being literal; literalness. **2.** a literal interpretation.

lit·er·al·ize (lit′ər ə līz′), *v.t.,* **-ized, -iz·ing.** to make literal; interpret literally. Also, *esp. Brit.,* **literalise.** —**lit′er·al·i·za′tion,** *n.* —**lit′er·al·iz′er,** *n.*

lit·er·al·ly (lit′ər ə lē), *adv.* **1.** in a literal manner; word for word: *to translate literally.* **2.** in the literal or strict sense: *What does the word mean literally?* **3.** without exaggeration or inaccuracy: *literally bankrupt.*

lit·er·al-mind·ed (lit′ər əl mīn′did), *adj.* unimaginative; prosaic; matter-of-fact.

lit·er·ar·y (lit′ə rer′ē), *adj.* **1.** pertaining to or of the nature of books and writings, esp. those classed as literature. **2.** pertaining to authorship: *literary style.* **3.** versed in or acquainted with literature; well-read. **4.** engaged in or having the profession of writing. **5.** stilted; pedantic. [< L *līterāri(us), litterārius* of reading and writing. See LETTER[1], -ARY] —**lit′er·ar′i·ly,** *adv.* —**lit′er·ar′i·ness,** *n.*

lit·er·ate (lit′ər it), *adj.* **1.** able to read and write. **2.** having an education; educated. **3.** having or showing knowledge of literature; writing, etc.; literary; well-read. **4.** (of writing, conversation, etc.) lucid; accomplished. —*n.* **5.** a person who can read and write. **6.** a learned person. [late ME < L *līterāt(us), litterātus* learned, scholarly. See LETTER[1], -ATE[1]] —**lit′er·ate·ly,** *adv.*

lit·e·ra·ti (lit′ə rä′tē, -rā′tī), *n.pl.* persons of scholarly or literary attainments; intellectuals; intelligentsia. [< L *līterāti* learned, scholarly people, n. use of pl. of *līterātus.* See LITERATE]

lit·e·ra·tim (lit′ə rā′tim), *adv.* letter for letter; literally. [< ML, a formation based on L *līterā(tus)* (see LITERATE), with adv. suffix *-tim*]

lit·er·a·ture (lit′ər ə chər, -chŏŏr′, li′trə-), *n.* **1.** writing regarded as having permanent worth through its intrinsic excellence. **2.** the entire body of writings of a specific language, period, people, etc. **3.** the writings dealing with a particular subject: *the literature of ornithology.* **4.** the profession of a writer or author. **5.** literary work or production. **6.** any kind of printed material, as circulars or prospectuses. **7.** *Archaic.* polite learning; literary culture; appreciation of letters and books. [late ME *litterature* < L *litterātūra* grammar. See LITERATE, -URE]
—**Syn.** **1.** LITERATURE, BELLES-LETTRES, LETTERS refer to artistic writings worthy of being remembered. In the broadest sense, LITERATURE includes any type of writings on any subject: *the literature of medicine;* usually, however, it means the body of artistic writings of a country or period that are characterized by beauty of expression and form and by universality of intellectual and emotional appeal: *English literature of the 16th century.* BELLES-LETTRES is a more specific term for writings of a light, elegant, or excessively refined character: *His talent is not for scholarship but for belles-lettres.* LETTERS refers to literature as a domain of study or artistic endeavor: *a man of letters.*

Lith, Lithuanian (def. 3).

lith-, var. of **litho-** before a vowel: *lithic.*

-lith, a noun termination meaning "stone" (*acrolith; megalith; paleolith*); sometimes occurring in words that are variant forms of *-lite* (*batholith; laccolith*). Cf. **-lite.** [see LITHO-]

Lith., **1.** Lithuania. **2.** Lithuanian.

lith., **1.** lithograph. **2.** lithography.

lith·arge (lith′ärj, li thärj′), *n.* a heavy, earthy, poisonous solid, PbO, used chiefly in the manufacture of storage batteries, pottery, lead glass, paints, enamels, and inks. Cf. **red lead.** [late ME (r. ME *litarge*) < MF *lit(h)arge,* apocopated var. of *litargire* < L *lithargyr(us)* < Gk *lithárgyros* spume of silver = *lith-* LITH- + *árgyros* silver]

lithe (līth), *adj.,* **lith·er, lith·est.** bending readily; pliant; limber; supple; flexible. Also, **lithe′some.** [ME *lith(e),* OE *līthe;* c. OLG *līthi,* G *lind* mild, L *lentus* slow] —**lithe′ly,** *adv.* —**lithe′ness,** *n.*

lith·i·a (lith′ē ə, lith′yə), *n.* a white oxide of lithium, Li_2O. [< NL]

li·thi·a·sis (li thī′ə sis), *n.* *Pathol.* the formation or presence of stony concretions, as calculi, in the body. [< NL < Gk]

lith·ic (lith′ik), *adj.* **1.** pertaining to or consisting of stone. **2.** *Pathol.* pertaining to stony concretions, or calculi, formed within the body, esp. in the bladder. **3.** *Chem.* of, pertaining to, or containing lithium. [< Gk *lithik(ós)* of stone] —**lith′i·cal·ly,** *adv.*

-lithic, an adjectival suffix identical with **lithic,** used esp. in archaeology: *paleolithic.*

lith·i·um (lith′ē əm), *n.* *Chem.* a soft, silver-white metallic element, the lightest of all metals, occurring combined in certain minerals. *Symbol:* Li; *at. wt.:* 6.939; *at. no.:* 3; *sp. gr.:* 0.53 at 20°C. [< NL]

lith·o (lith′ō), *n.* lithograph. [shortened form]

litho-, a learned borrowing from Greek meaning "stone," used in the formation of compound words: *lithography; lithophyte.* Also, *esp. before a vowel,* **lith-.** [< Gk, comb. form of *líthos*]

litho., **1.** lithograph. **2.** lithography. Also, **lithog.**

lith·o·graph (lith′ə graf′, -gräf′), *n.* **1.** a print produced by lithography. —*v.t.* **2.** to produce or copy by lithography. [back formation from LITHOGRAPHY]

li·thog·ra·pher (li thog′rə fər), *n.* a person who works at lithography.

li·thog·ra·phy (li thog′rə fē), *n.* the art or process of producing a figure or image on a flat, specially prepared stone or plate in such a way that it will absorb and print with special inks. Cf. **offset** (def. 6). [< NL *lithographia*] —**lith·o·graph·ic** (lith′ə graf′ik), **lith′o·graph′i·cal,** *adj.* —**lith′o·graph′i·cal·ly,** *adv.*

lith·oid (lith′oid), *adj.* resembling stone; stonelike; stony. Also, **li·thoi′dal.** [< Gk *lithoeid(ḗs)*]

lithol., lithology.

li·thol·o·gy (li thol′ə jē), *n.* **1.** the science dealing with the mineral composition and structure of rocks, esp. with such characters of structure as can be studied without high magnification. Cf. **petrography.** **2.** *Med.* the science treating of calculi in the human body. —**lith·o·log·ic** (lith′ə loj′ik), **lith′o·log′i·cal,** *adj.* —**lith′o·log′i·cal·ly,** *adv.*

lith·o·marge (lith′ə märj′), *n.* kaolin in compact, massive, usually impure form. [< NL *lithomarga* stone marl = *litho-* LITHO- + L *marga* marl]

lith·o·phyte (lith′ə fīt′), *n.* **1.** *Zool.* a polyp with a hard or stony structure, as a coral. **2.** *Bot.* any plant growing on the surface of rocks. —**lith·o·phyt·ic** (lith′ə fit′ik), *adj.*

lith·o·pone (lith′ə pōn′), *n.* a white pigment consisting of zinc sulfide, barium sulfate, and some zinc oxide, used as a pigment and filler in the manufacture of paints, inks, leather, paper, linoleum, and face powders. [LITHO- + Gk *pón(os)* a work, structure]

lith·o·print (lith′ə print′), *v.t.* **1.** to lithograph. —*n.* **2.** printed matter produced by lithography. —**lith′o·print′er,** *n.*

lith·o·sphere (lith′ə sfēr′), *n.* the crust of the earth.

li·thot·o·my (li thot′ə mē), *n., pl.* **-mies.** *Surg.* the operation or technique of cutting for stone in the urinary bladder. [< LL *lithotomia* < Gk *lithotomía*] —**lith·o·tom·ic** (lith′ə tom′ik), **lith′o·tom′i·cal,** *adj.* —**li·thot′o·mist,** *n.*

li·thot·ri·ty (li tho′tri tē), *n., pl.* **-ties.** *Surg.* the operation of crushing stone in the urinary bladder into particles that may be voided. [LITHO- + L *trīt(us)* rubbed, ground, crushed (ptp. of *terere*) + -Y[3]; see -ITY]

Lith·u·a·ni·a (lith′o͞o ā′nē ə), *n.* a constituent republic of the Soviet Union in Europe, in the W part, on the Baltic: an independent state 1918–40. 2,900,000 (est. 1965); 25,174 sq. mi. *Cap.:* Vilna. Lithuanian, **Lietuva.** Official name, **Lithua′nian So′viet So′cialist Repub′lic.** —**Lith·u·an·ic** (lith′o͞o an′ik), *adj., n.*

Lith·u·a·ni·an (lith′o͞o ā′nē ən), *adj.* **1.** of or pertaining to Lithuania, its inhabitants, or their language. —*n.* **2.** a native or inhabitant of Lithuania. **3.** a Baltic language, the official language of Lithuania. *Abbr.:* Lith, Lith.

lit·i·ga·ble (lit′ə gə bəl), *adj.* subject to litigation. [< L *lītigā(re)* (to) go to law (see LITIGATE) + -BLE]

lit·i·gant (lit′ə gənt), *n.* **1.** a person engaged in a lawsuit. —*adj.* **2.** litigating; engaged in a lawsuit. [< L *lītigant-* (s. of *lītigāns* going to law, prp. of *lītigāre*) = *līt-* (s. of *līs*) a lawsuit + *-ig-* (comb. form of *agere* to carry on) + *-ant-* -ANT]

lit·i·gate (lit′ə gāt′), *v.,* **-gat·ed, -gat·ing.** —*v.t.* **1.** to make the subject of a lawsuit; contest at law. **2.** *Archaic.* to dispute (a point, assertion, etc.). —*v.i.* **3.** to carry on a lawsuit. [< L *lītigāt(us)* (ptp. of *lītigāre*). See LITIGANT, -ATE[1]] —**lit′i·ga′tor,** *n.*

lit·i·ga·tion (lit′ə gā′shən), *n.* **1.** the act or process of litigating. **2.** a lawsuit. [< LL *lītigātiōn-* (s. of *lītigātiō*) a dispute]

li·ti·gious (li tij′əs), *adj.* **1.** of or pertaining to litigation. **2.** excessively inclined to litigate. **3.** inclined to dispute or disagree; argumentative. [ME < L *lītigiōs(us)* contentious = *lītigi(um)* a quarrel (see LITIGANT, -IUM) + *-ōsus* -OUS] —**li·ti′gious·ly,** *adv.* —**li·ti′gious·ness, li·ti·gi·os·i·ty** (li tij′ē os′i tē), *n.* —**Syn.** **3.** disputatious, quarrelsome.

lit·mus (lit′məs), *n.* a blue coloring matter obtained from certain lichens, esp. *Roccella tinctoria.* In alkaline solution litmus turns blue, in acid solution, red: widely used as an indicator. [earlier *lytmos* < Scand; cf. Icel *litmosi* dye moss (*lit-* color, dye + *mosi* moss), *litunarmosi* lichen for dyeing, *mosa* to dye with moss. The unique form *lygtmose* (1502) may reflect MD *lijcmoes* litmus]

lit′mus pa′per, a strip of paper impregnated with litmus, used as an indicator.

lit·o·ral (lit′ər əl), *adj.* littoral.

li·to·tes (lī′tə tēz′, -tō-, lit′ə-, lī tō′tēz), *n., pl.* **-tes.** *Rhet.* understatement, esp. that in which an affirmative is expressed by the negative of its contrary, as in "not bad at all." Cf. **hyperbole.** [< NL < Gk *lītótēs* a diminution < *lītós* plain, small, meager]

li·tre (lē′tər), *n.* *Chiefly Brit.* liter.

Litt.B., Bachelor of Letters; Bachelor of Literature. [< L *Lit(t)erārum Baccalaureus*]

Litt.D., Doctor of Letters; Doctor of Literature. [< L *Lit(t)erārum Doctor*]

lit·ten (lit′ən), *adj.* *Archaic.* lighted.

lit·ter (lit′ər), *n.* **1.** a variety of objects scattered about; scattered rubbish. **2.** a condition of disorder or untidiness. **3.** a number of young brought forth at one birth. **4.** a stretcherlike conveyance for a sick or wounded person. **5.** a vehicle carried by men or animals, consisting of a bed or couch, often covered and curtained, suspended between shafts. **6.** straw, hay, or the like, used as bedding for animals, protection for plants, etc. **7.** slightly decomposed organic material on the floor of a forest. **—*v.t.* 8.** to strew (a place) with scattered objects, rubbish, etc. **9.** to scatter (objects) in disorder. **10.** to be strewn about (a place) in disorder (often fol. by *up*). **11.** to give birth to (young), as a multiparous animal. **12.** to supply (an animal) with litter for a bed. **13.** to use (straw, hay, etc.) for litter. **14.** to cover (a floor or other area) with straw, hay, etc., for litter. **—*v.i.* 15.** to give birth to a litter. **16.** to strew objects about. [ME *litere* bed, litter < AF] **—Syn. 2.** clutter. **3.** See **brood. 8.** mess (up).

lit·te·rae hu·ma·ni·o·res (lit′ə rē′ hyōō man′ē ôr′ēz, -ôr′ēz), the humanities as a field of study. [< ML: lit., more humane letters]

lit·té·ra·teur (lit′ər ə tûr′; *Fr.* lē tā RA tœR′), *n., pl.* **-teurs** (-tûrz′; *Fr.* -tœR′). a writer of literary works. Also, **lit′te·ra·teur′.** [< F < L *litterātor* an (inferior) grammarian]

lit·te·ra·tim (lit′ə rā′tim), *adv.* *Obs.* literatim.

lit·ter·bag (lit′ər bag′), *n.* a small paper or plastic bag for trash or rubbish, esp. one used in an automobile.

lit·ter·bug (lit′ər bug′), *n.* a person who litters streets, buildings, etc., with wastepaper or other refuse.

lit·tle (lit′əl), *adj.,* **less** or **less·er, least** or **lit·tler, lit·tlest;** *adv.,* **less, least;** *n.* **—*adj.* 1.** not large or below the average in size. **2.** short in duration: *a little while.* **3.** few in number: *a little group of artists.* **4.** not much: *little hope.* **5.** of a certain amount (usually prec. by *a*): *a little difficulty.* **6.** of small importance, concern, influence, scope, etc. **7.** not strong, forceful, or loud: *a little voice.* **8.** mean, narrow, or illiberal: *a little mind.* **9.** endearingly or amusingly small or considered as such: *Bless your little heart!* **10.** contemptibly small, petty, mean, etc.: *filthy little tricks.* **—*adv.* 11.** not at all (used before a verb): *He little knows what awaits him.* **12.** in only a small amount or degree; not much; slightly. **13.** seldom; rarely; infrequently: *We see each other very little.* **—*n.* 14.** something not very appreciable; a small amount, quantity, or degree: *I did little to help.* **15.** a short distance: *It's down the road a little.* **16.** a short time: *Stay here for a little.* **17. in little,** on a small scale. **18. little by little,** by degrees; gradually. **19. make little of, a.** belittle. **b.** to understand or interpret only slightly. **20. think little of,** to treat casually; regard as trivial. [ME, OE *lȳtel* (*lȳt* few, small + *-el* dim. suffix); c. D *luttel,* OHG *luzzil*] **—lit·tlish** (lit′əlish, lit′lish), *adj.* **—lit′tle·ness,** *n.*
—Syn. 1–4. tiny, teeny, wee. LITTLE, SMALL, DIMINUTIVE, MINUTE refer to that which is not large or significant. LITTLE (the opposite of *big*) is very general, covering size, extent, number, quantity, amount, duration, or degree: *a little boy; a little time.* SMALL (the opposite of *large* and of *great*) can frequently be used interchangeably with LITTLE, but is esp. applied to what is limited or below the average in size: *small oranges.* DIMINUTIVE denotes (usually physical) size that is much less than the average or ordinary; it may suggest delicacy: *the baby's diminutive fingers; diminutive in size but autocratic in manner.* MINUTE suggests that which is so tiny it is difficult to discern: *a minute quantity.*

Lit′tle Amer′ica, a base in the Antarctic, on the Bay of Whales, S of the Ross Sea: established by Adm. Richard E. Byrd in 1929

Lit′tle Bear′, *Astron.* the constellation Ursa Minor.

Lit′tle Big′horn, a river flowing N from N Wyoming to S Montana into Bighorn River: Gen. Custer and troops massacred near its juncture by Indians 1876. 80 mi. long.

Lit′tle Di′omede. See under **Diomede Islands.**

Lit′tle Dip′per, *Astron.* dipper (def. 3b).

Lit′tle Dog′, *Astron.* the constellation Canis Minor.

lit′tle fin′ger, the finger farthest from the thumb, the smallest of the five fingers.

lit′tle hours′, *Rom. Cath. Ch.* the hours of prime, tierce, sext, and nones, and sometimes also vespers and complin.

Lit′tle League′, a baseball league consisting of teams whose players are not over 12 years of age. **—Lit′tle Lea′guer.**

lit·tle·neck (lit′əl nek′), *n.* the quahog clam, *Venus mercenaria,* when young and small. [named after *Little Neck* Bay, N.Y., where it was once plentiful]

lit′tle of′fice, (*sometimes caps.*) *Rom. Cath. Ch.* an office similar to but shorter than the divine office, in honor of a saint, a mystery, or, esp., of the Virgin Mary.

lit′tle peo′ple, 1. (in folklore) small, imaginary beings, as elves, fairies, leprechauns, etc. **2.** the common people.

Lit′tle Rock′, a city in and the capital of Arkansas, in the central part, on the Arkansas River. 132,483 (1970).

Lit′tle Rus′sia, a region in the SW Soviet Union in Europe, consisting mainly of the Ukraine but sometimes considered as including adjacent areas.

Lit′tle Rus′sian, 1. a member of a division of the Russian people dwelling in southern and southwestern Soviet Union in Europe and in adjoining regions. Cf. **Ruthenian. 2.** Ukrainian (def. 3).

lit′tle slam′, *Bridge.* the winning of twelve of the thirteen tricks of a deal. Also called **small slam.** Cf. **grand slam.**

Little St. Bernard. See **St. Bernard, Little.**

lit′tle the′ater, 1. noncommercial and experimental drama. **2.** amateur theatricals.

lit′tle toe′, the fifth, outermost, and smallest digit of the foot.

Lit·tle·ton (lit′əl tən), *n.* **1. Sir Thomas,** c1407–81, English jurist and author. **2.** a city in central Colorado, S of Denver. 26,466 (1970).

lit·to·ral (lit′ər əl), *adj.* **1.** pertaining to the shore of a lake, sea, or ocean. **—*n.* 2.** a littoral region. Also, **litoral.** [< L *littorāl(is),* var. of *lītorālis* of the shore = *lītor-* (s. of *lītus*) shore + *-ālis* -AL[1]]

li·tur·gi·cal (li tûr′ji kəl), *adj.* **1.** of or pertaining to formal public worship or liturgies. **2.** of or pertaining to the liturgy or Eucharistic service. **3.** of or pertaining to liturgics. Also, **li·tur′gic.** [< ML *lītūrgic(us)* < LGk *leitourgikós* ministering (*leitourg(ós)* minister + *-ikos* -IC; see LITURGY) + -AL[1]] **—li·tur′gi·cal·ly,** *adv.*

li·tur·gics (li tûr′jiks), *n.* (*construed as sing.*) the methods of conducting public worship. [pl. of *liturgic.* See LITURGICAL, -ICS]

lit·ur·gist (lit′ər jist), *n.* **1.** an authority on liturgies. **2.** a compiler of a liturgy or liturgies. **3.** a person who uses or favors the use of a liturgy. **—lit′ur·gism,** *n.* **—lit′ur·gis′tic,** *adj.*

lit·ur·gy (lit′ər jē), *n., pl.* **-gies. 1.** a form of public worship; ritual. **2.** a particular arrangement of services. **3.** the service of the Eucharist, esp. this service **(Divine Liturgy)** in the Eastern Church. [< eccl. L *lītūrgia* < Gk *leitourgía* public service, eccl. Gk: Eucharist = *leitourg(ós)* minister + *-ia* -Y[3]]

Lit·vi·nov (lit vē′nof), *n.* **Max·im Max·i·mo·vich** (mä ksēm′ mä′ksi mô′vich), 1876–1951, Russian communist leader and statesman.

liv·a·ble (liv′ə bəl), *adj.* **1.** suitable for living in; habitable; comfortable. **2.** that can be lived with; companionable (often used in combination with *with*). **3.** worth living; endurable: *something to make life seem more livable.* Also, **liveable. —liv′a·ble·ness, liv′a·bil′i·ty,** *n.*

live[1] (liv), *v.,* **lived** (livd), **liv·ing. —*v.i.* 1.** to have life, as an animal or plant; be capable of vital functions. **2.** to remain alive: *to live to a ripe old age.* **3.** to continue in existence, operation, memory, etc. **4.** to rely for one's maintenance (usually fol. by *on* or *upon*): *to live on one's income.* **5.** to feed or subsist (usually fol. by *on* or *upon*): *to live on rice.* **6.** to dwell or reside: *to live in a cottage.* **7.** to pass life in a specified manner: *They lived happily ever after.* **8.** to direct or regulate one's life. **9.** to experience or enjoy life to the full. **10.** to cohabit (usually fol. by *with*). **—*v.t.* 11.** to pass (one's life). **12.** to represent or exhibit in one's life: *to live a lie.* **13. live down,** to live so as to allow (a scandal, disgrace, etc.) to be forgotten or forgiven. **14. live high off the hog.** See **hog** (def. 6). **15. live in** or **out,** to reside at or away from the place of one's employment. **16. live it up,** *Informal.* to live in an extravagant, wild, or carefree manner. **17. live up to,** to live in accordance with some ideal or standard. [ME *live(n),* OE *lifian, libban;* c. D *leven,* G *leben,* Icel *lifa,* Goth *liban*]

live[2] (līv), *adj.,* **liv·er, liv·est** for 4–9, *adv.* **—*adj.* 1.** having life; alive. **2.** of, pertaining to, or during the life of a living being. **3.** characterized by or indicating the presence of living creatures. **4.** full of spirits, energy, or activity. **5.** *Informal.* (of a person) energetic; alert; up-to-date. **6.** *Chiefly U.S.* of current interest or importance, as a question or issue. **7.** burning or glowing, as a coal. **8.** vivid or bright, as color. **9.** having resilience or bounce: *a live tennis ball.* **10.** being in play, as a baseball or football. **11.** loaded or unexploded, as a cartridge or shell. **12.** *Elect.* electrically connected to a source of potential difference, or electrically charged so as to have a potential different from that of earth: *a live wire.* **13.** moving or imparting motion; powered. **14.** still in use, or to be used, as type set up or copy for printing. **15.** (of a radio or television program) broadcast or televised at the moment it is being presented at the studio. **16.** made up of actual persons: *a live audience.* **17. live one,** *U.S. Slang.* **a.** a person who spends money readily. **b.** a person easily imposed upon or made the dupe of others. **—*adv.* 18.** (of a radio or television program) at the moment of occurrence or performance: *brought to you live from New York.* [aph. var. of ALIVE, used attributively] **—live′ness,** *n.*

live·a·ble (liv′ə bəl), *adj.* livable. **—live′a·ble·ness, live′a·bil′i·ty,** *n.*

live·bear·er (līv′bâr′ər), *n.* any viviparous fish of the family *Poeciliidae,* often kept in home aquariums. **—live′-bear′ing,** *adj.*

live′ cen′ter (līv). See under **center** (def. 15).

lived (livd), *adj.* having life, a life, or lives, as specified (usually used in combination): *a many-lived cat.* [ME; see LIFE, -ED[3]]

live-for·ev·er (liv′fər ev′ər), *n.* an orpine.

live-in (liv′in′), *adj.* **1.** Also, **sleep-in.** residing at the place of one's employment: *a live-in maid.* **2.** requiring one's residing at the place where one is taught or trained. **3.** living with someone as husband or wife without being legally married: *She shared the apartment with her live-in boyfriend.* **—*n.* 4.** a person who lives in.

live·li·hood (līv′lē hŏŏd′), *n.* a means of maintaining life; maintenance; living. [earlier *livelihod,* metathetic var. of ME *livilod,* OE *līf(ge)lād* life course (see LIFE, LODE, LOAD); current form influenced by obs. *livelihood* liveliness] **—Syn.** sustenance, subsistence. See **living.**

live′ load′ (līv). See under **load** (def. 5).

live·long (liv′lông′, -long′), *adj.* (of a period of time) whole or entire, esp. when tediously long, slow in passing, etc. [alter. (by assoc. with LIVE[1]) of earlier *leeve long,* ME *leve longe* dear long. See LEIF, LONG[1]]

live·ly (līv′lē), *adj.,* **-li·er, -li·est,** *adv.* **—*adj.* 1.** full or suggestive of life or vital energy. **2.** animated, spirited, or sprightly: *a lively tune.* **3.** eventful, stirring, or exciting. 4. strong, keen, or distinct: *a lively recollection.* 5. striking, telling, or effective, as an expression or instance. 6. vivid or bright, as color or light. 7. sparkling, as wines. 8. fresh or invigorating, as air. 9. rebounding quickly; springing back; resilient. 10. (of a baseball) likely to travel a great distance when hit. 11. full of activity. —*adv.* 12. with activity, vigor, or animation; briskly: *to step lively.* [ME; OE *līflīc* vital. See LIFE, -LY] —**live′li·ly,** *adv.* —**live′li·ness,** *n.* —**Syn.** 1. alert, spry, nimble, agile, quick, pert. 2. gay, buoyant. —**Ant.** 1. inactive, torpid. 2. dull.

liv·en (lī′vən), *v.t.* 1. to put life or spirit into; rouse; cheer (often fol. by *up*). —*v.i.* 2. to become more lively; brighten (usually fol. by *up*). [aph. var. of ENLIVEN] —**liv′en·er,** *n.*

live′ oak′ (līv), 1. an evergreen oak, *Quercus virginiana,* of the southern U.S.: the state tree of Georgia. 2. any of various related trees. 3. the hard, durable wood of any of these trees.

liv·er[1] (liv′ər), *n.* 1. *Anat.* a large, reddish-brown, glandular organ located in the upper right side of the abdominal cavity, divided by fissures into five lobes, and functioning in the secretion of bile and various metabolic processes. 2. an organ in other animals similar to the human liver, often used as food. 3. a diseased condition of the liver. [ME; OE *lifer;* c. D *lever,* G *Leber,* Icel *lifr;* akin to Gk *liparós* fat]

liv·er[2] (liv′ər), *n.* 1. a person who lives in a manner specified: *He was always a high liver.* 2. a dweller or resident; inhabitant: *a liver in cities.* [LIVE[1] + -ER[1]]

liv·er[3] (lī′vər), *adj.* comparative of **live**[2]. [LIVE[2] + -ER[4]]

liv′er fluke′ (liv′ər), any of various trematodes, as *Fasciola hepatica,* parasitic in the liver and bile ducts of man and domestic animals.

liv·er·ied (liv′ə rēd, liv′rēd), *adj.* clad in livery, as servants: *a liveried footman.*

liv·er·ish (liv′ər ish), *adj.* 1. resembling liver, esp. in color. 2. having one's liver out of order. 3. bilious; disagreeable; melancholy. —**liv′er·ish·ness,** *n.*

Liv·er·more (liv′ər mōr′, -môr′), *n.* a city in W California. 37,703 (1970).

Liv·er·pool (liv′ər po͞ol′), *n.* a seaport in SW Lancashire, in W England, on the Mersey estuary. 747,490 (1961).

Liv·er·pud·li·an (liv′ər pud′lē ən), *n.* a native or inhabitant of Liverpool. [*Liverpuddle* (jocular alter. of LIVERPOOL) + -IAN]

liv·er·wort (liv′ər wûrt′), *n.* any mosslike or thalloid, cryptogamic plant of the class *Hepaticae,* growing chiefly on damp ground, in water, or on tree trunks. [ME; late OE *liferwyrt*]

liv·er·wurst (liv′ər wûrst′, -wo͝orst′), *n.* a sausage made with a large percentage of liver, esp. one made with pork liver and pork meat. [half trans., half adoption of G *Leberwurst*]

liv·er·y[1] (liv′ə rē, liv′rē), *n., pl.* **-er·ies.** 1. a distinctive dress, badge, or device formerly provided by a nobleman for his retainers. 2. a uniform worn by servants. 3. distinctive attire worn by an official, a member of a company or guild, etc. 4. Also called **liv′ery com′pany.** *Brit.* a guild or company of the City of London entitled to wear such livery. 5. characteristic dress, garb, or outward appearance: *the green livery of summer.* 6. the keep, feeding, stabling, etc., of horses for pay. 7. *Law.* formal delivery of possession. [ME *livere* < AF = OF *livree* allowance (of food, clothing, etc.), n. use of fem. ptp. of *livrer* to give over < L *līberāre;* see LIBERATE]

liv·er·y[2] (liv′ə rē), *adj.* liverish. [LIVER[1] + -Y[1]]

liv·er·y·man (liv′ə rē mən, liv′rē-), *n., pl.* **-men.** 1. a keeper of or an employee in a livery stable. 2. *Brit.* a freeman of the City of London, entitled to wear the livery of the ancient guild or city district to which he belongs. 3. *Obs.* a person in livery, esp. a servant.

liv′ery sta′ble, a stable where horses and vehicles are cared for or let out for pay.

lives (līvz), *n.* pl. of **life.**

live′ steam′ (līv), steam fresh from the boiler and at full pressure.

live·stock (līv′stok′), *n.* (*construed as sing. or pl.*) the horses, cattle, sheep, and other useful animals kept or raised on a farm or ranch.

live′ wire′ (līv), 1. *Elect.* a conductor, as a current-carrying wire, whose potential is not at ground potential. 2. *Slang.* an energetic, alert person.

liv·id (liv′id), *adj.* 1. having a discolored, bluish appearance due to a bruise, congestion of blood vessels, strangulation, etc. 2. dull blue; dark, grayish blue. 3. enraged. 4. deathly pale; ashen. [< L *līvid(us)* black and blue = *līv(ere)* (to) be livid (akin to Welsh *lliw* color) + *-idus* -ID[4]] —**liv′id·ly,** *adv.* —**liv′id·ness,** *n.*

liv·ing (liv′ing), *adj.* 1. being alive; not dead. 2. in actual existence or use: *living languages.* 3. active; strong: *a living faith.* 4. burning or glowing, as a coal. 5. flowing freely, as water. 6. lifelike; true to life, as a picture or narrative. 7. of or pertaining to living persons: *within living memory.* 8. pertaining to or sufficient for living: *a living wage.* 9. in its natural state and place; native: *living rock.* 10. very; absolute (used as an intensifier): *to scare the living daylights out of someone.* —*n.* 11. the act or condition of a person or thing that lives. 12. a particular manner or course of life: *luxurious living.* 13. the means of maintaining life; livelihood: *to earn one's living.* 14. *Brit.* the benefice of a clergyman. 15. (*construed as pl.*) living persons collectively (usually prec. by *the*). [ME *lyvynge,* earlier *liviende* (adj.), OE *lifgende* (adj.)] —**Syn.** 1. live, quick. 2. extant, surviving. 3. lively, vigorous. 13. sustenance, subsistence. LIVING, LIVELIHOOD, MAINTENANCE, SUPPORT refer, directly or indirectly, to what is earned or spent for subsistence. LIVING and LIVELIHOOD (a somewhat more formal word), both refer to what one earns to keep (oneself) alive, but are seldom interchangeable within the same phrase: *to earn one's living; to seek one's livelihood.* "To make a living" suggests making just enough to keep alive, and is particularly frequent in the negative: *You cannot make a living out of that.* "To make a livelihood out of something" suggests rather making a business of it: *to make a livelihood out of trapping foxes.* MAINTENANCE and SUPPORT refer usually to what is spent for the living of another: *to provide for the maintenance or support of someone.* MAINTENANCE occasionally refers to the allowance itself provided for livelihood: *They are entitled to a maintenance from this estate.* —**Ant.** 1. dead.

liv′ing death′, a life completely devoid of joy.

liv′ing pic′ture. See **tableau vivant.**

liv′ing room′, a room used, esp. by a family, for varied individual and shared social activities; parlor.

liv′ing stand′ard. See **standard of living.**

Liv·ing·ston (liv′ing stən), *n.* 1. **Robert R.,** 1746–1813, U.S. statesman and jurist. 2. a township in NE New Jersey. 30,127 (1970).

Liv·ing·stone (liv′ing stən), *n.* 1. **David,** 1813–73, Scottish missionary and explorer in Africa. 2. a town in SW Zambia, on the Zambesi River, near Victoria Falls: the former capital. 35,400 (est. 1964).

Li·vo·ni·a (li vō′nē ə), *n.* 1. a former Russian province on the Baltic: now part of the Latvian and Estonian republics of the Soviet Union. 2. a city in SE Michigan, near Detroit. 110,109 (1970). —**Li·vo′ni·an,** *adj., n.*

Li·vor·no (lē vôr′nô), *n.* Italian name of **Leghorn.**

li·vre (lē′vər; *Fr.* lē′vrᵊ), *n., pl.* **-vres** (-vərz; *Fr.* -vrᵊ). a former money of account and group of coins of France, discontinued in 1794. [< MF, OF < L *lībra* balance, pound]

Liv·y (liv′ē), *n.* (*Titus Livius*) 59 B.C.–A.D. 17, Roman historian.

lix·iv·i·ate (lik siv′ē āt′), *v.t.,* **-at·ed, -at·ing.** to treat with a solvent. [LIXIVI(UM) + -ATE[1]] —**lix·iv′i·a′tion,** *n.*

lix·iv·i·um (lik siv′ē əm), *n., pl.* **lix·iv·i·ums, lix·iv·i·a** (lik siv′ē ə). 1. the solution, containing alkaline salts, obtained by leaching wood ashes with water; lye. 2. any solution obtained by leaching. [< L: lye, n. use of neut. of *lixīvius* made into lye = *lix* ashes, lye + *-īvius,* var. of *-īvus* -IVE]

liz·ard (liz′ərd), *n.* 1. any of numerous reptiles of the suborder *Lacertilia (Sauria),* typically having a moderately elongate body, a tapering tail, and two pairs of legs, comprising terrestrial, fossorial, arboreal, and aquatic species. 2. any of various reptiles resembling a lizard, as a dinosaur or crocodile. 3. leather made from the skin of the lizard, used for shoes, purses, etc. 4. **The Lizard.** See **Lizard Head.** [ME *liserd,* var. of *lesard(e)* < MF *lesard* (masc.) *lesarde* (fem.) < L *lacertus, lacerta*]

Lizard, *Sceloperus undulatus* (Length 4 to 7¼ in.)

liz·ard·fish (liz′ərd fish′), *n., pl.* (*esp. collectively*) **-fish,** (*esp. referring to two or more kinds or species*) **-fish·es.** any of several large-mouthed fishes of the family *Synodontidae,* having a lizardlike head.

Liz′ard Head′, a promontory in SW Cornwall, in SW England: the southernmost point in England. Also called **The Lizard.**

Lju·blja·na (lyo͞o′blyä nä), *n.* a city in and the capital of Slovenia, in NW Yugoslavia. 178,000 (est. 1961). German, **Laibach.**

'll, 1. contraction of *will: What'll we do?* 2. *Informal.* contraction of *till*[1]: *Wait'll he comes.*

LL, 1. Late Latin. 2. Low Latin. Also, **L.L.**

ll., lines.

lla·ma (lä′mə), *n.* 1. a woolly-haired, South American ruminant of the genus *Lama,* believed to be a domesticated variety of the guanaco. 2. cloth made from the fine, soft fleece of the llama, often combined with wool. [< Sp < Quechuan]

Llama, *Lama guanicoe* (4 ft. high at shoulder; length 4 to 5 ft.)

Llan·e·lly (la nel′ē; *Welsh.* hla-ne′hlē), *n.* a seaport in S Wales. 29,994 (1961).

Lla·no Es·ta·ca·do (lä′nō es′tə kä′dō, lan′ō), a large plateau in the SW United States, in W Texas and SE New Mexico: cattle-grazing region. 1000–5000 ft. above sea level. Also called **Staked Plain.**

L. Lat., 1. Late Latin. 2. Low Latin.

LL.B., Bachelor of Laws. [< L *Legum Baccalaureus*]

LL.D., Doctor of Laws. [< L *Legum Doctor*]

LL.M., Master of Laws. [< L *Legum Magister*]

Lloyd (loid), *n.* 1. **Harold (Clay·ton)** (klāt′ᵊn), 1894–1971, U.S. film comedian. 2. **(John) Sel·wyn (Brooke)** (sel′win), 1904–78, British statesman.

Lloyd′ George′, David, 1st Earl of Du·for (do͞o′vôr), 1863–1945, British statesman, prime minister 1916–22.

Lloyd's (loidz), *n.* an association of English insurance underwriters, originally engaged in underwriting marine risks but now issuing policies on almost every type of insurance. [named after Edward *Lloyd,* owner of a London coffee house that was frequented by insurers against sea risk]

Llud (hlyd), *n.* *Welsh Legend.* a king of Britain who rid his kingdom of three plagues: noted for his generosity.

LM (lem), Lunar Module.

lm, *Optics.* lumen; lumens.

LMT, Local Mean Time.

ln, *Math.* See **natural logarithm.** [*l(ogarithm) n(atural)*]

LNG, liquefied natural gas.

lo (lō), *interj.* look; see; behold. [ME; OE *lā* oh! ah!; c. Goth *laian,* Icel *lā* blame]

L.O.A., *Naut.* length over all.

loach (lōch), *n.* any of several slender, European and Asian fishes of the family *Cobitidae* and related families, having several barbels around the mouth. [ME *loche* < MF]

load (lōd), *n.* 1. a quantity of material or number of objects that is, or is to be, conveyed or supported. 2. the normal maximum amount of something carried by a vehicle, vessel, etc., often used as a unit of measure (usually used in combination): *a wagonload of borax.* 3. something that burdens or oppresses like a heavy weight. 4. the demand on a person, business, mechanical system, etc., in terms of work. 5. *Engineering.* any of the forces that a structure is calculated to oppose, including any permanent force **(dead load),** any moving or temporary force **(live load),** wind or earthquake forces. 6. *Elect.* a. power output. b. a device

that receives power. **7.** an initial commission charged to buyers of mutual-fund shares. **8.** a charge for a firearm. **9.** *Slang.* liquor consumed by a person in quantity enough to make him drunk. **10. loads,** *Informal.* an enormous amount: *loads of fun.* **11. get a load of,** *Slang.* to look at or listen to. —*v.t.* **12.** to put a load on or in. **13.** to take on as a load. **14.** to put into (a device) something that it acts upon: *to load a gun.* **15.** to give (a person) something in lavish abundance: *They loaded us with gifts.* **16.** to burden or oppress (usually fol. by *down by, with,* etc.). **17.** to add to the weight of, esp. for purposes of fraud. **18.** to prejudice or cause to operate in a prejudicial manner. **19.** *Elect.* to add (a power-absorbing device) to an electric circuit. **20.** *Insurance.* to increase (the net premium) by adding charges, as for expenses.
—*v.i.* **21.** to put on or take on a load, as of passengers or goods. **22.** to load a firearm. **23.** to enter a carrier or conveyance (usually fol. by *into*): *The campers loaded into the buses.*
—*adv.* **24. loads,** *Informal.* very much; a great deal: *Thanks loads.* [ME *lode;* orig. the same word as LODE (OE *lād* way, course, carrying) but associated with LADE]
—**Syn. 3.** weight, encumbrance, onus. LOAD, BURDEN referred originally to something placed on a person or animal or put into a vehicle for conveyance; LOAD still retains this meaning; BURDEN has lost it, except in such fixed phrases as: *beast of burden,* and *a ship of 1500 tons burden* (carrying capacity). Both words have come to be used figuratively to refer to duties, cares, etc., that are oppressively heavy, and this is now the main meaning of BURDEN: *You have taken a load off my mind. Some children are a burden.* **12.** lade. **16.** weight, encumber. —**Ant. 16.** disburden.

load·ed (lō′did), *adj.* **1.** bearing a load; full. **2.** containing ammunition or an explosive charge. **3.** (of a word, statement, or argument) fraught with emotional or associative significance that hinders rational or unprejudiced consideration. **4.** (of dice) fraudulently weighted so as to fall in a particular way. **5.** *Slang.* drunk. **6.** *Slang.* very wealthy.

load·ing (lō′diṅg), *n.* **1.** the act of a person or thing that loads. **2.** that with which something is loaded; load; burden; charge. **3.** *Aeron.* the ratio of the gross weight of an airplane to engine power, wingspan, or wing area. **4.** *Insurance.* an addition to the net premium, to cover expenses and allow a margin for contingencies and profit.

load′ line′, *Naut.* any of various lines marked on the sides of a cargo vessel to indicate the depth to which a vessel may be immersed under certain conditions. Also called **Plimsoll line.**

Load line
AB, Official load line set by American Bureau of Shipping; TF, Tropical, fresh water; F, Fresh water; T, Tropical; S, Summer; W, Winter; WNA, Winter, North Atlantic

load′-line mark′ (lōd′līn′), *Naut.* any of various marks by which the allowable loading and the load line at load displacement are established for a merchant vessel. Also called **Plimsoll mark.**

load·star (lōd′stär′), *n.* lodestar.

load·stone (lōd′stōn′), *n.* **1.** a variety of magnetite that possesses magnetic polarity and attracts iron. **2.** a piece of this serving as a magnet. **3.** something that attracts. Also, **lodestone.** [*load* LODE + STONE]

loaf[1] (lōf), *n., pl.* **loaves** (lōvz). **1.** a portion of bread or cake baked in a mass of definite form. **2.** a shaped or molded mass of food, as of sugar or chopped meat. [ME *lo(o)f,* OE *hlāf* loaf, bread; c. G *Laib,* Icel *hleifr,* Goth *hlaifs*]

loaf[2] (lōf), *v.i.* **1.** to lounge or saunter lazily and idly. **2.** to idle away time. —*v.t.* **3.** to pass (time) by idling (usually fol. by *away*). [? back formation from LOAFER]

loaf·er (lō′fər), *n.* **1.** a person who loafs; a lazy person. **2.** a moccasinlike, slip-on shoe for casual wear. [? short for *land-loafer,* appar. var. of *landloper* vagabond (< MD; see LAND, LOPE), with *-f-* from its G synonym *Landläufer*]

loam (lōm), *n.* **1.** a rich, friable soil containing a relatively equal mixture of sand and silt and a somewhat smaller proportion of clay. **2.** *Archaic.* earth or soil. **3.** *Obs.* clay or clayey earth. —*v.t.* **4.** to cover or stop with loam. [late ME *lome,* ME *lam(e),* OE *lām;* c. D *leem,* G *Lehm* loam, clay; akin to LIME[1]] —**loam′i·ness,** *n.* —**loam′less,** *adj.* —**loam′y,** *adj.*

loan (lōn), *n.* **1.** the act of lending; a grant of the temporary use of something. **2.** something lent or furnished on condition of being returned, esp. a sum of money lent at interest. —*v.t.* **3.** to make a loan of; lend. **4.** to lend (money) at interest. —*v.i.* **5.** to make a loan or loans; lend. [ME *lon(e), lan(e),* OE *lān* < Scand; cf. Icel *lān;* r. its cognate, OE *lǣn* loan, grant, c. D *leen* loan, G *Leh(e)n* fief] —**loan′er,** *n.*

Lo·an·da (lō än′də), *n.* Luanda.

loan′ shark′, *Informal.* a person who lends money at excessive rates of interest; usurer.

loan′ transla′tion, a compound word or expression in one language derived by literal translation from one in another language, as *marriage of convenience* from French *mariage de convenance.*

loan′ word′, a word in one language that has been borrowed or taken over from another language, as *wine,* taken into Old English from Latin, or *blitz,* taken into Modern English from German. [trans. of G *Lehnwort*] Also, **loan·word** (lōn′wûrd′).

loath (lōth, lōth), *adj.* unwilling; reluctant. Also, **loth.** [ME *loth, lath,* OE *lāth* hostile, hateful; c. D *leed,* G *leid* sorry, Icel *leithr* hateful] —**loath′ness,** *n.* —**Syn.** disinclined, averse. See **reluctant.** —**Ant.** eager.

loathe (lōth), *v.t.,* **loathed, loath·ing,** to feel disgust or intense aversion for; abhor. [ME *loth(i)en, lath(i)en,* OE *lāthiān* < *lāth* LOATH] —**Syn.** detest, abominate, hate.

loath·ing (lō′thiṅg), *n.* strong dislike mingled with disgust; intense aversion. [ME *lathynge.* See LOATHE, -ING[1]] —**loath′ing·ly,** *adv.* —**Syn.** See **aversion.**

loath·ly[1] (lōth′lē, lōth′-), *adv.* reluctantly; unwillingly. [late ME *lothely,* early ME *lothliche,* OE *lāthlīce*]

loath·ly[2] (lōth′lē, lōth′-), *adj.* *Archaic.* loathsome; hideous; repulsive. [ME *loothly,* OE *lāthlīc*]

loath·some (lōth′səm, lōth′-), *adj.* such as to excite loathing. [ME *lothsom*] —**loath′some·ly,** *adv.* —**loath′some·ness,** *n.* —**Syn.** revolting, disgusting, offensive, detestable, abhorrent. —**Ant.** attractive.

loaves (lōvz), *n.* pl. of **loaf**[1].

lob[1] (lob), *v.,* **lobbed, lob·bing,** *n.* —*v.t.* **1.** *Tennis.* to hit (a ball) in a high arc to the back of the opponent's court. **2.** *Cricket.* to bowl (the ball) with a slow underhand motion. **3.** to fire (a missile, as a shell) in a high trajectory so that it drops onto a target. —*v.i.* **4.** *Tennis.* to lob a ball. —*n.* **5.** *Tennis, Cricket.* a lobbed ball. [orig. v.: to behave like a *lobbe* bumpkin, clumsy person (ME: pollack; OE: spider; basic sense, something pendulous); c. MLG, MD *lobbe* dangling part, stockfish, etc.]

lob[2] (lob), *n.* lobworm. [earlier *lobbe* (orig. something pendulous; see LOB[1])]

Lo·ba·chev·sky (lō′bə chef′skē; *Russ.* lo bä chef′ski), *n.* **Ni·ko·lai I·va·no·vich** (nē ko lī′ ē vä′no vich), 1793–1856, Russian mathematician.

lo·bar (lō′bər, -bär), *adj.* of or pertaining to a lobe, as of the lungs. [< NL *lobār(is)*]

lo·bate (lō′bāt), *adj.* **1.** having a lobe or lobes; lobed. **2.** having the form of a lobe. **3.** *Ornith.* noting or pertaining to a foot in which the individual toes have membranous flaps along the sides. Also, **lo′bat·ed.** [< NL *lobāt(us)*] —**lo′bate·ly,** *adv.*

lo·ba·tion (lō bā′shən), *n.* **1.** lobate formation. **2.** a lobe.

lob·by (lob′ē), *n., pl.* **-bies,** *v.,* **-bied, -by·ing.** —*n.* **1.** a corridor, vestibule, or entrance hall, as in a public building, often serving as an anteroom; foyer. **2.** a group of persons who conduct a campaign to influence the voting of legislators. —*v.i.* **3.** to try to influence the voting of legislators. —*v.t.* **4.** to influence (legislators) by lobbying. **5.** to urge or procure the passage of (a bill) by lobbying. [< ML *lobia, laubia* covered way < OHG **laubia* (later *lauba*) arbor < *laub* LEAF] —**lob′by·er,** *n.*

lob·by·ism (lob′ē iz′əm), *n.* *U.S.* the practices of persons who lobby. —**lob′by·ist,** *n.*

lobe (lōb), *n.* **1.** a roundish projection or division, as of an organ or a leaf. **2.** the soft, pendulous, lower part of the external ear. [< ML *lob(us)* (LL: hull, husk, pod) < Gk *lobós,* akin to L *legula* lobe of the ear]

lo·bec·to·my (lō bek′tə mē), *n., pl.* **-mies.** *Surg.* excision of a lobe of an organ or gland.

lobed (lōbd), *adj.* **1.** having a lobe or lobes; lobate. **2.** *Bot.* (of a leaf) having lobes or divisions extending less than halfway to the middle of the base.

lo·bel·ia (lō bēl′yə), *n.* any herbaceous or woody plant of the genus *Lobelia,* having blue, red, yellow, or white flowers. [< NL; named after Matthias de *Lobel* (1538–1616), Flemish botanist; see -IA]

lo·be·line (lō′bə lēn′, -lin, lō bē′lēn, -lin), *n.* *Pharm.* a poisonous alkaloid, $C_{22}H_{27}NO_2$, used chiefly in the form of its sulfate or hydrochloride as a respiratory stimulant, and as an agent to discourage tobacco smoking. [LOBEL(IA) + -INE[3]]

Lo·bi·to (lo͞o bē′to͞o, lo͝o bē′to͝o), *n.* a seaport in W Angola. 31,630 (est. 1955).

lob·lol·ly (lob′lol′ē), *n., pl.* **-lies.** **1.** a pine, *Pinus Taeda,* of the southern U.S. **2.** the wood of this tree. **3.** *U.S. Dial.* a mire; mudhole. **4.** *Brit. Dial.* a thick gruel. Also called **lob′lolly pine′** (for defs. 1, 2). [short for *loblolly pine* swamp pine, special use of nautical term *loblolly* thick gruel, whence also the American sense mudhole]

lo·bo (lō′bō), *n., pl.* **-bos.** the gray or timber wolf of the western U.S. [< Sp < L *lupus* wolf]

lo·bot·o·my (lō bot′ə mē, lə-), *n., pl.* **-mies.** *Surgery.* the cutting into or across a lobe of the brain, usually of the cerebrum, to alter brain function, esp. in the treatment of mental disorders. [< Gk *lobó(s)* LOBE + -TOMY]

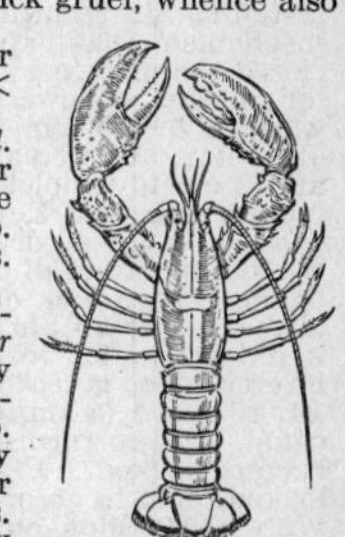
Lobster, *Homarus americanus* (Length 8 to 12 in.)

lob·ster (lob′stər), *n., pl.* (*esp. collectively*) **-ster,** (*esp. referring to two or more kinds or species*) **-sters.** **1.** any of various edible, marine, decapod crustaceans of the family *Homaridae,* esp. of the genus *Homarus.* **2.** See **spiny lobster.** **3.** any of various similar crustaceans, as certain crayfishes. [ME *lopster,* OE *loppestre,* lit., spidery creature]

lob·ster·ing (lob′stər iṅg), *n.* the act or process of capturing lobsters.

lob′ster New′burg, lobster cooked in a thick seasoned cream sauce flavored with sherry or brandy. Also, **lob′ster new′burg, lob′ster New′burgh.** Also called **lob′ster à la New′burg, lob′ster à la New′burgh.** [*Newburg* < ?]

lob′ster pot′, a trap, typically made of wooden slats, for catching lobsters.

lob′ster ther′midor, cooked lobster meat replaced in the shell with a cream sauce, grated cheese, and melted butter, and browned in the oven. [named by Napoleon after the month it was first served to him; see THERMIDOR]

lob·u·late (lob′yə lit, -lāt′), *adj.* consisting of, divided into, or having lobes. Also, **lob′u·lat′ed.** —**lob′u·la′tion,** *n.*

lob·ule (lob′yo͞ol), *n.* **1.** a small lobe. **2.** a subdivision of a lobe. [< NL *lobul(us)*] —**lob·u·lar** (lob′yə lər), *adj.*

lob·worm (lob′wûrm′), *n.* the lungworm. Also called **lob.**

lo·ca (lō′kə), *n.* a pl. of **locus.**

lo·cal (lō′kəl), *adj.* **1.** pertaining to or characterized by place or position in space. **2.** pertaining to, characteristic of, or restricted to a particular place or particular places. **3.** pertaining to or affecting a particular part or parts, as of a physical system or organism. **4.** stopping at all stations: *a local train.* —*n.* **5.** a local train, bus, etc. **6.** a local branch of a union, fraternity, etc. **7.** a local person or resident. **8.** *Brit. Informal.* a neighborhood pub or tavern. [late ME < LL *locāl(is).* See LOCUS, -AL[1]] —**lo′cal·ness,** *n.*

lo′cal col′or, distinctive characteristics or peculiarities of a place or period as represented in literature, drama, etc., or as observed in reality.

lo·cale (lō kal′, -käl′), *n.* **1.** a place or locality, esp. with reference to events or circumstances connected with it. **2.** the scene or setting, as of a play or motion picture. [earlier *local* < F, n. use of adj. See LOCAL] —**Syn. 1.** location, site, spot.

lo′cal gov′ernment, 1. the administration of the local affairs of a town or district by its inhabitants. **2.** the governing body of a town or district.

lo·cal·ism (lō′kə liz′əm), *n.* **1.** a custom, manner of speaking, etc., peculiar to one locality. **2.** excessive devotion to and promotion of the interests of a particular locality; sectionalism. —**lo′cal·ist,** *n.* —**lo′cal·is′tic,** *adj.*

lo·cal·i·ty (lō kal′i tē), *n., pl.* **-ties. 1.** a place or area. **2.** the property or fact of being at some specific place: *Every material object has locality.* [< LL *locālitās*]

lo·cal·ize (lō′kə līz′), *v.,* **-ized, -iz·ing.** —*v.t.* **1.** to confine or restrict to a particular place. —*v.i.* **2.** to gather in one locality. Also, *esp. Brit.,* **lo′cal·ise′.** —**lo′cal·iz′a·ble,** *adj.* —**lo′cal·i·za′tion,** *n.* —**lo′cal·iz′er,** *n.*

lo·cal·ly (lō′kə lē), *adv.* **1.** in a particular place, area, location, etc. **2.** with regard to place. [late ME *localliche*]

lo′cal op′tion, a right of choice exercised by a city, county, etc., esp. as to allowing the sale of liquor.

Lo·car·no (*It.* lô kär′nô), *n.* a town in S Switzerland, on Lake Maggiore. 10,155 (1960).

lo·cate (lō′kāt, lō kāt′), *v.,* **-cat·ed, -cat·ing.** —*v.t.* **1.** to discover the place or location of. **2.** to establish in a position, situation, or locality; place; settle. **3.** *U.S.* **a.** to survey and enter (a claim to a tract of land). **b.** to take possession of (land). **4.** to assign a particular location to (something), as by knowledge or opinion. —*v.i.* **5.** to establish oneself, one's business, or one's residence in a place; settle. [< L *locāt(us)* placed, ptp. of *locāre.* See LOCUS, -ATE[1]] —**lo·cat′a·ble,** *adj.* —**lo′cat·er,** *n.*

lo·ca·tion (lō kā′shən), *n.* **1.** the act of locating. **2.** the place where someone or something is at a given moment. **3.** the property or state of existing at some specific place at a given moment, or on a chronological or other scale. **4.** a site for a business, home, etc., esp. with reference to its environment: *a good location for a drugstore.* **5.** (in an electronic computer) any position on a register or memory device capable of storing one machine word. **6.** *Motion Pictures.* a place outside the studio suitable for filming a particular movie, scene, etc. (usually prec. by *on*). **7.** *Civil Law.* a letting or renting. [< L *locātiōn-* (s. of *locātiō*) a placing]

loc·a·tive (lok′ə tiv), *Gram.* —*adj.* **1.** noting a case that indicates place in or at which. —*n.* **2.** the locative case. **3.** a word in that case. [LOCATE + -IVE, modeled on *vocative*]

loc. cit. (lok′ sit′), in the place cited. [< L *locō citātō*]

loch (lok, lokh), *n. Scot.* **1.** a lake. **2.** a partially landlocked or protected bay; a narrow arm of the sea. [< Gael; r. ME *louch,* OE *luh* lake, pond < OWelsh *luch* (Welsh *llwch*) < OIr. See LOUGH]

Loch·in·var (lok′in vär′, lokh′-, lok′in vär′, lokh′-), *n.* the romantic hero of a ballad in the narrative poem *Marmion* (1808) by Sir Walter Scott.

Loch Ness (lok′ nes′, lokh′), a lake in NW Scotland, near Inverness: reputed home of creature resembling sea serpent. 23 mi. long.

lo·ci (lō′sī), *n.* a pl. of **locus.**

lock[1] (lok), *n.* **1.** a mechanical device for securing a door, window sash, etc., against intruders. **2.** any device for fastening or securing something. **3.** (in a firearm) the mechanism that explodes the charge; gunlock. **4.** an enclosed chamber in a canal, dam, etc., with gates at each end, for raising or lowering vessels by admitting or releasing water. **5.** an air lock or decompression chamber. **6.** *Wrestling.* any of various holds: *arm lock.* **7. lock, stock, and barrel,** completely; entirely; including every part. **8. under lock and key,** kept or confined in a secure place. —*v.t.* **9.** to fasten or secure (a door, window, building, etc.) by the operation of a lock or locks. **10.** to shut in a place fastened by a lock or locks, as for security or confinement (often fol. by *up*): *to lock up a prisoner.* **11.** to make fast or immovable. **12.** to join or unite firmly by interlinking or intertwining: *to lock arms.* **13.** to hold fast in an embrace. **14.** to move (a ship) by means of a lock or locks, as in a canal. **15.** to furnish with locks, as a canal. —*v.i.* **16.** to become locked. **17.** to become fastened, fixed, or interlocked. **18.** to go or pass by means of a lock or locks, as a vessel. **19. lock out, a.** to keep out by or as by a lock. **b.** to subject (employees) to a lockout. **20. lock up, a.** to imprison for a crime. **b.** to lock the doors and windows of a building, automobile, etc., as before leaving it. **c.** *Print.* to make (type) immovable in a chase by securing the quoins. [ME; OE *loc* fastening, bar; c. MLG *lok,* OHG *loh,* Icel *lok* lock, Goth *-luk* in *usluk* opening; akin to OE *lūcan* to shut] —**lock′a·ble,** *adj.*

lock[2] (lok), *n.* **1.** a tress or portion of hair. **2. locks,** the hair of the head. **3.** a flock or small portion of wool, cotton, flax, etc. [ME *locke,* OE *locc* lock of hair; c. Icel *lokkr,* D *lok* curl, G *Locke*]

lock·age (lok′ij), *n.* **1.** the use or operation of locks, as in a canal or stream. **2.** a toll paid for passage through a lock.

Locke (lok), *n.* **1. David Ross** ("*Petroleum V. Nasby*"), 1833–88, U.S. humorist and journalist. **2. John,** 1632–1704, English philosopher.

lock·er (lok′ər), *n.* **1.** a chest, drawer, compartment, closet, or the like, that may be locked. **2.** a refrigerated compartment, as in a locker plant, that may be rented for storing frozen foods. **3.** a person or thing that locks. [late ME *loker*]

lock′er plant′, an establishment for storing food under refrigeration, containing lockers for renting to users.

lock′er room′, a room containing lockers, as in a gymnasium, factory, school, etc., usually for the temporary storage and safekeeping of clothing and other personal belongings.

lock·et (lok′it), *n.* **1.** a small case for a portrait, lock of hair, or other keepsake, usually worn on a necklace. **2.** the uppermost mount of a scabbard. [ME *lokat* crossbar in a framework < AF *loquet,* dim. of *loc* latch < ME]

lock-in (lok′in′), *n.* **1.** an act or instance of becoming unalterable, unmovable, or rigid. **2.** commitment, binding, or restriction.

lock·jaw (lok′jô′), *n. Pathol.* tetanus in which the jaws become firmly locked together; trismus.

lock′ nut′, *Mach.* **1.** a nut specially constructed to prevent its coming loose. **2.** a thin supplementary nut screwed down upon a regular nut to prevent its loosening. Also, **lock′nut′.**

lock·out (lok′out′), *n.* the closing of a business or wholesale dismissal of employees by the employer because of a disagreement over terms.

Lock·port (lok′pōrt′, -pôrt′), *n.* a city in W New York, on the New York State Barge Canal. 25,399 (1970).

lock·smith (lok′smith′), *n.* a person who makes or repairs locks. [ME *lokismith*] —**lock′smith′er·y,** *n.* —**lock′smith′ing,** *n.*

lock′ step′, a mode of marching in very close file, in which the leg of each person moves with and closely behind the corresponding leg of the person ahead.

lock′ stitch′, a sewing-machine stitch in which two threads are locked together at small intervals.

lock·up (lok′up′), *n.* **1.** a jail. **2.** the act of locking up. **3.** *Print.* the act or procedure of locking up type and cuts in a chase.

lo·co (lō′kō), *n., pl.* **-cos,** *adj.* —*n.* **1.** locoweed. **2.** *Vet. Pathol.* locoism. —*adj.* **3.** *Slang.* crazy. [< Sp: insane]

loco-, a learned borrowing from Latin used, with the meaning "from place to place," in compound words: *locomotion.* [comb. form repr. L *locō,* abl. of *locus* place]

lo·co ci·ta·to (lō′kō ki tä′tō; *Eng.* lō′kō sī tā′tō, -tä′-). *Latin.* See **loc. cit.**

Lo·co·fo·co (lō′kō fō′kō), *n. U.S.* a member of the radical faction of the New York City Democrats, organized in 1835. Also, **lo′cofo′co.** [special use of *locofoco* (*cigar*) self-lighting, rhyming compound appar. based on LOCO(MOTIVE), taken to mean self-moving; *-foco,* alter. of It *fuoco* fire < L *focus* fireplace] —**Lo′co·fo′co·ism,** *n.*

lo·co·ism (lō′kō iz′əm), *n. Vet. Pathol.* a disease chiefly of sheep, horses, and cattle, caused by eating locoweed and characterized by weakness, impaired vision, and paralysis. Also called **loco, lo′co disease′.**

lo·co·mo·tion (lō′kə mō′shən), *n.* the act or power of moving from place to place.

lo·co·mo·tive (lō′kə mō′tiv), *n.* **1.** *Railroads.* a self-propelled vehicle for pulling trains. **2.** an organized group cheer, as at a football or basketball game, that begins slowly and progressively increases in speed in such a way as to suggest a steam locomotive. —*adj.* **3.** moving or traveling by means of its own mechanism or powers. **4.** of, pertaining to, or serving to produce such movement; adapted for or used in locomotion. **5.** of or pertaining to locomotives. —**lo′co·mo′tive·ly,** *adv.* —**lo′co·mo′tive·ness, lo′co·mo·tiv′i·ty,** *n.*

lo·co·mo·tor (lō′kə mō′tər), *adj.* of, pertaining to, or affecting locomotion. Also, **lo′co·mo′to·ry.**

locomo′tor atax′ia, *Pathol.* See **tabes dorsalis.**

lo·co·weed (lō′kō wēd′), *n.* any of various fabaceous plants of the genera *Astragalus* and *Oxytropis,* of the southwestern U.S., causing locoism.

loc. primo cit. (lok′ prī′mō sit′), in the place first cited. [< L *locō primō citātō*]

Lo·cris (lō′kris), *n.* either of two districts in the central part of ancient Greece. —**Lo′cri·an,** *n., adj.*

loc·u·lar (lok′yə lər), *adj. Biol.* having one or more loculi, chambers, or cells. [< NL *loculār(is)* kept in boxes]

loc·u·late (lok′yə lāt′, -lit), *adj. Biol.* having one or more loculi. Also, **loc′u·lat′ed.** [LOCUL(US) + -ATE[1]] —**loc′u·la′tion,** *n.*

loc·ule (lok′yo͞ol), *n. Chiefly Bot.* loculus.

loc·u·lus (lok′yə ləs), *n., pl.* **-li** (-lī′). **1.** *Biol., Anat.* a small compartment or chamber; cell. **2.** *Bot.* **a.** the cell of a carpel in which the seed is located. **b.** the cell of an anther in which the pollen is located. [< NL, special use of L *loculus.* See LOCUS, -ULE]

lo·cum te·nens (lō′kəm tē′nenz, ten′inz), *pl.* **lo·cum te·nen·tes** (lō′kəm tə nen′tēz). *Chiefly Brit.* a temporary substitute, esp. for a clergyman or doctor. Also called **locum.** [< ML: holding the place] —**lo·cum-te·nen·cy** (lō′kəm-tē′nən sē, -ten′ən-), *n.*

lo·cus (lō′kəs), *n., pl.* **-ci** (-sī), **-ca** (-kə). **1.** a place; locality. **2.** *Math.* the set of all points, lines, or surfaces that satisfies a given requirement. **3.** *Genetics.* the chromosomal position of a gene as determined by its linear order relative to the other genes on that chromosome. [< L; OL *stlocus* a place; akin to Gk *stéllein* to set up, Skt *sthalami* I stand. See STAND, STALL[1]]

lo·cust (lō′kəst), *n.* **1.** any of several grasshoppers of the family *Acrididae,* having short antennae and commonly migrating in swarms. **2.** any of various cicadas, as the seventeen-year locust. **3.** an American, fabaceous tree, *Robinia Pseudo-Acacia,* having thorny branches and white flowers. **4.** the durable wood of this tree. **5.** any of various other trees, as the carob or the honey locust. [ME < L *locusta* grasshopper] —**lo′cust·like′,** *adj.*

lo·cus·ta (lō kus′tə), *n., pl.* **-tae** (-tē). *Bot.* the spikelet of grasses. [< NL; see LOCUST] —**lo·cus′tal,** *adj.*

lo·cu·tion (lō kyo͞o′shən), *n.* **1.** a particular form of expression; phrase, expression, or idiom. **2.** a style of speech or verbal expression; phraseology. [< L *locūtiōn-* (s. of *locūtiō*) (style of) speech = *locūt(us)* spoken (ptp. of *loquī*) + *-iōn-* -ION]

lode (lōd), *n.* **1.** a veinlike deposit, usually metalliferous. **2.** any body of ore set off from adjacent rock formations. [ME; OE *lād* way, course, carrying; c. Icel *leith* way, route, OHG *leita* procession. See LOAD, LEAD[1]]

lo·den (lōd′ən), *n.* **1.** a thick, heavily fulled, waterproof fabric. **2.** Also called **lo′den green′.** the deep olive-green color of this fabric. [< G; OHG *lodo;* cf. OE *lotha* cloak, OIcel *lothi* fur cloak, *lothinn* shaggy]

lode·star (lōd′stär′), *n.* **1.** a star that shows the way. **2.** Polaris (def. 1). **3.** something that serves as a guide or on which the attention is fixed. Also, **loadstar.** [ME *loode sterre*]

lode·stone (lōd′stōn′), *n.* loadstone.

lodge (loj), *n., v.,* **lodged, lodg·ing.** —*n.* **1.** a roughly built shelter or hut, as in the woods. **2.** a cabin or cottage. **3.** a hotel building or main building at a resort or camp. **4.** a branch of a secret society, or its meeting place. **5.** a cottage for an employee on an estate or the like. **6.** an American-Indian dwelling. **7.** the den of an animal or group of animals, esp. beavers. —*v.i.* **8.** to have a habitation or quarters, esp. temporarily, in a hotel, another's house, etc. **9.** to be fixed, implanted, or caught in a place or position. —*v.t.* **10.** to furnish with a habitation or quarters, esp. temporarily; have as a lodger. **11.** to serve as a shelter or dwelling for; shelter; harbor. **12.** to put, place, or deposit for storage or keeping. **13.** to bring or send into a particular place or position. **14.** to house or contain. **15.** to vest (power, authority, etc.). **16.** to lay (information, a complaint, etc.) before a court or other authority. **17.** to beat down or lay flat, as vegetation in a storm. **18.** to track (a deer) to its lair. [ME *logge* < OF *loge* < OHG. See LOBBY] —**lodge′a·ble,** *adj.* —**Syn. 1, 2.** See **cottage. 10.** house, quarter.

Lodge (loj), *n.* **1. Henry Cabot,** 1850–1924, U.S. statesman and author: senator 1893–1924. **2.** his grandson, **Henry Cabot, Jr.,** 1902–85, U.S. journalist, statesman, and diplomat: ambassador to the United Nations 1953–60. **3. Thomas,** 1558?–1625, English poet and dramatist.

lodg·er (loj′ər), *n.* a person who lives in rented quarters in another's house. [ME *loger*]

lodg·ing (loj′ing), *n.* **1.** accommodation in a house, esp. in rooms for rent. **2.** a temporary place to stay; temporary quarters. **3. lodgings,** a room or rooms rented for residence in another's house. **4.** the act of lodging.

lodg·ment (loj′mənt), *n.* **1.** the act of lodging. **2.** the state of being lodged. **3.** something lodged or deposited. **4.** *Mil.* a position or foothold gained from an enemy, or an intrenchment made upon it. **5.** a lodging place; lodgings. Also, *esp. Brit.,* **lodge′ment.** [< MF *logement*]

Lo·di (lō′dē *for 1;* lō′dī *for 2, 3*), *n.* **1.** a town in N Italy, SE of Milan: Napoleon's defeat of the Austrians 1796. 38,321 (1961). **2.** a city in NE New Jersey. 25,213 (1970). **3.** a city in central California, near Sacramento. 28,691 (1970).

Łódź (lo͝oj), *n.* a city in central Poland, SW of Warsaw. 747,700 (est. 1968). Russian, **Lodz** (lôdz).

Loeb (lōb; *Ger.* lœb), *n.* **Jacques** (zhäk), 1859–1924, German physiologist and biologist in the U.S.

lo·ess (lō′es, les, lus; *Ger.* lœs), *n.* a loamy deposit formed by wind, usually yellowish and calcareous, common in the Mississippi valley and in Europe and Asia. [< G *Löss,* coined 1823 on basis of Alemannic *lösch* loose, light, akin to G *lösen* to loosen < *los* LOOSE] —**lo·ess′i·al, lo·ess′al,** *adj.*

Loe·wi (lō′ē), *n.* **Otto,** 1873–1961, U.S. physiologist and pharmacologist, born in Germany.

Loe·wy (lō′ē), *n.* **Raymond (Fer·nand)** (fər nand′), 1893–1986, U.S. industrial designer, born in France.

Lo′fo·ten Is′lands (lō′fo͞ot′ən), a group of islands NW of and belonging to Norway: rich fishing grounds. 474 sq. mi.

loft (lôft, loft), *n.* **1.** a room or the like under a sloping roof. **2.** a gallery or upper level in a church, hall, etc., having a special purpose: *a choir loft.* **3.** a hayloft. **4.** an upper story of a warehouse, mercantile building, or factory. **5.** *Golf.* **a.** the slope of the face of the head of a club backward from the vertical, tending to drive the ball upward. **b.** the act of lofting. **c.** a lofting stroke. **6.** the resiliency of wool. —*v.t.* **7.** to store in a loft. **8.** to hit or throw aloft. **9.** *Golf.* **a.** to slant the face of (a club). **b.** to hit (a golf ball) into the air or over an obstacle. **c.** to clear (an obstacle) in this manner. **10.** *Archaic.* to provide (a house, barn, etc.) with a loft. —*v.i.* **11.** to hit or throw something aloft. **12.** to go high into the air when hit, as a ball. [ME *lofte,* late OE *loft* < Scand; cf. Icel *lopt* upper chamber or region, the air, sky. See LIFT] —**loft′less,** *adj.*

Loft·ing (lôf′ting, lof′-), *n.* **Hugh,** 1886–1947, U.S. author of books for children, born in England.

loft·y (lôf′tē, lof′-), *adj.,* **loft·i·er, loft·i·est. 1.** extending high in the air; of imposing height; towering. **2.** exalted in rank, dignity, or character. **3.** elevated in style or sentiment, as writings or speech. **4.** haughty; proud; consciously superior or dignified. **5.** *Naut.* noting a rig of a sailing vessel having extraordinarily high masts. [late ME] —**loft′i·ly,** *adv.* —**loft′i·ness,** *n.* —**Syn. 1.** elevated. See **high. 3.** sublime. **4.** arrogant. —**Ant. 2.** lowly. **4.** humble.

log[1] (lôg, log), *n., v.,* **logged, log·ging.** —*n.* **1.** an unhewn length of the trunk or large limb of a felled tree. **2.** *Naut.* any of various devices for determining the speed of a vessel. **3.** any of various records concerning a trip made by a vessel or aircraft. **4.** any of various detailed records of the operation of a machine, progress of an activity, etc. —*v.t.* **5.** to cut (trees) into logs. **6.** to cut down the trees or timber on (land). **7.** to enter in a log; compile. **8.** to make (a certain speed), as a ship or airplane. **9.** to travel for (a certain distance or a certain amount of time), according to the record of a log. —*v.i.* **10.** to cut down trees and get logs from the forest for lumber. [ME *logge,* var. of *lugge* pole, limb of tree, now dial.; cf. obs. *logget* pole. See LUGSAIL]

log[2] (lôg, log), *n.* logarithm. [shortened form]

log-, var. of **logo-** before a vowel: *logarithm.*

-log, var. of **-logue:** *analog.*

log., logic.

Lo·gan (lō′gən), *n.* **Mount,** a mountain in Canada, in the Mount Elias Mountains: second highest peak in North America. 19,850 ft.

lo·gan·ber·ry (lō′gən ber′ē), *n., pl.* **-ries. 1.** the large, dark-red, acid fruit of a plant, *Rubus loganobaccus.* **2.** the plant itself. [named after James H. *Logan* (1841–1928), American horticulturist who first bred it; see BERRY]

lo·ga·ni·a·ceous (lō gā′nē ā′shəs), *adj.* belonging to the *Loganiaceae,* a family of herbs, shrubs, and trees of tropical and subtropical regions, including the nux vomica tree and other plants with poisonous properties. [< NL *Logani(a)* the typical genus (named after James *Logan,* 1674–1751, Irish-American botanist) + -ACEOUS]

log·a·oe·dic (lô′gə ē′dik, log′ə-), *Pros.* —*adj.* **1.** composed of dactyls and trochees or of anapests and iambs, producing a movement somewhat suggestive of prose. —*n.* **2.** a logaoedic verse. [< LL *logaoedic(us)* < Gk *logaoidikós.* See LOGO-, ODE, -IC]

log·a·rithm (lô′gə rit͟h′əm, -rit͟h′-, log′ə-), *n. Math.* the exponent of the power to which a base number must be raised to equal a given number: *The logarithm to the base 10 of 100 is 2. Abbr.:* log [< NL *logarithm(us)* < Gk *lóg(os)* LOG- + *arithmós* number; see ARITHMETIC]

log·a·rith·mic (lô′gə rit͟h′mik, -rit͟h′-, log′ə-), *adj. Math.* **1.** pertaining to a logarithm or logarithms. **2.** (of an equation) having a logarithm as one or more of its unknowns. Also, **log′a·rith′mi·cal.** —**log′a·rith′mi·cal·ly,** *adv.*

log·book (lôg′bo͝ok′, log′-), *n.* a book in which details of a trip made by a vessel or aircraft are recorded; log.

log′ bronc′, *Northwest U.S. Slang.* a one-man boat equipped with an outboard motor used to move logs in a lumber pond or pool.

loge (lōzh), *n.* **1.** a small enclosure; booth. **2.** a box in a theater or opera house. **3.** (in a theater) the front section of the lowest balcony, separated from the back section by an aisle or railing or both. [< F: see LODGE]

log·ger (lô′gər, log′ər), *n.* **1.** a person who logs; lumberjack. **2.** a tractor used in logging. **3.** a machine for loading logs.

log·ger·head (lô′gər hed′, log′ər-), *n.* **1.** a thickheaded or stupid person; blockhead. **2.** Also called **log′gerhead tur′tle.** a sea turtle, *Caretta caretta,* having a large head. **3. at loggerheads,** engaged in dispute; quarreling. [*logger* block of wood (first recorded in 18th century) + HEAD] —**log′ger·head′ed,** *adj.*

log·gia (loj′ə, lô′jē ə; *It.* lôd′jä), *n., pl.* **-gias,** *It.* **-gie** (-je). **1.** a gallery or arcade open to the air on at least one side. **2.** an enclosed area within the body of a building, open to the air on one side, that serves as an open-air room or as an entrance porch. [< It; see LODGE]

Loggia

log·ic (loj′ik), *n.* **1.** the science that investigates the principles governing correct or reliable inference. **2.** a particular method of reasoning or argumentation. **3.** reason or sound judgment, as in utterances or actions. **4.** the consistency to be discerned in a work of art, a system, etc. [ME *logik* < L *logica,* n. use of neut. pl. (in ML taken as fem. sing.) of Gk *logikós* of speech or reason. See LOGO-, -IC]

-logic, an element used in the formation of adjectives corresponding to nouns ending in *-logy: analogic.* [< Gk *-logikos.* See LOGIC]

log·i·cal (loj′i kəl), *adj.* **1.** according to or agreeing with the principles of logic. **2.** reasoning in accordance with the principles of logic. **3.** reasonable; reasonably to be expected: *the logical consequence of his actions.* **4.** of or pertaining to logic. [< ML *logicāl(is)*] —**log·i·cal·i·ty** (loj′i-kal′i tē), **log′i·cal·ness,** *n.* —**log′i·cal·ly,** *adv.*

-logical, an element used in the formation of adjectives corresponding to nouns with stems ending in *-logy: analogical.* Cf. **-logic.** [< Gk *-logik(os)* (see LOGIC) + -AL[1]]

log′ical pos′itivism, *Philos.* a movement that stresses philosophy as a method of criticizing and analyzing science and that rejects all transcendental metaphysics, statements of fact being held to be meaningful only if they have verifiable consequences in experience and statements of logic, mathematics, or philosophy, deriving their validity from the rules of language. Also called **log′ical empir′icism.**

lo·gi·cian (lō jish′ən), *n.* a person who is skilled in logic. [LOGIC + -IAN; r. ME *logicien* < MF]

log·i·cise (loj′i sīz′), *v.t., v.i.,* **-cised, -cis·ing.** *Chiefly Brit.* logicize.

log·i·cize (loj′i sīz′), *v.,* **-cized, -ciz·ing.** —*v.t.* **1.** to make logical; give logical form to. —*v.i.* **2.** to employ logic.

lo·gis·tic[1] (lō jis′tik), *adj.* of or pertaining to logistics. Also, **lo·gis′ti·cal.** [back formation from LOGISTICS] —**lo·gis′ti·cal·ly,** *adv.*

lo·gis·tic[2] (lō jis′tik), *n.* **1.** symbolic logic. **2.** *Archaic.* mathematical calculation. —*adj.* **3.** of or pertaining to logistic. [F *logistique* < LL *logisticus* of computation < Gk *logistikós* skilled in calculation, rational. See LOGO-, -IST, -IC]

lo·gis·tics (lō jis′tiks), *n.* (*construed as sing. or pl.*) the branch of military science dealing with the procurement, maintenance, and movement of equipment, supplies, and personnel. [< F *logistique* quartermaster's work = *log(er)* (to) LODGE, be quartered (said of troops) + *-istique* -ISTIC; see -ICS] —**lo·gis·ti·cian** (lō′ji stish′ən), *n.*

log·jam (lôg′jam′, log′-), *n.* **1.** an immovable tangle of logs, as in a river or stream during a drive. **2.** any blockage resembling this.

lo·go (lô′gō, log′ō), *n. Print.* logotype. [by shortening]

logo-, an element appearing in loan words from Greek, where it meant "word," "speech" (*logography*); on this model, used in the formation of new compound words (*logotype*). Also, *esp. before a vowel,* **log-.** Cf. **-log, -logic, -logical, -logue, -logy.** [< Gk *logo-,* comb. form of *lógos* LOGOS]

log·o·gram (lô′gə gram′, log′ə-), *n.* a conventional, abbreviated symbol for a frequently recurring word or phrase, as & for *and.* Also, **log·o·graph** (lô′gə graf′, -gräf′, log′ə-). —**log·o·gram·mat·ic** (lô′gə grə mat′ik, log′ə-), *adj.* —**log′o·gram·mat′i·cal·ly,** *adv.*

log·o·graph·ic (lô′gə graf′ik, log′ə-), *adj.* **1.** of, pertaining to, or using logograms: *logographic writing.* **2.** of or pertaining to logography. [< Gk *logographik(ós)*] —**log′o·graph′i·cal·ly,** *adv.*

lo·gog·ra·phy (lō gog′rə fē), *n.* **1.** printing with logotypes. **2.** a method of longhand reporting, each of several reporters in succession taking down a few words. [< Gk *logographía* speech writing] —**lo·gog′ra·pher,** *n.*

log·o·griph (lô′gə grif, log′ə-), *n.* an anagram or other word puzzle. [LOGO- + Gk *grîph(os)* a fishing basket, riddle] —**log′o·griph′ic,** *adj.*

lo·gom·a·chy (lō gom′ə kē), *n., pl.* **-chies. 1.** a dispute about or concerning words. **2.** a contention or debate marked by the reckless or incorrect use of words. **3.** a game played with cards, each bearing one letter, with which words are formed. [< Gk *logomachía*] —**log·o·mach·ic** (log′ə-mak′ik), **log′o·mach′i·cal,** *adj.* —**lo·gom′a·chist, log′o-mach′,** *n.*

log·or·rhe·a (lô′gə rē′ə, log′ə-), *n.* pathologically incoherent, repetitious speech. —**log′or·rhe′ic,** *adj.*

lo·gos (lō′gos, -gōs, log′os), *n.* **1.** (*often cap.*) *Philos.* the rational principle that governs and develops the universe. **2.** *Theol.* the divine word or reason incarnate in Jesus Christ. John 1:1–14. [< Gk: a word, saying, speech, discourse, thought, proportion, ratio, reckoning; akin to *légein* to speak]

log·o·ther·a·py (lô′gə ther′ə pē, log′ə-), *n.* a form of psychotherapy that stresses the nonmedical aspect, as by finding for a patient the meaning and aim of his existence as a human being.

log·o·type (lô′gə tīp′, log′ə-), *n.* **1.** a single piece of type bearing two or more uncombined letters, a syllable, or a word. **2.** a trademark or company name or device. **3.** nameplate (def. 2). Also called **logo.**

log·roll (lôg′rōl′, log′-), *Chiefly U.S.* —*v.t.* **1.** to procure the passage of (a bill) by logrolling. —*v.i.* **2.** to engage in political logrolling. [back formation from *logrolling*] —**log′roll′er,** *n.*

log·roll·ing (log′rō′ling, log′-), *n.* **1.** *Chiefly U.S.* the exchange of support or favors, esp. by legislators for mutual political gain. **2.** the action of rolling logs to a particular place. **3.** the action of rotating a log rapidly in the water, esp. as a competitive sport; birling.

Lo·gro·ño (lô grô′nyô), *n.* a city in N Spain. 63,781 (est. 1963).

-logue, a combining form denoting a specified kind of discourse, spoken or written: *analogue; monologue; travelogue.* Also, **-log.** [< F; r. ME *-loge* < L *-logus* < Gk *-logos.* See LOGOS]

log·way (lôg′wā′, log′-), *n.* gangway (def. 6).

log·wood (lôg′wŏŏd′, log′-), *n.* **1.** the heavy, brownish-red heartwood of a West Indian and Central American, caesalpiniaceous tree, *Haematoxylon campechianum,* used in dyeing. **2.** the tree itself.

lo·gy (lō′gē), *adj.,* **-gi·er, -gi·est.** lacking vitality; sluggish; dull; lethargic. [? < D *log* heavy, dull + -Y[1]] —**lo′gi·ly,** *adv.* —**lo′gi·ness, log′gi·ness,** *n.*

-logy, **1.** a combining form used in the names of sciences or bodies of knowledge: *paleontology; theology.* **2.** a termination of nouns referring to writing, discourses, collections, etc.: *trilogy; martyrology.* [ME *-logie* < L *-logia* < Gk *-logia.* See -LOGUE, -Y[3]]

Lo·hen·grin (lō′ən grin, -grēn′), *n.* *German Legend.* the son of Parzival, and a knight of the Holy Grail.

loid (loid), *v.t.* *Slang.* to open (a door) by sliding a thin piece of celluloid or plastic along the door edge to open a spring lock. [by shortening]

loin (loin), *n.* **1.** Usually, **loins.** the part or parts of the body of man or of a quadruped animal on either side of the spinal column, between the false ribs and hipbone. **2.** a cut of meat from this region of an animal, esp. a portion including the vertebrae of such parts. **3. loins,** *Chiefly Literary.* the area of the genitals regarded as the seat of strength and generative power. **4. gird up one's loins,** to prepare oneself for a test of strength or endurance. [ME *loyne* < MF *lo(i)gne,* perh. < VL **lumbea,* n. use of fem. of **lumbeus* of the loins = L *lumb(us)* loin + *-eus* -EOUS]

loin·cloth (loin′klôth′, -kloth′), *n.* a piece of cloth worn around the loins or hips, esp. by primitive inhabitants of tropical regions as the sole item of clothing.

Loire (lwar), *n.* a river in France, flowing S into the Atlantic: the longest river in France. 625 mi. long.

loi·ter (loi′tər), *v.i.* **1.** to linger aimlessly or as if aimlessly in or about a place. **2.** to move in a slow, idle manner. **3.** to waste time or dawdle over work. —*v.t.* **4.** to pass (time) in an idle or aimless manner (usually fol. by *away*). [late ME *loytre, lotere,* perh. < MD *loteren,* D *leuteren,* freq. of a verb akin to OE *lūtian* to lurk; see -ER[6]] —**loi′ter·er,** *n.* —**loi′ter·ing·ly,** *adv.*

—**Syn. 1.** LOITER, DALLY, DAWDLE, IDLE imply moving or acting slowly, stopping for unimportant reasons, and in general wasting time. To LOITER is to linger aimlessly: *to loiter until late.* To DALLY is to loiter indecisively or to delay sportively as if free from care or responsibility: *to dally on the way home.* To DAWDLE is to saunter, stopping often, and taking a great deal of time, or to fritter away time working in a half-hearted way: *to dawdle over a task.* To IDLE is to move slowly and aimlessly, or to spend a great deal of time doing nothing: *to idle away the hours.* **1–4.** loaf. **2, 3.** delay, tarry.

Lo·ki (lō′kē), *n.* *Scand. Myth.* a god of fire and the father of Fenrir, Hel, and the Midgard serpent: the god who instigated the death of Balder.

loll (lol), *v.i.* **1.** to recline or lean in a relaxed or indolent manner; lounge. **2.** hang loosely or droopingly; dangle. —*v.t.* **3.** to allow to hang, droop, or dangle. —*n.* *Archaic.* **4.** the act of lolling. **5.** a person or thing that lolls. [ME *lolle, lulle* (? imit.); cf. MD *lollen* to doze, sit over the fire] —**loll′er,** *n.* —**loll′ing·ly,** *adv.*

Lol·land (lol′ənd; *Dan.* lô′län), *n.* Laaland.

lol·la·pa·loo·za (lol′ə pə lōō′zə), *n.* *Slang.* an extraordinary or unusual thing, person, or event. Also, **lol′la-pa·loo′sa, lalapalooza, lallapalooza.** [?]

Lol·lard (lol′ərd), *n.* an English or Scottish follower of the religious teachings of John Wycliffe. [ME < MD *lollaerd* mumbler (of prayers) < *lollen* to mumble, hum. See LULL, -ARD] —**Lol′lard·y, Lol′lard·ry, Lol′lard·ism,** *n.*

lol·li·pop (lol′ē pop′), *n.* a piece of hard candy or taffy stuck on the end of a stick. Also, **lol′ly·pop′.** [? dial. *lolly* tongue + POP[1]]

lol·lop (lol′əp), *v.i.* **1.** *Brit. Dial.* to loll; lounge. **2.** to move forward with a bounding or leaping motion. [extended var. of LOLL; *-op* perh. to contrast with GALLOP]

lol·ly (lol′ē), *n., pl.* **-lies.** **1.** lollipop. **2.** *Brit. Informal.* **a.** a piece of candy, esp. hard candy. **b.** money. [shortening of LOLLYPOP]

lol·ly·gag (lol′ē gag′), *v.i.,* **-gagged, -gag·ging.** lallygag.

Lom·bard (lom′bərd, -bärd, lum′-), *n.* **1.** a native or inhabitant of Lombardy. **2.** a member of an ancient Germanic tribe in N Italy. —*adj.* **3.** Also, **Lom·bar′dic.** of or pertaining to the Lombards or Lombardy.

Lom·bard (lom′bərd, -bärd, lum′-; *Fr.* lôn bar′ *for 1;* lom′bärd *for 2*), *n.* **1. Peter** (*Petrus Lombardus*), c1100–64?, Italian theologian: bishop of Paris 1159–64?. **2.** a city in NE Illinois, near Chicago. 36,194 (1970).

Lom·bard·y (lom′bər dē, lum′-), *n.* a region and former kingdom in N Italy. 8,882,336; 9190 sq. mi.

Lom′bardy pop′lar, a poplar, *Populus nigra italica,* having a columnar, fastigiate manner of growth.

Lom·bok (lom bok′), *n.* an island in Indonesia, E of Java. 1,297,523 (est. 1961); 1826 sq. mi.

Lom·bro·so (lom brō′sō; *It.* lôm brô′sô), *n.* **Ce·sa·re** (che′zä re), 1836–1909, Italian physician and criminologist.

Lo·mé (lô mā′), *n.* a seaport in and the capital of Togo, on the Gulf of Guinea. 135,000.

lo·ment (lō′ment), *n.* *Bot.* a legume that is contracted in the spaces between the seeds, and breaks at maturity into one-seeded indehiscent joints. [late ME *lomente* < L *lōmentum* bean meal; see LOMENTUM] —**lo′ment·like′,** *adj.*

lo·men·ta·ceous (lō′mən tā′shəs), *adj.* *Bot.* resembling a loment; lomentlike.

lo·men·tum (lō men′təm), *n., pl.* **-ta** (-tə). *Bot.* loment. [< NL, special use of L: a face cream made of bean meal = *lō(tus)* washed (var. of *lautus,* ptp. of *lavāre;* see LAVE[1]) + *-mentum* -MENT]

Lo·mond (lō′mənd), *n.* **Loch,** a lake in W Scotland. 23 mi. long; 27 sq. mi.

Lom·poc (lom′pōk), *n.* a city in SW California, NW of Santa Barbara. 25,824 (1970).

lon., longitude.

Lon·don (lun′dən), *n.* **1. Jack,** 1876–1916, U.S. short-story writer and novelist. **2.** a metropolis in SE England, on the Thames: capital of the United Kingdom and the British Commonwealth. **3. City of,** a city in the central part of the former County of London: the ancient nucleus of the modern metropolis. 5400; 1 sq. mi. **4. County of,** a former administrative county comprising the City of London and the 28 metropolitan boroughs, now part of Greater London. **5. Greater,** an urban area comprising the City of London, London and Middlesex counties, and parts of Essex, Kent, Surrey, and Hertfordshire. 7,111,500; 609 sq. mi. **6.** a city in S Ontario, in SE Canada. 240,392.

Lon′don broil′, a broiled flank steak, crosscut into thin slices for serving.

Lon·don·der·ry (lun′dən der′ē), *n.* **1.** a county in N Northern Ireland. 111,536 (1961); 804 sq. mi. **2.** its county seat: a seaport. 53,762 (1961). Also called **Derry.**

Lon·don·er (lun′də nər), *n.* a native or inhabitant of London.

lone (lōn), *adj.* **1.** being alone; without company or accompaniment; solitary; unaccompanied. **2.** standing by itself or apart; isolated. **3.** sole; single. **4.** *Literary.* lonely; unfrequented. **5.** without companionship; lonesome. **6.** unmarried or widowed. [ME; aph. var. of ALONE, used attributively] —**lone′ness,** *n.* —**Syn. 1.** See **alone.**

lone′ hand′, **1.** someone who deliberately conducts his affairs without the advice or assistance of others. **2.** a stand or action taken independently.

lone·ly (lōn′lē), *adj.,* **-li·er, -li·est.** **1.** lone; solitary; without company; companionless. **2.** destitute of sympathetic or friendly companionship or relationships. **3.** remote from places of human habitation; unfrequented. **4.** standing apart; isolated. —**lone′li·ly,** *adv.* —**lone′li·ness,** *n.* —**Syn. 3.** sequestered.

lon·er (lō′nər), *n.* a person who remains alone or avoids the company of others.

lone·some (lōn′səm), *adj.* **1.** depressed or sad because of the lack of friends, companionship, etc.; lonely. **2.** attended with or causing such a state of feeling. **3.** lonely in situation; remote. —*n.* **4. on** or **by one's lonesome,** *Informal.* alone. —**lone′some·ly,** *adv.* —**lone′some·ness,** *n.*

Lone′ Star′ State′, Texas (used as a nickname).

lone′ wolf′, *Informal.* a person who chooses to live, act, or work alone.

long[1] (lông, long), *adj.,* **long·er** (lông′gər, long′-), **long·est** (lông′gist, long′-), *n., adv.* —*adj.* **1.** having considerable extent in space. **2.** having considerable duration. **3.** extending, lasting, or totaling a number of specified units: *eight miles long.* **4.** containing many items or units. **5.** requiring a considerable time to relate, read, etc. **6.** passing or seeming to pass slowly, because of the tedium or unpleasantness involved. **7.** reaching well into the past: *a long memory.* **8.** the longer of two or the longest of several: *He must have taken the long way home.* **9.** taking a long time; slow: *He's awfully long getting here.* **10.** extensive, broad, or thorough: *a long look ahead.* **11.** well-endowed or supplied with something (usually fol. by *on*): *long on brains.* **12.** having a considerable time to run, as a promissory note. **13.** higher or taller than usual. **14.** being against great odds; unlikely: *a long chance.* **15.** *Phonet.* **a.** lasting a relatively long time: *"Feed" has a longer sound than "feet" or "fit."* **b.** belonging to a class of sounds considered as usually longer in duration than another class, as the vowel of *bought* as compared to that of *but.* **c.** having the sound of the vowels in, conventionally, *mate, meet, mote,* and *moot,* and, popularly, in *mite* and *mute.* Cf. **short** (def. 14). **16.** *Pros.* (of a syllable in quantitative verse) lasting a relatively longer time than a short syllable. **17.** *Finance.* holding some commodity or stock in expectation of a profit from a rise in prices. —*n.* **18.** a long time: *They haven't been gone for long.* **19.** something that is long: *The signal was two longs and a short.* **20.** a size of clothing for tall men. **21.** *Finance.* a person who invests in stocks or commodities with the expectation of a rise in prices; a bull. **22. before long,** soon: *We should have news of her before long.* **23. the long and the short of,** the point or gist of; substance of. Also, **the long and short of.** —*adv.* **24.** for or through a great extent of space or, esp., time: *a reform long advocated.* **25.** for or throughout a specified extent, esp. of time: *How long did he stay?* **26.** (used elliptically in referring to the length of an absence, delay, etc.): *Don't be long.* **27.** throughout a specified period of time (usually used to emphasize a preceding noun): *It's been muggy all summer long.* **28.** at a point of time far distant from the time indicated: *long before.* **29. as long as.** See **as**[1] (def. 20). [ME *longe,* OE *lang, long;* c. D, G *lang,* Icel *langr,* Goth *langs,* L *longus*] —**long′ly,** *adv.* —**Syn. 1.** lengthy, extensive. **2.** protracted, prolonged, extended.

long[2] (lông, long), *v.i.* to have an earnest or strong desire; yearn; pine. [ME *long(en)*, OE *langian* to grow longer, yearn after, summon; see LONG[1]]

long[3] (lông, long), *v.i.* *Archaic.* to be suitable or fitting. [ME *long(en)*, OE *langian* to belong < *gelang* belonging to, dependent on; see ALONG]

long., longitude.

lon·gan (long′gən), *n.* **1.** the fruit of the large, evergreen, sapindaceous tree, *Euphoria Longan*, native to China and related to the litchi. **2.** the tree itself. Also, **lungan.** [< NL *longan(um)* < Chin *lung-yen* dragon's eye]

lon·ga·nim·i·ty (long′gə nim′i tē), *n.* patient endurance of hardship or injuries; fortitude; forbearance. [late ME *longanimyte* < LL *longanimitās* patience = *longanimi(s)* patient (see LONG[1], ANIMUS) + *-tās* -TY[2]] —**lon·gan·a·mous** (long gan′ə məs), *adj.*

Long′ Beach′, **1.** a city in SW California, S of Los Angeles: a seaside resort. 358,633 (1970). **2.** a city on SW Long Island, in SE New York. 33,127 (1970).

long·boat (lông′bōt′, long′-), *n.* *Naut.* (formerly) the largest boat carried by a sailing vessel.

long·bow (lông′bō′, long′-), *n.* a large bow drawn by hand, as that used by English archers from the 12th to the 16th centuries.

Long′ Branch′, a city in E New Jersey: seaside resort. 31,774 (1970).

long·cloth (lông′klôth′, long′kloth′), *n.* a fine, white plain-woven cotton cloth; high-grade muslin.

long′ dis′tance, telephone service between distant points. —**long′-dis′tance,** *adj.*

long′ divi′sion, *Math.* division, usually by a number of two or more digits, in which each step of the process is written down.

long-drawn (lông′drôn′, long′-), *adj.* drawn out; prolonged. Also, **long-drawn-out** (lông′drôn′out′, long′-).

longe (lunj, lonj), *n., v.,* **longed, longe·ing.** —*n.* **1.** a long rope used to guide a horse during training or exercise. —*v.t.* **2.** to train or exercise (a horse) by use of a longe. Also, **lunge.** [< F, OF, n. use of *longe* < L *longa*, fem. of *longus* LONG[1]]

lon·ge·ron (lon′jər ən), *n.* *Aeron.* a main longitudinal brace or support on an airplane. [< F: sidepiece = *longer* to skirt + *-on* n. suffix]

lon·gev·i·ty (lon jev′i tē), *n.* **1.** long life; great duration of life. **2.** the length or duration of life; *research in human longevity.* **3.** length of service, tenure, etc.; seniority. [< L *longaevitās.* See LONGEVOUS, -ITY]

lon·ge·vous (lon jē′vəs), *adj.* long-lived; living to a great age. [< L *longaevus* aged = *long(us)* long + *aev(um)* age + *-us* -OUS]

long′ face′, an unhappy or troubled expression. —**long′-faced′,** *adj.*

Long·fel·low (lông′fel′ō, long′-), *n.* **Henry Wads·worth** (wodz′wərth), 1807–82, U.S. poet.

Long·ford (lông′fərd, long′-), *n.* a county in Leinster, in the N Republic of Ireland. 30,642 (1961); 403 sq. mi. *Co. seat:* Longford.

long′ gal′lery, a large gallery, found esp. in the uppermost stories of Elizabethan and Jacobean manor houses, used as a family room and as a promenade.

long′ green′, *Slang.* paper money; cash.

long·hair (lông′hâr′, long′-), *Informal.* —*n.* **1.** *Sometimes Disparaging.* an intellectual. **2.** a person devoted to the arts, esp. a lover of classical music. —*adj.* **3.** Also, **long′-haired′.** of or characteristic of a longhair or his taste.

long·hand (lông′hand′, long′-), *n.* **1.** writing in which words are written out in full by hand. —*adj.* **2.** written in or employing longhand.

long·head (lông′hed′, long′-), *n.* *Anthropol.* **1.** a dolichocephalic person. **2.** a head with a low cephalic index.

long-head·ed (lông′hed′id, long′-), *adj.* **1.** *Anthropol.* dolichocephalic. **2.** of great discernment or foresight; farseeing or shrewd. Also, **long′head′ed.** —**long′-head′ed·ly, long′head′ed·ly,** *adv.* —**long′-head′ed·ness, long′head′ed·ness,** *n.*

long′ horn′, a moist Cheddar of cylindrical shape, weighing about 12 pounds.

Long·horn (lông′hôrn′, long′-), *n.* **1.** one of a nearly extinct English breed of beef cattle having long horns. **2.** (*l.c.*) See **Texas longhorn.** **3.** *Slang.* a Texan.

long′-horned bee′tle (lông′hôrnd′, long′-), any of numerous, often brightly colored beetles of the family *Cerambycidae,* usually with long antennae, the larvae of which bore into the wood of living or decaying trees.

long′-horned grass′hopper, any of numerous insects of the family *Tettigoniidae,* having long, threadlike antennae and well-developed stridulating organs on the forewings of the male.

long′ house′, **1.** a communal dwelling of the Iroquois and various other American-Indian peoples, consisting of a wooden, bark-covered framework often as much as 100 feet in length. **2.** (*caps.*) the league of the Iroquois.

long′ hun′dredweight, a hundredweight of 112 pounds, the usual hundredweight in Great Britain, but now rare in the U.S.

longi-, a learned borrowing from Latin meaning "long," used in the formation of compound words: *longicorn.* [< L, comb. form of *longus;* see -I-]

lon·gi·corn (lon′ji kôrn′), *Entomol.* —*adj.* **1.** having long antennae. **2.** belonging or pertaining to the *Cerambycidae,* comprising the long-horned beetles. —*n.* **3.** See **long-horned beetle.** [< NL *longicorn(is)* long-horned]

long·ing (lông′ing, long′-), *n.* **1.** prolonged, unceasing, or earnest desire. **2.** an instance of this. —*adj.* **3.** having or characterized by prolonged or earnest desire. [ME (n.); OE *langung* (n.). See LONG[2], -ING[1], -ING[2]] —**long′ing·ly,** *adv.* —**long′ing·ness,** *n.* —**Syn. 1.** See **desire.**

Lon·gi·nus (lon jī′nəs), *n.* **Dionysius Cas·sius** (kash′əs) A.D. 213?–273, Greek philosopher and rhetorician. —**Lon·gin·e·an** (lon jin′ē ən), *adj.*

long·ish (lông′ish, long′-), *adj.* somewhat long.

Long′ Is′land, an island in SE New York: the boroughs of Brooklyn and Queens of New York City are located at its W end. 118 mi. long; 12–20 mi. wide; 1682 sq. mi.

Long′ Is′land Sound′, an arm of the Atlantic between Connecticut and Long Island. ab. 90 mi. long.

lon·gi·tude (lon′ji to͞od′, -tyo͞od′), *n.* **1.** *Geog.* angular distance east or west on the earth's surface, measured by the angle contained between the meridian of a particular place and some prime meridian, as that of Greenwich, England, and expressed either in degrees or by some corresponding difference in time. **2.** *Astron.* See **celestial longitude.** [< L *longitūdō* length]

lon·gi·tu·di·nal (lon′ji to͞od′ənəl, -tyo͞od′-), *adj.* **1.** of or pertaining to longitude. **2.** *Zool.* pertaining to or extending along the long axis of the body, or the direction from front to back, or head to tail. **3.** pertaining to or extending in the direction of the length of a thing; lengthwise. —*n.* **4.** a longitudinal framing member, as in the hull of a ship. [< L *longitūdin-* (s. of *longitūdō*) LONGITUDE + -AL[1]] —**lon′gi·tu′di·nal·ly,** *adv.*

longitu′dinal wave′, *Physics.* a wave in which the direction of displacement is the same as the direction of propagation, as a sound wave. Cf. **transverse wave.**

long′ johns′, *Slang.* long underwear.

long′ jump′, *Chiefly Brit.* See **broad jump.**

long′leaf pine′ (lông′lēf′, long′-), **1.** an American pine, *Pinus palustris,* valued as a source of turpentine and for its timber. **2.** the wood of this tree.

long-lived (lông′līvd′, -livd′, long′-), *adj.* **1.** having a long life, existence, or duration. **2.** (of an object) lasting or functioning a long time. —**long′-lived′ness,** *n.*

long′ meas′ure. See **linear measure.**

Lon·go·bard (long′gō bärd′, -gə-), *n.* Lombard (def. 2).

Long′ Par′liament, *Eng. Hist.* the Parliament that assembled November 3, 1640, was expelled by Cromwell in 1653, reconvened in 1659, and was dissolved in 1660.

long′ pig′, (among the Maori and Polynesian peoples) human flesh eaten by cannibals.

long-play·ing (lông′plā′ing, long′-), *adj.* of or pertaining to disk records devised to be played at 33⅓ revolutions per minute.

long-range (lông′rānj′, long′-), *adj.* **1.** designed to fire a long distance. **2.** allowing for or extending into the more distant future.

long′ ri′fle. See **Kentucky rifle.**

long *s* (es), a style of the letter *s*, suggesting a lower-case *f* in form, formerly common in handwriting and in print.

long·ship (lông′ship′, long′-), *n.* a medieval ship used in northern Europe esp. by the Norse, having a narrow, open hull, a single square sail, and a large number of oars.

long·shore (lông′shôr′, -shōr′, long′-), *adj.* existing, found, or employed along the shore, esp. at or near a seaport. [aph. var. of ALONGSHORE]

long·shore·man (lông′shôr′mən, -shōr′-, -shôr′-, -shōr′-, long′-), *n., pl.* **-men.** a man employed on the wharves of a port, as in loading and unloading vessels.

long′ shot′, **1.** a selection, as of a race horse, that has very little chance of winning. **2.** an attempt or undertaking that offers great rewards as well as a great risk of failure. **3.** *Motion Pictures, Television.* a camera shot taken at a relatively great distance from the subject. Cf. **close-up** (def. 2). **4. by a long shot,** by any means: *They haven't finished by a long shot.*

long-sight·ed (lông′sī′tid, long′-), *adj.* **1.** far-sighted; hypermetropic. **2.** having great foresight; foreseeing remote results. —**long′-sight′ed·ness,** *n.*

Longs′ Peak′ (lôngz, longz), a peak in N Colorado, in the Rocky Mountain National Park. 14,255 ft.

long′ splice′, a splice for forming a united rope narrow enough to pass through a block, made by unlaying the ends of two ropes for a considerable distance, overlapping the strands so as to make pairs of one strand from each rope, unlaying one of each pair, twisting the other strand into its place in the united rope, and tucking the yarns of the unlaid strand separately into place. See illus. at **splice.**

long·spur (lông′spûr′, long′-), *n.* any of several fringillid birds of the genera *Calcarius* and *Rhynchophanes,* of tundra or prairie regions of North America, characterized by a long, spurlike hind claw on each foot.

long·stand·ing (lông′stan′ding, long′-), *adj.* existing or occurring for a long time.

Long·street (lông′strēt′, long′-), *n.* **James,** 1821–1904, Confederate general in the U.S. Civil War.

long-suf·fer·ing (lông′suf′ər ing, long′-), *adj.* **1.** enduring injury or provocation long and patiently. —*n.* **2.** long and patient endurance of injury or trouble. —**long′-suf′fer·ing·ly,** *adv.*

long′ suit′, *Cards.* **1.** the suit in which the most cards are held in a hand. **2.** *Bridge.* a suit in which four or more cards are held in a hand. **3.** the quality, activity, endeavor, etc., in which a person excels.

long′ sweet′ening, *Chiefly Southern and Midland U.S.* liquid sweetening, as maple syrup or molasses.

long-term (lông′tûrm′, long′-), *adj.* **1.** covering a relatively long period of time. **2.** *Finance.* maturing over a relatively long period of time.

long·time (lông′tīm′, long′-) *adj.* having existed, occurred, or continued for a long period of time.

long′ tom′, **1.** *Army Slang.* a large field gun, usually the 155-millimeter gun. **2.** a long heavy cannon formerly carried by small naval vessels.

long′ ton′. See under **ton**[1] (def. 1). *Abbr.:* L/T

long′ vaca′tion, *Brit.* the summer vacation given in the law courts and universities.

Long·view (lông′vyo͞o′, long′-), *n.* **1.** a city in NE Texas. 45,547 (1970). **2.** a city in SW Washington, on the Columbia. 28,373 (1970).

long-waist·ed (lông′wā′stid, long′-), *adj.* of more than average length between the shoulders and waistline; having a low waistline. Cf. **short-waisted.**

long-wind·ed (lông′win′did, long′-), *adj.* **1.** talking or writing at tedious length. **2.** continued to a tedious length in speech or writing. **3.** able to breathe deeply; not tiring easily. —**long′-wind′ed·ly,** *adv.* —**long′-wind′ed·ness,** *n.*

long·wise (lông′wīz′, long′-), *adj., adv.* lengthwise. Also, **long′ways′.**

Lönn·rot (len′rot, -ro͞ot; *Fin.* lœn′rôt), *n.* **E·lias** (e′lyäs), 1802–84, Finnish scholar and editor.

Lons-le-Sau·nier (lôɴ lə sō nyā′), *n.* a city in and the capital of Jura, in E France. 18,752 (1962).

loo[1] (lo͞o), *n., pl.* **loos,** *v.,* **looed, loo·ing.** —*n.* **1.** a game at cards in which forfeits are paid into a pool. **2.** the forfeit or sum paid into the pool. —*v.t.* **3.** to subject to a forfeit at loo. [short for *lanterloo* < D *lanterlu* < F *lantur(e)lu,* special use of meaningless refrain of an old song]

loo[2] (lo͞o), *n. Brit. Informal.* toilet; water closet. [? m. F *lieux d'aisances* privy, water closet]

loo·by (lo͞o′bē), *n., pl.* **-bies.** an awkward fellow, esp. one who is lazy or stupid; lout. [ME *loby.* See LOB[1], LUBBER]

loo·fa (lo͞o′fə), *n.* luffa. Also, **loo′fah.**

loo·ie (lo͞o′ē), *n. Slang.* a lieutenant of the armed forces. Also, **loo′ey, louie.** [LIEU(TENANT) + -IE]

look (lo͝ok), *v.i.* **1.** to set one's eyes upon something or in some direction in order to see. **2.** to glance or gaze in a manner specified: *to look questioningly at a person.* **3.** to use the sight in seeking, searching, examining, watching, etc. **4.** to tend, as in bearing or significance: *Conditions look toward war.* **5.** to appear or seem as specified: *to look pale.* **6.** to seem to the mind: *The case looks promising.* **7.** to direct the mental regard or attention: *to look at the facts.* **8.** to have an outlook or afford a view: *The window looks upon the street.* **9.** to face or front: *The house looks to the east.* —*v.t.* **10.** to give (someone) a look: *He looked me straight in the eye.* **11.** to have an appearance appropriate to or befitting (something): *The actor looked his part.* **12.** to try to find; seek (usually fol. by *up*). **13.** to express or suggest by looks. **14.** to view, inspect, or examine (often fol. by *over*). **15.** to appear to be; look like: *He looked a perfect fool.* **16.** *Archaic.* to bring, put, etc., by looks. **17. look after, a.** to follow with the eye, as someone or something moving away. **b.** to take care of; minister to. **18. look back,** to review past events; return in thought. **19. look daggers,** to look at someone with a furious, menacing expression. **20. look down on** or **upon,** to regard with scorn or disdain; have contempt for. **21. look down one's nose at,** to regard with an overbearing attitude of superiority, disdain, or censure. **22. look forward to,** to anticipate with eagerness or pleasure. **23. look in, a.** Also, **look into.** to look briefly inside of. **b.** Also, **look in on.** to visit (a person, place, etc.) briefly. **24. look into,** to inquire into; investigate; examine. **25. look on, a.** to be a spectator; watch: *The crowd looked on as the police moved in.* **b.** See **look** (def. 31a). **26. look out, a.** to look to the outside. **b.** to be on guard. **c.** to take watchful care; be concerned about: *to look out for one's health.* **27. look over,** to examine, esp. briefly or superficially. **28. look sharp,** to be alert and quick. **29. look to, a.** to give attention to. **b.** to direct one's expectations or hopes to. **c.** to depend or rely on. **30. look up, a.** to direct the eyes upward; raise one's glance. **b.** *Informal.* to become better or more prosperous; improve. **c.** to search for or seek out. **d.** *Naut.* (of a sailing vessel) to head more nearly in the direction of its destination after a favoring change of wind. **31. look upon, a.** Also, **look on.** to consider; regard: *They look upon gambling as a sin.* **b.** to observe or behold: *to look upon a beautiful picture.* **32. look up to,** to regard with admiration or respect; esteem. —*n.* **33.** the act or an instance of looking. **34.** an expressive glance. **35.** a visual search or examination. **36.** the way in which a person or thing appears to the eye or to the mind; aspect. **37. looks,** general aspect; appearance. [ME *lōk(i)e(n),* OE *lōcian;* c. MD *lœken,* akin to dial. G *lugen* to look out] —**Syn. 1.** See **watch. 6.** See **seem. 36.** appearance, air.

look·er (lo͝ok′ər), *n.* **1.** a person who looks. **2.** *Slang.* a very good-looking person, esp. a woman.

look·er-on (lo͝ok′ər on′), *n., pl.* **look·ers-on.** *Informal.* a person who looks on; spectator.

look-in (lo͝ok′in′), *n.* **1.** a brief glance. **2.** a short visit.

look′ing glass′, 1. a mirror made of glass with a metallic or amalgam backing. **2.** the glass used in a mirror.

look·out (lo͝ok′out′), *n.* **1.** the act of looking out or keeping watch. **2.** a watch kept, as for something that may come or happen. **3.** a person or group stationed or employed to keep such a watch. **4.** a station or place from which a watch is kept. **5.** *Chiefly Brit.* view; prospect; outlook. **6.** *Informal.* an object of care or concern: *That's not my lookout.*

Look′out Moun′tain, a mountain ridge in Georgia, Tennessee, and Alabama: Civil War battle fought here, near Chattanooga, Tennessee 1863; highest point, 2126 ft.

look-see (lo͝ok′sē′), *n. Slang.* a visual survey; look.

loom[1] (lo͞om), *n.* **1.** a hand-operated or power-driven apparatus for weaving fabrics. **2.** the art or the process of weaving. **3.** the part of an oar between the blade and the handle. —*v.t.* **4.** to weave (something) on a loom. [ME *lome,* OE *gelōma* tool, implement. See HEIRLOOM]

loom[2] (lo͞om), *v.i.* **1.** to come into view in indistinct and enlarged form: *The mountainous island loomed on the horizon.* **2.** to rise before the vision with an appearance of great or portentous size: *As we dashed round the corner, a police officer loomed in front of us.* **3.** to assume form as an impending event: *The convention looms as a political battle.* —*n.* **4.** a looming appearance, as of something seen indistinctly at a distance or through a fog. [?]

L.O.O.M., Loyal Order of Moose.

loon[1] (lo͞on), *n.* any of several large, short-tailed, web-footed, fish-eating diving birds of the genus *Gavia,* of the Northern Hemisphere. [var. of *loom* < Scand; cf. Icel *lōmr,* Sw *lom*]

loon[2] (lo͞on), *n.* a worthless, lazy, or stupid fellow. [late ME *lowen* < Scand; cf. Icel *lūinn* beaten, beat (ptp. of *lȳja* to beat), *lūalag* base conduct]

loon·ey (lo͞o′nē), *adj.* **loon·i·er, loon·i·est,** *n., pl.* **loon·ies.** loony.

loon·y (lo͞o′nē), *adj.,* **loon·i·er, loon·i·est,** *n., pl.* **loon·ies.** *Slang.* —*adj.* **1.** lunatic; insane. **2.** extremely foolish. —*n.* **3.** a lunatic. Also, **luny.** [LUN(ATIC) + -Y[2]] —**loon′i·ness,** *n.*

loon′y bin′, *Slang.* an insane asylum or the mental ward of a hospital.

loop[1] (lo͞op), *n.* **1.** a portion of a cord, ribbon, etc., folded or doubled upon itself so as to leave an opening between the parts. **2.** anything shaped more or less like a loop, as a line drawn on paper, a part of a letter, a part of a path, or a line of motion. **3.** a curved piece or a ring of metal, wood, or the like, used for the insertion of something, as a handle. **4.** *Aeron.* a maneuver executed by an airplane in such a manner that the airplane describes a closed curve in a vertical plane. **5.** a circular area at the end of a trolley line, railroad line, etc., where cars turn around. **6.** an arm of a cloverleaf where traffic may turn off or onto a main road or highway. **7.** *Physics.* the part of a vibrating string, column of air or other medium, etc., between two adjacent nodes. **8.** *Elect.* a closed electric or magnetic circuit. **9.** *Computer Technol.* **a.** reiteration of a set of instructions in a routine or program. **b.** a routine or program consisting of a set of iterative instructions. **10. the Loop,** the main business district of Chicago. **11. the Loop.** See **IUD.** —*v.t.* **12.** to form into a loop or loops. **13.** to make a loop or loops in. **14.** to enfold or encircle in or with something arranged in a loop. **15.** to fasten by forming into a loop, or by means of something formed into a loop (often fol. by *up*): *to loop up the new draperies.* **16.** to cause (a missile or projectile) to trace a looping or looplike trajectory through the air. **17.** to fly (an airplane) in a loop or series of loops. —*v.i.* **18.** to make or form a loop or loops: *The river loops around the two counties.* **19.** to move by forming loops, as a measuringworm. **20.** to perform a loop or series of loops in an airplane. [late ME *loupe;* perh. < Gael *lub* loop, bend]

loop[2] (lo͞op), *n. Archaic.* a small or narrow opening, as in a wall; loophole. [ME *loupe* window; cf. MD *lūpen* to peep, peer]

loop[3] (lo͞op), *n. Metalworking.* a hot bloom of pasty consistency, for working under a hammer or in rolls. [< F *loupe* (> G *Luppe*), special use of *loupe* wen, knob, gnarl << Gmc. See LOUPE]

looped (lo͞opt), *adj.* **1.** *Slang.* drunk; inebriated. **2.** having or consisting of loops.

loop·er (lo͞o′pər), *n.* **1.** a person or thing that loops. **2.** a measuringworm. **3.** the thread holder in a sewing machine using two threads.

loop·hole (lo͞op′hōl′), *n., v.,* **-holed, -hol·ing.** —*n.* **1.** a small or narrow opening, as in a wall, for looking through, for admitting light and air, or, particularly in a fortification, for the discharge of missiles against an enemy outside. **2.** an opening or aperture. **3.** a means of escape or evasion: *There are a number of loopholes in the tax laws whereby shrewd taxpayers can save money.* —*v.t.* **4.** to furnish with loopholes.

loop′ knot′, a knot made by doubling over a line at its end and tying both thicknesses into a square knot in such a way as to leave a loop. See illus. at **knot.**

loop′ stitch′, *Sewing.* any stitch that uses loops in the pattern or process of working.

loop-the-loop (lo͞op′thə lo͞op′), *n.* **1.** an airplane maneuver in which a plane, starting upward, makes one complete vertical loop. **2.** a ride in an amusement park that simulates this maneuver.

loose (lo͞os), *adj.,* **loos·er, loos·est,** *adv., v.,* **loosed, loos·ing.** —*adj.* **1.** free from anything that binds or restrains; unfettered. **2.** free or released from fastening or attachment: *a loose end.* **3.** uncombined, as a chemical element. **4.** not bound together: *to stack loose papers; to wear one's hair loose.* **5.** not put up in a package or other container: *loose mushrooms.* **6.** available for disposal; unemployed; unappropriated: *loose funds.* **7.** lacking in reticence or power of restraint: *a loose tongue.* **8.** lax, as the bowels. **9.** free from moral restraint; lax in principle or conduct: *loose morals; loose business practices.* **10.** sexually promiscuous or wanton; unchaste: *a loose woman.* **11.** not firm, taut, or rigid: *a loose tooth; a loose rein.* **12.** relaxed or limber in nature: *He runs with a loose, open stride.* **13.** not fitting closely or tightly: *a loose sweater.* **14.** not close or compact in structure or arrangement; open: *a loose weave.* **15.** imposing few restraints; allowing ample freedom for independent action: *a loose federation of city states.* **16.** (of earth, soil, etc.) not cohering: *loose sand.* **17.** not strict, exact, or precise: *loose thinking.* **18.** liberal; broad; generous: *a loose interpretation of the law.* **19. on the loose, a.** free; unconfined, as, esp., an escaped convict, circus animal, etc. **b.** *Informal.* unrestrained; dissolute. —*adv.* **20.** in a loose manner; loosely (usually used in combination): *loose-fitting; loose-jointed.* **21. break loose,** to free oneself; escape. **22. cut loose, a.** to release from domination or control. **b.** to become free, independent, etc. **c.** to abandon restraint. **23. let loose, a.** to free or become free. **b.** to yield; give way: *The guardrail let loose.* —*v.t.* **24.** to let loose; free from bonds or restraint. **25.** to release, as from constraint or obligation. **26.** to unfasten, undo, or untie, as a bond, fetter, or knot. **27.** to shoot or let fly: *to loose missiles at the invaders.* **28.** to make less tight; slacken or relax. —*v.i.* **29.** to let go a hold. **30.** to hoist anchor; get under way. **31.** to shoot or let fly an arrow, bullet, etc. (often fol. by *off*): *to loose off at a flock of ducks.* **32.** *Obs.* to become loose; loosen. [ME *los, loos* < Scand; cf. Icel *lauss* loose, free, empty; c. OE *lēas* (see -LESS), D, G *los* loose, free] —**loose′ly,** *adv.* —**loose′ness,** *n.*

—**Syn. 1.** untied, unrestricted, unconfined. **10.** libertine, dissolute, licentious. **17.** vague, general, indefinite. **24.** loosen, unbind. **25.** liberate. **28.** ease. —**Ant. 1.** bound. **10.** chaste. **28.** tighten.

loose′ end′, 1. a part or piece left hanging, unattached, or unused. **2.** an unsettled detail. **3. at loose ends, a.** in an uncertain or unsettled situation or position. **b.** having no immediate plans.

loose·fit·ting (lo͞os′fit′ing), *adj.* (of a garment) fitting loosely; not following the contours of the body.

loose-joint·ed (lo͞os′join′tid), *adj.* **1.** having loose joints. **2.** loosely built or framed; badly put together. **3.** having or marked by easy, free movement; limber: *a loose-jointed walk.*

loose-leaf (lo͞os′lēf′), *adj.* (of a book, notebook, etc.) consisting of individual leaves held in a binder (**loose′-leaf bind′er**) in such a way as to allow their removal without tearing.

loose-limbed (lo͞os′limd′), *adj.* having supple arms and legs: *a loose-limbed athlete.*

loos·en (lo͞o′sən), *v.t.* **1.** to unfasten or undo, as a bond or fetter. **2.** to make less tight; slacken or relax: *to loosen one's* *grasp.* **3.** to make less firmly fixed in place. **4.** to let loose or set free from bonds, restraint, or constraint. **5.** to make less close or compact in structure or arrangement. **6.** to make less dense or coherent: *to loosen the soil in a garden.* **7.** to relieve (the bowels) of a constipated condition. **8.** to relax in strictness or severity, as restraint or discipline: *to loosen restrictions on trade.* **—*v.i.*** **9.** to become loose or looser (sometimes fol. by *up*): *The shoes loosened up with wear.* [ME *loosne*] **—loos′en·er,** *n.*

loose′ sen′tence, a sentence that does not end with the completion of its main clause, but continues with one or more subordinate clauses or other modifiers. Cf. **periodic sentence.**

loose′ smut′, *Plant Pathol.* a disease of cereal grasses, characterized by uncovered, powdery masses of spores which replace the affected heads, caused by smut fungi of the genus *Ustilago.*

loose·strife (lo͞os′strīf′), *n.* **1.** any of several primulaceous plants of the genus *Lysimachia,* as *L. vulgaris,* having yellow flowers, or *L. quadrifolia,* having leaves in whorls of four or five. **2.** any of several lythraceous herbs of the genus *Lythrum,* as *L. Salicaria,* having purple flowers. [LOOSE + STRIFE, mistranslation of L *lysimachia* (< Gk; see LYSI-, -MACHY), plant said to be named after a certain *Lysimachos;* see -IA]

loose-tongued (lo͞os′tungd′), *adj.* unrestrained or irresponsible in speech; given to gossiping or chattering.

loot (lo͞ot), *n.* **1.** spoils or plunder taken by pillaging, as in war. **2.** anything taken by dishonesty, force, stealth, etc.: *a burglar's loot.* **3.** *Informal.* a collection of gifts, purchases, etc.: *The children opened their Christmas loot.* **4.** *Slang.* money. **5.** act of looting or plundering. **—*v.t.*** **6.** to carry off or take (something) as loot: *to loot a nation's art treasures.* **7.** to despoil by taking loot; plunder or pillage (a city, house, etc.), as in war. **8.** to rob, as by burglary, corrupt practice in public office, etc.: *conspiring to loot the public treasury.* **—*v.i.*** **9.** to take loot; plunder. [< Hindi *lūt,* akin to Skt *luṇṭati* he steals] **—loot′er,** *n.* **—Syn. 1.** booty. **7.** sack, ransack.

lop[1] (lop), *v.,* **lopped, lop·ping,** *n.* **—*v.t.*** **1.** to cut off (branches, twigs, etc.) from a tree or other plant. **2.** to cut off (a limb, part, or the like) from a person, animal, etc. **3.** to cut off the branches, twigs, etc., of (a tree or other plant). **4.** to eliminate as unnecessary or excessive: *They had to lop off whole pages of the report.* **5.** *Archaic.* to cut off the head, limbs, etc., of (a person). **—*v.i.*** **6.** to cut off branches, twigs, etc., as of a tree. **7.** to remove parts by or as by cutting. **—*n.*** **8.** parts or a part lopped off. **9.** (of trees) the smaller branches and twigs not useful as timber. [late ME *loppe* (n.) parts or part lopped off, etymologically identified with OE *loppe* spider, both objects being marked by many projecting parts. See LOBSTER] **—lop′per,** *n.*

lop[2] (lop), *v.,* **lopped, lop·ping,** *adj.* **—*v.i.*** **1.** to hang loosely or limply; droop. **2.** to sway, move, or go in a drooping or heavy, awkward way. **3.** to move in short, quick leaps: *a rabbit lopping through the garden.* **—*v.t.*** **4.** to let hang or droop: *He lopped his arms at his sides in utter exhaustion.* **—*adj.*** **5.** hanging down limply or droopingly: *a rabbit with lop ears.* [v. use of obs. *lop* spider or *lop* dangling part of a tree (see LOP[1]); lit., to behave like a *lop,* i.e., to dangle, hang loosely. See LOB[1]]

lope (lōp), *v.,* **loped, lop·ing,** *n.* **—*v.i.*** **1.** to move or run with bounding steps, as a quadruped, or with a long, easy stride, as a person. **2.** to canter leisurely with a rather long, easy stride, as a horse. **—*v.t.*** **3.** to cause to lope, as a horse. **—*n.*** **4.** the act or the gait of loping. **5.** a long, easy stride. [< D *lope(n)* (to) run; c. G *laufen* to run, Icel *hlaupa* to jump. See LEAP]

lop-eared (lop′ērd′), *adj.* having lop or drooping ears.

Lo·pe de Ve·ga (lō′pā də vā′gə; *Sp.* lô′pe t͟he ve′gä). See **Vega, Lope de.**

lop·er (lō′pər), *n.* a person or thing that lopes, as a horse with a loping gait.

Ló·pez (lō′pez; *Sp.* lô′pes), *n.* **Os·val·do** (ôs väl′dô), (*Osvaldo López Arellano*), born 1921, Honduran air force colonel: president of Honduras 1963–75.

loph·o·branch (lof′ə brangk′, lō′fə-), *adj.* **1.** belonging or pertaining to the *Lophobranchii,* the group of fishes comprising the pipefishes, sea horses, snipefishes, etc. **—*n.*** **2.** a lophobranch fish. [< NL *Lophobranch(iī)* name of the group < Gk *lópho(s)* crest, tuft + *bránchi(a)* BRANCHIA + L *-ī* nom. pl. n. suffix] **—loph·o·bran·chi·ate** (lof′ə brang′kē-it, -āt′, lō′fə-), *adj., n.*

lop·py (lop′ē), *adj.* **-pi·er, -pi·est.** lopping; hanging limply.

lop·sid·ed (lop′sī′did), *adj.* **1.** lopping or inclining to one side. **2.** heavier, larger, or more developed on one side than on the other; unevenly balanced; unsymmetrical. **—lop′sid′ed·ly,** *adv.* **—lop′sid′ed·ness,** *n.*

loq., loquitur.

lo·qua·cious (lō kwā′shəs), *adj.* **1.** talking or disposed to talk much or freely; talkative; garrulous. **2.** characterized by excessive talk; wordy: *the most loquacious play of the season.* **—lo·qua′cious·ly,** *adv.* **—lo·qua′cious·ness,** *n.* **—Syn.** verbose, voluble. See **talkative.**

lo·quac·i·ty (lō kwas′i tē), *n., pl.* **-ties. 1.** the state of being loquacious; talkativeness; garrulity. **2.** an instance of talkativeness or garrulity; a loquacious flow of talk. [< L *loquācitās* talkativeness = *loquāci-* (s. of *loquāx*) talkative + *-tās* -TY[2]]

lo·quat (lō′kwot, -kwat), *n.* a small, evergreen, malaceous tree, *Eriobotrya japonica,* native to China and Japan, but cultivated elsewhere for ornament and for its yellow, plumlike fruit. [< Chin (Cantonese) *lō-kwat,* lit., rush orange]

lo·qui·tur (lō′kwi to͝or′; *Eng.* lok′wi tər), *Latin.* he (or she) speaks.

Lo·rain (lō rān′, lô-), *n.* a port in N Ohio, on Lake Erie. 78,185 (1970).

lo·ran (lōr′ən, lôr′-), *n.* a device by which a navigator can locate his position by determining the time displacement between radio signals from two known stations. [*lo(ng) ra(nge) n(avigation)*]

Lor·ca (lôr′kə; *Sp.* lôr′kä), *n.* **1.** See **García Lorca. 2.** a city in SE Spain. 71,757 (est. 1956).

lord (lôrd), *n.* **1.** a person who has dominion over others; a master, chief, or ruler. **2.** a person who exercises authority from property rights; an owner or possessor of land, houses, etc. **3.** a person who is a leader in his profession: *one of the great lords of banking.* **4.** a feudal superior; the proprietor of a manor. **5.** a titled nobleman or peer; a person whose ordinary appellation contains by courtesy the title *Lord* or some higher title. **6. Lords,** the Lords Spiritual and Lords Temporal comprising the House of Lords. **7.** (*cap.*) *Brit.* **a.** the title of certain high officials (used with some other title or the like): *Lord Mayor of London.* **b.** the formally polite title of a bishop: *Lord Bishop of Durham.* **c.** the title informally substituted for marquis, earl, viscount, etc., as in the use of *Lord Kitchener* for *Earl Kitchener.* **8.** (*cap.*) the Supreme Being; God; Jehovah. **9.** (*cap.*) the Saviour, Jesus Christ. **10.** *Astrol.* a planet having dominating influence. **—*interj.*** **11.** (*often cap.*) (used in exclamatory phrases to express surprise, elation, etc.): *Lord, what a beautiful day!* **—*v.i.*** **12.** to play the lord; assume airs of importance and authority; domineer (usually fol. by *it*): *to lord it over someone.* [ME *lord, loverd,* OE *hlāford, hlāfweard,* lit., loaf-keeper. See LOAF[1], WARD] **—lord′less,** *adj.* **—lord′like′,** *adj.*

Lord′ Chan′cellor, the highest judicial officer of the British crown: law adviser of the ministry, keeper of the great seal, presiding officer in the House of Lords, etc. Also called **Lord′ High′ Chan′cellor.**

Lord′ Chief′ Jus′tice, the presiding judge of Britain's High Court of Justice, the superior court of record for both criminal and civil cases.

lord·ing (lôr′ding), *n.* *Archaic.* **1.** lord. **2.** Often, **lordings.** lords; sirs; gentlemen (often used as a term of address). [ME; OE *hlāfording* prince, lit., offspring of a lord = *hlāford* LORD + *-ing* patronymic suffix]

lord·ling (lôrd′ling), *n.* a young or unimportant lord; petty or insignificant lord. [ME; see LORD, -LING[1]]

lord·ly (lôrd′lē), *adj.,* **-li·er, -li·est,** *adv.* **—*adj.*** **1.** suitable for or befitting a lord; grand, magnificent, or elegant: *a lordly reception hall; lordly manners.* **2.** insolently imperious; haughty; arrogant; overbearing: *lordly contempt.* **3.** of or pertaining to a lord or lords. **4.** having the character or attributes of a lord. **—*adv.*** **5.** in the manner of a lord. [ME; OE *hlāfordlīc*] **—lord′li·ness,** *n.* **—Syn. 1.** majestic, regal, noble. **2.** domineering. **—Ant. 2.** meek.

Lord′ May′or, (in Britain) the mayor of certain cities or the chief municipal officer of certain boroughs.

Lord′ of hosts′, Jehovah; God. Also, **Lord′ of Hosts′.**

Lord′ of Misrule′, (in England) a person formerly chosen to direct the Christmas revels and sports.

lor·do·sis (lôr dō′sis), *n.* *Pathol.* forward curvature of the spine. [< NL < Gk: lit., a bending back = *lord(ós)* bent backwards + *-ōsis* -OSIS] **—lor·dot·ic** (lôr dot′ik), *adj.*

Lord′ Protec′tor, protector (def. 2a).

Lord's′ day′, the, Sunday.

lord·ship (lôrd′ship), *n.* **1.** (*often cap.*) a British term of respect used when speaking of or to judges or certain noblemen (usually prec. by *his* or *your*). **2.** the state or dignity of a lord. **3.** *Hist.* **a.** the authority or power of a lord. **b.** the domain of a lord. [ME; OE *hlāfordscipe*]

Lord′ Spir′itual, *pl.* **Lords Spiritual.** a bishop or archbishop belonging to the House of Lords. Cf. **Lord Temporal.** [late ME]

Lord's′ Prayer′, the, the prayer given by Jesus to His disciples, and beginning with the words *Our Father.* Matt. 6:9–13; Luke 11:2–4.

Lord's′ Sup′per, the, 1. the sacrament in commemoration of the Last Supper; Communion; Mass; Eucharist. **2.** See **Last Supper.**

Lord's′ ta′ble, the. See **communion table.**

Lord′ Tem′poral, *pl.* **Lords Temporal.** a member of the House of Lords who is not a member of the clergy. Cf. **Lord Spiritual.** [late ME]

lore[1] (lōr, lôr), *n.* **1.** the body of knowledge, esp. of a traditional, anecdotal, or popular nature, on a particular subject: *the lore of herbs.* **2.** learning, knowledge, or erudition. **3.** *Archaic.* **a.** the process or act of teaching; instruction. **b.** that which is taught; lesson. [ME; OE *lār;* c. D *leer,* G *Lehre* teaching. See LEARN] **—Syn. 1.** See **learning.**

lore[2] (lōr, lôr), *n.* *Zool.* the space between the eye and the bill of a bird, or a corresponding space in other animals, as serpents. [< NL *lōr(um),* special use of L: thong, strap]

Lor·e·lei (lôr′ə lī′; *Ger.* lō′ʀə lī′), *n.* a legendary nymph of the Rhine who lured sailors to shipwreck on her rock by singing. [< G, var. of *Lurlei,* cliff overlooking Rhine river, thought to be abode of a nymph: a creation of Klemens Brentano (1778–1842) in a poem of 1800]

Lo·rentz (lôr′ents, lōr′-; *Du.* lō′rents), *n.* **Hen·drik An·toon** (hen′drik än′tōn), 1853–1928, Dutch physicist: Nobel prize 1902.

lor·gnette (lôrn yet′), *n.* **1.** a pair of eyeglasses mounted on a handle. **2.** a pair of opera glasses for holding in the hand by a handle. [< F < *lorgn(er)* (to) eye furtively; see -ETTE]

lor·gnon (*Fr.* lôʀ nyôN′), *n., pl.* **-gnons** (*Fr.* -nyôN′). **1.** an eyeglass or a pair of eyeglasses. **2.** See **opera glasses.** [< F = *lorgn(er)* (see LORGNETTE) + *-on* n. suffix]

lo·ri·ca (lō rī′kə, lô-, -lə-), *n., pl.* **-cae** (-sē, -kē). **1.** *Zool.* a hard protective case or sheath, as the protective coverings secreted by certain infusorians. **2.** a cuirass or corselet, originally of leather. [def. 1: < NL, special use of L: corselet (orig. of leather), akin to *lōrum* thong; def. 2: < L]

lor·i·cate (lôr′ə kāt′, -kit, lor′-), *adj.* *Zool.* covered with a lorica. Also, **lor′i·cat′ed.** **—lor′i·ca′tion,** *n.*

Lo·rient (lô ʀyäN′), *n.* a seaport in NW France, on the Bay of Biscay. 63,924 (1962).

lor·i·keet (lôr′ə kēt′, lor′-, lôr′ə kēt′, lor′-), *n.* any of various small lories. [LORY + (PARA)KEET]

lor·i·mer (lôr′ə mər), *n.* a craftsman who makes hardware for harnesses and riding habits, as bits, spurs, etc. Also, **lor·i·ner** (lôr′ə nər). [ME < LL *lōrām(entum)* thong (L *lōrum* reins, thong + *-mentum* -MENT) + ME *-er* -ER[1]]

lo·ris (lōr′is, lôr′-), *n., pl.* **-ris. 1.** a small, slender, tailless, large-eyed, nocturnal lemur, *Loris gracilis,* of southern India and Ceylon. **2.** a similar but stockier lemur of the genus

Nycticebus, of southeastern Asia. [< NL < D *loeris* booby (now obs.), earlier *loerisch* clownish = *loer* stupid person (< F *lourd* < L *lūridus* LURID) + *-isch* -ISH[1]]

lorn (lôrn), *adj.* **1.** *Literary.* forsaken, bereft, or forlorn. **2.** *Obs.* lost, ruined, or undone. [ME; OE *loren,* ptp. of *-lēosan* LOSE (recorded in compounds)] —**lorn′ness,** *n.*

Lor·raine (lō rān′, lô-; *Fr.* lô ʀen′), *n.* **1.** Also, **Lorrain′. Claude,** (*Claude Gelée*), 1600–82, French painter. **2.** a medieval kingdom in W Europe along the Moselle, Meuse, and Rhine rivers. **3.** a region in NE France, once included in this kingdom: a former province. Cf. **Alsace-Lorraine.**

Lorraine′ cross′. See **cross of Lorraine.**

lor·ry (lôr′ē, lor′ē), *n., pl.* **-ries. 1.** *Brit.* a motor truck, esp. a large one. **2.** any of various vehicles running on rails, as for transporting material in a mine or factory. **3.** a long, low, horse-drawn wagon without sides, common in England. [akin to dial. *lurry* pull, drag, lug]

lo·ry (lōr′ē, lôr′ē), *n., pl.* **-ries.** any of several small, usually brilliantly colored, Australasian parrots having a brushlike fringe on the tongue for feeding on nectar and fruit juices. [< D, var. of *lori, loeri* < Malay *lūrī,* dial. var. of *nūrī*]

Los Al·a·mos (lôs al′ə mōs′, los), a town in central New Mexico: atomic research center. 11,310 (1970).

Los An·ge·le·no (lôs an′jə lē′nō, los), an inhabitant or native of Los Angeles. Also called **Los An·ge·le·an** (lôs an′jə lē′ən, los).

Los An·ge·les (lôs an′jə ləs, -lēz′, los *or, often,* lôs aŋ′gə ləs, -lēz′, los), a seaport in SW California. 2,809,596 (1970); 452 sq. mi.

lose (lo͞oz), *v.,* **lost, los·ing.** —*v.t.* **1.** to come to be without (something in one's possession or care), through accident, theft, etc., so that recovery is highly doubtful: *I'm sure I've merely misplaced my hat, not lost it.* **2.** to fail inadvertently to retain (something) in such a way that it cannot be immediately recovered: *I just lost a dime under this sofa.* **3.** to suffer the deprivation of: *to lose one's job; to lose one's life.* **4.** to be bereaved of by death: *to lose a sister.* **5.** to fail to keep, preserve, or maintain: *to lose one's balance; to lose one's figure.* **6.** to give up; forfeit the possession of: *to lose a fortune at the gaming table.* **7.** to cease to have, esp. as a result of will power, mastery, or the like: *to lose one's fear of the dark.* **8.** to bring to destruction or ruin (usually used passively): *Ship and crew were lost.* **9.** to have slip from sight, hearing, attention, etc.: *to lose a face in a crowd.* **10.** to stray from or become ignorant of (one's way, directions, etc.): *He lost his bearings in the strange city.* **11.** to leave far behind in a pursuit, race, etc.; outstrip. **12.** to use to no purpose; waste: *to lose time in waiting.* **13.** to fail to have, get, catch, etc.; miss: *to lose a bargain.* **14.** to fail to win (a prize, stake, etc.): *to lose a bet.* **15.** to be defeated in (a game, lawsuit, battle, etc.). **16.** to cause the loss of: *The delay lost the battle for them.* **17.** to let (oneself) go astray, miss the way, etc.: *We lost ourselves in the woods.* **18.** to allow (oneself) to become absorbed or engrossed in something and oblivious to all else: *I had lost myself in thought.* **19.** (of a physician) to fail to preserve the life of (a patient). **20.** (of a woman) to fail to be delivered of (a live baby), as because of miscarriage, complications in childbirth, etc. —*v.i.* **21.** to suffer loss: *to lose on a contract.* **22.** to suffer defeat in a contest, race, or the like: *We played well but we lost.* **23.** to depreciate in effectiveness or in some other essential quality: *a classic that loses in translation.* **24. lose out,** *Informal.* to suffer defeat or loss; fail to obtain something desired. [ME *lose(n),* OE *-lēosan,* r. ME *lesen,* OE *-lēosan* (cf. CHOOSE r. *chese*); c. G *(ver)lieren,* Goth *(fra)liusan* to lose. See LOSS] —**los′a·ble,** *adj.* —**los′a·ble·ness,** *n.*

lo·sel (lō′zəl, lo͞o′-, loz′əl), *Archaic.* —*n.* **1.** a worthless person; scoundrel. —*adj.* **2.** worthless or useless. [ME: lit., one who is lost = *los-* (ptp. s. of LOSE) + *-el* n. suffix of personalization]

los·er (lo͞o′zər), *n.* **1.** a person, team, nation, etc., that loses. **2.** *Slang.* someone or something that is marked by failure, consistently bad quality, performance, etc.

los·ing (lo͞o′ziŋ), *adj.* **1.** causing loss. **2.** characterized by or suffering defeat. —*n.* **3. losings,** losses, esp. at gambling. —**los′ing·ly,** *adv.*

los′ing haz′ard. See under **hazard** (def. 9).

loss (lôs, los), *n.* **1.** detriment or disadvantage from failure to keep, have, or get: *to bear the loss of a robbery.* **2.** an amount or number lost: *The loss from the robbery amounted to a week's salary.* **3.** the state of being deprived of or of being without something that one has had: *to suffer the loss of one's friends.* **4.** the accidental or inadvertent losing of something dropped, misplaced, stolen, etc.: *to discover the loss of a document.* **5.** a losing by defeat; failure to win: *the loss of a bet.* **6.** failure to make good use of something, as time; waste. **7.** failure to preserve or maintain: *loss of engine speed at high altitudes.* **8.** destruction or ruin: *the loss of a ship by fire.* **9.** a thing or a number of related things that are lost or destroyed to some extent: *Most buildings in the burned district were a total loss.* **10.** *Mil.* **a.** the losing of soldiers by death, capture, etc. **b.** Often, **losses.** the number of soldiers so lost. **11.** *Insurance.* the occurrence of an event, as death or damage of property, for which the insurer makes indemnity under the terms of a policy. **12. at a loss, a.** at less than cost; at a financial loss. **b.** in a state of bewilderment or uncertainty; perplexed: *We were completely at a loss for an answer.* [ME; OE *los* destruction; c. Icel *los* breaking up. See LOSE, LOOSE] —**Ant. 1.** gain.

loss′ lead′er, a popular article sold at a loss for the purpose of attracting trade to a retail store.

lost (lôst, lost), *adj.* **1.** no longer possessed or retained: *lost friends.* **2.** no longer to be found: *lost articles.* **3.** having gone astray or missed the way; bewildered as to place, direction, etc.: *Several lost children were reported.* **4.** not used to good purpose; wasted: *a lost advantage.* **5.** being that which someone has failed to win: *a lost prize.* **6.** attended with defeat: *a lost battle.* **7.** destroyed or ruined: *lost ships.* **8.** preoccupied; rapt: *He seems lost in thought.* **9.** distracted; distraught; desperate; hopeless: *His eyes had a frantic, lost look.* **10. lost to, a.** no longer belonging to. **b.** no longer possible or open to: *The opportunity was lost to him.* **c.** insensible to: *lost to all sense of duty.* —*v.t., v.i.* **11.** pt. and pp. of **lose.** —**Syn. 1.** forfeited, gone, missing. —**Ant. 1.** found.

lost′ cause′, a cause that has been defeated or for which defeat is inevitable.

Lost′ Genera′tion, 1. the generation of men and women who came of age during or immediately after World War I: viewed as being without cultural or emotional stability. **2.** a group of American writers of this generation, including Hemingway, Fitzgerald, and Dos Passos.

Lost′ Ple′iad. See under **Pleiades** (def. 1).

lost′ tribes′, the members of the 10 tribes of ancient Israel who were taken into captivity in 722 B.C. by Sargon II and are believed never to have returned to Palestine.

lot (lot), *n., v.,* **lot·ted, lot·ting.** —*n.* **1.** one of a set of objects, as straws or pebbles, drawn or thrown from a container to decide a question or choice by chance. **2.** the casting or drawing of such objects as a method of deciding something: *to choose a person by lot.* **3.** the decision or choice made by such a method. **4.** allotted share or portion: *to receive one's lot of an inheritance.* **5.** the portion in life assigned by fate or Providence; one's fate, fortune, or destiny: *Her lot had not been a happy one.* **6.** a distinct portion or piece of land: *a building lot.* **7.** a piece of land forming a part of a district, city, or other community. **8.** *Motion Pictures.* the site of a motion picture being filmed, esp. a studio. **9.** a distinct portion or parcel of anything, as of merchandise: *The furniture was auctioned off in 20 lots.* **10.** a number of things or persons collectively: *There's one more, and that's the lot.* **11.** *Informal.* kind of person; sort: *He's a bad lot.* **12.** Often, **lots.** *Informal.* a great many or a great deal: *a lot of books; lots of money.* **13.** *Chiefly Brit.* a tax or duty. **14. cast** or **cast in one's lot with,** to ally oneself with; share the life and fortunes of. **15. draw** or **cast lots,** to settle a question by the use of lots. —*v.t.* **16.** to divide or distribute by lot (sometimes fol. by *out*): *to lot furniture for sale.* **17.** to assign to one as his lot; allot. **18.** to divide into lots, as land. **19.** *Obs.* to cast or draw lots for. —*v.i.* **20.** to draw lots. [ME; OE *hlot;* c. D *lot,* Icel *hlutr;* akin to OE *hlīet,* G *Los,* Icel *hlaut,* Goth *hlauts*] —**Syn. 4.** part, quota. **7.** plot, parcel. **10.** group, crowd, gang.

Lot (lot), *n.* the nephew of Abraham. His wife was changed into a pillar of salt for looking back during their flight from Sodom. Gen. 13:1–12,19.

Lot (lôt), *n.* a river in S France, flowing W to the Garonne. 300 mi. long.

lo·ta (lō′tə), *n.* (in India) a small vessel for water, usually of brass or copper and round in shape. Also, **lo′tah.** [< Hindi *loṭā*]

loth (lōth, lōt͟h), *adj.* loath.

Lo·thair I (lō t͟hâr′, -târ′), A.D. 795?–855, king of Germany 840–843; emperor of the Holy Roman Empire 840–855. (son of Louis I).

Lothair II, ("*the Saxon*") c1070–1137, emperor of the Holy Roman Empire and king of the Germans 1125–37.

Lo·thar·i·o (lō t͟hâr′ē ō′), *n., pl.* **-thar·i·os.** (*sometimes l.c.*) a charming man who seduces and deceives women. [named after a young seducer in Nicholas Rowe's tragedy *The Fair Penitent* (1703)]

Lo·thi·ans, The (lō′t͟hē ənz, -t͟hē-), three counties in SW Scotland: East Lothian, Midlothian, West Lothian.

loth·some (lōt͟h′səm, lōth′-), *adj. Obs.* loathsome.

Lo·ti (lô tē′), *n.* **Pierre** (pyeʀ), (pen name of *Louis Marie Julien Viaud*), 1850–1923, French novelist.

lo·tion (lō′shən), *n.* **1.** *Pharm.* a liquid, usually aqueous or sometimes alcoholic preparation containing insoluble material in the form of a suspension or emulsion, intended for external application without rubbing, for skin conditions such as itching, infection, allergy, or the like. **2.** a liquid cosmetic, usually containing agents for soothing or softening the skin, esp. that of the face or hands: *after-shave lotion; hand lotion.* [< L *lōtiōn-* (s. of *lōtiō*) a washing = *lōt(us)* washed (see LOMENTUM) + *-iōn-* -ION]

lot·ter·y (lot′ə rē), *n., pl.* **-ter·ies. 1.** a gambling game or method of raising money, as for some public purpose, in which a large number of tickets are sold and a drawing is held for prizes. **2.** any scheme for the distribution of prizes by chance. [< MD *loterije* (> F *loterie*)]

lot·to (lot′ō), *n.* a game of chance in which a leader draws at random from a stock of numbered disks and the players cover the corresponding numbers on their cards, the winner being the first to cover five in a row. [< It < Gmc; see LOT]

lo·tus (lō′təs), *n., pl.* **-tus·es. 1.** a plant believed to be a jujube or elm, referred to in Greek legend as yielding a fruit that induced a state of dreamy and contented forgetfulness in those who ate it. **2.** the fruit itself. **3.** any aquatic, nymphaceous plant of the genus *Nelumbo,* having shieldlike leaves and showy, solitary flowers usually projecting above the water. **4.** any of several water lilies of the genus *Nymphaea.* **5.** a decorative motif derived from such a plant and used widely in ancient art, as on the capitals of Egyptian columns. **6.** any shrubby, leguminous herb of the genus *Lotus,* having red, pink, or white flowers. Also, **lo′tos.** [< L < Gk *lōtós* the lotus plant]

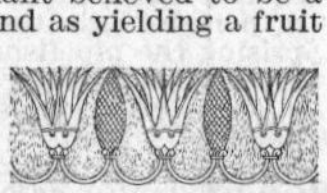

Lotus (def. 5)

lo·tus-eat·er (lō′təs ē′tər), *n.* **1.** *Class. Myth.* a member of a people whom Odysseus found existing in a state of languorous forgetfulness induced by their eating of the fruit of the legendary lotus. **2.** one who leads a life of dreamy, indolent ease, indifferent to the busy world; daydreamer. [sing. of *lotus-eaters,* trans. of Gk *Lōtophágoi,* n. use of masc. pl. of *lōtophágos* lotus-eating. See LOTUS, -PHAGOUS]

lo′tus posi′tion, (in Yoga) a sitting posture with the legs crossed and the hands resting on the thighs near the knees. Also called **lo′tus pos′ture.**

loud (loud), *adj.* **1.** striking strongly upon the organs of hearing, as sound, noise, the voice, etc.; strongly audible: *loud talking; loud thunder.* **2.** making, emitting, or uttering strongly audible sounds: *a quartet of loud trombones.* **3.** full of sound or noise; resounding: *They conversed in loud whispers.* **4.** clamorous, vociferous, or blatant: *a loud party; a loud demonstration.* **5.** emphatic or insistent: *to be loud in one's praises; a loud denial.* **6.** garish, conspicuous, or ostentatious, as colors, dress, the wearer of garish dress, etc.: *to have a penchant for loud ties.* **7.** obtrusively vulgar, as manners, persons, etc. —*adv.* **8.** loudly. [ME; OE *hlūd;* c. D *luid,* G *laut;* akin to Gk *klytós* famous] —**loud′ly,** *adv.* —**loud′ness,** *n.* —**loud′ish,** *adj.* —**Syn. 1.** resounding; deafening; stentorian.

loud·en (loud′ən), *v.t., v.i.* to make or become loud or louder.

loud-mouth (loud′mouth′), *n., pl.* **-mouths** (-mouthz′, -mouths′). a person who brags, gossips, or otherwise speaks foolishly or indiscreetly.

loud·mouth (loud′mouth′), *n., pl.* **-mouths** (-mouthz′, -mouths′). loud-mouth.

loud-mouthed (loud′mouthd′, -moutht′), *adj.* **1.** loud of voice or utterance; vociferous. **2.** Characterized by foolish, indiscreet, or vulgar speech. Also, **loud′mouthed′.**

loud·speak·er (loud′spē′kər), *n.* any of various electronic devices by which speech, music, etc., can be intensified and made audible throughout a room, hall, or the like.

lough (lok, lokH), *n. Irish Eng.* **1.** a lake. **2.** a partially landlocked bay. Cf. **loch.** [Anglo-Irish sp. of Ir *loch* lake; ME *lough* (south), *louch* (north). See LOUCH]

lou·ie (lo͞o′ē), *n.* looie.

lou·is (lo͞o′ē; *Fr.* lwē), *n., pl.* **lou·is** (lo͞o′ēz; *Fr.* lwē). See **louis d'or.**

Lou·is (lo͞o′is), *n.* **Joe** (*Joseph Louis Barrow*), 1914–81, U.S. boxer: world heavyweight champion 1937–49.

Lou·is I (lo͞o′ē, lo͞o′is; *Fr.* lwē), ("*le Débonnaire*"; "*the Pious*") A.D. 788–840, king of France and Germany 814–840; emperor of the Holy Roman Empire 814–840 (son of Charlemagne).

Louis II, **1.** German, **Ludwig II.** ("*the German*") A.D. 804–876, king of Germany 843–876 (son of Louis I). **2.** A.D. 822?–875, king of Italy 844–875, emperor of the Holy Roman Empire 855–875, king of Lorraine 872–875 (son of Lothair I).

Louis II de Bourbon. See **Condé, Prince de.**

Louis IV, ("*the Bavarian*") 1287?–1347, king of Germany and emperor of the Holy Roman Empire 1314–47.

Louis V, ("*le Fainéant*") A.D. 967?–987, king of France 986–987: last Carolingian to rule France.

Louis IX, **Saint,** 1214?–70, king of France 1226–70.

Louis XI, 1423–83, king of France 1461–83 (son of Charles VII).

Louis XII, ("*the Father of the People*") 1462–1515, king of France 1498–1515.

Louis XIII, 1601–43, king of France 1610–43 (son of Henry IV of Navarre).

Louis XIV, ("*the Great,*" "*the Sun King*") 1638–1715, king of France 1643–1715 (son of Louis XIII).

Louis XV, 1710–74, king of France 1715–74.

Louis XVI, 1754–93, king of France 1774–92 (grandson of Louis XV and husband of Marie Antoinette).

Louis XVII, ("*Louis Charles of France*") 1785–95, titular king of France 1793–95 (son of Louis XVI).

Louis XVIII, (*Louis Xavier Stanislas*) 1755–1824, king of France 1814–15, 1815–24 (brother of Louis XVI).

Lou·is·burg (lo͞o′is bûrg′), *n.* a seaport on SE Cape Breton Island, Nova Scotia, in SE Canada: French fortress captured by British 1745, 1758. 1417 (1961).

lou·is d'or (lo͞o′ē dôr′; *Fr.* lwē dôR′), *pl.* **lou·is d'or** (lo͞o′ēz dôr′; *Fr.* lwē dôR′). a former gold coin of France, issued from 1640 to 1795; pistole. Also called **louis.** [< F: lit., louis of gold; named after LOUIS XIII]

Lou·ise (lo͞o ēz′), *n.* **Lake,** a glacial lake in W Canada, in SW Alberta in the Canadian Rockies: resort. 5670 ft. above sea level.

Lou·i·si·an·a (lo͞o ē′zē an′ə, lo͞o′ə zē-, lo͞o′ē-), *n.* a state in the S United States. 3,643,180 (1970); 48,523 sq. mi. *Cap.:* Baton Rouge. *Abbr.:* La., LA —**Lou·i′si·an′an, Lou·i′si·an′i·an,** *adj., n.*

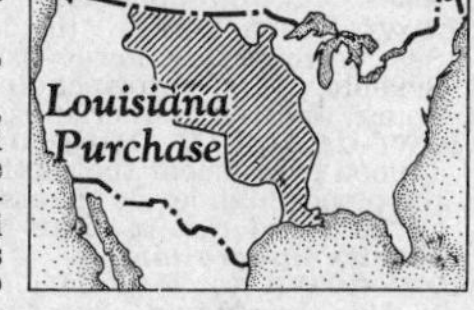

Loui′sian′a French′, Cajun (def. 2). *Abbr.:* LaF

Loui′sian′a Pur′chase, the territory that the United States purchased from France in 1803 for $15,000,000, extending from the Mississippi River to the Rocky Mountains and from the Gulf of Mexico to Canada.

Lou′is Napo′leon (lo͞o′ē, lo͞o′is; *Fr.* lwē). See **Napoleon III.**

Lou′is Philippe′, ("*Citizen King*") 1773–1850, king of France 1830–48.

Lou′is Qua·torze′ (kə tôrz′; *Fr.* KA tôRz′), noting or pertaining to the style of architecture, furnishings, and decoration prevailing in France about the time of Louis XIV, characterized by increasingly classicizing tendencies, and by an emphasis on dignity rather than comfort, and reflecting the influence of official and academic control over the arts.

Lou′is Quinze′ (kanz; *Fr.* KANZ), noting or pertaining to the Rococo style of architecture, furnishings, and decoration prevailing in France during the reign of Louis XV, characterized by fantasy, lightness, elegance, and comfort.

Lou·is·ville (lo͞o′ē vil′), *n.* a port in N Kentucky, on the Ohio River: Kentucky Derby. 361,958 (1970).

lounge (lounj), *v.,* **lounged, loung·ing,** *n.* —*v.i.* **1.** to pass time idly and indolently. **2.** to recline indolently; loll: *We lounged in the sun all afternoon.* **3.** to go or move in a leisurely, indolent manner; saunter (usually fol. by *around, along, off, etc.*). —*v.t.* **4.** to pass (time) in lounging (usually fol. by *away* or *out*): *to lounge away the afternoon at the seashore.* —*n.* **5.** a sofa for reclining, sometimes backless, having a headrest at one end. **6.** a place for sitting, waiting, smoking, etc., esp. a large public room, as in a hotel or theater. **7.** a place or section on a train, plane, or ship having various club or social facilities. **8.** a cocktail lounge. **9.** a public rest room. **10.** *Archaic.* the act or a period of lounging. **11.** *Archaic.* a lounging gait. [?] —**loung′er,** *n.* —**loung′y,** *adj.*

lounge′ car′. See **club car.**

lounge′ liz′ard, *Slang.* a foppish man who idles about the lounges of bars, cafés, hotels, etc., with or in search of women, esp. women who are willing to support him.

lounge′ suit′, *Chiefly Brit.* a man's suit, as opposed to formal attire.

loung·ing (loun′jing), *adj.* **1.** (of a garment) worn for leisure: *lounging jacket.* **2.** lacking energy; indolent.

loupe (lo͞op), *n.* any of several varieties of magnifying glasses used by jewelers and watchmakers, of from 2 to 20 power, esp. one intended to fit in the eye socket. [< F, orig. an imperfect gem, a mass of hot metal << Gmc; see LOB[1], LOOP[3]]

loup′ing ill′ (lou′ping, lō′-, lo͞o′-), *Vet. Pathol.* an acute, virus-induced infectious disease of sheep, affecting the nervous system and transmitted by a tick that also attacks man. [late ME *lowpynge* leaping = *loupe* to leap (< Scand, c. OE *hlēapan* to LEAP) + -ING[2]]

lour (lour, lou′ər), *v.i., n.* lower[2].

Lourdes (lo͝ord, lo͝ordz; *Fr.* lo͞oRd), *n.* a city in SW France: Roman Catholic shrine for miraculous cures. 16,376 (1962).

Lou·ren·ço Mar·ques (lō ren′sō mär′kes, lô-; *Port.* lō RENN′so͞o mäR′kəsh), former name of **Maputo,** in Mozambique.

lour·ing (lour′ing, lou′ər-), *adj.* lowering. —**lour′ing·ly,** *adv.* —**lour′ing·ness,** *n.*

lour·y (lour′ē, lou′ə rē), *adj.* lowery.

louse (lous), *n., pl.* **lice** (līs) for 1, 2, 3, **lous·es** for 4, *v.* —*n.* **1.** any small, wingless insect of the order *Anoplura* **(sucking louse),** parasitic on man and other mammals, having mouthparts adapted for sucking, as *Pediculus humanus* **(body louse** or **head louse)** and *Phthirius pubis* **(crab louse). 2.** any insect of the order *Mallophaga,* parasitic on birds and mammals, having mouthparts adapted for biting. **3.** See **plant louse. 4.** *Slang.* a contemptible person, esp. an unethical one. —*v.t.* **5.** to delouse. **6. louse up,** *Slang.* to spoil; botch; make a mess of. [ME *lows(e), lous(e),* OE *lūs,* pl. *lȳs;* c. D *luis,* G *Laus,* Icel *lūs*]

Body louse, *Pediculus humanus* (Length ⅛ in.)

louse·wort (lous′wûrt′), *n.* any scrophulariaceous herb of the genus *Pedicularis,* as the wood betony, formerly supposed to cause lice in sheep feeding on it.

lous·y (lou′zē), *adj.,* **lous·i·er, lous·i·est. 1.** infested with lice. **2.** *Informal.* **a.** mean or contemptible: *That was a lousy thing to do.* **b.** wretchedly bad; miserable: *He did a lousy job. I feel lousy.* **3. lousy with,** *Slang.* well supplied with: *He's lousy with money.* [ME *lousi*] —**lous′i·ly,** *adv.* —**lous′i·ness,** *n.*

lout (lout), *n.* **1.** an awkward, stupid person; clumsy, ill-mannered boor; oaf. —*v.t.* **2.** *Obs.* to flout; treat with contempt; scorn. [? special use of archaic *lout* (ME *louten*) to bend, stoop; akin to LITTLE]

lout·ish (lou′tish), *adj.* like or characteristic of a lout; awkward; clumsy; boorish. —**lout′ish·ly,** *adv.* —**lout′ish·ness,** *n.* —**Syn.** churlish, uncouth, vulgar, coarse.

lou·ver (lo͞o′vər), *n.* **1.** any of a series of narrow openings framed at their longer edges with slanting, overlapping fins or slats. **2.** a fin or slat framing such an opening. **3.** a ventilating turret or lantern, as on the roof of a medieval building. **4.** any of a system of slits formed in the hood of an automobile, the door of a metal locker, etc., used esp. for ventilation. **5.** a door, window, or the like, having louvers. [ME *lover* < MF *lovier* < MD *love* gallery. See LOBBY] —**lou′vered,** *adj.*

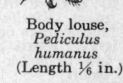

L, Louver

L'Ou·ver·ture (*Fr.* lo͞o veR tYR′), *n.* See **Toussaint L'Ouverture.**

Lou·vre (lo͞o′vRə), *n.* a building in Paris, France: formerly a royal palace; since 1793 a national museum of art.

Louys (lwē), *n.* **Pierre** (pyeR), 1870–1925, French poet and novelist.

lov·a·ble (luv′ə bəl), *adj.* of such a nature as to attract love; engaging. Also, **loveable.** [ME *lufabyll*] —**lov′a·bil′i·ty, lov′a·ble·ness,** *n.* —**lov′a·bly,** *adv.* —**Syn.** dear.

lov·age (luv′ij), *n.* a European, apiaceous herb, *Levisticum officinale,* cultivated in gardens. [ME *loveache* < AF *luvesche* (by assoc. with *ache* celery < L *apium*) < OE *lufes(ti)ce* (by syncope) < ML *levistica* r. LL *levisticum,* alter. of L *ligusticum* lovage, n. use of neut. of *Ligusticus* Ligurian]

love (luv), *n., v.,* **loved, lov·ing.** —*n.* **1.** a profoundly tender, passionate affection for a person of the opposite sex. **2.** a feeling of warm personal attachment or deep affection, as for a parent, child, or friend. **3.** sexual passion or desire, or its gratification. **4.** a person toward whom love is felt; beloved person; sweetheart. **5.** (used in direct address as a term of endearment.) **6.** a love affair; amour. **7.** (*cap.*) a personification of sexual affection, as Eros or Cupid. **8.** affectionate concern for the well-being of others: *the love of one's neighbor.* **9.** a strong predilection or liking for anything: *her love of books.* **10.** the object of this liking: *The theater was her great love.* **11.** the benevolent affection of God for His creatures, or the reverent affection due from them to God. **12.** *Chiefly Tennis.* a score of zero; nothing. **13. for the love of,** in consideration of; for the sake of: *For the love of mercy, stop that noise.* **14. in love (with),** feeling deep affection or passion for (a person, idea, occupation, etc.); enamored of: *in love with life; in love with one's work.* **15. make love, a.** to woo. **b.** to embrace and kiss as lovers. **c.** to engage in sexual intercourse. **16. no love lost,** dislike; animosity: *There was no love lost between the two brothers.* —*v.t.* **17.** to have love or affection for: *All her pupils love her.* **18.** to have a profoundly tender, passionate affection for (a person of the opposite sex). **19.** to have a strong liking for; take great pleasure in: *to love music.* **20.** to need or require; benefit greatly from: *Plants love sunlight.* **21.** to make love to; have sexual intercourse with. —*v.i.* **22.** to have love or affection, esp. for one of the opposite sex. [(n.) ME; OE *lufu;* c. OFris *luve,* OHG *luba,* Goth *lubō;* (v.) ME *lov(i)e(n),* OE *lufian;* c. OFris *luvia,* OHG *lubōn* to love, L *lubēre* (later *libēre*) to please; akin to LIEF]

—**Syn. 1.** tenderness, fondness, predilection, warmth. **1, 2.** LOVE, AFFECTION, DEVOTION all mean a deep and enduring emotional regard, usually for another person. LOVE may apply to various kinds of regard: the charity of the Creator, reverent adoration toward God or toward a person, the relation of parent and child, the regard of friends for each other, romantic feelings for one of the opposite sex, etc. AFFECTION is a fondness for persons of either sex, that is enduring and tender but calm. DEVOTION is an intense love for and a steadfast, enduring loyalty to a person; it may also imply consecration to a cause. **2.** liking.

love·a·ble (luv′ə bəl), *adj.* lovable. —**love′a·bil′i·ty, love′a·ble·ness,** *n.* —**love′a·bly,** *adv.*

love′ affair′, a romantic relationship or episode between lovers; an amour.

love′ ap′ple, (formerly) the tomato.

love′ ar′rows, fine needles of rutile crystals embedded in quartz.

love′ beads′, a necklace of small, often handmade beads, worn esp. by young persons as a symbol of peace and good will.

love·bird (luv′bûrd′), *n.* **1.** any of various small parrots, esp. of the genus *Agapornis,* of Africa, noted for the affection shown one another and often kept as pets. **2. lovebirds,** *Informal.* a pair of lovers, esp. a married couple who display close mutual affection and concern.

love′ child′, an illegitimate child.

love′ feast′, **1.** (among the early Christians) a meal eaten in token of brotherly love and charity. **2.** a rite in imitation of this, practiced by a number of modern denominations; a fellowship meal. **3.** a banquet or gathering of persons to promote good feeling, honor a special guest, etc.

love-in-a-mist (luv′in ə mist′), *n.* a ranunculaceous plant, *Nigella damascena,* having feathery dissected leaves and whitish or blue flowers.

love′ knot′, a stylized, decorative knot having four intertwined loops, often used as a token of love. [ME *love knotte*]

Love·lace (luv′lās′), *n.* **Richard,** 1618–56, English poet.

love·less (luv′lis), *adj.* **1.** devoid of or unattended with love: *a loveless marriage.* **2.** feeling no love. [ME *loveles*] —**love′less·ly,** *adv.* —**love′less·ness,** *n.*

love-lies-bleed·ing (luv′līz′blē′ding), *n.* an amaranth, esp. *Amaranthus caudatus,* having spikes of crimson flowers.

love·lock (luv′lok′), *n.* **1.** any lock of hair hanging or worn separately from the rest of the hair. **2.** (formerly) a long, flowing lock or curl dressed separately from the rest of the hair, worn by courtiers.

love·lorn (luv′lôrn′), *adj.* not loved; forsaken by one's lover. —**love′lorn′ness,** *n.*

love·ly (luv′lē), *adj.,* **-li·er, -li·est,** *adv.* —*adj.* **1.** charmingly or exquisitely beautiful: *a lovely flower.* **2.** having a beauty that appeals to the heart as well as to the eye, as a person, a face, etc. **3.** *Informal.* delightful; highly pleasing: *to have a lovely time.* **4.** of a great moral or spiritual beauty: *She is endowed with a lovely character.* —*adv.* **5.** *Colloq.* very well; splendidly: *That skirt and blouse go lovely together.* [ME *luvelich,* OE *luflīc* amiable] —**love′li·ness,** *n.*

love-mak·ing (luv′mā′king), *n.* **1.** the act of courting or wooing. **2.** sexual intercourse. [late ME]

love′ match′, a marriage entered into for love alone.

love′ po′tion, a potion believed to arouse love or sexual passion, esp. toward a specified person.

lov·er (luv′ər), *n.* **1.** a person who is in love, esp. a man in love with a woman. **2.** a person, esp. a man, who is involved in a nonmarital affair; paramour. **3. lovers,** a man and woman in love with each other or having a love affair. **4.** a person who has a strong predilection or liking for something, as specified: *a lover of music.* **5.** a person who loves, esp. a person who has affectionate regard for others: *a lover of mankind.* [ME] —**lov′er·like′,** *adj.* —**lov′er·ly,** *adj., adv.*

lov′ers′ lane′, a secluded lane, road, or parking area, as in a park, sought out by lovers for its privacy.

love′ seat′, an upholstered seat for two persons.

love·sick (luv′sik′), *adj.* **1.** languishing with love: *a lovesick adolescent.* **2.** expressive of such languishing: *a lovesick note.* —**love′sick′ness,** *n.*

lov·ing (luv′ing), *adj.* feeling or showing love; affectionate; fond: *loving glances.* [ME *lovyng,* r. *lovende,* OE *lufiende*] —**lov′ing·ly,** *adv.* —**lov′ing·ness,** *n.*

lov′ing cup′, **1.** a large cup, as of silver, usually with two or more handles, given as a prize, award, token of esteem or affection, etc. **2.** (formerly) a wine cup, usually of large size with several handles, passed from one person to another, as at a farewell gathering.

low[1] (lō), *adj.* **1.** situated or occurring not far above the ground, floor, or base: *a low shelf.* **2.** of small extent upward; not high or tall. **3.** not far above the horizon: *The moon was low in the sky.* **4.** lying or being below the general level: *low ground.* **5.** designating or pertaining to regions near sea level or the sea as opposed to highland or inland regions: *low countries.* **6.** bending or passing far downward; deep: *a low bow; a low swoop over a bomber target.* **7.** (of a garment) low-necked; décolleté. **8.** rising but slightly from a surface: *a low relief on a frieze.* **9.** of less than average or normal height or depth, as a liquid, stream, etc. **10.** lacking in customary strength or vigor; feeble; weak: *to feel low and listless.* **11.** providing little nourishment or strength, as a diet. **12.** of small amount, degree, force, etc.: *a low number; a low flame.* **13.** indicated or represented by a low number: *a low latitude.* **14.** assigning or attributing little worth, value, excellence, or the like: *a low estimate of a new book.* **15.** indicating something inferior or below an acceptable standard: *to receive low marks in school; low intelligence.* **16.** containing a relatively small amount: *a diet low in starches.* **17.** nearing depletion; not adequately supplied: *low on funds; Our stock of towels is low.* **18.** depressed or dejected: *low spirits.* **19.** far down in the scale of rank or estimation; humble: *low birth.* **20.** of inferior quality or character: *a low grade of fabric.* **21.** lacking in dignity or elevation, as of thought or expression. **22.** mean, base, or disreputable: *a low trick.* **23.** coarse or vulgar: *entertainment of a low sort.* **24.** *Boxing.* (of a blow) delivered below a contestant's belt. **25.** *Biol.* having a relatively simple structure. **26.** *Music.* produced by relatively slow vibrations, as sounds; grave in pitch. **27.** soft; subdued; not loud: *a low murmur.* **28.** indicating the bottom or the point farthest down; lowest: *He felt it was the low point in his creative life.* **29.** *Chiefly Brit.* holding to Low Church principles and practices. **30.** *Phonet.* (of a vowel) articulated with a relatively large opening above the tongue, as the vowels of *hat, hut, hot, ought,* etc. Cf. **high** (def. 23). **31.** *Auto.* of, pertaining to, or operating at the gear transmission ratio at which the drive shaft moves at the lowest speed; first: *low gear.* **32.** *Baseball.* (of a pitched ball) passing the plate at a level below that of the batter's knees. **33.** *Cards.* of relatively small value: *a low card.* —*adv.* **34.** in or to a low position, point, degree, etc. **35.** near the ground, floor, or base; not aloft. **36.** in or to a humble or abject state: *She swore she would bring him low.* **37.** in or to a condition of depletion, prostration, or death: *The gas in the tank is running low; a severe illness that brought him low.* **38.** at comparatively small cost; cheaply. **39.** at or to a low pitch, volume, intensity, etc.: *to sing low.* **40.** in a low tone; softly; quietly: *to speak low.* **41. lay low, a.** to overpower or kill: *to lay one's attackers low.* **b.** *Informal.* to lie low. **42. lie low, a.** to conceal oneself: *He had to lie low for a while.* **b.** to keep one's intentions concealed; bide one's time: *Until the merger is concluded, you had better lie low on drawing up any new contracts.* Also, *Informal,* **lay low.** —*n.* **43.** that which is low, as ground or prices. **44.** *Auto.* low gear; first gear. **45.** *Meteorol.* an atmospheric low-pressure system; cyclone. Cf. **high** (def. 38). **46.** *Cards.* **a.** the lowest trump card. **b.** the lowest score in a game. **47.** a point of deepest decline, vulgarity, etc.: *a new low in tastelessness.* [ME *lowe, lohe,* earlier *lāh* < Scand; cf. Icel *lāgr;* c. D *laag;* akin to LIE[2]] —**low′ish,** *adj.* —**low′ness,** *n.*

low[2] (lō), *v.i.* **1.** to utter the sound characteristic of cattle; moo. —*v.t.* **2.** to utter by or as by lowing. —*n.* **3.** the act or the sound of lowing: *the low of a distant herd.* [ME *low(en),* OE *hlōwan;* c. D *loeien,* OHG *hluoen,* OS *hlōian;* akin to Icel *Hlōi* proper name (lit., bellower, shouter), L *calāre* to call out]

Low (lō), *n.* **Juliette,** 1860–1927, founder of U.S. Girl Scouts.

Low′ Archipel′ago. See **Tuamotu Archipelago.**

low′ beam′, an automobile headlight beam providing short-range illumination. Cf. **high beam.**

low·born (lō′bôrn′), *adj.* of humble birth. [ME *lohiboren*]

low·boy (lō′boi′), *n.* *U.S. Furniture.* a low chest of drawers on short legs, resembling the lower part of a highboy.

Lowboy (18th century)

low·bred (lō′bred′), *adj.* characterized by or characteristic of low or vulgar breeding; ill-bred; coarse. —**Syn.** unrefined, rude. —**Ant.** noble.

low·brow (*n.* lō′brou′; *adj.* lō′brou′), *Informal.* —*n.* **1.** a person who is unconcerned, uninvolved, or uneducated in intellectual activities or pursuits. —*adj.* **2.** of, pertaining or proper to a lowbrow. —**low′brow′ism,** *n.*

low-cal (lō′kal′), *adj.* containing a small number of calories: *a low-cal diet.* [LOW + CAL(ORIE)]

Low′ Church′, pertaining or belonging to a party in the Anglican Church emphasizing evangelicalism and laying little stress on the sacraments, church rituals, and church authority. Cf. **High Church, Broad Church.** —**Low′ Church′man.**

low′ com′edy, comedy that depends on physical action, broadly humorous or farcical situations, and often bawdy jokes. Cf. **high comedy.** —**low′ come′dian.**

Low′ Coun′tries, the lowland region near the North Sea, forming the lower basin of the Rhine, Meuse, and Scheldt rivers: corresponding to modern Belgium, Luxembourg, and the Netherlands. —**low′-coun′try,** *adj.*

low′-den′si·ty lipopro′tein (lō′den′si tē), *Biochem.* a blood constituent that is the major carrier of cholesterol in the blood: high levels are associated with atherosclerosis and an increased risk of heart disease. *Abbr.:* LDL Cf. **high-density lipoprotein.**

low-down (*n.* lō′doun′; *adj.* lō′doun′), *Informal.* —*n.* **1.** Also, **low′down′.** the unadorned facts; the truth; inside information (usually prec. by *the*). —*adj.* **2.** contemptible; base; mean: *a low-down trick.*

Low′ Dutch′. See **Low German** (def. 1).

Low·ell (lō′əl), *n.* **1. Amy,** 1874–1925, U.S. poet and critic. **2. James Russell,** 1819–91, U.S. poet, essayist, and diplomat. **3. Percival,** 1855–1916, U.S. astronomer and author (brother of Amy Lowell). **4. Robert,** 1917–1977, U.S. poet. **5.** a city in NE Massachusetts, on the Merrimack River. 94,239 (1970).

low·er[1] (lō′ər), *v.t.* **1.** to cause to descend; let down: *to lower a flag.* **2.** to make lower in height or level: *to lower the water in a canal.* **3.** to reduce in amount, price, degree, force, etc. **4.** to make less loud, as the voice. **5.** to bring down in rank or estimation; degrade; humble; abase (oneself), as by some sacrifice of dignity: *I would not lower myself to do such a thing.* **6.** *Music.* to make lower in pitch; flatten. **7.** *Phonet.* to alter the articulation of (a vowel) by increasing the distance of the tongue downward from the palate: (ē) *is lowered to* (i) *before* (r). Cf. **low**[1] (def. 30). —*v.i.* **8.** to become lower, grow less, or diminish. **9.** to descend; sink: *the sun lowering in the west.* —*adj.* **10.** comparative of **low**[1]. **11.** (*often cap.*) *Stratig.* noting an early division of a period, system, or the like: *the lower Devonian.* —*n.* **12.** a denture for the lower jaw. **13.** a lower berth. [orig. comp. of LOW[1]] —**low′er·a·ble,** *adj.* —**Syn. 1.** drop. **3.** decrease, lessen.

low·er[2] (lou′ər, lour), *v.i.* **1.** to be dark and threatening, as the sky or the weather. **2.** to frown, scowl, or look sullen; glower. —*n.* **3.** a dark, threatening appearance, as of the sky or weather. **4.** a frown or scowl. Also, **lour.** [ME *lour* (n.), *loure* (v.) to frown, LURK; akin to G *lauern,* D *loeren*]

low′er ap′sis (lō′ər). See under **apsis.**

Low′er Aus′tria (lō′ər), a province in NE Austria. 1,371,911 (1961); 7092 sq. mi.

Low′er Califor′nia, a narrow peninsula in NW Mexico between the Gulf of California and the Pacific, forming two territories of Mexico. 604,346 (1960); 55,634 sq. mi. *Capitals:* Mexicali (Northern Territory) and La Paz (Southern Territory). Spanish, **Baja, Baja California.**

Low′er Can′ada, former name of Quebec province 1791–1841.

low′er case′ (lō′ər), *Print.* See under **case**[2] (def. 8).

low·er-case (lō′ər kās′), *adj.*, *v.*, **-cased, -cas·ing,** *n.* —*adj.* **1.** (of an alphabetical letter) of a particular form often different from and smaller than its corresponding capital letter and occurring after the initial letter of a proper name, of the first word in a sentence, etc., as a, b, q, r. **2.** *Print.* pertaining to or belonging in the lower case. Cf. **case**[2] (def. 8). —*v.t.* **3.** to print or write with a lower-case letter or letters. —*n.* **4.** a lower-case letter. Cf. **upper-case.**

low′er cham′ber (lō′ər). See **lower house.**

low·er·class·man (lō′ər klas′mən, -kläs′-), *n.*, *pl.* **-men.** underclassman.

low′er crit′icism (lō′ər). a form of Biblical criticism having as its object the reconstruction of the original texts of the books of the Bible. Also called **textual criticism.** Cf. **higher criticism.**

low′er house′ (lō′ər), the branch of a bicameral legislature that is generally more representative and has more members than the upper branch.

low·er·ing (lou′ər ing, lour′ing), *adj.* **1.** dark and threatening, as the sky, clouds, weather, etc.; gloomy. **2.** frowning or sullen, as the face, gaze, etc.; scowling; angry. Also, **louring.** [ME *louring*] —**low′er·ing·ly,** *adv.*

Low′er Mer′i·on (mer′ē ən), a town in SE Pennsylvania, near Philadelphia. 63,392 (1970).

Low′er Mich′igan, the southern part of Michigan, S of the Strait of Mackinac. Also called **Low′er Penin′sula.**

low·er·most (lō′ər mōst′ *or, esp. Brit.*, -məst), *adj.* lowest.

Low′er Palat′inate, Palatinate (def. 1).

Low′er Pa′leolith′ic. See under **Paleolithic.**

Low′er Sax′ony, a state in N West Germany. 6,761,000 (1963); 18,294 sq. mi. *Cap.:* Hanover. German, **Niedersachsen.**

low′er world′ (lō′ər), **1.** *Class. Myth.* the regions of the dead; Hades; the underworld. **2.** the earth, as distinguished from the heavenly bodies or from heaven.

low·er·y (lou′ə rē, lour′ē), *adj.* gloomy; threatening; dark: *a lowery sky.* Also, **loury.** [earlier *lowry*]

low′est com′mon denom′inator, *Math.* See **least common denominator.**

low′est com′mon mul′tiple, *Math.* the smallest number that is a common multiple of a given set of numbers. Also called **least common multiple.**

Lowes·toft (lōs′tôft, -toft, -təf), *n.* a seaport in NE Suffolk, in E England: famous for a type of china. 45,687 (1961).

low′ explo′sive, a relatively slow-burning explosive, usually set off by heat or friction, used for propelling charges in guns or for ordinary blasting.

low′ fre′quency, *Radio.* any frequency between 30 and 300 kilocycles per second. *Abbr.:* LF —**low′-fre′quency,** *adj.*

Low′ Ger′man, 1. the West Germanic languages not included in the High German group, as English, Dutch, Flemish, Plattdeutsch, etc. *Abbr.:* LG Cf. **High German** (def. 1). **2.** Plattdeutsch.

low-key (lō′kē′), *adj.* of reduced intensity; restrained; understated. Also, **low′-keyed′.**

low·land (lō′lənd), *n.* **1.** land that is low or level, with respect to the adjacent country. **2. the Lowlands,** a low, level region in S, central, and E Scotland. —*adj.* **3.** of, pertaining to, or characteristic of a lowland or lowlands.

Low·land·er (lō′lən dər, -lan′-), *n.* a native of the Lowlands.

Low′ Lat′in, any form of nonclassical Latin, as Late Latin, Vulgar Latin, or Medieval Latin.

low-level (lō′lev′əl), *adj.* **1.** undertaken by or composed of members having a low status: *a low-level discussion.* **2.** having low status: *low-level officials.* **3.** undertaken at or from a low altitude: *low-level bombing.*

low·life (lō′līf′), *n.*, *pl.* **-lifes.** *Slang.* a despicable person.

low·ly (lō′lē), *adj.*, **-li·er, -li·est,** *adv.* —*adj.* **1.** humble in station, condition, or nature: *a lowly cottage.* **2.** low in growth or position. **3.** humble in spirit; meek. —*adv.* **4.** in a low position, manner, or degree. **5.** in a lowly manner; humbly. **6.** in a quiet voice; softly: *to converse lowly.* [ME] —**low′li·ness,** *n.*

Low′ Mass′, a Mass that is said, rather than sung, by the celebrant, who is assisted by one server, and that has less ceremonial form than a High Mass, using no music or choir. Cf. **High Mass.**

low-mind·ed (lō′mīn′did), *adj.* having or showing a low, coarse, or vulgar mind. —**low′-mind′ed·ly,** *adv.* —**low′-mind′ed·ness,** *n.*

low-necked (lō′nekt′), *adj.* (of a garment) cut low so as to leave the neck and shoulders exposed; décolleté.

low-pitched (lō′picht′), *adj.* **1.** pitched in a low register or key: *a low-pitched aria for the basso.* **2.** soft in sound: *a low-pitched whistle.* **3.** (of a roof) having a low proportion of vertical to lateral dimensions.

low-pres·sure (lō′presh′ər), *adj.* **1.** having or involving a low or below-normal pressure, as steam or water. **2.** without vigor or persistence. **3.** quietly persuasive; subtle; indirect: *a low-pressure sales campaign.*

low′ pro′file, a deliberately inconspicuous, almost unnoticeable form or manner.

low′ relief′, bas-relief.

low·rid·er (lō′rī′dər, -rī′-), *n.* **1.** an individually decorated and customized car fitted with hydraulic jacks that permit lowering of the chassis nearly to the road. **2.** a person, usu. a teenage boy, who drives such a car.

low-spir·it·ed (lō′spir′i tid), *adj.* depressed; dejected. —**low′-spir′it·ed·ly,** *adv.* —**low′-spir′it·ed·ness,** *n.*

Low′ Sun′day, the first Sunday after Easter.

low-ten·sion (lō′ten′shən), *adj.* *Elect.* subjected to, or capable of operating under, relatively low voltage: *low-tension wire.*

low-test (lō′test′), *adj.* (of gasoline) boiling at a comparatively high temperature.

low′ tide′, 1. the tide at the point of maximum ebb. **2.** the time of low water. **3.** the lowest point of decline of anything: *His spirits were at low tide.*

low′ wa′ter, 1. water at its lowest level, as in a river. **2.** See **low tide.** —**low′-wa′ter,** *adj.*

low′-wa′ter mark′, 1. the lowest point reached by a low tide. **2.** the lowest or least admirable level that has been reached: *the low-water mark of political trickery.*

lox[1] (loks), *n.* a kind of smoked salmon. [< Yiddish *laks,* var. of G *Lachs* salmon; c. OE *leax,* Icel *lax*]

lox[2] (loks), *n.* **1.** See **liquid oxygen.** —*v.t.* **2.** to supply (a rocket) with this fuel. [*l(iquid) ox(ygen)*]

lox·o·drome (lok′sə drōm′), *n.* See **rhumb line.** [back formation from LOXODROMIC]

lox·o·drom·ic (lok′sə drom′ik), *adj.* **1.** noting, pertaining to, or according to loxodromes or rhumb lines. **2.** noting or pertaining to a map projection, as a Mercator projection, in which rhumb lines appear as straight lines. Also, **lox′o·drom′i·cal.** [< Gk *loxó(s)* slanting + *dromik(ós)* of a course; see -DROME, -IC] —**lox′o·drom′i·cal·ly,** *adv.*

lox·o·drom·ics (lok′sə drom′iks), *n.* (*construed as sing.*) the technique of navigating according to loxodromes or rhumb lines. Also, **lox·od·ro·my** (lok sod′rə mē).

loy·al (loi′əl), *adj.* **1.** faithful to one's allegiance, as to a sovereign, government, or state: *a loyal subject.* **2.** faithful to one's oath, commitments, or obligations: *to be loyal to a vow.* **3.** faithful to any person or thing conceived of as deserving fidelity or imposing obligations: *a loyal friend.* [< MF, OF *loial, le(i)al* < L *lēgālis* LEGAL] —**loy′al·ly,** *adv.* —**loy′al·ness,** *n.* —**Syn. 1.** patriotic. **2, 3.** See **faithful.**

loy·al·ist (loi′ə list), *n.* **1.** a person who is loyal; a supporter of the sovereign or of the existing government, esp. in time of revolt. **2.** (*sometimes cap.*) a person who remained loyal to the British during the American Revolution; Tory. **3.** (*cap.*) an adherent of the republic during the Spanish Civil War. —**loy′al·ism,** *n.*

loy·al·ty (loi′əl tē), *n.*, *pl.* **-ties. 1.** the state or quality of being loyal; faithfulness to commitments or obligations. **2.** faithful adherence to a sovereign, a government, cause, or the like. **3.** an example or instance of faithfulness, adherence, or the like: *a man with fierce loyalties.* [late ME *loyaltee* < MF *loialte*]
—**Syn. 2.** fealty, devotion, constancy. LOYALTY, ALLEGIANCE imply a sense of duty or of devoted attachment to something or someone. LOYALTY connotes sentiment and the feeling of devotion that one holds for one's country, creed, family, friends, etc. ALLEGIANCE applies particularly to a citizen's duty to his country, or, by extension, one's obligation to support a party, cause, leader, etc.

Loy·o·la (loi ō′lə), *n.* **Saint Ignatius** (*Iñigo Lōpez de Loyola*), 1491–1556, Spanish soldier and ecclesiastic: founder of the Society of Jesus.

loz·enge (loz′inj), *n.* **1.** a small flavored confection of sugar or syrup, often medicated, originally diamond-shaped. **2.** *Geom.* a four-sided equilateral figure whose opposing angles are equal; diamond. **3.** *Heraldry.* a diamond-shaped charge. [ME *losenge* < MF, OF, appar. < Gaulish **lausa* flat stone + Gmc *-inga* suffix of appurtenance]

LP, *pl.* **LPs, Lp's,** *Trademark.* a phonograph record designed to be played at 33⅓ revolutions per minute; a long-playing record. Also, **L-P**

L.P., 1. long primer. **2.** low pressure. Also, **l.p.**

LPG., See **liquefied petroleum gas.** Also, **LP gas.**

L.P.S., Lord Privy Seal.

lpW, lumen per watt; lumens per watt. Also, **l.p.w., L.P.W.**

LRBM, long-range ballistic missile.

L.S., 1. Licentiate in Surgery. **2.** the place of the seal, as on a document. [< L *locus sigilli*]

l.s.c., in the place cited above. [< L *locō suprā citātō*]

LSD, 1. Also called **LSD-25, lysergic acid diethylamide.** *Pharm.* a strongly hallucinogenic, psychedelic drug, $C_{15}H_{15}N_2CON(C_2H_5)_2$, the diethyl amide of lysergic acid: of use in medical research of mental disorders. **2.** See **least significant digit.**

L.S.D., pounds, shillings, and pence. Also, **£.s.d., l.s.d.** [< L *librae, solidi, denarii*]

LSI, a type of electronic microminiaturization in which approximately 1000 transistors and resistors may be concentrated on a single integrated-circuit chip. Cf. **MSI, SSI.** [L(ARGE-)S(CALE) I(NTEGRATION)]

LST, an ocean-going military vessel, used by amphibious forces for landing troops and heavy equipment on beaches. [*l(anding) s(hip) t(ank)*]

l.s.t., local standard time.

Lt., lieutenant.

l.t., 1. *Football.* left tackle. **2.** local time. **3.** long ton.

Lt. Col., Lieutenant Colonel.

Lt. Comdr., Lieutenant Commander. Also, **Lt. Com.**

Ltd., limited (def. 4). Also, **ltd.**

Lt. Gen., Lieutenant General.

Lt. Gov., Lieutenant Governor.

Lt. Inf., *Mil.* light infantry.

lt-yr, light-year; light-years.

Lu, *Chem.* lutetium.

Lu·a·la·ba (lo͞o′ä lä′bä), *n.* a river in SE Zaïre: a headstream of the Zaïre River. 400 mi. long.

Lu·an·da (lo͞o an′də), *n.* a seaport in and the capital of Angola, in SW Africa. 475,328. Also, **Loanda.** Also called **São Paulo de Luanda.**

Luang Pra·bang (lwäng′ prä bäng′), a city in N Laos, on the Mekong River: royal capital 1946–75. 45,000. Cf. **Vientiane.**

lu·au (lo͞o ou′, lo͞o′ou), *n.* **1.** a feast of Hawaiian food, usually accompanied by Hawaiian entertainment. **2.** a cooked dish of taro leaves, usually prepared with coconut cream and octopus or chicken. [< Hawaiian *lu'au*]

lub·ber (lub′ər), *n.* **1.** a big, clumsy, stupid person; lout. **2.** *Naut.* an awkward or unskilled seaman. —*adj.* **3.** clumsy; stupid. [ME *lobre.* See LOB[1], -ER[1]] —**lub′ber·ly,** *adj., adv.* —**lub′ber·li·ness,** *n.*

lub′ber line′, *Navig.* a reference mark on a compass or other navigational instrument, indicating the heading of a vessel. Also, **lub′ber's line′.** Also called **lub′ber's mark′, lub′ber's point′.**

Lub·bock (lub′ək), *n.* a city in NW Texas. 149,101 (1970).

lube (lo͞ob), *n.* *Informal.* **1.** lubricant. **2.** an application of a lubricant, as to a vehicle. [short form]

Lü·beck (lʏ′bek), *n.* a seaport in N West Germany: important Baltic port in the medieval Hanseatic League. 236,600 (1963).

Lüb·ke (lʏp′kə), *n.* **Hein·rich** (hīn′rɪкн), 1894–1972, German statesman: president of West Germany 1959–69. Also, **Luebke.**

Lu·blin (lyo͞o′blin), *n.* a city in E Poland. 194,000 (est. 1963). Russian, **Lyublin.**

lu·bric (lo͞o′brik), *adj.* *Archaic.* lubricous. [late ME *lubrik* < L *lūbric(us)* slippery, smooth, ML: lewd]

lu·bri·cant (lo͞o′brə kənt), *n.* **1.** a substance, as oil, grease, etc., for lessening friction, esp. in the working parts of a mechanism. —*adj.* **2.** capable of lubricating; used to lubricate. [< L *lūbricant-* (s. of *lūbricāns*) making slippery, prp. of *lūbricāre*]

lu·bri·cate (lo͞o′brə kāt′), *v.*, **-cat·ed, -cat·ing.** —*v.t.* **1.** to apply some oily or greasy substance to (a machine, parts of a mechanism, etc.) in order to diminish friction; oil or grease. **2.** to make slippery or smooth; apply a lubricant to: *to lubricate one's hands with a lotion.* —*v.i.* **3.** to act as a lubricant. **4.** to apply a lubricant to something. [< L *lūbricāt(us)* made slippery, ptp. of *lūbricāre*] —**lu′bri·ca′tion,** *n.* —**lu′bri·ca′tion·al,** *adj.* —**lu′bri·ca′tive,** *adj.* —**lu′bri·ca′tor,** *n.*

lu·bri·cious (lo͞o brish′əs), *adj.* lubricous. —**lu·bri′cious·ly,** *adv.*

lu·bric·i·ty (lo͞o bris′i tē), *n.* **1.** oily smoothness, as of a surface; slipperiness. **2.** ability to lubricate; capacity for lubrication: *the excellent lubricity of this new oil.* **3.** instability; shiftiness; fleetingness: *the lubricity of fame and fortune.* **4.** lewdness; wantonness. [late ME *lubrycyte* lewdness < ML *lubricitās* lechery, LL: slipperiness]

lu·bri·cous (lo͞o′brə kəs), *adj.* **1.** (of a surface, coating, etc.) having an oily smoothness; slippery. **2.** unstable; uncertain; shifty. **3.** sexually wanton; lewd; lecherous. Also, **lubricious.** [< L *lūbricus* slippery, LL: unstable. See LUBRIC] —**Syn. 2.** unsteady, wavering, undependable. **3.** lascivious, lustful, pornographic, obscene, filthy.

Lu·bum·ba·shi (lo͞o bo͞om′bä shē), *n.* a city in the S Democratic Republic of the Congo. 200,000 (est. 1964). Formerly, **Elisabethville.**

Lu·can (lo͞o′kən), *n.* (*Marcus Annaeus Lucanus*) A.D. 39–65, Roman poet, born in Spain.

Lu·ca·ni·a (lo͞o kā′nē ə), *n.* **1.** an ancient region in S Italy, NW of the Gulf of Taranto. **2.** a modern region in S Italy, comprising most of the ancient region. 648,085 (1961); 3856 sq. mi. Italian, **Basilicata.**

Lu·cas van Ley·den (lo͞o′käs vän līd′ən), (*Lucas Hugensz*) 1494–1533, Dutch painter and engraver.

Luc·ca (lo͞ok′kä), *n.* a city in NW Italy, W of Florence. 85,940 (1961).

luce (lo͞os), *n.* **1.** a pike, esp. the adult fish. **2.** *Heraldry.* a stylized representation of a pike. [ME < MF *lus* pike < LL *lūcius*]

Luce (lo͞os), *n.* **Henry (Robinson),** 1898–1967, U.S. publisher and editor.

lu·cent (lo͞o′sənt), *adj.* **1.** shining. **2.** translucent; clear. [< L *lūcent-* (s. of *lūcēns*) shining, prp. of *lūcēre*] —**lu′cen·cy;** *Rare.* **lu′cence,** *n.* —**lu′cent·ly,** *adv.*

Lu·cerne (lo͞o sûrn′; *Fr.* lʏ sern′), *n.* **1.** a city in central Switzerland, on Lake of Lucerne. 72,600 (est. 1964). **2. Lake of,** a lake in central Switzerland. 24 mi. long; 44 sq. mi. German, **Luzern.**

lu·ces (lo͞o′sēz), *n.* pl. of **lux.**

Lu·cian (lo͞o′shən), *n.* **1.** A.D. 117–c180, Greek rhetorician and satirist, born in Syria. **2.** ("*Lucian of Antioch*"; "*Lucian the Martyr*") A.D. c240–312, theologian and Biblical critic, born in Syria.

lu·cid (lo͞o′sid), *adj.* **1.** shining or bright. **2.** clear; pellucid; transparent. **3.** easily understood; intelligible or comprehensible: *a lucid explanation.* **4.** characterized by clear perception or understanding; rational or sane. [< L *lūcid(us)* = *lūc-* (s. of *lūx*) light + *-id-* -ID[4]] —**lu·cid′i·ty, lu′cid·ness,** *n.* —**lu′cid·ly,** *adv.* —**Syn. 1.** radiant, luminous. **2.** limpid. **3.** understandable. —**Ant. 1.** dim. **2, 3.** obscure. **4.** irrational.

Lu·ci·fer (lo͞o′sə fər), *n.* **1.** a proud, rebellious archangel, identified with Satan, expelled from heaven. **2.** the planet Venus when appearing as the morning star. **3.** (*l.c.*) Also called **lu′cifer match′.** See **friction match.** [< L: morning star, lit., light-bringing = *lūci-* (s. of *lūx*) light + *-fer* -FER]

lu·cif·er·ase (lo͞o sif′ə rās′), *n.* *Biochem.* an enzyme that is present in the luminous organs of fireflies and that produces luminosity when acting upon luciferin. [LUCIFER(IN) + -ASE]

lu·cif·er·in (lo͞o sif′ər in), *n.* *Biochem.* a pigment occurring in fireflies, luminous when acted upon by luciferase. [< L *lūcifer* (see LUCIFER) + -IN[2]]

lu·cif·er·ous (lo͞o sif′ər əs), *adj.* bringing or giving light. [< L *lūcifer* (see LUCIFER) + -OUS]

Lu·cil·i·us (lo͞o sil′ē əs), *n.* **Ga·ius** (gā′əs), c180–102? B.C., Roman satirist.

Lu·ci·na (lo͞o sī′nə), *n.* the ancient Roman goddess of childbirth. [< L, n. use of fem. of *lūcīnus* of light]

Lu·cite (lo͞o′sīt), *n.* *Trademark.* any of a class of methyl methacrylate ester polymers, used chiefly as substitutes for glass.

Lu·ci·us I (lo͞o′shē əs, -shəs), **Saint,** died A.D. 254, pope 253–254.

Lucius II, (*Gherardo Caccianemici dell' Orso*) died 1145, Italian ecclesiastic: pope 1144–45.

Lucius III, (*Ubaldo Allucingoli*) died 1185, Italian ecclesiastic: pope 1181–85.

luck (luk), *n.* **1.** the force that seems to operate for good or ill in a person's life, as in shaping circumstances, events, and opportunities. **2.** good fortune: *He had no luck finding work.* **3.** a combination of circumstances, events, etc., operating by chance to bring good or ill to a person: *He had wonderful luck in all his ventures.* **4. in luck,** lucky or fortunate on the occasion in question. **5. out of luck,** unlucky or unfortunate on the occasion in question. [late ME < MD *luc;* akin to D *geluk,* G *Glück*]

luck·i·ly (luk′ə lē), *adv.* by good luck; fortunately.

luck·less (luk′lis), *adj.* having no luck or attended with bad luck.

Luck·ner (luk′nər; *Ger.* lo͝ok′nər), *n.* **Count Fe·lix von** (fē′liks von; *Ger.* fā′liks fən), 1881–1966, German naval officer in World War I.

Luck·now (luk′nou), *n.* a city in S Uttar Pradesh, in N India: British were besieged (1857–58) during Sepoy Rebellion. 595,400 (1961).

luck·y (luk′ē), *adj.*, **luck·i·er, luck·i·est.** **1.** having or attended with good luck; fortunate: *a lucky day.* **2.** happening fortunately: *a lucky accident.* **3.** bringing or foretelling good luck: *a lucky penny.* —**luck′i·ness,** *n.* —**Syn. 1.** See **fortunate. 3.** auspicious, propitious. —**Ant. 1.** unfortunate.

lu·cra·tive (lo͞o′krə tiv), *adj.* profitable; moneymaking; remunerative: *a lucrative business; lucrative employment.* [< L *lucrātīv(us)* gainful = *lucrāt(us)* profited (ptp. of *lucrārī;* see LUCRE) + *-īvus* -IVE; r. late ME *lucratif* < MF] —**lu′cra·tive·ly,** *adv.* —**lu′cra·tive·ness,** *n.*

lu·cre (lo͞o′kər), *n.* monetary gain; money. [ME < L *lucr(um)* profit; akin to OE *lēan* reward, G *Lohn,* Goth, Icel *laun*]

Lu·cre·tia (lo͞o krē′shə, -shē ə), *n.* Also called **Lu·crece** (lo͞o krēs′). *Rom. Legend.* a Roman woman whose suicide, after her rape by a son of Tarquin the Proud, led to the expulsion of the Tarquins and the establishment of the Roman republic.

Lu·cre·tius (lo͞o krē′shəs), *n.* (*Titus Lucretius Carus*) 97?–54 B.C., Roman poet and philosopher. —**Lu·cre′tian,** *adj.*

lu·cu·brate (lo͞o′kyo͝o brāt′), *v.i.*, **-brat·ed, -brat·ing.** **1.** to work, write, or study laboriously, esp. at night. **2.** to write learnedly. [< L *lūcubrāt(us),* ptp. of *lūcubrāre* to work by artificial light; akin to LL *lūcubrum* dim light = *lūc-* (s. of *lūx*) light + *-brum* neut. suffix; see -ATE[1]] —**lu′cu·bra′tor,** *n.* —**lu′cu·bra′to·ry,** *adj.*

lu·cu·bra·tion (lo͞o′kyo͝o brā′shən), *n.* **1.** laborious work, study, etc., esp. at night. **2.** a pedantic literary composition. [< L *lūcubrātiōn-* (s. of *lūcubrātiō*)]

lu·cu·lent (lo͞o′kyo͝o lənt), *adj.* **1.** clear or lucid, as explanations or interpretations. **2.** convincing; cogent. [< L *lūculent(us)* bright = *lūc-* (s. of *lūx*) light + *-ulentus* -ULENT] —**lu′cu·lent·ly,** *adv.*

Lu·cul·lus (lo͞o kul′əs), *n.* **Lucius Li·cin·i·us** (li sin′ē əs), 110?–57? B.C., Roman general and epicure. —**Lu·cul′lan, Lu·cul·le·an** (lo͞o′kə lē′ən), **Lu·cul′li·an,** *adj.*

Lud·dite (lud′īt), *n.* a member of any of various bands of English workmen (1811–16) who destroyed industrial machinery in the belief that its use diminished employment. [after Ned *Ludd,* 18th-century Leicestershire worker who originated the idea; see -ITE[1]] —**Lud′dism, Lud′dit·ism,** *n.*

Lu·den·dorff (lo͞od′ən dôrf′), *n.* **E·rich Frie·drich Wil·helm von** (ā′rɪкн frē′drɪкн vil′helm fən), 1865–1937, German general in World War I.

Lü·der·itz (lʏ′dər its), *n.* a seaport in SW South-West Africa: diamond-mining center. 3925 (1951).

Lu·dhi·a·na (lo͝o′dē ä′nä), *n.* a city in central Punjab, in N India. 244,000 (1961).

lu·di·crous (lo͞o′də krəs), *adj.* provoking or deserving derision; amusingly absurd; ridiculous; comical; laughable: *a ludicrous incident.* [< L *lūdicrus* sportive = *lūdicr(um)* a show, public games (*lūdi-,* s. of *lūdere* to play + *-crum* n. suffix of instrument or result) + *-us* -OUS] —**lu′di·crous·ly,** *adv.* —**lu′di·crous·ness,** *n.* —**Syn.** farcical. See **funny.**

Lud·low (lud′lō), *n.* *Typesetting, Trademark.* a machine for casting slugs from matrices handset in a composing stick.

Ludwig II. See **Louis II** (def. 1).

Lud·wigs·ha·fen (lo͞ot′vɪкнs hä′fən, lo͞od′-), *n.* a city in W West Germany, on the Rhine opposite Mannheim. 171,500 (1963).

Lueb·ke (lʏp′kə), *n.* **Hein·rich** (hīn′rɪкн). See **Lübke, Heinrich.**

Luen·ing (lo͞o′ning), *n.* **Otto,** born 1900, U.S. composer, conductor, and flutist.

lu·es (lo͞o′ēz), *n.* *Pathol.* syphilis. [< NL, special use of L: contagious disease] —**lu·et·ic** (lo͞o et′ik), *adj.* —**lu·et′i·cal·ly,** *adv.*

luff (luf), *n.* *Naut.* **1.** the forward edge of a fore-and-aft sail. —*v.i.* **2.** to bring the head of a sailing vessel closer to or directly into the wind, with sails shaking. **3.** (of a sail) to shake from being set too close to the wind. —*v.t.* **4.** to set (the helm of a vessel) in such a way as to bring the head of the vessel into the wind. [ME *lof, loof* some kind of steering gear < OD (unrecorded), later D *loef* tholepin (of tiller); akin to Goth *lōfa,* Icel *lōfi* palm of the hand, OHG *lappo* palm of the hand, blade of a rudder]

luf·fa (luf′ə), *n.* **1.** Also called **dishcloth gourd, rag gourd.** the fruit of any cucurbitaceous plant of the genus *Luffa.* **2.** Also called **vegetable sponge.** the fibrous interior of the dried fruit, used as a sponge. Also, **loofa, loofah.** [< NL, name of genus < Ar *lūf*]

luff′ tack′le, *Naut.* a tackle composed of a fall rove through a double block and a single block and fastened to the single block, giving a mechanical advantage of three or four, neglecting friction. See diag. at **tackle.**

Luft·waf·fe (lo͝oft′väf′ə), *n.* *German.* the German air force during the Nazi regime. [lit., air weapon]

lug[1] (lug), *v.*, **lugged, lug·ging,** *n.* —*v.t.* **1.** to pull along or carry with force or effort: *to lug a suitcase upstairs.* **2.** (of a sailing vessel) to carry an excessive amount of (sail) for the conditions prevailing. —*v.i.* **3.** to pull; tug. —*n.* **4.** an act or instance of lugging; a forcible pull; haul. [ME *lugge(n)* < Scand; cf. Norw *lugge,* Sw *lugga* to pull by the hair]

lug[2] (lug), *n.* **1.** a projecting piece by which anything is held or supported. **2.** a leather loop hanging down from a saddle, through which a shaft is passed for support. **3.** *Slang.* **a.** an awkward, clumsy fellow. **b.** an average man; guy. [< Scand; cf. Norw, Sw *lugg* forelock. See LUG[1]]

lug[3] (lug), *n.* lugsail. [by shortening]

lug[4] (lug), *n.* lugworm. [? special use of LUG[2]]

Lu·gansk (lo͞o gänsk′), *n.* a city in the E Ukraine, in the S Soviet Union in Europe. 323,000 (est. 1964). Formerly, **Voroshilovgrad.**

Lu·ger (lo͞o′gər), *n.* *Trademark.* an automatic pistol of 9-millimeter caliber, made in Germany.

lug·gage (lug′ij), *n.* suitcases, trunks, valises, etc.; baggage. —**lug′gage·less,** *adj.*

lug·ger (lug′ər), *n.* *Naut.* a small vessel lug-rigged on two or three masts. [LUG(SAIL) + -ER[1]]

lug′ nut′, a large nut fitting over a heavy bolt, used esp. in attaching a wheel to an automobile.

Lu·go (lo͞o′gō), *n.* a city in NW Spain. 59,368 (1963).

lug-rigged (lug′rigd′), *adj.* *Naut.* rigged with a lugsail or lugsails.

lug·sail (lug′sāl′; *Naut.* lug′səl), *n. Naut.* a quadrilateral sail bent upon a yard that crosses the mast obliquely. Also called **lug.** See diag. at **sail.** [ME *lugge* pole (now dial.) + SAIL]

lu·gu·bri·ous (lo͝o go͞o′brē əs, -gyo͞o′-), *adj.* mournful or gloomy, esp. exaggeratedly so: *lugubrious tones of voice; a lugubrious expression.* [< L *lūgubri(s)* mournful (akin to *lūgēre* to mourn) + -OUS] —**lu·gu′bri·ous·ly,** *adv.* —**lu·gu′bri·ous·ness,** *n.* —**Syn.** sorrowful, melancholy.

lug·worm (lug′wûrm′), *n.* any burrowing, marine annelid of the genus *Arenicola*, having tufted gills, found in the sand and used as bait for fishing. Also called **lug.**

lug′ wrench′, a wrench for loosening or tightening lug nuts.

Luik (loik, lo͞ok), *n.* Flemish name of **Liège.**

Luke (lo͞ok), *n.* **1.** an early Christian disciple and companion of Paul, a physician and probably a gentile: traditionally believed to be the author of the Gospel of St. Luke and the Acts. **2.** the third Gospel.

luke·warm (lo͞ok′wôrm′), *adj.* **1.** moderately warm; tepid. **2.** having or showing little ardor or zeal; indifferent. [ME *lukewarme* tepid = *luke* tepid (*lew*, OE *gehlēow* tepid + *-k* suffix) + *warme* WARM] —**luke′warm′ly,** *adv.* —**luke′-warm′ness, luke′warmth′,** *n.*

Luks (luks), *n.* **George Benjamin,** 1867–1933, U.S. painter.

Lu·le·å (lo͞o′le ô′), *n.* a seaport in NE Sweden, on the Gulf of Bothnia. 33,983 (1965).

lull (lul), *v.t.* **1.** to put to sleep or rest by soothing means. **2.** to soothe or quiet. **3.** to give or lead to feel a false sense of safety. —*v.i.* **4.** to quiet down, let up, or subside. —*n.* **5.** a lulled condition; a temporary stillness: *a lull in a storm.* [ME *lulle(n)*, perh. imit.; cf. Sw *lulla*, G *lullen*, L *lallāre* to sing lullaby] —**lull′ing·ly,** *adv.*

lull·a·by (lul′ə bī′), *n., pl.* **-bies,** *v.,* **-bied, -by·ing.** —*n.* **1.** a song used to lull a child to sleep; cradlesong. —*v.t.* **2.** to lull with or as with a lullaby. [late ME (interj.) *lulla!* + *by!*]

Lul·ly (lo͞o′lē, *Fr.* ly lē′ *for 1;* lul′ē *for 2*), *n.* **1.** Italian, **Lul·li** (lo͞ol′lē). **Jean Bap·tiste** (zhäN bȧ tēst′), 1632–87, French composer, born in Italy. **2.** Catalan, **Lull** (lo͞ol). **Raymond** or **Ra·món** (rä môn′), 1235?–1315, Spanish theologian, philosopher, and author.

lu·lu (lo͞o′lo͞o), *n. Slang.* any outstanding person or thing. [after the proper name]

Lu·lua·bourg (lo͞ol′wä bo͝or′), *n.* a city in central Zaïre. 115,049 (est. 1959).

lumb-, a learned borrowing from Latin meaning "loin," used in the formation of compound words: *lumbar.* [comb. form repr. L *lumbus*]

lum·ba·go (lum bā′gō), *n. Pathol.* pain in the lower back or lumbar region, esp. chronic or recurring pain. [< LL = L *lumb(us)* the loin + *-āgō* n. suffix]

lum·bar (lum′bər, -bär), *adj.* **1.** of or pertaining to the loin or loins. —*n.* **2.** a lumbar vertebra, artery, or the like. [< NL *lumbār(is)*]

lum·ber[1] (lum′bər), *n.* **1.** timber sawed or split into planks, boards, etc. **2.** miscellaneous useless articles that are stored away. —*v.i.* **3.** to cut timber and prepare it for market. —*v.t.* **4.** to convert into or exploit for lumber. **5.** to heap together in disorder. **6.** to fill up or obstruct with miscellaneous useless articles; encumber. [orig. n. use of LUMBER[2]; i.e., useless goods that weigh one down, impede one's movements] —**lum′ber·er,** *n.* —**lum′ber·less,** *adj.*

lum·ber[2] (lum′bər), *v.i.* **1.** to move clumsily or heavily, esp. from great or ponderous bulk. **2.** *Obs.* to make a rumbling noise. [ME *lomere(n)*; cf. dial. Sw *lomra* to resound, *loma* to walk heavily]

lum·ber·ing[1] (lum′bər ing), *n.* the business of cutting and preparing timber. [LUMBER[1] + -ING[1]]

lum·ber·ing[2] (lum′bər ing), *adj.* **1.** moving clumsily or heavily. **2.** *Obs.* moving along with a rumbling noise. [LUMBER[2] + -ING[2]] —**lum′ber·ing·ly,** *adv.*

lum·ber·jack (lum′bər jak′), *n.* a person who works at lumbering; logger.

lum′ber jack′et, a short, straight, wool plaid jacket or coat, usually belted and having patch pockets.

lum·ber·man (lum′bər mən), *n., pl.* **-men. 1.** a person who deals in lumber. **2.** a person who cuts prepared logs into lumber. Cf. **logger** (def. 1).

lum·ber·mill (lum′bər mil′), *n.* a sawmill.

lum′ber room′, *Brit.* a room in a house used for storing odds-and-ends, esp. old furniture.

lum·ber·yard (lum′bər yärd′), *n.* a yard where lumber is stored for sale.

lum·bri·coid (lum′brə koid′), *adj.* resembling an earthworm. [< NL *lumbricoid(es)* < L *lumbrīc(us)* earthworm; see -OID]

lu·men (lo͞o′mən), *n., pl.* **-mi·na** (-mə nə). **1.** *Optics.* the unit of luminous flux, equal to the luminous flux emitted in a unit solid angle by a point source of one-candle intensity. *Abbr.:* lm **2.** *Anat.* the canal, duct, or cavity of a tubular organ. **3.** *Bot.* (of a cell) the cavity that the cell walls enclose. [< NL, special uses of L: light, window]

Lu·mi·nal (lo͞o′mə nəl), *n. Trademark.* phenobarbital.

lu·mi·nance (lo͞o′mə nəns), *n.* **1.** the state or quality of being luminous. **2.** Also called **luminosity.** the quality or condition of radiating or reflecting light. **3.** *Optics.* the quantitative measure of brightness of a light source or an illuminated surface, equal to luminous flux per unit solid angle emitted per unit projected area of the source or surface. [< L *lūmin-* (s. of *lūmen*) light + -ANCE]

lu·mi·nar·y (lo͞o′mə ner′ē), *n., pl.* **-nar·ies,** *adj.* —*n.* **1.** a celestial body, as the sun or moon. **2.** a body, object, etc., that gives light. **3.** a person of intellectual or moral eminence who is an inspiration to others. —*adj.* **4.** of, pertaining to, or characterized by light. [late ME *luminarye* < ML *lūmināria* lamp (fem. sing.), L: windows (neut. pl.). See LUMEN, -ARY]

lu·mi·nesce (lo͞o′mə nes′), *v.i.,* **-nesced, -nesc·ing.** to exhibit luminescence. [back formation from LUMINESCENT]

lu·mi·nes·cence (lo͞o′mə nes′əns), *n.* **1.** the emission of light occurring at a temperature below that of incandescent bodies. **2.** the light produced by such an emission. [< L *lūmin-* (see LUMEN) + -ESCENCE]

lu·mi·nes·cent (lo͞o′mə nes′ənt), *adj.* characterized by or pertaining to luminescence. [< L *lūmin-* (see LUMEN) + -ESCENT]

lu·mi·nif·er·ous (lo͞o′mə nif′ər əs), *adj.* producing light. [< L *lūmin-* (see LUMEN) + -I- + -FEROUS]

lu·mi·nos·i·ty (lo͞o′mə nos′i tē), *n., pl.* **-ties. 1.** luminance (def. 2). **2.** something luminous. **3.** *Astron.* the intrinsic brightness of a star in comparison with that of the sun, expressed as a multiple or fraction of the sun's brightness. [< L *lūminōs(us)* LUMINOUS + -ITY]

lu·mi·nous (lo͞o′mə nəs), *adj.* **1.** radiating or emitting light: *luminous paint.* **2.** reflecting or diffusing light. **3.** intellectually brilliant. **4.** clear; lucid. [< L *lūminōsus.* See LUMEN, -OUS] —**lu′mi·nous·ly,** *adv.* —**lu′mi·nous·ness,** *n.* —**Syn. 1.** radiant, resplendent, brilliant. **3.** bright, intelligent. **4.** understandable, perspicuous. —**Ant. 1, 2.** dark.

lu′minous flux′, *Optics.* the rate of transmission of luminous energy: expressed in lumens.

lu′minous inten′sity, *Optics.* the luminous flux in lumens emitted per unit solid angle by a light source, measured in candelas.

lu·mis·ter·ol (lo͞o mis′tə rôl′, -rōl′), *n. Biochem.* a water-insoluble compound, $C_{28}H_{44}O$, produced by the irradiation of ergosterol. [< L *lumi(n)-* (see LUMEN) + STEROL]

lum·mox (lum′əks), *n. Informal.* a clumsy, stupid person. [?]

lump[1] (lump), *n.* **1.** a piece or mass of solid matter of no particular shape. **2.** a protuberance or swelling. **3.** a heap or mass; clump. **4.** a small cube of granulated sugar. **5.** majority; plurality; multitude: *The great lump of voters are still undecided.* —*adj.* **6.** in the form of a lump or lumps: *lump sugar.* **7.** made up of a number of items taken together: *a lump sum.* —*v.t.* **8.** to unite into one aggregation, collection, or mass (often fol. by *together*): *lumping the Chinese and the Russians together.* **9.** to make into a lump or lumps. —*v.i.* **10.** to form or raise a lump or lumps. **11.** to move heavily and awkwardly. [ME *lumpe, lomp(e)*; c. early D *lompe* piece, Dan *lump(e)* lump, dial. Norw *lump* block] —**lump′ing·ly,** *adv.*

lump[2] (lump), *v.t. Informal.* to put up with; resign oneself to: *If you don't like it, you can lump it.* [?]

lum·pen (lum′pən), *adj.* of or pertaining to disfranchised and uprooted individuals or groups, esp. those who have lost status in their class. [< G *Lumpen-*, comb. form of *Lump* ragamuffin and *Lumpen* rag, as in *Lumpenproletariat*]

lump·fish (lump′fish′), *n., pl.* (*esp. collectively*) **-fish,** (*esp. referring to two or more kinds or species*) **-fish·es.** any of several thick-bodied, sluggish fishes of the family *Cyclopteridae*, found in northern seas, having the pelvic fins modified and united into a sucking disk, esp. *Cyclopterus lumpus*, of the North Atlantic.

lump·ish (lum′pish), *adj.* **1.** like a lump. **2.** having a heavy appearance; moving clumsily. **3.** having a sluggish mind; dull; stupid. [ME *lumpisch*] —**lump′ish·ly,** *adv.* —**lump′ish·ness,** *n.*

lump·y (lum′pē), *adj.,* **lump·i·er, lump·i·est. 1.** full of lumps: *lumpy gravy.* **2.** covered with lumps, as a surface. **3.** (of water) rough or choppy. —**lump′i·ly,** *adv.* —**lump′i·ness,** *n.*

lump′y jaw′, *Pathol., Vet. Pathol.* actinomycosis.

Lu·mum·ba (lo͝o mo͝om′bə), *n.* **Pa·trice (Em·er·gy)** (pə-trēs′ em′er zhē′), 1925–61, African political leader: premier of the Republic of the Congo 1960–61.

Lu·na (lo͞o′nə), *n.* **1.** the ancient Roman goddess personifying the moon, sometimes identified with Diana. **2.** (in alchemy) silver. [< L: moon]

lu·na·cy (lo͞o′nə sē), *n., pl.* **-cies. 1.** intermittent insanity, formerly believed to be related to phases of the moon. **2.** any form of insanity, sometimes not including idiocy. **3.** *Law.* unsoundness of mind sufficient to incapacitate a person for civil transactions. [LUNA(TIC) + -CY] —**Syn. 2.** derangement; madness, mania. —**Ant. 1, 2.** rationality, sanity.

lu′na moth′, a large, pale-green, American moth, *Actias luna*, having purple-brown markings, lunate spots, and long tails. Also, **Lu′na moth′.**

lu·nar (lo͞o′nər), *adj.* **1.** of or pertaining to the moon: *the lunar orbit.* **2.** measured by the moon's revolutions: *a lunar month.* **3.** of or pertaining to silver. —*n.* **4.** a lunar observation taken for purposes of navigation or mapping. [< L *lūnār(is)* of the moon]

lu′nar caus′tic, *Med., Chem.* silver nitrate, $AgNO_3$, esp. in a sticklike mold, used to cauterize tissues.

lu′nar day′, a division of time that is equal to the elapsed time between two consecutive returns of the same terrestrial meridian to the moon.

lu′nar eclipse′. See under **eclipse** (def. 1a).

lu′nar month′, month (def. 5).

lu′nar year′, year (def. 3a).

lu·nate (lo͞o′nāt), *adj.* crescent-shaped. Also, **lu′nat·ed.** [< L *lūnāt(us)*] —**lu′nate·ly,** *adv.*

lu·na·tic (lo͞o′nə tik), *n.* **1.** an insane person. **2.** a person who is extremely eccentric or reckless. —*adj.* **3.** insane; demented; crazy. **4.** characteristic or suggestive of lunacy. **5.** designated for or used by the insane: *a lunatic asylum.* Also, **lu·nat·i·cal** (lo͞o nat′i kəl) (for defs. 3, 4). [ME *lunatik* < OF *lunatique* < LL *lūnātic(us)* moonstruck. See LUNA, -ATIC] —**lu·nat′i·cal·ly,** *adv.*

lu′natic fringe′, members on the periphery of any group who hold extreme or fanatical views.

lu·na·tion (lo͞o nā′shən), *n.* the period of time from one new moon to the next, about 29½ days: a lunar month. [ME *lunacyon* < ML *lūnātiōn-* (s. of *lūnātiō*)]

lunch (lunch), *n.* **1.** a meal between breakfast and dinner; luncheon. **2.** any light meal or snack: *a box lunch; picnic lunch.* **3.** a lunchroom. —*v.i.* **4.** to eat lunch. —*v.t.* **5.** to provide lunch for. [short for LUNCHEON] —**lunch′er,** *n.* —**lunch′less,** *adj.*

lunch·eon (lun′chən), *n.* lunch, esp. a formal lunch held in connection with a special occasion. [dissimilated var. of *nuncheon* (now. dial.), ME *none(s)chench* noon drink = *none* NOON + *schench*, OE *scenc* a drink, cup, akin to OE *scencan* to pour out, give drink, c. D, G *schenken*] —**lunch′-eon·less,** *adj.*

lunch·eon·ette (lun′chə net′), *n.* a lunchroom or restaurant where light meals are served.

lunch·room (lunch′ro͞om′, -ro͝om′), *n.* **1.** a restaurant that specializes in serving light meals. **2.** a cafeteria or other room used as an eating place, as in a school.

lunch·time (lunch′tīm′), *n.* a period during which lunch is commonly eaten.

lune (lo͞on), *n.* **1.** anything shaped like a crescent or a half moon. **2.** a crescent-shaped figure bounded by two arcs of circles, either on a plane or a spherical surface. [< L *lūna* moon]

lu·nette (lo͞o net′), *n.* **1.** any of various objects or spaces of crescentlike or semicircular outline or section. **2.** *Archit.* (in the plane of a wall) an area framed by an arch or vault. **3.** a painting, sculpture, or window filling such an area. **4.** *Fort.* a work consisting of a salient angle with two flanks and an open gorge. **5.** *Ordn.* a towing ring in the trail plate of a towed vehicle, as a gun carriage. [< F; see LUNE, -ETTE]

Lu·né·ville (ly nā vēl′), *n.* a city in NE France, W of Strasbourg: treaty between France and Austria 1801. 24,463 (1962).

lung (lung), *n.* **1.** either of the two saclike respiratory organs in the thorax of man and the higher vertebrates. **2.** an analogous organ in certain invertebrates, as arachnids, terrestrial gastropods, etc. **3. at the top of one's lungs,** as loudly as possible; with full voice. [ME *lunge(n)*, OE *lungen;* c. G *Lunge;* akin to LIGHT[2], LIGHTS]

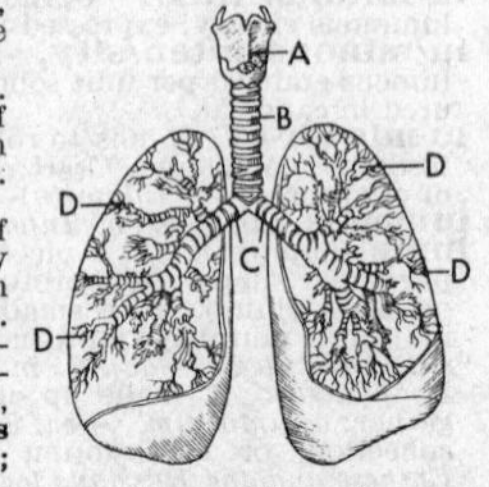

Lungs (Human)
A, Larynx; B, Trachea;
C, Bronchi; D, Ramifications of bronchial tubes

lun·gan (lung′gən), *n.* longan.

lunge[1] (lunj), *n., v.,* **lunged, lung·ing.** —*n.* **1.** a sudden forward thrust, as with a sword or knife; stab. **2.** any sudden forward movement; plunge. —*v.i.* **3.** to make a lunge or thrust; move with a lunge. —*v.t.* **4.** to thrust (something) forward; cause to move with a lunge. [earlier *longe* for F *allonge* (n.; misheard as *a longe*), *allonger* (v.) to lengthen, extend, deliver (blows) << LL *ēlongāre* to elongate]

lunge[2] (lunj), *n., v.,* **lunged, lung·ing.** longe.

lung·fish (lung′fish′), *n., pl.* (*esp. collectively*) **-fish,** (*esp. referring to two or more kinds or species*) **-fish·es.** any fish of the group *Dipnoi*, having a functional, lunglike air bladder as well as gills.

lun·gi (lo͝ong′gē, lo͝on′jē), *n.* a loincloth worn by men in India. Also, **lungyi.** [< Hindi *lungī* < Pers]

lung·worm (lung′wûrm′), *n.* **1.** any nematode worm of the superfamily *Metastrongylidae*, parasitic in the lungs of various mammals. **2.** a nematode worm of the genus *Rhabdias*, parasitic in the lungs of reptiles and amphibians.

lung·wort (lung′wûrt′), *n.* **1.** a European, boraginaceous plant, *Pulmonaria officinalis*, having blue flowers. **2.** a related American plant, *Mertensia virginica*, having blue flowers.

lun·gyi (lo͝ong′gē, lo͝on′jē), *n., pl.* **-gyis.** lungi.

luni-, a learned borrowing from Latin meaning "moon," used in the formation of compound words: *lunitidal.* [comb. form repr. L *lūna*]

Lu·nik (lo͞o′nik), *n.* one of a series of lunar probes fired by the Soviet Union. [< Russ, dim. of *luna* moon]

lu·ni·so·lar (lo͞o′ni sō′lər), *adj.* pertaining to or based upon the relations or joint action of the moon and the sun.

lu·ni·tid·al (lo͞o′ni tīd′ᵊl), *adj.* pertaining to the part of the tidal movement dependent upon the moon.

lu′nitid′al in′terval, the period of time between the moon's transit and the next high lunar tide.

lun·ker (lung′kər), *n.* **1.** something very large of its kind. **2.** *Angling.* a very large adult fish, esp. a bass. [?]

lunk·head (lungk′hed′), *n.* *Slang.* a dull or stupid person; blockhead. Also called **lunk.** [*lunk* (< ?) + HEAD] —**lunk′head′ed,** *adj.*

lunt (lunt, lo͞ont), *Scot.* —*n.* **1.** a match or torch; the flame used to light a fire. —*v.i.* **2.** to emit smoke or steam. [< D *lont* match, rag; akin to MLG *lunte* match, wick]

lu·nu·la (lo͞o′nyə lə), *n., pl.* **-lae** (-lē′). something shaped like a narrow crescent, as the small, white area at the base of the human fingernail. Also, **lu·nule** (lo͞o′nyo͞ol). [< L; see LUNA, -ULE]

lu·nu·lar (lo͞o′nyə lər), *adj.* crescent-shaped: *lunular markings.*

lu·nu·late (lo͞o′nyə lāt′), *adj.* **1.** having lunular markings. **2.** crescent-shaped. Also, **lu′nu·lat′ed.**

lun·y (lo͞o′nē), *adj.,* **lun·i·er, lun·i·est,** *n., pl.* **lun·ies.** loony.

Lu·per·ca·li·a (lo͞o′pər kā′lē ə, -kāl′yə), *n., pl.* **-li·a, -li·as.** (*sometimes construed as pl.*) an ancient Roman fertility festival. [< L, neut. pl. of *Lupercālis* of *Lupercus* a fertility god; see -AL[1]] —**Lu′per·ca′li·an,** *adj.*

lu·pine[1] (lo͞o′pin), *n.* any leguminous plant of the genus *Lupinus*, as *L. albus,* **(white lupine),** of Europe, bearing edible seeds, or *L. perennis*, of the eastern U.S., having blue, pink, or white flowers. [ME < L *lupīn(us)* or *lupīn(um)* plant name, n. use of masc. or neut. of *lupīnus* (adj.) LUPINE[2]]

lu·pine[2] (lo͞o′pīn), *adj.* **1.** pertaining to or resembling the wolf. **2.** related to the wolf. **3.** savage; ravenous; predatory. [< L *lupīn(us)* of a wolf = *lup(us)* wolf + *-īnus* -INE[1]]

lu·pu·lin (lo͞o′pyə lin), *n.* the glandular hairs of the hop, *Humulus Lupulus*, used in medicine. [< NL *lupul(us)* (dim. of L *lupus* the hop plant; see -ULE) + -IN[2]]

lu·pus (lo͞o′pəs), *n.* *Pathol.* See **lupus vulgaris.** [< ML (medical), special use of L: wolf] —**lu′pous,** *adj.*

lu′pus vul·ga′ris (vul gâr′əs), *Pathol.* tuberculosis of the skin characterized by brownish nodular tubercles, esp. about the nose and ears. Also called **lupus.** [< medical L: vulgar lupus]

lurch[1] (lûrch), *n.* **1.** an act or instance of swaying abruptly. **2.** a sudden tip or roll to one side, as of a ship or a staggering person. **3.** a swaying or staggering motion or gait. —*v.i.* **4.** to make a lurch, or move in lurches. [?] —**lurch′ing·ly,** *adv.*

lurch[2] (lûrch), *n.* **1.** a situation at the close of various games in which the loser scores nothing or is far behind his opponent. **2. leave in the lurch,** to leave in an uncomfortable or desperate situation; desert (someone) in time of trouble. [< MF *lourche* a game, n. use of *lourche* (adj.) discomfited < Gmc; cf. MHG *lurz* left (hand), OE *belyrtan* to deceive]

lurch[3] (lûrch), *v.t.* **1.** *Archaic.* to defraud; cheat. **2.** *Obs.* to steal; filch. —*v.i.* **3.** *Brit. Dial.* to lurk or prowl. —*n.* **4.** *Archaic.* the act of lurking or state of watchfulness. [late ME *lorche(n)*, appar. var. of *lurken* to LURK]

lurch·er (lûr′chər), *n.* *Archaic.* a person who lurks or prowls, as a petty thief or poacher.

lur·dan (lûr′dᵊn), *Archaic.* —*n.* **1.** a lazy, stupid, loutish fellow. —*adj.* **2.** lazy; stupid; worthless. [ME < MF *lourdin* dullard = *lourd* heavy, dull (<< L *lūridus* LURID) + *-in* -INE[1]]

lure (lo͝or), *n., v.,* **lured, lur·ing.** —*n.* **1.** anything that attracts, entices, or allures. **2.** the power of attracting or enticing. **3.** a decoy; live or esp. artificial bait used in angling or trapping. **4.** *Falconry.* a feathered decoy for attracting a hawk. **5. in lure,** *Heraldry.* noting a pair of wings joined with the tips downward (opposed to *a vol*). —*v.t.* **6.** to attract or entice. **7.** to draw, as by a lure or decoy. [ME < MF, OF *loire* < Gmc; cf. G *Luder* bait] —**lur′ing·ly,** *adv.* —**Syn. 1.** temptation. **6.** seduce.

lu·rid (lo͝or′id), *adj.* **1.** lighted or shining with an unnatural, fiery glow; wildly or garishly red: *a lurid sunset.* **2.** characterized by sensationalism or by a wildly dramatic quality: *lurid stories; lurid crimes.* **3.** gruesome; revolting: *the lurid details of an accident.* **4.** wan, pallid, or ghastly in hue; livid. [< L *lūrid(us)* sallow, ghastly; akin to *lūtum* yellowweed (see LUTEOUS); see -ID[4]] —**lu′rid·ly,** *adv.* —**lu′rid·ness,** *n.* —**Syn. 4.** pale, murky. —**Ant. 2.** mild.

lurk (lûrk), *v.i.* **1.** to lie or wait in concealment, as a person in ambush. **2.** to go furtively; slink. **3.** to exist unperceived or unsuspected. [ME *lurk(en)*, freq. of LOWER[2]; cf. Norw *lurka* to sneak away] —**lurk′er,** *n.* —**lurk′ing·ly,** *adv.* —**Syn. 1.** LURK, SKULK, SNEAK, PROWL suggest avoiding observation, often because of a sinister purpose. To LURK is to lie in wait for someone or to hide about a place, often without motion, for periods of time. SKULK suggests cowardliness and stealth of movement. SNEAK emphasizes the attempt to avoid being seen. It has connotations of slinking and of an abject meanness of manner, whether there exists a sinister intent or the desire to avoid punishment for some misdeed. PROWL implies the definite purpose of seeking for prey; it suggests continuous action in roaming or wandering, slowly and quietly but watchfully, as a cat hunting mice.

Lu·sa·ka (lo͞o sä′kə), *n.* a city in and the capital of Zambia, in the central part. 415,000.

Lu·sa·ti·a (lo͞o sā′shē ə, -shə), *n.* a region in E East Germany and SW Poland, between the Elbe and Oder rivers.

Lu·sa·tian (lo͞o sā′shən), *n.* **1.** a native or inhabitant of Lusatia. —*adj.* **2.** of or pertaining to Lusatia, its people or their language.

lus·cious (lush′əs), *adj.* **1.** highly pleasing to the taste or smell. **2.** sweet or attractive to the senses or the mind. **3.** *Archaic.* sweet to excess; cloying. [late ME *lucius*, unexplained var. of *licius*, aph. var. of DELICIOUS] —**lus′cious·ly,** *adv.* —**lus′cious·ness,** *n.*

lush[1] (lush), *adj.* **1.** (of vegetation, plants, grasses, etc.) luxuriant. **2.** characterized by luxuriant vegetation. **3.** characterized by luxuriousness, opulence, etc. [late ME *lusch* slack; akin to OE *lysu* bad, *lēas* lax, MLG *lasch* slack, Icel *löskr* weak, Goth *lasiws* weak] —**lush′ly,** *adv.* —**lush′ness,** *n.* —**Syn. 1.** luxurious, fresh. —**Ant. 1.** withered, stale.

lush[2] (lush), *n.* *Slang.* a person who drinks excessively and habitually; alcoholic; sot. [?]

Lu·si·ta·ni·a (lo͞o′si tā′nē ə), *n.* **1.** an ancient region and Roman province in the Iberian Peninsula, corresponding generally to modern Portugal. **2.** (*italics*) a British luxury liner sunk by the Germans in the North Atlantic on May 7, 1915: an event leading to U.S. entry into World War I.

lust (lust), *n.* **1.** sexual desire or appetite, esp. when uncontrolled or illicit. **2.** a passionate or overmastering desire (usually fol. by *for*): *a lust for power.* **3.** ardent enthusiasm; zest; relish. **4.** *Obs.* **a.** pleasure or delight. **b.** desire; inclination; wish. —*v.i.* **5.** to have strong sexual desire. **6.** to have a passionate yearning or desire (often fol. by *for* or *after*). [ME *luste*, OE *lust;* c. D, G *lust* pleasure, desire; akin to Icel *lyst* desire; see LIST[4]]

lus·ter[1] (lus′tər), *n.* **1.** the state or quality of shining by reflecting light; glitter, sparkle, sheen, or gloss. **2.** a substance, as a coating or polish, used to impart sheen or gloss. **3.** radiant or luminous brightness; brilliance; radiance. **4.** radiance of beauty, excellence, merit, etc. **5.** a shining ornament, as a cut-glass pendant. **6.** a chandelier, candleholder, etc., ornamented with cut-glass pendants. **7.** any natural or synthetic fabric with a lustrous finish. **8.** an iridescent metallic film produced on the surface of a ceramic glaze. **9.** *Mineral.* the nature of a mineral surface with respect to its reflective qualities: *greasy luster.* —*v.t.* **10.** to finish (fur, cloth, pottery, etc.) with a luster or gloss. —*v.i.* **11.** to be or become lustrous. Also, *esp. Brit.,* **lustre.** [< MF *lustre* < OIt *lustro*, akin to *lustrare* < L *lūstrāre* to illumine, purify. See LUSTRUM] —**lus′ter·less,** *adj.* —**Syn. 1.** See **polish.** —**Ant. 1.** dullness.

lus·ter[2] (lus′tər), *n.* lustrum (def. 1). Also, *esp. Brit.,* **lustre.** [ME *lustre* < L *lūstrum.* See LUSTRUM]

lus·ter[3] (lus′tər), *n.* a person who lusts: *a luster after power.* [LUST + -ER[1]]

lust·ful (lust′fəl), *adj.* **1.** full of or motivated by lust, greed, or the like. **2.** *Archaic.* lusty. [ME, OE] —**lust′ful·ly,** *adv.* —**lust′ful·ness,** *n.*

lus·tral (lus′trəl), *adj.* **1.** of, pertaining to, or employed in the rite of the lustrum. **2.** occurring every five years; quinquennial. [< L *lūstrāl(is)*]

lus·trate (lus′trāt), *v.t.,* **-trat·ed, -trat·ing.** to purify ceremonially. [< L *lūstrāt(us)* purified, illumined, ptp. of *lūstrāre.* See LUSTER[1], -ATE[1]] —**lus·tra′tion,** *n.* —**lus·tra·tive** (lus′trə tiv), *adj.*

lus·tre[1] (lus′tər), *n., v.t., v.i.,* **-tred, -tring.** *Chiefly Brit.* luster[1]. —**lus′tre·less,** *adj.*
lus·tre[2] (lus′tər), *n. Chiefly Brit.* luster[2].
lus·trous (lus′trəs), *adj.* **1.** having luster; shining; luminous. **2.** brilliant; splendid. [LUST(E)R[1] + -OUS] —**lus′trous·ly,** *adv.* —**lus′trous·ness,** *n.* —**Syn. 1.** gleaming, radiant, glowing, shimmering.
lus·trum (lus′trəm), *n., pl.* **-trums, -tra** (-trə). **1.** Also, **luster;** *esp. Brit.,* **lustre.** a period of five years. **2.** *Rom. Hist.* a lustration or ceremonial purification of the people, performed every five years, after the taking of the census. [< L, akin to *lūstrāre* to illumine, purify; see LUSTER[1]]
lust·y (lus′tē), *adj.,* **lust·i·er, lust·i·est. 1.** full of or characterized by healthy vigor. **2.** hearty, as a meal or the like. [ME] —**lust′i·ly,** *adv.* —**lust′i·ness,** *n.* —**Syn. 1.** robust, sturdy, stout. —**Ant. 1.** feeble, weak.
lu·tan·ist (lo͞ot′ᵊnist), *n.* lutenist.
lute[1] (lo͞ot), *n., v.,* **lut·ed, lut·ing.** —*n.* **1.** a stringed musical instrument having a long, fretted neck and a hollow, typically pear-shaped body with a vaulted back. —*v.i.* **2.** to play a lute. —*v.t.* **3.** to perform (music) on a lute. [ME < MF, OF < OPr *laut* < Ar *al ʿūd,* lit., the wood]

Lute

lute[2] (lo͞ot), *n., v.,* **lut·ed, lut·ing.** —*n.* **1.** luting. —*v.t.* **2.** to seal or cement with luting. [late ME < ML *lut(um),* special use of L: mud, clay]
lu·te·al (lo͞o′tē əl), *adj.* of, pertaining to, or involving the corpus luteum. [< L *lūte(us)* kind of yellow (see LUTEOUS) + -AL[1]]
lu·te·ci·um (lo͞o tē′shē əm), *n. Chem.* lutetium.
lu·te·in (lo͞o′tē in), *n. Biochem.* **1.** Also called **xanthophyll.** a yellow-red, carotenoid alcohol, $C_{40}H_{56}O_2$, found in the petals of certain flowers, egg yolk, algae, and corpora lutea: used chiefly in the study of the carotenoids. **2.** a preparation of dried and powdered corpora lutea from hogs. [< L *lūte(um)* egg yolk (n. use of neut. of *lūteus* yellow; see LUTEOUS) + -IN[2]]
lu·te·nist (lo͞ot′ᵊnist), *n.* a person who plays the lute. Also, **lutanist.** [< ML *lūtānist(a)* < *lūtāna* lute; see -IST]
lu·te·o·lin (lo͞o′tē ə lin), *n. Chem.* a yellow coloring, $C_{15}H_{10}O_6$, used in dyeing silk and, formerly, in medicine. [< NL (*Reseda*) *Lūteol(a)* the plant from which it is obtained < fem. of L *lūteolus* yellowish (dim. of *lūteus* yellow; see LUTEOUS) + -IN[2]]
lu·te·o·tro·pin (lo͞o′tē ə trō′pin), *n.* **1.** *Biochem.* an anterior pituitary hormone that, in mammals, regulates the production of progesterone and stimulates lactation of the mammary glands. **2.** *Pharm.* a commercial form of this substance, used to induce lactation and in the treatment of uterine bleeding. Also, **lu·te·o·tro·phin** (lo͞o′tē ə trō′fin). Also called **lu′te·o·trop′ic hor′mone** (lo͞o′tē ə trop′ik, lo͞o′-), **prolactin.** [LUTE(OUS) + -O- + -TROPIC + -IN[2]]
lu·te·ous (lo͞o′tē əs), *adj.* (of yellow) having a light to medium greenish tinge. [< L *lūteus* golden-yellow, lit., *lūtum*-colored = *lūt(um)* yellowweed + *-eus* -EOUS]
Lu·te′tia Pa·ris·i·o′rum (lo͞o tē′shə pə riz′ē ôr′əm, -ōr′-), an ancient name of **Paris.**
lu·te·ti·um (lo͞o tē′shē əm), *n. Chem.* a rare-earth, trivalent, metallic element. *Symbol:* Lu; *at. wt.:* 174.97; *at. no.:* 71. Also, **lutecium.** [< L *Lūtēt(ia)* Paris + -IUM]
Luth., Lutheran.
Lu·ther (lo͞o′thər; *Ger.* lo͝ot′ər), *n.* **Mar·tin** (mär′tᵊn; *Ger.* mär′tēn), 1483–1546, German theologian and author: leader, in Germany, of the Protestant Reformation.
Lu·ther·an (lo͞o′thər ən), *adj.* **1.** of or pertaining to Luther, adhering to his doctrines, or belonging to one of the Protestant churches that bears his name. —*n.* **2.** a follower of Luther, or an adherent of his doctrines; a member of the Lutheran Church. —**Lu′ther·an·ism, Lu·ther·ism** (lo͞o′thə riz′əm), *n.*
Lu·thu·li (lo͞o to͞o′lē, -tyo͞o′-), *n.* **Albert John,** 1898–1967, African leader in the Republic of South Africa and former Zulu chief: Nobel peace prize 1960.
lut·ing (lo͞o′ting), *n.* any of various readily molded substances for sealing joints, cementing objects together, or waterproofing surfaces. [ME *lute* (< ML *lutāre* to coat, stop, seal; see LUTE[2]) + -ING[1]]
lut·ist (lo͞o′tist), *n.* **1.** a lute player; lutenist. **2.** a maker of lutes.
Lu·tu·am·i·an (lo͞o′to͞o am′ē ən), *n. pl.* **-ans,** (*esp. collectively*) **-an.** a member of a group of American Indian peoples including the Modoc and the Klamath.
Lüt·zen (lʏ′tsən), *n.* a town in S East Germany, WSW of Leipzig: site of Napoleon's victory over the Russians in 1813.
Lüt′zow-Holm Bay′ (lʏ′tsôf hōlm′), an inlet of the Indian Ocean on the coast of Antarctica.
Lu·wi·an (lo͞o′ē ən), *n.* **1.** an extinct ancient Anatolian language written in cuneiform. —*adj.* **2.** of or pertaining to Luwian. [*Luwi* nation of ancient Asia Minor + -AN]
lux (luks), *n., pl.* **lu·ces** (lo͞o′sēz). *Optics.* a unit of illumination, equivalent to .0929 foot-candle and equal to the illumination produced by luminous flux of one lumen falling perpendicularly on a surface one meter square. [< L: light]
Lux., Luxembourg.
lux·ate (luk′sāt), *v.t.,* **-at·ed, -at·ing.** to put out of joint; dislocate. [< L *luxāt(us)* put out of joint (ptp. of *luxāre*) = *lux(us)* dislocated (c. Gk *loxós* oblique) + *-ātus* -ATE[1]] —**lux·a′tion,** *n.*
luxe (lo͝oks, luks; *Fr.* lʏks), *n.* luxury; elegance; sumptuousness. Cf. **deluxe.** [< F < L *lux(us)* excess]
Lux·em·bourg (luk′səm bûrg′; *Fr.* lʏk sän bo͞oʀ′), *n.* **1.** a grand duchy between Germany, France, and Belgium. 357,000; 999 sq. mi. **2.** a city in and the capital of this grand duchy. 78,400. Also, **Luxemburg.**
Lux·em·burg (luk′səm bûrg′; *Ger.* lo͝ok′səm bo͝oʀkh′), *n.* **1. Ro·sa** (rō′zə; *Ger.* ʀō′zä), ("*Red Rosa*"), 1870–1919, German socialist agitator, born in Poland. **2.** Luxembourg.
Lux·or (luk′sôr), *n.* a town in Upper Egypt, in the S Arab Republic of Egypt, on the Nile: ruins of ancient Thebes. ab. 15,000.
lux·u·ri·ance (lug zho͝or′ē əns, luk sho͝or′-), *n.* the condition of being luxuriant; luxuriant growth or productiveness.
lux·u·ri·ant (lug zho͝or′ē ənt, luk sho͝or′-), *adj.* **1.** abundant in growth, as vegetation. **2.** producing abundantly, as soil; fertile. **3.** richly abundant, profuse, or superabundant. **4.** florid, as ornamentation. [< L *luxuriant-* (s. of *luxuriāns*), prp. of *luxuriāre* to be rank] —**lux·u′ri·ant·ly,** *adv.* —**Syn. 1.** lush. **2.** fruitful, prolific.
lux·u·ri·ate (lug zho͝or′ē āt′, luk sho͝or′-), *v.i.,* **-at·ed, -at·ing. 1.** to enjoy oneself without stint; indulge in luxury; revel. **2.** to grow fully or abundantly; thrive. **3.** to take great delight. [< L *luxuriāt(us),* ptp. of *luxuriāre*] —**lux·u′ri·a′tion,** *n.*
lux·u·ri·ous (lug zho͝or′ē əs, luk sho͝or′-), *adj.* **1.** characterized by luxury. **2.** given to pleasure, esp. of the senses; voluptuous. **3.** present or occurring in great abundance; luxuriant. [< L *luxuriōs(us)*] —**lux·u′ri·ous·ly,** *adv.* —**lux·u′ri·ous·ness,** *n.* —**Syn. 1.** rich, sumptuous. **2.** sensual, self-indulgent. —**Ant. 1.** squalid.
lux·u·ry (luk′shə rē, lug′zhə-), *n., pl.* **-ries,** *adj.* —*n.* **1.** something enjoyed as an addition to the ordinary necessities and comforts of life. **2.** free or habitual indulgence in the pleasures afforded by such things. **3.** a foolish or worthless form of self-indulgence: *the luxury of self-pity.* **4.** *Archaic.* lasciviousness; lechery. —*adj.* **5.** of, pertaining to, or affording luxury or luxuries: *a luxury hotel.* [ME *luxurie* < L *luxuria* rankness, luxuriance = *luxur-* (comb. form of *luxus* extravagance) + *-ia* -Y[3]]
Lu·zern (lo͝o tsern′), *n.* German name of **Lucerne.**
Lu·zon (lo͞o zon′; *Sp.* lo͞o sôn′), *n.* the chief island of the Philippines, in the N part of the group. 12,000,000 (est. 1960); 40,420 sq. mi. *Cap.:* Manila.
LV., lev; leva.
lv., leave; leaves.
Lw, *Chem.* lawrencium.
lwop, leave without pay.
Lwów (*Pol.* lvo͞of), *n.* a city in W Ukraine, in the SW Soviet Union in Europe: formerly in Poland. 487,000 (est. 1964). German, **Lemberg.** Russian, **Lvov** (lvôf). Ukranian, **Lviv** (lvēf).
lx, lux; luces.
-ly, 1. a suffix forming adverbs from adjectives: *gladly; gradually; secondly.* **2.** a suffix meaning "every," attached to certain nouns denoting units of time: *hourly; daily.* **3.** an adjective suffix meaning "-like": *saintly; manly.* [ME *-li, -lich(e),* OE *-līce* (*-līc* adj. suffix + *-e* adv. suffix); in the sense of -like: ME *-li, -ly, -lich(e),* OE *-līc* (c. G *-lich*), suffixal use of *(ge)līc* LIKE[1]] —**Syn. 3.** See **-ish**[1].
Ly·all·pur (lī′əl po͝or′), *n.* a city in NE Pakistan. 820,000.
ly·am-hound (lī′əm hound′), *n. Archaic.* a bloodhound. [late ME *lyame* leash (< MF *liem* << L *ligāmen* a band, tie = *ligā(re)* (to) tie + *-men* n. suffix) + HOUND[1]]
Lyau·tey (lyō tē′), *n.* **Louis Hu·bert Gon·zalve** (lwē ʏ beʀ′ gôn zalv′), 1854–1934, French marshal and colonial administrator.
ly·can·thrope (lī′kən thrōp′, lī kan′thrōp), *n.* **1.** a person affected with lycanthropy. **2.** a werewolf. [< Gk *lykánthrōp(os)* wolf-man = *lýk(os)* wolf + *ánthrōpos* man]
ly·can·thro·py (lī kan′thrə pē), *n.* **1.** insanity in which a person imagines himself to be a wolf or other wild beast. **2.** the assumption of the form of a wolf by a human being. [< Gk *lykanthrōpía*] —**ly·can·throp·ic** (lī′kən throp′ik), *adj.*
Ly·ca·on (lī kā′on, -ən), *n. Class. Myth.* an Arcadian king transformed into a wolf for presuming to test the divinity of Zeus.
Lyc·a·o·ni·a (lik′ā ō′nē ə, -ōn′yə, lī′kā-), *n.* an ancient country in S Asia Minor: later a Roman province.
ly·cée (lē sā′), *n., pl.* **-cées** (-sāz′; *Fr.* -sā′). a secondary school, esp. in France, maintained by the state. [< F < L *lycēum* LYCEUM]
ly·ce·um (lī sē′əm), *n.* **1.** *U.S.* an institution for popular education, providing discussions, lectures concerts, etc. **2.** a building for public meetings, lectures, etc. **3.** (*cap.*) a gymnasium where Aristotle taught, in ancient Athens. [< L < Gk *Lýkeion* place in Athens, so named from the neighboring temple of Apollo; n. use of neut. of *lýkeios,* epithet of Apollo, variously explained]
lych′ gate′ (lich). See **lich gate.**
lych·nis (lik′nis), *n.* any showy-flowered, caryophyllaceous plant of the genus *Lychnis.* Cf. **scarlet lychnis.** [< L < Gk *lychnís* red flower, akin to *lýchnos* lamp]
Ly·ci·a (lish′ē ə), *n.* an ancient country in SW Asia Minor: later a Roman province.
Ly·ci·an (lish′ē ən), *adj.* **1.** of or pertaining to Lycia. —*n.* **2.** an inhabitant of Lycia. **3.** an Anatolian language of Lycia, written in a form of the Greek alphabet.
ly·co·po·di·um (lī′kə pō′dē əm), *n.* any erect or creeping, mosslike, evergreen plant of the genus *Lycopodium,* as the club moss or ground pine. Also, **ly·co·pod** (lī′kə pod′). [< NL < Gk *lýk(os)* wolf + *-podion* -PODIUM]
Ly·cur·gus (lī kûr′gəs), *n.* fl. 9th century B.C., Spartan lawgiver.
lydd·ite (lid′īt), *n. Chem.* a high explosive consisting chiefly of picric acid. [named after *Lydd,* borough in SE England near the site where it was first tested; see -ITE[1]]
Lyd·gate (lid′gāt′, -git), *n.* **John,** c1370–1451?, English monk, poet, and translator.
Lyd·i·a (lid′ē ə), *n.* an ancient kingdom in W Asia Minor.
Lyd·i·an (lid′ē ən), *adj.* **1.** of or pertaining to Lydia. —*n.* **2.** an inhabitant of Lydia. **3.** an Anatolian language of Lydia, written in a modified Greek alphabet.
lye (lī), *n. Chem.* **1.** a highly concentrated, aqueous solution of potassium hydroxide or sodium hydroxide. **2.** any solution resulting from leaching, percolation, or the like. [ME *lie, ley,* OE *lēag;* c. D *loog,* G *Lauge* lye, Icel *laug* warm bath. See LAVE[1]]
Ly·ell (lī′əl), *n.* **Sir Charles,** 1797–1875, English geologist.
ly·ing[1] (lī′ing), *n.* **1.** the telling of lies. —*adj.* **2.** deliberately untruthful: *a lying report.* [ME] —**ly′ing·ly,** *adv.*
ly·ing[2] (lī′ing), *v.* ppr. of **lie**[2]. —**ly′ing·ly,** *adv.*
ly·ing-in (lī′ing in′), *n., pl.* **lyings-in, lying-ins,** *adj.*

—*n.* **1.** the state of being in childbed; confinement. —*adj.* **2.** pertaining to or providing facilities for childbirth. [late ME *lyynge in*]

Lyl·y (lil′ē), *n.* **John,** 1554?–1606, English writer of romances and plays.

lymph (limf), *n.* **1.** *Anat., Physiol.* a yellowish, coagulable fluid, containing white blood cells in a plasmalike liquid which is derived from the body tissues and conveyed to the blood stream by the lymphatic vessels. **2.** *Archaic.* the sap of a plant. **3.** *Archaic.* a stream or spring of clear, pure water. [< L *lymph(a)* water, earlier **limpa* (see LIMPID); pseudo-Gk form, by assoc. with *nympha* < Gk *nýmphē* NYMPH]

lymph-, var. of **lympho-** before a vowel: *lymphoma.*

lym·phad·e·ni·tis (lim fad′ᵊnī′tis, lim′fə dᵊnī′-), *n.* *Pathol.* inflammation of a lymphatic gland. [LYMPH- + ADEN- + -ITIS]

lym·phat·ic (lim fat′ik), *adj.* **1.** pertaining to, containing, or conveying lymph. **2.** (of persons) having the characteristics, as flabbiness or sluggishness, formerly believed to be due to an excess of lymph in the system. —*n.* **3.** a lymphatic vessel. [< NL *lymphāticus(us)*] —**lym·phat′i·cal·ly,** *adv.*

lymph′ cell′, a lymphocyte.

lymph′ gland′, any of the glandlike masses of tissue in the lymphatic vessels containing cells that become lymphocytes. Also called **lymph′ node′, lymphat′ic gland′.**

lympho-, a combining form of **lymph:** *lymphocyte.* Also, *esp. before a vowel,* **lymph-.**

lym·pho·blast (lim′fə blast′), *n.* *Anat.* an immature lymphocyte. —**lym′pho·blas′tic,** *adj.*

lym·pho·cyte (lim′fə sīt′), *n.* *Anat.* a leukocyte, found in lymphoid tissue, having a large, spherical nucleus surrounded by a thin layer of nongranular cytoplasm. —**lym·pho·cyt·ic** (lim′fə sit′ik), *adj.*

lym·pho·cy·to·sis (lim′fə sī tō′sis), *n.* *Pathol.* an abnormal increase in the number of lymphocytes in the blood. —**lym·pho·cy·tot·ic** (lim′fō sī tot′ik), *adj.*

lym·pho·gran·u·lo·ma (lim′fə gran′yə lō′mə), *n., pl.* **-mas, -ma·ta** (-mə tə). *Pathol.* **1.** any of certain diseases characterized by granulomatous lesions of lymph nodes. **2.** *Obs.* See **Hodgkin's disease.**

lym·phoid (lim′foid), *adj.* **1.** of, pertaining to, or resembling lymph. **2.** of or pertaining to the tissue **(lym′phoid tis′sue)** that occurs esp. in the lymph glands, thymus, tonsils, and spleen and produces lymphocytes.

lym·pho·ma (lim fō′mə), *n.* *Pathol.* a tumor arising from any of the cellular elements of lymph nodes. [< NL] —**lym·pho′ma·toid′,** *adj.*

lyn·ce·an (lin sē′ən), *adj.* **1.** of or pertaining to a lynx; lynxlike. **2.** lynx-eyed; sharp-sighted. [< L *lyncē(us)* sharp-sighted (< *lync-,* s. of *lynx* LYNX) + -AN]

lynch (linch), *v.t.* to hang or otherwise kill (a person) by mob action and without legal authority, esp. for some real or presumed offense. [v. use of *lynch* in LYNCH LAW] —**lynch′er,** *n.* —**Syn.** See **hang.**

Lynch·burg (linch′bûrg), *n.* a city in central Virginia. 54,083 (1970).

lynch·ing (lin′ching), *n.* the act or an instance of a mob's killing of a person, esp. by hanging.

lynch′ law′, the administration of summary punishment, esp. death, by lynching. [orig. *Lynch's law;* perhaps named after Captain William *Lynch* (1742–1820) of Virginia]

Ly·nen (lē′nen), *n.* **Fe·o·dor** (fā ô′dôr), born 1911, German biochemist: Nobel prize in medicine 1964.

Lynn (lin), *n.* a seaport in E Massachusetts, on Massachusetts Bay. 90,294 (1970).

Lyn·wood (lin′wo͝od′), *n.* a city in SW California. 43,353 (1970).

lynx (lingks), *n., pl.* **lynx·es,** (*esp. collectively*) **lynx.** any of several wildcats of the genus *Lynx,* having long limbs, a short tail, and usually tufted ears, esp. *L. canadensis* **(Canada lynx),** of Canada and the northern U.S., having grayish-brown fur marked with white. [ME < L < Gk *lýnx*]

Canada lynx, *Lynx canadensis* (Length to 3½ ft.)

lynx-eyed (lingks′īd′), *adj.* sharp-sighted.

Ly·on (lī′ən *for 1;* lyôN *for 2*), *n.* **1. Mary,** 1797–1849, U.S. pioneer in providing advanced education for women. **2.** French name of **Lyons.**

Ly·on·nais (lē ô ne′), *n.* a former province in E France. Also, **Ly·o·nais′.** See map at **Savoy.**

ly·on·naise (lī′ə nāz′; *Fr.* lē ô nez′), *adj.* (of food, esp. fried potatoes) cooked with pieces of onion. [< F (*à la*) *Lyonnaise* (fem. adj.) in the manner of *Lyons*]

Ly·ons (lī′ənz), *n.* a city in E France at the confluence of the Rhone and Saône rivers. 535,784 (1962). French, **Lyon.**

ly·o·phil·ic (lī′ə fil′ik), *adj.* *Physical Chem.* noting a colloid whose particles have a strong affinity for the liquid in which they are dispersed. [*lyo-* (comb. form repr. Gk *lýein* to loose, dissolve, set free; see -o-) + -PHILIC]

ly·oph·i·lize (lī of′ə līz′), *v.t.,* **-lized, -liz·ing.** *Biochem.* (of tissue, blood, serum, or the like) to dry by freezing in a high vacuum. [LYOPHIL(IC) + -IZE] —**ly·oph′i·li·za′tion,** *n.*

ly·o·pho·bic (lī′ə fō′bik, -fob′ik), *adj.* *Physical Chem.* noting a colloid whose particles have little or no affinity for the liquid in which they are dispersed. [*lyo-* (see LYOPHILIC) + -PHOBIC]

Ly·ra (lī′rə), *n., gen.* **-rae** (-rē). *Astron.* the Lyre, a northern constellation between Cygnus and Hercules, containing the bright star Vega.

Lyrate leaf

ly·rate (lī′rāt, -rit), *adj.* **1.** *Bot.* (of a pinnate leaf) divided transversely into several lobes, the smallest at the base. **2.** *Zool.* lyre-shaped, as the tail of certain birds. Also, **ly′rat·ed.** [< NL *lyrāt(us)*] —**ly′rate·ly,** *adv.*

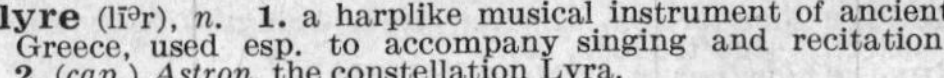

lyre (līᵊr), *n.* **1.** a harplike musical instrument of ancient Greece, used esp. to accompany singing and recitation. **2.** (*cap.*) *Astron.* the constellation Lyra. [ME *lire* < L *lyra* < Gk]

Lyre

lyre·bird (līᵊr′bûrd′), *n.* an Australian passerine bird of the genus *Menura,* the male of which has a long tail that is lyrate when spread.

lyr·ic (lir′ik), *adj.* Also, **lyr′i·cal. 1.** (of a poem) having the form and general effect of a song, esp. one expressing the poet's feelings. **2.** pertaining to or writing such poems. **3.** expressing or characterized by strong, spontaneous feeling. **4.** pertaining to, rendered by, or employing singing. **5.** pertaining, adapted, or sung to the lyre. **6.** (of a voice) relatively light of volume and modest in range. —*n.* **7.** a lyric poem. **8.** Often, **lyrics.** the words of a song. [< L *lyric(us)* < Gk *lyrikós.* See LYRE, -IC] —**lyr′i·cal·ly,** *adv.* —**lyr′i·cal·ness,** *n.*

lyr·i·cise (lir′i sīz′), *v.i., v.t.,* **-cised, -cis·ing.** *Chiefly Brit.* lyricize. —**lyr′i·ci·sa′tion,** *n.*

Lyrebird, *Menura novaehollandiae* (Length 3 ft; tail feathers 2 ft.)

lyr·i·cism (lir′i siz′əm), *n.* **1.** lyric character or style, as in poetry. **2.** lyric outpouring of feeling; enthusiasm. Also, **lyr·ism** (lir′is əm).

lyr·i·cist (lir′i sist), *n.* **1.** a person who writes the words for songs. **2.** a lyric poet.

lyr·i·cize (lir′i sīz′), *v.,* **-cized, -ciz·ing.** —*v.i.* **1.** to write lyrics. **2.** to sing the lyrics of a song. **3.** to write lyrically or in a lyric style. —*v.t.* **4.** to put into lyric form; treat in a lyric style. Also, *esp. Brit.,* **lyricise.** —**lyr′i·ci·za′tion,** *n.*

lyr·ist (līᵊr′ist *for 1;* lir′ist *for 2*), *n.* **1.** a person who plays the lyre. **2.** a lyric poet. [< L *lyrist(es)* < Gk. See LYRE, -IST]

Lys (lēs), *n.* a river in W Europe, in N France and W Belgium, flowing NE into the Scheldt River. 120 mi. long.

lys-, a learned borrowing from Greek meaning "loosening," "decomposition," used in the formation of compound words: *lysin.* Also, **lyso-.** Cf. **-lyse, -lysis, -lyte.** [< Gk]

Ly·san·der (lī san′dər), *n.* died 395 B.C., Spartan naval commander and statesman.

lyse (līs), *v.,* **lysed, lys·ing.** *Immunol., Biochem.* —*v.t.* **1.** to cause dissolution or destruction of cells by lysins. —*v.i.* **2.** to undergo lysis. [back formation from LYSIN OR LYSIS]

-lyse, *esp. Brit.,* var. of **-lyze.**

Ly·sen·ko (li seng′kō; *Russ.* li sen′ko), *n.* **Tro·fim De·ni·so·vich** (tro fēm′ de nē′so vich), 1898–1976, Russian biologist and agronomist.

Ly·sen·ko·ism (li seng′kō iz′əm), *n.* a genetic doctrine that heredity is not based on chromosomes and genes and that acquired characters are inherited. [named after T. D. LYSENKO; see -ISM]

ly·ser′gic ac′id (li sûr′jik, lī-), *Chem.* a crystalline solid, $C_{15}H_{15}N_2COOH$, obtained from ergot or synthesized: used in the synthesis of LSD. [LYS- + ERG(OT) + -IC]

lyser′gic ac′id di·eth′yl·a·mide (dī eth′əl ə mīd, -mid), *Pharm.* See **LSD** (def. 1).

Lys·i·as (lis′ē əs), *n.* c450–c380 B.C., Athenian orator.

Ly·sim·a·chus (lī sim′ə kəs), *n.* 361?–281 B.C., Macedonian general: king of Thrace 306–281.

ly·sin (lī′sin), *n.* *Immunol., Biochem.* an antibody causing the disintegration of erythrocytes or bacterial cells.

ly·sine (lī′sēn, -sin), *n.* *Biochem.* a basic amino acid, $H_2N(CH_2)_4CH(NH_2)COOH$, essential in the nutrition of man and animals.

Ly·sip·pus (lī sip′əs), *n.* fl. c360–c320 B.C., Greek sculptor

ly·sis (lī′sis), *n.* **1.** *Immunol., Biochem.* the dissolution or destruction of cells by lysins. **2.** *Med.* the gradual recession of a disease. [< NL < Gk: a loosening = *lý(ein)* (to) loose, release + *-sis* -SIS]

-lysis, an element of Greek origin, occurring esp. in scientific terms, denoting a breaking down, loosening, decomposition, etc.: *analysis; electrolysis; paralysis.* [< Gk; see LYSIS]

lyso-, var. of **lys-.**

ly·so·some (lī′sə sōm′) *n.* the part of a cell that contains lysins.

ly·so·zyme (lī′sə zīm′), *n.* *Biochem.* a bacteriolytic enzyme that serves as an antiseptic, found in tears, leukocytes, mucus, egg albumin, and certain plants. [LYSO- + (EN)ZYME]

-lyte[1], an element denoting something subjected to a certain process (indicated by a noun ending in *-lysis*): *electrolyte.* [< Gk *lyt(ós)* loosable, soluble, verbid of *lýein* to loose, dissolve; c. L *luere* to loose]

-lyte[2], var. of **-lite.**

lyth·ra·ceous (lith rā′shəs, lī thrā′-), *adj.* belonging to the *Lythraceae,* or loosestrife family of plants. [< NL *Lythr(um)* plant genus (< Gk *lýthron* gore, bloody gore) + -ACEOUS]

lyt·ic (lit′ik), *adj.* of, noting, or pertaining to lysis or a lysin. [< Gk *lytik(ós)* able to loosen]

-lytic, a termination of adjectives corresponding to nouns in **-lysis:** *analytic; paralytic.* [see LYTIC]

lyt·ta (lit′ə), *n., pl.* **lyt·tas, lyt·tae** (lit′ē). a long, wormlike cartilage in the tongue of the dog and other carnivorous animals. [< NL < Gk, Attic var. of *lýssa* rage, rabies; so named because cartilage was thought to cause rabies]

Lyt·ton (lit′ᵊn), *n.* **1. Edward George Earle Lytton Bulwer-, 1st Baron Lytton,** 1803–73, English novelist, dramatist, and politician. **2.** his son, **Edward Robert Bulwer-Lytton, 1st Earl Lytton** (pen name: *Owen Meredith*), 1831–91, English statesman and poet.

Lyu·blin (lyo͞o′blin), *n.* Russian name of **Lublin.**

-lyze, a word element used to form verbs from nouns with stems in **-lysis:** *catalyze.* Also, *esp. Brit.,* **-lyse.** [LY(SIS) + -(I)ZE]

M

DEVELOPMENT OF MAJUSCULE								
NORTH SEMITIC	GREEK		ETR.	LATIN		MODERN		
						GOTHIC	ITALIC	ROMAN
𐤌	𐌌	M	𐌌	M	M	𝔐	*M*	M

DEVELOPMENT OF MINUSCULE					
ROMAN CURSIVE	ROMAN UNCIAL	CAROL. MIN.	MODERN		
			GOTHIC	ITALIC	ROMAN
∼	m	m	𝔪	*m*	m

The thirteenth letter of the English alphabet developed from North Semitic *mem,* its form changing little through Greek *mu* (μ) to the modern capital and minuscule.

M, m (em), *n., pl.* **M's** or **Ms, m's** or **ms. 1.** the 13th letter of the English alphabet, a consonant. **2.** any spoken sound represented by the letter *M* or *m,* as in *my, summer,* or *him.* **3.** a written or printed representation of the letter *M* or *m.* **4.** a device, as a printer's type, for reproducing the letter *M* or *m.*

M, 1. mach. **2.** Medieval. **3.** Middle.

M, 1. the 13th in order or in a series, or, when *I* is omitted, the 12th. **2.** (*sometimes l.c.*) the Roman numeral for 1000. Cf. **Roman numerals. 3.** *Print.* em.

m, 1. medieval. **2.** medium. **3.** *Metric System.* meter; meters. **4.** middle.

M-, *U.S. Mil.* (used to designate the production model of military equipment, as the rifle M-1.)

m-, meta-.

M'-, var. of **Mac-.**

M., 1. Majesty. **2.** Manitoba. **3.** markka; markkaa. **4.** Marquis. **5.** Medicine. **6.** Medium. **7.** Meridian. **8.** noon. [< L *meridies*] **9.** Monday. **10.** *pl.* **MM.** Monsieur. **11.** mountain.

m., 1. male. **2.** (in Germany) mark; marks. **3.** married. **4.** masculine. **5.** *Mech.* mass. **6.** *Music.* measure. **7.** medium. **8.** noon. [< L *meridies*] **9.** meter. **10.** mile. **11.** minim. **12.** minute. **13.** (in prescriptions) mix. [< L *misce*] **14.** modification of. **15.** modulus. **16.** month. **17.** morning.

M-1 (em′wun′), *n., pl.* **M-1's.** a semiautomatic, clip-fed, .30-caliber rifle: the standard U.S. rifle in World War II and in the Korean War. Also called **Garand rifle.**

M-16 (em′siks′tēn′), *n., pl.* **M-16's.** a lightweight, fully automatic rifle shooting a small-caliber bullet at extremely high velocity: the standard U.S. rifle in the Vietnam War.

ma (mä), *n. Informal.* mother. [shortened var. of MAMMA[1]]

MA, 1. Massachusetts (approved esp. for use with zip code). **2.** *Psychol.* mental age.

mA, milliampere; milliamperes. Also, **ma**

mÅ, milliangstrom; milliangstroms.

M.A., 1. See **Master of Arts.** [< L *Magister Artium*] **2.** Military Academy.

ma'am (mam, mäm; *unstressed* məm), *n.* **1.** *Informal.* madam. **2.** (in Britain) a term used in addressing the Queen or a royal princess.

Maas (mäs), *n.* Dutch name of the **Meuse.**

Maas·tricht (mäs′trɪкнt), *n.* a city in the SE Netherlands, on the Maas River. 90,202 (est. 1960). Also, **Maestricht.**

Mab (mab), *n.* See **Queen Mab.**

mac (mak), *n. Brit. Informal.* mackintosh. [shortened form]

Mac-, a prefix found in many family names of Irish or Scots Gaelic origin: *MacDonald.* Also, **Mc-, Mᶜ-, M'-.** [< Gael *mac* name prefix meaning son of, OIr *macc* son; c. Welsh *mab,* OWelsh *map,* Cornish *mab*]

Mac., Maccabees.

ma·ca·bre (mə kä′brə, -käb′, -kä′bər), *adj.* **1.** gruesome; horrible; grim; ghastly. **2.** of, pertaining to, dealing with, or representing death. [< F; r. late ME (*daunce of*) *Machabree* < MF (*danse*) *Macabré* for *Maccabé* < LL *Maccabaeus* MACCABAEUS; the "dance of death," said to be so called after the medieval practice of praying for the dead before releasing them from their sins, as advocated in a passage so interpreted in the book of Maccabees]

mac·ad·am (mə kad′əm), *n.* **1.** a macadamized road or pavement. **2.** the broken stone used in making such a road. [named after J. L. *McAdam* (1756–1836), Scottish inventor]

mac·a·da·mi·a (mak′ə dā′mē ə), *n.* **1.** any Australian tree of the genus *Macadamia,* esp. *M. ternifolia,* having whorled leaves and white flowers. **2.** Also called **macada′mia nut′.** the edible, hard-shelled seed of this tree. [< NL, named after J. *Macadam* (d. 1865), Australian chemist; see -IA]

mac·ad·am·ise (mə kad′ə mīz′), *v.t.,* **-ised, -is·ing.** *Chiefly Brit.* macadamize. —**mac·ad′am·i·sa′tion,** *n.*

mac·ad·am·ize (mə kad′ə mīz′), *v.t.,* **-ized, -iz·ing.** to pave by laying and compacting successive layers of broken stone. —**mac·ad′am·i·za′tion,** *n.*

Ma·cao (mə kou′), *n.* **1.** a Portuguese overseas province in S China, in the delta of the Chu-Kiang River and including two small adjacent islands. 174,000 (est. 1964); 6 sq. mi. **2.** the seaport and capital of this territory. 161,252 (1960). Portuguese, **Macáu.**

Ma·ca·pa·gal (mä′kä pä gäl′), *n.* **Di·os·da·do** (dē′ôs dä′dô), born 1910, Philippine statesman: president 1961–1965.

ma·caque (mə käk′), *n.* any monkey of the genus *Macaca,* chiefly found in Asia and the East Indies, characterized by cheek pouches. [< F < Pg *macaco* monkey, of Afr orig.]

Macaque, *Macaca philippinensis* (Total length 5½ ft.; tail 2 ft.)

mac·a·ro·ni (mak′ə rō′nē), *n., pl.* **-nis, -nies** for 2. **1.** a wheat pasta in the form of dried, hollow tubes. **2.** an English dandy of the 18th century who affected Continental mannerisms. [earlier *maccaroni* < dial. It, pl. of *maccarone* (It *maccherone*). See MACAROON]

mac·a·ron·ic (mak′ə ron′ik), *adj.* **1.** composed of or characterized by Latin words mixed with vernacular words or non-Latin words terminated in Latin endings. **2.** composed of a mixture of languages. **3.** mixed; jumbled. —*n.* **4. macaronics,** macaronic language. **5.** a macaronic verse or composition. [< ML *macarōnic*(*us*) < dial. It *maccarone* MACARONI + L *-icus* -IC] —**mac′a·ron′i·cal·ly,** *adv.*

mac·a·roon (mak′ə ro͞on′), *n.* a cooky made of egg whites, sugar, almond paste or coconut, and sometimes, flour. [< MF *macaron* < dial. It *maccarone* cake or biscuit made of ground almonds; see MACARONI]

Mac·Ar·thur (mək är′thər, mə kär′-), *n.* **Douglas,** 1880–1964, U.S. general: commander of U.S. Armed Forces in the Far East 1941–51.

Ma·cas·sar (mə kas′ər), *n.* **1.** a seaport on SW Celebes, in central Indonesia. 384,159 (1961). **2. Strait of,** a strait between Borneo and Celebes. Dutch, **Makassar.**

Macas′sar oil′, 1. an oil derived from materials said to be obtained from Macassar, formerly used as a hairdressing. **2.** a similar oil or preparation for the hair.

Ma·cáu (mə kou′), *n.* Portuguese name of **Macao.**

Ma·cau·lay (mə kô′lē), *n.* **1. Dame Rose,** c1885–1958, English novelist. **2. Thomas Bab·ing·ton** (bab′ing tən), **1st Baron,** 1800–59, English historian, author, and statesman.

ma·caw (mə kô′), *n.* any of various large, long-tailed parrots, chiefly of the genus *Ara,* of tropical and subtropical America, noted for their brilliant plumage. [< Pg *macao* parrot, perh. < Tupi-Guarani *macaũ*(*ba*) macaw palm (< Arawak *maco*(*ya*) + Tupi-Guarani *ũba* tree); possibly brought into Brazilian Indian tongues by African slaves]

Macaw, *Ara macao* (Length 3 ft.)

Mac·beth (mək beth′, mak-), *n.* died 1057, king of Scotland 1040–57.

Macc., Maccabees.

Mac·ca·bae·us (mak′ə bē′əs), *n.* **Judas** or **Je·hu·dah** (jə ho͞o′də), ("*the Hammer*"), died 160 B.C., Judean patriot: military leader 166–160 (son of Mattathias).

Mac·ca·be·an (mak′ə bē′ən), *adj.* of or pertaining to the Maccabees or Judas Maccabaeus.

Mac·ca·bees (mak′ə bēz′), *n.* **1.** (*construed as pl.*) the members of the Hasmonean family of Jewish leaders, reigning in Judea from 167? to 137 B.C., esp. Judas Maccabaeus and his brothers, who defeated the Syrians under Antiochus IV in 165? and rededicated the Temple in Jerusalem. **2.** (*construed as sing.*) either of two books of the Apocrypha, I Maccabees or II Maccabees, that contain the history of the Maccabees.

mac·ca·boy (mak′ə boi′), *n.* a kind of snuff, usually rose-scented. Also, **mac′co·boy′.** [earlier *Maca*(*u*)*ba*(*o*) < F *macouba* a kind of aromatic tobacco; special use of *Macouba* place in northern Martinique, where made]

Mac·don·ald (mək don′əld), *n.* **Sir John Alexander,** 1815–91, Canadian statesman, born in Scotland; 1st prime minister 1867–73, 1878–91.

Mac·Don·ald (mək don′əld), *n.* **(James) Ramsay,** 1866–1937, British statesman and labor leader: prime minister 1924, 1929–35.

Mac·Don·ough (mək don′ə), *n.* **Thomas,** 1783–1825, U.S. naval officer: defeated British on Lake Champlain 1814.

Mac·Dow·ell (mək dou′əl), *n.* **Edward (Alexander),** 1861–1908, U.S. composer and pianist.

mace[1] (mās), *n.* **1.** a clublike weapon of war, often with a flanged or spiked metal head, used chiefly in the Middle Ages. **2.** a ceremonial staff carried before or by certain officials as a symbol of office. **3.** macebearer. [ME < OF (cf. F *masse*) large mallet < VL **mattea;* akin to L *matteola* kind of mallet, Skt *matya* harrow]

mace[2] (mās), *n.* a spice ground from the layer between a nutmeg shell and its outer husk. [ME, back formation from *macis* (taken as pl.) < MF < L *maccis* a spice]

Mace (mās), *n., v.,* **Maced, Mac·ing.** —*n.* **1.** Also called **Chemical Mace.** a nonlethal spray containing purified tear gas and chemical solvents which temporarily incapacitate a person by causing eye and skin irritations: used esp. as a means of subduing rioters. —*v.t.* **2.** (*sometimes l.c.*) to attack with Chemical Mace. [after MACE, a trademark]

mace·bear·er (mās′bâr′ər), *n.* an official, as of a city, who carries the ceremonial mace before dignitaries.

Maced., Macedonia.

mac·é·doine (mas′i dwän′; *Fr.* ma sā dwan′), *n., pl.* **mac·é·doines** (mas′i dwänz′; *Fr.* ma sā dwan′). **1.** a mixture of vegetables or fruits, often served as a salad. **2.** a medley. [< F, special use of *Macédoine,* MACEDONIA, prob. an allusion to the racial variety of the region]

Mac·e·do·ni·a (mas′i dō′nē ə, -dōn′yə), *n.* **1.** Also, **Mac·e·don** (mas′i don′). an ancient country in the Balkan Peninsula, N of ancient Greece. **2.** a region in S Europe, including parts of Greece, Bulgaria, and Yugoslavia.

Mac·e·do·ni·an (mas′i dō′nē ən), *n.* **1.** a Slavic language of modern Macedonia. **2.** an extinct language of ancient Macedonia, an Indo-European language of uncertain relationship within the Indo-European language family. —*adj.* **3.** of, pertaining to, or characteristic of Macedonia, its inhabitants, or their language.

Ma·cei·ó (mä′sä ô′), *n.* a seaport in and the capital of Alagoas, in E Brazil. 161,863 (1960).

mac·er (ma′sər), *n.* **1.** macebearer. **2.** (in Scotland) an officer who attends the highest civil court and carries out its orders. [ME < AF, c. MF *massier*]

mac·er·ate (mas′ə rāt′), *v.*, **-at·ed, -at·ing.** —*v.t.* **1.** to soften or separate (a substance) into parts by steeping in a liquid. **2.** to soften or decompose (food) by the action of a solvent. **3.** to cause to grow thin. —*v.i.* **4.** to undergo maceration. [< L *mācerāt(us)* made soft, weakened, steeped (ptp. of *mācerāre*) = *māc-* make soft or tender + *-er-* freq. suffix + *-ātus* -ATE[1]] —**mac′er·at′er, mac′er·a′tor,** *n.* —**mac′er·a′tive,** *adj.* —**mac′er·a′tion,** *n.*

mach (mäk), *n.* a number indicating the ratio of the speed of an object to the speed of sound in the medium through which the object is moving. *Abbr.:* M Also, **Mach.** Also called **mach number, Mach number.** [named after E. MACH]

Mach (mäk, mak; *Ger.* mäKH), *n.* **Ernst** (ernst), 1838–1916, Austrian physicist, psychologist, and philosopher.

mach., **1.** machine. **2.** machinery. **3.** machinist.

Ma·chaut (mA shō′), *n.* **Guil·laume de** (gē yōm′ də), 1300–77, French poet and composer. Also, **Ma·chault′.**

Mach·en (mak′ən), *n.* **Arthur,** 1863–1947, Welsh novelist and essayist.

ma chère (mA sheR′), *French.* (in addressing a woman or girl) my dear. Cf. **mon cher.**

ma·chet·e (mə shet′ē, -chet′ē; *Sp.* mä che′te), *n., pl.* **-chet·es** (-shet′ēz, -chet′ēz; *Sp.* -che′tes). a large heavy knife used as a tool in cutting sugar cane and clearing underbrush or as a weapon. [< Sp = *mach(o)* mallet (see MACE[1]) + *-ete* n. suffix]

Machete

Mach·i·a·vel·li (mak′ē ə vel′ē; *It.* mä′kyä vel′lē), *n.* **Nic·co·lò di Ber·nar·do** (nēk′kô lô′ dē beR näR′dô), 1469–1527, Italian statesman, philosopher, and author.

Mach·i·a·vel·li·an (mak′ē ə vel′ē ən), *adj.* **1.** of, like, or befitting Machiavelli. **2.** being or acting in accordance with the principles of government analyzed in Machiavelli's treatise, *The Prince* (1513), in which political expediency is placed above morality. **3.** characterized by unscrupulous cunning, deception, or dishonesty. —*n.* **4.** a follower of the principles analyzed or described in *The Prince.* Also, **Mach′i·a·vel′i·an.** —**Mach′i·a·vel′li·an·ism, Mach′i·a·vel′lism,** *n.* —**Mach′i·a·vel′li·an·ly,** *adv.*

ma·chic·o·late (mə chik′ə lāt′), *v.t.*, **-lat·ed, -lat·ing.** to provide with machicolations. [< ML *machico(l)lāt(us)* furnished with machicolations, ptp. of *machico(l)lāre,* Latinization of MF *machecoller* = *mache-* chew, crush (OF *ma(s)cher* < LL *masticāre;* see MASTICATE) + *coller* to flow, run < L *cōlāre* to filter]

ma·chic·o·la·tion (mə chik′ə lā′shən), *n.* *Archit.* **1.** an opening in the floor of a projecting gallery or parapet through which missiles, molten lead, etc., might be cast upon an enemy. **2.** a projecting gallery or parapet with such openings.

mach·i·nate (mak′ə nāt′), *v.*, **-nat·ed, -nat·ing.** to contrive or devise, esp. artfully or with evil purpose. [< L *māchināt(us)* skillfully contrived, adjusted, ptp. of *māchinārī*] —**mach′i·na′tor,** *n.*

mach·i·na·tion (mak′ə nā′shən), *n.* **1.** the act, an instance, or the process of machinating or plotting. **2.** Usually, **machinations.** crafty schemes; plots; intrigues. [< L *māchinātiōn-* (s. of *māchinātiō*)] —**Syn. 2.** stratagem.

ma·chine (mə shēn′), *n., v.*, **-chined, -chin·ing.** —*n.* **1.** an apparatus consisting of interrelated parts with separate functions, used in the performance of some kind of work: *a sewing machine.* **2.** a mechanical apparatus or contrivance; a mechanism. **3.** something operated by a mechanical apparatus, as an automobile or airplane. **4.** *Mech.* **a.** a device that transmits or modifies force or motion. **b.** Also called **simple machine.** any of six or more elementary mechanisms, as the lever, wheel and axle, pulley, screw, wedge, and inclined plane. **c.** a combination of simple machines. **5.** any complex agency or operating system. **6.** an organized group of persons that conducts or controls the activities of a political party or other organization. **7.** a person or thing that acts in a mechanical or automatic manner. —*v.t.* **8.** to make, prepare, or finish with a machine. [< F < L *māchina* < Doric Gk *māchanā́* pulley, akin to *mâchos* contrivance] —**ma·chine′less,** *adj.* —**ma·chine′-like′,** *adj.*

machine′ bolt′, a threaded fastener, used with a nut for connecting metal parts, having a thread diameter of ¼ inch or more and a square or hexagonal head for tightening by a wrench. Cf. **machine screw.** See illus. at **bolt**[1].

machine′ gun′, a small arm operated by a mechanism, able to deliver a rapid and continuous fire of bullets as long as the trigger is pressed.

ma·chine-gun (mə shēn′gun′), *v.t.*, **-gunned, -gun·ning.** to shoot at with a machine gun. —**ma·chine′ gun′ner.**

machine′ lan′guage, *Computer Technol.* the coding system for letters, numbers, and instructions that assigns actual storage locations and requires no translation by the computer for operation.

machine′ pis′tol, a fully automatic pistol. Also called **burp gun.**

machine′ ri′fle. See **automatic rifle.**

ma·chin·er·y (mə shē′nə rē), *n., pl.* **-er·ies. 1.** an assemblage of machines or mechanical apparatuses. **2.** the parts of a machine, collectively. **3.** the group or aggregate of literary devices, esp. those of supernatural agency in an epic poem. **4.** any system by which action, order, etc., is maintained: *the machinery of government.*

machine′ screw′, a threaded fastener, either used with a nut or driven into a tapped hole, usually having a diameter of about ¼ inch or less and a slotted head for tightening by a screwdriver. Cf. **machine bolt.**

machine′ shop′, a shop in which metal and other substances are cut, shaped, etc., by machine tools.

machine′ tool′, a power-operated machine, as a lathe, used for general cutting and shaping of metal. —**ma·chine′-tooled′,** *adj.*

machine′ transla′tion, *Computer Technol.* automatic translation or assistance in translation from one code or language into another by a computer or similar equipment.

ma·chine-wash (mə shēn′wosh, -wôsh), *v.t., v.i.* to launder by washing machine rather than by hand. —**ma·chine′-wash′a·ble,** *adj.*

machine′ word′, *Computer Technol.* a standard unit consisting of a fixed number of bits treated as a single entity by a computer.

ma·chin·ist (mə shē′nist), *n.* **1.** a person who operates machinery, esp. a highly trained, skilled operator of machine tools. **2.** a person who makes and repairs machines. **3.** *U.S. Navy.* a warrant officer whose duty is to assist the engineering officer in the engine room.

ma·chis·mo (mä chiz′mō), *n.* (in Hispanic cultures) maleness or virility; male domination. [< Sp *macho* male, he-man]

Mach·me·ter (mäk′mē′tər, mak′-), *n.* *Aeron.* a device that indicates airspeed relative to the speed of sound.

mach′ num′ber, mach. Also, **Mach′ num′ber.**

ma·cho (mä′chō), *n., pl.* **-chos** (chōs). *Mexican Spanish.* **1.** a strong, virile man; he-man. —*adj.* **2.** strong and manly.

ma·chree (mə krē′, mə KHRē′), *n.* *Irish Eng.* dear: *mother machree.* [< Ir *mo croidhe,* lit., my heart]

Ma·chu Pic·chu (mä′choo pēk′choo), the site of an ancient Incan and pre-Incan city, about 7000 feet above sea level in the Andes, in S central Peru.

-machy, a learned borrowing from Greek meaning "fighting," used in the formation of compound words: *logomachy.* [< Gk *-machia* = *mách(ē)* battle + *-ia* -Y[3]]

mach·zor (mäKH zôR′; *Eng.* mäKH′zôr, -zôr, -zər), *n., pl.* **mach·zo·rim** (mäKH zô Rēm′), *Eng.* **mach·zors.** *Hebrew.* mahzor.

mac·in·tosh (mak′in tosh′), *n.* mackintosh.

Mac·ken·zie (mə ken′zē), *n.* **1. Sir Alexander,** 1764?–1820, Scottish explorer in Canada. **2. Alexander,** 1822–92, Canadian statesman, born in Scotland: prime minister 1873–78. **3. William Lyon,** 1795–1861, Canadian political leader and journalist, born in Scotland. **4.** a river in NW Canada, flowing NW from the Great Slave Lake to the Arctic Ocean. 1120 mi. long; with tributaries 2525 mi. long. **5.** a district in the SW Northwest Territories of Canada. 527,490 sq. mi.

mack·er·el (mak′ər əl, mak′rəl), *n., pl.* (*esp. collectively*) **-el,** (*esp. referring to two or more kinds or species*) **-els. 1.** a swift food fish, *Scomber scombrus,* found in the North Atlantic, having wavy cross markings on the back. **2.** any of various similar fishes. [ME *makerel* < OF, perh. same word as MF *maquerel* pimp < MD *makelare* broker (by metathesis) = *makel(en)* (to) bring together + *-are* -ER[1]]

mack′erel sky′, **1.** a sky spotted with small, white, fleecy clouds. **2.** an extensive group of cirrocumulus or altocumulus clouds.

Mack·i·nac (mak′ə nô′, -ə nak′), *n.* **1. Straits of,** a strait between the peninsulas of Upper Michigan and Lower Michigan, connecting Lakes Huron and Michigan. **2.** Also called **Mack′inac Is′land.** an island in Lake Huron at the entrance of this strait. 517 (1970); 3 mi. long.

mack·i·naw (mak′ə nô′), *n.* a short coat of thick wool, usually plaid. [sp. var. of MACKINAC]

mack·in·tosh (mak′in tosh′), *n.* **1.** a raincoat made of rubberized cloth. **2.** such cloth. **3.** any raincoat. Also, **macintosh.** [named after Charles *Macintosh* (1766–1843), its inventor] —**mack′in·toshed′,** *adj.*

mack·le (mak′əl), *n., v.*, **-led, -ling.** —*n.* **1.** a blur in printing, as from a double impression. —*v.t., v.i.* **2.** to blur, as from a double impression in printing. Also, **macule.** [var. of earlier *macle, makle,* late ME *macule* spot, blemish < L *macula.* See MACULA]

Mac·Leish (mak lēsh′, mə klēsh′), *n.* **Archibald,** 1892–1982, U.S. poet and dramatist.

Mac·leod (mə kloud′), *n.* **Fi·o·na** (fē ô′nə). See **Sharp.**

Mac·Mil·lan (mək mil′ən), *n.* **Donald Bax·ter** (bak′stər), 1874–1970, U.S. arctic explorer.

Mac·Neice (mək nēs′), *n.* **Louis,** 1907–63, British poet and classical scholar, born in Ireland.

Ma·con (mā′kən), *n.* a city in central Georgia. 122,423 (1970).

Mâ·con (mä kôN′), *n.* a city in E central France. 27,669 (1962).

Mac·pher·son (mək fûr′sən), *n.* **James,** 1736–96, Scottish author and translator.

Mac·quar·ie (mə kwôr′ē, -kwor′ē), *n.* a river in SE Australia in New South Wales, flowing NW to the Darling River. 750 mi. long.

mac·ra·mé (mak′rə mā′), *n.* a knotted cotton trimming, usually in a geometrical pattern. Also called **mac′ramé lace′.** [< F < It *macramè* kind of fringe on hand towels < Turk *makrama* napkin, face towel < Ar *migrama* embroidered veil]

Mac·read·y (mə krē′dē), *n.* **William Charles,** 1793–1873, English actor.

macro-, a learned borrowing from Greek meaning "large," "long," "great," "excessive," used in the formation of compound words, contrasting with *micro-: macrocosm; macrograph; macroscopic.* Also, *esp. before a vowel,* **macr-.** [< Gk *makro-,* comb. form of *makrós;* c. L *macer* lean; see MEAGER]

mac·ro·bi·ot·ic (mak′rō bī ot′ik), *adj.* **1.** of or consisting primarily of grains and vegetables whose use is said to give long life: *a macrobiotic diet.* **2.** of, pertaining to, or serving such food: *macrobiotic cooking; a macrobiotic restaurant.* **3.** lengthening the life span. **4.** long-lived. [MACRO- + BIOTIC] —**mac′ro·bi·ot′i·cal·ly,** *adv.*

mac·ro·bi·ot·ics (mak′rō bī ot′iks), *n.* (*construed as sing.*) the art of lengthening life, esp. by a vegetarian diet.

mac·ro·ce·phal·ic (mak′rō sə fal′ik), *adj.* *Craniom.* being or having a skull with a large cranial capacity. Also, **mac·ro·ceph·al·ous** (mak′rō sef′ə ləs). [< Gk *makroképhal(os)* large-headed + -IC] —**mac·ro·ceph·a·ly** (mak′rō sef′ə lē), *n.*

mac·ro·ceph·a·lus (mak′rō sef′ə ləs), *n., pl.* **-li** (-lī′). **1.** a person with a macrocephalic skull. **2.** a macrocephalic skull. [< NL < Gk *makroképhalos.* See MACRO-, -CEPHALOUS]

mac·ro·cli·mate (mak′rə klī′mit), *n.* the general climate of a large area, as of a continent or country. Cf. **microclimate.** —**mac·ro·cli·mat·ic** (mak′rō klī mat′ik), *adj.*

mac·ro·cosm (mak′rə koz′əm), *n.* **1.** the great world or universe; the universe considered as a whole (opposed to *microcosm*). **2.** the total or entire complex structure of something: *the macrocosm of war.* **3.** a representation of a smaller unit or entity by a larger one, presumably of a similar structure. [< F *macrocosme* < ML *macrocosm(us).* See MACRO-, COSMOS] —**mac′ro·cos′mic,** *adj.* —**mac′ro·cos′mi·cal·ly,** *adv.*

mac·ro·cyte (mak′rə sīt′), *n. Pathol.* an abnormally large red blood cell. —**mac·ro·cyt·ic** (mak′rə sit′ik), *adj.*

mac·ro·e·co·nom·ics (mak′rō ē′kə nom′iks, -ek′ə-), *n.* (*construed as sing.*) the branch of economics dealing with the broad and general aspects of an economy, as the relationship between the income and investments of a country as a whole. Cf. **microeconomics.** —**mac′ro·e′co·nom′ic,** *adj.*

mac·ro·gam·ete (mak′rō gam′ēt, -gə mēt′), *n. Biol.* (in heterogamous reproduction) the larger and usually female of a pair of conjugating gametes; megagamete.

mac·ro·graph (mak′rə graf′, -gräf′), *n.* a photograph or other representation of an object that is of the same size as or larger than the object.

mac·ro·mol·e·cule (mak′rə mol′ə kyo͞ol′), *n. Chem.* a very large molecule, as a colloidal particle, protein, or esp. a polymer, composed of hundreds or thousands of atoms. Also, **mac·ro·mole** (mak′rə mōl′). —**mac·ro·mo·lec·u·lar** (mak′rō mə lek′yə lər), *adj.*

ma·cron (mā′kron, mak′ron), *n.* a horizontal line used as a diacritic over a vowel to indicate that it has a long sound, as in *fate* (fāt). [< Gk *makrón,* n. use of neut. of *makrós* long. See MACRO-]

mac·ro·phage (mak′rə fāj′), *n. Anat.* a large, amoeboid, phagocytic blood cell in connective tissue. [< NL *macrophag(us)*] —**mac·ro·phag·ic** (mak′rə faj′ik), *adj.*

mac·ro·scop·ic (mak′rə skop′ik), *adj.* visible to the naked eye. Cf. **microscopic** (def. 1). —**mac′ro·scop′i·cal·ly,** *adv.*

ma·cru·ran (mə kro͝or′ən), *adj.* **1.** Also, **ma·cru′ral, ma·cru′roid, ma·cru′rous.** belonging or pertaining to the suborder *Macrura,* comprising the lobsters, crayfishes, shrimps, and prawns. —*n.* **2.** a macruran crustacean. [< NL *macrūr(a)* (pl.) (see MACR-, -UR[2]) + -AN]

mac·u·la (mak′yə lə), *n., pl.* **-lae** (-lē′). **1.** a spot or blotch, esp. on one's skin; macule. **2.** any relatively small anatomical area that differs from its surroundings by virtue of color, consistency, etc. [late ME < L: spot, blemish] —**mac′u·lar,** *adj.*

mac·u·late (*v.* mak′yə lāt′; *adj.* mak′yə lit), *v.,* **-lat·ed, -lat·ing,** *adj.* —*v.t.* **1.** to mark with a spot or spots; stain. **2.** to sully or pollute. —*adj.* **3.** spotted; stained. [late ME < L *maculāt(us)* spotted, stained (ptp. of *maculāre*)]

mac·u·la·tion (mak′yə lā′shən), *n.* **1.** the act of spotting. **2.** a spotted condition. **3.** a marking of spots, as on an animal. **4.** a disfiguring spot or stain. **5.** defilement. [late ME *maculacion* < L *maculātiōn-* (s. of *maculātiō*)]

mac·ule (mak′yo͞ol), *n., v.,* **-uled, -ul·ing.** —*n.* **1.** mackle. **2.** macula. —*v.t., v.i.* **3.** mackle. [late ME; see MACKLE]

mad (mad), *adj.,* **mad·der, mad·dest,** *v.,* **mad·ded, mad·ding,** *n.* —*adj.* **1.** mentally disturbed or deranged; insane; demented. **2.** enraged or irritated; angry. **3.** (of animals) **a.** abnormally furious. **b.** affected with rabies; rabid. **4.** wildly excited; frantic. **5.** extremely foolish or unwise; imprudent; irrational. **6.** overcome by desire, eagerness, enthusiasm, etc.; excessively fond; infatuated. **7.** wildly gay or merry; enjoyably hilarious. **8. like mad,** *Slang.* with great haste, impulsiveness, energy, or enthusiasm. **9. mad as a hatter,** completely mad; deranged; batty. —*v.t.* **10.** *Archaic.* to make mad. —*v.i.* **11.** *Archaic.* to be, become, or act mad. —*n.* **12.** *Informal.* a period or spell of anger or ill temper. [ME; OE *gemǣd(e)d* maddened, ptp. of **gemǣdan,* akin to *gemād* mad, foolish; c. OS *gemēd,* OHG *gimeit* foolish] —**mad′dish,** *adj.*

—**Syn. 1.** lunatic, maniacal, crazed, crazy. **2.** furious, exasperated, raging, irate. **4.** frenzied. **5.** ill-advised; dangerous, perilous. MAD, CRAZY, INSANE are used to characterize wildly impractical or foolish ideas, actions, etc. MAD suggests senselessness and excess: *The scheme of buying the bridge was absolutely mad.* In informal usage, CRAZY suggests recklessness and impracticality: *a crazy young couple.* INSANE is used with some opprobrium to express unsoundness and possible harmfulness: *The new traffic system is simply insane.* —**Ant. 5.** sensible, practical; sound, safe.

—**Usage. 2.** Careful users of English object to the use of MAD to mean "irritated, angry, annoyed." However, MAD is widely used with this meaning by educated speakers even though they will avoid such a vague, general term in writing.

Madag., Madagascar.

Mad·a·gas·car (mad′ə gas′kər), *n.* an island republic in the Indian Ocean, about 240 mi. off the SE coast of Africa: formerly a French colony; now an independent member of the French Community. 8,000,000; 227,800 sq. mi. *Cap.:* Tananarive. Former name, **Malagasy Republic.** —**Mad′a·gas′can,** *n., adj.*

mad·am (mad′əm), *n.* **1.** a polite term of address to a woman, originally used only to a woman of rank or authority. **2.** the woman in charge of a brothel. [ME *madame* < OF, orig. *ma dame* my lady; see DAME]

mad·ame (mad′əm; mə dam′, -däm′, ma-; *Fr.* MA DAM′), *n., pl.* **mes·dames** (mā dam′, -däm′; *Fr.* me DAM′). a conventional title of respect used in speaking to or of a married woman, esp. one of rank or distinction who is not of American or British origin. *Abbr.:* Mme. [< F; see MADAM]

Ma·da·ria·ga (mä′thä RYä′gä), *n.* **Sal·va·dor de** (säl′vä-thôR′ the), (*Salvador de Madariaga y Rojo*), 1886–1979, Spanish diplomat, historian, and writer in England.

mad·cap (mad′kap′), *adj.* **1.** wildly impulsive; reckless; rash. —*n.* **2.** a madcap person, esp. a girl. [MAD + CAP[1]]

mad·den (mad′ᵊn), *v.t.* **1.** to make mad or insane. **2.** to infuriate. —*v.i.* **3.** to become mad; act as if mad; rage. —**Syn. 2.** provoke, enrage, anger, exasperate; irritate, vex, annoy. —**Ant. 2.** calm, mollify.

mad·den·ing (mad′ᵊning), *adj.* **1.** driving to madness or frenzy. **2.** infuriating; exasperating. —**mad′den·ing·ly,** *adv.* —**mad′den·ing·ness,** *n.*

mad·der[1] (mad′ər), *n.* **1.** any rubiaceous plant of the genus *Rubia,* esp. a climbing herb, *R. tinctorum,* of Europe, having panicles of small, yellowish flowers. **2.** the root of this plant, used in dyeing. **3.** the dye itself. [ME *mad(d)er,* OE *mæd(e)re;* c. Icel *madhra,* OHG *matara*]

mad·der[2] (mad′ər), *adj.* comparative of **mad.**

mad·dest (mad′ist), *adj.* superlative of **mad.**

mad·ding (mad′ing), *adj.* **1.** mad; acting madly or senselessly; frenzied. **2.** making mad. [*mad* (ME *maden,* OE *gemǣdan* to hurt, drive MAD) + -ING[2]]

made (mād), *v.* **1.** pt. and pp. of **make.** —*adj.* **2.** produced by making, preparing, etc., in a particular way (often used in combination): *handmade garments.* **3.** artificially produced. **4.** invented or made-up. **5.** assured of success or fortune: *a made man.*

Ma·dei·ra (mə dēr′ə, -der′ə; *Port.* mä de′Rə), *n.* **1.** a group of volcanic islands off the NW coast of Africa, part of Portugal. 270,000; 308 sq. mi. *Cap.:* Funchal. **2.** the chief island of this group. 286 sq. mi. **3.** (*often l.c.*) a rich, strong white wine, resembling sherry, made there. **4.** a river in W Brazil flowing NE to the Amazon: chief tributary of the Amazon. 2100 mi. long.

mad·e·moi·selle (mad′ə mə zel′, mad′mwə-; *Fr.* MAD-MWA zel′), *n., pl.* **mad·e·moi·selles** (mad′ə mə zelz′, mad′mwə-), **mes·de·moi·selles** (mā′də mə zel′, mād′mwə-zel′; *Fr.* mād MWA zel′). a title of respect used in speaking to or of a girl or unmarried woman who is not of American or British origin: *Abbr.:* Mlle. [< F; OF *ma damoisele* my noble young lady; see MADAME, DAMSEL]

Ma·de·ro (mä the′Rô), *n.* **Fran·cis·co In·da·le·cio** (fRän sēs′kô ēn′dä le′syô), 1873–1913, Mexican revolutionary and political leader: president 1911–13.

made-to-or·der (mād′to͞o ôr′dər, -tə-), *adj.* made in or as in accordance with individual specifications or requirements. Cf. **ready-to-wear.**

made-up (mād′up′), *adj.* **1.** concocted; invented. **2.** being in make-up; wearing facial cosmetics. **3.** put together; finished.

mad·house (mad′hous′), *n., pl.* **-hous·es** (-hou′ziz). **1.** an insane asylum. **2.** a wild, confused, and often noisy place, set of circumstances, etc.

Madh·ya Pra·desh (mud′yə prə dāsh′, prä′desh), a state in central India. 48,230,000; 171,201 sq. mi. *Cap.:* Bhopal.

Mad·i·son (mad′i sən), *n.* **1. Dol·ly** or **Dol·ley** (dol′ē), (*Dorothea Payne*), 1768–1849, wife of James Madison. **2. James,** 1751–1836, 4th president of the U.S. 1809–17. **3.** a city in and the capital of Wisconsin, in the S part. 172,007 (1970). **4.** a city in NE New Jersey. 16,710 (1970).

Mad′ison Av′enue, a street in New York City on or near which many advertising firms are located and that has become a symbol of their attitudes, methods, etc.

Mad′ison Heights′, a city in SE Michigan, N of Detroit. 38,599 (1970).

mad·ly (mad′lē), *adv.* **1.** insanely or wildly. **2.** with desperate haste or intensity; furiously. **3.** foolishly. [ME]

mad·man (mad′man′, -mən), *n., pl.* **-men** (-men′, -mən). an insane man; lunatic; maniac. [ME]

mad′ mon′ey, *Slang.* a small sum of money kept in reserve or carried by a woman or girl for an emergency or for minor expenses.

mad·ness (mad′nis), *n.* **1.** the state of being mad; insanity. **2.** rabies. **3.** senseless folly: *It is sheer madness to speak as you do.* **4.** frenzy; rage. **5.** intense excitement or enthusiasm. [ME]

Ma·doe·ra (mä do͞o′Rä), *n.* Dutch name of **Madura.**

Ma·don·na (mə don′ə), *n.* **1.** the Virgin Mary (usually prec. by *the*). **2.** a picture or statue representing the Virgin Mary. **3.** (*l.c.*) *Archaic.* an Italian title of formal address to a woman. [< It: my lady]

Madon′na lil′y, a lily, *Lilium candidum,* having pure white flowers.

mad·ras (mad′rəs, mə dras′, -dräs′), *n.* **1.** a light cotton fabric with cords set at intervals or with woven stripes or figures, often of another color, for shirts, dresses, etc. **2.** a thin curtain fabric of a light, gauzelike weave with figures of heavier yarns. **3.** a large, brightly colored kerchief, of silk or cotton, often used for turbans. [after MADRAS]

Ma·dras (mə dras′, -dräs′), *n.* **1.** former name of **Tamil Nadu. 2.** a seaport in and the capital of Tamil Nadu, in the NE part, on the Bay of Bengal. 2,470,288 (1971).

ma·dre (mä′thRe; *Eng.* mä′drā), *n., pl.* **-dres** (-thRes; *Eng.* -drāz). *Spanish.* mother.

Ma·dre de Dios (mä′thRe the dyôs′), a river in Peru and Bolivia, flowing E to the Beni River. 900 mi. long.

mad·re·pore (mad′rə pōr′, -pôr′), *n.* any true or stony coral of the order *Madreporaria,* forming reefs or islands in tropical seas. [< F *madrépore* reef-building coral < It *madrepora* = *madre* mother (< L *māter*) + *-pora* for *poro* < Gk *pôros* kind of stone] —**mad·re·por·ic** (mad′rə pôr′ik, -por′-), **mad·re·po·rit·ic** (mad′rə pə rit′ik, mə drep′ə-), **mad·re·po·ri·an** (mad′rə pōr′ē ən, -pôr′-), *adj.*

Ma·drid (mə drid′; *Sp.* mä thReth′), *n.* a city in and the capital of Spain, in the central part. 3,500,000. —**Mad·ri·le·ni·an** (ma′drə lē′nē ən, -lēn′yən), *adj., n.*

mad·ri·gal (mad′rə gəl), *n.* **1.** a part song usually for five or six voices, making abundant use of contrapuntal imitation. **2.** a lyric poem suitable for being set to music, usually short and often of amatory character. [< It *madrigale* < ML *mātricāle* something simple, n. use of neut. of LL *mātricālis,* lit., of the womb. See MATRIX, -AL[1]] —**mad′ri·gal·esque′,** *adj.* —**mad·ri·gal·i·an** (mad′rə gal′ē ən, -gal′yən, -gā′lē ən), *adj.*

mad·ri·gal·ist (mad′rə gə list), *n.* a composer or a singer of madrigals.

mad·ri·lène (mad′rə len′, -lān′; *Fr.* MA dRē len′), *n.* a consommé flavored with tomato, frequently jelled and served cold. [< F (*consommé*) *madrilène,* lit., Madrid consommé]

ma·dro·ño (mə drōn′yō), *n., pl.* **-ños.** an evergreen, ericaceous tree or shrub, *Arbutus Menziesii,* of western North America, yielding a hard wood, having a smooth bark, and bearing a yellow, edible berry. Also, **ma·dro·ña** (mə drōn′yə), **ma·dro·ne** (mə drō′nə). [< Sp]

mad′ stag′gers, *Vet. Pathol.* stagger (def. 10).

Ma·du·ra (mä do͝or′ä *for 1;* maj′o͝o rə *for 2*), *n.* **1.** Dutch, **Madoera.** an island in Indonesia, off the NE coast of Java. 2112 sq. mi. **2.** Also, **Ma·du·rai** (mad′yo͝o rī′). a city in S Madras, in S India. 424,800 (1961).

ma·du·ro (mə do͝or′ō), *adj.* (of cigars) strong and darkly colored. [< Sp < L *mātūrus* ripe]

mad·wo·man (mad′wo͝om′ən), *n., pl.* **-wom·en.** an insane woman.

mad·wort (mad′wûrt′), *n.* **1.** one of the alyssum plants, *Alyssum saxatille.* **2.** a boraginaceous plant, *Asperugo procumbens.*

mae (mā), *adj., n., adv. Scot.* more. [ME (north), OE *mā;* c. G *mehr,* Icel *meir,* Goth *mais.* See MORE]

Mae·an·der (mē an′dər), *n.* ancient name of the **Menderes.**

Ma·e·ba·shi (mä′e bä′shē), *n.* a city in the central part of Honshu, in central Japan. 190,000 (est. 1963).

Mae·ce·nas (mē sē′nəs, mī-), *n.* **1. Gaius Cil·ni·us** (sil′nē-əs). c70–8 B.C., Roman statesman: patron of Horace and Vergil. **2.** a generous patron or supporter of the arts.

mael·strom (māl′strəm), *n.* **1.** a large, powerful, or violent whirlpool. **2.** a restless, disordered, or tumultuous state of affairs. [< early D *maelstroom* (now *maalstroom*), lit., grinding stream. See MEAL[2], STREAM]

mae·nad (mē′nad), *n.* **1.** bacchante. **2.** any frenzied or raging woman. [< L *Maenad-* (s. of *Maenas*) < Gk: madwoman] **—mae·nad′ic,** *adj.* **—mae′nad·ism,** *n.*

ma·es·to·so (mī stō′sō; *It.* mä′es tô′sô), *adj., adv.* majestically (used as a musical direction). [< It: stately, majestic = *maest(à)* (< L *mājestās* MAJESTY) + *-oso* -OSE[1]]

Maes·tricht (*Du.* mäs′trikht), *n.* Maastricht.

maes·tro (mī′strō; *It.* mä es′trô), *n., pl.* **maes·tros,** *It.* **ma·es·tri** (mä es′trē). **1.** an eminent composer, teacher, or conductor of music. **2.** (*cap.*) a title of respect used in addressing or referring to such a person. **3.** a master of any art. [< It: master]

Mae·ter·linck (mā′tər lingk′; *Fr.* ma ter laN′; *Du.* mä′-ter lingk′), *n.* **Comte Mau·rice** (*Fr.* mō rēs′), 1862–1947, Belgian poet, dramatist, and essayist: Nobel prize 1911.

Mae′ West′, an inflatable life jacket for emergency use. [named after *Mae West* (b. 1892), American actress]

Maf·e·king (mä′fə king′), *n.* a town in the Republic of South Africa: besieged by Boers 1899–1900. 6965 (1951).

Ma·fi·a (mä′fē ə; *It.* mä′fē ä), *n.* **1.** (in the U.S.) a secret organization of persons, generally assumed to be of Sicilian and mainland Italian origin, engaged in criminal activities. **2.** (in Sicily) **a.** (*l.c.*) a popular spirit of hostility to legal restraint and to the law, often manifesting itself in criminal acts. **b.** a secret society that acts in this spirit. Also, **Maf′fi·a.** [< It (Sicilian) *mafia* boldness; perh. < Ar *mahyah* boasting]

Ma·fi·o·so (mä fē ō′sō), *n., pl.,* **-si** (sē). a reputed member of the Mafia. [< It]

ma foi (ma fwa′), *French.* my word! really! [lit.: my faith]

maf·tir (mäf tēr′; *Eng.* mäf′tēr), *n. Hebrew.* the concluding section of a Parashah. [lit.: dismisser]

mag (mag), *n. Informal.* magazine. [shortened form]

mag., **1.** magazine. **2.** magnetism. **3.** magnitude.

Ma·ga·lla·nes (*Sp.* mä′gä yä′nes), *n.* See **Punta Arenas.**

mag·a·zine (mag′ə zēn′, mag′ə zēn′), *n.* **1.** *Publishing.* a publication that is issued periodically, usually bound in a paper cover, and typically containing stories, essays, poems, etc., by many writers, and often photographs and drawings, frequently specializing in a particular subject or area. **2.** a room or place for keeping gunpowder and other explosives, as in a fort or on a warship. **3.** a building or place for keeping military stores, as arms or provisions. **4.** a quickly replaceable metal receptacle for a number of cartridges, for inserting into certain types of automatic weapons. **5.** *Photog.* cartridge (def. 4). [< F *magasin* < It *magazzino* storehouse < Ar *makhāzin,* pl. of *makhzan* storehouse]

Mag·da·le·na (mag′də lā′nə, -lē′-; *Sp.* mäg′thä le′nä), *n.* a river in SW Colombia, flowing N to the Caribbean. 1060 mi. long.

Mag′dale′na Bay′, a bay in NW Mexico, on the SW coast of Lower California. 17 mi. long; 12 mi. wide.

Mag·da·lene (mag′də lēn′, mag′də lē′nē), *n.* **1.** the. See **Mary Magdalene. 2.** (*l.c.*) a reformed prostitute. Also, **Mag·da·len** (mag′də lən).

Mag·da·le·ni·an (mag′də lē′nē ən), *adj.* noting the period or culture in the Old World Stone Age in which Cro-Magnon man reached his highest level of industry and art. [< F *Magdalénien* < Latinization of *La Madeleine,* in SW France, where artifacts were found; see -IAN]

Mag·de·burg (mag′də bûrg′; *Ger.* mäg′də bo͝ork′), *n.* a city in W. East Germany. 265,141 (1964).

mage (māj), *n. Archaic.* a magician. [ME < MF < L *mag(us).* See MAGUS]

Ma·gel·lan (mə jel′ən), *n.* **1. Ferdinand,** c1480–1521, Portuguese navigator: discoverer of the Straits of Magellan 1520 and the Philippines 1521. **2. Strait of,** a strait near the S tip of South America between the mainland of Chile and Tierra del Fuego and other islands, connecting the Atlantic and the Pacific. 360 mi. long; 2½–17 mi. wide.

Mag′ellan′ic cloud′, *Astron.* either of two irregular galactic clusters in the southern heavens that are the nearest independent star system to the Milky Way.

Ma·gen Da·vid (mô′gən dô′vid, dā′vid; *Heb.* mä gān′ dä vēd′), *Judaism.* See **Star of David.** [< Heb: lit., Shield of David]

ma·gen·ta (mə jen′tə), *n.* **1.** fuchsin. **2.** reddish purple. [named after MAGENTA]

Ma·gen·ta (mə jen′tə), *n.* a town in N Italy, W of Milan: the French and Sardinians defeated the Austrians here 1859. 18,533 (1961).

Mag·gio·re (mə jôr′ē, -jōr′ē; *It.* mäd jô′re), *n.* **Lake,** a lake in N Italy and S Switzerland. 83 sq. mi.

mag·got (mag′ət), *n.* **1.** a soft-bodied, legless larva of certain dipterous insects. **2.** *Archaic.* an odd fancy; whim. [ME *magot, magat,* unexplained var. of *maddock,* early ME *mathek* < Scand; cf. Icel *mathkr,* Dan *maddik* maggot; akin to OE *matha, mathu* grub, maggot, OHG *mado* maggot] **—mag′got·y,** *adj.*

Ma·ghrib (mu′grib), *n.* the Arabic name for the countries of NW Africa: Morocco, Algeria, and Tunisia.

Ma·gi (mā′jī), *n.pl., sing.* **-gus** (-gəs). (*sometimes l.c.*) **1.** the three wise men who paid homage to the infant Jesus. Matt. 2:1–12. **2.** the class of Zoroastrian priests in ancient Media and Persia, reputed to possess supernatural powers. [pl. of MAGUS] **—Ma·gi·an** (mā′jē ən), *adj.* **—Ma′gi·an·ism,** *n.*

mag·ic (maj′ik), *n.* **1.** the art of producing a desired effect or result through the use of various techniques, as incantation, that presumably assure human control of supernatural agencies or the forces of nature. **2.** the exercise of this art. **3.** the effects produced. **4.** power or influence exerted through this art. **5.** any extraordinary or irresistible influence, charm, power, etc. **6.** the art of causing illusions as entertainment by the use of sleight of hand, deceptive devices, etc.; legerdemain; conjuring. **—*adj.*** Also, **mag′i·cal. 7.** employed in magic. **8.** mysteriously enchanting: *magic beauty.* **9.** of, pertaining to, or due to magic. **10.** producing the effects of magic; like magic. [ME *magik(e)* witchcraft < LL *magica,* L *magicē* < Gk *magikḗ,* n. use of fem. of *magikós.* See MAGUS, -IC] **—mag′i·cal·ly,** *adv.*

—Syn. 1. enchantment. MAGIC, NECROMANCY, SORCERY, WITCHCRAFT imply producing results through mysterious influences or unexplained powers. MAGIC may have glamorous and attractive connotations; the other terms suggest the harmful and sinister. MAGIC is an art employing some occult force of nature. NECROMANCY is an art of prediction, supposedly based on communication with the dead. SORCERY, originally divination by casting lots, came to mean supernatural knowledge gained through the aid of evil spirits and used for evil ends. WITCHCRAFT esp. suggests a malign kind of magic used against innocent victims.

ma·gi·cian (mə jish′ən), *n.* **1.** a person skilled in magic. **2.** an entertainer skilled in causing illusion by sleight of hand, deceptive devices, etc.; conjurer. [MAGIC + -IAN; r. ME *magicien* < MF]

mag′ic lan′tern, a device for projecting images mounted on slides or films.

mag′ic num′ber, *Physics.* the atomic number or neutron number of an exceptionally stable nuclide.

mag′ic square′, a square containing integers arranged in an equal number of rows and columns so that the sum of the integers in any row, column, or diagonal is the same.

10	3	8
5	7	9
6	11	4

Magic square

Ma′gi·not line′ (mazh′ə nō′; *Fr.* ma zhē nō′), a zone of French fortifications erected along the French-German border in the years preceding World War II. [named after André *Maginot* (1877–1932), French minister of war]

mag·is·te·ri·al (maj′i stēr′ē əl), *adj.* **1.** of, pertaining to, or befitting a master; authoritative; weighty; of importance or consequence. **2.** imperious; domineering. **3.** of or befitting a magistrate or his office. [< ML *magisteriāl(is)* of control] **—mag′is·te′ri·al·ly,** *adv.* **—mag′is·te′ri·al·ness,** *n.*

mag·is·ter·y (maj′i ster′ē, -stə rē), *n., pl.* **-ter·ies. 1.** an agency or substance, as in alchemy, to which faculties of healing, transformation, etc., are ascribed. **2.** mastership. [< L *magisteri(um)*]

mag·is·tra·cy (maj′i strə sē), *n., pl.* **-cies. 1.** the office or function of a magistrate. **2.** a body of magistrates. **3.** the district under a magistrate. Also, **mag·is·tra·ture** (maj′i strā′chər).

mag·is·tral (maj′i strəl), *adj.* **1.** *Pharm.* prescribed or prepared for a particular occasion, as a remedy. Cf. **officinal** (def. 1). **2.** *Fort.* principal; main. **3.** *Rare.* magisterial. [< L *magistrāl(is)* of a master. See MASTER, -AL[1]] **—mag′is·tral′i·ty,** *n.* **—mag′is·tral·ly, mag·is·trat·i·cal·ly** (maj′i strat′ik lē), *adv.*

mag·is·trate (maj′i strāt′, -strit), *n.* **1.** a civil officer charged with the administration of the law. **2.** a minor judicial officer, as a justice of the peace, having jurisdiction to try minor criminal cases. [ME *magistrat* < L *magistrāt(us)* magistracy, magistrate. See MASTER, -ATE[1], -ATE[3]]

mag·ma (mag′mə), *n., pl.* **-mas, -ma·ta** (-mə tə). **1.** any crude mixture of finely divided mineral or organic matter. **2.** *Geol.* molten material beneath or within the earth's crust, from which igneous rock is formed. **3.** *Chem., Pharm.* a paste composed of solid and liquid matter. [< L: dregs, leavings < Gk: kneaded mass, salve = *mag-* (base of *massein* to knead, press) + *-ma* n. suffix of result] **—mag·mat·ic** (mag mat′ik), *adj.* **—mag′ma·tism,** *n.*

magn-, var. of **magni-** before a vowel: *magnanimous.*

Mag·na Char·ta (mag′nə kär′tə), **1.** the "great charter" of English liberties, forced from King John by the English barons, and sealed at Runnymede, June 15, 1215. **2.** any fundamental constitution or law guaranteeing rights. Also, **Mag′na Car′ta.** [< ML]

mag·na cum lau·de (mäg′nə ko͝om lou′dā, -də, -dē; mag′nə kum lô′dē), with great praise: used in diplomas to grant the next-to-highest of three special honors for grades above the average. Cf. **cum laude, summa cum laude.** [< L]

Mag·na Grae·ci·a (mag′nə grē′shē ə; *Lat.* mäg′nä grī′ki ä′), the ancient colonies of Greece in S Italy.

mag·na·nim·i·ty (mag′nə nim′i tē), *n., pl.* **-ties** for 2. **1.** the quality of being magnanimous. **2.** a magnanimous act. [ME *magnanimite* < L *magnanimitās*]

mag·nan·i·mous (mag nan′ə məs), *adj.* **1.** generous in forgiving an insult or injury; free from petty resentfulness or vindictiveness. **2.** high-minded; noble. **3.** proceeding from or revealing nobility of mind, character, etc. [< L *magnanimus* great-souled. See MAGN-, ANIMUS, -OUS] **—mag·nan′i·mous·ly,** *adv.* **—mag·nan′i·mous·ness,** *n.*

mag·nate (mag′nāt, -nit), *n.* a person of great influence, importance, or standing in a particular enterprise, field of business, etc. [back formation from ME *magnates* (pl.) < LL = L *magn(us)* MAGN- + *-ātēs,* pl. of *-ās* n. suffix] **—mag′nate·ship′,** *n.*

mag·ne·sia (mag nē′zhə, -shə), *n.* a white, tasteless substance, magnesium oxide, MgO, used in medicine as an antacid and laxative. Cf. **milk of magnesia.** [ME < ML < Gk (*hē*) *Magnēsíē* (*líthos*) (the stone) of MAGNESIA] **—mag·ne′sian, mag·ne·sic** (mag nē′sik), **mag·ne′sial,** *adj.*

Mag·ne·si·a (mag nē′shē ə, -zhē ə), *n.* ancient name of **Manisa.**

mag·ne·site (mag′ni sīt′), *n.* a mineral, magnesium

carbonate, $MgCO_3$, usually occurring in white masses. [MAGNES(IA) + -ITE[1]; cf. F *magnésite*]

mag·ne·si·um (mag nē′zē əm, -zhəm, -shē əm), *n. Chem.* a light, ductile, silver-white metallic element which burns with a dazzling white light, used in lightweight alloys, flares, in the manufacture of optical mirrors and precision instruments, and as a zinc substitute in batteries. *Symbol:* Mg; *at. wt.:* 24.312; *at. no.:* 12; *sp. gr.:* 1.74 at 20°C. [< NL; see MAGNESIA, -IUM]

magne′sium ar′senate, *Chem.* a white powder, $Mg_3(AsO_4)_2 \cdot nH_2O$, used chiefly as an insecticide.

magne′sium hydrox′ide, *Chem.* a white powder, $Mg(OH)_2$, used as an antacid and as a laxative.

magne′sium ox′ide, *Chem.* magnesia.

magne′sium sul′fate, *Chem.* a white salt, $MgSO_4$, used chiefly in medicine and in the processing of leather and textiles. Cf. **Epsom salt.**

magne′sium trisil′icate, *Chem.* a white powder, $2MgO \cdot 3SiO_2 \cdot nH_2O$, used industrially to absorb odors and decolorize and, pharmaceutically, as an antacid.

mag·net (mag′nit), *n.* **1.** a body, as a piece of iron or steel, that possesses the property of attracting certain substances, as iron. **2.** a loadstone. **3.** a thing or person that attracts, as by some inherent power or charm. [late ME *magnete* < L *magnēta* < Gk, acc. of *mágnēs,* short for *ho Mágnēs líthos* the stone of Magnesia]

magnet-, var. of **magneto-** before some vowels: *magneton.*

mag·net·ic (mag net′ik), *adj.* **1.** of or pertaining to a magnet or magnetism. **2.** having the properties of a magnet. **3.** capable of being magnetized or attracted by a magnet. **4.** pertaining to the magnetic field of the earth. **5.** exerting a strong attractive power or charm. **6.** noting or pertaining to various bearings and measurements as indicated by a magnetic compass. Also, **mag·net′i·cal.** [< LL *magnēticus*] —**mag·net′i·cal·ly,** *adv.*

magnet′ic core′, *Computer Technol.* core[1] (def. 7).

magnet′ic course′, *Navig.* a course whose bearing is given relative to the magnetic meridian of the area. Cf. **compass course, true course.**

magnet′ic declina′tion, *Navig.* variation (def. 8).

magnet′ic dip′, dip (def. 26).

magnet′ic drum′, *Computer Technol.* a revolving cylinder in a computer, having a magnetized surface on which information can be stored as small polarized spots.

magnet′ic equa′tor. See **aclinic line.**

magnet′ic field′, a condition of space in the vicinity of a magnetic or current-carrying substance, manifesting itself as a force on a moving charge or magnetic pole within that space.

magnet′ic flux′, *Physics.* the total number of lines of induction through a given cross section of a surface, expressed in maxwells or webers.

magnet′ic induc′tion, *Physics.* **1.** the process by which a body becomes magnetized by a magnetic field. **2.** a vector quantity used as a measure of a magnetic field, directly proportional to the force on a moving conductor in the field and inversely proportional to the product of the charge on the conductor and the velocity of the conductor. *Symbol:* B

magnet′ic nee′dle, a magnetized steel rod that indicates the direction of the earth's magnetic fields or the approximate position of north and south.

magnet′ic north′, north as indicated by a magnetic compass, differing in most places from true north.

magnet′ic pole′, **1.** the region of a magnet toward which the lines of induction converge **(south pole)** or from which the lines of induction diverge **(north pole).** **2.** either of the two points on the earth's surface where the dipping needle of a compass stands vertical, one in the arctic, the other in the antarctic.

magnet′ic res′onance im′aging. See **MRI.**

mag·net·ics (mag net′iks), *n.* (*construed as sing.*) the science of magnetism. [see MAGNETIC, -ICS]

magnet′ic storm′, a temporary disturbance of the earth's magnetic field, induced by radiation and streams of charged particles from the sun.

magnet′ic tape′, a ribbon of material, usually with a plastic base, coated on one side **(single tape)** or both sides **(double tape)** with a substance containing iron oxide, to make it sensitive to impulses from an electromagnet. Also called **tape.**

magnet′ic varia′tion, *Navig.* variation (def. 8).

mag·net·ise (mag′ni tīz′), *v.t.,* **-ised, -is·ing.** *Chiefly Brit.* magnetize. —**mag′net·i·sa′tion,** *n.* —**mag′net·is′er,** *n.*

mag·net·ism (mag′ni tiz′əm), *n.* **1.** the properties of attraction possessed by magnets; the molecular properties common to magnets. **2.** the agency producing magnetic phenomena. **3.** the science dealing with magnetic phenomena. **4.** magnetic or attractive power or charm. [< NL *magnētismus*]

mag·net·ite (mag′ni tīt′), *n.* a very common black iron oxide, Fe_3O_4, strongly attracted by magnets: an important iron ore.

mag·net·iz·a·ble (mag′ni tī′zə bəl), *adj.* susceptible to magnetization. —**mag′ne·tiz′a·bil′i·ty,** *n.*

mag·net·ize (mag′ni tīz′), *v.t.,* **-ized, -iz·ing.** **1.** to make a magnet of or impart the properties of a magnet to. **2.** to exert an attracting or compelling influence upon. **3.** *Archaic.* to mesmerize. Also, *esp. Brit.,* **magnetise.** —**mag′net·i·za′tion,** *n.* —**mag′net·iz′er,** *n.*

mag·ne·to (mag nē′tō), *n., pl.* **-tos.** *Elect.* a small electric generator the armature of which rotates in a magnetic field provided by permanent magnets. [short for *magnetoelectric generator*]

magneto-, a combining form of **magnetic, magnetism:** *magnetochemistry.* Also, *esp. before a vowel,* **magnet-.**

mag·ne·to·chem·is·try (mag nē′tō kem′i strē), *n.* the study of magnetic and chemical phenomena in their relation to one another. —**mag·ne′to·chem′i·cal,** *adj.*

mag·ne·to·e·lec·tric·i·ty (mag nē′tō i lek tris′i tē, -ē′-lek-), *n.* electricity developed by the action of magnets.

mag·ne·to·hy·dro·dy·nam·ic (mag nē′tō hī′drō dī-nam′ik, -di-), *adj. Physics.* of or pertaining to the phenomena associated with the motion of an electrically conducting fluid, as liquid metal or ionized gas, in a magnetic field. —**mag·ne′to·hy′dro·dy·nam′i·cal·ly,** *adv.*

mag·ne·to·hy·dro·dy·nam·ics (mag nē′tō hī′drō dī-nam′iks, -di-), *n.* (*construed as sing.*) *Physics.* the branch of physics that deals with magnetohydrodynamic phenomena. Also called **hydromagnetics.**

mag·ne·tom·e·ter (mag′ni tom′i tər), *n.* an instrument for measuring the intensity of a magnetic field, esp. the earth's magnetic field. —**mag·ne·to·met·ric** (mag′nē tō-me′trik), *adj.* —**mag′ne·tom′e·try,** *n.*

mag·ne·to·mo·tive (mag nē′tō mō′tiv), *adj.* producing magnetic effects.

magne′tomo′tive force′, *Elect.* the force that gives rise to a magnetic field, equal to the product of magnetic flux and reluctance.

mag·ne·ton (mag′ni ton′), *n. Physics.* a unit of magnetic moment, used in measuring the magnetic moment of atomic and subatomic particles.

mag·ne·to·stric·tion (mag nē′tō strik′shən), *n. Physics.* a change in dimensions exhibited by ferromagnetic materials when subjected to a magnetic field. [MAGNETO- + (CON)-STRICTION] —**mag·ne·to·stric·tive** (mag nē′tə strik′tiv), *adj.*

mag·ne·tron (mag′ni tron′), *n. Electronics.* a two-element vacuum tube in which the flow of electrons is under the influence of an external magnetic field, used to generate extremely short radio waves. [MAGNE(T) + (ELEC)TRON]

magni-, an element appearing in loan words from Latin, where it meant "large," "great": *magnify.* Also, *esp. before a vowel,* **magn-.** [< L, comb. form of *magnus*]

mag·nif·ic (mag nif′ik), *adj. Archaic.* magnificent; imposing. Also, **mag·nif′i·cal.** [< L *magnific(us)* grand (see MAGNI-, -FIC); r. late ME *magnyfyque* < MF] —**mag·nif′i·cal·ly,** *adv.*

Mag·nif·i·cat (mag nif′ə kat′, mag nif′ə kät′, män yif′-), *n.* **1.** (*italics*) the hymn of the Virgin Mary in Luke, 1:46–55, beginning "My soul doth magnify the Lord," used as a canticle at evensong or vespers. **2.** a musical setting for this. [ME < L: (it) magnifies (from the first word of the hymn)]

mag·ni·fi·ca·tion (mag′nə fə kā′shən), *n.* **1.** the act of magnifying. **2.** the state of being magnified. **3.** the power to magnify. **4.** a magnified copy or reproduction. [< LL *magnificātiōn-* (s. of *magnificātiō*)]

mag·nif·i·cence (mag nif′i səns), *n.* **1.** the quality or state of being magnificent; splendor; grandeur. **2.** impressiveness of surroundings. [ME < L *magnificentia.* See MAGNIFIC, -ENCE] —**Syn. 1.** sumptuousness, pomp, majesty. **2.** luxury, luxuriousness. —**Ant. 1, 2.** squalor.

mag·nif·i·cent (mag nif′i sənt), *adj.* **1.** making a splendid appearance or show; of surpassing beauty, size, etc. **2.** extraordinarily fine; superb. **3.** noble; sublime. **4.** (*usually cap.*) (now used only as a title) great; grand. [< MF < L *magnificent-* (recorded in comp., superl., and other forms) for *magnificus.* See MAGNIFIC] —**mag·nif′i·cent·ly,** *adv.* —**mag·nif′i·cent·ness,** *n.*

—**Syn. 1, 2.** luxurious, lavish; exquisite; showy. MAGNIFICENT, GORGEOUS, SPLENDID, SUPERB are terms of high admiration and all are used informally in weak exaggeration. That which is MAGNIFICENT is beautiful, princely, grand, or ostentatious: *a magnificent display of paintings.* That which is GORGEOUS moves one to admiration by the richness and (often colorful) variety of its effects: *a gorgeous array of gifts.* That which is SPLENDID is dazzling or impressive in its brilliance, radiance, or excellence: *splendid jewels; a splendid body of scholars.* That which is SUPERB is above others in, or is of the highest degree of, excellence, elegance, or (less often, today) grandeur: *a superb rendition of a song; superb wines.* —**Ant. 1, 2.** modest; poor.

mag·nif·i·co (mag nif′ə kō′), *n., pl.* **-coes.** **1.** a Venetian grandee. **2.** any grandee or great personage. [< It (adj.) < L *magnificus*]

mag·ni·fy (mag′nə fī′), *v.,* **-fied, -fy·ing.** —*v.t.* **1.** to increase the apparent size of, as a lens does. **2.** to make greater in actual size; enlarge. **3.** to cause to seem greater or more important; attribute too much importance to; exaggerate. **4.** to make more exciting; intensify; dramatize; heighten. **5.** *Archaic.* to extol; praise. —*v.i.* **6.** to increase or be able to increase the apparent or actual size of an object. [ME *magnifie(n)* < L *magnific(āre).* See MAGNI-, -FY] —**mag′ni·fi′a·ble,** *adj.* —**mag′ni·fi′er,** *n.* —**Syn. 2.** augment, increase, amplify. **3.** overstate.

mag·nil·o·quent (mag nil′ə kwənt), *adj.* speaking or expressed in a lofty or grandiose style; bombastic; pompous. [back formation from L *magniloquentia* elevated language = *magniloqu(us)* speaking grandly (*magni-* MAGNI- + *loqu(ī)* (to) speak + *-us* adj. suffix) + *-entia* -ENCE] —**mag·nil′o·quence,** *n.* —**mag·nil′o·quent·ly,** *adv.*

Mag·ni·to·gorsk (mäg ni to gôrsk′), *n.* a city in the W RSFSR, in the W Soviet Union in Asia, on the Ural River. 333,000 (est. 1962).

mag·ni·tude (mag′ni to͞od′, -tyo͞od′), *n.* **1.** size; extent; dimensions. **2.** great amount, importance, etc. **3.** greatness; great size. **4.** moral greatness. **5.** *Astron.* **a.** the brightness of a star or other celestial body as viewed by the unaided eye from the earth and expressed by a mathematical ratio of 2.512: a star of the first magnitude is approximately 2½ times as bright as one of the second magnitude and 100 times as bright as one of the sixth magnitude. **b.** See **absolute magnitude.** **6.** *Math.* a number characteristic of a quantity and forming a basis for comparison with similar quantities, as length. [ME < L *magnitūdō*] —**mag·ni·tu·di·nous** (mag′ni to͞od′ᵊnəs, -tyo͞od′-), *adj.*

mag·no·lia (mag nōl′yə, -nō′lē ə), *n.* **1.** any shrub or tree of the genus *Magnolia,* having large, usually fragrant flowers and an aromatic bark, much cultivated for ornament. **2.** the blossom of any such shrub or tree, as of the evergreen magnolia tree: the state flower of Louisiana and Mississippi. [< NL, named after Pierre *Magnol* (1638–1715), French botanist; see -IA]

mag·no·li·a·ceous (mag nō′lē ā′shəs), *adj.* belonging to the *Magnoliaceae,* or magnolia family of plants, including the magnolias, the tulip trees, etc.

Magno′lia State′, Mississippi (used as a nickname).
mag·num (mag′nəm), *n.* a large bottle for wine or spirits, containing about 50 ounces. [< L: large, great]
mag′num o′pus, a great work, esp. the chief work of a writer or artist. [< L]
Mag′nus hitch′ (mag′nəs), a knot similar to a clove hitch but taking one more turn around the object to which the line is being bent; rolling hitch. [named after H. G. *Magnus* (1802–70), German scientist]
Ma·gog (mā′gog), *n.* a people descended from Japheth. Gen. 10:2; Ezek. 38, 39. Cf. **Gog and Magog.**
mag·pie (mag′pī′), *n.* **1.** either of two corvine birds, *Pica pica,* of Eurasia and North America, or *P. nuttalli,* of California, having long, graduated tails, black-and-white plumage, and noisy, mischievous habits. **2.** a chatterbox. [*Mag* Margaret + PIE²]

Magpie, *Pica pica* (Length 18 in.)

Ma·gritte (*Fr.* MA GRĒT′), *n.* **Re·né** (*Fr.* Rə nā′), 1898–1967, Belgian painter.
Mag·say·say (mäg sī′sī), *n.* **Ra·món** (rä mōn′; *Sp.* RÄ mōn′), 1907–57, Philippine statesman: president 1953–57.
mag·uey (mag′wā, mə gā′; *Sp.* mä gā′), *n.* **1.** any of several amaryllidaceous plants of the genus *Agave,* esp. *A. Cantala,* or of the related genus *Furcraea.* **2.** the fiber from these plants. [< Sp < Taino]
Ma·gus (mā′gəs), *n., pl.* **-gi** (-jī). **1.** (*sometimes l.c.*) one of the Magi. **2.** (*l.c.*) an astrologer, wizard, sorcerer, or the like. **3.** (*sometimes l.c.*) a Zoroastrian priest. Cf. **Magi** (def. 2). [< L < Gk *mágos* < OPers *magus* seer, wizard. See MAGIC]
Mag·yar (mag′yär; *Hung.* mo′dyoR), *n.* **1.** a member of a people speaking a Finno-Ugric language, which forms the predominant element of the population of Hungary. **2.** Hungarian (def. 3). —*adj.* **3.** of or pertaining to the Magyars or their language; Hungarian.
Ma·gyar·or·szág (mo′dyoR ôR′säg), *n.* Hungarian name of **Hungary.**
Ma·ha·ba·li·pur·am (mə hä′bə lē po͝or′əm), *n.* a village in NE Madras, in SE India: Hindu temples; early Dravidian architecture. Also, **Ma·ha′ba·li·pur′, Mamallapuram.**
Ma·ha·bha·ra·ta (mə hä′bär′ə tə), *n.* *Hinduism.* an epic poem of India, one of the Puranas, dealing mainly with the conflict between the Pandavas and the Kauravas; includes the Bhagavad-Gita. Also, **Ma·ha·bha·ra·tum** (mə hä′bär′ə təm). [< Skt = *mahā-* great + *Bhārata* descendant of a king or tribe named Bharata]
Ma·hal·la el Ku·bra (mə hal′ə el ko͞o′brə), a city in the N United Arab Republic, in the Nile delta. 198,900 (est. 1962).
Ma·ha·ma·ya (mə hä′mä′yə), *n.* *Hinduism.* maya (def. 4). [< Skt = *mahā-* great + *māyā* MAYA]
ma·ha·ra·jah (mä′hə rä′jə; *Hind.* mə hä′RÄ′jə), *n.* the title of a ruling prince in India, esp. of one of the major states. Also, **ma′ha·ra′ja.** [< Hindi *mahārājā* great king]
ma·ha·ra·nee (mä′hə rä′nē; *Hind.* mə hä′RÄ′nē), *n.* **1.** the wife of a maharajah. **2.** an Indian princess who is sovereign in her own right. Also, **ma′ha·ra′ni.** [< Hindi *mahārānī* great queen]
Ma·ha·rash·tra (mä′hə räsh′trə; *Hind.* mə hä′RÄsh′tRə), *n.* a state in SW India. 39,553,718 (1961); 118,903 sq. mi. *Cap.:* Bombay.
ma·hat·ma (mə hät′mə, -hat′-), *n.* (*sometimes cap.*) **1.** a Brahmansage. **2.** (in Theosophy) a great sage who has renounced further spiritual development in order to aid those who are less advanced. [< Skt *mahātma(n)* high-souled; magnanimous = *mah(ā)-* great + *ātmán* ATMAN] —**ma·hat′ma·ism,** *n.*
Mahat′ma Gan′dhi. See **Gandhi, Mohandas Karamchand.**
Ma·ha·ya·na (mä′hə yä′nə; *Hind.* mə hä′yä′nə), *n.* the later of the two great schools of Buddhism, characterized by eclecticism and a general belief in a common search for salvation, sometimes thought to be attainable through faith alone. Cf. **Hinayana.** [< Skt = *mahā-* great + *yāna* vehicle] —**ma·ha·ya·nist** (mä′hə yä′nist), *n.*
Mah·di (mä′dē), *n., pl.* **-dis. 1.** (in Muslim, esp. Shiite, usage) the title of an expected spiritual and temporal ruler destined to establish a reign of righteousness throughout the world. **2.** any of various claimants, esp. Muhammad Ahmed, who established an independent government in the Anglo-Egyptian Sudan which lasted until 1898. [< Ar *mahdīy* he who is guided] —**Mah·dism** (mä′diz əm), *n.*
Ma·hen·dra (mä hen drä′), *n.* (*Mahendra Bir Bikram Shah Deva*) 1920–72, king of Nepal 1955–72.
Mah·goub (mä go͞ob′), *n.* **Mohammed Ahmed,** born 1908, Sudanese lawyer and politician: prime minister 1965–69.
Ma·hi·can (mə hē′kən), *n., pl.* **-cans,** (*esp. collectively*) **-can. 1.** a tribe or confederacy of North American Indians of Algonquian speech, centralized formerly in the upper Hudson valley. **2.** an Indian of this confederacy. **3.** Mohegan (def. 1). Also, **Mohican.** [< AmerInd (Algonquian): lit., wolf]
mah-jongg (mä′jông′, -jong′, -zhông′, -zhong′), *n.* a game of Chinese origin usually played by four persons with 144 dominolike tiles marked in suits, counters, and dice, the object being to build a winning combination of pieces. Also, **mah′-jong′.** [formerly trademark]
Mah·ler (mä′lər), *n.* **Gus·tav** (go͞os′täf), 1860–1911, Austrian composer and conductor, born in Bohemia.
mahl·stick (mäl′stik′, môl′-), *n.* a painter's stick, held in one hand as a support for the other, which holds the brush. Also, **maulstick.** [< D *maalstok,* lit., paint-stick. See MOLE¹, STOCK]
Mah·mud II (mä mo͞od′), 1785–1839, sultan of Turkey 1809–39.
ma·hog·a·ny (mə hog′ə nē), *n., pl.* **-nies,** *adj.* —*n.* **1.** any of several tropical American, meliaceous trees, esp. *Swietenia Mahogoni* and *S. macrophylla,* yielding a hard, reddish-brown wood used for making furniture. **2.** the wood itself. **3.** a reddish-brown color. —*adj.* **4.** pertaining to or made of mahogany. [? < some non-Carib WInd tongue]
Ma·hom·et (mə hom′it), *n.* Muhammad. Also, **Ma·hom·ed** (mə hom′id).
Ma·hom·e·tan (mə hom′i tᵊn), *n., adj.* Muslim. —**Ma·hom′et·an·ism,** *n.*
Ma·hound (mə hound′, -ho͞ond′), *n.* **1.** *Archaic.* Muhammad. **2.** *Scot.* Satan; the devil. [early ME *Mahun, Mahum* < OF, short for MAHOMET; *-d* by assoc. with HOUND¹]
ma·hout (mə hout′), *n.* the keeper or driver of an elephant, esp. in India. [< Hindi *mahāut,* var. of *mahāvat*]
Mah·rat·ta (mə rat′ə), *n.* a member of a Hindu people inhabiting central and western India. Also, **Maratha.**
Mah·rat·ti (mə rat′ē), *n.* Marathi.
Mäh·ren (me′Rən), *n.* German name of **Moravia.**
Mäh·risch-Os·trau (me′Rish ôs′tRou), *n.* German name of **Moravská Ostrava.**
mah·zor (mäKH zôR′; *Eng.* mäKH′zôr, -zôr -zər), *n., pl.* **mah·zo·rim** (mäKH zô Rēm′), *Eng.* **mah·zors.** *Hebrew.* a Jewish prayer book designed for use on festivals and holy days. Also, **machzor.** Cf. **siddur.**
Ma·ia (mā′yə, mī′ə), *n.* *Class. Myth.* the eldest of the Pleiades and the mother of Hermes by Zeus.
maid (mād), *n.* **1.** a girl; young unmarried woman. **2.** a female servant. **3.** *Rare.* a spinster; old maid. **4.** *Archaic.* a virgin. [apocopated var. of MAIDEN] —**maid′ish,** *adj.* —**maid′ish·ness,** *n.* —**Syn. 1.** lass; maiden.
maid·en (mād′ᵊn), *n.* **1.** a girl; young unmarried woman; maid. **2.** an instrument resembling the guillotine, formerly used in Scotland. **3.** a maiden horse. **4.** a maiden race. —*adj.* **5.** of, pertaining to, or befitting a girl or unmarried woman. **6.** unmarried. **7.** made, tried, appearing, etc., for the first time. **8.** virgin. **9.** (of a horse) never having won a race or a prize. **10.** (of a prize or a race) offered for or open only to maiden horses. **11.** untried, as a knight, soldier, or weapon. [ME; OE *mægden* = *mægd* (c. Goth *magaths,* [G *Magd*) + *-en* -EN⁵] —**maid′en·li·ness,** *n.* —**maid′en·ly,** *adj.* —**maid′en·ship′,** *n.*
maid·en·hair (mād′ᵊn hâr′), *n.* any fern of the genus *Adiantum,* the cultivated species of which have fine, glossy stalks and delicate, finely divided fronds. [ME]
maid·en·head (mād′ᵊn hed′), *n.* **1.** maidenhood; virginity. **2.** the hymen. [ME *maidenhed*]
maid·en·hood (mād′ᵊn ho͝od′), *n.* the state or time of being a maiden; virginity. [ME; OE *mægdenhād*]
maid′en name′, a woman's surname before marriage.
maid′en voy′age, *Naut.* the first scheduled voyage of a vessel after its completion.
maid-in-wait·ing (mād′in wā′ting), *n., pl.* **maids-in-wait·ing.** an unmarried woman who acts as an attendant to a queen or princess; a lady-in-waiting.
Maid′ Mar′ian, 1. Queen of the May, one of the characters in the old morris dance. **2.** See **morris dance.**
maid′ of hon′or, 1. the chief unmarried attendant of a bride. **2.** an unmarried woman, usually of noble birth, attendant on a queen or princess.
Maid′ of Or′leans. See **Joan of Arc.**
maid·ser·vant (mād′sûr′vənt), *n.* a female servant.
Maid·stone (mād′stōn′, -stən), *n.* a city in and the county seat of Kent, in SE England. 59,761 (1961).
ma·ieu·tic (mā yo͞o′tik), *adj.* noting the method used by Socrates in bringing forth knowledge by interrogation and insistence on close and logical reasoning. [< Gk *maieutik(ós)* of, pertaining to midwifery = *maieú(esthai)* (to) serve as a midwife (akin to *maîa* midwife) + *-tikos* -TIC]
mai·gre (mā′gər; *Fr.* me′gRᵊ), *adj.* containing neither flesh nor its juices, as food permissible on days of religious abstinence. [< F; see MEAGER]
mai·hem (mā′hem), *n.* mayhem.
mail¹ (māl), *n.* **1.** letters, packages, etc., that are sent or delivered by means of the post office. **2.** a single collection of such letters, packages, etc., as sent or delivered. **3.** Also, **mails.** the system, usually operated by the national government, for sending or delivering letters, packages, etc.; postal system. **4.** a train, boat, person, etc., as a carrier of postal matter. —*adj.* **5.** of or pertaining to mail: *mail delivery.* —*v.t.* **6.** to send by mail; place in a post office or mailbox for transmission. [ME *male* < OF *malle* < Gmc; cf. OHG *mal(a)ha* satchel, bag]

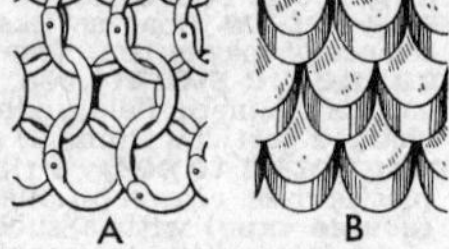

Mail
A, (def. 1); B, (def. 2)

mail² (māl), *n.* **1.** flexible armor of interlinked rings. **2.** (loosely) any flexible armor, as one having a protective exterior of scales or small plates. —*v.t.* **3.** to clothe or arm with mail. [ME *maille* one of the rings of which armor was composed < OF < L *macula* spot, mesh of a net] —**mail′less,** *adj.*
mail³ (māl), *n.* *Scot.* monetary payment or tribute, esp. rent or tax. [ME (north) *mal(e),* OE *māl* agreement < Scand; cf. Icel *māl* agreement, speech, c. OE *mǣl* speech]
mail·a·ble (mā′lə bəl), *adj.* legally acceptable as mail. —**mail′a·bil′i·ty,** *n.*
mail·bag (māl′bag′), *n.* **1.** a large bag used by mailmen for carrying mail. **2.** a large bag or pouch used in transporting mail in bulk.
mail·box (māl′boks′), *n.* *U.S.* **1.** Also called **postbox.** a public box in which mail is placed for delivery by the post office; letterbox. **2.** a private box, as at a home, into which mail is delivered by the mailman. Also called, *Brit.,* **letter-box.**
mailed (māld), *adj.* clad or armed with mail: *a mailed knight.* [ME]
mailed′ fist′, 1. superior force, esp. when presented as a threat. **2.** brutal or naked power, esp. coercive force.
mail·er (mā′lər), *n.* a person who mails or prepares material for mailing.
Mail·er (mā′lər), *n.* **Norman,** born 1923, U.S. writer.
Mail·lol (mA yôl′), *n.* **A·ris·tide** (A Rēs tēd′), 1861–1944, French sculptor.
mail·lot (mä yō′; *Fr.* mA yō′), *n., pl.* **mail·lots** (mä-yōz′; *Fr.* mA yō′) **1.** tights worn by dancers, acrobats, etc. **2.** a close-fitting, one-piece bathing suit for women. **3.** a close-fitting knitted shirt. [< F: bathing costume, tights, swaddling clothes, var. of earlier *maillol* < *maille* MAIL²]

mail·man (māl′man′), *n., pl.* **-men.** a man, usually employed by the post office, who delivers mail; postman.
mail′ or′der, an order received or shipped by mail.
mail′-order house′, a firm that conducts all or most of its business through mail orders.
maim (mām), *v.t.* **1.** to deprive of the use of some part of the body by wounding or the like; cripple. **2.** to impair; make essentially defective. **—***n. Obs.* **3.** a physical injury, esp. a loss of a limb. **4.** an injury or defect; blemish; lack. [ME *mayme(n)* (v.) < *mayme* MAYHEM] **—maimed′ness,** *n.* **—maim′er,** *n.*
—Syn. 1. MAIM, LACERATE, MANGLE, MUTILATE indicate the infliction of painful and severe injuries on the body. To MAIM is to injure by giving a disabling wound, or by depriving a person of one or more members or their use: *maimed in an accident.* To LACERATE is to inflict severe cuts and tears on the flesh or skin: *to lacerate an arm.* To MANGLE is to chop undiscriminatingly or to crush or rend by blows or pressure, as if by machinery: *bodies mangled in a train wreck.* To MUTILATE is to injure the completeness or beauty of a body, esp. by cutting off an important member: *to mutilate a statue, a tree, a person.* **2.** injure, disable, deface, mar.
Mai·mon·i·des (mī mon′i dēz′), *n.* (*Moses ben Maimon*) ("*RaMBaM*") 1135–1204, Jewish scholastic philosopher and rabbi, born in Spain: one of the major theologians of Judaism. **—Mai·mon′i·de′an,** *adj., n.*
main[1] (mān), *adj.* **1.** chief; principal; leading; most important. **2.** sheer; utmost, as strength or force. **3.** of or pertaining to a broad expanse: *main sea.* **4.** *Gram.* syntactically independent; capable of use in isolation. In *I walked out when the bell rang, I walked out* is the main clause. Cf. **dependent** (def. 4), **independent** (def. 12). **5.** *Naut.* of or pertaining to a mainmast. **6.** *Obs.* having momentous or important results; essential. **—***n.* **7.** a principal pipe or duct in a system used to distribute water, gas, etc. **8.** strength; force; violent effort. **9.** the chief or principal part or point. **10.** *Literary.* the open ocean; high sea: *the bounding main.* **11.** the mainland. **12. in the main,** for the most part; chiefly. [ME *meyn,* OE *mægen* strength, power; c. Icel *megin* strength] **—Syn. 1.** cardinal, prime. **2.** pure, direct. **7.** conduit. **8.** power, might. **—Ant. 1.** secondary, least. **8.** weakness.
main[2] (mān), *n.* a cockfight. [? special use of MAIN[1]]
Main (mān; *Ger.* mīn), *n.* a river in central and W Germany, flowing W from N Bavaria into the Rhine at Mainz, in West Germany. 305 mi. long.
main′ clause′, *Gram.* a clause that can stand alone as a sentence, containing a subject, a predicate of a finite verb, and sometimes a direct object, as *I was there* in the sentence *I was there when he arrived.* Cf. **subordinate clause.**
main′ course′ 1. *U.S.* the principal dish of a meal. Cf. **entrée** (def. 5). **2.** *Naut.* a square mainsail. See diag. at **ship.**
main′ deck′, *Naut.* the uppermost weatherproof deck, running the full length of a vessel.
Maine (mān *for 1, 3;* men *for 2*), *n.* **1.** a state in the NE United States, on the Atlantic coast. 993,663 (1970); 33,215 sq. mi. *Cap.:* Augusta. *Abbr.:* Me., ME **2.** a former province in NW France. See map at **Picardy. 3.** (*italics*) a U.S. battleship blown up in the harbor of Havana, Cuba, on February 15, 1898.
main·frame (mān′frām′), *n.* the device within a computer which contains the central control and arithmetic units, responsible for the essential control and computational functions. Also called **central processing unit.**
main·land (mān′land′, -lənd), *n.* the principal land of a country, region, etc., as distinguished from adjacent islands. [ME] **—main′land′er,** *n.*
Main·land (mān′land′, -lənd), *n.* **1.** the largest of the Shetland Islands. ab. 200 sq. mi. **2.** Pomona (def. 3).
main′ line′, the principal line of a railroad. **2.** *Slang.* a prominent and readily accessible vein that may be used for a narcotic's injection.
main·line (mān′līn′, -līn′), *v.t., v.i.,* **-lined, -lin·ing.** *Slang.* to inject (a drug, esp. heroin) into a vein. **—main′-lin′er,** *n.*
main·ly (mān′lē), *adv.* **1.** chiefly; principally; for the most part; in the main; to the greatest extent. **2.** *Obs.* greatly; abundantly. [ME *maynliche, maynly*]
main·mast (mān′mast′, -mäst′; *Naut.* mān′məst), *n.* *Naut.* **1.** the second mast from forward in any vessel or dandy. **2.** the larger forward mast of a yawl, ketch, or dandy. **3.** the sole mast of any of various vessels, as sloops or cutters.
main·sail (mān′sāl′; *Naut.* mān′səl), *n.* *Naut.* the lowermost sail on a mainmast. See diag. at **ship.** [ME]
main·sheet (mān′shēt′), *n.* *Naut.* a sheet of a mainsail. [ME]
main·spring (mān′spring′), *n.* **1.** the principal spring in a mechanism, as in a watch. **2.** the chief motive power of something; impelling cause.
main·stay (mān′stā′), *n.* **1.** a person or thing that acts as a chief support or part of something. **2.** *Naut.* the stay that secures the mainmast forward. [ME]
main·stream (mān′strēm′), *n.* **1.** the principal or dominant course, tendency, or trend. **2.** a river having tributaries.
main·tain (mān tān′), *v.t.* **1.** to keep in existence or continuance; preserve; retain. **2.** to keep in due condition, operation, or force; keep unimpaired. **3.** to keep in a specified state, position, etc. **4.** to affirm; assert; declare. **5.** to support in speech or argument, as a statement or proposition. **6.** to keep or hold against attack. **7.** to provide for the upkeep or support of; carry the expenses of. [ME *mainteine(n)* < OF *mainten(ir)* < ML *manūtenēre,* L *manū tenēre,* lit., to hold in hand = *manū,* abl. of *manus* hand (see MANUAL) + *tenēre* to hold (see TENET)] **—main·tain′a·ble,** *adj.* **—main·tain′er,** *n.* **—Syn. 1.** continue. **4.** aver, asseverate, state, hold, allege. **5.** uphold, defend, vindicate, justify. **7.** See **support. —Ant. 1.** discontinue. **5.** contradict.
main·te·nance (mān′t[ə]nəns), *n.* **1.** the act of maintaining. **2.** the state of being maintained: *the maintenance of friendly relations with England.* **3.** means of upkeep, support, or subsistence; livelihood. **4.** *Law.* an officious meddling in a suit in which the meddler has no interest, esp. by providing funds to aid the prosecution or defense. [ME *maintenaunce* < MF *maintenance*] **—Syn. 3.** See **living.**
Main·te·non (maɴt[ə] nôɴ′), *n.* **Marquise de** (*Françoise d'Aubigné*), 1635–1719, second wife of Louis XIV.
main′ yard′, *Naut.* a yard for a square mainsail.
Mainz (mīnts), *n.* a port in W West Germany, at the confluence of the Rhine and Main rivers. 139,400 (1963).
ma·iol·i·ca (mə yol′ə kə), *n.* majolica.
mai·son de san·té (me zôɴ də säɴ tā′), *pl.,* **mai·sons de san·té** (me zôɴ də säɴ tā′). *French.* a private hospital or sanitarium for the sick or insane. [lit., house of health]
mai·son·ette (mā′zə net′), *n.* *Chiefly Brit.* a small apartment, esp. part of a private house rented as an apartment. Also, **mai′son·nette′.** [< F, OF, dim. of *maison* house]
mai tai (mī′ tī′), a cocktail of rum and lemon and pineapple juice, sweetened and served with ice. [< Tahitian: *maita'i* good]
Mait·land (māt′lənd), *n.* **Fredrick William,** 1850–1906, English jurist and legal historian.
maî·tre d' (mā′tər dē′, mā′trə), *pl.* **maî·tre d's.** *Informal.* See **maître d'hôtel** (defs. 1, 2).
maî·tre d'hô·tel (mā′tər dō tel′, mā′trə; *Fr.* me′tʀ[ə] dō tel′), *pl.* **maî·tres d'hô·tel** (mā′tərz dō tel′, mā′trəz; *Fr.* me′tʀ[ə] dō tel′). **1.** a headwaiter or steward. **2.** the owner or manager of a hotel. **3.** *Cookery.* a sauce of melted butter, minced parsley, and lemon juice or vinegar. [< F: master of (the) hotel]
maize (māz), *n.* **1.** (chiefly in British and technical usage) corn[1] (def. 1). **2.** a pale yellow resembling the color of corn. **—***adj.* **3.** of the color of maize. [< Sp *maíz* < Hispaniolan Taino *mahís*]
maize′ oil′. See **corn oil.**
Maj., Major.
ma·jes·tic (mə jes′tik), *adj.* characterized by or possessing majesty; of lofty dignity or imposing aspect; stately; grand: *a majestic manner; the majestic Alps.* Also, **ma·jes′ti·cal.** **—ma·jes′ti·cal·ly,** *adv.* **—Syn.** magnificent, regal, royal.
maj·es·ty (maj′i stē), *n., pl.* **-ties** for 2–4. **1.** regal, lofty, or stately dignity; imposing character; grandeur. **2.** supreme greatness or authority; sovereignty. **3.** a royal personage. **4.** (*usually cap.*) a title used when speaking of or to a sovereign (usually prec. by *his, her,* or *your*). [ME *majeste* < MF < L *mājestāt-* (s. of *mājestās*) sovereignty, greatness, grandeur = **mājes-* (akin to *mājus;* see MAJOR) + *-tāt-* -TY[2]]
Maj. Gen., Major General.
ma·jol·i·ca (mə jol′ə kə, mə yol′-), *n.* **1.** Italian earthenware covered with an opaque glaze of tin oxide and usually highly decorated. **2.** any pottery, as faïence or delft, resembling this. Also, **maiolica.** [earlier *maiolica* < It < ML, var. of LL *Mājorica* MAJORCA, where it was made]
ma·jor (mā′jər), *n.* **1.** *Mil.* a commissioned officer ranking next below a lieutenant colonel and next above a captain. **2.** a subject or discipline upon which a college student concentrates a large share of his efforts: *History was his major.* **3.** *Music.* a major interval, chord, scale, etc. **4.** a person of superior rank, ability, etc., in a specified class. **5.** a person of full legal age (opposed to *minor*). **6. the majors,** *Sports.* the major leagues. **—***adj.* **7.** greater, as in size, amount, extent, or rank. **8.** great, as in rank or importance: *a major question; a major artist.* **9.** of or pertaining to the majority: *the major opinion.* **10.** *Music.* **a.** (of an interval) being between the tonic and the second, third, sixth, and seventh degrees of a major scale. **b.** (of a chord) having a major third between the root and the note next above it. **11.** of full legal age. **—***v.i.* **12.** to follow a major subject: *to major in math.* [< L, comp. of *magnus* great; r. ME *majour* < AF]
Ma·jor·ca (mə jôr′kə, -yôr′-), *n.* a Spanish island in the W Mediterranean: the largest of the Balearic Islands. 350,000 (est. 1965); 1405 sq. mi. *Cap.:* Palma. Spanish, **Mallorca. —Ma·jor′can,** *adj., n.*
ma·jor-do·mo (mā′jər dō′mō), *n., pl.* **-mos. 1.** a man in charge of a great household, as that of a sovereign; chief steward. **2.** a steward or butler. [< Sp *mayordomo* < ML *mājordomūs* head of the house = *major* MAJOR + *domūs,* gen. of *domus* house; see DOME]
ma·jor·ette (mā′jə ret′), *n.* See **drum majorette.**
ma′jor gen′eral, *Mil.* an officer ranking next below a lieutenant general and next above a brigadier general. **—ma′jor-gen′er·al·ship′,** *n.*
ma·jor·i·ty (mə jôr′i tē, -jor′-), *n., pl.* **-ties,** *adj.* **—***n.* **1.** the greater part or number; any number larger than half the total, as opposed to the minority: *the majority of mankind.* **2.** a number of voters or votes, jurors, or others in agreement constituting more than half of the total number. **3.** the amount by which the greater number, as of votes, surpasses the remainder (distinguished from *plurality*). **4.** the party or faction with the majority vote. **5.** the state or time of being of full legal age. **6.** the military rank or office of a major. **—***adj.* **7.** of, pertaining to, or being a majority. [< ML *mājoritās*]
major′ity lead′er, *U.S. Govt.* the party member who directs the activities of the majority party on the floor of either the Senate or the House of Representatives.
ma′jor league′, 1. either of the two main professional baseball leagues in the U.S. **2.** a league of corresponding stature in any of certain other sports.
ma′jor or′der, *Rom. Cath. Ch.* the degree or grade of priesthood, diaconate, or subdiaconate. Cf. **minor order.**
ma′jor prem′ise, *Logic.* See under **syllogism** (def. 1).
Ma′jor Proph′ets, Isaiah, Jeremiah, and Ezekiel. Cf. **Minor Prophets.**
ma′jor scale′, *Music.* a scale consisting of a series of whole steps except for half steps between the third and fourth and the seventh and eighth degrees.
ma′jor suit′, *Bridge.* hearts or spades, esp. with reference to their higher point values. Cf. **minor suit.**
ma′jor term′, *Logic.* See under **syllogism** (def. 1).
Ma·jun·ga (mə jung′gə), *n.* a seaport on W Madagascar. 34,119 (1960).
ma·jus·cule (mə jus′kyo͞ol, maj′ə skyo͞ol′), *adj.* **1.** (of letters) capital. **2.** large, as either capital or uncial letters. **3.** written in such letters. **—***n.* **4.** a majuscule letter. Cf. **minuscule.** [< L *mājuscula* (*littera*) a somewhat bigger

(letter) = *mājus-*, s. of *mājor* MAJOR + *-cula* -CULE] —**ma·jus′cu·lar,** *adj.*

Ma·ka·lu (muk′ə lo͞o′), *n.* a mountain in the Himalayas, on the boundary between Nepal and Tibet. 27,790 ft.

Ma·kar·i·os III (mə kar′ē əs, -ōs′; *Gk.* mä kä′rē ôs), (*Michael Christedoulos Mouskos*) 1913–77, Cypriote statesman and Greek Orthodox prelate: archbishop and patriarch of Cyprus 1950–77; president 1960–77 (in exile 1974).

Ma·kas·sar (mə käs′ər), *n.* Dutch name of **Macassar.**

make (māk), *v.*, **made, mak·ing,** *n.* —*v.t.* **1.** to bring into existence by shaping or changing material, combining parts, etc.: *to make a dress; to make a chair; to make a work of art.* **2.** to produce; cause to exist; bring about: *to make trouble; to make war.* **3.** to cause to be or become; render: *to make someone happy.* **4.** to put in the proper condition or state, as for use; fix; prepare: *to make a meal.* **5.** to bring into a certain form: *to make bricks out of clay.* **6.** to convert from one state, condition, category, etc., to another: *to make a liquid into a solid.* **7.** to cause, induce, or compel. **8.** to give rise to; occasion. **9.** to produce, earn, or win for oneself: *to make a good salary.* **10.** to write or compose, as a poem. **11.** to draw up, as a legal document: *to make a will.* **12.** to do; effect: *to make a bargain.* **13.** to establish or enact; put into existence: *to make laws.* **14.** to appoint or name; elevate to a particular position: *The President made him his special envoy. Queen Elizabeth made him a baronet.* **15.** to become by development; prove to be: *He will make a good lawyer.* **16.** to form in the mind, as a judgment or estimate. **17.** to judge or interpret, as to the truth, nature, meaning, etc. (often fol. by *of*): *What do you make of it?* **18.** to estimate as being; reckon: *to make the distance ten miles.* **19.** to bring together separate parts so as to produce a whole; compose; form: *to make a matched set.* **20.** to bring to; bring up the total to: *to make an even dozen.* **21.** to be equal to: *Two plus two makes four.* **22.** to serve as: *to make good reading.* **23.** to be sufficient to constitute; be adequate to: *That makes a good answer!* **24.** to assure the success or fortune of. **25.** to deliver or utter; put forth: *to make a stirring speech.* **26.** to go or travel at a particular speed: *to make 60 miles an hour.* **27.** to arrive at or reach: *The ship made port on Friday.* **28.** to arrive in time for: *If you hurry, you can make the next flight.* **29.** *Informal.* to gain or acquire a position within: *He made the big time.* **30.** to receive mention or appear in or on: *to make the front page.* **31.** *Cards.* **a.** to name (the trump). **b.** to take a trick with (a card). **c.** *Bridge.* to fulfill or achieve (a contract or bid). **d.** to mix up or shuffle (the cards). **32.** to earn, as a score: *make a home run.* **33.** to close (an electric circuit).
—*v.i.* **34.** to show oneself to be in action or behavior (usually fol. by an adjective): *to make merry.* **35.** to be made, as specified: *This toy stove makes easily: just fold on the dotted lines.* **36.** to rise, as the tide or water in a ship. **37. make a play for,** to try to get. **38. make believe,** to pretend; imagine: *The little girl made believe she was a princess.* **39. make book,** *Slang.* to take bets and give odds. **40. make do,** to function or manage, despite a lack of something: *During the war we had no butter or coffee, but we made do.* **41. make fast,** to fasten or secure. **42. make for, a.** to go toward; approach. **b.** to lunge at; attack. **c.** to help to promote or maintain: *This incident will not make for peace.* **43. make good, a.** to provide restitution or reparation for. **b.** to succeed: *He has talent and he'll make good.* **c.** to fulfill, as a promise (sometimes fol. by *on*). **44. make it,** *Informal.* **a.** to achieve a specific goal: *to make it to the train; to make it through college.* **b.** to succeed in general: *He'll make it, he's got a rich daddy.* **45. make like,** *Slang.* to try or pretend to be like; imitate. **46. make off,** to run away; depart hastily. **47. make off with,** to carry away; steal: *Thieves made off with many of their valuables.* **48. make out, a.** to write out or complete, as a bill or check. **b.** to establish; prove. **c.** to decipher; discern; comprehend. **d.** to imply, suggest, or impute: *He made me out to be a liar.* **e.** *Informal.* to manage; succeed: *How are you making out in your new job?* **f.** *Slang.* to engage in kissing and caressing; neck. **49. make over, a.** to remodel; alter: *to make over a dress; make over a page.* **b.** to transfer the title of (property); convey: *The old lady made over her property to her children.* **50. make time.** See **time** (def. 40). **51. make up, a.** (of parts) to constitute; form. **b.** to put together; construct; compile. **c.** to concoct; invent. **d.** Also, **make up for.** to compensate for; make good. **e.** to complete. **f.** to put in order; arrange. **g.** to conclude; decide. **h.** to settle amicably, as differences. **i.** to become reconciled, as after a quarrel. **j.** to dress in appropriate costume and apply cosmetics for a part on the stage. **k.** to apply cosmetics. **52. make up to, a.** *Informal.* to try to become friendly with; fawn on. **b.** to make advances to; flirt with.
—*n.* **53.** style or manner of being made; form; build. **54.** production with reference to the maker; brand: *our own make.* **55.** disposition; character; nature. **56.** act or process of making. **57.** quantity made; output. **58.** *Cards.* act of naming the trump, or the suit named as trump. **59. on the make,** *Informal.* **a.** seeking to improve one's social or financial position at the expense of others or of principle. **b.** increasing; advancing. **c.** *Slang.* seeking amorous relations. [ME *make(n)*, OE *macian;* c. LG, D *maken*, G *machen*] —**mak′a·ble,** *adj.*
—**Syn. 1.** form; build; produce; fabricate, create, fashion, mold. MAKE, CONSTRUCT, MANUFACTURE mean to produce, to put into definite form, or to put parts together to make a whole. MAKE is the general term: *Bees make wax.* CONSTRUCT, more formal, means to put parts together, usually according to a plan or design: *to construct a building.* MANUFACTURE usually refers to producing something from material that requires conversion from one state or condition to another, now almost entirely by means of machinery in a relatively complex process: *to manufacture automobile tires.* **6.** transform, change, turn. **7.** force. **9.** get, gain, acquire, obtain, secure, procure. **12.** perform, execute. **18.** judge, gauge.

make-be·lieve (māk′bi lēv′), *n.* **1.** pretense, esp. of an innocent kind, as in the imaginative play of children. **2.** a pretender; one who pretends. —*adj.* **3.** pretended; made-up; unreal.

Ma·ke·ev·ka (*Russ.* mä ke′yəf kä′), *n.* Makeyevka.

make·fast (māk′fast′, -fäst′), *n.* *Naut.* any structure to which a vessel is tied up, as a bollard or buoy.

mak·er (mā′kər), *n.* **1.** a person or thing that makes. **2.** (*cap.*) God. **3.** a person who executes and signs a promissory note. **4.** *Cards.* the person who first names the successful bid. **5. go to** or **meet one's Maker,** to die. [ME]

make-read·y (māk′red′ē), *n.* the process of preparing a form for printing by overlays or underlays to equalize the impression.

mak′er's mark′, the personal mark of a goldsmith or silversmith, struck on pieces coming from his shop.

make·shift (māk′shift′), *n.* **1.** a temporary expedient or substitute. —*adj.* **2.** serving as, or of the nature of, a makeshift. [n., adj. use of v. phrase *make shift*] —**Syn. 1.** contrivance. **2.** emergency, temporary, improvised.

make-up (māk′up′), *n.* **1.** facial cosmetics, as lipstick, powder, etc., used by women to enhance their features. **2.** cosmetics used on other parts of the body, as to make the skin appear darker. **3.** the application of cosmetics. **4.** the effect created by such application: *Her make-up is too showy.* **5.** the total ensemble, consisting of cosmetics, costumes, etc., used by a performer. **6.** the manner of being made up or put together; composition. **7.** physical or mental constitution: *the make-up of a criminal.* **8.** the appearance of a page, book, or the like, resulting from the disposition and the variation in size and style of the printed elements. **9.** *Print.* the arrangement of set type, cuts, etc., into columns or pages. **10.** (in education) an examination taken in substitution for an examination that one failed to pass or from which one was absent. Also, **make′up′.**

make-work (māk′wûrk′), *n.* unnecessary work invented to keep workers from being idle.

Ma·ke·yev·ka (mä ke′yəf kä′), *n.* a city in the SE Ukraine, in the SW Soviet Union in Europe, N of the Sea of Azov. 440,000. Also, **Makeevka.**

Ma·khach·ka·la (mə käch′kə lä′; *Russ.* mä khäch′kä-lä′), *n.* a seaport in the W RSFSR, in the S Soviet Union in Europe, on the Caspian Sea. 248,000.

mak·ing (mā′king), *n.* **1.** the act of a person or thing that makes. **2.** structure; constitution; make-up. **3.** the means or cause of success or advancement: *to be the making of someone.* **4.** Usually, **makings.** capacity or potential: *He has the makings of a first-rate officer.* **5. makings,** material of which something may be made: *the makings of a cigarette.* **6.** something made. **7.** the quantity made: *a making of butter.* **8. in the making,** in the process of being made; developing; growing. [ME; OE *macung*]

Mak·kah (mak′ə, -kä), *n.* Mecca (def. 1).

mal-, a prefix meaning "bad," "wrongful," "ill," occurring originally in loan words from French (*malapert*); on this model, used in the formation of other words (*malfunction; malcontent*). Cf. **male-.** [ME < OF, repr. *mal*, adv. (<< L *male* badly, ill), or *mal*, adj. (<< L *malus* bad)]

Mal., **1.** Malachi. **2.** Malayan.

Mal′a·bar Coast′ (mal′ə bär′), a region along the entire SW coast of India, extending from the Arabian Sea inland to the Western Ghats. Also called **Mal′abar′.**

Ma·la·bo (mə lä′bō), *n.* a town in and the capital of Equatorial Guinea, on N Fernando Po Island. 20,000. Formerly, **Santa Isabel.**

Ma·lac·ca (mə lak′ə), *n.* **1.** a state in Malaysia, on the SW Malay Peninsula: formerly a part of the British Straits Settlements and of the Federation of Malaya. 404,125; 640 sq. mi. **2.** a seaport in and the capital of this state. 87,160. **3. Strait of,** a strait between Sumatra and the Malay Peninsula. 35–185 mi. wide. —**Ma·lac′can,** *adj., n.*

Malac′ca cane′, a cane or walking stick made of the brown, often mottled or clouded stem of an East Indian rattan palm, *Calamus Scipionum.*

ma·la·ceous (mə lā′shəs), *adj.* belonging to the *Malaceae*, or apple family of plants, comprising the apple, pear, quince, medlar, loquat, hawthorn, etc. [< L *māl(um)* apple (c. Gk *mâlon*, var. of *mêlon*) + -ACEOUS]

Mal·a·chi (mal′ə kī′), *n.* **1.** a Minor Prophet of the 5th century B.C. **2.** the book of the Bible bearing his name.

mal·a·chite (mal′ə kīt′), *n.* a green mineral, basic copper carbonate, $Cu_2CO_3(OH)_2$, an ore of copper, used for making ornamental articles. [< Gk *maláchē* MALLOW + -ITE[1]; r. ME *melochites* < L *molochītēs* < Gk *molóchē* mallow]

malaco-, a learned borrowing from Greek, meaning "soft," used in the formation of compound words: *malacopterygian.* [< Gk *malako-*, comb. form of *malakós*]

mal·a·col·o·gy (mal′ə kol′ə jē), *n.* the science dealing with the study of mollusks. [< F *malacologie*, syncopated var. of *malacozoologie*] —**mal·a·co·log·i·cal** (mal′ə kə loj′i-kəl), *adj.* —**mal′a·col′o·gist,** *n.*

mal·a·cop·te·ryg·i·an (mal′ə kop′tə rij′ē ən), *adj.* belonging or pertaining to the *Malacopterygii* (*Malacopteri*), a division of soft-finned, teleost fishes. [< NL *Malacopterygi(i)* (MALACO- + Gk *pteryg-* s. of *ptéryx* wing, fin + L *-ii* masc. pl. ending) + -AN]

mal·a·cos·tra·can (mal′ə kos′trə kən), *adj.* **1.** belonging or pertaining to the subclass *Malacostraca*, which includes the lobsters, shrimps, crabs, etc. —*n.* **2.** a malacostracan crustacean. [< NL *Malacostrac(a)* order of crustacea (< Gk *malakóstrakos* soft-shelled; see MALACO-, OSTRACIZE) + -AN]

mal·ad·just·ed (mal′ə jus′tid), *adj.* badly or unsatisfactorily adjusted, esp. in relationship to one's circumstances, environment, etc.

mal·ad·just·ment (mal′ə just′mənt), *n.* bad or unsatisfactory adjustment.

mal·ad·min·is·ter (mal′əd min′i stər), *v.t.* to manage badly or inefficiently. —**mal′ad·min′is·tra′tion,** *n.*

mal·a·droit (mal′ə droit′), *adj.* lacking in adroitness; unskillful: awkward; bungling; tactless. [< F, MF] —**mal′a·droit′ly,** *adv.* —**mal′a·droit′ness,** *n.* —**Syn.** clumsy.

mal·a·dy (mal′ə dē), *n.*, *pl.* **-dies.** **1.** any disorder or disease of the body, esp. one that is chronic or deep-seated. **2.** any undesirable or disordered condition: *social maladies; a malady of the spirit.* [ME *maladie* < OF = *malade* sick (< LL *male habitus*, lit., ill-conditioned) + *-ie* -Y[3]] —**Syn. 1.** illness, sickness, ailment. See **disease.**

ma·la fi·de (mä′lä fē′de; *Eng.* mā′lə fī′dē), *Latin.* in bad faith; not genuine.

Mal·a·ga (mal′ə gə), *n.* **1.** a strong, sweet dessert wine produced chiefly in Málaga, Spain. **2.** any of the grapes used to make Malaga wine.

Mál·a·ga (mal′ə gə; *Sp.* mä′lä gä′), *n.* **1.** a province in S Spain, in Andalusia. 775,167 (1960); 2813 sq. mi. **2.** a seaport in S Spain, on the Mediterranean. 324,949 (1965).

Mal·a·gas·y (mal′ə gas′ē), *n., pl.* **-gas·y, -gas·ies** for 1. **1.** a native of the Malagasy Republic. **2.** the Malayo-Polynesian language of Madagascar.

Malagas′y Repub′lic, former official name of **Madagascar.** French, **République Malgache.**

ma·laise (ma lāz′; *Fr.* MA lez′), *n.* **1.** a condition of general bodily weakness or discomfort. **2.** an unfocused feeling of mental uneasiness or discomfort. [< F, OF; see MAL-, EASE]

Mal·a·mud (mal′ə məd, -mo͝od′), *n.* **Bernard,** 1914–86, U.S. novelist and short-story writer.

mal·a·mute (mal′ə myo͞ot′), *n.* (*sometimes cap.*) See **Alaskan malamute.** Also, **malemute.** [var. of *Malemute,* Eskimo tribe that bred the dogs]

Ma·lan (mä län′), *n.* **Daniel Fran·çois** (frän swä′), 1874–1959, South African editor and political leader: prime minister 1948–54.

mal·an·ders (mal′ən dərz), *n.* (*construed as sing.*) *Vet. Pathol.* a dry, scabby or scurfy eruption or scratch behind the knee in a horse's foreleg. Also, **mallanders, mallenders.** [late ME *malawnder* < MF *malander* < L *malandria* blister on a horse's neck]

Ma·lang (mä läng′), *n.* a city on E Java, in S Indonesia. 341,452 (1961).

mal·a·pert (mal′ə pûrt′), *adj. Archaic.* unbecomingly bold or saucy. [late ME: insolent < MF: unskillful. See MAL-, PERT] —**mal′a·pert′ly,** *adv.* —**mal′a·pert′ness,** *n.*

mal·a·prop·ism (mal′ə prop iz′əm), *n.* **1.** the act or habit of misusing words ridiculously, esp. by the confusion of words that are similar in sound. **2.** an instance of this, as in "Lead the way and we'll precede." [named after Mrs. Malaprop, a character in Sheridan's comedy *The Rivals* (1775), noted for her misapplication of words]

mal·ap·ro·pos (mal′ap rə pō′), *adj.* **1.** inappropriate. —*adv.* **2.** inappropriately. [< F *mal à propos* badly (suited) to the purpose]

ma·lar (mā′lər), *Anat.* —*adj.* **1.** of or pertaining to the cheek or zygomatic bone. —*n.* **2.** Also, **ma′lar bone′.** See **zygomatic bone.** [< NL *mālār(is)* of, pertaining to the cheek = L *māl(a)* cheek, jaw + *-āris* -AR[1]]

Mä·lar (mā′lər, -lär), *n.* **Lake,** a lake in S Sweden, extending W from Stockholm toward the Baltic Sea. 440 sq. mi. Swedish, **Mä·lar·en** (me′lä Rən).

ma·lar·i·a (mə lâr′ē ə), *n.* **1.** *Pathol.* any of a group of diseases characterized by attacks of chills, fever, and sweating: caused by parasitic protozoans that are transferred to the human bloodstream by mosquitoes of the genus *Anopheles* and that occupy and destroy the red blood corpuscles. **2.** *Archaic.* unwholesome or poisonous air. [< It, contr. of *mala aria* bad air] —**ma·lar′i·al, ma·lar′i·an, ma·lar′i·ous,** *adj.*

ma·lar·key (mə lär′kē), *n. Informal.* speech or writing designed to obscure, mislead, or impress; bunkum. [?]

mal·ate (mal′āt, mā′lāt), *n. Chem.* a salt or ester of malic acid. [MAL(IC) + -ATE[2]]

Mal·a·thi·on (mal′ə thī′on), *n. Chem., Trademark.* a liquid, $C_{10}H_{19}O_6PS_2$, used as an insecticide.

Ma·la·tya (mä′lä tyä′), *n.* a city in central Turkey. 150,397. Ancient, **Melitene.**

Ma·la·wi (mä lä′wē), *n.* a republic in SE Africa, on the W and S shores of Lake Nyasa: formerly a British protectorate and part of the Federation of Rhodesia and Nyasaland; gained independence 1964; a member of the British Commonwealth of Nations. 5,400,000; 49,177 sq. mi. *Cap.:* Lilongwe. Formerly, **Nyasaland.**

Ma·lay (mā′lā, mə lā′), *adj.* **1.** of or pertaining to the Malays or their country or language. **2.** *Phys. Anthropol.* of, pertaining to, or characteristic of a racially intermixed, brown-skinned people of the Malay Peninsula who are marked generally by short stature, roundish skull, and wavy to straight black hair; Malayo-Indonesian. —*n.* **3.** a member of the dominant people of the Malay Peninsula and adjacent islands. **4.** a Malayo-Polynesian language widespread in the East Indies as a language of commerce and serving as the first language of a large population in the Malay Peninsula.

Ma·lay·a (mə lā′ə), *n.* **1.** See **Malay Peninsula. 2.** Formerly, **Federation of Malaya, Malay States, Malay′an Un′ion.** a part of Malaysia, in the S Malay Peninsula: formerly an independent federation of 11 states; a British protectorate 1948–57. 50,690 sq. mi. *Cap.:* Kuala Lumpur. Cf. **Malaysia** (def. 1).

Mal·a·ya·lam (mal′ə yä′ləm), *n.* a Dravidian language spoken in extreme southwestern India.

Ma·lay·an (mə lā′ən), *adj.* **1.** Malay. —*n.* **2.** a Malay. **3.** (no longer current) Indonesian (def. 3).

Ma′lay Archipel′ago, an extensive island group in the Indian and Pacific oceans, SE of Asia: includes Sumatra, the Moluccas, Borneo, the Philippines, Celebes, and Timor. Also called **Malaysia.**

Malayo-, a combining form of **Malay.**

Ma·lay·o-In·do·ne·sian (mə lā′ō in′də nē′zhən, -shən, -dō-), *adj.* Malay (def. 2).

Ma·lay·o-Pol·y·ne·sian (mə lā′ō pol′ə nē′zhən, -shən), *adj.* **1.** of or belonging to a family of languages including those of the indigenous inhabitants of most of Oceania, the Philippines, Formosa, the East Indies, the Malay Peninsula, and Madagascar; Austronesian. —*n.* **2.** Also called **Austronesian.** the family of Malayo-Polynesian languages.

Ma′lay Penin′sula, a peninsula in SE Asia, consisting of Malaya and the S part of Thailand. Also called **Malaya.**

Ma·lay·sia (mə lā′zhə, -shə), *n.* **1.** an independent federation of SE Asia, comprising the former British territories of Malaya, Sabah, Sarawak, and, formerly, Singapore: member of the British Commonwealth of Nations. 12,100,000; 126,310 sq. mi. *Cap.:* Kuala Lumpur. **2.** See **Malay Archipelago.**

Ma·lay·sian (mə lā′zhən, -shən), *n.* **1.** a native of Malaysia. **2.** Indonesian (def. 1). **3.** Malay (def. 3). —*adj.* **4.** of, pertaining to, or characteristic of Malaysia or its inhabitants.

Ma′lay States′, former name of Malaya.

mal·con·tent (mal′kən tent′), *adj.* **1.** not happy about currently prevailing conditions or circumstances; discontented; dissatisfied. **2.** dissatisfied with the existing government, administration, system, etc. —*n.* **3.** a malcontent person. [< MF, OF]

mal de mer (MAl də MER′), *French.* seasickness.

Mal·den (môl′dən), *n.* a city in E Massachusetts, near Boston. 56,127 (1970).

Mal·dives (mal′dīvz), *n.* a group of 2000 islands constituting a republic in the Indian Ocean, SW of Sri Lanka: British protectorate 1887–1965. 140,000; 115 sq. mi. *Cap.:* Malé. Also called **Mal′dive Is′lands** (mal′dīv).

male (māl), *adj.* **1.** of or belonging to the sex that begets young by fertilizing the female. **2.** pertaining to or characteristic of this sex; masculine. **3.** composed of males: *a male choir.* **4.** *Bot.* **a.** designating or pertaining to any reproductive structure producing or containing elements that bring about the fertilization of the female element. **b.** (of seed plants) staminate. **5.** *Mach.* noting a part, thread, etc., fitting into a corresponding female part. —*n.* **6.** a person of the male sex; man or boy. **7.** any animal of male sex. **8.** *Bot.* a staminate plant. [ME < MF *ma(s)le* < L *mascul(us).* See MASCULINE] —**male′ness,** *n.*
—**Syn. 1.** MALE, MASCULINE are descriptive of one belonging to the paternal sex. MALE always refers to sex, whether of human beings, animals, or plants: *Male animals are often larger than the females.* MASCULINE applies to the qualities that properly characterize human males: *a masculine love of sports.* The term may be applied to women, suggesting some incongruity (as, *a masculine appearance*), or with complimentary or ambivalent implications: *She has a masculine mind.* **2.** manly. —**Ant. 1, 2, 4–8.** female.

Ma·lé (mä′lē), *n.* a city in and the capital of the Maldives. 17,000.

male-, a prefix meaning "evil," occurring in loan words from Latin: *malediction.* Cf. **mal-.** [< L]

ma·le·ate (mə lē′it), *n. Chem.* a salt or ester of maleic acid. [MALE(IC ACID) + -ATE[2]]

Male·branche (MAl BRÄNSH′), *n.* **Ni·co·las de** (nē kô-lä′ də), 1638–1715, French philosopher.

mal·e·dict (mal′i dikt), *Archaic.* —*adj.* **1.** accursed. —*v.t.* **2.** to put a curse on. [< L *maledict(us)* abused, slandered (LL: accursed), ptp. of *maledīcere.* See MALEDICTION]

mal·e·dic·tion (mal′i dik′shən), *n.* **1.** a curse or the utterance of a curse; imprecation. **2.** slander. [late ME *malediccion* < L *maledictiōn-* (s. of *maledictiō*) slander (LL: curse)] —**mal′e·dic′tive, mal·e·dic·to·ry** (mal′i dik′tə rē), *adj.* —**Syn. 1.** damning, execration. —**Ant. 1.** benediction.

mal·e·fac·tion (mal′ə fak′shən), *n.* an evil deed; crime; wrongdoing. [MALEFACT(OR) + -ION]

mal·e·fac·tor (mal′ə fak′tər), *n.* **1.** a person who violates the law; criminal. **2.** a person who does evil. Also, *referring to a woman,* **mal·e·fac·tress** (mal′ə fak′tris). [late ME *malefactour* < L *malefactor* = *malefact(um)* evil deed (see MALE-, FACT) + *-or* -OR[2]] —**Syn. 1.** felon, culprit. —**Ant. 1, 2.** benefactor.

ma·lef·ic (mə lef′ik), *adj.* productive of evil; malign; baneful. [L *malefic(us)* evildoing, wicked. See MALE-, -FIC]

ma·lef·i·cence (mə lef′i səns), *n.* **1.** the doing of evil or harm. **2.** evil or harmful character. [< L *maleficentia.* See MALEFIC, -ENCE]

ma·lef·i·cent (mə lef′i sənt), *adj.* doing evil or harm; malicious. [back formation from L *maleficentia* MALEFICENCE; see -ENT]

ma·le′ic ac′id (mə lē′ik), *Chem.* a solid, HOOC-CH=CHCOOH, used in the manufacture of synthetic resins, the dyeing and finishing of textiles, and as a preservative for fats and oils. [< F *maléique,* alter. of *malique* MALIC]

mal·e·mute (mal′ə myo͞ot′), *n.* (*sometimes cap.*) See **Alaskan malamute.**

Ma·len·kov (mä′lən kôf′; *Russ.* mä len kôf′), *n.* **Ge·or·gi Ma·xi·mi·lia·no·vich** (gā ôR′gi mä′ksi mi lyä′no vich), born 1902, Russian political leader: premier of the Soviet Union 1953–55.

mal·en·ten·du (MAl äN tän dY′), *n., pl.* **-dus** (-dY′). *French.* a misunderstanding; mistake.

ma·lev·o·lence (mə lev′ə ləns), *n.* the state of being malevolent; ill will; malice; hatred. [< L *malevolentia* (see MALEVOLENT, -ENCE); r. late ME *malivolence* < MF] —**Syn.** maliciousness, spite, spitefulness.

ma·lev·o·lent (mə lev′ə lənt), *adj.* **1.** wishing evil to another or others; showing ill will; ill-disposed; vindictive; malicious. **2.** evil; harmful; injurious. [< L *malevolent-* (s. of *malevolēns*) ill-disposed, spiteful = *male-* MALE- + *volent-* (s. of *volēns*) wishing, prp. of *velle;* see WILL[1], -ENT] —**ma·lev′o·lent·ly,** *adv.*

mal·fea·sance (mal fē′zəns), *n. Law.* the performance by a public official of an act that is legally unjustified, harmful, or contrary to law. Cf. **misfeasance** (def. 2), **nonfeasance.** [earlier *malefeasance.* See MALE-, FEASANCE] —**mal·fea′sant,** *adj., n.*

mal·for·ma·tion (mal′fôr mā′shən), *n.* faulty or anomalous formation or structure, esp. in a living body.

mal·formed (mal fôrmd′), *adj.* faultily formed.

mal·func·tion (mal fungk′shən), *n.* **1.** failure to function properly. —*v.i.* **2.** to fail to function properly.

mal·gré lui (MAl GRĀ lwē′), *French.* in spite of himself; despite his action or intent.

Mal·herbe (MAl ERB′), *n.* **Fran·çois de** (FRÄN SWA′ də), 1555–1628, French poet and critic.

Ma·li (mä′lē), *n.* **Republic of,** a republic in W Africa: a member of the French Community; formerly a territory of France. 5,600,000; 463,500 sq. mi. *Cap.:* Bamako. Formerly, **French Sudan.**

mal·ic (mal′ik, mā′lik), *adj.* **1.** pertaining to or derived from apples. **2.** *Chem.* of or derived from malic acid. [< F *malique* < L *māl(um)* apple + F *-ique* -IC]

mal′ic ac′id, *Chem.* a solid, $HOOCCH_2CH(OH)COOH$, occurring in apples and other fruits and as an intermediate in animal metabolism.

mal·ice (mal′is), *n.* **1.** a desire to inflict injury or suffering on another, esp. when based on deep-seated meanness. **2.** *Law.* evil intent on the part of a person who commits a wrongful act injurious to others. [ME < OF < L *malitia*] —**Syn. 1.** animosity, enmity; malevolence; rancor. See **grudge.** —**Ant. 1.** benevolence, good will.

mal′ice afore′thought, *Law.* a predetermination to commit an unlawful act without just cause or provocation (applied chiefly to cases of first-degree murder).

ma·li·cious (mə lish′əs), *adj.* **1.** full of, characterized by, or showing malice; malevolent; spiteful: *malicious gossip.* **2.** *Law.* motivated by vicious, wanton, or mischievous purposes. [ME *malicius* < OF < L *malitiōs(us)*] —**ma·li′cious·ly,** *adv.* —**ma·li′cious·ness,** *n.*

ma·lign (mə līn′), *v.t.* **1.** to speak harmful untruths about; slander; defame. —*adj.* **2.** evil in effect; pernicious; baleful; injurious. **3.** having or showing an evil disposition; malevolent; malicious. [ME *maligne* < MF < L *malīgn(us).* See MAL-, BENIGN] —**ma·lign′er,** *n.* —**ma·lign′ly,** *adv.* —**Syn. 1.** libel; disparage; revile, vilify. —**Ant. 1.** praise.

ma·lig·nan·cy (mə lig′nən sē), *n., pl.* **-cies** for 2, 3. **1.** the quality or condition of being malignant. **2.** malignant character, behavior, action, or the like: *the malignancies of war.* **3.** a malignant tumor. Also, **ma·lig′nance** (for defs. 1, 2). [MALIGN(ANT) + -ANCY]

ma·lig·nant (mə lig′nənt), *adj.* **1.** disposed to cause harm, suffering, or distress deliberately; feeling or showing ill will or hatred. **2.** very dangerous; harmful in influence or effect. **3.** *Pathol.* deadly; tending to produce death, as a disease or tumor. [< LL *malīgnant-* (s. of *malīgnāns*), prp. of *malīgnāre* to act maliciously] —**ma·lig′nant·ly,** *adv.* —**Syn. 1.** spiteful, malevolent. **2.** perilous, hurtful. —**Ant. 1–3.** benign.

ma·lig·ni·ty (mə lig′ni tē), *n., pl.* **-ties** for 2. **1.** the state or character of being malign; malevolence; intense ill will; spite. **2.** a malignant feeling, action, etc. [ME *malignitee* < L *malignitās*]

ma·li·hi·ni (mä′lē hē′nē), *n., pl.* **-hi·nis.** a newcomer to Hawaii. [< Hawaiian]

Mal·i·ki (mal′ə kē), *n.* *Islam.* one of the four teachings of the Sunna sect and the one that incorporates custom into its law. Cf. **Hanafi, Hanbali, Shafii.**

ma·lines (mə lēn′; *Fr.* mȧ lēn′), *n.* **1.** Also, **ma·line′.** a delicate net resembling tulle. **2.** See **Mechlin lace.** [after MALINES]

Ma·lines (mȧ lēn′; *Eng.* mə lēnz′), *n.* French name of **Mechlin.**

ma·lin·ger (mə liŋ′gər), *v.i.* to pretend illness, esp. in order to avoid duty, work, etc. [< F *malingre* sickly, ailing = *mal* MAL- + OF *heingre* haggard (perh. < Gmc)] —**ma·lin′ger·er,** *n.*

Ma·li·now·ski (mä′li nôf′skē), *n.* **Bro·ni·slaw Kas·per** (brô nē′släf käs′pər), 1884–1942, Polish anthropologist in the U.S.

mal·i·son (mal′i zən, -sən), *n.* *Archaic.* a curse. [ME *maliso(u)n* < OF *maleison* < L *maledictiōn-* (s. of *maledictiō*) MALEDICTION]

mal·kin (mô′kin, môl′-, mal′-), *n.* *Brit. Dial.* **1.** an untidy or lewd woman. **2.** a scarecrow or grotesque effigy. **3.** a cat. **4.** a hare. [ME, dim. of *Mal,* var. of *Molly* Mary; see -KIN]

mall (môl, mäl, mal), *n.* **1.** a large area, usually lined with shade trees and shrubbery, used as a public walk or promenade. **2.** a strip of land separating lanes of opposite traffic, as on a highway. **3.** the mallet used in the game of pall-mall. **4.** the game itself. **5.** the place or alley where pall-mall was played. **6.** *Rare.* maul. —*v.t.* **7.** *Rare.* to maul. [contr. of PALL-MALL]

Mallard (Length 2 ft.)

mal·lan·ders (mal′ən dərz), *n.* (*construed as sing.*) *Vet. Pathol.* malanders.

mal·lard (mal′ərd), *n., pl.* **-lards,** (*esp. collectively*) **-lard.** a common, almost cosmopolitan, wild duck, *Anas platyrhynchos,* from which the domestic ducks descended. [ME < MF, OF *mallart,* ? < OHG *Madelhart,* thought to be name given to duck as character in fable]

Mal·lar·mé (mȧ lȧr mā′), *n.* **Sté·phane** (stā fȧn′), 1842–1898, French poet.

mal·le·a·ble (mal′ē ə bəl), *adj.* **1.** capable of being extended or shaped by hammering or by pressure from rollers. **2.** adaptable or tractable: *the malleable mind of a child.* [ME *malliable* < ML *malleābil(is)* = *malle(āre)* (to) hammer (see MALLEUS) + *-ābilis* -ABLE] —**mal′le·a·bil′i·ty, mal′le·a·ble·ness,** *n.*

mal·lee (mal′ē), *n.* **1.** any of various dwarf Australian eucalyptuses, as *Eucalyptus dumosa* and *E. oleosa,* that sometimes form large tracts of brushwood. **2.** the brushwood itself. [< native Austral]

mal·le·muck (mal′ə muk′), *n.* *Dial.* any of various oceanic birds, as the fulmar or albatross. [< D *mallemok* = *malle,* var. of *mal* foolish + *mok* < Norw *måk* MEW²]

mal·len·ders (mal′ən dərz), *n.* (*construed as sing.*) *Vet. Pathol.* malanders.

mal·let (mal′it), *n.* **1.** a hammerlike tool, usually of wood, used for driving any tool with a wooden handle, as a chisel. **2.** the long-handled wooden implement used to strike the balls in croquet. **3.** *Polo.* the long-handled stick, or club, used to drive the ball. [late ME *maillet* < MF = *mail* MAUL + *-et* -ET]

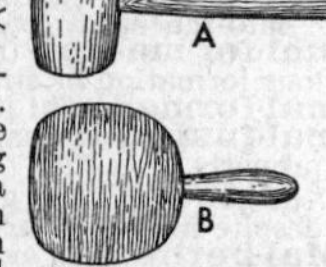

A, Mallet; B, Stone-cutter's mallet

mal·le·us (mal′ē əs), *n., pl.* **mal·le·i** (mal′ē ī′). *Anat.* the outermost of a chain of three small bones in the middle ear of man and other mammals. Also called **hammer.** Cf. **incus** (def. 1), **stapes.** [< L: hammer]

Ma·llor·ca (mä lyôr′kä, -yôr′-; *Eng.* mä yôr′kə), *n.* Spanish name of **Majorca.**

mal·low (mal′ō), *n.* **1.** any herb of the genus *Malva,* having angularly lobed or dissected leaves and purple, pink, or white flowers. **2.** any malvaceous plant, as the marsh mallow. [ME *malue,* OE *mealwe* < L *malva*]

malm (mäm), *n.* **1.** a soft, friable limestone. **2.** a chalk-bearing soil of southeastern England. [ME *malme,* OE *mealm-* (in *mealmiht* sandy, *mealmstān* sandstone); c. Goth *malma* sand, Icel *malmr* metal (in granular form); akin to OS, OHG *melm* dust. See MEAL²]

Mal·mé·dy (mȧl mā dē′), *n.* See **Eupen and Malmédy.**

Malm·ö (mal′mō; *Swed.* mälm′œ′), *n.* a seaport in S Sweden, on the sound opposite Copenhagen, Denmark. 245,565 (1965).

malm·sey (mäm′zē), *n.* a strong, sweet wine with a strong flavor, made in Madeira. [late ME *malmesye* < MLG << *Monemvasia* Greek town where it was originally produced]

mal·nu·tri·tion (mal′no͞o trish′ən, -nyo͞o-), *n.* lack of proper nutrition; inadequate or unbalanced nutrition.

mal·oc·clu·sion (mal′ə klo͞o′zhən), *n.* *Dentistry.* faulty occlusion; irregular contact of opposing teeth in the upper and lower jaws. —**mal′oc·clud′ed,** *adj.*

mal·o·dor (mal ō′dər), *n.* an unpleasant odor. —**mal·o′dor·ous,** *adj.*

ma·lo′nic ac′id (mə lō′nik, -lon′ik), *Chem.* a dibasic acid, $CH_2(COOH)_2$, used chiefly as an intermediate in the synthesis of barbiturates. [< F *malonique,* alter. of *malique* MALIC]

mal·o·nyl·u·re·a (mal′ə nil yo͝o rē′ə, -yo͝or′ē ə, -nēl-), *n.* *Chem.* See **barbituric acid.** [MALON(IC) + -YL + UREA]

Mal·o·ry (mal′ə rē), *n.* **Sir Thomas,** c1400–71, English author.

Mal·pi·ghi (mäl pē′gē), *n.* **Mar·cel·lo** (mär chel′lô), 1628–94, Italian anatomist. —**Mal·pigh·i·an** (mal pig′ē ən), *adj.*

mal·pigh·i·a·ceous (mal pig′ē ā′shəs), *adj.* belonging or pertaining to the *Malpighiaceae,* a large family of tropical plants. [< NL *Malpighi(a)* the typical genus (named after MALPIGHI) + -ACEOUS]

Malpigh′ian cor′puscle, *Anat.* the structure at the beginning of a vertebrate nephron, consisting of a glomerulus and its surrounding membrane. Also called **Malpigh′ian bod′y.**

Malpigh′ian lay′er, *Anat.* the deep, germinative layer of the epidermis.

Malpigh′ian tube′, one of a group of long, slender excretory tubules at the anterior end of the hindgut in insects and other terrestrial arthropods. Also called **Malpigh′ian tu′bule, Malpigh′ian ves′sel.**

mal·po·si·tion (mal′pə zish′ən), *n.* faulty or wrong position.

mal·prac·tice (mal prak′tis), *n.* **1.** *Law.* failure of a professional person, as a physician or lawyer, to render proper services through reprehensible ignorance or negligence or through criminal intent, esp. when injury or loss follows. **2.** any improper, negligent practice; misconduct or misuse.

Mal·raux (mȧl rō′), *n.* **An·dré** (äN drā′), 1901–76, French novelist, critic, and government official.

malt (môlt), *n.* **1.** germinated grain, usually barley, used in brewing and distilling. **2.** See **malted milk** (def. 2). —*v.t.* **3.** to convert (grain) into malt. **4.** to treat or mix with malt, malt extract, etc. **5.** to make (liquor) with malt. —*v.i.* **6.** to become malt. **7.** to produce malt from grain. [ME; OE *mealt;* c. Icel *malt,* G *Malz;* akin to MELT]

Mal·ta (môl′tə), *n.* **1.** an island in the Mediterranean between Sicily and Africa. 95 sq. mi. **2.** a former British colony consisting of this island and two small adjacent islands: now an independent sovereign state and a member of the British Commonwealth. 297,622; 122 sq. mi. *Cap.:* Valletta.

Mal′ta fe′ver, *Pathol.* brucellosis.

malt·ase (môl′tās), *n.* *Biochem.* an enzyme that converts maltose into dextrose and causes similar cleavage of many other glucosides.

malt′ed milk′ (môl′tid), **1.** a soluble powder made of dehydrated milk and malted cereals. **2.** Also called **malt′ed.** a beverage made by dissolving this powder, usually in milk, often with ice cream and flavoring added.

Mal·tese (môl tēz′, -tēs′), *adj., n., pl.* **-tese.** —*adj.* **1.** of or pertaining to Malta, its people, or their language. —*n.* **2.** a native or inhabitant of Malta. **3.** the Arabic dialect spoken in Malta.

Mal′tese cat′, a bluish-gray variety of the domestic cat.

Mal′tese cross′, **1.** a cross having four equal arms that expand in width outward. See illus. at **cross.** **2.** See **scarlet lychnis.**

Mal′tese dog′, one of a breed of toy dogs having a long, straight, silky, white coat.

mal·tha (mal′thə), *n.* **1.** any of various natural mixtures of hydrocarbons, as ozocerite. **2.** a viscous mineral liquid or semiliquid bitumen; a mineral tar. [< Gk: mixed wax and pitch; r. late ME *malthe*]

Mal·thus (mal′thəs), *n.* **Thomas Robert,** 1766–1834, English economist and clergyman.

Mal·thu·si·an (mal tho͞o′zē ən), *adj.* **1.** of or pertaining to the theories of T. R. Malthus, which state that population tends to increase faster than the means of subsistence, resulting in an inadequate supply of food and necessary goods, unless war, famine, or disease reduce the population, or the increase of population is slowed. —*n.* **2.** a follower of Malthus. —**Mal·thu′si·an·ism,** *n.*

malt′ liq′uor, an alcoholic beverage, as beer, fermented from malt.

malt·ol (môl′tôl, -tōl, -tol), *n.* *Chem.* a compound, $C_6H_6O_3$, obtained from larch bark, pine needles, chicory, or roasted malt, used for enhancing flavors and aromas.

malt·ose (môl′tōs), *n.* *Chem.* a white, crystalline, water-soluble sugar, $C_{12}H_{22}O_{11} \cdot H_2O$, formed by the action of diatase, esp. from malt, on starch: used chiefly as a nutrient, as a sweetener, and in culture media. Also called **malt′ sug′ar, mal·to·bi·ose** (môl′tō bī′ōs).

mal·treat (mal trēt′), *v.t.* to treat badly; handle roughly; abuse. [earlier *maltrait* < F *maltrait(er)*] —**mal·treat′er,** *n.* —**mal·treat′ment,** *n.* —**Syn.** mistreat, injure.

malt·ster (môlt′stər), *n.* a maker of or dealer in malt. [ME *malt(e)stere*]

malt·y (môl′tē), *adj.,* **malt·i·er, malt·i·est.** of, like, or containing malt. —**malt′i·ness,** *n.*

mal·va·ceous (mal vā′shəs), *adj.* belonging to the *Malvaceae,* or mallow family of plants, comprising the abutilon, althea, hollyhock, okra, cotton plant, etc. [< L *malvāceus.* See MALLOW, -ACEOUS]

mal·va·si·a (mal′və sē′ə), *n.* malmsey. [< It, for *Monemvasia.* See MALMSEY] —**mal′va·si′an,** *adj.*

Mal·vern (môl′vərn, mô′-), *n.* an urban area in W Worcestershire, in W England, SW of Birmingham: comprises several small towns; mineral springs. 24,373 (1961).

Mal′vern Hill′ (mal′vərn), a plateau in E Virginia, SE of Richmond: battle 1862.

Mal′vern Hills′ (môl′vərn, mô′-), a range of hills in W England, between Worcestershire and Herefordshire.

mal·ver·sa·tion (mal′vər sā′shən), *n. Chiefly Law.* improper or corrupt behavior in office, esp. in public office. [< MF = *malvers(er)* (to) embezzle (< L *male versārī* to behave badly = *male* badly (see MAL-) + *versārī*, deponent of *versāre* to turn (see VERSATILE)) + *-ation* -ATION]

Mal·vi·nas (mäl vē′näs), *n.* **Is·las** (ēz′läz), Spanish name of the **Falkland Islands.**

mal·voi·sie (mal′voi zē, -və-), *n.* **1.** malmsey. **2.** the malvasia grape. [< F; r. ME *malvesie* < MF < It *malvasia.* See MALMSEY]

ma·ma (mä′mə, mə mä′), *n. Informal.* mamma[1].

Ma·mal·la·pur·am (mə mä′lə po͝or′əm), *n.* Mahabalipuram.

mam·ba (mäm′bä), *n.* any of several long, slender, arboreal snakes of the genus *Dendroaspis*, of central and southern Africa, the bite of which often causes death. [< SAfr (Kaffir) *m′namba*]

mam·bo (mäm′bō), *n., pl.* **-bos,** *v.* **—***n.* **1.** a fast ballroom dance of Haitian origin. **—***v.i.* **2.** to dance the mambo. [prob. < Creole of Hispaniola]

Mam·e·luke (mam′ə lo͞ok′), *n.* **1.** a member of a military class that ruled Egypt 1250–1517. **2.** (*l.c.*) (in Muslim countries) a slave. [< Ar *mamlūk*, lit., slave, n. use of ptp. of *malaka* to possess]

mam·ma[1] (mä′mə, mə mä′), *n. Informal.* mother. Also, **mama.** [nursery word based on baby's meaningless syllable *ma* in repetitive babbling. Cf. F *maman*, L *mamma*, Gk *mámmē*, Russ, Lith *mama*]

mam·ma[2] (mam′ə), *n., pl.* **mam·mae** (mam′ē) for 1; **mam·ma** for 2. **1.** *Anat., Zool.* the organ, characteristic of mammals, that in the female secretes milk; breast or udder. **2.** (*construed as pl.*) hanging, breastlike protuberances on the under surface of a cloud. [< L: breast, teat (> OE *mamme* teat). See MAMMA[1]]

mam·mal (mam′əl), *n.* any vertebrate of the class *Mammalia*, including man, that feeds its young with milk from the female mammary glands, that has the body more or less covered with hair, and that, with the exception of the monotremes, brings forth living young rather than eggs. [back formation from NL *Mammālia*, n. use of neut. pl. of LL *mammālis* of the breast. See MAMMA[2], -AL[1]]

mam·ma·li·an (mə mā′lē ən, -māl′yən), *n.* **1.** an animal of the class *Mammalia;* mammal. **—***adj.* **2.** belonging or pertaining to the class *Mammalia;* characteristic of mammals. [< NL *Mammāli(a)* (see MAMMAL) + -IAN] **—mam·mal·i·ty** (mə mal′i tē), *n.*

mam·mal·o·gy (mə mal′ə jē), *n.* the science dealing with mammals.

mam·ma·ry (mam′ə rē), *adj. Anat., Zool.* of or pertaining to the mamma or breast; mammalike.

mam·ma·to-cu·mu·lus (mə mā′tō kyo͞o′myə ləs), *n., pl.* **-lus.** *Meteorol. Obs.* mamma[2] (def. 2). [< NL = L *mammāt(us)* of, like the breast (see MAMMA[2], -ATE[1]) + *-o-* -o- + *cumulus* CUMULUS]

mam·m·ifer·ous (ma mif′ər əs), *adj.* having mammae; mammalian.

mam·mil·la (ma mil′ə), *n., pl.* **-mil·lae** (-mil′ē). **1.** *Anat.* the nipple of the mamma, or breast. **2.** any nipplelike process or protuberance. [< L: breast, teat, dim. of *mamma* MAMMA[2]] **—mam′mil·lar′y,** *adj.*

mam·mil·late (mam′ə lāt′), *adj.* having a mamilla or mammillae. Also, **mam′mil·lat′ed.** [< LL *mammillāt(us)*] **—mam′mil·la′tion,** *n.*

mam·mo·gram (mam′ə gram′), *n.* the x-ray photograph obtained by mammography. [MAMM(A)[2] + -O- + -GRAM]

mam·mog·ra·phy (ma mog′rə fē), *n.* x-ray photography of the breast, esp. for early detection of cancer. [MAMM(A)[2] + -O- + -GRAPHY] **—mam·mo·graph·ic** (mam′ə graf′ik), *adj.*

mam·mon (mam′ən), *n.* **1.** *New Testament.* riches or material wealth. Matt. 6:24; Luke 16:9, 11, 13. **2.** (*cap.*) a personification of riches as an evil spirit or deity. [ME *mammona* < LL < Gk *mam(m)ōnâs* < Aram *māmōnā* riches] **—mam′mon·ish,** *adj.*

mam·mon·ism (mam′ə niz′əm), *n.* the greedy pursuit of riches. **—mam′mon·ist, mam′mon·ite′,** *n.*

Mammoth, *Mammuthus primigenius* (11 ft. high at shoulder; tusks to 13 ft. long)

mam·moth (mam′əth), *n.* **1.** any large, elephantlike mammal of the extinct genus *Mammuthus*, from the Pleistocene epoch, having a hairy skin and ridged molar teeth. **—***adj.* **2.** huge; enormous; immensely large. [< Russ *mamont*] **—Syn. 2.** See **gigantic.**

Mam′moth Cave′, a large limestone cavern in central Kentucky: noted for its onyx formations; in Mammoth Cave National Park. 79 sq. mi.

mam·my (mam′ē), *n., pl.* **-mies. 1.** *Informal.* mother. **2.** (in the southern U.S.) a Negro woman engaged as a nurse to white children or as a servant to a white family. [MAMM(A)[1] + -Y[2]]

Ma·mo·ré (mä′mô rā′), *n.* a river in Bolivia, flowing N to the Beni River on the border of Brazil to form the Madeira River. 700 mi. long.

man[1] (man), *n., pl.* **men,** *v.,* **manned, man·ning,** *interj.* **—***n.* **1.** an adult male person, as distinguished from a boy or woman. **2.** the creature, *Homo sapiens*, at the highest level of animal development, characterized esp. by a highly developed brain. **3.** the human race; mankind. **4.** a person (usually used in contexts in which sexual distinctions are not relevant): *When the sale started, it was every man for himself.* **5.** an individual; someone; one (usually prec. by *a*): *to give a man a chance.* **6.** a husband: *man and wife.* **7.** a male follower, subordinate, or employee: *officers and men.* **8.** a male having manly qualities or virtues: *Be a man. The army will make a man of you.* **9.** a male servant; valet. **10.** a term of familiar address to a man; fellow: *Now, now, my good man, please calm down.* **11.** *Slang.* a term of address to a man or woman: *Hey, man, don't you dig that music?* **12.** one of the pieces used in playing certain games, as chess or checkers; counter. **13.** *Hist.* a liegeman; vassal. **14.** *Obs.* manly character or courage. **15. as one man,** unanimously. **16. be one's own man,** to be independent. **17. man and boy,** during and since childhood. **18. the Man,** *Slang.* a white man, esp. one in a position of authority, as a policeman or employer (used by Negroes). **19. to a man,** with no exception; everyone; all. **—***v.t.* **20.** to furnish with men, as for service or defense. **21.** to take one's place at for service, as at a gun or post: *to man the ramparts.* **—***interj.* **22.** *Slang.* (used as an expression of surprise, enthusiasm, or other strong feeling): *Man, what a ball game!* [(n.) ME; OE *man(n)*; c. Goth *manna*, G *Mann*, D *man*, Icel *mathr;* (v.) ME *manne(n)*, OE *mannian*]

man[2] (män, man; *unstressed* mən), *aux. v. Scot.* maun.

Man (man), *n.* **Isle of,** an island of the British Isles, in the Irish Sea. 58,773; 227 sq. mi. *Cap.:* Douglas.

Man., 1. Manila. **2.** Manitoba.

ma·na (mä′nä), *n. Anthropol.* a generalized, supernatural force or power, which may be concentrated in objects or persons. [< Polynesian, Melanesian]

man′ about town′, a socially active, sophisticated man.

man·a·cle (man′ə kəl), *n., v.,* **-cled, -cling. —***n.* **1.** a shackle for the hand; handcuff. **2.** Usually, **manacles.** restraints; checks. **—***v.t.* **3.** to handcuff; fetter. **4.** to hamper; restrain. [ME, var. of *manicle* < MF: handcuff < L *manicula* a small hand. See MANUS, -I-, -CLE]

Ma·na·do (mä nä′dō), *n.* Menado.

man·age (man′ij), *v.,* **-aged, -ag·ing. —***v.t.* **1.** to bring about; succeed in accomplishing: *He managed to see the governor.* **2.** to have charge of or responsibility for: *to manage an estate.* **3.** to dominate or influence (a person) by tact or artifice. **4.** to handle, direct, govern, or control in action or use. **5.** to wield (a weapon, tool, etc.). **6.** to contrive to bring about or accomplish despite hardship or difficulty: *Somehow we must manage the suppression of our baser instincts.* **7.** *Archaic.* to handle or train (a horse) in the exercises of the manège. **8.** *Archaic.* to use sparingly or with judgment, as health, money, etc.; husband. **—***v.i.* **9.** to conduct business, commercial affairs, etc.; be in charge: *Who will manage while the boss is away?* **10.** to continue to function, progress, or succeed, usually despite hardship or difficulty; get along: *How will she manage with her husband gone?* [earlier *manege* < It *manegg(iare)* (to) handle, train (horses) < *man(o)* < L *manus* hand] **—Syn. 1.** arrange, contrive. **4.** guide, conduct, regulate, engineer. See **rule. 5.** handle.

man·age·a·ble (man′i jə bəl), *adj.* that can be managed; governable; contrivable; tractable. **—man′age·a·bil′i·ty, man′age·a·ble·ness,** *n.* **—man′age·a·bly,** *adv.*

man·age·ment (man′ij mənt), *n.* **1.** the act or manner of managing; handling, direction, or control. **2.** skill in managing; executive ability. **3.** the person or persons controlling and directing the affairs of an institution, business, etc. **4.** executives collectively, considered as a class. **—Syn. 1.** administration; charge, conduct, guidance.

man′agement informa′tion sys′tem, a system in which data is collected and organized, usually using a computer, for the use of business management. *Abbr.:* MIS

man·ag·er (man′i jər), *n.* **1.** a person who manages: *the manager of our track team.* **2.** a person charged with the control or direction of an institution, business, or the like. **3.** a person who controls and manipulates resources and expenditures, as of a household. **—man′ag·er·ship′,** *n.*

man·ag·er·ess (man′i jər is; *Brit.* man′i jə res′), *n. Chiefly Brit.* a female manager.

man·a·ge·ri·al (man′i jēr′ē əl), *adj.* pertaining to management or a manager. **—man′a·ge′ri·al·ly,** *adv.*

man′aging ed′itor, an editor assigned to the supervision of certain editorial activities of a newspaper, magazine, book publishing company, and the like.

Ma·na·gua (mä nä′gwä), *n.* **1. Lake,** a lake in W Nicaragua. 390 sq. mi. **2.** a city in and the capital of Nicaragua, in the W part, on Lake Managua. 556,470.

man·a·kin (man′ə kin), *n.* manikin.

Ma·na·la (mä′nə lə), *n.* Tuonela.

Ma·na·ma (*Pers.* ma na′mə, -ma), *n.* a city in and the capital of Bahrain on N Bahrain island. 94,697.

ma·ña·na (mä nyä′nä; *Eng.* mə nyä′nə), *Spanish.* **—***n.* **1.** tomorrow; the (indefinite) future. **—***adv.* **2.** tomorrow; in the (indefinite) future.

Ma·náos (mä nous′), *n.* a port in and the capital of Amazonas, in N Brazil, on the Río Negro near its confluence with the Amazon. 248,118. Also, **Manaus.**

Ma·nas·sas (mə nas′əs), *n.* a town in NE Virginia: battles of Bull Run 1861, 1862. 9164 (1970).

Ma·nas·seh (mə nas′ə), *n.* **1.** the first son of Joseph. Gen. 41:51. **2.** the tribe of Israel traditionally descended from him. Gen. 48:14–19. **3.** a king of Judah of the 7th century B.C. II Kings 21. Also, *Douay Bible,* **Ma·nas·ses** (mə nas′ēz).

man-at-arms (man′ət ärmz′), *n., pl.* **men-at-arms. 1.** a soldier. **2.** a heavily armed soldier on horseback.

Manatee, *Trichechus manatus* (Length 8 to 13 ft.)

man·a·tee (man′ə tē′, man′ə tē′), *n.* any of several herbivorous, gregarious sirenians of the genus *Trichechus*, of West Indian, Floridian, and Gulf Coast waters, having two flippers in front and a spoon-shaped tail. [< Sp *manatí* < Carib, but assoc.

with L *manātus* provided with hands] **—man′a·toid′,** *adj.*

Ma·naus (mä nous′), *n.* Manáos.

manche (mänch), *n. Heraldry.* a conventional representation of a sleeve with a flaring end, used as a charge. [ME < MF < L *manicae* (pl.) long sleeves, gloves, handcuffs < *man(us)* hand. See MANACLE]

Man·ches·ter (man′ches′tər, -chi stər), *n.* **1.** a city in SE Lancashire, in NW England: connected with the Mersey estuary by a ship canal. 661,041 (1961). **2.** a city in S New Hampshire. 87,754 (1970). **3.** a town in central Connecticut. 47,994 (1970).

Man′chester ter′rier, one of a breed of slender terriers having a short, glossy, black-and-tan coat.

man·chet (man′chit), *n. Archaic.* a kind of white bread made from the finest flour. [late ME *manchete*]

man-child (man′chīld′), *n., pl.* **men-chil·dren.** a male child; boy; son.

man·chi·neel (man′chə nēl′), *n.* a tropical American, euphorbiaceous tree or shrub, *Hippomane Mancinella,* having a milky, highly caustic, poisonous sap. [earlier *mançanilla* < Sp *manzanilla,* dim. of *manzana* apple << L (*māla*) *Matiāna* (apples) of *Matius* (1st century B.C.), Roman author of a cooking manual]

Man·chu (man chōō′), *n., pl.* **-chus,** (*esp. collectively*) **-chu,** *adj.* **—***n.* **1.** a member of a Mongolian people of Manchuria who conquered China in the 17th century and established a dynasty there (**Manchu′ dy′nasty** or **Ch′ing**) 1644–1912. **2.** a Tungusic language spoken by the Manchus. **—***adj.* **3.** of or pertaining to the Manchus, their country, or their language.

Man·chu·kuo (man′chōō′kwō′; *Chin.* män′jō′kwô′), *n.* a former country (1932–45) in E Asia, under Japanese control: included Manchuria and parts of Inner Mongolia; now a part of China. Also, **Man′chou′kuo′.**

Man·chu·ri·a (man chŏŏr′ē ə), *n.* a historic region in NE China: ancestral home of the Manchus. ab. 413,000 sq. mi. **—Man·chu′ri·an,** *adj., n.*

man·ci·ple (man′sə pəl), *n.* an officer or steward of a monastery, college, etc., authorized to purchase provisions. [ME < ML *mancip(ius)* buyer, agent, peddler (r. L *manceps,* lit., one who takes (something) in hand) + OF *manciple,* var. of *mancipe* < L *mancip(ium)* a purchase, possession, slave]

-mancy, a combining form meaning "divination": *necromancy.* [ME *-manci(e), -mancy(e)* < OF *-mancie* < L *-mantīa* < Gk *manteía* divination. See MANTIC, -Y]

Man·dae·an (man dē′ən), *n.* **1.** a member of a Gnostic sect extant in Iraq. **2.** the Aramaic language of the Mandaean sacred books. **—***adj.* **3.** of or pertaining to the Mandaeans. Also, **Mandean.** [< Mandaean *mandayy(ā)* Gnostics (lit., the knowing ones) + -AN] **—Man·dae′an·ism,** *n.*

man·da·la (mun′dᵊlə), *n. Oriental Art.* a schematized representation of the cosmos, chiefly characterized by a concentric organization of geometric shapes, each of which contains an image or attribute of a deity. [< Skt *maṇḍala* circle]

Man·da·lay (man′dᵊlā′, man′dᵊlā′), *n.* a city in central Burma, on the Irrawaddy River: the former capital of Upper Burma. 212,873 (est. 1963).

man·da·mus (man dā′məs), *n., pl.* **-mus·es.** *Law.* a writ from a superior court commanding that a specified thing be done. [< L: we command]

Man·dan (man′dan, -dən), *n., pl.* **-dans,** (*esp. collectively*) **-dan. 1.** a member of a Siouan people of North Dakota. **2.** the Siouan language of the Mandan Indians.

man·da·rin (man′də rin), *n.* **1.** (in the Chinese Empire) a member of any of the nine ranks of public officials. **2.** (*cap.*) the standard Chinese language. **3.** (*cap.*) the north China language, esp. that of Peking. **4.** the flattish, yellow to reddish-orange, loose-skinned fruit of a Chinese citrus tree, *Citrus reticulata,* cultivated in many varieties. **5.** the tree itself. Also called **man′darin or′ange** (for defs. 4, 5). [< pidgin English < Pg *mandarim,* alter. of Malay *mĕntĕri* < Skt *mantrin* councilor < *mantra* counsel; akin to MIND]

man·da·tar·y (man′də ter′ē), *n., pl.* **-tar·ies.** a person or nation holding a mandate. Also, **mandatory.** [< LL *mandātāri(us)*]

man·date (*n.* man′dāt, -dit; *v.* man′dāt), *n., v.,* **-dat·ed, -dat·ing.** **—***n.* **1.** (in the League of Nations) a commission given to a nation to administer the government and affairs of a former Turkish territory or German colony. **2.** a mandated territory or colony. **3.** *Politics.* a directive or authorization, usually implied, as by a vote, given by the electorate to its representative. **4.** a command from a superior court or official to an inferior one. **5.** any authoritative order or command: *a royal mandate.* **—***v.t.* **6.** to consign (a territory, colony, etc.) to the charge of a particular nation under a mandate. **7.** to authorize or decree (a particular action), as by the enactment of a law. [< L *mandāt(um),* n. use of neut. of *mandātus,* ptp. of *mandāre* to commission, lit., to give into (someone's) hand. See MANUS, DATE[1]] **—man·da′tor,** *n.* **—Syn. 5.** fiat, decree, injunction, edict, ruling.

man·da·to·ry (man′də tōr′ē, -tôr′ē), *adj., n., pl.* **-ries.** **—***adj.* **1.** pertaining to, of the nature of, or containing a command. **2.** authoritatively ordered; obligatory. **3.** (of a nation) having received a mandate. **—***n.* **4.** mandatary. [< LL *mandātōri(us)*] **—man′da·to′ri·ly,** *adv.*

Man·de·an (man dē′ən), *n., adj.* Mandaean.

Man·de·la (man del′ə), *n.* **Nelson (Ro·lih·lah·la)** (rô′lē lä′lə), born 1918, and his wife, **Win·nie** (win′ē), born 1936?, South African black activists.

Man·de·ville (man′də vil), *n.* **1. Bernard de** (də), c1670–1733, English physician and satirist, born in Holland. **2. Sir John,** died 1372, English compiler of a book of travels.

man·di·ble (man′də bəl), *n.* **1.** the bone of the lower jaw. **2.** (in birds) **a.** the lower part of the bill. **b. mandibles,** the upper and lower parts of the bill. **3.** (in arthropods) one of the first pair of mouthpart appendages, typically a jawlike biting organ, but styliform or setiform in piercing and sucking species. [< LL *mandibula* jaw = *mandi-* (s. of *mandere* to chew) + *-bula* n. suffix of means] **—man·dib·u·lar** (man dib′yə lər), *adj.*

Man·din·go (man ding′gō), *n., pl.* **-gos, -goes.** a member of any of a number of Negro peoples forming an extensive linguistic group in western Africa.

man·do·lin (man′dᵊlin, man′dᵊlin′), *n.* a musical instrument with a pear-shaped wooden body (smaller than that of the lute) and a fretted neck, usually having metal strings plucked with a plectrum. [< It *mandolin(o),* dim. of *mandola,* var. of *mandora,* alter. of *pandora* BANDORE] **—man′do·lin′ist,** *n.*

Mandolin

man·drag·o·ra (man drag′ər ə, man′drə gōr′ə, -gôr′ə), *n.* **1.** mandrake (def. 1). **2.** a mandrake root. [ME, OE < ML < L, Gk *mandragoras*]

man·drake (man′drāk, -drik), *n.* **1.** a narcotic, short-stemmed, European, solanaceous herb, *Mandragora officinarum,* having a fleshy, often forked root thought to resemble a human form. **2.** *U.S.* the May apple. [ME, var. of *mandrage* (short for MANDRAGORA), taken (by folk etym.) as MAN[1] + DRAKE[2]]

man·drel (man′drəl), *n.* **1.** *Mach.* a shaft or bar the end of which is inserted into a workpiece to hold it during machining. **2.** the driving spindle in the headstock of a lathe. **3.** a spindle on which a circular saw or grinding wheel rotates. Also, **man′dril.** [? akin to F *mandrin*]

man·drill (man′dril), *n.* a large, ferocious-looking baboon, *Papio sphinx,* of W Africa, the male of which has the face marked with blue and scarlet and the muzzle ribbed. [MAN[1] + DRILL[4]]

Mandrill (20 in. high at shoulder; length 3 ft.)

mane (mān), *n.* the long hair growing on the back of or about the neck and neighboring parts of some animals, as the horse and lion. [ME; OE *manu;* c. Icel *mön,* G *Mähne,* D *manen*] **—maned,** *adj.* **—mane′less,** *adj.*

man-eat·er (man′ē′tər), *n.* **1.** a human cannibal. **2.** an animal, esp. a tiger, lion, or shark, that eats or is said to eat human flesh. **3.** See **great white shark.** **—man′-eat′ing,** *adj.*

ma·nège (ma nezh′, -nāzh′), *n.* **1.** the art of training and riding horses. **2.** the action or movements of a trained horse. **3.** a school for training horses and teaching horsemanship. Also, **ma·nege′.** [< F < It *maneggio;* see MANAGE]

ma·nes (mā′nēz; *Lat.* mä′nes), *n.* **1.** (*construed as pl.*) *Rom. Religion.* the souls of the dead; shades. **2.** (*construed as sing.*) the spirit or shade of a particular dead person. Also, **Ma′nes.** [< L: lit., the good ones; akin to OL *mānus* good]

Ma·nes (mā′nēz), *n.* A.D. 216?–276?, Persian prophet: founder of Manicheanism. Also called **Manicheus, Mani.**

Ma·net (ma nā′; *Fr.* MA ne′), *n.* **É·douard** (ā dwAR′), 1832–83, French painter.

ma·neu·ver (mə nōō′vər), *n., v.,* **-vered, -ver·ing.** **—***n.* **1.** a planned and regulated movement or evolution of troops, war vessels, etc. **2. maneuvers,** a series of tactical exercises usually carried out in the field by large bodies of troops in imitation of war. **3.** an adroit move, skillful proceeding, etc., esp. as characterized by craftiness: *political maneuvers.* **—***v.t.* **4.** to change the position of (troops, vessels, etc.) by a maneuver. **5.** to bring, put, drive, or make by maneuvers: *He maneuvered his way into the confidence of the enemy.* **6.** to manipulate or manage with skill or adroitness: *to maneuver a conversation.* **—***v.i.* **7.** to perform a maneuver or maneuvers. **8.** to scheme; intrigue. Also, **manoeuvre.** [< F *manoeuvre,* MF *manuevre* handwork < OF *manuvrer* < L *manū operāre* to do handwork = *manū* (abl. of *manus* hand) + *operāre* to work (see OPERATE)] **—ma·neu′ver·a·ble,** *adj.* **—ma·neu′ver·a·bil′i·ty,** *n.* **—ma·neu′ver·er,** *n.* **—Syn. 3.** stratagem, procedure, scheme, plot, plan. **8.** plot, plan.

man′ Fri′day, a male administrative assistant with diverse duties. [after a character in Daniel Defoe's novel *Robinson Crusoe* (1719)]

man·ful (man′fəl), *adj.* having or showing manly spirit; resolute; bold; courageous. [ME] **—man′ful·ly,** *adv.* **—man′ful·ness,** *n.*

man·ga·bey (mang′gə bā′), *n., pl.* **-beys.** any of several slender, long-tailed monkeys of the genus *Cercocebus,* found in forests of Africa. [after *Mangabey,* Madagascar]

mangan-, var. of **mangano-** before a vowel: *manganic.*

man·ga·nate (mang′gə nāt′), *n. Chem.* a salt of manganic acid, as potassium manganate, K_2MnO_4.

man·ga·nese (mang′gə nēs′, -nēz′), *n. Chem.* a hard, brittle, grayish-white, metallic element, an oxide of which, MnO_2 (**man′ganese diox′ide**), is a valuable oxidizing agent: used chiefly as an alloying agent in steel to give it toughness. *Symbol:* Mn; *at. wt.:* 54.938; *at. no.:* 25; *sp. gr.:* 7.2 at 20°C. [< F *manganèse* < It *manganese,* metathetic var. of ML *magnesia* MAGNESIA]

man·gan·ic (man gan′ik), *adj. Chem.* of or containing manganese, esp. in the trivalent state.

mangan′ic ac′id, *Chem.* a hypothetical acid, H_2MnO_4, occurring only in the form of its salts and in solution.

man·ga·nite (mang′gə nīt′), *n.* **1.** a mineral, hydrous manganese oxide, MnO(OH). **2.** *Chem.* any of a series of salts containing tetravalent manganese and derived from either of two acids, H_4MnO_4 or H_2MnO_3.

mangano-, a combining form of **manganese.** Also, **mangan-, mangani-.** [< G *Mangan* manganese + -o-]

man·ga·nous (mang′gə nəs, man gan′əs), *adj. Chem.* containing bivalent manganese.

mange (mānj), *n. Vet. Pathol.* any of various skin diseases caused by parasitic mites, affecting animals and sometimes man and characterized by loss of hair and scabby eruptions. [late ME *manjewe* itch < MF *mangeue* an eating, itch < *mangier* to eat; see MANGER]

man·gel-wur·zel (mang′gəl wûr′zəl), *n. Chiefly Brit.* a variety of the beet *Beta vulgaris,* cultivated as food for livestock. Also called **man′gel.** [< G, var. of *Mangoldwurzel* (*Mangold* beet + *Wurzel* root)]

man·ger (mān′jər), *n.* **1.** a box or trough from which horses or cattle eat. 2. *Naut.* a. a space at the bow of a vessel, having a partition for confining water entering at the hawseholes until it can be drained. b. a sunken bottom in a chain locker, covered by a grating and used to collect water from the anchor chain. [ME < MF *maingeure* < *mangier* to eat < L *manducāre* to chew, eat]

man·gey (mān′jē), *adj.*, **-gi·er, -gi·est.** mangy.

man·gle[1] (maŋ′gəl), *v.t.*, **-gled, -gling.** 1. to cut, slash, or crush so as to disfigure. 2. to spoil; ruin; mar badly. [late ME < AF *mangler*, perh. dissimilated var. of OF *mangonner* to mangle; akin to MANGONEL] —**man′gler,** *n.* —**Syn. 1.** See **maim. 2.** deface; destroy.

man·gle[2] (maŋ′gəl), *n., v.*, **-gled, -gling.** —*n.* 1. a machine for smoothing or pressing cloth, household linen, etc., by means of rollers. —*v.t.* 2. to smooth with a mangle. 3. *Metalworking.* to squeeze (metal plates) between rollers. [< D *mangel* < LL *mangan(um)* (by dissimilation). See MANGONEL]

man·go (maŋ′gō), *n., pl.* **-goes, -gos.** 1. the oblong, slightly acid fruit of a tropical, anacardiaceous tree, *Mangifera indica*, eaten ripe, or preserved or pickled. 2. the tree itself. [< Pg *manga* < Malay *mangā* < Tamil *mān-kāy* fruit (*kāy*) of mango tree (*mān*)]

man·go·nel (maŋ′gə nel′), *n.* any of various former military engines for throwing large stones and darts. [ME < OF (dim.) < LL *manganum* < Gk *mánganon* engine of war]

man·go·steen (maŋ′gə stēn′), *n.* 1. the juicy, edible fruit of an East Indian tree, *Garcinia Mangostana*. 2. the tree itself. [< Malay *mangustan*]

man·grove (maŋ′grōv, man′-), *n.* 1. any tropical tree or shrub of the genus *Rhizophora*, the species of which are mostly low trees noted for a copious development of interlacing adventitious roots above the ground. 2. any of various similar plants. [alter. (by folk etym.) of earlier *mangrow* < Pg *mangue* << Taino]

man·gy (mān′jē), *adj.*, **-gi·er, -gi·est.** 1. having, caused by, or like the mange. 2. contemptible; mean: *a mangy trick.* 3. squalid; shabby: *a mangy little suburb.* Also, **mangey.**

man·han·dle (man′han′dᵊl, man han′dᵊl), *v.t.*, **-dled, -dling.** 1. to handle roughly. 2. to move by human strength, without the use of mechanical appliances.

Man·hat·tan (man hat′ᵊn, *esp. for 1, 2,* mən-), *n.* 1. Also called **Man·hat′tan Is′land.** an island in New York City surrounded by the Hudson, East, and Harlem rivers. 13½ mi. long; 2½ mi. greatest width; 22¼ sq. mi. 2. a borough of New York City approximately coextensive with Manhattan Island: commercial center. 1,539,233 (est. 1970). 3. a city in NE Kansas, on the Kansas River. 27,575 (1970). 4. a cocktail of whiskey and sweet vermouth.

Manhat′tan Beach′, a city in SW California, SW of Los Angeles. 35,352 (1970).

Manhat′tan clam′ chow′der, a chowder made from clams, salt pork, tomatoes, and other vegetables. Cf. **New England clam chowder.**

Man·hat·tan·ite (man hat′ᵊnīt′, mən-), *n.* a native or inhabitant of the borough of Manhattan.

Manhat′tan Proj′ect, *U.S.* the code designation for the secret program that led to the development of the first atomic bomb during World War II.

man·hole (man′hōl′), *n.* a hole, usually with a cover, affording entrance to a sewer, drain, steam boiler, etc.

man·hood (man′hŏŏd), *n.* 1. the state of being a man or an adult male person. 2. manly qualities: *He proved his manhood in the war.* 3. men collectively. 4. state of being human. [ME]

man-hour (man′our′, -ou′ər), *n.* an hour of work by one man, used as an industrial time unit. *Abbr.:* man-hr

man·hunt (man′hunt′), *n.* 1. an intensive search for a criminal, suspect, escaped convict, etc., as by the law enforcement agencies of a country. 2. any intensive search for a man. —**man′ hunt′er.**

Ma·ni (mä′nē), *n.* Manes.

ma·ni·a (mā′nē ə, mān′yə), *n.* 1. excessive excitement or enthusiasm: *She has a mania for bizarre cocktails.* 2. *Psychiatry.* a form of insanity characterized by great excitement, with or without delusions, and in its acute stage by great violence. [late ME < L < Gk: madness; akin to MAENAD, MIND]

-mania, a combining form of **mania** (*megalomania*); extended to mean exaggerated desire or love for (*bibliomania*).

ma·ni·ac (mā′nē ak′), *n.* 1. a raving or violently insane person; madman; lunatic. —*adj.* 2. raving with madness; mad. [< ML *maniac(us)* of, pertaining to madness]

ma·ni·a·cal (mə nī′ə kəl), *adj.* of or pertaining to mania or a maniac. —**ma·ni′a·cal·ly,** *adv.*

man·ic (man′ik, mā′nik), *adj.* pertaining to or affected by mania. [< Gk *manik(ós)* inclined to madness]

man·ic-de·pres·sive (man′ik di pres′iv), *Psychiatry.* —*adj.* 1. having a mental disorder marked by alternating extremes of excitement and depression. —*n.* 2. a person suffering from this disorder.

Man·i·che·an (man′ə kē′ən), *n.* 1. Also, **Man·i·chee** (man′ə kē′). an adherent of the dualistic religious system of Manes, a combination of Gnostic Christianity, Buddhism, Zoroastrianism, and various other elements, with a basic doctrine of a conflict between light and dark, matter being regarded as dark and evil. —*adj.* 2. of or pertaining to the Manicheans or their doctrines. Also, **Man′i·chae′an.** [ME *Manichee* (< LL *Manichae(us)* < LGk *Manichaîos* of Manes) + -AN] —**Man′i·che′an·ism, Man′i·che′ism, Man′i·chae′an·ism, Man′i·chae′ism,** *n.*

Man·i·che·us (man′ə kē′əs), *n.* Manes.

ma·ni·cot·ti (man′ə kot′ē; *It.* mä′nē kôt′tē), *n.* *Italian Cookery.* a dish consisting of large, tubular noodles stuffed with a mild cheese and baked in a tomato sauce. [< It: muffs, pl. of *manicotto*, dim. of *manica* sleeve. See MANCHE]

man·i·cure (man′ə kyŏŏr′), *n., v.*, **-cured, -cur·ing.** —*n.* 1. a professional treatment of the hands and fingernails for removing cuticle, trimming and shaping nails, etc. 2. a manicurist. —*v.t., v.i.* 3. to take care of (the hands and fingernails) by means of manicure treatment. [< F < L *mani-* (comb. form of *manus* hand) + *cūra* care]

man·i·cur·ist (man′ə kyŏŏr′ist), *n.* a person, esp. a woman, who gives manicures.

man·i·fest (man′ə fest′), *adj.* 1. readily perceived by the eye or the understanding; evident; obvious; apparent; plain: *a manifest error.* 2. *Psychoanal.* of or pertaining to conscious feelings, ideas, and impulses that contain repressed psychic material. —*v.t.* 3. to make manifest to the eye or the understanding; show plainly. 4. to prove; put beyond doubt or question. 5. to record in a ship's manifest. —*n.* 6. a list of the cargo carried by a vessel. 7. a list of the cargo or passengers carried on an airplane. [ME < L *manifest(us)*, var. of *manufestus* evident, lit., struck with the hand. See MANUS, INFEST] —**man′i·fest′ly,** *adv.* —**man′i·fest′ness,** *n.* —**Syn. 1.** clear, distinct, unmistakable. **3.** reveal, disclose, evince. See **display.** —**Ant. 1.** obscure. **3.** conceal.

man·i·fes·tant (man′ə fes′tənt), *n.* a person who initiates or participates in a manifestation or public demonstration. [< L *manifestant-* (s. of *manifestāns*), prp. of *manifestāre* to MANIFEST; see -ANT]

man·i·fes·ta·tion (man′ə fe stā′shən), *n.* 1. the act of manifesting. 2. the state of being manifested. 3. a means of manifesting; indication. 4. a public demonstration, as for political effect. 5. *Spiritualism.* a materialization. [< LL *manifestātiōn-* (s. of *manifestātiō*)]

Man′ifest Des′tiny, the 19th-century belief or doctrine that it was the destiny of the U.S. to expand across the continent of North America.

man·i·fes·to (man′ə fes′tō), *n., pl.* **-toes.** a public declaration of intentions, opinions, objectives, or motives, as one issued by a government, sovereign, or organization. [< It; see MANIFEST]

man·i·fold (man′ə fōld′), *adj.* 1. of many kinds; numerous and varied: *manifold duties.* 2. having many different parts, elements, features, forms, etc.: *a manifold program for social reform.* 3. doing or operating several things at once. —*n.* 4. something having many different parts or features. 5. a copy or facsimile, as of something written. 6. *Mach.* a chamber having several outlets through which a liquid or gas is distributed or gathered. —*v.t.* 7. to make copies of, as with carbon paper. [ME; OE *manigf(e)ald.* See MANY, -FOLD] —**man′i·fold′ly,** *adv.* —**man′i·fold′ness,** *n.*

man·i·fold·er (man′ə fōl′dər), *n.* a machine for making manifolds or copies, as of writing.

man·i·kin (man′ə kin), *n.* 1. a little man; dwarf; pygmy. 2. mannequin. 3. a model of the human body for teaching anatomy, demonstrating surgical operations, etc. Also, **manakin, mannikin.** [< D *mannekin*, dim. of *man* MAN[1]. See -KIN, MANNEQUIN]

Ma·nil·a (mə nil′ə), *n.* 1. a seaport in and the capital of the Philippines, on S Luzon. 1,339,000 (est. 1965). Cf. **Quezon City.** 2. See **Manila hemp.** 3. See **Manila paper.**

Manil′a Bay′, a bay in the Philippines, in W Luzon Island: the American fleet under Admiral Dewey defeated the Spanish fleet 1898.

Manil′a hemp′, a fibrous material obtained from the leaves of the abaca, *Musa textilis*, used for making ropes, fabrics, etc. Also called **Manila, manilla.**

Manil′a pa′per, strong, light-brown or buff paper, originally made from Manila hemp but now also from wood pulp substitutes and various other fibers. Also called **Manila, manilla.**

Manil′a rope′, rope manufactured from Manila hemp.

ma·nil·la (mə nil′ə), *n.* 1. See **Manila hemp.** 2. See **Manila paper.**

man′ in the street′, the average citizen.

man·i·oc (man′ē ok′, mā′nē-), *n.* cassava. [< Tupi *man(d)ioca*; r. *manihot* < MF < Guarani *man(d)io*]

man·i·ple (man′ə pəl), *n.* 1. (in ancient Rome) a subdivision of a legion, consisting of 60 or 120 men. 2. *Eccles.* one of the Eucharistic vestments, consisting of an ornamental band or strip worn on the left arm near the wrist. See illus. at **chasuble.** [< ML *manipul(us)* sudarium, L: infantry company, lit., handful = *mani-* (comb. form of *manus* hand) + *-pulus* -FUL]

ma·nip·u·la·ble (mə nip′yə lə bəl), *adj.* that can be manipulated. —**ma·nip·u·la·bil·i·ty** (mə nip′yə lə bil′i tē), *n.*

ma·nip·u·lar (mə nip′yə lər), *adj.* 1. of or pertaining to the Roman maniple. 2. of or pertaining to manipulation. [< L *manipulār(is)*]

ma·nip·u·late (mə nip′yə lāt′), *v.t.*, **-lat·ed, -lat·ing.** 1. to handle, manage, or use, esp. with skill, in some process of treatment or performance. 2. to manage or influence by artful skill: *to manipulate a person.* 3. to adapt or change (accounts, figures, etc.) to suit one's purpose or advantage. [back formation from MANIPULATION] —**ma·nip′u·lat′a·ble,** *adj.* —**ma·nip·u·la·tive** (mə nip′yə lā′tiv, -yə lə tiv), *adj.* —**ma·nip′u·la′tive·ly,** *adv.* —**ma·nip′u·la′tive·ness,** *n.* —**ma·nip′u·la′tor,** *n.* —**ma·nip·u·la·to·ry** (mə nip′yə lə tōr′ē, -tôr′ē), *adj.* —**Syn. 3.** juggle, falsify.

ma·nip·u·la·tion (mə nip′yə lā′shən), *n.* 1. skillful or artful management. 2. the act of manipulating. 3. the state or fact of being manipulated. [< F = *manipule* handful (of grains, etc.; see MANIPLE) + *-ation* -ATION]

Ma·ni·pur (mun′i pŏŏr′), *n.* a union territory in NE India between Assam and Burma. 780,037 (1961); 8620 sq. mi. *Cap.:* Imphal.

Ma·ni·sa (mä′ni sä′), *n.* a city in W Turkey, near the Aegean: battle 190 B.C. 59,675 (1960). Ancient, **Magnesia.**

Man·i·to·ba (man′i tō′bə), *n.* 1. a province in central Canada. 921,686 (1961); 246,512 sq. mi. *Cap.:* Winnipeg. **2. Lake,** a lake in the S part of this province. 120 mi. long; 1817 sq. mi. —**Man′i·to′ban,** *adj., n.*

man·i·tou (man′i tōō′), *n., pl.* **-tous,** (*esp. collectively*) **-tou.** (among the Algonquian Indians) a supernatural being that controls nature; a spirit, deity, or object having supernatural power. Also, **manitu.** [< Algonquian; cf. Ojibwa *manito* spirit, god]

Man·i·tou·lin (man′i tōō′lin), *n.* an island in N Lake Huron belonging to Canada. 80 mi. long. Also called **Manitou′lin Is′land.**

Man·i·to·woc (man′i tə wok′), *n.* a port in E Wisconsin, on Lake Michigan. 33,430 (1970).

man·i·tu (man′i tōō′), *n., pl.* **-tus,** (*esp. collectively*) **-tu.** manitou.

Ma·ni·za·les (mä′nē sä′les), *n.* a city in W Colombia. 186,910 (est. 1964).

Man·ka·to (man kā′tō), *n.* a city in S Minnesota, on the Minnesota River. 30,895 (1970).

man·kind (man′kīnd′ *for 1;* man′kīnd′ *for 2*), *n.* **1.** the human race; human beings collectively. **2.** men, as distinguished from women. [ME]

man·like (man′līk′), *adj.* **1.** resembling a man. **2.** manly. [late ME]

man·ly (man′lē), *adj.*, **-li·er, -li·est,** *adv.* **—***adj.* **1.** having the qualities usually considered desirable in a man; virile. **2.** pertaining to or befitting a man: *manly sports.* **—***adv.* **3.** *Archaic.* in a manly manner. [ME (adj., adv.); OE *manlīce* (adv.)] **—man′li·ness,** *n.*
—Syn. 1. masculine, male. MANLY, MANNISH mean possessing the qualities of a man. MANLY implies possession of the most valuable or desirable qualities a man can have, as dignity, honesty, directness, courage, strength, and fortitude: *manly determination.* MANNISH applies to that which resembles a man: *a boy with a mannish voice.* Applied to a woman, the term is derogatory, suggesting the possession of masculine characteristics: *a mannish stride.*

man-made (man′mād′), *adj.* produced, formed, or made by man; artificial; not natural.

Mann (män, man *for 1, 3;* man *for 2*), *n.* **1. Hein·rich** (hīn′rik; *Ger.* hīn′RIKH), 1871–1950, German novelist and dramatist, in the U.S. after 1940 (brother of Thomas Mann). **2. Horace,** 1796–1859, U.S. educational reformer. **3. Thom·as** (tom′əs; *Ger.* tō′mäs), 1875–1955, German novelist and critic, in the U.S. after 1937: Nobel prize 1929.

man·na (man′ə), *n.* **1.** the food miraculously supplied to the Israelites in the wilderness. Ex. 16:14–36. **2.** divine or spiritual food. **3.** the exudation of the ash *Fraxinus Ornus* and related plants: source of mannitol. [ME, OE < LL < Gk < Heb *mān*]

Mann′ Act′ (man), *U.S.* an act of Congress in 1910 making it a federal offense to aid or participate in the transportation of a woman from one state to another for immoral purposes. Also called **White Slave Act.**

man′na grass′, any aquatic or marsh grass of the genus *Glyceria,* of Europe, Asia, and North America.

man·ne·quin (man′ə kin), *n.* **1.** a model of the human figure used for displaying clothing, and by tailors, dress designers, etc., for fitting or making clothes. **2.** a girl or woman employed to model clothes. **3.** See **lay figure** (def. 1). Also, **manikin.** [< F < D *mannekijn, manneken;* see MANIKIN]

man·ner (man′ər), *n.* **1.** way of doing, being done, or happening; mode of action, occurrence, etc. **2.** characteristic or customary way of acting or doing. **3. manners, a.** the prevailing customs, ways of living, and the like, of a people, class, period, etc. **b.** ways of behaving with reference to polite standards. **4.** a person's characteristic behavior in a social situation. **5.** (*construed as pl.*) kind; sort: *All manner of things were happening.* **6.** characteristic style in art, literature, or the like: *verses in the manner of Spenser.* **7.** *Obs.* **a.** nature; character. **b.** guise; fashion. **8. by all manner of means,** by all means; certainly. **9. in a manner of speaking,** as it were; so to speak. **10. to the manner born, a.** accustomed by birth to a high position. **b.** used to a particular custom from birth. [ME *manere* < AF; OF *maniere* << LL *manuāria,* fem. of *manuārius* of, pertaining to the hand]
—Syn. 1. method. **2.** mode, fashion, style; habit, custom. **4.** demeanor, deportment. MANNER, AIR, BEARING all refer to a person's outward aspect or behavior. MANNER applies to a distinctive mode of behavior or social attitude toward others: *a gracious manner.* AIR applies to outward appearance insofar as this is distinctive or indicative: *an air of martyrdom.* BEARING applies esp. to carriage: *a noble bearing.*

man·nered (man′ərd), *adj.* **1.** having manners as specified (usually used in combination): *ill-mannered people.* **2.** having mannerisms; affected: *a mannered walk.* [ME *manered*]

man·ner·ism (man′ə riz′əm), *n.* **1.** marked or excessive adherence to an unusual or a particular manner, esp. an affectation. **2.** (*usually cap.*) a style in the fine arts developed first in Italy and afterward in the rest of Europe during the 16th century, characterized by spatial complexity and elongation of forms. **3.** a habitual or characteristic manner, mode, or way of doing something. **—man′ner·ist,** *n.* **—man′ner·is′tic,** *adj.* **—man′ner·is′ti·cal·ly,** *adv.*

man·ner·less (man′ər lis), *adj.* without good manners; discourteous; impolite. [ME *manerles*] **—man′ner·less·ness,** *n.*

man·ner·ly (man′ər lē), *adj.* **1.** having or showing good manners; polite. **—***adv.* **2.** with good manners; politely. [ME *manerly*] **—man′ner·li·ness,** *n.*

Mann·heim (man′hīm; *Ger.* män′hīm), *n.* a city in SW West Germany, on the Rhine: major inland port and transportation center. 323,972 (est. 1964).

man·ni·kin (man′ə kin), *n.* manikin.

man·nish (man′ish), *adj.* (of a woman or her behavior, attributes, etc.) resembling, characteristic of, natural to, or appropriate for a man. [ME] **—man′nish·ly,** *adv.* **—man′nish·ness,** *n.* **—Syn.** See **manly.**

man·ni·tol (man′i tōl′, -tôl′, -tol′), *n. Chem.* a carbohydrate alcohol, $HOCH_2(CHOH)_4CH_2OH$, occurring in three optically different forms, the common one being found in the manna of the ash *Fraxinus Ornus* and in other plants: used chiefly in the manufacture of resins, electrolytic condensers for radios, plasticizers, and as a pill excipient. [MANN(OSE) + -ITE[1] + -OL[1]]

man·nose (man′ōs), *n. Chem.* a hexose, $C_6H_{12}O_6$, obtained from the hydrolysis of the ivory nut, and yielding mannitol upon reduction. [MANN(A) + -OSE[2]]

mano a mano (mä′nō ə mä′nō), *pl.* **mano a manos** for 1. *Spanish.* **1.** a confrontation or conflict. **2.** alone or in a small informal group. [< Sp: lit., hand by hand]

ma·noeu·vre (mə nōō′vər), *n., v.t., v.i.,* **-vred, -vring.** maneuver.

man′ of God′, 1. a saint, prophet, etc. **2.** a clergyman.

Man′ of Sor′rows, (in Christian exegesis) an appellation of Jesus Christ as the suffering Savior. Isa. 53:3.

man′ of straw′. See **straw man.**

man′ of the cloth′, a clergyman or other ecclesiastic.

man′ of the world′, a worldly, sophisticated man.

man-of-war (man′əv wôr′), *n., pl.* **men-of-war. 1.** a warship. **2.** See **Portuguese man-of-war.**

Ma·no·le·te (mä′nô le′te), *n.* (*Manuel Laureano Rodríguez y Sánchez*) 1917–47, Spanish matador.

ma·nom·e·ter (mə nom′i tər), *n.* an instrument for measuring the pressure of a fluid, consisting of a tube filled with a liquid so that the level of the liquid is determined by the fluid pressure and the height of the liquid may be read from a scale. [< F *manomètre* = *mano-* (< Gk *manós* loose, rare, sparse) + *-mètre* -METER] **—man·o·met·ric** (man′ə me′trik), **man′o·met′ri·cal,** *adj.* **—man′o·met′ri·cal·ly,** *adv.* **—ma·nom′e·try,** *n.*

man′ on horse′back, a military figure who presents himself as the savior of the country during a crisis and either assumes or threatens to assume dictatorial powers.

man·or (man′ər), *n.* **1.** a landed estate or territorial unit, consisting of a lord's demesne and of lands within which he has the right to exercise certain privileges, exact certain fees, etc. **2.** the mansion of a lord with the land belonging to it. **3.** the main house or mansion on an estate, plantation, etc. [ME *maner* < OF *manoir,* n. use of *manoir* to remain, dwell < L *manēre* to remain; see MANSION] **—ma·no·ri·al** (mə nōr′ē əl, -nôr′-), *adj.*

man′or house′, the house of the lord of a manor. Also called **mansion.**

ma·no·ri·al·ism (mə nōr′ē ə liz′əm, -nôr′-), *n.* the medieval manorial organization or its principles and practices.

man′-o′-war′ bird′ (man′ə wôr′). See **frigate bird.**

man′ pow′er, 1. the power supplied by the physical exertions of a man or men. **2.** a unit of power, assumed to be equal to the rate at which a man can do mechanical work, and commonly taken as 1/10 horsepower. **3.** manpower.

man·pow·er (man′pou′ər), *n.* **1.** a labor force, or a number of workers contributing to or needed for such a force: *The company suspended the project for lack of manpower.* **2.** total military personnel available, as of a nation in time of war: *French manpower.*

man·qué (män kā′; *Eng.* mäng kā′), *adj. French.* having failed, missed, or fallen short, esp. because of circumstances or a defect of character; unfulfilled: *a poet* manqué.

man·rope (man′rōp′), *n. Naut.* a rope placed at the side of a gangway, ladder, or the like, to serve as a rail.

man·sard (man′särd), *n.* a form of curb roof whose lower slope approaches the vertical and usually contains dormer windows, while the upper slope is nearly flat. Also called **man′sard roof′.** See illus. at **roof.** [< F *mansarde,* named after N. F. MANSART]

Man·sart (män SAR′; *Eng.* man′särt), *n.* **1. Jules Hardouin-** (zhyl AR dwAN′-), (*Jules Hardouin*), 1646–1708, French architect: chief architectural director for Louis XIV. **2.** his grand-uncle, **(Ni·co·las) Fran·çois** (nē kô lä′ fRÄN-SWA′), 1598–1666, French architect. Also, **Man·sard** (mäN-SAR′; *Eng.* man′särd).

manse (mans), *n.* **1.** the house and land occupied by a minister or parson. **2.** *Obs.* a manor house. [ME *manss* < ML *mānsus* farm, dwelling, n. use of ptp. of L *manēre* to dwell. See REMAIN]

man·serv·ant (man′sûr′vənt), *n., pl.* **men·serv·ants.** a male servant, esp. a valet.

Mans·field (manz′fēld), *n.* **1. Katherine** (pen name of *Kathleen Beauchamp Murry*), 1888–1923, English short-story writer, born in New Zealand. **2. Michael Joseph** (*Mike*), born 1903, U.S. politician and diplomat: senator 1953–77; ambassador to Japan since 1977. **3.** a city in W Nottinghamshire, in central England. 53,222 (1961). **4.** a city in N Ohio. 55,047 (1970). **5. Mount,** a mountain in N Vermont: highest peak of Green Mountains, 4393 ft.

man·sion (man′shən), *n.* **1.** a very large, impressive, or stately residence. **2.** See **manor house. 3.** *Oriental and Medieval Astron.* each of 28 divisions of the ecliptic occupied by the moon on successive days. **4.** *Archaic.* a place of abode, as in John 14:2. [ME < L *mānsiōn-* (s. of *mānsiō*) an abiding, abode]

man-sized (man′sīzd′), *adj. Informal.* **1.** of a size suitable for a man: *a nourishing, man-sized meal.* **2.** challenging one's abilities: *a man-sized job.*

man·slaugh·ter (man′slô′tər), *n.* **1.** the killing of a human being by another; homicide. **2.** *Law.* the killing of a human being unlawfully but without malice aforethought, as in an accident.

man·sue·tude (man′swi tōōd′, -tyōōd′), *n.* mildness; gentleness: *the mansuetude of Christian love.* [ME < L *mansuētūdō* tameness, mildness = *mansuēt(us)* tamed, gentle, lit., accustomed to the (guiding) hand (*man(us)* hand + *suētus,* ptp. of *suēscere* to grow accustomed) + *-ūdō* abstract n. suffix; see -TUDE]

Man·sur, al- (al′man sōōr′), (*'Abdullāh al-Mansūr*) A.D. 712?–775, Arab caliph 754–775: founder of Baghdad 764.

Man·sû·ra (man sōōr′ə; *Arab.* mon sōō′RÄ), *n.* See **El Mansûra.**

man·ta (man′tə; *Sp.* män′tä), *n., pl.* **-tas** (-təz; *Sp.* -täs). **1.** (in Spain and Spanish America) a cloak or wrap. **2.** the type of blanket or cloth used on a horse or mule, as for covering the load on a packsaddle. **3.** See **manta ray.** [< Sp < Pr: blanket. See MANTLE]

man-tai·lored (man′tā′lərd), *adj.* (of women's clothing) tailored in the manner and with the details of men's clothing.

man′ta ray′, a huge ray common in tropical waters, reaching a width of 20 feet and having earlike flaps on each side of the head.

man·teau (man′tō, man tō′; *Fr.* mäN tō′), *n., pl.* **-teaus** (-tōz, -tōz′), *Fr.* **-teaux** (-tō′). *Obs.* a mantle or cloak, esp. one worn by women. [< F; see MANTLE]

Man·te·gna (män te′nyä), *n.* **An·dre·a** (än dRe′ä), 1431–1506, Italian painter and engraver.

man·tel (man′tᵊl), *n.* **1.** a construction framing the opening of a fireplace and usually covering part of the chimney breast in a more or less decorative manner. **2.** a shelf above a fireplace opening, often used to display ornaments, candelabra, and the like. Also, **mantle.** Also called **mantelpiece, mantlepiece.** [late ME *mantell* mantelet; var. of MANTLE]

man·tel·et (man′tᵊlet′, mant′lit), *n.* **1.** a short mantle. **2.** Also, **mantlet.** *Mil.* a movable shelter, as one formerly used by besiegers when storming a fortress or city. **3.** any of various bulletproof shelters or screens. [ME < MF]

man·tel·let·ta (man′tᵊlet′ə), *n. Rom. Cath. Ch.* a silk or woolen sleeveless vestment reaching to the knees. [< It, prob. < ML *mantelletum,* dim. of L *mantellum* MANTLE]
man·tel·piece (man′tᵊl pēs′), *n.* mantel.
man·tel·tree (man′tᵊl trē′), *n.* **1.** a wooden or stone lintel over the opening of a fireplace. **2.** a masonry arch used in place of such a lintel. Also, **mantletree.** [late ME]
man·tic (man′tik), *adj.* **1.** of or pertaining to divination. **2.** having the power of divination. [< Gk *mantik(ós)* of, for a soothsayer, prophetic. See MANTIS, -IC] —**man′ti·cal·ly,** *adv.*
-mantic, a combining form of **mantic,** used in the formation of adjectives corresponding to nouns with stems in *-mancy: necromantic.*
man·til·la (man til′ə, -tē′ə), *n.* **1.** a silk or lace head scarf, usually covering the shoulders, worn esp. in Spain and Latin America. **2.** a short mantle or light cape. [< Sp; dim. of MANTA]

Mantilla

Man·ti·ne·a (man′tə nē′ə), *n.* an ancient city in S Greece, in Arcadia: battles 362 B.C., 223 B.C.
man·tis (man′tis), *n., pl.* **-tis·es, -tes** (-tēz). any of several predaceous insects of the order *Mantidae,* having a long prothorax and typically holding the forelegs in an upraised position as if in prayer. Also called **praying mantis, praying mantid.** [< NL < Gk: prophet, kind of insect; akin to MANIA]
man·tis·sa (man tis′ə), *n. Math.* the decimal part of a common logarithm. Cf. **characteristic** (def. 3a). [< L, var. of *mantīsa* makeweight, said to be from Etruscan]
man′tis shrimp′, any stomatopod crustacean having a pair of appendages modified for grasping prey and resembling those of a mantis.
man·tle (man′tᵊl), *n., v.,* **-tled, -tling.** —*n.* **1.** a loose, sleeveless cloak. **2.** something that covers, envelops, or conceals: *the mantle of darkness.* **3.** *Zool.* a single or paired outgrowth of the body wall that lines the inner surface of the valves of the shell in mollusks and brachiopods. **4.** an incombustible network hood for a gas jet, kerosene wick, etc., that gives off a brilliant light when incandescent. **5.** *Ornith.* the back, scapular, and inner wing plumage, esp. when of the same color. **6.** Also called **man·tle·piece** (man′tᵊl pēs′). mantel. **7.** *Geol.* the portion of the earth, about 1800 miles thick, between the crust and the core. Cf. **core**[1] (def. 5), **crust** (def. 6). —*v.t.* **8.** to cover with or as with a mantle; envelop; conceal. —*v.i.* **9.** to spread like a mantle, as a blush over the face. **10.** to flush; blush. **11.** to be or become covered with a coating, as a liquid; foam. [ME *mantel,* OE *mæntel* < L *mantell(um),* dim. of *mantum* cloak]

Mantis, *Mantis religiosa* (Length 2 in.)

Man·tle (man′tᵊl), *n.* **Mickey (Charles),** born 1931, U.S. baseball player.
man′tle rock′, *Phys. Geog.* the layer of disintegrated and decomposed rock fragments, including soil, just above the solid rock of the earth's crust; regolith.
mant·let (mant′lit), *n. Mil.* mantelet (def. 2).
man·tle·tree (man′tᵊl trē′), *n.* manteltree.
man·tling (mant′ling), *n. Heraldry.* a decorative piece of cloth represented as hanging from a torse so as to cover the sides and rear of a helmet and often so as to frame the escutcheon below. Also called **lambrequin.**
man-to-man (man′tə man′), *adj.* characterized by directness, openness, etc.: *a man-to-man talk.*
man′-to-man′ defense′, *Sports.* a method of defense, esp. in basketball and football, in which each member of the defensive team is designated to guard a particular member of the offensive team. Cf. **zone defense.**
Man·toux′ test′ (man to͞o′, man′to͞o; *Fr.* mäN to͞o′), *Med.* a test for tuberculosis in which a hypersensitive reaction to an intracutaneous injection of tuberculin indicates a tubercular condition. [named after C. *Mantoux* (b. 1877), French physician]
man·tra (man′trə, mun′-), *n. Hinduism.* a word or formula to be recited or sung. [< Skt: speech]
man·tu·a (man′cho͞o ə), *n.* **1.** a loose gown worn by women in the 17th and 18th centuries. **2.** a mantle. [var. of MANTEAU, by assoc. with MANTUA]
Man·tu·a (man′cho͞o ə), *n.* a city in E Lombardy, in N Italy: birthplace of Vergil. 61,580 (1961). Italian, **Man·to·va** (män′tô vä). —**Man′tu·an,** *adj., n.*
man·u·al (man′yo͞o əl), *adj.* **1.** of or pertaining to the hand or hands. **2.** operated by hand. **3.** involving or using work with the hands. **4.** of the nature of a manual or handbook. —*n.* **5.** a small book, esp. one giving information or instructions; handbook. **6.** *Mil.* prescribed drill in handling a rifle. **7.** *Music.* a keyboard, esp. one of several belonging to a pipe organ. [< L *manuāl(is)* (adj.), *manuāle* (n.) (something) that can be held in the hand (*manu(s)* hand + *-ālis, -āle* -AL[1]); r. late ME *manuel* < MF] —**man′u·al·ly,** *adv.*
man′ual train′ing, training in the various manual arts and crafts, esp. woodworking.
ma·nu·bri·um (mə no͞o′brē əm, -nyo͞o′-), *n., pl.* **-bri·a** (-brē ə), **-bri·ums. 1.** *Anat., Zool.* a segment, bone, cell, etc., resembling a handle. **2.** *Anat.* **a.** the uppermost of the three portions of the sternum. Cf. **gladiolus** (def. 2), **xiphisternum. b.** the long process of the malleus. [< NL, L: a handle. See MANUS] —**ma·nu′bri·al,** *adj.*
manuf., 1. manufacture. **2.** manufacturer. **3.** manufacturing.
man·u·fac·to·ry (man′yə fak′tə rē), *n., pl.* **-ries.** *Archaic.* a factory. [obs. *manufact* handmade (< LL *manūfact(us)*; see MANUS, FACT) + -ORY[2]]
man·u·fac·ture (man′yə fak′chər), *v.,* **-tured, -tur·ing,** *n.* —*v.t.* **1.** to make (objects or materials), esp. by machinery and on a large scale. **2.** to make anything. **3.** to convert (material) into a useful form or useful objects. **4.** to invent fictitiously; fabricate. **5.** to produce in a mechanical way without inspiration or originality. —*n.* **6.** the making of objects or materials, esp. by machinery on a large scale. **7.** something that is manufactured: *a museum of arts and manufactures.* **8.** the creation of anything: *the manufacture of blood corpuscles.* [obs. *manufact* (see MANUFACTORY) + -URE] —**man′u·fac′tur·a·ble,** *adj.* —**man′u·fac′tur·al,** *adj.* —**man′u·fac′tur er,** *n.*
—**Syn. 1.** build. MANUFACTURE, ASSEMBLE, FABRICATE apply to processes in industry. MANUFACTURE, originally to make by hand, now means to make by machine or by industrial process: *to manufacture rubber tires.* To ASSEMBLE is to fit together the manufactured parts of something mechanical: *to assemble an automobile.* To FABRICATE is to construct or build by fitting standardized parts together: *to fabricate houses.* See also **make. 4.** compose. —**Ant. 1.** destroy.
man·u·mis·sion (man′yə mish′ən), *n.* the act of manumitting. [late ME < L *manūmissiōn-* (s. of *manūmissiō*)]
man·u·mit (man′yə mit′), *v.t.,* **-mit·ted, -mit·ting.** to release from slavery or servitude. [late ME < L *manūmitt(ere),* earlier *manū ēmittere* to emit from (one's) hand, i.e., to set free] —**man′u·mit′ter,** *n.*
ma·nure (mə no͝or′, -nyo͝or′), *n., v.,* **-nured, -nur·ing.** —*n.* **1.** any natural or artificial substance for fertilizing the soil. **2.** excrement, esp. of animals, or other refuse used as fertilizer. —*v.t.* **3.** to treat (land) with fertilizing matter; apply manure to. [late ME *manour* (v.) < MF *manouvrer* to do manual work. See MANEUVER]
ma·nus (mā′nəs), *n., pl.* **-nus. 1.** *Anat., Zool.* the distal segment of the forelimb of a vertebrate, including the carpus and the forefoot or hand. **2.** *Roman Law.* power over persons, as that of the husband over the wife. [< L: hand]
man·u·script (man′yə skript′), *n.* **1.** a book, document, letter, etc., written by hand. **2.** an author's copy of his work that is used as the basis for typesetting. **3.** writing, as distinguished from print. —*adj.* **4.** written by hand or typed. [< ML *manūscript(um)* something written by hand = L *manū* by hand (abl. of *manus*) + *scriptum* written; see SCRIPT]
Ma·nu·ti·us (mə no͞o′shē əs, -nyo͞o′-), *n.* **Al·dus** (ôl′dəs, al′-), (*Teobaldo Mannucci* or *Manuzio*), 1450–1515, Italian printer and classical scholar.
Manx (mangks), *adj.* **1.** of or pertaining to the Isle of Man, its inhabitants, or their language. —*n.* **2.** (*construed as pl.*) the inhabitants of the Isle of Man. **3.** the Gaelic of the Isle of Man, virtually extinct. [metathetic and syncopated form of earlier *Manisk(e)* (< Scand; cf. Icel *manskr* of the Isle of Man) = *man* MAN[1] + *-sk* -ISH[1]]
Manx′ cat′, a tailless variety of domestic cat.
Manx·man (mangks′mən), *n., pl.* **-men.** a native or inhabitant of the Isle of Man.

Manx cat

man·y (men′ē), *adj.,* **more, most,** *n., pron.* —*adj.* **1.** constituting or forming a large number: *many people,* **2.** noting each one of a large number (usually fol. by *a* or *an*): *For many a day it rained.* —*n.* **3.** a large or considerable number of persons or things: *A good many of the beggars were blind.* **4. the many,** the greater part of mankind. —*pron.* **5.** many persons or things: *Many of the beggars were blind.* [ME *mani, meni,* OE *manig, menig;* akin to OS, OHG *manag, menig,* Goth *manags,* Dan *mange*]
—**Syn. 1.** multifarious, multitudinous, myriad; divers. MANY, NUMEROUS, INNUMERABLE imply the presence or succession of a large number of units. MANY is a popular and common word for this idea; *many times* NUMEROUS, a more formal word, refers to a great number, or to containing very many units: *letters too numerous to mention.* INNUMERABLE denotes number that is beyond count, or, more loosely, what is extremely difficult to count: *the innumerable stars in the sky.* —**Ant. 1.** few, single.
man·y·plies (men′ē plīz′), *n.* (*construed as sing.*) *Zool.* the omasum: so called from the many plies or folds of its membrane.
man·y-sid·ed (men′ē sī′did), *adj.* **1.** having many sides. **2.** having many aspects. **3.** having many interests, qualities, etc.; versatile. —**man′y-sid′ed·ness,** *n.*
man·za·nil·la (man′zə nēl′yə, -nē′ə), *n.* a pale, very dry sherry from Spain. [< Sp; see MANCHINEEL]
man·za·ni·ta (man′zə nē′tə), *n.* **1.** any ericaceous shrub of the genus *Arctostaphylos,* of the western U.S. **2.** the fruit of one of these shrubs. [< Sp, dim. of *manzana* apple]
Man·zo·ni (män dzô′nē), *n.* **A·les·san·dro (Fran·ces·co Tom·ma·so An·to·nio)** (ä′les sän′drô frän ches′kô tôm-mä′zô än tô′nyô), 1785–1873, Italian novelist, poet, and dramatist.
Mao·ism (mou′iz əm), *n.* the political, social, economic, and military theories and policies advocated by Mao Tse-tung, esp. those concerning revolutionary movements, guerrilla warfare, etc. —**Mao′ist,** *n., adj.*
Ma·o·ri (mä′ō rē, -ô rē, mou′rē, mä′rē), *n., pl.* **-ris,** (*esp. collectively*) **-ri,** *adj.* —*n.* **1.** a member of a brown-skinned Polynesian people of New Zealand. **2.** a Polynesian language, the language of the Maoris. —*adj.* **3.** of or pertaining to the Maoris or their language.
mao tai (mou′ tī′), a very strong, colorless Chinese liquor distilled from sorghum. [after *Maotai,* Kweichow, where produced]
Mao Tse-tung (mou′ dzu′do͝ong′; *Eng.* mou′ dzə-do͝ong′, tsə to͝ong′), 1893–1976, Chinese communist leader: chairman of the People's Republic of China 1949–59; chairman of the Chinese Communist party 1943–76.

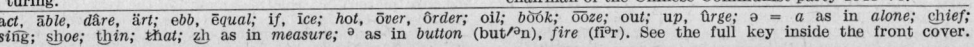

map (map), *n.*, *v.*, **mapped, map·ping.** —*n.* **1.** a representation, usually on a flat surface, of the features of an area of ground, a portion of the heavens, etc., showing them in their correct forms, sizes, and relationships, according to some convention of representation. **2.** *Math.* function (def. 4). **3.** *Slang.* the face. **4. off the map,** out of existence; into oblivion. —*v.t.* **5.** to represent or delineate on or as on a map. **6.** to sketch or plan (often fol. by *out*): *to map out a new career.* [< ML *mapp(a) (mundī)* map (of the world); special use of L: napkin, of Sem. orig.] —**map′pa·ble,** *adj.* —**Syn. 1.** plan, outline, diagram. MAP, CHART, GRAPH refer to representations of surfaces, areas, or facts. MAP most commonly refers to a representation of the surface of the earth or a section of it, or an area of the sky: *a map of England.* A CHART may be an outline map with symbols conveying information superimposed on it, a map designed esp. for navigators on water or in the air, a diagram, or a table giving information in an orderly form: *a chart of the shoals off a coast.* A GRAPH may be a diagram representing a set of interrelated facts by means of dots or lines on a coordinate background; or it may use small figures (people, animals, machines, etc.) appropriate to the facts being represented, each figure standing for a specific number in statistics being given: *a graph of the rise in population from 1900 to 1940.*

Map (map), *n.* **Walter,** c1140–1209?, Welsh ecclesiastic, poet, and satirist. Also, **Mapes** (māps, mā′pēz).

ma·ple (mā′pəl), *n.* **1.** any of numerous trees or shrubs of the genus *Acer,* species of which are grown as shade or ornamental trees, for timber, or for sap. **2.** the wood of any such tree. [ME *mapel,* OE *mapul-,* in *mapultrēow, mapulder* maple tree, c. OS *mapulder*]

Ma′ple Heights′, a city in NE Ohio, near Cleveland. 34,093 (1970).

ma′ple sug′ar, a yellowish-brown sugar produced by boiling down maple syrup.

ma′ple syr′up, **1.** a syrup produced by partially boiling down the sap of the sugar maple or of any of several other maple trees. **2.** a commercial variety of such syrup.

Ma·ple·wood (mā′pəl wo͝od′), *n.* a city in SE Minnesota, near St. Paul. 25,222 (1970).

map·ping (map′ing), *n.* **1.** the act of a person who maps. **2.** *Math.* function (def. 4).

Ma·pu·to (mə po͞o′tō), *n.* a seaport in and the capital of Mozambique, on Delagoa Bay. 383,775.

ma·quis (mä kē′; *Fr.* MA kē′), *n.*, *pl.* **-quis** (-kē′). (*often cap.*) a member of the French underground movement in World War II. [< F, special use of *maquis, makis* wild, bushy land (Corsican dial.) < It *macchie,* pl. of *macchia* a thicket < L *macula* spot]

mar (mär), *v.t.*, **marred, mar·ring. 1.** to damage or spoil to a certain extent. **2.** to disfigure; deface. [ME *merre(n),* OE *merran* to hinder, waste; c. OS *merrian,* OHG *merren* to hinder, Icel *merja* to bruise, Goth *marzjan* to offend] —**Syn.** flaw, injure; blot. MAR, DEFACE, DISFIGURE, DEFORM agree in applying to some form of injury. MAR is general, but usually refers to an external or surface injury, if it is a physical one: *The table top was marred by dents and scratches.* DEFACE refers to a surface injury that may be temporary or easily repaired: *a tablecloth defaced by penciled notations.* DISFIGURE applies to external injury of a more permanent and serious kind: *A birthmark disfigured one side of his face.* DEFORM suggests that something has been distorted or internally injured so severely as to change its normal form or qualities, or else that some fault has interfered with its proper development: *deformed by an accident that had crippled him; to deform feet by binding them.* —**Ant.** enhance, adorn.

Mar., March.

mar., **1.** maritime. **2.** married.

mar·a·bou (mar′ə bo͞o′), *n.* **1.** any of three large storks of the genus *Leptoptilus,* as *L. crumeniferus,* of Africa, *L. javanicus,* of the East Indies, and the adjutant stork, *L. dubius,* having under the wings and tail soft, downy feathers that are used in millinery and for making a furlike trimming or material. **2.** a feather from one of these storks. **3.** the trimming or material made of the feathers. **4.** a fine raw silk that can be dyed without removal of the natural gum. Also, **marabout.** [< F *marabout,* lit., MARABOUT]

Marabou, *Leptoptilus crumeniferus* (Length 5 ft.)

mar·a·bout (mar′ə bo͞ot′, -bo͞o′), *n.* **1.** *Islam.* a hermit or holy man, esp. in N Africa, often credited with supernatural powers. **2.** marabou. [< F < Pg *marabuto* < Ar *murābiṭ*]

ma·rac·a (mə rä′kə, -rak′ə), *n.* a gourd or a gourd-shaped rattle filled with seeds or pebbles and used, often in a pair, as a rhythm instrument. [< Pg < Tupi]

Mar·a·cai·bo (mar′ə kī′bō; *Sp.* mä′RÄ kī′vô), *n.* **1.** a seaport in NW Venezuela. 786,389. **2. Gulf of,** a gulf on the NW coast of Venezuela. **3. Lake,** a lake in NW Venezuela. 100 mi. long; 75 mi. wide.

Mar·a·can·da (mar′ə kan′də), *n.* ancient name of **Samarkand.**

Ma·ra·cay (mä′RÄ kī′), *n.* a city in N central Venezuela. 255,134.

Ma·ra·jó (mä′RÄ zhô′), *n.* an island in N Brazil, at the mouth of the Amazon. 19,000 sq. mi.

Ma·ra·nhão (mä′RƏ nyouN′), *n.* a state in NE Brazil. 2,883,211; 125,312 sq. mi. *Cap.:* São Luiz.

Ma·ra·ñón (mä′RÄ nyôn′), *n.* a river in Peru, flowing N and then E, joining the Ucayali to form the Amazon. 1000 mi. long.

ma·ras·ca (mə ras′kə), *n.* a wild cherry, *Prunus Cerasus Marasca,* yielding a small, bitter fruit, from which maraschino is made. [< It < *amaro* < L *amārus* bitter]

mar·a·schi·no (mar′ə skē′nō, -shē′-). *n.* a cordial or liqueur distilled from marascas. [< It; see MARASCA, -INE[1]]

mar′aschi′no cher′ry, a cherry cooked in colored syrup and flavored with maraschino, used as a garnish.

ma·ras·mus (mə raz′məs), *n.* *Pathol.* gradual loss of flesh and strength from no apparent cause, occurring chiefly in infants. [< NL < Gk *marasmós* a wasting away, akin to *marainein* to weaken, waste away] —**ma·ras′mic,** *adj.* —**ma·ras′moid,** *adj.*

Ma·rat (MA RA′), *n.* **Jean Paul** (zhäN pôl), 1743–93, French politician and journalist: leader in the Revolution.

Ma·ra·tha (mə rä′tə), Mahratta.

Ma·ra·thi (mə rä′tē, -rat′ē), *n.* an Indic language of Bombay and vicinity. Also, **Mahratti.**

mar·a·thon (mar′ə thon′, -thən), *n.* **1.** any long-distance race. **2.** a foot race on a course measuring 26 miles 385 yards. **3.** any long contest with endurance as the primary factor: *a dance marathon.* [allusion to the 26-mile run of Pheidippides from *Marathon* to Athens to carry news of the Greek victory over the Persians]

Mar·a·thon (mar′ə thon′), *n.* a plain in SE Greece, in Attica: site of Athenian victory over the Persians 490 B.C. —**Mar·a·tho·ni·an** (mar′ə thō′nē ən), *adj.*

ma·raud (mə rôd′), *v.i.* **1.** to rove in quest of plunder; make a raid for booty. —*v.t.* **2.** to raid for plunder. —*n.* **3.** *Archaic.* the act of marauding. [< F *maraud(er)* < *maraud* rogue, vagabond] —**ma·raud′er,** *n.* —**Syn. 1, 2.** invade, attack; ravage, harry.

mar·a·ve·di (mar′ə vā′dē), *n.*, *pl.* **-dis.** a former gold coin issued by the Moors in Spain. [< Sp *maravedí* < Ar *Murābiṭīn* relating to the Almoravides, Moorish dynasty (11th–12th centuries), pl. of *Murābit:* see MARABOUT]

mar·ble (mär′bəl), *n.*, *adj.*, *v.*, **-bled, -bling.** —*n.* **1.** limestone in a more or less crystalline state and capable of taking a high polish, occurring in many varieties. **2.** a work of sculpture in this stone. **3.** an imitation of this stone, or a natural stone falsely associated with it. **4.** a little ball made of glass or agate for use in games. **5. marbles, a.** (*construed as sing.*) a game for children in which a marble is propelled by the thumb to hit other marbles, so as to drive them out of a circle drawn on the ground. **b.** *Slang.* wits; common sense. —*adj.* **6.** consisting of marble. **7.** like marble, as in hardness, coldness, smoothness, etc. **8.** of variegated or mottled color. —*v.t.* **9.** to color or stain like variegated marble. **10.** to apply a variegated pattern to (paper, the edges of a book, etc.). [ME *marbel* < OE *marmel* (in *marmelstān* marble stone) < L *marmor* < Gk *mármaros*] —**mar′bler,** *n.*

Mar·ble (mär′bəl), *n.* **Alice,** born 1913, U.S. tennis player.

mar′ble cake′, a loaf cake given a marblelike appearance by the incomplete mixing of dark and light batters.

Mar·ble·head (mär′bəl hed′, mär′bəl hed′), *n.* a city in NE Massachusetts: resort. 21,295 (1970).

mar·ble·ize (mär′bə līz′), *v.t.*, **-ized, -iz·ing.** marble (def. 9). —**mar′ble·i·za′tion,** *n.*

mar·bling (mär′bling), *n.* **1.** the act, process, or art of coloring or staining in imitation of variegated marble. **2.** a decoration or pattern resembling variegated marble.

mar·bly (mär′blē), *adj.* resembling marble in appearance, hardness, coldness, etc. [late ME]

Mar·burg (mär′bo͝ork; *Eng.* mär′bûrg), *n.* **1.** a city in central West Germany. 72,000. **2.** German name of **Maribor.**

marc (märk; *Fr.* MAR), *n.* **1.** the residue of grapes after the juice is expressed. **2.** (in France) the brandy distilled from grape pomace. **3.** *Pharm.* the residue that remains following the extraction of active principles from a vegetable drug by means of a solvent. [< MF, akin to *marcher* to tread; see MARCH[1]]

Marc (märk; *Ger.* märk), *n.* **Franz** (fränts), 1880–1916, German painter.

Marc′ An′tony (märk). See **Antony, Mark.**

mar·ca·site (mär′kə sīt′), *n.* **1.** a common mineral, iron disulfide, FeS_2, chemically similar to pyrite but crystallizing in the orthorhombic system. **2.** (formerly) any of the crystallized forms of iron pyrites, much used in the 18th century for ornaments. [late ME *markasit* < ML *marcasīta* = *marcas-* (< ?) + *-īta* -ITE[1]] —**mar·ca·sit·i·cal** (mär′kə-sit′i kəl), *adj.*

mar·cel (mär sel′), *v.*, **-celled, -cel·ling,** *n.* —*v.t.* **1.** to wave (the hair) by means of special irons, producing the effect of regular, continuous waves (**marcel′ waves′**). —*n.* **2.** the act or an instance of marcelling. [named after *Marcel* Grateau (1852–1936), French hairdresser who originated it] —**mar·cel′ler,** *n.*

Mar·cel·li·nus (mär′sə lī′nəs), *n.* **Saint,** died A.D. 304, pope 296–304.

Mar·cel·lus (mär sel′əs), *n.* **Marcus Claudius,** 268?–208 B.C., Roman general and consul.

Marcellus I, Saint, died A.D. 309, pope 308–309.

Marcellus II, (*Marcello Cervini*) 1501–55, Italian ecclesiastic; pope 1555.

march[1] (märch), *v.i.* **1.** to walk with regular and measured tread, as soldiers. —*v.t.* **2.** to cause to march. —*n.* **3.** the act or course of marching. **4.** the distance covered in a single period of marching. **5.** advance; forward movement: *the march of science.* **6.** a piece of music with a rhythm suited to marching. [< MF *march(i)er,* OF *marchier* to tread < ?]

march[2] (märch), *n.* **1.** a tract of land along a border of a country; frontier. **2. marches,** the border districts between England and Scotland, or England and Wales. —*v.i.* **3.** to touch at the border; border. [ME *marche,* OE *(ge)mearc,* *gem(i)erce* boundary + OF *marche* < Gmc; cf. Goth *marka* boundary]

March (märch *for 1;* märkh *for 2*), *n.* **1. Pey·ton Con·way** (pāt′ən kon′wā), 1864–1955, U.S. army officer. **2.** German name of the **Morava.**

March (märch), *n.* the third month of the year, containing 31 days. [ME *March(e)* < AF *Marche;* r. OE *Martius* < L, short for *Martius mēnsis* month of Mars (*Marti-,* s. of *Mars,* + *-us* adj. suffix)]

March., Marchioness.
Mär·chen (meʀ′ᴋʜən), *n., pl.* **-chen.** *German.* fairy story; folk tale.
march·er[1] (mär′chər), *n.* a person who marches on foot: *a line of marchers.* [MARCH[1] + -ER[1]]
march·er[2] (mär′chər), *n. Hist.* an inhabitant of a march or border territory. [late ME; see MARCH[2], -ER[1]]
March·es, The (mär′chiz), a region in central Italy, bordering the Adriatic. 1,347,234 (1961); 3743 sq. mi. Italian, **Le Mar·che** (le mär′ke).
mar·che·sa (mäʀ ke′zä), *n., pl.* **-se** (-ze). an Italian noblewoman, equivalent in rank to a marchioness. [< It; fem. of MARCHESE]
mar·che·se (mäʀ ke′ze), *n., pl.* **-si** (-ze). an Italian nobleman, equivalent in rank to a marquis. [< It; see MARQUIS]
Mar·chesh·van (mär ᴋʜesh′vən, -hesh′-; *Heb.* mäʀ-ᴋʜesh vän′), *n.* Heshvan.
mar·chion·ess (mär′shə nis, mär′shə nes′), *n.* **1.** the wife or widow of a marquis. **2.** a lady holding in her own right the rank equal to that of a marquis. [< ML *marchiōnissa = marchiōn-* (s. of *marchiō*) MARQUIS (lit., man of the border) + *-issa* -ESS]
march·land (märch′land′, -lənd), *n.* borderland.
march·pane (märch′pān′), *n.* marzipan. [< F, dial. var. of *massepain, marcepain* < It *marzapane,* orig. sugar-candy box < Ar *mautabān* glazed vessel]
Mar·co·ni (mär kō′nē; *It.* mäʀ kô′nē), *n.* **Gu·gliel·mo** (gōō lyel′mô), **Marchese,** 1874–1937, Italian electrical engineer and inventor, esp. in the field of wireless telegraphy.
Marco′ni rig′, *Naut.* a rig of triangular sails for a yacht. Also called **Bermuda rig, Bermudan rig, Bermudian rig.**
Mar·co Po·lo (mär′kō pō′lō). See **Polo, Marco.**
Mar·cos (mär′kōs; *Sp.* mäʀ′kôs), *n.* **Ferdinand E·dra·lin** (e thʀä lēn′), born 1917, Philippine political leader: president 1965–86.
Mar·cus (mär′kəs), *n.* **Saint,** died A.D. 336, pope 336. Also, **Mark.**
Mar′cus Au·re·li·us (ô rē′lē əs, ô rēl′yəs), (*Marcus Annius Verus*) A.D. 121–180, Stoic philosopher and writer: emperor of Rome 161–180. Also called **Mar′cus Aure′lius An·to·ni·nus** (an′tə nī′nəs).
Mar·cy (mär′sē), *n.* **Mount,** a mountain in NE New York: highest peak of the Adirondack Mountains, 5344 ft.
Mar del Pla·ta (mäʀ′ thel plä′tä), a city in E Argentina: seaside resort. 141,886 (est. 1958).
Mar·di gras (mär′dē grä′, grä′), the day before Lent, often celebrated as a day of carnival; Shrove Tuesday. [< F: lit., fat Tuesday]
Mar·duk (mär′dŏŏk), *n. Babylonian Religion.* the chief of the Babylonian deities.
mare[1] (mâr), *n.* a fully mature female horse or other equine animal. [ME, var. of *mere,* OE *m(i)ere; c.* Icel *merr,* D *merrie,* G *Mähre;* akin to OE *mearh,* Icel *marr.* See MARSHAL]
mare[2] (mâr), *n. Obs.* nightmare (def. 3). [ME, OE; c. G *Mahre,* Icel *mara*]
ma·re[3] (mär′ā, mâr′ē), *n., pl.* **ma·ri·a** (mär′ē ə, mâr′-). *Astron.* any of the several large, dark plains on the moon, believed by Galileo to be seas when he first saw them through a telescope. [< L: sea]
Ma′re Acidal′ium (mär′ā, mâr′ē), an area in the northern hemisphere of Mars, appearing as a dark region when viewed telescopically from the earth.
ma·re clau·sum (mâr′ē klô′səm; *Lat.* mä′ʀe klou′-sŏŏm), a body of navigable water under the sole jurisdiction of a nation. [< L: closed sea]
Ma′re Fecundita′tis (mär′ā, mâr′ē), a dark plain in the fourth quadrant and extending into the first quadrant of the face of the moon. ab. 160,000 sq. mi. Also called **Sea of Fertility, Sea of Plenty.**
Ma′re Frigo′ris (mär′ā, mâr′ē), a dark plain in the northern hemisphere, in the first and second quadrants, of the face of the moon: ab. 55 mi. wide at its narrowest width and 750 mi. long: ab. 67,000 sq. mi. Also called **Sea of Cold.**
Ma′re Im′brium (mär′ā, mâr′ē), a dark plain in the second quadrant of the face of the moon. ab. 340,000 sq. mi. Also called **Sea of Showers, Sea of Rains.**
Mare′ Is′land (mâr), an island in the N part of San Francisco Bay, California: U.S. navy yard.
ma·re li·be·rum (mâr′ē lib′ər əm; *Lat.* mä′ʀe lē′be-ʀŏŏm′), a body of navigable water to which all nations have unrestricted access. [< L: free sea]
ma·rem·ma (mə rem′ə), *n., pl.* **-rem·me** (-rem′ē). a marshy region near the seashore. [< It < L *maritima,* fem. of *maritimus* MARITIME]
Ma·ren·go (mə reng′gō; *for 1 also It.* mä ʀeng′gô), *n., pl.* **-gos** for 2. **1.** a village in Piedmont, in NW Italy: battle 1800. 2034 (1961). **2.** a former gold coin of Italy, issued by Napoleon after the battle of Marengo.
ma·re nos·trum (mä′ʀe nōs′tʀŏŏm; *Eng.* mâr′ē nos′-trəm), *Latin.* our sea: the Mediterranean to the ancient Romans.
Ma′re Serenita′tis (mär′ā, mâr′ē), a dark plain in the first quadrant of the face of the moon. ab. 120,000 sq. mi. Also called **Sea of Serenity.**
mare's-nest (mârz′nest′), *n.* **1.** something thought to be an extraordinary discovery but proving to be a delusion or a hoax. **2.** an extremely confused or disordered place, situation, etc.
mares′ of Diome′des, *Class. Myth.* wild mares owned by Diomedes, a Thracian king, who fed them on human flesh; captured by Hercules in fulfillment of one of his labors.
mare's-tail (mârz′tāl′), *n.* **1.** an erect, aquatic, Old World plant, *Hippuris vulgaris,* having crowded whorls of narrow, hairlike leaves. **2.** a cirrus cloud resembling a horse's tail.
Ma′re Tranquillita′tis (mär′ā, mâr′ē), a dark plain in the first quadrant of the face of the moon. ab. 110,000 sq. mi. Also called **Sea of Tranquillity.**
marg., **1.** margin. **2.** marginal.
Mar′garet of An′jou, 1430–82, queen of Henry VI of England.
Mar′garet of Navarre′, 1492–1549, queen of Navarre 1544–49. Also called **Mar′garet of An·gou·lême′** (äng′-gŏŏ lem′; *Fr.* äɴ gōō lem′).
Mar′garet of Valois′, ("*Queen Margot*") 1533–1615, 1st wife of Henry IV of France: queen of Navarre (daughter of Henry II of France and Catherine de' Medici). Also called **Mar′garet of France′.**
Mar′garet Rose′, born 1930, English princess (daughter of George VI; sister of Elizabeth II).
mar·gar′ic ac′id (mär gar′ik, -gär′-), *Chem.* a fatty acid, $CH_3(CH_2)_{15}COOH$, obtained from lichens or synthetically. [< Gk *márgar(on)* pearl + -IC]
mar·ga·rine (mär′jər in, -jə rēn′, märj′rin), *n.* **1.** a butterlike product made of refined vegetable oils, sometimes blended with animal fats, and emulsified with milk. **2.** oleomargarine. Also, **mar·ga·rin** (mär′jər in, märj′rin). [MARGAR(IC ACID) + -INE[2]]
Mar·ga·ri·ta (mär′gə rē′tə), *n.* a cocktail made of tequila, lime or lemon juice, and an orange-flavored liqueur. [< AmSp: Margaret]
Mar·gate (mär′git), *n.* a city in E Kent, in SE England: seaside resort. 45,780 (1961).
mar·gay (mär′gā), *n.* a small tiger cat, *Felis tigrina,* of tropical America. [< F, alter. of *margaia* < Pg *maracajá* < Tupi *mbaracaiá*]
marge (märj), *n. Archaic.* margin; edge. [< MF < L *margō;* see MARGIN]
mar·gin (mär′jin), *n.* **1.** a border or edge. **2.** the space around the printed or written matter on a page. **3.** a limit in condition, capacity, etc., beyond or below which something ceases to exist, or to be desirable or possible. **4.** an amount allowed or available beyond what is actually assumed to be necessary: *a margin of safety.* **5.** *Finance.* **a.** security deposited with a broker as a provision against loss on transactions. **b.** the amount representing the customer's investment or equity in such an account. **6.** the difference between the amount of a loan and the market value of the collateral. **7.** *Com.* the difference between the cost and the selling price. **8.** *Econ.* the point of monetary return below which production is unprofitable. —*v.t.* **9.** to provide with a margin or border. **10.** to furnish with marginal notes, as a document. **11.** *Finance.* to deposit a margin upon. [ME < L *margin-* (s. of *margō*) border; akin to MARCH[2]] —**Syn. 1.** rim, verge, brink. See **edge. 3.** confine, bound. —**Ant. 1.** center.
mar·gin·al (mär′jə nəl), *adj.* **1.** pertaining to a margin. **2.** situated on the border or edge. **3.** at the outer or lower limits; minimal for requirements. **4.** written or printed in the margin of a page. **5.** marked by contact with disparate cultures, and acquiring some but not all of the traits or values common to any one of them. **6.** *Econ.* **a.** selling goods at a price that just equals the additional cost of producing the last unit supplied. **b.** of or pertaining to goods produced and marketed at margin: *marginal profits.* [< ML *marginālis* of, pertaining to an edge] —**mar′gin·al′i·ty,** *n.* —**mar′gin·al·ly,** *adv.*
mar·gi·na·li·a (mär′jə nā′lē ə, -nāl′yə), *n.pl.* marginal notes. [< NL, n. use of neut. pl. of ML *marginālis* MARGINAL]
mar·gin·ate (mär′jə nāt′), *adj., v.,* **-at·ed, -at·ing.** —*adj.* Also, **mar′gin·at′ed. 1.** having a margin. **2.** *Entomol.* having the margin of a distinct color. —*v.t.* **3.** to furnish with a margin; border. [< L *margināt(us)* furnished with a border, bordered, ptp. of *margināre*] —**mar′gin·a′tion,** *n.*
mar·gra·vate (mär′grə vāt′), *n.* the province or territory of a margrave. Also, **mar·gra·vi·ate** (mär grā′vē āt′).
mar·grave (mär′grāv), *n.* **1.** the hereditary title of the rulers of certain states. **2.** *Hist.* a hereditary German title, equivalent to marquis. **3.** (originally) a German military governor of a mark, or border province. [earlier *marcgrave* < MD = *marc* border (c. MARCH[2]) + *grave* count (c. REEVE[1])] —**mar·gra′vi·al,** *adj.*
mar·gra·vine (mär′grə vēn′), *n.* the wife of a margrave. [earlier *margravinne* < MD *marcgravinne,* fem. of MARGRAVE]
mar·gue·rite (mär′gə rēt′), *n.* **1.** the European daisy, *Bellis perennis.* **2.** any of several daisylike flowers, esp. *Chrysanthemum frutescens,* cultivated for its numerous white-rayed, yellow-centered flowers. [< F: daisy, pearl < L *margarīta* pearl < Gk *margarī́tēs = márgar(on)* pearl + *-ītēs* -ITE[1]]
Mar·hesh·van (mär hesh′vən, -ᴋʜesh′-; *Heb.* mäʀ ᴋʜesh-vän′), *n.* Heshvan.
mar·i·a·chi (mä′rē ä′chē), *adj.* **1.** pertaining to Mexican dance music, usually played by a small band of strolling musicians dressed in native costumes. —*n.* **2.** a member of such a band. [< MexSp *mariache,* a Mexican dance]
Ma·ri·a de Me·di·ci (*It.* mä ʀē′ä de me′dē chē). See **Marie de Médicis.**
ma·riage de con·ve·nance (mᴀ ʀʏᴀzh′ də kôɴ və-näɴs′), *French.* See **marriage of convenience.**
Ma·ri·a Lu·i·sa (*Ger.* mä ʀē′ä lōō ē′zä). See **Marie Louise.**
Mar·i·an (mâr′ē ən), *adj.* **1.** of or pertaining to the Virgin Mary. **2.** of or pertaining to some other Mary, as Mary Tudor of England or Mary, Queen of Scots. —*n.* **3.** a person who has a particular devotion to the Virgin Mary.
Mar·i·a′na Is′lands (mâr′ē an′ə, mar′-; *Sp.* mä′ʀē-ä′nä), a group of 15 small islands in the Pacific, E of the Philippines: except Guam, formerly mandated to Japan; now under U.S. trusteeship. 9640 (1970); 453 sq. mi. Also called **Mar′ia′nas.** Formerly, **Ladrone Islands, Ladrones.**
Mar′ian′a Trench′, a depression in the ocean floor of the Pacific, S and W of the Mariana Islands: site of greatest known depth of any ocean. 36,198 ft. deep.
Ma·ri·a·na·o (mä′ʀē ä nä′ô), *n.* a city in NW Cuba, a part of Havana.
Mar·i·anne (mâr′ē an′, mar′-), *n.* the French Republic, personified as a woman.
Ma·ri·án·ské Láz·ně (mä′ri yän ske läz′nye), Czech name of **Marienbad.**
Ma·ri·a The·re·sa (mə rē′ə tə rē′sə, -zə, mə rī′ə), 1717–1780, archduchess of Austria; queen of Hungary and Bohemia 1740–80 (wife of Francis II; mother of Joseph II, Leopold II, Marie Antoinette). German, **Ma·ri·a The·re·si·a** (mä ʀē′ä te ʀä′zē ä).
Mari′a There′sa tha′ler, a former silver coin of Austria, issued between 1740 and 1780 and used or imitated for trade with Ethiopia and other countries; Levant dollar.

Ma·ri·bor (mär′i bôr), *n.* a city in N Yugoslavia, on the Drava River. 91,000 (1961). German, **Marburg.**

Ma·rie An·toi·nette (mə rē′ an′twə net′; *Fr.* mᴀ ʀē′ äɴ twᴀ net′), (*Josèphe Jeanne Marie Antoinette*) 1755–93, queen of France 1774–93: wife of Louis XVI; executed in the French Revolution (daughter of Maria Theresa).

Ma·rie′ Byrd′ Land′ (mə rē′ bûrd′), former name of **Byrd Land.**

Ma·rie de Mé·di·cis (mᴀ ʀē′ də mā dē sēs′), 1573–1642, queen of Henry IV of France: regent 1610–17. Italian, **Maria de Medici.**

Ma·rie Lou·ise (mə rē′ lo͞o ēz′; *Fr.* mᴀ ʀē′ lwēz′), 1791–1847, 2nd wife of Napoleon I: empress of France (daughter of Francis II of Austria; mother of Napoleon II). German, **Maria Luisa.**

Ma·ri·en·bad (mâr′ē ən bad′, mar′-; *Ger.* mä ʀē′ən bät′), *n.* a spa and resort town in W Bohemia, in W Czechoslovakia. 8417 (1947). Czech, **Mariánské Lázně.**

Mar·i·et·ta (mâr′ē et′ə), *n.* a city in NW Georgia. 27,216 (1970).

mar·i·gold (mar′ə gōld′), *n.* **1.** any of several chiefly golden-flowered, composite plants, esp. of the genus *Tagetes,* as *T. erecta,* having strong-scented foliage. **2.** any of several other, unrelated plants, esp. of the genus *Calendula,* as *C. officinalis,* the pot marigold. [ME; see Mary (the Virgin), gold]

ma·ri·jua·na (mar′ə wä′nə, -hwä′-, mär′-), *n.* **1.** the Indian hemp, *Cannabis sativa.* **2.** its dried leaves and flowers, used as a hallucinogen. Also, **ma′ri·hua′na.** [< Mex Sp *mariguana, marihuana*]

ma·rim·ba (mə rim′bə), *n.* a musical instrument consisting of a set of graduated wooden bars, often with resonators beneath to reinforce the sound, struck with mallets. [< WAfr]

Marimba

Mar·in (mär′in), *n.* **John,** 1870–1953, U.S. painter.

ma·ri·na (mə rē′nə), *n.* a boat basin offering dockage and other service for small craft. [< It, Sp, n.use of fem. of *marino* < L *marīnus* marine]

mar·i·nade (*n.* mar′ə nād′, mar′ə nād′; *v.* mar′ə nād′), *n., v.,* **-nad·ed, -nad·ing.** —*n.* **1.** a seasoned liquid in which meat, fish, vegetables, etc., are steeped before cooking. **2.** meat or fish steeped in it. —*v.t.* **3.** to marinate. [< F < *marin(er)* (to) marinate + *-ade* -ade[1]]

ma·ri·na·ra (mär′ə när′ə, mar′ə nar′ə), *Italian Cookery.* —*n.* **1.** a highly seasoned sauce of tomatoes, garlic, and spices. —*adj.* **2.** garnished or served with marinara: *shrimps marinara.* [< It; see marinate]

mar·i·nate (mar′ə nāt′), *v.t.,* **-nat·ed, -nat·ing.** to let stand in a seasoned vinegar-oil mixture; marinade. [prob. < It *marinato,* ptp. of *marinare* to pickle] —**mar′i·na′tion,** *n.*

Ma·rin·du·que (*Sp.* mä′ʀin do͞o′ke), *n.* an island of the Philippines, between Luzon and Mindora islands. 107,150 (est. 1960); 347 sq. mi.

ma·rine (mə rēn′), *adj.* **1.** of or pertaining to the sea; existing in or produced by the sea. **2.** pertaining to navigation or shipping; nautical; maritime. **3.** adapted for use at sea or on vessels. **4.** of or belonging to the marines. —*n.* **5.** (*sometimes cap.*) a member of the U.S. Marine Corps. **6.** one of a class of naval troops serving both on shipboard and on land. **7.** seagoing vessels collectively, esp. with reference to nationality or class; shipping in general. **8.** a seascape. **9.** the department of naval affairs, as in France. [ME *maryne* < MF *marin* (fem. *marine*) < L *marīn(us)* of the sea < *mare* sea; see -ine[1]]

Marine′ Corps′. See **United States Marine Corps.**

marine′ insur′ance. See **ocean marine insurance.**

mar·i·ner (mar′ə nər), *n.* **1.** a person who directs or assists in the navigation of a ship. **2.** (*cap.*) *U.S.* one of a series of unmanned spacecraft for flights to Mars and Venus. [ME < AF; OF *marinier*] —**Syn. 1.** seafarer. See **sailor.**

mar′iner's com′pass, a compass used for navigational purposes, consisting of a pivoted compass card in a gimbal-mounted, nonferrous metal bowl.

Ma·ri·ni (mə rē′nē; *It.* mä ʀē′nē), *n.* **Giam·bat·tis·ta** (jäm′bät tēs′tä), ("*il Cavalier Marino*"), 1569–1625, Italian poet. Also, **Ma·ri·no** (mə rē′nō; *It.* mä ʀē′nō).

Ma·ri·nus I (mə rī′nəs), died A.D. 884, pope 882–884. Also called **Martin II.**

Marinus II, died A.D. 946, pope 942–946. Also called **Martin III.**

Mar·i·ol·a·try (mâr′ē ol′ə trē), *n.* excessive and proscribed veneration of the Virgin Mary. —**Mar′i·ol′a·ter,** *n.* —**Mar′i·ol′a·trous,** *adj.*

Mar·i·ol·o·gy (mâr′ē ol′ə jē), *n.* **1.** the body of belief, doctrine, and opinion concerning the Virgin Mary. **2.** the study of the Virgin Mary. —**Mar′i·ol′o·gist,** *n.*

Mar·i·on (mar′ē ən, mâr′-), *n.* **1. Francis** ("*the Swamp Fox*"), 1732?–95, American Revolutionary general. **2.** a city in central Indiana. 39,607 (1970). **3.** a city in central Ohio. 38,646 (1970).

mar·i·on·ette (mar′ē ə net′), *n.* a puppet manipulated from above by strings attached to its jointed limbs. [< F *marionnette* = *Marion* (dim. of *Marie* Mary) + *-ette* -ette]

mar·i·po·sa lil′y (mar′ə pō′sə, -zə), any liliaceous plant of the genus *Calochortus,* of the western U.S. and Mexico, having tuliplike flowers of various colors. Also called **mar′i·po′sa, maripo′sa tu′lip.** [< Sp *mariposa* butterfly, moth; so named because blooms were likened to butterflies]

mar·ish (mar′ish), *n. Archaic.* a marsh. [ME *mareis* < MF < Gmc. See morass, marsh]

Mar·i·sol (mar′i sol′), *n.* (*Marisol Escubar*) born 1930, Venezuelan artist, in U.S. since 1950.

Mar·ist (mâr′ist), *n. Rom. Cath. Ch.* a member of a religious order founded in Lyons, France, in 1816 for missionary and educational work in the name of the Virgin Mary. [< F *Mariste.* See Mary, -ist]

Ma·ri·tain (mᴀ ʀē taɴ′), *n.* **Jacques** (zhäk), 1882–1973, French philosopher, theologian, and diplomat.

mar·i·tal (mar′i t^{ə}l), *adj.* **1.** of or pertaining to marriage; conjugal; connubial; matrimonial: *marital discord.* **2.** *Archaic.* of or pertaining to a husband. [< L *marītāl(is)* of married people < *marīt(us)* of marriage. See marry[1], -al[1]] —**mar′i·tal·ly,** *adv.*

mar·i·time (mar′i tīm′), *adj.* **1.** of or pertaining to the navigation of seas or to seagoing vessels. **2.** adapted for use at sea or on vessels; marine. **3.** of, pertaining to, or living in the sea; marine. **4.** bordering on or making a living from the sea: *a maritime state.* [< L *maritim(us)* pertaining to the sea = *mari-* (s. of *mare*) sea + *-timus* adj. suffix]

Mar′itime Alps′, a range of the Alps in SE France and NW Italy.

Mar′itime Prov′inces, the Canadian provinces of Nova Scotia, New Brunswick, and Prince Edward Island.

Ma·ri·tsa (mä′ʀe tsä′), *n.* a river in S Europe, flowing from S Bulgaria along the boundary between Greece and European Turkey and into the Aegean. 300 mi. long.

Ma·ri·u·pol (*Russ.* mä′ʀe o͞o′pol′y^ə), *n.* former name of **Zhdanov.**

Mar·i·us (mâr′ē əs), *n.* **Gaius,** c155–86 B.C., Roman general and consul: opponent of Lucius Cornelius Sulla.

Ma·ri·vaux (mᴀ ʀē vō′), *n.* **Pierre Car·let de Cham·blain de** (pyeʀ kᴀʀ le′ də shäɴ blaɴ′ də), 1688–1763, French dramatist and novelist.

mar·jo·ram (mär′jər əm), *n.* any of several mints of the genera *Origanum* and *Majorana,* as sweet marjoram. [ME *majorane* < ML *majorana,* var. of *majoraca,* alter. of L *amāracus* < Gk *amárakos*]

mark[1] (märk), *n.* **1.** something appearing distinctly on a surface, as a line, spot, scar, or dent. **2.** a conspicuous object or sign used in measuring, finding one's way, etc. **3.** a symbol or character, written, printed, or affixed, as for punctuation, in lieu of a signature, as an indication of ownership or manufacture, etc. **4.** something indicative of one's condition, feelings, etc.: *to bow as a mark of respect.* **5.** a symbol used in rating conduct, proficiency, etc., as of pupils. **6.** a recognized or required standard of quality, accomplishment, etc.; norm: *His dissertation was below the mark.* **7.** distinction or importance; repute; note. **8.** an object aimed at a goal or target. **9.** an object of derision, scorn, hostile schemes, swindling, or the like. **10.** *Track.* the starting line. **11.** *Boxing.* the middle of the stomach. **12.** *Lawn Bowling.* jack[1] (def. 5). **13.** *Bowling.* a strike or spare. **14.** *Naut.* any of the distinctively marked points on a deep-sea lead line. Cf. **deep** (def. 26). **15.** a tract of land that was held in common by a primitive or medieval community of freemen in Germany. **16.** *Archaic.* a boundary; frontier. **17. beside the mark,** not pertinent; irrelevant. **18. make one's mark,** to attain success; achieve one's ambition. **19. wide of the mark,** inaccurate or irrelevant. —*v.t.* **20.** to be a distinguishing feature of. **21.** to put a mark or marks on. **22.** to furnish with figures, signs, tags, etc., to indicate price, quality, brand name, or the like. **23.** to trace or form by or as by marks (often fol. by *out*): *to mark out a plan of attack.* **24.** to indicate or designate by or as by marks. **25.** to single out; destine. **26.** to record, as a score. **27.** to make manifest: *to mark approval with a nod.* **28.** to give heed or attention to: *Mark my words!* **29.** to notice or observe. —*v.i.* **30.** to take notice; give attention; consider. **31. mark down,** to reduce the price of. **32. mark time.** See **time** (def. 42). **33. mark up, a.** to mar or deface with marks. **b.** to mark with notations or symbols. **c.** to fix the selling price of (an article) by adding the seller's expenses and desired profit to cost. [ME; OE *mearc* mark, sign, banner, dividing line, borderland; c. Icel *mörk* forest (orig. border-land), unit of weight, Goth *marka* boundary, borderland, G *Mark* borderland, unit of weight, L *margō* margin] —**Syn. 7.** eminence, consequence. **8.** purpose, objective. **24.** identify, label, tag. **27, 28.** note. **29.** eye, regard, spot.

mark[2] (märk), *n.* **1.** the monetary unit of Germany since 1871: originally a silver coin. Cf. **Deutsche mark, ostmark, reichsmark. 2.** the markka of Finland. **3.** Also, **merk.** a former silver coin of Scotland. **4.** a former money of account of England. **5.** a former European unit of weight, esp. for gold and silver, generally equal to 8 ounces. [ME; OE *marc* unit of weight < ML *marca* < Gmc; see mark[1]]

Mark (märk), *n.* **1.** one of the four Evangelists: traditionally believed to be the author of the second Gospel. **2.** the second Gospel. **3. King,** *Arthurian Romance.* ruler of Cornwall, husband of Iseult and uncle of Sir Tristram. **4. Saint.** See **Marcus, Saint.**

Mark An·to·ny (märk an′tə nē). See **Antony, Mark.**

mark·down (märk′doun′), *n.* **1.** a reduction in price. **2.** the amount by which a price is reduced.

marked (märkt), *adj.* **1.** strikingly noticeable; conspicuous: *with marked success.* **2.** watched as an object of suspicion or vengeance: *a marked man.* **3.** having a mark or marks. **4.** *Linguistics.* characterized by the presence of a feature that distinguishes the members of a minimal pair. [OE *gemearcodan*] —**mark·ed·ly** (mär′kid lē), *adv.* —**mark′·ed·ness,** *n.*

mark·er (mär′kər), *n.* **1.** a person or thing that marks. **2.** something used as a mark or indication.

mar·ket (mär′kit), *n.* **1.** a meeting of people for selling and buying. **2.** a place used for selling and buying. **3.** a store for the sale of food. **4.** trade or traffic in a particular commodity. **5.** a body of persons carrying on extensive transactions in a specified commodity. **6.** the field of trade or business. **7.** demand for a commodity. **8.** a particular group of potential buyers: *hats for the Peruvian market.* **9.** current price or value. **10. in the market for,** ready to buy; seeking to buy: *in the market for a motor scooter.* **11. on the market,** for sale; available. —*v.i.* **12.** to buy or sell in a market; deal. —*v.t.* **13.** to carry or send to market for disposal: *to market produce many miles.* **14.** to dispose of in a market; sell. [ME, late OE < VL *marcāt(us),* L *mercātus* trading, traffic, market]

mar·ket·a·ble (mär′ki tə bəl), *adj.* **1.** readily salable. **2.** of or pertaining to selling or buying. —**mar′ket·a·bil′i·ty, mar′ket·a·ble·ness,** *n.* —**mar′ket·a·bly,** *adv.*

mar′ket gar′den, a garden or farm for growing vegetables to be shipped esp. to local or nearby markets. Cf. **truck farm.** —**mar′ket gar′dener.** —**mar′ket gar′dening.**

mar·ket·ing (mär′ki ting), *n.* **1.** the act of buying or selling in a market. **2.** the total of activities by which transfer of title or possession of goods from seller to buyer is effected, including advertising, shipping, storing, and selling.

mar′ket or′der, an order to purchase or sell at the current market price.

mar·ket·place (mär′kit plās′), *n.* **1.** an open area or a building where goods are offered for sale, often by many independent merchants. **2.** the world of commerce. **3.** the area of collective evaluation in which ideas, values, etc., are considered as competing for recognition: *the literary marketplace.* Also, **mar′ket place′.** [ME]

mar′ket research′, the gathering and studying of data relating to consumer preferences, purchasing power, etc., esp. preliminary to introducing a product on the market.

mar′ket town′, a town in which a public market is held. [late ME]

mar′ket val′ue, the value of a business, property, etc., in terms of what it can be sold for on the open market; current value (distinguished from *book value*).

Mark·ham (mär′kəm), *n.* **1. (Charles) Edwin,** 1852–1940, U.S. poet. **2. Mount,** a mountain in Antarctica, SW of the Ross Sea. 15,100 ft.

mar·khoor (mär′ko͝or), *n., pl.* **-khoors,** (*esp. collectively*) **-khoor.** markhor.

mar·khor (mär′kôr), *n., pl.* **-khors,** (*esp. collectively*) **-khor.** a wild goat, *Capra falconeri,* found in mountainous regions from Afghanistan to India, having large, compressed, spiral horns and long, shaggy hair. Also, **markhoor.** [< Pers = *mār* snake + *-khōr* eating]

mark·ing (mär′king), *n.* **1.** a mark, or a number or pattern of marks, as on a bird or other animal. **2.** the act of a person or thing that marks. [ME]

mark·ka (märk′kä), *n., pl.* **-kaa** (-kä). a cupronickel or bronze coin and monetary unit of Finland, equal to 100 pennia; finmark. *Abbr.:* F.Mk., M. [< Finn; see MARK[2]]

Mar·ko·va (mär kō′və), *n.* **Alicia** (*Alice Marks*), born 1910, English ballet dancer and choreographer.

marks·man (märks′mən), *n., pl.* **-men. 1.** a person skilled in shooting at a mark. **2.** *U.S. Mil.* the lowest rating in rifle marksmanship. —**marks′man·ship′,** *n.*

marks·wom·an (märks′wo͝om′ən), *n., pl.* **-wom·en.** a woman skilled at marksmanship.

mark·up (märk′up′), *n.* **1.** *Com.* **a.** the amount added by a seller to the cost of a commodity to cover his expenses and profit in fixing the selling price. **b.** the difference between the cost price and the selling price, computed as a percentage of either the selling price or the cost price. **2. a.** an increase in price, as of a commodity. **b.** the amount by which a price is increased.

marl[1] (märl), *n.* **1.** a friable earthy deposit consisting of clay and calcium carbonate, used esp. as a fertilizer for soils deficient in lime. **2.** *Archaic.* earth. —*v.t.* **3.** to fertilize with marl. [ME *marle* < MFlem < OF < LL *margila,* dim. of L *marga* < Celtic] —**mar·la·cious** (mär lā′shəs), **marl′y,** *adj.*

marl[2] (märl), *v.t. Naut.* to wind (a rope) with marline, every turn being secured by a hitch. [late ME *marlyn* to tie; akin to OE *mārels* cable. See MOOR[2]]

marl·ber·ry (märl′ber′ē, -bə rē), *n., pl.* **-ries.** a shrub or small tree, *Ardisia paniculata,* of southern Florida, having oblong leaves, white flowers, and shiny, black fruit. [dial. *marl* (contr. of MARBLE) + BERRY]

Marl·bor·o (märl′bûr ō, -bur ō), *n.* a city in E Massachusetts. 27,936 (1970).

Marl·bor·ough (märl′bûr ō, -bur ō, -brə, môl′-), *n.* **John Churchill, 1st Duke of.** See **Churchill, John, 1st Duke of Marlborough.**

mar·lin[1] (mär′lin), *n., pl.* (*esp. collectively*) **-lin,** (*esp. referring to two or more kinds or species*) **-lins.** any large, saltwater game fish of the genus *Makaira,* having the upper jaw elongated into a spearlike structure. [short for MARLINESPIKE]

mar·lin[2] (mär′lin), *n.* marline.

mar·line (mär′lin), *n. Naut.* small stuff of two fiber strands, sometimes tarred, laid up left-handed. Also, **marlin, mar·ling** (mär′ling). [late ME *marlyne.* See MARL[2], LINE[1]]

mar·line·spike (mär′lin spīk′), *n. Naut.* a pointed iron implement used in separating the strands of rope in splicing, marling, etc. Also, **mar′lin·spike′, mar·ling·spike** (mär′ling spīk′). [orig. *marling spike.* See MARL[2], SPIKE]

marl·ite (mär′līt), *n.* a variety of marl resistant to the action of the air. —**mar·lit·ic** (mär lit′ik), *adj.*

Mar·lowe (mär′lō), *n.* **Christopher,** 1564–93, English dramatist and poet.

mar·ma·lade (mär′mə lād′, mär′mə lād′), *n.* a jellylike preserve containing small pieces of fruit and fruit rind, as of oranges. [< Pg *marmelada* quince jam < *marmelo* quince < L *melimēlum* a kind of apple < Gk *melímēlon* (*méli* honey + *mêlon* a fruit); see -ADE[1]]

Mar·ma·ra (mär′mər ə), *n.* **Sea of,** a sea in NW Turkey, between European and Asian Turkey, connected with the Black Sea by the Bosporus, and with the Aegean by the Dardanelles. 4300 sq. mi. Also, **Mar·mo·ra** (mär′mər ə, mär môr′ə, -mōr′ə).

Mar·mo·la·da (mär′mô lä′dä), *n.* a mountain in N Italy: highest peak of the Dolomites, 11,020 ft.

mar·mo·re·al (mär môr′ē əl, -mōr′-), *adj.* of or like marble. Also, **mar·mo′re·an.** [< L *marmore(us)* made of marble (see MARBLE, -EOUS) + -AL[1]] —**mar·mo′re·al·ly,** *adv.*

mar·mo·set (mär′mə zet′), *n.* any of several small South and Central American monkeys of the genera *Callithrix, Leontocebus,* etc., having soft fur and a long, nonprehensile tail, and somewhat resembling a squirrel in body form. [ME *marmuset* < MF *marmouse* grotesque image]

Marmoset, *Callithrix jacchus* (Total length 21 in.; tail 11½ in.)

mar·mot (mär′mət), *n.* **1.** any bushy-tailed, stocky rodent of the genus *Marmota,* as the woodchuck. **2.** any of certain related animals, as the prairie dogs. [< F *marmotte*]

Marmot, *Marmota caligata* (Total length 2½ ft.; tail 10 in.)

Marne (märn; *Fr.* MARN), *n.* a river in NE France, flowing W to the Seine near Paris: battles 1914, 1918, 1944. 325 mi. long.

Ma·roc (MA RôK′), *n.* French name of **Morocco.**

ma·roon[1] (mə ro͞on′), *adj.* dark brownish-red. [< F *marron* < It *marrone* chestnut]

ma·roon[2] (mə ro͞on′), *v.t.* **1.** to put ashore and leave on a desolate island or coast. **2.** to isolate without resources or hope. —*n.* **3.** any of a group of Negroes, descended from fugitive slaves of the 17th and 18th centuries, living in the West Indies and Guiana. [< AmerSp (*ci*)*marrón* wild; first used in reference to domestic animals that escaped into the woods, later to fugitive slaves]

Ma·ros (mo′rôsh), *n.* Hungarian name of **Mures.**

mar·plot (mär′plot′), *n.* a person who mars or defeats a plan, design, or project by officious interference.

Marq., **1.** Marquess. **2.** Marquis.

marque (märk), *n.* **1.** See **letter of marque. 2.** *Obs.* seizure by way of reprisal or retaliation. [ME *mark* < MF < Pr *marca* seizure by warrant (orig. token) < Gmc; see MARK[1]]

mar·quee (mär kē′), *n.* **1.** a rooflike shelter, as of glass, projecting above an outer door and over a sidewalk or a terrace. **2.** a similar projection above a theater entrance, usually containing the names of a currently featured play or film and its stars. **3.** *Chiefly Brit.* a large tent or tentlike shelter with open sides. [assumed sing. of MARQUISE, taken as pl.]

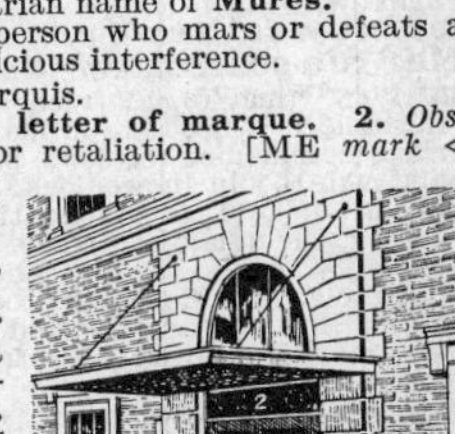

Marquee (def. 1)

Mar·que′sas Is′lands (mär kā′zəz, -səz, -səs), a group of islands in French Polynesia. 4170 (1960); 480 sq. mi. —**Mar·que′san,** *n., adj.*

mar·quess (mär′kwis), *n. Chiefly Brit.* marquis.

mar·que·try (mär′ki trē), *n., pl.* **-tries,** inlaid work of variously colored woods or other materials, esp. in furniture. Also, **mar·que·te·rie** (mär′ki trē). [< MF *marqueterie,* inlaid work = *marquet(er)* (to) speckle, spot, inlay (lit., make marks < Gmc; see MARK[1]) + *-erie* -ERY]

Mar·quette (mär ket′; *Fr.* MAR ket′), *n.* **Jacques** (zhäk), ("*Père Marquette*"), 1637–75, French Jesuit missionary and explorer in America.

mar·quis (mär′kwis, mär kē′; *Fr.* MAR kē′), *n., pl.* **-quis·es, -quis** (-kēz′; *Fr.* -kē′). a nobleman ranking next below a duke and above an earl or count. Also, *esp. Brit.,* **marquess.** [ME *markis* < MF *marquis* < It *marchese* < Pr *marques;* r. ME *marchis* < MF. See MARCH[2], -ESE]

Mar·quis (mär′kwis), *n.* **Don(ald Robert Perry),** 1878–1937. U.S. humorist and poet.

mar·quis·ate (mär′kwi zit), *n.* **1.** the rank of a marquis. **2.** the territory ruled by a marquis or a margrave. [modeled on F *marquisat,* It *marchesato*]

mar·quise (mär kēz′; *Fr.* MAR kēz′), *n., pl.* **-quis·es** (-kē′ziz; *Fr.* -kēz′). **1.** the wife or widow of a marquis. **2.** a lady holding the rank equal to that of a marquis. **3.** a gem, esp. a diamond, having the form of a low, pointed oval with many facets. [< F]

mar·qui·sette (mär′ki zet′, -kwi-), *n.* a lightweight open fabric of leno weave in cotton, rayon, silk, or nylon. [< F, dim. of *marquise*]

Mar′quis of Queens′ber·ry rules′ (kwēnz′ber′ē, -bə rē), *Boxing.* a set of basic rules for modern boxing, requiring the use of gloves instead of bare knuckles, the 10-second count for a knockout, etc.: named after Sir John Sholto Douglas (1844–1900), 8th Marquis of Queensberry, an English sportsman who originated the rules in 1867. Also called **Queensberry rules.**

Mar·ra·kech (mə rä′kesh, mar′ə kesh′), *n.* a city in W Morocco: former capital of Southern Sultanate. 243,134 (1960). Also, **Mar·ra′kesh.** Also called **Morocco.**

Mar·ra·no (mə rä′nō), *n., pl.* **-nos.** (in late-medieval Spain or Portugal) a Jew who had been converted to Christianity under duress but who adhered to Judaism in secret. [< Sp: lit., pig, from the Jewish law forbidding pork]

Mar·re·ro (mə rer′ō), *n.* a town in SE Louisiana, near New Orleans. 29,015 (1970).

mar·riage (mar′ij), *n.* **1.** the social institution under which a man and woman establish their decision to live as husband and wife by legal commitments, religious ceremonies, etc. **2.** the state, condition, or relationship of being married; wedlock: *a happy marriage.* **3.** the legal or religious ceremony that formalizes the decision of a man and woman to live as husband and wife. **4.** any close or intimate association or union: *the marriage of form and content.* **5.** *Cards.* a meld of the king and queen of a suit, as in pinochle. [ME *mariage* < OF = *mari(er)* (to) MARRY[1] + *-age* -AGE]
—**Syn. 3.** matrimony. MARRIAGE, WEDDING, NUPTIALS are terms for the ceremony uniting couples in wedlock. MARRIAGE is the simple and usual term, without implications as to circumstances and without emotional connotations: *to announce the marriage of a daughter.* WEDDING has strong emotional, even sentimental, connotations, and suggests the accompanying festivities, whether elaborate or simple:

a beautiful wedding; a reception after the wedding. NUPTIALS is a formal and lofty word applied to the ceremony and attendant social events; it does not have emotional connotations but strongly implies surroundings characteristic of wealth, rank, pomp, and grandeur: *royal nuptials.*

mar·riage·a·ble (mar′i jə bəl), *adj.* suitable for marriage. —**mar′riage·a·bil′i·ty, mar′riage·a·ble·ness,** *n.*

mar′riage of conven′ience, a marriage for some advantage or expediency, esp. one for the sake of money or social position.

mar′riage por′tion, dowry.

mar·ried (mar′ēd), *adj.* **1.** united in wedlock; wedded. **2.** of or pertaining to marriage or married persons. —*n.* **3.** Usually, **marrieds.** married people: *Young marrieds are prime buyers of furniture.* [ME]

mar·ron (mar′ən, mə rōn′; *Fr.* MA RÔN′), *n.* a chestnut, esp. as used in cookery: candied or preserved in syrup. [< F]

mar·rons gla·cés (*Fr.* MA RÔN′ GLA SĀ′), chestnuts glazed or coated with sugar eaten as a confection; candied chestnuts. [< F]

mar·row (mar′ō), *n.* **1.** a soft, fatty, vascular tissue in the interior cavities of bones. **2.** the inmost or essential part. **3.** strength or vitality. [ME *mar(o)we,* OE *mearg;* c. D *merg,* G *Mark,* Icel *mergr*] —**mar′row·ish,** *adj.* —**mar′row·less,** *adj.* —**mar′row·y,** *adj.*

mar·row·bone (mar′ō bōn′), *n.* a bone containing edible marrow. [ME]

mar·row·fat (mar′ō fat′), *n.* a large-seeded variety of pea.

Mar·rue·cos (mär RWE′kōs), *n.* Spanish name of **Morocco.**

mar·ry[1] (mar′ē), *v.,* **-ried, -ry·ing.** —*v.t.* **1.** to take as a husband or wife; take in marriage. **2.** to perform the marriage ceremonies for (two people who wish to be husband and wife); join in wedlock. **3.** to give in marriage (often fol. by *off*). **4.** to unite intimately. **5.** *Naut.* **a.** to lay together (the unlaid strands of two ropes) to be spliced. **b.** to seize (two ropes) together end to end for use as a single line. **c.** to seize (parallel ropes) together at intervals. —*v.i.* **6.** to take a husband or wife; wed. [ME *marie(n)* < OF *marie(r)* < L *marītāre* to wed < *marīt(us)* conjugal, akin to *mās* male (person)] —**mar′ri·er,** *n.*

mar·ry[2] (mar′ē), *interj.* *Archaic.* (used as an exclamation of surprise, astonishment, etc.) [euphemistic var. of MARY (the Virgin)]

Mar·ry·at (mar′ē ət), *n.* **Frederick,** 1792–1848, English naval officer and novelist.

Mars (märz), *n.* **1.** the ancient Roman god of war, identified with the Greek god Ares. **2.** *Astron.* the planet fourth in order from the sun, having a diameter of 4230 miles, a mean distance from the sun of 142,000,000 miles, a period of revolution of 686.9 days, and two satellites.

Mar·sa·la (mär sä′lə; *It.* mär sä′lä), *n.* **1.** a seaport in W Sicily. 81,426 (1961). **2.** a sweet, dark, fortified wine made near Marsala, or a similar wine made elsewhere.

marse (märs), *n.* *Southern U.S.* (used chiefly in representation of southern Negro speech) master. Also, **massa.**

Mar·seil·laise (mär′sə lāz′, -sā ez′; *Fr.* MAR se yez′), *n.* the French national anthem, written in 1792 by Rouget de Lisle.

mar·seilles (mär sālz′), *n.* a thick cotton fabric woven in figures or stripes with an embossed effect, chiefly for bedspreads and other coverings. [after MARSEILLES]

Mar·seilles (mär sā′; *older* mär sālz′), *n.* French, **Marseille** (MAR se′yᵊ). a seaport in SE France. 783,738 (1962).

marsh (märsh), *n.* a tract of low wet land, often treeless and periodically inundated. [ME *mershe,* OE *mer(i)sc* (c. G *Marsch*). See MERE[2], -ISH[1]] —**marsh′like′,** *adj.*

Marsh (märsh), *n.* **Reginald,** 1898–1954, U.S. painter and illustrator.

mar·shal (mär′shəl), *n., v.,* **-shaled, -shal·ing** or (*esp. Brit.*) **-shalled, -shal·ling.** —*n.* **1.** a military officer of the highest rank, as in the French and some other armies. Cf. **field marshal. 2.** an administrative officer of a U.S. judicial district who performs duties similar to those of a sheriff. **3.** a court officer engaged chiefly in serving processes. **4.** the police officer in some communities. **5.** a higher officer of a royal household or court. **6.** a person charged with the arrangement or regulation of ceremonies, parades, etc. —*v.t.* **7.** to arrange in proper order; set out in an orderly manner; arrange clearly: *to marshal the facts.* **8.** to array, as for battle. **9.** to usher or lead. [ME, syncopated var. of *mareschal* < OF < Gmc; cf. OHG *marahscalh* groom = *marah* horse (see MARE[1]) + *scalh* servant, c. OE *scealc*] —**mar′shal·cy, mar′shal·ship′,** *n.* —**mar′shal·er;** *esp. Brit.,* **mar′shal·ler,** *n.* —**Syn. 7.** order; convoke. See **gather.**

Mar·shall (mär′shəl), *n.* **1. George C(at·lett)** (kat′lit), 1880–1959, U.S. general and statesman: Secretary of State 1947–49; Nobel peace prize 1953. **2. John,** 1755–1835, U.S. jurist and statesman: Chief Justice of the U.S. 1801–35. **3. Thomas Riley,** 1854–1925, vice president of the U.S. 1913–21. **4. Thur·good** (thûr′go͝od), born 1908, associate justice of the U.S. Supreme Court since 1967.

Mar′shall Is′lands, a group of 24 atolls in the N Pacific: now under U.S. trusteeship. 22,888 (1970); 74 sq. mi.

Mar′shall Plan′. See **European Recovery Program.**

Mar·shal·sea (mär′shəl sē′), *n.* *Brit. Hist.* **1.** the court of the marshal of the royal household. **2.** a debtors' prison in London, abolished 1842. [ME *marchalsye.* See MARSHAL, -CY]

marsh′ el′der, *U.S.* any of various composite plants of the genus *Iva,* as *I. frutescens,* which grows in salt marshes.

marsh′ gas′, a gaseous decomposition product of organic matter, consisting primarily of methane.

marsh′ hen′, any of various rails or raillike birds.

marsh·land (märsh′land′), *n.* a region, area, district, etc., characterized by marshes, swamps, bogs, or the like. [ME *mershland,* OE *merscland*]

marsh′ mal′low, 1. an Old World mallow, *Althaea officinalis,* having pink flowers, found in marshy places. **2.** the rose mallow, *Hibiscus Moscheutos.* [ME *marshmalue,* OE *merscmealwe*]

marsh·mal·low (märsh′mel′ō, -mal′ō), *n.* **1.** a sweetened paste or confection made from the root of the marsh mallow. **2.** a similar confection containing gum arabic or gelatin, sugar, corn syrup, and flavoring. —**marsh′mal′low·y,** *adj.*

marsh′ mar′igold, a yellow-flowered, ranunculaceous plant, *Caltha palustris,* growing in marshes and meadows; cowslip.

marsh·y (mär′shē), *adj.,* **marsh·i·er, marsh·i·est. 1.** soft and wet, as a marsh; boggy. **2.** pertaining to a marsh. **3.** consisting of or constituting a marsh. [ME *mershi*] —**marsh′i·ness,** *n.*

mar·si·po·branch (mär′sə pō brangk′), *adj.* **1.** belonging to the *Marsipobranchii* or *Cyclostomata,* a group or class of vertebrates comprising the cyclostomes. —*n.* **2.** a marsipobranch fish. [back formation from NL *Marsipobranchia* a class of vertebrates < Gk *mársipo(s)* bag, pouch (see MARSUPIUM) + *bránchia* gills]

Mars·ton (mär′stən), *n.* **John,** c1575–1634, English dramatist and satirical poet.

Mars′ton Moor′, a former moor in NE England, west of York: Cromwell's defeat of the Royalists 1644.

mar·su·pi·al (mär so͞o′pē əl), *adj.* **1.** pertaining to, resembling, or having a marsupium. **2.** of or pertaining to the marsupials. —*n.* **3.** any viviparous, nonplacental mammal of the order *Marsupialia,* comprising the opossums, kangaroos, wombats, etc., most of which have a marsupium containing the mammary glands and serving as a receptacle for the young. [< NL *marsupiāl(is)* pertaining to a pouch. See MARSUPIUM, -AL[1]]

mar·su·pi·um (mär so͞o′pē əm), *n., pl.* **-pi·a** (-pē ə). the pouch or fold of skin on the abdomen of a female marsupial. [< NL, var. of L *marsuppium* pouch, purse < Gk *marsýpion,* dim. of *mársipos* bag, pouch]

mart (märt), *n.* **1.** marketplace; trading center; trade center. **2.** *Archaic.* a fair. [late ME < MD, var. of *markt* MARKET]

Mar·ta·ban (mär′tə bän′), *n.* **Gulf of,** an inlet of the Bay of Bengal, in Burma.

Mar·tel′lo tow′er (mär tel′ō), *Fort.* a circular, towerlike fort with guns on the top. Also, **martel′lo tow′er.** Also called **martel′lo, Martel′lo.** [named after Cape *Mortella,* Corsica, where a tower of this kind was taken by British forces in 1794]

Marten, *Martes americana* (Total length about 2½ ft.; tail 9 in.)

mar·ten (mär′tᵊn, -tin), *n., pl.* **-tens,** (*esp. collectively*) **-ten. 1.** any of several slender, chiefly arboreal carnivores of the genus *Martes,* found in northern forests, having a long, glossy coat and bushy tail. **2.** the fur of such an animal, generally a dark brown. [< MLG = *mart* marten (c. OE *mearth*) + *-en* -EN[5]; r. late ME *martren* < MF *martrine* marten fur, n. use of fem. of *martrin* pertaining to a marten = *martre* marten (< Gmc; cf. G *Marder*) + *-in* -IN[1]]

Mar·tha (mär′thə), *n.* the sister of Mary and Lazarus. Luke 10:38–42; John 11:1–44.

Mar′tha's Vine′yard, an island off SE Massachusetts: summer resort. 108¾ sq. mi.

Mar·tí (mär tē′), *n.* **Jo·sé** (hō se′), 1853–1895, Cuban patriot and writer.

mar·tial (mär′shəl), *adj.* **1.** inclined or disposed to war; warlike; brave. **2.** pertaining to or appropriate for war: *martial music.* **3.** characteristic of or befitting a warrior: *a martial stride.* **4.** pertaining to or connected with the army or navy. [ME < L *Martiāl(is)* of, belonging to Mars = *Marti-* (s. of *Mars*) + *-ālis* -AL[1]] —**mar′tial·ism,** *n.* —**mar′tial·ist,** *n.* —**mar′tial·ly,** *adv.* —**mar′tial·ness,** *n.* —**Syn. 2, 3.** military, soldierly.

Mar·tial (mär′shəl), *n.* (*Marcus Valerius Martialis*) A.D. 43?–104?, Roman poet and epigrammatist, born in Spain.

mar′tial law′, the law imposed upon an area by military forces when civil authority has broken down.

Mar·tian (mär′shən), *adj.* **1.** pertaining to the planet Mars. —*n.* **2.** a supposed inhabitant of the planet Mars. [< L *Marti(us)* of, belonging to Mars]

mar·tin (mär′tᵊn, -tin), *n.* any of several swallows. Cf. **purple martin.** [named after St. MARTIN of Tours, supposedly because it migrates south at Martinmas or thereafter]

Mar·tin (mär′tᵊn, -tin), *n.* **1. Glenn Luther,** 1886–1955, U.S. airplane designer and manufacturer. **2. Homer Dodge,** 1836–97, U.S. painter. **3. Joseph W(illiam) Jr.,** 1884–1968, U.S. political leader and publisher: Speaker of the House 1947–49, 1953–55. **4. Saint,** A.D. 316?–397, French prelate: bishop of Tours 370?–397.

Martin I, Saint, died A.D. 655, Italian ecclesiastic: pope 649–655.

Martin II. See **Marinus I.**

Martin III. See **Marinus II.**

Martin IV, (*Simon de Brie* or *Simon de Brion*) c1210–85, French ecclesiastic: pope 1281–85.

Martin V, (*Oddone Colonna*) 1368–1431, Italian ecclesiastic: pope 1417–31.

Mar·tin du Gard (MAR TAN′ DY GAR′), **Ro·ger** (RÔ-ZHĀ′), 1881–1958, French novelist: Nobel prize 1937.

Mar·ti·neau (mär′ti nō′, -tᵊnō′), *n.* **1. Harriet,** 1802–1876, English novelist and economist. **2.** her brother, **James,** 1805–1900, English theologian and philosopher.

mar·ti·net (mär′tᵊnet′, mär′tᵊnet′), *n.* a strict disciplinarian, esp. a military one. [named after General Jean *Martinet* (d. 1672), French inventor of a system of drill] —**mar′ti·net′ish,** *adj.* —**mar′ti·net′ism,** *n.*

mar·tin·gale (mär′tᵊn gāl′), *n.* **1.** Also called **standing martingale.** part of the tack or harness of a horse, consisting of a strap that fastens to the girth, passes between the forelegs and through a loop in the neckstrap or hame, and fastens to the noseband: used to steady or hold down the horse's head. **2.** Also called **running martingale.** a similar device that divides at the chest into two branches, each ending in a ring through which the reins pass. **3.** *Naut.* **a.** a stay from the end of a jib boom or spike bowsprit to some part of a martingale boom. **b.** See **martingale boom. 4.** any of a number of systems of gambling in which the stakes are doubled or otherwise raised after each loss. [< MF < ?]

mar′tingale boom′, *Naut.* a strut, extending downward, that reinforces the jib boom or bowsprit against the upward pull of headstays. Also called **martingale, dolphin striker.**

mar·ti·ni (mär tē′nē), *n., pl.* **-nis.** a cocktail made with gin or vodka and dry vermouth. [appar. special use of the name *Martini*]

Mar·ti·ni (mär tē′nē; *It.* mär tē′nē), *n.* **Si·mo·ne** (sē mô′ne), 1283–1344, Italian painter.

Mar·ti·nique (mär′tᵊnēk′), *n.* an island in the E West Indies: an overseas department of France. 342,000; 425 sq. mi. *Cap.:* Fort-de-France.

Mar·tin·mas (mär′tᵊn məs, -tin-), *n.* a church festival, November 11, in honor of St. Martin. [ME *Martinmasse.* See Saint MARTIN, -MAS]

mart·let (märt′lit), *n. Brit. Dial.* a small, European swallow. [< MF *martelet,* var. of *martinet,* dim. of MARTIN]

mar·tyr (mär′tər), *n.* **1.** a person who chooses to suffer death rather than renounce his religion. **2.** a person who is put to death or endures great suffering on behalf of any belief, principle, or cause. **3.** a person who undergoes severe or constant suffering. **4.** a person who seeks sympathy or attention by feigning or exaggerating pain, deprivation, etc. **—*v.t.* 5.** to make a martyr of, esp. by putting to death. **6.** to torment or torture. [(n.) ME *marter,* OE *martyr* < LL < LGk, var. of Gk *mártys* a witness; (v.) ME *martire(n),* OE *martyrian* < n.] **—mar′tyr·ly,** *adv., adj.*

mar·tyr·dom (mär′tər dəm), *n.* **1.** the condition, sufferings, or death of a martyr. **2.** extreme suffering. [ME *martirdom,* OE *martyrdōm*]

mar·tyr·ise (mär′tə rīz′), *v.t.,* **-ised, -is·ing.** *Chiefly Brit.* martyrize. **—mar′tyr·i·sa′tion,** *n.*

mar·tyr·ize (mär′tə rīz′), *v.t.,* **-ized, -iz·ing. 1.** to make a martyr of. **2.** to torment. [ME *martirize(n)* < ML *martyriz(āre)*] **—mar′tyr·i·za′tion,** *n.*

mar·tyr·ol·o·gy (mär′tə rol′ə jē), *n., pl.* **-gies. 1.** the branch of knowledge dealing with the lives of martyrs. **2.** an account or history of martyrs. **3.** such histories collectively. **4.** a list of martyrs. [< ML *martyrologi(um)* history of martyrs < LGk *martyrológion*] **—mar·tyr·o·log·i·cal** (mär′tər ə loj′i kəl), **mar′tyr·o·log′ic,** *adj.* **—mar′tyr·ol′o·gist,** *n.*

mar·tyr·y (mär′tə rē), *n., pl.* **-tyr·ies.** a shrine, chapel, or the like, erected in honor of a martyr. [< eccl. L *martyri(um)* martyrdom, martyr's grave < LGk *martýrion*]

mar·vel (mär′vəl), *n., v.,* **-veled, -vel·ing** or (*esp. Brit.*) **-velled, -vel·ling. —*n.* 1.** a person or thing that arouses wonder, admiration, or astonishment. **2.** *Archaic.* the feeling of wonder; astonishment. **—*v.t.* 3.** to wonder at (usually fol. by a clause as object): *I marvel that you were able to do it.* **4.** to wonder or be curious about (usually fol. by a clause as object). **—*v.i.* 5.** to be affected with wonder, as at something surprising or extraordinary. [ME *mervel* < OF *merveil(l)e* < LL *mīrābilia* marvels, n. use of neut. pl. of L *mīrābilis* marvelous. See ADMIRABLE] **—mar′vel·ment,** *n.*

Mar·vell (mär′vəl), *n.* **Andrew,** 1621–78, English poet and satirist.

mar·vel·ous (mär′və ləs), *adj.* **1.** tending to arouse wonder, admiration, or astonishment; surprising; extraordinary. **2.** superb or excellent; great. **3.** improbable or incredible. Also, *esp. Brit.,* **mar′vel·lous.** [ME *merve(il)lous* < MF *merveilleus*] **—mar′vel·ous·ly;** *esp. Brit.,* **mar′vel·lous·ly,** *adv.* **—mar′vel·ous·ness;** *esp. Brit.,* **mar′vel·lous·ness,** *n.* **—Syn. 1.** wondrous, amazing, miraculous. **2.** wonderful.

Mar·war (mär′wär), *n.* Jodhpur (def. 1).

Marx (märks; *Ger.* märks), *n.* **Karl (Hein·rich)** (kärl hīn′rik; *Ger.* kärl hīn′riᴋʜ), 1818–83, German socialist and political theorist: originator of communist doctrines. **—Marx′i·an,** *adj.* **—Marx′i·an·ism,** *n.*

Marx·ism (märk′siz əm), *n.* the system of thought developed by Karl Marx, along with Friedrich Engels, esp. a set of economic and political doctrines characterized chiefly by the theories of dialectical materialism, surplus value, and class struggle. **—Marx′ist,** *n., adj.*

Mar·y (mâr′ē), *n.* **1.** Also called **Virgin Mary.** the mother of Jesus. **2.** the sister of Lazarus and Martha. Luke 10:39–42; John 11:1,2. **3.** (*Princess Victoria Mary of Teck*) 1867–1953, queen of England 1910–36 (wife of George V). [ME *Marie,* OE *Maria* < L < Gk < Heb *Miryām*]

Mary I, (*Mary Tudor*) (*"Bloody Mary"*) 1516–58, queen of England 1553–58 (wife of Philip II of Spain; daughter of Henry VIII).

Mary II, 1662–94, queen of England 1689–94: joint ruler with her husband William III (daughter of James II).

Mar′y Jane′, *U.S. Slang.* marijuana. Also, **mar′y·jane′.**

Mar·y·land (mer′ə lənd), *n.* a state in the E United States, on the Atlantic coast. 3,922,399 (1970); 10,577 sq. mi. *Cap.:* Annapolis. *Abbr.:* Md., MD

Mar′y Mag′dalene, Mary of Magdala: traditionally identified with the repentant woman whom Jesus forgave. Luke 7:37–50.

Mar′y, Queen′ of Scots′, (*Mary Stuart*) 1542–87, queen of Scotland 1542–67: beheaded for plotting to assassinate her cousin Queen Elizabeth I.

mar·zi·pan (mär′zə pan′), *n.* a confection made with almond milk and egg whites. Also called **marchpane.** [< G < It *marzapane.* See MARCHPANE]

-mas, a combining form of **Mass,** occurring in certain names of holidays and Christian feasts: *Michaelmas.*

mas., masculine.

Ma·sac·cio (mä sät′chô; *Eng.* mə sä′chē ō′), *n.* (*Tommaso Guidi*) 1401–28?, Italian painter.

Ma·sa·da (mä sä′dä), *n.* a mountainous fortress on the W shore of the Dead Sea where 960 Jewish zealots chose suicide rather than surrender to the Romans in 73 A.D.

Ma·sai (mə sī′), *n., pl.* **-sais,** (*esp. collectively*) **-sai.** a member of a pastoral African people inhabiting the highlands of Kenya and Tanzania.

Ma·sa·ryk (mas′ə rik; *Czech.* mä′sä rik), *n.* **1. Jan** (yän), 1886–1948, Czech statesman. **2.** his father, **To·máš Gar·rigue** (tô′mäsh gə rēg′), 1850–1937, Czech statesman: 1st president of Czechoslovakia 1918–35.

Mas·ba·te (mäs bä′tə), *n.* one of the central islands of the Philippines. 492,868; 1262 sq. mi.

masc., masculine.

Mas·ca·gni (mäs kä′nyē), *n.* **Pie·tro** (pye′trô), 1863–1945, Italian opera composer.

mas·car·a (ma skar′ə), *n.* a substance used as a cosmetic to color the eyelashes and sometimes the eyebrows. [< Sp: mask; see MASQUERADE]

mas·con (mas′kon′), *n.* a massive concentration of heavy material beneath the surface of the moon, caused by the uneven gravity field of the moon. [MAS(S) + CON(CENTRATION)]

mas·cot (mas′kət, -kot), *n.* a person, animal, or thing whose presence or association is considered as bringing good luck. [< F *mascotte* < Pr *mascoto* talisman, charm, dim. of *masco* witch < ML *mascus* ghost. See MASK]

mas·cu·line (mas′kyə lin), *adj.* **1.** having the qualities or characteristics of a man; manly; virile. **2.** pertaining to or characteristic of a man or men. **3.** *Gram.* noting or pertaining to the gender that has among its members most nouns referring to males. **4.** (of a woman) mannish. **—*n.*** *Gram.* **5.** the masculine gender. **6.** a noun or other element in that gender. [ME *masculin* < L *masculīn(us)* = *mascul-(us)* male (*mās* male + *-culus* -CULE) + *-īnus* -INE[1]] **—mas′cu·line·ly,** *adv.* **—mas′cu·lin′i·ty, mas′cu·line·ness,** *n.* **—Syn. 1.** See **male.**

mas′culine caesu′ra, *Pros.* a caesura occurring immediately after a stressed or a long syllable.

mas′culine rhyme′, *Pros.* a rhyme of but a single stressed syllable, as in *disdain, complain.*

mas·cu·lin·ise (mas′kyə lə nīz′), *v.t.,* **-ised, -is·ing.** *Chiefly Brit.* masculinize. **—mas′cu·lin·i·sa′tion,** *n.*

mas·cu·lin·ize (mas′kyə lə nīz′), *v.t.,* **-ized, -iz·ing.** *Med.* to produce certain male secondary sex characteristics in (a female). **—mas′cu·lin·i·za′tion,** *n.*

Mase·field (mās′fēld′, māz′-), *n.* **John,** 1878–1967, English poet, playwright, and critic: poet laureate 1930–67.

ma·ser (mā′zər), *n.* a device for amplifying electrical impulses by stimulated emission of radiation. [*m(icrowave) a(mplification by) s(timulated) e(mission of) r(adiation)*]

Mas·e·ru (maz′ə ro͞o′), *n.* a town in and the capital of Lesotho, in the NW part. 29,000.

mash (mash), *n.* **1.** a soft, pulpy mass. **2.** pulpy condition. **3.** a mess of boiled grain, bran, meal, etc., fed warm to horses and cattle. **4.** crushed malt or meal of grain mixed with hot water to form wort. **—*v.t.* 5.** to crush. **6.** to reduce to a soft, pulpy mass, as by heating or pressure, esp. in the preparation of food. **7.** to mix (crushed malt or meal of grain) with hot water to form wort. [ME; OE *mǣsc-, masc-* (in compounds); c. G *Maische*]

Ma·shar·brum (mush′ər bro͝om′), *n.* a mountain in N India, in the Himalayas. 25,660 ft. Also, **Ma′sher·brum′.**

mash·er (mash′ər), *n.* **1.** a person or thing that mashes. **2.** *Slang.* a man who makes amorous advances, esp. to women he does not know.

Mash·had (mash had′), *n.* Persian name of **Meshed.**

mash·ie (mash′ē), *n. Golf.* a club with an iron head, the face of which has more slope than a mashie iron but less slope than a mashie niblick. Also, **mashy.** [perh. < F *massue* club < VL **matteuca* = **matte(a)* MACE[1] + *-uca,* n. use of fem. of L *-ūcus* suffix of appurtenance]

mash′ie i′ron, *Golf.* an iron that has more slope than a mid-mashie but less slope than a mashie.

mash′ie nib′lick, *Golf.* a club with an iron head, the face of which has more slope than a mashie but less slope than a pitcher.

mash·y (mash′ē), *n., pl.* **mash·ies.** *Golf.* mashie.

Mas·i·nis·sa (mas′ə nis′ə), *n.* 238–149 B.C., king of Numidia c210–149. Also, **Massinissa.**

mas·jid (mus′jid), *n. Arabic.* a mosque. Also, **musjid.**

mask (mask, mäsk), *n.* **1.** a covering for all or part of the face, usually worn to conceal one's identity; false face. **2.** a molded or carved covering for the face of an actor, representing the character portrayed, as in Greek drama. **3.** anything that disguises or conceals; a pretense. **4.** a person wearing a mask; masker. **5.** a masquerade or revel. **6.** masque (defs. 1, 2). **7.** a likeness of a face, as one cast in a mold formed on the face. Cf. **death mask, life mask. 8.** the face or head, as of a fox. **9.** a representation of a face or head, generally grotesque, used as an ornament. **10.** a covering of wire, gauze, etc., to protect the face, as from splinters, dust, a pitched ball, etc. **11.** See **gas mask. 12.** *Fort.* a screen, as of earth or brush, for concealing or protecting a battery or any military operation. **13.** any protective covering, as paper, cardboard, etc., used for masking an area of something, as of a photograph or window. **14.** the dark shading on the muzzle of certain dogs. **—*v.t.* 15.** to disguise; conceal. **16.** to cover with a mask. **—*v.i.* 17.** to put on a mask; disguise oneself. [< MF *masque* < ML *masc(us), masco* ghost, *masca* witch < ?] **—mask′like′,** *adj.* **—Syn. 5.** mummery. **15.** veil, cloak, shroud, cover.

mas·ka·longe (mas′kə lonj′), *n., pl.* **-long·es,** (*esp. collectively*) **-longe.** muskellunge.

mas·ka·nonge (mas′kə nonj′), *n., pl.* **-nong·es,** (*esp. collectively*) **-nonge.** muskellunge.

masked (maskt, mäskt), *adj.* **1.** employing or wearing a mask or masks: *a masked burglar.* **2.** disguised or concealed; hidden. **3.** *Zool.* having markings that resemble a mask.

masked′ ball′, a ball at which masks and other disguises are worn.

mask·er (mas′kər, mä′skər), *n.* a person who masks, esp. one who takes part in a masque. Also, **masquer.**

mask′ing tape′, an adhesive tape used for protecting surfaces that are not to be painted, sprayed, etc.

mas·ki·nonge (mas′kə nonj′), *n., pl.* **-nong·es,** (*esp. collectively*) **-nonge.** muskellunge.

mas·och·ism (mas′ə kiz′əm, maz′-), *n.* **1.** *Psychiatry.* the condition in which sexual gratification depends on suffering, physical pain, and humiliation, esp. inflicted on oneself. **2.** gratification gained from pain, deprivation, etc., inflicted or imposed on oneself. [named after L. von SACHER-MASOCH, who described it] —**mas′och·ist,** *n.* —**mas′-och·is′tic,** *adj.* —**mas′och·is′ti·cal·ly,** *adv.*

ma·son (mā′sən), *n.* **1.** a person whose trade is building with stones, bricks, etc., usually with the use of mortar or cement as a bonding agent. **2.** a person who dresses stones or bricks. **3.** (*often cap.*) a Freemason. —*v.t.* **4.** to construct of or strengthen with masonry. [ME < OF *maçon* < Frankish **makjo* < **makan* to MAKE]

Ma·son (mā′sən), *n.* **Charles,** 1730–87, English astronomer and surveyor.

Ma′son Cit′y, a city in N Iowa. 30,379 (1970).

Ma′son-Dix′on line′ (mā′sən dik′sən), the boundary between Pennsylvania and Maryland, partly surveyed by Charles Mason and Jeremiah Dixon between 1763 and 1767: popularly regarded as the dividing line between North and South. Also called **Ma′son and Dix′on line′.**

ma·son·ic (mə son′ik), *adj.* (*often cap.*) pertaining to or characteristic of Freemasons or Freemasonry. —**ma·son′i·cal·ly,** *adv.*

Ma·son·ite (mā′sə nīt′), *n. Trademark.* a wood-fiber material, pressed in sheets and used for partitions, insulation, etc.

Ma′son jar′, a glass jar with an airtight screw top, much used in home canning. [named after John L. *Mason,* 19th-century American who patented it in 1857]

ma·son·ry (mā′sən rē), *n., pl.* **-ries. 1.** the art or occupation of a mason. **2.** work constructed by a mason, esp. stonework. **3.** (*often cap.*) Freemasonry. [ME *masonerie* < MF *maçonnerie*]

Ma·so·rah (mə sôr′ə, -sōr′ə; *Heb.* mi sô RÄ′), *n.* a collection of critical and explanatory notes on the Hebrew text of the Old Testament, compiled from the 7th? to 10th centuries A.D. and traditionally accepted as an authoritative exegetic guide, chiefly in matters of pronunciation and grammar. Also, **Ma·so′ra, Massorah, Massora.** [< Heb: tradition]

Mas·o·rete (mas′ə rēt′), *n.* **1.** one of the writers or compilers of the Masorah. **2.** a person versed in the Masorah. Also, **Massorete, Mas·o·rite** (mas′ə rīt′). [earlier *mas(s)oreth* < Heb *māsōreth*]

Mas·o·ret·ic (mas′ə ret′ik), *adj.* of or pertaining to the Masorah or the Masoretes. Also, **Mas′o·ret′i·cal, Massoretic, Massoretical.**

Mas·qat (mus kat′), *n.* Arabic name of **Muscat.**

masque (mask, mäsk), *n.* **1.** an elaborate entertainment in England in the 16th and 17th centuries, performed chiefly by amateur actors. **2.** a dramatic composition for such entertainment. **3.** a masquerade; revel. Also, **mask** (for defs. 1, 2). [var. of MASK]

mas·quer (mas′kər, mä′skər), *n.* masker.

mas·quer·ade (mas′kə rād′), *n., v.,* **-ad·ed, -ad·ing.** —*n.* **1.** a festive gathering of persons wearing masks and other disguises, and often elegant, historical, or fantastic costumes. **2.** disguise such as is worn at such an assembly. **3.** false outward show; disguise; pretense. —*v.i.* **4.** to go about under false pretenses or a false character; assume the character of another person: *to masquerade as a former Russian count.* **5.** to disguise oneself. **6.** to take part in a masquerade. [earlier *masquerada* < Sp *mascarada* = *máscar(a)* mask (? < Ar *maskhara* clown) + *-ada* -ADE[1]] —**mas′quer·ad′er,** *n.*

mass (mas), *n.* **1.** a body of coherent matter, usually of indefinite shape and often of considerable size: *a mass of dough.* **2.** a collection of incoherent particles, parts, or objects regarded as forming one body: *a mass of sand.* **3.** a considerable assemblage, number, or quantity. **4.** *Fine Arts.* **a.** *Painting.* an expanse of color or tone that defines form or shape in general outline rather than in detail. **b.** a three-dimensional shape or volume that has or gives the illusion of having great density and bulk. **5.** the main body, bulk, or greater part of anything. **6.** bulk, size, or massiveness. **7.** *Physics.* a fundamental property of a body, giving a measure of the acceleration the body will have when a given force is applied, usually considered constant and a measure of the matter in the body although mass varies with the velocity of the body. **8.** *Pharm.* a preparation from which pills are made. **9. the masses,** the great body of the common people, esp. the working classes. —*adj.* **10.** of, pertaining to, or affecting the masses; widespread: *mass hysteria.* **11.** done repeatedly or in great quantity: *mass attacks; mass suicides.* —*v.i.* **12.** to come together in or form a mass or masses. —*v.t.* **13.** to gather into or dispose in a mass or masses; assemble. **14. mass in,** *Fine Arts.* to sketch or indicate (forms, colors, etc.) in a broad or generalized manner rather than in detail. [ME *masse* < L *massa* < Gk *mâza* barley cake, akin to *mássein* to knead] —**mass·ed·ly** (mas′id lē, mast′lē), *adv.* —**Syn. 2.** aggregate, heap. **3.** collection, accumulation, pile. **5.** majority. **6.** magnitude, dimension. See **size**[1]. **9.** proletariat, plebeians.

Mass (mas), *n.* **1.** the celebration of the Eucharist. Cf. **High Mass, Low Mass. 2.** (*sometimes l.c.*) a musical setting of certain parts of this service, as the Kyrie eleison, Gloria, Credo, Sanctus, Benedictus, and Agnus Dei. [ME *masse,* OE *mæsse* < VL **messa,* eccl. L *missa;* orig. application of Latin term is uncertain]

Mass., Massachusetts.

mas·sa (mas′ə), *n.* marse.

Mas·sa (mäs′sä), *n.* a city in W Italy, near the Ligurian Sea: important marble industry. 55,626 (1959).

Mas·sa·chu·set (mas′ə chōō′sit), *n., pl.* **-sets,** (*esp. collectively*) **-set. 1.** a member of an Algonquian Indian people. **2.** the extinct Algonquian language of the Massachuset and Wampanoag Indians. Also, **Massachusetts.** [< Algonquian: lit., at or about the biggish hill]

Mas·sa·chu·setts (mas′ə chōō′sits), *n.* **1.** a state in the NE United States, on the Atlantic coast. 5,689,170 (1970); 8257 sq. mi. *Cap.:* Boston. *Abbr.:* MA, Mass. **2.** Massachuset.

Mas′sachu′setts Bay′, an inlet of the Atlantic, off the E coast of Massachusetts.

Mas′sachu′setts Bay′ Com′pany, a company, chartered in England in 1629 to establish a colony on Massachusetts Bay, that founded Boston in 1630.

mas·sa·cre (mas′ə kər), *n., v.,* **-cred, -cring.** —*n.* **1.** the unnecessary, indiscriminate killing of a number of human beings, as in barbarous warfare or persecution, or for revenge or plunder. —*v.t.* **2.** to kill indiscriminately, esp. a large number of human beings. [< MF < OF *macecler* to butcher < *mache-col* butcher = *mach(er)* (to) smash (see MASH) + *col* neck (< L *collum*); also influenced by *masselier* butcher < L *macellār(ius)*] —**mas′sa·crer** (mas′ə krər), *n.* —**Syn. 1.** carnage, extermination, butchery. **2.** slay.

mas·sage (mə säzh′, -säj′ *or, esp. Brit.,* mas′äzh), *n., v.,* **-saged, -sag·ing.** —*n.* **1.** the act or technique of treating the body by rubbing, kneading, or the like, to stimulate circulation, increase suppleness, etc. —*v.t.* **2.** to treat by massage. [< F = *mass(er)* (to) massage (< Ar *massa* to handle) + *-age* -AGE] —**mas·sag′er, mas·sag′ist,** *n.*

massage′ par′lor, a commercial establishment most often for the massage of males by masseuses, who are sometimes allegedly also engaged in illegal sexual activities.

Mas·sa·pe·qua (mas′ə pē′kwə), *n.* a town on SW Long Island, in SE New York. 26,821 (1970).

Mas·sa·soit (mas′ə soit′), *n.* c1580–1661, North American Indian leader: sachem of the Wampanoag tribe; negotiator of peace treaty with the Pilgrim Fathers 1621 (father of King Philip).

Mas·sa·ua (mäs sä′wä), *n.* a seaport in E Eritrea, in N Ethiopia, on the Red Sea. 26,627 (est. 1956). Also, **Mas-sa′wa.**

mass′ de′fect, *Physics.* the amount by which the mass of an atomic nucleus is less than the sum of the masses of its constituent particles, being the mass equivalent of the energy released in the formation of the nucleus. Cf. **binding energy.**

mas·sé (ma sā′ *or, esp. Brit.,* mas′ē), *n. Billiards.* a stroke made by hitting the cue ball with the cue held almost or quite perpendicular to the table. Also called **massé′ shot′.** [< F: lit., hammered, i.e., struck from above, straight down = *masse* sledge hammer (OF *mace;* see MACE[1]) + *-é* -EE]

Mas·sé·na (MA sā NA′), *n.* **An·dré** (äN DRĀ′), **duc de Ri·vo·li** (*Fr.* RĒ vô lē′; *It.* RĒ′vô lē) and **Prince d'Ess·ling** (des′liNG), 1758–1817, French marshal under Napoleon I.

mass′-en′er·gy equa′tion (mas′en′ər jē), *Physics.* the equation, $E = mc^2$, formulated by Albert Einstein, expressing the equivalence between mass and energy, where E is energy, m is mass, and c is the velocity of light.

Mas·se·net (mas′ə nā′; *Fr.* MAS[ə]NE′), *n.* **Jules É·mile Fré·dé·ric** (zhyl ā mēl′ frā dā rēk′), 1842–1912, French composer.

mas·se·ter (ma sē′tər), *n. Anat.* a short, thick, masticatory muscle, the action of which assists in closing the jaws by raising the mandible or lower jaw. [< NL < Gk *masētḗr* a chewer = *mas(âsthai)* (to) chew + *-ē-* connecting vowel + *-tēr* agentive suffix] —**mas·se·ter·ic** (mas′i ter′ik), *adj.*

mas·seur (mə sûr′; *Fr.* MA SŒR′), *n., pl.* **-seurs** (-sûrz′; *Fr.* -SŒR′). a man who provides massage as a profession or occupation. [< F; see MASSAGE, -OR[2]]

mas·seuse (mə sōōs′, -sōōz′; *Fr.* MA SŒZ′), *n., pl.* **-seus·es** (-sōō′siz, -sōō′ziz; *Fr.* -SŒZ′). a woman who provides massage as a profession or occupation. [< F; fem. of MASSEUR]

Mas·sey (mas′ē), *n.* **Vincent,** 1887–1967, Canadian statesman: governor general 1952–59.

mas·si·cot (mas′ə kot′), *n.* monoxide of lead, PbO, in the form of a yellow powder, used as a pigment and drier. Also, **mas′si·cot·ite′.** [< F < It *massicotto* < Sp *mazacote* soda ash, mortar, alter. of Ar *shabb kubṭī* coptic alum]

mas·sif (mas′if; *Fr.* MA sēf′), *n.* **1.** a compact portion of a mountain range, containing one or more summits. **2.** a band or zone of the earth's crust raised or depressed as a unit and bounded by faults. [< F, n. use of *massif* MASSIVE]

Mass·if Cen·tral (MA sēf′ säN TRAL′), a great mountainous plateau and the chief water divide of France, in the central part.

Mas·sil·lon (mas′ə lon′), *n.* a city in NE Ohio. 32,539 (1970).

Mas·sine (mä sēn′), *n.* **Lé·o·nide** (lā ô nēd′), 1896–1979, U.S. ballet dancer and choreographer, born in Russia.

Mas·sin·ger (mas′ən jər), *n.* **Philip,** 1583–1640, English dramatist: collaborated with John Fletcher.

Mas·si·nis·a (mas′ə nis′ə), *n.* Masinissa.

mas·sive (mas′iv), *adj.* **1.** consisting of or forming a large mass; bulky and heavy. **2.** large, as the head or forehead. **3.** solid or substantial; great or imposing. **4.** *Mineral.* having no outward crystal form, although sometimes crystalline in internal structure. **5.** *Geol.* without stratification or lamination; homogenous. **6.** *Med.* affecting a large, continuous mass of bodily tissue. [late ME; r. ME *massif* < MF] —**mas′-sive·ly,** *adv.* —**mas′sive·ness, mas·siv′i·ty,** *n.*

mass·less (mas′lis), *adj. Physics.* having no mass. —**mass′less·ness,** *n.*

mass′ me′dia, media[1] (def. 2).

mass′ meet′ing, a large or general assembly to discuss or hear discussed some matter of common interest.

mass′ move′ment, 1. a movement through space involving large numbers of people: *mass movement of troops.* **2.** *Sociol.* a loosely organized effort by a large number of people, esp. those not forming part of the elite of a given society, to bring about pervasive changes in existing social, economic, or political institutions.

mass′ noun′, *Gram.* a noun that typically refers to an indefinitely divisible substance or an abstract notion, and that in English cannot be used, in such a sense, with the indefinite article or in the plural, as *water, air, happiness.* Cf. **count noun.**

mass′ num′ber, *Physics.* the integer nearest in value to the atomic weight of an atom and equal to the number of nucleons in the nucleus of the atom. *Symbol:* A

Mas·so·rah (mə sôr′ə, -sōr′ə; *Heb.* mi sô RÄ′), *n.* Masorah. Also, **Mas·so′ra.**

Mas·so·rete (mas′ə rēt′), *n.* Masorete.

Mas·so·ret·ic (mas′ə ret′ik), *adj.* Masoretic. Also, **Mas′-so·ret′i·cal.**

mas·so·ther·a·py (mas′ō ther′ə pē), *n. Med.* treatment by massage. [MASS(AGE) + -O- + THERAPY] —**mas′so-ther′a·pist,** *n.*

mass-pro·duce (mas′prə dōōs′, -dyōōs′), *v.t.,* **-duced, -duc·ing.** to produce or manufacture goods in large quantities, esp. by machinery. —**mass′-pro·duc′er,** *n.*

mass′ produc′tion, the production or manufacture of goods in large quantities by machinery.
mass′ spec′trograph, *Physics.* a mass spectroscope for recording a mass spectrum on a photographic plate.
mass′ spectrom′eter, *Physics.* a device for identifying the various kinds of particles present in a given substance, by ionizing the particles and subjecting a beam of the ionized particles to an electric or magnetic field such that the field deflects the particles in angles directly proportional to the masses of the particles.
mass′ spec′troscope, *Physics.* an instrument used to determine the masses of small, electrically charged particles. —**mass′ spectros′copy.**
mass′ spec′trum, *Physics.* a spectrum of charged particles, arranged in accordance with their masses or mass-to-charge ratios.
mass·y (mas′ē), *adj.*, **mass·i·er, mass·i·est.** massive. [ME] —**mass′i·ness,** *n.*
mast[1] (mast, mäst), *n.* **1.** *Naut.* **a.** a spar or structure rising above the hull and upper portions of a vessel to hold sails, rigging, etc., at some point on the fore-and-aft line, as a foremast or mainmast. **b.** any of a number of individual spars composing such a structure, as a topmast supported on trestletrees at the head of a lower mast. **c.** any of various portions of a single spar that are beside particular sails, as a topgallant mast and royal mast formed as a single spar. **2.** the upright support of a jib crane. **3.** any upright pole, as a support for an aerial, a post in certain cranes, etc. **4. before the mast,** *Naut.* as an unlicensed seaman. —*v.t.* **5.** to provide with a mast or masts. [ME; OE *mæst;* c. G *Mast;* akin to L *mālus* pole] —**mast′less,** *adj.* —**mast′like′,** *adj.*
mast[2] (mast, mäst), *n.* the fruit of the oak and beech or other forest trees, used as food for hogs and other animals. [ME; OE *mæst;* c. G *Mast;* akin to MEAT]
mast-, var. of **masto-** before a vowel: *mastectomy.*
mas·ta·ba (mas′tə bə), *n.* an ancient Egyptian tomb, rectangular in plan, with sloping sides and a flat roof. Also, **mas′ta·bah.** [< Ar: bench]
mas·tec·to·my (ma stek′tə mē), *n., pl.* **-mies.** *Surg.* the operation of removing the breast or mamma.
mas·ter (mas′tər, mä′stər), *n.* **1.** a person with the ability or power to use, control, or dispose of something. **2.** an employer of workmen or servants. **3.** a person who commands a merchant vessel; captain. **4.** the male head of a household. **5.** an owner of a slave, animal, etc. **6.** a presiding officer. **7.** *Chiefly Brit.* a male teacher, tutor, or schoolmaster. **8.** a person whose teachings one accepts or follows: *a master of Zen.* **9.** a victor or conqueror. **10.** a workman qualified to teach apprentices and to carry on his trade independently. **11.** a man eminently skilled in something, as an occupation, art, or science. **12.** an assistant judge who takes testimony, makes a report, etc. **13.** *Educ.* a person having a master's degree. **14.** a boy or young man (used chiefly as a term of address). **15.** Also called **matrix.** something to be mechanically reproduced. **16.** a device for controlling another device operating in a similar way. Cf. **slave** (def. 4). —*adj.* **17.** being master; exercising mastery. **18.** chief or principal. **19.** directing or controlling. **20.** dominating or predominant. **21.** being a master carrying on his trade independently, rather than a workman employed by another. **22.** being a master of some occupation, art, etc.; eminently skilled. **23.** characteristic of a master; showing mastery. —*v.t.* **24.** to conquer or subdue; reduce to subjection. **25.** to rule or direct as master. **26.** to make oneself master of; become an adept in. [ME *maistre, maister,* OE *magister* < L, akin to *magnus* great] —**mas′ter·dom,** *n.* —**mas′ter·hood′,** *n.* —**mas′ter·less,** *adj.* —**Syn. 1.** adept, expert. **19.** main, leading, cardinal. **24.** subjugate, overcome, overpower. **25.** govern, manage.
mas·ter-at-arms (mas′tər ət ärmz′, mä′stər-), *n., pl.* **mas·ters-at-arms. 1.** *Navy.* a petty officer in charge of discipline on a ship. **2.** an officer of a fraternal organization, veterans' society, or the like, empowered to maintain order, exclude unauthorized persons, etc.
mas′ter build′er, 1. a building contractor. **2.** an architect.
mas·ter·ful (mas′tər fəl, mä′stər-), *adj.* **1.** having or showing the qualities of a master; authoritative; domineering; self-willed; imperious. **2.** showing mastery or skill; masterly. [ME] —**mas′ter·ful·ly,** *adv.* —**mas′ter·ful·ness,** *n.* —**Syn. 2.** consummate; adept, expert, skilled, skillful.
mas′ter hand′, 1. an expert. **2.** great expertness.
mas′ter key′, a key that will open a number of locks, the proper keys of which are not interchangeable.
mas·ter·ly (mas′tər lē, mä′stər-), *adj.* **1.** like or befitting a master, as in skill or art; worthy of a master; very skillful. —*adv.* **2.** in a masterly manner. [ME *maisterly*] —**mas′ter·li·ness,** *n.*
mas′ter ma′son, 1. (*often caps.*) a Freemason who has reached the third degree. **2.** an expert mason.
mas′ter mechan′ic, a thoroughly skilled mechanic, esp. in charge of other mechanics.
mas·ter·mind (mas′tər mīnd′, mä′stər-), *v.t.* **1.** to plan and direct activities skillfully. —*n.* **2.** a person who originates or is primarily responsible for the execution of a particular idea, project, or the like.
Mas′ter of Arts′, a master's degree given usually in a specific branch of the humanities or social sciences. *Abbr.:* A.M., M.A. [late ME]
mas′ter of cer′emonies, a person who directs the entertainment at a party, dinner, or the like. *Abbr.:* M.C.
mas′ter of fox′hounds, the person responsible for the conduct of a hunt and to whom all members of the hunt and its staff are responsible.
Mas′ter of Sci′ence, a master's degree given usually in a specific branch of the natural sciences, mathematics, or technology. *Abbr.:* M.S., M.Sc., S.M., Sc.M.
mas·ter·piece (mas′tər pēs′, mä′stər-), *n.* **1.** a person's most excellent production, as in an art. **2.** any production of masterly skill. **3.** a piece made by a journeyman or other craftsman aspiring to the rank of master in a guild or other craft organization as a proof of his competence. [MASTER + PIECE, modeled on D *meesterstuk,* G *Meisterstück*]
mas′ter point′, a point awarded to a bridge player who has won or placed in an officially recognized tournament.
mas′ter race′, a race or nation, as Germany under Hitler, whose members consider themselves superior to all other peoples and therefore justified in conquering and ruling them.
Mas·ters (mas′tərz, mä′stərz), *n.* **Edgar Lee,** 1869–1950, U.S. poet and novelist.
mas′ter's degree′, a degree awarded by a graduate school or department, usually to a person who has completed at least one year of graduate study.
mas′ter ser′geant, *U.S.* **1.** *Army, Air Force, Marine Corps.* a noncommissioned officer ranking next to the highest noncommissioned officer. **2.** *Air Force.* a noncommissioned officer of one of the three top enlisted grades.
mas·ter·ship (mas′tər ship′, mä′stər-), *n.* **1.** the office, function, or authority of a master. **2.** control; command. **3.** masterly skill or knowledge. [ME]
mas′ter stroke′, a masterly action or achievement; an extremely skillful or effective action.
mas·ter·work (mas′tər wûrk′, mä′stər-), *n.* masterpiece.
mas′ter work′man, 1. a workman in charge. **2.** a person who is master of his craft.
mas·ter·y (mas′tə rē, mä′stə-), *n., pl.* **-ter·ies** for 2–5. **1.** the state of being master; power of command or control. **2.** command or grasp, as of a subject. **3.** victory. **4.** the act of mastering. **5.** expert skill or knowledge. [MASTER + -Y[3]; r. ME *maistre* < OF]
mast·head (mast′hed′, mäst′-), *n.* **1.** *Naut.* **a.** the head of a mast. **b.** (loosely) the uppermost point of a mast. **2.** Also called **flag.** a statement in a newspaper, magazine, or the like, giving the publication's name, the names of the owner and staff, etc. **3.** nameplate (def. 2). —*v.t.* **4.** *Naut.* to hoist to the truck of a mast, as a flag. —*adj.* **5.** *Naut.* run up to the head of a mast: *masthead rig.*
mas·tic (mas′tik), *n.* **1.** Also, **mas·ti·che** (mas′ti kē), **mastix.** an aromatic, astringent resin obtained from a small anacardiaceous evergreen tree, *Pistacia Lentiscus,* native to the Mediterranean region: used in making varnish. **2.** any similar resin, esp. one yielded by other trees of the same genus. **3.** a tree yielding a mastic, esp. *Pistacia Lentiscus.* [ME *mastyk* < L *masticē* < Gk *mastíchē* chewing gum, akin to *mastichân* to gnash the teeth]
mas·ti·cate (mas′tə kāt′), *v.t., v.i.,* **-cat·ed, -cat·ing. 1.** to chew. **2.** to reduce to a pulp by crushing or kneading, as rubber. [< LL *masticāt(us)* chewed, ptp. of *masticāre*] —**mas·ti·ca·ble** (mas′tə kə bəl), *adj.* —**mas′ti·ca′tion,** *n.* —**mas′ti·ca′tor,** *n.*
mas·ti·ca·to·ry (mas′tə kə tōr′ē, -tôr′ē), *adj., n., pl.* **-ries.** —*adj.* **1.** of, pertaining to, or used in or for mastication. —*n.* **2.** *Pharm.* a medicinal substance to be chewed, as to promote the secretion of saliva. [< NL *masticātōri(us)*]
mas·tiff (mas′tif, mä′stif), *n.* one of a breed of large, powerful, short-haired dogs having an apricot, fawn, or brindled coat. [ME *mastif* << VL **mansuetīvus* = L *mansuēt(us)* tamed (see MANSUETUDE) + *-īvus* -IVE]

Mastiff
(30 in. high at shoulder)

mas·ti·goph·o·ran (mas′tə gof′ər-ən), *n.* **1.** Also, **mas·ti·go·phore** (mas′tə gə fōr′, -fôr′). a protozoan of the class *Mastigophora* (*Flagellata*), comprising the flagellates. —*adj.* **2.** Also, **mas·ti·goph′o·rous,** belonging or pertaining to the *Mastigophora.* [< NL *Mastigophor(a)* name of the class (< Gk *mastīgophóros* whip-bearing = *mástīg(ion),* dim. of *mástix* whip + *-o-* -O- + *-phoros* -PHORE) + -AN]
mas·ti·tis (ma stī′tis), *n.* **1.** *Pathol.* inflammation of the breast. **2.** *Vet. Pathol.* inflammation of the udder, esp. of cows; garget. —**mas·tit·ic** (ma stit′ik), *adj.*
mas·tix (mas′tiks), *n.* mastic (def. 1).
masto-, a learned borrowing from Greek meaning "breast," used in the formation of compound words: *mastodon.* Also, *esp. before a vowel,* **mast-.** [comb. form repr. Gk *mastós*]
mas·to·don (mas′tə don′), *n.* any large, elephant-like mammal of the genera *Mammut, Mastodon,* etc., from the Oligocene and Pleistocene epochs, having conical projections on the molar teeth. [< NL < Gk *mas-t(ós)* breast + *odṓn* tooth] —**mas′to·don′ic,** *adj.*

Mastodon, *Mammut americanum*
(7 to 9½ ft. high at shoulder)

mas·toid (mas′toid), *adj.* **1.** resembling a breast or nipple. **2.** denoting the nipplelike process of the temporal bone behind the ear. **3.** of or pertaining to the mastoid process. —*n.* **4.** the mastoid process. [< NL *mastoīd(ēs)* < Gk *mastoeidḗs*]
mas·toid·ec·to·my (mas′toi dek′tə mē), *n., pl.* **-mies.** *Surg.* the removal of part of a mastoid bone, usually for draining an infection.
mas·toid·i·tis (mas′toi dī′tis), *n.* *Pathol.* inflammation of the mastoid process of the temporal bone of the skull.
mas·tur·bate (mas′tər bāt′), *v.,* **-bat·ed, -bat·ing.** —*v.i.* **1.** to engage in masturbation. —*v.t.* **2.** to practice masturbation upon. [< L *masturbāt(us)* engaged in masturbation, ptp. of *masturbārī* < ?] —**mas′tur·ba′tor,** *n.*
mas·tur·ba·tion (mas′tər bā′shən), *n.* **1.** the stimulation or manipulation of one's own or another's genitals to achieve orgasm. **2.** sexual self-gratification. —**mas′tur·ba′tion·al,** *adj.* —**mas·tur·ba·to·ry** (mas′tər bə tōr′ē, -tôr′ē), *adj.*
Ma·su·ri·a (mə zo͝or′ē ə), *n.* a region in NE Poland, formerly in East Prussia, Germany: German defeat of Russians 1914–15. German, **Ma·su·ren** (mä zo͞o′rən).
mat[1] (mat), *n., v.,* **mat·ted, mat·ting.** —*n.* **1.** a piece of

fabric made of some pliant material, as rubber, used as a protective covering on a floor or other surface. **2.** a smaller piece of material, often ornamental, set under a dish of food, a lamp, vase, etc. **3.** *Sports.* a floor covering for the protection of contestants or performers, as wrestlers or tumblers. **4.** a thickly growing or thick and tangled mass, as of hair or weeds. —*v.t.* **5.** to cover with or as with mats or matting. **6.** to form into a mat, as by interweaving. —*v.i.* **7.** to become entangled; form tangled masses. [ME, OE *matte* < LL *matta* mat of rushes < Sem (Punic)] —**mat′less,** *adj.*

mat[2] (mat), *n., v.,* **mat·ted, mat·ting.** —*n.* **1.** a piece of cardboard or other material placed over or under a drawing, painting, photograph, etc., to serve as a frame or provide a border between the picture and the frame. —*v.t.* **2.** to provide (a picture) with a mat. [special use of MAT[3] and MAT[1]]

mat[3] (mat), *adj., n., v.,* **mat·ted, mat·ting.** —*adj.* **1.** lusterless and dull in surface. —*n.* **2.** a dull or dead surface, without luster, produced on metals, as gold or silver, by a special operation. **3.** a tool for producing it. —*v.t.* **4.** to finish with a mat surface. Also, **matt, matte.** [earlier *matte* < G *matt* < ML *matt(us)* stupid, downcast; orig. disputed]

mat[4] (mat), *n. Print.* **1.** the intaglio, usually of papier-mâché, impressed from type or a cut, from which a stereotype plate is cast. **2.** *Informal.* matrix (def. 7). [shortened form of MATRIX]

mat., **1.** matinée. **2.** matins. **3.** maturity.

Mat·a·be·le (mat′ə bē′lē), *n., pl.* **-les,** (*esp. collectively*) **-le.** a member of a Bantu-speaking people of Rhodesia and formerly of the Transvaal. Also called **Ndebele.**

mat·a·dor (mat′ə dôr′), *n.* **1.** the bullfighter who kills the bull in a bullfight; a torero. **2.** one of the principal cards in skat and certain other games. **3.** (*cap.*) *U.S.* a surface-to-surface, pilotless aircraft. [< Sp < L *mactātor* slayer < *mactāre* to kill; see -ATE[1], -OR[2]]

Ma·ta Ha·ri (mä′tə här′ē, mat′ə har′ē), (*Gertrud Margarete Zelle*) 1876–1917, Dutch dancer in France: executed as a spy by the French.

Mat·a·mo·ros (mat′ə mōr′əs, -môr′-; *Sp.* mä′tä mô′rôs), *n.* a seaport in NE Mexico, on the Rio Grande opposite Brownsville, Texas. 131,576 (est. 1965).

Mat·a·nus·ka (mat′ə no͞os′kə), *n.* **1.** a river in S Alaska flowing SW to Cook Inlet. 90 mi. long. **2.** a village in the valley of this river, NE of Anchorage: site of federal experiment in rural resettlement in 1935.

Ma·tan·zas (mə tan′zəs; *Sp.* mä tän′säs), *n.* a seaport on the NW coast of Cuba. 82,619 (1960).

Mat·a·pan (mat′ə pan′), *n.* **Cape,** a cape in S Greece, at the S tip of the Peloponnesus.

match[1] (mach), *n.* **1.** a short, slender piece of wood or other material tipped with a chemical substance that produces fire when rubbed on a rough or chemically prepared surface. **2.** a wick, cord, or the like, prepared to burn at an even rate, used to fire cannon, gunpowder, etc. [ME *macche* wick < MF *meiche,* OF *mesche* < VL **mesca* lamp wick, metathetic var. of L *myxa* < Gk: mucus, nostril, nozzle of a lamp]

match[2] (mach), *n.* **1.** a person or thing that equals or resembles another in some respect. **2.** a person or thing that is an exact counterpart of another. **3.** a person or thing able to cope with another as an equal: *to meet one's match.* **4.** a corresponding or suitably associated pair. **5.** *Chiefly Brit.* a contest or game. **6.** an engagement for a contest or game. **7.** a person considered with regard to suitability as a partner in marriage: *a good match.* **8.** a matrimonial compact or alliance. —*v.t.* **9.** to equal; be equal to: *My talent does not match his.* **10.** to be the match or counterpart of. **11.** to cause to correspond; adapt: *to match one's actions to one's beliefs.* **12.** to fit together, as two things: *matching the tongue and groove of adjoining floorboards.* **13.** to procure or produce an equal to. **14.** to place in opposition or conflict. **15.** to provide with an adversary or competitor of equal power: *The teams were well matched.* **16.** to encounter as an adversary with equal power. **17.** to prove a match for. **18.** to unite in marriage; procure a matrimonial alliance for. —*v.i.* **19.** to be equal or suitable. **20.** to correspond; be of corresponding size, shape, color, pattern, etc.: *These gloves do not match.* **21.** to ally oneself in marriage. [ME *macche,* OE *gemæcca* mate, fellow] —**match′a·ble,** *adj.* —**match′er,** *n.*

match·board (mach′bōrd′, -bôrd′), *n.* a board having a tongue formed on one edge and a groove of the same dimensions cut into the other, used with similar boards to compose floors, dados, etc.

match·book (mach′bo͝ok′), *n.* a small cardboard folder into which several rows of paper matches are stapled.

match·box (mach′boks′), *n.* a small box, usually of cardboard, for matches.

match·less[1] (mach′lis), *adj.* having no equal; peerless; unequaled; incomparable: *matchless courage.* [MATCH[2] + -LESS] —**match′less·ly,** *adv.* —**match′less·ness,** *n.*

match·less[2] (mach′lis), *adj.* **1.** lacking a safety match or matches. **2.** made so as to be lighted or ignited without a match: *a matchless gas range.* [MATCH[1] + -LESS]

match·lock (mach′lok′), *n.* **1.** an old form of gunlock in which the priming was ignited by a slow match. **2.** a hand gun, usually a musket, with such a lock.

match·mak·er[1] (mach′mā′kər), *n.* **1.** a person who arranges or tries to arrange marriages by introducing possible mates. **2.** a person who arranges matches for athletic contests, esp. prizefights and wrestling matches. [MATCH[2] + MAKER] —**match′mak′ing,** *n., adj.*

match·mak·er[2] (mach′mā′kər), *n.* a person who makes matches for burning. [MATCH[1] + MAKER] —**match′mak′ing,** *n., adj.*

match′ play′, *Golf.* play in which the score is reckoned by counting the holes won by each side. Cf. **medal play.** —**match′ play′er.**

match·wood (mach′wo͝od′), *n.* **1.** wood suitable for making matches. **2.** splinters; tiny pieces.

mate[1] (māt), *n., v.,* **mat·ed, mat·ing.** —*n.* **1.** one of a pair: *I can't find the mate to this glove.* **2.** a counterpart. **3.** husband or wife; spouse. **4.** one of a pair of mated animals. **5.** a habitual associate; fellow worker; comrade; partner (often used in combination): *classmate.* **6.** *Naut.* See **first mate.** **7.** an assistant to a warrant officer or other functionary on a ship. —*v.t.* **8.** to join as a mate or as mates. **9.** to match or marry. **10.** to bring (animals) together for breeding purposes. **11.** to join or associate suitably, as one thing with another. —*v.i.* **12.** to associate as a mate or as mates. **13.** to marry. **14.** (of animals) to copulate. **15.** *Archaic.* to consort; keep company. [ME < MLG; r. ME *mette,* OE *gemetta* messmate, guest. See MEAT] —**mate′less,** *adj.* —**mate′ship,** *n.*

mate[2] (māt), *n., v.t.,* **mat·ed, mat·ing,** *interj. Chess.* checkmate (def. 1). [ME *mat* defeated (adj.), defeat (n.) < OF << Pers; see CHECKMATE]

ma·te[3] (mä′tā, mat′ā), *n.* maté.

ma·té (mä′tā, mat′ā), *n.* a tealike South American beverage made from the leaves of a species of holly. Also, **mate.** [< Sp *mate,* orig. the vessel in which the herb is steeped < Quechua *mati* calabash]

mat·e·lote (mat′ᵊlōt′; *Fr.* mAt° lôt′), *n.* a highly seasoned fish stew made with wine. [< F, special fem. use of *matelot* sailor]

ma·ter (mā′tər), *n., pl.* **-ters, -tres** (-trēz). *Brit. Informal.* mother. [< L]

ma·ter·fa·mil·i·as (mā′tər fə mil′ē əs), *n.* the mother of a family. [< L; cf. PATERFAMILIAS]

ma·te·ri·al (mə tēr′ē əl), *n.* **1.** the substance or substances of which a thing is made or composed. **2.** any constituent element of a thing. **3.** anything that serves as crude or original matter to be used or developed: *building material.* **4.** a group of related facts, ideas, or data that may serve as the basis for some integrated work: *to gather material for a history of North Carolina.* **5.** a textile fabric. **6. materials,** the articles or apparatus needed to make or do something: *writing materials.* —*adj.* **7.** formed or consisting of matter; physical; corporeal: *the material world.* **8.** relating to, concerned with, or involving matter: *material force.* **9.** pertaining to the physical rather than the spiritual or intellectual aspect of things. **10.** of substantial import; of much consequence; important: *Your support will make a material difference in the success of our program.* **11.** *Law.* likely to influence the determination of a case: *material evidence.* **12.** *Philos.* of or pertaining to matter as distinguished from form. [ME < LL *māteriāl(is)* of, belonging to matter] —**ma·te′ri·al·ness,** *n.* —**Syn. 10.** essential, vital.

ma·te·ri·al·ise (mə tēr′ē ə līz′), *v.t., v.i.,* **-ised, -is·ing.** *Chiefly Brit.* materialize. —**ma·te′ri·al·i·sa′tion,** *n.* —**ma·te′ri·al·is′er,** *n.*

ma·te·ri·al·ism (mə tēr′ē ə liz′əm), *n.* **1.** the philosophical theory that regards matter and its motions as constituting the universe, and all phenomena, including those of mind, as due to material agencies. **2.** attention to or emphasis on material objects, needs, and considerations, with a disinterest in or rejection of spiritual values. [< NL *māteriālism(us)*]

ma·te·ri·al·ist (mə tēr′ē ə list), *n.* **1.** an adherent of philosophical materialism. **2.** a person who is markedly more concerned with material things than with spiritual values. [< NL *māteriālista*] —**ma·te′ri·al·is′tic,** *adj.* —**ma·te′ri·al·is′ti·cal·ly,** *adv.*

ma·te·ri·al·i·ty (mə tēr′ē al′i tē), *n., pl.* **-ties.** for 2. **1.** material nature or quality. **2.** something material. [< ML *māteriālitās*]

ma·te·ri·al·ize (mə tēr′ē ə līz′), *v.,* **-ized, -iz·ing.** —*v.t.* **1.** to give material form to; realize. **2.** to invest with material attributes. **3.** to make physically perceptible; cause (a spirit or the like) to appear in bodily form. **4.** to render materialistic. —*v.i.* **5.** to assume material or bodily form; become corporeal: *The ghost materialized before Hamlet.* **6.** to come into perceptible existence; appear; become actual fact; be realized or carried out: *Our plans never materialized.* Also, *esp. Brit.,* **materialise.** —**ma·te′ri·al·i·za′tion,** *n.* —**ma·te′ri·al·iz′er,** *n.*

ma·te·ri·al·ly (mə tēr′ē ə lē), *adv.* **1.** to an important degree; considerably: *His work didn't help materially.* **2.** with reference to matter or material things and conditions; physically. **3.** *Philos.* with regard to matter or substance as distinguished from form.

mate′rials han′dling, the loading and unloading of goods, esp. by the aid of mechanical devices.

ma·te·ri·a med·i·ca (mə tēr′ē ə med′ə kə), **1.** the remedial substances employed in medicine. **2.** Also called **pharmacognosy.** the science dealing with the sources, physical characteristics, uses, and doses of drugs. [< ML: medical material]

ma·te·ri·el (mə tēr′ē el′), *n.* **1.** the aggregate of things used or needed in any business, undertaking, or operation (distinguished from *personnel*). **2.** *Mil.* arms, ammunition, and equipment in general. Also, **ma·té′ri·el′.** [< F; see MATERIAL]

ma·ter·nal (mə tûr′nᵊl), *adj.* **1.** of, pertaining to, having the qualities of, or befitting a mother. **2.** derived from a mother. **3.** related through a mother. [late ME < ML *māternāl(is)* = L *mātern(us)* (*māter* mother + *-nus* adj. suffix) + *-ālis* -AL[1]] —**ma·ter′nal·ism,** *n.* —**ma·ter′nal·is′tic,** *adj.* —**ma·ter′nal·ly,** *adv.*

ma·ter·ni·ty (mə tûr′ni tē), *n.* **1.** the state of being a mother; motherhood. **2.** motherliness. —*adj.* **3.** of, pertaining to, or for the period in which a woman is pregnant or has just given birth to a child. [< ML *māternitās.* See MATERNAL, -ITY]

mate·y[1] (mā′tē), *n., pl.* **mate·ys.** *Chiefly Brit. Informal.* comrade; chum; buddy. [MATE[1] + -Y[2]] —**mate′y·ness, mat′i·ness,** *n.*

mate·y[2] (mā′tē), *adj. Chiefly Brit. Informal.* sociable or friendly: *a matey chat.* [MATE[1] + -Y[1]]

math (math), *n. Informal.* mathematics. [shortened form]

math., **1.** mathematical. **2.** mathematics.

math·e·mat·i·cal (math′ə mat′i kəl), *adj.* **1.** of, pertaining to, or employing mathematics: *mathematical study; mathematical analysis.* **2.** employed in the operations of mathematics: *mathematical instruments.* **3.** having the exactness or precision of mathematics. Also, **math′e·mat′ic.** —**math′e·mat′i·cal·ly,** *adv.*

mathemat′ical expecta′tion, *Statistics.* the summation or integration over all values of a variate, of the product of the variate and its probability or its probability density.

mathemat′ical log′ic. See **symbolic logic.**

math·e·ma·ti·cian (math′ə mə tish′ən), *n.* an expert in mathematics. [late ME *mathematicion* (? misspelling)]

math·e·mat·ics (math/ə mat/iks), *n.* **1.** (*construed as sing.*) the systematic treatment of magnitude, relationships between figures and forms, and relations between quantities expressed symbolically. **2.** (*construed as sing. or pl.*) mathematical procedures, operations, or properties. [n. use of *mathematic* < L *mathēmatic(a ars)* < Gk *mathēmatikē (téchnē)* scientific (craft) = *mathēmat-* (s. of *máthēma*) science, knowledge + *-ikē*, fem. of *-ikos* -IC]

Math·er (math/ər, math/-), *n.* **1. Cotton,** 1663–1728, American clergyman and author. **2.** his father, **In·crease** (in/krēs), 1639–1723, American clergyman and author.

Math·ew·son (math/yo͞o sən), *n.* **Christopher** ("*Christy*"), 1880–1925, U.S. baseball player.

Ma·thu·ra (mut/o͝o rə), *n.* a city in W Uttar Pradesh, in N India: Hindu shrine and holy city: reputed birthplace of Krishna. 123,096 (est. 1964). Formerly, **Muttra.**

ma·til·da (mə til/də), *n. Australian.* swag[2] (def. 2). [special use of proper name *Matilda*]

mat·in (mat/ᵊn, mat/in), *n.* **1. matins.** Also, *esp. Brit.*, **mattins.** (*usually construed as sing.*) *Eccles.* **a.** the first of the seven canonical hours. **b.** the service for it, properly beginning at midnight, but sometimes beginning at daybreak. **c.** Also called **Morning Prayer.** the service of public prayer, said in the morning, in the Anglican Church. **2.** a morning song, as of birds. —*adj.* **3.** Also, **mat/in·al.** pertaining to the morning or to matins. [ME *matyn* (pl. *matines*) < OF *matin* < L *mātūtīn(us)* MATUTINAL]

mat·i·née (mat/ᵊnā/; *esp. Brit.* mat/ᵊnā/), *n.* an entertainment, esp. a dramatic or musical performance, held in the daytime, usually in the afternoon. Also, **mat/i·nee/.** [< F: morning. See MATIN]

matinée/ i/dol, an actor, esp. a leading man, idolized by female audiences.

Ma·tisse (mᴀ tēs/), *n.* **Hen·ri** (äɴ ʀē/), 1869–1954, French painter.

Ma·to Gros·so (mä/to͝o gʀô/so͝o; *Eng.* mat/ə grō/sō), **1.** a plateau in SW Brazil. **2.** a state in SW Brazil. 910,262 (1960); 475,378 sq. mi. *Cap.:* Cuiabá. Also, **Matto Grosso.**

matri-, a learned borrowing from Latin meaning "mother," used in the formation of compound words: *matrilineal.* [< L, comb. form of *māter*]

ma·tri·arch (mā/trē ärk/), *n.* a woman holding a position analogous to that of a patriarch, as in a family or tribe. —**ma/tri·ar/chal, ma/tri·ar/chic,** *adj.* —**ma/tri·ar/chal·ism,** *n.*

ma·tri·ar·chate (mā/trē är/kit, -kāt), *n.* **1.** a matriarchal system or community. **2.** a social order believed to have preceded patriarchal tribal society in the early period of human communal life, embodying rule by the mothers or by all adult women.

ma·tri·ar·chy (mā/trē är/kē), *n., pl.* **-chies.** a form of social organization, as in certain primitive tribes, in which the mother is head of the family, and in which descent is reckoned in the female line, the children belonging to the mother's clan; a matriarchal system.

ma·tri·ces (mā/tri sēz/, ma/tri-), *n.* a pl. of **matrix.**

mat·ri·cide (ma/tri sīd/, mā/-), *n.* **1.** the act of killing one's mother. **2.** a person who kills his mother. [< L *mātrīcīd(ium)*, *mātrīcīd(a)*] —**mat/ri·cid/al,** *adj.*

ma·tric·u·lant (mə trik/yə lənt), *n.* a person who matriculates; a candidate for matriculation. [< LL *mātrīcul(a)* list (dim. of *mātrix* list; see MATRIX, -ULE) + -ANT]

ma·tric·u·late (*v.* mə trik/yə lāt/; *n.* mə trik/yə lit), *v.,* **-lat·ed, -lat·ing,** *n.* —*v.t.* **1.** to enroll, or admit to membership and privileges by enrolling, esp. in a college or university. —*v.i.* **2.** to be matriculated. —*n.* **3.** a person who has been matriculated. [< ML *mātrīculāt(us)* keeper, lit., person listed (for some specific duty). See MATRICULANT, -ATE[1]] —**ma·tric/u·la/tion,** *n.* —**ma·tric/u·la/tor,** *n.*

mat·ri·lin·e·al (ma/trə lin/ē əl, mā/-), *adj.* inheriting or determining descent through the female line. —**mat/ri·lin/e·al·ly,** *adv.*

mat·ri·lo·cal (ma/trə lō/kəl, mā/-), *adj. Anthropol.* of or pertaining to residence with the family or tribe of one's wife; uxorilocal. Cf. **patrilocal.** —**mat/ri·lo·cal/i·ty,** *n.*

mat·ri·mo·ni·al (ma/trə mō/nē əl), *adj.* of or pertaining to matrimony; marital; nuptial; connubial; conjugal. [< LL *mātrimōniāl(is)*] —**mat/ri·mo/ni·al·ly,** *adv.*

mat·ri·mo·ny (ma/trə mō/nē), *n., pl.* **-nies** for 1. **1.** the rite, ceremony, or sacrament of marriage. **2.** the state of marriage; wedlock. [ME < L *mātrimōni(um)* wedlock]

mat/rimony vine/, any solanaceous plant of the genus *Lycium*, species of which are cultivated for their foliage, flowers, and berries. Also called **boxthorn.**

ma·trix (mā/triks, ma/-), *n., pl.* **ma·tri·ces** (mā/tri sēz/, ma/-), **ma·trix·es,** *v.,* **ma·trixed, ma·trix·ing.** —*n.* **1.** that which gives origin or form to a thing, or which serves to enclose it: *Rome was the matrix of Western civilization.* **2.** *Anat.* a formative part, as the corium beneath a nail. **3.** *Biol.* the intercellular substance of a tissue. **4.** the fine-grained portion of a rock in which coarser crystals or rock fragments are embedded. **5.** *Mining.* gangue. **6.** *Metall.* a crystalline phase in an alloy in which other phases are embedded. **7.** *Print.* a mold for casting type faces. **8.** master (def. 15). **9.** (in a press or stamping machine) a multiple die or perforated block on which the material to be formed is placed. **10.** *Math.* the rectangular arrangement into rows and columns of the elements of a set. **11.** (in the circuit of an electronic computer) an array of components and parts, as relays, diodes, etc., for translating from one code to another. **12.** matrixing. **13.** *Archaic.* the womb. —*v.t.* **14.** to produce (a phonograph record) by electronic matrixing. [< L: female beast kept for breeding (LL: register, orig. of such beasts), womb, parent stem (of plants) < *māter* mother]

ma·trix·ing (mā/trik sing, ma/-), *n.* an electronic method of processing four-channel, or quadraphonic, sound for recording in a two-channel form, for reconversion to four channels when played back.

ma·tron (mā/trən), *n.* **1.** a married woman, esp. one with children, or one who has an established social position. **2.** a woman who has charge of the domestic affairs of an institution. **3.** a woman serving as a guard, warden, or attendant for women or girls, as in a female prison. [ME *matrone* < L *mātrōna* wife, lady < *māter* mother] —**ma·tron·al** (mā/trə nᵊl, ma/-), *adj.* —**ma/tron·hood/, ma/tron·ship/,** *n.*

ma·tron·ly (mā/trən lē), *adj.* **1.** of, pertaining to, or having the characteristics of a matron; maturely dignified and socially respected. **2.** characteristic of or suitable for a matron. —**ma/tron·li·ness,** *n.*

ma/tron of hon/or, a married woman acting as the principal attendant of the bride at a wedding.

mat·ro·nym·ic (ma/trə nim/ik), *adj.* metronymic.

MATS (mats), *n.* Military Air Transport Service.

Ma·tsu (mat so͞o/, mat/so͞o; *Chin.* mä/dzo͞o/), *n.* an island off the SE coast of China, in the East China Sea: part of Nationalist China. 11,002 (est. 1956); 17 sq. mi. Cf. **Quemoy.**

Ma·tsu·ya·ma (mä/tso͞o yä/mä), *n.* a seaport on NW Shikoku, in SW Japan. 238,514 (1960).

matt (mat), *adj., n., v.t.* mat[3].

Matt., Matthew.

Mat·ta·thi·as (mat/ə thī/əs), *n.* died 167? B.C., Jewish priest in Judea (father of Judas Maccabaeus).

matte (mat), *adj., n., v.,* **mat·ted, mat·ting.** —*adj.* **1.** (of paper) having a dull surface. Cf. **glossy** (def. 3). **2.** mat[3] (def. 1). —*n.* **3.** *Metall.* an unfinished metallic product of the smelting of certain sulfide ores, esp. those of copper. **4.** mat[3] (defs. 2, 3). —*v.t.* **5.** mat[3] (def. 4). [< F < G *matt* MAT[3]]

mat·ted[1] (mat/id), *adj.* **1.** covered with a dense growth or a tangled mass. **2.** covered with mats or matting. **3.** formed into a mat; entangled in a thick mass. **4.** formed of mats, or of plaited or woven material. [MAT[1] + -ED[2]]

mat·ted[2] (mat/id), *adj.* having a dull finish, matte. [MAT[3] + -ED[2]]

mat·ter (mat/ər), *n.* **1.** the substance or substances of which any physical object consists or is composed. **2.** physical or corporeal substance in general, whether solid, liquid, or gaseous, esp. as distinguished from incorporeal substance, as spirit or mind, or from qualities, actions, and the like. **3.** something that occupies space. **4.** a particular kind of substance: *coloring matter.* **5.** a substance discharged by a living body, esp. pus. **6.** the material or substance of a discourse, book, etc., often as distinguished from the form. **7.** something written or printed: *postal matter.* **8.** a situation, state, affair, or business: *a trivial matter.* **9.** an amount or extent reckoned approximately: *a matter of 10 miles.* **10.** something of consequence: *matter for serious thought.* **11.** importance or significance. **12.** difficulty or trouble (usually prec. by *the*). **13.** ground, reason, or cause: *a matter for complaint.* **14.** *Philos.* **a.** that which by integrative organization forms chemical substances and living things. **b.** *Aristotelianism.* that which relates to form as potentiality does to actuality. **15.** *Print.* **a.** material for work; copy. **b.** type set up. **16. a matter of life and death,** something of vital importance. **17. as a matter of fact,** in reality; actually; truthfully. **18. for that matter,** as far as that is concerned; as for that. Also, **for the matter of that. 19. no matter,** it is unimportant; it makes no difference. —*v.i.* **20.** to be of importance; signify: *It matters little.* **21.** *Pathol.* to suppurate. [ME *mater*, back formation from early ME *materie* < L *māteria* stuff, matter, wood of trees] —**mat/ter·ful,** *adj.* —**mat/ter·less,** *adj.*

Mat·ter·horn (mat/ər hôrn/), *n.* a mountain on the border of Switzerland and Italy, in the Pennine Alps. 14,780 ft. French, **Mont Cervin.**

mat/ter of course/, something that follows in logical or customary sequence: *After such reprisals, war followed as a matter of course.*

mat·ter-of-course (mat/ər əv kōrs/, -kôrs/), *adj.* **1.** occurring or proceeding in or as if in the natural course of things; expected or inevitable. **2.** accepting things as occurring in their natural course.

mat/ter of fact/, **1.** *Law.* a statement or allegation to be judged on the basis of the evidence. **2.** something of a factual nature, as an actual occurrence.

mat·ter-of-fact (mat/ər əv fakt/), *adj.* **1.** adhering strictly to fact; not imaginative. **2.** prosaic; commonplace. —**mat/ter-of-fact/ly,** *adv.* —**mat/ter-of-fact/ness,** *n.*

Mat·thew (math/yo͞o), *n.* **1.** one of the four Evangelists: one of the 12 apostles. Matt. 9:9–13. **2.** the first Gospel.

Mat/thew of Par/is, c1200–59, English chronicler. Also called **Mat/thew Par/is.**

Mat·thi·as (mə thī/əs), *n.* a disciple chosen to take the place of Judas Iscariot as one of the apostles. Acts 1:23–26.

mat·ting[1] (mat/ing), *n.* **1.** a coarse fabric of rushes, grass, straw, hemp, or the like, used for wrapping, covering floors, etc. **2.** material for mats. [MAT[1] + -ING[1]]

mat·ting[2] (mat/ing), *n.* a dull, slightly roughened surface, free from polish. [MAT[3] + -ING[1]]

mat·tins (mat/ᵊnz, -inz), *n.* (*usually construed as sing.*) *Chiefly Brit.* matin (def. 1).

mat·tock (mat/ək), *n.* an instrument for loosening the soil in digging, shaped like a pickax, but having one end broad instead of pointed. [ME *mattok*, OE *mattuc*]

Mat·to Gros·so (mä/to͝o gʀô/so͝o; *Eng.* mat/ə grō/sō). See **Mato Grosso.**

mat·tress (ma/tris), *n.* **1.** a large pad used as or on a bed, consisting of a case, usually of heavy cloth, that contains hair, straw, cotton, foam rubber, etc., or a framework of metal springs. **2.** a mat woven of brush, poles, or similar material, used to prevent erosion of the surface of dikes, jetties, etc. [ME *materas* < OF < It *materass(o)* < Ar *(al-) maṭrah* (the) mat, cushion]

mat·u·rate (mach/o͝o rāt/, mat/yo͝o-), *v.i.,* **-rat·ed, -rat·ing. 1.** *Pathol.* to suppurate. **2.** to mature. [< L *mātūrāt(us)* ripe, brought to maturity, ptp. of *mātūrāre*] —**ma·tur·a·tive** (mə cho͝or/ə tiv, mach/o͝o rā/-, mat/yo͝o-), *adj.*

mat·u·ra·tion (mach/o͝o rā/shən, mat/yo͝o-), *n.* **1.** the act or process of maturating. **2.** *Biol.* the second phase of gametogenesis, resulting in the production of mature eggs and sperms from oogonia and spermatogonia. [< medical L *mātūrātiōn-* (s. of *mātūrātiō*)] —**mat/u·ra/tion·al,** *adj.*

ma·ture (mə to͝or′, -tyo͝or′, -cho͝or′), *adj.*, *v.*, **-tured, -tur·ing.** —*adj.* **1.** complete in natural growth or development, as plant and animal forms. **2.** ripe, as fruit, or fully aged, as cheese, wine, etc. **3.** fully developed in body or mind, as a person. **4.** pertaining to or characteristic of full development. **5.** completed, perfected, or elaborated in full by the mind: *mature plans.* **6.** *Phys. Geog.* (of topographical features) exhibiting the stage of maximum stream development, as in the process of erosion of a land surface. —*v.t.* **7.** to make mature; ripen. **8.** to bring to full development. **9.** to complete or perfect. —*v.i.* **10.** to become mature; ripen. **11.** to come to full development. **12.** *Finance.* to become due, as a note. [late ME < L *mātūr(us)* ripe, timely, early; akin to MANES] —**ma·ture′ly,** *adv.* —**ma·ture′ness,** *n.* —**Syn. 1, 3.** aged, grown, adult. **2.** See **ripe.**

Ma·tu·rín (mä′to͞o rēn′), *n.* a city in NE Venezuela. 98,188.

ma·tu·ri·ty (mə to͝or′i tē, -tyo͝or′-, -cho͝or′-), *n.* **1.** the state of being mature; ripeness. **2.** full development; perfected condition. **3.** *Finance.* **a.** the state of being due. **b.** the time when a note or bill of exchange becomes due. [ME *maturite* < L *mātūritās* ripeness]

ma·tu·ti·nal (mə to͞ot′ᵊnᵊl, -tyo͞ot′-), *adj.* pertaining to or occurring in the morning; early in the day. [< LL *mātūtīnāl(is)* of, belonging to the morning, early = L *mātūtīn(us)* of the morning (*Mātūt(a)* goddess of dawn + *-īnus* -INE[1]) + *-ālis* -AL[1]] —**ma·tu′ti·nal·ly,** *adv.*

mat·zah (mät′sə; *Heb.* mä tsä′), *n.*, *pl.* **mat·zahs,** *Heb.* **ma·tzoth** (mä tsôt′). matzo.

mat·zo (mät′sə, -sō; *Heb.* mä tsä′), *n.*, *pl.* **mat·zos** (mät′səz, -sōs); *Heb.* **ma·tzoth** (mä tsôt′). **1.** unleavened bread in the form of large crackers, typically square and corrugated, eaten by Jews during Passover. **2.** one of these crackers. Also, **matzah.** [< Yiddish *matse* < Heb *maṣṣāh*]

mat′zo ball′, a dumpling made from matzo meal.

mat′zo meal′, ground matzos.

maud·lin (môd′lin), *adj.* **1.** tearfully or weakly emotional; mawkishly sentimental: *a maudlin story of a little orphan and her lost doggy.* **2.** mawkishly drunk or pertaining to mawkish drunkenness. [special use of *Maudlin,* ME *Maudelen* << LL *Magdalene* < Gk *Magdalēnē* Mary Magdalene, portrayed in art as a weeping penitent] —**maud′lin·ism,** *n.* —**maud′lin·ly,** *adv.* —**maud′lin·ness,** *n.*

Maugham (môm), *n.* **W(illiam) Som·er·set** (sum′ər set′, -sit), 1874–1965, English novelist, dramatist, and short-story writer.

mau·gre (mô′gər), *prep.* *Archaic.* in spite of; notwithstanding. Also, **mau′ger.** [ME < MF: lit., spite, ill will. See MAL-, GREE[2]]

Ma·u·i (mä′o͞o ē′; *Eng.* mou′ē), *n.* an island in central Hawaii. 728 sq. mi.

maul (môl), *n.* **1.** a heavy hammer, as for driving piles. **2.** *Archaic.* a heavy club or mace. —*v.t.* **3.** to handle or use roughly. **4.** to injure by a rough beating, shoving, or the like; bruise. **5.** *U.S.* to split with a maul and wedge. Also, **mall.** [ME *malle* (n.) < OF *mail* mallet, hammer < L *malle(us)* hammer; ME *malle(n)* (v.) < OF *maill(ier)* < n.] —**maul′er,** *n.*

Maul·main (mōl mān′, môl-), *n.* Moulmein.

maul·stick (môl′stik′), *n.* mahlstick.

Mau Mau (mou′ mou′), *pl.* **Mau Maus,** (*esp. collectively*) **Mau Mau.** a member of a revolutionary tribal society in Kenya that engaged in terrorist activities in an attempt to drive out Europeans: active from 1952 to 1956. [<Kikuyu]

mau·met (mô′mit), *n.* *Obs.* an idol; a false god. [ME < OF *mahommet* idol, special use of *Mahommet* MOHAMMED, whose image was thought to be an object of worship]

maun (män, môn), *auxiliary v.* *Scot.* must. Also, **man.** [ME *man* < Scand; cf. Icel *man* must, shall, will]

Mau·na Ke·a (mou′nə kā′ə, mô′nə kē′ə; *Hawaiian.* mä′o͞o nä′ kā′ä), an extinct volcano on the island of Hawaii. 13,784 ft.

Mau·na Lo·a (mou′nə lō′ə, mô′nə; *Hawaiian.* mä′o͞o nä′ lō′ä), an active volcano on the island of Hawaii. 13,680 ft.

maund (mônd), *n.* a unit of weight in India and other parts of Asia, varying greatly according to locality: in India, from about 25 to 82.286 pounds (the latter being the government maund). [< Hindi *man* < Skt *manā*]

maun·der (môn′dər), *v.i.* **1.** to talk in a rambling, foolish, or meaningless way. **2.** to move, go, or act in an aimless, confused manner. [?] —**maun′der·er,** *n.*

maund·y (môn′dē), *n.* the ceremony of washing the feet of the poor, esp. commemorating Jesus' washing of His disciples' feet on Maundy Thursday. [ME *maunde* < OF *mande* < L *mandāt(um)* command, MANDATE (from the opening phrase *novum mandātum* (Vulgate) of Jesus' words to the disciples after he had washed their feet)]

Maun′dy Thurs′day, the Thursday of Holy Week, commemorating Jesus' Last Supper and His washing of the disciples' feet upon that day.

Mau·pas·sant (mō′pə sänt′; *Fr.* mō pa säN′), *n.* **(Hen·ri Re·né Al·bert) Guy de** (äN rə′ rə nā′ al ber′ gē də), 1850–93, French short-story writer and novelist.

Mau·re·ta·ni·a (môr′i tā′nē ə), *n.* an ancient kingdom in NW Africa: it included the territory that is modern Morocco and part of Algeria. Also, **Mauritania.** —**Mau′re·ta′ni·an,** *adj.*, *n.*

Mau·riac (mō ryäk′), *n.* **Fran·çois** (fräN swa′), 1885–1970, French novelist: Nobel prize 1952.

Mau·rice (môr′is, mor′-, mō rēs′), *n.* **1.** German, **Moritz.** 1521–53, German general: elector of Saxony 1547–53. **2. of Nassau,** 1567–1625, Dutch statesman.

Mau·ri·ta·ni·a (môr′i tā′nē ə), *n.* **1.** Official name, **Islamic Republic of Mauritania.** a republic in W Africa, largely in the Sahara Desert: formerly a French colony; now an independent member of the French Community. 1,500,000; 418,120 sq. mi. *Cap.:* Nouakchott. **2.** Mauretania. —**Mau′ri·ta′ni·an,** *adj.*, *n.*

Mau·ri·tius (mô rish′əs, -rish′ē əs), *n.* **1.** an island in the Indian Ocean, E of Madagascar. 880,781; 720 sq. mi. **2.** a republic consisting of this island and dependencies: formerly a British colony. 900,000; 809 sq. mi. *Cap.:* Port Louis. —**Mau·ri′tian,** *adj.*, *n.*

Mau·rois (mō rwa′), *n.* **An·dré** (äN drā′), (pen name of *Émile Solomon Wilhelm Herzog*), 1885–1967, French biographer and novelist.

Mau·ry (môr′ē, mor′ē), *n.* **Matthew Fon·taine** (fon tān′, fon′tān), 1806–73, U.S. naval officer and scientist.

mau·so·le·um (mô′sə lē′əm, -zə-), *n.*, *pl.* **-le·ums, -le·a** (-lē′ə). **1.** a sepulchral or stately monument, often architecturally noteworthy. **2.** a structure for the interment of many bodies. **3.** (*cap.*) the tomb erected at Halicarnassus in Asia Minor in 350? B.C. Cf. **Seven Wonders of the World.** [< L < Gk *mausōleîon* the tomb of *Mausolus,* king of Caria] —**mau′so·le′an,** *adj.*

mauve (mōv), *n.* **1.** pale bluish purple. **2.** a purple dye obtained from aniline, discovered in 1856; the first of the coal-tar dyes. —*adj.* **3.** of the color of mauve: *a mauve dress.* [< F: lit., mallow < L *malva* MALLOW]

mauve′ dec′ade, the 1890's as a social and cultural period, characterized by prosperity and complacency.

mav·er·ick (mav′ər ik, mav′rik), *n.* **1.** *Southwestern U.S.* an unbranded calf, cow, or steer, esp. a motherless calf. **2.** a person who takes an independent stand apart from his associates. [after Samuel A. *Maverick* (1803–70), Texas pioneer who did not brand his cattle]

ma·vin (mā′vən), *n.* an expert, esp. in everyday matters. Also, **ma′ven.** [< Yiddish < Heb: connoisseur]

ma·vis (mā′vis), *n.* a common European songbird, *Turdus philomelos.* [ME *mavys* thrush < MF *mauvis* < ?]

ma·vour·neen (mə vo͝or′nēn, -vōr′-, -vôr′-), *n.* *Irish English.* darling; dear. Also, **ma·vour′nin.** [< Ir *mo mhuirnín*]

maw[1] (mô), *n.* **1.** the mouth, throat, or gullet of an animal, esp. a carnivorous mammal. **2.** the crop or craw of a fowl. **3.** the stomach, esp. that of an animal. **4.** a cavernous opening that resembles the jaws of an animal. [ME *mawe,* OE *maga;* c. D *maag,* G *Magen,* Icel *magi*]

maw[2] (mô), *n.* *Dial.* mother. [var. of MA]

mawk·ish (mô′kish), *adj.* **1.** having a faint sickly flavor; insipid. **2.** sickly sentimental; feebly emotional. [obs. *mawk* MAGGOT (late ME < Scand; cf. Icel *mathkr* maggot) + -ISH[1]] —**mawk′ish·ly,** *adv.* —**mawk′ish·ness,** *n.*

max., maximum.

max·i (mak′sē), *n.* *Informal.* a maxiskirt. [by shortening]

maxi-, a combining form of **maximum,** used with the following particular meanings: "very long," "very large" (*maxiskirt*); "of the greatest scope or intensity" (*maxiservice*).

max·il·la (mak sil′ə), *n.*, *pl.* **max·il·lae** (mak sil′ē). **1.** a jaw or jawbone, esp. the upper. **2.** one of the paired appendages immediately behind the mandibles of arthropods. [< NL, special use of L: lower jaw, dim. of *māla* (earlier **maxla*) upper jaw, cheekbone]

max·il·lar·y (mak′sə ler′ē, mak sil′ə rē), *adj.*, *n.*, *pl.* **-lar·ies.** —*adj.* **1.** of or pertaining to a jaw, jawbone, or maxilla. —*n.* **2.** a maxilla or maxillary bone. [< L *maxillār(is)* of, belonging to the jaw]

max·il·li·ped (mak sil′ə ped′), *n.* one member of the three pairs of appendages situated immediately behind the maxillae of crustaceans. —**max′il·li·ped′a·ry,** *adj.*

max·im (mak′sim), *n.* **1.** an expression of a general truth or principle, esp. an aphoristic or sententious one. **2.** a principle of conduct. [ME *maxime* < MF < ML *maxima* (orig. in phrase *maxima prōpositiō* axiom, lit., greatest proposition), fem. of L *maximus;* see MAXIMUM] —**Syn. 1.** aphorism, saying, adage. See **proverb.**

Max·im (mak′sim), *n.* **1. Hiram Percy,** 1869–1936, U.S. inventor. **2.** his father, **Sir Hiram Stevens,** 1840–1916, English inventor, born in the U.S. **3. Hudson,** 1853–1927, U.S. inventor and explosives expert (brother of Sir Hiram).

max·i·ma (mak′sə mə), *n.* a pl. of **maximum.**

max·i·mal (mak′sə məl), *adj.* of or being a maximum; greatest possible. [MAXIM(UM) + -AL[1]] —**max′i·mal·ly,** *adv.*

Max·i·mil·ian (mak′sə mil′yən), *n.* 1832–67, archduke of Austria: emperor of Mexico 1864–67.

Maximilian I, 1459–1519, emperor of the Holy Roman Empire 1493–1519.

Maximilian II, 1527–76, emperor of the Holy Roman Empire 1564–76.

max·i·mise (mak′sə mīz′), *v.t.*, **-mised, -mis·ing.** *Chiefly Brit.* maximize. —**max′i·mi·sa′tion, max′i·ma′tion,** *n.*

max·i·mize (mak′sə mīz′), *v.t.*, **-mized, -miz·ing.** to increase to the greatest possible amount or degree. —**max′i·mi·za′tion, max′i·ma′tion,** *n.* —**max′i·miz′er,** *n.*

max·i·mum (mak′sə məm), *n.*, *pl.* **-mums, -ma** (-mə), *adj.* —*n.* **1.** the greatest quantity or amount possible, assignable, attained, etc. (opposed to *minimum*). **2.** *Math.* **a.** the value of a function at a certain point in its domain greater than or equal to the values at all other points in the immediate vicinity of the point. Cf. **absolute maximum. b.** the point in the domain at which a maximum occurs. —*adj.* **3.** amounting to a maximum; greatest possible; highest. **4.** pertaining to a maximum or maximums. [< L, n. use of neut. of *maximus,* superl. of *magnus* great, large. See MUCH] —**max′i·mum·ly,** *adv.*

max·well (maks′wəl, -wel), *n.* *Elect.* the centimeter-gram-second unit of magnetic flux, equal to the magnetic flux through one square centimeter normal to a magnetic field of one gauss. *Abbr.:* Mx Also called **line.** [named after J. C. MAXWELL]

Max·well (maks′wəl, -wel), *n.* **James Clerk** (klärk), 1831–79, Scottish physicist.

Max′well de′mon, *Physics.* a hypothetical agent or device of arbitrarily small mass that is considered selectively to admit or block the passage of individual molecules from one compartment to another according to their speed: constituting a violation of the second law of thermodynamics. [named after J. C. MAXWELL]

may[1] (mā), *v.*, *pres. sing. 1st pers.* **may,** *2nd* **may** or (*Archaic*) **may·est** or **mayst,** *3rd* **may;** *pres. pl.* **may;** *past* **might. 1.** (used to express wish or prayer): *May you live long!* **2.** (used to express contingency, esp. in clauses indicating condition, result, etc.): *I may be wrong, but I think you would be wise to go.* **3.** (used to express possibility, opportunity, or permission): *It may rain. You may enter.* **4.** *Archaic.* (used to express ability or power.) [OE *mæg,* 1st and 3rd pers. sing. pres. ind. of *magan,* c. G *mögen*] —**Syn. 3.** See **can[1].**

may[2] (mā), *n.* *Archaic.* a maiden.

May (mā), *n.* **Cape,** a cape at the SE tip of New Jersey, on Delaware Bay.

May (mā), *n.* **1.** the fifth month of the year, containing 31 days. **2.** the early part of one's life, esp. the prime. **3.** the festivities of May Day. **4.** (*l.c.*) *Brit.* the hawthorn. —*v.i.* **5.** (*l.c.*) to gather flowers in the spring. [ME; OE *Maius* < L, short for *Maius mēnsis* Maia's month]

ma·ya (mä′yä, -yə), *n.* *Hinduism.* **1.** the power, as of a god, to produce illusions. **2.** the production of an illusion. **3.** (in Vedantic philosophy) the illusion of the reality of sensory experience and of the experienced qualities and attributes of oneself. **4.** (*cap.*) Also called **Mahamaya.** a goddess personifying the power that creates phenomena. [< Skt] —**ma′yan,** *adj.*

Ma·ya (mä′yə), *n., pl.* **-yas,** (*esp. collectively*) **-ya. 1.** a member of a highly civilized Amerindian people of pre-Columbian Yucatán. **2.** the historical and modern language of the Mayas, of Mayan stock.

Ma·ya·güez (mä′yä gwes′), *n.* a seaport in W Puerto Rico. 68,872 (1970).

Ma·yan (mä′yən), *adj.* **1.** of or pertaining to the Mayas. —*n.* **2.** a member of the Mayan tribe. **3.** a linguistic stock of southern Mexico, Guatemala, and British Honduras, including Maya and Quiché, and probably related to Penutian.

May′ ap′ple, 1. a perennial, American herb, *Podophyllum peltatum,* bearing an edible, yellowish, egg-shaped fruit. **2.** the fruit itself.

may·be (mā′bē), *adv.* perhaps; possibly: *Maybe I'll go too.* [late ME *may be,* short for *it may be*]

May′ Day′, the first day of May, long celebrated with various festivities, as the crowning of the May queen, dancing around the Maypole, and, in recent years, often marked by labor parades and political demonstrations. [late ME] —**May′-day′,** *adj.*

May·day (mā′dā′), *n.* the international radiotelephone distress signal, used by ships and aircraft. [< pseudo-F *m'aidez* help me]

may·est (mā′ist), *v.* *Archaic.* 2nd pers. sing. pres. indic. of **may.**

May·fair (mā′fâr′), *n.* a fashionable locality in London, England, E of Hyde Park.

May·flow·er (mā′flou′ər), *n.* **1.** (*italics*) the ship in which the Pilgrim Fathers sailed from England to America in 1620. **2.** any of various plants that blossom in May, as the trailing arbutus, hepatica, or anemone in the U.S., and the hawthorn or cowslip in England.

may·fly (mā′flī′), *n., pl.* **-flies. 1.** any insect of the order *Ephemeroptera,* having delicate, membranous wings with the front pair much larger than the rear and having an aquatic larval stage and a brief, terrestrial adult stage. **2.** *Angling.* an artificial fly made to resemble this insect. Also, **May′ fly′.**

Mayfly, *Hexagenia limbata* (Body length 1 in.)

may·hap (mā′hap′, mā′hap′), *adv.* *Archaic.* perhaps. [short for *it may hap*]

may·hem (mā′hem, mā′əm), *n.* *Law.* the crime of willfully inflicting a bodily injury on another so as to make him less able to defend himself or, under modern statutes, so as to cripple or mutilate him. Also, **maihem.** [ME *maheym, maim* < AF *mahem,* etc. < Gmc; akin to MHG *meidem* gelding, Icel *meitha* to injure. See MAIM]

May·ing (mā′ing), *n.* the celebration of May Day. [late ME]

may·n't (mā′ənt, mānt), contraction of *may not.*

may·o (mā′ō), *n.* *Informal.* mayonnaise. [by shortening]

May·o (mā′ō), *n.* **1. Charles Horace,** 1865–1939, and his brother **William James,** 1861–1939, U.S. surgeons. **2.** a county in NW Connaught province, in the NW Republic of Ireland. 123,330 (1961); 2084 sq. mi. *Co. seat:* Castlebar.

Ma·yon (mä yôn′), *n.* an active volcano in the Philippines, on SE Luzon Island. 7926 ft.

may·on·naise (mā′ə nāz′, mā′ə nāz′), *n.* a thick dressing of egg yolks, vinegar or lemon juice, seasonings, and oil, used for salads, sandwiches, vegetable dishes, etc. [< F = *mayon* (? var. of *Mahón,* town in Minorca) + *-aise* -ESE]

may·or (mā′ər, mâr), *n.* **1.** the chief executive official of a city, town, or village. **2.** the chief magistrate of a city or borough. [< ML *māior,* sp. var. of *mājor* MAJOR; r. ME *mer, mair* < OF *maire*] —**may′or·al,** *adj.* —**may′or·ship′,** *n.*

may·or·al·ty (mā′ər əl tē, mâr′əl-), *n., pl.* **-ties.** the office or tenure of a mayor. [alter. of ME *mairaltee* < MF *mairalte*]

may·or·ess (mā′ər is, mâr′is), *n.* **1.** a woman mayor. **2.** *Brit.* a woman chosen by the mayor to be a town's first lady, usually the mayor's wife, daughter, sister, etc. [MAYOR + -ESS; r. ME *meyresse*]

Ma·yotte (*Fr.* MA yôt′), *n.* one of the Comoro Islands, in the Indian Ocean, NW of Madagascar: an overseas department of France. 52,000; 143 sq. mi.

May·pole (mā′pōl′), *n.* (*often l.c.*) a high pole, decorated with flowers and ribbons, around which revelers dance during May Day celebrations.

may·pop (mā′pop′), *n.* **1.** the edible fruit of a passion flower, *Passiflora incarnata,* of the southern U.S. **2.** the plant itself. [? repr. a Virginia var. of Algonquian *maracock*]

May′ queen′, a girl or young woman crowned with flowers and honored as queen in the sports of May Day.

Mays (māz), *n.* **Willie (Howard),** born 1931, U. S. baseball player.

mayst (māst), *v.* *Archaic.* 2nd pers. sing. pres. indic. of **may.**

May·time (mā′tīm′), *n.* the month of May. Also called **May·tide** (mā′tīd′).

may′ tree′, *Brit.* the hawthorn.

may·weed (mā′wēd′), *n.* a composite herb, *Anthemis Cotula,* native to Europe and Asia but naturalized in North America, having pungent, rank-scented foliage and flower heads with a yellow disk and white rays. [obs. *may(th)* mayweed (OE *mægtha*) + WEED^1]

May′ wine′, a punch consisting esp. of Alsatian, Moselle, or Rhine wine, flavored with woodruff.

May·wood (mā′wo͝od′), *n.* a city in NE Illinois, near Chicago. 29,019 (1970).

ma·zal tov (mä′zəl tôv′, tôf′, tōv′). See **mazel tov.**

maz·ard (maz′ərd), *n.* **1.** *Archaic.* **a.** head. **b.** face. **2.** *Obs.* a mazer. [MAZ(ER) + -ARD]

Maz·a·rin (maz′ə rin, maz′ə rēn′; *Fr.* MA ZA RAN′), *n.* **Jules** (jo͞olz; *Fr.* zhYl), (*Giulio Mazarini*), 1602–61, French cardinal and statesman, born in Italy.

Ma·zat·lán (mä′sät län′), *n.* a seaport in S Sinaloa, in W Mexico. 169,500.

Maz·da (maz′də), *n.* *Zoroastrianism.* See **Ahura Mazda.**

Maz·da·ism (maz′də iz′əm), *n.* Zoroastrianism.

maze (māz), *n., v.,* **mazed, maz·ing.** —*n.* **1.** a confusing network of intercommunicating paths or passages; a labyrinth. **2.** a state of bewilderment, confusion, or perplexity. **3.** a winding movement, as in dancing. —*v.t.* **4.** *Chiefly Dial.* to stupefy or daze. [ME *mase,* aph. var. of *amase(n)* (to) AMAZE] —**mazed·ly** (māzd′lē, mā′zid-), *adv.* —**mazed′ness,** *n.* —**maze′like′,** *adj.*

ma·zel tov (mä′zel tôv′, tôf′, tōv′), a Jewish expression of congratulations and best wishes. Also, **mazal tov.** [< Yiddish < Heb: lit., good luck]

ma·zer (mā′zər), *n.* a large metal drinking bowl or cup, formerly of wood. [early ME: kind of wood (prob. maple), OE *mæser-* (in adj. *mæseren* = *mæser* maple + *-en* -EN^2); c. Icel *mösurr* maple, MHG *maser* maple, drinking cup]

ma·zu·ma (mə zo͞o′mə), *n.* *Slang.* money. [< Yiddish *mezumen* < Heb *mezūmān* set, fixed]

ma·zur·ka (mə zûr′kə, -zo͝or′-), *n.* **1.** a lively Polish dance in moderately quick triple meter. **2.** music for, or in the rhythm of, this dance. Also, **ma·zour′ka.** [< Pol = *Mazur* Mazovia (district in northern Poland) + *-ka* suffix of appurtenance]

ma·zy (mā′zē), *adj.,* **-zi·er, -zi est.** full of confusing turns, passages, etc.; like a maze; labyrinthine. —**ma′zi·ly,** *adv.* —**ma′zi·ness,** *n.*

maz·zard (maz′ərd), *n.* a wild sweet cherry, *Prunus avium,* used as a rootstock for cultivated varieties of cherries. [earlier *mazer;* cf. obs. *mazers* spots, MEASLES]

Maz·zi·ni (mät tsē′nē; *Eng.* mat sē′nē, mad zē′-), *n.* **Giu·sep·pe** (jo͞o zep′pe), 1805–72, Italian patriot and revolutionary. —**Maz·zi·ni·an** (mat sē′nē ən, mad zē′-), *adj., n.*

mb, 1. millibar; millibars. **2.** millibarn; millibarns.

M.B., *Chiefly Brit.* Bachelor of Medicine. [< L *Medicinae Baccalaureus*]

M'Ba (ᵊmbä), *n.* **Lé·on** (le ôN′), 1902–67, African statesman: president of the Republic of Gabon 1961–67.

M.B.A., Master of Business Administration.

Mba·ba·ne (ᵊmbä bä′nä), *n.* a city in and the capital of Swaziland, in the NW part. 8400 (1963).

M·ban·da·ka (ᵊmbän′dä kä), *n.* a city in W Zaïre. 134,495. Formerly, **Coquilhatville.**

M.B.E., Member of the Order of the British Empire.

MBFR, *Mil.* Mutual and Balanced Force Reductions.

Mbo·mu (ᵊmbō′mo͞o), *n.* Bomu.

Mboy·a (ᵊmboi′ə), *n.* **Tom** (*Thomas Joseph Mboya*), 1930–69, African political leader in Kenya.

MC, 1. Marine Corps. **2.** Medical Corps. **3.** Member of Congress.

Mc, 1. megacurie; megacuries. **2.** megacycle; megacycles.

mc, 1. megacycle; megacycles. **2.** millicurie; millicuries.

Mc-, var. of **Mac-.** Also, **M**^{c}**-.**

M.C., 1. Master Commandant. **2.** See **master of ceremonies. 3.** Medical Corps. **4.** Member of Congress. **5.** *Brit.* Military Cross.

Mc·A·doo (mak′ə do͞o′), *n.* **William Gibbs,** 1863–1941, U.S. lawyer and statesman: Secretary of the Treasury 1913–18.

Mc·Al·len (mə kal′ən), *n.* a city in S Texas, on the Rio Grande. 37,636 (1970).

Mc·Car·thy (mə kär′thē), *n.* **1. Joseph R(aymond)** ("*Joe*"), 1909–57, U.S. politician: investigated alleged Communist influence and infiltration into government. **2. Mary (Therese),** born 1912, U.S. writer.

Mc·Car·thy·ism (mə kär′thē iz′əm), *n.* *U.S.* **1.** the practice of making accusations of disloyalty, esp. of pro-Communist activity, often unsupported or based on doubtful evidence. **2.** the attempt to restrict individual dissent or political criticism by claiming that it is pro-Communistic or unpatriotic. [J. R. MCCARTHY + -ISM]

Mc·Clel·lan (mə klel′ən), *n.* **George Brin·ton** (brin′tən, tᵊn), 1826–85, Union general in the U.S. Civil War.

Mc·Cloy (mə kloi′), *n.* **John Jay,** born 1895, U.S. lawyer, banker, and government official.

Mc·Cor·mack (mə kôr′mik), *n.* **1. John,** 1884–1945, U.S. tenor, born in Ireland. **2. John William,** 1891–1980, U.S. politician: Speaker of the House 1962–70.

Mc·Cor·mick (mə kôr′mik), *n.* **Cyrus Hall,** 1809–84, U.S. inventor, esp. of harvesting machinery.

Mc·Coy (mə koi′), *n.* *Slang.* the genuine thing or person as promised, stated, or implied (usually prec. by *the* or *the real*): *Those other paintings are copies, but this one is the McCoy.* [said to refer to a U.S. pugilist, Kid *McCoy,* distinguishing him from an obscure or inferior boxer of the same name]

Mc·Cul·lers (mə kul′ərz), *n.* **Car·son** (kär′sən), 1917–67, U.S. novelist and short-story writer.

Mc·Dow·ell (mək dou′əl), *n.* **Irvin,** 1818–85, Union general in the U.S. Civil War.

Mcf, one thousand cubic feet.

Mc·Fee (mək fē′), *n.* **William,** 1881–1966, English writer.

Mc·Graw (mə grô′), *n.* **John Joseph,** 1873–1934, U.S. baseball player and manager.

Mc·Guf·fey (mə guf′ē), *n.* **William Holmes,** 1800–73, U.S. educator: editor of children's readers.

Mc·Hen·ry (mək hen′rē, mə ken′-), *n.* **Fort.** See **Fort McHenry.**

MCi, megacurie; megacuries.

mCi, millicurie; millicuries.

Mc·In·tosh (mak′in tosh′), *n.* a variety of red apple that ripens in early autumn. [named after John *McIntosh* of Ontario, Canada, who first cultivated it (1796)]

Mc·In·tyre (mak′in tīər′), *n.* **James Francis Aloysius,** 1886–1979, U.S. Roman Catholic clergyman: cardinal from 1953; archbishop of Los Angeles 1948–70.

Mc·Kees·port (mə kēz′pôrt′, -pōrt′), *n.* a city in SW Pennsylvania, near Pittsburgh. 37,977 (1970).

Mc·Kin·ley (mə kin′lē), *n.* **1. William,** 1843–1901, 25th president of the U.S. 1897–1901. **2. Mount,** a mountain in central Alaska: highest peak in North America. 20,300 ft.

Mc·Leod′ gauge′ (mə kloud′), a device for determining very low gas pressures by measuring the pressure of a sample after compressing it to a known fraction of its original volume. [named after H. *McLeod* (1841–1932), English chemist]

Mc·Lu·han (mə klo͞o′ən), *n.* **Marshall,** 1911–80, Canadian cultural historian and mass-communications theorist.

Mc·Mur′do Sound′ (mək mûr′dō), an inlet of Ross Sea, in Antarctica, N of Victoria Land.

Mc·Na·ma·ra (mak′nə mar′ə), *n.* **Robert Strange** (strānj), born 1916, U.S. business executive and government official.

MD, 1. Maryland (approved esp. for use with zip code). 2. Middle Dutch.

Md, *Chem.* mendelevium.

Md., Maryland.

M.D., 1. Doctor of Medicine. [< L *Medicinae Doctor*] 2. Middle Dutch.

M-day (em′dā′), *n.* *Mil.* mobilization day: a day assumed by the Department of Defense as the first day of mobilization, used by the military for planning purposes.

mdse., merchandise.

me (mē), *pron.* **1.** the objective case of **I,** both as direct and as indirect object: *They asked me to the party. Give me your hand.* **2.** *Informal.* (used instead of the pronoun *my* in gerundive constructions): *Did you hear about me getting promoted?* [ME *me,* OE *mē* (dat. sing.); c. D *mij, mir;* akin to L *mē* (acc.)]
—Usage. 2. In traditional grammar a gerund, being considered syntactically identical to a noun, requires modification by the genitive form of the noun or pronoun preceding it. Hence, traditional grammarians insist on constructions like: *She likes my* (rather than *me*) *singing her to sleep.* This is true of all pronominal constructions (HIS, HER, ITS, OUR, THEIR, and YOUR), as well as of noun-gerund combinations (*He hates the carpenter's making so much noise*). However, many writers and speakers do not follow this tradition.

ME, 1. Maine (approved esp. for use with zip code). 2. Middle English. 3. Middle East.

Me., Maine.

M.E., 1. (*often l.c.*) managing editor. 2. Master of Education. 3. Master of Engineering. 4. Mechanical Engineer. 5. Methodist Episcopal. 6. Middle English. 7. Mining Engineer.

me·a cul·pa (me′ä ko͝ol′pä; *Eng.* mē′ə kul′pə), *Latin.* through my fault; my fault.

mead[1] (mēd), *n.* an alcoholic liquor made by fermenting honey and water. [ME *mede,* OE *meodu;* c. D *mee,* G *Met,* Icel *mjöthr* mead, Skt *madhu* honey, Gk *méthy* wine]

mead[2] (mēd), *n.* *Archaic.* meadow. [ME *mede,* OE *mǣd.* See MEADOW]

Mead (mēd), *n.* **1. Margaret,** 1901–78, U.S. anthropologist. **2. Lake,** a lake in NW Arizona and SE Nevada, formed by Boulder Dam. 115 mi. long; 227 sq. mi.

Meade (mēd), *n.* **George Gordon,** 1815–72, Union general in the U.S. Civil War.

mead·ow (med′ō), *n.* **1.** a tract of grassland used for pasture or serving as a hayfield. **2.** a tract of grassland in an upland area near the timber line. [ME *medwe,* OE *mǣdw-,* in inflectional forms of *mǣd* MEAD[2]; akin to G *Matte*] **—mead′ow·less,** *adj.*

mead′ow grass′, any grass of the genus *Poa,* esp. *P. pratensis,* the Kentucky bluegrass.

mead·ow·lark (med′ō lärk′), *n.* any of several American songbirds of the genus *Sturnella,* of the family *Icteridae,* esp. *S. magna* and *S. neglecta,* having a brownish and black back and wings and a yellow breast, noted for their clear, tuneful song.

Meadowlark, *Sturnella neglecta* (Length 9 in.)

mead′ow mouse′, any of numerous short-tailed rodents of the genus *Microtus* and allied genera, found chiefly in fields and meadows of the temperate Northern Hemisphere.

mead′ow mush′room. See under **mushroom** (def. 2).

mead′ow rue′, a ranunculaceous plant of the genus *Thalictrum,* having leaves resembling those of rue, esp. *T. dioicum,* of North America.

mead·ow·sweet (med′ō swēt′), *n.* **1.** any rosaceous plant of the genus *Spiraea,* esp. *S. latifolia,* having white or pink flowers. **2.** any plant of the closely related genus *Filipendula* (or *Ulmaria*).

mea·ger (mē′gər), *adj.* **1.** deficient in quantity or quality; lacking fullness or richness; poor; scanty: *a meager salary; a meager harvest.* **2.** having little flesh; lean; thin: *a body meager with hunger.* **3.** maigre. Also, *esp. Brit.,* **mea′gre.** [ME *megre* < OF *maigre* < L *macer* lean] **—mea′ger·ly;** *esp. Brit.,* **mea′gre·ly,** *adv.* **—mea′ger·ness;** *esp. Brit.,* **mea′gre·ness,** *n.* **—Syn. 1.** See **scanty. —Ant. 1.** abundant.

meal[1] (mēl), *n.* **1.** one of the regular occasions during the day when food is taken. **2.** the food served or eaten at such occasions. [ME; OE *mǣl* measure, fixed time, occasion, meal; c. G *Mal* time, *Mahl* meal, ON *māl,* Goth *mēl* time, hour] **—meal′less,** *adj.*

meal[2] (mēl), *n.* **1.** a coarse, unsifted powder ground from the edible seeds of any grain: *wheat meal.* **2.** any ground or powdery substance, as of nuts or seeds, resembling this. [ME *mele,* OE *melu;* c. G *Mehl,* D *meel,* Icel *mjöl;* akin to Goth *malan,* L *molere* to grind. See MILL[1]] **—meal′less,** *adj.*

-meal, a native English combining form, now largely obsolete, denoting a fixed measure at a time: *piecemeal.* [ME *-mele,* OE *-mǣlum,* comb. form repr. *mǣl* MEAL[1]]

meal·ie (mē′lē), *n.* (in Africa) **1. mealies,** corn[1] (def. 1a). **2.** an ear of corn. [< SAfrD *mielie* < Pg *milho* maize, millet < L *milium* MILLET]

meal′ tick′et, **1.** a ticket that entitles the bearer to meals in a specified restaurant, esp. at reduced rates. **2.** *Slang.* someone upon whom one is dependent for one's income or livelihood.

meal·time (mēl′tīm′), *n.* the usual time for a meal. [ME *meeltyme*]

meal·worm (mēl′wûrm′), *n.* the larva of any of several darkling beetles of the genus *Tenebrio,* which infests granaries.

meal·y (mē′lē), *adj.,* **meal·i·er, meal·i·est. 1.** having the qualities of meal; powdery. **2.** of the nature of or containing meal; farinaceous. **3.** covered with or as with meal or powder. **4.** colored as if flecked with meal; spotty. **5.** pale, as the complexion; sallow. **6.** mealy-mouthed. **—meal′i·ness,** *n.*

meal·y·bug (mē′lē bug′), *n.* any of several scalelike, homopterous insects of the family *Pseudococcidae* that are covered with a powdery, waxy secretion.

meal·y-mouthed (mē′lē mouthd′, -moutht′), *adj.* avoiding the use of direct and plain language, as from timidity, excessive delicacy, or hypocrisy. **—meal·y-mouth·ed·ly** (mē′lē mou′thid lē, -thid-, -moutht′-), *adv.* **—meal′y-mouth′ed·ness,** *n.*

mean[1] (mēn), *v.,* **meant, mean·ing.** **—*v.t.* 1.** to have in mind as one's purpose or intention; intend: *I mean to talk to him about the show.* **2.** to intend for a particular purpose, destination, etc.: *They were meant for each other.* **3.** to intend to express or indicate: *What do you mean by "liberal"?* **4.** to have as the sense or signification; signify: *The word "freedom" means many things to many people.* **5.** to bring, cause, or produce as a result: *This bonus means that we can take a trip to Florida.* **6.** to have (certain intentions) toward a person. **7.** to have the value of; assume the importance of: *Money means everything to him.* **—*v.i.* 8.** to be minded or disposed; have intentions. **9. mean well,** to have good intentions; try to be kind or helpful. [ME *mene(n),* OE *mǣnan;* c. G *meinen,* D *meenen*] **—Syn. 1.** contemplate. **2.** destine, foreordain. **4.** denote, indicate; import, imply, connote.

mean[2] (mēn), *adj.* **1.** inferior in grade, quality, or character: *no mean scholar.* **2.** low in station, rank, or dignity. **3.** of little importance or consequence: *mean little details.* **4.** unimposing or shabby. **5.** small-minded or ignoble. **6.** penurious, stingy, or miserly. **7.** offensive, selfish, or unaccommodating. **8.** *Informal.* troublesome or vicious, as a horse. **9.** *Slang.* skillful or impressive: *He blows a mean trumpet.* [ME *mene,* aph. var. of *imene,* OE *gemǣne;* c. G *gemein,* D *gemeen* common, Goth *gemains* in common]
—Syn. 2. common, humble; plebeian. **3.** inconsequent, insignificant, petty. **4.** squalid, poor. **5.** contemptible, despicable. MEAN, LOW, BASE, VILE all refer to ignoble characteristics worthy of dislike, contempt, or disgust. MEAN suggests pettiness and small-mindedness: *to take a mean advantage.* Low suggests coarseness and vulgarity: *low company.* BASE suggests selfish cowardice or moral depravity: *base motives.* VILE suggests disgusting foulness or repulsiveness: *vile insinuation; a vile creature.* **6.** niggardly, close, tight, parsimonious, selfish. **—Ant. 1.** superior. **2.** exalted. **3.** important. **6.** generous.

mean[3] (mēn), *n.* **1.** Usually, **means.** (*often construed as sing.*) an agency, instrument, or method used to attain an end. **2. means, a.** available resources, esp. money. **b.** considerable financial resources; riches: *a man of means.* **3.** something midway between two extremes. **4.** *Math.* **a.** a quantity having a value intermediate between the values of other quantities; an average, esp. the arithmetic mean. **b.** either the second or third term in a proportion of four terms. **5.** *Statistics.* See **expected value.** Cf. **arithmetic mean, geometric mean, harmonic mean. 6.** *Logic.* the middle term in a syllogism. **7. by all means, a.** at any cost; without fail. **b.** (in emphasis) certainly. **8. by means of,** with the help of; through the use of: *We crossed the stream by means of a log.* **9. by no means,** in no way; not at all. **10. not by any means,** not in any way; absolutely not. **—*adj.* 11.** occupying a middle position or an intermediate place, as in kind or quality. [ME *mene* < MF *meen,* var. of *meien* < L *mediān(us);* see MEDIAN] **—Syn. 1.** mode, way. **2.** funds. **3.** middle, center, midpoint, median. **11.** middling, average.

me·an·der (mē an′dər), *v.i.* **1.** to proceed by a winding or indirect course. **2.** to wander aimlessly; ramble: *The talk meandered on.* **—*n.* 3.** Usually, **meanders.** turnings or windings. **4.** a circuitous movement or journey. **5.** an intricate variety of fret or fretwork. [< L *maeander* < Gk *maíandros* a winding, special use of *Maíandros,* the Menderes river, noted for its winding course] **—me·an′der·er,** *n.* **—me·an′der·ing·ly,** *adv.* **—me·an′drous,** *adj.* **—Syn. 1.** wind, turn.

Me·an·der (mē an′dər), *n.* an ancient name of the **Menderes.**

mean′ devia′tion, *Statistics.* a measure of dispersion, computed by taking the arithmetic mean of the absolute values of the deviations of the functional values from some central value, usually the mean or median. Also called **average deviation.**

mean·ie (mē′nē), *n.* *Informal.* meany.

mean·ing (mē′ning), *n.* **1.** that which is intended to be, or actually is, expressed or indicated; signification; import. **2.** the end, purpose, or significance of something: *What is the meaning of life?* **—*adj.* 3.** intentioned (usually used in combination): *She's a well-meaning person.* **4.** full of significance; expressive: *a meaning look.* [ME (n.)] **—mean′ing·ly,** *adv.*
—Syn. 1. tenor, gist, drift, trend. MEANING, PURPORT, SENSE, SIGNIFICANCE denote that which is expressed or indicated by something. MEANING is the general word denoting that which is intended to be or actually is expressed or indicated: *the meaning of a word.* PURPORT is mainly limited to the meaning of a formal document, speech, important conversation, etc., and refers to the gist of something fairly complicated: *the purport of his letter to the editor.* SENSE may be used to denote one particular meaning of a word or phrase: *The word is frequently used in this sense.* SENSE may also be used loosely to refer to intelligible meaning: *There's no sense in what he says.* SIGNIFICANCE refers particularly to a meaning that is implied rather than expressed: *the significance of her glance;* or to a meaning the importance of which may not be easy to perceive immediately: *The real significance of his words was not grasped at the time.*

mean·ing·ful (mē′ning fəl), *adj.* full of meaning; significant. —**mean′ing·ful·ly,** *adv.* —**mean′ing·ful·ness,** *n.*
mean·ing·less (mē′ning lis), *adj.* without meaning, significance, or value; purposeless. —**mean′ing·less·ly,** *adv.* —**mean′ing·less·ness,** *n.*
mean·ly[1] (mēn′lē), *adv.* **1.** in a poor, lowly, or humble manner. **2.** in a base, contemptible, or shabby manner. **3.** in a stingy, miserly manner. [MEAN[2] + -LY]
mean·ly[2] (mēn′lē), *adv.* *Obs.* moderately. [ME; see MEAN[3], -LY]
mean·ness (mēn′nis), *n.* **1.** the state or quality of being mean. **2.** a mean act.
mean′ so′lar day′, day (def. 3a).
mean′ so′lar time′, *Astron.* time measured by the hour angle of the mean sun. Also called **mean′ time′.**
means′ test′, **1.** *Brit.* an inquiry into the income of a person who receives unemployment relief. **2.** any investigation into the financial position of a person applying for aid from public funds.
mean′ sun′, *Astron.* an imaginary sun moving uniformly in the celestial equator and taking the same time to make its annual circuit as the true sun does in the ecliptic.
meant (ment), *v.* pt. and pp. of **mean**[1].
mean·time (mēn′tīm′), *n.* **1.** the intervening time. —*adv.* **2.** in the intervening time; during the interval. **3.** at the same time. [ME]
mean·while (mēn′hwīl′, -wīl′), *n., adv.* meantime. [ME]
mean·y (mē′nē), *n., pl.* **mean·ies.** *Informal.* a small-minded, mean, or malicious person. Also, **meanie.** [MEAN + -Y[2]]
Mean·y (mē′nē), *n.* **George,** 1894–1980, U.S. labor leader: president of the AFL-CIO 1955–79.
meas., measure.
mea·sle (mē′zəl), *n.* sing. of **measles** (def. 3).
mea·sled (mē′zəld), *adj.* (of swine or other livestock) affected with measles. [ME *meseled*]
mea·sles (mē′zəlz), *n.* **1.** (*construed as sing. or pl.*) *Pathol.* **a.** an acute infectious disease occurring mostly in children, characterized by catarrhal and febrile symptoms and an eruption of small red spots; rubeola. **b.** any of certain other eruptive diseases. Cf. **German measles. 2.** *Vet. Pathol.* a disease in swine and other animals caused by the larvae of certain tapeworms of the genus *Taenia*. **3.** (*construed as pl.*) the larvae that cause measles in swine and other animals, and that upon maturation produce trichinosis in man. [ME *mesels,* mutated var. of *maseles* (pl.); c. D *maselen* (pl.), MD *masel;* akin to G *Masern* measles]
mea·sly (mē′zlē), *adj.,* **-sli·er, -sli·est. 1.** infected with measles. **2.** pertaining to or resembling measles. **3.** *Informal.* wretchedly poor or unsatisfactory: *a measly performance; a measly payment.* [MEASL(ES) + -Y[1]]
meas·ur·a·ble (mezh′ər ə bəl), *adj.* capable of being measured. [ME *mesurable* < MF < LL *mensūrābil(is)* that can be measured] —**meas′ur·a·bil′i·ty, meas′ur·a·ble·ness,** *n.* —**meas′ur·a·bly,** *adv.*
meas·ure (mezh′ər), *n., v.,* **-ured, -ur·ing.** —*n.* **1.** the act or process of ascertaining the extent, dimensions, quantity, etc., of something, esp. by comparison with a standard; measurement. **2.** size, dimensions, quantity, etc., as thus ascertained. **3.** an instrument, as a graduated rod or a vessel of standard capacity, for measuring. **4.** a unit or standard of measurement. **5.** a definite or known quantity measured out: *to drink a measure of wine.* **6.** a system of measurement. **7.** any standard of comparison, estimation, or judgment. **8.** a quantity, degree, or proportion. **9.** a moderate amount. **10.** reasonable bounds or limits: *to know no measure.* **11.** a legislative bill or enactment. **12.** Usually, **measures.** actions or procedures intended as a means to an end: *to take measures to avert suspicion.* **13.** a short rhythmical movement or arrangment, as in poetry or music. **14.** a particular kind of such arrangement. **15.** a metrical unit. **16.** the music contained between two bar lines; bar. **17.** a slow, dignified dance. **18. measures,** *Geol.* beds; strata. **19. for good measure,** as an extra. **20. have** or **take one's measure,** to judge or assess someone's character, capabilities, etc.; size up. **21. in a measure,** to some extent or degree: *His view is correct in a measure.* —*v.t.* **22.** to ascertain the extent, dimensions, quantity, capacity, etc., of, esp. by comparison with a standard. **23.** to mark off or deal out by way of measurement (often fol. by *off* or *out*): *to measure out martinis.* **24.** to estimate the relative amount, value, etc., of, by comparison with some standard: *to measure the importance of an issue.* **25.** to judge or appraise by comparison with something or someone else: *to measure Pope against Dryden.* **26.** to serve as the measure of. **27.** to adjust or proportion. **28.** to travel over; traverse. —*v.i.* **29.** to take measurements. **30.** to admit of measurement. **31.** to be of a specified measure. **32. measure one's length,** to fall or be knocked down; fall flat. **33. measure swords, a.** to test one's preparedness for a contest or encounter. **b.** to battle with swords. **c.** to fight, compete, etc. **34. measure up, a.** to reach a specified standard: *The exhibition didn't measure up to last year's.* **b.** to be capable or qualified: *As an administrator he couldn't quite measure up.* [ME *mesure* < MF < L *mensūra* = *mēns(us)* (ptp. of *mētīrī* to measure, mete) + *-ūra* -URE] —**meas′ur·er,** *n.*

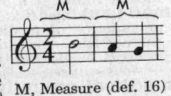

M M

M, Measure (def. 16)

meas·ured (mezh′ərd), *adj.* **1.** ascertained or apportioned by measure. **2.** accurately regulated or proportioned. **3.** regular or uniform, as in movement. **4.** deliberate and restrained: *measured terms.* **5.** in the form of meter or verse; metrical. [ME] —**meas′ured·ly,** *adv.* —**meas′ured·ness,** *n.*
meas·ure·less (mezh′ər lis), *adj.* without limits or bounds; unlimited: *a measureless fall; measureless contempt.* [ME *measureles*] —**meas′ure·less·ly,** *adv.* —**meas′ure·less·ness,** *n.* —**Syn.** boundless, limitless, infinite.
meas·ure·ment (mezh′ər mənt), *n.* **1.** the act of measuring. **2.** a measured dimension. **3.** extent, size, etc., ascertained by measuring. **4.** a system of measuring or measures: *liquid measurement.* **5. measurements,** *Informal.* the dimensions of a woman's bust, waist, and hips, in that order, expressed in inches: *The starlet's measurements were 38–24–36.*
meas′urement ton′. See under **ton**[1] (def. 5).
meas′uring cup′, a graduated cup, often of glass or plastic, used esp. in cooking for measuring ingredients.
meas·ur·ing·worm (mezh′ər ing wûrm′), *n.* the larva of any geometrid moth, which progresses by bringing the rear end of the body forward and then advancing the front end. Also called **inchworm, looper, spanworm.**
meat (mēt), *n.* **1.** the flesh of animals as used for food. **2.** food in general: *meat and drink.* **3.** the edible part of anything, as a fruit or nut. **4.** the essential point or part; gist; crux. **5.** *Informal.* a favorite occupation, activity, etc.: *Chess is his meat.* **6.** *Archaic.* the principal meal. [ME, OE *mete;* c. Icel *matr,* Goth *mats,* OHG *maz* food] —**meat′less,** *adj.*
meat′ and pota′toes, *U.S. Slang.* the essential or most important part. —**meat′-and-pota′toes,** *adj.*
meat′ ax′, cleaver (def. 2).
meat-ax (mēt′aks′), *adj.* *U.S. Slang.* **1.** drastic or severe: *meat-ax defense cuts.* **2.** favoring or advocating elimination or drastic reductions: *a meat-ax approach to the budget.*
meat·ball (mēt′bôl′), *n.* chopped meat, esp. beef, molded or shaped into a ball before cooking.
Meath (mēth, mēth), *n.* a county in Leinster, in the E Republic of Ireland. 65,106 (1961); 902 sq. mi. *Co. seat:* Trim.
meat·head (mēt′hed′), *n.* *Slang.* blockhead; dunce; fool.
me·a·tus (mē ā′təs), *n., pl.* **-tus·es, -tus.** *Anat.* an opening or foramen, esp. in a bone or bony structure, as the opening of the ear, nose, etc. [< L: course, channel (4th decl.), n. use of ptp. of *meāre* to go] —**me·a′tal,** *adj.*
meat·y (mē′tē), *adj.,* **meat·i·er, meat·i·est. 1.** of or like meat. **2.** abounding in meat. **3.** rich in matter; full of substance; pithy. —**meat′i·ly,** *adv.* —**meat′i·ness,** *n.*
Mec·ca (mek′ə), *n.* **1.** Also, **Makkah, Mekka.** a city in and the capital of Hejaz, in W Saudi Arabia: the religious capital of Saudi Arabia; birthplace of Muhammad; spiritual center of Islam. 366,801. **2.** (*often l.c.*) any place that many people visit or hope to visit. —**Mec′can,** *adj., n.*
mech., 1. mechanical. **2.** mechanics. **3.** mechanism.
me·chan·ic (mə kan′ik), *n.* **1.** a skilled worker with tools, machines, etc. **2.** a person who repairs machinery, motors, etc. [< L *mēchanic(us)* a mechanic < Gk *mēchanikós*]
me·chan·i·cal (mə kan′i kəl), *adj.* **1.** having to do with machinery: *a mechanical failure.* **2.** being a machine, or including machinery: *a mechanical toy.* **3.** caused by or derived from machinery: *mechanical propulsion.* **4.** using machine parts only: *mechanical, hydraulic, or compressed-air brakes.* **5.** brought about by friction, abrasion, etc.: *mechanical erosion.* **6.** pertaining to the design or contrivance of tools or machinery: *a mechanical genius.* **7.** working with tools or machinery. **8.** pertaining to the use or comprehension of tools, machinery, or the like: *mechanical ability.* **9.** produced by such means. **10.** acting or performed without spirit, individuality, etc. **11.** habitual or routine; automatic. **12.** belonging or pertaining to the subject matter of mechanics. **13.** pertaining to, or controlled or effected by, physical forces. **14.** (of a philosopher or philosophical theory) explaining phenomena as due to mechanical action or the material forces of the universe. **15.** unspiritual; materialistic. —*n.* **16.** *Print.* a sheet of stiff paper on which has been pasted artwork, type proofs, or both, for making a printing plate; pastewor up. **17.** *Archaic.* a manual worker. [late ME *mechanicall* < L *mēchanic(us)* MECHANIC; see -AL[1]] —**me·chan′i·cal·ly,** *adv.* —**me·chan′i·cal·ness, me·chan′i·cal′i·ty,** *n.*
mechan′ical advan′tage, *Mech.* the ratio of output force to the input force applied to a mechanism.
mechan′ical draw′ing, drawing, as of machinery, done with the aid of rulers, scales, compasses, etc.
mechan′ical engineer′ing, the branch of engineering dealing with the design and production of machinery. —**mechan′ical engineer′.**
mechan′ical equiv′alent of heat′, (in any system of physical units) the number of units of work or energy equal to one unit of heat, as 4.1858 joules, which equals one small calorie.
mech·a·ni·cian (mek′ə nish′ən), *n.* a person skilled in constructing, working, or repairing machines.
me·chan·ics (mə kan′iks), *n.* **1.** (*construed as sing.*) the science that deals with the action of forces on bodies and with motion: comprises kinetics, statics, and kinematics. **2.** (*construed as sing.*) the theoretical and practical application of this science to machinery, mechanical appliances, etc. **3.** (*usually construed as pl.*) the technical aspect or working part; mechanism; structure. **4.** (*usually construed as pl.*) routine methods, procedures, or details. [see MECHANIC, -ICS]
Me·chan·ics·ville (mə kan′iks vil′), *n.* a village in E Virginia, near Richmond: Civil War battle 1862.
mech·a·nise (mek′ə nīz′), *v.t.,* **-nised, -nis·ing.** *Chiefly Brit.* mechanize. —**mech′a·ni·sa′tion,** *n.* —**mech′a·nis′er,** *n.*
mech·an·ism (mek′ə niz′əm), *n.* **1.** an assembly of moving parts performing a complete functional motion. **2.** the agency or means by which an effect is produced or a purpose is accomplished. **3.** machinery or mechanical appliances in general. **4.** the structure or arrangement of parts of a machine or similar device, or of anything analogous. **5.** the mechanical part of something; any mechanical device: *the mechanism of a clock.* **6.** routine methods or procedures. **7.** mechanical execution, as in painting or music; technique. **8.** the theory that everything in the universe is produced by matter in motion; materialism. Cf. **dynamism** (def. 1), **vitalism** (def. 1). **9.** *Philos.* **a.** the view that all natural processes are explicable in terms of Newtonian mechanics. **b.** the view that all biological processes may be described in physiochemical terms. **10.** *Psychoanal.* the operation and interaction of psychological forces (used as an analogy drawn from mechanics). [< NL *mēchanism(us);* LL *mēchanism(a)* a contrivance < Gk *mēchan(ḗ)* machine + *-ismus, -isma* -ISM] —**mech′a·nis′mic,** *adj.*
mech·a·nist (mek′ə nist), *n.* **1.** a person who believes in the theory of mechanism. **2.** *Rare.* a mechanician. [MECHAN(IC) + -IST]
mech·a·nis·tic (mek′ə nis′tik), *adj.* **1.** of or pertaining to the theory of mechanism or to mechanists. **2.** of or pertaining to mechanics. —**mech′a·nis′ti·cal·ly,** *adv.*

mech·a·nize (mek′ə nīz′), *v.t.*, **-nized, -niz·ing.** **1.** to make mechanical. **2.** to operate or perform by or as if by machinery. **3.** to introduce machinery into (an industry, enterprise, etc.). **4.** *Mil.* to equip with tanks and other armored vehicles. Also, *esp. Brit.*, **mechanise.** [MECHAN(IC) + -IZE] —**mech′a·ni·za′tion,** *n.* —**mech′a·niz′er,** *n.*

Mech·lin (mek′lin), *n.* **1.** French, **Malines.** Flemish, **Mech·e·len** (meKH′ə lən). a city in N Belgium. 65,388 (est. 1964). **2.** See **Mechlin lace.**

Mech′lin lace′, **1.** a bobbin lace with raised cord, originally made in Mechlin. **2.** a similar lace made by machine. Also called **Mechlin, malines.** [after MECHLIN]

Mech·ni·kov (mech nē kôf′), *n.* See **Metchnikoff.**

Meck·len·burg (mek′lən bûrg′; *Ger.* mek′lən bŏŏRK′, mā′klən-), *n.* a former state in NE Germany, formed in 1934 from two states **(Mecklenburg-Schwerin** and **Mecklenburg-Strelitz).**

Meck·len·burg-Schwe·rin (mek′lən bûrg′shwer′ən; *Ger.* mek′lən bŏŏRK′shvā Rēn′, mā′klən-), *n.* See under **Mecklenburg.**

Meck·len·burg-Stre·litz (mek′lən bûrg′shtrā′lits; *Ger.* mek′lən bŏŏRK′shtRā′lits, mā′klən-), *n.* See under **Mecklenburg.**

med., **1.** medical. **2.** medicine. **3.** medieval. **4.** medium.

med·al (med′əl), *n.*, *v.*, **-aled, -al·ing** or (*esp. Brit.*) **-alled, -al·ling.** —*n.* **1.** a flat piece of metal, in any of various shapes, issued to commemorate a person, action, or event, or given as a reward for bravery, merit, or the like. —*v.t.* **2.** to decorate or honor with a medal. [earlier *medaille* < MF < It *medaglia* copper coin < VL **medalia*, var. (by dissimilation) of LL *mediālia*, neut. pl. of *mediālis* MEDIAL]

med·al·ist (med′əlist), *n.* **1.** a designer, engraver, or maker of medals. **2.** a person to whom a medal has been awarded. **3.** (in a golf tournament) the winner at medal play. Also, *esp. Brit.*, **med′al·list.** [< F *médailliste* < It *medaglista*]

me·dal·lion (mə dal′yən), *n.* **1.** a large medal. **2.** *Archit.* **a.** a tablet, usually rounded, often bearing decorations in relief. **b.** a decorative design resembling a panel. **3.** *U.S.* an official permit to operate a taxicab, usually represented by a small metal disk attached to the car. [< F *médaillon* < It *medaglione*, aug. of *medaglia* MEDAL]

Med′al of Hon′or, *U.S.* the nation's highest military decoration, awarded in the name of Congress to a member of the armed forces who distinguishes himself in combat, at the risk of life and beyond the call of duty.

med′al play′, *Golf.* play in which the score is reckoned by counting the strokes taken to complete the round.

Me·dan (me dän′), *n.* a city in NE Sumatra, in W Indonesia. 624,000 (1972).

med·dle (med′əl), *v.i.*, **-dled, -dling.** to involve oneself in a matter without right or invitation; interfere officiously without being asked or required to. [ME *medle(n)* < MF *medler*, var. of OF *mes(d)ler* < VL *misculāre*, freq. of L *miscēre* to mix] —**med′dler,** *n.* —**med′dling·ly,** *adv.*

med·dle·some (med′əl səm), *adj.* given to meddling; interfering. —**med′dle·some·ly,** *adv.* —**med′dle·some·ness,** *n.* —**Syn.** intrusive. See **curious.**

Mede (mēd), *n.* a native or inhabitant of Media. [ME *Medis* (pl.), OE *Mēdas* < L *Mēdī* < Gk *Mêdoi* (pl.), *Mêdos* (sing.) < OPers *Māda*]

Me·de·a (mi dē′ə), *n.* *Gk. Legend.* a sorceress, daughter of Aeëtes, king of Colchis, and wife of Jason, whom she assisted in obtaining the Golden Fleece.

Me·del·lín (me the yēn′), *n.* a city in W Colombia. 1,400,000 (est. 1970).

med·e·vac (med′ə vak′), *n.*, *v.*, **-vacked, -vack·ing.** *U.S. Mil.* —*n.* **1.** a helicopter for evacuating the wounded from a battlefield. —*v.t.* **2.** to transport (the wounded) by a medevac. [*med(ical-)evac(uation helicopter)*]

Med·ex (med′eks), *n.*, *pl.* **Med·ex.** *U.S.* a former medical corpsman trained to assist a physician by taking over his routine medical functions. [MEDI(CAL CORPSMAN) + EX(TENSION)]

med·fly (med′flī′), *n.*, *pl.* **-flies.** (*often cap.*) See **Mediterranean fruit fly.**

Med·ford (med′fərd), *n.* **1.** a city in E Massachusetts. 64,397 (1970). **2.** a city in SW Oregon. 28,454 (1970).

medi-, an element occurring in loan words from Latin, where it meant "middle": *mediate.* Also, **medio-.** [comb. form of L *medius* MID[1]]

me·di·a[1] (mē′dē ə), *n.* **1.** a pl. of **medium. 2. the media.** Also called **mass media.** the means of communication, as radio and television, newspapers, magazines, etc., that reach very large numbers of people.

me·di·a[2] (mē′dē ə), *n.*, *pl.* **-di·ae** (-dē ē′). **1.** *Gk. Grammar.* a voiced plosive, as *β*, *δ*, *γ*. **2.** *Anat.* the middle layer of an artery or lymphatic vessel. [< LL (grammar sense only), n. use of fem. sing. of L *medius* MID[1]]

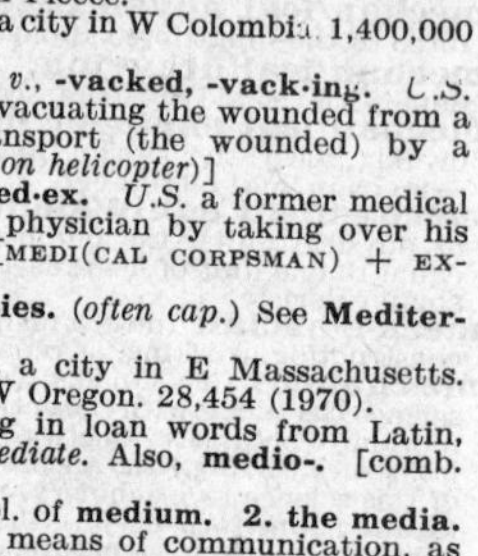

Me·di·a (mē′dē ə), *n.* an ancient country in W Asia, S of the Caspian Sea, corresponding generally to NW Iran. *Cap.:* Ecbatana.

me·di·ae·val (mē′dē ē′vəl, med′ē-, mid′ē, mid ē′vəl), *adj.* medieval. —**me′di·ae′val·ism,** *n.* —**me′di·ae′val·ist,** *n.*

me·di·al (mē′dē əl), *adj.* **1.** situated in or pertaining to the middle; median; intermediate. **2.** pertaining to a mean or average. **3.** ordinary or average. **4.** *Phonet.* within a word or syllable; neither initial nor final, as the *t*, *a*, and *n* in *stand.* **5.** *Phonet.* media[2] (def. 1). [< LL *mediāl(is)* middle] —**me′di·al·ly,** *adv.*

me·di·an (mē′dē ən), *adj.* **1.** noting or pertaining to a plane dividing something into two equal parts, esp. one dividing an animal into right and left halves. **2.** situated in or pertaining to the middle; medial. —*n.* **3.** *Arith., Statistics.* the middle number in a given sequence, or the average of the two middle numbers when the sequence has an even number of numbers: *4 is the median of 1, 3, 4, 8, 9.* **4.** *Geom.* a straight line from a vertex of a triangle to the midpoint of the opposite side. **5.** a dividing strip, often landscaped, between opposing lanes of highway traffic. [< L *mediān(us)* that is in the middle, middle] —**me′di·an·ly,** *adv.*

Me·di·an (mē′dē ən), *adj.* **1.** of or pertaining to Media, the Medes, or their language. —*n.* **2.** a Mede.

me·di·ant (mē′dē ənt), *n.* the third degree of a major or minor musical scale. [< It *mediante* < LL *mediant-* (s. of *mediāns*), prp. of *mediāre* to be in the middle]

me·di·as·ti·num (mē′dē ə stī′nəm), *n.*, *pl.* **-as·ti·na** (-ə stī′nə). *Anat.* **1.** a median septum or partition between two parts of an organ or paired cavities of the body. **2.** the partition separating the right and left thoracic cavities, formed of the two inner pleural walls, and, in man, comprising all the viscera of the thorax except the lungs. [< medical L, neut. of ML *mediastīn(us)* medial, L: drudge (n.) = *medias-* mid + *-tīnus* adj., n. suffix] —**me′di·as·ti′nal,** *adj.*

me·di·ate (*v.* mē′dē āt′; *adj.* mē′dē it), *v.*, **-at·ed, -at·ing,** *adj.* —*v.t.* **1.** to bring about (an agreement, peace, etc.) as an intermediary between parties. **2.** to settle (disputes, strikes, etc.) as an intermediary between parties; reconcile. **3.** to effect (a result) or convey (a message, gift, etc.) by or as by an intermediary. —*v.i.* **4.** to act between parties as an intermediary. **5.** to occupy an intermediate position. —*adj.* **6.** acting through or involving an intermediate agency; not direct or immediate. [ME < LL *mediāt(us)* divided in the middle, ptp. of *mediāre*] —**me′di·ate·ly,** *adv.* —**me′di·ate·ness,** *n.* —**Syn. 1, 2.** arbitrate.

me·di·a·tion (mē′dē ā′shən), *n.* action in mediating between parties, as to effect an agreement or reconciliation. [ME *mediacioun* < ML *mediātiōn-* (s. of *mediātiō*)] —**Syn.** MEDIATION, ARBITRATION designate processes for bringing about agreement or reconciliation between opponents in a dispute. MEDIATION implies deliberation that results in solutions that may or may not be accepted by the contending parties. ARBITRATION involves a more formal deliberation, it being understood that the results will be binding on the contending parties.

me·di·a·tive (mē′dē ā′tiv, -ə tiv), *adj.* mediatory.

me·di·a·tor (mē′dē ā′tər), *n.* a person who mediates. [< LL; r. ME *mediatour* < AF] —**me·di·a·to·ri·al** (mē′dē ə tôr′ē əl, -tôr′-), *adj.*

me·di·a·to·ry (mē′dē ə tôr′ē, -tôr′ē), *adj.* **1.** pertaining to mediation. **2.** having the function of mediating. [< LL *mediātōri(us)*]

me·di·a·trix (mē′dē ā′triks), *n.*, *pl.* **-a·tri·ces** (-ə trī′sēz, -ā′tri sēz′), **-a·trix·es.** *Obs.* a female mediator [late ME < LL; fem. of MEDIATOR]

med·ic[1] (med′ik), *n.* *Slang.* a doctor, medical student, or medical corpsman. [shortened form of MEDICAL]

med·ic[2] (med′ik), *n.* any fabaceous plant of the genus *Medicago.* Cf. **alfalfa.** [< L *mēdica* < Gk (*póa*) *Mēdikḗ*, lit., Median (grass)]

med·i·ca·ble (med′ə kə bəl), *adj.* susceptible of medical treatment; curable. [< L *medicābil(is)* healing, curative] —**med′i·ca·bly,** *adv.*

Med·i·caid (med′ə kād′), *n.* *U.S.* a government program, financed by federal, state, and local funds, of hospitalization and medical insurance for persons of all ages within certain income limits. Cf. **Medicare.** [MEDIC(AL) + AID]

med·i·cal (med′i kəl), *adj.* **1.** of or pertaining to the science or practice of medicine. **2.** *Rare.* curative or medicinal; therapeutic: *medical properties.* [< ML *medicāl(is)*, L *medicus* medical (adj.), physician (n.) = *med(ērī)* (to) heal + *-icus* -IC; see -AL[1]] —**med′i·cal·ly,** *adv.*

med′ical exam′iner, **1.** an official, as a physician or other person trained in medicine, who performs autopsies on the bodies of persons supposed to have died from unnatural causes. **2.** a physician retained by an insurance company, industrial firm, or the like, to give medical examinations to its clients or employees.

me·dic·a·ment (mə dik′ə mənt, med′ə kə-), *n.* a healing substance; medicine; remedy. [< L *medicāment(um)* remedy, physic = *medicā(rī)* (to) cure + *-mentum* -MENT. See MEDICATE] —**med·i·ca·men·tal** (med′ə kə men′təl), **med′i·ca·men′ta·ry, med′i·ca·men′tous,** *adj.*

Med·i·care (med′ə kâr′), *n.* *U.S.* a federal program of hospitalization insurance and voluntary medical insurance for persons aged 65 and over. Also, **med′i·care′.** Cf. **Medicaid.** [MEDI(CAL) + CARE]

med·i·cate (med′ə kāt′), *v.t.*, **-cat·ed, -cat·ing.** **1.** to treat with medicine or medicaments. **2.** to impregnate with a medicine. [< L *medicāt(us)* medicated (ptp. of *medicāre*), healed (ptp. of *medicārī*)]

med·i·ca·tion (med′ə kā′shən), *n.* **1.** the use or application of medicine. **2.** a medicinal substance; medicament. [< L *medicātiōn-* (s. of *medicātiō*)]

Med·i·ci (med′i chē; *It.* me′dē chē), *n.* **1. Catherine de′.** See **Catherine de Médicis. 2. Cos·mo** (kŏz′mō) or **Co·si·mo, de′** (kô′zē mô de), ("*the Elder*"), 1389–1464, Italian banker, statesman, and patron of art and literature. **3. Cosmo** or **Cosimo, de′** ("*the Great*"), 1519–74, duke of Florence and first grand duke of Tuscany. **4. Gio·van·ni de′** (jô vän′nē de). See **Leo X. 5. Giu·lio de′** (jōō′lyô de). See **Clement VII. 6. Lo·ren·zo de′** (lô Ren′tsô de), ("*Lorenzo the Magnificent*"), 1449–92, poet and patron of the arts; ruler of Florence 1478–92 (father of Leo X). **7. Ma·ri·a de′** (mə rē′ə də; *It.* mä Rē′ä de). See **Marie de Médicis.**

me·dic·i·nal (mə dis′ə nəl), *adj.* of, pertaining to, or having the properties of a medicine; curative; remedial. [ME < L *medicīnāl(is)*] —**me·dic′i·nal·ly,** *adv.*

med·i·cine (med′i sin *or, esp. Brit.*, med′sin), *n.*, *v.*, **-cined, -cin·ing.** —*n.* **1.** any substance or substances used in treating disease or illness; remedy. **2.** the art or science of restoring or preserving health or due physical condition: often divided into medicine proper, surgery, and obstetrics. **3.** the art or science of treating disease with drugs or curative substances, as distinguished from surgery and obstetrics. **4.** the medical profession. **5.** any object or practice regarded by primitive peoples as of magical efficacy. **6. give someone a taste** or **dose of his own medicine,** to repay or punish a person for an injury by use of his own methods. **7. take one's medicine.** to undergo or accept punishment, esp. as the result of one's own actions. —*v.t.* **8.** to administer medicine to. [ME *medicin* < L *medicīna* (*ars*) the healing (art), fem. of *medicīnus* pertaining to a physician]

med′icine ball′, a large, solid, heavy, leather-covered ball, thrown for exercise.

Med′icine Bow′ Range′ (bō), a range of the Rocky Mountains, in Wyoming and Colorado. Highest peak, Elk Mountain, 11,162 ft.

Med′icine Hat′, a city in SE Alberta, in SW Canada. 32,811.

med′icine lodge′, **1.** a structure used for various ceremonials of the North American Indians. **2.** (*caps.*) the most important religious society among the Central Algonquian tribes of North America.

med′icine man′, (esp. among American Indians) a man supposed to possess supernatural powers.

med′icine show′, a traveling troupe that offers entertainment to attract customers for the patent medicines or purported cures proffered for sale.

med·i·co (med′ə kō′), *n., pl.* **-cos.** *Slang.* a doctor. [< Sp *médico,* It *medico* < L *medicus* physician]

medico-, a combining form meaning "medical." [comb. form repr. L *medicus* of, pertaining to healing; see MEDICAL]

me·di·e·val (mē′dē ē′vəl, med′ē-, mid′ē-, mid ē′vəl), *adj.* of, pertaining to, characteristic of, or in the style of the Middle Ages. **2.** *Informal.* old-fashioned. Also, **mediaeval.** [earlier *mediaeval* < NL *medi(um) aev(um)* the middle age + -AL[1]. See MEDIUM, AGE] —**me′di·e′val·ly,** *adv.*

Medie′val Greek′, the Greek language of the Middle Ages, usually dated A.D. 700 to 1500. *Abbr.:* MGk, MGk., MGr. Also called **Middle Greek.**

me·di·e·val·ism (mē′dē ē′və liz′əm, med′ē-, mid′ē-, mid ē′və-), *n.* **1.** the spirit, practices, or methods of the Middle Ages. **2.** devotion to or adoption of medieval ideals or practices. **3.** a medieval belief, practice, or the like. Also, **mediaevalism.**

me·di·e·val·ist (mē′dē ē′və list, med′ē-, mid′ē-, mid-ē′və-), *n.* **1.** an expert in medieval history, literature, philosophy, etc. **2.** a person who is devoted to the art, culture, spirit, etc., of the Middle Ages. Also, **mediaevalist.**

Medie′val Lat′in, the Latin language of the literature of the Middle Ages, usually dated A.D. 700 to 1500. *Abbr.:* ML, M.L. Also called **Middle Latin.**

Me·di·na (mə dē′nə), *n.* a city in W Saudi Arabia, where Muhammad was first accepted as the supreme Prophet of Allah and where his tomb is located. 150,000.

Me·di·na as-Shaab (me dē′nä äs s͟häb′), a city in and the former capital of South Yemen, in the SW part: established 1965. Formerly **Al Ittihad.**

medio-, var. of **medi-.**

me·di·o·cre (mē′dē ō′kər, mē′dē ō′kər), *adj.* of only ordinary quality; neither good nor bad; barely adequate. [< MF < L *mediocr(is)* in a middle state, lit., at middle height = *medi-* MEDI- + OL *ocris* rugged mountain, c. Gk *ókris,* akin to *ákros* apex] —**Syn.** average, commonplace.

me·di·oc·ri·ty (mē′dē ok′ri tē), *n., pl.* **-ties** for 2, 3. **1.** the state or quality of being mediocre. **2.** mediocre ability or accomplishment. **3.** a person of but moderate ability. [late ME *mediocrite* < MF < L *mediocritāt-* (s. of *mediocritās*) a middle state, moderation]

Medit., Mediterranean.

med·i·tate (med′i tāt′), *v.,* **-tat·ed, -tat·ing.** —*v.i.* **1.** to think contemplatively; muse; reflect. —*v.t.* **2.** to intend to do or achieve; plan: *to meditate revenge.* [< L *meditāt(us),* ptp. of *meditārī*] —**med′i·tat′ing·ly,** *adv.* —**med′i·ta′tor,** *n.* —**Syn. 1.** ruminate; cogitate, think. **2.** contemplate.

med·i·ta·tion (med′i tā′s͟hən), *n.* **1.** the act of meditating. **2.** thought; reflection; contemplation. [< L *meditātiōn-* (s. of *meditātiō*) a thinking over; r. ME *meditacioun* < AF]

med·i·ta·tive (med′i tā′tiv), *adj.* given to, characterized by, or indicative of meditation; contemplative. [< LL *meditātīv(us)*] —**med′i·ta′tive·ly,** *adv.* —**med′i·ta′tive·ness,** *n.* —**Syn.** thoughtful. See **pensive.**

Med·i·ter·ra·ne·an (med′i tə rā′nē ən), *n.* **1.** See **Mediterranean Sea.** **2.** a person whose physical characteristics are considered typical of the peoples native to or inhabiting the Mediterranean area. —*adj.* **3.** pertaining to, situated on or near, or dwelling about the Mediterranean Sea. **4.** *Anthropol.* of or belonging to the Caucasoid peoples distributed chiefly in the areas surrounding the Mediterranean Sea. [< L *mediterrāne(us)* midland, inland + -AN]

Med′iterra′nean fe′ver, *Pathol.* brucellosis.

Med′iterra′nean fruit′ fly′, a small, irregularly banded two-winged fly, *Ceratus capitata,* inhabiting many warm regions and having larvae that feed within citrus and other succulent fruits. Also called **medfly.**

Med′iterra′nean Sea′, a sea surrounded by Africa, Europe, and Asia. 2400 mi. long; 1,145,000 sq. mi.; greatest known depth 14,436 ft.

me·di·um (mē′dē əm), *n., pl.* **-di·a** (-dē ə) for 1–9, **-di·ums** for 1–10, *adj.* —*n.* **1.** a middle state or condition; mean. **2.** something intermediate in nature or degree. **3.** an intervening substance, as air, through which a force acts or an effect is produced. **4.** the element that is the natural habitat of an organism. **5.** surrounding objects, conditions, etc.; environment. **6.** an agency, means, or instrument, usually of something specified: *a communications medium.* **7.** *Biol.* the substance in which specimens are displayed or preserved. **8.** Also called **culture medium.** *Bacteriol.* a liquid or solidified nutrient material suitable for the cultivation of microorganisms. **9.** *Fine Arts.* **a.** *Painting.* a liquid with which pigments are mixed. **b.** the material or technique with which an artist works. **10.** a person serving, or conceived of as serving, as an instrument through which another personality or a supernatural agency manifests itself. —*adj.* **11.** about halfway between extremes, as of degree, quality, or size. [< L: the middle, neut. of *medius* middle. See MID[1]] —**Syn. 11.** average, mean, middling, mediocre.

me′dium artil′lery, *U.S. Mil.* guns and howitzers of more than 105-millimeter and less than 155-millimeter caliber, sometimes including the 155-millimeter howitzers. Cf. **heavy artillery, light artillery.**

me′dium bomb′er, *Mil.* a moderately large airplane capable of carrying large bomb loads for moderate distances at medium altitudes, esp. one weighing 100,000 to 250,000 pounds loaded. Cf. **heavy bomber, light bomber.**

me′dium fre′quency, *Radio.* any frequency between 300 and 3,000 kilohertz. *Abbr.:* MF, mf

me′dium of exchange′, anything generally accepted as representing a standard of value and exchangeable for goods or services.

me′dium-scale′ in′tegra′tion (mē′dē əm skāl′). See **MSI.**

me·di·us (mē′dē əs), *n., pl.* **-di·i** (-dē ī′). *Anat.* the middle finger. [< L: middle]

med·lar (med′lər), *n.* **1.** a small, malaceous tree, *Mespilus germanica,* the fruit of which is edible in the early stages of decay. **2.** any of certain other malaceous trees. **3.** the fruit of any of these trees. [ME *medler* < MF: medlar tree = **medle* (var. of *mesle* the fruit < L *mespil(um)* < Gk *méspilon*)]

med·ley (med′lē), *n., pl.* **-leys,** *adj.* —*n.* **1.** a piece of music combining airs or passages from various sources. **2.** a mixture, esp. of heterogeneous elements; jumble. —*adj.* **3.** *Archaic.* mixed; mingled. [ME *medlee* < MF, n. use of fem. of ptp. of *medler* to mix, fight; see MEDDLE]

Mé·doc (mā dok′; *Fr.* mā dôk′), *n.* **1.** a wine-growing region in Gironde, SW France. **2.** a claret produced there.

me·dul·la (mi dul′ə), *n., pl.* **-dul·las, -dul·lae** (-dul′ē). **1.** *Anat.* **a.** the marrow of the bones. **b.** the soft, marrowlike center of an organ, as the adrenal gland or kidneys. **c.** See **medulla oblongata.** **2.** *Bot.* the pith of plants. [< L: marrow, innermost part, dim. of *medius* middle; see MEDIUM]

medul′la oblonga′ta (ob′lôn̄g gä′tə, -lon̄g-), *pl.* **medulla oblongatas, medullae oblongatae** (-tē). *Anat.* the lowest or hindmost part of the brain, continuous with the spinal cord. [< NL: the long medulla; see OBLONG, -ATE[1]]

med·ul·lar·y (med′ᵊler′ē, mej′ə ler′ē, mi dul′ə rē), *adj.* pertaining to, consisting of, or resembling the medulla of an organ or the medulla oblongata.

med′ullary ray′, *Bot.* (in the stems of exogenous plants) one of the vertical bands or plates of parenchymatous tissue that radiate between the pith and the bark.

med′ullary sheath′, **1.** *Bot.* a narrow zone made up of the innermost layer of woody tissue immediately surrounding the pith in plants. **2.** *Anat.* See **myelin sheath.**

me·du·sa (mə dōō′sə, -zə, -dyōō′-), *n., pl.* **-sas, -sae** (-sē, -zē). *Zool.* a jellyfish. [special use of MEDUSA, alluding to the Gorgon's snaky locks]

Me·du·sa (mə dōō′sə, -zə, -dyōō′-), *n., pl.* **-sas.** *Class. Myth.* the only mortal of the three Gorgons, killed by Perseus. [< L < Gk *Médousa,* special use of fem. of *médōn* ruler]

me·du·san (mə dōō′sən, -zən, -dyōō′-), *adj.* **1.** pertaining to a medusa or jellyfish. —*n.* **2.** a medusa or jellyfish.

meed (mēd), *n. Archaic.* a reward or recompense. [ME *mede,* OE *mēd;* c. G *Miete* hire; akin to OE *meord*]

meek (mēk), *adj.* **1.** humbly patient or submissive. **2.** overly patient or submissive; spiritless; tame. **3.** *Obs.* gentle; kind. [ME *meke, meoc* < Scand; cf. Icel *mjūkr* soft, mild, meek] —**meek′ly,** *adv.* —**meek′ness,** *n.*

meer·schaum (mēr′s͟həm, -s͟hôm, -shoum), *n.* **1.** a mineral, hydrous magnesium silicate, $H_4Mg_2Si_3O_{10}$, occurring in white, claylike masses, used for carvings, for pipe bowls, etc.; sepiolite. **2.** a tobacco pipe with the bowl made of this substance. [< G: lit., sea foam]

Mee·rut (mēr′ət), *n.* a city in W Uttar Pradesh, in N India. 367,281.

meet[1] (mēt), *v.,* **met, meet·ing,** *n.* —*v.t.* **1.** to come upon; encounter. **2.** to become or to make oneself acquainted with. **3.** to join at an appointed place or time: *Meet me in St. Louis.* **4.** to be present at the arrival of. **5.** to come to or before (one's notice, or a means of noticing, as the eyes or ears): *A peculiar sight met my eyes.* **6.** to face, eye, etc., directly or without avoidance. **7.** to come into physical contact, juxtaposition, or collision. **8.** to encounter in opposition, conflict, or contest. **9.** to oppose. **10.** to cope or deal effectively with (an objection, difficulty, etc.). **11.** to satisfy (needs, obligations, demands, etc.). **12.** to conform with (wishes, expectations, views, etc.). **13.** to encounter in experience. —*v.i.* **14.** to come together, face to face, or into company. **15.** to assemble for action or conference, as a committee. **16.** to become personally acquainted. **17.** to come into contact or form a junction, as lines, planes, areas, etc. **18.** to be conjoined or united. **19.** to concur or agree. **20.** to come together in opposition or conflict, as adversaries, hostile forces, etc. **21. meet halfway, a.** to concede in part, as to the demands of an opposing faction or person. **b.** to anticipate another's actions and conduct oneself accordingly. **22. meet with, a.** to come across; encounter. **b.** to experience; undergo; receive. **23. well met,** *Archaic.* welcome. —*n.* **24.** an assembly, as of persons and hounds for a hunt, swimmers or runners for a race or series of races, etc. **25.** those assembled. **26.** the place of such an assembling. [ME *mete(n),* OE *(ge)mētan;* c. Icel *moeta,* OLG *mōtian.* See MOOT] —**meet′er,** *n.* —**Syn. 6.** confront. **7.** join, intersect, cross.

meet[2] (mēt), *adj.* suitable; fitting; proper. [ME *mete,* repr. OE (dial.); r. OE *gemǣte* suitable, c. G *gemäss* conformable] —**meet′ly,** *adv.* —**meet′ness,** *n.* —**Syn.** apt, appropriate.

meet·ing (mē′tin̄g), *n.* **1.** the act of coming together. **2.** an assembly of persons for a specific purpose. **3.** the body of persons present at an assembly. **4.** a hostile encounter; a duel. **5.** an assembly for religious worship, esp. of Quakers. **6.** See **meeting house.** **7.** a place or point of contact; junction; union. [ME]

meet′ing house′, a house or building for religious worship, esp. for Quakers.

mega-, a learned borrowing from Greek meaning "large," "great" (*megalith*); specialized in physics to mean 1,000,000 times a given unit (*megahertz*). Also, *esp. before a vowel,* **meg-.** Cf. **megalo-.** [comb. form repr. Gk *mégas* large, great, vast, powerful]

meg·a·bit (meg′ə bit′), *n. Computer Technol.* **1.** 1024 kilobits, or 1,048,576 bits. **2.** (loosely) one million bits.

meg·a·byte (meg′ə bīt′), *n. Computer Technol.* **1.** 1024 kilobytes, or 1,048,576 bytes. **2.** (loosely) one million bytes.

meg·a·ce·phal·ic (meg′ə sə fal′ik), *adj.* **1.** *Craniom.* having a skull with a large cranial capacity or one exceeding the mean. Cf. **microcephalic** (def. 1). **2.** large-headed. Also, **meg·a·ceph·a·lous** (meg′ə sef′ə ləs). —**meg′a·ceph′a·ly,** *n.*

meg·a·cu·rie (meg′ə kyŏŏr′ē, -kyŏŏ rē′), *n.* one million curies. *Abbr.:* MCi, Mc

meg·a·cy·cle (meg′ə sī′kəl), *n.* a unit equal to one million cycles per second: largely replaced in technical usage by the term megahertz. *Abbr.:* Mc, mc

Me·gae·ra (mə jēr′ə), *n. Class. Myth.* one of the Furies.

meg·a·ga·mete (meg′ə gə mēt′, -gam′ēt), *n.* macrogamete.

meg·a·hertz, (meg′ə hûrts′), *n., pl.* **-hertz.** *Elect.* a unit equal to one million cycles per second. *Abbr.:* MHz [MEGA- + HERTZ]

-megalia, var. of **-megaly:** *splenomegalia.*

meg·a·lith (meg′ə lith), *n. Archaeol.* a stone of great size, esp. in ancient construction work. **—meg′a·lith′ic,** *adj.*

megalo-, a learned borrowing from Greek indicating bigness, exaggeration, extravagance: *megalomania.* Also, *esp. before a vowel,* **megal-.** Cf. **mega-.** [< Gk, comb. form of *megal-* (s. of *mégas*) great, large]

meg·a·lo·ce·phal·ic (meg′ə lō sə fal′ik), *adj.* megacephalic. Also, **meg·a·lo·ceph·a·lous** (meg′ə lō sef′ə ləs). **—meg′a·lo·ceph′a·ly, meg·a·lo·ce·pha·li·a** (meg′ə lō sə fā′lē ə, -fāl′yə), *n.*

meg·a·lo·ma·ni·a (meg′ə lō mā′nē ə), *n.* **1.** *Psychiatry.* a form of mental illness marked by delusions of greatness, wealth, etc. **2.** an obsession with doing extravagant or grand things. **—meg′a·lo·ma′ni·ac′,** *n.* **—meg·a·lo·ma·ni·a·cal** (meg′ə lō mə nī′ə kəl), *adj.*

meg·a·lop·o·lis (meg′ə lop′ə lis), *n.* **1.** an outsize city, as Tokyo. **2.** (loosely) an urban region, esp. one consisting of several large, adjoining cities. Also, **me·gap·o·lis** (mə gap′ə lis).

meg·a·lo·pol·i·tan (meg′ə lō pol′i tən), *adj.* **1.** of, pertaining to, or characteristic of a megalopolis. **—***n.* **2.** an inhabitant of a megalopolis. [from MEGALOPOLIS, modeled after *metropolis: metropolitan*] **—meg′a·lo·pol′i·tan·ism,** *n.*

meg·a·lo·saur (meg′ə lə sôr′), *n.* any gigantic carnivorous dinosaur of the genus *Megalosaurus.* [< NL *megalosaur(us)*] **—meg′a·lo·sau′ri·an,** *adj., n.*

-megaly, a suffix indicating enlargement: *acromegaly.* Also, **-megalia.** [< NL *-megalia.* See MEGALO-, -Y³]

meg·a·phone (meg′ə fōn′), *n.* a device, usually funnel-shaped, for magnifying or directing the sound of the voice. **—meg·a·phon·ic** (meg′ə fon′ik), *adj.* **—meg′a·phon′i·cal·ly,** *adv.*

meg·a·pod (meg′ə pod′), *adj.* having large feet.

Meg·a·ra (meg′ər ə), *n.* a city in ancient Greece: the chief city of Megaris. **—Me·gar·i·an, Me·gar·e·an** (mə gar′ē ən, me-), **Me·gar′ic,** *adj.*

Meg·a·ris (meg′ər is), *n.* a district in ancient Greece, between the Gulf of Corinth and the Saronic Gulf.

meg·a·spo·ran·gi·um (meg′ə spō ran′jē əm, -spô-), *n., pl.* **-gi·a** (-jē ə). *Bot.* a sporangium containing megaspores.

meg·a·spore (meg′ə spōr′, -spôr′), *n. Bot.* **1.** the larger of the two kinds of spores produced by some pteridophytes. **2.** the embryo sac of a flowering plant. **—meg·a·spor·ic** (meg′ə spōr′ik, -spor′-), *adj.*

meg·a·spo·ro·phyll (meg′ə spōr′ə fil, -spôr′-), *n. Bot.* a sporophyll producing megasporangia only.

me·gass (mə gas′, -gäs′), *n.* bagasse. Also, **me·gasse′.** [unexplained var.]

meg·a·struc·ture (meg′ə struk′chər), *n.* a complex of huge, usually high-rise buildings for many purposes, such as apartments, offices, stores, theaters, athletic facilities, etc.

meg·a·there (meg′ə thēr′), *n.* any of the huge, slothlike animals of the extinct genus *Megatherium.* [< NL *megathēr(ium)* = Gk *megā-* MEGA- + *thērion* wild beast]

Megathere, genus *Megatherium* (Length 20 ft.)

meg·a·ton (meg′ə tun′), *n.* **1.** one million tons. **2.** an explosive force equal to that of one million tons of TNT, as that of atomic or hydrogen bombs. *Abbr.:* MT **—meg·a·ton·ic** (meg′ə ton′ik), *adj.*

meg·a·volt (meg′ə vōlt′), *n. Elect.* a unit of electromotive force, equal to one million volts. *Abbr.:* MV, Mv

meg·a·volt-am·pere (meg′ə vōlt′am′pēr, -am pēr′), *n.* one million volt-amperes. *Abbr.:* MVA, Mva

meg·a·watt (meg′ə wot′), *n. Elect.* a unit of power, equal to one million watts. *Abbr.:* Mw

meg·a·watt-hour (meg′ə wot′our′, -ou′ər), *n.* a unit of energy equal to one million watt-hours. *Abbr.:* MWh, Mwhr

Me·gid·do (mə gid′ō), *n.* an ancient city in N Israel, on the plain of Esdraelon.

me·gil·lah (mə gil′ə; *for 2 also Heb.* mi gē lä′), *n., pl.* **-gil·lahs** for 1, **-gil·loth** (-gē lôt′) for 2. **1.** *Slang.* a lengthy explanation or account. **2.** (*italics*) *Hebrew.* a scroll, esp. one containing the Book of Esther or of Ecclesiastes, the Song of Solomon, the Book of Ruth, or the Book of Lamentations.

me·grim (mē′grim), *n.* **1. megrims,** low spirits; the blues. **2.** *Archaic.* a whim or caprice. **3.** *Obs.* migraine. [ME *mygrame* a type of headache < MF *migraine* (by misreading, *in* taken as *m*); see MIGRAINE]

Me·hem·et A·li (mi hem′et ä lē′, ä′lē, mā′met), 1769–1849, viceroy of Egypt 1805–48. Also, **Mohammed Ali.**

Mei·ji (mā′jē′), *n. Japanese Hist.* the period from 1867 to 1912, during which the Emperor Mutsuhito reigned. [< Jap: lit., enlightened peace]

mein·y (mā′nē), *n., pl.* **mein·ies.** *Archaic.* **1.** *Scot.* a multitude; crowd. **2.** a group or suite of attendants, followers, etc. Also, **mein′ie.** [ME *meynee* household < OF *meyne, mesnie, mesnede* < VL **mansiōnāta.* See MANSION, -ATE¹]

mei·o·sis (mī ō′sis), *n.* **1.** *Biol.* the maturation process of gametes, consisting of chromosome conjugation and two cell divisions, in the course of which the diploid chromosome number becomes reduced to the haploid. **2.** *Rhet.* expressive understatement, esp. litotes. [< Gk: a lessening = *mei(oûn)* (to) lessen (< *meîōn* less) + *-ōsis* -OSIS] **—mei·ot·ic** (mī ot′ik), *adj.*

Me·ir (mā ēr′), *n.* **Gol·da** (gōl′də), 1898–1978, Israeli stateswoman, born in Russia: premier 1969–74.

Meis·sen (mī′sən), *n.* a city in SE East Germany, on the Elbe River: famous for fine porcelain. 44,110.

Meis·ter·sing·er (mī′stər siŋ′ər, -ziŋ′-), *n., pl.* **-sing·er, -sing·ers.** an artisan, poet, or musician who was a member of one of the craft guilds during the 14th–16th centuries in Germany. [< G: master singer]

Meit·ner (mīt′nər), *n.* **Li·se** (lē′zə), 1878–1968, Austrian nuclear physicist.

Mé·ji·co (me′hē kô), *n.* Spanish name of **Mexico.**

Mek·ka (mek′ə), *n.* Mecca (def. 1).

Mek·nès (mek nes′), *n.* a city in N Morocco: former capital of Morocco. 244,520.

Me·kong (mā′koŋ′; *Thai.* ma kôŋ′), *n.* a river whose source is in SW China, flowing SE along the boundary between Thailand and Laos to the South China Sea. 2600 mi. long. Chinese, **Lantsang.**

Me′kong Del′ta, the delta of the Mekong River in S Vietnam.

mel·a·mine (mel′ə mēn′, mel′ə mēn′), *n.* **1.** *Chem.* a solid, $C_3N_3(NH_2)_3$, used chiefly in organic synthesis and in the manufacture of resins, esp. melamine resins. **2.** any of the melamine resins. [< G *Melamin* < *Melam* distillate of ammonium thiocyanate (arbitrary coinage, but *-am* repr. AMMONIUM); see -INE²]

mel′amine res′in, *Chem.* any of the class of thermosetting resins formed by the interaction of melamine and formaldehyde: used chiefly as adhesives for laminated materials and as coatings for paper, plastics, and textiles.

melan-, var. of **melano-** before a vowel: *melanism.*

mel·an·cho·li·a (mel′ən kō′lē ə, -kōl′yə), *n. Psychiatry.* mental disease characterized by great depression of spirits and gloomy forebodings. [< LL; see MELANCHOLY] **—mel·an·cho·li·ac** (mel′ən kō′lē ak′), *adj., n.* **—mel·an·chol·ic** (mel′ən kol′ik), *adj.* **—mel′an·chol′i·cal·ly,** *adv.*

mel·an·chol·y (mel′ən kol′ē), *n., pl.* **-chol·ies,** *adj.* **—***n.* **1.** a gloomy state of mind, esp. when habitual or prolonged; depression. **2.** sober thoughtfulness; pensiveness. **3.** *Archaic.* **a.** condition of having too much black bile. **b.** the bile itself. **—***adj.* **4.** affected with, characterized by, or showing melancholy; mournful; depressed: *a melancholy mood.* **5.** causing melancholy or sadness. **6.** soberly thoughtful; pensive. [ME *melancholie* < LL *melancholia* < Gk: black bile] **—mel′an·chol′i·ly** *adv.* **—mel′an·chol′i·ness,** *n.* **—Syn. 1.** sadness, despondency. **4.** despondent, gloomy, blue, dispirited, downcast, glum. See **sad. —Ant. 1.** cheer, happiness. **5.** happy.

Me·lanch·thon (mə laŋk′thən; *Ger.* mā länkʜ′tôn), *n.* **Phil·ipp** (fil′ip; *Ger.* fē′lip), (*Philipp Schwarzert*), 1497–1560, German Protestant reformer.

Mel·a·ne·sia (mel′ə nē′zhə, -shə), *n.* one of the three principal divisions of Oceania, comprising the island groups in the S Pacific NE of Australia.

Mel·a·ne·sian (mel′ə nē′zhən, -shən), *adj.* **1.** of or pertaining to Melanesia, its inhabitants, or their languages. **—***n.* **2.** *Anthropol.* a member of any of the dark-skinned, frizzy-haired peoples inhabiting Melanesia and New Guinea. **3.** the Malayo-Polynesian languages of Melanesia, taken collectively.

mé·lange (*Fr.* mā läɴzh′), *n., pl.* **-langes** (*Fr.* -läɴzh′). a mixture; medley. [< F; see MEDLEY]

me·lan·ic (mə lan′ik), *adj.* **1.** *Pathol.* melanotic. **2.** of or pertaining to melanism.

mel·a·nin (mel′ə nin), *n. Biochem.* a dark pigment in the body of man and certain animals, as that occurring in the hair, epidermis, etc.

mel·a·nism (mel′ə niz′əm), *n. Ethnol., Zool.* the condition of having a high amount of dark or black pigment granules in the skin, hair, eyes, plumage, etc. Cf. **melanin. —mel′a·nis′tic,** *adj.*

mel·a·nite (mel′ə nīt′), *n. Mineral.* a deep black variety of andradite garnet.

melano-, a learned borrowing from Greek meaning "black," used in the formation of compound words: *melanoma.* Also, *esp. before a vowel,* **melan-.** [< Gk, comb. form of *mélas*]

mel·a·noch·ro·i (mel′ə nok′rō ī′), *n.pl.* (*often cap.*) light-complexioned Caucasoids with dark hair. [< NL < Gk **melánōchroi* black pale ones = *melan-* MELAN- + *-ōchroi,* pl. of *ōchrós* pale] **—mel·a·noch·roid** (mel′ə nok′roid), **mel·a·no·chro·ic** (mel′ə nō krō′ik), *adj.*

mel·a·noid (mel′ə noid′), *adj.* **1.** of or characterized by melanosis. **2.** resembling melanin; darkish.

mel·a·no·ma (mel′ə nō′mə), *n., pl.* **-mas, -ma·ta** (-mə tə). *Pathol.* a darkly pigmented tumor, esp. of the skin or eye, of cells containing melanin.

mel·a·no·sis (mel′ə nō′sis), *n. Pathol.* **1.** abnormal deposition or development of black or dark pigment in the tissues. **2.** a discoloration caused by this. [< NL < LGk: a becoming black] **—mel·a·not·ic** (mel′ə not′ik), *adj.*

mel·an·tha·ceous (mel′ən thā′shəs), *adj.* belonging to the *Melanthaceae,* a family of bulbless plants related to and sometimes classified in the lily family, comprising the bellwort, white hellebore, etc. [< NL *Melanth(ium)* name of typical genus (< Gk *mél(as)* black + *ánth(os)* flower + *-ium,* n. suffix) + -ACEOUS]

mel·a·phyre (mel′ə fīər′), *n. Obs.* any of various dark-colored igneous rocks of porphyritic texture. [< F *mélaphyre* = *méla-* (< Gk *méla(s)* black) + *(por)phyre* PORPHYRY]

Mel·ba (mel′bə), *n.* **(Dame) Nellie** (*Helen Porter Mitchell Armstrong*), 1861–1931, Australian operatic soprano.

Mel′ba sauce′, a clear raspberry sauce, used esp. as a dessert topping. [named after Nellie MELBA]

Mel′ba toast′, bread sliced thin and toasted until crisp. [named after Nellie MELBA]

Mel·bourne (mel′bərn), *n.* **1. 2nd Viscount.** See **Lamb, William. 2.** a seaport in and the capital of Victoria, in SE Australia. 2,319,700 (1968). **3.** a city in E Florida. 40,236 (1970). **—Mel·bur·ni·an** (mel bûr′nē ən), *n., adj.*

Mel·chi·a·des (mel kī′ə dēz′), *n.* **Saint,** died A.D. 314, pope 310–314. Also, **Miltiades.**

Mel·chior (mel′kyôr, mel′kē ôr′), *n.* **1.** one of the three Magi. **2. Lau·ritz (Leb·recht Hom·mel)** (lou′rits lib′rekt hom′əl, lôr′its; *Dan.* lou′rits lib′rekʜt hom′el), 1890–1973, U.S. operatic tenor, born in Denmark.

Mel·chite (mel′kīt), *n.* any Christian in Egypt and Syria who accepted the definition of faith adopted by the Council of Chalcedon in A.D. 451. [< ML *Melchīta* < MGk *Melchī́tēs* royalist = *melch-* king (< Sem) + *-ītēs* -ITE¹]

Mel·chiz·e·dek (mel kiz′i dek′), *n.* a priest and king of Salem. Gen. 14:18. Also, *Douay Bible,* **Mel·chis′e·dech′.**

meld[1] (meld), *Cards.* —*v.t., v.i.* **1.** to announce and display (a counting combination of cards in the hand) for a score. —*n.* **2.** the act of melding. **3.** any combination of cards to be melded. [< G *meld(en)* (to) announce; akin to OE *meldian*]

meld[2] (meld), *v.t., v.i.* to merge; blend. [MEL(T + WEL)D[1]]

Mel·e·a·ger (mel′ē ā′jər), *n. Gk. Legend.* the heroic son of Althaea, an Argonaut and the slayer of the Calydonian boar.

me·lee (mā′lā, mā lā′, mel′ā), *n.* **1.** a confused, general, hand-to-hand fight. **2.** confusion; turmoil; jumble. Also, **mê·lée.** [< F *mêlée.* See MEDLEY]

-melia, an element indicating a specified condition of the limbs: *phocomelia.* [< NL, comb. form repr. Gk *mélos* limb; see -IA]

me·li·a·ceous (mē′lē ā′shəs), *adj.* belonging to the *Meliaceae,* a family of trees and shrubs comprising the azedarach, mahogany, Spanish cedar, etc. [< NL *Meli(a)* name of genus (< Gk: ash) + -ACEOUS]

Me·li·ae (mē′lē ē′), *n.pl. Class. Myth.* the nymphs born from the blood of Uranus at the time of his mutilation by Cronus; the nymphs of ash trees. [< Gk *melíai* < *melía* manna, ash]

mel·ic (mel′ik), *adj.* **1.** intended to be sung. **2.** noting or pertaining to the more elaborate form of Greek lyric poetry, as distinguished from iambic and elegiac poetry. [< Gk *melik(ós)* = *mél(os)* limb, song + *-ikos* -IC]

mel·i·lite (mel′ə līt′), *n.* a mineral group, chiefly of sodium, calcium, and aluminum silicates, occurring in igneous rocks. [< NL *melilith(us)* = Gk *méli* honey + *líthos* -LITE]

Me·lil·la (mā lēl′yä), *n.* a seaport belonging to Spain on the NE coast of Morocco, in NW Africa. 79,056 (1961).

mel·i·lot (mel′ə lot′), *n.* any cloverlike, fabaceous herb of the genus *Melilotus.* [ME *mellilot* < L *melilōt(os)* < Gk: a clover = *méli* honey + *lōtós* LOTUS]

mel·io·rate (mēl′yə rāt′, mē′lē ə-), *v.t., v.i.,* **-rat·ed, -rat·ing.** to ameliorate. [< L *meliōrāt(us)* made better, improved (ptp. of *meliōrāre*) = *meliōr-* (s. of *melior*) better + *-ātus* -ATE[1]] —**mel·io·ra·ble** (mēl′yər ə bəl, mē′lē ər ə-), *adj.* —**mel′io·ra′tion,** *n.* —**mel·io·ra·tive** (mēl′yə rā′tiv, -yər ə tiv, mē′lē ə rā′-, -ər ə-), *adj.* —**mel′io·ra′tor,** *n.*

mel·io·rism (mēl′yə riz′əm, mē′lē ə-), *n.* the doctrine that the world tends to become better or may be made better by human effort. [< L *melior* better + -ISM] —**mel′io·rist,** *n., adj.* —**mel′io·ris′tic,** *adj.*

mel·ior·i·ty (mēl yôr′i tē, -yor′-, mē′lē ôr′-, -or′-), *n.* superiority. [< ML *meliōritās* = L *meliōr-* (s. of *melior*) better + *-itās* -ITY]

Mel·i·te·ne (mel′i tē′nē), *n.* ancient name of **Malatya.**

Me·li·to·pol (mel′ə tô′pəl; *Russ.* me li tô′pol), *n.* a city in the SE Ukraine, in the SW Soviet Union in Europe, NW of the Sea of Azov: battles 1941, 1943. 104,000 (est. 1962).

mel·lif·er·ous (mə lif′ər əs), *adj.* yielding or producing honey. [< L *mellifer* honey-bearing (*melli-,* s. of *mel* honey, + *-fer* -FER) + -OUS]

mel·lif·lu·ent (mə lif′lo͞o ənt), *adj.* mellifluous. [< LL *mellifluent-* (s. of *mellifluēns*) = L *melli-* (s. of *mel*) honey + *fluent-* FLUENT] —**mel·lif′lu·ence,** *n.* —**mel·lif′lu·ent·ly,** *adv.*

mel·lif·lu·ous (mə lif′lo͞o əs), *adj.* **1.** sweetly or smoothly flowing; sweet-sounding: *a mellifluous voice; mellifluous tones.* **2.** flowing with honey; sweetened with or as with honey. [< LL *mellifluus* = L *melli-* (s. of *mel*) honey + *-flu(ere)* (to) flow + *-us* -OUS] —**mel·lif′lu·ous·ly,** *adv.* —**mel·lif′lu·ous·ness,** *n.*

Mel·lon (mel′ən), *n.* **Andrew William,** 1855–1937, U.S. financier: Secretary of the Treasury 1921–32.

mel·lo·phone (mel′ə fōn′), *n.* althorn. [MELLO(W) + -PHONE]

mel·low (mel′ō), *adj.* **1.** soft and full-flavored from ripeness, as fruit. **2.** well-matured, as wines. **3.** softened, toned down, or improved, as by aging or ripening. **4.** soft and rich, as sound, tones, color, light, etc. **5.** genial; jovial. **6.** friable or loamy, as soil. **7.** *Informal.* mildly intoxicated. —*v.t., v.i.* **8.** to make or become mellow; soften by aging or ripening. [late ME *mel(o)we,* alter. of ME *meruw,* OE *meru* soft (? by dissimilation, in phrase *meruw fruit*)] —**mel′low·ly,** *adv.* —**mel′low·ness,** *n.* —**Syn. 1.** See **ripe. 8.** mature. —**Ant. 1.** immature, raw, green. **4.** harsh.

me·lo·de·on (mə lō′dē ən), *n.* **1.** a small reed organ. **2.** a kind of accordion. [< G, formed on *Melodie* melody]

me·lod·ic (mə lod′ik), *adj.* **1.** melodious. **2.** pertaining to melody as distinguished from harmony and rhythm. [< LL *melōdic(us)* < Gk *melōidikós*] —**me·lod′i·cal·ly,** *adv.*

melod′ic in′terval. See under **interval** (def. 5).

melod′ic mi′nor scale′, *Music.* See **minor scale** (def. 2).

me·lo·di·ous (mə lō′dē əs), *adj.* **1.** of the nature of or characterized by melody; tuneful. **2.** producing melody; sweet-sounding; musical. [ME < ML *melōdiōs(us)*] —**me·lo′di·ous·ness,** *n.*

mel·o·dist (mel′ə dist), *n.* a composer or a singer of melodies.

mel·o·dize (mel′ə dīz′), *v.,* **-dized, -diz·ing.** —*v.t.* **1.** to make melodious. —*v.i.* **2.** to make melody. **3.** to blend melodiously. Also, *esp. Brit.,* **mel′o·dise′.** —**mel′o·diz′er,** *n.*

mel·o·dra·ma (mel′ə drä′mə, -dram′ə), *n.* a dramatic form in which exaggeration of effect and emotion is produced and plot or action is emphasized at the expense of characterization. [< F *mélodrame* = *mélo-* (< Gk *mélo(s)* song) + *drame* DRAMA] —**mel·o·dram·a·tist** (mel′ə dram′ə tist, -drä′mə-), *n.*

mel·o·dra·mat·ic (mel′ə drə mat′ik), *adj.* **1.** of, like, or befitting melodrama; sentimental and exaggerated. —*n.* **2. melodramatics,** melodramatic writing or behavior. —**mel′o·dra·mat′i·cal·ly,** *adv.*

mel·o·dram·a·tize (mel′ə dram′ə tīz′, -drä′mə-), *v.t.,* **-tized, -tiz·ing. 1.** to make melodramatic. **2.** to turn (a novel, story, etc.) into a melodrama. Also, *esp. Brit.,* **mel′o·dram′a·tise′.**

mel·o·dy (mel′ə dē), *n., pl.* **-dies. 1.** musical sounds in agreeable succession or arrangement. **2.** *Music.* **a.** the succession of single tones in musical compositions, as distinguished from harmony and rhythm. **b.** the principal part in a harmonic composition; the air. **c.** a rhythmical succession of single tones producing a distinct musical phrase or idea. **3.** a poem suitable for singing. [ME *melodie* < eccl. L *melōdia* < Gk *melōidía* (choral) singing. See MELIC, ODE, -Y[3]] —**mel′o·dy·less,** *adj.* —**Syn. 1.** See **harmony. 2.** tune, song, theme.

mel·oid (mel′oid), *n.* **1.** a beetle of the family *Meloidae,* comprising the blister beetles. —*adj.* **2.** belonging or pertaining to the family *Meloidae.* [< NL *Meloid(ae)* name of the family = *Melo(ē)* typical genus + *-idae* -ID[2]]

mel·on (mel′ən), *n.* **1.** the fruit of any of various cucurbitaceous plants, as the muskmelon or watermelon. **2.** *Slang.* **a.** a large extra dividend to be distributed to stockholders. **b.** any large sum of money, as profit, a bonus, prize money, etc., for distribution. [ME < LL *mēlōn-* (s. of *mēlō*), short for *mēlopepō* < Gk *mēlopépōn* apple-shaped melon = *mêlo(n)* apple + *pépōn* melon, see PEPO]

Me·los (mē′los, -lōs, mel′os, -ōs; *Gk.* mē′lôs), *n.* a Greek island in the Cyclades, in the SW Aegean. 5586 (1951); 51 sq. mi. Also, **Milo, Milos.** —**Me·li·an** (mē′lē ən, mēl′yən), *adj., n.*

Mel·pom·e·ne (mel pom′ə nē′), *n. Class. Myth.* the Muse of tragedy. [< L < Gk, special use of fem. of prp. of *mélpesthai* to sing]

Mel·rose (mel′rōz), *n.* **1.** a city in E Massachusetts, near Boston. 33,180 (1970). **2.** a village in SE Scotland, on the Tweed River: ruins of a famous abbey.

melt[1] (melt), *v.,* **melt·ed, melt·ed** or **mol·ten, melt·ing,** *n.* —*v.i.* **1.** to become liquefied by heat. **2.** to become liquid; dissolve: *Let the cough drop melt in your mouth.* **3.** to pass away, dwindle, or fade gradually (often fol. by *away*): *His fortune slowly melted away.* **4.** to pass, change, or blend gradually (often fol. by *into*): *Night melted into day.* **5.** to become softened in feeling by pity, sympathy, love, or the like. —*v.t.* **6.** to reduce to a liquid state by heat; fuse. **7.** to cause to pass away, dwindle, or fade gradually. **8.** to cause to pass, change, or blend gradually. **9.** to soften in feeling, as a person, the heart, etc. —*n.* **10.** the act or process of melting. **11.** the state of being melted. **12.** that which is melted. **13.** a quantity melted at one time. **14.** Also, **milt.** the spleen, esp. that of a cow, pig, etc. [ME *melte(n),* OE *meltan* (v.i.), *m(i)elten* (v.t.) to melt, digest; c. Icel *melta* to digest, Gk *méldein* to melt] —**melt′a·bil′i·ty,** *n.* —**melt′a·ble,** *adj.* —**melt′ing·ly,** *adv.* —**melt′·ing·ness,** *n.*

—**Syn. 1.** MELT, DISSOLVE, FUSE, THAW imply reducing a solid substance to a liquid state. To MELT is to bring a solid to a liquid condition by the agency of heat: *to melt butter.* To DISSOLVE is to bring a solid into contact with a liquid so that the particles of the solid become distributed throughout the liquid: *to dissolve a solid in alcohol.* To FUSE is to subject a solid to a very high temperature; it applies esp. to melting or blending metals together: *Bell metal is made by fusing copper and tin.* To THAW is to reduce a frozen liquid to its liquid or a semiliquid state by raising its temperature above the freezing point: *Sunshine will thaw ice in a lake.* It is also applied to reducing a frozen solid, such as food, to its normal soft or pliable state. **4.** dwindle. **9.** gentle, mollify, relax. —**Ant. 1.** freeze. **2.** solidify, crystallize.

melt[2] (melt), *n.* the spleen, esp. that of a cow, pig, etc. Also, **milt.** [ME, OE *milte,* c. OHG *milzi,* G *Milz,* ON *milti;* prob. akin to MELT[1]]

melt·down (melt′doun′), *n.* the melting of a significant portion of a nuclear-reactor core due to inadequate cooling of the fuel elements, potentially resulting in escape of radiation. [n. use of v. phrase *melt down*]

melt′ing point′, *Physical Chem.* the temperature at which a solid substance melts or fuses.

melt′ing pot′, 1. a country, locality, or situation in which a blending of races and cultures is taking place. **2.** a pot in which metals or other substances are melted or fused.

mel′ton cloth′ (mel′tən), *n.* a smooth, heavy woolen cloth, for overcoats, hunting jackets, etc. Also called **mel′ton.** [after *Melton* Mowbray, town in Leicestershire, England]

Mel·ville (mel′vil), *n.* **Herman,** 1819–91, U.S. novelist.

Mel′ville Is′land, an island in the Arctic Ocean, N of Canada: belonging to Canada. 200 mi. long; 130 mi. wide.

Mel′ville Penin′sula, a peninsula in N Canada, SE of the Gulf of Boothia. 250 mi. long.

mem (mem; *Heb.* mem), *n.* the 13th letter of the Hebrew alphabet. [< Heb: lit., water]

mem., 1. member. **2.** memoir. **3.** memorandum.

mem·ber (mem′bər), *n.* **1.** any of the persons composing a society, party, community, or other body. **2.** *Govt.* a member of a legislative body, esp. the U.S. House of Representatives or the British House of Commons. **3.** a part or organ of an animal body; a limb, as a leg, arm, or wing. **4.** a constituent part of any structural or composite whole, as a subordinate architectural feature of a building or the like. **5.** *Math.* **a.** either side of an equation. **b.** an element of a set —*adj.* **6.** being a member of or having membership in an association, organization, etc.: *a member bank; member countries of the United Nations.* [ME *membre* < L *membr(um)*] —**mem′ber·less,** *adj.* —**Syn. 4.** element, portion.

mem·ber·ship (mem′bər ship′), *n.* **1.** the state of being a member, as of a society. **2.** the status of a member. **3.** the total number of members belonging to an organization, society, etc.

mem·brane (mem′brān), *n. Biol.* **1.** a thin, pliable sheet or layer of animal or vegetable tissue, serving to line an organ, connect parts, etc. **2.** the thin, limiting covering of a cell or cell part. [earlier *membraan* parchment < L *membrāna.* See MEMBER, -ANE] —**mem′brane·less,** *adj.*

mem′brane bone′, a bone that develops from membranous tissue. Cf. **cartilage bone.**

mem·bra·nous (mem′brə nəs), *adj.* **1.** consisting of, of the nature of, or resembling membrane. **2.** characterized by the formation of a membrane. Also, **mem·bra·na·ceous** (mem′brə nā′shəs). [cf. F *membraneux*] —**mem′bra·nous·ly,** *adv.*

Me·mel (mā′məl, mem′əl), *n.* **1.** a seaport in NW Lithuania, in the W Soviet Union in Europe. 89,000 (1959). **2.** a territory including this seaport: ceded to Germany by Lithuania 1939; incorporated into the Soviet Union 1945. 933 sq. mi. **3.** the lower course of the Niemen River. Cf. **Niemen.** Lithuanian, **Klaipeda** (for defs. 1, 2).

me·men·to (mə men′tō), *n., pl.* **-tos, -toes. 1.** something that serves as a reminder of what is past or gone; souvenir.

2. something serving as a reminder or warning of a future event. [< L *mementō*, impv. of *meminisse* to remember]
me·men·to mo·ri (mə men′tō mōr′ī, môr′ī, mōr′ē, môr′ē; *for 1 also Lat.* me men′tō mōʀ′ē), *pl.* **memento mori** for 2. **1.** (*italics*) *Latin.* remember that thou must die. **2.** an object, as a skull, serving as a reminder of death.
Mem·ling (mem′liŋg), *n.* **Hans** (häns), c1430–94?, Flemish painter. Also, **Mem·linc** (mem′liŋgk).
Mem·non (mem′non), *n. Class. Myth.* an Oriental or Ethiopian hero slain by Achilles in the Trojan War.
mem·o (mem′ō), *n., pl.* **mem·os.** *Informal.* memorandum. [by shortening]
mem·oir (mem′wär, -wôr), *n.* **1. memoirs, a.** records of facts or events in connection with a particular subject, historical period, etc., as known to the writer or gathered from special sources. **b.** records of one's life and experiences. **c.** a collection of reports made to a scientific or other learned society. **2.** a biography. [< F *mémoire* < L *memoria* MEMORY]
mem·oir·ist (mem′wär ist, -wôr-), *n.* a writer or author of a memoir or memoirs.
mem·o·ra·bil·i·a (mem′ər ə bil′ē ə, -bil′yə), *n.pl., sing.* **-o·rab·i·le** (-ə rab′ə lē). matters or events worthy to be remembered. [< L: things to be remembered, neut. pl. of *memorābilis* MEMORABLE]
mem·o·ra·ble (mem′ər ə bəl), *adj.* **1.** worthy of being remembered; notable: *a memorable speech.* **2.** easily remembered. [late ME < L *memorābil(is)* worth mentioning = *memorā(re)* (to) mention + *-bilis* -BLE] —**mem′o·ra·bil′i·ty, mem′o·ra·ble·ness,** *n.* —**mem′o·ra·bly,** *adv.*
mem·o·ran·dum (mem′ə ran′dəm), *n., pl.* **-dums, -da** (-də). **1.** a note designating something to be remembered, esp. something to be done or acted upon in the future; reminder. **2.** a record or written statement of something. **3.** an informal message, esp. one sent between two or more employees of the same company. **4.** *Law.* a writing, usually informal, containing the terms of a transaction. **5.** *Diplomacy.* an informal official communication. [< L: something to be noted, neut. of *memorandus* notable, orig. ger. of *memorāre* to mention, tell]
me·mo·ri·al (mə mōr′ē əl, -môr′-), *n.* **1.** something designed to preserve the memory of a person, event, etc., as a monument or a periodic observance. **2.** a written statement of facts presented to a sovereign, a legislative body, etc., as the ground of a petition. —*adj.* **3.** preserving the memory of a person or thing; commemorative: *memorial services.* **4.** of or pertaining to the memory. [ME < LL *memoriāle,* n. use of neut. of L *memoriālis* for memoranda] —**me·mo′ri·al·ly,** *adv.*
Memo′rial Day′, *U.S.* **1.** Also called **Decoration Day.** a day, May 30, set aside in most states for observances in memory of dead servicemen of all wars: now officially observed on last Monday in May. **2.** any of several days, as April 26, May 10, or June 3, similarly observed in various southern states.
me·mo·ri·al·ise (mə mōr′ē ə līz′, -môr′-), *v.t.,* **-ised, -is·ing.** *Chiefly Brit.* memorialize. —**me·mo′ri·al·i·sa′tion,** *n.* —**me·mo′ri·al·is′er,** *n.*
me·mo·ri·al·ist (mə mōr′ē ə list, -môr′-), n. **1.** a person who writes memorials. **2.** a person who writes memoirs.
me·mo·ri·al·ize (mə mōr′ē ə līz′, -môr′-), *v.t.,* **-ized, -iz·ing. 1.** to commemorate. **2.** to present a memorial to. Also, *esp. Brit.,* **memorialise.** —**me·mo′ri·al·i·za′tion,** *n.* —**me·mo′ri·al·iz′er,** *n.*
mem·o·rize (mem′ə rīz′), *v.t.,* **-rized, -riz·ing.** to commit to memory; learn by heart: *to memorize a poem.* —**mem′o·riz′a·ble,** *adj.* —**mem′o·ri·za′tion,** *n.* —**mem′o·riz′er,** *n.*
mem·o·ry (mem′ə rē), *n., pl.* **-ries. 1.** the mental capacity or faculty of retaining and reviving impressions, or of recalling or recognizing previous experiences. **2.** this faculty as possessed by a particular individual: *to have a good memory.* **3.** the act or fact of retaining mental impressions; remembrance; recollection. **4.** the length of time over which recollection extends: *a time within the memory of living men.* **5.** a mental impression retained; recollection: *one's earliest memories.* **6.** the reputation of a person or thing, esp. after death; fame: *a ruler of beloved memory.* **7.** the state or fact of being remembered. **8.** a person or thing remembered. **9.** commemorative remembrance; commemoration: *a monument in memory of Columbus.* **10.** Also called **storage.** *Computer Technol.* **a.** the capacity of a computer to store information subject to recall. **b.** the set of components of the computer, in which such information is stored. [ME *memorie* < L *memoria* = *memor* remembering + *-ia* -Y[3]]
Mem·phi·an (mem′fē ən), *n.* **1.** Egyptian (def. 3). **2.** a native or resident of Memphis, Tennessee.
Mem·phis (mem′fis), *n.* **1.** a port in SW Tennessee, on the Mississippi. 623,530 (1970). **2.** a ruined city in Upper Egypt, on the Nile, S of Cairo: the ancient capital of Egypt. See map at **Goshen.**
Mem·phite (mem′fīt), *adj.* **1.** Also, **Mem·phit·ic** (mem fit′ik). of or pertaining to the ancient Egyptian city of Memphis. —*n.* **2.** a native or inhabitant of the ancient Egyptian city of Memphis. [<< Gk *Memphītēs* inhabitant of Memphis; see -ITE[1]]
Mem·phre·ma·gog (mem′frē mā′gog), *n.* **Lake,** a lake on the boundary between the U.S. and Canada, between N Vermont and S Quebec. 30 mi. long.
mem·sa·hib (mem′sä′ib, -ēb, -sä′hib, -hēb), *n.* (formerly in India) a term of respect for a European woman. [< Hindi = *mem* (< E MA'AM) + *sāhib* master]
men (men), *n.* pl. of **man.**
men·ace (men′is), *n., v.,* **-aced, -ac·ing.** —*n.* **1.** something that threatens to cause evil, harm, etc.; threat. —*v.t.* **2.** to utter or direct a threat against; threaten. **3.** to serve as a probable threat to; imperil. —*v.i.* **4.** to appear or act as a threat or danger. [late ME < MF < L *mināci̇a* = *mināc-* (s. of *mināx*) jutting out, threatening + *-ia* -IA] —**men′ac·er,** *n.* —**men′ac·ing·ly,** *adv.*
Me·na·do (me nä′dō), *n.* a seaport on NE Celebes, in NE Indonesia. 127,614 (1961). Also, **Manado.**
mé·nage (mā näzh′; *Fr.* mā nazh′), *n., pl.* **-nages** (-nä′zhiz; *Fr.* -nazh′). **1.** a domestic establishment; household. **2.** housekeeping. Also, **me·nage′.** [< F << VL **mansiōnāticum.* See MANSION, -AGE]
mé·nage à trois (mā nazh a trwä′), *French.* a domestic arrangement involving a married couple and the lover of one of them, in which all three occupy the same household. [lit., household of three]
me·nag·er·ie (mə naj′ə rē, -nazh′-), *n.* **1.** a collection of wild or strange animals, esp. for exhibition. **2.** a place where they are kept or exhibited. [< F: lit., housekeeping]
Men′ai Strait′ (men′ī), a strait between Anglesey island and the mainland of NW Wales. 14 mi. long.
Me·nam (me näm′), *n.* a river in N Thailand, flowing S to the Gulf of Siam. 150 mi. long. Also called **Chao Phraya, Nam.**
Me·nan·der (mə nan′dər), *n.* 342?–291 B.C., Greek writer of comedies.
men·ar·che (mə när′kē, me-), *n. Physiol.* the first menstrual period; the establishment of menstruation. [< Gk *mēn* month + *archē* beginning] —**men·ar′che·al, men·ar′chi·al,** *adj.*
men-chil·dren (men′chil′drən, -drin), *n.* pl. of **man-child.**
Men·ci·us (men′shē əs, -shəs), *n.* c380–289 B.C., Chinese philosopher. Also called **Mêng-tzŭ, Meng-tse.**
Menck·en (meŋ′kən), *n.* **H(enry) L(ouis),** 1880–1956, U.S. author, editor, and critic.
mend (mend), *v.t.* **1.** to make (something broken, worn, torn, or otherwise damaged) whole, sound, or usable by repairing: *to mend clothes.* **2.** to remove or correct defects or errors in. **3.** to remove or correct. **4.** to set right; make better; improve: *to mend matters.* —*v.i.* **5.** to progress toward recovery, as a sick person. **6.** to improve, as conditions, affairs, etc. —*n.* **7.** the act of mending; repair or improvement. **8.** a mended place. **9. on the mend,** recovering from an illness; recuperating. [aph. var. of AMEND] —**mend′a·ble,** *adj.* —**Syn. 1.** fix, restore, retouch. **2.** rectify, amend, emend. **4.** ameliorate, meliorate. **5.** heal, recover.
men·da·cious (men dā′shəs), *adj.* **1.** false or untrue: *a mendacious report.* **2.** lying; untruthful; dishonest. [< L *mendāci-* (see MENDACITY) + -OUS] —**men·da′cious·ly,** *adv.* —**men·da′cious·ness,** *n.*
men·dac·i·ty (men das′i tē), *n., pl.* **-ties** for 2. **1.** the quality of being mendacious; untruthfulness; tendency to lie. **2.** an instance of lying; falsehood. [< LL *mendācitās* falsehood = L *mendāci-* (s. of *mendāx*) given to lying, false + *-tās* -TY[2]]
Men·del (men′dᵊl), *n.* **Gre·gor Jo·hann** (greg′ər yō′hän; *Ger.* gʀā′gôʀ yō′hän), 1822–84, Austrian monk and botanist: pioneer in the science of genetics.
Men·de·le·ev (men′dᵊlā′əf; *Russ.* men′də le′yəf), *n.* **Dmi·tri I·va·no·vich** (dmē′tʀi i vä′no vich), 1834–1907, Russian chemist: helped develop the periodic law. Also, **Men′de·ley′ev, Men′de·lej′eff.**
men·de·le·vi·um (men′dᵊlē′vē əm), *n. Chem.* a synthetic, radioactive element. *Symbol:* Md, Mv; *at. no.:* 101. [named after D. I. MENDELEEV; see -IUM]
Men·de·li·an (men dē′lē ən, -dēl′yən), *adj.* **1.** of or pertaining to Gregor Mendel or to his laws of heredity. —*n.* **2.** a follower of Gregor Mendel; a person who accepts Mendelism.
Men·del·ism (men′dᵊliz′əm), *n.* the theories of heredity advanced by Gregor Mendel. Also, **Men·de·li·an·ism** (men dē′lē ə niz′əm).
Men′del's laws′, *Genetics.* the basic principles of heredity discovered by Gregor Mendel, showing that alternative hereditary factors of hybrids exhibit a clean-cut separation or segregation from one another and that different pairs of hereditary traits are independently sorted from each other.
Men·dels·sohn (men′dᵊl sən; *Ger.* men′dəl zōn′), *n.* **1. Fe·lix** (fē′liks; *Ger.* fā′liks), (*Jacob Ludwig Felix Mendelssohn-Bartholdy*), 1809–47, German composer. **2.** his grandfather, **Mo·ses** (mō′ziz, -zis; *Ger.* mō′zes), 1729–86, German philosopher.
Men·de·res (men′de res′), *n.* **1. Ad·nan** (äd′nän), 1899–1961, Turkish political leader: premier 1950–60. **2.** Ancient, **Maeander, Meander.** a river in W Asia Minor, flowing into the Aegean near Samos. 240 mi. long. **3.** Ancient, **Scamander.** a river in NW Asia Minor, flowing across the Trojan plain into the Dardanelles. 60 mi. long.
Men·dès-France (men′dis frans′, -fräns′; *Fr.* mäɴ des fʀäɴs′), *n.* **Pierre** (pyeʀ), 1907–82, French statesman and economist: premier 1954–55.
men·di·can·cy (men′də kən sē), *n.* **1.** the practice of begging. **2.** the state or condition of being a beggar. [MENDIC(ANT) + -ANCY]
men·di·cant (men′də kənt), *adj.* **1.** begging; living on alms. **2.** pertaining to or characteristic of a beggar. —*n.* **3.** a person who lives by begging; beggar. **4.** a mendicant friar. [late ME < L *mendīcant-* (s. of *mendīcāns*) begging (prp. of *mendīcāre*) = *mendīc(us)* beggarly, needy + *-ant-* -ANT]
men·dic·i·ty (men dis′i tē), *n.* mendicancy. [late ME *mendicite* < L *mendīcitās* beggary = *mendīc(us)* needy, beggarly + *-itās* -ITY]
Men·do·ci·no (men′də sē′nō), *n.* **Cape,** a cape in NW California: the westernmost point in California.
Men·do·za (men dō′zə; *Sp.* men dô′sä *or, for 1,* -thä), *n.* **1. Pe·dro de** (pe′thʀô the), 1487?–1537, Spanish soldier and explorer: founder of the first colony of Buenos Aires about 1536. **2.** a city in W central Argentina. 194,921 (est. 1965).
Men·e·la·us (men′ᵊlā′əs), *n. Class. Myth.* a king of Sparta, the husband of Helen and brother of Agamemnon, to whom he appealed for an army with which to attack Troy in order to recover Helen from her abductor, Paris.
me·ne, me·ne, tek·el, u·phar·sin (mē′nē, mē′nē, tek′əl, yōō fär′sin), *Aramaic.* numbered, numbered, weighed, divided: the miraculous writing on the wall interpreted by Daniel as foretelling the destruction of Belshazzar and his kingdom. Dan. 5:25–31.
Me·nén·dez de A·vi·lés (me nen′deth the ä′vē les′), **Pe·dro** (pe′thʀô), 1519–74, Spanish admiral and colonizer: founder of St. Augustine, Florida, 1565.
Me·nes (mē′nēz), *n.* fl. c3200 B.C., 1st king of Egypt: founder of the 1st dynasty.
men·folk (men′fōk′), *n.pl.* men, esp. those of a family or community. Also, **men′folks′.**
Meng·tze (muŋg′dzu′), *n.* a city in SE Yünnan, in SW China. ab. 200,000. Also, **Meng′tseu′, Meng′tsu′, Meng′tzu′.**
Mêng-tzu (muŋg′dzu′), *n.* Mencius. Also, **Meng-tse** (muŋg′dzu′).
men·ha·den (men hād′ᵊn), *n., pl.* **-den.** any marine clupeoid fish of the genus *Brevoortia,* esp. *B. tyrannus,* re-

sembling a shad but with a more compressed body, found along the eastern coast of the U.S. and used for making oil and fertilizer. [< Algonquian; cf. Narragansett *munnawhatteaûg*, lit., fertilizer]

men·hir (men′hir), *n.* *Archaeol.* an upright monumental stone, standing either alone or with others, as in a cromlech, found chiefly in Cornwall. [< Breton phrase *men hir* = *men* stone + *hir* long]

me·ni·al (mē′nē əl, mēn′yəl), *adj.* **1.** pertaining or proper to domestic servants. **2.** servile; degrading: *a menial occupation.* —*n.* **3.** a domestic servant. **4.** a servile person. [ME *meynyal* < AF *me(i)nial.* See MEINY, -AL[1]] —**me′ni·al·ly,** *adv.* —**Syn. 2.** See **servile. 3.** attendant, flunky, underling.

Mé·nière's′ syn′drome (mān yârz′), *Pathol.* a disease of the labyrinth of the ear, characterized by deafness, ringing in the ears, dizziness, nausea, and vomiting. Also called **Ménière's′ disease′.** [named after Prosper *Ménière* (1799–1862), French physician]

me·nin·ges (mi nin′jēz), *n.pl., sing.* **me·ninx** (mē′ningks). *Anat.* the three membranes investing the brain and spinal cord. Cf. **arachnoid** (def. 2), **dura mater, pia mater.** [< NL < Gk, pl. of *mēninx* membrane] —**me·nin·ge·al** (mi nin′jē əl), *adj.*

men·in·gi·tis (men′in jī′tis), *n.* *Pathol.* inflammation of the meninges, esp. of the pia mater and arachnoid. [< NL] —**men·in·git·ic** (men′in jit′ik), *adj.*

me·nis·cus (mi nis′kəs), *n., pl.* **-nis·ci** (-nis′ī), **-nis·cus·es. 1.** a crescent or a crescent-shaped body. **2.** *Optics.* a lens with a crescent-shaped section; a concavo-convex or convexo-concave lens. **3.** the convex or concave upper surface of a column of liquid, the curvature of which is caused by surface tension. **4.** *Anat.* a disk of cartilage between the articulating ends of the bones in a joint. [< NL < Gk *mēnískos* crescent, dim. of *mḗnē* moon]

A B

Menisci (def. 3)
A, Concave
B, Convex

men·i·sper·ma·ceous (men′i spər mā′shəs), *adj.* belonging to the *Menispermaceae*, a family of chiefly woody, climbing plants. [< NL *Mēnisperm(um)* the typical genus, moonseed (< Gk *mḗnē* moon + *spérma* seed) + -ACEOUS]

Men′lo Park′ (men′lō), **1.** a city in W California, near San Francisco. 26,906 (1970). **2.** a village in central New Jersey, SE of Plainfield: site of Thomas Edison's laboratory 1876–87. 10,000 (1970).

Men·ning·er (men′ing ər), *n.* **Karl Augustus,** born 1893, and his brother **William Claire,** 1899–1966, U.S. psychiatrists.

Men·non·ite (men′ə nīt′), *n.* a member of an evangelical Protestant sect that practices baptism of believers only, restricts marriage to members of the denomination, and is noted for simplicity of living and plain dress. [< G *Mennonit;* named after *Menno* Simons (1492–1559), Frisian religious leader; see -ITE[1]] —**Men′no·nit′ism,** *n.*

me·no (mā′nō; *It.* me′nô), *adv.* *Music.* less: *meno mosso.* [< It < L *minus* less]

meno-, a learned borrowing from Greek, where it meant "month"; often used with reference to menstruation in the formation of compound words: *menopause.* [< Gk *mēno-*, comb. form of *mḗn* month]

me·nol·o·gy (mi nol′ə jē), *n., pl.* **-gies. 1.** a calendar of the months. **2.** a record or account, as of saints, arranged in the order of a calendar. [< NL *mēnologi(um)* < LGk *mēnológion*]

Me·nom′o·nee Falls′ (mə nom′ə nē), a city in SE Wisconsin, NW of Milwaukee. 31,697 (1970).

men·o·pause (men′ə pôz′), *n.* *Physiol.* the period of permanent cessation of menstruation, usually occurring between the ages of 45 and 50. [< F *ménopause*] —**men′o·pau′sic, men′o·pau′sal,** *adj.*

me·nor·ah (mə nōr′ə, -nôr′ə), *n.* *Judaism.* **1.** a candelabrum having eight branches and a shammash, used during Hanukkah. **2.** a candelabrum having seven branches. [< Heb: lit., candlestick]

Menorah

Me·nor·ca (me nôr′kä), *n.* Spanish name of **Minorca.**

men·or·rha·gi·a (men′ə rā′jē ə, -jə), *n.* *Pathol.* excessive menstrual discharge. —**men·or·rhag·ic** (men′ə raj′ik), *adj.*

Me·not·ti (mə not′ē; *It.* me nôt′tē), *n.* **Gian Car·lo** (jän kär′lō; *It.* jän kär′lô), born 1911, Italian composer.

men·sa (men′sə), *n., pl.* **-sas, -sae** (-sē). the flat stone forming the top of the altar in a Roman Catholic church. Also called **altar stone, altar slab.** [< L: table]

men·sal[1] (men′səl), *adj.* monthly. [< L *mens(is)* month + -AL[1]]

men·sal[2] (men′səl), *adj.* of, pertaining to, or used at the table. [< L *mensāl(is).* See MENSA, -AL[1]]

mensch (mensh, mench), *n., pl.* **mensch·en** (mensh′ən, mench′ən). *U.S. Slang.* a decent, sincere, mature, and respectable person. [< Yiddish < G *Mensch* human being]

men·ser·vants (men′sûr′vənts), *n.* pl. of **manservant.**

men·ses (men′sēz), *n.* (*construed as sing. or pl.*) *Physiol.* the periodic flow of blood and mucosal tissue from the uterus. [< L, pl. of *mensis* month]

Men·she·vik (men′shə vik; *Russ.* men′she vēk′), *n., pl.* **-viks, -vik·i** (-vik′ē, -vē′kē; *Russ.* -vi kē′). (in Russia) a member of the Social Democratic party in opposition to the Bolsheviks and advocating gradual development of full socialism through parliamentary government and cooperation with bourgeois parties: absorbed into the Communist party formed in 1918. Also, **men′she·vik.** [< Russ: minority = *men'she* less + *-vik* n. suffix] —**Men·she·vism, men·she·vism** (men′shə viz′əm), *n.* —**Men′she·vist, men′she·vist,** *adj.*

men's′ room′, a public lavatory for men. Also called **men's′ lounge′.**

mens sa·na in cor·po·re sa·no (mens sä′nä in kôr′pō re′ sä′nō; *Eng.* menz sā′nə in kôr′pə rē′ sā′nō), *Latin.* a sound mind in a sound body.

men·stru·al (men′strōō əl, -strəl), *adj.* **1.** of or pertaining to menstruation or to the menses. **2.** monthly. [ME *menstruall* < L *mēnstruāl(is)* having monthly courses = *mēnstru(a)* monthly courses (n. use of neut. pl. of *mēnstruus* monthly) + *-ālis* -AL[1]]

men·stru·ate (men′strōō āt′), *v.i.,* **-at·ed, -at·ing.** to undergo menstruation. [v. use of ME *menstruate* menstruous < LL *mēnstruāt(us)*]

men·stru·a·tion (men′strōō ā′shən), *n.* **1.** the act of periodically discharging blood and mucosal tissue from the uterus, occurring approximately monthly from puberty to menopause. **2.** the period of menstruating. —**men′stru·ous,** *adj.*

men·stru·um (men′strōō əm), *n., pl.* **-stru·ums, -stru·a** (-strōō ə). a solvent. [special use of ME: monthly period < ML (in L only pl. *mēnstrua* occurs)]

men·sur·a·ble (men′shər ə bəl), *adj.* measurable. [< LL *mēnsūrābil(is).* See MEASURE, -BLE] —**men′sur·a·bil′i·ty,** *n.*

men·su·ral (men′shər əl), *adj.* pertaining to measure. [< LL *mēnsūrāl(is).* See MEASURE, -AL[1]]

men·su·ra·tion (men′shə rā′shən), *n.* **1.** the branch of geometry that deals with the measurement of length, area, or volume. **2.** the act or process of measuring. [< LL *mēnsūrātiōn-* (s. of *mēnsūrātiō*) a measuring. See MEASURE, -ATION] —**men′su·ra′tion·al,** *adj.*

mens·wear (menz′wâr′), *n.* clothing or suits for men.

-ment, a suffix of nouns, often concrete, denoting an action or resulting state (*abridgment; refreshment*), a product (*fragment*), or means (*ornament*). [< F < L *-mentum,* suffix forming nouns, usually from verbs]

men·tal[1] (men′tᵊl), *adj.* **1.** of or pertaining to the mind. **2.** characterized by a disorder of the mind: *a mental patient.* **3.** providing care for persons with disordered minds, emotions, etc.: *mental hospital.* **4.** performed by or existing in the mind: *mental arithmetic.* [late ME < LL *mentāl(is)* = L *ment-* (s. of *mēns*) mind + *-ālis* -AL[1]]

men·tal[2] (men′tᵊl), *adj.* of or pertaining to the chin. [< L *ment(um)* the chin + -AL[1]]

men′tal age′, *Psychol.* the level of native mental ability or capacity of an individual in relation to the chronological age of the average individual at this level.

men′tal defi′ciency, *Psychol.* lack of powers associated with normal intellectual development, resulting in an inability of the individual to function adequately in everyday life.

men′tal disease′, any of the various forms of insanity or severe neurosis. Also called **men′tal disor′der, men′tal ill′ness.**

men′tal heal′ing, the healing of a physical ailment or disorder by mental concentration or suggestion. —**men′tal heal′er.**

men·tal·ism (men′tᵊliz′əm), *n.* the doctrine that objects of knowledge have no existence except in the mind of the perceiver. —**men′tal·is′tic,** *adj.* —**men′tal·is′ti·cal·ly,** *adv.*

men·tal·ist (men′tᵊlist), *n.* a mind reader.

men·tal·i·ty (men tal′i tē), *n., pl.* **-ties.** mental capacity or endowment; intellectual character.

men·tal·ly (men′tᵊlē), *adv.* **1.** in or with the mind or intellect; intellectually. **2.** with regard to the mind.

men′tal retarda′tion. See **mental deficiency.**

men·tha·ceous (men thā′shəs), *adj.* belonging to the *Menthaceae* (usually included in the *Labiatae*) or mint family of plants, comprising the horsemint, peppermint, pennyroyal, savory, etc. [< L *menth(a)* MINT[1] + -ACEOUS]

men·thene (men′thēn), *n.* *Chem.* **1.** any of several isomeric, monocyclic terpenes having the formula $C_{10}H_{18}$. **2.** a colorless, liquid terpene, $C_{10}H_{18}$, found in certain essential oils and prepared from menthol. [< NL *Menth(a)* (see MINT[1]) + -ENE]

men·thol (men′thōl, -thôl, -thol), *n.* **1.** *Chem., Pharm.* a colorless alcohol, $CH_3C_6H_9(C_3H_7)OH$, obtained from peppermint oil or synthesized: used chiefly in perfumes, confections, liqueurs, and for colds and nasal disorders because of its cooling effect on mucous membranes. **2.** *Informal.* a mentholated cigarette. —*adj.* **3.** *Informal.* mentholated: *menthol cigarettes.* [< NL *Menth(a)* (see MINT[1]) + -OL[1]]

men·tho·lat·ed (men′thə lā′tid), *adj.* **1.** covered or treated with menthol. **2.** containing menthol.

men·tion (men′shən), *v.t.* **1.** to refer briefly to; refer to by name incidentally; name, specify, or speak of. **2.** to cite formally for a meritorious act or achievement. **3. not to mention,** in addition to: *We were served French champagne, not to mention the usual cocktails.* —*n.* **4.** a direct or incidental reference. **5.** formal recognition for a meritorious act or achievement. [< L *mentiōn-* (s. of *mentiō*) a calling to mind, a touching upon (see MENTAL[1], -ION); r. ME *mencioun* < AF] —**men′tion·a·ble,** *adj.* —**men′tion·er,** *n.* —**Syn. 1.** indicate, identify.

Men·ton (men tōn′; *Fr.* mäɴ tôɴ′), *n.* a city in SE France, on the Mediterranean: winter resort. 20,069 (1962). Italian, **Men·to·ne** (men tô′ne).

Men·tor (men′tər, -tôr), *n.* **1.** (in the *Odyssey*) a loyal adviser of Odysseus entrusted with the care and education of Telemachus. **2.** (*l.c.*) a wise and trusted counselor.

Men·tor (men′tər), *n.* a city in NE Ohio, near Cleveland. 36,912 (1970).

men·u (men′yōō, mā′nyōō), *n.* **1.** a list of the dishes or foods available in a restaurant; bill of fare. **2.** the dishes served, as at a banquet. [< F: detailed list, n. use of *menu* small, detailed < L *minūt(us)* MINUTE[2]]

Men·u·hin (men′yōō in), *n.* **Ye·hu·di** (yə hōō′dē), born 1916, U.S. violinist.

me·ow (mē ou′, myou), *n.* **1.** the sound a cat makes. —*v.i.* **2.** to make such a sound. Also, **miaow, miaou, miaul.** [imit.]

me·per·i·dine (mə per′i dēn′, -din), *n.* *Pharm.* a narcotic compound, $C_2H_5OOCC(C_6H_5)CH_2CH_2N(CH_3)CH_2CH_2$, used in the form of its hydrochloride as an analgesic and sedative. [ME(THYL + PI)PERIDINE]

Meph·i·stoph·e·les (mef′i stof′ə lēz′), *n.* *Medieval Demonology.* one of the seven chief devils. Also called **Me·phis·to** (mə fis′tō). —**Meph·is·to·phe·li·an, Meph·is·to·phe·le·an** (mef′i stō fē′lē ən), *adj.*

me·phit·ic (mə fit′ik), *adj.* **1.** offensive to the smell. **2.** noxious; pestilential; poisonous. [< LL *mephītic(us).* See MEPHITIS, -IC] —**me·phit′i·cal·ly,** *adv.*

me·phi·tis (mə fī′tis) *n.* **1.** a noxious or pestilential exhalation from the earth, as poison gas. **2.** any noisome or poisonous stench. [< L < Oscan *mefītis*]

me·pro·ba·mate (mə prō′bə māt′, mep′rō bam′āt), *n.* *Pharm.* a powder, $CH_3(C_3H_7)C(CH_2OOCNH_2)_2$, used as a tranquilizer for treating anxiety, tension, and skeletal muscle spasm. [ME(THYL) + PRO(PYL + CAR)BAMATE]

-mer, *Chem.* a combining form denoting a member of a particular group: *isomer.* Cf. **-mere, -merous.** [comb. form repr. Gk *méros* part, portion]

mer., **1.** meridian. **2.** meridional.

mer·bro·min (mər brō′min), *n.* *Pharm.* a powder, $C_{20}H_8Br_2HgNa_2O_6$, used as an antiseptic and as a germicide. [MER(CURIC) + BROM(O) + -IN[2]]

merc., **1.** mercantile. **2.** mercurial. **3.** mercury.

Mer·ca (mer′kä), *n.* a city in the S Somali Republic. 59,300 (1956).

mer·can·tile (mûr′kən tēl′, -tīl′, -til), *adj.* **1.** of or pertaining to merchants or trade; commercial. **2.** engaged in trade or commerce: *a mercantile nation.* **3.** *Econ.* of or pertaining to the mercantile system. [< F < It: pertaining to merchants = *mercant(e)* merchant (< L *mercant-,* s. of *mercāns* buyer, n. use of prp. of *mercārī* to buy) + *-ile* -ILE]

mer′cantile sys′tem, *Econ.* a political and economic system or policy, evolving with the modern national state, seeking to secure a nation's supremacy over other states by the accumulation of precious metals and by exporting the largest possible quantity of products while importing as little as possible.

mer·can·til·ism (mûr′kən ti liz′əm, -tē-, -tī-), *n.* **1.** the mercantile spirit. **2.** See **mercantile system.** [< F *mercantilisme*] —**mer′can·til·ist,** *n., adj.*

mer·cap·tan (mər kap′tan), *n.* *Chem.* **1.** any of a class of sulfur-containing compounds having the type formula RSH, in which R represents a radical: many have an extremely offensive odor. **2.** a flammable liquid, CH_3CH_2SH, having a characteristic penetrating odor. [< L, short for phrase *corpus mercurium captāns* a body capturing quicksilver]

mer·cap·to (mər kap′tō), *adj.* *Chem.* containing the mercapto group; sulfhydryl; thiol. [MERCAPT(AN) + -O-]

mercap′to group′, *Chem.* the univalent group, -SH. Also called **mercap′to rad′ical.**

mer·cap·to·pu·rine (mər kap′tō pyŏŏr′ēn), *n.* *Pharm.* a yellow, crystalline powder, $C_5H_4N_4S$, used in the treatment of leukemia.

Mer·ca·tor (mər kā′tər; *Flem.* mer kä′tôr), *n.* **1. Ger·har·dus** (jər här′dəs), (*Gerhard Kremer*), 1512–94, Flemish cartographer and geographer. —*adj.* **2.** noting, pertaining to, or according to the principals of the Mercator projection: *a Mercator chart.*

Merca′tor projec′tion, *Cartog.* a map projection on which any rhumb line is represented as a straight line, used chiefly in navigation: the scale varies with latitude and areal size and the shapes of large areas are distorted. Also, **Mer·ca′tor's projec′tion.**

mer·ce·nar·y (mûr′sə ner′ē), *adj., n., pl.* **-nar·ies.** —*adj.* **1.** working or acting merely for money or other reward; venal. **2.** fighting for a cause solely for pay or remuneration: *a mercenary army; a mercenary soldier.* —*n.* **3.** a professional soldier serving in a foreign army solely for pay or remuneration. **4.** any hireling. [ME *mercenarie* < L *mercēnāri(us)* hireling (n.), hired, paid (adj.) = *mercēd-* (s. of *mercēs* wages, akin to *merx* goods) + *-ārius* -ARY] —**mer·ce·nar·i·ly** (mûr′sə nâr′ə lē, mûr′sə ner′-), *adv.* —**mer′ce·nar′i·ness,** *n.* —**Syn. 1.** grasping; avaricious, covetous.

mer·cer (mûr′sər), *n.* *Brit.* a dealer in textile fabrics. [early ME < AF; OF *mercier* merchant = *merci-* (< L, s. of *merx* goods) + *-er* -ER[2]]

mer·cer·ize (mûr′sə rīz′), *v.t.,* **-ized, -iz·ing.** to treat (cotton yarns or fabric) with caustic alkali under tension in order to increase strength, luster, and affinity for dye. [named after John *Mercer* (1791–1866), English calico printer, the patentee (1850) of the process; see -IZE]

mer·cer·y (mûr′sə rē), *n., pl.* **-cer·ies.** *Brit.* **1.** a mercer's shop. **2.** mercers' wares. [ME *mercerie* < OF]

mer·chan·dise (*n.* mûr′chən dīz′, -dīs′; *v.* mûr′chən dīz′), *n., v.,* **-dised, -dis·ing.** —*n.* **1.** goods, esp. manufactured goods; commodities. —*v.i.* **2.** to carry on trade. —*v.t.* **3.** to buy and sell; deal in; trade. **4.** to plan for and promote the sales of. [ME *marchandise* < OF. See MERCHANT, -ICE] —**mer′chan·dis′er,** *n.*

mer·chan·dis·ing (mûr′chən dī′zing), *n.* the total planning, advertising, and other activities involved in promoting the sales of a product. Also called **mer′chan·dise plan′ning.** [ME]

mer·chan·dize (*n.* mûr′chən dīz′, -dīs′; *v.* mûr′chən-dīz′), *n., v.i., v.t.,* **-dized, -diz·ing.** merchandise. —**mer′chan·diz′er,** *n.*

mer·chant (mûr′chənt), *n.* **1.** a person who buys and sells commodities for profit; dealer; trader. **2.** a storekeeper; retailer. —*adj.* **3.** pertaining to or used for trade or commerce: *a merchant ship.* **4.** pertaining to the merchant marine: *a merchant seaman.* [ME *marchant* < OF *marcheant* < VL **mercātant-* (s. of **mercātāns*), prp. of **mercātāre,* freq. of L *mercārī* to trade < *merx* goods] —**mer′chant·like′,** *adj.*

mer·chant·a·ble (mûr′chən tə bəl), *adj.* marketable. [ME *marchandabull*]

mer′chant bank′, *Finance. Brit.* a private banking firm engaged chiefly in accepting bills of exchange in foreign trade and investing in new issues of securities.

mer·chant·man (mûr′chənt mən), *n., pl.* **-men.** a commercial ship that primarily carries freight. [ME *marchandman*]

mer′chant marine′, **1.** the vessels of a nation that are engaged in commerce. **2.** the officers and crews of such vessels.

mer′chant prince′, a very wealthy or influential merchant.

mer·ci (mer sē′), *interj. French.* thank you.

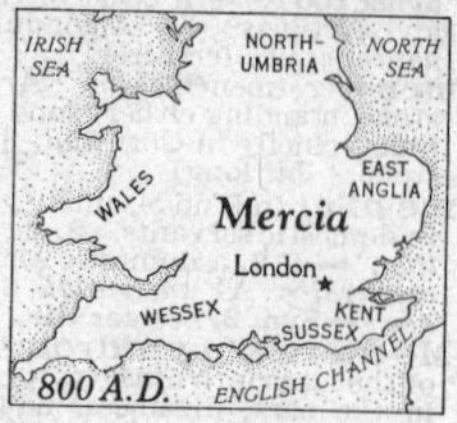

Mer·ci·a (mûr′shē ə, -shə), *n.* an early English kingdom in central Britain.

Mer·ci·an (mûr′shən), *adj.* **1.** of or pertaining to Mercia, its inhabitants, or their dialect. —*n.* **2.** a native or inhabitant of Mercia. **3.** the dialect of Anglo-Saxon spoken in Mercia.

mer·ci beau·coup (mer sē′ bō kōō′), *French.* thank you very much.

Mer·cier (*Fr.* mer syā′), *n.* **Dé·si·ré Jo·seph** (dā zē rā′ zhō zef′), 1851–1926, Belgian cardinal and patriot.

mer·ci·ful (mûr′si fəl), *adj.* full of mercy; characterized by or exercising mercy; compassionate. [ME] —**mer′ci·ful·ly,** *adv.* —**mer′ci·ful·ness,** *n.* —**Syn.** forgiving, tender. —**Ant.** cruel.

mer·ci·less (mûr′si lis), *adj.* without mercy; pitiless: *a merciless king.* [ME *mercyles*] —**mer′ci·less·ly,** *adv.* —**mer′ci·less·ness,** *n.* —**Syn.** cruel. —**Ant.** compassionate.

mercur-, a combining form of **mercury:** *mercuric.* Also, **mercuro-.**

mer·cu·rate (mûr′kyə rāt′), *n., v.,* **-rat·ed, -rat·ing.** *Chem.* —*n.* **1.** Also, **mer·cu·ri·ate** (mər kyŏŏr′ē it, -āt′). any salt in which bivalent mercury is part of a complex anion. —*v.t.* **2.** to introduce mercury into (an organic compound); treat with mercury. —**mer′cu·ra′tion,** *n.*

mer·cu·ri·al (mər kyŏŏr′ē əl), *adj.* **1.** pertaining to, containing, or caused by the metal mercury. **2.** (*cap.*) of or pertaining to the god Mercury. **3.** (*cap.*) of or pertaining to the planet Mercury. **4.** active; lively; sprightly; volatile. **5.** changeable; fickle; flighty; erratic: *a mercurial nature.* —*n.* **6.** *Pharm.* a preparation of mercury used as a drug. [< L *mercuriāl(is)* of, pertaining to the god or planet Mercury] —**mer·cu′ri·al·ness, mer·cu′ri·al′i·ty,** *n.*

mercu′rial barom′eter. See **mercury barometer.**

mer·cu·ric (mər kyŏŏr′ik), *adj.* *Chem.* of or containing mercury, esp. in the bivalent state.

mercu′ric chlo′ride, *Chem.* a strongly acrid, highly poisonous solid, $HgCl_2$, used chiefly as an antiseptic. Also called **mercury bichloride, corrosive sublimate.**

mercuro-, var. of **mercur-:** *Mercurochrome.*

Mer·cu·ro·chrome (mər kyŏŏr′ə krōm′), *n.* *Pharm., Trademark.* merbromin.

mer·cu·rous (mər kyŏŏr′əs, mûr′kyər əs), *adj.* *Chem.* containing univalent mercury, Hg^{+1} or Hg^{+2}.

mercu′rous chlo′ride, *Pharm.* calomel.

mer·cu·ry (mûr′kyə rē), *n., pl.* **-ries. 1.** *Chem.* a heavy, silver-white, metallic element, noted for its fluidity at ordinary temperatures: used in barometers, thermometers, pesticides, pharmaceutical preparations, reflecting surfaces of mirrors, and dental fillings, in certain switches, lamps, and other electric apparatus, and as a laboratory catalyst; quicksilver. *Symbol:* Hg; *at. wt.:* 200.59; *at. no.:* 80; *sp. gr.:* 13.546 at 20°C; *freezing point:* −38.9°C; *boiling point:* 357°C. **2.** *Pharm.* this metal, used in medicine, in the form of various compounds, usually for skin infections. **3.** (*cap.*) the ancient Roman god who served as messenger of the gods and was also the god of commerce, thievery, eloquence, and science, identified with the Greek god Hermes. **4.** (*cap.*) *Astron.* the planet nearest the sun, having a diameter of 3000 miles, a mean distance from the sun of 36,000,000 miles, a period of revolution of 88 days, and having no satellites: the smallest planet in the solar system. **5.** a messenger; carrier of news. **6.** any euphorbiaceous herb of the genus *Mercurialis,* esp. the poisonous, weedy *M. perennis.* **7.** (*cap.*) *U.S.* a one-man spacecraft launched by an Atlas booster. [ME *Mercurie* < ML, L *Mercurius,* akin to *merx* goods]

Mercury (def. 3)

mer′cury barom′eter, a barometer in which the weight of a column of mercury in a glass tube with a sealed top is balanced against that of the atmosphere pressing on an exposed cistern of mercury at the base of the mercury column, the height of the column varying with atmospheric pressure. Also called **mercurial barometer.** Cf. **aneroid barometer.**

mer′cury bichlo′ride, *Chem.* See **mercuric chloride.**

mer′cury chlo′ride, **1.** *Chem.* See **mercuric chloride. 2.** calomel.

mer′cu·ry-va′por lamp′ (mûr′kyə rē vā′pər), *Elect.* a lamp producing a light with a high actinic and ultraviolet content by means of an electric arc in mercury vapor.

mer·cy (mûr′sē), *n., pl.* **-cies** for 4, 5. **1.** compassionate or kindly forbearance shown toward an offender, an enemy, or other person in one's power; compassion, pity, or benevolence. **2.** the disposition to be merciful: *an adversary wholly without mercy.* **3.** the discretionary power of a judge to pardon or to mitigate punishment, esp. to send to prison rather than invoke the death penalty. **4.** an act of kindness, compassion, or favor. **5.** *Dial.* something that gives evidence of divine favor; blessing: *It was just a mercy I was there when it happened.* **6. at the mercy of,** subject to; entirely in the power of. [ME *merci* < OF, earlier *mercit* < L *mercēd-* (s. of *mercēs*) wages < *merx* goods] —**Syn. 1.** forgiveness, clemency, leniency, lenity, mildness. —**Ant. 1.** cruelty.

mer′cy kill′ing, euthanasia (def. 1).

mer′cy seat′, *Bible.* **1.** the gold covering on the ark of the covenant, regarded as the resting place of God. Ex. 25:17–22. **2.** the throne of God.

mere (mēr), *adj., superl.* **mer·est. 1.** being nothing more nor better than what is specified: *He is still a mere child.* **2.** *Obs.* pure and unmixed, as wine, a people, or a language. **3.** *Obs.* fully as much as what is specified. [ME < L *mer(us)* pure, unmixed, mere] **—Ant. 1.** abundant.

mère (mer; *Eng.* mâr), *n., pl.* **mères** (mer; *Eng.* mârz). *French.* mother.

-mere, a learned borrowing from Greek meaning "part," used in the formation of compound words: *blastomere.* Cf. **-mer, -merous.** [comb. form repr. Gk *méros*]

Mer·e·dith (mer′i dith), *n.* **1. George,** 1828–1909, English novelist and poet. **2. Owen.** See **Bulwer-Lytton.**

mere·ly (mēr′lē), *adv.* **1.** only as specified, and nothing more; simply: *merely a matter of form.* **2.** *Obs.* without admixture; purely: *not mixedly but merely true and good.* **3.** *Obs.* altogether; entirely: *His love is merely mine.*

me·ren·gue (mə reng′gā; *Sp.* me reng′ge), *n., pl.* **-gues** (-gāz; *Sp.* -ges). a ballroom dance of Dominican and Haitian origin, characterized by a stiff-legged, limping step. [< AmerSp]

mer·e·tri·cious (mer′i trish′əs), *adj.* **1.** alluring by a show of flashy or vulgar attractions; tawdry. **2.** based on pretense, deception, or insincerity. [< L *meretrīcius* of, pertaining to harlots = *meretrīci-* (s. of *meretrīx* harlot, lit., earner = *mere-,* (s. of *merēre* to earn) + *-trīx* -TRIX) + *-us* -OUS] **—mer′e·tri′cious·ly,** *adv.* **—mer′e·tri′cious·ness,** *n.* **—Syn. 1.** showy, gaudy. **2.** spurious, sham, false.

mer·gan·ser (mər gan′sər), *n., pl.* **-sers,** (*esp. collectively*) **-ser.** any of several fish-eating diving ducks of the subfamily *Merginae,* having a narrow bill hooked at the tip and serrated at the edges. [< NL = L *merg(us)* diver, a kind of water bird + *anser* goose]

merge (mûrj), *v.,* **merged, merg·ing.** **—*v.t.* 1.** to cause to combine or coalesce; unite. **2.** to combine, blend, or unite gradually so as to blur the individuality of (often fol. by *in* or *into*). **—*v.i.* 3.** to become combined, united, or absorbed; lose identity by uniting or blending (often fol. by *in* or *into*): *This stream merges into the river up ahead.* **4.** (of two or more enterprises, bodies, etc.) to combine or unite into a single unit: *The two firms merged last year.* [< L *merge(re)* (to) dip immerse, plunge into water] **—mer′gence,** *n.* **—Syn. 1–3.** amalgamate, consolidate.

Mer·gen·tha·ler (mûr′gən thô′lər; *Ger.* mer′gən tä′lər), *n.* **Ott·mar** (ot′mär; *Ger.* ôt′mär), 1854–99, U.S. inventor of the Linotype, born in Germany.

merg·er (mûr′jər), *n.* **1.** a combination of two or more business enterprises into a single enterprise. **2.** a statutory combination of two or more corporations by the transfer of the properties to one surviving corporation. **3.** the act or an instance of merging.

Mer·gui (mûr gwē′), *n.* a seaport in S Burma, on the Andaman Sea. 33,697 (1953).

Mé·ri·da (me′rē thä′), *n.* **1.** a city in and the capital of Yucatán, in SE Mexico. 187,015 (est. 1965). **2.** a city in W Venezuela. 34,143 (est. 1955).

Mer·i·den (mer′i dᵊn), *n.* a city in central Connecticut. 55,959 (1970).

me·rid·i·an (mə rid′ē ən), *n.* **1.** *Geog.* **a.** a great circle of the earth passing through the poles and any given point on the earth's surface. **b.** the half of such a circle included between the poles. **2.** *Astron.* the great circle of the celestial sphere that passes through its poles and the observer's zenith. **3.** a point or period of highest development, greatest prosperity, or the like. **—*adj.* 4.** of or pertaining to a meridian. **5.** of or pertaining to midday or noon: *the meridian hour.* **6.** pertaining to a period of greatest prosperity, splendor, elevation, etc.; culminating. [ME < L *merīdiān(us)* of noon = *merīdi(ēs)* midday (dissimilated var. of *medīdiēs,* orig. *medii-,* comb. form of *medius* MID¹ + *diēs* day) + *-ānus* -AN]

Me·rid·i·an (mə rid′ē ən), *n.* a city in E Mississippi. 45,083 (1970).

mé·ri·di·enne (mə rid′ē en′, mə rid′ē en′; *Fr.* mā rē dyen′), *n., pl.* **mé·ri·di·ennes** (mə rid′ē enz′, mə rid′ē enz′; *Fr.* mā rē dyen′). *Fr. Furniture.* a short daybed of the Empire period, having ends of unequal height connected by a back with a sloping top. See illus. at **Empire.** [< F, special use of fem. of *méridien* MERIDIAN (adj.)]

me·rid·i·o·nal (mə rid′ē ə nᵊl), *adj.* **1.** of, pertaining to, or resembling a meridian. **2.** characteristic of the south or people inhabiting the south, esp. of France. **3.** southern; southerly. **—*n.* 4.** an inhabitant of the south, esp. of France. [ME < LL *merīdiōnāl(is)* southern, modeled on *septentriōnālis* SEPTENTRIONAL. See MERIDIAN, -AL¹] **—me·rid′i·o·nal·ly,** *adv.*

Mé·ri·mée (mā rē mā′), *n.* **Pros·per** (prô sper′), 1803–1870, French short-story writer, novelist, and essayist.

me·ringue (mə rang′), *n.* **1.** a frothy topping of beaten egg whites and sugar. **2.** a pastry or pastry shell made by baking such a mixture, sometimes filled with fruit, whipped cream, etc. [< F]

me·ri·no (mə rē′nō), *n., pl.* **-nos. 1.** (*cap.*) one of a breed of sheep, raised originally in Spain, valued for its fine wool. **2.** wool from such sheep. **3.** a knitted fabric of wool or wool and cotton. [< Sp < L (*ariēs*) *mājōrīn(us)* (male sheep) of the larger sort. See MAJOR, -INE¹]

Merino, *Ovis aries* (2 ft. high at shoulder)

Mer·i·on·eth·shire (mer′ē on′ith shēr′, -shər), *n.* a county in N Wales. 39,007 (1961); 660 sq. mi. *Co. seat:* Dolgelly. Also called **Mer′i·on′eth.**

mer·i·sis (mer′i sis), *n.* *Biol.* growth, esp. growth resulting from cell division. Cf. **auxesis.** [< Gk *meri-* (comb. form of *merís* part, portion) + -SIS]

mer·i·stem (mer′i stem′), *n.* *Bot.* embryonic tissue; undifferentiated, growing, actively dividing cells. [< Gk *merist(ós)* divided, distributed (< *merízein* to divide into parts < *merís* part, share) + *-em,* var. of -EME] **—meri·ste·mat·ic** (mer′i stə mat′ik), *adj.*

me·ris·tic (mə ris′tik), *adj.* *Biol.* of, pertaining to, or divided into segments or somites. [< Gk *meristik(ós)* of division. See MERISTEM, -IC]

mer·it (mer′it), *n.* **1.** claim to commendation; excellence; worth. **2.** something that entitles a person to a reward or commendation; a commendable quality, act, etc.: *The book's only merit is its sincerity.* **3. merits,** the intrinsic right and wrong of a matter, as a law case, unobscured by procedural details, technicalities, personal feelings, etc.: *The case will be decided on its merits alone.* **4.** Often, **merits.** the state or fact of deserving; desert: *to treat someone according to his merits.* **—*v.t.* 5.** to be worthy of; deserve. [ME < L *meri-t(um)* act worthy of praise (or blame), n. use of *meritus* earned, ptp. of *merēre*] **—mer′it·less,** *adj.* **—Syn. 1.** value.

mer·i·toc·ra·cy (mer′i tok′rə sē), *n.* *Chiefly Brit.* a class of persons making their way on their own ability and talent rather than because of class privileges.

mer·i·to·crat (mer′i tə krat′), *n.* *Chiefly Brit.* a member of a meritocracy.

mer·i·to·ri·ous (mer′i tōr′ē əs, -tôr′-), *adj.* possessing merit; deserving praise, reward, esteem, etc.; praiseworthy. [late ME < L *meritōrius* on hire] **—mer′i·to′ri·ous·ly,** *adv.* **—mer′i·to′ri·ous·ness,** *n.*

mer′it sys′tem, (in the U.S. civil service) a system or practice in which persons are hired or promoted on the basis of ability rather than patronage.

merk (merk), *n.* *Scot.* mark² (def. 3).

merle (mûrl), *n.* *Chiefly Scot.* the blackbird, *Turdus merula.* Also, **merl.** [late ME < MF < L *merul(us), merula* ousel, blackbird]

mer·lin (mûr′lin), *n.* **1.** a small, bold, European falcon, *Falco columbarius aesalon.* **2.** the pigeon hawk. [ME *merlioun* < AF *merilun,* OF *esmerillon,* aug. of *esmeril* < Gmc; akin to G *Schmerl,* Icel *smyrill*]

Mer·lin (mûr′lin), *n.* *Arthurian Romance.* a venerable magician and seer.

mer·lon (mûr′lən), *n.* (in a battlement) the solid part between two crenels. [< F < It *merlone,* aug. of *merlo* (in pl., *merli* battlements) < ?]

mer·maid (mûr′mād′), *n.* an imaginary female marine creature, having the head, torso, and arms of a woman and the tail of a fish. [ME *mermayde* = *mere* lake, pond, body of sea water (OE; c. G *Meer,* Ir *muir,* L *mare*) + *mayde* MAID]

Mer′maid Tav′ern, a former London inn, meeting place for Elizabethan writers.

mer·man (mûr′man′), *n., pl.* **-men.** an imaginary male marine creature, having the head, torso, and arms of a man and the tail of a fish. [ME; see MERMAID, MAN¹]

mero-, a learned borrowing from Greek meaning "part," "partial," used in the formation of compound words: *meroblastic.* [< Gk *méros* part]

mer·o·blas·tic (mer′ə blas′tik), *adj.* *Embryol.* (of certain eggs) undergoing partial cleavage. Cf. **holoblastic. —mer′-o·blas′ti·cal·ly,** *adv.*

Mer·o·ë (mer′ō ē′), *n.* a ruined city in Sudan, on the Nile, NE of Khartoum: a capital of ancient Ethiopia.

-merous a suffix meaning "having parts (of a specified number or type)," "partite": *dimerous.* Cf. **-mer, -mere.** [< Gk *méros* part, portion, share; see -OUS]

Mer·o·vin·gi·an (mer′ə vin′jē ən, -jən), *adj.* **1.** of or pertaining to the Frankish dynasty established by Clovis, which reigned in Gaul and Germany from about A.D. 500 to 751. **—*n.* 2.** a member or supporter of the Merovingian dynasty. [< F *mérovingien* = *méroving-* (< ML < Gmc; cf. OE *Merewīowing* offspring of *Merewīg,* grandfather of Clovis) + *-ien* -IAN]

mer·o·zo·ite (mer′ə zō′īt), *n.* (in the asexual reproduction of certain sporozoans) a cell developed from a schizont which parasitizes an erythrocyte in the host.

Mer·rick (mer′ik), *n.* a town on SW Long Island, in SE New York. 25,904 (1970).

Mer·ri·mack (mer′ə mak′), *n.* a river in central New Hampshire and NE Massachusetts, flowing S and NE to the Atlantic. 110 mi. long.

Mer·ri·mack (mer′ə mak′), *n.* the first ironclad warship: used by the Confederates in a battle against the *Monitor* in Hampton Roads, Virginia in 1862.

mer·ri·ment (mer′i mənt), *n.* **1.** merry gaiety; mirth; hilarity; laughter. **2.** *Obs.* a cause of mirth; a jest, entertainment, etc. **—Syn. 1.** See **mirth.**

Mer′ritt Is′land (mer′it), a town in E Florida. 29,233 (1970).

mer·ry (mer′ē), *adj.,* **mer·ri·er, mer·ri·est. 1.** full of cheerfulness or gaiety; joyous in disposition or spirit: *a merry little man.* **2.** laughingly gay; mirthful; festively joyous; hilarious: *a merry time at the party.* **3.** *Archaic.* causing happiness; pleasant; delightful. **4. make merry,** to be gay or festive; celebrate; party. [ME *meri(e), myrie, murie,* OE *myr(i)ge, mer(i)ge* pleasant, delightful] **—mer′-ri·ly,** *adv.* **—Syn. 1.** happy, blithe, cheery, glad. See **gay. 2.** jolly, jovial, gleeful. **—Ant. 1.** sad. **2.** solemn.

mer·ry-an·drew (mer′ē an′drōō), *n.* a clown; buffoon. [MERRY + *Andrew,* the name]

mer·ry-go-round (mer′ē gō round′), *n.* **1.** Also called **carrousel, carousel.** a revolving, circular platform fitted with wooden horses or other animals on which persons, esp. children, may ride, usually to the accompaniment of music, in amusement parks, carnivals, etc. **2.** a rapid whirl; a busy round, as of social life, business affairs, etc.

mer·ry·mak·er (mer′ē mā′kər), *n.* a person who makes merry; reveler.

mer·ry·mak·ing (mer′ē mā′king), *n.* **1.** the act of taking part gaily or enthusiastically in some festive or merry celebration. **2.** a merry festivity; revel. **—*adj.* 3.** producing mirth; gay; festive.

mer·ry·thought (mer′ē thôt′), *n.* *Chiefly Brit.* the wishbone or furcula of a fowl. [so called from the custom of two persons pulling the bone until it breaks; the person gaining the longer (sometimes shorter) piece will supposedly marry first or will be granted a wish made at the time]

Mer·sey (mûr′zē), *n.* a river in W England, flowing W from Derbyshire to the Irish Sea. 70 mi. long.

Mer·thi·o·late (mər thī′ə lāt′), *n.* *Pharm., Trademark.* thimerosal.

Mer·thyr Tyd·fil (mûr′thər tid′vil; *Welsh.* mûʀ′thəʀ tud′vil), a city in SE Wales. 59,008 (1961).

mes-, var. of **meso-** before some vowels: *mesencephalon.*

me·sa (mā′sə; *Sp.* me′sä), *n.* a land formation having a flat top and steep rock walls: common in arid and semiarid parts of the U.S. and Mexico. [< Sp: table < L *mēnsa*]

Me·sa (mā′sə), *n.* a city in central Arizona, near Phoenix. 62,853 (1970).

mé·sal·li·ance (mā′zə lī′əns, mā zal′ē əns; *Fr.* mā zᴀʟyäɴs′), *n., pl.* **mé·sal·li·anc·es** (mā′zə lī′ən sis, mā zal′ē ən sis; *Fr.* mā zᴀʟ yäɴs′). a marriage with a social inferior; misalliance. [< F]

mes·arch (mez′ärk, mes′-, mē′zärk, -särk), *adj. Ecol.* (of a sere) originating in a mesic habitat.

Me·sa Ver·de (mā′sə vûrd′; *Sp.* me′sä veʀ′the), a national park in SW Colorado: ruins of cliff dwellings. 80 sq. mi.

mes·cal (me skal′), *n.* **1.** either of two species of cactus, *Lophophora Williamsii* or *L. Lewinni,* of Texas and northern Mexico. **2.** an intoxicating beverage distilled from the fermented juice of certain species of agave. **3.** any agave yielding this spirit. [< AmerSp < Nahuatl *mexcalli* mescal = *me(tl)* maguey + *(i)xcalli* stew]

mescal′ but′tons, the dried, buttonlike tops of a mescal of the genus *Lophophora,* used as a hallucinogen, esp. by the Indians during religious ceremonies; peyote.

mes·ca·line (mes′kə lēn′, -lin), *n. Pharm.* a hallucinogenic drug, $C_{11}H_{17}NO_3$, obtained from mescal buttons; peyote. Also, **mezcaline.**

mes·dames (mā däm′, -dam′; *Fr.* mā dᴀm′), *n.* pl. of **madame.**

mes·de·moi·selles (mā′də mə zel′, mād′mwə zel′; *Fr.* mād mwᴀ zel′), *n.* pl. of **mademoiselle.**

me·seems (mē sēmz′), *v. impers.; pt.* **me·seemed.** *Archaic.* it seems to me. [orig. two words: *me seems*]

mes·en·ceph·a·lon (mes′en sef′ə lon′, mez′-), *n., pl.* **-la** (-lə), **-lons.** the midbrain. —**mes·en·ce·phal·ic** (mes′en sə fal′ik, mez′-), *adj.*

mes·en·chyme (mes′eng kīm′, mez′-), *n. Embryol.* an aggregation of cells of mesodermal origin that are capable of developing into connective tissues, blood, and lymphatic and blood vessels. [var. of *mesenchyma* < NL < Gk = *mes-* ᴍᴇs- + *énchyma* infusion] —**mes·en·chy·mal** (mes eng′kə məl, mez-), **mes·en·chym·a·tous** (mes′eng kim′ə təs, mez′-), *adj.*

mes·en·ter·on (mes en′tə ron′, mez-), *n., pl.* **-ter·a** (-tər ə). *Obs.* midgut.

mes·en·ter·y (mes′ən ter′ē, mez′-), *n., pl.* **-ter·ies.** *Anat.* the membrane, consisting of a double layer of peritoneum, that invests the intestines, attaching them to the posterior wall of the abdomen, maintaining them in position in the abdominal cavity, and supplying them with blood vessels, nerves, and lymphatics, esp. the part of this membrane investing the jejunum and ileum. [< NL *mesenteri(um)* < Gk *mesentérion* (*mes-* ᴍᴇs- + *entérion,* neut. of *entérios* of the bowel; see ᴇɴᴛᴇʀᴏɴ)] —**mes′en·ter′ic,** *adj.*

mesh (mesh), *n.* **1.** one of the open spaces in a net or other network, as a screen. **2. meshes, a.** the lines, threads, or the like, that bind such spaces. **b.** the means of catching or holding fast: *to be caught in the meshes of the law.* **3.** an interwoven or intertwined structure; network. **4.** any knit, woven, or knotted fabric of open texture. **5.** *Mach.* the engagement of gear teeth. **6.** any arrangement of interlocking metal links or wires with evenly-spaced, uniform small openings between, as used in jewelry, sieves, etc. —*v.t.* **7.** to catch or entangle in or as in a net; enmesh. **8.** to form with meshes, as a net. **9.** *Mach.* to engage, as gear teeth. **10.** to cause to match, coordinate, or interlock. —*v.i.* **11.** to become enmeshed. **12.** *Mach.* to become or be engaged, as the teeth of one gear with those of another. **13.** to match, coordinate, or interlock. [appar. back formation from OE *mǣscre* mesh; akin to OHG *māsca,* etc.]

Me·shach (mē′shak), *n.* a companion of Daniel. Cf. **Shadrach.**

Me·shed (me shed′), *n.* a city in NE Iran: Muslim shrine. 409,616 (est. 1967). Persian, **Mashhad.**

mesh·work (mesh′wûrk′), *n.* meshed work; network.

mesh·y (mesh′ē), *adj.,* **mesh·i·er, mesh·i·est.** formed with meshes; meshed.

me·si·al (mē′zē əl, -sē-, mez′ē əl, mes′-), *adj.* medial. —**me′si·al·ly, me′sal·ly,** *adv.*

me·sic (mez′ik, mes′-, mē′zik, -sik), *adj.* of, pertaining to, or adapted to an environment having a balanced supply of moisture. [ᴍᴇs- + -ɪᴄ] —**mes′i·cal·ly,** *adv.*

me·sit·y·lene (mi sit′ᵊlēn′, mes′itᵊlēn′), *n. Chem.* a colorless, liquid, aromatic hydrocarbon, $C_6H_3(CH_3)_3$, occurring naturally in coal tar and prepared from acetone: used chiefly as a chemical intermediate. [*mesityl* (< NL *mesīt(a)* (< Gk *mesī́tēs* mediator; see ᴍᴇs-, -ɪᴛᴇ[1]) + -ʏʟ) + -ᴇɴᴇ]

Mes·mer (mez′mər; *Ger.* mes′məʀ), *n.* **Franz** (frants, franz; *Ger.* fʀänts) or **Frie·drich An·ton** (frē′drik an′tᵊn, -ton; *Ger.* fʀē′dʀiᴋʜ än′tōn), 1733–1815, Austrian physician.

mes·mer·ise (mez′mə rīz′), *v.t.,* **-ised, -is·ing.** *Chiefly Brit.* mesmerize. —**mes′mer·i·sa′tion,** *n.* —**mes′mer·is′er,** *n.*

mes·mer·ism (mez′mə riz′əm, mes′-), *n.* **1.** hypnosis as induced by F.A. Mesmer through animal magnetism. **2.** hypnotism. **3.** a compelling attraction; fascination. —**mes·mer·ic** (mez mer′ik, mes-), *adj.* —**mes′mer·ist,** *n.*

mes·mer·ize (mez′mə rīz′, mes′-), *v.t.,* **-ized, -iz·ing. 1.** to hypnotize. **2.** to spellbind; fascinate. **3.** to compel by fascination. Also, *esp. Brit.,* **mesmerise.** —**mes′mer·i·za′tion,** *n.* —**mes′mer·iz′er,** *n.*

mesne (mēn), *adj. Law.* intermediate or intervening. [< legal AF, sp. var. of *meen* ᴍᴇᴀɴ[3]]

mesne′ lord′, (in old English law) an intermediate feudal lord; the tenant of a chief lord and a lord to his own tenants.

meso-, a learned borrowing from Greek meaning "middle," used in the formation of compound words: *mesocephalic.* Also, **mes-.** [comb. form repr. Gk *mésos* middle, in the middle; akin to L *medius*]

Mes·o·a·mer·i·ca (mez′ō ə mer′i kə, mes′-, mē′zō-, -sō-), *n. Chiefly Archaeol.* See **Central America.** —**Mes′o·a·mer′i·can,** *adj., n.*

mes·o·blast (mez′ə blast′, mes′-, mē′zə-, -sə-), *n. Embryol.* **1.** the mesoderm. **2.** the primordial middle layer of a young embryo before the segregation of the germ layers, capable of becoming the mesoderm. —**mes′o·blas′tic,** *adj.*

mes·o·carp (mez′ə kärp′, mes′-, mē′zə-, -sə-), *n. Bot.* the middle layer of pericarp, as the fleshy part of certain fruits. See diag. at **pericarp.**

mes·o·ce·phal·ic (mez′ō sə fal′ik, mes′-, mē′zō-, -sō-), *adj. Cephalom.* having a head with a cephalic index between that of dolichocephaly and brachycephaly. —**mes·o·ceph·al** (mez′ə sef′əl, mes′-, mē′zə-, -sə-), *n.* —**mes′o·ceph′al·y,** *n.*

mes·o·cra·nic (mez′ə krā′nik, mes′-, mē′zə-, -sə-), *adj. Craniom.* having a skull with a cranial index between that of dolichocranic and brachycranic skulls.

mes·o·crat·ic (mez′ə krat′ik, mes′-, mē′zə-, -sə-), *adj. Geol.* composed of light and dark minerals in nearly equal amounts.

mes·o·derm (mez′ə dûrm′, mes′-, mē′zə-, -sə-), *n. Embryol.* the middle germ layer of a metazoan embryo. —**mes′o·der′mal, mes′o·der′mic,** *adj.*

mes·o·gle·a (mez′ə glē′ə, mes′-, mē′zə-, -sə-), *n.* the noncellular, gelatinous material between the inner and outer body walls of a coelenterate or sponge. Also, **mes′o·gloe′a.** [< NL = *meso-* ᴍᴇsᴏ- + Gk *gloía* glue] —**mes′o·gle′al, mes′o·gloe′al,** *adj.*

me·sog·na·thous (mi zog′nə thəs, -sog′-), *adj. Anthropol.* **1.** having medium, slightly protruding jaws. **2.** having a moderate or intermediate gnathic index, from 98 to 103. Also, **mes·og·nath·ic** (mez′əg nath′ik, mes′-, mē′zəg-, -səg-). —**me·sog′na·thism, me·sog′na·thy,** *n.*

Mes·o·lith·ic (mez′ə lith′ik, mes′-, mē′zə-, -sə-), *adj.* of, pertaining to, or characteristic of a transitional period of the Stone Age intermediate between the Paleolithic and the Neolithic periods.

Me·so·lon·ghi (*Gk.* me′sô lông′gē), *n.* Missolonghi.

mes·o·morph (mez′ə môrf′, mes′-, mē′zə-, -sə-), *n.* a person of the mesomorphic type.

mes·o·mor·phic (mez′ə môr′fik, mes′-, mē′zə-, -sə-), *adj.* having or pertaining to a muscular or sturdy body build characterized by the relative prominence of structures developed from the embryonic mesoderm (contrasted with *ectomorphic, endomorphic*). —**mes′o·mor′phism,** *n.* —**mes′o·mor′phy,** *n.*

me·son (mē′zon, -son, mez′on, mes′-), *n. Physics.* any of several elementary particles having a mass intermediate between that of an electron and a proton, being either neutral or positively or negatively charged, and having a spin of ½ or 0. Cf. **mu meson, pi meson.** [ᴍᴇs- + -ᴏɴ[1]]

mes·o·neph·ros (mez′ə nef′ros, mes′-, mē′zə-, -sə-), *n., pl.* **-roi** (-roi). *Embryol.* one of the three embryonic excretory organs of vertebrates, becoming the functional kidney of fishes and amphibians and becoming part of the epididymis in higher vertebrates. Cf. **metanephros, pronephros.** [< NL = *meso-* ᴍᴇsᴏ- + Gk *nephrós* kidney] —**mes′o·neph′ric,** *adj.*

mes·o·pause (mez′ə pôz′, mes′-, mē′zə-, -sə-), *n. Meteorol.* the boundary or transition zone between the mesosphere and the ionosphere.

mes·o·phyll (mez′ə fil, mes′-, mē′zə-, -sə-), *n. Bot.* the parenchyma, usually containing chlorophyll, that forms the interior parts of a leaf. —**mes′o·phyl′lic, mes′o·phyl′lous,** *adj.*

mes·o·phyte (mez′ə fīt′, mes′-, mē′zə-, -sə-), *n.* a plant growing under conditions of well-balanced moisture supply. —**mes·o·phyt·ic** (mez′ə fit′ik, mes′-, mē′zə-, -sə-), *adj.*

Mes·o·po·ta·mi·a (mes′ə pə tā′mē ə), *n.* an ancient country in W Asia between the Tigris and Euphrates rivers: now part of Iraq. —**Mes′o·po·ta′mi·an,** *adj., n.*

mes·o·sphere (mez′ə sfēr′, mes′-, mē′zə-, -sə-), *n.* **1.** (in the classification of the earth's atmosphere by chemical properties) the region between the ionosphere and the exosphere. **2.** the region of the earth's atmosphere between the stratosphere and the thermosphere. —**mes·o·spher·ic** (mez′ə sfer′ik, mes′-, mē′zə-, -sə-), *adj.*

mes·o·the·li·um (mez′ə thē′lē əm, mes′-, mē′zə-, -sə-), *n., pl.* **-li·a** (-lē ə). *Anat., Embryol.* epithelium of mesodermal origin, which lines the body cavities. [ᴍᴇsᴏ- + (ᴇᴘɪ)ᴛʜᴇʟɪᴜᴍ] —**mes′o·the′li·al,** *adj.*

mes·o·tho·rax (mez′ə thôr′aks, -thōr′-, mes′-, mē′zə-, -sə-), *n., pl.* **-tho·rax·es, -tho·ra·ces** (-thôr′ə sēz′, -thōr′-). the middle segment of the three divisions of the thorax of an insect, bearing the second pair of legs and the first pair of wings. —**mes·o·tho·rac·ic** (mez′ə thō ras′ik, -thô-, mes′-, mē′zə-, -sə-), *adj.*

Mes·o·zo·ic (mez′ə zō′ik, mes′-, mē′zə-, -sə-), *Geol.* —*adj.* **1.** noting or pertaining to an era occurring between 70,000,000 and 220,000,000 years ago, characterized by the appearance of flowering plants and by the appearance and extinction of dinosaurs. See table at **era.** —*n.* **2.** the Mesozoic era or group of systems.

mes·quite (me skēt′, mes′kēt), *n.* **1.** a mimosaceous tree or shrub, *Prosopis glandulosa,* of the southwestern U.S. and Mexico, bearing beanlike pods that are rich in sugar and are used for fodder. **2.** any plant of the genus *Prosopis.* Also, **mes·quit′.** [< AmerSp *mezquite* < Nahuatl *mizquitl*]

Mes·quite (me skēt′, mi-), *n.* a city in NE Texas, E of Dallas. 55,131 (1970).

mess (mes), *n.* **1.** a dirty or untidy condition. **2.** a dirty or untidy accumulation of matter or objects. **3.** a state of embarrassing confusion. **4.** an unpleasant or difficult situation. **5.** a group regularly taking meals together. **6.** the meal so taken. **7.** See **mess hall. 8.** a quantity of food sufficient for a dish or a single occasion. **9.** a dish or quantity of soft or liquid food. **10.** *Informal.* a person whose life or affairs are in a state of confusion. —*v.t.* **11.** to make dirty or untidy (often fol. by *up*): *Don't mess up my clean floor.* **12.** to make a mess or muddle of (affairs, responsibilities, etc.) (often fol. by *up*): *They messed up the whole* *deal.* —*v.i.* **13.** to eat in company, esp. as a member of a mess. **14.** to make a dirty or untidy mess. **15. mess around** or **about, a.** *Informal.* to busy oneself without purpose or plan. **b.** *Slang.* to waste time; loaf. **c.** *Slang.* to involve or associate oneself with someone or something. [ME *mes* < OF: a course at a meal < LL *miss(us)* what is sent (put on the table), n. use of ptp. of L *mittere* to send]

mes·sage (mes′ij), *n.* **1.** a communication by means of an intermediary or by telegraph, radio, mail, etc. **2.** an official communication: *the President's message to Congress.* **3.** the inspired utterance of a prophet or sage. **4.** (in automated information and data processing) one or more words taken as a unit. **5.** an idea or maxim to be inferred from a play, novel, etc. [ME < OF < VL **missāticum* = L *miss(us)* sent (ptp. of *mittere* to send) + *-āticum* -AGE]

mes′sage u′nit, *U.S.* a measurement used in charging for telephone calls within a designated area, subject to variations depending on the destination and length of each call placed.

Mes·sa·li·na (mes′ə lī′nə), *n.* **Va·le·ri·a** (və lēr′ē ə), died A.D. 48, 3rd wife of Claudius I.

mes·sa·line (mes′ə lēn′, mes′ə lēn′), *n.* a thin, soft silk with a twill or satin weave. [< F]

Mes·sei·gneurs (*Fr.* mā se nyœr′), *n.* (*sometimes l.c.*) pl. of **Monseigneur.**

Mes·se·ne (me sē′nē), *n.* an ancient city in the SW Peloponnesus; capital of ancient Messenia.

mes·sen·ger (mes′ən jər), *n.* **1.** a person who conveys messages or parcels. **2.** *Archaic.* a herald, precursor, or harbinger. [ME *messager, messangere* < OF *messagier.* See MESSAGE, -ER[2]]

Mes·se·ni·a (mə sē′nē ə, -sēn′yə), *n.* a division of ancient Greece, in the SW Peloponnesus: an important center of Mycenaean culture.

Mes·ser·schmitt (mes′ər shmit′), *n.* any of several types of fighter aircraft used by the German air force in World War II, esp. the ME-109. [named after Willy *Messerschmitt* (1898–1978), German aircraft designer]

mess′ hall′, a place in which a group eats regularly, esp. a dining hall in a military camp, post, etc.

Mes·si·ah (mi sī′ə), *n.* **1.** the promised and expected deliverer of the Jewish people. **2.** Jesus Christ, regarded by Christians as fulfilling this promise and expectation. John 4:25, 26. **3.** (*usually l.c.*) any expected deliverer. [< Heb *māshīah* anointed] —**Mes·si·an·ic** (mes′ē an′ik), *adj.* —**Mes′si·an′i·cal·ly,** *adv.*

Mes·si·dor (me sē dôr′), *n.* (in the French Revolutionary calendar) the 10th month of the year, from June 19 to July 18. [< F < L *messi(s)* harvest + Gk *dôr(on)* gift]

Mes·sier (me syā′), *n.* **Charles** (sharl), 1730–1817, French astronomer.

mes·sieurs (mes′ərz; *Fr.* me syœ′), *n.* pl. of **monsieur.**

Mes·si·na (me sē′nə), *n.* **1.** a seaport in NE Sicily: totally destroyed by an earthquake 1908. 251,423 (1961). **2. Strait of,** a strait between Sicily and Italy. 2½ mi. wide.

Mes·sines (*Fr.* me sēn′), *n.* a village in W Belgium, near Ypres: battles 1914, 1917.

mess′ jack′et, a short, close-fitting jacket, worn by men, esp. as part of a uniform.

mess′ kit′, a portable metal kit used for eating meals when camping out. Also called **mess′ gear′.**

mess·man (mes′mən), *n., pl.* **-men.** *Naval.* an enlisted man who serves in a mess hall.

mess·mate (mes′māt′), *n.* a person, esp. a friend, who is a member of a group regularly taking meals together, as in an army camp.

Messrs. (mes′ərz), pl. of **Mr.** Also, *esp. Brit.,* **Messr**

mes·suage (mes′wij), *n.* *Law.* a dwelling house with its adjacent buildings and lands. [ME < AF, misreading (*n* taken as *u*) of OF *mesnage* MÉNAGE]

mess·y (mes′ē), *adj.,* **mess·i·er, mess·i·est. 1.** characterized by a dirty, untidy, or confused condition. **2.** causing a mess. **3.** embarrassing, difficult, or unpleasant: *a messy situation.* **4.** *Informal.* characterized by a confused moral or psychological outlook. —**mess′i·ly,** *adv.* —**mess′i·ness,** *n.*

mes·tee (me stē′), *n.* mustee.

mes·ti·zo (me stē′zō, mi-), *n., pl.* **-zos, -zoes. 1.** a person of mixed blood. **2.** (in Spanish America) a person of mixed Spanish and Amerindian blood. **3.** a person of mixed European and East Indian, Negro, or Malay blood. **4.** a person of mixed Philippine and foreign ancestry. Also, *referring to a woman,* **mes·ti·za** (me stē′zə, mi-). [< Sp, n. use of adj. *mestizo* mixed < LL *mixtīcius* of mixed race]

Meš·tro·vić (mesh′trə vich; *Serbo-Croatian.* mesh′trô-vich′), *n.* **I·van** (ī′vən; *Serbo-Croatian.* ē′vän), 1883–1962, Yugoslav sculptor, in the U.S. after 1946.

met (met), *v.* pt. and pp. of **meet**[1].

met-, var. of **meta-** before a vowel: *metempirical.*

met., **1.** metaphor. **2.** metaphysics. **3.** metropolitan.

met·a (met′ə), *adj.* *Chem.* pertaining to or occupying two positions in the benzene ring that are separated by one carbon atom. Cf. **ortho, para**[2]. See diag. at **ortho.** [separate use of META-]

meta-, **1.** a learned borrowing from Greek meaning "after," "along with," "beyond," "among," "behind," and often denoting change, used in the formation of compound words: *metacarpus; metagenesis; metalinguistics.* **2.** *Chem.* **a.** (of acids, salts, or their organic derivatives) a combining form denoting the least hydrated of a series: *meta-antimonic,* $HSbO_3$; *meta-antimonous,* $HSbO_2$. Cf. **ortho-, pyro-. b.** a combining form designating the meta position in the benzene ring. *Abbr.:* m-. Cf. **ortho-, para-**[1]. Also, *esp. before a vowel,* **met-.** [< Gk, prefix and prep.; c. OE *mid* with, G *mit*]

met·a·bol·ic (met′ə bol′ik), *adj.* **1.** of, pertaining to, or affected by metabolism. **2.** undergoing metamorphosis. [< Gk *metabolik(ós)* changeable. See METABOLISM, -IC] —**met′a·bol′i·cal·ly,** *adv.*

me·tab·o·lise (mə tab′ə līz′), *v.t., v.i.,* **-lised, -lis·ing.** *Chiefly Brit.* metabolize.

me·tab·o·lism (mə tab′ə liz′əm), *n.* *Biol., Physiol.* the sum of the physical and chemical processes in an organism by which protoplasm is produced, maintained, and destroyed, and by means of which energy is made available. Cf. anabolism, catabolism. [< Gk *metabol(ḗ)* transition (akin to *metabállein* to change = *meta-* META- + *bállein* to throw) + -ISM]

me·tab·o·lite (mə tab′ə līt′), *n.* *Biol., Physiol.* a product of metabolic action. [METABOL(ISM) + -ITE[1]]

me·tab·o·lize (mə tab′ə līz′), *v.t., v.i.,* **-lized, -liz·ing.** to subject to metabolism; change by metabolism. Also, *esp. Brit.,* **metabolise.** —**me·tab′o·liz′a·bil′i·ty,** *n.* —**me·tab′o·liz′a·ble,** *adj.*

met·a·car·pal (met′ə kär′pəl), *adj.* **1.** of or pertaining to the metacarpus. —*n.* **2.** a metacarpal bone.

met·a·car·pus (met′ə kär′pəs), *n., pl.* **-pi** (-pī). *Anat.* the part of a hand or forelimb, esp. of its bony structure, included between the wrist, or carpus, and the fingers, or phalanges. [< NL (see META-, CARPUS), r. *metacarpium* < Gk *metakárpion*]

met·a·cen·ter (met′ə sen′tər), *n.* *Naval Archit.* the intersection between two vertical lines, one through the center of buoyancy of a hull in equilibrium, the other through the center of buoyancy when the hull is inclined slightly to one side or toward one end: the distance of this intersection above the center of gravity is an indication of the initial stability of the hull. Also, *esp. Brit.,* **met′a·cen′tre.** [< F *métacentre*] —**met′a·cen′tric,** *adj.*

M, Metacenter of a boat; G, Center of gravity; B, Center of buoyancy; B′, Center of buoyancy when boat is displaced

met·a·chro·ma·tism (met′ə krō′mə tiz′əm), *n.* change of color, esp. that due to variation in the temperature of a body. —**met·a·chro·mat·ic** (met′ə krō mat′ik, -krə-), *adj.*

met·a·eth·ics (met′ə eth′iks), *n.* the branch of philosophy dealing with the foundations of ethics, esp. the meaning of ethical terms and the nature of moral discourse.

met·a·gal·ax·y (met′ə gal′ək sē), *n., pl.* **-ax·ies.** *Astron.* the complete system of galaxies including the Milky Way. —**met·a·ga·lac·tic** (met′ə gə lak′tik), *adj.*

met·a·gen·e·sis (met′ə jen′i sis), *n.* *Biol.* reproduction characterized by the alternation of a sexual generation and a generation that reproduces asexually. —**met·a·ge·net·ic** (met′ə jə net′ik), —**met′a·gen′ic,** *adj.* —**met′a·ge·net′i·cal·ly,** *adv.*

me·tag·na·thous (mə tag′nə thəs), *adj.* *Ornith.* having the tips of the mandibles crossed, as the crossbills. —**me·tag′na·thism,** *n.*

Me·tairie (me′trē), *n.* a town in SE Louisiana, W of New Orleans. 136,477 (1970).

met·al (met′ᵊl), *n., v.,* **-aled, -al·ing** or (*esp. Brit.*) **-alled, -al·ling.** —*n.* **1.** any of a class of elementary substances, as gold, silver, or copper, all of which are crystalline when solid and many of which are characterized by opacity, ductility, conductivity, and a peculiar luster when freshly fractured. **2.** *Chem.* **a.** such a substance in its pure state, as distinguished from alloys. **b.** an element yielding positively charged ions in aqueous solutions of its salts. **3.** an alloy or mixture composed wholly or partly of such substances. **4.** *Print.* **a.** See **type metal. b.** the state of being set in type. **5.** molten glass in the pot or melting tank. **6.** *Heraldry.* either of the tinctures or or argent, represented respectively by gold or yellow, and silver or white. —*v.t.* **7.** to furnish or cover with metal. [ME (< OF) < L *metall(um)* quarry, metal < Gk *métallon* mine, quarry, metal] —**met′al·like′,** *adj.*

metal., **1.** metallurgical. **2.** metallurgy.

met·a·lin·guis·tics (met′ə ling gwis′tiks), *n.* (*construed as sing.*) the study of the relation of language to its cultural context. —**met′a·lin·guis′tic,** *adj.* —**met′a·lin·guis′ti·cal·ly,** *adv.*

met·al·ist (met′ᵊlist), *n.* **1.** a person who works with metals. **2.** a person who advocates the use of metallic money exclusively. Also, **metallist.**

met·al·ize (met′ᵊlīz′), *v.t.,* **-ized, -iz·ing.** to make metallic; give the characteristics of metal to. Also, **metallize;** *esp. Brit.,* **metallise.** —**met′al·i·za′tion,** *n.*

metall-, var. of **metallo-** esp. before a vowel: *metallurgy.*

metall., metallurgy.

met·alled (met′ᵊld), *adj.* *Brit.* (of a road) paved.

metalli-, a combining form of Latin origin meaning "metal": *metalliferous.* [< L, comb. form of *metallum*]

me·tal·lic (mə tal′ik), *adj.* **1.** of, pertaining to, or consisting of metal. **2.** of the nature of metal, as in luster, resonance, or hardness. **3.** *Chem.* **a.** (of a metal element) being in the free or uncombined state: *metallic iron.* **b.** containing or yielding metal. [< L *metallic(us)* < Gk *metallikós* of, for mines] —**me·tal′li·cal·ly,** *adv.* —**met·al·lic·i·ty** (met′ᵊlis′i tē), **met·al·le·i·ty** (met′ᵊlē′i tē), *n.*

met·al·lif·er·ous (met′ᵊlif′ər əs), *adj.* containing or yielding metal. [< L *metallifer* (see METALLI-, -FER) + -OUS]

met·al·line (met′ᵊlin, -ᵊlīn′), *adj.* **1.** metallic. **2.** containing one or more metals or metallic salts. [ME *mettaline* < ML *metallīn(us)* of metal]

met·al·lise (met′ᵊlīz′), *v.t.,* **-lised, -lis·ing.** *Chiefly Brit.* metallize. —**met′al·li·sa′tion,** *n.*

met·al·list (met′ᵊlist), *n.* metalist.

met·al·lize (met′ᵊlīz′), *v.t.,* **-lized, -liz·ing.** metalize. —**met′al·li·za′tion,** *n.*

metallo-, a combining form of Greek origin meaning "metal": *metallography.* Also, *esp. before a vowel,* **metall-.** [< Gk, comb. form of *métallon*]

met·al·log·ra·phy (met′ᵊlog′rə fē), *n.* **1.** the study of the structure of metals and alloys by means of microscopy. **2.** a lithographic process employing metal plates. [< NL *metallographia*] —**met′al·log′ra·pher, met′al·log′ra·phist** *n.* —**me·tal·lo·graph·ic** (mə tal′ə graf′ik), *adj.*

met·al·loid (met′ᵊloid′), *n.* **1.** a nonmetal. **2.** an element that is both metallic and nonmetallic, as arsenic, silicon, or bismuth. —*adj.* **3.** of or pertaining to a metalloid. **4.** resembling both a metal and a nonmetal.

met·al·lur·gy (met′ᵊlûr′jē *or, esp. Brit.,* mə tal′ər jē), *n.* **1.** the technique or science of separating metals from their ores. **2.** the technique or science of making and compounding alloys. **3.** the technique or science of working or heat-treating metals. [< NL *metallurgia* < Gk *metallourgós* working in metals, mines] —**met′al·lur′gic, met′al·lur′gi·cal,** *adj.* —**met′al·lur′gi·cal·ly,** *adv.* —**met·al·lur·gist** (met′ᵊlûr′jist, mə tal′ər jist), *n.*

met·al·smith (met′ᵊl smith′), *n.* a person skilled in fashioning articles of metal.

met·al·ware (met′ᵊl wâr′), *n.* work of metal, esp. utensils, flatware, etc.

met·al·work·ing (met′ᵊl wûr′king), *n.* the act or technique of making metal objects.

met·a·math·e·mat·ics (met′ə math′ə mat′iks), *n.* (*construed as sing.*) the logical analysis of the fundamental concepts of mathematics, as number, function, etc. —**met′a·math′e·mat′i·cal,** *adj.* —**met·a·math·e·ma·ti·cian** (met′ə math′ə mə tish′ən), *n.*

met·a·mer (met′ə mər), *n.* *Chem.* a compound exhibiting metamerism with one or more other compounds.

met·a·mere (met′ə mēr′), *n.* a somite.

met·a·mer·ic (met′ə mer′ik), *adj.* **1.** *Zool.* **a.** consisting of metameres. **b.** pertaining to metamerism. **2.** *Chem.* of, pertaining to, or characteristic of metamerism. —**met′a·mer′i·cal·ly,** *adv.*

me·tam·er·ism (mə tam′ə riz′əm), *n.* **1.** *Zool.* **a.** division into metameres, the developmental process of somite formation. **b.** existence in a metameric state. **2.** *Chem.* isomerism resulting from the attachment of different groups to the same atom, as $C_2H_5NHC_2H_5$ and $CH_3NHC_3H_7$.

met·a·mor·phic (met′ə môr′fik), *adj.* **1.** pertaining to or characterized by change of form, or metamorphosis. **2.** *Geol.* pertaining to or exhibiting structural change or metamorphism.

met·a·mor·phism (met′ə môr′fiz əm), *n.* **1.** metamorphosis. **2.** *Geol.* a change in the structure or constitution of a rock due to natural agencies, as pressure and heat, esp. when the rock becomes harder and more completely crystalline.

met·a·mor·phose (met′ə môr′fōz, -fōs), *v.*, **-phosed, -phos·ing.** —*v.t.* **1.** to change the form or nature of; transform. **2.** to subject to metamorphosis or metamorphism. —*v.i.* **3.** to undergo or be capable of undergoing a change in form or nature. [back formation from METAMORPHOSIS] —**Syn. 1, 3.** mutate, transmute.

met·a·mor·pho·sis (met′ə môr′fə sis), *n.*, *pl.* **-ses** (-sēz′). **1.** a complete change of form, structure, or substance, as transformation by magic or witchcraft. **2.** any complete change in appearance, character, circumstances, etc. **3.** a form resulting from any such change. **4.** *Zool.* a change or successive changes of form during the postembryonic growth of an animal by which it is adapted to a new or special environment or way of living. **5.** *Bot.* the structural or functional modification of a plant organ or structure during its development. [< L < Gk: transformation] —**Syn. 2.** mutation, transmutation. —**Ant. 1, 2.** stasis.

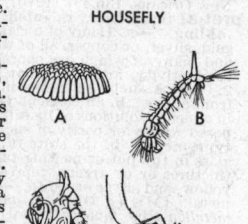

HOUSEFLY

MOSQUITO

Metamorphosis (def. 4)
A, Eggs; B, Larva; C, Pupa; D, Adult

met·a·mor·phous (met′ə môr′fəs), *adj.* metamorphic.

met·a·neph·ros (met′ə nef′ros), *n.*, *pl.* **-roi** (-roi). *Embryol.* one of the three embryonic excretory organs of higher vertebrates, becoming the permanent and functional kidney. Cf. **mesonephros, pronephros.** [< NL < Gk *meta-* META- + *nephrós* kidney] —**met′a·neph′ric,** *adj.*

metaph., **1.** metaphysical. **2.** metaphysics.

met·a·phase (met′ə fāz′), *n.* *Biol.* the stage in mitosis in which the duplicated chromosomes lie on the equatorial plane of the spindle.

met·a·phor (met′ə fôr′, -fər), *n.* the application of a word or phrase to an object or concept it does not literally denote, in order to suggest comparison with another object or concept, as in "A mighty fortress is our God." Cf. **mixed metaphor, simile** (def. 1). [< L *metaphora* < Gk: a transfer, akin to *metaphérein* to transfer] —**met·a·phor·i·cal** (met′ə fôr′i kəl, -for′-), **met′a·phor′ic,** *adj.* —**met′a·phor′i·cal·ly,** *adv.* —**met′a·phor′i·cal·ness,** *n.*

met′a·phos·phor′ic ac′id (met′ə fos fôr′ik, -for′-), *Chem.* an acid, HPO_3, derived from phosphorous pentoxide, and containing the smallest amount of water of the phosphoric acids. Cf. **phosphoric acid.**

met·a·phrase (met′ə frāz′), *n.*, *v.*, **-phrased, -phras·ing.** —*n.* **1.** a translation. —*v.t.* **2.** to translate, esp. literally. **3.** to change the phrasing or literary form of. [< Gk *metáphras(is)* a paraphrasing, change of phrasing]

met·a·phrast (met′ə frast′), *n.* a person who translates or changes a literary work from one form to another, as prose into verse. [< MGk *metaphrást(ēs)* a person who translates, akin to *metaphrázein* to translate] —**met′a·phras′tic, met′a·phras′ti·cal,** *adj.* —**met′a·phras′ti·cal·ly,** *adv.*

metaphys., metaphysics.

met·a·phys·ic (met′ə fiz′ik), *Rare.* —*n.* **1.** metaphysics. —*adj.* **2.** metaphysical. [ME *metaphesik* < ML *metaphysica* (neut. pl., taken as fem. sing.); see METAPHYSICS]

met·a·phys·i·cal (met′ə fiz′i kəl), *adj.* **1.** *Philos.* pertaining to or of the nature of metaphysics. **2.** highly abstract or abstruse. **3.** of or pertaining to a highly philosophical school of poetry in 17th-century England. **4.** *Archaic.* imaginary. [ME < ML *metaphysicāl(is)*] —**met′a·phys′i·cal·ly,** *adv.*

met·a·phy·si·cian (met′ə fi zish′ən), *n.* a person who creates or develops metaphysical theories. Also, **met·a·phys·i·cist** (met′ə fiz′i sist). [prob. < MF *metaphysicien* = *metaphysique* METAPHYSIC + *-ien* -IAN]

met·a·phys·ics (met′ə fiz′iks), *n.* (*construed as sing.*) **1.** the branch of philosophy that treats of first principles or the ultimate nature of existence, reality, and experience, esp. as developed in self-contained conceptual systems. **2.** philosophy, esp. in its more abstruse branches. [< ML *metaphysic(a)* < MGk *(tà) metaphysiká* (neut. pl.), Gk *tà metà tà physiká* the (works) after the physics; with reference to the arrangement of Aristotle's writings]

met·a·plasm (met′ə plaz′əm), *n.* **1.** *Biol.* the nonliving matter or inclusions, as starch or pigments, in the protoplasm of a cell. **2.** *Gram.* a change in the structure of a word or sentence made by adding, removing, or transposing the constituent letters or words. [< L *metaplasm(us)* a grammatical change, irregularity < Gk *metaplasmós* reforming, remodeling < *metaplás(ein)* (to) mold differently, remodel] —**met′a·plas′mic,** *adj.*

met·a·pro·tein (met′ə prō′tēn, -tē in), *n.* *Biochem.* a hydrolytic derivative of protein, insoluble in water but soluble in dilute acids or alkalies.

met·a·psy·chol·o·gy (met′ə sī kol′ə jē), *n.* *Psychol.* **1.** speculative thought dealing systematically with concepts extending beyond the limits of psychology as an empirical science. **2.** (in psychoanalytic theory) the conception of mental processes as subsumed under the three major categories of causal relations, structural placement, and functional value. —**met·a·psy·cho·log·i·cal** (met′ə sī′kə loj′i kəl), *adj.*

met·a·so·ma·tism (met′ə sō′mə tiz′əm), *n.* *Geol.* **1.** the series of processes whereby minerals or rocks are replaced by others of different chemical composition as a result of the introduction of material, usually in very hot aqueous solutions, from sources external to the formation undergoing change. **2.** replacement (def. 4). Also, **met·a·so·ma·to·sis** (met′ə sō′mə tō′sis). —**met·a·so·mat·ic** (met′ə sō mat′ik), *adj.*

me·ta·sta·ble (met′ə stā′bəl, met′ə stā′-), *adj.* **1.** *Metall.* chemically unstable in the absence of certain conditions that would induce stability, but not liable to spontaneous transformation. **2.** *Physics, Chem.* pertaining to a body or system existing at an energy level above that of a more stable state and requiring the addition of a small amount of energy to induce a transition to the more stable state. —**met·a·sta·bil·i·ty** (met′ə stə bil′i tē), *n.*

Me·ta·sta·sio (me′tä stä′zyô), *n.* (*Pietro Antonio Domenico Bonaventura Trapassi*) 1698–1782, Italian poet and dramatist.

me·tas·ta·sis (mə tas′tə sis), *n.*, *pl.* **-ses** (-sēz′). **1.** *Pathol.* **a.** the transference of disease-producing organisms or of malignant or cancerous cells to other parts of the body by way of the blood vessels, lymphatics, or membranous surfaces. **b.** the condition produced by this. **2.** transformation (def. 3). [< Gk: a changing] —**met·a·stat·ic** (met′ə stat′ik), *adj.* —**met′a·stat′i·cal·ly,** *adv.*

me·tas·ta·size (mə tas′tə sīz′), *v.i.*, **-sized, -siz·ing.** *Pathol.* (of malignant cells or disease-producing organisms) to spread to other parts of the body by way of the blood vessels, lymphatics, or membranous surfaces.

met·a·tar·sal (met′ə tär′səl), *adj.* **1.** of or pertaining to the metatarsus. —*n.* **2.** a bone in the metatarsus.

met·a·tar·sus (met′ə tär′səs), *n.*, *pl.* **-si** (-sī). *Anat.*, *Zool.* the part of a foot or hind limb, esp. its bony structure, included between the tarsus and the toes or phalanges. [< NL]

me·tath·e·sis (mə tath′i sis), *n.*, *pl.* **-ses** (-sēz′). **1.** the transposition of letters, syllables, or sounds in a word. **2.** *Chem.* See **double decomposition.** [< LL: transposition of letters of a word < Gk *metáthesis* transposition] —**met·a·thet·ic** (met′ə thet′ik), **met′a·thet′i·cal,** *adj.*

me·tath·e·sise (mə tath′i sīz′), *v.t.*, *v.i.*, **-sised, -sis·ing.** *Chiefly Brit.* metathesize.

me·tath·e·size (mə tath′i sīz′), *v.t.*, *v.i.*, **-sized, -siz·ing.** to undergo or cause to undergo metathesis.

met·a·tho·rax (met′ə thôr′aks, -thōr′-), *n.*, *pl.* **-tho·rax·es, -tho·ra·ces** (-thôr′ə sēz′, -thōr′-). the posterior division of the thorax of an insect, bearing the third pair of legs and the second pair of wings. —**met·a·tho·rac·ic** (met′ə thō ras′ik, -thô-), *adj.*

met·a·to·lu·i·dine (met′ə tə lo͞o′i dēn′, -din), *n.* *Chem.* a liquid, $CH_3C_6H_4NH_2$, the meta isomer of toluidine, used in the manufacture of dyes and other organic compounds.

Me·ta·xas (mə tak′səs; *Gk.* me′tä ksäs′), *n.* **Jo·an·nes** (yô ä′nyēs), 1871–1941, Greek general and political leader: dictator 1936–40.

met·a·xy·lem (met′ə zī′lem), *n.* *Bot.* the part of the primary xylem that is the last to be formed, usually having weblike or pitted surfaces.

Met·a·zo·a (met′ə zō′ə), *n.* a zoological division comprising the multicellular animals. —**met′a·zo′an,** *adj.*, *n.* —**met′a·zo′ic, met′a·zo′al,** *adj.*

Metch·ni·koff (mech′nē kôf′), *n.* **É·lie** (ā lē′), 1845–1916, Russian zoologist and bacteriologist in France: Nobel prize for medicine 1908. Russian, **Mechnikov.**

mete[1] (mēt), *v.t.*, **met·ed, met·ing.** **1.** to distribute or apportion by measure; allot (usually fol. by *out*): *to mete out punishment.* **2.** *Archaic.* to measure. [ME; OE *metan*; c. D *meten*, Icel *meta*, Goth *mitan*, G *messen* to measure, Gk *médesthai* to ponder] —**Syn. 1.** dole, deal, measure, parcel.

mete[2] (mēt), *n.* **1.** a limiting mark. **2.** a limit or boundary. [late ME < MF < L *mēta* goal, turning post]

met·em·pir·i·cal (met′em pir′i kəl), *adj.* **1.** beyond or outside the field of experience. **2.** of or pertaining to metempirics. Also, **met′em·pir′ic.** —**met′em·pir′i·cal·ly,** *adv.*

met·em·pir·ics (met′em pir′iks), *n.* (*construed as sing.*) the philosophy dealing with the existence of things outside or beyond experience. Also, **met′em·pir′i·cism.** —**met′em·pir′i·cist,** *n.*

me·tem·psy·cho·sis (mə tem′sə kō′sis, -temp′-, met′əm sī-), *n.*, *pl.* **-ses** (-sēz). the transmigration of the soul, esp. the passage of the soul after death from a human or animal to some other human or animal body. [< LL < Gk = *metempsȳch(oûsthai)* to pass from one body into another (see META-, EM-[3], PSYCHO-) + *-ōsis* -OSIS] —**met·em·psy-**

chic (met′əm sī′kik), **me·tem′psy·cho′sic, me·tem′psy·cho′si·cal,** *adj.*

met·en·ceph·a·lon (met′en sef′ə lon′), *n., pl.* **-lons, -la** (-lə). *Anat.* the anterior section of the hindbrain, comprising the cerebellum and pons. **—met·en·ce·phal·ic** (met′en sə fal′ik), *adj.*

me·te·or (mē′tē ər), *n.* **1.** a meteoroid or meteorite. **2.** a transient fiery streak in the sky produced by a meteoroid passing through the earth's atmosphere. **3.** *Obs.* any atmospheric phenomenon, as hail, a typhoon, etc. [< ML *meteor(um)* < Gk *meteōron* meteor, a thing in the air, n. use of neut. of *meteōros* raised in the air = *met-* MET- + *eōr-* (var. s. of *aeírein* to raise) + *-os* adj. suffix] **—me′te·orlike′,** *adj.*

meteor., 1. meteorological. **2.** meteorology.

me·te·or·ic (mē′tē ôr′ik, -or′-), *adj.* **1.** of, pertaining to, or like a meteor or meteors. **2.** consisting of meteors: *a meteoric shower.* **3.** suggesting a meteor, as in transient brilliance: *a meteoric career.* **4.** of the atmosphere; meteorological. [< ML *meteoric(us)*] **—me′te·or′i·cal·ly,** *adv.*

me·te·or·ite (mē′tē ə rīt′), *n.* **1.** a mass of stone or metal that has reached the earth from outer space; a fallen meteoroid. **2.** a meteoroid. **—me·te·or·it·ic** (mē′tē ə rit′ik), **me′te·or·it′i·cal, me·te·or·it·al** (mē′tē ə rīt′əl), *adj.*

me·te·or·it·ics (mē′tē ə rit′iks), *n.* (*construed as sing.*) *Astron.* the science that deals with meteors. **—me·te·or·it·i·cist** (mē′tē ə rit′i sist), *n.*

me·te·or·o·graph (mē′tē ôr′ə graf′, -gräf′, -or′-, mē′tē ər ə-), *n.* an instrument for automatically recording various meteorological conditions simultaneously. [METEORO(LOGY) + -GRAPH] **—me·te·or·o·graph·ic** (mē′tē ôr′ə graf′ik, -or′-, mē′tē ər ə-), *adj.*

me·te·or·oid (mē′tē ə roid′), *n.* *Astron.* any of the small bodies, often remnants of comets, traveling through space.

meteorol., 1. meteorological. **2.** meteorology.

me·te·or·o·log·i·cal (mē′tē ər ə loj′i kəl), *adj.* pertaining to meteorology or to phenomena of the atmosphere. Also, **me′te·or·o·log′ic.** [< Gk *meteōrologik(ós)* pertaining to celestial phenomena + -AL[1]] **—me′te·or·o·log′i·cal·ly,** *adv.*

me·te·or·ol·o·gy (mē′tē ə rol′ə jē), *n.* the science dealing with the atmosphere and its phenomena, including weather and climate. [< Gk *meteōrología* a treatise on the heavenly bodies] **—me′te·or·ol′o·gist,** *n.*

me′teor show′er, *Astron.* the profusion of meteors observed when the earth passes through a meteor swarm.

me·ter[1] (mē′tər), *n.* the fundamental unit of length in the metric system, equivalent to 39.37 U.S. inches, now defined as 1,650,763.73 wavelengths of the orange-red radiation of krypton 86 under specified conditions. *Abbr.:* m Also, *esp. Brit.,* **metre.** [< F *mètre* < Gk *métron* measure]

me·ter[2] (mē′tər), *n.* **1.** *Pros.* **a.** poetic measure; an arrangement of words in rhythmic lines or verses. **b.** a particular form of such an arrangement, depending on both the kind and the number of feet constituting the verse (usually used in combination): *iambic trimeter.* **2.** *Music.* **a.** the rhythmic element as measured by division into parts of equal time value. **b.** the unit of measurement, in terms of number of beats, adopted for a given piece of music. Cf. **measure** (def. 16). Also, *esp. Brit.,* **metre.** [ME *metir, metur,* OE *mēter* < L *metr(um)* poetic meter, verse < Gk *métron* measure; r. ME *metre* < MF]

me·ter[3] (mē′tər), *n.* **1.** an instrument that automatically measures and registers a quantity consumed, distance traveled, degree of intensity, etc. **—***v.t.* **2.** to measure by means of a meter. [ME; see METE[1], -ER[1]]

-meter, a learned borrowing from Latin and Greek meaning "measure," used in the names of instruments measuring quantity, extent, degree, etc.: *altimeter; barometer.* Cf. **-metry.** [< NL *-metrum* < Gk *métron* measure]

me·ter-kil·o·gram-sec·ond (mē′tər kil′ə gram′ sek′ənd), *adj.* of or pertaining to the system of units in which the meter, kilogram, and second are the principal units of length, mass, and time. *Abbr.:* MKS, mks, m.k.s.

me′ter maid′, *U.S.* a uniformed female employee in a municipal traffic department whose chief duty is the issuance of tickets for parking violations.

meth-, a combining form of **methyl:** *methenamine.*

Meth., Methodist.

meth·ac·ry·late (meth ak′rə lāt′), *n.* *Chem.* an ester or salt derived from methacrylic acid.

methac′rylate res′in, *Chem.* an acrylic resin formed by polymerizing the esters or amides of methacrylic acid.

meth′a·cryl′ic ac′id (meth′ə kril′ik, meth′-), *Chem.* a liquid acid, $CH_2{=}C(CH_3)COOH$, whose methyl ester, methyl methacrylate, polymerizes to yield a clear plastic. Cf. **Lucite, plexiglass.**

meth·a·done (meth′ə dōn′), *n.* *Pharm.* a synthetic narcotic drug, $(C_6H_5)_2C(COC_2H_5)CH_2CH(CH_3)N(CH_3)_2$, that blocks the effects of heroin and may be used as a heroin substitute in the treatment of heroin addiction and as a painkiller. Also, **meth·a·don** (meth′ə don′). [METH- + A(MINO) + D(IPHENYL) + -ONE]

meth·ane (meth′ān), *n.* *Chem.* a colorless, odorless, flammable gas, CH_4, the main constituent of marsh gas and the firedamp of coal mines, obtained commercially from natural gas: the first member of the methane, or alkane, series of hydrocarbons.

meth′ane se′ries, *Chem.* See **alkane series.**

meth·a·nol (meth′ə nōl′, -nôl′, -nol′), *n.* *Chem.* See **methyl alcohol.**

meth·a·qua·lone (meth′ə kwo′lōn), *n.* *Pharm.* a nonbarbiturate sedative-hypnotic drug, $C_{16}H_{14}N_2O$, used to induce sleep. [METH- + A-[6] + QU(ININE) + A(ZO)L(E) + -ONE]

Meth·e·drine (meth′ə drēn′, -drin), *n.* *Trademark.* a stimulating drug similar in its effects to amphetamine.

me·theg·lin (mə theg′lin), *n.* mead. [< Welsh *meddyglyn* = *meddyg* healing (< L *medicus;* see MEDICAL) + *llyn* liquor]

met·he·mo·glo·bin (met hē′mə glō′bin, -hem′ə-, -hē′mə glō′-, -hem′ə-), *n.* *Biochem.* a brownish compound of oxygen and hemoglobin, formed in the blood, as by the use of certain drugs. Also, **met·hae′mo·glo′bin.** Also called **hemiglobin.**

me·the·na·mine (me thē′nə mēn′, -min), *n.* *Chem.* hexamethylenetetramine. [METH- + -ENE + AMINE]

me·thinks (mi thingks′), *v. impers.; pt.* **me·thought.** *Archaic.* it seems to me. [ME *me thinketh,* OE *me thyncth.* See ME, THINK[2]]

me·thi·o·nine (me thī′ə nēn′, -nin), *n.* *Biochem.* an amino acid, $CH_3SCH_2CH_2CH(NH_2)COOH$, found in casein, wool, and other proteins or prepared synthetically: used as a supplement to a high-protein diet in the prevention and treatment of certain liver diseases. [METH- + THIONINE]

meth·od (meth′əd), *n.* **1.** a plan or system of action, inquiry, analysis, etc. **2.** order or system in one's actions. **3.** Often, **methods.** the manner in which one acts, esp. in conducting a business. **4.** an order or system, as of classification or arrangement. **5. the Method.** Also called **Stanislavski Method, Stanislavski System.** a theory and technique of acting in which the performer identifies with the character to be portrayed. [< L *method(us)* < Gk *méthodos* systematic course. See META-, -ODE[2]] **—meth′od·less,** *adj.*
—Syn. 1. means, technique. METHOD, MODE, WAY imply a manner in which a thing is done or in which it happens. METHOD refers to a settled kind of procedure, usually according to a definite, established, logical, or systematic plan: *the open-hearth method of making steel.* MODE is a more formal word that implies a customary or characteristic fashion of doing something: *Kangaroos have a peculiar mode of carrying their young.* WAY, a word in popular use for the general idea, is equivalent to various more specific words: *someone's way* (manner) *of walking; the best way* (method) *of rapid calculating; the way* (mode) *of holding a pen.*

me·thod·i·cal (mə thod′i kəl), *adj.* **1.** performed, disposed, or acting in a systematic way. **2.** painstaking; deliberate. Also, **me·thod′ic.** [< L *methodic(us)* (< Gk *methodikós;* see METHOD, -IC) + -AL[1]] **—me·thod′i·cal·ly,** *adv.* **—me·thod′i·cal·ness,** *n.* **—Syn. 1.** See **orderly.**

meth·od·ise (meth′ə dīz′), *v.t.,* **-ised, -is·ing.** *Chiefly Brit.* methodize. **—meth′od·is′er,** *n.*

Meth·od·ism (meth′ə diz′əm), *n.* **1.** the doctrines and beliefs of the Methodists. **2.** (*l.c.*) *Rare.* the act or practice of working, proceeding, etc., according to some method or system. **3.** (*l.c.*) *Rare.* an excessive use of or preoccupation with methods, systems, or the like.

Meth·od·ist (meth′ə dist), *n.* **1.** a member of a leading Protestant denomination, which grew out of the revival of religion led by John Wesley: stresses both personal and social morality and has an Arminian doctrine and, in the U.S., a modified episcopal polity. **2.** (*l.c.*) *Rare.* a person who uses methods or a particular method, esp. habitually or excessively. **—***adj.* **3.** Also, **Meth′od·is′tic, Meth′od·is′ti·cal.** of or pertaining to the Methodists or Methodism. **—Meth′od·is′ti·cal·ly,** *adv.*

Me·tho·di·us (mə thō′dē əs), *n.* **Saint** (*Apostle of the Slavs*), A.D. c825–885, Greek missionary in Moravia (brother of Saint Cyril).

meth·od·ize (meth′ə dīz′), *v.t.,* **-ized, -iz·ing. 1.** to reduce to a method. **2.** to arrange according to a method. Also, *esp. Brit.,* **methodise. —meth′od·iz′er,** *n.*

meth·od·ol·o·gy (meth′ə dol′ə jē), *n., pl.* **-gies. 1.** a system of methods, principles, and rules, as those of an art or science. **2.** *Philos.* **a.** the underlying principles and rules of organization of a philosophical system or inquiry procedure. **b.** the study of the principles underlying the organization of the various sciences and the conduct of scientific inquiry. **3.** *Educ.* the analysis and evaluation of subjects to be taught and the study of the methods of teaching them. [< NL *methodologia*] **—meth·od·o·log·i·cal** (meth′ə də loj′i kəl), *adj.* **—meth′od·o·log′i·cal·ly,** *adv.* **—meth′od·ol′o·gist,** *n.*

me·thought (mi thôt′), *v.* pt. of **methinks.**

meth·ox·ide (meth ok′sīd, -sid), *n.* *Chem.* methylate (def. 1).

me·thox·y (mə thok′sē), *adj.* *Chem.* containing the methoxy group. Also, **meth·ox·yl** (mə thok′sil). [METH- + OXY(GEN)]

methoxy-, a combining form representing the methoxy group: *methoxychlor.*

me·thox·y·chlor (mə thok′si klōr′, -klôr′), *n.* *Chem.* a solid, $Cl_3CCH(C_6H_4OCH_3)_2$, used as an insecticide. [METHOXY- + CHLOR(INE)]

methox′y group′, *Chem.* the univalent group, CH_3O–. Also called **methox′y rad′ical.**

Me·thu·en (mə thōō′ən), *n.* a town in NE Massachusetts, near Lawrence. 35,456 (1970).

Me·thu·se·lah (mə thōō′zə lə, -thōōz′lə), *n.* **1.** a patriarch, said to have lived 969 years. Gen. 5:27. **2.** a wine bottle holding 6½ quarts.

meth·yl (meth′əl), *adj.* *Chem.* containing the methyl group. **—me·thyl·ic** (me thil′ik, mə-), *adj.*

methyl-, a combining form indicating the presence of the methyl group: *methylamine.*

meth′yl ac′etate, *Chem.* a colorless, flammable, volatile liquid, CH_3COOCH_3, used chiefly as a solvent.

meth·yl·al (meth′ə lal′, meth′ə lal′), *n.* *Chem.* a flammable, volatile liquid, $CH_3OCH_2OCH_3$, having a chloroformlike odor: used chiefly as a solvent, in perfumery, and in organic synthesis. Also called **formal.**

meth′yl al′cohol, *Chem.* a colorless, volatile, water-soluble, poisonous liquid, CH_3OH, used chiefly as a solvent, a fuel, and an automobile antifreeze and in the synthesis of formaldehyde. Also called **methanol, wood alcohol, wood spirit.**

meth·yl·a·mine (meth′ə lə mēn′, -əl am′in), *n.* *Chem.* any of three derivatives of ammonia in which one or all of the hydrogen atoms are replaced by methyl groups, esp. a gas, CH_3NH_2, with an ammonialike odor, the simplest alkyl derivative of ammonia.

meth·yl·ate (meth′ə lāt′), *n., v.,* **-at·ed, -at·ing.** *Chem.* **—***n.* **1.** Also called **methoxide.** any derivative of methyl alcohol, as sodium methylate, CH_3ONa. **2.** any compound containing the methyl group. **—***v.t.* **3.** (in a compound) to replace one or more hydrogen atoms with the methyl group. **4.** to mix with methyl alcohol, as in the denaturation of ethyl alcohol. **—meth′yl·a′tor,** *n.*

meth′ylated spir′its, ethyl alcohol denatured with

methyl alcohol for the purpose of preventing its use as an alcoholic beverage. Also, **meth′ylated spir′it.**

meth·yl·ben·zene (meth′əl ben′zēn, -ben zēn′), *n. Chem.* toluene.

meth′yl bro′mide, *Chem.* a colorless, poisonous gas, CH_3Br, used chiefly as a solvent, refrigerant, and fumigant and in organic synthesis.

meth′yl chlo′ride, *Chem.* a poisonous gas, CH_3Cl, used chiefly as a solvent, as a refrigerant, and in organic synthesis.

meth·yl·ene (meth′ə lēn′), *adj. Chem.* containing the methylene group.

meth′ylene blue′, *Chem., Pharm.* a dark-green crystalline compound, $C_{16}H_{18}ClN_3S \cdot 3H_2O$, that dissolves in water to form a deep-blue solution: used chiefly as a dye, as a bacteriological and biological stain, and as an antidote for cyanide poisoning.

meth′ylene group′, *Chem.* the bivalent group, $> CH_2$, derived from methane. Also called **meth′ylene rad′ical.**

meth′yl group′, *Chem.* the univalent group, CH_3-, derived from methane. Also called **meth′yl rad′ical.** —**me·thyl·ic** (mə thil′ik), *adj.*

meth′yl i·so·cy′a·nate (ī′sə sī′ə nāt′), *Chem.* a highly toxic, flammable, colorless liquid, CH_3NCO, used in the manufacture of pesticides: in 1984, the accidental release of a cloud of this chemical in Bhopal, India, caused many deaths and injuries.

meth′yl methac′rylate, *Chem.* a volatile, flammable liquid, unsaturated ester, $CH_2{=}C(CH_3)COOCH_3$, that polymerizes readily to a clear plastic. Cf. **Lucite, plexiglass.**

meth′yl meth′ane, ethane.

meth·yl·naph·tha·lene (meth′əl naf′thə lēn′, -nap′-), *n. Chem.* a compound, $C_{10}H_7CH_3$, whose alpha isomer, a colorless liquid, is used in determining cetane numbers.

meth′yl or′ange, *Chem.* an orange-yellow powder, $(CH_3)_2NC_6H_4N{=}NC_6H_4SO_3Na$, used chiefly as an acid-base indicator. Cf. **methyl red.**

meth·yl·par·a·ben (meth′əl par′ə ben′), *n. Chem.* a needlelike substance, $HOC_6H_4COOCH_3$, used chiefly as a preservative in foods and pharmaceuticals. [METHYL- + PARA-² + BEN(ZOIC ACID)]

meth′yl red′, *Chem.* a solid occurring as a dark-red powder or violet crystals, $(CH_3)_2NC_6H_4N{=}NC_6H_4COOH$, used chiefly as an acid-base indicator. Cf. **methyl orange.**

meth′yl·ros·an′i·line chlo′ride (meth′əl rō zan′ə lin, -līn′, meth′-). See **gentian violet.**

meth′yl salic′ylate, *Chem.* a liquid, $HOC_6H_4COOCH_3$, used chiefly in perfumery and flavoring, and in medicine as a counterirritant in external preparations. Also called **oil of wintergreen, wintergreen oil.**

meth·y·pry·lon (meth′i prī′lon), *n. Pharm.* a bitter powder, $C_{10}H_{17}NO_2$, used as a sedative and hypnotic. [METHY(L)- + P(IPE)R(IDINE + DIETH)YL + *-on,* var. of -ONE]

me·tic·u·lous (mə tik′yə ləs), *adj.* extremely careful about minute details. [< L *meticulōs(us)* full of fear, fearful = *meti-* for *metu-* (s. of *metus* fear) + *-cul(us)* -CULE + *-ōsus* -OUS] —**me·tic′u·lous·ly,** *adv.* —**me·tic′u·lous·ness, me·tic·u·los·i·ty** (mə tik′yə los′i tē), *n.* —**Syn.** exact, precise.

mé·tier (mā′tyā, mā tyā′), *n.* **1.** a field of work; occupation, trade, or profession. **2.** a field of work or other activity in which a person has special ability, training, etc.; forte. [< F << L *minister(ium)* MINISTRY]

mé·tis (mā tēs′, -tē′), *n., pl.* **-tis** (-tēs′, -tēz′). **1.** any person of mixed ancestry. **2.** *Canadian.* a half-breed of white, esp. French, and Indian parentage. [< F, MF: MESTIZO]

Me·ton′ic cy′cle (mi ton′ik), *Astron.* a 19-year cycle after which the new moon occurs on the same day of the year as at the beginning of the cycle. [named after *Meton,* 5th-century B.C. Athenian astronomer]

met·o·nym (met′ə nim), *n.* a word used in metonymy. [back formation from METONYMY]

me·ton·y·my (mi ton′ə mē), *n. Rhet.* the use of the name of one object or concept for that of another to which it is related, or of which it is a part, as "scepter" for "sovereignty." [< LL *metōnymia* < Gk: change of name] —**met′o·nym′i·cal, met′o·nym′ic,** *adj.* —**met′o·nym′i·cal·ly,** *adv.*

met·o·pe (met′ə pē′, -ōp), *n. Archit.* any of the square spaces between triglyphs in the Doric frieze. [< Gk]

me·tre (mē′tər), *n. Chiefly Brit.* meter.

met·ric¹ (me′trik), *adj.* pertaining to the meter or to the metric system. [< F *métrique*]

met·ric² (me′trik), *adj.* metrical. [< L *metric(us)* < Gk *metrikós* of, relating to measuring. See METER², -IC]

-metric, a word element used to form adjectives from nouns with stems in **-meter** (*barometric*) or **-metry** (*geometric*). [MET(E)R or -METR(Y) + -IC]

met·ri·cal (me′tri kəl), *adj.* **1.** pertaining to meter or poetic measure. **2.** composed in meter or verse. **3.** pertaining to measurement. [late ME < LL *metric(us)* (see METRIC²) + -AL¹] —**met′ri·cal·ly,** *adv.*

met′ric hun′dredweight, a unit of weight equivalent to 50 kilograms.

me·tri·cian (mi trish′ən), *n.* a metrist. [late ME *metricion*]

met·rics (me′triks), *n.* (*construed as sing.*) **1.** the science of meter. **2.** the art of metrical composition.

met′ric sys′tem, a decimal system of weights and measures, universally used in science and used for all purposes in a large number of countries. The basic units are the meter (39.37 inches) for length and the gram (15.432 grains) for mass or weight. Derived units are the liter (0.908 U.S. dry quart, or 1.0567 U.S. liquid quarts) for capacity, and the are (119.6 square yards) for area. Names for units larger and smaller than these are formed with the following prefixes: kilo, 1000; hecto, 100; deca, 10; deci, 0.1; centi, 0.01; milli, 0.001; micro, 0.000001.

met′ric ton′, a unit of 1000 kilograms, equivalent to 2204.62 avoirdupois pounds.

met·rist (me′trist, mē′trist), *n.* a person who is skilled in the use of poetic meters. [< ML *metrist(a)*]

met·ro (me′trō), *n., pl.* **-ros.** (*often cap.*) a subway, esp. in Paris, France or Montreal, Canada. Also, **mé·tro** (*Fr.* mā tʀō′). [< F *métro,* short for *chemin de fer métropolitain* metropolitan railway]

metro-¹, a learned borrowing from Greek meaning "measure," used in the formation of compound words: *metronome.* [comb. form repr. Gk *métron* measure]

metro-², a learned borrowing from Greek meaning "uterus," used in the formation of compound words. Also, *esp. before a vowel,* **metr-.** [comb. form repr. Gk *mētra* womb]

Met·ro·lin·er (me′trō lī′nər), *n. U.S.* **1.** a high-speed, reserved-seat train run by Amtrak, esp. between New York and Washington, D.C., with stops en route. **2.** any of the cars in such a train. [METRO(POLITAN) + LINER]

me·trol·o·gy (mi trol′ə jē), *n., pl.* **-gies.** the science of measures and weights. —**met·ro·log·i·cal** (me′trə loj′i kəl), *adj.* —**met′ro·log′i·cal·ly,** *adv.* —**me·trol·o·gist,** *n.*

met·ro·nome (me′trə nōm′), *n.* an instrument for marking time, used esp. as an aid in practicing music by making clicking sounds at regular, predetermined intervals. [METRO-¹ + Gk *nóm(os)* rule, law] —**met·ro·nom·ic** (me′trə nom′ik), **met′ro·nom′i·cal,** *adj.* —**met′ro·nom′i·cal·ly,** *adv.*

Metronome

me·tro·nym·ic (mē′trə nim′ik, me′-), *adj.* **1.** derived from the name of a mother or other female ancestor. —*n.* **2.** a metronymic name. Also, **matronymic.** [< Gk *mētrōnymik(ós)* named after one's mother]

me·trop·o·lis (mə trop′ə lis), *n., pl.* **-lis·es. 1.** the chief city of a country, state, or region. **2.** any large, busy city. **3.** a city that is the center of a certain trade or activity. **4.** the mother city or parent state of an ancient Greek colony. [< LL < Gk: a mother state or city]

met·ro·pol·i·tan (me′trə pol′i tᵊn), *adj.* **1.** of, noting, or characteristic of a metropolis or its inhabitants; urban. —*n.* **2.** a person who inhabits a metropolis, or one who has the manners and tastes associated with a metropolis. **3.** the head of an ecclesiastical province in the Eastern Orthodox Church or the Church of England. **4.** *Rom. Cath. Ch.* an archbishop who has authority over one or more suffragan sees. [< LL *mētropolītān(us)* of, belonging to a metropolis < Gk *mētropolít(ēs)* (see METROPOLIS, -ITE¹) + L *-ānus* -AN] —**met′ro·pol′i·tan·ism,** *n.*

met·ro·port (me′trō pōrt′, -pôrt′), *n.* an airport for helicopters, in a downtown area, sometimes on a rooftop. [METRO(POLITAN + AIR)PORT]

-metry, a combining form denoting the process of measuring: *anthropometry; chronometry.* [< Gk *-metria* = *-metr(ēs)* measurer (< *métron* measure; see METER¹) + *-ia* -Y³]

Met·ter·nich (met′əʀ niᴋʜ; *Eng.* met′ər nik), *n.* **Prince Klé·mens Wen·zel Ne·po·muk Lo·thar von** (klā′mens ven′tsəl nā′pô mo͝ok lō′täʀ fən, lō täʀ′), 1773–1859, Austrian statesman and diplomat.

met·tle (met′ᵊl), *n.* **1.** characteristic disposition or temperament. **2.** spirit; courage. **3. on one's mettle,** in the position of being incited to do one's best. [var. of METAL]

met·tle·some (met′ᵊl səm), *adj.* spirited; courageous.

Metz (mets; *Fr.* mes), *n.* a city in NE France: fortress; battles 1870, 1918, 1940, 1944. 109,678 (1962).

meu·nière (mən yâr′; *Fr.* mœ nyeʀ′), *adj.* (of food, esp. fish) dipped in flour, browned on both sides in butter, and sprinkled with lemon juice and parsley. [< F: lit., miller's wife (fem. of *meunier*)]

Meur·sault (mûr sō′; *Fr.* mœʀ sō′), *n.* a dry, white wine from the parish of Meursault in Burgundy.

Meuse (myo͞oz; *Fr.* mœz), *n.* a river in W Europe, flowing from NE France through E Belgium and S Netherlands into the North Sea. 575 mi. long. Dutch, **Maas.**

MeV (mev), *Physics.* million electron-volts. Also, **Mev, mev**

mew¹ (myo͞o), *n.* **1.** the sound a cat makes. —*v.i.* **2.** to make this sound. [imit.]

mew² (myo͞o), *n.* a sea gull, esp. the common gull, *Larus canus,* of Europe. [OE; c. G *Möwe*]

mew³ (myo͞o), *n.* **1.** a cage for hawks, esp. while molting. **2.** a pen in which poultry is fattened. **3.** a place of retirement or concealment. **4. mews,** (*usually construed as sing.*) *Chiefly Brit.* an area of stables, carriage houses, and living quarters built around a yard, court, or street. —*v.t.* **5.** to shut up in or as in a mew; confine; conceal (often fol. by *up*). [ME *mue* < MF; akin to *muer* to molt. See MEW⁴]

mew⁴ (myo͞o), *v.t., v.i.* to shed; molt. [ME *mewe(n)* < OF *mue(r)* (to) molt < L *mūtāre* to change]

Me·war (me wär′), *n.* Udaipur (def. 2).

mewl (myo͞ol), *v.i.* to cry, as a baby, young child, or the like; whimper. [imit.] —**mewl′er,** *n.*

Mex., 1. Mexican. **2.** Mexico.

Mex·i·cal·i (mek′sə kal′ē; *Sp.* me′hē kä′lē), *n.* a city in and the capital of Lower California, in NW Mexico, on the Mexican-U.S. border. 288,601 (est. 1965).

Mex·i·can (mek′sə kən), *adj.* **1.** of Mexico or its people. —*n.* **2.** a native or inhabitant of Mexico. [< Sp *mexican(o)*]

Mex′ican bean′ bee′tle, a ladybird beetle, *Epilachna varivestis,* introduced into the U.S. from Mexico, that feeds on the foliage of the bean plant.

Mex′ican hair′less, one of a breed of small dogs having no hair except for a tuft on the head and tail.

Mex′ican jump′ing bean′. See **jumping bean.**

Mex·i·ca·no (mek′sə kä′nō; *Sp.* me′hē kä′nô), *n. Informal.* the Nahuatl language. [< Sp: MEXICAN]

Mex′ican Span′ish, Spanish as used in Mexico.

Mex′ican stand′-off, an impasse.

Mex′ican War′, the war between the U.S. and Mexico, 1846–48.

Mex·i·co (mek′sə kō′), *n.* **1.** a republic in S North America. 63,000,000; 761,530 sq. mi. *Cap.:* Mexico City. **2.** a state in central Mexico. 6,245,000; 8268 sq. mi. *Cap.:* Toluca. **3. Gulf of.** Mexican, **Gol·fo de Mé·xi·co** (gôl′fô ᵺe me′hē kô′). an arm of the Atlantic between the U.S., Cuba, and Mexico. 700,000 sq. mi.; greaest depth 12,714 ft. Mexican, **Mé·xi·co** (me′hē kô′) (for defs. 1, 2). Spanish, **Méjico** (for defs. 1, 2).

Mex′ico Cit′y, a city in and the capital of Mexico, in the central part. 8,906,000; ab. 7400 ft. above sea level. Official name, **Mé·xi·co Dis·tri·to Fe·de·ral** (me′hē kô′ dēs tʀē′tô fe ᵺe ʀäl′).

MexSp, Mexican Spanish.

Mey·er·beer (mī′ər bēr′; *Ger.* mī′əʀ bāʀ′), *n.* **Gia·co·mo** (jä′kô mô), (*Jakob Liebmann Beer*), 1791–1864, German composer.

Mey·nell (men′ᵊl), *n.* **Alice Christiana, nee Thompson,** 1850–1922, English poet and essayist.

mez·ca·line (mez′kə lēn′, -lin), *n.* *Pharm.* mescaline.

me·ze·re·on (mi zēr′ē on′), *n.* an Old World, thymelaeaceous shrub, *Daphne Mezereum,* cultivated for its fragrant purplish-pink flowers, which appear in early spring. Also, **me·ze·re·um** (mi zēr′ē əm), *n.* [late ME *mizerion* < ML *mezereon* < Ar *māzaryūn*]

me·zu·za (mə zŏŏz′ə; *Heb.* mə zōō zä′), *n., pl.* **-zas,** *Heb.* **-zu·zoth** (-zōō zôt′). mezuzah.

me·zu·zah (mə zŏŏz′ə; *Heb.* mə zōō zä′), *n., pl.* **-zahs,** *Heb.* **-zu·zoth** (-zōō zôt′). *Judaism.* a small case that contains a piece of parchment inscribed with verses 4–9 of Deut. 6 and 13–21 of Deut. 11, traditionally attached to one or more doorposts of the home. [< Heb: lit., doorpost]

mez·za·nine (mez′ə nēn′, mez′ə nēn′), *n.* **1.** a low story between two main stories in a building. **2.** the lowest balcony or forward part of such a balcony in a theater. [< F < It *mezzanino,* dim. of *mezzano* middle < L *mediānus* MEDIAN]

mez·za vo·ce (met′sə vō′chā, mez′ə; *It.* med′dzä vô′che), with half the power of the voice (used as a musical direction). [< It: lit., half voice]

mez·zo (met′sō, mez′ō; *It.* med′dzô), *adj., n., pl.* **-zos.** —*adj.* **1.** middle; medium; half. —*n.* **2.** a mezzo-soprano. [< It < L *medius* middle]

mez′zo for′te (fôr′tā; *It.* fôr′te), *Music.* moderately loud. [< It: lit., half loud]

mez′zo pia′no (pē ä′nō; *It.* pyä′nô), *Music.* moderately soft. [< It: lit., half soft]

mez·zo-re·lie·vo (met′sō ri lē′vō, mez′ō-), *n., pl.* **-vos** (-vōz). sculptured relief intermediate between high relief and bas-relief.

mez·zo-ri·lie·vo (med′dzô rē lye′vô; *Eng.* met′sō ri lē′vō, mez′ō-), *n., pl.* **mez·zi-ri·lie·vi** (med′dzē rē lye′vē; *Eng.* met′sē ri lē′vē, mez′ē-). *Italian.* mezzo-relievo.

mez·zo-so·pran·o (met′sō sə pran′ō, -prä′nō, mez′ō-), *n., pl.* **-pran·os, -pran·i** (-pran′ē, -prä′nē), *adj. Music.* —*n.* **1.** a voice or voice part intermediate between soprano and contralto. **2.** a person having such a voice. —*adj.* **3.** of, pertaining to, or suitable for a mezzo-soprano. [< It]

mez·zo·tint (met′sō tint′, mez′ō-), *n.* **1.** a method of engraving on copper or steel by burnishing or scraping away a uniformly roughened surface. **2.** a print produced by this method. —*v.t.* **3.** to engrave in mezzotint. [< It *mezzotint(o)* half-tint]

MF, **1.** See **medium frequency. 2.** Middle French.

mf, See **medium frequency.**

mf., **1.** *Music.* mezzo forte. **2.** microfarad; microfarads.

M.F., Middle French.

M.F.A., Master of Fine Arts.

mfd., **1.** manufactured. **2.** microfarad; microfarads.

mfg., manufacturing.

MFlem, Middle Flemish.

mfr., **1.** manufacture. **2.** *pl.* **mfrs.** manufacturer.

M.Fr., Middle French.

mg, milligram; milligrams.

Mg., *Chem.* magnesium.

MGB, Soviet Ministry of State Security. [< Russ *Ministerstvo Gosudarstvennoi Bezopasnosti*]

MGk, Medieval Greek. Also, **MGk.**

MGr., Medieval Greek.

mgr., **1.** manager. **2.** Monseigneur. **3.** Monsignor. Also, **Mgr.**

mgt., management.

mH, millihenry; millihenries. Also, **mh**

M.H., Medal of Honor.

MHG, Middle High German. Also, **M.H.G.**

mho (mō), *n., pl.* **mhos.** *Elect.* the meter-kilogram-second unit of electric conductance, equal to the conductance of a conductor in which a potential difference of one volt maintains a current of one ampere. [reversed sp. of OHM]

M.H.R., Member of the House of Representatives.

M.H.W., mean high water. Also, **m.h.w.**

MHz, *Elect.* megahertz; megahertz.

MI, Michigan (approved esp. for use with zip code).

mi (mē), *n. Music.* **1.** the syllable used for the third tone of a diatonic scale. **2.** (in the fixed system of solmization) the tone E. Cf. **sol-fa** (def. 1). [see GAMUT]

mi, *Linear Measure.* mile; miles.

mi., **1.** *Linear Measure.* mile; miles. **2.** mill; mills.

M.I., Military Intelligence.

M.I.A., *Mil.* missing in action. Also, **MIA**

Mi·am·i (mī am′ē, -am′ə), *n., pl.* **-am·is** (*esp. collectively*) **-am·i. 1.** a member of a North American Indian tribe of the Algonquian family, now extinct as a tribe. **2.** their dialect of the Illinois language.

Mi·am·i (mī am′ē, -am′ə), *n.* **1.** a city in SE Florida: seaside winter resort. 334,859 (1970). **2.** a river in W Ohio, flowing S into the Ohio River. 160 mi. long. —**Mi·am′i·an,** *n.*

Miam′i Beach′, a city in SE Florida on an island 2½ mi. across Biscayne Bay from Miami. 87,072 (1970).

mi·aow (mē ou′, myou), *n., v.i.* meow. Also, **mi·aou′.**

mi·as·ma (mī az′mə, mē-), *n., pl.* **-ma·ta** (-mə tə), **-mas. 1.** noxious exhalations from putrescent organic matter; poisonous effluvia or germs infecting the atmosphere. **2.** a dangerous, foreboding, or deathlike influence or atmosphere. [< NL < Gk: stain, pollution, akin to *miaínein* to pollute, stain] —**mi·as′mal, mi·as·mat·ic** (mī′az mat′ik), **mi′as·mat′i·cal, mi·as′mic,** *adj.*

mib (mib), *n. Chiefly Dial.* **1.** a playing marble, esp. one that is not used as a shooter. **2. mibs,** (*construed as sing.*) the game of marbles. [shortened var. of MARBLE]

Mic., Micah.

mi·ca (mī′kə), *n.* any member of a group of minerals, hydrous disilicates of aluminum with other bases, that separate readily into thin, tough, often transparent, and usually elastic laminae; isinglass. [< L: crumb, morsel, grain]

mi·ca·ceous (mī kā′shəs), *adj.* **1.** consisting of, containing, or resembling mica. **2.** of or pertaining to mica.

Mi·cah (mī′kə), *n.* **1.** a Minor Prophet of the 8th century B.C. **2.** a book of the Bible bearing his name.

mice (mīs), *n.* pl. of **mouse.**

mi·celle (mi sel′), *n. Physical Chem.* an electrically charged particle formed by an aggregate of molecules and occurring in certain colloidal electrolyte solutions, as those of soaps and detergents. [< NL *mīcella,* dim. of L *mīca* crumb, morsel] —**mi·cel′lar,** *adj.* —**mi·cel′lar·ly,** *adv.*

Mich., **1.** Michaelmas. **2.** Michigan.

Mi·chael (mī′kəl), *n.* a militant archangel. Dan. 10:13.

Mich·ael·mas (mik′əl məs), *n. Chiefly Brit.* a festival celebrated on September 29 in honor of the archangel Michael. Also called **Mich′aelmas Day′.** [OE (*Sanct*) *Michaeles masse* (St.) Michael's mass]

Mich′aelmas dai′sy, *Brit.* an aster.

Mi·chel·an·ge·lo (mī′kəl an′jə lō′, mik′əl-; *It.* mē′kel-än′je lô), *n.* (*Michelangelo Buonarroti*) 1475–1564, Italian sculptor, painter, architect, and poet.

Mi·che·let (mēshᵊ lā′), *n.* **Jules** (zhyl), 1798–1874, French historian.

Mi·chel·son (mī′kəl sən), *n.* **Albert Abraham,** 1852–1931, U.S. physicist, born in Germany: Nobel prize 1907.

Mi′chel·son-Mor′ley exper′iment (mī′kəl sən môr′lē), *Physics.* an experiment (1881), that showed the velocity of light is not influenced by any motion of the medium through which it passes. [named after MICHELSON and Edward *Morley* (1838–1923), U.S. chemist and physicist]

Mich·e·ner (mich′ə nər), *n.* **1. James A(lbert),** born 1907, U.S. novelist. **2. Roland,** born 1900, Canadian politician: governor general 1967–74.

Mich·i·gan (mish′ə gən), *n.* **1.** a state in the N central United States. 8,875,083 (1970); 58,216 sq. mi. *Cap.:* Lansing. *Abbr.:* MI, Mich. **2. Lake,** a lake in the N central U.S., between Wisconsin and Michigan: one of the five Great Lakes. 22,400 sq. mi. —**Mich·i·gan·der** (mish′ə gan′dər), **Mich·i·gan·ite** (mish′ə gə nīt′), *n.*

Mich′igan Cit′y, a port in NW Indiana, on Lake Michigan. 39,369 (1970).

Mi·cho·a·cán (mē′chô ä kän′), *n.* a state in SW Mexico. 1,862,568 (1960); 23,196 sq. mi. *Cap.:* Morelia.

Mick (mik), *n. Offensive.* Irishman. [from name *Michael*]

Mick·ey (mik′ē), *n., pl.* **-eys.** *Slang.* a drink, usually of liquor, containing a drug, purgative, or the like, that renders the drinker helpless. Also called **Mick′ey Finn′.**

Mic·kie·wicz (mits kye′vich), *n.* **A·dam** (ä′däm), 1798–1855, Polish poet.

mick·le (mik′əl), *adj. Archaic.* great; large; much. [ME *mikel* < Scand (cf. Icel *mykill*); r. ME *michel,* OE *micel* MUCH; c. OHG *mihil,* Goth *mikils,* akin to L *magnus,* Gk *mégas*]

Mic·mac (mik′mak), *n., pl.* **-macs,** (*esp. collectively*) **-mac** for **1. 1.** a member of a tribe of Algonquian Indians inhabiting the southern shores of the Gulf of St. Lawrence. **2.** the Algonquian language of these Indians.

mi·cra (mī′krə), *n.* a pl. of **micron.**

mi·cri·fy (mī′krə fī′), *v.t.,* **-fied, -fy·ing.** to make small or insignificant.

micro-, a learned borrowing from Greek, where it meant "small" (*microcosm*), used to mean "enlarging (something small)" (*microphone*), as a combining form of **microscopic** (*microorganism*), and to represent a millionth part of a unit (*microgram*). Also, *esp. before a vowel,* **micr-.** [comb. form repr. Gk *mīkrós*]

mi·cro·am·me·ter (mī′krō am′mē tər), *n.* an instrument for measuring extremely small electric currents, calibrated in microamperes.

mi·cro·am·pere (mī′krō am′pēr, -am pēr′), *n. Elect.* a unit of electric current, equal to one millionth of an ampere. *Symbol:* μA

mi·cro·a·nal·y·sis (mī′krō ə nal′i sis), *n., pl.* **-ses** (-sēz′). *Chem.* the analysis of very small samples of substances. —**mi·cro·an·a·lyst** (mī′krō an′ᵊlist), *n.* —**mi·cro·an·a·lyt·i·cal** (mī′krō an′ᵊlit′i kəl), **mi′cro·an′a·lyt′ic,** *adj.*

mi·cro·ang·strom (mī′krō‿aŋ′strəm), *n.* one millionth of an angstrom. *Symbol:* μÅ

mi·cro·bac·te·ri·um (mī′krō bak tēr′ē əm), *n., pl.* **-te·ri·a** (-tēr′ē ə). *Bacteriol.* any of several rod-shaped, thermoduric, saprophytic bacteria of the genus *Microbacterium,* found chiefly in dairy products.

mi·cro·bal·ance (mī′krə bal′əns), *n. Chem.* a balance for weighing minute quantities of material.

mi·cro·bar (mī′krə bär′), *n.* a centimeter-gram-second unit of pressure, equal to one millionth of a bar; one dyne per square centimeter.

mi·cro·bar·o·graph (mī′krə bär′ə graf′, -gräf′), *n. Meteorol.* a barograph for recording minute fluctuations of atmospheric pressure.

mi·crobe (mī′krōb), *n.* a microorganism, esp. a pathogenic bacterium. [< F < Gk *mīkro-* MICRO- + *bíos* life] —**mi′crobe·less,** *adj.* —**mi·cro′bi·al, mi·cro′bic, mi·cro′bi·an,** *adj.*

mi·cro·bi·cide (mī krō′bi sīd′), *n.* a substance or preparation for killing microbes. —**mi·cro′bi·cid′al,** *adj.*

mi·cro·bi·ol·o·gy (mī′krō bī ol′ə jē), *n.* the science dealing with the structure, function, uses, etc., of microscopic organisms. —**mi·cro·bi·o·log·i·cal** (mī′krō bī′ə loj′i kəl), **mi′cro·bi′o·log′ic,** *adj.* —**mi′cro·bi′o·log′i·cal·ly,** *adv.* —**mi′cro·bi·ol′o·gist,** *n.*

mi·cro·ce·phal·ic (mī′krō sə fal′ik), *adj.* **1.** *Craniom.* having a skull with a small cranial capacity. Cf. **megacephalic** (def. 1). **2.** *Pathol.* having an abnormally small skull. Also, **mi·cro·ceph·a·lous** (mī′krō sef′ə ləs). [< NL *mīcrocephalic(us)*] —**mi′cro·ceph′a·lism, mi′cro·ceph′a·ly,** *n.*

mi·cro·chem·is·try (mī′krō kem′i strē), *n.* the branch of chemistry dealing with minute quantities of substances. —**mi·cro·chem·i·cal** (mī′krō kem′i kəl), *adj.*

mi·cro·cir·cuit (mī′krō sûr′kit), *n.* a compact electronic circuit whose miniaturized components form an inseparable unit, usually on a silicon chip.

mi·cro·cli·mate (mī′krə klī′mit), *n.* the climate of a small area, as of houses, of plant communities, or of urban communities. Cf. **macroclimate.** —**mi·cro·cli·mat·ic** (mī′krō klī mat′ik), —**mi′cro·cli·mat′i·cal·ly,** *adv.*

mi·cro·cli·ma·tol·o·gy (mī′krō klī′mə tol′ə jē), *n.* the study of the local climatic conditions of a small area, esp. the analysis of climatic profiles of the lowest stratum of the atmosphere, as of confined spaces, of plants and plant communities, or of urban communities. —**mi·cro·cli·ma·to·log·ic** (mī′krō klī′mə tᵊloj′ik), **mi′cro·cli′ma·to·log′i·cal,** *adj.* —**mi′cro·cli′ma·tol′o·gist,** *n.*

mi·cro·cline (mī′krə klīn′), *n.* a mineral of the feldspar group, potassium aluminum silicate, $KAlSi_3O_8$, used in making porcelain. [MICRO- + Gk *klīn(ein)* (to) cause to slant]

mi·cro·coc·cus (mī′krə kok′əs), *n., pl.* **-coc·ci** (-kok′sī). *Bacteriol.* any spherical bacterium of the genus *Micrococcus,* occurring in irregular masses, many species of which are pigmented and are saprophytic or parasitic. [< NL] —**mi′cro·coc′cal, mi·cro·coc·cic** (mī′krə kok′sik), *adj.*

mi·cro·com·put·er (mī′krō kəm pyōō′tər, mī′krō kəm-pyōō′tər), *n.* a compact and inexpensive computer, relatively limited in capability and capacity, consisting of a microprocessor and other components of a computer, miniaturized where possible: now increasingly used in small business, by hobbyists, etc.

mi·cro·cop·y (mī′krə kop′ē), *n., pl.* **-cop·ies.** a greatly reduced photographic copy of a printed page or the like.

mi·cro·cosm (mī′krə koz′əm), *n.* **1.** a little world; a world in miniature (opposed to *macrocosm*): *The atom is a microcosm.* **2.** man regarded as epitomizing the universe. **3.** anything viewed as an epitome of the world or universe. Also called **mi·cro·cos·mos** (mī′krə koz′məs, -mōs). [late ME *microcosme* < ML *mīcrocosm(us)* < Gk *mīkros kósmos* small world] —**mi′cro·cos′mic,** *adj.*

mi·cro·crys·tal (mī′krə kris′tᵊl), *n.* a microscopic crystal. —**mi·cro·crys·tal·line** (mī′krō kris′tᵊlin, -tᵊlīn′), *adj.*

mi·cro·cu·rie (mī′krə kyŏŏr′ē, mī′krō kyŏŏ rē′), *n. Physics, Chem.* a unit of radioactivity, equal to one millionth of a curie; 3.70×10^4 disintegrations per second. *Symbol:* μCi; μc

mi·cro·cyte (mī′krə sīt′), *n.* **1.** a minute cell or corpuscle. **2.** *Pathol.* an abnormally small red blood cell, usually deficient in hemoglobin. —**mi·cro·cyt·ic** (mī′krə sit′ik), *adj.*

mi·cro·dont (mī′krə dont′), *adj.* having abnormally small teeth. Also, **mi′cro·don′tic, mi′cro·don′tous.**

mi·cro·e·co·nom·ics (mī′krō ē′kə nom′iks, -ek′ə-), *n.* (*construed as sing.*) the branch of economics dealing with particular aspects of an economy, as the price-cost relationship of a firm. Cf. **macroeconomics.** —**mi′cro·e′co·nom′ic,** *adj.*

mi·cro·e·lec·tron·ics (mī′krō i lek tron′iks, -ē′lek-), *n.* (*construed as sing.*) the branch of electronics dealing with the design, manufacture, and use of miniaturized electronic components and circuits.

mi·cro·el·e·ment (mī′krō el′ə mənt), *n. Biochem.* See **trace element.**

mi·cro·far·ad (mī′krə far′əd, -ad), *n. Elect.* a unit of capacitance, equal to one millionth of a farad. *Abbr.:* mf, mfd. *Symbol:* μF, μf

mi·cro·fiche (mī′krə fēsh′), *n.* a flat sheet of microfilm, typically 4 x 6 inches. [MICRO- + F *fiche* small card]

mi·cro·film (mī′krə film′), *n.* **1.** a film bearing a miniature photographic copy of printed or other graphic matter, made for a library, archive, or the like. —*v.t.* **2.** to make a microfilm of.

mi·cro·form (mī′krə fôrm′), *n.* any form or type of film or paper containing microphotographic images.

mi·cro·gam·ete (mī′krō gam′ēt, -krō gə mēt′), *n. Biol.* (in heterogamous reproduction) the smaller and, usually, the male of two conjugating gametes.

mi·cro·gram¹ (mī′krə gram′), *n.* a unit of mass or weight equal to one millionth of a gram, used chiefly in microchemistry. *Symbol:* μg Also, *esp. Brit.,* **mi′cro·gramme′.**

mi·cro·gram² (mī′krə gram′), *n.* micrograph (def. 2).

mi·cro·graph (mī′krə graf′, -gräf′), *n.* **1.** an instrument for executing minute writing or engraving. **2.** *Optics.* a photograph taken through a microscope or a drawing of an object as seen through a microscope.

mi·crog·ra·phy (mī krog′rə fē), *n.* **1.** the description or delineation of microscopic objects. **2.** examination or study with the microscope. **3.** the technique or practice of using the microscope. **4.** the art or practice of writing in very small characters. —**mi·crog′ra·pher,** *n.* —**mi·cro·graph·ic** (mī′krə graf′ic), *adj.* —**mi′cro·graph′i·cal·ly,** *adv.*

mi·cro·groove (mī′krə grōōv′), *n.* the narrow needle groove on a long-playing record.

mi·cro·hen·ry (mī′krə hen′rē), *n., pl.* **-ries, -rys.** *Elect.* a unit of inductance, equal to one millionth of a henry. *Symbol:* μH, μh

mi·crohm (mī′krōm′), *n. Elect.* a unit of resistance, equal to one millionth of an ohm. *Symbol:* $\mu\Omega$

mi·cro·inch (mī′krō inch′), *n.* a unit of length equal to one millionth of an inch. *Symbol:* μin

mi·cro·lite (mī′krə līt′), *n.* **1.** *Mineral.* any microscopic crystal. **2.** a mineral, principally calcium pyrotantalate, $Ca_2Ta_2O_7$, usually including niobium and fluorine.

mi·cro·li·ter (mī′krə lē′tər), *n.* a unit of capacity equal to one millionth of a liter, used esp. in microchemistry. *Symbol:* μl Also, *esp. Brit.,* **mi′cro·li′tre.**

mi·crol·o·gy (mī krol′ə jē), *n.* excessive attention to petty details or distinctions. [< Gk *mikrología* minute discussion, frivolity] —**mi·cro·log·i·cal** (mī′krə loj′i kəl), **mi′cro·log′ic,** *adj.* —**mi·crol′o·gist,** *n.*

mi·cro·me·te·or·ite (mī′krō mē′tē ə rīt′), *n. Astron.* a very small meteorite, usually one having a diameter of less than a millimeter.

mi·crom·e·ter¹ (mī krom′i tər), *n.* **1.** any of various devices for measuring minute distances, angles, etc., as in connection with a telescope or microscope. **2.** See **micrometer caliper.** —**mi·crom′e·try,** *n.* —**mi·cro·met·ri·cal** (mī′krō me′tri-kəl), **mi′cro·met′ric,** *adj.* —**mi′cro·met′ri·cal·ly,** *adv.*

mi·cro·me·ter² (mī′krə mē′tər), *n.* a unit of length equal to one millionth of a meter; micron. *Symbol:* μm

microm′eter cal′iper, a precision caliper with a spindle moved by a finely threaded screw, for the measurement of thicknesses and short lengths.

Micrometer caliper

mi·cro·mho (mī′krə mō′), *n., pl.* **-mhos.** *Elect.* a unit of conductance, equal to one millionth of a mho. *Symbol:* μmho

micromicro-, pico-.

mi·cro·mi·cro·cu·rie (mī′krō mī′krō kyŏŏr′ē, -kyŏŏ rē′), *n.* picocurie.

mi·cro·mi·cro·far·ad (mī′krō mī′krō far′əd, -ad), *n.* picofarad. *Abbr.:* mmf *Symbol:* $\mu\mu$f

mi·cro·mi·cron (mī′krō mī′kron), *n., pl.* **-crons, -cra** (-krə). *Metric System.* one millionth of a micron. *Symbol:* $\mu\mu$

mi·cro·mil·li·me·ter (mī′krō mil′ə mē′tər), *n. Metric System.* the millionth part of a millimeter.

mi·cro·min·i·a·ture (mī′krō min′ē ə chər, -min′ə chər), *adj.* built on an extremely small scale, smaller than subminiature, esp. of electronic equipment with small solid-state components in the place of vacuum tubes.

mi·cro·min·i·a·tur·i·za·tion (mī′krō min′ē ə chər i zā′-shən *or, esp. Brit.,* -chə rī-), *n.* extreme miniaturization, esp. of electronic equipment smaller than subminiature and involving the substitution of solid-state components for vacuum tubes.

mi·cron (mī′kron), *n., pl.* **-crons, -cra** (-krə). **1.** *Metric System.* the millionth part of a meter. *Symbol:* μ, mu **2.** *Physical Chem.* a colloidal particle whose diameter is between .2 and 10 microns. Also, **mikron.** [< Gk *mīkrón* small, little, neut. sing. of *mīkrós*]

Mi·cro·ne·sia (mī′krə nē′zhə, -shə), *n.* one of the three principal divisions of Oceania, comprising the small Pacific islands N of the equator and E of the Philippines, whose main groups are the Mariana Islands, the Caroline Islands, and the Marshall Islands, which are U.S. Trust Territories.

Mi·cro·ne·sian (mī′krə nē′zhən, -shən), *adj.* **1.** of or pertaining to Micronesia, its inhabitants, or their languages. —*n.* **2.** a native of Micronesia. **3.** the Malayo-Polynesian languages of Micronesia, taken collectively.

mi·cro·or·gan·ism (mī′krō ôr′gə niz′əm), *n.* a microscopic plant or animal. Also, **mi′cro·ör′gan·ism.** —**mi·cro·or·gan·ic, mi·cro·ör·gan·ic** (mī′krō ôr gan′ik), **mi′-cro·or′gan·is′mal, mi′cro·ör′gan·is′mal,** *adj.*

mi·cro·pa·le·on·tol·o·gy (mī′krō pā′lē ən tol′ə jē, -pal′-ē-), *n.* the branch of paleontology dealing with the study of microscopic fossils. —**mi·cro·pa·le·on·to·log·i·cal** (mī′krō-pā′lē on′tᵊloj′i kəl, -pal′ē-), **mi′cro·pa′le·on′to·log′ic,** *adj.* —**mi′cro·pa′le·on·tol′o·gist,** *n.*

mi·cro·par·a·site (mī′krō par′ə sīt′), *n.* a parasitic microorganism. —**mi·cro·par·a·sit·ic** (mī′krō par′ə sit′ik), *adj.*

mi·cro·phage (mī′krə fāj′), *n. Anat.* a small phagocytic cell in blood or lymph, esp. a polymorphonuclear leukocyte.

mi·cro·phone (mī′krə fōn′), *n.* an instrument capable of transforming sound waves into changes in electric currents or voltage, used in recording or transmitting sound.

mi·cro·pho·to·graph (mī′krə fō′tə graf′, -gräf′), *n.* **1.** microfilm (def. 1). **2.** a small photograph requiring optical enlargement to render it visible in detail. **3.** a photomicrograph. —*v.t.* **4.** to make a microphotograph of. —**mi·cro·pho·to·graph·ic** (mī′krə fō′tə graf′ik), *adj.* —**mi·cro·pho·tog·ra·phy** (mī′krō fə tog′rə fē), *n.*

mi·cro·phys·ics (mī′krə fiz′iks), *n.* (*construed as sing.*) the branch of physics dealing with physical objects that are not large enough to be observed and treated directly, as elementary particles, atoms, and molecules. —**mi′cro·phys′i·cal,** *adj.*

mi·cro·print (mī′krə print′), *n.* a microphotograph reproduced in print for reading by a magnifying device.

mi·cro·proc·es·sor (mī′krō pros′es-ər *or, esp. Brit.,* -prō′ses-; mī′krō-pros′es ər *or, esp. Brit.,* -prō′ses-), *n. Computer Technol.* a miniaturized integrated circuit that performs all of the functions of a central processing unit.

mi·cro·pyle (mī′krə pīl′), *n.* **1.** *Zool.* any minute opening in an ovum through which a spermatozoon can enter, as in many insects. **2.** *Bot.* the minute orifice or opening in the integuments of an ovule. [MICRO- + Gk *pýlē* gate] —**mi′cro·py′lar,** *adj.*

mi·cro·py·rom·e·ter (mī′krō pī-rom′i tər), *n.* an optical pyrometer to measure the temperature of small glowing bodies.

micros., microscopy.

mi·cro·scope (mī′krə skōp′), *n.* an optical instrument having a magnifying lens or a combination of lenses for inspecting objects too small to be seen or seen distinctly by the naked eye. [< NL *mīcroscop(ium)*]

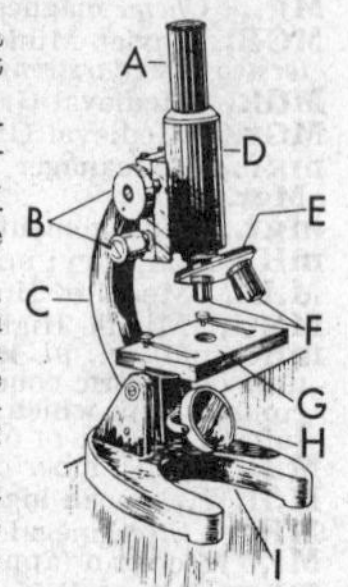

Microscope (Monocular) A, Eyepiece; B, Adjusting screws; C, Arm; D, Tube; E, Revolving nosepiece; F, Objectives; G, Stage; H, Illuminating mirror; I, Stand

mi·cro·scop·ic (mī′krə skop′ik), *adj.* **1.** so small as to be invisible or indistinct without the use of the microscope. Cf. **macroscopic. 2.** very small; tiny. **3.** of, pertaining to, or involving a microscope. **4.** suggesting microscopy, as in attention to minute details. Also, **mi′cro·scop′i·cal.** —**mi′cro·scop′i·cal·ly,** *adv.*

mi·cros·co·py (mī kros′kə pē), *n.* **1.** the use of the microscope. **2.** microscopic investigation. —**mi·cros·co·pist** (mī kros′kə pist), *n.*

mi·cro·sec·ond (mī′krə sek′ənd), *n. Metric System* a. unit of time equal to one millionth of a second. *Symbol :* μsec

mi·cro·seism (mī′krə sī′zəm, -səm), *n. Geol.* a feeble, recurrent vibration of the ground recorded by seismographs and believed to be due to an earthquake or a storm at sea. —**mi·cro·seis·mic** (mī′krə sīz′mik, -sīs′-), *adj.*

mi·cro·sie·mens (mī′krə sē′mənz, -zē′-), *n.* one millionth of a siemens. *Symbol:* μs

mi·cro·some (mī′krə sōm′), *n. Biol.* a small inclusion, consisting of ribosomes and fragments of the endoplasmic reticulum, in the protoplasm of a cell. —**mi′cro·so′mal, mi′cro·so′mi·al, mi′cro·so′mic,** *adj.*

mi·cro·spo·ran·gi·um (mī′krō spō ran′jē əm, -spô-), *n., pl.* **-gi·a** (-jē ə). *Bot.* a sporangium containing microspores.

mi·cro·spore (mī′krə spōr′, -spôr′), *n. Bot.* **1.** the smaller of two kinds of spores produced by some pteridophytes. **2.** a pollen grain. —**mi·cro·spor·ic** (mī′krə spôr′ik, -spor′-), **mi·cro·spor·ous** (mī′krə spôr′əs, -spôr′-, mī kros′pər əs), *adj.*

mi·cro·spo·ro·phyll (mī′krə spōr′ə fil, -spôr′-), *n. Bot.* a sporophyll bearing microsporangia.
mi·cro·struc·ture (mī′krō struk′chər), *n. Metall.* the structure of a metal or alloy as observed, after etching and polishing, under a high degree of magnification.
mi·cro·sur·ger·y (mī′krə sûr′jə rē), *n.* surgery in which the surgeon works with a microscope and very small instruments to repair or attach blood vessels, nerves, etc.: *to reattach a severed hand by means of microsurgery.* —**mi′cro·sur′gi·cal,** *adj.*
mi·cro·tome (mī′krə tōm′), *n.* an instrument for cutting very thin sections, as of organic tissue, for microscopic examination.
mi·crot·o·my (mī krot′ə mē), *n., pl.* **-mies.** the cutting of very thin sections with the microtome. —**mi·cro·tom·ic** (mī′krə tom′ik), **mi′cro·tom′i·cal,** *adj.* —**mi·crot′o·mist,** *n.*
mi·cro·tone (mī′krə tōn′), *n.* any musical interval smaller than a semitone, specifically, a quarter tone. —**mi′cro·ton′al,** *adj.* —**mi′cro·to·nal′i·ty,** *n.* —**mi′cro·ton′al·ly,** *adv.*
mi·cro·volt (mī′krə vōlt′), *n. Elect.* a unit of electromotive force or potential difference equal to one millionth of a volt. *Symbol:* μV, μv
mi·cro·watt (mī′krō wot′), *n. Elect.* a unit of power equal to one millionth of a watt. *Symbol:* μW, μw
mi·cro·wave (mī′krō wāv′), *n.* an electromagnetic wave of extremely high frequency, usually one having wavelength of from 1 mm. to 50 cm.
mi′crowave ov′en, an electrically operated oven using high-frequency electromagnetic waves that penetrate food, causing its molecules to vibrate and generating heat within the food to cook it in a very short time.
mi′crowave spectros′copy, *Physics.* the determination of those microwave frequencies of the microwave spectrum that are selectively absorbed by certain materials, providing information about atomic, molecular, and crystalline structure. —**mi′crowave spec′troscope.**
mic·tu·rate (mik′chə rāt′), *v.i.,* **-rat·ed, -rat·ing.** to pass urine; urinate. [< L *mictur(īre)* (to) desire to make water (*mict(us),* ptp. of *mingere* to make water + *-ur-* desiderative suffix) + -ATE[1]] —**mic·tu·ri·tion** (mik′chə rish′ən), *n.*
mid[1] (mid), *adj.* **1.** being at or near the middle point of: *in mid autumn.* **2.** being or occupying a middle place or position: *the mid East.* **3.** *Phonet.* (of a vowel) articulated with an opening above the tongue relatively intermediate between those for high and low: the vowels of *beet, bet,* and *hot* are respectively high, mid, and low. Cf. **high** (def. 23), **low** (def. 30). —*n.* **4.** *Archaic.* the middle. [ME, OE *midd;* c. OHG *mitti,* Icel *mithr,* Goth *midjis,* L *medius,* Gk *mésos*]
mid[2] (mid), *prep.* amid. Also, **'mid.**
mid-, a combining form meaning "middle," "middle part of": *midday; mid-Victorian.* [ME, OE; see MID[1]]
mid., middle.
mid·air (mid âr′), *n.* any point in the air not close to the earth or other underlying surface.
Mi·das (mī′dəs), *n.* **1.** *Class. Myth.* a Phrygian king who had the power of turning whatever he touched into gold. **2.** a man of great wealth or great moneymaking ability.
mid·brain (mid′brān′), *n. Anat.* the mesencephalon, being the middle of the three primary divisions of the brain in the embryo of a vertebrate or the part of the adult brain derived from this tissue.
mid·day (mid′dā′), *n.* **1.** the middle of the day; noon or the time around noon. —*adj.* **2.** pertaining to or happening during the middle part of the day. [ME; OE *middæg*]
mid·den (mid′ᵊn), *n.* **1.** *Brit. Dial.* a dunghill or refuse heap. **2.** See **kitchen midden.** [ME *midding* < Scand; cf. Dan *mödding* = *mög* muck, dung + *dynge* heap, dunghill]
mid·dle (mid′ᵊl), *adj.* **1.** halfway between extremes or outer limits. **2.** being intermediate on some basis of reckoning, as of sizes, quantities, or historical periods. **3.** avoiding or remote from extremes. **4.** (*cap.*) (in the history of a language) intermediate between periods classified as Old and New or Modern: *Middle English.* **5.** *Gram.* (in some languages) noting a voice in verb inflection in which the subject is represented as acting on or for itself, in contrast to the active and passive voices. —*n.* **6.** the point, part, position, etc., equidistant from extremes or limits. **7.** the middle part of the human body, esp. the waist. **8.** a mean; something intermediate. **9.** (in farming) the ground between two rows of plants. [ME, OE *middel;* c. G *mittel*]
—**Syn. 1.** equidistant, halfway, medial, midway. **6.** midpoint. MIDDLE, CENTER, MIDST indicate something from which two or more other things are (approximately or exactly) equally distant. MIDDLE denotes, literally or figuratively, the point or part equidistant from or intermediate between extremes or limits in space or in time: *the middle of a road.* CENTER, a more precise word, is ordinarily applied to a point within circular, globular, or regular bodies: *the center of the earth;* it may also be used metaphorically (still suggesting the core of a sphere): *center of interest.* MIDST usually suggests that a person or thing is closely surrounded or encompassed on all sides, esp. by that which is thick or dense: *the midst of a storm.* —**Ant. 1.** extreme. **6.** extremity.
mid′dle age′, the period of human life between youth and old age, sometimes considered as the years between 45 and 65 or thereabout. [ME]
mid·dle-aged (mid′ᵊl ājd′), *adj.* **1.** being of the age intermediate between youth and old age, roughly between 45 and 65. **2.** characteristic of or suitable for persons of this age. —**mid·dle-a·ged·ly** (mid′ᵊl ā′jid lē, -ājd′-), *adv.* —**mid′dle-a′ged·ness,** *n.*
Mid′dle Ag′es, the time in European history between classical antiquity and the Italian Renaissance, from the late 5th century A.D. to c1350; sometimes restricted to the part of this period after 1100 and sometimes extended to 1450 or 1500. [pl. of *Middle Age,* trans. of NL *Medium Aevum*]
Mid′dle Amer′ica, **1.** continental North America S of the U.S., comprising Mexico, Central America, and usually the West Indies. 92,000,000; 1,060,118 sq. mi. **2.** the average, middle-class Americans as a group, as opposed to the rich or poor or to extreme radicals or conservatives. —**Mid′dle Amer′ican.**
Mid′dle Atlan′tic States′, New York, New Jersey, and Pennsylvania. Also called **Middle States.**
mid·dle·break·er (mid′ᵊl brā′kər), *n.* lister (def. 1).
mid·dle·brow (mid′ᵊl brou′), *n.* a person of conventional or widely accepted tastes and cultural interests. —**mid′dle·brow′ism,** *n.*
mid·dle·bust·er (mid′ᵊl bus′tər), *n.* lister (def. 1).
middle C, *Music.* the note indicated by the first leger line above the bass staff and the first below the treble staff.
mid′dle class′, **1.** a class of people intermediate in social, economic, and cultural standing. **2.** the class traditionally intermediate between the aristocratic class and the laboring class. **3.** an intermediate class. —**mid′dle-class′,** *adj.*
mid′dle dis′tance, *Fine Arts.* the represented space between the foreground and background in paintings, drawings, etc. Also called **mid′dle ground′, middle plane.**
Mid′dle Dutch′, the Dutch language of the period 1100–1500. *Abbr.:* MD
mid′dle ear′, *Anat.* the middle portion of the ear, consisting of the tympanic membrane and an air-filled chamber lined with mucous membrane, which contains the malleus, incus, and stapes. Cf. **ear**[1] (def. 1).
Mid′dle East′, (loosely) the area from Libya to Afghanistan, usually including the Arab Republic of Egypt, Sudan, Israel, Jordan, Lebanon, Syria, Turkey, Iraq, Iran, and the countries of the Arabian Peninsula. Also called **Mideast.** —**Mid′dle East′ern.**
Mid′dle Eng′lish, the English language of the period c1150–c1475. *Abbr.:* ME
mid′dle fin′ger, the finger between the forefinger and the third finger.
Mid′dle Flem′ish, the Flemish language of the 14th, 15th, and 16th centuries. *Abbr.:* MFlem
Mid′dle French′, the French language of the 14th, 15th, and 16th centuries. *Abbr.:* MF, M.F.
Mid′dle Greek′. See **Medieval Greek.**
Mid′dle High′ Ger′man, the High German language of the period 1100–1500. *Abbr.:* MHG, M.H.G.
Mid′dle I′rish, the Irish language of the later Middle Ages. *Abbr.:* MIr
Mid′dle King′dom, **1.** Also called **Mid′dle Em′pire.** the period of the XI–XIV dynasties in the history of ancient Egypt, c2000–1785 B.C. Cf. **New Kingdom, Old Kingdom.** **2.** *Hist.* the 18 inner provinces of China, taken collectively.
Mid′dle Lat′in. See **Medieval Latin.**
Mid′dle Low′ Ger′man, Low German of the period 1100–1500. *Abbr.:* MLG
mid·dle·man (mid′ᵊl man′), *n., pl.* **-men.** a person who acts as an intermediary, esp. in the movement of goods from the producer to the consumer.
mid·dle·most (mid′ᵊl mōst′), *adj.* midmost. [ME]
mid′dle name′, a person's name occurring between the first and family names, as a second forename.
mid·dle-of-the-road (mid′ᵊl əv thə rōd′), *adj.* not favoring any extreme position; moderate. —**mid′dle-of-the-road′er,** *n.*
Mid′dle Paleolith′ic. See under **Paleolithic.**
mid′dle pas′sage, *Hist.* the part of the Atlantic Ocean between Africa and the West Indies: longest part of the journey made by slave ships. Also, **Mid′dle Pas′sage.**
Mid′dle Path′, *Hinduism, Buddhism.* the conduct of life by a religious person in such a way as to avoid the extremes of luxury and asceticism.
Mid′dle Per′sian, the Persian language from c300 B.C. to c1100 A.D. *Abbr.:* MPers
mid′dle plane′. See **middle distance.**
Mid·dles·brough (mid′ᵊlz brə), *n.* a seaport in NE England, on the Tees estuary. 153,300.
mid′dle school′, a scholastic division, esp. in a private school, including the upper elementary grades and leading to the final secondary grades.
Mid·dle·sex (mid′ᵊl seks′), *n.* a county in SE England, bordering W and N London. 2,230,093 (1961); 232 sq. mi.
Mid′dle States′. See **Middle Atlantic States.**
Mid′dle Tem′ple, **1.** See under **Inns of Court** (def. 1). **2.** See under **temple**[1] (def. 7).
mid′dle term′. See under **syllogism** (def. 1).
Mid·dle·ton (mid′ᵊl tən), *n.* **Thomas,** c1570–1627, English dramatist.
Mid·dle·town (mid′ᵊl toun′), *n.* **1.** a city in SW Ohio on the Miami River. 48,767 (1970). **2.** a township in E New Jersey. 54,623 (1970). **3.** a city in central Connecticut, on the Connecticut River. 36,924 (1970). **4.** a town in E Pennsylvania. 30,512 (1970). **5.** a city in SE New York. 22,607 (1970). **6.** a city in S Rhode Island. 29,290 (1970).
mid·dle·weight (mid′ᵊl wāt′), *n.* **1.** a person of average weight. **2.** a boxer or other contestant intermediate in weight between a welterweight and a light heavyweight, esp. a boxer weighing from 147 to 160 pounds. —*adj.* **3.** *Boxing.* of or pertaining to a middleweight or middleweights.
Mid′dle West′, the region of the United States bounded on the W by the Rocky Mountains, on the S by the Ohio River and the S extremities of Missouri and Kansas, and on the E, variously, by the Allegheny Mountains, the E border of Ohio, or the E border of Illinois. Also called **Midwest.** —**Mid′dle West′erner.**
Mid′dle West′ern, of or pertaining to the Middle West. Also called **Midwestern.**
mid·dling (mid′ling), *adj.* **1.** medium in size, quality, grade, rank, etc. **2.** *Dial.* in fairly good health. —*adv.* **3.** moderately; fairly. —*n.* **4.** **middlings,** any of various products or commodities of intermediate quality, grade, size, etc. [late ME (north)] —**mid′dling·ly,** *adv.*
mid·dy (mid′ē), *n., pl.* **-dies.** **1.** *Informal.* a midshipman. **2.** See **middy blouse.** [MID(SHIPMAN) + -Y[2]]
mid′dy blouse′, any of various loose blouses with a sailor collar, as worn by sailors, children, young girls, etc.
Mid·east (mid′ēst), *n.* See **Middle East.** —**Mid·east′ern,** *adj.*
Mid·gard (mid′gärd), *n. Scand. Myth.* the abode of mankind, located between Niflheim and Muspelheim. Also, **Mid·garth** (mid′gärth). [< Icel *mithgarthr*]

midge (mij), *n.* **1.** any of numerous minute dipterous insects, esp. of the family *Chironomidae*, somewhat resembling a mosquito. **2.** a tiny person. [ME *mygge*, OE *mycg(e)*; c. G *Mücke*, Icel *mȳ*; akin to Gk *myîa*, L *musca* fly]

midg·et (mij′it), *n.* **1.** an extremely small person. **2.** any animal or thing very small of its kind. —*adj.* **3.** very small or of a class below the usual size. —**midg′et·ism,** *n.* —**Syn. 1.** See **dwarf.**

mid·gut (mid′gut′), *n.*, *Embryol., Zool.* the middle part of the embryonic alimentary canal from which the intestines develop. Cf. **foregut, hindgut.**

mid·i (mid′ē), *n. Informal.* a midiskirt. [by shortening]

midi-, a combining form meaning "of a mid-calf length": *midiskirt.* [alter. of MID-, modeled on MINI-]

Mi·di (mē dē′), *n.* the south of France. [< F: lit., midday = *mi-* half (< L *medius* MID[1]) + *-di* day (< L *diēs*)]

Mid·i·an (mid′ē ən), *n.* a son of Abraham. Gen. 25:1–4.

Mid·i·an·ite (mid′ē ə nīt′), *n.* **1.** a member of an ancient desert people of northwest Arabia near the Gulf of Aqaba, believed to have descended from Midian. —*adj.* **2.** of or pertaining to the Midianites. —**Mid′i·an·it′ish,** *adj.*

mid·i·nette (mid′ᵊnet′; *Fr.* mē dē net′), *n., pl.* **-nettes** (-nets′; *Fr.* -net′). a Parisian salesgirl or seamstress. [< F: lit., little meal at noon = *mi(di)* noon (see MIDI) + *dînette* (see DINE, -ETTE); the girls were so called because they had time for only a light meal at noon]

mid·i·ron (mid′ī′ərn), *n. Golf.* a club with an iron head the face of which has more slope than a driving iron but less slope than a mid-mashie.

mid·land (mid′lənd), *n.* **1.** the middle or interior part of a country. **2.** (*cap.*) the dialect of English spoken in the central part of England. **3.** (*cap.*) the dialect of English spoken in the southern parts of Illinois, Indiana, Ohio, Pennsylvania, and New Jersey, and in West Virginia, Kentucky, and eastern Tennessee, and throughout the southern Appalachians. —*adj.* **4.** in or of the midland; inland. **5.** (*cap.*) of or pertaining to Midland.

Mid·land (mid′lənd), *n.* **1.** a city in W Texas. 59,463 (1970). **2.** a city in central Michigan. 35,176 (1970).

Mid·lands (mid′ləndz), *n.pl.* the central part of England; the midland counties.

Mid·lo·thi·an (mid lō′t͟hē ən, -t͟hē-), *n.* a county in SE Scotland. 580,332 (1961); 366 sq. mi. *Co. seat:* Edinburgh. Formerly, **Edinburgh.**

mid-mash·ie (mid′mash′ē), *n. Golf.* a club with an iron head, the face of which has more slope than a midiron but less slope than a mashie iron.

mid·most (mid′mōst′), *adj.* **1.** being in the very middle. **2.** at or near the middle part or point of. —*adv.* **3.** in the midmost part; in the midst. [r. ME, OE *midmest*]

mid·night (mid′nīt′), *n.* **1.** the middle of the night, at or around twelve o'clock. —*adj.* **2.** of or pertaining to midnight. **3.** resembling midnight, as in darkness. **4. burn the midnight oil,** to study or work far into the night. [ME; OE *midniht*] —**mid′night′ly,** *adj., adv.*

mid′night sun′, the sun visible at midnight in midsummer in arctic and antarctic regions.

mid′ off′, *Cricket.* the position of a fielder on the off side of the wicket. Also, **mid′-off′.** Also called **mid wicket off.**

mid′ on′, *Cricket.* the position of a fielder on the on side of the wicket. Also, **mid′-on′.** Also called **mid wicket on.**

mid·point (mid′point′), *n.* **1.** a point at or near the middle of something, as a line. **2.** *Geom.* the point on a line segment or an arc that is equidistant, when measured along the line or the arc, from both endpoints. **3.** a point in time halfway between a beginning and a termination.

mid·rash (mid′räsh; *Heb.* mē dräsh′), *n., pl.* **mid·ra·shim** (mi drō′shim; *Heb.* mē drä shēm′). **1.** an early Jewish interpretation of or commentary on a Biblical text. **2.** (*cap.*) a collection of such interpretations or commentaries. [< Heb: explanation] —**mid·rash·ic** (mid rash′ik), *adj.*

mid·rib (mid′rib′), *n. Bot.* the central or middle rib of a leaf.

M, Midrib

mid·riff (mid′rif), *n.* **1.** the diaphragm of the human body. **2.** the middle part of the body, between the chest and the waist. **3.** the part of a dress or bodice, usually close-fitting, that covers this part of the body. **4.** a garment that exposes this part of the body. [ME *mydryf*, OE *midhrif* = *midd* MID[1] + *hrif* belly, c. L *corpus* body]

mid·sec·tion (mid′sek′shən), *n.* **1.** the middle section or part of anything. **2.** *Informal.* the solar plexus; midriff.

mid·ship (mid′ship′), *adj.* in or belonging to the middle part of a ship.

mid·ship·man (mid′ship′mən, mid ship′-), *n., pl.* **-men.** **1.** a student, as at the U.S. Naval Academy, in training for commission as ensign in the Navy or second lieutenant in the Marine Corps. Cf. **cadet** (def. 2). **2.** *Brit. Navy.* **a.** (*often cap.*) a recent graduate of a government naval school, having officer rank. **b.** (formerly) a young candidate for officer rank.

mid·ships (mid′ships′), *adv.* amidships.

midst[1] (midst), *n.* **1.** the part of a number of persons or things, or of an area, that is well within the outer limits (usually prec. by *the*): *in the midst of a crowd.* **2.** the time during which a thing or things exist or happen with full intensity (usually prec. by *the*): *in the midst of the crisis.* **3.** the figurative area within which a group of persons are gathered: *a traitor in our midst.* **4.** the figurative domain of any kind of environmental condition or influence (usually prec. by *the*): *In the midst of plenty there is want.* [ME *middes* (aph. var. of *amiddes* AMIDST) + excrescent *-t*]

midst[2] (midst), *prep.* amidst.

mid·stream (mid′strēm′), *n.* the middle of a stream. [ME *myddstreme*]

mid·sum·mer (mid′sum′ər, -sum′-), *n.* **1.** the middle of summer. —*adj.* **2.** of, pertaining to, or occurring in the middle of the summer. [ME, OE]

Mid′summer Day′, *Chiefly Brit.* the saint's day of St. John the Baptist, celebrated on June 24, being one of the four quarter days in England. Also called **St. John's Day.**

Mid′summer Eve′, *Chiefly Brit.* the evening preceding Midsummer Day: formerly believed to be a time when witches caused mischief. Also called **Mid′summer Night′, St. John's Eve, St. John's Night.**

mid′summer mad′ness, a temporary lapse into foolishness, senseless behavior, folly, etc., esp. during the summer.

mid·term (mid′tûrm′), *n.* **1.** the middle or halfway point of a term, as a school term or term of office. **2.** Usually, **midterms,** examinations taken halfway through an academic semester. —*adj.* **3.** pertaining to or occurring at this point.

mid·town (mid′toun′, -toun′), *n.* **1.** the part of a city or town between uptown and downtown. —*adj.* **2.** of, pertaining to, or situated in this part.

mid-Vic·to·ri·an (mid′vik tōr′ē ən, -tôr′-), *adj.* **1.** of, pertaining to, or characteristic of the middle portion of the reign of Queen Victoria. —*n.* **2.** a person, as a writer, belonging to the mid-Victorian time. **3.** a person of mid-Victorian tastes, standards, ideas, etc. —**mid′-Vic·to′ri·an·ism,** *n.*

mid·way (*adv., adj.* mid′wā′; *n.* mid′wā′), *adv., adj.* **1.** in the middle of the way or distance; halfway. —*n.* **2.** a place or part situated midway. **3.** (*often cap.*) the place or way, as at a fair, on or along which side shows and similar amusements are located. [ME *midwei*, OE *midweg*]

Mid·way (mid′wā′), *n.* several U.S. islets in the N Pacific, about 1200 mi. NW of Hawaii: Japanese defeated in a naval battle June, 1942. 2355 (1970); 2 sq. mi.

mid·week (mid′wēk′), *n.* **1.** the middle of the week. **2.** (*cap.*) (among the Quakers) Wednesday. —*adj.* **3.** of, pertaining to, or occurring in the middle of the week.

mid·week·ly (mid′wēk′lē), *adj.* **1.** midweek. —*adv.* **2.** in the middle of the week.

Mid·west (mid′west′), *U.S.* —*n.* **1.** See **Middle West.** —*adj.* **2.** Also, **Mid·west′ern.** See **Middle Western.** —**Mid′west′ern·er,** *n.*

Mid′west Cit′y, a city in central Oklahoma, near Oklahoma City. 48,212 (1970).

mid′ wick′et off′, *Cricket.* See **mid off.**

mid′ wick′et on′, *Cricket.* See **mid on.**

mid·wife (mid′wīf′), *n., pl.* **-wives** (-wīvz′). **1.** a woman who assists women in childbirth. **2.** a person or thing that assists in a creative process. [ME *midwif;* OE *mid* with + *wif* woman; see WIFE]

mid·wife·ry (mid′wī′fə rē, -wīf′rē), *n.* the art or practice of assisting women in childbirth. [late ME]

mid·win·ter (mid′win′tər), *n.* **1.** the middle of winter. —*adj.* **2.** of, pertaining to, or occurring in the middle of the winter. [ME, OE]

mid·year (mid′yēr′), *n.* **1.** the middle of the academic or calendar year. **2.** *Informal.* an examination at the middle of the academic year. **3. midyears,** *Informal.* a series of school examinations at midyear. —*adj.* **4.** of, pertaining to, or occurring in the middle of the academic or calendar year.

mien (mēn), *n.* air, bearing, or aspect, as showing character, feeling, etc.: *a man of noble mien.* [prob. aph. var. of obs. *demean* bearing, n. use of DEMEAN[2]; sp. with *-ie-* to distinguish it from MEAN[2]] —**Syn.** appearance, look; carriage.

Mies van der Ro·he (mēz′ van dər rō′ə, fän, mēs′), **Lud·wig** (lud′wig), 1886–1969, U.S. architect, born in Germany. Also, **Mi·ës van der Ro·he** (mē′əs van dər rō′ə, fän, mēz′, mēs′).

miff (mif), *v.t. Informal.* to give offense to; offend. [? imit. of exclamation of disgust; cf. G *muffen* to sulk]

miffed (mift), *adj.* offended and irritable.

mig (mig), *n. Chiefly Dial.* **1.** a playing marble, esp. one not used as a shooter. **2. migs,** (*construed as sing.*) the game of marbles. Also, **migg.** [? var. of MIB with *-g* from GAME[1]]

Mig (mig), *n.* any of several Russian-built fighter aircraft. [after *Mi(koyan)* & *G(urevich)*, Russian aircraft designers]

might[1] (mīt), *v.* pt. of **may.**

might[2] (mīt), *n.* **1.** power or ability to do or accomplish; capacity. **2.** physical strength. **3.** superior power or strength; force. **4. with might and main,** with all the vigor, force, or energy at one's command. [ME *myghte*, OE *miht, meaht;* c. G *Macht*, Goth *mahts;* akin to MAY] —**Syn. 1–3.** See **strength.** —**Ant. 1–3.** weakness.

might·i·ly (mīt′ᵊlē), *adv.* **1.** in a mighty manner; powerfully; vigorously. **2.** to a great extent or degree; very much: *to desire something mightily.* [ME; OE *mihtiglīce*]

might·y (mī′tē), *adj.,* **might·i·er, might·i·est,** *adv.* —*adj.* **1.** having, characterized by, or showing might or power. **2.** of great size; huge: *a mighty oak.* **3.** great in amount, extent, degree, or importance; exceptional: *a mighty accomplishment.* —*adv.* **4.** *Informal.* very: *I'm mighty pleased.* [ME; OE *mihtig*] —**might′i·ness,** *n.* —**Syn. 1.** strong, puissant. See **powerful. 2.** immense, tremendous. —**Ant. 1.** feeble.

mi·gnon (min yon′, -yun′, min′yon, -yun; *Fr.* mē nyôɴ′), *adj.* small and pretty. Also, *referring to a woman,* **mi·gnonne** (min yon′, min′yon; *Fr.* mē nyôn′). [< F; see MINION]

mi·gnon·ette (min′yə net′), *n.* a plant, *Reseda odorata,* common in gardens, having racemes of small, fragrant, greenish-white flowers with prominent reddish-yellow or brownish anthers. [< F]

mi·graine (mī′grān), *n.* a paroxysmal headache usually confined to one side of the head and often accompanied by nausea. [< F; see MEGRIM]

mi·grant (mī′grənt), *adj.* **1.** migrating; migratory. —*n.* **2.** a person or thing that migrates, as a migratory worker. [< L *migrant-* (s. of *migrāns*), prp. of *migrāre*]

mi·grate (mī′grāt), *v.i.,* **-grat·ed, -grat·ing.** **1.** to go from one country, region, or place of abode to settle in another. **2.** to pass periodically from one region to another, as certain birds, fishes, and animals. [< L *migrāt(us)* changed, moved, ptp. of *migrāre*] —**mi′gra·tor,** *n.*

—**Syn. 1.** move, resettle. MIGRATE, EMIGRATE, IMMIGRATE are used of changing one's abode from one country or part of a country to another. To MIGRATE is to make such a move either once or repeatedly and is applied both to people and to animals: *to migrate from Ireland to the United States; Ducks migrate every fall.* To EMIGRATE is to leave a country, usually one's own (and take up residence in another): *Each year many people emigrate from Europe.* To IMMIGRATE is to enter and settle in a country not one's own: *There are many inducements to immigrate to Australia.* —**Ant. 1.** remain.

mi·gra·tion (mī grā′shən), *n.* **1.** the act, process, or an instance of migrating. **2.** a migratory movement. **3.** a number or body of persons or animals migrating together. **4.** *Chem.*

a movement or change of position of atoms within a molecule. [< L *migrātiōn-* (s. of *migrātiō*)]

mi·gra·to·ry (mī′grə tôr′ē, -tōr′ē), *adj.* **1.** migrating currently. **2.** that migrates periodically: *migratory birds.* **3.** pertaining to a migration; *migratory movements of birds.* **4.** roving; nomadic; wandering. [< NL *migrātōri(us)*]

mi·ka·do (mi kä′dō), *n., pl.* **-dos.** (*sometimes cap.*) a title of the emperor of Japan. [< Jap = *mi-* honorable + *kado* gate, door (of the imperial palace)]

mike (mīk), *n.* **1.** *Informal.* a microphone. **2.** *Informal.* a micrometer. **3.** a word used in communications to represent the letter *M.* [by shortening in defs. 1, 2; arbitrary in def. 3]

Mi·ko·yan (mē ko yän′), *n.* **A·nas·tas I·va·no·vich** (ä näs täs′ i vä′no vich), 1895–1978, Russian government official: first deputy chairman of the Council of Ministers 1958–64; president of the Soviet Union 1964–65.

mi·kron (mī′kron), *n., pl.* **-krons, -kra** (-krə). micron.

mik·vah (mēk vä′; *Eng.* mik′və), *n., pl.* **-voth** (-vōt′), *Eng.* **-vahs.** *Hebrew.* a public establishment for ritual bathing by Orthodox Jews. Also, **mik′veh.**

mil (mil), *n.* **1.** a unit of length equal to .001 of an inch, used in measuring the diameter of wires. **2.** a military unit of angular measurement equal to the angle subtended by $^1/_{6400}$ of a circumference. **3.** (used formerly in pharmaceutical prescriptions) milliliter or cubic centimeter. [short for L *millēsimus* thousandth. See MILLESIMAL]

mil., **1.** military. **2.** militia.

mi·la·dy (mi lā′dē), *n., pl.* **-dies.** **1.** an English noblewoman (often used as a term of address). **2.** a woman regarded as having fashionable or expensive tastes (used abstractly): *shoes to match milady's spring wardrobe.* Also, **mi·la′di.** [< F < E, contr. of phrase *my lady*]

mil·age (mī′lij), *n.* mileage.

Mi·lan (mi lan′, -län′), *n.* a city in central Lombardy, in N Italy. 1,580,978 (1961). Italian, **Mi·la·no** (mē lä′nô).

mil·a·naise (mil′ə nāz′; *Fr.* mē lA nez′), *adj.* *French Cookery.* served with macaroni, or sometimes spaghetti, that has been flavored with tomatoes, mushrooms, shredded meat, etc.: *veal cutlets à la milanaise.* [< F, fem. of *milanais* of Milan]

Mil·an·ese (mil′ə nēz′, -nēs′), *n., pl.* **-ese,** *adj.* **—***n.* **1.** a native or inhabitant of Milan, Italy. **2.** the Italian dialect spoken in Milan. **—***adj.* **3.** of, pertaining to, or characteristic of Milan, Italy, its inhabitants, or their dialect of Italian. **4.** *Italian Cookery.* **a.** (esp. of meats) coated with flour or bread crumbs and browned in hot oil or butter. **b.** (esp. of pasta) having a sauce of tomatoes, mushrooms, grated cheese, shredded meat, and truffles. [< It]

Mil′anese chant′. See **Ambrosian chant.**

Mi·laz·zo (mē lät′tsô), *n.* a seaport in NE Sicily, in Italy. 24,083 (1961).

mild (mīld), *adj.* **1.** gentle or temperate in feeling or behavior toward others. **2.** characterized by or showing such feeling or behavior. **3.** not severe or extreme: *a mild winter.* **4.** not sharp, pungent, or strong: *a mild flavor.* **5.** moderate in intensity, degree, or character: *mild regret.* **6.** *Brit. Dial.* comparatively soft and easily worked, as soil, wood, stone, etc. **7.** *Obs.* kind or gracious. [ME, OE *milde;* c. G *mild;* akin to Gk *malthakós* soft] **—mild′ly,** *adv.* **—mild′ness,** *n.* **—Syn. 1.** soft, pleasant. See **gentle. 3.** temperate, moderate. **4.** bland. **—Ant. 1.** forceful. **3.** severe, harsh.

mild·en (mīl′d^{ə}n), *v.t., v.i.* to make or become mild or milder.

mil·dew (mil′dōō′, -dyōō′), *n.* **1.** *Plant Pathol.* a disease of plants, characterized by a cottony, usually whitish coating caused by any of various fungi. **2.** any of these fungi. **3.** any of similar coatings or discolorations, caused by fungi in a moist environment. **—***v.t., v.i.* **4.** to affect or become affected with mildew. [ME; OE *mildēaw* = *mil-* honey (c. Goth *milith,* akin to L *mel,* Gk *méli,* etc.) + *dēaw* DEW] **—mil′-dew′y,** *adj.*

mil·dew·proof (mil′dōō prōōf′, -dyōō-), *adj.* able to withstand or repel the effect of mildew.

mild′ steel′, low-carbon steel, containing no more than 10.25 percent carbon.

mile (mīl), *n.* **1.** Also called **statute mile.** a unit of distance on land in English-speaking countries equal to 5280 feet, or 1760 yards. *Abbr.:* mi, mi. **2.** Also called **geographical mile, nautical mile.** a unit of distance equal to 6080 feet. **3.** Also called **international nautical mile, international air mile.** a unit of distance in sea and air navigation equal to 1.852 kilometers, or 6076.1155 feet. **4.** any of various other units of distance or length. Cf. **Roman mile. 5.** a large gap, distance, or margin. [ME; OE *mīl* < L *mīlia* (*passuum*) a thousand (paces)]

mile·age (mī′lij), *n.* **1.** the aggregate number of miles traveled over in a given time. **2.** length, extent, or distance in miles. **3.** an allowance for traveling expenses at a fixed rate per mile. **4.** a fixed charge per mile, as for railroad transportation. **5.** the number of miles or relative distance that a vehicle can travel on a quantity of fuel. Also, **milage.**

mile·post (mīl′pōst′), *n.* any of a series of posts set up to mark distance by miles, as along a highway, or an individual post showing the distance to or from a place.

mil·er (mī′lər), *n.* **1.** a participant in a one-mile race. **2.** an athlete who specializes in races of one mile.

mi·les glo·ri·o·sus (mē′les glō′RE ō′sōōs; *Eng.* mī′lēz glōr′ē ō′səs, -glôr′-), *pl.* ***mi·li·tes glo·ri·o·si*** (mē′li tes′ glō′RE ō′sē; *Eng.* mil′i tēz′ glōr′ē ō′sī, -glôr′-). *Latin.* a boastful soldier, esp. as a figure of comedy.

mile·stone (mīl′stōn′), *n.* **1.** a stone functioning as a milepost. **2.** a significant event, as in history or in a person's life.

Mi·le·tus (mī lē′təs), *n.* an ancient city in Asia Minor, on the Aegean.

mil·foil (mil′foil′), *n.* yarrow (def. 1). [ME < OF < L *mīlifol(ium),* var. of *millefolium* = *mille* thousand + *folium* leaf]

Mil·ford (mil′fərd), *n.* a city in S Connecticut, on Long Island Sound. 50,858 (1970).

Mil′ford Ha′ven, **1.** a bay in SW Wales. **2.** a seaport on the N side of this bay. 12,802 (1961).

Mi·lhaud (mē yō′), *n.* **Da·rius** (dA RYYS′), 1892–1974, French composer, in U.S. after 1940.

mil·ia·ren·sis (mil′yə ren′sis), *n., pl.* **-ses** (-sēz). a silver coin of ancient Rome, introduced by Constantine I as the 14th part of a solidus. [< LL < L *mille* thousand; see -ESE]

mil·i·ar·i·a (mil′ē âr′ē ə), *n.* *Pathol.* an inflammatory disease of the skin, located about the sweat glands, marked by the formation of vesicles or papules resembling millet seeds; prickly heat. [< NL, L, fem. of *miliārius* MILIARY]

mil·i·ar·y (mil′ē er′ē, mil′yə rē), *adj.* **1.** resembling a millet seed or seeds. **2.** *Pathol.* accompanied by papules or vesicles resembling millet seeds: *miliary fever.* [< L *miliāri(us)* of millet. See MILIUM, -ARY]

mi·lieu (mil yōō′, mēl-; *Fr.* mē lyœ′), *n., pl.* **-lieus,** *Fr.* **-lieux** (-lyœ′). an environment, medium, or condition. [< F = *mi-* (< L *medius* middle; see MEDIUM) + *lieu* LIEU]

milit., military.

mil·i·tant (mil′i tənt), *adj.* **1.** vigorously active, aggressive, or combative. **2.** engaged in warfare; warring. **—***n.* **3.** a militant person. [late ME < L *mīlitant-* (s. of *mīlitāns*), prp. of *mīlitāre* to serve as a soldier. See MILITATE, -ANT] **—mil′i·tan·cy, mil′i·tant·ness,** *n.* **—mil′i·tant·ly,** *adv.*

mil·i·ta·rise (mil′i tə rīz′), *v.t.,* **-rised, -ris·ing.** *Chiefly Brit.* militarize. **—mil′i·ta·ri·sa′tion,** *n.*

mil·i·ta·rism (mil′i tə riz′əm), *n.* **1.** a strong military spirit or policy. **2.** the principle of maintaining a large military establishment. **3.** the tendency to regard military efficiency as the supreme ideal of the state. [< Fr *militarisme*]

mil·i·ta·rist (mil′i tər ist), *n.* **1.** a person imbued with militarism. **2.** a person skilled in military affairs. **—mil′i·ta·ris′tic,** *adj.* **—mil′i·ta·ris′ti·cal·ly,** *adv.*

mil·i·ta·rize (mil′i tə rīz′), *v.t.,* **-rized, -riz·ing.** **1.** to equip with armed forces, military supplies, etc.; make military. **2.** to imbue with militarism. Also, *esp. Brit.,* **militarise. —mil′i·ta·ri·za′tion,** *n.*

mil·i·tar·y (mil′i ter′ē), *adj., n., pl.* **-tar·ies, -tar·y. —***adj.* **1.** of, for, or pertaining to armed forces, soldiers, affairs of war, or a state of war. **2.** befitting or characteristic of a soldier. **3.** pertaining to the life of a soldier: *a military career.* **—***n.* **4.** the military establishment of a nation; the armed forces. [< L *mīlitāri(s)* = *mīlit-* (s. of *mīles*) soldier + *-āris* -ARY] **—mil·i·tar·i·ly** (mil′i târ′ə lē, mil′i ter′ə lē), *adv.*

mil′itary acad′emy, **1.** a private school organized somewhat along the lines of and following some of the procedures of military life. **2.** a school that trains men for military careers as army officers, usually as part of a college education. Also called **military school.**

mil′itary attaché′, a military officer who is assigned to a diplomatic post to gather military information concerning the country in which he is stationed.

mil′itary brush′, one of a pair of matched hairbrushes having no handles, used esp. by men.

mil′itary law′, the body of laws relating to the government of the armed forces.

mil′itary pace′, a pace, equal to a single step, used to coordinate the marching of soldiers, equal in the U.S. to 2½ feet for quick time and 3 feet for double time.

mil′itary police′, soldiers who perform police duties within the army.

mil′itary school′. See **military academy.**

mil′itary sci′ence, the study of the causative factors and tactical principles of warfare.

mil·i·tate (mil′i tāt′), *v.i.,* **-tat·ed, -tat·ing.** **1.** to operate against or in favor of something. **2.** *Obs.* **a.** to be a soldier. **b.** to take part in warfare. **c.** to take a stand, as for a belief or movement. [< L *mīlitāt(us)* served as a soldier, taken part in warfare (ptp. of *mīlitāre*). See MILITARY, -ATE^1] **—mil′i·ta′tion,** *n.*

mi·li·tes glo·ri·o·si (mē′li tes′ glō′RE ō′sē; *Eng.* mil′i-tēz′ glōr′ē ō′sī, glôr′-), *Latin.* pl. of **miles gloriosus.**

mi·li·tia (mi lish′ə), *n.* **1.** a body of men enrolled for military service, and called out periodically for drill and exercise but serving full time only in emergencies. **2.** *U.S.* al able-bodied males of each state between 18 and 45 yearslof age considered eligible for military service. **3.** a body ofcitizen soldiers as distinguished from professional soldiers. [< L: soldiery = *mīlit-* (s. of *mīles*) soldier + *-ia* -IA]

mi·li·tia·man (mi lish′ə mən), *n., pl.* **-men.** a person serving in the militia.

mil·i·um (mil′ē əm), *n., pl.* **mil·i·a** (mil′ē ə). *Pathol.* a small nodule resembling a millet seed, .produced in the skin by the retention of sebaceous secretion [< NL, L: millet]

milk (milk), *n.* **1.** an opaque white or bluish-white liquid secreted by the mammary glands of female mammals, serving for the nourishment of their young. **2.** this liquid as secreted by cows, goats, or certain other animals and used for food by human beings. **3.** any liquid resembling this, as the liquid within a coconut, the juice or sap of certain plants, or various pharmaceutical preparations. **4. cry over spilt milk,** to lament what cannot be changed. **—***v.t.* **5.** to press or draw from the udder of (a cow or other animal). **6.** to drain strength, information, wealth, etc., from. **—***v.i.* **7.** to yield milk, as a cow. **8.** to milk a cow or other animal. [ME; OE *milc* (Anglian); c. G *Milch,* Goth *miluks,* Icel *mjolk;* akin to L *mulgēre,* Gk *amélgein* to milk]

milk′ and hon′ey, **1.** extraordinary fertility and abundance: *America used to be called a land of milk and honey.* **2.** *Informal.* abundantly easy, carefree conditions.

milk′ bar′, a restaurantlike establishment that sells milk drinks, sandwiches, and other light refreshments.

milk′ choc′olate, candy made of or coated with chocolate diluted with milk.

milk·er (mil′kər), *n.* **1.** a person who milks. **2.** See **milking machine. 3.** a cow or other animal that gives milk.

milk′ fe′ver, *Vet. Pathol.* a febrile condition often affecting dairy cows immediately after calving, causing somnolence and paralysis.

milk′ glass′, an opaque white glass. Also called **opaline.**

milk′ing machine′, an electric machine for milking cows. Also called **milker.**

milk′ing stool′, a low, three-legged stool with a flat seat in the shape of a half circle.

milk′ leg′, *Pathol.* a painful swelling of the leg, due to thrombosis of the large veins, occurring most frequently in connection with childbirth. Also called **white leg.**

milk·maid (milk′mād′), *n.* a woman who milks cows or who is employed in a dairy.

milk·man (milk′man′), *n., pl.* **-men.** a man who sells or delivers milk.

milk′ of magne′sia, a milky white suspension in water of magnesium hydroxide, $Mg(OH)_2$, used as an antacid or laxative.

milk′ punch′, a beverage containing milk and alcoholic liquor with sugar, flavoring, etc.

milk′ run′, *Slang.* a routine trip or undertaking, esp. one presenting little danger or difficulty: *The reconnaissance flight was a milk run.*

milk′ shake′, a frothy drink made of cold milk, flavoring, and usually ice cream, shaken together or blended in a mixer.

milk′ sick′ness, *Pathol.* a disease of man, formerly common in some parts of the Middle West, caused by consuming milk from cattle that have been poisoned by eating certain kinds of snakeroot.

milk′ snake′, a brightly marked kingsnake, *Lampropeltis doliata,* of eastern North America. [so called because it is mistakenly believed to suck the milk from cows]

milk·sop (milk′sop′), *n.* an unmanly or effeminate man or youth.

milk′ sug′ar, lactose.

milk′ toast′, toast, usually buttered, served in hot milk with sugar or with salt and pepper.

milk-toast (milk′tōst′), *adj.* **1.** (of a man) extremely mild or ineffectual. —*n.* **2.** milquetoast.

milk′ tooth′, one of the temporary teeth of a mammal that are replaced by the permanent teeth. Also called **deciduous tooth.**

milk′ train′, *Slang.* a local train running through the early hours of the morning.

milk′ vetch′, **1.** a European, fabaceous herb, *Astragalus Glycyphyllos,* believed to increase the secretion of milk in goats. **2.** any herb of certain allied genera.

milk·weed (milk′wēd′), *n.* **1.** any of several asclepiadaceous plants that secrete a milky juice or latex, esp. those of the genus *Asclepias,* as *A. syriaca.* **2.** any of various other plants having a milky juice, as certain spurges.

milk·wood (milk′wo͝od′), *n.* any of various trees having a milky juice, as *Pseudomedia spuria,* of Jamaica.

milk·wort (milk′wûrt′), *n.* any herb or shrub of the genus *Polygala,* formerly supposed to increase the secretion of milk.

milk·y (mil′kē), *adj.,* **milk·i·er, milk·i·est.** **1.** of or like milk. **2.** white or whitish in color. **3.** giving a good supply of milk. **4.** meek, tame, or spiritless. [ME] —**milk′i·ly,** *adv.* —**milk′i·ness,** *n.*

milk′y disease′, a disease affecting Japanese beetle larvae, characterized by a milky appearance of the blood and caused by the bacteria *Bacillus popilliae* or *Bacillus lentimorbus.*

Milk′y Way′, *Astron.* the faintly luminous band stretching across the heavens, composed of innumerable stars too distant to be seen clearly with the naked eye; the galaxy containing the earth, sun, and solar system. [ME, trans. of L *via lactea*]

mill[1] (mil), *n.* **1.** a building or establishment in which any of various mechanical operations or forms of manufacture is carried on. **2.** a building or establishment for converting grain into flour and other cereal products. **3.** a machine for grinding, crushing, or pulverizing any solid substance. **4.** a machine that works materials in some way. **5.** an establishment that handles important matters in a perfunctory or routine manner; *a divorce mill; a diploma mill.* **6. through the mill,** *Informal.* undergoing or having undergone severe difficulties and trouble. —*v.t.* **7.** to grind, work, treat, or shape in or with a mill. **8.** *Coining.* **a.** to make a raised edge on (a coin or the like). **b.** to make narrow, radial grooves on the raised edge of (a coin or the like). **9.** *Slang.* to beat or strike; fight; overcome. —*v.i.* **10.** to move around aimlessly or confusedly, as a herd of cattle (often fol. by *about* or *around*). [ME *mille,* OE *myl(e)n* < LL *molīna,* n. use of fem. of *molīnus* of a mill = L *mol(a)* mill(stone) + *-īnus* -INE[1]] —**mill′a·ble,** *adj.*

mill[2] (mil), *n.* a unit of monetary value equal to .001 of a U.S. dollar; one tenth of a cent: used in various times and places in the U.S. as a money of account, esp. in paying sales taxes. [short for L *mill(ēsimus)* thousandth; see MIL]

Mill (mil), *n.* **1. James,** 1773–1836, English philosopher, historian, and economist; born in Scotland. **2.** his son, **John Stuart,** 1806–73, English philosopher and economist.

mil·lage (mil′ij), *n.* the tax rate, as for property, assessed in mills per dollar. [MILL[2] + -AGE]

Mil·lais (mi lā′), *n.* **Sir John Everett,** 1829–96, English painter.

Mil·lay (mi lā′), *n.* **Edna St. Vincent,** 1892–1950, U.S. poet and playwright.

mill·board (mil′bōrd′, -bôrd′), *n. Bookbinding.* a strong, thick pasteboard used to make book covers. [MILL(ED) + BOARD]

Mill·burn (mil′bərn), *n.* a township in NE New Jersey. 21,307 (1970).

mill·dam (mil′dam′), *n.* a dam built in a stream to furnish a head of water for turning a mill wheel. [ME]

milled (mild), *v.* **1.** pt. and pp. of **mill**[1]. —*adj.* **2.** having undergone the operations of a mill.

mil·le·nar·i·an (mil′ə nâr′ē ən), *adj.* **1.** of or pertaining to a thousand, esp. the thousand years of the prophesied millennium. —*n.* **2.** a believer in the millennium.

mil·le·nar·y (mil′ə ner′ē), *adj., n., pl.* **-nar·ies.** —*adj.* **1.** consisting of or pertaining to a thousand, esp. a thousand years. **2.** pertaining to the millennium. —*n.* **3.** an aggregate of a thousand. **4.** millennium. **5.** millenarian. [< LL *millēnāri(us)* of a thousand = *millēn(ī)* a thousand each (L *mill(e)* thousand + *-ēnī* distributive suffix) + *-ārius* -ARY]

mil·len·ni·al (mi len′ē əl), *adj.* **1.** of or pertaining to a millennium or the millennium. **2.** worthy or suggestive of the millennium.

mil·len·ni·um (mi len′ē əm), *n., pl.* **-ni·ums, -ni·a** (-nē ə). **1.** a period of one thousand years. **2.** a thousandth anniversary. **3. the millennium,** the period of a thousand years during which Christ will reign on earth. Rev. 20:1–7. **4.** a period of general righteousness and happiness, esp. in the indefinite future. [< NL; see MILL[2], BIENNIUM]

mil·le·pede (mil′ə pēd′), *n.* millipede.

mil·le·pore (mil′ə pōr′, -pôr′), *n.* a coralline hydrozoan of the genus *Millipora,* having a smooth calcareous surface with many perforations. [< NL *millepora.* See MILL[2], PORE[2]]

mill·er (mil′ər), *n.* **1.** a person who owns or operates a mill, esp. a grain mill. **2.** See **milling machine. 3.** any moth, esp. of the family *Noctuidae,* having wings that appear powdery. [ME *millere,* assimilated var. of *milnere*]

Mill·er (mil′ər), *n.* **1. Arthur,** born 1915, U.S. playwright and novelist. **2. Henry,** 1891–1980, U.S. novelist. **3. Joa·quin** (wä kēn′), (*Cincinnatus Heine Miller*), 1841–1913, U.S. poet. **4. Joe** (*Joseph* or *Josias Miller*), 1684–1738, English actor after whom *Joe Miller's Jestbook* (1739) was named. **5. William,** 1782–1849, U.S. religious leader: founder of the Adventist Church.

Mill′er in′dex, *Crystall.* one of three integers giving the orientation and position of the face of a crystal. [named after W. H. *Miller* (1801–80), British mineralogist]

Mill·er·ite (mil′ə rīt′), *n.* a follower of William Miller who believed that the Second Coming of Christ was to occur in 1843. [William MILLER + -ITE[1]]

mill·er's-thumb (mil′ərz thum′), *n.* any of several small, fresh-water sculpins of the genus *Cottus,* as *C. gobio,* of Europe. [ME; the fish is so called from its thumblike head]

mil·les·i·mal (mi les′ə məl), *adj.* **1.** thousandth. —*n.* **2.** a thousandth part. [< L *millēsim(us)* thousandth (*mill(e)* thousand + *-ēsimus* ordinal suffix) + -AL[1]]

mil·let (mil′it), *n.* **1.** a cereal grass, *Setaria italica,* extensively cultivated in the East and in southern Europe for its small seed, or grain, used as food for man and fowls, but in the U.S. grown chiefly for fodder. **2.** any of various related or similar grasses. **3.** the grain of any of these grasses. [ME *milet* < MF. See MILIUM, -ET]

Mil·let (mi lā′; *Fr.* mē le′), *n.* **Jean Fran·çois** (zhäɴ fräɴ swa′), 1814–75, French painter.

milli-, a learned borrowing from Latin meaning "thousand" (*millipede*): in the metric system, used to indicate one thousandth of the specified unit (*millimeter*). [< F < L, comb. form of *mille* thousand]

mil·li·am·me·ter (mil′ē am′mē tər), *n.* an instrument for measuring small electric currents, calibrated in milliamperes. [MILLIAM(PERE) + -METER]

mil·li·am·pere (mil′ē am′pēr), *n. Elect.* one thousandth of an ampere. *Abbr.:* mA, ma. [< F]

mil·li·ang·strom (mil′ē ang′strəm), *n.* one thousandth of an angstrom. *Abbr.:* mÅ

mil·liard (mil′yərd, -yärd), *n. Brit.* one thousand millions: equivalent to U.S. billion. [< F]

mil·li·are (mil′ē âr′, -är′), *n. Metric System.* a unit of area equal to one thousandth of an are. [< F]

mil·li·ar·y (mil′ē er′ē), *adj.* **1.** of, pertaining to, or designating the ancient Roman mile of a thousand paces. **2.** marking a mile. [< L *milliāri(us)* having a thousand]

mil·li·bar (mil′ə bär′), *n.* a unit of pressure equal to one thousandth of a bar or 1000 dynes per square centimeter: used to measure barometric pressure. *Abbr.:* mb

mil·li·barn (mil′ə bärn′), *n.* one thousandth of a barn. *Abbr.:* mb

mil·li·cur·ie (mil′ə kyo͝or′ē, -kyo͝o rē′), *n. Physics, Chem.* a unit of radioactivity equal to one thousandth of a curie; 3.70×10^7 disintegrations per second. *Abbr.:* mCi, mc

mil·lieme (mēl yem′, mē yem′), *n.* any of the copper coins equal to the thousandth part of the pound, or the tenth part of the piaster, of Libya, Sudan, and the Arab Republic of Egypt. [< F *millième* << L *millēsim(us)* MILLESIMAL]

mil·lier (mēl yā′), *n.* 1000 kilograms; a metric ton. Also called **tonneau.** [< F < L *milliār(ius)* MILLIARY]

mil·li·gram (mil′ə gram′), *n. Metric System.* a unit of weight equal to one thousandth of a gram, and equivalent to 0.0154 grain. *Abbr.:* mg Also, *esp. Brit.,* **mil′li·gramme′.** [< F *milligramme*]

mil·li·hen·ry (mil′ə hen′rē), *n., pl.* **-ries, -rys.** *Elect.* a unit of inductance equal to one thousandth of a henry. *Abbr.:* mH, mh

Mil·li·kan (mil′ə kən), *n.* **Robert Andrews,** 1868–1953, U.S. physicist: Nobel prize 1923.

mil·li·lam·bert (mil′ə lam′bərt), *n. Optics.* a unit of luminance equal to one thousandth of a lambert. *Abbr.:* mL

mil·li·li·ter (mil′ə lē′tər), *n. Metric System.* a unit of capacity equal to one thousandth of a liter, and equivalent to 0.033815 fluid ounce, or 0.061025 cubic inch. *Abbr.:* ml Also, *esp. Brit.,* **mil′li·li′tre.** [< F *millilitre*]

mil·lime (mil′im, -ēm), *n.* an aluminum coin of Tunisia, the thousandth part of a dinar. [appar. alter. of F *millième* thousandth]

mil·li·me·ter (mil′ə mē′tər), *n. Metric System.* a unit of length equal to one thousandth of a meter and equivalent to 0.03937 inch. *Abbr.:* mm Also, *esp. Brit.,* **mil′le·me′tre.** [< F *millimètre*] **mil·li·met·ric** (mil′ə me′trik), *adj.*

mil·li·mho (mil′ə mō′), *n., pl.* **-mhos.** *Elect.* a unit of conductance equal to .001 mho. *Abbr.:* mmho

mil·li·mi·cron (mil′ə mī′kron), *n., pl.* **-crons, -cra** (-krə). a unit of length equal to one thousandth of a micron or 10^{-7} centimeter. *Symbol:* mμ

mil·li·mole (mil′ə mōl′), *n.* one thousandth of a mole. *Abbr.:* mM

mil·line (mil′līn′, mil līn′), *n.* **1.** one agate line of advertising one column in width appearing in one million copies of a periodical. **2.** Also called **mil′line rate′.** the charge or cost per milline. [MIL(LION) + LINE[1]]

mil·li·ner (mil′ə nər), *n.* a person who designs, makes, or sells hats for women. [var. of obs. *Milaner* native of Milan, dealer in goods from Milan; see -ER[1]]

mil·li·ner·y (mil′ə ner′ē, -nə rē), *n.* **1.** women's hats and other articles made or sold by milliners. **2.** the business or trade of a milliner.

mill·ing (mil′ing), *n.* **1.** the act or an instance of subjecting something to the operation of a mill. **2.** the act or process of producing plane or shaped surfaces with a milling machine. **3.** the grooved edge on a coin.

mill′ing machine′, a machine tool for rotating a cutter to produce plane or formed surfaces on a workpiece, usually by moving the work past the cutter.

mil·li·ohm (mil′ē ōm′), *n. Elect.* a unit of resistance equal to one thousandth of an ohm.

mil·lion (mil′yən), *n., pl.* **-lions,** (*as after a numeral*) **-lion,** *adj.* —*n.* **1.** a cardinal number, a thousand times one thousand. **2.** a symbol for this number, as 1,000,000 or M. **3.** the amount of a thousand thousand in the currency units of a specified country. **4.** a very great number: *a million things to do.* **5. the million,** the mass of the common people. **6. millions,** the numbers between 1,000,000 and 999,999,999, as in referring to an amount of money. —*adj.* **7.** amounting to one million in number. [ME < MF < early It *millione* = *mille* thousand (< L) + *-one* aug. suffix]

mil·lion·aire (mil′yə nâr′), *n.* **1.** a person whose wealth amounts to a million or more in the currency units of a specified country. **2.** (loosely) any very rich person. Also, **mil′lion·naire′.** [< F *millionnaire.* See MILLION, -ARY]

mil·lionth (mil′yənth), *adj.* **1.** coming last in a series of a million. **2.** being one of a million equal parts. —*n.* **3.** the millionth member of a series. **4.** a millionth part, esp. of one (1/1,000,000).

Millipede, *Cambala annulata* (Length 1 in.)

mil·li·pede (mil′ə pēd′), *n.* any terrestrial arthropod of the class *Diplopoda,* having a cylindrical body composed of from 20 to over 100 segments, each with two pairs of legs. Also, **millepede.** [< L *millepeda* the wood louse = *mille* thousand + *-peda* -PED]

mil·li·rem (mil′ə rem′), *n.* one thousandth of a rem. *Abbr.:* mrem

mil·li·roent·gen (mil′ə rent′gən, -jən, -runt′-), *n.* a unit of radiation equal to one thousandth of a roentgen.

mil·li·sec·ond (mil′i sek′ənd), *n.* one thousandth of a second. *Abbr.:* msec

mil·li·sie·mens (mil′ə sā′mənz, -zē′-), *n.* a unit of conductance equal to one thousandth of a siemens. *Abbr.:* mS

mil·li·volt (mil′ə vōlt′), *n. Elect.* a unit of electromotive force equal to one thousandth of a volt. *Abbr.:* mV, mv

mil·li·watt (mil′ə wot′), *n.* a unit of power equal to one thousandth of a watt. *Abbr.:* mW, mw

mill·pond (mil′pond′), *n.* a pond for supplying water to drive a mill wheel.

mill·race (mil′rās′), *n.* **1.** the channel in which the current of water driving a mill wheel flows to the mill. **2.** the current itself.

mill·stone (mil′stōn′), *n.* **1.** either of a pair of heavy circular stones between which grain or another substance is ground, as in a mill. **2.** any heavy emotional, financial, or other burden. [ME *mylneston,* OE *mylenstān*]

mill·stream (mil′strēm′), *n.* the stream in a millrace.

mill′ wheel′, a water wheel for driving a mill. [ME *myln whele,* OE *mylenhwēol*]

mill·work (mil′wûrk′), *n.* **1.** ready-made carpentry work from a mill. **2.** work done in a mill. **3.** profiled or finished woodwork, as moldings, lattices, etc.. Also, **mill′ work′.**

mill·wright (mil′rīt′), *n.* a person who erects the machinery of a mill.

Milne (miln), *n.* **A(lan) A(lexander),** 1882–1956, English novelist, playwright, and author of prose and verse for children.

Mi·lo (mī′lō; *Gk.* mē′lō), *n.* Melos. Also, **Mi·los** (*Gk.* mē′lôs).

mi·lord (mi lôrd′), *n.* an English nobleman (often used as a term of address). [< F < E, contr. of phrase *my lord*]

Mi·losz (mē′wôsh; *Eng.* mē′losh), *n.* **Czes·law** (ches′wäf; *Eng.* ches′lô), born 1911, Polish writer and poet; self-exiled in U.S. since 1960: Nobel prize 1980.

Mil·pi·tas (mil pē′təs), *n.* a city in W California. 27,149 (1970).

milque·toast (milk′tōst′), *n.* a man who is easily dominated or intimidated. [after Caspar *Milquetoast,* a character in *The Timid Soul,* comic strip by H. T. Webster, 20th-century American cartoonist]

mil·reis (mil′rās′; *Port.* mēl RĀS′), *n. pl.* **-reis. 1.** a silver coin and former monetary unit of Brazil, equal to 1000 reis, discontinued in 1942. **2.** a gold coin and former monetary unit of Portugal, equal to 1000 reis, discontinued in 1910. [< Pg: a thousand reis. See MILLI-, REIS]

Mil·stein (mil′stīn), *n.* **Nathan,** born 1904, U.S. violinist, born in Russia.

milt[1] (milt), *n.* **1.** the secretion of the male generative organs of fishes. **2.** the organs themselves. [ME *mylke* MILK, milt + *mille* milt, spleen, with confusion in form and sense prob. influenced by MD *milte* milt, spleen]

milt[2] (milt), *n.* melt[2].

milt·er (mil′tər), *n.* a male fish in breeding time.

Mil·ti·a·des (mil tī′ə dēz′), *n.* **1.** c540–488? B.C., Athenian general. **2.** Melchiades.

Mil·ton (mil′tᵊn), *n.* **1. John,** 1608–74, English poet. **2.** a town in E Massachusetts, near Boston. 27,190 (1970).

Mil·ton·ic (mil ton′ik), *adj.* **1.** of or pertaining to the poet Milton or his writings. **2.** resembling Milton's majestic style. Also, **Mil·to·ni·an** (mil tō′nē ən).

Mil·town (mil′toun′), *n. Pharm., Trademark.* meprobamate.

Mil·wau·kee (mil wô′kē), *n.* a port in SE Wisconsin, on Lake Michigan. 717,372 (1970). —**Mil·wau′kee·an,** *n.*

mim (mim), *adj. Brit. Dial.* primly modest or demure. [? M(UM[2] + PR)IM]

mim·bar (mim′bär), *n.* a pulpit in a mosque. [< Ar]

mime (mīm, mēm), *n., v.,* **mimed, mim·ing.** —*n.* **1.** the art or technique of portraying a character, mood, idea, or narration by gestures and bodily movements; pantomime. **2.** a performer specializing in this art. **3.** an ancient Greek or Roman farce of a slapstick character. **4.** a performer in such a farce. **5.** mimic (def. 4). **6.** a jester, clown, or comedian. —*v.t.* **7.** to mimic. —*v.i.* **8.** to play a part by mimicry, esp. without words. [OE *mīma* < L *mīmus* < Gk *mîmos* imitator, mime] —**mim′er,** *n.*

mim·e·o (mim′ē ō′), *n., v.t. Informal.* mimeograph. [by shortening]

mim·e·o·graph (mim′ē ə graf′, -gräf′), *n.* **1.** a printing device in which a waxed paper stencil, cut by a typewriter or stylus, rotates on a drum, ink from which penetrates the cut areas and is deposited on a sheet of paper with each revolution. —*v.t.* **2.** to make copies of (something) using a mimeograph. [formerly trademark]

mi·me·sis (mi mē′sis, mī-), *n.* **1.** *Rhet.* imitation or reproduction of the supposed words of another. **2.** *Biol.* imitation. **3.** *Zool.* mimicry. [< Gk: imitation = *mīmē-* (var. s. of *mīmeîsthai* to copy) + *-sis* -SIS]

mi·met·ic (mi met′ik, mī-), *adj.* **1.** characterized by exhibiting, or of the nature of mimicry. **2.** mimic; make-believe. [< Gk *mīmētik(ós)* imitative. See MIMESIS, -TIC] —**mi·met′i·cal·ly,** *adv.*

mim·e·tite (mim′i tīt′, mī′mi-), *n.* a mineral, lead chloroarsenate, $Pb_5As_3O_{12}Cl$, a minor ore of lead. [< Gk *mīmēt(ēs)* imitator (*mīmē-* imitate + *-tēs* agent suffix) + -ITE[1]]

mim·ic (mim′ik), *v.,* **-icked, -ick·ing,** *n., adj.* —*v.t.* **1.** to imitate or copy in action, speech, etc., often playfully or derisively. **2.** to imitate servilely or unintelligently; ape. **3.** to be an imitation of; simulate; resemble closely. —*n.* **4.** a person who is clever at or skilled in mimicking the voices and gestures of others. **5.** a person or thing that imitates or mimics. **6.** a performer in a mime. —*adj.* **7.** being merely an imitation or reproduction of the true thing, often on a smaller scale. **8.** apt at or given to imitating. [< L *mīmic(us)* < Gk *mīmikós* of a mime or mimic. See MIME, -IC] —**mim′ick·er,** *n.* —**Syn. 7** mock, simulated.

mim·i·cal (mim′i kəl), *adj. Archaic.* mimic. —**mim′i·cal·ly,** *adv.*

mim·ic·ry (mim′ik rē), *n., pl.* **-ries. 1.** the act, practice, or art of mimicking. **2.** *Zool.* the close external resemblance, as if from imitation or simulation, of an animal to some different animal or to surrounding objects, esp. as serving for protection or concealment. **3.** an instance, performance, or result of mimicking.

Mi·mir (mē′mir), *n. Scand. Myth.* the god of the open sea.

mi·mo·sa (mi mō′sə, -zə), *n.* any of numerous herbs, shrubs, or trees of the genus *Mimosa,* native to tropical or warm regions, having small flowers in globular heads or cylindrical spikes and often sensitive leaves. [< NL = L *mīm(us)* MIME + *-ōsa,* fem. of *-ōsus* -OSE[1]]

mim·o·sa·ceous (mim′ə sā′shəs, mī′mə-), *adj.* belonging to the *Mimosaceae,* or mimosa family of plants, usually included in the family *Leguminosae.* [< NL *mīmosāce(ae)* name of the family (see MIMOSA, -ACEAE) + -OUS]

Mims (mimz), *n.* **Fort.** See **Fort Mims.**

min, minim; minims.

min., **1.** mineralogical. **2.** mineralogy. **3.** minim. **4.** minimum. **5.** mining. **6.** minor. **7.** minute; minutes.

mi·na (mī′nə), *n., pl.* **-nae** (-nē), **-nas.** an ancient unit of weight and value equal to the sixtieth part of a talent. [< L < Gk *mnâ* < Sem; cf. Heb *māneh* mina]

min·a·ret (min′ə ret′, min′ə ret′), *n.* a slender tower or turret attached to a mosque and from which the muezzin calls the people to prayer. [< F < Turk *menaret* < Ar *manārah* lighthouse, akin to *nār* fire] —**min′a·ret′ed,** *adj.*

Mi′nas Ba′sin (mī′nəs), a bay in E Canada, the easternmost arm of the Bay of Fundy, in N Nova Scotia: noted for its high tides.

Mi·nas Ge·rais (mē′nəs zhi RīS′), a state in E Brazil. 11,279,872; 224,701 sq. mi. *Cap.:* Belo Horizonte.

min·a·to·ry (min′ə tôr′ē, -tōr′ē), *adj.* menacing; threatening. Also, **min′a·to′ri·al.** [< LL *minātōri(us)* = L *mināt(us)* menaced (ptp. of *minārī* to threaten) + *-ōrius* -ORY[1]] —**min′a·to′ri·ly,** *adv.*

mince (mins), *v.,* **minced, minc·ing,** *n.* —*v.t.* **1.** to cut into very small pieces. **2.** to subdivide minutely. **3.** to soften or moderate (one's words), esp. for the sake of decorum or courtesy. **4.** to perform or utter with affected elegance. —*v.i.* **5.** to walk or move with short, affectedly dainty steps. **6.** to act, behave, or speak with affected elegance. —*n.* **7.** something cut up very small; mincemeat. [ME *mince(n)* < MF *minc(i)er* < VL **minūtiāre* to mince] —**minc′er,** *n.*

mince·meat (mins′mēt′), *n.* **1.** a mixture composed of minced apples, suet, and sometimes meat, together with raisins, currants, candied citron, etc. **2.** anything cut up very small, esp. meat.

mince′ pie′, a pie having a filling of mincemeat.

minc·ing (min′sing), *adj.* **1.** (of the gait or speech, behavior, etc.) affectedly dainty or elegant. **2.** walking, acting, or speaking in an affectedly nice or elegant manner. —**minc′ing·ly,** *adv.*

mind (mīnd), *n.* **1.** the agency or part in a human or other conscious being that reasons, understands, wills, perceives, experiences emotions, etc. **2.** *Psychol.* the totality of conscious and unconscious mental processes and activities of the organism. **3.** the faculty of reasoning or understanding; intelligence. **4.** a person considered with relation to his intellectual powers: *the great minds of the day.* **5.** reason or sanity: *to lose one's mind.* **6.** opinion or intentions: *to change one's mind.* **7.** inclination or desire. **8.** psychic or spiritual being, as opposed to matter. **9.** a conscious or intelligent agency or being: *an awareness of a mind ordering the universe.* **10.** remembrance or recollection: *Former days were called to mind.* **11.** attention; thoughts: *He can't keep his mind on his studies.* **12.** *Rom. Cath. Ch.* a commemoration of a person's death, esp. by a Requiem Mass. **13.** (*cap.*) *Christian Science.* the noncorporeal as the single source of life, substance, and intelligence. **14. a piece of one's mind,** *Informal.* a frank expression of one's anger or disapproval. **15. bear** or **keep in mind,** to remember: *Bear in mind that tomorrow is a holiday.* **16. have a good mind to,** to feel strongly inclined to. **17. in mind, a.** in one's conscious thoughts. **b.** as a plan or intention. **18. know one's own mind,** to be firm in one's intentions, opinions, or plans. **19. make up one's mind,** to decide or resolve, as on a course of action. **20. on one's mind,** constantly in one's thoughts. **21. out of one's mind, a.** insane. **b.** totally distracted: *out of her mind with worry.* **22. presence of mind,** ability to think clearly in a crisis. **23. to one's mind,** in accord with one's judgment or opinion: *To my mind, she'll always be unpleasant.* —*v.t.* **24.** to pay attention to, heed, or obey (a person, instructions, etc.). **25.** to apply oneself or attend to: *to mind one's own business.* **26.** to look after; take care of: *Who's minding*

the store? **27.** to be careful, cautious, or wary concerning. **28.** to feel concern at; care about. **29.** to feel disturbed or inconvenienced by; object to (usually used in negative or interrogative constructions): *Would you mind handing me that book?* **30.** to regard as concerning oneself or as mattering: *Don't mind his bluntness.* **31.** *Dial.* to perceive or notice. —*v.i.* **32.** to obey. **33.** to take notice, observe, or understand (used chiefly in the imperative): *Mind now, I want you home by twelve.* **34.** to be careful or wary. **35.** to care, feel concern, or object (often used in negative or interrogative constructions): *Do you mind if I go?* **36.** to regard a thing as concerning oneself or as mattering: *You mustn't mind about their gossiping.* **37. never mind,** give it no further thought. [ME *mynd(e),* OE *gemynd* commemoration]
—**Syn. 1.** reason. MIND, INTELLECT, INTELLIGENCE refer to mental equipment or qualities. MIND is the part of man that thinks, feels, and wills, as contrasted with body: *His mind remained active in spite of his physical deterioration.* INTELLECT is reasoning power as distinguished from feeling; it is often used in a general sense to characterize high mental ability: *to appeal to the intellect rather than to the emotions.* INTELLIGENCE is ability to learn and to understand; it is also mental alertness or quickness of understanding: *A dog has more intelligence than many other animals.* **3.** MIND, BRAIN, BRAINS may refer to mental capacity. MIND is the philosophical and general term for the center of mental activity, and is therefore used of intellectual powers: *a brilliant mind.* BRAIN is properly the physiological term for the organic structure that makes mental activity possible (*The brain is the center of the nervous system.*), but it is often applied, like mind, to intellectual capacity: *a fertile brain.* BRAINS is the anatomical word (*the brains of an animal used for food*), but, in popular usage, it is applied to intelligence (particularly of a shrewd, practical nature).

Min·da·na·o (min′dä nä′ō, -nou′; *Sp.* mēn′dä nä′ô), *n.* the second largest island of the Philippines, in the S part of the group. 7,292,691; 36,537 sq. mi.

mind-blow·ing (mīnd′blō′ing), *n. Slang.* —*adj.* **1.** astounding; astonishing; overwhelming. **2.** producing an effect similar to that of hallucinogenic drugs. —*n.* **3.** the taking of hallucinogenic drugs.

mind·ed (mīn′did), *adj.* **1.** having a certain kind of mind (in combination): *strong-minded.* **2.** inclined or disposed.

mind·ful (mīnd′fəl), *adj.* attentive or careful (usually fol. by *of*). [ME *myndeful*] —**mind′ful·ly,** *adv.* —**mind′ful·ness,** *n.*

mind·less (mīnd′lis), *adj.* **1.** without intelligence; senseless. **2.** unmindful, careless, or heedless. [ME *myndles,* OE *gemyndlēas*] —**mind′less·ly,** *adv.* —**mind′less·ness,** *n.*

Min·do·ro (min dōr′ō, -dôr′ō; *Sp.* mēn dô′rô), *n.* a central island of the Philippines. 473,940; 3922 sq. mi.

mind′ read′ing, the professed or reputed ability to discern the unexpressed thoughts of others, as through telepathy. —**mind′ read′er.**

mind-set (mīnd′set′), *n.* **1.** an intention or inclination. **2.** a disposition or mood.

mind's′ eye′, the hypothetical site of visual recollection or imagination.

mine[1] (mīn), *pron.* **1.** a form of the possessive case of *I* used as a predicate adjective: *The yellow sweater is mine.* **2.** that which belongs to me: *Mine is the car with the flat tire.* **3.** *Archaic.* my (used before a word beginning with a vowel or a silent *h,* or following a noun): *mine eyes; lady mine.* [ME, OE *mīn;* c. Icel *mīn,* G *mein,* Goth *meina;* see ME]

mine[2] (mīn), *n., v.,* **mined, min·ing.** —*n.* **1.** an excavation made in the earth for the purpose of extracting ores, precious stones, coal, etc. **2.** a natural deposit of such minerals. **3.** an abundant source; store: *a mine of information.* **4.** *Mil.* **a.** a subterranean passage beneath the enemy's fortifications. **b.** an enclosed explosive charge for destroying ships, land vehicles, or personnel. **5.** a passageway in the parenchyma of a leaf, made by certain insects. —*v.i.* **6.** to dig in the earth for the purpose of extracting ores, coal, etc.; make a mine. **7.** to extract ores, etc., from a mine. **8.** to make subterranean passages. **9.** to dig or lay mines, as in military operations. —*v.t.* **10.** to dig in (earth, rock, etc.) in order to obtain ores, coal, etc. **11.** to extract (ore, coal, etc.) from a mine. **12.** to make subterranean passages in or under; burrow. **13.** to make (passages, tunnels, etc.) by digging or burrowing. **14.** to dig away or remove the foundations of. **15.** to attack, ruin, or destroy by secret or slow methods. **16.** to dig or lay military mines under. [ME < MF, perh. < OF *miniere* mine] —**min′a·ble, mine′a·ble,** *adj.*

mine·field (mīn′fēld′), *n. Mil., Naval.* an area of land or water throughout which explosive mines have been laid.

mine·lay·er (mīn′lā′ər), *n.* a naval vessel specially equipped for laying mines in the water.

min·er (mī′nər), *n.* **1.** a person who works in a mine. **2.** (formerly) a person who digs or lays military mines. [r. ME *minour* < AF; see -OR[2]]

min·er·al (min′ər əl, min′rəl), *n.* **1.** any of a class of substances occurring in nature, usually comprising inorganic substances, as quartz or feldspar, of definite chemical composition and usually of definite crystal structure, but sometimes also including rocks formed by these substances as well as certain natural products of organic origin, as asphalt or coal. **2.** a substance obtained by mining; ore. **3. minerals,** *Brit.* See **mineral water.** —*adj.* **4.** of, pertaining to, or of the nature of a mineral or minerals. **5.** containing a mineral or minerals. [late ME < ML *minerāle* (n.), *minerālis* (adj.)]

mineral., **1.** mineralogical. **2.** mineralogy.

min·er·al·ize (min′ər ə līz′, min′rə-), *v.,* **-ized, -iz·ing.** —*v.t.* **1.** to convert into a mineral substance. **2.** to transform (a metal) into an ore. **3.** to impregnate or supply with mineral substances. —*v.i.* **4.** to study or collect the minerals of a region. —**min′er·al·i·za′tion,** *n.* —**min′er·al·iz′er,** *n.*

min′eral king′dom, minerals collectively. Cf. **animal kingdom, plant kingdom.**

min·er·al·o·gist (min′ə rol′ə jist, -ral′ə-), *n.* a specialist in mineralogy.

min·er·al·o·gy (min′ə rol′ə jē, -ral′ə-), *n.* the science or study of minerals. —**min·er·al·og·i·cal** (min′ər ə loj′i kəl), **min′er·al·og′ic,** *adj.* —**min′er·al·og′i·cal·ly,** *adv.*

min′eral oil′, a colorless, oily, almost tasteless, water-insoluble liquid, consisting of mixtures of hydrocarbons obtained from petroleum by distillation: used chiefly as a lubricant, in the manufacture of cosmetics, and as a laxative.

min′eral spring′, a spring of water that contains a significant amount of dissolved minerals.

min′eral tar′ bitumen of the consistency of tar; maltha.

min′eral wa′ter, **1.** water containing dissolved mineral salts or gases, esp. such water for medicinal use. **2. mineral waters,** *Brit.* **a.** carbonated water; soda water. **b.** artificially flavored, bottled soft drinks; soda pop.

min′eral wax′, ozocerite.

min′eral wool′, a woollike material for heat and sound insulation, made by blowing steam or air through molten slag or rock. Also called **rock wool.**

Mi·ner·va (mi nûr′və), *n.* the ancient Roman goddess of wisdom and arts, identified with Greek goddess Athena.

min·e·stro·ne (min′i strō′nē; *It.* mē′ne strô′ne), *n. Italian Cookery.* a thick soup of vegetables and chicken or meat and bits of pasta. [< It = *minestr(a)* kind of soup (lit., something served; see MINISTER) + *-one* aug. suffix]

mine·sweep·er (mīn′swē′pər), *n. Navy.* a vessel or ship used for dragging a body of water in order to remove enemy mines. —**mine′sweep′ing,** *n.*

Ming (ming), *n.* **1.** a dynasty in China, 1368–1644, marked by the development of the arts, esp. in porcelain, textiles, and painting. —*adj.* **2.** noting the fine porcelains produced in the Ming dynasty, esp. those produced before 1620.

min·gle (ming′gəl), *v.,* **-gled, -gling.** —*v.i.* **1.** to become mixed, blended, or united. **2.** to associate or mix in company. **3.** to take part with others; participate. —*v.t.* **4.** to mix or combine; put together in a mixture; blend. **5.** to unite, join, or conjoin. **6.** to cause to associate in company. **7.** to form by mixing; compound; concoct. [ME *mengle,* freq. (with -LE suffix) of *mengen,* OE *mengan* to mix; c. D, G *mengen*] —**min′gle·ment,** *n.* —**min′gler,** *n.*

ming′ tree′ (ming), an artificially dwarfed tree resembling a bonsai. [? after MING]

Mi·nho (mē′nyōō), *n.* a river in SW Europe, flowing SSW from NW Spain along the N boundary of Portugal into the Atlantic. 171 mi. long. Spanish, **Miño.**

Min·how (min′hō′), *n.* Foochow.

min·i (min′ē), *n. Informal.* **1.** miniskirt. **2.** anything that is smaller than is normal or customary. **3.** subcompact (def. 2). [by shortening]

mini-, a combining form of **miniature,** used with the following particular meanings: "very short" (*miniskirt*); "small," "lightweight" (*minicar*); "on a small scale," "in reduced size" (*minicomputer; minicalculator*); "of limited scope or intensity" (*minirecession*).

min·i·a·ture (min′ē ə chər, min′ə chər), *n.* **1.** a representation or image of something on a small or reduced scale. **2.** a greatly reduced or abridged form. **3.** a very small painting, esp. a portrait, on ivory, vellum, or the like. **4.** the art of executing such paintings. **5.** an illumination in an illuminated manuscript or book. **6. in miniature,** in a greatly reduced size. —*adj.* **7.** being, on, or represented on a very small scale; reduced. **8.** pertaining to a system of photography using 35-millimeter film. [< It *miniatura* < ML = *miniāt(us)* rubricated, illuminated, L: colored with red lead (see MINIUM, -ATE[1]) + *-ūra* -URE]

min′iature cam′era, *Photog.* a small camera using a 35-millimeter film.

min′iature golf′, a game or amusement modeled on golf and played with a putter and golf ball, in which each very short, grassless "hole" constitutes an obstacle course, through which the ball must be driven.

min′iature photog′raphy, photography with a camera using 35-millimeter film.

min·i·a·tur·ize (min′ē ə chə rīz′, min′ə-), *v.t.,* **-ized, -iz·ing.** **1.** to make in an extremely small size in order to keep volume and weight to a minimum: *to miniaturize the electronic equipment in a spacecraft.* **2.** to produce an exact working copy on a very small scale. —**min′i·a·tur·i·za′tion,** *n.*

min·i·bike (min′ē bīk′), *n.* a small, low-frame motorcycle.

min·i·bus (min′ē bus)′, *n., pl.* **-bus·es, -bus·ses.** a small bus.

Min·i·cam (min′ē kam′), *n. Trademark.* a small, portable electronic camera using microwave transmission for relaying its television pictures to a studio for broadcasting.

min·i·com·put·er (min′ē kəm pyōō′tər), *n.* a computer with processing and storage capabilities smaller than those of a full-sized computer, used by small businesses, in manufacturing processes, scientific research, etc.

Min′ié ball′ (min′ē, min′ē ā′; *Fr.* mē nyā′), a conical bullet with a hollow base that expanded when fired, used in the 19th century. [named after C. E. *Minié* (1814–79), French officer who invented it]

min·i·fy (min′ə fī′), *v.t.,* **-fied, -fy·ing.** **1.** to make less. **2.** to minimize. [< L *min(us)* less + -IFY, modeled on MAGNIFY] —**min′i·fi·ca′tion,** *n.*

min·i·kin (min′ə kin), *n.* **1.** a person who or object that is delicate or diminutive. —*adj.* **2.** delicate; dainty; mincing. [< MD *minneken* = *minne* love + *-ken* -KIN]

min·im (min′əm), *n.* **1.** the smallest unit of liquid measure, the sixtieth part of a fluid dram, roughly equivalent to one drop. *Symbol:* M, ♏ *Abbr.:* min, min. **2.** *Music.* a note, formerly the shortest in use, but now equivalent in time value to one half of a semibreve; half note. See illus. at **note.** **3.** the least quantity of anything. **4.** something very small or insignificant. —*adj.* **5.** smallest; very small. [late ME]

min·i·ma (min′ə mə), *n.* a pl. of **minimum.**

min·i·mal (min′ə məl), *adj.* **1.** pertaining to or being a minimum. **2.** least possible. **3.** smallest; very small. —**min′i·mal·ly,** *adv.*

min′imal art′, a style in painting and sculpture characterized by an impersonality and formal simplicity, subsequently applied to architecture, design, dance, theater, and music. Also called **min′i·mal·ism.**

min′imal pair′, *Linguistics.* a pair of words, as *pin* and *bin,* or *bet* and *bed,* differing only by one phonemic feature in the same position in each word.

min·i·mize (min′ə mīz′), *v.t.,* **-mized, -miz·ing.** **1.** to reduce to the smallest possible amount or degree. **2.** to belittle. —**min′i·mi·za′tion,** *n.* —**min′i·miz′er,** *n.*

min·i·mum (min′ə məm), *n., pl.* **-mums, -ma** (-mə), *adj.* —*n.* **1.** the least quantity or amount possible, allowable, etc. **2.** the lowest amount, value, or degree attained or recorded (opposed to *maximum*). 3. *Math.* a. the value of a function at a certain point in its domain that is less than or equal to the values at all other points in the immediate vicinity of the point. Cf. **absolute minimum.** b. the point in the domain at which a minimum occurs. —*adj.* 4. noting or pertaining to a minimum or minimums. [< L, neut. of *minimus* smallest, least. See MINOR]

min′imum wage′, the lowest fixed wage payable to employees of a particular group according to law or to union agreement.

min·ing (mī′niŋ), *n.* 1. the act, process, or industry of extracting ores, coal, etc., from mines. 2. the laying of explosive mines.

min′ing engineer′ing, the branch of engineering dealing with the location and appraisal of mineral deposits and the laying out, equipment, and management of mines. —**min′ing engineer′.**

min·ion (min′yən), *n.* 1. a servile follower or subordinate of a person in power. 2. any favored or highly regarded person. 3. a minor official. 4. *Print.* a 7-point type. [< MF *mignon,* r. OF *mignot* dainty < ?]

min·i·park (min′ēpärk), *n.* See **pocket park.**

min·i·se·ries (min′ē sēr′ēz), *n., pl.* **-ries.** 1. a short series of things, as events or presentations. 2. *Television.* a special program, dramatic presentation, etc., that is shown in three or more installments, often on successive evenings. Also, **min′i·se′ries.**

min·ish (min′ish), *v.t., v.i.* *Archaic.* to diminish or lessen. [late ME, var. of *menuse* < MF *menu(i)sier* < VL **minūtiāre* to lessen. See MINUTE[2], MINCE]

min·i·skirt (min′ē skûrt′), *n.* a very short skirt, esp. one ending three or more inches above the knee. [MINI- + SKIRT] —**min′i·skirt′ed,** *adj.*

min·is·ter (min′i stər), *n.* 1. a person authorized to conduct religious worship; clergyman; pastor. 2. a person authorized to administer sacraments, as at Mass. 3. (*often cap.*) (chiefly in Europe) a person appointed to some high office of state, esp. to that of head of an administrative department: *Minister of Transport.* 4. a diplomatic representative ranking below an ambassador. Cf. **envoy**[1] (def. 1). 5. a person acting as the agent or instrument of another. —*v.i.* 6. to perform the functions of a religious minister. 7. to give service, care, or aid. 8. to contribute, as to comfort, happiness, etc. —*v.t.* 9. to administer or apply. 10. *Archaic.* to furnish, supply. [< L: servant = *minis-* less (var. of *minor*) + *-ter* n. suffix; r. ME *menistre* < OF]

min·is·te·ri·al (min′i stēr′ē əl), *adj.* 1. pertaining to the ministry of religion, or to a minister or clergyman. 2. (chiefly in Europe) pertaining to a ministry or minister of state. 3. pertaining to or invested with delegated executive authority. 4. of ministry or service. 5. serving as an instrument or means; instrumental. [< LL *ministeriāl(is)*] —**min′is·te′ri·al·ly,** *adv.*

min′ister plenipoten′tiary, plenipotentiary (def. 1).

min′ister without′ portfo′lio, *pl.* **ministers without portfolios.** a minister of state who is not appointed to any specific department.

min·is·trant (min′i strənt), *adj.* 1. ministering. —*n.* 2. a person who ministers. [< L *ministrant-* (s. of *ministrāns*) serving, prp. of *ministrāre*]

min·is·tra·tion (min′i strā′shən), *n.* the act or an instance of ministering care, aid, religious service, etc. [< L *ministrātiōn-* (s. of *ministrātiō*) service = *ministrāt(us)* served (ptp. of *ministrāre*) + *-iōn-* -ION] —**min′is·tra′tive,** *adj.*

min·is·try (min′i strē), *n., pl.* **-tries.** 1. the service, functions, or profession of a minister of religion. 2. the body or class of ministers of religion; clergy. 3. the service, function, or office of a minister of state. 4. the body of ministers of state. 5. (*usually cap.*) any of the administrative departments of certain countries. 6. (*usually cap.*) the building that houses such an administrative department. 7. the term of office of a minister. 8. ministration; service. [ME < L *ministeri(um).* See MINISTER, -Y[3]]

min·i·track (min′i trak′), *n.* the procedure of tracing the orbit of an artificial satellite and of recording its signals by telemeter. [MINI(ATURE) + TRACK]

min·i·um (min′ē əm), *n.* See **red lead.** [ME < L: cinnabar, red lead < Iberian; cf. Basque *armineā* cinnabar]

min·i·ver (min′ə vər), *n.* 1. (in the Middle Ages) a white fur used for linings and trimmings. Cf. **vair** (def. 1). 2. any white fur, particularly that of the ermine, used esp. on robes of state. [ME *meniver* < MF *menu vair* small VAIR; see MENU]

Mink, *Mustela vison* (Total length 2 ft.; tail to 9 in.)

mink (miŋk), *n., pl.* **minks,** (*esp. collectively*) **mink.** 1. a semiaquatic weasellike animal of the genus *Mustela,* esp. the North American *M. vison.* 2. the valuable fur of this animal, brownish with lustrous outside hairs and a thick, soft undercoat. 3. a garment made of this fur, as a woman's coat or stole. [late ME; akin to or < Sw *mänk*]

Min·kow·ski (miŋ kôf′skē), *n.* **Her·mann** (hûr′mən; *Ger.* heʀ′män), 1864–1909, German mathematician.

Minkow′ski world′, *Math.* a four-dimensional space in which the fourth coordinate is time and in which a single event is represented as a point. Also called **Minkow′ski u′niverse.** [named after H. MINKOWSKI]

Minn., Minnesota.

Min·ne·ap·o·lis (min′ē ap′ə lis), *n.* a city in SE Minnesota, on the Mississippi. 434,400 (1970). —**Min·ne·a·pol·i·tan** (min′ē ə pol′i tᵊn), *n.*

min·ne·sing·er (min′i siŋ′ər), *n.* one of a class of German lyric poets and singers of the 12th, 13th, and 14th centuries. [< G = *Minne* love + *Singer* singer]

Min·ne·so·ta (min′i sō′tə), *n.* 1. a state in the N central United States. 3,805,069 (1970); 84,068 sq. mi. *Cap.:* St. Paul. *Abbr.;* Minn., MN 2. a river flowing SE from the W border of Minnesota into the Mississippi near St. Paul. 332 mi. long. —**Min′ne·so′tan,** *adj., n.*

Min·ne·ton·ka (min′i toŋ′kə), *n.* 1. a city in E Minnesota, near Minneapolis. 35,737 (1970). 2. **Lake,** a lake in SE Minnesota, W of Minneapolis. 10 mi. long.

min·now (min′ō), *n., pl.* (*esp. referring to two or more kinds or species*) **-nows,** (*esp. collectively, Rare*) **-now.** 1. a small, European cyprinoid fish, *Phoxinus phoxinus.* 2. any other fish of the family *Cyprinidae,* including the carps, goldfishes, etc. 3. any of various other small fishes. [ME *minwe,* OE **mynwe* (fem.), *myne* (masc.); c. OHG *munewa* kind of fish]

Mi·ño (mē′nyô), *n.* Spanish name of **Minho.**

Mi·no·an (mi nō′ən), *adj.* 1. of or pertaining to the ancient civilization of the island of Crete, dating from about 3000 to 1100 B.C. —*n.* 2. a native or inhabitant of ancient Crete. [MINO(S) + -AN]

mi·nor (mī′nər) *adj.* 1. being the lesser, in some respect, of two persons or things. 2. being among the lesser, or less important, things or persons of a specified kind: *a minor composer; a minor wound.* 3. being under legal age (opposed to *major*). 4. *Music.* a. (of an interval) smaller by a chromatic half step than the corresponding major interval. b. (of a chord) having a minor third between the root and the note next above it. 5. of or pertaining to the minority. 6. *Educ.* of or pertaining to a student's minor field of study. —*n.* 7. a person under legal age. 8. a person of inferior rank or importance in a specified group, class, etc. 9. *Educ.* a subject or a course of study pursued subordinately or supplementarily to a major subject or course. 10. *Music.* a minor interval, chord, scale, etc. 11. **the minors,** *Sports.* the minor leagues. —*v.i.* 12. to choose and follow a specific minor course of study: *He minored in Greek literature.* [ME < L: smaller, less; akin to Icel *minni* smaller, Goth *minniza* younger, Skt *minâti* lessens] —**Syn.** 2. smaller, secondary, petty, unimportant, small. —**Ant.** 1. major.

Mi·nor·ca (mi nôr′kə), *n.* 1. Spanish, **Menorca.** one of the Balearic Islands, in the W Mediterranean. 50,217; 271 sq. mi. 2. one of a Mediterranean breed of white-skinned chickens.

Mi·nor·can (mi nôr′kən), *adj.* 1. of or pertaining to Minorca. —*n.* 2. a native or inhabitant of Minorca.

Mi·nor·ite (mī′nə rīt′), *n.* See **Friar Minor.** [(*friars*) MINOR (< ML *frātrēs minōrēs,* lit., inferior brothers, a name emphasizing their humility); see -ITE[1]]

mi·nor·i·ty (mi nôr′i tē, -nor′-, mī-), *n., pl.* **-ties,** *adj.* —*n.* 1. the smaller part or number; less than half of the whole. 2. a smaller party or group opposed to a majority, as in voting or other action. 3. Also called **minor′ity group′.** a group differing, esp. in race, religion, or ethnic background, from the majority of a population. 4. the state or period of being a minor or under legal age. —*adj.* 5. of or pertaining to a minority or minorities. [< ML *minōritās*]

minor′ity lead′er, *U.S. Govt.* the party member who directs the activities of the minority party on the floor of either the Senate or the House of Representatives.

mi′nor key′, *Music.* a key based on a minor scale.

mi′nor league′, *U.S.* any association of professional sports teams other than the acknowledged major leagues. —**mi′nor-league′,** *adj.* —**mi′nor-lea′guer,** *n.*

mi′nor mode′, *Music.* a scale or key in which the third degree is a minor third above the tonic.

mi′nor or′der, *Rom. Cath. Ch.* the degree or grade of acolyte, exorcist, lector, or ostiary. Cf. **major order.**

mi′nor plan′et, *Astron.* asteroid.

mi′nor prem′ise, *Logic.* See under **syllogism** (def. 1).

Mi′nor Proph′ets, Hosea, Joel, Amos, Obadiah, Jonah, Micah, Nahum, Habakkuk, Zephaniah, Haggai, Zechariah, and Malachi. Cf. **Major Prophets.**

mi′nor scale′, 1. Also called **harmonic minor scale.** a scale having half steps between the second and third, fifth and sixth, and seventh and eighth degrees, with whole steps for the other intervals. 2. Also called **melodic minor scale.** a scale having the third degree lowered a half step when ascending, and the seventh, sixth, and third degrees lowered a half step when descending.

mi′nor suit′, *Bridge.* diamonds or clubs. Cf. **major suit.**

mi′nor term′, *Logic.* See under **syllogism** (def. 1).

mi′nor tri′ad, *Music.* a triad consisting in root position of a root tone with a minor third and a perfect fifth above.

Mi·nos (mī′nəs, -nos), *n.* *Class. Myth.* a king of Crete, and husband of Pasiphaë: he ordered Daedalus to build the Labyrinth.

Mi·not (mī′nət), *n.* a city in N North Dakota. 32,290 (1970).

Min·o·taur (min′ə tôr′), *n.* *Class. Myth.* a monster, half bull and half man: housed in the Cretan Labyrinth, killed by Theseus. [< L *Mīnōtaur(us)* < Gk *Mīnṓtauros* = *Mīnṓ(s)* MINOS + *taûros* bull]

Minsk (minsk; *Russ.* mēnsk), *n.* a city in and the capital of Byelorussia, in the W Soviet Union in Europe. 1,273,000.

min·ster (min′stər), *n.* *Chiefly Brit.* 1. a church actually or historically connected with a monastery. 2. any large or important church, as a cathedral. [ME, OE *mynster* < VL **monister(ium),* var. of LL *monastērium* MONASTERY]

min·strel (min′strəl), *n.* 1. a medieval musician who sang or recited to the accompaniment of instruments. 2. a musician, singer, or poet. 3. one of a troupe of comedians, usually white men made up as black performers, presenting songs, jokes, etc. [ME *ministrel* < OF < LL *ministeriāl(is)* servant]

min′strel show′, stage entertainment featuring highly stylized comic dialogue, song, and dance performed by a troupe of actors in blackface.

min·strel·sy (min′strəl sē), *n.* 1. the art or practice of a minstrel. 2. minstrels' songs, ballads, etc. [ME *minstralcie*]

mint[1] (mint), *n.* 1. any aromatic, labiate herb of the genus *Mentha,* having opposite leaves and small, verticillate flowers, as the spearmint, peppermint, and horsemint. 2. any plant of the mint family, *Labiatae.* 3. a peppermint-flavored candy. —*adj.* 4. made or flavored with mint: *mint tea; mint jelly.* [ME, OE *minte* < L *ment(h)a* < Gk *mínthē*]

mint[2] (mint), *n.* 1. a place where money is produced under government authority. 2. *Informal.* a vast amount, esp. of money. —*adj.* 3. as issued to the public, without having been used: *a mint stamp; a book in mint condition.* **—*v.t.*** **4.** to make (coins, money, etc.) by stamping metal. **5.** to turn (metal) into coins. [ME *mynt,* OE *mynet* coin < L *monēta* coin, mint, after the temple of Juno *Monēta,* where Roman money was coined] **—mint′er,** *n.*

mint·age (min′tij), *n.* **1.** the act or process of minting. **2.** the output of a mint; coinage. **3.** the charge for or cost of minting or coining.

mint′ ju′lep, a tall, frosted drink made with bourbon, sugar, and ice and garnished with sprigs of mint.

mint·y (min′tē), *adj.,* **mint·i·er, mint·i·est.** having the flavor or aroma of mint.

min·u·end (min′yo͞o end′), *n. Arith.* a number from which another is subtracted. Cf. **subtrahend.** [< L *minuend(us)* (*numerus*) (the number) to be diminished or made smaller, (ger. of *minuere*) = *minu-* (see MINUS) + *-endus* ger. suffix]

min·u·et (min′yo͞o et′), *n.* **1.** a slow, stately dance in triple meter, popular in the 17th and 18th centuries. **2.** a piece of music for such a dance or in its rhythm. [< F *menuet,* (see MENU, -ET); so called from the shortness of the dancers' steps]

Min·u·it (min′yo͞o it), *n.* **Peter,** 1580–1638, Dutch colonial administrator in America: director general of New Netherland 1626–31.

mi·nus (mī′nəs), *prep.* **1.** less by the subtraction of; decreased by: *ten minus six.* **2.** lacking or without: *a book minus its title page.* **—*adj.*** **3.** involving or noting subtraction. **4.** algebraically negative: *a minus quantity.* **—*n.*** **5.** See **minus sign. 6.** a minus quantity. **7.** a deficiency or loss. [< L, neut. of *minor* less; see MINOR]

mi·nus·cule (min′ə skyo͞ol′, mi nus′kyo͞ol), *adj.* **1.** very small. **2.** (of letters or writing) small; not capital or majuscule. **—*n.*** **3.** a minuscule letter. **4.** a small cursive script developed in the 7th century A.D. from the uncial, which it afterward superseded. [< L *minuscul(us)* smallish] **—mi·nus′cu·lar,** *adj.*

mi′nus sign′, *Arith.* the symbol (–) denoting subtraction or a negative quantity.

min·ute[1] (min′it), *n., v.,* **-ut·ed, -ut·ing,** *adj.* **—*n.*** **1.** the sixtieth part of an hour; sixty seconds. **2.** an indefinitely short period of time: *I'll be with you in a minute.* **3.** a rough draft, summary, or memorandum. **4. minutes,** an official record of the meeting of an organization. **5.** *Geom.* the sixtieth part of a degree of angle or arc, often represented by the sign (′): *12°10′ equals twelve degrees, ten minutes.* **6. up to the minute,** modern; up-to-date. **—*v.t.*** **7.** to time to the minute. **8.** to record in a minute. **—*adj.*** **9.** quickly prepared; taking but little time to prepare: *minute rice.* [ME < ML *minūta,* n. use of fem. of *minūtus* MINUTE[2]] **—Syn. 2.** jiffy, second, instant, moment.

mi·nute[2] (mī no͞ot′, -nyo͞ot′, mi-), *adj.,* **-nut·er, -nut·est. 1.** extremely small in size, amount, extent, or degree. **2.** of minor importance; insignificant; trifling. **3.** attentive to or concerned with small details: *a minute examination.* [ME < L *minūt(us)* lessened, made smaller, hence, small (ptp. of *minuere*). See MINUS] **—mi·nute′ness,** *n.* **—Syn. 1.** infinitesimal, minuscule. See **little. 3.** detailed, exact, precise. **—Ant. 1.** large. **3.** cursory.

min′ute hand′ (min′it), the hand that indicates the minutes on a clock or watch.

min·ute·ly[1] (min′it lē), *adj.* **1.** occurring every minute. **—*adv.*** **2.** every minute; minute by minute. [MINUTE[1] + -LY]

mi·nute·ly[2] (mī no͞ot′lē, -nyo͞ot′-, mi-), *adv.* in a minute manner, form, or degree; in minute detail. [MINUTE[2] + -LY]

Min·ute·man (min′it man′), *n., pl.* **-men. 1.** (*sometimes l.c.*) one of a group of American militiamen during the Revolutionary period who held themselves in readiness for immediate military service. **2.** *U.S.* an intercontinental ballistic missile with three stages. **3.** a member of a small, secret, reactionary organization having the declared purpose of conducting guerrilla warfare in the event of a communist invasion of the U.S.

min′ute steak′ (min′it), a thin piece of beefsteak that can be cooked quickly.

mi·nu·ti·ae (mi no͞o′shē ē′, -nyo͞o′-), *n.pl., sing.* **-ti·a** (-shē ə, -shə). small or trivial details; trifling circumstances or matters. [< L, pl. of *minūtia* smallness] **—mi·nu′ti·al,** *adj.*

minx (mingks), *n.* a pert, impudent, or flirtatious girl. [? < LG *minsk* man, impudent woman; c. G *Mensch;* see MANNISH] **—minx′ish,** *adj.*

min·yan (mēn yän′; *Eng.* min′yən), *n., pl.* **min·ya·nim** (mēn yä nēm′), *Eng.* **min·yans.** *Hebrew.* the minimum number required to be present for the lawful conduct of a public Jewish service: 10 Jewish males at least 13 years of age. [lit., number, reckoning]

Mi·o·cene (mī′ə sēn′), *Geol.* **—*adj.*** **1.** noting or pertaining to an epoch of either the Tertiary or Neocene period, characterized by the presence of grazing mammals. See table at **era. —*n.*** **2.** the Miocene epoch or series. [*mio-* (< Gk *meíōn* less) + -CENE]

mi·o·sis (mī ō′sis), *n., pl.* **-ses** (-sēz). *Pathol.* excessive constriction of the pupil of the eye, as a result of drugs, disease, or the like. Also, **myosis.** Cf. **mydriasis.** [var. of *myosis* < Gk *mý(ein)* (to) shut (the eyes) + *-ōsis* -OSIS]

mi·ot·ic (mī ot′ik), *adj.* **1.** pertaining to or producing miosis. **—*n.*** **2.** a miotic drug. Also, **myotic.**

Miq·ue·lon (mik′ə lon′; *Fr.* mēkə lôɴ′), *n.* See **St. Pierre and Miquelon.**

mir (mēʀ), *n., pl.* **mi·ri** (mē′ʀi). *Russian.* a Russian village commune. [lit., world, peace]

MIr., Middle Irish. Also, **M.Ir.**

Mi·ra (mī′rə), *n. Astron.* a bright variable star in the constellation Cetus, having an average period of 330 days: the first known variable star.

Mir·a·beau (mir′ə bō′; *Fr.* mē ʀa bō′), *n.* **Ho·no·ré Ga·bri·el Vic·tor Ri·que·ti** (ô nô ʀā′ ga brē el′ vēk tôʀ′ ʀēkə tē′), **Count de,** 1749–91, French Revolutionary statesman and orator.

mi·ra·bi·le dic·tu (mē rä′bi le′ dik′to͞o; *Eng.* mi rab′ə lē dik′to͞o, -tyo͞o), *Latin.* strange to say; marvelous to relate.

mi·ra·cid·i·um (mī′rə sid′ē əm), *n., pl.* **-cid·i·a** (-sid′ē ə). the larva that hatches from the egg of a trematode worm or fluke. [< NL < LL *miracidion* < Gk *meirak-* (s. of *meîrax*) boy, girl + *-idion* -IDION] **—mi′ra·cid′i·al,** *adj.*

mir·a·cle (mir′ə kəl), *n.* **1.** an event in the physical world that surpasses all known human or natural powers and is ascribed to a divine or supernatural cause. **2.** a wonder; marvel. [ME; late OE *miracul* < L *mīrācul(um)* = *mīrā(rī)* (to) wonder at + *-culum* -CLE]

mir′acle drug′. See **wonder drug.**

mir′acle play′, a medieval dramatic form dealing with religious subjects such as Biblical stories or saints' lives, usually presented in a series or cycle by the craft guilds. Cf. **morality play, mystery play.**

mi·rac·u·lous (mi rak′yə ləs), *adj.* **1.** of the nature of a miracle; marvelous. **2.** having or seeming to have the power to work miracles: *miraculous drugs.* [< ML *mīrāculōs(us)*] **—mi·rac′u·lous·ly,** *adv.* **—mi·rac′u·lous·ness,** *n.*

—Syn. 1. wonderful, extraordinary. MIRACULOUS, PRETERNATURAL, SUPERNATURAL refer to that which seems to transcend the laws of nature. MIRACULOUS usually refers to an individual event that apparently contravenes known laws governing the universe: *a miraculous cure.* PRETERNATURAL suggests the possession of supernormal gifts or qualities: *Dogs have a preternatural sense of smell.* SUPERNATURAL suggests divine or superhuman properties: *supernatural aid in battle.* **—Ant. 1.** natural; prosaic, commonplace.

Mi·ra·flo·res (mir′ə flôr′əs, -flōr′-; *Sp.* mē′ʀä flô′ʀes), *n.pl.* the locks of the Panama Canal, near the Pacific entrance.

mi·rage (mi räzh′), *n.* **1.** an optical phenomenon by which reflected images of distant objects are seen, often inverted, when the air close to the ground is denser than the air above. **2.** something illusory, without substance, or without foundation in reality. [< F = (*se*) *mir(er)* (to) look at (oneself), be reflected (< L *mīrārī* to wonder at) + *-age* -AGE]

mire (mīər), *n., v.,* **mired, mir·ing. —*n.*** **1.** a section of wet, swampy ground; bog; marsh. **2.** slimy soil, deep mud, or the like. **—*v.t.*** **3.** to cause to stick fast in mire. **4.** to involve in difficulties. **5.** to soil or bespatter with mire or filth. **—*v.i.*** **6.** to sink in mire or mud; stick. [ME < Scand; cf. Icel *mýrr* bog. c. OE *mēos* moss]

Mir·i·am (mir′ē əm), *n.* the sister of Moses and Aaron. Num. 26:59.

mirk (mûrk), *n., adj.* murk.

mirk·y (mûr′kē), *adj.,* **mirk·i·er, mirk·i·est.** murky.

Mi·ró (mē rō′; *Sp.* mē ʀô′), *n.* **Joan** (hwän), 1893–1983, Spanish painter.

mir·ror (mir′ər), *n.* **1.** a reflecting surface, usually of glass with a metallic or amalgam backing and set in a frame. **2.** any reflecting surface, as the surface of calm water. **3.** *Optics.* a surface that is either plane, concave, or convex and that reflects rays of light. **4.** something that gives a faithful representation. **5.** a pattern for imitation; exemplar. **—*v.t.*** **6.** to reflect in or as in a mirror. **7.** to be or give a faithful representation of. [ME *mirour* < OF *mireo(u)r* = *mir-* (see MIRAGE) + *-eo(u)r* < L *-ātor;* see -OR[2]] **—mir′ror·like′,** *adj.*

mir′ror im′age, an image of an object, as it would appear if viewed in a mirror, with right and left reversed.

mirth (mûrth), *n.* **1.** rejoicing; gaiety or jollity. **2.** amusement or laughter. [ME *mirthe,* OE *myrigth.* See MERRY, -TH[1]] **—mirth′ful,** *adj.* **—mirth′ful·ly,** *adv.* **—mirth′ful·ness,** *n.* **—mirth′less,** *adj.* **—mirth′less·ly,** *adv.* **—mirth′less·ness,** *n.*

—Syn. MIRTH, GLEE, HILARITY, MERRIMENT, JOLLITY, JOVIALITY refer to the gaiety characterizing people who are enjoying the companionship of others. MIRTH suggests spontaneous amusement or gaiety, manifested briefly in laughter: *uncontrolled outbursts of mirth.* GLEE suggests an effervescence of high spirits or exultation, often manifested in playful or ecstatic gestures; it may apply also to a malicious rejoicing over mishaps to others: *glee over the failure of a rival.* HILARITY implies noisy and boisterous mirth, often exceeding the limits of reason or propriety: *hilarity aroused by practical jokes.* MERRIMENT suggests fun, good spirits, and good nature rather than the kind of wit and funmaking that cause hilarity: *The house resounded with music and sounds of merriment.* JOLLITY and JOVIALITY may refer either to a general atmosphere of mirthful festivity or to the corresponding traits of individuals. JOLLITY implies an atmosphere of easy and convivial gaiety, a more hearty merriment or a less boisterous hilarity: *The holiday was a time of jollity.* JOVIALITY implies a more masculine merriment generated by people who are hearty, generous, benevolent, and high-spirited: *the joviality of friends.*

MIRV (mûrv), *n.* a guided missile that carries several warheads, each of which can be aimed at a different target. [*m(ultiple) i(ndependently targeted) r(eentry) v(ehicle)*]

mir·y (mīər′ē), *adj.,* **mir·i·er, mir·i·est. 1.** of the nature of mire; swampy: *miry ground.* **2.** abounding in mire; muddy. **3.** covered or bespattered with mire; dirty. [ME] **—mir′i·ness,** *n.*

MIS, See **management information system.** Also, **M.I.S.**

mis-[1], a prefix applied to various parts of speech, meaning "ill," "mistaken," "wrong," "wrongly," "incorrectly," or simply negating: *mistrial; misprint; mistrust.* [ME; OE *mis(se)-*; c. G *miss-,* Goth *missa-* (see MISS[1]); often r. ME *mes-* < OF < WGmc *mis(s)-*]

mis-[2], var. of **miso-** before some vowels: *misanthrope.*

mis·ad·ven·ture (mis′əd ven′chər), *n.* **1.** an instance of bad fortune; mishap. **2.** bad fortune. [MIS-[1] + ADVENTURE; r. ME *mesaventure* < OF] **—Syn. 1.** mischance, accident; disaster, calamity. **2.** misfortune.

mis·al·li·ance (mis′ə lī′əns), *n.* an improper alliance or association, esp. in marriage; mésalliance. [modeled on F *mésalliance*]

mis·an·thrope (mis′ən thrōp′, miz′-), *n.* a hater of mankind. Also, **mis·an·thro·pist** (mis an′thrə pist, miz-). [< Gk *mīsánthrōp(os)* hating mankind, misanthropic] **—mis·an·throp·ic** (mis′ən throp′ik, miz′-), **mis′an·throp′i·cal,** *adj.* **—mis′an·throp′i·cal·ly,** *adv.*

mis·an·thro·py (mis an′thrə pē, miz-), *n.* hatred, dislike, or distrust of mankind. [< Gk *mīsanthrōpía*]

---

mis·act′, *v.i.*
mis·add′, *v.*
mis′ad·dress′, *v.t.*
mis′ad·just′, *v.*
mis′ad·just′ment, *n.*
mis′ad·min′is·tra′tion, *n.*
mis′ad·vise′, *v.t.,* **-vised, -vis·ing.**
mis′a·lign′ment, *n.*
mis′al·lot′ment, *n.*
mis′al·ly′, *v.t.,* **-lied, ly·ing.**
mis·al′pha·bet·ize′, *v.t.,* **-ized, -iz·ing.**
mis·an′a·lyze′, *v.t.,* **-lyzed, -lyz·ing.**

mis·ap·pre·hend (mis′ap ri hend′), *v.t.* to misunderstand. —**mis′ap·pre·hend′ing·ly,** *adv.*

mis·ap·pre·hen·sion (mis′ap ri hen′shən), *n.* misunderstanding; misconception. —**mis′ap·pre·hen′sive,** *adj.* —**mis′ap·pre·hen′sive·ly,** *adv.* —**mis′ap·pre·hen′sive·ness,** *n.*

mis·ap·pro·pri·ate (mis′ə prō′prē āt′), *v.t.,* **-at·ed, -at·ing.** to put to a wrong use, as funds entrusted to one's care. —**mis′ap·pro′pri·a′tion,** *n.*

mis·be·come (mis′bi kum′), *v.t.,* **-came, -come, -com·ing.** to be unsuitable, unbecoming, or unfit for.

mis·be·got·ten (mis′bi got′ən), *adj.* **1.** Also, **mis′be·got′.** unlawfully or irregularly begotten; illegitimate. **2.** ill-conceived.

mis·be·have (mis′bi hāv′), *v.,* **-haved, -hav·ing.** —*v.i.* **1.** to behave badly or improperly. —*v.t.* **2.** to conduct (oneself) without regard for good manners or accepted moral standards. [late ME] —**mis′be·hav′er,** *n.*

mis·be·ha·vior (mis′bi hāv′yər), *n.* improper, inappropriate, or bad behavior. Also, *esp. Brit.,* **mis′be·hav′iour.** [ME]

mis·be·lief (mis′bi lēf′), *n.* **1.** erroneous belief; false opinion. **2.** erroneous or unorthodox religious belief. [ME]

mis·be·lieve (mis′bi lēv′), *v.,* **-lieved, -liev·ing.** *Obs.* —*v.i.* **1.** to believe wrongly; hold an erroneous belief. —*v.t.* **2.** to disbelieve; doubt. [ME] —**mis′be·liev′er,** *n.* —**mis′be·liev′ing·ly,** *adv.*

misc., **1.** miscellaneous. **2.** miscellany.

mis·cal·cu·late (mis kal′kyə lāt′), *v.t., v.i.,* **-lat·ed, -lat·ing.** to calculate or judge incorrectly: *to miscalculate the time required for a job.* —**mis′cal·cu·la′tion,** *n.* —**mis·cal′cu·la′tor,** *n.*

mis·call (mis kôl′), *v.t.* to call by a wrong name. [ME] —**mis·call′er,** *n.*

mis·car·riage (mis kar′ij *or, for 3,* mis′kar-), *n.* **1.** failure to attain the just, proper, or desired result: *a miscarriage of justice.* **2.** failure of something sent, as a letter, to reach its destination. **3.** the expulsion of a fetus before it is viable, esp. between the third and seventh months of pregnancy. Cf. **abortion** (def. 1).

mis·car·ry (mis kar′ē), *v.i.,* **-ried, -ry·ing. 1.** to fail to attain the right or desired end; be unsuccessful. **2.** to go astray or be lost in transmission. **3.** to have a miscarriage of a fetus. [ME *miscarie(n)*]

mis·cast (mis kast′, -käst′), *v.t.,* **-cast, -cast·ing.** to cast ineptly or with poor judgment: *to miscast a play; to miscast an actor.*

mis·ce·ge·na·tion (mis′i jə nā′shən, mi sej′ə-), *n.* **1.** marriage or cohabitation between a man and woman of different races. **2.** interbreeding between members of different races. [< L *miscē(re)* (to) mix + *gen(us)* race, stock, species + -ATION] —**mis·ce·ge·net·ic** (mis′i jə net′ik, mi sej′ə-), *adj.*

mis·cel·la·ne·a (mis′ə lā′nē ə), *n.pl.* miscellaneous writings, papers, or objects. [< L: hash, hodgepodge, n. use of neut. pl. of *miscellāneus* MISCELLANEOUS]

mis·cel·la·ne·ous (mis′ə lā′nē əs), *adj.* **1.** consisting of members or elements of different kinds. **2.** having various qualities or aspects. **3.** dealing with various subjects: *a miscellaneous discussion.* [< L *miscellāneus* mixed, of all sorts = *miscell(us)* mixed + *-āneus* -ANEOUS] —**mis′cel·la′ne·ous·ly,** *adv.* —**Syn. 1.** varied. **2.** heterogeneous, diversified.

mis·cel·la·ny (mis′ə lā′nē; *Brit.* mi sel′ə nē), *n., pl.* **-nies. 1.** a miscellaneous collection or group of various or unselected items. **2.** a volume of literary pieces by several authors, dealing with various topics. **3.** Often, **miscellanies,** a miscellaneous collection of articles or entries, as in a book. [Anglicized var. of MISCELLANEA]

mis·chance (mis chans′, -chäns′), *n.* a mishap or misfortune. [r. ME *mescheance* < OF]

mis·chief (mis′chif), *n.* **1.** a tendency or disposition to tease or annoy. **2.** conduct or actions resulting from this disposition. **3.** conduct or actions resulting in harm or trouble: *malicious mischief.* **4.** a source of harm or trouble. **5.** harm or trouble: *to come to mischief.* [ME *meschef* < OF, back formation from *meschever* to end badly, come to grief. See MIS-[1], ACHIEVE] —**Syn. 5.** hurt. See **damage.**

mis·chief-mak·er (mis′chif mā′kər), *n.* a person who makes mischief, as one who stirs up discord by gossiping. —**mis′chief-mak′ing,** *adj., n.*

mis·chie·vous (mis′chə vəs), *adj.* **1.** harmful or injurious. **2.** having or revealing a disposition to cause mischief. [ME *mischevous* < AF *meschevous*] —**mis′chie·vous·ly,** *adv.* —**mis′chie·vous·ness,** *n.*

mis·ci·ble (mis′ə bəl), *adj.* capable of being mixed: *miscible ingredients.* [< L *misc(ēre)* (to) mix, mingle + -IBLE] —**mis′ci·bil′i·ty,** *n.*

mis·con·ceive (mis′kən sēv′), *v.t., v.i.,* **-ceived, -ceiv·ing.** to conceive wrongly; misunderstand. [ME] —**mis′con·ceiv′er,** *n.*

mis·con·cep·tion (mis′kən sep′shən), *n.* an erroneous conception; mistaken notion.

mis·con·duct (*n.* mis kon′dukt; *v.* mis′kən dukt′), *n.* **1.** improper conduct; wrong behavior. **2.** unlawful conduct by an official in regard to his office. —*v.t.* **3.** to mismanage. **4.** to misbehave (oneself).

mis·con·struc·tion (mis′kən struk′shən), *n.* the act or an instance of misconstruing; misinterpretation.

mis·con·strue (mis′kən strōō′ *or, esp. Brit.,* mis kon′strōō), *v.t.,* **-strued, -stru·ing.** to misunderstand the meaning of; take in a wrong sense; misinterpret. [ME] —**Syn.** misread, misapprehend, misjudge.

mis·count (mis kount′), *v.t., v.i.* **1.** to count or calculate erroneously. —*n.* **2.** an erroneous counting or miscalculation. [r. ME *mesconten* < MF *mesconter*]

mis·cre·ance (mis′krē əns), *n.* a wrong belief, misbelief, or false religious faith. [ME < MF *mescreance* = *mes-* MIS-[1] + *creance* < VL **crēdentia* CREDENCE]

mis·cre·an·cy (mis′krē ən sē), *n.* **1.** the state or condition of a miscreant; villainy. **2.** *Archaic.* miscreance.

mis·cre·ant (mis′krē ənt), *adj.* **1.** depraved, villainous, or base. **2.** misbelieving; holding a false or unorthodox religious belief. —*n.* **3.** a vicious person; villain. **4.** a misbelieving person, as a heretic or an infidel. [ME < MF *mescreant* unbelieving = *mes-* MIS-[1] + *creant* < L *crēdent-* CREDENT]

mis·cre·ate (*v.* mis′krē āt′; *adj.* mis′krē it, -āt′), *v.,* **-at·ed, -at·ing,** *adj.* —*v.t., v.i.* **1.** to create amiss or deformed. —*adj.* **2.** *Archaic.* miscreated. —**mis′cre·a′tion,** *n.*

mis·cre·at·ed (mis′krē ā′tid), *adj.* wrongly created; misshapen; monstrous.

mis·cue[1] (mis kyōō′), *n., v.,* **-cued, -cu·ing.** —*n.* **1.** *Informal.* a mistake. —*v.i.* **2.** *Informal.* to make a mistake. **3.** *Theat.* to fail to answer one's cue or to answer another's cue. [MIS-[1] + CUE[1]]

mis·cue[2] (mis kyōō′), *n., v.,* **-cued, -cu·ing.** *Billiards, Pool.* —*n.* **1.** a stroke in which the cue fails to make solid contact with the cue ball. —*v.i.* **2.** to make a miscue. [MIS-[1] + CUE[2]]

mis·date (mis dāt′), *v.,* **-dat·ed, -dat·ing,** *n.* —*v.t.* **1.** to assign or affix a wrong date to. —*n.* **2.** a wrong date.

mis·deal (mis dēl′), *v.,* **-dealt, -deal·ing,** *n.* —*v.t., v.i.* **1.** to deal wrongly, esp. to deal the wrong number at cards. —*n.* **2.** an incorrect deal. —**mis·deal′er,** *n.*

mis·deed (mis dēd′), *n.* an immoral or wicked deed. [ME *misdede,* OE *misdǣd*]

mis·de·mean (mis′di mēn′), *v.t.* *Rare.* to misbehave (oneself). [late ME; see MIS-[1], DEMEAN[2]]

mis·de·mean·ant (mis′di mē′nənt), *n.* **1.** a person who is guilty of misbehavior. **2.** *Law.* a person who has been convicted of a misdemeanor.

mis·de·mean·or (mis′di mē′nər), *n.* **1.** misbehavior or an instance of it. **2.** *Law.* a criminal offense defined as less serious than a felony. Also, *esp. Brit.,* **mis′de·mean′our.** —**Syn. 1.** transgression, fault; offense.

mis·do (mis dōō′), *v.t.,* **-did, -done, -do·ing.** to do wrongly; botch. [ME *misdo(n),* OE *misdōn*] —**mis·do′er,** *n.*

mis·doubt (mis dout′), *v.t., v.i.* **1.** to doubt or suspect. —*n.* **2.** doubt or suspicion.

mise (mēz, mīz), *n.* **1.** a settlement or agreement. **2.** *Law.* the issue in a proceeding instituted on a writ of right. [late ME < AF: a putting, setting down (e.g., of expenses), n. use of fem. of *mis* < L *miss(us)* sent, bestowed, ptp. of *mittere*]

mis·ease (mis ēz′), *n.* **1.** *Archaic.* discomfort or distress; suffering. **2.** *Obs.* poverty. [ME *misese* < OF *mesaise*]

mise en scène (mē zäN sen′), *French.* **1.** the act or art of placing actors, scenery, properties, etc., on stage. **2.** the stage setting of a play. **3.** surroundings; environment.

Mi·se·no (mē ze′nō), *n.* a cape in SW Italy, on the N shore of the Bay of Naples: ruins of ancient Roman naval station and resort.

mi·ser (mī′zər), *n.* **1.** a person who lives in wretched circumstances in order to save and hoard money. **2.** a niggardly, avaricious person. **3.** *Obs.* a wretched or unhappy person. [< L: wretched] —**Syn. 2.** niggard, skinflint, tightwad, pinchpenny.

mis·er·a·ble (miz′ər ə bəl, miz′rə-), *adj.* **1.** wretchedly unhappy or impoverished. **2.** of wretched character or quality; contemptible. **3.** attended with or causing misery: *a miserable existence.* **4.** revealing or expressing misery. **5.** worthy of pity; deplorable: *a miserable failure.* [late ME < L *miserābil(is)* = *miserā(rī)* (to) pity (< *miser* wretched) + *-bilis* -BLE] —**mis′er·a·ble·ness,** *n.* —**mis′er·a·bly,** *adv.* —**Syn. 1.** disconsolate, doleful, distressed. **2.** despicable, mean, low. **5.** pitiable, lamentable. —**Ant. 1.** happy.

Mis·e·re·re (miz′ə rår′ē, -rēr′ē), *n.* **1.** the 51st Psalm, or the 50th in the Douay Bible. **2.** a musical setting for it. **3.** (*l.c.*) a prayer or expression of appeal for mercy. **4.** (*l.c.*) misericord (def. 1). [< L: lit., have pity (impv.), first word of the Psalm]

mis·er·i·cord (miz′ər ə kôrd′, mi zer′ə kôrd′), *n.* **1.** a small projection on the underside of a hinged seat of a church stall that gives support, when the seat is lifted, to a person standing in the stall. **2.** a medieval dagger, used for the *coup de grâce* to a wounded foe. Also, **mis′er·i·corde′.** [ME *misericorde* < MF < L *misericordia* pity = *misericord-* (s. of *misericors*) compassionate (*miseri-,* s. *of miserēre* to pity + *cor* heart) + *-ia* -Y[3]]

mis·er·i·cor·di·a (mis′er i kōr′dē ä′; *Eng.* miz′ər ə kôr′dē ə), *n.* *Latin.* compassion; mercy.

mi·ser·ly (mī′zər lē), *adj.* of, like, or befitting a miser; penurious; niggardly. —**mi′ser·li·ness,** *n.* —**Syn.** stingy, parsimonious. —**Ant.** generous.

mis·er·y (miz′ə rē), *n., pl.* **-er·ies. 1.** wretchedness of condition or circumstances. **2.** distress caused by need, privation, or poverty. **3.** great distress of mind; extreme unhappiness. **4.** a cause or source of distress. **5.** *Dial.* **a.** a pain: *a misery in my left side.* **b.** rheumatism. **c.** Often, **miseries.** a case or period of despondency or gloom. [ME *miserie* < L *miseria* = *miser* wretched + *-ia* -Y[3]] —**Syn. 1.** tribulation, suffering. **3.** grief, anguish, woe. —**Ant. 3.** happiness.

mis·fea·sance (mis fē′zəns), *n.* *Law.* the wrongful per-

mis′ap·pel·la′tion, *n.*
mis′ap·pli·ca′tion, *n.*
mis′ap·ply′, *v.t.,* **-plied, -ply·ing.**
mis′ap·praise′, *v.t.,* **-praised, -prais·ing.**
mis′ar·range′, *v.t.,* **-ranged, -rang·ing.**
mis′ar·range′ment, *n.*
mis·cat′e·go·rize′, *v.t.,* **-rized, -riz·ing.**
mis·char′ac·ter·ize′, *v.t.,* **-ized, -iz·ing.**
mis·charge′, *v.,* **-charged, -charg·ing.**
mis′ci·ta′tion, *n.*
mis·cite′, *v.t.,* **-cit·ed, -cit·ing.**
mis·claim′, *v.t.*
mis′clas·si·fi·ca′tion, *n.*
mis·clas′si·fy′, *v.t.,* **-fied, -fy·ing.**
mis·col′or, *v.t.*
mis′com·pu·ta′tion, *n.*
mis′con·jec′ture, *v.,* **-tured, -tur·ing;** *n.*
mis·con′ju·gate′, *v.,* **-gat·ed, -gat·ing.**
mis·cop′y, *v.,* **-cop·ied, -cop·y·ing.**
mis′de·fine′, *v.t.,* **-fined, -fin·ing.**
mis′de·rive′, *v.i.,* **-rived, -riv·ing.**
mis′di·rect′, *v.t.*
mis′di·rec′tion, *n.*
mis·ed′u·cate′, *v.t.,* **-cat·ed, -cat·ing.**
mis′ed·u·ca′tion, *n.*
mis′em·ploy′, *v.t.*
mis′es·teem′, *v.t., n.*
mis·es′ti·mate′, *v.t.,* **-mat·ed, -mat·ing.**
mis·es′ti·mate, *n.*
mis·es′ti·ma′tion, *n.*

formance of a normally lawful act. Cf. **malfeasance, nonfeasance.** [< AF *mesfesance*] —**mis·feas′or,** *n.*

mis·file (mis fīl′), *v.t.*, **-filed, -fil·ing.** to file (papers, documents, records, etc.) incorrectly.

mis·fire (mis fīər′), *v.*, **-fired, -fir·ing,** *n.* —*v.i.* **1.** (of a gun, internal-combustion engine, or the like) to fail to fire. **2.** *Informal.* to fail to produce the intended effect. —*n.* **3.** a failure to fire on the part of a gun, internal-combustion engine, or the like.

mis·fit (mis′fit, mis fit′), *n.* **1.** a bad fit, as a garment that is too large or too small. **2.** a person who is badly adjusted to his environment.

mis·for·tune (mis fôr′chən), *n.* **1.** adverse fortune; bad luck. **2.** an instance of this; mischance; mishap.

mis·give (mis giv′), *v.*, **-gave, -giv·en, -giv·ing.** —*v.t.* **1.** (of one's mind, heart, etc.) to give doubt or apprehension to (oneself). —*v.i.* **2.** to be apprehensive.

mis·giv·ing (mis giv′ing), *n.* a feeling of doubt, distrust, or apprehension. —**mis·giv′ing·ly,** *adv.* —**Syn.** suspicion, mistrust. See **apprehension.**

mis·gov·ern (mis guv′ərn), *v.t.* to govern or manage badly. [late ME *misgoverne*] —**mis·gov′ern·ment,** *n.*

mis·guide (mis gīd′), *v.t.*, **-guid·ed, -guid·ing.** to direct wrongly; mislead. [MIS-[1] + GUIDE; r. ME *misgye(n)*; see GUY[2]] —**mis·guid′ance,** *n.*

mis·guid·ed (mis gī′did), *adj.* misled; mistaken: *misguided charity.* —**mis·guid′ed·ly,** *adv.*

mis·han·dle (mis han′dəl), *v.t.*, **-dled, -dling.** **1.** to treat or handle badly. **2.** to manage badly: *to mishandle an estate.*

mis·hap (mis′hap, mis hap′), *n.* an unfortunate accident. [ME]

Mish·a·wa·ka (mish′ə wô′kə), *n.* a city in N Indiana, near South Bend. 35,517 (1970).

mis·hear (mis hēr′), *v.t.*, **-heard, -hear·ing.** to hear incorrectly or imperfectly. [ME *misher(en)*, OE *mishīeran*]

mish·mash (mish′mosh′, -mash′), *n.* a confused mess; hodgepodge; jumble. Also, **mish·mosh** (mish′mosh′). [late ME; gradational formation based on MASH]

Mish·na (mish′nə; *Heb.* mēsh nä′), *n.*, *pl.* **Mish·na·yoth** (mish nä′yōt; *Heb.* mēsh nä yōt′). *Judaism.* Mishnah.

Mish·nah (mish′nə; *Heb.* mēsh nä′), *n.*, *pl.* **Mish·na·yoth** (mish nä′yōt; *Heb.* mēsh nä yōt′). *Judaism.* **1.** the section of the Talmud consisting of the collection of oral laws edited by Rabbi Judah ha-Nasi (A.D. c135–c210). **2.** an article of this section. [< Heb: teaching by oral repetition] —**Mish·na·ic** (mish nā′ik), **Mish′nic, Mish′ni·cal,** *adj.*

mis·in·form (mis′in fôrm′), *v.t.* to give false or misleading information to. [ME *misenfourme(n)*] —**mis′in·form′ant, mis′in·form′er,** *n.* —**mis·in·for·ma·tion** (mis′in fər mā′shən), *n.*

mis·in·ter·pret (mis′in tûr′prit), *v.t.* to interpret, explain, or understand incorrectly. —**mis′in·ter′pre·ta′tion,** *n.* —**mis′in·ter′pret·er,** *n.*

mis·join·der (mis join′dər), *n.* *Law.* a joining in one suit or action of causes or of parties not permitted to be so joined.

mis·judge (mis juj′), *v.t.*, *v.i.*, **-judged, -judg·ing.** to judge, estimate, or value wrongly or unjustly. —**mis·judg′er,** *n.* —**mis·judg′ing·ly,** *adv.* —**mis·judg′ment;** *esp. Brit.*, **mis·judge′ment,** *n.*

Mis·kolc (mish′kôlts), *n.* a city in N Hungary. 165,000 (est. 1964).

mis·la·bel (mis lā′bəl), *v.t.*, **-beled, -bel·ing** or (*esp. Brit.*) **-belled, -bel·ling.** to label wrongly or misleadingly: *to mislabel a bottle of medicine; to mislabel a package.*

mis·lay (mis lā′), *v.t.*, **-laid, -lay·ing.** **1.** to put in a place afterward forgotten. **2.** to lay or place wrongly, as a rug. [ME *mysse laye(n)*] —**mis·lay′er,** *n.*

mis·lead (mis lēd′), *v.t.*, **-led, -lead·ing.** **1.** to lead or guide wrongly; lead astray. **2.** to lead into error of conduct, thought, or judgment. [ME *mislede(n)*, OE *mislǣdan*] —**mis·lead′er,** *n.* —**Syn. 1.** misdirect. **2.** delude, deceive.

mis·lead·ing (mis lē′ding), *adj.* deceptive; tending to mislead. —**mis·lead′ing·ly,** *adv.*

mis·like (mis līk′), *v.t.*, **-liked, -lik·ing.** **1.** to dislike. **2.** *Archaic.* to displease. [ME *mislike(n)*, OE *mislīcian*]

mis·man·age (mis man′ij), *v.t.*, **-aged, -ag·ing.** to manage incompetently or dishonestly. —**mis·man′age·ment,** *n.*

mis·mar·riage (mis mar′ij), *n.* an unsuitable or unhappy marriage.

mis·match (mis mach′), *v.t.* **1.** to match badly or unsuitably. —*n.* **2.** a bad or unsatisfactory match.

mis·mate (mis māt′), *v.t.*, *v.i.*, **-mat·ed, -mat·ing.** to mate unsuitably or wrongly.

mis·no·mer (mis nō′mər), *n.* **1.** a misapplied name or designation. **2.** an error in naming a person or thing. [late ME < AF, MF *mesnomer* to misname = *mes-* MIS-[1] + *nomer* < L *nōmināre*; see NOMINATE]

miso-, a combining form referring to hate: *misogyny.* Also, **mis-.** [< Gk, comb. form of *mīseîn* to hate, *mîsos* hatred]

mi·sog·a·my (mi sog′ə mē, mī-), *n.* hatred of marriage. —**mis·o·gam·ic** (mis′ə gam′ik, mī′sə-), *adj.* —**mi·sog′a·mist,** *n.*

mi·sog·y·ny (mi soj′ə nē, mī-), *n.* hatred of women. [< Gk *mīsogynía* hatred of women. See MISO-, GYN-, -Y[3]] —**mi·sog′y·nic, mi·sog′y·nous, mi·sog′y·nis′tic,** *adj.* —**mi·sog′y·nist,** *n.*

mi·sol·o·gy (mi sol′ə jē, mī-), *n.* distrust or hatred of reason or reasoning. —**mi·sol′o·gist,** *n.*

mis·o·ne·ism (mis′ō nē′iz əm, mī′sō-), *n.* hatred or dislike of what is new or represents change. [< It *misoneismo(o)*. See MISO-, NEO-, -ISM] —**mis′o·ne′ist,** *n.* —**mis′o·ne·is′tic,** *adj.*

mis·pick·el (mis′pik′əl), *n.* arsenopyrite. [< G]

mis·place (mis plās′), *v.t.*, **-placed, -plac·ing.** **1.** to put in a wrong or forgotten place. **2.** to place or bestow improperly, unsuitably, or unwisely: *to misplace one's trust.* —**mis·place′ment,** *n.* —**Syn. 1.** mislay, lose. **2.** misapply.

mis′placed mod′ifier, *Gram.* a word, phrase, or clause that modifies an unintended word because of its placement or construction in a sentence, as, *When a small boy* in *When a small boy, a girl is of little interest.* Cf. **dangling participle.**

mis·play (mis plā′), *Sports, Games.* —*n.* **1.** a wrong play. **2.** a play prohibited by the rules. —*v.t.* **3.** to make an error or incorrect play on or with; play wrongly.

mis·plead·ing (mis plē′ding), *n.* *Law.* a mistake in pleading.

mis·print (*n.* mis′print′, mis print′; *v.* mis print′), *n.* **1.** a mistake in printing. —*v.t.* **2.** to print incorrectly.

mis·pri·sion (mis prizh′ən), *n.* *Law.* **1.** a violation of official duty by one in office. **2.** failure by one not an accessory to prevent or notify of treason or felony. **3.** a contempt against the government, monarch, or courts, as sedition or contempt of court. [ME < AF, OF *mesprision* = *mes-* MIS-[1] + *prision* < L *prēnsiōn-*, var. of *prehēnsiōn-* (s. of *prehēnsiō*) PREHENSION]

mis·prize (mis prīz′), *v.t.*, **-prized, -priz·ing.** **1.** to despise. **2.** to undervalue. [late ME *misprise* < MF *mesprisie(r)*]

mis·pro·nounce (mis′prə nouns′), *v.t.*, *v.i.*, **-nounced, -nounc·ing.** to pronounce incorrectly. —**mis·pro·nun·ci·a·tion** (mis′prə nun′sē ā′shən), *n.*

mis·quo·ta·tion (mis′kwō tā′shən), *n.* **1.** the act of misquoting. **2.** an instance or occasion of misquoting or of being misquoted.

mis·quote (mis kwōt′), *v.*, **-quot·ed, -quot·ing,** *n.* —*v.t.*, *v.i.* **1.** to quote incorrectly. —*n.* **2.** a quotation that is incorrect.

mis·read (mis rēd′), *v.t.*, **-read** (red), **-read·ing.** to read wrongly; misinterpret. [OE *misrǣdan*]

mis·re·mem·ber (mis′ri mem′bər), *v.t.*, *v.i.* **1.** to remember incorrectly. **2.** *Dial.* to fail to remember.

mis·rep·re·sent (mis′rep ri zent′), *v.t.* **1.** to represent incorrectly or falsely. **2.** to represent in an unsatisfactory manner. —**mis′rep·re·sen·ta′tion,** *n.* —**mis′rep·re·sen′ta·tive,** *adj.* —**mis′rep·re·sent′er,** *n.*

mis·rule (mis ro͞ol′), *n.*, *v.*, **-ruled, -rul·ing.** —*n.* **1.** bad or unwise rule; misgovernment. **2.** disorder or lawless tumult. —*v.t.* **3.** to misgovern. [ME *misreulen* (v.), *misreule* (n.)]

miss[1] (mis), *v.t.* **1.** to fail to hit or strike. **2.** to fail to encounter, meet, catch, etc.: *to miss a train.* **3.** to fail to take advantage of: *to miss a chance.* **4.** to fail to be present at or for: *to miss a day of school.* **5.** to notice the absence or loss of: *When did you first miss your wallet?* **6.** to regret the absence or loss of: *I miss you all dreadfully.* **7.** to escape or avoid: *He just missed being caught.* **8.** to fail to perceive or understand: *to miss the point of a remark.* —*v.i.* **9.** to fail to hit something. **10.** to fail of effect or success; be unsuccessful. **11. miss fire.** See **fire** (def. 20). —*n.* **12.** a failure to hit something. **13.** a failure of any kind. **14.** an omission. [ME *miss(en)*, OE *missan*; c. G *missen*]

miss[2] (mis), *n.*, *pl.* **miss·es.** **1.** (*cap.*) the conventional title of respect for an unmarried woman, prefixed to the name. **2.** (used by itself as a term of address, esp. to an unmarried woman): *Just one moment, miss!* **3.** a young unmarried woman; girl. [short for MISTRESS]

Miss., Mississippi.

mis·sal (mis′əl), *n.* **1.** (*sometimes cap.*) *Rom. Cath. Ch.* the book containing the prayers and rites of the Mass. **2.** any book of prayers or devotions. [ME < ML *missāle*, n. use of neut. of *missālis*. See MASS, -AL[1]]

mis·say (mis sā′), *v.*, **-said, -say·ing.** *Archaic.* —*v.t.* **1.** to say or speak ill of; abuse; slander. **2.** to say wrongly. —*v.i.* **3.** to speak wrongly or incorrectly. [ME *misseye(n)*]

mis·shape (mis shāp′, mish-), *v.t.*, **-shaped, -shaped** or **-shap·en, -shap·ing.** to shape badly or wrongly; deform. [late ME]

mis·shap·en (mis shā′pən, mish-), *adj.* badly shaped; deformed: *a misshapen body.* [late ME] —**mis·shap′en·ly,** *adv.* —**mis·shap′en·ness,** *n.*

mis·sile (mis′əl *or, esp. Brit.*, -īl), *n.* **1.** an object or weapon that is thrown, shot, or otherwise propelled to a target. **2.** See **guided missile.** —*adj.* **3.** capable of being used as a missile. **4.** used or designed for discharging missiles. [< L, neut. of *missilis*. See MISSION, -ILE]

mis·sile·man (mis′əl man′, -mən′), *n.*, *pl.* **-men.** **1.** a person who launches or operates guided missiles. **2.** a technician or scientist whose work pertains to missilery. Also called **mis·sil·eer** (mis′ə lēr′).

mis·sile·ry (mis′əl rē), *n.* the science of the construction and use of guided missiles. Also, **mis′sil·ry.**

miss·ing (mis′ing), *adj.* lacking, absent, or not found.

miss′ing link′, **1.** a hypothetical primate forming an evolutionary connection between the anthropoid apes and man. **2.** anything lacking for the completion of a series or sequence.

mis·sion (mish′ən), *n.* **1.** a group of persons acting on behalf of a government in a foreign country or outside their own territory. **2.** a specific task that a person or group of persons is sent to perform. **3.** a permanent diplomatic establishment abroad. **4.** *Mil.* an operational task, usually assigned by a higher headquarters. **5.** *Rocketry.* **a.** a rocket flight or trip. **b.** the tasks, tests, experiments, etc., that such a flight or its astronauts are to perform. **6.** a body of persons sent by a church to carry on religious work, esp. evangelization in foreign lands. **7.** the place of operation of such persons, or the territory for which they are responsible. **8.** a place for evangelical and philanthropic work, esp. in the poorer urban areas. **9.** a church or a region with a nonresident minister or priest. **10.** a series of special religious services for increasing religious devotion and for conversion. **11.** an assigned or self-imposed duty or task. —*adj.* **12.** (*usually cap.*) noting or pertaining to a style of American furniture of the early 20th century, created in supposed imitation of the furnishings of the Spanish missions of California and characterized by the use of dark, stained wood, by heaviness, and by extreme plainness. [< L *missiōn-* (s. of *missiō*) a sending off = *miss(us)* sent (ptp. of *mittere*) + *-iōn-* -ION]

mis·sion·ar·y (mish′ə ner′ē), *n.*, *pl.* **-ar·ies,** *adj.* —*n.* Also, **mis′sion·er. 1.** a person sent into a newly settled or

---

mis·gauge′, *v.t.*, **-gauged, -gaug·ing.**
mis′i·den′ti·fi·ca′tion, *n.*
mis′i·den′ti·fy′, *v.*, **-fied, -fy·ing.**
mis′in·struct′, *v.t.*
mis′in·struc′tion, *n.*
mis·name′, *v.t.*, **-named, -nam·ing.**
mis′nav·i·ga′tion, *n.*
mis·num′ber, *v.*
mis·phrase′, *v.t.*, **-phrased, -phras·ing.**
mis′pro·por′tion, *n.*
mis·reck′on, *v.*
mis′re·late′, *v.*, **-lat·ed, -lat·ing.**
mis′re·port′, *v.t.*, *n.*
mis′re·port′er, *n.*
mis·rhymed′, *adj.*

foreign region to carry on religious, educational, or medical work. **2.** a person who attempts to persuade or convert others to his position or principles. **3.** a person who is sent on a mission. **—adj. 4.** pertaining to or connected with religious missions. **5.** characteristic of a missionary.

Mis′sionary Ridge′, a ridge in NW Georgia and SE Tennessee: Civil War battle 1863.

mis·sis (mis′iz, -is), *n. Informal.* wife: *I'll have to ask the missis.* Also, **missus.** [var. of MISTRESS]

Mis·sis·sip·pi (mis′i sip′ē), *n.* **1.** a state in the S United States. 2,216,912 (1970); 47,716 sq. mi. *Cap.:* Jackson. *Abbr.:* Miss., MS **2.** a river flowing S from N Minnesota to the Gulf of Mexico: the principal river of the U.S. 2470 mi. long; from the headwaters of the Missouri to the Gulf of Mexico 3988 mi. long.

Mis·sis·sip·pi·an (mis′i sip′ē ən), *adj.* **1.** of or pertaining to the state of Mississippi or the Mississippi River. **2.** *Geol.* noting or pertaining to a period of the Paleozoic era, occurring from about 300 million to 350 million years ago and characterized by the increase of land areas and the development of winged insects: sometimes considered an epoch of the Carboniferous period. See table at **era.** **—n. 3.** a native or inhabitant of Mississippi. **4.** *Geol.* the Mississippian period or system.

mis·sive (mis′iv), *n.* **1.** a written message; letter. **—adj. 2.** sent or about to be sent, esp. of a letter from an official source. [late ME (*letter*) *missive* < ML (*littera*) *missīva* sent (letter). See MISSION, -IVE]

Mis·so·lon·ghi (mis′ə lông′gē), *n.* a town in W Greece, on the Gulf of Patras: Byron died here 1824. 13,837 (1951). Also, **Mesolonghi.**

Mis·sou·la (mi zo͞o′lə), *n.* a city in W Montana. 29,497 (1970).

Mis·sour·i (mi zo͝or′ē, -zo͝or′ə), *n.* **1.** a state in the central United States. 4,677,399 (1970); 69,674 sq. mi. *Cap.:* Jefferson City. *Abbr.:* Mo., MO **2.** a river flowing from SW Montana into the Mississippi N of St. Louis, Missouri. 2723 mi. long. **3. from Missouri,** *Informal.* unwilling to accept without proof; skeptical. **—Mis·sour′i·an,** *adj., n.*

Missour′i Com′promise, *U.S. Hist.* a proviso attached to a bill passed by Congress in 1820, by which slavery was to be excluded in any state formed from the Louisiana Territory north of latitude 36°30′N, except Missouri.

mis·speak (mis spēk′), *v.t., v.i.,* **-spoke, -spok·en, -speak·ing.** to speak, utter or pronounce incorrectly.

mis·spell (mis spel′), *v.t., v.i.,* **-spelled** or **-spelt, -spell·ing.** to spell incorrectly.

mis·spend (mis spend′), *v.t.,* **-spent, -spend·ing.** to spend improperly; squander; waste. [ME *misspende(n)*]

mis·state (mis stāt′), *v.t.,* **-stat·ed, -stat·ing.** to state wrongly or misleadingly; make a wrong statement about. **—mis·state′ment,** *n.*

mis·step (mis step′), *n.* **1.** a wrong step. **2.** an error or slip in conduct.

mis·sus (mis′əz, -əs), *n. Informal.* missis.

miss·y (mis′ē), *n., pl.* **miss·ies.** *Informal.* young miss; girl.

mist (mist), *n.* **1.** a cloudlike aggregation of minute globules of water suspended in the atmosphere at or near the earth's surface. **2.** a cloud of particles resembling this. **3.** *Meteorol.* a very thin fog in which the horizontal visibility is greater than one kilometer; drizzle. **4.** a haze before the eyes. **—v.i. 5.** to become misty. **6.** to rain in very fine drops; drizzle: *It was misting a while ago.* **—v.t. 7.** to make misty. [ME, OE; c. D, LG, Sw *mist;* akin to Gk *omíchlē* fog, Skt *megha* cloud] **—Syn. 1.** See **cloud.**

mis·tak·a·ble (mi stā′kə bəl), *adj.* capable of being or liable to be mistaken or misunderstood. **—mis·tak′a·bly,** *adv.*

mis·take (mi stāk′), *n., v.,* **-took, -tak·en, -tak·ing.** **—n. 1.** an error caused by a lack of skill, attention, knowledge, etc. **2.** a misunderstanding or misconception. **—v.t. 3.** to regard or identify wrongly (usually fol. by *for*): *I mistook him for the mayor.* **4.** to understand, interpret, or evaluate wrongly; misunderstand. **—v.i. 5.** to be in error. [ME < Scand; cf. Icel *mistaka* to take in error] **—mis·tak′er,** *n.* **—mis·tak′ing·ly,** *adv.* **—Syn. 1.** inaccuracy, erratum, fault, oversight. **4.** misjudge, err. **—Ant. 2.** understanding.

mis·tak·en (mi stā′kən), *adj.* **1.** being a mistake: *a mistaken idea.* **2.** making a mistake: *In that idea, you're mistaken.* **—mis·tak′en·ly,** *adv.* **—mis·tak′en·ness,** *n.* **—Syn. 1.** inaccurate, misconceived.

Mis·tas·si·ni (mis′tə sē′nē), *n.* a lake in E Canada, in Quebec province. 840 sq. mi.

mist·bow (mist′bō′), *n.* fogbow.

mis·ter (mis′tər), *n.* **1.** (*cap.*) the conventional title of respect for a man, prefixed to the name and to certain official designations (usually written *Mr.*). **2.** *Informal.* sir (used in direct address, omitting the name of the man addressed): *Watch it, mister!* **3.** the informal or social title used in addressing certain military, naval, or merchant-marine officers or cadets. [var. of MASTER]

Mis′ter Char′lie (chär′lē), *U.S. Slang* (*used derogatively by blacks*). the white man individually or collectively. Also, **Mis′ter Char′ley** (chär′lē), **Mr. Charlie, Mr. Charley.**

mist·flow·er (mist′flou′ər), *n.* a North American, composite plant, *Eupatorium* (*Conoclinium*) *coelestinum,* having heads of blue flowers.

mis·think (mis thingk′), *v.i.,* **-thought, -think·ing.** *Archaic.* to think incorrectly or unfavorably. [ME *misthenke(n)*]

Mis·ti (mēs′tē), *n.* See **El Misti.**

mis·time (mis tīm′), *v.t.,* **-timed, -tim·ing.** to time badly; perform, say, etc., at a bad or inappropriate time. [ME *mistime(n),* OE *mistīmian*]

mis·tle·toe (mis′əl tō′), *n.* **1.** a European plant, *Viscum album,* having yellowish flowers and white berries, growing parasitically on various trees, used in Christmas decorations. **2.** any of several other related, similar plants, as *Phoradendron flavescens,* of the U.S.: the state flower of Oklahoma. [ME *mistilto,* appar. back formation from OE *mistiltān* (*mistil* mistletoe, basil + *tān* twig), the *-n* being taken as pl. ending; c. Icel *mistilteinn*]

Mistletoe, *Phoradendron flavescens*

mis·took (mi sto͝ok′), *v.* pt. of **mistake.**

mis·tral (mis′trəl, mi sträl′), *n.* a cold, dry, northerly wind common in southern France and neighboring regions. [< MF < Pr; OPr *maistral* < L *magistrāl(is)* MAGISTRAL]

Mis·tral (mē stral′ *for 1;* mēs träl′ *for 2*), *n.* **1. Fré·dé·ric** (frā dā rēk′), 1830–1914, French Provençal poet. **2. Ga·bri·e·la** (gä′vrē e′lä), (*Lucila Godoy Alcayaga*), 1889–1957, Chilean poet and educator.

mis·trans·late (mis′trans lāt′, -tranz-, mis trans′lāt, -tranz′-), *v.t., v.i.,* **-lat·ed, -lat·ing.** to translate incorrectly. **—mis′trans·la′tion,** *n.*

mis·treat (mis trēt′), *v.t.* to treat badly or abusively. [late ME *mistrete*] **—mis·treat′ment,** *n.*

mis·tress (mis′tris), *n.* **1.** a woman in authority, as over a household, an institution, or a servant. **2.** the female owner of an animal. **3.** a woman who has the power of controlling or disposing of something. **4.** *Brit.* a female teacher; schoolmistress. **5.** a woman who has a continuing, illicit sexual relationship with a man. **6.** *Archaic.* sweetheart. **7.** *Archaic.* (used as a term of address preceding the full name of a married or unmarried woman.) [ME *maistresse* < MF, OF. See MASTER, -ESS]

mis′tress of cer′emonies, a woman who acts as master of ceremonies.

mis·tri·al (mis trī′əl, -trīl′), *n. Law.* **1.** a trial terminated without conclusion on the merits of the case because of some error in the proceedings. **2.** an inconclusive trial, as where the jury cannot agree.

mis·trust (mis trust′), *n.* **1.** lack of trust or confidence; distrust. **—v.t. 2.** to regard with mistrust; distrust. **3.** to suspect or surmise. **—v.i. 4.** to be distrustful. [ME *mistruste(n)*] **—mis·trust′ing·ly,** *adv.*

mis·trust·ful (mis trust′fəl), *adj.* full of mistrust; suspicious. **—mis·trust′ful·ly,** *adv.* **—mis·trust′ful·ness,** *n.*

mist·y (mis′tē), *adj.,* **mist·i·er mist·i·est. 1.** consisting of, abounding in, or clouded by mist. **2.** appearing as if seen through mist; indistinct; obscure; vague. [ME; OE *mistig*] **—mist′i·ly,** *adv.* **—mist′i·ness,** *n.*

mist·y-eyed (mis′tē īd′), *adj.* easily moved to the point of tears; sentimental.

mis·un·der·stand (mis′un dər stand′), *v.t., v.i.,* **-stood, -stand·ing. 1.** to misinterpret. **2.** to understand wrongly. [ME *misunderstonde(n)*]

mis·un·der·stand·ing (mis′un dər stan′ding), *n.* **1.** a failure to understand; mistake as to meaning. **2.** disagreement or dissension. [late ME] **—mis′un·der·stand′ing·ly,** *adv.* **—Syn. 1.** misapprehension, error. **2.** discord, difference, difficulty, quarrel. **—Ant. 2.** concord.

mis·un·der·stood (mis′un dər sto͝od′), *adj.* **1.** improperly interpreted. **2.** misjudged; unappreciated.

mis·us·age (mis yo͞o′sij, -zij), *n.* **1.** wrong or improper usage, as of words. **2.** bad or abusive treatment.

mis·use (*n.* mis yo͞os′; *v.* mis yo͞oz′), *n., v.,* **-used, -us·ing.** **—n. 1.** wrong or improper use; misapplication. **2.** *Obs.* illusage. **—v.t. 3.** to use wrongly or improperly; misapply. **4.** to treat abusively; maltreat. [ME]

mis·us·er[1] (mis yo͞o′zər), *n. Law.* abuse of a right; unlawful use of an office, franchise, benefit, etc. [n. use of MF *mesuser* to MISUSE]

mis·us·er[2] (mis yo͞o′zər), *n.* a person who misuses. [MIS-[1] + USER]

mis·val·ue (mis val′yo͞o), *v.t.,* **-ued, -u·ing.** to value wrongly, esp. to undervalue.

Mitch·ell (mich′əl), *n.* **1. Maria,** 1818–89, U.S. astronomer. **2. William,** 1879–1936, U.S. general: pioneer in the field of aviation. **3. Mount,** a mountain in W North Carolina: highest peak in the E United States, 6684 ft.

mite[1] (mīt), *n.* any of numerous small or minute arachnids of the order *Acarina,* including species that are parasitic on animals and plants or that are free-living, feeding on decaying matter and stored foods. [ME *myte,* OE *mīte;* c. MD *mīte,* OHG *miza* midge]

mite[2] (mīt), *n.* **1.** a very small sum of money. **2.** a very small object, creature, or bit of something. **3.** a coin of very small value. **—adv. 4.** to a small extent; somewhat (often prec. by *a*): *He's a mite selfish.* [ME *myte* < MD *mīte;* ult. identical with MITE[1]]

mi·ter (mī′tər), *n.* **1.** the official headdress of a bishop in the Western Church, a tall cap having an archlike outline in the front and back. **2.** *Judaism.* the official headdress of the high priest. **3.** an oblique surface formed on a piece of wood or the like so as to butt against an oblique surface on another piece to be joined with it. **—v.t. 4.** to bestow a miter upon, or raise to a rank entitled to it. **5.** to join with a miter joint. **6.** to cut to a miter. Also, *esp. Brit.,* **mitre.** [ME *mitre* < L *mitra* < Gk: turban, headdress]

Miter (def. 1) A, Lappet

mi′ter box′, *Carpentry.* a troughlike box with slotted sides for guiding a saw in making miters or cross cuts.

mi′ter joint′, a joint, between two pieces of wood or the like, each with a miter on the end.

mi′ter square′, *Carpentry.* an instrument for laying out miter joints.

mi·ter·wort (mī′tər wûrt′), *n.* **1.** any saxifragaceous herb of the genus *Mitella,* having a capsule that resembles a bishop's miter. **2.** a low, loganiaceous plant, *Cynoctonum Mitreola,* of the southwestern U.S.

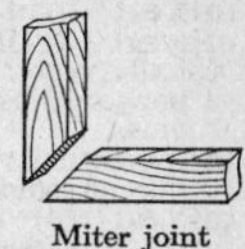

Miter joint

Mith·rae·um (mi thrē′əm), *n., pl.* **Mith-**

mis·sort′, *v.* **mis·term′,** *v.t.* **mis·ti′tle,** *v.t.,* **-tled, -tling.** **mis·trace′,** *v.,* **-traced, -trac·ing.** **mis·tune′,** *v.,* **-tuned, -tun·ing.** **mis·type′,** *n.,* **-typed, -typ·ing.** **mis·typed′,** *adj.* **mis·word′,** *n.*

rae·a (mi thrē′ə), **Mith·rae·ums.** a temple of Mithras. [< NL < Gk *Mithraîon* = *Mīthrās* MITHRAS + *-aion* suffix of place]
Mith·ra·ism (mith′rə iz′əm), *n.* an ancient religion of Persian origin, in which Mithras was worshiped. Also, **Mith·ra·i·cism** (mith rā′i siz′əm). —**Mith·ra·ic** (mith-rā′ik), **Mith′ra·is′tic,** *adj.* —**Mith′ra·ist,** *n.*
Mith·ras (mith′ras), *n.* *Persian Myth.* the god of light and truth, later of the sun. Also, **Mith·ra** (mith′rə). [< L < Gk < OPers *Mithra*]
Mith·ri·da·tes VI (mith′ri dā′tēz), ("*the Great*") 132?–63 B.C., king of Pontus 120–63. Also called **Mith·ri·da′tes Eu′pa·tor** (yōō′pə tôr′).
mith·ri·da·tism (mith′ri dā′tiz əm), *n.* the production of immunity against the action of a poison by taking the poison in gradually increased doses. [after MITHRIDATES VI, said to have so immunized himself] —**mith·ri·dat·ic** (mith′ri-dat′ik), *adj.*
mit·i·cide (mit′i sīd′), *n.* *Chem.* a substance or preparation for killing mites. —**mit′i·cid′al,** *adj.*
mit·i·gate (mit′ə gāt′), *v.*, **-gat·ed, -gat·ing.** —*v.t.* **1.** to make less severe, intense, painful, etc. **2.** *Rare.* to make (a person) milder or more gentle; mollify; appease. —*v.i.* **3.** to become milder. [< L *mītigāt(us)* calmed, softened, soothed (ptp. of *mītigāre*) = *mīt(is)* mild, soft, gentle + *-ig-* (var. of *ag-*, root of *agere* to make) + *-ātus* -ATE[1]] —**mit·i·ga·ble** (mit′ə gə bəl), *adj.* —**mit′i·gat′ed·ly,** *adv.* —**mit′i·ga′tion,** *n.* —**mit′i·ga′tive,** *adj.* —**mit′i·ga′tor,** *n.*
mi·tis (mī′tis, mē′-), *n.* **1.** Also called **mi′tis met′al.** wrought iron melted and cast. —*adj.* **2.** noting or pertaining to mitis. [< L: soft; see MITIGATE]
mi·to·chon·dri·on (mī′tə kon′drē ən, mit′ə-), *n.*, *pl.* **-dri·a** (-drē ə). *Biol.* one of the minute, granular, rodlike or threadlike bodies occurring in the cytoplasm of cells and functioning in cellular metabolism. Also called **chondriosome.** [< Gk *mîto(s)* a thread + *chóndrion* small grain] —**mi′to·chon′dri·al,** *adj.*
mi·to·sis (mī tō′sis, mi-), *n.* *Biol.* the usual method of cell division, characterized typically by the resolving of the chromatin of the nucleus into a threadlike form that separates into segments or chromosomes, each of which separates longitudinally into two parts, one part of each chromosome being retained in each of two new cells resulting from the original cell. [< Gk *mít(os)* a thread + -OSIS] —**mi·tot·ic** (mī tot′ik, mi-), *adj.* —**mi·tot′i·cal·ly,** *adv.*
mi·tral (mī′trəl), *adj.* **1.** of or resembling a miter. **2.** *Anat.* of, pertaining to, or situated near a mitral valve.
mi′tral valve′, *Anat.* the valve between the left atrium and ventricle of the heart, consisting of two triangular flaps of tissue, that prevents the blood from flowing back into the atrium. Also called **bicuspid valve.** Cf. **tricuspid valve.**
mi·tre (mī′tər), *n.*, *v.t.*, **-tred, -tring.** *Chiefly Brit.* miter.
mits·vah (mēts vä′; *Eng.* mits′və), *n.*, *pl.* **-voth** (-vôt′), *Eng.* **-vahs.** *Hebrew.* mitzvah.
mitt (mit), *n.* **1.** *Baseball.* a mittenlike hand protector worn esp. by a catcher. Cf. **baseball glove. 2.** a mitten. **3.** *Slang.* a hand. **4.** a long glove that leaves the fingers bare, worn by women. [short for MITTEN]
Mit·tel·eu·ro·pa (mit′əl oi rō′pä), *n.* *German.* central Europe.
mit·ten (mit′ən), *n.* **1.** a hand covering enclosing the four fingers together and the thumb separately. **2.** mitt (def. 4). [ME *miteyn* < MF, OF *mitaine* = *mite* mitten (< ?) + *-aine* -AN] —**mit′ten·like′,** *adj.*
Mit·te·rand (mēt[ə] RäN; *Eng.* mē′tə rand′, mit′ə-), *n.* **Fran·çois** (fRäN swA′), born 1916, French political leader: president since 1981.
mit·ti·mus (mit′ə məs), *n.*, *pl.* **-mus·es.** *Law.* a warrant of commitment to prison. [late ME < L: we send, first word of writ in Latin]
mitz·vah (mēts vä′; *Eng.* mits′və), *n.*, *pl.* **-voth** (-vôt′), *Eng.* **-vahs.** *Hebrew.* **1.** *Judaism.* any of the 613 precepts that are present in or derived from the Bible. **2.** a good or praiseworthy deed. Also, **mitsvah.** [lit., commandment]
mix (miks), *v.*, **mixed** or **mixt, mix·ing,** *n.* —*v.t.* **1.** to put (various materials, objects, etc.) together in a homogeneous or reasonably uniform mass. **2.** to add as an ingredient of such a mass: *Mix some salt into the flour.* **3.** to form by mixing ingredients: *to mix mortar.* **4.** to put together indiscriminately or confusedly (often fol. by *up*). **5.** to combine, unite, or join: *to mix business and pleasure.* **6.** to crossbreed. —*v.i.* **7.** to become or admit of being mixed: *a paint that mixes easily with water.* **8.** to associate, as in company. **9.** to crossbreed. —*n.* **10.** the act or an instance of mixing. **11.** the result of mixing; mixture. **12.** a commercially prepared blend of dry ingredients to be mixed with a liquid to obtain a desired consistency: *a cake mix.* **13.** Also, **mixer.** *Informal.* soda, ginger ale, fruit juice, or water for adding to whiskey or other liquor in making a highball. **14.** the proportion of ingredients in a mixture; formula: *a mix of two to one.* [late ME, back formation from *mixt* MIXED] —**mix′a·bil′i·ty,** *n.* —**mix′a·ble, mix′i·ble,** *adj.* —**Syn. 1, 7.** commingle, jumble, amalgamate, fuse. **7.** coalesce. **11.** concoction.
mixed (mikst), *adj.* **1.** put together or formed by mixing. **2.** composed of or containing different kinds of persons, materials, elements, etc. **3.** *Law.* involving more than one issue or aspect. **4.** *Phonet.* (of a vowel) central. [late ME *mixt* < L *mixt(us)*, ptp. of *miscēre* to mingle]
mixed′ bless′ing, something that offers great advantages but also has serious disadvantages.
mixed′ bud′. See under **bud**[1] (def. 1a).
mixed′ grill′, several kinds of broiled or grilled meats, and usually vegetables, served together, as a lamb chop, bacon, a pork sausage, a piece of liver, a grilled tomato, and mushrooms.
mixed′ mar′riage, a marriage between persons of different religions or races.
mixed′ me′dia, the integrated use of several media, such as films, slides, books, tape recorders, etc., to teach, advertise, entertain, etc. —**mixed′-me′di·a,** *adj.*
mixed′ met′aphor, the use in the same expression of two or more metaphors that are incongruous or illogical in combination, as in "The president will put the ship of state on its feet."
mixed′ num′ber, *Arith.* a number consisting of a whole number and a fraction, as 4½ or 4.5.
mixed-up (mikst′up′), *adj.* suffering from or revealing mental confusion.
mix·er (mik′sər), *n.* **1.** a person or thing that mixes. **2.** *Informal.* a person, with reference to his sociability: *a good mixer.* **3.** an electrical kitchen appliance, resembling an eggbeater, for use in mixing and beating foodstuffs. Cf. **blender** (def. 2). **4.** an informal dance or gathering. **5.** *Informal.* mix (def. 13). **6.** an electrical system, as in a broadcasting studio, providing for the blending, fading, substituting, etc., of sounds from various sources, as from microphones, recordings, etc.
mixt (mikst), *v.* a pt. and pp. of **mix.**
Mix·tec (mēs′tek), *n.*, *pl.* **-tecs,** (*esp. collectively*) **-tec** for 1. **1.** a member of an Amerindian people of Guerrero, Oaxaca, and Puebla, in Mexico. **2.** the language spoken by this Indian tribe. —**Mix·tec′an,** *adj.*, *n.*
Mix·te·co (mēs tek′ō), *n.*, *pl.* **-cos,** (*esp. collectively*) **-co.** Mixtec.
mix·ture (miks′chər), *n.* **1.** a product of mixing. **2.** any combination of contrasting elements, qualities, etc. **3.** *Chem.*, *Physics.* an aggregate of two or more substances that are not chemically united and that exist in no fixed proportion to each other. Cf. **compound** (def. 8). **4.** a fabric woven of yarns combining various colors. **5.** the act of mixing. **6.** the state of being mixed. [late ME < L *mixtūra.* See MIXED, -URE] —**Syn. 1.** blend, combination; compound. **2.** miscellany, medley, mélange.
mix-up (miks′up′), *n.* a confused state of things; muddle; tangle.
Mi·ya·za·ki (mē′yä zä′kē), *n.* a city on SE Kyushu, in Japan. 185,000 (est. 1963).
Miz·ra·chi (miz Rä′KHē), *n.* **1.** an Israeli religious group organized in 1902 as a wing of the orthodox Zionist movement, chiefly devoted to furthering traditional Judaism. —*adj.* **2.** of or pertaining to the Mizrachi. Also, **Miz·ra′hi.** [< Heb *Mizrāḥi*, lit., of the east]
miz·zen (miz′ən), *Naut.* —*n.* **1.** a fore-and-aft sail set on a mizzenmast. Cf. **crossjack, spanker** (def. 1a). See diag. at **ship. 2.** mizzenmast. —*adj.* **3.** of or pertaining to a mizzenmast. Also, **miz′en.** [late ME *meson*, prob. < It *mezzana* < Ar *mazzān* mast]
miz·zen·mast (miz′ən mast′, -mäst′; *Naut.* miz′ən məst), *n.* *Naut.* **1.** the third mast from forward in a vessel having three or more masts. **2.** the after and shorter mast of a yawl, ketch, or dandy; jiggermast. Also, **miz′en·mast′.** [late ME *meson mast*]
mk., *pl.* **mks.** mark[2] (def. 1).
MKS, meter-kilogram-second. Also, **mks, m.k.s.**
mkt., market.
ML, Medieval Latin. Also, **M.L.**
mL, millilambert; millilamberts.
ml, milliliter; milliliters. Also, **ml.**
MLA, Modern Language Association.
MLG, Middle Low German. Also, **M.L.G.**
Mlle., *pl.* **Mlles.** mademoiselle. Also, **Mlle**
mM, millimole; millimoles.
mm, millimeter; millimeters.
MM., messieurs.
mm., **1.** thousands. [< L *millia*] **2.** millimeter; millimeters.
Mme., *pl.* **Mmes.** madame.
mmf, *Elect.* micromicrofarad; micromicrofarads.
mmho, millimho; millimhos.
MN, Minnesota (approved esp. for use with zip code).
Mn, *Chem.* manganese.
mne·mon·ic (nē mon′ik, ni-), *adj.* **1.** assisting or intended to assist the memory. **2.** of or pertaining to mnemonics or memory. [< Gk *mnēmonik(ós)* of, relating to memory = *mnēmon-* (s. of *mnḗmōn*) mindful + *-ikos* -IC] —**mne·mon′i·cal·ly,** *adv.*
mne·mon·ics (nē mon′iks, ni-), *n.* (*construed as sing.*) the process or technique of improving or developing the memory. Also called **mne·mo·tech·nics** (nē′mō tek′niks).
Mne·mos·y·ne (nē mos′ə nē′, -moz′-, ni-), *n.* the ancient Greek goddess of memory. [< Gk: lit., memory]
-mnesia, a combining form denoting a certain type of memory: *paramnesia.* [comb. form abstracted from AMNESIA]
Mngr., Monsignor.
mngr., manager.
MO, Missouri (approved esp. for use with zip code).
Mo, *Chem.* molybdenum.
-mo, a suffix occurring in a series of compounds that describe book sizes according to the number of leaves formed by the folding of a single sheet of paper: *sixteenmo.* [comb. form abstracted from DUODECIMO]
Mo., **1.** Missouri. **2.** Monday.
mo., *pl.* **mos., mo.** month.
M.O., **1.** mail order. **2.** Medical Officer. **3.** method of working. [< L *modus operandi*] **4.** money order.
m.o., **1.** mail order. **2.** money order.
mo·a (mō′ə), *n.* any of several extinct, flightless birds of the family *Dinornithidae*, of New Zealand, related to the kiwis but resembling the ostrich. [< Maori]

Moa, *Dinornis maximus* (Height 10 ft.)

Mo·ab (mō′ab), *n.* an ancient kingdom E of the Dead Sea, in what is now Jordan. See map at **Philistia.** —**Mo·ab·ite** (mō′ə bīt′), *n.*, *adj.*
moan (mōn), *n.* **1.** a prolonged, low, inarticulate sound uttered from or as from physical or mental suffering. **2.** any similar sound: *the moan of the wind.* **3.** *Archaic.* complaint or lamentation. —*v.i.* **4.** to utter or produce moans. **5.** to utter with a moan. **6.** to lament or bemoan. [ME *mone, man(e)*, OE **mān*, inferred from its deriv. *mǣnan* to mourn] —**moan′ful,** *adj.* —**moan′ful·ly,** *adv.* —**moan′ing·ly,** *adv.*

moat (mōt), *n.* *Fort.* a deep, wide trench, usually filled with water, surrounding a fortified place. [ME *mote* < OF: clod, mound, perh. < Gmc]

mob (mob), *n., adj., v.,* **mobbed, mob·bing.** —*n.* **1.** a disorderly, riotous, or lawless crowd of people. **2.** *Sociol.* a group of persons stimulating one another to excitement and losing ordinary rational control over their activity. **3.** *Sometimes Disparaging.* any group or collection of persons, animals, or things. **4.** the mass of common people; the populace or multitude. **5.** a criminal gang. —*adj.* **6.** of, pertaining to, or characteristic of a disorderly, riotous, or lawless crowd of people: *mob rule.* **7.** directed at or reflecting the lowest intellectual level: *mob appeal.* —*v.t.* **8.** to crowd around noisily. **9.** to attack violently or riotously in or as in a mob. [short for L *mōbile vulgus* the movable (i.e., changeable, inconstant) common people]

mob·cap (mob′kap′), *n.* (formerly) a large, full, indoor cap for women, often tying under the chin. [*mob* woman (? var. of *Mab* for *Mabel*) + CAP[1]]

mo·bile (mō′bəl *or, esp. for 6,* mō′bēl), *adj.* **1.** movable; capable of moving readily. **2.** flowing freely, as a liquid. **3.** changeable or changing easily in expression, mood, purpose, etc., as the human face. **4.** quickly responding to impulses, emotions, etc., as the mind. **5.** *Sociol.* **a.** characterized by or permitting the mixing of social groups. **b.** characterized by or permitting individual progress from one social group to another. —*n.* **6.** a piece of sculpture having delicately balanced units that move independently, as when stirred by a breeze. Cf. **stabile** (def. 2). [< L *mōbilis* movable = *mō-* (ptp. s. of *movēre* to MOVE) + *-bilis* -BLE]

Mo·bile (mō′bēl, mō bēl′), *n.* a seaport in SW Alabama, on Mobile Bay. 190,026 (1970).

Mo′bile Bay′, a bay of the Gulf of Mexico, in SW Alabama: Civil War naval battle 1864. 36 mi. long.

mo′bile home′, a large house trailer, designed for year-round living in one place.

mo·bi·lise (mō′bə līz′), *v.t., v.i.,* **-lised, -lis·ing.** *Chiefly Brit.* mobilize. —**mo′bi·lis′a·ble,** *adj.* —**mo′bi·li·sa′tion,** *n.*

mo·bil·i·ty (mō bil′i tē), *n.* **1.** the quality of being mobile. **2.** *Sociol.* the movement of people in a population, as from place to place, from job to job, or from one social class to another. [< L *mōbilitās*]

mo·bi·lize (mō′bə līz′), *v.,* **-lized, -liz·ing.** —*v.t.* **1.** to assemble (armed forces) into readiness for active service. **2.** to organize or adapt (industries, transportation facilities, etc.) for service to the government in time of war. **3.** to marshal, bring together, prepare (power, wealth, etc.) for action or use. —*v.i.* **4.** to be or become assembled, organized, etc., as for war. Also, *esp. Brit.,* **mobilise.** [back formation from *mobilization*] —**mo′bi·liz′a·ble,** *adj.* —**mo′bi·li·za′tion,** *n.*

Mö′bi·us strip′ (mœ′bē əs, mā′-, mē′-; *Ger.* mœ′bē ŏŏs), *Geom.* a continuous, one-sided surface formed by twisting one end of a rectangular strip through 180° about the longitudinal axis of the strip and attaching this end to the other. [named after A. F. *Möbius* (1790–1868), German mathematician]

mob·oc·ra·cy (mob ok′rə sē), *n., pl.* **-cies. 1.** political control by a mob; mob rule. **2.** the mob as a ruling class. —**mob·o·crat** (mob′ə krat′), *n.* —**mob′o·crat′ic,** *adj.*

mob·ster (mob′stər), *n.* a member of a criminal gang.

Mo·çam·bi·que (mō′səm bē′kə), *n.* Portuguese name of **Mozambique.**

moc·ca·sin (mok′ə sin, -zən), *n.* **1.** a shoe made entirely of soft leather, as deerskin, worn originally by the American Indians. **2.** a hard-soled shoe or slipper resembling this. **3.** any of several snakes of the genus *Ancistrodon,* esp. the cottonmouth. [< Algonquian (Va.) *mockasin*]

moc′casin flow′er, 1. the lady's-slipper. **2.** a cypripedium, *Cypripedium reginae,* of the U.S.

mo·cha (mō′kə), *n.* **1.** a choice variety of coffee. **2.** a flavoring obtained from a coffee infusion or a combined infusion of chocolate and coffee. **3.** a brownish chocolate color. **4.** a fine grade of glove leather, often made from Arabian goatskins.

Mo·cha (mō′kə), *n.* a seaport in S Yemen. 25,000.

mo·chi·la (mō c͟hē′lə; *Sp.* mô c͟hē′lä), *n.* a leather covering on the seat of a saddle. [< Sp: lit., knapsack < *mochil* errand boy < Basque *motxil,* dim. of *motil* boy < L *mutilus* mutilated (from the custom of shaving boys' heads)]

mock (mok), *v.t.* **1.** to assail or treat with ridicule, contempt, or derision. **2.** to ridicule by mimicry of action or speech; mimic derisively. **3.** to dismiss; defy: *His actions mock convention.* **4.** to deceive, delude, or disappoint. —*v.i.* **5.** to use ridicule or derision; scoff; jeer. **6. mock up,** to build a mock-up of. —*n.* **7.** a mocking or derisive action or speech; mockery or derision. **8.** something mocked or derided; an object of derision. **9.** an imitation. —*adj.* **10.** being an imitation, semblance, or counterfeit of: *a mock battle.* [late ME *mokke(n)* < MF *mocque(r)*] —**mock′a·ble,** *adj.* —**mock′er,** *n.* —**mock′ing·ly,** *adv.* —**Syn. 1.** deride; taunt, flout, gibe; chaff, tease. See **ridicule. 4.** cheat, dupe.

mock·er·y (mok′ə rē), *n., pl.* **-er·ies. 1.** ridicule, contempt, or derision. **2.** a derisive action or speech. **3.** a subject or occasion of derision. **4.** an imitation, esp. of a ridiculous or unsatisfactory kind. **5.** a mocking pretense; travesty: *a mockery of justice.* **6.** something absurdly or offensively inadequate or unfitting. [ME *moquerie* < MF]

mock-he·ro·ic (mok′hi rō′ik), *adj.* **1.** imitating or burlesquing that which is heroic, as in manner, character, or action: *mock-heroic dignity.* **2.** *Literature.* of or pertaining to a form of satire in which trivial subjects, characters, and events are treated in the ceremonious manner and with the elevated language and elaborate devices characteristic of the heroic style. —*n.* **3.** an imitation or burlesque of something heroic. —**mock′-he·ro′i·cal·ly,** *adv.*

mock·ing·bird (mok′ing bûrd′), *n.* any of several gray, black, and white songbirds of the genus *Mimus,* esp. *M. polyglottos,* of the southern U.S. and Mexico, noted for their ability to mimic the songs of other birds.

mock′ or′ange, the syringa, *Philadelphus coronarius.*

mock′ tur′tle soup′, a rich clear soup prepared to resemble turtle soup, made with a calf's head or other meat, seasonings, and often with wine.

mock-up (mok′up′), *n.* a model, often full-scale, for study, testing, or teaching. Also, **mock′up′.**

Moc·te·zu·ma (*Sp.* môk′te sōō′mä), *n.* See **Montezuma II.**

mod (mod), *adj.* **1.** of or pertaining to a style of dress characterized by bold and unconventional design, colors, and patterns, as miniskirts, iridescent shirts, or the like. —*n.* **2.** (*sometimes cap.*) a British teen-ager who affects a sophisticated, aloof manner and wears an ultramodern version of Edwardian dress. [short for MODERN]

mod., 1. moderate. **2.** *Music.* moderato. **3.** modern.

mod·a·cryl·ic (mod′ə kril′ik), *n.* any of various man-made copolymer fibers used in textiles, containing less than 85% but at least 35% of acrylonitrile. Also called **mod′acryl′ic fi′ber.** [MOD(IFIED) + ACRYLIC]

mod·al (mōd′ᵊl), *adj.* **1.** of or pertaining to mode, manner, or form. **2.** *Music.* **a.** pertaining to mode, as distinguished from key. **b.** based on a scale other than major or minor. **3.** *Gram.* noting or pertaining to mood. **4.** *Philos.* pertaining to a mode of a thing, as distinguished from one of its basic attributes or from its substance or matter. **5.** *Logic.* exhibiting or expressing some phase of modality. [< ML *modāl(is)*] —**mod′al·ly,** *adv.*

mod′al auxil′iary, *Gram.* any of the group of English auxiliary verbs, including *can, dare, do, may, must, need, shall, will,* that are used with the base form of another verb to express distinctions of mood.

mo·dal·i·ty (mō dal′i tē), *n., pl.* **-ties. 1.** the quality or state of being modal. **2.** a modal attribute or circumstance. **3.** Also called **mode.** *Logic.* the classification of propositions according to whether they are contingently true or false, possible, impossible, or necessary. **4.** *Med.* the application of a therapeutic agent, usually a physical therapeutic agent. **5.** one of the primary forms of sensation, as vision or touch. [< ML *modālitās*]

mode[1] (mōd), *n.* **1.** manner of acting or doing; method; way. **2.** the natural disposition or the manner of existence or action of anything; form. **3.** *Philos.* **a.** appearance, form, or disposition taken by a thing or by one of its essential properties or attributes. **b.** (in the philosophy of Kant) any of the three categories, actuality, possibility, or existence. **4.** *Logic.* **a.** modality (def. 3). **b.** mood[2] (def. 2). **5.** *Music.* any of various arrangements of the diatonic tones of an octave, differing from one another in the order of the whole steps and half steps; scale. **6.** *Gram.* mood[2] (def. 1). **7.** *Statistics.* the value of the variate at which a relative or absolute maximum occurs in the frequency distribution of the variate. **8.** *Petrog.* the actual mineral composition of a rock, expressed in percentages by weight. [ME < L *mod(us)* manner]

mode[2] (mōd), *n.* **1.** customary or conventional usage in manners, dress, etc., esp. as observed by persons of fashion. **2.** a style or fashion. [< F < L *mod(us)* manner]

mod·el (mod′ᵊl), *n., adj., v.,* **-eled, -el·ing** or (*esp. Brit.*) **-elled, -el·ling.** —*n.* **1.** a standard or example for imitation or comparison. **2.** a representation, generally in miniature, to show the structure or serve as a copy of something. **3.** an image in clay, wax, or the like, to be reproduced in more durable material. **4.** a person or thing that serves as a subject for an artist, sculptor, writer, etc. **5.** a person, esp. an attractive young woman, whose profession is posing with, wearing, using, or demonstrating a product for purposes of display or advertising. **6.** a pattern or mode of structure or formation. **7.** a typical form or style. —*adj.* **8.** serving as a model: *a model apartment.* **9.** worthy of serving as a model; exemplary: *a model student.* —*v.t.* **10.** to form or plan according to a model. **11.** to give shape or form to; fashion. **12.** to make a representation of. **13.** to display, esp. by wearing: *to model dresses.* —*v.i.* **14.** to construct models. **15.** to produce designs in some plastic material. **16.** to serve or be employed as a model. [earlier *modell* < It *modell(o),* dim. of *modo* MODE[1]] —**mod′el·er;** *esp. Brit.,* **mod′el·ler,** *n.* —**Syn. 1.** prototype, archetype, mold. See **ideal.**

mod·el·ing (mod′ᵊling), *n.* **1.** the act, art, or profession of a person who models. **2.** the process of producing sculptured form with plastic material, as clay. **3.** the technique of rendering the illusion of volume on a two-dimensional surface by shading. **4.** the treatment of volume in sculpture. Also, *esp. Brit.,* **mod′el·ling.**

mod·el·ist (mod′ə list), *n.* a person who makes models, as of airplanes.

mo·dem (mō′dəm, -dem), *n.* *Computer Technol.* an electronic device, either built into a control unit or separate from it, that makes possible the transmission of data to or from a computer via telephone or other communication lines. [MO(DULATOR) + DEM(ODULATOR)]

Mo·de·na (mōd′ᵊnə; *It.* mô′de nä), *n.* a city in N Italy, NW of Bologna. 178,959.

mod·er·ate (*adj., n.* mod′ər it, mod′rit; *v.* mod′ə rāt′), *adj., n., v.,* **-at·ed, -at·ing.** —*adj.* **1.** kept or keeping within reasonable or proper limits; not extreme, excessive, or intense. **2.** of medium quantity, extent, etc.: *a moderate income.* **3.** mediocre; fair. **4.** of or pertaining to moderates, as in politics or religion. —*n.* **5.** a person who is moderate in opinion or opposed to extreme views and actions, esp. in politics or religion. **6.** (*usually cap.*) a member of a political party advocating moderate reform. —*v.t.* **7.** to reduce the excessiveness of; make less violent, severe, or rigorous. **8.** to preside over or at (a public forum, debate, etc.). —*v.i.* **9.** to become less violent, severe, or rigorous. **10.** to act as moderator; preside. [< L *moderāt(us)* restrained, controlled (ptp. of *moderārī*). See MODEST, -ATE[1]] —**mod′er·ate·ly,** *adv.* —**mod′er·ate·ness,** *n.* —**Syn. 1.** reasonable, temperate. **2.** average. **7.** calm, mitigate, diminish, reduce.

mod′erate breeze′, *Meteorol.* (on the Beaufort scale) a wind of 13–18 miles per hour.

mod′erate gale′, *Meteorol.* (on the Beaufort scale) a wind of 32–38 miles per hour.

mod·er·a·tion (mod′ə rā′s͟hən), *n.* **1.** the quality of being moderate; restraint; avoidance of extremes; temperance. **2.** the act of moderating. **3. in moderation,** without excess; temperately. [ME *moderacion* < L *moderātiōn-*]

mod·e·ra·to (mod′ə rä′tō), *adj.* *Music.* moderate; in moderate time. [< It < L *moderātus*]

mod·er·a·tor (mod′ə rā′tər), *n.* **1.** a person or thing that moderates. **2.** a presiding officer, as over a public forum, a legislative body, or an ecclesiastical body in the Presbyterian Church. **3.** a radio or television performer who presides over a quiz show or panel discussion. **4.** *Physics.* a substance, as graphite or heavy water, used to slow neutrons from the high speeds at which they are released in fission to lower ones, more efficient in causing fission. [ME < L] —**mod·er·a·to·ri·al** (mod′ər ə tōr′ē əl, -tôr′-), *adj.*

mod·ern (mod′ərn), *adj.* **1.** of or pertaining to present and recent time; not ancient or remote. **2.** of or pertaining to the historical period following the Middle Ages: *modern history.* **3.** of, pertaining to, or characteristic of contemporary styles of art, literature, music, etc., that reject traditionally accepted or sanctioned forms and emphasize individual experimentation and sensibility. **4.** characteristic of present and recent time; not antiquated or obsolete: *modern viewpoints.* —*n.* **5.** a person of modern times. **6.** a person whose views and tastes are modern. **7.** *Print.* a type style differentiated from old style by heavy vertical strokes and straight serifs. [< LL *modern(us)* = L *mod(o),* *modō* lately, just now (orig. abl. sing. of *modus* MODE[1]) + *-ernus* adj. suffix of time] —**mod′ern·ly,** *adv.* —**mod′ern·ness,** *n.*

mod′ern dance′, a form of contemporary theatrical and concert dance employing a special technique for using the entire body in movements that express abstract ideas.

mo·derne (mo′dern′), *adj.* *Disparaging.* self-consciously or tastelessly modern. [< F]

Mod′ern Eng′lish, the English language since c1475.

Mod′ern French′, the French language since c1600.

Mod′ern Greek′, the Greek language since c1500. *Abbr.:* ModGk, Mod. Gk., Mod. Gr.

Mod′ern He′brew, the language of modern Israel, a revived form of ancient Hebrew. *Abbr.:* ModHeb

mod·ern·ise (mod′ər nīz′), *v.t., v.i.,* **-ised, -is·ing.** *Chiefly Brit.* modernize. —**mod′ern·i·sa′tion,** *n.* —**mod′ern·is′er,** *n.*

mod·ern·ism (mod′ər niz′əm), *n.* **1.** modern character or tendencies; sympathy with what is modern. **2.** a modern usage or characteristic. **3.** (*cap.*) *Theol.* **a.** the movement in Roman Catholic thought that interpreted the teachings of the Church in the light of modern philosophic and scientific conceptions: condemned by Pope Pius X in 1907. **b.** the liberal theological tendency in 20th-century Protestantism. —**mod′ern·ist,** *n., adj.*

mod·ern·is·tic (mod′ər nis′tik), *adj.* **1.** modern. **2.** of modernism or modernists. —**mod′ern·is′ti·cal·ly,** *adv.*

mo·der·ni·ty (mo dûr′ni tē, mō-), *n., pl.* **-ties.** **1.** the quality of being modern. **2.** something modern.

mod·ern·ize (mod′ər nīz′), *v.,* **-ized, -iz·ing.** —*v.t.* **1.** to make modern; give a new or modern character or appearance to. —*v.i.* **2.** to become modern; adopt modern ways, views, etc. Also, *esp. Brit.,* **modernise.** —**mod′ern·i·za′tion,** *n.* —**mod′ern·iz′er,** *n.*

mod′ern jazz′, jazz evolved since the early 1940's and marked generally by increasing harmonic and rhythmic complexity. Also called **progressive jazz.**

mod·est (mod′ist), *adj.* **1.** having or showing a moderate or humble estimate of one's merits, importance, etc. **2.** free from ostentation or showy extravagance: *a modest house.* **3.** moderate: *to pay a modest sum.* **4.** having or showing regard for the decencies of behavior, speech, dress, etc.; decent: *a modest neckline on a dress.* [< L *modest(us)* moderate = *modes-* (*mod(us)* MODE[1] + *-es-,* var. of *-er-;* see MODERATE) + *-tus* adj. suffix] —**mod′est·ly,** *adv.*
—**Syn. 1.** unassuming. **1, 2.** unpretentious, unobtrusive. **4.** pure, virtuous. MODEST, DEMURE, PRUDISH imply conformity to propriety and decorum, and a distaste for anything coarse or loud. MODEST implies a becoming shyness and proper behavior: *a modest, self-respecting person.* DEMURE implies a bashful, quiet simplicity and decorum, but can also indicate an assumed or affected modesty: *a demure young chorus girl.* PRUDISH suggests an exaggeratedly self-conscious modesty or propriety in behavior or conversation of one who wishes to be thought of as easily shocked and who often is intolerant: *a prudish objection to a harmless remark.*

Mo·des·to (mə des′tō), *n.* a city in central California. 61,712 (1970).

mod·es·ty (mod′i stē), *n., pl.* **-ties.** **1.** the quality of being modest; freedom from vanity, boastfulness, etc. **2.** regard for decency of behavior, speech, dress, etc. **3.** simplicity; moderation. [< L *modestia*]

ModGk, Modern Greek. Also, **Mod. Gk., Mod. Gr.**

ModHeb, Modern Hebrew.

mod·i·cum (mod′ə kəm), *n.* a moderate or small quantity: *He hasn't even a modicum of common sense.* [late ME < L, neut. of *modicus* limited, measured. See MODE[1], -IC]

mod·i·fi·cand (mod′ə fə kand′), *n.* *Gram.* a word that is modified, or qualified, by another. In *red books, books* is a modificand. [< L *modificand(um)* (a thing) to be measured or limited, neut. of ger. of *modificāre* to MODIFY]

mod·i·fi·ca·tion (mod′ə fə kā′shən), *n.* **1.** the act or an instance of modifying. **2.** the state of being modified. **3.** a modified form; variant. **4.** *Biol.* a change in a living organism acquired from its own activity or environment and not transmitted to its descendants. **5.** limitation or qualification. **6.** *Gram.* **a.** the use of a modifier in a construction. **b.** the meaning of a modifier. **c.** a change in the shape of a morpheme, word, or other form, as the change of *not* to *-n't* in *doesn't.* [< L *modificātiōn-* (s. of *modificātiō*) = *modificāt(us)* measured (ptp. of *modificāre;* see MODIFY) + *-iōn-* -ION]

mod·i·fi·ca·to·ry (mod′ə fə kā′tə rē), *adj.* modifying. Also, **mod′i·fi·ca′tive.** [< L *modificāt(us)* (see MODIFY) + -ORY[1]]

mod·i·fi·er (mod′ə fī′ər), *n.* **1.** a person or thing that modifies. **2.** *Gram.* a word or phrase that modifies another element in the same construction: *Adjectives are modifiers.*

mod·i·fy (mod′ə fī′), *v.,* **-fied, -fy·ing.** —*v.t.* **1.** to change somewhat the form or qualities of; alter partially: *to modify a design.* **2.** *Gram.* (of a word or phrase) to stand in a syntactically subordinate relation to (another word or phrase), usually with descriptive, limiting, or particularizing meaning; be a modifier. In *a good man, good* modifies *man.* **3.** to change (a vowel) by umlaut. **4.** to reduce in degree; moderate; qualify: *to modify one's statement.* —*v.i.* **5.** to be or become modified. [ME *modifie(n)* < MF *modifie(r)* < L *modificāre* to limit, measure] —**mod′i·fi′a·bil′i·ty, mod′i·fi′a·ble·ness,** *n.* —**mod′i·fi′a·ble,** *adj.*
—**Syn. 1.** vary, adjust, shape, reform. **4.** MODIFY, QUALIFY, TEMPER suggest altering an original statement, condition, or the like, so as to avoid anything excessive or extreme. To MODIFY is to alter in one or more particulars, generally in the direction of leniency or moderation: *to modify demands, rates.* To QUALIFY is to restrict or limit by exceptions or conditions: *to qualify one's praise, hopes.* To TEMPER is to alter the quality of something, generally so as to diminish its force or harshness: *to temper one's criticism with humor.*

Mo·di·glia·ni (mō dē′lē ä′nē; *It.* mô′dē lyä′nē), *n.* **A·me·de·o** (ä′me de′ō), 1884–1920, Italian painter and sculptor in France.

mo·dil·lion (mō dil′yən, mə-), *n.* *Archit.* an ornamental cantilever beneath the corona or similar member of a cornice, stringcourse, etc. [< It *modiglione* < VL **mutiliōnem,* var. of *mūtuliōnem,* acc. of **mūtuliō.* See MUTULE, -ION]

Modillion

mod·ish (mō′dish), *adj.* in accordance with the prevailing mode; fashionable; stylish. —**mod′ish·ly,** *adv.* —**mod′ish·ness,** *n.*

mo·diste (mō dēst′; *Fr.* mô dēst′), *n., pl.* **-distes** (-dēsts′; *Fr.* -dēst′). a maker of or dealer in articles of fashionable attire, esp. women's dresses and millinery. [< F]

Mo·doc (mō′dok), *n., pl.* **-docs,** (*esp. collectively*) **-doc.** a member of an American Indian people ranging from southern Oregon to northern California.

Mo·dred (mō′drid), *n.* *Arthurian Romance.* the treacherous nephew, or son, and slayer of Arthur. Also, **Mordred.**

mod·u·lar (moj′ə lər, mod′yə-), *adj.* **1.** of or pertaining to a module or a modulus. **2.** composed of standardized units or sections for easy construction or flexible arrangement: *a modular home.* [< NL *modulār(is)*]

mod·u·late (moj′ə lāt′, mod′yə-), *v.,* **-lat·ed, -lat·ing.** —*v.t.* **1.** to regulate by or adjust to a certain measure or proportion; soften; tone down. **2.** to adapt (the voice) to the circumstances. **3.** *Music.* **a.** to attune to a certain pitch or key. **b.** to vary the volume of (tone). **4.** *Radio.* to cause the amplitude, frequency, phase, or intensity of (a carrier wave) to vary in accordance with a sound wave or other signal. —*v.i.* **5.** *Radio.* to modulate a carrier wave. **6.** *Music.* to pass from one key to another. [< L *modulāt(us)* measured, regulated (ptp. of *modulārī*). See MODULE, -ATE[1]] —**mod·u·la·bil·i·ty** (moj′ə lə bil′i tē, mod′yə-), *n.* —**mod′u·la′tive,** *adj.* —**mod′u·la′tor,** *n.* —**mod·u·la·to·ry** (moj′ə lə tōr′ē, -tôr′ē, mod′yə-), *adj.*

mod·u·la·tion (moj′ə lā′shən, mod′yə-), *n.* **1.** the act of modulating. **2.** the state of being modulated. **3.** *Gram.* **a.** the use of a particular distribution of stress or pitch in a construction, as the use of rising pitch on *here* in *John is here?* **b.** the feature of a construction resulting from such use. [ME *modulacion* < L *modulātiōn-* (s. of *modulātiō*) rhythmical measure]

mod·ule (moj′o͞ol, mod′yo͞ol), *n.* **1.** a standard or unit for measuring. **2.** a selected unit of measure, ranging in size from a few inches to several feet, used as a basis for the planning and standardization of building materials. **3.** a separable component, frequently one that is interchangeable with others, for assembly into units of differing size, complexity, or function. **4.** any of the individual, self-contained segments of a spacecraft, designed to perform a particular task in space: *a command module of the Apollo spacecraft; a lunar module.* [< L *modulus.* See MODE[1], -ULE]

mod·u·lo (moj′ə lō′, mod′yə-), *adv.* *Math.* with respect to a modulus: *6 is congruent to 11, modulo 5.* [< NL, abl. of *modulus*]

mod·u·lus (moj′ə ləs, mod′yə-), *n., pl.* **-li** (-lī). **1.** *Physics.* a coefficient pertaining to a physical property. **2.** *Math.* **a.** the number by which the logarithms in one system are multiplied to yield the logarithms in another. **b.** a quantity by which two given quantities can be divided to yield the same remainders. [< L: a little unit of measure]

mo·dus o·pe·ran·di (mō′do͝os ō′pe rän′dē; *Eng.* mō′dəs op′ə ran′dī), *pl.* **mo·di o·pe·ran·di** (mō′dē ō′pe rän′dē; *Eng.* mō′dī op′ə ran′dī). *Latin.* mode of operating or working.

mo·dus vi·ven·di (mō′do͝os wē wen′dē; *Eng.* mō′dəs vi ven′dī), *pl.* **mo·di vi·ven·di** (mō′dē wē wen′dē; *Eng.* mō′dī vi ven′dī). **1.** (*italics*) *Latin.* manner of living. **2.** a temporary arrangement between persons or parties pending a settlement of matters in debate.

Moe·si·a (mē′shē ə), *n.* an ancient country in SE Europe, S of the Danube: later a Roman province.

Moe·so·goth (mē′sō goth′, -sə-), *n.* one of the Christianized Goths who settled in Moesia in the 4th century A.D. [MOES(IA) + -O- + GOTH] —**Moe·so·goth·ic** (mē′sō goth′ik), *adj.*

mo·fette (mō fet′; *Fr.* mô fet′), *n.* **1.** a noxious emanation, consisting chiefly of carbon dioxide, escaping from the earth in regions of nearly extinct volcanic activity. **2.** one of the openings or fissures from which this emanation issues. Also, **mof·fette′.** [< F < It (Neapolitan) *mofeta;* cf. dial. G *muffezen* to emit a rotten smell]

Mo·ga·di·scio (mog′ə dish′ē ō′, -dish′ō; *It.* mô′gä dē′shô), *n.* a seaport in and the capital of the Somali Republic, in the S part. 400,000. Also, **Mo·ga·di·shu** (mô′gä dē′sho͞o).

Mog·a·dor (mog′ə dōr′, -dôr′; *Fr.* mô GA DÔR′), *n.* a seaport in W Morocco. 30,061.

Mo·gen Da·vid (mô′gən dô′vid, dā′vid, mō′gən; *Heb.* mä gen′ dä vēd′), *Judaism.* See **Star of David.**

Mo·gi·lev (mō′gi lef′; *Russ.* mo gi lyôf′), *n.* a city in E Byelorussia, in the W Soviet Union in Europe, on the Dnieper. 151,000 (est. 1964).

mo·gul (mō′gəl), *n.* a bump or mound of hard snow on a ski slope. [< Norw]

Mo·gul (mō′gul, -gəl, mō gul′), *n.* **1.** one of the Mongol conquerors of India who established an empire that lasted from 1526 to 1857. **2.** one of their descendants. **3.** a Mongol or

Mongolian. **4.** (*l.c.*) an important, powerful, or influential person: *a mogul of the movie industry.* [< Pers *Mugul* MONGOL]

mo·hair (mō′hâr′), *n.* **1.** the coat or fleece of an Angora goat. **2.** a fabric made of yarn from this fleece. [var. (by folk etym.) of *mocayare* < It *moccaiaro* < Ar *mukhayyar*, lit., chosen, choice, ptp. of *khayyara* to choose]

Moham., Mohammedan.

Mo·ham·med (mō ham′id), *n.* Muhammad.

Mohammed II, (*"the Conqueror"*) 1430–81, sultan of Turkey 1451–81: conqueror of Constantinople 1453.

Moham′med A·li′ (ä lē′, ä′lē). See **Mehemet Ali.**

Mo·ham·med·an (mō ham′i dᵊn), *adj., n.* Muslim.

Mo·ham·med·an·ism (mō ham′i dᵊniz′əm), *n.* the Muslim religion; Islam.

Mo·ham·med·an·ize (mō ham′i dᵊnīz′), *v.t.*, **-ized, -iz·ing.** Islamize.

Mo·har·ram (mō har′əm), *n.* Muharram.

Mo·ha·ve (mō hä′vē), *n., pl.* **-ves,** (*esp. collectively*) **-ve,** *adj.* —*n.* **1.** a member of a North American Indian tribe belonging to the Yuman linguistic family, formerly located in the Colorado River valley of Arizona and California. —*adj.* **2.** of or pertaining to a Mohave or the Mohave tribe. Also, **Mojave.**

Moha′ve Des′ert. See **Mojave Desert.**

Mo·hawk (mō′hôk), *n., pl.* **-hawks,** (*esp. collectively*) **-hawk.** **1.** a member of a tribe of the most easterly of the Five Nations, formerly resident along the Mohawk River, New York. **2.** the language of the Mohawk Indians, an Iroquoian language. **3.** a river flowing E from central New York to the Hudson. 148 mi. long.

Mo·he·gan (mō hē′gən), *n., pl.* **-gans,** (*esp. collectively*) **-gan.** **1.** a member of a tribe of Algonquian-speaking North American Indians dwelling chiefly along the Thames River, in Connecticut, in the 17th century. **2.** Mahican (defs. 1, 2).

mo·hel (mô hāl′; *Eng.* mō′əl, -hel, moi′-), *n., pl.* **mo·ha·lim** (mô hä lēm′), *Eng.* **mo·hels.** *Hebrew, Judaism.* the person who performs the circumcision of a male child eight days after birth.

Mo·hen·jo-Da·ro (mō hen′jō där′ō), *n.* an archaeological site in West Pakistan, near the Indus River.

Mo·hi·can (mō hē′kən), *n., pl.* **-cans,** (*esp. collectively*) **-can.** Mahican.

Moh·ism (mō′iz əm), *n.* the doctrines and beliefs of Motze, characterized by advocacy of universal love of mankind and government by an absolute monarch. [Mo(-TZE) + -*h*- connective + -ISM] —**Moh′ist,** *n., adj.*

Mo·hock (mō′hok), *n.* (in early 18th-century London) one of a group of aristocratic ruffians who attacked persons on the streets at night. [var. of MOHAWK] —**Mo′hock·ism,** *n.*

Mo·hole (mō′hōl′), *n.* a hole bored through the earth's crust into the region below the Mohorovičić discontinuity for purposes of geological research. [*Mo(horovičić)* (see MOHOROVIČIĆ DISCONTINUITY) + HOLE]

Mo·ho·ro′vi·čić discontinu′ity (mō′hō rō′və chich, -hô-), *Geol.* the discontinuity between the crust and the mantle of the earth, occurring at depths that average about 22 miles beneath the continents and about 6 miles beneath the ocean floor. Also called **Mo·ho** (mō′hō). [named after A. *Mohorovičić* (1857–1936) Yugoslav geologist]

Mohs′ scale′ (mōz), a scale of hardness used in mineralogy. Its degrees are: talc 1; gypsum 2; calcite 3; fluorite 4; apatite 5; feldspar 6; quartz 7; topaz 8; sapphire 9; diamond 10. [named after F. *Mohs* (1733–1839), German mineralogist]

mo·hur (mō′hər), *n.* a gold coin of British India. [earlier *muhr* < Urdu < Pers: seal, gold coin; akin to Skt *mudrā*]

moi·dore (moi′dōr, -dôr), *n.* a former gold coin of Portugal and Brazil. [< Pg *moeda de ouro* coin of gold < L *monēta dē aurō*]

moi·e·ty (moi′i tē), *n., pl.* **-ties.** **1.** a half. **2.** an indefinite portion. **3.** *Anthropol.* one of two units into which a tribe is divided on the basis of unilateral descent. [late ME *moite* < MF < L *medietāt-* (s. of *medietās*) the middle = *medi(us)* mid + *-etāt-*, var. of *-itāt-* -ITY]

moil (moil), *v.i.* **1.** to work hard; toil; drudge. —*n.* **2.** toil or drudgery. **3.** confusion, turmoil, or trouble. [ME *moille(n)* (to) make or get wet and muddy < MF *moillie(r)* < VL **molliāre* < L *moll(is)* soft] —**moil′er,** *n.*

Moi·ra (moi′rə), *n., pl.* **-rai** (-rī). *Class. Myth.* the personification of fate.

moire (mwär, mōr, môr), *n.* any moiré fabric. [< F, for MOHAIR]

moi·ré (mwä rā′, mōr′ā, môr′ā; *Fr.* MWA RĀ′), *adj.* **1.** (of silks and other fabrics) presenting a watery or wavelike appearance. —*n.* **2.** a design pressed on silk, rayon, etc., by engraved rollers. **3.** any fabric with a watery or wavelike appearance. [< F]

Moi·se·yev (moi se′yev, -yəf), *n.* **I·gor A·le·xan·dro·vich** (ē′gôr ä le ksän′drô vich), born 1906, Russian dancer, choreographer, and ballet master.

moist (moist), *adj.* **1.** moderately or slightly wet; damp. **2.** (of the eyes) tearful. **3.** accompanied by or connected with liquid or moisture. [ME *moiste* < MF; connected with L *mūcidus* MUCID] —**moist′ful,** *adj.* —**moist′less,** *adj.* —**moist′ly,** *adv.* —**moist′ness,** *n.*

mois·ten (moi′sən), *v.t., v.i.* to make or become moist. —**moist′en·er,** *n.*

mois·ture (mois′chər, moish′-), *n.* **1.** condensed or diffused liquid, esp. water. **2.** a small quantity of liquid, esp. water; enough liquid to moisten. [ME; cf. MF *moistour*] —**mois′ture·less,** *adj.*

mois·tur·ize (mois′chə rīz′, moish′-), *v.*, **-ized, -iz·ing.** —*v.t.* **1.** to impart or restore moisture to (something). —*v.i.* **2.** to supply moisture. —**mois′tur·iz′er,** *n.*

Mo·ja·ve (mō hä′vē), *n., pl.* **-ves,** (*esp. collectively*) **-ve,** *adj.* Mohave.

Moja′ve Des′ert, a desert in S California: part of the Great Basin. ab. 13,500 sq. mi. Also, **Mohave Desert.**

Mo·ji (mô′jē′), *n.* a seaport on N Kyushu, in SW Japan. 152,081 (1964).

Mok·po (môk′pō), *n.* a seaport in SW South Korea. 154,241 (est. 1964). Japanese, **Moppo.**

mol (mōl), *n. Chem.* mole[4].

mol., **1.** molecular. **2.** molecule.

mo·la (mō′lə), *n., pl.* (*esp. collectively*) **-la,** (*esp. referring to two or more kinds or species*) **-las.** any of several thin, silvery fishes of the family *Molidae*, found in tropical and temperate seas. [< L: millstone; so called from its shape]

mo·lal (mō′ləl), *adj. Chem.* **1.** noting or pertaining to gram-molecular weight. **2.** noting or pertaining to a solution containing one mole of solute per 1000 grams of solvent.

mo·lal·i·ty (mō lal′i tē), *n., pl.* **-ties.** *Chem.* the number of moles of solute per liter of solvent.

mo·lar[1] (mō′lər), *n.* **1.** Also called **mo′lar tooth′.** a tooth having a broad biting surface adapted for grinding: in man, one of twelve, there being three on each side of the upper and lower jaws. —*adj.* **2.** adapted for grinding, as teeth. **3.** pertaining to such teeth. [< L *molār(is)* grinder, short for (*dēns*) *molāris* grinding (tooth)]

mo·lar[2] (mō′lər), *adj.* **1.** *Physics.* pertaining to a body of matter as a whole (contrasted with *molecular* and *atomic*). **2.** *Chem.* pertaining to a solution containing one mole of solute per liter of solution. [< L *mōl(ēs)* a mass + -AR[1]]

mo·lar·i·ty (mō lar′i tē), *n. Chem.* the number of moles of solute per liter of solution.

mo·las·ses (mə las′iz), *n.* any of various thick, dark-colored syrups produced during the refining of sugar or from sorghum. [< Pg *melaço* (< L *mellāceum* must, neut. of **mellāceus* honeylike = *mell-*, s. of *mel* honey, + *-āceous* -ACEOUS) + *-es* pl. suffix]

mold[1] (mōld), *n.* **1.** a hollow form or matrix for giving a particular shape to something in a molten or plastic state. **2.** that on or about which something is formed or made. **3.** something formed in or on a mold: *a mold of jelly.* **4.** the shape imparted to a thing by a mold. **5.** shape or form. **6.** a prototype, example, or precursor. **7.** a distinctive nature, character, or type. **8.** *Archit.* a molding. —*v.t.* **9.** to work into a required shape or form; shape. **10.** to shape or form in or on a mold. **11.** *Foundry.* to form a mold of or from, in order to make a casting. **12.** to produce by or as by shaping material; form. **13.** to have influence in forming: *to mold the character of a child; to mold public opinion.* **14.** to ornament with moldings. Also, *esp. Brit.*, **mould.** [ME *molde* < OF *modle* < L *modul(us)* MODULE] —**mold′a·bil′i·ty,** *n.* —**mold′a·ble,** *adj.*

mold[2] (mōld), *n.* **1.** a growth of minute fungi forming on vegetable or animal matter, commonly as a downy or furry coating, and associated with decay. **2.** any of the fungi that produce such a growth. —*v.t.* **3.** to cause to become overgrown with mold. —*v.i.* **4.** to become overgrown with mold. Also, *esp. Brit.*, **mould.** [ME *mowlde*, appar. var. of *mowled*, ptp. of *moulen*, *mawlen*, c. dial. Dan *mugle* to grow moldy]

mold[3] (mōld), *n.* **1.** loose, friable earth, esp. when rich in organic matter and favorable to the growth of plants. **2.** *Brit. Dial.* ground; earth. Also, *esp. Brit.*, **mould.** [ME, OE *molde* earth, dust, ground; c. Goth *mulda* dust; akin to MEAL[2], MILL[1]]

Mol·dau (môl′dou, mōl′-), *n.* a river in Czechoslovakia, flowing N through the Bohemian Forest to the Elbe. 270 mi. long. Czech, **Vltava.**

Mol·da·vi·a (mol dā′vē ə, -vyə), *n.* **1.** a region in NE Rumania: formerly a principality that united with Wallachia to form Rumania. *Cap.:* Jassy. **2.** Official name, **Molda′vian So′viet So′cialist Repub′lic.** a constituent republic of the Soviet Union in Europe, in the SW part: formed in 1940 from the former autonomous republic of Moldavia and the ceded Rumanian territory of Bessarabia. 3,300,000 (est. 1965); 13,100 sq. mi. *Cap.:* Kishinev. —**Mol·da′vi·an,** *adj., n.*

mol·da·vite (mol′də vīt′), *n.* a green natural glass found in Bohemia and thought to be of meteoritic origin. [MOLDAV(IA) + -ITE[1]]

mold·board (mōld′bōrd′, -bôrd′), *n.* **1.** the curved metal plate in a plow that turns over the earth from the furrow. **2.** a large blade mounted on the front of a bulldozer to push loose earth. **3.** a board forming one side or surface of a mold for concrete.

mold·er[1] (mōl′dər), *v.i.* **1.** to turn to dust by natural decay; crumble; waste away: *a house that had been left to molder.* —*v.t.* **2.** to cause to molder. Also, *esp. Brit.*, **moulder.** [obs. *mold* to crumble (v. use of MOLD[3]) + -ER[6]]

mold·er[2] (mōl′dər), *n.* a person who molds; a maker of molds. Also, *esp. Brit.*, **moulder.** [late ME]

mold·ing (mōl′ding), *n.* **1.** the act or process of molding or shaping. **2.** something molded. **3.** (in architecture, furniture, etc.) **a.** any of various long, narrow, ornamental surfaces having a strikingly modeled profile that casts strong shadows: used on frames, tables, etc., and certain architectural members, as cornices, stringcourses, or bases. **b.** a strip of wood, stone, etc., having such a surface. **4.** a strip of contoured wood or other material placed on a wall, as just below the juncture with the ceiling. Also, *esp. Brit.*, **moulding.** [ME]

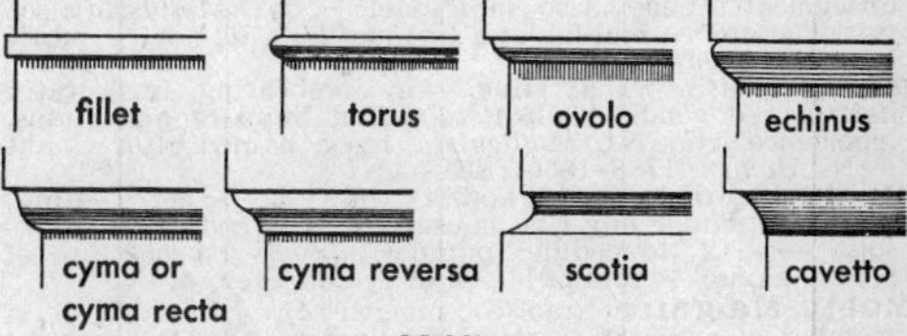

Moldings

mold′ing board′, a board upon which bread is kneaded, cookies prepared, etc.

mold·y (mōl′dē), *adj.*, **mold·i·er, mold·i·est.** **1.** overgrown or covered with mold. **2.** musty, as from decay or age. Also, *esp. Brit.*, **mouldy.** [ME] —**mold′i·ness,** *n.*

mole[1] (mōl), *n.* **1.** a small, congenital spot or blemish on the human skin, usually of a dark color, slightly elevated, and often hairy. **2.** a pigmented nevus. [ME; OE *māl;* c. OHG *meil* spot, Goth *mail* wrinkle]

mole[2] (mōl), *n.* any of various small insectivorous mammals, esp. of the family *Talpidae,* living chiefly underground and having velvety fur, very small eyes, and strong, fossorial forefeet. [ME *molle;* akin to MD, MLG *mol*]

Mole[2], *Scalopus aquaticus* (Total length to 8 in.; tail to 1½ in.)

mole[3] (mōl), *n.* **1.** a massive structure, esp. of stone, set up in the water, as for a breakwater or a pier. **2.** an anchorage or harbor protected by such a structure. [< L *mōlēs* mass, dam, mole]

mole[4] (mōl), *n.* *Chem.* the molecular weight of a substance expressed in grams; gram molecule. Also, **mol.** [< G *Mol,* short for *Molekül* MOLECULE]

mole[5] (mōl), *n.* *Pathol.* a fleshy mass in the uterus formed by a hemorrhagic dead ovum. [< medical L *mola,* special use of *mola* millstone]

Mo·lech (mō′lek), *n.* Moloch (defs. 1, 2).

mo·lec·u·lar (mō lek′yə lər, mə-), *adj.* pertaining to, caused by, or consisting of molecules. **—mo·lec′u·lar·ly,** *adv.*

molec′ular beam′, *Physics.* a stream of molecules that are freed from a substance, usually a salt, by evaporation and are then passed through a narrow slit for focusing: used for investigating the properties of nuclei, atoms, and molecules. Also called **molec′ular ray′.**

molec′ular film′, *Physical Chem.* a film or layer one molecule thick. Also called **monolayer.**

molec′ular for′mula, *Chem.* a chemical formula that indicates the kinds of atoms and the number of each kind in a molecule of a compound. Cf. **empirical formula, structural formula.**

mo·lec·u·lar·i·ty (mō lek′yə lar′i tē, mə-), *n.* *Chem.* the number of molecules or atoms that participate in a chemical process.

molec′ular weight′, *Chem.* the average weight of a molecule of an element or compound measured in units based on $^1/_{12}$ the weight of the carbon-12 atom; the sum of the atomic weights of all the atoms in a molecule. *Abbr.:* mol. wt.

mol·e·cule (mol′ə kyōōl′), *n.* **1.** *Chem., Physics.* the smallest physical unit of an element or compound, consisting of one or more like atoms in an element and two or more different atoms in a compound. **2.** a quantity of a substance, the weight of which, measured in any chosen unit, is numerically equal to the molecular weight; gram molecule. [earlier *molecula* < NL. See MOLE[3], -CULE]

mole·hill (mōl′hil′), *n.* **1.** a small mound or ridge of earth raised up by burrowing moles. **2.** something insignificant, esp. a small obstacle or difficulty. [late ME]

mole·skin (mōl′skin′), *n.* **1.** the soft, deep-gray, fragile fur of the mole. **2.** a stout, napped, twilled cotton fabric. **3.** **moleskins,** a garment, esp. trousers, of this fabric.

mo·lest (mə lest′), *v.t.* **1.** to bother, interfere with, or annoy. **2.** to make indecent sexual advances to. [ME *moleste(n)* < L *molest(āre)* (to) irk < *molest(us)* irksome = *mōlēs* mass, burden, trouble + *-tus* adj. suffix] **—mo·les·ta·tion** (mō′le stā′shən, mol′e-), *n.* **—mo·lest′er,** *n.*

Mo·lière (mōl yâr′; *Fr.* mô lyer′), *n.* (*Jean Baptiste Poquelin*) 1622–73, French actor and playwright.

Mo·li·na (mō lē′nə, mə-; *Sp.* mô lē′nä), *n.* **1. Lu·is** (lōō ēs′), 1535–1600, Spanish Jesuit theologian. **2. Tirso de.** See **Tirso de Molina.**

mo·line (mō′lin, mō līn′), *adj.* *Heraldry.* (of a cross) having arms of equal length, split and curved back at the ends. See illus. at **cross.** [< AF **moliné* = *molin* MILL[1] + *-é* -ED[3]]

Mo·line (mō lēn′), *n.* a city in NW Illinois, on the Mississippi. 46,237 (1970).

moll (mol), *n.* *Slang.* See **gun moll.** [special use of *Moll* proper name]

mol·lah (mô′lə), *n.* mullah.

mol·les·cent (mə les′ənt), *adj.* softening or tending to soften. [< L *mollescent-* (s. of *mollescēns*) softening (prp. of *mollescere*) = *moll(is)* soft + *-escent-* -ESCENT] **—mol·les′cence,** *n.*

mol·li·fy (mol′ə fī′), *v.t.,* **-fied, -fy·ing.** **1.** to soften in feeling or temper, as a person; pacify; appease. **2.** to mitigate or reduce: *to mollify one's demands.* [ME *mollifie(n)* < MF *mollifie(r)* < LL *mollificāre* = L *molli(s)* soft + *-ficāre* -FY] **—mol′li·fi·ca′tion,** *n.* **—mol′li·fi′er,** *n.*

mol·lus·coid (mə lus′koid), *adj.* belonging or pertaining to the phylum *Molluscoidea,* in certain classifications comprising the bryozoans and brachiopods. [< NL *Mollus-coid(ea)* = L *mollusc(us)* soft (see MOLLESCENT) + *-oidea* -OID]

mol·lusk (mol′əsk), *n.* any invertebrate of the phylum *Mollusca* comprising the chitons, snails, bivalves, squids, octopuses, etc., typically having a calcareous shell of one, two, or more pieces that wholly or partly encloses the soft, unsegmented body. Also, **mol′lusc.** [< NL *Mollusc(a);* see MOLLUSCOID] **—mol·lus·can** (mə lus′kən), *adj., n.* **—mol′lusk·like′,** *adj.*

mol·ly (mol′ē), *n., pl.* **-lies.** any livebearing, fresh-water fish of the genus *Mollienisia,* often kept in aquariums. [shortened from NL *Mollienisia,* irreg. named after Count F. N. *Mollien* (1758–1850); see -IA]

mol·ly·cod·dle (mol′ē kod′əl), *n., v.,* **-dled, -dling.** **—***n.* **1.** a man or boy who is used to being coddled; a milksop. **—***v.t.* **2.** to coddle; pamper. [*molly* (special use of proper name) + CODDLE] **—mol′ly·cod′dler,** *n.*

Mol·ly Ma·guire (mol′ē mə gwīər′), *Irish Hist.* a member of a secret society organized in 1843 to prevent evictions by terrorizing law-enforcement officials.

Mol·nar (mōl′när; *Hung.* môl′när), *n.* **Fe·renc** (fe′rents), 1878–1952, Hungarian playwright and novelist.

Mo·loch (mō′lok, mol′ək), *n.* **1.** a deity whose worship was marked by the sacrificial burning of children. II Kings 23:10; Jer. 32:35. **2.** anything conceived of as requiring appalling sacrifice. **3.** (*l.c.*) a spiny lizard, *Moloch horridus,* of Australian deserts, that resembles the horned lizard. Also, **Molech** (for defs. 1, 2). [< LL (Vulgate) < Gk (Septuagint) < Heb *Mōlokh,* var. of *mělekh* king]

Mo·lo·ka·i (mō′lō kä′ē), *n.* an island in central Hawaii: leper colony. 5089 (1970); 259 sq. mi.

Mo·lo·tov (mol′ə tôf′, -tof′, mōl′-; *Russ.* mô′lo tof), *n.* **1. Vya·che·slav Mi·khai·lo·vich** (vyä′che släf′ mi khī′lo vich), (*Vyacheslav Mikhailovich Skryabin*), 1890–1986, Russian statesman: commissar of foreign affairs 1939–49, 1953–56. **2.** former name of **Perm.**

Mo′lotov cock′tail, a crude incendiary grenade consisting of a bottle filled with a flammable liquid and a saturated wick that is ignited before throwing. [named after V. M. MOLOTOV]

molt (mōlt), *v.i.* **1.** (of birds, insects, reptiles, etc.) to cast or shed the feathers, skin, etc., that will be succeeded by a new growth. **—***v.t.* **2.** to cast or shed (feathers, skin, etc.) in the process of renewal. **—***n.* **3.** the act, process, or instance of molting. **4.** that which is dropped in molting. Also, *esp. Brit.,* **moult.** [earlier *moult* (with analogical *-l-* as in *could*), ME *mouten,* OE *-mūtian* to change (in *bimūtian* to exchange for) < L *mūtāre* to change; see MUTATE] **—molt′er,** *n.*

mol·ten (mōl′tən), *v.* **1.** a pp. of **melt.** **—***adj.* **2.** liquefied by heat; in a state of fusion: *molten lead; molten lava.* **3.** produced by melting and casting. [ME] **—mol′ten·ly,** *adv.*

Molt·ke (môlt′kə), *n.* **1. Hel·muth Jo·han·nes** (hel′mōōt yō hä′nəs), **Count von,** 1848–1916, German general: chief of staff 1906–14. **2.** his uncle, **Helmuth Karl** (kärl), 1800–1891, Prussian field marshal: chief of staff 1858–88.

mol·to (mōl′tō; *It.* môl′tô), *adv.* *Music.* very: *molto allegro.* [< It < L *multum,* adv. use of acc. sing. neut. of *multus* much]

Mo·luc·cas (mō luk′əz, mə-), *n.* (*construed as pl.*) a group of islands in Indonesia, between Celebes and New Guinea. 797,000 (est. 1961); ab. 30,000 sq. mi. Also called **Mo·luc′ca Is′lands, Spice Islands.**

mol. wt., See **molecular weight.**

mo·ly (mō′lē), *n., pl.* **-lies.** *Class. Myth.* an herb given to Odysseus by Hermes to counteract the spells of Circe. [< L < Gk]

mo·lyb·date (mə lib′dāt), *n.* *Chem.* a salt of any molybdic acid.

mo·lyb·de·nite (mə lib′də nīt′, mol′ib dē′nīt), *n.* a soft, graphitelike mineral, molybdenum sulfide, MoS_2, occurring in foliated masses or scales: the principal ore of molybdenum. [obs. *molybden(a)* MOLYBDENUM + -ITE[1]]

mo·lyb·de·nous (mə lib′də nəs, mol′ib dē′nəs), *adj.* *Chem.* containing bivalent molybdenum.

mo·lyb·de·num (mə lib′də nəm, mol′ib dē′nəm), *n.* *Chem.* a silver-white, metal element, used as an alloy with iron in making cutting tools. *Symbol:* Mo; *at. wt.:* 95.94; *at. no.:* 42; *sp. gr.:* 10.2. [< NL, alter. of earlier *molybdēna* < L *molybdaena* < Gk *molýbdaina* galena = *mólybd(os)* lead + *-aina* suffix of appurtenance]

mo·lyb·dic (mə lib′dik), *adj.* *Chem.* of or containing molybdenum, esp. in the trivalent or hexavalent state, as molybdic acid, H_2MoO_4.

mom (mom), *n.* *Informal.* mother. [short for MOMMA]

mom-and-pop (mom′ən pop′), *adj.* *Informal.* of or pertaining to a small retail store or business, usually owned and operated by a family, with few or no employees: *a mom-and-pop grocery.*

Mom·ba·sa (mom bä′sä, -bas′ə), *n.* **1.** an island in S Kenya. **2.** a seaport on this island. 179,575 (1962).

mome (mōm), *n.* *Archaic.* a fool; blockhead. [?]

mo·ment (mō′mənt), *n.* **1.** an indefinitely short space of time; an instant. **2.** the present or any other particular instant (usually prec. by *the*): *He is busy at the moment.* **3.** a definite period or stage, as in a course of events; juncture. **4.** importance or consequence: *a decision of great moment.* **5.** *Statistics.* the mean or expected value of the product formed by multiplying together a set of one or more variates or variables each to a specified power. **6.** *Philos.* an aspect of a thing. **7.** *Mech.* **a.** a tendency to produce motion, esp. about an axis. **b.** the product of a physical quantity and its perpendicular distance from an axis. [ME < L *mōment(um)* motion, cause of motion, hence, influence, importance = *mō-* (ptp. s. of *movēre* to MOVE) + *-mentum* -MENT]

mo·men·tar·i·ly (mō′mən târ′ə lē, mō′mən ter′-), *adv.* **1.** for a moment; briefly: *to pause momentarily.* **2.** every moment; from moment to moment: *Our danger is increasing momentarily.* **3.** imminently; at any moment.

mo·men·tar·y (mō′mən ter′ē), *adj.* **1.** lasting but a moment; very brief. **2.** occurring at any moment; imminent: *to live in fear of momentary annihilation.* **3.** *Rare.* effective or recurring at every moment; constant. [< L *mōmentāri(us)*] **—mo′men·tar′i·ness,** *n.*

mo·ment·ly (mō′mənt lē), *adv.* **1.** from moment to moment. **2.** for a moment. **3.** at any moment.

mo′ment of truth′, **1.** the moment in a bullfight at which the matador is about to make the kill. **2.** the moment at which a person is put to an extreme test; critical moment.

mo·men·tous (mō men′təs), *adj.* of great consequence: *a momentous event.* **—mo·men′tous·ness,** *n.* **—Syn.** critical, crucial, serious. See **heavy.** **—Ant.** trivial, trifling.

mo·men·tum (mō men′təm), *n., pl.* **-ta** (-tə), **-tums.** **1.** force or speed of movement; impetus. **2.** *Physics.* a quantity expressing the motion of a body or system, equal to the product of the mass of a body and its velocity. *Symbol:* p **3.** *Philos.* moment (def. 6). [< L; see MOMENT]

mom·ism (mom′iz əm), *n.* (*sometimes cap.*) *U.S.* excessive dependence on maternal affection or care, often resulting in absence or loss of maturity and independence.

mom·ma (mom′ə), *n.* *Informal.* mamma[1].

Mo·mus (mō′məs), *n., pl.* **-mus·es, -mi** (-mī) for 2. **1.** Also, **Mo·mos** (mō′mos). *Class. Myth.* the god of censure and ridicule. **2.** (*sometimes l.c.*) a faultfinder; carping critic. [< L < Gk *Mômos,* special use of *mômos* blame, ridicule]

mon (mon), *n.* *Scot. and North Eng.* man[1].

Mon (mōn), *n.* an Austroasiatic language used chiefly in Burma, esp. in the vicinity of Moulmein.

mon-, var. of **mono-** before a vowel: *monacid.*

Mon., **1.** Monday. **2.** Monsignor.

Mo·na·can (mon′ə kən, mə nä′kən), *n.* **1.** a native or inhabitant of Monaco. **—***adj.* **2.** of or pertaining to Monaco. Also called **Monegasque.**

mon·a·chal (mon′ə kəl), *adj.* pertaining to or characteristic of monks or their life; monastic. [< LL *monachāl(is)*]

mon·a·chism (mon′ə kiz′əm), *n.* monasticism. [< LL *monach(us)* MONK + -ISM] —**mon′a·chist,** *adj.*

mon·ac·id (mon as′id), *adj., n. Chem.* monoacid. —**mon′-a·cid′ic,** *adj.*

Mon·a·co (mon′ə kō′, mə nä′kō; *Fr.* mô NA kō′; *It.* mô′nä-kô′), *n.* **1.** a principality on the Mediterranean coast, bordering SE France. 25,000; ½ sq. mi. **2.** the capital of this principality. 1685.

mon·ad (mon′ad, mō′nad), *n.* **1.** *Biol.* **a.** any simple, single-celled organism. **b.** a small, flagellate, colorless, naked amoeboid with one to three flagella. **2.** *Chem.* an element, atom, or group having a valence of one. Cf. **dyad** (def. 3), **triad** (def. 2a). **3.** *Philos.* **a.** (in the metaphysics of Leibniz) an unextended, indivisible, and indestructible entity that is the basic or ultimate constituent of the universe and a microcosm of it. **b.** (in the philosophy of Giordano Bruno) a basic and irreducible metaphysical unit that is spatially and psychically individuated. **c.** any basic metaphysical entity, esp. having an autonomous life. **4.** a single unit or entity. [< LL *monad-* (s. of *monas*) < Gk: unity] —**mo·nad·ic** (mə-nad′ik), **mo·nad′i·cal, mo·nad′al,** *adj.* —**mo·nad′i·cal·ly,** *adv.*

mon·a·del·phous (mon′ə del′fəs), *adj. Bot.* **1.** (of stamens) united into one bundle or set by their filaments. **2.** (of a plant or flower) having the stamens so united.

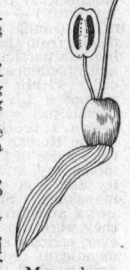

Monadelphous flower of hollyhock, *Althaea rosea*

mon·ad·ism (mon′ə diz′əm, mō′nad iz′-əm), *n. Philos.* the doctrine of monads as ultimate units of being, esp. as expounded by Leibniz. Also called **mon·ad·ol·o·gy** (mon′ə dol′ə jē, mō′na dol′-). —**mon′ad·is′tic,** *adj.*

mo·nad·nock (mə nad′nok), *n.* **1.** *Phys. Geog.* a residual hill or mountain standing well above the surface of a surrounding peneplain. **2.** (*cap.*) **Mount,** a mountain peak in SW New Hampshire. 3186 ft. [< AmerInd: (object) standing out, isolated]

Mon·a·ghan (mon′ə gən, -han), *n.* a county in the NE Republic of Ireland. 47,088 (1961); 498 sq. mi. *Co. seat:* Monaghan.

mo·nan·drous (mə nan′drəs), *adj.* **1.** of, pertaining to, or characterized by monandry. **2.** *Bot.* **a.** (of a flower) having only one stamen. **b.** (of a plant) having such flowers. [< Gk *mónandros*]

mo·nan·dry (mə nan′drē), *n.* the practice or condition of having but one husband at a time (distinguished from *polyandry*).

Mo′na Pas′sage (mō′nə; *Sp.* mô′nä), a strait between Hispaniola and Puerto Rico. 80 mi. wide.

mon·arch (mon′ərk), *n.* **1.** a hereditary sovereign with more or less limited powers, as a king, queen, or emperor. **2.** a sole and absolute ruler of a state. **3.** a person or thing that holds a dominant position: *a monarch of international shipping.* **4.** a large, reddish-brown butterfly, *Danaus plexippus,* having black and white markings, the larvae of which feed on the leaves of milkweed. [late ME < LL *monarcha* < Gk *monárchēs* ruling alone] —**mo·nar·chal** (mə när′kəl), **mo·nar·chi·al** (mə när′kē əl), *adj.* —**mo·nar′chal·ly,** *adv.*

Monandrous flower of mare's-tail, *Hippuris vulgaris*

Mo·nar·chi·an·ism (mə när′kē ə niz′əm), *n. Theol.* any of several doctrines of the Christian church in the 2nd and 3rd centuries A.D., emphasizing the unity of God by maintaining that the Father, the Son, and the Holy Ghost are three manifestations or aspects of God. [*monarchian* (< LL *monarchiān(us)*; see MONARCHY, -AN) + -ISM] —**Mo-nar′chi·an,** *adj., n.* —**Mo·nar′chi·an·ist,** *n.*

mo·nar·chi·cal (mə när′ki kəl), *adj.* **1.** of, like, or pertaining to a monarch or monarchy. **2.** characterized by or favoring monarchy. Also, **mo·nar′chic.** [< Gk *monarchik(ós)* + -AL¹] —**mo·nar′chi·cal·ly,** *adv.*

mon·ar·chism (mon′ər kiz′əm), *n.* **1.** the principles of monarchy. **2.** the advocacy of monarchical rule. [MONARCH(Y) + -ISM; cf. F *monarchisme,* G *Monarchismus*] —**mon′ar·chist,** *n., adj.* —**mon′ar·chist′ic,** *adj.*

mon·ar·chy (mon′ər kē), *n., pl.* **-chies.** **1.** a government or state in which the supreme power is actually or nominally lodged in a monarch. **2.** supreme power or sovereignty held by a single person. [ME *monarchie* < Gk *monarchía*]

mo·nar·da (mə när′də), *n.* any aromatic, erect, labiate herb of the genus *Monarda,* of North America, including horsemint, Oswego tea, etc. [< NL, named after N. *Monardés* (1493–1588), Spanish botanist]

mon·as·ter·y (mon′ə ster′ē), *n., pl.* **-ter·ies.** **1.** a house or place of residence occupied by a community of persons, esp. monks, living in seclusion under religious vows. **2.** the community itself. [ME < LL *monastēri(um)* < LGk *monastḗrion* monk house, orig. hermit's cell. See MONASTIC] —**mon·as·te·ri·al** (mon′ə stēr′ē əl), *adj.*

mo·nas·tic (mə nas′tik), *adj.* Also, **mo·nas′ti·cal.** **1.** of, pertaining to, or characteristic of monks or monasteries: *monastic vows; a monastic library.* **2.** of or pertaining to a secluded or harshly austere manner of living. —*n.* **3.** a member of a monastic community or order; monk. [< LL *monastic(us)* < LGk *monastikós* = *monast-* (verbal s. of *monázein* to be alone; see MON-) + *-ikos* -IC] —**mo·nas′ti·cal·ly,** *adv.* —**mo·nas·ti·cism** (mə nas′ti siz′əm), *n.*

Mo·na·stir (mô′nä stēr′), *n.* Turkish name of **Bitolj.**

mon·a·tom·ic (mon′ə tom′ik), *adj. Chem.* **1.** having one atom in the molecule. **2.** containing one replaceable atom or group. **3.** having a valence of one. Also, **monoatomic.**

mon·au·ral (mon ôr′əl), *adj.* monophonic (def. 2). —**mon·au′ral·ly,** *adv.*

mon·ax·i·al (mon ak′sē əl), *adj. Bot.* **1.** uniaxial. **2.** having flowers that grow on the primary axis.

mon·a·zite (mon′ə zīt′), *n.* a reddish- or yellowish-brown mineral, a phosphate of cerium and lanthanum, (Ce,La)PO_4; the principal ore of thorium. [< G *Monazit*]

Mön·chen·glad·bach (mœn′KHən glät′bäKH), *n.* a city in W North Rhine-Westphalia, in W West Germany. 260,700. Formerly, **München-Gladbach.**

mon cher (môN sher′), *French.* (in addressing a man) my dear. Cf. **ma chère.**

Monck (muŋk), *n.* **George** (*1st Duke of Albemarle* and *Earl of Torrington*), 1608–70, English general. Also, **Monk.**

Monc·ton (muŋk′tən), *n.* a city in SE New Brunswick, in E Canada. 55,934.

Mon·dale (mon′dāl′), *n.* **Walter F(rederick)** ("*Fritz*"), born 1928, 42nd vice president of the U.S. 1977–81.

Mon·day (mun′dē, -dā), *n.* the second day of the week, following Sunday. [ME *Mone(n)day,* OE *mōn(an)dæg,* trans. of LL *lūnae diēs* moon's day]

Mon′day-morn′ing quar′terback, *Informal.* a person who criticizes the actions or decisions of others after the fact, using hindsight to assess situations infallibly or to offer solutions to problems. —**Mon′day-morn′ing quar′-ter·back·ing.**

Mon·days (mun′dēz, -dāz), *adv.* on Mondays.

mon·do (mon dō′), *n., pl.* **-dos.** *Zen.* a question to a student for which an immediate answer is demanded, the spontaneity of which is often illuminating. [< Jap = *mon* questions + *do* answers]

Mon·dri·an (môn′drē än′, mon′-; *Du.* mon′drē än′), *n.* **Piet** (pēt), (*Pieter Cornelis Mondriaan*) 1872–1944, Dutch painter.

mo·ne·cious (mə nē′shəs, mō-), *adj.* monoecious.

Mon·e·gasque (mon′ə gask′), *n., adj.* Monacan. [< F *monégasque* < Pr *mounegasc* < *Mounegue* Monaco]

Mo·nel′ met′al (mō nel′), *Trademark.* a corrosion-resistant alloy consisting mainly of nickel and copper.

Mo·net (mō nā′; *Fr.* mô ne′), *n.* **Claude** (klōd; *Fr.* klōd), 1840–1926, French painter.

mon·e·tar·ism (mon′i ter′iz əm), *n. Econ.* a theory or doctrine that changes in the money supply determine the direction of a nation's economy. —**mon′e·tar′ist,** *n., adj.*

mon·e·tar·y (mon′i ter′ē, mun′-), *adj.* **1.** of or pertaining to the coinage or currency of a country. **2.** of or pertaining to money; pecuniary. [< LL *monētāri(us)*] —**mon·e·tar·i·ly** (mon′i târ′ə lē, mun′-, mon′i ter′ə lē, mun′-), *adv.*

mon′etary u′nit, the standard unit of value of the currency of a country, as the dollar in the U.S.

mon·e·tize (mon′i tīz′, mun′-), *v.t.,* **-tized, -tiz·ing.** **1.** to legalize as money. **2.** to coin into money: *to monetize gold.* Also, *Brit.,* **mon′e·tise′.** [< L *monēt(a)* MONEY + -IZE] —**mon′e·ti·za′tion,** *n.*

mon·ey (mun′ē), *n., pl.* **mon·eys, mon·ies,** *adj.* —*n.* **1.** gold, silver, or other metal in pieces of convenient form stamped by government authority and issued as a medium of exchange and measure of value. **2.** See **paper money.** **3.** any circulating medium of exchange, including coins, paper money, and demand deposits. **4.** any article or substance used as a medium of exchange, measure of wealth, or means of payment, as checks, wampum, etc. **5.** a particular form or denomination of currency. **6.** See **money of account.** **7.** property considered with reference to its pecuniary value. **8.** an amount or sum of money: *Can you lend me some money?* **9.** wealth considered in terms of money: *Her family has money.* **10. moneys** or **monies,** *Law.* pecuniary sums. **11.** pecuniary profit. **12. for one's money,** *Informal.* with respect to one's opinion, choice, or wish: *For my money, there's nothing to be gained by waiting.* **13. in the money,** *Slang.* first, second, or third place in a contest, esp. a horse or dog race. **14. make money,** to make a profit or become rich. [ME *moneie* < MF < L *monēta* MINT²] —**mon′ey·less,** *adj.* —**Syn. 1.** coin, cash, currency. **7.** capital, assets, wealth.

mon·ey·bag (mun′ē bag′), *n.* **1.** a bag for money. **2. moneybags,** (*construed as sing.*) *Informal.* a wealthy person.

mon′ey box′, **1.** *Chiefly Brit.* a small, lidded receptacle for keeping, collecting, or saving coins, usually with a slot for insertion. **2.** cashbox.

mon·ey·chang·er (mun′ē chān′jər), *n.* **1.** a person whose business is the exchange of currency at an official or prevailing rate. **2.** a device consisting of four mechanical barrels for holding coins of different sizes and dispensing change. [ME]

mon·eyed (mun′ēd), *adj.* having money; wealthy. [late ME]

mon·ey·er (mun′ē ər), *n. Archaic.* a person employed in the authorized coining of money. [ME < OF *monier*]

mon·ey·lend·er (mun′ē len′dər), *n.* a person whose business it is to lend money at interest.

mon·ey·mak·er (mun′ē mā′kər), *n.* **1.** a person engaged in or successful at acquiring money. **2.** something that yields pecuniary profit. [late ME]

mon·ey·mak·ing (mun′ē mā′kiŋ), *adj.* **1.** profitable: *a moneymaking scheme.* **2.** capable of making money: *the moneymaking part of the deal.* —*n.* **3.** the making of money.

mon′ey-mar′ket fund′ (mun′ē mär′kit), a mutual fund that invests in short-term credit instruments, such as Treasury bills, commercial paper, etc., which yield a relatively high interest rate. Also called **mon′ey-mar′ket mu′tual fund′.**

mon′ey of account′, a monetary denomination used in reckoning, esp. one not issued as paper money or coin, as the U.S. mill or English guinea.

mon′ey or′der, an order for the payment of money, as one issued by one bank or post office and payable at another.

mon′ey supply′, *Econ.* the sum of demand or checking-account deposits and currency in the hands of the public.

mon′ey tree′, **1.** a legendary or imaginary tree that, when shaken, sheds coins or paper money. **2.** *Informal.* a good source of money, funds, or revenues.

mon·ey·wort (mun′ē wûrt′), *n.* a creeping, primulaceous herb, *Lysimachia Nummularia,* having roundish leaves and yellow flowers.

mon·ger (muŋ′gər, moŋ′-), *n.* **1.** *Chiefly Brit.* a dealer or trader in a commodity (usually used in combination): *cheesemonger.* **2.** a person who busies himself with or promotes something considered petty or contemptible (usually used in combination): *a slandermonger.* [ME, OE *mongere* = *mong-* (< L *mango* salesman) + *-ere* -ER¹; c. Icel, OHG *mangari*] —**mon′ger·ing,** *n., adj.*

mon·go (moŋ′gō), *n., pl.* **-gos.** mungo. Also, **mon′goe.**

Mon·gol (moŋ′gəl, -gol, -gōl, mon′-), *n.* **1.** a member of a pastoral people now living chiefly in Mongolia. **2.** a person having Mongoloid characteristics. **3.** any Mongolian language. **4.** (*often l.c.*) *Pathol.* a person affected with Mongolism. —*adj.* **5.** Mongolian. **6.** (*often l.c.*) *Pathol.* of, pertaining to, or characteristic of Mongolism.

Mon′gol Em′pire, an empire founded in the 12th century by Genghis Khan, which reached its greatest territorial extent in the 13th century, encompassing the larger part of Asia and extending westward to the Dnieper River in eastern Europe.

Mon·go·li·a (moŋ gō′lē ə, mon-), *n.* **1.** a region in Asia including Inner Mongolia, the Mongolian People's Republic, and the Tuva Autonomous Soviet Socialist Republic. **2. Inner.** Offical name, **In′ner Mongo′lian Auton′omous Re′gion.** the S part of Mongolia, generally including the provinces of Jehol, Chahar, Suiyüan, and Ningsia: under China's control; boundaries frequently change. 13,000,000; 454,420 sq. mi. **3. Outer,** former name of **Mongolian People's Republic.**

Mon·go·li·an (moŋ gō′lē ən, mon-), *adj.* **1.** pertaining to Mongolia. **2.** of or pertaining to the Mongol people of inner Asia. **3.** *Anthropol.* Mongoloid. **4.** (*often l.c.*) (formerly) Mongoloid (def. 3). **5.** of or pertaining to Mongolian, a branch of the Altaic family of languages. —*n.* **6.** a native or inhabitant of the Mongolian People's Republic. **7.** a native or inhabitant of Inner Mongolia. **8.** Also, **Mongolic.** a group of languages constituting a branch of the Altaic family. **9.** any of the languages of this branch, esp. Khalkha. **10.** a member of the Mongoloid peoples of Asia.

Mongo′lian fold′, epicanthus.

Mongo′lian id′iocy, (formerly) Down's syndrome. —**Mongo′lian id′iot.**

Mongo′lian Peo′ple's Repub′lic, a republic in E central Asia, in N Mongolia. 1,380,000; ab. 600,000 sq. mi. *Cap.:* Ulan Bator. Formerly, **Outer Mongolia.**

Mon·gol·ic (moŋ gol′ik, mon-), *adj.* **1.** Mongolian. —*n.* **2.** Mongolian (def. 8).

Mon·gol·ism (moŋ′gə liz′əm, mon′-), *n.* (*often l.c.*) *Pathol.* the abnormal condition of a child born with a wide, flattened skull, narrow, slanting eyes, and generally a mental deficiency. Also, **Mon·go·li·an·ism** (moŋ gō′lē ə niz′əm, mon-). Also called **Mongolian idiocy.**

Mon·gol·oid (moŋ′gə loid′, mon′-), *adj.* **1.** resembling the Mongols. **2.** *Anthropol.* of, pertaining to, or characteristic of a major racial division of mankind marked by epicanthic folds, prominent cheekbones, straight black hair, a small nose, and a broad face, usually including the Mongols, Manchus, Chinese, Koreans, Japanese, Vietnamese, Siamese, Burmese, Tibetans, Eskimos, and certain American Indians. **3.** (*often l.c.*) (not in technical use) of, pertaining to, or affected with Down's syndrome. —*n.* **4.** a member of a Mongoloid people. **5.** (*often l.c.*) (not in technical use) a person affected with Down's syndrome.

mon·goose (moŋ′gōōs′, mon′-), *n., pl.* **-goos·es. 1.** a slender, ferretlike carnivore, *Herpestes edwardsii,* of India, that feeds on rodents, birds, eggs, etc., noted esp. for its ability to kill cobras and other venomous snakes. **2.** any of several other animals of this genus or related genera. [< Marathi *mangūs*]

Mongoose,
Herpestes edwardsii
(Total length 2½ ft.; tail 14 in.)

mon·grel (muŋ′grəl, moŋ′-), *n.* **1.** any animal or plant resulting from the crossing of different breeds or varieties. **2.** any cross between different things, esp. if inharmonious or indiscriminate. **3.** a dog of mixed or indeterminate breed. —*adj.* **4.** of mixed breed, nature, etc. [obs. *mong* mixture (OE *gemang*) + -REL] —**mon′grel·ism, mon′grel·ness,** *n.* —**mon′grel·ly,** *adv.* —**Syn. 1.** cross; half-breed. **3.** mutt. See **hybrid.**

mon·grel·ise (muŋ′grə līz′, moŋ′-), *v.t.,* **-ised, -is·ing.** *Chiefly Brit.* mongrelize. —**mon′grel·i·sa′tion,** *n.* —**mon′grel·is′er,** *n.*

mon·grel·ize (muŋ′grə līz′, moŋ′-), *v.t.,* **-ized, -iz·ing. 1.** to subject (a breed, race, etc.) to crossbreeding, esp. with a breed or race considered inferior. **2.** to mix the kinds, classes, types, characters, or sources of origin of (people, animals, or things). —**mon′grel·i·za′tion,** *n.* —**mon′grel·iz′er,** *n.*

mongst (muŋst), *prep. Literary.* amongst. Also, **'mongst.**

mon·ies (mun′ēz), *n.* a pl. of **money.**

mon·i·ker (mon′ə kər), *n. Slang.* a person's name, esp. a nickname. Also, **mon′ick·er.** [MONO(GRAM + MAR)KER]

mo·nil·i·form (mō nil′ə fôrm′), *adj.* **1.** *Bot., Zool.* consisting of or characterized by a series of beadlike swellings alternating with contractions, as certain roots, stems, etc. **2.** resembling a string of beads in shape. [< L *monīli-* (s. of *monīle* necklace) + -FORM]

Moniliform fruits of pagoda tree, *Sophora japonica*

mon·ism (mon′iz əm, mō′niz əm), *n.* **1.** *Philos.* **a.** (in metaphysics) any of various theories holding that there is only one basic substance or principle as the ground of reality or that reality consists of a single element. Cf. **dualism** (def. 2), **pluralism** (def. 1a). **b.** (in epistemology) a theory that the object and datum of cognition are identical. Cf. **pluralism** (def. 1b). **2.** the reduction of all processes, structures, etc., to a single governing principle. **3.** the conception that there is only one causal factor in history. [< G *Monism(us)*] —**mon′ist,** *n.* —**mo·nis·tic** (mə nis′tik, mō-), **mo·nis′ti·cal,** *adj.*

mo·ni·tion (mō nish′ən, mə-), *n.* **1.** admonition; warning; caution. **2.** an official or legal notice. **3.** *Law.* (in admiralty practice) a court order summoning a party to appear and answer. [late ME *monicio(u)n* < L *monitiōn-* warning = *monit(us)* warned (ptp. of *monēre;* see -ITE[2]) + *-iōn-* -ION]

mon·i·tor (mon′i tər), *n.* **1.** a pupil appointed to assist in the conduct of a class or school, as to help keep order. **2.** something that serves to remind or give warning. **3.** a device or arrangement for observing or recording the operation of a machine or system. **4.** *Naut.* **a.** *U.S. Hist.* a steam-propelled, armored warship of very low freeboard, formerly used for coastal defense. **b.** (*cap., italics*) the first of such vessels, used against the Confederate ironclad warship *Merrimack* at Hampton Roads, Virginia, in 1862. **5.** any of several large lizards of the family *Varanidae,* of Africa, southern Asia, the East Indies, and Australia, reputed to give warning of the presence of crocodiles. **6.** *Radio and Television.* a receiving apparatus used in a control room or studio for monitoring transmission. **7.** a person who admonishes, esp. with reference to conduct. —*v.t.* **8.** *Radio and Television.* **a.** to listen to (transmitted signals) on a receiving set in order to check the quality of the transmission. **b.** to view or listen to (a televised program, broadcast, or the like) in order to determine video or audio quality, for purposes of censorship, etc. **9.** to observe, record, or detect (an operation or condition) with instruments. **10.** to observe critically; oversee; supervise. —*v.i.* **11.** to serve as a monitor, or detector, supervisor, etc. [< L: prompter, adviser = *monit(us)* warned (see MONITION) + *-or* -OR[2]] —**mon′i·tor·ship′,** *n.*

mon·i·to·ri·al (mon′i tōr′ē əl, -tôr′-), *adj.* **1.** of or pertaining to a monitor. **2.** monitory. —**mon′i·to′ri·al·ly,** *adv.*

mon·i·to·ry (mon′i tōr′ē, -tôr′ē), *adj., n., pl.* **-ries.** —*adj.* **1.** serving to admonish or warn; admonitory. **2.** giving monition. —*n.* **3.** a letter containing a monition. [< L *monitōri(us)* reminding, warning = *monit(us)* warned (see MONITION) + *-orius* -ORY[1]]

monk (muŋk), *n.* **1.** (in Christianity) a man who has withdrawn from the world for religious reasons and lives according to a particular rule and under vows of poverty, chastity, and obedience. **2.** a man who is a member of a monastic order within any religion: *a Buddhist monk.* [ME; OE *munuc* < LL *monach(us)* < Gk *monachós* solitary (adj.), hermit (n.) = *món(os)* alone + *-achos* adj. suffix]
—**Syn. 1.** brother. MONK, FRIAR refer to special male groups in the Roman Catholic Church whose lives are devoted to the service of the church. A MONK is properly a member of a monastery, under a superior; he is bound by a vow of stability and is a co-owner of the community property of the monastery. Since the Reformation, MONK and FRIAR have been used as if they were the same. A FRIAR is, however, strictly speaking, a member of a mendicant order, whose members are not attached to a monastery and own no community property.

Monk (muŋk), *n.* **1. The·lo·ni·ous** (thə lō′nē əs) (**Sphere**), 1917–82, U.S. jazz pianist and composer. **2. George.** See **Monck, George.**

monk·er·y (muŋ′kə rē), *n., pl.* **-ies.** the mode of life of monks; monasticism.

mon·key (muŋ′kē), *n., pl.* **-keys,** *v.,* **-keyed, -key·ing.** —*n.* **1.** any mammal of the order *Primates,* including the guenons, macaques, langurs, capuchins, etc., but excluding man, the anthropoid apes, and, usually, the lemurs. **2.** a person likened to such an animal, as a mischievous child. **3. make a monkey out of,** to cause to appear ridiculous; make a fool of. Also, **make a monkey of.** —*v.i.* **4.** *Informal.* to play or trifle idly; fool (often fol. by *around* or *with*). —*v.t.* **5.** to imitate; ape; mimic. [appar. < LG; cf. MLG *Moneke* (name of son of Martin the Ape in the story of Reynard) = *mone-* (akin to obs. F *monne* she-ape, Sp, Pg *mono* ape, of Dravidian orig.; cf. Malayalam *monna* monkey) + *-ke* dim. suffix]

Rhesus monkey,
Macaca mulatta
(Total length 2½ ft.; tail 10 in.)

mon′key bread′, **1.** the gourdlike fruit of the baobab, eaten by monkeys. **2.** the tree itself.

mon′key busi′ness, *U.S. Slang.* **1.** improper or underhanded conduct. **2.** frivolous or mischievous behavior.

mon′key flow′er, any scrophulariaceous plant of the genus *Mimulus,* as *M. cardinalis,* having spotted, bilabiate flowers that resemble a face.

mon′key jack′et, a man's short, close-fitting jacket. [so called because like jacket worn by organ grinder's monkey]

mon′key nut′, *Chiefly Brit. Slang.* a peanut.

mon·key·pot (muŋ′kē pot′), *n.* the woody, operculate seed vessel of any of certain large South American trees of the genus *Lecythis.* [so called because potlike in shape and big enough for a monkey to use]

mon′key puz′zle, a South American, coniferous tree, *Araucaria imbricata,* having candelabralike branches, stiff, sharp leaves, and edible nuts. [? from its intertwined limbs]

mon·key·shine (muŋ′kē shīn′), *n.* Usually, **monkeyshines.** *Slang.* a trick or mischievous prank; a bit of monkey business.

mon′key suit′, *Slang.* a man's dress suit.

mon′key wrench′, **1.** Also called, *Brit.,* **adjustable spanner.** a wrench having an adjustable jaw at right angles to the handle. **2.** *U.S. Informal.* something that interferes with functioning: *He threw a monkey wrench into our plans.*

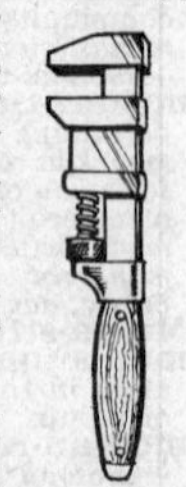
Monkey wrench

Mon-Khmer (mōn′kmer′), *adj.* **1.** of or pertaining to a group of related languages that includes Mon, of Burma, and Khmer, the official language of Cambodia. —*n.* **2.** the Mon-Khmer languages collectively.

monk·hood (mungk′ho͝od), *n.* **1.** the condition or profession of a monk. **2.** monks collectively. [late ME *monkehode,* OE *munuchade*]

monk·ish (mung′kish), *adj.* *Usually Derogatory.* of, pertaining to, characteristic of, or resembling a monk: *a monkish manner.* —**monk′ish·ly,** *adv.* —**monk′ish·ness,** *n.*

monk's′ cloth′, a heavy cotton fabric in a basket weave, used for curtains, bedspreads, etc.

monks·hood (mungks′ho͝od′), *n.* a plant of the genus *Aconitum,* esp. *A. Napellus,* the flowers of which have a large, hood-shaped sepal.

Mon·mouth (mon′məth), *n.* **1. James Scott, Duke of,** 1649–85, illegitimate son of Charles II of England and pretender to the throne of James II. **2.** Monmouthshire. **3.** former name of **Freehold.**

Mon·mouth·shire (mon′məth shēr′, -shər), *n.* a county in E Wales. 443,689 (1961); 543 sq. mi. *Co. seat:* Monmouth. Also called **Monmouth.**

Mon·net (mō nā′; *Fr.* mô ne′), *n.* **Jean** (zhäN), 1888–1979, French economist.

mon·o[1] (mon′ō), *n.* *Informal.* See **infectious mononucleosis.** [by shortening]

mon·o[2] (mon′ō), *adj.* monophonic (def. 2). [by shortening]

mono-, a learned borrowing from Greek meaning "alone," "single," "one" (*monogamy*); specialized in some scientific terms to denote a monomolecular thickness (*monolayer*) and adapted in chemistry to apply to compounds containing one atom of a particular element (*monohydrate*). Also, *esp. before a vowel,* **mon-.** [< Gk, comb. form of *mónos* alone, perh. akin to *mānós* thin]

mon·o·ac·id (mon′ō as′id, mon′ō as′id), *Chem.* —*adj.* Also, **monacidic. 1.** having one replaceable hydrogen atom or hydroxyl radical. **2.** capable of reacting with only one equivalent weight of an acid. —*n.* **3.** an acid having one replaceable hydrogen atom. Also, **monacid.**

mon·o·a·tom·ic (mon′ō ə tom′ik), adj. *Chem.* monatomic.

mon·o·ba·sic (mon′ə bā′sik), *adj.* **1.** *Chem.* (of an acid) containing one replaceable hydrogen atom. **2.** *Biol.* monotypic. —**mon·o·ba·sic·i·ty** (mon′ə bā sis′i tē), *n.*

mon·o·car·pel·lar·y (mon′ə kär′pə ler′ē), *adj.* *Bot.* consisting of a single carpel.

mon·o·car·pic (mon′ə kär′pik), *adj.* *Bot.* producing fruit only once and then dying.

mon·o·car·pous (mon′ə kär′pəs), *adj.* *Bot.* **1.** having a gynoecium which forms only a single ovary. **2.** monocarpic.

mon·o·chlo·ride (mon′ə klôr′īd, -klōr′-), *n.* *Chem.* a chloride containing one atom of chlorine with one atom of another element or with a group.

mon·o·chord (mon′ə kôrd′), *n.* an acoustical instrument dating from antiquity, consisting of an oblong wooden sounding box, usually with a single string, used for the mathematical determination of musical intervals. [ME *monocorde* < ML *monochord(um)* < Gk *monóchordon,* n. use of neut. of *monóchordos* with one string]

mon·o·chro·mat (mon′ə krō′mat), *n.* *Ophthalm.* a person who has monochromatism. Also, **mon·o·chro·mate** (mon′ə-krō′māt). [<< Gk *monochrōmat(os)* of one color]

mon·o·chro·mat·ic (mon′ə krō mat′ik, -ō krə-), *adj.* **1.** of or having one color. **2.** of, pertaining to, or having tones of one color in addition to the ground hue: *a monochromatic painting.* **3.** *Optics.* of, producing, or pertaining to one color or to a very limited range of wavelengths. **4.** *Ophthalm.* of or pertaining to monochromatism. —**mon′o·chro·mat′i·cal·ly,** *adv.* —**mon·o·chro·ma·tic·i·ty** (mon′ə krō′mə tis′i tē), *n.*

mon·o·chro·ma·tism (mon′ə krō′mə tiz′əm), *n.* **1.** a monochromatic quality, as in a work of art. **2.** *Ophthalm.* a defect of vision in which the retina fails to perceive color. Cf. **dichromatism** (def. 2), **trichromatism** (def. 3).

mon·o·chrome (mon′ə krōm′), *n.* **1.** a painting or drawing in different shades of a single color. **2.** the art or technique of producing such a painting or drawing. —*adj.* **3.** monochromatic (def. 2). [< ML *monochrōma*] —**mon′o·chro′mic, mon′o·chro′mi·cal,** *adj.* —**mon′o·chrom′ist,** *n.*

mon·o·cle (mon′ə kəl), *n.* an eyeglass for one eye. [< F < LL *monocul(us)* one-eyed = *mon-* MON- + *oculus* eye] —**mon′o·cled,** *adj.*

mon·o·cli·nal (mon′ə klīnᵊl), *Geol.* —*adj.* **1.** noting, pertaining to, or composed of strata dipping in only one direction. —*n.* **2.** monocline. [MONO- + Gk *klīn(ein)* (to) incline + -AL[1]] —**mon′o·cli′nal·ly,** *adv.*

mon·o·cline (mon′ə klīn′), *n.* *Geol.* a monoclinal structure or fold. [back formation from MONOCLINAL]

mon·o·clin·ic (mon′ə klin′ik), *adj.* *Crystall.* noting or pertaining to crystallization in which the crystals have three unequal axes, with one oblique intersection. Cf. **system** (def. 11). [MONO- + Gk *klīn(ein)* (to) incline + -IC]

mon·o·cli·nous (mon′ə klī′nəs, mon′ə klī′nəs), *adj.* *Bot.* (of a plant, species, etc.) having both the stamens and pistils in the same flower. [MONO- + Gk *klīn(ē)* bed + -OUS] —**mon′o·cli′nism,** *n.*

mon′o·clo′nal an′tibody (mon′ə klōn′əl, mon′-), *Biotech.* antibody that is produced by a laboratory-grown cell clone and is more abundant and uniform than natural antibody: used as an analytic tool in scientific research and medical diagnosis to bind to a chosen protein site or reveal previously unknown sites. *Abbr.:* MAb

mon·o·cot (mon′ə kot′), *n.* a monocotyledon. Also, **mon·o·cot·yl** (mon′ə kot′ᵊl). [shortened form]

mon·o·cot·y·le·don (mon′ə kot′ᵊlēd′ᵊn), *n.* an angiospermous plant of the subclass *Monocotyledoneae,* characterized by the production of seeds with one cotyledon and an endogenous manner of growth. Cf. **dicotyledon.** [< NL]

mon·o·cot·y·le·don·ous (mon′ə kot′ᵊlēd′ᵊnəs), *adj.* belonging or pertaining to the *Monocotyledoneae,* characterized by possession of a single cotyledon.

mo·noc·ra·cy (mō nok′rə sē, mə-), *n.,* *pl.* **-cies.** government by a single person; autocracy. [MONO- + -CRACY; modeled on *aristocracy, democracy*] —**mon·o·crat** (mon′ə-krat′), *n.* —**mon′o·crat′ic,** *adj.*

mo·noc·u·lar (mə nok′yə lər), *adj.* **1.** having only one eye. **2.** of, pertaining to, intended for, or involving the use of only one eye: *a monocular microscope.* [< LL *monocul(us)* one-eyed (see MONOCLE) + -AR[1]] —**mo·noc′u·lar·ly,** *adv.*

mon·o·cul·ture (mon′ə kul′chər), *n.* *Agric.* the use of land for growing only one type of crop. —**mon′o·cul′tur·al,** *adj.*

mon·o·cy·cle (mon′ə sī′kəl), *n.* unicycle.

mon·o·cy·clic (mon′ə sī′klik, -sik′lik), *adj.* **1.** having one cycle. **2.** *Chem.* containing one ring. —**mon′o·cy′cly,** *n.*

mon·o·cyte (mon′ə sīt′), *n.* *Anat.* a large, phagocytic leukocyte, formed in bone marrow and in the spleen, that has an oval or horseshoe-shaped nucleus. —**mon·o·cyt·ic** (mon′ə sit′ik), *adj.* —**mon′o·cy′toid,** *adj.*

mo·nod·ic (mə nod′ik), *adj.* *Music.* of or relating to monody. [< Gk *monōidik(ós)*] —**mo·nod′i·cal·ly,** *adv.*

mon·o·dy (mon′ə dē), *n.,* *pl.* **-dies. 1.** a Greek ode sung by a single voice, as in a tragedy; lament. **2.** a poem in which one person laments another's death. **3.** *Music.* **a.** a style of composition in which one part or melody predominates; homophony, as distinguished from polyphony. **b.** a piece in this style. **c.** monophony (def. 1). [< LL *monōdia* < Gk *monōidía* a solo = *monōid(ós)* singing alone (see MON-, ODE) + *-ia* -Y[3]] —**mon·o·dist** (mon′ə dist), *n.*

mo·noe·cious (mə nē′shəs), *adj.* **1.** *Biol.* having both male and female organs in the same individual; hermaphroditic. **2.** *Bot.* (of a plant, species, etc.) having the stamens and the pistils in separate flowers on the same plant. Also, **monecious, monoicous.** [MON- + Gk *oikí(on),* dim. of *oîkos* house + -OUS] —**mo·noe′cious·ly,** *adv.* —**mo·noe′cism** (mə nē′siz-əm), **mo·noe′cy,** *n.*

Monoecious branch of walnut, *Juglans quadrangulata* A, Staminate flowers; B, Pistillate flowers

mon·o·fil·a·ment (mon′ə fil′ə mənt), *n.* **1.** Also called **mon·o·fil** (mon′ə-fil′). a single large filament of synthetic fiber. —*adj.* **2.** made of such a filament: *a monofilament fishing line.*

mo·nog·a·mist (mə nog′ə mist), *n.* a person who practices or advocates monogamy.

mo·nog·a·mous (mə nog′ə məs), *adj.* **1.** practicing or advocating monogamy. **2.** pertaining to monogamy. Also, **mon·o·gam·ic** (mon′ə gam′ik). [< LL *monogamus* < Gk *monógamos* marrying only once] —**mo·nog′a·mous·ly,** *adv.* —**mo·nog′a·mous·ness,** *n.*

mo·nog·a·my (mə nog′ə mē), *n.* **1.** marriage with only one person at a time. Cf. **bigamy, polygamy** (def. 1). **2.** *Zool.* the practice of having only one mate. **3.** the practice of marrying only once during life. Cf. **digamy.** [< LL *monogamia* < Gk]

mon·o·gen·e·sis (mon′ə jen′i sis), n. **1.** the hypothetical descent of the human race from a single pair. **2.** the hypothetical descent of all living things from a single cell. Also, **mo·nog·e·ny** (mə noj′ə nē).

mon·o·ge·net·ic (mon′ō jə net′ik), *adj.* **1.** of or pertaining to monogenesis. **2.** (of certain trematode worms) having only one generation in the life cycle, without an intermediate asexual generation. **3.** *Geol.* resulting from one genetic process. Also, **mo·nog·e·nous** (mə noj′ə nəs).

mon·o·gen·ic (mon′ə jen′ik), *adj.* *Genetics.* pertaining to a character controlled by one pair of genes.

mon·o·gram (mon′ə gram′), *n.* a character consisting of two or more letters combined or interlaced, commonly one's initials, often printed on stationery, embroidered on clothing, etc. [< LL *monogram(ma)* < LGk] —**mon·o·gram·mat·ic** (mon′ə grə mat′ik), **mon′o·gram·mat′i·cal,** *adj.*

mon·o·graph (mon′ə graf′, -gräf′), *n.* **1.** a learned treatise on a particular subject. **2.** an account of a single thing or class of things. —*v.t.* **3.** to write a monograph about. —**mo·nog·ra·pher** (mə nog′rə fər), **mo·nog′ra·phist,** *n.* —**mon·o·graph·ic** (mon′ə graf′ik), **mon′o·graph′i·cal,** *adj.*

mo·nog·y·ny (mə noj′ə nē), *n.* the practice or condition of having only one wife at a time. Cf. **polygyny** (def. 1). —**mo·nog′y·nous, mon·o·gyn·ic** (mon′ə jin′ik), **mon′o·gyn′i·ous,** *adj.* —**mo·nog′y·nist,** *n.*

mon·o·hy·drate (mon′ə hī′drāt), *n.* *Chem.* a hydrate that contains one molecule of water, as ammonium carbonate, $(NH_4)_2CO_3 \cdot H_2O$. —**mon′o·hy′drat·ed,** *adj.*

mon·o·hy·dric (mon′ə hī′drik), *adj.* *Chem.* (esp. of alcohols and phenols) monohydroxy. [MONO- + HYDR(OXYL) + -IC]

mon·o·hy·drox·y (mon′ə hī drok′sē), *adj.* *Chem.* (of a molecule) containing one hydroxyl group.

mo·noi·cous (mə noi′kəs), *adj.* monoecious.

mo·nol·a·try (mə nol′ə trē), *n.* the worship of but one god when other gods are recognized as existing. —**mo·nol·a·ter** (mə nol′ə tər), *n.* —**mo·nol′a·trous,** *adj.*

mon·o·lay·er (mon′ə lā′ər), *n.* See **molecular film.**

mon·o·lin·gual (mon′ə ling′gwəl), *adj.* **1.** knowing or able to use only one language. **2.** spoken or written in only one language. —*n.* **3.** a monolingual person.

mon·o·lith (mon′ə lith), *n.* **1.** a single block of stone of considerable size. **2.** an obelisk, column, statue, etc., formed of a single block of stone. **3.** something having a uniform, massive, or intractable quality or character. [< L *monolith(us)* < Gk *monólithos* made of one stone]

mon·o·lith·ic (mon′ə lith′ik), *adj.* **1.** of or pertaining to a monolith. **2.** made of only one stone: *a monolithic column.* **3.** characterized by massiveness, total uniformity, and intractability: *a monolithic society; a monolithic state.* —**mon′o·lith′i·cal·ly,** *adv.*

mon·o·logue (mon′ə lôg′, -log′), *n.* **1.** a prolonged talk or discourse by a single speaker. **2.** any composition, as a poem, in which a single person speaks alone. **3.** a dramatic soliloquy. Also, **mon′o·log′.** [< F < Gk *monólog(os)* speaking alone] —**mon·o·log·ic** (mon′ə loj′ik), **mon′o·log′i·cal,** *adj.* —**mon·o·log·ist** (mon′ə lôg′ist, -log′-, mə nol′ə jist), **mon·o·logu·ist** (mon′ə lôg′ist, -log′-), *n.*

mon·o·ma·ni·a (mon′ə mā′nē ə, -mān′yə), *n.* **1.** partial insanity in which the psychotic thinking is confined to one idea or group of ideas. **2.** an exaggerated zeal for or interest in a single thing, idea, subject, or the like; obsession. [< NL]

—**mon·o·ma·ni·ac** (mon′ə mā′nē ak′), *n.* —**mon·o·ma·ni·a·cal** (mon′ə mə nī′ə kəl), *adj.*
mon·o·mer (mon′ə mər), *n.* *Chem.* a molecule of low molecular weight capable of reacting with identical or different molecules of low molecular weight to form a polymer. —**mon·o·mer·ic** (mon′ə mer′ik), *adj.*
mo·nom·er·ous (mə nom′ər əs), *adj.* consisting of one part. [< Gk *monomer(ḗs)* consisting of one part; see -OUS]
mon·o·me·tal·lic (mon′ō mə tal′ik), *adj.* of or using one metal.
mon·o·met·al·lism (mon′ə met′əliz′əm), *n.* the use of one metal only, as gold or silver, as a monetary standard. [MONO- + (BI)METALLISM] —**mon′o·met′al·list,** *n.*
mo·nom·e·ter (mə nom′i tər), *n.* *Pros.* a line of verse of one measure or foot. [< LL < Gk *monómetr(os).* See MONO-, METER[2]] —**mon·o·met·ri·cal** (mon′ə me′tri kəl), **mon′o·met′ric,** *adj.*
mo·no·mi·al (mō nō′mē əl, mə-), *adj.* **1.** *Algebra.* consisting of one term only. **2.** *Biol.* noting or pertaining to a name that consists of a single word or term. —*n.* **3.** *Algebra.* a monomial expression or quantity. [MON- + (BIN)OMIAL]
mon·o·mo·lec·u·lar (mon′ō mə lek′yə lər), *adj.* **1.** noting or pertaining to a thickness of one molecule. **2.** having a thickness of one molecule.
mon·o·mor·phic (mon′ə môr′fik), *adj.* **1.** *Biol.* having only one form. **2.** of the same or of an essentially similar type of structure. Also, **mon′o·mor′phous.**
Mo·non·ga·he·la (mə nong′gə hē′lə), *n.* a river flowing from N West Virginia through SW Pennsylvania into the Ohio River. 128 mi. long.
mon·o·nu·cle·ar (mon′ə no͞o′klē ər, -nyo͞o′-), *adj.* having only one nucleus.
mon·o·nu·cle·o·sis (mon′ə no͞o′klē ō′sis, -nyo͞o′-), *n.* *Pathol.* **1.** the presence of an abnormally large number of mononuclear leukocytes, or monocytes, in the blood. **2.** See **infectious mononucleosis.** [MONONUCLE(AR) + -OSIS]
mon·o·phon·ic (mon′ə fon′ik), *adj.* **1.** *Music.* of or pertaining to monophony. **2.** Also, **monaural.** of or noting a sound-reproducing system that produces a single output signal from one or more input signals. Cf. **stereophonic.**
mo·noph·o·ny (mə nof′ə nē), *n., pl.* **-nies.** **1.** a musical style employing a single melodic line without accompaniment. **2.** monody (def. 3a).
mon·oph·thong (mon′əf thông′, -thong′), *n.* *Phonet.* a vowel of apparently unvarying quality. [< LGk *monóphthong(os)* (n. use of adj.) with one sound = *mono-* MONO- + *phthóngos* sound] —**mon·oph·thon·gal** (mon′əf thông′gəl, -thong′-), *adj.*
mon·o·phy·let·ic (mon′ō fī let′ik), *adj.* **1.** of or pertaining to a single tribe or stock. **2.** developed from a single ancestral type, as a group of animals.
Mo·noph·y·site (mə nof′i sīt′), *n.* *Theol.* a person who maintains that Christ has one nature, partly divine and partly human. [< LL *monophysīta* < LGk *monophysī́tēs* = *mono-* MONO- + *phý̆s(is)* nature + *-ī́tēs* -ITE[1]] —**Mon·o·phy·sit·ic** (mon′ə fi sit′ik), *adj.* —**Mo·noph′y·sit′ism, Mo·noph′y·sism,** *n.*
mon·o·plane (mon′ə plān′), *n.* an airplane with one main sustaining surface, or one set of wings.
mon·o·ple·gi·a (mon′ə plē′jē ə, -plē′jə), *n.* *Pathol.* paralysis of only one extremity, muscle, or muscle area. —**mon·o·ple·gic** (mon′ə plē′jik, -plej′ik), *adj.*
mon·o·ploid (mon′ə ploid′), *Biol.* —*adj.* **1.** having the basic or haploid number of chromosomes. —*n.* **2.** a monoploid cell or organism.
mon·o·pode (mon′ə pōd′), *adj.* **1.** having only one foot. —*n.* **2.** a creature having only one foot. [< LL *monopod(ius)* one-footed = *monopod-* (< Gk; see MONO-, -POD) + *-ius* adj. suffix]
mon·o·po·di·um (mon′ə pō′dē əm), *n., pl.* **-di·a** (-dē ə). *Bot.* a single main axis that continues to extend at the apex in the original line of growth, giving off lateral branches beneath in acropetal succession. —**mon′o·po′di·al,** *adj.* —**mon′o·po′di·al·ly,** *adv.*
mo·nop·o·dy (mə nop′ə dē), *n., pl.* **-dies.** *Pros.* a measure consisting of one foot. [< Gk *monopodía*] —**mon·o·pod·ic** (mon′ə pod′ik), *adj.*
mo·nop·o·lise (mə nop′ə līz′), *v.t.,* **-lised, -lis·ing.** *Chiefly Brit.* monopolize. —**mo·nop′o·li·sa′tion,** *n.* —**mo·nop′o·lis′er,** *n.*
mo·nop·o·lism (mə nop′ə liz′əm), *n.* the existence or prevalence of monopolies.
mo·nop·o·list (mə nop′ə list), *n.* **1.** a person who has a monopoly. **2.** an advocate of monopoly. —**mo·nop′o·lis′tic,** *adj.* —**mo·nop′o·lis′ti·cal·ly,** *adv.*
mo·nop·o·lize (mə nop′ə līz′), *v.t.,* **-lized, -liz·ing.** **1.** to acquire, have, or exercise a monopoly of. **2.** to obtain exclusive possession of; keep entirely to oneself. Also, *esp. Brit.,* **monopolise.** —**mo·nop′o·li·za′tion,** *n.* —**mo·nop′o·liz′er,** *n.*
mo·nop·o·ly (mə nop′ə lē), *n., pl.* **-lies.** **1.** exclusive control of a commodity or service in a particular market, or a control that makes possible the manipulation of prices. **2.** an exclusive privilege to carry on a traffic or service, granted by a sovereign power. **3.** the exclusive possession or control of something. **4.** something that is the subject of such control, as a commodity, service, etc. **5.** a company or the like having such control. **6.** the market condition that exists when there is only one seller. [< L *monopōli(um)* < Gk *monopṓlion* right of exclusive sale = *mono-* MONO- + *pōl(eîn)* (to) sell + *-ion* n. suffix]
mo·nop·so·ny (mə nop′sə nē), *n., pl.* **-nies.** the market condition that exists when there is one buyer. [MON- + Gk *opsōní(a)* purchase of provisions, catering] —**mo·nop′so·nist,** *n.* —**mo·nop′so·nis′tic,** *adj.*
mon·o·rail (mon′ə rāl′), *n.* **1.** a railroad the rolling stock of which is balanced upon or suspended from a single rail. **2.** the rail of such a railroad.
mon·o·sac·cha·ride (mon′ə sak′ə rīd′, -ər id), *n.* *Chem.* a carbohydrate that does not hydrolyze, as glucose, fructose, ribose, or other simple sugars: occurring naturally or obtained by the hydrolysis of glycosides or polysaccharides. Also, **mon·o·sac·cha·rose** (mon′ə sak′ə rōs′).
mon·o·sep·al·ous (mon′ə sep′ə ləs), *adj.* *Bot.* having only one sepal, as a calyx.
mon·o·so·di·um glu·ta·mate (mon′ə sō′dē əm gloo͞′tə māt′), *Chem.* a white, crystalline, water-soluble powder, $HOOC(CH_2)_2CH(NH_2)COONa$, used chiefly to intensify the flavor of meat. Also called **MSG, sodium glutamate.** Cf. **glutamic acid.**
mon·o·some (mon′ə sōm′), *n.* *Genetics.* **1.** a chromosome having no homologue, esp. an unpaired X chromosome. **2.** a monosomic individual.
mon·o·so·mic (mon′ə sō′mik), *adj.* *Genetics.* having one less than the usual diploid number of chromosomes.
mon·o·stich (mon′ə stik′), *n.* **1.** a poem or epigram consisting of a single metrical line. **2.** a single line of poetry. [< LL *monostich(um)* < Gk *monóstichon,* n. use of neut. of *monóstichos* consisting of one line of verse] —**mon′o·stich′ic,** *adj.*
mon·o·stome (mon′ə stōm′), *adj.* having a single mouth, pore, or stoma. Also, **mo·nos·to·mous** (mə nos′tə məs).
mo·nos·tro·phe (mə nos′trə fē, mon′ə strōf′), *n.* a poem in which all the strophes or stanzas are of the same metrical form. [< Gk *monóstroph(os)* consisting of one strophe]
mon·o·stroph·ic (mon′ə strof′ik, -strō′fik), *adj.* **1.** of or consisting of a monostrophe. —*n.* **2.** **monostrophics,** monostrophic verses. [< Gk *monostrophik(ós)*]
mon·o·sty·lous (mon′ə stī′ləs), *adj.* *Bot.* having only one style.
mon·o·syl·lab·ic (mon′ə si lab′ik), *adj.* **1.** having only one syllable, as the word *no.* **2.** having a vocabulary composed exclusively of monosyllables. **3.** expressed in or employing monosyllables. [< ML *monosyllabic(us)* = LL *monosyllab(on)* monosyllable (< Gk, n. use of neut. of *monosýllabos* monosyllabic) + *-icus* -IC] —**mon′o·syl·lab′i·cal·ly,** *adv.*
mon·o·syl·la·bism (mon′ə sil′ə biz′əm), *n.* **1.** the quality of being monosyllabic. **2.** the use of monosyllables. [< LL *monosyllab(on)* monosyllable (see MONOSYLLABIC) + -ISM]
mon·o·syl·la·ble (mon′ə sil′ə bəl), *n.* a word of one syllable, as *yes* or *no.*
mon·o·sym·met·ric (mon′ə si me′trik), *adj.* **1.** *Crystall.* monoclinic. **2.** *Biol., Bot.* zygomorphic (def. 1). Also, **mon′o·sym·met′ri·cal.** —**mon′o·sym·met′ri·cal·ly,** *adv.* —**mon·o·sym·met·ry** (mon′ə sim′i trē), *n.*
mon·o·the·ism (mon′ə thē iz′əm, mon′ə thē′iz əm), *n.* the doctrine or belief that there is only one God. [MONO- + (POLY)THEISM] —**mon′o·the′ist,** *n., adj.* —**mon′o·the·is′tic, mon′o·the·is′ti·cal,** *adj.* —**mon′o·the·is′ti·cal·ly,** *adv.*
mon·o·tint (mon′ə tint′), *n.* monochrome.
mon·o·tone[1] (mon′ə tōn′), *n.* **1.** a vocal utterance in one unvaried tone of voice. **2.** a single tone without harmony or variation in pitch. **3.** recitation or singing of words in such a tone. **4.** sameness of style, as in composition or writing.
mon·o·tone[2] (mon′ə tōn′), *adj.* **1.** monotonous. **2.** consisting of or characterized by a uniform tone of one color. [< F *monotone* < LGk *monóton(os)* MONOTONOUS]
mon·o·ton·ic (mon′ə ton′ik), *adj.* **1.** of, pertaining to, or uttered in a monotone. **2.** *Math.* (of a function or of a particular set of values of a function) increasing or decreasing. —**mon′o·ton′i·cal·ly,** *adv.*
mo·not·o·nous (mə not′ənəs), *adj.* **1.** lacking in variety; tiresomely uniform. **2.** characterizing a sound continuing on one note. **3.** having very little inflection; limited to a narrow pitch range. [< LGk *monótonos*] —**mo·not′o·nous·ly,** *adv.* —**mo·not′o·nous·ness,** *n.* —**Syn. 1.** tedious, humdrum, boring, dull. —**Ant. 1.** interesting, diverting.
mo·not·o·ny (mə not′ənē), *n.* **1.** wearisome uniformity or lack of variety. **2.** the continuance of an unvarying sound; monotone. **3.** sameness of tone or pitch, as in speaking. [< LGk *monotonía.* See MONOTONOUS, -Y[3]]
mon·o·treme (mon′ə trēm′), *n.* any oviparous animal of the *Monotremata,* the lowest order of mammals, comprising only the duckbill and the echidnas of the Australian region. [back formation from NL *Monotrēmata,* neut. pl. of *monotrēmatus* one-holed = *mono-* MONO- + *trēmat-* (< Gk, s. of *trêma* hole) + *-us* -OUS] —**mon·o·tre·ma·tous** (mon′ə trē′mə təs), *adj.*
mo·not·ri·chate (mə no′trə kit), *adj.* (of bacteria) having a single flagellum at one pole. Also, **mo·not′ri·chous, mon·o·trich·ic** (mon′ə trik′ik).
Mon·o·type (mon′ə tīp′), *n.* **1.** *Print., Trademark.* a machine for setting and casting individual types that uses a paper tape containing holes in a coded pattern. **2.** (*l.c.*) *Biol.* the only type of its group, as a single species constituting a genus. —**mon′o·typ′er,** *n.*
mon·o·typ·ic (mon′ə tip′ik), *adj.* **1.** having only one type. **2.** *Biol.* having only one representative, as a genus with a single species.
mon·o·va·lent (mon′ə vā′lənt), *adj.* **1.** *Chem.* univalent. **2.** *Bacteriol.* (of an immune serum) containing only one kind of antibody. —**mon′o·va′lence, mon′o·va′len·cy,** *n.*
mon·ox·ide (mon ok′sīd, mə nok′-), *n.* *Chem.* an oxide containing one oxygen atom in each molecule.
Mon·roe (mən rō′), *n.* **1. Harriet,** 1861?–1936, U.S. editor and poet. **2. James,** 1758–1831, 5th president of the U.S. 1817–25. **3.** a city in N Louisiana. 56,374 (1970).
Monroe′ Doc′trine, the doctrine, contained in a message of President Monroe to Congress in 1823, proscribing European intervention in the affairs of Spanish-American states and closing future colonization to European countries.
Mon·roe·ville (mən rō′vil), *n.* a city in SW Pennsylvania, near Pittsburgh. 29,011 (1970).
Mon·ro·vi·a (mən rō′vē ə), *n.* **1.** a seaport in and the capital of Liberia, in W Africa. 204,000. **2.** a city in SW California. 30,015 (1970).
mons (monz), *n., pl.* **mon·tes** (mon′tēz). *Anat.* a rounded prominence of fatty tissue, covered with hair, over the pubic symphysis of the adult human. [< NL, L: mountain, hill; see MOUNT[2]]
Mons., Monsieur.
Mon·sei·gneur (môɴ se nyœr′), *n., pl.* **Mes·sei·gneurs** (mā se nyœr′). **1.** a French title of honor given to princes, bishops, and other persons of eminence. **2.** a person bearing this title. Also, **mon·sei·gneur′.** [< F: my lord; see SEIGNEUR]
mon·sieur (mə syœ′), *n., pl.* **mes·sieurs** (*Fr.* me syœ′; *Eng.* mes′ərz). the conventional French title of respect and term of address for a man, corresponding to *Mr.* or *Sir.* [< F: lit., my lord (orig. applied only to men of high station); see SIEUR]
Mon·si·gnor (mon sē′nyər; *It.* môn′sē nyôr′), *n., pl.*

Mon·si·gnors, *It.* **Mon·si·gno·ri** (môn′sē nyô′RE). *Rom. Cath. Ch.* **1.** a title conferred upon certain prelates. **2.** a person bearing this title. Also, **mon·si′gnor, Monsignore.** [< It < F; see MONSEIGNEUR, SIGNOR]

Mon·si·gno·re (*It.* môn′sē nyô′RE), *n., pl.* **Mon·si·gno·ri** (*It.* môn′sē nyô′RE). Monsignor.

mon·soon (mon so͞on′), *n.* **1.** the seasonal wind of the Indian Ocean and southern Asia, blowing from the southwest in summer and from the northeast in winter. **2.** (in India and nearby lands) the season during which the southwest monsoon blows, commonly marked by heavy rains. **3.** any wind that changes direction with the seasons. **4.** any persistent wind established between water and adjoining land. [< D *monssoen* (now obs.) < Pg *monção*, earlier *moução* < Ar *mawsim* season] —**mon·soon′al,** *adj.*

mon·ster (mon′stər), *n.* **1.** a fabled animal combining human and animal features, as a centaur, griffin, or sphinx. **2.** any creature so ugly as to appall or frighten people. **3.** any animal or human grotesquely deviating from the normal. **4.** anything unnatural or monstrous. **5.** *Biol.* an animal or plant of abnormal form or structure, as from marked malformation, the absence of certain parts or organs, etc. **6.** a person who excites horror, as by wickedness or cruelty. **7.** any animal or thing of huge size. —*adj.* **8.** huge; enormous. [ME *monstre* < L *monstr(um)*, orig. a portent = *mon(ēre)* (to) warn + *-strum* n. suffix] —**mon′ster·like′,** *adj.* —**Syn. 6.** fiend, brute, devil.

mon·strance (mon′strəns), *n. Rom. Cath. Ch.* a receptacle in which the consecrated Host is exposed for adoration. [ME < ML *monstrantia* = *monstr(āre)* (to) show + *-antia* -ANCE]

mon·stros·i·ty (mon stros′i tē), *n., pl.* **-ties. 1.** the state or character of being monstrous. **2.** a monster or something monstrous. [< LL *monstrōsitās*]

mon·strous (mon′strəs), *adj.* **1.** frightful or hideous, esp. in appearance. **2.** shocking or revolting; outrageous. **3.** extraordinarily great; huge. **4.** deviating grotesquely from what is natural or normal. **5.** having the nature or appearance of a fabulous monster. [late ME < L *monstrōs(us)*] —**mon′strous·ly,** *adv.* —**mon′strous·ness,** *n.* —**Syn. 1, 2.** horrible.

mons ve·ne·ris (monz′ ven′ər is), *pl.* **mon·tes ve·ne·ris** (mon′tēz ven′ər is). *Anat.* the mons of the human female. [< NL: mons of Venus]

Mont., Montana.

mon·tage (mon täzh′; *Fr.* môN TAZH′), *n., pl.* **-tag·es** (-täzh′iz; *Fr.* -TAZH′). **1.** the technique of combining in a single photographic composition elements from various sources, as parts of different photographs **(photomontage),** by superimposition, juxtaposition, etc. **2.** a photographic image produced by this technique. **3.** *Motion Pictures, Television.* **a.** juxtaposition or partial superimposition of several shots to form a single image. **b.** a technique of film editing in which this is used to present an idea or set of interconnected ideas. **4.** any combination of disparate elements that forms or is felt to form a unified whole, single image, etc. [< F = *mont(er)* (to) MOUNT[1] + *-age* -AGE]

Mon·ta·gnard (mon′tən yärd′, -yär′), *n., pl.* **-gnards,** (*esp. collectively*) **-gnard,** *adj.* —*n.* **1.** a member of an Athapaskan Indian tribe inhabiting the Canadian Rockies. **2.** (*sometimes l.c.*) a member of a dark-skinned people of mixed ethnic origins inhabiting the highland areas of both South and North Vietnam. —*adj.* **3.** (*sometimes l.c.*) of or pertaining to a Montagnard or Montagnards. [< F: lit., mountaineer. See MOUNTAIN, -ARD]

Mon·ta·gu (mon′tə gyo͞o′), *n.* **1. Charles, 1st Earl of Halifax,** 1661–1715, British statesman: prime minister 1714–15. **2. Lady Mary Wort·ley** (wûrt′lē), nee **Pierrepont,** 1689–1762, English author.

Mon·taigne (mon tān′; *Fr.* môN ten′yᵊ), *n.* **Mi·chel Ey·quem** (mē shel′ e kem′), **Seigneur de,** 1533–92, French essayist.

Mon·tan·a (mon tan′ə), *n.* a state in the NW United States. 694,409 (1970); 147,138 sq. mi. *Cap.:* Helena. *Abbr.:* Mont., MT —**Mon·tan′an,** *adj., n.*

mon·tane (mon′tān), *Ecol.* —*adj.* **1.** pertaining to mountain conditions. —*n.* **2.** the lower vegetation belt on mountains. [< L *montān(us)*. See MOUNT[2], -ANE]

mon·ta·ni sem·per li·be·ri (mōn tä′nē sem′peR lē′be RE; *Eng.* mon tā′nī sem′pər lib′ə rī′), *Latin.* mountaineers (are) always freemen: motto of West Virginia.

mon′tan wax′ (mon′tan), a dark-brown bituminous wax extracted from lignite and peat: used chiefly in polishes and waxes for furniture, shoes, etc. [< L *montān(us)* of a mountain]

Mon·tau·ban (môN tō bäN′), *n.* a city in S France, N of Toulouse. 43,401 (1962).

Mon′tauk Point′ (mon′tôk), the E end of Long Island, in SE New York.

Mont Blanc (môN bläN′), a mountain in SW Europe, on the boundary between France and Italy: highest peak of the Alps, 15,781 ft. Italian, **Mon·te Bian·co** (môn′te byäng′kô).

Mont·calm (mont käm′; *Fr.* môN KALM′), *n.* **Louis Joseph** (lwē zhô zef′), 1712–59, French general in Canada.

Mont Cer·vin (môN SER VAN′), French name of **Matterhorn.**

Mont·clair (mont clâr′), *n.* a city in NE New Jersey. 44,043 (1970).

mont-de-pié·té (môNdᵊ pyā tā′), *n., pl.* **monts-de-pié·té** (môNdᵊ pyā tā′). *French.* a public pawnbroking establishment for lending money on reasonable terms, esp. to the poor. [< It *monte di pietà* bank of pity]

mon·te (mon′tē, mōn′tā; *Sp.* môn′te), *n. Cards.* a gambling game played with a 40-card pack. Also called **mon′te bank′.** [< Sp: mountain, hence, heap (of cards); see MOUNT[2]]

Mon·te·bel·lo (mon′tə bel′ō), *n.* a city in SW California, SE of Los Angeles. 42,807 (1970).

Mon·te Car·lo (mon′tē kär′lō; *It.* môn′te käR′lô), a town in Monaco principality, in SE France: gambling resort. 10,000.

Mon·te Cas·si·no (môn′te käs sē′nô), a monastery at Cassino: founded c A.D. 530 by St. Benedict and destroyed by Allied bombings in 1944.

Mon·te Cor·no (môn′te kôR′nô), a mountain in central Italy: highest peak in the Apennines, 9585 ft.

Mon·te′go Bay′ (mon tē′gō), a city on NW Jamaica: seaside resort. 50,000.

mon·teith (mon tēth′), *n.* a large punch bowl, usually of silver, having a notched rim for suspending punch cups. [named after its 17th-century Scottish inventor]

Mon·te·ne·gro (mon′tə nē′grō; *It.* môn′te ne′gRô), *n.* a constituent republic of Yugoslavia, in the S part: an independent kingdom 1878–1918. 471,894 (1961); 5345 sq. mi. *Cap.:* Cetinje. —**Mon·te·ne·grin** (mon′tə nē′grin), *adj., n.*

AUSTRIA-HUNGARY · SERBIA · Sarajevo · Montenegro · ADRIATIC SEA · ALBANIA · ITALY · GREECE · 1878-1918

Mon·te·rey (mon′tə rā′), *n.* a city in W California, on Monterey Bay: the capital of California until 1847. 26,302 (1970).

Mon′terey Bay′, an inlet of the Pacific in W California. 26 mi. long.

Mon′terey Park′, a city in SW California, E of Los Angeles. 49,166 (1970).

mon·te·ro (mon târ′ō; *Sp.* môn te′Rô), *n., pl.* **-ros** (-rōz; *Sp.* -Rôs). a huntsman's cap, round in shape and having a flap. [< Sp, special use of *montero* huntsman, lit., mountaineer]

Mon·ter·rey (mon′tə rā′; *Sp.* môn′teR Rā′), *n.* a city in and the capital of Nuevo Leon, in NE Mexico: battle 1846. 1,500,000.

Mon·tes·pan (mon′tə span′; *Fr.* môN tes päN′), *n.* **Marquise de** (*Françoise Athénaïs de Rochechouart*), 1641–1707, mistress of Louis XIV of France.

Mon·tes·quieu (mon′te skyo͞o′; *Fr.* môN tes kyœ′), *n.* (*Charles Louis de Secondat, Baron de la Brède et de Montesquieu*) 1689–1755, French philosophical writer.

Mon·tes·so·ri (mon′ti sōr′ē, -sôr′ē; *It.* môn′tes sô′RE), *n.* **Ma·ri·a** (mə rē′ə; *It.* mä RE′ä), 1870–1952, Italian educator.

Montesso′ri meth′od, a system for training and instructing young children, of which the fundamental aim is self-education by the children themselves accompanied by special emphasis on the training of the senses. Also called **Montesso′ri sys′tem.** [named after Maria MONTESSORI]

Mon·teux (mon tœ′; *Fr.* môN tœ′), *n.* **Pierre** (pyeR), 1875–1964, U.S. orchestra conductor, born in France.

Mon·te·ver·di (mon′tə vâr′dē; *It.* môn′te veR′dē), *n.* **Clau·dio** (klou′dyô), 1567–1643, Italian composer.

Mon·te·vi·de·o (mon′tə vi dā′ō, -vid′ē ō′; *Sp.* môn′te-vē the′ô), *n.* a seaport in and the capital of Uruguay. 1,229,748.

Mon·te·zu·ma II (mon′ti zo͞o′mə), c1470–1520, last Aztec emperor of Mexico 1502–20. Also, **Moctezuma.**

Mon′tezu′ma's revenge′, *Facetious.* (in Mexico) diarrhea. [with reference to the killing of Montezuma by the invading Spanish]

Mont·fort (mont′fərt; *Fr.* môN fôR′), *n.* **1. Si·mon de** (sē môN′ də), c1160–1218, French leader of the crusade against the Albigenses. **2.** his son **Simon de, Earl of Leicester,** 1208?–65, English soldier and statesman.

mont·gol·fi·er (mont gol′fē ər; *Fr.* môN gôl fyā′), *n., pl.* **-fi·ers** (-fē ərz; *Fr.* -fyā′). a hot-air balloon in which the air is heated by a fire carried beneath it. [named after Joseph and Jacques MONTGOLFIER]

Mont·gol·fi·er (mont gol′fē ər; *Fr.* môN gôl fyā′), *n.* **Jacques É·tienne** (zhäk ā tyen′), 1745–99, and his brother **Jo·seph Mi·chel** (zhô zef′ mē shel′), 1740–1810, French aeronauts: inventors of the first practical balloon 1783.

Mont·gom·er·y (mont gum′ə rē, -gum′rē), *n.* **1. Bernard Law, 1st Viscount Montgomery of Alamein** ("*Monty*"), 1887–1976, British field marshal. **2. Richard,** 1736–75, American Revolutionary general. **3.** a city in and the capital of Alabama, in the central part, on the Alabama River. 133,386 (1970). **4.** Montgomeryshire.

Mont·gom·er·y·shire (mont gum′ə rē shēr′, -shər), *n.* a county in central Wales. 44,228 (1961); 797 sq. mi. *Co. seat:* Montgomery. Also called **Montgomery.**

month (munth), *n.* **1.** Also called **solar month.** one twelfth of a solar or tropical year. **2.** any of the twelve parts, as January, February, etc., into which the calendar year is divided. **3.** the time from any day of one calendar month to the corresponding day of the next. **4.** a period of about four weeks. **5.** Also called **lunar month.** the period of a complete revolution of the moon around the earth, as the period between successive conjunctions with a star **(sidereal month),** equal to 27.322 days. [ME; OE *mōnath;* c. OHG *mānōd,* Icel *mānathr.* See MOON]

month·ly (munth′lē), *adj., n., pl.* **-lies,** *adv.* —*adj.* **1.** pertaining to a month. **2.** happening, falling due, etc., once a month. **3.** continuing or lasting for a month. —*n.* **4.** a periodical published once a month. —*adv.* **5.** once a month; by the month.

Mon·ti·cel·lo (mon′ti sel′ō, -chel′-), *n.* the estate of Thomas Jefferson, near Charlottesville, Virginia.

mon·ti·cule (mon′tə kyo͞ol′), *n.* **1.** a small mountain, hill, or mound. **2.** a subordinate volcano cone. [< LL *monticul(us).* See MOUNT[2], -CULE]

Mont·lu·çon (môN lʏ sôN′), *n.* a city in central France. 58,855 (1962).

Mont·mar·tre (môN MAR′tRᵊ), *n.* a hilly section in the N part of Paris, France: noted for its cafés and the artists who have frequented and lived in the area.

Mont·mo·ren·cy (mont′mə ren′sē; *Fr.* môN mô RäN sē′), *n.* **Anne** (an; *Fr.* AN), **Duc de,** 1493–1567, French marshal: constable of France 1537.

Mont·par·nasse (môN PAR NAS′), *n.* a district in S Paris, France, on the left bank of the Seine: noted for its cafés and artists.

Mont·pel·ier (mont pēl′yər), *n.* a city in and the capital of Vermont, in the central part. 8609 (1970).

Mont·pel·lier (môN pe lyā′), *n.* a city in S France, near the Mediterranean. 123,367 (1962).

Mon·tra·chet, Le (lə mōN′trä shā′, -trə-; *Fr.* lə môN-ʀa she′), a full-bodied white wine from Burgundy.

Mont·re·al (mon′trē ôl′, mun′-), *n.* a seaport in S Quebec, in SE Canada, on an island in the St. Lawrence. 1,080,546. French, **Mont·ré·al** (mōN rā al′). —**Mont′re·al′er,** *n.*

Mon·treuil (môN tʀœ′yᵊ), *n.* a suburb of Paris, in N France. 96,684.

Mont·rose (mon trōz′), *n.* **James Graham, Marquis of,** 1612–50, Scottish supporter of Charles I.

Mont-Saint-Mi·chel (môN saN mē shel′), *n.* a rocky islet near coast of NW France, in inlet of Gulf of St. Malo: famous abbey and fortress. Also, **Mont Saint Mi·chel′.**

Mont·ser·rat (mont′sə rat′; *for 2 also Sp.* mônt′seʀ rät′), *n.* **1.** an island in the central Leeward Islands, in the E West Indies: a British colony. 12,162; 32½ sq. mi. *Cap.:* Plymouth. **2.** a mountain in NE Spain, NW of Barcelona: the site of Montserrat Monastery. 4058 ft.

mon·u·ment (mon′yə mənt), *n.* **1.** something built or placed to commemorate a person, event, etc. **2.** something shown or maintained for its historical, aesthetic, or scenic interest, as a building or site. **3.** a person or thing that exemplifies an outstanding quality or attribute. **4.** a written tribute to a person, esp. after his death. **5.** an object that marks property lines or the like. **6.** *Obs.* a statue. [ME < L *monument(um)* = *monu-* (var. of *moni-,* comb. form of *monēre* to remind) + *-mentum* -MENT]

mon·u·men·tal (mon′yə men′tᵊl), *adj.* **1.** resembling a monument, as in being massive or imposing. **2.** of historical or enduring significance. **3.** of or pertaining to a monument or monuments. **4.** serving as a monument. **5.** conspicuously great: *monumental stupidity.* **6.** *Fine Arts.* of heroic scale. [< LL *monumentāl(is)*] —**mon′u·men′tal·ism,** *n.* —**mon′u·men·tal′i·ty,** *n.* —**mon′u·men′tal·ly,** *adv.*

mon·u·men·tal·ise (mon′yə men′tᵊlīz′), *v.t.,* **-ised, -is·ing.** *Chiefly Brit.* monumentalize.

mon·u·men·tal·ize (mon′yə men′tᵊlīz′), *v.t.,* **-ized, -iz·ing.** to establish an enduring memorial or record of.

-mony, a noun suffix indicating result or condition (*parsimony*), but sometimes having the same function as **-ment.** [< L *-mōnia, -mōnium*]

Mon·za (mon′zə; *It.* môn′tsä), *n.* a city in N Italy, N of Milan. 121,155.

mon·zo·nite (mon′zə nīt′), *n.* any of a group of granular igneous rocks having approximately equal amounts of orthoclase and plagioclase feldspar, intermediate in composition between syenite and diorite. [< G *Monzonit,* named after *Monzoni,* mountain in Tyrol; see -ITE¹] —**mon·zo·nit·ic** (mon′zə nit′ik), *adj.*

moo (mo͞o), *v.,* **mooed, moo·ing,** *n., pl.* **moos.** —*v.i.* **1.** to utter the characteristic sound of a cow; low. —*n.* **2.** a mooing sound. [imit.]

mooch (mo͞och), *Slang.* —*v.t.* **1.** scrounge (defs. 1, 2). —*v.i.* **2.** scrounge (def. 4). **3.** to beg. [late ME, appar. var. of ME *michen* < OF *muchie(r)* (to) skulk, hide] —**mooch′er,** *n.*

mood¹ (mo͞od), *n.* **1.** a person's emotional state or outlook at a particular moment. **2.** a person's disposition in dealing with others at a particular moment. **3.** an emotional response or attitude toward something seen, heard, or otherwise experienced. **4. moods,** fits of emotion, esp. of sullenness or gloom. [ME; OE *mōd* mind, spirit, courage] —**Syn. 1.** temper, humor, disposition, inclination.

mood² (mo͞od), *n.* **1.** *Gram.* a set of categories for a verb, used chiefly to indicate the attitude of a speaker toward what he is saying, as certainty or uncertainty, wish or command, emphasis or hesitancy, and usually inflected or involving the use of auxiliary words, as *can, may, might: the Latin indicative mood.* **2.** *Logic.* any of the various forms of valid syllogisms. Also called **mode.** [special use of MOOD¹ by influence of MODE¹]

mood·y (mo͞o′dē), *adj.,* **mood·i·er, mood·i·est. 1.** given to gloomy or sullen moods. **2.** revealing such a mood: *a moody silence.* **3.** exhibiting sharply varying moods. [ME *mody,* OE *mōdig*] —**mood′i·ly,** *adv.* —**mood′i·ness,** *n.*

Moo·dy (mo͞o′dē), *n.* **1. Dwight Ly·man** (lī′mən), 1837–1899, U.S. evangelist. **2. William Vaughn** (vôn), 1869–1910, U.S. poet and playwright.

Moog′ syn′thesiz′er (mōg), *Music.* a type of synthesizer that electronically produces a much wider range of timbres than can be done by conventional instruments. Also called **Moog.** [after Robert A. *Moog* (b. 1934), U.S. engineer]

mool (mo͞ol), *n.* *Scot. and North Eng.* **1.** soft, crumbly soil rich in mold or humus. **2.** earth from or for a grave. **3.** a grave. [var. of MOLD³]

moo·la (mo͞o′lə), *n.* *U.S. Slang.* money. Also, **moo′lah.** [?]

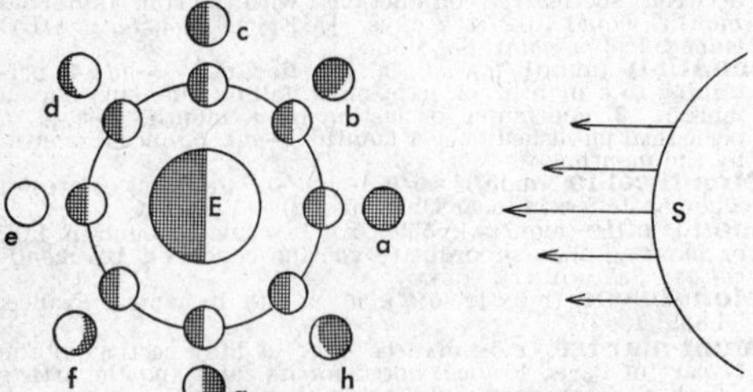

Phases of the moon
Figures on the inner circle show the moon in its orbit; those on the outer circle represent the moon's corresponding phases as seen from the earth; a, New moon (invisible); b, Crescent (waxing moon); c, First quarter (half-moon); d, Gibbous; e, Full moon; f, Gibbous; g, Last quarter (half moon); h, Crescent (waning moon); S, Sun; E, Earth

moon (mo͞on), *n.* **1.** the earth's natural satellite, orbiting the earth at a mean distance of 238,857 miles and having a diameter of 2160 miles. **2.** this body as it appears at a given moment or during a given phase. **3.** a month. **4.** any planetary satellite. **5.** something shaped like an orb or a crescent. —*v.i. Informal.* **6.** to indulge in sentimental reveries. **7.** to gaze dreamily or sentimentally at something or someone. —*v.t.* **8.** *Informal.* to spend (time) idly: *to moon the afternoon away.* [ME *mone,* OE *mōna;* c. OHG *māno,* Icel *māni,* Goth *mena,* Gk *mḗnē* moon] —**moon′less,** *adj.*

moon·beam (mo͞on′bēm′), *n.* a ray of moonlight.

moon-blind (mo͞on′blīnd′), *adj.* *Vet. Pathol.* (of horses) afflicted with moon blindness.

moon′ blind′ness, *Vet. Pathol.* a specific, probably noninfectious disease of horses in which the eyes suffer from recurring attacks of inflammation, and which eventually results in opacity and blindness.

moon·bow (mo͞on′bō′), *n.* a rainbow caused by the refraction and reflection of light from the moon. [MOON + (RAIN)BOW]

moon·calf (mo͞on′kaf′, -käf′), *n., pl.* **-calves. 1.** a congenital imbecile. **2.** a foolish person. **3.** a person who spends much time idly daydreaming.

moon-faced (mo͞on′fāst′), *adj.* having a very round face, regarded as resembling a full moon.

moon·fish (mo͞on′fish′), *n., pl.* (*esp. collectively*) **-fish,** (*esp. referring to two or more kinds or species*) **-fish·es. 1.** any of several silvery, marine fishes of the genus *Vomer,* having a very compressed body. **2.** the opah. **3.** any of various other rounded, silvery fishes.

moon·flow·er (mo͞on′flou′ər), *n.* a convolvulaceous plant, *Calonyction aculeatum,* having fragrant, white flowers that bloom at night.

Moon·ie (mo͞o′nē), *n.* *Informal.* a member or follower of the Unification Church, a religious sect headed by the Rev. Sun Myung Moon, esp. a young person living in a communal center sponsored by this sect. [after Sun Myung *Moon,* b. 1920, South Korean evangelist in the U.S.; see -IE]

moon·ish (mo͞o′nish), *adj.* **1.** capricious; inconstant. **2.** fully round or plump and soft. [ME *monish*] —**moon′ish·ly,** *adv.*

moon·light (mo͞on′līt′), *n., adj., v.,* **-light·ed, -light·ing.** —*n.* **1.** the light of the moon. —*adj.* **2.** pertaining to moonlight. **3.** illuminated by moonlight. **4.** occurring by moonlight, or by night. —*v.i.* **5.** *Informal.* to practice moonlighting. [ME *monelight*]

moon·light·ing (mo͞on′lī′ting), *n.* *Informal.* working at an additional job, usually at night, after one's regular, full-time employment. —**moon′light′er,** *n.*

moon·lit (mo͞on′lit′), *adj.* lighted by the moon.

moon·rak·er (mo͞on′rā′kər), *n.* **1.** Also called **moonsail** (mo͞on′səl, -sāl′). *Naut.* a light square sail set above a skysail. **2.** a simpleton.

moon·rise (mo͞on′rīz′), *n.* **1.** the rising of the moon above the horizon. **2.** the time at which this occurs.

moon·scape (mo͞on′skāp′), *n.* **1.** the general appearance of the surface of the moon. **2.** an artistic representation of it. [MOON + (LAND)SCAPE]

moon·seed (mo͞on′sēd′), *n.* any climbing herb of the genus *Menispermum,* having greenish-white flowers and crescent-shaped seeds.

moon·shine (mo͞on′shīn′), *n.* **1.** *U.S. Informal.* smuggled or illicitly distilled liquor, esp. corn whiskey as illegally made in rural areas of the southern states. **2.** the light of the moon. **3.** empty or foolish talk, ideas, etc.; nonsense.

moon·shin·er (mo͞on′shī′nər), *n.* *U.S. Informal.* a person who distills or sells liquor illegally, esp. corn whiskey in rural areas of the southern states.

moon·shot (mo͞on′shot′), *n.* **1.** the act or procedure of launching a missile to the moon. **2.** the missile itself.

moon·stone (mo͞on′stōn′), *n.* a semitransparent or translucent, opalescent, pearly-blue variety of adularia, used as a gem.

moon·struck (mo͞on′struk′), *adj.* harmed in mind or body,s upposedly by the influence of the moon. Also, **moon·strick·en** (mo͞on′strik′ən).

moon·wort (mo͞on′wûrt′), *n.* **1.** any fern of the genus *Botrychium,* esp. *B. Lunaria,* having fronds with crescent-shaped pinnae. **2.** honesty (def. 4).

moon·y (mo͞o′nē), *adj.,* **moon·i·er, moon·i·est. 1.** resembling the moon or moonlight. **2.** moonlit. —**moon′i·ly,** *adv.* —**moon′i·ness,** *n.*

moor¹ (mo͝or), *n.* *Chiefly Brit.* a tract of open, peaty, wasteland, often overgrown with heather. [ME *more,* OE *mōr;* c. D *moer,* G *Moor* marsh] —**moor′y,** *adj.*

moor² (mo͝or), *v.t.* **1.** to secure (a ship, dirigible, etc.) in a particular place. **2.** to fix firmly; secure. —*v.i.* **3.** to moor one's ship, dirigible, etc. **4.** to be made secure by cables or the like. —*n.* **5.** the act of mooring. [late ME *more,* akin to OE *mǣrels-* in *mǣrelstrāp* mooring rope; see MARLINE]

Moor (mo͝or), *n.* **1.** a Muslim of the mixed Berber and Arab people inhabiting NW Africa. **2.** (formerly, in European use) a Muslim. [ME *More* < MF, var. of *Maure* < L *Maur(us)* < Gk *Maûros*]

moor·age (mo͝or′ij), *n.* **1.** a place for mooring. **2.** a charge or payment for the use of moorings. **3.** the act or an instance of mooring. **4.** the state of being moored.

Moore (mo͝or, mōr, môr), *n.* **1. Douglas Stuart,** 1893–1969, U.S. composer. **2. George,** 1852–1933, Irish novelist, critic, and dramatist. **3. G(eorge) E(dward),** 1873–1958, English philosopher. **4. Henry,** 1898–1986, English sculptor. **5. Sir John,** 1761–1809, British general. **6. Marianne (Craig)** (krāg), 1887–1972, U.S. poet and critic. **7. Thomas,** 1779–1852, Irish poet.

Moor·head (mōr′hed′, môr′-, mo͝or′-), *n.* a city in W Minnesota. 29,687 (1970).

moor·hen (mo͝or′hen′), *n.* a common, European gallinule, *Gallinula chloropus.* [ME *mor-hen*]

moor·ing (mo͝or′ing), *n.* **1.** the act of a person or thing that moors. **2.** Usually, **moorings.** the means by which a vessel is moored.

Moor·ish (mo͝or′ish), *adj.* of, pertaining to, or resembling the Moors. [late ME *morys*]

moor·land (mo͝or′land′), *n.* *Chiefly Brit.* an area of moors, esp. country abounding in heather. [ME *more lond,* OE *morlond*]

moor·wort (mo͝or′wûrt′), *n.* a low, ericaceous shrub, *Andromeda polifolia,* having pink or white flowers, native to swamplands in the Northern Hemisphere.

moose (mōōs), *n., pl.* **moose.** **1.** a large animal, *Alces americanus,* of the deer family, inhabiting Canada and the northern U.S., the male of which has enormous palmate antlers, long legs, and a large head. **2.** a similar species, *A. gigas,* found in Alaska. **3.** the European elk, *A. machlis.* [< Algonquian; kindred forms in Narragansett, Delaware, etc., meaning "he strips or eats off (trees and shrubs)"]

Moose, *Alces americanus* (5½ ft. high at shoulder; length 9 ft.)

Moose′head Lake′ (mōōs′hed′), a lake in central Maine. 36 mi. long; 120 sq. mi.

Moose′ Jaw′, a city in S Saskatchewan, in SW Canada. 32,581.

moose·milk (mōōs′milk′), *n. Canadian Dial.* **1.** homemade or bootleg whiskey. **2.** a cocktail having a base of rum and milk.

moot (mōōt), *adj.* **1.** subject to argument or discussion; debatable; doubtful: *a moot point.* **2.** of little or no practical value or meaning; purely academic. **3.** not actual; theoretical or hypothetical. **—*v.t.*** **4.** to present or introduce for discussion. **5.** to reduce or remove the practical significance of (a question). **—*n.*** **6.** an early English assembly of the people, exercising administrative powers. **7.** (in some English towns) the town hall. **8.** an argument or discussion, esp. of a hypothetical legal case. [ME *mote,* OE (*ge*)*mōt* meeting, assembly: c. Icel *mōt,* D *gemoet* meeting. See MEET[1]] **—Syn. 1.** disputable, disputed, unsettled.

moot′ court′, a mock court for the conduct of hypothetical legal cases, as for students of law.

mop[1] (mop), *n., v.,* **mopped, mop·ping.** **—*n.*** **1.** a bundle of absorbent material, as yarn or cloth, fastened at the end of a stick or handle and used for washing floors, dishes, etc. **2.** *Slang.* a thick mass of hair. **—*v.t.*** **3.** to rub or wipe with or as with a mop. **4. mop up, a.** *Mil.* to clear of surviving enemy combatants. **b.** *Informal.* to complete or finish. [earlier *map,* late ME *mappe* < ML *mappula* a cloth]

mop[2] (mop), *v.,* **mopped, mop·ping,** *n.* **—*v.i.*** **1.** to make a disappointed or unhappy face. **—*n.*** **2.** a wry face; grimace. [? akin to D *moppen* to pout]

mop·board (mop′bōrd′, -bôrd′), *n.* baseboard (def. 1). [so called because it adjoins the floor surface, which is cleaned by a mop]

mope (mōp), *v.,* **moped, mop·ing,** *n.* **—*v.i.*** **1.** to be sunk in listless apathy or dull dejection. **—*v.t.*** **2.** to make listless and dispirited. **—*n.*** **3.** a person who mopes or is given to moping. **4. mopes,** low spirits; blues. [? var. of MOP[2]] **—mop′er,** *n.* **—mop′ing·ly,** *adv.*

mo·ped (mō′ped), *n.* a low-powered, heavily built motorized bicycle. [MO(TOR) + PED(AL)] **—mo′ped′er,** *n.*

mop·ish (mō′pish), *adj.* given to moping; listless and dejected. **—mop′ish·ly,** *adv.* **—mop′ish·ness,** *n.*

mop·pet (mop′it), *n. Informal.* a young child. [obs. *mop* rag doll, baby (see MOP[1]) + -ET]

Mop·po (môp′ō), *n.* Japanese name of **Mokpo.**

mop-up (mop′up′), *n.* the act, process, or an instance of mopping up; completion of an operation or action.

mo·quette (mō ket′), *n.* a type of fabric with a thick, velvety pile, used for carpets and in upholstering. [< F = *moc*(*ade*) imitation velvet + *-ette* -ETTE]

mor., morocco.

mo·ra (mōr′ə, môr′ə), *n., pl.* **mo·rae** (mōr′ē, môr′ē), **mo·ras.** *Pros.* the unit of time equivalent to the ordinary or normal short sound or syllable. [< L: delay, hence, space of time]

mo·ra·ceous (mō rā′shəs, mô-), *adj.* belonging to the *Moraceae,* or mulberry family of plants, comprising the mulberry, fig, hemp, hop, Osage orange, etc. [< NL *Mor*(*us*) the typical genus (L: mulberry tree) + -ACEOUS]

Mo·ra·da·bad (mōr′ə də bad′, môr′-, mō′rä dä bäd′, mô′-), *n.* a city in N Uttar Pradesh, in N India. 272,355.

mo·raine (mə rān′), *n.* **1.** a ridge, mound, or irregular mass of boulders, gravel, sand, and clay, carried in or on a glacier. **2.** a deposit of such material left on the ground by a glacier. [< F < dial. (Savoy) *morêna;* cf. ML *morena* embankment of stakes] **—mo·rain′al, mo·rain′ic,** *adj.*

mor·al (môr′əl, mor′-), *adj.* **1.** of, pertaining to, or concerned with right conduct or its principles. **2.** being in accordance with such principles. **3.** conforming to these principles rather than to law, custom, etc.: *a moral obligation.* **4.** expressing such principles, as a literary work. **5.** capable of recognizing and conforming to such principles: *Man is a moral being.* **6.** behaving according to such principles; not immoral or amoral. **7.** virtuous in sexual matters; chaste. **8.** of, pertaining to, or acting on the mind: *moral support.* **9.** depending upon what is observed, as of human nature, rather than upon factual evidence: *moral evidence.* **—*n.*** **10.** the moral teaching or practical lesson contained in a story or experience. **11. morals,** principles or habits with respect to right or wrong conduct. [ME < L *mōrāl*(*is*) = *mōr-* (s. of *mōs*) usage, custom + *-ālis* -AL[1]] **—Syn. 6.** upright, honest, virtuous, honorable. **11.** standards. MORALS, ETHICS refer to rules and standards of conduct and practice. MORALS refers to generally accepted customs of conduct and right living in a society, and to the individual's practice in relation to these: *the morals of our civilization.* ETHICS now implies high standards of honest and honorable dealing, and of methods used, esp. in the professions or in business: *ethics of the medical profession.*

mo·rale (mə ral′), *n.* the moral or mental condition of a person or group with respect to cheerfulness, confidence, etc. [< F, n. use of fem. of *moral* MORAL]

mor·al·ise (môr′ə līz′, mor′-), *v.i., v.t.,* **-ised, -is·ing.** *Chiefly Brit.* moralize. **—mor′al·i·sa′tion,** *n.* **—mor′al·is′er,** *n.* **—mor′al·is′ing·ly,** *adv.*

mor·al·ism (môr′ə liz′əm, mor′-), *n.* **1.** the habit of moralizing. **2.** a moral maxim. **3.** the practice of morality, as distinct from religion.

mor·al·ist (môr′ə list, mor′-), *n.* **1.** a person who teaches or inculcates morality. **2.** a person who practices morality. **3.** a person who believes in regulating the morals of others, as by imposing censorship. **—mor′al·is′tic,** *adj.* **—mor′al·is′ti·cal·ly,** *adv.*

mo·ral·i·ty (mə ral′i tē, mô-), *n., pl.* **-ties** for 4–6. **1.** conformity to the rules of right conduct; moral or virtuous conduct. **2.** moral quality or character. **3.** virtue in sexual matters; chastity. **4.** a doctrine or system of morals. **5.** moral instruction; a moral lesson or precept. **6.** See **morality play.** [late ME *moralite* < LL *mōrālitās*]

moral′ity play′, an allegorical form of the drama current from the 14th to 16th centuries and employing personified abstractions, as of virtues and vices. Cf. **miracle play, mystery play.**

mor·al·ize (môr′ə līz′, mor′-), *v.,* **-ized, -iz·ing.** **—*v.i.*** **1.** to make moral reflections. **—*v.t.*** **2.** to explain in a moral sense, or draw a moral from. **3.** to improve the morals of. Also, *esp. Brit.,* **moralise.** [late ME *moralise* < ML *mōrāliz*(*āre*)] **—mor′al·i·za′tion,** *n.* **—mor′al·iz′er,** *n.* **—mor′al·iz′ing·ly,** *adv.*

mor·al·ly (môr′ə lē, mor′-), *adv.* **1.** in a moral manner. **2.** from a moral point of view. **3.** virtuously. **4.** virtually; practically. [late ME]

Mor′al Major′ity, a political action group formed mainly of Protestant fundamentalists to spread strict conservative morality, as through strong antiabortion laws, school prayer, the teaching of creationism in public schools, the defeat of liberal politicians, and the curbing of books and TV programs considered antireligious or immoral. **—Mo′ral Major′itar′ian.**

Mor′al Re-Ar′ma·ment (rē är′mə mənt), a worldwide movement initiated by Frank Buchman in 1938 as a successor to the Oxford Group, and maintaining that high morality in public and private life is the key to world betterment. *Abbr.:* MRA

mor′al sense′, the ability to judge the rightness or wrongness of actions.

mor′al tur′pitude, **1.** conduct that is regarded as immoral or depraved. **2.** an act or instance of such conduct.

mo·rass (mə ras′), *n.* **1.** a tract of low, soft, wet ground. **2.** a marsh or bog. **3.** marshy ground. [< D *moeras,* alter. (by assoc. with *moer* marsh) of MD *maras* < OF *mareis*]

mor·a·to·ri·um (môr′ə tōr′ē əm, -tôr′-, mor′-), *n., pl.* **-to·ri·a** (-tōr′ē ə, -tôr′-), **-to·ri·ums.** **1.** a legal authorization to delay the performance of some legal obligation, esp. the payment of debts, as in an emergency. **2.** the period during which such authorization is in effect. **3.** a temporary cessation of activity, esp. of an activity considered hostile or dangerous. [< NL, LL, n. use of neut. of *morātōrius* MORATORY]

mor·a·to·ry (môr′ə tōr′ē, -tôr′ē, mor′-), *adj.* authorizing delay of payment. [< LL *morātōri*(*us*) dilatory = *morāt*(*us*) delayed (ptp. of *morārī;* see MORA) + *-ōrius* -ORY[1]]

Mo·ra·va (*Czech., Serbo-Croatian.* mô′RÄ vä), *n.* **1.** German, **March.** a river flowing S from N Czechoslovakia to the Danube. 240 mi. long. **2.** a river in E Yugoslavia, flowing N to the Danube. 134 mi. long. **3.** Czech name of **Moravia.**

Mo·ra·vi·a (mō rā′vē ə, -rä′-, mô-), *n.* a former province of Austria: part of Czechoslovakia since 1918. Czech, **Morava.**

Mo·ra·vi·an (mō rā′vē ən, mô-), *adj.* **1.** pertaining to Moravia or its inhabitants. **2.** of or pertaining to the religious denomination of Moravians. **—*n.*** **3.** a native or inhabitant of Moravia. **4.** a member of a Christian denomination descended from the Bohemian Brethren. **5.** a dialect of Czech, spoken in Moravia. **—Mo·ra′vi·an·ism,** *n.*

Mora′vian Gate′, a mountain pass between the Sudeten Mountains and the Tatra range of the Carpathians, leading from S Poland into Moravia, Czechoslovakia.

Mo·rav·ská Os·tra·va (mô′räf skä ôs′trä vä), former name of **Ostrava.** German, **Mährisch-Ostrau.**

mo·ray (mōr′ā, môr′ā; mō rā′, mô-), *n., pl.* **-rays.** any of numerous chiefly tropical eels of the family *Muraenidae,* having porelike gill openings and no pectoral fins. Also, called **mo′ray eel′.** [< Pg *moréi*(*a*) < L *mūraena* < Gk *mýraina* lamprey]

Mor·ay (mûr′ē), *n.* a county in NE Scotland, on Moray Firth. 49,156 (1961); 476 sq. mi. *Co. seat:* Elgin. Formerly, **Elgin.**

Mor′ay Firth′, an arm of the North Sea projecting into the NE coast of Scotland. Inland portion ab. 30 mi. long.

mor·bid (môr′bid), *adj.* **1.** suggesting an unhealthy mental state; unwholesomely gloomy, sensitive, etc.: *a morbid interest in death.* **2.** affected by, caused by, causing, or characteristic of disease. **3.** pertaining to diseased parts: *morbid anatomy.* **4.** gruesome; grisly. [< L *morbid*(*us*) sickly = *morb*(*us*) sickness + *-idus* -ID[4]] **—mor′bid·ly,** *adv.* **—mor′bid·ness,** *n.* **—Syn. 2.** diseased. **—Ant. 1.** cheerful.

mor·bid·i·ty (môr bid′i tē), *n.* **1.** a morbid state or quality. **2.** the percentage of deaths resulting from any specific disease. **3.** the proportion of sickness or of a specific disease in a geographical locality.

mor·bil·li (môr bil′ī), *n.* (*construed as sing.*) *Pathol.* measles (def. 1). [< ML, pl. of *morbillus,* dim. of L *morbus* sickness]

mor·da·cious (môr dā′shəs), *adj.* biting or given to biting. [*mordaci*(*ty*) biting power (< L *mordācitās* = *mordāci-* (s. of *mordāx* given to biting) + *-tās* -TY[2]) + -OUS] **—mor·da′cious·ly,** *adv.* **—mor·dac·i·ty** (môr das′i tē), *n.*

mor·dant (môr′dᵊnt), *adj.* **1.** caustic or sarcastic, as in expression. **2.** having the property of fixing colors, as in dyeing. **—*n.*** **3.** a substance used in dyeing to fix the coloring matter. **4.** an acid or other corrosive substance used in etching. **5.** *Music.* mordent. **—*v.t.*** **6.** to impregnate or treat with a mordant. [late ME < MF, prp. of *mordre* to bite < L *mordēre;* see -ANT] **—mor′dan·cy,** *n.* **—mor′dant·ly,** *adv.*

Mor·de·cai (môr′də kī′, môr′də kā′ī), *n.* the uncle and guardian of Esther who delivered the Jews from the destruction planned by Haman. Esther 2–8.

mor·dent (môr′dᵊnt), *n. Music.* a melodic embellishment consisting of a rapid alternation of a principal tone with the tone a half or a whole step below it. Also, **mordant.** [< G < It *mordente* biting < L *mordent-*, s. of *mordēns*, prp. of *mordēre* to bite; see -ENT]

Mordents
A, Single; B, Double

Mor·dred (môr′dred), *n.* Modred.

more (mōr, môr), *adj., compar. of* **much** *or* **many** *with* **most** *as superl.* **1.** in addition to that or those already observed, given, taken, used, etc.: *more time; more pencils.* —*n.* **2.** an additional quantity, amount, or number. **3.** a greater quantity, amount, or degree. **4.** something of greater worth, scope, etc. (usually fol. by *than*): *His report is more than a survey.* **5.** (*construed as pl.*) a greater number of persons or of things previously specified: *More will attend than ever before.* **6. the more** or **all the more,** even more than one would otherwise: *I like him all the more for his reticence.* —*adv., compar. of* **much** *with* **most** *as superl.* **7.** in or to a greater extent or degree: *more rapid.* **8.** in addition; further; longer; again: *Let's talk more another time. We couldn't stand it any more.* **9.** moreover. **10. more and more,** to an increasing extent or degree. **11. more or less, a.** to some extent. **b.** in substance; approximately. [ME; OE *māra;* c. OHG *mēro,* Icel *meiri,* Goth *maiza.* See MOST]

More (mōr, môr), *n.* **1. Hannah,** 1745–1833, English writer on religious subjects. **2. Sir Thomas,** 1478–1535, English humanist, statesman, and author: lord chancellor 1529–32: canonized in 1935.

Mo·re·a (mō rē′ə, mô-), *n.* Peloponnesus.

Mo·reau (mô rō′; *Fr.* mô ʀō′), *n.* **1. Gus·tave** (gʏs tav′), 1826–98, French painter. **2. Jean Vic·tor** (zhäɴ vēk tôʀ′), 1763–1813, French general.

mo·reen (mə rēn′), *n.* a heavy fabric of wool, or wool and cotton, commonly watered, used for curtains, petticoats, etc. [*mor-* (? var. of MOIRE) + (VELVET)EEN]

mo·rel[1] (mə rel′), *n.* any edible mushroom of the genus *Morchella,* esp. *M. esculenta.* [< F *morille* < Gmc; cf. OHG *morhila,* dim. of *morha* carrot, c. OE *more*]

mo·rel[2] (mə rel′), *n.* any of several nightshades, esp. the black nightshade. Also, **mo·relle′.** [ME *morele* < OF < VL **maurella,* dim. of L *Maurus* Moor]

Mo·re·lia (mô ʀe′lyä), *n.* a city in and the capital of Michoacán in central Mexico. 127,816 (est. 1965).

mo·rel·lo (mə rel′ō), *n., pl.* **-los.** a variety of sour cherry having dark skin and juice. [perh. < It *amarello* AMARELLE, confused (in E) with It *morello* blackish. See MOREL[2]]

Mo·re·los (mô ʀe′lôs), *n.* a state in S central Mexico. 386,264 (1960); 1916 sq. mi. *Cap.:* Cuernavaca.

more·o·ver (mōr ō′vər, môr-, mōr′ō′vər, môr′-), *adv.* beyond what has been said; further; besides. [ME *more over*] —**Syn.** See **besides.**

mo·res (mōr′āz, -ēz, môr′-), *n.pl. Sociol.* folkways of central importance accepted without question and embodying the fundamental moral views of a group. [< L, pl. of *mōs* usage, custom]

Mo·resque (mə resk′), *adj.* Moorish. [< MF < It *moresco.* See MOOR, -ESQUE]

Mor·ga·gni (môr gä′nyē), *n.* **Gio·van·ni Bat·tis·ta** (jô-vän′nē bät tēs′tä), 1682–1771, Italian anatomist.

Mor·gain le Fay (môr′gān lə fā′, môr′gən). See **Morgan le Fay.**

Mor·gan (môr′gən), *n.* **1. Daniel,** 1736–1802, American Revolutionary general. **2. Sir Henry,** 1635?–88, Welsh buccaneer in the Americas. **3. John Hunt,** 1826–64, Confederate general in the U.S. Civil War. **4. J(ohn) P(ier·pont)** (pēr′pont), 1837–1913, U.S. financier and philanthropist. **5.** his son **John Pierpont,** 1867–1943, U.S. financier. **6. Thomas Hunt,** 1866–1945, U.S. zoologist.

Mor·gan (môr′gən), *n.* one of a breed of light saddle horses. [named after the original sire owned by Justin *Morgan* (1747–1798), a New England teacher]

mor·ga·nat·ic (môr′gə nat′ik), *adj.* designating or pertaining to a form of marriage in which a man of high rank marries a woman of lower station with the stipulation that neither she nor their children, if any, will have any claim to his rank or property. [< NL *morganātic(us)* (adj.), for ML phrase (*mātrimōnium*) *ad morganāticam* (marriage) to the extent of morning-gift (*morganātica* repr. OHG **morgangeba* (fem.); c. OE *morgengiefu* gift from husband to wife on day after wedding); ML also had *morganāticum* (neut.) < OHG *morgan* MORN + L *-āticum* -AGE] —**mor′ga·nat′i·cal·ly,** *adv.*

mor·gan·ite (môr′gə nīt′), *n.* rose-colored beryl. [named after J. P. MORGAN (1837–1913); see -ITE[1]]

Mor·gan le Fay (môr′gən lə fā′), *Celtic and Arthurian Legend.* the fairy sister of King Arthur. Also, **Morgain le Fay.**

Mor·gan·town (môr′gən toun′), *n.* a city in N West Virginia. 29,431 (1970).

mor·gen (môr′gən), *n.* **1.** a unit of land measure equal to about two acres, formerly in use in Holland and the Dutch colonies and still used in South Africa. **2.** a unit equal to about two thirds of an acre, formerly used in Prussia, Norway, and Denmark. [< D, G *Morgen* morning (as much land as one plows in a morning)]

morgue (môrg), *n.* **1.** a place in which bodies are kept, esp. the bodies of unidentified dead persons pending identification or burial. **2.** *Journalism.* a library or file of clippings, photographs, etc., kept for reference. [< F; name of building in Paris housing dead bodies not identified]

mor·i·bund (môr′ə bund′, mor′-), *adj.* **1.** in a dying state; near death. **2.** on the verge of extinction or termination. **3.** not progressing; stagnant. [< L *moribund(us)* dying = *mori-* (s. of *morī* to die) + *-bundus* adj. suffix] —**mor′i·bun′di·ty,** *n.* —**mor′i·bund′ly,** *adv.*

mo·ri·on[1] (mōr′ē on′, môr′-), *n.* an open helmet of the 16th and early 17th centuries, usually having a flat or turned-down brim and a crest from front to back. See illus. at **corselet.** [< MF < Sp *morrión* = *morr(a)* top of head + *-ión* n. suffix]

mo·ri·on[2] (mōr′ē on′, môr′-), *n.* a variety of smoky quartz of a dark-brown or nearly black color. [< L *mōrion* a misreading of *mormorion* a kind of crystal]

Mo·ris·co (mə ris′kō), *adj., n., pl.* **-cos, -coes.** —*adj.* **1.** Moorish. —*n.* **2.** a Moor. **3.** one of the Moors of Spain. [< Sp; see MOOR, -ESQUE]

Mor·i·son (môr′i sən, mor′-), *n.* **Samuel Eliot,** 1887–1976, U.S. historian.

Mo·ritz (*Ger.* mō′ʀits), *n.* Maurice (def. 1).

mo·ri·tu·ri te sa·lu·ta·mus (mō′ʀi to͞o′ʀē te sä′lo͞o tä′-mo͝os; *Eng.* môr′i tyo͝or′ī tē sal′yo͞o tā′məs), *Latin.* we who are about to die salute thee: said by Roman gladiators to the emperor before their contest in the arena.

Mor·ley (môr′lē), *n.* **1. Edward Williams,** 1838–1923, U.S. chemist and physicist. **2. Thomas,** 1557–1603?, English composer, esp. of madrigals.

Mor·mon (môr′mən), *n.* **1.** a member of the Church of Jesus Christ of Latter-day Saints **(Mor′mon Church′),** founded in the U.S. in 1830 by Joseph Smith. **2.** See under **Book of Mormon.** —*adj.* **3.** of or pertaining to the Mormons or their belief. —**Mor′mon·ism,** *n.*

morn (môrn), *n. Chiefly Literary.* morning. [ME *morn(e),* OE *morne* (dat. of *morgen* morning); c. D, G *Morgen*]

Mor·nay (môʀ nā′), *n.* **Phi·lippe de** (fē lēp′ də), **Seigneur du Ples·sis-Mar·ly** (sε nyœʀ′ dʏ ple sē′maʀ lē′), ("*Pope of the Huguenots*"), 1549–1623, French statesman and Protestant leader. Also called **Duplessis-Mornay.**

morn·ing (môr′ning), *n.* **1.** the beginning of day; dawn. **2.** the first part or period of the day, extending from dawn, or from midnight, to noon. **3.** the first or early period of anything. —*adj.* **4.** of or pertaining to morning. [ME, modeled on *evening*] —**Syn. 1.** morn, daybreak, sunrise.

morn′ing af′ter, *pl.* **mornings after.** a period, usually in the morning, when the aftereffects of excessive self-indulgence, esp. drinking alcoholic beverages, are felt.

morn′ing-af′ter pill′, a contraceptive pill for use by women within a few hours after sexual intercourse.

morn′ing coat′, a man's cutaway for wear as part of morning dress.

morn′ing dress′, formal daytime apparel for men. Cf. **evening dress.**

morn·ing-glo·ry (môr′ning glōr′ē, -glôr′ē), *n., pl.* **-ries.** any of various convolvulaceous plants, esp. of the genera *Ipomoea* and *Convolvulus,* as *I. purpurea,* a twining plant having cordate leaves and funnel-shaped flowers of various colors.

Morn′ing Prayer′ (prâr), matin (def. 1c).

morn·ings (môr′ningz), *adv.* in or during the morning regularly.

morn′ing sick′ness, nausea occurring in the early part of the day, as a characteristic symptom in the first months of pregnancy.

morn′ing star′, **1.** any bright planet seen in the east immediately before sunrise. **2.** an annual plant, *Mentzelia Lindleyi,* of California, having bright-yellow flowers.

Mo·ro (mōr′ō, môr′ō), *n., pl.* **-ros,** (*esp. collectively*) **-ro.** a member of any of the various tribes of Muslim Malays in the southern Philippines. [< Sp < L *Maurus* MOOR]

Mo·roc·co (mə rok′ō), *n.* **1.** French, **Maroc.** Spanish, **Marruecos.** a kingdom in NW Africa: formed from two former protectorates **(French Morocco** and **Spanish Morocco)** and an international zone. 17,000,000; 172,684 sq. mi. *Cap.:* Rabat. Cf. **Tangier Zone. 2.** Marrakech. **3.** (*l.c.*) Also called **moroc′co leath′er.** a fine, pebble-grained leather, originally made in Morocco from goatskin tanned with sumac. —**Mo·roc·can** (mə rok′ən), *adj., n.*

mo·ron (mōr′on, môr′-), *n.* **1.** a person having an I.Q. of 50–69 and judged incapable of developing beyond a mental age of 8–12. **2.** *Informal.* any stupid person or a person lacking in good judgment. [< Gk, neut. of *mōrós* foolish] —**mo·ron·ic** (mə ron′ik), *adj.* —**mo·ron′i·cal·ly,** *adv.* —**mo′ron·ism, mo·ron·i·ty** (mə ron′i tē), *n.*

mo·rose (mə rōs′), *adj.* gloomily or sullenly ill-humored, as a person, mood, etc. [< L *mōrōs(us)* fretful, peevish, willful = *mōr-* (s. of *mōs*) will, inclination + *-ōsus* -OSE[1]] —**mo·rose′ly,** *adv.* —**mo·rose′ness, mo·ros·i·ty** (mə ros′i tē), *n.* —**Syn.** moody, sour, sulky, surly. —**Ant.** cheerful.

morph (môrf), *n. Linguistics.* a sequence of phonemes constituting a minimal unit of grammar or syntax, and, as such, a representation, member, or contextual variant of a morpheme in a specific environment. Cf. **allomorph** (def. 2). [back formation from MORPHEME]

morph-, var. of **morpho-** before a vowel: *morpheme.*

-morph, var. of **morpho-** as final element in compound words: *isomorph.*

mor·pheme (môr′fēm), *n. Linguistics.* any of the minimal grammatical units of a language that cannot be divided into smaller independent grammatical parts, as *the, write,* or the *-ed* of *waited.* Cf. **allomorph** (def. 2), **morph.** —**mor·phem′ic,** *adj.* —**mor·phem′i·cal·ly,** *adv.*

mor·phe·mics (môr fē′miks), *n.* (*construed as sing.*) **1.** the study of the classification, description, and functions of morphemes. **2.** the manner by which morphemes combine to form words.

Mor·phe·us (môr′fē əs, -fyo͞os), *n.* **1.** *Class. Myth.* a son of Hypnos and the god of dreams. **2. in the arms of Morpheus,** asleep; in deep sleep. [ME < L < Gk *morphḗ* form + L *-eus* n. suffix (coined by Ovid, with allusion to the forms seen in dreams)] —**Mor′phe·an,** *adj.*

-morphic, an element used as an adjective termination corresponding to **-morph:** *anthropomorphic.*

mor·phine (môr′fēn), *n. Pharm.* a white, bitter, crystalline alkaloid, $C_{17}H_{19}NO_3 \cdot H_2O$, the most important narcotic principle of opium: used chiefly in medicine in the form of its sulfate, hydrochloride, or other salt to dull pain, as a sedative, and to induce sleep. Also **mor·phi·a** (môr′fē ə). [< G *Morphin.* See MORPHEUS, -INE[2]]

mor·phin·ism (môr′fə niz′əm), *n. Pathol.* a morbid condition induced by the habitual use of morphine.

-morphism, an element forming abstract nouns denoting the state of having a specified form: *anthropomorphism.*

morpho-, a learned borrowing from Greek meaning "form," used in the formation of compound words: *morphology.* Also, *esp. before a vowel,* **morph-.** Cf. **-morph,**

-morphic, -morphism, -morphous. [< Gk, comb. form of *morphḗ*]

mor·pho·gen·e·sis (môr′fə jen′i sis), *n.* *Biol.* the structural evolution or development of forms of life, or of an organism or part. —**mor·pho·ge·net·ic** (môr′fō jə net′ik), **mor′pho·gen′ic,** *adj.*

mor·phol·o·gy (môr fol′ə jē), *n.* **1.** the branch of biology dealing with the form and structure of plants and animals. **2.** the form and structure of an organism considered as a whole. **3.** *Gram.* **a.** the patterns of word formation in a particular language, including inflection, derivation, and composition. **b.** the study and description of such patterns. **4.** *Phys. Geog.* geomorphology. **5.** the form or structure of anything. **6.** the study of the form or structure of anything. —**mor·pho·log·ic** (môr′fə loj′ik), **mor′pho·log′i·cal,** *adj.* —**mor′pho·log′i·cal·ly,** *adv.* —**mor·phol′o·gist,** *n.*

mor·pho·pho·neme (môr′fə fō′nēm, môr′fō-), *n.* *Linguistics.* **1.** an abstract phonological unit representing corresponding phonemes in different allomorphs of one morpheme. In English the symbol *F* may be used to represent a morphophoneme occurring in two related allomorphs, as *f* in *leaf,* but *v* in the plural *leaves.* **2.** a phonological entity comprising a bundle of distinctive features used in the representation of a morpheme. [MORPH(EME) + -O- + PHONEME]

mor·pho·pho·ne·mic (môr′fō fə nē′mik, -fō nē′-), *adj.* *Linguistics.* noting or pertaining to morphophonemics or morphophonemes.

mor·pho·pho·ne·mics (môr′fō fə nē′miks, -fō nē′-), *n.* (*construed as sing.*) *Linguistics.* **1.** the study of the relations between morphemes and their phonological realizations, components, or mappings. **2.** the body of data concerning these relations in a given language. [see MORPHOPHONEMIC, -ICS]

-morphous, an element used as an adjective termination corresponding to **-morph**: *polymorphous.* [< Gk *-morphos.* See MORPHO-, -OUS]

Mor′rill Act′ (môr′il, mor′-), *U.S.* **1.** an act of Congress (1862) granting each state 30,000 acres of land for each member it had in Congress, 90 percent of the gross proceeds of which were to be used for the endowment and maintenance of colleges and universities teaching agricultural and mechanical arts and other subjects. **2.** either of two supplementary acts (1890 and 1907) in which Congress made direct financial grants to assist the land-grant colleges and universities. [named after Justin Smith *Morrill* (1810–98), congressman and senator from Vermont]

Mor·ris (môr′is, mor′-), *n.* **1. Gouv·er·neur** (guv′ər nēr′), 1752–1816, U.S. statesman. **2. Robert,** 1734–1806, U.S. financier and statesman, born in England. **3. William,** 1834–96, English painter, furniture designer, poet, and socialist writer.

Mor′ris chair′, a large armchair having an adjustable back and loose, removable cushions. [named after William MORRIS]

Morris chair

mor′ris dance′ (môr′is, mor′-), a rural folk dance of north English origin, performed in costume by persons who originally represented characters of the Robin Hood legend, common in England, esp. in May Day festivities. Also called **mor′ris.** [late ME *moreys daunce* Moorish dance; see MOORISH]

Mor·ris·town (môr′is toun′, mor′-), *n.* a city in N New Jersey: Washington's winter headquarters 1776–77, 1779–1780. 17,662 (1970).

mor·ro (môr′ō, mor′ō; *Sp.* môʀ′ʀō), *n., pl.* **-ros** (-rōz; *Sp.* -ʀōs). a rounded hill, hillock, or promontory. [< Sp: rounded, projecting object. See MORION[1]]

Mor′ro Cas′tle (môr′ō, mor′ō; *Sp.* môʀ′ʀō), a historic fort at the entrance to the harbor of Havana, Cuba.

mor·row (mor′ō, môr′ō), *n.* **1.** the day next after this or after some other particular day or night. **2.** *Archaic.* morning. [ME *morwe,* var. of *morwen,* OE *morgen* morning. See MORN]

Morse (môrs), *n.* **1. Samuel F(in·ley) B(reese)** (fin′lē brēz), 1791–1872, U.S. artist and inventor. **2. Wayne Ly·man** (lī′mən), 1900–74, Democratic Senator from Oregon 1945–69. **3.** See **Morse code.**

Morse′ code′, either of two signal codes of dots, dashes, and spaces used esp. in telegraphy and for blinker signaling. Also called **Morse′ al′phabet.** [named after S. F. B. MORSE]

mor·sel (môr′səl), *n., v.,* **-seled, -sel·ing** or (*esp. Brit.*) **-selled, -sel·ling.** —*n.* **1.** a bite, mouthful, or small portion of food, candy, etc. **2.** a small piece, quantity, or amount of anything; scrap; bit. —*v.t.* **3.** to distribute in or divide into tiny portions (often fol. by *out*). [ME < OF = *mors* a bite (< L *morsum* something bitten off, n. use of neut. of *morsus,* ptp. of *mordēre* to bite) + *-el* < L *-ellus* dim. suffix]

mort[1] (môrt), *n.* **1.** *Hunting.* the note played on a horn signifying that the animal hunted has been killed. **2.** *Obs.* death. [ME < MF < L *mort-* (s. of *mors*) death]

mort[2] (môrt), *n.* a three-year-old salmon. [?]

mor·tal (môr′tᵊl), *adj.* **1.** subject to death. **2.** of or pertaining to man as subject to death. **3.** belonging to this world. **4.** of or pertaining to death. **5.** involving spiritual death (opposed to *venial*): *mortal sin.* **6.** causing or liable to cause death. **7.** to the death: *mortal combat.* **8.** deadly or implacable: *a mortal enemy.* **9.** severe; dire: *in mortal fear.* —*n.* **10.** a human being. [ME < L *mortāl(is).* See MORT[1], -AL[1]] —**mor′tal·ly,** *adv.* —**Syn. 6.** See **fatal.**

mor·tal·i·ty (môr tal′i tē), *n., pl.* **-ties. 1.** the state or condition of being subject to death. **2.** mortal beings collectively; humanity. **3.** the relative frequency of death in a district or community. **4.** death or destruction on a large scale. **5.** *Obs.* death. [ME *mortalite* < MF < L *mortālitās*]

mortal′ity ta′ble, *Insurance.* an actuarial table showing the number of persons who die at any given age. Also called **life table.**

mor′tal sin′, *Rom. Cath. Ch.* a willfully committed, serious transgression against the law of God, depriving the soul of divine grace. Cf. **venial sin.**

mor·tar[1] (môr′tər), *n.* **1.** a vessel having a bowl-shaped cavity in which substances are powdered with a pestle. **2.** any of various mechanical appliances in which substances are pounded or ground. **3.** a cannon very short in proportion to its bore, for throwing shells at high angles. **4.** some similar contrivance, as for throwing pyrotechnic bombs or a life line. [ME, OE *mortere* < L *mortār(ium)* vessel to make mortar in (see MORTAR[2]); in defs. 3, 4, trans. of F *mortier*]

A, Mortar[1]
B, Pestle

mor·tar[2] (môr′tər), *n.* **1.** a mixture of lime or cement or a combination of both with sand and water, used as a bonding agent between bricks, stones, etc. —*v.t.* **2.** to plaster or fix with mortar. [ME *morter* < OF *mortier* < L *mortār(ium)* contents of vessel. See MORTAR[1]] —**mor′tar·less,** *adj.* —**mor′tar·y,** *adj.*

mor·tar·board (môr′tər bōrd′, -bôrd′), *n.* **1.** a board, usually square, used by masons to hold mortar. **2.** a close-fitting cap with a square, flat top and a tassel, worn as part of academic costume.

Mortarboard

mort·gage (môr′gij), *n., v.,* **-gaged, -gag·ing.** —*n.* *Law.* **1.** a conveyance of property to a creditor as security. **2.** the deed by which such a transaction is effected. **3.** the rights conferred by it. —*v.t.* **4.** *Law.* to convey or place (property) under a mortgage. **5.** to obligate or pledge. [ME *morgage* < MF, OF = *mort* dead (< L *mortuus,* ptp. of *morī* to die) + *gage* pledge, GAGE[1]]

mort·ga·gee (môr′gə jē′), *n.* a person to whom property is mortgaged.

mort·ga·gor (môr′gə jər), *n.* a person who mortgages property. Also, **mort′gag·er.**

mor·tice (môr′tis), *n., v.t.,* **-ticed, -tic·ing.** mortise.

mor·ti·cian (môr tish′ən), *n.* undertaker (def. 2). [MORT(UARY) + -ICIAN, modeled on *physician*]

mor·ti·fi·ca·tion (môr′tə fə kā′shən), *n.* **1.** humiliation in feeling, as by some wound to pride. **2.** a cause or source of such humiliation. **3.** the practice of asceticism by penitential discipline to overcome desire for sin and to strengthen the will. **4.** *Pathol.* the death of one part of the body while the rest is alive; gangrene. [ME *mortificacion* < eccl. L *mortificātiōn-* (s. of *mortificātiō*) = *morti-* (see MORTIFY) + *-ficātiōn-* -FICATION] —**Syn. 1.** See **shame.**

mor·ti·fy (môr′tə fī′), *v.,* **-fied, -fy·ing.** —*v.t.* **1.** to humiliate, as by a blow to the pride or self-respect. **2.** to subjugate (the body, passions, etc.) by disciplinary austerities. **3.** *Pathol.* to affect with gangrene or necrosis. —*v.i.* **4.** to practice mortification or disciplinary austerities. **5.** *Pathol.* to undergo mortification, or become gangrened or necrosed. [ME *mortifie(n)* < MF *mortifie(r)* < LL *mortificāre* to put to death = L *morti-* (s. of *mors*) death + *-ficāre* -FY] —**mor′ti·fied′ly,** *adv.* —**mor′ti·fi′er,** *n.* —**mor′ti·fy′ing·ly,** *adv.* —**Syn. 1.** humble, abase.

Mor·ti·mer (môr′tə mər), *n.* **Roger de** (də), **8th Baron of Wig·more** (wig′mōr′, -môr′) and **1st Earl of March,** 1287–1330, English rebel leader: paramour of Isabella, queen of Edward II of England.

mor·tise (môr′tis), *n., v.,* **-tised, -tis·ing.** —*n.* **1.** a hole or slot made in a piece of wood to receive a tenon. —*v.t.* **2.** to secure with a mortise and tenon. **3.** to cut or form a mortise in (a piece of wood). **4.** *Print.* to cut out metal from a plate and insert (new material) in its place. Also, **mortice.** [ME *mortays* < MF *mortaise,* perh. < Ar *murtazza* made fast] —**mor′tis·er,** *n.*

mor′tise joint′, any of various joints between two pieces of timber in which a tenon is housed in a mortise. Also called **mor′tise and ten′on joint′, mor′tise-and-ten′on joint′.**

Mortise joint
M, Mortise
T, Tenon

mort·main (môrt′mān′), *n.* *Law.* **1.** the condition of lands or tenements held without right of alienation, as by an ecclesiastical corporation. **2.** the perpetual holding of land, esp. by a corporation or charitable trust. [ME *mort(e)mayn(e)* < MF *mortemain,* trans. of ML *mortua manus* dead hand]

Mor·ton (môr′tᵊn), *n.* **1. Jelly Roll** (*Ferdinand Joseph La Menthe*), 1885–1941, U.S. jazz pianist and composer. **2. Le·vi Par·sons** (lē′vī pär′sənz), 1824–1920, vice president of the U.S. 1889–93. **3. William Thomas Green,** 1819–68, U.S. dentist: first to employ ether as an anesthetic.

Mor′ton Grove′, a city in NE Illinois, near Chicago. 26,369 (1970).

mor·tu·ar·y (môr′cho͞o er′ē), *n., pl.* **-ar·ies,** *adj.* —*n.* **1.** See **funeral home.** —*adj.* **2.** of or pertaining to the burial of the dead. **3.** pertaining to or connected with death. [ME *mortuarie* < ML *mortuāri(um),* n. use of neut. of L *mortuārius* of the dead = *mortu(us)* dead (ptp. of *morī* to die) + *-ārius* -ARY]

mor·u·la (môr′o͝o lə, -yo͝o-), *n., pl.* **-las, -lae** (-lē′). *Embryol.* the mass of cells resulting from the cleavage of the ovum before the formation of a blastula. [< NL = L *mōr(um)* mulberry + *-ula* -ULE] —**mor′u·lar,** *adj.*

MOS, *Electronics.* **1.** metal-oxide semiconductor. **2.** metal-oxide silicon.

mos., months.

mo·sa·ic (mō zā′ik), *n.* **1.** a picture or decoration made of small pieces of inlaid stone, glass, etc. **2.** the technique of producing such a picture or decoration. **3.** an assembly of aerial photographs matched so as to show a continuous photographic representation of an area (**mosa′ic map′**). **4.** Also called **mosa′ic disease′.** *Plant Pathol.* any of several diseases of plants, characterized by mottled green or green and yellow areas on the leaves, caused by certain viruses. —*adj.* **5.** pertaining to, resembling, or used for making a mosaic or mosaic work. [ME < ML *mosaic(um)* (*opus*), r. L *mūsīvum* (*opus*) < Gk *mouseîon* mosaic (work), lit., work pertaining to the Muses. See MUSE, -IC]

Mo·sa·ic (mō zā′ik), *adj.* of or pertaining to Moses or the writings, laws, and principles attributed to him. Also, **Mo·sa′i·cal.** [< NL *Mosaic(us)* = L *Mōs(ēs)* MOSES + *-aicus,* after *Hebraicus* Hebraic]

mosa′ic gold′, **1.** See **stannic sulfide.** **2.** ormolu (def. 1). [so called because used in mosaic work]

mo·sa·i·cist (mō zā′i sist), *n.* **1.** a maker or designer of mosaics. **2.** a dealer in mosaics.

Mosa′ic Law′. See **Law of Moses.**

Mos·by (mōz′bē), *n.* **John Sin·gle·ton** (sing′gəl tən), 1833–1916, Confederate colonel in the U.S. Civil War.

mos·cha·tel (mos′kə tel′, mos′kə tel′), *n.* a small plant, *Adoxa Moschatellina,* having greenish or yellowish flowers with a musky odor. [< F *moscatelle* < It *moscatella,* dim. of *moscato* musk; *-h-* from botanical name]

Mos·cow (mos′kō *or, for 1,* -kou), *n.* **1.** Russian, **Moskva.** a city in and the capital of the Soviet Union and of the RSFSR, located in the central part of the Soviet Union in Europe. 7,911,000. **2.** Also called **Grand Duchy of Moscow.** Muscovy (def. 1).

Mo·selle (mō zel′), *n.* **1.** Also, **Mo·sel′.** a river in W central Europe, flowing from the Vosges Mountains in NE France into the Rhine in W West Germany. 320 mi. long. **2.** a light, white wine of West Germany.

Mo·ses (mō′ziz, -zis), *n.* **1.** the Hebrew patriarch who led the Israelites out of Egypt and was their leader and lawgiver during their years of wandering in the wilderness. **2. Anna Mary Robertson** ("*Grandma Moses*"), 1860–1961, U.S. painter.

mo·sey (mō′zē), *v.i.,* **-seyed, -sey·ing.** *U.S. Informal.* **1.** to leave quickly; decamp. **2.** to shuffle about leisurely; stroll; saunter (often fol. by *along* or *about*). [?]

Mos·kva (mos kvä′), *n.* Russian name of **Moscow.**

Mos·lem (moz′ləm, mos′-), *adj., n., pl.* **-lems, -lem.** Muslim.

Mos·lem·ism (moz′lə miz′əm, mos′-), *n.* the Muslim religion; Islam.

mosque (mosk, môsk), *n.* a Muslim place of public worship. [? back formation from earlier *mosquee* < MF < It *moschea* << Ar *masjid* < *sajada* to worship, lit., prostrate oneself; the *-ee* seems to have been taken as dim. suffix and dropped]

Mosque

mos·qui·to (mə skē′tō), *n., pl.* **-toes.** any of numerous dipterous insects of the family *Culicidae,* the females of which suck the blood of animals and man. [< Sp, dim. of *mosca* fly < L *musca*]

mosqui′to boat′. See **PT boat.**

mosqui′to hawk′, *U.S. Dial.* nighthawk (def. 1). [so called from its nocturnal habits]

mosqui′to net′, a screen, curtain, or canopy of net, gauze, or the like, for keeping out mosquitoes.

Mosquito, *Culex pipiens* (Length ¼ in.)

mosqui′to net′ting, netting used in the making of mosquito nets.

moss (môs, mos), *n.* **1.** any small, leafy-stemmed, cryptogamic plant of the class *Musci,* growing in tufts, sods, or mats on moist ground, tree trunks, rocks, etc. **2.** a growth of such plants. **3.** any of various similar plants, as Iceland moss or club moss. **4.** *Chiefly Scot. and North Eng.* a swamp or bog. [ME *mos(se),* OE *mos* moss, bog; akin to G *Moos,* Icel *mýrr* MIRE]

moss′ ag′ate, a kind of agate or chalcedony containing brown or black mosslike dendritic markings from various impurities.

moss·back (môs′bak′, mos′-), *n.* **1.** *Informal.* **a.** an extreme conservative. **b.** a rustic or backwoodsman. **2.** *U.S.* **a.** an old turtle. **b.** *Angling.* a large and old fish, as a bass. **c.** a wild bull or cow.

Möss·bau·er (môs′bou ər, mos′-; *Ger.* mœs′bou′ər), *n.* **Ru·dolf L.** (ro͞o′dôlf), born 1929, German physicist.

Möss′bauer effect′, *Physics.* the phenomenon in which an atom in a crystal undergoes no recoil when emitting a gamma ray, giving all the emitted energy to the gamma ray, resulting in a sharply defined wavelength. [named after Rudolf MÖSSBAUER]

moss·bunk·er (môs′bung′kər, mos′-), *n.* the menhaden. [< D *marsbanker*]

mos·so (mô′sō; *It.* môs′sô), *adj. Music.* rapid; fast. [< It, ptp. of *muovere* to MOVE]

moss′ pink′, a phlox, *Phlox subulata,* of the eastern U.S., having showy pink to purple flowers.

moss·troop·er (môs′tro͞o′pər, mos′-), *n.* **1.** one of a class of 17th-century marauders along the border between England and Scotland. **2.** any marauder.

moss·y (mô′sē, mos′ē), *adj.,* **moss·i·er, moss·i·est.** **1.** overgrown with or abounding in moss. **2.** appearing as if covered with moss. **3.** resembling moss. —**moss′i·ness,** *n.*

most (mōst), *adj., superl. of* **much** *or* **many** *with* **more** *as compar.* **1.** in the greatest number, amount, or degree: *the most votes; the most coal; the most talent.* **2.** in the majority of instances: *Most exercise is beneficial.* **3. for the most part.** See **part** (def. 16). —*n.* **4.** the greatest quantity, amount, or degree. **5.** the greatest number or greater part of what is specified: *Most of his writing is rubbish.* **6.** the greatest number: *The most this room will seat is 150.* **7.** the majority of persons: *to be happier than most.* **8.** the best that is possible: *the most one can hope for; to make the most of something.* **9. at the most,** at the maximum. Also, **at most.** **10. the most,** *U.S. Slang.* the ultimate in something. —*adv., superl. of* **much** *with* **more** *as compar.* **11.** in or to the greatest extent or degree (in this sense often used before adjectives and adverbs, and regularly before those of more than two syllables,

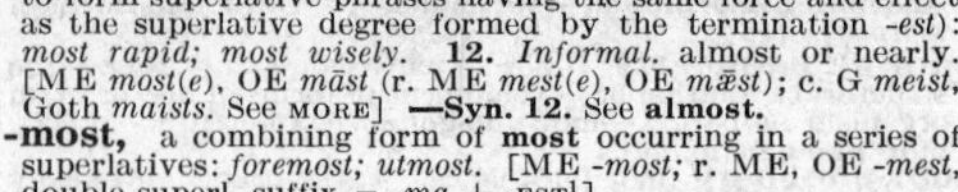

to form superlative phrases having the same force and effect as the superlative degree formed by the termination *-est*): *most rapid; most wisely.* **12.** *Informal.* almost or nearly. [ME *most(e),* OE *māst* (r. ME *mest(e),* OE *mǣst*); c. G *meist,* Goth *maists.* See MORE] —**Syn. 12.** See **almost.**

-most, a combining form of **most** occurring in a series of superlatives: *foremost; utmost.* [ME *-most;* r. ME, OE *-mest,* double superl. suffix = *-ma* + -EST[1]]

most·ly (mōst′lē), *adv.* **1.** for the most part; in the main. **2.** chiefly. **3.** generally; customarily. —**Syn. 2.** especially, particularly. —**Ant. 3.** seldom.

most′ signif′icant dig′it, the digit farthest to the left in a number. *Abbr.:* MSD Cf. **least significant digit.**

Mo·sul (mō so͞ol′), *n.* a city in N Iraq, on the Tigris, opposite the ruins of Nineveh. 215,882 (est. 1963).

mot (mō), *n.* **1.** a pithy or witty remark. **2.** *Archaic.* a note blown on a horn, bugle, etc. [< F < L *mutt(um)* utterance. See MOTTO]

mote[1] (mōt), *n.* a particle or speck, esp. of dust. [ME, OE *mot* speck; c. D *mot* grit, sawdust, Norw *mutt* speck] —**mote′y,** *adj.*

mote[2] (mōt), *v., pt.* **moste** (mōst). *Archaic.* may or might. [ME *mot(e),* OE *mōt* pres. tense (1st sing.); c. G *muss.* See MUST[1]]

mo·tel (mō tel′), *n.* a hotel designed to provide travelers with lodging and free parking facilities, typically a roadside hotel having bedrooms adjacent to a parking space or an urban hotel offering free parking within the building. Also called **motor court, motor hotel, motor inn, motor lodge.** [M(OTOR + H)OTEL]

mo·tet (mō tet′), *n. Music.* a vocal composition in polyphonic style, on a Biblical or similar prose text, intended for use in a church service. [ME < MF; see MOT, -ET]

moth (môth, moth), *n., pl.* **moths** (môthz, mothz, môths, moths). any of numerous insects of the order *Lepidoptera,* generally distinguished from the butterflies by having antennae of various types, usually not clubbed, and by having nocturnal or crepuscular habits. [ME *mothe,* OE *moththe;* akin to G *Motte,* Icel *motti*]

moth·ball (môth′bôl′, moth′-), *n.* **1.** a small ball of naphthalene or sometimes of camphor for placing in closets or other storage areas to repel moths. **2. in mothballs.** in a state or condition of being in disuse or in storage. —*v.t.* **3.** to put into storage or reserve; inactivate. —*adj.* **4.** inactive; unused; stored away.

moth-eat·en (môth′ēt′ən, moth′-), *adj.* **1.** eaten or damaged by or as by moths. **2.** decayed; decrepit. **3.** out of fashion.

moth·er[1] (muth′ər), *n.* **1.** a female parent. **2.** (*often cap.*) a person's female parent. **3.** *Informal.* a mother-in-law, stepmother, or adoptive mother. **4.** See **mother superior.** **5.** a woman looked upon as a mother or exercising control or authority like that of a mother. **6.** the qualities characteristic of a mother, as maternal affection. **7.** something that gives rise to or exercises protective care over something else. **8.** *U.S. Slang* (*usually vulgar*). motherfucker. —*adj.* **9.** being a mother: *a mother bird.* **10.** of, pertaining to, or characteristic of a mother: *mother love.* **11.** derived from one's mother; native: *mother dialect.* **12.** bearing a relation like that of a mother, as in giving origin or rise, or in exercising protective care: *mother earth.* —*v.t.* **13.** to be the mother of; give origin or rise to. **14.** to acknowledge oneself the author of; assume as one's own. **15.** to care for or protect as a mother does; act maternally toward. [ME *moder,* OE *mōdor;* c. D *moeder,* G *Mutter,* Icel *mōthir,* L *māter,* Gk *mḗtēr,* Skt *mātar-.* As in *father,* late substitution of *th* for *d,* possibly on pattern of *brother*] —**moth′er·less,** *adj.*

moth·er[2] (muth′ər), *n.* a mucilaginous substance that forms on the surface of a fermenting liquid and causes fermentation when added to other liquids, as in changing wine or cider to vinegar. Also called **mother of vinegar.** [prob. special use of MOTHER[1], but perh. another word, akin to D *modder* dregs, MLG *moder* swampy land; see MUD]

Moth′er Car′ey's chick′en (kâr′ēz), any of various small petrels, esp. the stormy petrel, *Oceanites oceanicus.* [?]

moth′er church′, **1.** a church from which other churches have had their origin or derived their authority. **2.** a cathedral or a metropolitan church. [ME *moder chirche*]

moth′er coun′try, **1.** the country of one's birth or ancestry. **2.** the country of origin of settlers or colonists.

moth·er·fuck·er (muth′ər fuk′ər), *n. U.S. Slang* (*usually vulgar*). **1.** a mean, despicable, or vicious person. **2.** (used as an exclamation of contempt, anger, etc.).

Moth′er Goose′, a made-up name for the author of the collection of nursery rhymes first published in English (1760) under the title of *Mother Goose's Melody.*

moth·er·hood (muth′ər ho͝od′), *n.* **1.** the state of being a mother; maternity. **2.** mothers collectively. **3.** the qualities or spirit of a mother.

Moth′er Hub′bard (hub′ərd), a full, loose dress for women, named after the heroine of a nursery rhyme.

moth·er-in-law (muth′ər in lô′), *n., pl.* **moth·ers-in-law.** the mother of one's husband or wife. [late ME *modyr in lawe*]

moth·er·land (muth′ər land′), *n.* **1.** a person's native land. **2.** the land of one's ancestors.

moth′er lode′, *Mining.* a rich or important lode.

moth·er·ly (muth′ər lē), *adj.* **1.** pertaining to, characteristic of, or befitting a mother: *motherly solicitude.* **2.** like a mother. —*adv.* **3.** in the manner of a mother. [ME *moderly,* OE *mōdorlīc*] —**moth′er·li·ness,** *n.*

Moth′er of God′, a title of the Virgin Mary. [late ME]

moth·er-of-pearl (muth′ər əv pûrl′), *n.* **1.** a hard, iridescent substance forming the inner layer of certain shells, as that of the pearl oyster; nacre. —*adj.* **2.** of or having the qualities of mother-of-pearl. [cf. It *madreperla,* obs. F *mère perle*]

moth′er of vin′egar, mother[2].

Moth′er's Day′, (in the U.S. and Canada) a day, usually the second Sunday in May, devoted to honoring mothers.

moth′er ship′, an ocean-going vessel or a space vehicle that services other vessels or vehicles operating far from a home port or center.

moth′er supe′rior, *pl.* **mother superiors, mothers superior.** the head of a Christian religious community for women.

moth′er tongue′, 1. a person's native language. 2. a parent language. [ME *moder tonge*]
Moth·er·well (muth′ər wəl, -wel′), *n.* **Robert,** born 1915, U.S. painter and writer.
moth′er wit′, natural or practical intelligence, wit, or sense. [late ME *moderis wytte*]
moth·er·wort (muth′ər wûrt′), *n.* a European, labiate plant, *Leonorus cardica,* an introduced weed in the U.S., having cut leaves with a whorl of flowers in the axils. [ME *moderwort* (see MOTHER[1], WORT[2]), so called because believed helpful for diseases of the womb]
moth·proof (môth′proof′, moth′-), *adj.* 1. resistant to attack by moths. —*v.t.* 2. to render (fabric, clothing, etc.) mothproof.
moth·y (mô′thē, moth′ē), *adj.,* **moth·i·er, moth·i·est.** 1. containing moths. 2. moth-eaten.
Mo Ti (*Chin.* mô′ dē′), Mo-tze.
mo·tif (mō tēf′), *n.* 1. a recurring subject, theme, idea, etc., esp. in an artistic work, as a musical composition or a novel. 2. a distinctive and recurring form, shape, figure, etc., in a design. 3. a dominant idea or feature. 4. a standard, often recurring narrative element in folklore and literature. [< F]
mo·tile (mōt′əl, mō′til), *adj.* 1. *Biol.* moving or capable of moving spontaneously: *motile cells or spores.* —*n.* 2. *Psychol.* a person in whose mind motor images, rather than visual or auditory images, are predominant or unusually distinct. [< L *mōt(us)* moved (see MOTION) + -ILE] —**mo·til·i·ty** (mō til′i tē), *n.*
mo·tion (mō′shən), *n.* 1. the action or process of moving or of changing place or position. 2. a movement. 3. power of movement, as of a living body. 4. the manner of moving the body in walking; gait. 5. a bodily movement or change of posture; a gesture. 6. a formal proposal, esp. one made to a deliberative assembly. 7. *Law.* an application made to a court or judge for an order, ruling, or the like. 8. an inward prompting or impulse; inclination. 9. *Music.* melodic progression, as the change of a voice part from one pitch to another. 10. *Mach.* **a.** a piece of mechanism with a particular action or function. **b.** the action of such a mechanism. 11. **in motion,** in active operation; moving. —*v.t.* 12. to direct by a significant motion or gesture, as with the hand. —*v.i.* 13. to make a significant motion, as with the hand; gesture; signal. [ME *mocio(u)n* < L *mōtiōn-* (s. of *mōtiō*) = *mōt(us)* moved (ptp. of *movēre*) + *-iōn-* -ION] —**mo′tion·al,** *adj.* —**mo′tion·er,** *n.*
—**Syn. 1.** MOTION, MOVE, MOVEMENT refer to change of position in space. MOTION denotes change of position, either considered apart from or as a characteristic of that which moves: *perpetual motion.* The chief uses of MOVE are founded upon the idea of moving a piece, in chess or a similar game, for winning the game, and hence the word denotes any change of position, condition, or circumstances for the accomplishment of some end: *a shrewd move to win votes.* MOVEMENT is always connected with the person or thing moving, and is usually a definite or particular motion: *the movements of a dance.* 4. bearing, carriage. —**Ant. 1.** stasis.
mo·tion·less (mō′shən lis), *adj.* without motion or incapable of motion: *a motionless statue.* —**mo′tion·less·ly,** *adv.* —**mo′tion·less·ness,** *n.* —**Syn.** stationary, unmoving.
mo′tion pic′ture, 1. a sequence of consecutive pictures of objects photographed in motion by a specially designed camera (**mo′tion-pic′ture cam′era**) and thrown on a screen by a projector (**mo′tion-pic′ture projec′tor**) in such rapid succession as to give the illusion of natural movement. 2. a play, event, or the like, presented in this form. 3. **motion pictures,** the art, technique, or business of producing motion pictures. —**mo′tion-pic′ture,** *adj.*
mo′tion sick′ness, *Pathol.* a feeling of nausea and dizziness resulting from stimulation by motion of the semicircular canals of the ear during travel by ship, airplane, car, train, etc.
mo′tion stud′y. See **time and motion study.**
mo·ti·vate (mō′tə vāt′), *v.t.,* **-vat·ed, -vat·ing.** to provide with a motive or motives.
mo·ti·va·tion (mō′tə vā′shən), *n.* 1. the act or an instance of motivating. 2. the state or condition of being motivated. 3. something that motivates; inducement; incentive. —**mo′ti·va′tion·al,** *adj.* —**mo′ti·va′tive,** *adj.*
motiva′tion research′, the application of the knowledge and techniques of the social sciences, esp. psychology and sociology, to understanding consumer attitudes and behavior: used as a guide in advertising and marketing. *Abbr.:* MR, M.R. Also, **motiva′tional research′.**
mo·tive (mō′tiv), *n., adj., v.,* **-tived, -tiv·ing.** —*n.* 1. something that prompts a person to act in a certain way or that determines volition; incentive. 2. the goal or object of one's actions. 3. (in art, literature, and music) a motif. —*adj.* 4. causing or tending to cause motion. 5. pertaining to motion. 6. prompting to action. 7. constituting a motive or motives. —*v.t.* 8. to motivate. 9. *Obs.* to relate to a motif in a work of art. [ME < ML *mōtīv(um)* that which moves someone to do something, n. use of neut. of *mōtīvus* serving to move = L *mōt(us)* moved (ptp. of *movēre*) + *-īvus* -IVE] —**mo′tive·less,** *adj.* —**mo′tive·less·ly,** *adv.* —**mo′tive·less·ness,** *n.*
—**Syn. 1.** motivation, incitement; influence, ground, cause. MOTIVE, INDUCEMENT, INCENTIVE apply to whatever moves a person to action. MOTIVE is applied mainly to an inner urge that moves or prompts a person to action, though it may also apply to a contemplated result, the desire for which moves the person: *His motive was a wish to be helpful.* INDUCEMENT is never applied to an inner urge, and seldom to a goal, but is that which leads a person on; it is used mainly of opportunities offered by another person or by the factors of a situation: *The salary offered me was a great inducement.* INCENTIVE was once used of anything inspiring or stimulating the emotions or imagination; it has retained its connotations of that which inspires a person, but is today applied only to something offered as a reward or to stimulate competitive activity: *to create incentives for higher achievement.* 2. See **reason.**
mo′tive pow′er, 1. any power used to impart motion. 2. a source of mechanical energy.
mo·tiv·i·ty (mō tiv′i tē), *n.* the power of initiating or producing motion.
mot juste (mō zhyst′), *pl.* **mots justes** (mō zhyst′). *French.* the exact or appropriate word.
mot·ley (mot′lē), *adj., n., pl.* **-leys.** —*adj.* 1. exhibiting great diversity of elements; heterogeneous. 2. being of different colors combined; parti-colored. 3. wearing a parti-colored garment. —*n.* 4. a combination of different colors. 5. the parti-colored garment of a court jester. 6. a heterogeneous assemblage. 7. a medley. [ME; see MOTE[1], -LY]
Mot·ley (mot′lē), *n.* **John Lo·throp** (lō′thrəp), 1814–77, U.S. historian and diplomat.
mot·mot (mot′mot), *n.* any of several tropical and subtropical American birds of the family *Momotidae,* related to the kingfishers, having a serrate bill and chiefly greenish and bluish plumage. [< AmerSp; repetitive compound, imitating the bird's note]
mo·to·cross (mō′tō krôs′, -kros′), *n.* a sports competition in which lightweight motorcycles are raced over a course of very rough terrain. [MOTO(RCYCLE) + CROSS(-COUNTRY)]
mo·tor (mō′tər), *n.* 1. a comparatively small and powerful engine, esp. an internal-combustion engine in an automobile, motorboat, etc. 2. any self-powered vehicle. 3. something that imparts motion, esp. a contrivance, as a steam engine, which receives and modifies energy from some natural source in order to utilize it in driving machinery. 4. *Elect.* a machine that converts electrical energy into mechanical energy. 5. **motors,** stocks or bonds in automobile companies. —*adj.* 6. causing or imparting motion. 7. pertaining to or operated by a motor. 8. of, for, by, or pertaining to motor vehicles: *motor freight.* 9. *Physiol.* conveying an impulse that results or tends to result in motion, as a nerve. 10. *Psychol., Physiol.* of, pertaining to, or involving muscular movement: *a motor response; motor images.* —*v.i.* 11. to ride or travel in an automobile. [< L: mover = *mōt(us)* moved (ptp. of *movēre*) + *-or* -OR[2]]
mo·tor·bike (mō′tər bīk′), *n.* 1. a bicycle that is propelled by an attached motor. 2. a small, lightweight motorcycle.
mo·tor·boat (mō′tər bōt′), *n.* 1. a boat propelled by an inboard or outboard motor. —*v.i.* 2. to travel in or operate a motorboat.
mo·tor·bus (mō′tər bus′), *n.* a passenger bus powered by a motor. Also called **mo′tor coach′.**
mo·tor·cade (mō′tər kād′), *n.* a procession or parade of automobiles. [MOTOR + (CAVAL)CADE]
mo·tor·car (mō′tər kär′), *n.* 1. an automobile. 2. *Railroads, U.S.* a self-propelled car for freight or passengers.
mo′tor court′, *U.S.* motel.
mo·tor·cy·cle (mō′tər sī′kəl), *n., v.,* **-cled, -cling.** —*n.* 1. a two-wheeled vehicle, similar to but heavier than a bicycle, driven by a gasoline engine and chiefly for one rider. —*v.i.* 2. to ride on or operate a motorcycle. —**mo·tor·cy·clist** (mō′tər sī′klist), *n.*
mo·tor·drome (mō′tər drōm′), *n.* a rounded course or track for automobile and motorcycle races.
mo·tored (mō′tərd), *adj.* having a motor or motors, esp. of a specified number or type (usually used in combination): *a bimotored airplane.*
mo′tor home′, a small bus with a roomlike or apartmentlike area behind the driver's seat, outfitted as living quarters for use in camping, extended motor excursions, etc.
mo·tor·ing (mō′tər ing), *n.* traveling in or driving a car.
mo·tor·ise (mō′tə rīz′), *v.t.,* **-ised, -is·ing.** *Chiefly Brit.* motorize. —**mo′tor·i·sa′tion,** *n.*
mo·tor·ist (mō′tər ist), *n.* a person who drives or travels in an automobile.
mo·tor·ize (mō′tə rīz′), *v.t.,* **-ized, -iz·ing.** 1. to furnish with a motor or motors. 2. to supply with motor-driven vehicles. Also, *esp. Brit.,* **motorise.** —**mo′tor·i·za′tion,** *n.*
mo′tor lodge′, *U.S.* motel. Also called **mo′tor inn′, mo′tor hotel′.**
mo·tor·man (mō′tər mən), *n., pl.* **-men.** 1. a person who operates an electric vehicle, as a streetcar or subway train. 2. a person who operates a motor.
mo′tor scoot′er, scooter (def. 2).
mo′tor ship′, a ship driven by a diesel or other internal-combustion engine or engines. Also, **mo′tor·ship′.**
mo′tor truck′, truck[1] (def. 1).
mo′tor ve′hicle, any transportation vehicle designed for use on highways, as an automobile, bus, or truck.
Mott (mot), *n.* 1. **John Raleigh,** 1865–1955, U.S. religious leader: Nobel peace prize 1946. 2. **Lucretia Coffin,** 1793–1880, U.S. social reformer: advocate of women's rights.
mot·tle (mot′əl), *v.,* **-tled, -tling,** *n.* —*v.t.* 1. to diversify with spots or blotches of a different color or shade. —*n.* 2. a diversifying spot or blotch of color. 3. mottled coloring or pattern. [back formation from MOTLEY] —**mot′tle·ment,** *n.*
mot·tled (mot′əld), *adj.* spotted or blotched in coloring.
mot·to (mot′ō), *n., pl.* **-toes, -tos.** 1. a maxim adopted as an expression of one's guiding principle. 2. a sentence, phrase, or word attached to or inscribed on anything as appropriate to it. [< It < L *muttum* utterance. See MOT]
Mo·tze (mô′dzu′), *n.* (*Mo Ti*) fl. 5th century B.C., Chinese philosopher. Also, **Mo Ti, Mo′ Tzu′.**
moue (moo), *n., pl.* **moues** (moo). *French.* a pouting grimace.
mouf·lon (moof′lon), *n.* a wild sheep, *Ovis musimon,* inhabiting the mountainous regions of Sardinia, Corsica, etc., the male of which has large curving horns. Also, **mouf′flon.** [< F < Corsican *mufrone* < LL *mufrōni-* (s. of *mufrō*)]
mouil·lé (moo yā′), *adj.* *Phonet.* 1. palatal or palatalized, esp. referring to sounds spelled *ll* and *ñ* in Spanish, *gl* and *gn* in Italian, etc. 2. (of French sounds) spelled *l* or *ll* and pronounced as a *y* sound. [< F, ptp. of *mouiller* to wet < VL **molliāre* to soften by wetting < L *moll(is)* soft; see MOLLIFY]
mou·jik (moo zhik′, moo′zhik), *n.* muzhik.
Mouk·den (mook′den′, mook′-), *n.* Mukden.
mou·lage (moo läzh′), *n.* 1. the making of a mold, esp. with plaster of Paris, of objects, footprints, tire tracks, etc., as for the purpose of identification. 2. the mold itself. [< F]
mould (mōld), *n., v.t., v.i.* *Chiefly Brit.* mold. —**mould′a·bil′i·ty,** *n.* —**mould′a·ble,** *adj.*
mould·er (mōl′dər), *v.i., v.t., n.* *Chiefly Brit.* molder.
mould·ing (mōl′ding), *n.* *Chiefly Brit.* molding.

mould·y (mōl′dē), *adj.*, **mould·i·er, mould·i·est.** *Chiefly Brit.* moldy. —**mould′i·ness,** *n.*

mou·lin (mo͞o laN′), *n.* a nearly vertical shaft or cavity worn in a glacier by surface water falling through a crack in the ice. [< F < LL *molīn(um)* MILL[1]]

Moul·mein (mo͞ol mān′, mōl-), *n.* a seaport in S Burma at the mouth of the Salween River. 171,767. Also, **Maulmain.**

Moul·oud (mo͞ol′o͞od), *n.* *Islam.* a Muslim holiday celebrating the birth of Muhammad, occurring on the twelfth day of the fourth month of the Muslim calendar.

moult (mōlt), *v.i., v.t., n.* *Chiefly Brit.* molt. —**moult′er,** *n.*

Moul·trie (mōl′trē, mo͞ol′-), *n.* **1. William,** 1730–1805, U.S. general. **2. Fort.** See **Fort Moultrie.**

mound[1] (mound), *n.* **1.** an elevation formed of earth, sand, stones, etc., esp. over a grave or ruins. **2.** a tumulus or other raised work of earth dating from a prehistoric or long-past period. **3.** a natural elevation of earth; a hillock or knoll. **4.** an artificial elevation of earth, as for a defense work, a dam or barrier, etc.; an embankment. **5.** a heap or raised mass. **6.** *Baseball.* the slightly elevated ground from which the pitcher delivers the ball. Cf. **rubber**[1] (def. 9). —*v.t.* **7.** to furnish with a mound of earth, as for a defense. **8.** to form into a mound; heap up. [OE *mund* hand, hence protection, protector; in 16th century, protective barrier, e.g., fence, earthwork; c. Icel *mund,* MD *mond* protection]

mound[2] (mound), *n.* a golden globe topped with a cross that symbolizes power and constitutes part of the regalia of an English sovereign. [ME < L *mund(us)* world]

Mound′ Build′ers, the various Indian tribes who, in prehistoric and early historic times, erected the burial mounds and other earthworks of the Mississippi drainage basin and southeastern U.S.

mount[1] (mount), *v.t.* **1.** to go up; climb; ascend: *He mounted the stairs slowly.* **2.** to get up on (a platform, a horse, etc.). **3.** to set or place at an elevation: *to mount a house on stilts.* **4.** to furnish with a horse or other animal for riding. **5.** to set or place (a person) on horseback. **6.** to raise or put into position for use, as a gun. **7.** (of a fortress or vessel) to have or carry (guns) in position for use. **8.** to go or put on guard, as a sentry or watch. **9.** to fix on or in a support, backing, setting, etc: *to mount a photograph.* **10.** to provide (a play, musical comedy, etc.) with scenery, costumes, and other equipment for production. **11.** to prepare (an animal body or skeleton) as a specimen. **12.** (of a male animal) to climb upon (a female) for copulation. **13.** *Micros.* **a.** to prepare (a slide) for microscopic investigation. **b.** to prepare (a sample) for examination by a microscope, as by placing it on a slide. —*v.i.* **14.** to rise or go to a higher position, level, degree, etc.; ascend. **15.** to rise in amount. **16.** to get up on the back of a horse or other animal for riding. **17.** to get up on something, as a platform. —*n.* **18.** the act or a manner of mounting. **19.** a horse, other animal, or sometimes a vehicle, as a bicycle, used, provided, or available for riding. **20.** an act or occasion of riding a horse, esp. in a race. **21.** a support, backing, setting, or the like, on or in which something is, or is to be, mounted or fixed. **22.** *Micros.* a prepared slide. **23.** *Philately.* hinge (def. 4). [ME *mounte(n)* < OF *munte(r), monte(r)* < VL **montāre* < L *mont-* (s. of *mōns*) MOUNT[2]] —**mount′a·ble,** *adj.* —**mount′less,** *adj.* —**Syn. 1.** scale. See **climb. 19.** steed, charger. —**Ant. 1, 14.** descend.

mount[2] (mount), *n.* a hill or mountain. [ME, OE *munt* < L *mont-* (s. of *mōns*) mountain, hill]

moun·tain (moun′tᵊn), *n.* **1.** a natural elevation of the earth's surface rising more or less abruptly to a summit, and attaining an altitude greater than that of a hill. **2.** a large mass of something resembling this, as in shape or size. **3.** a huge amount. **4.** a formidable obstacle. **5. the Mountain,** *Fr. Hist.* (in the revolutionary legislatures) an extremist faction led by Danton and Robespierre, whose members occupied the topmost seats or benches in the legislatures. —*adj.* **6.** of or pertaining to mountains. **7.** living, growing, or located in the mountains. **8.** resembling or suggesting a mountain, as in size. [ME *mountaine* < OF *montaigne* < VL **montāneus* = L *montān(us)* mountainous (see MOUNT[2], -AN) + *-eus* -EOUS] —**moun′tain·less,** *adj.*

moun′tain ash′, 1. any of several small, rosaceous trees of the genus *Sorbus,* having small, white, corymbose flowers and bright-red to orange berries. **2.** any of certain other trees, as several Australian species of eucalyptus.

moun′tain cat′, 1. a cougar. **2.** a bobcat.

moun′tain chain′, 1. a connected series of mountains. **2.** See **mountain range.**

moun′tain cran′berry, a vacciniaceous shrub, *Vaccinium Vitis-Idaea,* having evergreen leaves, prostrate stems, and tart, red berries edible after cooking.

moun′tain dew′, *Facetious.* any whiskey, esp. illegally distilled corn whiskey.

moun·tain·eer (moun′tᵊnēr′), *n.* **1.** an inhabitant of a mountainous district. **2.** a climber of mountains. —*v.i.* **3.** to climb mountains.

moun′tain goat′. See **Rocky Mountain goat.**

moun′tain lau′rel, a North American laurel, *Kalmia latifolia,* having terminal clusters of rose to white flowers: the state flower of Connecticut and Pennsylvania.

moun′tain li′on, cougar.

moun·tain·ous (moun′tᵊnəs), *adj.* **1.** abounding in or composed of mountains. **2.** of the nature of a mountain. **3.** resembling a mountain or mountains, as being large and high. [late ME *mounteynous*] —**moun′tain·ous·ly,** *adv.* —**moun′tain·ous·ness,** *n.*

moun′tain oys′ter, the testis of a calf, sheep, pig, etc., used as food. Cf. **prairie oyster.**

moun′tain range′, 1. a series of more or less connected mountains ranged in a line. **2.** a series of mountains, or of more or less parallel lines of mountains, closely related, as in origin. **3.** an area in which the greater part of the land surface is in considerable degree of slope, upland summits are small or narrow, and there are great differences in elevations within the area (commonly over 2000 feet).

moun′tain sheep′, 1. the bighorn. **2.** any of various wild sheep inhabiting mountains.

moun′tain sick′ness, *Pathol.* a condition characterized by difficult breathing, headache, nausea, etc., caused by the rarefaction of the air at high altitudes.

Moun′tain State′, Montana (used as a nickname).

Moun′tain time′. See under **standard time.**

moun·tain·top (moun′tᵊn top′), *n.* **1.** the top of a mountain. —*adj.* **2.** situated at the top of a mountain: *a mountaintop house.*

Moun′tain View′, a city in central California, S of San Francisco. 54,206 (1970).

Mount′ Ar′arat, Ararat.

Mount·bat·ten (mount bat′ᵊn), *n.* **Louis, 1st Earl Mountbatten of Burma,** 1900–79, British admiral: viceroy of India 1947; governor general of India 1947–48.

Mount′ Des′ert Is′land (dez′ərt, di zûrt′), an island off the coast of E central Maine: summer resort. 14 mi. long; 8 mi. wide.

moun·te·bank (moun′tə baŋgk′), *n.* **1.** a huckster who sells quack medicines from a platform in public places, appealing to his audience by tricks, storytelling, etc. **2.** any charlatan or quack. —*v.i.* **3.** to play the mountebank. [< It *montimbanco* one who climbs on a bench = *mont(are)* (to) climb (see MOUNT[1]) + *-im-* var. of *in* on + *banco* bench (see BANK[2])] —**moun·te·bank·er·y** (moun′tə baŋgk′ə rē), *n.* —**Syn. 1.** pitchman. **2.** phony, pretender, fraud.

mount·ed (moun′tid), *adj.* **1.** seated or riding on a horse or other animal. **2.** serving on horseback, or on some special mount, as soldiers or police. **3.** *Mil.* (formerly) permanently equipped with horses or vehicles for transport. **4.** fixed on or in a support, backing, setting, or the like. **5.** put into position for use, as guns. —**Ant. 1.** afoot.

Moun·tie (moun′tē), *n.* *Informal.* a law-enforcement officer of the Royal Canadian Mounted Police. Also, **Mounty.** [MOUNT(ED) + -IE]

mount·ing (moun′tiŋg), *n.* **1.** the act of a person or thing that mounts. **2.** something that serves as a mount, support, setting, or the like: *a new mounting for an heirloom jewel.* [ME]

Mount′ Leb′anon, a town in SW Pennsylvania, SW of Pittsburgh. 39,596 (1970).

Mount′ McKin′ley Na′tional Park′, a national park in central Alaska, including Mounts McKinley and Foraker. 3030 sq. mi. Official name, **Denali National Park.**

Mount′ Pros′pect, a city in NE Illinois, near Chicago. 34,995 (1970).

Mount′ Rainier′. See **Rainier, Mount.**

Mount′ Rainier′ Na′tional Park′, a national park in W Washington, including Mount Rainier. 378 sq. mi.

Mount′ Rob′son Park′ (rob′sən), a national park in the Rocky Mountains of E British Columbia, Canada.

Mount′ St. Hel′ens. See **St. Helens, Mount.**

Mount′ Ver′non, 1. the home and tomb of George Washington in NE Virginia, on the Potomac, 15 mi. below Washington, D.C. **2.** a city in SE New York, near New York City. 72,778 (1970).

Mount·y (moun′tē), *n., pl.* **Mount·ies.** *Informal.* Mountie.

mourn (mōrn, môrn), *v.i.* **1.** to feel or express sorrow or grief. **2.** to grieve or lament for the dead. **3.** to show the conventional or usual signs of sorrow over a person's death. —*v.t.* **4.** to feel or express sorrow or grief over (misfortune, loss, or anything regretted); deplore. **5.** to grieve or lament over (the dead). **6.** to utter in a sorrowful manner. [ME *mo(u)rne(n),* OE *murnan;* c. OHG *mornēn,* Icel *morna,* Goth *maurnan*] —**Syn. 1.** bewail, bemoan. See **grieve.** —**Ant. 1.** laugh, rejoice.

mourn·er (mōr′nər, môr′-), *n.* **1.** a person who mourns. **2.** a person who attends a funeral as a mourning friend or relative of the deceased. **3.** *U.S.* (at religious revival meetings) a person who professes penitence. [ME]

mourn′ers' bench′, *U.S.* (at religious revival meetings) a bench, seat, or room set apart for mourners.

mourn·ful (mōrn′fəl, môrn′-), *adj.* **1.** having, expressing, or showing sorrow or grief; sorrowful; sad. **2.** of or pertaining to mourning for the dead. **3.** causing or attended with sorrow or mourning. **4.** gloomy, somber, or dreary, as in appearance or character. —**mourn′ful·ly,** *adv.* —**mourn′ful·ness,** *n.*

mourn·ing (mōr′niŋg, môr′-), *n.* **1.** the act of a person who mourns; sorrowing or lamentation. **2.** the conventional manifestation of sorrow for a person's death, esp. by the wearing of black, the hanging of flags at half-mast, etc. **3.** the outward tokens of such sorrow, as black garments. —*adj.* **4.** of, pertaining to, or used in mourning. [ME (n., adj.); OE *murnung* (n.)] —**mourn′ing·ly,** *adv.*

mourn′ing band′, a piece of black material which is worn, esp. as a band encircling the upper arm, to indicate mourning.

mourn′ing cloak′, a butterfly, *Nymphalis antiopa,* widely distributed in Europe and North America, having velvety, dark-brown wings with purple spots and pale-yellow edges. Also called **mourn′ing cloak′ but′terfly.**

mourn′ing dove′, a dove, *Zenaidura macroura,* of North America, noted for its plaintive cooing.

mouse (*n.* mous; *v.* mouz), *n., pl.* **mice** (mīs), *v.,* **moused, mous·ing.** —*n.* **1.** any of numerous small rodents of the family *Muridae,* esp. of the genus *Mus,* introduced into the U.S. from the Old World and of wide distribution. **2.** any similar animal of another family. **3.** a quiet, timid person. **4.** *Computer Technol.* a palm-sized device used to move the cursor on a CRT. **5.** *Informal.* a swelling under the eye, caused by a blow; black eye. —*v.t.* **6.** to hunt out, as a cat hunts out mice. **7.** *Naut.* to secure with a mousing. —*v.i.* **8.** to hunt for or catch mice. **9.** to prowl about, as if in search of something. [ME *mous,* OE *mūs* (pl. *mӯs*)]

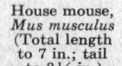

House mouse, *Mus musculus* (Total length to 7 in.; tail to 3½ in.)

mouse′ deer′, chevrotain.

mouse-ear (mous′ēr′), *n.* any of various plants having small, hairy leaves, as the hawkweed, *Hieracium Pilosella,* the forget-me-not, *Myosotis palustris,* etc. [ME *mouse-ere*]

mous·er (mou′zər), *n.* an animal that catches mice. [ME]
mouse·trap (mous′trap′), *n.* a trap for mice, usually consisting of a rectangular wooden base on which a metal spring is mounted.
mous·ey (mou′sē, -zē), *adj.*, **mous·i·er, mous·i·est.** mousy. —**mous′i·ly,** *adv.* —**mous′i·ness,** *n.*
mous·ing (mou′zing), *n. Naut.* a wrapping of several turns of small stuff around the shank end of a hook.
mousse (mo͞os), *n. Cookery.* **1.** a sweetened preparation with whipped cream as a base, often stabilized with gelatin and chilled in a mold. **2.** a similar preparation, unsweetened and containing meat, vegetables, or fish. [< F: moss, froth < Gmc; see MOSS]
mousse·line (mo͞os lēn′), *n. French.* muslin.
Mous·sorg·sky (mə zôrg′skē; *Russ.* mo͝o sôrg′ski), *n.* **Mo·dest Pe·tro·vich** (mo dest′ pe trô′vich), 1839–81, Russian composer. Also, **Mous·sorg′ski, Mussorgski, Mussorgsky.**
mous·tache (mə stash′, mus′tash), *n.* mustache. —**mous·tached′,** *adj.*
Mous·te·ri·an (mo͞o stēr′ē ən), *adj. Anthropol.* of or pertaining to the middle Paleolithic culture, during which time flint tools were refined. Also, **Mous·tie′ri·an.** [< F *moust(i)érien* (so called from tools found in the sands of *Moustier,* France) see -IAN]
mous·y (mou′sē, -zē), *adj.*, **mous·i·er, mous·i·est. 1.** resembling or suggesting a mouse, as in color, odor, etc. **2.** drab and colorless. **3.** quiet; noiseless: *a mousy tread.* **4.** infested with mice. Also, **mousey.** —**mous′i·ly,** *adv.* —**mous′i·ness,** *n.*
mouth (*n.* mouth; *v.* mouth), *n., pl.* **mouths** (mouthz), *v.* —*n.* **1.** *Anat., Zool.* **a.** the opening through which an animal or man takes in food. **b.** the cavity containing the structures used in mastication. **c.** the structures enclosing or being within this cavity, considered as a whole. **2.** the masticating and tasting apparatus. **3.** a person or animal considered as requiring food or dependent on someone for food or for food and other necessities: *another mouth to feed.* **4.** the oral opening or cavity considered as the source of vocal utterance. **5.** utterance or expression: *to give mouth to one's thoughts.* **6.** talk, esp. loud, empty, or boastful talk, or an inclination to such talk: *That man is all mouth.* **7.** a grimace made with the lips. **8.** an opening leading out of or into any cavity or hollow place or thing. **9.** a part of a river or the like where its waters are discharged into some other body of water. **10.** the opening between the jaws of a vise or the like. **11.** the lateral hole of an organ pipe. **12.** the lateral blowhole of a flute. **13. down in the mouth,** *Informal.* having a sad countenance; depressed; disheartened. **14. word of mouth,** speaking rather than writing; oral transmission. —*v.t.* **15.** to utter in a sonorous or pompous manner, or with excessive mouth movements: *to mouth a speech.* **16.** to put or take into the mouth, as food. **17.** to press, rub, or chew at with the mouth or lips. **18.** to accustom (a horse) to the use of the bit and bridle. —*v.i.* **19.** to speak sonorously and oratorically, or with excessive mouth movements. **20.** to grimace with the lips. [ME; OE *mūth;* c. Icel *muthr, munnt,* G *Mund*] —**mouth′less,** *adj.*

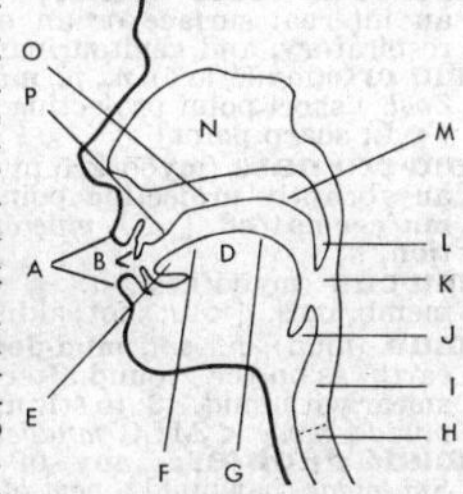

Mouth and nose (section) A, Lips; B, Teeth; C, Oral cavity; D, Tongue; E, Tip; F, Front; G, Back; H, Vocal cords; I, Larynx; J, Epiglottis; K, Pharynx; L, Uvula; M, Soft palate; N, Nasal cavity; O, Hard palate; P, Alveolar ridge

mouth·breed·er (mouth′brē′dər), *n.* any of several fishes of the genera *Tilapia* and *Haplochromis,* that hatch and care for their young in the mouth.
mouth·ful (mouth′fo͝ol′), *n., pl.* **-fuls. 1.** as much as a mouth can hold. **2.** as much as is taken into the mouth at one time. **3.** a small quantity.
mouth′ or′gan, harmonica.
mouth·part (mouth′pärt′), *n.* Usually, **mouthparts.** the appendages surrounding or associated with the mouth in arthropods.
mouth·piece (mouth′pēs′), *n.* **1.** a piece placed at or forming the mouth, as of a receptacle, tube, etc. **2.** a piece or part, as of an instrument, to which the mouth is applied or that is held in the mouth: *a trumpet mouthpiece.* **3.** the part of a bit or bridle, as for a horse, that passes through the animal's mouth. **4.** a person, newspaper, etc., that conveys the opinions or sentiments of another or others; spokesman. **5.** *Slang.* a lawyer.
mouth·wash (mouth′wôsh′, -wosh′), *n.* a solution containing germicidal and breath-sweetening agents used for cleansing the mouth.
mouth-wa·ter·ing (mouth′wô′tər ing, -wot′ər-), *adj.* so appetizing in appearance, aroma, or description as to cause the saliva to flow.
mouth·y (mou′thē, -thē), *adj.*, **mouth·i·er, mouth·i·est.** loud-mouthed; ranting; bombastic. —**mouth′i·ly,** *adv.* —**mouth′i·ness,** *n.*
mou·ton (mo͞o′ton), *n.* sheepskin processed to resemble seal or beaver. [< F: sheep, sheepskin; see MUTTON]
mou·ton·née (mo͞ot′ᵊnā′), *adj. Phys. Geog.* designating scattered knobs of rock rounded and smoothed by glacial action. Also, **mou′ton·néed′.** [< F: sheep-shaped. See MOUTON, -EE]
mov·a·ble (mo͞o′və bəl), *adj.* **1.** capable of being moved; not fixed in one place, position, or posture. **2.** *Law.* (of property) personal, as distinguished from real. **3.** changing from one date to another in different years: *a movable holiday.* **4.** (of type or matrices) able to be rearranged. —*n.* **5.** an article of furniture that is not fixed in place. **6. movables,** *Law.* movable property. Also, **moveable.** [ME *mevable, movable* < AF *movable*] —**mov′a·bil′i·ty, mov′a·ble·ness,** *n.* —**mov′a·bly,** *adv.*
mov′able feast′, a religious feast that does not occur on the same day each year.
move (mo͞ov), *v.,* **moved, mov·ing,** *n.* —*v.i.* **1.** to pass from one place or position to another. **2.** to go from one place of residence to another. **3.** to advance or progress. **4.** to have a regular motion, as an implement or a machine; turn; revolve. **5.** *Com.* to be disposed of by sale, as goods in stock. **6.** *Informal.* to start off or leave. **7.** (of the bowels) to evacuate. **8.** to be active in a particular sphere: *to move in society.* **9.** to take action; proceed. **10.** to make a formal request, application, or proposal. —*v.t.* **11.** to change from one place or position to another. **12.** to set or keep in motion. **13.** to prompt, actuate, or impel to some action. **14.** to cause (the bowels) to evacuate. **15.** to arouse or excite the feelings or passions of; affect with emotion (usually fol. by *to*): *to move someone to anger.* **16.** to affect with tender or compassionate emotion; touch. **17.** *Com.* to dispose of (goods in stock) by sale. **18.** to propose formally, as to a court or judge, or for consideration by a deliberative assembly. **19.** to submit a formal request or proposal to (a sovereign, a court, etc.). —*n.* **20.** the act or an instance of moving; movement. **21.** a change of abode or residence. **22.** an action toward an end; step: *a move in the right direction.* **23.** (in chess, checkers, etc.) **a.** a player's right or turn to make a play. **b.** the play itself. **24. get a move on,** *Informal.* to begin; act; hurry. **25. on the move,** *Informal.* **a.** busy; active. **b.** going from place to place. **c.** advancing; progressing. [ME *meve(n), move(n)* < AF *move(r)* < L *movēre*] —**move′less,** *adj.* —**move′less·ly,** *adv.* —**move′less·ness,** *n.* —**mov′er,** *n.* —**Syn. 2.** remove. **4.** spin, rotate. **11.** shift, transfer. **12.** agitate. **13.** influence, induce, incite. **20.** See **motion.** —**Ant. 11.** fix.
move·a·ble (mo͞o′və bəl), *adj., n.* movable. —**move′a·bil′i·ty, move′a·ble·ness,** *n.* —**move′a·bly,** *adv.*
move·ment (mo͞ov′mənt), *n.* **1.** the act, process, or result of moving. **2.** a particular manner of moving. **3.** Usually, **movements.** actions or activities, as of a person or a body of persons. **4.** *Mil.* a change of position or location of troops, ships, etc. **5.** rapid progress of events, or abundance of events or incidents. **6.** the progress of events, as in a narrative or drama. **7.** *Fine Arts.* the suggestion of motion in a work of art, either by represented gesture in figurative painting or sculpture or by the relationship of structural elements in a design or composition. **8.** a progressive development of ideas toward a particular conclusion. **9.** a series of actions or activities directed or tending toward a particular end. **10.** the course, tendency, or trend of affairs in a particular field. **11.** a diffusely organized or heterogeneous group of people or organizations tending toward or favoring a generalized common goal. **12.** See **bowel movement** (defs. 1, 2). **13.** the working parts or a distinct portion of the working parts of a mechanism, as of a watch. **14.** *Music.* **a.** a principal division or section of a sonata, symphony, or the like. **b.** motion; rhythm; time; tempo. **15.** *Pros.* rhythmical structure or character. [ME < MF] —**Syn. 1.** See **motion.**
mov·ie (mo͞o′vē), *n. Informal.* **1.** See **motion picture. 2.** a motion-picture theater. **3. movies, a.** motion pictures, as an industry (usually prec. by *the*). **b.** motion pictures, as a genre of art or entertainment. **c.** the exhibition of a motion picture: *an evening at the movies.* [MOV(ING PICTURE) + -IE]
mov·ie·go·ing (mo͞o′vē gō′ing), *n.* **1.** the practice or act of going to see motion pictures. —*adj.* **2.** characterized by going to see motion pictures often. —**mov′ie·go′er,** *n.*
mov·ing (mo͞o′ving), *adj.* **1.** that moves: *a moving target.* **2.** causing or producing motion. **3.** actuating, instigating, or impelling. **4.** exciting the feelings or affecting the emotions, esp. touchingly or pathetically. [ME *moeving*] —**mov′ing·ly,** *adv.*
mov′ing pic′ture. See **motion picture.**
mov′ing stair′case, escalator. Also called **mov′ing stair′way.**
mow[1] (mō), *v.,* **mowed, mowed** or **mown, mow·ing.** —*v.t.* **1.** to cut down (grass, grain, etc.) with a scythe or a machine. **2.** to cut grass, grain, etc., from: *to mow an overgrown lawn.* **3.** to destroy or kill indiscriminately or in great numbers, as men in battle. —*v.i.* **4.** to cut down grass, grain, etc. [ME *mowe(n),* OE *māwan;* c. G *mähen*] —**mow′er,** *n.*
mow[2] (mou), *n.* **1.** the place in a barn where hay, sheaves of grain, etc., are stored. **2.** a heap or pile of hay or of sheaves of grain in a barn. [ME *mow(e),* OE *mūwa, mūha, mūga;* c. Icel *mūgi* swath]
mow[3] (mou, mō), *Archaic.* —*n.* **1.** a wry or derisive grimace. —*v.i.* **2.** to make mows, mouths, or grimaces. [ME *mowe* < MF *moue* lip, pout < Gmc; cf. MD *mouwe* protruded lip]
mown (mōn), *v.* a pp. of **mow**[1].
mox·a (mok′sə), *n.* a flammable substance or material obtained from the leaves of certain Chinese and Japanese wormwood plants, esp. *Artemisia moxa.* [< Jap *mogusa* for *moe gusa* burning herb]
mox·ie (mok′sē), *n. Slang.* **1.** vigor; pep. **2.** courage or nerve. [after *Moxie,* a trademark (name of a soft drink)]
mo·yen âge (mwa ye näzh′), *French.* See **Middle Ages.**
Mozamb., Mozambique.
Mo·zam·bique (mō′zəm bēk′), *n.* **1.** a republic in SE Africa; formerly an overseas province of Portugal; independent since 1975. 9,900,000; 297,731 sq. mi. *Cap.:* Maputo. Formerly, **Portuguese East Africa. 2.** a seaport on an island just off the NE coast of this country. 55,000. Portuguese, **Moçambique.**
Mo′zambique′ Chan′nel, a channel in SE Africa, between Mozambique and Madagascar. 950 mi. long; 250–550 mi. wide.
Moz·ar·ab (mō zar′əb), *n.* a Christian in Moorish Spain. [< Sp *mozárabe* < Ar *musta'rib* a would-be Arab]
Moz·ar·a·bic (mō zar′ə bik), *adj.* **1.** of or pertaining to the Mozarabs. **2.** of or pertaining to a style of Spanish church architecture from the 9th to 15th centuries, characterized by the horseshoe-shaped arch.

Mo·zart (mōt′särt), *n.* **Wolf·gang A·ma·de·us** (wŏŏlf′gang am′ə dā′əs; *Ger.* vôlf′gäng ä′mä dā′ŏŏs), 1756–91, Austrian composer. —**Mo·zar′te·an, Mo·zar′ti·an,** *adj.*

moz·za·rel·la (mot′sə rel′ə, mōt′-), *n.* a mild, white, semisoft Italian cheese. [< It = *mozza* a kind of cheese (lit., a cut; cf. *mozzare* to cut off) + *-rella* -REL]

moz·zet·ta (mō zet′ə; *It.* môt tset′tä), *n., pl.* **-tas,** *It.* **moz·zet·te** (môt tset′te). *Rom. Cath. Ch.* a short, hooded cape that can be buttoned over the breast. Also, **mo·zet′ta.** [< It, aph. var. of *almozzetta* = *almozz(a)* (cf. ML *almutia* AMICE[1]) + *-etta* -ETTE]

MP, 1. Military Police. 2. Mounted Police.

mp., melting point.

M.P., 1. Member of Parliament. 2. Military Police. 3. Mounted Police.

MPers, Middle Persian.

mpg, miles per gallon.

mph, miles per hour. Also, **m.p.h.**

MR, See **motivation research.** Also, **M.R.**

mR, milliroentgen. Also, **mr**

Mr. (mis′tər), *pl.* **Messrs.** (mes′ərz). Mister: a title prefixed to a man's name or position. Also, *esp. Brit.,* **Mr**

MRA, See **Moral Re-Armament.**

Mr. Bones, the end man in a minstrel troupe who plays the bones.

Mr. Charlie (chär′lē), *U.S. Slang.* See **Mister Charlie.** Also, **Mr. Charley** (chär′lē).

Mr. Clean, *Informal.* a person with an impeccable record or background, esp. one in or running for public office.

mrem, millirem; millirems.

MRI, *Med.* magnetic resonance imaging: a noninvasive diagnostic procedure employing a body-encircling magnet and weak radio waves to obtain detailed images of body organs and tissues.

Mrs. (mis′iz, miz′-), *pl.* **Mrs., Mmes.** (mā däm′, -dam′). a title prefixed to the name of a married woman: *Mrs. Jones.* Also, *esp. Brit.,* **Mrs** [abbr. of MISTRESS]

MS, 1. Mississippi (approved esp. for use with zip code). 2. motor ship. 3. See **multiple sclerosis.**

Ms. (miz), *n.* a title prefixed to a woman's name or position: unlike Miss or Mrs., it does not depend upon or indicate her marital status. Also, **Ms** [M(ISS + MR)S.]

M/S, 1. *Com.* months after sight. 2. motor ship.

m/s, 1. meters per second. 2. meters per second per second.

MS., *pl.* **MSS.** manuscript.

ms., *pl.* **mss.** manuscript.

M.S., 1. See **Master of Science.** 2. motor ship. 3. See **multiple sclerosis.**

M.Sc., See **Master of Science.**

MSD, See **most significant digit.**

msec, millisecond; milliseconds.

MSG, See **monosodium glutamate.**

Msgr., Monsignor.

M.Sgt., master sergeant.

MSH, See **Mohs scale.**

MSI, a type of electronic microminiaturization in which between 100 and 1000 transistors and resistors may be concentrated on a single integrated-circuit chip. Cf. **LSI, SSI.** [(MEDIUM-)-S(CALE) I(NTEGRATION)]

m.s.l., mean sea level. Also, **M.S.L.**

MST, Mountain Standard Time. Also, **M.S.T., m.s.t.**

MT, 1. megaton; megatons. 2. Montana (approved esp. for use with zip code).

Mt., 1. mount: *Mt. Rainier.* 2. mountain. Also, **mt.**

M.T., 1. metric ton. 2. Mountain Time.

mtg., 1. meeting. 2. mortgage.

mtge., mortgage.

mtn., mountain. Also, **Mtn.**

Mt. Rev., Most Reverend.

Mts., mountains. Also, **mts.**

mu (myo͞o, mo͞o), *n.* the 12th letter of the Greek alphabet (M, μ). [< Gk]

Mu·ba·rak (mo͞o bär′ək), *n.* **(Mohammed) Hos·ni** (hoz′nē, hos′-), born 1928, Egyptian political leader: president since 1981.

muc-, var. of **muco-** before a vowel: *mucin.*

much (much), *adj.,* **more, most,** *n., adv.,* **more, most.** —*adj.* 1. being of great quantity, amount, measure, or degree. —*n.* 2. a great quantity or amount; a great deal. 3. a great, important, or notable thing or matter. 4. **make much of, a.** to treat, represent, or consider as of great importance. **b.** to treat with great consideration. —*adv.* 5. to a great extent or degree; greatly; far. 6. nearly, approximately, or about. [ME *muche, moche,* apocopated var. of *muchel, mochel,* OE *mycel;* r. ME *miche(l),* OE *micel* great, much, c. Icel *mikill,* Goth *mikils,* Gk *mégalos* great]

much·ness (much′nis), *n. Archaic.* greatness, as in quantity, measure, or degree. [ME *mochenesse*]

mu′cic ac′id (myo͞o′sik), *Chem.* a powder, $HOOC(CHOH)_4COOH$, used chiefly in organic synthesis.

mu·ci·lage (myo͞o′sə lij), *n.* 1. any of various preparations of gum, glue, or the like, for causing adhesion. 2. any of various gummy secretions or gelatinous substances present in plants. [ME *muscilage* < LL *mūcilāgō* a musty juice]

mu·ci·lag·i·nous (myo͞o′sə laj′ə nəs), *adj.* 1. of, pertaining to, or secreting mucilage. 2. of the nature of or resembling mucilage; moist, soft, and viscid. [< LL *mūcilāgin-* (s. of *mūcilāgō*) MUCILAGE + -OUS] —**mu′ci·lag′i·nous·ly,** *adv.*

mu·cin (myo͞o′sin), *n. Biochem.* any of a group of nitrogenous substances found in mucous secretions. —**mu′cin·oid′,** *adj.* —**mu·ci·nous** (myo͞o′sə nəs), *adj.*

muck (muk), *n.* 1. farmyard dung, decaying vegetable matter, etc., in a moist state; manure. 2. a highly organic, dark or black soil, less than 50 percent combustible, often used as a manure. 3. filth; dirt. 4. a confused state or condition. 5. *Chiefly Brit. Informal.* trash. 6. (esp. in mining) earth, rock, or other useless matter to be removed in order to get out the mineral or other substances sought. —*v.t.* 7. to manure. 8. to make dirty; soil. 9. to remove muck from. 10. *Brit. Slang.* to ruin or bungle. —*v.i.* 11. **muck about,** *Brit. Slang.* to idle; putter. [ME *muc, muk* < Scand; cf. Icel *myki* cow dung]

muck·er (muk′ər), *n. Brit. Slang.* a vulgar, ill-bred person.

muck·ing (muk′ing), *adj., adv. Brit. Slang.* damned.

muck·le (muk′əl), *adj. Brit. Dial.* mickle. [ME, var. of *muchel;* see MUCH]

muck·luck (muk′luk), *n.* mukluk.

muck·rake (muk′rāk′), *v.i.,* **-raked, -rak·ing.** to search for and expose real or alleged corruption, scandal, or the like, esp. in politics. [obs. *muck rake* a rake for use on muck or dung] —**muck′rak′er,** *n.*

muck·y (muk′ē), *adj.,* **muck·i·er, muck·i·est.** 1. of or like muck. 2. filthy; dirty. 3. *Brit. Informal.* **a.** nasty; mean. **b.** (of weather) oppressively humid.

muc·luc (muk′luk), *n.* mukluk.

muco-, a combining form representing **mucus** or **mucous:** *mucoprotein.* Also, **muc-.**

mu·coid (myo͞o′koid), *n.* 1. *Biochem.* any of a group of substances resembling the mucins, occurring in connective tissue, cysts, etc. —*adj.* 2. Also, **mu·coi·dal** (myo͞o koid′əl). resembling mucus. [MUC(IN) + -OID]

mu·co·lyt·ic (myo͞o′kō lit′ik), *adj.* noting or pertaining to enzymes that hydrolyze mucopolysaccharides.

mu·co·pol·y·sac·cha·ride (myo͞o′kō pol′ē sak′ə rīd′, -rid), *n.* any of a class of polysaccharides derived from hexosamine that form mucins when dispersed in water.

mu·co·pro·tein (myo͞o′kə prō′tēn, -tē in), *n. Biochem.* a protein yielding carbohydrates and amino acids on hydrolysis.

mu·co·sa (myo͞o kō′sə), *n., pl.* **-sae** (-sē). *Anat.* See **mucous membrane.** [< NL, n. use of fem. of L *mūcōsus* MUCOUS]

mu·cous (myo͞o′kəs), *adj.* 1. pertaining to, consisting of, or resembling mucus. 2. containing or secreting mucus. [< L *mūcōs(us)* slimy, mucous. See MUCUS, -OUS] —**mu·cos·i·ty** (myo͞o kos′i tē), *n.*

mu′cous mem′brane, a lubricating membrane lining an internal surface or an organ, such as the alimentary, respiratory, and genitourinary canals.

mu·cro (myo͞o′krō), *n., pl.* **mu·cro·nes** (myo͞o krō′nēz). *Bot., Zool.* a short point projecting abruptly, as at the end of a leaf. [< L: sharp point]

mu·cro·nate (myo͞o′krō nit, -nāt′), *adj. Bot., Zool.* having an abruptly projecting point, as a feather, leaf, etc. Also, **mu′cro·nat′ed.** [< L *mūcrōnāt(us)* pointed] —**mu′cro·na′tion,** *n.*

mu·cus (myo͞o′kəs), *n.* a viscid secretion of the mucous membranes. [< L: snot; akin to Gk *myktḗr* nose, *mýxa* slime]

mud (mud), *n., v.t.,* **mud·ded, mud·ding.** —*n.* 1. wet, soft earth, as on the ground after rain; mire. —*v.t.* 2. to cover or smear with mud. 3. to stir up the mud or sediment in. [ME *mudde, mode* < MLG *mudde.* See MOTHER[2]]

mud′ daub′er, any of several wasps of the family *Sphecidae* that build a nest of mud cells and provision it with spiders or insects.

mud·der (mud′ər), *n.* a race horse able to perform well on a muddy track.

mud·dle (mud′əl), *v.,* **-dled, -dling,** *n.* —*v.t.* 1. to mix up in a confused or bungling manner; jumble. 2. to cause to become mentally confused. 3. to cause to become confused or stupid with or as with intoxicating drink. 4. to mix or stir (a cocktail, chocolate, etc.). 5. to make muddy or turbid, as water. —*v.i.* 6. to think or act in a confused or bungling manner. 7. **muddle through,** to come to a successful conclusion without much purposeful effort or planned direction: *to muddle through college.* —*n.* 8. a state or condition of being muddled, esp. a confused mental state. 9. a confused, disordered, or embarrassing state of affairs; a mess. [MUD + -LE; c. MD *moddelen* to muddy] —**mud′dled·ness, mud′dle·ment,** *n.* —**mud′dling·ly,** *adv.*

mud·dle·head·ed (mud′əl hed′id), *adj.* confused in one's thinking; blundering: *a muddleheaded assertion.*

mud·dler (mud′lər), *n.* 1. a stick for stirring drinks. 2. a person who muddles or muddles through.

mud·dy (mud′ē), *adj.,* **-di·er, -di·est,** *v.,* **-died, -dy·ing.** —*adj.* 1. abounding in or covered with mud. 2. not clear or pure, as color. 3. dull, as the complexion. 4. not clear mentally. 5. obscure or vague, as thought or expression. —*v.t.* 6. to make muddy; soil with mud. 7. to make turbid. 8. to render confused or obscure. 9. to slander; defame: *to muddy a candidate's name.* —*v.i.* 10. to become muddy. [late ME *moddy*] —**mud′di·ly,** *adv.* —**mud′di·ness,** *n.*

Mu·dé·jar (*Sp.* mo͞o ᵺe′häʀ), *n., pl.* **-ja·res** (-hä ʀes′), *adj.* —*n.* 1. a Muslim permitted to remain in Spain after the Christian reconquest. —*adj.* 2. of or pertaining to a style of Spanish architecture from the 13th to 16th centuries, a fusion of the Romanesque and Gothic with the Arabic. [< Sp < Ar *muddājjan* permitted to stay]

mud′ flat′, 1. a mud-covered, gently sloping tract of land, alternately covered and left bare by tidal waters. 2. the muddy, nearly level bed of a dry lake.

mud·guard (mud′gärd′), *n.* a shield so placed as to protect riders or passengers from mud thrown by the wheel of a bicycle, automobile, or the like.

mud·lark (mud′lärk′), *n. Chiefly Brit. Informal.* a gutter urchin; street Arab.

mud·pup·py (mud′pup′ē), *n., pl.* **-pies.** 1. any of several large, aquatic salamanders of the genus *Necturus,* of eastern North America, having bushy, red gills and well-developed limbs. 2. any of several North American salamanders of the genus *Ambystoma.*

Mudpuppy, *Necturus maculosus* (Length 8 in.)

mud·sling·ing (mud′sling′ing), *n.* an attempt to discredit one's opponent, by malicious personal attacks, as in political campaigning. —**mud′sling′er,** *n.*

mud·stone (mud′stōn′), *n.* a clayey rock of nearly uniform texture throughout, with little or no lamination.

mud′ tur′tle, any of several small, fresh-water turtles of the family *Kinosternidae,* of the New World, as the dark-brown *Kinosternum subrubrum,* of the eastern U.S.

muen·ster (mo͝on′stər, mun′-, min′-, mʏn′-), *n.* a white, semisoft, mild cheese made from whole milk. [after *Muenster* in France (Haut Rhin)]

mu·ez·zin (myo͞o ez′in, mo͞o-), *n.* (in Islamic communities) the crier who, from a minaret or other high part of a mosque, at stated hours five times daily, intones aloud the call summoning the faithful to prayer. [< Ar *mu'adhdhin*]

muff (muf), *n.* **1.** a thick, tubular case for the hands, often covered with fur. **2.** a tuft of feathers on the sides of the head of certain fowls. **3.** *Sports.* a failure to catch a ball that may reasonably be expected to be caught. **4.** any failure. —*v.t.* **5.** *Informal.* to bungle; handle clumsily. **6.** *Sports.* to fail to catch (a ball that may reasonably be expected to be caught); fumble. [< D *mof,* earlier *moffel* mitten, muff < MF *moufle* mitten]

muf·fin (muf′in), *n.* **1.** a small, round bread made with wheat flour, corn meal, or the like, and eaten with butter. **2.** See **English muffin.** [?]

muf′fin stand′, a small stand having several tiers for holding plates and a tea service.

muf·fle (muf′əl), *v.,* **-fled, -fling,** *n.* —*v.t.* **1.** to wrap or envelop in a shawl, coat, etc., esp. to keep warm or protect the face and neck (often fol. by *up*). **2.** to wrap with something to deaden or prevent sound. **3.** to deaden (sound) by wrappings or other means. **4.** to wrap (oneself) in a garment or other covering: *muffled in silk.* —*n.* **5.** something that muffles. **6.** muffled sound. **7.** an oven or arched chamber in a furnace or kiln, used for heating substances without direct contact with the fire. **8.** the thick, bare part of the upper lip and nose of ruminants and rodents. [ME *mufle(n),* prob. < MF; cf. MF *emmoufle* wrapped up]

muf·fler (muf′lər), *n.* **1.** a heavy neck scarf. **2.** any of various devices for deadening sound, as the sound of escaping gases of an internal-combustion engine. **3.** anything used for muffling.

muf·ti (muf′tē), *n., pl.* **-tis.** **1.** civilian dress, as opposed to military or other uniform, or as worn by a person who usually wears a uniform. **2.** the religious head of a Muslim community. **3.** a Muslim legal adviser consulted in applying the religious law. **4.** (*cap.*) See **Grand Mufti.** [< Ar: lit., one who delivers a judgment, orig. a Muslim legal adviser; def. 1 arises from legal adviser being a civil official]

mug (mug), *n., v.,* **mugged, mug·ging.** —*n.* **1.** a drinking cup, usually cylindrical in shape, having a handle, and often of a heavy substance, as earthenware. **2.** the quantity it holds. **3.** *Slang.* the face. **4.** *Slang.* a thug; ruffian. —*v.t.* **5.** to assault (a victim), usually with intent to rob. —*v.i.* **6.** *Slang.* to grimace voluntarily. [prob. < Scand; cf. Sw *mugg,* Norw, Dan *mugge* drinking cup]

Mu·ga·be (mo͞o gä′bē, -bā), *n.* **Robert,** born 1925, Zimbabwe political leader: prime minister since 1980.

mug·ger¹ (mug′ər), *n.* **1.** a person who mugs, esp. one who assaults another person in order to rob him. **2.** a person, as an actor, who grimaces, esp. for comic effect. [MUG + -ER¹]

mug·ger² (mug′ər), *n.* a broad-snouted crocodile, *Crocodylus palustris,* of southern Asia, that grows to a length of about 12 feet. Also, **mug′gar, mug′gur.** [< Hindi *magar*]

mug·gy (mug′ē), *adj.,* **-gi·er, -gi·est.** (of the atmosphere, weather, etc.) humid and oppressive; damp and close. [*mug* drizzle (n. and v.) (< Scand; cf. Icel *mugga* mist, drizzle) + -Y¹] —**mug′gi·ly,** *adv.* —**mug′gi·ness,** *n.* —**Ant.** dry.

mug·wump (mug′wump′), *n. U.S.* **1.** a Republican who refused to support the party nominee, James G. Blaine, in the presidential campaign of 1884. **2.** a person who is neutral on a controversial issue. [< Algonquian (Massachusetts): lit., great man] —**mug′wump′er·y, mug′wump′ism,** *n.* —**mug′wump′i·an,** *adj.* —**mug′wump′ish,** *adj.*

Mu·ham·mad (mo͝o ham′əd), *n.* ("*the Prophet*") A.D. 570–632, founder of Islam. Also, **Mohammed, Mahomet.**

Muham′mad Ah′med (ä′məd), ("*the Mahdi*") 1844–1885, Muslim leader in Anglo-Egyptian Sudan.

Muham′mad Ali′. See **Ali, Muhammad.**

Mu·ham·mad·an (mo͝o ham′ə dᵊn), *adj., n.* Muslim. Also, **Mu·ham′med·an.**

Muham′mad Ri·za′ Pah·la·vi′ (ri zä′ pä lä vē′, pal′ə vē), 1919–80, shah of Iran 1941–79: in exile from 1979. Also called **Mu·ham′mad Re·za′ Shah′ Pahlavi′, Mu·ham′mad Re·za′ Shah′ Pah·le·vi′** (pä le vē′, pal′ə vē).

Mu·har·ram (mo͞o har′əm), *n.* the first month of the Islamic calendar. Also, **Moharram.** [< Ar: lit., holy]

Muh·len·berg (myo͞o′lən bûrg′), *n.* **1. Frederick Augustus Conrad,** 1750–1801, U.S. clergyman and statesman: first Speaker of the House 1789–91, 1793–95. **2.** his father, **Henry Mel·chi·or** (mel′kē ôr′), 1711–87, American Lutheran clergyman, born in Germany.

Muir (myo͝or), *n.* **John,** 1838–1914, U.S. naturalist, explorer, and writer.

Muir′ Gla′cier, a glacier in SE Alaska, flowing SE from Mount Fairweather. 350 sq. mi.

mu·jik (mo͞o zhik′, mo͞o′zhik), *n.* muzhik.

Muk·den (mo͝ok′den′, mo͝ok′-), *n.* a city in S Manchuria, in NE China: former capital of Manchuria; battle 1905. 3,000,000. Also, **Moukden.** Also called **Fengtien, Shenyang.**

muk·luk (muk′luk), *n.* **1.** a soft boot worn by Eskimos, usually of sealskin or reindeer skin. **2.** a similar boot with a soft sole, usually worn for lounging. Also, **mucluc, muckluck.** [< Eskimo *muklok* big seal]

mu·lat·to (mə lat′ō, myo͞o-), *n., pl.* **-toes,** *adj.* —*n.* **1.** the offspring of one white parent and one Negro parent. **2.** a person whose racial ancestry is mixed Negroid and Caucasoid, esp. one with light-brown skin. —*adj.* **3.** of a light-brown color, as resembling the skin of a mulatto. [< Sp *mulato* young mule = *mul(o)* MULE¹ + *-ato* < ?]

mul·ber·ry (mul′ber′ē, -bə rē), *n., pl.* **-ries.** **1.** the edible, berrylike collective fruit of any tree of the genus *Morus.* **2.** a tree of this genus, as *M. rubra* bearing dark-purple fruit, *M. nigra* bearing dark-colored fruit, and *M. alba* bearing nearly white fruit and having leaves used as food for silkworms. [ME *mulberie,* dissimilated var. of *murberie,* OE *mōrberie* = *mōr-* (< L *mōrum* mulberry) + *berie* BERRY]

mulch (mulch), *Hort.* —*n.* **1.** a covering, as of straw, leaves, manure, etc., spread or left on the ground around plants to prevent excessive evaporation or erosion, enrich the soil, etc. —*v.t.* **2.** to cover with mulch. [n. use of obs. *mulch* (adj.), ME *molsh* soft, OE *myl(i)sc* mellow]

mulct (mulkt), *n.* **1.** a fine; penalty. —*v.t.* **2.** to punish (a person) by fine or forfeiture. **3.** to obtain (money or the like) by fraud, extortion, etc. **4.** to deprive (someone) of something, as by fraud. [< L *mulct(a)* a fine]

mule¹ (myo͞ol), *n.* **1.** the offspring of a male donkey and a mare, valued as a work animal. **2.** any hybrid between the donkey and the horse. **3.** *Biol.* a hybrid, esp. a hybrid between the canary and some other finch. **4.** Also called **spinning mule.** a machine for spinning cotton or other fibers into yarn and winding the yarn on spindles. **5.** *Informal.* a stubborn person. [ME < OF < L *mūla* she-mule; r. OE *mūl* < L *mūlus*]

Mule, *Equus asinus x caballus* (5 ft. high at shoulder)

mule² (myo͞ol), *n.* a backless slipper for a woman, esp. such a slipper for informal wear at home. [< MF < L *mulleus* red shoe]

mule′ deer′, a deer, *Odocoileus hemionus,* of western North America, having large ears.

mule′ skin′ner, *Informal.* a muleteer.

mu·le·ta (mo͞o lā′tə, -let′ə), *n.* a red cloth, for use by a matador in guiding the course of the bull's attack in the stage of the fight preparatory to the kill. [< Sp: prop, support, muleta, dim. of *mula* (fem.) MULE¹]

mu·le·teer (myo͞o′lə tēr′), *n.* a driver of mules. [< MF *muletier* = *mulet* (see MULE¹, -ET) + *-ier* -EER]

mu·ley (myo͞o′lē, mo͝ol′ē), *adj., n., pl.* **-leys.** —*adj.* **1.** (of cattle) hornless; polled. —*n.* **2.** any cow. Also, **mulley.** [var. of dial. *moiley* < Ir *maol* or Welsh *moel* bald, hornless + -EY²]

Mule deer (3½ ft. high at shoulder; total length 6 ft.; tail 7½ in.)

Mul·ha·cén (mo͞ol′ä then′), *n.* a mountain in S Spain: the highest peak in Spain, 11,411 ft.

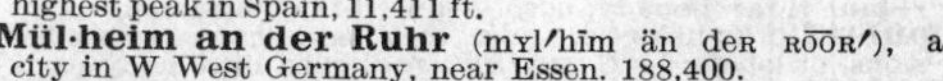

Mül·heim an der Ruhr (myl′hīm än dɛʀ ʀo͞oʀ′), a city in W West Germany, near Essen. 188,400.

Mul·house (my lo͞oz′), *n.* a city in E France, near the Rhine. 119,326. German, **Mül·hau·sen** (myl hou′zən).

mu·li·eb·ri·ty (myo͞o′lē eb′ri tē), *n.* **1.** womanly nature or qualities. **2.** womanhood. [< LL *muliēbritās* womanhood = *muliēbri(s)* womanly (< *mulier* woman) + *-tās* -TY²] —**mu′li·eb′ral,** *adj.*

mul·ish (myo͞o′lish), *adj.* stubborn, obstinate, or intractable. —**mul′ish·ly,** *adv.* —**mul′ish·ness,** *n.*

mull¹ (mul), *v.i.* to study or ruminate; ponder (often fol. by *over*): *to mull over a decision.* [appar. var. of MUDDLE]

mull² (mul), *v.t.* to heat, sweeten, and spice for drinking, as ale, wine, etc.: *mulled cider.* [?]

mull³ (mul), *n.* a soft, thin muslin. [earlier *mulmul* < Hindi *malmal*]

Mull (mul), *n.* an island in the Hebrides, in W Scotland. 2149 (1961).

mul·lah (mul′ə, mo͝ol′ə, mo͞o′lə), *n.* **1.** (in Islamic countries) a title of respect for a person who is learned in, teaches, or expounds the sacred law. **2.** (in Turkey) a provincial judge. Also, **mul′la, mollah.** [< Pers or Urdu *mullā* < Ar *mawlā*]

Mu·lla Mus·ta·fa el-Bar·za·ni (mo͞o′lä mo͝os′tä fä′ el-bär zä′nē), born 1904, Kurdish leader in Iraq.

mul·lein (mul′ən), *n.* **1.** an Old World weed, *Verbascum Thapsus,* having coarse, woolly leaves and dense spikes of yellow flowers, introduced into North America. **2.** any similar plant. Also, **mul′len.** [ME *moleine* < AF, perh. < *mol* soft < L *moll(is)*]

mul·ler (mul′ər), *n.* **1.** an implement of stone or other substance with a flat base for grinding paints, powders, etc., on a slab of stone or the like. **2.** any of various mechanical devices for grinding. [perh. formed on ME *mull* powder, OE *myl* dust; see -ER¹]

Mul·ler (mul′ər), *n.* **Hermann Joseph,** 1890–1967, U.S. geneticist: Nobel prize for medicine 1946.

Mül·ler (mul′ər; *Ger.* my′lər), *n.* **1. Frie·drich Max** (frē′drik maks; *Ger.* frē′drikн mäks), 1823–1900, English Sanskrit scholar and philologist born in Germany. **2. Jo·hann** (yō′hän), ("*Regiomontanus*"), 1436–76, German mathematician and astronomer.

mul·let¹ (mul′it), *n., pl.* (*esp. collectively*) **-let,** (*esp. referring to two or more kinds or species*) **-lets.** **1.** any of several marine or fresh-water, usually gray fishes of the family *Mugilidae,* having a nearly cylindrical body. **2.** a goatfish. **3.** a sucker, esp. of the genus *Moxostoma.* [late ME *mulet* < MF < L *mull(us)* red mullet; see -ET]

mul·let² (mul′it), *n. Heraldry.* a starlike charge having five points unless a greater number is specified, used esp. as the cadency mark of a third son. [ME *molet* < OF *molette* rowel of spur]

mul·ley (mo͝ol′ē), *adj., n., pl.* **-leys.** muley.

mul·li·gan (mul′ə gən), *n. U.S. Slang.* a kind of stew containing meat, vegetables, etc. Also called **mul′ligan stew′.** [special use of proper name]

mul·li·ga·taw·ny (mul′ə gə tô′nē), *n.* a curry-flavored soup of East Indian origin, often made with chicken stock. [< Tamil *milakutanni,* lit., pepper water]

Mul·li·ken (mul′ə kən), *n.* **Robert S(an·der·son)** (san′dər-sən), 1896–1986, U.S. physicist, chemist, and teacher: Nobel prize for chemistry 1966.

mul·lion (mul′yən), *n.* *Archit.* a vertical member, as of stone or wood, between the lights of a window, the panels in wainscoting, or the like. [metathetic var. of archaic *monial* < MF *moinel* < ?]

mul·lock (mul′ək), *n.* (in Australasia) refuse or rubbish, as rock, earth, or the like, from a mine; muck. [ME *mullok.* See MULLER, -OCK] **—mul′lock·y,** *adj.*

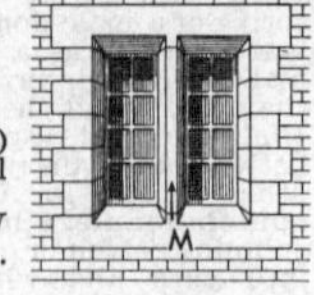

M, Mullion

Mu·lock (myo͞o′lok), *n.* **Dinah Maria.** See **Craik, Dinah Maria Mulock.**

Mul·ro·ney (mul rō′nē), *n.* **(Martin) Brian,** born 1939, Canadian political leader: prime minister since 1984.

Mul·tan (mo͝ol tän′), *n.* a city in W Punjab, in central Pakistan. 575,000.

mul·tan·gu·lar (mul tang′gyə lər), *adj.* having many angles; polyangular. Also, **mul·ti·an·gu·lar** (mul′tē ang′gyə lər, mul′tī-). [< L *multangul(us)* many-cornered (see MULT-, ANGLE[1]) + -AR[1]]

mul·tan·gu·lum (mul tang′gyə ləm), *n., pl.* **-la** (-lə). *Anat.* either of two bones of the carpus, one **(greater multangular bone)** articulating with the metacarpal bone of the thumb or one **(lesser multangular bone)** articulating with the metacarpal bone of the forefinger. [< NL: polygon]

multi-, an element of Latin origin meaning "many," "much," "multiple," "many times," "more than one," "more than two," "composed of many like parts," "in many respects," used in the formation of compound words: *multiply; multivitamin.* Also, *esp. before a vowel,* **mult-.** [ME < L, comb. form of *multus* much, many]

mul·ti·col·or (mul′ti kul′ər), *n.* **1.** an arrangement or design of many colors. **—***adj.* **2.** (of a printing press) capable of printing more than two colors simultaneously or in a single operation. **3.** multicolored. [back formation from MULTICOLORED]

mul·ti·col·ored (mul′ti kul′ərd, mul′ti kul′ərd), *adj.* of many colors.

mul·ti·dis·ci·pli·nar·y (mul′tē dis′ə plə ner′ē, mul′tī-), *adj.* composed or made up of several specialized branches of learning, as for achieving a common aim.

mul·ti·fac·et·ed (mul′tē fas′i tid, mul′tī-), *adj.* **1.** having many facets, as a gem. **2.** having many aspects or phases. **3.** possessing many talents.

mul·ti·far·i·ous (mul′tə fâr′ē əs), *adj.* **1.** having many different parts, elements, forms, etc. **2.** numerous and varied; manifold: *multifarious activities.* [< LL *multifārius* many-sided, manifold = L *multifāri(am)* on many sides + *-us* -OUS] **—mul′ti·far′i·ous·ly,** *adv.* **—mul′ti·far′i·ous·ness,** *n.*

mul·ti·fid (mul′tə fid), *adj.* cleft into many parts, divisions, or lobes. [< L *multifid(us)* divided into many parts]

mul·ti·fold (mul′tə fōld′), *adj.* manifold.

mul·ti·form (mul′tə fôrm′), *adj.* having many forms. [< L *multiform(is)*] **—mul·ti·for·mi·ty** (mul′tə fôr′mi tē), *n.*

Mul·ti·graph (mul′tə graf′, -gräf′), *n.* *Trademark.* a rotary typesetting and printing machine, commonly used in making many copies of written matter.

mul·ti·lat·er·al (mul′ti lat′ər əl), *adj.* **1.** having many sides; many-sided. **2.** *Govt.* participated in by two or more states: *multilateral treaty.* **—mul′ti·lat′er·al·ly,** *adv.*

mul·ti·lin·gual (mul′ti ling′gwəl), *adj.* **1.** able to speak more than two languages with approximately equal facility. **2.** spoken or written in more than two languages.

Mul·ti·lith (mul′ti lith), *n.* *Trademark.* a small photo-offset printing machine.

mul·ti·me·di·a (mul′ti mē′dē ə), *n.pl.* (*construed as sing.*) the simultaneous, combined use of several media at once, as films, slides, flashing lights, and music.

mul·ti·mil·lion·aire (mul′tē mil′yə nâr′, mul′tī-), *n.* a person who has several million dollars, pounds, francs, etc.

mul·ti·na·tion·al (mul′ti nash′ə nᵊl), *n.* **1.** a giant, usually diversified corporation with operations and subsidiaries in many foreign countries. **—***adj.* **2.** of, pertaining to, or composed of many nations or nationalities. **3.** noting or pertaining to a multinational or multinationals.

mul·ti·nu·cle·ar (mul′ti no͞o′klē ər, -nyo͞o′-), *adj.* having many or several nuclei, as a cell. Also, **mul·ti·nu·cle·ate** (mul′ti no͞o′klē āt′, -nyo͞o′-).

mul·tip·a·ra (mul tip′ər ə), *n., pl.* **-a·rae** (-ə rē′). *Obstet.* a woman who has borne two or more children, or who is parturient for the second time. [n. use of fem. of NL *multiparus* MULTIPAROUS]

mul·tip·a·rous (mul tip′ər əs), *adj.* **1.** producing many, or more than one, at a birth. **2.** *Bot.* (of a cyme) having many lateral axes. [< NL *multipar(us)* bearing many young at a birth] **—mul·ti·par·i·ty** (mul′ti par′i tē), *n.*

mul·ti·par·tite (mul′ti pär′tīt), *adj.* **1.** divided into many parts; having many divisions. **2.** *Govt.* multilateral (def. 2). [< L *multipartīt(us)* divided into many parts]

mul·ti·ped (mul′tə ped′), *adj.* **1.** having many feet. **—***n.* **2.** *Rare.* a many-footed animal as a centipede. Also, **mul·ti·pede** (mul′tə pēd′). [< L *multiped-* (s. of *multipēs*) many-footed]

mul·ti·phase (mul′ti fāz′), *adj.* having many phases. **—mul′ti·pha′sic,** *adj.*

mul·ti·ple (mul′tə pəl), *adj.* **1.** consisting of, having, or involving many individuals, parts, elements, relations, etc.; manifold. **2.** *Elect.* **a.** (of circuits) arranged in parallel. **b.** (of a circuit or circuits) having a number of points at which connection can be made. **3.** *Bot.* (of a fruit) collective. **—***n.* **4.** *Math.* a number which contains another number an integral number of times without a remainder: *12 is a multiple of 3.* [< F < LL *multipl(us)* manifold. See MULTIPLEX]

mul′tiple alleles′, *Genetics.* a series of three or more alternative or allelic forms of a gene, only two of which can exist in any normal, diploid individual. **—mul′tiple allel′ism.**

mul·ti·ple-choice (mul′tə pəl chois′), *adj.* consisting of several possible answers from which the correct one must be selected: *a multiple-choice examination.*

mul′tiple fac′tors, *Genetics.* a series of two or more pairs of genes responsible for the development of complex, quantitative characters such as size, yield, etc.

mul′tiple in′tegral, *Math.* an integral in which the integrand involves a function of more than one variable, requiring repeated integration for evaluation.

mul′tiple personal′ity. See **split personality.**

mul′tiple sclero′sis, *Pathol.* a progressive neurological disease, chiefly of young adults, characterized by speech disturbances, muscular incoordination, weakness, and nystagmus, and caused by sclerotic patches in the brain and spinal cord.

mul′tiple star′, *Astron.* three or more stars lying close together in the celestial sphere and usually united in a single gravitational system.

mul′tiple vot′ing, the casting of ballots by a voter in more than one constituency in an election.

mul·ti·plex (mul′tə pleks′), *adj.* **1.** manifold; multiple. **2.** of, pertaining to, or using a telegraph or telephone circuit, or radio or television transmitting and receiving equipment capable of carrying two or more distinct signals simultaneously. **—***v.t.* **3.** *Elect.* to arrange a circuit for use by multiplex telegraphy. **4.** to transmit (two or more signals or messages) by a multiplex system, circuit, or the like. **—***v.i.* **5.** to send several messages or signals simultaneously, as by multiplex telegraphy. **—***n.* **6.** a multiplex electronics system. **7.** (in map making) a device that gives a three-dimensional effect to a combined topographical image when seen through stereoscopic glasses. [< L: manifold = *multi-* MULTI- + *-plex* -fold; see PLY[2]] **—mul′ti·plex′er,** *n.*

mul·ti·pli·a·ble (mul′tə plī′ə bəl), *adj.* capable of being multiplied. Also, **mul·ti·plic·a·ble** (mul′tə plik′ə bəl). [MULTIPLY[1] + -ABLE]

mul·ti·pli·cand (mul′tə pli kand′), *n.* *Arith.* a number to be multiplied by another. [< L *multiplicand(um),* n. use of neut. of *multiplicandus* to be multiplied, ger. of *multiplicāre* to MULTIPLY[1]]

mul·ti·pli·cate (mul′tə pli kāt′), *adj.* multiple; manifold. [ME *multiplicat* < L *multiplicāt(us)* multiplied, increased, ptp. of *multiplicāre*]

mul·ti·pli·ca·tion (mul′tə plə kā′shən), *n.* **1.** the act or process of multiplying. **2.** the state of being multiplied. **3.** *Arith.* a mathematical operation signifying, when *a* and *b* are positive integers, that *a* is to be added to itself as many times as there are units in *b.* **4.** *Math.* any generalization of this operation applicable to numbers other than integers, such as fractions, irrational numbers, etc. [ME *multiplicacio(u)n* < L *multiplicātiōn-* (s. of *multiplicātiō*)] **—mul′ti·pli·ca′tion·al,** *adj.*

multiplica′tion sign′, *Arith.* the symbol (·) or (×) between two mathematical expressions, denoting multiplication of the second expression by the first; times sign.

multiplica′tion ta′ble, *Arith.* a tabular listing of the products of any two numbers of a set, usually of the integers 1 through 10 or 1 through 12.

mul·ti·pli·ca·tive (mul′tə plə kā′tiv, mul′tə plik′ə-), *adj.* **1.** tending to multiply or increase. **2.** having the power of multiplying. [< ML *multiplicātīv(us)*] **—mul′ti·pli·ca′tive·ly,** *adv.*

mul·ti·plic·i·ty (mul′tə plis′i tē), *n., pl.* **-ties.** **1.** a multitude or great number. **2.** the state of being multiplex or manifold. [< LL *multiplicitās* = *multiplic-* (s. of *multiplex*) MULTIPLEX + *-itās* -ITY]

mul·ti·pli·er (mul′tə plī′ər), *n.* **1.** a person or thing that multiplies. **2.** *Arith.* a number by which another is multiplied. **3.** *Physics.* a device for intensifying some effect. [ME]

mul·ti·ply[1] (mul′tə plī′), *v.,* **-plied, -ply·ing.** **—***v.t.* **1.** to make many or manifold; increase the number, quantity, etc., of. **2.** *Arith.* to find the product of by multiplication. **3.** to procreate or increase by procreation. **—***v.i.* **4.** to grow in number, quantity, etc.; increase. **5.** *Arith.* to perform the process of multiplication. **6.** to increase in number by procreation or natural generation. [ME *multiplie(n)* < OF *multiplie(r)* < L *multiplicāre*]

mul·ti·ply[2] (mul′tə plē), *adv.* in a multiple manner; manifoldly. [MULTIP(LE) + -LY]

mul·ti·pur·pose (mul′ti pûr′pəs), *adj.* able to be used for several purposes.

mul·ti·stage (mul′ti stāj′), *adj.* (of a rocket or guided missile) having more than one stage.

mul·ti·tude (mul′ti to͞od′, -tyo͞od′), *n.* **1.** a great number of persons or things. **2.** a crowd or throng. **3.** the state or character of being many. **4. the multitude,** the common people. [ME < L *multitūdō*] **—Syn. 2.** mass. See **crowd**[1].

mul·ti·tu·di·nous (mul′ti to͞od′ᵊnəs, -tyo͞od′-), *adj.* **1.** forming a multitude or great number; existing, occurring, or present in great numbers. **2.** comprising many items, parts, or elements. [< L *multitūdin-* (s. of *multitūdō*) + -OUS] **—mul′ti·tu′di·nous·ly,** *adv.* **—mul′ti·tu′di·nous·ness,** *n.*

mul·ti·va·lent (mul′tə vā′lənt, mul tiv′ə lənt), *adj.* *Chem.* having a valence of three or higher. **—mul′ti·va′lence,** *n.*

mul·ti·valve (mul′ti valv′), *adj.* **1.** (of a shell) composed of more than two valves or pieces. **—***n.* **2.** a multivalve mollusk or its shell.

mul·ti·vi·ta·min (mul′tə vī′tə min), *adj.* **1.** containing or consisting of a combination of several vitamins. **—***n.* **2.** a compound of many vitamins.

mul·tiv·o·cal (mul tiv′ə kəl), *adj.* having many or different meanings of equal probability or validity.

mul·tum in par·vo (mo͝ol′to͝om in pär′wō; *Eng.* mul′təm in pär′vō), *Latin.* much in little; a great deal in a small space or in brief.

mul·ture (mul′chər), *n.* *Scots Law.* a toll or fee given to the proprietor of a mill for the grinding of grain. [ME *multir* < OF *molture* < ML *molitūra* a grinding = L *molit(us)* ground (ptp. of *molere*) + *-ūra* -URE]

mum[1] (mum), *adj.* **1.** silent; not saying a word: *to keep mum.* **—***interj.* **2.** say nothing! be silent! **3. mum's the word,** do not reveal what you know. [ME *momme,* imit.]

mum[2] (mum), *v.i.,* **mummed, mum·ming.** to act as a mummer. Also, **mumm.** [ME *momme(n),* v. use of MUM[1]; cf. MD *mommen* to act the mummer's part]

mul′ti·ax′i·al, *adj.;* **-ly,** *adv.*
mul′ti·birth′, *n.*
mul′ti·branched′, *adj.*
mul′ti·cel′lu·lar, *adj.*
mul′ti·chan′neled, *adj.*
mul′ti·di·men′sion·al, *adj.*
mul′ti·di·rec′tion·al, *adj.*
mul′ti·en′gined, *adj.*
mul′ti·faced′, *adj.*
mul′ti·lam′i·nar, *adj.*
mul′ti·lam′i·nate′, *adj.*
mul′ti·lin′e·al, *adj.*
mul′ti·lobed′, *adj.*
mul′ti·lob′u·lar, *adj.*
mul′ti·mo·lec′u·lar, *adj.*
mul′ti·mo′tored, *adj.*
mul′ti·o′vu·lar, *adj.*
mul′ti·po′lar, *adj.*
mul′ti·ra′cial, *adj.*
mul′ti·ra′di·al, *adj.*

mum[3] (mum), *n. Informal.* chrysanthemum. [shortened form]
mum[4] (mum), *n. Chiefly Brit. Informal.* mother. [nursery word; see MOM]
mum[5] (mum), *n.* a strong beer or ale. [< G *Mumme,* said to have been named after the brewer who made it]
mum·ble (mum′bəl), *v.,* **-bled, -bling,** *n.* —*v.i.* **1.** to speak indistinctly or unintelligibly, as with partly closed lips; mutter low, indistinct words. **2.** to chew ineffectively, as from loss of teeth. —*v.t.* **3.** to utter indistinctly, as with partly closed lips. **4.** to chew, or try to eat, with difficulty, as from loss of teeth. —*n.* **5.** a low, indistinct utterance or sound. [ME *momele(n)* freq. based on MUM[1]; see -LE] —**mum′bler,** *n.* —**mum′bling·ly,** *adv.* —**Syn. 3.** See **murmur.**
mum·ble·ty·peg (mum′bəl tē peg′), *n.* a children's game played with a pocketknife, the object being to cause the blade to stick in the ground or a wooden surface by flipping the knife in a number of prescribed ways or from a number of prescribed positions. Also, **mum·ble-dy·peg** (mum′bəl dē peg′), **mum′ble peg′, mum·ble-the-peg** (mum′bəl *th*ə peg′). [from phrase *mumble the peg* (see MUMBLE); so named because the losing player was formerly required to pull a peg from the ground with his teeth]
mum·bo jum·bo (mum′bō jum′bō), *pl.* **mum·bo jum·bos. 1.** a meaningless incantation or ritual. **2.** senseless or pretentious language, usually designed to confuse. [rhyming alter. of Mandingo *Mama Dyumbo* a tribal god]
mu′ me′son, *Physics.* a meson having a mass approximately 207 times that of an electron, with positive or negative charge and spin of ½. Also called **muon.**
Mu-met·al (mo͞o′met′ᵊl, myo͞o′-), *n.* an alloy containing nickel, iron, and copper, characterized by high magnetic permeability and low hysteresis losses. [short for *Muntz metal;* named after its inventor, G. F. *Muntz,* 19th-century English metallurgist and manufacturer]
Mum·ford (mum′fərd), *n.* **Lewis,** born 1895, U.S. author and social scientist.
mumm (mum), *v.i.* mum[2].
mum·mer (mum′ər), *n.* **1.** a person who wears a mask or fantastic disguise, esp. in some localities at Christmas, New Year's, and other festive seasons. **2.** an actor. **3.** a pantomimist. [late ME *mommer*]
mum·mer·y (mum′ə rē), *n., pl.* **-mer·ies. 1.** performance of mummers. **2.** an empty or ostentatious ceremony or performance.
mum·mi·fy (mum′ə fī′), *v.,* **-fied, -fy·ing.** —*v.t.* **1.** to make (a dead body) into a mummy. **2.** to make (something) resemble a mummy, as by drying or shriveling. —*v.i.* **3.** to dry or shrivel up. —**mum′mi·fi·ca′tion,** *n.*
mum·my[1] (mum′ē), *n., pl.* **-mies,** *v.,* **-mied, -my·ing.** —*n.* **1.** the dead body of a human being or animal preserved by embalming. **2.** a dead body dried and preserved by the agencies of nature. —*v.t.* **3.** to mummify. [ME *mummie* < ML *mummia* < Ar *mūmiyah* mummy, lit., asphalt]
mum·my[2] (mum′ē), *n., pl.* **-mies.** *Chiefly Brit. Informal.* mother. [MUM[4] + -Y[2]]
mumps (mumps), *n.* (*construed as sing.*) *Pathol.* an infectious disease characterized by inflammatory swelling of the parotid and usually other salivary glands, and sometimes by inflammation of the testes, ovaries, etc. [*mump* (dial.) to grin (imit.) + -S[3]]
mun., **1.** municipal. **2.** municipality.
munch (munch), *v.t.* **1.** to chew with steady or vigorous working of the jaws, and often audibly. —*v.i.* **2.** to chew steadily or vigorously, and often audibly. [ME *monche;* imit.]
Munch (mo͝ongk), *n.* **Ed·vard** (ed′värd), 1863–1944, Norwegian painter and graphic artist.
Mün·chen (myn′kʜən), *n.* German name of **Munich.**
Mün·chen-Glad·bach (myn′kʜən glät′bäkʜ), *n.* former name of **Mönchengladbach.**
Münch·hau·sen (myngkʜ′hou′zən), *n.* **Karl Frie·drich Hi·e·ro·ny·mus** (kärl frē′drikʜ hē′ā rō′ny mo͝os′), **Baron von** (fən), 1720–97, German soldier, adventurer, and raconteur. English, **Mun·chau·sen** (mun′chou′zən, munch′hou′-, mun chô′-).
munch·y (mun′chē), *adj.,* **munch·i·er, munch·i·est,** *n., pl.* **munch·ies** (mun′chēz). —*adj.* **1.** (of food) suitable for munching as snacks, as crackers, popcorn, or the like. —*n.* **2. munchies, a.** *Informal.* food suitable or meant for snacking: *Drinks and munchies were served before dinner.* **b.** *Slang.* hunger, esp. for snacks or sweets: *an attack of the munchies.* —**munch′i·ness,** *n.*
Mun·cie (mun′sē), *n.* a city in E Indiana. 69,082 (1970).
mun·dane (mun dān′, mun′dān), *adj.* **1.** of or pertaining to the world. **2.** noting or pertaining to the everyday concerns of this world rather than to spiritual matters. **3.** common; ordinary; banal. [< LL *mundān(us)* (see MOUND[2], -ANE); r. ME *mondeyne* < MF *mondain*] —**mun·dane′ly,** *adv.* —**Syn. 2.** secular, temporal. See **earthly.**
mung′ bean′ (mung), **1.** the green or yellow, edible seed of an Asian bean, *Phaseolus aureus:* often used as bean sprouts. **2.** the plant itself. [*mung* < Tamil *mūngu* << Skt *mudga*]
mun·go (mung′gō), *n., pl.* **-gos.** a low-grade wool from felted rags or waste. Also, **mongo, mongoe.** Cf. **shoddy** (def. 1). [?]
Mu·nich (myo͞o′nik), *n.* a city in and the capital of Bavaria, in SW West Germany. 1,311,300. German, **München.**
Mu′nich Pact′ the pact signed by Germany, Great Britain, France, and Italy on September 29, 1938, by which the Sudetenland was ceded to Germany. Also called **Mu′nich Agree′ment.**
mu·nic·i·pal (myo͞o nis′ə pəl), *adj.* **1.** of or pertaining to the local government of a town or city. **2.** *Archaic.* pertaining to the internal affairs of a state. [< L *mūnicipāl(is)* = *mūnicip-* (s. of *mūniceps*) citizen of a free town (*mūni(a)* duties + *-cip-,* var. s. of *capere* to take) + *-ālis* -AL[1]] —**mu·nic′i·pal·ly,** *adv.*
mu·nic·i·pal·ism (myo͞o nis′ə pə liz′əm), *n.* **1.** the principle or system of home rule by a municipality. **2.** advocacy of such a principle or system. —**mu·nic′i·pal·ist,** *n.*
mu·nic·i·pal·i·ty (myo͞o nis′ə pal′i tē), *n., pl.* **-ties. 1.** a city, town, or other district possessing corporate existence. **2.** the governing body of such a district. [< F *municipalité*]
mu·nic·i·pal·ize (myo͞o nis′ə pə līz′), *v.t.,* **-ized, -iz·ing.** to bring under municipal ownership or control. —**mu·nic′i·pal·i·za′tion,** *n.*
mu·nif·i·cent (myo͞o nif′i sənt), *adj.* characterized by or displaying great generosity: *a munificent bequest.* [back formation from L *mūnificentia* generosity = *mūnific(us)* generous (*mūni-,* comb. form of *mūnus* gift + *-ficus* -FIC) + *-entia* -ENCE] —**mu·nif′i·cence, mu·nif′i·cent·ness,** *n.* —**mu·nif′i·cent·ly,** *adv.* —**Syn.** bountiful, bounteous.
mu·ni·ment (myo͞o′nə mənt), *n.* **1. muniments,** *Law.* a title deed, a charter, etc., by which rights or privileges are defended. **2.** *Rare.* a defense or protection. [ME < ML *mūnīment(um)* document for use in defense against a claimant < L = *mūnī(re)* (to) fortify + *-mentum* -MENT]
mu·ni·tion (myo͞o nish′ən), *n.* **1.** Usually, **munitions.** materials used in war, esp. weapons and ammunition. **2.** material or equipment for carrying on any undertaking. —*v.t.* **3.** to provide with munitions. [< L *mūnītiōn-* (s. of *mūnītiō*) a fortifying = *mūnīt(us)* fortified (ptp. of *mūnīre*) + *-iōn-* -ION]
Mu·ñoz Ma·rín (mo͞o nyôs′ mä rēn′), **Luis** (lwēs), 1898–1980, Puerto Rican political leader: governor 1948–64.
Mun·ro (mən rō′), *n.* **H(ector) H(ugh)** (pen name: *Saki*), 1870–1916, Scottish short-story writer and novelist, born in Burma.
Mun·roe′ effect′ (mun rō′), *Mil.* the reinforcement of shock waves in a hollow charge, concentrating the effect of the explosion along the axis of the charge. [named after C. E. *Munroe* (1849–1938), U.S. chemist]
Mun·ster (mun′stər), *n.* a province in SW Republic of Ireland. 882,002; 9316 sq. mi.
mün·ster (mo͝on′stər, mun′-, min′-, myn′-), *n.* muenster.
Mün·ster (myn′stər), *n.* a city in NW West Germany: treaty of Westphalia 1648. 264,200.
mun·tin (mun′tᵊn), *n.* a bar for holding the edges of window panes within the sash. [var. of *munting* < MF *montant,* n. use of prp. of *monter* to MOUNT[1] with -ING[1] for -ANT]
munt·jac (munt′jak), *n.* **1.** any of various small deer of the genus *Muntiacus,* of southern and eastern Asia and the adjacent islands, esp. *M. muntjac,* of Java, India, etc., having well-developed horns on bony pedicels. **2.** any of the small deer of the related genus *Elaphodus,* of China and Tibet, having minute horns. Also, **munt′jak.** [< an unrecorded var. of Javanese *mindjangan* deer]
mu·on (myo͞o′on), *n. Physics.* See **mu meson.** [by shortening]
mu·rae·nid (myo͝o rē′nid), *n.* any fish of the family *Muraenidae,* comprising the morays. [< NL *Muraenid(ae)* name of the family = L *muraen(a)* + *-idae* -ID[2]]
mu·ral (myo͝or′əl), *adj.* **1.** of, pertaining to, or resembling a wall. **2.** executed on or affixed to a wall. —*n.* **3.** a painting executed on or permanently affixed to a wall. [< L *mūrāl(is)* = *mūr(us)* wall + *-ālis* -AL[1]]
mu·ral·ist (myo͝or′ə list), *n.* an artist who paints murals.
Mu·ra·no (mo͝o rä′nō; *It.* mo͞o rä′nô), *n.* an insular suburb of Venice: glass manufacture. 30,614 (1961).
Mu·ra·sa·ki Shi·ki·bu (mo͞o′rä sä′kē shē′kē bo͞o′), **Baroness,** 978?–1031?, Japanese poet and novelist.
Mu·rat (my ra′), *n.* **Jo·a·chim** (zhô a kēm′), 1767?–1815, French marshal: king of Naples 1808–15.
Mu·rat (mo͝o rät′), *n.* a river in E Turkey, flowing W to the Euphrates. 425 mi. Also called **Mu·rad Su** (mo͝o räd′so͞o′).
Mur·cia (mo͝or′shə; *Sp.* mo͞or′thyä), *n.* **1.** a city in SE Spain. 243,759. **2.** a region in SE Spain: formerly a kingdom.
mur·der (mûr′dər), *n.* **1.** *Law.* the unlawful killing of a human being with malice aforethought. **2.** *Slang.* something extremely difficult or perilous: *That final exam was murder!* —*v.t.* **3.** *Law.* to kill by an act constituting murder. **4.** to kill or slaughter inhumanly or barbarously. **5.** to spoil or mar through incompetence: *to murder a tune.* —*v.i.* **6.** to commit murder. [ME; var. of MURTHER] —**mur′der·er;** *referring to a woman,* **mur′der·ess,** *n.* —**Syn. 1.** homicide.
mur·der·ous (mûr′dər əs), *adj.* **1.** of the nature of or involving murder. **2.** guilty of, bent on, or capable of murder. **3.** extremely difficult, dangerous, or trying. —**mur′der·ous·ly,** *adv.* —**mur′der·ous·ness,** *n.*
Mu·res (mo͝or′esh), *n.* a river in SE central Europe, flowing W from the Carpathian Mountains in central Rumania to the Tirsza River in S Hungary. 400 mi. long. Hungarian, **Maros.** Rumanian, **Mu·reș** (mo͝o′resh).
mu·rex (myo͝or′eks), *n., pl.* **mu·ri·ces** (myo͝or′i sēz′), **mu·rex·es.** any marine gastropod of the genus *Murex,* common in tropical seas, certain species of which yielded the royal purple dye of the ancients. [< NL, L]

Murex, *Murex tenuispina* (Shell length 4 to 5 in.)

Mur·frees·bor·o (mûr′frēz bûr′ō, -bur′ō), *n.* a city in central Tennessee: battle of Stone River (or Murfreesboro) 1862. 26,360 (1970).
mu·ri·ate (myo͝or′ē āt′, -it), *n.* (not in scientific use) any chloride, esp. potassium chloride, KCl, used as a fertilizer. [back formation from *muriatic;* see MURIATIC ACID]
mu′ri·at′ic ac′id (myo͝or′ē at′ik, myo͝or′-), (not in scientific use) See **hydrochloric acid.** [< L *muriātic(us)* pickled = *muri(a)* brine + *-āticus;* see -ATE[1], -IC]
mu·ri·cate (myo͝or′ə kāt′), *adj. Bot., Zool.* covered with short, sharp points. Also, **mu′ri·cat′ed.** [< L *mūricāt(us)* murexlike = *mūric-* (s. of *mūrex*) MUREX + *-ātus* -ATE[1]]
Mu·ril·lo (myo͝o ril′ō; *Sp.* mo͞o rē′lyô), *n.* **Bar·to·lo·mé Es·te·ban** (bär′tô lô me′ es te′vän), 1617–82, Spanish painter.
mu·rine (myo͝or′īn, -in), *adj.* **1.** belonging or pertaining to the *Muridae,* the family of rodents that includes the mice and rats, or to the *Murinae,* the subfamily that includes the domestic species. —*n.* **2.** a murine rodent. [< L *mūrīn(us)* of mice = *mūr-* (s. of *mūs*) MOUSE + *-īnus* -INE[1]]

murk (mûrk), *n.* **1.** darkness; gloom. **2.** mist or haze. —*adj.* **3.** dark; with little light; murky. Also, **mirk.** [ME *mirke* < Scand; cf. Icel *myrkr* dark, darkness, c. OE *myrce* dark]

murk·y (mûr′kē), *adj.*, **murk·i·er, murk·i·est. 1.** intensely dark or gloomy. **2.** obscure or thick with mist, haze, etc. Also, **mirky.** [ME *mirky*] —**murk′i·ly,** *adv.* —**murk′i·ness,** *n.* —**Syn. 1.** See **dark. 2.** cloudy, dusky, lowering, misty, hazy. —**Ant. 1, 2.** bright, clear.

Mur·man′ Coast′ (mŏŏr män′), an arctic coastal region in the NW Soviet Union in Europe, on the Kola Peninsula.

Mur·mansk (mŏŏr mänsk′), *n.* a seaport and railroad terminus in the NW RSFSR, in the NW Soviet Union, on the Murman Coast. 262,000 (est. 1964).

mur·mur (mûr′mər), *n.* **1.** any low, continuous sound, as of low, indistinct voices. **2.** a guarded expression of discontent. **3.** Also called **heart murmur.** *Med.* a sound heard on listening to the heart, usually through a stethoscope, produced by the abnormal opening and closing of deformed valves. —*v.i.* **4.** to make a low or indistinct sound, as in speaking. **5.** to complain in a guarded manner. —*v.t.* **6.** to express in murmurs. [(n.) ME < L; (v.) ME *murmure(n)* < L *murmurāre*] —**mur′mur·er,** *n.* —**mur′mur·ing,** *adj., n.* —**mur′mur·ing·ly,** *adv.*
—**Syn. 1.** mumble, mutter. **4.** MURMUR, MUMBLE, MUTTER mean to make sounds that are not fully intelligible. To MURMUR is to utter sounds or words in a low, almost inaudible tone, as in expressing affection, dissatisfaction, etc.: *to murmur disagreement.* To MUMBLE is to utter imperfect or inarticulate sounds with the mouth partly closed, so that the words can be distinguished only with difficulty: *to mumble the answer to a question.* To MUTTER is to utter words in a low, grumbling way, often voicing complaint or discontent, not meant to be fully audible: *to mutter complaints.* **5.** grumble, grouse.

mur·mur·ous (mûr′mər əs), *adj.* **1.** abounding in or characterized by murmurs. **2.** murmuring: *murmurous waters.* —**mur′mur·ous·ly,** *adv.*

Mur·phy (mûr′fē), *n.* **William Par·ry** (par′ē), born 1892, U.S. physician: Nobel prize for medicine 1934.

Mur′phy bed′, a bed constructed so that it can be folded or swung into a closet. [named after William L. *Murphy*, 20th-century American inventor]

mur·rain (mûr′in), *n.* **1.** *Vet. Pathol.* any of various diseases of cattle, as anthrax, foot-and-mouth disease, or tick fever. **2.** *Obs.* a plague or pestilence. [ME *moreine, moryne* < MF *morine* plague = *mor(ir)* (to) die (< L *morī*) + *-ine* -INE[1]]

Mur·ray (mûr′ē, mur′ē), *n.* **1. (George) Gilbert (Ai·mé)** (ā mā′), 1866–1957, English classical scholar, born in Australia. **2. Sir James Augustus Henry,** 1837–1915, Scottish lexicographer and philologist. **3. Lind·ley** (lin′lē, lind′-), 1745–1826, English grammarian, born in the U.S. **4. Philip,** 1886–1952, U.S. labor leader: president of the CIO 1940–52. **5.** a river in SE Australia, flowing W along the border between Victoria and New South Wales, through SE South Australia into the Indian Ocean. 1200 mi. long.

murre (mûr), *n.* **1.** either of two black and white diving birds of the genus *Uria*, of northern seas, *U. aalge* or *U. lomvia.* **2.** See **razor-billed auk.** [?]

Mur·rum·bidg·ee (mûr′əm bij′ē), *n.* a river in SE Australia, flowing W through New South Wales to the Murray River. 1050 mi. long.

mur·ther (mûr′thər), *n., v.t., v.i. Obs.* murder. [ME *morther*, OE *morthor*; c. Goth *maurthr*. See MORTAL]

mus., 1. museum. **2.** music. **3.** musical. **4.** musician.

mu·sa·ceous (myōō zā′shəs), *adj.* belonging to the *Musaceae*, or banana family of plants. [< NL *Mūsāce(ae)* family name (*Mūs(a)* genus name (< Ar *mawzah* banana) + *-āceae* -ACEAE) + -OUS]

Mus.B., Bachelor of Music. Also, **Mus. Bac.** [< L *Musicae Baccalaureus*]

mus·ca·del (mus′kə del′), *n.* muscatel. Also, **mus′ca·delle′.**

mus·ca·dine (mus′kə din, -dīn′), *n.* a grape, *Vitis rotundifolia*, of the southern U.S., having dull purple, thick-skinned musky fruit and being the origin of many grape varieties. [MUSCAD(EL) + -INE[1]]

mus·cae vo·li·tan·tes (mus′ē vol′i tan′tēz), *Ophthalm.* specks that seem to dance in the air before the eyes, due to defects in the vitreous humor of the eye or to other causes. [< NL: lit., flying flies]

mus·ca·rine (mus′kər in, -kə rēn′), *n. Chem.* a poisonous compound, $C_8H_{19}NO_3$, found as an alkaloid in certain mushrooms, esp. fly agaric, and as a ptomaine in decaying fish. [< L *muscār(ius)* of flies (*musc(a)* fly + *-ārius* -ARY) + -INE[1]] —**mus·ca·rin·ic** (mus′kə rin′ik), *adj.*

mus·cat (mus′kət, -kat), *n.* **1.** a variety of grape having a pronounced pleasant sweet aroma and flavor, used for making wine. **2.** the vine bearing the fruit. [short for *muscat wine* or *grape* < MF *muscat* musky < OPr = *musc* (< L *muscus* MUSK) + *-at* -ATE[1]]

Mus·cat (mus kat′), *n.* a seaport in and the capital of Oman, in SE Arabia. 70,000. Arabic, **Masqat.**

Muscat′ and Oman′, former name of the Sultanate of Oman.

mus·ca·tel (mus′kə tel′, mus′kə tel′), *n.* **1.** a sweet wine made from muscat grapes. **2.** muscat. Also, **muscadel, muscadelle.** [< MF = *muscat* MUSCAT + *-el* n. suffix; r. ME *muscadell* < MF *muscad-* (< OPr *muscade*, fem. of *muscat* musky) + *-elle*, fem. of *-el* n. suffix]

mus·ca·va·do (mus′kə vā′dō, -vä′-), *n.* muscovado.

mus·cid (mus′id), *adj.* **1.** belonging or pertaining to the *Muscidae*, the family of dipterous insects that includes the common housefly. —*n.* **2.** any muscid fly. [< NL *Muscid(ae)* = *musc(a)* fly + *-idae* -ID[2]]

mus·cle (mus′əl), *n., v.,* **-cled, -cling.** —*n.* **1.** a tissue composed of cells or fibers, the contraction of which produces movement in the body. **2.** an organ, composed of muscle tissue, that contracts to effect a particular movement. **3.** muscular strength; brawn. —*v.t.* **4.** to strengthen or toughen; put muscle into. —*v.i.* **5.** *Informal.* to make one's way by force or fraud (often fol. by *in*). [< medical L *muscul(us)* lit., little mouse (from fancied looks of some muscles) = *mūs* mouse + *-culus* -CLE] —**mus′cly,** *adj.*

mus·cle·bound (mus′əl bound′), *adj.* having enlarged and somewhat inelastic muscles, as from excessive exercise.

mus′cle car′, *U.S. Slang.* an automobile, esp. a sports car, having high performance in power and speed.

mus·cle·man (mus′əl man′, -mən′), *n. U.S. Slang.* **1.** a strong-arm man, as one employed to eject disorderly customers. **2.** a bodyguard.

Mus′cle Shoals′, former rapids of the Tennessee River in SW Alabama, changed into a lake: part of the Tennessee Valley Authority.

mus·co·va·do (mus′kə vā′dō, -vä′-), *n.* raw or unrefined sugar, obtained from the juice of the sugar cane by evaporating and draining off the molasses. Also, **muscavado.** [short for *muscovado sugar* < Pg *açucar mascavado* raw sugar, lit., sugar separated (from molasses); *mascavado*, ptp. of *mascavar* = *mas-* from (? < L *minus* less) + *-cavar* take (< VL **capāre* for L *capere*)]

Mus·co·vite (mus′kə vīt′), *n.* **1.** a native or inhabitant of Moscow, U.S.S.R. **2.** a native or inhabitant of the Grand Duchy of Muscovy. **3.** (*l.c.*) common light-colored mica, essentially $KAl_3Si_3O_{10}(OH)_2$, used as an electrical insulator. **4.** *Archaic.* a Russian. —*adj.* **5.** of, pertaining to, or characteristic of Moscow, Muscovy, or the Muscovites.

Mus·co·vit·ic (mus′kə vit′ik), *adj.* of, pertaining to, or characteristic of czarist Russia.

Mus·co·vy (mus′kə vē), *n.* **1.** Also called **Grand Duchy of Muscovy.** a former principality founded c1271 around the ancient city of Moscow. **2.** *Archaic.* Russia (def. 1).

Mus′covy duck′, a large, crested, wild duck, *Cairina moschata*, of tropical America, which has been widely domesticated. Also called **musk duck.**

mus·cu·lar (mus′kyə lər), *adj.* **1.** of or pertaining to muscle or the muscles. **2.** dependent on or affected by the muscles: *muscular strength.* **3.** having well-developed muscles; brawny. [< L *muscul(us)* MUSCLE + -AR[1]] —**mus·cu·lar·i·ty** (mus′kyə lar′i tē), *n.* —**mus′cu·lar·ly,** *adv.* —**Syn. 3.** strong, powerful; sturdy.

mus′cular dys′trophy, *Pathol.* a disease of unknown origin that produces a progressive muscular deterioration and wasting.

mus·cu·la·ture (mus′kyə lə chər), *n.* the muscular system of the body or of its parts. [*musculat(ion)* muscular system (see MUSCLE, -ATION) + -URE]

Mus.D., Doctor of Music. Also, **Mus.Doc., Mus.Dr.** [< L *Musicae Doctor*]

muse (myōōz), *v.,* **mused, mus·ing.** —*v.i.* **1.** to reflect or meditate in silence, as on some subject. **2.** to gaze meditatively or wonderingly. —*v.t.* **3.** to meditate on. [ME *muse(n)* (to) mutter, gaze meditatively on, be astonished < MF *muse(r)* < ML *musus* mouth, snout] —**mus′er,** *n.* —**Syn. 1.** cogitate, ruminate, think; dream. **1, 3.** ponder.

Muse (myōōz), *n.* **1.** *Class. Myth.* any of the nine daughters of Zeus and Mnemosyne who presided over various arts: Calliope (epic poetry), Clio (history), Erato (lyric poetry), Euterpe (music), Melpomene (tragedy), Polyhymnia (religious music), Terpsichore (dance), Thalia (comedy), and Urania (astronomy); identified by the Romans with the Camenae. **2.** (*sometimes l.c.*) the goddess or the power regarded as inspiring a poet. **3.** (*l.c.*) the genius or powers characteristic of a poet. [ME < L *Mūsa* < Gk *Moûsa*]

muse·ful (myōōz′fəl), *adj. Archaic.* deeply thoughtful; pensive. —**muse′ful·ly,** *adv.*

mu·sette (myōō zet′; *Fr.* MY zet′), *n., pl.* **-settes** (-zets′; *Fr.* -zet′). **1.** a French bagpipe of the 17th and early 18th centuries, with several chambers and drones, and with the wind supplied by a bellows rather than a blowpipe. **2.** a short musical piece with a drone bass, often forming the middle section of a gavotte. [ME < MF = *muse* bagpipe (< *muser* to play the bagpipe; see MUSE) + *-ette* -ETTE]

musette′ bag′, a small leather or canvas bag for personal belongings of army officers, carried by a shoulder strap.

mu·se·um (myōō zē′əm), *n.* a building or place where works of art or other objects of permanent value are kept and displayed. [< L < Gk *Mouseîon* = *Moûs(a)* MUSE + *-eion* suffix of place]

muse′um piece′, 1. something regarded as old-fashioned or decrepit. **2.** something suitable for keeping in a museum.

mush[1] (mush *or, esp. Dial.,* mŏŏsh), *n.* **1.** *U.S.* meal, esp. corn meal, boiled in water or milk until it forms a thick, soft mass, or until it is stiff enough to mold into a loaf for slicing and frying. **2.** any thick, soft mass. **3.** mawkish sentimentality or amorousness. [obs. *moose* porridge (OE *mōs* food) + (MA)SH]

mush[2] (mush), *v.i.* **1.** to go or travel, esp. over snow with a dog team and sled. —*interj.* **2.** used as an order to start or speed up a dog team.) [? < CanF *mouche(r)* (to) make haste < F *mouche* fly < L *musca*]

mush·room (mush′rōōm, -rŏŏm), *n.* **1.** any of various fleshy fungi including the toadstools, puffballs, coral fungi, morels, etc. **2.** any of several edible species, esp. of the family *Agaricaceae*, as *Agaricus campestris* (**meadow mushroom** or **field mushroom**), cultivated for food in the U.S. **3.** anything suggesting these, as in shape or rapid growth. —*adj.* **4.** of, consisting of, or containing mushrooms. **5.** resembling a mushroom in shape or form. **6.** of rapid growth and often brief duration. —*v.i.* **7.** to gather mushrooms. **8.** to have or assume the shape of a mushroom. **9.** to spread, grow, or develop quickly. [alter. (by folk etym.) of ME *muscheron, mushroom* < MF *mousseron* << LL *mussiriōn-* (s. of *mussiriō*)] —**mush′room·like′,** *adj.*

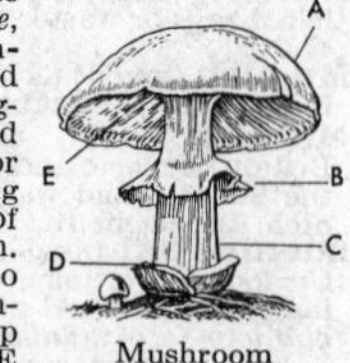

Mushroom
A, Pileus; B, Annulus; C, Stem; D, Volva; E, Gills

mush′room an′chor, *Naut.* a stockless anchor having a mushroom-shaped head. See illus. at **anchor.**

mush′room cloud′, a large, mushroom-shaped cloud resulting from the explosion of a nuclear bomb above the surface of the earth.

mush·y (mush′ē *or, esp. Dial.*, mo͝osh′ē), *adj.*, **mush·i·er, mush·i·est.** **1.** resembling mush; pulpy. **2.** *Informal.* overly emotional or sentimental. —**mush′i·ly,** *adv.* —**mush′i·ness,** *n.*

mu·sic (myo͞o′zik), *n.* **1.** the art of combining and regulating sounds of varying pitch to produce compositions expressive of various ideas and emotions. **2.** a sequence of sounds or a composition produced according to this art. **3.** a number of such compositions, esp. as the product of a certain composer, period, nation, etc. **4.** the written or printed score of a musical composition. **5.** any sweet, pleasing, or harmonious sounds or sound: *the music of the waves.* **6. face the music,** *Informal.* to be accountable for or accept the consequences of one's mistakes, actions, etc. [ME *musike* < L *mūsica* < Gk *mousikḗ* (the art) of the Muse, fem. of *mousikós.* See MUSE, -IC]

mu·si·cal (myo͞o′zi kəl), *adj.* **1.** of, pertaining to, or producing music. **2.** of the nature of or resembling music; melodious; harmonious. **3.** fond of or skilled in music. **4.** set to or accompanied by music. —*n.* **5.** See **musical comedy.** [ME < ML *mūsicāl(is)*] —**mu′si·cal·ly,** *adv.* —**mu′si·cal′i·ty, mu′si·cal·ness,** *n.*

mu′sical chairs′, a children's game in which players march to music around two rows of chairs placed back to back, there being one chair less than the number of players, the object being to find a seat when the music stops abruptly.

mu′sical com′edy, a play with music, often of a whimsical or satirical nature, based on a slight plot with singing and dancing in solos and groups.

mu·si·cale (myo͞o′zə kal′), *n.* a program of music forming part of a social occasion. [< F, short for *soirée musicale* (fem.) musical evening]

mu′sic box′, a box or case containing an apparatus for producing music mechanically.

mu′sic dra′ma, an opera having more or less continuous musical and dramatic activity.

mu′sic hall′, **1.** a hall for musical entertainments. **2.** *Chiefly Brit.* a vaudeville or variety theater.

mu·si·cian (myo͞o zish′ən), *n.* **1.** a person who makes music a profession, esp. as a performer or composer. **2.** a person skilled in playing a musical instrument. [ME *musicien* < MF] —**mu·si′cian·ly,** *adj.*

mu·si·cian·ship (myo͞o zish′ən ship′), *n.* knowledge, skill, and artistic sensitivity in performing music.

mu′sic of the spheres′, a music, imperceptible to human ears, formerly supposed to be produced by the movements of the spheres or heavenly bodies.

mu·si·col·o·gy (myo͞o′zə kol′ə jē), *n.* the scholarly or scientific study of music, as in historical research, musical theory, etc. —**mu·si·co·log·i·cal** (myo͞o′zə kə loj′i kəl), *adj.* —**mu′si·co·log′i·cal·ly,** *adv.* —**mu′si·col′o·gist,** *n.*

mu′sic roll′, a roll of perforated paper for actuating a player piano.

mu′sic stand′, a standing rack, usually adjustable to various heights, for holding music in position for reading.

mus·ing (myo͞o′zing), *adj.* **1.** absorbed in thought; meditative. —*n.* **2.** contemplation; reflection. [ME] —**mus′ing·ly,** *adv.*

mu·sique con·crète (my zēk kôN kret′), *French.* tape-recorded musical and natural sounds, often electronically distorted, arranged in planned combinations, sequences, and rhythmic patterns to create an artistic work.

mus·jid (mus′jid), *n. Arabic.* masjid.

musk (musk), *n.* **1.** a substance secreted in a glandular sac under the skin of the abdomen of the male musk deer, having a strong odor, and used in perfumery. **2.** an artificial imitation of the substance. **3.** a similar secretion of other animals, as the civet, muskrat, otter, etc. **4.** the odor of musk, or some similar odor. **5.** *Bot.* any of several plants, as the monkey flower, having a musky fragrance. [ME *muske,* var. of *musco* < LL, abl. sing. of *muscus* < LGk *móschos* < Pers *mushk*]

mus·kal·longe (mus′kə lonj′), *n., pl.* **-longe.** muskellunge.

musk′ bag′, the musk-secreting gland of a male musk deer. Also called **musk gland.**

musk′ deer′, a small, hornless deer, *Moschus moschiferus,* of central Asia, the male of which secretes musk.

musk′ duck′, **1.** See **Muscovy duck.** **2.** an Australian duck, *Biziura lobata,* having a musky odor.

mus·keg (mus′keg), *n.* a bog of northern North America, commonly having sphagnum mosses, sedge, and sometimes stunted black spruce and tamarack trees. [< Algonquian (Ojibwa): grassy bog]

Mus·ke·gon (mus kē′gən), *n.* a port in W Michigan, on Lake Michigan. 44,631 (1970).

mus·kel·lunge (mus′kə lunj′), *n., pl.* **-lunge.** a large game fish, *Esox masquinongy,* of the pike family, found in the lakes and rivers of eastern and middle western North America. Also, **maskalonge, maskanonge, maskinonge, muskallonge.** [dissimilated var. of Ojibwa *mashkinonge* great pike]

mus·ket (mus′kit), *n.* a heavy, large-caliber hand gun for infantry soldiers, introduced in the 16th century: the predecessor of the modern rifle. [< MF *mousquet* < It *moschett(o)* crossbow arrow, later musket, orig. kind of hawk = *mosch(a)* fly (< L *musca*) + *-etto* -ET]

mus·ket·eer (mus′ki tēr′), *n.* a soldier armed with a musket. [MUSKET + -EER; cf. F *mousquetaire* = *mousquet* musket + *-aire* -ARY]

mus·ket·ry (mus′ki trē), *n.* **1.** *Mil.* the technique of bringing fire from a group of rifle and automatic weapons to bear on specified targets. **2.** muskets or musketeers collectively. [< F *mousqueterie*]

musk′ gland′. See **musk bag.**

mus·kie (mus′kē), *n.* muskellunge. [MUSK(ELLUNGE) + -IE]

musk′ mal′low, **1.** Also called **musk rose.** a European mallow, *Malva moschata,* introduced into North America, having musk-scented foliage. **2.** abelmosk.

musk·mel·on (musk′mel′ən), *n.* **1.** a round or oblong melon, occurring in many varieties, having a juicy, sweet, yellow, white, or green, edible flesh. **2.** the plant, *Cucumis Melo,* bearing this fruit. **3.** cantaloupe (def. 1).

Mus·ko·ge·an (mus kō′gē ən), *n.* a family of American Indian languages of the southeastern U.S., including Choctaw, Creek, and several less well-known languages. Also, **Mus·kho′ge·an.**

Mus·ko·gee (mus kō′gē), *n., pl.* **-gees,** (*esp. collectively*) **-gee** for 2. **1.** a city in E Oklahoma. 37,331 (1970). **2.** a member of an American Indian people living in Oklahoma. **3.** Creek (def. 2).

musk′ ox′, a large bovine ruminant, *Ovibos moschatus,* of arctic regions of North America, that is related to the goat and the antelope. [so called from its musky odor]

Musk ox (4 to 5 ft. high at shoulder; length 8 ft.)

musk·rat (musk′rat′), *n., pl.* **-rats,** (*esp. collectively*) **-rat.** **1.** a large, aquatic, North American rodent, *Ondatra zibethica,* having a musky odor. **2.** its thick, light-brown fur, used esp. for women's coats. [folk-etymological var. of MUSQUASH]

musk′ rose′, **1.** a rose, *Rosa moschata,* of the Mediterranean region, having white, musk-scented flowers. **2.** See **musk mallow** (def. 1).

Muskrat (Total length about 2 ft.; tail to 11 in.)

musk′ tur′tle, any of several aquatic turtles of the genus *Sternotherus,* of North and Central America, that emit a musky secretion when molested or frightened. [so called from its musky odor]

musk·y[1] (mus′kē), *adj.*, **musk·i·er, musk·i·est.** of or like musk, as an odor. [MUSK + -Y[1]] —**musk′i·ness,** *n.*

mus·ky[2] (mus′kē), *n., pl.* **-kies.** muskellunge. [var. of MUSKIE]

Mus·lem (muz′ləm, mo͝oz′-, mo͝os′-), *adj., n., pl.* **-lems, -lem.** Muslim.

Mus·lim (muz′lim, mo͝oz′-, mo͝os′-), *adj., n., pl.* **-lims, -lim.** —*adj.* **1.** of or pertaining to the religion, law, or civilization of Islam. —*n.* **2.** an adherent of Islam. **3.** See **Black Muslim.** Also, **Moslem, Muslem** (for defs. 1, 2). [< Ar: one who submits. See ISLAM]

Mus′lim cal′endar, the lunar calendar used by Muslims that is reckoned from A.D. 622 and was established by Muhammad, the calendar year varying between 354 and 355 days.

mus·lin (muz′lin), *n.* a cotton fabric made in various degrees of fineness, and often printed, woven, or embroidered in patterns, esp. a cotton fabric of plain weave, used for sheets and for a variety of other purposes. [< F *mousseline* < It *mussolina* = *Mussol(o)* Mosul, Iraq (where first made), + *-ina* -INE[1]]

Mus.M., Master of Music. [< L *Musicae Magister*]

Mus·pel·heim (mo͞os′pəl hām′), *n. Scand. Myth.* a region of fire, the heat of which turns the ice of Niflheim to mist. Also, **Mus·pels·heim, Mus·pells·hiem** (mo͞os′pəls hām′). Also called **Mus·pell** (mo͞os′pəl).

mus·quash (mus′kwosh), *n.* a muskrat. [< Algonquian (Virginia): it is red]

muss (mus), *n.* **1.** *Informal.* a state of disorder, untidiness, or confusion. —*v.t.* **2.** to put into disorder; make messy; rumple (often fol. by *up*). [appar. b. MESS and FUSS]

mus·sel (mus′əl), *n.* any bivalve mollusk, esp. an edible marine bivalve of the family *Mytilidae* and a fresh-water clam of the family *Unionidae.* [ME, OE *muscle* < VL **muscula,* var. of L *musculus* little mouse, sea-mussel. See MUSCLE]

Mus·set (my sā′), *n.* **(Louis Charles) Al·fred de** (lwē sharl al fred′ də), 1810–57, French poet, dramatist, and novelist.

Mus·so·li·ni (mo͞os′ə lē′nē, mo͞o′sə-; *It.* mo͞os′sô lē′nē), *n.* **Be·ni·to** (bə nē′tō; *It.* be nē′tô), ("*Il Duce*"), 1883–1945, Italian Fascist leader: premier of Italy 1922–43.

Mus·sorg·sky (mə zôrg′skē; *Russ.* mo͞o′sôrg ski), *n.* **Mo·dest Pe·tro·vich** (mo dest′ pe trô′vich). See **Moussorgsky, Modest Petrovich.** Also, **Mus·sorg′ski.**

Mus·sul·man (mus′əl mən), *n., pl.* **-mans.** a Muslim. [< Pers *Musulmān* (pl.) < Ar *Muslimūn,* pl. of *Muslim* MUSLIM]

muss·y (mus′ē), *adj.*, **muss·i·er, muss·i·est.** *Informal.* untidy, messy, or rumpled. —**muss′i·ly,** *adv.* —**muss′i·ness,** *n.*

must[1] (must), *auxiliary verb.* **1.** to be compelled to, as by instinct or natural law: *One must eat.* **2.** to be required to, as because of coercion, moral obligation, or the promptings of reason or good sense: *You must not smoke here. You must keep your spirits up.* **3.** to feel a strong urge to: *I must try some of that pudding.* **4.** to be obliged to, in order to bring about certain results: *To succeed, you must have tried.* **5.** to be reasonably expected to; be bound to: *It must have stopped raining.* **6.** to be inevitably certain to: *Man must die.* —*v.i.* **7.** to be obliged; feel compelled: *Do I have to go? I must, I suppose.* **8.** *Archaic.* (sometimes used with ellipsis of *go, get,* or some similar verb readily understood from the context): *We must away.* —*n.* **9.** anything necessary or vital. [ME *most(e),* OE *mōste* past tense; c. G *musste.* See MOTE[2]]
—**Syn. 1.** MUST, OUGHT, SHOULD express necessity or duty. MUST expresses necessity, or compulsion: *All men must die. I must attend to those patients first. Soldiers must obey orders.* OUGHT (weaker than MUST) expresses obligation, duty, desirability: *You ought to tell your mother.* SHOULD expresses obligation, expectation, or probability: *You are not behaving as you should. Children should be taught to speak the truth. They should arrive at one o'clock.* It also expresses the conditional: *I should be glad to play if I could;* and future intention: *I said I should be home next week.*

must[2] (must), *n.* new wine; the unfermented juice as pressed from the grape or other fruit. [ME, OE < L *must(um),* short for *vīnum mustum* new wine]

must[3] (must), *n.* mold; moldiness or mustiness. [back formation from MUSTY]

must[4] (must), *n.* musth.

mus·tache (mus′tash, mə stash′), *n.* **1.** the hair growing on the upper lip of men, or either half of such a growth of hair. **2.** such hair when allowed to grow and usually trimmed in any of various shapes. **3.** hairs or bristles growing near the mouth of an animal. Also, **moustache.** [< MF *moustache* < It *mostaccio;* see MUSTACHIO] —**mus′tached,** *adj.*

mus′tache cup′, a cup having a straight piece inside, just below the rim, for holding back a man's mustache while he is drinking.

mus·ta·chio (mə stä′shō, -shē ō′, -stash′ō, -stash′ē ō′), *n., pl.* **-chios.** a mustache. [< Sp *mostacho* and its source, It *mostaccio,* var. of *mostacchio* < MGk *moustáki* < DoricGk *mýstak-* (s. of *mýstax*) upper lip, mustache] —**mus·ta′chioed,** *adj.*

Mus·ta·fa Ke·mal (mo͝os′tä fä kə mäl′). See **Kemal Atatürk.**

Mus·tagh (mo͞os täkh′), *n.* Karakoram (def. 1).

mus·tang (mus′tang), *n.* the small, hardy horse of the American plains, descended from Spanish stock. [< Sp *mestengo* stray or ownerless beast, n. use of masc. adj.: pertaining to a mixed lot of beasts = *mest(a)* such a mixed lot (< L *(animālia) mixta* mixed (beasts), neut. pl. adj., taken as fem. sing. n.; see MIXED) + *-engo* adj. suffix]

mus·tard (mus′tərd), *n.* **1.** a pungent powder or paste prepared from the seed of the mustard plant, much used as a food seasoning or condiment, and medicinally in plasters, poultices, etc. **2.** any of various brassicaceous plants, esp. of the genus *Brassica,* as *B. nigra* **(black mustard),** the chief source of commercial mustard, *B. hirta* **(white mustard),** or *B. juncea* **(leaf mustard),** the leaves of which are used for food. [ME < OF *moustarde* a relish orig. made of mustard seed and must = *mouste* MUST[2] + *-arde* -ARD]

mus′tard gas′, a liquid chemical-warfare agent, $(ClCH_2CH_2)_2S$, producing burns, blindness, and death. Also called **dichlorodiethyl sulfide.** [so called from its mustard-like effects on eyes and lungs]

mus′tard oil′, oil expressed from the seed of mustard, esp. a carbylamine: used chiefly in making soap.

mus′tard plas′ter, a black, powdered mixture of mustard and rubber in solution, placed on a cloth and used as a counterirritant.

mus·tee (mu stē′, mus′tē), *n.* **1.** the offspring of a white person and a quadroon; octoroon. **2.** a half-breed. [short var. of MESTIZO]

mus·te·line (mus′tᵊlīn′, -tᵊlin), *adj.* **1.** belonging or pertaining to the family *Mustelidae,* including the martens, skunks, minks, and weasels. **2.** resembling a weasel. **3.** tawny or brown, like a weasel in summer. [< L *mustēlīn(us)* = *mustēl(a)* weasel (*mūs* mouse + *-tēla* < ?) + *-īnus* -INE[1]]

mus·ter (mus′tər), *v.t.* **1.** to assemble (troops, a ship's crew, etc.), as for battle or inspection. **2.** to gather or summon (often fol. by *up*): *to muster up one's courage.* —*v.i.* **3.** to assemble for inspection, service, etc. **4.** to come together; collect; gather. **5. muster in** or **out,** to enlist into or discharge from military service. —*n.* **6.** an assembling of troops or men for inspection or other purposes. **7.** an assemblage or collection. **8.** the act of mustering. **9. pass muster,** to meet a certain standard of appearance or performance. [ME *mostre(n)* < OF *mostre(r)* < L *monstrāre* to show < *monstr(um)* portent; see MONSTER] —**Syn. 1.** convoke. See **gather. 1, 4.** convene; congregate. **7.** gathering, assembly.

musth (must), *n.* a state or condition of violent, destructive frenzy occurring somewhat periodically in male elephants. Also, **must.** [< Urdu *mast* < Pers: lit., drunk]

must·n't (mus′ənt), contraction of *must not.*

mus·ty (mus′tē), *adj.,* **-ti·er, -ti·est. 1.** having an odor or flavor suggestive of mold. **2.** made obsolete by time; antiquated: *musty laws.* **3.** dull; apathetic. [? var. of *moisty* (ME) with loss of *i* before *s* as in *master,* etc.] —**mus′ti·ly,** *adv.* —**mus′ti·ness,** *n.*

mu·ta·ble (myo͞o′tə bəl), *adj.* **1.** liable or subject to change or alteration. **2.** given to changing, or constantly changing. [ME < L *mūtābil(is)* = *mūtā(ve)* (to) change + *-bilis* -BLE] —**mu′ta·bil′i·ty, mu′ta·ble·ness,** *n.* —**mu′ta·bly,** *adv.* —**Syn. 1.** changeable, variable. **2.** unstable, vacillating, wavering, unsteady. —**Ant. 2.** stable.

mu·ta·gen·ic (myo͞o′tə jen′ik), *adj.* capable of inducing a mutation. —**mu′ta·gen′i·cal·ly,** *adv.*

mu·tant (myo͞ot′ᵊnt), *adj.* **1.** undergoing mutation; resulting from mutation. —*n.* **2.** a new type of organism produced by mutation. [< L *mūtant-* (s. of *mūtāns*) changing, prp. of *mūtāre;* see -ANT]

mu·tate (myo͞o′tāt), *v.,* **-tat·ed, -tat·ing.** —*v.t.* **1.** to change; alter. **2.** *Phonet.* to change by umlaut. —*v.i.* **3.** to change; undergo mutation. [< L *mūtāt(us)* changed, ptp. of *mūtāre;* see -ATE[1]] —**mu·ta·tive** (myo͞o′tə tiv), *adj.*

mu·ta·tion (myo͞o tā′shən), *n.* **1.** the act or process of changing. **2.** a change or alteration. **3.** *Biol.* **a.** a sudden departure from the parent type, as when an individual differs from its parents in one or more heritable characteristics, caused by a change in a gene or a chromosome. **b.** an individual, species, or the like, resulting from such a departure. **4.** *Phonet.* umlaut. [ME *mutacio(u)n* < L *mūtātiōn-* (s. of *mūtātiō*) a changing] —**mu·ta′tion·al,** *adj.* —**mu·ta′tion·al·ly,** *adv.*

mu·ta·tis mu·tan·dis (mo͞o tä′tēs mo͞o tän′dēs; *Eng.* myo͞o tā′tis myo͞o tan′dis), *Latin.* the necessary changes having been made.

mutch·kin (much′kin), *n. Scot.* a unit of liquid measure equal to a little less than a U.S. liquid pint. [ME *muchekyn* < MD *mudseken* = *mudse-* (dim. of *mudde* << *modius,* a grain measure) + *-ken* -KIN]

mute (myo͞ot), *adj., n., v.,* **mut·ed, mut·ing.** —*adj.* **1.** refraining from speech or utterance; silent. **2.** not emitting or having sound of any kind. **3.** incapable of speech; dumb. **4.** (of letters) silent; not pronounced. **5.** *Law.* making no plea when arraigned, or refusing to stand trial: *to stand mute.* —*n.* **6.** a person unable to utter words. **7.** *Law.* a person who remains mute when arraigned. **8.** Also called **sordino.** a mechanical device of various shapes and materials for muffling the tone of a musical instrument. **9.** *Phonet.* a stop. —*v.t.* **10.** to deaden or muffle the sound of. **11.** to reduce the intensity of (a color) by the addition of another color. [< L *mūt(us)* dumb; r. ME *muet* < MF = OF *mu* (< L *mūtus*) + unexplained suffix *-et;* cf. -ET] —**mute′ly,** *adv.* —**mute′ness,** *n.* —**Syn. 3.** See **dumb.**

mute′ swan′, a commonly domesticated white swan, *Cygnus olor,* of Europe and Asia. See illus. at **swan.**

mu·ti·late (myo͞ot′ᵊlāt′), *v.t.,* **-lat·ed, -lat·ing. 1.** to deprive (a person or animal) of a limb or other essential part. **2.** to injure, disfigure, or make imperfect by removing or irreparably damaging parts. [< L *mutilāt(us)* cut off, maimed (ptp. of *mutilāre*) = *mutil(us)* maimed, mutilated + *-ātus* -ATE[1]] —**mu′ti·la′tion,** *n.* —**mu′ti·la′tive, mu·ti·la·to·ry** (myo͞ot′ᵊlə tôr′ē, -tōr′ē), *adj.* —**mu′ti·la′tor,** *n.* —**Syn. 1.** See **maim. 2.** damage, mar, cripple.

mu·ti·neer (myo͞ot′ᵊnēr′), *n.* a person who mutinies. [< MF *mutinier* = *mutin* mutiny, mutinous (< *meut(e)* mutiny < VL **movita,* fem. of **movitus,* var. of L *mōtus* ptp. of *movēre* to MOVE + *-in* -INE[1]) + *-ier* -EER]

mu·ti·nous (myo͞ot′ᵊnəs), *adj.* **1.** disposed to, engaged in, or involving revolt against authority. **2.** characterized by mutiny; rebellious. **3.** difficult to control. [obs. *mutine* mutiny (< MF *mutin;* see MUTINEER) + -OUS] —**mu′ti·nous·ly,** *adv.* —**Syn. 1.** seditious, revolutionary, insurgent. **2.** refractory, insubordinate. —**Ant. 2.** obedient.

mu·ti·ny (myo͞ot′ᵊnē), *n., pl.* **-nies,** *v.,* **-nied, -ny·ing,** —*n.* **1.** revolt or rebellion against constituted authority, esp. by seamen or soldiers against their officers. —*v.i.* **2.** to commit mutiny; revolt against authority. [obs. *mutine* to mutiny (< MF *mutine(r)* < *mutin* mutiny; see MUTINEER) + -Y[3]]

mutt (mut), *n. Slang.* **1.** a dog, esp. a mongrel. **2.** a stupid person. [short for MUTTON-HEAD]

mut·ter (mut′ər), *v.i.* **1.** to utter words indistinctly or in a low tone, often in talking to oneself; murmur. **2.** to make a low, rumbling sound. —*v.t.* **3.** to utter indistinctly or in a low tone. —*n.* **4.** the act or utterance of a person who mutters. [ME *motere(n),* perh. freq. of MOOT (OE *mōtian* to speak); see -ER[6]] —**mut′ter·er,** *n.* —**mut′ter·ing·ly,** *adv.* —**Syn. 1.** See **murmur.**

mut·ton[1] (mut′ᵊn), *n.* **1.** the flesh of sheep, used as food. **2.** the flesh of the full-grown or more mature sheep, as distinguished from lamb. [ME *moton* sheep < OF < Celt; cf. MIr *molt* wether] —**mut′ton·y,** *adj.*

mut·ton[2] (mut′ᵊn), *n. Print.* em (def. 2). [code term, coined to differentiate the pronunciation of *em quad* from *en quad*]

mut·ton·chops (mut′ᵊn chops′), *n.pl.* side whiskers that are narrow at the top and broad and trimmed short at the bottom, the chin being shaved both in front and beneath. Also called **mut′tonchop whisk′ers.** [so called from shape]

mut·ton-head (mut′ᵊn hed′), *n. Informal.* a slow or stupid person; dolt. —**mut′ton-head′ed,** *adj.*

Mut·tra (mu′trə), *n.* former name of **Mathura.**

mu·tu·al (myo͞o′cho͞o əl), *adj.* **1.** possessed, experienced, performed, etc., by each of two or more with respect to the other or others; reciprocal. **2.** having the same relation each toward the other or others: *to be mutual enemies.* **3.** of or pertaining to each of two or more, or having in common: *mutual acquaintances.* **4.** pertaining to mutual insurance: *a mutual company.* [ME < MF *mutuel* < L *mūtu(us)* interchanged, reciprocal (akin to *mūtāre;* see MUTATE) + *-el* (< L *-ālis*) -AL[1]] —**mu′tu·al·ly,** *adv.*
—**Syn. 1.** MUTUAL, RECIPROCAL agree in the idea of an exchange or balance between two or more persons or groups. MUTUAL indicates an exchange of a feeling, obligation, etc.: *mutual esteem; in mutual agreement.* RECIPROCAL indicates a relation in which one act, thing, feeling, etc., balances or is given in return for another: *reciprocal promises or favors.*

mu′tual fund′. See **open-end investment company.**

mu′tual insur′ance, insurance in which those insured become members of a company who reciprocally engage, by payment of certain amounts into a common fund, to indemnify one another against loss.

mu·tu·al·ise (myo͞o′cho͞o ə līz′), *v.t., v.i.,* **-ised, -is·ing.** *Chiefly Brit.* mutualize. —**mu′tu·al·i·sa′tion,** *n.*

mu·tu·al·ism (myo͞o′cho͞o ə liz′əm), *n.* a relationship between two species of organisms in which both benefit from the association. —**mu′tu·al·is′tic,** *adj.*

mu·tu·al·i·ty (myo͞o′cho͞o al′i tē), *n.* the condition or quality of being mutual; reciprocity.

mu·tu·al·ize (myo͞o′cho͞o ə līz′), *v.,* **-ized -iz·ing.** —*v.t.* **1.** to make mutual. **2.** to incorporate with employee or customer ownership of the major or controlling portion of issued shares. —*v.i.* **3.** to become mutual. Also, *esp. Brit.,* **mutualise.** —**mu′tu·al·i·za′tion,** *n.*

mu′tual sav′ings bank′, a noncapitalized savings bank that distributes its available net earnings to depositors.

mu·tu·el (myo͞o′cho͞o əl), *n.* pari-mutuel.

mu·tule (myo͞o′cho͞ol), *n. Archit.* a projecting flat block under the corona of the Doric cornice, corresponding to the modillion of other orders. [< L *mūtul(us)* modillion] —**mu·tu·lar** (myo͞o′chə lər), *adj.*

muu·muu (mo͞o′mo͞o′), *n.* **1.** a loose dress, often brightly colored or patterned, worn esp. by Hawaiian women. **2.** a similar dress worn as a house dress. [< Hawaiian, name of the dress, lit., cut-off; so called because of its originally lacking a yoke]

mu·zhik (mo͞o zhik′, mo͞o′zhik), *n.* a Russian peasant. Also, **moujik, mujik, mu·zjik′.** [< Russ: lit., little man, dim. of *muzh* man]

muz·zle (muz′əl), *n., v.,* **-zled -zling.** —*n.* **1.** the mouth, or end for discharge, of a gun, pistol, etc. **2.** the projecting part of the head of an animal, including jaws, mouth, and nose. **3.** a device placed over an animal's mouth to prevent biting, eating, etc. —*v.t.* **4.** to put a muzzle on (an animal or its mouth). **5.** to restrain, as from speech or the expression of opinion. [ME *musel* < MF = VL **mūsus* snout + *-el* -LE; cf. ML *musellum,* dim. of *musum* snout < ?]

muz·zle·load·er (muz′əl lō′dər), *n.* a firearm that is loaded through the muzzle. Also, **muz′zle-load′er.** —**muz′zle·load′ing, muz′zle-load′ing,** *adj.*

MV, **1.** *Elect.* megavolt; megavolts. **2.** motor vessel.

Mv, *Elect.* megavolt; megavolts.

Mv, *Chem.* mendelevium.

mV, millivolt; millivolts. Also, **mv**

m.v., *Music.* mezza voce.

MVA, megavolt-ampere; megavolt-amperes. Also, **Mva**

MVD, the secret police of the U.S.S.R. since 1943. Cf. **Cheka, G.P.U., NKVD.** [< Russ *M(inisterstvo) V(nutrennikh) D(el)* Ministry of Home Affairs]

Mw, *Elect.* megawatt; megawatts.

mW, *Elect.* milliwatt; milliwatts. Also, **mw**

Mwan·za (mwän′zä), *n.* a city in N Tanzania, on Lake Victoria. 35,000.

Mwe·ru (mwā′ro͞o), *n.* a lake in S Africa, between Zaïre and Zambia. 68 mi. long.

MWh, *Elect.* megawatt-hour; megawatt-hours. Also, **Mwhr**

Mx, *Elect.* maxwell; maxwells.

MX, a land-based intercontinental U.S. ballistic missile having a solid-fuel propellant and carrying 10 independently targeted nuclear warheads. [M(issile) X(-experimental; see x, def. 3)]

my (mī), *pron.* **1.** (a form of the possessive case of **I** used as an attributive adjective): *My soup is cold.* —*interj.* **2.** *Informal.* (used as an exclamation of surprise): *My, what a big house!* [ME *mī*, var. of *mīn*, OE *mīn;* see MINE[1]] —**Usage.** See **me.**

my-, var. of **myo-** before some vowels: *myalgia.*

my·al·gi·a (mī al′jē ə, -jə), *n. Pathol.* pain in the muscles; muscular rheumatism. —**my·al′gic,** *adj.*

my·as·the·ni·a (mī′əs thē′nē ə), *n. Pathol.* muscle weakness. —**my·as·then·ic** (mī′əs then′ik), *adj.*

myasthe′nia gra′vis, *Pathol.* a disease characterized by muscular weakness, affecting esp. the muscles of the face, tongue, and neck, but not involving atrophy. [< NL]

myc-, var. of **myco-** before a vowel: *mycelium.*

my·ce·li·um (mī sē′lē əm), *n., pl.* **-li·a** (-lē ə). *Bot.* the vegetative part or thallus of the fungi, being composed of one or more filamentous elements or hyphae. [MYC- + Gk *(h)ēl(os)* wart, nail + -IUM] —**my·ce′li·al,** *adj.*

My·ce·nae (mī sē′nē), *adj.* an ancient city in S Greece, in Argolis.

My·ce·nae·an (mī′si nē′ən), *adj.* **1.** of or pertaining to the ancient city of Mycenae. **2.** noting or pertaining to the civilization at Mycenae, dating from c1950 to c1100 B.C.

-mycetes, an element meaning "fungi," used esp. in the names of classes: *Myxomycetes.* Also, **-mycete.** [< NL < Gk *mykētes*, pl. of *mýkēs* mushroom, fungus. See MYCO-]

myceto-, a combining form meaning "fungus": *mycetozoan.* [comb. form repr. Gk *mykēt-*, s. of *mýkēs;* see MYCO-]

my·ce·to·zo·an (mī sē′tə zō′ən), *adj.* **1.** of or pertaining to the order *Mycetozoa*, the classification used by those considering the true slime molds to be animals, or to the class *Myxomycetes*, the classification used by those considering the true slime molds to be plants. —*n.* **2.** a slime mold; myxomycete.

myco-, a learned borrowing from Greek meaning "fungus," used in the formation of compound words: *mycology.* Also, *esp. before a vowel,* **myc-.** [comb. form repr. Gk *mýkēs* mushroom, fungus]

my·co·bac·te·ri·um (mī′kō bak tēr′ē əm), *n., pl.* **-te·ri·a** (-tēr′ē ə). *Bacteriol.* any of several rod-shaped aerobic bacteria of the genus *Mycobacterium*, certain species of which, as *M. tuberculosis*, are pathogenic for man and animals.

my·col·o·gy (mī kol′ə jē), *n.* **1.** the branch of botany dealing with fungi. **2.** the fungi found in an area. —**my·co·log·i·cal** (mī′kə loj′i kəl), **my′co·log′ic,** *adj.* —**my′co·log′i·cal·ly,** *adv.* —**my·col′o·gist,** *n.*

my·cor·rhi·za (mī′kō rī′zə, -kō-), *n., pl.* **-zae** (-zē), **-zas.** *Plant Pathol.* a symbiotic association of the mycelium of a fungus, esp. a basidiomycete, with the roots of certain plants, in which the hyphae form a closely woven mass around the rootlets or penetrate the cells of the root. Also, **my′co·rhi′za.** —**my′cor·rhi′zal, my′co·rhi′zal,** *adj.*

my·co·sis (mī kō′sis), *n. Pathol.* **1.** the presence of parasitic fungi in or on any part of the body. **2.** the condition caused by the presence of such fungi.

my·dri·a·sis (mi drī′ə sis, mī-), *n. Med.* excessive dilatation of the pupil of the eye, as the result of disease, drugs, or the like. Cf. **miosis.** (def. 1). [< L < Gk]

myd·ri·at·ic (mid′rē at′ik), *adj.* **1.** pertaining to or producing mydriasis. —*n.* **2.** a mydriatic drug.

myel-, var. of **myelo-** before a vowel: *myelitis.*

my·e·len·ceph·a·lon (mī′ə lən sef′ə lon′), *n., pl.* **-lons, -la** (-lə). *Anat.* the posterior section of the hindbrain comprising the medulla oblongata. —**my·e·len·ce·phal·ic** (mī′ə lən sə fal′ik), *adj.*

my·e·lin (mī′ə lin), *n. Anat.* a soft, white, fatty substance encasing the axis cylinder of certain nerve fibers. Also, **my·e·line** (mī′ə lēn′). —**my′e·lin′ic,** *adj.*

my′elin sheath′, *Anat.* the sheath of myelin surrounding the axons or fibers of certain nerves. Also called **medullary sheath.**

my·e·li·tis (mī′ə lī′tis), *n. Pathol.* **1.** inflammation of the substance of the spinal cord. **2.** inflammation of the bone marrow.

myelo-, a learned borrowing from Greek meaning "marrow," "of the spinal cord," used in the formation of compound words. Also, *esp. before a vowel,* **myel-.** [comb. form repr. Gk *myelós*]

my·e·loid (mī′ə loid′), *adj. Anat.* **1.** pertaining to the spinal cord. **2.** marrowlike. **3.** pertaining to marrow.

my·ia·sis (mī′ə sis), *n., pl.* **-ses** (-sēz′). *Pathol.* any disease that results from the infestation of tissues or cavities of the body by larvae of flies. [*myi-* (< Gk *myîa* fly) + -ASIS]

My·lit·ta (mi lit′ə), *n.* Ishtar.

my·lo·nite (mī′lə nīt′, mil′ə-), *n.* a rock that has been crushed and rolled out to such an extent that the original structure has been destroyed. [*mylon-* (< Gk: mill) + -ITE[1]]

my·na (mī′nə), *n.* any of several Asian birds of the starling family *Sturnidae*, esp. those of the genera *Acridotheres* and *Gracula*, certain species of which have the ability to mimic speech. Also, **my′nah.** [< Hindi *mainā*]

Myn·heer (mīn hâr′, -hēr′), *n.* the Dutch term of address and title of respect corresponding to *sir* and *Mr.* [sp. var. of D *mijnheer* = *mijn* MINE[1] + *heer* lord, sir, Mr.; see HERR]

myo-, a learned borrowing from Greek meaning "muscle," used in the formation of compound words: *myology.* Also, *esp. before a vowel,* **my-.** [comb. form repr. Gk *mŷs* mouse, muscle]

my·o·car·di·o·graph (mī′ə kär′dē ə graf′, -gräf′), *n.* an instrument for recording the movements of the heart.

my·o·car·di·tis (mī′ō kär dī′tis), *n. Pathol.* inflammation of the myocardium.

my·o·car·di·um (mī′ə kär′dē əm), *n., pl.* **-di·a** (-dē ə). *Anat.* the muscular substance of the heart. [< NL < Gk *myo-* MYO- + *-kardion*, dim. of *kardía* heart] —**my′o·car′di·al,** *adj.*

my·o·gen·ic (mī′ə jen′ik), *adj.* originating in muscle, as an impulse or sensation. —**my·o·ge·nic·i·ty** (mī′ə jə nis′i tē), *n.*

my·o·glo·bin (mī′ə glō′bin, mī′ə glō′-), *n. Biochem.* hemoglobin of muscle, weighing less and carrying more oxygen and less carbon monoxide than blood hemoglobin.

my·o·graph (mī′ə graf′, -gräf′), *n.* an instrument for recording the contractions and relaxations of muscles. —**my·o·graph·ic** (mī′ə graf′ik), *adj.* —**my′o·graph′i·cal·ly,** *adv.* —**my·og·ra·phy** (mī og′rə fē), *n.*

my·ol·o·gy (mī ol′ə jē), *n.* the science or branch of anatomy dealing with muscles. [< NL *myologia*] —**my·o·log·ic** (mī′ə loj′ik), **my′o·log′i·cal,** *adj.* —**my·ol′o·gist,** *n.*

my·ope (mī′ōp), *n.* a person who is nearsighted. [< F < LL *myops* < Gk *mýōps* nearsighted. See MYOPIA]

my·o·pi·a (mī ō′pē ə), *n.* **1.** *Ophthalm.* a condition of the eye in which parallel rays are focused in front of the retina, objects being seen distinctly only when near to the eye; nearsightedness (opposed to *hypermetropia*). **2.** *Informal.* lack of knowledge, tolerance, or foresight. [< NL < Gk *myōp-* (s. of *mýōps*) nearsighted, lit., blinking (*mý(ein)* to shut + *ṓps* eye) + *-ia* -IA]

my·op·ic (mī op′ik), *adj.* **1.** *Ophthalm.* pertaining to or having myopia; nearsighted. **2.** lacking knowledge, tolerance, or foresight: *a myopic viewpoint.* —**my·op′i·cal·ly,** *adv.*

my·o·scope (mī′ə skōp′), *n.* an instrument for observing muscular contraction.

my·o·sin (mī′ə sin), *n. Biochem.* a globulin occurring in muscle plasma. [MY + -OSE[2] + -IN[2]]

my·o·sis (mī ō′sis), *n. Med.* miosis.

my·o·so·tis (mī′ə sō′tis), *n.* any boraginaceous plant of the genus *Myosotis*, as the forget-me-not. Also, **my·o·sote** (mī′ə sōt′). [< NL, L < Gk: the plant mouse-ear = *myós* (gen. of *mŷs*) MOUSE + *-ōt-* (s. of *oûs*) ear + *-is* n. suffix]

my·ot·ic (mī ot′ik), *adj., n.* miotic.

my·o·tome (mī′ə tōm′), *n. Embryol.* the part of a mesodermal somite contributing to the development of the skeletal muscles.

my·o·to·ni·a (mī′ə tō′nē ə), *n. Pathol.* tonic muscle spasm or muscular rigidity. [*myoton(ic)* (see MYO-, TONIC) + -IA] —**my·o·ton·ic** (mī′ə ton′ik) *adj.*

My·ra (mī′rə), *n.* an ancient city in Lycia.

Myr·dal (mēr′däl, -dôl, mûr′-), *n.* **1. Alva (Rei·mer)** (rā′mər), 1902–86, Swedish sociologist and diplomat: Nobel peace prize 1982. **2. (Karl) Gun·nar** (kärl gun′ər, go͝on′-), 1898–1987, Swedish economist and sociologist: Nobel prize in economics 1974 (husband of Alva Myrdal).

myr·i·ad (mir′ē əd), *n.* **1.** an indefinitely great number. **2.** a very great number of persons or things. **3.** ten thousand. —*adj.* **4.** of an indefinitely great number; innumerable. **5.** having innumerable phases, aspects, etc. **6.** ten thousand. [< Gk *myriad-* (s. of *myriás*) ten thousand; see -AD[1]]

myr·i·a·pod (mir′ē ə pod′), *n.* **1.** any arthropod of the group *Myriapoda*, having an elongated, segmented body with numerous, paired, jointed legs, formerly classified as a class comprising the centipedes and millipedes. —*adj.* **2.** Also, **myr·i·ap·o·dous** (mir′ē ap′ə dəs). belonging or pertaining to the *Myriapoda.* **3.** having very numerous legs. Also, **myr′i·o·pod′.** [< NL *Myriapod(a).* See MYRIAD, -POD]

myrmeco-, a combining form meaning "ant": *myrmecology.* [< Gk *myrmēk-* (s. of *mýrmēx*)]

myr·me·col·o·gy (mûr′mə kol′ə jē), *n.* the branch of entomology dealing with the ants. —**myr·me·co·log·i·cal** (mûr′mə kə loj′i kəl), *adj.* —**myr′me·col′o·gist,** *n.*

myr·me·coph·a·gous (mûr′mə kof′ə gəs), *adj.* adapted for feeding on ants, as the jaws or teeth of various anteaters.

Myr·mi·don (mûr′mi don′, -dən), *n., pl.* **Myr·mi·dons, Myr·mid·o·nes** (mûr mid′ənēz′). **1.** *Class. Myth.* one of the warlike people of ancient Thessaly who accompanied Achilles, their king, to the Trojan War. **2.** (*l.c.*) a person who executes without scruple his master's commands.

my·rob·a·lan (mī rob′ə lən, mi-), *n.* the dried plumlike fruit of certain tropical trees of the genus *Terminalia*, used in dyeing, tanning, and making ink. [ME < L *myrobalan(um)* < Gk *myrobálanos* kind of fruit = *mýro(n)* balsam + *bálanos* acorn]

My·ron (mī′rən), *n.* fl. c450 B.C., Greek sculptor.

myrrh (mûr), *n.* an aromatic resinous exudation from certain plants of the genus *Commiphora*, esp. *C. Myrrha*, a spiny shrub: used for incense, perfume, etc. [ME, OE *myrre* < L *myrrha* < Gk *mýrra*] —**myrrh′ic,** *adj.*

Myr·rha (mēr′ə), *n. Class. Myth.* a king's daughter who had incestuous relations with her father and was changed into a myrrh tree by the gods. Their child, Adonis, was born from the split trunk of the tree. Also called **Smyrna.**

myr·ta·ceous (mûr tā′shəs), *adj.* **1.** belonging to the *Myrtaceae*, or myrtle family of plants, comprising the myrtle, the clove and allspice trees, the guava, the eucalyptus, etc. **2.** of, pertaining to, or resembling the myrtle. [< NL *Myrtāce(ae)* (L *myrt(us)* MYRTLE + *-āceae* -ACEAE) + -OUS]

myr·tle (mûr′təl), *n.* **1.** any plant of the genus *Myrtus*, esp. *M. communis*, a shrub of southern Europe having evergreen leaves, fragrant white flowers, and aromatic berries. This plant is used as an emblem of love and was anciently held sacred to Venus. **2.** *U.S.* any of certain unrelated plants, as the periwinkle, *Vinca minor*, and California laurel, *Umbellularia californica.* [ME *mirtile* < ML *myrtill(us)*, dim. of L *myrtus* < Gk *mýrtos*]

my·self (mī self′), *pron., pl.* **our·selves** (our selvz′). **1.** (used as an intensifier of *me* or *I*): *I myself told her.* **2.** (used reflexively as a substitute for *me*): *She wanted John and myself to go.* **3.** (used as the direct or indirect object of a verb.) **4.** my normal or customary self: *A short nap and I was myself again.* [r. ME *meself*, OE *mē selfum* (dat.)] —**Usage.** It is considered nonstandard to use any reflexive pronoun (MYSELF, YOURSELF, HIMSELF, HERSELF, ITSELF, OURSELF, OURSELVES, THEMSELVES) in place of the objective form where the latter would normally occur: *He gave it to me* (not *myself*).

My·si·a (mish′ē ə), *n.* an ancient country in NW Asia Minor. —**My′si·an,** *adj., n.*
My·sore (mī sōr′, -sôr′), *n.* **1.** a state in S India; enlarged in 1956 in conformance with linguistic boundaries. 23,586,722 (1961); 74,326 sq. mi. *Cap.:* Bangalore. **2.** a city in the S part of this state. 257,999 (est. 1965).
mys·ta·gogue (mis′tə gôg′, -gog′), *n.* a person who instructs persons before initiation into religious mysteries or before participation in sacraments. [< L *mystagōg(us)* < Gk *mystagōgós.* See MYSTIC, -AGOGUE] —**mys·ta·go·gy** (mis′tə gō′jē), *n.* —**mys·ta·gog·ic** (mis′tə goj′ik), **mys′-ta·gog′i·cal,** *adj.* —**mys′ta·gog′i·cal·ly,** *adv.*
mys·te·ri·ous (mi stēr′ē əs), *adj.* **1.** full of, characterized by, or involving mystery. **2.** of obscure nature, meaning, origin, etc.; puzzling; inexplicable. **3.** implying or suggesting a mystery. —**mys·te′ri·ous·ly,** *adv.* —**mys·te′ri·ous·ness,** *n.* —**Syn. 1.** secret, occult, cryptic. **2.** unfathomable, unintelligible, incomprehensible.
mys·ter·y[1] (mis′tə rē, -trē), *n., pl.* **-ter·ies. 1.** something that is secret or impossible to understand. **2.** something that arouses curiosity through its obscure nature. **3.** secrecy, or the quality of being obscure or enigmatic: *to assume an air of mystery.* **4.** Also called **mys′tery sto′ry.** a work of fiction concerned with the identification and capture of a criminal or criminals. **5.** any truth unknowable except by divine revelation. **6.** (in the Christian religion) **a.** a sacramental rite. **b.** the Eucharist. **7.** an incident or scene in connection with the life or passion of Christ, or with the life of the Virgin Mary. **8. mysteries, a.** ancient religions that admitted candidates by secret rites and rituals understood only by initiates. **b.** any rites or secrets known only to initiates. **c.** (in the Christian religion) the Eucharistic elements. **9.** See **mystery play.** [ME *mysterie* < L *mystēri(um)* < Gk *mystḗrion* = *mýst(ēs)* (see MYSTIC) + *-ērion* n. suffix]
mys·ter·y[2] (mis′tə rē), *n., pl.* **-ter·ies.** *Archaic.* **1.** a craft or trade. **2.** a guild. [ME *mistery* < ML *mistēri(um),* var. of L *ministerium* MINISTRY]
mys′tery play′, a medieval dramatic form based on a Biblical story, usually about the life, death, and resurrection of Christ. Cf. **miracle play, morality play.**
mys·tic (mis′tik), *adj.* **1.** spiritually significant or symbolic. **2.** of occult or mysterious character, power, or significance: *a mystic formula.* **3.** of or pertaining to mystics or mysticism. —*n.* **4.** a person initiated into mysteries. **5.** a person who attains, or believes in the possibility of attaining insight into mysteries transcending ordinary human knowledge, as by immediate intuition in a state of spiritual ecstasy. [ME *mystik* < L *mystic(us)* < Gk *mystikós* = *myst-* (s. of *mýstēs*) an initiate into the mysteries, akin to *myeîn* to initiate + *-ikos* -IC] —**mys·tic·i·ty** (mi stis′i tē), *n.* —**mys′tic·ly,** *adv.*
Mys·tic (mis′tik), *n.* a town in SE Connecticut: maritime museum. 2568 (1970).
mys·ti·cal (mis′ti kəl), *adj.* **1.** mystic; occult. **2.** of or pertaining to mystics or mysticism: *mystical writings.* **3.** spiritually symbolic. **4.** *Rare.* obscure in meaning; mysterious. —**mys′ti·cal·ly,** *adv.*
mys·ti·cism (mis′ti siz′əm), *n.* **1.** the beliefs, ideas, or mode of thought of mystics. **2.** the doctrine of an immediate spiritual intuition of truths believed to transcend ordinary understanding, or of a direct, intimate union of the soul with God through contemplation and love. **3.** obscure thought or speculation.
mys·ti·fy (mis′tə fī′), *v.t.,* **-fied, -fy·ing. 1.** to cause bewilderment in. **2.** to impose on (a person) by bewildering him purposely. **3.** to involve in mystery or obscurity. [< F *mystifie(r)* = *mysti-* (irreg. < *mistique* MYSTIC or *mystère* MYSTERY[1]) + *-fier* -FY] —**mys′ti·fi·ca′tion,** *n.* —**mys′ti-fied′ly,** *adv.* —**mys′ti·fi′er,** *n.* —**mys′ti·fy′ing·ly,** *adv.*
mys·tique (mi stēk′), *n.* **1.** a framework of doctrines, ideas, beliefs, or the like, constructed around a person or object, endowing him or it with enhanced value or profound meaning. **2.** an aura of mystery or mystical power surrounding a particular occupation or pursuit. [< F (adj.); see MYSTIC]
myth (mith), *n.* **1.** a traditional or legendary story, usually concerned with deities or demigods and the creation of the world and its inhabitants. **2.** a story or belief that attempts to express or explain a basic truth; an allegory or parable. **3.** a belief or a subject of belief whose truth or reality is accepted uncritically. **4.** such stories or beliefs collectively. [< LL *mӯth(os)* < Gk *mŷthos* story, word] —**Syn. 1.** See **legend.**
myth., 1. mythological. **2.** mythology.
myth·i·cal (mith′i kəl), *adj.* **1.** pertaining to, of the nature of, or involving a myth or myths. **2.** dealt with in myth, as a period. **3.** dealing with myths, as a writer. **4.** existing only in myth, as a person. **5.** without foundation in fact; imaginary; fictitious. Also, **myth′ic.** [< LL *mӯthic(us)* (< Gk *mӯthikós* of myths; see MYTH, -IC) + -AL[1]] —**myth′i-cal·ly,** *adv.*
myth·i·cise (mith′i sīz′), *v.t.,* **-cised, -cis·ing.** *Chiefly Brit.* mythicize.
myth·i·cize (mith′i sīz′), *v.t.,* **-cized, -ciz·ing.** to turn into, treat, or explain as a myth.
mytho-, a combining form of **myth:** *mythographer.* [< Gk, comb. form of *mŷthos* MYTH]
my·thog·ra·pher (mi thog′rə fər), *n.* a person who collects or records myths in writing. Also, **my·thog′ra·phist.** [< Gk *mӯthográph(os)* mythographer + -ER[1]]
mythol., 1. mythological. **2.** mythology.
myth·o·log·i·cal (mith′ə loj′i kəl), *adj.* of or pertaining to mythology. Also, **myth′o·log′ic.** [< LL *mythologic(us)* (< Gk *mӯthologikós;* see MYTHOLOGY, -IC) + -AL[1]] —**myth′-o·log′i·cal·ly,** *adv.*
my·thol·o·gise (mi thol′ə jīz′), *v.i., v.t.,* **-gised, -gis·ing.** *Chiefly Brit.* mythologize. —**my·thol′o·gi·sa′tion,** *n.*
my·thol·o·gist (mi thol′ə jist), *n.* **1.** an expert in mythology. **2.** a writer of myths. [< Gk *mӯthológ(os)* storyteller (see MYTHO-, LOGO-) + -IST]
my·thol·o·gize (mi thol′ə jīz′), *v.,* **-gized, -giz·ing.** —*v.i.* **1.** to classify, explain, or write about myths. **2.** to construct or narrate myths. —*v.t.* **3.** to make into or explain as a myth; make mythical. Also, *esp. Brit.,* **mythologise.** [MYTHOLOG(Y) + -IZE; cf. F *mythologiser*] —**my·thol′o-gi·za′tion,** *n.*
my·thol·o·gy (mi thol′ə jē), *n., pl.* **-gies. 1.** a body of myths having a common source or subject. **2.** myths collectively. **3.** the science or study of myths. [ME *mythologie* < LL *mӯthologia* < Gk]
myth·o·ma·ni·a (mith′ə mā′nē ə), *n. Psychiatry.* lying or exaggerating to an abnormal degree. —**myth·o·ma·ni·ac** (mith′ə mā′nē ak′), *n., adj.*
myth·o·poe·ia (mith′ə pē′ə), *n.* a mythopoeic act, circumstance, characteristic, etc. [< LL < Gk *mӯthopoiīa* making of fables, invention = *mytho-* MYTHO- + *-poiia* (*poi(eîn)* (to) make + *-ia* n. suffix)]
myth·o·poe·ic (mith′ə pē′ik), *adj.* **1.** of or pertaining to the making of myths. **2.** causing, producing, or giving rise to a myth or myths. [< Gk *mӯthopoi(ós)* making tales (*mytho-* MYTHO- + *-poios* making = *poi(eîn)* (to) make + *-os* adj. suffix) + -IC] —**myth′o·poe′ism,** *n.* —**myth′o·poe′ist,** *n.*
Myt·i·le·ne (mit′əlē′nē; *Gk.* mē′tē lē′nē), *n.* **1.** Also called **Lesbos.** a Greek island in the NE Aegean. 140,251 (1961); 836 sq. mi. **2.** Also called **Kastros.** the capital of this island. 27,125 (1951).
myx·e·de·ma (mik′si dē′mə), *n. Pathol.* a condition characterized by thickening of the skin, blunting of the senses and intellect, labored speech, etc., associated with diminished functional activity of the thyroid gland. Also, **myx′-oe·de′ma.** —**myx·e·dem·a·tous, myx·oe·dem·a·tous** (mik′-si dem′ə təs, -dē′mə-), *adj.* —**myx·e·dem·ic, myx·oe·dem·ic** (mik′si dem′ik), *adj.*
myxo-, a learned borrowing from Greek, where it meant "mucus," "slime," used in the formation of compound words: *myxomycete.* Also, *esp. before a vowel,* **myx-.** [comb. form repr. Gk *mýxa*]
myx·o·ma (mik sō′mə), *n., pl.* **-mas, -ma·ta** (-mə tə). *Pathol.* a soft tumor composed of connective and mucoid tissue. [< NL] —**myx·om·a·tous** (mik som′ə təs), *n.*
myx·o·ma·to·sis (mik′sə mə tō′sis), *n. Vet. Pathol.* a highly infectious viral disease of rabbits: artificially introduced into Great Britain and Australia to reduce the rabbit population. [< NL *myxomat-* (s. of *myxoma;* see MYX-, -OMA) + -OSIS]
myx·o·my·cete (mik′sō mī sēt′), *n.* an organism of the class *Myxomycetes,* the classification used by those considering the true slime molds to be plants. [back formation from NL *myxomycētes*] —**myx′o·my·ce′tous,** *adj.*

N

DEVELOPMENT OF MAJUSCULE								
NORTH SEMITIC	GREEK		ETR.	LATIN		MODERN		
						GOTHIC	ITALIC	ROMAN
𐤍	𐌍	N	𐌍	N	N	𝔑	*N*	N

DEVELOPMENT OF MINUSCULE					
ROMAN CURSIVE	ROMAN UNCIAL	CAROL. MIN.	MODERN		
			GOTHIC	ITALIC	ROMAN
~	N	n	𝔫	*n*	n

The fourteenth letter of the English alphabet developed from North Semitic *nun,* has preserved its original form, with little change, through Greek *nu* (ν). It has usually followed M, and during most of its history, paralleling that letter, it has retained its similarity to it.

N, n (en), *n., pl.* **N's** or **Ns, n's** or **ns. 1.** the 14th letter of the English alphabet, a consonant. **2.** any spoken sound represented by the letter *N* or *n,* as in *now, dinner,* or *son.* **3.** a written or printed representation of the letter *N* or *n.* **4.** a device, as a printer's type, for reproducing the letter *N* or *n.*

N, 1. north. **2.** northern.

N, 1. the 14th in order or in a series, or, when *I* is omitted, the 13th. **2.** *Chem.* nitrogen. **3.** *Math.* an indefinite, constant whole number, esp. the degree of a quantic or an equation, or the order of a curve. **4.** *Chess.* knight. **5.** *Print.* en. **6.** See **Avogadro's number.**

n, 1. *Optics.* See **index of refraction. 2.** *Physics.* neutron.

'n (ən), *conj. Informal.* and: *Stop 'n save. Look 'n listen.* Also, **'n'.**

-n, var. of **-an** after a vowel: *Virginian.*

N., 1. Nationalist. **2.** Navy. **3.** New. **4.** Noon. **5.** *Chem.* Normal (strength solution). **6.** Norse. **7.** north. **8.** northern. **9.** November.

n., 1. born. [< L *nātus*] **2.** nephew. **3.** neuter. **4.** new. **5.** nominative. **6.** noon. **7.** *Chem.* normal (strength solution). **8.** north. **9.** northern. **10.** noun. **11.** number.

Na, *Chem.* sodium. [< NL *natrium*]

n/a, no account.

N.A., North America.

NAACP, National Association for the Advancement of Colored People. Also, **N.A.A.C.P.**

nab (nab), *v.t.,* **nabbed, nab·bing.** *Informal.* to capture or arrest. [earlier *nap;* perh. < Scand; cf. Dan *nappe,* Sw *nappa* to snatch]

Nab·a·tae·an (nab′ə tē′ən), *n.* a subject of an ancient Arab kingdom in Palestine that became a Roman province in A.D. 106. Also, **Nab′a·te′an.**

Na·bis (nä′bēz), *n. Fine Arts.* (*sometimes l.c.*) a group of French artists of the late 19th century whose paintings were characterized chiefly by an emphasis on flat shapes and the use of high-key colors. [< F < Heb *nābhi* prophet]

Na·blus (nä blo͞os′), *n.* modern name of **Shechem.**

na·bob (nā′bob), *n.* **1.** Also, **nawab.** a person, esp. a European, who has made a large fortune in India or another country of the East. **2.** any very wealthy or powerful person. [< Hindi *nawwāb.* See NAWAB]

Na·bo·kov (nä bô′kof, nä′bo kôf′), *n.* **Vla·di·mir Vla·di·mi·ro·vich** (vlä dē′mir vlä dē′mi rô′vich), 1899–1977, U.S. novelist, short-story writer, and poet, born in Russia.

Na·both (nā′both, -bōth), *n.* a man of Jezreel whose vineyard was secured for the covetous Ahab by the scheming of Jezebel. I Kings 21.

na·celle (nə sel′), *n.* **1.** the enclosed part of an airplane, dirigible, etc., in which the engine is housed or in which cargo or passengers are carried. **2.** the car of a balloon. [< F: a small boat < LL *nāvicella,* r. L *nāvicula.* See NAVE[1], -CULE]

na·cre (nā′kər), *n.* mother-of-pearl. [< ML *nacrum, nacer,* var. of *nacara* < OIt *naccara* kind of drum, nacre < Ar *naqqārah* drum]

na·cred (nā′kərd), *adj.* lined with or resembling nacre.

na·cre·ous (nā′krē əs), *adj.* **1.** of or pertaining to nacre. **2.** resembling nacre; lustrous; pearly.

Na-De·ne (nä dā′nē, nä′dā nā′), *n.* a language stock including Athapaskan, Haida, and Tlingit. Cf. **stock** (def. 13). Also, **Na·de′ne.**

Na·der (nā′dər), *n.* **Ralph,** born 1934, U.S. lawyer, author, and consumer advocate.

na·dir (nā′dər, -dēr), *n.* **1.** *Astron.* the point on the celestial sphere directly beneath a given position or observer and diametrically opposite to the zenith. **2.** the lowest point: *the nadir of our hopes.* [ME << Ar *naẓīr* over against, opposite to (the zenith)] —**na′dir·al,** *adj.*

nae (nā), *Scot. and North Eng.* —*adv.* **1.** no; not. —*adj.* **2.** no.

nae·thing (nā′thing), *n., adv. Scot.* nothing.

nae·vus (nē′vəs), *n., pl.* **-vi** (-vī). *Med.* nevus. —**nae·void** (nē′void), *adj.*

nag[1] (nag), *v.,* **nagged, nag·ging,** *n.* —*v.t.* **1.** to torment with persistent demands or complaints. **2.** to keep in a state of troubled awareness or anxiety, as a recurrent pain, problem, etc.: *She had certain misgivings that nagged at her.* —*v.i.* **3.** to find fault or complain in an irritating or relentless manner. **4.** to cause persistent discomfort or distress (often fol. by *at*): *This headache has been nagging at me all day.* —*n.* **5.** the act or an instance of nagging. **6.** Also, **nagger.** a person who nags, esp. habitually. [< Scand; cf. Icel *nagga* to rub, grumble, quarrel; akin to MLG *naggen* to irritate. See GNAW] —**Syn. 1.** pester, harass, annoy, vex.

nag[2] (nag), *n.* **1.** an old, inferior, or worthless horse. **2.** *Slang.* any horse, esp. a racehorse. **3.** a small riding horse or pony. [late ME *nagge;* c. obs. D *neg;* akin to NEIGH]

Na·ga (nä′gə), *n. Hindu Myth.* a water spirit, half human and half serpent, supposed to bring safety and prosperity.

Na·ga·land (nä′gə land′), *n.* a state in E India. 516,449, 6366 sq. mi. *Cap.:* Kohima.

na·ga·na (nə gä′nə), *n. Vet. Pathol.* **1.** a disease of horses and other animals that occurs only in certain parts of Africa and is caused by the organism *Trypanosoma brucei,* transmitted by a variety of tsetse fly. **2.** certain other African trypanosomal diseases of animals. Also, **n'gana.** [< Zulu *unakane*]

Na·ga·no (nä gä′nô), *n.* a city on central Honshu, in central Japan. 307,000.

Na·ga·ri (nä′gə rē), *n.* **1.** a group of related scripts, including Devanagari, derived from Brahmi and used for the writing of many of the languages of India. **2.** Devanagari.

Na·ga·sa·ki (nä′gə sä′kē, nag′ə sak′ē; *Jap.* nä′gä sä′kē), *n.* a seaport on W Kyushu, in SW Japan. 450,000.

nag·ger (nag′ər), *n.* nag[1] (def. 6).

Na·go·ya (nä′gô yä′), *n.* a city on S Honshu, in central Japan. 2,080,000.

Nag·pur (nag po͝or′), *n.* a city in NE Maharashtra, in central India. 866,144.

Na·gy·vá·rad (nod′yə vä′rod, noj′-), *n.* Hungarian name of **Oradea.**

Nah., Nahum.

Na·hua (nä′wä), *n., pl.* **-huas,** (*esp. collectively*) **-hua,** *adj.* Nahuatl.

Na·hua·tl (nä′wät[ə]l), *n., pl.* **-hua·tls,** (*esp. collectively*) **-hua·tl,** *adj.* —*n.* **1.** a member of any of various peoples of ancient origin ranging from southeastern Mexico to parts of Central America and including the Aztecs. **2.** a Uto-Aztecan language spoken by over half a million people mostly in central Mexico. Cf. **Aztec** (def. 2). —*adj.* **3.** of or pertaining to any of these languages or peoples. [< Nahuatl = *Nahua* NAHUA + *-tl* sing. suffix]

Na·hua·tlan (nä′wät lən), *n.* **1.** Nahuatl in all its dialects, often taken as a group of languages, spoken in large areas of central Mexico and El Salvador and in various small, widely dispersed areas throughout southern Mexico and Central America. —*adj.* **2.** of or pertaining to Nahuatl or Nahuatlan.

Na·hum (nā′həm), *n.* **1.** a Minor Prophet of the 7th century B.C. **2.** a book of the Bible bearing his name.

nai·ad (nā′ad, -əd, nī′-), *n., pl.* **-ads, -a·des** (-ə dēz′). **1.** (*sometimes cap.*) *Class. Myth.* any of a class of nymphs presiding over rivers and springs. **2.** *Bot.* a plant of the genus *Naias,* or the family *Naiadaceae.* [< L *nāiad-* (s. of *nāias*) < Gk: a water nymph]

na·ïf (nä ēf′), *adj.* naïve. Also, **na·if′.** [< MF; masc. of NAÏVE]

nail (nāl), *n.* **1.** a small, rodlike piece of metal, typically having a pointed tip and a flattened head, usually hammered into wood or other material as a fastener or support. **2.** *Anat.* a thin, horny plate, consisting of modified epidermis, growing on the upper side of the end of a finger or toe. **3.** a measure of length for cloth, equal to 2¼ inches. **4. hit the nail on the head,** to say or do exactly the right thing. —*v.t.* **5.** to fasten with a nail or nails. **6.** to enclose or confine by nailing. **7.** to make fast or keep firmly in one place or position: *Surprise nailed him to the spot.* **8.** *Informal.* to catch or seize. **9.** *Slang.* to hit (a person). **10.** *Obs.* to stud with or as with nails. **11. nail down,** *Informal.* to make final; settle once and for all. [ME; OE *nægl;* c. D, G *Nagel;* akin to L *unguis,* Gk *ónyx*]

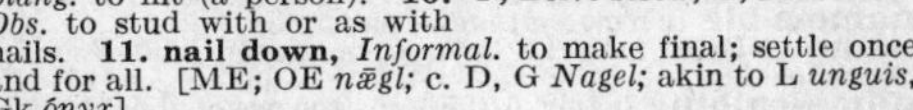

Nails (def. 1)
A, Common nail; B, Finishing nail; C, Brad; D, Cut nail; E, Roofing nail; F, Drive screw; G, Boat nail

nail·brush (nāl′brush′), *n.* a small brush with stiff bristles, used to clean the fingernails.

nail′ file′, a small file for smoothing or shaping the fingernails.

nail·head (nāl′hed′), *n.* **1.** the enlarged top of a nail, usually flattened but sometimes rounded. **2.** an ornament that suggests or resembles this.

nail′ pol′ish, a polish of quick-drying lacquer used by women to paint the fingernails. Also called **nail′ enam′el.**

nail′ set′, a short rod of steel used to drive a nail below, or flush with, a surface.

nain·sook (nān′so͝ok, nan′-), *n.* a fine, soft-finished cotton fabric, usually white, used for lingerie and infants' wear. [< Urdu (Hindi) *nainsukh* = *nain* the eye + *sukh* pleasure]

Nairn (nârn), *n.* a county in N Scotland. 8421 (1960); 163 sq. mi. *Co. seat:* Nairn. Also called **Nairn·shire** (nârn′shēr′, -shər).

Nai·ro·bi (nī rō′bē), *n.* a city in and the capital of Kenya, in the SW part. 650,000.

Nai·smith (nā′smith′), *n.* **James,** 1861–1939, U.S. physical-education professor and originator of basketball, born in Canada.

nais·sance (nā′səns), *n.* a birth, an origination, or a growth, as that of a person, an organization, an idea, or a movement. [< F, MF = *nais-* (s. of *naître* to be born < L *nascere,* var. of *nascī;* see NATION) + *-ance* -ANCE]

na·ïve (nä ēv′), *adj.* **1.** having or showing natural simplicity of nature; unsophisticated; ingenuous. **2.** having or showing a lack of experience, judgment, or information. Also, **na·ive′.** [< F, fem. of *naïf*, OF *naif* natural, instinctive < L *nātīv(us)* NATIVE] —**na·ïve′ly, na·ive′ly,** *adv.* —**Syn. 1.** unaffected; unsuspecting. —**Ant. 1.** sophisticated.

naïve′ re′alism, *Philos.* the theory that the world is perceived exactly as it is.

na·ïve·té (nä ēv tā′), *n.* **1.** Also called **na·ïve′ness.** the quality or state of being naïve; artless simplicity. **2.** a naïve action, remark, etc. Also, **na·ive·té′, na·ïve·te′.** [< F]

na·ïve·ty (nä ēv′tē), *n., pl.* **-ties.** naïveté.

Na·ka·so·ne (nä′kä sô′ne), *n.* **Ya·su·hi·ro** (yä′sŏŏ hē′rô), born 1918, Japanese prime minister since 1982.

na·ked (nā′kid), *adj.* **1.** without clothing or covering; nude. **2.** without adequate clothing. **3.** bare of any covering, overlying matter, or the like. **4.** bare, stripped, or destitute (usually fol. by *of*): *The trees were left naked of leaves.* **5.** without the customary covering, container, furnishings, etc. **6.** (of the eye, sight, etc.) unassisted by an optical instrument. **7.** defenseless; unprotected; exposed. **8.** simply and candidly revealed; fully apparent. **9.** unconcealed or unmodified. **10.** *Law.* unsupported, as by authority or consideration. **11.** *Bot.* **a.** (of seeds) not enclosed in an ovary. **b.** (of flowers) without a calyx or perianth. **c.** (of stalks, branches, etc.) without leaves. **d.** (of stalks, leaves, etc.) without hairs or pubescence. **12.** *Zool.* having no covering of hair, feathers, shell, etc. [ME *naked(e)*, OE *nacod;* c. D *naakt*, G *nackt*, Goth *naqths;* akin to Icel *nakinn*, L *nūdus*, Gk *gymnós*, Skt *nagnás*] —**na′ked·ly,** *adv.* —**na′ked·ness,** *n.*

Nam (näm), *n.* Menam.

NAM, National Association of Manufacturers. Also, **N.A.M.**

nam·a·ble (nā′mə bəl), *adj.* **1.** capable of being or liable of being named or revealed. **2.** capable of being said or discussed without shocking a person's sensibilities or sense of decency. Also, **nameable.** —**nam′a·bil′i·ty, name′a·bil′i·ty,** *n.*

Na·man·gan (nä′män gän′), *n.* a city in E Uzbekistan, in the SW Soviet Union in Asia. 150,000 (est. 1965).

Na·ma·qua·land (nə mä′kwə land′), *n.* a coastal region in the S part of South-West Africa, extending into the Cape of Good Hope province of the Republic of South Africa: inhabited by Hottentots. Also called **Na·ma·land** (nä′mä land′).

nam·by-pam·by (nam′bē pam′bē), *adj., n., pl.* **-bies** for 5. —*adj.* **1.** weakly sentimental, pretentious, or affected; insipid. **2.** lacking in character, directness, or moral or emotional strength: *namby-pamby behavior.* **3.** without firm methods or policy; weak or indecisive. —*n.* **4.** namby-pamby verse or prose. **5.** a namby-pamby person. **6.** namby-pamby sentiment. [special use of nickname *Namby Pamby* for Ambrose Philips; first used 1726 by Henry Carey as title of poem ridiculing Philips's verses]

name (nām), *n., v.,* **named, nam·ing,** *adj.* —*n.* **1.** a word or a combination of words by which a person, place, idea, etc., is known or designated. **2.** mere designation, as distinguished from fact: *He was a ruler in name only.* **3.** something that a person is said to be, esp. by way of insult or reproach: *to call a person names.* **4.** reputation of any kind: *to protect someone's good name.* **5.** a distinguished reputation: *to make a name for oneself.* **6.** a widely known or famous person: *She's a name in show business.* **7.** (*cap.*) a symbol of divinity. **8.** a body of persons grouped under one name, as a family or race. **9. by name, a.** by one's own name: *to address someone by name.* **b.** not personally; by repute: *I know him only by name.* **10. in the name of, a.** with appeal to: *In the name of mercy, stop that screaming!* **b.** by the authority of: *Open, in the name of the law!* **c.** on behalf of. **d.** under the name of: *money deposited in the name of a son.* **11. to one's name,** in one's possession: *I haven't a penny to my name.* —*v.t.* **12.** to give a name to: *Have they named the new baby yet?* **13.** to call by a specified name. **14.** to identify, specify, or mention by name. **15.** to designate for some duty or office. **16.** to specify; suggest: *Name a price.* **17.** to give the name of. **18. name names,** to specify people by name. —*adj.* **19.** famous; widely known: *a name actor.* **20.** designed for or carrying a name: *a name tag.* **21.** giving its name or title to a collection. [ME; OE *nama;* c. G *Name* Goth *namō;* akin to Icel *nafn*, L *nōmen*, Gk *ónoma*]
—**Syn. 1.** NAME, TITLE both refer to the label by which a person is known. NAME is the simpler and more general word for appellation: *The name is John.* A TITLE is an official or honorary term bestowed on a person or the specific designation of a book, article, etc.: *He now has the title of Doctor.* Treasure Island *is the title of a book.* **4.** repute.

name·a·ble (nā′mə bəl), *adj.* namable.

name-call·er (nām′kô′lər), *n.* a person who resorts to name-calling.

name-call·ing (nām′kô′liṅg), *n.* the use of abusive names in a political campaign, an argument, etc.

name′ day′, the day of the saint after whom a person is named.

name-drop·ping (nām′drop′iṅg), *n.* the introduction into one's conversation, letters, etc., of the names of famous people as alleged friends or associates in order to impress others. —**name′-drop′per,** *n.*

name·less (nām′lis), *adj.* **1.** unknown to fame; obscure. **2.** having no name. **3.** left unnamed, as for purposes of concealment. **4.** anonymous. **5.** having no legitimate paternal name, as a child born out of wedlock. **6.** difficult or impossible to specify or describe: *a nameless charm.* **7.** too shocking or vile to be specified. [ME] —**name′less·ly,** *adv.* —**name′less·ness,** *n.*

name·ly (nām′lē), *adv.* that is to say: *an item of legislation, namely, the housing bill.* [ME *namely, nameliche*]

name′ of the game′, *Informal.* the central purpose, method, or quality: *Profit is the name of the game in business.*

name·plate (nām′plāt′), *n.* **1.** a plate lettered with a name. **2.** Also called **masthead.** *Journalism.* a line of type on the front page of a newspaper or the cover of a periodical giving the name of the publication.

name·sake (nām′sāk′), *n.* a person given the same name as another. [alter. of *name's sake*]

name·tag (nām′tag′), *n.* an identification tag or label, usually showing one's name and other information, either attached to an article of clothing or worn around the neck or wrist.

Nam·hoi (näm′hoi′), *n.* Nanhai.

Na·mib·i·a (nə mib′ē ə), *n.* official (UN) name of **South-West Africa.** —**Na·mib′i·an,** *adj., n.*

Nam·pu·la (nam pōō′lə), *n.* a city in E Mozambique. 146,916 (est. 1955).

Na·mur (nä mŏŏr′; *Fr.* NA MYR′), *n.* **1.** a province in S Belgium. 375,634 (est. 1964); 1413 sq. mi. **2.** a city in and the capital of this province, on the Sambre and Meuse rivers. 32,467 (est. 1964).

nan-, var. of **nano-** before a vowel.

Na·nak (nä′nək), *n.* ("*Guru*") 1469–1538, Indian religious leader: founder of Sikhism.

Nan·chang (nän′chäng′), *n.* a city in and the capital of Kiangsi, in SE China. 508,000 (est. 1957).

Nan·cy (nan′sē; *Fr.* näN sē′), *n.* a city in NE France: battles 1477, 1914, 1944. 695,733 (1962).

Nan·da De·vi (nun′dä dā′vē), a mountain in N India, in Uttar Pradesh: a peak of the Himalayas. 25,661 ft.

Nan·ga Par·bat (nuṅg′gə pur′but), a mountain in NW Kashmir, in the Himalayas. 26,660 ft.

Nan·hai (nän′hī′), *n.* a city in W Kwantung, in SE China, near Canton. 96,000 (est. 1950). Also, **Namhoi.** Also called **Fatshan, Foshan.**

nan·keen (nan kēn′), *n.* **1.** a firm, durable, yellow or buff fabric, originally made from a natural-colored Chinese cotton. **2. nankeens,** garments made of this material. **3.** Also called **Nan′keen por′celain, Nan′king chi′na, Nan-king′ ware′.** a type of Chinese porcelain having blue ornament on a white ground. Also, **nan·kin** (nan′kin). [after *Nankin* NANKING, where first made]

Nan·king (nan′kiṅg′; *Chin.* nän′kiṅg′), *n.* a port in and the capital of Kiangsu, in E China, on the Yangtze: a former capital of China. 1,419,000 (est. 1957).

Nan Ling (nän′ liṅg′), a mountain range in S China. Also called **Nan Shan.**

Nan·ning (nan′niṅg′; *Chin.* nän′niṅg′), *n.* a city in and the capital of Kwangsi, in S China. 264,000 (est. 1957). Formerly, **Yungning.**

nan·ny (nan′ē), *n., pl.* **-nies.** *Chiefly Brit.* a child's nursemaid. [special use of given name *Nanny*]

nan′ny goat′, a female goat.

nano-, a learned borrowing from Latin meaning "dwarf"; specialized in certain measurements to mean "one billionth": *nanocurie; nanosecond.* Also, *esp. before a vowel,* **nan-.** [comb. form repr. L *nānus* dwarf < Gk *nânos*]

na·no·cu·rie (nā′nə kyŏŏr′ē, nan′ə-), *n.* one billionth (10^{-9}) of a curie. *Abbr.:* nC, nc

na·no·far·ad (nā′nə far′əd, -ad, nan′ə-), *n.* one billionth (10^{-9}) of a farad. *Abbr.:* nF, nf

na·no·hen·ry (nā′nə hen′rē, nan′ə-), *n., pl.* **-ries, -rys.** one billionth (10^{-9}) of a henry. *Abbr.:* nH, nh

na·no·me·ter (nā′nə mē′tər, nan′ə-), *n.* *Metric System.* one millionth of a millimeter. *Abbr.:* nm

na·no·sec·ond (nā′nə sek′ənd, nan′ə-), *n.* one billionth (10^{-9}) of a second. *Abbr.:* ns, nsec

na·no·watt (nā′nə wot′, nan′ə-), *n.* one billionth (10^{-9}) of a watt. *Abbr.:* nW, nw

Nan′sen bot′tle, *Oceanog.* a waterproof container for collecting samples of ocean water at predetermined depths. [named after Fridtjof *Nansen* (1861–1930), Norwegian arctic explorer]

Nan Shan (nän′ shän′), **1.** a mountain range in W China. **2.** See **Nan Ling.**

Nantes (nants; *Fr.* näNt), *n.* **1.** a seaport in W France, on the Loire River. 246,227 (1962). **2. Edict of,** *Fr. Hist.* a law, promulgated by Henry IV in 1598, granting considerable religious and civil liberty to the Huguenots: revoked by Louis XIV in 1685.

Nan·tuck·et (nan tuk′it), *n.* **1.** an island off SE Massachusetts: summer resort; 15 mi. long. **2.** a town on this island. 3774 (1970).

Naoi·se (nē′shə, nā′-), *n.* *Irish Legend.* the husband of Deirdre and a nephew of Conchobar, by whom he was treacherously killed.

Na·o·mi (nā ō′mē, -mī, nā′ō mī′, -mē′), *n.* the mother-in-law of Ruth. Ruth 1.

na·os (nā′os), *n., pl.* **-oi** (-oi). **1.** a temple. **2.** *Archit.* cella. [< Gk: the dwelling of a god, the inner part of a shrine]

nap[1] (nap), *v.,* **napped, nap·ping,** *n.* —*v.i.* **1.** to sleep for a short time; doze. **2.** to be off one's guard: *to catch someone napping.* —*v.t.* **3.** to sleep or doze through (a period of time) (usually fol. by *away*): *I napped the afternoon away.* —*n.* **4.** a brief period of sleep. [ME *nappe(n)*, OE *hnappian;* c. MHG *napfen*]

nap[2] (nap), *n., v.,* **napped, nap·ping.** —*n.* **1.** the short fuzzy ends of fibers on the surface of cloth, drawn up in napping. **2.** any downy coating, as on plants. —*v.t.* **3.** to raise a nap on. [late ME *noppe*, OE *-hnoppa* (as in *wullcnoppa*, mistake for *wullhnoppa* tuft of wool), c. MD, MLG *noppe;* akin to OE *hnoppian* to pluck]

nap[3] (nap), *n.* napoleon (defs. 2, 3). [shortened form]

Nap·a (nap′ə), *n.* a city in W California. 35,978 (1970).

na·palm (nā′päm), *Mil.* —*n.* **1.** a highly inflammable jellylike substance used in fire bombs, flame throwers, etc. —*v.t.* **2.** to drop bombs containing napalm on (troops, a city, or the like). [NA(PHTHENE) + PALM(ITATE)]

nape (nāp, nap), *n.* the back of the neck (usually used in the phrase *nape of the neck*). [ME]

na·per·y (nā′pə rē), *n.* **1.** table linen, as tablecloths, napkins, etc. **2.** any linen for household use. [ME *naprye* < MF. See NAPKIN, -ERY]

Naph·ta·li (naf′tə lī′), *n.* **1.** a son of Jacob and Bilhah. Gen. 30:7,8. **2.** one of the 12 tribes of Israel, traditionally descended from Naphtali.

naphth-, a combining form of **naphtha** or **naphthalene:** *naphthol.*

naph·tha (naf′thə, nap′-), *n.* **1.** a colorless, volatile petroleum distillate, usually an intermediate product between gasoline and benzine, used as a solvent, fuel, etc. **2.** any of various similar liquids distilled from other products. [< L < Gk; akin to Avestan *napta* wet] —**naph′thous,** *adj.*

naph·tha·lene (naf′thə lēn′, nap′-), *n.* *Chem.* a white, crystalline, water-insoluble hydrocarbon, $C_{10}H_8$, usually obtained from coal tar: used in making dyes, as a moth repellant, etc. Also, **naph′tha·line′, naph·tha·lin** (naf′thə lin, nap′-). [NAPHTH- + -AL³ + -ENE] —**naph·thal·ic** (naf-thal′ik, nap-), **naph·tha·len·ic** (naf′thə len′ik, nap′-), *adj.*

naph·tha·lize (naf′thə līz′, nap′-), *v.t.*, **-lized, -liz·ing.** to mix or saturate with naphtha.

naph·thene (naf′thēn, nap′-), *n. Chem.* any of a group of hydrocarbon ring compounds of the general formula, C_nH_{2n}, derivatives of cyclopentane and cyclohexane, found in certain petroleums. —**naph·the·nic** (naf thē′nik, -then′ik, nap-), *adj.*

naph·thol (naf′thōl, -thôl, -thol, nap′-), *n. Chem.* **1.** one of two isomeric derivatives of naphthalene, $C_{10}H_7OH$, used chiefly in the manufacture of dyes and perfumes; 1-naphthol. **2.** one of two isomeric derivatives of naphthalene, $C_{10}H_7OH$, used chiefly in the manufacture of dyes, drugs, perfumes, fats, oils, etc., and as an antiseptic; 2-naphthol. **3.** any of certain hydroxyl derivatives of naphthalene.

naph·thyl (naf′thil, nap′-), *adj. Chem.* containing the naphthyl group.

Na·pi·er (nā′pē ər *or, for 1–3,* nə pēr′), *n.* **1. Sir Charles James,** 1782–1853, British general. **2.** Also, **Neper. John,** 1550–1617, Scottish mathematician. **3. Robert Cornelis** (*1st Baron Napier of Magdala*), 1810–90, English field marshal. **4.** a seaport on E North Island, in New Zealand. 32,716 (1961).

Na·pier′i·an log′arithm (na pēr′ē ən), *Math.* See **natural logarithm.**

na·pi·form (nā′pə fôrm′), *adj.* turnip-shaped, as a root. [< L *nāp(us)* a kind of turnip + -I- + -FORM]

nap·kin (nap′kin), *n.* **1.** a rectangular piece of cloth or paper for use in wiping the lips and fingers and to protect the clothes while eating. **2.** a small towel of linen or cotton cloth. **3.** *Chiefly Brit.* a diaper. **4.** *North Eng. and Scot.* a handkerchief. **5.** *Scot.* a kerchief or neckerchief. [ME < MF *nappe* tablecloth (< L *mappa* napkin); see -KIN]

nap′kin ring′, a ring or band of metal, wood, etc., through which a folded napkin is inserted, often as part of a place setting.

Na·ples (nā′pəlz), *n.* **1.** Italian, **Napoli.** a seaport in SW Italy on the Bay of Naples. 1,220,639 (1964). **2. Bay of.** Italian, **Gol·fo di Na·po·li** (gôl′fô dē nä′pô lē). a bay in SW Italy. 22 mi. long.

na·po·le·on (nə pō′lē ən, -pōl′yən), *n.* **1.** a pastry consisting of thin layers of puff paste interlaid with a cream filling. **2.** a former gold coin of France, equal to 20 francs and bearing a portrait either of Napoleon I or of Napoleon III. **3.** *Cards.* **a.** a game in which the players bid for the privilege of naming the trump, stating the number of tricks they propose to win. **b.** a bid in this game to take all five tricks of a hand. [< F]

Na·po·le·on (nə pō′lē ən), *n.* **Louis** (lo͞o′ē; *Fr.* lwē). See **Napoleon III.**

Napoleon I, (*Napoleon Bonaparte*) (*"the Little Corporal"*) 1769–1821, French general born in Corsica: emperor of France 1804–15.

Napoleon II, (*Napoleon Bonaparte*) (*Duke of Reichstadt*) 1811–32, titular king of Rome (son of Napoleon I).

Napoleon III, (*Louis Napoleon Bonaparte*) 1808–73, president of France 1848–52, emperor of France 1852–70.

Na·po·le·on·ic (nə pō′lē on′ik), *adj.* pertaining to, resembling, or suggestive of Napoleon I or his dynasty. —**Na·po′le·on′i·cal·ly,** *adv.*

Napo′leon′ic Code′, See **Code Napoléon.**

Napo′leon′ic Wars′, the intermittent wars (1796–1815) waged by France principally against England, Prussia, Austria, and Russia.

Na·po·li (nä′pô lē), *n.* Italian name of **Naples.**

nappe (nap), *n. Geom.* one of the two equal sections of a cone. [< F: lit., tablecloth, cloth. See NAPKIN]

nap·per¹ (nap′ər), *n.* **1.** a textile worker who naps cloth. **2.** a machine for putting a nap on cloth. [NAP² + -ER¹]

nap·per² (nap′ər), *n.* a person who dozes. [NAP¹ + -ER¹]

nap·py¹ (nap′ē), *adj.*, **-pi·er, -pi·est. 1.** *Brit. Informal.* (of ale and other malt liquors) foaming and hearty. **2.** *Chiefly Scot. Informal.* mildly drunk; tipsy. [late ME *noppy*]

nap·py² (nap′ē), *n., pl.* **-pies.** a small dish, usually round and often of glass, with a flat bottom and sloping sides, for serving food. Also, **nap′pie.** [*nap* (ME; OE *hnæp* bowl) + -Y²]

nap·py³ (nap′ē), *adj.*, **-pi·er, -pi·est.** covered with nap; downy. [NAP² + -Y¹] —**nap′pi·ness,** *n.*

Na·ra (nä rä′), *n.* a city on S Honshu, in central Japan: chief Buddhist center of ancient Japan. 152,610 (1964).

Nar·ba·da (nər bud′ə), *n.* a river flowing W from central India to the Arabian Sea. 800 mi. long. Also, **Nerbudda.**

Nar·bonne (NAR bôn′), *n.* a city in S France: an important port in Roman times. 35,899 (1962).

narc (närk), *n. U.S. Slang.* a government narcotics agent or detective. [shortened form of NARCOTICS AGENT]

narc-, var. of **narco-** before a vowel: *narcose.*

nar·cis·sism (när′si siz′əm), *n.* **1.** egocentricity. **2.** *Psychoanal.* erotic gratification derived from admiration of one's own physical or mental attributes. Also, **nar·cism** (när′siz əm). [< G *Narzissismus*] —**nar′cis·sist, nar′-cist,** *n.* —**nar′cis·sis′tic, nar·cis′tic,** *adj.*

nar·cis·sus (när sis′əs), *n., pl.* **-cis·sus, -cis·sus·es, -cis·si** (-sis′ē, -sis′ī) for 1, 2. **1.** any bulbous amaryllidaceous plant of the genus *Narcissus,* having showy flowers with a cup-shaped corona. **2.** the flower of any of these plants. **3.** (*cap.*) *Class. Myth.* a youth who fell in love with his own image reflected in a pool and wasted away from unsatisfied desire, whereupon he was transformed into the flower. [< L < Gk *nárkissos* plant name, connected, by virtue of plant's narcotic effects, with *nárkē* numbness, torpor. See NARCOTIC]

nar·co (när′kō), *n., pl.* **nar·cos.** *U.S. Slang.* narc.

narco-, a combining form meaning "stupor," "narcosis": *narcolepsy.* Also, *esp. before a vowel,* **narc-.** [< Gk *nárk(ē)* numbness, stiffness + -o-]

nar·co·lep·sy (när′kə lep′sē), *n. Pathol.* a condition characterized by a frequent and uncontrollable need for short periods of deep sleep. [NARCO- + (EPI)LEPSY] —**nar′co-lep′tic,** *adj., n.*

nar·cose (när′kōs), *adj.* characterized by stupor; stuporous.

nar·co·sis (när kō′sis), *n.* **1.** a state of sleep or drowsiness. **2.** a state of unconsciousness or drowsiness produced by a drug, or by heat, cold, or electricity. [< NL < Gk *nárkōsis*]

nar·co·syn·the·sis (när′kō sin′thi sis), *n.* a treatment for psychiatric disturbances that uses narcotics.

nar·cot·ic (när kot′ik), *adj.* **1.** having the power to produce narcosis, as a drug. **2.** pertaining to or of the nature of narcosis. **3.** pertaining to narcotics or their use. **4.** used by, or in the treatment of, narcotic addicts. —*n.* **5.** any of a class of addictive substances, as opium and morphine, that blunt or distort the senses and in large quantities produce euphoria, stupor, or coma: used in medicine to relieve pain, cause sedation, and induce sleep. **6.** an individual inclined toward the habitual use of such substances. **7.** anything that exercises a soothing or numbing effect or influence. [ME *narcotik(e)* < ML *narcōticum* < Gk *narkōtikón,* n. use of neut. of *narkōtikós* benumbing = *narkō-* (var. s. of *narkoûn* to benumb; see NARCO-) + *-tikos* -TIC] —**nar·cot′i·cal·ly,** *adv.*

nar·co·tise (när′kə tīz′), *v.t., v.i.*, **-tised, -tis·ing.** *Chiefly Brit.* narcotize. —**nar′co·ti·sa′tion,** *n.*

nar·co·tism (när′kə tiz′əm), *n.* **1.** habitual use of narcotics. **2.** the action or influence of narcotics. **3.** narcosis. **4.** an abnormal inclination to sleep. [earlier *narcoticism*] —**nar′co·tist,** *n.*

nar·co·tize (när′kə tīz′), *v.*, **-tized, -tiz·ing.** —*v.t.* **1.** to subject to a narcotic; stupefy. **2.** to make dull; deaden the awareness of: *to narcotize one's anxieties.* —*v.i.* **3.** to act as a narcotic. Also, *esp. Brit.,* **narcotise.** —**nar′co·ti·za′tion,** *n.*

nard (närd), *n.* **1.** an aromatic, Himalayan plant, believed to be the spikenard, *Nardostachys Jatamansi,* the source of an ointment used by the ancients. **2.** the ointment. [ME *narde* < L *nardus* < Gk *nárdos* < Sem (cf. Heb *nērd*), or through Sem < Skt *nálada*] —**nar·dine** (när′din, -dīn), *adj.*

nar·es (nâr′ēz), *n.pl., sing.* **nar·is** (nâr′is). *Anat.* the nostrils or the nasal passages. [< L, pl. of *nāris* a nostril]

Na·rew (nä′REf), *n.* a river in NE Poland, flowing S and SW into the Bug River: battle 1915. 290 mi. long. Russian, **Na·rev** (nä′REf).

nar·ghi·le (när′gə lē, -lā′), *n.* hookah. Also, **nar′gi·le, nar′gi·leh.** [< Turk *nargile* < Pers *nārgīleh* < *nārgīl* coconut, of which the bowl was formerly made]

nar·i·al (nâr′ē əl), *adj. Anat.* of or pertaining to the nares or nostrils. Also, **nar·ine** (nâr′in, -īn). [< L *nāri(s)* nostril + -AL¹]

nark (närk), *n.* **1.** *Brit. Slang.* See **stool pigeon** (def. 2). **2.** *Chiefly Australian Slang.* an annoying person, esp. a kill-joy. —*v.i.* **3.** *Chiefly Australian Slang.* to become annoyed. [< Gypsy *nāk* nose]

Nar·ra·gan·sett (nar′ə gan′sit), *n., pl.* **-setts,** (*esp. collectively*) **-sett. 1.** a member of a North American Indian tribe of the Algonquian family formerly located in Rhode Island but now extinct. **2.** an Algonquian language, the language of the Narragansett Indians.

Nar′ragan′sett Bay′, an inlet of the Atlantic in E Rhode Island. 28 mi. long.

nar·rate (nar′āt, na rāt′), *v.*, **-rat·ed, -rat·ing.** —*v.t.* **1.** to give an account or tell the story of (events, experiences, etc.). —*v.i.* **2.** to relate or recount events, experiences, etc., in speech or writing. [< L *narrāt(us)* made known, told (ptp. of *narrāre*) = *nār(us)* knowing, acquainted with (var. of *gnārus*) + *-ātus* -ATE¹] —**nar′rat·a·ble,** *adj.* —**nar′ra·tor, nar′rat·er,** *n.* —**Syn. 1.** detail, recite.

nar·ra·tion (na rā′shən), *n.* **1.** something that is narrated; an account or story; narrative. **2.** the act or process of narrating. [late ME *narracion* < L *narrātiōn-* (s. of *narrātiō*)] —**nar·ra′tion·al,** *adj.*

nar·ra·tive (nar′ə tiv), *n.* **1.** a story of events, experiences, or the like; narration. **2.** a written or spoken work containing such a story. **3.** the art, technique, or process of narrating. —*adj.* **4.** consisting of or being a narrative. **5.** of or pertaining to narration. [< L *narrātīv(us)* suitable for narration] —**nar′ra·tive·ly,** *adv.*

—**Syn. 1.** chronicle, tale. NARRATIVE, ACCOUNT, RECITAL, HISTORY are terms for a story of an event or events. NARRATIVE is the general term for a story long or short; of the past, present, or future; factual or imagined; told for any purpose; and with or without much detail. The other three terms apply primarily to factual stories of time already past. An ACCOUNT is usually told informally, often for entertainment, with emphasis on details of action, whether about an incident or a series of happenings. A RECITAL is an extended narrative, usually with an informative purpose, emphasizing accuracy and exhaustive details of facts and figures. A HISTORY, usually written and at some length, is characterized by a tracing of causes and effects, and by an attempt to estimate, evaluate, and interpret facts.

nar·row (nar′ō), *adj.* **1.** of little breadth or width. **2.** affording little room: *narrow quarters.* **3.** limited in range or scope. **4.** lacking breadth of view or sympathy. **5.** limited in amount; meager: *narrow resources.* **6.** straitened, as circumstances. **7.** barely adequate or successful: *a narrow escape.* **8.** careful or minute, as a scrutiny, search, or inquiry. **9.** *Brit. Dial.* stingy or thrifty; parsimonious. **10.** *Phonet.* (of a vowel) articulated with the tongue laterally constricted, as the *ee* of *beet,* the *oo* of *boot,* etc.; tense. Cf. **lax** (def. 6). **11.** (of livestock feeds) proportionately rich in protein. —*v.i.* **12.** to become narrower. —*v.t.* **13.** to make narrower. **14.** to limit or restrict increasingly (often fol. by *down*): *to narrow down a contest to three competitors.* **15.** to make narrow-minded. —*n.* **16.** a narrow part, place, or thing. **17.** a narrow part of a valley, passage, or road. **18. narrows,** (*construed as sing. or pl.*) a narrow part of a strait, river, ocean current, etc. [ME; OE *nearu;* c. OS *naru* narrow, D *naar* unpleasant; akin to G *Narbe* scar, lit., narrow mark] —**nar′row·ish,** *adj.* —**nar′row·ly,** *adv.* —**nar′row·ness,** *n.*

nar′row gauge′. See under **gauge** (def. 11). —**nar′row-gauge′;** *esp. in technical use,* **nar′row-gage′,** *adj.* —**nar′row-gauged′;** *esp. in technical use,* **nar′row-gaged′,** *adj.*

nar′row-leaved bot′tle tree′ (nar′ō lēvd′). See under **bottle tree.**

nar·row-mind·ed (nar′ō mīn′did), *adj.* having or showing a prejudiced or an extremely conservative and morally self-righteous mind. —**nar′row-mind′ed·ly,** *adv.* —**nar′-row-mind′ed·ness,** *n.* —**Syn.** biased, bigoted, partial.

nar·thex (när′theks), *n.* *Archit.* an enclosed passage between the main entrance and the nave of a church. [< LGk, Gk: giant fennel; so named from its shape]

Nar·va (när′vä), *n.* a seaport in Estonia, in the W Soviet Union in Europe, on the Gulf of Finland: Swedish defeat of Russians 1700. 72,000.

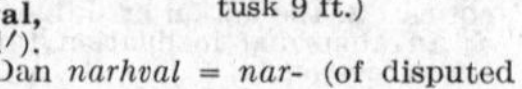
Narwhal (Total length 23 ft.; tusk 9 ft.)

Nar·vá·ez (när vä′eth, -vä′-es), *n.* **Pán·fi·lo de** (pän′fē-lô′ the), 1478?–1528, Spanish soldier and adventurer in America.

nar·whal (när′wəl), *n.* an arctic cetacean, *Monodon monoceros,* the male of which has a long, spirally twisted tusk extending forward from the upper jaw. Also, **nar′wal, nar·whale** (när′hwāl′, -wāl′). [< Scand; cf. Norw, Sw, Dan *narhval* = *nar-* (of disputed orig.) + *hval* WHALE[1]]

nar·y (nâr′ē), *adj.* *Dial.* not any; no; never a. [var. of *ne'er a* never a]

N.A.S., National Academy of Sciences. Also, **NAS**

NASA (nas′ə, nā′sə), *n.* National Aeronautics and Space Administration.

na·sal[1] (nā′zəl), *adj.* **1.** of or pertaining to the nose: *the nasal cavity.* **2.** *Phonet.* pronounced with the voice issuing through the nose, either partly, as in French nasal vowels, or entirely (as in *m, n,* or the *ng* of *song*). —*n.* **3.** *Phonet.* a nasal speech sound. [< F < LL **nāsāl(is).* See NASO-, -AL[1]] —**na·sal·i·ty** (nā zal′i tē), *n.* —**na′sal·ly,** *adv.*

na·sal[2] (nā′zəl), *n.* *Armor.* a bar or narrow plate used with an open helmet as a defense for the nose. [late ME < ML *nāsāle,* n. use of neut. of LL **nāsālis* NASAL[1]; r. ME *nasel* < MF < LL **nāsāle*]

na′sal gleet′, *Vet. Pathol.* gleet (def. 2).

na·sal·ise (nā′zə līz′), *v.t., v.i.,* **-ised, -is·ing.** *Chiefly Brit.* nasalize. —**na′sal·i·sa′tion,** *n.*

na·sal·ize (nā′zə līz′), *v.,* **-ized, -iz·ing.** *Phonet.* —*v.t.* **1.** to pronounce as a nasal sound. —*v.i.* **2.** to nasalize normally oral sounds. —**na′sal·i·za′tion,** *n.*

Nas·by (naz′bē), *n.* **Petroleum V.** See **Locke, David Ross.**

nas·cent (nas′ənt, nā′sənt), *adj.* **1.** beginning to exist or develop; young or developing: *the nascent republic.* **2.** *Chem.* (of an element) in the nascent state. [< L *nascent-* (s. of *nascēns,* prp. of *nasci*) being born, arising = *nā(tus)* born (var. of *gnātus*) + *-sc-* inceptive suffix + *-ent-* -ENT] —**nas′cence, nas′cen·cy,** *n.*

nas′cent state′, *Chem.* the condition of an element at the instant it is set free from a combination in which it has previously existed. Also called **nas′cent condi′tion.**

NASDAQ (naz′dak′), *n.* *Trademark.* a computerized system that makes bid and asked quotations on over-the-counter stocks instantly available across the country. [*N(ational) A(ssociation of) S(ecurities) D(ealers) A(utomated) Q(uotations)*]

Nase·by (nāz′bē), *n.* a village in W Northamptonshire, in central England: Royalist defeat 1645.

Nash (nash), *n.* **1. John,** 1752–1835, English architect and city planner. **2. Ogden,** 1902–71, U.S. writer of humorous verse. **3.** Also, **Nashe. Thomas,** (pen name: *Pasquil*), 1567–1601, English dramatist, novelist, and satirical pamphleteer.

Nash·u·a (nash′o͞o ə), *n.* a city in S New Hampshire, on the Merrimack River. 55,820 (1970).

Nash·ville (nash′vil), *n.* a city in and the capital of Tennessee, in the central part: battle 1864. 447,877 (1970).

naso-, a learned borrowing from Latin meaning "nose," used in the formation of compound words: *nasopharynx.* [comb. form repr. L *nāsus* the nose; see -O-]

na·so·phar·ynx (nā′zō far′ingks), *n., pl.* **-pha·ryn·ges** (-fə rin′jēz), **-phar·ynx·es.** *Anat.* the part of the pharynx behind and above the soft palate, directly continuous with the nasal passages. —**na·so·pha·ryn·ge·al** (nā′zō fə rin′jē-əl, -jəl, -far′ən jē′əl), *adj.*

Nas·sau (nas′ô; *for 2, also Ger.* nä′sou), *n.* **1.** a seaport on New Providence island: capital of the Bahamas; seaside resort. 100,000. **2.** a district in central West Germany: formerly a duchy, now a part of Hesse.

Nas′sau Moun′tains, a range in West Irian. Highest peak, Carstensz, 16,404 ft.

Nas·ser (nä′sər, nas′ər), *n.* **Ga·mal Ab·del** (gə mäl′ ab′del), 1918–70, Egyptian military and political leader.

Nast (nast), *n.* **Thomas,** 1840–1902, U.S. cartoonist.

nas·tic (nas′tik), *adj.* *Plant Physiol.* of or showing sufficiently greater cellular force or growth on one side of an axis to change the form or position of the axis. [< Gk *nast(ós)* pressed close, stamped down + -IC]

-nastic, a suffix forming adjectives of nouns with stems in **-nasty:** *hyponastic.* [see NASTIC]

na·stur·tium (na stûr′shəm, nə-), *n.* **1.** any plant of the genus *Tropaeolum,* cultivated for its showy flowers or for its fruit, which is pickled and used like capers. **2.** the flower. [< L: a kind of cress, lit., something that wrings the nose (referring to its acrid smell). See NOSE, TORT]

nas·ty (nas′tē), *adj.,* **-ti·er, -ti·est.** **1.** disgustingly unclean. **2.** offensive to taste or smell. **3.** highly objectionable: *a nasty habit.* **4.** morally filthy; obscene. **5.** vicious, spiteful, or ugly. **6.** bad to deal with or experience: *a nasty cut; a nasty accident.* [late ME] —**nas′ti·ly,** *adv.* —**nas′ti·ness,** *n.* —**Syn. 1.** foul, loathsome. **2.** nauseating, sickening, repulsive. —**Ant. 1.** clean, pure. **2.** delightful.

-nasty, a combining form indicating irregularity of cellular growth because of some pressure: *hyponasty.* [< Gk *nast(ós)* pressed close, stamped down, (see NASTIC) + -Y[3]]

nat., **1.** national. **2.** native. **3.** natural. **4.** naturalist.

na·tal (nāt′əl), *adj.* **1.** of or pertaining to one's birth. **2.** presiding over or affecting a person at birth. [< L *nātāl(is)* of, belonging to one's birth, natal = *nāt(us)* born (var. of *gnātus,* ptp. of *nasci*) + *-ālis* -AL[1]]

Na·tal (nə tal′, -täl′ *for 1;* nə täl′, -tôl′ *for 2*), *n.* **1.** a province in the E part of the Republic of South Africa. 4,236,700; 35,284 sq. mi. *Cap.:* Pietermaritzburg. **2.** a seaport in E Brazil. 250,787. —**Na·tal′i·an,** *adj., n.*

na·tal·i·ty (nā tal′i tē), *n.* See **birth rate.**

na·tant (nāt′ənt), *adj.* **1.** swimming; floating. **2.** *Bot.* floating on water, as the leaf of an aquatic plant. [< L *natant-* (s. of *natāns*), prp. of *natāre;* see -ANT] —**na′tant·ly,** *adv.*

na·ta·tion (nā tā′shən, na-), *n.* the act or art of swimming. [< L *natātiōn-* (s. of *natātiō*) = *natā(us)* swum (ptp. of *natāre*) + *-iōn-* -ION]

na·ta·to·ri·al (nā′tə tōr′ē əl, -tôr′-, nat′ə-), *adj.* pertaining to, adapted for, or characterized by swimming: *natatorial birds.* Also, **na′ta·to′ry.** [NATAT(ION) + -ORIAL]

na·ta·to·ri·um (nā′tə tōr′ē əm, -tôr′-, nat′ə-), *n., pl.* **-to·ri·ums, -to·ri·a** (-tōr′ē ə, -tôr′-). a swimming pool, esp. one that is indoors. [< LL: swimming-place = L *natāt(us)* (see NATATION) + *-ōrium* -ORIUM]

Natch·ez (nach′iz), *n., pl.* **-ez** for 2. **1.** a port in SW Mississippi, on the Mississippi River. 19,704 (1970). **2.** a member of an extinct Muskhogean Indian tribe once living on the lower Mississippi River.

na·tes (nā′tēz), *n.pl.* buttocks; rump. [< L: the rump, buttocks, pl. of *natis;* generally used in the pl.; akin to Gk *nōton* the back]

Na·than (nā′thən), *n.* **1.** a prophet during the reigns of David and Solomon. II Sam. 12; I Kings 1:34. **2. George Jean,** 1882–1958, U.S. drama critic, author, and editor.

Na·than·a·el (nə than′ē əl, -than′yəl), *n.* a disciple of Jesus. John 1:45–51.

nathe·less (nāth′lis, nath′-), *adv.* *Archaic.* nevertheless. Also, **nath·less** (nath′lis). [ME; OE *nāthelǣs,* var. of *nāthylǣs* = *nā* never + *thȳ* for that + *lǣs* less]

Na·tick (nā′tik), *n.* a town in E Massachusetts, W of Boston. 31,057 (1970).

na·tion (nā′shən), *n.* **1.** a body of people, associated with a particular territory, that is sufficiently conscious of its unity to seek or to possess a government peculiarly its own. **2.** the territory or country itself. **3.** a member tribe of an Indian confederation. **4.** an aggregation of persons of the same ethnic family, often speaking the same language or cognate languages. [ME < L *nātiōn-* (s. of *nātiō*) birth, tribe = *nāt(us)* born (see NATAL) + *-iōn-* -ION] —**na′tion-hood′,** *n.* —**na′tion·less,** *adj.* —**Syn. 1.** See **race**[2]. **2.** state, kingdom, realm.

Na·tion (nā′shən), *n.* **Carry** or **Carrie (Amelia Moore),** 1846–1911, U.S. temperance leader.

na·tion·al (nash′ə nəl), *adj.* **1.** of, pertaining to, or maintained by a whole nation. **2.** peculiar or common to the whole people of a country. **3.** devoted to one's own nation, its interests, etc.; patriotic: *national pride.* **4.** nationalist. **5.** concerning or encompassing an entire nation. **6.** limited to one nation. —*n.* **7.** a citizen or subject of a particular country. —**na′tion·al·ly,** *adv.*

na′tional bank′, **1.** *U.S.* a bank chartered by the national government. **2.** a bank owned and administered by a government.

na′tional cem′etery, *U.S.* a cemetery, maintained by the federal government, for persons who have served honorably in the armed forces.

na′tional church′, an independent church within a country, usually representing the prevalent religion. Cf. **established church.**

Na′tional Cit′y, a city in SW California, near San Diego. 43,184 (1970).

Na′tional Conven′tion, **1.** *Fr. Hist.* the legislature of France 1792–95. **2.** *U.S.* a convention held every four years by each of the major political parties to nominate a presidential candidate.

na′tional debt′, the financial debt of a national government resulting from deficit spending. Also called **public debt.**

na′tional for′est, *U.S.* a forest maintained and preserved by the federal government.

Na′tional Guard′, *U.S.* state military forces, in part equipped, trained, and quartered by the U.S. government, and paid by the U.S. government, that become an active component of the army when called or ordered into federal service by the President under the authority of the Constitution and implementing laws. Cf. **militia** (def. 2).

na′tional hol′iday, **1.** a holiday that is observed throughout a nation. **2.** a holiday that is legally established by a national government rather than by a municipal or state government.

na′tional in′come, the total net earnings from the production of goods and services in a country over a period of time, and consisting essentially of wages, salaries, rent, profits, etc. Cf. **gross national product, net national product.**

na·tion·al·ise (nash′ə nəlīz′), *v.t., v.i.,* **-ised, -is·ing.** *Chiefly Brit.* nationalize. —**na′tion·al·i·sa′tion,** *n.*

na·tion·al·ism (nash′ə nəliz′əm), *n.* **1.** national spirit or aspirations. **2.** devotion to the interests of one's own nation. **3.** desire for national advancement or independence. **4.** a movement, as in the arts, based upon the folk idioms, history, aspirations, etc., of a nation. **5.** an idiom or trait peculiar to a nation.

na·tion·al·ist (nash′ə nəlist), *n.* **1.** a person devoted to nationalism. **2.** an advocate of national independence. **3.** (*cap.*) a member of a political group advocating or fighting for national independence, a strong national government, etc. —*adj.* **4.** Also, **na′tion·al·is′tic.** of, pertaining to, or promoting nationalism. **5.** (*cap.*) of, pertaining to, or noting a group advocating or fighting for national independence, a strong national government, etc. —**na′tion·al·is′ti·cal·ly,** *adv.*

Na′tionalist Chi′na. See **China, Republic of.**

na·tion·al·i·ty (nash′ə nal′i tē), *n., pl.* **-ties** for 1, 2, 5, 6. **1.** membership in a particular nation or country. **2.** the relationship of property to a particular nation: *the nationality of a ship.* **3.** nationalism. **4.** existence as an independent nation. **5.** a nation or people. **6.** a national quality or character.

na·tion·al·ize (nash′ə nəlīz′), *v.,* **-ized, -iz·ing.** —*v.t.* **1.** to bring under the control or ownership of a nation, as industries or land. **2.** to make national in extent or scope. **3.** to grant citizenship to; naturalize. **4.** to make into a nation. —*v.i.* **5.** to become nationalized or naturalized. Also, *esp. Brit.,* **nationalise.** —**na′tion·al·i·za′tion,** *n.*

Na′tional Libera′tion Front′, 1. the name taken by nationalist, insurgent groups in various countries. 2. Also called **Na′tional Libera′tion Front′ of South′ Vietnam′.** a political organization formed by the Vietcong in South Vietnam in 1960 to carry out an insurgent policy.

na′tional mon′ument, a monument, as a historic site, geographical area, etc., maintained in the public interest by the federal government.

na′tional park′, an area of scenic beauty, historical importance, or the like, maintained by a national government for the use of the people.

Na′tional So′cialism, the principles and practices of the Nazi party in Germany. —**Na′tional So′cialist.**

Na′tional Weath′er Serv′ice, an agency in the U.S. Department of Commerce that makes weather forecasts, issues storm and flood warnings, etc. Formerly, **Weather Bureau.**

na·tion·hood (nā′shən ho͝od′), *n.* the state or quality of having status as a separate and independent nation.

na·tion·wide (nā′shən wīd′), *adj.* extending throughout the nation.

na·tive (nā′tiv), *adj.* 1. being the place of origin of a person or thing: *one's native land.* 2. belonging to a person at his birth or a thing at its origin: *native intelligence.* 3. originating in and being characteristic of a specified region. 4. belonging to a people regarded as natives, esp. nonwhites. 5. of or pertaining to such a people. 6. being so at one's birth: *a native American.* 7. belonging or pertaining to a person by reason of his birthplace: *one's native language.* 8. remaining or growing in a natural state; unadorned or unchanged. 9. originating naturally in a particular country or region, as animals or plants. 10. found in nature rather than produced artificially, as a mineral substance. 11. occurring in nature pure or uncombined, as minerals. 12. *Archaic.* belonging to a person as a birthright. 13. *Archaic.* closely related, as by birth. 14. **go native,** *Informal.* (esp. of a tourist or resident) to affect the manners or imitate the way of life of a country. —*n.* 15. one of the original inhabitants of a place or country, esp. as distinguished from strangers or foreigners. 16. a person born in a particular place or country: *a native of Ohio.* 17. an animal or plant indigenous to a particular region. [< L *nātīv(us)* inborn, natural = *nāt(us)* born + *-īvus* -IVE; r. ME *natif* < MF] —**na′tive·ly,** *adv.* —**na′tive·ness,** *n.* —**Syn.** 2. inherited, innate, inbred.

na·tive-born (nā′tiv bôrn′), *adj.* born in the place or country indicated: *a native-born Australian.*

Na′tive States′. See **Indian States and Agencies.**

na·tiv·ism (nā′ti viz′əm), *n.* 1. the policy of protecting the interests of native inhabitants against those of immigrants. 2. *Philos.* the doctrine that innate ideas exist. —**na′tiv·ist,** *n.* —**na′tiv·is′tic,** *adj.*

na·tiv·i·ty (nə tiv′i tē, nā-), *n., pl.* **-ties.** 1. birth. 2. birth with reference to place or attendant circumstances. 3. (*cap.*) the birth of Christ. 4. (*cap.*) Christmas. 5. (*cap.*) a representation of the birth of Christ, as in art. 6. *Astrol.* a horoscope of a person's birth. [ME *nativite(th)* < OF *nativite(d)* < ML *nātīvitāt-* (s. of *nātīvitās*)]

natl., national.

NATO (nā′tō), *n.* an organization formed in Washington, D.C. (1949), comprising the 12 nations of the North Atlantic Treaty together with Greece, Turkey, and the Federal Republic of Germany, for the purpose of collective defense against aggression. Also, **Na′to.** Cf. **Warsaw Treaty Organization.** [*N(orth) A(tlantic) T(reaty) O(rganization)*]

na·tri·um (nā′trē əm), *n. Obs.* sodium. [< NL]

nat·ro·lite (na′trə līt′, nā′-), *n.* a zeolite mineral, a hydrous silicate of sodium and aluminum, $Na_2Al_2Si_3O_{10}\cdot 2H_2O$, occurring usually in white or colorless, often acicular crystals. [NATRO(N) + -LITE]

na·tron (nā′tron), *n.* a mineral, hydrated sodium carbonate, $Na_2CO_3\cdot 10H_2O$. [< F < Sp < Ar *natrūn,* var. of *nitrūn* < Gk *nítron* NITER]

nat·ter (nat′ər), *v.i.* 1. *Brit.* to complain; grumble. 2. *Australian.* to chatter. —*n.* 3. *Brit.* a chat. 4. *Canadian.* gossip. [var. of earlier *gnatter* < ?]

nat·ty (nat′ē), *adj.,* **-ti·er, -ti·est.** neatly smart in dress or appearance. [? var. of NEAT + -Y[1]] —**nat′ti·ly,** *adv.* —**nat′ti·ness,** *n.*

nat·u·ral (nach′ər əl, nach′rəl), *adj.* 1. of or pertaining to nature. 2. existing in or formed by nature. 3. in accordance with the principles of nature. 4. as formed by nature without human intervention. 5. in accordance with human nature. 6. in accordance with the nature of things; to be expected or reckoned with. 7. without affectation or constraint. 8. inborn; native: *natural ability.* 9. being such because of one's inborn nature: *a natural mathematician.* 10. reproducing the original or the original state closely: *a natural likeness.* 11. of or pertaining to the natural sciences. 12. having a real or physical existence. 13. based upon the innate moral feeling of mankind: *natural justice.* 14. related only by birth; of no legal relationship; illegitimate: *a natural son.* 15. unenlightened or unregenerate: *the natural man.* 16. *Music.* **a.** neither sharp nor flat; without sharps or flats. **b.** changed in pitch by the sign ♮. **c.** (of a horn or trumpet) having neither side holes nor valves. —*n.* 17. *Informal.* any person or thing that is well-qualified in some way. 18. *Music.* **a.** a white key on a piano, organ, or the like. **b.** the sign ♮, placed before a note, canceling the effect of a previous sharp or flat. **c.** a note affected by a ♮, or a tone thus represented. 19. an idiot. 20. *Cards.* blackjack (def. 5b). 21. (in craps) a winning combination of seven or eleven made on the first cast. [ME < L *nātūrāl(is)* (see NATURE, -AL[1]); r. ME *naturel* < MF] —**nat′u·ral·ly,** *adv.* —**nat′u·ral·ness,** *n.*

Nat′ural Bridge′, a natural limestone bridge in western Virginia. 215 ft. high; 90 ft. span.

nat′ural child′birth, childbirth, involving little or no use of drugs, for which the mother has been psychologically prepared by an explanation of pertinent facts concerning the birth process and sometimes by special exercises.

nat′ural death′, death that occurs from natural internal causes, as disease or old age.

nat′ural gas′, *Chem.* combustible gas formed naturally in the earth, as in regions yielding petroleum, consisting usually of over 80 percent of methane together with minor amounts of ethane, propane, butane, nitrogen, and, sometimes, helium: used as a fuel and to make carbon black and acetylene.

nat′ural gen′der, *Gram.* gender based on the sex or, for neuter, the lack of sex of the referent of a noun. Cf. **grammatical gender.**

nat′ural his′tory, 1. the sciences, as botany, zoology, etc., dealing with the study of all objects in nature: used esp. in reference to the beginnings of these sciences in former times. 2. the study of these sciences, esp. of a nontechnical nature. —**nat′ural histo′rian.**

nat·u·ral·ise (nach′ər ə līz′, nach′rə-), *v.t., v.i.,* **-ised, -is·ing.** *Chiefly Brit.* naturalize. —**nat′u·ral·i·sa′tion,** *n.*

nat·u·ral·ism (nach′ər ə liz′əm, nach′rə-), *n.* 1. *Literature.* a technique reflecting a deterministic view of human nature and attempting a nonidealistic, detailed, quasi-scientific observation of events. 2. a technique of rendering an artistic subject so as to reproduce its natural appearance in detail. 3. the theory of literary or artistic naturalism. 4. action arising from or based on natural instincts and desires alone. 5. *Philos.* **a.** the view that all objects and events are capable of being accounted for by scientific explanation, usually allied with the ontological claim that there are no nonnatural objects, processes, causes, etc. **b.** the view that moral judgments are factual statements and refer to empirically verifiable phenomena. 6. *Theol.* the doctrine that all religious truth is derived from a study of natural processes and not from revelation. 7. adherence or attachment to what is natural.

nat·u·ral·ist (nach′ər ə list, nach′rə-), *n.* 1. a person who is versed in or devoted to natural history, esp. a zoologist or botanist. 2. an adherent of naturalism in literature or art.

nat·u·ral·is·tic (nach′ər ə lis′tik, nach′rə-), *adj.* 1. imitating nature or the usual natural surroundings. 2. pertaining to naturalists or natural history. 3. pertaining to naturalism, esp. in art. —**nat′u·ral·is′ti·cal·ly,** *adv.*

nat·u·ral·ize (nach′ər ə līz′, nach′rə-), *v.,* **-ized, -iz·ing.** —*v.t.* 1. to invest (an alien) with the rights and privileges of a citizen. 2. to introduce (animals or plants) into a region and cause them to flourish as if native. 3. to introduce or adopt (foreign practices, words, etc.). 4. to bring into conformity with nature. 5. to regard or explain as natural rather than supernatural. 6. to adapt or accustom to a place or to new surroundings. —*v.i.* 7. to become naturalized. 8. to adapt oneself or itself as if native to a new environment, set of circumstances, etc. Also, *esp. Brit.,* **naturalise.** —**nat′u·ral·i·za′tion,** *n.*

nat′ural law′, a principle or body of laws considered as derived from nature, right reason, or religion and as ethically binding in human society.

nat′ural log′arithm, *Math.* a logarithm having *e* as a base. *Symbol:* ln. Also called **Napierian logarithm.** Cf. **common logarithm.**

nat′ural num′ber, a positive integer or zero.

nat′ural philos′ophy, 1. See **natural science.** 2. See **physical science.** —**nat′ural philos′opher.**

nat′ural re′sources, the natural wealth of a country, consisting of land, forests, mineral deposits, water, etc.

nat′ural rub′ber, rubber[1] (def. 1).

nat′ural sci′ence, a science or knowledge of objects or processes observable in nature, as biology, physics, etc., as distinguished from the abstract or theoretical sciences, as mathematics, philosophy, etc.

nat′ural selec′tion, a process in nature resulting in the survival and perpetuation of only those forms of plant and animal life having certain favorable characteristics that best enable them to adapt to a specific environment. Cf. **Darwinism.**

nat′ural theol′ogy, the theology of natural religion. —**nat′ural theolo′gian.**

nat′ural vir′tue, (esp. among the scholastics) any moral virtue of which man is capable, esp. the cardinal virtues. Cf. **theological virtue.**

na·ture (nā′chər), *n.* 1. the particular combination of qualities belonging to a person, animal, thing, or class by birth, origin, or constitution. 2. the instincts or inherent tendencies directing conduct. 3. character, kind, or sort: *two recent books of the same nature.* 4. the material world, esp. that part unaffected by man. 5. plants, animals, geographical features, etc., or the places where these exist largely free of human influence. 6. the universe, with all its phenomena. 7. the sum total of the forces at work throughout the universe. 8. the true appearance of anything: *a portrait true to nature.* 9. the biological functions or the urges to satisfy their requirements. 10. the laws and principles believed to be followed naturally and rightly by living beings: *an act that is against nature.* 11. the original, natural, uncivilized condition of man. 12. a primitive, wild condition; an uncultivated state. 13. **by nature,** as a result of inherent qualities; innately. [ME *natur(e)* < L *nātūra* blood-kinship, quality, character, natural order, world = *nāt(us)* born (see NATAL) + *-ūra* -URE]

-natured, a combining form of **nature** used in compound adjectives to indicate a specified character, temperament, etc.: *good-natured.*

na′ture stud′y, the study of the physical world, esp. as a combination of basic botany, zoology, etc., as taught at the primary school level.

na′ture wor′ship, a system of religion based on the deification and worship of natural forces and phenomena. —**na′ture wor′ship·er.**

na·tur·ist (nā′chər ist′), *n.* a person who appreciates the beauty and benefits of nature. —**na′tur·ism′,** *n.*

na·tur·op·a·thy (nā′chə rop′ə thē, nach′ə-), *n.* a method of treating disease, using food, exercise, heat, etc., to assist the natural healing processes. —**na·tur·o·path·ic** (nā′chər ə path′ik, nach′ər-), *adj.*

Nau·cra·tis (nô′krə tis), *n.* an ancient Greek city in N Egypt, on the Nile delta. Greek, **Nau′kra·tis.**

Nau·ga·hyde (nô′gə hīd′), *n. Trademark.* a strong vinyl fabric, used for upholstery, luggage, etc.

naught (nôt), *n.* 1. a cipher (0); zero. 2. nothing. 3.

complete failure: *Her efforts came to naught.* **4. set at naught,** to regard or treat as of no importance. **—***adj.* **5.** *Obs.* morally bad; wicked. Also, **nought.** [ME; OE *nauht, nāwiht.* See NO[1], WIGHT[1], WHIT]

naugh·ty (nô′tē), *adj.*, **-ti·er, -ti·est. 1.** disobedient; mischievous (used esp. in speaking to or about children). **2.** improper; obscene: *a naughty word.* **3.** *Obs.* wicked; evil. [ME] **—naugh′ti·ly,** *adv.* **—naugh′ti·ness,** *n.*

nau·ma·chi·a (nô mā′kē ə), *n., pl.* **-chi·ae** (-kē ē′), **-chi·as. 1.** (in ancient Rome) a mock sea fight. **2.** a place for such a fight. [< L: mock naval battle < Gk: a sea fight = *naû(s)* a ship + *-machia* -MACHY]

nau·ma·chy (nô′mə kē), *n., pl.* **-chies.** naumachia.

nau·pli·us (nô′plē əs), *n., pl.* **-pli·i** (-plē ī′). (in many crustaceans) a larval form with three pairs of appendages and a single median eye, occurring usually as the first stage of development after leaving the egg. [< L: a kind of shellfish, special use of proper name] **—nau′pli·al, nau′pli·oid′,** *adj.*

Na·u·ru (nä o͞o′ro͞o), *n.* **Republic of,** an island republic in the Pacific, near the equator, W of the Gilbert Islands, administered by Australia before 1968. 4613 (1961); 8¼ sq. mi. Formerly, **Pleasant Island. —Na·u′ru·an,** *n.*

nau·se·a (nô′zē ə, -zhə, -sē ə, -shə), *n.* **1.** sickness at the stomach, esp. when accompanied by a loathing for food and an involuntary impulse to vomit. **2.** extreme disgust; loathing; repugnance. [< L, var. of *nausia* < Gk: seasickness < *naûs* ship; see -IA]

nau·se·ant (nô′zē ənt, -zhē-, -sē-, -shē-), *n.* *Med.* an agent for inducing nausea. [< L *nauseant-* (s. of *nauseāns*) being seasick, prp. of *nauseāre*]

nau·se·ate (nô′zē āt′, -zhē-, -sē-, -shē-), *v.,* **-at·ed, -at·ing.** **—***v.t.* **1.** to affect with nausea; sicken. **2.** to cause to feel extreme disgust. **—***v.i.* **3.** to become affected with nausea. [< L *nauseāt(us)* having been seasick (ptp. of *nauseāre*). See NAUSEA, -ATE[1]] **—nau′se·a′tion,** *n.* **—Syn. 2.** revolt. **—Ant. 2.** attract, delight.

nau·se·at·ing (nô′zē ā′ting, -zhē-, -sē-, -shē-), *adj.* **1.** such as to cause contempt, disgust, loathing, etc. **2.** causing extreme physical revulsion or loathing. **—nau′se·at′ing·ly,** *adv.*

nau·seous (nô′shəs, -zē əs), *adj.* **1.** causing nausea; sickening. **2.** *Informal.* ill or affected with nausea. [< L *nauseōsus.* See NAUSEA, -OUS] **—nau′seous·ly,** *adv.* **—nau′seous·ness,** *n.* **—Syn. 1.** revolting, repellent, abhorrent; despicable, offensive. **—Ant. 1.** delightful.

—Usage. 2. Although it is often used in this sense, NAUSEOUS is frowned upon by educated speakers and writers as a substitute for NAUSEATED.

Nau·sic·a·ä (nô sik′ē ə, -ā ə, nou-), *n.* *Class. Myth.* a Phaeacian princess who discovered the shipwrecked Odysseus and directed him to the palace of her father, King Alcinoüs.

naut., nautical.

nautch (nôch), *n.* (in India) an exhibition of dancing by professional dancing girls. [< Urdu *nāch* < Prakrit *nachcha* dancing]

nau·ti·cal (nô′ti kəl), *adj.* of or pertaining to seamen, ships, or navigation: *nautical terms.* [< L *nautic(us)* pertaining to ships or sailors (< Gk *nautikós* = *naû(s)* ship + *-tikos* -TIC) + -AL[1]] **—nau′ti·cal·ly,** *adv.*

nau′tical mile′, mile (def. 2).

nau·ti·lus (nôt′əl əs), *n., pl.* **nau·ti·lus·es, nau·ti·li** (nôt′əl ī′). **1.** Also called **chambered nautilus, pearly nautilus.** any cephalopod of the genus *Nautilus,* having a spiral, chambered shell with pearly septa. **2.** See **paper nautilus.** [< L: lit., sailor < Gk *nautílos.* See NAUTICAL]

Pearly nautilus, *Nautilus macromphalus* (Shell length 8 in.)

nav., **1.** naval. **2.** navigation.

Nav·a·ho (nav′ə hō′, nä′və-), *n., pl.* **-hos, -hoes,** (*esp. collectively*) **-ho** for 1, *adj.* **—***n.* **1.** a member of the principal tribe of the southern division of the Athapaskan stock, located in New Mexico and Arizona. **2.** the Athapaskan language of the Navaho Indians. **—***adj.* **3.** of, pertaining to, or characteristic of the Navaho Indians or their language.

Nav·a·jo (nav′ə hō′, nä′və-), *n., pl.* **-jos, -joes,** (*esp. collectively*) **-jo,** *adj.* Navaho.

na·val (nā′vəl), *adj.* **1.** of or pertaining to warships. **2.** of or pertaining to ships: *naval architecture.* **3.** belonging to, pertaining to, or connected with a navy. **4.** possessing a navy: *the great naval powers.* [< L *nāvāl(is)* = *nāv(is)* ship + *-ālis* -AL[1]] **—na′val·ly,** *adv.*

na′val acad′emy, a collegiate institution for training naval officers.

na′val ar′chitecture, the science of designing ships and other kinds of waterborne craft. **—na′val ar′chitect.**

Nav·a·ri·no (nav′ə rē′nō), *n.* a seaport in the SW Peloponnesus, in SW Greece: Turkish and Egyptian fleets defeated near here in a naval battle 1827. Greek, **Pylos, Pilos.**

Na·varre (nə vär′), *n.* a former kingdom in SW France and N Spain. Spanish, **Na·var·ra** (nä vär′rä). **—Na·var·rese** (nav′ə rēz′, -rēs′, nä′və-), *adj., n.*

nave[1] (nāv), *n.* the principal longitudinal area of a church, extending from the main entrance or narthex to the chancel, usually flanked by aisles of less height and breadth: generally used only by the congregation. [< ML *nāvis,* L: ship; from the resemblance in shape]

nave[2] (nāv), *n.* the central part of a wheel; hub. [ME; OE *nafu;* c. D *naaf,* Icel *nöf,* G *Nabe;* akin to Skt *nābhi* nave, NAVEL]

na·vel (nā′vəl), *n.* **1.** umbilicus (def. 1). **2.** the central point or middle of any thing or place. [ME; OE *nafela;* c. D *navel,* G *Nabel,* Icel *nafli;* akin to Skt *nābhīla,* L *umbilīcus,* Gk *omphalós*]

na′vel or′ange, a variety of orange having at the apex a navellike formation containing a small secondary fruit.

na·vette (na vet′; *Fr.* NA vet′), *n., pl.* **-vettes** (-vets′; *Fr.* -vet′). *Jewelry.* a gem, esp. one not a diamond, cut as a marquise. [< F: weaver's shuttle, lit., little ship]

nav·i·cert (nav′i sûrt′), *n.* a document, issued by a British consular officer in wartime, certifying that a vessel of a neutral country is carrying noncontraband cargo and is not liable to search or seizure by British naval ships. [NAVI(GATION) + CERT(IFICATE)]

na·vic·u·lar (nə vik′yə lər), *Anat.* **—***adj.* **1.** boat-shaped, as certain bones. **—***n.* Also, **na·vic·u·lar·e** (nə vik′yə lâr′ē, -lär′ē). **2.** the bone at the radial end of the proximal row of the bones of the carpus. **3.** the bone in front of the talus, or anklebone, on the inner side of the foot. [< LL *nāviculār(is)* of, relating to shipping = *nāvicul(a)* (*nāvi(s)* ship + *-cula* -CULE) + *-āris* -AR[1]]

navig., navigation.

nav·i·ga·ble (nav′ə gə bəl), *adj.* **1.** (of a body of water) deep and wide enough to afford passage to ships. **2.** capable of being steered or guided, as a vessel, aircraft, or missile. [< L *nāvigābil(is)*] **—nav′i·ga·bil′i·ty, nav′i·ga·ble·ness,** *n.* **—nav′i·ga·bly,** *adv.*

nav′igable sem′icircle, *Naut.* the less violent half of a cyclone; the half blowing in the direction opposite to that in which the cyclone is moving and in which a vessel can run before the wind.

nav·i·gate (nav′ə gāt′), *v.,* **-gat·ed, -gat·ing. —***v.t.* **1.** to traverse (the sea, a river, country, etc.) in a vessel or aircraft. **2.** to direct or manage (a ship, aircraft, or guided missile) on its course. **3.** to ascertain or plot and control the course or position of (a ship, aircraft, etc.). **4.** to pass over or along (a body of water), as a ship does. **5.** *Informal.* to walk in or across safely and soberly. **—***v.i.* **6.** to direct or manage a ship, aircraft, or guided missile on its course. **7.** to pass over the water, as a ship does. **8.** *Informal.* to walk or find one's way safely and soberly. [< L *nāvigāt(us)* sailed, prp. of *nāvigāre* to sail (*nāv(is)* ship + *-igāre,* comb. form of *agere* to drive)]

nav·i·ga·tion (nav′ə gā′shən), *n.* **1.** the act or process of navigating. **2.** the art or science of plotting, ascertaining, or directing the course of a ship or aircraft. [< L *nāvigātiōn-* (s. of *nāvigātiō*) a voyage] **—nav′i·ga′tion·al,** *adj.*

nav·i·ga·tor (nav′ə gā′tər), *n.* **1.** a person who practices, or is skilled in, navigation. **2.** a person who conducts explorations by sea. **3.** *Brit.* a navvy or laborer. [< L: a sailor, mariner]

Nav′igator Is′lands, former name of **Samoa.**

Náv·pak·tos (näf′päk tôs), *n.* Greek name of **Lepanto.**

nav·vy (nav′ē), *n., pl.* **-vies.** *Brit. Informal.* a manual laborer employed in excavating for or building railroads, roads, canals, etc. [short for NAVIGATOR]

na·vy (nā′vē), *n., pl.* **-vies. 1.** the whole body of warships and auxiliaries belonging to a country or ruler. **2.** the department of government charged with their management. **3.** (*often cap.*) the complete body of such warships together with their officers and men, equipment, yards, etc. **4.** Also called **na′vy blue′.** a dark blue. **5.** *Archaic.* a fleet of warships; armada. [ME *navie* < MF < VL **navia* = L *nāv(is)* ship + *-ia* -Y[3]]

na′vy bean′, a small, white bean, dried for prolonged storage and prepared for eating by soaking and cooking. [so called from wide use in U.S. Navy]

Na′vy Cross′, *U.S. Navy.* a decoration awarded for outstanding heroism in operations against an enemy.

na′vy yard′, a government dockyard where naval vessels are built, repaired, and fitted out, and naval supplies and munitions are laid up.

na·wab (nə wôb′), *n.* nabob (def. 1). [< Urdu *nawwāb* < Ar, pl of *nā'ib* deputy, viceroy]

Nax·os (nak′sos, -sōs; *Gk.* nä′ksôs), *n.* a Greek island in the S Aegean: the largest of the Cyclades group. 18,593 (1951); 169 sq. mi.

nay (nā), *adv.* **1.** no (used in dissent, denial, or refusal). **2.** and not only so, but; indeed: *many good, nay, noble qualities.* **—***n.* **3.** a denial or refusal. **4.** a negative vote or voter. [ME *nai, nei* < Scand; cf. Icel *nei* no = *ne* not + *ei* ever; see AY[1]]

na·ya pai·sa (nə yä′ pī sä′), *pl.* **na·ye pai·se** (nə yā′ pī sā′). **1.** a copper coin of India, the 100th part of a rupee; paisa; pice. **2.** the 100th part of a gulf rupee. **3.** the 100th part of the rupee of Oman. [< Hindi: lit., new pice]

Na·ya·rit (nä′yä RĒt′), *n.* a state in W Mexico. 391,970 (1960); 10,442 sq. mi. *Cap.:* Tepic.

Naz·a·rene (naz′ə rēn′, naz′ə rēn′), *n.* **1.** a native or inhabitant of Nazareth. **2.** one of a sect of early Jewish converts to Christianity who retained the Mosaic ritual. **3. the Nazarene,** Jesus Christ. **4.** *Obs.* (among Jews and Muslims) a Christian. **—***adj.* **5.** of or pertaining to Nazareth or the Nazarenes. [< LL *Nazarēn(us)* < Gk *Nazarēnós* < *Nazarét* NAZARETH]

Naz·a·reth (naz′ər əth, -ə rith), *n.* a town in N Israel: the childhood home of Jesus. 26,400 (est. 1963).

Naz·a·rite (naz′ə rīt′), *n.* **1.** (among the ancient Hebrews) a religious devotee who had taken certain strict vows. **2.** *Rare.* Christ. Also, **Naz′i·rite′.** [< LL *Nāzar(aeus)* (< Gk *Nāzeraîos* = *nazēr* (< Heb *nāzīr* consecrated person) + *-aios* suffix) + -ITE[1]] **—Naz·a·rit·ic** (naz′ə rit′ik), **Naz·a·rit·ish** (naz′ə rī′tish), *adj.*

Naze (nāz), *n.* **The,** Lindesnes.

Na·zi (nä′tsē, nat′sē), *n., pl.* **-zis,** *adj.* **—***n.* **1.** a member of the National Socialist German Workers' party, which in 1933, under Adolf Hitler, seized political control of Germany. **2.** (*often l.c.*) a person who holds similar views elsewhere. **—***adj.* **3.** of or pertaining to the Nazis. [< G *Nazi(onalsozialist)* National Socialist] **—Na·zism** (nä′tsiz-əm, nat′siz-, nä′tsē iz′əm, nat′sē-), **Na·zi·ism** (nä′tsē-iz′əm, nat′sē-), *n.*

NB, note well; take notice. [< L *notā bene*]

Nb, *Chem.* niobium.

N.B., 1. New Brunswick. **2.** note well; take notice. [< L *notā bene*]

NBA, 1. National Basketball Association. 2. National Boxing Association.
NbE, See **north by east.**
NBS, National Bureau of Standards. Also, **N.B.S.**
NbW, See **north by west.**
NC, 1. North Carolina (approved esp. for use with zip code). 2. numerical control (used in machine-tool computerization). 3. *Mil.* Nurse Corps.
N.C., North Carolina.
NCAA, National Collegiate Athletic Association. Also, **N.C.A.A.**
nCi, nanocurie; nanocuries. Also, **nc**
N.C.O., Noncommissioned Officer.
ND, North Dakota (approved esp. for use with zip code).
Nd, *Chem.* neodymium.
n.d., no date.
N.Dak., North Dakota. Also, **N.D.**
Nde·be·le (ən′də bē′lē), *n., pl.* **-les,** (*esp. collectively*) **-le.** Matabele.
N'Dja·me·na (ənjä′mə nə), *n.* a city in and the capital of Chad, in the SW part. 192,962. Formerly, **Fort-Lamy.**
Ndo·la (əndō′lə), *n.* a city in N Zambia. 131,600 (est. 1968).
NE, 1. Nebraska (approved esp. for use with zip code). 2. northeast. 3. northeastern. Also, **n.e.** (for defs. 2, 3).
Ne, *Chem.* neon.
ne-, var. of **neo-,** esp. before a vowel: *Nearctic.*
N.E., 1. New England. 2. northeast. 3. northeastern.
N.E.A., National Education Association. Also, **NEA**
Ne·an·der·thal (nē an′dər thôl′, -tôl′, -täl′; nā än′dər täl′), *adj.* 1. *Anthropol.* of or pertaining to Neanderthal man. —*n.* 2. *Anthropol.* See **Neanderthal man.** [after *Neanderthal,* valley in Germany, near Düsseldorf, where evidence of Neanderthal man was first found]
Nean′derthal man′, *Anthropol.* a type of powerfully built Paleolithic man who inhabited Europe and western and central Asia. See illus. at **Pithecanthropus.**
Ne·an·der·thal·oid (nē an′dər thô′loid, -tô′-, -tä′-; nā än′dər tä′loid), *Anthropol.* —*adj.* 1. resembling or characteristic of the physical type of Neanderthal man. —*n.* 2. a fossil man having characteristics like those of Neanderthal man.
neap[1] (nēp), *adj.* 1. designating those tides, midway between spring tides, that attain the least height. —*n.* 2. neap tide. See **tide[1].** [ME *neep,* OE *nēp-,* in *nēpflōd* neap tide]
neap[2] (nēp), *n. Dial.* the tongue of a cart, wagon, etc. [?]
Ne·a·pol·i·tan (nē′ə pol′i tən), *adj.* 1. of, pertaining to, or characteristic of Naples. —*n.* 2. a native or inhabitant of Naples. [< L *Neāpolītān(us)*]
near (nēr), *adv.* 1. at or to a place a relatively short distance away from a specified person or thing, or from oneself: *This hotel is near the terminal. Come nearer, please.* 2. close in time: *Easter draws near.* 3. in or toward a specified state or position: *Every lesson brings me nearer to proficiency.* 4. almost; nearly: *near dead from exhaustion.* 5. *Naut.* close to the wind. —*adj.* 6. being close by; not distant. 7. being relatively closer: *the near side of the road.* 8. having a relatively direct relation or correspondence: *a near translation.* 9. being of one's immediate family, circle of acquaintances, etc. 10. that narrowly misses or avoids: *The fire was a near catastrophe.* 11. with little margin of safety: *a near escape.* 12. (of horses or horse-drawn vehicles) on the left side (opposed to *off*): *the near foreleg.* 13. **near at hand, a.** in the immediate vicinity. **b.** in the near future. —*prep.* 14. at, to, or within a relatively short distance from. 15. close upon in time. 16. close upon a condition or state: *He is near death.* —*v.t., v.i.* 17. to come or draw near; approach. [ME *nere,* OE *nēar,* comp. of *nēah* NIGH] —**near′ness,** *n.*
near′ beer′, a malt beverage that has an alcoholic content of less than ½ percent.
near·by (nēr′bī′), *adj.* 1. close at hand; not far off; adjacent; neighboring. —*adv.* 2. in the near vicinity.
Ne·arc·tic (nē ärk′tik, -är′-), *adj. Zoogeog.* belonging or pertaining to a geographical division comprising temperate and arctic North America and Greenland.
Near′ East′, an indefinite geographical or regional term, usually referring to the countries of SW Asia, the Arab Republic of Egypt, and sometimes the Balkan States. Cf. **Middle East.** —**Near′ East′ern.**
near·ly (nēr′lē), *adv.* 1. all but; almost: *nearly dead with cold.* 2. with close approximation: *a nearly perfect likeness.* 3. with close agreement or resemblance: *a plan nearly like our own.* 4. with close kinship, interest, or connection; closely. 5. *Archaic.* with parsimony; stingily.
near′ rhyme′. See **slant rhyme.**
near·sight·ed (nēr′sī′tid), *adj.* seeing distinctly at a short distance only; myopic. —**near′sight′ed·ly,** *adv.* —**near′sight′ed·ness,** *n.*
near-term (nēr′tûrm′), *adj.* for, covering, or involving the very near future: *the near-term prospects of lower interest rates.*
neat (nēt), *adj.* 1. in a pleasingly orderly condition. 2. orderly in personal appearance or habits. 3. of a simple, pleasing appearance. 4. cleverly effective: *a neat plan.* 5. *Slang.* great; wonderful. 6. (of liquor) unadulterated or undiluted; straight. 7. net: *neat profits.* —*adv.* 8. *Informal.* neatly. [ME *net* spruce, trim, clean < MF < L *nitidus* shining, polished, handsome, spruce = *nit(ēre)* (to) shine + *-idus* -ID[4]] —**neat′ly,** *adv.* —**neat′ness,** *n.* —**Syn. 1, 2.** spruce, smart. —**Ant. 1, 2.** sloppy. 4. maladroit
neat·en (nēt′ən), *v.t.* to make (something) neat.
neath (nēth, nēth), *prep. Dial.* beneath. Also, **'neath.**
neat's′-foot oil′ (nēts′fo͝ot′), a pale-yellow fixed oil made by boiling the feet and shinbones of cattle, used chiefly as a dressing for leather. [*neat* any bovine animal (ME *neet,* OE *nēat;* akin to *nēotan* to use)]
neb (neb), *n.* 1. a bill or beak, as of a bird. 2. *Chiefly Scot.* a person's mouth. 3. the nose, esp. of an animal. 4. the tip or pointed end of anything. 5. the nib of a pen. [ME *nebbe,* OE *nebb;* c. MD, MLG *nebbe,* Icel *nef.* See NIB]
Neb., Nebraska.
neb·bish (neb′ish), *n. Slang.* a drab, insignificant person who is generally ignored. [< Yiddish; ? *neb* (var. of obs. *nib* freshman) + -ISH[1]]
NEbE, See **northeast by east.**
Ne·bi·im (nə bē ēm′; *Eng.* neb′ē ēm′), *n. Hebrew.* the Prophets, being the second of the three Jewish divisions of the Old Testament. Also, **Neviim.** Cf. **Tanach.**
NEbN, See **northeast by north.**
Ne·bo (nē′bō), *n.* **Mount.** See under **Pisgah.**
Nebr., Nebraska.
Ne·bras·ka (nə bras′kə), *n.* a state in the central United States. 1,483,791 (1970); 77,237 sq. mi. *Cap.:* Lincoln. *Abbr.:* NE, Nebr., Neb.
Ne·bras·kan (nə bras′kən), *adj.* 1. of or pertaining to Nebraska. 2. *Geol.* of or pertaining to the Nebraskan. —*n.* 3. a native or inhabitant of Nebraska. 4. *Geol.* the first stage of the glaciation of North America during the Pleistocene.
Neb·u·chad·nez·zar (neb′ə kəd nez′ər, neb′yo͝o-), *n.* a king of Babylonia, 604?–561? B.C., and conqueror of Jerusalem. II Kings 24, 25. Also, **Neb·u·chad·rez·zar** (neb′ə kəd rez′ər, neb′yo͝o-).
neb·u·la (neb′yə lə), *n., pl.* **-lae** (-lī′), **-las.** 1. *Astron.* **a.** a cloudlike, luminous or dark mass composed of gases and small amounts of dust. **b.** Also called **planetary nebula.** a central star surrounded by a gaseous envelope. **c.** Also called **extragalactic nebula.** an exterior galaxy. 2. *Pathol.* **a.** a faint opacity in the cornea. **b.** cloudiness in the urine. [< L: mist, vapor, cloud; akin to Gk *nephélē* cloud, G *Nebel* fog, haze] —**neb′u·lar,** *adj.*
neb′ular hypoth′esis, *Astron.* Laplace's theory, prominent in the 19th century, that the solar system evolved from a mass of nebular matter.
neb·u·lat·ed (neb′yə lā′tid), *adj.* having dim or indistinct markings, as a bird or other animal. [< LL *nebulāt(us)*]
neb·u·lé (neb′yə lā′, -lē′), *adj. Heraldry.* 1. (of a partition line) having deep indentations so as to form a continuous S-curve. 2. (of a charge, as an ordinary) having the border or borders so indented: *a fess nebulé.* Also, **nebuly.** [< MF: lit., clouded]
neb·u·lise (neb′yə līz′), *v.t.,* **-lised, -lis·ing.** *Chiefly Brit.* nebulize. —**neb′u·li·sa′tion,** *n.* —**neb′u·lis′er,** *n.*
neb·u·lize (neb′yə līz′), *v.t.,* **-lized, -liz·ing.** to reduce to fine spray; atomize. —**neb′u·li·za′tion,** *n.* —**neb′u·liz′er,** *n.*
neb·u·lose (neb′yə lōs), *adj.* 1. cloudlike; nebulous. 2. hazy or indistinct; nebulous. 3. having cloudlike markings. [< L *nebulōsus* full of mist, foggy, cloudy]
neb·u·los·i·ty (neb′yə los′i tē), *n., pl.* **-ties.** 1. nebulous or nebular matter. 2. a nebulous form, shape, or mass. 3. the state or condition of being nebulous. [< LL *nebulōsitās*]
neb·u·lous (neb′yə ləs), *adj.* 1. hazy, vague, indistinct, or confused. 2. cloudy or cloudlike. 3. of or resembling a nebula or nebulae; nebular. [< L *nebulōsus* full of mist, foggy, cloudy] —**neb′u·lous·ly,** *adv.* —**neb′u·lous·ness,** *n.*
neb·u·ly (neb′yə lē), *adj.* nebulé.
nec·es·sar·i·ly (nes′i sâr′ə lē, nes′i ser′-), *adv.* 1. by or of necessity: *You don't necessarily have to attend.* 2. as a necessary result: *That conclusion doesn't follow necessarily from the foregoing.* [late ME]
nec·es·sar·y (nes′i ser′ē), *adj., n., pl.* **-sar·ies.** —*adj.* 1. being essential, indispensable, or requisite: *a necessary law.* 2. happening or existing by necessity: *a necessary makeshift.* 3. acting or proceeding from compulsion or necessity; not free; involuntary: *a necessary agent.* 4. *Logic.* **a.** (of a proposition) such that a denial of it involves a self-contradiction. **b.** (of an inference or argument) such that it cannot be false if its supporting premises are true. **c.** (of a condition) such that it must exist if a given event is to occur or a given thing is to exist. Cf. **sufficient** (def. 2). —*n.* 5. something necessary or requisite; necessity. 6. **necessaries,** *Law.* food, clothing, etc., required by a dependent or incompetent. 7. *Chiefly New Eng.* a privy or water closet. [ME *necessarie* < L *necessārius* unavoidable, inevitable, needful = *necess(e)* (neut. indecl. adj.) unavoidable, necessary + *-ārius* -ARY] —**nec′es·sar′i·ness,** *n.*
—**Syn. 1.** required, needed. NECESSARY, INDISPENSABLE, ESSENTIAL, REQUISITE indicate something vital for the fulfillment of a need. NECESSARY applies to that without which a condition cannot be fulfilled or to an inevitable consequence of certain events, conditions, etc.: *Food is necessary to life. Multiplicity is a necessary result of division.* INDISPENSABLE applies to that which cannot be done without or removed from the rest of a unitary condition: *Food is indispensable to living things. He made himself indispensable as a companion.* That which is ESSENTIAL forms a vitally necessary condition of something: *Air is essential to red-blooded animals. It is essential to understand the matter clearly.* REQUISITE applies to what is thought necessary to complete or perfect something: *He had all the requisite qualifications.*
ne·ces·si·tar·i·an (nə ses′i târ′ē ən), *n.* 1. a person who advocates or supports necessitarianism. —*adj.* 2. pertaining to necessitarians or necessitarianism.
ne·ces·si·tar·i·an·ism (nə ses′i târ′ē ə niz′əm), *n.* the doctrine that all events, including acts of the will, are determined by antecedent causes; determinism.
ne·ces·si·tate (nə ses′i tāt′), *v.t.,* **-tat·ed, -tat·ing.** 1. to make necessary or unavoidable. 2. to compel, oblige, or force. [< ML *necessitāt(us)* having been unavoidable, needful, ptp. of *necessitāre*] —**ne·ces′si·ta′tion,** *n.* —**ne·ces′si·ta′tive,** *adj.*
ne·ces·si·tous (nə ses′i təs), *adj.* 1. being in or involving necessity; needy; indigent. 2. being essential or unavoidable. 3. requiring immediate attention; urgent. —**ne·ces′si·tous·ly,** *adv.* —**ne·ces′si·tous·ness,** *n.*
ne·ces·si·ty (nə ses′i tē), *n., pl.* **-ties.** 1. something necessary or indispensable: *the necessities of life.* 2. the fact of being necessary or indispensable; indispensability: *the necessity of adequate housing.* 3. an imperative requirement or need for something: *the necessity for a quick decision.* 4. the state or fact of being necessary or inevitable: *to face the necessity of appearing in court.* 5. an unavoidable need or compulsion to do something: *not by choice but by necessity.* 6. a state of being in difficulty or need; poverty: *a family in dire necessity.* 7. *Philos.* the quality of following inevitably from logical, physical, or moral laws. 8. **of necessity,** as an inevitable result; unavoidably: *That discussion must of neces-*

sity be postponed for a while. [ME *necessite* < L *necessitās* = *necess(e)* needful + *-itās* -ITY]

neck (nek), *n.* **1.** the part of the body of an animal or man that connects the head and the trunk. **2.** the part of a garment encircling, partly covering, or lying closest to the neck; neckline. **3.** the slender part near the top of a bottle, vase, or similar object. **4.** any narrow, connecting, or projecting part suggesting the neck of an animal. **5.** a narrow strip of land, as an isthmus or a cape. **6.** a strait. **7.** the longer and more slender part of a violin or similar stringed instrument, extending from the body to the head. **8.** *Anat.* a constricted part of a bone, organ, or the like. **9.** *Dentistry.* the slightly narrowed region of a tooth between the crown and the root. **10.** *Print.* beard (def. 5). **11.** *Archit.* a cylindrical continuation of the shaft of a column above the lower astragal of the capital, as in the Roman Doric and Tuscan orders. **12.** *Geol.* the solidified lava or igneous rock filling a conduit leading either to a vent of an extinct volcano or to a laccolith. **13. break one's neck,** *Informal.* to make a great effort. **14. neck and neck,** just even or very close; indeterminate as to the outcome. **15. stick one's neck out,** *Slang.* to take a risk; expose oneself to danger or condemnation. **16. win by a neck, a.** to win by a small amount. **b.** *Racing.* to be first by a head and neck; finish closely. **—*v.i.* 17.** *Informal.* (of two persons of opposite sex) to kiss and fondle one another. **—*v.t.* 18.** to kiss and fondle. **19.** to strangle or behead. [ME *nekke,* OE *hnecca,* c. D *nek* nape of neck; akin to G *Nacken,* Icel *hnakki* nape of neck] **—neck′less,** *adj.* **—neck′like′,** *adj.*

Neck·ar (nek′ər; *Ger.* ne′käʀ), *n.* a river in SW Germany, flowing N and NE from the Black Forest, then W to the Rhine River. 246 mi. long.

neck·band (nek′band′), *n.* **1.** a band of cloth at the neck of a garment. **2.** a band, esp. one of ornamental design, worn around the neck. [late ME *nekband*]

neck·cloth (nek′klôth′, -kloth′), *n., pl.* **-cloths** (-klôthz′, -klothz′, -klôths′, -kloths′). *Obs.* cravat (def. 2).

Neck·er (nek′ər; *Fr.* ne keʀ′), *n.* **Jacques** (zhäk), 1732–1804, French financier and statesman, born in Switzerland.

neck·er·chief (nek′ər chif), *n.* a cloth worn around the neck by women or men. [ME]

neck·ing (nek′ing), *n.* **1.** *Informal.* the act of kissing and fondling. **2.** *Archit.* a molding or group of moldings between the projecting part of a capital of a column and the shaft.

neck·lace (nek′lis), *n.* jewelry consisting of a string of stones, beads, jewels, or the like, for wearing around the neck.

neck·line (nek′līn′), *n.* the contour of the neck of a garment, esp. of a woman's garment.

neck·piece (nek′pēs′), *n.* a scarf, esp. one of fur.

neck·tie (nek′tī′), *n.* a decorative band of fabric worn around the neck, under the collar, by men, esp. a four-in-hand. **—neck′tie′less,** *adj.*

neck·wear (nek′wâr′), *n.* articles of dress, as neckties or scarves, to be worn around or at the neck.

necro-, a learned borrowing from Greek used, with the meaning "dead," "corpse," "death," in the formation of compound words: *necrology.* Also, *esp. before a vowel,* **necr-.** [< Gk *nekro-,* comb. form of *nekrós* dead body or person]

ne·crol·a·try (nə krol′ə trē, ne-), *n.* worship of the dead.

ne·crol·o·gy (nə krol′ə jē, ne-), *n., pl.* **-gies. 1.** a notice of death; obituary. **2.** a list of persons who have died within a certain time. **—nec·ro·log·i·cal** (nek′rə loj′i kəl), **nec′ro·log′ic,** *adj.* **—ne·crol′o·gist,** *n.*

nec·ro·man·cy (nek′rə man′sē), *n.* **1.** magic, esp. that practiced by a witch or sorcerer; witchcraft; conjuration. **2.** the alleged art of divination through communication with the dead; the black art. [r. ME *nigromancie* < ML *nigromantīa* for LL *necromantīa* < Gk *nekromanteía;* by folk etym. *nigro-* (comb. form of L *niger* black) was substituted in ML for orig. *necro-*] **—nec′ro·man′cer,** *n.* **—nec′ro·man′tic,** *adj.*

ne·croph·a·gous (nə krof′ə gəs, ne-), *adj.* feeding on carrion. [< Gk *nekrophágos*] **—ne·croph·a·gy** (nə krof′ə jē, ne-), *n.*

nec·ro·phil·i·a (nek′rə fil′ē ə, -fēl′yə), *n. Psychiatry.* an erotic attraction to corpses. Also, **ne·croph·i·lism** (nə krof′ə liz′əm, ne-). [< NL] **—nec·ro·phile** (nek′rə fīl′), *n.* **—nec·ro·phil·i·ac** (nek′rə fil′ē ak′), **nec′ro·phil′ic,** *adj., n.*

nec·ro·pho·bi·a (nek′rə fō′bē ə), *n. Psychiatry.* **1.** an abnormal fear of death. **2.** an abnormal fear of dead bodies. [< NL]

ne·crop·o·lis (nə krop′ə lis, ne-), *n., pl.* **-lis·es.** a cemetery, esp. a large one. [< Gk *nekrópolis* burial place (lit., city of the dead)] **—nec·ro·pol·i·tan** (nek′rə pol′i tᵊn), *adj.*

nec·rop·sy (nek′rop sē), *n., pl.* **-sies.** the examination of a body after death; autopsy. [NECR- + *-opsy* (< Gk *ópsis* sight, viewing; see -OPSIS)]

ne·crose (ne krōs′, nek′rōs), *v.t., v.i.,* **-crosed, -cros·ing.** *Pathol.* to affect or be affected with necrosis. [back formation from NECROSIS]

ne·cro·sis (nə krō′sis, ne-), *n.* **1.** death of a circumscribed piece of tissue or of an organ. **2.** *Plant Pathol.* a diseased condition in plants resulting from the death of the tissue. [< NL < Gk *nékrōsis* a making dead, deadness] **—ne·crot·ic** (nə krot′ik, ne-), *adj.*

nec·ro·tise (nek′rə tīz′), *v.i., v.t.,* **-tised, -tis·ing.** *Chiefly Brit.* necrotize.

nec·ro·tize (nek′rə tīz′), *v.,* **-tized, -tiz·ing. —*v.i.* 1.** to undergo necrosis. **—*v.t.* 2.** to cause necrosis in (a tissue, an organ, etc.). [NECROT(IC) + -IZE]

nec·tar (nek′tər), *n.* **1.** *Bot.* the saccharine secretion of a plant, which attracts the insects or birds that pollinate the flower. **2.** *Class. Myth.* the life-giving drink of the gods. Cf. **ambrosia** (def. 1). **3.** the juice of a fruit, esp. when not diluted, or a blend of fruit juices. **4.** any delicious drink. [< L < Gk *néktar* nectar] **—nec′tar·like′,** *adj.*

nec·tar·ine (nek′tə rēn′, nek′tə rēn′), *n.* a peach having a smooth, downless skin.

nec·tar·ise (nek′tə rīz′), *v.t.,* **-ised, -is·ing.** *Chiefly Brit.* nectarize.

nec·tar·ize (nek′tə rīz′), *v.t.,* **-ized, -iz·ing.** to mix or saturate with nectar; sweeten.

nec·tar·ous (nek′tər əs), *adj.* **1.** of the nature of or resembling nectar. **2.** delicious; sweet. Also, **nec·tar·e·ous** (nek târ′ē əs), **nec·tar′e·an.**

nec·ta·ry (nek′tə rē), *n., pl.* **-ries. 1.** *Bot.* an organ or part that secretes nectar. **2.** *Entomol.* a cornicle (formerly thought to secrete honeydew). [< NL *nectarium*] **—nec′ta·ried,** *adj.*

nee (nā), *adj.* born (placed after the name of a married woman to introduce her maiden name): *Madame de Staël, nee Necker.* Also, **née.** [< F, fem. of *né* (ptp. of *naître* to be born << L *nascī*)]

need (nēd), *n.* **1.** a requirement, necessary duty, or obligation, or a lack of something wanted or deemed necessary. **2.** urgent want, as of something requisite: *He has no need of your charity.* **3.** necessity arising from the circumstances of a case: *There is no need to worry.* **4.** a situation or time of difficulty; exigency: *to help a friend in need; to be a friend in need.* **5.** a condition marked by the lack of something requisite: *the need for leadership.* **6.** destitution; extreme poverty. **7. if need be,** should the necessity arise. **—*v.t.* 8.** to have need of; require: *to need money.* **—*v.i.* 9.** to be under a necessity (used as an auxiliary, always in a question or in a negative statement, and fol. by an infinitive, in certain cases without *to;* in the 3d pers. sing. the form is *need,* not *needs*): *He need not go.* **10.** to be in need or want. **11.** *Archaic.* to be necessary: *There needs no apology.* [ME *nede,* OE *nēd, nīed, nēad,* c. G *Not,* Icel *nauth,* Goth *nauths*] **—need′er,** *n.* **—Syn. 4.** emergency. **6.** neediness, indigence, privation.

need·ful (nēd′fəl), *adj.* **1.** being necessary or required: *needful supplies.* **2.** *Archaic.* needy. **3. the needful,** *Slang.* money, esp. immediately available cash. [ME] **—need′ful·ly,** *adv.* **—need′ful·ness,** *n.*

Need·ham (nē′dəm), *n.* a town in E Massachusetts, near Boston. 29,748 (1970).

need·i·ness (nē′dē nis), *n.* a state of need; indigence.

nee·dle (nēd′ᵊl), *n., v.,* **-dled, -dling. —*n.* 1.** a small, slender, rodlike instrument, usually of polished steel, with a sharp point at one end and an eye or hole for thread at the other, for passing thread through cloth to make stitches in sewing. **2.** any of various similar, usually considerably larger, implements for making stitches, as one for use in knitting or one hooked at the end for use in crocheting. **3.** *Med.* **a.** a slender, pointed, steel instrument used in sewing or piercing tissues, as in suturing. **b.** See **hypodermic needle. 4.** *Informal.* an injection of a drug or medicine; shot. **5.** a small, slender, pointed instrument, usually of polished steel or some other material, used to transmit vibrations, as from a phonograph record. **6.** *Elect.* See **magnetic needle. 7.** a pointed instrument, or stylus, used in various recording instruments and for engraving, etching, etc. **8.** *Bot.* a needle-shaped leaf, as of a conifer: *a pine needle.* **9.** *Zool.* a slender, sharp spicule. **10.** *Chem., Mineral.* a needlelike crystal. **11.** a sharp-pointed mass or pinnacle of rock. **12.** an obelisk, or a tapering, four-sided shaft of stone. **—*v.t.* 13.** to sew or pierce with or as with a needle. **14.** *Informal.* **a.** to prod or goad (someone) to a specified action: *We needled her into going with us.* **b.** to tease, heckle, or annoy. **—*v.i.* 15.** to work with a needle. [ME *nedle,* OE *nǣdl,* c. G *Nadel;* akin to L *nēre* to spin]

nee·dle·craft (nēd′ᵊl kraft′, -kräft′), *n.* needlework. [ME *nedle craft*]

nee·dle·fish (nēd′ᵊl fish′), *n., pl.* (*esp. collectively*) **-fish,** (*esp. referring to two or more kinds or species*) **-fish·es. 1.** any fish of the family *Belonidae,* found in warm seas and coastal fresh waters, having a sharp beak and needlelike teeth. **2.** a pipefish.

nee·dle·point (nēd′ᵊl point′), *n.* **1.** Also, **nee′dle point′.** embroidery upon canvas, usually with uniform spacing of stitches in a pattern. **—*adj.* 2.** Also, **nee′dle-point′.** noting a lace (**nee′dlepoint lace′**) in which a needle works out the design upon parchment or paper.

need·less (nēd′lis), *adj.* unnecessary; not needed or wanted: *a needless waste of food.* [ME *nedles*] **—need′less·ly,** *adv.* **—need′less·ness,** *n.*

nee′dle valve′, *Mach.* a valve with a needlelike part, a fine adjustment, or a small opening, esp. a valve in which the opening is controlled by a needlelike or conical point that fits into a conical seat.

nee·dle·wom·an (nēd′ᵊl wo͝om′ən), *n., pl.* **-wom·en.** a woman who does needlework.

nee·dle·work (nēd′ᵊl wûrk′), *n.* **1.** the art or process of working with a needle, esp. in embroidery or needlepoint. **2.** the product of such art or process. **3.** the occupation or employment of a person skilled in embroidery, needlepoint, etc. Also called **needlecraft.** [ME *nedle werk*]

need·n't (nēd′ᵊnt), contraction of *need not.*

needs (nēdz), *adv. Obs.* of necessity; necessarily (often prec. or fol. by *must*): *It must needs be so. It needs must be.* [ME *nedis,* OE *nēdes,* adv. gen. of *nēd* NEED; see -s[1]]

need·y (nē′dē), *adj.,* **need·i·er, need·i·est.** in a state of need or want; without means of subsistence; extremely poor; destitute. [ME *nedi*] **—need′i·ly,** *adv.*

neep (nēp), *n. Brit. Dial.* a turnip. [ME *nepe,* OE *nǣp,* *nǣp* < L *nāpus* turnip]

ne'er (nâr), *adv. Archaic.* never.

ne'er-do-well (nâr′do͞o wel′), *n.* **1.** an idle, worthless, or ineffectual person; good-for-nothing. **—*adj.* 2.** worthless; ineffectual; good-for-nothing.

ne·far·i·ous (ni fâr′ē əs), *adj.* extremely wicked; iniquitous: *nefarious deeds.* [< L *nefārius* impious, abominable, wicked = *nefās* wickedness (*ne* not + *fās* law, right) + *-ius* -IOUS] **—ne·far′i·ous·ly,** *adv.* **—ne·far′i·ous·ness,** *n.* **—Syn.** heinous, infamous; vile, atrocious. **—Ant.** good.

Nef·er·ti·ti (nef′ər tē′tē), *n.* fl. early 14th century B.C., Egyptian queen: wife of Amenhotep IV. Also, **Nef·re·te·te** (nef′ri tē′tē), **Nofretete.**

neg., **1.** negative. **2.** negatively.

ne·gate (ni gāt′, neg′āt, nē′gāt), *v.,* **-gat·ed, -gat·ing. —*v.t.* 1.** to nullify or invalidate (something). **2.** to deny the existence, evidence, or truth of (something). **—*v.i.* 3.** to deny or nullify: *a pessimism which always negates.* [< L *negāt(us)* denied, refused (ptp. of *negāre*) = *neg-* (var. of *nec* not; see NEGLECT) + *-ā-* v. suffix + *-tus* ptp. suffix] **—ne·ga′tor, ne·gat′er,** *n.*

ne·ga·tion (ni gā′shən), *n.* **1.** the act of denying: *He shook his head in negation of the charge.* **2.** a denial: *a negation of one's former beliefs.* **3.** that which is without existence; nonentity. **4.** the absence or opposite of that which is actual, positive, or affirmative: *Darkness is the negation of light.* **5.** a negative statement, idea, concept, doctrine, etc.;

contradiction, refutation, or rebuttal. [< L *negātiōn-* (s. of *negātiō*) denial] —**ne·ga′tion·al,** *adj.* —**ne·ga′tion·ist,** *n.*

neg·a·tive (neg′ə tiv), *adj., n., v.,* **-tived, -tiv·ing.** —*adj.* **1.** expressing or containing negation or denial: *a negative statement.* **2.** expressing refusal to do something: *He maintained a negative attitude about cooperating.* **3.** refusing consent, as to a proposal: *a negative reply to my request.* **4.** prohibitory, as a command or order. **5.** characterized by the absence of distinguishing or marked qualities or features; lacking positive attributes (opposed to *positive*): *a dull, lifeless, negative character.* **6.** lacking in constructiveness, helpfulness, optimism, cooperativeness, or the like: *a man of negative viewpoint.* **7.** being without rewards, results, or effectiveness; fruitless. **8.** *Math., Physics.* **a.** involving or noting subtraction; minus. **b.** measured or proceeding in the direction opposite to that which is considered as positive. **9.** *Bacteriol.* failing to show a positive result in a test for a specific disease caused by either bacteria or viruses. **10.** *Photog.* noting an image in which the brightness values of the subject are reproduced so that the lightest areas are shown as the darkest. **11.** *Physiol.* responding in a direction away from the stimulus. **12.** *Elect.* of, pertaining to, or characterized by negative electricity. **13.** of, pertaining to, or noting the south pole of a magnet. **14.** *Chem.* (of an element or group) tending to gain electrons and become negatively charged; acid. **15.** *Logic.* (of a proposition) denying the truth of the predicate with regard to the subject. —*n.* **16.** a negative statement, answer, word, gesture, etc. **17.** a refusal of assent. **18.** the negative form of statement (opposed to *affirmative*). **19.** a person or number of persons arguing against a resolution, statement, etc. **20.** a negative quality or characteristic. **21.** *Math.* **a.** a minus sign. **b.** a negative quantity or symbol. **22.** *Photog.* a negative image, as on a film, used chiefly for making positives. **23.** *Archaic.* a veto or right of veto. **24. in the negative,** in expression of refusal or repudiation; no: *The reply, when it finally came, was in the negative.* —*v.t.* **25.** to deny; contradict. **26.** to refute or disprove (something). **27.** to refuse assent or consent to; veto. **28.** to neutralize or counteract. [< L *negātīv(us)* denying (see NEGATE, -IVE), r. ME *negatif* < MF] —**neg′a·tive·ly,** *adv.* —**neg′a·tive·ness, neg′a·tiv′i·ty,** *n.*

neg′ative in′come tax′, a system of welfare or public assistance whereby families or individuals are paid a guaranteed annual income of a predetermined amount: under most plans income earned by the recipients is taxed at a specified rate and a break-even point occurs where the income given by the government is equal to the tax paid out.

neg·a·tiv·ism (neg′ə ti viz′əm), *n.* **1.** *Psychol.* a tendency to resist external commands, suggestions, or expectations, or internal stimuli, as hunger, by doing nothing or something contrary or unrelated to the stimulus. **2.** any negative philosophy, as extreme skepticism. —**neg′a·tiv·ist,** *n.* —**neg′a·tiv·is′tic,** *adj.*

neg·a·tron (neg′ə tron′), *n.* electron (def. 1). [NEGA(TIVE + ELEC)TRON]

Neg·ev (neg′ev), *n.* a partially reclaimed desert region and district in S Israel, bordering on the Sinai Peninsula. 4700 sq. mi. *Cap.:* Beersheba. Also, **Neg′eb.**

ne·glect (ni glekt′), *v.t.* **1.** to pay no attention or too little attention to; disregard or slight. **2.** to be remiss in care for or treatment of: *to neglect one's appearance.* **3.** to omit, as through indifference or carelessness: *to neglect to reply to an invitation.* **4.** to fail to carry out or perform (orders, duties, etc.). **5.** to fail to take or use: *to neglect no precaution.* —*n.* **6.** the fault or an instance of neglecting; disregard; negligence. **7.** the fact or state of being neglected. [< L *neglect(us),* var. of *neclectus* slighted (ptp. of *neg-, neclegere*) = *nec* not + *lec-* (var. of *leg-,* base of *legere* to pick up) + *-tus* ptp. suffix] —**ne·glect′ed·ly,** *adv.* —**ne·glect′ed·ness,** *n.* —**ne·glect′er, ne·glec′tor,** *n.*
—**Syn. 1.** ignore. See **slight. 6, 7.** default, inattention, heedlessness. NEGLECT, NEGLIGENCE, DERELICTION, REMISSNESS imply carelessness, failure, or some important omission in the performance of one's duty, a task, etc. NEGLECT and NEGLIGENCE are occasionally interchangeable, but NEGLECT commonly refers to an instance, NEGLIGENCE to the habit or trait, of failing to attend to or perform what is expected or required: *gross neglect of duty; negligence in handling traffic problems.* DERELICTION implies culpable or reprehensible neglect or failure in the performance of duty: *dereliction in a position of responsibility.* REMISSNESS implies the omission or the careless or indifferent performance of a duty: *Remissness was the sole cause of his tardiness.*

ne·glect·ful (ni glekt′fəl), *adj.* characterized by neglect; disregardful; careless; negligent (often fol. by *of*). —**ne·glect′ful·ly,** *adv.* —**ne·glect′ful·ness,** *n.* —**Syn.** remiss, heedless, thoughtless. —**Ant.** careful, thoughtful.

neg·li·gee (neg′li zhā′, neg′li zhā′), *n.* **1.** a woman's dressing gown or robe, usually with soft, flowing lines. **2.** easy, informal attire. Also, **neg′li·gée′.** [< F *négligé* undress, lit., neglected, ptp. of *négliger* < L *neglig(ere),* var. of *negleg(ere)* (to) NEGLECT]

neg·li·gence (neg′li jəns), *n.* **1.** the state or fact of being negligent; neglect. **2.** an instance of being negligent. **3.** *Law.* the failure to exercise such care as would normally be expected of a reasonable man. —*adj.* **4.** pertaining to or involving a civil action for compensation for damages, injury, or loss arising from another's negligence. [ME; var. of *necligence* < L *neg-, necligentia, -legentia*] —**Syn. 1.** See **neglect.**

neg·li·gent (neg′li jənt), *adj.* **1.** guilty of or characterized by neglect, as of duty. **2.** indifferent, careless, or casual: *a negligent grace that was part of her charm.* [ME; var. of *necligent* < L *neg-, necligent-,* s. of *negligēns,* prp. of *negligere,* var. of *neglegere* to NEGLECT; see -ENT] —**neg′li·gent·ly,** *adv.* —**Syn. 1.** neglectful.

neg·li·gi·ble (neg′li jə bəl), *adj.* being so small or trifling that it may safely be disregarded: *negligible expenses.* [< L *neglig(ere)* slight, not attend|to (see NEGLECT) + -IBLE] —**neg′li·gi·bil′i·ty, neg′li·gi·ble·ness,** *n.* —**neg′li·gi·bly,** *adv.*

ne·go·ti·a·ble (ni gō′shē ə bəl, -shə bəl), *adj.* **1.** (of bills securities, etc.) transferable by delivery, with or without endorsement, according to the circumstances, the title passing to the transferee. **2.** capable of being negotiated. —**ne·go′ti·a·bil′i·ty,** *n.*

ne·go·ti·ant (ni gō′shē ənt), *n.* a person who negotiates; negotiator. [< L *negōtiant-* (s. of *negōtiāns*) trading (adj.), trader (n.), prp. of *negōtiārī*]

ne·go·ti·ate (ni gō′shē āt′), *v.,* **-at·ed, -at·ing.** —*v.i.* **1.** to deal or bargain with another or others. —*v.t.* **2.** to arrange for or bring about by discussion and settlement of terms: *to negotiate a loan.* **3.** to manage; transact; conduct: *He negotiated an important business deal.* **4.** to move through, around, or over in a satisfactory manner. **5.** to dispose of by sale or transfer: *to negotiate securities.* **6.** to transfer (negotiable paper) by assignment or delivery. [< L *negōtiātus* (ptp. of *negōtiārī*) traded] —**ne·go′ti·a′tor,** *n.*

ne·go·ti·a·tion (ni gō′shē ā′shən), *n.* **1.** Often, **negotiations.** mutual discussion aiming at agreement; parley; conference. **2.** the act or process of negotiating. **3.** an instance or the result of negotiating. [< L *negōtiātiōn-* (s. of *negōtiātiō*) a doing of business]

Ne·gress (nē′gris), *n.* *Usually Offensive.* a black woman. [< F *négresse.* See NEGRO, -ESS]

Ne·gril·lo (ni gril′ō), *n., pl.* **-los,** (*esp. collectively*) **-lo.** Pygmy (def. 1a). [< Sp *negrillo,* dim. of *negro* black]

Ne·gri Sem·bi·lan (nā′grē sem bē′län, sem′bē län′, nə grē′), a state in Malaysia, on the SW Malay Peninsula. 481,563; 2580 sq. mi.

Ne·gri·to (ni grē′tō), *n., pl.* **-tos, -toes. 1.** *Anthropol.* any of various dark-skinned, short-statured peoples of the Philippines, the Malay Peninsula, the Andaman Islands, and southern India. **2.** Pygmy (def. 1a). [< Sp *negrito* = *negr(o)* black + *-ito* dim. suffix]

Neg·ri·tude (neg′ri to͞od′, -tyo͞od′), *n.* the historical, cultural, and social background considered common to blacks collectively. [*Negri-* (comb. form of NEGRO) + -TUDE]

Ne·gro (nē′grō), *n., pl.* **-groes,** *adj.* —*n.* **1.** *Anthropol.* one of the major races of mankind, including esp. the indigenous peoples of Africa south of the Sahara, characterized generally by brown to black pigmentation, broad, flat noses, everted lips, and short, thick, curly hair. **2.** a person of Negro ancestry. —*adj.* **3.** of or pertaining to Negroes. [< Sp and Pg *negro* black < L *nigr-,* s. of *niger* black]
—**Usage.** Many people today prefer the term BLACK to NEGRO, esp. in ethnic or cultural contexts.

Ne·gro (nā′grō; *Sp.* ne′gʀô), *n.* **Rí·o** (rē′ō; *Sp.* ʀē′ô), **1.** a river in NW South America, flowing SE from E Colombia through N Brazil into the Amazon. 1400 mi. long. **2.** a river in S Argentina, flowing E from the Andes to the Atlantic. 700 mi. long.

Ne·groid (nē′groid), *adj.* **1.** of, pertaining to, or having the characteristics of the Negro race. —*n.* **2.** a Negro.

Ne·gro·ism (nē′grō iz′əm), *n.* **1.** the doctrine or advocacy of civil rights and civil liberties for blacks equal to those enjoyed by others, esp. whites. **2.** a quality or manner, as a pronunciation, considered characteristic of blacks.

Ne·gro·phile (nē′grə fīl′, -fil), *n.* (*sometimes l.c.*) a Caucasoid or other non-Negro who is esp. sympathetic to blacks and Negroism. Also, **Ne·gro·phil** (nē′grə fil).

Ne·gro·phobe (nē′grə fōb′), *n.* (*sometimes l.c.*) a person who fears or strongly dislikes blacks.

Ne·gro·pho·bi·a (nē′grə fō′bē ə), *n.* (*sometimes l.c.*) fear or strong dislike of blacks.

Neg·ro·pont (neg′rō pont′), *n.* Euboea. Italian, **Ne·gro·pon·te** (ne′gʀô pôn′te).

Ne·gros (nā′grōs; *Sp.* ne′gʀôs), *n.* an island of the central Philippines. 2,307,493; 5043 sq. mi.

ne·gus[1] (nē′gəs), *n., pl.* **-gus·es. 1.** a title of Ethiopian royalty. **2.** (*cap.*) the Emperor of Ethiopia. [< Amharic: king]

ne·gus[2] (nē′gəs), *n.* a beverage made of wine and hot water, with sugar, nutmeg, and lemon. [named after Colonel Francis *Negus* (d. 1732), Englishman who invented it]

Neh., Nehemiah.

Ne·he·mi·ah (nē′ə mī′ə), *n.* **1.** a Hebrew leader of the 5th century B.C. **2.** a book of the Bible bearing his name.

Neh·ru (nā′ro͞o, ne′ro͞o), *n.* **Ja·wa·har·lal** (jə wə hər läl′), 1889–1964, Hindu political leader in India: prime minister of the republic of India 1950–64 (father of Indira Gandhi).

neigh (nā), *v.i.* **1.** to utter the cry of a horse; whinny. —*n.* **2.** the cry of a horse; whinny. [ME *nege(n),* OE *hnǣgan,* c. Icel *hneggja.* See NAG[2]]

neigh·bor (nā′bər), *n.* **1.** a person who lives near another. **2.** a person or thing that is near another. **3.** one's fellow human being; a fellow-man. **4.** a person who shows kindliness or helpfulness toward his fellow-men: *to be a neighbor to someone in distress.* **5.** (used as a term of address, esp. as a friendly greeting to someone whose name one does not know.) —*adj.* **6.** living or situated near another: *one of our neighbor nations.* —*v.t.* **7.** to live or be situated near to; adjoin; border on. **8.** to place or bring near. —*v.i.* **9.** to live or be situated nearby. **10.** to associate on neighborly terms; be friendly. Also, *esp. Brit.,* **neigh′bour.** [ME; OE *neahgebūr, nēahbūr* (*nēah* NIGH + *(ge)būr* farmer]

neigh·bor·hood (nā′bər ho͝od′), *n.* **1.** the region surrounding or near some place or thing; vicinity. **2.** a district or locality, often with reference to its character or inhabitants: *a fashionable neighborhood.* **3.** a number of persons living near one another or in a particular locality: *The whole neighborhood was there.* **4.** nearness; proximity. **5. in the neighborhood of,** *Informal.* approximately; about. Also, *esp. Brit.,* **neigh′bour·hood′.** [late ME *neighborehode*]

neigh·bor·ing (nā′bər ing), *adj.* living or situated near; adjacent. Also, *esp. Brit.,* **neigh′bour·ing.**

neigh·bor·ly (nā′bər lē), *adj.* having or showing qualities befitting a neighbor; friendly. Also, *esp. Brit.,* **neigh′bour·ly.** —**neigh′bor·li·ness;** *esp. Brit.,* **neigh′bour·li·ness,** *n.*

Neis·se (nī′sə), *n.* a river in N Europe, flowing N from NW Czechoslovakia along part of the boundary between East Germany and Poland to the Oder River. 145 mi. long.

nei·ther (nē′thər, nī′-), *conj.* **1.** not either, as of persons or things specified (usually fol. by *nor*): *Neither John nor Betty is at home.* **2.** nor; nor yet; no more: *Bob can't go, and neither can I.* —*adj.* **3.** not either; not the one or the other: *Neither statement is true.* —*pron.* **4.** not either; not one person or the other; not one thing or the other: *Neither of the suggestions will do. Neither is to be trusted.* [ME = *ne* not + EITHER; r. ME *nawther,* OE *nāwther, nāhwæther* (*nā* not + *hwæther* which of two; see WHETHER)]

Nejd (nejd, nād), *n.* one of the two major regions of Saudi Arabia in the E central part: formerly a sultanate of Arabia; inhabited by Wahabis. ab. 3,000,000; ab. 414,000 sq. mi.

nek·ton (nek′ton), *n.* (in a body of water) the aggregate of actively swimming aquatic organisms able to move independently of currents. [< G < Gk *nēktón* swimming, neut. of *nēktós* (verbal of *nḗchein* to swim)] —**nek·ton′ic,** *adj.*

nel·son (nel′sən), *n. Wrestling.* any of four holds, in which pressure is applied to the head, back of the neck, and one arm (**half nelson, quarter nelson, three-quarter nelson**) or both arms (**full nelson**) of an opponent. [special use of name *Nelson*]

Nel·son (nel′sən), *n.* **1. Viscount Horatio,** 1758–1805, British admiral. **2.** a river in central Canada, flowing NE from Lake Winnipeg to Hudson Bay. 400 mi. long.

ne·lum·bo (nə lum′bō), *n., pl.* **-bos.** lotus (def. 3). [< NL < Singhalese *nelumbu*] —**ne·lum′bi·an,** *adj.*

Ne·man (nem′ən; *Russ.* ne′män), *n.* Russian name of **Niemen.**

nemat-, var. of **nemato-** before a vowel or *h: nemathelminth.*

nem·a·thel·minth (nem′ə thel′minth), *n.* any worm of the phylum *Nemathelminthes* (now usually divided into several phyla), including the nematodes and hairworms, having an elongated, unsegmented, cylindrical body.

nemato-, a learned borrowing from Greek, where it meant "thread," used in combination to refer to threadlike things: *nematocyst.* Also, *esp. before a vowel or h,* **nemat-.** [comb. form repr. Gk *nēmat-* (s. of *nēma*) thread, yarn, that which is spun]

nem·a·to·cyst (nem′ə tə sist, ni mat′ə-), *n. Zool.* an organ in coelenterates consisting of a minute capsule containing a thread capable of being ejected and causing a sting, used for protection and for capturing prey. —**nem′a·to·cys′tic,** *adj.*

nem·a·tode (nem′ə tōd′), *n.* **1.** any unsegmented worm of the phylum or class *Nematoda,* having an elongated, cylindrical body; roundworm. —*adj.* **2.** belonging or pertaining to this phylum or class.

Nem·bu·tal (nem′byə tôl′), *n. Pharm., Trademark.* pentobarbital.

Ne·me·a (nē′mē ə), *n.* a valley in SE Greece, in ancient Argolis. —**Ne·me·an** (ni mē′ən, nē′mē-), *adj.*

Neme′an Games′, a festival of ancient Greece, held at Nemea in the second and fourth year of each Olympiad.

Neme′an li′on, *Class. Myth.* a powerful lion strangled by Hercules as one of his labors.

ne·mer·te·an (ni mûr′tē ən), *n.* **1.** any unsegmented, marine worm of the phylum *Nemertea* (*Nemertinea* or *Nemertina*), having a protrusible proboscis; ribbon worm. —*adj.* **2.** belonging or pertaining to any of these worms. [< NL *Nemertea* (< Gk *Nēmertḗ(s)* a Nereid + *-a* neut. pl. ending) + -AN]

nem·e·sis (nem′i sis), *n., pl.* **-ses** (-sēz′) for 2–4. **1.** (*cap.*) *Class. Myth.* the goddess of divine retribution. **2.** an agent or act of retribution or punishment. **3.** that which a person cannot conquer, achieve, etc.: *The performance test proved to be my nemesis.* **4.** an opponent or rival whom a person cannot best. [< L < Gk: lit., a dealing out]

ne·mi·ne con·tra·di·cen·te (ne′mi ne′ kōn′trä di ken′te; *Eng.* nem′ə nē′ kon′trə di sen′tē), *Latin.* no one contradicting; unanimously.

ne·mi·ne dis·sen·ti·en·te (ne′mi ne′ di sen′tē en′te; *Eng.* nem′ə nē′ di sen′shē en′tē), *Latin.* no one dissenting; unanimously.

Ne·mu·nas (nye′mo͝o näs′), *n.* Lithuanian name of **Niemen.**

N. Eng., Northern England.

Nen·ni (nen′nē), *n.* **Pie·tro** (pye′trô), 1891–1980, Italian socialist leader and author.

neo-, **1.** a learned borrowing from Greek meaning "new," "recent," used freely in the formation of compound words: *Neo-Darwinism; neolithic; neoorthodoxy; neophyte.* **2.** *Chem.* a combining form indicating an isomer having a carbon atom attached to four carbon atoms: *neoarsphenamine.* [< Gk *neo-* new, fresh, recent, young (comb. form of *néos*); akin to NEW]

ne·o·ars·phen·a·mine (nē′ō ärs fen′ə mēn′, -fə nam′in), *n. Pharm.* a medicinal powder, $H_2NC_6H_3(OH)As_2C_6H_3$-$(OH)NHCH_2OSNa$, that is less toxic than arsphenamine.

Ne·o·cene (nē′ə sēn′), *Geol.* —*adj.* **1.** noting or pertaining to a division of the Tertiary period including the Pliocene and Miocene epochs. See table at **era.** —*n.* **2.** the Neocene division of the Tertiary period or its associated rock series.

ne·o·clas·sic (nē′ō klas′ik), *adj.* **1.** belonging or pertaining to a revival or adaptation of a classic style, as in art, literature, music, or architecture. **2.** (*usually cap.*) *Fine Arts.* designating a European style of painting and sculpture developed principally from the mid-18th through the mid-19th centuries. **3.** *Archit.* of, pertaining to, or designating Neoclassicism. Also, **ne′o·clas′si·cal, ne′o·clas′sic, ne′o-clas′si·cal.** —**ne′o·clas′si·cist, ne′o-clas′si·cist,** *n.*

Ne·o·clas·si·cism (nē′ō klas′i siz′əm), *n.* **1.** *Archit.* the trend or movement prevailing in the architecture of Europe, America, and various European colonies at various periods during the late 18th and early 19th centuries, characterized by the introduction and widespread use of Greek orders and decorative motifs. **2.** (*often l.c.*) the principles of the neoclassic style in art, literature, etc. **3.** (*sometimes l.c.*) any of various movements based on neoclassic principles in the arts, literature, etc., of the late-17th to mid-19th centuries. Also, **Ne′o-Clas′si·cism, Ne′o-clas′si·cism.**

ne·o·co·lo·ni·al·ism (ne′ō kə lō′nē ə liz′əm), *n.* the policy of a strong nation in seeking political and economic hegemony over an independent nation or extended geographical area without necessarily reducing the subordinate nation or area to the legal status of a colony. —**ne′o·co·lo′ni·al,** *adj.* —**ne′o·co·lo′ni·al·ist,** *n.*

Ne·o-Dar·win·ism (nē′ō där′wi niz′əm), *n. Biol.* the theory of evolution as expounded by later students of Charles Darwin, who hold that natural selection accounts for evolution and deny the inheritance of acquired characters. —**Ne′o-Dar·win′i·an,** *adj., n.* —**Ne′o-Dar′win·ist,** *n.*

ne·o·dym·i·um (nē′ō dim′ē əm), *n. Chem.* a rare-earth, metallic, trivalent element occurring with cerium and other rare-earth metals, and having rose- to violet-colored salts. *Symbol:* Nd; *at. wt.:* 144.24; *at. no.:* 60; *sp. gr.:* 6.9 at 20°C. [< NL; see NEO-, DIDYMIUM]

ne·o·fas·cism (nē′ō fash′iz əm), *n.* **1.** any of various political movements or beliefs inspired by or reminiscent of fascism or Nazism. **2. neo-Fascism,** an Italian political movement that seeks to reestablish Fascism. —**ne′o-fas′cist, ne′o-Fas′cist,** *adj., n.*

Ne·o·gae·a (nē′ə jē′ə), *n.* a biogeographical division comprising the Neotropical region. Also, **Ne′o·ge′a.** [< NL; see NEO-, GAEA] —**Ne′o·gae′an, Ne′o·ge′an,** *adj.*

Ne·o-Im·pres·sion·ism (nē′ō im presh′ə niz′əm), *n. Fine Arts.* Pointillism. Also, **ne′o-impres′sion·ism.** —**Ne′o-Im·pres′sion·ist, ne′o-im·pres′sion·ist,** *n., adj.*

Ne·o-La·marck·ism (nē′ō lə mär′kiz əm), *n. Biol.* Lamarckism as expounded by later biologists who hold especially that some acquired characters of organisms may be transmitted to descendants, but that natural selection also is a factor in evolution. —**Ne′o-La·marck′i·an,** *adj., n.*

Ne·o-Lat·in (nē′ō lat′ən), *n.* **1.** Also called **New Latin.** the Latin that became current, notably in scientific literature, after the Renaissance, c1500. **2.** romance[1] (def. 8). —*adj.* **3.** romance[1] (def. 12). *Abbr.:* NL

ne·o·lith (nē′ə lith), *n.* a neolithic stone implement. [back formation from NEOLITHIC]

Ne·o·lith·ic (nē′ə lith′ik), *adj. Anthropol.* noting or pertaining to the final stage of the Stone Age, characterized by the use of polished stone implements and the beginning of agriculture.

ne·ol·o·gise (nē ol′ə jīz′), *v.i.,* **-gised, -gis·ing.** *Chiefly Brit.* neologize.

ne·ol·o·gism (nē ol′ə jiz′əm), *n.* **1.** a new word, usage, or phrase. **2.** the introduction or use of new words or new senses of words. **3.** a new doctrine, esp. a new interpretation of sacred writings. [< F *néologisme*] —**ne·ol′o·gist,** *n.* —**ne·ol′o·gis′tic, ne·ol′o·gis′ti·cal,** *adj.*

ne·ol·o·gize (nē ol′ə jīz′), *v.i.,* **-gized, -giz·ing. 1.** to make or use new words or create new meanings for words. **2.** to devise or accept new religious doctrines. Also, *esp. Brit.,* **neologise.**

ne·ol·o·gy (nē ol′ə jē), *n., pl.* **-gies.** neologism. [< F *néologie*] —**ne·o·log·i·cal** (nē′ə loj′i kəl), **ne′o·log′ic,** *adj.*

ne·o·my·cin (nē′ō mī′sin), *n. Pharm.* an antibiotic produced by an actinomycete, *Streptomyces fradiae,* administered orally or locally, used chiefly for skin and eye infections and as an intestinal antiseptic in surgery.

ne·on (nē′on), *n.* **1.** *Chem.* a chemically inert gaseous element occurring in small amounts in the earth's atmosphere, used chiefly in orange-red, tubular electrical discharge lamps. *Symbol:* Ne; *at. wt.:* 20.183; *at. no.:* 10; *weight of one liter of the gas at 0°C and at 760 mm pressure:* 0.9002 gr. **2.** a sign, as for advertising, formed from neon lamps. —*adj.* **3.** using or containing the gas neon. **4.** made of or formed by a neon lamp or lamps: *a neon sign.* **5.** *Informal.* of, pertaining to, or characteristic of a tawdry urban district or cheap, gaudy nighttime entertainment. [< NL < Gk *néon* new, recent]

ne·o·nate (nē′ə nāt′), *n.* a newborn child, or one in its first 28 days. [NEO- + L *nāt(us)* born; see NATIVE] —**ne′o·na′tal,** *adj.* —**ne′o·na′tal·ly,** *adv.*

ne·o·na·tol·o·gy (nē′ō nā tol′ə jē), *n.* the branch of medicine that specializes in the care of newborn children, esp. those that are premature. —**ne′o·na·tol′o·gist,** *n.*

ne·o-Na·zi (nē′ō nä′tsē, -nat′sē), *n., pl.* **-zis.** (since 1945) a person who belongs to a political organization whose beliefs are inspired by or reminiscent of Nazism.

ne·o·or·tho·dox·y (nē′ō ôr′thə dok′sē), *n.* a 20th-century movement in Protestant theology reacting against liberal theology and reaffirming certain doctrines of the Reformation. Also, **ne′o-or′tho·dox′y.** —**ne′o·or′tho·dox′, ne′o-or′tho·dox′,** *adj.*

Ne·o·pa·le·o·zo·ic (nē′ō pā′lē ə zō′ik, -pal′ē-), *n. Geol.* the portion of the Paleozoic comprising the Permian, Pennsylvanian, Mississippian, and Devonian periods.

ne·o·phyte (nē′ə fīt′), *n.* **1.** a person newly converted to a belief, as a heathen, heretic, nonbeliever, etc.; proselyte. **2.** *Primitive Church.* a person newly baptized. **3.** *Rom. Cath. Ch.* a novice. **4.** a beginner; tyro. [< LL *neophytus* newly planted < Gk *neóphytos*] —**ne·o·phyt·ic** (nē′ə fit′ik), *adj.* —**ne·o·phyt·ism** (nē′ə fītiz′əm), *n.*

ne·o·plasm (nē′ə plaz′əm), *n. Pathol.* a new growth of different or abnormal tissue; tumor. —**ne·o·plas·tic** (nē′ə-plas′tik), *adj.*

ne·o·plas·ty (nē′ə plas′tē), *n.* the repairing or restoration of a part by plastic surgery.

Ne·o·pla·to·nism (nē′ō plāt′ənniz′əm), *n.* a philosophical system, originated in the 3rd century A.D. by Plotinus, founded chiefly on Platonic doctrine and Oriental mysticism, with later influences from Christianity. It holds that all existence consists of emanations from the One with whom the soul may be reunited. Also, **Ne′o-Pla′to·nism.** —**Ne·o·pla·ton·ic, Ne·o-Pla·ton·ic** (nē′ō plə ton′ik), *adj.* —**Ne′-o·pla′to·nist, Ne′o-Pla′to·nist,** *n.*

ne·o·prene (nē′ə prēn′), *n. Chem.* an oil-resistant synthetic rubber made by polymerizing chloroprene: used chiefly in paints, putties, linings for tanks and chemical apparatus, and in crepe soles for shoes. [NEO- + (CHLORO)PRENE]

Ne·op·tol·e·mus (nē′op tol′ə məs), *n. Class. Myth.* the son of Achilles and slayer of Priam. Also called **Pyrrhus.**

Ne·o-Re·al·ism (nē′ō rē′ə liz′əm), *n.* **1.** any of various movements in literature, motion-picture directing, etc., considered as representing a return to a more realistic style. **2.** *Philos.* See **New Realism.** —**Ne′o-Re′al·ist,** *n., adj.*

Ne·o-Ro·man·ti·cism (nē′ō rō man′ti siz′əm), *n.* any of various movements or styles in literature, motion-picture directing, architecture, etc., considered as representing a return to a more romantic style. Also, **ne′o-Ro·man′ti·cism, Ne′o·ro·man′ti·cism, ne′o·ro·man′ti·cism.**

Ne·o-Scho·las·ti·cism (nē′ō skə las′ti siz′əm), *n. Philos., Theol.* a contemporary application of Scholasticism to modern problems and life. —**Ne′o-Scho·las′tic,** *adj.*

ne·ot·e·ny (nē ot′ənē), *n. Zool.* the capacity or phenomenon of becoming sexually mature in the larval state. [< Gk *neo-* NEO- + *teín(ein)* (to) stretch] —**ne·ot′e·nous,** *adj.*

ne·o·ter·ic (nē′ə ter′ik), *adj.* **1.** modern; new. —*n.* **2.** a modern writer, thinker, etc. [< LL *neōteric(us)* new, modern

< Gk *neōterikós* young, youthful = *neṓter(os)* younger, newer (comp. degree of *néos*) + *-ikos* -IC] —**ne/o·ter/i·cal·ly,** *adv.*

Ne·o·trop·i·cal (nē/ō trop/i kəl), *adj.* *Biogeog.* belonging or pertaining to a geographical division comprising that part of the New World extending from the tropic of Cancer southward.

Ne·o·zo·ic (nē/ə zō/ik), *adj.*, *n.* *Obs.* Cenozoic.

NEP (nep), *n.* New Economic Policy. Also, **Nep, N.E.P.**

Ne·pal (nə pôl/, -päl/, -pal/, nā-), *n.* a constitutional monarchy (since 1951) in the Himalayas between N India and Tibet. 13,000,000; ab. 54,000 sq. mi. *Cap.:* Katmandu.

Nep·a·lese (nep/ə lēz/, -lēs/), *adj.*, *n.*, *pl.* **-lese** for 2. —*adj.* **1.** of or pertaining to Nepal, its inhabitants, or their language. —*n.* **2.** a native or inhabitant of Nepal.

ne·pen·the (ni pen/thē), *n.* **1.** a drug or drink used by the ancients to bring forgetfulness of sorrow or trouble. **2.** anything inducing a pleasurable sensation of forgetfulness [< L *nēpenthe(s)* < Gk *nēpenthés* herb for soothing, n. use of neut. of *nēpenthḗs* sorrowless = *nē-* not + *pénth(os)* sorrow + *-ēs* adj. suffix] —**ne·pen/the·an,** *adj.*

ne·pen·thes (nə pen/thēz), *n.*, *pl.* **-thes.** nepenthe.

Ne·per (nā/pər), *n.* **John.** See **Napier, John.**

Neph·e·le (nef/ə lē), *n.* *Class. Myth.* a woman whom Zeus formed from a cloud as a counterfeit of Hera.

neph·e·line (nef/ə lin), *n.* a feldspathoid mineral, essentially sodium aluminum silicate, $NaAlSiO_4$, occurring in alkali-rich volcanic rocks. Also, **neph·e·lite** (nef/ə līt/). [< F *néphéline* = *néphél-* (< Gk *nephélē* cloud) + *-ine* -INE[2]]

neph·e·lin·ite (nef/ə lə nīt/), *n.* *Petrog.* a fine-grained, dark rock of volcanic origin, essentially a basalt containing nepheline but no feldspar and little or no olivine. —**neph·e·li·nit·ic** (nef/ə lə nit/ik), *adj.*

neph·e·lom·e·ter (nef/ə lom/i tər), *n.* **1.** *Bacteriol.* an apparatus containing a series of barium chloride standards used to determine the number of bacteria in a suspension. **2.** *Physical Chem.* an instrument for studying the density of suspended particles in a liquid by measuring scattered light. [*nephel-* (comb. form repr. Gk *nephélē* cloud; see NEBULA) + -o- + -METER] —**neph·e·lo·met·ric** (nef/ə lə me/trik), **neph/e·lo·met/ri·cal,** *adj.* —**neph/e·lom/e·try,** *n.*

neph·ew (nef/yōō *or, esp. Brit.,* nev/yōō), *n.* **1.** a son of one's brother or sister. **2.** a son of one's husband's or wife's brother or sister. **3.** *Obs.* a direct descendant, esp. a grandson. [ME *neveu* < OF < L *nepōt-* (s. of *nepōs* nephew, grandson); akin to OE *nefa,* Icel *nefi,* D *neef,* G *Neffe*]

nepho-, a learned borrowing from Greek meaning "cloud," used in the formation of compound words: *nephology.* [< Gk *népho(s)* a cloud, mass of clouds; see NEBULA]

neph·o·gram (nef/ə gram/), *n.* a photograph of a cloud or clouds.

neph·o·graph (nef/ə graf/, -gräf/), *n.* an instrument for photographing clouds.

ne·phol·o·gy (ne fol/ə jē), *n.* the branch of meteorology that treats of clouds. —**neph·o·log·i·cal** (nef/ə loj/i kəl), *adj.* —**ne·phol/o·gist,** *n.*

neph·o·scope (nef/ə skōp/), *n.* an instrument for determining the altitude, velocity, and direction of clouds.

nephr-, var. of **nephro-** before a vowel: *nephrectomy.*

ne·phrec·to·my (nə frek/tə mē), *n.*, *pl.* **-mies.** *Surg.* excision of a kidney.

ne·phrid·i·um (nə frid/ē əm), *n.*, *pl.* **-phrid·i·a** (-frid/ē ə). *Zool.* the excretory organ of many invertebrates, consisting of a tubule with an open or closed motile apparatus at its inner end. [< NL] —**ne·phrid/i·al,** *adj.*

neph·rite (nef/rīt), *n.* a mineral, a compact or fibrous variety of actinolite, varying from whitish to dark green: a form of jade. [< G *Nephrit*]

ne·phri·tis (nə frī/tis), *n.* *Pathol.* inflammation of the kidneys, esp. in Bright's disease. [< LL *nephrītis* a disease of the kidneys < Gk] —**ne·phrit·ic** (nə frit/ik), *adj.*

nephro-, a learned borrowing from Greek meaning "kidney," used in the formation of compound words: *nephrotomy.* Also, *esp. before a vowel,* **nephr-.** [comb. form repr. Gk *nephr(ós)* kidney, kidneys]

neph·ron (nef/ron), *n.* *Anat., Zool.* an excretory unit of vertebrate kidneys. [< G; alter. of Gk *nephrós* kidney]

ne·phro·sis (nə frō/sis), *n.* *Pathol.* kidney disease, esp. marked by noninflammatory degeneration of the tubular system. [< NL] —**ne·phrot·ic** (nə frot/ik), *adj.*

ne·phrot·o·my (nə frot/ə mē), *n.*, *pl.* **-mies.** *Surg.* incision into the kidney, as for the removal of a calculus. [< NL *nephrotomia*]

ne plus ul·tra (ne plōōs ōōl/trä; *Eng.* nē plus ul/trə), *Latin.* the highest point; acme.

Ne·pos (nē/pos, nep/os), *n.* **Cornelius,** 99?–24? B.C., Roman biographer and historian.

nep·o·tism (nep/ə tiz/əm), *n.* patronage bestowed or favoritism shown on the basis of family relationship, as in business or politics. [< It *nepotismo.* See NEPHEW, -ISM] —**ne·pot·ic** (nə pot/ik), **nep/o·tis/tic, nep/o·tis/ti·cal,** *adj.* —**nep/o·tist,** *n.*

Nep·tune (nep/tōōn, -tyōōn), *n.* **1.** the ancient Roman god of the sea, identified with the Greek god Poseidon. **2.** the sea or ocean: *Neptune's mighty roar.* **3.** *Astron.* the planet eighth in order from the sun, having a diameter of 39,930 miles, a mean distance from the sun of 2,793,500,000 miles, and a period of revolution of 164.8 years, and having two satellites. **4.** a township in E New Jersey. 27,863 (1970).

Nep·tu·ni·an (nep tōō/nē ən, -tyōō/-), *adj.* **1.** pertaining to Neptune or the sea. **2.** pertaining to the planet Neptune. **3.** (*often l.c.*) *Geol.* formed by the action of water.

nep·tu·ni·um (nep tōō/nē əm, -tyōō/-), *n.* *Chem.* a radioactive transuranic element, not found in nature, produced artificially by the neutron bombardment of U-238. It decays rapidly to plutonium and then to U-235. *Symbol:* Np; *at. no.:* 93; *at. wt.:* 237.

Ner·bud·da (nər bud/ə), *n.* Narbada.

nerd (nûrd), *n.* *Slang.* a dull, foolish, or unattractive person. [?]

Ne·re·id (nēr/ē id), *n.* (*sometimes l.c.*) *Class. Myth.* any of the 50 daughters of Nereus; a sea nymph. [< L *Nērēid-* (s. of *Nērēis*) < Gk, s. of *Nērēís.* See NEREUS, -ID[1]]

Ne·re·us (nēr/ē əs, -ōōs), *n.* *Class. Myth.* a sea god, the father of the Nereids.

Ne·ri (nâr/ē; *It.* ne/rē), *n.* **Saint Philip** (*Filippo Neri*), 1515–95, Italian priest: founder of Congregation of the Oratory.

ne·rit·ic (nə rit/ik), *adj.* of or pertaining to the region of shallow water along a seacoast. [? < L *nērīt(a)* a sea mussel (< Gk *nērítēs* < *Nēreús* NEREUS) + -IC]

Ne·ro (nēr/ō), *n.* (*Lucius Domitius Ahenobarbus*) ("*Nero Claudius Caesar Drusus Germanicus*") A.D. 37–68, emperor of Rome 54–68.

ner/o·li oil/ (ner/ə lē, nēr/-), a brown essential oil derived from the flowers of the orange tree, *Citrus Bigaradia,* used in the manufacture of perfumes. [< It *Neroli,* title of Anne Marie de la Tremoïlle, a 17th-century Italian princess of French birth, said to have discovered it]

Ne·ro·nise (nēr/ō nīz/), *v.t.*, **-nised, -nis·ing.** *Chiefly Brit.* Neronize.

Ne·ro·nize (nēr/ō nīz/), *v.t.*, **-nized, -niz·ing.** **1.** to characterize (a person) as resembling Nero. **2.** to make depraved in the manner of Nero. **3.** to rule over, tyrannize, or oppress in the manner of Nero. [< L *Nērōn-* (s. of NERO) + -IZE]

nerts (nûrts), *interj.* *Slang.* nuts (def. 1). Also, **nertz.** [by alter.]

Ne·ru·da (ne rōō/thä), *n.* **Pa·blo** (pä/vlô), (pen name of *Ricardo Eliezer Neftali Reyes Basoalto*), 1904–73, Chilean poet and diplomat: Nobel prize 1971.

NERVA (nûr/və), nuclear engine for rocket-vehicle application.

Ner·va (nûr/və), *n.* **Marcus Coc·ce·ius** (kok sē/yəs), A.D. 32?–98, emperor of Rome 96–98.

ner·va·tion (nûr vā/shən), *n.* venation. Also, **ner·va·ture** (nûr/və chōōr/, -chər).

nerve (nûrv), *n.*, *v.*, **nerved, nerv·ing.** —*n.* **1.** one or more bundles of fibers forming part of a system that conveys impulses of sensation, motion, etc., between the brain or spinal cord and other parts of the body. **2.** (not in technical use) pulp tissue of a tooth. **3.** a sinew or tendon: *to strain every nerve.* **4.** strength, vigor, or energy. **5.** firmness or courage under trying circumstances. **6. nerves,** nervousness: *an attack of nerves.* **7.** *Informal.* impertinence; audacity: *He had the nerve to say that?* **8.** *Bot.* a vein, as in a leaf. **9.** a line, or one of a system of lines, extending across something. **10. get on one's nerves,** to irritate or provoke one. —*v.t.* **11.** to give strength, vigor, or courage to. [< L *nervus* sinew, tendon; akin to Gk *neûron* (see NEURON); r. ME *nerf* < MF] —**Syn. 4.** power, force. **5.** steadfastness, fortitude, resolution. **11.** strengthen, fortify. —**Ant. 4.** weakness. **11.** weaken.

nerve/ cell/, *Anat., Physiol.* **1.** any of the cells constituting the cellular element of nerve tissue. **2.** one of the essential cells of a nerve center.

nerve/ cen/ter, 1. a group of nerve cells closely connected with one another and acting together in the performance of some function. **2.** a source of authority or information, as of some military or business enterprise; command post; headquarters.

nerve/ fi/ber, *Anat., Physiol.* a process, axon, or dendrite of a nerve cell.

nerve/ gas/, *Chem. Warfare.* any of several poison gases, derived chiefly from phosphoric acid, that weaken or paralyze the nervous system, esp. that part of the system controlling respiration.

nerve/ im/pulse, *Physiol.* a progressive wave of electric and chemical activity along a nerve fiber that stimulates or inhibits the action of a muscle, gland, or other nerve cell.

nerve·less (nûrv/lis), *adj.* **1.** without nerves, or nervousness, as in emergencies; cool, calm, and collected. **2.** lacking strength or vigor; feeble; weak. **3.** lacking firmness or courage; spiritless; cowardly. **4.** *Anat., Bot.* having no nerves. —**nerve/less·ly,** *adv.* —**nerve/less·ness,** *n.*

nerve-rack·ing (nûrv/rak/ing), *adj.* extremely irritating or trying. Also, **nerve/-wrack/ing.**

ner·vine (nûr/vēn, -vīn), *adj.* **1.** of or pertaining to the nerves. **2.** acting on or soothing the nerves. —*n.* **3.** a nervine medicine. [< NL *nervīnus*]

nerv·ing (nûr/ving), *n.* *Vet. Med.* the excision of part of a nerve trunk.

nerv·ous (nûr/vəs), *adj.* **1.** highly excitable; unnaturally or acutely uneasy or apprehensive: *to become nervous under stress.* **2.** of or pertaining to the nerves: *nervous tension.* **3.** having or containing nerves. **4.** affecting the nerves: *nervous diseases.* **5.** suffering from, characterized by, or originating in disordered nerves. **6.** characterized by or attended with acute uneasiness or apprehension: *a nervous moment for us all.* **7.** sinewy or strong. [< L *nervōsus* full of sinews, nervous] —**nerv/ous·ly,** *adv.* —**nerv/ous·ness,** *n.* —**Syn. 1.** fearful, timid. —**Ant. 1.** confident, bold.

nerv/ous break/down, a case of neurasthenia.

nerv/ous prostra/tion, *Pathol.* neurasthenia.

nerv/ous sys/tem, *Anat., Zool.* **1.** the system of nerves and nerve centers in an animal or man, including the brain, spinal cord, nerves, and ganglia. **2.** a particular part of this system. Cf. **autonomic nervous system, central nervous system.**

ner·vure (nûr/vyōōr), *n.* *Bot., Zool.* a vein, as of the wing of an insect. [< F: rib. See NERVE, -URE]

nerv·y (nûr/vē), *adj.*, **nerv·i·er, nerv·i·est. 1.** *Informal.* brashly presumptuous or insolent. **2.** having or showing courage: *the nervy feats of the mountaineers.* **3.** strong; sinewy; vigorous. **4.** *Chiefly Brit.* straining one's patience or forbearance; trying. **5.** nervous; excitable; on edge. —**nerv/i·ly,** *adv.* —**nerv/i·ness,** *n.*

nes·cience (nesh/əns, nesh/ē əns), *n.* **1.** lack of knowledge; ignorance. **2.** agnosticism. [< LL *nescientia* ignorance = *ne-* not + *scientia* knowledge; see SCIENCE] —**nes/cient,** *adj.*

ness (nes), *n.* *Archaic.* a headland; promontory; cape. [< Scand; cf. Icel *nes,* c. OE *næs* headland, akin to NOSE]

-ness, a native English suffix attached to adjectives and participles, forming abstract nouns denoting quality and state (and often, by extension, something exemplifying a quality or state): *darkness; goodness; kindness; obligingness; preparedness.* [ME, OE *-nes, -nis,* c. G *-nis,* Goth *-(n)assus;* suffix orig. *-assus; -n-* by false division in words like *evenness*]

Nes·sel·rode (nes′əl rōd′; *Russ.* nes′sel rô′de), *n.* **Count Karl Rob·ert** (kärl rob′ərt; *Russ.* kärl ro bert′, rô′bert), 1780–1862, Russian diplomat and statesman.
Nes·sel·rode (nes′əl rōd′), *n.* a mixture of preserved fruits, nuts, etc., used as a sauce or in puddings, pies, ice cream, or the like. [said to have been invented by chef of COUNT NESSELRODE]
Nes·sus (nes′əs), *n.* *Class. Myth.* a centaur who, on attempting to seduce Deianira, the wife of Hercules, was killed by Hercules. Before Nessus died, he gave to Deianira the poisoned tunic that ultimately caused Hercules' death.
nest (nest), *n.* **1.** a pocketlike, usually more or less circular structure of twigs, grass, mud, etc., formed by a bird, often high in a tree, as a place in which to lay and incubate its eggs and rear its young. **2.** a place used by insects, fishes, turtles, rabbits, or the like, for similar purposes. **3.** a number of birds or animals inhabiting one such place. **4.** a snug retreat or refuge; resting place. **5.** an assemblage of things lying or set close together or within one another: *a nest of tables.* **6.** a place where something bad is fostered or flourishes: *a robbers' nest.* **7.** the occupants or frequenters of such a place. —*v.t.* **8.** to settle or place (something) in or as if in a nest: *to nest dishes in excelsior.* **9.** to fit or place one within another. —*v.i.* **10.** to build or have a nest. **11.** to settle in or as in a nest. **12.** to fit together or within one another, as boxes, pots and pans, dishes, small tables, or the like. **13.** to search for or collect birds' nests: *to go nesting.* [ME, OE, c. D, G *nest;* akin to L *nīdus* nest, Skt *nīda* lair. Basic meaning: sitting-place; see NETHER, SIT] —**nest′er,** *n.*
n'est-ce pas (nes pä′), *French.* isn't that so?
nest′ egg′, **1.** money saved and held in reserve for emergencies, retirement, etc. **2.** a natural or artificial egg left in a nest to induce a hen to continue laying eggs there.
nes·tle (nes′əl), *v.,* **-tled, -tling.** —*v.i.* **1.** to lie close and snug, like a bird in a nest; snuggle or cuddle. **2.** to lie or be located in a sheltered spot; be naturally or pleasantly situated. **3.** *Archaic.* **a.** to make or have a nest. **b.** to make one's home; settle in a home. —*v.t.* **4.** to provide with or settle in a nest, as a bird. **5.** to settle snugly. **6.** to put or press confidingly or affectionately: *She nestled her head on his shoulder.* [ME *nestle(n),* OE *nestlian,* c. D *nestelen*] —**nes′tler,** *n.*
nest·ling (nest′ling, nes′ling), *n.* **1.** a young bird not yet old enough to leave the nest. **2.** a young child. [ME]
Nes·tor (nes′tər), *n.* *Class. Myth.* the wisest and oldest of the Greeks in the Trojan War.
Nes·to·ri·an (ne stôr′ē ən, -stōr′-), *n.* one of a sect of Christians, followers of Nestorius, who denied the hypostatic union and were represented as maintaining the existence of two distinct persons in Christ. [< LL *Nestoriān(us)*] —**Nes·to′ri·an·ism,** *n.*
Nes·to·ri·us (ne stôr′ē əs, -stōr′-), *n.* died A.D. 451?, Syrian ecclesiastic: patriarch of Constantinople 428–431.
net[1] (net), *n., v.,* **net·ted, net·ting.** —*n.* **1.** a lacelike fabric with a uniform mesh of cotton, silk, rayon, nylon, etc., often forming the foundation of any of various laces. **2.** a piece of meshed fabric designed to serve a specific purpose, as to divide a court in racket games or protect against insects. **3.** a bag or other contrivance of strong thread or cord worked into an open, meshed fabric, for catching fish, birds, or other animals: *a butterfly net.* **4.** anything serving to catch or ensnare: *a police net to trap the bank robber.* **5.** any network or reticulated system of filaments, veins, etc. —*v.t.* **6.** to cover, screen, or enclose with a net or netting. **7.** to take with a net: *to net fish.* **8.** to catch or ensnare. **9.** (in tennis, badminton, etc.) to hit (the ball) into the net. [ME *net(te),* OE *net(t),* c. D, Icel *net,* Goth *nati,* G *Netz*] —**net′ta·ble,** *adj.*
net[2] (net), *adj., n., v.,* **net·ted, net·ting.** —*adj.* **1.** remaining after deductions, as for charges, expenses, etc. (opposed to *gross*): *net income.* **2.** (of weight) after deduction of tare, tret, or both. **3.** final; totally conclusive: *the net result.* —*n.* **4.** net income, profit, or the like. —*v.t.* **5.** to gain or produce as clear profit. [var. of NEAT] —**net′ta·ble,** *adj.*
Neth., Netherlands.
neth·er (neth′ər), *adj.* **1.** lying, or believed to lie, beneath the earth's surface; infernal: *the nether regions.* **2.** lower or under: *his nether lip.* [ME *nethere,* OE *neothera, nithera* < *nither* down (c. G *nieder*), lit., further down = *ni-* down + *-ther* comp. suffix] —**neth′er·ward,** *adj.*
Neth·er·lands, the (neth′ər ləndz), (*construed as sing. or pl.*) a kingdom in W Europe, bordering on the North Sea, West Germany, and Belgium. 13,733,578; 13,433 sq. mi. *Capitals:* Amsterdam *and* The Hague. Also called **Holland.** —**Neth·er·land·er** (neth′ər lan′dər), *n.* —**Neth′er·land′i·an, Neth′er·land′ic,** *adj.*
Neth′erlands Antil′les, a Netherlands overseas territory in the Caribbean Sea, N and NE of Venezuela; includes the islands of Aruba, Bonaire, Curaçao, Saba, and St. Eustatius and the S part of St. Martin: considered an integral part of the Dutch realm. 234,374; 366 sq. mi. *Cap.:* Willemstad. Also called **Curaçao.** Formerly, **Neth′erlands West′ In′dies, Dutch West Indies.**
Neth′erlands East′ In′dies, a former name of the Republic of Indonesia.
Neth′erlands Guian′a, Surinam.
Neth′erlands New′ Guin′ea, a former name of West Irian.
Neth′erlands Ti′mor, former name of Indonesian Timor.
neth·er·most (neth′ər mōst′, -məst), *adj.* lowest.
neth′er world′, **1.** the infernal regions; hell. **2.** the afterworld, or hereafter.
Né·thou (*Fr.* nā to͞o′), *n.* **Pic de** (*Fr.* pēk də), a mountain in NE Spain: highest peak of the Pyrenees. 11,165 ft.
net′ na′tional prod′uct, the gross national product less allowance for depreciation of capital goods. *Abbr.:* NNP Cf. **national income.**
net′ prof′it, the actual profit made on a business transaction, sale, etc., or during a specific period of business activity, after deducting all costs from gross receipts.
ne·tsu·ke (net′skē, -skā; *Jap.* ne′tso͞o ke′), *n.* (on Japanese clothing) a small figure of ivory, wood, metal, or ceramic, originally used as a buttonlike fixture on a man's sash, from which small personal belongings were hung. [< Jap]
net·ting (net′ing), *n.* any of various kinds of net fabric.
net·tle (net′əl), *n., v.,* **-tled, -tling.** —*n.* **1.** any herb of the genus *Urtica,* covered with stinging hairs. **2.** any of various similar plants. —*v.t.* **3.** to irritate or provoke. [ME; OE *netele,* c. D *netel,* Norw *netla,* G *Nessel*] —**net′tly,** *adj.*
net′tle cell′, *Zool.* a nematocyst.
net′tle rash′, *Pathol.* urticaria resulting from contact with various plants causing local irritation.
net·tle·some (net′əl səm), *adj.* **1.** causing irritation or annoyance. **2.** easily provoked or annoyed.
net′ ton′. See **short ton.**
net′ ton′nage, the taxable gross tonnage of a merchant ship.
net·work (net′wûrk′), *n.* **1.** any netlike combination of filaments, lines, veins, passages, or the like. **2.** a system of interrelated buildings, offices, stations, etc., esp. over a large area. **3.** a netting or net. **4.** *Radio, Television.* a group of transmitting stations linked by wire or microwave relay so that the same program can be broadcast or telecast by all. **5.** any widespread, highly organized system or activity: *a crime network.* **6.** a system of computer terminals interconnected with one or more computers.
net·work·ing (net′wûr′king), *n.* **1.** a supportive system of sharing information and services among individuals and groups having a common interest: *Working mothers in the community use networking to help themselves manage successfully.* **2.** the design, establishment, or utilization of a computer network.
Neu·châ·tel (*Fr.* nœ shä tel′), *n.* **1.** a city on the Lake of Neuchâtel. 33,430 (1960). **2. Lake of,** a lake in W Switzerland. 85 sq. mi. German, **Neu·en·burg** (noi′ən bo͝ork′).
Neuf·châ·tel (no͞o′shə tel′, no͞o′shə tel′; *Fr.* nœ shä tel′), *n.* a soft, white cheese similar to cream cheese, made from skimmed milk. Also called **Neuf′châtel cheese′.**
Neuil·ly (nœ yē′), *n.* a suburb of Paris, in N France: treaty of peace between the Allies and Bulgaria 1919. 73,315 (1962). Also called **Neuil·ly-sur-Seine** (nœ yē syr sen′).
neume (no͞om, nyo͞om), *n.* **1.** any of various symbols used to indicate relative pitch in the music of the early Middle Ages. **2.** any of various symbols employed in the notation of Gregorian chant. [late ME < ML *neuma* < Gk *pneûma* breath] —**neu·mat·ic** (no͞o mat′ik, nyo͞o-), **neu′mic,** *adj.*

Neumes (def. 2)

neur-, var. of **neuro-** before a vowel: *neuritis.*
neu·ral (no͝or′əl, nyo͝or′-), *adj.* of or pertaining to a nerve or the nervous system. —**neu′ral·ly,** *adv.*
neu·ral·gia (no͝o ral′jə, nyo͝o-), *n.* *Pathol.* sharp and paroxysmal pain along the course of a nerve. —**neu·ral′gic,** *adj.*
neu·ras·the·ni·a (no͝or′əs thē′nē ə, nyo͝or′-), *n.* *Pathol.* nervous debility and exhaustion, as from overwork or prolonged mental strain; nervous prostration; nervous breakdown. —**neu·ras·then·ic** (no͝or′əs then′ik, nyo͝or′-), *adj., n.* —**neu′ras·then′i·cal·ly,** *adv.*
neu·rec·to·my (no͝o rek′tə mē, nyo͝o-), *n., pl.* **-mies.** *Surg.* the removal of part or all of a nerve.
neu·ri·lem·ma (no͝or′ə lem′ə, nyo͝or′-), *n.* *Anat.* the delicate, membranous sheath of a nerve fiber. [alter. of F *névrilème* (< Gk *neur-* NEUR- + *eilēma* covering), by assoc. with LEMMA[2]] —**neu′ri·lem′mal,** *adj.*
neu·ri·tis (no͝o rī′tis, nyo͝o-), *n.* *Pathol.* **1.** inflammation of a nerve. **2.** continuous pain in a nerve, associated with paralysis and sensory disturbances. —**neu·rit·ic** (no͝o rit′ik, nyo͝o-), *adj.*
neuro-, a learned borrowing from Greek used, with the meaning "nerve," "sinew," "tendon," in the formation of compound words: *neurology.* Also, *esp. before a vowel,* **neur-.** [< Gk *neuro-,* comb. form of *neûron,* akin to L *nervus*]
neu·ro·blast (no͝or′ə blast′, nyo͝or′-), *n.* *Embryol.* one of the cells in the embryonic brain and spinal cord of vertebrates that develop into nerve cells. —**neu′ro·blas′tic,** *adj.*
neu·ro·coele (no͝or′ə sēl′, nyo͝or′-), *n.* *Embryol.* the system of cavities of the embryonic brain and spinal cord.
neu·ro·gen·ic (no͝or′ə jen′ik, nyo͝or′-), *adj.* *Med.* originating in a nerve or nerve tissue.
neu·rog·li·a (no͝o rog′lē ə, nyo͝o-), *n.* *Anat.* the delicate connective tissue that supports and binds together the essential elements of nerve tissue in the central nervous system. [NEURO- + LGk *glía* glue] —**neu·rog′li·al, neu·rog·li·ac** (no͝o rog′lē ak′, nyo͝o-), **neu·rog′li·ar, neu·rog′lic,** *adj.*
neu·ro·hu·mor (no͝or′ō hyo͞o′mər, -yo͞o-, nyo͝or′-), *n.* a substance produced by a neuron that activates neighboring nerve or muscle tissue.
neu·rol·o·gist (no͝o rol′ə jist, nyo͝o-), *n.* a physician specializing in neurology.
neu·rol·o·gy (no͝o rol′ə jē, nyo͝o-), *n.* the science of the nerves and the nervous system, esp. of the diseases affecting them. [< NL *neurologia*] —**neu·ro·log·i·cal** (no͝or′ə loj′i kəl, nyo͝or′-), *adj.*
neu·ro·ma (no͝o rō′mə, nyo͝o-), *n., pl.* **-mas, -ma·ta** (-mə tə). *Pathol.* a tumor formed of nerve tissue. [< NL] —**neu·rom·a·tous** (no͝o rom′ə təs, nyo͝o-), *adj.*
neu·ro·mus·cu·lar (no͝or′ə mus′kyə lər, nyo͝or′-), *adj.* pertaining to or affecting both nerves and muscles.
neu·ron (no͝or′on, nyo͝or′-), *n.* *Anat.* a nerve cell with its processes, constituting the structural and functional unit of nerve tissue. Also, **neu·rone** (no͝or′ōn, nyo͝or′-). [< Gk *neûron* sinew, cord, nerve] —**neu·ron·ic** (no͝o ron′ik, nyo͝o-), *adj.*

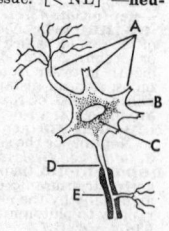

A B C D E

Neuron
A, Dendrites;
B, Cell body;
C, Nucleus; D, Axon;
E, Myelin sheath

neu·ro·path (no͝or′ə path′, nyo͝or′-), *n.* *Psychiatry.* a person subject to or affected with a functional nervous disease; a neurotic person.
neu·ro·pa·thol·o·gy (no͝or′ō pə thol′ə jē, nyo͝or′-), *n.* the pathology of the nervous system. —**neu′ro·pa·thol′o·gist,** *n.*
neu·rop·a·thy (no͝o rop′ə thē, nyo͝o-), *n.* any diseased condition of the nervous system. —**neu·ro·path·ic** (no͝or′ə path′ik, nyo͝or′-), *adj.* —**neu′ro·path′i·cal·ly,** *adv.*
neu·ro·phys·i·ol·o·gy (no͝or′ə fiz′ē ol′ə jē, nyo͝or′-), *n.* the branch of physiology dealing with the nervous sys-

tem. —**neu·ro·phys·i·o·log·i·cal** (no͝or′ō fiz′ē ə loj′i kəl, nyo͝or′-), **neu′ro·phys′i·o·log′ic,** *adj.* —**neu′ro·phys′i·o·log′i·cal·ly,** *adv.* —**neu′ro·phys′i·ol′o·gist,** *n.*

neu·ro·psy·chi·a·try (no͝or′ō sī kī′ə trē, nyo͝or′-), *n.* the branch of medicine dealing with diseases involving the mind and nervous system. —**neu·ro·psy·chi·at·ric** (no͝or′ō sī′kē a′trik, nyo͝or′-), *adj.* —**neu′ro·psy·chi′a·trist,** *n.*

neu·ro·psy·cho·sis (no͝or′ō sī kō′sis, nyo͝or′-), *n.* *Pathol.* mental derangement in association with nervous disease. —**neu·ro·psy·chot·ic** (no͝or′ō sī kot′ik, nyo͝or′-), *adj.*

neu·rop·ter·ous (no͝o rop′tər əs, nyo͝o-), *adj.* *Entomol.* belonging or pertaining to the *Neuroptera*, an order of insects characterized by four membranous wings having netlike venation, including the antlions and lacewings. [< NL *Neuropter(a)* + -OUS] —**neu·rop′ter·on,** *n.*

neu·ro·sis (no͝o rō′sis, nyo͝o-), *n.*, *pl.* **-ses** (-sēz). psychoneurosis.

neu·ro·sur·ger·y (no͝or′ō sûr′jə rē, nyo͝or′-), *n.* the branch of medicine dealing with the surgery of the brain and nerve tissue. —**neu·ro·sur·geon** (no͝or′ō sûr′jən, nyo͝or′-), *n.* —**neu′ro·sur′gi·cal,** *adj.*

neu·rot·ic (no͝o rot′ik, nyo͝o-), *adj.* **1.** having a psychoneurosis. **2.** *Pathol.* pertaining to the nerves or to nerve disease. —*n.* **3.** a person affected with psychoneurosis. [NEURO(SIS) + -TIC] —**neu·rot′i·cal·ly,** *adv.*

neu·rot·o·my (no͝o rot′ə mē, nyo͝o-), *n.*, *pl.* **-mies.** *Surg.* the cutting of a nerve, as to relieve neuralgia. —**neu·ro·tom·i·cal** (no͝or′ə tom′i kəl, nyo͝or′-), *adj.* —**neu·rot′o·mist,** *n.*

neu·ro·vas·cu·lar (no͝or′ə vas′kyə lər, nyo͝or′-), *adj.* of, pertaining to, or involving nerves and blood vessels.

Neus·tri·a (no͞o′strē ə, nyo͞o′-), *n.* the western Frankish kingdom, corresponding roughly to north and northwest France. Cf. **Austrasia.** —**Neus′tri·an,** *adj.*

neut., neuter.

neu·ter (no͞o′tər, nyo͞o′-), *adj.* **1.** *Gram.* **a.** noting or pertaining to the gender containing words not classed as masculine, feminine, or common. **b.** (of a verb) intransitive. **2.** having no organs of reproduction; without sex; asexual. **3.** *Zool.* having imperfectly developed sexual organs, as the worker bees and ants. **4.** siding with no one, neutral. —*n.* **5.** *Gram.* **a.** the neuter gender. **b.** a noun or other element in that gender. **c.** an intransitive verb. **6.** an animal made sterile by castration. **7.** *Zool.* a neuter insect. **8.** a person who is neutral. **9.** *Bot., Zool.* a plant with neither stamens nor pistils. —*v.t.* **10.** to spay or castrate (as a dog or cat). [< L *neuter* neither (of two) = *ne* not + *uter* either (of two); r. ME *neutre* < MF]

neu·tral (no͞o′trəl, nyo͞o′-), *adj.* **1.** (of a person or government) not taking part or giving assistance in a dispute or war between others. **2.** of no particular kind, characteristics, etc.; indefinite: *a neutral personality.* **3.** (of a color or shade) **a.** gray; without hue; of zero chroma; achromatic. **b.** matching well with many or most other colors or shades, as white or a pastel. **4.** *Bot., Zool.* neuter. **5.** *Chem.* exhibiting neither acid nor alkaline qualities: *neutral salts.* **6.** *Elect., Magnetism.* neither positive nor negative; not electrified; not magnetized. —*n.* **7.** a person or state that remains neutral. **8.** a citizen of a neutral nation during a war. **9.** *Mach.* the position or state of disengaged interconnecting parts, as gears: *in neutral.* [< L *neutrāl(is)* neuter] —**neu′tral·ly,** *adv.*

neu′tral acrifla′vine, *Chem.* acriflavine.

neu·tral·ise (no͞o′trə līz′, nyo͞o′-), *v.t., v.i.,* **-ised, -is·ing.** *Chiefly Brit.* neutralize.

neu·tral·ism (no͞o′trə liz′əm, nyo͞o′-), *n.* the policy or practice of maintaining strict neutrality in foreign affairs. —**neu′tral·ist,** *n.*

neu·tral·i·ty (no͞o tral′i tē, nyo͞o-), *n.* **1.** the state of being neutral. **2.** the policy or status of a nation that does not participate in a war between other nations. **3.** neutral status.

neu·tral·ize (no͞o′trə līz′, nyo͞o′-), *v.*, **-ized, -iz·ing.** —*v.t.* **1.** to make neutral. **2.** to make (something) ineffective; counteract; nullify. **3.** *Mil.* to put out of action or make incapable of action. **4.** to declare neutral; invest with neutrality. **5.** *Chem.* to add acid to an alkaline solution or an alkali to an acid solution until neutral. **6.** *Elect.* to render electrically or magnetically neutral. —*v.i.* **7.** to become neutral or neutralized; undergo neutralization. Also, *esp. Brit.,* **neutralise.** —**neu·tral·i·za·tion** (no͞o′trə li zā′shən, nyo͞o′- or, *esp. Brit.,* -lī-), *n.* —**neu′tral·iz′er,** *n.*

neu′tral spir′its, nonflavored alcohol of 95 percent, or 190 proof, used for blending with straight whiskies and in the making of gin, cordials, liqueurs, and the like.

neu′tral zone′, an area of land set aside, as by a treaty, to separate two hostile nations.

neu·tri·no (no͞o trē′nō, nyo͞o-), *n.*, *pl.* **-nos.** *Physics.* an elementary particle having zero rest mass and charge and spin of ½, emitted with electrons and positrons in certain radioactive-decay processes. [NEUTR(ON) + It *-ino* adj. suffix]

neutro-, a combining form meaning "neutral": *neutrosphere.* [< LL < L *neutr-.* See NEUTER, -O-]

neu·tron (no͞o′tron, nyo͞o′-), *n.* *Physics.* an elementary particle having no charge, mass slightly greater than that of a proton, and spin of ½: a constituent of the nuclei of all atoms except those of hydrogen. *Symbol:* n [NEUTR(O)- + -ON[1]]

neu′tron bomb′, a nuclear bomb releasing a shower of life-destroying neutrons but having relatively little blast and contamination, so that the target area may be occupied and used shortly after the detonation of the bomb.

neu·tro·phil (no͞o′trə fil, nyo͞o′-), *adj.* **1.** (of a cell or cell part) having an affinity for neutral dyes. —*n.* **2.** *Anat.* a phagocytic leukocyte having a lobulate nucleus and neutrophil granules in the cytoplasm. Also, **neu·tro·phile** (no͞o′trə fīl′, nyo͞o′-).

Nev., Nevada.

Ne·va (nē′və; *Russ.* ni vä′), *n.* a river in the NW Soviet Union in Europe, flowing from Lake Ladoga through Leningrad into the Gulf of Finland: canalized for ships. 40 mi. long.

Ne·va·da (nə vad′ə, -vä′də), *n.* a state in the W United States. 488,738 (1970); 110,540 sq. mi. *Cap.:* Carson City. *Abbr.:* Nev., NV —**Ne·va′dan,** *adj., n.*

Ne·va·do del Ru·iz (ne vä′thô del ro͞o ēs′), a volcano in W central Colombia, in the Andes: major eruptions 1985. 17,720 ft.

né·vé (nā vā′), *n.* **1.** granular snow accumulated on high mountains and subsequently compacted into glacial ice. **2.** a field of such snow. Also called **firn.** [< F, alter. of SwissF *nevé* < LL **nivātum*, n. use of neut. of L *nivātus* snow-cooled = *niv-* (s. of *nix* snow) + *-ātus* -ATE[1]]

nev·er (nev′ər), *adv.* **1.** not ever; at no time: *Such an idea never occurred to me.* **2.** not at all; absolutely not: *Go back there again? Never!* **3.** to no extent or degree: *He was never the wiser for his experience.* [ME; OE *nǣfre* = *ne* not + *ǣfre* EVER]

nev·er·mind (nev′ər mīnd′, nev′ər mīnd′), *n.* *Dial.* attention; heed; notice (usually used in negative constructions): *Pay him no nevermind.*

nev·er·more (nev′ər mōr′, -môr′), *adv.* never again: *And nevermore were the elves seen in that town.* [ME]

nev·er-nev·er (nev′ər nev′ər), *n.* **1.** Also called **nev′er-nev′er land′.** an unreal, imaginary, or ideal state, condition, place, etc. **2.** *Brit. Slang.* See **hire-purchase system.** —*adj.* **3.** not real or true; imaginary; illusory.

Ne·vers (nə ver′), *n.* a city in central France, on the Loire River: Romanesque church. 41,051 (1962).

nev·er·the·less (nev′ər t͟hə les′), *adv.* nonetheless; notwithstanding; however; in spite of that. [ME] —**Syn.** See **but**[1].

Ne·vi·im (nə vē ēm′), *n.* *Hebrew.* Nebiim.

Nev·ille (nev′il), *n.* **Richard.** See **Warwick, Earl of.**

Ne·vis (nē′vis, nev′is), *n.* **1.** one of the Leeward Islands, in the E West Indies: a member of the West Indies Associated States; formerly a British colony. 12,761 (1960); 50 sq. mi. Cf. **St. Kitts-Nevis-Anguilla.** **2. Ben.** See **Ben Nevis.**

ne·vus (nē′vəs), *n.*, *pl.* **-vi** (-vī). *Med.* any congenital anomaly of the skin, including various types of birthmarks and all types of moles. Also, **naevus.** [sp. var. of L *naevus:* mole[1]] —**ne·void** (nē′void), *adj.*

new (no͞o, nyo͞o), *adj.* **1.** of recent origin, production, purchase, etc.; having but lately come or been brought into being: *a new book.* **2.** of a kind now existing or appearing for the first time; novel: *a new concept of the universe.* **3.** having but lately or but now become known: *a new chemical element.* **4.** unfamiliar or strange (often fol. by *to*): *ideas new to us.* **5.** having but lately come to a place, position, status, etc.: *a reception for our new minister.* **6.** unaccustomed (usually fol. by *to*): *men new to such work.* **7.** coming or occurring afresh; further; additional: *new gains.* **8.** fresh or unused: *to start a new sheet of paper.* **9.** (of physical or moral qualities) different and better: *The vacation made a new man of him.* **10.** other than the former or the old: *a new era.* **11.** being the later or latest of two or more things of the same kind: *a new edition.* **12.** (*cap.*) (of an ancient language) of the form in use at the present time: *New High German.* —*adv.* **13.** recently or lately (usually used in combination): *new-planted crops.* **14.** freshly; anew or afresh (often used in combination): *roses new washed with dew; the refreshing smell of new-mown hay.* —*n.* **15.** something that is new; a new object, quality, condition, etc.: *Ring out the old, ring in the new.* [ME *newe,* OE *nēowe,* var. of *nīewe,* c. D *nieuw,* G *neu,* Icel *nȳr,* Goth *niujis,* Gk *neíos;* akin to L *novus,* Gk *néos,* Skt *návas*] —**new′ness,** *n.*

—**Syn. 1.** modern; late. NEW, FRESH, NOVEL describe that which is not old. NEW applies to that which has not been long in existence: *a new broom, dress* (one recently made or bought). FRESH suggests a condition of newness, not yet affected by use or the passage of time: *a fresh towel, dress* (newly clean). NOVEL suggests newness that has an unexpected quality, or is strange or striking, but generally pleasing: *a novel experience, dress* (a dress of unusual design, or the like).

New′ Al′bany, a city in S Indiana, on the Ohio River. 38,402 (1970).

New′ Am′ster·dam (am′stər dam′), a former Dutch town on Manhattan Island, founded 1625: the capital of New Netherland; renamed New York by the British in 1664.

New·ark (no͞o′ərk, nyo͞o′-), *n.* **1.** a city in NE New Jersey, on Newark Bay. 382,288 (1970). **2.** a city in central Ohio. 41,836 (1970). **3.** a city in W California. 27,153 (1970).

New′ Bed′ford, a seaport in SE Massachusetts: formerly a chief whaling port. 101,777 (1970).

New′ Ber′lin, a city in SE Wisconsin, near Milwaukee. 26,910 (1970).

new·born (no͞o′bôrn′, nyo͞o′-), *adj., n., pl.* **-born, -borns.** —*adj.* **1.** recently or only just born. **2.** reborn: *a newborn faith.* —*n.* **3.** a newborn infant; neonate. [ME]

New′ Brit′ain, **1.** a city in central Connecticut. 83,441 (1970). **2.** an island in the S Pacific, NE of New Guinea: the largest island in the Bismarck Archipelago. 118,796 including adjacent islands (est. 1961); ab. 14,600 sq. mi. *Cap.:* Rabaul.

New′ Bruns′wick, **1.** a province in SE Canada, E of Maine. 623,000 (est. 1965); 27,985 sq. mi. *Cap.:* Fredericton. **2.** a city in central New Jersey. 41,885 (1970).

New·burg (no͞o′bûrg, nyo͞o′-), *adj.* (of seafood) cooked in a sauce of cream, egg yolk, butter, and wine or brandy. [after *Newburgh* a fishing village in Scotland]

New·burgh (no͞o′bûrg, nyo͞o′-), *n.* a city in SE New York, on the Hudson. 26,219 (1970).

New′ Cal·e·do′ni·a (kal′i dō′nē ə, -dōn′yə), **1.** an island in the S Pacific, ab. 800 mi. E of Australia. 46,643 (1952); 6224 sq. mi. **2.** an overseas territory of France comprising this island and other smaller islands: formerly a penal colony. 78,000 (est. 1960); 7200 sq. mi. *Cap.:* Nouméa.

New′ Cas·tile′ (ka stēl′), a region in central Spain: formerly a province. 27,933 sq. mi. Spanish, **Castilla la Nueva.**

New′ Cas′tle, a city in W Pennsylvania. 38,559 (1970).

New·cas·tle (no͞o′kas′əl, -kä′səl, nyo͞o′-), *n.* **1.** Also called **New·cas·tle-up·on-Tyne** (no͞o′kas′əl ə pon′tīn′, -ə-pôn′-, -kä′səl-, nyo͞o′-). a seaport in SE Northumberland, in NE England, on the Tyne River. 269,389 (1961). **2.** a seaport in E New South Wales, in SE Australia: a traditional coaling port. 208,630 (1961). **3. carry coals to Newcastle,** to provide something already present in abundance.

New′castle disease′, *Vet. Pathol.* a specific virus-induced disease of birds and domestic fowl, as chickens, marked by loss of egg production in old birds and by paralysis in chicks. [after NEWCASTLE-UPON-TYNE]

New′ Church′. See **New Jerusalem Church.**
New·chwang (no͞o′chwäng′, nyo͞o′-), *n.* Yingkow.
New′ Cit′y, a town in S New York. 27,344 (1970).
new·com·er (no͞o′kum′ər, nyo͞o′-), *n.* a person who has recently arrived; new arrival.
new′ crit′icism, (*sometimes caps.*) an approach to the critical study of literature which concentrates on textual explication and considers historical and biographical study as secondary to an understanding of the total formal organization of a work (often prec. by *the*). —**new′ crit′ic, New′ Crit′ic.**
New′ Deal′, the domestic policies and administration of President Franklin D. Roosevelt. Cf. **Fair Deal, Great Society, New Frontier.** —**New′ Deal′er.**
New′ Del′hi, a city in and the capital of India, in the N part, adjacent to Delhi. 301,800. Cf. **Delhi** (def. 2).
new·el (no͞o′əl, nyo͞o′-), *n.* **1.** a central pillar or upright from which the steps of a winding stair radiate. **2.** See **newel post.** [earlier *neul,* ME *nowel* < MF *no(u)el* kernel, newel < LL **nucāle,* n. use of neut. of *nucālis* of a nut, nutlike. See NUCLEAR, -AL[1]]

N, Newel

new′el post′, a post supporting one end of a handrail at the top or bottom of a flight of stairs.

N, Newel post

New′ Em′pire. See **New Kingdom.**
New′ Eng′land, an area in the NE United States, including Connecticut, Maine, Massachusetts, New Hampshire, Rhode Island, and Vermont. —**New′ Eng′lander.**
New′ Eng′land boiled′ din′ner. See **boiled dinner.**
New′ Eng′land clam′ chow′der, a thick chowder made from clams, onions, potatoes, and milk or cream. Cf. **Manhattan clam chowder.**
new·fan·gled (no͞o′fang′gəld, nyo͞o′-), *adj.* **1.** of a new kind or fashion: *newfangled ideas.* **2.** fond of or given to novelty. [ME *newefangel* taken by what is new (*newe* NEW + *-fangel,* OE **-fangol* = *fang-* take + *-ol* adj. suffix) + -ED[3]] —**new′fan′gled·ness,** *n.*
New′ For′est, a forest region in S England, in Hampshire: national park. 145 sq. mi.
New·found·land (no͞o′fənd land′, -lənd, -fən-, nyo͞o′-; no͞o found′lənd, nyo͞o-; no͞o′fənd land′, nyo͞o′-), *n.* **1.** a large island in E Canada. 444,319 (1961); 42,734 sq. mi. **2.** a province in E Canada, composed of Newfoundland island and Labrador. 498,000 (est. 1965); 155,364 sq. mi. *Cap.:* St. John's. **3.** one of a breed of large, powerful dogs having a dense, oily, usually black coat, raised originally in Newfoundland.

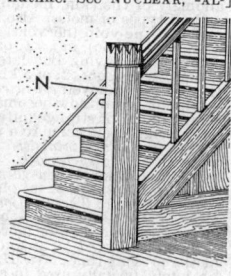

Newfoundland (28 in. high at shoulder)

New·found·land·er (no͞o′found lən′dər, nyo͞o′-), *n.* a native or inhabitant of Newfoundland.
new′ franc′, franc (def. 1).
New′ France′, the French colonies and possessions in North America up to 1763.
New′ Frontier′, the principles of the liberal wing of the Democratic party under the leadership of President John F. Kennedy. Cf. **Fair Deal, Great Society, New Deal.**
New·gate (no͞o′gāt′, -git, nyo͞o′-), *n.* a prison in London, England: torn down 1902.
New′ Geor′gia, **1.** a group of islands in the Solomon Islands: a British protectorate. **2.** the chief island of this group. 50 mi. long; 20 mi. wide.
new′ gram′mar, grammar using symbols from mathematics and logic to analyze the language at the sentence level, rather than to analyze parts of speech as in traditional grammar.
New′ Grana′da, **1.** a former Spanish viceroyalty in NW South America, comprising the present republics of Ecuador, Venezuela, Colombia, and Panama. **2.** early name of Colombia (before the secession of Panama).
New′ Guin′ea, **1.** a large island N of Australia, divided into the Indonesian province of West Irian and the independent country of Papua New Guinea. ab. 317,000 sq. mi. **2. Territory of,** an administrative division until 1975 of the former Australian trusteeship of Papua, including North East New Guinea, the Bismarck Archipelago, Bougainville, and other islands: now part of Papua New Guinea. 92,160 sq. mi. (69,095 sq. mi. mainland). *Cap.:* Port Moresby.
new′ half′penny, halfpenny (def. 2).
New′ Hamp′shire, **1.** a state in the NE United States. 737,681 (1970); 9304 sq. mi. *Cap.:* Concord. *Abbr.:* N.H., NH **2.** one of an American breed of chestnut-red chickens raised for meat and eggs.
New′ Han′over, a township in S New Jersey. 27,410 (1970).
New′ Har′mony, a town in SW Indiana: socialistic community established by Robert Owen 1825. 971 (1970).
New′ Ha′ven (hā′vən), a seaport in S Connecticut, on Long Island Sound. 137,707 (1970).
New′ Heb′ri·des (heb′ri dēz′), an island group in the S Pacific, ab. 1000 mi. NE of Australia: under joint British and French administration 1906–80; independent since 1980. 112,596; ab. 5700 sq. mi. *Cap.:* Vila. Official name, Republic of **Vanuatu.**
New′ High′ Ger′man, the High German language since c1500.
New′ Ibe′ria, a city in S Louisiana. 30,147 (1970).
Ne Win (ne′win′), **U** (o͞o), (*Maung Shu Maung*) born 1911, Burmese statesman: prime minister 1958–60, 1962–74; president 1974–81.
New·ing·ton (no͞o′ing tən, nyo͞o′-), *n.* a city in central Connecticut. 26,037 (1970).
New′ Ire′land, an island in the S Pacific, in the Bismarck Archipelago, NE of New Guinea: part of Papua New Guinea. ab. 3800 sq. mi.
new·ish (no͞o′ish, nyo͞o′-), *adj.* rather new.
New′ Jer′sey, a state in the E United States, on the Atlantic coast. 7,168,164 (1970); 7836 sq. mi. *Cap.:* Trenton. *Abbr.:* N.J., NJ —**New′ Jer′sey·ite** (jûr′zē īt′).
New′ Jeru′salem, the abode of God and His saints; heaven. Rev. 21:2. Also called **Heavenly City.**
New′ Jeru′salem Church′, the church composed of the followers of Swedenborg; the Swedenborgian church. Also called **New Church.**
New′ King′dom, the period of the XVIII–XX dynasties in ancient Egypt 1580–1085 B.C. Also called **New Empire.** Cf. **Middle Kingdom** (def. 1), **Old Kingdom.**
New′ Lat′in, Neo-Latin (def. 1).
new′ learn′ing, the humanist revival of classical Greek and Latin studies and the development of Biblical scholarship, esp. in the 15th and 16th centuries.
New′ Left′, *U.S.* (since 1960) a group of liberals, esp. young intellectuals, that has advocated complete racial equality, disarmament, nonintervention in foreign affairs, and radical changes in the political and economic system.
New′ Lon′don, a seaport in SE Connecticut, on the Thames River: naval base. 31,630 (1970).
new·ly (no͞o′lē, nyo͞o′-), *adv.* **1.** recently; lately. **2.** anew or afresh. **3.** in a new manner or form. [ME; OE *nīwlice*]
new·ly·wed (no͞o′lē wed′, nyo͞o′-), *n.* a person who has recently married.
New·man (no͞o′mən, nyo͞o′-), *n.* **John Henry, Cardinal,** 1801–90, English theologian and author.
New·mar·ket (no͞o′mär′kit, nyo͞o′-), *n.* **1.** a town in SE Cambridgeshire, in E England, E of Cambridge: horse races. 20,887 (1961). **2.** (*often l.c.*) a long, close-fitting coat of the 19th century.
new′ math′, a unified, sequential system of teaching arithmetic and mathematics in accord with set theory: used in some U.S. schools since the 1950's. Also called **new′ mathemat′ics.**
New′ Mex′ico, a state in the SW United States. 1,016,000 (1970); 121,666 sq. mi. *Cap.:* Santa Fe. *Abbr.:* N.M., NM, N. Mex. —**New′ Mex′i·can.**
new′ moon′, **1.** the moon either when in conjunction with the sun or soon after, being either invisible or visible only as a slender crescent. **2.** the phase of the moon at this time. See diag. at **moon.**
New′ Neth′erland, a Dutch colony in North America (1613–64), comprising the area along the Hudson and lower Delaware rivers. *Cap.:* New Amsterdam.
New′ Or′le·ans (ôr′lē ənz, ôr lēnz′, ôr′lənz), a seaport in SE Louisiana, on the Mississippi: British defeated by Americans under Andrew Jackson 1815. 593,471 (1970).
new′ pen′ny, penny (def. 3).
New·port (no͞o′pōrt′, -pôrt′, nyo͞o′-), *n.* **1.** a seaport in S Monmouthshire, in SE Wales, near the Severn estuary. 133,500. **2.** a seaport and summer resort in SE Rhode Island: naval base. 34,562 (1970). **3.** a city in N Kentucky, on the Ohio River, opposite Cincinnati, Ohio. 25,998 (1970). **4.** a city on the Isle of Wight, in S England. 22,286.
New′port Beach′, a city in SW California, SE of Los Angeles. 49,422 (1970).
New′port News′, a seaport in SE Virginia. 138,177 (1970).
New′ Prov′idence, an island in the W Bahamas. 80,907 (1963); 58 sq. mi.
New′ Re′alism, *Philos.* a movement of the early 20th century opposing Idealism and seeking to establish the independence of the object known from the mind of the knower.
New′ Ro·chelle′ (rə shel′, rō-), a city in SE New York, near New York City. 75,385 (1970).
New′ Rom′ney, a town in E Kent, in SE England: one of the Cinque Ports. 3480 (est. 1965). Formerly, **Romney.**
news (no͞oz, nyo͞oz), *n.* (*construed as sing. or pl.*) **1.** a report of a recent event; intelligence; information. **2.** a report on current events in a newspaper or other periodical or on radio or television. **3.** such reports taken collectively: *There's good news tonight.* **4.** a person, event, etc., considered as a choice subject for journalistic treatment. [ME; OE *nīwes,* n. use of gen. sing. of *nīwe* NEW; see -S[1]]
news′ a′gency, **1.** a business organization that gathers news for transmittal to its subscribers. **2.** a business that sells newspapers at retail.
news·boy (no͞oz′boi′, nyo͞oz′-), *n.* a boy who sells or delivers newspapers.
news·cast (no͞oz′kast′, -käst′, nyo͞oz′-), *n.* a broadcast of news on radio or television. [NEWS + (BROAD)CAST] —**news′cast′er,** *n.*
news·deal·er (no͞oz′dē′lər, nyo͞oz′-), *n.* a person who sells newspapers and periodicals.
New′ Sibe′rian Is′lands, a group of islands in the Arctic Ocean, N of the Soviet Union in Asia: part of the Yakutsk Autonomous Republic.
news·let·ter (no͞oz′let′ər, nyo͞oz′-), *n.* **1.** a written report, prepared by or for a group or institution, to present information to employees, stockholders, etc., and often to the press and public. **2.** a written report and analysis, often providing forecasts, typically directed at a special audience.
news·mak·er (no͞oz′mā′kər), *n.* *U.S.* a person, thing, or event that is newsworthy.
news·man (no͞oz′man′, nyo͞oz′-), *n., pl.* **-men.** **1.** a person employed to gather or report news, as for a newspaper; newspaperman. **2.** a newsdealer.
news·mon·ger (no͞oz′mung′gər, -mong′-, nyo͞oz′-), *n.* a person who spreads gossip or idle talk; a gossip.
New′ South′ Wales′, a state in SE Australia. 3,917,013 (1961); 309,433 sq. mi. *Cap.:* Sydney.

New′ Spain′, the former Spanish possessions in the Western Hemisphere, at one time including South America (except Brazil), Middle America, Florida, and most of the land in the U.S. west of the Mississippi River.

news·pa·per (no͞oz′pā′pər, nyo͞oz′-), *n.* **1.** a publication printed on newsprint, usually issued daily or weekly, and commonly containing news, comment, features, photographs, and advertising. **2.** a business organization publishing such a publication. **3.** a single issue or copy of such a publication. **4.** newsprint.

news·pa·per·man (no͞oz′pā′pər man′, nyo͞oz′-), *n., pl.* **-men. 1.** a man employed by a newspaper or wire service as a reporter, writer, editor, etc. **2.** the owner or operator of a newspaper or news service.

new·speak (no͞o′spēk′, nyo͞o′-), *n.* an official or semi-official style of writing or saying something in the guise of its opposite, esp. in order to serve a political or ideological cause. [coined by George Orwell in his novel, *1984*]

news·print (no͞oz′print′, nyo͞oz′-), *n.* a low-grade, machine-finished paper used chiefly for newspapers.

news·reel (no͞oz′rēl′, nyo͞oz′-), *n.* a short motion picture presenting current events.

news′ release′. See **press release.**

news′ room′, a room in the offices of a newspaper, news service, or broadcasting organization in which the news is processed.

news·stand (no͞oz′stand′, nyo͞oz′-), *n.* a stall or other place at which newspapers and often periodicals are sold.

New′ Stone′ Age′, the Neolithic period.

New′ Style′, time reckoned according to the Gregorian calendar. Cf. **old style** (def. 2).

news·wor·thy (no͞oz′wûr′thē, nyo͞oz′-), *adj.* of sufficient potential interest to warrant press coverage.

news·y (no͞o′zē, nyo͞o′-), *adj.,* **news·i·er, news·i·est.** *Informal.* **1.** full of news: *a newsy letter.* **2.** gossipy. **—news′i·ness,** *n.*

newt (no͞ot, nyo͞ot), *n.* **1.** any of several brilliantly colored salamanders of the genus *Triturus,* of North America, Europe, and northern Asia. **2.** (loosely) any of various small salamanders. [ME *newte, ewte* (*an ewte* being taken as *a newte*), var. of *evet,* OE *efete* EFT[1]]

Newt, *Triturus* (*Diemictylus*) *viridescens* (Length 3½ in.)

New Test., New Testament.

New′ Tes′tament, 1. the collection of the books of the Bible that were produced by the early Christian church, comprising the Gospels, Acts of the Apostles, the Epistles, and the Revelation of St. John the Divine. **2.** the covenant between God and man in which the dispensation of grace is revealed through Jesus Christ.

new′ theol′ogy, a movement away from orthodox or fundamentalist theological thought, originating in the late 19th century and aimed at reconciling modern concepts and discoveries in science and philosophy with theology.

New′ Thought′, a system of doctrine and practice originating in the 19th century and stressing the power of thought to control physical and mental events. **—New′ Thought′er, New′ Thought′ist.**

new·ton (no͞ot′ən, nyo͞ot′-), *n.* *Physics.* the standard meter-kilogram-second unit of force, equal to the force that produces an acceleration of one meter per second per second on a mass of one kilogram. [named after Sir Isaac NEWTON]

New·ton (no͞ot′ən, nyo͞ot′-), *n.* **1. Sir Isaac,** 1642–1727, English philosopher and mathematician: formulator of the law of gravitation. **2.** a city in E Massachusetts, near Boston. 91,263 (1970).

New′ton's laws′ of mo′tion, *Physics.* See **law of motion.**

new′ wave′, 1. a movement or trend, as in art, literature, or politics, that breaks with traditional concepts. **2.** a group of leaders or representatives of such a movement. Also, **New′ Wave′.**

New′ Wind′sor, Windsor (def. 3).

New′ World′. See **Western Hemisphere** (def. 1).

New′ World′ mon′key, a platyrrhine monkey.

new′ year′, 1. the year approaching or newly begun. **2.** See **New Year's Day. 3. New Year,** the first few days of a year. [ME]

New′ Year's′, *Chiefly U.S.* **1.** See **New Year's Day. 2.** See **New Year's Eve.**

New′ Year's′ Day′, January 1. [ME]

New′ Year's′ Eve′, the night of December 31, usually observed with merrymaking. [ME]

New′ York′, 1. Also called **New′ York′ State′.** a state in the NE United States. 18,241,266 (1970); 49,576 sq. mi. *Cap.:* Albany. *Abbr.:* N.Y., NY **2.** Also called **New′ York′ Cit′y.** a seaport in SE New York at the mouth of the Hudson: largest city in Western Hemisphere, comprised of boroughs of Manhattan, Queens, Brooklyn, the Bronx, and Richmond. 7,895,563 (1970). **—New′ York′er.**

New′ York′ Bay′, a bay of the Atlantic at the mouth of the Hudson River.

New′ York′ cut′, *Chiefly Western and Midwestern U.S.* a porterhouse steak with the fillet and often the bone removed.

New′ York′ State′ Barge′ Canal′, 1. a New York State waterway system. 575 mi. long. **2.** the main canal of this system, between the Hudson River and Lake Erie: consists of the rebuilt Erie Canal. 352 mi. long.

New′ Zea′land (zē′lənd), a country in the S Pacific, SE of Australia, consisting of North Island, South Island, and adjacent small islands: a member of the British Commonwealth. 3,129,383; 103,416 sq. mi. *Cap.:* Wellington. **—New′ Zea′land·er.**

Nex·ö (nek′sœ), *n.* **Mar·tin An·der·sen** (mär′ten ä′nər-sən), 1869–1954, Danish novelist.

next (nekst), *adj.* **1.** immediately following in time, order, importance, etc.: *the next day.* **2.** nearest in place or position: *the next room.* **3.** nearest in relationship or kinship. **4. next door to,** in an adjacent house; neighboring. **—*adv.* 5.** in the nearest place, time, importance, etc. **6.** on the first occasion to follow: *when next we meet.* **7. next to,** almost; nearly: *next to impossible.* **—*prep.* 8.** adjacent to; nearest: *next the cathedral.* [ME *next(e),* OE *nēxt, nēhst,* superl. of *nēah* NIGH; c. Icel *næstr,* G *nächst*]

next-door (*adv.* neks′dôr′, -dôr′, nekst′-; *adj.* neks′dôr′, -dôr′, nekst′-), *adv.* **1.** to, at, or in the next building, house, apartment, etc.: *Go next-door.* **—*adj.* 2.** Also, **next′door′.** being, situated, or living in the next building, house, apartment, etc: *next-door neighbors.*

next′ friend′, *Law.* a person other than a duly appointed guardian who acts on behalf of an infant or other person not fully qualified by law to act on his own behalf. [ME *neist frend,* OE *niehstan friend*]

next′ of kin′, 1. a person's nearest relative or relatives. **2.** *Law.* the nearest relative or relatives who share in the estate of a person who dies intestate. [OE *nexte cun*]

nex·us (nek′səs), *n., pl.* **nex·us. 1.** a means of connection; tie; link. **2.** a connected series or group. [< L: a binding, joining, fastening (ptp. of *nectere* to bind, fasten, tie)]

Ney (nā), *n.* **Mi·chel** (mē shel′), **Duke of El·ching·en** (el′кнiŋ ən), 1769–1815, French revolutionary and Napoleonic military leader: marshal of France 1805–15.

Nez Percé (nez′ pûrs′; *Fr.* nā per sā′), *pl.* **Nez Per·cés** (nez′ pûr′siz; *Fr.* nā per sā′), (*esp. collectively*) **Nez Percé** for **1. 1.** a member of a North American Indian people of the Sahaptin family. **2.** the Sahaptin language of the Nez Percé Indians. [< F: lit., pierced nose]

NF, 1. no funds. **2.** Norman French.

nF, nanofarad; nanofarads. Also, **nf**

n/f, no funds. Also, **N/F**

N.F., 1. Newfoundland. **2.** no funds. **3.** Norman French.

NFD., Newfoundland.

NFL, National Football League.

NG, *Chem.* nitroglycerin.

N.G., 1. National Guard. **2.** New Guinea. **3.** no good.

n.g., no good.

n'ga·na (nə gä′nə), *n.* *Vet. Pathol.* nagana.

Ngan·hwei (*Chin.* ənŋän′hwā′), *n.* Anhwei.

NGk., New Greek. Also, **N.Gk.**

Ngo Dinh Diem (əŋgō′ dēn′ dyem′, dzyem′, nō′), 1901–1963, South Vietnamese leader: president 1956–1963.

Ngu·yen Van Thieu (əŋgo͞o′yen′ vän′ tyo͞o′, no͞o′-), born 1923, South Vietnamese leader: president 1967–75.

NH, New Hampshire (approved esp. for use with zip code).

nH, nanohenry; nanohenries. Also, **nh**

N.H., New Hampshire.

N. Heb., New Hebrides.

N.H.I., *Brit.* National Health Insurance. Also, **NHI**

Ni, *Chem.* nickel.

N.I., Northern Ireland.

ni·a·cin (nī′ə sin) *n.* *Biochem.* See **nicotinic acid.** [NI(COTINIC) AC(ID) + -IN[2]]

Ni·ag·a·ra (nī ag′rə, -ag′ər ə), *n.* **1.** a river on the boundary between W New York and Ontario, Canada, flowing from Lake Erie into Lake Ontario. 34 mi. long. **2.** See **Niagara Falls. 3. Fort,** a fort in W New York, at the mouth of the Niagara River.

Niag′ara Falls′, 1. the falls of the Niagara River: in Canada, the Horseshoe Falls, 158 ft. high; 2600 ft. wide; American Falls, 167 ft. high; 1400 ft. wide. **2.** a city in W New York, on the U.S. side of the falls. 85,615 (1970). **3.** a city in SE Ontario, on the Canadian side of the falls. 22,351 (1961).

Nia·mey (nyä mā′), *n.* a port in and the capital of Niger, in the SW part, on the Niger River. 102,000.

nib (nib), *n., v.,* **nibbed, nib·bing. —*n.* 1.** a bill or beak, as of a bird; neb. **2.** a penpoint. **3.** a point of anything: *a cutting tool with a diamond nib.* **—*v.t.* 4.** to mend or trim the nib of. [OE *nybba* (in a place-name); c. Icel *nibba* sharp point, MLG *nibbe* beak. See NIBBLE] **—nib′like′,** *adj.*

nib·ble (nib′əl), *v.,* **-bled, -bling,** *n.* **—*v.i.* 1.** to eat or bite off small pieces: *She nibbled on a cracker.* **2.** to bite slightly or gently (usually fol. by *at*). **—*v.t.* 3.** to eat or bite off small bits of (something). **4.** to bite or nip gently. **—*n.* 5.** a small morsel or bit. **6.** the act or an instance of nibbling. [*nib* to peck, pick (see NIB) + -LE (freq. suffix); akin to MLG *nibbelen* to pick with the beak] **—nib′bler,** *n.*

Ni·be·lung·en·lied (nē′bə lo͝oŋ′ən lēt′), *n.* a Middle High German epic of c1200, related to the Scandinavian *Volsunga Saga* and telling of the life of Siegfried, his marriage to Kriemhild, his wooing of Brunhild on behalf of Gunther, his murder by Hagen, and the revenge of Kriemhild. [< G; see NIBELUNGS, LIED]

Ni·be·lungs (nē′bə lo͝oŋz′), *n.pl., sing.* **Ni·be·lung.** *Teutonic Legend.* **1.** a race of dwarfs who possessed a treasure captured by Siegfried. **2.** the followers of Siegfried. **3.** (in the *Nibelungenlied*) the family of Gunther.

nib·lick (nib′lik), *n.* *Golf.* a club with an iron head the face of which has the greatest slope of all the irons, for hitting the ball with maximum loft. [? NIBBLE + *-ick,* var. of -OCK]

nibs (nibz), *n.* *Slang.* **1.** a person in authority. **2. his nibs,** *Often Disparaging.* a haughty or tyrannical person. [?]

ni-cad (nī′kad′), *n.* nickel-cadmium. Also, **ni′cad′.** [by shortening]

Ni·cae·a (nī sē′ə), *n.* an ancient city in NW Asia Minor: Nicene Creed formulated here A.D. 325.

Ni·cae·an (nī sē′ən), *adj.* Nicene.

Nic·a·ra·gua (nik′ə rä′gwə), *n.* **1.** a republic in Central America. 2,253,095; 57,143 sq. mi. *Cap.:* Managua. **2. Lake,** a lake in SW Nicaragua. 92 mi. long, 34 mi. wide. **—Nic′a·ra′guan,** *n., adj.*

nic·co·lite (nik′ə līt′), *n.* a pale copper-red mineral, nickel arsenide, NiAs. [< NL *niccol(um)* nickel + -ITE[1]]

nice (nīs), *adj.,* **nic·er, nic·est. 1.** pleasing; agreeable; delightful: *a nice visit.* **2.** amiably pleasant; kind. **3.** characterized by or requiring great accuracy, precision, skill, or delicacy: *nice workmanship.* **4.** showing minute differences; minutely accurate, as instruments. **5.** minute, fine, or subtle: *a nice distinction.* **6.** refined as to manners, language, etc. **7.** virtuous; respectable; decorous: *a nice girl.* **8.** suitable or proper. **9.** carefully neat as to dress, habits, etc.; dainty or fussy. **10.** *Obs.* coy, shy, or reluctant. **11.** *Obs.* unimportant; trivial. [ME: foolish < OF < L *nescius* ignorant, incapable = *ne* not + *sci-* (s. of *scīre* to know) + *-us* adj. suffix] —**nice′ly,** *adv.* —**nice′ness,** *n.* —**Syn. 2.** friendly. **3.** delicate, exact, exacting. **6.** polite. **9.** fastidious, finical, finicky. —**Ant. 1.** unpleasant. **2.** unkind. **3.** careless. **8.** improper.

—**Usage.** The semantic history of NICE is varied, as the etymology and the obsolete senses attest, and any attempt to insist on only one of its senses as correct will not be in keeping with the facts of the way the word is used. If any criticism is valid, it might be that the word is used too often and has become a cliché lacking the qualities of precision and intensity embodied in many of its synonyms.

Nice (nēs), *n.* a port in SE France, on the Mediterranean: resort. 294,976 (1962).

Ni·cene (nī′sēn, nī sēn′), *adj.* of or pertaining to Nicaea. Also, **Nicaean.** [< LL *Nicēn(us)*, var. of *Nicaenus* < Gk *Nīkaîos (Nīkai(a)* Nicea + *-os* adj. suffix), with *-n-* from L adj. suffix *-ānus* -AN]

Ni′cene Coun′cil, either of two church councils which met at Nicaea, the first in A.D. 325 to deal with the Arian heresy, the second in A.D. 787 to consider the question of the veneration of images.

Ni′cene Creed′, **1.** a formal statement of the chief tenets of Christian belief, adopted by the first Nicene Council. **2.** a later creed of closely similar form referred, perhaps erroneously, to the Council of Constantinople (A.D. 381), received universally in the Eastern Church and, with an addition introduced in the 6th century A.D., accepted generally throughout western Christendom.

nice′ nel′ly (nel′ē), a person, esp. a girl or woman, who professes or exhibits excessive modesty, prudishness, or the like. Also, **nice′ Nel′ly, nice′ nel′lie, nice′ Nel′lie.**

nice-nel·ly·ism (nīs′nel′ē iz′əm), *n.* **1.** excessive modesty; prudishness. **2.** a euphemism. Also **nice′-Nel′ly·ism.**

ni·ce·ty (nī′si tē), *n., pl.* **-ties. 1.** a delicate or fine point; a punctilio: *niceties of protocol.* **2.** a fine distinction; subtlety; detail. **3.** Usually, **niceties.** a refinement or elegance, as of manners or living. **4.** the quality of being nice; niceness. **5.** delicacy of character, as of something requiring care or tact. **6. to a nicety,** to the last detail; precisely. [ME < OF *nicete*]

niche (nich), *n., v.,* **niched, nich·ing.** —*n.* **1.** an ornamental recess, usually set in a wall, for a statue or other decorative object. **2.** a place or position suitable or appropriate for a person or thing. **3.** *Ecol.* the position or function of an organism in a community of plants and animals. —*v.t.* **4.** to place (something) in a niche. [< F, MF, back formation from *nicher* < VL **nīdicāre* to make a nest. See NEST]

Niche (def. 1)

Nich·o·las (nik′ə ləs), *n.* **1. of Cu·sa** (kyōō′zə). German, **Nikolaus von Cusa.** Latin, **Nicolaus Cusanus.** 1401–1464, German cardinal, mathematician, and philosopher. **2. Saint,** fl. 4th century A.D., bishop in Asia Minor: patron saint of Russia; protector of children and prototype of the legendary Santa Claus.

Nicholas I, 1. Saint ("*Nicholas the Great*"), died A.D. 867, Italian ecclesiastic: pope 858–867. **2.** 1796–1855, emperor of Russia 1825–55.

Nicholas II, 1. (*Gerard*) died 1061, pope 1058–61. **2.** 1868–1918, emperor of Russia 1894–1917.

Nicholas III, (*Giovanni Gaetani Orsini*) died 1280, Italian ecclesiastic: pope 1277–80.

Nicholas IV, (*Girolamo Masci*) died 1292, Italian ecclesiastic: pope 1288–92.

Nicholas V, (*Thomas Parentucelli*) 1397?–1455, Italian ecclesiastic: pope 1447–55.

Nich·ol·son (nik′əl sən), *n.* **Sir Frances,** 1655–1728, English colonial administrator in America.

Ni·chrome (nī′krōm′), *n.* *Trademark.* a nickel-base alloy, containing chromium and iron, having high electrical resistance and stability at high temperatures.

nicht wahr (nikht vär′), *German.* isn't that so?

Ni·ci·as (nish′ē əs), *n.* died 413 B.C., Athenian statesman and general.

nick (nik), *n.* **1.** a notch, groove, chip, or the like, cut into or existing in a thing. **2.** a small groove on one side of the shank of a printing type, serving as a guide in setting or to distinguish different types. **3. in the nick of time,** at the propitious or vital moment. —*v.t.* **4.** to make a nick or nicks in (something); notch. **5.** to record by means of a notch or notches. **6.** to cut into or through. **7.** to hit or injure slightly. **8.** to hit, guess, catch, etc., exactly. **9.** to trick, cheat, or defraud. **10.** *Brit. Slang.* to catch (a criminal or suspect). [late ME *nyke;* akin to OE *gehnycned* wrinkled, Icel *hnykla* to wrinkle]

Nick (nik), *n.* See **Old Nick.**

nick·el (nik′əl), *n., v.,* **-eled, -el·ing** or (*esp. Brit.*) **-elled, -el·ling.** —*n.* **1.** *Chem.* a hard, silvery-white, ductile and malleable metallic element, allied to iron and cobalt, not readily oxidized: used chiefly in alloys, in electroplating, and as a catalyst in organic synthesis. *Symbol:* Ni; *at. wt.:* 58.71; *at. no.:* 28; *sp. gr.:* 8.9 at 20°C. **2.** a cupronickel coin of the U.S., the 20th part of a U.S. dollar, equal to five cents. —*v.t.* **3.** to cover or coat with nickel; nickel-plate. [< Sw, abstracted from *kopparnickel* < G *Kupfernickel* niccolite, lit., copper demon (so called because though looking like copper it yielded none); *nickel* demon, special use of *Nickel,* short for *Nikolaus* proper name]

nick·el·ic (ni kel′ik, nik′ə lik), *adj.* *Chem.* of or containing nickel, esp. in the trivalent state.

nick·el·o·de·on (nik′ə lō′dē ən), *n.* **1.** (formerly) a motion-picture theater, admission to which cost 5 cents. **2.** an early jukebox that operated when a nickel was inserted into a slot. [NICKEL + (MEL)ODEON]

nick·el·ous (nik′ə ləs), *adj.* *Chem.* containing bivalent nickel

nick′el ox′ide, *Chem.* a green powder, NiO, used in the manufacture of nickel salts and in green pigments. Also called **nick′elous ox′ide.**

nick′el plate′, a thin coating of nickel deposited on the surface of a piece of metal, as by electroplating.

nick·el-plate (nik′əl plāt′), *v.t.,* **-plat·ed, -plat·ing.** to coat with nickel, as by electroplating.

nick′el sil′ver. See **German silver.**

nick·er[1] (nik′ər), *n.* a person or thing that nicks. [NICK + -ER[1]]

nick·er[2] (nik′ər), *v.i., n.* *Chiefly Dial.* **1.** neigh. **2.** laugh; snicker. [appar. var. of *nicher, neigher,* freq. of NEIGH]

nick·er[3] (nik′ər), *n., pl.* **-er, -ers** for 1. **1.** *Brit. Slang.* one pound sterling. **2.** *Australian.* money. [? special use of *nicker;* see NICK, -ER[1]]

nick·nack (nik′nak′), *n.* knickknack.

nick·name (nik′nām′), *n., v.,* **-named, -nam·ing.** —*n.* **1.** a name added to or substituted for the proper name of a person, place, etc., as in ridicule or familiarity. **2.** a familiar form of a proper name, as *Jim* for *James.* —*v.t.* **3.** to give a nickname to (a person, town, etc.); call by a nickname. **4.** to miscall; misname. [late ME *nekename,* for *ekename* (*an ekename* being taken as *a nekename*). See EKE[2], NAME, NEWT] —**nick′nam′er,** *n.*

Nic′o·bar Is′lands (nik′ə bär′). See **Andaman and Nicobar Islands.**

Nic·o·de·mus (nik′ə dē′məs), *n.* a Pharisee and member of the Sanhedrin who became a secret follower of Jesus. John 3:1–21; 7:50–52; 19:39.

Ni·co·laus Cu·sa·nus (nē′ko lous′ kōō sä′nŏŏs), Nicholas (def. 1).

Nic·ol·son (nik′əl sən), *n.* **1. Sir Harold George,** 1886–1968, English diplomat, biographer, and journalist. **2. Marjorie Hope,** born 1894, U.S. scholar, educator, and author.

Nic·o·si·a (nik′ə sē′ə), *n.* a city on and the capital of Cyprus, in the central part. 115,700.

ni·co·ti·a·na (ni kō′shē ā′nə, -an′ə, -ä′nə), *n.* any plant of the genus *Nicotiana,* esp. one grown for its ornamental value, as flowering tobacco. [< NL (*herba*) *nicotiana* Nicot's (herb) (named after Jacques *Nicot* (1530–1600), said to have introduced tobacco into France); see -IANA]

nic·o·tin·a·mide (nik′ə tin′ə mīd′, -mid), *n.* *Biochem.* a solid, $C_5H_4NCONH_2$, the amide of nicotinic acid, and a component of the vitamin-B complex, found in meat, liver, fish, whole wheat, and eggs: used as an agent for preventing or treating human pellagra. Also called **nicotin′ic ac′id am′ide.**

nic·o·tine (nik′ə tēn′, -tin, nik′ə tēn′), *n.* *Chem.* a colorless, highly toxic, liquid alkaloid, $C_{10}H_{14}N_2$, obtained from tobacco. [< NL (*herba*) *nicot(iana)* NICOTIANA + F *-ine* -INE[2]] —**nic·o·tin·ic** (nik′ə tin′ik), *adj.*

nic′otin′ic ac′id, *Biochem.* an acid, $(C_5H_4N)COOH$, that is a component of the vitamin-B complex, found in fresh meat, yeast, etc.: used in the prevention and treatment of pellagra. Also called **niacin.**

nic·o·tin·ism (nik′ə tē niz′əm, -ti-, nik′ə tē′niz-), *n.* a pathological condition caused by excessive use of tobacco.

nic·tate (nik′tāt), *v.i.,* **-tat·ed, -tat·ing.** nictitate. —**nicta′tion,** *n.*

Nic·the·roy (nik′te roi′), *n.* Niteroi.

nic·ti·tate (nik′ti tāt′), *v.i.,* **-tat·ed, -tat·ing.** to wink. Also, **nictate.** [< ML *nictitāt(us)* (ptp. of *nictitāre*), freq. of L *nictāre* to wink, freq. of *nicere* to beckon; see -ATE[1]] —**nic′ti·ta′tion,** *n.*

nic′titating mem′brane, a thin membrane, or inner or third eyelid, present in many animals, capable of being drawn across the eyeball, as for protection.

Ni·da·ros (nē′dä rōs′), *n.* former name of **Trondheim.**

nid·der·ing (nid′ər ing), *Archaic.* —*n.* **1.** a cowardly or base person. —*adj.* **2.** cowardly; base. Also, **nid′er·ing.** [erroneous archaism based on OE *nīthing* < Scand; cf. Icel *nīthingr* = *nīth(a)* to act basely (< *nīth* defamation; c. OE *nīth* spite, G *Neid* envy) + *-ingr* -ING[1]]

nide (nīd), *n.* *Rare.* a nest or brood, esp. of pheasants. [< L *nīdus* nest]

ni·dic·o·lous (nī dik′ə ləs), *adj.* *Ornith.* remaining in the nest for a period after hatching. Cf. **nidifugous.** [< L *nīd-* (s. of *nīdus*) a nest + -I- + -COLOUS]

nid·i·fi·cate (nid′ə fə kāt′), *v.i.,* **-cat·ed, -cat·ing.** to build a nest. [< L *nīdificāt(us)* (ptp. of *nīdificāre*) having built a nest. See NIDIFY, -ATE[1]] —**nid′i·fi·ca′tion,** *n.*

ni·dif·u·gous (nī dif′yə gəs), *adj.* *Ornith.* leaving the nest shortly after hatching. Cf. **nidicolous.** [< L *nīd-* (s. of *nīdus*) a nest + *-i-* -I- + *fug(ere)* (to) flee, take flight + -OUS]

nid·i·fy (nid′ə fī′), *v.i.,* **-fied, -fy·ing.** nidificate. [< L *nīdificāre*) (to) build a nest = *nīd-* (s. of *nīdus*) a nest + *-ificāre* -IFY]

ni·dus (nī′dəs), *n., pl.* **-di** (-dī). **1.** a nest, esp. one in which insects, spiders, etc., deposit their eggs. **2.** a place or point in an organism where a germ or other organism can develop or breed. [< L: nest] —**ni′dal,** *adj.*

Nie·buhr (nē′bŏŏr; *for 1 also Ger.* nē′bōōʀ), *n.* **1. Barthold Ge·org** (bär′tōlt gā ôʀk′), 1776–1831, German historian. **2. Rein·hold** (rīn′hōld), 1892–1971, U.S. theologian and philosopher.

niece (nēs), *n.* **1.** a daughter of one's brother or sister. **2.** a daughter of one's husband's or wife's brother or sister. [ME *nece* < OF < VL *neptia* for L *neptis* granddaughter; r. ME *nifte* (OE *nift*) niece]

Nie·der·sach·sen (nē′dər zäkh′zən), *n.* German name of **Lower Saxony.**

ni·el·lo (nē el′ō), *n., pl.* **ni·el·li** (nē el′ē), *v.,* **-loed, -lo·ing.** —*n.* **1.** a black metallic substance, consisting of silver, copper, lead, and sulfur, with which an incised design or ground is filled to produce an ornamental effect on metal. **2.** ornamental work so produced. **3.** a specimen of such work. —*v.t.* **4.** to decorate by means of niello. [< It < L *nigellus* blackish, dim. of *niger* black] —**ni·el′list,** *n.*

Niel·sen (nēl′sən), *n.* **1. Carl Au·gust** (käʀl ou′gŏŏst), 1865–1931, Danish composer. **2.** See **Nielsen rating.**

Niel′sen rat′ing, an estimate of the number of viewers of a television program based on monitoring the sets of a selected sample of viewers. Also called **Nielsen.** [after the A.C. *Nielsen* Co., its originator]

Nie·men (nē′mən; *Pol.* nye′men), *n.* a river in the W Soviet Union in Europe, flowing into the Baltic: called Memel in its lower course. 565 mi. long. Lithuanian, **Nemunas.** Russian, **Neman, Nyeman.**

Nie·mey·er (nē′mī ər), *n.* **Oscar,** born 1907, Brazilian architect.

Nie·moel·ler (nē′mœ lər), *n.* **Mar·tin** (mär′tēn), 1892–1984, German clergyman: opposed Nazism. Also, **Nie′möl·ler.**

Nie·tzsche (nē′chə, -chē), *n.* **Frie·drich Wil·helm** (frē′drikh vil′helm), 1844–1900, German philosopher.

Nie·tzsche·ism (nē′chē iz′əm), *n.* the philosophy of Nietzsche, emphasizing the will to power as the chief motivating force of both the individual and society. Also, **Nie′tzsche·an·ism.** —**Nie′tzsche·an,** *n., adj.*

Ni·fl·heim (niv′əl hām′), *n.* *Scand. Myth.* a place of eternal cold, darkness, and fog: a place of punishment for the dead. [< Icel *Niflheimr* = *nifl* mist + *heimr* HOME]

nif·ty (nif′tē), *adj.*, **-ti·er, -ti·est.** *Informal.* smart, stylish; fine; clever. [orig. theatrical slang]

Ni·ger (nī′jər), *n.* **1** a republic in NW Africa: formerly part of French West Africa. 4,239,000; 458,976 sq. mi. *Cap.:* Niamey. **2.** a river in W Africa, rising in S Guinea, flowing NE through Mali, and then SE through Nigeria into the Gulf of Guinea. 2600 mi. long.

Ni·ger-Con·go (nī′jər koŋ′gō), *n.* a group of African languages including Ewe, Ibo, Yoruba, and the Bantu languages.

Ni·ger·i·a (nī jēr′ē ə), *n.* a republic in W Africa: member of the British Commonwealth; formerly a British colony and protectorate. 75,000,000; 360,000 sq. mi. *Cap.:* Lagos. Official name, **Fed′eral Repub′lic of Nige′ria.** —**Ni·ge′ri·an,** *adj., n.*

Ni′ger seed′, the black seed of a tropical African, composite plant, *Guizotia abyssinica,* yielding an oil used as food, in the manufacture of soap, etc.

nig·gard (nig′ərd), *n.* **1.** an extremely stingy person. —*adj.* **2.** niggardly; stingy. [ME *nyggard* = *nig* niggard (< Scand; cf. dial. Sw *nygg;* akin to OE *hnēaw* stingy) + -ARD]

nig·gard·ly (nig′ərd lē), *adj.* **1.** reluctant to give or spend; stingy. **2.** meanly small or scanty: *a niggardly tip to a waiter.* —*adv.* **3.** in the manner of a niggard. —**nig′gard·li·ness,** *n.* —**Syn. 1.** penurious, miserly. —**Ant. 1.** generous.

nig·ger (nig′ər), *n.* *Offensive and Disparaging.* **1.** a Negro. **2.** a member of any dark-skinned race. [var. of *neger* < F *nègre* < Sp *negro* black, NEGRO]

nig·gle (nig′əl), *v.i.*, **-gled, -gling. 1.** to spend excessive time on inconsequential details; trifle. **2.** to criticize constantly in a petty manner. [< Scand; cf. Norw *nigla*] —**nig′gler,** *n.*

nig·gling (nig′liŋ), *adj.* **1.** petty; inconsequential. **2.** demanding excessive care, attention, etc. **3.** fussy. —*n.* **4.** petty or inconsequential work. —**nig′gling·ly,** *adv.*

nigh (nī), *adv., adj.*, **nigh·er, nigh·est,** *v.* —*adv.* **1.** near in space, time, or relation (often fol. by *on, onto,* etc.). **2.** nearly or almost. —*adj.* **3.** being near in relationship; not distant. **4.** short or direct. —*v.i., v.t.* **5.** *Archaic.* to approach. [ME *nigh(e), neye,* OE *nēah, nēh;* c. D *na,* Icel *nā-,* Goth *nehw, nehwa,* G *nahe*]

night (nīt), *n.* **1.** the period of darkness between sunset and sunrise. **2.** the beginning of night; nightfall. **3.** the darkness of night; the dark. **4.** a state or time of obscurity, ignorance, misfortune, etc. **5.** (*sometimes cap.*) an evening used or set aside for a particular event or special purpose. **6. night and day,** tirelessly; unceasingly; continually. —*adj.* **7.** of or pertaining to night: *the night hours.* **8.** occurring, appearing, or seen at night. **9.** used or designed to be used at night. **10.** working at night: *night nurse.* [ME; OE *niht, neaht;* c. G *Nacht,* Goth *nahts,* L *nox* (s. *noct-*), Gk *nýx* (s. *nykt-*)] —**night′less,** *adj.* —**night′like′,** *adj.*

night′ blind′ness, nyctalopia. —**night′blind′,** *adj.*

night′-bloom·ing ce′reus (nīt′blōō′miŋ), either of two American cactuses, *Selenicereus grandiflorus* or *S. pteranthus,* having large, fragrant flowers that open at night.

night·cap (nīt′kap′), *n.* **1.** a cap worn with nightwear. **2.** *Informal.* an alcoholic drink taken at bedtime. **3.** *Sports. Informal.* the last event of the program for the day. [ME]

night′ clothes′, garments for wear in bed.

night′ club′, a restaurant that is open until early in the morning and provides food, drink, music, etc. Also, **night′club′.** Also called **nightspot.** —**night′club′ber,** *n.*

night′ crawl′er, *U.S. Dial.* a large earthworm that emerges from its burrow at night.

night·fall (nīt′fôl′), *n.* the coming of night.

night·gown (nīt′goun′), *n.* **1.** a loose gown, worn in bed by women or children. **2.** a man's nightshirt. Also called **night·dress** (nīt′dres′). [ME]

night·hawk (nīt′hôk′), *n.* **1.** any of several long-winged, American goatsuckers of the genus *Chordeiles,* related to the whippoorwill, esp. *C. minor,* having variegated black, white, and buff plumage. **2.** the European goatsucker or nightjar, *Caprimulgus europaeus.*

night′ her′on, any of several thick-billed, crepuscular or nocturnal herons of the genus *Nycticorax* and related genera, as *Nycticorax nycticorax,* of the Old and New Worlds, and *Nyctanassa violacea,* of America.

night·ie (nī′tē), *n.* a nightgown. Also, **nighty.** [NIGHT(GOWN) + -IE]

night·in·gale (nīt′ən gāl′, nī′tiŋ-), *n.* any of several small, Old World, migratory birds of the thrush family, esp. *Luscinia megarhyncha,* of Europe, noted for the melodious song of the male. [ME *nightyngale,* nasalized var. of *nightegale,* OE *nihtegale* (c. G *Nachtigall,* lit., night singer); cf. OE *galan* to sing, akin to YELL]

Nightingale, *Luscinia megarhyncha* (Length 6½ in.)

Night·in·gale (nīt′ən gāl′, nī′tiŋ-), *n.* **Florence** (*"the Lady with the Lamp"*), 1820–1910, English nurse, reformer of hospital conditions and procedures; reorganizer of nurse's training programs.

night·jar (nīt′jär′), *n.* *Ornithol.* any Old World goatsucker, esp. the common species, *Caprimulgus europaeus.* [NIGHT + JAR² (from its harsh cry)]

night′ latch′, a door lock operated from the inside by a knob and from the outside by a key.

night′ let′ter, a telegram, sent at night for delivery the following morning, that is cheaper than a regular telegram.

night′ light′, a usually dim light kept burning at night, as in a child's bedroom or a hallway.

night·long (nīt′lôŋ′, -loŋ′), *adj.* **1.** lasting all night. —*adv.* **2.** throughout the night. [OE *nihtlang*]

night·ly (nīt′lē), *adj.* **1.** coming, occurring, appearing, or active at night: *nightly revels.* **2.** coming or occurring each night: *his nightly walk.* **3.** of, pertaining to, or characteristic of night: *the nightly gloom.* —*adv.* **4.** at or by night. **5.** on every night: *performances given nightly.* [ME; OE *nihtlīc*]

night·mare (nīt′mâr′), *n.* **1.** a terrifying dream in which the dreamer experiences feelings of helplessness, extreme anxiety, sorrow, etc. **2.** a condition, thought, or experience suggestive of a nightmare in sleep. **3.** (formerly) a monster or evil spirit believed to oppress persons during sleep. [ME; see NIGHT, MARE²] —**night′mar′ish,** *adj.* —**Syn. 1.** phantasmagoria.

night′ owl′, *Informal.* a person who often stays up late at night.

night·rid·er (nīt′rī′dər), *n.* **1.** *Southern U.S.* one of a band of mounted men, esp. during the Reconstruction, who commit deeds of violence for vengeance or intimidation. **2.** a member of the Ku Klux Klan. —**night′rid′ing,** *n.*

night′ robe′, nightgown. —**night′-robed′,** *adj.*

nights (nīts), *adv.* at or during the night regularly: *He works nights.* [ME *nightes,* OE *nihtes* (gen. sing.). See NIGHT, -S¹]

night′ school′, a school held in the evening, esp. for those unable to attend school during the day.

night·shade (nīt′shād′), *n.* **1.** any of various plants of the genus *Solanum,* esp. the black nightshade or the bittersweet. **2.** any of various other solanaceous plants, as the deadly nightshade. [ME; OE *nihtscada*]

night′ shift′, **1.** the work force, as of a factory, scheduled to work during the nighttime. **2.** the scheduled period of labor for this work force.

night·shirt (nīt′shûrt′), *n.* a loose shirt reaching to the knees or lower, for wearing in bed.

night′ soil′, human excrement used as fertilizer.

night·spot (nīt′spot′), *n.* *Informal.* See **night club.**

night′ stick′, a heavy stick or long club carried by a policeman; billy.

night′ ta′ble, bedstand. Also called **night·stand** (nīt′stand′).

night·time (nīt′tīm′), *n.* the time between evening and morning. Also, *Literary,* **night·tide** (nīt′tīd′). [late ME *nyght time*]

night·walk·er (nīt′wô′kər), *n.* a person who walks or roves about at night, as a thief, prostitute, etc.

night′ watch′, **1.** a watch or guard kept during the night. **2.** a person or the persons keeping such a watch. **3.** Usually, **night watches.** the periods or divisions into which the night was divided in ancient times. [ME *niht wecche,* OE *niht wæccan*]

night′ watch′man, a watchman who is on duty at night.

night·y (nī′tē), *n., pl.* **night·ies.** nightie.

night·y-night (nī′tē nīt′), *interj.* *Informal.* See **good night.** [redupl. of (*good*) *night;* see -Y²]

ni·gres·cent (nī gres′ənt), *adj.* tending toward black; blackish. [< L *nigrescent-* (s. of *nigrescēns*), prp. of *nigrescere.* See NEGRO, -ESCE, -ENT] —**ni·gres′cence,** *n.*

nig·ri·tude (nig′ri tōōd′, -tyōōd′, nī′gri-), *n.* **1.** utter or complete darkness; blackness. **2.** *Archaic.* something black or of blackened reputation. [< L *nigritūdō.* See NEGRO, -I-, -TUDE] —**nig·ri·tu·di·nous** (nig′ri tōōd′ənəs, -tyōōd′-), *adj.*

nig·ro·sine (nī′grə sēn′, -sin), *n.* *Chem.* any of the class of deep blue or black dyes obtained by the oxidation of aniline. Also, **ni·gro·sin** (nī′grə sin). [< L *nigr-* (s. of *niger*) black, dark + -OSE¹ + -INE¹]

ni·hil (ni′hil; *Eng.* nī′hil, nē′-), *n.* *Latin.* nothing; a thing of no value.

ni·hil·ism (nī′ə liz′əm, nē′-), *n.* **1.** total rejection of established laws and institutions. **2.** *Philos.* extreme skepticism, esp. with regard to value statements or moral judgments. **3.** (*usually cap.*) the principles of a Russian revolutionary group, active in the latter half of the 19th century, that often employed terrorism, assassination, etc., as a means of enforcing its program. **4.** anarchy, terrorism, or other revolutionary activity. **5.** total and absolute destructiveness toward the world at large and oneself. —**ni′hil·ist,** *n., adj.* —**ni′hil·is′tic,** *adj.*

ni·hil·i·ty (nī hil′i tē, nē-), *n.* the state of being nothing; nothingness.

ni·hil ob·stat (nē′hil ob′stat), *Rom. Cath. Ch.* official permission to publish a book that is certified to contain nothing contrary to faith or morals. [< L: lit., nothing stands in the way]

Ni·hon (nē′hon′), *n.* a Japanese name of **Japan.**

Ni·i·ga·ta (nē′ē gä′tä), *n.* a seaport on NW Honshu, in central Japan. 844,846 (1964).

Ni·i·ha·u (nē′ē hä′ōō), *n.* an island in NW Hawaii, W of Kauai. 237 (1970); 72 sq. mi.

Ni·jin·sky (ni zhin′skē, -jin′-; *Russ.* ni zhēn′ski), *n.* **Vas·lav** or **Was·law** (väts′läf), 1890–1950, Russian ballet dancer and choreographer.

Nij·me·gen (nī′mā′gən; *Du.* nī′mā′khən), *n.* a city in the E Netherlands, on the Waal River: peace treaty 1678. 136,111 (1962). German, **Nimwegen.** Formerly, **Nymwegen.**

-nik, a suffix of nouns that refer, usually derogatorily, to persons who support or are concerned or associated with a particular political cause or group, cultural attitude, or the like: *filmnik; no-goodnik; peacenik; protestnik.* [< Yiddish < Russ. n. suffix of agency or connection]

Ni·ke (nī′kē), *n.* **1.** the ancient Greek goddess of victory, often identified with Athena: identified by the Romans with Victoria. **2.** one of a series of antiaircraft or antimissile missiles having two or three rocket stages. [< Gk: victory]

Nik·ko (nēk′kô), *n.* a city on NE Honshu, in central Japan: famous for shrines and temples. 32,753 (1964).

Ni·ko·la·ev (ni/kô lä′yef), *n.* a city in the S Ukraine, in the SW Soviet Union in Europe. 280,000 (est. 1965). Formerly, **Vernoleninsk.**

Ni·ko·laus von Cu·sa (*Ger.* nē′kō lous fən ko͞o′zä *or, often,* nē′kō lä′o͞os), Nicholas (def. 1).

nil (nil), *n.* nothing; naught; zero. [< L, var. (by apocope) of *nīlum,* contr. of *nihilum* nothing = *ni* (var. of *ne* not) + *hīlum* trifle]

Nile (nīl), *n.* the longest river in Africa, flowing N from Lake Victoria to the Mediterranean Sea. 3485 mi. long. Latin, **Nilus.** Cf. **Blue Nile, White Nile.**

Nile′ blue′, pale greenish blue.

Nile′ green′, pale bluish green.

Niles (nīlz), *n.* a city in NE Illinois, near Chicago. 31,432 (1970).

nil·gai (nil′gī), *n., pl.* **-gais, -gai.** a large, Indian antelope, *Boselaphus tragocomelus,* the male of which is bluish gray with small horns, the female tawny and hornless. Also, **nylghai, nylghau.** [< Hindi: lit., blue cow]

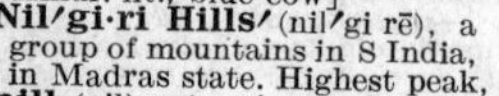

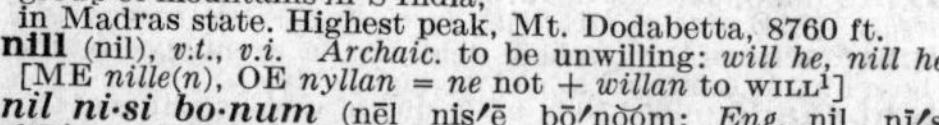

Nilgai
(4½ ft. high at shoulder; length 6½ ft.)

Nil′gi·ri Hills′ (nil′gi rē), a group of mountains in S India, in Madras state. Highest peak, Mt. Dodabetta, 8760 ft.

nill (nil), *v.t., v.i. Archaic.* to be unwilling: *will he, nill he.* [ME *nille(n),* OE *nyllan* = *ne* not + *willan* to WILL[1]]

nil ni·si bo·num (nēl nis′ē bō′no͝om; *Eng.* nil nī′sī bō′nəm), *Latin.* See **de mortuis nil nisi bonum.**

Ni·lot·ic (nī lot′ik), *adj.* of or pertaining to the Nile River or the inhabitants of the Nile region. [< L *Nīlōtic(us)* < Gk *Neilōtikós.* See NILUS, -OTIC]

nil si·ne nu·mi·ne (nēl sin′e no͞o′mi ne; *Eng.* nil sī′nī no͞o′mi nē, nyo͞o′-), *Latin.* nothing without the divine will: motto of Colorado.

Ni·lus (nē′lo͝os; *Eng.* nī′ləs), *n.* Latin name of the **Nile.**

nim·ble (nim′bəl), *adj.,* **-bler, -blest. 1.** quick and light in movement; agile; active. **2.** quick in apprehending, devising, etc.: *a nimble mind.* [late ME *nymel,* ME *nemel,* OE *nǣmel* capable = *nǣm-* (var. s. of *niman* to take; see NUMB) + *-el* -LE] —**nim′ble·ness,** *n.* —**nim′bly,** *adv.*

nimbo-, a combining form of **nimbus:** *nimbostratus.*

nim·bo·stra·tus (nim′bō strā′təs, -strat′əs), *n., pl.* **-tus.** a formless, dark-gray cloud layer.

nim·bus (nim′bəs), *n., pl.* **-bi** (-bī), **-bus·es. 1.** *Class. Myth.* a shining cloud sometimes surrounding a deity when on earth. **2.** a cloud, aura, atmosphere, etc., surrounding a person or thing. **3.** halo (def. 1). **4.** *Obs.* a cloud that yields rain or snow. [< L: a rainstorm, rain cloud, cloud, akin to *nebula* and Gk *nephélē, néphos* cloud] —**nim′bused,** *adj.*

Nîmes (nēm), *n.* a city in S France: Roman ruins. 105,199 (1962).

ni·mi·e·ty (ni mī′i tē), *n., pl.* **-ties.** excess; overabundance. [< LL *nimietās* = *nimi(us)* too much + *-etās,* var. of *-itās* -ITY]

Nim·itz (nim′its), *n.* **Chester William,** 1885–1966, U.S. admiral.

Nim·rod (nim′rod), *n.* the great-grandson of Noah: noted as a great hunter. Gen. 10:8–10.

Nim·we·gen (nim′vā′gən), *n.* German name of **Nijmegen.**

Ni·ña (nēn′yə, nē′nə; *Sp.* nē′nyä), *n.* one of the three ships under the command of Columbus when he made his first voyage of discovery to America in 1492.

nin·com·poop (nin′kəm po͞op′, ning′-), *n.* a fool. [?]

nine (nīn), *n.* **1.** a cardinal number, eight plus one. **2.** a symbol for this number, as 9 or IX. **3.** a set of this many persons or things. **4.** a baseball team. **5.** a playing card with nine pips. **6. the Nine,** the nine Muses. —*adj.* **7.** amounting to nine in number. [ME; OE *nigan, nigon;* c. D *negen;* akin to Icel *nīu,* Goth *niun,* G *neun,* L *novem,* Gk *ennéa,* Skt *nava*]

nine·fold (nīn′fōld′), *adj.* **1.** having nine elements or parts. **2.** nine times as great or as much. —*adv.* **3.** to or by nine times as much. [OE *nigonfeald*]

nine·pen·ny (nīn′pen′ē), *adj.* noting a nail 2¾ inches long. *Abbr.:* 9d

nine·pins (nīn′pinz′), *n.* **1.** (*construed as sing.*) tenpins played without the head pin. **2. ninepin,** a pin used in this game.

nine·teen (nīn′tēn′), *n.* **1.** a cardinal number, ten plus nine. **2.** a symbol for this number, as 19 or XIX. **3.** a set of this many persons or things. —*adj.* **4.** amounting to nineteen in number. [ME *nintene,* OE *nigontȳne*]

nine·teenth (nīn′tēnth′), *adj.* **1.** next after the eighteenth; being the ordinal number for 19. **2.** being one of 19 equal parts. —*n.* **3.** a nineteenth part, esp. of one (1/19). **4.** the nineteenth member of a series. [ME *nyntenthe* (see NINETEEN, -TH[2]); r. *nientethe,* OE *nigontēotha;* see NINE, TITHE]

nine·ti·eth (nīn′tē ith), *adj.* **1.** next after the eighty-ninth; being the ordinal number for 90. **2.** being one of 90 equal parts. —*n.* **3.** a ninetieth part, esp. of one (1/90). **4.** the ninetieth member of a series. [ME *nyntithe,* OE *nigenteotha*]

nine·ty (nīn′tē), *n., pl.* **-ties,** *adj.* —*n.* **1.** a cardinal number, ten times nine. **2.** a symbol for this number, as 90 or XC. **3.** a set of this many persons or things. **4. nineties,** the numbers, years, degrees, or the like, between 90 and 99, as in referring to numbered streets, indicating the years of a lifetime or of a century, or degrees of temperature. —*adj.* **5.** amounting to 90 in number. [ME *nineti,* OE *nigontig*]

Nin·e·veh (nin′ə və), *n.* the ancient capital of Assyria, on the Tigris River, in N Iraq. —**Nin·e·vite** (nin′ə vīt′), *n.* —**Nin·e·vit·i·cal** (nin′ə vit′i kəl), *adj.* —**Nin·e·vit·ish** (nin′ə vī′tish), *adj.*

Ning·po (ning′pō′), *n.* a seaport in E Chekiang, in E China. 237,500 (1953).

Ning·sia (ning′shyä′), *n.* former province in NW China.

nin·ny (nin′ē), *n., pl.* **-nies.** a fool; simpleton. [? *(a)n inn(ocent)* + -Y[2]] —**nin′ny·ish,** *adj.*

ni·non (nē nôN′), *n.* a sturdy chiffon or voile, used esp. for women's garments, curtains, and drapery. [< F: special use of nickname for Anne]

ninth (nīnth), *adj.* **1.** next after the eighth; being the ordinal number for nine. **2.** being one of nine equal parts. —*n.* **3.** a ninth part, esp. of one (1/9). **4.** the ninth member of a series. **5.** *Music.* **a.** a tone distant from another tone by an interval of an octave and a second. **b.** the interval between such tones. **c.** harmonic combination of such tones. [ME *ninthe* (see NINE, -TH[2]), r. ME *niend* (OE *nigend*), *neogethe, nigethe* (OE *nigotha*), etc.; akin to OS *nigutho,* Icel *nīundi,* Goth *niunda*] —**ninth′ly,** *adv.*

ninth′ chord′, *Music.* a chord formed by the superposition of four thirds.

Ninth′ of Ab′, *Judaism.* See **Tishah b'Ab.**

Ni·nus (nī′nəs), *n.* the legendary husband of Semiramis and founder of Nineveh.

Ni·o·be (nī′ō bē′), *n. Class. Myth.* the daughter of Tantalus and wife of Amphion of Thebes; her children were slain and Zeus turned her into stone, in which state she continued to weep over her loss. —**Ni′o·be′an,** *adj.*

ni·o·bi·um (nī ō′bē əm), *n. Chem.* a steel-gray metallic element resembling tantalum in its chemical properties; used chiefly in alloy steels. *Symbol:* Nb; *at. no.:* 41; *at. wt.:* 92,906; *sp. gr.:* 8.4 at 20°C. [< NL; named after NIOBE; see -IUM] —**ni·o·bic** (nī ō′bik, -ob′ik), *adj.*

ni·o·bous (nī ō′bəs), *adj.* **1.** *Chem.* containing trivalent niobium, as niobous chloride, $NbCl_3$. **2.** of niobium.

Ni·o·brar·a (nī′ə brâr′ə), *n.* a river flowing E from E Wyoming through Nebraska to the Missouri. 431 mi. long.

Niord (nyôrd), *n. Scand. Myth.* the god of winds, navigation, and prosperity, and the father of Frey and Freya; king of the Vanir.

Niort (nyôR), *n.* a city in W France. 39,165 (1962).

nip[1] (nip), *v.,* **nipped, nip·ping,** *n.* —*v.t.* **1.** to compress tightly between two surfaces or points; pinch; bite. **2.** to sever by pinching, biting, or snipping. **3.** to check in growth or development. **4.** to affect sharply and painfully or injuriously, as cold does. —*v.i.* **5.** *Chiefly Brit. Slang.* to leave stealthily; sneak away; flee. **6. nip in the bud.** See **bud**[1] (def. 5). —*n.* **7.** the act or an instance of nipping; a pinch. **8.** a sharp or biting remark. **9.** sharp cold; a sharp touch of frost. **10.** the biting taste or tang in cheese. **11.** a small bit or quantity of anything. **12.** Usually, **nips.** nipper (def. 2). **13. nip and tuck,** *U.S. Informal.* (of a race or other contest) very close: *It was nip and tuck until the final round.* [ME *nyppe* pinch < Scand; cf. Icel *hnippa* poke in the ribs]

nip[2] (nip), *n., v.,* **nipped, nip·ping.** —*n.* **1.** a small drink of liquor; sip. **2.** *Brit.* a small tankard of ale, about a half pint. —*v.t., v.i.* **3.** to drink (liquor) in small sips, esp. repeatedly. [short for *nipperkin* vessel holding half pint or less, small amount, ? < D; cf. *nippertje* nip and tuck; see -KIN]

Nip (nip), *n., adj. Disparaging.* Japanese. [short for NIPPONESE]

ni·pa (nē′pə, nī′-), *n.* a palm, *Nipa fruticans,* of the East Indies, Philippines, etc., whose foliage is used for thatching, basketry, etc. [< NL < Malay *nīpah*]

Nip·is·sing (nip′i sing), *n.* a lake in SE Canada, in Ontario, N of Georgian Bay. 330 sq. mi.

nip·per (nip′ər), *n.* **1.** a person or thing that nips. **2.** Usually, **nippers.** a device for nipping, as pincers or forceps. **3.** one of the large claws of a crustacean. **4.** *Chiefly Brit. Informal.* a small child, esp. a boy.

nip·ping (nip′ing), *adj.* **1.** characterized by nips. **2.** sharp or biting, as cold. **3.** sarcastic; caustic; bitter. —**nip′ping·ly,** *adv.*

nip·ple (nip′əl), *n.* **1.** a protuberance of the mamma or breast where, in the female, the milk ducts discharge; teat. **2.** something resembling it, as the mouthpiece of a nursing bottle, a sugar-tit, pacifier, etc. **3.** a short piece of pipe with threads on each end. [OE *nypel* proboscis, orig., projecting part; akin to Dan *nip* point] —**nip′ple·less,** *adj.*

Nip·pon (nē pôn′; *Eng.* ni pon′, nip′on), *n.* a Japanese name of **Japan.**

Nip·pon·ese (nip′ə nēz′, -nēs′), *n., pl.* **-ese,** *adj.* Japanese

Nip·pur (nip po͝or′), *n.* an ancient Sumerian and Babylonian city in SE Iraq.

nip·py (nip′ē), *adj.,* **-pi·er, -pi·est.** tending to nip; sharp; biting: *a nippy taste.*

nip-up (nip′up′), *n.* a calisthenic routine of springing to one's feet from a supine posture.

nir·va·na (nir vä′nə, -van′ə, nər-), *n.* **1.** (*often cap.*) *Buddhism.* freedom from the endless cycle of personal reincarnations, with their consequent suffering, as a result of the extinction of individual passion, hatred, and delusion: attained by the Arhat as his goal, but postponed by the Bodhisattva. **2.** (*often cap.*) *Hinduism.* salvation through the union of Atman with Brahma; moksha. **3.** a state of freedom from pain, worry, and the external world. [< Skt *nirvāṇa* a blowing out] —**nir·va′nic,** *adj.*

Niš (nēsh), *n.* a city in SE Serbia, in E Yugoslavia: a former capital of Serbia. 95,000 (est. 1964). Also, **Nish.**

Ni·san (nis′ən; *Heb.* nē sän′), *n.* the seventh month of the Jewish calendar. Also, **Nissan.** Cf. **Jewish calendar.**

Ni·sei (nē′sā′), *n., pl.* **-sei.** a person of Japanese descent, born and educated in the U.S. (distinguished from *Kibei*). Also, **ni′sei′.** Cf. **Issei, Sansei.** [< Jap = *ni* second + *sei* generation]

Ni·sha·pur (nē′shä po͝or′), *n.* a town in NE Iran: the birthplace of Omar Khayyám. 24,270 (est. 1949).

Ni·shi·no·mi·ya (nē′shē nô′mē yä′), *n.* a city on S Honshu, in central Japan. 262,608 (1964).

ni·si (nī′sī), *adj., conj.* not yet final or absolute (used, esp. in law, to indicate that a judgment or decree will become final on a particular date unless set aside or invalidated by certain specified contingencies): *to grant a decree nisi.* [< L: if not, unless (conj.)]

ni·si pri·us (nī′sī prī′əs), *Law.* **1.** Also called **ni′si pri′us court′.** a trial court for the hearing of civil cases before a judge and jury. **2.** *Brit. Law.* **a.** a writ commanding a sheriff of a county to summon a jury and bring it to the court in Westminster on a certain day, unless the judges of assizes previously have come to that county. **b.** the clause with the words "nisi prius" introducing this writ. **c.** the system of judicial circuits to which judges are assigned for local trials of civil and criminal cases. [< L: lit., unless previously, unless before] **—ni′si-pri′us,** *adj.*

Nis·san (nis′ən; *Heb.* nē sän′), *n.* Nisan.

Nis·tru (nē′strōō), *n.* Rumanian name of **Dniester.**

ni·sus (nī′səs), *n., pl.* **-sus.** a striving toward a particular goal or attainment; effort; impulse. [< L: effort = *nīs-*, ptp. s. of *nītī* to exert oneself + *-us* n. suffix (4th decl.)]

nit (nit), *n.* **1.** the egg of a parasitic insect, esp. of a louse. **2.** the young of such an insect. [ME *nite*, OE *hnitu*]

ni·ter (nī′tər), *n.* **1.** potassium nitrate, a white salt, KNO_3, used in the manufacture of gunpowder, fireworks, etc.; saltpeter. **2.** sodium nitrate, a white salt, $NaNO_3$, used as a fertilizer, in dynamite, etc.; Chile saltpeter. Also, *esp. Brit.,* **ni′tre.** [late ME *nitre* < L *nitrum* < Gk *nítron* natron]

Ni·te·roi (nē′tə roi′), *n.* a seaport in and the capital of Rio de Janeiro state, in SE Brazil. 229,025 (1960). Also, **Nictheroy.**

nit·er·y (nit′ə rē), *n., pl.* **-er·ies.** *U.S. Informal.* See **night club.** [*nite* (alter. for NIGHT) + -ERY]

nit·pick (nit′pik′), *v.i. Slang.* to be excessively concerned with inconsequential details. **—nit′pick′er,** *n.* **—nit′pick′ing,** *adj., n.*

nitr-, var. of **nitro-** before a vowel: *nitrate.*

ni·trate (nī′trāt), *n., v.,* **-trat·ed, -trat·ing.** **—*n.* 1.** *Chem.* a salt or ester of nitric acid, or any compound containing the univalent group $-ONO_2$ or $-NO_3$. **2.** fertilizer consisting of potassium nitrate or sodium nitrate. **—*v.t.* 3.** to treat with nitric acid or a nitrate. **4.** to convert into a nitrate. **—ni·tra′tion,** *n.*

ni·tric (nī′trik), *adj.* **1.** *Chem.* containing nitrogen, usually in the pentavalent state. **2.** of or pertaining to niter. [NITR- + -IC, modeled on F *nitrique*]

ni′tric ac′id, *Chem.* a caustic, corrosive, water-soluble liquid, HNO_3, having powerful oxidizing properties: used chiefly in the manufacture of explosives, fertilizers, and in organic synthesis. Also called **aqua fortis.**

ni′tric bacte′ria, nitrobacteria.

ni′tric ox′ide, *Chem.* a colorless, slightly water-soluble gas, NO, used chiefly as an intermediate in the manufacture of nitric acid from ammonia.

ni·tride (nī′trīd, -trid), *n. Chem.* a compound, containing two elements only, of which the more electronegative one is nitrogen. [NIT(E)R + -IDE]

ni·tri·fi·ca·tion (nī′trə fə kā′shən), *n.* the act of nitrifying.

ni·tri·fy (nī′trə fī′), *v.t.,* **-fied, -fy·ing.** **1.** to oxidize (ammonia, ammonium compounds, or atmospheric nitrogen) to nitrites, nitrates, or their respective acids, esp. by bacterial action. **2.** to impregnate with nitrogen or nitrogen compounds. [< F *nitrifier*] **—ni′tri·fi′a·ble,** *adj.*

ni·trile (nī′tril, -trīl), *n. Chem.* any of a class of organic compounds with the general formula $RC{\equiv}N$.

ni·trite (nī′trīt), *n. Chem.* a salt or ester of nitrous acid.

nitro-, *Chem.* **1.** a combining form indicating the nitro group: *nitroglycerin.* **2.** (erroneously) a combining form indicating the nitrate group: *nitrocellulose.* Also, *esp. before a vowel,* **nitr-.** [comb. form of Gk *nítron.* See NITER]

ni·tro·bac·te·ri·a (nī′trō bak tēr′ē ə), *n.pl., sing.* **-te·ri·um** (-tēr′ē əm). certain bacteria in the soil involved in nitrifying processes.

ni·tro·ben·zene (nī′trō ben′zēn, -ben zēn′), *n. Chem.* a toxic liquid, $C_6H_5NO_2$, used chiefly in the manufacture of aniline. Also called **essence of mirbane.**

ni·tro·cel·lu·lose (nī′trə sel′yə lōs′), *n. Chem.* See **cellulose nitrate.** **—ni′tro·cel′lu·los′ic,** *adj.*

ni·tro·chlo·ro·form (nī′trə klōr′ə fôrm′, -klôr′-), *n. Chem.* chloropicrin.

ni·tro·gen (nī′trə jən), *n. Chem.* a colorless, odorless, gaseous element that constitutes about four fifths of the volume of the atmosphere and is present in combined form in animal and vegetable tissues, esp. in proteins: used chiefly in the manufacture of ammonia, nitric acid, cyanide, explosives, fertilizer, dyes, as a cooling agent, etc. *Symbol:* N; *at. wt.:* 14.0067; *at. no.:* 7; *weight of one liter at 760 mm pressure and 0° C:* 1.2506 g. [< F *nitrogène*] **—ni·trog·e·nous** (nī troj′ə nəs), *adj.*

ni′trogen cy′cle, the continuous sequence of changes by which atmospheric nitrogen and nitrogenous compounds in the soil are converted, as by nitrification and nitrogen fixation, into substances that can be utilized by green plants, the substances returning to their previous state as a result of the decay of the plants and denitrification.

ni′trogen diox′ide, *Chem.* a poisonous gas, NO_2, used in the manufacture of nitric and sulfuric acids, and as a nitrating and oxidizing agent.

ni′trogen fixa′tion, **1.** any process of combining atmospheric nitrogen with other elements, either by chemical means or by bacterial action: used chiefly in the preparation of fertilizers, industrial products, etc. **2.** this process as performed by certain bacteria found in the nodules of leguminous plants, which make the resulting nitrogenous compounds available to their host plants. **—ni′tro·gen-fix′ing,** *adj.*

ni′trogen mus′tard, *Chem.* any of the class of poisonous, blistering compounds, as $(ClCH_2CH_2)_2NCH_3$, analogous in composition to mustard gas: used in the treatment of cancer and similar diseases.

ni′trogen tetrox′ide, *Chem.* a poisonous compound, N_2O_4: used chiefly as an oxidizer, esp. in rocket fuels, as a nitrating agent, and in the manufacture of nitric acid.

ni·tro·glyc·er·in (nī′trə glis′ər in), *n. Chem., Pharm.* a highly explosive liquid, $CH_2NO_3CHNO_3CH_2NO_3$, used chiefly as a constituent of dynamite and other explosives, in rocket propellants, and as a vasodilator in the treatment of angina pectoris. Also, **ni·tro·glyc·er·ine** (nī′trə glis′ər in, -ə rēn′). Also called **glyceryl trinitrate, trinitroglycerin.**

ni′tro group′, *Chem.* the univalent group, $-NO_2$. Also called **ni′tro rad′ical.** **—ni·tro** (nī′trō), *adj.*

ni·trol·ic (nī trol′ik), *adj. Chem.* of or noting a series of acids of the type $RC(=NOH)NO_2$ whose salts form deep-red solutions. [NITR- + -OL[1] + -IC]

ni·trom·e·ter (nī trom′i tər), *n.* an apparatus for determining the amount of nitrogen or nitrogen compounds in a substance or mixture. **—ni·tro·met·ric** (nī′trō me′trik), *adj.*

ni·tro·meth·ane (nī′trə meth′ān), *n. Chem.* a poisonous liquid, CH_3NO_2, used as a solvent and in organic synthesis.

ni·tro·par·af·fin (nī′trə par′ə fin), *n. Chem.* any of a class of compounds derived from the methane series replacing a hydrogen atom by the nitro group.

ni·tros·a·mine (nī tros′ə mēn′, -min), *n. Chem.* any of a series of compounds with the type formula R_2NNO.

ni·tro·so (nī trō′sō), *adj. Chem.* (esp. of organic compounds) containing the nitroso group; nitrosyl. [special use of *nitroso-*, repr. L *nitrōs(us)* full of natron. See NITER, -OSE[1]]

nitro′so group′, *Chem.* the univalent group, $O{=}N-$. Also called **nitro′so rad′ical.**

ni·tro·syl (nī′trə sil, nī′trə sēl′, nī trō′sil), *adj. Chem.* nitroso. [NITROS(O) + -YL]

ni·trous (nī′trəs), *adj. Chem.* **1.** pertaining to compounds obtained from niter, usually containing less oxygen than the corresponding nitric compounds. **2.** containing nitrogen, usually in the trivalent state. [< L *nitrōsus* full of natron]

ni′trous ac′id, *Chem.* an acid, HNO_2, known only in solution.

ni′trous bacte′ria, nitrobacteria that convert ammonia derivatives into nitrites by oxidation.

ni′trous ox′ide, *Chem., Pharm.* a sweet-smelling, sweet-tasting, nonflammable gas, N_2O, that sometimes produces a feeling of exhilaration when inhaled: used chiefly as an anesthetic, in the manufacture of chemicals, and as an aerosol. Also called **laughing gas.**

nit·ty-grit·ty (nit′ē grit′ē), *n. Slang.* the crux of a matter or of a problem. [perh. rhyming compound based on GRITTY]

nit·wit (nit′wit′), *n.* a slow-witted or foolish person. [*nit* (< G; dial. var. of *nicht* not) + WIT]

Ni·u·e (nē ōō′ā), *n.* an island in the S Pacific between Tonga and Cook Islands: possession of New Zealand. 4781 (est. 1960); ab. 100 sq. mi. Also called **Savage Island.** **—Ni·u·an** (nē ōō′ən), *adj., n.*

ni·val (nī′vəl), *adj.* of or growing in snow: *nival flora.* [< L *nivāl(is)* of, belonging to snow, snowy = *niv-* (s. of *nix*) snow + *-ālis* -AL[1]]

niv·e·ous (niv′ē əs), *adj.* resembling snow, esp. in whiteness; snowy. [< L *niveus* snowy, snow-white, of, from snow = *niv-* (s. of *nix*) snow + *-eus* -EOUS]

Ni·ver·nais (nē ver ne′), *n.* a former province in central France. *Cap.:* Nevers.

Ni·vôse (nē vōz′), *n.* (in the French Revolutionary calendar) the fourth month of the year, extending from December 21 to January 19. [< F < L *nivōsus* snowy = *niv-* (s. of *nix*) snow + *-ōsus* -OSE[1]]

nix[1] (niks), *Slang.* **—*n.* 1.** nothing. **—*adv.* 2.** no. **—*interj.* 3.** (used as an exclamation of disagreement, warning, etc.) **—*v.t.* 4.** to veto; refuse to agree to; prohibit: *to nix the project.* [< G: var. of *nichts* nothing]

nix[2] (niks), *n., pl.* **nix·es.** *Germanic Folklore.* a water spirit, usually small, and either good or bad. Also, *referring to a female,* **nix·ie** (nik′sē). [< G *Nix*, OHG *nihhus*, c. OE *nicor* sea monster]

nix·ie (nik′sē), *n., pl.* **nix·ies.** *U.S.* a letter or parcel that is undeliverable by the post office because of a faulty or illegible address. [NIX[1] + -IE]

Nix·on (nik′sən), *n.* **Richard M(il·hous)** (mil′hous), born 1913, 37th president of the U.S. 1969–74 (resigned).

Ni·zam (ni zäm′, -zam′), *n.* **1.** the title of the ruler of Hyderabad from the beginning of the 18th century to 1950. **2.** (*l.c.*) the Turkish regular army or any member of it. [(def. 1) < Urdu *Nizām-al-mulk* governor of the realm; (def. 2) < Turk *nizāmiye* regular army; both < Ar *nizām* order, arrangement, etc.]

Nizh·ni Nov·go·rod (*Russ.* nēzh′ni nôv′go rot), former name of the city of **Gorki.**

Nizh′ni Ta·gil′ (tä gēl′), a city in the W RSFSR, in the W Soviet Union in Asia, on the E slope of the Ural Mountains. 370,000 (est. 1965).

NJ, New Jersey (approved esp. for use with zip code).

N.J., New Jersey.

Nkru·mah (ənkrōō′mə, əng krōō′-), *n.* **Kwa·me** (kwä′mē), 1909–72, president of Ghana 1960–66.

NKVD, (formerly) the secret police of the Soviet Union (1935–43). Also, **N.K.V.D.** Cf. **Cheka, G.P.U., MVD.** [< Russ *N(arodnii) K(ommissariat) V(nutrennikh) D(el)* People's Commissariat of Internal Affairs]

NL, New Latin; Neo-Latin. Also, **NL.**

N.L., **1.** *Baseball.* National League. **2.** New Latin; Neo-Latin.

n.l., **1.** See **non licet.** **2.** See **non liquet.**

N. Lat., north latitude. Also, **N. lat.**

N.L.F., See **National Liberation Front.**

NLRB, National Labor Relations Board. Also, **N.L.R.B.**

NM, New Mexico (approved esp. for use with zip code).

nm, **1.** nanometer. **2.** nautical mile. **3.** nonmetallic.

N.M., New Mexico. Also, **N. Mex.**

N.M.U., National Maritime Union. Also, **NMU**

NNE, north-northeast. Also, **N.N.E.**

NNP, See **net national product.**

NNW, north-northwest. Also, **N.N.W.**

no[1] (nō), *adv., n., pl.* **noes, nos.** **—*adv.* 1.** (a negative used to express dissent, denial, or refusal, as in response to a question, request, etc.) **2.** (used to emphasize or introduce a negative statement): *None of the girls came to the party, no, not a one.* **3.** not in any degree; not at all (used with a comparative). *He is no better.* **4.** not: *whether or no.* **—*n.* 5.** an utterance of the word "no." **6.** a denial or refusal. **7.** a negative vote or voter. [ME; OE *nā* = *ne* not + *ā* ever; see AY[1]]

no[2] (nō), *adj.* **1.** not any: *no money.* **2.** not at all; far from being: *He is no genius.* [var. of NONE[1]]

No, *Chem.* nobelium.

Nō (nō), *n.* the classic drama of Japan, developed chiefly in the 14th century, employing verse, prose, choral song, and dance in highly conventionalized formal and thematic patterns derived from religious sources and folk myths.

Also, **No, Noh.** Cf. **kabuki.** [< Jap: lit., ability, capacity]

no., 1. north. 2. northern. 3. number. Also, **No.**

No·a·chi·an (nō ā′kē ən), *adj.* of or pertaining to the patriarch Noah or his time. Also, **No·ach·ic** (nō ak′ik, -ā′kik), **No·ach′i·cal, No·ah·ic** (nō ā′ik). [*Noach* (var. of NOAH) + -IAN]

No·ah (nō′ə), *n.* the patriarch who built a vessel (**No′ah's Ark′**) in which he, his family, and animals of every species survived the Flood. Gen. 5–9.

nob[1] (nob), *n.* *Cribbage.* the jack of the same suit as the card turned up, counting one to the holder. [? var. of KNOB]

nob[2] (nob), *n.* *Chiefly Brit. Slang.* a person of wealth or social distinction. [? special use of NOB[1]]

nob·ble (nob′əl), *v.t.*, **-bled, -bling.** *Brit. Slang.* **1.** to drug or disable (a race horse) to prevent its winning a race. **2.** to convince (a person) by fraudulent methods. [back formation from *nobbler,* var. of HOBBLER (*an 'obbler* being taken as *a nobbler*)] —**nob′bler,** *n.*

nob·by (nob′ē), *adj.*, **-bi·er, -bi·est.** *Brit. Slang.* **1.** fashionable or elegant. **2.** excellent; first-rate. —**nob′bi·ly,** *adv.*

No·bel (nō bel′), *n.* **1. Al·fred Bern·hard** (äl′frĕd bern′-närd), 1833–96, Swedish engineer, manufacturer, and philanthropist. **2.** See **Nobel prize.**

No·bel·ist (nō bel′ist), *n.* a person who is awarded a Nobel prize.

no·be·li·um (nō bē′lē əm), *n.* *Chem.* a synthetic, radioactive element. *Symbol:* No; *at. no.:* 102. [< NL; named after *Nobel* Institute where first discovered; see -IUM]

No′bel prize′, one of a group of prizes awarded annually from the bequest of Alfred B. Nobel for achievement during the preceding year in physics, chemistry, medicine or physiology, literature, and the promotion of peace; an annual award in economics was established in 1969 from private funds. Also called **Nobel.**

no·bil·i·ty (nō bil′i tē), *n., pl.* **-ties** for 1, 5, 6. **1.** the noble class or the body of nobles in a country. **2.** (in Britain) the peerage. **3.** the state or quality of being noble. **4.** noble birth or rank. **5.** nobleness of mind or spirit; exalted moral excellence. **6.** grandeur or magnificence. [late ME *nobilite* < L *nōbilitās*]

no·ble (nō′bəl), *adj.*, **-bler, -blest,** *n.* —*adj.* **1.** distinguished by rank or title. **2.** pertaining to persons so distinguished. **3.** of, belonging to, or constituting a hereditary class possessing special social or political status in a country or state; of or pertaining to the aristocracy. **4.** of an exalted moral character or excellence. **5.** imposing in appearance; magnificent. **6.** of an admirably high quality. **7.** *Chem.* inert; chemically inactive. —*n.* **8.** a person of noble birth or rank; nobleman. **9.** a former gold coin of England equal to half a mark or 6s. 8d. **10.** (in Britain) a peer. [ME < OF < L (*g*)*nōbilis* notable, of high rank = (*g*)*nō-* KNOW + *-bilis* -BLE] —**no′ble·ness,** *n.*
—**Syn. 3.** highborn, aristocratic. **4.** lofty, honorable. NOBLE, HIGH-MINDED, MAGNANIMOUS agree in referring to lofty principles and loftiness of mind or spirit. NOBLE implies a loftiness of character or spirit that scorns the petty, mean, base, or dishonorable: *a noble deed.* HIGH-MINDED implies having elevated principles and consistently adhering to them: *a high-minded pursuit of legal reforms.* MAGNANIMOUS suggests greatness of mind or soul, esp. as manifested in generosity or in overlooking injuries: *magnanimous toward his former enemies.* **5.** grand, lordly, splendid, stately.

no·ble·man (nō′bəl mən), *n., pl.* **-men.** a man of noble birth or rank; noble.

no·blesse o·blige (nō bles′ ō blēzh′; *Fr.* nô bles′ ô blēzh′), the moral obligation of the rich or highborn to display honorable or charitable conduct. [< F: lit., nobility obliges]

no·ble·wom·an (nō′bəl wŏŏm′ən), *n., pl.* **-wom·en.** a woman of noble birth or rank.

no·bly (nō′blē), *adv.* **1.** in a noble manner. **2.** courageously; bravely; gallantly. **3.** splendidly; superbly; magnificently. **4.** of noble ancestry: *nobly born.* [ME *nobliche*]

no·bod·y (nō′bod′ē, -bə dē), *pron., n., pl.* **-bod·ies.** —*pron.* **1.** no person; not anyone; no one. —*n.* **2.** *Informal.* a person of no importance, esp. socially. [ME]

nock (nok), *n.* **1.** a notch or groove at the end of an arrow into which the bowstring fits. **2.** a notch or groove at each end of the bow, to hold the bowstring in place. **3.** *Naut.* throat (def. 6). —*v.t.* **4.** to furnish with a nock. **5.** to adjust (the arrow) to the bowstring, in readiness to shoot. [ME *nocke;* akin to D *nok,* LG *nok*(*ke*) tip]

noct-, var. of **nocti-** before a vowel.

noc·tam·bu·lism (nok tam′byə liz′əm), *n.* somnambulism. Also, **noc·tam′bu·la′tion.** [NOCT- + L *ambul*(*āre*) (to) walk + -ISM] —**noc·tam′bu·list,** *n.*

nocti-, a learned borrowing from Latin meaning "night," used in the formation of compound words: *noctilucent.* Also, *esp. before a vowel,* **noct-.** [< L *nocti-,* comb. form of *nox* night]

noc·ti·lu·ca (nok′tə lŏŏ′kə), *n., pl.* **-cae** (-sē). a dinoflagellate of the genus *Noctiluca,* capable of producing light and, in groups, of causing a luminous appearance of the sea. [< L *noctilūca* shiner by night = *nocti-* NOCTI- + *-lūca* shiner, akin to *lūcēre* to shine] —**noc′ti·lu′can,** *adj.*

noc·ti·lu·cent (nok′tə lŏŏ′sənt), *adj.* *Meteorol.* (of high-altitude clouds) visible during the short night of summer.

noc·tu·id (nok′chŏŏ id), *n.* **1.** any of numerous moths of the family *Noctuidae,* comprising dull-colored moths, the larvae of which include the armyworms and cutworms. —*adj.* **2.** belonging or pertaining to the family *Noctuidae.* [< NL *Noctuid*(*ae*) = *noctu-* (s. of L *noctua* a nocturnal owl; see NOCTI-) + *-idae* -ID[2]]

noc·turn (nok′tûrn), *n.* *Rom. Cath. Ch.* a division of the office of matins. [ME *nocturne* < ML *nocturna,* n. use of fem. of L *nocturnus* by night; r. OE *noctern*]

noc·tur·nal (nok tûr′nəl), *adj.* **1.** of or pertaining to the night. **2.** done, occurring, or coming by night. **3.** active by night, as animals (opposed to *diurnal*). **4.** opening by night and closing by day, as certain flowers (opposed to *diurnal*). [< LL *nocturnāl*(*is*)] —**noc·tur·nal·i·ty** (nok′tər nal′i tē), *n.* —**noc·tur′nal·ly,** *adv.*

noc·turne (nok′tûrn), *n.* **1.** a musical composition appropriate to the night or evening. **2.** a composition, esp. of music, of a dreamy character. [< F; see NOCTURN]

noc·u·ous (nok′yŏŏ əs), *adj.* likely to cause damage or injury; noxious. [< L *nocuus* harmful, injurious = *nocu-* (perf. s. of *nocēre* to harm) + *-us* -OUS] —**noc′u·ous·ly,** *adv.* —**noc′u·ous·ness,** *n.*

nod (nod), *v.*, **nod·ded, nod·ding,** *n.* —*v.i.* **1.** to make a slight, quick inclination of the head, as in assent or greeting. **2.** to let the head fall forward with a sudden, involuntary movement when sleepy. **3.** to become careless; make an error or mistake through lack of attention. **4.** (of trees, flowers, plumes, etc.) to droop, bend, or incline with a swaying motion. —*v.t.* **5.** to incline (the head) in a short, quick movement, as of assent or greeting. **6.** to express or signify by such a movement. **7.** to summon, bring, or send by a nod of the head. —*n.* **8.** a short, quick inclination of the head, as in assent, greeting, command, or drowsiness. **9.** a brief period of sleep; nap. **10.** a bending or swaying movement of anything. [ME *nodde* < ?] —**nod′ding·ly,** *adv.*

Nod (nod), *n.* See **land of Nod.**

nod·al (nōd′əl), *adj.* pertaining to or of the nature of a node. —**no·dal·i·ty** (nō dal′i tē), *n.*

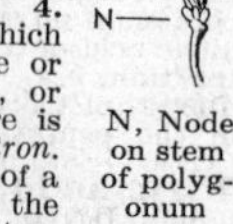

N, Node on stem of polygonum

nod·dy (nod′ē), *n., pl.* **-dies.** **1.** any of several dark-bodied terns found about the coasts and islands in warm seas of both the New and Old Worlds, often so tame as to seem stupid. **2.** a fool or simpleton; noodle. [? n. use of *noddy* (adj.) silly. See NOD, -Y[1]]

node (nōd), *n.* **1.** a knot, protuberance, or knob. **2.** a centering point of component parts. **3.** *Bot.* **a.** a joint in a stem. **b.** a part of a stem that normally bears a leaf. **4.** *Geom.* a point on a curve or surface at which there can be more than one tangent line or tangent plane. **5.** *Physics.* a point, line, or region in a standing wave at which there is relatively little or no vibration. **6.** *Astron.* either of the two points at which the orbit of a heavenly body intersects a given plane, esp. the plane of the ecliptic or of the celestial equator. **7.** *Anat.* a knotlike mass of tissue: *lymph nodes.* **8.** *Pathol.* circumscribed swelling. **9.** nodus. [< L *nōdus* a knot]

nod·i·cal (nod′i kəl, nō′di-), *adj.* *Astron.* of or pertaining to a node or the nodes.

no·dose (nō′dōs, nō dōs′), *adj.* having nodes. Also, **no·dous** (nō′dəs). [< L *nōdōsus* full of knots, knotty] —**no·dos·i·ty** (nō dos′i tē), *n.*

nod·u·lar (noj′ə lər), *adj.* **1.** of, pertaining to, or characterized by nodules. **2.** shaped like or occurring in nodules.

nod·ule (noj′ŏŏl), *n.* **1.** a small node, knot, or knob. **2.** a small, rounded mass or lump. **3.** *Bot.* a tubercle. [< L *nōdulus* a little knot]

nod·u·lous (noj′ə ləs), *adj.* having nodules. Also, **nod·u·lose** (noj′ə lōs′, noj′ə lōs′).

no·dus (nō′dəs), *n., pl.* **-di** (-dī). a difficult or intricate point, situation, plot, etc. [< L *nōdus* a knot]

No·el (nō el′), *n.* **1.** the Christmas season; yuletide. **2.** (*l.c.*) a Christmas song or carol. [< F << L *nātālis* birthday, n. use of *nātālis* NATAL]

no·e·sis (nō ē′sis), *n.* (in Greek philosophy) the exercise of reason. [< Gk *nóēsis* thought, intelligence = *noē-* (verbid s. of *noeîn* to think) + *-sis* -SIS]

no·et·ic (nō et′ik), *adj.* **1.** of or pertaining to the mind. **2.** originating in or apprehended by the reason. [< Gk *noētikós* intelligent = *noē*(*sis*) NOESIS + *-tikos* -TIC]

no-fault (nō′fôlt′), *n.* a form of automobile insurance enabling the policyholder in case of an accident to collect a certain basic compensation promptly for his economic loss from his own insurance company without determination of liability. Also called **no′-fault′ in·sur′ance.**

Nof·re·te·te (nof′ri tē′tē), *n.* Nefertiti.

no-frills (nō′frilz′), *adj.* not providing or including normally expected or available features or comfort; reduced to essentials: *a no-frills air fare.*

nog[1] (nog), *n.* **1.** *U.S.* any beverage made with beaten eggs, usually with alcoholic liquor; eggnog. **2.** a kind of strong ale. Also, **nogg.** [?]

nog[2] (nog), *n.* a block of wood, as one inserted into brickwork to provide a hold for nails. [? var. of *knag,* ME *knagge* spur, peg]

nog·gin (nog′ən), *n.* **1.** a small cup or mug. **2.** a small amount of liquor, usually a gill. **3.** *Informal.* the head. [?]

nog·ging (nog′ing), *n.* **1.** (in frame construction) the act of filling the spaces between studs or nogs with small masonry, as bricks. **2.** masonry employed in nogging.

No·gu·chi (nô gŏŏ′chē), *n.* **1. Hi·de·yo** (hē′de yô′), 1876–1928, Japanese physician and bacteriologist in the U.S. **2. I·sa·mu** (ē′sä mŏŏ′), born 1904, U.S. sculptor and designer.

Noh (nō), *n.* Nō.

no·how (nō′hou′), *adv.* *Chiefly Dial.* in no manner; not at all: *I can't learn this nohow.*

-noia, an element appearing in loan words from Greek, where it meant "thought": *paranoia.* [< Gk *-noia,* = *nó*(*os*) mind + *-ia* -Y[3]]

noil (noil), *n.* a short fiber of cotton, wool, worsted, etc., separated from the long fibers in combing. [?] —**noil′y,** *adj.*

noise (noiz), *n., v.,* **noised, nois·ing.** —*n.* **1.** sound, esp. of a loud, harsh, or confused kind. **2.** a sound of any kind. **3.** loud shouting or clamor. **4.** an electric disturbance in a communications system that interferes with or prevents reception of a signal or of information. **5.** *Obs.* rumor or common talk, esp. slander. —*v.t.* **6.** to spread as a report or rumor. —*v.i.* **7.** to talk much or publicly. **8.** to make a noise or clamor. [ME < OF < L *nausea* seasickness. See NAUSEA]
—**Syn. 1.** clatter, blare, uproar. NOISE, CLAMOR, HUBBUB, RACKET refer to unmusical or confused sounds. NOISE is the general word and is applied equally to soft or loud, confused or inharmonious sounds: *street noises.* CLAMOR and HUBBUB are alike in referring to loud noises resulting from shouting, cries, animated or excited tones, and the like; but in CLAMOR the emphasis is on the meaning of the shouting, and in HUBBUB the emphasis is on the confused mingling of sounds: *the clamor of an angry crowd; His voice could be heard above the hubbub.* RACKET suggests a loud, confused noise of the kind produced by clatter or percussion: *She always makes such a racket when she cleans up the dishes.* **2.** See **sound**[1].

noise·less (noiz′lis), *adj.* accompanied by or making no noise; silent; quiet. —**noise′less·ly,** *adv.* —**noise′less·ness,** *n.* —**Syn.** inaudible, soundless. See **still**[1].

noise·mak·er (noiz′mā′kər), *n.* a person or thing that makes noise, as a reveler on New Year's Eve, or a rattle, horn, or similar device. —**noise′mak′ing,** *n., adj.*

noise·proof (noiz′pro͞of′), *adj.* soundproof.

noi·some (noi′səm), *adj.* **1.** offensive or disgusting, as an odor. **2.** harmful, injurious, or noxious. [ME *noy* (aph. var. of ANNOY) + -SOME[1]] —**noi′some·ly,** *adv.* —**noi′some·ness,** *n.* —**Syn. 1.** putrid, rotten, stinking. **2.** hurtful, pernicious, deleterious. —**Ant. 2.** healthful.

nois·y (noi′zē), *adj.,* **nois·i·er, nois·i·est. 1.** making much noise. **2.** abounding in or full of noise. —**nois′i·ly,** *adv.* —**nois′i·ness,** *n.* —**Syn. 1.** clamorous, vociferous.

no′-load′ fund′ (nō′lōd′), a mutual fund that carries no sales charge. Also called **no′-load′.**

no·lens vo·lens (nō′lāns wō′lāns; *Eng.* nō′lens vō′lens), *Latin.* whether willing or not; willy-nilly.

no·li me tan·ge·re (nō′lī mē tan′jə rē; *Lat.* nō′lē me täng′ge re′), **1.** a person or thing that must not be touched or interfered with. **2.** a picture representing Jesus appearing to Mary Magdalene after His resurrection. **3.** Also, **no′li-me-tan′ge·re.** the touch-me-not. [< L: touch me not]

nol·le pros·e·qui (nol′ē pros′ə kwī′), *Law.* an entry made upon the records of a court when the plaintiff or prosecutor will proceed no further in a suit or action. *Abbr.:* nol. pros. [< L: be unwilling to pursue, do not prosecute]

no·lo con·ten·de·re (nō′lō kən ten′də rē), *Law.* (in a criminal case) a defendant's pleading that does not admit guilt but subjects him to punishment as though he had pleaded guilty. [< L: I am unwilling to contend]

nol-pros (nol′pros′), *v.t.,* **-prossed, -pros·sing.** *Law.* to end by a nolle prosequi.

nol. pros., *Law.* See **nolle prosequi.**

nom., nominative.

no·ma (nō′mə), *n., pl.* **-mas.** *Pathol.* a gangrenous ulceration of the mouth and cheeks and sometimes other parts, occurring mainly in debilitated children. [< NL = L *nom(ē)* a sore, ulcer < Gk *nomḗ* a feeding, grazing (akin to *némein* to feed, graze, consume) + L *-a* n. suffix]

no·mad (nō′mad, nom′ad), *n.* **1.** a member of a people or tribe that has no fixed abode, but moves about from place to place according to the state of the pasturage or food supply. **2.** any wanderer. —*adj.* **3.** nomadic. [< L *nomad-* < Gk, s. of *nomás* pasturing flocks, akin to *némein* to pasture] —**no′mad·ism,** *n.*

no·mad·ic (nō mad′ik), *adj.* of, pertaining to, or characteristic of nomads. —**no·mad′i·cal·ly,** *adv.* [< Gk *nomadikós*]

no′ man's′ land′, 1. a tract of land between opposing armies, over which no control has been established. **2.** an unowned or unclaimed tract of usually barren land.

nom·arch (nom′ärk), *n.* the governor of a nome or a nomarchy. [< Gk *nomárch(ēs)* the chief of a province = *nom(ós)* a province, district + *árch(ein)* (to) rule + *-ēs* n. suffix]

nom·ar·chy (nom′är kē), *n., pl.* **-chies.** one of the provinces into which modern Greece is divided. [< Gk *nomarchía* rule of a province]

nom·bril (nom′bril), *n.* *Heraldry.* the point in an escutcheon between the middle of the base and the fess point. [< F: lit., navel]

nom de guerre (nôN də ger′; *Eng.* nom′ də gâr′), *pl.* **noms de guerre** (nôN də ger′; *Eng.* nomz′ də gâr′). *French.* an assumed name; pseudonym. [lit., war name]

nom de plume (nom′ də plo͞om′; *Fr.* nôN də plym′), *pl.* **noms de plume** (nomz′ də plo͞om′; *Fr.* nôN də plym′). See **pen name.** [coined in E < F words: lit., pen name]

nome (nōm), *n.* **1.** one of the provinces of ancient Egypt. **2.** nomarchy. [< Gk *nom(ós)* a pasture, district, akin to *némein* to pasture]

Nome (nōm), *n.* **1.** a seaport in W Alaska. 2488 (1970). **2. Cape,** a cape in W Alaska, on Seward Peninsula, W of Nome.

no·men (nō′men), *n., pl.* **nom·i·na** (nom′ə nə). (in ancient Rome) the second name of a citizen, indicating his gens, as "Gaius *Julius* Caesar." [< L: a NAME]

no·men·cla·tor (nō′mən klā′tər), *n.* *Archaic.* **1.** a person who calls or announces things or persons by their names. **2.** a person who assigns names, as in scientific classification; classifier. [< L: var. of *nōmenculātor* one who announces names = *nōmen* NAME + *-culātor,* var. of *calātor* a crier (*calā(re)* (to) call + *-tor* agent suffix)]

no·men·cla·ture (nō′mən klā′chər, nō men′klə-), *n.* **1.** a set or system of names or terms, as those used in a particular science or art, by an individual or community, etc. **2.** the names or terms comprising a set or system. [< L *nōmenclātūra* a calling by name, list of names. See NOMENCLATOR, -URE] —**no′men·cla′tur·al, no·men·cla·to·ri·al** (nō′mən klə tōr′ē əl, -tôr′-), **no·men·cla·tive** (nō′mən klā′tiv), *adj.*

nom·i·nal (nom′ə nəl), *adj.* **1.** being such in name only; so-called. **2.** (of a price, consideration, etc.) named as a mere matter of form, being trifling in comparison with the actual value. **3.** of, pertaining to, or constituting a name or names. **4.** *Gram.* of, pertaining to, functioning as, or producing a noun or nouns: *a nominal suffix.* **5.** assigned to a person by name: *nominal shares of stock.* **6.** containing, bearing, or giving a name. [< L *nōmināl(is)* of, belonging to a name = *nōmin-* (s. of *nōmen*) a name + *-ālis* -AL[1]]

nom·i·nal·ism (nom′ə nəliz′əm), *n.* (in medieval philosophy) the doctrine that general or abstract words, or universals, do not stand for objectively existing entities, and that universals are no more than names assigned to individual physical particulars which alone have objective existence. Cf. **conceptualism, realism** (def. 5a). [< F *nominalisme*] —**nom′i·nal·ist,** *n.* —**nom′i·nal·is′tic,** *adj.* —**nom′i·nal·is′ti·cal·ly,** *adv.*

nom·i·nal·ize (nom′ə nəlīz′), *v.t.,* **-ized, -iz·ing.** to convert (another part of speech) into a noun.

nom·i·nal·ly (nom′ə nəlē), *adv.* by or as regards name; in name; ostensibly.

nom′inal val′ue, book or par value, as of securities; face value.

nom′inal wag′es, *Econ.* wages measured in terms of money and not by their ability to command goods and services. Cf. **real wages.**

nom·i·nate (*v.* nom′ə nāt′; *adj.* nom′ə nit), *v.,* **-nat·ed, -nat·ing,** *adj.* —*v.t.* **1.** to propose (someone) as a proper person for appointment or election to an office. **2.** to appoint to a duty or office. **3.** *Archaic.* to entitle; name; designate. **4.** *Obs.* to specify. —*adj.* **5.** having a particular name. [< L *nōmindruc(us)* (see below)]

—**nom′i·na′tor,** *n.*

nom·i·na·tion (nom′ə nā′shən), *n.* **1.** the act or an instance of nominating, esp. to office. **2.** the state of being nominated, esp. to office. [< L *nōminātiōn-* (s. of *nōminātiō*) a naming]

nom·i·na·tive (nom′ə nə tiv, -nā′tiv, nom′nə-), *adj.* **1.** *Gram.* **a.** (in certain inflected languages, as Sanskrit, Latin, and Russian) noting a case having as its function the indication of the subject of a finite verb. **b.** similar to such a case in function or meaning. **2.** nominated; appointed by nomination. **3.** made out in a person's name, as a certificate or security. —*n.* *Gram.* **4.** the nominative case. **5.** a word in the nominative case. **6.** a form or construction of similar function or meaning. [< L *nōminātīv(us)* (see NOMINATE, -IVE), r. ME *nominatif* < MF] —**nom′i·na·tive·ly,** *adv.*

nom·i·nee (nom′ə nē′), *n.* a person nominated, as to run for elective office, fill a particular post, etc. [NOMIN(ATE) + -EE]

nomo-, a learned borrowing from Greek meaning "custom," "law," used in the formation of compound words: *nomology.* [< Gk *nomo-,* comb. form of *nómos* law, custom; akin to *nėm(ein)* (to) manage, control]

nom·o·gram (nom′ə gram′, nō′mə-), *n.* **1.** a graph, usually containing three parallel scales graduated for different variables so that when a straight line connects values of any two, the related value may be read directly from the third at the point intersected by the line. **2.** any similar graph used to show the relation between quantities, values, numbers, and so on. Also called **nom·o·graph** (nom′ə graf′, -gräf′, nō′mə-).

no·mog·ra·phy (nō mog′rə fē), *n., pl.* **-phies** for 1. **1.** the art of or a treatise on drawing up laws. **2.** the art of making and using nomograms. [< Gk *nomographía* the writing of laws] —**no·mog′ra·pher,** *n.* —**nom·o·graph·ic** (nom′ə graf′ik), **nom′o·graph′i·cal,** *adj.* —**nom′o·graph′i·cal·ly,** *adv.*

no·mol·o·gy (nō mol′ə jē), *n.* **1.** the science of law. **2.** the science of the laws of the mind. —**nom·o·log·i·cal** (nom′ə loj′i kəl), *adj.* —**no·mol′o·gist,** *n.*

nom·o·thet·ic (nom′ə thet′ik), *adj.* **1.** lawgiving; legislative. **2.** founded upon or derived from law. **3.** pertaining to or involving the study or formulation of general or universal laws (opposed to *idiographic*). [< Gk *nomothetik(ós)*]

No·mu·ra (nô′mo͞o rä′), *n.* **Ki·chi·sa·bu·ro** (kē′chē sä′bo͞o rō′), 1877–1964, Japanese diplomat.

-nomy, a combining form of Greek origin meaning "distribution," "arrangement," "management," or having reference to laws or government: *astronomy; economy; taxonomy.* [< Gk *-nomía* law. See NOMO-, -Y[3]]

non-, a combining form meaning "not," freely used as an English formative, usually with a simple negative force as implying mere negation or absence of something (rather than the opposite or reverse of it, as often expressed by **un-**[1]): *nonadherence; noninterference; nonpayment; nonprofessional.* [comb. form repr. L adv. *nōn* not]

no·na (nō′nə), *n.* *Pathol.* See **sleeping sickness** (def. 2). [< L *nōna* (*hōra*) ninth (hour); i.e., late stage in life of patient]

non·age (non′ij, nō′nij), *n.* **1.** the period of legal minority. **2.** any period of immaturity. [late ME < MF (see NON-, AGE), r. ME *nownage* < AF *nounage*]

non·a·ge·nar·i·an (non′ə jə nâr′ē ən, nō′nə jə-), *adj.* **1.** of the age of 90 years, or between 90 and 100 years old. —*n.* **2.** a nonagenarian person. [< L *nōnāgēnāri(us)* that contains ninety, that consists of ninety (*nōnāgēn(i)* ninety each + *-ārius* -ARY) + -AN]

non·ag·gres·sion (non′ə gresh′ən), *n.* **1.** abstention from aggression, esp. by a nation. —*adj.* **2.** of or pertaining to abstention from aggression. —**non′ag·gres′sive,** *adj.* —**non′ag·gres′sive·ly,** *adv.* —**non′ag·gres′sive·ness,** *n.*

140°

Nonagon (Regular)

non·a·gon (non′ə gon′), *n.* a polygon having nine angles and nine sides. Also called **enneagon.** [< L *nōnā-,* comb. form of *nōn(us)* ninth + -GON] —**non·ag·o·nal** (non ag′ə nəl), *adj.*

non·a·ligned (non′ə līnd′), *adj.* **1.** not aligned. **2.** (of a nation or national policy) not aligned with or favoring the U.S., the U.S.S.R., or Communist China: *a nonaligned African nation.* —**non′a·lign′ment,** *n.*

non·al·ler·gen·ic (non′al ər jen′ik), *adj.* not causing an allergic reaction: *nonallergenic cosmetics.*

non·ap·pear·ance (non′ə pēr′əns), *n.* failure or neglect to appear, as in a court.

non·as·sess·a·ble (non′ə ses′ə bəl), *adj.* (of stock) exempting the investor from any expense or liability beyond

non′a·bra′sive, *adj.;* **-ly,** *adv.;* **-ness,** *n.*
non·ab′so·lute′, *adj., n.;* **-ly,** *adv.;* **-ness,** *n.*
non′ab·sorb′a·ble, *adj.*
non′ab·sorb′ent, *adj., n.*
non′ab·stain′er, *n.*
non′ab·sten′tion, *n.*
non′ac·a·dem′ic, *adj., n.*
non′ac·cept′ance, *n.*
non·ac′tive, *adj., n.*
non′a·dap′tive, *adj.*
non′ad·dict′ing, *adj.*
non′ad·dic′tive, *adj.*
non′ad·her′ence, *n.*
non′ad·he′sive, *adj.*
non′ad·ja′cent, *adj.*
non′ad·just′a·ble, *adj.*
non′ad·min′is·tra′tive, *adj.;* **-ly,** *adv.*
non′ad·mis′sion, *n.*
non′a·dult′, *adj., n.*
non′ad·van·ta′geous, *adj.;* **-ly,** *adv.*
non′af·fil′i·at′ed, *adj.*
non′a·gree′ment, *n.*
non′ag·ri·cul′tur·al, *adj.*
non′al·co·hol′ic, *adj.*
non′al·lel′ic, *adj.*
non′an·a·lyt′ic, *adj.*
non·ap′pli·ca·ble, *adj.*
non′a·quat′ic, *adj.*
non-Ar′y·an, *n., adj.*
non·as′pi·rat′ed, *adj.*
non′as·ser′tive, *adj.;* **-ly,** *adv.*

the amount of his investment. —**non′as·sess′a·bil′i·ty,** *n.*

non·be·liev·er (non′bi lē′vər), *n.* a person who lacks faith, esp. in God.

non·bel·lig·er·ent (non′bə lij′ər ənt), *adj.* **1.** of or pertaining to a nation not officially involved in a war, esp. one that favors and aids one of the belligerents. —*n.* **2.** a nonbelligerent nation. —**non′bel·lig′er·en·cy,** *n.*

non·ca·non·i·cal (non′kə non′i kəl), *adj.* **1.** not included within a canon or group of rules. **2.** not belonging to the canon of Scripture.

nonce (nons), *n.* the present, or immediate, occasion or purpose (usually used in the phrase *for the nonce*). [ME *nones,* in phrase *for the nones,* by faulty division of *then ones* the once (ME *then* dat. sing. of THE + *ones* ONCE)]

nonce′ word′, a word coined and used only for the particular occasion.

non·cha·lance (non′shə läns′, non′shə ləns), *n.* the state or quality of being nonchalant; cool indifference or lack of concern. [< F]

non·cha·lant (non′shə länt′, non′shə lənt), *adj.* coolly unconcerned, indifferent, or unexcited; casual. [< F *nonchalant,* prp. of obs. *nonchaloir* to lack warmth (of heart), be indifferent = *non-* NON- + *chaloir* < L *calēre* to be warm; see -ANT] —**Syn.** cool, calm, collected. —**Ant.** excitable.

non·com (non′kom′), *n.* *Informal.* a noncommissioned officer. [by shortening]

non·com·bat (non kom′bat), *adj.* not including or requiring combat: *noncombat duty.*

non·com·bat·ant (non kom′bə tənt, non′kəm bat′ənt), *n.* **1.** a person who is not a combatant; a civilian in time of war. **2.** a person connected with a military force in some capacity other than that of a fighter. —*adj.* **3.** not constituting, designed for, or engaged in combat.

non·com·bus·ti·ble (non′kəm bus′tə bəl), *adj.* **1.** not flammable. —*n.* **2.** a noncombustible substance. —**non′com·bus′ti·bil′i·ty,** *n.*

non′com·mis′sioned of′ficer (non′kə mish′ənd, non′-), *Mil.* an enlisted person holding any of various ranks below commissioned or warrant officers.

non·com·mit·tal (non′kə mit′əl), *adj.* not committing oneself, or not involving committal, to a particular view, course, or the like. —**non′com·mit′tal·ly,** *adv.*

non·com·mu·ni·ca·ble (non′kə myo͞o′nə kə bəl), *adj.* not communicable, esp. with reference to a disease that is not transmitted through contact with an infected or afflicted person.

non·com·pli·ance (non′kəm plī′əns), *n.* failure or refusal to comply. —**non′com·pli′ant,** *n.*

non com·pos men·tis (nōn kōm′pōs men′tis; *Eng.* non kom′pəs men′tis), *Latin.* not of sound mind; mentally incapable.

non·con·duc·tor (non′kən duk′tər), *n.* a substance that does not readily conduct heat, sound, or electricity. —**non′con·duc′ting,** *adj.*

non·con·form·ing (non′kən fôr′ming), *adj.* noting or pertaining to nonconformists or nonconformity.

non·con·form·ist (non′kən fôr′mist), *n.* **1.** a person who refuses to conform, as to established customs. **2.** (*often cap.*) a Protestant in England who is not a member of the Church of England; dissenter. —**non′con·form′ism,** *n.*

non·con·form·i·ty (non′kən fôr′mi tē), *n.* **1.** lack of conformity or agreement. **2.** failure or refusal to conform, as with established customs. **3.** (*often cap.*) refusal to conform to the Church of England.

non·co·op·er·a·tion (non′kō op′ə rā′shən), *n.* **1.** failure or refusal to cooperate. **2.** a method of showing opposition to acts or policies of the government by refusing to participate in civic and political life. Also, **non′co-op′er·a′tion, non′co·öp′er·a′tion.** —**non′co·op′er·a′tive, non′co-op′er·a′tive, non′co·öp′er·a′tive,** *adj.* —**non′co·op′er·a′tor, non′co-op′er·a′tor, non′co·öp′er·a′tor,** *n.* —**non′co·op′er·a′tion·ist, non′co-op′er·a′tion·ist, non′co·öp′er·a′tion·ist,** *n.*

non·de·script (non′di skript′), *adj.* **1.** of no recognized, definite, or particular type or kind: *a nondescript color.* —*n.* **2.** a person or a thing of no particular type or kind. [NON- + L *dēscript(us)* described, defined, represented (ptp. of *dēscrībere;* see DESCRIBE)] —**Syn. 1.** amorphous, indistinct; indescribable.

non·dis·junc·tion (non′dis jungk′shən), *n.* *Biol.* the failure of chromosomes to follow normal separation into daughter cells at division.

non·dis·tinc·tive (non′di stingk′tiv), *adj.* *Linguistics.* not serving to distinguish meanings. —**non′dis·tinc′tive·ly,** *adv.*

none[1] (nun), *pron.* **1.** no one; not one: *None of the members is going.* **2.** not any, as of something indicated: *That is none of your business.* **3.** no part; nothing. **4.** (*construed as pl.*) no or not any persons or things: *None were left when I came.* —*adv.* **5.** to no extent; in no way; not at all. —*adj.* **6.** *Archaic.* not any; no (usually used only before a vowel or *h*): *Thou shalt have none other gods but me.* [ME *non,* OE *nān* = *ne* not + *ān* one]

—**Usage.** Since many construe NONE in its etymological sense of "not one," they insist that precision demands its being treated as a singular, followed by a singular verb, as in def. 1, above. However, the word is very often felt to have the sense of def. 4, and there is ample evidence for such use dating back to the earliest English writings.

none[2] (nōn), *n.* nones[1]. [ME; OE *nōn* < L *nōna* (*hōra*) ninth (hour). See NOON]

non·ef·fec·tive (non′i fek′tiv), *adj.* **1.** not effective. **2.** not fit for duty or active service, as a soldier or sailor. —*n.* **3.** a noneffective person.

non·e·go (non ē′gō, -eg′ō), *n.* *Metaphys.* all that is not the ego or conscious self; object as opposed to subject.

non·en·ti·ty (non en′ti tē), *n., pl.* **-ties. 1.** a person or thing of no importance. **2.** something that does not exist, or exists only in imagination.

nones[1] (nōnz), *n.* *Eccles.* the fifth of the seven canonical hours, or the service for it, originally fixed for the ninth hour of the day (or 3 P.M.). [pl. of NONE[2]]

nones[2] (nōnz), *n.* (*construed as sing. or pl.*) (in the ancient Roman calendar) the ninth day before the ides. [ME < L *nōnae,* orig. fem. pl. of *nōnus* ninth]

non·es·sen·tial (non′i sen′shəl), *adj.* **1.** not essential; not necessary. —*n.* **2.** a nonessential thing or person.

non est (non′ est′), *Law.* the returning of a sheriff's writ when the person to be arrested or served with it cannot be found in the sheriff's jurisdiction. [< L short for *non est inventus* he was not found]

none·such (nun′such′), *n.* a person or thing without equal; paragon. Also, **nonsuch.** —**Syn.** ideal, nonpareil.

none·the·less (nun′thə les′), *adv.* however; nevertheless.

non-Eu·clid·e·an (non′yo͞o klid′ē ən), *adj.* differing from or based upon postulates other than those employed by Euclid.

non′-Euclid′ean geom′etry, geometry based upon one or more postulates that differ from those of Euclid.

non·fea·sance (non fē′zəns), *n.* *Law.* the omission of

non′as·sim′i·la′tion, *n.*
non′ath·let′ic, *adj.*
non′at·tend′ance, *n.*
non′at·trib′u·tive, *adj.;* **-ly,** *adv.*
non′au·thor′i·ta′tive, *adj.;* **-ly,** *adv.*
non′au·to·bi′o·graph′i·cal, *adj.;* **-ly,** *adv.*
non·au′to·mat′ed, *adj.*
non′au·to·mat′ic, *adj.*
non·ba′sic, *adj.*
non·be′ing, *n.*
non·break′a·ble, *adj.*
non·cak′ing, *adj.*
non′ca·lor′ic, *adj.*
non′car·bo·hy′drate, *n.*
non·car′bo·nat′ed, *adj.*
non′car·niv′o·rous, *adj.*
non-Cath′o·lic, *adj., n.*
non′-Cau·ca′sian, *adj., n.*
non·caus′al, *adj.;* **-ly,** *adv.*
non′cau·sal′i·ty, *n.*
non′cau·sa′tion, *n.*
non′ce·les′tial, *adj.*
non·cel′lu·lar, *adj.*
non·cen′tral, *adj.;* **-ly,** *adv.*
non·cer′e·bral, *adj.*
non′cer·e·mo′ni·al, *adj.;* **-ly,** *adv.*
non·charge′a·ble, *adj.*
non-Chris′tian, *adj., n.*
non·cit′i·zen, *n.*
non·civ′i·lized′, *adj.*
non·clas′si·cal, *adj.;* **-ly,** *adv.*
non·clas′si·fied′, *adj.*
non·cler′i·cal, *adj.;* **-ly,** *adv.*
non·clin′i·cal, *adj.;* **-ly,** *adv.*
non′co·ag′u·lat′ing, *adj.*
non′co·he′sive, *adj.;* **-ly,** *adj.;* **-ness,** *n.*
non′col·laps′a·ble, *adj.*
non′col·laps′i·ble, *adj.*
non′col·lect′i·ble, *adj.*
non′com·bin′ing, *adj.*
non′com·mer′cial, *adj., n.;* **-ly,** *adv.*
non′com·mis′sioned, *adj.*
non′com·mu′ni·ca′tive, *adj.*
non·com′mu·nist, *n., adj.*
non′com·pet′i·tive, *adj.*
non′com·ply′ing, *adj., n.*
non′con·cil′i·at′ing, *adj.*
non′con·cil′i·a·to′ry, *adj.*
non′con·clu′sive, *adj.;* **-ly,** *adv.;* **-ness,** *n.*
non′con·cur′rence, *n.*
non′con·cur′rent, *adj., n.;* **-ly,** *adv.*
non′con·dens′ing, *adj.*
non′con·duc′tive, *adj.*
non·con′fi·dence, *n.*
non′con·fi·den′tial, *adj.*
non′con·flict′ing, *adj.*
non′con·geal′ing, *adj.*
non′con·gen′i·tal, *adj.*
non′con·nec′tive, *adj.*
non′con·sec′u·tive, *adj.*
non′con·sent′ing, *adj.*
non′con·sti·tu′tion·al, *adj.*
non′con·strain′ing, *adj.*
non′con·struc′tive, *adj.;* **-ly,** *adv.*
non′con·sump′tion, *n.*
non′con·ta′gious, *adj.*
non′con·tem′po·rar′y, *adj.*
non′con·tig′u·ous, *adj.;* **-ly,** *adv.*
non′con·tin′u·ance, *n.*
non′con·tin′u·a′tion, *n.*
non′con·tin′u·ous, *adj.*
non·con′tra·band′, *n., adj.*
non′con·trac′tion, *n.*
non′con·tra·dic′to·ry, *adj.*
non′con·tras′tive, *adj.*
non′con·trib′u·ting, *adj.*
non′con·trib′u·to′ry, *adj.*
non′con·trol′la·ble, *adj.;* **-ly,** *adv.*
non′con·trolled′, *adj.*
non′con·trol′ling, *adj.*
non′con·tro·ver′sial, *adj.;* **-ly,** *adv.*
non′con·ven′tion·al, *adj.*
non′con·ver′gent, *adj.*
non′con·ver′san·cy, *n.*
non′con·ver′sant, *adj.;* **-ly,** *adv.*
non′con·vert′i·ble, *adj.*
non′cor·rob′o·ra′tive, *adj.*
non′cor·rod′ing, *adj.*
non′cor·ro′sive, *adj.*
non′cre·a′tive, *adj.*
non·crim′i·nal, *adj.*
non·crit′i·cal, *adj.*
non·crys′tal·line, *adj.*
non·cul′ti·vat′ed, *adj.*
non′cul·ti·va′tion, *n.*
non·cur′rent, *adj.*
non·cy′cli·cal, *adj.*
non′de·cid′u·ous, *adj.;* **-ly,** *adv.;* **-ness,** *n.*
non′de·duct′i·ble, *adj.*
non′de·fer′a·ble, *adj.*
non′de·fer′ra·ble, *adj.*
non′de·fin′ing, *adj.*
non′dem·o·crat′ic, *adj.*
non′de·mon′stra·ble, *adj.*
non′de·nom′i·na′tion·al, *adj.*
non′de·part·men′tal, *adj.*
non′de·pend′ence, *n.*
non′de·pre′ci·at′ing, *adj.*
non′de·riv′a·tive, *adj.*
non′de·scrip′tive, *adj.*
non′de·struc′tive, *adj.;* **-ly,** *adv.;* **-ness,** *n.*
non′de·tach′a·ble, *adj.*
non·det′o·nat′ing, *adj.*
non′dic·ta·to′ri·al, *adj.*
non′dif·fer·en′ti·a′tion, *n.*
non′dif·fus′ing, *adj.*
non′dip·lo·mat′ic, *adj.*
non′di·rec′tion·al, *adj.*
non′di·rec′tive, *adj.*
non·dir′i·gi·ble, *adj., n.*
non·dis′ci·pli·nar′y, *adj.*
non′dis·crim′i·nat′ing, *adj.*
non′dis·crim′i·na′tion, *n.*
non′dis·crim′i·na·to′ry, *adj.*
non′dis·cur′sive, *adj.;* **-ly,** *adv.*
non′di·vis′i·ble, *adj.*
non·doc′tri·nal, *adj.*
non′dog·mat′ic, *adj.*
non′do·mes′ti·cat′ed, *adj.*
non′dra·mat′ic, *adj.*
non·drink′a·ble, *adj.*
non·drink′er, *n.*
non·dry′ing, *adj.*
non′dy·nas′tic, *adj.*
non·earn′ing, *adj., n.*
non′ec·cle′si·as′ti·cal, *adj.*
non′e·co·nom′ic, *adj.*
non·ed′i·ble, *adj.*
non·ed′u·ca·ble, *adj.*
non′ed·u·ca′tion·al, *adj.*
non′ef·fer·ves′cent, *adj.;* **-ly,** *adv.*
non′e·las′tic, *adj.*
non′e·lec′tion, *n.*
non′e·lec′tive, *adj.*
non·el′i·gi·ble, *adj.*
non′e·mo′tion·al, *adj.;* **-ly,** *adv.*
non′em·pir′i·cal, *adj.;* **-ly,** *adv.*
non′en·force′ment, *n.*
non·e′qual, *adj., n.*
non′e·quiv′a·lent, *adj., n.*
non′es·tab′lish·ment, *n.*
non·eth′i·cal, *adj.;* **-ly,** *adv.;* **-ness,** *n.*
non′ex·change′a·ble, *adj.*
non′ex·clu′sive, *adj.*
non′ex·empt′, *adj., n.*
non′ex·ist′ence, *n.*
non′ex·ist′ing, *adj.*
non′ex·pend′a·ble, *adj.*
non′ex·plan′a·to′ry, *adj.*
non′ex·plo′sive, *adj., n.*
non′ex·port′a·ble, *adj.*
non′ex·tant′, *adj.*
non·ex′tra·dit′a·ble, *adj.*
non·fac′tu·al, *adj.;* **-ly,** *adv.*
non′fa·nat′i·cal, *adj.;* **-ly,** *adv.*
non·fas′cist, *n., adj.*
non·fa′tal, *adj.;* **-ly,** *adv.*

some act which ought to have been performed. Cf. **malfeasance, misfeasance.**

non·fer·rous (non fer′əs), *adj.* **1.** (of a metal) containing no iron or very little. **2.** noting or pertaining to metals other than iron or steel.

non·fic·tion (non fik′shən), *n.* **1.** the branch of literature comprising works of prose dealing with or offering facts or theory (contrasted with *fiction* and distinguished from *poetry* and *drama*). **2.** works of this class. **—non·fic′tion·al,** *adj.* **—non·fic′tion·al·ly,** *adv.*

non·fig·ur·a·tive (non fig′yər ə tiv), *adj.* nonrepresentational (def. 2).

non·flam·ma·ble (non flam′ə bəl), *adj.* not combustible or easily set on fire; not flammable; not inflammable.

no·nil·lion (nō nil′yən), *n., pl.* **-lions,** (*as after a numeral*) **-lion,** *adj.* **—***n.* **1.** a cardinal number represented in the U.S. and France by one followed by 30 zeros, and in Great Britain and Germany, by one followed by 54 zeros. **—***adj.* **2.** amounting to one nonillion in number. [< F = *non-* (< L *nōnus* ninth) + (*m*)*illion*] **—no·nil′lionth,** *n., adj.*

non·in·ter·fer·ence (non′in tər fēr′əns), *n.* the policy or practice of refraining from interference, esp. in political affairs. **—non′in·ter·fer′er,** *n.*

non·in·ter·ven·tion (non′in tər ven′shən), *n.* **1.** abstention by a state from interference in the affairs of other states. **2.** failure or refusal to intervene. **—non′in·ter·ven′tion·al,** *adj.* **—non′in·ter·ven′tion·al·ist, non′in·ter·ven′tion·ist,** *n.*

non·join·der (non join′dər), *n. Law.* failure to join, as of a person who should have been a party to an action.

non·ju·ror (non jŏŏr′ər), *n.* **1.** a person who refuses to take a required oath, as of allegiance. **2.** (*often cap.*) *Eng. Hist.* an Anglican clergyman who refused to swear allegiance to William and Mary.

non·lead·ed (non′led′id), *adj.* (of gasoline) containing no tetraethyl lead, which on combustion produces a toxic pollutant. Also, **unleaded.**

non·le·gal (non lē′gəl), *adj.* not related to, qualified for, or phrased in the manner of the practice of law (distinguished from *illegal*).

non li·cet (non lī′sit), it is not permitted or lawful. *Abbr.:* n.l.

non li·quet (non lī′kwit), *Roman Law.* (of evidence, a cause, etc.) it is not clear or evident. *Abbr.:* n.l.

non·lit·er·ate (non lit′ər it), *adj. Anthropol.* lacking a written language: *a nonliterate people.*

non·ma·te·ri·al (non′mə tēr′ē əl), *adj.* **1.** not material or composed of matter. **2.** of or pertaining to the spirit or soul; spiritual: *to minister to man's nonmaterial needs.* **3.** cultural, aesthetic, or the like.

non·met·al (non′met′ᵊl), *n. Chem.* **1.** an element not having the character of a metal, as carbon, nitrogen, etc. **2.** an element incapable of forming simple positive ions in solution. **—non·me·tal·lic** (non′mə tal′ik), *adj.*

non·mor·al (non môr′əl, -mor′-), *adj.* having no relation to morality; neither moral nor immoral. **—non′mo·ral′i·ty,** *n.* **—non·mor′al·ly,** *adv.* **—Syn.** See **immoral.**

no-no (nō′nō′), *n., pl.* **no-nos, no-no's.** *U.S. Slang.* anything that is forbidden, usually because it is offensive, unsafe, unwise, or undesirable. [prob. babytalk based on *No! No!*]

non·ob·jec·tive (non′əb jek′tiv), *adj. Fine Arts.* abstract; nonrepresentational.

non ob·stan·te (nōn ōb stän′te; *Eng.* non ob stan′tē), *Latin.* notwithstanding. [late ME < AL]

non·pa·reil (non′pə rel′), *adj.* **1.** having no equal; peerless. **—***n.* **2.** a person or thing having no equal. **3.** a small pellet of colored sugar for decorating candy, cake, and cookies. **4.** a flat, round, bite-sized piece of chocolate covered with this sugar. **5.** *Print.* **a.** a 6-point type. **b.** a slug occupying 6 points of space between lines. [late ME *nonparaille* < MF *nonpareil* = *non-* NON- + *pareil* equal < VL **pariculum* (L *pari-* (s. of *pār*) equal + *-culum* -CULE)]

non·par·ous (non par′əs), *adj. Physiol.* having borne no children.

non·par·tic·i·pat·ing (non′pär tis′ə pā′ting), *adj. Insurance.* having or imparting no right to dividends or to a distribution of surplus.

non·par·tic·i·pa·tion (non′pär tis′ə pā′shən), *n.* absence of participation: *nonparticipation of citizens in local government.* **—non′par·tic′i·pant,** *n.*

non·par·ti·san (non pär′ti zən), *adj.* **1.** not partisan; objective. **2.** not supporting any of the established or regular parties. **—***n.* **3.** a person who is nonpartisan. Also, **non·par′ti·zan.** **—non·par′ti·san·ship′, non·par′ti·zan·ship′,** *n.*

non·pay·ment (non pā′mənt), *n.* failure or neglect to pay. [late ME]

non·per·form·ance (non′pər fôr′məns), *n.* failure or neglect to perform. **—non′per·form′ing,** *adj.*

non·per·ish·a·ble (non per′i shə bəl), *adj.* **1.** not subject to rapid deterioration or decay. **—***n.* **2.** Usually, **nonperishables.** articles or items, esp. of food, not subject to rapid spoilage.

non·per·son (non′pûr′sən), *n.* a person whose importance, influence, or rights are minimized, denied, or glossed over.

non·plus (non plus′, non′plus), *v.,* **-plused, -plus·ing** or (*esp. Brit.*) **-plussed, -plus·sing,** *n.* **—***v.t.* **1.** to make utterly perplexed; puzzle completely. **—***n.* **2.** a state of utter perplexity. [< L *nōn plūs:* lit., not more, no further]

non pos·su·mus (nōn pōs′ŏŏ mŏŏs′; *Eng.* non pos′ə-məs), *Latin.* we cannot.

non·pro·duc·tive (non′prə duk′tiv), *adj.* **1.** not producing goods directly, as employees in charge of personnel, inspectors, etc. **2.** not productive. **—non′pro·duc′tive·ly,** *adv.* **—non′pro·duc′tive·ness, non·pro·duc·tiv·i·ty** (non′-prō duk tiv′i tē), *n.*

non·pro·fes·sion·al (non′prə fesh′ən^əl), *adj.* **1.** not a member of or trained in a specific profession. **2.** *Sports.* not participating as a means of livelihood or for any financial gain; amateur. **—***n.* **3.** a person who is not a professional. **4.** an amateur athlete.

non·prof·it (non prof′it), *adj.* not yielding a return; not entered into for profit: *a nonprofit association.*

non·pro·lif·er·a·tion (non′prō lif′ə rā′shən), *n.* **1.** failure or refusal to proliferate, as in budding or cell division. **2.** the action or practice of curbing or controlling an excessive, rapid spread: *nonproliferation of nuclear weapons.*

non·pros (non′pros′), *v.t.,* **-prossed, -pros·sing.** *Law.* to adjudge (a plaintiff) in default. [shortened form of NON PROSEQUITUR]

non pros., non prosequitur.

non pro·se·qui·tur (non′ prō sek′wi tər), *Law.* a judgment entered against the plaintiff in a suit when he does not appear in court to prosecute it. [< L: lit., he does not pursue]

non·fed′er·al, *adj.*
non·fed′er·at′ed, *adj.*
non′fic·ti′tious, *adj.*
non·fil′ter·a·ble, *adj.*
non·fi′nite, *adj., n.;* **-ly,** *adv;* **-ness,** *n.*
non·fis′cal, *adj.;* **-ly,** *adv.*
non·fis′sion·a·ble, *adj.*
non·flex′i·ble, *adj.*
non·flow′er·ing, *adj.*
non·flu′id, *n.*
non·fly′ing, *adj.*
non·for′feit·a·ble, *adj.*
non·for′fei·ture, *adj., n.*
non′for·ma′tion, *n.*
non·freez′ing, *adj.*
non′ful·fill′ment, *n.*
non·func′tion·al, *adj.*
non·fu′si·ble, *adj.*
non·gas′e·ous, *adj.*
non′gov·ern·men′tal, *adj.*
non′gre·gar′i·ous, *adj.*
non·guilt′, *n.*
non·hab′it·a·ble, *adj.*
non′ha·bit′u·al, *adj.*
non′ha·bit′u·at·ing, *adj.*
non·haz′ard·ous, *adj.*
non′he·red′i·tar′y, *adj.*
non·her′it·a·ble, *adj.*
non′his·tor′ic, *adj.*
non′his·tor′i·cal, *adj.;* **-ly,** *adv.;* **-ness,** *n.*
non′ho·mo·ge′ne·ous, *adj.*
non·hu′man, *adj.*
non′i·den′ti·cal, *adj.*
non′i·den′ti·ty, *n.*
non′i·de·o·log′i·cal, *adj.*
non′id·i·o·mat′ic, *adj.*
non′im·mu′ni·ty, *n., pl.* **-ties.**
non·im′mu·nized′, *adj.*
non′in·clu′sion, *n.*
non′in·crim′i·nat′ing, *adj.*
non′in·de·pend′ent, *adj.*
non′in·dict′a·ble, *adj.*
non′in·dus′tri·al, *adj.*
non′in·fec′tious, *adj.*
non′in·flam′ma·ble, *adj.*
non′in·flect′ed, *adj.*
non′in·flec′tion·al, *adj.*
non′in·for′ma·tive, *adj.;* **-ly,** *adv.*
non′in·hab′it·a·ble, *adj.*
non′in·her′ent, *adj.*
non′in·her′it·a·ble, *adj.*
non′in·ju′ri·ous, *adj.;* **-ly,** *adv.;* **-ness,** *n.*
non′in·stinc′tive, *adj.*
non′in·stinc′tu·al, *adj.*
non′in·sti·tu′tion·al, *adj.*
non′in·tel·lec′tu·al, *adj., n.;* **-ly,** *adv.*
non′in·ter·change′a·ble, *adj.*
non′in·ter·sect′ing, *adj.*
non′in·tox′i·cant, *adj., n.*
non′in·tox′i·cat′ing, *adj.*
non·ir′ri·ga·ble, *adj.*
non·ir′ri·tant, *adj.*
non·ir′ri·tat′ing, *adj.*
non-Jew′ish, *adj.*
non·ko′sher, *adj., n.*
non·le′thal, *adj.*
non′li·a·bil′i·ty, *n., pl.* **-ties.**
non·lin′e·ar, *adj.*
non·lit′er·ar′y, *adj.*
non′li·tur′gi·cal, *adj.;* **-ly,** *adv.*
non·lo′cal, *adj., n.;* **-ly,** *adv.*
non·log′i·cal, *adj.*
non·lu′mi·nous, *adj.*
non′mag·net′ic, *adj.*
non′ma·li′cious, *adj.;* **-ly,** *adv.*
non′ma·lig′nant, *adj.*
non·mal′le·a·ble, *adj.*
non·mar′i·tal, *adj.;* **-ly,** *adv.*
non·mar′tial, *adj.*
non′ma·te′ri·al·is′tic, *adj.*
non′ma·ter′nal, *adj.;* **-ly,** *adv.*
non′math·e·mat′i·cal, *adj.*
non·meas′ur·a·ble, *adj.*
non′me·chan′i·cal, *adj.;* **-ly,** *adv.*
non′mech·a·nis′tic, *adj.*
non·med′i·cal, *adj.;* **-ly,** *adv.*
non′me·lod′ic, *adj.*
non·mem′ber, *n.*
non·mem′ber·ship′, *n.*
non·met′ri·cal, *adj.;* **-ly,** *adv.*
non·mi′gra·to′ry, *adj.*
non·mil′i·tant, *adj., n.;* **-ly,** *adv.*
non′min·is·te′ri·al, *adj.;* **-ly,** *adv.*
non·mis′chie·vous, *adj.;* **-ly,** *adv.*
non·mor′tal, *adj.*
non·mo′tile, *adj.*
non·moun′tain·ous, *adj.*
non′mu·nic′i·pal, *adj.;* **-ly,** *adv.*
non·mus′cu·lar, *adj.;* **-ly,** *adv.*
non·mys′ti·cal, *adj.;* **-ly,** *adv.*
non·myth′i·cal, *adj.;* **-ly,** *adv.*
non·na′tion·al, *adj.*
non·na·tion·al·is′tic, *adj.*
non·na′tive, *adj.*
non·nat′u·ral, *adj.*
non·nav′i·ga·ble, *adj.*
non′ne·ces′si·ty, *n., pl.* **-ties.**
non′ne·go′ti·a·ble, *adj.*
non′ni·trog′e·nous, *n.*
non·nu·tri′tious, *adj.*
non′o·be′di·ence, *n.*
non′ob·lig′a·to′ry, *adj.*
non′ob·serv′ance, *n.*
non′oc·cur′rence, *n.*
non·o′dor·ous, *adj.*
non′of·fi′cial, *adj.;* **-ly,** *adv.*
non·op′er·a·ble, *adj.*
non·op′er·at′ing, *adj.*
non·op′er·a′tive, *adj.*
non′or·gan′ic, *adj.*
non·or′tho·dox′, *adj.*
non′os·ten′sive, *adj.*
non·own′er, *n.*
non·pal′a·tal, *adj.*
non′pal·a·tal·i·za′tion, *n.*
non·par′al·lel′, *adj.*
non′par·a·sit′ic, *adj.*
non′pa·ren′tal, *adj.*
non′pa·rish′ion·er, *n.*
non′par·lia·men′ta·ry, *adj.*
non′pa·ro′chi·al, *adj.;* **-ly,** *adv.*
non·pas′ser·ine, *adj.*
non′pa·ter′nal, *adj.;* **-ly,** *adv.*
non·pay′ing, *adj.*
non·per′ma·nent, *adj.*
non·per′me·a·ble, *adj.*
non′phil·o·soph′i·cal, *adj.;* **-ly,** *adv.*
non′pho·ne′mic, *adj.*
non′pho·ne′mi·cal·ly, *adv.*
non·phys′i·cal, *adj.;* **-ly,** *adv.*
non·phys·i·o·log′i·cal, *adj.;* **-ly,** *adv.*
non′po·et′ic, *adj.*
non·poi′son·ous, *adj.*
non′po·lit′i·cal, *adj.;* **-ly,** *adv.*
non·po′rous, *adj.*
non′pos·ses′sion, *n.*
non′pos·ses′sive, *adj.;* **-ly,** *adv.;* **-ness,** *n.*
non·po′ta·ble, *adj.*
non·prac′ti·cal, *adj.*
non·pre′cious, *adj.*
non·pred′a·to′ry, *adj.*
non·pred′i·ca′tive, *adj.;* **-ly,** *adv.*
non′pre·dict′a·ble, *adj.*
non′prej·u·di′cial, *adj.;* **-ly,** *adv.*
non′pre·scrip′tive, *adj.*
non′pre·serv′a·ble, *adj.*
non′pres·er·va′tion, *n.*
non′pro·duc′er, *n.*
non′pro·duc′ing, *adj.*
non′pro·gres′sive, *adj.*
non′pro·por′tion·al, *adj.;* **-ly,** *adv.*
non′pro·pri′e·tar′y, *adj., n., pl.* **-tar·ies.**
non′pro·tec′tive, *adj.;* **-ly,** *adv.*
non·pun′ish·a·ble, *adj.*

non′rel·a·tiv·is′tic quan′tum mechan′ics (non′-rel ə ti vis′tik, non′-), *Physics.* See under **quantum mechanics** (def. 1).

non rep., non repetatur.

non re·pe·ta·tur (non rep′i tā′tər), (in prescriptions) do not repeat. [< L]

non·rep·re·sen·ta·tion·al (non′rep ri zen tā′shə nəl), *adj.* **1.** not representational. **2.** designating a style of fine art in which natural objects or forms are not represented or depicted. —**non′rep·re·sen·ta′tion·al·ism,** *n.*

non·res·i·dent (non rez′i dənt), *adj.* **1.** not resident in a particular place. **2.** not residing where official duties require a person to reside. —*n.* **3.** a person who is nonresident. —**non·res′i·dence, non·res′i·den·cy,** *n.*

non·re·sis·tance (non′ri zis′təns), *n.* the policy or practice of not resisting violence or tyrannical authority by force.

non·re·sis·tant (non′ri zis′tənt), *adj.* **1.** not resistant; passively obedient. —*n.* **2.** a person who does not resist authority or force. **3.** a person who maintains that violence should not be resisted by force.

non·re·stric·tive (non′ri strik′tiv), *adj.* *Gram.* descriptive of a modified element rather than limiting of the element's meaning. Cf. **restrictive** (def. 4).

non′restric′tive clause′, *Gram.* See **descriptive clause.**

non·rig·id (non rij′id), *adj.* **1.** not rigid. **2.** designating a type of airship that lacks a supporting structure and is held in shape only by the pressure of the gas within.

non·sched·uled (non skej′o͞old; *Brit.,* non shed′yo͞old), *adj.* not scheduled; not entered on or having a schedule; unscheduled.

non′scheduled air′line, an airline authorized to carry passengers or freight between specified points as demand warrants, rather than on a regular schedule.

non·sec·tar·i·an (non′sek târ′ē ən), *adj.* not affiliated with any specific religious denomination.

non·sense (non′sens), *n.* **1.** that which makes no sense or is lacking in sense. **2.** words without sense or conveying absurd ideas. **3.** senseless or absurd action; foolish conduct, notions, etc. **4.** something absurd; an absurdity. **5.** anything of trifling importance or of little or no use. —**non·sen·si·cal** (non sen′si kəl), *adj.* —**non·sen′si·cal·ly,** *adv.* —**non·sen′si·cal·ness, non·sen·si·cal·i·ty** (non′sen si kal′-it ē), *n.* —**Syn. 1.** twaddle, balderdash, folly.

non seq., non sequitur.

non se·qui·tur (non sek′wi tər; *Lat.* nōn se′kwi to͝or′), an inference or a conclusion that does not follow from the premises. [< L: it does not follow]

non·sked (non sked′), *n.* *Informal.* a nonscheduled airline. [NON- + *sked* (short for SCHEDULE)]

non·skid (non′skid′), *adj.* designed to be skid-resistant, as a tire, rug pad, etc.

non·stand·ard (non′stan′dərd), *adj.* differing in usage from the speech or writing that is generally considered to be correct or preferred.

non·stop (non′stop′), *adj., adv.* without a single stop en route.

non·such (non′such′), *n.* nonesuch.

non·suit (non′so͞ot′), *Law.* —*n.* **1.** a judgment given against a plaintiff who neglects to prosecute, or who fails to show a legal cause of action. —*v.t.* **2.** to subject to a nonsuit. [r. ME *nounsuyt* < AF *nounsute*]

non·sup·port (non′sə pōrt′, -pôrt′), *n.* *Law.* failure to support a dependent as required by law.

non trop·po (non trop′ō; *It.* nôn trôp′pô), *Music.* not too much: *allegro non troppo* [< It]

non-U (non yo͞o′), *adj.* *Informal.* not characteristic of or appropriate to the upper class, esp. of Great Britain. [NON- + U (initial of *upper*)]

non·un·ion (non yo͞on′yən), *adj.* **1.** not belonging to, in accordance with, or recognizing a trade union or union policy. —*n.* **2.** *Med.* failure of a broken bone to heal.

non·un·ion·ism (non yo͞on′yə niz′əm), *n.* disregard of or opposition to trade unions. —**non·un′ion·ist,** *n.*

non·vi·o·lence (non vī′ə ləns), *n.* the policy or practice of refraining from the use of violence, as in reaction to oppressive authority. —**non·vi′o·lent,** *adj.* —**non·vi′o·lent·ly,** *adv.*

non·vot·er (non vō′tər), *n.* **1.** a person who does not vote. **2.** a person who is not eligible to vote.

non·white (non hwīt′, -wīt′), *n.* **1.** a person who is not Caucasoid. —*adj.* **2.** not Caucasoid.

noo·dle[1] (no͞od′əl), *n.* a narrow strip of unleavened egg dough that has been rolled thin and dried, usually boiled and served in soups, casseroles, etc.; a ribbon-shaped pasta. [< G *Nudel*]

noo·dle[2] (no͞od′əl), *n., v.,* **-dled, -dling.** —*n.* **1.** *Slang.* the head. **2.** a fool or simpleton. —*v.i.* **3.** to play idly on a musical instrument. [? var. of *noddle* the head]

nook (no͝ok), *n.* **1.** a corner, as in a room. **2.** any retired or obscure corner. **3.** any small recess. **4.** a remote spot. [ME *nok*] —**nook′like′,** *adj.*

noon (no͞on), *n.* **1.** midday. **2.** twelve o'clock in the daytime. **3.** the highest, brightest, or finest point or part. **4.** *Chiefly Literary.* midnight. [ME *none,* OE *nōn* < L *nōna* ninth hour. See NONE[2]]

noon·day (no͞on′dā′), *adj.* **1.** of or at noonday: *the noonday meal.* —*n.* **2.** midday; noon.

no′ one′, no person; not anyone; nobody: *No one is home.* Also, **no′-one′.**

noon·ing (no͞o′ning), *n.* *Chiefly Dial.* **1.** noontime. **2.** an interval at noon for rest or food. **3.** a rest or meal at noon.

noon·tide (no͞on′tīd′), *n.* noon. [ME *nonetyde,* OE *nōntīd*]

noon·time (no͞on′tīm′), *n.* noon; noontide; noonday. [ME *none tyme*]

noose (no͞os), *n., v.,* **noosed, noos·ing.** —*n.* **1.** a loop with a running knot, as in a snare, lasso, or hangman's halter, that tightens as the rope is pulled. **2.** a tie or bond; snare. —*v.t.* **3.** to secure by or as by a noose. **4.** to make a noose with or in (a rope or the like). [late ME *nose* < ?] —**noos′er,** *n.*

Noot·ka (no͞ot′kə, no͝ot′-), *n., pl.* **-kas,** (*esp. collectively*) **-ka.** **1.** a Wakashan language spoken in SW Canada on the western coast of Vancouver Island. **2.** a member of an Indian people of Washington and Vancouver Island speaking this language.

no·pal (nō′pəl), *n.* any cactus or fruit of the genera *Opuntia* and *Nopalea.* [< Sp < Nahuatl *nopālli*]

no-par (nō′pär′), *adj.* without par or face value: *no-par stock.* [special use of phrase *no par (value)*]

nope (nōp), *adv.* *Informal.* no.

nor (nôr; *unstressed* nər), *conj.* **1.** (used in negative phrases, esp. after *neither,* to introduce the second member in a series, or any subsequent member): *They won't wait for you, nor for me, nor for anybody.* **2.** (used to continue the force of a negative, as *not, no, never,* etc., occurring in a preceding clause): *I never saw him again, nor did I regret it.* **3.** (used after an affirmative clause, or as a continuative, in the sense of *and not*): *They are happy, nor need we worry.* **4.** *Dial.* than. **5.** *Archaic.* (used without a preceding *neither,* the negative force of which is understood): *He nor I was there.* **6.** *Archaic.* (used instead of *neither* as correlative to a following *nor*): *Nor he nor I was there.* [ME; contr. of *nother,* OE *nōther* = *ne* not + *ōther* (contr. of *ōhwæther*) either]

Nor., **1.** Norman. **2.** North. **3.** Northern. **4.** Norway. **5.** Norwegian.

nor., **1.** north. **2.** northern.

Nor·dau (nôr′dou), *n.* **Max Si·mon** (mäks zē′môn), 1849–1923, Hungarian author and Zionist leader.

Nor′den·skjöld Sea′ (no͞or′dən shœld′). See **Laptev Sea.** [named after N. A. E. *Nordenskjöld* (1832–1901), Swedish explorer and geographer]

Nord·hau·sen (nôrt′hou′zən), *n.* a city in SW East Germany. 39,200 (est. 1959).

Nor·dic (nôr′dik), *adj.* *Anthropol.* of, pertaining to, or characteristic of a Caucasoid people, generally marked by tall stature, blond hair, blue eyes, and elongated head, exemplified by North Europeans and their descendants. [< F *nordique* = *nord* north + *-ique* -IC] —**Nor·dic·i·ty** (nôr-dis′i tē), *n.*

Nord′kyn Cape′ (nôr′kyn), a cape in N Norway: the northernmost point of the European mainland.

nor′east·er (nôr′ē′stər), *n.* northeaster.

no-re·turn (nō′ri tûrn′), *adj.* (of beverage bottles) that need not be returned when empty for refund of a deposit.

Nor·folk (nôr′fək), *n.* **1.** a county in E England. 561,980 (1961); 2054 sq. mi. *Co. seat:* Norwich. **2.** a seaport in SE Virginia: naval base. 307,951 (1970).

---

non′rab·bin′i·cal, *adj.*
non·ra′cial, *adj.*
non·rad′i·cal, *adj.*
non′ra·di·o·ac′tive, *adj.*
non·rat′ed, *adj.*
non·ra′tion·al, *adj.;* **-ly,** *adv.*
non′re·ac′tive, *adj.*
non·read′er, *n.*
non′re·al·is′tic, *adj.*
non′re·cip′ro·cal, *adj., n.;* **-ly,** *adv.*
non′re·cip′ro·cat′ing, *adj.*
non′rec·og·ni′tion, *n.*
non′re·cov′er·a·ble, *adj.*
non′re·cur′rent, *adj.*
non′re·cur′ring, *adj.*
non′re·deem′a·ble, *adj.*
non′re·duc′i·ble, *adj.*
non′re·fill′a·ble, *adj.*
non′re·flec′tive, *adj.*
non·reg′i·ment′ed, *adj.*
non·reg′is·tered, *adj.*
non′re·li′gious, *adj.*
non′re·mu′ner·a′tive, *adj.*
non′re·new′a·ble, *adj.*
non′rep·re·sent′a·tive, *n.*
non′res·i·den′tial, *adj.*
non′re·strict′ed, *adj.*
non′re·ten′tion, *n.*
non′ret·ro·ac′tive, *adj.;* **-ly,** *adv.*
non′re·turn′a·ble, *adj.*
non′re·vers′i·ble, *adj.*
non·rhyth′mic, *adj.*
non·rhyth′mi·cal, *adj.;* **-ly,** *adv.*
non·ru′ral, *adj.;* **-ly,** *adv.*
non·sal′a·ble, *adj.*
non′scho·las′tic, *adj.*
non′sci·en·tif′ic, *adj.*
non·sea′son·al, *adj.*
non·se′cret, *adj.;* **-ly,** *adv.*
non·sec′u·lar, *adj.*
non·seg′re·gat′ed, *adj.*
non′se·lec′tive, *adj.*
non·sen′si·tive, *adj.;* **-ly,** *adv.*
non·sen′su·al, *adj.;* **-ly,** *adv.*
non·sen′su·ous, *adj.;* **-ly,** *adv.;* **-ness,** *n.*
non·sex′u·al, *adj.;* **-ly,** *adv.*
non·shrink′a·ble, *adj.*
non′sig·nif′i·cant, *adj.*
non·sink′a·ble, *adj.*
non·skilled′, *adj.*
non·smok′er, *n.*
non·so′cial, *adj.*
non·sol′u·ble, *adj.*
non·speak′ing, *adj.*
non·spe′cial·ist, *n.*
non·spe′cial·ized′, *adj.*
non′spe·cif′ic, *adj.*
non·spec′u·la′tive, *adj.;* **-ly,** *adv.;* **-ness,** *n.*
non·spir′it·u·al, *adj.*
non·sport′ing, *adj.;* **-ly,** *adv.*
non·sta′ble, *adj.*
non·stain′a·ble, *adj.*
non·stain′ing, *adj.*
non·stand′ard·ized′, *adj.*
non·start′er, *n.*
non′sta·tis′ti·cal, *adj.;* **-ly,** *adv.*
non·stim′u·lat′ing, *adj.*
non′stra·te′gic, *adj.*
non·strik′er, *n.*
non·strik′ing, *adj.*
non·struc′tur·al, *adj.;* **-ly,** *adv.*
non′sub·mis′sive, *adj.;* **-ly,** *adv.;* **-ness,** *n.*
non′sub·scrib′er, *n.*
non′suc·cess′, *n.*
non′suc·ces′sive, *adj.;* **-ly,** *adv.;* **-ness,** *n.*
non′sug·ges′tive, *adj.*
non′sul′fur·ous, *adj.*
non′sup·pres′sion, *n.*
non·sur′gi·cal, *adj.*
non′sus·cep′ti·bil′i·ty, *n.*
non′sus·cep′ti·ble, *adj.*
non·sus′pect, *n., adj.*
non′sus·tain′ing, *adj.*
non′sym·bol′ic, *adj.*
non′sys·tem·at′ic, *adj.*
non′sys·tem·at′i·cal, *adj.;* **-ly,** *adv.*
non·tar′nish·a·ble, *adj.*
non·tax′a·ble, *adj.*
non·teach′a·ble, *adj.*
non·tech′ni·cal, *adj.;* **-ly,** *adv.*
non·tem′po·ral, *adj.*
non′ter·ri·to′ri·al, *adj.*
non′the·at′ri·cal, *adj.*
non′the·o·log′i·cal, *adj.;* **-ly,** *adv.*
non·think′ing, *adj.*
non·tox′ic, *adj.*
non′tra·di′tion·al, *adj.;* **-ly,** *adv.*
non·trans′fer·a·ble, *adj.*
non′trans·par′ent, *adj.*
non·trop′i·cal, *adj.*
non·typ′i·cal, *adj.;* **-ly,** *adv.*
non′ty·ran′ni·cal, *adj.;* **-ly,** *adv.*
non·u′ni·fied′, *adj.*
non·u′ni·form′, *adj.*
non′u·nit′ed, *adj.*
non·us′er, *n.*
non·vas′cu·lar, *adj.;* **-ly,** *adv.*
non·ven′om·ous, *adj.*
non·ver′bal, *adj.*
non·ver′i·fi′a·ble, *adj.*
non·ver′ti·cal, *adj.;* **-ly,** *adv.*
non·vi′a·ble, *adj.*
non′vi·o·la′tion, *n.*
non·vis′i·ble, *adj.*
non·vis′u·al, *adj.*
non·vo′cal, *adj.*
non′vo·ca′tion·al, *adj.*
non·vol′a·tile, *adj.*
non·vol′un·tar′y, *adj.*
non·vot′ing, *adj.*
non·work′er, *n.*
non·work′ing, *adj.*

Nor′folk Is′land, an island in the S Pacific between New Caledonia and New Zealand: a territory of Australia. 844 (est. 1961); 13 sq. mi.

Nor′folk jack′et, a man's loosely belted single-breasted jacket. Also called **Nor′folk coat′.** [named after NORFOLK county in England]

Nor·ge (nôʀ′gə), *n.* Norwegian name of **Norway.**

no·ri·a (nōr′ē ə, nôr′-), *n.* a device consisting of a series of buckets on a wheel, used in Spain and the Orient for raising water. [< Sp < Ar *nā'ūra*]

Nor·i·cum (nôr′i kəm, nor′-), *n.* an ancient Roman province in central Europe, roughly corresponding to the part of Austria south of the Danube.

nor·ite (nôr′īt), *n.* a granular rock, the lighter minerals of which are calcic plagioclase feldspars, and the darker minerals of which are orthorhombic pyroxenes. [< Norw *norit.* See NORWAY, -ITE[1]] —**nor·it·ic** (nô rit′ik), *adj.*

nor·land (nôr′lənd), *n. Chiefly Dial.* northland. —**nor′-land·er,** *n.*

norm (nôrm), *n.* **1.** standard, model, or pattern. **2.** general level or average. **3.** *Educ.* **a.** a designated standard of average performance of people of a given age, background, etc. **b.** a standard based on the past average performance of a given individual. **4.** *Math.* **a.** a real-valued, nonnegative function whose domain is a vector space. **b.** the greatest difference between two successive points of a given partition. [< L *norm(a)* a carpenter's square, a rule, pattern] —**norm′-less,** *adj.*

Norm., Norman.

nor·mal (nôr′məl), *adj.* **1.** conforming to the standard or the common type; usual; not abnormal; regular; natural. **2.** serving to fix a standard. **3.** *Psychol.* **a.** approximately average in any psychological trait, as intelligence, personality, or emotional adjustment. **b.** free from any mental disorder; sane. **4.** *Math.* **a.** being at right angles, as a line; perpendicular. **b.** of the nature of or pertaining to a mathematical normal. **5.** *Chem.* **a.** (of a solution) containing one equivalent weight of the constituent in question in one liter of solution. **b.** pertaining to an aliphatic hydrocarbon having a straight unbranched carbon chain, each carbon atom of which is joined to no more than two other carbon atoms. **c.** of or pertaining to a neutral salt in which any replaceable hydroxyl groups or hydrogen atoms have been replaced by other groups or atoms, as sodium sulfate, Na_2SO_4. **6.** *Biol., Med.* **a.** free from any infection or other form of disease or malformation, or from experimental therapy or manipulation. **b.** of natural occurrence. —*n.* **7.** the standard or type. **8.** the normal form or state; the average or mean. **9.** *Math.* **a.** a perpendicular line or plane, esp. one perpendicular to a tangent line of a curve, or a tangent plane of a surface, at the point of contact. **b.** the portion of this perpendicular line included between its point of contact with the curve and the *x*-axis. [< L *normāl(is)* made according to a carpenter's square, a rule, pattern = *norm(a)* (see NORM) + *-ālis* -AL[1]] —**nor·mal·i·ty** (nôr mal′i tē), **nor′mal·ness,** *n.*

Nor·mal (nôr′məl), *n.* a city in central Illinois. 26,396 (1970).

nor′mal curve′, *Statistics.* a bell-shaped curve showing a distribution of probability associated with different values of a variate. Also called **Gaussian curve.**

nor·mal·cy (nôr′məl sē), *n.* the character or state of being normal, as the general economic, political, and social conditions of a nation; normality.

nor′mal distribu′tion, *Statistics.* a theoretical frequency distribution represented by a normal curve. Also called **Gaussian distribution.**

nor·mal·ise (nôr′mə līz′), *v.t., v.i.,* **-ised, -is·ing.** *Chiefly Brit.* normalize. —**nor′mal·i·sa′tion,** *n.*

nor·mal·ize (nôr′mə līz′), *v.,* **-ized, -iz·ing.** —*v.t.* **1.** to make normal. —*v.i.* **2.** to become normal; resume a normal state. —**nor′mal·i·za′tion,** *n.*

nor·mal·ly (nôr′mə lē), *adv.* according to rule, general custom, etc.; as a rule.

nor′mal school′, a school giving a two-year course to high-school graduates preparing to be teachers.

Nor·man (nôr′mən), *n.* **1.** a member of that branch of the Northmen or Scandinavians who in the 10th century conquered Normandy. **2.** Also called **Norman French.** one of the mixed Scandinavian and French people who inhabited Normandy and conquered England in 1066. **3.** a native or inhabitant of Normandy. **4.** See **Norman French** (def. 1). **5.** a city in central Oklahoma. 52,117 (1970). —*adj.* **6.** of or pertaining to the Normans. **7.** noting or pertaining to a variety of Romanesque architecture built by the Normans, esp. in England after 1066. [< ME < OF *Normant* < ON *Northmathr* Northman]

Nor′man Con′quest, the conquest of England by the Normans under William the Conqueror, in 1066.

Nor·man·dy (nôr′mən dē), *n.* a region in N France along the English Channel: invaded and settled by Scandinavians in the 10th century, becoming a duchy in A.D. 911; later a province, the capital of which was Rouen; Allied invasion in World War II began here June 6, 1944.

Nor′man French′, **1.** Also called **Norman.** the French of the Normans or of Normandy. **2.** Norman (def. 2). —**Nor′man-French′,** *adj.*

Nor·man·ise (nôr′mə nīz′), *v.t., v.i.,* **-ised, -is·ing.** *Chiefly Brit.* Normanize. —**Nor′man·i·sa′tion,** *n.* —**Nor′man-is′er,** *n.*

Nor·man·ize (nôr′mə nīz′), *v.t., v.i.,* **-ized, -iz·ing.** to make or become Norman in customs, language, etc. —**Nor′-man·i·za′tion,** *n.* —**Nor′man·iz′er,** *n.*

nor·ma·tive (nôr′mə tiv), *adj.* **1.** of or pertaining to a norm, esp. an assumed norm regarded as the standard of correctness in behavior, speech, writing, etc. **2.** tending or attempting to establish such a norm, esp. by the application of rules: *normative grammar.* **3.** reflecting the assumption of such a norm, or favoring its establishment. [NORM + -ATIVE] —**nor′ma·tive·ly,** *adv.* —**nor′ma·tive·ness,** *n.*

Norn (nôrn), *n. Scand. Myth.* a personification of fate, usually in the form of a virgin goddess. Cf. **Skuld, Urd, Urdar, Verdandi.**

No·ro·dom Si·ha·nouk (nôr′ə dom′ sē′ä no͞ok′), **Prince,** born 1922, Cambodian statesman: premier 1952–60; chief of state 1960–70, 1975–76.

Nor·ris (nôr′is, nor′-), *n.* **1. Frank,** 1870–1902, U.S. novelist. **2. George William,** 1861–1944, U.S. senator 1913–43.

Nor·ris·town (nôr′is toun′, nor′-), *n.* a borough in SE Pennsylvania, near Philadelphia. 38,169 (1970).

Norr·kö·ping (nôʀ′chœ′ping), *n.* a seaport in SE Sweden. 93,161 (1965).

Norse (nôrs), *adj.* **1.** belonging or pertaining to Norway, esp. ancient Norway with its colonies, or to ancient Scandinavia generally. —*n.* **2.** (*construed as pl.*) the Norwegians. **3.** (*construed as pl.*) the ancient Norwegians. **4.** (*construed as pl.*) the Northmen or ancient Scandinavians generally. **5.** the Norwegian language, esp. in its older forms. Cf. **Old Norse.** [perh. < D *noorsch,* obs. var. of *noordsch* (now *noords*) = *noord* NORTH + *-sch* -ISH[1]. Cf. Norw, Sw, Dan *Norsk* Norwegian, Norse]

Norse·man (nôrs′mən), *n., pl.* **-men.** Northman.

Nor·stad (nôr′stad, -städ), *n.* **Lau·ris** (lōr′is, lôr′-), born 1907, U.S. Air Force general: Supreme Allied Commander of NATO 1956–63.

north (nôrth), *n.* **1.** a cardinal point of the compass, lying in the plane of the meridian and to the left of a person facing the rising sun. *Abbr.:* N **2.** the direction in which this point lies. **3.** (*usually cap.*) a region or territory situated in this direction. **4.** (*cap.*) the northern area of the United States, esp. the states that fought to preserve the Union in the Civil War, lying to the north of the Ohio River, and usually including Missouri and Maryland. —*adj.* **5.** lying toward or situated in the north: *the north end of town.* **6.** in the direction of or toward the north. **7.** coming from the north, as a wind. —*adv.* **8.** toward the north: *heading north.* **9.** from the north. [ME, OE, c. D *noord,* Icel *northr,* G *nord*]

North (nôrth), *n.* **1. Christopher,** pen name of John Wilson. **2. Frederick, 2nd Earl of Guil·ford** (gil′fərd) ("*Lord North*"), 1732–92, British statesman: prime minister 1770–1782. **3. Sir Thomas,** 1535?–1601?, English translator.

North′ Af′rica, the northern part of Africa, esp. the region north of the tropical rain forest, comprising Morocco, Algeria, Tunisia, Libya, and that part of the Arab Republic of Egypt west of the Gulf of Suez. —**North′ Af′rican.**

North′ Amer′ica, the northern continent of the Western Hemisphere, extending from Central America to the Arctic Ocean. Highest point, Mt. McKinley, 20,300 ft.; lowest, Death Valley, 276 ft. below sea level. (including Central America) 316,000,000; ab. 8,440,000 sq. mi. —**North′ Amer′ican.**

North·amp·ton (nôr thamp′tən, nôrth hamp′-), *n.* **1.** a city in and the county seat of Northamptonshire, in central England. 105,361 (1961). **2.** Northamptonshire. **3.** a city in central Massachusetts. 29,664 (1970).

North·amp·ton·shire (nôr thamp′tən shēr′, -shər, nôrth-hamp-′), *n.* a county in central England. 398,132 (1961); 914 sq. mi. *Co. seat:* Northampton. Also called **Northampton.**

North′ Atlan′tic Cur′rent, an ocean current formed by the convergence of the Gulf Stream and the Labrador Current SE of Newfoundland and that flows NE toward the British Isles. Also called **North′ Atlan′tic Drift′.**

North′ Atlan′tic Trea′ty, the treaty (1949) signed by 12 countries, providing for the establishment of NATO. Also called **North′ Atlan′tic Pact′.**

North′ Atlan′tic Trea′ty Organiza′tion. See **NATO.**

North′ Bab′ylon, a town on S Long Island, in SE New York. 39,526 (1970).

North′ Ber′gen, a township in NE New Jersey. 47,751 (1970).

North′ Bor′neo, a former name of **Sabah.**

north·bound (nôrth′bound′), *adj.* going toward the north: *northbound traffic.*

North·brook (nôrth′bro͝ok′), *n.* a city in NE Illinois. 27,297 (1970).

north′ by east′, *Navig., Survey.* a point on the compass 11°15′ east of north. *Abbr.:* NbE

north′ by west′, *Navig., Survey.* a point on the compass 11°15′ west of north. *Abbr.:* NbW

North′ Cape′, **1.** a point of land on an island at the N tip of Norway: the northernmost point of Europe. **2.** the northern end of North Island, New Zealand.

North′ Caroli′na, a state in the SE United States, on the Atlantic coast. 5,082,059 (1970); 52,712 sq. mi. *Cap.:* Raleigh. *Abbr.:* N.C., NC —**North′ Carolin′ian.**

North′ Cau′casus, a region in the S Soviet Union in Europe, E of the Black Sea.

North′ Chan′nel, a strait between SW Scotland and NE Ireland. 14 mi. wide at the narrowest point.

North′ Chica′go, a city in NE Illinois, on Lake Michigan. 47,275 (1970).

North·cliffe (nôrth′klif), *n.* **Viscount.** See **Harmsworth.**

North′ Coun′try, **1.** the part of England north of the Humber estuary. **2.** Alaska and the Yukon territory of Canada (as a geographical and economic unit).

North′ Dako′ta, a state in the N central United States. 617,761 (1970); 70,665 sq. mi. *Cap.:* Bismarck. *Abbr.:* N. Dak., N.D., ND —**North′ Dako′tan.**

north·east (nôrth′ēst′; *Naut.* nôr′ēst′), *n.* **1.** a point on the compass midway between north and east. *Abbr.:* NE **2.** a region in this direction. **3. the Northeast,** the northeastern part of the U.S., esp. the New England states. —*adj.* **4.** lying toward or situated in the northeast: *the northeast end of town.* **5.** in the direction of or toward the northeast. **6.** coming from the northeast, as a wind. —*adv.* **7.** toward the northeast: *heading northeast.* **8.** from the northeast. Also, **north′east′ern** (for defs. 4, 5). [OE]

northeast′ by east′, *Navig., Survey.* a point on the compass 11°15′ east of northeast. *Abbr.:* NEbE

northeast′ by north′, *Navig., Survey.* a point on the compass 11°15′ north of northeast. *Abbr.:* NEbN

north·east·er (nôrth′ē′stər; *Naut.* nôr′ē′stər), *n.* a wind or gale from the northeast. Also, **nor′easter.**

north·east·er·ly (nôrth′ē′stər lē; *Naut.* nôr′ē′stər lē), *adj.* **1.** of, pertaining to, or situated in the northeast. **2.** in the direction of or toward the northeast. **3.** coming from the northeast, as a wind. —*adv.* **4.** toward the northeast. **5.** from the northeast.

north·east·ern·er (nôrth/ē′stər nər), *n.* **1.** a native or inhabitant of the northeast. **2.** (*cap.*) a native or inhabitant of the northeastern U.S.

North′east Pas′sage, a ship route along the N coast of Europe and Asia, between the North Sea and the Pacific.

north·east·ward (nôrth′ēst′wərd; *Naut.* nôr′ēst′wərd), *adj.* **1.** moving, facing, or situated toward the northeast. —*adv.* **2.** toward the northeast. —*n.* **3.** the northeast.

north·east·ward·ly (nôrth′ēst′wərd lē; *Naut.* nôr′ēst′-wərd lē), *adj., adv.* toward the northeast.

north·east·wards (nôrth′ēst′wərdz; *Naut.* nôr′ēst′-wərdz), *adv.* northeastward.

north·er (nôr′thər), *n.* **1.** (in the U.S. Gulf Coast region) a cold gale from the north. **2.** a wind or storm from the north.

north·er·ly (nôr′thər lē), *adj., adv., n., pl.* **-lies.** —*adj.* **1.** of, pertaining to, or situated in the north. **2.** in the direction of or toward the north. **3.** coming from the north, as a wind. —*adv.* **4.** toward the north. **5.** from the north, as a wind. —*n.* **6.** a northerly wind. [NORTH + *erly,* modeled on *easterly*] —**north′er·li·ness.** *n.*

north·ern (nôr′thərn), *adj.* **1.** lying toward or situated in the north. **2.** directed or proceeding northward. **3.** coming from the north, as a wind. **4.** (*often cap.*) of or pertaining to the North, esp. the northern U.S. **5.** *Astron.* north of the celestial equator or of the zodiac: *a northern constellation.* —*n.* **6.** a person living in a northern region or country. [ME, OE] —**north′ern·ness,** *n.*

North′ern Cameroons′. See under **Cameroons** (def. 2).

North′ern Coal′sack, *Astron.* See under **Coalsack.**

North′ern Cross′, *Astron.* six stars in the constellation Cygnus, arranged in the form of a cross.

North′ern Crown′, *Astron.* the constellation Corona Borealis.

North·ern·er (nôr′thər nər), *n.* (*sometimes l.c.*) a native or inhabitant of the North, esp. of the northern U.S.

North′ern Hem′isphere, the half of the earth between the North Pole and the equator.

North′ern Ire′land, a political division of the United Kingdom, in the NE part of the island of Ireland. 1,458,000 (est. 1964); 5238 sq. mi. *Cap.:* Belfast.

north′ern lights′. See **aurora borealis.**

North′ern Mich′igan. See **Upper Peninsula.**

north·ern·most (nôr′thərn mōst′ *or, esp. Brit.,* -məst), *adj.* farthest north.

North′ern Rhode′sia, former name of **Zambia.**

North′ern Spy′, **1.** an American variety of red-striped apple that ripens in autumn or early winter. **2.** the tree bearing this fruit.

North′ern Ter′ritories, a former British protectorate in W Africa: now a part of N Ghana.

North′ern Ter′ritory, a territory in N Australia. 27,095 (1961); 523,620 sq. mi. *Cap.:* Darwin.

North′ Frig′id Zone′, the part of the earth's surface between the Arctic Circle and the North Pole.

North′ German′ic, the subbranch of Germanic that includes the languages of Scandinavia and Iceland. Also called **Scandinavian.**

North′ Glenn′, a city in central Colorado. 27,937 (1970).

North′ High′lands, a town in central California, near Sacramento. 31,854 (1970).

North′ Hol′land, a province in the W Netherlands. 2,054,509 (est. 1960); 1163 sq. mi. *Cap.:* Haarlem.

north·ing (nôr′thing, -thing), *n.* **1.** northward movement or deviation. **2.** distance due north. **3.** distance due north made on any course tending northward.

North′ Is′land, the northernmost principal island of New Zealand. 1,684,139 (est. 1961); 44,281 sq. mi.

North′ Kings′town′ (kingz′toun′), a city in S Rhode Island. 29,793 (1970).

North′ Kore′a, a country in E Asia: formed 1948 after the division of the former country of Korea at 38° N. 16,000,000; 50,000 sq. mi. *Cap.:* Pyongyang. Official name, **Democrat′ic Peo′ple's Repub′lic of Kore′a.** Cf. **Korea** (def. 1).

north·land (nôrth′lənd), *n.* **1.** the land or region in the north. **2.** the northern part of a country. **3.** (*cap.*) the peninsula containing Norway and Sweden. [ME, OE] —**north′land·er,** *n.*

North′ Las′ Ve′gas, a city in S Nevada. 36,216 (1970).

North′ Lit′tle Rock′, a city in central Arkansas, on the Arkansas River. 60,040 (1970).

North·man (nôrth′mən), *n., pl.* **-men.** one of the ancient Scandinavians, esp. a member of the group that from about the 8th to the 11th century established settlements in Great Britain, Ireland, many parts of continental Europe, and probably in parts of North America. [OE]

North′ Miam′i, a city in SE Florida. 34,767 (1970).

North′ Miam′i Beach′, a city in SE Florida. 30,833 (1970).

north-north·east (nôrth′nôrth′ēst′; *Naut.* nôr′nôr′ēst′), *n.* **1.** the point on the compass midway between north and northeast. —*adj.* **2.** in the direction of or toward this point. **3.** coming from this point, as a wind. —*adv.* **4.** toward this point. **5.** from this point. *Abbr.:* NNE [late ME *northnorthest*]

north-north·west (nôrth′nôrth′west′; *Naut.* nôr′nôr′-west′), *n.* **1.** the point on the compass midway between north and northwest. —*adj.* **2.** in the direction of or toward this point. **3.** coming from this point, as a wind. —*adv.* **4.** toward this point. **5.** from this point. *Abbr.:* NNW [ME]

North′ Olm′sted, a city in NE Ohio, near Cleveland. 34,861 (1970).

North′ Pacif′ic cur′rent, a warm, eastward-flowing ocean current formed by the convergence of the Japan and Oyashio currents along the E coast of Japan.

North′ Platte′, a river flowing from N Colorado through SE Wyoming and W Nebraska into the Platte. 618 mi. long.

North′ Pole′, **1.** *Geog.* the end of the earth's axis of rotation marking the northernmost point on the earth. **2.** *Astron.* the point at which the extended axis of the earth cuts the northern half of the celestial sphere, about 1° from the North Star; the north celestial pole. **3.** (*l.c.*) See under **magnetic pole** (def. 1).

North′ Rhine′-West·pha′li·a (rīn′west fā′lē ə, -fāl′-yə), a state in W West Germany; formerly a part of Rhine province. 16,280,000 (1963); 13,111 sq. mi. *Cap.:* Düsseldorf.

North′ Rid′ing (rī′ding), an administrative division of Yorkshire, in N England. 354,382 (1961); 2127 sq. mi. *Co. seat:* Northallerton.

North′ Riv′er, a part of the Hudson River between NE New Jersey and SE New York.

North′ Sea′, an arm of the Atlantic between Great Britain and the European mainland. ab. 201,000 sq. mi.; greatest depth, 1998 ft. Formerly, **German Ocean.**

North′ Slope′, the northern coastal area of Alaska where rich reserves of oil and natural gas were discovered in 1968: so called because it is N of the Brooks Range sloping down to the Arctic Ocean.

North′ Star′, *Astron.* Polaris (def. 1).

North′ Tem′perate Zone′, the part of the earth's surface between the tropic of Cancer and the Arctic Circle.

North′ Ton·a·wan·da (ton′ə won′də), a city in W New York. 36,012 (1970).

North·um·ber·land (nôr thum′bər lənd), *n.* a county in NE England. 818,988 (1961); 2019 sq. mi. *Co. seat:* Newcastle.

North·um·bri·a (nôr thum′brē ə), *n.* an early English kingdom extending N from the Humber to the Firth of Forth. See map at **Mercia.**

North·um·bri·an (nôr thum′brē ən), *adj.* **1.** of or pertaining to Northumbria, Northumberland, or the inhabitants or dialect of either. —*n.* **2.** a native or inhabitant of Northumbria or Northumberland. **3.** the English dialect of Northumbria or Northumberland.

North′ Vietnam′, a former country in SE Asia, that comprised Vietnam above 17°N: now part of reunified Vietnam. Cf. **South Vietnam, Vietnam.**

north·ward (nôrth′wərd; *Naut.* nôr′thərd), *adj.* **1.** moving, facing, or situated toward the north. —*adv.* **2.** Also, **north′wards.** toward the north. —*n.* **3.** the north. Also, **north′ward·ly** (for defs. 1, 2). [ME; OE *northweard*]

north·west (nôrth′west′; *Naut.* nôr′west′), *n.* **1.** a point on the compass midway between north and west. *Abbr.:* NW **2.** a region in this direction. **3. the Northwest, a.** the northwestern part of the United States, esp. Washington, Oregon, and Idaho. **b.** the northwestern part of the United States when its western boundary was the Mississippi River. **c.** the northwestern part of Canada. —*adj.* **4.** lying toward or situated in the northwest: *the northwest end of town.* **5.** in the direction of or toward the northwest. **6.** coming from the northwest, as a wind. —*adv.* **7.** toward the northwest: *heading northwest.* **8.** from the northwest. Also, **north′-west′ern** (for defs. 4, 5). [ME, OE]

northwest′ by north′, *Navig., Survey.* a point on the compass, 11°15′ north of northwest. *Abbr.:* NWbN

northwest′ by west′, *Navig., Survey.* a point on the compass, 11°15′ west of northwest. *Abbr.:* NWbW

north·west·er (nôrth′wes′tər; *Naut.* nôr′wes′tər), *n.* a wind or gale from the northwest. Also, **nor′wester.**

north·west·er·ly (nôrth′wes′tər lē; *Naut.* nôr′wes′tər lē), *adj.* **1.** of, pertaining to, or situated in the northwest. **2.** in the direction of or toward the northwest. **3.** coming from the northwest, as a wind. —*adv.* **4.** toward the northwest. **5.** from the northwest, as a wind.

north·west·ern·er (nôrth′wes′tər nər), *n.* **1.** a native or inhabitant of the northwest. **2.** (*cap.*) a native or inhabitant of the northwestern U.S.

North′-West Frontier′ Prov′ince (nôrth′west′, -west′), **1.** a province in Pakistan, bordering Punjab and Kashmir on the west: included in Pakistan province 1955; a former province of British India. 13,560 sq. mi. *Cap.:* Peshawar. **2.** the former agencies and tribal areas between this province and Afghanistan. 25,699 sq. mi.

North′west Mount′ed Police′, official name, before 1904, of Royal Canadian Mounted Police.

North′west Pas′sage, a ship route along the Arctic coast of Canada and Alaska, joining the Atlantic and Pacific oceans.

North′west Ter′ritories, a territory of Canada lying N of the provinces and extending E from Yukon territory to Davis Strait. 22,998 (1961); 1,304,903 sq. mi.

North′west Ter′ritory, the region north of the Ohio River and east of the upper Mississippi River, organized by Congress in 1787.

Northwest Territory
Mississippi R.
Ohio River
ATLANTIC OCEAN
GULF OF MEXICO

north·west·ward (nôrth′-west′wərd; *Naut.* nôr′west′-wərd), *adj.* **1.** moving, facing, or situated toward the northwest. —*adv.* **2.** Also, **north-westwards.** toward the northwest. —*n.* **3.** the northwest. Also, **north′west′ward·ly** (for defs. 1, 2). [ME]

north·west·wards (nôrth′west′wərdz; *Naut.* nôr′west′-wərdz), *adv.* northwestward.

Norw, Norwegian (def. 3).

Norw., **1.** Norway. **2.** Norwegian.

Nor·walk (nôr′wôk), *n.* **1.** a city in SW California. 91,827 (1970). **2.** a city in SW Connecticut. 79,113 (1970).

Nor·way (nôr′wā), *n.* a kingdom in N Europe, in the W part of the Scandinavian Peninsula. 4,017,101; 124,555 sq. mi. *Cap.:* Oslo. Norwegian, **Norge.**

Nor′way ma′ple, a European maple, *Acer platanoides,* having bright green leaves, grown as a shade tree in the U.S.

Nor′way rat′, an Old World rat, *Rattus norvegicus,* having a grayish-brown body with whitish underparts and a long, scaly tail, now common in the U.S. in or near homes, barns, wharves, etc. Also called **brown rat.**

Nor′way salt′peter, *Chem.* See **ammonium nitrate.**

Nor′way spruce′, a European spruce, *Picea abies,* grown as an ornamental.

Nor·we·gian (nôr wē′jən), *adj.* **1.** of or pertaining to Norway, its inhabitants, or their language. —*n.* **2.** a native or inhabitant of Norway. **3.** the speech of Norway in any of its forms, whether Dano-Norwegian, the local dialects, or the standard language based on these, all being closely related to one another and to the other Scandinavian languages. *Abbr.:* Norw [earlier *Norvegian* < ML *Norvegi(a)* NORWAY + -AN]

Norwe′gian elk′hound, one of a breed of dogs having a short, compact body, short, pointed ears, and a thick, gray coat, raised originally in Norway for hunting elk and other game.

Norwe′gian salt′peter, *Chem.* See **calcium nitrate.**

Norwe′gian Sea′, part of the Arctic Ocean between Greenland and Norway and N of Iceland.

nor′west·er (nôr wes′tər), *n.* **1.** southwester (def. 3). **2.** northwester. [NOR(TH)WESTER]

Nor·wich (nôr′ich, -ij, nor′- *for 1;* nôr′wich *for 2*), *n.* **1.** a city in E Norfolk, in E England: cathedral. 119,904 (1960). **2.** a city in SE Connecticut, on the Thames River. 41,739 (1970).

Nor·wood (nôr′wo͝od′), *n.* **1.** a city in SW Ohio, near Cincinnati. 30,420 (1970). **2.** a town in E Massachusetts. 30,815 (1970).

nos-, var. of **noso-** before a vowel.

nos., numbers. Also, **Nos.**

nose (nōz), *n., v.,* **nosed, nos·ing.** **—***n.* **1.** the part of the face or facial region in man and certain animals that contains the nostrils and the organs of smell, and functions as the usual passageway for air in respiration and, in man, in the modification or modulation of the voice. **2.** this part as the organ of smell. **3.** the sense of smell. **4.** a faculty of perceiving or detecting. **5.** something regarded as resembling the nose of a person or animal, as a spout or nozzle. **6.** the prow of a ship. **7.** the forward end of an aircraft. **8.** the forward edge of the head of a golf club. **9.** a projecting part of anything. **10.** the human nose regarded as a symbol of meddling or prying. **11.** the length of a nose, as of a horse. **12. by a nose,** *Slang.* by a very narrow margin. **13. cut off one's nose to spite one's face,** to create a disadvantage to oneself through one's own spiteful action. **14. on the nose,** *Slang.* **a.** precisely; correctly. **b.** exactly on time. **c.** (of a bet) for win only. **15. pay through the nose,** to pay an excessive price. **—***v.t.* **16.** to perceive by or as by the nose or the sense of smell. **17.** to approach the nose to, as in smelling or examining; sniff. **18.** to move or push forward with or as with the nose. **19.** to touch or rub with the nose; nuzzle. **—***v.i.* **20.** to smell or sniff. **21.** to seek by or as by smelling or scent. **22.** to move or push forward: *to nose into the wind.* **23.** to meddle or pry (often fol. by *about, into,* etc.): *to nose about in someone else's business.* [ME; OE *nosu,* akin to D *neus,* G *Nase,* L *nāsus,* Skt *nāsā*] **—nose′less,** *adj.* **—nose′like′,** *adj.*

nose′ bag′. See **feed bag** (def. 1).

nose·band (nōz′band′), *n.* the part of a bridle or halter that passes over the animal's nose. **—nose′band′ed,** *adj.*

nose·bleed (nōz′blēd′), *n.* bleeding from the nose.

nose′ cone′, *Rocketry.* the cone-shaped forward section of a rocket or guided missile, including a heat shield and containing the payload.

nose′ dive′, **1.** a plunge of an aircraft with the forward part pointing downward. **2.** any sudden drop or decline: *Market values took a nose dive.*

nose-dive (nōz′dīv′), *v.i.,* **-dived** or **-dove, -dived, -div·ing.** to go into a nose dive.

nose·gay (nōz′gā′), *n.* a small bunch of flowers; bouquet; posy. [late ME; a *gay* (obs., something pretty) for the NOSE (i.e., to smell)]

nose·piece (nōz′pēs′), *n.* **1.** a protective cover for the nose. **2.** the part of a microscope to which the objectives are attached. **3.** a noseband. **4.** the part of a frame for eyeglasses that passes over the bridge of the nose.

nos·ey (nō′zē), *adj.,* **nos·i·er, nos·i·est.** nosy.

nosh (nosh), *v.i.* to eat between meals, esp. to nibble at tidbits. [< Yiddish; cf. G *naschen* to nibble, eat on the sly; c. Dan *naske,* Sw *snaska*] **—nosh′er,** *n.*

no-show (nō′shō′), *n. Informal.* a person who makes a reservation on a plane, ship, etc., and neither uses nor cancels it.

nos·ing (nō′zing), *n. Archit.* a projecting edge, as the part of the tread of a step extending beyond the riser or a projecting part of a buttress.

noso-, a learned borrowing from Greek meaning "disease," used in the formation of compound words: *nosology.* Also, *esp. before a vowel,* **nos-.** [comb. form repr. Gk *nóso(s)* disease, sickness, malady]

no·sol·o·gy (nō sol′ə jē), *n.* **1.** the systematic classification of diseases. **2.** the knowledge of a disease. [< NL *nosologia*] **—nos·o·log·i·cal** (nos′ə loj′i kəl), *adj.* **—nos′o·log′i·cal·ly,** *adv.* **—no·sol′o·gist,** *n.*

nos·tal·gia (no stal′jə, -jē ə, nə-), *n.* a longing for experiences, things, or acquaintanceships belonging to the past. [< NL < Gk *nóst(os)* a return home + *-algia* -ALGIA] **—nos·tal′gic,** *adj.* **—nos·tal′gi·cal·ly,** *adv.*

nos·toc (nos′tok), *n.* any fresh-water, blue-green alga of the genus *Nostoc,* often found in jellylike colonies in moist places. [< NL, coined by Paracelsus]

nos·tol·o·gy (no stol′ə jē), *n.* geriatrics. [< Gk *nósto(s)* a return home + -LOGY] **—nos·to·log·ic** (nos′tə loj′ik), *adj.*

Nos·tra·da·mus (nos′trə dā′məs, -dä′-), *n.* (*Michel de Nostredame*) 1503–66, French astrologer. **—Nos·tra·dam·ic** (nos′trə dam′ik), *adj.*

nos·tril (nos′trəl), *n.* one of the external openings of the nose. [ME *nostrill,* OE *nosterl,* var. of *nosthyrl* = *nosu* nose + *thyrel* hole; see THIRL]

nos·trum (nos′trəm), *n.* **1.** a patent medicine. **2.** a quack medicine. **3.** a pet scheme, theory, device, etc., esp. one to remedy social or political ills; panacea. [< L *nostrum* our, ours (neut. sing. of *noster*); referring to the seller's calling the drug "our" drug]

nos·y (nō′zē), *adj.,* **nos·i·er, nos·i·est.** *Informal.* prying; inquisitive. Also, **nosey.** **—nos′i·ly,** *adv.* **—nos′i·ness,** *n.*

Nos·y Par·ker (nō′zē pär′kər), *Informal.* a nosy, prying person; busybody.

not (not), *adv.* (used to express negation, denial, refusal, or prohibition): *It's not far from here. You must not do that.* [ME; weak var. of NOUGHT]

no·ta be·ne (nō′tä be′ne; *Eng.* nō′tə bē′nē, bā′nā), *Latin.* note well; take notice.

no·ta·bil·i·ty (nō′tə bil′i tē), *n., pl.* **-ties** for 2. **1.** the state or quality of being notable. **2.** *Chiefly Brit.* a notable person. [ME *notabilite*]

no·ta·ble (nō′tə bəl), *adj.* **1.** worthy of note or notice; noteworthy. **2.** prominent, important, or distinguished, as persons. **3.** *Archaic.* capable, thrifty, and industrious. **—***n.* **4.** a notable or prominent person. **5.** (*usually cap.*) *Fr. Hist.* one of a number of prominent men, usually of the aristocracy, called by the king on extraordinary occasions. **6.** *Obs.* a notable fact or thing. [ME *notab(i)le* < L *notābilis*] **—no′ta·bly,** *adv.* **—Syn. 1, 2.** memorable, remarkable, outstanding. **2.** celebrated, famous. **—Ant. 1.** ordinary. **2.** unknown.

no·tar·i·al (nō târ′ē əl), *adj.* **1.** of, pertaining to, or characteristic of a notary. **2.** drawn up or executed by a notary. **—no·tar′i·al·ly,** *adv.*

no·ta·rize (nō′tə rīz′), *v.t.,* **-rized, -riz·ing.** to certify (a document, contract, etc.) or cause to become certified through a notary public.

no·ta·ry (nō′tə rē), *n., pl.* **-ries.** See **notary public.** [ME < L *notārius* clerk = *not(āre)* (to) note, mark + *-ārius* -ARY] **—no′ta·ry·ship′,** *n.*

no′tary pub′lic, *pl.* **notaries public.** a public officer or other person authorized to authenticate contracts, take affidavits, etc.

no·tate (nō′tāt), *v.t.,* **-tat·ed, -tat·ing.** to put into notation. [back formation from NOTATION]

no·ta·tion (nō tā′shən), *n.* **1.** a system of graphic symbols for a specialized use: *musical notation.* **2.** the process of noting by means of a special system of signs or symbols. **3.** the act of making notes in writing. **4.** a note, jotting, or record. [< L *notātiōn-* (s. of *notātiō*) a marking = *notāt(us)* noted (ptp. of *notāre*) + *-iōn-* -ION] **—no·ta′tion·al,** *adj.*

notch (noch), *n.* **1.** an angular cut, indentation, or hollow in an object, surface, or edge. **2.** a cut or nick made in an object as a record, score, etc. **—***v.t.* **3.** to cut or make a notch or notches in. [*a notch* (by false division) for *an* **otch* < OF *oche* notch]

note (nōt), *n., v.,* **not·ed, not·ing.** **—***n.* **1.** a brief written record. **2.** a brief written comment, instruction, reminder, etc. **3.** a short, informal letter: *a thank-you note.* **4.** a formal diplomatic or official communication. **5. notes,** a written summary or outline of something that has been observed, studied, etc. **6.** a printed paper accepted as money. **7.** a written promise to pay a stated amount. **8.** notice, observation, or heed: *to take note of a sign; a play worthy of note.* **9.** reputation or prominence: *a person of note.* **10.** importance or consequence: *Has anything of note happened?* **11.** a hint or underlying expression of a quality, emotion, etc.: *a note of whimsy in an essay; a speech ending on a note of triumph.* **12.** a musical sound or tone. **13.** *Music.* **a.** a sign or character used to represent a tone, its position and form indicating the pitch and duration of the tone. **b.** a key, as of a piano. **14.** a sound of musical

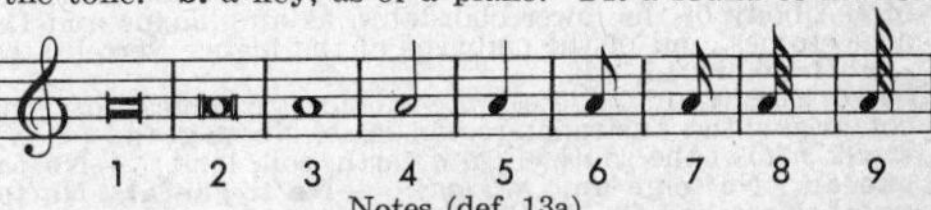

Notes (def. 13a)

1, 2, Breve; 3, Whole note or semibreve; 4, Half note or minim; 5, Quarter note or crotchet; 6, Eighth note or quaver; 7, Sixteenth note or semiquaver; 8, Thirty-second note or demisemiquaver; 9, Sixty-fourth note or hemidemisemiquaver

quality. **15.** *Archaic.* a melody, tune, or song. **16. compare notes,** to exchange views, ideas, or impressions. **—***v.t.* **17.** to mark down, as in writing; make a record or memorandum of. **18.** to annotate. **19.** to observe carefully; give attention or heed to. **20.** to take notice of; perceive. **21.** to set down in or furnish with musical notes. **22.** to indicate or designate; signify; denote. [ME < ML *nota* sign for musical tone, L, mark] **—Syn. 1.** memorandum, minute. **2.** commentary, annotation. See **remark. 6.** bill. **9.** repute, celebrity, fame, renown. **17.** register, record. **20.** see, spot, remark.

note·book (nōt′bo͝ok′), *n.* **1.** a book of or for notes. **2.** a book in which promissory notes are entered, registered, recorded, etc.

note·case (nōt′kās′), *n. Chiefly Brit.* billfold.

not·ed (nō′tid), *adj.* celebrated; famous; renowned. **—not′ed·ly,** *adv.* **—Syn.** distinguished, eminent. **—Ant.** obscure, unknown.

note·less (nōt′lis), *adj.* **1.** of no note. **2.** unmusical or voiceless.

note′ of hand′. See **promissory note.**

note·pap·er (nōt′pā′pər), *n.* writing paper, esp. that used in personal correspondence.

note·wor·thy (nōt′wûr′thē), *adj.* worthy of notice or attention; notable; remarkable. **—note′wor′thi·ly,** *adv.*

noth·ing (nuth′ing), *n.* **1.** no thing; not anything; naught: *She sat there all the evening and said nothing.* **2.** no item, part, quantity, trace, etc., of something implied or mentioned: *The searchers found nothing in the woods. Say nothing of our talk.* **3.** no matter of any kind: *A perfect vacuum would consist literally of nothing.* **4.** a complete absence of reward, value to be received or given, meaning, etc.: *hopes that come to nothing; an antique worth next to nothing; to expect something for nothing.* **5.** something of no importance: *Oh, my headache is nothing now.* **6.** a zero quantity: *Nothing from nine leaves nine.* **7.** a trivial utterance: *to say sweet nothings.* **8.** no great effort, trouble, etc.: *There's nothing to fixing this if you know how.* **9. nothing but,** nothing other than; only. **10. nothing doing, a.** emphatically no; certainly not. **b.** no perceptible activity of note: *There was nothing doing in town.* **—***adv.* **11.** in no respect or degree; not at all: *Nothing dismayed, he repeated his question.* [orig. two words: *no thing*]

noth·ing·ness (nuth′ing nis), *n.* **1.** lack of being; nonexistence. **2.** absence of worth or significance. **3.** unconsciousness or death.

no·tice (nō′tis), *n., v.,* **-ticed, -tic·ing.** —*n.* **1.** information or warning of something: *to give notice of storms approaching; to serve notice that smoking is not allowed.* **2.** a printed or written statement of such information or warning. **3.** notification to another that an arrangement with him is to end at a specified time: *to give an employer notice.* **4.** attention or observation (often prec. by *take*): *to take notice of one's surroundings.* **5.** a review or critique. —*v.t.* **6.** to be aware of or observe. **7.** to comment on. **8.** to give polite attention to. [late ME < MF < L *nōtitia* a knowing] —**Syn. 1.** advice, news, notification, announcement. **2.** sign, poster. **4.** note, cognizance. **6.** see, regard, observe; note, mark; distinguish, discriminate, recognize. NOTICE, DISCERN, PERCEIVE imply becoming aware of, and paying attention to, something. To NOTICE is to become aware of something that has caught one's attention: *to notice a newspaper headline.* DISCERN suggests distinguishing (sometimes with difficulty) and recognizing a thing for what it is, discriminating it from its surroundings: *In spite of the fog, we finally discerned the outline of the harbor.* PERCEIVE, often used as a formal substitute for see or notice, may convey also the idea of understanding meanings and implications: *After examining the evidence he perceived its significance.*

no·tice·a·ble (nō′ti sə bəl), *adj.* **1.** able to attract notice or attention. **2.** deserving of notice or attention. —**no′tice·a·bil′i·ty,** *n.* —**no′tice·a·bly,** *adv.* —**Syn.** conspicuous, prominent, notable. —**Ant.** inconspicuous.

no·ti·fi·ca·tion (nō′tə fə kā′shən), *n.* the act or an instance of notifying, making known, or giving notice. [ME *notificacioun* < ML *notificātiōn-* (s. of *notificātiō*)]

no·ti·fy (nō′tə fī′), *v.t.,* **-fied, -fy·ing. 1.** to inform or give notice of (something). **2.** *Chiefly Brit.* to make known; give information of: *The sale was notified in the newspapers.* [ME *notifien* < MF *notifier* < L *nōtificāre* = (*g*)*nōt*(*us*) known (ptp. of (*g*)*nōscere* to come to know) + *-ificāre* -IFY] —**no′ti·fi′a·ble,** *adj.* —**no′ti·fi′er,** *n.* —**Syn. 1.** apprise.

no·tion (nō′shən), *n.* **1.** a general, vague, or imperfect conception or idea. **2.** an opinion, view, or belief. **3.** a fanciful or foolish idea; whim. **4.** an ingenious article; device; contrivance. **5. notions,** *U.S.* small articles for sale, as buttons, thread, ribbon, etc. [< L *nōtiōn-* (s. of *nōtiō*) examination, idea] —**no′tion·less,** *adj.* —**Syn. 1.** See **idea.**

no·tion·al (nō′shə nəl), *adj.* **1.** pertaining to or expressing a notion or idea. **2.** of the nature of a notion or idea. **3.** abstract, theoretical, or speculative, as reflective thought. **4.** not real or actual; ideal or imaginary. **5.** *Gram.* relating to the meaning expressed by a linguistic form. Cf. **relational** (def. 3). **6.** *Semantics.* belonging to a class of words that express concepts rather than relations between concepts; presentive. Cf. **symbolic** (def. 4). —**no′tion·al·ly,** *adv.*

noto-, a learned borrowing from Greek meaning "the back," used in the formation of compound words: *notochord.* [comb. form repr. Gk *nōton* the back]

no·to·chord (nō′tə kôrd′), *n.* *Biol., Embryol.* a rodlike cord of cells that forms the chief axial supporting structure of the body of the lower chordates, as amphioxus and the cyclostomes, and of the embryos of the higher vertebrates. —**no′to·chord′al,** *adj.*

No·to·gae·a (nō′tə jē′ə), *n.* a biogeographical division comprising the Australian region. Also, **No′to·ge′a.** [< NL < Gk *nōto*(*s*) the south + *gaîa* earth, soil, land] —**No′to·gae′an, No′to·ge′an,** *n., adj.* —**No′to·gae′al, No′to·ge′al, No′to·gae′ic, No′to·ge′ic,** *adj.*

no·to·ri·e·ty (nō′tə rī′i tē), *n., pl.* **-ties** for 2. **1.** the state or character of being notorious or widely known, esp. unfavorably. **2.** *Chiefly Brit.* a notorious person, esp. one of bad repute. [< ML *nōtōrietās* = *nōtōri*(*us*) NOTORIOUS + *-etās,* var. of *-itās* -ITY]

no·to·ri·ous (nō tōr′ē əs, -tôr′-), *adj.* **1.** widely but unfavorably known: *a notorious criminal.* **2.** generally known. [< ML *nōtōrius* evident = *nōt*(*us*) known, recognized (ptp. of *nōscere*) + *-ōrius* -ORY¹] —**no·to′ri·ous·ly,** *adv.*

no·tor·nis (nō tôr′nis), *n.* any of several rare, flightless, birds of the genus *Notornis,* of New Zealand. [< NL: name of the genus < Gk *nót*(*os*) the south + *órnis* a bird]

no-trump (nō′trump′), *Bridge.* —*adj.* **1.** (of a hand, bid, or contract) without a trump suit; noting a bid or contract to be played without naming a trump suit. —*n.* **2.** the bid to play a no-trump contract.

no-trump·er (nō′trum′pər), *n.* *Bridge.* the player who bids or plays a no-trump contract.

Not·ting·ham (not′ing əm), *n.* **1.** a city in SW Nottinghamshire, in central England. 287,800. **2.** Nottinghamshire.

Not·ting·ham·shire (not′ing əm shēr′, -shər), *n.* a county in central England. 982,700; 844 sq. mi. *Co. seat:* Nottingham. Also called **Nottingham, Notts** (nots).

not·tur·no (nə tŏŏr′nō, nō-; *It.* nôt tōōR′nô), *n., pl.* **-ni** (-nē). *Music.* nocturne. [< It: of the night. See NOCTURN]

no·tum (nō′təm), *n., pl.* **-ta** (-tə). a dorsal plate or sclerite of the thorax of an insect. [< NL < Gk *nōton* the back] —**no′tal,** *adj.*

No·tus (nō′təs), *n.* the ancient Greek personification of the south wind. Cf. **Auster.** [< L < Gk *Nótos* the south wind, the south]

not·with·stand·ing (not′with stan′ding, -wi*th*-), *prep.* **1.** in spite of. —*conj.* **2.** in spite of the fact that; although. —*adv.* **3.** nevertheless; anyway; yet. [ME] —**Syn. 1.** NOTWITHSTANDING, DESPITE, IN SPITE OF imply that something is true even though there are obstacles or opposing conditions. The three expressions may be used practically interchangeably. NOTWITHSTANDING suggests, however, a hindrance of some kind: *Notwithstanding the long delay, I shall still go.* DESPITE indicates that there is an active opposition: *Despite procrastination and disorganization, they finished the project.* IN SPITE OF, the informal equivalent of DESPITE, also implies meeting strong opposing forces or circumstances that must be taken into account; *He succeeded in spite of many discouragements.* **3.** however.

Nouak·chott (nwäk shot′), *n.* a city in and the capital of Mauritania, on the W coast. 130,000.

nou·gat (nōō′gət, nōō′gä), *n.* a chewy or brittle confection containing almonds or other nuts and sometimes fruit. [< F < Pr << L *nucātum, n. use of neut. of *nucātus = nuc- (s. of *nux*) nut + *-ātus* -ATE¹]

nought (nôt), *n., adj.* naught. [ME; OE *nōht,* contr. of *nōwiht* = *ne* not + *ōwiht* OUGHT³]

Nou·mé·a (nōō mā′ə), *n.* a city in and the capital of New Caledonia, on the SW coast. 59,869.

nou·me·non (nōō′mə non′, nou′-), *n., pl.* **-na** (-nə). **1.** the object, itself inaccessible to experience, to which a phenomenon is referred for the basis or cause of its sense content. **2.** a thing in itself, as distinguished from a phenomenon or thing as it appears. **3.** *Kantianism.* that which can be the object only of a purely intellectual, nonsensuous intuition. Cf. **thing-in-itself.** [< Gk *nooúmenon* a thing being perceived, n. use of neut. of prp. passive of *noeîn* to perceive; akin to NOUS] —**nou′me·nal,** *adj.* —**nou′me·nal·ism,** *n.* —**nou′me·nal·ist,** *n.* —**nou′me·nal′i·ty,** *n.* —**nou′me·nal·ly,** *adv.*

noun (noun), *n.* **1.** *Gram.* any member of a class of words distinguished chiefly by having plural and possessive endings, by functioning as subject or object in a construction, and by designating persons, places, things, states, or qualities. —*adj.* **2.** Also, **noun′al.** of or resembling a noun. [ME *nowne* < AF *noun* < L *nōmen* NAME] —**noun′al·ly,** *adv.* —**noun′less,** *adj.*

nour·ish (nûr′ish, nur′-), *v.t.* **1.** to sustain with food or nutriment. **2.** to strengthen or promote. [ME *norisshe* < OF *noriss-,* long s. of *norir* < L *nūtrīre* to feed; see -ISH²] —**nour′ish·er,** *n.* —**nour′ish·ing·ly,** *adv.*

nour·ish·ment (nûr′ish mənt, nur′-), *n.* **1.** something that nourishes; food; sustenance. **2.** the act of nourishing. **3.** the state of being nourished. [late ME *norysshement* < MF *norissement*]

nous (nōōs, nous), *n.* *Gk. Philos.* mind or intellect. [< Gk *noûs,* contracted var. of *nóos* mind]

nou·veau riche (nōō vō RESH′; *Eng.* nōō′vō rēsh′), *pl.* **nou·veaux riches** (nōō vō RESH′; *Eng.* nōō′vō rēsh′). *French. Usually Disparaging.* a person who is newly rich.

nou·velle cui·sine (nōō vel kwē zēn′), (*sometimes caps.*) *French.* a modern style of French cooking that emphasizes the use of the finest and freshest ingredients simply and imaginatively prepared, often with fresh herbs, the artful arrangement and presentation of food, and the use of reduced stocks in place of flour-thickened sauces. [lit., new cooking]

Nov., November.

no·va (nō′və), *n., pl.* **-vae** (-vē), **-vas.** *Astron.* a star that suddenly becomes thousands of times brighter and then gradually fades. Cf. **supernova.** [< NL: n. use of fem. of L *novus* NEW]

no·vac·u·lite (nō vak′yə līt′), *n.* *Petrog.* a very hard rock, probably sedimentary, composed essentially of microcrystalline quartz. [< L *novācul*(*a*) a sharp knife, razor + -ITE¹]

No·va·lis (nō vä′lis), *n.* (pen name of *Friedrich von Hardenberg*) 1772–1801, German poet.

No·va Lis·bo·a (*Port.* nô′və lēzh bô′ə), a city in central Angola. 89,000 (est. 1971). Formerly, **Huambo.**

No·va·ra (nō vär′ə; *It.* nô vä′rä), *n.* a city in NE Piedmont, in NW Italy. 102,135.

No·va Sco·tia (nō′və skō′shə), a peninsula and province in SE Canada: once a part of the French province of Acadia. 812,127; 21,068 sq. mi. *Cap.:* Halifax. —**No′va Sco′tian.**

no·va·tion (nō vā′shən), *n.* *Law.* the substitution of a new obligation for an old one. [< L *novātiōn-* (s. of *novātiō*) a renewing = *novāt*(*us*) renewed (ptp. of *novāre;* see NOVA) + *-iōn-* -ION]

No·va·to (nō vä′tō, nə-), *n.* a city in W California, N of San Francisco. 31,006 (1970).

No·va·ya Zem·lya (nô′vä yä zem lyä′), two large islands in the Arctic Ocean, N of the Soviet Union, to which they belong: nuclear test center. 35,000 sq. mi. Also, **No·va Zem·bla** (nô′vä zem blä′).

nov·el¹ (nov′əl), *n.* **1.** a fictitious prose narrative of considerable length. **2.** (formerly) novella. [< It *novella* < L: short for *novella narrātiō* new kind of story. See NOVEL²]

nov·el² (nov′əl), *adj.* of a new or different kind: *a novel idea.* [late ME < L *novellus* fresh, young, novel, dim. of *novus* NEW] —**nov′el·ly,** *adv.* —**Syn.** See **new.**

nov·el³ (nov′əl), *n.* *Roman Law.* an enactment subsequent and supplementary to an imperial code. [< LL *novella* (*constitūtiō*) a new (regulation, order). See NOVEL²]

nov·el·ette (nov′ə let′), *n.* a short novel; novella

nov·el·ise (nov′ə līz′), *v.t.,* **-ised, -is·ing.** *Chiefly Brit.* novelize. —**nov′el·i·sa′tion,** *n.*

nov·el·ist (nov′ə list), *n.* a person who writes novels.

nov·el·is·tic (nov′ə lis′tik), *adj.* of, pertaining to, or characteristic of novels. —**nov′el·is′ti·cal·ly,** *adv.*

nov·el·ize (nov′ə līz′), *v.t.,* **-ized, -iz·ing.** to put into the form of a novel. Also, *esp. Brit.,* **novelise.** —**nov′el·i·za′tion,** *n.*

no·vel·la (nō vel′ə; *It.* nô vel′lä), *n., pl.* **-vel·las, -vel·le** (-vel′ā; *It.* -vel′le). a fictional prose narrative that is longer and more complex than a short story; a short novel. [< It]

nov·el·ty (nov′əl tē), *n., pl.* **-ties,** *adj.* —*n.* **1.** the state or quality of being novel; newness. **2.** a novel occurrence, experience, etc. **3.** an article of trade having mainly amusement value and whose appeal is often transitory. —*adj.* **4.** *Textiles.* (of a weave) consisting of a combination of basic weaves. **5.** of or pertaining to novelties as articles of trade. [ME *novelte* < MF *novelete* < LL *novellitās* newness]

nov′elty sid′ing. See **drop siding.**

No·vem·ber (nō vem′bər), *n.* **1.** the eleventh month of the year, containing 30 days. **2.** a word used in communications to represent the letter *N.* [ME, OE < L *novembris* the ninth month of the early Roman calendar]

no·ve·na (nō vē′nə, nə-), *n., pl.* **-nae** (-nē). *Rom. Cath. Ch.* a devotion consisting of prayers or services on nine consecutive days. [< ML, n. use of fem. sing. of L *novēnus* nine each]

Nov·go·rod (nôv′go rot), *n.* a city in the W RSFSR, in the NW Soviet Union in Europe, SE of Leningrad: a former capital of Russia. 185,000.

nov·ice (nov′is), *n.* **1.** a person who is new to the circumstances, work, etc., in which he is placed. **2.** a person who has been received into a religious order or congregation for a period of probation before taking vows. **3.** a person newly become a church member. [ME *novyce* < MF *novice* < ML *novītius* convent novice, var. of L *novīcius* newly come into a particular status < *novus* new; see -ITIOUS] —**nov′ice·hood′**, *n.* —**Syn. 1.** newcomer. **1, 2.** neophyte.

No·vi Sad (nô′vē säd′), a city in NE Yugoslavia, on the Danube. 102,469 (1961).

no·vi·ti·ate (nō vish′ē it, -āt′), *n.* **1.** the state or period of being a novice. **2.** the quarters occupied by religious novices during probation. **3.** a novice. Also, **no·vi′ci·ate.** [< ML = *novīti(us)* NOVICE + *-ātus* -ATE[1]]

No·vo·caine (nō′və kān′), *n. Pharm., Trademark.* procaine.

No·vo·kuz·netsk (nô′vo ko͝oz netsk′), *n.* a city in the S RSFSR, in the E Soviet Union in Asia. 475,000 (est. 1965). Formerly, **Stalinsk.**

No·vo·mos·kovsk (nô′vo mos kôfsk′), *n.* a city in the W RSFSR, in the central Soviet Union in Europe, S of Moscow. 123,000 (est. 1965).

No·vo·ros·siysk (nô′vo ʀo sēsk′), *n.* a seaport in the SW RSFSR, in the S Soviet Union in Europe, on the Black Sea. 115,000 (est. 1965). Also, **No′vo·ros·siisk′.**

No·vo·si·birsk (nô′vo si bēʀsk′), *n.* a city in the SW RSFSR, in the W Soviet Union in Asia, on the Ob. 1,029,000 (est. 1965). Formerly, **No·vo·ni·ko·la·evsk** (nô′vo ni ko lä′yefsk).

No·vot·ný (nô′vôt nē′), *n.* **An·to·nín** (än′tô nyēn′), 1904–75, Czech political leader: president 1957–68.

no·vus or·do se·clo·rum (nō′wo͝os ōʀ′dō se klō′ʀo͞om; *Eng.* nō′vəs ôr′dō se klôr′əm, -klōr′-), *Latin.* a new order of the ages (is born): motto on the reverse of the great seal of the United States (adapted from Vergil's *Eclogues* IV:5).

now (nou), *adv.* **1.** at this time or moment. **2.** without delay; immediately: *Shall I work on this now?* **3.** at the time or juncture being referred to: *It was now one o'clock. Having washed, they were now ready to eat.* **4.** in the very recent past (usually prec. by *just* or *only*). **5.** nowadays: *You rarely hear a waltz now.* **6.** under the present or existing circumstances; as matters stand: *I see now what you meant.* **7.** (used to introduce a statement or question): *Now, you don't really mean that.* **8.** (used to strengthen a command, entreaty, or the like): *Now stop that!* **9. now and again,** occasionally. Also, **now and then. 10. now that,** inasmuch as; since. —*conj.* **11.** inasmuch as; since. —*n.* **12.** the present time or moment. [ME; OE *nū*, c. Icel, Goth *nū*; akin to G *nun*, L *num*, Skt *nu*, Gk *nŷ*, *nŷn*]

now·a·days (nou′ə dāz′), *adv.* **1.** in these present times. —*n.* **2.** the present: *the manners of nowadays.* [ME *nou adaies*, OE *nū on dæge*; see -S[1]]

no·way (nō′wā′), *adv.* in no way, respect, or degree; not at all. Also, **no′ways′.** [ME]

no·where (nō′hwâr′, -wâr′), *adv.* **1.** in, at, or to no place; not anywhere. —*n.* **2.** the state of actual or apparent nonexistence. **3.** anonymity or obscurity. [ME; OE *nāhwær*, *nōhwær*]

no·wheres (nō′hwârz, -wârz), *adv. U.S. Dial.* nowhere.

no·whith·er (nō′hwith′ər, -with′-), *adv.* to no place; nowhere. [ME *nohwider*, OE *nāhwider*]

no·wise (nō′wīz′), *adv.* in no wise; not at all.

nowt (nōt), *n. Brit. Dial.* naught; nothing.

Nox (noks), *n.* the ancient Roman goddess personifying night.

nox·ious (nok′shəs), *adj.* **1.** harmful or injurious to health or physical well-being. **2.** morally harmful; pernicious. [< L *noxius* harmful, hurtful, injurious = *nox(a)* harm, hurt, injury (akin to *noc(ēre)* (to) do harm, inflict injury) + *-ius* -IOUS] —**nox′ious·ly,** *adv.* —**Syn. 1.** unhealthy, detrimental, deleterious. **1, 2.** unwholesome. —**Ant. 1, 2.** harmless.

Noyes (noiz), *n.* **1. Alfred,** 1880–1958, English poet. **2. John Humphrey,** 1811–86, U.S. social reformer: founder of the Oneida Community.

noz·zle (noz′əl), *n.* **1.** a projecting spout, terminal discharging pipe, or the like, as of a bellows or a hose. **2.** the socket of a candlestick. **3.** the spout of a teapot. [NOSE + -LE (dim. suffix)]

NP, neuropsychiatric.

Np, *Chem.* neptunium.

N.P., 1. new paragraph. **2.** See **nisi prius. 3.** Notary Public.

n.p., 1. new paragraph. **2.** See **nisi prius. 3.** See **notary public.**

n.p. or d., no place or date.

n.p.t., normal pressure and temperature. Also, **npt**

nr., near.

NRA, National Recovery Administration. Also, **N.R.A.**

NS, 1. not sufficient (funds). **2.** nuclear ship.

Ns, nimbo-stratus.

ns, nanosecond; nanoseconds. Also, **nsec**

N.S., 1. New Style. **2.** Nova Scotia.

n.s., not specified.

NSA, National Standards Association.

NSC, National Security Council.

NSF, 1. National Science Foundation. **2.** not sufficient funds. Also, **N.S.F.**

N/S/F, not sufficient funds.

N.S.P.C.A., National Society for the Prevention of Cruelty to Animals.

N.S.P.C.C., National Society for the Prevention of Cruelty to Children.

N.S.W., New South Wales.

NT, New Testament. Also, **NT.**

-n't, an adverbial combining form of **not:** *didn't; won't; mustn't.* [by contr.]

N.T., 1. New Testament. **2.** Northern Territory.

nth (enth), *adj.* **1.** being the last in a series of infinitely decreasing or increasing values, amounts, etc. **2.** *Informal.* being the latest, or most recent of a lengthy series: *This is the nth time I've told you to eat slowly.* **3. the nth degree** or **power, a.** a high degree or power. **b.** the utmost degree or extent.

nt. wt., net weight.

nu (no͞o, nyo͞o), *n.* the 13th letter of the Greek alphabet (Ν, ν). [< Gk < Sem; cf. Heb *nun*]

nu·ance (no͞o′äns, nyo͞o′-, no͞o äns′, nyo͞o-; *Fr.* ɴʏ äɴs′), *n., pl.* **-anc·es** (-än siz, -än′siz; *Fr.* -äɴs′). a subtle shade of color, expression, or variation, etc. [< F: shade, hue = *nu(er)* (to) shade (lit., to cloud < VL **nūba*, r. L *nūbēs* cloud) + *-ance* -ANCE]

nub (nub), *n.* **1.** a knob or protuberance. **2.** a lump or small piece: *a nub of coal.* **3.** *Informal.* the gist of something. **4.** a small knot of fibers introduced into yarn during the spinning process. [var. of *knub* < MLG *knubbe* KNOB]

nub·bin (nub′in), *n.* an undeveloped fruit. [? NUB + *-in*, var. of -ING[1]]

nub·ble (nub′əl), *n.* **1.** a small lump or piece. **2.** a small knob or protuberance. [NUB + -LE (dim. suffix)]

nub·bly (nub′lē), *adj.*, **-bli·er, -bli·est. 1.** full of small protuberances. **2.** in the form of small lumps.

nub·by (nub′ē), *adj.*, **-bi·er, -bi·est.** having nubs.

Nu·bi·a (no͞o′bē ə, nyo͞o′-), *n.* **1.** a region in the S United Arab Republic and the Sudan, N of Khartoum, extending from the Nile to the Red Sea. **2.** an ancient kingdom in NE Africa.

Nu·bi·an (no͞o′bē ən, nyo͞o′-), *n.* **1.** a member of a Negroid people of mixed descent inhabiting Nubia. **2.** a language of the Nile valley below Khartoum. **3.** a Nubian or Negro slave. **4.** a Nubian horse. —*adj.* **5.** of, pertaining to, or characteristic of Nubia, its people, or their language.

Nu′bian Des′ert, an arid region in the NE Sudan.

nu·bile (no͞o′bil, nyo͞o′-), *adj.* (of a girl or young woman) suitable for marriage, esp. in regard to age or physical development. [< L *nūbilis* = *nūb(ere)* (to) marry + *-ilis* -ILE] —**nu·bil′i·ty,** *n.*

nu·cel·lus (no͞o sel′əs, nyo͞o-), *n., pl.* **-cel·li** (-sel′ī). *Bot.* the central cellular mass of the body of the ovule, containing the embryo sac. [< NL: alter. of L *nucella* little nut = *nuc-* (s. of *nux*) nut + *-ella* dim. suffix] —**nu·cel′lar,** *adj.*

nucle-, var. of **nucleo-** before a vowel: *nuclear.*

nu·cle·ar (no͞o′klē ər, nyo͞o′-), *adj.* **1.** of, pertaining to, or forming a nucleus. **2.** pertaining to or involving atomic weapons. **3.** operated or powered by atomic energy: *a nuclear submarine.* **4.** (of a nation or a group of nations) possessing atomic bombs: *the nuclear powers.* [cf. F *nucléaire*]

nu′clear cross′ sec′tion, *Physics.* See **cross section** (def. 8).

nu′clear en′ergy. See **atomic energy.**

nu′clear fam′ily, *Anthropol.* a social unit composed of father, mother, and children.

nu′clear fis′sion, fission (def. 3).

nu′clear fu′sion, fusion (def. 5).

nu′clear i′somer, isomer (def. 2).

nu′clear isom′erism, isomerism (def. 2).

nu′clear phys′ics, the branch of physics that deals with the behavior, structure, and component parts of atomic nuclei. —**nu′clear phys′icist.**

nu′clear reac′tion, reaction (def. 8).

nu′clear reac′tor, reactor (def. 4).

nu·cle·ase (no͞o′klē ās′, nyo͞o′-), *n. Biochem.* any of the class of enzymes comprising the nucleinases, nucleotidases, and nucleosidases, and that serve to break down nucleic acids, found in plant and animal tissue.

nu·cle·ate (no͞o′klē it, -āt′, nyo͞o′-), *adj., v.,* **-at·ed, -at·ing.** —*adj.* **1.** having a nucleus. —*v.t.* **2.** to form (something) into a nucleus. —*v.i.* **3.** to form a nucleus. [< L *nucleātus* having a kernel or stone] —**nu·cle·a·tion** (no͞o′klē ā′shən, nyo͞o′-), *n.* —**nu′cle·a′tor,** *n.*

nu·cle·i (no͞o′klē ī′, nyo͞o′-), *n.* pl. of **nucleus.**

nu·cle′ic ac′id (no͞o klē′ik, nyo͞o-), *Biochem.* any of a group of complex acids occurring in all living cells, esp. as a component of cell-nucleus proteins, and composed of a phosphoric acid group, a carbohydrate, two purines, and two pyrimidines. Cf. **DNA, RNA.**

nu·cle·in (no͞o′klē in, nyo͞o′-), *n. Biochem.* any of a class of phosphorus-containing protein substances occurring in cell nuclei.

nu·cle·in·ase (no͞o′klē ə nās′, nyo͞o′-), *n. Biochem.* any of a class of enzymes that split nucleic acids into nucleotides.

nucleo-, a combining form of **nucleus, nuclear,** or **nucleic acid:** *nucleoprotein.* Also, *esp. before a vowel,* **nucle-.**

nucleol-, a combining form of **nucleolus:** *nucleolated.*

nu·cle·o·lar (no͞o klē′ə lər, nyo͞o-), *adj.* of, pertaining to, or forming a nucleolus.

nu·cle·o·lat·ed (no͞o′klē ə lā′tid, nyo͞o′-), *adj.* containing a nucleolus or nucleoli. Also, **nu′cle·o·late′.**

nu·cle·o·lus (no͞o klē′ə ləs, nyo͞o-), *n., pl.* **-li** (-lī′). *Biol.* a conspicuous, often rounded body within the nucleus of a cell. Also, **nu·cle·ole** (no͞o′klē ōl′, nyo͞o′-). [< L, dim. of *nucleus* kernel, NUCLEUS] —**nu·cle′o·loid′,** *adj.*

nu·cle·on (no͞o′klē on′, nyo͞o′-), *n. Physics.* a proton or neutron, esp. when considered as a component of a nucleus.

nu·cle·on·ics (no͞o′klē on′iks, nyo͞o′-), *n.* (*construed as sing.*) the branch of science that deals with atomic nuclei, esp. practical applications.

nu·cle·o·plasm (no͞o′klē ə plaz′əm, nyo͞o′-), *n. Biol.* karyoplasm. —**nu′cle·o·plas′mic, nu·cle·o·plas·mat·ic** (no͞o′klē ō plaz mat′ik, nyo͞o′-), *adj.*

nu·cle·o·pro·tein (no͞o′klē ə prō′tēn, -tē in, nyo͞o′-), *n. Biochem.* any of the class of conjugated proteins found in plant and animal cells and consisting of a protein combined with a nucleic acid, essential for cell division and reproduction.

nu·cle·o·sid·ase (no͞o′klē ə sī′dās, nyo͞o′-), *n. Biochem.* any of the class of enzymes that catalyze the hydrolysis of nucleosides.

nu·cle·o·side (no͞o′klē ə sīd′, nyo͞o′-), *n. Biochem.* any of the class of compounds derived by the hydrolysis of nucleic acids or nucleotides, consisting typically of deoxyribose or ribose combined with adenine, or guanine and cytosine, uracil, or thymine.

nu·cle·o·tid·ase (no͞o′klē ə tī′dās, nyo͞o′-), *n. Biochem.* any of the class of enzymes that catalyze the hydrolysis of nucleotides into nucleosides and phosphoric acid. Also called **nu·cle·o·phos·pha·tase** (no͞o′klē ō fos′fə tās′, nyo͞o′-), **phosphonuclease.**

nu·cle·o·tide (no͞o′klē ə tīd′, nyo͞o′-), *n. Biochem.* any of the class of esters formed by the interaction of phosphoric acid and a nucleoside or by the partial hydrolysis of nucleic acids. [alter. of NUCLEOSIDE]

nu·cle·us (no͞o′klē əs, nyo͞o′-), *n., pl.* **-cle·i** (-klē ī′), **-cle·us·es.** **1.** a central part or group around which others are grouped; core. **2.** *Biol.* a specialized, usually spherical mass of protoplasm encased in a membrane and found in most living cells, forming an essential element in their growth, metabolism, and reproduction, and in the transmission of genic characters. **3.** *Anat.* a mass of gray matter in the brain and spinal cord in which incoming nerve fibers form connections with outgoing fibers. **4.** *Chem.* a fundamental arrangement of atoms, as the benzene ring, that may occur in many compounds by substitution of atoms without a change in structure. **5.** *Physics.* the positively charged mass within an atom, composed of neutrons and protons, and possessing most of the mass but occupying only a small fraction of the volume of the atom. **6.** *Astron.* the condensed portion of the head of a comet. [< L: kernel, syncopated var. of *nuculeus* = *nucul(a)* little nut (*nuc-*, s. of *nux* nut + *-ula* -ULE) + *-eus* adj. suffix] —**Syn. 1.** center, kernel.

nu·clide (no͞o′klīd, nyo͞o′-), *n.* *Physics.* **1.** an atomic species in which all atoms have the same atomic number and mass number. **2.** an individual atom in such a species. [NUCL- + *-ide* < Gk *eîdos* shape]

nude (no͞od, nyo͞od), *adj.* **1.** naked or unclothed, as a person or the body. **2.** without the usual coverings, furnishings, etc.; bare. **3.** *Law.* unsupported. —*n.* **4.** a nude figure in art. **5.** an unclothed human figure. **6. the nude,** the condition of being unclothed. [< L *nūdus* NAKED] —**nude′ly,** *adv.* —**Syn. 1.** uncovered, unclothed, undressed, undraped.

nudge (nuj), *v.,* **nudged, nudg·ing,** *n.* —*v.t.* **1.** to push slightly or jog, esp. with the elbow. —*v.i.* **2.** to give a nudge. —*n.* **3.** a slight push or jog. [var. of dial. *(k)nidge,* akin to OE *cnucian, cnocian* to KNOCK] —**nudg′er,** *n.*

nudi-, a learned borrowing from Latin meaning "naked," "bare," used in the formation of compound words: *nudibranch.* [comb. form repr. L *nūd(us)* naked]

nu·di·branch (no͞o′də braŋk′, nyo͞o′-), *n.* a shell-less, marine snail of the suborder *Nudibranchia,* having external, often branched respiratory appendages on the back and sides. [< F *nudibranche* = *nudi* NUDI- + *branche* gills (< L *branchia* BRANCHIA)]

nu·di·bran·chi·ate (no͞o′də braŋ′kē it, -āt′, nyo͞o′-), *n.* **1.** nudibranch. —*adj.* **2.** of or pertaining to the *Nudibranchia.* Also, **nu·di·bran·chi·an** (no͞o′də braŋ′kē ən, nyo͞o′-). [< NL *Nudibranchiata* name of suborder of mollusks]

nud·ie (no͞o′dē, nyo͞o′-), *n.* *Slang.* **1.** a show or motion picture in which a nude or nearly nude female or females perform. **2.** a nude or nearly nude female performer or model.

nud·ism (no͞o′diz əm, nyo͞o′-), *n.* the practice of going nude. —**nud′ist,** *n., adj.*

nu·di·ty (no͞o′di tē, nyo͞o′-), *n., pl.* **-ties** for 2. **1.** the state or fact of being nude; nakedness. **2.** something nude or naked. [< L *nūditās*]

nud·nik (no͝od′nik), *n.* *Slang.* a bothersome, boring person; pest. [< Yiddish < Russ]

Nu·e·ces (no͞o ā′sās), *n.* a river in S Texas, flowing SE to Corpus Christi Bay, on the Gulf of Mexico. 338 mi. long.

Nue·vo La·re·do (nwe′vô lä re′thô), a city in NE Mexico, on the Rio Grande. 117,728 (est. 1965).

Nue·vo Le·ón (nwā′vō lā ōn′, no͞o ā′-; *Sp.* nwe′vô le ôn′), a state in NE Mexico. 1,078,848 (1960); 25,136 sq. mi. *Cap.:* Monterrey.

nu·ga·to·ry (no͞o′gə tōr′ē, -tôr′ē, nyo͞o′-), *adj.* **1.** trifling; of no real value. **2.** of no force or effect; futile. [< L *nūgātōrius* worthless, useless, trifling = *nūgāt(us)* (ptp. of *nūgārī* to trifle) + *-ōrius* -ORY[1]] —**Syn. 1.** trivial, frivolous.

nug·get (nug′it), *n.* a lump, esp. of native gold or other precious metal. [? dim. of obs. *nug* small piece, var. of NOG[2]; see -ET] —**nug′get·y,** *adj.*

nui·sance (no͞o′səns, nyo͞o′-), *n.* **1.** an obnoxious or annoying person, thing, practice, etc. **2.** *Law.* something offensive or annoying to individuals or to the community. [late ME *nu(i)sa(u)nce* < AF = *nuis(er)* (to) harm (< L *nocēre*) + *-ance* -ANCE]

nui′sance tax′, a tax paid in small amounts, usually by consumers.

nuke (no͞ok, nyo͞ok), *Slang.* —*n.* **1.** a nuclear weapon. **2.** a thermonuclear weapon. **3.** a nuclear-powered generating plant. —*adj.* **4.** of or pertaining to a nuclear or thermonuclear weapon.

null (nul), *adj.* **1.** without value, effect, consequence, or significance. **2.** being or amounting to nothing; lacking; nonexistent. **3.** *Math.* (of a set) containing no elements. **4.** being or amounting to zero. **5. null and void,** without legal force; not valid. [< L *nullus* = *n(e)* not + *ullus* any]

nul·lah (nul′ə), *n.* (in the East Indies) **1.** an intermittent watercourse. **2.** a gully. [< Hindi *nālā* brook, ravine]

nulli-, a combining form meaning "none," "null": *nullify.* [< LL *nulli-* not any, none, no (comb. form of *null(us)* NULL)]

nul·li·fi·ca·tion (nul′ə fə kā′shən), *n.* **1.** the act or an instance of nullifying. **2.** the state of being nullified. **3.** (*often cap.*) *U.S.* failure of a state to aid in enforcement of federal laws within its limits. [< LL *nullificātiōn-* (s. of *nullificātiō*) contempt = *nullificāt(us)* despised (ptp. of *nullificāre*) + *-iōn-* -ION. See NULLIFY] —**nul′li·fi·ca′tor,** *n.*

nul·li·fy (nul′ə fī′), *v.t.,* **-fied, -fy·ing. 1.** to deprive of value or effectiveness. **2.** to render or declare legally void or inoperative. [< LL *nullificāre* to despise] —**nul′li·fi′er,** *n.* —**Syn.** invalidate, annul, void.

nul·lip·a·ra (nu lip′ər ə), *n., pl.* **-a·rae** (-ə rē′). *Obstet.* a woman who has never borne a child. [< NL: *nulli-* NULLI- + *-para,* fem. of *-parus* -PAROUS] —**nul·li·par·i·ty** (nul′ə-par′i tē), *n.* —**nul·lip′a·rous,** *adj.*

nul·li·ty (nul′i tē), *n., pl.* **-ties** for 2, 3. **1.** the state or quality of being null; nothingness; invalidity. **2.** something that is null. **3.** something of no legal force or validity. [< ML *nullitas*]

Num., Numbers.

num., **1.** number. **2.** numeral; numerals.

Nu·man·ti·a (no͞o man′shē ə, -shə, nyo͞o-), *n.* an ancient city in N Spain.

Nu·ma Pom·pil·i·us (no͞o′mə pom pil′ē əs, nyo͞o′mə), died 673? B.C., the second legendary Sabine king of Rome 715–673?.

numb (num), *adj.* **1.** deprived of or deficient in the physical or mental power of sensation and movement. **2.** of the nature of numbness: *a numb sensation.* —*v.t.* **3.** to make numb. [ME *nome,* lit., taken, seized, var. of *nomen, numen,* OE *numen,* ptp. of *niman* to take] —**numb′ness,** *n.*

num·ber (num′bər), *n.* **1.** a mathematical unit, as in a numerical series, having precise relations with other such units: *Six is an even number.* **2.** the sum, total, or aggregate of such units: *What number of people are you expecting?* **3.** a numeral assigned to an object, person, size, etc., for purposes of identification or classification: *locomotive number 396; a number 3 can.* **4.** that which bears such a numeral: *Go to number 20 Commerce Street.* **5.** a numeral, word, symbol, etc., representing a number. **6.** a group or quantity of indefinite size: *a number of persons.* **7.** a single item in a series. **8.** a single item on the program of a show or concert. **9.** a single issue of a periodical or serial. **10. numbers, a.** a considerable amount or quantity; many. **b.** numerical strength or superiority: *victory through sheer weight of numbers.* **c.** metrical feet; verse. **d.** musical periods, measures, or groups of notes. **e.** See **numbers game. f.** *Obs.* arithmetic. **11.** *Gram.* a category of substantival and verbal inflection that indicates whether a word has one or more than one referent, as singular, dual, and plural. **12.** *Informal.* **a.** a girl or young woman. **b.** the numerals of a license plate, a street address, or a telephone. **13. get** or **have someone's number,** *Slang.* to discover someone's real character, intentions, etc. **14. without number,** countless; vast. —*v.t.* **15.** to ascertain the number of. **16.** to mark with or distinguish by a number or numbers. **17.** to count or mention one by one; enumerate. **18.** to fix the number of; limit in number. **19.** to consider or include in a group or number. **20.** to live or have lived (a number of years). **21.** to amount to or comprise in number; total. **22.** to apportion or divide. —*v.i.* **23.** to be numbered or included. **24.** to make a total; reach an amount: *Casualties numbered in the thousands.* [ME; var. of *nombre* < OF < L *numerus*]
—**Syn. 2.** NUMBER, SUM both imply the total of two or more units. NUMBER applies to the result of a count or estimate in which the units are considered as individuals; it is used of groups of persons or things: *to have a number of items on the agenda.* SUM applies to the result of addition, in which only the total is considered: *a large sum of money.* **5.** digit, figure.

num·ber-crunch·er (num′bər krun′chər), *n.* *Informal.* one who or that which performs number crunching, as a financial analyst, statistician, computer, or computer program.

num′ber crunch′ing, *Informal.* the process of performing a great many numerical calculations. —**num′ber-crunch′ing,** *adj.*

num·ber·less (num′bər lis), *adj.* **1.** innumerable; countless; myriad. **2.** without a number or numbers.

num′ber one′, *Informal.* **1.** one's own well-being; oneself: *He's always looking out for number one.* **2.** of the best quality; first-rate.

Num·bers (num′bərz), *n.* (*construed as sing.*) the fourth book of the Old Testament, containing the census of the Israelites after the Exodus from Egypt.

num′bers game′, an illegal lottery in which money is wagered on the appearance of certain numbers in some statistical listing or tabulation published in a daily newspaper, racing form, etc. Also called **numbers, num′bers pool′, num′bers rack′et.**

num′ber the′ory, *Math.* the study of integers and their relation to one another.

numb·fish (num′fish′), *n., pl.* (*esp. collectively*) **-fish,** (*esp. referring to two or more kinds or species*) **-fish·es.** an electric ray: so called from its power of numbing its prey by means of electric shocks.

numb·ing (num′iŋ), *adj.* causing numbness or insensibility; paralyzing; stupefying. —**numb′ing·ly,** *adv.*

num·bles (num′bəlz), *n.pl.* *Archaic.* certain of the inward parts of an animal, esp. of a deer, used as food. [ME < MF *nombles* fillet of venison, pl. of *nomble,* dissimilated var. of **lomble* < L *lumbulus,* dim. of *lumbus* loin; see -ULE]

numb·skull (num′skul′), *n.* numskull.

nu·men (no͞o′min, nyo͞o′-), *n., pl.* **-mi·na** (-mə nə). a deity, esp. one presiding locally or believed to inhabit a particular object. [< L: a nod, command; divine will, power, or being; akin to *nūtāre* to nod again and again]

nu·mer·a·ble (no͞o′mər ə bəl, nyo͞o′-), *adj.* capable of being numbered or counted. [< L *numerābilis* that can be counted = *numer(āre)* (to) number + *-ābilis* -ABLE] —**nu′mer·a·bly,** *adv.*

nu·mer·al (no͞o′mər əl, nyo͞o′-), *n.* **1.** one or more words or symbols expressing a number. —*adj.* **2.** of, pertaining to, or consisting of numbers. **3.** expressing or noting a number or numbers. [< LL *numerālis* of, belonging to number = L *numer(us)* number + *-ālis* -AL[1]]

nu·mer·ar·y (no͞o′mə rer′ē, nyo͞o′-), *adj.* of or pertaining to a number or numbers. [< ML *numerārius* (LL: arithmetician, accountant) = L *numer(us)* number + *-ārius* -ARY]

nu·mer·ate (no͞o′mə rāt′, nyo͞o′-), *v.t.,* **-at·ed, -at·ing. 1.** to number; count; enumerate. **2.** to read (a numerical expression) in words. [< L *numerātus* numbered, counted, reckoned (ptp. of *numerāre*) = *numer-* number + *-ātus* -ATE[1]]

nu·mer·a·tion (no͞o′mə rā′shən, nyo͞o′-), *n.* **1.** the act, process, or result of numbering or counting. **2.** the process or a method of reckoning or calculating. **3.** the act or process of expressing or reading off numbers set down in numerals. [< L *numerātiōn-* (s. of *numerātiō*) a counting out, paying] —**nu′mer·a′tive,** *adj.*

nu·mer·a·tor (no͞o′mə rā′tər, nyo͞o′-), *n.* **1.** *Arith.* the term of a fraction, usually above the line, that indicates the number of equal parts to be added together; the dividend placed over a divisor: *The numerator of the fraction* $\frac{2}{3}$ *is 2.* **2.** a person or thing that numbers. [< LL *numerātor* a counter, numberer]

nu·mer·i·cal (no͞o mer′i kəl, nyo͞o-), *adj.* **1.** of or pertaining to numbers; of the nature of a number. **2.** indicating a number, as a symbol. **3.** bearing or designated by a number. **4.** expressed in numbers. **5.** noting or pertaining to skill at working with numbers. **6.** *Math.* absolute (def. 11). Also, **nu·mer′ic.** [< L *numer(us)* number + -ICAL] —**nu·mer′i·cal·ly,** *adv.*

nu·mer·ol·o·gy (no͞o′mə rol′ə jē, nyo͞o′-), *n.* the study of numbers, as the figures designating the year of one's birth, to determine their supposed influence on one's life, future, etc. [< L *numer(us)* a number + -o- + -LOGY] —**nu·mer·o·log·i·cal** (no͞o′mər ə loj′i kəl, nyo͞o′-), *adj.*

nu·mer·ous (no͞o′mər əs, nyo͞o′-), *adj.* **1.** many; being or existing in considerable quantity. **2.** consisting of or comprising a great number: *a numerous gathering.* [< L *numerōsus* consisting of a great number, numerous = *numer(us)* a number + *-ōsus* -OUS] —**nu′mer·ous·ly,** *adv.* —**nu′mer·ous·ness, nu·me·ros·i·ty** (no͞o′mə ros′i tē, nyo͞o′-), *n.* —**Syn. 1.** See **many.**

Nu·mid·i·a (no͞o mid′ē ə, nyo͞o-), *n.* an ancient country in N Africa, corresponding roughly to modern Algeria. —**Nu·mid′i·an,** *adj., n.*

nu·mi·na (no͞o′mə nə, nyo͞o′-), *n.* pl. of **numen.**

nu·mi·nous (no͞o′mə nəs, nyo͞o′-), *adj.* **1.** of, pertaining to, or like a numen; spiritual or supernatural. **2.** surpassing comprehension; mysterious. **3.** arousing elevated or spiritual emotions. [< L *nūmin-* (s. of *nūmen*) NUMEN + -OUS]

numis., **1.** numismatic. **2.** numismatics.

nu·mis·mat·ic (no͞o′miz mat′ik -mis-, nyo͞o′-), *adj.* **1.** of, pertaining to, or consisting of coins, medals, or the like. **2.** pertaining to numismatics. Also, **nu′mis·mat′i·cal.** [< NL *numismatic(us)* < Gk *nomismat-* (s. of *nómisma*) currency + *-ikos* -IC; akin to *nómos* usage, law] —**nu′mis·mat′i·cal·ly,** *adv.*

nu·mis·mat·ics (no͞o′miz mat′iks, -mis-, nyo͞o′-), *n.* (*construed as sing.*) the study or collecting of coins, medals, and the like. Also, **nu·mis·ma·tol·o·gy** (no͞o miz′mə tol′ə jē, -mis′-, nyo͞o-). —**nu·mis′ma·tol′o·gist,** *n.*

nu·mis·ma·tist (no͞o miz′mə tist, -mis′-, nyo͞o-), *n.* **1.** a specialist in numismatics. **2.** a person who collects numismatic items, esp. coins.

num·ma·ry (num′ə rē), *adj.* of or pertaining to coins or money. [< L *nummārius* of, belonging to money = *nummus* coin + *-ārius* -ARY]

num·mu·lar (num′yə lər), *adj.* having the shape of a coin; disklike. [< L *nummul(ī)* petty cash, small change (*numm(us)* money + *-ulī,* pl. of *-ulus* -ULE) + -AR[1]]

num·mu·lite (num′yə līt′), *n.* a fossil foraminifer of the genus *Camerina* (*Nummulites*), having a calcareous, usually disklike shell. [NUMMUL(AR) + -ITE[1]] —**num·mu·lit·ic** (num′yə lit′ik), *adj.*

num·skull (num′skul′), *n.* *Informal.* a dull-witted person; dunce. Also, **numbskull.** [NUM(B) + SKULL]

nun[1] (nun), *n.* a woman bound to a religious order, esp. one living in a convent under solemn vows of poverty, chastity, and obedience. [ME, OE *nunne* < eccl. L *nonna,* fem. of *nonnus* monk] —**nun′like′,** *adj.*

nun[2] (no͝on; *Heb.* no͞on), *n.* the 14th letter of the Hebrew alphabet. [< Heb; cf. NU]

Nun (no͞on), *n.* the major channel of the Niger River, in W Africa.

nun′ buoy′ (nun), an unlighted buoy having a conical form above water, used as a channel marker. Cf. **can buoy.** See illus. at **buoy.** [obs. *nun* spinning top + BUOY]

Nunc Di·mit·tis (no͝ongk′ di mit′is, no͞ongk′), the canticle beginning with the words of Simeon, in Luke 2:29–32, "Lord, now lettest thou thy servant depart in peace." [< L: now lettest thou]

nun·ci·a·ture (nun′shē ə chər), *n.* the office or the term of service of a nuncio. [< It *nunziatura*]

nun·ci·o (nun′shē ō), *n., pl.* **-ci·os.** a permanent diplomatic representative of the pope. [< It *nuncio, nunzio* < L *nuncius, nuntius* messenger]

nun·cle (nung′kəl), *n.* *Chiefly Brit. Dial.* uncle. [*mine uncle,* taken as *my nuncle;* cf. NEWT]

nun·cu·pa·tive (nung′kyə pā′tiv, nung kyo͞o′pə tiv), *adj.* (esp. of a will) oral; not written. [< LL *nuncupātīv(us)* so-called, specified by name = *nuncupāt(us)* named (ptp. of *nuncupāre* for *nōmen capere* to take a name, i.e., utter it publicly) + *-īvus* -IVE]

Nun·kiang (no͝on′kyäng′), *n.* a former province in Manchuria, in NE China. 25,856 sq. mi. *Cap.:* Tsitsihar.

nun·ner·y (nun′ə rē), *n., pl.* **-ner·ies.** a religious house for nuns; convent. [ME *nonnerie*]

nup·tial (nup′shəl), *adj.* **1.** of or pertaining to marriage or the marriage ceremony. —*n.* **2.** Usually, **nuptials.** a wedding or marriage. [< L *nuptiāl(is)* of, belonging to a marriage < *nuptiae* a marriage, wedding = *nūpt(a)* married, lit., veiled (fem. ptp. of *nūbere* to cover) + *-iae* pl. of *-ia* -IA. See -AL[1]] —**nup′tial·ly,** *adv.* —**Syn. 2.** See **marriage.**

Nu·rem·berg (no͝or′əm bûrg′, nyo͝or′-), *n.* a city in central Bavaria, in SE West Germany: site of trials (1945–46) of Nazis accused of war crimes. 466,100 (1963). German, **Nürn·berg** (NYRN′berk).

Nu·re·yev (no͝o rā′ef, -ev; *Russ.* no͞o RE′yef), *n.* **Rudolf (Ha·me·to·vich)** (hä me′to vich), born 1938, Russian ballet dancer.

Nu·ri·stan (no͝or′i stan′), *n.* a mountainous region in NE Afghanistan. 5000 sq. mi. Formerly, **Kafiristan.**

nurl (nûrl), *n., v.t.* knurl.

Nur·mi (nûr′mē; *Fin.* no͝oR′mē), *n.* **Paa·vo Jo·han·nes** (pä′vô yô hän′nes), 1897–1973, Finnish athlete.

nurse (nûrs), *n., v.,* **nursed, nurs·ing.** —*n.* **1.** a person, esp. a woman, who takes care of the sick or infirm. **2.** a woman who has the general care of a child or children; dry nurse. **3.** *Entomol.* a worker that attends the young in a colony of social insects. —*v.t.* **4.** to attend to the needs of (the sick or infirm). **5.** to seek to cure (an ailment) by taking care of oneself: *to nurse a cold.* **6.** to suckle (an infant). **7.** to handle carefully or fondly. **8.** to preserve in an active or flourishing state: *to nurse a grudge.* **9.** to feed or tend in infancy. —*v.i.* **10.** to act as nurse; tend the sick or infirm. **11.** to suckle a child, esp. one's own. **12.** (of a child) to suckle. [ME, var. of *nurice* < OF < LL *nūtrīcia,* n. use of fem. of L *nūtrīcius* NUTRITIOUS] —**Syn. 9.** rear, raise.

nurse·ling (nûrs′ling), *n.* nursling.

nurse·maid (nûrs′mād′), *n.* a maidservant employed to take care of children. Also called **nurs′er·y·maid′.**

nurs·er·y (nûr′sə rē), *n., pl.* **-er·ies.** **1.** a room or place set apart for young children. **2.** a nursery school or day nursery. **3.** a place where young trees or other plants are raised for transplanting or for sale. [ME *norcery*]

nurs·er·y·man (nûr′sə rē mən), *n., pl.* **-men.** a person who owns or conducts a nursery for plants.

nurs′ery rhyme′, a short, simple poem or song for very young children.

nurs′ery school′, a prekindergarten school.

nurs′ing bot′tle, a bottle with a rubber nipple, from which an infant sucks milk, water, etc.

nurs′ing home′, **1.** a private residence or the like equipped to care for the aged or infirm. **2.** *Chiefly Brit.* a small, privately owned hospital.

nurs·ling (nûrs′ling), *n.* **1.** an infant, child, or young animal being nursed. **2.** any person or thing under fostering care. Also, **nurseling.**

nur·ture (nûr′chər), *v.,* **-tured, -tur·ing,** *n.* —*v.t.* **1.** to promote the development of by providing nourishment, support, encouragement, etc., during the stages of growth. **2.** to bring up; train; educate. —*n.* **3.** upbringing; training; breeding. **4.** education; tutelage. **5.** something that nourishes; nourishment; food. [ME < MF, var. of *nourriture* < LL *nūtrītūra* a nourishing = L *nūtrīt(us)* nourished (ptp. of *nūtrīre*) + *-ūra* -URE] —**nur′tur·a·ble,** *adj.* —**nur′ture·less,** *adj.* —**nur′tur·er,** *n.*

nut (nut), *n., v.,* **nut·ted, nut·ting.** —*n.* **1.** a dry fruit consisting of an edible kernel or meat enclosed in a woody or leathery shell. **2.** the kernel itself. **3.** *Bot.* a hard, indehiscent, one-seeded fruit, as the chestnut or the acorn. **4.** *Slang.* an insane or highly eccentric person. **5.** *Slang.* an enthusiast or buff. **6.** a block, usually of metal, perforated with a threaded hole so that it can be screwed onto a bolt to hold together objects through which the bolt passes. **7.** *Music.* (in instruments of the violin family) **a.** the ledge at the upper end of the finger board over which the strings pass. **b.** the movable piece at the lower end of the bow, by means of which the hairs may be slackened or tightened. **8.** *Print.* en (def. 2). **9.** *Slang* (*vulgar*). a testis. —*v.i.* **10.** to seek for or gather nuts. [ME *nute,* OE *hnutu;* c. D *noot,* Icel *hnot,* G *Nuss;* akin to L *nux*] —**nut′like′,** *adj.*

nu·tant (no͞ot′ənt, nyo͞ot′-), *adj.* *Bot.* drooping; nodding. [< L *nūtant-* (s of *nūtāns*) nodding often, prp. of *nūtāre.* See NUTATION, -ANT]

nu·ta·tion (no͞o tā′shən, nyo͞o-), *n.* **1.** the act or an instance of nodding one's head, esp. involuntarily or spasmodically. **2.** *Bot.* spontaneous movements of plant parts during growth. **3.** *Astron.* the periodic oscillation observed in the precession of the earth's axis and the precession of the equinoxes. **4.** the variation of the inclination of the axis of a gyroscope to the vertical. [< L *nūtātiōn-* (s. of *nūtātiō*) = *nūtāt(us)* (ptp. of *nūtāre* to nod repeatedly; *nū-* nod + *-tā-* freq. suffix + *-re* inf. ending) + *-iōn-* -ION] —**nu·ta′tion·al,** *adj.*

nut·crack·er (nut′krak′ər), *n.* an instrument for cracking nuts.

nut·gall (nut′gôl′), *n.* a nutlike gall or excrescence, esp. one formed on an oak.

nut′ grass′, any of various sedges of the genus *Cyperus,* esp. *C. rotundus,* bearing small, nutlike tubers.

nut·hatch (nut′hach′), *n.* any of numerous small, short-tailed, sharp-beaked birds of the family *Sittidae* that creep on trees and feed on small nuts and insects. [ME *notehache, nuthagge, nuthak,* lit., nut hacker. See NUT, HACK[1]]

Nuthatch
Sitta carolinensis
(Length 6 in.)

nut·let (nut′lit), *n.* **1.** a small nut or nutlike fruit or seed. **2.** the stone of a plum or other drupe.

Nut·ley (nut′lē), *n.* a city in NE New Jersey. 31,913 (1970).

nut·meat (nut′mēt′), *n.* the edible kernel of a nut.

nut·meg (nut′meg), *n.* **1.** the hard, aromatic seed of the fruit of an East Indian tree, *Myristica fragrans,* used as a spice. **2.** the similar product of certain other trees of the same genus or other genera. **3.** a tree bearing such seeds. [ME *notemug(g)e,* perh. back formation from **notemugede* (*-ede* being taken as -ED[3]) = *note* NUT + *mugede* < OF < LL *muscāta* musky; see MUSK, -ATE[1]]

Nut′meg State′, Connecticut (used as a nickname).

nut·pick (nut′pik′), *n.* a sharp-pointed table device for removing the meat from nuts.

nut′ pine′, any of various trees of the southwestern U.S. and Rocky Mountains, as *Pinus monophylla, P. edulis,* etc., bearing edible nuts.

nu·tri·a (no͞o′trē ə, nyo͞o′-), *n.* **1.** the coypu. **2.** the fur of the coypu, resembling beaver, used esp. for women's coats. [< Sp: otter, var. of *lutria* < ML, r. L *lutra*]

nu·tri·ent (no͞o′trē ənt, nyo͞o′-), *adj.* **1.** containing or conveying nutriment. **2.** nourishing; providing nourishment or nutriment. —*n.* **3.** a nutrient substance. [< L *nūtrient-* (s. of *nūtriēns*) feeding, prp. of *nūtrīre;* see -ENT]

nu·tri·lite (no͞o′trə līt′, nyo͞o′-), *n.* *Biochem.* any of several substances that serve as nutrients for microorganisms. [NUTRI(MENT + METABO)LITE]

nu·tri·ment (no͞o′trə mənt, nyo͞o′-), *n.* something that nourishes; food. [< L *nūtrīment(um)* nourishment = *nūtrī(re)* (to) nourish, feed + *-mentum* -MENT] —**nu·tri·men·tal** (no͞o′trə men′tᵊl, nyo͞o′-), *adj.*

nu·tri·tion (no͞o trish′ən, nyo͞o-), *n.* **1.** the act or process of nourishing or of being nourished. **2.** the process by which plants and animals take in and utilize food material. **3.** food; nutriment. **4.** the science or study of the nourishment of humans or other creatures. [< LL *nūtrītiōn-* (s. of *nūtrītiō*) a feeding = L *nūtrīt(us)* fed (ptp. of *nūtrīre*) + *-iōn-* -ION] —**nu·tri′tion·al, nu·tri′tion·ar′y,** *adj.* —**nu·tri′tion·al·ly,** *adv.*

nu·tri·tion·ist (no͞o trish′ə nist, nyo͞o-), *n.* a person whose occupation is nutrition.

nu·tri·tious (no͞o trish′əs, nyo͞o-), *adj.* providing nourishment, esp. to a high degree; nourishing. [< L *nūtrīti(us)* that suckles, nourishes, var. of *nūtrīcius* = *nūtrīc-* (s. of *nūtrix*) NURSE + *-us* -OUS] —**nu·tri′tious·ly,** *adv.* —**nu·tri′tious·ness,** *n.*

nu·tri·tive (no͞o′tri tiv, nyo͞o′-), *adj.* **1.** serving to nourish; providing nutriment; nutritious. **2.** of, pertaining to, or concerned with nutrition. —*n.* **3.** an item of nourishing food. [< ML *nūtrītīv(us)* = *nūtrīt-* (see NUTRITION) + *-īvus* -IVE; r. late ME *nutritif* < MF] —**nu′tri·tive·ly,** *adv.*

nuts (nuts), *Slang.* —*interj.* **1.** Also, **nerts, nertz.** (used to express defiance, disgust, disapproval, despair, etc.) —*adj.* **2.** crazy; insane. **3. be nuts about** or **on,** to be wildly enthusiastic about. [pl. of NUT]

nuts′ and bolts′, the most essential or fundamental aspects: *to learn the nuts and bolts of a new job.* —**nuts′-and-bolts′,** *adj.*

nut·shell (nut′shel′), *n.* **1.** the shell of a nut. **2. in a nutshell,** in brief. [ME *nutescell*]

nut·ty (nut′ē), *adj.,* **-ti·er, -ti·est. 1.** abounding in or producing nuts. **2.** nutlike, esp. in taste. **3.** *Informal.* silly or ridiculous. **4.** *Slang.* insane. —**nut′ti·ly,** *adv.* —**nut′ti·ness,** *n.*

nut·wood (nut′wo͝od′), *n.* **1.** any of various nutbearing trees, as the hickory, walnut, etc. **2.** the wood of such a tree.

nux vom·i·ca (nuks vom′ə kə), **1.** the seed of the orange-like fruit of an East Indian loganiaceous tree, *Strychnos Nux-vomica,* containing strychnine, used in medicine. **2.** the tree itself. [< NL: lit., vomiting nut]

nuz·zle (nuz′əl), *v.,* **-zled, -zling,** *n.* —*v.i.* **1.** to burrow or root with the nose, as an animal does. **2.** to thrust the nose (fol. by *at, up, against,* etc.). **3.** to lie close to or cuddle or snuggle up with someone or something. —*v.t.* **4.** to root up with the nose or snout. **5.** to touch or rub with the nose. **6.** to thrust the nose against or into. **7.** to thrust (the nose or head) into something. **8.** to lie close to or snuggle or cuddle up to. —*n.* **9.** an affectionate embrace or cuddle. [ME *nosele.* See NOSE, -LE]

NV, Nevada (approved esp. for use with zip code).

NW, 1. northwest. **2.** northwestern. Also, **N.W., n.w.**

nW, nanowatt; nanowatts. Also, **nw**

NWbN, See **northwest by north.**

NWbW, See **northwest by west.**

n. wt., net weight.

N.W.T., Northwest Territories (Canada).

NY, New York (approved esp. for use with zip code).

N.Y., New York.

NYA, National Youth Administration. Also, **N.Y.A.**

Nya·sa (nyä′sä, nī as′ə), *n.* a lake in SE Africa, between Malawi, Tanzania, and Mozambique. 11,000 sq. mi. Also, **Nyas′sa.**

Nya·sa·land (nyä′sä land′, nī as′ə-), *n.* former name of **Malawi.**

N.Y.C., New York City.

nyct-, a combining form meaning "night": *nyctalopia.* [< Gk *nykt-,* s. of *nýx* night]

nyc·ta·gi·na·ceous (nik′tə jə nā′shəs), *adj.* belonging to the *Nyctaginaceae,* or four-o'clock family of plants. [< NL *Nyctāgin-* (s. of *Nyctāgō* old name of genus = *nyct-* NYCT- + L *-āgō* n. suffix) + -ACEOUS]

nyc·ta·lo·pi·a (nik′tᵊlō′pē ə), *n.* *Ophthalm.* a condition of the eyes in which sight is abnormally poor or wholly gone at night or in a dim light. Also called **night blindness.** [< LL < Gk *nykt-* NYCT- + *al(aós)* blind + *-ōpia* -OPIA] —**nyc·ta·lop·ic** (nik′tᵊlop′ik), *adj.*

nycto-, var. of **nyct-.**

nyc·to·pho·bi·a (nik′tə fō′bē ə), *n.* *Psychiatry.* an abnormal fear of night or darkness.

Nye (nī), *n.* **Edgar Wilson** ("*Bill Nye*"), 1850–96, U.S. humorist.

Nye·man (nye′män), *n.* Russian name of **Niemen.**

Nye·re·re (*Swahili.* nye ʀe′ʀe; *Eng.* ni râr′ē), *n.* **Julius Kam·ba·ra·ge** (*Swahili.* käm bä′rä gə), born 1921, Tanzanian political leader: president 1964–85.

Nyí·regy·há·za (nyē′ʀedyᵊ hä′zo), *n.* a city in NE Hungary. 59,000 (est. 1962).

nyl·ghai (nil′gī), *n., pl.* **-ghais,** (*esp. collectively*) **-ghai.** nilgai.

nyl·ghau (nil′gô), *n., pl.* **-ghaus,** (*esp. collectively*) **-ghau.** nilgai.

ny·lon (nī′lon), *n.* **1.** any of a class of thermoplastic polyamides capable of extrusion when molten: used for yarn, as for hosiery, for bristles, as for brushes, etc. **2. nylons,** stockings made of nylon. [formerly a trademark]

nymph (nimf), *n.* **1.** one of a numerous class of lesser deities of mythology, conceived of as beautiful maidens inhabiting the sea, rivers, woods, trees, mountains, etc., and frequently mentioned as attending a superior deity. **2.** a beautiful or graceful young woman. **3.** the young of an insect that undergoes incomplete metamorphosis. [ME *nimphe* < L *nympha* < Gk *nýmphē* bride, nymph] —**nym′phal, nym·phe·an** (nim′fē ən), *adj.* —**Syn. 1.** naiad, nereid, dryad, hamadryad. See **sylph.**

nym·pha (nim′fə), *n., pl.* **-phae** (-fē). **1.** *Anat.* one of the inner labia of the vulva. **2.** nymph (def. 3). [< L *nympha* a bride, young woman, NYMPH]

nym·phae·a·ceous (nim′fē ā′shəs), *adj.* belonging to the *Nymphaeaceae,* or water-lily family of plants. [< L *nymphae(a)* the water lily (< Gk *nymphaîa,* n. use of fem. of *nymphaîos,* sacred to the nymphs) + -ACEOUS]

nym·pha·lid (nim′fə lid), *n.* **1.** a butterfly of the family *Nymphalidae,* comprising the brush-footed butterflies. —*adj.* **2.** belonging or pertaining to the family *Nymphalidae.* [< NL *Nymphalid(ae)* name of family = *Nymphāl(is)* name of genus (= L *nymph(a)* NYMPH + *-ālis* -AL[1]) + *-idae* -ID[2]]

nymph·et (nim fet′, nim′fit), *n.* a sexually attractive young girl. [< MF *nymphette*]

nym·pho (nim′fō), *n., pl.* **-phos.** *adj.* *Slang.* nymphomaniac. [by shortening]

nym·pho·lep·sy (nim′fə lep′sē), *n., pl.* **-sies. 1.** an ecstasy supposed by the ancients to be inspired by nymphs. **2.** a frenzy of emotion, as for something unattainable. [b. NYMPHOLEPT and EPILEPSY] —**nym·pho·lep·tic** (nim′fə lep′tik), *adj.*

nym·pho·lept (nim′fə lept′), *n.* a person seized with nympholepsy. [< Gk *nymphólēpt(os)* caught by nymphs = *nýmph(ē)* NYMPH + *-o-* -O- + *lēptos,* verbid of *lambánein* to seize]

nym·pho·ma·ni·a (nim′fə mā′nē ə), *n.* *Pathol.* abnormal and uncontrollable sexual desire in women. [< Gk *nympho-* (comb. form of *nýmphē* NYMPH) + -MANIA] —**nym·pho·ma·ni·ac** (nim′fə mā′nē ak′), *adj., n.* —**nym·pho·ma·ni·a·cal** (nim′fō mə nī′ə kəl), *adj.*

Nym·we·gen (nim′vā gən), *n.* former name of **Nijmegen.**

Ny·norsk (ny′nôshk′; *Eng.* nē′nōrsk, -nôrsk), *n.* *Norwegian.* a literary language based on western Norwegian dialects and Old Norse and in 1885 adopted as one of the two official languages of Norway. Also called **Landsmål.** Cf. **Bokmål.** [lit., new Norse]

nys·tag·mus (ni stag′məs), *n.* *Pathol.* an involuntary oscillation of the eyeball, usually lateral but sometimes rotatory or vertical. [< NL < Gk *nystagm(ós)* nodding, akin to *nystázein* to nod] —**nys·tag′mic,** *adj.*

Nyx (niks), *n.* an ancient Greek goddess personifying night.

N.Z., New Zealand. Also, **N. Zeal.**

DEVELOPMENT OF MAJUSCULE							
NORTH SEMITIC	GREEK		ETR.	LATIN	MODERN		
					GOTHIC	ITALIC	ROMAN
O	O	O	O	O	O	*O*	O

DEVELOPMENT OF MINUSCULE					
ROMAN CURSIVE	ROMAN UNCIAL	CAROL. MIN.	MODERN		
			GOTHIC	ITALIC	ROMAN
o	o	o	o	*o*	o

The fifteenth letter of the English alphabet descended from the Greek vowel *omicron* (ο). In form, however, the letter was adopted in Greek from the North Semitic consonant *ayin*, North Semitic having no vowel symbols. Since its appearance in Greek, this sign has changed little throughout its history.

O, o (ō), *n., pl.* **O's** or **Os; o's** or **os** or **oes. 1.** the 15th letter of the English alphabet, a vowel. **2.** any spoken sound represented by the letter *O* or *o*, as in *box, note,* or *do.* **3.** something having the shape of an O. **4.** a written or printed representation of the letter *O* or *o.* **5.** a device, as a printer's type, for reproducing the letter *O* or *o.*

O (ō), *interj., n., pl.* **O's.** —*interj.* **1.** (used before a name in direct address, esp. in solemn or poetic language, to lend earnestness to an appeal): *Hear, O Israel!* **2.** (used as an expression of surprise, pain, annoyance, longing, gladness, etc.) —*n.* **3.** the exclamation "O."

O, Old.

O, 1. the 15th in order or in a series. **2.** the Arabic cipher; zero. **3.** a major blood group or type usually enabling a person whose blood is of this group to donate blood to persons of group O, A, B, or AB and to receive blood from persons of group O. **4.** *Chem.* oxygen.

o' (ə, ō), *prep.* **1.** an abbreviated form of *of,* now chiefly dialectal or informal except in *o'clock, will-o'-the-wisp,* etc. **2.** an abbreviated form of *on.* [ME; by alter.]

O', a prefix meaning "descendant of," in Irish family names: *O'Brien; O'Connor.* [repr. Ir ō descendant, OIr *au*]

o-[1], *Chem.* an abridgment of **ortho-.**

o-[2], var. of **ob-** before *m: omission.*

-o-, the typical ending of the first element of compounds of Greek origin (as **-i-** is in compounds of Latin origin), used regularly in forming new compounds with elements of Greek origin and often used in English as a connective irrespective of etymology: *Franco-Italian; geography; seriocomic; speedometer.* Cf. **-i-.** [ME (< OF) < L < Gk]

O., 1. Ocean. **2.** octavo. **3.** October. **4.** Ohio. **5.** Old. **6.** Ontario. **7.** Oregon.

o., 1. pint. [< L *octārius*] **2.** octavo. **3.** off. **4.** old. **5.** only. **6.** order. **7.** *Baseball.* out; outs.

oaf (ōf), *n.* **1.** a simpleton; dunce; blockhead. **2.** a clumsy, stupid person; lout. **3.** a deformed or mentally deficient child. **4.** a changeling. [var. of *auf,* ME *alfe,* OE *ælf* ELF; c. G *Alp* nightmare] —**oaf′ish,** *adj.* —**oaf′ish·ly,** *adv.* —**oaf′ish·ness,** *n.* —**Syn. 1.** dolt, ninny. **2.** churl, boor.

O·a·hu (ō ä′ho͞o), *n.* an island in central Hawaii: location of Honolulu. 629,176 (1970); 589 sq. mi.

oak (ōk), *n.* **1.** any fagaceous tree or shrub of the genus *Quercus,* bearing the acorn as fruit. **2.** the hard, durable wood of such a tree, used in making furniture and in construction. **3.** the leaves of this tree, esp. as worn in a chaplet. [ME *ook,* OE *āc;* c. D *eik,* G *Eiche*] —**oak′like′,** *adj.*

oak′ ap′ple, any of various roundish galls produced on oaks. Also called **oak′ gall′.** [ME]

oak·en (ō′kən), *adj.* **1.** made of oak. **2.** of or pertaining to the oak tree. [ME]

Oak·land (ōk′lənd), *n.* a seaport in W California, on San Francisco Bay. 361,561 (1970).

Oak′ Lawn′, a city in NE Illinois, near Chicago. 60,305 (1970).

oak′-leaf′ clus′ter (ōk′lēf′), a U.S. military decoration in the form of a small bronze twig bearing four oak leaves and three acorns, worn on the ribbon of another decoration to signify a second award of the same medal. Also, **oak′leaf′ clus′ter, Oak′ Leaf′ clus′ter.**

Oak·ley (ōk′lē), *n.* **Annie** (*Phoebe Anne Oakley Mozee*), 1860–1926, U.S. markswoman.

Oak′ Park′, 1. a city in NE Illinois, near Chicago. 62,511 (1970). **2.** a city in SE Michigan, near Detroit. 36,762 (1970).

Oak′ Ridge′, a city in E Tennessee, near Knoxville: atomic research center. 28,319 (1970).

oa·kum (ō′kəm), *n.* loose fiber obtained by untwisting and picking apart old ropes, used for caulking the seams of ships. [ME *okome,* OE *ācum(a),* var. of *ācumba,* lit., offcombings = *ā-* separative prefix + *-cumba* (see COMB[1])]

OAO, Orbiting Astronomical Observatory.

oar (ōr, ôr), *n.* **1.** a long shaft with a broad blade at one end, used as a lever for rowing or otherwise propelling or steering a boat. **2.** an oarsman. —*v.t.* **3.** to propel with or as with oars; row. —*v.i.* **4.** to row. **5.** to move or advance by or as by rowing. [ME *ore,* OE *ār;* c. Icel *ār*] —**oar′less,** *adj.* —**oar′like′,** *adj.*

oar·fish (ōr′fish′, ôr′-), *n., pl.* (*esp. collectively*) **-fish,** (*esp. referring to two or more kinds or species*) **-fish·es.** any pelagic fish of the genus *Regalecus,* having a compressed, tapelike body from 12 to over 20 feet long.

O, Oarlock

oar·lock (ōr′lok′, ôr′-), *n.* any of various devices providing a pivot for an oar in rowing, esp. a swiveling, crutchlike or ringlike metal device projecting above a gunwale. [ME *orlok,* OE *ārloc*]

oars·man (ōrz′mən, ôrz′-), *n., pl.* **-men.** a person who rows a boat or other vessel; rower. —**oars′man·ship′,** *n.*

OAS, 1. Organization of American States: an economic, political, and military organization composed of the U.S., Mexico, Haiti, the Dominican Republic, and the republics of Central and South America. **2.** an army organization in Algeria composed of French officers who refused to recognize Algerian independence. [< F *O(rganisation de l')a(rmée) s(ecrete),* lit., secret army organization] **3.** On Active Service.

o·a·sis (ō ā′sis, ō′ə sis), *n., pl.* **-ses** (-sēz, -sēz′). **1.** a fertile or green area in a desert region, usually having a spring or well. **2.** something serving as a pleasant relief, refuge, or change. [< LL < Gk; ? < Egypt *wāh*]

oast (ōst), *n.* *Chiefly Brit.* a kiln for drying hops or malt. [ME *ost,* OE *āst;* c. D *eest*]

oat (ōt), *n.* **1.** a cereal grass, *Avena sativa,* cultivated for its edible seed. **2.** Usually, **oats.** the seed of this plant, used as a food for man and animals. **3.** any of several plants of the same genus, as the wild oat. **4.** *Archaic.* a musical pipe regarded as made of an oat straw. **5. feel one's oats,** *Informal.* **a.** to feel gay or lively. **b.** to become aware of and use one's importance or power. **6. sow one's wild oats.** See **wild oat** (def. 2). [ME *ote,* OE *āte*] —**oat′like′,** *adj.*

oat·cake (ōt′kāk′), *n.* a cake, usually thin and brittle, made of oatmeal.

-oate, *Chem.* a combining form indicating the presence of the ester or >C=O group: *benzoate.* [*-o(ic)* (as in *benzoic*) + -ATE[2]]

oat·en (ōt′ən), *adj.* of, pertaining to, or made of oats, oatmeal, or oat straw. [ME]

Oates (ōts), *n.* **Titus,** 1649–1705, English impostor: instigator of the Popish Plot scare.

oat′ grass′, 1. any of certain oatlike grasses. **2.** any wild species of oat.

oath (ōth), *n., pl.* **oaths** (ōt͟hz, ōths). **1.** a solemn appeal to God or to some revered person or thing to witness one's determination to speak the truth or to keep a promise. **2.** a statement or promise strengthened by such an appeal. **3.** a formally affirmed statement or promise accepted as an equivalent of an appeal to God or a revered person or thing; affirmation. **4.** any established or set form of statement or promise: *the oath of office.* **5.** an irreverent or blasphemous use of the name of God or anything sacred. **6.** any profane expression; curse. **7. on, upon,** or **under oath,** bound by or under the obligation imposed by an oath. **8. take oath,** to swear solemnly; vow. [ME *ooth,* OE *āth;* c. G *Eid*] —**Syn. 2.** vow, pledge. **5.** profanity.

oat·meal (ōt′mēl′, -mēl′), *n.* **1.** meal made from oats. **2.** a cooked breakfast food made from this. —*adj.* **3.** made with or containing oatmeal: *oatmeal cookies.* [ME]

Oa·xa·ca (wä hä′kä; *Eng.* wə hä′kə), *n.* **1.** a state in S Mexico. 1,727,266 (1960); 36,375 sq. mi. **2.** a city in and the capital of this state, in the central part. 74,370 (1960).

Ob (ôp), *n.* **1.** a river in the W Soviet Union in Asia, flowing NW to the Gulf of Ob. 2500 mi. long. **2. Gulf of,** an inlet of the Arctic Ocean. ab. 500 mi. long.

ob-, a prefix meaning "toward," "to," "on," "over," "against," orig. occurring in loan words from Latin, but now used also, with the sense of "reversely," "inversely," to form Neo-Latin and English scientific terms: *object; obligate; oblanceolate.* Also, **o-, oc-, of-, op-.** [ME (< OF) < L, repr. *ob* (prep.); in some scientific terms < NL, L *ob-*]

ob., 1. obiit. **2.** incidentally. [< L *obiter*] **3.** oboe.

Obad., Obadiah.

O·ba·di·ah (ō′bə dī′ə), *n.* **1.** a Minor Prophet. **2.** a book of the Bible bearing his name.

obb., obbligato.

ob·bli·ga·to (ob′lə gä′tō; *It.* ôb′blē gä′tô), *adj., n., pl.* **-tos,** *It.* **-ti** (-tē). *Music.* —*adj.* **1.** (used as a musical direction) obligatory or indispensable; so important that it cannot be omitted (opposed to *ad libitum*). —*n.* **2.** an obbligato part or accompaniment. **3.** a continuing or persistent subordinate or background motif. Also, **obligato.** [< It: bound, obliged < L *obligāt(us);* see OBLIGATE]

ob·cor·date (ob kôr′dāt), *adj.* *Bot.* heart-shaped, with the attachment at the pointed end, as a leaf.

obdt., obedient.

ob·du·rate (ob′do͝o rit, -dyo͝o-), *adj.* **1.** unmoved by persuasion, pity, or tender feelings; unyielding. **2.** stubbornly resistant to moral influence; persistently impenitent: *an obdurate sinner.* [ME *obdurat* < L *obdūrāt(us)* hardened (ptp. of *obdūrāre*) = *ob-* OB- + *dūr(us)* hard + *-ātus* -ATE[1]] —**ob′du·rate·ly,** *adv.* —**ob′du·ra·cy, ob′du·rate·ness,** *n.* —**Syn. 1.** obstinate, unbending. **2.** unregenerate.

O.B.E., 1. Officer (of the Order) of the British Empire. **2.** Order of the British Empire.

o·be·ah (ō′bē ə), *n.* obi[2]. —**o′be·ah·ism,** *n.*

o·be·di·ence (ō bē′dē əns), *n.* **1.** the state or quality of being obedient. **2.** the act or practice of obeying; dutiful or submissive compliance. **3.** a sphere of authority or jurisdiction, esp. ecclesiastical. **4.** *Chiefly Eccles.* conformity to a monastic rule or the authority of a religious superior. [ME < OF < L *oboedientia.* See OBEDIENT, -ENCE]

o·be·di·ent (ō bē′dē ənt), *adj.* obeying or willing to obey;

complying with authority. [ME < OF < L *oboedient-* (s. of *oboediēns*), prp. of *oboedīre* to OBEY; see -ENT] —**Syn.** compliant, docile, tractable, willing. —**Ant.** recalcitrant.

O·beid (ō bād′), *n.* See **El Obeid.**

o·bei·sance (ō bā′səns, ō bē′-), *n.* **1.** a movement of the body expressing deep respect or deferential courtesy, as before a superior; a bow, curtsy, or similar gesture. **2.** deference or homage. [ME *obeisaunce* < MF *obeissance* < OF *obeissant*, prp. of *obeir* to OBEY: see -ANCE] —**o·bei′sant,** *adj.* —**o·bei′sant·ly,** *adv.*

ob·e·lise (ob′ə līz′), *v.t.*, **-lised, -lis·ing.** *Chiefly Brit.* obelize.

ob·e·lisk (ob′ə lisk), *n.* **1.** a four-sided shaft of stone, usually monolithic, that tapers slightly from bottom to top and has a pyramidal apex. **2.** an obelus. **3.** *Print.* dagger (def. 2). [< L *obelisc(us)* < Gk *obelískos* small spit = *obel(ós)* spit, pointed pillar + *-iskos* dim. suffix] —**ob′e·lis′cal,** *adj.* —**ob′e·lis′koid,** *adj.*

ob·e·lize (ob′ə līz′), *v.t.*, **-lized, -liz·ing.** to mark (a word or passage) with an obelus. Also, *esp. Brit.*, **obelise.** [< Gk *obelíz(ein)* = *obel(ós)* OBELUS + *-izein* -IZE] —**ob′e·lism,** *n.*

ob·e·lus (ob′ə ləs), *n.*, *pl.* **-li** (-lī′). **1.** a mark (– or ÷) used in ancient manuscripts to point out spurious, corrupt, doubtful, or superfluous words or passages. **2.** *Print.* dagger (def. 2). [< LL < Gk *obelós* spit, pointed pillar]

Obelisk

O·ber·am·mer·gau (ō′bər ä′mər-gou′), *n.* a village in S West Germany, SW of Munich: famous for the passion play performed every ten years. 4603 (1961).

O·ber·hau·sen (ō′bər hou′zən), *n.* a city in W West Germany, in the lower Ruhr valley. 259,800 (1963).

O·ber·land (ō′bər land′; *Ger.* ō′bər länt′), *n.* a mountain region in central Switzerland, mostly in S Bern canton.

O·ber·lin (*Fr.* ô ber lan′ *for 1;* ō′bər lin *for 2*), *n.* **1. Jean Fré·dé·ric** (*Fr.* zhäN frā dā rēk′), 1740–1826, Alsatian clergyman. **2.** a village in N Ohio. 8761 (1970).

O·ber·on (ō′bə ron′), *n.* (in medieval folklore) the king of the fairies and husband of their queen, Titania.

o·bese (ō bēs′), *adj.* extremely fat; corpulent; overweight. [< L *obēs(us)*, ptp. of *obēdere* to eat away = *ob-* OB- + *ēdere* to EAT] —**o·bese′ly,** *adv.* —**o·bese′ness, o·bes·i·ty** (ō bē′si tē), *n.*

o·bey (ō bā′), *v.t.* **1.** to comply with or follow the commands, restrictions, wishes, or instructions of. **2.** to comply with or follow (a command, restriction, guiding principle, etc.). **3.** (of things) to respond to: *The car obeyed the slightest touch of the wheel.* —*v.i.* **4.** to be obedient: *to love, honor, and obey.* [ME *obeie(n)* < OF *obei(r)* < L *oboedīre* = *ob-* OB- + *audīre* to hear] —**o·bey′a·ble,** *adj.* —**o·bey′er,** *n.* —**o·bey′ing·ly,** *adv.*

ob·fus·cate (ob fus′kāt, ob′fə skāt′), *v.t.*, **-cat·ed, -cat·ing.** **1.** to confuse, bewilder, or stupefy. **2.** to make obscure: *to obfuscate a problem with extraneous information.* **3.** to darken. [< LL *obfuscāt(us)* darkened (ptp. of *obfuscāre*) = L *ob-* OB- + *fusc(us)* dark + *-ātus* -ATE[1]] —**ob′fus·ca′tion,** *n.* —**Syn. 1.** muddle, perplex. **2.** cloud. —**Ant. 1.** clarify.

o·bi[1] (ō′bē; *Jap.* ô′bē), *n.*, *pl.* **o·bis,** *Jap.* **o·bi.** a long, broad sash, worn around the waist over a Japanese kimono. [< Jap]

o·bi[2] (ō′bē), *n.*, *pl.* **o·bis** for 2. **1.** a kind of sorcery practiced by some Negroes in Africa, the West Indies, and elsewhere. **2.** a fetish or charm used in it. Also called **obeah.** [< WAfr] —**o′bi·ism,** *n.*

o·bi·it (ō′bi it; *Eng.* ō′bē it, ob′ē-), *Latin.* he (or she) died.

o·bit (ō′bit, ob′it), *n.* *Informal.* obituary. [ME *obite* < L *obit(us)* dead = *ob-* OB- + *-i-* go + *-tus* ptp. suffix]

ob·i·ter dic·tum (ob′i tər dik′təm), *pl.* **ob·i·ter dic·ta** (ob′i tər dik′tə). **1.** an incidental or passing remark, opinion, etc. **2.** *Law.* an incidental or supplementary opinion by a judge, not essential to a decision and therefore not binding. [< L: (a) saying by the way]

o·bit·u·ar·y (ō bich′o͞o er′ē), *n.*, *pl.* **-ar·ies,** *adj.* —*n.* **1.** a notice of the death of a person, usually with a brief biographical sketch, as in a newspaper. —*adj.* **2.** of, pertaining to, or recording a death or deaths. [< ML *obituāri(us)* = L *obitu(s)* death (see OBIT) + *-ārius* -ARY]

obj., **1.** object. **2.** objection. **3.** objective.

ob·ject (*n.* ob′jikt, -jekt; *v.* əb jekt′), *n.* **1.** anything that is visible or tangible and is stable in form. **2.** anything that may be apprehended intellectually: *objects of thought.* **3.** a person or thing with reference to the impression made on the mind or the feeling: *an object of pity.* **4.** a thing, person, or matter to which thought or action is directed: *an object of medical investigation.* **5.** the end toward which effort is directed; goal; purpose. **6.** *Gram.* a noun, noun phrase, or noun substitute representing by its syntactical position either the goal of the action of a verb with which it combines to form a verb phrase or the goal of a preposition in a prepositional phrase, as *ball* in *John hit the ball,* or *Venice* in *He came to Venice, coin* and *her* in *He gave her a coin.* Cf. **direct object, indirect object.** —*v.i.* **7.** to offer a reason or argument in opposition. **8.** to express or feel disapproval, dislike, or distaste; be averse. —*v.t.* **9.** to state, claim, or cite in opposition; put forward in objection. [ME < LL *object(us)* act of placing before or opposite, n. use of L *objectus* (ptp. of *objicere*) = *ob-* OB- + *jec-* (comb. form of *jac-* throw; see JET[1]) + *-tus* ptp. suffix] —**ob·jec′tor,** *n.* —**Syn. 5.** objective, target, destination, intent. See **aim.**

object., **1.** objection. **2.** objective.

ob′ject ball′, *Billiards, Pool.* **1.** the first ball struck by the cue ball in making a carom. **2.** a ball to be struck by the cue ball; any ball except the cue ball.

ob′ject glass′, *Optics.* objective (def. 3).

ob·jec·ti·fy (əb jek′tə fī′), *v.t.*, **-fied, -fy·ing.** to present as an object, esp. of sight, touch, or other physical sense; make objective; externalize. [< ML *object(um)* OBJECT + -IFY] —**ob·jec′ti·fi·ca′tion,** *n.*

ob·jec·tion (əb jek′shən), *n.* **1.** something said or offered in disagreement, opposition, refusal, or disapproval. **2.** the act of objecting. **3.** a ground or cause for objecting. **4.** a feeling of disapproval, dislike, or disagreement. [ME *objeccioun* < LL *objectiōn-* (s. of *objectiō*) = L *object(us)* OBJECT + *-iōn-* -ION]

ob·jec·tion·a·ble (əb jek′shə nə bəl), *adj.* **1.** causing or tending to cause objection, disapproval, or protest. **2.** offensive, as to good taste. **3.** offensive or insulting, esp. to a religious or ethnic group. —**ob·jec′tion·a·bil′i·ty, ob·jec′tion·a·ble·ness,** *n.* —**ob·jec′tion·a·bly,** *adv.*

ob·jec·tive (əb jek′tiv), *n.* **1.** something that one's efforts are intended to attain or accomplish; purpose; goal; target. **2.** *Gram.* **a.** Also called **objec′tive case′.** (in English and some other languages) a case specialized for the use of a form as the object of a transitive verb or of a preposition, as *him* in *The boy hit him* or *me* in *He comes to me with his troubles.* **b.** a word in that case. **3.** Also called **object glass, objective lens, object lens.** *Optics.* (in a telescope, microscope, camera, or other optical system) the lens or combination of lenses that first receives the rays from the object and forms the image in the focal plane of the eyepiece or on a plate or screen. —*adj.* **4.** being or belonging to the object of perception or thought (opposed to *subjective*): *objective characteristics.* **5.** not affected by personal feelings or prejudice; based on facts; unbiased. **6.** being the object or goal of one's endeavors or actions. **7.** intent upon or dealing with things external to the mind rather than with thoughts or feelings, as a person, a book, etc. **8.** of or pertaining to something that can be known, or to something that is an object or a part of an object. **9.** being part of or pertaining to an object to be drawn. **10.** *Gram.* **a.** pertaining to the use of a form as the object of a transitive verb or of a preposition. **b.** (in English and some other languages) noting the objective case. **c.** similar to such a case in meaning. [< ML *objectīv(us)* = L *object(us)* (see OBJECT) + *-īvus* -IVE] —**ob·jec′tive·ly,** *adv.* —**ob·jec′tive·ness,** *n.* —**Syn. 1.** object, destination. **5.** impartial, fair, impersonal, disinterested. —**Ant. 5.** subjective, personal.

objec′tive com′plement, *Gram.* a word or a group of words used in the predicate following a factitive verb to modify or qualify its direct object, as *chairman* in *We appointed him chairman.* Also called **objec′tive pred′icate, predicate objective.**

objec′tive correl′ative, *Literature.* a completely depicted situation or chain of events that objectifies a particular emotion in such a way as to produce or evoke that emotion in the reader.

objec′tive lens′, *Optics.* objective (def. 3). Also called **ob′ject lens′.**

ob·jec·tiv·ism (əb jek′tə viz′əm), *n.* **1.** a tendency to lay stress on the objective or external elements of cognition. **2.** the tendency, as of a writer, to deal with things external to the mind rather than thoughts or feelings. **3.** a doctrine characterized by this tendency. —**ob·jec′tiv·ist,** *n., adj.* —**ob·jec′ti·vis′tic,** *adj.*

ob·jec·tiv·i·ty (ob′jek tiv′i tē), *n.* **1.** the state or quality of being objective. **2.** intentness on objects external to the mind. **3.** external reality.

ob·ject·less (ob′jikt lis), *adj.* **1.** not directed toward any end or goal; purposeless; aimless. **2.** having no object.

ob′ject les′son, a practical or concrete illustration of a principle.

ob·jet d'art (ôb zhe dar′), *pl.* **ob·jets d'art** (ôb zhe dar′). *French.* an object of artistic worth or curiosity, esp. a small object.

ob·jur·gate (ob′jər gāt′, əb jûr′gāt), *v.t.*, **-gat·ed, -gat·ing.** to reproach or denounce vehemently; upbraid harshly; berate sharply. [< L *objurgāt(us)* rebuked, ptp. of *objurgāre* = *ob-* OB- + *jurgāre* to rebuke (*jur-* (s. of *jus*) law + *(a)g-* do, drive) + *-ātus* -ATE[1]] —**ob′jur·ga′tion,** *n.* —**ob′jur·ga′tor,** *n.* —**ob·jur′ga·to′ry, ob·jur′ga·tive,** *adj.*

obl., **1.** oblique. **2.** oblong.

ob·lan·ce·o·late (ob lan′sē ə lit, -lāt′), *adj.* *Bot.* inversely lanceolate, as a leaf.

ob·last (ob′last, -läst; *Russ.* ôb′läst), *n.*, *pl.* **-lasts,** *Russ.* **-las·ti** (-läs tē). (in the Soviet Union) an administrative division corresponding to an autonomous province. [< Russ *oblast'* < OSlav = *ob-* against, on + *vlast'* administration]

ob·late[1] (ob′lāt, o blāt′), *adj.* flattened at the poles (opposed to *prolate*). See diag. at **prolate.** [< NL *oblāt(us)* lengthened = L *ob-* OB- + *lātus* carried] —**ob′late·ly,** *adv.*

ob·late[2] (ob′lāt, o blāt′), *n.* **1.** a person serving and living in a monastery, but not under monastic vows or full monastic rule. **2.** a layman of any of various Roman Catholic societies devoted to special religious work. [< ML *oblāt(us)* offered, ptp. of *offerre* to OFFER]

ob·la·tion (o blā′shən), *n.* **1.** the offering to God of the elements of bread and wine in the Eucharist. **2.** the whole office of the Eucharist. **3.** the act of making an offering, esp. to God or a deity. **4.** any offering for religious or charitable uses. [ME *oblacion* < LL *oblātiōn-* (s. of *oblātiō*) = *oblāt(us)* offered (see OBLATE[2]) + *-iōn-* -ION] —**ob·la·to·ry** (ob′lə tōr′ē, -tôr′ē), **ob·la′tion·al,** *adj.*

ob·li·gate (*v.* ob′lə gāt′; *adj.* ob′lə git, -gāt′), *v.*, **-gat·ed, -gat·ing,** *adj.* —*v.t.* **1.** to oblige or bind morally or legally. **2.** to pledge, commit, or bind (funds, property, etc.) to meet an obligation. —*adj.* **3.** necessary; essential. **4.** *Biol.* restricted to a particular condition of life (opposed to *facultative*): *an obligate parasite.* [ME *obligat* < L *obligāt(us)* bound (ptp. of *obligāre*) = *ob-* OB- + *ligātus;* see LIGATE] —**ob·li·ga·ble** (ob′lə gə bəl), *adj.* —**ob·li·gate·ly** (ob′lə-git′lē), *adv.* —**ob′li·ga′tor,** *n.*

ob·li·ga·tion (ob′lə gā′shən), *n.* **1.** something by which a person is bound to do certain things and which arises out of a sense of duty or results from custom, law, etc. **2.** something that is done or is to be done for such reasons: *to fulfill one's obligations.* **3.** a binding promise, contract, sense of duty, etc. **4.** the act of binding oneself by a promise, contract, etc. **5.** *Law.* **a.** an agreement enforceable by law. **b.** a document containing such an agreement. **c.** a bond containing a penalty, with a condition for performance annexed. **d.** any bond, note, or the like, as of a government, serving as evidence of indebtedness. **6.** a moral or legal indebtedness or an amount of indebtedness. **7.** a favor, service, or benefit for which gratitude is due. **8.** a debt of gratitude. **9.** the state of being morally or legally indebted. [ME *obligacioun* < OF *obligation* < L *obligātiōn-* (s. of *obligātiō*) a binding = *obligāt(us)* bound (see OBLIGATE) + *-iōn-* -ION] —**ob·li·ga·tive** (ob′lə gā′tiv), *adj.* —**Syn. 1.** responsibility. See **duty. 5.** contract.

ob·li·ga·to (ob′lə gä′tō), *adj., n., pl.* **-tos, -ti** (-tē). obbligato.

ob·lig·a·to·ry (ə blig′ə tôr′ē, -tōr′ē, ob′lə gə-), *adj.* **1.** imposing moral or legal obligation; binding. **2.** required as a matter of obligation; mandatory. **3.** incumbent or compulsory (usually fol. by *on* or *upon*): *duties obligatory on all.* **4.** creating or recording an obligation, as a document. [ME < LL *obligātōri(us)* binding] —**ob·lig·a·to·ri·ly** (ə blig′ə tôr′ə lē, -tōr′-, ob′lə gə-; ə blig′ə tôr′ə lē, -tōr′-, ob′lə gə-), *adv.*

o·blige (ə blīj′), *v.,* **o·bliged, o·blig·ing.** —*v.t.* **1.** to require or constrain. **2.** to bind morally or legally, as by a promise or contract. **3.** to make (an action, policy, etc.) necessary or obligatory: *Your recalcitrance obliges firmness on my part.* **4.** to place under a debt of gratitude; obligate. **5.** to favor or accommodate: *Mr. Weems will oblige us with a song.* —*v.i.* **6.** to be kindly accommodating; help out. [ME *oblige(n)* < OF *obligie(r)* < L *obligāre* to bind. See OBLIGATE] —**o·blig·ed·ly** (ə blī′jid lē), *adv.* —**o·blig′ed·ness,** *n.* —**o·blig′er,** *n.* —**Syn. 1.** compel, force. **2.** obligate. **5.** OBLIGE, ACCOMMODATE imply making a gracious and welcome gesture of some kind. OBLIGE emphasizes the idea of conferring a favor or benefit (and often of taking some trouble to do it): *to oblige someone with a loan.* ACCOMMODATE emphasizes doing a service or furnishing a convenience: *to accommodate someone with lodgings and meals.*

ob·li·gee (ob′lə jē′), *n.* **1.** *Law.* **a.** a person to whom another is bound. **b.** a person to whom a bond is given. **2.** a person who is under obligation.

o·blig·ing (ə blī′jing), *adj.* willing or eager to do favors, perform services, etc.; accommodating. —**o·blig′ing·ly,** *adv.* —**o·blig′ing·ness,** *n.* —**Syn.** helpful, kind, friendly.

ob·li·gor (ob′lə gôr′, ob′lə gôr′), *n.* *Law.* **1.** a person who is bound to another. **2.** a person who gives a bond.

ob·lique (ə blēk′; *Mil.* ə blīk′), *adj., adv., v.,* **-liqued, -liqu·ing,** *n.* —*adj.* **1.** neither perpendicular nor parallel to a given line or surface; slanting; sloping. **2.** *Geom.* (of a solid) not having the axis perpendicular to the plane of the base. **3.** diverging from a given straight line or course. **4.** indirectly stated or expressed; not straightforward. **5.** indirectly aimed at or reached, as ends or results; deviously achieved. **6.** devious or underhand; perverse. **7.** *Gram.* noting or pertaining to any case of noun inflection except nominative, vocative, and, sometimes, accusative. **8.** *Anat.* (of muscles) running or situated obliquely. **9.** *Bot.* having unequal sides, as a leaf. **10.** *Drafting.* designating a method of projection **(oblique′ projec′tion)** in which a three-dimensional object is represented by a drawing **(oblique′ draw′ing)** in which the face, usually parallel to the picture plane, is represented in accurate or exact proportion and all other faces are shown at any convenient angle other than 90°. Cf. **axonometric, cabinet** (def. 17), **isometric** (def. 4). See illus. at **isometric.** —*adv.* **11.** *Mil.* at an angle of 45°. —*v.i.* **12.** to have or take an oblique direction; slant. —*n.* **13.** *Gram.* the oblique case. **14.** something that is oblique, as an oblique muscle. [ME *oblike* < L *oblīqu(us)* slanting = *ob-* OB- + OL *līquus* < ?] —**ob·lique′ly,** *adv.* —**ob·lique′ness,** *n.*

oblique′ an′gle, any acute or obtuse angle.

ob·liq·ui·ty (ə blik′wi tē), *n., pl.* **-ties. 1.** the state of being oblique. **2.** divergence from moral rectitude; immorality or dishonesty. **3.** an instance of such divergence. **4.** an inclination or a degree of inclination. **5.** a confusing or obscure statement or passage of writing, esp. one deliberately made obscure; obfuscation. **6.** Also called **obliq′uity of the eclip′tic.** *Astron.* the angle between the plane of the earth's orbit and that of the earth's equator, equal to 23°27′; the inclination of the earth's equator. [ME *obliquitee* < MF *obliquite* < L *oblīquitāt-* (s. of *oblīquitās*) = *obliqu(us)* OBLIQUE + *-itāt-* -ITY] —**ob·liq′ui·tous,** *adj.*

ob·lit·er·ate (ə blit′ə rāt′), *v.t.,* **-at·ed, -at·ing. 1.** to remove all traces of; do away with; destroy completely. **2.** to blot out or render undecipherable; cancel; efface. [< L *oblitterāt(us)* blotted out (ptp. of *oblitterāre*) = *ob-* OB- + *litter(a)* letter + *-ātus* -ATE¹] —**ob·lit·er·a·ble** (ə blit′ər ə-bəl), *adj.* —**ob·lit′er·a′tion,** *n.* —**ob·lit·er·a·tive** (ə blit′ə-rā′tiv, -ər ə tiv), *adj.* —**Syn. 2.** expunge. See **cancel.**

ob·liv·i·on (ə bliv′ē ən), *n.* **1.** the state of being forgotten, as by the public: *a former screen star now in oblivion.* **2.** the state of forgetting or of being mentally withdrawn: *His nap gave him 30 minutes of oblivion.* **3.** official disregard or overlooking of offenses; pardon; amnesty. [ME < MF < L *oblīviōn-* (s. of *oblīviō*) = *obliv(iscī)* (to) forget (*ob-* OB- + *līv-,* s. of *livēre* to darken, forget) + *-iōn-* -ION]

ob·liv·i·ous (ə bliv′ē əs), *adj.* **1.** unmindful or unconscious; unaware (usually fol. by *of* or *to*): *She was oblivious of his admiration.* **2.** forgetful; without remembrance or memory (usually fol. by *of*): *to be oblivious of past failures.* **3.** *Archaic.* inducing forgetfulness. [ME < L *oblīviōs(us)* forgetful = *oblīvi(scī)* (to) forget (see OBLIVION) + *-ōsus* -OUS] —**ob·liv′i·ous·ly,** *adv.* —**ob·liv′i·ous·ness,** *n.*

ob·long (ob′lông′, -long′), *adj.* **1.** elongated, usually from the square or circular form. **2.** in the form of a rectangle one of whose dimensions is greater than the other. —*n.* **3.** an oblong figure. [ME *oblonge* < L *oblong(us)* rather long] —**ob′long·ish,** *adj.* —**ob′long·ly,** *adv.* —**ob′long·ness,** *n.*

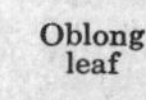

Oblong leaf

ob·lo·quy (ob′lə kwē), *n., pl.* **-quies. 1.** bad repute resulting from public censure. **2.** censure or abusive language, esp. as inflicted by numerous persons or by the general public. [< LL *obloqui(um)* contradiction = L *obloqu(ī)* (to) contradict (*ob-* OB- + *loquī* to speak) + *-ium* -Y³] —**ob·lo·qui·al** (o blō′-kwē əl), *adj.* —**Syn. 1.** disgrace. **2.** reproach, calumny; aspersion, revilement. —**Ant. 1.** credit, renown. **2.** praise.

ob·nox·ious (əb nok′shəs), *adj.* **1.** objectionable or offensive. **2.** *Archaic.* exposed or liable to harm, evil, or anything objectionable. **3.** *Obs.* meriting punishment or censure; reprehensible. [< L *obnoxiōs(us)* harmful] —**ob·nox′ious·ly,** *adv.* —**ob·nox′ious·ness,** *n.* —**Syn. 1.** See **hateful.**

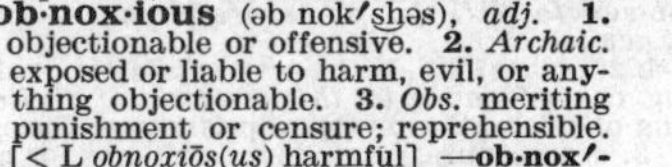

Oboe

o·boe (ō′bō), *n.* **1.** a woodwind instrument having a slender conical body and a double-reed mouthpiece. **2.** (*cap.*) a word formerly used in communication to represent the letter *O.* [< It < F *hautbois* = *haut* high + *bois* wood]

o·bo·ist (ō′bō ist), *n.* a player of the oboe.

ob·ol (ob′əl), *n.* **1.** a silver coin of ancient Greece, the sixth part of a drachma. **2.** obole. [see OBOLUS]

ob·ole (ob′ōl), *n.* a silver-alloy coin of France issued during the Middle Ages, the 24th part of a sol, or one-half denier. Also, **obol, obolus.** [< F < L *obol(us)* OBOLUS]

ob·o·lus (ob′ə ləs), *n., pl.* **-li** (-lī′). **1.** a modern Greek unit of weight equal to 0.1 gram. **2.** obole. [< L < Gk *obolós* small coin, weight]

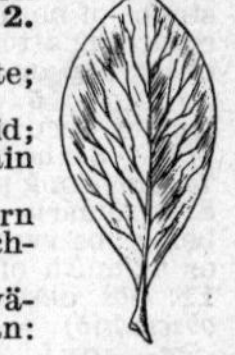

Obovate leaf

ob·o·vate (ob ō′vāt), *adj.* inversely ovate; ovate with the narrow end at the base.

ob·o·void (ob ō′void), *adj.* inversely ovoid; ovoid with the narrow end at the base, as certain fruits.

O'Boyle (ō boil′), *n.* **Patrick Aloysius,** born 1896, U.S. Roman Catholic clergyman: archbishop of Washington, D.C., since 1947.

O·bre·gón (ō′vre gôn′), *n.* **Al·va·ro** (äl′vä-rō), 1880–1928, Mexican general and statesman: president 1920–24.

OBrit, Old British.

obs., 1. observation. **2.** observatory. **3.** obsolete. Also, **Obs.**

ob·scene (əb sēn′), *adj.* **1.** offensive to modesty or decency; indecent; lewd. **2.** causing or intended to cause sexual excitement or lust. **3.** abominable or disgusting; repulsive: *an obscene exhibition of public discourtesy.* [< L *obscēn(us),* *obscaen(us),* prob. akin to *caenum, cēnum* dirt, filth] —**ob·scene′ly,** *adv.* —**ob·scene′ness,** *n.*

ob·scen·i·ty (əb sen′i tē, -sē′ni-), *n., pl.* **-ties** for 2, 3. **1.** the character or quality of being obscene; indecency. **2.** something obscene. **3.** an obscene word or expression, esp. when used as an invective. [< F *obscenité* < L *obscenitāt-* (s. of *obscenitās*)]

ob·scu·rant (əb skyŏŏr′ənt), *n.* **1.** a person who strives to prevent the increase and spread of knowledge. **2.** a person who obscures meaning. —*adj.* **3.** pertaining to or characteristic of obscurants. [< L *obscūrant-* (s. of *obscūrāns,* prp. of *obscūrāre*) = *obscūr(us)* dark + *-ant-* -ANT]

ob·scu·rant·ism (əb skyŏŏr′ən tiz′əm, ob′skyŏŏ ran′tiz-əm), *n.* **1.** opposition to the increase and spread of knowledge. **2.** deliberate obscurity or evasion of clarity. [< F *obscurantisme*] —**ob·scu′rant·ist,** *n., adj.*

ob·scu·ra·tion (ob′skyŏŏ rā′shən), *n.* **1.** the act of obscuring. **2.** the state of being obscured. [< L *obscūrātiōn-* (s. of *obscūrātiō*) a darkening = *obscūrāt(us),* ptp. of *obscūrāre,* (*obscūr(us)* dark + *-ātus* -ATE¹) + *-iōn-;* see -ATION]

ob·scure (əb skyŏŏr′), *adj.,* **-scur·er, -scur·est,** *v.,* **-scured, -scur·ing,** *n.* —*adj.* **1.** (of meaning) not clear or plain; uncertain. **2.** (of language, style, a speaker, etc.) not expressing the meaning clearly or plainly. **3.** inconspicuous or unnoticeable. **4.** of little or no prominence. **5.** far from worldly affairs; remote: *an obscure little town.* **6.** indistinct to the sight or any other sense; faint. **7.** (of a vowel) having the reduced or neutral sound usually represented by the schwa (ə). **8.** lacking in light or illumination; dark; dim; murky: *an obscure back room.* **9.** enveloped in or concealed by darkness. **10.** dull or darkish, as color or appearance. **11.** not clear to the understanding. —*v.t.* **12.** to conceal physically; hide or cover. **13.** to make confusing or oblique, as the meaning of a statement. **14.** to make dark, dim, indistinct, etc. **15.** to reduce (a vowel) to the sound usually represented by a schwa (ə). —*n.* **16.** *Rare.* obscurity. [ME < OF *oscur, obscur* < L *obscūr(us)* dark] —**ob·scur·ed·ly** (əb skyŏŏr′-id lē), **ob·scure′ly,** *adv.* —**ob·scure′ness,** *n.* —**Syn. 1.** doubtful, vague, ambiguous. **4.** undistinguished, unknown. **5.** inconspicuous, unnoticed. **6.** blurred, veiled. **8.** cloudy, dusky, somber. See **dark.** —**Ant. 1.** certain. **6.** clear. **8.** bright.

ob·scu·ri·ty (əb skyŏŏr′i tē), *n., pl.* **-ties** for 2. **1.** the state or quality of being obscure. **2.** a person or thing that is obscure. [< MF *obscurite* < L *obscūritāt-* (s. of *obscūritās*)]

ob·se·crate (ob′sə krāt′), *v.t.,* **-crat·ed, -crat·ing.** to entreat solemnly; beseech; supplicate. [< L *obsecrāt(us)* supplicated (ptp. of *obsecrāre*) = *ob-* OB- + *secr-* sacred (var. of *sacr-,* s. of *sacer*) + *-ātus* -ATE¹] —**ob′se·cra′tion,** *n.*

ob·se·quence (ob′sə kwəns), *n.* willingness or eagerness to serve, comply, please, etc.; the state of being obsequious. Also, **ob·se·que·ence** (ob sē′kwē əns). [< L *obsequentia* = *obsequent-* (s. of *obsequēns*) obsequious, prp. of *obsequī* to comply (*ob-* OB- + *sequī* to follow) + *-ia* -IA; see -ENCE]

ob·se·qui·ous (əb sē′kwē əs), *adj.* **1.** servilely compliant or deferential. **2.** characterized by or showing servile complaisance or deference: *an obsequious bow.* **3.** *Archaic.* obedient; dutiful. [< L *obsequiōs(us)* = *obsequi(um)* compliance (< *obsequī;* see OBSEQUENCE) + *-ōsus* -OUS] —**ob·se′qui·ous·ly,** *adv.* —**ob·se′qui·ous·ness,** *n.* —**Syn. 1.** cringing, submissive. See **servile. 2.** fawning, sycophantic, flattering.

ob·se·quy (ob′sə kwē), *n., pl.* **-quies.** Usually, **obsequies.** a funeral rite or ceremony. [ME *obseque* < MF < LL *obsequi(ae)* alter. (by confusion with *exsequiae* funeral rites) of *obsequia,* pl. of L *obsequium;* see OBSEQUIOUS]

ob·serv·a·ble (əb zûr′və bəl), *adj.* **1.** capable of being observed; noticeable; visible; discernible. **2.** worthy of being celebrated, followed, or observed: *an observable holiday.* **3.** deserving of attention; noteworthy. [< L *observābil(is)* remarkable] —**ob·serv′a·bil′i·ty, ob·serv′a·ble·ness,** *n.* —**ob·serv′a·bly,** *adv.*

ob·serv·ance (əb zûr′vəns), *n.* **1.** the act or an instance of following, obeying, or conforming to: *the observance of traffic laws.* **2.** a keeping or celebration by appropriate procedure, ceremonies, etc. **3.** a procedure, ceremony, or rite, as for a particular occasion: *patriotic observances.* **4.** a rule or custom to be followed or obeyed; a customary practice. **5.** *Rom. Cath. Ch.* a rule or discipline for a religious house or order. **6.** the act or an instance of watching, noting, or perceiving; observation. [ME *observaunce* < OF < LL *observantia,* L: esteem, attention < *observant-* (s. of *observāns*), prp. of *observāre.* See OBSERVE, -ANCE]

ob·serv·ant (əb zûr′vənt), *adj.* **1.** observing or regarding attentively; watchful. **2.** quick to notice or perceive; alert. **3.** careful in the observing of a law, custom, religious ritual, or the like. —*n.* **4.** an observer of law or rule. **5.** (*cap.*) Also, **Ob·ser·van·tine** (ob zûr′vən tin, -tēn′). a member of a Franciscan order observing the strict rule of St. Francis. [< F, prp. of *observer*] —**ob·serv′ant·ly,** *adv.* —**Syn. 1.** heedful, aware. **2.** perceptive. **3.** obedient. —**Ant. 1.** heedless. **2.** dull, slow.

ob·ser·va·tion (ob′zûr vā′shən), *n.* **1.** the act or an instance of noticing or perceiving. **2.** the act or an instance of regarding attentively or watching. **3.** the faculty or habit of observing or noticing. **4.** notice: *to escape a person's observation.* **5.** the act or an instance of viewing or noting a fact or occurrence for some scientific or other special purpose. **6.** the information or record obtained by such an act. **7.** something that is learned in the course of observing things. **8.** a remark, comment, or statement. **9.** the condition of being observed. **10.** *Navig.* the measurement of the altitude or azimuth of a heavenly body for navigational purposes. **11.** *Obs.* observance, as of the law. [< L *observātiōn-* (s. of *observātiō*) = *observāt(us)* (ptp. of *observāre* OBSERVE) + *-iōn-* -ION] —**ob′ser·va′tion·al,** *adj.* —**ob′ser·va′tion·al·ly,** *adv.* —**Syn. 3.** attention. **8.** pronouncement. See **remark.**

observa′tion car′, a railroad passenger car, usually at the end of a train, having a platform or lounge from which the scenery may be observed.

observa′tion post′, *Mil.* a forward position, usually on high ground, from which enemy activity can be observed and, particularly, from which artillery or mortar fire can be directed.

ob·serv·a·to·ry (əb zûr′və tōr′ē, -tôr′ē), *n., pl.* **-ries. 1.** a place or building equipped and used for making observations of astronomical or other natural phenomena, esp. a domed structure equipped with a powerful telescope for observing the planets and stars. **2.** an institution that controls or carries on the work of such a place. **3.** a place or structure for affording an extensive view; lookout. [< L *observāt(us)* (see OBSERVATION) + -ORY[2]]

ob·serve (əb zûrv′), *v.,* **-served, -serv·ing.** —*v.t.* **1.** to see, watch, perceive, or notice. **2.** to regard with attention so as to see or learn something, esp. for a scientific or official purpose: *to observe an eclipse.* **3.** to state by way of comment; remark. **4.** to keep or maintain in one's action, conduct, etc.: *You must observe quiet.* **5.** to obey, comply with, or conform to, as a law. **6.** to show regard for by some appropriate procedure, ceremonies, etc.: *to observe a holiday.* —*v.i.* **7.** to notice. **8.** to act as an observer. **9.** to remark or comment. [ME *observe(n)* < MF *observe(r)* < L *observāre* to watch, regard, attend to = *ob-* OB- + *servāre* to keep, save, pay heed to] —**ob·serv′ing·ly,** *adv.*
—**Syn. 1.** discover, detect. **2.** note. OBSERVE, WITNESS imply paying strict attention to what one sees or perceives. To OBSERVE is to mark or be attentive to something seen, heard, etc.; to consider carefully; to watch steadily: *to observe the behavior of birds, to observe a person's pronunciation.* To WITNESS, formerly to be present when something was happening, has added the idea of having observed with sufficient care to be able to give an account as evidence: *to witness an accident.* **5.** follow, fulfill. **6.** celebrate, keep. —**Ant. 1, 2, 5, 6.** ignore.

ob·serv·er (əb zûr′vər), *n.* **1.** a person or thing that observes. **2.** a person who maintains observation in an aircraft during flight. **3.** Also called **air observer.** *U.S. Army.* a person who serves in an aircraft as a reconnoiterer and directs artillery fire. **4.** a delegate to an assembly who observes and reports but does not participate officially in its activities.

ob·sess (əb ses′), *v.t.* to dominate or preoccupy the thoughts or feelings of (a person); beset, trouble, or haunt persistently or abnormally: *Suspicion obsessed him.* [< L *obsess(us),* ptp. of *obsidēre* to besiege] —**ob·sess′ing·ly,** *adv.* —**ob·ses′sor,** *n.*

ob·ses·sion (əb sesh′ən), *n.* **1.** the domination of one's thoughts or feelings by a persistent idea, image, desire, etc. **2.** the idea, image, etc., itself. **3.** the state of being obsessed. **4.** the act of obsessing. [< L *obsessiōn-* (s. of *obsessiō*) blockade, siege = *obsess(us)* (see OBSESS) + *-iōn-* -ION] —**ob·ses′sion·al,** *adj.*

ob·ses·sive (əb ses′iv), *adj.* **1.** being, pertaining to, or resembling an obsession: *obsessive fears.* **2.** causing an obsession. [OBSESS(ION) + -IVE]

ob·sid·i·an (əb sid′ē ən), *n.* a volcanic glass similar in composition to granite, usually dark but transparent in thin pieces and having a good conchoidal fracture. [< L *Obsidiān(us),* prop. *Obsiānus* pertaining to *Obsius,* the discoverer (according to Pliny) of a similar mineral in Ethiopia; see -AN]

obsolesc., obsolescent.

ob·so·lesce (ob′sə les′), *v.i.,* **-lesced, -lesc·ing.** to be or become obsolete or obsolescent. [< L *obsolesc(ere)*]

ob·so·les·cence (ob′sə les′əns), *n.* the state, process, or condition of being or becoming obsolete. [OBSOLESC(ENT) + -ENCE]

ob·so·les·cent (ob′sə les′ənt), *adj.* **1.** becoming obsolete; passing out of use, as a word. **2.** *Biol.* gradually disappearing or imperfectly developed, as vestigial organs. [< L *obsolescent-* (s. of *obsolescēns,* prp. of *obsolescere* to grow old). See OBSOLETE, -ESCENT] —**ob′so·les′cent·ly,** *adv.*

ob·so·lete (ob′sə lēt′, ob′sə lēt′), *adj.* **1.** no longer in general use; fallen into disuse. **2.** of a discarded or outmoded type; out of date. **3.** (of a word or other linguistic unit) no longer in use, esp., out of use for at least a century. Cf. **archaic** (def. 2), **obsolescent** (def. 1). **4.** *Biol.* imperfectly developed or rudimentary in comparison with the corresponding character in other individuals, as of the opposite sex or of a related species. [< L *obsolēt(us)* worn out, ptp. of *obsolescere* (*obs-* toward + *ol-* age, c. OLD + *-esc(ere)* -ESCE)] —**ob′so·lete′ly,** *adv.* —**ob′so·lete′ness,** *n.*
—**Syn. 2.** antiquated, ancient, old. —**Ant. 1, 2.** new, modern.

ob·sta·cle (ob′stə kəl), *n.* something that stands in the way or obstructs progress. [ME < OF < L *obstācul(um)* = *ob-* OB- + *stā-* stand + *-culum* -CLE]
—**Syn.** OBSTACLE, OBSTRUCTION, HINDRANCE, IMPEDIMENT refer to that which interferes with or prevents action of progress. An OBSTACLE is something that stands in the way of progress: *Lack of imagination is an obstacle to one's advancement.* An OBSTRUCTION is something that more or less completely blocks a passage: *A blood clot is an obstruction to the circulation.* A HINDRANCE keeps back or delays by interfering: *Interruptions are a hindrance to one's work.* An IMPEDIMENT interferes with proper functioning: *an impediment in one's speech.*

ob′stacle course′, a military training area having obstacles, as hurdles, ditches, walls, etc., that must be surmounted or crossed in succession.

ob′stacle race′, a race in which the contestants are prevented in a specific way from covering the full course at top speed, as by having hurdles to jump or sacks enclosing the legs. —**ob′stacle rac′er.**

obstet., 1. obstetric. **2.** obstetrics.

ob·stet·ric (əb ste′trik), *adj.* of or pertaining to childbirth or obstetrics. Also, **ob·stet′ri·cal.** [< NL *obstetrīc(us)* pertaining to a midwife, alter. of L *obstetrīcius* < *obstetrix* = *ob-* OB- + *ste-* (var. s. of *stāre*) stand + *-trix* -TRIX] —**ob·stet′ri·cal·ly,** *adv.*

ob·ste·tri·cian (ob′sti trish′ən), *n.* a physician who specializes in obstetrics. [< L *obstetrīci(a)* midwifery (n. use of fem. of *obstetrīcius;* see OBSTETRIC) + -AN]

ob·stet·rics (əb ste′triks), *n.* (*construed as sing.*) the branch of medical science concerned with childbirth and caring for and treating women in or in connection with childbirth. [see OBSTETRIC, -ICS]

ob·sti·na·cy (ob′stə nə sē), *n., pl.* **-cies** for 2. **1.** the quality or state of being obstinate. **2.** an instance of being obstinate. [ME < ML *obstinātia* < L *obstinātus* OBSTINATE; see -CY]

ob·sti·nate (ob′stə nit), *adj.* **1.** adhering firmly or perversely to one's purpose, opinion, etc.; unyielding. **2.** characterized by such firm or perverse adherence: *obstinate advocacy of high tariffs.* **3.** not easily controlled, overcome, or remedied: *the obstinate growth of weeds; an obstinate cough.* [< L *obstināt(us)* determined (ptp. of *obstināre*) = *ob-* OB- + *stin-* (var. s. of *stāre*) stand + *-ātus* -ATE[1]] —**ob′sti·nate·ly,** *adv.* —**ob′sti·nate·ness,** *n.* —**Syn. 1.** See **stubborn.**

ob·strep·er·ous (əb strep′ər əs), *adj.* **1.** resisting control in a noisy and difficult manner; unruly. **2.** noisy, clamorous, or boisterous. [< L *obstreperus* clamorous, akin to *obstrepere* to make a noise at (*ob-* OB- + *strepere* to rattle); see -OUS] —**ob·strep′er·ous·ly,** *adv.* —**ob·strep′er·ous·ness,** *n.* —**Syn. 1.** uncontrolled. —**Ant. 1.** obedient. **2.** calm.

ob·struct (əb strukt′), *v.t.* **1.** to block or close up with an obstacle or obstacles, as a road. **2.** to interrupt, hinder, or oppose the passage, progress, course, etc., of. **3.** to block from sight. [< L *obstruct(us)* built against (ptp. of *obstruere*). See OB-, CONSTRUCT] —**ob·struct′er, ob·struc′tor,** *n.* —**ob·struct′ing·ly,** *adv.* —**ob·struc′tive,** *adj.* —**ob·struc′tive·ness, ob·struc·tiv·i·ty** (ob′struk tiv′i tē), *n.* —**Syn. 1.** stop, clog. **2.** impede; check. —**Ant. 2.** encourage, further.

ob·struc·tion (əb struk′shən), *n.* **1.** something that obstructs; obstacle or hindrance: *obstructions to navigation.* **2.** the act or an instance of obstructing. **3.** the deliberate delaying or preventing of business before a legislative body, as by parliamentary contrivances. **4.** the state of being obstructed. [< L *obstructiōn-* (s. of *obstructiō*) barrier] —**Syn. 1.** barrier, bar. See **obstacle.**

ob·struc·tion·ist (əb struk′shə nist), *n.* a person who deliberately delays or prevents progress, esp. of business before a legislative body. —**ob·struc′tion·ism,** *n.* —**ob·struc′tion·is′tic,** *adj.*

ob·stru·ent (ob′stro͞o ənt), *adj.* **1.** *Med.* (of a substance) producing an obstruction. **2.** *Phonet.* having the properties of a speech sound in which the breath is wholly or partly obstructed, as a fricative, affricate, or occlusive. Cf. **sonorant** (def. 2). —*n.* **3.** *Med.* a medicine that closes the natural passages of the body. **4.** *Phonet.* an obstruent speech sound. Cf. **sonorant** (def. 1). [< L *obstruent-* (s. of *obstruēns,* prp. of *obstruere* to OBSTRUCT); see -ENT]

ob·tain (əb tān′), *v.t.* **1.** to come into possession of; get or acquire; procure, as through an effort or by a request: *to obtain some information.* **2.** *Archaic.* to attain or reach. —*v.i.* **3.** to be prevalent, customary, or in vogue: *the morals that obtained in Rome.* **4.** *Archaic.* to succeed or win success. [ME *obtein(en)* < MF *obten(ir)* < L *obtinēre* to take hold of = *ob-* OB- + *-tinēre* (comb. form of *tenēre* to hold)] —**ob·tain′a·ble,** *adj.* —**ob·tain′er,** *n.* —**ob·tain′ment,** *n.* —**Syn. 1.** gain, achieve, earn, win, attain. See **get.** —**Ant. 1.** lose, forgo.

ob·tect (ob tekt′), *adj.* (of a pupa) having the antennae, legs, and wings glued to the surface of the body by a hardened secretion. Also, **ob·tect′ed.** [< L *obtect(us)* covered over (ptp. of *obtegere,* var. of *obtigere*) = *ob-* OB- + *teg-* cover (see THATCH, TOGA) + *-tus* ptp. suffix]

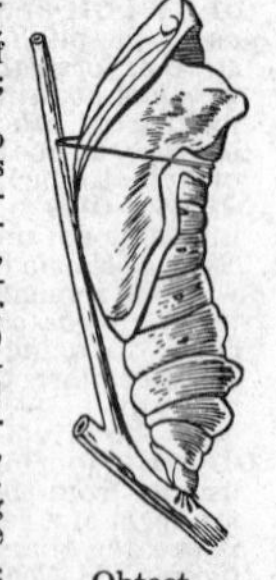
Obtect pupa of swallowtail, genus *Papilio*

ob·test (ob test′), *v.t.* **1.** to invoke as witness. **2.** to supplicate earnestly; beseech with fervor; beg. —*v.i.* **3.** to protest. [< L *obtest(ārī)* = *ob-* OB- + *test-* bear witness + *-ārī* inf. suffix] —**ob′tes·ta′tion,** *n.*

ob·trude (əb tro͞od′), *v.,* **-trud·ed, -trud·ing.** —*v.t.* **1.** to thrust (something) forward or upon a person, esp. without warrant or invitation. **2.** to thrust forth; push out. **—*v.i.*** **3.** to thrust oneself or itself forward, esp. unduly; intrude. [< L *obtrūde(re)* (to) thrust against = *ob-* OB- + *trūd-* THRUST + *-ere* inf. suffix] **—ob·trud′er,** *n.* **—ob·tru·sion** (əb tro͞o′zhən), *n.* **—Syn. 1.** impose, force. **3.** shove, push.

ob·tru·sive (əb tro͞o′siv), *adj.* **1.** tending to obtrude. **2.** (of a thing) obtruding itself: *an obtrusive error.* **3.** protruding. [< L *obtrūs(us)* thrust against (ptp. of *obtrūdere;* see OBTRUDE) + -IVE] **—ob·tru′sive·ly,** *adv.* **—ob·tru′sive·ness,** *n.* **—Syn. 2.** blatant.

ob·tu·rate (ob′tə rāt′, -tyə-), *v.t.,* **-rat·ed, -rat·ing.** to stop up; close. [< L *obtūrāt(us)* stopped up (ptp. of *obtūrāre*) = *ob-* OB- + *tūr-* stop + *-ātus* -ATE[1]] **—ob′tu·ra′tion,** *n.* **—ob′tu·ra′tor,** *n.*

ob·tuse (əb to͞os′, -tyo͞os′), *adj.* **1.** not sharp, acute, or pointed; blunt in form. **2.** (of a leaf, petal, etc.) rounded at the extremity. **3.** dull in perception, feeling, or intellect. **4.** indistinctly felt or perceived, as pain, sound, etc. [< L *obtūs(us)* dulled (ptp. of *obtundere*) = *ob-* OB- + *tū(d)-* beat + *-sus* ptp. suffix] **—ob·tuse′ly,** *adv.* **—ob·tuse′ness,** *n.* **—Syn. 3.** tactless, insensitive; imperceptive, unobservant.

obtuse′ an′gle, an angle greater than 90° but less than 180°. See diag. at **angle.** **—ob·tuse′-an′gled, ob·tuse′-an′gu·lar,** *adj.*

obtuse′ tri′angle, *Geom.* a triangle with one obtuse angle. See diag. at **triangle.**

OBulg, Old Bulgarian. Also, **OBulg.**

ob·verse (*n.* ob′vûrs; *adj.* ob vûrs′, ob′vûrs), *n.* **1.** the side of a coin, medal, etc., that bears the principal design (opposed to *reverse*). **2.** the front or principal surface of anything. **3.** a counterpart. **4.** *Logic.* a proposition obtained from another by obversion. **—*adj.*** **5.** turned toward or facing the observer. **6.** corresponding to something else as a counterpart. **7.** having the base narrower than the top, as a leaf. [< L *obvers(us)* turned toward, against (ptp. of *obvertere*) = *ob-* OB- + *ver(t)-* turn + *-sus* ptp. suffix]

ob·ver·sion (ob vûr′zhən, -shən), *n.* **1.** the act or an instance of obverting. **2.** the state of being obverted. **3.** something that is obverted. **4.** *Logic.* a form of inference in which a negative proposition is obtained from an affirmative or vice versa, as "No men are immortal" is obtained by obversion from "All men are mortal." [< LL *obversiōn-* (s. of *obversiō*) a turning toward]

ob·vert (ob vûrt′), *v.t.* **1.** to turn (something) so as to show a different surface. **2.** *Logic.* to change (a proposition) by obversion. [< L *obvert(ere)* (to) turn toward = *ob-* OB- + *vertere* to turn]

ob·vi·ate (ob′vē āt′), *v.t.,* **-at·ed, -at·ing.** to prevent or eliminate (difficulties, disadvantages, etc.) by effective measures; render unnecessary. [< L *obviāt(us)* prevented, opposed (ptp. of *obviāre*) = *ob-* OB- + *vi(am)* the way + *-ātus* -ATE[1]] **—ob·vi·a·ble** (ob′vē ə bəl), *adj.* **—ob′vi·a′tion,** *n.* **—ob′vi·a′tor,** *n.* **—Syn.** preclude, avert.

ob·vi·ous (ob′vē əs), *adj.* **1.** easily seen, recognized, or understood; open to view or knowledge: *an obvious advantage.* **2.** lacking in subtlety: *a play with rather obvious characterizations.* **3.** *Obs.* being or standing in the way. [< L *obvius* in the way, meeting = *ob-* OB- + *vi(a)* way + *-us* -OUS] **—ob′vi·ous·ly,** *adv.* **—ob′vi·ous·ness,** *n.* **—Syn. 1.** evident, clear, unmistakable. See **apparent.** **—Ant. 1.** hidden.

ob·vo·lute (ob′və lo͞ot′), *adj.* rolled or turned in. [< L *obvolut(us)* wrapped up (ptp. of *obvolvere*) = *ob-* OB- + *vol-* roll + *-ū-* v. suffix + *-tus* ptp. suffix; see VOLUTE]

oc-, var. of **ob-** (by assimilation) before *c: occident.*

Oc., ocean. Also, **oc.**

o.c., in the work cited. [< L *opere citāto*]

oc·a·ri·na (ok′ə rē′nə), *n.* a simple musical wind instrument shaped somewhat like an elongated egg and having a mouthpiece and finger holes. Also called, *Informal,* **sweet potato.** [< It, dim. of *oca* goose < LL **avica* = *auc(a)* (L *avis* bird) + *-ica* dim. suffix]

O'Ca·sey (ō kā′sē), *n.* **Sean** (shôn, shän), 1880–1964, Irish playwright.

Oc·cam (ok′əm), *n.* **William of,** died 1349?, English scholastic philosopher. Also, **Ockham.**

Ocarina

Oc′cam's ra′zor, the maxim that assumptions introduced to explain a thing must not be multiplied beyond necessity. Also, **Ockham's razor.** [after William of OCCAM]

occas., **1.** occasional. **2.** occasionally.

oc·ca·sion (ə kā′zhən), *n.* **1.** a particular time, esp. as marked by certain circumstances or occurrences: *They met on three occasions.* **2.** a special or important time, event, ceremony, celebration, etc.: *His birthday will be quite an occasion.* **3.** a convenient or favorable time or juncture; opportunity. **4.** the ground, reason, or incidental cause of some action or result. **5. occasions,** *Obs.* **a.** needs or necessities. **b.** necessary business matters. **6. on occasion,** now and then; occasionally. **—*v.t.*** **7.** to cause or bring about. [ME *occasioun* < OF *occasion* < L *occāsiōn-* (s. of *occāsiō*) = *oc-* OC- + *cās(us)* (ptp. of *cadere* to fall) + *-iōn-* -ION] **—Syn. 3.** chance, opening. **4.** motive, inducement. See **cause.** **7.** motivate, originate, create.

oc·ca·sion·al (ə kā′zhə nəl), *adj.* **1.** occurring or appearing at irregular or infrequent intervals: *an occasional publication.* **2.** intended for supplementary use when necessary: *an occasional chair.* **3.** pertaining to, arising out of, or intended for the occasion: *occasional verses.* **4.** acting or serving for the occasion or on particular occasions: *an occasional servant.* **5.** serving as the occasion or incidental cause.

oc·ca·sion·al·ism (ə kā′zhə nəliz′əm), *n.* *Philos.* a theory that there is no natural interaction between mind and matter, but that God makes mental events correspond to physical perceptions and actions. **—oc·ca′sion·al·is′tic,** *adj.*

oc·ca·sion·al·ly (ə kā′zhə nəlē), *adv.* at times; now and then: *He enjoys playing the piano occasionally.*

Oc·ci·dent (ok′si dənt), *n.* **1. the Occident, a.** the West; the countries of Europe and America. **b.** See **Western Hemisphere.** **2.** (*l.c.*) the west; the western regions. [ME < MF < L *occident-* (s. of *occidēns,* prp. of *occidere* to set) = *oc-* OC- + *cid-* fall (comb. form of *cadere*) + *-ent-* -ENT]

Oc·ci·den·tal (ok′si den′təl), (*sometimes l.c.*) **—*adj.*** **1.** of, pertaining to, or characteristic of the Occident or its natives and inhabitants; Western. **—*n.*** **2.** a native or inhabitant of the Occident. [ME < L *occidentāl(is)* western] **—oc·ci·den·tal·i·ty** (ok′si den tal′i tē), *n.* **—oc′ci·den′tal·ly,** *adv.*

Oc·ci·den·tal·ise (ok′si den′təlīz′), *v.t.,* **-ised, -is·ing.** *Chiefly Brit.* Occidentalize. **—Oc′ci·den′tal·i·sa′tion,** *n.*

Oc·ci·den·tal·ism (ok′si den′təliz′əm), *n.* Occidental character or characteristics. **—Oc′ci·den′tal·ist,** *n., adj.*

Oc·ci·den·tal·ize (ok′si den′təlīz′), *v.t.,* **-ized, -iz·ing.** to make Occidental. Also, *esp. Brit.,* **Occidentalise.** **—Oc′ci·den′tal·i·za′tion,** *n.*

oc·cip·i·tal (ok sip′i təl), *Anat.* **—*adj.*** **1.** of, pertaining to, or situated near the occiput or the occipital bone. **—*n.*** **2.** any of several parts of the occiput, esp. the occipital bone. [< ML *occipitāl(is)* = L *occipit-* (s. of *occiput*) OCCIPUT + *-ālis* -AL[1]] **—oc·cip′i·tal·ly,** *adv.*

occip′ital bone′, *Anat.* a curved, compound bone forming the back and part of the base of the skull.

occipito-, a combining form of "occiput." [< NL, comb. form of L *occipit-* (s. of *occiput*) + *-o-* -O-]

oc·ci·put (ok′sə put′, -pət), *n., pl.* **oc·ci·puts, oc·cip·i·ta** (ok sip′i tə). *Anat.* the back part of the head or skull. [< L = *oc-* OC- + *-ciput,* comb. form of *caput* head]

oc·clude (ə klo͞od′), *v.,* **-clud·ed, -clud·ing.** **—*v.t.*** **1.** to close, shut, or stop up (a passage, opening, etc.). **2.** to shut in, out, or off. **3.** *Physical Chem.* (of certain metals and other solids) to incorporate (gases and other foreign substances), as by absorption or adsorption. **—*v.i.*** **4.** *Dentistry.* to meet with the cusps of the opposing teeth of the upper and lower jaws fitting together. **5.** *Meteorol.* to form an occluded front. [< L *occlūd(ere)* (to) shut up, close up = *oc-* OC- + *clūd-* shut (var. of *claud-*)] **—oc·clud′ent,** *adj.*

occlud′ed front′, *Meteorol.* a composite front formed when a cold front overtakes a warm front and forces it aloft. Also called **occlusion.**

oc·clu·sion (ə klo͞o′zhən), *n.* **1.** the act or state of occluding. **2.** the state of being occluded. **3.** *Phonet.* momentary complete closure at some area in the vocal tract, causing stoppage of the breath stream and accumulation of pressure. **4.** *Meteorol.* See **occluded front.** [prob. < NL **occlūsiōn-* (s. of **occlūsiō*) = *occlūs(us)* (ptp. of *occlūdere* to OCCLUDE) + *-iōn-* -ION] **—oc·clu·sal** (ə klo͞o′səl), *adj.*

oc·clu·sive (ə klo͞o′siv), *adj.* **1.** occluding or tending to occlude. **2.** *Phonet.* characterized by or having occlusion. **—*n.*** **3.** *Phonet.* a stop that is unreleased, as the *p*-sound in *stop,* or deviously released, as the *k*-sound in *acme.* [< L *occlus(us)* (see OCCLUSION) + -IVE] **—oc·clu′sive·ness,** *n.*

oc·cult (ə kult′, ok′ult), *adj.* **1.** beyond the range of ordinary knowledge; mysterious. **2.** secret; disclosed or communicated only to the initiated. **3.** of or pertaining to magic, astrology, and other alleged sciences claiming use or knowledge of secret, mysterious, or supernatural agencies. **4.** hidden from view. **—*n.*** **5.** occult studies or sciences (usually prec. by *the*). **6.** the supernatural or supernatural agencies and affairs considered as a whole (usually prec. by *the*). **—*v.t.*** **7.** to block or shut off (an object) from view; hide. **8.** *Astron.* to hide (a body) by occultation. **—*v.i.*** **9.** to become hidden or shut off from view. [< L *occult(us)* covered over, concealed (ptp. of *occulere*) = *oc-* OC- + *cul-* hide (var. of *cel-*) + *-tus* ptp. suffix] **—oc·cult′er,** *n.* **—oc·cult′ly,** *adv.* **—oc·cult′ness,** *n.* **—Syn. 1.** metaphysical, supernatural. **2.** concealed, unrevealed; veiled, shrouded; mystical, cabalistic.

oc·cul·ta·tion (ok′ul tā′shən), *n.* **1.** *Astron.* the passage of one celestial body in front of a second, thus hiding the second from view: applied esp. to the moon's coming between an observer and a star or planet. **2.** disappearance from view or notice. **3.** the act of blocking or hiding from view. **4.** the resulting hidden or concealed state. [ME < L *occultātiōn-* (s. of *occultātiō*) a hiding = *occultāt(us)* hidden, ptp. of *occultāre* (*oc-* OC- + *cult-* hide + *-ātus* -ATE[1]) + *-iōn-* -ION]

oc·cult·ism (ə kul′tiz əm), *n.* belief in the existence of certain secret, mysterious, or supernatural agencies with which human beings can communicate. **—oc·cult′ist,** *n., adj.*

oc·cu·pan·cy (ok′yə pən sē), *n., pl.* **-cies.** **1.** the act, state, or condition of being or becoming a tenant or of living in or taking up quarters or space in or on something. **2.** the possession or tenancy of a property. **3.** the act of taking possession, as of a property. **4.** the term during which a person is an occupant. **5.** the use to which property is put. **6.** exercise of dominion over unowned property so as to become the legal owner.

oc·cu·pant (ok′yə pənt), *n.* **1.** a person who or family, group, or organization that lives in, occupies, or has quarters or space in or on something: *the occupants of a taxicab.* **2.** a tenant of a house, estate, office, etc. **3.** *Law.* an owner through occupancy. [< MF *occupant,* prp. of *occuper*]

oc·cu·pa·tion (ok′yə pā′shən), *n.* **1.** a person's usual or principal work or business. **2.** any activity in which a person is engaged. **3.** possession, settlement, or use of land or property. **4** the act of occupying. **5.** the state of being occupied. **6.** tenure of an office or official function. **7.** the seizure and control of an area, esp. a foreign territory, by military forces. **8.** the term of control of a territory by foreign military forces. [ME *occupacioun* < MF *occupation* < L *occupātiōn-* (s. of *occupātiō*) = *occupāt(us)* occupied (ptp. of *occupāre;* see OCCUPY) + *-iōn-* -ION]

—Syn. 1. vocation, employment. OCCUPATION, BUSINESS, PROFESSION, TRADE refer to the activity to which a person regularly devotes himself, esp. his regular work, or means of getting a living. OCCUPATION is the general word: *a pleasant occupation.* BUSINESS esp. suggests a commercial or mercantile occupation: *the printing business.* PROFESSION implies an occupation requiring special knowledge and training in some field of science or learning: *the profession of teaching.*

TRADE suggests an occupation involving manual training and skill: *one of the building trades.* **3.** occupancy.

oc·cu·pa·tion·al (ok′yə pā′shə nᵊl), *adj.* **1.** of or pertaining to occupation: *occupational risks.* **2.** of or pertaining to an occupation, trade, or calling: *occupational guidance.* —**oc′cu·pa′tion·al·ly,** *adv.*

occupa′tional disease′, a disease caused by the conditions or hazards of a particular occupation.

oc′cupa′tional haz′ard, a danger to workers that is inherent in a particular occupation.

oc′cupa′tional ther′apy, *Med.* therapy consisting of light work that provides mental diversion for the patient and frequently serves to exercise an affected part of the body or to give vocational training.

oc·cu·py (ok′yə pī′), *v.*, **-pied, -py·ing.** —*v.t.* **1.** to take or fill up (space, time, etc.). **2.** to engage or employ (the mind, one's attention, etc.). **3.** to take possession and control of (a place), as by military invasion. **4.** to hold (a position, office, etc.). **5.** to be a resident or tenant of; dwell in. —*v.i.* **6.** *Obs.* to take or hold possession. [ME *occupie(n)* < MF *occup(er)* < L *occupāre* to seize] —**oc′cu·pi′a·ble,** *adj.* —**oc′cupi′er,** *n.* —**Syn. 1-4.** See **have.**

oc·cur (ə kûr′), *v.i.*, **-curred, -cur·ring.** **1.** to happen; come to pass. **2.** to be met with or found; present itself; appear. **3.** to suggest itself in thought (usually fol. by *to*): *An idea occurred to me.* [< L *occurr(ere)* (to) run to]

oc·cur·rence (ə kûr′əns, ə kur′-), *n.* **1.** the action or fact of occurring. **2.** something that happens, esp. unexpectedly; event; incident. [prob. OCCURR(ENT) + -ENCE] —**oc·cur′rent,** *adj.* —**Syn. 2.** circumstance. See **event.**

OCD, Office of Civil Defense.

OCDM, Office of Civil and Defense Mobilization.

o·cean (ō′shən), *n.* **1.** the vast body of salt water that covers almost three fourths of the earth's surface. **2.** any of the geographical divisions of this body, commonly given as the Atlantic, Pacific, Indian, Arctic, and Antarctic oceans. **3.** a vast expanse or quantity. [ME < L *ōcean(us)* ocean < Gk *Ōkeanós* OCEANUS] —**o′cean·like′,** *adj.*

o·cea·naut (ō′shə nôt′, -not′), *n.* aquanaut (def. 1). [OCEA(N) + (AERO)NAUT]

o·cean·front (ō′shən frunt′), *n.* **1.** the land along the shore of an ocean in a particular place, as a resort town. —*adj.* **2.** located on such land: *an oceanfront hotel.*

o·cean-go·ing (ō′shən gō′ing), *adj.* **1.** (of a vessel) designed and equipped to go on the open sea. **2.** noting or pertaining to sea transportation: *ocean-going traffic.*

O·ce·an·i·a (ō′shē an′ē ə, -ä′nē ə), *n.* the islands of the central and S Pacific, including Micronesia, Melanesia, Polynesia, and sometimes Australasia and the Malay Archipelago. Also, **O·ce·an·i·ca** (ō′shē an′ə kə). —**O′ce·an′i·an,** *adj., n.*

o·ce·an·ic (ō′shē an′ik), *adj.* **1.** of, living in, belonging to, or produced by the ocean; pelagic. **2.** immensely large; vast. [< ML *ōceanic(us)*]

O·ce·a·nid (ō sē′ə nid), *n., pl.* **O·ce·a·nids, O·ce·an·i·des** (ō′sē an′i dēz′). *Class. Myth.* any of the daughters of Oceanus and Tethys; a sea nymph. [< Gk *Ōkeanid(es)* daughter(s) of Oceanus]

o′cean lin′er, a vessel for carrying a large number of passengers and a small amount of freight on ocean voyages.

O′cean of Storms′. See **Oceanus Procellarum.**

oceanog., oceanography.

o·ce·a·nog·ra·phy (ō′shē ə nog′rə fē, ō′shə nog′-), *n.* the body of science dealing with the ocean. —**o′ce·a·nog′ra·pher,** *n.* —**o·ce·a·no·graph·ic** (ō′shē ə nə graf′ik, ō′shə nə-), **o′ce·a·no·graph′i·cal,** *adj.*

o·cea·nol·o·gy (ō′shə nol′ə jē), *n.* oceanography. —**o·cea·no·log·i·cal** (ō′shə nə loj′i kəl), *adj.*

o′cean pout′, an eelpout, *Macrozoarces americanus,* found along the northeastern coast of North America.

O·cean·side (ō′shən sīd′), *n.* **1.** a town on SW Long Island, in SE New York. 35,372 (1970). **2.** a city in SW California. 40,494 (1970).

O·ce·a·nus (ō sē′ə nəs), *n.* *Class. Myth.* **1.** a Titan who was the son of Uranus and Gaea, the consort of Tethys, and the father of the river gods and Oceanids. **2.** a great stream of water encircling the earth and believed to be the source of all rivers, lakes, etc.

O·ce·a·nus Pro·cel·la·rum (ō′shē ä′nəs prō′se lär′əm, -an′əs), the largest dark plain on the face of the moon, in the second and third quadrants. ab. 2,000,000 sq. mi. Also called **Ocean of Storms.**

Ocellated marking on peacock feather

o·cel·lar (ō sel′ər), *adj.* pertaining to an ocellus.

oc·el·lat·ed (os′ə lā′tid, ō sel′ā tid), *adj.* **1.** (of a spot or marking) eyelike. **2.** having ocelli, or eyelike spots. Also, **oc·el·late** (os′ə lāt′, ō sel′it, -āt). [< L *ocellāt(us)* (*ocell(us)* OCELLUS + *-ātus* -ATE[1]) + -ED[3]]

oc·el·la·tion (os′ə lā′shən), *n.* an eyelike spot or marking.

o·cel·lus (ō sel′əs), *n., pl.* **o·cel·li** (ō sel′ī). **1.** a type of eye common to invertebrates, consisting of retinal cells, pigments, and nerve fibers. **2.** an eyelike spot, as on a peacock feather. [< L: little eye = *oc-* (s. of *oculus*) EYE + *-ellus* dim. suffix]

Ocelot (Total length about 4 ft.; tail 14 in.)

o·ce·lot (ō′sə lot′, os′ə-), *n.* a spotted, leopardlike cat, *Felis pardalis,* ranging from Texas through South America. [< F < Nahuatl *ocelotl* jaguar] —**o′ce·loid′,** *adj.*

o·cher (ō′kər), *n.* **1.** any of a class of natural earths, mixtures of hydrated oxide of iron with various earthy materials, ranging in color from pale yellow to orange and red, and used as pigments. **2.** a color ranging from pale yellow to reddish yellow. Also, **ochre.** [ME *oker* < OF *ocre* < L *ōchra* < Gk: yellow ocher] —**o′cher·ous, o′cher·y,** *adj.* —**o·chroid** (ō′kroid), *adj.*

och·loc·ra·cy (ok lok′rə sē), *n.* government by the mob; mob rule. [< Gk *ochlokratía* = *óchlo(s)* mob + *-kratia* -CRACY] —**och·lo·crat** (ok′lə krat′), *n.* —**och′lo·crat′ic, och′lo·crat′i·cal,** *adj.*

O·cho·a (ō chō′ə; *Sp.* ô chô′ä), *n.* **Se·ve·ro** (sə vâr′ō; *Sp.* se ve′rô), born 1905, U.S. biochemist, born in Spain: Nobel prize for medicine 1959.

o·chre (ō′kər), *n.* ocher. —**o·chre·ous** (ō′kər əs, ō′krē əs), **o·chrous** (ō′krəs), **o·chry** (ō′krē), *adj.*

och·re·a (ok′rē ə), *n., pl.* **-re·ae** (-rē ē′). ocrea.

Ochs (oks), *n.* **Adolph Simon,** 1858–1935, U.S. newspaper publisher.

-ock, a native English suffix of nouns, used to form descriptive names (*ruddock,* lit., the red one), diminutives (*hillock*), etc. [ME *-ok,* OE *-oc, -uc*]

Ock·ham (ok′əm), *n.* Occam.

o'clock (ə klok′), *adv.* **1.** of, by, or according to the clock (used in specifying the hour of the day): *It is now 1 o'clock.* **2.** according to a method for indicating relative position whereby a plane in space is considered to be numbered as a clock's face, with 12 o'clock considered as directly ahead or straight up: *Enemy aircraft were approaching at 6 o'clock.*

O'Con·nell (ō kon′ᵊl), *n.* **Daniel,** 1775–1847, Irish nationalist leader and orator.

O'Con·nor (ō kon′ər), *n.* **Sandra Day,** born 1930, U.S. jurist: associate justice of the U.S. Supreme Court since 1981; appointed by President Reagan.

o·co·til·lo (ō′kə tēl′yō; *Sp.* ô′kô tē′yô), *n., pl.* **-til·los** (-tēl′yōz; *Sp.* -tē′yôs). a spiny, woody shrub, *Fouquieria splendens,* of arid regions of Mexico and the southwestern U.S. [< MexSp, dim. of *ocote* kind of pine < Aztec *ocotl*]

OCR, *Computer Technol.* **1.** optical character reader. **2.** optical character recognition.

oc·re·a (ok′rē ə, ō′krē ə), *n., pl.* **oc·re·ae** (ok′rē ē′, ō′krē ē′). *Bot., Zool.* a sheathing part, as a pair of stipules united about a stem. Also, **ochrea.** [< L: greave, legging < Gk *ōkris* prominence, crag, c. *ākris* peak]

O, Ocrea

oc·re·ate (ok′rē it, -āt′, ō′krē-), *adj.* having an ocrea or ocreae; sheathed. [< L *ocreāt(us)* greaved = *ocre(a)* greave (see OCREA) + *-ātus* -ATE[1]]

OCS, **1.** officer candidate school. **2.** Old Church Slavonic.

oct-, var. of **octa-** or **octo-** before a vowel: *octad.*

Oct., October.

oct., octavo.

octa-, an element occurring in loan words from Greek and Latin, where it meant "eight" (*octagon; octameter*); on this model, used in the formation of compound words and in chemical terms specialized to mean "having eight atoms." Also, **oct-, octo-.** [< Gk *okta-,* comb. form of *oktṓ* EIGHT]

oc·tad (ok′tad), *n.* **1.** a group or series of eight. **2.** *Chem.* an element, atom, or group having a valence of eight. [< Gk *oktad-* (s. of *oktás*) group of eight = *okt-* OCT- + *-ad* -AD[1]] —**oc·tad′ic,** *adj.*

135°

Octagon (Regular)

oc·ta·gon (ok′tə gon′, -gən), *n.* a polygon having eight angles and eight sides. Also called **octangle.** [< L *octagōn(os)* eight-cornered (sp. var. of *octōgōnos*) < Gk *oktágōnos* octangular = *okta-* OCTA- + *gōn(ía)* angle; see -GON]

oc·tag·o·nal (ok tag′ə nᵊl), *adj.* having eight angles and eight sides. [< NL *octōgōnāl(is)* = L *octōgōn(um)* OCTAGON + *-ālis* -AL[1]] —**oc·tag′o·nal·ly,** *adv.*

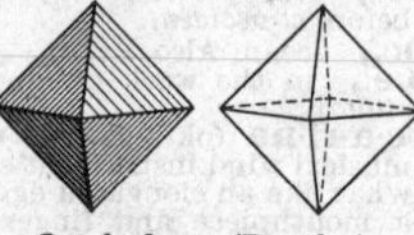

Octahedrons (Regular)

oc·ta·he·drite (ok′tə hē′drīt), *n.* anatase. [< LL *octahedr(os)* eight-sided < Gk *oktáedr(on)* (see OCTAHEDRON) + -ITE[1]]

oc·ta·he·dron (ok′tə hē′drən), *n., pl.* **-drons, -dra** (-drə). a solid figure having eight faces. [< Gk *oktáedron* eight-sided (neut. of *oktáedros*)] —**oc′ta·he′dral,** *adj.*

oc·tam·er·ous (ok tam′ər əs), *adj.* **1.** consisting of or divided into eight parts. **2.** *Bot.* (of flowers) having eight members in each whorl. [< Gk *oktamer(ḗs)* having eight parts + -OUS]

oc·tam·e·ter (ok tam′i tər), *Pros.* —*adj.* **1.** consisting of eight measures or feet. —*n.* **2.** an octameter verse. [< LL < Gk *oktámetr(os)*]

oc·tane (ok′tān), *n.* *Chem.* any of 18 isomeric saturated hydrocarbons having the formula C_8H_{18}, some of which are obtained in the distillation and cracking of petroleum.

oc′tane num′ber, (of gasoline) a designation of antiknock quality, numerically equal to the percentage of isooctane by volume in a mixture of isooctane and normal heptane that matches the given gasoline in antiknock characteristics. Also called **oc′tane rat′ing.**

oc·tan·gle (ok′tang gəl), *adj.* **1.** octangular. —*n.* **2.** octagon. [< LL *octangul(us)* eight-angled]

oc·tan·gu·lar (ok tang′gyə lər), *adj.* having eight angles. [< LL *octangul(us)* (see OCTANGLE) + -AR[1]] —**oc·tan′gu·lar·ness,** *n.*

oc·tant (ok′tənt), *n.* **1.** the eighth part of a circle. **2.** *Math.* any of the eight parts into which three mutually perpendicular planes divide space. **3.** an instrument having an arc of 24°, used by navigators for measuring angles up to 90°. **4.** the position of one heavenly body when 45° distant from another. [< L *octant-* (s. of *octāns*) = *oct-* OCT- + *-āns* (see -ANT)] —**oc·tan·tal** (ok tan′tᵊl), *adj.*

oc·tave (ok′tiv, -tāv), *n.* **1.** *Music.* **a.** a tone on the eighth degree from a given tone. **b.** the interval encompassed by such tones. **c.** the harmonic combination of such tones. **d.** a series of tones, or of keys of an instrument, extending through this interval. **2.** a pipe-organ stop whose pipes give tones an octave above the normal pitch of the keys used. **3.** Also called **octet.** *Pros.* **a.** a group of eight lines of verse, esp. the first eight lines of a sonnet in the Petrarchan form. Cf. **sestet** (def. 1). **b.** a stanza of eight lines. **4.** *Eccles.* **a.** the eighth day from a feast day, counting the feast day as the first. **b.** the period of eight days beginning with a feast day. **5.** one eighth of a pipe of wine or other liquid. **6.**

Fencing. the eighth of eight defensive positions. —*adj.* **7.** *Music.* pitched an octave higher. [< OF < L *octāva* eighth, fem. of *octāvus* = *oct-* OCT- + *-āvus* adj. suffix] —**oc·ta·val** (ok tā′vəl, ok′tə-), *adj.*

Oc·ta·vi·a (ok tā′vē ə), *n.* died 11 B.C., sister of Roman emperor Augustus and wife of Mark Antony.

Oc·ta·vi·an (ok tā′vē ən), *n.* Augustus.

oc·ta·vo (ok tā′vō, -tä′-), *n., pl.* **-vos** for 2, *adj.* —*n.* **1.** a book size of about 6 × 9 inches, determined by printing on sheets folded to form 8 leaves or 16 pages. *Abbr.:* 8vo, 8° **2.** a book of this size. —*adj.* **3.** in octavo. [short for NL *in octāvō* in an eighth (of a sheet)]

oc·tet (ok tet′), *n.* **1.** a company of eight singers or musicians. **2.** a musical composition for eight voices or instruments. **3.** *Pros.* octave (def. 3). **4.** any group of eight. Also, **oc·tette′.** [OCT- + *-et,* as in *duet*]

oc·til·lion (ok til′yən), *n., pl.* **-lions,** (*as after a numeral*) **-lion,** *adj.* —*n.* **1.** a cardinal number represented in the U.S. and France by a one followed by 27 zeros, and in Great Britain and Germany by a one followed by 48 zeros. —*adj.* **2.** amounting to one octillion in number. [< F = *oct-* OCT- + *-illion,* as in *million*] —**oc·til′lionth,** *n., adj.*

octo-, var. of **octa-:** *octosyllabic.*

Oc·to·ber (ok tō′bər), *n.* **1.** the tenth month of the year, containing 31 days. **2.** *Brit.* ale brewed in this month. [ME, OE < L: the eighth month of the early Roman year = *octō-* OCTO- + *-ber* adj. suffix]

Octo′ber Revolu′tion. See **Russian Revolution** (def. 2).

Oc·to·brist (ok tō′brist), *n.* **1.** a member of a Russian political party that advocated constitutional monarchism, organized after the Czar's manifesto in October, 1905. **2.** a member of a communist organization in the Soviet Union for children ranging in age from 8 to 10. [trans. of Russ *oktyabrist*]

oc·to·de·cil·lion (ok′tō di sil′yən), *n., pl.* **-lions,** (*as after a numeral*) **-lion,** *adj.* —*n.* **1.** a cardinal number represented in the U.S. and France by a one followed by 57 zeros, and in Great Britain and Germany by a one followed by 108 zeros. —*adj.* **2.** amounting to one octodecillion in number. [< L *octodec(im)* eighteen + *-illion,* as in *million*] —**oc′to·de·cil′lionth,** *adj., n.*

oc·to·dec·i·mo (ok′tə des′ə mō′), *n., pl.* **-mos** for 2, *adj.* —*n.* **1.** a book size of about 4 × 6¼ inches, determined by printing on sheets folded to form 18 leaves or 36 pages. *Abbr.:* 18mo, 18° **2.** a book of this size. —*adj.* **3.** in octodecimo. Also called **eighteenmo.** [short for NL *in octōdecimō* in an eighteenth (of a sheet)]

oc·to·ge·nar·i·an (ok′tə jə nâr′ē ən), *adj.* Also, **oc·tog·e·nar·y** (ok toj′ə ner′ē). **1.** of the age of 80 years. **2.** between 80 and 90 years old. —*n.* **3.** an octogenarian person. [< L *octōgēnāri(us)* belonging to eighty = *octōgēn(ī)* eighty each + *-ārius* -ARY + -AN]

oc·to·nar·y (ok′tə ner′ē), *adj., n., pl.* **-nar·ies.** —*adj.* **1.** pertaining to the number 8. **2.** consisting of eight. —*n.* **3.** a group of eight; ogdoad. **4.** *Pros.* a stanza of eight lines. [< L *octōnāri(us)* consisting of eight = *octō-* OCTO- + *-n-* connective + *-ārius* -ARY]

oc·to·pod (ok′tə pod′), *n.* any eight-armed cephalopod of the order or suborder *Octopoda,* including the octopuses and paper nautiluses. [< NL *Octopod(a)* < Gk *oktṓpoda* neut. pl. of *oktṓpous* eight-footed]

oc·to·pus (ok′tə pəs), *n., pl.* **-pus·es, -pi** (-pī′). **1.** any animal of the genus *Octopus,* having a soft, oval body and eight sucker-bearing arms, living mostly at the bottom of the sea. **2.** any octopod. **3.** something likened to an octopus, as an organization or person of far-reaching influence or control. [< NL < Gk *oktṓpous* eight-footed]

Octopus, *Octopus vulgaris* (Radial span about 10 ft.)

oc·to·roon (ok′tə ro͞on′), *n.* a person having one-eighth Negro ancestry; the offspring of a quadroon and a white. [OCTO- + *-roon,* modeled on *quadroon*]

oc·to·syl·lab·ic (ok′tō si lab′ik), *adj.* **1.** consisting of or pertaining to eight syllables. —*n.* **2.** an octosyllable. [< LL *octosyllab(us)* (< Gk *okta-* OCTO- + *-syllabos* syllabic) + -IC]

oc·to·syl·la·ble (ok′tə sil′ə bəl), *n.* a word or line of verse of eight syllables. [part trans. of L *octōsyllabus*]

oc·troi (ok′troi; *Fr.* ôk TRWA′), *n., pl.* **-trois** (-troiz; *Fr.* -TRWA′). (formerly esp. in France and Italy) a tax levied on certain articles on their entry into a city. [< F, back formation from *octroyer* to grant, OF *otreier* < ML *auctorizāre;* see AUTHORIZE]

oc·tu·ple (ok′to͝o pəl, -tyo͝o-; ok to͞o′pəl, -tyo͞o′-), *adj., v.,* **-pled, -pling.** —*adj.* **1.** eightfold; eight times as great. **2.** having eight effective units or elements. —*v.t.* **3.** to make eight times as great. [< L *octupl(us)* = *octō-* OCTO- + *-plus* -FOLD]

oc·tup·let (ok tup′lit, -to͞o′plit, -tyo͞o′-; ok′to͝o plit, -tyo͝o-), *n.* a group, series, or combination of eight items.

oc·tu·plex (ok′to͝o pleks′, -tyo͝o-, ok to͞o′pleks, -tyo͞o′-, -tup′leks), *adj.* eightfold; octuple. [< L *octu-* (as in *octuplus* OCTUPLE) + *-plex* -FOLD]

oc·tu·pli·cate (*n., adj.* ok to͞o′plə kit, -kāt′, -tyo͞o′-, -tup′lə-; *v.* ok to͞o′plə kāt′, -kit, -tyo͞o′-, -tup′lə-), *n., adj., v.,* **-cat·ed, -cat·ing.** —*n.* **1.** a group, series, or set of eight identical copies (usually prec. by *in*). —*adj.* **2.** having or consisting of eight identical parts; eightfold. **3.** noting the eighth copy or item. —*v.t.* **4.** to make eight copies of. **5.** to make eight times as great, as by multiplying. [< L *octuplicāt(us)* = *octupl(us)* OCTUPLE + *-ātus* -ATE[1], modeled after *quadruplus, quadruplicatus*]

ocul-, var. of **oculo-** before a vowel: *oculist.*

oc·u·lar (ok′yə lər), *adj.* **1.** of, for, or pertaining to the eye or eyes: *ocular movements.* **2.** of the nature of an eye: *an ocular organ.* **3.** performed or perceived by the eye or eyesight. —*n.* **4.** *Optics.* eyepiece. [< L *oculār(is)* = *ocul(us)* eye + *-āris* -AR[1]] —**oc′u·lar·ly,** *adv.*

oc·u·list (ok′yə list), *n.* **1.** an ophthalmologist. **2.** (loosely) an optometrist. [< F *oculiste*] —**oc′u·lis′tic,** *adj.*

oculo-, a learned borrowing from Latin meaning "eye," "ocular," used in the formation of compound words: *oculomotor.* Also, *esp. before a vowel,* **ocul-.** [comb. form of L *oculus* eye; see -O-]

oc·u·lo·mo·tor (ok′yə lō mō′tər), *adj.* moving the eyeball.

oculomo′tor nerve′, *Anat.* either one of the third pair of cranial nerves, consisting chiefly of motor fibers that innervate most of the muscles of the eyeball.

Od (od), *interj. Archaic.* (a euphemistic form of *God,* used as a mild oath.) Also, **'Od, Odd.**

OD, **1.** See **officer of the day.** **2.** Old Dutch. **3.** Ordnance Department. **4.** outside diameter.

OD (ō′dē′), *n., v.,* **OD'd, OD'ing.** *Slang.* —*n.* **1.** an overdose, esp. of a narcotic drug. —*v.i.* **2.** to take an overdose, esp. of a narcotic drug, to such an extent as to cause death. Also, **O.D.** [shortened form of OVERDOSE]

od, **1.** on demand. **2.** outside diameter. **3.** overdraft. **4.** overdrawn.

OD., Old Dutch.

O.D., **1.** Doctor of Optometry. **2.** (in prescriptions) the right eye. [< L *oculus dexter*] **3.** See **officer of the day.** **4.** Old Dutch. **5.** (of a military uniform) olive drab. **6.** See **ordinary seaman.** **7.** outside diameter. **8.** overdraft. **9.** overdrawn.

o.d., **1.** (in prescriptions) the right eye. [< L *oculus dexter*] **2.** olive drab. **3.** on demand. **4.** outside diameter.

o·da·lisque (ōd′ᵊlisk), *n.* a female slave or concubine in a harem, esp. in that of the Sultan of Turkey. Also, **o′da·lisk.** [< F, misspelling (with orig. mute *s*) of Turk *odalik* concubine = *oda* room + *-lik* n. suffix]

odd (od), *adj.* **1.** differing in nature from what is ordinary, usual, or expected. **2.** singular or peculiar in a freakish or eccentric way. **3.** close to, esp. more than, an amount that is specified (usually used in combination with a round number): *I owe 300-odd dollars.* **4.** being a small amount in addition to what is counted or specified: *I have five gross and a few odd dozens.* **5.** being part of a pair, set, or series of which the rest is lacking: *an odd glove.* **6.** left over after all others are used, consumed, etc. **7.** (of a pair) not matching. **8.** (of a number) leaving a remainder of 1 when divided by 2, as 3, 15, or 19 (opposed to *even*). **9.** not forming part of any particular group, set, or class: *to pick up odd bits of information.* **10.** (of a job, chore, or the like) not being part of a full-time assignment; occasional; incidental. —*n.* **11.** something that is odd. **12.** *Golf.* a stroke more than the opponent has played. [ME *odde* < Scand; cf. Icel *odda-tala* odd number] —**odd′ly,** *adv.* —**odd′ness,** *n.* —**Syn. 1.** extraordinary, unusual, rare, uncommon. See **strange.** —**Ant. 1.** ordinary, usual, common.

odd·ball (od′bôl′), *U.S. Slang.* —*n.* **1.** an eccentric or nonconformist. —*adj.* **2.** eccentric or atypical: *an oddball scheme.*

Odd′ Fel′low, a member of a large fraternal society, the Independent Order of Odd Fellows.

odd·i·ty (od′i tē), *n., pl.* **-ties** for 1, 3. **1.** an odd or remarkably unusual person, thing, or event. **2.** the quality of being odd; singularity, strangeness, or eccentricity. **3.** an odd characteristic; peculiarity.

odd′ job′ber, a person who works at brief, impermanent jobs that usually require little or no special skill.

odd′ lot′, **1.** a quantity or amount less than the conventional unit of trading. **2.** *Stock Exchange.* (in a transaction) a quantity of stock less than the established 100-share unit for active issues or the 10-share unit for designated inactive issues. —**odd′-lot′,** *adj.*

odd′ man′ out′, **1.** a method of selecting or isolating a person from a group, as by matching coins, esp. as a game or in preparation for playing a game. **2.** the person so selected or isolated.

odd·ment (od′mənt), *n.* an odd or extra article, bit, remnant, etc.; leftover.

odd-pin·nate (od′pin′āt, -it), *adj. Bot.* pinnate with an odd terminal leaflet.

odds (odz), *n.* (*usually construed as pl.*) **1.** the probability that something is so or will occur rather than something else: *The odds are that it will rain today.* **2.** the ratio of probability that something is so or will occur rather than something else: *The odds are two-to-one that it won't rain today.* **3.** the ratio of probability that a contestant will win or lose a contest, esp. as reflected in betting: *Track odds on the seven horse are nine-to-five.* **4.** an equalizing allowance, as that given the weaker person or team in a contest; handicap. **5.** an advantage favoring one of two contestants. **6.** an amount or degree by which one thing is better or worse than another. **7. at odds,** at variance; in disagreement. **8. by all odds,** in every respect; by far; undoubtedly. Also, **by long odds, by odds.** [special use of ODD]

odds′ and ends′, **1.** miscellaneous articles; remnants; scraps. **2.** miscellaneous items, as of business.

odds-on (odz′on′, -ôn′), *adj.* **1.** (of a race horse, team, or other contestant) being even money or less in the betting on a specific event; rated at one-to-one odds or less. **2.** being the one more or most likely to win, succeed, attain or achieve something, etc.

ode (ōd), *n.* **1.** a lyric poem typically of elaborate or irregular metrical form and expressive of exalted or enthusiastic emotion. **2.** (originally) a poem intended to be sung. Cf. **Horatian ode, Pindaric ode.** [< MF < LL *ōd(a)* < Gk *ōidḗ,* contr. of *aoidḗ* song < *aeíd(ein)* (to) sing]

-ode[1], a suffix of nouns, appearing in loan words from Greek, where it meant "like"; used in the formation of compound words: *phyllode.* Cf. **-oid.** [< Gk *-ōdēs,* contr. of *-oeidēs* -OID]

-ode[2], a learned borrowing from Greek meaning "way," "road," used in the formation of compound words: *anode; electrode.* [< Gk *-odos,* comb. form of *hodós*]

O·den·se (ō′t͟hən sə), *n.* a city on Fyn island, in S Denmark. 129,833 (1960).

O·der (ō′dər), *n.* a river in central Europe, flowing from the Carpathians in N Czechoslovakia through SW Poland and along the border between East Germany and Poland into the Baltic. 562 mi. long.

O′der-Neis′se Line′ (ō′dər nī′sə), the de facto boundary between Poland and East Germany.

O·des·sa (ō des′ə; *Russ.* o de′sä), *n.* **1.** a seaport in the S Ukraine, in the SW Soviet Union in Europe, on the Black Sea: the principal export center of Ukrainian grain. 735,000 (1965). **2.** a city in W Texas. 78,380 (1970).

O·dets (ō dets′), *n.* **Clifford,** 1906–63, U.S. dramatist.

o·de·um (ō dē′əm), *n., pl.* **o·de·a** (ō dē′ə). **1.** a hall or structure for musical or dramatic performances. **2.** (in ancient Greece and Rome) a roofed building for musical performances. [< L: music hall < Gk *ōideîon* = *ōid(ḗ)* song, ODE + *-eion* suffix denoting place]

od·ic (ō′dik), *adj.* of an ode.

O·din (ō′din), *n. Scand. Myth.* the ruler of the Aesir and god of war, poetry, knowledge, and wisdom; Wotan.

o·di·ous (ō′dē əs), *adj.* **1.** deserving or causing hatred; hateful; repugnant; detestable. **2.** highly offensive; disgusting. [ME < L *odiōs(us)* = *od(ium)* hate, ODIUM + *-ōsus* -OUS] —**o′di·ous·ly,** *adv.* —**o′di·ous·ness,** *n.* —**Syn. 1.** abominable, objectionable, despicable, execrable. See **hateful. 2.** loathsome, repellent, repulsive. —**Ant. 1.** attractive, lovable.

o·di·um (ō′dē əm), *n.* **1.** intense hatred or dislike, esp. toward someone or something regarded as contemptible, despicable, or repugnant. **2.** the reproach, discredit, or opprobrium attaching to something hated or repugnant. **3.** the state or quality of being hated. [< L: hate, cf. *ōdī* I hate] —**Syn. 1.** detestation, abhorrence, antipathy. **2.** obloquy. —**Ant. 1, 2.** love.

O·do·a·cer (ō′dō ā′sər), *n.* A.D. 434?–493, first barbarian ruler of Italy 476–493. Also, **Odovacar.**

o·do·graph (ō′də graf′, -gräf′), *n.* **1.** a recording odometer. **2.** a pedometer. [var. of *hodograph* < Gk *hodó(s)* way + -GRAPH]

o·dom·e·ter (ō dom′i tər), *n.* an instrument for measuring distance passed over, as by an automobile. Also, **hodometer.** [var. of *hodometer* < Gk *hodó(s)* way + -METER]

odont-, var. of **odonto-** before a vowel: *odontoid.*

-odont, var. of **odonto-** as final element of compounds.

o·don·tal·gia (ō′don tal′jə, -jē ə), *n. Dentistry.* pain in a tooth; toothache. —**o′don·tal′gic,** *adj.*

odonto-, a learned borrowing from Greek meaning "tooth," used in the formation of compound words: *odontology.* Also, **odont-, -odont.** Cf. **denti-, -odus.** [< Gk *odont-,* s. of *odoús* or *odṓn* tooth]

o·don·to·blast (ō don′tə blast′), *n. Anat.* one of a layer of cells, lining the pulp cavity of a tooth, from which dentin is formed.

o·don·to·glos·sum (ō don′tə glos′əm), *n.* any epiphytic orchid of the genus *Odontoglossum,* of the mountainous regions from Bolivia to Mexico. [< NL < Gk *odonto-* ODONTO- + *glôss(a)* tongue + NL *-um* neut. n. suffix]

o·don·toid (ō don′toid), *adj.* **1.** of or resembling a tooth; toothlike. **2.** *Anat.* of or pertaining to the odontoid process. —*n.* **3.** See **odontoid process.** [< Gk *odontoeid(ḗs)* toothlike]

odon′toid proc′ess, *Anat.* a toothlike process of the axis or second cervical vertebra upon which the atlas rotates.

o·don·tol·o·gy (ō′don tol′ə jē, od′on-), *n.* the science dealing with the study of the teeth and their surrounding tissues and with the prevention and cure of their diseases. —**o·don·to·log·i·cal** (ō don′t[ə]loj′i kəl), *adj.* —**o′don·tol′o·gist,** *n.*

o·don·to·phore (ō don′tə fōr′, -fôr′), *n. Zool.* a structure in the mouth of most mollusks over which the radula is drawn backward and forward in the process of breaking up food. [< Gk *odontophór(os)* bearing teeth]

o·dor (ō′dər), *n.* **1.** the property of a substance that affects the sense of smell. **2.** a sensation perceived by the sense of smell; scent. **3.** an agreeable scent; fragrance. **4.** a disagreeable smell. **5.** a quality or property characteristic or suggestive of something; hint. **6.** repute or estimation. Also, *esp. Brit.,* **o′dour.** [ME < OF < L] —**o′dor·ful;** *esp. Brit.,* **o′dour·ful,** *adj.* —**o′dor·less;** *esp. Brit.,* **o′dour·less,** *adj.* —**Syn. 3.** aroma, redolence, perfume.

o·dor·ant (ō′də rənt), *n.* an odorous substance or product. [ME *odourant* < MF < L *odōrant-* (s. of *odōrāns,* prp. of *odōrāre* to perfume)]

o·dor·if·er·ous (ō′də rif′ər əs), *adj.* yielding or diffusing an odor, esp. a fragrant one. [ME < L *odōrifer* bringing odors = *odōr-* ODOR + *-i-* -I- + *-fer* -FER + -OUS] —**o′dor·if′er·ous·ly,** *adv.* —**o′dor·if′er·ous·ness,** *n.* —**Syn.** odorous, fragrant, aromatic, perfumed, redolent.

o·dor·ous (ō′dər əs), *adj.* odoriferous. [< L *odōrus* fragrant] —**o′dor·ous·ly,** *adv.* —**o′dor·ous·ness,** *n.*

O·do·va·car (ō′dō vā′kər), *n.* Odoacer.

Ods·bod·i·kins (odz bod′ə kinz), *interj.* Gadsbodikins. Also, **Ods·bod·kins** (odz bod′kinz).

-odus, *Zool.* a suffix occurring in names of genera, used to mean "having a (certain kind of) tooth": *ceratodus.* [< NL, comb. form repr. Gk *odoús* tooth. See ODONTO-]

od·yl (od′il, ō′dil), *n.* od. Also, **od′yle.**

-odynia, a learned borrowing from Greek meaning "pain," used in the formation of compound words: *pododynia.* Cf. **-algia.** [< NL < Gk = *odýn(ē)* pain + *-ia* -Y[3]]

O·dys·se·us (ō dis′ē əs, ō dis′yōōs), *n. Class. Myth.* the son of Laertes, husband of Penelope, and father of Telemachus: king of Ithaca and wisest and shrewdest of the Greek leaders in the Trojan War. Latin, **Ulysses.**

Od·ys·sey (od′i sē), *n.* **1.** (*italics*) an epic poem attributed to Homer, describing Odysseus' adventures in his ten-year attempt to return home to Ithaca after the Trojan War. **2.** (*often l.c.*) any long series of wanderings, esp. when filled with notable experiences, hardships, etc. —**Od′ys·se′an,** *adj.*

Od·zooks (od zo͝oks′, -zo͞oks′), *interj.* Gadzooks. Also, **Od·zook·ers** (od zo͝ok′ərz, -zo͞o′kərz).

OE, Old English (def. 1). Also, **OE.**

Oe, oersted; oersteds.

oe-, var. spelling of **e-,** appearing in some words of Latin and Greek origin: *oecology; oenology; oesophagus.* [< L, repr. Gk *oi-,* as in *oîkos* house (see ECONOMY), *oînos* wine (see OENOLOGY)]

O.E., **1.** Old English. **2.** *Com.* omissions excepted.

o.e., *Com.* omissions excepted. Also, **oe**

OECD, Organization for Economic Cooperation and Development. Also, **O.E.C.D.**

oe·col·o·gy (i kol′ə jē), *n.* ecology. —**oec·o·log·i·cal** (ek′ə loj′i kəl, ē′kə-), **oec′o·log′ic,** *adj.* —**oec′o·log′i·cal·ly,** *adv.* —**oe·col′o·gist,** *n.*

oec·u·men·i·cal (ek′yo͝o men′i kəl *or, esp. Brit.,* ē′kyo͝o-), *adj.* ecumenical. Also, **oec′u·men′ic.**

oe·de·ma (i dē′mə), *n., pl.* **-ma·ta** (-mə tə). *Pathol.* edema.

oed·i·pal (ed′ə pəl, ē′də-), *adj.* (*often cap.*) of, characterized by, or resulting from the Oedipus complex. [OEDIP(US COMPLEX) + -AL[1]]

Oed·i·pus (ed′ə pəs, ē′də-), *n. Gk. Legend.* a king of Thebes, the son of Laius and Jocasta, and the father by Jocasta of Eteocles, Polynices, and Antigone: as was prophesied at his birth, he unwittingly killed his father and married his mother, and blinded and exiled himself for having done so.

Oed′ipus com′plex, *Psychoanal.* the unresolved desire of a child for sexual gratification through the parent of the opposite sex, esp. the desire of a son for his mother. This involves, first, identification with and, later, hatred for the parent of the same sex, who is considered by the child as a rival. Cf. **Electra complex.**

oeil-de-boeuf (œ′y[ə] də bœf′), *n., pl.* **oeils-de-boeuf** (œ′y[ə] də bœf′). *French.* a comparatively small round or oval window, as in a frieze. [lit., bull's eye]

Oe·ne·us (ē′nē əs, -no͞os, -nyo͞os), *n. Class. Myth.* a king of Calydon believed to have been the first grower of grapes.

oe·nol·o·gy (ē nol′ə jē), *n.* the science of viniculture. Also, **enology.** [< Gk *oin-* (s. of *oînos*) wine + -LOGY] —**oe·no·log·i·cal** (ēn′[ə]loj′i kəl), *adj.* —**oe·nol′o·gist,** *n.*

Oe·no·ma·us (ē′nə mā′əs), *n. Class. Myth.* a Pisan king.

oe·no·mel (ē′nə mel′, en′ə-), *n.* **1.** a drink made of wine mixed with honey. **2.** something combining strength with sweetness. [< LL *oenomel(um)* (sp. var. of *oenomeli*) < Gk *oinómel(i)* = *oîno(s)* wine + *méli* honey]

Oe·no·ne (ē nō′nē), *n. Class. Myth.* the wife of Paris, deserted by him for Helen.

oe·no·phile (ē′nə fīl′), *n.* a person who enjoys wines, usually as a connoisseur. [< Gk *oîno(s)* wine + PHILE]

OEO, Office of Economic Opportunity.

OEP, Office of Emergency Preparedness.

o'er (ōr, ôr), *prep., adv. Literary.* over.

oer·sted (ûr′sted), *n. Elect.* a centimeter-gram-second unit of magnetic intensity, equal to the magnetic pole of unit strength when undergoing a force of one dyne in a vacuum. *Abbr.:* Oe [named after H. C. *Oersted* (1777–1851), Danish physicist]

Oe·sel (œ′zəl), *n.* German name of **Saaremaa.**

oesophag-, var. of **esophag-.**

oe·soph·a·ge·al (i sof′ə jē′əl, ē′sə faj′ē əl), *adj.* esophageal.

oe·soph·a·gus (i sof′ə gəs), *n., pl.* **-gi** (-jī′). esophagus.

oes·tra·di·ol (es′trə dī′ōl, -ôl, -ol, ē′strə-), *n. Biochem.* estradiol.

oes·trin (es′trin, ē′strin), *n. Biochem.* estrone.

oes·tri·ol (es′trē ōl′, -ôl′, -ol′, ē′strē-), *n. Biochem.* estriol.

oes·tro·gen (es′trə jən, ē′strə-), *n. Biochem.* estrogen.

oes·trone (es′trōn, ē′strōn), *n. Biochem.* estrone.

oes·trous (es′trəs, ē′strəs), *adj.* estrous.

oes·trus (es′trəs, ē′strəs), *n.* estrus.

oeu·vre (œ′vʀ[ə]), *n., pl.* **oeu·vres** (œ′vʀ[ə]). *French.* **1.** the works of a writer, painter, or the like, taken as a whole. **2.** any one of the works of a writer, painter, or the like.

of[1] (uv, ov; *unstressed* əv), *prep.* **1.** (used to indicate distance or direction from, separation, deprivation, etc.): *within a mile of the church; south of Tahiti; to be robbed of one's money.* **2.** (used to indicate derivation, origin, or source): *the plays of O'Neill.* **3.** (used to indicate cause, motive, occasion, or reason): *to die of hunger.* **4.** (used to indicate material, components, or content): *a dress of silk; an apartment of three rooms; a package of cheese.* **5.** (used to indicate apposition or identity): *Is that idiot of a salesman calling again?* **6.** (used to indicate specific identity or a particular item within a category): *the city of Chicago.* **7.** (used to indicate authority or ownership): *the king of France; the property of the church.* **8.** (used to indicate inclusion within a group, class, or greater whole): *one of us.* **9.** (used to indicate the objective relation, the object of the action noted by the preceding noun or the application of a verb or adjective): *the ringing of bells.* **10.** (used to indicate reference or respect): *talk of peace.* **11.** (used to indicate qualities or attributes): *a man of tact.* **12.** (used to indicate time): *They arrived of an evening.* **13.** before; until: *twenty minutes of five.* **14.** on the part of: *It was very mean of you to insult her.* **15.** in respect to: *to be fleet of foot.* **16.** *Archaic.* (used to indicate the agent by whom or by which an action is carried through): *consumed of worms.* [ME, OE; c. G, L *ab,* Gk *apo.* See OFF]

of[2] (əv), *auxiliary v. Nonstandard.* have: *He should of gone.*

OF, Old French. Also, **OF., O.F., OFr.**

of-, var. of **ob-** (by assimilation) before *f: offend.*

O'Fao·láin (ō fā′lən, ō fal′ən), *n.* **Seán** (shôn), born 1900, Irish writer and teacher.

o·fay (ō′fā), *n. Disparaging.* a white person. [?]

off (ôf, of), *adv.* **1.** so as to be no longer supported or attached. **2.** so as to be no longer covering or enclosing: *Take your hat off.* **3.** away from a place: *to run off.* **4.** away from a path, course, etc: *This road branches off to Dayton.* **5.** so as to be away or on one's way: *to start off early; to cast off.* **6.** away from what is considered normal, regular, standard, or the like: *to go off on a tangent.* **7.** from a charge or price: *10 percent off for cash.* **8.** at a distance in space or future time: *They live two blocks off. Summer is only a week off.* **9.** out of operation or effective existence: *Turn the lights off.* **10.** so as to interrupt continuity or cause discontinuance: *Negotiations have been broken off.* **11.** in absence from work, service, a job, etc. **12.** completely; utterly: *to kill off.* **13.** with prompt or ready performance: *to dash a letter off.* **14.** to fulfillment, or into execution or effect: *The contest came off on the day fixed.* **15.** so as to be delineated, divided, or apportioned: *Mark it off into three equal parts.* **16.** away from a state of consciousness: *I must have dozed off.* **17.** *Naut.* away from the land, a ship, the wind, etc. **18. be off,** to depart; leave. **19. off and on,** with intervals between;

intermittently. Also, **on and off.** **20. off with,** take away! remove!: *Off with his head!*
—*prep.* **21.** so as to be no longer supported by or attached to: *Break off a piece of bread.* **22.** deviating from: *off balance.* **23.** below or less than the usual or expected level or standard: *25 percent off the marked price.* **24.** away, disengaged, or resting from: *off duty.* **25.** *Informal.* refraining or abstaining from: *I'm off liquor.* **26.** away from; apart or distant from: *a village off the main road.* **27.** leading into or away from: *an alley off 12th Street.* **28.** not fixed on or directed toward, as the gaze, eyes, etc. **29.** *Informal.* from: *I bought it off him.* **30.** from or of, indicating material or component parts: *to make a meal off fish.* **31.** so as to be no longer covering or enclosing: *Take the lid off the box.* **32.** *Naut.* at some distance to seaward of: *off Cape Hatteras.*
—*adj.* **33.** in error; wrong. **34.** slightly abnormal or not quite sane. **35.** not up to standard; not so good or satisfactory as usual. **36.** no longer in effect or operation: *The agreement is off.* **37.** in a specified state, circumstances, etc.: *to be badly off for money.* **38.** free from work or duty: *a pastime for one's off hours.* **39.** of less than the ordinary activity, liveliness, or lively interest: *an off season.* **40.** more distant; farther: *the off side of a wall.* **41.** (in riding or driving) on the right (opposed to *near*). **42.** starting to go away: *I'm off to Europe on Monday.* **43.** *Naut.* noting one of two like things that is the farther from the shore; seaward. **44.** *Cricket.* noting or pertaining to that side of the wicket or of the field opposite that on which the batsman stands.
—*n.* **45.** the state or fact of being off. **46.** *Cricket.* the off side.
—*interj.* **47.** be off! stand off! off with you! [ME, OE *of*, var. of OF[1] when stressed]
—**Usage.** Despite the frequency with which it is heard, OFF OF in a construction like, *I asked him to keep off of the freshly varnished floor,* is considered nonstandard, largely because it is redundant and poor style. OFF, without OF, is sufficient to express the same notion.

off., 1. offered. 2. office. 3. officer. 4. official.

of·fal (ô′fəl, of′əl), *n.* **1.** the parts of a butchered animal that are considered inedible by human beings; carrion. **2.** refuse in general; rubbish; garbage. [ME; see OFF, FALL]

off·beat (*adj.* ôf′bēt′, of′-; *n.* ôf′bēt′, of′-), *adj.* **1.** differing from the usual or expected; unconventional. —*n.* **2.** *Music.* an unaccented beat of a measure.

off′ Broad′way, (in New York City) experimental and low-budget drama, as produced in theaters other than the traditional commercial theaters in the Broadway area. —**off′-Broad′way,** *adj.*

off·cast (ôf′kast′, -käst′, of′-), *adj.* **1.** discarded or rejected; castoff: *his offcast suits.* —*n.* **2.** a castoff person or thing.

off-cen·ter (ôf′sen′tər, of′-), *adj.* Also, **off′-cen′tered. 1.** missing or diverging from the exact center. **2.** out of balance or alignment. —*adv.* **3.** so as to be out of balance or alignment.

off′ chance′, a very slight possibility or likelihood.

off-col·or (ôf′kul′ər, of′-), *adj.* **1.** not having the usual or standard color. **2.** of doubtful propriety or taste; risqué: *an off-color joke.* **3.** not in one's usual health. Also, *esp. Brit.,* **off′-col′our.**

Of·fen·bach (ô′fən bäk′, of′ən-; *for 1 also Fr.* ô fen bak′; *for 2 also Ger.* ôf′ən bäkh′), *n.* **1. Jacques** (zhäk), 1819–80, French composer, born in Germany. **2.** a city in S Hesse, in central West Germany, on the Main River, near Frankfurt. 118,000 (1963).

of·fence (ə fens′, ô′fens, of′ens), *n.* offense.

of·fend (ə fend′), *v.t.* **1.** to cause resentful displeasure in. **2.** to affect (the sense, taste, etc.) disagreeably. **3.** to violate or transgress, as a religious or moral law. **4.** to hurt or cause pain to. **5.** (in Biblical use) to cause to fall into sinful ways. —*v.i.* **6.** to cause resentful displeasure. **7.** to err in conduct. [ME *offend(en)* < MF *offend(re)* < L *offendere* to strike against, displease = *of-* OF- + *fendere* to strike] —**of·fend′a·ble, of·fend′i·ble,** *adj.* —**of·fend′er,** *n.* —**Syn. 1.** provoke, nettle, affront, insult. **7.** transgress. —**Ant. 1.** please.

of·fense (ə fens′ *or, esp. for 7, 8,* ô′fens, of′ens), *n.* **1.** a violation or breaking of a law or rule; transgression; sin; crime. **2.** a violation of the criminal law, esp. one that is not a felony. **3.** a cause of transgression or wrong. **4.** something that offends or displeases. **5.** the act of offending or displeasing. **6.** a feeling of resentful displeasure: *to give offense.* **7.** the act of attacking; attack or assault: *weapons of offense.* **8.** a person, side, team, army, etc., attacking. **9.** *Obs.* injury, harm, or hurt. Also, **offence.** [ME *offence, offense* < MF *offense* < L *offēns(a),* fem. ptp. of *offendere* to strike against (see OFFEND)] —**Syn. 1.** See **crime. 6.** umbrage, resentment. **7.** aggression. **8.** attackers. —**Ant. 7.** defense.

of·fense·less (ə fens′lis), *adj.* **1.** without offense. **2.** incapable of offense or attack. **3.** not offensive. Also, **offence′less.** —**of·fense′less·ly,** *adv.*

of·fen·sive (ə fen′siv, ô′fen-, of′en-), *adj.* **1.** causing resentful displeasure. **2.** unpleasant or disagreeable to the senses. **3.** repugnant, as to the moral sense or good taste. **4.** pertaining to or characterized by offense or attack: *offensive movements.* —*n.* **5.** the position or attitude of offense or attack. **6.** an aggressive movement or attack. [< ML *offensīv(us)*] —**of·fen′sive·ly,** *adv.* —**of·fen′sive·ness,** *n.* —**Syn. 1.** displeasing, vexing, unpleasant. See **hateful. 2, 3.** distasteful, disgusting, revolting, repellent. **4.** attacking. —**Ant. 1, 2.** pleasing. **4.** defensive.

of·fer (ô′fər, of′ər), *v.t.* **1.** to present for acceptance or rejection. **2.** to propose for consideration: *to offer a suggestion.* **3.** to make a show of willingness to perform or give. **4.** to present or volunteer (oneself) to someone as a spouse. **5.** to present solemnly as an act of worship or devotion. **6.** to give, make, or promise: *The doctor offered no hope.* **7.** to attempt to inflict, do, or make: *to offer battle.* **8.** to do, make, or threaten (violence, resistance, etc.). **9.** to introduce or present for exhibition or performance. **10.** to present for sale. **11.** to tender or bid, as a price. **12.** to render (homage, thanks, etc.). —*v.i.* **13.** to make a proposal or suggestion. **14.** to present itself, as an opportunity; occur. **15.** *Archaic.* to make an attempt (fol. by *at*). —*n.* **16.** the act or an instance of offering. **17.** a proposal of marriage. **18.** a proposal or bid to give or pay something. **19.** the condition of being offered: *an offer for sale.* **20.** something offered. **21.** *Law.* a proposal which requires only acceptance in order to create a contract. **22.** an attempt or endeavor. **23.** a show of intention or willingness. [ME *offre(n),* OE *offrian* < L *offerre* = *ob-* OB- + *ferre* to BEAR[1]] —**of′fer·a·ble,** *adj.* —**of′fer·er, of′fe·ror,** *n.*
—**Syn. 1.** OFFER, PROFFER, TENDER mean to present for acceptance or refusal. OFFER is a common word in general use for presenting something to be accepted or rejected: *to offer assistance.* PROFFER, with the same meaning, is now chiefly a literary word: *to proffer one's services.* TENDER is a ceremonious term for a more or less formal or conventional act: *to tender one's resignation.* **2.** give, move, propose. —**Ant. 1.** withdraw, withhold.

of·fer·ing (ô′fər ing, of′ər-), *n.* **1.** something offered in worship or devotion. **2.** a contribution given to or through a church. **3.** anything offered as a gift. **4.** something presented for inspection or sale. **5.** the act of a person who offers. [ME; OE *offrung*]

of·fer·to·ry (ô′fər tôr′ē, -tōr′ē, of′ər-), *n., pl.* **-ries. 1.** (*sometimes cap.*) the offering of the unconsecrated elements that is made to God by the celebrant at Mass. **2.** *Eccles.* **a.** the verses, anthem, or music said, sung, or played while the offerings of the people are received at a religious service. **b.** that part of a service at which offerings are made. **c.** the offerings themselves. [ME *offertorie* < ML *offertōri(um)* place to which offerings were brought, offering, oblation = L *offert(us)* (ptp. of *offerre* to OFFER) + *-ōrium* -ORY[2]] —**of′fer·to′ri·al,** *adj.*

off·hand (ôf′hand′, of′-), *adv.* **1.** without previous thought or preparation. **2.** cavalierly, curtly, or brusquely. —*adj.* **3.** Also, **off′hand′ed.** done or made offhand. **4.** informal or casual. —**off′hand′ed·ly,** *adv.* —**off′hand′ed·ness,** *n.* —**Syn. 2.** short, shortly, abruptly. **3, 4.** impromptu, extempore. —**Ant. 3.** considered.

off-hour (*n.* ôf′our′, -ou′ər, -our′, -ou′ər, of′-; *adj.* ôf′our′, -ou′ər, of′-), *n.* **1.** an hour or other period off duty. **2.** a period outside the hours of greatest activity. —*adj.* **3.** of, pertaining to, or during an off-hour.

of·fice (ô′fis, of′is), *n.* **1.** a place where business is transacted. **2.** a room assigned to a specific person or a group of persons in such a place. **3.** a business or professional organization: *He went to work in an architect's office.* **4.** (*cap.*) **a.** *U.S.* an operating agency or division of certain departments of the federal government: *Office of Education.* **b.** *Brit.* a major administrative unit of the national government: *the Scottish Office.* **5.** the staff that works in a place of business. **6.** a position of duty, trust, or high authority: *the office of president.* **7.** employment or position as an official: *to seek office.* **8.** the duty, function, or part of a particular person or agency: *to act in the office of adviser.* **9.** a service or task to be performed. **10.** Often, **offices.** something, whether good or bad, done or said for or to another: *the good offices of a friend.* **11.** *Eccles.* **a.** the prescribed order or form for a service of the church or for devotional use. **b.** the services so prescribed. **c.** Also called **divine office.** the prayers, readings from the Scriptures, and psalms that must be recited every day by all who are in major orders. **d.** a ceremony or rite, esp. for the dead. **12. offices,** *Chiefly Brit.* the parts of a house, as the kitchen or laundry, devoted to household work. [ME < OF < L *offic(ium)* service, duty, ceremony = *op(us)* work + *-fic* + -FIC + *-ium* n. suffix] —**Syn. 6.** post, station, berth, situation. See **appointment. 8.** responsibility, charge, trust. **9.** chore.

of′fice boy′, a boy employed in an office to run errands, do odd jobs, etc.

of·fice·hold·er (ô′fis hōl′dər, of′is-), *n.* a person filling a governmental position.

of′fice hours′, the hours of work in an office.

of·fic·er (ô′fi sər, of′i-), *n.* **1.** a person appointed to a position of authority or command in the armed services, esp. one holding a commission. **2.** a person appointed or elected to a position of responsibility or authority in an organization. **3.** a policeman or constable. **4.** a person licensed to take full or partial responsibility for the operation of a ship. **5.** (in some honorary orders) a member of any rank except the lowest. **6.** *Obs.* an agent. —*v.t.* **7.** to furnish with officers. [ME < MF *officier* < ML *officiār(ius)*] —**of·fi·ce·ri·al** (ô′fi sēr′ē əl, of′i-), *adj.*

of′ficer of the day′, *Mil.* an officer who has charge, on an assigned day, of the guard and security of a post or other installation. *Abbr.:* OD, O.D.

of′ficer of the guard′, *Mil.* an officer, acting under the officer of the day, who is responsible for the instruction, discipline, and performance of duty of the guard. *Abbr.:* OG, O.G.

of′fice seek′er, a person who seeks public office.

of·fi·cial (ə fish′əl), *n.* **1.** a person charged with certain duties in an organization, esp. in the government. —*adj.* **2.** of or pertaining to an office of duty or authority. **3.** appointed, authorized, or approved by a government or organization. **4.** formal and public, as a ceremony. **5.** holding office. **6.** *Pharm.* noting drugs or drug preparations that are recognized by and that conform to the standards of the *United States Pharmacopoeia* or the *National Formulary.* [< LL *officiāl(is)* of duty. See OFFICE, -AL[1]] —**of·fi′cial·ly,** *adv.*

of·fi·cial·dom (ə fish′əl dəm), *n.* the domain or class of officials.

of·fi·cial·ese (ə fish′ə lēz′, -lēs′), *n.* a style of language used in official pronouncements that is typically hard to understand and is full of polysyllabic jargon and obscure, pretentiously wordy phrasing.

of·fi·cial·ism (ə fish′ə liz′əm), *n.* **1.** official methods or systems. **2.** excessive attention to official regulations and routines. **3.** officials collectively.

of·fi·ci·ant (ə fish′ē ənt), *n.* a person who officiates at a religious service or ceremony. [< ML *officiant-* (s. of *officiāns,* prp. of *officiāre*) officiating]

of·fi·ci·ar·y (ə fish′ē er′ē), *adj.* **1.** pertaining to or derived from an office, as a title. **2.** having a title or rank derived from an office, as a dignitary. [< L *offici(um)* OFFICE + -ARY]

of·fi·ci·ate (ə fish′ē āt′), *v.,* **-at·ed, -at·ing.** —*v.i.* **1.** to perform the duties or function of some office or position. **2.** to perform the office of a priest or minister, as at a divine service. —*v.t.* **3.** to perform, carry out, or fulfill (an official duty or function). **4.** to serve as the priest or minister of (a divine service, religious ceremony, etc.). **5.** to act as a referee, umpire, or the like, for (a sports contest or game). [< ML *officiāt(us)* officiated (ptp. of *officiāre*)] —**of·fi′ci·a′tion,** *n.* —**of·fi′ci·a′tor,** *n.*

of·fic·i·nal (ə fis′ə nᵊl), *adj.* **1.** kept in stock by apothecaries, as a drug. Cf. **magistral** (def. 1). **2.** official (def. 6). —*n.* **3.** an officinal medicine. [< ML *officīnāl(is)* of a storeroom = L *officīn(a)* workshop, sp. var. of *opificīna* (*opific-*, s. of *opifex* artisan = *opi-*, var. s. of *opus* work + *-fic* -FIC + *-ina* -INE[1]) + *-ālis* -AL[1]] —**of·fic′i·nal·ly,** *adv.*

of·fi·cious (ə fish′əs), *adj.* **1.** objectionably forward in offering unrequested and unwanted services, help, or advice. **2.** marked by such forwardness. **3.** *Obs.* ready to serve; obliging. [< L *officiōs(us)* obliging, dutiful] —**of·fi′cious·ly,** *adv.* —**of·fi′cious·ness,** *n.* —**Syn. 1.** interfering.

off·ing (ô′fing, of′ing), *n.* **1.** the more distant part of the sea seen from the shore. **2.** a position at a distance from shore. **3. in the offing, a.** at a distance but within sight. **b.** in the anticipated future.

off·ish (ô′fish, of′ish), *adj. Informal.* aloof; unapproachable. —**off′ish·ly,** *adv.* —**off′ish·ness,** *n.*

off-key (ôf′kē′, of′-), *adj.* **1.** deviating from the correct tone or pitch. **2.** irregular, abnormal, or incongruous. **3.** mildly obscene; risque.

off-lim·its (ôf′lim′its, of′-), *adj.* forbidden to be entered or patronized by certain persons, as soldiers.

off-line (ôf′līn′, of′-), *adj.* (in data processing) operating independently of the main computer.

off-load (ôf′lōd′), *v.t., v.i.* to unload. Also, **off′load′.**

off·print (ôf′print′, of′-), *n.* **1.** Also called **separate.** a reprint in separate form of an article that originally appeared as part of a larger publication. —*v.t.* **2.** to reprint separately, as an article from a larger publication. [trans. of G *Abdruck*]

off-ramp (ôf′ramp′, of′-), *n.* an exit lane for traffic from a turnpike or freeway to a street. Cf. **on-ramp.**

off·screen (ôf′skrēn′, of′-), *adj.* **1.** occurring, existing, or done away from the motion-picture screen: *an offscreen voice.* **2.** in actual life rather than on the motion-picture screen.

off-sea·son (ôf′sē′zən, of′-), *adj.* **1.** being of a time of year other than the regular or busiest one for a specific activity. —*adv.* **2.** in or during the off-season. —*n.* **3.** of a time of year other than the regular or busiest one for a specific activity.

off·set (*n., adj.* ôf′set′, of′-; *v.* ôf′set′, of′-), *n., adj., v.,* **-set, -set·ting.** —*n.* **1.** something that compensates for something else. **2.** a start, beginning, or outset. **3.** a short lateral shoot by which certain plants are propagated. **4.** an offshoot or branch. **5.** *Geol.* (in faults) the magnitude of separation between two previously aligned bodies of rock. **6.** Also called **off′set lithog′raphy.** *Lithog.* **a.** a process in which a lithographic stone or metal or paper plate is used to make an inked impression on a rubber blanket which transfers it to the paper being printed. **b.** the impression itself. **7.** any part of a line, surface, or object that deviates from an otherwise prevailing straightness or flatness. **8.** Also called **off′set line′.** *Survey.* a line a short distance from and parallel to a main survey line. —*adj.* **9.** of, noting, or pertaining to an offset. **10.** *Lithog.* pertaining to, printed by, or suitable for printing by, offset. **11.** placed off a center line; off-center. **12.** placed at an angle to something. —*v.t.* **13.** to juxtapose with something else, as for purposes of comparison. **14.** to compensate for: *The gains offset the losses.* **15.** *Print.* **a.** to make an offset of. **b.** to print by the process of offset lithography. —*v.i.* **16.** to project as an offset or branch. **17.** *Print.* to make an offset.

off·shoot (ôf′shōōt′, of′-), *n.* **1.** a branch or lateral shoot from a main stem, as of a plant. **2.** anything conceived of as springing or proceeding from a main stock.

off·shore (ôf′shôr′, -shōr′, of′-), *adv.* **1.** off or away from the shore. **2.** at a distance from the shore. —*adj.* **3.** moving or tending away from the shore. **4.** located or operating at some distance from the shore. **5.** *U.S.* **a.** of or denoting an American-owned investment company that is registered outside the country and that offers shares only to foreigners: *an offshore mutual fund.* **b.** of, for, or involving a business that is based outside the United States and operated mostly by American citizens: *an offshore automobile plant.*

off·side (ôf′sīd′, of′-), *adj., adv. Sports.* illegally beyond a prescribed line or area or in advance of the ball or puck at the beginning of or during play or a play.

off·spring (ôf′spring′, of′-), *n., pl.* **-spring, -springs. 1.** children or young of a particular parent or progenitor. **2.** a child or animal in relation to its parent or parents. **3.** a descendant. **4.** descendants collectively. **5.** a product, result, or effect. [ME, OE]

off·stage (ôf′stāj′, of′-), *adv.* **1.** off the stage or in the wings; away from the view of the audience (opposed to *onstage*). —*adj.* **2.** not in view of the audience; backstage, in the wings, etc. **3.** of or pertaining to actual life rather than the theater: *The offstage life of the actor is not glamorous.*

off-the-cuff (ôf′thə kuf′, of′-), *adj. U.S. Informal.* with little or no preparation.

off-the-re·cord (ôf′thə rek′ərd, of′-), *adj.* **1.** not for publication; not to be quoted. **2.** unofficial or confidential.

off-the-shelf (ôf′thə shelf′, of′-), *adj.* **1.** readily available from merchandise in stock. **2.** suitable or easily adaptable for a new or special purpose.

off-the-wall (ôf′thə wôl′, of′-), *adj. Slang.* **1.** surprisingly unusual or unconventional: *an off-the-wall remark.* **2.** bizarre; freakish: *off-the-wall behavior.* **3.** impromptu; unexpected.

off·track (ôf′trak′, of′-), *adj.,* of or pertaining to a system of betting, esp. on horse races, in legalized locations away from the race track: *offtrack betting; offtrack parlors.*

off-white (ôf′hwīt′, -wīt′, of′-), *adj.* **1.** white mixed with a small amount of gray, yellow, or other light color. —*n.* **2.** an off-white color.

off′ year′, *U.S.* **1.** a year marked by reduced or inferior production or activity. **2. a.** a year without a major election on a state or local level. **b.** a year without a presidential election. —**off′-year′,** *adj.*

OFlem, Old Flemish. Also, **OFlem.**

OFr., Old French.

OFris, Old Frisian. Also, **OFris.**

oft (ôft, oft), *adv. Literary.* often. [ME *oft(e)*, OE *oft;* c. G *oft*]

of·ten (ô′fən, of′ən *or, sometimes,* ôf′tən, of′-), *adv.* **1.** many times; frequently. **2.** in many cases. —*adj.* **3.** *Archaic.* frequent. [ME *oftin,* var. before vowels of *ofte* OFT] —**of′ten·ness,** *n.*

—**Syn. 1, 2.** repeatedly, customarily. OFTEN, FREQUENTLY, GENERALLY, USUALLY refer to experiences that are customary. OFTEN and FREQUENTLY may be used interchangeably in most cases, but OFTEN implies numerous repetitions and, sometimes, regularity of recurrence: *We often go there;* FREQUENTLY suggests esp. repetition at comparatively short intervals: *It happens frequently.* GENERALLY refers to place and means universally: *It is generally understood. He is generally liked;* but it is often used as a colloquial substitute for USUALLY. In this sense, GENERALLY, like USUALLY, refers to time, and means in numerous instances. GENERALLY, however, extends in range from the merely numerous to a majority of possible instances; whereas USUALLY means practically always: *The train is generally on time. We usually have hot summers.* —**Ant. 1, 2.** seldom.

of·ten·times (ô′fən tīmz′, of′ən- *or, sometimes,* ôf′tən, of′-), *adv.* often. Also, **oft·times** (ôft′tīmz′, oft′-, ôf′-, of′-). [ME]

OG, See **officer of the guard.**

O.G., 1. See **officer of the guard. 2.** *Philately.* See **o.g.**

o.g., *Philately.* original gum: the gum on the back of a stamp when it is issued to the public.

og·am (og′əm, ô′gəm), *n.* ogham.

O·ga·sa·wa·ra Ji·ma (ô′gä sä wä′rä jē′mä), Japanese name of **Bonin Islands.**

O gauge, 1. a model railroad gauge of 1¼ inches, used either with a scale of ¼ inch or 17/64 inch to the foot. **2.** Also called **Q gauge.** a model railroad gauge of 1 3/16 inches with a scale of ¼ inch to the foot.

Og·bo·mo·sho (og′bə mō′shō), *n.* a city in SW Nigeria. 319,881 (1963).

Og·den (ôg′den, og′-), *n.* a city in N Utah. 69,478 (1970).

og·do·ad (og′dō ad′), *n.* a group of eight. [< LL *ogdoad-* (s. of *ogdoas*) < Gk *ogdoás.* See OCTO-, -AD[1]]

o·gee (ō jē′, ō′jē), *n.* **1.** a double curve, resembling the letter S, formed by the union of a concave and a convex line. **2.** *Archit.* a molding with such a curve. [var. of OGIVE]

o′gee arch′, *Archit.* an arch each haunch of which is an ogee with the concave side uppermost.

og·ham (og′əm, ô′gəm), *n.* an Old Irish alphabet used from about the 5th to the 10th centuries A.D., consisting of 20 characters representing vowels and consonants. Also, **ogam.** [< Ir; MIr, OIr *ogam, ogum*]

o·give (ō′jīv, ō jīv′), *n.* **1.** *Archit.* **a.** a diagonal vaulting rib. **b.** a pointed arch. **2.** *Statistics.* the distribution curve of an accumulative frequency distribution. **3.** *Rocketry.* the curved nose of a missile or rocket. [ME < MF *ogive, augive* < ?]

o·gle (ō′gəl), *v.,* **o·gled, o·gling,** *n.* —*v.t.* **1.** to look at amorously, flirtatiously, or impertinently. **2.** to eye; look or stare at. —*v.i.* **3.** to look amorously, flirtatiously, or impertinently. **4.** to look or stare. —*n.* **5.** an amorous, flirtatious, or impertinent glance. [appar. < freq. (cf. LG *oegeln,* G *äugeln*) of D *oogen* to eye < *oog* eye]

O·gle·thorpe (ō′gəl thôrp′), *n.* **James Edward,** 1696–1785, British general: founder of the colony of Georgia.

Og·pu (og′pōō), *n.* See **G.P.U.**

o·gre (ō′gər), *n.* **1.** a monster in fairy tales and popular legend, usually represented as a hideous giant who feeds on human flesh. **2.** a monstrously ugly, cruel, or barbarous person. [< F, ? < L *Orcus* ORCUS] —**o·gre·ish** (ō′gər ish), **o·grish** (ō′grish), *adj.* —**o′gre·ish·ly, o′grish·ly,** *adv.* —**o′gre·ism, o′grism,** *n.*

o·gress (ō′gris), *n.* a female ogre. [< F *ogresse*]

O·gyg·i·a (ō jij′ē ə), *n. Gk. Legend.* the island of Calypso.

OH, Ohio (approved esp. for use with zip code).

oh (ō), *interj., n., pl.* **oh's, ohs,** *v.* —*interj.* **1.** (used as an expression of surprise, pain, disapprobation, etc.) **2.** (used in direct address to attract the attention of the person spoken to): *Oh, John, will you take these books?* —*n.* **3.** the exclamation "oh." —*v.i.* **4.** to exclaim "oh." [ME *o*]

O'Har·a (ō hâr′ə, ō har′ə), *n.* **John (Henry),** 1905–70, U.S. journalist, author, and scenarist.

O. Hen·ry (ō hen′rē), (pen name of *William Sydney Porter*) 1862–1910, U.S. short-story writer.

OHG, Old High German. Also, **OHG., O.H.G.**

O'Hig·gins (ō hig′inz; *Sp.* ô ē′gēns), *n.* **1. Am·bro·sio** (äm brô′syô), (*Marqués de Osorno*), 1720?–1801, Irish soldier and administrator in South America. **2.** his son, **Ber·nar·do** (ber när′thô), ("*Liberator of Chile*"), 1778–1842, Chilean general and statesman.

O·hi·o (ō hī′ō), *n.* **1.** a state in the NE central United States: a part of the Midwest. 10,652,017 (1970); 41,222 sq. mi. *Cap.:* Columbus. *Abbr.:* O., OH **2.** a river formed by the confluence of the Allegheny and Monongahela rivers, flowing SW from Pittsburgh, Pennsylvania, to the Mississippi in S Illinois. 981 mi. long. —**O·hi′o·an,** *adj., n.*

Ohi′o buck′eye. See under **buckeye** (def. 1).

ohm (ōm), *n. Elect.* the meter-kilogram-second unit of resistance, equal to the resistance in a conductor in which one volt of potential difference produces a current of one ampere. *Symbol:* Ω [named after G. S. OHM] —**ohm·ic** (ō′mik), *adj.*

Ohm (ōm), *n.* **Ge·org Si·mon** (gā ôrk′ zē′môn), 1787–1854, German physicist.

ohm·age (ō′mij), *n. Elect.* electric resistance in ohms.

ohm·me·ter (ōm′mē′tər), *n. Elect.* an instrument for measuring electric resistance in ohms.

O.H.M.S., On His (or Her) Majesty's Service.

Ohm's′ law′, *Elect.* the law that for any circuit the electric current is directly proportional to the voltage and inversely proportional to the resistance. [after G. S. OHM]

o·ho (ō hō′), *interj.* (used as an exclamation to express surprise, taunting, exultation, etc.) [ME]

O·hře (*Czech.* ô′hrzhe), *n.* a river in central Europe, flowing NE from S West Germany to Czechoslovakia to the Elbe. 193 mi. long. German, **Eger.**

Ohr·mazd (ôr′məzd), *n.* See **Ahura Mazda.**

OIcel, Old Icelandic.

-oid, a learned borrowing from Greek meaning "resembling," "like," used in the formation of adjectives and nouns (and often implying an incomplete or imperfect resemblance to what is indicated by the preceding element): *alkaloid; ovoid.* Cf. **-ode**[1]. [< Gk *-oeidēs* = *-o-* -o- + *-eidēs* having the form of < *eîdos* form]

-oidea, a suffix used in naming zoological classes or entomological superfamilies. [< NL < *-oïdes* -OID]

oil (oil), *n.* **1.** any of a large class of substances typically unctuous, viscous, combustible, liquid at ordinary temperatures, and soluble in ether or alcohol but not in water, used for lubricating, illuminating, etc. **2.** a substance of this or similar consistency. **3.** petroleum. **4.** See **crude oil. 5.** *Painting.* **a.** See **oil color. b.** See **oil painting. 6. pour oil on troubled waters,** to pacify; calm. **7. strike oil,** to discover a petroleum deposit. **—*v.t.* 8.** to smear, lubricate, or supply with oil. **9.** to convert into oil by melting, as butter. **—*adj.* 10.** pertaining to or resembling oil. **11.** concerned with the production or use of oil. **12.** made with oil. **13.** using oil, esp. as a fuel. **14.** obtained from oil. [ME *olie, oile* < OF < L *oleum* (olive) oil < *olea* olive tree < Gk *elaía* OLIVE]

oil′ bee′tle, any of several blister beetles of the genus *Meloe* that exude an oily fluid from the joints of their legs.

oil′ cake′, a cake or mass of linseed, cottonseed, soybean, or the like, from which the oil has been extracted or expressed, used as food for livestock.

oil·can (oil′kan′), *n.* a can having a long spout through which oil is poured or squirted to lubricate machinery, etc.

oil·cloth (oil′klôth′, -kloth′), *n., pl.* **-cloths** (-klôthz′, -klothz′, -klôths′, -kloths′) for 2. **1.** a cotton fabric made waterproof by being treated with oil and pigment, for use as tablecloths, shelf coverings, and the like. **2.** a piece of this fabric.

oil′ col′or, a paint made by grinding a pigment in oil, usually linseed oil.

oil·cup (oil′kup′), *n.* a closed cup or can supplying lubricant to a bearing or bearings. Also called **grease cup.**

oil·er (oi′lər), *n.* **1.** a person or thing that oils. **2.** a workman employed to oil machinery. **3.** an oilcan. **4.** an oil tanker, esp. one for refueling other ships at sea.

oil′ field′, an area having large deposits of oil.

oil·man (oil′man′, -mən), *n., pl.* **-men** (-men′, -mən). **1.** a person who owns or operates oil wells. **2.** a person who retails or delivers oil.

oil′ of cade′. See under **cade**[1].

oil′ of tur′pentine, a colorless, flammable, volatile essential oil having a penetrating odor and a pungent, bitter taste: used in paints and varnishes, and as a carminative, vermifuge, expectorant, rubefacient, and, formerly, as a diuretic. Also called **spirits of turpentine, turpentine.**

oil′ of vit′riol, *Chem.* See **sulfuric acid.**

oil′ of win′tergreen. See **methyl salicylate.**

oil′ paint′, **1.** See **oil color. 2.** a commercial paint in which a drying oil is the vehicle.

oil′ paint′ing, **1.** the art or technique of painting with oil colors. **2.** a painting in oil colors. **—oil′ paint′er.**

Oil′ Riv′ers, a region in W Africa, comprising the vast Niger River delta: formerly a British protectorate; now a part of Nigeria.

oil·skin (oil′skin′), *n.* **1.** a cotton fabric made waterproof by treatment with oil and used for rain gear and fishermen's clothing. **2.** a piece of this. **3.** Often, **oilskins.** a garment made of this.

oil′ slick′, a smooth area on the surface of water caused by the presence of oil.

oil·stone (oil′stōn′), *n.* a block of fine-grained stone, usually oiled, for putting the final edge on certain cutting tools by abrasion.

oil′ well′, a well that yields petroleum.

oil·y (oi′lē), *adj.,* **oil·i·er, oil·i·est,** *adv.* **—*adj.* 1.** of or pertaining to oil. **2.** full of or containing oil. **3.** smeared or covered with oil. **4.** of the nature of, consisting of, or resembling oil. **5.** smooth or unctuous, as in manner or speech. **—*adv.* 6.** in an oily manner. **—oil′i·ness,** *n.*

oint·ment (oint′mənt), *n. Pharm.* a soft, unctuous preparation, often medicated, for application to the skin; an unguent. [obs. *oint* (aph. var. of ANOINT) + -MENT; r. ME *oignement* < OF < VL **unguiment(um)* for L *unguentum;* see UNGUENT] **—Syn.** salve, balm.

OIr, Old Irish. Also, **OIr., OIrish.**

Oise (WAZ), *n.* a river in W Europe, flowing SW from S Belgium through N France to the Seine, near Paris. 186 mi. long.

Oi·sin (u shēn′), *n.* Ossian.

OIt, Old Italian.

O·jib·wa (ō jib′wā, -wə), *n., pl.* **-was,** (*esp. collectively*) **-wa. 1.** a member of a large tribe of North American Indians divided geographically between the U.S. and Canada in the Lake Superior region. **2.** an Algonquian language used by the Ojibwa, Algonquin, and Ottawa Indians. Also, **Ojibway.** Also called **Chippewa.** [< AmerInd (Algonquian) *ojibway* to roast until puckered up = *ojib* to pucker up + *ub-way* to roast < *wāy* heat, with reference to the puckered seams on their moccasins]

O·jib·way (ō jib′wā), *n., pl.* **-ways,** (*esp. collectively*) **-way.** Ojibwa.

OK, **1.** See **O.K. 2.** Oklahoma (approved esp. for use with zip code).

O.K. (ō′kā′, ō′kā′), *adj., adv., v.,* **O.K.'d, O.K.'ing,** *n., pl.* **O.K.'s.** *Informal.* **—*adj., adv.* 1.** all right; all correct: *O.K., I'll get it for you. Everything is O.K.* **—*v.t.* 2.** to endorse or approve by saying or writing "O.K." **—*n.* 3.** an approval, agreement, or endorsement. Also, **OK, okay.** [prob. after the *O.K. Club,* formed in 1840 by partisans of Martin Van Buren, who allegedly named their organization in allusion to "Old Kinderhook," his birthplace being Kinderhook, New York; but cf. also the Bostonian phrase *all correct*]

o·ka (ō′kə), *n.* **1.** a unit of weight in Turkey and neighboring countries, equal to about 2¾ pounds. **2.** a unit of liquid measure, equal to about 1⅓ U.S. liquid quarts. Also, **oke.** [< It *occa* < Turk *ōqa* < Ar (cf. *ūqiyya*) < Gk *ounkía;* c. L *uncia;* see OUNCE[1]]

O·ka (o kä′), *n.* a river in the central Soviet Union in Europe, flowing NE to the Volga River at Gorki. ab. 950 mi. long.

o·ka·pi (ō kä′pē), *n., pl.* **-pis,** (*esp. collectively*) **-pi.** an African mammal, *Okapia johnstoni,* closely related to and resembling the giraffe, but smaller and with a much shorter neck. [< a Central Afr language]

O·ka·van·go (ō′kä väng′gō), *n.* Okovanggo.

o·kay (ō′kā′, ō′kā′), *adj., adv., v.t., n.* O.K.

O·ka·ya·ma (ô′kä yä′mä), *n.* a city on SW Honshu, in SW Japan. 301,438 (1964).

O·ka·za·ki (ô′kä zä′kē), *n.* a city on S central Honshu, in central Japan. 188,603 (1964).

oke[1] (ōk), *n.* oka.

oke[2] (ōk), *adj. Informal.* all right; O.K.

O·kee·cho·bee (ō′kē chō′bē), *n.* **Lake,** a lake in S Florida, in the N part of the Everglades. 35 mi. long; 30 mi. wide.

O'Keeffe (ō kēf′), *n.* **Georgia,** 1887–1986, U.S. painter.

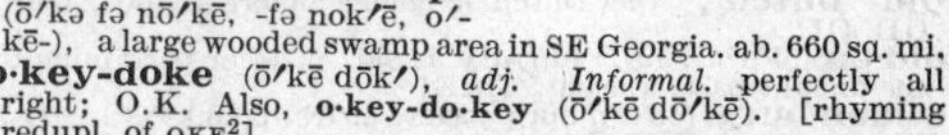

Okapi,
(5 ft. high at shoulder;
total length 7½ ft.;
tail 16 in.)

O·ke·fe·no′kee Swamp′ (ō′kə fə nō′kē, -fə nok′ē, ō′kē-), a large wooded swamp area in SE Georgia. ab. 660 sq. mi.

o·key-doke (ō′kē dōk′), *adj. Informal.* perfectly all right; O.K. Also, **o·key-do·key** (ō′kē dō′kē). [rhyming redupl. of OKE[2]]

O·khotsk (ō kotsk′; *Russ.* o khôtsk′), *n.* **Sea of,** an arm of the N Pacific, E of the Soviet Union in Asia. 582,000 sq. mi.

O·kie (ō′kē), *n. Usually Disparaging.* **1.** a migrant farm worker from Oklahoma. **2.** any migrant farm worker. [OK(LAHOMA) + -IE]

O·ki·na·wa (ō′kə nou′wə, -nä′wə; *Jap.* ô′kē nä′wä), *n.* the largest of the Ryukyu Islands, in the N Pacific, SW of Japan: occupied by the U.S. 1945–1972; returned to Japan 1972. 718,500 (est. 1959); 544 sq. mi. **—O′ki·na′wan,** *adj., n.*

Okla., Oklahoma.

O·kla·ho·ma (ō′klə hō′mə), *n.* a state in the S central United States. 2,559,253 (1970); 69,919 sq. mi. *Cap.:* Oklahoma City. *Abbr.:* OK, Okla. **—O′kla·ho′man,** *adj., n.*

O′klaho′ma Cit′y, a city in and the capital of Oklahoma, in the central part. 368,856 (1970).

O·ko·vang·go (ō′kə vang′gō), *n.* a river in central Africa, flowing SE from Angola to Botswana. ab. 1000 mi. long. Also, **Okavango.** Also called **Kubango.**

o·kra (ō′krə), *n.* **1.** a malvaceous shrub, *Hibiscus esculentus,* bearing beaked, mucilaginous pods. **2.** the pods, used in soups, stews, etc. **3.** a dish made with the pods; gumbo. [< a WAfr language]

OL, Old Latin. Also, **OL.**

-ol[1], a suffix used in the names of chemical derivatives, representing "alcohol" (*glycerol; naphthol; phenol*), or sometimes "phenol" or less definitely assignable phenol derivatives (*resorcinol*). [short for ALCOHOL OR PHENOL]

-ol[2], var. of **-ole.**

O.L., **1.** Also, **o.l.** (in prescriptions) the left eye. [< L *oculus laevus*] **2.** Old Latin.

O·laf I (ō′läf; *Eng.* ō′ləf), (*Olaf Tryggvessön*) A.D. 969–1000, king of Norway 995–1000. Also, **O·lav I** (ō′läv).

Olaf II, Saint (*Olaf Haraldssön*), A.D. 995–1030, king of Norway 1016–29; patron saint of Norway. Also, **Olav II.**

Olaf V, born 1903, king of Norway since 1957. Also, **Olav V.**

Ö·land (œ′länd′), *n.* an island in SE Sweden, separated by Kalmar Sound. 25,534 (1964); 519 sq. mi.

old (ōld), *adj.,* **old·er, old·est** or **eld·er, eld·est,** *n.* **—*adj.* 1.** far advanced in years or life: *an old man; an old horse.* **2.** of or pertaining to the latter part of the life or term of existence of a person or thing: *old age.* **3.** as if or appearing to be far advanced in years: *Worry had made him old.* **4.** having lived, existed, or matured for a specified time: *a man thirty years old.* **5.** having lived, existed, or matured as specified with relation to younger or newer persons or things: *Jim is our oldest boy. This is a fine old brandy.* **6.** long known or in use: *the same old excuse.* **7.** belonging to the past: *the good old days.* **8.** no longer in general use: *This typewriter is an old model.* **9.** having been replaced or supplanted. **10.** belonging to the historical or remote past. **11.** belonging to the earliest stage of development: *Old French.* **12.** having been such for a long time: *an old trouper.* **13.** (of colors) dull, faded, or subdued: *old rose.* **14.** deteriorated through age or long use. **15.** *Phys. Geog.* (of topographical features) far advanced in reduction by erosion or the like. **16.** sedate, sensible, or wise, as if from mature years. **17.** (used to indicate affection, familiarity, disparagement, or a personalization): *good old Bob; that dirty old thing.* **18.** *Informal.* (used as an intensive) great; uncommon: *a high old time.* **19.** having been so formerly: *a dinner for old Etonians.* **—*n.* 20.** (*construed as pl.*) old persons collectively (usually prec. by *the*): *care for the old.* **21.** a person or animal of a specified age or age group (used in combination): *a class for six-year-olds.* **22. of old,** in the past. [ME; OE *eald, ald;* c. D *old,* G *alt,* Goth *altheis;* akin to OIcel *ala* to nourish, L *-ul-* of *adultus* ADULT] **—old′ish,** *adj.* **—old′ness,** *n.*

—Syn. 1. OLD, AGED, ELDERLY all mean well along in years. An OLD person has lived long, nearly to the end of the usual period of life. An AGED person is very far advanced in years, and is usually afflicted with the infirmities of age. An ELDERLY person is somewhat old, but usually has the mellowness, satisfactions, and joys of age before him. **6.** olden.

Old′ Ad′am, (in theology) man in his unredeemed state.
old′ age′, the last period of human life, generally considered to be the years after 65. [ME]
Old′ Bai′ley (bā′lē), the main criminal court of London.
old boy (ōld′ boi′ *for 1;* ōld′ boi′ *for 2;* ōld′ boi′ *for 3*), 1. a vivacious, elderly man. 2. *Brit.* an alumnus, esp. of a preparatory or public school. 3. *Chiefly Brit.* See **old chap.**
Old′ Bridge′, a town in central New Jersey. 25,176 (1970).
Old′ Brit′ish, Brythonic as used before A.D. c800.
Old′ Bulgar′ian, the Bulgarian language of the Middle Ages. *Abbr.:* OBulg, OBulg. Cf. **Old Church Slavonic.**
Old′ Cas·tile′ (ka stēl′), a region in N Spain: formerly a province. Spanish, **Castilla la Vieja.**
Old·cas·tle (ōld′kas′əl, -kä′səl), *n.* **Sir John,** 1377–1417, English Lollard leader, executed for treason and heresy: model of Shakespeare's Falstaff.
old′ chap′, *Chiefly Brit.* (used in direct address to a close friend.) Also called **old boy.**
Old′ Church′ Slavon′ic, the oldest attested Slavic language, an ecclesiastical language that represents the South Slavic, Bulgarian dialect of 9th-century Salonika with considerable addition of other South and West Slavic elements. *Abbr.:* OCS Also called **Old′ Church′ Slavic′, Old Slavic, Old Slavonic.** Cf. **Church Slavic.**
old′ coun′try, *U.S.* the original home country of an immigrant or a person's ancestors.
Old′ Del′hi, Delhi (def. 2).
Old′ Domin′ion, the State of Virginia (used as a nickname).
Old′ Dutch′, the Dutch language before c1100. *Abbr.:* OD, OD.
old·en (ōl′dᵊn), *adj. Literary.* 1. old. 2. of or pertaining to the distant past; ancient. [ME]
Ol·den·burg (ōl′dᵊn bûrg′; Ger. ōl′dᵊn bŏŏʀk′), *n.* 1. a former state in NW Germany: now a part of Lower Saxony. 2. a city in NW West Germany. 126,200 (1963).
Old′ Eng′lish, 1. Also called **Anglo-Saxon.** the English language of A.D. c450–c1150. *Abbr.:* OE, OE. 2. *Print.* a style of black letter.
Old′ Eng′lish sheep′dog, one of an English breed of medium-sized dogs having a long, shaggy, gray or merle-and-white coat that hangs over the eyes.
old·er (ōl′dər), *adj.* a comparative of **old.**
—Syn. OLDER, ELDER imply having greater age than something or someone else. OLDER is the usual form of the comparative of old: *This building is older than that one.* ELDER is used chiefly to indicate seniority in age between any two people but esp. priority of birth between children born of the same parents: *The elder brother became king.*
old·est (ōl′dist), *adj.* a superlative of **old.**
Old′ Fash′ioned, a cocktail made with whiskey, bitters, water, and sugar, garnished with citrus fruit slices and a cherry.
old-fash·ioned (ōld′fash′ənd), *adj.* reflecting the styles, customs, or methods of the past; out-of-date; antiquated. **—old′-fash′ioned·ly,** *adv.* **—old′-fash′ioned·ness,** *n.* **—Syn.** outmoded, obsolete. See **ancient**[1].
Old′ Flem′ish, the Flemish language before c1300. *Abbr.:* OFlem, OFlem.
old′ fo′gy, a person who is excessively conservative or old-fashioned in ideas, manners, etc. Also, **old′ fo′gey. —old′-fo′gy·ish, old′-fo′gey·ish,** *adj.*
Old′ Franco′nian, the Franconian language before 1100; Frankish.
Old′ French′, the French language of the 9th through 13th centuries. *Abbr.:* OF, OF., O.F., OFr.
Old′ Fri′sian, the Frisian language before c1500. *Abbr.:* OFris, OFris.
Old′ Glo′ry. See **Stars and Stripes.**
old′ goat′, *Slang.* 1. an elderly man who is disliked, esp. for being mean to younger people. 2. a lecherous old man.
Old′ Guard′, 1. *U.S.* the conservative element of any political party. 2. (*usually l.c.*) the influential, established, more conservative members of any group. [trans. of F *Vieille Garde*] **—Old′ Guard′ism.**
Old·ham (ōl′dəm; *locally* ou′dəm), *n.* a city in SE Lancashire, in NW England, near Manchester. 115,426 (1961).
old′ hand′, a person who is knowledgeable about something, esp. from long experience.
Old′ Har′ry, Satan.
old′ hat′, *Informal.* old-fashioned; trite from having long been used or known.
Old′ High′ Ger′man, High German before c1100. *Abbr.:* OHG, OHG., O.H.G.
Old′ Icelan′dic, Old Norse as used in Iceland. *Abbr.:* OIcel
old·ie (ōl′dē), *n. Informal.* a popular song, joke, movie, etc. that was in vogue at a time considerably in the past.
Old′ Ion′ic, epic (def. 9).
Old′ I′rish, the Irish language before the 11th century. *Abbr.:* OIr, OIr., OIrish.
Old′ I′ronsides, the U.S. frigate *Constitution* (used as a nickname).
old·ish (ōl′dish), *adj.* somewhat old: *an oldish man.*
Old′ Ital′ian, the Italian language of the 10th to the 14th centuries. *Abbr.:* OIt
Old′ King′dom, the period of the III–VI dynasties in the history of ancient Egypt, 2780-2280 B.C. Cf. **Middle Kingdom** (def. 1), **New Kingdom.**
old′ la′dy, *Informal.* 1. a mother, usually one's own. 2. a wife, esp. a man's own.
Old′ La′dy of Thread′nee·dle Street′ (thred′nēd-ᵊl), the Bank of England (used as a nickname).
Old′ Lat′in, the Latin language found in written records of the 7th to the 1st centuries B.C. *Abbr.:* OL, OL., O.L.
old-line (ōld′līn′), *adj.* 1. following or supporting conservative or traditional ideas, beliefs, customs, etc. 2. long established; traditional: *old-line society.* **—old′-lin′er,** *n.*
Old′ Low′ Fran·co′ni·an (frang kō′nē ən), a Low German dialect of the Franks of the lower Rhine valley before c1100. Also called **Old′ Low′ Frank′ish.**
Old′ Low′ Ger′man, the language of the German lowlands before c1100. *Abbr.:* OLG, O.L.G.
old′ maid′, 1. an elderly or confirmed spinster. 2. a fussy, timid, or prudish person. 3. *Cards.* a. a simple game in which the players draw from one another to match pairs and the one holding an odd queen at the end loses. b. the loser of such a game. 4. *Facetious.* the person who takes the last portion of food from a serving platter.
old-maid·ish (ōld′mā′dish), *adj.* resembling an old maid, esp. in being prudish, fussy, etc.
old′ man′, *Informal.* 1. a father, esp. a person's own. 2. a husband, esp. a woman's own. 3. (*sometimes caps.*) a person in a position of authority, as an employer or a commanding officer. 4. southernwood.
old′ mas′ter, 1. an eminent artist of an earlier period, esp. 15th–18th centuries. 2. a painting by such an artist.
Old′ Nick′, Satan.
Old′ Norse′, the Germanic language of medieval Scandinavia. *Abbr.:* ON, ON., O.N.
Old′ North′ French′, the dialect of Old French spoken in northern France. *Abbr.:* ONF, ONFr.
Old′ Per′sian, an ancient West Iranian language attested by cuneiform inscriptions. *Abbr.:* OPers
Old′ Pretend′er. See **Stuart, James Francis Edward.**
Old′ Provençal′, the Provençal language as found in documents from the 11th to the 16th centuries. *Abbr.:* OPr
Old′ Prus′sian, a Baltic language extinct since the 17th century. *Abbr.:* OPruss
Old′ Rus′sian, Russian as used in documents c1300–c1600. *Abbr.:* ORuss
Old′ Sax′on, the Saxon dialect of Low German as spoken before c1100. *Abbr.:* OS, OS.
old′ school′, advocates or supporters of established custom or of conservatism. **—old′-school′,** *adj.*
old′ school′ tie′, 1. a necktie whose markings indicate that the wearer is the alumnus of an English public school. 2. the clannishness, conservatism, or personal influence believed to prevail among alumni of such schools.
Old′ Scratch′, Satan.
old-shoe (ōld′shōō′), *adj. Informal.* comfortably familiar or unpretentious.
Old′ Slav′ic. See **Old Church Slavonic.** Also called **Old′ Slavon′ic.** *Abbr.:* OSlav
Old′ South′, the U.S. South before the Civil War.
Old′ Span′ish, the Spanish language of the 12th to the 16th centuries. *Abbr.:* OSp
old′ stag′er, stager (def. 1).
old·ster (ōld′stər), *n. Informal.* an old or elderly person.
Old′ Stone′ Age′, the Paleolithic period.
old′ style′, 1. Also, **old·style** (ōld′stīl′). *Print.* a type style differentiated from modern by the more or less uniform thickness of all strokes and by slanted serifs. 2. (*caps.*) time reckoned according to the Julian calendar. Cf. **New Style. —old′-style′,** *adj.*
Old Test., Old Testament.
Old′ Tes′tament, 1. the first of the two main divisions of the Christian Bible, regarded as the complete Bible of the Jews, and comprising the Law, the Prophets, and the Hagiographa. 2. the covenant between God and Israel on Mount Sinai, constituting the basis of the Hebrew religion. Ex. 19–24; Jer. 31:31–34; II Cor. 3:6, 14. [ME, trans. of LL *Vetus Testament(um),* trans. of Gk *Palaiā Diathḗkē*]
old-time (ōld′tīm′), *adj.* 1. belonging to or characteristic of old or former times. 2. being long established.
old-tim·er (ōld′tī′mər), *n. Informal.* 1. a person whose residence, membership, or experience dates from long ago. 2. an elderly person; oldster. 3. (used as a form of familiar direct address to an elderly man.)
Ol′du·vai Gorge′ (ōl′dōō vī′), a gorge in Tanzania in which Australopithecine and human remains are located.
old·wife (old′wīf′), *n., pl.* **-wives.** any of various fishes, as the alewife, the menhaden, etc.
old′ wives′ tale′, a superstitious belief, story, or idea.
old-wom·an·ish (ōld′wŏŏm′ə nish), *adj.* characteristic of an old woman, as excessive fussiness.
Old′ World′, 1. Europe, Asia, and Africa. 2. See **Eastern Hemisphere.**
old-world (ōld′wûrld′), *adj.* 1. of or pertaining to the ancient world or to a former period of history. 2. of or pertaining to the Old World. **—old′-world′ly,** *adj.*
Old′ World′ mon′key, any of the monkeys indigenous to the Eastern Hemisphere: characterized by close-set, downward-opening nostrils and a nonprehensile tail.
o·lé (ō lā′), *n.* 1. a shout of approval, acclamation, etc. *—interj.* 2. (used as a shout of approval or encouragement to a bullfighter, performer, etc.) [< Sp < Ar *wa-llāh* = *wa-* and *allāh* God, ALLAH]
-ole, var. of **oleo-** as final element of compounds: *thiazole.* Also, **-ol.**
o·le·a·ceous (ō′lē ā′shəs), *adj.* belonging to the *Oleaceae,* or olive family of plants, comprising the ash, jasmine, etc. [< NL *Oleāce(ae)* (see OIL, -ACEAE) + -OUS]
o·le·ag·i·nous (ō′lē aj′ə nəs), *adj.* 1. having the nature or qualities of oil. 2. containing oil. 3. producing oil. 4. oily in manner. [< L *oleāginus* of the olive < *olea* olive tree; see OIL]
o·le·an·der (ō′lē an′dər, ō′lē an′-), *n.* any apocynaceous plant of the genus *Nerium,* esp. the poisonous evergreen *N. Oleander,* having showy rose-colored or white flowers or *N. odorum,* of India, having fragrant flowers. [< ML < ? Cf. LL *lorandrum,* var. of L *rhododendron* RHODODENDRON]
o·le·as·ter (ō′lē as′tər), *n.* an ornamental shrub or small tree, *Elaeagnus angustifolia,* of southern Europe and western Asia, having fragrant yellow flowers and an olivelike fruit. [ME < L: wild olive tree < *olea* olive tree; see OIL]
o·le·ate (ō′lē āt′), *n. Chem.* an ester or a salt of oleic acid. [OLE(IC) + -ATE[2]]
o·lec·ra·non (ō lek′rə non′, ō′lə krā′non), *n. Anat.* the part of the ulna beyond the elbow joint. [< NL < Gk *ōlékrānon* point of the elbow, short for *ōlenókrānon* = *ōlénē* elbow + *krānion* head; see CRANIUM] **—o·lec·ra·nal** (ō lek′rə nᵊl, ō′lə krān′ᵊl), **o′le·cra′ni·al, o′le·cra′ni·an, o′le·cra′ni·oid′,** *adj.*

o·le·fin (ō′lə fin), *n.* *Chem.* any member of the alkene series. Also, **o·le·fine** (ō′lə fin, -fēn′). [< F *oléf(iant)* (*olé-* OLEO- + *-fiant;* see -FY, -ANT) + -IN²] —**o′le·fin′ic,** *adj.*

o′lefin se′ries, *Chem.* See **alkene series.**

o·le·ic (ō lē′ik, ō′lē ik), *adj.* *Chem.* pertaining to or derived from oleic acid. [< L *ole(um)* OIL + -IC]

ole′ic ac′id, *Chem.* a water-insoluble liquid unsaturated acid, $CH_3(CH_2)_7CH{=}CH(CH_2)_7COOH$, used chiefly in the manufacture of soap and cosmetics.

o·le·in (ō′lē in), *n.* *Chem.* **1.** an oily liquid, $(C_{17}H_{33}COO)_3$-C_3H_5, the triglyceride of oleic acid. **2.** the oily or lower-melting fractions of a fat as distinguished from the solid or higher-melting constituents. [< F *oléine.* See OLEO-, -IN²]

o·le·o (ō′lē ō), *n.* oleomargarine. [by shortening]

oleo-, a learned borrowing from Latin meaning "oil," used in the formation of compound words: *oleograph.* Also, **-ol, -ole.** [< L, comb. form repr. *oleum* OIL]

o·le·o·graph (ō′lē ə graf′, -gräf′), *n.* a chromolithograph printed in oil colors on canvas or cloth. —**o·le·o·graph·ic** (ō′lē ə graf′ik), *adj.* —**o·le·og·ra·phy** (ō′lē og′rə fē), *n.*

o·le·o·mar·ga·rine (ō′lē ō mär′jə rin, -rēn′, -märj′-rin, -rēn), *n.* a butter substitute used as a cooking and table fat, made by combining animal oils such as oleo oil and refined lard, and sometimes cottonseed oil, with milk. Also, **o′le·o·mar′ga·rin.** Also called **margarine.** [< F *oléomargarine*] —**o·le·o·mar·gar·ic** (ō′lē ō mär gär′ik), *adj.*

o′leo oil′, a product obtained from beef fat and consisting chiefly of a mixture of olein and palmitin, used for making butterlike foods.

o·le·o·res·in (ō′lē ō rez′ən), *n.* **1.** a mixture of an essential oil and a resin, found in nature. **2.** *Pharm.* an oil holding resin in solution, extracted from a substance, as ginger, by means of alcohol, ether, or acetone. —**o′le·o·res′in·ous,** *adj.*

ol·er·i·cul·ture (ol′ər ə kul′chər), *n.* the cultivation of vegetables. [< L *oleri-* (s. of *olus* or *holus*) vegetable, kitchen herb + CULTURE] —**ol′er·i·cul′tur·al,** *adj.* —**ol′er·i·cul′tur·al·ly,** *adv.* —**ol′er·i·cul′tur·ist,** *n.*

o·le·um (ō′lē əm), *n., pl.* **o·le·a** (ō′lē ə), *Pharm.* oil. [< L: OIL]

ol·fac·tion (ol fak′shən), *n.* **1.** the act of smelling. **2.** the sense of smell. [< L *olfact(us)* smelled (see OLFACTORY) + -ION]

ol·fac·to·ry (ol fak′tə rē, -trē), *adj., n., pl.* **-ries.** —*adj.* **1.** of or pertaining to the sense of smell: *olfactory organs.* —*n.* **2.** Usually, **olfactories.** an olfactory organ. **3.** See **olfactory nerve.** [< L *olfactōri(us)* < *olfact(us)* smelled, ptp. of *olfacere* (*ol(ere)* (to) smell + *facere* to make, do) + *-ōrius* -ORY¹] —**ol·fac′to·ri·ly,** *adv.*

olfac′tory nerve′, *Anat.* either one of the first pair of cranial nerves, consisting of sensory fibers that conduct to the brain the impulses from the mucous membranes of the nose.

OLG, Old Low German. Also, **O.L.G.**

o·lib·a·num (ō lib′ə nəm), *n.* frankincense. [ME < ML, var. of LL *liban(us)* < Gk *líbanos,* of Sem orig.; cf. Heb *lebhonāh*]

ol·i·garch (ol′ə gärk′), *n.* one of the rulers in an oligarchy. [< Gk *oligárch(ēs)*]

ol·i·gar·chic (ol′ə gär′kik), *adj.* of, pertaining to, or having the form of an oligarchy. Also, **ol′i·gar′chi·cal.** [< Gk *oligarchik(ós).* See OLIGARCHY, -IC] —**ol′i·gar′chi·cal·ly,** *adv.*

ol·i·gar·chy (ol′ə gär′kē), *n., pl.* **-chies.** **1.** a form of government in which the power is vested in a few persons. **2.** a state or organization so ruled. **3.** the persons or class so ruling. [< ML *oligarchia* < Gk *oligarchía*]

oligo-, a learned borrowing from Greek meaning "few," "little," used in the formation of compound words: *oligopoly.* Also, *esp. before a vowel,* **olig-.** [< Gk, comb. form of *olígos* little (in pl., few)]

Ol·i·go·cene (ol′ə gō sēn′), *Geol.* —*adj.* **1.** noting or pertaining to an epoch either of the Tertiary or Paleogene period, occurring from 25,000,000 to 40,000,000 years ago and characterized by the presence of saber-toothed cats. See table at **era.** —*n.* **2.** the Oligocene epoch or series.

ol·i·go·chaete (ol′ə gō kēt′), *n.* any of a group of annelids, including earthworms and certain small, fresh-water species, having locomotory setae sunk directly in the body wall. [< NL *Oligochaet(a).* See OLIGO-, CHAETA] —**ol′i·go·chae′tous,** *adj.*

ol·i·go·clase (ol′ə gō klās′), *n.* *Mineral.* a kind of plagioclase feldspar occurring commonly in crystals of white color, sometimes shaded with gray, green, or red. [OLIGO- + Gk *klás(is)* a breaking]

ol·i·gop·o·ly (ol′ə gop′ə lē), *n.* the market condition that exists when there are few sellers. [OLIGO- + (MONO)POLY] —**ol·i·gop·o·lis·tic** (ol′ə gop′ə lis′tik), *adj.*

ol·i·gop·so·ny (ol′ə gop′sə nē), *n.* the market condition that exists when there are few buyers. [OLIG- + Gk *opsōnía* purchase of victuals] —**ol′i·gop′so·nis′tic,** *adj.*

ol·i·go·sac·cha·ride (ol′ə gō sak′ə rīd′, -ər id), *n.* *Chem.* any carbohydrate yielding few monosaccharides on hydrolysis, as two, three, or four.

ol·i·go·troph·ic (ol′ə gō trof′ik), *adj.* *Ecol.* (of a lake) characterized by a low accumulation of dissolved nutrient salts, supporting but a sparse plant and animal life, and having a high oxygen content owing to the low organic content. —**ol·i·got·ro·phy** (ol′ə go′trə fē), *n.*

o·li·o (ō′lē ō′), *n., pl.* **o·li·os.** **1.** a dish of many ingredients. **2.** a medley or potpourri, as of musical or literary selections; miscellany. [< Sp *olla* pot, stew < LL: pot, jar]

ol·i·va·ceous (ol′ə vā′shəs), *adj.* olive in color. [< NL *olīvāceus*]

ol·i·va·ry (ol′ə ver′ē), *adj.* **1.** shaped like an olive. **2.** of or pertaining to an olivary body. [< L *olīvāri(us)* belonging to olives]

o′livary bod′y, *Anat.* one of two oval bodies or prominences composed of nerve tissue, one on each side of the anterior surface of the medulla oblongata.

ol·ive (ol′iv), *n.* **1.** an evergreen tree, *Olea europaea,* of Mediterranean and other warm regions. **2.** the fruit of this tree, a small oval drupe, used as a relish and as a source of oil. **3.** any of various related or similar trees. **4.** the foliage of this tree. **5.** a wreath of this foliage. **6.** See **olive branch. 7.** an ocher green or dull yellow green. —*adj.* **8.** of, pertaining to, or made of olives, their foliage, or their fruit. **9.** of or tinged with the color olive. [ME < OF < L *olīv(a);* akin to Gk *elaía* olive tree. See OIL]

ol′ive branch′, **1.** a branch of the olive tree as an emblem of peace. **2.** something offered as a token of peace.

ol′ive drab′, *pl.* **olive drabs** for 3. **1.** a deep olive color. **2.** woolen cloth of this color used for U.S. Army uniforms. **3.** a uniform made from this cloth.

ol·ive-green (ol′iv grēn′), *n., adj.* green with a yellowish or brownish tinge.

o·liv·en·ite (ō liv′ə nīt′, ol′ə və-), *n.* a mineral, basic copper arsenate, $Cu_4As_2O_8(OH)_2$, usually olive-green in color. [< G *Oliven(erz)* olive (ore) + -ITE¹]

ol′ive oil′, an oil expressed from the olive fruit, used with food, in medicine, etc.

Ol·i·ver (ol′ə vər), *n.* one of the 12 paladins of Charlemagne. Cf. **Roland.**

Ol·ives (ol′ivz), *n.* **Mount of,** a small ridge E of Jerusalem, in what is now Jordan: part of the territory occupied by Israel 1967. Highest point, 2680 ft. Also, **Ol·i·vet** (ol′ə vet′, -vit).

ol·i·vine (ol′ə vēn′, ol′ə vēn′), *n.* **1.** a common mineral, magnesium iron silicate, $(Mg,Fe)_2SiO_4$, occurring commonly in olive-green to gray-green masses as an important constituent of basic igneous rocks. **2.** a rare, transparent variety of this, used as a gem; peridot. Also called **chrysolite.** [< G *Olivin* = *Olive* OLIVE + *-in* -INE²]

o·lla (ō′lyä, ô′yä; *Eng.* ol′ə), *n.* *Spanish.* an earthen pot or jar for holding water, cooking, etc.

ol·la po·dri·da (ol′ə pə drē′də; *Sp.* ô′lyä pô thrē′thä, ô′yä-), **1.** a Spanish stew of meat and vegetables. **2.** an incongruous mixture; miscellany. [< Sp: lit., rotten pot]

Olm·sted (ōm′stid, -sted), *n.* **Frederick Law,** 1822–1903, U.S. landscape architect: designer of Central Park, N.Y.C.

O·lo·mouc (ô′lô mōts), *n.* a city in central Moravia, in Czechoslovakia. 73,591 (1963). German, **Ol·mütz** (ôl′mʏts).

Ol·wen (ol′wen), *n.* *Welsh Legend.* a princess, the daughter of Yspadaden Penkawr.

O·lym·pi·a (ō lim′pē ə), *n.* **1.** a plain in ancient Elis, Greece, where the Olympic Games were held. **2.** a city in and the capital of Washington, in the W part, on Puget Sound. 23,111 (1970).

o·lym·pi·ad (ō lim′pē ad′), *n.* (*often cap.*) **1.** a period of four years reckoned from one celebration of the Olympic Games to the next, by which the Greeks computed time from 776 B.C. **2.** a celebration of the modern Olympic Games. [ME < L *Olympiad-* (s. of *Olympias*) < Gk] —**O·lym′pi·ad′ic,** *adj.*

O·lym·pi·an (ō lim′pē ən), *adj.* **1.** pertaining to Mount Olympus or dwelling thereon, as the gods of classical Greece. **2.** of, characteristic of, or suitable to the gods of Olympus, as in being majestic, aloof, or disdainful. **3.** of or pertaining to the Olympic Games. —*n.* **4.** an Olympian deity. **5.** a contender in the Olympic Games. [< LL *Olympiān(us)* = L *Olympi(us)* (< Gk *Olýmpios* < *Ólymp(os)* OLYMPUS) + *-iānus* -IAN]

O·lym·pic (ō lim′pik), *adj.* **1.** of or pertaining to the Olympic Games. —*n.* **2. Olympics.** See **Olympic Games.** [< L *Olympic(us)* of Olympus, of Olympia < Gk *Olympikós*]

Olym′pic Games′, **1.** Also called **Olym′pian Games′.** the greatest of the games or festivals of ancient Greece, held every four years in honor of Zeus. **2.** a modern revival of these games consisting of athletic and sports contests involving amateur participants from nations throughout the world, held every four years, each time in a different country.

Olym′pic Moun′tains, a mountain system in NW Washington, part of the Coast Range. Highest peak, Mt. Olympus, 7954 ft.

Olym′pic Na′tional Park′, a national park in NW Washington. 1323 sq. mi.

Olym′pic-size′ pool′ (ō lim′pik sīz′), a large swimming pool, typically 25 meters in length, esp. one attached to a resort hotel or apartment house. Also called **Olym′pic pool′.**

O·lym·pus (ō lim′pəs), *n.* **Mount, 1.** a mountain in NE Greece, on the boundary between Thessaly and Macedonia: mythical abode of the greater Grecian gods. 9730 ft. **2.** a mountain in NW Washington: highest peak of the Olympic Mountains. 7954 ft.

O·lyn·thus (ō lin′thəs), *n.* an ancient city in NE Greece, on Chalcidice Peninsula. —**O·lyn·thi·ac** (ō lin′thē ak′), **O·lyn′thi·an,** *adj., n.*

Om., ostmark; ostmarks.

O.M., *Brit.* Order of Merit.

-oma, *pl.* **-omas, -omata.** a noun suffix appearing in loan words from Greek, specialized in terms from pathology to indicate a tumor: *carcinoma; glaucoma; sarcoma.* [< Gk *-ōma*]

O·ma·ha (ō′mə hô′, -hä′), *n., pl.* **-has,** (*esp. collectively*) **-ha** for 2. **1.** a city in E Nebraska, on the Missouri River. 346,929 (1970). **2.** a member of a Siouan people formerly living in northeastern Nebraska.

O·man (ō män′), *n.* **1. Sultanate of.** Formerly, **Muscat and Oman.** an independent absolute monarchy in SE Arabia. 800,000; ab. 82,000 sq. mi. *Cap.:* Muscat. **2. Gulf of,** a NW arm of the Arabian Sea, at the entrance to the Persian Gulf.

O·mar Khay·yám (ō′mär kī yäm′, -yam′, ō′mər), died 1123?, Persian poet and mathematician.

o·ma·sum (ō mā′səm), *n., pl.* **-sa** (-sə). the third stomach of a ruminant, between the reticulum and the abomasum; the manyplies. [< NL, L: bullock's tripe]

O·may·yad (ō mī′ad), *n., pl.* **-yads, -ya·des** (-ə dēz′). **1.** a member of the dynasty that ruled at Damascus A.D. 661–750. **2.** a member of the dynasty of caliphs, closely related to the Damascus dynasty, that ruled in southern Spain, A.D. 756–1031. Also, **Ommiad, Umayyad.**

om·ber (om′bər), *n.* **1.** a card game popular in the 17th and 18th centuries and played, usually by three persons, with forty cards. **2.** the player undertaking to win the pool in this game. Also, **hombre;** *esp. Brit.,* **om′bre.** [< F *(h)ombre*

< Sp *hombre,* lit., man < L *homin-* (s. of *homō*) man. See HOMAGE]

om·buds·man (om′bo͝odz man′; *Sw.* ôm′bʏdz män′), *n., pl.* **-men,** *Sw.* **-man** (-men′). **1.** a commissioner appointed by a legislature, as in some Scandinavian countries, to hear and investigate complaints by private citizens against government officials or agencies. **2.** any official patterned after this, in other countries. [< Sw: commissioner]

Om·dur·man (om′do͝or män′), *n.* a city in the central Sudan, on the White Nile opposite Khartoum: British victory over the Mahdi, 1898. 171,000 (est. 1964).

o·me·ga (ō mē′gə, -mā′-, ō meg′ə, ō′meg ə), *n.* **1.** the 24th letter of the Greek alphabet (Ω, ω). **2.** the last of any series; the end. [< Gk *ō méga,* lit., great *o.* Cf. OMICRON]

ome′ga mi′nus, *Physics.* a subatomic particle that decays into a cascade particle on collision with a pi meson.

o·me′ga-3 fat′ty ac′id (ō mē′gə thrē′, ō mā′-, ō-meg′ə-), a polyunsaturated fatty acid, abundant in fish of northern seas, that influences various metabolic pathways, resulting in lowered cholesterol and triglyceride levels, inhibited platelet clotting, and reduced inflammatory reactions. [so named because its 1st double bond occurs after the 3rd carbon atom counting from the methyl or *omega* end of the molecule]

om·e·let (om′ə lit, om′lit), *n.* eggs beaten until frothy, and cooked until set, often with other ingredients added, as cheese, herbs, jelly, or chopped ham. Also, **om′e·lette.** [< F *omelette,* earlier *amelette,* metathetic form of *alemette,* var. of *alemelle,* lit., thin plate, var. of OF *lemelle* < L *lamella.* See LAMELLA, -ET]

o·men (ō′mən), *n.* **1.** any event believed to portend something good or evil. **2.** prophetic significance; presage: *a bird of ill omen.* —*v.t.* **3.** to be an omen of; portend. [< L; OL *osmen* < ?] —**Syn. 1.** augury, foreboding. See **sign.**

o·men·tum (ō men′təm), *n., pl.* **-ta** (-tə). *Anat.* a fold or duplication of the peritoneum passing between certain of the viscera. [< L: fat skin] —**o·men′tal,** *adj.*

o·mer (ō′mər), *n.* a Hebrew unit of dry measure, the tenth part of an ephah. [< Heb *'ōmer*]

om·i·cron (om′ə kron′, ō′mə-), *n.* the 15th letter of the Greek alphabet (O, ο). [< Gk *ō mikrón,* lit., small *o*]

om·i·nous (om′ə nəs), *adj.* **1.** portending evil or harm; threatening. **2.** having the significance of an omen. [< L *ōminōs(us)* portentous = *ōmin-* (s. of *ōmen*) OMEN + *-ōsus* -OUS] —**om′i·nous·ly,** *adv.* —**om′i·nous·ness,** *n.* —**Syn. 1.** portentous, unpropitious.

o·mis·si·ble (ō mis′ə bəl), *adj.* capable of being or allowed to be omitted. [< L *omiss(us)* let go (see OMISSION) + -IBLE]

o·mis·sion (ō mish′ən), *n.* **1.** the act of omitting. **2.** the state of being omitted. **3.** something omitted. [ME < LL *omissiōn-* (s. of *omissiō*) = *omiss(us)* let go (ptp. of *omittere;* see OMIT) + *-iōn-* -ION; see MISSION]

o·mis·sive (ō mis′iv), *adj.* neglecting; leaving out. [< L *omiss(us)* let go (see OMISSION) + -IVE]

o·mit (ō mit′), *v.t.,* **o·mit·ted, o·mit·ting. 1.** to leave out; not include or mention. **2.** to forbear or fail to do, make, use, send, etc. [ME *omitt(en)* < L *omitt(ere)* (to) let go = *o-* O-[2] + *mitt-* send]

om·ma·tid·i·um (om′ə tid′ē əm), *n., pl.* **-tid·i·a** (-tid′ē ə). *Zool.* one of the radial elements composing a compound eye. [< NL < Gk *ommat-* (s. of *ómma* eye) + *-idion* -IDION] —**om′ma·tid′i·al,** *adj.*

om·mat·o·phore (ə mat′ə fōr′, -fôr′), *n. Zool.* a tentacle or movable stalk bearing an eye, as in certain snails. [< Gk *ommat-* (s. of *ómma* eye) + -o- + -PHORE] —**om·ma·toph·or·ous** (om′ə tof′ər əs), *adj.*

Om·mi·ad (ō mī′ad), *n., pl.* **-ads, -a·des** (-ə dēz′). Omayyad.

omni-, an element of Latin origin meaning "all," used in combination with various words: *omnifarious; omnipotence; omniscient.* [< L, comb. form of *omnis*]

om·ni·a vin·cit a·mor (ôm′nē ä′ wen̄g′kit ä′môr; *Eng.* om′nē ə vin′sit ā′môr), *Latin.* love conquers all.

om·ni·bus (om′nə bus′, -bəs), *n., pl.* **-bus·es,** *adj.* —*n.* **1.** bus (def. 1). **2.** a volume of reprinted works of a single author or of works related in interest or theme. —*adj.* **3.** pertaining to or dealing with numerous objects or items at once. [< F < L: for all (dat. pl. of *omnis*)]

om·ni·far·i·ous (om′nə fâr′ē əs), *adj.* of all forms, varieties, or kinds. [< LL *omnifārius* < L *omnifāriam* on all sides) = L *omni-* OMNI- + *-fārius* -fold] —**om′ni·far′i·ous·ly,** *adv.* —**om′ni·far′i·ous·ness,** *n.*

om·nif·i·cent (om nif′i sənt), *adj.* creating all things; having all powers of creation. [OMNI- + *-ficent,* as in *beneficent*]

om·nip·o·tence (om nip′ə təns), *n.* the quality or state of being omnipotent. [< LL *omnipotentia.* See OMNIPOTENT]

om·nip·o·tent (om nip′ə tənt), *adj.* **1.** almighty, or infinite in power, as God or a deity. **2.** having very great or unlimited authority or power. —*n.* **3. the Omnipotent,** God. [ME < L *omnipotent-* (s. of *omnipotēns*). See OMNI-, POTENT[1]] —**om·nip′o·tent·ly,** *adv.*

om·ni·pres·ent (om′nə prez′ənt), *adj.* present everywhere at the same time. [< ML *omnipraesent-* (s. of *omnipraesēns*)] —**om′ni·pres′ence,** *n.*

om·nis·cience (om nish′əns), *n.* **1.** the quality or state of being omniscient. **2.** infinite knowledge. **3.** extensive knowledge. [< ML *omniscientia.* See OMNI-, SCIENCE]

om·nis·cient (om nish′ənt), *adj.* **1.** having complete or infinite knowledge, awareness, or understanding; perceiving all things. **2.** having extensive knowledge: *Goethe was omniscient in his era.* —*n.* **3.** an omniscient being. [< NL *omniscient-* (s. of *omnisciēns*) = L *omni-* OMNI- + *scient-* (s. of *sciēns*) knowing; see SCIENCE] —**om·nis′cient·ly,** *adv.*

om·ni·um-gath·er·um (om′nē əm gath′ər əm), *n., pl.* **-ums.** a miscellaneous collection. [< L *omnium* of all (gen. pl. of *omnis*) + *gatherum* a gathering, pseudo-L < GATHER]

om·ni·vore (om′nə vōr′, -vôr′), *n.* **1.** a person or thing that is omnivorous. **2.** an omnivorous animal. [< NL *Omnivor(a)* name of the group, n. use of neut. pl. of L *omnivorus* OMNIVOROUS]

om·niv·or·ous (om niv′ər əs), *adj.* **1.** eating all kinds of foods indiscriminately. **2.** eating both animal and plant foods. **3.** taking in everything, as with the mind. [< L *omnivorus*] —**om·niv′o·rous·ly,** *adv.* —**om·niv′o·rous·ness,** *n.*

om·pha·cite (om′fə sīt′), *n. Mineral.* a pale-green variety of pyroxene similar to olivine, found in eclogite rocks. [< G *Omphazit* < Gk *omphakît(ēs)* green stone = *omphak-* (s. of *ómphax*) unripe grape + *-ītēs* -ITE[1]]

om·pha·los (om′fə ləs), *n.* **1.** the navel. **2.** the central point. **3.** a conical stone in the temple of Apollo at Delphi, believed by the ancients to mark the center of the earth. [< Gk: lit., navel]

Omsk (ômsk), *n.* a city in the S central RSFSR, in the W Soviet Union in Asia, on the Irtish River. 722,000 (1965).

O·mu·ta (ō′mo͞o tä′), *n.* a seaport on W Kyushu, in SW Japan. 158,431 (1964). Also, **O·mu·da** (ō′mo͞o dä′).

on (on, ôn), *prep.* **1.** so as to be or remain supported by: *a book on a table; a hat on a hook.* **2.** so as to be attached to or unified with: *a picture on a wall.* **3.** so as to be a covering or wrapping for: *Put the blanket on the baby.* **4.** in connection, association, or cooperation with: *to serve on a jury.* **5.** so as to have as a supporting part or base: *a painting on canvas.* **6.** (used to indicate place, location, situation, etc.): *a scar on the face.* **7.** (used to indicate immediate proximity): *a house on the lake.* **8.** in the direction of: *on the starboard bow; to sail on a southerly course.* **9.** (used to indicate a means of conveyance or a means of supporting or supplying movement): *on the wing.* **10.** by the agency or means of: *drunk on wine; I saw it on television.* **11.** with respect or regard to: *Let's play a joke on him. Write a term paper on Shakespeare.* **12.** in a state, condition, or process of: *The house is on fire!* **13.** (used to indicate a source or agent): *She depends on her father for money.* **14.** (used to indicate a basis or ground): *on my word of honor.* **15.** (used to indicate risk or liability): *on pain of death.* **16.** (used to indicate time or occasion): *on Sunday; We demand cash on delivery.* **17.** (used to indicate the object or end of motion): *to march on the capital.* **18.** (used to indicate the object or end of action, thought, desire, etc.): *to gaze on a scene.* **19.** (used to indicate an encounter): *to happen on a person.*
—*adv.* **20.** in or into a position of being supported. **21.** in or into a position of covering or wrapping: *Put your clothes on.* **22.** fast to a thing, as for support: *Hold on!* **23.** toward a place, point, activity, or object: *to look on while others work.* **24.** forward, onward, or along, as in any course or process: *further on.* **25.** with continuous activity: *to work on.* **26.** into or in active operation or performance: *Turn the gas on.* **27. on and off.** See **off** (def. 19). **28. on and on,** at great length, so as to become tiresome.
—*adj.* **29.** operating or in use: *The television set was on.* **30.** taking place; occurring: *Don't you know there's a war on?* **31.** scheduled or planned: *Anything on after supper?* **32.** *Cricket.* noting that side of the wicket, or of the field, on which the batsman stands. **33. on to,** *Informal.* aware of the true nature, motive, or meaning of.
—*n.* **34.** the state or fact of being on. **35.** *Cricket.* the on side. [ME *on, an,* OE: on, in, to; c. D *aan,* G *an,* OIcel *ā,* Goth *ana;* akin to Gk *aná* on, upon. See ANA-]

On (on), *n.* Biblical name of **Heliopolis.**

ON, Old Norse. Also, **ON., O.N.**

-on[1], a formal element used in the naming of elementary particles: *neutron; proton.* [abstracted from such words as ION, ELECTRON]

-on[2], a formal element used in the naming of inert gaseous elements: *neon.* [<< Gk *-on,* neut. of *-os,* masc. sing. adj. ending]

on·a·ger (on′ə jər), *n., pl.* **-gri** (-grī′), **-gers. 1.** a wild ass, *Equus hemionus,* of southwestern Asia. **2.** an ancient and medieval engine of war for throwing stones. [ME (LL: scorpion (colloquial), hence machine for throwing projectiles) < L, var. of *onagrus* wild ass < Gk *ónagr(os)* = *ón(os)* ass + *-agros* field]

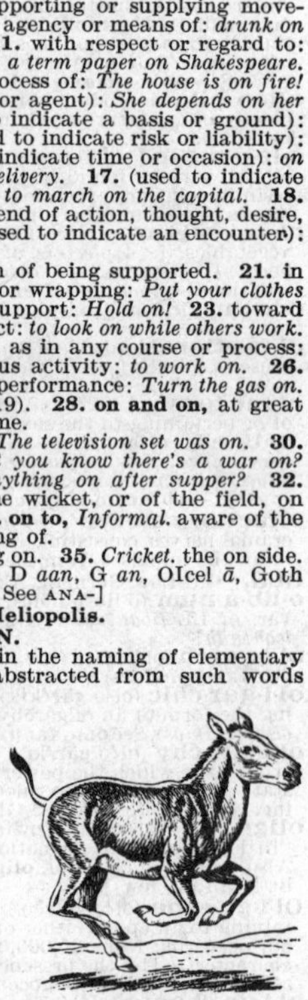

Onager
(4½ ft. high at shoulder)

on·a·gra·ceous (on′ə grā′shəs), *adj.* belonging to the *Onagraceae,* or evening-primrose family of plants. [< NL *Onagrāce(ae)* (L *onagr(a),* fem. of *onagrus* wild ass (see ONAGER) + *-āceae* -ACEAE) + -OUS]

o·nan·ism (ō′nə niz′əm), *n.* **1.** withdrawal in sexual intercourse so that ejaculation takes place outside the vagina. **2.** masturbation. [after *Onan,* son of Judah (Gen. 38:9); see -ISM] —**o′nan·ist,** *n.* —**o′nan·is′tic,** *adj.*

once (wuns), *adv.* **1.** at one time in the past; formerly. **2.** a single time: *once a week.* **3.** even a single time: *Once a liar, always a liar.* **4.** by a single step, degree, or grade: *a cousin once removed.* **5. once and for all,** decisively; finally. Also, **once for all. 6. once in a while,** at intervals; occasionally. **7. once or twice,** a very few times; infrequently. **8. once upon a time,** at some unspecified past time, esp. a long time ago. —*adj.* **9.** former; having at one time been. —*conj.* **10.** if or when at any time; if ever. **11.** whenever: *Once you're finished, go to bed.* —*n.* **12.** a single occasion; one time only: *Once is enough.* **13. all at once, a.** simultaneously. **b.** suddenly. **14. at once, a.** immediately; promptly. **b.** at the same time; simultaneously. [ME *ones,* OE *ānes* (adv.), orig. gen. of *ān* ONE; r. ME *enes,* OE *ǣnes* once = *ǣne* once + *-es* adv. suffix]

once-o·ver (wuns′ō′vər), *n. Informal.* **1.** a quick examination. **2.** a quick, superficial job.

once-o·ver-light·ly (wuns′ō′vər līt′lē), *n. Informal.* a hasty or superficial treatment, look, examination, etc.

on·col·o·gy (on̄g kol′ə jē), *n.* the branch of medical science dealing with tumors. [< Gk *ónko(s)* mass, bulk + -LOGY] —**on·co·log·ic** (on̄g′kə loj′ik), **on′co·log′i·cal,** *adj.*

on·com·ing (on′kum′ing, ôn′-), *adj.* **1.** approaching; nearing: *the oncoming train.* —*n.* **2.** approach; onset: *the oncoming of winter.*

on·do·gram (on′də gram′), *n.* an autographic record made on an ondograph. [prob. < F *onde* wave (< L *unda*) + -o- + -GRAM[1]]

on·do·graph (on′də graf′, -gräf′), *n.* an instrument for graphically recording oscillatory variations, as in alternating currents. [< F *ondographe.* See ONDOGRAM, -GRAPH]

on·dom·e·ter (on dom′i tər), *n.* an instrument for measuring the wavelengths of radio waves. [< F *onde* wave (< L *unda*) + -o- + -METER]

one (wun), *adj.* **1.** being or amounting to a single unit or individual or entire thing, item, or object. **2.** being unique in kind for a particular reason: *You're the one man I can trust.* **3.** noting some indefinite time: *one evening this week.* **4.** shared by or common to all or everywhere within understood limits: *one nation, indivisible.* **5.** a certain: *One John Smith was chosen.* —*n.* **6.** the first and lowest whole number, being a cardinal number; unity. **7.** a symbol of this number, as 1 or I. **8.** a single person or thing: *one at a time.* **9.** something, as a domino face, that signifies one unit. **10.** *Informal.* a one-dollar bill. **11.** (*cap.*) *Neoplatonism.* the ultimate reality, seen as a central source of being by whose emanations all entities have their existence. **12. at one,** in a state of unity or harmony. —*pron.* **13.** a person or thing of a number or kind: *one of the poets.* **14.** a person: *He's a quiet one.* **15.** some indefinite person, taken as a typical example: *In time, one just gets fed up.* **16. all one, a.** all the same. **b.** insignificant. **17. one with,** in agreement with. [ME *oon,* OE *ān;* c. D *een,* G *ein,* Goth *ains,* L *ūnus* (OL *oinos*); akin to Gk *oínē* ace on a die]

-one, a noun suffix of Greek origin, specialized in chemical terminology to indicate chemical derivatives, esp. ketones. [< Gk, abstracted from fem. patronymics in *-ōnē*]

1-A (wun′ā′), *n.* **1.** a U.S. Selective Service classification designating a person available for military service. **2.** a person so classified. Also, **I-A.**

one′ anoth′er, one of two or more; each other.

1-A-O (wun′ā′ō′), *n.* **1.** a U.S. Selective Service classification designating a conscientious objector available for noncombatant military service only. **2.** a person so classified. Also, **I-A-O.**

one′-armed ban′dit (wun′ärmd′), *Informal.* See **slot machine** (def. 1). Also, **one′-arm ban′dit.**

one-bag·ger (wun′bag′ər), *n. Slang.* single (def. 20).

one′-base hit′ (wun′bās′), *Baseball.* single (def. 20).

1-C (wun′sē′), *n.* **1.** a U.S. Selective Service classification designating a member of the U.S. armed forces, the U.S. Coast and Geodetic Survey, or the U.S. Public Health Service. **2.** a person so classified. Also, **I-C.**

1-D (wun′dē′), *n.* **1.** a U.S. Selective Service classification designating a qualified member of a reserve unit or a student taking military training. **2.** a person so classified. Also, **I-D.**

O·ne·ga (ō nē′gə; *Russ.* o ne′gä), *n.* **Lake,** a lake in the NW Soviet Union in Europe. 3764 sq. mi.

one-horse (wun′hôrs′, -hôrs′), *adj.* **1.** using or having only a single horse: *a one-horse shay.* **2.** *Informal.* small and unimportant; limited: *a one-horse town.*

O·nei·da (ō nī′də), *n., pl.* **-das,** (*esp. collectively*) **-da** for 1. **1.** a member of an Iroquois people formerly inhabiting the region east of Oneida Lake. **2.** the Iroquoian language of the Oneida Indians, noted for its complex system of verbs. [< Iroquois *tiionenyote* a rock set up long ago and still standing (with reference to a boulder near an ancient village)]

Onei′da Lake′, a lake in central New York. 20 mi. long; 5 mi. wide.

O'Neill (ō nēl′), *n.* **Eugene (Gladstone),** 1888–1953, U.S. playwright: Nobel prize 1936.

o·nei·ric (ō nī′rik), *adj.* of or pertaining to dreams. [< Gk *óneir(os)* dream + -IC]

o·nei·ro·man·cy (ō nī′rə man′sē), *n.* divination through dreams. [< Gk *óneiro(s)* dream + -MANCY] —**o·nei′ro·man′cer,** *n.*

one-lin·er (wun′lī′nər), *n. U.S.* a brief, very witty or humorous remark.

one·ness (wun′nis), *n.* **1.** the quality of being one. **2.** unity of thought, feeling, aim, etc.

one′-night stand′ (wun′nīt′), *U.S.* a single performance given at a specific place.

1-O (wun′ō′), *n.* **1.** a U.S. Selective Service classification designating a conscientious objector available for civilian work in the national interest. **2.** a person so classified. Also, **I-O.**

on·er·ous (on′ər əs, ō′nər-), *adj.* **1.** burdensome, oppressive, or troublesome: *onerous duties.* **2.** having or involving obligations or responsibilities, esp. legal ones, that outweigh the advantages. [ME < L *onerōs(us)* = *oner-* (s. of *onus*) burden + *-ōsus* -OUS] —**on′er·ous·ly,** *adv.* —**on′er·ous·ness,** *n.*

one·self (wun self′, wunz-), *pron.* **1.** a person's self (often used for emphasis or reflexively): *One hurts oneself by such methods.* **2. be oneself, a.** to be in one's normal state of mind or physical condition. **b.** to be unaffected and sincere. **3. by oneself, a.** without a companion; alone. **b.** through one's own efforts. **4. come to oneself.** Also, **come to.** to regain one's self-possession; to come to one's senses. Also, **one's′ self′.** [orig. *one's self*]

one′ shot′, *U.S. Informal.* **1.** a magazine published but one time and devoted to one subject. **2.** a single appearance by a performer.

one-sid·ed (wun′sī′did), *adj.* **1.** considering but one side of a matter or question; partial. **2.** *Law.* involving the action of one person only. **3.** with all the advantage on one side: *a one-sided fight.* **4.** having but one side, or but one fully developed side. **5.** having the parts all on one side, as an inflorescence. —**one′-sid′ed·ly,** *adv.* —**one′-sid′ed·ness,** *n.*

one-step (wun′step′), *n.* a round dance performed by couples to ragtime.

one-time (wun′tīm′), *adj.* having been such at one time; former: *his one-time partner.* Also, **one′time′.**

one-to-one (wun′tə wun′), *adj.* **1.** (of the relationship between two or more groups of things) corresponding element by element. **2.** *Math.* associating with each element in one set a unique element in a second set: *a one-to-one function.*

one-track (wun′trak′), *adj.* **1.** having only one track. **2.** *Informal.* able to concentrate on only one thing at a time.

one′ up′, **1.** having gained an advantage, esp. over rivals. **2.** leading an opponent by one point or one scoring unit. **3.** one each: *The score was one up in the ninth inning.*

one-up (wun′up′), *v.t.,* **-upped, -up·ping.** to get the better of; be a point, move, advantage, etc., ahead of (someone). [back formation from ONE-UPMANSHIP]

one-up·man·ship (wun′up′mən ship′), *n.* the art or practice of getting a superior or advantageous position in a competitive social, business, or personal relationship, usually by an ingenious maneuver. [ONE UP + *-manship,* as in *swordsmanship*]

1-W (wun′dub′əl yōō′), *n.* **1.** a U.S. Selective Service classification designating a conscientious objector performing civilian work in the national interest, or one who has performed such work. **2.** a person so classified. Also, **I-W.**

one-way (wun′wā′), *adj.* **1.** moving, or allowing movement, in one direction only: *one-way traffic; a one-way street.* **2.** without anything offered in return. **3.** *U.S.* valid or providing travel in one direction only: *a one-way ticket.*

ONF, Old North French. Also, **ONFr.**

on·go·ing (on′gō′ing, ôn′-), *adj.* continuing without termination or interruption.

on·ion (un′yən), *n.* **1.** a liliaceous plant, *Allium cepa,* having an edible, succulent, pungent bulb. **2.** any of certain similar plants. **3.** the bulb of the onion plant. **4.** the flavor or odor of this bulb. —*adj.* **5.** containing or cooked with onions: *onion omelet.* **6.** of, pertaining to, or resembling an onion. [ME *onyon* < OF *oignon* < L *ūniōn-* (s. of *ūniō*) large pearl, onion; see UNION]

on′ion dome′, *Archit.* a bulbous, domelike roof ending in a sharp point, characteristically used in Russian Orthodox Church architecture.

on·ion·skin (un′yən skin′), *n.* a translucent, glazed paper.

on-lim·its (on′lim′its, ôn′-), *adj. U.S.* open or not prohibited to certain persons, as military personnel.

on-line (on′līn′, ôn′-), *adj.* (in data processing) operating as part of or directly connected with the main computer.

on·look·er (on′lŏŏk′ər, ôn′-), *n.* spectator.

on·look·ing (on′lŏŏk′ing, ôn′-), *adj.* looking on; observing; perceiving.

on·ly (ōn′lē), *adv.* **1.** with no other one or anything else besides: *Only he remained.* **2.** no more than; merely; just: *If it were only true!* **3.** as recently as: *I saw him only yesterday.* **4.** as a final result: *You will only make matters worse.* **5.** as the only one: *the only begotten Son of God.* **6. only too, a.** as a matter of fact, extremely: *I am only too glad to go.* **b.** unfortunately, very: *It is only too likely to happen.* —*adj.* **7.** being the single one or the relatively few of the kind: *He was the only child in the room.* **8.** having no sibling or no sibling of the same sex: *an only child; an only son.* **9.** unique: *the one and only Joe Louis.* —*conj.* **10.** except that (introducing a single restriction, restraining circumstance, or the like): *I would have gone, only you objected.* **11.** *Chiefly Dial.* except; but: *Only for him you would not be here.* [ME *oonlich,* OE *ānlich, ǣnlich.* See ONE, -LY] —**Syn. 5.** uniquely. **7.** lone.
—**Usage.** The placement of ONLY can change the entire meaning of even the simplest sentence. For example, *Only he sees the book* means "He, and no other person, sees the book." *He only sees the book* means "He sees the book (but does not or cannot touch it, feel it, smell it, read it, etc.)." *He sees only the book* means "He sees the book and nothing else." *He sees the only book* means "He sees the single, solitary book that can be seen." *He sees the book only* means "He sees or is capable of seeing the book and nothing but the book."

on·o·mas·tic (on′ə mas′tik), *adj.* **1.** of or pertaining to onomastics. **2.** of or pertaining to proper names. **3.** *Law* (of a signature) written in a handwriting other than that of the document, instrument, etc., to which it is appended. [< Gk *onomastik(ós)* = *onomast(ós)* named (ptp. of *onomázein* < *ónoma* NAME) + *-ikos* -IC]

on·o·mas·tics (on′ə mas′tiks), *n.* (*construed as sing.*) the study of the origin and history of proper names. [< F *onomastique,* n. use of *onomastique* (adj.) ONOMASTIC; see -ICS]

on·o·ma·tol·o·gy (on′ō mə tol′ə jē), *n.* onomastics. [< MGk *onomatología* = Gk *onomatológ(os)* word-gathering (*onomato-,* comb. form of *ónoma* NAME + *-logos*) + *-ia;* see -LOGY] —**on·o·mat·o·log·ic** (on′ə mat′əloj′ik), **on′o·mat′o·log′i·cal,** *adj.* —**on′o·ma·tol′o·gist,** *n.*

on·o·mat·o·poe·ia (on′ə mat′ə pē′ə, -mät′-), *n.* **1.** the formation of a word, as *cuckoo* or *boom,* by imitation of a sound made by or associated with its referent. **2.** *Rhet.* the use of imitative and naturally suggestive words for rhetorical effect. [< LL < Gk *onomatopoiía* making of words = *onomato-* (comb. form of *ónoma* NAME) + *poi-* make (s. of *poieîn* to make) + *-ia* -IA] —**on′o·mat′o·poe′ic, on·o·mat·o·po·et·ic** (on′ə mat′ə pō et′ik, -mät′-), *adj.* —**on′o·mat′o·poe′i·cal·ly, on′o·mat′o·po·et′i·cal·ly,** *adv.*

On·on·da·ga (on′ən dô′gə, -dä′-), *n., pl.* **-gas,** (*esp. collectively*) **-ga** for 1. **1.** a member of a tribe of Iroquoian Indians formerly inhabiting the region of Onondaga Lake. **2.** the dialect of the Seneca language spoken by these Indians. [< Iroquois *ononytā'geh* on top of hill] —**On′on·da′gan,** *adj.*

On′onda′ga Lake′, a lake in central New York, near Syracuse. 5 mi. long; 1 mi. wide.

on-ramp (on′ramp′, ôn′-), *n.* an entrance lane for traffic going from a street onto a freeway or turnpike. Cf. **off-ramp.**

on·rush (on′rush′, ôn′-), *n.* a strong forward rush, flow, etc. —**on′rush′ing,** *adj.*

on·set (on′set′, ôn′-), *n.* **1.** a beginning or start: *the onset of winter.* **2.** an assault or attack.

on·shore (on′shôr′, -shōr′, ôn′-), *adv.* **1.** onto or in the direction of the shore. **2.** close to or parallel with the shore: *to sail a boat onshore.* **3.** on land, esp. within the area adjoining a port. —*adj.* **4.** moving or proceeding toward shore or onto land. **5.** located on or close to the shore: *an onshore lighthouse; an onshore buoy.* **6.** done or taking place on land.

on·side (on′sīd′, ôn′-), *adj., adv. Sports.* not offside; being within the prescribed line or area at the beginning of or during play or a play.

on·slaught (on′slôt′, ôn′-), *n.* an onset, assault, or attack, esp. a vigorous or furious one. [< D *aanslag* plot, attack; c. G *Anschlag* (*-t* possibly by influence of *slaughter*)]

on·stage (on′stāj′, ôn′-), *adv.* **1.** on or onto the stage (opposed to *offstage*). —*adj.* **2.** of, pertaining to, or used in the acting area of a stage.

on-stream (on′strēm′, ôn′-), *adv.* in or into manufacturing operation: *The new plant went on-stream last month.*

Ont., Ontario.

On·tar·i·o (on târ′ē ō′), *n.* **1.** a province in S Canada, bordering on the Great Lakes. 6,731,000 (est. 1965); 412,582 sq. mi. *Cap.:* Toronto. **2. Lake,** a lake between the NE United States and S Canada, between New York and Ontario province: the smallest of the Great Lakes. 193 mi. long; 7540 sq. mi. **3.** a city in SW California, E of Los Angeles. 64,118 (1970). —**On·tar′i·an,** *adj., n.*

on·to (on′to͞o, ôn′-; *unstressed* on′tə, ôn′-), *prep.* **1.** to a place or position upon; on: *to get onto a horse.* **2.** *Informal.* in or into a state of awareness about: *I'm onto your tricks.*

onto-, a learned borrowing from Greek meaning "being," used in the formation of compound words: *ontogeny.* [< NL < Gk *ont-* (s. of *ṓn,* neut. prp. of *eînai* to be) + *-o-* -o-]

on·tog·e·ny (on toj′ə nē), *n. Biol.* the development or developmental history of an individual organism. Also, **on·to·gen·e·sis** (on′tə jen′i sis). Cf. **phylogeny.** —**on·to·ge·net·ic** (on′tō jə net′ik), **on′to·ge·net′i·cal, on′to·gen′·ic,** *adj.*

on′tolog′ical ar′gument, *Philos.* an a priori argument for the existence of God, asserting that as existence is a perfection, and as God is conceived of as the most perfect being, it follows that God must exist.

on·tol·o·gy (on tol′ə jē), *n.* **1.** the branch of metaphysics that studies the nature of existence. **2.** (loosely) metaphysics. [< NL *ontologia*] —**on·to·log·i·cal** (on′tᵊloj′i kəl), *adj.* —**on·tol′o·gist,** *n.*

o·nus (ō′nəs), *n., pl.* **o·nus·es.** a burden; a responsibility. [< L: load, burden]

o·nus pro·ban·di (ō′nōōs prō bän′dē; *Eng.* ō′nəs prō-ban′dī, -dē), *Latin.* the burden of proof.

on·ward (on′wərd, ôn′-), *adv.* Also, **on′wards. 1.** toward a point ahead or in front; forward, as in space or time. **2.** at a position or point in advance. —*adj.* **3.** directed or moving onward or forward; forward. [ME] —**Syn. 1.** See **forward.**

-onym, a combining form of Greek origin, meaning "word," "name": *pseudonym.* [< Gk *-onym(os),* comb. form of *ónoma* NAME]

on·yx (on′iks, ō′niks), *n.* **1.** a variety of chalcedony having straight parallel bands of alternating colors. **2.** (not used technically) an unbanded chalcedony dyed for ornamental purposes. **3.** black, esp. a pure or jet black. **4.** *Med.* a nail of a finger or toe. —*adj.* **5.** black, esp. jet-black. [ME *onix* < L *onyx* < Gk: nail, claw, veined gem]

oo-, a learned borrowing from Greek meaning "egg," used in the formation of compound words: *oogamous.* Also, **oö-.** [< Gk *ōio-,* comb. form of *ōión* EGG[1]]

o·o·cyte (ō′ə sīt′), *n. Biol.* a female germ cell in the maturation stage. Also, **o′ö·cyte′.**

oo·dles (o͞od′ᵊlz), *n.* (*sometimes construed as sing.*) *Informal.* a large quantity: *oodles of money.* [?]

o·og·a·mous (ō og′ə məs), *adj. Biol.* **1.** having structurally dissimilar gametes, the female gamete being large and nonmotile and the male gamete being small and motile. **2.** reproducing by the union of such gametes. Also, **o·ög′a·mous.** —**o·og′a·my, o·ög′a·my,** *n.*

OO gauge, a model railroad gauge of 19 millimeters.

o·o·gen·e·sis (ō′ə jen′i sis), *n. Biol.* the origin and development of the ovum. Also, **o′ö·gen′e·sis.** —**o·o·ge·net·ic, o·ö·ge·net·ic** (ō′ə jə net′ik), *adj.*

o·o·go·ni·um (ō′ə gō′nē əm), *n., pl.* **-ni·a** (-nē ə), **-ni·ums. 1.** *Biol.* one of the undifferentiated germ cells giving rise to oocytes. **2.** *Bot.* the one-celled female reproductive organ in certain thallophytic plants, usually a more or less spherical sac containing one or more eggs. Also, **o′ö·go′ni·um.** [< NL] —**o′o·go′ni·al, o′ö·go′ni·al,** *adj.*

o·o·lite (ō′ə līt′), *n. Geol.* a limestone composed of minute rounded concretions resembling fish roe, in some places altered to ironstone by replacement with iron oxide. Also, **o′ölite′.** [earlier *oolites* < NL] —**o·o·lit·ic, o·ö·lit·ic** (ō′ə lit′ik), *adj.*

o·ol·o·gy (ō ol′ə jē), *n.* the branch of ornithology dealing with the study of birds' eggs. Also, **o·öl′o·gy.** —**o·o·log·i·cal, o·ö·log·i·cal** (ō′ə loj′i kəl), *adj.* —**o·ol′o·gist, o·öl′o·gist,** *n.*

oo·long (o͞o′lông′, -long′), *n.* a brown or amber tea, grown in China and Taiwan and partially fermented before being dried. [< Chin *wu-lung,* lit., black dragon]

oo·mi·ak (o͞o′mē ak′), *n.* umiak. Also, **oo′mi·ac′.**

Oom Paul (o͞om pō′o͝ol). See **Kruger.**

oomph (o͝omf), *n. U.S. Slang.* **1.** vitality. **2.** sex appeal. [perh. based on hum of admiration]

-oon, a word element occurring in several words borrowed from French and other Romance languages (*bassoon; balloon; dragoon; pontoon*), and on this model occasionally used in the formation of new nouns in English (*spittoon*). [as an English formative (e.g., in *spittoon*), abstracted from words of various origins (*buffoon, lagoon,* etc.) but repr. chiefly F *-on* in words stressed on the final syllable; cf. Sp. *-on,* It. *-one,* L *-ōn-*]

oophor-, a learned borrowing from Greek meaning "ovary," used in the formation of compound words: *oophoritis.* Also, **oöphor-.** [< NL < Gk *ōophor(ós)* bearing eggs. See OO-, -PHORE]

o·o·pho·rec·to·my (ō′ə fə rek′tə mē), *n., pl.* **-mies.** *Surg.* ovariotomy. Also, **o′ö·pho·rec′to·my.**

o·o·pho·ri·tis (ō′ə fə rī′tis), *n. Pathol.* inflammation of an ovary, usually combined with an inflammation of the Fallopian tubes; ovaritis. Also, **o′ö·pho·ri′tis.** [< NL]

o·o·phyte (ō′ə fīt′), *n. Bot.* the gametophyte of a moss, fern, or liverwort, resulting from the development of a fertilized egg. Also, **o′ö·phyte′.** —**o·o·phyt·ic, o·ö·phyt·ic** (ō′ə fit′ik), *adj.*

oops (o͝ops, o͞ops), *interj.* (used to express mild dismay, chagrin, surprise, etc., as at one's own mistake.) [?]

o·o·sperm (ō′ə spûrm′), *n. Biol.* a fertilized egg; zygote. Also, **o′ö·sperm′.**

o·o·sphere (ō′ə sfēr′), *n. Bot.* an unfertilized egg within an oogonium. Also, **o′ö·sphere′.**

o·o·spore (ō′ə spōr′, -spôr′), *n. Bot.* a fertilized egg within an oogonium. Also, **o′ö·spore′.** —**o·o·spor·ic, o·ö·spor·ic** (ō′ə spōr′ik, -spor′-), **o·os·por·ous, o·ös·por·ous** (ō os′pər-əs, ō′ə spōr′əs, -spôr′-), *adj.*

o·o·the·ca (ō′ə thē′kə), *n., pl.* **-cae** (-sē). a case or capsule containing eggs, as that of certain gastropods and insects. Also, **o′ö·the′ca.** [< NL] —**o′o·the′cal, o′ö·the′cal,** *adj.*

o·o·tid (ō′ə tid), *n. Biol.* the cell that results from the meiotic divisions of an oocyte and matures into an ovum. Also, **o′ö·tid.** [OO- + (SPERMA)TID]

ooze[1] (o͞oz), *v.,* **oozed, ooz·ing,** *n.* —*v.i.* **1.** (of moisture, liquid, etc.) to flow or exude slowly, as through holes or small openings. **2.** (of air, sound, etc.) to pass slowly or gradually as if through pores or small openings. **3.** (of a substance) to exude moisture. **4.** (of something abstract, as courage) to disappear slowly or imperceptibly. —*v.t.* **5.** to exude (moisture, air, etc.) slowly. —*n.* **6.** the act of oozing. **7.** something that oozes. **8.** an infusion of oak bark, sumac, etc., used in tanning. [ME *wose(n)* < *wos* (n.), OE *wōs* juice, moisture]

ooze[2] (o͞oz), *n.* **1.** a calcareous mud composed chiefly of the shells of small organisms, covering parts of the ocean bottom. **2.** soft mud or slime. **3.** a marsh or bog. [ME *wose,* OE *wāse* mud]

ooze′ leath′er, leather prepared from calfskin or other skin and having a soft, velvety finish on the flesh side.

ooz·y[1] (o͞o′zē), *adj.,* **ooz·i·er, ooz·i·est. 1.** exuding moisture. **2.** damp with moisture. [OOZE[1] + -Y[1]]

ooz·y[2] (o͞o′zē), *adj.,* **ooz·i·er, ooz·i·est.** of or like ooze, soft mud, or slime. [ME *wosi.* See OOZE[2], -Y[1]] —**ooz′·i·ly,** *adv.* —**ooz′i·ness,** *n.*

op (op), *n.* See **op art.**

op-, var. of **ob-** (by assimilation) before *p: oppose.*

Op., opus.

op., **1.** opera. **2.** operation. **3.** opposite. **4.** opus.

O.P., 1. Order of Preachers (Dominican). [< L *Ordō Praedicātōrum*] **2.** Also, **o.p.** out of print.

OPA, *U.S. Govt.* Office of Price Administration: the World War II agency (1941–46) regulating rents, prices, etc.

o·pac·i·fy (ō pas′ə fī′), *v.,* **-fied, -fy·ing.** —*v.t.* **1.** to cause to become opaque. —*v.i.* **2.** to become opaque. [< L *opāc(us)* shaded + -IFY] —**o·pac′i·fi·ca′tion,** *n.* —**o·pac′·i·fi′er,** *n.*

o·pac·i·ty (ō pas′i tē), *n., pl.* **-ties. 1.** the state or quality of being opaque. **2.** something opaque. **3.** the degree to which a substance is or may be opaque. **4.** *Photog.* the proportion of the light that is absorbed by the emulsion on any given area of a negative. **5.** obscurity of meaning. **6.** mental dullness. [< L *opācitās* shade]

o·pah (ō′pə), *n.* a large, deep-bodied, brilliantly colored, oceanic food fish, *Lampris regius.* [< WAfr (Niger-Congo coast)]

o·pal (ō′pəl), *n.* **1.** a mineral, an amorphous form of silica, SiO_2 with some water of hydration, found in many varieties and colors, including a form that is milky white. **2.** a gem composed of an iridescent variety of this. [< L *opal(us)* < Gk *opállios* opal, gem < Skt *úpala* stone]

o·pal·esce (ō′pə les′), *v.i.,* **-esced, -esc·ing.** to exhibit a play of colors like that of the opal. [back formation from OPALESCENT]

o·pal·es·cent (ō′pə les′ənt), *adj.* **1.** exhibiting a play of colors like that of the opal. **2.** having a milky iridescence. —**o′pal·es′cence,** *n.*

o·pal·ine (ō′pə lin, -līn′), *adj.* **1.** like opal; opalescent. —*n.* **2.** See **milk glass.**

o·paque (ō pāk′), *adj., n., v.,* **o·paqued, o·paqu·ing.** —*adj.* **1.** not transparent or translucent; not allowing light to pass through. **2.** not transmitting radiation, sound, heat, etc. **3.** not shining or bright; dark; dull. **4.** hard to understand; not clear or lucid. **5.** dull or unintelligent. —*n.* **6.** something that is opaque. **7.** *Photog.* coloring used to render parts of a negative opaque. —*v.t.* **8.** to make opaque. **9.** *Photog.* to render parts of (a negative) opaque. [late ME *opake* < L *opāc(us)* shaded] —**o·paque′ly,** *adv.* —**o·paque′ness,** *n.*

opaque′ projec′tor, a machine for projecting opaque objects, as books, on a screen, by means of reflected light.

op′ art′, a style of abstract art in which forms and space are organized in such a way as to provide optical illusions of an ambiguous nature, as alternately advancing and receding squares on a flat surface. Also called **op.** [OP(TICAL)] —**op′ art′ist.**

op. cit. (op′ sit′), in the work cited. [< L *opere citātō*]

ope (ōp), *adj., v.t., v.i.,* **oped, op·ing.** *Archaic.* open.

OPEC (ō′pek), Organization of Petroleum Exporting Countries.

Op-Ed (op′ed′), *n. U.S.* a newspaper page devoted to signed articles by commentators, essayists, humorists, etc., of varying viewpoints: *the Op-Ed page of today's* New York Times. Also called **Op′-Ed′ page′.** [*op(posite) ed(itorial page)*]

o·pen (ō′pən), *adj.* **1.** not closed or barred at the time, as a doorway or passageway by a door. **2.** (of a barrier, as a door) set so as to permit passage through the opening it otherwise closes. **3.** having no means of being enclosed. **4.** having the interior immediately accessible, as a drawer that is pulled out. **5.** relatively free of obstructions: *an open floor plan.* **6.** constructed so as not to be fully enclosed: *an open boat.* **7.** having relatively large or numerous voids or intervals: *open ranks of soldiers.* **8.** relatively unoccupied by buildings, fences, trees, etc.: *open country.* **9.** extended or unfolded: *an open newspaper.* **10.** without restrictions as to who may participate: *an open competition.* **11.** available; accessible, as for trade: *Which job is open? It's an open port. The store is open on Saturday.* **12.** not restricted as to the hunting of game: *open season.* **13.** free from frost: *an open winter.* **14.** *Informal.* without effective or enforced legal, commercial, or moral regulations: *an open town.* **15.** undecided; unsettled: *several open questions.* **16.** liable or subject: *open to question.* **17.** receptive, as to ideas. **18.** exposed to general view without concealment: *open disregard of rules.* **19.** unreserved, candid, or frank, as persons or their speech, aspect, etc. **20.** generous, liberal, or bounteous: *to give with an open hand.* **21.** free of navigational obstructions or hazards: *an open coast.* **22.** noting the part of the sea beyond headlands or enclosing areas of land. **23.** *Print.* **a.** (of type) in outline form. **b.** widely spaced or leaded, as printed matter. **24.** not yet balanced or adjusted, as an account. **25.** *Music.* **a.** (of an organ pipe) not closed at the far end. **b.** (of a string) not stopped by a finger. **c.** (of a note) produced by an open pipe or string or, on a wind instrument, without the aid of a slide, key, etc. **26.** *Phonet.* **a.** (of a vowel) articulated with a relatively large opening above the tongue or with a relatively large oral aperture, as the vowel sound of *cot* compared with that in *caught.* **b.** (of a syllable) ending with a vowel. **c.** (of a consonant) continuant. Cf. **stop** (def. 36).
—*v.t.* **27.** to move (a door, window sash, etc.) from a shut or

closed position. **28.** to render (a doorway, window, etc.) unobstructed. **29.** to render the interior of (a box, drawer, etc.) readily accessible. **30.** to make accessible or available: *to open a port for trade.* **31.** to recall or revoke (a judgment, decree, etc.) for the purpose of allowing further contest or delay. **32.** to clear of obstructions. **33.** to uncover, lay bare, or expose to view. **34.** to disclose, reveal, or divulge, as one's inner feelings. **35.** to render (the mind) accessible, as to ideas. **36.** to expand, unfold, or spread out: *to open a map.* **37.** to make less compact or less closely spaced: *to open ranks.* **38.** to establish for business purposes or for public use: *to open an office.* **39.** to set in action or commence (sometimes fol. by *up*): *to open a campaign.* **40.** to make an opening in. **41.** to make or produce (an opening): *to open a way through a crowd.* **42.** *Law.* to make the first statement of (a case) to the court or jury.
—*v.i.* **43.** to become open. **44.** to afford access to or be connected with a place: *This door opens onto a garden.* **45.** (of a building) to open its doors to the public. **46.** to commence; be in effect: *When will school open? Deer-hunting season opens Tuesday. The meeting opened with a prayer for our country.* **47.** to part or seem to part: *At last the cliffs opened to show us a way out.* **48.** to become disclosed or revealed. **49.** to come into view, or become more visible or plain. **50.** (of the mind) to become receptive. **51.** to spread out or expand, as the hand or a fan. **52.** to turn to a page of a book, newspaper, etc.: *Open to page 32.* **53.** to become less compact, less closely spaced, or the like: *The ranks began to open.* **54.** *Hunting.* (of hounds) to begin to bark, as on the scent of game. **55.** *Cards.* to make the first bet, bid, or lead in beginning a hand. **56. open up,** *Slang.* **a.** to go into action, esp. to begin firing. **b.** to become familiar. **c.** to disclose confidential information. **d.** to increase speed or the speed of (a vehicle).
—*n.* **57.** an open or clear space. **58.** the open air. **59.** the open water, as of the sea. **60.** a contest or tournament in which both amateurs and professionals may compete, esp. in golf. **61. the open, a.** the unenclosed or unobstructed country. **b.** the outdoors: *vacations in the open.* **c.** the condition of being unconcealed or publicly known: *The scandal is now out in the open.* [ME, OE; c. D *open*, G *offen*, OIcel *opinn;* based on root of UP] **—o′pen·ly,** *adv.* **—o′pen·ness,** *n.*

o′pen air′, the unconfined atmosphere; outdoors.

o·pen-air (ō′pən âr′), *adj.* existing in, taking place in, or characteristic of the open air; outdoor.

o·pen-and-shut (ō′pən ən shut′), *adj.* *Informal.* immediately obvious upon consideration.

o′pen book′, a person, thing, or situation obvious or easy to know or interpret.

o′pen chain′, *Chem.* a series of atoms linked in a chain not joined together at its ends, and so represented in its structural formula. Cf. **closed chain. —o′pen-chain′,** *adj.*

o′pen cit′y, *Mil.* a city that is officially declared to be demilitarized and that is by official agreement not to be subject to attack during war.

o′pen cou′plet, a couplet that concludes with a run-on line. Cf. **closed couplet.**

o′pen diapa′son. See under **diapason** (def. 4).

o′pen door′, the policy of admitting all nations or people of all nationalities to a country upon equal terms, as for trade or immigration. **—o′pen-door′,** *adj.*

o·pen-end (ō′pən end′), *adj.* not having fixed limits; permitting a broad interpretation: *open-end agreements.* Also, **o′pen-end′ed.**

o′pen-end invest′ment com′pany, an investment company that issues its shares continuously and without limit and is obliged to redeem or repurchase them from owners on demand. Also called **mutual fund.** Cf. **closed-end investment company.**

o·pen·er (ō′pə nər), *n.* **1.** a person or thing that opens. **2.** a device for opening sealed containers: *a can opener.* **3.** the first in a series of events. **4. openers,** *Poker.* cards in a hand, as a pair of jacks or better, that are worth enough to enable the holder to make the first bet of a deal.

o·pen-eyed (ō′pən īd′), *adj.* **1.** having the eyes open. **2.** having the eyes wide open, as in wonder. **3.** watchful; alert. **4.** done or experienced with full awareness.

o·pen-faced (ō′pən fāst′), *adj.* **1.** having a frank or ingenuous face. **2.** (of a watch) having the dial covered only by the crystal. **3.** (of a pie, sandwich, etc.) without a layer of dough, crust, bread, etc., on top.

o′pen frac′ture. See **compound fracture.**

o·pen-hand·ed (ō′pən han′did), *adj.* generous; liberal. Also, **o′pen·hand′ed. —o′pen-hand′ed·ly, o′pen·hand′ed·ly,** *adv.* **—o′pen-hand′ed·ness, o′pen·hand′ed·ness,** *n.*

o·pen-heart·ed (ō′pən-här′tid), *adj.* **1.** unreserved, candid, or frank: *open-hearted advice.* **2.** kindly; benevolent: *an open-hearted gift to charity.* **—o′pen-heart′ed·ly,** *adv.* **—o′pen-heart′ed·ness,** *n.*

o·pen-hearth (ō′pən-härth′), *adj.* noting, pertaining to, used in, or produced by the open-hearth process.

o′pen-hearth′ proc′ess, a process of steelmaking in which the charge is laid in a furnace (**o′pen-hearth′ fur′nace**) on a shallow hearth over which play flames of burning gas and hot air.

A A B A
C C
D E E D

Open-hearth furnace
(Cross section)
A, Charging door; B, Hearth;
C, Checkers; D, Air; E, Gas

o′pen house′, **1.** a party or a time during which a person's home is open to all friends and relatives. **2.** a time during which a school, institution, etc., is open to the public for exhibition or for some other specific purpose. **3. keep open house,** to be prepared to entertain visitors at any time.

o′pen hous′ing, *U.S.* the elimination of racial discrimination in the sales and rentals of private housing. Also called **fair housing. —o′pen-hous′ing,** *adj.*

o·pen·ing (ō′pə ning), *n.* **1.** the act or an instance of making or becoming open. **2.** an unobstructed or unoccupied space or place. **3.** a hole or void in something solid; aperture. **4.** the act of beginning an activity. **5.** the first part or initial stage of anything. **6.** the beginning of a prolonged activity or event, or of a series of events. **7.** a celebration marking this. **8.** an unfilled position or job. **9.** an opportunity. **10.** a mode of beginning a game: *a manual of chess openings.* [ME] **—Syn. 3.** orifice; slit, breach, rift, chasm, cleft, fissure, rent. **—Ant. 1.** closing.

o′pen let′ter, a letter, usually of protest or criticism, addressed to a specific person but meant to be brought to widespread public attention.

o·pen-mind·ed (ō′pən mīn′did), *adj.* **1.** having or showing a mind receptive to new ideas or arguments. **2.** unprejudiced. **—o′pen-mind′ed·ly,** *adv.* **—o′pen-mind′ed·ness,** *n.*

o·pen-mouthed (ō′pən mouthd′, -moutht′), *adj.* **1.** having the mouth open. **2.** gaping, as with surprise or astonishment. **3.** having a wide mouth, as a pitcher or jar. **—o·pen-mouth·ed·ly** (ō′pən mou′thid lē, -mouth′tlē), *adv.*

o′pen or′der, *Mil.* a troop formation having intervals greater than those in close order.

o′pen pri′mary, *U.S.* a direct primary election in which voters need not meet a test of party membership.

o′pen se′cret, something supposedly secret but actually known quite generally.

o′pen ses′ame, any marvelously effective means for bringing about a desired result. [from the use of these words by Ali Baba, hero of an Arabian folk tale, to open the door of the robbers' den]

o·pen-shelf (ō′pən shelf′), *adj.* open-stack.

o′pen shop′, a shop in which a union acts as representative of all the employees, but in which union membership is not a condition of employment. **—o′pen-shop′,** *adj.*

o′pen sight′, (on a firearm) a rear sight consisting of a notch across which the gunner aligns the front sight on the target. Cf. **peep sight.**

o·pen-stack (ō′pən stak′), *adj.* of or pertaining to a system of library management in which patrons have direct access to bookshelves; open-shelf.

o′pen stock′, *Com.* merchandise sold in sets with individual pieces available from stock for future purchase.

o·pen·work (ō′pən wûrk′), *n.* any kind of work, esp. ornamental, showing openings through its substance.

OPer., Old Persian.

op·er·a[1] (op′ər ə, op′rə), *n.* **1.** an extended dramatic composition in which all parts are sung to instrumental accompaniment. Cf. **comic opera, grand opera. 2.** the art form represented by such compositions. **3.** a performance of one: *to go to the opera.* **4.** (*sometimes cap.*) an opera house: *the Paris Opera.* [< It: work, opera < L: service, work, a work, pl. of *opus*]

o·per·a[2] (ō′pər ə, op′ər ə), *n.* *Chiefly Music.* a pl. of **opus.**

op·er·a·ble (op′ər ə bəl), *adj.* **1.** capable of being put into use, operation, or practice. **2.** admitting of a surgical operation without undue risk. Cf. **inoperable** (def. 2). [< LL *operābil(is)* = *operā(rī)* (to) work + *-bilis* -BLE] **—op′er·a·bil′i·ty,** *n.* **—op′er·a·bly,** *adv.*

o·pé·ra bouffe (op′ər ə bo͞of′, op′rə; *Fr.* ô pā RA bo͞of′), *pl.* **o·pé·ra bouffes, o·pé·ras bouffe,** *Fr.* **o·pé·ras bouffes** (ô pā RA bo͞of′). a comic, usually farcical, opera. [< F]

o·pe·ra buf·fa (op′ər ə bo͞o′fə, op′rə; *It.* ô′pe rä bo͞of′fä), *pl.* **o·pe·ra buf·fas, o·pe·ras buf·fa,** *It.* **o·pe·re buf·fe** (ô′pe re bo͞of′fe). an Italian farcical comic opera. [< It]

o·pé·ra co·mique (op′ər ə ko mēk′, op′rə; *Fr.* ô pā RA kô mēk′), *pl.* **o·pé·ra co·miques, o·pé·ras co·mique,** *Fr.* **o·pé·ras co·miques** (ô pā RA kô mēk′). **1.** an opera with spoken dialogue. **2.** See **comic opera.** [< F]

op′era glass′es, a small, low-power pair of binoculars for use at plays, concerts, and the like. Also, **op′era glass′.**

op′era hat′, a man's tall, collapsible silk hat.

op′era house′, **1.** a theater devoted chiefly to operas. **2.** *U.S. Dial.* a theater or exhibition hall.

op·er·and (op′ə rand′), *n.* *Math.* a quantity upon which a mathematical operation is performed. [< L *operand(um)*, neut. of ger. of *operārī* to OPERATE]

op·er·ant (op′ər ənt), *adj.* **1.** operating; producing effects. **2.** *Psychol.* (of a response) identifiable or definable in terms of its consequences rather than by its stimulus, which may be unknown. **—***n.* **3.** a person or thing that operates. [< L *operant-* (s. of *operāns*, prp. of *operārī*). See OPERATE, -ANT]

o·pe·ra se·ria (op′ər ə sēr′ē ə, op′rə; *It.* ô′pe rä se′ryä), *pl.* **o·pe·ra se·rias, o·pe·ras se·ria,** *It.* **o·pe·re se·rie** (ô′pe re se′rye). Italian dramatic opera of the 18th century characterized by extensive use of the aria da capo and recitative. [< It: lit., serious opera]

op·er·ate (op′ə rāt′), *v.,* **-at·ed, -at·ing. —***v.i.* **1.** to work, perform, or function, as a machine does. **2.** to exert force or influence. **3.** to perform some process of work or treatment. **4.** *Surg.* to act with instruments upon the body of a patient to remedy or remove deformity, injury, or disease. **5.** *Mil.* **a.** to carry on operations in war. **b.** to give orders and accomplish military acts, as distinguished from doing staff work. **6.** to carry on transactions in securities or commodities, esp. speculatively or on a large scale. **—***v.t.* **7.** to manage or use (a machine, device, etc.). **8.** to put or keep in operation: *He operates a ranch.* **9.** to bring about, effect, or produce, as by the exertion of force or influence. [< L *operāt(us)* having done work (ptp. of *operārī*) = *oper-* (s. of *opus*) work + *-ātus* -ATE[1]] **—op′er·at′a·ble,** *adj.*

op·er·at·ic (op′ə rat′ik), *adj.* **1.** of, pertaining to, or resembling opera. **2.** suitable for opera: *an operatic tenor.* **—***n.* **3.** Usually, **operatics.** (*construed as sing. or pl.*) **a.** the technique of producing or staging operas. **b.** wildly exaggerated or melodramatic behavior. [OPERA[1] + -TIC, after *drama, dramatic*] **—op′er·at′i·cal·ly,** *adv.*

op·er·a·tion (op′ə rā′shən), *n.* **1.** the act or an instance, process, or manner of functioning or operating. **2.** the state of something that operates or is in effect (usually prec. by *in* or *into*): *a rule no longer in operation.* **3.** the exertion of force or influence: *the operation of alcohol on the mind.* **4.** a process of a practical or mechanical nature. **5.** *Surg.* a process or act of operating on the body of a patient. **6.** *Math.* a mathematical process, as addition, multiplication, etc., or an instance of its application. **7.** *Mil.* **a.** a campaign, mission, maneuver, or action. **b.** Usually, **operations.** the conduct of a campaign, mission, etc. **c. operations,** a place from which a military campaign or the like is planned and controlled. **8.** a business transaction in securities or commodities, esp. one of a speculative nature or on a large scale. [ME *operacioun* < L *operātiōn-* (s. of *operātiō*)]

op·er·a·tion·al (op′ə rā′shə nəl), *adj.* **1.** able to function or be used. **2.** *Mil.* **a.** of, pertaining to, or involved in military operations. **b.** in actual operation or ready to execute an operation. **3.** of or pertaining to operations or an operation. —**op′er·a′tion·al·ly,** *adv.*

op·er·a·tion·al·ism (op′ə rā′shə nəliz′əm), *n.* *Philos.* the doctrine that the meaning of a scientific term, concept, or proposition consists of the operation or operations performed in defining or demonstrating it. Also, **op′er·a′tion·ism.**

opera′tions research′, the analysis, usually involving mathematical treatment, of a process, problem, or operation to determine its purpose and effectiveness and to gain maximum efficiency.

op·er·a·tive (op′ə rā′tiv, -ər ə tiv, op′rə tiv), *n.* **1.** a person engaged in some branch of work, esp. industrial work. **2.** *U.S. Informal.* **a.** a detective. **b.** a secret agent; spy. —*adj.* **3.** operating, or exerting force or influence. **4.** being in effect or operation: *laws operative in this city.* **5.** effective or efficacious. **6.** pertaining to work or productive activity. [< MF *operatif* < L *operāt(us)* having done work (see OPERATE) + MF *-if* -IVE] —**op′er·a′tive·ly,** *adv.* —**op′er·a′tive·ness, op·er·a·tiv·i·ty** (op′ər ə tiv′i tē), *n.* —**Syn. 2.** investigator, agent.

op·er·a·tor (op′ə rā′tər), *n.* **1.** a person who operates a machine, apparatus, or the like. **2.** a person who operates a telephone switchboard. **3.** a person who conducts an industrial establishment. **4.** a person who trades in securities, esp. speculatively. **5.** a person who performs a surgical operation. **6.** *Math.* **a.** a symbol for expressing a mathematical operation. **b.** a function, esp. one transforming a function, set, etc., into another: *a differential operator.* **7.** *Slang.* a person who accomplishes his purposes by cleverness of method, persuasiveness, etc. [< LL]

o·per·cu·late (ō pûr′kyə lit, -lāt′), *adj.* having an operculum. Also, **o·per′cu·lat′ed.**

o·per·cu·lum (ō pûr′kyə ləm), *n., pl.* **-la** (-lə), **-lums. 1.** *Bot., Zool.* a part or organ serving as a lid or cover, as a covering flap on a seed vessel. **2.** *Zool.* **a.** the gill cover of fishes and amphibians. **b.** (in many gastropods) a horny plate that closes the opening of the shell when the animal is retracted. [< NL, L: lid, cover = *oper(īre)* (to) cover + *-culum* -CULE] —**o·per′cu·lar,** *adj.*

o·pe·re ci·ta·to (ō′pe RE′ ki tä′tō; *Eng.* op′ə rē′ sī tā′tō), *Latin.* See **op. cit.**

op·er·et·ta (op′ə ret′ə), *n.* a short opera, commonly of a light, amusing character. [< It, dim. of *opera* OPERA[1]] —**op′er·et′tist,** *n.*

op·er·ose (op′ə rōs′), *adj.* industrious. [< L *operōs(us)* busy, active = *oper-* (s. of *opus*) work + *-ōsus* -OSE[1]] —**op′er·ose′ly,** *adv.* —**op′er·ose′ness,** *n.*

OPers, Old Persian.

oph·i·cleide (of′ə klīd′), *n.* a musical wind instrument, a development of the old wooden serpent, consisting of a conical metal tube bent double. [< F *ophicléide* < Gk *óphi(s)* serpent + *kleid-* (s. of *kleís*) key]

o·phid·i·an (ō fid′ē ən), *adj.* **1.** belonging or pertaining to the suborder *Ophidia,* comprising the snakes. —*n.* **2.** a snake. [< NL *Ophidi(a)* (pl.) name of the suborder (< Gk *ophídion,* dim. of *óphis* serpent) + -AN]

oph·i·ol·o·gy (of′ē ol′ə jē, ō′fē-), *n.* the branch of herpetology dealing with snakes. [< Gk *óphi(s)* snake + -o- + -LOGY] —**oph′i·ol′o·gist,** *n.*

O·phir (ō′fər), *n.* a country of uncertain location, possibly southern Arabia or the eastern coast of Africa, from which gold, precious stones, and timber were brought for Solomon. I Kings 10:11.

oph·ite (of′īt, ō′fīt), *n.* *Mineral.* an ophitic diabase. [< L *ophīt(ēs)* serpentine stone < Gk *ophítēs* (*líthos*) serpentine (stone) = *óph(is)* serpent + *-ītēs* -ITE[1]]

o·phit·ic (ō fit′ik), *adj.* noting or pertaining to a rock texture exhibited by certain ophites, in which elongate feldspar crystals are embedded in a matrix.

ophthalm., ophthalmology. Also, **ophthalmol.**

oph·thal·mi·a (of thal′mē ə, op-), *n.* inflammation of the eye, esp. of its membranes or external structures. [< LL < Gk] —**oph·thal·mi·ac** (of thal′mē ak′), *n.*

oph·thal·mic (of thal′mik, op-), *adj.* of or pertaining to the eye; ocular. [< L *ophthalmic(us)* < Gk *ophthalmikós*]

ophthalmo-, a learned borrowing from Greek meaning "eye," used in the formation of compound words: *ophthalmology.* Also, *esp. before a vowel,* **ophthalm-.** [< Gk, comb. form of *ophthalmós*]

oph·thal·mol·o·gist (of′thal mol′ə jist, -thəl-, -thə-, op′-), *n.* a doctor of medicine specializing in ophthalmology.

oph·thal·mol·o·gy (of′thal mol′ə jē, -thəl-, -thə-, op′-), *n.* the branch of medical science dealing with the anatomy, functions, and diseases of the eye. —**oph·thal·mo·log·i·cal** (of thal′mə loj′i kəl, op-), **oph·thal′mo·log′ic,** *adj.*

oph·thal·mo·scope (of thal′mə skōp′, op-), *n.* an instrument for viewing the interior of the eye or examining the retina. —**oph·thal·mo·scop·ic** (of thal′mə skop′ik, op-), **oph·thal′mo·scop′i·cal,** *adj.*

oph·thal·mos·co·py (of′thal mos′kə pē, op′-), *n., pl.* **-pies.** the use of or technique of using an ophthalmoscope. —**oph′thal·mos′co·pist,** *n.*

-opia, a learned borrowing from Greek, added to nouns indicating a condition of sight or of the visual organs: *diplopia; hemeralopia; myopia.* [< Gk *-ōpia* < *ṓps* eye]

o·pi·ate (*n., adj.* ō′pē it, -āt′; *v.* ō′pē āt′), *n., adj., v.,* **-at·ed, -at·ing.** —*n.* **1.** a medicine containing opium, used for inducing sleep and relieving pain. **2.** *Informal.* any sedative, soporific, or narcotic. **3.** anything that soothes or dulls the mind. —*adj.* **4.** mixed or prepared with opium. **5.** inducing sleep. **6.** causing dullness or inaction. —*v.t.* **7.** to subject to an opiate; stupefy. **8.** to dull or deaden. [< ML *opiāt(us)* bringing sleep. See OPIUM, -ATE[1]] —**Syn. 2.** drug. **3.** anodyne. **5.** sedative. —**Ant. 2.** stimulant.

o·pine (ō pīn′), *v.,* **o·pined, o·pin·ing.** —*v.t.* **1.** to hold as an opinion. —*v.i.* **2.** to express an opinion. [< L *opīn(ārī)* (to) think, deem]

o·pin·ion (ə pin′yən), *n.* **1.** a belief or judgment that rests on grounds insufficient to produce certainty. **2.** beliefs or judgments shared by many: *social opinion.* **3.** the expression of a personal attitude or judgment: *to give an opinion on tariffs.* **4.** the expression of a formal or professional judgment. **5.** *Law.* the formal statement by a judge or court of the reasoning and the principles of law. **6.** a judgment or estimate of a person or thing with respect to character, merit, etc.: *to forfeit someone's good opinion.* **7.** a favorable estimate; esteem: *I haven't much of an opinion of him.* [ME < OF < L *opīniōn-* (s. of *opīniō*), akin to *opīnārī* to OPINE]

—**Syn. 1.** persuasion, notion, idea, impression. OPINION, SENTIMENT, VIEW are terms for a person's conclusion about something. An OPINION is a belief or judgment that falls short of absolute conviction, certainty, or positive knowledge; it is a conclusion that certain facts, ideas, etc., are probably true or likely to prove so: *political opinions; an opinion about art; In my opinion this is true.* SENTIMENT (usually *pl.*) refers to an opinion or judgment arrived at as the result of deliberation and representing a rather fixed conviction; it usually has a tinge of emotion about it: *These are my sentiments.* VIEW is an estimate of something, an intellectual judgment, a critical survey based on a mental examination, particularly of a public matter: *views on governmental planning.*

o·pin·ion·at·ed (ə pin′yə nā′tid), *adj.* obstinate or conceited with regard to one's opinions. —**o·pin′ion·at′ed·ly,** *adv.* —**o·pin′ion·at′ed·ness,** *n.* —**Syn.** prejudiced, biased; bigoted; stubborn.

o·pin·ion·a·tive (ə pin′yə nā′tiv), *adj.* **1.** of, pertaining to, or of the nature of opinion. **2.** opinionated. —**o·pin′ion·a′tive·ly,** *adv.* —**o·pin′ion·a′tive·ness,** *n.*

op·is·thog·na·thous (op′is thog′nə thəs), *adj.* *Zool.* having receding jaws. [< Gk *ópisth(en)* behind + -o- + -GNATHOUS] —**op′is·thog′na·thism,** *n.*

o·pi·um (ō′pē əm), *n.* **1.** the inspissated juice of the opium poppy that has a narcotic, soporific, analgesic, and astringent effect and contains morphine, codeine, papaverine, and other alkaloids now used in medicine in their isolated or derived forms: a narcotic substance, poisonous in large doses. **2.** anything that causes dullness or inaction or soothes the mind or emotions. [ME < L < Gk *ópion* poppy juice, dim. of *opós* sap, juice]

o′pium pop′py, a Eurasian poppy, *Papaver somniferum,* having white, pink, red, or purple flowers, cultivated as the source of opium, for its oily seeds, and as an ornamental.

O·por·to (ō pōr′tō, ō pôr′-), *n.* a port in NW Portugal, near the mouth of the Douro River. 303,424 (1960). Portuguese, **Porto.**

o·pos·sum (ə pos′əm, pos′əm), *n., pl.* **-sums,** (*esp. collectively*) **-sum. 1.** a prehensile-tailed marsupial, *Didelphis virginiana,* of the eastern U.S., the female having an abdominal pouch in which its young are carried: noted for the habit of feigning death when in danger. **2.** any of various animals of related genera. [< Algonquian; cf. Lenape (Virginia) *apăssum* white beast, Ojibwa *wabăsim* white dog]

Opossum, *Didelphis virginiana* (Total length about 3 ft.; tail 13 in.)

opos′sum shrimp′, a shrimplike crustacean of the order *Mysidacea,* that carries its eggs in a pouch between the legs.

Opp., opuses; opera.

opp., **1.** opposed. **2.** opposite.

Op·pen·heim (op′ən hīm′), *n.* **E(dward) Phillips,** 1866–1946, English novelist.

Op·pen·heim·er (op′ən hī′mər), *n.* **J(ulius) Robert,** 1904–67, U.S. nuclear physicist.

op·pi·dan (op′i dən), *adj.* **1.** of a town; urban. —*n.* **2.** a townsman. [< L *oppidān(us)* = *oppid(um)* town (OL *oppedum,* prob. = L *op-* OP- + *pedum* field < Gk *pédon*) + *-ānus* -AN]

op·pi·late (op′ə lāt′), *v.t.,* **-lat·ed, -lat·ing.** to stop up; fill with obstructing matter; obstruct. [< L *oppīlāt(us)* stopped up (ptp. of *oppīlāre*) = *op-* OP- + *pīl-* ram + *-ātus* -ATE[1]] —**op′pi·la′tion,** *n.*

op·po·nen·cy (ə pō′nən sē), *n.* **1.** the act or an instance of opposing. **2.** the state of being an opponent.

op·po·nent (ə pō′nənt), *n.* **1.** a person who is on an opposing side in a contest, controversy, or the like. —*adj.* **2.** being opposite, as in position. **3.** opposing; adverse; antagonistic. **4.** *Anat.* bringing parts together or into opposition, as a muscle. [< L *oppōnent-* (s. of *oppōnēns,* prp. of *oppōnere*) = *op-* OP- + *pōn-* place + *-ent-* -ENT]

—**Syn. 1.** antagonist; contestant. OPPONENT, COMPETITOR, RIVAL refer to persons engaged in a contest. OPPONENT is the most impersonal, meaning merely a person who opposes; perhaps one who continually blocks and frustrates or one who happens to be on the opposite side in a temporary contest: *an opponent in a debate.* COMPETITOR emphasizes the action in striving against another or others for a definite, common goal: *competitors in business.* RIVAL has both personal and emotional connotations; it emphasizes the idea that (usually) two persons are struggling to attain the same object: *rivals for an office.* —**Ant. 1.** ally, friend.

op·por·tune (op′ər to͞on′, -tyo͞on′), *adj.* **1.** appropriate, favorable, or suitable. **2.** occurring or coming at an appropriate time. [ME < L *opportūn(us)* convenient = *op-* OP- + *port(us)* access, PORT[1] + *-ūnus* adj. suffix] —**op′por·tune′ly,** *adv.* —**op′por·tune′ness,** *n.*

—**Syn. 1.** apt; fortunate, propitious. **2.** convenient. OPPORTUNE, SEASONABLE, TIMELY refer to something that is particularly fitting or suitable for a certain time. OPPORTUNE refers to something that is well-timed and meets exactly the demands of the time or occasion: *an opportune remark.* That which is SEASONABLE is right or proper for the time, season, or occasion: *seasonable weather.* That which is TIMELY occurs or is done at an appropriate time, esp. in time to meet some need: *timely intervention.*

op·por·tun·ism (op′ər to͞o′niz əm, -tyo͞o′-), *n.* the policy or practice of exploiting opportunities without regard to ethical or moral principles. [< It *opportunism(o)*] —**op′por·tun′ist,** *n.* —**op′por·tun·is′tic,** *adj.* —**op′por·tun·is′ti·cal·ly,** *adv.*

op·por·tu·ni·ty (op′ər to͞o′ni tē, -tyo͞o′-), *n., pl.* **-ties. 1.** an appropriate or favorable time or occasion. **2.** a situation or condition favorable for attainment of a goal. **3.** a good position, chance, or prospect for self-advancement. [ME *opportunite* < MF < L *opportūnitāt-* (s. of *opportūnitās*) fitness]

op·pos·a·ble (ə pō′zə bəl), *adj.* **1.** capable of being placed opposite to something else. **2.** capable of being resisted, fought, or opposed. —**op·pos′a·bil′i·ty,** *n.*

op·pose (ə pōz′), *v.,* **-posed, -pos·ing.** —*v.t.* **1.** to resist forcefully; combat. **2.** to stand in the way of; hinder or obstruct. **3.** to set in a situation of conflict: *to oppose armies.* **4.** to have an adverse opinion concerning. **5.** to cause to have an adverse opinion concerning (usually used passively). **6.** to offer arguments against. **7.** to compare or contrast with one another or with another. **8.** to place over against or opposite something. —*v.i.* **9.** to be or act in opposition. [ME < OF *oppose(r),* b. L *oppōnere* to set against and OF *poser* to POSE[1]] —**op·pos′er,** *n.* —**op·pos′ing·ly,** *adv.*

—**Syn. 1.** confront, contravene. OPPOSE, RESIST, WITHSTAND imply setting up a force against something. The difference between OPPOSE and RESIST is somewhat that between offensive and defensive action: to OPPOSE is mainly to fight against, in order to thwart, certain tendencies, procedures, or what one does not approve: *He opposed the passage of the bill.* RESIST suggests that the subject is already threatened by the forces, or by the imminent possibility, against which a person struggles: *to resist temptation.* Whereas OPPOSE always suggests an attitude of great disapproval, RESIST may imply an inner struggle in which the will is divided: *She tried unsuccessfully to resist his charm.* WITHSTAND generally implies successful resistance; it may refer to endurance that allows a person to emerge unharmed (*to withstand a shock*), as well as to active resistance: *to withstand an attack.* —**Ant. 1.** support, help.

op·po·site (op′ə zit, -sit), *adj.* **1.** situated with regard to another or to each other so that the greater part of their location is between the two: *the opposite ends of a room.* **2.** suggesting this in differing radically in some related way: *opposite sides in a controversy.* **3.** *Bot.* **a.** situated on diametrically opposed sides of an axis, as leaves when there are two on one node. **b.** having one organ vertically above another; superimposed. —*n.* **4.** a person or thing that is opposite or contrary. **5.** an antonym. **6.** *Archaic.* an opponent; antagonist. —*prep.* **7.** across from; facing. **8.** in a role parallel or complementary to: *to play opposite a leading lady.* —*adv.* **9.** on opposite sides. [ME < MF < L *opposit(us)* set against, ptp. of *oppōnere.* See OPPOSE, -ITE[2]] —**op′po·site·ly,** *adv.* —**op′po·site·ness,** *n.*

Opposite leaves (def. 3a)

—**Syn. 1.** facing. **2.** unlike, differing. OPPOSITE, CONTRARY, REVERSE imply that two things differ from each other in such a way as to indicate a definite kind of relationship. OPPOSITE suggests symmetrical antithesis in position, action, or character: *opposite ends of a pole, views.* CONTRARY sometimes adds to OPPOSITE the idea of conflict or antagonism: *contrary statements, beliefs.* REVERSE suggests something that faces or moves in the opposite direction: *the reverse side of a coin; a reverse gear.* —**Ant. 2.** same, like.

op·po·si·tion (op′ə zish′ən), *n.* **1.** the action of opposing, resisting, or combating. **2.** antagonism or hostility. **3.** a person or group of persons opposing, criticising, or protesting something, someone, or another group. **4.** the major political party that is opposed to the party in power: *His Majesty's loyal opposition.* **5.** the act of placing opposite. **6.** the state of being placed opposite. **7.** the act of opposing by way of comparison or contrast. **8.** the state of being so opposed. **9.** *Logic.* the relation between two propositions which have the same subject and predicate, but which differ in quantity or quality, or in both. **10.** *Astron.* the situation of two heavenly bodies when their longitudes or right ascensions differ by 180°: *The moon is in opposition to the sun when the earth is directly between them.* [< L *oppositiōn-* (s. of *oppositiō*); r. ME *opposicioun* < OF *opposicion*] —**op′po·si′tion·al,** *adj.*

op·press (ə pres′), *v.t.* **1.** to be as a heavy burden to: *Care and sorrow oppressed them.* **2.** to subject to a burdensome or harsh exercise of authority or power. **3.** to weigh down, as sleep or weariness does. **4.** *Archaic.* to put down, subdue or suppress. **5.** *Obs.* to press upon or against; crush. [ME *oppress(en)* < MF *oppress(er)* < ML *oppressāre* (freq.) < = L *oppress(us)* crushed, ptp. of *opprimere* = *op-* OP- + *-primere* (comb. form of *premere*) to PRESS[1]] —**op·pres′sor,** *n.*

—**Syn. 1, 2.** OPPRESS, DEPRESS, both having the literal meaning to press down upon, to cause to sink, are today mainly limited to figurative applications. To OPPRESS is usually to subject (a people) to burdens, to undue exercise of authority, and the like; its chief application, therefore, is to a social or political situation: *The tyrant oppressed his subjects.* DEPRESS suggests mainly the psychological effect upon the individual of unpleasant conditions, situations, etc., that temporarily sadden and discourage: *depressed by the news.* When OPPRESS is sometimes used in this sense, it suggests a psychological attitude of more complete or permanent hopelessness: *oppressed by a sense of failure.* **2.** maltreat, persecute. —**Ant. 1.** uphold, encourage.

op·pres·sion (ə presh′ən), *n.* **1.** the burdensome, unjust exercise of authority or power. **2.** the act or an instance of oppressing. **3.** the state of being oppressed. **4.** the feeling of being oppressed in mind or body. [< MF < L *oppressiōn-* (s. of *oppressiō*) a pressing down] —**Syn. 1.** tyranny, despotism, persecution. —**Ant. 1.** kindness, justice.

op·pres·sive (ə pres′iv), *adj.* **1.** unjustly harsh or tyrannical. **2.** causing discomfort: *oppressive heat.* **3.** distressing or grievous: *oppressive sorrows.* [< ML *oppressīv(us)*] —**op·pres′sive·ly,** *adv.* —**op·pres′sive·ness,** *n.*

op·pro·bri·ous (ə prō′brē əs), *adj.* **1.** conveying or expressing opprobrium. **2.** disgraceful or shameful: *opprobrious conduct.* [ME < LL *opprobriōs(us)* See OPPROBRIUM, -OUS] —**op·pro′bri·ous·ly,** *adv.* —**op·pro′bri·ous·ness,** *n.* —**Syn. 1.** reproachful, abusive, vituperative, contemptuous. **2.** dishonorable, ignominious. —**Ant. 1.** laudatory. **2.** reputable.

op·pro·bri·um (ə prō′brē əm), *n.* **1.** the disgrace or the reproach incurred by conduct considered outrageously shameful; infamy. **2.** a cause or object of such disgrace or reproach. [< L: reproach = *op-* OP- + *probr(um)* infamy, disgrace + *-ium* -IUM]

op·pugn (ə pyo͞on′), *v.t.* **1.** to assail by criticism, argument, or action. **2.** to call in question; dispute. [ME < L *oppugn(āre)* (to) oppose, attack = *op-* OP- + *pugn-* fight < *pugnus* fist; see PUGILISM]

op·pug·nant (ə pug′nənt), *adj.* opposing; antagonistic; contrary. [< L *oppugnant-* (s. of *oppugnāns*) opposing, prp. of *oppugnāre.* See OPPUGN, -ANT] —**op·pug′nan·cy,** *n.*

OPr, Old Provençal.

OPruss, Old Prussian.

Ops (ops), *n.* *Class. Myth.* the ancient Roman goddess of plenty, and the wife of Saturn and mother of Jupiter: identified with the Greek goddess Rhea.

-opsis, a learned borrowing from Greek indicating apparent likeness: *coreopsis.* [< Gk *ópsis* appearance, sight]

op·son·ic (op son′ik), *adj.* *Bacteriol.* of, pertaining to, or influenced by opsonin. [OPSON(IN) + -IC]

opson′ic in′dex, the ratio of the number of bacteria taken up by phagocytes in the blood serum of a patient or test animal to the number taken up in normal blood serum.

op·so·nin (op′sə nin), *n.* *Bacteriol.* a constituent of normal or immune blood serum that makes invading bacteria more susceptible to the destructive action of the phagocytes. [< L *opsōn(ium)* victuals, hors d'oeuvre < Gk *opsṓnion* < *opsōn(eîn)* (to) buy provisions]

op·so·nize (op′sə nīz′), *v.t.,* **-nized, -niz·ing.** *Immunol.* to increase the susceptibility of (bacteria) to ingestion by phagocytes. [OPSON(IN) + -IZE]

opt (opt), *v.i.* to make a choice; choose (usually fol. by *for* or by an infinitive clause). [< F *opt(er)* (to) choose, divide < L *optāre* to select]

opt., 1. optative. **2.** optical. **3.** optician. **4.** optics.

op·ta·tive (op′tə tiv), *Gram.* —*adj.* **1.** designating or pertaining to a verb mood that expresses a wish. —*n.* **2.** the optative mood. **3.** a verb in it. [< LL *optātīv(us)* = L *optāt(us)* (ptp. of *optāre;* see OPT) + *-īvus* -IVE]

op·tic (op′tik), *adj.* **1.** of or pertaining to the eye or sight. **2.** optical. —*n.* **3.** a lens of an optical instrument. **4.** *Informal.* the eye. [< ML *optic(us)* < Gk *optikós* (cf. *optḗr* spy) = *opt(ós)* seen (verbid of *ópesthai*) + *-ikos* -IC]

op·ti·cal (op′ti kəl), *adj.* **1.** of, pertaining to, or applying optics or the principles of optics. **2.** constructed to assist sight or to correct defects in vision. **3.** of or pertaining to sight or vision; visual: *optical illusions.* **4.** of or pertaining to the eye. **5.** dealing with or skilled in optics.

op′tical activ′ity, *Physical Chem.* the ability of a substance to rotate the plane of polarization of light.

op′tical dou′ble star′. See under **double star.**

op′tical glass′, *Optics.* any of several types of high-quality, homogeneous, color-free glass, as flint or crown glass, having specified refractive properties, used in lenses and other components of optical systems.

op′tical isom′erism, *Chem.* stereoisomerism in which the isomers differ in their effect on the rotation of the plane of polarization of polarized light. —**op′tical i′somer.**

op′tical rota′tion, *Physical Chem.* the angle at which the plane of polarized light is rotated when passed through an optically active substance.

op′tical scan′ning, *Computer Technol.* a process for recording impulses on magnetic tape by using a photoelectric device capable of reading characters and converting the information to electric impulses. —**op′tical scan′ner.**

op′tic ax′is, *Crystall.* (in a crystal exhibiting double refraction) the direction or directions, uniaxial or biaxial respectively, along which the doubly refracting phenomenon does not occur.

op·ti·cian (op tish′ən), *n.* **1.** a person who makes or sells glasses for remedying defects of vision in accordance with the prescriptions of oculists. **2.** a maker or seller of optical glasses and instruments. [< F *opticien* < ML *optic(a)* (see OPTICS) + F *-ien* -IAN]

op·ti·cist (op′ti sist), *n.* a person engaged in the fields of theoretical or applied optics.

op′tic nerve′, *Anat.* either one of the second pair of cranial nerves, consisting of sensory fibers that conduct impulses from the retina to the brain.

op·tics (op′tiks), *n.* (*construed as sing.*) the branch of physical science that deals with the properties and phenomena of both visible and invisible light and with vision. [< ML *optic(a)* (pl.) < Gk *optikā́,* neut. pl. of *optikós;* see OPTIC] —**op′tic·ly,** *adv.*

op′tic thal′amus, thalamus (def. 1).

op·ti·mal (op′tə məl), *adj.* best; most desirable. [OPTIM(UM) + -AL[1]]

op·ti·mise (op′tə mīz′), *v.i., v.t.,* **-mised, -mis·ing.** *Chiefly Brit.* optimize. —**op′ti·mi·sa′tion,** *n.*

op·ti·mism (op′tə miz′əm), *n.* **1.** a disposition or tendency to look on the more favorable side of happenings or possibilities. **2.** the belief that good ultimately predominates over evil in the world. **3.** the doctrine that the existing world is the best of all possible worlds. **4.** the belief that goodness pervades reality. [< F *optimisme.* See OPTIMUM, -ISM]

op·ti·mist (op′tə mist), *n.* **1.** an optimistic person. **2.** a person who holds the belief or the doctrine of optimism. [< F *optimiste.* See OPTIMUM, -IST]

op·ti·mis·tic (op′tə mis′tik), *adj.* **1.** disposed to take a favorable view of happenings or possibilities. **2.** reflecting optimism: *an optimistic plan.* **3.** of or pertaining to optimism. Also, **op′ti·mis′ti·cal.** —**op′ti·mis′ti·cal·ly,** *adv.*

op·ti·mize (op′tə mīz′), *v.,* **-mized, -miz·ing.** —*v.i.* **1.** to be optimistic. —*v.t.* **2.** to make as effective, perfect, or useful as possible. **3.** to make the best of. **4.** *Computer Technol.* to rewrite (a program) to obtain maximum efficiency. Also, *esp. Brit.*, **optimise.** —**op′ti·mi·za′tion,** *n.*

op·ti·mum (op′tə məm), *n., pl.* **-ma** (-mə), **-mums,** *adj.* —*n.* **1.** the best or most favorable conditions for obtaining a given result. **2.** the greatest degree or best result obtained or obtainable under specific conditions. —*adj.* **3.** best or most favorable: *optimum distribution.* [< L: best, neut. of *optimus,* superl. of *bonus* good]

op·tion (op′shən), *n.* **1.** the power or right of choosing. **2.** something that may be or is chosen; choice. **3.** the act of choosing. **4.** a privilege of demanding, within a specified time, the carrying out of a transaction upon stipulated terms. [< L *optiōn-* (s. of *optiō*) choice. See OPT, -ION] —**Syn. 2.** See **choice. 2, 3.** selection, election.

op·tion·al (op′shə nᵊl), *adj.* **1.** left to one's choice; not mandatory. **2.** leaving something to choice. —**op·tion·al·i·ty** (op′shə nal′i tē), *n.* —**op′tion·al·ly,** *adv.*

op·tion·ee (op′shə nē′), *n.* a person who acquires or holds a legal option.

opto-, a learned borrowing from Greek meaning "optic," "vision," used in the formation of compound words: *optometry.* [< Gk *optó(s),* verbal of *ópsesthai* to be about to see]

op·tom·e·ter (op tom′i tər), *n.* any of various instruments for measuring the refractive error of an eye.

op·tom·e·trist (op tom′i trist), *n.* a person skilled in optometry.

op·tom·e·try (op tom′i trē), *n.* the practice or profession of testing the eyes for defects of vision in order to prescribe corrective glasses. —**op·to·met·ri·cal** (op′tə me′tri kəl), *adj.*

op·u·lence (op′yə ləns), *n.* **1.** wealth, riches, or affluence. **2.** abundance, as of resources, goods, etc.; plenty. **3.** the state of being opulent. Also, **op′u·len·cy.** [< L *opulentia* wealth. See OPULENT, -ENCE]

op·u·lent (op′yə lənt), *adj.* **1.** rich; affluent. **2.** abundant or plentiful: *opulent sunshine.* [< L *opulent(us)* wealthy = *op-* (s. of *opēs* wealth, pl. of *ops* power) + *-ulentus* -ULENT] —**op′u·lent·ly,** *adv.* —**Syn. 1.** See **rich.**

o·pun·ti·a (ō pun′shē ə, -shə), *n.* any cactaceous fleshy herb, shrubby plant, or tree of the genus *Opuntia,* having branches usually composed of flattened or globose joints, and having usually yellow flowers and pear-shaped or ovoid, often edible fruit. [< NL, L, after *Opuntius* pertaining to *Opūs* a town in Locris, Greece; see -IA]

o·pus (ō′pəs), *n., pl.* **o·pus·es** or, esp. for 2, **o·pe·ra** (op′ər ə). **1.** a literary work or composition, as a book. **2.** a musical composition, esp. one numbered to show its place in the composer's published work. *Abbr.:* op. [< L: work, labor, a work]

o·pus·cule (ō pus′kyōōl), *n.* a small or minor work. [< F < L *opuscul(um).* See OPUS, -CULE] —**o·pus′cu·lar,** *adj.*

-opy, var. of **-opia.**

OR, 1. See **operations research. 2.** Oregon (approved esp. for use with zip code).

or¹ (ôr; *unstressed* ər), *conj.* **1.** (used to connect words, phrases, or clauses representing alternatives): *to be or not to be.* **2.** (used to connect alternative terms for the same thing): *the Hawaiian or Sandwich Islands.* **3.** (used in correlation): *either . . . or; or . . . or; whether . . . or.* **4.** (used to correct or rephrase what was previously said): *His autobiography, or rather memoirs, is ready for publication.* [ME, orig. unstressed member of correlative *other . . . or,* earlier *other . . . other,* OE *āther, ā-hwæther (oththe) . . . oththe* either . . . or]

or² (ôr), *prep., conj. Archaic.* before; ere. [ME, OE *ār* soon, early; c. OIcel *ār,* Goth *air* early; cf. OE *ǣr* soon,before, ERE]

or³ (ôr), *Heraldry.* —*n.* **1.** the tincture, or metal, gold: represented either by gold or by yellow. —*adj.* **2.** of the tincture, or metal, gold: *a lion or.* [ME < MF < L *aur(um)* gold]

-or¹, a formal element appearing in nouns (of various origins) denoting action, state or condition, result, a quality or property, etc.: *ardor; honor; tremor.* [< L; in some cases r. ME *-our* < AF (F *-eur*) << L]

-or², a suffix of nouns denoting a person or thing that does something, or has some particular function or office (*actor; elevator; traitor*). It occurs chiefly in nouns originally Latin or formed from Latin stems. In some cases it is used as an alternative or substitute for the homonymous native English suffix **-er¹,** esp. in legal terms (often correlative with forms in **-ee**) or with some other differentiation of use (*assignor; grantor; lessor*). [< L; in some cases r. ME *-our* < AF *-(e)our* (F *-eur*) << L *-or, -ātor,* etc.]

O.R., *Com.* owner's risk. Also, **O.R.**

o·ra (ôr′ə, ôr′ə), *n.* pl. of **os².**

or·ach (ôr′əch, or′-), *n.* any plant of the genus *Atriplex,* esp. *A. hortensis,* cultivated for use like spinach. Also, **or′ache.** [ME *orage, arage* < OF *arache* < VL **atripica,* var. of L *atriplic-* (s. of *atriplex*) < Gk *atráphaxys*]

or·a·cle (ôr′ə kəl, or′-), *n.* **1.** (esp. in ancient Greece) a divine utterance made by a god through a priest or priestess in response to an inquiry. **2.** the agency or medium of such responses, or the shrine or place at which they were made. **3.** a divine communication or revelation. **4. oracles,** the Scriptures. **5.** the holy of holies of the temple built by Solomon in Jerusalem. I Kings 6:16, 19–23. **6.** any person or thing serving as an agency of divine communication. **7.** a person who delivers authoritative, wise, or highly regarded and influential pronouncements. [ME < OF < L *ōrācul(um)* = *ōrā(re)* (to) plead (see ORATION) + *-culum* -CLE]

o·rac·u·lar (ō rak′yə lər, ô rak′-), *adj.* **1.** of the nature of or suggesting an oracle. **2.** giving forth utterances or decisions as if by special inspiration or authority. **3.** ambiguous or obscure. [< L *ōrācul(um)* ORACLE + -AR¹] —**o·rac′u·lar·ly,** *adv.* —**Syn. 1.** prophetic. **2.** authoritative; dogmatic.

O·ra·dea (ô rä′dyä), *n.* a city in NW Rumania. 110,719 (est. 1964). Also called **Ora′dea Ma′re** (mä′re). German, **Grosswardein.** Hungarian, **Nagyvárad.**

o·ral (ōr′əl, ôr′-), *adj.* **1.** uttered by the mouth; spoken. **2.** of or using speech: *oral methods of teaching.* **3.** of or pertaining to the mouth: *the oral cavity.* **4.** administered through the mouth: *an oral dose of medicine.* **5.** *Zool.* pertaining to that surface of polyps and marine animals that contains the mouth and tentacles. **6.** *Phonet.* articulated with none of the voice issuing through the nose, as the normal English vowels and the consonants *b* and *v.* **7.** *Psychoanal.* of or pertaining to the first stage of libidinal development in which sexual desire is undifferentiated from the desire for food. —*n.* **8.** *Informal.* an examination, esp. for an advanced degree, that requires spoken answers. [< L *ōr-* (s. of *ōs*) mouth (c. Skt *āsya*) + -AL¹] —**o′ral·ly,** *adv.*

—**Syn. 1.** vocal. ORAL, VERBAL are not properly synonyms. ORAL is properly applied to that which is spoken, as opposed to what is conveyed in writing: *oral message.* VERBAL is often used for oral: *a verbal agreement.* Literally, however, VERBAL applies to the words, spoken or written, in which thought or feeling is conveyed: *a verbal picture.*

O·ran (ō ran′, ô ran′; *Fr.* ô RäN′), *n.* a seaport in NW Algeria. 392,637 with suburbs (1960).

o·rang (ō rang′, ô rang′), *n.* orang-utan.

or·ange (ôr′inj, or′-), *n.* **1.** a globose, reddish-yellow, bitter or sweet, edible citrus fruit. **2.** any of the white-flowered, evergreen rutaceous trees of the genus *Citrus,* bearing this fruit, as *C. aurantium* **(bitter orange, Seville orange,** or **sour orange)** and *C. sinensis* **(sweet orange)** cultivated in warm countries. **3.** any of several other citrus trees, as the trifoliate orange. **4.** any of several trees or fruits resembling an orange. **5.** a color between yellow and red in the spectrum; reddish yellow. —*adj.* **6.** of or pertaining to the orange. **7.** made or prepared with oranges or orangelike flavoring: *orange sherbet.* **8.** of the color orange; reddish-yellow. [ME < OF (b. with *or* gold), c. Sp *naranja* < Ar *nāranj* < Pers *nārang* < Skt *nāraṅga*] —**or′ang·y, or′ang·ey,** *adj.*

Or·ange (ôr′inj, or′-; *Fr.* ô RäNzh′ *for 6*), *n.* **1.** a member of a European princely family ruling in the United Kingdom from 1689 to 1702 and in the Netherlands since 1815. **2.** a river in the Republic of South Africa, flowing W from Lesotho to the Atlantic. 1300 mi. long. **3.** a former small principality of W Europe: now in the SE part of France. **4.** a city in NE New Jersey, near Newark. 32,566 (1970). **5.** a city in SW California, near Los Angeles. 77,365 (1970). **6.** a town in SE France, near Avignon: Roman ruins. 21,450 (1962). **7. Fort.** See **Fort Orange.**

or·ange·ade (ôr′inj ād′, -in jād′, or′-), *n.* a beverage consisting of orange juice, sweetener, and water, sometimes carbonated. [< F]

or′ange blos′som, the white flower of an orange tree, esp. of the genus *Citrus,* much used in wreaths, bridal bouquets, etc.: the state flower of Florida.

Or′ange Free′ State′, a province in the central Republic of South Africa: a Boer republic 1854–1900; a British colony **(Or′ange Riv′er Col′ony)** 1900–10. 1,373,790 (1960); 49,647 sq. mi. *Cap.:* Bloemfontein.

Or·ange·man (ôr′inj mən, or′-), *n., pl.* **-men. 1.** a member of a secret Protestant society formed in the north of Ireland in 1795. **2.** a Protestant of Northern Ireland.

Or′ange Moun′tains, a range in E central West Irian, on the island of New Guinea. Highest peak, Wilhelmina, 15,584 ft.

or′ange pe′koe, 1. a black tea composed of only the smallest top leaves and grown in India and Ceylon. **2.** any India or Ceylon tea of good quality.

or·ange·ry (ôr′inj rē, or′-), *n., pl.* **-ries.** a place, as a greenhouse, in which orange trees are cultivated in cool climates. [< F *orangerie* = *orang(er)* orange tree (< *orange* ORANGE) + *-erie* -ERY]

or′ange stick′, a pencil-like stick, typically of orangewood, used in manicuring and having one round and one pointed end.

or·ange·wood (ôr′inj-wŏŏd′, or′-), *n.* the hard, fine-grained, yellowish wood of the orange tree, used in inlaid work and fine turnery.

o·rang·u·tan (ō rang′ŏŏ-tan′, ô rang′-), *n.* a large, long-armed anthropoid ape, *Pongo pygmaeus,* of arboreal habits, found in Borneo and Sumatra. Also, **o·rang′-u·tan′, o·rang′u·tang′, o·rang-ou·tang** (ō rang′ŏŏ tang′, ō-rang′-, ə rang′-). Also called **orang.** [< Malay: man of the woods]

Orangutan
(4½ ft. high; arm spread 7½ ft.)

o·ra pro no·bis (ō′rä prō nō′bis; *Eng.* ōr′ä prō nō′bis, ôr′ä), *Latin.* pray for us.

o·rate (ō rāt′, ô rāt′, ōr′āt, ôr′āt), *v.i., v.t.,* **-rat·ed, -rat·ing.** to speak pompously or formally; declaim. [back formation from ORATION]

o·ra·tion (ō rā′shən, ô rā′-), *n.* a formal speech, esp. one delivered on a special occasion. [ME *oracion* < L *ōrātiōn-* (s. of *ōrātiō*) speech, prayer = *ōrāt(us)* pleaded (ptp. of *ōrāre* < *ōr-,* s. of *ōs,* mouth) + *-iōn-* -ION] —**Syn.** See **speech.**

or·a·tor (ôr′ə tər, or′-), *n.* **1.** a person who delivers an oration or orations. **2.** *Law. Obs.* a plaintiff in a case in a court of equity. [< L: speaker, suppliant (see ORATION, -OR²); r. ME *oratour* < AF]

Or·a·to·ri·an (ôr′ə tōr′ē ən, -tôr′-, or′-), *Rom. Cath. Ch.* —*n.* **1.** a member of an Oratory. —*adj.* **2.** of or pertaining to the Oratorians.

or·a·tor·i·cal (ôr′ə tôr′i kəl, or′ə tor′-), *adj.* of, pertaining to, or suggesting an orator or oratory. [ORATOR, ORATOR(Y)¹ + -ICAL] —**or′a·tor′i·cal·ly,** *adv.*

or·a·to·ri·o (ôr′ə tōr′ē ō′, -tôr′-, or′-), *n., pl.* **-ri·os.** an extended choral and orchestral composition with a text more or less dramatic in character and usually based upon a religious theme. [< It: small chapel < LL *ōrātōri(um)* ORATORY²; so named from the musical services in the church of the Oratory of St. Philip Neri in Rome]

or·a·to·ry¹ (ôr′ə tōr′ē, -tôr′ē, or′-), *n.* the art or speech of an orator. [< L *ōrātōri(a),* n. use of fem. of *ōrātōrius* of an orator. See ORATOR, -Y³]

or·a·to·ry² (ôr′ə tōr′ē, -tôr′ē or′-), *n., pl.* **-ries. 1.** a small chapel or a room for private devotions. **2.** (*cap.*) *Rom. Cath. Ch.* any of the religious societies of secular priests who live communally but do not take vows. [ME < LL *ōrātōri(um)* place of prayer, n. use of neut. of L *ōrātōrius* oratorical. See ORATOR, -ORY²]

or·a·trix (ôr′ə triks, or′-), *n., pl.* **or·a·tri·ces** (ôr′ə trī′sēz, or′-). a female orator. Also called **or·a·tress** (ôr′ə tris, or′-). [< L; see ORATOR, -TRIX]

orb (ôrb), *n.* **1.** any of the heavenly bodies. **2.** a sphere or globe. **3.** the eyeball or eye. **4.** a globe bearing a cross, used as an emblem of sovereignty. **5.** *Archaic.* a circle or something circular. **6.** *Astron. Obs.* the orbit of a heavenly body. **7.** *Obs.* the earth. **—***v.t.* **8.** to form into a circle or sphere. **9.** *Archaic.* to encircle; enclose. **—***v.i.* **10.** to move in an orbit. **11.** to form into an orb or globe; round out. [< L *orb-* (s. of *orbis*) circle, disk, orb] **—Syn. 2.** See **ball**[1].

or·bic·u·lar (ôr bik′yə lər), *adj.* like an orb; rounded. [ME < LL *orbiculār(is)* circular = L *orbicul(us)* small disk (see ORB, -CULE) + *-āris* -AR[1]] **—or·bic′u·lar′i·ty,** *n.*

or·bic·u·late (ôr bik′yə lit, -lāt′), *adj.* orbicular; rounded. Also, **or·bic′u·lat′ed.** [< L *orbiculāt(us)* gone round in a circle (ptp. of *orbiculārī*). See ORBICULAR, -ATE[1]] **—or·bic′u·late·ly,** *adv.* **—or·bic′u·la′tion,** *n.*

or·bit (ôr′bit), *n.* **1.** the curved path, usually elliptical, described by a planet, satellite, etc., about a celestial body, as the sun. **2.** the usual course of a person's life or range of activities. **3.** *Anat.* **a.** the bony cavity of the skull that contains the eye; eye socket. **b.** the eye. **4.** *Zool.* the part surrounding the eye of a bird or insect. **5.** *Physical Chem.* the path traced by an electron revolving around the nucleus of an atom. **—***v.t.* **6.** to move or travel around in an orbital or elliptical path. **7.** to send into orbit, as a satellite. **—***v.i.* **8.** to go or travel in an orbit. [< L *orbit(a)* wheel track, course, circuit] **—or′bit·er,** *n.*

or·bit·al (ôr′bit^{ə}l), *adj.* **1.** of or pertaining to an orbit or orbits. **—***n.* **2.** *Chem.* a solution of the Schrödinger wave equation corresponding to a region of space in which an electron of given energy is likely to be located.

or′bital veloc′ity, the minimum velocity at which a body must move to maintain a given orbit.

ORC., Organized Reserve Corps.

or·ca (ôr′kə), *n.* the killer whale, *Grampus orca.* [< NL, L: whale]

orch., orchestra.

or·chard (ôr′chərd), *n.* **1.** an area, often enclosed, devoted to the cultivation of fruit trees. **2.** a group or collection of such trees. [ME *orch(i)ard,* OE *orceard;* r. *ortyard,* ME *ortyerd,* OE *ortigeard* (cf. Goth *aurtigards* garden) = *ort-* (cf. L *hortus* garden) + *geard* YARD[2]]

or·char·dist (ôr′chər dist), *n.* a person who cultivates an orchard.

or·ches·tra (ôr′ki strə), *n.* **1.** a company of performers on various musical instruments, including esp. stringed, brass, and percussion instruments, for playing concert music, as symphonies or operas. **2.** (in a modern theater) **a.** the space reserved for the musicians, usually the front part of the main floor (**or′chestra pit′**). **b.** *U.S.* the entire main-floor space for the audience. **c.** *U.S.* the front section of seats on the main floor. **3.** (in the ancient Greek theater) the circular space in front of the stage, allotted to the chorus. **4.** (in the Roman theater) a similar space reserved for persons of distinction. [< L < Gk: the space on which the chorus danced < *orcheîsthai* to dance] **—or·ches·tral** (ôr kes′trəl), *adj.* **—or·ches′tral·ly,** *adv.*

or·ches·trate (ôr′ki strāt′), *v.t., v.i.,* **-trat·ed, -trat·ing.** to compose or arrange (music) for performance by an orchestra. [< F *orchestr(er)* (< *orchestre* ORCHESTRA) + -ATE[1]] **—or′ches·tra′tion,** *n.* **—or′ches·tra′tor, or′ches·trat′er,** *n.*

orchi-, var. of **orchido-.**

or·chid (ôr′kid), *n.* **1.** any terrestrial or epiphytic, perennial herb of the family *Orchidaceae,* of temperate and tropical regions, having usually showy flowers. **2.** a bluish to reddish purple. [< NL *Orchid(eae)* (later *Orchidaceae*). See ORCHIS, -ID[2]]

Orchid, genus *Cattleya*

orchid-, var. of **orchido-** before a vowel: *orchidology.*

or·chi·da·ceous (ôr′ki dā′shəs), *adj.* belonging to the *Orchidaceae,* or orchid family of plants. [< NL *Orchidace(ae).* See ORCHID-, -ACEOUS]

orchido-, a combining form meaning "orchid," "testicle," used in the formation of compound words: *orchidology.* Also, **orchi-, orchid-.** [*orchid-* (erroneously supposed s. of Gk *órchis* ORCHIS) + -o-]

or·chid·ol·o·gy (ôr′ki dol′ə jē), *n.* the branch of botany or horticulture dealing with orchids. **—or′chid·ol′o·gist,** *n.*

or·chil (ôr′kil, -chil), *n.* **1.** a violet coloring matter obtained from certain lichens, chiefly species of *Roccella.* **2.** any lichen yielding this dye. Also, **archil.** [late ME < OF]

or·chis (ôr′kis), *n.* **1.** any orchid. **2.** any of various terrestrial orchids, esp. of the genus *Orchis,* of temperate regions, having spicate flowers. **3.** See **fringed orchis.** [< L < Gk: testicle, plant with roots like testicles]

or·ci·nol (ôr′sə nōl′, -nôl′, -nol′), *n. Chem.* a white, crystalline, water-soluble solid, $CH_3C_6H_3(OH)_2 \cdot H_2O$, sweet but unpleasant in taste, that reddens on exposure to air: obtained from many lichens or produced synthetically and used chiefly as a reagent for certain carbohydrates. Also, **or·cin** (ôr′sin). [< NL *orcin(a)* (< It *orcello* ORCHIL, by alter.) + -OL[2]]

Or·cus (ôr′kəs), *n.* **1.** the ancient Roman god of the underworld, identified with the Greek Pluto. **2.** the ancient Roman underworld; Hades.

Or·czy (ôrt′sē), *n.* **Em·mus·ka** (em′mo͝osh kə), **Baroness,** 1865–1947, English novelist, born in Hungary.

ord., **1.** order. **2.** ordinal. **3.** ordinance. **4.** ordinary. **5.** ordnance.

or·dain (ôr dān′), *v.t.* **1.** *Eccles.* to invest with ministerial or sacerdotal functions; confer holy orders upon. **2.** to enact or establish by law, edict, etc. **3.** to decree or give orders (that something should be done). **4.** (of God, fate, etc.) to destine or predestine. **—***v.i.* **5.** to order or command: *Thus do the gods ordain.* [ME *ordein(en)* < OF *ordene(r)* < L *ordināre* to order, arrange, appoint. See ORDINATION] **—or·dain′a·ble,** *adj.* **—or·dain′ment,** *n.* **—Syn. 3.** order, prescribe, determine. **4.** predetermine.

or·deal (ôr dēl′, -dē′əl, ôr′dēl), *n.* **1.** any extremely severe or trying test, experience, or trial. **2.** a primitive form of trial to determine guilt or innocence by subjecting the accused person to physical danger, the result being regarded as a divine judgment. [ME *ordal,* OE *ordāl;* c. D *oordeel,* G *Urteil.* See DOLE[1]]

or·der (ôr′dər), *n.* **1.** an authoritative communication by which the person addressed is directed to do something; command. **2.** a system of arrangement, classification, or coordination of persons or things, as by sequence or rank: *alphabetical order.* **3.** the state of being arranged or classified under such a system: *Put these cards in order.* **4.** a state of efficiency, neatness, or the like: *to put one's affairs in order.* **5.** a state of effective operation: *a wrist watch in working order.* **6.** a state of public peace or conformity to law: *to maintain order at a beach.* **7.** a general classification according to quality or standing: *talents of a high order.* **8.** a social class: *the lower orders.* **9.** a customary mode of procedure. **10.** conformity to this, esp. in parliamentary procedure. **11.** a political or other system that prevails in or is familiar to a certain period. **12.** a request or set of instructions according to which goods or services are sold, made, or furnished. **13.** something sold, made, or furnished according to a request or set of instructions. **14.** *Gram.* the sequential arrangement of elements in a construction or sentence. **15.** *Biol.* the usual major subdivision of a class or subclass in the classification of plants and animals, consisting of several families. **16.** a group or body of persons of the same profession, occupation, or pursuits. **17.** a body or society of persons living by common consent under the same religious, moral, or social regulations. **18.** *Eccles.* any of the degrees or grades of clerical office. Cf. **major order, minor order.** **19.** any of the nine grades of angels in medieval angelology. Cf. **angel** (def. 1). **20. orders,** the rank or status of an ordained Christian minister. **21.** Usually, **orders.** the rite or sacrament of ordination. **22.** *Hist.* (esp. during the Middle Ages) a society of combined military and monastic character, as the Knights Templars. **23.** an honorary institution or society, or the decoration conferred by it. **24.** a written direction to pay money or deliver goods, given by a person legally entitled to the disposition. **25.** *Archit.* **a.** any arrangement of columns with an entablature. **b.** any of five such arrangements typical of classical architecture, includ-

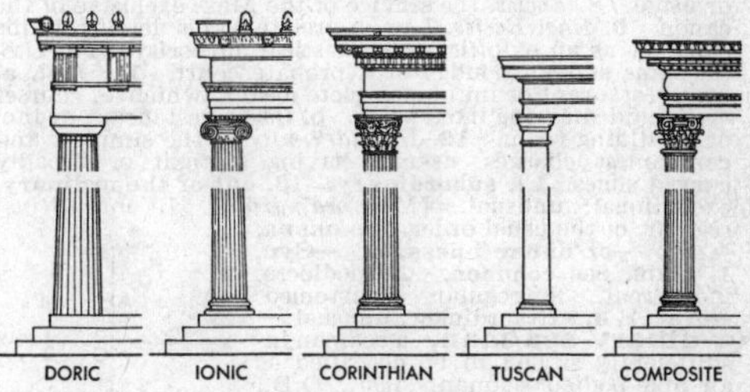

Orders (def. 25b)

ing the Doric, Ionic, Corinthian, Tuscan, and Composite. **c.** any of several concentric rings composing an arch, esp. when each projects beyond the one below. **26.** *Math.* **a.** degree, as in algebra. **b.** the number of rows or columns of a square matrix or determinant. **c.** the number of times a function has been differentiated to produce a given derivative: *a second order derivative.* **d.** the order of the highest derivative appearing in a given differential equation: $\frac{d^2y}{dx^2} + 3y\frac{dy}{dx} - 6 = 0$ is a differential equation of order two. **e.** the number of elements of a given group. **27. call to order,** to begin (a meeting). **28. in order, a.** fitting; appropriate. **b.** in a state of proper arrangement or preparation. **c.** correct according to the rules of parliamentary procedure. **29. in order that,** to the end that. **30. in order to,** as a means to; with the purpose of. **31. in short order,** with promptness or speed; rapidly. **32. on order,** requested or ordered but not yet received. **33. on the order of,** resembling to some extent; like. **34. out of order, a.** inappropriate; unsuitable. **b.** not operating properly; in disrepair. **c.** incorrect according to the rules of parliamentary procedure. **—***v.t.* **35.** to give an order to; command. **36.** to command to come or go as specified: *to order someone out of one's house.* **37.** to give an order for: *Have you ordered your meal yet?* **38.** to urge authoritatively, as a doctor does. **39.** to put in order. **40.** to invest with clerical rank or authority; ordain. **41.** *Math.* to arrange (the elements of a set) so that if one element precedes another, it cannot be preceded by the other or by elements that the other precedes. **—***v.i.* **42.** to give or issue orders, instructions, etc. [ME *ordre* < OF < L *ordin-* (s. of *ordō*) row, rank, regular arrangement] **—or′der·a·ble,** *adj.* **—or′dered·ness,** *n.* **—or′der·er,** *n.* **—or′der·less,** *adj.*
—Syn. 1. prescription, instruction. **17.** fraternity, community. **35.** instruct, bid, require. See **direct. 39.** arrange, systematize.

or′der arms′, *Mil.* **1.** a position, in the manual of arms in close-order drill, in which the rifle is held at the right side, with its butt on the ground. **2.** (as an interjection) the command to move the rifle to this position.

or·der·ly (ôr′dər lē), *adj., adv., n., pl.* **-lies.** **—***adj.* **1.** arranged or disposed in a neat, tidy manner or in a regular sequence: *an orderly desk.* **2.** observant of or governed by system or method, as persons, the mind, etc. **3.** characterized by or observant of law, rule, or discipline; law-abiding. **4.** pertaining to or charged with the communication or execution of orders. **—***adv.* **5.** according to established order or rule. **—***n.* **6.** *Mil.* an enlisted man selected to perform various menial chores for an officer or officers. **7.** a hospital attendant, usually male. [ME (adv.)] **—or′der·li·ness,** *n.*
—Syn. 1, 2. ORDERLY, METHODICAL, SYSTEMATIC characterize that which is neat, in order, and planned. These three words are sometimes used interchangeably. However, ORDERLY emphasizes neatness of arrangement: *an orderly array of books.* METHODICAL suggests a logical plan, a definite order of actions or method from beginning to end: *a methodical*

examination. Systematic suggests thoroughness, an extensive and detailed plan, together with regularity of action: *a systematic review.* **—Ant. 1.** chaotic, haphazard.

or′derly of′ficer, *Brit.* See **officer of the day.**

or′der of the day′, **1.** the agenda for an assembly, meeting, etc. **2.** *Mil.* a specific command or proclamation issued by a commanding officer to his troops.

Or′der of the Gar′ter, the highest order of British knighthood, instituted by Edward III about 1348.

or·di·nal[1] (ôr′dᵊnᵊl), *adj.* **1.** of or pertaining to an order, as of animals or plants. —*n.* **2.** an ordinal number. [< LL *ordināl(is)* in order. See order, -al[1]] **—or′di·nal·ly,** *adv.*

or·di·nal[2] (ôr′dᵊnᵊl), *n.* **1.** a directory of ecclesiastical services. **2.** a book containing the forms for the ordination of priests, consecration of bishops, etc. [ME < ML, m. LL *ordināle* in order (neut. of *ordinālis*). See ordinal[1]]

or′dinal num′ber, any of the numbers that express degree, quality, or position in a series, as *first, second, third,* etc. (distinguished from *cardinal number*). Also called **or′dinal nu′meral.**

or·di·nance (ôr′dᵊnəns), *n.* **1.** an authoritative rule or law; a decree or command. **2.** a public injunction or regulation. **3.** *Eccles.* an established rite or ceremony. [ME *ordinaunce* < OF *ordenance,* ML *ordinantia* < L *ordinant-* (s. of *ordināns*) arranging, prp. of *ordināre.* See ordination, -ance] **—Syn. 1.** order.

or·di·nar·i·ly (ôr′dᵊnâr′ə lē, ôr′dᵊner′ə lē), *adv.* **1.** in ordinary cases; usually. **2.** in an unexceptional manner or fashion; modestly. **3.** to the usual extent; reasonably.

or·di·nar·y (ôr′dᵊner′ē), *adj., n., pl.* **-nar·ies.** —*adj.* **1.** of the usual kind; not exceptional; commonplace. **2.** somewhat inferior or below average: *very ordinary manners.* **3.** customary; normal. **4.** (of jurisdiction) immediate, as contrasted with that which is delegated. **5.** (of officials) belonging to the regular staff or the fully recognized class. —*n.* **6.** the commonplace or average condition, degree, etc.: *ability above the ordinary.* **7.** something regular, customary, or usual. **8.** *Eccles.* the service of the Mass exclusive of the canon. **9.** *Eng. Eccles. Law.* a prelate or his deputy, in his capacity as an ex-officio ecclesiastical authority. **10.** *U.S.* (in some states) a judge of a probate court. **11.** *Brit.* **a.** (in a restaurant or inn) a complete meal in which all courses are included at one fixed price. **b.** *Obs.* a restaurant or inn, or its dining room. **12.** *Heraldry.* any of the simplest and commonest charges, usually having straight or broadly curved edges. Cf. **subordinary. 13. out of the ordinary,** exceptional; unusual. [ME *ordinarie* < L *ordinār(ius)* regular, of the usual order. See order, -ary] **—or′di·nar′i·ness,** *n.* **—Syn. 1.** plain. See **common. 2.** mediocre, indifferent. **3.** regular, accustomed. **—Ant. 1, 3.** extraordinary, unusual.

or′dinary sea′man, a seaman insufficiently skilled to be classified as an able-bodied seaman. *Abbr.:* O.D., O.S., o.s.

or·di·nate (ôr′dᵊnāt′, -dᵊnit), *n. Math.* (in plane Cartesian coordinates) the y-coordinate of a point: its distance from the x-axis measured parallel to the y-axis. Cf. **abscissa.** [abstracted from NL (*linea*) *ordināte* (*applicāta*) line applied in order; NL *ordināte* (adv.) < L *ordinātus* arranged. See ordination]

Ordinate
P, Any point; AO and PB, Ordinate of P; YY, Axis of ordinates; OB and AP, Abscissa of P; XX, Axis of abscissas

or·di·na·tion (ôr′dᵊnā′shən), *n.* **1.** *Eccles.* the ceremony of ordaining. **2.** the fact of being ordained. **3.** a decreeing. **4.** the act of arranging. **5.** the resulting state; disposition. [ME *ordinacioun* < LL *ordinātiōn-* (s. of *ordinātiō*) ordainment; L: an ordering = *ordināt(us)* ordered (ptp. of *ordināre* to order, arrange < *ordin-,* s. of *ordō* order) + *-iōn-* -ion]

ordn., ordnance.

ord·nance (ôrd′nəns), *n.* **1.** cannon or artillery. **2.** military weapons of all kinds with their equipment, ammunition, etc. **3.** the branch of an army that procures, stores, and issues weapons, munitions, and combat vehicles. [syncopated var. of ordinance]

or·do (ôr′dō), *n., pl.* **or·di·nes** (ôr′dᵊnēz′). *Rom. Cath. Ch.* a booklet containing short and abbreviated directions for the contents of the office and Mass of each day in the year. [< ML, L: series, row, order]

or·don·nance (ôr′dᵊnəns; *Fr.* ôʀ dô näɴs′), *n., pl.* **-donnanc·es** (-dᵊnən siz; *Fr.* -dô näɴs′). **1.** arrangement or disposition of parts, as of a building, a picture, or a literary composition. **2.** an ordinance, decree, or law. [< F, alter. of MF *ordenance* ordinance, by influence of *donner* to give] **—or′don·nant,** *adj.*

Or·do·vi·cian (ôr′də vish′ən), *Geol.* —*adj.* **1.** noting or pertaining to a period of the Paleozoic era, occurring 440,000,000 to 500,000,000 years ago, and characterized by the advent of conodonts and ostracods and the presence of algae and seaweeds. See table at **era.** —*n.* **2.** the Ordovician period or system. [named after the *Ordovic(es)* (pl.) (< L) an ancient British tribe in northern Wales; see -ian]

or·dure (ôr′jər, -dyŏŏr), *n.* dung; manure; excrement. [ME < OF = *ord* filthy (< L *horrid(us)* horrid) + *-ure* -ure] **—or′dur·ous,** *adj.*

Or·dzho·ni·kid·ze (ôʀ jo ni kēd′ze), *n.* a city in the RSFSR, in the S Soviet Union in Europe. 208,000 (est. 1965). Also, **Orjonikidze.** Formerly, **Vladikavkaz.**

ore (ōr, ôr), *n.* **1.** a metal-bearing mineral or rock, or a native metal, esp. when of value. **2.** a mineral or natural product serving as a source of some nonmetallic substance, as sulfur. [ME *oor* metal, ore, OE *ār* brass]

ö·re (œ′ʀə), *n., pl.* **ö·re. 1.** a bronze coin of Norway, the 100th part of a krone. **2.** a zinc coin of Denmark, the 100th part of a krone. **3.** a bronze coin of Sweden, the 100th part of a krona. Also, **øre** (for defs. 1, 2). [all << L *aureus* a gold coin]

Ore., Oregon.

o·re·ad (ōr′ē ad′, ôr′-), *n. Class. Myth.* any of a group of mountain nymphs who were the companions of Artemis. [< L *Oread-* (s. of *Oreas*) < Gk *oreiad-* (s. of *oreiás*). See oro-[1], -ad[1]]

Ö·re·bro (œ′ʀə bʀōō′), *n.* a city in S Sweden. 79,727 (1965).

ore′ dress′ing, *Metall.* the art of separating the valuable minerals from an ore without chemical changes.

Oreg., Oregon.

o·reg·a·no (ə reg′ə nō′, ô reg′-), *n.* any menthaceous plant of the genus *Origanum,* related to but spicier than marjoram, used in cookery. [< AmerSp *orégano,* Sp: wild marjoram < L *origan(um).* See origan]

Or·e·gon (ôr′ə gən, -gon′, or′-), *n.* a state in the NW United States, on the Pacific coast. 2,091,385 (1970); 96,981 sq. mi. *Cap.:* Salem. *Abbr.:* OR, Oreg., Ore. **—Or·e·go·ni·an** (ôr′ə gō′nē ən, or′-), *adj., n.*

Or′egon grape′, **1.** an evergreen shrub, *Mahonia aquifolium,* of the western coast of the U.S., having yellow flowers and small, blue, edible berries: the state flower of Oregon. **2.** the berry itself.

Or′egon pine′. See **Douglas fir.**

Or′egon Trail′, *U.S.* a route used during the westward migrations, from Missouri to Oregon. ab. 2000 mi. long.

O·re·kho·vo-Zu·ye·vo (o-ʀe′ĸʜo vo zōō′ye vo), *n.* a city in the W RSFSR, in the central Soviet Union in Europe, E of Moscow. 116,000 (est. 1965).

O·rel (ō rel′, ô rel′; *Russ.* o ʀyôl′), *n.* a city in the W RSFSR, in the central Soviet Union in Europe, S of Moscow. 197,000 (est. 1965).

O·rem (ōr′əm, ôr′-), *n.* a city in N Utah. 25,729 (1970).

O·ren·burg (ōr′ən bûrg′, ôr′-; *Russ.* o ʀen bŏŏʀk′), *n.* Chkalov.

O·ren·se (ô ʀen′se), *n.* a city in N Spain. 66,403 (est. 1963).

Or·e·o (ôr′ē ō′), *n., pl.* **Oreos.** *Derogatory.* a black person who thinks and acts like a white one. [from trademark name of a cookie consisting of a white filling between two chocolate layers]

O·res·tes (ō res′tēz, ô res′-), *n. Class. Myth.* the son of Agamemnon and Clytemnestra, and the brother of Electra and Iphigenia: avenged the murder of Agamemnon by killing Clytemnestra and her lover, Aegisthus.

Ö·re·sund (œ′ʀə sŏŏnd′), *n.* Swedish and Danish name of The Sound.

-orexia, an element occurring in loan words from Greek and used with the meaning "desire," "appetite," in the formation of compound words: *anorexia.* [< Gk = *órex(is)* desire (*orég(ein)* (to) desire + *-sis* -sis) + *-ia* -y[3]]

org., **1.** organic. **2.** organized.

or·gan (ôr′gən), *n.* **1.** Also called **pipe organ.** a musical instrument consisting of one or more sets of pipes sounded by means of compressed air, played by means of one or more keyboards, and capable of producing a wide range of musical effects. **2.** any of various similar instruments, as an electronic organ. **3.** a barrel organ or hand organ. **4.** a differentiated part or member having a specific function in a plant or animal. **5.** an instrument or means, as of action or performance. **6.** a newspaper, magazine, or other publication representing a special group. [ME < L *organ(um)* < Gk *órganon* implement, tool, bodily organ, musical instrument]

or·ga·na[1] (ôr′gə nə), *n.* a pl. of **organon.**

or·ga·na[2] (ôr′gə nə), *n.* a pl. of **organum.**

or·gan·dy (ôr′gən dē), *n.* a fine, thin, cotton fabric usually having a crisp finish: used for blouses, curtains, etc. Also, **or′gan·die.** [< F *organdi* < ?]

or·gan·elle (ôr′gə nel′, ôr′gə nel′), *n. Biol.* a specialized part of a cell having some specific function; a cell organ.

or′gan grind′er, a street musician who earns his living by playing a hand organ or hurdy-gurdy.

or·gan·ic (ôr gan′ik), *adj.* **1.** noting or pertaining to a class of compounds that formerly comprised only those existing in or derived from plants or animals, but that now includes all other compounds of carbon. Cf. **inorganic** (def. 3). **2.** characteristic of, pertaining to, or derived from living organisms. **3.** of or pertaining to an organ or the organs of an animal or a plant. **4.** of, pertaining to, or affecting living tissue: *organic pathology.* **5.** *Psychol.* caused by structural impairment or change: *organic disorder.* Cf. **functional** (def. 6). **6.** characterized by the systematic arrangement of parts; organized; systematic. **7.** of or pertaining to the constitution or structure of a thing. **8.** growing and developing in the manner of living organisms: *a view that history is organic.* **9.** of, pertaining to, involving, or grown with the use of fertilizers or pesticides of animal or vegetable origin. **10.** *Law.* noting or pertaining to the constitutional or essential law or laws organizing the government of a state. **11.** *Archit.* noting or pertaining to architecture regarded as having the directness of form and economy of material common to organisms. —*n.* **12.** a substance, as a fertilizer or pesticide, of animal or vegetable origin. [< L *organic(us)* instrumental < Gk *organikós*] **—or·ga·nic·i·ty** (ôr′gə nis′i tē), *n.* **—Syn. 7.** inherent, essential.

or·gan·i·cal·ly (ôr gan′ik lē), *adv.* **1.** in an organic manner. **2.** with reference to organic structure.

organ′ic chem′istry, the branch of chemistry dealing with the compounds of carbon.

organ′ic disease′, *Pathol.* a disease in which there is a structural alteration (opposed to *functional disease*).

or·gan·i·cism (ôr gan′i siz′əm), *n.* **1.** *Biol., Philos.* the theory that vital activities arise not from any one part of an organism but from its autonomous composition. **2.** *Pathol.* the doctrine that all symptoms arise from organic disease. **3.** a view of society as an autonomous entity analogous to an organism. **—or·gan′i·cis′tic,** *adj.* **—organ′i·cist,** *n.*

or·gan·ise (ôr′gə nīz′), *v.t., v.i.,* **-ised, -is·ing.** *Chiefly Brit.* organize. **—or′gan·is′a·ble,** *adj.*

or·gan·ism (ôr′gə niz′əm), *n.* **1.** a form of life composed of mutually dependent parts that maintain various vital processes. **2.** any form of animal or plant life. **3.** any organized body or system conceived of as analogous to a living being: *the governmental organism.* **4.** any complex thing or system having properties and functions determined by the character of the whole as well as of the parts and by the relations of the parts to the whole. **—or′gan·is′mic, or′gan·is′mal,** *adj.* **—or′gan·is′mi·cal·ly,** *adv.*

or·gan·ist (ôr′gə nist), *n.* a person who plays the organ. [< ML *organist(a)*]

or·gan·i·za·tion (ôr′gə ni zā′shən *or, esp. Brit.,* -nī-), *n.* **1.** the act or process of organizing. **2.** the state or manner of being organized. **3.** something that is organized. **4.** organic structure; composition. **5.** a body of persons organized for some end or work. Also, *esp. Brit.,* **or′gan·i·sa′tion.** [late ME *organizacion* < ML *organizātiōn-* (s. of *organizātiō*) = *organizāt(us)* organized (ptp. of *organizāre;* see ORGANIZE) + *-iōn-* -ION] **—or′gan·i·za′tion·al;** *esp. Brit.,* **or′gan·i·sa′tion·al,** *adj.* **—or′gan·i·za′tion·al·ly;** *esp. Brit.,* **or′gan·i·sa′tion·al·ly,** *adv.*

Organiza′tion of Amer′ican States′. See **OAS.**

or·gan·ize (ôr′gə nīz′), *v.,* **-ized, -iz·ing.** **—***v.t.* **1.** to form as or into a whole consisting of interdependent or coordinated parts: *to organize a committee.* **2.** to systematize: *to organize the files of an office.* **3.** to give organic structure or character to. **4.** to build a labor union among. **5.** to enlist the employees of (a business) into a labor union. **6.** *Informal.* to put (oneself) in a state of mental competence to perform a task. **—***v.i.* **7.** to combine in an organization. **8.** to assume organic structure. Also, *esp. Brit.,* **organise.** [ME *organyse(n)* < ML *organiz(āre)*] **—or′gan·iz′a·ble,** *adj.* **—Syn. 1.** dispose, frame. **2.** order. **—Ant. 1.** destroy.

or′ganized la′bor, all workers who are organized in labor unions.

or·gan·iz·er (ôr′gə nī′zər), *n.* **1.** a person who organizes, esp. one who enlists employees into membership in a union. **2.** a multiple folder in which correspondence, papers, etc., are sorted for systematic handling. **3.** *Embryol.* any part of an embryo that stimulates the development and differentiation of another part. Also, *esp. Brit.,* **or′gan·is′er.**

organo-, an element of Greek origin meaning "organ (of the body)," or "organic," used in the formation of compound words: *organology.* [< Gk, comb. form of *órganon* ORGAN]

or·ga·nog·ra·phy (ôr′gə nog′rə fē), *n., pl.* **-phies.** the description of the organs of animals or plants. **—or·ga·no·graph·ic** (ôr′gə nə graf′ik), **or′ga·no·graph′i·cal,** *adj.* **—or′ga·nog′ra·phist,** *n.*

or·ga·nol·o·gy (ôr′gə nol′ə jē), *n.* **1.** the branch of biology that deals with the structure and functions of the organs of animals or plants. **2.** the study of musical instruments. **3.** phrenology. **—or·ga·no·log·ic** (ôr′gə nəloj′ik), **or′ga·no·log′i·cal,** *adj.* **—or′ga·nol′o·gist,** *n.*

or·ga·no·me·tal·lic (ôr′gə nō mə tal′ik, ôr gan′ō-), *adj. Chem.* pertaining to or noting an organic compound containing a metal or a metalloid linked to carbon.

or·ga·non (ôr′gə non′), *n., pl.* **-na** (-nə), **-nons. 1.** an instrument of thought or knowledge. **2.** *Philos.* a system of rules or principles of demonstration or investigation. [< Gk; see ORGAN]

or·ga·no·ther·a·peu·tics (ôr′gə nō ther′ə pyōō′tiks, ôr gan′ō-), *n.* (*construed as sing.*) organotherapy.

or·ga·no·ther·a·py (ôr′gə nō ther′ə pē, ôr gan′ō-), *n.* the branch of therapeutics that deals with the use of remedies prepared from the organs of animals.

or′gan pipe′, one of the pipes of a pipe organ.

or·ga·num (ôr′gə nəm), *n., pl.* **-na** (-nə), **-nums. 1.** an organon. **2.** *Music.* **a.** the doubling, or simultaneous singing, of a melody at an interval of either a fourth, a fifth, or an octave. **b.** the second part in such singing. [<L; see ORGAN]

or·gan·za (ôr gan′zə), *n.* a sheer rayon, nylon, or silk fabric for evening dresses, trimmings, etc. [?]

or·gan·zine (ôr′gən zēn′), *n.* silk that has been additionally twisted in opposite directions, used warpwise in weaving silk fabrics. Cf. **tram**[3]. [< F *organsin* < It *organzin(o)*]

or·gasm (ôr′gaz əm), *n.* **1.** the physical and emotional sensation experienced at the culmination of a sexual act. **2.** an instance of experiencing this. **3.** intense or unrestrained excitement. [< NL *orgasm(us)* < Gk *orgasmós* excitement < *orgâ(ein)* (to) swell, be excited] **—or·gas′mic, or·gas′tic,** *adj.*

or·geat (ôr′zhat; *Fr.* ôʀ zhA′), *n.* a syrup or drink made originally from barley but later from almonds, prepared with sugar and an extract of orange flowers. [< F < Pr *orjat* < *orge* barley < L *horde(um)*]

Or·get·o·rix (ôr jet′ə riks), *n.* fl. c60 B.C., Helvetian chieftain.

or·gi·as·tic (ôr′jē as′tik), *adj.* **1.** of, pertaining to, or having the nature of an orgy. **2.** tending to arouse or excite unrestrained emotion: *orgiastic rhythms.* [< Gk *orgiastik(ós)* < *orgiáz(ein)* (to) celebrate orgies]

or·gy (ôr′jē), *n., pl.* **-gies. 1.** wild, drunken, or licentious festivity or revelry. **2.** a party characterized by public promiscuous sexual intercourse. **3.** any proceedings marked by unbridled indulgence of passions: *an orgy of killing.* **4. orgies,** esoteric religious rituals in ancient Greece, used esp. in the worship of Demeter and Dionysus, characterized in later times by wild dancing, singing, and drinking. [< MF *orgie* < L *orgia* (neut. pl.) < Gk *órgia,* akin to *érgon* work]

-orial, a suffix used to form adjectives from nouns with stems in **-or** or **-ory:** *professorial; purgatorial.* [ME *-oriale.* See -OR[2], -ORY[2], -AL[1]]

or·i·bi (ôr′ə bē, or′-), *n., pl.* **-bis.** a small tan-colored antelope, *Ourebia ourebi,* of South and East Africa, with spikelike horns. [< SAfrD < Hottentot *arab*]

o·ri·el (ōr′ē əl, ôr′-), *n.* a bay window, esp. one cantilevered or corbeled out from a wall. [ME < OF *oriol* porch, passage, gallery << L *aureol(us)* gilded]

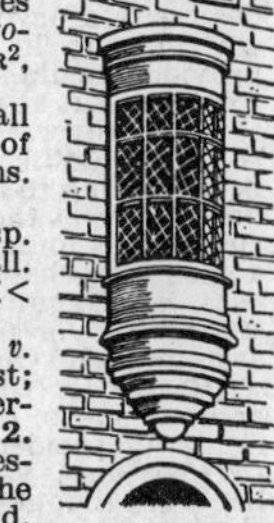
Oriel

o·ri·ent (*n., adj.* ōr′ē ənt, ōr′ē ent′, ôr′-; *v.* ōr′ē ent′, ôr′-), *n.* **1. the Orient, a.** the East; the countries to the E and SE of the Mediterranean. **b.** See **Eastern Hemisphere. 2.** *Jewelry.* **a.** an orient pearl. **b.** the iridescence of a pearl. **3.** *Archaic.* the east; the eastern region of the heavens or the world. **—***adj.* **4.** oriental (def. 4b). **5.** *Archaic.* eastern or oriental. **6.** *Archaic.* rising or appearing, esp. as from beneath the horizon: *the orient sun.* **—***v.t.* **7.** to bring into due relation to surroundings, circumstances, facts, etc.: *to orient one's ideas to new conditions.* **8.** to familiarize (a person) with new surroundings, circumstances, or the like. **9.** to place in any definite position with reference to the points of the compass or other locations. **10.** to determine the position of in relation to the points of the compass; get the bearings of. **11.** to place with all important parts facing in certain standard directions: *to orient a church.* **—***v.i.* **12.** to turn toward the east or in any specified direction. [ME < MF < L *orient-* (s. of *oriēns*) the east, sunrise, n. use of prp. of *orīrī* to rise; see -ENT]

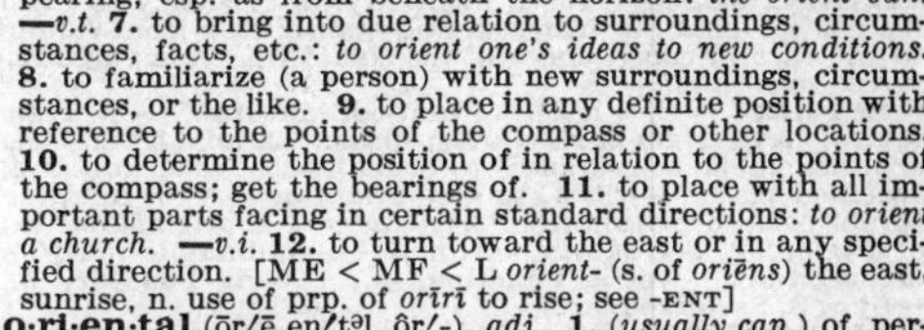

o·ri·en·tal (ōr′ē en′tᵊl, ôr′-), *adj.* **1.** (*usually cap.*) of, pertaining to, or characteristic of the Orient or East. **2.** (*cap.*) *Zoogeog.* belonging to a geographical division comprising southern Asia and the Malay Archipelago as far as and including the Philippines, Borneo, and Java. **3.** of the orient or east; eastern. **4.** *Jewelry.* **a.** (*usually cap.*) designating various gems that are varieties of corundum: *Oriental ruby.* **b.** (of a gem or pearl) fine or precious; orient. **—***n.* **5.** (*usually cap.*) a native or inhabitant of the Orient, esp. one belonging to a native race. [ME < MF < L *orientāl(is).* See ORIENT, -AL[1]] **—o′ri·en′tal·ly,** *adv.*

O·ri·en·ta·li·a (ōr′ē ən tā′lē ə, -tāl′yə, ôr-′), *n.pl.* objects pertaining to the Orient and Oriental art, culture, history, folklore, or the like. [< NL, n. use of neut. pl. of L *orientālis* ORIENTAL]

O·ri·en·tal·ism (ōr′ē en′tᵊliz′əm, ôr′-), *n.* (*often l.c.*) **1.** a peculiarity or idiosyncrasy of the Oriental peoples. **2.** the character or characteristics of the Oriental peoples. **3.** the knowledge and study of Oriental languages, literature, etc. **—O′ri·en′tal·ist,** *n.*

O·ri·en·tal·ize (ōr′ē en′tᵊlīz′, ôr′-), *v.t., v.i.,* **-ized, -iz·ing.** (*often l.c.*) to make or become Oriental. Also, *esp. Brit.,* **O′ri·en′tal·ise′. —O′ri·en′tal·i·za′tion,** *n.*

O′rien′tal rug′, a rug or carpet woven usually in Asia and characterized by hand-knotted pile, used in the Orient as a rug, blanket, wall hanging, etc., and in the U.S. chiefly as a floor covering. Cf. **Persian carpet.**

o·ri·en·tate (ōr′ē en tāt′, ôr′-, ōr′ē en′tāt, ôr′-), *v.t., v.i.,* **-tat·ed, -tat·ing.** to orient. [< F *orient(er)*]

o·ri·en·ta·tion (ōr′ē en tā′shən, ôr′-), *n.* **1.** the act or process of orienting. **2.** the state of being oriented. **3.** *Psychol., Psychiatry.* the ability to locate oneself in one's environment with reference to time, place, and people. **4.** the ascertainment of one's true position, as in a novel situation. **5.** an introduction, as to guide a person in adjusting to new surroundings, employment, or the like. **6.** *Chem.* **a.** the relative positions of certain atoms or groups, esp. in aromatic compounds. **b.** the determination of the position of substituted atoms or groups in a compound. **—o′ri·en·ta′tive,** *adj.*

O·ri·en·te (ô′ʀē en′te), *n.* **1.** a region in Ecuador, E of the Andes: the border long disputed by Peru. **2.** a province in E Cuba. 2,443,600; 14,132 sq. mi. *Cap.:* Santiago de Cuba.

o·ri·en·teer·ing (ōr′ē en tēr′ing, ôr′-), *n.* a race in which the competitors run cross-country through an unknown area to find various checkpoints by using a compass and topographical map. [alter. of Sw *orientering* (conformed to -EER), equiv. to *orienter(a)* ORIENT (v.) + *-ing* -ING[1]]

or·i·fice (ôr′ə fis, or′-), *n.* a mouth or mouthlike opening. [< MF < LL *ōrific(ium).* See ORO-[2], -FIC, -IUM] **—or·i·fi·cial** (ôr′ə fish′əl, or′-), *adj.*

or·i·flamme (ôr′ə flam′, or′-), *n.* the red banner of St. Denis, near Paris, carried before the early kings of France as a military ensign. [late ME *oriflam* < MF *oriflamme,* OF = *orie* golden (< L *aurea,* fem. of *aureus* < *aurum* gold) + *flamme* FLAME]

orig., 1. origin. **2.** original. **3.** originally. **4.** originated.

o·ri·ga·mi (ôr′ə gä′mē), *n., pl.* **-mis** for 2. **1.** a technique of folding paper into decorative or representational forms. **2.** an object made by this technique. [< Jap]

or·i·gan (ôr′ə gən, or′-), *n.* marjoram, esp. the Old World wild marjoram, *Origanum vulgare.* [ME < L *origan(um).* See OREGANO]

Or·i·gen (ôr′i jen′, -jən, or′-), *n.* (*Origenes Admantius*) A.D. 185?–254?, Alexandrian writer, Christian theologian, and teacher. **—Or′i·gen′i·an,** *adj., n.* **—Or′i·gen′ism,** *n.*

or·i·gin (ôr′i jin, or′-), *n.* **1.** the source from which anything arises or is derived. **2.** the rise or derivation of something from a particular source. **3.** the first stage of existence; beginning. **4.** birth or parentage; extraction: *Scottish origin.* **5.** *Anat.* **a.** the point of derivation. **b.** the more fixed portion of a muscle. **6.** *Math.* **a.** the point in a Cartesian coordinate system where the axes intersect. **b.** the point from which rays designating specific angles originate in a polar coordinate system with no axes. [ME < L *orīgin-* (s. of *orīgo*) beginning, source, rise < *orīrī* to rise] **—Syn. 1.** root, foundation. **4.** ancestry, lineage, descent. **—Ant. 1.** destination, end.

o·rig·i·nal (ə rij′ə nᵊl), *adj.* **1.** belonging or pertaining to the origin or beginning of something, or to a thing at its beginning. **2.** having originality; inventive or creative: *an original thinker.* **3.** showing originality; new; fresh: *an original viewpoint.* **4.** noting the first presentation, performance, or version of something. **5.** being that from which a copy, a translation, or the like is made. **—***n.* **6.** a primary form or type from which varieties are derived. **7.** an original work, writing, or the like, as opposed to any copy or imitation. **8.** the person or thing represented by a picture, description, etc. **9.** a person who is original in his ways of thinking or acting. **10.** *Archaic.* an eccentric person. [ME < L *orīgināl(is)* (ML *orīgināle,* n. use of neut. adj.)] **—Syn. 1.** primary, primordial, primitive, aboriginal. **6.** archetype, pattern, prototype, model. **—Ant. 1.** secondary. **6.** copy.

orig′inal gum′, *Philately.* See **o.g.**

o·rig·i·nal·i·ty (ə rij′ə nal′i tē), *n.* **1.** the quality or state of being original. **2.** ability to think or express oneself independently and individually. **3.** freshness or novelty, as of an idea, method, or performance. [< F *originalité*]

o·rig·i·nal·ly (ə rij′ə nᵊlē), *adv.* **1.** with respect to origin; by origin. **2.** at the origin; at first. **3.** in an original, novel, or distinctively individual manner. **4.** *Archaic.* from the beginning; from the first; inherently.

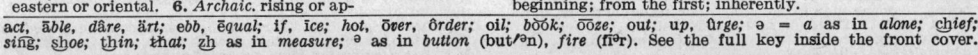

orig′inal sin′, *Theol.* a depravity, or tendency to evil, held to be innate in mankind and transmitted from Adam to the race in consequence of his sin. [ME; trans. of ML *peccātum orīginale*]

o·rig·i·nate (ə rij′ə nāt′), *v.*, **-nat·ed, -nat·ing.** —*v.i.* **1.** to take or have origin or rise; arise; spring. **2.** (of a train, bus, or other public conveyance) to begin its scheduled run at a specified place. —*v.t.* **3.** to give origin or rise to; initiate. [prob. back formation from *origination* < L *orīginātiōn-* (s. of *orīginātiō*). See ORIGIN, -ATION] —**o·rig·i·na·ble** (ə rij′ə-nə bəl), *adj.* —**o·rig′i·na′tion,** *n.* —**o·rig′i·na′tor,** *n.* —**Syn. 3.** See **discover.**

o·rig·i·na·tive (ə rij′ə nā′tiv), *adj.* having or characterized by the power of originating. —**o·rig′i·na′tive·ly,** *adv.*

o·ri·na·sal (ôr′ē nā′zəl, ōr′-), *Phonet.* —*adj.* **1.** pronounced with the voice issuing through the mouth and the nose simultaneously, as in the nasalized vowels of French. —*n.* **2.** an orinasal sound. [OR (o)-² + -I- + NASAL¹] —**o′ri·na′sal·ly,** *adv.*

O·ri·no·co (ôr′ə nō′kō, ōr′-; *Sp.* ô′rē nô′kô), *n.* a river in N South America, flowing N from the border of Brazil, along the E border of Colombia, and NE through Venezuela to the Atlantic. 1600 mi. long.

o·ri·ole (ôr′ē ōl′, ōr′-), *n.* **1.** any of several usually brightly colored passerine birds of the family *Oriolidae,* of the Old World. **2.** any of several brightly colored passerine birds of the family *Icteridae,* of America. [< F, OF *oriol* < ML *oriol(us),* var. of L *aureolus* golden = *aure(us)* golden (< *aurum* gold) + *-olus* dim. suffix]

O·ri·on (ō rī′ən, ô rī′-), *n., gen.* **Or·i·o·nis** (ôr′ē ō′nis, or′-, ə rī′ə nis) for 2. **1.** *Class. Myth.* a giant-sized hunter who pursued the Pleiades, was eventually slain by Artemis, and was then placed in the sky as a constellation. **2.** *Astron.* the Hunter, a constellation lying on the celestial equator between Canis Major and Taurus, containing the bright stars Betelgeuse and Rigel.

or·i·son (ôr′i zən, or′-), *n.* a prayer. [ME < OF < LL *ōrātiōn-* (s. of *ōrātiō*). See ORATION]

O·ris·sa (ō ris′ə, ô ris′ə), *n.* a state in E India. 17,548,846 (1961); 60,136 sq. mi. *Cap.:* Bhubaneswar.

-orium, a suffix occurring in loan words from Latin, denoting a place or an instrument: *emporium; moratorium.* See **-ory².** Cf. **-arium.** [< L]

O·ri·ya (ô rē′yə), *n.* the Indic language of Orissa.

O·ri·za·ba (ôr′ə zä′bə, ōr′-; *Sp.* ô′rē sä′vä), *n.* **1.** Also called **Citlaltepetl.** an inactive volcano in SE Mexico, in Veracruz state. 18,546 ft. **2.** a city near this peak. 55,531 (1960).

Or·jo·ni·kid·ze (*Russ.* ôʀ jo ni kēd′ze), *n.* Ordzhonikidze.

Ork′ney Is′lands (ôrk′nē), an island group off the NE tip of Scotland, constituting a county in Scotland. 18,743 (1961); 376 sq. mi. *Co. seat:* Kirkwall.

Or·lan·do (ôr lan′dō; *for 1 also It.* ôʀ län′dô), *n.* **1. Vit·to·rio E·ma·nu·e·le** (vēt tô′ʀyô e′mä nōō e′le), 1860–1952, Italian statesman. **2.** a city in central Florida: resort. 99,006 (1970).

orle (ôrl), *n. Heraldry.* **1.** a charge in the form of a narrow band following the form of the escutcheon within the edge, so that the extreme outer edge of the escutcheon is of the field tincture. **2.** an arrangement in orle of small charges: *azure, an orle of bezants.* **3. in orle,** (of small charges) arranged within the edge of an escutcheon in the manner of an orle. [< MF: border, edge < VL **ōrul(us),* dim. of L *ōra* border]

Or·lé·a·nais (ôʀ lā ᴀ ne′), *n.* a former province in N France. *Cap.:* Orleans. See map at **Picardy.**

Or·le·an·ist (ôr′lē ə nist), *n.* a supporter of the Orleans branch of the former French royal family. [< F *Orléaniste,* after ORLÉANS; see -IST] —**Or′le·an·ism,** *n.*

Or·lé·ans (ôr′lē ənz; *Fr.* ôʀ lā äɴ′), *n.* a city in central France, SSW of Paris: English siege of the city raised by Joan of Arc 1428. 88,105 (1962).

Or·lé·ans, d′ (dôʀ lā äɴ′), *n.* **Louis Phi·lippe Jo·seph** (lwē fē lēp′ zhô zef′), **Duc** (*Philippe Égalité*), 1747–93, French political leader.

Or·lon (ôr′lon), *n. Trademark.* a synthetic, acrylic textile fiber of light weight, good wrinkle resistance, and high resistance to weathering and many chemicals.

or·lop (ôr′lop), *n. Naut.* the lowermost of four or more decks above the space at the bottom of a hull. Also called **or′lop deck′.** [late ME < MLG *overlōp* covering, lit., an over-leap = *over-* OVER- + *-loop(en)* (to) run, extend; see LEAP]

Or·ly (ôr′lē; *Fr.* ôʀ lē′), *n.* a suburb SE of Paris, France: international airport. 18,469 (1962).

Or·man·dy (ôr′mən dē), *n.* **Eugene,** 1899–1985, U.S. conductor and violinist, born in Hungary.

Or·mazd (ôr′məzd), *n.* See **Ahura Mazda.** Also, **Or′muzd.**

or·mer (ôr′mər), *n.* **1.** an abalone, *Haliotis tuberculata,* found in the Channel Islands. **2.** any abalone. [< F *ormier* < L *auris maris* ear of the sea]

or·mo·lu (ôr′mə lōō′), *n.* **1.** an alloy of copper and zinc used to imitate gold. **2.** gilded metal, esp. brass or bronze. [< F *or moulu* ground gold = *or* (< L *aurum*) + *moulu,* ptp. of *moudre* to grind < L *molere*]

Or·muz (ôr′muz), *n.* **Strait of.** See **Hormuz, Strait of.**

or·na·ment (*n.* ôr′nə mənt; *v.* ôr′nə ment′), *n.* **1.** an object or feature intended to improve the appearance of something to which it is added or of which it is part. **2.** a group, category, or system of such objects or features: *a book on Gothic ornament.* **3.** anything or anyone that adds to the credit or glory of a society, era, etc. **4.** the act of adorning. **5.** the state of being adorned. **6.** mere outward display. **7.** *Music.* a tone or group of tones applied as decoration to a principal melodic tone. —*v.t.* **8.** to furnish with ornaments. **9.** to be an ornament to. [< L *ornāment(um)* equipment, ornament = *ornā(re)* (to) equip + *-mentum* -MENT; r. ME *ornement* < OF < L] —**Syn. 1.** embellishment. **2.** decoration. **8.** embellish, trim. **8, 9.** decorate, adorn, grace.

or·na·men·tal (ôr′nə men′tᵊl), *adj.* **1.** used or grown for ornament: *ornamental plants.* **2.** such as to ornament; decorative. **3.** of or pertaining to ornament. —*n.* **4.** something ornamental. **5.** a plant cultivated for decorative purposes. —**or′na·men·tal′i·ty,** *n.* —**or′na·men′tal·ly,** *adv.*

or·na·men·ta·tion (ôr′nə men tā′shən), *n.* **1.** the act of ornamenting. **2.** the state of being ornamented. **3.** ornaments, taken collectively.

or·nate (ôr nāt′), *adj.* **1.** elaborately or sumptuously adorned, often excessively or showily so. **2.** embellished with rhetoric; florid or high-flown. [ME < L *ornāt(us)* adorned, ptp. of *ornāre* to equip; see -ATE¹] —**or·nate′ly,** *adv.* —**or·nate′ness,** *n.* —**Syn. 1.** showy, ostentatious; rich, lavish.

or·ner·y (ôr′nə rē), *adj.* **1.** *Informal.* ugly in disposition or temper. **2.** *Chiefly Dial.* inferior or common; ordinary. [contr. of ORDINARY] —**or′ner·i·ness,** *n.*

ornith., **1.** ornithological. **2.** ornithology.

or·nith·ic (ôr nith′ik), *adj.* of or pertaining to birds. [< Gk *ornīthik(ós)* birdlike]

or·ni·thine (ôr′nə thēn′), *n. Biochem.* an amino acid, $H_2N(CH_2)_3CH(NH)_2COOH$, obtained by the hydrolysis of arginine. [*ornith(uric acid),* secreted by birds + -INE²]

or·nith·is·chi·an (ôr′nə this′kē ən), *n.* **1.** any herbivorous dinosaur of the order *Ornithischia,* having a pelvis resembling that of a bird. Cf. **saurischian.** —*adj.* **2.** belonging or pertaining to the *Ornithischia.* [< NL *Ornithischi(a)* (*ornith-* ORNITH- + *-ischia* < Gk *ischíon* ISCHIUM) + -AN]

ornitho-, a learned borrowing from Greek meaning "bird," used in the formation of compound words: *ornithology.* Also, *esp. before a vowel,* **ornith-.** [comb. form repr. Gk *ornīth-* (s. of *órnis*) bird]

or·ni·thoid (ôr′nə thoid′), *adj.* resembling a bird.

ornithol., **1.** ornithological. **2.** ornithology.

or·ni·thol·o·gy (ôr′nə thol′ə jē), *n.* the branch of zoology that deals with birds. [< NL *ornithologia*] —**or·ni·tho·log·i·cal** (ôr′nə thə loj′i kəl), **or′ni·tho·log′ic,** *adj.* —**or′ni·tho·log′i·cal·ly,** *adv.* —**or′ni·thol′o·gist,** *n.*

or·ni·tho·pod (ôr′nə thə pod′, ôr nī′thə-), *n.* any herbivorous dinosaur of the suborder *Ornithopoda* whose members usually walked erect on their hind legs. [< NL *Ornithopod(a)* (pl.)]

or·ni·thop·ter (ôr′nə thop′tər), *n.* a heavier-than-air craft sustained in and propelled through the air by flapping wings. Also, **orthopter.**

or·ni·tho·rhyn·chus (ôr′nə thə ring′kəs), *n.* the duckbill. [ORNITHO- + Gk *rhýnchos* bill]

or·ni·tho·sis (ôr′nə thō′sis), *n. Vet. Pathol.* psittacosis, esp. of birds other than those of the parrot family. [< NL]

oro-¹, a learned borrowing from Greek meaning "mountain," used in the formation of compound words: *orography.* [< Gk, comb. form of *óros*]

oro-², a learned borrowing from Latin meaning "mouth," used in the formation of compound words. [< L, comb. form of *ōs*]

or·o·ban·cha·ceous (ôr′ō bang kā′shəs, or′ō-), *adj.* belonging to the *Orobanchaceae,* the broomrape family of parasitic herbs. [< L *orobanch(ē)* broomrape (< Gk *orobánchē*) + -ACEOUS]

o·rog·e·ny (ō roj′ə nē, ô roj′-), *n. Geol.* the process of mountain formation or upheaval. —**or·o·gen·ic** (ôr′ə jen′ik, or′ə-), **or′o·ge·net′ic,** *adj.*

o·rog·ra·phy (ō rog′rə fē, ô rog′-), *n.* the branch of physical geography dealing with mountains. —**or·o·graph·ic** (ôr′ə graf′ik, or′ə-), **or′o·graph′i·cal,** *adj.* —**or′o·graph′i·cal·ly,** *adv.*

o·ro·ide (ōr′ō īd′, ôr′-), *n.* an alloy containing copper, tin, etc., used to imitate gold. [< F *or* gold (< L *aurum*) + *-oide* -OID]

o·rol·o·gy (ō rol′ə jē, ô rol′-), *n.* the science of mountains. —**or·o·log·i·cal** (ôr′ə loj′i kəl, or′ə-), *adj.* —**o·rol′o·gist,** *n.*

o·rom·e·ter (ō rom′i tər, ô rom′-), *n.* an aneroid barometer with a scale giving elevations above sea level, used to determine altitudes of mountains, volcanoes, etc.

O·ron·tes (ō ron′tēz, ô ron′-), *n.* a river in W Asia, flowing N from Lebanon through NW Syria and then SW past Antioch, Turkey, to the Mediterranean. 250 mi. long.

o·ro·tund (ōr′ə tund′, ôr′-), *adj.* **1.** (of the voice or speech) characterized by strength, fullness, richness, and clearness. **2.** (of a style of speaking) pompous or bombastic. [< L *ōre rotundō,* lit., with round mouth] —**o·ro·tun·di·ty** (ōr′ə-tun′di tē, ôr′-), *n.*

o·ro y pla·ta (ô′ʀô ē plä′tä; *Eng.* ôr′ō ē plä′tə), *Spanish.* gold and silver: motto of Montana.

O·roz·co (ô ʀôs′kô), *n.* **Jo·sé Cle·men·te** (hô sā′ kle-men′te), 1883–1949, Mexican painter.

or·phan (ôr′fən), *n.* **1.** a child who has lost both parents through death, or, less commonly, one parent. **2.** a young animal that has been deserted by or has lost its mother. **3.** a person or thing that is without protection, sponsorship, etc. —*adj.* **4.** bereft of parents. **5.** of or for orphans: *an orphan home.* —*v.t.* **6.** to deprive of parents or a parent. [late ME < LL *orphan(us)* destitute, without parents (akin to L *orbus* bereaved) < Gk *orphanós* bereaved] —**or′phan·hood′,** *n.*

or·phan·age (ôr′fə nij), *n.* **1.** an institution for the housing and care of orphans. **2.** the state of being an orphan; orphanhood. **3.** *Archaic.* orphans collectively.

or′phans′ court′, a probate court in certain U.S. states.

Or·phe·us (ôr′fē əs, -fyōōs), *n. Class Myth.* a poet and musician, a son of Calliope by Apollo, who followed his dead wife, Eurydice, to the underworld. By charming Hades with music, he obtained permission to lead her away, provided he did not look back at her until they had returned to earth. But at the last moment he looked, and she was lost to him forever. —**Or·phe·an** (ôr fē′ən, ôr′fē ən), *adj.*

Or·phic (ôr′fik), *adj.* **1.** of or pertaining to Orpheus. **2.** pertaining to a religious or philosophical school maintaining a form of the cult of Dionysus, or Bacchus, ascribed to Orpheus as founder: *Orphic mysteries.* **3.** (of music) casting a spell, like that of Orpheus. [< Gk *Orphik(ós)* (c. L *Orphicus*). See ORPHEUS, -IC] —**Or′phi·cal·ly,** *adv.*

Or·phism (ôr′fiz əm), *n.* the religious or philosophical system of the Orphic school.

or·phrey (ôr′frē), *n., pl.* **-phreys.** **1.** an ornamental band or border, esp. on an ecclesiastical vestment. **2.** a piece of richly embroidered material. [ME *orfreis* < OF < LL *aurifris(ium),* var. of L *aurumphrygium* gold embroidery, lit., Phrygian gold] —**or′phreyed,** *adj.*

or·pi·ment (ôr′pə mənt), *n.* a mineral, arsenic trisulfide, As_2S_3, used as a pigment. [ME < OF < L *auripigment(um)* pigment of gold; see PIGMENT]

or·pine (ôr′pin), *n.* a perennial, crassulaceous herb, *Sedum Telephium,* having purplish flowers. Also, **or′pin.** [ME < MF, back formation from *orpiment* ORPIMENT]

Or·ping·ton (ôr′ping tən), *n.* one of a breed of large, white-skinned chickens. [after *Orpington*, town in Kent, England]

or·rer·y (ôr′ə rē, or′-), *n., pl.* **-rer·ies.** **1.** an apparatus for representing the motions and phases of the planets, satellites, etc., in the solar system. **2.** any of certain similar machines, as a planetarium. [named after Charles Boyle, Earl of *Orrery* (1676–1731), for whom it was first made]

or·ris (ôr′is, or′-), *n.* an iris, esp. *Iris florentina*, having a fragrant rootstock. Also, **or′rice.** [unexplained alter. of IRIS]

Orsk (ôrsk), *n.* a city in the S RSFSR, in the E Soviet Union in Europe, on the Ural River. 210,000 (est. 1965).

ort (ôrt), *n.* Usually, **orts.** a fragment of food left at a meal. [ME; c. LG *ort*, early D *oorete* = *oor-* rejected (lit., out, from) + *ete*, food; cf. OE *or-*, *æt*]

Or·te·gal (ôʀ′te gäl′), *n.* **Cape,** a cape in NW Spain, on the Bay of Biscay.

Or·te·ga Sa·a·ve·dra (ôʀ te′gä sä′ä ve′tʜrä), **(Jo·sé) Da·niel** (hô se′ dä nyel′), born 1945, Nicaraguan political leader: president since 1985.

Or·te·ga y Gas·set (ôr tā′gə ē gä set′; *Sp.* ôʀ te′gä ē gäs set′), **Jo·sé** (hô se′), 1883–1955, Spanish philosopher, journalist, and critic.

Orth., Orthodox.

or·thi·con (ôr′thə kon′), *n.* *Television.* a camera tube, in which a beam of low-velocity electrons scans a photoemissive mosaic. Also called **or·thi·con·o·scope** (ôr′thə-kon′ə skōp′). [ORTH- + ICON(OSCOPE)]

or·tho (ôr′thō), *adj.* *Chem.* pertaining to or occupying two adjacent positions in the benzene ring. Cf. **meta²**, **para²**. [independent use of ORTHO-]

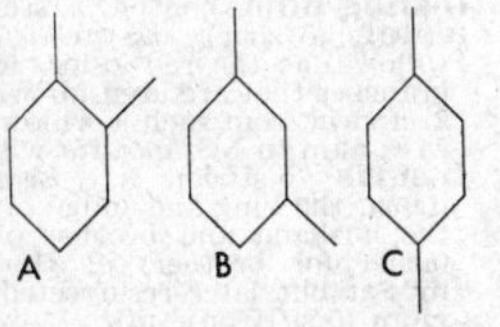

A B C

A, Ortho; B, Meta; C, Para

ortho-, **1.** an element occurring in loan words from Greek, where it meant "straight," "upright," "right," "correct" (*orthodox*) and on this model used in the formation of compound words (*orthopedic*). **2.** *Chem.* **a.** a prefix indicating that acid of a series that contains most water (*orthoboric acid*). Cf. **meta-**, **pyro-**. **b.** a prefix applied to a salt of one of these acids: if the acid ends in *-ic*, the corresponding salt ends in *-ate* (*orthoboric acid* (H_3BO_3) and *potassium orthoborate* (K_3BO_3)); if the acid ends in *-ous*, the corresponding salt ends in *-ite* (*orthoantimonous acid* (H_3SbO_3) and *potassium orthoantimonite* (K_3SbO_3)). **c.** a prefix designating the 1, 2 position in the benzene ring. Also, *esp. before a vowel,* **orth-.** [< Gk, comb. form of *orthós* straight, correct]

or′tho·bo′ric ac′id (ôr′thə bōr′ik, -bôr′-, ôr′thə-), *Chem.* See **boric acid** (def. 1). Cf. **ortho-** (def. 2).

or·tho·cen·ter (ôr′thə sen′tər), *n.* *Geom.* the point of intersection of the three altitudes of a triangle.

or·tho·ce·phal·ic (ôr′thō sə fal′ik), *adj.* having the relation between the height of the skull and the breadth or the length medium or intermediate. Also, **or·tho·ceph·a·lous** (ôr′thə sef′ə ləs). [< NL *orthocephal(us)*] —**or′tho·ceph′a·ly,** *n.*

or·tho·chro·mat·ic (ôr′thə krō mat′ik, -thō krə-), *adj.* *Photog.* **1.** representing correctly the relations of colors as found in a subject. **2.** (of an emulsion) sensitive to all visible colors except red. Also, **isochromatic.**

or·tho·clase (ôr′thə klās′, -klāz′), *n.* a common mineral of the feldspar group, $KAlSi_3O_8$, having two good cleavages at right angles. [ORTHO- + Gk *klás(is)* cleavage, breaking]

or·tho·clas·tic (ôr′thə klas′tik), *adj.* *Crystall.* (of a crystal) having cleavages at right angles to each other. [< G *orthoklastisch*]

or·tho·don·tics (ôr′thə don′tiks), *n.* (*construed as sing.*) the branch of dentistry dealing with the prevention and correction of irregular dentition. Also, **or·tho·don·tia** (ôr′thə don′shə, -shē ə). [ORTH- + -ODONT + -ICS] —**or′tho·don′tic,** *adj.*

or·tho·don·tist (ôr′thə don′tist), *n.* a specialist in orthodontics.

or·tho·dox (ôr′thə doks′), *adj.* **1.** sound or correct in opinion or doctrine, esp. theological or religious doctrine. **2.** conforming to the Christian faith as represented in the creeds of the early church. **3.** (*cap.*) of, pertaining to, or designating the Eastern Church, esp. the Greek Orthodox Church. **4.** of, pertaining to, or conforming to beliefs, attitudes, or modes of conduct that are generally approved. **5.** customary or conventional, as a means or method. [< LL *orthodox(us)* < Gk *orthódoxos* right in opinion < *orthodox(ein)* (to) have the right opinion < *ortho-* ORTHO- + *dóx(a)* belief, opinion]

Or′thodox Church′, **1.** the Christian church comprising the local and national Eastern churches that are in communion with the ecumenical patriarch of Constantinople; Byzantine Church. **2.** (originally) the Christian church of those countries formerly comprising the Eastern Roman Empire and of countries evangelized from it; Greek Orthodox Church.

Or′thodox Jew′, a Jew who adheres faithfully to the principles and practices of traditional Judaism as evidenced chiefly by a devotion to and study of the Torah, daily synagogue attendance if possible, and strict observance of the Sabbath, festivals, holy days, and the dietary laws. Cf. **Conservative Jew, Reform Jew.** —**Or′thodox Ju′daism.**

or·tho·dox·y (ôr′thə dok′sē), *n., pl.* **-dox·ies** for 1. **1.** orthodox belief or practice. **2.** orthodox character. [< LL *orthodoxia* < Gk *orthodoxía*]

or·tho·e·py (ôr thō′ə pē, ôr′thō ep′ē), *n.* the study of correct pronunciation. Also, **or·tho′ë·py.** [< Gk *orthoépeia* correctness of diction = *ortho-* ORTHO- + *epe-* (s. of *épos*) word + *-ia* -Y³] —**or·tho·ep·ic** (ôr′thō ep′ik), **or′tho·ep′i·cal,** *adj.* —**or′tho·ep′i·cal·ly,** *adv.* —**or·tho′e·pist,** *n.*

or·tho·gen·e·sis (ôr′thə jen′i sis), *n.* **1.** *Biol.* the evolution of species in definite lines which are predetermined by the constitution of the germ plasm. **2.** *Sociol.* a hypothetical parallelism between the stages through which every culture necessarily passes, in spite of secondary conditioning factors. [< NL] —**or·tho·ge·net·ic** (ôr′thō jə net′ik), *adj.*

or·tho·gen·ic (ôr′thə jen′ik), *adj.* *Psychol.* of, concerned with, or providing corrective treatment for mentally retarded or seriously disturbed children.

or·thog·na·thous (ôr thog′nə thəs), *adj.* *Craniom.* straight-jawed; having the profile of the face vertical or nearly so. Also, **or·thog·nath·ic** (ôr′thəg nath′ik, -thog-). See diag. at **facial angle.** —**or·thog·na·thism** (ôr thog′nə thiz′əm), **or·thog′na·thy,** *n.*

or·thog·o·nal (ôr thog′ə nᵊl), *adj.* **1.** *Math.* pertaining to or involving right angles or perpendiculars. **2.** *Crystall.* referable to a rectangular set of axes. **3.** (in drafting) noting a projection **(orthog′onal projec′tion** or **orthograph′ic projec′tion)** in which the subject is placed with a principal face parallel to the picture plane and in which all rays from the subject are perpendicular to the picture plane, so that a scale drawing results; orthographic. [obs. *orthogon(ium)* (< LL < Gk *orthogṓnion* (neut.) right-angled. See ORTHO-, -GON, -AL¹] —**or·thog·o·nal·i·ty** (ôr thog′ə nal′i tē), *n.* —**or·thog′o·nal·ly,** *adv.*

or·tho·graph·ic (ôr′thə graf′ik), *adj.* **1.** of or pertaining to orthography. **2.** orthogonal (def. 3). Also, **or′tho·graph′i·cal.** —**or′tho·graph′i·cal·ly,** *adv.*

or·thog·ra·phy (ôr thog′rə fē), *n., pl.* **-phies** for 3, 4. **1.** the art of spelling words according to accepted usage. **2.** the part of grammar that treats of letters and spelling. **3.** a method of spelling. **4.** a system of symbols for spelling. [ME *ortografye* < L *orthographia* correct writing, orthogonal projection < Gk] —**or·thog′ra·pher, or·thog′ra·phist,** *n.*

or·tho·hy·dro·gen (ôr′thə hī′drə jən), *n.* *Physics, Chem.* the form of molecular hydrogen in which the nuclei of the two hydrogen atoms contained in the molecule have spins in the same direction. Cf. **parahydrogen.**

or·tho·pe·dic (ôr′thə pē′dik), *adj.* of or pertaining to orthopedics. Also, **or′tho·pae′dic.** [ORTHO- + Gk *paid-* (s. of *paîs*) child + -IC] —**or′tho·pe′di·cal·ly, or′tho·pae′di·cal·ly,** *adv.*

or·tho·pe·dics (ôr′thə pē′diks), *n.* (*construed as sing.*) the correction or cure of deformities and diseases of the spine, bones, joints, muscles, etc., of the skeletal system, esp. in children. Also, **or′tho·pae′dics, or′tho·pe′dy, or′tho·pae′dy.** [see ORTHOPEDIC, -ICS]

or·tho·pe·dist (ôr′thə pē′dist), *n.* a person who specializes in orthopedics. Also, **or′tho·pae′dist.**

or·tho·phos·phate (ôr′thə fos′fāt), *n.* a salt or ester of orthophosphoric acid, or any compound containing the trivalent group $-PO_4$.

or′thophosphor′ic ac′id, *Chem.* a colorless, solid, H_3PO_4, the tribasic acid of pentavalent phosphorus: used in fertilizers, as a source of phosphorus salts, and in soft drinks as an acidulating and flavoring agent. —**or·tho·phos·phor·ic** (ôr′thō fos fôr′ik, -for′-), *adj.*

or·thop·ter (ôr thop′tər), *n.* ornithopter. [< F *orthoptère*. See ORTHO-, HELICOPTER]

or·thop·ter·an (ôr thop′tər ən), *adj.* **1.** orthopterous. —*n.* **2.** an orthopterous insect. [< NL *Orthopter(a)* + -AN]

or·thop·ter·on (ôr thop′tə ron′, -tər ən), *n., pl.* **-ter·a** (-tər ə). orthopteran. [< NL, sing. of *Orthoptera* name of the order]

or·thop·ter·ous (ôr thop′tər əs), *adj.* belonging or pertaining to the *Orthoptera*, an order of insects comprising the crickets, grasshoppers, cockroaches, etc., characterized by leathery forewings and membranous hind wings. [< NL *orthopterus* straight-winged]

or·tho·rhom·bic (ôr′thə rom′bik), *adj.* *Crystall.* noting or pertaining to a system of crystallization characterized by three unequal axes intersecting at right angles; rhombic; trimetric. Cf. **system** (def. 11).

or·tho·scop·ic (ôr′thə skop′ik), *adj.* *Ophthalm.* pertaining to, characterized by, or produced by normal vision; presenting objects correctly to the eye.

or·tho-to·lu·i·dine (ôr′thō tə lo͞o′i dēn′, -din), *n.* *Chem.* a light-yellow liquid, $CH_3C_6H_4NH_2$, the ortho isomer of toluidine: used in the manufacture of dyes, saccharin, and other organic compounds, and in textile printing.

or·tho·trop·ic (ôr′thə trop′ik), *adj.* *Bot.* noting, pertaining to, or exhibiting a mode of growth that is more or less vertical.

or·thot·ro·pous (ôr tho′trə pəs), *adj.* *Bot.* (of an ovule) straight and symmetrical, with the chalaza at the evident base and the micropyle at the opposite extremity. [< NL *orthotropus*]

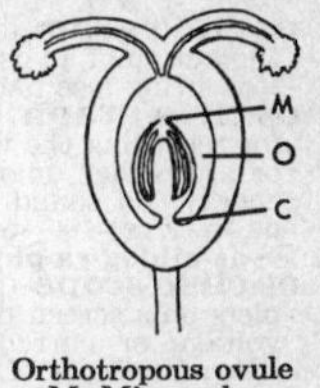

M O C

Orthotropous ovule M, Micropyle; C, Chalaza; O, Ovule

Or·thrus (ôr′thrəs), *n.* *Class. Myth.* a two-headed monster guarding the cattle of Geryon, killed by Hercules.

Ort·ler (ôrt′lər), *n.* **1.** a range of the Alps in N Italy. **2.** the highest peak of this range. 12,802 ft.

or·to·lan (ôr′tᵊlən), *n.* **1.** an Old World bunting, *Emberiza hortulana*, valued as a food. **2.** the bobolink. **3.** the sora. [< F < Pr: lit., gardener (i.e., frequenting gardens) < L *hortulān(us)* = *hortul(us)* little garden (*hort(us)* garden + *-ulus* -ULE) + *-ānus* -AN]

O·ru·ro (ô ʀo͞o′ʀô), *n.* a city in W Bolivia: a former capital. 94,000 (est. 1965); over 12,000 ft. high.

ORuss, Old Russian.

Or·vi·e·to (ôr′vē ā′tō; *It.* ôʀ vye′tô), *n.* an Italian white wine.

Or·well (ôr′wel, -wəl), *n.* **George** (pen name of *Eric Arthur Blair*), 1903–50, English novelist and essayist.

Or·well·i·an (ôr wel′ē ən), *adj.* of, pertaining to, or characteristic of George Orwell, his works, or the totalitarian future described in his anti-utopian novel *1984* (1949).

-ory¹, a suffix of adjectives borrowed from Latin, meaning "having the function or effect of": *compulsory; contributory; declaratory; illusory.* [< L *-ōri(us)*, suffix of adjectives associated esp. with agent nouns in *-or*. See -OR²]

-ory², a suffix of nouns borrowed from Latin, denoting esp. a place or an instrument: *crematory; dormitory.* [< L *-ōri(um)*, neut. of *-ōrius* -ORY¹]

o·ryx (ôr′iks, ōr′-), *n., pl.* **o·ryx·es,** (*esp. collectively*) **o·ryx.** a large African antelope, *Oryx beisa,* grayish with black markings and having long, nearly straight horns. [ME < L < Gk: pickax, oryx]

os[1] (os), *n., pl.* **os·sa** (os′ə). *Anat., Zool.* a bone. [< L]

os[2] (os), *n., pl.* **o·ra** (ōr′ə, ôr′ə). *Anat.* a mouth, opening, or entrance. [< L: mouth]

os[3] (ōs), *n., pl.* **o·sar** (ō′sär). *Geol.* an esker, esp. when of great length. [< Sw *ås* (pl. *åsar*) ridge]

OS, Old Saxon. Also, **OS.**

Os, *Chem.* osmium.

O/S, (of the calendar) Old Style.

o/s, **1.** (of the calendar) Old Style. **2.** out of stock. **3.** (in banking) outstanding.

O.S., **1.** (in prescriptions) the left eye. [< L *oculus sinister*] **2.** Old Saxon. **3.** Old School. **4.** Old Series. **5.** (of the calendar) Old Style. **6.** See **ordinary seaman.**

o.s., **1.**(in prescriptions) the left eye. [< L *oculus sinister*] **2.** See **ordinary seaman.**

O.S.A., Order of St. Augustine (Augustinian).

O·sage (ō′sāj, ō sāj′), *n., pl.* **O·sag·es,** (*esp. collectively*) **O·sage.** **1.** a dialect mutually intelligible with Ponca and belonging to the Siouan language family. **2.** a member of an American Indian people speaking this dialect. **3.** a river flowing E from E Kansas to the Missouri River in central Missouri. 500 mi. long.

O′sage or′ange, **1.** an ornamental, moraceous tree, *Maclura pomifera,* native to Arkansas and adjacent regions, used for hedges. **2.** its fruit, which resembles a warty orange.

O·sa·ka (ō sä′kə; *Jap.* ô′sä kä′), *n.* a city on S Honshu, in S Japan. 3,214,330 (1964).

o·sar (ō′sär), *n.* pl. of **os**[3].

O.S.B., Order of St. Benedict (Benedictine).

Os·borne (oz′bərn), *n.* **John (James),** born 1929, English playwright.

Os·can (os′kən), *n.* **1.** one of an ancient people of south-central Italy. **2.** the Indo-European, probably Italic, language of the Oscans. [< L *Osc(ī)* the Oscans + -AN]

Os·car (os′kər), *n.* one of a group of statuettes awarded annually by the Academy of Motion Picture Arts and Sciences for professional achievements in motion-picture production and performance. [said to have been named in 1931 by an employee of the Academy after her uncle]

Os·car (os′kər), *n.* a word used in communications to represent the letter *O.*

Oscar II, 1829–1907, king of Sweden 1872–1907; king of Norway 1872–1905.

Os·ce·o·la (os′ē ō′lə, ō′sē-), *n.* 1804–38, U.S. Indian leader: chief of the Seminole tribe.

os·cil·late (os′ə lāt′), *v.,* **-lat·ed, -lat·ing.** —*v.i.* **1.** to swing or move to and fro, as a pendulum does; vibrate. **2.** to fluctuate between differing beliefs, opinions, conditions, etc. **3.** *Physics.* to have, produce, or generate oscillations. —*v.t.* **4.** to cause to move to and fro; vibrate. [< L *oscillāt(us)* swung (ptp. of *oscillāre*) = *oscill(um)* swing + *-ātus* -ATE[1]] —**Syn. 1.** See **swing**[1]. **2.** vacillate, vary.

os·cil·la·tion (os′ə lā′shən), *n.* **1.** the act or fact of oscillating. **2.** a single swing or movement in one direction by an oscillating body. **3.** fluctuation between beliefs, conditions, etc. **4.** *Physics.* **a.** an effect expressible as a quantity that repeatedly and regularly fluctuates above and below some mean value, as the pressure of a sound wave or the voltage of an alternating current. **b.** a single fluctuation between maximum and minimum values in such an effect. [< L *oscillātiōn-* (s. of *oscillātiō*) a swinging]

os·cil·la·tor (os′ə lā′tər), *n.* **1.** a device or machine producing oscillations. **2.** an electronic circuit that produces an alternating output current of a frequency determined by the characteristics of the circuit components. **3.** a person or thing that oscillates. [< NL]

os·cil·la·to·ry (os′ə lə tōr′ē, -tôr′ē), *adj.* characterized by or involving oscillation. [< NL *oscillātōri(us).* See OSCILLATE, -ORY[1]]

os·cil·lo·gram (ə sil′ə gram′), *n.* the record produced by the action of an oscillograph or oscilloscope. [< L *oscill(āre)* (to) swing (see OSCILLATE) + -o- + -GRAM[1]]

os·cil·lo·graph (ə sil′ə graf′, -gräf′), *n.* *Elect.* a device for recording the wave forms of changing currents, voltages, or any other quantity that can be translated into electric energy, as sound waves. [< L *oscill(āre)* (to) swing (see OSCILLATE) + -o- + -GRAPH] —**os·cil′lo·graph′ic,** *adj.* —**os·cil·log·ra·phy** (os′ə log′rə fē), *n.*

os·cil·lo·scope (ə sil′ə skōp′), *n.* *Elect.* a device that depicts on a screen periodic changes in an electric quantity, as voltage or current, using a cathode-ray tube or similar instrument. [< L *oscill(āre)* (to) swing (see OSCILLATE) + -o- + -SCOPE]

os·cine (os′in, -īn), *adj.* **1.** of, belonging to, or pertaining to the suborder *Oscines,* of the order *Passeriformes,* comprising the songbirds that have highly developed vocal organs. —*n.* **2.** an oscine bird. [back formation from NL *Oscines* name of the suborder = L *oscin-* (s. of *oscen*) songbird + *-es* nom. pl. n. suffix]

os·ci·tant (os′i tənt), *adj.* **1.** yawning, as with drowsiness; gaping. **2.** drowsy; inattentive. **3.** dull; lazy or negligent. [< L *ōscitant-* (s. of *ōscitāns*) yawning (prp. of *ōscitāre*) = *ōscit-* open the mouth wide (*ōs* mouth + *cit-* put in motion) + *-ant-* -ANT] —**os′ci·tan·cy, os′ci·tance,** *n.*

Os·co-Um·bri·an (os′kō um′brē ən), *n.* a major division of languages, usually classified as Italic, that contains Oscan and Umbrian.

os·cu·lant (os′kyə lənt), *adj.* **1.** united by certain common characteristics. **2.** *Zool.* adhering closely; embracing. [< L *ōsculant-* (s. of *ōsculāns*) kissing (prp. of *ōsculārī;* see OSCULATE) + *-ant-* -ANT]

os·cu·lar (os′kyə lər), *adj.* **1.** of or pertaining to an osculum. **2.** of or pertaining to the mouth or kissing: *oscular stimulation.* [< NL *ōsculār(is).* See OSCULUM, -AR[1]] —**os·cu·lar·i·ty** (os′kyə lar′i tē), *n.*

os·cu·late (os′kyə lāt′), *v.,* **-lat·ed, -lat·ing.** —*v.i.* **1.** *Geom.* (of a curve) to touch another curve or another part of the same curve so as to have the same tangent and curvature at the point of contact. **2.** to kiss. —*v.t.* **3.** *Geom.* (of a curve) to touch (another curve or another part of the same curve) in osculation. **4.** to kiss. [< L *ōsculāt(us)* kissed (ptp. of *ōsculārī*). See OSCULUM, -ATE[1]] —**os·cu·la·to·ry** (os′kyə lə tōr′ē, -tôr′ē), *adj.*

os·cu·la·tion (os′kyə lā′shən), *n.* **1.** the act of kissing. **2.** a kiss. **3.** *Geom.* the contact between two osculating curves or the like. [< L *ōsculātiōn-* (s. of *ōsculātiō*) a kissing]

os·cu·lum (os′kyə ləm), *n., pl.* **-la** (-lə). a small mouthlike aperture, as of a sponge. [< NL, L. See OS[2], -CULE]

OSD Office of the Secretary of Defense.

O.S.D., Order of St. Dominic (Dominican).

-ose[1], a suffix occurring in adjectives borrowed from Latin, meaning "full of," "abounding in," "given to," "like": *jocose; otiose; verbose.* [< L *-ōs(us).* Cf. -OUS]

-ose[2], a suffix used in chemical terminology to form the names of sugars and other carbohydrates (*amylose; fructose; hexose; lactose*), and of protein derivatives (*proteose*). [abstracted from GLUCOSE]

Ö·sel (œ′zəl), *n.* German name of **Saaremaa.**

O·se·tian (o sē′shən), *adj., n.* Ossetian.

O·set·ic (o set′ik), *adj., n.* Ossetic.

O.S.F., Order of St. Francis (Franciscan).

Osh·kosh (osh′kosh), *n.* a city in E Wisconsin, on Lake Winnebago. 53,221 (1970).

O·shog·bo (ō shog′bō), *n.* a city in SW Nigeria. 210,384 (1963).

o·sier (ō′zhər), *n.* *Chiefly Brit.* **1.** any of various willows, as the red osier, having tough, flexible twigs or branches that are used for wickerwork. **2.** a twig from such a willow. [ME < MF; akin to ML *ausaria* willow bed]

Osiris

O·si·ris (ō sī′ris), *n.* *Egyptian Religion.* the king and judge of the dead, the husband and brother of Isis and father (or brother) of Horus, killed by Set but later resurrected. —**O·si·ri·an** (ō sī′rē ən), *adj.*

-osis, a suffix occurring in loan words from Greek, where it denoted action, process, state, condition (*metamorphosis*); used in the formation of many pathological terms (*tuberculosis*). [< Gk, suffix forming nouns from verbs with infinitives in *-oein, -oun*]

-osity, a combination of **-ose** (or **-ous**) and **-ity,** used to form nouns from stems in **-ose** (or **-ous**): *verbosity; generosity.* [repr. L *-ōsitas* and F *-osité*]

OSlav, Old Slavic.

Os·ler (ōs′lər, ōz′-), *n.* **Sir William,** 1849–1919, Canadian physician and professor of medicine.

Os·lo (oz′lō, os′-, ōs′-; *Norw.* ōōs′lōō), *n.* a seaport in and the capital of Norway, in the SE part, at the head of Oslo Fiord. 463,022. Formerly, **Christiania.**

Os′lo Fiord′, an inlet of the Skagerrak, in SE Norway. 75 mi. long.

osm-, a learned borrowing from Greek meaning "smell," used in the formation of compound words: *osmium.* [< Gk, comb. form of *osmḗ*]

Os·man (oz′mən, os′-; *Turk.* os män′), *n.* 1259–1326, Turkish emir 1299–1326: founder of the Ottoman dynasty. Also, **Othman.**

Os·man·li (oz man′lē, os-), *n., pl.* **-lis,** *adj.* —*n.* **1.** an Ottoman. **2.** the language of the Ottoman Turks. —*adj.* **3.** Ottoman.

os·mic (oz′mik), *adj.* *Chem.* of or containing osmium in its higher valences, esp. the tetravalent state.

os·mi·ous (oz′mē əs), *adj.* *Chem.* of or containing osmium in its lower valences.

os·mi·rid·i·um (oz′mə rid′ē əm), *n.* iridosmine. [< G; see OSMIUM, IRIDIUM]

os·mi·um (oz′mē əm), *n.* *Chem.* a hard, heavy, metallic element having the greatest density of the known elements and forming octavalent compounds, as OsO_4 and OsF_8: used chiefly as a catalyst, in alloys, and in the manufacture of electric-light filaments. *Symbol:* Os; *at. wt.:* 190.2; *at. no.:* 76; *sp. gr.:* 22.57. [< NL, named from the penetrating odor of one of its oxides]

os·mom·e·try (oz mom′i trē), *n.* *Physical Chem.* measurement of osmotic pressure. —**os·mom′e·ter,** *n.* —**os·mo·met·ric** (oz′mə me′trik), *adj.* —**os′mo·met′ri·cal·ly,** *adv.*

os·mose (oz′mōs, os′-), *v.,* **-mosed, -mos·ing.** —*v.i.* **1.** to undergo osmosis. —*v.t.* **2.** to subject to osmosis. [abstracted from *endosmose* and *exosmose* as representing the common element; cf. Gk *ōsmós* a push, thrust]

os·mo·sis (oz mō′sis, os-), *n.* **1.** *Physical Chem.* **a.** the passage of a fluid through a semipermeable membrane into a solution where its concentration is lower, thus equalizing the conditions on both sides of the membrane. **b.** the diffusion of fluids through membranes or porous partitions. Cf. **endosmosis, exosmosis.** **2.** a subtle or gradual absorption or mingling suggesting such diffusion. [< NL < Gk *ōsmó(s)* a push, thrust + *-sis* -SIS] —**os·mot·ic** (oz mot′ik, os-), *adj.* —**os·mot′i·cal·ly,** *adv.*

osmot′ic pres′sure, *Physical Chem.* the force that a dissolved substance exerts on a semipermeable membrane, through which it cannot penetrate, when separated by it from pure solvent.

os·mund (oz′mənd, os′-), *n.* any fern of the genus *Osmunda,* esp. the royal fern. [ME *osmunde* < ?]

Os·na·brück (oz′nə brŏŏk′; *Ger.* ôs′nä brʏk′), *n.* a city in N West Germany, in Hanover. 141,000 (1963).

Os·na·burg (oz′nə bûrg′), *n.* a heavy, coarse cotton in a plain weave, for grain sacks and sportswear and also finished into cretonne. [irreg. after OSNABRÜCK, known for its linen]

O·sor·no (ô sôr′nô), *n.* a city in S Chile. 78,187.

Osprey (Length 2 ft.; wingspread 4½ ft.)

OSp, Old Spanish.

os·prey (os′prē), *n., pl.* **-preys.** a large hawk, *Pandion haliaetus,* that feeds on fish. Also called **fish hawk.** [ME *ospray(e)* < MF *orfraie, offraie* < L *ossifraga,* lit., bone breaker. See OSSIFRAGE]

OSS, Office of Strategic Services. Also, **O.S.S.**
os·sa (os′ə), *n.* pl. of **os**[1].
Os·sa (os′ə), *n.* a mountain in E Greece, in Thessaly. 6490 ft.
os·se·in (os′ē in), *n.* *Biochem.* the organic basis of bone, remaining after the removal of mineral matter. [< L *osse(us)* OSSEOUS + -IN[2]]
os·se·ous (os′ē əs), *adj.* **1.** composed of, containing, or resembling bone; bony. **2.** ossiferous. [< L *osseus* bony = *oss-* (s. of *os*) bone + *-eus* -EOUS] —**os′se·ous·ly,** *adv.*
Os·set (os′it), *n.* a member of a tall Aryan people of Ossetia. Also, **Os·sete** (os′ēt), **Ossetian.**
Os·se·tia (o sē′shə; *Russ.* o se′tyä), *n.* a region in the S Soviet Union in Europe, in Caucasia.
Os·se·tian (ō sē′shən), *adj.* **1.** Also, **Ossetic.** of, pertaining to, or characteristic of Ossetia or the Ossets. —*n.* **2.** Osset.
Os·set·ic (o set′ik), *adj.* **1.** Ossetian. —*n.* **2.** the Indo-European, Iranian language of the Ossets.
Os·sian (osh′ən, os′ē ən), *n.* *Gaelic Legend.* a legendary hero and poet who is supposed to have lived during the 3rd century A.D. Also, **Oisin.** —**Os·si·an·ic** (osh′ē an′ik, os′ē-), *adj.*
os·si·cle (os′i kəl), *n.* a small bone. [< L *ossicul(um)* = *ossi-* (s. of *os*) bone + *-culum* -CLE] —**os·sic·u·lar** (o sik′yə lər), **os·sic·u·late** (o sik′yə lit), *adj.*
os·sif·er·ous (o sif′ər əs), *adj.* containing bones, esp. fossile bones. [< L *ossi-* (s. of *os*) bone + -FEROUS]
os·si·fi·ca·tion (os′ə fə kā′shən), *n.* **1.** the act or process of ossifying. **2.** the state of being ossified. **3.** something that has ossified. [< NL **ossificātiōn-* (s. of **ossificātiō*) = **ossificāt(us)* (ptp. of **ossificāre* to OSSIFY) + L *-iōn-* -ION]
os·si·fied (os′ə fīd′), *adj.* **1.** hardened like or into bone. **2.** *Slang.* drunk.
os·si·frage (os′ə frij), *n.* **1.** the lammergeier. **2.** *Rare.* the osprey. [< L *ossifraga* sea eagle, lit., bone breaker (fem. of *ossifragus*) = *ossi-* (s. of *os*) bone + *frag-* break + *-a* fem. n. suffix]
os·si·fy (os′ə fī′), *v.,* **-fied, -fy·ing.** —*v.t.* **1.** to convert into or cause to harden like bone. —*v.i.* **2.** to become bone or harden like bone. **3.** to become rigid or inflexible in habits, attitudes, opinions, etc. [< NL **ossificāre* = L *ossi-* (s. of *os*) bone + *-ficāre* -FY] —**os′si·fi′er,** *n.*
Os·si·ning (os′ə ning), *n.* a city in SE New York, on the Hudson: the site of Sing Sing, a state prison. 21,659 (1970).
os·su·ar·y (osh′o͞o er′ē, os′-), *n., pl.* **-ar·ies.** a place or receptacle for the bones of the dead. [< LL *ossuāri(um),* var. of *ossārium* = *oss-* (s. of *os*) bone + *-ārium* -ARY]
oste-, var. of **osteo-** before a vowel: *osteitis.*
os·te·al (os′tē əl), *adj.* osseous.
Os·te·ich·thy·es (os′tē ik′thē ēz′), *n.* the class comprising the bony fishes. [< NL < Gk *ostéo(on)* OSTE- + *ichthýes* fish (pl. of *ichthýs*)]
os·te·i·tis (os′tē ī′tis), *n.* *Pathol.* inflammation of the substance of bone. —**os·te·it·ic** (os′tē it′ik), *adj.*
Ost·end (os tend′), *n.* a seaport in NW Belgium. 57,063 (est. 1964). French, **Os·tende** (ôs tänd′).
os·ten·si·ble (o sten′sə bəl), *adj.* **1.** given out or outwardly appearing as such; professed; pretended. **2.** apparent; conspicuous: *the ostensible truth of his theories.* [< F < L *ostens(us)* displayed (see OSTENTATION) + F *-ible* -IBLE] —**os·ten′si·bil′i·ty,** *n.* —**os·ten′si·bly,** *adv.*
os·ten·sive (o sten′siv), *adj.* **1.** clearly or manifestly demonstrative. **2.** ostensible (def. 1). [< ML *ostensīv(us)* = L *ostens(us)* displayed (see OSTENTATION) + *-īvus* -IVE] —**os·ten′sive·ly,** *adv.*
os·ten·ta·tion (os′ten tā′shən), *n.* **1.** pretentious display. **2.** *Archaic.* the act of showing or exhibiting. [ME *ostentacioun* < MF *ostentation* < L *ostentātiōn-* (s. of *ostentātiō*) = *ostentāt(us)* displayed, ptp. of *ostentāre* (*ostent(us),* ptp. of *ostendere* = *os-,* var of *ob-* OB- + *tendere* to stretch, + *-ātus* -ATE[1]) + *-iōn-* -ION] —**Syn. 1.** pretension. See **show.**
os·ten·ta·tious (os′ten tā′shəs), *adj.* **1.** characterized by or given to ostentation. **2.** (of actions, manner, etc.) intended to attract notice. —**os′ten·ta′tious·ly,** *adv.*
osteo-, a learned borrowing from Greek meaning "bone," used in the formation of compound words: *osteoclasis.* Also, *esp. before a vowel,* **oste-.** [< Gk, comb. form of *ostéon*]
os·te·o·blast (os′tē ə blast′), *n.* *Anat.* a bone-forming cell. —**os′te·o·blas′tic,** *adj.*
os·te·oc·la·sis (os′tē ok′lə sis), *n.* *Anat.* **1.** the breaking down or absorption of osseous tissue. **2.** *Surg.* the fracturing of a bone to correct deformity.
os·te·o·clast (os′tē ə klast′), *n.* **1.** *Anat.* one of the large multinuclear cells in growing bone concerned with the absorption of osseous tissue, as in the formation of canals. **2.** *Surg.* an instrument for effecting osteoclasis. [OSTEO- + Gk *klast(ós)* broken] —**os′te·o·clas′tic,** *adj.*
os·te·oid (os′tē oid′), *adj.* resembling bone; bonelike.
os·te·ol·o·gy (os′tē ol′ə jē), *n.* the branch of anatomy dealing with the skeleton. [< NL *osteologia*] —**os·te·o·log·i·cal** (os′tē ə loj′i kəl), **os′te·o·log′ic,** *adj.* —**os′te·o·log′i·cal·ly,** *adv.* —**os′te·ol′o·gist, os′te·ol′o·ger,** *n.*
os·te·o·ma (os′tē ō′mə), *n., pl.* **-mas, -ma·ta** (-mə tə). *Pathol.* a tumor composed of osseous tissue.
os·te·o·ma·la·cia (os′tē ō mə lā′shə, -shē ə, -sē ə), *n.* *Pathol.* a condition, esp. of women during pregnancy, characterized by a softening of the bones with subsequent flexibility, deformity, weakness, and pain, caused by a deficiency of calcium, phosphorus, and vitamin D. [< NL < OSTEO- + Gk *malakía* softness; see MALACO-, -IA] —**os′te·o·ma·la′cial, os·te·o·ma·lac·ic** (os′tē ō mə las′ik), *adj.*
os·te·o·my·e·li·tis (os′tē ō mī′ə lī′tis), *n.* *Pathol.* a purulent inflammation of the bone.
os·te·o·path (os′tē ə path′), *n.* a person who practices osteopathy. Also, **os·te·op·a·thist** (os′tē op′ə thist). [back formation from OSTEOPATHY]
os·te·op·a·thy (os′tē op′ə thē), *n.* a therapeutic system based upon the premise that restoring or preserving health can best be accomplished by manipulation of the skeleton and muscles. —**os·te·o·path·ic** (os′tē ə path′ik), *adj.* —**os′te·o·path′i·cal·ly,** *adv.*
os·te·o·phyte (os′tē ə fīt′), *n.* *Pathol.* a small osseous excrescence or outgrowth on bone. —**os·te·o·phyt·ic** (os′tē ə fit′ik), *adj.*
os·te·o·plas·tic (os′tē ə plas′tik), *adj.* **1.** *Surg.* pertaining to osteoplasty. **2.** *Physiol.* pertaining to bone formation.
os·te·o·plas·ty (os′tē ə plas′tē), *n.* *Surg.* the transplanting or inserting of bone, or surgical reconstruction of bone, to repair a defect or loss.
os·te·o·tome (os′tē ə tōm′), *n.* *Surg.* a double-beveled chisellike instrument for cutting or dividing bone. [< NL *osteotom(us)*]
os·te·ot·o·my (os′tē ot′ə mē), *n., pl.* **-mies.** *Surg.* the dividing of a bone, or the excision of part of it.
Ös·ter·reich (œ′stər rīkh′), *n.* German name of **Austria.**
Os·ti·a (os′tē ə; *It.* ô′styä), *n.* a town in central Italy, SW of Rome: ruins from 4th century B.C.; site of ancient port of Rome. 2364 (1951).
os·ti·ar·y (os′tē er′ē), *n., pl.* **-ar·ies. 1.** *Rom. Cath. Ch.* **a.** a member of the lowest-ranking of the four minor orders. **b.** the order itself. Cf. **acolyte** (def. 2), **exorcist** (def. 2), **lector** (def. 2). **2.** a doorkeeper, as of a church. [< L *ostiāri(us)* doorkeeper = *osti(um)* door + *-ārius* -ARY]
os·ti·na·to (os′ti nä′tō; *It.* ôs′tē nä′tô), *n., pl.* **-tos.** *Music.* a constantly recurring melodic fragment. [< It: lit., obstinate < L *obstināt(us)* OBSTINATE]
os·ti·ole (os′tē ōl′), *n.* a small opening or orifice. [< L *ostiol(um)* little door, dim. of *ostium* door] —**os·ti·o·lar** (os′tē ə lər, o stī′-), *adj.*
ost·ler (os′lər), *n.* hostler.
ost·mark (ôst′märk′, ost′-), *n.* a cupronickel coin and monetary unit of East Germany, equal to 100 pfennigs. Cf. **Deutsche mark.** [< G: east mark]
os·to·sis (o stō′sis), *n.* *Physiol.* the formation of bone; ossification. [< NL; see OSTE-, -OSIS]
Ost·preus·sen (ôst′proi′sən), *n.* German name of **East Prussia.**
os·tra·cise (os′trə sīz′), *v.t.,* **-cised, -cis·ing.** *Chiefly Brit.* ostracize.
os·tra·cism (os′trə siz′əm), *n.* **1.** the act of ostracizing. **2.** the fact or state of being ostracized. **3.** (in ancient Greece) temporary banishment of a citizen, decided upon by popular vote. [< NL *ostracism(us)* < Gk *ostrakismós* banishment. See OSTRACIZE, -ISM]
os·tra·cize (os′trə sīz′), *v.t.,* **-cized, -ciz·ing. 1.** to exclude, by general consent, from society, privileges, etc. **2.** to banish (a person) from his native country; expatriate. **3.** (in ancient Greece) to banish (a citizen) temporarily by popular vote. Also, *esp. Brit.,* **ostracise.** [< Gk *ostrakíz(ein)* = *óstrak(on)* potsherd, tile, ballot (akin to *óstreion* OYSTER, shell) + *-izein* -IZE] —**os′tra·ciz′a·ble,** *adj.* —**os′tra·ci·za′tion,** *n.* —**os′tra·ciz′er,** *n.* —**Syn. 1.** exile.
os·tra·cod (os′trə kod′), *n.* any of numerous minute, marine and fresh-water crustaceans of the subclass *Ostracoda,* having the body enclosed in a hinged, bivalve shell. [< NL *Ostracod(a)* < Gk *ostrakṓdēs* = *óstrak(on)* shell (see OSTRACIZE) + *-ōdēs* -ODE[1]] —**os·tra·co·dan** (os′trə kōd′ən), **os′tra·co′dous,** *adj.*
O·stra·va (*Czech.* ô′strä vä), *n.* a city in N Moravia, in N Czechoslovakia. 251,959 (est. 1963). Formerly, **Moravská Ostrava.**
os·trich (ô′strich, os′trich), *n.* **1.** a large, two-toed, swift-footed, flightless bird, *Struthio camelus,* indigenous to Africa and Arabia, domesticated for its plumage: the largest of living birds. **2.** (not used scientifically) a rhea. **3.** a person who is unwilling to face unpleasant facts. [ME *ostrice* < OF *ostruce* < VL **avi(s) strūthio* ostrich (LL *strūthio* < Gk *strouthíōn*)]

Ostrich, *Struthio camelus*
(Height 8 ft.; length 6 ft.)

Os·tro·goth (os′trə goth′), *n.* a member of the easterly division of the Goths, maintaining a monarchy in Italy, A.D. 493–555. Cf. **Visigoth.** [< LL *Ostrogoth(ī)* (pl.) < Goth] —**Os′tro·goth′ic, Os′tro·goth′i·an,** *adj.*
Os·ty·ak (os′tē ak′), *n.* **1.** an Ugric language of the Uralic family of languages, spoken in NW Siberia in the Ob River basin. **2.** a member of a Finnic people dwelling in western Siberia and the Ural Mountains.
Os·wald (oz′wôld), *n.* **Lee Harvey,** 1939–63, assassin of President John F. Kennedy.
Os·we·go (o swē′gō), *n.* a port in W New York, on Lake Ontario. 20,913 (1970).
Oswe′go tea′, a North American, labiate herb, *Monarda didyma,* having showy, bright-red flowers.
Oś·wię·cim (ôsh vyan′tsim), *n.* Polish name of **Auschwitz.**
OT, Old Testament. Also, **OT., O.T.**
ot-, var. of **oto-** before a vowel: *otic.*
o·tal·gi·a (ō tal′jē ə, -jə), *n.* *Pathol.* earache. [< NL < Gk *ōtalgía*] —**o·tal′gic,** *adj.*
O·ta·ru (ô′tä ro͞o′), *n.* a city on W Hokkaido, in N Japan. 206,620 (1964).
OTB, offtrack betting.
OTC, 1. Officer in Tactical Command. **2.** *Stock Exchange.* over-the-counter.
O.T.C., *Brit.* Officers' Training Corps.
O tem·po·ra! O mo·res! (ō tem′pō rä′ ō mō′rās; *Eng.* ō tem′pər ə ō mōr′ēz, môr′-), *Latin.* O times! O customs!
-oth, a plural ending of feminine nouns occurring in loan words from Hebrew: *Sabaoth.*
oth·er (uth′ər), *adj.* **1.** additional or further: *he and one other person.* **2.** different or distinct from the one or ones mentioned or implied: *in some other city.* **3.** different in nature or kind: *I would not have him other than he is.* **4.** being the remaining one of two or more: *the other hand.* **5.** (used with plural nouns) being the remaining ones of a

number: *the other men.* **6.** former: *sailing ships of other days.* **7. every other,** every alternate. **8. the other day (night, evening,** etc.), a day (night, evening, etc.) or two ago; lately: *That thunderstorm the other night frightened the baby.* —*n.* **9.** the other one: *Each praises the other.* —*pron.* **10.** Usually, **others.** other persons or things: *others in the medical profession; others who follow his example.* **11.** some person or thing else: *Surely some friend or other will help me.* —*adv.* **12.** otherwise; differently (usually fol. by *than*): *We can't collect the rent other than by suing the tenant.* [ME; OE *ōther;* c. G *ander,* Goth *anthar;* akin to Skt *antara-*] —**oth′er·ness,** *n.*

oth·er-di·rect·ed (uŧħ′ər di rek′tid), *adj.* guided by a set of values that is derived from current trends or outward influences rather than from within oneself. Cf. **inner-directed.** —**oth′er-di·rect′ed·ness,** *n.* —**oth′er-di·rec′tion,** *n.*

oth·er·guess (uŧħ′ər ges′), *adj. Archaic.* of another kind; different. [var. of *othergets,* var. of ME *othergates.* See OTHER, GATE², -S¹]

oth·er·where (uŧħ′ər hwâr′, -wâr′), *adv. Archaic.* elsewhere.

oth·er·while (uŧħ′ər hwīl′, -wīl′), *adv. Archaic.* at another time or other times. [ME *otherwhil, otherwhiles*]

oth·er·wise (uŧħ′ər wīz′), *adv.* **1.** under other circumstances: *Otherwise they may get broken.* **2.** in another manner; differently. **3.** in other respects: *an otherwise happy life.* —*adj.* **4.** other or different; of another nature or kind: *We hoped his behavior would be otherwise.* **5.** in other or different circumstances. [ME; OE (*on*) *ōthre wīsan* (in) other manner]

oth′er world′, the world after death.

oth·er·world·ly (uŧħ′ər wûrld′lē), *adj.* of, pertaining to, or devoted to another world, as the world of imagination or the world to come. —**oth′er·world′li·ness,** *n.*

Oth·man (oth′mən; *for 1 also Arab.* ŏŏth män′), *n., pl.* **-mans. 1.** Osman. **2.** Ottoman (defs. 2, 3).

O·tho I (ō′thō). See **Otto I.**

o·tic (ō′tik, ot′ik), *adj. Anat.* of or pertaining to the ear; auricular. [< Gk *ōtik(ós)*]

-otic, an adjective suffix of Greek origin, often corresponding to nouns with stems in *-osis,* denoting a relationship to an action, process, state, or condition indicated by the preceding element: *hypnotic; neurotic.* See **-tic.** Cf. **-osis.** [< Gk *-ōtikos*]

o·ti·ose (ō′shē ōs′, ō′tē-), *adj.* **1.** leisured; idle or indolent. **2.** ineffective or futile. **3.** superfluous or useless. [< L *ōtiōs(us)* at leisure = *ōti(um)* leisure + *-ōsus* -OSE¹] —**o′ti·ose′ly,** *adv.* —**o·ti·os·i·ty** (ō′shē os′i tē, ō′tē-), **o′ti·ose′ness,** *n.* —**Syn. 1.** lazy, slothful. **2.** idle, vain, profitless. **3.** redundant, worthless, pointless.

O·tis (ō′tis), *n.* **1. Elisha Graves,** 1811–61, U.S. inventor. **2. James,** 1725–83, American patriot.

o·ti·tis (ō tī′tis), *n. Pathol.* inflammation of the ear.

oto-, a learned borrowing from Greek meaning "ear," used in the formation of compound words: *otology.* Also, *esp. before a vowel,* **ot-.** [< Gk, comb. form of *oûs*]

o·to·cyst (ō′tə sist), *n.* a statocyst. —**o·to·cys·tic** (ō′tə-sis′tik), *adj.*

o·to·lar·yn·gol·o·gy (ō′tō lar′ing gol′ə jē), *n.* otorhinolaryngology. —**o′to·lar′yn·gol′o·gist,** *n.* —**o·to·la·ryn·go·log·i·cal** (ō′tō lə ring′gə loj′i kəl), *adj.*

o·to·lith (ōt′əlith), *n.* **1.** *Anat., Zool.* a calcareous concretion in the internal ear of vertebrates. **2.** statolith.

o·tol·o·gy (ō tol′ə jē), *n.* the science of the ear and its diseases. —**o·to·log·i·cal** (ōt′əloj′i kəl), *adj.* —**o·tol′o·gist,** *n.*

o·to·plas·ty (ō′tə plas′tē), *n.* plastic surgery of the external ear. —**o′to·plas′tic,** *adj.*

o·to·rhi·no·lar·yn·gol·o·gy (ō′tō rī′nō lar′ing gol′ə jē), *n.* the branch of medicine that deals with the anatomy, function, and diseases of the ear, nose, and throat. Also, **otolaryngology.** —**o·to·rhi·no·la·ryn·go·log·i·cal** (ō′tō-rī′nō lə ring′gə loj′i kəl), **o′to·rhi′no·la·ryn′go·log′ic,** *adj.* —**o′to·rhi′no·lar′yn·gol′o·gist,** *n.*

o·to·scope (ō′tə skōp′), *n. Med.* **1.** an instrument for examining the external canal and tympanic membrane of the ear. **2.** an instrument for auscultation in the ear. —**o·to·scop·ic** (ō′tə skop′ik), *adj.* —**o·tos·co·py** (ō tos′-kə pē), *n.*

O·tran·to (ō trän′tō; *It.* ô′trän tô), *n.* **Strait of,** a strait between SE Italy and Albania, connecting the Adriatic and the Mediterranean. 44 mi. wide.

ot·tar (ot′ər), *n.* attar (def. 1).

ot·ta·va (ō tä′və; *It.* ôt tä′vä), *adv. Music.* (of notes in a score) at an octave higher than written (when placed above the staff) or lower than written (when placed below the staff). *Abbr.:* 8va. [< It: OCTAVE]

ot·ta·va ri·ma (ō tä′və rē′mə), *pl.* **ot·ta·va ri·mas.** an Italian stanza of eight lines, each of eleven syllables (or, in the English adaptation, of ten or eleven syllables), the first six lines rhyming alternately and the last two forming a couplet with a different rhyme. [< It: octave rhyme]

Ot·ta·wa (ot′ə wə), *n., pl.* **-was,** (*esp. collectively*) **-wa** for 3. **1.** a city in and the capital of Canada, in SE Ontario. 304,462. **2.** a river in SE Canada, flowing SE along the boundary between Ontario and Quebec into the St. Lawrence at Montreal. 685 mi. long. **3.** a member of a tribe of Algonquian Indians of Canada, forced into the Lake Superior and Lake Michigan regions by the Iroquois confederacy. **4.** the Ojibwa language as used by the Ottawa Indians.

Otter, *Lutra canadensis* (Total length about 4 ft.; tail to 1½ ft.)

ot·ter (ot′ər), *n., pl.* **-ters,** (*esp. collectively*) **-ter.** any of several aquatic, fur-bearing, carnivorous, musteline mammals of the genus *Lutra* and related genera, having webbed feet and a long, slightly flattened tail. [ME *otter, oter,* OE *otor, ottor;* c. D, G *otter;* akin to Gk *hýdrā,* Skt *udrā-* water serpent. See HYDRA]

Ot·ter (ot′ər), *n.* (in the *Volsunga Saga*) a son of Hreidmar, who assumed the form of an otter when fishing, and who was killed by Loki while in that form.

Ot·ter·bein (ot′ər bīn′), *n.* **Philip William,** 1726–1813, American clergyman, born in Germany: originator of the United Brethren.

Ot·ter·burn (ot′ər bûrn′), *n.* a village in central Northumberland, in NE England: defeat of English by Scots 1388.

ot·to (ot′ō), *n.* attar (def. 1).

Ot·to I (ot′ō; *Ger.* ôt′ō), ("*the Great*") A.D. 912–973, king of the Germans 936–973; emperor of the Holy Roman Empire 962–973. Also, **Otho I.**

Ot·to·man (ot′ə mən), *adj., n., pl.* **-mans.** —*adj.* **1.** of or pertaining to the Ottoman Empire. —*n.* **2.** a Turk. **3.** a Turk of the family or tribe of Osman. **4.** (*l.c.*) a kind of sofa or seat, with or without a back. **5.** (*l.c.*) a cushioned footstool. **6.** (*l.c.*) a corded silk or rayon fabric with large cotton cord for filling. Also, **Othman** (for defs. 2, 3). [< F < It *ottoman(o),* after the founder of the empire (Ar *'othmān*); in defs. 4, 5, 6 < F *ottomane* (fem.)] —**Ot′to·man·like′,** *adj.*

Ot′toman Em′pire, a former Turkish empire 1300–1919: replaced by the republic of Turkey. *Cap.:* Constantinople. Also called **Turkish Empire.**

Ot′to Stru′ve. See **Struve, O.**

Ot·tum·wa (ə tum′wə), *n.* a city in SE Iowa, on the Des Moines River. 29,610 (1970).

Ot·way (ot′wā), *n.* **Thomas,** 1652–85, English dramatist.

oua·ba·in (wä bä′in), *n. Pharm.* a glycoside, $C_{29}H_{44}O_{12}$, obtained from the seeds of a shrub, *Strophanthus gratus,* or from the wood of a tree, *Acokanthera schimperi:* used chiefly as a cardiac stimulant. [< F *ouaba(ïo)* (< Somali *waba yo* the name of a tree) + -IN²]

Ouach·i·ta (wosh′i tô, wô′shi-), *n.* a river flowing SE from W Arkansas through NE Louisiana to the Red River. 605 mi. long.

Ouach′ita Moun′tains, a range extending from SE Oklahoma to W Arkansas.

Oua·ga·dou·gou (wä′gə dōō′gōō), *n.* a city in and the capital of Burkina Faso, in the central part. 124,779.

Ou·ban·gi (ōō bäɴ gē′), *n.* French name of **Ubangi.**

Ou·ban·gi-Cha·ri (ōō bäɴ gē′shA ʀē′), *n.* French name of **Ubangi-Shari.**

ou·bli·ette (ōō′blē et′), *n.* a secret dungeon with an opening only at the top, as in certain old castles. [< F, MF = *oubli(er)* (to) forget, OF *oblider* < VL **oblītāre* < L *oblīt(us)* forgotten (ptp. of *oblīvīscī;* see OBLIVION) + MF *-ette* -ETTE]

ouch¹ (ouch), *interj.* (an exclamation expressing sudden pain.) [< G *autsch*]

ouch² (ouch), *n. Archaic.* **1.** a clasp, buckle, or brooch, esp. one worn for ornament. **2.** the setting of a precious stone. [ME *ouche,* for *nouche* (*a nouche* taken as *an ouche;* cf. APRON) < OF *nosche* << Gmc]

Oudh (oud), *n.* a former part of the United Provinces of Agra and Oudh in N India: now part of Uttar Pradesh.

Oues·sant (we säɴ′), *n.* French name of **Ushant.**

ought¹ (ôt), *auxiliary verb.* **1.** (used to express duty or moral obligation): *Every citizen ought to help.* **2.** (used to express justice, moral rightness, or the like): *He ought to be punished.* **3.** (used to express propriety, appropriateness, etc.): *You ought to be home early.* **4.** (used to express probability or natural consequence): *That ought to be the postman.* —*n.* **5.** duty or obligation. [ME *ought, aught,* OE *āhte,* pret. of *āgan* to OWE] —**Syn. 1.** See **must**¹.

ought² (ôt), *n., adv.* aught¹. [var. of NOUGHT, *a nought* being taken as *an ought;* cf. OUCH²]

ought³ (ôt), *n.* aught².

ought·n't (ôt′ənt), contraction of *ought not.*

oui (wē), *adv., n. French.* yes.

Oui·da (wē′də), *n.* See **Ramée, Louise de la.**

Oui·ja (wē′jə, -jē), *n. Trademark.* a device consisting of a small board, or planchette, resting on a larger board marked with words and letters, used to spell out messages in spiritualistic communication. Also, **oui′ja.** Also called **oui′ja board′.**

Ouj·da (ōōj dä′), *n.* a city in NE Morocco. 649,400.

Ou·lu (ou′lōō), *n.* a city in W Finland, on the Gulf of Bothnia. 78,545 (est. 1965).

ounce¹ (ouns), *n.* **1.** a unit of weight equal to 437.5 grains or 1/16 pound avoirdupois. **2.** a unit of 480 grains, 1/12 pound troy or apothecaries' weight. *Abbr.:* oz, oz. **3.** a fluid ounce. **4.** a small quantity or portion. [ME *unce* < MF < L *uncia* twelfth part, inch, ounce < *unus* ONE]

ounce² (ouns), *n.* a long-haired, leopardlike feline, *Panthera uncia,* of mountain ranges of central Asia. Also called **snow leopard.** [ME < OF, var. of *lonce* (taken as *l'once* the ounce) < VL **luncea* < L *lync-* (s. of *lynx*) LYNX]

ouphe (ouf, ōōf), *n.* an elf or goblin. [scribal var. of OAF]

our (our, ou′ər; *unstressed* är), *pron.* (a form of the possessive case of *we* used as an attributive adjective): *Our team is going to win.* Cf. **ours.** [ME *oure,* OE *ūre,* gen. pl. See US] —**Usage.** See **me.**

ou·ra·ri (ōō rär′ē), *n.* curare.

Our′ Fa′ther. See **Lord's Prayer.**

Our′ La′dy, a title of the Virgin Mary. [ME]

ours (ourz, ou′ərz *or, often,* ärz), *pron.* **1.** (a form of the possessive case of *we* used as a predicate adjective): *Which house is ours?* **2.** that or those belonging to us. [ME *ures, oures*]

our·self (är self′, our-, ou′ər-), *pron.* **1.** (a form corresponding to *ourselves,* used of a single person, esp. in the regal or formal style, as *we* for *I*): *We have taken unto ourself such powers as may be necessary.* **2.** one's own person, individuality, etc., considered as private and apart from others. [ME *oure self;* modeled on OURSELVES] —**Usage.** See **myself.**

our·selves (är selvz′, our-, ou′ər-), *pron.pl.* **1.** (used reflexively as the direct or indirect object of a verb or as the object of a preposition): *Give us a moment to ourselves.* **2.** (used as an intensive with *we*): *We ourselves would never say such a thing.* **3.** (used as an intensive in place of *us*): *Nobody likes it but ourselves.* **4.** (used for emphasis in place of *we* or *we ourselves*): *The ones who really want it are ourselves. No one loves it more than ourselves.* **5.** our healthy, normal selves: *After a good rest, we're almost ourselves again.* [ME *oure selven*] —**Usage.** See **myself.**

-ous, 1. an adjective suffix, occurring with stems of any origin, meaning "full of," "abounding in," "given to," "characterized by," "having," "like," etc. (*glorious; joyous; mucous; nervous; sonorous; wondrous*). **2.** a suffix in chemical terms, specialized in opposition to corresponding terms in *-ic* to mean the lower of two possible valences (*stannous chloride*, $SnCl_2$, and *stannic chloride*, $SnCl_4$). Also, **-eous, -ious.** [ME < OF < L *-ōsus;* often repr. L *-us* (adj.), Gk *-os* (adj.); in some words (e.g., *wondrous*), attached to native stems]

Ouse (o͞oz), *n.* **1.** a river in NE England, in Yorkshire, flowing SE to the Humber. 57 mi. long. **2.** Also called **Great Ouse.** a river in E England, flowing NE to the Wash. 160 mi. long. **3.** a river in SE England, flowing S to the English Channel. 30 mi. long.

ou·sel (o͞o′zəl), *n.* ouzel.

oust (oust), *v.t.* **1.** to expel from a place or position occupied. **2.** *Law.* to eject; dispossess. [< AF *oust(er)* (to) remove = OF *oster* < L *obstāre* to stand in the way, oppose (*ob-* OB- + *stāre* to stand)]

oust·er (ou′stər), *n.* **1.** expulsion from a place or position occupied. **2.** *Law.* **a.** an ejection; dispossession. **b.** a wrongful exclusion from real property. [< AF, n. use of inf. See OUST]

out (out), *adv.* **1.** away from, or not in, the normal or usual place, position, state, etc. **2.** away from one's home, country, work, etc., as specified: *to go out of town.* **3.** in or into the outdoors: *to go out for a walk.* **4.** to exhaustion, extinction, or depletion: *to pump a well out.* **5.** to the end or conclusion; to a final decision or resolution. **6.** to a point or into a state of extinction, nonexistence, etc.: *The lamp went out.* **7.** in or into a state of neglect, disuse, etc.; not in vogue or fashion. **8.** in or into public notice or knowledge. **9.** seeking openly and energetically to do or have: *to be out for a good time.* **10.** in or into society, as a result of one's debut. **11.** not in present or personal possession or use, as on loan: *The librarian said that the book was still out.* **12.** on strike. **13.** so as to project or extend: *to stretch out.* **14.** in or into activity, existence, or outward manifestation: *A rash broke out on her arm.* **15.** from a source or material, as specified: *made out of scraps.* **16.** from a state of composure, satisfaction, or harmony: *to be put out over trifles.* **17.** in or into a state of confusion, vexation, dispute, variance, or unfriendliness: *to fall out about trifles.* **18.** so as to deprive or be deprived: *to cheat out of money.* **19.** so as to use the last of: *to run out of coal.* **20.** from a number, stock, or store: *to pick out.* **21.** aloud or loudly: *to call out.* **22.** with completeness or effectiveness: *to fill out.* **23.** thoroughly; completely; entirely: *The children tired me out.* **24.** so as to obliterate or make undecipherable: *to paint out; to ink out.* **25.** *Sports.* in a manner resulting in an out: *to strike out.* **26. all out,** *Informal.* with maximum effort: *They went all out to finish on time.* **27. out and away,** to a surpassing degree; by far. **28. out from under,** *Informal.* out of a difficult situation: *The bankrupt tried to get out from under but couldn't make it.* —*adj.* **29.** exposed; made bare, as by holes in one's clothing: *out at the knees.* **30.** beyond fixed or regular limits: *The ball was declared out.* **31.** beyond the usual range, size, weight, etc. (often in combination): *an outsize bed.* **32.** incorrect or inaccurate: *His calculations are out.* **33.** not in practice; unskillful from lack of practice: *Your bow hand is out.* **34.** having a pecuniary loss to an indicated extent. **35.** wanting; lacking; without (often fol. by *of*): *We are out of butter.* **36.** removed from or not in effective operation, play, or the like, as in a game. **37.** unconscious; senseless: *Two drinks and he's usually out.* **38.** *Baseball.* **a.** (of a batter) not succeeding in getting on base. **b.** (of a base runner) not successful in an attempt to advance a base or bases. **39.** no longer having or holding (a public office, a job, etc.); unemployed; disengaged (usually fol. by *of*): *to be out of work.* **40.** at variance; at odds; unfriendly. **41.** finished; ended. **42.** inoperative; extinguished. **43.** not in power, authority, or the like. **44.** moving or directed outward; outgoing: *an out box for mail.* **45.** of or pertaining to the playing of the first nine holes of an eighteen-hole golf course. **46.** not stylish or fashionable. **47.** not available, plentiful, etc.: *Mums are out till next fall.* **48.** *Obs.* external; exterior; outer. **49.** *Obs.* located at a distance; outlying. **50. out of, a.** foaled by (a dam). **b.** as a result of; from: *She did it out of pity.* **51. out of trim,** *Naut.* (of a vessel) drawing excessively at the bow or stern. **52. out of whack.** See **whack** (def. 6). —*prep.* **53.** (used to indicate movement or direction from the inside to the outside of something): *He looked out the window. He ran out the door.* **54.** (used to indicate movement away from a central point): *Let's drive out the old mill road.* —*interj.* **55.** begone!; away! **56.** *Archaic.* (used as an exclamation of indignation, reproach, etc.) (usually fol. by *upon*): *Out upon you!* —*n.* **57.** something that is out, as a projecting corner. **58.** a means of escape, as from a place, punishment, retribution, responsibility, etc. **59.** a person who lacks status or authority, esp. in relation to a particular group or situation. **60.** *Baseball.* a put-out. **61.** (in tennis, squash, handball, etc.) a return or service that does not land within the inbounds limits of a court or section of a court (opposed to *in*). **62.** Usually, **outs.** persons not in office or political power. **63.** *Print.* **a.** the omission of a word or words. **b.** the word or words omitted. **64.** *Dial.* an outing. **65. be on the** or **at outs with,** *Informal.* to be estranged from (another person); be on bad terms with. —*v.i.* **66.** to go or come out. **67.** to become public, evident, etc.: *The truth will out.* **68.** to make known; tell; utter (fol. by *with*): *Out with the truth!* —*v.t.* **69.** *Archaic.* to oust. [ME; OE *ūt;* c. D *uit,* G *aus,* Icel, Goth *ūt;* akin to Skt *ud-*]

out-, a prefixal use of **out,** *adv.*, occurring in various senses in compounds (*outcast; outside*), and serving also to form many transitive verbs denoting a going beyond, surpassing, or outdoing in the particular action indicated (*outlast; outlive; outstay*). [ME; OE *ūt*]

out·age (ou′tij), *n.* **1.** a stoppage in the functioning of a machine or mechanism due to a failure in the supply of power or electricity. **2.** a period during which such a failure in the supply of power or electricity occurs. **3.** the quantity of goods lost or lacking from a shipment.

out-and-out (out′ənout′, -ənd out′), *adj.* thoroughgoing; thorough; complete; unqualified. [ME]

out·back (*n.* out′bak′; *adj., adv.* out′bak′), *Australian.* —*n.* **1.** (*often cap.*) the back country or remote settlements; the bush (usually prec. by *the*). —*adj.* **2.** (*sometimes cap.*) of, pertaining to, or located in the back country. —*adv.* **3.** (*sometimes cap.*) in or to the back country.

out·bal·ance (out′bal′əns), *v.t.*, **-anced, -anc·ing.** to outweigh.

out·bid (out′bid′), *v.t.*, **-bid, -bid·den** or **-bid, -bid·ding.** to outdo in bidding.

out·board (out′bōrd′, -bôrd′), *adj.* **1.** located on the exterior of a hull or aircraft. **2.** located farther from the center. **3.** (of a motorboat) having an outboard motor. —*adv.* **4.** outside or away from the center of a hull or aircraft. Cf. **inboard** (def. 4). —*n.* **5.** an outboard motor. **6.** a boat equipped with an outboard motor.

out′board mo′tor, a portable gasoline engine with propeller and tiller, clamped on the stern of a boat.

out·bound (out′bound′), *adj.* outward bound.

out·break (out′brāk′), *n.* **1.** a breaking out; an outburst. **2.** a sudden and active manifestation. **3.** a public disturbance; insurrection; riot.

out·breed (out′brēd′), *v.t.*, **-bred, -breed·ing.** to breed outside the limits of the family, within a breed or variety.

out·build·ing (out′bil′diŋ), *n.* a detached building subordinate to a main building.

out·burst (out′bûrst′), *n.* **1.** a bursting forth; eruption. **2.** a sudden and violent outpouring: *an outburst of tears.* **3.** a sudden spell of activity, energy, etc.

out·by (out′bī′), *adv.* *Scot. and North Eng.* outside; outdoors. Also, **out′bye′.** [ME (Scot)]

out·cast (out′kast′, -käst′), *n.* **1.** a person who is rejected or cast out, as from home or society. **2.** a homeless wanderer; vagabond. —*adj.* **3.** cast out, as from one's home or society. **4.** pertaining to or characteristic of an outcast. **5.** rejected or discarded. [ME]

out·caste (out′kast′, -käst′), *n.* **1.** a person of no caste. **2.** (in India) a person who has forfeited membership in his caste.

out·class (out′klas′, -kläs′), *v.t.* to surpass in class or quality; be superior.

out·come (out′kum′), *n.* that which results from something; consequence. [ME *utcume*] —**Syn.** See **end**[1].

out·crop (*n.* out′krop′; *v.* out′krop′), *n.*, *v.*, **-cropped, -crop·ping.** —*n.* **1.** a cropping out, as of a stratum or vein at the surface of the earth. **2.** the emerging part. **3.** something that emerges suddenly or violently in the manner of an outcrop; outbreak: *an outcrop of student demonstrations.* —*v.i.* **4.** to crop out, as strata.

out·cross (*v.* out′krôs′, -kros′; *n.* out′krôs′, -kros′), *v.t.* **1.** to produce (a hybrid) by outcrossing. —*n.* **2.** a hybrid animal or plant so produced. **3.** an act of outcrossing.

out·cross·ing (out′krô′siŋ, -kros′iŋ), *n.* the crossing of animals or plants that are of different strains but usually, esp. of livestock, within the same breed.

out·cry (*n.* out′krī′; *v.* out′krī′), *n., pl.* **-cries,** *v.* **-cried, -cry·ing.** —*n.* **1.** a crying out. **2.** a cry of distress, indignation, or the like. **3.** loud clamor. —*v.t.* **4.** to outdo in crying; cry louder than. [ME]

out·curve (out′kûrv′), *n.* *Baseball.* a pitch that breaks outward from the batter. Also called **outshoot.** Cf. **incurve**[2].

out·date (out′dāt′), *v.t.*, **-dat·ed, -dat·ing.** to put out of date; make antiquated or obsolete.

out·dis·tance (out′dis′təns), *v.t.*, **-tanced, -tanc·ing.** to leave behind, as in running; outstrip.

out·do (out′do͞o′), *v.t.*, **-did, -done, -do·ing.** to surpass in execution or performance. [ME] —**Syn.** See **excel.**

out·door (out′dōr′, -dôr′), *adj.* characteristic of, located, or belonging outdoors. Also, **outdoors.** [earlier *out (of) door*]

out·doors (out′dōrz′, -dôrz′), *adv.* **1.** out of doors; in the open air. —*n.* **2.** (*construed as sing.*) the world outside of houses; open air. —*adj.* **3.** outdoor. [earlier *out (of) doors*]

out·draw (out′drô′), *v.t.*, **-drew, -drawn, -draw·ing.** **1.** to draw a gun, revolver, etc., faster than (one's opponent or competitor). **2.** to excel in drawing power; prove a greater attraction than: *She outdraws all male stars at the box office.*

out·er (ou′tər), *adj.* of, pertaining to, or situated on or toward the outside; farther out; external; exterior. [ME] —**out′er·ness,** *n.*

out′er bar′, *Eng. Law.* a body of the junior counsel who sit and plead outside the dividing bar in the court, ranking below the King's Counsel or Queen's Counsel. Also, **utter bar.** Cf. **inner bar.**

Out′er Heb′rides. See under **Hebrides.**

out′er jib′, *Naut.* a headsail next forward from an inner jib and aft of a flying jib. See diag. at **ship.**

Out′er Mongo′lia, former name of **Mongolian People's Republic.**

out·er·most (ou′tər mōst′ *or, esp. Brit.,* -məst), *adj.* farthest out; remotest from the interior or center.

out′er prod′uct, *Math.* See **vector product.**

out′er space′, space beyond the atmosphere of the earth.

out·face (out′fās′), *v.t.*, **-faced, -fac·ing.** **1.** to face or stare down. **2.** to face or confront boldly; defy.

out·fall (out′fôl′), *n.* the outlet or place of discharge of a river, drain, sewer, etc.

out·field (out′fēld′), *n.* **1.** *Baseball.* **a.** the part of the field beyond the diamond. **b.** the positions played by the right, center, and left fielders. **c.** the outfielders considered as a

out′ar′gue, *v.t.*
out′bar′gain, *v.t.*
out′bet′ter, *v.t.*
out′bluff′, *v.t.*
out′blus′ter, *v.t.*
out′boast′, *v.t.*
out′box′, *v.t.*
out′brave′, *v.t.*, **-braved, -brav·ing.**
out′cheat′, *v.t.*
out′curse′, *v.t.*, **-cursed, -curs·ing.**
out′dance′, *v.t.*, **-danced, -danc·ing.**
out′dare′, *v.t.*, **-dared, -dar·ing.**
out′dodge′, *v.t.*, **-dodged, -dodg·ing.**
out′drink′, *v.t.*, **-drank** or (*Nonstandard*) **-drunk; -drunk** or (*Nonstandard*) **-drank; -drink·ing.**
out′eat′, *v.t.*, **-ate, -eat·en, -eat·ing.**

group (contrasted with *infield*). **2.** *Cricket.* the part of the field farthest from the batsman.

out·field·er (out′fē′ldər), *n.* *Sports.* one of the players stationed in the outfield.

out·fit (out′fit′), *n.*, *v.*, **-fit·ted, -fit·ting.** —*n.* **1.** an assemblage of articles for fitting out or equipping: *an explorer's outfit.* **2.** a complete costume, esp. for a woman, usually including shoes, coat, hat, dress, and other matching or harmonious accessories; ensemble: *a new spring outfit.* **3.** a set of articles for any purpose: *a cooking outfit.* **4.** *Informal.* **a.** a group associated in an undertaking requiring close cooperation, as a military unit. **b.** a business firm engaged in a particular form of commercial enterprise: *a construction outfit.* **5.** the act of fitting out or equipping for any purpose, as for a voyage, journey, or expedition. —*v.t.* **6.** to furnish with an outfit; fit out; equip. **7.** *Naut.* to finish equipping (a vessel) at a dock. —*v.i.* **8.** to furnish oneself with an outfit. —**out′fit′ter,** *n.* —**Syn. 1, 3.** kit. **6.** appoint, supply, rig.

out·flank (out′flangk′), *v.t.* **1.** to go or extend beyond the flank of (an opposing military unit); turn the flank of. **2.** to get around (an opposing force); outmaneuver; bypass.

out·flow (out′flō′), *n.* **1.** the act of flowing out. **2.** that which flows out. **3.** any outward movement.

out·foot (out′fo͝ot′), *v.t.* to outdo or excel (another boat) in speed; outstrip.

out·fox (out′foks′), *v.t.* to outwit; outsmart.

out·gen·er·al (out′jen′ər əl), *v.t.*, **-aled, -al·ing** or (*esp. Brit.*) **-alled, -al·ling.** to outdo in generalship.

out·go[1] (out′gō′), *n.*, *pl.* **-goes. 1.** the act or process of going out. **2.** money paid out; expenditure. **3.** that which goes out; outflow. [n. use of OUTGO[2]]

out·go[2] (out gō′), *v.t.*, **-went, -gone, -go·ing. 1.** to go beyond; outdistance. **2.** to surpass, excel, or outdo. **3.** *Archaic.* to go faster than. [OUT- + GO[1]]

out·go·ing (out′gō′ing), *adj.* **1.** going out; departing: *outgoing trains.* **2.** interested in and responsive to others: *an outgoing personality.* **3.** of or pertaining to simple food or beverages prepared and wrapped by a restaurant for consumption elsewhere, as sandwiches, coffee, etc. [ME (n.)]

out·group (out′gro͞op′), *n.* *Sociol.* people outside one's own group, esp. as considered to be inferior or alien. Cf. **ingroup.**

out·grow (out′grō′), *v.*, **-grew, -grown, -grow·ing.** —*v.t.* **1.** to grow too large for. **2.** to leave behind or lose in the changes incident to development or the passage of time. **3.** to surpass in growing. —*v.i.* **4.** *Archaic.* to grow out; burst forth; protrude.

out·growth (out′grōth′), *n.* **1.** a development, product, or result. **2.** an additional, supplementary result. **3.** a growing out or forth. **4.** that which grows out; offshoot; excrescence.

out·guess (out′ges′), *v.t.* to outwit.

out·haul (out′hôl′), *n.* *Naut.* a rope used for hauling out a sail on a boom, yard, etc.

out-Her·od (out′her′əd), *v.t.* to outdo in extravagance or excess. [OUT- + HEROD (ANTIPAS)]

out·house (out′hous′), *n.*, *pl.* **-hous·es** (-hou′ziz). **1.** an outbuilding. **2.** an outbuilding with one or more seats and a pit serving as a toilet.

out·ing (ou′ting), *n.* **1.** a pleasure trip, picnic, or the like. **2.** the part of the sea out from the shore. [ME]

out′ing flan′nel, a light cotton flannel with a short, dense nap.

out·laid (out′lād′), *v.* pt. and pp. of **outlay.**

out·land (*n.* out′land′; *adj.* out′land′, -lənd), *n.* **1.** Usually, **outlands.** the outlying districts or remote regions of a country; provinces. **2.** (formerly) the outlying land of a feudal estate, usually granted to tenants. **3.** *Archaic.* a foreign land. —*adj.* **4.** outlying, as districts. **5.** *Archaic.* foreign. [ME; OE *ūtland*]

out·land·er (out′lan′dər), *n.* a foreigner; alien.

out·land·ish (out lan′dish), *adj.* **1.** freakishly or grotesquely strange or odd, as dress, objects, ideas, practices, etc.; bizarre. **2.** having a foreign appearance. **3.** out-of-the-way, as a place. **4.** *Archaic.* foreign. [ME; OE *ūtlendisc*] —**out·land′ish·ly,** *adv.* —**out·land′ish·ness,** *n.* —**Syn. 1.** peculiar, queer, eccentric, curious. **3.** remote.

out·last (out′last′, -läst′), *v.t.* to last longer than.

out·law (out′lô′), *n.* **1.** a person, group, or thing excluded from the benefits and protection of the law. **2.** a person under sentence of outlawry. **3.** a habitual criminal. **4.** a horse that cannot be broken; a mean, intractable horse. **5.** any rogue animal. —*v.t.* **6.** to deprive of the benefits and protection of the law. **7.** to make unlawful. **8.** to remove from legal jurisdiction. **9.** to prohibit. [ME *outlawe*, OE *ūtlage* < Scand; cf. Icel *ūtlagi*] —**Syn. 3.** robber, thief; bandit, brigand. **9.** proscribe.

out·law·ry (out′lô′rē), *n.*, *pl.* **-ries** for 1, 3. **1.** the act or process of outlawing. **2.** the state of being outlawed. **3.** disregard or defiance of the law. [ME *outlagerie*, *outlagarie* < AF *utlagerie*, ML *utlagāria* < ME *outlage* OUTLAW + AF *-erie* -RY, ML *-āria* -ARY]

out·lay (*n.* out′lā′; *v.* out′lā′), *n.*, *v.*, **-laid, -lay·ing.** —*n.* **1.** an expending or expenditure, as of money. **2.** an amount expended. —*v.t.* **3.** to expend, as money.

out·let (out′let, -lit), *n.* **1.** an opening or passage by which anything is let out; a vent or exit. **2.** *Elect.* **a.** a point on a wiring system at which current is taken to supply electric devices. **b.** Also called **out′let box′.** the metal box or receptacle designed to facilitate connections to a wiring system. **3.** *Com.* **a.** a market for goods. **b.** a retail store selling the goods of a particular manufacturer. **4.** a means of expression or satisfaction: *an outlet for one's artistic inclinations.* **5.** a local radio or television station that broadcasts the programs of a large network. **6.** a river or stream flowing from a body of water, as a lake or pond. **7.** the channel such a river or stream follows. **8.** the lower end or mouth of a river where it meets a large body of water, as a lake or the sea. [early ME *utlete*]

out·li·er (out′lī′ər), *n.* **1.** a person or thing that lies outside. **2.** a person residing outside the place of his business, duty, etc. **3.** *Geol.* a part of a formation left detached through the removal of surrounding parts by denudation.

out·line (out′līn′), *n.*, *v.*, **-lined, -lin·ing.** —*n.* **1.** the line by which a figure or object is defined or bounded; contour. **2.** a drawing or sketch restricted to line without shading or modeling of form. **3.** a general sketch, account, or report, indicating only the main features, as of a book, subject, project, etc. **4. outlines,** the essential features or main aspects of something under discussion. —*v.t.* **5.** to draw the outline of or draw in outline, as a figure or object. **6.** to give an outline of; sketch the main features of. —**Syn. 1.** See **form. 3.** plan, draft. **5, 6.** delineate, draft.

out·live (out′liv′), *v.t.*, **-lived, -liv·ing. 1.** to live longer than; survive (a person, period, etc.). **2.** to outlast; live or last through. [ME *outleve(n)*] —**out′liv′er,** *n.* —**Syn. 1.** See **survive.**

out·look (out′lo͝ok′), *n.* **1.** the view or prospect from a place. **2.** mental view: *one's outlook on life.* **3.** prospect of the future: *the political outlook.* **4.** the place from which an observer looks out; lookout. **5.** the act or state of looking out. **6.** a watch kept; vigilance; lookout. —**Syn. 1, 3.** scene. **2.** attitude, picture, approach.

out·ly·ing (out′lī′ing), *adj.* **1.** lying at a distance from the center or the main body; remote; out-of-the-way. **2.** lying outside the boundary or limit.

out·ma·neu·ver (out′mə no͞o′vər), *v.t.* to outdo in or get the better of by maneuvering.

out·ma·noeu·vre (out′mə no͞o′vər), *v.t.*, **-vred, -vring.** outmaneuver.

out·match (out′mach′), *v.t.* to surpass; outdo.

out·mode (out′mōd′), *v.t.*, **-mod·ed, -mod·ing.** to make obsolete or cause to go out of style. [*out (of) mode*]

out·mod·ed (out′mō′did), *adj.* **1.** gone out of style; no longer fashionable. **2.** not acceptable by present standards; no longer usable; obsolete. [*out (of) mode* + -ED[2]]

out·most (out′mōst′ *or, esp. Brit.*, -məst), *adj.* farthest out; outermost. [ME]

out·num·ber (out′num′bər), *v.t.* to exceed in number.

out-of-bounds (out′əv boundz′), *adj.* **1.** *Sports.* being beyond the limits within which something is legally in play. **2.** further than or beyond established limits, as of behavior, thought, etc.

out-of-date (out′əv dāt′), *adj.* gone out of style; outmoded; obsolete. —**out′-of-date′ness,** *n.*

out′ of doors′, in the open air; not within a house or building; outdoors.

out-of-doors (out′əv dōrz′, -dôrz′), *adj.* **1.** Also, **out′-of-door′.** outdoor. —*n.* **2.** (*construed as sing.*) outdoors.

out-of-pock·et (out′əv pok′it), *adj.* **1.** paid out or owed in cash: *out-of-pocket expenses.* **2.** without funds or assets.

out′ of print′, no longer published.

out-of-the-way (out′əv thə wā′), *adj.* **1.** remote from much-traveled, frequented, or populous regions; secluded. **2.** seldom encountered; unusual. **3.** giving offense; improper.

out-of-town·er (out′əv tou′nər), *n.* *Informal.* a stranger or visitor from another town.

out·pa·tient (out′pā′shənt), *n.* a patient receiving treatment at a hospital but not being an inmate.

out·place·ment (out′plās′mənt), *n.* counseling and assistance in finding a new job, offered by a company to personnel being discharged.

out·point (out′point′), *v.t.* **1.** to excel in number of points, as in a competition or contest. **2.** *Naut.* to sail closer to the wind than (another vessel).

out·post (out′pōst′), *n.* **1.** a station established at a distance from the main body of an army to protect it from surprise attack. **2.** the body of troops stationed there.

out·pour (*n.* out′pōr′, -pôr′; *v.* out′pōr′, -pôr′), *n.* **1.** outpouring. —*v.t.* **2.** to pour out. —**out′pour′er,** *n.*

out·pour·ing (out′pōr′ing, -pôr′-), *n.* that which pours out or is poured out; an outflow, overflow, or effusion.

out·put (out′po͝ot′), *n.* **1.** the act of turning out; production. **2.** the quantity or amount produced, as in a given time: *to increase one's daily output.* **3.** the product or yield, as of a mine. **4.** the current, voltage, power, or signal produced by an electrical or electronic circuit or device. Cf. **input** (def. 3). **5.** *Computer Technol.* **a.** information in a form suitable for transmission from internal to external units of a computer, or to an outside apparatus. **b.** the process of transferring data from internal storage to an external device. **6.** the power or force produced by a machine.

out·rage (out′rāj), *n.*, *v.*, **-raged, -rag·ing.** —*n.* **1.** an act of wanton violence; any gross violation of law or decency. **2.** anything that outrages the feelings. **3.** *Obs.* passionate or violent behavior or language; fury or insolence. —*v.t.* **4.** to subject to grievous violence or indignity. **5.** to anger or offend; make resentful; shock. **6.** to offend against (right, decency, feelings, etc.) grossly or shamelessly. **7.** to rape (a woman). [ME < OF *outrage*, *ultrage* = *outr(er)* (to) push beyond bounds (< *outre* beyond < L *ultrā*) + *-age* -AGE]

out·ra·geous (out rā′jəs), *adj.* **1.** of the nature of or involving gross injury or wrong: *an outrageous slander.* **2.** grossly offensive to the sense of right or decency. **3.** passing reasonable bounds; intolerable or shocking. **4.** violent in action or temper. **5.** highly unusual or unconventional; extravagant. [ME < MF *outrageus*] —**out·ra′geous·ly,** *adv.* —**out·ra′geous·ness,** *n.* —**Syn. 2.** insulting, shocking.

out·ran (out′ran′), *v.* pt. of **outrun.**

out·rank (out′rangk′), *v.t.* to rank above.

ou·tré (o͞o trā′), *adj.* *French.* passing the bounds of what is usual or considered proper.

out·reach (*v.* out′rēch′; *n.* out′rēch′), *v.t.* **1.** to reach beyond; exceed. **2.** *Archaic.* to reach out; extend. —*v.i.* **3.** to reach out. —*n.* **4.** the act or an instance of reaching out. **5.** length of reach.

out·ride (*v.* out′rīd′; *n.* out′rīd′), *v.*, **-rode, -rid·den, -rid·ing,** *n.* —*v.t.* **1.** to outdo or outstrip in riding. **2.** to come safely through (a storm) by lying to, as a vessel. —*v.i.* **3.**

out′fight′, *v.t.*, **-fought, -fight·ing.**
out′fly′, *v.t.*, **-flew, -flown, -fly·ing.**
out′gun′, *v.t.*, **-gunned, -gun·ning.**
out′hit′, *v.t.*, **-hit, -hit·ting.**
out′jump′, *v.t.*
out′jut′, *v.i.*, **-jut·ted, -jut·ting.**
out′kick′, *v.t.*
out′laugh′, *v.t.*
out′leap′, *v.t.*, **-leaped** or **-leapt, -leap·ing.**
out′march′, *v.t.*
out′per·form′, *v.t.*
out′play′, *v.t.*
out′poll′, *v.t.*
out′pro·duce′, *v.t.*, **-duced, -duc·ing.**
out′race′, *v.t.*, **-raced, -rac·ing.**
out′range′, *v.t.*
out′rea′son, *v.t.*

to act as an outrider. —*n.* **4.** *Pros.* an unaccented syllable or syllables added to a metrical foot, esp. in sprung rhythm.

out·rid·er (out′rī′dər), *n.* **1.** a mounted attendant riding before or beside a carriage. **2.** someone who goes in advance of an automobile or person to clear a passage. **3.** a person who leads the way or is a member of a vanguard. **4.** a man who rides out or forth, esp. a scout, cowboy, ranch hand, or the like. [ME: official in a monastery]

out·rig·ger (out′rig′ər), *n.* **1.** a framework supporting a float extended outboard from the side of a boat for adding stability, as on South Pacific canoes. **2.** a bracket extending outward from the side of a racing shell, to support an oarlock. **3.** the shell itself. **4.** a spar rigged out from a ship's rail or the like, as for extending a sail. **5.** any of various projecting frames or parts on an airplane, as for supporting a rudder. **6.** a projecting beam, as for supporting a hoisting tackle.

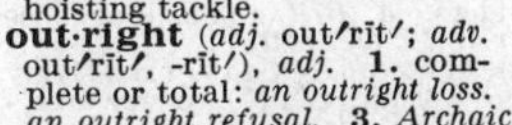

O, Outrigger (def. 1)

out·right (*adj.* out′rīt′; *adv.* out′rīt′, -rīt′), *adj.* **1.** complete or total: *an outright loss.* **2.** downright or unqualified: *an outright refusal.* **3.** *Archaic.* directed straight out or on. —*adv.* **4.** completely; entirely. **5.** without restraint, reserve, or concealment; openly. **6.** at once; instantly: *to be killed outright.* **7.** *Archaic.* straight out or ahead; directly onward. [ME] —**out′right′ness,** *n.*

out·root (out′ro͞ot′, -ro͝ot′), *v.t.* to root out; eradicate.

out·run (out′run′), *v.t.*, **-ran, -run, -run·ning. 1.** to run faster or farther than. **2.** to escape by or as by running. **3.** to exceed; excel; surpass.

out·run·ner (out′run′ər), *n.* **1.** a person or thing that runs out or outside. **2.** an attendant who runs before or beside a carriage. **3.** a forerunner.

out·rush (out′rush′), *n.* a rapid or intense outflow: *an outrush of water from a bursting pipe.*

out·sat (out′sat′), *v.* pt. and pp. of **outsit.**

out·sell (out′sel′), *v.t.*, **-sold, -sell·ing. 1.** to exceed in volume of sales; sell more than. **2.** to exceed in value of sales. **3.** *Archaic.* to obtain a higher price than.

out·sert (out′sûrt′), *n.* *Bookbinding.* an additional folded signature or sheet into which another is bound. Also called **outset, wraparound.** [OUT- + (IN)SERT]

out·set (out′set′), *n.* **1.** the beginning or start. **2.** outsert.

out·shine (out′shīn′), *v.*, **-shone, -shin·ing.** —*v.t.* **1.** to surpass in shining. **2.** to surpass in splendor, excellence, etc. —*v.i.* **3.** *Archaic.* to shine out or forth.

out·shoot (*v.* out′sho͞ot′; *n.* out′sho͞ot′), *v.*, **-shot, -shoot·ing,** *n.* —*v.t.* **1.** to surpass in shooting. **2.** to shoot beyond. **3.** to shoot (something) out; send forth. —*v.i.* **4.** to shoot forth; project. —*n.* **5.** the act or an instance of shooting out. **6.** something that shoots out. **7.** *Baseball.* outcurve.

out·side (*n.* out′sīd′, -sīd′; *adj.* out′sīd′, out′-; *adv.* out′-sīd′; *prep.* out′sīd′, out′sīd′), *n.* **1.** the outer side, surface, or part; the exterior. **2.** the external aspect or appearance. **3.** something merely external. **4.** the space without or beyond an enclosure, boundary, etc. **5. at the outside,** at the utmost limit; at the maximum. —*adj.* **6.** being, acting, done, or originating beyond an enclosure, boundary, etc.: *outside noises.* **7.** situated on or pertaining to the outside; exterior; external. **8.** not belonging to or connected with a specified institution, society, etc.: *outside influences.* **9.** extremely unlikely or remote: *an outside chance for recovery.* **10.** *Baseball.* (of a pitched ball) passing, but not going over, home plate on the side opposite the batter. —*adv.* **11.** on or to the outside, exterior, or space without: *Take the dog outside.* —*prep.* **12.** on or toward the outside of: *There was a noise outside the door.* **13.** *Informal.* with the exception of; aside from. **14. outside of,** *Informal.* other than; exclusive of; excepting.

out·sid·er (out′sī′dər), *n.* **1.** a person or thing not within an enclosure, boundary, etc. **2.** a person not belonging to a particular group, set, party, etc. **3.** a person unconnected or unacquainted with the matter in question. **4.** a race horse, sports team, etc., not classified among the best or among those expected to win.

out·size (out′sīz′), *n.* **1.** an uncommon or irregular size. **2.** a garment of such a size, esp. if larger than average. —*adj.* **3.** Also, **out′sized′.** unusually or abnormally large, heavy, extensive, etc.

out·skirt (out′skûrt′), *n.* **1.** Often, **outskirts.** the outlying district or region, as of a city, metropolitan area, or the like. **2.** Usually, **outskirts.** the border or fringes of a specified quality, condition, or the like.

out·smart (out′smärt′), *v.t.* **1.** to get the better of (someone); outwit. **2. outsmart oneself,** to defeat oneself unintentionally by intrigue, elaborate scheming, or the like.

out·sold (out′sōld′), *v.* pt. and pp. of **outsell.**

out·sole (out′sōl′), *n.* the outer sole of a shoe.

out·spent (out′spent′), *adj.* worn-out; exhausted.

out·spo·ken (out′spō′kən), *adj.* **1.** uttered or expressed with frankness or lack of reserve: *outspoken criticism.* **2.** free or unreserved in speech: *outspoken people.* —*v.* **3.** pp. of **outspeak.** —**out′spo′ken·ly,** *adv.* —**out′spo′ken·ness,** *n.* —**Syn. 1.** See **frank.** —**Ant. 1.** taciturn.

out·spread (*v.* out′spred′; *adj.* out′spred′; *n.* out′spred′), *v.*, **-spread, -spread·ing,** *adj.*, *n.* —*v.t.*, *v.i.* **1.** to spread out; extend. —*adj.* **2.** spread out; stretched out. **3.** diffused abroad; widely disseminated. —*n.* **4.** the act of spreading out; expansion. **5.** that which is spread out; an expanse. [ME *outspredd(en)* (v.)]

out·stand (out′stand′), *v.*, **-stood, -stand·ing.** —*v.i.* **1.** (of a ship) to sail out to sea. —*v.t.* *Archaic.* **2.** to stay or remain beyond: *to outstand the hour.* **3.** to withstand.

out·stand·ing (out′stan′ding), *adj.* **1.** prominent or conspicuous; striking. **2.** continuing in existence; remaining unsettled, unpaid, etc. **3.** (of capital stocks) issued and sold or in circulation. **4.** standing out; projecting; detached. **5.** *Archaic.* resisting or opposing. —**out′stand′ing·ly,** *adv.* —**out′stand′ing·ness,** *n.* —**Syn. 1.** eminent. **2.** owing, due.

out·stare (out′stâr′), *v.t.*, **-stared, -star·ing. 1.** to outdo in staring; stare down. **2.** to cause (someone) discomfort or embarrassment.

out·sta·tion (out′stā′shən), *n.* an auxiliary station, esp. on the outskirts of a district.

out·stay (out′stā′), *v.t.* **1.** to stay longer than. **2.** to stay beyond the time or duration of: *to outstay one's welcome.*

out·stretch (out′strech′), *v.t.* **1.** to stretch forth; extend. **2.** to stretch beyond. **3.** to stretch out; expand. **4.** *Obs.* to strain. —**out′stretch′er,** *n.*

out·strip (out′strip′), *v.t.*, **-stripped, -strip·ping. 1.** to outdo; surpass; excel. **2.** to outdo or pass in running or swift travel. **3.** to get ahead of or leave behind in a race or in any course of competition.

out·talk (out′tôk′), *v.t.* to outdo or overcome in talking.

out·think (out′thingk′), *v.t.*, **-thought, -think·ing. 1.** to excel in thinking; think faster, more accurately, or more perceptively than. **2.** to get the advantage of (someone) by quick or clever thinking; outwit.

out·throw (out′thrō′), *v.t.*, **-threw, -thrown, -throw·ing. 1.** to throw out; extend. **2.** to surpass in throwing; throw farther and more accurately than. [ME]

out·thrown (out′thrōn′), *adj.* thrown or extended outward: *arms outthrown in greeting.*

out·thrust (*v.*, *adj.* out′thrust′; *n.* out′thrust′), *v.*, **-thrust, -thrust·ing,** *adj.*, *n.* —*v.t.*, *v.i.* **1.** to thrust out or extend. —*adj.* **2.** thrust or extended outward. —*n.* **3.** something that thrusts or extends outward.

out·turn (out′tûrn′), *n.* **1.** a quantity produced; output. **2.** the quality or condition of something produced.

out·vote (out′vōt′), *v.t.*, **-vot·ed, -vot·ing.** to outdo or defeat in voting.

out·wait (out′wāt′), *v.t.* **1.** to surpass in waiting or expecting. **2.** *Archaic.* to lie in ambush longer than.

out·ward (out′wərd), *adj.* **1.** pertaining to or being what is seen or apparent, as distinguished from the underlying nature, facts, etc.; pertaining to surface qualities only; superficial: *outward appearances.* **2.** pertaining to the outside of the body; external. **3.** pertaining to the body, as opposed to the mind or spirit. **4.** belonging or pertaining to external actions or appearances, as opposed to inner feelings, mental states, etc. **5.** belonging or pertaining to what is external to oneself: *outward influences.* **6.** proceeding or directed toward the outside or exterior, or away from a central point. **7.** lying toward the outside; located on the outer side: *an outward court.* **8.** of or pertaining to the outside, outer surface, or exterior. **9.** *Archaic.* not directly concerned or interested. —*n.* **10.** *Archaic.* that which is without; the external or material world. **11.** *Archaic.* outward appearance. —*adv.* Also, **out′wards. 12.** toward the outside; out. **13.** visibly expressing one's inner feelings, mental state, etc. **14.** away from port: *a ship bound outward.* **15.** *Obs.* on the outside; without. [ME; OE *ūtweard*] —**out′ward·ness,** *n.*

out·ward·ly (out′wərd lē), *adv.* **1.** as regards appearance or outward manifestation. **2.** toward the outside. **3.** on the outside or outer surface; externally. [ME]

out·wash (out′wash′, -wôsh′), *n.* *Geol.* the material, chiefly sand or gravel, washed from a glacier by the action of meltwater.

out·watch (out′woch′, -wôch′), *v.t.* **1.** to outdo in watching. **2.** to watch, or maintain a vigil, until the end of: *The mourners had outwatched the night.*

out·wear (out′wâr′), *v.t.*, **-wore, -worn, -wear·ing. 1.** to wear or last longer than; outlast. **2.** to outlive or outgrow. **3.** to wear out; destroy by wearing. **4.** to exhaust in strength or endurance. **5.** to pass (time).

out·weigh (out′wā′), *v.t.* **1.** to exceed in value, importance, influence, etc. **2.** to be too heavy or burdensome for. **3.** to exceed in weight.

out·went (out′went′), *v.* pt. of **outgo.**

out·wind (out′wind′), *v.t.* to cause to be out of breath: *A fierce race had outwinded the runners.*

out·wit (out′wit′), *v.t.*, **-wit·ted, -wit·ting. 1.** to get the better of by superior ingenuity or cleverness: *to outwit a dangerous opponent.* **2.** *Archaic.* to surpass in wisdom or knowledge. —**Syn. 1.** outmaneuver, outthink, finesse.

out·work (*v.* out′wûrk′; *n.* out′wûrk′), *v.t.*, **-worked** or **-wrought, -work·ing,** *n.* —*v.t.* **1.** to surpass in working; work harder or faster than. **2.** to work out or carry on to a conclusion; finish. **3.** *Archaic.* to outdo in workmanship. —*n.* **4.** a minor defense lying outside the principal fortification limits. [ME: to complete] —**out′work′er,** *n.*

out·worn (out′wōrn′, -wôrn′), *adj.* **1.** out-of-date; obsolete, as opinions, ideas, etc. **2.** worn-out, as clothes. **3.** exhausted in strength or endurance, as persons. —*v.* **4.** pp. of **outwear.**

out·write (out′rīt′), *v.t.*, **-wrote** or (*Archaic*) **-writ; -written** or (*Archaic*) **-writ; -writ·ing. 1.** to write more or better than. **2.** to surmount or dispel by writing: *to outwrite one's melancholy.*

ou·zel (o͞o′zəl), *n.* any of several black, European thrushes, esp. *Turdus torquatus,* having a band of white across the chest. Also, **ousel.** [ME *osel,* OE *ōsle;* c. G *Amsel,* perh. also L *merula;* see MERLE]

ou·zo (o͞o′zō; *Gk.* o͞o′zô), *n.* an anise-flavored liqueur of Greece. [< NGk *oúzo(n)*]

o·va (ō′və), *n.* pl. of **ovum.**

o·val (ō′vəl), *adj.* **1.** having the general form, shape, or outline of an egg; egg-shaped. **2.** ellipsoidal or elliptical. —*n.* **3.** any of various objects of oval shape. **4.** a body or plane figure that is oval in shape or outline. **5.** *Informal.* a foot-

out′ri′val, *v.t.*, **-valed, -val·ing** or (*esp. Brit.*) **-valled, -val·ling.**
out′score′, *v.t.*, **-scored, -scor·ing.**
out′shout′, *v.t.*
out′sing′, *v.t.*, **-sang, -sung, -sing·ing.**
out′sleep′, *v.t.*, **-slept, -sleep·ing.**
out′so·phis′ti·cate′, *v.t.*, **-cat·ed, -cat·ing.**
out′spell′, *v.t.*
out′swim′, *v.t.*, **-swam, -swum, -swim·ming.**
out′thun′der, *v.t.*
out′trade′, *v.t.*, **-trad·ed, -trad·ing.**
out′walk′, *v.t.*
out′yell′, *v.t.*

ball. [< NL *ōvāl(is).* See OVUM, -AL[1]] —**o′val·ly,** *adv.* —**o′val·ness, o·val·i·ty** (ō val′i tē), *n.*

O′val Of′fice, 1. the office of the President of the United States, located in the White House. **2.** this office regarded as the seat of executive power in the federal government. [so called because of its shape]

o·var·i·ot·o·my (ō vâr′ē ot′ə mē), *n., pl.* **-mies.** *Surg.* incision into or removal of an ovary. [< NL *ōvāriotomia*]

o·va·ri·tis (ō′və rī′tis), *n. Pathol.* oophoritis. [< NL]

o·va·ry (ō′və rē), *n., pl.* **-ries. 1.** *Anat., Zool.* the female gonad or reproductive gland, in which the ova and the hormones that regulate female secondary sex characteristics develop. **2.** *Bot.* the enlarged lower part of the pistil in angiospermous plants, enclosing the ovules or young seeds. [< NL *ōvāri(um).* See OVUM, -ARY] —**o·var·i·an** (ō vâr′ē ən), *adj.*

o·vate (ō′vāt), *adj.* **1.** egg-shaped. **2.** *Bot.* **a.** having a plane figure like the longitudinal section of an egg. **b.** having such a figure with the broader end at the base, as a leaf. [< L *ōvāt(us).* See OVUM, -ATE[1]] —**o′vate·ly,** *adv.*

Ovate leaf

o·va·tion (ō vā′shən), *n.* **1.** an enthusiastic public reception of a person; enthusiastic applause. **2.** *Rom. Hist.* the ceremonial entrance into Rome of a commander whose victories did not warrant a triumph. Cf. **triumph** (def. 3). [< L *ovātiōn-* (s. of *ovātiō*) a rejoicing, shouting] —**o·va′tion·al,** *adj.*

ov·en (uv′ən), *n.* **1.** a heated chamber or compartment, as in a stove, for baking, roasting, heating, drying, etc. **2.** a primitive oven usually made of mud and in the shape of a mound about three ft. high. [ME; OE *ofen;* c. G *Ofen,* Icel *ofn*] —**ov′en·like′,** *adj.*

ov·en·bird (uv′ən bûrd′), *n.* **1.** an American warbler, *Seiurus aurocapillus,* that builds an oven-shaped nest of leaves, twigs, etc., on the forest floor. **2.** any of several South American passerine birds of the genus *Furnarius* or of the family *Furnariidae,* certain species of which build an oven-shaped nest.

ov·en·ware (uv′ən wâr′), *n.* heat-resistant dishes of glass, pottery, etc., for baking and serving food.

o·ver (ō′vər), *prep.,* **1.** above in place or position: *the roof over one's head.* **2.** above and to the other side of: *to leap over a wall.* **3.** above in authority, rank, power, etc. **4.** so as to rest on or cover; on or upon: *Throw a sheet over the bed.* **5.** on or upon, so as to cause an apparent change in one's mood, attitude, etc.: *I can't imagine what has come over her.* **6.** on or on top of: *to hit someone over the head.* **7.** here and there on or in. **8.** through all parts of; all through. **9.** from side to side of; to the other side of; across: *to go over a bridge.* **10.** on the other side of; across: *lands over the sea.* **11.** reaching higher than, so as to submerge. **12.** in excess of; more than. **13.** above in degree, quantity, etc. **14.** in preference to. **15.** throughout the length of. **16.** until after the end of: *to adjourn over the holidays.* **17.** throughout the duration of: *over a long period of years.* **18.** in reference to, concerning, or about: *to quarrel over a matter.* **19.** while engaged in or occupied with: *to fall asleep over one's work.* **20.** across; to the other side of: *to sell drugs over the counter.* **21.** (used to indicate a means of communication): *I heard it over the radio.* **22. over and above,** in addition to; besides. —*adv.* **23.** beyond the top or upper surface or edge of something: *a roof that hangs over.* **24.** so as to cover the surface or affect the whole surface. **25.** through a region, area, etc. **26.** at some distance, as in a direction indicated: *He lives over by the hill.* **27.** from side to side; across; to the other side: *to sail over.* **28.** across an intervening space. **29.** from beginning to end; throughout: *to read a thing over.* **30.** from one person, party, etc., to another. **31.** on the other side, as of a sea, a river, or any space: *over in Europe.* **32.** *U.S.* from or to Europe by crossing the Atlantic, esp. as an emigrant from Europe: *Her ancestors came over on the* Mayflower. **33.** so as to displace from an upright position: *to knock over a glass of milk.* **34.** once more; again: *to do a thing over.* **35.** in repetition or succession: *twenty times over.* **36.** in excess or addition. **37.** in excess of or beyond a certain amount: *Five goes into seven once, with two over.* **38.** throughout or beyond a period of time: *to stay over till Monday.* **39.** to one's residence, office, or the like. **40. all over, a.** over the entire surface of; everywhere. **b.** thoroughly; entirely. **c.** finished. **41. all over with,** ended; finished. **42. over again,** in repetition; once more. **43. over and over,** several times; repeatedly. **44. over there,** *U.S. Informal.* (during and after World War I) in or to Europe. —*adj.* **45.** upper; higher up. **46.** higher in authority, station, etc. **47.** serving, or intended to serve, as an outer covering; outer. **48.** remaining or additional, surplus; extra. **49.** too great; excessive (usually used in combination). **50.** ended; done; past: *when the war was over.* —*n.* **51.** an amount in excess or addition; extra. **52.** *Mil.* a shot that strikes or bursts beyond the target. **53.** *Cricket.* **a.** the number of balls, usually six, delivered between successive changes of bowlers. **b.** the part of the game played between such changes. [ME; OE *ofer;* c. D *over,* G *ober;* akin to L *super,* Gk *hypér,* Skt *upari.* See UP, HYPER-]

over-, a prefixal use of **over,** *prep., adv.,* or *adj.,* occurring in various senses in compounds (*overboard; overcoat; overhang; overlap; overlord; overrun; overthrow*), and esp. employed, with the sense of "over the limit," "to excess," "too much," "too;" to form verbs, adjectives, adverbs, and nouns (*overact; overcapitalize; overcrowd; overfull; overmuch; oversupply; overweight*), and many others, mostly self-explanatory: a hyphen, which is commonly absent from old or well-established formations, is often used in new coinages or in any words whose component parts it may be desirable to set off distinctly. [ME; OE *ofer-.* See OVER]

o·ver·a·bun·dance (ō′vər ə bun′dəns), *n.* an excessive amount or abundance; surfeit. [ME] —**o′ver·a·bun′dant,** *adj.* —**o′ver·a·bun′dant·ly,** *adv.*

o·ver·a·chieve (ō′vər ə chēv′), *v.i.,* **-a·chieved, -a·chiev·ing.** *Educ.* (of a student) to perform academically above the potential indicated by his scores on tests of mental ability. —**o′ver·a·chieve′ment,** *n.* —**o′ver·a·chiev′er,** *n.*

o·ver·act (ō′vər akt′), *v.t., v.i.* to act in an exaggerated manner, esp. as in a dramatic performance.

o·ver·ac·tive (ō′vər ak′tiv), *adj.* active to excess; too active. —**o′ver·ac·tiv′i·ty, o′ver·ac′tive·ness,** *n.*

o·ver·age[1] (ō′vər āj′), *adj.* beyond the required or desired age: *overage for the draft.* [OVER- + AGE]

o·ver·age[2] (ō′vər ij), *n. Com.* an excess supply of merchandise. [OVER- + -AGE]

o·ver·all (*adv.* ō′vər ôl′; *adj., n.* ō′vər ôl′), *adv., adj.* **1.** from one extreme limit of a thing to the other. **2.** covering or including everything. —*n.* **3. overalls,** a man's loose work trousers, usually with a part covering the chest and having straps over the shoulders. **4.** *Brit.* a smock or loose housedress. [ME *overal* (adv.), OE *ofer eall*]

o·ver·anx·ious (ō′vər angk′shəs, -ang′-), *adj.* excessively anxious. —**o·ver·anx·i·e·ty** (ō′vər ang zī′i tē), **o′ver·anx′ious·ness,** *n.* —**o′ver·anx′ious·ly,** *adv.*

o·ver·arm (ō′vər ärm′), *adj.* thrown or performed with the arm above the shoulder.

o·ver·ate (ō′vər āt′), *v.* pt. of **overeat.**

o·ver·awe (ō′vər ô′), *v.t.,* **-awed, -aw·ing.** to restrain or subdue by inspiring awe; intimidate.

o·ver·bal·ance (*v.* ō′vər bal′əns; *n.* ō′vər bal′əns), *v.,* **-anced, -anc·ing,** *n.* —*v.t.* **1.** to outweigh: *The opportunity overbalances the disadvantages.* **2.** to cause to lose balance or to fall or turn over. —*n.* **3.** an excessive weight or amount.

o·ver·bear (ō′vər bâr′), *v.,* **-bore, -borne, -bear·ing.** —*v.t.* **1.** to bear over or down by weight or force. **2.** to overcome or overwhelm. **3.** to prevail over or overrule (wishes, objections, etc.). **4.** to treat in a domineering way; dominate. —*v.i.* **5.** to produce fruit or progeny so abundantly as to impair the health. —**o′ver·bear′er,** *n.*

o·ver·bear·ing (ō′vər bâr′ing), *adj.* domineering; dictatorial; haughtily or rudely arrogant. —**o′ver·bear′ing·ly,** *adv.* —**o′ver·bear′ing·ness,** *n.*

o·ver·bid (*v.* ō′vər bid′; *n.* ō′vər bid′), *v.,* **-bid, -bid·ding,** *n.* —*v.t.* **1.** to bid more than the value of (a thing). **2.** to outbid. —*v.i.* **3.** to bid more than the actual value or worth. —*n.* **4.** a higher bid.

o·ver·bite (ō′vər bīt′), *n. Dentistry.* occlusion in which the upper incisor teeth overlap the lower.

o·ver·blow (ō′vər blō′), *v.,* **-blew, -blown, -blow·ing.** —*v.t.* **1.** to give excessive importance or value to. **2.** to blow (a wind instrument or an organ pipe) in such a way as to produce overtones. —*v.i.* **3.** *Music.* to blow a wind instrument with extra pressure in order to produce specific overtones instead of the fundamental tones. [ME]

o·ver·blown[1] (ō′vər blōn′), *adj.* **1.** overdone or excessive. **2.** of unusually large size or proportions. **3.** overinflated; turgid; bombastic; pretentious. —*v.* **4.** pp. of **overblow.**

o·ver·blown[2] (ō′vər blōn′), *adj.* (of a flower) more than full-blown: *an overblown rose.*

o·ver·board (ō′vər bōrd′, -bôrd′), *adv.* **1.** over the side of a ship or boat, esp. into or in the water: *to fall overboard.* **2. go overboard,** to go to extremes, esp. in regard to approval or disapproval of a person or thing. [ME *over bord,* OE *ofer bord*]

o·ver·borne (ō′vər bōrn′, -bôrn′), *adj.* **1.** overcome; crushed; oppressed. —*v.* **2.** pp. of **overbear.**

o·ver·buy (ō′vər bī′), *v.,* **-bought, -buy·ing.** —*v.t.* **1.** to purchase in excessive quantities. **2.** *Finance.* to buy on margin in excess of one's ability to provide added security in an emergency, as in a falling market. —*v.i.* **3.** to buy regardless of one's financial ability. [ME *overbiggen*]

o·ver·call (*n.* ō′vər kôl′; *v.* ō′vər kôl′, ō′vər kôl′), *Cards.* **1.** a bid higher than the previous bid. **2.** *Bridge.* a bid higher than the previous bid of an opponent that was not followed by a bid or double by one's partner. —*v.t.* **3.** to bid higher than. —*v.i.* **4.** to make an overcall.

o·ver·came (ō′vər kām′), *v.* pt. of **overcome.**

o·ver·cap·i·tal·ise (ō′vər kap′i t^əlīz′), *v.t.,* **-ised, -is·ing.** *Chiefly Brit.* overcapitalize. —**o′ver·cap′i·tal·i·sa′tion,** *n.*

o·ver·cap·i·tal·ize (ō′vər kap′i t^əlīz′), *v.t.,* **-ized, -iz·ing. 1.** to fix the nominal value of the capital of (a company) in excess of the limits set by law or by sound financial policy. **2.** to provide an excessive amount of capital to or for (a business enterprise). —**o′ver·cap′i·tal·i·za′tion,** *n.*

o·ver·cast (*adj.* ō′vər kast′, -käst′, ō′vər kast′, -käst′; *v.* ō′vər kast′, -käst′, ō′vər kast′, -käst′; *n.* ō′vər kast′, -käst′), *adj., v.,* **-cast, -cast·ing,** *n.* —*adj.* **1.** overspread or covered with clouds; cloudy: *an overcast sky.* **2.** *Meteorol.* (of the sky) more than 95 percent covered by clouds. **3.** dark; gloomy. **4.** *Sewing.* sewn by overcasting. —*v.t.* **5.** to overcloud, darken, or make gloomy. **6.** to stitch (material) at intervals over an edge to prevent raveling. —*v.i.* **7.** to become cloudy or dark. —*n.* **8.** *Meteorol.* the condition of the sky when more than 95 percent covered by clouds. [ME (v.)]

o·ver·cast·ing (ō′vər kas′ting, -kä′sting), *n. Sewing.* **1.** the act of sewing along the edges of material with long, spaced stitches to prevent raveling. **2.** a series of stitches done in this manner.

o·ver·charge (*v.* ō′vər chärj′; *n.* ō′vər chärj′), *v.,* **-charged, -charg·ing,** *n.* —*v.t.* **1.** to charge (someone) too

o′ver·a·bound′, *n.*
o′ver·ac·cen′tu·ate′, *v.t.,* **-at·ed, -at·ing.**
o′ver·ac·cu′mu·la′tion, *n.*
o′ver·a·dorned′, *adj.*
o′ver·ad·vance′, *v.,* **-vanced, -vanc·ing,** *n.*
o′ver·af·fect′, *v.t.*
o′ver·ag·gres′sive, *adj.*
o′ver·am·bi′tious, *adj.;* **-ly,** *adv.*
o′ver·an′a·lyze′, *v.,* **-lyzed, -lyz·ing.**
o′ver·an′gry, *adj.*
o′ver·an′i·mat′ed, *adj.;* **-ly,** *adv.*
o′ver·an′i·ma′tion, *n.*
o′ver·ap·pre′ci·a′tion, *n.*
o′ver·ap·pre′ci·a′tive, *adj.*
o′ver·ap′pre·hen′sive, *adj.;* **-ly,** *adv.;* **-ness,** *n.*
o′ver·arch′, *v.*
o′ver·ar′gu·men′ta·tive, *adj.*
o′ver·as·sert′, *v.t.*
o′ver·as·ser′tion, *n.*
o′ver·as·ser′tive, *adj.;* **-ly,** *adv.;* **-ness,** *n.*
o′ver·as·sess′ment, *n.*
o′ver·as·sured′, *adj.*
o′ver·at·tached′, *adj.*
o′ver·at·ten′tive, *adj.;* **-ly,** *adv.;* **-ness,** *n.*
o′ver·big′, *adj.*
o′ver·bold′, *adj.*
o′ver·brave′, *adj.*
o′ver·bul′ky, *adj.*
o′ver·bur′den, *v.t.*
o′ver·bur′den·some, *adj.*
o′ver·bus′y, *adj.*
o′ver·ca·pac′i·ty, *n.*
o′ver·care′ful, *adj.*
o′ver·cas′u·al, *adj.*
o′ver·cau′tious, *adj.*
o′ver·cen′tral·i·za′tion, *n.*
o′ver·ce·re′bral, *adj.*

high a price. **2.** to fill too full; overload. **3.** to exaggerate. **—*v.i.* 4.** to make an excessive charge; charge too much for something. **—*n.* 5.** a charge in excess of a just price. **6.** an act of charging excessively. **7.** an excessive load. [ME] **—o′ver·charg′er,** *n.*

o·ver·check (ō′vər chek′), *n.* a checkrein passing from the bit, over a horse's head, to the saddle of a harness.

o·ver·clothes (ō′vər klōz′, -klōthz′), *n.* (*construed as pl.*) clothing worn outside other garments.

o·ver·cloud (ō′vər kloud′), *v.t.* **1.** to overspread with or as with clouds. **2.** to darken; obscure; make gloomy. **—*v.i.* 3.** to become clouded over or overcast.

o·ver·coat (ō′vər kōt′), *n.* a coat worn over the ordinary clothing, as in cold weather; a greatcoat.

o·ver·come (ō′vər kum′), *v.*, **-came, -come, -com·ing. —*v.t.* 1.** to get the better of in a struggle or conflict; conquer; defeat. **2.** to prevail over (opposition, objections, temptations, etc.); surmount. **3.** to overpower or overwhelm in body or mind, as does liquor, a drug, emotion, etc. **4.** *Archaic.* to overspread or overrun. **—*v.i.* 5.** to gain the victory; win; conquer. [ME; OE *ofercuman*] **—o′ver·com′er,** *n.* **—Syn. 1.** vanquish. See **defeat.**

o·ver·com·pen·sa·tion (ō′vər kom′pən sā′shən), *n.* *Psychoanal.* an exaggerated striving to neutralize and conceal a strong but unacceptable character trait by substituting for it an opposite trait. **—o·ver·com·pen·sa·to·ry** (ō′vər kəm pen′sə tōr′ē, -tôr′ē), *adj.*

o·ver·con·fi·dent (ō′vər kon′fi dənt), *adj.* too confident. **—o′ver·con′fi·dence,** *n.* **—o′ver·con′fi·dent·ly,** *adv.*

o·ver·crowd (ō′vər kroud′), *v.t., v.i.* to crowd to excess.

o·ver·de·vel·op (ō′vər di vel′əp), *v.t., v.i.* to develop to excess: *to overdevelop a photograph; to overdevelop feelings of responsibility.* **—o′ver·de·vel′op·ment,** *n.*

o·ver·do (ō′vər do͞o′), *v.*, **-did, -done, -do·ing. —*v.t.* 1.** to do to excess: *to overdo exercise.* **2.** to carry to excess or beyond the proper limit. **3.** to overact (a part); exaggerate. **4.** to overtax the strength of; fatigue; exhaust. **5.** to cook too much or too long; overcook. **—*v.i.* 6.** to do too much; go to an extreme. [ME *overdo(n)*, OE *oferdōn*] **—o′ver·do′er,** *n.*

o·ver·done (ō′vər dun′), *v.* **1.** pp. of **overdo. —*adj.* 2.** (of food) cooked too much or too long. **3.** excessive; exaggerated. **4.** overtaxed; exhausted.

o·ver·dose (*n.* ō′vər dōs′; *v.* ō′vər dōs′), *n., v.*, **-dosed, -dos·ing. —*n.* 1.** Also, **o′ver·dos′age.** an excessive dose. **—*v.t.* 2.** to give an overdose to; dose to excess.

o·ver·draft (ō′vər draft′, -dräft′), *n.* **1.** a draft in excess of one's credit balance, or the amount of the excess. **2.** the action of overdrawing an account, as at a bank. **3.** a draft made to pass over a fire, as in a furnace.

o·ver·draw (ō′vər drô′), *v.*, **-drew, -drawn, -draw·ing. —*v.t.* 1.** to draw upon (an account, allowance, etc.) in excess of the balance standing to one's credit or at one's disposal. **2.** to strain, as a bow, by drawing too far. **3.** to exaggerate in drawing, depicting, or describing. **—*v.i.* 4.** to overdraw an account or the like. **5.** (of a stove, fireplace, etc.) to draw excessively; have too strong an updraft. [ME]

o·ver·dress (*v.* ō′vər dres′; *n.* ō′vər dres′), *v.*, **-dressed, -dress·ing,** *n.* **—*v.t., v.i.* 1.** to dress too warmly or with too much display. **—*n.* 2.** a dress worn over another which it covers either partially or completely.

o·ver·drive (*v.* ō′vər drīv′; *n.* ō′vər drīv′), *v.*, **-drove, -driv·en, -driv·ing,** *n.* **—*v.t.* 1.** to push or carry to excess; overwork. **2.** to drive too hard. **—*n.* 3.** *Mach.* a device containing a gear set at such ratio and arrangement as to provide a drive-shaft speed greater than the engine crankshaft speed. [ME *overdrive(n)* (v.)]

o·ver·due (ō′vər do͞o′, -dyo͞o′), *adj.* **1.** past due, as a belated train or a bill not paid by the designated date; late. **2.** too long awaited; needed or expected for an undue length of time. **3.** more than sufficiently advanced, mature, or ready.

o·ver·ea·ger (ō′vər ē′gər), *adj.* excessively or unduly eager: *overeager for riches.* **—o′ver·ea′ger·ly,** *adv.* **—o′ver·ea′ger·ness,** *n.*

o·ver·eat (ō′vər ēt′), *v.*, **-ate, -eat·en, -eat·ing. —*v.i.* 1.** to eat too much. **—*v.t.* 2.** to eat more than is good for (oneself). **—o′ver·eat′er,** *n.*

o·ver·e·lab·o·rate (*adj.* ō′vər i lab′ər it; *v.* ō′vər i lab′ə rāt′), *adj., v.*, **-rat·ed, -rat·ing. —*adj.* 1.** excessively or fussily elaborate, ornate, detailed, etc. **—*v.t.* 2.** to fill or supply with excessive or fussy detail: *He so overelaborates his jokes that they lose their humor.* **—*v.i.* 3.** to add excessive details, as in writing or speaking. **—o′ver·e·lab′o·rate·ly,** *adv.* **—o′ver·e·lab′o·ra′tion, o′ver·e·lab′o·rate·ness,** *n.*

o·ver·es·ti·mate (*v.* ō′vər es′tə māt′; *n.* ō′vər es′tə mit), *v.*, **-mat·ed, -mat·ing,** *n.* **—*v.t.* 1.** to estimate at too high a value, amount, rate, or the like. **—*n.* 2.** an estimate that is too high. **—o′ver·es′ti·ma′tion,** *n.*

o·ver·ex·ert (ō′vər ig zûrt′), *v.t.* to exert excessively. **—o′ver·ex·er′tion,** *n.*

o·ver·ex·pose (ō′vər ik spōz′), *v.t.*, **-posed, -pos·ing. 1.** to expose too much, as to the sun, cold, light rays, etc. (often used reflexively). **2.** *Photog.* to expose (a film or the like) for too long a time.

o·ver·ex·po·sure (ō′vər ik spō′zhər), *n.* excessive exposure, esp. of photographic film or a sensitized plate to light rays.

o·ver·ex·tend (ō′vər ik stend′), *v.t.* to extend (credit, welcome, etc.) beyond a reasonable or established limit.

o·ver·fish (ō′vər fish′), *v.t.* **1.** to fish (an area) excessively; exhaust the supply of usable fish in (certain waters). **—*v.i.* 2.** to fish so as to deplete the supply of fish in certain waters.

o·ver·flight (ō′vər flīt′), *n.* an air flight that passes over a specific area, territory, country, etc.

o·ver·flow (*v.* ō′vər flō′; *n.* ō′vər flō′), *v.*, **-flowed, -flown, -flow·ing,** *n.* **—*v.i.* 1.** to flow or run over, as rivers, water, etc. **2.** to have the contents flowing over, as an overfull vessel. **3.** to pass from one place or part to another as if flowing from an overfull space: *The population overflowed into the adjoining territory.* **4.** to be filled or supplied with in great measure. **—*v.t.* 5.** to flow over; flood; inundate. **6.** to flow over or beyond (the brim, banks, borders, etc.). **7.** to cause to overflow. **8.** to flow over the edge or brim of (a vessel, container, etc.). **9.** to fill to the point of running over. **—*n.* 10.** an overflowing. **11.** that which flows or runs over. **12.** an excess or superabundance. **13.** a portion crowded out of an overfilled place. **14.** an outlet for excess liquid. [ME *overflowe(n)*, OE *oferflōwan*] **—o′ver·flow′a·ble,** *adj.* **—o′ver·flow′ing·ly,** *adv.*

o·ver·fly (ō′vər flī′), *v.*, **-flew, -flown, -fly·ing. —*v.t.* 1.** to fly over (a specific area, territory, country, etc.). **2.** to fly farther than or beyond; overshoot. **—*v.i.* 3.** to fly over a specific area, territory, country, etc.

o·ver·full (ō′vər fo͝ol′), *adj.* excessively full. [ME; OE *oferfull*] **—o′ver·full′ness,** *n.*

o·ver·gar·ment (ō′vər gär′mənt), *n.* an outer garment.

o·ver·gild (ō′vər gild′), *v.t.*, **-gild·ed** or **-gilt, -gild·ing. 1.** to cover with gilding. **2.** to tint with a golden color. [ME *overgild(en)*, OE *ofergyldan*]

o·ver·glaze (*n., adj.* ō′vər glāz′; *v.* ō′vər glāz′, ō′vər-glāz′), *n., v.*, **-glazed, -glaz·ing,** *adj.* *Ceram.* **—*n.* 1.** a color or glaze applied to an existing glaze. **—*v.t.* 2.** to cover or decorate (a ceramic object) with an overglaze. **—*adj.* 3.** used as an overglaze.

o·ver·graze (ō′vər grāz′, ō′vər grāz′), *v.t.*, **-grazed, -graz·ing.** to graze (land) to excess.

o·ver·grow (ō′vər grō′, ō′vər grō′), *v.*, **-grew, -grown, -grow·ing. —*v.t.* 1.** to grow over; cover with a growth of something. **2.** to outdo in growing; choke or supplant by a more exuberant growth. **3.** to grow beyond, grow too large for, or outgrow. **—*v.i.* 4.** to grow to excess; grow too large. **5.** to grow over, as with weeds; become grown over. [ME *overgrow(en)*]

o·ver·growth (ō′vər grōth′), *n.* **1.** a growth overspreading or covering something. **2.** excessive growth.

o·ver·hand (ō′vər hand′), *adv.* Also, **o′ver·hand′ed. 1.** with the hand over the object: *to grasp one's fork overhand.* **2.** with the hand and part or all of the arm raised above the shoulder: *to pitch overhand.* **3.** (in sewing and embroidery) with close, shallow stitches over two edges. **—*adj.* 4.** thrown or performed overhand: *overhand stroke.* **5.** overarm. **—*n.* 6.** an overhand stroke or delivery. **—*v.t.* 7.** to sew overhand.

o′verhand knot′, a simple knot of various uses that slips easily. See illus. at **knot.**

o·ver·hang (*v.* ō′vər hang′; *n.* ō′vər hang′), *v.*, **-hung, -hang·ing,** *n.* **—*v.t.* 1.** to hang or be suspended over. **2.** to extend, project, or jut over. **3.** to impend over, or threaten, as danger or evil. **4.** to spread throughout; permeate; pervade. **—*v.i.* 5.** to hang over; project or jut out over something below. **—*n.* 6.** something that extends or juts out over; projection. **7.** the extent of projection, as of the bow of a vessel. **8.** an excess or surplus, as of securities, currencies, raw materials in inventory, etc.

o·ver·haul (*v.* ō′vər hôl′, ō′vər hôl′; *n.* ō′vər hôl′), *v.t.* **1.** to investigate or examine thoroughly, as for repair, re-

o′ver·civ′il, *adj.*
o′ver·civ′i·lize′, *v.t.*, **-lized, -liz·ing.**
o′ver·clean′, *adj.*
o′ver·com′mon, *adj.*
o′ver·com·pet′i·tive, *adj.*
o′ver·com·pla′cen·cy, *n.*
o′ver·com·pla′cent, *adj.*
o′ver·com·plex′, *adj.*
o′ver·com′pli·cate′, *v.t.*, **-cat·ed, -cat·ing.**
o′ver·con′cen·trate′, *v.t.*, **-trat·ed, -trat·ing.**
o′ver·con′cen·tra′tion, *n.*
o′ver·con·cern′, *n.*
o′ver·con′sci·en′tious, *adj.*
o′ver·con·serv′a·tive, *adj.*
o′ver·con·sid′er·ate, *adj.*
o′ver·con·sume′, *v.*, **-sumed, -sum·ing.**
o′ver·con·sump′tion, *n.*
o′ver·cook′, *v.t.*
o′ver·cool′, *adj., v.t.*
o′ver·cor·rect′ *adj., v.*
o′ver·cost′ly, *adj.*
o′ver·crit′i·cal, *adj.*
o′ver·crit′i·cize′, *v.*, **-cized, -ciz·ing.**
o′ver·cul′ti·vate′, *v.t.*, **-vat·ed, -vat·ing.**
o′ver·cun′ning, *adj.*
o′ver·cu′ri·ous, *adj.*
o′ver·dec′o·rate′, *v.t.*, **-rat·ed, -rat·ing.**
o′ver·de·fen′sive, *adj.*
o′ver·def′er·en′tial, *adj.*
o′ver·de·lib′er·ate′, *v.*, **-at·ed, -at·ing.**
o′ver·de·lib′er·ate, *adj.*
o′ver·del′i·cate, *adj.*
o′ver·de·pend′ent, *adj.*
o′ver·de·sir′ous, *adj.*
o′ver·de·tailed′, *adj.*
o′ver·dil′i·gent, *adj.*; **-ly,** *adv.*
o′ver·di·lute′, *v.*, **-lut·ed, -lut·ing;** *adj.*
o′ver·dis′ci·pline, *v.t.*, **-plined, -plin·ing.**
o′ver·dis′tant, *adj.*
o′ver·di·ver′si·fi·ca′tion, *n.*
o′ver·di·ver′si·fy′, *v.*, **-fied, -fy·ing.**
o′ver·di·ver′si·ty, *n.*
o′ver·dram′a·tize′, *v.t.*, **-tized, -tiz·ing.**
o′ver·drink′, *v.*
o′ver·ear′nest, *adj.*
o′ver·ed′u·cate′, *v.t.*, **-cat·ed, -cat·ing.**
o′ver·ef·fu′sive, *adj.*
o′ver·e·late′, *v.t.*, **-lat·ed, -lat·ing.**
o′ver·em·bel′lish, *v.t.*
o′ver·em·broi′der, *v.t.*
o′ver·e·mo′tion·al, *adj.*
o′ver·e·mo′tion·al·ize′, *v.t.*, **-ized, -iz·ing.**
o′ver·em′pha·sis, *n.*
o′ver·em′pha·size′, *v.t.*, **-sized, -siz·ing.**
o′ver·em·phat′ic, *adj.*
o′ver·em′u·la′tion, *n.*
o′ver·en·thu′si·asm, *n.*
o′ver·en·thu′si·as′tic, *adj.*
o′ver·ex·act′ing, *adj.*
o′ver·ex·cit′a·ble, *adj.*; **-cit′a·bly,** *adv.*
o′ver·ex·cite′, *v.t.*, **-cit·ed, -cit·ing.**
o′ver·ex′er·cise′, *v.t.*, **-cised, -cis·ing;** *n.*
o′ver·ex·pand′, *v.*
o′ver·ex·pan′sion, *n.*
o′ver·ex·pect′ant, *adj.*
o′ver·ex·pend′, *v.t.*
o′ver·ex·pen′di·ture, *n.*
o′ver·ex·plic′it, *adj.*
o′ver·ex·pres′sive, *adj.*; **-ly,** *adv.*; **-ness,** *n.*
o′ver·fac′ile, *adj.*
o′ver·fa·mil′iar, *adj.*
o′ver·fa·mil′i·ar′i·ty, *n.*
o′ver·fan′ci·ful, *adj.*
o′ver·far′, *adj., adv.*
o′ver·fas·tid′i·ous, *adj.*
o′ver·fa·tigue′, *v.t.*, **-tigued, -ti·guing.**
o′ver·fear′ful, *adj.*
o′ver·feed′, *v.*, **-fed, -feed·ing.**
o′ver·fill′, *v.*
o′ver·fond′, *adj.*
o′ver·frag′ile, *adj.*
o′ver·fur′nish, *v.t.*
o′ver·gen′er·al·i·za′tion, *n.*
o′ver·gen′er·al·ize′, *v.t.*, **-ized, -iz·ing.**
o′ver·gen′er·ous, *adj.*
o′ver·hast′ily, *adv.*
o′ver·hast′i·ness, *n.*
o′ver·hast′y, *adj.*

vision, etc. **2.** to make necessary repairs on; restore to serviceable condition. **3.** to haul or turn over for examination. **4.** to gain upon or overtake, as in a race. **5.** *Naut.* **a.** to slacken (a rope) by hauling in the opposite direction to that in which it was drawn taut. **b.** to release the blocks of (a tackle). —*n.* **6.** Also, **o′ver·haul′ing.** a general examination and repair. —**o′ver·haul′er,** *n.*

o·ver·head (*adv.* ō′vər hed′; *adj., n.* ō′vər hed′), *adv.* **1.** over one's head; aloft; up in the air or sky, esp. near the zenith. **2.** so as to be completely submerged or deeply involved. —*adj.* **3.** situated, operating, or passing above, aloft, or over the head. **4.** general; average; not specific or particular. —*n.* **5.** the general cost of running a business. **6.** *Accounting.* that part of manufacturing costs for which cost per unit produced is not readily assignable. **7.** *Tennis, Badminton.* a stroke in which the ball or shuttlecock is hit with a downward motion from above the head; smash.

o·ver·hear (ō′vər hēr′), *v.t.*, **-heard, -hear·ing.** to hear (speech or a speaker) without the speaker's intention or knowledge. —**o′ver·hear′er,** *n.*

o·ver·heat (ō′vər hēt′), *v.t.* **1.** to heat to excess. **2.** to excite or agitate; make vehement. —*v.i.* **3.** to become overheated. —*n.* **4.** the state or condition of being overheated; excessive heat, agitation, or vehemence. [ME *overhet(en)*]

o·ver·hung (*v.* ō′vər hung′; *adj.* ō′vər hung′), *v.* **1.** pt. and pp. of **overhang.** —*adj.* **2.** hung or suspended from above: *an overhung door.*

O·ver·ijs·sel (ō′vər ī′səl), *n.* a province in the E Netherlands. 835,494 (1962); 1254 sq. mi. *Cap.:* Zwolle.

o·ver·in·dulge (ō′vər in dulj′), *v.t., v.i.*, **-dulged, -dulg·ing.** to indulge to excess: *to overindulge one's fondness for candy.* —**o′ver·in·dul′gence,** *n.* —**o′ver·in·dul′gent,** *adj.* —**o′ver·in·dul′gent·ly,** *adv.*

o·ver·is·sue (ō′vər ish′o͞o *or, esp. Brit.,* -is′yo͞o), *n.* an excessive issue of stocks or bonds.

o·ver·joy (ō′vər joi′), *v.t.* to cause to feel great joy.

o·ver·kill (ō′vər kil′), *n.* **1.** the capacity of a nation to destroy, by nuclear weapons, more of an enemy than would be necessary for a military victory. **2.** any effect or result that far exceeds what is necessary or intended.

o·ver·lade (ō′vər lād′), *v.t.*, **-lad·ed, -lad·en** or **-lad·ed, -lad·ing.** to overload (usually used in pp. *overladen*): *a table overladen with rich food.* [ME *overlade(n)* = *over* OVER- + *laden* to load; see LADE]

o·ver·land (ō′vər land′, -lənd), *adv.* **1.** by land. **2.** over or across the land. —*adj.* **3.** proceeding, performed, or carried on overland: *overland transportation.* [ME *overlond*]

O·ver·land (ō′vər lənd), *n.* a city in E Missouri, near St. Louis. 24,949 (1970).

O′verland Park′, a city in E Kansas, near Kansas City. 79,034 (1970).

o′verland stage′, a stagecoach used in the Western U.S. during the middle of the 19th century.

o·ver·lap (*v.* ō′vər lap′; *n.* ō′vər lap′), *v.*, **-lapped, -lap·ping,** *n.* —*v.t.* **1.** to lap over (something else or each other); extend over and cover a part of. **2.** to cover and extend beyond (something else). **3.** to coincide in part with; have in common with. —*v.i.* **4.** to lap over. —*n.* **5.** the act or an instance of overlapping. **6.** the extent or amount of overlapping. **7.** an overlapping part. **8.** the place of overlapping.

o·ver·lay[1] (*v.* ō′vər lā′; *n.* ō′vər lā′), *v.*, **-laid, -lay·ing,** *n.* —*v.t.* **1.** to lay or place (one thing) over or upon another. **2.** to cover, overspread, or surmount with something. **3.** to finish with a layer or applied decoration of something: *wood richly overlaid with gold.* **4.** *Print.* to put an overlay upon. —*n.* **5.** something laid over something else; covering. **6.** a layer or decoration of something applied: *an overlay of gold.* **7.** *Print.* a shaped piece of paper, or a sheet of paper reinforced at the proper places by shaped pieces, put on the tympan of a press to increase or equalize the impression. **8.** a transparent sheet giving special military information not ordinarily shown on maps, used by being placed over the map on which it is based. [ME]

o·ver·lay[2] (ō′vər lā′), *v.* pt. of **overlie.**

o·ver·leaf (ō′vər lēf′), *adv.* on the other side of the page or sheet: *continued overleaf.*

o·ver·leap (ō′vər lēp′), *v.t.* **-leaped** or **-leapt, -leap·ing.** **1.** to leap over or across. **2.** to overreach (oneself) by leaping too far. **3.** to pass over or omit. **4.** *Archaic.* to leap farther than; outleap. [ME *overlep(en),* OE *oferhlēapan*]

o·ver·lie (ō′vər lī′), *v.t.*, **-lay, -lain, -ly·ing.** **1.** to lie over or upon, as a covering, stratum, etc. **2.** to smother (an infant) by lying upon it, as in sleep. [ME *overlie(n), overligg(en)*]

o·ver·live (ō′vər liv′), *v.*, **-lived, -liv·ing.** *Archaic.* —*v.t.* **1.** to live or last longer than (another person, an era, etc.); outlast. —*v.i.* **2.** to survive or continue to live; live too long. [ME *overlive(n),* OE *oferlibben*] —**o′ver·liv′er,** *n.*

o·ver·load (*v.* ō′vər lōd′; *n.* o′vər lod′), *v.t.* **1.** to load to excess; overburden. —*n.* **2.** an excessive load.

o·ver·look (*v.* ō′vər lo͝ok′; *n.* ō′vər lo͝ok′), *v.t.* **1.** to fail to notice, perceive, or consider. **2.** to disregard or ignore indulgently, as faults, misconduct, etc. **3.** to look over, as from a higher position. **4.** to afford a view down over. **5.** to rise above. **6.** to excuse; pardon. **7.** to look over in inspection, examination, or perusal. **8.** to look after, oversee, or supervise. **9.** *Archaic.* to look upon with the evil eye; bewitch. —*n.* **10.** terrain, as on a cliff, that affords a view. [ME] —**Syn. 1.** miss. See **slight.**

o·ver·lord (ō′vər lôrd′), *n.* **1.** a person who is lord over another or over other lords. **2.** a person of great influence, authority, power, or the like. —*v.t.* **3.** to rule or govern arbitrarily or tyrannically; domineer. [ME] —**o′ver·lord′ship,** *n.*

o·ver·ly (ō′vər lē), *adv.* overmuch; excessively; too: *a voyage not overly dangerous.* [ME; OE *oferlīce*]

o·ver·ly·ing (ō′vər lī′ing), *v.* pp. of **overlie.**

o·ver·man (*n.* ō′vər mən *for 1, 2,* ō′vər man′ *for 3; v.* ō′vər man′), *n., pl.* **-men** (-mən *for 1, 2;* -men′ *for 3*), *v.*, **-manned, -man·ning.** —*n.* **1.** a foreman or overseer. **2.** *Chiefly Scot.* a person who arbitrates a dispute; an arbiter or umpire. **3.** *Archaic.* a superman. —*v.t.* **4.** to oversupply with men, esp. for service. [ME]

o·ver·mas·ter (ō′vər mas′tər, -mä′stər), *v.t.* to gain mastery over; overpower. [ME *overmaistre(n)*] —**o′ver·mas′ter·ing·ly,** *adv.*

o·ver·match (ō′vər mach′), *v.t.* **1.** to outmatch; surpass; defeat. **2.** to match (a competitor) against another of superior strength, ability, or the like. [ME *overmacche(n)*]

o·ver·much (ō′vər much′), *adj., n., adv.* too much. [ME]

o·ver·nice (ō′vər nīs′), *adj.* excessively particular; too fastidious: *He was unhampered by overnice manners.* [ME] —**o′ver·nice′ly,** *adv.* —**o′ver·nice′ness,** *n.*

o·ver·night (*adv.* ō′vər nīt′; *adj., n.* ō′vər nīt′), *adv.* **1.** for or during the night: *to stay overnight.* **2.** on the previous evening: *Preparations were made overnight.* **3.** very quickly; suddenly: *New suburbs sprang up overnight.* —*adj.* **4.** done, occurring, or continuing during the night: *an overnight stop.* **5.** staying for one night: *a group of overnight guests.* **6.** designed to be used on a trip or for a journey lasting one night or a very few nights: *an overnight bag.* **7.** valid for one night: *The corporal got an overnight pass.* **8.** of or pertaining to the previous evening: *an overnight decision.* **9.** occurring suddenly or within a very short time. —*n.* **10.** *Archaic.* the previous evening. [ME]

o·ver·night·er (ō′vər nīt′ər), *n.* a small, light suitcase adequate for use on a short trip. Also called **o′ver·night′ bag′.**

o·ver·op·ti·mism (ō′vər op′tə miz′əm), *n.* excessive or unfounded optimism. —**o′ver·op′ti·mist,** *n.* —**o′ver·op′ti·mis′tic,** *adj.* —**o′ver·op′ti·mis′ti·cal·ly,** *adv.*

o·ver·or·gan·ize (ō′vər ôr′gə nīz′), *v.t.*, **-ized, -iz·ing.** —*v.t.* **1.** to stress status, rules, and details excessively. —*v.i.* **2.** to become overorganized. —**o′ver·or′gan·i·za′tion,** *n.* —**o′ver·or′gan·iz′er,** *n.*

o·ver·pass (*n.* ō′vər pas′, -päs′; *v.* ō′vər pas′, -päs′), *n., v.*, **-passed** or **-past, -pass·ing.** —*n.* **1.** a highway or railway bridge crossing some barrier, as another highway or railroad tracks. —*v.t.* **2.** to pass over or traverse (a region, space, etc.). **3.** to pass beyond (specified limits, bounds, etc.); exceed; overstep; transgress. **4.** to get over (obstacles, difficulties, etc.); surmount. **5.** to go beyond, exceed, or surpass. **6.** to pass through (time, experiences, etc.). **7.** to overlook; disregard; omit. —*v.i.* **8.** to pass over; pass by. [ME]

o·ver·pay (ō′vər pā′), *v.t.*, **-paid, -pay·ing.** **1.** to pay more than (an amount due): *I received a credit after overpaying the bill.* **2.** to pay (a person) in excess: *We were certain we had overpaid him for helping us.* —**o·ver·pay·ment** (ō′vər pā′mənt, ō′vər pā′mənt), *n.*

o·ver·per·suade (ō′vər pər swād′), *v.t.*, **-suad·ed, -suad·ing.** to persuade (a person) against his inclination or intention. —**o′ver·per·sua′sion,** *n.*

o·ver·play (ō′vər plā′), *v.t.* **1.** to exaggerate or overemphasize (one's performance in a play, an emotion, an effect, etc.). **2.** to overstress the value or importance of. —*v.i.* **3.** to exaggerate one's part, an effect, etc.; overact. **4.** *Golf.* to hit (the ball) past the putting green.

o·ver·plus (ō′vər plus′), *n.* an excess over a particular amount; surplus. [ME; partial trans. of OF *surplus* SURPLUS]

o·ver·pop·u·late (ō′vər pop′yə lāt′), *v.t.*, **-lat·ed, -lat·ing.** to fill with an excessive number of people. —**o′ver·pop′u·la′tion,** *n.*

o·ver·pow·er (ō′vər pou′ər), *v.t.* **1.** to overcome or overwhelm in feeling; affect or impress excessively. **2.** to overcome, master, or subdue by superior force. **3.** to overmaster the bodily powers or mental faculties of. **4.** to furnish or equip with excessive power. —**Syn. 2.** vanquish, subjugate, conquer, defeat, beat.

o·ver·pow·er·ing (ō′vər pou′ər ing), *adj.* that overpowers; overwhelming. —**o′ver·pow′er·ing·ly,** *adv.*

o·ver·print (*v.* ō′vər print′; *n.* ō′vər print′), *v.t.* **1.** *Print.* to print additional material or another color on a form or sheet previously printed. —*n.* **2.** *Print.* a quantity of printing in excess of that desired; overrun. **3.** *Philately.* **a.** any word, inscription, or device written or printed on the face of a stamp that alters, limits, or describes its use, place of issue, or character. **b.** a stamp so marked.

o·ver·pro·duce (ō′vər prə do͞os′, -dyo͞os′), *v.t., v.i.*, **-duced, -duc·ing.** to produce in excess of demand or of a stipulated amount.

o·ver·pro·duc·tion (ō′vər prə duk′shən), *n.* excessive production; production in excess of the demand.

o·ver·pro·nounce (ō′vər prə nouns′), *v.*, **-nounced, -nounc·ing.** —*v.t.* **1.** to pronounce (a word, syllable, etc.) in an exaggerated, affected, or overcareful manner. —*v.i.* **2.** to pronounce or speak overcarefully, affectedly, exaggeratedly, etc. —**o·ver·pro·nun·ci·a·tion** (ō′vər prə nun′sē ā′shən), *n.*

o·ver·proof (ō′vər pro͞of′), *adj.* containing a greater proportion of alcohol than proof spirit does.

o·ver·pro·por·tion (*v.* ō′vər prə pōr′shən, -pôr′-; *n.* ō′vər prə pōr′shən, -pôr′-), *v.t.* **1.** to make or measure in excess of the true or desired proportion. —*n.* **2.** the exces-

o′ver·hunt′, *v.t.*
o′ver·hur′ried, *adj.*
o′ver·i·de′al·is′tic, *adj.*
o′ver·i·de′al·ize′, *v.*, **-ized, -iz·ing.**
o′ver·im·ag′i·na′tive, *adj.*
o′ver·im·press′, *v.t.*
o′ver·im·pres′sion·a·ble, *adj.*
o′ver·in·cline′, *v.*, **-clined, -clin·ing.**
o′ver·in·dus′tri·al·ize′, *v.*, **-ized, -iz·ing.**
o′ver·in·flate′, *v.t.*, **-flat·ed, -flat·ing.**
o′ver·in′flu·ence, *v.t.*, **-enced, -enc·ing.**
o′ver·in′flu·en′tial, *adj.*
o′ver·in·sist′ence, *n.*
o′ver·in·sist′ent, *adj.*; **-ly,** *adv.*
o′ver·in·sure′, *v.t.*, **-sured, -sur·ing.**
o′ver·in′tel·lec′tu·al, *adj.*; **-ly,** *adv.*
o′ver·in·tense′, *adj.*; **-ly,** *adv.*
o′ver·in′ter·est, *n.*
o′ver·in·vest′, *v.*
o′ver·large′, *adj.*
o′ver·lav′ish, *adj.*
o′ver·long′, *adj., adv.*
o′ver·mag′ni·fi·ca′tion, *n.*
o′ver·mag′ni·fy′, *v.t.*, **-fied, -fy·ing.**
o′ver·meas′ure, *n.*
o′ver·mod′est, *adj.*; **-ly,** *adv.*
o′ver·mod′i·fy′, *v.*, **-fied, -fy·ing.**
o′ver·mort′gage, *v.t.*, **-gaged, -gag·ing.**
o′ver·par·tic′u·lar, *adj.*
o′ver·pes′si·mis′tic, *adj.*
o′ver·pow′er·ful, *adj.*
o′ver·praise′, *v.t.*, **-praised, -prais·ing.**
o′ver·pre·cise′, *adj.*
o′ver·price′, *v.t.*, **-priced, -pric·ing.**
o′ver·prom′i·nent, *adj.*
o′ver·prompt′, *adj.*, **-ly,** *adv.*

siveness of something in relation to another or to what is considered correct, desirable, or normal. —**o′ver·pro·por′tion·ate,** *adj.* —**o′ver·pro·por′tion·ate·ly,** *adv.* —**o′ver·pro·por′tioned,** *adj.*

o·ver·pro·tect (ō′vər prə tekt′), *v.t.* **1.** to protect (esp. a child) to the point of inhibiting appropriate action or development. **2.** to protect to excess. —**o′ver·pro·tec′tion,** *n.*

o·ver·proud (ō′vər proud′), *adj.* excessively proud. [ME *over prowde,* OE *ofer-prūt*] —**o′ver·proud′ly,** *adv.*

o·ver·ran (ō′vər ran′), *v.* pt. of **overrun.**

o·ver·rate (ō′vər rāt′), *v.t.,* **-rat·ed, -rat·ing.** to rate too highly; overestimate.

o·ver·reach (ō′vər rēch′), *v.t.* **1.** to reach or extend over or beyond. **2.** to reach for or aim at but go beyond, as a thing sought or a mark. **3.** to stretch to excess, as by a straining effort. **4.** to defeat (oneself) by overdoing matters, often by excessive eagerness or cunning. **5.** to strain or exert (oneself or itself) to the point of exceeding the purpose. **6.** to get the better of, esp. by deceit or trickery; outwit. —*v.i.* **7.** to reach or extend over something. **8.** to reach too far. **9.** to cheat others. **10.** (of a horse) to strike, or strike and injure, the forefoot with the hind foot. [ME]

o·ver·re·fine (ō′vər ri fīn′), *v.t.,* **-fined, -fin·ing.** to refine excessively, as with oversubtle distinctions. —**o′ver·re·fine′ment,** *n.*

o·ver·ride (*v.* ō′vər rīd′; *n.* ō′vər rīd′), *v.,* **-rode, -rid·den, -rid·ing,** *n.* —*v.t.* **1.** to trample or crush by riding over. **2.** to assert one's will, authority, etc., over; dominate: *to override one's advisers.* **3.** to prevail over; supersede; annul: *a decision that overrides all previous decisions.* **4.** to ride (a horse) too much; exhaust by excessive riding. **5.** to pass or extend over. **6.** *Surg.* to overlap, as one piece of a fractured bone over another. —*n.* **7.** a commission, as that paid on sales or profits. [ME *override(n),* OE *oferrīdan*]

o·ver·rid·ing (ō′vər rī′diŋ), *adj.* taking precedence over all other considerations: *an overriding national interest.*

o·ver·ripe (ō′vər rīp′), *adj.* too ripe; more than ripe: *overripe fruit.* —**o′ver·ripe′ly,** *adv.* —**o′ver·ripe′ness,** *n.*

o·ver·ruff (ō′vər ruf′), *v.t., v.i. Cards.* to overtrump.

o·ver·rule (ō′vər ro͞ol′), *v.t.,* **-ruled, -rul·ing.** **1.** to rule against or disallow the arguments of (a person). **2.** to rule or decide against (a plea, argument, etc.); disallow. **3.** to prevail over so as to change the purpose or action. **4.** to exercise rule or influence over. —**o′ver·rul′er,** *n.* —**o′ver·rul′ing·ly,** *adv.*

o·ver·run (*v.* ō′vər run′; *n.* ō′vər run′), *v.,* **-ran, -run, -run·ning,** *n.* —*v.t.* **1.** to rove over (a country, region, etc.); invade; ravage. **2.** to swarm over in great numbers, as animals, esp. vermin. **3.** to spread or grow rapidly over, as plants, esp. vines, weeds, etc. **4.** to attack and defeat decisively; overwhelm; crush. **5.** to spread rapidly throughout, as a new idea, spirit, etc. **6.** to run beyond. **7.** to exceed. **8.** to run over; overflow. **9.** *Print.* to print copies of (a book, brochure, etc.) in excess of those ordered. **10.** *Print.* to print additional copies of (a magazine, special article, etc.) so as to meet an abnormally heavy demand. **11.** *Archaic.* to outrun; overtake in running. —*v.i.* **12.** to run over; overflow. **13.** to exceed the proper, desired, or normal limit. —*n.* **14.** the act or an instance of overrunning. **15.** an amount in excess; surplus. [ME *overrin(en),* OE *oferyrnan*]

o·ver·score (ō′vər skōr′, -skôr′), *v.t.,* **-scored, -scor·ing.** to score over, as with strokes or lines.

o·ver·seas (*adv., n.* ō′vər sēz′; *adj.* ō′vər sēz′), *adv.* **1.** over, across, or beyond the sea; abroad: *to be sent overseas.* —*adj.* **2.** of or pertaining to passage over the sea: *overseas travel.* **3.** situated beyond the sea. **4.** pertaining to countries beyond the sea. —*n.* **5.** (*construed as sing.*) countries or territories across the sea; foreign lands. Also, *esp. Brit.,* **o·ver·sea** (*adv.* ō′vər sē′; *adj.* ō′vər sē′) (for defs. 1–4). [late ME *over see,* OE *ofersǣwisc* (see OVER-, SEA) + -S³]

overseas′ cap′, *U.S. Mil.* a wedge-shaped cap of cotton or woolen fabric, worn as part of the service uniform. Also called **garrison cap.**

o·ver·see (ō′vər sē′), *v.t.,* **-saw, -seen, -see·ing.** **1.** to direct (work or workers); supervise; manage. **2.** to see or observe secretly or unintentionally. **3.** *Archaic.* to survey or watch, as from a higher position. **4.** *Archaic.* to look over; inspect. [ME *oversee(n),* OE *oferseōn*]

o·ver·se·er (ō′vər sē′ər, -sēr′), *n.* **1.** a person who oversees; supervisor: *the overseer of a plantation.* **2.** (in Britain) a minor parish official, appointed annually, who performs various administrative details and is in charge of relief to the poor. [ME]

o·ver·sell (ō′vər sel′), *v.,* **-sold, -sell·ing.** —*v.t.* **1.** to sell more of (a stock, product, etc.) than can be delivered. **2.** to sell aggressively, as by using high-pressure merchandising techniques. **3.** to emphasize the good points of excessively. —*v.i.* **4.** to sell something aggressively. **5.** to make extreme claims for something or someone.

o·ver·set (*v.* ō′vər set′; *n.* ō′vər set′), *v.,* **-set, -set·ting,** *n.* —*v.t.* **1.** to upset or overturn; overthrow. **2.** to throw into confusion; disorder physically or mentally. —*v.i.* **3.** to become upset, overturned, or overthrown. **4.** *Print.* **a.** (of type or copy) to set in or to excess. **b.** (of space) to set too much type for. —*n.* **5.** the act or fact of oversetting; an upset or overturn. [ME] —**o′ver·set′ter,** *n.*

o·ver·sexed (ō′vər sekst′), *adj.* having or showing excessive interest in or need for sexual activity.

o·ver·shade (ō′vər shād′), *v.t.,* **-shad·ed, -shad·ing.** **1.** to cast shade over. **2.** to make dark or gloomy. [OE *ofer sceadath* (ptp.)]

o·ver·shad·ow (ō′vər shad′ō), *v.t.* **1.** to diminish the importance of, or render insignificant in comparison. **2.** to cast a shadow over; cover with shadows, clouds, darkness, etc. **3.** to make dark or gloomy. **4.** *Archaic.* to shelter or protect. [ME *overschadew(en),* OE *ofersceadwian*] —**o′ver·shad′ow·er,** *n.* —**o′ver·shad′ow·ing·ly,** *adv.*

o·ver·shine (ō′vər shīn′), *v.t.,* **-shone** or **-shined, -shin·ing.** **1.** to outshine. **2.** to surpass in splendor, excellence, etc. **3.** *Archaic.* to shine over or upon. [OE *oferscīn(an)*]

o·ver·shoe (ō′vər sho͞o′), *n.* a shoe or boot usually worn over another and intended for protection against wet or cold weather, esp. one that is waterproof.

o·ver·shoot (ō′vər sho͞ot′), *v.,* **-shot, -shoot·ing.** —*v.t.* **1.** to shoot or go over, beyond, or above; miss. **2.** to pass or go by or beyond (a point, limit, etc.). **3.** to shoot or pour down over. **4.** to overreach (oneself or itself); go further than is intended or proper; go too far. **5.** *Aeron.* to fly too far along (a landing strip) in attempting to land. —*v.i.* **6.** to fly or go beyond. **7.** to shoot over or above a mark. [ME]

o·ver·shot (ō′vər shot′), *adj.* **1.** driven over the top of, as by water passing over from above. **2.** having the upper jaw projecting beyond the lower, as a dog. —*v.* **3.** pt. and pp. of **overshoot.**

o′vershot wheel′, a water wheel in which the water enters the buckets tangentially near the top of the wheel.

Overshot wheel

o·ver·side (ō′vər sīd′), *adv.* **1.** over the side, as of a ship. **2.** on the opposite side (of a phonograph record). —*adj.* **3.** effected over the side of a vessel. **4.** placed or located on the opposite side (of a phonograph record). —*n.* **5.** the opposite side (of a phonograph record). [short for *over the side*]

o·ver·sight (ō′vər sīt′), *n.* **1.** failure to notice or consider. **2.** an omission or error due to carelessness. **3.** supervision; watchful care. [ME] —**Syn. 1.** lapse, neglect, inattention. **1, 2.** mistake, blunder, slip. **2.** erratum. **3.** control; surveillance.

o·ver·signed (*adj.* ō′vər sīnd′; *n.* ō′vər sīnd′), *adj.* **1.** of or pertaining to a signature at the top or beginning of a document, letter, etc. —*n.* **2.** the person whose signature appears at the top or beginning of a document, letter, etc.

o·ver·sim·pli·fy (ō′vər sim′plə fī′), *v.t.,* **-fied, -fy·ing.** to simplify to the point of obscurity or error. —**o′ver·sim′pli·fi·ca′tion,** *n.*

o·ver·size (*adj.* ō′vər sīz′; *n.* ō′vər sīz′), *adj.* Also, **o′ver·sized′. 1.** of excessive size; unusually large: *a man smoking an oversize cigar.* **2.** of a size larger than is necessary or required. —*n.* **3.** something that is oversize; an oversize article or object. **4.** a size larger than the proper or usual size.

o·ver·skirt (ō′vər skûrt′), *n.* an outer skirt.

o·ver·slaugh (ō′vər slô′), *v.t.* to pass over or disregard (a person) by giving a promotion, position, etc., due him to another. [< D *overslag,* akin to *overslaan* to pass over, omit]

o·ver·sleep (ō′vər slēp′), *v.,* **-slept, -sleep·ing.** —*v.i.* **1.** to sleep beyond the proper time of waking. —*v.t.* **2.** to sleep beyond (a certain hour). **3.** to let (oneself) sleep past the hour of arising. [ME]

o·ver·slip (ō′vər slip′), *v.t.,* **-slipped** or **-slipt, -slip·ping.** *Obs.* **1.** to leave out; miss. **2.** to elude; evade. [late ME]

o·ver·sold (ō′vər sōld′), *v.* pt. and pp. of **oversell.**

o·ver·soul (ō′vər sōl′), *n. Philos.* (esp. in transcendentalism) a supreme reality or mind; the spiritual unity of all being.

o·ver·spend (ō′vər spend′), *v.,* **-spent, -spend·ing.** —*v.i.* **1.** to spend more than one can afford. —*v.t.* **2.** to spend in excess of. **3.** to spend beyond one's means (used reflexively). **4.** *Archaic.* to wear out; exhaust.

o·ver·spill (*v.* ō′vər spil′; *n.* ō′vər spil′), *v.,* **-spilled** or **-spilt, -spill·ing,** *n.* —*v.i.* **1.** to spill over. —*n.* **2.** the act of spilling over. **3.** that which spills over.

o·ver·spread (ō′vər spred′), *v.t.,* **-spread, -spread·ing.** to spread or diffuse over. [ME; OE *ofersprǣdan*]

o·ver·state (ō′vər stāt′), *v.t.,* **-stat·ed, -stat·ing.** to state too strongly; exaggerate: *to overstate one's position in a controversy.* —**o′ver·state′ment,** *n.*

o·ver·stay (ō′vər stā′), *v.t.* **1.** to stay beyond the time or duration of; outstay: *to overstay one's welcome.* **2.** *Finance Informal.* to remain in (the market) beyond the point of the greatest profit.

o·ver·step (ō′vər step′), *v.t.,* **-stepped, -step·ping.** to step or pass over or beyond: *to overstep one's authority.* [ME *overstepp(en),* OE *ofersteppan*]

o·ver·stock (*v.* ō′vər stok′; *n.* ō′vər stok′), *v.t.* **1.** to stock to excess: *We are overstocked on this item.* —*n.* **2.** a stock in excess of need or demand.

o·ver·stretch (ō′vər strech′), *v.t.* **1.** to stretch excessively. **2.** to stretch or extend over. [ME]

o·ver·stride (ō′vər strīd′), *v.t.,* **-strode, -strid·den, -strid·ing.** **1.** to surpass. **2.** to stand or sit astride of; bestride. **3.** to tower over; dominate. **4.** to stride or step over or across. **5.** to stride more rapidly than or beyond. [ME]

o·ver·strung (ō′vər struŋ′), *adj.* too highly strung.

o·ver·stuff (ō′vər stuf′), *v.t.* **1.** to force too much into. **2.** *Furniture.* to envelop completely with deep upholstery.

o·ver·stuffed (ō′vər stuft′), *adj.* **1.** *Furniture.* having the entire frame covered by stuffing and upholstery, so that only decorative woodwork or the like is exposed: *an overstuffed sofa.* **2.** overlong; filled with tedious or extraneous material. **3.** obese; corpulent.

o·ver·sub·scribe (ō′vər səb skrīb′), *v.t.,* **-scribed, -scrib·ing.** to subscribe for in excess of what is available or required. —**o′ver·sub·scrib′er,** *n.* —**o·ver·sub·scrip·tion** (ō′vər səb skrip′shən), *n.*

o·ver·sup·ply (*n.* ō′vər sə plī′; *v.* ō′vər sə plī′), *n., pl.*

o′ver·pub′li·cize′, *v.t.,* **-cized, -ciz·ing.**
o′ver·ra′tion·al·ize′, *v.,* **-ized, -iz·ing.**
o′ver·right′eous, *adj.;* **-ly,** *adv.;* **-ness,** *n.*
o′ver·rig′id, *adj.*
o′ver·rig′or·ous, *adj.*
o′ver·roast′, *v.t.*
o′ver·ro·man′ti·cize′, *v.,* **-cized, -ciz·ing.**
o′ver·salt′, *v.t.*
o′ver·scru′pu·lous, *adj.*
o′ver·sen′si·tive, *adj.*
o′ver·se·vere′, *adj.*
o′ver·sharp′, *adj.*
o′ver·skep′ti·cal, *adj.*
o′ver·so·lic′i·tous, *adj.*
o′ver·so·phis′ti·cat′ed, *adj.*
o′ver·spar′ing, *adj.*
o′ver·spe′cial·i·za′tion, *n.*
o′ver·spe′cial·ize′, *v.,* **-ized, -iz·ing.**
o′ver·stim′u·late′, *v.,* **-lat·ed, -lat·ing.**
o′ver·strict′, *adj.*
o′ver·sub′tle, *adj.*
o′ver·sub′tle·ty, *n., pl.* **-ties.**

-plies, *v.,* **-plied, -ply·ing.** **—***n.* **1.** an excessive supply. **—***v.t.* **2.** to supply in excess.

o·vert (ō vûrt′, ō′vûrt), *adj.* open to view or knowledge; not concealed or secret: *overt hostility.* [ME < OF, ptp. of *ouvrir* to open < VL **ōperīre,* var. of L *aperīre*] **—o·vert′ly,** *adv.*

o·ver·take (ō′vər tāk′), *v.,* **-took, -tak·en, -tak·ing.** **—***v.t.* **1.** to catch up with in traveling or in pursuit. **2.** to catch up with or pass in any course of action. **3.** to happen to or befall suddenly or unexpectedly, as death, night, a storm, etc. **4.** *Chiefly Brit.* to pass (another vehicle). **—***v.i.* **5.** *Chiefly Brit.* to pass another vehicle. [ME]

o·ver·tax (ō′vər taks′), *v.t.* **1.** to tax too heavily. **2.** to make too great demands on. **—o′ver·tax·a′tion,** *n.*

o·ver-the-coun·ter (ō′vər t͟hə koun′tər), *adj.* **1.** (of stocks and securities) sold or purchased other than on an organized securities exchange; unlisted. **2.** *Pharm.* noting drugs that may be sold legally without a prescription.

o·ver-the-road (ō′vər t͟hə rōd′), *adj.* of, for, or pertaining to long-distance transportation on public highways: *over-the-road trucks.*

o·ver·throw (*v.* ō′vər thrō′; *n.* ō′vər thrō′), *v.,* **-threw, -thrown, -throw·ing,** *n.* **—***v.t.* **1.** to depose, as from a position of power; overcome, defeat, or vanquish. **2.** to put an end to by force, as governments or institutions. **3.** to throw over; upset; overturn. **4.** to knock down and demolish. **5.** to throw (something) too far. **6.** *Archaic.* to destroy the sound condition of (the mind). **—***v.i.* **7.** to throw too far. **—***n.* **8.** the act of overthrowing. **9.** the state or condition of being overthrown. **10.** deposition from power. **11.** defeat; destruction; ruin. [ME] **—o′ver·throw′er,** *n.* **—Syn. 1.** conquer, overpower. **4.** destroy, raze, level.

o·ver·thrust (ō′vər thrust′), *n.* *Geol.* **1.** a thrust fault with a deep dip and a large slip. **2.** a thrust fault in which the hanging wall was the one that moved (opposed to *underthrust*).

o·ver·time (*n., adv., adj.* ō′vər tīm′; *v.* ō′vər tīm′), *n., adv., adj., v.,* **-timed, -tim·ing.** **—***n.* **1.** the time during which a person works before or after regularly scheduled working hours; extra working time. **2.** pay for such time (distinguished from *straight time*). **3.** time in excess of a prescribed period. **4.** *Sports.* an additional unit of play for deciding the winner of a tied game. **—***adv.* **5.** during extra time: *to work overtime.* **—***adj.* **6.** of or pertaining to overtime: *overtime pay.* **—***v.t.* **7.** to give too much time to (a photographic exposure).

o·ver·tone (ō′vər tōn′), *n.* **1.** *Music.* an acoustical frequency that is higher in frequency than the fundamental. **2.** an additional, usually subsidiary and implicit, meaning or quality. [trans. of G *Oberton*]

o·ver·took (ō′vər to͝ok′), *v.* pt. of **overtake.**

o·ver·top (ō′vər top′), *v.t.,* **-topped, -top·ping.** **1.** to rise over or above the top of. **2.** to rise above in authority; take precedence over; override. **3.** to surpass or excel.

o·ver·trade (ō′vər trād′), *v.i.,* **-trad·ed, -trad·ing.** to trade in excess of one's capital.

o·ver·train (ō′vər trān′), *v.t., v.i.* to train to excess, as an athlete.

o·ver·trick (ō′vər trik′), *n.* *Bridge.* a trick won by declarer in excess of the number of tricks necessary to make his contract. Cf. **undertrick.**

o·ver·trump (ō′vər trump′, ō′vər trump′), *v.t., v.i.* *Cards.* to play a higher trump than has already been played.

o·ver·ture (ō′vər chər, -cho͝or′), *n., v.,* **-tured, -tur·ing.** **—***n.* **1.** an opening or initiating move toward negotiations, establishment of a relationship, etc.; a formal or informal proposal or offer. **2.** *Music.* **a.** an orchestral composition forming the prelude or introduction to an opera, oratorio, etc. **b.** an independent piece of similar character. **3.** an introductory part, as of a poem. **—***v.t.* **4.** to submit as an overture or proposal; make an overture or proposal to. [ME < OF; see OVERT, -URE]

o·ver·turn (*v.* ō′vər tûrn′; *n.* ō′vər tûrn′), *v.t.* **1.** to destroy the power of; overthrow; defeat; vanquish. **2.** to turn over on its side, face, or back; upset: *to overturn a vase.* **—***v.i.* **3.** to turn on its side, face, or back; upset; capsize. **—***n.* **4.** the act of overturning. **5.** the state of being overturned. [ME] **—o′ver·turn′a·ble,** *adj.* **—Syn. 1.** conquer.

o·ver-un·der (ō′vər un′dər), *adj.* **1.** (of double-barreled firearms) with one barrel mounted over the other. **—***n.* **2.** such a firearm.

o·ver·use (*v.* ō′vər yo͞oz′; *n.* ō′vər yo͞os′), *v.,* **-used, -us·ing,** *n.* **—***v.t.* **1.** to use too much or too often. **—***n.* **2.** excessive use.

o·ver·view (ō′vər vyo͞o′), *n.* **1.** a general idea or outline of a subject. **2.** an over-all impression, as of a field of activity or study; survey.

o·ver·watch (ō′vər woch′, -wôch′), *v.t.* **1.** to watch over. **2.** *Archaic.* to weary by keeping awake. **—o′ver·watch′er,** *n.*

o·ver·wear (ō′vər wâr′), *v.t.,* **-wore, -worn, -wear·ing.** to use or wear excessively; wear out; exhaust.

o·ver·wea·ry (*adj.* ō′vər wēr′ē; *v.* ō′vər wēr′ē), *adj., v.,* **-ried, -ry·ing.** **—***adj.* **1.** excessively weary; tired out. **—***v.t.* **2.** to weary to excess; overcome with weariness.

o·ver·ween (ō′vər wēn′), *v.i.* *Archaic.* to be conceited or arrogant. [ME] **—o′ver·ween′er,** *n.*

o·ver·ween·ing (ō′vər wē′ning), *adj.* **1.** (of a person) conceited, overconfident, or presumptuous. **2.** (of opinions, pretensions, characteristics, etc.) exaggerated, excessive, or arrogant. [ME] **—o′ver·ween′ing·ly,** *adv.* **—o′ver·ween′ing·ness,** *n.*

o·ver·weigh (ō′vər wā′), *v.t.* **1.** to exceed in weight; overbalance or outweigh. **2.** to weigh down; oppress. [ME]

o·ver·weight (ō′vər wāt′), *n.* **1.** extra or excess weight above what law or regulation allows, as of baggage or freight. **2.** weight in excess of that considered normal, proper, healthful, etc. **3.** greater effect or importance; preponderance. **—***adj.* **4.** weighing too much or more than is considered normal, proper, etc.

o·ver·whelm (ō′vər hwelm′, -welm′), *v.t.* **1.** to overpower, esp. with superior forces; destroy; crush. **2.** to overcome completely in mind or feeling. **3.** to load, heap, treat, or address with an overpowering or excessive amount of anything. **4.** to cover or bury beneath a mass of something, as flood waters, debris, an avalanche, etc. **5.** *Archaic.* to overthrow. [ME]

o·ver·whelm·ing (ō′vər hwel′ming, -wel′-), *adj.* **1.** that overwhelms: *The temptation is overwhelming.* **2.** so great as to render opposition useless: *an overwhelming force.* **—o′ver·whelm′ing·ly,** *adv.* **—o′ver·whelm′ing·ness,** *n.*

o·ver·wind (ō′vər wīnd′), *v.t.,* **-wound, -wind·ing.** to wind beyond the proper limit; wind too far, as a watch.

o·ver·word (ō′vər wûrd′), *n.* a word that is repeated, as a refrain in a song.

o·ver·wore (ō′vər wōr′, -wôr′), *v.* pt. of **overwear.**

o·ver·work (*v.* ō′vər wûrk′; *n.* ō′vər wûrk′), *v.,* **-worked** or **-wrought, -work·ing,** *n.* **—***v.t.* **1.** to cause to work too hard or too long; weary or exhaust with work (often used reflexively). **2.** to work up, stir up, or excite excessively. **3.** to employ or elaborate to excess. **4.** to work or decorate all over; decorate the surface of. **—***v.i.* **5.** to work too hard; work to excess. **—***n.* **6.** work beyond one's strength or capacity. **7.** extra or excessive work. [OE *oferwyrc(an)*]

o·ver·worn (ō′vər wōrn′, -wôrn′), *v.* pp. of **overwear.**

o·ver·write (ō′vər rīt′), *v.,* **-wrote, -writ·ten, -writ·ing.** **—***v.t.* **1.** to write in too elaborate, burdensome, diffuse, or prolix a style. **2.** to write in excess of the requirements, esp. so as to defeat the original intention. **3.** to write on or over; cover with writing. **—***v.i.* **4.** to write too elaborately.

o·ver·wrought (ō′vər rôt′, ō′vər-), *adj.* **1.** worked up or excited excessively. **2.** elaborated to excess; overworked. **3.** *Archaic.* wearied or exhausted by overwork. **—***v.* **4.** a pt. and pp. of **overwork.**

o·ver·zeal·ous (ō′vər zel′əs), *adj.* too zealous. **—o′ver·zeal′ous·ly,** *adv.* **—o′ver·zeal′ous·ness,** *n.*

ovi-, a learned borrowing from Latin meaning "egg," used in the formation of compound words: *oviferous.* [< L, comb. form of *ōvum*]

Ov·id (ov′id), *n.* (*Publius Ovidius Naso*) 43 B.C.–A.D. 17?, Roman poet. **—O·vid·i·an** (ō vid′ē ən), *adj.*

o·vi·duct (ō′vi dukt′), *n.* *Anat., Zool.* either of a pair of tubes that transport the ova from the ovary to the exterior, the distal ends of which are fused to form the uterus and vagina in higher mammals. [< NL *ōviduct(us)*] **—o·vi·du·cal** (ō′vi do͞o′kəl, -dyo͞o′-), **o′vi·duc′tal,** *adj.*

O·vie·do (ô vye′dô), *n.* a city in NW Spain. 134,424 (est. 1960).

o·vif·er·ous (ō vif′ər əs), *adj.* *Anat., Zool.* bearing eggs.

o·vi·form (ō′və fôrm′), *adj.* having a shape resembling that of an egg; egg-shaped.

o·vine (ō′vīn, ō′vin), *adj.* pertaining to, of the nature of, or like sheep. [< LL *ovīn(us)* = L *ov(is)* sheep + *-īnus* -INE[1]]

o·vip·a·ra (ō vip′ər ə), *n.pl.* *Zool.* egg-laying animals. [< NL, L, neut. pl. of *ōviparus* OVIPAROUS]

o·vip·a·rous (ō vip′ər əs), *adj.* *Zool.* producing eggs that mature and hatch after being expelled from the body, as birds, most reptiles and fishes, certain mammals, etc. [< L *ōviparus*] **—o·vi·par·i·ty** (ō′vi par′i tē), **o·vip′a·rous·ness,** *n.* **—o·vip′a·rous·ly,** *adv.*

o·vi·pos·it (ō′vi poz′it, ō′vi poz′-), *v.i.* to deposit or lay eggs, esp. by means of an ovipositor. [OVI- + L *posit(us)* placed; see POSIT] **—o·vi·po·si·tion** (ō′vi pə zish′ən), *n.*

o·vi·pos·i·tor (ō′vi poz′i tər), *n.* *Entomol.* (in certain female insects) an organ at the end of the abdomen, by which eggs are deposited.

o·vi·sac (ō′vi sak′), *n.* *Zool.* a sac or capsule containing an ovum or ova.

o·void (ō′void), *adj.* **1.** egg-shaped; having the solid form of an egg. **2.** ovate (def. 2). **—***n.* **3.** an ovoid body. [< NL *ōvoid(es).* See OVI-, -OID]

o·vo·lo (ō′və lō′), *n., pl.* **-li** (-lī′). *Archit.* a convex molding forming or approximating in section a quarter of a circle or ellipse. See illus. at **molding.** [< It, var. (now obs.) of *uovolo,* dim. of *uovo* egg < L *ōvum*]

o·vo·vi·vip·a·rous (ō′vō vī vip′ər əs), *adj.* *Zool.* producing eggs that are hatched within the body, so that the young are born alive but without placental attachment, as certain reptiles, fishes, etc. **—o′vo·vi·vip′a·rism, o·vo·vi·vi·par·i·ty** (ō′vō vī′və par′i tē), **o′vo·vi·vip′a·rous·ness,** *n.* **—o′vo·vi·vip′a·rous·ly,** *adv.*

o·vu·lar (ō′vyə lər), *adj.* pertaining to or of the nature of an ovule. [< NL *ōvulār(is)*]

o·vu·late (ō′vyə lāt′, ov′yə-), *v.i.,* **-lat·ed, -lat·ing.** *Biol.* to shed eggs from an ovary or ovarian follicle. **—o′vu·la′tion,** *n.*

o·vule (ō′vyo͞ol), *n.* **1.** *Bot.* **a.** a rudimentary seed. **b.** the body that contains the embryo sac and hence the female germ cell, which after fertilization develops into a seed. **2.** *Biol.* a small egg. [< L *ōvul(um)* little egg. See OVUM, -ULE]

o·vum (ō′vəm), *n., pl.* **o·va** (ō′və). *Biol.* **1.** the female reproductive cell or gamete of animals, which is capable of developing, usually only after fertilization, into a new individual. **2.** the female reproductive cell or gamete of plants. [< L: egg; c. Gk *ōión*]

ow (ou), *interj.* (used esp. as an expression of intense or sudden pain.)

owe (ō), *v.,* **owed, ow·ing.** **—***v.t.* **1.** to be indebted or beholden for (usually fol. by *to*): *to owe one's fame to good fortune.* **2.** to be under obligation for the payment or repayment of (often fol. by an indirect object). **3.** to be in debt to. **4.** to have or cherish (a certain feeling) toward a person. **5.** *Obs.* to own. **—***v.i.* **6.** to be in debt. [ME *owe(n),* OE *āgan;* c. OHG *eigan,* OIcel *eiga.* See OWN, OUGHT[1]]

Ow·en (ō′in), *n.* **1. Robert,** 1771–1858, Welsh social reformer. **2. Wilfred,** 1893–1918, English poet.

Ow·ens·bor·o (ō′inz bûr′ō, -bur′ō), *n.* a city in NW Kentucky, on the Ohio River. 50,329 (1970).

O′wen Stan′ley, a mountain range in SE New Guinea. Highest peak, Mt. Victoria, 13,240 ft.

OWI, *U.S.* Office of War Information: federal agency (1942–45) charged with disseminating war information.

ow·ing (ō′ing), *adj.* **1.** owed or due: *to pay what is owing.* **2.** *Archaic.* that owes or is under obligation. **3.** *Archaic.* indebted. **4. owing to,** attributable to; because of. [ME]

owl (oul), *n.* any of numerous, chiefly nocturnal birds of prey, of the order *Strigiformes,* having a broad

---

o′ver·sus·cep′ti·ble, *adj.*
o′ver·sus·pi′cious, *adj.*
o′ver·sys′tem·at′ic, *adj.*
o′ver·tech′ni·cal, *adj.*
o′ver·tire′, *v.t.,* **-tired, -tir·ing.**
o′ver·val′ue, *v.t.,* **-ued, -u·ing.**
o′ver·vi′o·lent, *adj.*
o′ver·weal′thy, *n.*
o′ver·will′ing, *adj.,* **-ly,** *adv.*
o′ver·wise′, *adj.*

head with large eyes that are usually surrounded by disks of modified feathers and directed forward. [ME *oule,* OE *ūle;* c. LG *ūle,* D *uil;* akin to Icel *ugla,* G *Eule*] —**owl′like′,** *adj.*

owl·et (ou′lit), *n.* a young owl.

owl·ish (ou′lish), *adj.* resembling an owl. —**owl′ish·ly,** *adv.* —**owl′ish·ness,** *n.*

own (ōn), *adj.* **1.** of, pertaining to, or belonging to oneself or itself (usually used after a possessive to emphasize the idea of ownership, interest, or relation conveyed by the possessive): *He spent only his own money.* **2.** (used as an intensifier to indicate oneself as the sole agent of some activity or action, prec. by a possessive): *He insists on being his own doctor. She does her own housework.* —*n.* **3.** that which belongs to one (prec. by a possessive adjective): *This car is my own.* **4. come into one's own, a.** to take possession of that which is due one. **b.** to receive the recognition which one's abilities merit. **5. hold one's own, a.** to maintain one's position or condition. **b.** to be equal to the opposition; be a match for. **6. of one's own,** belonging to oneself. **7. on one's own,** *Informal.* **a.** on one's own responsibility or resources; independently. **b.** being on one's own responsibility or resources; independent. —*v.t.* **8.** to have or hold as one's own; possess. **9.** to acknowledge or admit: *to own a fault.* **10.** to acknowledge as one's own; recognize as having full claim, authority, power, dominion, etc. —*v.i.* **11.** to confess (often fol. by *to* or *up*): *I own to being uncertain about that.* [(adj.) ME *owen,* OE *āgen* (c. G *eigen,* Icel *eigenn*), orig. ptp. of *āgan* to have, possess. See OWE; (v.) ME *own(en),* OE *āgnian, āhnian* < *āgen* own (adj.)] —**Syn. 8.** See **have.**

Great horned owl, *Bubo virginianus* (Length 2 ft.)

own·er (ō′nər), *n.* a person who owns; proprietor. [ME]

own·er·ship (ō′nər ship′), *n.* **1.** the state or fact of being an owner. **2.** legal right of possession; proprietorship.

ox (oks), *n., pl.* **ox·en** for 1, 2, **ox·es** for 3. **1.** the adult castrated male of the genus *Bos,* used as a draft animal and for food. **2.** any member of the bovine family. **3.** a clumsy, stupid fellow. [ME *oxe,* OE *oxa;* c. G *Ochse*]

ox-, *Chem.* a combining form meaning "containing oxygen": *oxazine.* [short for OXYGEN]

Ox., Oxford. [< ML *Oxonia*]

oxa-, *Chem.* a combining form denoting oxygen when it replaces carbon. [var. of ox- or OXY-¹]

ox·a·late (ok′sə lāt′), *n.* *Chem.* a salt or ester of oxalic acid. [OXAL(IC) + -ATE²]

ox·al′ic ac′id (ok sal′ik), *Chem.* a poisonous acid, $HOOCCOOH{\cdot}2H_2O$, used chiefly for bleaching, as a cleanser, and as a laboratory reagent. [< F *oxalique.* See OXALIS, -IC]

ox·a·lis (ok′sə lis, ok sal′is), *n.* any plant of the genus *Oxalis,* comprising the wood sorrels. [< L: garden sorrel, sour wine < Gk < *oxýs* sharp]

ox·a·zine (ok′sə zēn′, -zin), *n.* *Chem.* any of a group of 13 compounds having the formula C_4H_5NO arranged in a six-membered ring.

ox·blood (oks′blud′), *n.* a deep dull red color. Also called **ox′blood red′.**

ox·bow (oks′bō′), *n.* **1.** a U-shaped piece of wood placed under and around the neck of an ox with its upper ends in the bar of the yoke. **2.** *Phys. Geog. U.S.* **a.** a bow-shaped bend in a river, or the land embraced by it. **b.** a bow-shaped lake formed in an abandoned channel of a river. [ME]

ox′bow front′, *Furniture.* a front, as of a chest of drawers, having a horizontal compound curve with a concave section between two convex ones.

Ox·bridge (oks′brij′), *Brit.* —*n.* **1.** Oxford or Cambridge University, or both. **2.** upper-class intellectual life in England. —*adj.* **3.** of, pertaining to, or characteristic of Oxford and Cambridge: *to voice the proper Oxbridge sentiments.*

Oxbow front (England, 1720)

ox·cart (oks′kärt′), *n.* an ox-drawn cart.

ox·en (ok′sən), *n.* a pl. of **ox.**

Ox·en·stier·na (ŏŏk′sən shēr′nä), *n.* **Count Ax·el** (äk′səl), 1583–1654, Swedish statesman. Also, **Ox′en·stjer′na.**

ox·eye (oks′ī′), *n., pl.* **-eyes.** any of various plants having flowers composed of a disk with marginal rays, as the mayweed and the oxeye daisy. [late ME]

ox-eyed (oks′īd′), *adj.* having large, round eyes similar to those of an ox.

ox′eye dai′sy, a composite plant, *Chrysanthemum leucanthemum,* having flowers with white rays and a yellow disk.

ox·ford (oks′fərd), *n.* **1.** a low shoe laced over the instep. **2.** Also called **ox′ford cloth′.** a rayon or cotton fabric, in plain, twill, or basket weave, constructed on a pattern of two fine yarns woven as one warpwise and one loosely twisted yarn woven weftwise, for shirts, skirts, and summer sportswear. [after OXFORD (def. 2)]

Ox·ford (oks′fərd), *n.* **1. 1st Earl of.** See **Harley, Robert. 2.** a city in S Oxfordshire, in S England, NW of London: university, founded in 12th century. 106,124 (1961). **3.** Oxfordshire. **4.** Also called **Ox′ford Down′.** one of an English breed of large, hornless sheep, noted for its market lambs and heavy fleece of medium length.

Ox′ford Group′, an organization founded at Oxford University in 1921 by Frank Buchman, advocating absolute morality in public and private life. Cf. **Moral Re-Armament.**

Ox′ford move′ment, the movement toward High Church principles within the Church of England, originating at Oxford University in 1833 in opposition to liberalizing, rationalizing, and evangelical tendencies and emphasizing the principles of primitive and patristic Christianity as well as the historic and catholic character of the church. Cf. **Tractarianism.**

Ox·ford·shire (oks′fərd shēr′, -shər), *n.* a county in S England. 309,458 (1961); 749 mi. *Co. seat:* Oxford. Also called **Oxford, Oxon.**

ox·heart (oks′härt′), *n.* any large, heart-shaped variety of sweet cherry.

ox·i·dant (ok′si dənt), *n.* a chemical agent that oxidizes.

ox·i·dase (ok′si dās′, -dāz′), *n.* *Biochem.* any of a class of oxidoreductase enzymes that catalyze the oxidation of molecular oxygen. —**ox·i·da·sic** (ok′si dā′sik, -zik), *adj.*

ox·i·date (ok′si dāt′), *v.t., v.i.,* **-dat·ed, -dat·ing.** *Chem.* to oxidize. —**ox′i·da′tion,** *n.* —**ox′i·da′tion·al, ox′i·da′tive,** *adj.*

oxida′tion poten′tial, *Chem.* the potential of the electrode in a galvanic cell at which oxidation occurs.

ox·ide (ok′sīd, -sid), *n.* *Chem.* **1.** a compound containing oxygen and one or more elements, as mercuric oxide, HgO. **2.** a compound containing oxygen and one or more groups, as ethyl oxide, $(C_2H_5)_2O$. Also, **ox·id** (ok′sid). [< F (now *oxyde*), b. *oxygène* and *acide.* See OXYGEN, ACID] —**ox·id·ic** (ok sid′ik), *adj.*

ox·i·dim·e·try (ok′si dim′i trē), *n.* a technique of analytical chemistry that utilizes oxidizing agents for titration. —**ox·i·di·met·ric** (ok′si di me′trik), *adj.*

ox·i·dise (ok′si dīz′), *v.t., v.i.,* **-dised, -dis·ing.** *Chiefly Brit.* oxidize. —**ox′i·dis′a·bil′i·ty,** *n.* —**ox′i·dis′a·ble,** *adj.* —**ox′i·di·sa′tion,** *n.* —**ox′i·dis′er,** *n.*

ox·i·dize (ok′si dīz′), *v.,* **-dized, -diz·ing.** *Chem.* —*v.t.* **1.** to convert (an element) into its oxide; combine with oxygen. **2.** to cover with a coating of oxide, or rust. **3.** to take away hydrogen, as by the action of oxygen; add oxygen or any nonmetal. **4.** to increase the valence of (an element). **5.** to remove electrons from. —*v.i.* **6.** to become oxidized. —**ox′i·diz′a·bil′i·ty,** *n.* —**ox′i·diz′a·ble, ox·i·da·ble** (ok′si də bəl), *adj.* —**ox′i·di·za′tion,** *n.* —**ox′i·diz′er,** *n.*

ox·i·do·re·duc·tase (ok′si dō ri duk′tās), *n.* *Biochem.* any of a class of enzymes that act as a catalyst, some of them conjointly, causing the oxidation and reduction of compounds. Also, **ox′i·do-re·duc′tase.**

ox·ime (ok′sēm, -sim), *n.* *Chem.* any of a group of compounds containing the group >C=NOH produced by the condensation of ketones or aldehydes with hydroxylamine. [OX(YGEN) + IM(ID)E]

ox·lip (oks′lip′), *n.* a primrose, *Primula elatior,* having pale-yellow flowers. [ME; OE *oxan slyppe,* lit., ox's slime. See SLIP³ and cf. COWSLIP]

Ox·nard (oks′närd), *n.* a city in SW California, NW of Los Angeles. 71,225 (1970).

Ox·on (ok′son), *n.* Oxfordshire.

Oxon., **1.** Oxford. [< ML *Oxonia*] **2.** of Oxford. [< ML *Oxoniensis*]

Ox·o·ni·an (ok sō′nē ən), *adj.* **1.** of or pertaining to Oxford, England, or to Oxford University. —*n.* **2.** a member or graduate of Oxford University. **3.** a native or inhabitant of Oxford. [< ML *Oxoni(a)* Oxford + -AN]

ox·tail (oks′tāl′), *n.* the skinned tail of an ox or steer, used as an ingredient in soup, stew, etc. [ME]

ox·tongue (oks′tung′), *n.* any of various plants having rough, tongue-shaped leaves, as the bugloss, *Anchusa officinalis.* [ME]

Ox·us (ok′səs), *n.* See **Amu Darya.**

oxy-¹, a learned borrowing from Greek used, with the meaning "sharp," "acute," "keen," "pointed," "acid," in the formation of compound words: *oxygen; oxymoron.* [< Gk, comb. form of *oxýs* sharp, keen, acid]

oxy-², a combining form of **oxygen,** sometimes used as an equivalent of *hydroxy-: oxycalcium.*

ox·y·a·cet·y·lene (ok′sē ə set′ᵊlēn′, -ᵊlin), *adj.* noting or pertaining to a mixture of oxygen and acetylene used in a blowpipe for cutting steel plates or the like.

ox·y·ac·id (ok′sē as′id), *n.* *Chem.* an inorganic acid containing oxygen. Also called **ox′ygen ac′id.**

ox·y·cal·ci·um (ok′si kal′sē əm), *adj.* pertaining to or produced by oxygen and calcium.

oxycal′cium light′. See **calcium light.**

ox·y·chlo·ride (ok′si klōr′īd, -id, -klôr′-), *n.* *Chem.* a compound having oxygen and chlorine atoms bonded to another element, as bismuth oxychloride, BiOCl. [OXY-² + CHLORIDE] —**ox′y·chlo′ric,** *adj.*

ox·y·gen (ok′si jən), *n.* *Chem.* a colorless, odorless, gaseous element constituting about one fifth of the volume of the atmosphere and present in a combined state in nature. It is the supporter of combustion in air. *Symbol:* O; *at. wt.:* 15.9994; *at. no.:* 8; *weight of 1 liter at 0°C and 760 mm pressure:* 1.4290 grams. [< F *oxygène* = *oxy-* OXY-¹ + *-gène* -GEN] —**ox·y·gen·ic** (ok′si jen′ik), **ox·yg·e·nous** (ok sij′ə nəs), *adj.* —**ox′y·gen·ic′i·ty,** *n.*

ox·y·gen·ate (ok′si jə nāt′), *v.t.,* **-at·ed, -at·ing.** to treat, combine, or enrich with oxygen: *to oxygenate the blood.* —**ox′y·gen·a′tion,** *n.* —**ox′y·gen·a′tor,** *n.*

ox·y·gen·ize (ok′si jə nīz′), *v.t.,* **-ized, -iz·ing.** oxygenate. —**ox′y·gen·iz′a·ble,** *adj.* —**ox′y·ge·niz′er,** *n.*

ox′ygen mask′, a masklike device placed or worn over the nose and mouth when inhaling supplementary oxygen from an attached tank.

ox′ygen tent′, a small tentlike canopy for placing over a sick person for delivering and maintaining a flow of oxygen at critical periods.

ox·y·he·mo·glo·bin (ok′si hē′mə glō′bin, -hem′ə-, -hē′mə glō′-, -hem′ə-), *n.* *Biochem.* See under **hemoglobin.** *Symbol:* HbO_2

ox·y·hy·dro·gen (ok′si hī′drə jən), *adj.* **1.** pertaining to or involving a mixture of oxygen and hydrogen. —*n.* **2.** a mixture of oxygen and hydrogen, used in a blowpipe for cutting steel plates or the like.

ox·y·mo·ron (ok′si mōr′on, -môr′-), *n., pl.* **-mo·ra** (-mōr′ə, -môr′ə). *Rhet.* a figure of speech by which a locution produces an effect by seeming self-contradiction, as in "cruel kindness" or "to make haste slowly." [< NL < Gk: pointedly foolish, neut. of *oxýmōros* = *oxý(s)* OXY-¹ + *mōrós* foolish]

ox·y·salt (ok′si sôlt′), *n.* *Chem.* any salt of an oxyacid.

ox·y·sul·fide (ok′si sul′fīd, -fid), *n.* *Chem.* a sulfide in which part of the sulfur is replaced by oxygen.

ox·y·te·tra·cy·cline (ok′si te′trə sī′klīn, -klin), *n*

Pharm. a dull yellow, antibiotic powder, $C_{22}H_{24}N_2O_9$, used in treating infections caused by streptococci, staphylococci, rickettsiae, and by certain protozoans and viruses.

ox·y·to·cic (ok′si tō′sik, -tos′ik), *Med.* —*adj.* **1.** of or causing the stimulation of the involuntary muscle of the uterus. **2.** promoting or accelerating childbirth. —*n.* **3.** an oxytocic substance or drug. [< NL *oxytoc(ia)* (*oxy-* OXY-[1] + *toc-* (< Gk *tókos* childbirth) + *-ia* -IA) + -IC]

ox·y·to·cin (ok′si tō′sən), *n.* **1.** *Biochem.* a polypeptide hormone, produced by the posterior lobe of the pituitary gland, that stimulates contraction of the smooth muscle of the uterus. **2.** *Pharm.* a commercial form of this substance, obtained from beef and hog pituitary glands or esp. by synthesis, and used chiefly in obstetrics to induce labor and to control postnatal hemorrhage. [OXYTOC(IC) + -IN[2]]

ox·y·tone (ok′si tōn′), *Classical Gk. Gram.* —*adj.* **1.** having an acute accent on the last syllable. —*n.* **2.** an oxytone word. [< Gk *oxýton(os)* shrill-toned]

oy (oi), *interj.* (used to express dismay, pain, annoyance, grief, etc.)

o·yer and ter·mi·ner (ō′yər ən tûr′mə nər, oi′ər), *Law.* **1.** *U.S.* (in some states) any of various higher criminal courts. **2.** *Brit.* a writ directing the holding of a court to try offenses. Also called **o′yer.** [ME < AF: lit., to hear and determine; *oyer* < L *audīre; terminer* < L *termināre*]

o·yez (ō′yes, ō′yez), *interj.* **1.** hear!; attend! (a cry uttered usually three times by a court crier to command silence before making a proclamation). —*n.* **2.** a cry of "oyez." Also, **o′yes.** [< AF, 2nd pers. pl. impv. of *oyer.* See OYER AND TERMINER]

oys·ter (oi′stər), *n.* **1.** any of several edible, marine bivalve mollusks of the family *Ostreidae,* having an irregularly shaped shell, found on the bottom or adhering to rocks or other objects in shallow water. **2.** the oyster-shaped bit of dark meat in the front hollow of the side bone of a fowl. **3.** something from which one may extract or derive advantage: *The world was his oyster.* **4.** *Slang.* a taciturn person. —*v.i.* **5.** to dredge for or otherwise take oysters. [ME *oistre* < MF < L *ostrea* < Gk *óstreon*]

oys′ter bed′, a place where oysters breed or are cultivated.

oys·ter·catch·er (oi′stər kach′ər), *n.* any of several long-billed wading birds of the genus *Haematopus* that have chiefly black and white plumage and that feed on oysters, clams, mussels, etc. Also, **oys′ter catch′er.**

oys′ter crab′, a pea crab, *Pinnotheres ostreum,* the female of which lives as a commensal within the mantle cavity of oysters.

oys′ter crack′er, a small, round, usually salted cracker, served with oysters, soup, etc.

oys′ter fork′, a small, three-pronged fork, used esp. in eating raw oysters or clams, shrimp, etc.

oys·ter·man (oi′stər mən), *n., pl.* **-men. 1.** a man who gathers, cultivates, or sells oysters. **2.** a boat specially equipped for gathering oysters. Also called **oys′ter·er.**

oys′ter plant′, salsify.

oys′ter white′, a slightly grayish white; off-white.

oz., ounce; ounces.

Oz·a·lid (oz′ə lid), *n. Trademark.* a process for reproducing line drawings, manuscripts, and the like, on a sensitized paper developed by ammonia vapor.

oz. ap., *Pharm.* ounce apothecary's.

O′zark Moun′tains (ō′zärk), a group of low mountains in S Missouri, N Arkansas, and NE Oklahoma. Also called **O′zarks.**

oz. av., ounce avoirdupois.

O·zen·fant (ō zäɴ fäɴ′), *n.* **A·mé·dée** (ᴀ mā dā′), 1886–1966, French painter and writer, in the U.S. after 1938.

ozo-, an element of Greek origin meaning "smell," used in the formation of compound words: *ozocerite.* [< Gk comb. form of *ózōn* smelling (prp. of *ózein*); akin to L *odor* ODOR]

o·zo·ce·rite (ō zō′kə rīt′, -sə rīt′, ō′zō sēr′īt), *n.* wax-like mineral resin; mineral wax. Also, **o·zo·ke·rite** (ō zō′kə rīt′, ō′zō kēr′īt). [< G *Ozokerit* < Gk *ozo-* OZO- + *kēr(ós)* wax + G *-it* -ITE[1]]

ozon-, var. of **ozono-** before a vowel: *ozonide.*

o·zone (ō′zōn, ō zōn′), *n.* **1.** a form of oxygen, O_3, having three atoms to the molecule, with a peculiar odor suggesting that of weak chlorine, produced when an electric spark is passed through air or oxygen: a powerful oxidizing agent, used for bleaching, sterilizing water, etc. **2.** *Informal.* clear, fresh, invigorating air [< G *Ozon.* See OZO-, -ONE] —**o·zon·ic** (ō zon′ik, ō zō′nik), *adj.*

o′zone lay′er, ozonosphere.

o·zo·nide (ō′zō nīd′), *n. Chem.* any compound, usually explosive, formed by the addition of ozone to the double or triple bond of an organic compound.

o·zo·nif·er·ous (ō′zō nif′ər əs), *adj.* containing ozone.

o·zo·nise (ō′zō nīz′), *v.t., v.i.,* **-ised, -is·ing.** *Chiefly Brit.* ozonize.

o·zo·ni·za·tion (ō′zō ni zā′shən *or, esp. Brit.,* -nī-), *n.* **1.** the treatment of a compound with ozone. **2.** the conversion of oxygen into ozone. Also, *esp. Brit.,* **o′zo·ni·sa′tion.**

o·zo·nize (ō′zō nīz′), *v.,* **-ized, -iz·ing.** —*v.t.* **1.** to impregnate or treat with ozone. **2.** to convert (oxygen) into ozone. —*v.i.* **3.** (of oxygen) to be converted into ozone. Also, *esp. Brit.,* **ozonise.**

ozono-, a combining form of **ozone:** *ozonosphere.* Also, *esp. before a vowel,* **ozon-.**

o·zo·nol·y·sis (ō′zō nol′i sis), *n. Chem.* the reaction of ozone with hydrocarbons.

o·zo·no·sphere (ō zō′nə sfēr′), *n.* the region in the upper atmosphere where most atmospheric ozone is concentrated. Also called **ozone layer.**

ozs., ounces.

oz. t., ounce troy.

DEVELOPMENT OF MAJUSCULE								
NORTH SEMITIC	GREEK			ETR.	LATIN		MODERN		
							GOTHIC	ITALIC	ROMAN
𐤐	⅂	Π	⅂	Γ	P	𝔓	*P*	P

DEVELOPMENT OF MINUSCULE					
ROMAN CURSIVE	ROMAN UNCIAL	CAROL. MIN.	MODERN		
			GOTHIC	ITALIC	ROMAN
p	p	p	𝔭	*p*	p

The sixteenth letter of the English alphabet developed from the North Semitic letter *pe*, which means "mouth," but even in its earliest extant form, the shape of the letter has no obvious connection with this meaning. Its further history can be traced through Greek *pi* (π), Etruscan, and Latin, but except in the case of the last, its present form bears little if any resemblance to its earlier forms. The minuscule (p) is derived from the capital by lengthening the descender.

P, p (pē), *n., pl.* **P's** or **Ps, p's** or **ps. 1.** the sixteenth letter of the English alphabet, a consonant. **2.** any spoken sound represented by the letter *P* or *p*, as in *pet, supper*, or *top.* **3.** a written or printed representation of the letter *P* or *p.* **4.** a device, as a printer's type, for reproducing the letter *P* or *p.* **5. mind one's p's and q's,** to be careful of one's behavior.

P, 1. passing. **2.** *Chess.* pawn. **3.** *Physics.* poise. **4.** poor.

P, 1. the 16th in order or in a series, or, when *I* is omitted, the 15th. **2.** *Genetics.* parental. **3.** *Chem.* phosphorus. **4.** *Physics.* **a.** power. **b.** pressure.

p, 1. new penny; new pence. **2.** *Music.* softly. [< It *piano*] **3.** *Physics.* poise.

p, *Physics.* momentum.

P-, *U.S.* (in designations of fighter aircraft) pursuit: *P-38.*

p-, *Chem.* para-[1].

P., 1. pastor. **2.** father. [< L *Pater*] **3.** peseta; pesetas. **4.** (in Mexico and Cuba) peso; pesos. **5.** post. **6.** president. **7.** pressure. **8.** priest. **9.** prince. **10.** progressive.

p., 1. page. **2.** part. **3.** participle. **4.** past. **5.** father. [< L *pater*] **6.** *Chess.* pawn. **7.** penny. **8.** per. **9.** peseta. **10.** peso. **11.** *Music.* softly. [< It. *piano*] **12.** pint. **13.** pipe. **14.** *Baseball.* pitcher. **15.** pole. **16.** population. **17.** after. [< L *post*]

pa (pä), *n. Informal.* father. [short for PAPA]

PA, 1. Pennsylvania (approved esp. for use with zip code). **2.** press agent. **3.** public-address system.

Pa, *Chem.* protactinium.

Pa., Pennsylvania.

P.A., 1. passenger agent. **2.** post adjutant. **3.** power of attorney. **4.** press agent. **5.** purchasing agent.

p.a., 1. participial adjective. **2.** per annum. **3.** press agent.

PABA, para-aminobenzoic acid.

Pab·lum (pab′ləm), *n.* **1.** *Trademark.* a cereal for infants. **2.** (*l.c.*) banal ideas or writings; intellectual pap.

pab·u·lum (pab′yə ləm), *n.* **1.** something that nourishes an animal or vegetable organism; food. **2.** material for intellectual nourishment. **3.** banalities; pablum. [< L: food, nourishment = *pā(scere)* to feed (akin to FOOD) + *-bulum* n. suffix of means, instrument]

PABX, *Teleph.* private automatic branch exchange.

Paca
(Length 2½ ft.)

Pac., Pacific.

pa·ca (pä′kə, pak′ə), *n.* a large, white-spotted, almost tailless rodent, *Cuniculus paca*, of Central and South America. Also called **spotted cavy.** [< Sp or Pg < Tupi]

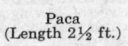

pace[1] (pās), *n., v.,* **paced, pac·ing.** —*n.* **1.** a rate of movement, esp. in stepping, walking, etc.: *to hike at a rapid pace.* **2.** a rate of activity, progress, performance, etc.; tempo. **3.** any of various standard lineal measures representing the space naturally measured by the movement of the feet in walking. Cf. **military pace. 4.** a single step: *She took three paces forward.* **5.** the distance covered in a step. **6.** a manner of stepping; gait. **7.** a gait of a horse or other animal in which the feet on the same side are lifted and put down together. **8. put someone through his paces,** to cause to prove ability or show skill. **9. set the pace,** to act as an example for others to rival; be the most progressive or successful. —*v.t.* **10.** to set, establish, or regulate the pace for, as in racing. **11.** to traverse or go over with steps: *He paced the floor nervously.* **12.** to measure by paces. **13.** to train to a certain pace. **14.** (of a horse) to run (a distance) at a pace: *to pace a mile.* —*v.i.* **15.** to take slow, regular steps. **16.** to walk up and down nervously, as to expend nervous energy. **17.** (of a horse) to travel at a pace. [ME *pas* < OF < L *pass(us)* step, n. use of ptp. of *pandere* to spread (the legs)] —**Syn. 15, 16.** PACE, PLOD, TRUDGE refer to a steady and monotonous kind of walking. PACE suggests steady, measured steps, as of someone lost in thought or impelled by some distraction: *to pace up and down.* PLOD implies a slow, heavy, laborious, weary walk: *The mailman plods his weary way.* TRUDGE implies a spiritless but usually steady and doggedly persistent walk: *The farmer trudged to the village to buy supplies.* —**Ant. 15.** scurry, scamper.

pa·ce[2] (pā′sē; *Lat.* pä′ke), *prep.* with the permission of (a courteous form used in mentioning one who disagrees): *I do not, pace my rival, hold with the ideas of the reactionaries.* [< L *pāce* in peace, by favor (abl. sing. of *pāx*)]

paced (pāst), *adj.* **1.** having a specified or indicated pace (usually used in combination): *slow-paced.* **2.** counted out or measured by paces. **3.** run at a pace set by a pacemaker.

pace·mak·er (pās′mā′kər), *n.* **1.** a person or thing that sets the pace, as in racing. **2.** a person, group, etc., that serves as a model to be imitated, followed, or the like. **3.** *Med.* an instrument implanted beneath the skin for providing a normal heartbeat by electrical stimulation of the heart muscle, used in certain heart conditions. Also called **pacesetter** (for defs. 1, 2). —**pace′mak′ing,** *n.*

pac·er (pā′sər), *n.* **1.** a standard-bred horse used for pacing in harness racing. **2.** a person or thing that paces. **3.** a pacemaker.

pace·set·ter (pās′set′ər), *n.* pacemaker (defs. 1, 2).

pa·cha (pə shä′, pash′ə), *n.* pasha. —**pa·cha′dom,** *n.*

pa·chi·si (pə chē′zē, pä-), *n.* a game similar to backgammon, played in India. [< Hindi < *pachis* twenty-five (the highest throw in the game)]

pach·ou·li (pach′o͞o lē, pə cho͞o′lē), *n.* patchouli.

Pa·chu·ca (pä cho͞o′kä), *n.* a city in and the capital of Hidalgo, in central Mexico: silver mines. 69,432 (1960).

pach·y·derm (pak′i dûrm′), *n.* **1.** any of the thick-skinned, nonruminant ungulates, esp. the elephant. **2.** a person who is thick-skinned or insensitive to criticism, ridicule, etc. [back formation from NL *Pachydermata* < Gk *pachý(s)* thick + *dérma* skin + NL *-ata* -ATA] —**pach′y·der′mal, pach′y·der′mous, pach′y·der′mic, pach′y·der′moid,** *adj.*

pach·y·der·ma·tous (pak′i dûr′mə təs), *adj.* **1.** of, pertaining to, or characteristic of pachyderms. **2.** thick-skinned; insensitive: *a pachydermatous indifference to insults.* [< NL *Pachydermat(a)* a classification of mammals (see PACHYDERM) + -OUS]

pach·y·san·dra (pak′i san′drə), *n.* any plant of the genus *Pachysandra*, often used as a ground cover in the U.S. [< NL = Gk *pachýs* thick + NL *-andra*, fem. of *-andrus* -ANDROUS]

pa·cif·ic (pə sif′ik), *adj.* **1.** tending to make peace; conciliatory. **2.** not warlike; peaceable; mild. **3.** at peace; peaceful: *a pacific era in history.* **4.** calm; tranquil: *The Wabash is a pacific river.* **5.** (*cap.*) of or pertaining to the Pacific Ocean. **6.** (*cap.*) of or pertaining to the region bordering on the Pacific Ocean: *the Pacific states.* —*n.* **7.** (*cap.*) See **Pacific Ocean.** [< L *pācific(us)*, lit., peacemaking = *pāci-* (s. of *pāx*) peace + *-ficus* -FIC] —**pa·cif′i·cal·ly,** *adv.* —**Syn. 1.** appeasing. PACIFIC, PEACEABLE, PEACEFUL describe that which is in a state of peace. That which is PACIFIC tends toward the making, promoting, or preserving of peace: *pacific intentions.* That which is PEACEABLE desires to be at peace or is free from the disposition to quarrel: *peaceable citizens.* That which is PEACEFUL is in a calm state or is characteristic of or characterized by peace: *a peaceful death.* —**Ant. 1, 2.** hostile. **2.** aggressive, bellicose.

Pa·cif·i·ca (pə sif′i kə), *n.* a city in W California, S of San Francisco. 36,020 (1970).

pa·cif·i·cal (pə sif′i kəl), *adj. Archaic.* pacific (defs. 1–4). [< L *pācific(us)* + -AL[1]]

pa·cif·i·cate (pə sif′ə kāt′), *v.t.,* **-cat·ed, -cat·ing.** to pacify. [< L *pācificāt(us)* made peace (ptp. of *pācificāre*). See PACIFY, -ATE[1]] —**pac·i·fi·ca·tion** (pas′ə fə kā′shən), *n.* —**pa·cif′i·ca′tor,** *n.* —**pa·cif·i·ca·to·ry** (pə sif′ə kə tôr′ē, -tōr′ē), *adj.*

Pacif′ic Is′lands, Trust Territory of the, a U.S. trust territory in the Pacific Ocean, comprising the Mariana, Marshall, and Caroline Islands. 94,900 (1970); 717 sq. mi.

pa·cif·i·cism (pə sif′i siz′əm), *n. Brit.* pacifism. —**pacif′icist,** *n.* —**pa·cif′i·cis′tic,** *adj.* —**pa·cif′i·cis′ti·cal·ly,** *adv.*

Pacif′ic O′cean, an ocean bordered by the American continents, Asia, and Australia: largest ocean in the world; divided by the equator into the North Pacific and the South Pacific. 70,000,000 sq. mi.; greatest known depth, 35,433 ft.

Pacif′ic time′. See under **standard time.**

pac·i·fi·er (pas′ə fī′ər), *n.* **1.** a person or thing that pacifies. **2.** any rubber or plastic device, often shaped into a nipple, for a baby to suck on. **3.** See **teething ring.**

pac·i·fism (pas′ə fiz′əm), *n.* **1.** opposition to war or violence. **2.** the principle or policy of establishing and maintaining universal peace or such relations among all nations that all differences may be adjusted without recourse to war. **3.** nonresistance to aggression. Also, *Brit.,* **pacificism.**

pac·i·fist (pas′ə fist), *n.* Also, *Brit.,* **pacificist. 1.** a person who believes in pacifism or is opposed to war or to violence of any kind. **2.** a man whose personal belief in pacifism causes him to resist being drafted into military service. Cf. **conscientious objector. 3.** a person who refuses to resist violence or aggression. —*adj.* **4.** pacifistic. [< F *pacifiste*]

pac·i·fis·tic (pas′ə fis′tik), *adj.* of pacifism or pacifists. Also, *Brit.,* **pacificistic.** —**pac′i·fis′ti·cal·ly,** *adv.*

pac·i·fy (pas′ə fī′), *v.t.,* **-fied, -fy·ing. 1.** to bring or restore to a state of peace or tranquillity; quiet; calm. **2.** to appease. **3.** to reduce to a submissive state; subdue. [late ME < L *pācific(āre)* (to) make peace]

pack[1] (pak), *n.* **1.** a group of things wrapped or tied up for easy handling or carrying, esp. for carrying on the back of an animal or a person; bundle. **2.** a definite quantity or standard measure of merchandise together with its wrapping or package: *a pack of cigarettes.* **3.** a container or package for an item of merchandise. **4.** the quantity of something that is packaged at one time: *last year's salmon pack.* **5.** a group of people or things: *a pack of fools.* **6.** a group of certain animals of the same kind, esp. predatory ones: *a pack of wolves* **7.** *Hunting.* a number of hounds, regularly used together in a hunt. **8.** a complete set of playing cards, usually 52 in number; deck. **9.** See **pack ice. 10.** *Med.* **a.** a wrapping of the body in cloths for therapeutic purposes. **b.** the cloths used. **11.** a cosmetic material, usually of a pastelike consistency, applied either to the face or to the hair and scalp: *a mud pack.* **12.** *Obs.* a low or worthless person. —*v.t.* **13.** to make into a pack or bundle. **14.** to form into a group or compact mass. **15.** to fill compactly with anything: *to pack a trunk.* **16.** to put in a case, box, or the like, as for storage or carrying. **17.** to press or crowd together within; cram: *The crowd packed the gallery.* **18.** to prepare for marketing by putting into containers or packages. **19.** to make airtight, vaportight, or watertight by stuffing. **20.** to cover or envelop with something pressed closely around. **21.** to load, as with packs or luggage. **22.** to carry or wear, esp. as part of one's usual equipment: *to pack a gun.* **23.** to send off summarily (sometimes fol. by *off, away,* etc.): *We packed her off to her mother.* **24.** *Slang.* to be able to deliver (a blow, punch, etc.). —*v.i.* **25.** to pack goods in compact form, as for transporting or storage (often fol. by *up*). **26.** to adapt to compact storage or packing, usually as specified: *articles that pack well.* **27.** to move as a pack, or crowded together, as persons. **28.** to become compacted: *Wet snow packs readily.* **29.** to leave hastily (usually fol. by *off, away,* etc.). —*adj.* **30.** used in transporting a pack: *pack animals.* **31.** compressed into a pack; packed. **32.** used in or adapted for packing: *pack equipment.* [ME *pak, packe* < MFlem *pac*] —**pack′a·ble,** *adj.*

—**Syn. 1.** knapsack. See **package. 5.** band, company, crew. **6.** See **flock**[1].

pack[2] (pak), *v.t.* to choose, collect, arrange, or manipulate (cards, persons, facts, etc.) so as to serve one's own purposes: *to pack a jury.* [? var. of PACT]

pack·age (pak′ij), *n., v.,* **-aged, -ag·ing.** —*n.* **1.** a bundle of something, usually of small or medium size, that is packed and wrapped or boxed; parcel. **2.** a container, as a box or case in which something may be packed. **3.** *Informal.* a person or thing conceived of as a compact unit having particular characteristics: *She's a neat little package.* **4.** the packing of goods, freight, etc. **5.** a finished product contained in a unit that is suitable for immediate installation and operation, as a power or heating unit. **6.** a group, combination, or series of related parts or elements to be accepted or rejected as a single unit. **7.** a complete program produced for the theater, television, etc., or a series of these, sold as a unit. —*v.t.* **8.** to put into wrappings or a container. **9.** to design and manufacture a package for (a product or series of related products): *They package their soaps in eye-catching wrappers.* **10.** to group or combine (a series of related parts) into a single unit. [< D *pakkage*]

—**Syn. 1.** PACKAGE, PACK, PACKET, PARCEL refer to a bundle or to something fastened together. A PACKAGE is a bundle of things packed and wrapped: *a package from the drugstore.* A PACK is a large bundle or bale of things put or fastened together, usually wrapped up or in a bag, case, etc., to be carried by a person or a beast of burden: *a peddler's pack.* A PACKET, originally a package of letters or dispatches, is a small package or bundle: *a packet of gems.* A PARCEL is an object or set of objects wrapped up to form a single, small bundle: *a parcel containing two dresses.* **2.** carton.

pack′age store′, a store selling sealed bottles of alcoholic beverages for consumption off the premises.

pack·er (pak′ər), *n.* **1.** a person or thing that packs. **2.** a person or organization that engages in packing, esp. a company that packs food for market: *a major meat packer.*

pack·et (pak′it), *n.* **1.** a small pack or package of anything. **2.** a boat that carries mail, passengers, and goods regularly on a fixed route. [< MF *pacquet* = *pacq(uer)* (to) PACK[1] + *-et* -ET] —**Syn. 1.** See **package.**

pack·horse (pak′hôrs′), *n.* a horse used for carrying goods, freight, supplies, etc.

pack′ ice′, a large area of floating ice formed over a period of many years and consisting of pieces of ice driven together by wind, currents, etc. Also called **ice pack.**

pack·ing (pak′ing), *n.* **1.** the act or work of a person or thing that packs. **2.** the preparation and packaging of foodstuffs, esp. to be sold at wholesale. **3.** the way in which something is packed. **4.** the act or an instance of transporting supplies, goods, etc., on the backs of horses, mules, or men. **5.** material used to cushion or protect goods packed in a container. **6.** material compressed inside a stuffing box or the like to prevent leakage around a moving shaft. [ME *pakking*]

pack′ing frac′tion, *Physics.* a measure of the stability of an atomic nucleus, equal to the quotient of the difference of the mass number and the mass of the atom divided by the mass number.

pack′ing house′, an establishment for processing and packing foods to be sold at wholesale, esp. meat.

pack·man (pak′mən), *n., pl.* **-men.** a peddler.

pack′ rat′, 1. a large, bushy-tailed rodent, *Neotoma cinerea,* of North America, noted for carrying away small articles which it stores in its nest. **2.** *Informal.* **a.** an old prospector or guide. **b.** a person who collects, saves, or hoards useless small items.

pack·sack (pak′sak′), *n.* a leather or canvas carrying bag, usually one that can be strapped over the shoulders, used to carry food and personal items when a person is traveling.

pack·sad·dle (pak′sad′əl), *n.* a saddle specifically designed for supporting the load on a pack animal. [ME *pakke saddil*]

pack·thread (pack′thred′), *n.* a strong thread or twine for sewing or tying up packages. [ME *pakthrede*] —**pack′thread′ed,** *adj.*

pack·train (pak′trān′), *n.* a train of pack animals, as mules, used to transport supplies.

pact (pakt), *n.* **1.** an agreement, covenant, or compact. **2.** an agreement or treaty between two or more nations. [late ME *pact(e)* < MF < L *pact(um),* n. use of neut. of ptp. of *pacīscī* to make a bargain, contract] —**Syn. 1.** contract, bond. **2.** league, alliance.

pac·tion (pak′shən), *n. Rare.* an agreement. [late ME *pactyon* < L *pactiōn-* (s. of *pactiō*) bargain, agreement] —**pac′tion·al,** *adj.* —**pac′tion·al·ly,** *adv.*

Pac·to·lus (pak tō′ləs), *n.* a small river in ancient Lydia: famous for the gold washed from its sands.

pad[1] (pad), *n., v.,* **pad·ded, pad·ding.** —*n.* **1.** a cushionlike mass of soft material used for comfort, protection, or stuffing. **2.** a soft, stuffed cushion used as a saddle; a padded leather saddle without a tree. **3.** a number of sheets of paper held together at one edge to form a tablet. **4.** a soft, ink-soaked block of absorbent material for inking a rubber stamp. **5.** one of the cushionlike protuberances on the underside of the feet of dogs, foxes, and some other animals. **6.** the foot of such an animal. **7.** a piece or fold of gauze or other absorbent material for use as a surgical dressing or a protective covering. **8.** *Zool.* a pulvillus, as on the tarsus or foot of an insect. **9.** the large floating leaf of the water lily. **10.** *Slang.* **a.** an apartment; home. **b.** one's bed. —*v.t.* **11.** to furnish, protect, fill out, or stuff with a pad or padding. **12.** to expand with unnecessary, bogus, or fraudulent material: *to pad a term paper; to pad one's expense account.* [special uses of obs. *pad* bundle to lie on, ? b. PACK[1] and BED]

pad[2] (pad), *n., v.,* **pad·ded, pad·ding.** —*n.* **1.** a dull sound, as of footsteps on the ground. **2.** a road horse, as distinguished from a hunter or workhorse. **3.** *Brit. Dial.* a path, lane, or road. **4.** *Archaic.* a highwayman. —*v.t.* **5.** to travel along on foot. **6.** to beat down by treading. —*v.i.* **7.** to travel on foot; walk. **8.** to walk so that one's footsteps make a dull sound. [(n.) < D; c. PATH; (v.) < MD *pad(en)* (to) make or follow a path; c. OE *pæthhan* to traverse. See FOOTPAD]

PaD, Pennsylvania Dutch.

Pa·dang (pä däng′), *n.* a seaport in W central Sumatra, in W Indonesia. 143,699 (1961).

pa·dauk (pə douk′), *n.* See **padouk wood.**

pad·ding (pad′ing), *n.* **1.** material, as cotton or straw, used to pad something. **2.** unnecessary verbal material used deliberately to lengthen a speech, essay, etc. **3.** fraudulent expense listed on one's expense account or the like. **4.** the act of a person or thing that pads.

Pad·ding·ton (pad′ing tən), *n.* a residential borough of W London, England. 115,322 (1961).

pad·dle[1] (pad′əl), *n., v.,* **-dled, -dling.** —*n.* **1.** a short, flat-bladed oar for propelling and steering a canoe, usually held in both hands and moved through a vertical arc. **2.** any of various similar implements used for mixing, stirring, or beating. **3.** an implement with a short handle and a wide, rounded blade, used as a racket in table tennis. **4.** a similar instrument used for spanking a child or in hazing freshmen, initiates to a fraternity, etc. **5.** Also called **float.** a blade of a paddle wheel. **6.** See **paddle wheel. 7.** a flipper or limb of a penguin, turtle, whale, etc. **8.** an act of paddling. —*v.i.* **9.** to propel or travel in a canoe or the like by using a paddle. **10.** to row lightly or gently with oars. **11.** to move by means of paddle wheels, as a steamer. —*v.t.* **12.** to propel with a paddle. **13.** to spank with or as with a paddle. **14.** to stir, mix, or beat with or as with a paddle. **15.** to convey by paddling, as in a canoe. **16.** to hit (a table-tennis ball or the like) with a paddle. [late ME *padell*] —**pad′dler,** *n.*

pad·dle[2] (pad′əl), *v.i.,* **-dled, -dling. 1.** to move the feet or hands playfully in shallow water; dabble. **2.** to toddle. **3.** *Archaic.* to toy with the fingers. [?] —**pad′dler,** *n.*

pad·dle·fish (pad′əl fish′), *n., pl.* **-fish·es,** (*esp. collectively*) **-fish.** a large ganoid fish, *Polyodon spathula,* found in the Mississippi River and its larger tributaries, having a long, flat, paddlelike snout.

pad′dle ten′nis, a variety of tennis played with wooden paddles and a ball of sponge rubber on a court about half the size of a tennis court.

pad′dle wheel′, an engine-driven wheel for propelling a vessel, having a number of horizontal paddles entering the water more or less perpendicularly. —**pad′dle-wheel′,** *adj.*

pad·dock[1] (pad′ək), *n.* **1.** a small, usually enclosed field near a stable or barn for pasturing or exercising animals. **2.** *Horse Racing.* the enclosure in which the horses are saddled and mounted. [var. of ME *parrok,* OE *pearroc* enclosure, orig. fence. See PARK]

pad·dock[2] (pad′ək), *n. Scot. and North Eng.* a frog or toad. [ME *paddok(e)* < early ME *pad* toad; akin to D, LG *pad,* Icel *padda;* see -OCK]

pad·dy (pad′ē), *n., pl.* **-dies. 1.** a rice field. **2.** rice. **3.** rice in the husk, uncut or gathered. [< Malay *pādī*]

Pad·dy (pad′ē), *n., pl.* **-dies.** *Slang.* an Irishman or one of Irish descent. [familiar var. of Ir *Padraig* Patrick]

pad′dy wag′on, *Slang.* See **patrol wagon.** [prob. PADDY (policeman)]

pad·dy·whack (pad′ē hwak′, -wak′), *v.t. Informal.* to spank or beat. Also, **pad·dy·wack** (pad′ē wak′).

Pa·de·rew·ski (pä′de ref′skī; *Eng.* pad′ə ref′skē, -rev′-), *n.* **I·gnace** (*Fr.* ē nyAs′) or **Ig·na·cy Jan** (*Pol.* ig nä′tse yän), 1860–1941, Polish pianist, composer, patriot, and statesman.

Pa·di·shah (pä′di shä′), *n.* great king; emperor (a title applied esp. to the Shah of Iran or the Sultan of Turkey). Also, **pa′di·shah′.** [< Pers (poetical form) = *pādi-* (earlier *pati*) lord + *shāh* SHAH]

pad·lock (pad′lok′), *n.* **1.** a portable or detachable lock with a pivoted or sliding shackle that can be passed through a staple, link, ring, or the like. —*v.t.* **2.** to fasten with or as if with a padlock. [ME *padlok.* See POD[3], LOCK[1]]

pa·douk′ wood′ (pə douk′), an ornamental wood, mottled in shades of yellowish red, from a Malaysian tree, *Pterocarpus indicus,* used in inlaying, etc. Also called **pa·douk′, padauk.** [*padouk* < Burmese native name]

Pa·do·va (pä′dô vä), *n.* Italian name of **Padua.**

pa·dre (pä′drā, -drē; *Sp.* pä′thre; *It.* pä′dre), *n., pl.* **-dres** (-drāz, -drēz; *Sp.* -thres), *It.* **-dri** (-drē). **1.** father (used esp. in addressing or referring to a priest or clergyman). **2.** *U.S. Mil. Informal.* a chaplain. [< Sp, Pg, It: father < L *pater*]

pa·dro·ne (pə drō′nē, -nā; *It.* pä drô′ne), *n., pl.* **-nes** (-nēz, -nāz), *It.* **-ni** (-nē). **1.** a master; head. **2.** an employer who almost entirely controls the lives of his employees for exploitative purposes. **3.** the master or captain of a ship. **4.** an innkeeper. [< It; see PATRON] —**pa·dro·nism** (pə drō′niz əm), *n.*

Pad·u·a (paj′o͞o ə, pad′yo͞o ə), *n.* a city in NE Italy. 198,403 (1961). Italian, **Padova.** —**Pad′u·an,** *adj.*

pad·u·a·soy (paj′ōō ə soi′), *n., pl.* **-soys.** **1.** a smooth, strong, silk fabric. **2.** a garment made of this. [alter. of F *pou de soie* (var. of *poult de soie,* lit., pelt of silk) by assoc. with PADUA]

Pa·du·cah (pə dōō′kə, -dyōō′-), *n.* a city in W Kentucky, at the junction of the Tennessee and Ohio rivers. 31,627 (1970).

Pa·dus (pā′dəs), *n.* ancient name of **Po.**

pae·an (pē′ən), *n.* **1.** any song of praise, joy, or triumph. **2.** a hymn of invocation or thanksgiving to Apollo or some other ancient Greek deity. [< L: religious or festive hymn, special use of *Paean* appellation of Apollo < Gk *Paiā́n* physician of the gods] —**pae′an·ism,** *n.*

paed-, var. of **ped-**[1]. Also, **paedo-.**

paed·a·go·gy (ped′ə gō′jē, -goj′ē, pē′də-), *n.* pedagogy.

paed·er·as·ty (ped′ə ras′tē, pē′də-), *n.* pederasty.

pae·di·at·rics (pē′dē a′triks, ped′ē-), *n.* (*construed as sing.*) *Chiefly Brit.* pediatrics. —**pae′di·at′ric,** *adj.*

paedo-, var. of **pedo-**[1]. Also, *esp. before a vowel,* **paed-.**

pae·do·gen·e·sis (pē′də jen′i sis), *n.* reproduction by animals in the larval state, often by parthenogenesis. [< NL] —**pae·do·ge·net·ic** (pē′dō jə net′ik), **pae′do·gen′ic,** *adj.*

pa·el·la (pä ā′lə, -el′ə, pə-; *Sp.* pä e′lyä, -e′yä), *n.* a Spanish dish prepared by simmering together chicken, rice, vegetables, saffron and other seasonings, and often meat and shellfish. [< Sp < Catalan: lit., frying pan, pot < MF *paelle* < L *patella* pan]

pae·on (pē′ən), *n. Class. Pros.* a foot of one long and three short syllables in any order. [< L < Gk *paiṓn,* Attic var. of *paiā́n* PAEAN]

Paes·tum (pes′təm), *n.* an ancient coastal city of Lucania, in S Italy: extant ruins include three Greek temples.

PaG, Pennsylvania German.

pa·gan (pā′gən), *n.* **1.** one of a people or community professing a polytheistic religion. **2.** a person who is not a Christian, Jew, or Muslim. **3.** an irreligious or hedonistic person. —*adj.* **4.** pertaining to pagans or their religion. **5.** of or characteristic of pagans. **6.** irreligious and hedonistic. [ME < ML, LL (eccl.) *pāgānus* worshiper of false gods, civilian (i.e., not a soldier of Christ), L: peasant, n. use of *pāgānus* (adj.) < *pāgus* village, rural district (akin to *pangere* to fix, make fast); see -AN] —**pa′gan·ish,** *adj.* —**pa′gan·ish·ly,** *adv.* —**Syn. 5.** See **heathen.**

pa·gan·dom (pā′gən dəm), *n.* pagans collectively.

Pa·ga·ni·ni (pag′ə nē′nē; *It.* pä′gä nē′nē), *n.* **Nic·co·lò** (nēk′kô lô′), 1784–1840, Italian composer and violinist.

pa·gan·ise (pā′gə nīz′), *v.t., v.i.,* **-ised, -is·ing.** *Chiefly Brit.* paganize. —**pa′ga·ni·sa′tion,** *n.* —**pa′ga·nis′er,** *n.*

pa·gan·ism (pā′gə niz′əm), *n.* **1.** pagan spirit or attitude in religious or moral questions. **2.** the beliefs or practices of pagans. **3.** the state of being a pagan. [ME *pāgānysme* < LL *pāgānism(us)*] —**pa′gan·ist,** *adj., n.* —**pa′gan·ist′ic,** *adj.*

pa·gan·ize (pā′gə nīz′), *v.,* **-ized, -iz·ing.** —*v.t.* **1.** to make pagan. —*v.i.* **2.** to become pagan. Also, *esp. Brit.,* **paganise.** —**pa′gan·i·za′tion,** *n.* —**pa′gan·iz′er,** *n.*

page[1] (pāj), *n., v.,* **paged, pag·ing.** —*n.* **1.** one side of a leaf of something printed or written, as a book. **2.** the entire leaf. **3.** a noteworthy event or period: *a bright page in English history.* —*v.t.* **4.** to paginate. —*v.i.* **5.** to turn pages (usually fol. by *through*). [< MF < L *pāgina,* akin to *pangere* to fix, make fast]

page[2] (pāj), *n., v.,* **paged, pag·ing.** —*n.* **1.** a boy servant or attendant. **2.** a youth in attendance on a person of rank or, in medieval times, a youth being trained for knighthood. **3.** a young male attendant or employee, who carries messages, ushers guests, runs errands, etc. —*v.t.* **4.** to summon formally by calling out the name of repeatedly. [ME < OF < ?]

Page (pāj), *n.* **1. Thomas Nelson,** 1853–1922, U.S. novelist and diplomat. **2. Walter Hines** (hīnz), 1855–1918, U.S. journalist, editor, and diplomat.

pag·eant (paj′ənt), *n.* **1.** an elaborate public spectacle illustrative of the history of a place, institution, etc. **2.** a costumed procession, masque, allegorical tableau, or the like forming part of public or social festivities. **3.** something comparable to such a spectacle or procession in its colorful variety or grandeur: *the pageant of Renaissance history.* **4.** a pretentious display. [ME *pagyn* < AL *pāgina* a stage for plays, scene, platform, special use of L *pāgina* PAGE[1]]

pag·eant·ry (paj′ən trē), *n., pl.* **-ries.** **1.** spectacular display; pomp. **2.** mere show; empty display. **3.** pageants collectively; pageants and the performance of pageants.

page·boy (pāj′boi′), *n.* a woman's hair style in which the hair is rolled under at shoulder length. Also, **page′ boy′.**

pag·er (pāj′ər), *n.* **1.** a loudspeaker for paging people. **2.** a very small portable radio-operated device that receives a beep or similar signal indicating the recipient should report in by telephone or in person. [PAGE[2] + -ER[1]]

pag·i·nal (paj′ə nᵊl), *adj.* **1.** of or pertaining to pages. **2.** consisting of pages. [< LL *pāginālis*) of, belonging to a page]

pag·i·nate (paj′ə nāt′), *v.t.,* **-nat·ed, -nat·ing.** to indicate the sequence of pages in (a book, manuscript, etc.) by placing numbers or other characters on each leaf. [< L *pāgin(a)* PAGE[1] + -ATE[1]]

pag·i·na·tion (paj′ə nā′shən), *n. Bibliog.* **1.** the number of pages or leaves in a book. **2.** the figures by which pages are numbered. **3.** the act of paginating. [< L *pāgin(a)* PAGE[1] + -ATION]

pa·go·da (pə gō′də), *n.* **1.** (in India, Burma, China, etc.) a temple or sacred building, usually a pyramidlike tower and typically having upward-curving roofs over the individual stories. **2.** any of several former gold or silver coins of southern India. [< Pg *pagode* temple << Pers *butkadah* (*but* idol + *kadah* temple, dwelling)]

Pagoda (Chinese), 11th century

Pa·go Pa·go (päng′ō päng′ō), the chief harbor and town of American Samoa, on Tutuila island: naval station. 2451 (1970). Also, **Pa′go·pa′go, Pango Pango.**

pa·gu·ri·an (pə gyŏŏr′ē ən), *n.* a hermit crab, esp. of the genus *Pagurus.* [< NL *Pagūr(us)* the typical genus (L: crab < Gk *págouros* = *pág(os)* rock, something hard + *our(á)* tail + *-os* adj. suffix) + -IAN]

pa·gu·rid (pə gyŏŏr′id, pag′yə rid), *n.* pagurian. [back formation from NL *Pagūridae* name of the family < *Pagūr(us)* (see PAGURIAN) + *-idae* -ID[2]]

pah (pä, pa), *interj.* (exclamation of disgust or disbelief.)

Pa·hang (pä häng′), *n.* a state in Malaysia, on the SE Malay Peninsula. 354,316 (est. 1961); 13,820 sq. mi. *Cap.:* Kuala Lipis.

Pa·ha·ri (pə här′ē), *n., pl.* **-ris,** (esp. collectively) **-ri.** **1.** any of several hill peoples inhabiting the area in India southwest of the Ganges river. **2.** a member of any of these peoples. **3.** a group of Indic languages or dialects spoken by these peoples. [< Hindi: *pahārī* mountaineer]

Pah·la·vi (pä′lə vē′), *n., pl.* **-vis** for 2, 3. **1.** See **Muhammad Riza Pahlavi.** **2.** a member of the dynasty ruling in Iran from 1925 to 1979. **3.** (*l.c.*) a former gold coin of Iran, equal to 100 rials. Also, **Pah′le·vi′.**

Pah·la·vi (pä′lə vē′), *n.* **1.** the Indo-European, Iranian language of the Zoroastrian literature of the 3rd to the 10th centuries. **2.** the script used in writing this language, derived from the Aramaic alphabet. [< Pers: Parthian]

paid (pād), *v.* a pt. and pp. of **pay**[1].

paido-, var. of **pedo-**[1].

pail (pāl), *n.* **1.** a cylindrical or nearly cylindrical container with a semicircular handle, used for holding liquids or solids; bucket. **2.** pailful. [ME *payle* wooden vessel, OE *pægel* wine vessel, liquid measure < ML *pagella* liquid measure >> G *Pegel* water gauge]

pail·ful (pāl′fŏŏl′), *n., pl.* **-fuls.** a quantity sufficient to fill a pail.

pail·lasse (pal yas′, pal′yas), *n. Chiefly Brit.* a mattress of straw; pallet. Also, **palliasse.** [< F < It *pagliaccio* straw pallet = *pagli(a)* straw (< L *palea* chaff) + *-accio* pejorative n. suffix]

pail·lette (pal yet′, pə let′; *Fr.* pä yet′), *n., pl.* **paillettes** (pal yets′, pə lets′; *Fr.* pä yet′). a spangle for ornamenting a costume. [< F; see PALLET[1]] —**pail·let′ted,** *adj.*

pain (pān), *n.* **1.** bodily suffering or distress, as due to injury or illness. **2.** a distressing sensation in a particular part of the body: *a back pain.* **3.** mental or emotional suffering or torment. **4. pains, a.** laborious or careful efforts; assiduous care. **b.** the suffering of childbirth. **5. on** or **upon pain of,** liable to the penalty of: *on pain of death.* Also, **under pain of.** —*v.t.* **6.** to cause physical pain to; hurt. **7.** to cause (someone) mental or emotional pain; distress: *Her sarcasm pained him.* —*v.i.* **8.** to have or give pain. [ME *peine* < OF < L *poena* penalty, pain < Gk *poinḗ* penalty] —**Syn. 1–3.** torture, misery. PAIN, ACHE, AGONY, ANGUISH are terms for sensations causing suffering or torment. PAIN and ACHE usually refer to physical sensations (except *heartache*); AGONY and ANGUISH may be physical or mental. PAIN suggests a sudden sharp twinge: *a pain in one's ankle.* ACHE applies to a continuous pain, whether acute or dull: *headache; muscular aches.* AGONY implies a continuous, excruciating, scarcely endurable pain: *in agony from a wound.* ANGUISH suggests not only extreme and long-continued pain, but also a feeling of despair. **2.** pang, twinge, stitch. **7.** torment.

Paine (pān), *n.* **1. Albert Big·e·low** (big′ə lō′), 1861–1937, U.S. author and editor. **2. Robert Treat** (trēt), 1731–1814, U.S. jurist and statesman. **3. Thomas,** 1737–1809, U.S. patriot and writer on government and religion, born in England.

pain·ful (pān′fəl), *adj.* **1.** affected with, causing, or characterized by pain. **2.** laborious; exacting; difficult: *a painful life.* **3.** *Archaic.* painstaking; careful. [ME] —**pain′ful·ly,** *adv.* —**pain′ful·ness,** *n.* —**Syn. 1.** distressing, agonizing, tormenting, excruciating. **2.** arduous. —**Ant. 1.** pleasant.

pain·kil·ler (pān′kil′ər), *n. Informal.* something that relieves pain, esp. an analgesic.

pain·less (pān′lis), *adj.* **1.** without pain; causing no pain: *painless dentistry.* **2.** *Informal.* not difficult; requiring little or no hard work or exertion. —**pain′less·ly,** *adv.* —**pain′less·ness,** *n.*

pains·tak·ing (pānz′tā′king, pān′stā′-), *adj.* **1.** taking or characterized by taking pains, or trouble; careful: *a painstaking craftsman; painstaking research.* —*n.* **2.** careful and diligent effort. —**pains′tak′ing·ly,** *adv.* —**pains′tak′ing·ness,** *n.*

paint (pānt), *n.* **1.** a substance composed of solid coloring matter suspended in a liquid medium, for application to various surfaces as a protective or decorative coating or to canvas or other materials in producing a work of art. **2.** an application of this. **3.** the dried surface pigment: *Don't scuff the paint.* **4.** the solid coloring matter alone; pigment. **5.** facial cosmetics designed to heighten natural color. **6.** *Chiefly Western U.S.* a pied, calico, or spotted horse or pony; pinto. —*v.t.* **7.** to coat, cover, or decorate (something) with or as with paint. **8.** to produce (a picture, design, etc.) in paint: *to paint a portrait.* **9.** to represent in paint: *to paint a sunset.* **10.** to describe vividly in words. —*v.i.* **11.** to coat or cover anything with paint. **12.** to engage in painting as an art. **13.** to put on or use facial cosmetics. **14. paint the town red,** *Slang.* to celebrate boisterously, esp. by making a round of stops at bars and night clubs. Also, **paint the town.** [ME *peint(n)* < OF *peint,* ptp. of *peindre* < L *pingere* to paint] —**paint′less,** *adj.*

paint·brush (pānt′brush′), *n.* **1.** any brush for applying paint. **2.** any plant of the figwort family.

paint·ed (pān′tid), *adj.* **1.** reproduced or represented in paint: *a painted image.* **2.** covered with a coating of paint: *a painted chair.* **3.** unreal; artificial. **4.** exaggerated or misrepresented. [ME]

paint′ed bunt′ing, a brilliantly colored bunting, *Passerina ciris,* of the southern U.S.

paint′ed cup′, any of several plants of the genus *Castilleja,* having highly colored, dilated bracts about the flowers.
Paint′ed Des′ert, a region in N central Arizona, E of the Colorado River: many-colored rock surfaces.
paint′ed wom′an, 1. a prostitute. 2. a promiscuous and cynical woman.
paint·er[1] (pān′tər), *n.* 1. an artist who paints pictures. 2. a person who coats walls or other surfaces with paint, esp. as an occupation. [r. ME *peyntour* < AF *peintour*]
paint·er[2] (pān′tər), *n.* a rope, usually at the bow, for fastening a boat to a ship, stake, etc. [ME *paynter,* prob. < MF *pentoir* rope, cord for hanging things on. See PEND, -ER[2]]
paint·er[3] (pān′tər), *n.* cougar. [var. of PANTHER]
paint·er·ly (pān′tər lē), *adj.* characteristic of a painter or of the art of painting, esp. in reference to color and tonal relationships.
paint′er's col′ic, *Pathol.* lead poisoning causing intense intestinal pain.
paint·ing (pān′ting), *n.* 1. a picture or design executed in paints. 2. the act, art, or work of a person who paints. 3. the works of art painted in or at a particular place or period: *a book on Flemish painting.* [ME]
pair (pâr), *n., pl.* **pairs, pair,** *v.* —*n.* 1. two identical, similar, or corresponding things that are matched for use together: *a pair of gloves.* 2. something consisting of or regarded as having two parts or pieces joined together: *a pair of scissors; a pair of slacks.* 3. two people or animals who are similar or in some way associated: *a pair of liars; a pair of horses.* 4. a married, engaged, or dating couple. 5. *Govt.* a. two members on opposite sides in a deliberative body who, for convenience, as to permit absence, arrange together to forgo voting on a given occasion. b. the arrangement thus made. 6. *Cards.* a. two cards of the same denomination without regard to suit or color. b. **pairs,** two players who are matched together against different contestants. 7. *Mech.* two parts or pieces so connected that they mutually constrain relative motion. —*v.t.* 8. to arrange or designate in pairs or groups of two. 9. to form into a pair, as by matching or joining; match; couple. 10. to cause (animals) to mate. —*v.i.* 11. to separate into pairs or groups of two (usually fol. by *off*): *to pair off for a procession.* 12. to form a pair or pairs. 13. to be a member of a pair. 14. (of animals) to mate. [ME *paire* < OF < L *pāria,* pl. (taken as fem. sing.) of *pār* a pair. See PAR]
—**Syn.** 1. PAIR, BRACE, COUPLE, SPAN, YOKE are terms for groups of two. PAIR is used of two things naturally or habitually associated in use, or necessary to each other to make a complete set: *a pair of dice.* It is used also of one thing composed of two similar and complementary parts: *a pair of trousers.* BRACE is a hunter's term, used of a pair of dogs, ducks, etc., or a pair of pistols or slugs: *a brace of partridges.* In COUPLE the idea of combination or interdependence has become greatly weakened; it may be used loosely for two of anything and even for more than two (= several): *a couple of apples; I have to see a couple of people.* SPAN is used of a matched pair of horses harnessed together side by side. YOKE applies to two animals hitched together under a yoke for drawing and pulling: *a yoke of oxen.*
pair′ annihila′tion, *Physics.* annihilation (def. 3a).
pair-oar (pâr′ōr′, -ôr′), *n.* a racing shell having two oarsmen with one oar each.
pair′ produc′tion, *Physics.* the simultaneous creation of a particle and its antiparticle by a nucleus or particle in an excited state, as when a photon is absorbed.
pai·sa (pī′sä), *n., pl.* **-se** (-sā). 1. See **naya paisa.** 2. a money of account of Pakistan, the 100th part of a rupee. [< Hindi *paisā*]
pai·sa·no (pī sä′nō; *Sp.* pī sä′nô), *n., pl.* **-nos** (-nōz; *Sp.* -nôs). *Slang.* 1. pal; comrade. 2. compatriot. [< Sp < F *paysan.* See PEASANT]
pais·ley (pāz′lē), *n., pl.* **-leys,** *adj.* —*n.* 1. a soft woolen fabric woven with a pattern of colorful and minutely detailed figures. 2. a shawl, scarf, or other article made of this fabric. 3. Also called **pais′ley print′.** a pattern resembling the paisley design. —*adj.* 4. made of paisley. 5. having the pattern of a paisley. [after PAISLEY]
Pais·ley (pāz′lē), *n.* a city in central Renfrew, SW Scotland, W of Glasgow: thread factories. 95,753 (1961).
Pai·ute (pī o͞ot′), *n., pl.* **-utes,** (*esp. collectively*) **-ute.** 1. a member of a group of North American Indians of Uto-Aztecan family dwelling in California, Nevada, Utah, and Arizona. 2. either of two mutually unintelligible Shoshonean dialects. Also, **Piute.**
pajam′a par′ty, a party at which teen-age girls dress in night clothes and stay overnight at a friend's home.
pa·jam·as (pə jä′məz, -jam′əz), *n.* (*construed as pl.*). 1. night clothes consisting of loose-fitting trousers and jacket. 2. loose trousers, usually of silk or cotton, worn in the Orient. Also, *esp. Brit.,* **pyjamas.** [pl. of *pajama* < Hindi, var. of *pāejāma* < Pers *pāe* leg + *jāma* garment] —**pa·ja′maed,** *adj.*
Pa·ki·stan (pak′i stan′, pä′ki stän′), *n.* 1. **Islam′ic Repub′lic of,** a republic in S Asia, W of India: formerly part of India; from 1947–71 divided into West Pakistan and East Pakistan (now Bangladesh). 76,800,000; 310,236 sq. mi. *Cap.:* Islamabad. 2. (before 1947) the predominantly Muslim areas of the peninsula of India as distinguished from Hindustan, the predominantly Hindu areas.
Pa·ki·sta·ni (pä′ki stä′nē), *n., pl.* **-nis, -ni,** *adj.* —*n.* 1. a native or inhabitant of Pakistan. —*adj.* 2. of, pertaining to, or characteristic of Pakistan or its inhabitants.
PAL (pal), *n.* a special air service for sending parcels from 5 to 30 pounds to overseas servicemen: only the regular parcel-post rate to the U.S. port of shipment plus $1 is charged. Cf. **SAM** (def. 1). [*P*(*arcel*) *A*(*ir*) *L*(*ift*)]
pal (pal), *n., v.,* **palled, pal·ling.** *Informal.* —*n.* 1. a comrade; chum. —*v.i.* 2. to associate as comrades or chums. [< E Gypsy: brother, mate, dissimilated var. of continental Gypsy *pral, plal* << Skt *bhrātr* brother]
Pal., Palestine.
pal., 1. paleography. 2. paleontology.
pal·ace (pal′is), *n.* 1. the official residence of a sovereign, bishop, or other exalted personage. 2. any mansion or large and stately building, esp. as found in Europe. 3. a large and ornate place for entertainment, exhibitions, etc. [late ME < ML *palātium,* sing. of L *palātia* palace (L *Palātium* was name of a hill on which many early emperors' residences were situated; hence pl. meaning); r. ME *paleis* < OF << L *Palāt*(*ium*)] —**pal′aced,** *adj.* —**pal′ace·like′,** *adj.*
pal′ace guard′, 1. an imperial bodyguard. 2. a group of highly trusted and influential advisers or assistants who seem to control access to a king, president, or the like.
pal·a·din (pal′ə din), *n.* 1. any of the 12 legendary peers or knightly champions in attendance on Charlemagne. 2. any champion of a noble cause. [< F < It *paladin*(*o*) < LL *palātīnus* imperial functionary, n. use of adj.; see PALATINE[1]]
palae-, var. of **pale-.** Also, *esp. before a consonant,* **palaeo-.**
palaeo-, var. of **paleo-.** Also, *before some vowels,* **palae-.**
pa·lae·o·bi·ol·o·gy (pā′lē ō bī ol′ə jē, pal′ē-), *n.* paleobiology.
pa·lae·o·bot·a·ny (pā′lē ō bot′ᵊnē, pal′ē-), *n.* paleobotany.
Pa·lae·o·cene (pā′lē ə sēn′, pal′ē-), *n., adj.* Paleocene.
Pa·lae·o·gene (pā′lē ə jēn′, pal′ē-), *adj., n.* Paleogene.
Pa·lae·o·lith·ic (pā′lē ə lith′ik, pal′ē-), *adj.* Paleolithic.
pa·lae·on·tol·o·gy (pā′lē ən tol′ə jē, pal′ē-), *n., pl.* **-gies.** paleontology.
Pa·lae·o·zo·ic (pā′lē ə zō′ik, pal′ē-), *n., adj.* Paleozoic.
pa·laes·tra (pə les′trə), *n., pl.* **-tras, -trae** (-trē). *Gk. Antiq.* palestra. —**pa·laes′tral, pa·laes′tric,** *adj.*
pa·lais (pa le′), *n., pl.* **-lais.** *French.* a palace, esp. a French government or municipal building.
Pal·a·me·des (pal′ə mē′dēz), *n.* *Class. Myth.* a lieutenant of Agamemnon who tricked Odysseus into going to the Trojan War, later killed through the plotting of Odysseus.
pal·an·quin (pal′ən kēn′), *n.* (in India and other Eastern countries) a passenger carriage consisting of a covered or boxlike litter carried by several men. Also, **pal′an·keen′.** [< MF < D *pallankin* < Pg *palanquim* << Pali *palanki* palanquin < Prakrit *pallanka* couch, bed]
pal·at·a·ble (pal′ə tə bəl), *adj.* 1. pleasing or acceptable to the palate or taste. 2. pleasing or acceptable to the mind or feelings. —**pal′at·a·bil′i·ty, pal′at·a·ble·ness,** *n.* —**pal′at·a·bly,** *adv.* —**Syn.** 1. edible. 2. satisfactory.
pal·a·tal (pal′ə tᵊl), *adj.* 1. *Anat.* of or pertaining to the palate. 2. *Phonet.* articulated with the blade of the tongue held close to or touching the hard palate. —*n.* 3. *Phonet.* a palatal consonant. [< F] —**pal′a·tal·ism, pal·a·tal·i·ty** (pal′ə tal′i tē), *n.* —**pal′a·tal·ly,** *adv.*
pal·a·tal·ise (pal′ətᵊlīz′), *v.,* **-ised, -is·ing.** *Chiefly Brit.* palatalize. —**pal′a·tal·i·sa′tion,** *n.*
pal·a·tal·ize (pal′ətᵊlīz′), *v.,* **-ized, -iz·ing.** *Phonet.* —*v.t.* 1. to articulate (a consonant other than a normal palatal) as a palatal or with relatively more contact between the blade of the tongue and the hard palate, as in certain pronunciations of the *l*-sound in *million.* —*v.i.* 2. (of a consonant) to undergo palatalization. —**pal′a·tal·i·za′tion,** *n.*
pal·ate (pal′it), *n.* 1. *Anat.* the roof of the mouth, consisting of an anterior bony portion **(hard palate)** and a posterior muscular portion **(soft palate)** that separate the oral cavity from the nasal cavity. 2. the sense of taste. 3. intellectual or aesthetic taste; mental appreciation. [ME *palat* < L *palāt*(*um*) roof of the mouth] —**pal′ate·less,** *adj.*
pa·la·tial (pə lā′shəl), *adj.* 1. of, pertaining to, or resembling a palace: *a palatial home.* 2. befitting or suitable for a palace; stately; magnificent. [< L *palāti*(*um*) PALACE + -AL[1]] —**pa·la′tial·ly,** *adv.* —**pa·la′tial·ness,** *n.*
Pa·lat·i·nate (pə lat′ᵊnāt′, -ᵊnit), *n.* 1. **The.** Also called **Lower Palatinate, Rhine Palatinate.** German, **Pfalz.** a district in SW Germany, W of the Rhine: belonged to Bavaria until 1945; formerly, with portions of the neighboring territory **(Upper Palatinate),** constituted an electorate of the Holy Roman Empire; now part of Rhineland-Palatinate state. 2. a native or inhabitant of the Palatinate. 3. (*l.c.*) the territory under a palatine. —**pa·lat′i·nal,** *adj.*
pal·a·tine[1] (pal′ə tīn′, -tin), *adj.* 1. having royal privileges. 2. of or pertaining to a count palatine, earl palatine, or county palatine. 3. of or pertaining to a palace; palatial: *a palatine chapel.* 4. (*cap.*) of or pertaining to the Palatinate. —*n.* 5. a vassal exercising royal privileges in a province; a count or earl palatine. 6. an important officer of an imperial palace. 7. a high official of an empire. 8. (*cap.*) a native or inhabitant of the Palatinate. 9. (*cap.*) one of the seven hills on which ancient Rome was built. 10. (formerly) a shoulder cape of fur or lace. [late ME < ML, L *palātīn*(*us*) of the imperial house, imperial; orig., of the hill *Palātium* in Rome, where the emperor's palace was situated. See PALADIN, -INE[1]]
pal·a·tine[2] (pal′ə tīn′, -tin), *adj.* of, near, or in the palate; palatal: *the palatine bones.* [< F *palatin, -ine*]
Pal·a·tine (pal′ə tīn′), *n.* a city in NE Illinois. 25,904 (1970).
Pa·lau′ Is′lands (pä lou′), a group of Pacific islands in the W part of the Caroline group: taken by U.S. forces in 1944; formerly a Japanese mandate, now under U.S. trusteeship. 11,210 (1970); 171 sq. mi. Also, **Pelew Islands.**
pa·lav·er (pə lav′ər, -lä′vər), *n.* 1. a long parley, esp. one with primitive natives. 2. profuse and idle talk; chatter. 3. flattery or cajolery. —*v.i.* 4. to talk profusely and idly. 5. to parley or confer. —*v.t.* 6. to cajole. [< Pg *palavra* word, speech, talk < LL *parabola* PARABLE] —**pa·lav′er·er,** *n.*
Pa·la·wan (pä lä′wän), *n.* an island in the SW Philippines. 232,322; 5697 sq. mi. *Cap.:* Puerto Princesa.
pa·laz·zo (pä lät′sô), *n., pl.* **-laz·zi** (-lät′sē). *Italian.* an impressive public building or private residence; palace.
pale[1] (pāl), *adj.,* **pal·er, pal·est,** *v.,* **paled, pal·ing.** —*adj.* 1. lacking intensity of color; colorless or whitish: *a pale complexion.* 2. of a low degree of chroma, saturation, or purity; approaching white or gray: *pale yellow.* 3. not bright or brilliant; dim: *the pale moon.* 4. lacking vigor; faint; feeble: *a pale protest.* —*v.t., v.i.* 5. to make or become pale. [ME < MF < L *pallid*(*us*) PALLID] —**pale′ly,** *adv.* —**pale′ness,** *n.*
—**Syn.** 1. ashy, ashen. PALE, PALLID, WAN imply an absence of color, esp. from the human countenance. PALE implies a faintness or absence of color that may be natural when applied to things (*the pale blue of a violet*) but when used to refer to the human face usually means an unnatural and often temporary absence of color, as arising from sickness or sudden emotion: *pale cheeks.* PALLID implies an excessive paleness induced by intense emotion, disease, or death: *the pallid lips of the dying man.* WAN implies a sickly paleness, as after

a long illness: *wan and thin;* the suggestion of weakness may be more prominent than that of lack of color: *a wan smile.*

pale[2] (pāl), *n., v.,* **paled, pal·ing.** —*n.* **1.** a stake or picket, as of a fence. **2.** an enclosing or confining barrier; enclosure. **3.** an enclosed area. **4.** limits; bounds. **5.** a district or region within fixed bounds. **6.** (*cap.*) Also called **English Pale, Irish Pale.** a district in E Ireland included in the Angevin Empire of King Henry II and his successors. **7.** *Heraldry.* an ordinary in the form of a broad vertical stripe at the center of an escutcheon. **8. beyond the pale,** beyond the limits of propriety, courtesy, protection, safety, etc. **9. in pale,** *Heraldry.* **a.** (of two charges) with one directly over the other. **b.** (of a single charge) placed upright at the center of the escutcheon. **10. per pale,** *Heraldry.* from top to bottom at the center. —*v.t.* **11.** to enclose with pales; fence. **12.** to encircle or encompass. [ME (north), OE *pāl* < L *pāl(us)* stake. See POLE]

pale-, var. of **paleo-** before most vowels: *paleethnology.* Also, **palae-.**

pa·le·a (pā′lē ə), *n., pl.* **-le·ae** (-lē ē′). *Bot.* **1.** a chafflike scale or bract. **2.** the scalelike, membranous organ in the flowers of grasses that is situated upon a secondary axis in the axil of the flowering glume and envelops the stamens and pistil. [< NL, special use of L *palea* chaff] —**pa·le·a·ceous** (pā′lē ā′shəs), **pa·le·ate** (pā′lē it, -āt′), *adj.*

pa·le·eth·nol·o·gy (pā′lē eth nol′ə jē, pal′ē-), *n.* the branch of ethnology concerned with the earliest or most primitive races of mankind. —**pa·le·eth·no·log·ic** (pā′lē-eth′nəloj′ik, pal′ē-), **pa′le·eth·no·log′i·cal,** *adj.* —**pa′le-eth·nol′o·gist,** *n.*

pale·face (pāl′fās′), *n. Sometimes Disparaging.* a white person as distinguished from a North American Indian. [expression attributed to North American Indians]

Pa·lem·bang (pä′lem bäng′), *n.* a city in SE Sumatra, in W Indonesia. 582,961.

Pa·len·que (pä leng′ke), *n.* a village in SE Mexico, in Chiapas state: ruins of ancient Mayan city.

paleo-, a learned borrowing from Greek meaning "old," used in the formation of compound words: *paleobotany.* Also, *esp. before a vowel,* **pale-.** [< Gk *palaio-,* comb. form of *palaiós*]

pa·le·o·bi·ol·o·gy (pā′lē ō bī ol′ə jē, pal′ē-), *n.* the branch of paleontology dealing with fossil plants and animals, esp. with reference to their origin, growth, structure, etc. Also, **palaeobiology.** —**pa·le·o·bi·o·log·i·cal** (pā′lē ō-bī′ə loj′i kəl, pal′ē-), **pa′le·o·bi′o·log′ic,** *adj.* —**pa′le·o-bi·ol′o·gist,** *n.*

pa·le·o·bot·a·ny (pā′lē ō bot′ənē, pal′ē-), *n.* the branch of paleontology dealing with fossil plants. Also, **palaeo-botany.** —**pa·le·o·bo·tan·i·cal** (pā′lē ō bə tan′i kəl, pal′ē-), **pa′le·o·bo·tan′ic,** *adj.* —**pa′le·o·bot′a·nist,** *n.*

Pa·le·o·cene (pā′lē ə sēn′, pal′ē-), *Geol.* —*adj.* **1.** noting or pertaining to an epoch of the Tertiary period, occurring from 60,000,000 to 70,000,000 years ago, characterized by the advent of birds and the placental mammals. See table at **era.** —*n.* **2.** the Paleocene epoch or series. Also, **Palaeocene.**

paleog., paleography.

Pa·le·o·gene (pā′lē ə jēn′, pal′ē-), *Geol.* —*adj.* **1.** noting or pertaining to the earlier part of the Cenozoic era, in a system adopted by some geologists, occurring from 25,000,000 to 70,000,000 years ago and including the Oligocene, Eocene, and Paleocene epochs: corresponds to the earlier part of the Tertiary period in the system generally used in the U.S. See table at **era.** Cf. **Neocene.** —*n.* **2.** the Paleogene period or system. Also, **Palaeogene.** [< G *Paläogen,* equiv. to *paläo-* PALEO- + *-gen* (< Gk *genésthai* be born)]

pa·le·o·gen·e·sis (pā′lē ō jen′i sis, pal′ē-), *n. Biol.* palingenesis (def. 2). —**pa·le·o·ge·net·ic** (pā′lē ō jə net′ik, pal′ē-), *adj.*

pa·le·o·ge·og·ra·phy (pā′lē ō jē og′rə fē, pal′ē-), *n.* the science of representing the earth's geographic features belonging to any part of the geologic past. —**pa′le·o·ge·og′ra·pher,** *n.* —**pa·le·o·ge·o·graph·ic** (pā′lē ō jē′ə graf′ik, pal′ē-), **pa′le·o·ge′o·graph′i·cal,** *adj.* —**pa′le·o·ge′o·graph′i·cal·ly,** *adv.*

pa·le·o·ge·ol·o·gy (pā′lē ō jē ol′ə jē, pal′ē-), *n.* the science of representing geologic conditions of some given time in earth history. —**pa·le·o·ge·o·log·ic** (pā′lē ō jē′ə loj′ik, pal′ē-), *adj.* —**pa′le·o·ge·ol′o·gist,** *n.*

pa·le·og·ra·phy (pā′lē og′rə fē, pal′ē-), *n.* **1.** ancient forms of writing, as in documents and inscriptions. **2.** the study of ancient writing, including decipherment and determination of origin and date. —**pa′le·og′ra·pher,** *n.* —**pa·le·o·graph·ic** (pā′lē ə graf′ik, pal′ē-), **pa′le·o·graph′i·cal,** *adj.* —**pa′le·o·graph′i·cal·ly,** *adv.*

pa·le·o·lith (pā′lē ə lith, pal′ē-), *n.* a Paleolithic stone implement.

Pa·le·o·lith·ic (pā′lē ə lith′ik, pal′ē-), *adj.* of, pertaining to, or characteristic of the cultures of the Pleistocene epoch: usually divided into three periods **(Lower Paleolithic,** c500,000 B.C.–c250,000 B.C.; **Middle Paleolithic,** c250,000 B.C.–c60,000 B.C.; and **Upper Paleolithic,** c60,000 B.C. –c10,000 B.C.). Also, **Palaeolithic.**

pa·le·ol·o·gy (pā′lē ol′ə jē, pal′e-), *n.* the study of antiquities. —**pa·le·o·log·i·cal** (pā′lē ə loj′i kəl, pal′ē-), *adj.* —**pa′le·ol′o·gist,** *n.*

pa·le·o·mag·net·ism (pā′lē ō mag′ni tiz′əm), *n.* the magnetization acquired by a rock at the time of its formation. —**pa·le·o·mag·net·ic** (pā′lē ō mag net′ik), *adj.*

pa·le·on·tog·ra·phy (pā′lē ən tog′rə fē, pal′ē-), *n.* descriptive paleontology. [< F *paléontographie*] —**pa′le·on-tog′ra·pher,** *n.* —**pa·le·on·to·graph·ic** (pā′lē on′tə graf′ik, pal′ē-), **pa′le·on′to·graph′i·cal,** *adj.*

paleontol., paleontology. Also, **paleon.**

pa·le·on·tol·o·gy (pā′lē ən tol′ə jē, pal′ē-), *n., pl.* **-gies** for 2. **1.** the science of the forms of life existing in former geologic periods, as represented by fossil animals and plants. **2.** a treatise on paleontology. Also, **palaeontology.** [< F *paléontologie*] —**pa·le·on·to·log·ic** (pā′lē on′təloj′ik, pal′ē-), **pa′le·on′to·log′i·cal,** *adj.* —**pa′le·on′to·log′i·cal·ly,** *adv.* —**pa′le·on·tol′o·gist,** *n.*

Pa·le·o·zo·ic (pā′lē ə zō′ik, pal′ē-), *Geol.* —*adj.* **1.** noting or pertaining to an era occurring between 220,000,000 and 600,000,000 years ago, characterized by the appearance of fish, insects, and reptiles. See table at **era.** —*n.* **2.** the Paleozoic era or group of systems. Also, **Palaeozoic.** [PALEO- + ZO(O)- + -IC]

pa·le·o·zo·ol·o·gy (pā′lē ō zō ol′ə jē, pal′ē-), *n.* the branch of paleontology dealing with fossil animals. Also, **pa′le·o·zo·öl′o·gy.** —**pa·le·o·zo·o·log·i·cal, pa·le·o·zo·ö-log·i·cal** (pā′lē ō zō′ə loj′i kəl, pal′ē-), **pa′le·o·zo′o·log′ic, pa′le·o·zo′ö·log′ic,** *adj.* —**pa′le·o·zo·ol′o·gist, pa′le·o-zo·öl′o·gist,** *n.*

Pa·ler·mo (pə lâr′mō, -lûr′-; *It.* pä ler′mô), *n.* a seaport in and the capital of Sicily, in the NW part. 587,063 (1961).

Pal·es·tine (pal′i stīn′), *n.* **1.** Also called **Holy Land.** Biblical name, **Canaan.** an ancient country in SW Asia, on the E coast of the Mediterranean. **2.** a former British mandate comprising part of this country, divided between Israel, Jordan, and Egypt in 1948: the Jordanian and Egyptian parts were occupied by Israel in 1967.

Pal·es·tin·i·an (pal′i stin′ē ən), *n.* **1.** a native or inhabitant of Palestine. **2.** Also called **Palestin′ian Ar′ab.** an Arab formerly living in Palestine who advocates the establishment of an Arab homeland there. —*adj.* **3.** of or pertaining to Palestine or Palestinians. **4.** of or pertaining to Palestinian Arabs: *Palestinian guerrillas.*

pa·les·tra (pə les′trə), *n., pl.* **-tras, -trae** (-trē). *Gk. Antiq.* a school for athletics. Also, **palaestra.** [late ME *palestre* < L *palaestra* a wrestling school, gymnasium < Gk *palaístra* = *palaí(ein)* (to) wrestle + *-stra* n. suffix of place]

Pa·le·stri·na (pal′i strē′nə; *It.* pä′le strē′nä), *n.* **Gio·van·ni Pier·lu·i·gi da** (jô vän′nē pyer′lo͞o ē′jē dä), 1526?–94, Italian composer.

pal·e·tot (pal′i tō′, pal′tō), *n.* **1.** a loose overcoat. **2.** a close-fitting jacket differing in material from the rest of a costume, worn by women, esp. in the 19th century. [< F, MF, var. of *paletoc* < ME *paltok* a jacket, peasant's coat]

pal·ette (pal′it), *n.* **1.** a thin and usually oval or oblong board or tablet with a thumb hole at one end, used by painters for holding and mixing colors. **2.** any other flat surface used by a painter for this purpose. **3.** the set of colors on such a board or surface. **4.** the range of colors used by a particular artist. **5.** the elements of any art considered as to quality or range: *a musical palette.* [< F, MF < It *paletta,* dim. of *pala* shovel < L; see -ETTE] —**pal′ette·like′,** *adj.*

pal′ette knife′, *Painting.* a thin blade of varying flexibility set in a handle and used for mixing colors or applying them to a canvas.

pal·frey (pôl′frē), *n., pl.* **-freys.** **1.** a riding horse, as distinguished from a war horse. **2.** a saddle horse, particularly a gentle one suitable for a woman. [ME *palefret* < OF, earlier *palefreid* < LL *paraverēd(us)* post horse < Gk *pará* near, beside (see PARA-) + L *verēdus* swift hunting horse < Celt]

Pal·grave (pôl′grāv, pal′-), *n.* **Francis Turner,** 1824–97, English critic, poet, and anthologist.

Pa·li (pä′lē), *n.* the Prakrit language of the Buddhist scriptures. [short for Skt *pāli-bhāṣa* language of the canonical texts = *pāli* line, row, canon + *bhāṣa* language]

pal·i·mo·ny (pal′ə mō′nē), *n. Informal.* a form of alimony awarded, usually to a woman, after the breakup of a relationship in which two unmarried people have lived together as husband and wife for a considerable length of time. [PAL + (AL)IMONY]

pal·imp·sest (pal′imp sest′), *n.* a parchment or the like from which writing has been partially or completely erased to make room for another text. [< L *palimpsēst(us)* < Gk *palímpsēstos* rubbed again (*pálin* again + *psēstós* scraped, rubbed, < *psên* to rub smooth)]

pal·in·drome (pal′in drōm′), *n.* a word, line, verse, etc., reading the same backward as forward, as *Madam, I'm Adam* or *Poor Dan is in a droop.* [< Gk *palíndrom(os)* recurring = *pálin* again, back + *-dromos* -DROME]

pal·ing (pā′ling), *n.* **1.** a fence of pales. **2.** a pale or picket for a fence. **3.** pales collectively. **4.** the act of one who builds a fence with pales. [ME]

pal·in·gen·e·sis (pal′in jen′i sis), *n.* **1.** rebirth; regeneration. **2.** *Biol.* the development of an individual which reproduces the ancestral features (opposed to *cenogenesis*). **3.** the doctrine of transmigration of souls. [< NL < Gk *pálin* again + *génesis* GENESIS] —**pal·in·ge·ne·si·an** (pal′in jə nē′zhē-ən), **pal·in·ge·net·ic** (pal′in jə net′ik), *adj.*

pal·i·node (pal′ə nōd′), *n.* **1.** a poem in which the poet retracts something said in an earlier poem. **2.** a recantation. [< LL *palinōd(ia)* < Gk *palinōidía* a singing again, especially a recanting = *pálin* again, back + *ōid(ḗ)* ODE + *-ia* -IA]

pal·i·sade (pal′i sād′), *n., v.,* **-sad·ed, -sad·ing.** —*n.* **1.** a fence of pales or stakes set firmly in the ground, as for enclosure or defense. **2.** any of a number of pales pointed at the top and set in a row to form a defense. **3. palisades,** a line of cliffs. —*v.t.* **4.** to furnish or fortify with a palisade. [< F *palissade* < OPr *palissad(a)* = *paliss(a)* paling (< *pal* stake < L *pālus*) + *-ada* -ADE[1]]

Pal·i·sades (pal′i sādz′), *n.* the line of cliffs in NE New Jersey and SE New York extending along the W bank of the lower Hudson River; ab. 40 mi. long.

pall[1] (pôl), *n.* **1.** a cloth, often of velvet, for spreading over a coffin, bier, or tomb. **2.** a coffin. **3.** something that covers, shrouds, or overspreads, esp. with darkness or gloom. **4.** *Eccles.* **a.** pallium (def. 2). **b.** a linen cloth or a square cloth-covered piece of cardboard used to cover a chalice. **5.** *Archaic.* a cloth spread upon an altar; corporal. **6.** *Archaic.* a garment, esp. a robe, cloak, or the like. —*v.t.* **7.** to cover with or as with a pall. [ME; OE *pæll* < L *pall(ium)* cloak] —**pall′-like′,** *adj.*

pall[2] (pôl), *v.i.* **1.** to have a wearying effect. **2.** to become distasteful or unpleasant. **3.** to become satiated or cloyed with something. —*v.t.* **4.** to satiate or cloy. **5.** to make dull, distasteful, or unpleasant. [ME *palle(n)*; aph. var. of APPALL] —**Syn. 4.** glut, sate, surfeit. **5.** weary.

Pal·la·di·an (pə lā′dē ən), *adj.* pertaining to or in the style of Andrea Palladio.

Pal·la·di·an (pə lā′dē ən), *adj.* **1.** of or pertaining to the goddess Pallas. **2.** pertaining to wisdom, knowledge, or study. [< L *Palladi(us)* of Pallas (< Gk *Pallădios;* see PALLADIUM) + -AN]

Palla′dian win′dow, a window in the form of an archway with two narrow, flat-headed side compartments.

Palladian window

pal·lad·ic (pə lad′ik, -lā′dik), *adj. Chem.* of or containing palladium, esp. in the tetravalent state.

pal·la·di·nize (pal′ə-dᵊnīz′), *v.t.,* **-ized, -iz·ing.** palladiumize. [irreg. < NL *pallad(ium)*; see -IZE]

Pal·la·dio (päl lä′dyô), *n.* **An·dre·a** (än dre′ä), 1508–80, Italian architect.

pal·la·di·um (pə lā′dē əm), *n. Chem.* a rare metallic element of the platinum group, silver-white, ductile, and malleable, harder and fusing more readily than platinum: used chiefly as a catalyst and in dental and other alloys. *Symbol:* Pd; *at. wt.:* 106.4; *at. no.:* 46; *sp. gr.:* 12 at 20°C. [special use of PALLADIUM; named (1803) after the asteroid PALLAS, then newly discovered; see -IUM]

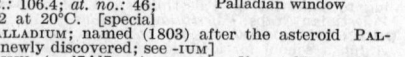

Pal·la·di·um (pə lā′dē əm), *n., pl.* **-di·a** (-dē ə). **1.** a statue of Pallas Athene, esp. one on the citadel of Troy. **2.** (*usually l.c.*) anything believed to provide protection or safety; safeguard. [< L *Palladium* < Gk *Pallădion,* n. use of neut. of *Pallădios* of Pallas = *Pallad-* (s. of *Pallás*) PALLAS + *-ios* adj. suffix]

pal·la·di·um·ize (pə lā′dē ə mīz′), *v.t.,* **-ized, -iz·ing.** to treat or cover (a surface) with palladium. Also, **palladinize, palladize.**

pal·la·dize (pal′ə dīz′), *v.t.,* **-dized, -diz·ing.** palladiumize. [PALLAD(IUM) + -IZE]

pal·la·dous (pə lā′dəs, pal′ə dəs), *adj. Chem.* containing bivalent palladium.

Pal·las (pal′əs), *n.* **1.** Also called **Pal′las Athen′a.** *Class. Myth.* Athena. **2.** *Astron.* the second largest and one of the four brightest asteroids.

pal·las·ite (pal′ə sīt′), *n. Mineral.* a type of meteorite containing crystals of olivine embedded in nickel iron. [named after Peter S. *Pallas* (d. 1811), German naturalist; see -ITE[1]]

pall·bear·er (pôl′bâr′ər), *n.* one of several persons who carry or attend the coffin at a funeral.

pal·let[1] (pal′it), *n.* **1.** a bed or mattress of straw. **2.** a small or makeshift bed. [ME *pailet* < AF *paillete* = OF *paille* straw (< L *palea* chaff) + *-ete* -ETTE]

pal·let[2] (pal′it), *n.* **1.** a shaping tool used by potters and consisting of a flat blade or plate with a handle at one end. **2.** a flat board or metal plate used to support ceramic articles during drying. **3.** *Horol.* **a.** a lever with three projections, two intermittently looking and receiving impulses from the escape wheel and one transmitting the impulses to the balance. **b.** either of the two projections of this lever that engage and release the escape wheel. **4.** (on a pawl) a lip, or projection, that engages with the teeth of a ratchet wheel. **5.** a platform on which goods are placed for storage or transportation. [< MF *palette* small shovel. See PALETTE]

pal·let·ize (pal′i tīz′), *v.t.,* **-ized, -iz·ing.** to place (materials) upon pallets for handling or transportation. —**pal′let·i·za′tion,** *n.*

pal′let knife′, *Cookery.* a small, flat utensil for picking up and handling pastry paste.

pal·li·al (pal′ē əl), *adj.* **1.** of or pertaining to the mantle of a mollusk. **2.** of or pertaining to the cerebral cortex. [PALLI(UM) + -AL[1]]

pal·liasse (pal yas′, pal′yas), *n. Chiefly Brit.* paillasse.

pal·li·ate (pal′ē āt′), *v.t.,* **-at·ed, -at·ing.** **1.** to attempt to mitigate or conceal the gravity of (an offense) by excuses, apologies, etc.; extenuate. **2.** to relieve without curing, as a disease; mitigate; alleviate. [< LL *palliāt(us)* cloaked, covered. See PALLIUM, -ATE[1]] —**pal′li·a′tion,** *n.* —**pal′li·a′tor,** *n.*

pal·li·a·tive (pal′ē ā′tiv, -ē ə tiv), *adj.* **1.** serving to palliate. —*n.* **2.** something that palliates. [< F *palliatif*] —**pal′li·a′tive·ly,** *adv.*

pal·lid (pal′id), *adj.* **1.** pale; wan; faint or deficient in color: *a pallid face.* **2.** lacking in vitality or interest: *a pallid musical performance.* [< L *pallid(us)* sallow = *pall(ēre)* (to) be pale + *-idus* -ID[4]] —**pal′lid·ly,** *adv.* —**pal′lid·ness,** *n.* —**Syn. 1.** See **pale**[1].

Pal·li·ser (pal′i sər), *n.* **John,** 1807–87, Canadian geographer and explorer, born in Ireland.

pal·li·um (pal′ē əm), *n., pl.* **pal·li·a** (pal′ē ə), **pal·li·ums.** **1.** a large, rectangular mantle worn by men in ancient Greece and Rome. **2.** *Eccles.* a woolen vestment worn by the pope and by archbishops, consisting of a narrow band resting on the shoulders, with a lappet in front and behind. **3.** *Anat.* the entire cortex of the cerebrum. **4.** *Zool.* a mantle. [ME, OE < L; see PALL[1]]

Pall Mall (pel′ mel′, pal′ mal′, pôl′ môl′), a street in London, England, famed for its social clubs.

pall-mall (pel′mel′), *n.* **1.** a game, popular in the 17th century, in which a ball of boxwood was struck with a mallet in an attempt to drive it through a raised iron ring at the end of a playing alley. **2.** the playing alley. [< MF *pallemaille* < It *pallamaglio* = *palla* ball (< Langobardish) + *maglio* mallet (< L *malleus*). See BALL[1], MALL]

pal·lor (pal′ər), *n.* unnatural paleness, as from fear, ill health, or death; wanness. [< L: paleness = *pall(ēre)* (to) be pale + *-or* -OR[1]]

palm[1] (päm), *n.* **1.** the part of the inner surface of the hand that extends from the wrist to the bases of the fingers. **2.** the corresponding part of the forefoot of an animal. **3.** the part of a glove covering this part of the hand. **4.** Also called **sailmaker's palm.** a stiff rawhide or metal shield worn over this part of the hand by sailmakers to serve as a thimble. **5.** a linear measure of from three to four inches, based on the breadth of the hand. **6.** a linear measure of from seven to ten inches, based on the length of the hand. **7.** the flat, expanded part of the horn or antler of a deer. **8.** a flat, widened part at the end of an armlike projection. **9.** *Naut.* **a.** the blade of an oar. **b.** the inner face of an anchor fluke. **c.** (loosely) an anchor fluke. **10. cross** or **grease someone's palm,** to give money to, esp. as a bribe. —*v.t.* **11.** to conceal in the palm, as a playing card used in cheating. **12.** to pick up stealthily. **13.** to hold in the hand. **14.** to touch or stroke with the palm or hand. **15. palm off,** to dispose of by fraud; substitute (something) with intent to deceive: *to palm off a forged painting.* [< L *palm(a)* (c. OE *folm* hand); r. ME *paume* < MF < L *palma*]

Royal palm, *Roystonea regia*

palm[2] (päm), *n.* **1.** any of numerous plants of the family *Palmaceae,* most species being tall, unbranched trees surmounted by a crown of large pinnate or palmately cleft leaves. **2.** any of various other trees or shrubs that resemble them. **3.** a leaf or branch of any of these trees, esp. as formerly borne to signify victory or as used on festive occasions. **4.** a representation of such a leaf or branch, as on a military or other decoration of honor. **5.** the reward of honor due a victor. **6.** victory; triumph; success: *He carried off the palm by sheer perseverance.* [ME, OE < L *palma* palm tree, special use of *palma* PALM[1]] —**palm′like′,** *adj.*

Pal·ma (päl′mä), *n.* a seaport in and the capital of the Balearic Islands, on W Majorca. 164,963 (est. 1963). Also called **Pal·ma de Ma·llor·ca** (Sp. päl′mä the mä lyôʀ′kä).

pal·ma·ceous (pal mā′shəs, päl-, pä mā′-), *adj.* belonging to the *Palmaceae,* or palm family of plants.

pal·mar (pal′mər, päl′-, pä′mər), *adj.* of, pertaining to, or located in or on the palm of the hand or the corresponding part of the forefoot of an animal. [< L *palmār(is)* a hand's breadth]

pal·ma·ry (pal′mə rē, päl′-, pä′mə-), *adj.* having or deserving to have the palm of victory or success; praiseworthy: *a palmary achievement.* [< L *palmāri-(us)* of, belonging to palms]

Pal·mas (päl′mäs), *n.* **Las.** See **Las Palmas.**

Palmate leaf

pal·mate (pal′māt, -mit, päl′-, pä′-māt), *adj.* **1.** shaped like an open palm or like a hand with the fingers extended, as a leaf or an antler. **2.** *Bot.* lobed or divided so that the sinuses point to or reach the apex of the petiole irrespective of the number of lobes. **3.** *Zool.* webbed, as the anterior toes of certain aquatic birds. Also, **pal′mat·ed.** [< L *palmāt(us)* marked with or shaped like the palm of a hand] —**pal′mate·ly,** *adv.*

pal·ma·tion (pal mā′shən, päl-, pä mā′-), *n.* **1.** a palmate state or formation. **2.** a palmate structure.

Palm′ Beach′, a town in SE Florida: seaside winter resort. 9086 (1970).

palm·er (pä′mər, päl′mər), *n.* **1.** a pilgrim, esp. of the Middle Ages, who had returned from the Holy Land, in token of which he bore a palm branch. **2.** any religious pilgrim. [ME *palmer(e)* < AF *palmer* = OF *palmier* < ML *palmār(ius),* special use of L *palmārius* PALMARY]

Pal·mer (pä′mər), *n.* **Daniel David,** 1845–1913, Canadian originator of chiropractic medicine.

Palm′er Land′, the southern part of the Antarctic Peninsula.

Palm′er Penin′sula, former name of **Antarctic Peninsula.**

Palm·er·ston (pä′mər stən), *n.* **Henry John Temple, 3rd Viscount,** 1784–1865, British statesman: prime minister 1855–58; 1859–65.

palm·er·worm (pä′mər wûrm′), *n.* the larva of a tineid moth, *Dichomeris ligulella,* of the eastern U.S., that feeds on the leaves of apple and other fruit trees.

pal·mette (pal met′), *n.* a conventionalized shape in the form of palmately spread leaves or sections, used as ornamentation. Cf. **anthemion, lotus** (def. 5). [< F]

pal·met·to (pal met′ō), *n., pl.* **-tos, -toes.** any of various palms having fan-shaped leaves, as of the genera *Sabal, Serenoa,* and *Thrinax.* [earlier *palmito* < Sp, dim. of *palma* PALM[2], *-etto* by assoc. with -ETTE]

Palmet′to State′, South Carolina (used as a nickname).

Pal·mi·ra (päl mē′ʀä), *n.* a city in W Colombia. 148,510 (est. 1964).

palm·is·try (pä′mi strē), *n.* the art or practice of telling fortunes and interpreting character by the lines and configurations of the palm of the subject's hand. [late ME *pawmestry* = *pawm* PALM[1] + *-estr-* (var. of *-istr-* < MF *-istre*) + *-y* -Y[3]] —**palm′ist,** *n.*

pal·mi·tate (pal′mi tāt′, päl′-, pä′mi-), *n. Chem.* a salt or ester of palmitic acid. [PALMIT(IN) + -ATE[2]]

pal·mit′ic ac′id (pal mit′ik, päl-, pä mit′-), *Chem.* a solid, $CH_3(CH_2)_{14}COOH$, obtained by hydrolysis from palm oil and natural fats, and from spermaceti: used in the manufacture of soap. [< F *palmitique.* See PALM[2], -ITE[1], -IC]

pal·mi·tin (pal′mi tin, päl′-, pä′mi-), *n. Chem.* a powder, $(C_{15}H_{31}COO)_3C_3H_5$, prepared from glycerol and palmitic acid: used in the manufacture of soap. [< F *palmitine.* See PALM[2], -ITE[1], -IN[2]]

palm′ oil′, **1.** a yellow, butterlike oil derived from the fruit of the oil palm and used as an edible fat and for making soap, candles, etc. **2.** oil obtained from various species of palm.

Palm′ Springs′, a city in S California: resort. 20,936 (1970).

Palm′ Sun′day, the Sunday before Easter, celebrating Christ's triumphal entry into Jerusalem. [ME *palmesonday,* OE *palmsunnandæg*]

palm·y (pä′mē), *adj.,* **palm·i·er, palm·i·est.** **1.** glorious, prosperous, or flourishing: *the palmy days of yesteryear.* **2.** abounding in or shaded with palms: *palmy islands.*

pal·my·ra (pal mī′rə), *n.* a tropical Asian fan palm, *Borassus flabellifer.* [alter. of Pg *palmeira* PALM[2]]

Pal·my·ra (pal mī′rə), *n.* an ancient city in central Syria, NE of Damascus: reputedly built by Solomon.

Pal·o Al·to (pal′ō al′tō *for 1;* pä′lō äl′tō *for 2*), **1.** a city in W California, SE of San Francisco. 56,181 (1970). **2.** a battlefield 12 mi. NE of Brownsville, Texas: first battle of Mexican War 1846.

pal·o·mi·no (pal′ə mē′nō), *n., pl.* **-nos.** one of a breed of horses developed chiefly in the southwestern U.S. and characterized by a golden color and a flaxen mane and tail. [< AmerSp, special use of Sp *palomino* of, resembling a dove < L *palumbīnus* = *palumb(ēs)* dove + *-īnus* -INE[1]]

pa·loo·ka (pə lo͞o′kə), *n. Slang.* an athlete, esp. a boxer, lacking in ability, experience, or competitive spirit. [?]

Pa·los (pä′lôs), *n.* a seaport in SW Spain: starting point of Columbus' first voyage westward. 3500 (1961).

Pal′os Ver′des Penin′sula (pal′əs vûr′dəs), a town in SW California. 38,918 (1970).

palp (palp), *n.* a palpus.

pal·pa·ble (pal′pə bəl), *adj.* **1.** readily or plainly seen, heard, perceived, etc.; obvious; evident. **2.** capable of being touched or felt; tangible. [ME < LL *palpābil(is)* that can be touched = *palpā(re)* (to) touch + *-bilis* -BLE] —**pal′pa·bil′i·ty, pal′pa·ble·ness,** *n.* —**pal′pa·bly,** *adv.* —**Syn. 1.** manifest, plain. **2.** material, corporeal.

pal·pate[1] (pal′pāt), *v.t.,* **-pat·ed, -pat·ing.** *Med.* to examine by touch. [< L *palpāt(us)*, ptp. of *palpāre* to feel, touch; see -ATE[1]] —**pal·pa′tion,** *n.* —**pal·pa·to·ry** (pal′pə tōr′ē, -tôr′ē), *adj.*

pal·pate[2] (pal′pāt), *adj. Zool.* having a palpus or palpi. [PALP(US) + -ATE[1]]

pal·pe·bral (pal′pə brəl), *adj.* of or pertaining to the eyelids. [< LL *palpebrāl(is)* of, on the eyelids = L *palpebr(a)* eyelid (sp. var. of *palpebrum*) + *-ālis* -AL[1]]

pal·pe·brate (pal′pə brāt′, pal pē′brit), *adj.* having eyelids. [< NL *palpebrāt(us)* = L *palpebr(a)* eyelid + *-ātus* -ATE[1]]

pal·pi (pal′pī), *n.* pl. of **palpus.**

pal·pi·tant (pal′pi tənt), *adj.* palpitating. [< L *palpitant-* (s. of *palpitāns*) throbbing, prp. of *palpitāre*]

pal·pi·tate (pal′pi tāt′), *v.i.,* **-tat·ed, -tat·ing. 1.** to pulsate, as the heart, with unnatural rapidity from exertion, emotion, disease, etc.; flutter. **2.** to pulsate; quiver; throb; tremble. [< L *palpitāt(us)* throbbed, ptp. of *palpitāre*, freq. of *palpāre* to stroke. See PALPUS, -ATE[1]] —**pal′pi·tat′ing·ly,** *adv.* —**Syn. 1.** See **pulsate.**

pal·pi·ta·tion (pal′pi tā′shən), *n.* **1.** the act of palpitating. **2.** an abnormally rapid or violent beating of the heart. [< L *palpitātiōn-* (s. of *palpitātiō*) a throbbing]

pal·pus (pal′pəs), *n., pl.* **-pi** (-pī). an appendage attached to an oral part and serving as an organ of sense, as in insects and crustaceans. [< NL, special use of L *palpus* a stroking, caress, akin to FEEL]

pals·grave (pôlz′grāv, palz′-), *n.* a German count palatine. [< D *paltsgrave* (now *paltsgraaf*); c. G *Pfalzgraf* imperial count. See MARGRAVE, PALATINE[1]]

pals·gra·vine (pôlz′grə vēn′, palz′-), *n.* the wife or widow of a palsgrave. [< D *paltsgravin*]

pal·sy (pôl′zē), *n., pl.* **-sies,** *v.,* **-sied, -sy·ing.** —*n.* **1.** paralysis (def. 1). **2.** any of a variety of atonal muscular conditions characterized by tremors of the body parts, as of the hands, arms, or legs, or of the entire body. —*v.t.* **3.** to paralyze. [ME, var. of *parlesie* < MF *paralisie* < L *paralysis* PARALYSIS] —**pal′sy·like′,** *adj.*

pal·sy-wal·sy (pal′zē wal′zē), *adj. Slang.* friendly or appearing to be friendly in an intimate or hearty way. [rhyming compound, based on *palsy*, extended form of PAL; see -S[3], -Y[1]]

pal·ter (pôl′tər), *v.i.* **1.** to talk or act insincerely; lie or use trickery. **2.** to bargain; haggle. [earliest sense: to speak indistinctly; perh. alter. of FALTER in same sense, with *p-* from PALSY] —**pal′ter·er,** *n.*

pal·try (pôl′trē), *adj.,* **-tri·er, -tri·est. 1.** trifling; petty. **2.** trashy or worthless: *paltry rags.* **3.** mean or contemptible: *a paltry coward.* [< LG *paltrig* ragged = *palter* rag (dial. G *Palter*) + *-ig* -Y[1]] —**pal′tri·ly,** *adv.* —**pal′tri·ness,** *n.* —**Syn. 1.** insignificant. See **petty.** —**Ant. 1.** important.

pa·lu·dal (pə lo͞od′əl, pal′yə dəl), *adj.* **1.** of or pertaining to marshes. **2.** produced by marshes, as miasma or disease. [< L *palūd-* (s. of *palus*) swamp, marsh + -AL[1]]

pal·u·dism (pal′yə diz′əm), *n. Pathol.* malaria. [< L *palūd-* (s. of *palus*) swamp, marsh + -ISM]

Pa′lus Som′ni (pä′ləs som′nē), a hilly area in the first quadrant of the face of the moon at the edge of Mare Tranquillitatis. ab. 11,000 sq. mi. Also, **Pa′lus Som′ni·i** (som′nē ē′). Also called **Marsh of Sleep.**

pal·y[1] (pā′lē), *adj. Archaic.* pale[1]. [PALE[1] + -Y[1]]

pal·y[2] (pā′lē), *adj. Heraldry.* divided palewise into equal parts of alternating tinctures. [ME < MF *pale.* See PALE[2], -EE]

pam., pamphlet.

Pa·mirs, the (pä mērz′), a plateau in central Asia, where the Hindu Kush, Tien Shan, and Himalaya mountain ranges converge. Highest peaks, ab. 25,000 ft. Also **the Pa·mir′.**

Pam′li·co Sound′ (pam′lə kō′), a sound between the North Carolina mainland and coastal islands.

pam·pas (pam′pəz; *attributively* pam′pəs; *Sp.* päm′päs), *n.pl., sing.* **-pa** (-pə; *Sp.* -pä). the vast grassy plains of S South America, esp. in Argentina. [< AmerSp, pl. of *pampa* < Quechua *bamba* plain] —**pam·pe·an** (pam pē′ən, pam′pē ən), *adj.*

pam′pas grass′, a tall, ornamental grass, *Cortaderia Sellona,* native to South America, having large, thick, feathery, silvery-white panicles.

Pam·pe·lu·na (päm′pe lo͞o′nä), *n.* Pamplona.

pam·per (pam′pər), *v.t.* to treat or gratify with extreme or excessive indulgence, kindness, or care: *to pamper a child; to pamper one's stomach.* [ME *pamper(en)*, prob. < MFlem; cf. Flem *pamperen*] —**pam′pered·ly,** *adv.* —**pam′pered·ness,** *n.* —**pam′per·er,** *n.* —**Syn.** humor, coddle, baby, spoil.

pam·pe·ro (päm pâr′ō; *Sp.* päm pe′rō), *n., pl.* **-ros** (-rōz; *Sp.* -rōs). a cold, dry, southwesterly wind that sweeps over the pampas of Argentina. [< AmerSp: lit., of the pampas]

pamph., pamphlet.

pam·phlet (pam′flit), *n.* **1.** a short treatise or essay, generally a controversial tract, on some subject of contemporary interest: *a political pamphlet.* **2.** a complete, unbound publication of generally less than 80 pages stitched or stapled together. [ME *pamflet* < AL *panflet(us)*, syncopated var. of *Pamphiletus*, dim. of ML *Pamphilus*, title of a 12th-century Latin comedy (< Gk *Pámphilos* man's name); see -ET] —**pam′phlet·ar′y,** *adj.*

pam·phlet·eer (pam′fli tēr′), *n.* **1.** a writer of pamphlets. —*v.i.* **2.** to write and issue pamphlets.

Pam·plo·na (pam plō′nə; *Sp.* päm plô′nä), *n.* a city in N Spain. 105,397 (est. 1963). Also, **Pampeluna.**

pan[1] (pan), *n., v.,* **panned, pan·ning.** —*n.* **1.** a broad, shallow, metal container used in various forms for frying, baking, washing, etc. **2.** any of various open or closed vessels used in industrial or mechanical processes. **3.** *Slang.* the face. **4.** a drifting piece of flat, thin ice. **5.** a natural or excavated depression in the ground. **6.** (in old guns) the depressed part of the lock, holding the priming. —*v.t.* **7.** to wash (gravel, sand, etc.) in a pan to separate gold or other heavy valuable metal. **8.** to separate by such washing. **9.** *Informal.* to criticize severely, as in a review of a play. —*v.i.* **10.** to wash gravel, sand etc., in a pan in seeking gold or the like. **11.** to yield gold or the like, as gravel washed in a pan. **12. pan out,** *Informal.* to develop or conclude with a specific result: *His new job is panning out well for him.* [ME, OE *panne;* c. D *pan,* G *Pfanne,* Icel *panna*]

pan[2] (pän), *n.* **1.** the leaf of the betel. **2.** a substance, esp. betel nut or a betel-nut mixture, used for chewing. [< Hindi < Skt *parṇa* feather, leaf]

pan[3] (pan), *v.,* **panned, pan·ning.** *Motion Pictures, Television.* —*v.i.* **1.** to photograph or televise a scene or moving subject while rotating the camera through a wide angle. **2.** (of a camera) to be moved or manipulated in such a manner. —*v.t.* **3.** to move (a camera) in such a manner. [shortening of PANORAMA]

Pan

Pan (pan), *n.* the ancient Greek god of forests, flocks, and shepherds, represented with the head, chest, and arms of a man and the legs and sometimes the horns and ears of a goat.

pan-, a learned borrowing from Greek meaning "all," occurring originally in loan words from Greek (*panacea; panoply*), but now used freely as a general formative (*panleukopenia; panorama; pantheism*), and esp. in terms, formed at will, implying the union of all branches of a group (*Pan-American, Pan-Slavism*). The hyphen and the second capital tend with longer use to be lost (*Panhellenic*), unless they are retained in order to set off clearly the component parts. Also, **pant-, panto-.** [< Gk *pan-* comb. form of *pâs* all]

Pan., Panama.

pan·a·ce·a (pan′ə sē′ə), *n.* **1.** a remedy for all disease or ills; cure-all. **2.** an answer for all problems or solution to all difficulties. [< L < Gk *panákeia* = *panakē(s)* all-healing (*pan-* PAN- + *akēs* a cure) + *-ia* -IA]

Pan·a·ce·a (pan′ə sē′ə), *n.* an ancient Greek goddess of healing.

pa·nache (pə nash′, -näsh′), *n.* **1.** an ornamental plume, esp. of feathers, usually worn on a helmet or cap. **2.** a grand or flamboyant manner; verve; style. [var. (after F) of *pennache* < MF < early It *pennachio* < LL *pinnāculum*, dim. of *pinna* wing; identical in form with *pinnāculum* PINNACLE]

Pan-Af·ri·can·ism (pan′af′rə kə niz′əm), *n.* the idea or advocacy of a political alliance of all the African nations. —**Pan′-Af′ri·can,** *adj., n.* —**Pan′-Af′ri·can·ist,** *n.*

Pan·a·ma (pan′ə mä′), *n.* **1.** a republic in S Central America, enclosing but not including the Panama Canal. 1,900,000; 28,575 sq. mi. **2.** Also called **Panama City.** a city in and the capital of Panama, at the Pacific end of the Panama Canal, though not in the Canal Zone. 438,000. **3. Isthmus of.** Formerly, **Isthmus of Darien.** an isthmus between North and South America. **4. Gulf of,** the portion of the Pacific in the bend of the Isthmus of Panama. **5.** (*sometimes l.c.*) See **Panama hat.** Spanish, **Pa·na·má** (pä′nä mä′) (for defs. 1, 2). —**Pan·a·ma·ni·an** (pan′ə mā′nē ən, -mä′-), *adj., n.*

Pan′ama Canal′, a canal extending SE from the Atlantic to the Pacific across the Isthmus of Panama. 40 mi. long.

Pan′ama Canal′ Zone′. See **Canal Zone.**

Pan′ama Cit′y, 1. Panama (def. 2). **2.** a city in NW Florida. 32,096 (1970).

Pan′ama hat′, a hat made of finely plaited young leaves of a palmlike plant, *Carludovica palmata,* of Central and South America. Also called **Panama.**

Pan-A·mer·i·can (pan′ə mer′i kən), *adj.* of, pertaining to, or representing all the countries or people of North, Central, and South America.

Pan-A·mer·i·can·ism (pan′ə mer′i kə niz′əm), *n.* **1.** the idea or advocacy of a political alliance of all the countries of North, Central, and South America. **2.** a movement for or the idea or advocacy of close economic, cultural, and military cooperation among these countries.

Pan′ Amer′ican Un′ion, a former organization of American republics dedicated to furthering understanding and peace.

Pan′a·mint Moun′tains (pan′ə mint), a mountain range in E California. Highest peak, Telescope Peak, 11,045 ft.

Pan-Ar·a·bism (pan′ar′ə biz′əm), *n.* the idea or advocacy of a political alliance or union of all the Arab nations. —**Pan′-Ar′ab, Pan′-Ar′ab·ic,** *adj., n.*

pan·a·tel·la (pan′ə tel′ə), *n.* panetella. Also, **pan′a·tel′a.**

Pa·nay (pä nī′), *n.* an island in the Central Philippines. 1,813,000 (est. 1965); 4446 sq. mi. *Cap.:* Iloilo.

pan-broil (pan′broil′), *v.t., v.i.* to cook in an uncovered frying pan over direct heat using little or no fat.

pan·cake (pan′kāk′), *n., v.,* **-caked, -cak·ing.** —*n.* **1.** a flat cake of batter cooked in a pan or on a griddle; griddlecake or flapjack. **2.** an airplane landing made by pancaking. **3.** Also called **pan′cake make′-up.** a make-up in cake form, used alone or with powder, applied with a damp sponge. —*v.i.* **4.** (of an airplane or the like) to drop flat to the ground after leveling off a few feet above it. —*v.t.* **5.** to cause (an airplane) to pancake. [late ME]

Pan·chai·a (pän kē′ə), *n.* an area in the northern hemisphere of Mars, appearing as a dark region when viewed telescopically from the earth.

Pan′chen La′ma (pän′chen). See **Tashi Lama.** Also called **Pan′chen Rim·po′che** (rim pō′chā).

pan·chro·mat·ic (pan′krō mat′ik, -krə-), *adj.* sensitive to all visible colors, as a photographic film. —**pan·chro·ma·tism** (pan krō′mə tiz′əm), *n.*

pan·cre·as (pan′krē əs, paŋ′-), *n.* *Anat., Zool.* a gland, situated near the stomach, which secretes a digestive fluid into the intestine through one or more ducts and also secretes the hormone insulin. Cf. **islet of Langerhans, pancreatic juice.** [< NL < Gk *pánkreas* sweetbread = *pan-* PAN- + *kréas* flesh, meat] —**pan·cre·at·ic** (pan′krē at′ik, paŋ′-), *adj.*

pancreat-, var. of **pancreato-** before a vowel: *pancreatin.*

pancreat′ic juice′, *Biochem.* a thick, colorless, very alkaline fluid secreted by the pancreas, containing enzymes that break down protein, fat, and starch.

pan·cre·a·tin (pan′krē ə tin, paŋ′-), *n.* **1.** *Biochem.* a substance containing the pancreatic enzymes, trypsin, amylase, and lipase. **2.** a commercial preparation of this substance, used chiefly as a digestive.

pancreato-, a combining form of **pancreas.** Also, *esp. before a vowel,* **pancreat-.** [< NL < Gk *pankreat-* (s. of *pánkreas*); see -o-]

Giant panda, *Ailuropoda melanoleuca* (2 ft. high at shoulder; length 5 ft.)

pan·da (pan′də), *n.* **1.** Also called **lesser panda.** a reddish-brown carnivore, *Ailurus fulgens,* of the Himalayas, having the face marked with white and a long, bushy tail marked with pale rings. **2.** Also called **giant panda.** a large, bearlike carnivore, *Ailuropoda melanoleuca,* of Tibet and southwestern China, white with black limbs, shoulders, and ears, and with a black ring around each eye. [after a Nepalese name for the animal]

pan·da·na·ceous (pan′də nā′shəs), *adj.* belonging to the *Pandanaceae,* or pandanus family of trees and shrubs. [PANDAN(US) + -ACEOUS]

pan·da·nus (pan dā′nəs), *n., pl.* **-nus·es.** any plant of the genus *Pandanus,* comprising the screw pines. [< NL < Malay *pandan*]

Pan·da·rus (pan′dər əs), *n.* *Class. Myth.* a Trojan who, at the instigation of Athena, attempted to assassinate Menelaus, thereby violating a truce between the Greeks and the Trojans and prolonging the Trojan War: in medieval accounts, he is the procurer of Cressida for Troilus.

Pan·da·vas (pun′də vəz), *n.* (*construed as pl.*) (in the *Mahabharata*) the family of Arjuna, at war with their cousins, the Kauravas.

Pan·de·an (pan dē′ən), *adj.* of or pertaining to the god Pan. [irreg. PAN + *-e-* (< L *-aeus*) + -AN]

pan·dect (pan′dekt), *n.* **1. pandects,** a complete body or code of laws. **2.** a comprehensive digest. **3. Pandects,** *Roman Law.* digest (def. 12). [< LL *Pandect(ēs)* < Gk *pandéktēs* all-receiver (*pan-* PAN- + *déktēs* receiver, container), in pl., encyclopedia]

pan·dem·ic (pan dem′ik), *adj.* **1.** (of a disease) prevalent throughout an entire country, continent, or the whole world. **2.** general; universal: *pandemic fear of atomic war.* —*n.* **3.** a pandemic disease. [< LL *pandēm(us)* < Gk *pándēmos* common (*pan-* PAN- + *dêm(os)* people + *-os* adj. suffix) + -IC]

pan·de·mo·ni·um (pan′də mō′nē əm), *n.* **1.** wild lawlessness or uproar; tumult or chaos. **2.** a place or scene of riotous uproar or utter chaos. **3.** (*often cap.*) the abode of all the demons. **4.** hell. [after *Pandaemonium,* Milton's name for the capital of hell; see PAN-, DEMON] —**pan′de·mo′ni·an,** *adj., n.* —**pan·de·mon·ic** (pan′də mon′ik), *adj.*

pan·der (pan′dər), *n.* Also, **pan′der·er. 1.** a go-between in amorous intrigues. **2.** a procurer; pimp. **3.** a person who caters to or profits from the weaknesses or vices of others. —*v.i.* **4.** to act as a pander; cater basely: *to pander to the tastes of vulgar persons.* —*v.t.* **5.** to act as a pander for. [earlier *pandar(e)* < ME *Pandare* PANDARUS]

pan·dit (pun′dit; *spelling pron.* pan′dit), *n.* (in India) a man held in high respect for his great wisdom or learning; scholar. [< Hindi < Skt *paṇḍita*]

P. and L., profit and loss. Also, **P. & L., p. and l.**

pan·do·ra (pan dōr′ə, -dôr′ə), *n.* bandore. Also, **pan·dore** (pan dōr′, -dôr′, pan′dōr, -dôr).

Pan·do·ra (pan dōr′ə, -dôr′ə), *n.* *Class. Myth.* the first woman, created by Hephaestus, endowed by the gods with all the graces and treacherously presented with a box in which were confined all the evils that could trouble mankind. As the gods had anticipated, Pandora opened the box, allowing the evils to escape. [< L < Gk: lit., all-gifted = *pan-* PAN- + *dôron* gift]

Pan·do·rae Fre·tum (pan dōr′ē frē′təm, -dôr′ē), an area in the southern hemisphere of Mars.

Pando′ra's box′, a source of extensive and unforeseen troubles or problems.

pan·dow·dy (pan dou′dē), *n., pl.* **-dies.** *U.S.* a pudding or deep pie made with apples, and usually sweetened with molasses. Also called **apple pandowdy.** [? var. of obs. dial. (Somerset) *pan-doulde* custard; see PAN¹]

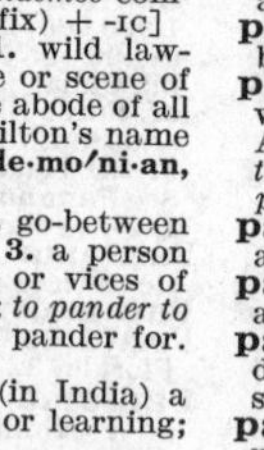

P&S, purchase and sales (of stocks in a brokerage house).

Pandurate leaf

pan·du·rate (pan′dyə rāt′), *adj.* shaped like a fiddle or like the blade of a paddle, as a leaf. Also, **pan·du·ri·form** (pan do͝or′ə fôrm′, -dyo͝or′-). [< LL *pandūr(a)* musical instrument (see BANDORE) + -ATE¹]

pan·dy (pan′dē), *n., pl.* **-dies.** *Chiefly Scot.* a stroke on the palm of the hand with a cane or strap, given as a punishment in school. [< L *pande* stretch out! (impv. of *pandere*), i.e., open your hand to take the blow]

pane (pān), *n.* **1.** one of the divisions of a window or the like, consisting of a single plate of glass in a frame. **2.** a plate of glass for such a division. **3.** a panel, as of a wainscot, ceiling, door, etc. **4.** a flat section, side, or surface, as one of the sides of a bolthead. **5.** *Philately.* a sheet of stamps or any large portion of one, as a half or a quarter, as issued by the post office. [ME *pane, pan* strip of cloth, section < MF *pan* < L *pann(us)* cloth; akin to OE *fana* flag; see VANE]

paned (pānd), *adj.* having panes (usually used in combination): *a small-paned window.*

pan·e·gyr·ic (pan′i jir′ik, -jī′rik), *n.* **1.** an oration, discourse, or writing in praise of a person or thing; eulogy. **2.** a formal or elaborate commendation. [< L, n. use of *panegyric(us)* of, belonging to a public assembly < Gk *panē-gyrikós* = *panḗgyr(is)* solemn assembly (*pan-* PAN- + *ágyris* gathering) + *-ikos* -IC] —**pan′e·gyr′i·cal,** *adj.* —**pan′e·gyr′i·cal·ly,** *adv.*

pan·e·gy·rise (pan′i jə rīz′), *v.t., v.i.,* **-rised, -ris·ing.** *Chiefly Brit.* panegyrize.

pan·e·gyr·ist (pan′i jir′ist, -jī′rist, pan′i jir′ist, -jī′rist), *n.* a person who panegyrizes; eulogist. [< LL *panēgyrist(a)* < Gk *panēgyristḗs* one who takes part in a public festival or assembly = *panēgyr(ízein)* (to) celebrate a public festival + *-istēs* -IST]

pan·e·gy·rize (pan′i jə rīz′), *v.,* **-rized, -riz·ing.** —*v.t.* **1.** to speak or write a panegyric about; eulogize. —*v.i.* **2.** to indulge in panegyric; bestow praises. Also, *esp. Brit.,* **panegyrise.** [< Gk *panēgyríz(ein)* (to) celebrate a public festival = *panḗgyr(is)* (see PANEGYRIC) + *-izein* -IZE]

pan·el (pan′əl), *n., v.,* **-eled, -el·ing** or (*esp. Brit.*) **-elled, -el·ling.** —*n.* **1.** an area of a wall, door, ceiling, etc., that is distinct from the surrounding or adjoining areas. **2.** any of various flat, thin pieces of material joined to form a surface or solid. **3.** *Painting.* **a.** a flat, broad piece of wood on which a picture is painted. **b.** the picture itself. **4.** a photograph much longer in one dimension than the other. **5.** a broad, vertical strip of fabric set on a dress, skirt, etc. **6.** *Law.* **a.** a list of persons summoned for service as jurors. **b.** the body of persons composing a jury. **7.** a group of persons gathered to conduct a public discussion, serve as advisers, participate in a quiz game, or the like. **8.** a public discussion by such a group. **9.** a mount for or surface or section of a machine containing the controls and dials. **10.** *Elect.* a switchboard or control board, or a division of a switchboard or control board containing a set of related cords, jacks, relays, etc. **11.** *Engineering, Building Trades.* an area or section of a truss bounded by principal web members and chords. **12.** *Aeron.* **a.** a lateral subdivision of an airfoil with internal girder construction. **b.** a section of the hull of a rigid airship marked off by a set of transverse and lateral girders. —*v.t.* **13.** to arrange in or furnish with a panel or panels. **14.** to set in a frame as a panel. [ME < OF *panel* a piece (of anything), dim. of *pan* piece of cloth or the like. See PANE]

pan′el discus′sion, an organized discussion before an audience, for which the topic, speakers, etc., have been selected in advance.

pan′el heat′ing, heating of a room or building by means of wall, ceiling, floor, or baseboard panels containing heating pipes or electric conductors.

pan·el·ing (pan′əliŋ), *n.* **1.** wood or other material made into panels. **2.** a surface of panels, esp. of decorative wood or woodlike panels. **3.** panels collectively. Also, *esp. Brit.,* **pan′el·ling.**

pan·el·ist (pan′əlist), *n.* a member of a small group of persons gathered for public discussion, judging, playing a quiz or guessing game, etc.

pan·el·ized (pan′əlīzd′), *adj.* composed of prefabricated sections of walls, floors, or roofs that can be assembled at the building site: *a panelized house.* Cf. **modular** (def. 2).

pan′el truck′, a small truck having a fully enclosed body, used mainly to deliver light or small objects.

pan·e·tel·la (pan′i tel′ə), *n.* a long, slender cigar, usually with straight sides and tapering to a point at the closed end. Also, **pan′e·tel′a, panatella, panatela.** [< AmerSp *panetela* < *panatela* a kind of bread, long, slender biscuit < It *panatella,* dim. of *pane* (< L *panis*) bread]

pan·fish (pan′fish′), *n., pl.* **-fish·es,** (*esp. collectively*) **-fish.** a small, fresh-water food fish that is usually pan-fried.

pan-fry (pan′frī′), *v.t.,* **-fried, -fry·ing.** to fry in a small amount of fat, as in a skillet or shallow pan; sauté.

pang (paŋ), *n.* **1.** a sudden feeling of mental or emotional distress or longing. **2.** a sudden, brief, sharp pain or physical sensation; spasm. [?]

pan·ga (päŋ′gə), *n.* a large, broad-bladed African knife used as a weapon or as an implement for cutting heavy jungle growth, sugar cane, etc.; machete. [< native African name]

pan·gen·e·sis (pan jen′i sis), *n.* *Biol.* the theory that a reproductive cell or body contains gemmules or undetectable germs that were derived from the individual cells from every part of the organism and are the bearers of hereditary attributes. —**pan·ge·net·ic** (pan′jə net′ik), *adj.* —**pan′ge·net′i·cal·ly,** *adv.*

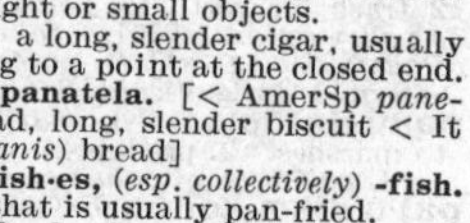

Pangolin, genus *Manis* (Total length 4 ft.; tail 2 ft.)

Pan-Ger·man·ism (pan′jûr′mə niz′əm), *n.* the idea of a union of all the German peoples in one political body. —**Pan′-Ger′man,** *adj., n.* —**Pan-Ger·man·ic** (pan′jər man′ik), *adj.*

pan·go·lin (paŋ gō′lin), *n.* any mammal of the order *Pholidota,* of Africa and tropical Asia, having a covering of broad, overlapping, flattened, horny scales and feeding largely on ants and termites. Also called **scaly anteater.** [< Malay *pengg͝oling* roller]

Pang·o Pang·o (päŋ′ō päŋ′ō). See **Pago Pago.**

pan′ gra′vy, meat juices, as from a roast, seasoned but not thickened.

pan·han·dle¹ (pan′han′dəl), *n.* **1.** the handle of a pan. **2.** (*sometimes cap.*) a long, narrow, projecting strip of territory that is not a peninsula, esp. such a part of a specified state: *the Texas panhandle.*

pan·han·dle² (pan′han′dəl), *v.,* **-dled, -dling.** *Informal.* —*v.i.* **1.** to accost passers-by on the street and beg from them. —*v.t.* **2.** to accost and beg from. **3.** to obtain by accosting and begging from someone. [back formation from PANHANDLER; so called from the resemblance of the extended arm to a PANHANDLE[1]] —**pan′han′dler,** *n.*

Pan′handle State′, West Virginia (used as a nickname).

Pan·hel·len·ic (pan′hə len′ik), *adj.* **1.** of or pertaining to all Greeks or to Panhellenism. **2.** of, pertaining to, or noting collegiate fraternities and sororities. Also, **pan′hel·len′ic.**

Pan·hel·len·ism (pan hel′ə niz′əm), *n.* the idea or advocacy of a union of all Greeks in one political body. —**Pan·hel′len·ist,** *n.*

pan·ic[1] (pan′ik), *n., adj., v.,* **-icked, -ick·ing.** —*n.* **1.** a sudden overwhelming fear that produces hysterical or irrational behavior, and that often spreads quickly through a group of persons or animals. **2.** an instance, outbreak, or period of such fear. **3.** *Finance.* a sudden widespread fear concerning financial affairs, leading to credit contraction and widespread sale of securities at lowered prices. **4.** *Slang.* someone or something that is considered hilariously funny: *The comedian was an absolute panic.* —*adj.* **5.** of the nature of, caused by, or indicating panic: *a wave of panic buying shook the stock market.* **6.** (*cap.*) of or pertaining to the god Pan. —*v.t.* **7.** to affect with panic. **8.** *Slang.* to keep (an audience or the like) highly amused. —*v.i.* **9.** to be stricken with panic. [earlier *panique* < F < Gk *Panik(ós)* of PAN; see -IC] —**pan′ick·y,** *adj.* —**Syn. 1.** See **terror.**

pan·ic[2] (pan′ik), *n.* **1.** Also called **pan′ic grass′.** any grass of the genus *Panicum,* many species of which bear edible grain. **2.** the grain. [late ME < L *pānic(um)* a kind of millet, appar. back formation from *pānicula,* dim. of *pānus* ear of millet. See PANICLE]

pan·i·cle (pan′i kəl), *n.* *Bot.* **1.** a compound raceme. **2.** any loose, diversely branching flower cluster. [< L *pānicul(a)* tuft (on plants), dim. of *pānus* thread wound on a bobbin, a swelling, ear of millet < Doric Gk *pânos,* var. of Attic *pênos* a web; see -I-, -CLE] —**pan′i·cled,** *adj.*

pan·ic-strick·en (pan′ik strik′ən), *adj.* overcome with or characterized by panic. Also, **pan·ic-struck** (pan′ik struk′).

pa·nic·u·late (pə nik′yə lāt′, -lit), *adj.* *Bot.* arranged in panicles. Also, **pa·nic′u·lat′ed.** [< NL *pāniculāt(us)*] —**pa·nic′u·late′ly,** *adv.*

pan·ier (pan′yər), *n.* pannier.

Pa·ni·ni (pä′nē nē), *n.* fl. c400 B.C., Indian grammarian of Sanskrit.

Pan·ja·bi (pun jä′bē), *n., pl.* **-bis. 1.** Punjabi (def. 1). **2.** Also, **Punjabi.** an Indic language of the Punjab.

pan·jan·drum (pan jan′drəm), *n.* a self-important or pretentious official. [pseudo-Latin word (based on PAN-) made up by Samuel Foote (1720–77), English dramatist and actor, for a nonsensical context]

Pank·hurst (paŋk′hûrst), *n.* **Em·me·line (Goul·den)** (em′ə lēn′, -līn′ gōōl′dᵊn), 1858–1928, English suffragist leader.

pan·leu·ko·pe·ni·a (pan′lōō kə pē′nē ə), *n.* *Vet. Pathol.* distemper[1] (def. 1c). Also, **pan′leu·co·pe′ni·a.**

pan·lo·gism (pan′lə jiz′əm), *n.* *Philos.* the doctrine that the universe is a realization or act of the logos. [< G *Panlogism(us).* See PAN-, LOGOS, -ISM] —**pan·log·i·cal** (pan loj′i kəl), **pan′lo·gis′tic, pan′lo·gis′ti·cal,** *adj.* —**pan′lo·gist,** *adj., n.*

Pan·mun·jom (pän′mōōn′jom′), *n.* a small community along the boundary between North Korea and South Korea: site of truce talks following the Korean War.

panne (pan), *n.* a soft, lustrous, lightweight velvet with flattened pile. [< F, OF, var. of *pen(n)e* = ML *panna, penna* skin, fur, appar. special use of L *penna* feather; cf. MHG *federe* kind of fur]

pan·nier (pan′yər, -ē ər), *n.* **1.** a basket, esp. a large one, to be carried on a person's back. **2.** one of a pair of baskets to be slung across the back of a beast of burden. **3.** (on a dress, skirt, etc.) a puffed arrangement of drapery at the hips. **4.** an oval framework formerly used for distending the skirt of a woman's dress at the hips. Also, **panier.** [ME *panier* < MF < L *pānār(ium)* breadbasket = *pān(is)* bread + *-ārium* -ER[2]] —**pan′niered,** *adj.*

pan·ni·kin (pan′ə kin), *n.* *Chiefly Brit.* a small pan or metal cup.

Pan·no·ni·a (pə nō′nē ə), *n.* an ancient country and Roman province in central Europe, S and W of the Danube, the territory of which is now mostly occupied by Hungary and Yugoslavia. —**Pan·no′ni·an,** *adj., n.*

pa·no·cha (pə nō′chə), *n.* **1.** Also, **penuche.** a coarse grade of sugar made in Mexico. **2.** penuche (def. 1). Also, **pa·no·che** (pə nō′chē). [< MexSp, dim. of Sp *pan* bread]

Pa·nof·sky (pa nof′skē), *n.* **Erwin,** 1892–1968, U.S. art historian, born in Germany.

pan·o·ply (pan′ə plē), *n., pl.* **-plies. 1.** a complete suit of armor. **2.** a complete covering or array of something. [< Gk *panoplía* = *pan-* PAN- + *hópl(a)* armor (pl. of *hóplon* tool) + *-ia* -Y[3]]

pan·op·tic (pan op′tik), *adj.* permitting the viewing of all parts or elements. Also, **pan·op′ti·cal.** [< Gk *panóptēs* all-seeing] —**pan·op′ti·cal·ly,** *adv.* —**Syn.** panoramic.

pan·o·ram·a (pan′ə ram′ə, -rä′mə), *n.* **1.** an unobstructed and wide view of an extensive area. **2.** an extended pictorial representation of a landscape or other scene, often exhibited a part at a time before the spectators. **3.** a continuously passing or changing scene or unfolding of events: *the panorama of recent history.* **4.** a comprehensive survey, as of a subject. [PAN- + Gk *hórama* view, sight < *horân* to see, look] —**pan′o·ram′ic,** *adj.* —**pan′o·ram′i·cal·ly,** *adv.*

pan·pipe (pan′pīp′), *n.* a primitive wind instrument consisting of a series of hollow pipes of graduated length, the tones being produced by blowing across the upper ends. Also, **Pan's′ pipes′, pan′pipes′.**

Panpipe

pan·psy·chism (pan sī′kiz əm), *n.* *Philos.* the doctrine that each object in the universe has either a mind or a psyche. —**pan·psy′chic,** *adj.* —**pan·psy′chist,** *n.* —**pan′psy·chis′tic,** *adj.*

Pan-Slav·ism (pan′slä′viz əm, -slav′iz-), *n.* the idea or advocacy of a political union of all the Slavic races. —**Pan′-Slav′, Pan′-Slav′ic,** *adj.*

pan·soph·ism (pan′sə fiz′əm), *n.* a claim or pretension to pansophy. [< Gk *pánsoph(os)* all-wise + -ISM] —**pan′so·phist,** *n.*

pan·so·phy (pan′sə fē), *n.* universal wisdom or knowledge. —**pan·soph·ic** (pan sof′ik), **pan·soph′i·cal,** *adj.* —**pan·soph′i·cal·ly,** *adv.*

pan·sy (pan′zē), *n., pl.* **-sies. 1.** a violet, *Viola tricolor hortensis,* cultivated in many varieties, having richly and variously colored flowers. **2.** *Slang.* a male homosexual. [< MF *pensée* pansy, lit., thought, n. use of fem. of ptp. of *penser* to think < L *pēnsāre* to weigh, consider. See PENSIVE]

pant (pant), *v.i.* **1.** to breathe hard and quickly, as after exertion. **2.** to emit steam or the like in loud puffs. **3.** to long or yearn: *to pant for revenge.* **4.** to throb or heave violently or rapidly; palpitate. **5.** *Naut.* (of the bow or stern of a vessel) to work with the shock of contact with a succession of waves. —*v.t.* **6.** to breathe or utter gaspingly. —*n.* **7.** a short, quick, labored effort at breathing; gasp. **8.** a puff, as of an engine. **9.** a throb or heave, as of the breast. [late ME *pant(en)* < MF *pant(a)is(i)er* < LL **phantasiāre* to have visions < Gk *phantasioûn* to have or form images. See FANTASY] —**pant′ing·ly,** *adv.*

—**Syn. 1.** puff, blow. PANT, GASP suggest breathing with more effort than usual. PANT suggests rapid, convulsive breathing, as from violent exertion or excitement: *to pant after a run for the train.* GASP suggests catching one's breath in a single quick intake, as from amazement, terror, and the like, or a series of such quick intakes of breath as in painful breathing: *to gasp with horror; to gasp for breath.* **3.** thirst, hunger.

pant-, var. of **panto-** before a vowel.

pan·ta·graph (pan′tə graf′, -gräf′), *n.* pantograph (def. 1).

Pan·tag·ru·el (pan tag′rōō el′; *Fr.* päN TA GRY el′), *n.* (in Rabelais' satirical novels *Gargantua* (1534) and *Pantagruel* (1532)) the huge son of Gargantua, represented as dealing with serious matters in a spirit of rough and somewhat cynical good humor. Cf. **Gargantua.** —**Pan·ta·gru·el·i·an** (pan′tə grōō el′ē ən), *adj.*

pan·ta·lets (pan′tᵊlets′), *n.pl.* long ruffled drawers extending below the skirt, worn in the mid-19th century. Also, **pan′ta·lettes′.** Also called **trousers.** [PANTAL(OON) + -ET + -S[3]] —**pan′ta·let′ted,** *adj.*

pan·ta·loon (pan′tᵊlōōn′), *n.* **1. pantaloons,** a man's close-fitting trousers, worn esp. in the 19th century. **2.** (in the modern pantomime) a foolish, vicious old man, the butt and accomplice of the clown. **3.** (*usually cap.*) Also, **Pan·ta·lo·ne** (pan′tᵊlō′nā, pän′-; *It.* pän′tä lô′ne). (in commedia dell'arte) a foolish old Venetian merchant, generally lascivious, and frequently deceived in the course of lovers' intrigues. [< MF *Pantalon* < It *Pantalone* (Venetian dial.) nickname for a Venetian, var. of *Pantaleone,* name of a 4th-century saint once a favorite with the Venetians]

pan·tech·ni·con (pan tek′nə kon′, -kən), *n.* *Brit.* **1.** a warehouse, esp. a furniture warehouse. **2.** Also called **pantech′nicon van′.** a moving van. [PAN- + Gk *technikón* artistic, skillful (neut. of *technikós*); see TECHNIC]

Pan·tel·le·ri·a (pän tel′le RĒ′ä), *n.* an Italian island in the Mediterranean between Sicily and Tunisia. 9598 (1961); 32 sq. mi. Ancient name, **Cosyra.**

pan·the·ism (pan′thē iz′əm), *n.* **1.** the doctrine that God is the transcendent reality of which the material universe and man are only manifestations. **2.** any religious belief or philosophical doctrine that identifies God with the universe. [< F *panthéisme*] —**pan′the·ist,** *n.* —**pan′the·is′tic, pan′the·is′ti·cal,** *adj.* —**pan′the·is′ti·cal·ly,** *adv.*

pan·the·on (pan′thē on′, -ən, pan thē′ən), *n.* **1.** a public building containing tombs or memorials of the illustrious dead of a nation. **2.** a temple dedicated to all the gods. **3.** the gods of a particular mythology considered collectively. **4.** the realm of the heroes or persons venerated by any group: *a place in the pantheon of American literature.* [ME *panteon* < L *Panthēon* < Gk *Pántheion,* n. use of neut. of *pántheios* of all gods = *pan-* PAN- + *the(ós)* god + *-ios* adj. suffix]

pan·ther (pan′thər), *n., pl.* **-thers,** (*esp. collectively*) **-ther. 1.** cougar. **2.** the leopard, *Panthera pardus.* **3.** any leopard in the black color phase. Also, *referring to a female,* **pan·ther·ess** (pan′thər is). [< L *panthēr(a)* < Gk *pánthēr;* r. ME *pantere* (< OF) and OE *pandher* (< L)]

pant·ies (pan′tēz), *n.* (construed as pl.) underpants or undershorts for women and children. Also, **pan′tie, panty.** [pl. of PANTY]

pan·tile (pan′tīl′), *n.* **1.** a roofing tile straight in its length but curved in its width to overlap the next tile. **2.** a tapered, semi-cylindrical roofing tile laid convex side up to overlap the edges of similar tiles laid concave side up.

Pantiles

panto-, a combining form synonymous with **pan-:** *pantology.* Also, *esp. before a vowel,* **pant-.** [comb. form repr. Gk *pant-* all (s. of *pân,* neut. of *pâs*)]

pan·to·fle (pan′tə fəl, pan tof′əl, -tōō′fəl), *n.* a slipper. Also, **pan′tof·fle.** [late ME *pantufle* < MF *pantoufle* < OIt *pantofola* < MGk *pantophellos* cork shoe, lit., all-cork. See PANTO-, PHELLOGEN]

pan·to·graph (pan′tə graf′, -gräf′), *n.* **1.** an instrument for the mechanical copying of plans, diagrams, etc., on any desired scale. **2.** *Elect.* a current collector for transferring current from an overhead wire to a vehicle, usually consisting of two parallel, hinged, double-diamond frames. —**pan·tog·ra·pher** (pan tog′rə fər), *n.* —**pan·to·graph·ic** (pan′tə graf′ik), *adj.* —**pan′to·graph′i·cal·ly,** *adv.* —**pan·tog′ra·phy,** *n.*

pan·tol·o·gy (pan tol′ə jē), *n.* a systematic view of all human knowledge. —**pan·to·log·ic** (pan′tᵊloj′ik), **pan′to·log′i·cal,** *adj.* —**pan·tol′o·gist,** *n.*

pan·to·mime (pan′tə mīm′), *n., v.,* **-mimed, -mim·ing.** —*n.* **1.** a play or entertainment in which the performers express themselves mutely by gestures, often to the accompaniment of music. **2.** *Brit.* highly elaborate theatrical spectacle, principally for children and common in England during the Christmas season. **3.** an actor in dumb show, as in ancient Rome. **4.** significant gesture without speech. **5.** the art or technique of conveying emotions, actions, feelings, etc., by mute gestures. —*v.t.* **6.** to represent or express in pantomime. —*v.i.* **7.** to express oneself in pantomime. [earlier *pantomimus* < L < Gk *pantómīmos*] —**pan·to·mim·ic** (pan′tə-mim′ik), *adj.*

pan·to·mim·ist (pan′tə mī′mist), *n.* **1.** a person who acts in pantomime. **2.** the author of a pantomime.

pan′to·then′ic ac′id (pan′tə then′ik, pan′-), *Biochem.* an oily, hydroxy acid, $HOCH_2C(CH_3)_2CHOHCONHCH_2CH_2COOH$, found in plant and animal tissues, rice, bran, etc., and essential for cell growth. [< Gk *pántothen* from all quarters (*panto-* PANTO- + *-then* suffix of motion from) + -IC]

pan·try (pan′trē), *n., pl.* **-tries. 1.** a room or closet for storing food, dishes, utensils, etc. **2.** a room in which food is prepared for serving. [ME *panetrie* < AF, OF *paneterie* bread room = *panet(er)* (to) bake bread (< *pan* bread < L *pānis*) + *-erie* -ERY]

pants (pants), *n.pl.* **1.** trousers (def. 1). **2.** underpants, esp. for women and children; panties. **3.** *Brit.* men's underpants, esp. long drawers. **4. wear the pants,** to have the principal authority, as in a household. [short for PANTALOONS]

pant·suit (pant′so͞ot′), *n.* See **slack suit** (def. 2). Also, **pant′ suit′, pants′ suit′.**

pant·y (pan′tē), *n., pl.* **pant·ies.** panties. [PANT(S) + -Y²]

pant′y gir′dle, a girdle with a crotch.

pant′y hose′, a one-piece, skintight garment worn by women, combining panties and stockings.

pant·y·waist (pan′tē wāst′), *n.* **1.** a child's two-piece undergarment, buttoned together at the waist. **2.** *Informal.* a cowardly or effeminate boy or man; sissy.

Pan·za (pan′zə; *Sp.* pän′thä), *n.* See **Sancho Panza.**

pan·zer (pan′zər; *Ger.* pän′tsər), *adj.* **1.** of or belonging to a panzer division. —*n.* **2.** a vehicle, esp. a tank, forming part of a panzer division. [< G; MHG *panzier* < OF *panciere* coat of mail, lit., belly piece. See PAUNCH, -ER²]

pan′zer divi′sion, an armored division of the German army, esp. in World War II, consisting chiefly of tanks and organized for making sudden, rapid attacks.

Pão de A·çú·car (poun′ də ä so͞o′kər), Portuguese name of **Sugarloaf Mountain.**

Pao·ting (bou′ding′), *n.* former name of **Tsingyuan.**

pap¹ (pap), *n.* **1.** soft food for infants or invalids, as bread soaked in water or milk. **2.** ideas, speech, writing, etc., without substance or real value. [late ME; imit. of a baby's call for food; c. D *pap*, G *Pappe*, It *pappa*, L *pappa*, etc.]

pap² (pap), *n.* *Chiefly Dial.* **1.** a teat; nipple. **2.** something resembling a teat or nipple. [ME *pap(pe)*; a nursery word identical in origin with PAP¹; cf. dial. Norw, Sw *pappe*, L *papilla* nipple]

pa·pa¹ (pä′pə, pə pä′), *n.* **1.** father. **2.** (*cap.*) a word used in communications to represent the letter *P.* [< F; MF *pappa* (nursery word); cf. L *pāpa* father (see POPE), Icel *pāpi, pabbi* father. See PAP¹]

pa·pa² (pä′pä), *n.* *Rare.* the Roman Catholic pontiff; pope. [< It: pope]

pa·pa·cy (pā′pə sē), *n., pl.* **-cies.** *Rom. Cath. Ch.* **1.** the office, dignity, or jurisdiction of the pope. **2.** the system of Roman Catholic ecclesiastical government. **3.** the period during which a specific pope is in office. **4.** the succession or line of the popes. [ME *papacie* < ML *pāpātia.* See POPE, -ACY]

pa·pa·in (pə pā′in, -pī′in, pā′pə-), *n.* **1.** *Chem.* a proteolytic enzyme found in the fruit of the papaya tree, *Carica Papaya.* **2.** *Pharm.* a commercial preparation of this used as a meat tenderizer and in medicine as a digestant. [PA-PA(YA) + -IN²]

pa·pal (pā′pəl), *adj.* **1.** of or pertaining to the pope or the papacy. **2.** of or pertaining to the Roman Catholic Church. [ME < ML *pāpāl(is).* See POPE, -AL¹] —**pa′pal·ly,** *adv.*

pa′pal cross′, a cross with three horizontal crosspieces. See illus. at **cross.**

Pa′pal States′, the areas comprising a large district in central Italy ruled as a temporal domain by the popes A.D. 755–1860. Also called **States of the Church.** Cf. **Vatican City.**

Pa·pan·dre·ou (pä′pən drā′o͞o), *n.* **George,** 1888–1968, Greek statesman: premier 1944, 1963–65.

pa·pav·er·a·ceous (pə pav′ə rā′shəs), *adj.* belonging to the *Papaveraceae*, or poppy family of plants. [< NL, L *papāver* poppy + -ACEOUS]

pa·pav·er·ine (pə pav′ə rēn′, -ər in, pə pā′və rēn′, -vər in), *n.* *Pharm.* a crystalline, non-narcotic, alkaloidal powder, $C_{20}H_{21}NO_4$, obtained from opium, but not habit-forming: used esp. in the treatment of spasms of the stomach, bronchi, and arteries. [< L *papāver* poppy + -INE²]

pa·paw (pô′pô, pə pô′), *n.* **1.** the small fleshy fruit of a temperate North American bush or small tree, *Asimina triloba.* **2.** the tree itself. Also, **pawpaw.** [unexplained var. of PAPAYA]

pa·pa·ya (pə pä′yə), *n.* the large, yellow, melonlike fruit of a tropical American shrub or small tree, *Carica Papaya.* [< Sp < Carib (Hispaniola)] —**pa·pa′yan,** *adj.*

Pa·pe·e·te (pä′pē ā′tā), *n.* a city on NW Tahiti, in the Society Islands: capital of the Society Islands and of French Polynesia. 20,302 (1962).

Pa·pen (pä′pən), *n.* **Franz von** (fränts fən), 1879–1969, German diplomat, statesman, and soldier.

pa·per (pā′pər), *n.* **1.** a substance made from rags, straw, wood, or other fibrous material, usually in thin sheets, used to bear writing or printing or for wrapping things, decorating walls, etc. **2.** a piece, sheet, or leaf of this. **3.** a written or printed document or the like. **4.** negotiable notes, bills, etc. **5.** Often, **papers.** a document establishing or verifying identity, status, or the like: *citizenship papers.* **6.** any written piece of schoolwork. **7.** an essay, article, or dissertation on a particular topic. **8.** a newspaper or journal. **9.** wallpaper. **10.** *Slang.* a free pass to a place of entertainment. **11. on paper, a.** in written or printed form. **b.** in theory rather than in practice. **c.** in a preliminary state; in a plan or design. —*v.t.* **12.** to line, cover, or wrap with paper. **13.** to supply with paper. **14.** *Slang.* to fill (a theater or the like) by means of free tickets or passes. —*v.i.* **15.** to apply wallpaper to walls. —*adj.* **16.** made of paper or paperlike material: *a paper bag.* **17.** pertaining to or carried on by means of letters, articles, books, etc.: *a paper war.* **18.** existing on paper only and not in reality: *paper profits.* **19.** indicating the first event of a series, as a wedding anniversary. [ME, OE < L *papȳr(us)* PAPYRUS]

pa·per·back (pā′pər bak′), *n.* **1.** a book bound in a flexible paper cover, often a low-priced edition of a hardcover book. —*adj.* **2.** (of a book) bound in a flexible paper cover: *a paperback edition of Chaucer's works.* **3.** of or pertaining to paperbacks: *a paperback bookstore.* Cf. **hardcover.** Also, **pa·per-bound** (pā′pər bound′).

pa′per birch′, a North American birch, *Betula papyrifera*, having a tough bark and yielding a valuable wood: the state tree of New Hampshire.

pa·per·board (pā′pər bōrd′, -bôrd′), *n.* **1.** a thick, stiff cardboard composed of layers of paper or paper pulp compressed together; pasteboard. —*adj.* **2.** of, pertaining to, or made of paperboard.

pa′per clip′, a flat wire clip bent so that it can clasp sheets of paper together. Also called **clip.**

pa′per cut′ter, any device for cutting or trimming many sheets of paper at once. —**pa′per-cut′ting,** *adj.*

pa′per doll′, **1.** a paper or cardboard, usually two-dimensional, representation of the human figure, used as a child's toy. **2.** Usually, **paper dolls.** a connected series of doll-like figures cut from folded paper.

pa·per·er (pā′pər ər), *n.* **1.** a paperhanger. **2.** a person who lines or covers something with paper.

pa′per gold′, *Informal.* See **special drawing rights.**

pa·per·hang·er (pā′pər hang′ər), *n.* a person whose job is covering walls with wallpaper. Also, **pa′per hang′er.** —**pa′per·hang′ing,** *n.*

pa·per-mâ·ché (pā′pər mə shā′, -ma-), *n., adj.* papier-mâché.

pa′per mon′ey, currency in paper form, as government and bank notes.

pa′per mul′berry, a moraceous tree, *Broussonetia papyrifera*, of eastern Asia, grown as a shade tree. [so called because its bark is used to make paper]

pa′per nau′tilus, any dibranchiate cephalopod of the genus *Argonauta*, the female of which has a delicate, white shell.

pa′per ti′ger, a person or thing that has the appearance of strength or power but is actually weak or ineffectual.

pa·per·weight (pā′pər wāt′), *n.* a small, heavy object laid on papers to keep them from scattering.

pa·per·work (pā′pər wûrk′), *n.* written or clerical work, as records, reports, etc., forming an incidental but necessary part of some work or job. Also, **pa′per work′.**

pa·per·y (pā′pə rē), *adj.* like paper; thin or flimsy. —**pa′per·i·ness,** *n.*

pap·e·terie (pap′i trē; *Fr.* pap^ə trē′), *n., pl.* **-teries** (-trēz; *Fr.* -trē′). a case or box of paper and other materials for writing. [< F = *papet(ier)* papermaker or dealer (irreg. < *papier* PAPER; see -ER²) + *-erie* -ERY]

Pa·phi·an (pā′fē ən), *adj.* **1.** of or pertaining to Paphos, sacred to Aphrodite. **2.** of or pertaining to love, esp. illicit sexual love. **3.** noting or pertaining to Aphrodite or to her worship or service. [< L *Paphi(us)* (< Gk *Páphios* of Paphos, of Aphrodite) + -AN]

Paph·la·go·ni·a (paf′lə gō′nē ə), *n.* an ancient country and Roman province in N Asia Minor, on the S coast of the Black Sea.

Pa·phos (pā′fos), *n.* **1.** an ancient city in SW Cyprus. **2.** Also, **Pa·phus** (pā′fəs). *Class. Myth.* the son of Pygmalion and Galatea who inherited the throne of Cyprus from his father.

pa·pier-mâ·ché (pā′pər mə shā′; *Fr.* pa pyā′ma shā′), *n.* a substance made of pulped paper or paper pulp mixed with glue and other materials or of layers of paper glued and pressed together, molded when moist to form various articles, and becoming hard and strong when dry. Also, **paper-mâché.** [< F: lit., chewed paper]

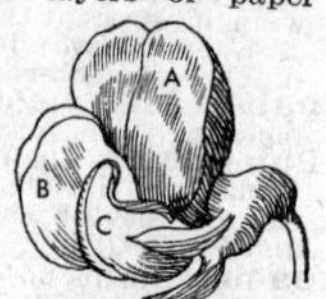

Papilionaceous flower of bean, *Phaseolus vulgaris* A, Vexillum; B, Wing; C, Keel or carina

pa·pil·i·o·na·ceous (pə pil′ē ə nā′shəs), *adj.* *Bot.* **1.** having an irregular corolla shaped somewhat like a butterfly, as the pea and other leguminous plants. **2.** belonging to the family *Papilionaceae* (*Fabaceae*), often included as part of the *Leguminosae.* [< L *pāpiliōn-* (s. of *pāpiliō*) butterfly + -ACEOUS]

pa·pil·la (pə pil′ə), *n., pl.* **-pil·lae** (-pil′ē). **1.** any small, nipplelike process or projection. **2.** one of certain small protuberances concerned with the senses of touch, taste, and smell: *the papillae of the tongue.* **3.** a small vascular process at the root of a hair. **4.** a papule or pimple. [< L: nipple, teat, akin to *papula* pimple. See PAP²] —**pap·il·lar** (pap′ə lər, pə pil′ər), *adj.* —**pap·il·lose** (pap′ə lōs′), *adj.* —**pap·il·los·i·ty** (pap′ə los′i tē), *n.*

pap·il·lar·y (pap′ə ler′ē, pə pil′ə rē), *adj.* **1.** of, pertaining to, or of the nature of a papilla or papillae. **2.** having or covered with papillae.

pap·il·lo·ma (pap′ə lō′mə), *n., pl.* **-ma·ta** (-mə tə), **-mas.** *Pathol.* a tumor of skin or mucous membrane consisting of a hypertrophied papilla or group of papillae, as a wart or a corn. [< NL] —**pap′il·lo′ma·to′sis,** *n.* —**pap·il·lo·ma·tous** (pap′ə lō′mə təs, -lom′ə-), *adj.*

pap·il·lon (pap′ə lon′), *n.* one of a breed of toy spaniels having a long, silky coat and large, erect ears held so that they resemble the wings of a butterfly. [< F: butterfly < L *pāpiliōn-* (s. of *pāpiliō*)]

pap·il·lote (pap′ə lōt′), *n.* **1.** a decorative curled paper placed over the end of the bone of a cutlet or chop. **2.** See **en papillote.** [< F, irreg. < *papillon* butterfly]

pa·pist (pā′pist), *Usually Disparaging.* —*n.* **1.** a Roman Catholic. —*adj.* **2.** papistical. [earlier *papista* < NL. See POPE, -IST]

pa·pis·ti·cal (pā pis′ti kəl, pə-), *adj.* *Usually Disparaging.* of or pertaining to the Roman Catholic Church. Also, **pa·pis′tic.** [prob. < MF *papistique* (see PAPIST, -IC) + -AL¹]

pa·pist·ry (pā′pi strē), *n.* *Usually Disparaging.* Roman Catholicism.

pa·poose (pa po͞os′, pə-), *n.* a North American Indian baby or young child. Also, **pap·poose′.** [< Algonquian (New England) *papeisses* < *peisses* child]

pap·pose (pap′ōs), *adj.* *Bot.* **1.** having or forming a pappus. **2.** downy. Also, **pap·pous** (pap′əs).

pap·pus (pap′əs), *n., pl.* **pap·pi** (pap′ī). *Bot.* a downy, bristly, or other tuftlike appendage of the achene of certain plants, as the dandelion and the thistle. [< NL < Gk *páppos* down, lit., grandfather (taken as greybeard, white hairs, down)]

pap·py[1] (pap′ē), *adj.*, **-pi·er, -pi·est.** like pap; mushy. [PAP[1] + -Y[1]]

pap·py[2] (pap′ē), *n., pl.* **-pies.** *Chiefly Midland and Southern U.S.* father. [PAP(A)[1] + -Y[2]]

pap·ri·ka (pa prē′kə, pə-, pap′rə kə), *n.* a red, powdery condiment derived from dried, ripe sweet peppers. [< G < Hung < Croatian < *papar* PEPPER]

Pap′ smear′ (pap), *Med.* a test for malignancy based on the analysis of bodily secretions, esp. of the female genital tract. Also called **Pap′ test′.** [named after G.N. *Papanicolaou* (1883–1962), U.S. anatomist, born in Greece]

Pap·u·a (pap′yo͞o ə, pä′po͞o ä′), *n.* **1. Territory of.** Formerly, **British New Guinea.** a former Australian territory on SE New Guinea, including the adjacent islands: merged with the Territory of New Guinea 1945; now a part of Papua New Guinea. 86,100 sq. mi. **2. Gulf of,** a gulf of the Coral Sea, off the SE coast of New Guinea.

pap·u·an (pap′yo͞o ən), *adj.* **1.** of or pertaining to Papua. **2.** noting or pertaining to the native Negroid race of New Guinea, characterized by a black or sooty-brown complexion and crisp, frizzled hair. **3.** of or pertaining to any of the unaffiliated languages indigenous to New Guinea and other islands nearby, esp. Timor, the Bismarck Archipelago, the Moluccas, and the Solomons. **—*n.* 4.** a native or inhabitant of New Guinea.

Pap′ua New′ Guin′ea, an independent country in the W Pacific, comprising the E part of New Guinea and numerous adjacent islands: former territory of Australia, independent since 1975. 3,000,000; 178,260 sq. mi. *Cap.:* Port Moresby.

pap·ule (pap′yo͞ol), *n.* *Pathol.* a small, somewhat pointed elevation of the skin, usually inflammatory but nonsuppurative. [< L *papul(a)* pimple, pustule, akin to *papilla* nipple. See PAP[2], -ULE] **—pap′u·lar,** *adj.* **—pap·u·lose** (pap′yə lōs′), *adj.*

pap·y·ra·ceous (pap′ə rā′shəs), *adj.* papery. [< L *papȳr(us)* PAPYRUS + -ACEOUS]

pa·py·rus (pə pī′rəs), *n., pl.* **-py·ri** (-pī′rī), **-rus·es. 1.** a tall, aquatic, cyperaceous plant, *Cyperus papyrus,* of the Nile valley. **2.** an ancient paperlike material, made by pressing together thin strips of the pith of this plant. **3.** an ancient document, as a manuscript or scroll, written on this material. [< L < Gk *pāpyros*] **—pa·py′ral, pa·pyr·i·an** (pə pir′ē ən), **pap·y·rine** (pə pī′rin), *adj.* **—pap·y·ri·tious** (pap′ə rish′əs), *adj.*

Papyrus, *Cyperus papyrus* (Height 3 to 10 ft.)

par (pär), *n.* **1.** an equality in value or standing; a level of equality: *The gains and the losses are on a par.* **2.** an average or normal amount, quality, condition, etc.: *below par.* **3.** *Finance.* **a.** the legally established value of the monetary unit of one country in terms of that of another using the same metal as a standard of value. **b.** the state of the shares of any business, undertaking, loan, etc., when they may be purchased at the original price or at their face value. **4.** *Golf.* the number of strokes set as a standard for a hole or a complete course. **5. at par,** *Finance.* (of a share) purchasable at issue par or nominal par. **—*adj.* 6.** average or normal. **7.** *Finance.* at or pertaining to par: *the par value of a bond.* [< L: equal, equal to]

par-, var. of **para-**[1] before a vowel: *parenchyma.*

par., **1.** paragraph. **2.** parallel. **3.** parenthesis. **4.** parish.

pa·ra[1] (pä rä′, pä′rä), *n., pl.* **-ras, -ra.** a money of account of Yugoslavia, the 100th part of a dinar. [< Serbo-Croatian < Turk < Pers *pārah,* lit., piece]

par·a[2] (par′ə), *adj.* *Chem.* pertaining to or occupying two positions in the benzene ring that are separated by two carbon atoms. Cf. **meta, ortho.** [independent form of PARA-[1]]

Pa·rá (pä rä′), *n.* **1.** Belém. **2.** an estuary in N Brazil: an arm of the Amazon. 200 mi. long; 40 mi. wide. **3.** See **Pará rubber.**

para-[1], **1.** an element appearing in loan words from Greek, where it meant "beside" (*paradigm; paragraph*); on this model, used also with the meanings "near," "beyond," "aside," "amiss," and sometimes implying alteration or modification (*paragenesis; parapsychology*). **2.** *Chem.* a combining form designating the para position in the benzene ring. *Abbr.:* p-. Cf. **meta-** (def. 2b), **ortho-** (def. 2b). Also, *esp. before a vowel,* **par-.** [< Gk *para-,* comb. form repr. *pará* (prep.) beside, alongside of, by, beyond]

para-[2], a combining form meaning "guard against," used in a few words: *parachute; parasol.* [< F < It *para-,* s. of *parare* to prepare against, ward off < L *parāre* to prepare]

Para., Paraguay.

par′a-am·i·no·ben·zo′ic ac′id (par′ə ə mē′nō ben zō′ik, -am′ə nō-), *Chem.* a white or yellowish solid, $H_2NC_6H_4COOH$, the para isomer of aminobenzoic acid: used chiefly in the manufacture of dyes and pharmaceuticals.

par·a·bi·o·sis (par′ə bī ō′sis), *n.* *Biol.* experimental or natural physiological and anatomical union of two individuals. **—par·a·bi·ot·ic** (par′ə bī ot′ik), *adj.*

par·a·blast (par′ə blast′), *n.* *Biol.* the nutritive yolk of a meroblastic ovum or egg. **—par′a·blas′tic,** *adj.*

par·a·ble (par′ə bəl), *n.* **1.** a short allegorical story designed to convey a truth or moral lesson. **2.** a statement or comment that conveys a meaning indirectly by the use of comparison, analogy, or the like. [ME *parabil* < LL *parabol(a)* comparison, parable, word < Gk *parabolḗ* comparison] **—pa·rab·o·list** (pə rab′ə list), *n.*

pa·rab·o·la (pə rab′ə lə), *n.* *Geom.* a plane curve formed by the intersection of a right circular cone with a plane parallel to a generator of the cone; the set of points in a plane that are equidistant from a fixed line and a fixed point in the same plane or in a parallel plane. See diag. at **conic section.** [< NL < Gk *parabolḗ* a putting aside. See PARABLE]

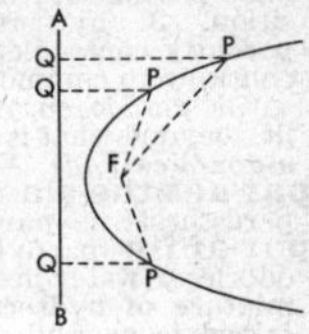

Parabola AB, Directrix; F, Focus, P, Point on parabola; PQ, Always equal to PF

par·a·bol·ic[1] (par′ə bol′ik), *adj.* **1.** having the form, outline, or section of a parabola. **2.** of, pertaining to, or resembling a parabola.

par·a·bol·ic[2] (par′ə bol′ik), *adj.* of, pertaining to, or involving a parable. Also, **par′a·bol′i·cal.** [< LL *parabolic(us)* metaphoric < LGk *parabolikós* figurative. See PARABLE, -IC] **—par′a·bol′i·cal·ism,** *n.* **—par′a·bol′i·cal·ly,** *adv.*

pa·rab·o·lise (pə rab′ə līz′), *v.t.,* **-lised, -lis·ing.** *Chiefly Brit.* parabolize.

pa·rab·o·lize[1] (pə rab′ə līz′), *v.t.,* **-lized, -liz·ing.** to tell or explain in a parable or parables. [< LL *parabol(a)* PARABLE + -IZE]

pa·rab·o·lize[2] (pə rab′ə līz′), *v.t.,* **-lized, -liz·ing.** to form as a parabola or paraboloid. [PARABOL(A) + -IZE] **—pa·rab′o·li·za′tion,** *n.*

pa·rab·o·loid (pə rab′ə loid′), *n.* *Geom.* a solid or surface generated by the revolution of a parabola about its axis, or a surface of the second degree some of whose plane sections are parabolas. **—pa·rab·o·loi·dal** (pə rab′ə loid′əl, par′ə bə-), *adj.*

Paraboloids A, Hyperbolic; B, Elliptic

Par·a·cel·sus (par′ə sel′səs), *n.* **Phi·lip·pus Au·re·o·lus** (fi lip′əs ô rē′ō ləs), (*Theophrastus Bombastus von Hohenheim*), 1493?–1541, Swiss physician and alchemist.

pa·rach·ro·nism (pa rak′rə niz′əm), *n.* a chronological error in which a person, event, etc., is assigned a date later than the actual one. Cf. **anachronism, prochronism. —par·ach′ro·nis′tic,** *adj.*

par·a·chute (par′ə sho͞ot′), *n., v.,* **-chut·ed, -chut·ing. —*n.* 1.** a large, umbrellalike device of cloth that opens in midair and, by offering resistance to the air, allows a man, object, etc., suspended from it to descend at a safe rate of speed, as from an airplane, balloon, or the like. **2.** any similar device for reducing forward speed, as of an airplane. **—*v.t.* 3.** to drop or deliver by parachute. **—*v.i.* 4.** to descend by parachute. [< F = *para-* PARA-[2] + *chute* fall] **—par′a·chut′ist, par′a·chut′er,** *n.*

par′achute spin′naker, *Naut.* a large spinnaker that assumes a nearly hemispherical form when filled.

par·a·clete (par′ə klēt′), *n.* **1.** a person called in to aid; an advocate or intercessor. **2.** (*cap.*) the Holy Spirit; the Comforter. [< eccl. L *Paraclēt(us)* < LGk *Paráklētos* comforter, lit., (person) called in (to help)]

par·a·cy·mene (par′ə sī′mēn), *n.* *Chem.* a colorless liquid, $CH_3C_6H_4CH(CH_3)_2$, obtained as a by-product of paper making. Cf. **cymene.** [PARA-[1] + CYMENE]

pa·rade (pə rād′), *n., v.,* **-rad·ed, -rad·ing. —*n.* 1.** a large public procession, usually of a festive nature and accompanied by band music. **2.** a military ceremony involving the formation and marching of troop units. **3.** the orderly assembly of troops for inspection or display. **4.** a place where troops regularly assemble for parade. **5.** an ostentatious display: *to make a parade of one's beliefs.* **6.** *Chiefly Brit.* **a.** a group or procession of promenaders. **b.** a promenade. **7.** *Fort.* the level space forming the interior or enclosed area of a fortification. **8.** *Fencing.* a parry. **—*v.t.* 9.** to walk up and down on or in. **10.** to display ostentatiously. **11.** to cause to march or proceed for display. **—*v.i.* 12.** to march in a procession. **13.** to promenade in a public place, esp. for the purpose of showing off. **14.** to assemble in military order for display. [< F, MF < Sp *parada* a stop, stopping place, n. use of fem. of *parado,* ptp. of *parar* to stop, end < L *parāre* to set. See COMPARE, PARRY, -ADE[1]] **—pa·rad′er** *n.* **—Syn. 10.** show, flaunt, flourish.

parade′ rest′, *Mil.* a position in which the feet are 12 inches apart, the hands are clasped behind the back, and the head is held motionless and facing forward.

par·a·di·chlor·o·ben·zene (par′ə dī klôr′ō ben′zēn, -ben zēn′, -klôr′-), *n.* *Chem.* a white solid, $C_6H_4Cl_2$, of the benzene series, having a penetrating odor: used chiefly as a moth repellent. Also, **par′a-di·chlor′o·ben′zene.** Also called **PDB.**

par·a·did·dle (par′ə did′əl, par′ə did′əl), *n.* (on a snare drum) a pattern or series of syncopated drumbeats in which the right and left drumsticks alternate strokes. [partly imit.; cf. DIDDLE[2]]

par·a·digm (par′ə dim, -dīm′), *n.* **1.** *Gram.* a set of all inflected forms based on a single stem or theme, as *boy, boy's, boys, boys'.* **2.** an example; pattern. [late ME < LL *paradīgm(a)* < Gk *parádeigma* pattern, akin to *paradeiknýnai* to show side by side = *para-* PARA-[1] + *deiknýnai* to show; see DEICTIC] **—par·a·dig·mat·ic** (par′ə dig mat′ik), *adj.* **—Syn. 2.** model, mold, ideal, standard, paragon.

par·a·di·sa·i·cal (par′ə di sā′i kəl, -zā′-), *adj.* paradisiacal. Also, **par′a·di·sa′ic.** [PARADISE + *-aic* (suffix abstracted from words like *prosaic, algebraic,* etc.) + -AL[1]] **—par′a·di·sa′i·cal·ly,** *adv.*

par·a·dise (par′ə dīs′, -dīz′), *n.* **1.** heaven, as the final abode of the righteous. **2.** an intermediate place for the departed souls of the righteous awaiting resurrection. **3.** Eden. **4.** a place of extreme beauty, delight, or happiness. **5.** supreme happiness or a state of supreme happiness. [ME, OE *paradīs* < LL *paradīs(us)* < Gk *parádeisos* park, pleasure grounds < Iranian; cf. Avestan *pairidaēza-* enclosure = *pairi-* PERI- + *daēza-* wall]

par·a·di·si·a·cal (par′ə di sī′ə kəl, -zī′-), *adj.* of, like, or befitting paradise. Also, **par·a·dis·i·ac** (par′ə dis′ē ak′), **paradisaical.** [< LL *paradīsiac(us)* < Gk *paradeisiakós* (see PARADISE, -AC) + -AL[1]] **—par′a·di·si′a·cal·ly,** *adv.*

par·a·dos (par′ə dos′), *n. Fort.* the bank behind a trench for protecting men from enemy fire and from being seen against the skyline. [< F; see PARA-², REREDOS]

par·a·dox (par′ə doks′), *n.* **1.** a statement or proposition seemingly self-contradictory or absurd but in reality expressing a possible truth. **2.** a self-contradictory and false proposition. **3.** any person, thing, or situation exhibiting an apparently contradictory nature. **4.** an opinion or statement contrary to commonly accepted opinion. [< L *paradox(um)* < Gk *parádoxon,* n. use of neut. of *parádoxos* unbelievable, lit., beyond what is thought. See PARA-¹, ORTHODOX] —**par′a·dox′i·cal,** *adj.* —**par′a·dox′i·cal·ly,** *adv.*

par·aes·the·sia (par′is thē′zhə, -zhē ə, -zē ə), *n. Pathol.* paresthesia. —**par·aes·thet·ic** (par′is thet′ik), *adj.*

par·af·fin (par′ə fin), *n.* **1.** a white or colorless, tasteless, odorless, water-insoluble, solid substance, consisting of a mixture of hydrocarbons chiefly of the alkane series, obtained from crude petroleum: used in candles, for forming preservative coatings and seals, for waterproofing paper, etc. **2.** *Chem.* **a.** any member of the alkane series. **b.** one of the higher members of the alkane series, solid at ordinary temperatures, having a boiling point above 300°C, that largely constitutes the commercial form of this substance. **3.** Also called **par′affin oil′.** *Brit.* kerosene. —*v.t.* **4.** to cover or impregnate with paraffin. [< G < L *par(um)* barely + *affin(is)* connected; so called from its slight affinity for other substances; see AFFINITY]

par·af·fine (par′ə fin, -fēn′), *n., v.t.,* **-fined, -fin·ing.** paraffin.

par·af·fin·ize (par′ə fi nīz′), *v.t.,* **-ized, -iz·ing.** paraffin (def. 4).

par′affin se′ries, *Chem.* See **alkane series.**

par′affin wax′, paraffin in its solid state.

par·a·form·al·de·hyde (par′ə fôr mal′də hīd′), *n. Chem.* a solid, $(HCOH)_n$, having the odor of formaldehyde, used chiefly as an antiseptic. Also called **par·a·form** (par′ə-fôrm′).

par·a·gen·e·sis (par′ə jen′i sis), *n. Geol.* the origin of minerals or mineral deposits in contact so as to affect one another's formation. Also, **par·a·ge·ne·sia** (par′ə jə nē′zhə, -zhē ə, -zē ə). [< NL; see PARA-¹, GENESIS] —**par·a·ge·net·ic** (par′ə jə net′ik), *adj.*

par·a·go·ge (par′ə gō′jē), *n.* the addition of a sound or group of sounds at the end of a word, as *height-th* for *height.* [< LL *paragōgē* addition to a word, lengthening of a word < Gk *paragōgḗ* a leading by, alteration, change < *parágein* to lead by, past. See PARA-¹, -AGOGUE] —**par·a·gog·ic** (par′ə-goj′ik), **par′a·gog′i·cal,** *adj.* —**par′a·gog′i·cal·ly,** *adv.*

par·a·gon (par′ə gon′, -gən), *n.* **1.** a model or pattern of excellence or of a particular excellence. **2.** *Print.* a 20-point type. **3.** a perfect diamond weighing 100 carats or more. **4.** an unusually large, round pearl. —*v.t.* **5.** *Archaic.* to compare; parallel. **6.** *Archaic.* to be a match for; rival. **7.** *Obs.* to surpass. [< MF < OIt *paragone* comparison, ? < Gk *parágōn,* prp. of *parágein* to bring side by side]

par·a·graph¹ (par′ə graf′, -gräf′), *n.* **1.** a distinct portion of written or printed matter dealing with a particular idea, usually beginning with an indentation on a new line. **2.** a note, item, or brief article, as in a newspaper. —*v.t.* **3.** to divide into paragraphs. **4.** to write or publish paragraphs about, as in a newspaper. [earlier *paragraphe* < Gk *paragraphḗ* marked passage] —**par·a·graph·ic** (par′ə graf′ik), **par′a·graph′i·cal,** *adj.* —**par′a·graph′i·cal·ly,** *adv.*

par·a·graph² (par′ə graf′, -gräf′), *n.* a character, usually ¶, used to indicate the beginning of a distinct or separate portion of a text, or as a mark of reference. [earlier *paragraf(f)e* < ML *paragraph(us)* < Gk *parágraphos* mark made beside (usually below) to set off part of a text]

Par·a·guay (par′ə gwā′, -gwī′; *Sp.* pä′rä gwī′), *n.* **1.** a republic in central South America bordered by Bolivia, Brazil, and Argentina. 2,600,000; 157,047 sq. mi. *Cap.:* Asunción. **2.** a river in central South America, flowing S from W Brazil through Paraguay to the Paraná. 1500 mi. long. —**Par′a·guay′an,** *adj., n.*

par·a·hy·dro·gen (par′ə hī′drə jən), *n. Physics, Chem.* the form of molecular hydrogen in which the nuclei of the two hydrogen atoms contained in the molecule have spins in opposite directions. Cf. **orthohydrogen.**

Pa·ra·í·ba (pä′rä ē′bə), *n.* a state in E Brazil. 2,675,100; 21,760 sq. mi. *Cap.:* João Pessoa.

par·a·keet (par′ə kēt′), *n.* any of numerous small, slender parrots, usually having a long, graduated tail and noted for their ability to mimic speech. Also, **parrakeet.** [earlier *parrachito* < It *parochito* (Florio), var. of *parrochetto,* dim. of *parroco* parson. See PAROCHIAL, -ET]

Parakeet (Budgerigar), *Melopsittacus undulatus* (Length 7 in.)

par·al·de·hyde (pə ral′də hīd′), *n. Chem., Pharm.* a liquid, cyclic compound, $C_6H_{12}O_3$, used chiefly in the manufacture of organic chemicals and as a sedative and hypnotic.

par·a·lep·sis (par′ə lep′sis), *n., pl.* **-ses** (-sēz). paralipsis.

par·a·lip·sis (par′ə lip′sis), *n., pl.* **-ses** (-sēz). *Rhet.* the suggestion, by deliberately concise treatment of a topic, that much of significance is being omitted, as in "not to mention other faults." Also, **paralepsis.** [< LL *paralīpsis* < Gk *paráleipsis* an omitting = *paraleíp(ein)* (to) leave on one side (*para-* PARA-¹ + *leípein* to leave) + *-sis* -SIS]

Parallax (geocentric) of the moon
P, Parallax; O, Observer; E, Center of earth; M, Moon; E′, Image of E; O′, Image of O

par·al·lax (par′ə laks′), *n.* **1.** the apparent displacement of an observed object due to the difference between two points of view. **2.** *Astron.* the apparent displacement of a celestial body due to its being observed from the surface instead of from the center of the earth **(diurnal parallax** or **geocentric parallax)** or due to its being observed from the earth instead of from the sun **(annual parallax** or **heliocentric parallax). 3.** the difference between the view of an object as seen through the picture-taking lens of a camera and the view as seen through a separate viewfinder. [< Gk *parállax(is)* change = *parallak-* (verbid s. of *parallássein: para-* PARA-¹ + *allássein* to vary, akin to *állos* other; see ELSE, ALIEN) + *-sis* -SIS] —**par·al·lac·tic** (par′ə lak′-tik), *adj.* —**par′al·lac′ti·cal·ly,** *adv.*

par·al·lel (par′ə lel′), *adj., n., v.,* **-leled, -lel·ing** or (*esp. Brit.*) **-lelled, -lel·ling.** —*adj.* **1.** extending in the same direction, equidistant at all points, and never converging or diverging: *parallel rows of trees.* **2.** having the same direction, course, nature, or tendency: *parallel interests.* **3.** *Geom.* **a.** (of straight lines) lying in the same plane but never meeting no matter how far extended. **b.** (of planes) having common perpendiculars. **c.** (of a single line, plane, etc.) equidistant from another or others at all corresponding points (usually fol. by *to* or *with*). **4.** *Music.* (of two voice parts) progressing so that the interval between them remains the same. **5.** *Elect.* consisting of or having component parts connected in parallel: *a parallel circuit.* —*n.* **6.** anything parallel or comparable in action, effect, nature, or tendency to something else. **7.** correspondence or analogy, as one thing with another. **8.** a comparison made between two things. **9.** a parallel line or plane. **10.** Also called **parallel of latitude.** *Geog.* an imaginary circle on the earth's surface formed by the intersection of a plane parallel to the plane of the equator, designated in degrees of latitude north or south of the equator along the arc of any meridian. **11.** a parallel direction or course. **12.** *Print.* a pair of vertical parallel lines (‖) used as a mark for reference. **13.** *Elect.* an arrangement of the components, as resistances, of a circuit in such a way that all positive terminals are connected to one point and all negative terminals are connected to a second point, the same voltage being applied to each component. Cf. **series** (def. 5). **14.** *Fort.* a trench cut in the ground before a fortress, parallel to its defenses, for the purpose of covering a besieging force. —*v.t.* **15.** to make parallel. **16.** to form a parallel to; match; equal. **17.** to go or be in a parallel course, direction, etc., to. [< L *parallēl(us)* < Gk *parállēlos* side by side = *para-* PARA-¹ + *állēlos* one another; see ELSE] —**Syn. 2.** like, alike. **7.** similarity, likeness, resemblance. —**Ant. 2.** divergent; unlike. **7.** dissimilarity.

par′allel ax′iom, *Geom.* See **parallel postulate.**

par′allel bars′, *Gymnastics.* an apparatus consisting of two wooden bars on uprights, adjustable in height and distance apart and used for exercising.

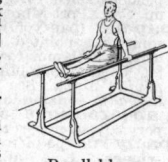

Parallel bars

par·al·lel·e·pi·ped (par′ə lel′ə pī′pid, -pip′id), *n.* a prism with six faces, all parallelograms. Also, **par·al·lel·e·pip·e·don** (par′ə lel′ə pip′i don′, -dən), **par′al·lel′o·pi′ped.** [< Gk *parallēlepíped(on)* body with parallel surfaces = *parállēl(os)* PARALLEL + *epípedon* plane, n. use of neut. of *epípedos* flat (*epi-* EPI- + *pédon* ground)] —**par·al·lel·e·pip·e·dic** (par′ə-lel′ə pip′i dik), *adj.*

Parallelepiped

par′allel forc′es, *Mech.* forces acting in parallel lines of action.

par·al·lel·ise (par′ə lel īz′, -lə līz′), *v.t.,* **-ised, -is·ing.** *Chiefly Brit.* parallelize. —**par′al·lel′i·sa′tion,** *n.*

par·al·lel·ism (par′ə lel′iz əm), *n.* **1.** the position or relation of parallels. **2.** agreement, as in tendency or character. **3.** a parallel or comparison. **4.** *Metaphys.* the doctrine that mental and bodily processes each vary with variation of the other, but that there is no causal relation in their interaction. —**par′al·lel′ist,** *n.* —**par·al·lel·is·tic** (par′ə-lel is′tik, -lə lis′-), *adj.*

par·al·lel·ize (par′ə lel īz′, -lə līz′), *v.t.,* **-ized, -iz·ing. 1.** to make parallel; place so as to be parallel. **2.** to draw an analogy between. Also, *esp. Brit.,* **parallelise.** [< Gk *parallēlíz(ein)*] —**par′al·lel′i·za′tion,** *n.*

par′allel of lat′itude, parallel (def. 10).

par·al·lel·o·gram (par′ə lel′ə-gram′), *n.* a quadrilateral having both pairs of opposite sides parallel to each other. [< LL *parallēlogramm(um)* < Gk *parallēlógrammon*] —**par′al·lel′-o·gram·mat′ic, par′al·lel′o·gram′mic,** *adj.*

Parallelograms

parallel′ogram of forc′es, *Physics.* a parallelogram in which two adjacent sides represent the forces acting on a body, and the diagonal between them represents their resultant.

par′allel pos′tulate, *Geom.* the axiom in Euclidean geometry that only one line can be drawn through a given point so that the line is parallel to a given line that does not contain the point. Also called **parallel axiom.**

par′allel rul′ers, a pair of straightedges connected by two pivoted crosspieces of equal length so as to be parallel at all times, used for various navigational purposes, esp. for transferring the bearing of a plotted course to a compass rose.

pa·ral·o·gism (pə ral′ə jiz′əm), *n. Logic.* a violation of principles of valid reasoning. [< LL *paralogism(us)* < Gk *paralogismós.* See PARA-¹, LOGO-, -ISM] —**pa·ral′o·gis′tic,** *adj.*

par·a·lyse (par′ə līz′), *v.t.,* **-lysed, -lys·ing.** *Chiefly Brit.* paralyze. —**par′a·lys′er,** *n.* —**par′a·lys′ing·ly,** *adv.*

pa·ral·y·sis (pə ral′i sis), *n., pl.* **-ses** (-sēz′). **1.** *Pathol.* **a.** a loss or impairment of sensation or esp. of muscle function, caused by injury or disease of the nerves, brain, or spinal cord. **b.** a disease characterized by this, esp. palsy. **2.** a crippling or stoppage, as of powers or activities. [< L < Gk = *paralý(ein)* (to) loosen (i.e., disable) on one side (*para-* PARA-¹ + *lýein* to loosen) + *-sis* -SIS]

paral′ysis ag′i·tans (aj′i tanz′), *Pathol.* See **Parkinson's disease.** [< NL: lit., shaking paralysis]

par·a·lyt·ic (par′ə lit′ik), *n.* **1.** a person affected with paralysis. —*adj.* **2.** affected with or subject to paralysis. **3.** of or pertaining to paralysis. [ME *paralitik* < L *paralyticus* < Gk *paralytikós* = *paraly̆(ein)* (to) disable on one side (see PARALYSIS) + *-tikos* -TIC] —**par′a·lyt′i·cal·ly,** *adv.*

par·a·lyze (par′ə līz′), *v.t.*, **-lyzed, -lyz·ing. 1.** to affect with paralysis. **2.** to bring to a condition of helpless inactivity. Also, *esp. Brit.*, **paralyse.** [back formation from PARALYSIS] —**par′a·lyz′er,** *n.* —**par′a·lyz′ing·ly,** *adv.*

par·a·mag·net (par′ə mag′nit), *n. Physics.* a body or substance having paramagnetic properties. [back formation from PARAMAGNETIC] —**par′a·mag′net·ism,** *n.*

par·a·mag·net·ic (par′ə mag net′ik), *adj. Physics.* noting or pertaining to a substance in which the magnetic moments of the atoms have random directions until placed in a magnetic field, when they possess magnetization in direct proportion to the field strength. Cf. **antiferromagnetic, diamagnetic, ferromagnetic.**

Par·a·mar·i·bo (par′ə mar′ə bō′), *n.* a seaport in and the capital of Surinam, in NE South America. 150,000.

Par·am·at·man (pur′ə mät′mən), *n. Hinduism.* absolute Atman. [< Skt: lit., beyond Atman]

par·a·mat·ta (par′ə mat′ə), *n.* a light, twilled dress fabric of wool and either silk or cotton. Also, **parramatta.** [named after *Parramatta*, town in New South Wales]

par·a·me·ci·um (par′ə mē′shē əm, -sē əm), *n., pl.* **-ci·a** (-shē ə, -sē ə). any ciliated fresh-water protozoan of the genus *Paramecium*, having an oval body and a long, deep oral groove. [< NL < Gk *paramḗk(ēs)* oblong, oval; see -IUM]

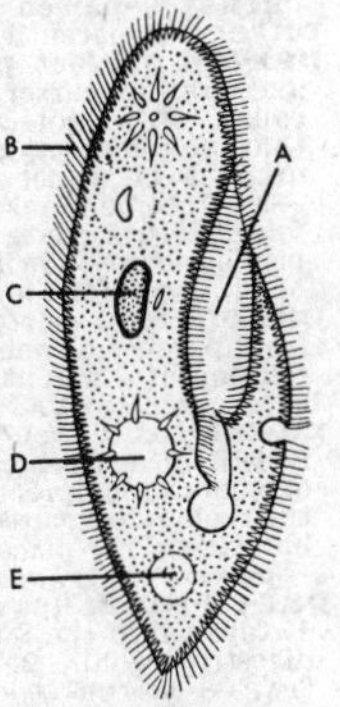

A B C D E

Paramecium
A, Oral groove; B, Cilia; C, Nucleus; D, Contractile vacuole; E, Food vacuole

par·a·med·ic (*n.* par′ə med′ik; *adj.* par′ə med′ik), *n.* **1.** *Mil.* a medic in the paratroops. **2.** a doctor who parachutes into remote areas to give medical care. —*adj.* **3.** of or pertaining to a paramedic or to paramedics. [PARA(CHUTE) + MEDIC[1]]

par·a·med·i·cal (par′ə med′i kəl), *adj.* related to the medical profession in a secondary or supplementary capacity.

pa·ram·e·ter (pə ram′i tər), *n.* **1.** *Math.* **a.** a constant or variable term in a function that determines the specific form of the function but not its general nature, as *a* in $f(x) = ax$, where *a* determines only the slope of the line described by $f(x)$. **b.** one of the independent variables in a set of parametric equations. **2.** *Statistics.* a variable entering into the mathematical form of any distribution such that the possible values of the variable correspond to different distributions. **3.** a determining factor, characteristic, etc.: *the basic parameters of their foreign policy.* [< NL *parametrum*] —**par·a·met·ric** (par′ə me′trik), **par′a·met′ri·cal,** *adj.*

par·a·mil·i·tar·y (par′ə mil′i ter′ē), *adj.* noting or pertaining to an organization operating as, in place of, or as a supplement to a regular military force: *a paramilitary police unit.* [PARA-[1] + MILITARY]

par·am·ne·sia (par′am nē′zhə, -zhē ə, -zē ə), *n. Psychiatry.* a distortion of memory in which fact and fantasy are confused. [< NL]

par·a·morph (par′ə môrf′), *n. Mineral.* a pseudomorph formed by a change in crystal structure but not in chemical composition. —**par′a·mor′phic, par′a·mor′phous,** *adj.*

par·a·mount (par′ə mount′), *adj.* **1.** chief in importance; supreme; preeminent. **2.** above others in rank or authority; superior in power or jurisdiction. —*n.* **3.** an overlord; supreme ruler. [< AF *paramont* above = *par* PER- + *a mont* < L *ad montem* to the mountain, hence, in OF: upward, above; see AD-, MOUNT[2]] —**par′a·mount′ly,** *adv.*

Par·a·mount (par′ə mount′), *n.* a city in SW California, near Los Angeles. 34,734 (1970).

par·a·mour (par′ə mo͝or′), *n.* **1.** an illicit lover, esp. of a married person. **2.** any lover. [ME, from the phrase *par amour* by or through love < OF]

Pa·ram·us (pə ram′əs), *n.* a city in NE New Jersey. 28,381 (1970).

Pa·ra·ná (par′ə nä′; *Port.* pä′rə nä′), *n.* **1.** a river in central South America, flowing from S Brazil along the SE boundary of Paraguay and through E Argentina into the Río de la Plata. 2050 mi. long. **2.** a city in E Argentina, on the Paraná River: the capital of Argentina 1852–61. 184,000.

par·a·noi·a (par′ə noi′ə), *n. Psychiatry.* mental disorder characterized by systematized delusions and the projection of personal conflicts, that are ascribed to the supposed hostility of others. [< NL < Gk: madness. See PARA-, NOUS, -IA] —**par′a·noid′, par·a·noi·ac** (par′ə noi′ak), *adj., n.*

par·a·nymph (par′ə nimf′), *n.* **1.** a groomsman or a bridesmaid. **2.** (in ancient Greece) **a.** a friend who accompanied the bridegroom when he went to bring home the bride. **b.** the bridesmaid who escorted the bride to the bridegroom. [< LL *paranymph(us)* < Gk *paránymphos* (common gender) groomsman, bridesmaid]

par·a·pet (par′ə pit, -pet′), *n.* **1.** *Fort.* a defensive wall or elevation in a fortification. **2.** any low protective wall or barrier at the edge of a balcony, roof, bridge, or the like. [< It *parapett(o)*. See PARA-[2], PETTO] —**par′a·pet·ed,** *adj.*

par·aph (par′əf), *n.* a flourish made after a signature, as in a document, originally as a precaution against forgery. [ME *paraf* < MF *paraphe* PARAGRAPH[2] (by syncope)]

par·a·pher·nal·ia (par′ə fər nāl′yə, -fə nāl′-), *n.* **1.** (*construed as pl.*) personal belongings. **2.** (*construed as pl.*) *Law.* the personal articles, apart from dower, reserved by law to a married woman. **3.** (*sometimes construed as sing.*) equipment, apparatus, or furnishing. [< ML *paraphernālia* (*bona*) a bride's goods, beyond her dowry = LL *paraphern(a)* a bride's property (< Gk *parápherna* = *para-* PARA-[1] + *phern(ē)* dowry < *phérein* to carry) + L *-ālia*, neut. pl. (n.) of *-ālis* -AL[1]] —**par′a·pher·na′li·an, par·a·pher·nal** (par′ə fûr′nəl), *adj.* —**Syn. 1.** effects. **3.** appurtenances, trappings.

par·a·phrase (par′ə frāz′), *n., v.,* **-phrased, -phras·ing.** —*n.* **1.** a restatement of a text or passage giving the meaning in another form, as for clearness; rewording. **2.** the act or process of restating or rewording. —*v.t.* **3.** to render the meaning of in a paraphrase. —*v.i.* **4.** to make a paraphrase or paraphrases. [< MF < L *paraphrasis* < Gk] —**par′a·phras′er,** *n.* —**par·a·phras·tic** (par′ə fras′tik) *adj.* —**par′a·phras′ti·cal·ly,** *adv.* —**Syn. 3.** summarize; explain.

par·a·phrast (par′ə frast′), *n.* a person who paraphrases. [< LL *paraphrast(ēs)* < Gk < *paraphrázein* to retell in other words = *para-* PARA-[1] + *phrázein* to tell, declare]

pa·raph·y·sis (pə raf′i sis), *n., pl.* **-ses** (-sēz′). *Bot.* one of the sterile, usually filamentous, outgrowths often occurring among the reproductive organs in many cryptogamous plants. [< NL < Gk: lit., a growing beside, by-growth]

par·a·ple·gi·a (par′ə plē′jē ə, -jə), *n. Pathol.* paralysis of the legs and lower part of the body, due to spinal disease or injury. [< NL < Gk *paraplēgía*] —**par·a·ple·gic** (par′ə plē′jik, -plej′ik), *adj., n.*

par·a·pro·fes·sion·al (par′ə prə fesh′ə nəl), *n.* **1.** a person trained to assist a professional, such as a doctor's assistant or a part-time teaching assistant. —*adj.* **2.** of or pertaining to paraprofessionals.

par·a·psy·chol·o·gy (par′ə sī kol′ə jē), *n.* the branch of psychology that deals with the investigation of psychic phenomena, as clairvoyance, extrasensory perception, telepathy, and the like. —**par′a·psy·chol′o·gist,** *n.*

par·a·quat (par′ə kwät′), *n.* a toxic herbicide spray, $C_{12}H_{14}N_2$ combined with chloride or dimethyl sulfate, applied as a crop defoliant and weed killer. [PARA- + QUAT(ERNARY)]

Pará′ rhat′any. See under **rhatany** (def. 1).

Pará′ rub′ber, rubber obtained chiefly from the euphorbiaceous tree *Hevea brasiliensis* of tropical South America.

par·a·sail·ing (par′ə sā′ling), *n.* the sport of soaring while harnessed to a special parachute (**par′a·sail′**) towed by a motorboat, car, or other fast-moving vehicle, from which one often releases oneself to float freely.

par·a·sang (par′ə sang′), *n.* a Persian unit of distance, of varying length, anciently about 3⅖ miles. [< L *parasang(a)* < Gk *parasángēs* < OPers; akin to Pers *farsang*]

par·a·se·le·ne (par′ə si lē′nē), *n., pl.* **-nae** (-nē). *Meteorol.* a bright moonlike spot on a lunar halo; a mock moon. Cf. **parhelion.** [< NL = *para-* PARA-[1] + Gk *selḗnē* the moon] —**par·a·se·le·nic** (par′ə si lē′nik, -len′ik), *adj.*

Par·a·shah (pär′ə shä′; *Heb.* pä rä shä′), *n., pl.* **Par·a·shoth** (pär′ə shōt′; *Heb.* pä rä shōt′), **Par·a·shi·oth** (pär′ə shē′ōt; *Heb.* pä rä shē ōt′). *Judaism.* **1.** a portion of the Torah chanted or read each week in the synagogue on the Sabbath. **2.** a selection from such a portion, chanted or read in the synagogue on Mondays, Thursdays, and holy days. [< Heb: division]

par·a·site (par′ə sīt′), *n.* **1.** an animal or plant that lives on or in an organism of another species from whose body it obtains nutriment. **2.** a person who receives support, advantage, or the like, from another or others without giving any useful or proper return. **3.** (in ancient Greece) a person who received free meals for his amusing conversation. [< L *parasīt(us)* < Gk *parásītos* one who eats at another's table, orig. adj.: feeding beside = *para-* PARA-[1] + *sît(os)* grain, food + *-os* adj. suffix] —**Syn. 2.** sycophant, hanger-on.

par·a·sit·ic (par′ə sit′ik), *adj.* of, pertaining to, or characteristic of parasites. Also, **par′a·sit′i·cal.** [< L *parasīticus* < Gk *parasitikós*] —**par′a·sit′i·cal·ly,** *adv.*

par·a·sit·i·cide (par′ə sit′i sīd′), *adj.* **1.** destructive to plant or animal parasites. —*n.* **2.** an agent or preparation that destroys parasites. —**par′a·sit′i·cid′al,** *adj.*

par·a·sit·ism (par′ə sī′tiz əm), *n.* **1.** a parasitic mode of life or existence. **2.** *Zool., Bot.* a relation between organisms in which one lives as a parasite on another. **3.** *Pathol.* a diseased condition due to parasites.

par·a·si·tize (par′ə si tīz′, -sī-), *v.t.*, **-tized, -tiz·ing.** to live on (a host) as a parasite. Also, *esp. Brit.*, **par′a·si·tise′.**

par·a·sit·ol·o·gy (par′ə sī tol′ə jē, -si-), *n.* the branch of biology dealing with parasites and the effects of parasitism. —**par·a·si·to·log·i·cal** (par′ə sīt′əloj′i kəl), *adj.* —**par′a·si·tol′o·gist,** *n.*

par·a·sol (par′ə sôl′, -sol′), *n.* a woman's small or light sun umbrella. [< F, MF < It *parasole.* See PARA-[2], SOL]

par·a·sym·pa·thet·ic (par′ə sim′pə thet′ik), *Anat., Physiol.* —*adj.* **1.** pertaining to that part of the autonomic system consisting of nerves and ganglia that arise from the cranial and sacral regions and function in opposition to the sympathetic system, as in inhibiting heart beat, contracting the pupil of the eye, etc. —*n.* **2.** a nerve of the parasympathetic system.

par·a·syn·ap·sis (par′ə si nap′sis), *n. Biol.* the conjugation of chromosomes side by side; synapsis. —**par′a·syn·ap′tic,** *adj.* —**par′a·syn·ap′tist,** *n.*

par·a·syn·the·sis (par′ə sin′thi sis), *n. Gram.* **1.** the formation of a word by the addition of both a prefix and a derivational suffix to a word or stem, as *demoralize.* **2.** the formation of a word by the addition of a derivational suffix to a phrase or compound, as *great-hearted*, which is *great heart* plus *-ed.* —**par·a·syn·thet·ic** (par′ə sin thet′ik), *adj.*

par·a·tax·is (par′ə tak′sis), *n.* the placing together of sentences, clauses, or phrases without a conjunctive word, as *Hurry up, it's getting late.* [< NL < Gk: an arranging in order for battle] —**par·a·tac·tic** (par′ə tak′tik), **par′a·tac′ti·cal,** *adj.* —**par′a·tac′ti·cal·ly,** *adv.*

par·a·thi·on (par′ə thī′on), *n. Chem.* a poisonous liquid, $(C_2H_5O)_2P(S)OC_6H_4NO_2$, used as an insecticide.

par·a·thy·roid (par′ə thī′roid), *Anat.* —*adj.* **1.** situated near the thyroid gland. —*n.* **2.** See **parathyroid gland.**

parathy′roid gland′, *Anat.* any of several small glands or oval masses of epitheloid cells usually lying near or embedded in the thyroid gland, the internal secretions of which control the calcium content of the blood.

par·a·to·lu·i·dine (par′ə tə lo͞o′i dēn′, -din), *n. Chem.* a white solid, $CH_3C_6H_4NH_2$, the para isomer of toluidine, used in the manufacture of dyes and in organic synthesis.

par·a·troop (par′ə tro͞op′), *adj.* **1.** of or pertaining to a paratrooper or a parachute unit: *paratroop boots.* —*n.*

paratroops, 2. a unit of paratroopers. **3.** paratroopers collectively. [back formation from PARATROOPER]

par·a·troop·er (par′ə tro͞o′pər), *n. Mil.* a member of an army infantry unit trained to attack or land in combat areas by parachuting from airplanes. [PARA(CHUTE) + TROOPER]

par·a·ty·phoid (par′ə tī′foid), *Pathol.* —*n.* **1.** Also called **paraty′phoid fe′ver.** an infectious disease, similar in some of its symptoms to typhoid but usually milder, caused by the paratyphoid bacillus. —*adj.* **2.** of or pertaining to paratyphoid. **3.** resembling typhoid.

par·a·vane (par′ə vān′), *n.* a device for cutting the moorings of underwater mines, consisting of a pair of torpedo-shaped vanes streamed from the bow of a ship at the ends of cables bearing cutting edges.

par a·vion (PA RA vyôN′), *French.* by plane (used esp. as a designation on matter to be sent by air mail).

par·boil (pär′boil′), *v.t.* to boil partially, or for a short time; precook. [late ME *parboyle(n)* (to) boil partly, earlier, boil fully < MF *parboill(ir)* < LL *perbullīre* to boil through and through (see PER-, BOIL[1]); change of meaning by confusion of *par-* with *part*]

par·buck·le (pär′buk′əl), *n., v.,* **-led, -ling.** —*n.* **1.** a tackle for raising or lowering a cask or similar object along an inclined plane or a vertical surface, consisting of a rope looped over a post or the like, with its two ends passing around the object to be moved. **2.** a kind of double sling made with a rope, as around a cask to be raised or lowered. —*v.t.* **3.** to raise, lower, or move with a parbuckle. [earlier *parbunkel* < ?]

par·cel (pär′səl), *n., v.,* **-celed, -cel·ing** or (*esp. Brit.*) **-celled, -cel·ling,** *adv.* —*n.* **1.** an object, container, or quantity of something wrapped or packed up; package; bundle. **2.** a quantity or unit of something, as of a commodity for sale; a lot. **3.** any group or assemblage of persons or things. **4.** a distinct portion or tract of land. **5.** a part, portion, or fragment. —*v.t.* **6.** to divide into or distribute in parcels or portions (usually fol. by *out*): *to parcel out land for homesites.* **7.** to make into a parcel or wrap as a parcel. **8.** *Naut.* to cover or wrap (a rope) with strips of canvas. —*adv.* **9.** in part; partially. [ME < MF *parcelle* < LL **particella* for L *particula;* see PARTICLE] —**Syn. 1.** See **package. 6.** mete.

par·cel·ing (pär′sə ling), *n.* **1.** the act of separating or dividing into parts and distributing; allotting or apportioning. **2.** *Naut.* odd strips of canvas for wrapping around a rope.

par′cel post′, 1. a branch of a postal service charged with conveying parcels. **2.** the service this branch renders. **3.** parcels handled by this branch.

par·ce·nar·y (pär′sə ner′ē), *n. Law.* the undivided holding of land by two or more coheirs; coheirship. [< AF *parcenarie,* OF *parçonerie.* See PARCENER, -ARY]

par·ce·ner (pär′sə nər), *n. Law.* a joint heir; coheir. [ME < AF = *parcen* (OF *parçon* < VL **partion-* for L *partitiōn-* PARTITION) + *-er* -ER[2]]

parch (pärch), *v.t.* **1.** to make excessively or completely dry, as heat, sun, and wind do. **2.** to make dry, hot, or thirsty. **3.** to dry (peas, beans, etc.) by exposure to heat without burning; to toast or roast slightly: *to parch corn.* **4.** to dry or shrivel with cold. —*v.i.* **5.** to suffer from heat or thirst. **6.** to become dry. [ME *perche(n)* < ?] —**parch′a·ble,** *adj.* —**parch′ing·ly,** *adv.*

par·chee·si (pär chē′zē), *n. Trademark.* a simplified form of pachisi.

parch·ment (pärch′mənt), *n.* **1.** the skin of sheep, goats, etc., prepared for use as a material on which to write. **2.** a manuscript or document on such material. **3.** a paper resembling this material. **4.** a diploma. [late ME *parchment* < MF, OF *parche* (< L *Parthica (pellis)* Parthian (leather); see -MENT and cf. ML *percamentum,* D *perkament*); r. ME *parchemin* < OF (*-min* < ML *(perga)mīnum,* var. of *pergamēnum* for LL *Pergamēna charta* paper of PERGAMUM)] —**parch′ment·like′,** *adj.*

parch′ment pa′per, a waterproof and grease-resistant paper produced by treating unsized paper with concentrated sulfuric acid.

pard[1] (pärd), *n. Archaic.* a leopard or panther. [ME *parde,* OE *pardus* < L < Gk *pārdos* (masc.) < *pārdalis* (fem.)] —**pard·ine** (pär′dīn, -din), *adj.*

pard[2] (pärd), *n. Slang.* partner; companion. [by alter. and shortening of PARTNER]

par·dah (pûr′də), *n.* purdah.

par·di (pär dē′), *adv., interj. Archaic.* verily; indeed. Also, **par·die′, pardy, perdie.** [late ME *pardie,* ME *parde* < OF *par De* < L *per Deum* by God]

pard·ner (pärd′nər), *n. U.S. Dial.* **1.** (in direct address) friend. **2.** partner. [alter. of PARTNER]

par·don (pär′dᵊn), *n.* **1.** kind indulgence, as in forgiveness of an offense or discourtesy, or in tolerance of an inconvenience: *I beg your pardon.* **2.** *Law.* **a.** a release from the penalty of an offense. **b.** the warrant by which such remission is declared. **3.** forgiveness of an offense or offender. **4.** *Obs.* a papal indulgence. —*v.t.* **5.** to remit the penalty of (an offense). **6.** to release (a person) from liability for an offense. **7.** to make courteous allowance for or to excuse: *Pardon me, madam.* [ME < OF: remission, indulgence, back formation from *pardoner* < ML *perdōnāre* to remit, overlook = L *per-* FOR- + *dōnāre* to give; see DONATE. ML v. perh. a trans. of Gmc] —**par′don·a·ble,** *adj.* —**par′don·a·bly,** *adv.* —**par′don·less,** *adj.* —**Syn. 3.** absolution. **5.** forgive. **6.** acquit. See **excuse.**

par·don·er (pär′dᵊnər), *n.* **1.** a person who pardons. **2.** *Obs.* an ecclesiastical official authorized to sell indulgences.

par·dy (pär dē′), *adv., interj. Archaic.* pardi.

pare (pâr), *v.t.,* **pared, par·ing. 1.** to cut off the outer coating, layer, or part of. **2.** to remove (an outer layer or part) by cutting. **3.** to reduce or remove by or as by cutting; diminish or decrease gradually. [ME *pare(n)* < MF *par(er)* (to) make ready, trim < L *parāre* to prepare] —**par′er,** *n.* —**Syn. 1.** See **peel**[1].

Pa·ré (PA RĀ′), *n.* **Am·broise** (äN BRWAZ′), 1510–90, French surgeon.

pa·re·cious (pə rē′shəs), *adj. Bot.* paroicous.

par·e·gor·ic (par′ə gôr′ik, -gor′-), *Pharm.* —*n.* **1.** a soothing medicine; anodyne. **2.** a camphorated tincture of opium, used chiefly to check diarrhea in children. —*adj.* **3.** assuaging pain; soothing. [< LL *parēgoric(us)* < Gk *parēgorikós* soothing = *parēgor(os)* pertaining to consolatory speech (see PARA-[1], AGORA) + *-ikos* -IC]

pa·rei·ra (pə râr′ə), *n.* the root of a South American vine, *Chondodendron tomentosum,* used as a source of curare, a diuretic, etc. [short for PAREIRA BRAVA]

parei′ra bra′va (brä′və, brā′-), pareira. [< Pg *parreira brava,* lit., wild vine]

paren., parenthesis.

pa·ren·chy·ma (pə reng′kə mə), *n.* **1.** *Bot.* the fundamental tissue of plants, composed of thin-walled cells. **2.** *Anat., Zool.* the specific tissue of an animal organ as distinguished from its connective or supporting tissue. **3.** *Zool.* a type of connective tissue in certain lower animals, consisting of a spongy mass of cells. [< NL < Gk: lit., something poured in beside = *par-* PAR- + *énchyma* infusion; see EN-[2], CHYME] —**par·en·chym·a·tous** (par′eng kim′ə təs), *adj.*

parens., parentheses.

par·ent (pâr′ənt, par′-), *n.* **1.** a father or a mother. **2.** an ancestor, precursor, or progenitor. **3.** a source, origin, or cause. **4.** a protector or guardian. **5.** *Biol.* any organism that produces or generates another. —*adj.* **6.** being the original or supervising source: *the parent organization.* —*v.t.* **7.** to be the parent of; bear or rear: *The couple parented four children.* [late ME <L *parent-* (s. of *parēns*), n. use of prp. of *parere* to bring forth, breed; in obs. sense, kinsman < MF] —**par′ent·less,** *adj.* —**par′ent·like′,** *adj.*

par·ent·age (pâr′ən tij, par′-), *n.* **1.** derivation or descent from parents or ancestors; origin or lineage. **2.** the state or relation of a parent. [< MF] —**Syn. 1.** descent, ancestry, extraction, stock.

pa·ren·tal (pə ren′tᵊl), *adj.* **1.** of, pertaining to, or characteristic of a parent. **2.** *Genetics.* pertaining to the sequence of generations preceding the filial generation, each generation being designated by a P followed by a subscript number indicating its place in the sequence. [< L *parentāl(is)*] —**pa·ren′tal·ly,** *adv.*

par·en·ter·al (pa ren′tər əl), *adj. Anat., Med., Physiol.* **1.** taken into the body in a manner other than through the digestive canal. **2.** not within the intestine; not intestinal. [PAR- + ENTER- + -AL[1]] —**par·en′ter·al·ly,** *adv.*

pa·ren·the·sis (pə ren′thi sis), *n., pl.* **-ses** (-sēz′). **1.** either or both of a pair of signs ( ) used to indicate a parenthetic remark. **2.** *Gram.* a qualifying, explanatory, or appositive word, phrase, clause, sentence, or other sequence that interrupts a syntactic construction without otherwise affecting it. **3.** an interval. [< LL < Gk; see PARENTHETIC, -SIS]

pa·ren·the·sise (pə ren′thi sīz′), *v.t.,* **-sised, -sis·ing.** *Chiefly Brit.* parenthesize.

pa·ren·the·size (pə ren′thi sīz′), *v.t.,* **-sized, -siz·ing. 1.** to insert (a word, phrase, etc.) as a parenthesis. **2.** to put between marks of parenthesis. **3.** to interlard with parenthetic remarks, as a speech.

par·en·thet·ic (par′ən thet′ik), *adj.* **1.** of or pertaining to a parenthesis: *several unnecessary parenthetic remarks.* **2.** characterized by the use of parentheses. Also, **par′en·thet′i·cal.** [back formation from *parenthetical* < Gk *parénthet(os)* putting in beside (verbid of *parentithénai* = *par-* PAR- + *en-* EN-[2] + *tithénai* to put) + -IC + -AL[1]] —**par′en·thet′i·cal·ly,** *adv.*

par·ent·hood (pâr′ənt ho͝od′, par′-), *n.* the state, position, or relation of a parent.

pa·ren·ti·cide (pə ren′ti sīd′), *n.* **1.** a person who kills one or both of his or her parents. **2.** the act of killing one's parent or parents.

par′ent-teach′er asso′ciation (pâr′ənt tē′chər, par′-), an organization of teachers and the parents of their students, as within a public school, to promote mutual understanding and to increase the effectiveness of the educational program. *Abbr.:* PTA, P.T.A.

pa·re·sis (pə rē′sis, par′i sis), *n. Pathol.* partial motor paralysis. [< NL < Gk: paralysis, a letting go = *pare-* (var. s. of *pariénai* to let go; see PAR-) + *-sis* -SIS]

par·es·the·sia (par′is thē′zhə, -zhē ə, -zē ə), *n. Pathol.* an abnormal sensation, as prickling, itching, etc. Also, **paraesthesia.** [< NL] —**par·es·thet·ic** (par′is thet′ik), *adj.*

pa·ret·ic (pə ret′ik, pə rē′tik), *Pathol.* —*n.* **1.** a person who has general paresis. —*adj.* **2.** pertaining to or affected with paresis. [< NL *paretic(us)* < Gk *páret(os)* relaxed, palsied (verbid of *pariénai*) + *-ikos* -IC] —**pa·ret′i·cal·ly,** *adv.*

Pa·re·to (pä RE′tô), *n.* **Vil·fre·do** (vēl FRE′dô), 1848–1923, Italian sociologist and economist in Switzerland.

pa·re·u (pä′rā o͞o′), *n.* lava-lava. [< Tahitian]

pa·re·ve (pär′və, pär′ə və), *adj. Judaism.* parve.

par ex·cel·lence (PA REK sə LäNS′; *Eng.* pär ek′sə läns′), *French.* being an example of excellence; superior; preeminent: *a chef* par excellence.

par·fait (pär fā′), *n.* **1.** a dessert made of layers of ice cream and fruit, syrup, etc., usually topped with whipped cream. **2.** a rich frozen dessert of whipped cream and egg, variously flavored. [< F: lit., perfect < L *perfect(us).* See PERFECT]

par·fleche (pär′flesh, pär flesh′), *n.* **1.** a rawhide that has been dried after having been soaked in a solution of lye and water to remove the hair. **2.** an article or object, as a case, pouch, etc., made of such rawhide. [< CanF *parflèche* = F *par(er)* to parry (see PARA-[2]) + *flèche* arrow]

par·get (pär′jit), *n., v.,* **-get·ed, -get·ing** or (*esp. Brit.*) **-get·ted, -get·ting.** —*n.* **1.** any of various plasters or roughcasts for covering walls or other surfaces, esp. a mortar of lime, hair, and cow dung. **2.** gypsum. **3.** pargeting (defs. 2, 3). —*v.t.* **4.** to cover or decorate with parget or pargeting. [ME < MF *parget(er)* = *par-* PER- + *geter,* sp. var. of *jeter* JET[1]]

par·get·ing (pär′ji ting), *n.* **1.** the act of one who pargets. **2.** ornamental plasterwork, esp. exterior plasterwork bearing designs in low relief. **3.** a lining of mortar or plaster for a chimney flue or the like. Also, *esp. Brit.,* **par′get·ting, parget** (for defs. 2, 3). [ME]

parhe′lic cir′cle, *Meteorol.* a white, horizontal band passing through the sun, either incomplete or extending around the horizon, produced by the reflection of the sun's rays from the vertical faces of ice prisms in the atmosphere. Also called **par′heli′acal ring′.**

par·he·li·on (pär hē′lē ən), *n., pl.* **-li·a** (-lē ə). *Meteorol.* a bright circular spot on a solar halo; a mock sun. Also called **sundog.** [etym. alter. of L *parēlion* < Gk, n. use of neut. of *parélios* beside the sun] —**par·he·li·a·cal** (pär′hi lī′ə kəl), **par·he·lic** (pär hē′lik, -hel′ik), *adj.*

pari-, a learned borrowing from Latin meaning "equal," used in the formation of compound words: *paripinnate.* [comb. form repr. L *pari-* (s. of *pār*). See PAR]

pa·ri·ah (pə rī′ə, par′ē ə, pär′-), *n.* **1.** an outcast. **2.** any person or animal generally despised. **3.** (*cap.*) a member of a low caste in southern India. [< Tamil *paraiyar,* pl. of *paraiyan,* lit., drummer (from a hereditary duty of the caste) < *parai* a festival drum]

Par·i·an (pâr′ē ən, par′-), *adj.* **1.** of or pertaining to Paros, noted for its white marble. **2.** noting or pertaining to a fine, unglazed porcelain resembling this marble. —*n.* **3.** a native or inhabitant of Paros. **4.** Also called **Par′ian ware′.** a hard, white porcelain used mainly for making statuettes. [< L *Pari(us)* of PAROS + -AN]

Pa·ri·cu·tín (pä rē ko͞o tēn′), *n.* a volcano in W central Mexico: first eruption 1943; now dormant. 8200 ft.

par·i·es (pâr′ē ēz′), *n., pl.* **pa·ri·e·tes** (pə rī′i tēz′). Usually, **parietes.** *Biol.* a wall, as of a hollow organ; an investing part. [< NL, special use of L: a wall, partition]

pa·ri·e·tal (pə rī′i tᵊl), *adj.* **1.** *Anat.* of, pertaining to, or situated near the side and top of the skull or the parietal bone. **2.** *Biol.* of or pertaining to parietes or structural walls. **3.** *Bot.* pertaining to or arising from a wall: usually applied to ovules when they proceed from or are borne on the walls or sides of the ovary. **4.** pertaining to or having authority over residence within the walls of a college. —*n.* **5.** *Anat.* any of several parts in the parietal region of the skull, esp. the parietal bone. [< LL *parietāl(is)* of, belonging to walls = L *pariet-* (s. of *pariēs*) wall + *-ālis* -AL[1]]

pari′etal bone′, *Anat.* either of a pair of membrane bones forming, by their union at the sagittal suture, part of the sides and top of the skull.

par·i-mu·tu·el (par′i myo͞o′cho͞o əl), *n.* **1.** a form of betting on horse races in which those holding winning tickets divide the total amount bet less a percentage for the management, taxes, etc. **2.** Also called **pari-mu′tuel machine′.** a machine that registers bets in pari-mutuel betting and calculates the changing odds and final payoffs. Also, **par′i·mu′·tu·el.** [< F: lit., mutual bet]

par·ing (pâr′ing), *n.* **1.** the act of a person or thing that pares. **2.** a piece or part pared off: *apple parings.* [ME]

pa·ri pas·su (pä′rē päs′so͞o; *Eng.* pâr′ī pas′o͞o, par′ē), *Latin.* **1.** with equal pace or progress; side by side. **2.** without partiality; equably; fairly.

par·i·pin·nate (par′i pin′āt), *adj. Bot.* **1.** evenly pinnate. **2.** pinnate without an odd terminal leaflet.

Par·is (par′is; *for 2 also Fr.* PA RĒ′), *n.* **1. Matthew.** See **Matthew of Paris. 2.** Ancient, **Lutetia Parisiorum, Pa·ris·i·i** (pə riz′ē ī′). a city in and the capital of France, in the N part, on the Seine. 2,317,227.

Par·is (par′is), *n. Class. Myth.* a Trojan prince, son of Priam and Hecuba, whose abduction of Helen led to the Trojan War.

Par′is Com′mune, commune[3] (def. 7).

Par′is green′, *Chem.* an emerald-green, poisonous powder having the approximate formula, $3Cu(AsO_2)_2 \cdot Cu(C_2H_3O_2)_2$, used as a pigment, insecticide, and wood preservative.

par·ish (par′ish), *n.* **1.** an ecclesiastical district having its own church and clergyman. **2.** a local church with its field of activity. **3.** *Chiefly Brit.* a civil district or administrative division. **4.** (in Louisiana) a county. **5.** the people of an ecclesiastical or civil parish. [ME, var. of *parosshe* < MF *paroisse* < LL *parochia,* alter. of *paroecia* < LGk *paroikía* < Gk *pároikos* neighbor (see PAROICOUS), in Christian usage, sojourner; see -IA]

par′ish house′, a building used by a church chiefly for administrative and social purposes.

pa·rish·ion·er (pə rish′ə nər), *n.* a member or inhabitant of a parish. [earlier *parishion,* ME *paroschian, -ien, -en* < OF *paroissien*]

Pa·ri·sian (pə rē′zhən, -rizh′ən, -riz′ē ən), *n.* **1.** a native or inhabitant of Paris, France. —*adj.* **2.** of, pertaining to, or characteristic of Paris, France. [< F *parisien*]

par·i·ty[1] (par′i tē), *n.* **1.** equality, as in amount, status, or character. **2.** equivalence; correspondence; similarity; analogy. **3.** *Physics.* a type of symmetry analogous to that which exists between the left and right hands. **4.** *Finance.* **a.** equivalence in value in the currency of another country. **b.** equivalence in value at a fixed ratio between moneys of different metals. **5.** *U.S.* a system of regulating prices of farm commodities to provide farmers with the same purchasing power they had in a selected base period. [< LL *pāritās.* See PAR, -ITY]

par·i·ty[2] (par′i tē), *n. Obstet.* the condition or fact of having borne offspring. [< L *par(ere)* (to) bring forth + -ITY]

park (pärk), *n.* **1.** a public area of land, usually in a natural state, having facilities for rest and recreation. **2.** an enclosed area or a stadium used for sports: *a baseball park.* **3.** a considerable extent of land forming the grounds of a country house. **4.** *Brit.* a tract of land reserved for wild animals; game preserve. **5.** *U.S.* a broad valley in a mountainous region. **6.** a space where vehicles, esp. automobiles, may be assembled or stationed. **7.** *Mil.* **a.** the space occupied by the assembled guns, tanks, or vehicles of a military unit. **b.** the assemblage so formed. —*v.t.* **8.** to halt (one's vehicle) with the intention of not using it again immediately. —*v.i.* **9.** to park a car, bicycle, etc. [ME < OF *parc* enclosure < LL **parric(us)* < Gmc. See PADDOCK[1]] —**park′like′,** *adj.*

par·ka (pär′kə), *n.* **1.** a fur coat, shirtlike and hooded, for wear in arctic regions. **2.** a similar garment, of wool or other wind-resistant material, worn for winter sports, by the military, etc. [< Aleut < Russ: pelt < Samoyed]

Park′ Av′enue, a street in New York City which, because of its large, expensive apartment houses, has come to represent luxury and fashion.

Par·ker (pär′kər), *n.* **1. Dorothy (Rothschild),** 1893–1967, U.S. author. **2. Matthew,** 1504–75, English theologian.

Par′ker House′ roll′, a bread roll made by folding a flat disk of dough in half. [after the *Parker House* hotel in Boston, which originally served the rolls]

Par·kers·burg (pär′kərz bûrg′), *n.* a city in NW West Virginia, on the Ohio River. 44,208 (1970).

Park′ For′est, a city in NE Illinois. 30,638 (1970).

park·ing (par′king), *n.* **1.** the act of a person or thing that parks, esp. a vehicle. **2.** space in which to park vehicles.

park′ing me′ter, a mechanical device for registering and collecting payment for the length of time that a motor vehicle occupies a parking space, consisting typically of a coin-operated timer mounted on a pole.

park′ing ramp′, apron (def. 3).

Park′in·son's disease′ (pär′kin sənz), *Pathol.* a nerve disease, characterized by tremors, esp. of fingers and hands, rigidity of muscles, slowness of movements and speech, and a masklike, expressionless face. Also called **Par′kin·son·ism, paralysis agitans, shaking palsy.** [named after James *Parkinson* (1755–1824), English physician who first described it]

park·land (pärk′land′), *n.* a grassland region with isolated or grouped trees, usually in temperate regions.

Park·man (pärk′mən), *n.* **Francis,** 1823–93, U.S. historian.

Park′ Range′, a range of the Rocky Mountains in central Colorado. Highest peak, Mt. Lincoln, 14,287 ft.

Park′ Ridge′, a city in NE Illinois. 42,614 (1970).

Park·ville (pärk′vil), *n.* a town in central Maryland, near Baltimore. 33,589 (1970).

park·way (pärk′wā′), *n.* a broad thoroughfare with a dividing strip or side strips planted with grass, trees, etc.

Park′way′-Sac′ramen′to South′ (pärk′wā′), a town in central California, near Sacramento. 28,574 (1970).

Parl., **1.** Parliament. **2.** Parliamentary. Also, **parl.**

par·lance (pär′ləns), *n.* **1.** a way or manner of speaking; vernacular; idiom: *legal parlance.* **2.** speech, esp. a formal discussion or debate. **3.** *Archaic.* talk; parley. [< AF; see PARLE, -ANCE]

par·lan·do (pär län′dō), *adj. Music.* sung or played as though speaking or reciting (a musical direction). [< It, prp. of *parlare* to speak; see PARLE]

par·lay (pär′lē, pär lā′), *U.S.* —*v.t.* **1.** to bet (an original amount and its winnings) on a subsequent race, contest, etc. **2.** *Informal.* to use (one's money, talent, or other assets) to obtain spectacular wealth or success: *He parlayed a modest inheritance into a fortune.* —*n.* **3.** a bet of an original sum and the subsequent winnings. [alter. of earlier *paroli* < F < Neapolitan It, pl. of *parolo,* ? < *paro* equal < L *pār;* see PAIR]

parle (pärl), *n., v.i.,* **parled, parl·ing.** *Archaic.* talk; parley. [ME *parle(n)* < MF *parle(r)* (to) speak < LL *parabolāre*]

par·ley (pär′lē), *n., pl.* **-leys,** *v.,* **-leyed, -ley·ing.** —*n.* **1.** a discussion or conference. **2.** an informal conference between enemies under truce, to discuss terms. —*v.i.* **3.** to hold an informal conference with an enemy, under a truce. **4.** to speak, talk, or confer. [earlier *parlee* < MF, n. use of fem. of *parle,* ptp. of *parler* to PARLE] —**par′ley·er,** *n.*

Par·ley (pär′lē), *n.* See **Goodrich, Samuel Griswold.**

par·lia·ment (pär′lə mənt), *n.* **1.** (*usually cap.*) the legislature of Great Britain, consisting of the House of Lords and the House of Commons. **2.** (*usually cap.*) the legislature of certain British Commonwealth countries. **3.** any legislative body in other countries. **4.** *Fr. Hist.* any of several high courts of justice in France before 1789. **5.** a meeting or assembly for conference on public or national affairs. **6.** *Cards.* fan-tan (def. 1). [late ME < AL *parliament(um),* alter. of ML *parlāmentum* < OF *parlement* a speaking, conference (see PARLE, -MENT); r. ME *parlement* < OF]

par·lia·men·tar·i·an (pär′lə men târ′ē ən), *n.* **1.** a person who is expert in parliamentary rules and procedures. **2.** (*sometimes cap.*) *Brit.* a member of Parliament. **3.** (*cap.*) a partisan of the British Parliament in opposition to Charles I.

par·lia·men·tar·i·an·ism (pär′lə men târ′ē ə niz′əm), *n.* advocacy of a parliamentary system of government.

par·lia·men·ta·ry (pär′lə men′tə rē, -trē), *adj.* **1.** of, pertaining to, or characteristic of a parliament. **2.** enacted by a parliament. **3.** having a parliament. **4.** in accordance with the rules governing deliberative bodies.

par·lor (pär′lər), *n.* **1.** a room for the reception and entertainment of visitors; living room. **2.** a semiprivate room in a hotel, club, or the like, for relaxation, conversation, etc.; lounge. **3.** *U.S.* a room or building forming a business place: *billiard parlor.* Also, *esp. Brit.,* **parlour.** [ME *parlur* < AF; OF *parleor* = *parl(er)* (to) speak (see PARLE) + *-eor* -ATORY]

par′lor car′, *U.S.* a railroad passenger car having individual reserved seats and more comfortable than a day coach.

par′lor game′, any game usually played indoors, esp. in the living room or parlor, as a word game or a quiz, requiring little or no physical activity.

par·lor·maid (pär′lər mād′), *n.* a maid who answers the door, waits on guests, etc.

par·lour (pär′lər), *n. Chiefly Brit.* parlor.

par·lous (pär′ləs), *Archaic.* —*adj.* **1.** perilous; dangerous. **2.** clever; shrewd. —*adv.* **3.** to a large extent; greatly. [ME, var. of *perlous;* syncopated var. of PERILOUS] —**par′lous·ly,** *adv.* —**par′lous·ness,** *n.*

parl. proc., parliamentary procedure.

Par·ma (pär′mə; *for 1 also It.* päR′mä), *n.* **1.** a city in N Italy, SE of Milan. 140,844 (1961). **2.** a city in NE Ohio. 100,216 (1970).

Par′ma Heights′ (pär′mə), a city in NE Ohio, near Cleveland. 27,192 (1970).

Par·men·i·des (pär men′i dēz′), *n.* fl. c450 B.C., Greek Eleatic philosopher. —**Par·me·nid·e·an** (pär′mə nid′ē ən), *adj.*

Par·me·san (pär′mi zan′, -zän′, -zən, pär′mi zan′, -zän′), *adj.* **1.** of or from Parma, in northern Italy. —*n.* **2.** Also called **Par′mesan cheese′.** a hard, dry variety of Italian cheese made from skim milk: usually grated and sprinkled over pasta dishes and soups. [< MF < It *parmigiano* pertaining to Parma]

par·mi·gia·na (pär′mə zhä′nə; *It.* päR′mē jä′nä), *adj. Italian Cookery.* cooked with Parmesan cheese: *veal parmigiana.* Also, **par·mi·gia·no** (pär′mə zhä′nō; *It.* päR′mē-jä′nō). [< It, fem. of *parmigiano* Parmesan]

Par·na·í·ba (päR′nə ē′bə), *n.* a river in NE Brazil, flowing NE to the Atlantic. 900 mi. long. Also, **Par′na·hi′ba, Par′na·hy′ba.**

Par·nas·si·an (pär nas′ē ən), *adj.* **1.** pertaining to Mount Parnassus. **2.** pertaining to poetry. **3.** pertaining to a school of French poets of the latter half of the 19th century who emphasized metrical form rather than emotion. —*n.* **4.** a member of the Parnassian school of French poets. [< L *Parnāsi(us)* of PARNUSSUS + -AN] —**Par·nas′si·an·ism, Par·nas′sism,** *n.*

Par·nas·sus (pär nas′əs), *n.* **1. Mount.** Modern, **Lia·koura.** a mountain in central Greece, N of the Gulf of Corinth, formerly considered sacred to Apollo and the Muses. 8062 ft. **2.** a collection of poems or of elegant literature. **3.** any center of poetry or artistic activity.

Par·nell (pär′nəl, pär nel′), *n.* **Charles Stewart,** 1846–91, Irish political leader. —**Par′nell·ite′,** *n.*

pa·ro·chi·al (pə rō′kē əl), *adj.* **1.** of or pertaining to a parish or parishes. **2.** of or pertaining to parochial schools or the education they provide. **3.** of very limited or narrow scope; provincial. [late ME *parochialle* < LL *parochiāl(is)* (see PARISH, -AL[1]); r. ME *parochiele* < AF *parochiel*] —**pa·ro′chi·al·ly,** *adv.*

pa·ro·chi·al·ise (pə rō′kē ə līz′), *v.t., v.i.,* **-ised, -is·ing.** *Chiefly Brit.* parochialize.

pa·ro·chi·al·ism (pə rō′kē ə liz′əm), *n.* a parochial character, spirit, or tendency; excessive narrowness of interests or view; provincialism. —**pa·ro′chi·al·ist,** *n.*

pa·ro·chi·al·ize (pə rō′kē ə līz′), *v.,* **-ized, -iz·ing.** —*v.t.* **1.** to make parochial. —*v.i.* **2.** to work in or for a parish. Also, *esp. Brit.,* **parochialise.** —**pa·ro′chi·al·i·za′tion,** *n.*

paro′chial school′, an elementary or high school maintained and operated by a religious organization.

par·o·dos (păr′ə dos′), *n., pl.* **-doi** (-doi′). *Greek.* (in ancient Greek drama) an ode sung by the chorus at their entrance, usually beginning the play.

par·o·dy (par′ə dē), *n., pl.* **-dies,** *v.,* **-died, -dy·ing.** —*n.* **1.** a humorous or satirical imitation of a serious piece of literature, musical composition, person, event, etc. **2.** the genre of literary composition represented by such imitations. **3.** a poor or feeble imitation; travesty. —*v.t.* **4.** to imitate (a composition, author, etc.) for purposes of ridicule or satire. **5.** to imitate poorly or feebly; travesty. [< L *parōdia* < Gk *parōidía* burlesque song or poem. See PAR-, ODE, -Y[3]] —**pa·rod·ic** (pə rod′ik), **pa·rod′i·cal,** *adj.* —**par′o·dist,** *n.* —**Syn. 1, 2.** See **burlesque.**

pa·roi·cous (pə roi′kəs), *adj. Bot.* (of certain mosses) having the male and female reproductive organs beside or near each other. Also, **parecious, pa·roe·cious** (pə rē′shəs). [< Gk *pároikos* dwelling beside (adj.), neighbor (n.) = *par-* PAR- + *oîk(os)* house + *-os* -OUS]

pa·rol (pə rōl′, par′əl), *Law.* —*n.* **1.** something stated or declared. **2. by parol,** by word of mouth; orally. —*adj.* **3.** given by word of mouth; oral. Also, **parole.** [late ME *parole* < AF, OF < VL **paraula,* syncopated var. of **paravola,* for L *parabola* PARABLE]

pa·role (pə rōl′), *n., v.,* **-roled, -rol·ing,** *adj.* —*n.* **1.** *Penol.* **a.** the conditional release of a person from prison prior to the end of the maximum sentence imposed. **b.** such release or its duration. **c.** an official document authorizing such a release. **2.** *Mil.* **a.** the promise of a prisoner of war that if he is released he either will return to custody at a specified time or will not again take up arms against his captors. **b.** (formerly) a password given by authorized personnel in passing by a guard. **3.** word of honor. **4.** *Law.* parol. —*v.t.* **5.** to put on parole. —*adj.* **6.** of or pertaining to parole or parolees: *a parole record.* **7.** *Law.* parol. [< MF, short for *parole d'honneur* word of honor. See PAROL] —**pa·rol′a·ble,** *adj.*

pa·rol·ee (pə rō lē′), *n.* a person released from prison on parole.

par·o·no·ma·sia (par′ə nō mā′zhə, -zhē ə, -zē ə), *n. Rhet.* a play on words; pun. [< L < Gk: a slight name-change < *paronomázein* to make such a change (*par-* PAR- + *onomázein* to name < *ónoma* a name); see -IA] —**par·o·no·mas·tic** (par′ə nə mas′tik), *adj.* —**par′o·no·mas′ti·cal·ly,** *adv.*

par·o·nych·i·a (par′ə nik′ē ə), *n. Pathol.* inflammation of the folds of skin bordering a nail of a finger or toe, usually characterized by infection and pus formation; felon. [< L *parōnychia* < Gk *parōnychía* whitlow = *par-* PARA-[1] + *onych-* (s. of *ónyx*) claw, nail + *-ia* -IA] —**par′o·nych′i·al,** *adj.*

par·o·nym (par′ə nim), *n. Gram.* a word containing the same root as another; cognate: "*Wise*" *and* "*wisdom*" *are paronyms.* [< Gk *parṓnym(on),* neut. of *parṓnymos*] —**par′o·nym′ic, pa·ron·y·mous** (pə ron′ə məs), *adj.*

Par·os (pâr′os; *Gk.* pä′rôs), *n.* a Greek island of the Cyclades, in the S Aegean: noted for its white marble. 9022 (1951); 77 sq. mi.

pa·ro·tic (pə rō′tik, -rot′ik), *adj. Anat., Zool.* situated about or near the ear. [< NL *parōtic(us).* See PAR-, OTIC]

pa·rot·id (pə rot′id), *Anat.* —*n.* **1.** a salivary gland situated at the base of each ear. —*adj.* **2.** of, pertaining to, or situated near either parotid. [< NL *parōtid-* (s. of *parōtis*) parotid gland; L, Gk: tumor near the ear. See PAR-, OTO-, -ID[1]]

par·o·ti·tis (par′ə tī′tis), *n. Pathol.* **1.** inflammation of a parotid. **2.** mumps. Also, **pa·rot·i·di·tis** (pə rot′i dī′tis). —**par·o·tit·ic** (par′ə tit′ik), *adj.*

pa·ro·toid (pə rō′toid), *Zool.* —*adj.* **1.** resembling a parotid. **2.** denoting certain cutaneous glands forming warty masses or excrescences near the ear in certain salientians, as toads. —*n.* **3.** a parotoid gland.

-parous, a learned borrowing from Latin meaning "bearing," "producing," used in the formation of compound words: *oviparous; viviparous.* [< L *-parus* bearing = *par(ere)* (to) bear, bring forth + *-us* -OUS]

par·ox·ysm (par′ək siz′əm), *n.* **1.** any sudden, violent outburst, as of action or emotion: *a paroxysm of grief.* **2.** *Pathol.* a severe attack or an increase in violence of a disease, usually recurring periodically. [earlier *paroxismos* < Gk *paroxysmós* irritation < *paroxýnein* to irritate. See PAR-, OXY-[1], -ISM] —**par′ox·ys′mal, par′ox·ys′mic,** *adj.* —**par′ox·ys′mal·ly,** *adv.*

par·ox·y·tone (pa rok′si tōn′), *Classical Gk. Gram.* —*adj.* **1.** having an acute accent on the next-to-the-last syllable. —*n.* **2.** a paroxytone word. [< NL *paroxyton(us)* < Gk *paroxýtonos*] —**par·ox·y·ton·ic** (par′ok si ton′ik), *adj.*

par·quet (pär kā′, -ket′), *n., v.,* **-queted -quet·ing.** —*n.* **1.** a floor of inlaid design. **2.** the main floor of a theater, opera house, etc., between the musicians' area and the parquet circle or, esp. in the U.S., the entire floor space for spectators. —*v.t.* **3.** to construct (a floor) of parquetry. [< F, dim. of *parc* PARK; see -ET]

parquet′ cir′cle, the part of the main floor of a theater, opera house, etc., behind the parquet, often including the area under the galleries. Also called **parterre.**

par·quet·ry (pär′ki trē), *n.* mosaic work of wood used for floors, wainscoting, etc.; marquetry. [< F *parqueterie*]

Parquetry

parr (pär), *n., pl.* **parrs,** (*esp. collectively*) **parr. 1.** a young salmon, having dark crossbars on its sides. **2.** the young of certain other fishes, as the codfish. [?]

Parr (pär), *n.* **Catherine,** 1512–48, 6th wife of Henry VIII: queen of England 1543–47.

par·ra·keet (par′ə kēt′), *n.* parakeet.

par·ra·mat·ta (par′ə mat′ə), *n.* paramatta.

par·rel (par′əl), *n. Naut.* a sliding ring or collar of rope, wood, or metal, that confines a yard or the jaws of a gaff to the mast but allows vertical movement. Also, **par′ral.** [late ME *perell,* var. of ME *parail,* aph. var. of *aparail* APPAREL]

par·ri·cide (par′i sīd′), *n.* **1.** the act of killing one's father, mother, or other close relative. **2.** a person who commits such an act. [< L *parricīd(um)* act of kin-murder, *parricīd(a)* kin-killer, var. of OL *pāricīdum, -a* = *pāri-* (akin to Gk *pāós,* Attic *pēós* kinsman) + *-cīdum, -a* -CIDE] —**par′ri·cid′al,** *adj.*

Par·ring·ton (par′ing tən), *n.* **Vernon Louis,** 1871–1929, U.S. literary historian and critic.

Par·rish (par′ish), *n.* **(Frederick) Max·field** (maks′fēld), 1870–1966, U.S. painter and illustrator.

par·rot (par′ət), *n.* **1.** any of numerous hook-billed, often brilliantly colored birds of the order *Psittaciformes,* as the cockatoo, lory, macaw, parakeet, etc., having the ability to mimic speech and often kept as pets. **2.** a person who, without thought or understanding, merely repeats the words or imitates the actions of another. —*v.t.* **3.** to repeat or imitate without thought or understanding. [unexplained var. of PARAKEET] —**par′rot·like′,** *adj.* —**par′rot·y,** *adj.*

par′rot fe′ver, *Pathol.* psittacosis. Also called **par′rot disease′.**

par·rot·fish (par′ət fish′), *n., pl.* (*esp. collectively*) **-fish,** (*esp. referring to two or more kinds or species*) **-fish·es.** any of various chiefly tropical marine fishes, esp. of the families *Scaridae* and *Labridae:* so called because of their coloring or the shape of their jaws.

par·ry (par′ē), *v.,* **-ried, -ry·ing,** *n., pl.* **-ries.** —*v.t.* **1.** to ward off (a thrust, blow, etc.), as in fencing; avert. **2.** to evade; avoid; dodge: *to parry an embarrassing question.* —*v.i.* **3.** to parry a thrust, blow, etc. —*n.* **4.** a defensive movement in fencing. **5.** an adroit or skillful answer; evasion. [< F *parez,* impv. of *parer* to ward off, set off < L *parāre* to set. See PARADE] —**Syn. 2.** avert; elude.

Par·ry (par′ē), *n.* **William Edward,** 1790–1855, English arctic explorer.

parse (pärs, pärz), *v.t.,* **parsed, pars·ing.** *Gram.* to describe (a word or series of words) grammatically, telling the part of speech, inflectional form, syntactic relations, etc. [< L *pars* part, as in *pars ōrātiōnis* part of speech] —**pars′a·ble,** *adj.* —**pars′er,** *n.*

par·sec (pär′sek′), *n. Astron.* a unit of distance equal to that required to cause a heliocentric parallax of one second of an arc, equivalent to 206,265 times the distance from the earth to the sun, or 3.26 light-years. [PAR(ALLAX) + SEC(OND)[2]]

Par·see (pär′sē, pär sē′), *n.* **1.** an Indian Zoroastrian descended from Persian Zoroastrians who came to India in the 7th and 8th centuries to escape Muslim persecution. **2.** the Middle Persian dialect of the Parsee scriptures. Also, **Par′si.** [< Pers *Pārsī* Persian = *Pārs* Persia + *-ī* suffix of appurtenance] —**Par′see·ism, Par′si·ism,** *n.*

Par·si·fal (pär′sə fəl, -fäl′), *n. Teutonic Legend.* Percival.

par·si·mo·ni·ous (pär′sə mō′nē əs), *adj.* characterized by or showing parsimony; sparing or frugal, esp. to excess. —**par′si·mo′ni·ous·ly,** *adv.* —**par′si·mo′ni·ous·ness,** *n.* —**Syn.** stingy, tight, close, niggardly, miserly, penurious. —**Ant.** generous.

par·si·mo·ny (pär′sə mō′nē), *n.* extreme or excessive economy or frugality; stinginess or niggardliness. [late ME *parcimony* < L *parcimōnia,* var. of *parsimōnia* frugality, thrift = *parsi-* (comb. form of *parsus,* ptp. of *parcere* to economize) or *parci-* (comb. form of *parcus* sparing) + *-mōnia* -MONY]

pars·ley (pärs′lē), *n.* **1.** a garden herb, *Petroselinum crispum,* having aromatic leaves used to garnish or season food. **2.** any of certain allied or similar plants. —*adj.* **3.** cooked or garnished with parsley: *parsley potatoes.* [ME *persely,* b. OE *petersilie* + OF *persil,* both < LL **petrosilium,* alter. of L *petroselīnum* < Gk *petrosélīnon* rock parsley. See PETRO-, CELERY]

pars·nip (pär′snip), *n.* **1.** a plant, *Pastinaca sativa,* cultivated varieties of which have a large, whitish, edible root. **2.** the root of this plant. [ME *pas(t)nep(e)* < L *past(ināca)* parsnip < *pastinum* forked dibble]

par·son (pär′sən), *n.* a clergyman; minister; preacher. [ME *persone* < ML *persōna* parish priest, L: personage. See PERSON] —**par·son·ic** (pär son′ik), **par·son′i·cal,** *adj.* —**par′son·ish, par′son·like′,** *adj.*

par·son·age (pär′sə nij), *n.* the residence of a parson or clergyman, as provided by the parish or church. [ME *personage* < AF; ML *persōnāticum* benefice]

par′son bird′, tui.

Par·sons (pär′sənz), *n.* **Tal·cott** (tôl′kot, tal′-), 1902–79, U.S. sociologist and author.

part (pärt), *n.* **1.** a portion or division of a whole that is separate either in reality or in thought only; a piece, fragment, fraction, or section; constituent: *the rear part of the house.* **2.** an essential or integral attribute or quality: *A sense of humor is part of a healthy personality.* **3.** a section or division of a literary work. **4.** a portion, member, or organ of an animal body. **5.** one of a number of equal quantities

that compose a whole: *Use two parts sugar to one part cocoa.* **6.** an allotted portion; share. **7.** Usually, **parts. a.** a region, quarter, or district. **b.** a quality or attribute establishing the possessor as a person of importance or superior worth: *a man of parts.* **8.** one of the opposing sides in a contest, question, agreement, etc. **9.** the dividing line formed in parting the hair. **10.** a constituent piece of a machine or tool either included at the time of manufacture or set in place as a replacement for the original piece. **11.** *Music.* **a.** a voice, either vocal or instrumental. **b.** a written or printed score for a performer's use: *a horn part.* **c.** a section or division of a composition. **12.** participation, interest, or concern in something: *The Commies have some part in this!* **13.** one's share in some action; a duty, function, or office. **14.** a character or role acted in a play or sustained in real life. **15. for one's part,** as far as concerns one: *For my part, you can do whatever you please.* **16. for the most part,** usually; mostly. **17. in good part, a.** without offense; amiably. **b.** to a great extent; largely. **18. in part,** in some measure or degree; to some extent: *The crop failure was due in part to the drought.* **19. on the part of,** so far as pertains to or concerns a person: *He expressed appreciation on the part of himself and his colleagues.* Also, **on one's part. 20. part and parcel,** an essential or integral part: *Her love for her child was part and parcel of her life.* **21. take part,** to participate; partake. **22. take someone's part,** to align oneself with; support; defend.
—*v.t.* **23.** to divide (a thing) into parts; break; cleave. **24.** to comb (the hair) away from a dividing line. **25.** to dissolve (a connection, relationship, etc.): *They parted company.* **26.** to divide into shares; apportion. **27.** to put or keep apart; separate. **28.** *Metall.* to separate (silver) from gold in refining. **29.** *Obs.* to leave.
—*v.i.* **30.** to be or become divided into parts; break or cleave. **31.** to go apart, separate from one another, as persons or things. **32.** to be or become separated from something else (usually fol. by *from*). **33.** *Naut.* to break or become torn apart, as a cable. **34.** to depart. **35.** to die. **36. part with,** to give up; relinquish. [ME, OE < L *part-* (s. of *pars*) piece, portion]
—**Syn. 1.** component, ingredient, sector. PART, PIECE, PORTION, SEGMENT, SECTION, refer to that which is less than the whole. PART is the general word: *part of a house.* A PIECE suggests a part that is itself a complete unit, often of standardized form: *a piece of pie.* A PORTION is a part allotted or assigned to a person, purpose, etc.: *a portion of food.* A SEGMENT is often a part into which something separates naturally: *a segment of an orange.* SECTION suggests a relatively substantial, clearly separate part that fits closely with other parts to form a whole: *a section of a fishing rod, a book.* **6.** apportionment, lot. **13.** responsibility. **23.** sever, sunder, dissociate, disconnect, disjoin, detach. —**Ant. 1.** whole. **23.** join.

part., **1.** participle. **2.** particular.

par·take (pär tāk′), *v.*, **-took, -tak·en, -tak·ing.** —*v.i.* **1.** to take part or have a share; participate. **2.** to receive, take, or have a share (usually fol. by *of*): *to partake of a meal.* **3.** to have something of the nature or character (usually fol. by *of*): *feelings partaking of both joy and regret.* —*v.t.* **4.** to take or have a part in; share. [back formation from *partaking,* ME *part taking,* trans. of L *participātiō* participation] —**par·tak′er,** *n.* —**Syn. 1.** See **share**[1].

part·ed (pär′tid), *adj.* **1.** divided into parts; cleft. **2.** set or kept apart; separated. **3.** *Bot.* (of a leaf) separated into rather distinct portions by incisions that extend nearly to the midrib or the base. **4.** *Heraldry.* party (def. 10). **5.** *Archaic.* deceased. [ME] —**part′ed·ness,** *n.*

par·terre (pär târ′), *n.* **1.** See **parquet circle. 2.** an ornamental arrangement of flower beds of different shapes and sizes. [< F, n. use of phrase *par terre* on the ground] —**par·terred′,** *adj.*

par·the·no·gen·e·sis (pär′thə nō jen′i sis), *n.* *Biol.* development of an egg without fertilization. [< Gk *parthéno(s)* maiden + GENESIS] —**par·the·no·ge·net·ic** (pär′thə nō jə net′ik), *adj.* —**par′the·no·ge·net′i·cal·ly,** *adv.*

Par·the·non (pär′thə non′, -nən), *n.* the temple of Athena Parthenos on the Acropolis at Athens, completed c438 B.C.: regarded as the first and finest peripteral Doric temple.

Par·the·no·pae·us (pär′thə nō pē′əs), *n.* *Class. Myth.* a son of Hippomenes and Atalanta, and one of the Seven against Thebes.

Par·then·o·pe (pär then′ə pē′), *n.* *Class. Myth.* a siren who drowned herself when Odysseus escaped from the influence of the sirens' singing. —**Par·then·o·pe·an** (pär′thə nə pē′ən), *adj.*

Par·the·nos (pär′thə nos′, -nōs′), *n.* an epithet of certain ancient Greek deities, esp. Athena, meaning "virgin."

Par·thi·a (pär′thē ə), *n.* an ancient country in W Asia, SE of the Caspian Sea: conquered by the Iranians A.D. 226; now a part of NE Iran. —**Par′thi·an,** *n., adj.*

Par′thian shot′, **1.** a rearward shot by a fleeing mounted archer. **2.** a sharp, telling remark made in departing. [so called from the custom of the ancient Parthian cavalry of shooting arrows while in real or feigned flight]

par·tial (pär′shəl), *adj.* **1.** pertaining to or affecting a part. **2.** being such in part only; not total or general; incomplete: *partial blindness; a partial payment.* **3.** being a part; component; constituent. **4.** biased or prejudiced in favor of a person, group, side, etc. **5.** *Bot.* secondary or subordinate. **6. partial to,** having a liking for; particularly fond of: *I'm partial to chocolate cake.* —*n.* **7.** *Acoustics, Music.* See **partial tone.** [late ME *parcial* biased, particular < MF < LL *partiāl(is)* pertaining to a part = L *parti-* (s. of *pars*) PART + *-ālis* -AL[1]] —**par′tial·ly,** *adv.* —**par′tial·ness,** *n.* —**Syn. 2.** unfinished, imperfect, limited. **4.** one-sided, unfair, unjust. —**Ant. 2.** complete. **4.** unbiased, fair.

par′tial deriv′ative, *Math.* the derivative of a function with respect to one of its variables with all other variables held constant.

par′tial differen′tial, *Math.* an expression obtained from a given function of several variables by taking the partial derivative with respect to one of the variables and multiplying by the increment in that variable.

par′tial frac′tion, *Algebra.* one of the fractions into which a given fraction can be resolved, the sum of such simpler fractions being equal to the given fraction.

par·tial·i·ty (pär shal′i tē, pär′shē al′-), *n., pl.* **-ties** for 2, 3. **1.** the state or character of being partial. **2.** a favorable bias or prejudice: *the partiality of parents for their own children.* **3.** a special fondness or liking. [late ME *parcialite* < ML *partiālitās*] —**Syn. 2.** favoritism. **3.** leaning, inclination, bent, predilection. —**Ant. 2.** justice. **3.** dislike.

par′tial pres′sure, *Physics, Chem.* the pressure that a gas in a mixture of gases would exert if it occupied the same volume as the mixture at the same temperature.

par′tial tone′, *Acoustics, Music.* one of the pure tones forming a part of a complex tone; the fundamental tone or a harmonic. Also called **partial.**

part·i·ble (pär′tə bəl), *adj.* capable of being divided or separated; divisible. [< LL *partibil(is)* divisible = L *par-t(īrī)* (to) divide, PART + *-ibilis* -IBLE] —**part′i·bil′i·ty,** *n.*

par·ti·ceps cri·mi·nis (pär′ti seps′ krim′ə nis), *Law.* an accomplice in a crime. [< L]

par·tic·i·pant (pär tis′ə pənt), *n.* **1.** a person who participates; partaker. —*adj.* **2.** participating; sharing. [< L *participant-* (s. of *participāns*), prp. of *participāre*]

par·tic·i·pate (pär tis′ə pāt′), *v.*, **-pat·ed, -pat·ing.** —*v.i.* **1.** to take or have a part, as with others; partake; share (fol. by *in*): *to participate in profits; to participate in a play.* —*v.t.* **2.** to take or have a part or share in; partake in; share. [< L *participāt(us)* shared (ptp. of *participāre*) = *particip-* (s. of *particeps*) taking part, partner (see PARTICIPLE) + *-ātus* -ATE[1]] —**par·tic′i·pa′tive,** *adj.* —**par·tic′i·pa′tor,** *n.* —**Syn. 1.** See **share**[1].

par·tic·i·pa·tion (pär tis′ə pā′shən), *n.* **1.** the act or an instance of participating; a taking part. **2.** a sharing, as in benefits or profits. Also, **par·tic·i·pance** (pär tis′ə pəns), **par·tic′i·pan·cy.** [< LL *participātiōn-,* s. of *participātiō* (see PARTICIPATE, -ION); r. ME *participacioun* < AF]

par·ti·cip·i·al (pär′ti sip′ē əl), *Gram.* —*adj.* **1.** of or pertaining to a participle. **2.** similar to or formed from a participle. —*n.* **3.** a participle. [< L *participiāl(is).* See PARTICIPLE, -AL[1]] —**par′ti·cip′i·al·ly,** *adv.*

par·ti·ci·ple (pär′ti sip′əl, -sə pəl), *n.* *Gram.* an adjective or complement to certain auxiliaries that is regularly derived from the verb in many languages and refers to participation in the action or state of the verb; a verbal form used as in an adjective. It does not specify person or number in English, but may have a subject or object, show tense, etc., as *burning* in *a burning candle,* or *devoted* in *his devoted friend.* [ME < MF, var. of *participe* < L *particip(ium)* < *particeps* taking part = *parti-* (s. of *pars*) PART + *-cep-* (var. s. of *capere* to take) + *-s* nom. sing. ending]

par·ti·cle (pär′ti kəl), *n.* **1.** a minute portion, piece, or amount; a very small bit: *a particle of dust.* **2.** *Physics.* **a.** one of the extremely small constituents of matter, as in an atom or nucleus. **b.** a body considered as possessing finite mass but infinitesimal dimensions. **c.** a body in which the internal motion is negligible. **3.** a clause or article, as of a document. **4.** *Rom. Cath. Ch.* a small piece of the Host given to each lay communicant. **5.** *Gram.* **a.** a prefix or suffix, as *re-* or *-wise.* **b.** a small word of functional or relational use, such as an article, preposition, interjection, or conjunction. [ME < L *particula*] —**Syn. 1.** mite, whit, iota, jot, tittle, grain, speck.

par·ti-col·ored (pär′tē kul′ərd), *adj.* having different colors in different parts; variegated: *a parti-colored dress.* Also, **party-colored;** *esp. Brit.,* **par′ti-col′oured, party-coloured.** [ME *parti* variegated < MF << L *partī(tus)* divided, ptp. of *partīre.* See PARTY]

par·tic·u·lar (pər tik′yə lər), *adj.* **1.** of or pertaining to a single or specific person, thing, occasion, etc.; special rather than general: *one's particular interests.* **2.** distinguished from the ordinary; noteworthy; unusual; exceptional or especial: *Take particular pains with this job.* **3.** being such in an exceptional degree: *a particular friend of mine.* **4.** dealing with or giving details; detailed; minute; circumstantial. **5.** exceptionally selective, attentive, or exacting; fussy; fastidious: *to be particular about one's food.* **6.** *Logic.* not general; referring to an indefinite part of a whole class. **7.** *Law.* noting an estate that precedes a future or ultimate ownership. —*n.* **8.** an individual or distinct part, as an item of a list. **9.** Usually, **particulars.** specific points, details, or circumstances: *the particulars of a case.* **10.** *Logic.* an individual or a specific group within a general class. **11. in particular,** particularly; especially. [ME *particuler* < MF < LL *particulār(is).* See PARTICLE, -AR[1]] —**Syn. 1.** specific; distinct; discrete. See **special. 2.** notable. **4.** scrupulous, careful, exact, precise. **5.** discriminating; finical, finicky. **8.** feature, particularity. —**Ant. 2.** ordinary. **4.** inexact. **5.** undiscriminating.

par·tic·u·lar·ise (pər tik′yə lə rīz′), *v.t., v.i.,* **-ised, -is·ing.** *Chiefly Brit.* particularize. —**par·tic′u·lar·i·sa′tion,** *n.* —**par·tic′u·lar·is′er,** *n.*

par·tic·u·lar·ism (pər tik′yə lə riz′əm), *n.* **1.** exclusive attention or devotion to one's own particular interests, party, etc. **2.** the principle of leaving each state of a federation free to promote its interests. **3.** *Theol.* the doctrine that divine grace is provided only for the elect. [< F *particularisme*] —**par·tic′u·lar·ist,** *n.* —**par·tic′u·lar·is′tic,** *adj.* —**par·tic′u·lar·is′ti·cal·ly,** *adv.*

par·tic·u·lar·i·ty (pər tik′yə lar′i tē), *n., pl.* **-ties. 1.** the quality or state of being particular. **2.** a special, peculiar, or individual character. **3.** detailed, minute, or circumstantial character, as of description or statement. **4.** attention to details; special care. **5.** fastidiousness. **6.** a particular or characteristic feature or trait. [< MF *particularite* < LL *particulāritāt-* (s. of *particulāritās*) state of being apart]

par·tic·u·lar·ize (pər tik′yə lə rīz′), *v.*, **-ized, -iz·ing.** —*v.t.* **1.** to make particular. **2.** to mention or indicate specifically; specify. **3.** to state or treat in detail. —*v.i.* **4.**

to speak or treat particularly or specifically. Also, *esp. Brit.*, **particularise.** [< MF *particularis(er)*] —**par·tic′u·lar·i·za′tion,** *n.* —**par·tic′u·lar·iz′er,** *n.*

par·tic·u·lar·ly (pər tik′yə lər lē), *adv.* **1.** in a particular or to an exceptional degree; especially: *He read it with particularly great interest.* **2.** in a particular manner; specifically; individually. **3.** in detail; minutely. [ME *particulerly*] —**Syn. 1.** exceptionally, specially. See **especially. 3.** scrupulously. —**Ant. 1.** generally; commonly.

par·tic·u·late (pər tik′yə lit, -lāt′), *adj.* of, pertaining to, or composed of distinct particles. [< NL *particulāt(us).* See PARTICLE, -ATE[1]]

part·ing (pär′ting), *n.* **1.** the act of a person or thing that parts. **2.** a division or separation. **3.** a departure; leave-taking. **4.** death. **5.** a place of division or separation. **6.** something that serves to part or separate things. —*adj.* **7.** given or done at parting: *a parting remark.* **8.** of or pertaining to parting, leave-taking, or death. **9.** departing: *the parting day.* **10.** dividing; separating. [ME *partyng* (n.)]

part′ing shot′, a witty or slighting retort or an aggressive action made upon leaving.

par·ti pris (PAR tē PRē′), *French.* a position or attitude resolved upon or taken in advance.

par·ti·san[1] (pär′ti zən), *n.* **1.** an adherent or supporter of a person, party, or cause. **2.** *Mil.* a member of a party of light or irregular troops engaged in harassing an enemy; guerrilla. —*adj.* **3.** of, pertaining to, or characteristic of partisans; partial to a specific party, person, etc.: *partisan politics.* **4.** of, pertaining to, or carried on by military partisans or guerrillas. Also, **partizan.** [< MF < It *partigiano.* See PARTY, -IAN] —**par′ti·san·ship′,** *n.* —**Syn. 3.** biased.

par·ti·san[2] (pär′ti zən), *n.* a shafted weapon having as a head a long spear blade with a pair of curved lobes at the base. Also, **partizan.** [< MF *partisane* < It *partigiana* halberd < OHG *part(a)* halberd + It suffix; see PARTISAN[1]]

par·ti·ta (pär tē′tə; *It.* pär tē′tä), *n., pl.* **-tas,** *It.* **-te** (-te). *Music.* **1.** an instrumental suite, esp. of the 18th century. **2.** a variation or set of variations. [< It, fem. of *partito* divided. See PARTY]

par·tite (pär′tīt), *adj.* **1.** divided into parts (usually used in combination): *a tripartite agreement.* **2.** *Bot.* parted. [< L *partīt(us)* divided (ptp. of *partīrī*)]

par·ti·tion (pär tish′ən), *n.* **1.** a division into or distribution in portions or shares. **2.** a separation, as of two or more things. **3.** something that separates or divides. **4.** a part, division, or section. **5.** an interior wall or barrier dividing a room, enclosure, etc. **6.** a septum or dissepiment, as in a plant or animal structure. **7.** *Law.* a division of property among joint owners. **8.** *Logic.* the separation of a whole into its integrant parts. **9.** *Math.* a mode of separating a positive whole number into a sum of positive whole numbers. —*v.t.* **10.** to divide into parts or portions. **11.** to divide or separate by a partition. **12.** *Law.* to divide property among several owners. [< L *partītiōn-* (s. of *partītiō*)] —**par·ti′tion·er, par·ti′tion·ist,** *n.* —**par·ti′tion·ment,** *n.* —**Syn. 1.** See **division. 10.** portion, apportion. —**Ant. 10.** unite.

parti′tion line′, *Heraldry.* a plain or figured edge between two adjacent areas of an escutcheon, between an ordinary and the field of an escutcheon, or between two adjacent ordinaries. Also called **boundary line.**

par·ti·tive (pär′ti tiv), *adj.* **1.** serving to divide into parts. **2.** *Gram.* noting part of a whole: *the Latin partitive genitive.* —*n.* **3.** *Gram.* a partitive word or formation, as *of the men* in *half of the men.* [< ML *partītīv(us)* divisive. See PARTITE, -IVE] —**par′ti·tive·ly,** *adv.*

par·ti·zan (pär′ti zən), *n., adj.* partisan.

part·let (pärt′lit), *n.* a 16th-century garment for the neck and shoulders, usually having a collar and ruffles. [unexplained var. of late ME *patelet* < MF *patelette* strip of cloth, band, lit., little paw = OF *pate* paw + *-lete* -LET]

part·ly (pärt′lē), *adv.* in part; to some extent or degree; not wholly: *His statement is partly true.*

part′ mu′sic, music, esp. vocal music, with parts for two or more independent performers.

part·ner (pärt′nər), *n.* **1.** a sharer or partaker; associate. **2.** *Law.* a person associated with another or others as a principal or a contributor of capital in a business or a joint venture. **3.** See **silent partner. 4.** a husband or a wife; spouse. **5.** one's companion in a dance. **6.** a player on the same side or team as another. **7. partners,** *Naut.* a framework of timber around a hole in a ship's deck, to support a mast, capstan, pump, etc. —*v.t.* **8.** to associate as a partner or partners with. [ME *partener;* alter. of PARCENER by assoc. with PART] —**part′ner·less,** *adj.* —**Syn. 1.** colleague, accessory, accomplice.

part·ner·ship (pärt′nər ship′), *n.* **1.** the state or condition of being a partner; participation; association; joint interest. **2.** *Law.* **a.** the relation subsisting between partners. **b.** the contract creating this relation. **c.** an association of persons joined as partners in business.

part′ of speech′, *Gram.* any of the major form classes into which words have traditionally been divided, chiefly on the basis of syntactic function, as, in English, noun, pronoun, verb, adverb, adjective, preposition, conjunction, and interjection.

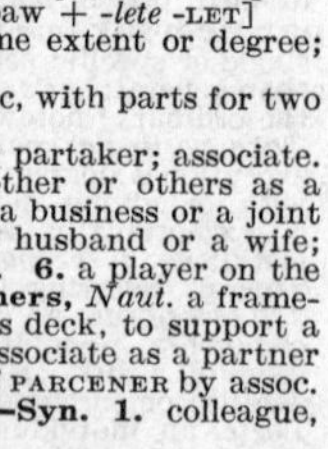

par·took (pär to͝ok′), *v.* pt. of **partake.**

par·tridge (pär′trij), *n., pl.* **-tridg·es,** (*esp. collectively*) **-tridge. 1.** any of several Old World, gallinaceous game birds of the subfamily *Perdicinae,* esp. *Perdix perdix* of Europe. **2.** *Chiefly New England.* the ruffled grouse. **3.** *Southern U.S.* bobwhite. **4.** any of several other North American, gallinaceous game birds. **5.** any of various South and Central American tinamous. [ME *partrich,* var. of *pertrich* < MF *pertris,* var. of *perdris,* OF *perd(r)iz* < L *perdix* < Gk] —**par′tridge·like′,** *adj.*

Partridge,
Perdix perdix
(Length 1 to 1½ ft.)

par·tridge·ber·ry (pär′trij ber′ē), *n., pl.* **-ries.** a North American, trailing, rubiaceous plant, *Mitchella repens,* having roundish evergreen leaves, fragrant white flowers, and scarlet berries.

part′ song′, a song with parts for several voices, esp. one meant to be sung without accompaniment.

part-time (pärt′tīm′), *adj.* **1.** employed to work less than the usual or full time: *a part-time clerk.* **2.** of, pertaining to, or noting such work: *part-time employment.* —*adv.* **3.** on a part-time basis: *to work part-time.* Cf. **full-time.**

par·tu·ri·ent (pär to͝or′ē ənt, -tyo͝or′-), *adj.* **1.** bringing forth or about to bring forth young; travailing. **2.** pertaining to parturition. **3.** bringing forth or about to produce something, as an idea. [< L *parturient-* (s. of *parturiēns*) being in labor, lit., desiring to bring forth (prp. of *parturīre*) = *part(us)* brought forth, born (ptp. of *parere*) + *-uri-* desiderative suffix + *-ent-* -ENT] —**par·tu′ri·en·cy,** *n.*

par·tu·ri·tion (pär′to͝o rish′ən, -tyo͝o-, -cho͝o-), *n.* the act of bringing forth young; childbirth. [< LL *parturītiōn-* (s. of *parturītiō*) travail = L *parturīt(us)* (ptp. of *parturīre;* see PARTURIENT) + *-iōn-* -ION]

par·ty (pär′tē), *n., pl.* **-ties,** *adj., v.,* **-tied, -ty·ing.** —*n.* **1.** a social gathering for conversation, refreshments, entertainment, etc. **2.** a group gathered for some special purpose or task: *a search party.* **3.** a detachment or detail of troops assigned to perform some particular service. **4.** a group of persons with common purposes or opinions, esp. a political group organized for gaining governmental control: *the Republican party.* **5.** *Law.* one of the litigants in a legal proceeding. **6.** a person who or group that participates in some action, affair, plan, etc.; participant: *He was a party to the deal.* **7.** *Informal.* a specific individual. —*adj.* **8.** of or pertaining to a party or faction; partisan: *party politics.* **9.** of or for a social gathering: *a party dress.* **10.** being shared by or pertaining to two or more persons or things. **11.** *Heraldry.* (of an escutcheon) having the field divided into a number of parts, usually two; parted. —*v.i.* **12.** *Informal.* to go to parties, esp. a series of parties. **13.** *Slang.* to enjoy oneself thoroughly and without restraint. [ME *partie* < OF, n. use of fem. of *parti* (ptp. of *partir*) < L *partītus, -a-, -um* divided, PARTITE] —**par′ty·less,** *adj.* —**Syn. 1.** gathering, assemblage. See **company. 4.** faction, circle, coterie, ring. —**Usage.** PARTY is considered poor style when used in place of "person," "man," etc., as in def. 7, and is avoided by writers and speakers who are careful about their forms of expression.

par·ty-col·ored (pär′tē kul′ərd), *adj.* parti-colored. Also, *esp. Brit.,* **par′ty-col′oured.**

par·ty line (pär′tē līn′ *for 1, 2;* pär′tē līn′ *for 3, 4*), **1.** a telephone line connecting the telephones of a number of subscribers. **2.** the boundary line separating adjoining properties. **3.** the authoritatively announced policies and practices of a political party or group, esp. of the Communist party. **4.** the guiding policy, tenets, or practices of a political party: *The delegates voted along party lines.*

par′ty wall′, *Law.* a wall used, or usable, as a part of contiguous structures.

par′ty whip′, *Politics.* whip (def. 19a).

pa·rure (pə ro͝or′; *Fr.* PA RYR′), *n., pl.* **-rures** (-ro͝orz′; *Fr.* -RYR′). a matching set of jewels or ornaments. [< F: lit., adornment; OF *pareure* peeling < L *parātūra* (*parāt-,* ptp. s. of *parāre* to prepare + *-ūra* -URE)]

par′ val′ue. See **face value** (def. 1).

Par·va·ti (pär′və tē), *n.* *Hinduism.* Devi (def. 2).

par·ve (pär′və), *adj.* *Judaism.* permissible for use with both meat and dairy meals; neutral: *parve soup.* Also, **pareve.** [< Yiddish *parev*]

par·ve·nu (pär′və no͞o′, -nyo͞o′), *n.* **1.** a person who has suddenly acquired wealth or importance, but lacks the proper social qualifications; an upstart. —*adj.* **2.** being or resembling a parvenu. **3.** characteristic of a parvenu. [< F: upstart, n. use of ptp. of *parvenir* to arrive, reach < L *pervenīre* = *per-* PER- + *venīre* to come]

Par·zi·val (pär′tsi fäl′), *n.* *Teutonic Legend.* Percival. Also, **Par·zi·fal** (pär′tsi fäl′).

pas (pä), *n., pl.* **pas. 1.** a step or series of steps in ballet. **2.** right of precedence. [< F < L *pass(us).* See PACE[1]]

Pas·a·de·na (pas′ə dē′nə), *n.* **1.** a city in SW California, near Los Angeles. 112,981 (1970). **2.** a city in SE Texas, near Houston. 89,277 (1970).

Pa·sar·ga·dae (pə sär′gə dē′), *n.* an ancient ruined city in S Iran, NE of Persepolis: tomb of Cyrus the Great.

Pas·ca·gou·la (pas′kə go͞o′lə), *n.* a city in SE Mississippi, on the Gulf of Mexico. 27,264 (1970).

Pas·cal (pas kal′, pas′kəl; *Fr.* PA SKAL′), *n.* **Blaise** (blez), 1623–62, French philosopher and mathematician.

Pasch (pask), *n.* *Archaic.* **1.** the Jewish festival of Passover. **2.** Easter. [early ME < eccl. L *Pascha* < Gk < Aram: Passover, var. of Heb *Pesakh* PESACH]

pas·chal (pas′kəl), *adj.* **1.** of or pertaining to the Passover. **2.** of or pertaining to Easter. —*n.* **3.** a paschal candle or candlestick. [ME *paschall* < LL *paschāl(is)*]

Pas·chal I (pas′kəl), died A.D. 824, pope 817–824.

Paschal II, (*Ranieri*) died 1118, Italian ecclesiastic: pope 1099–1118.

pas′chal flow′er, pasqueflower.

pas′chal lamb′, 1. *Jewish Hist.* a lamb slaughtered and eaten on the eve of the first day of Passover. Ex. 12:3–11. **2.** (*caps.*) Christ. **3.** (*caps.*) any of several symbolic representations of Christ, as the Agnus Dei.

Pas de Ca·lais (päd[e] KA le′), French name of the Strait of Dover.

pas de deux (*Fr.* pä də dœ′), *pl.* **pas de deux.** *Ballet.* a dance for two persons. [< F: lit., step for two]

pas de trois (*Fr.* pä də TRWÄ′), *pl.* **pas de trois.** *Ballet.* a dance for three persons. [< F: lit., step for three]

pa·se·o (pä sā′ō), *n., pl.* **-se·os. 1.** a slow, idle, or leisurely walk or stroll. **2.** a public place or path designed for walking; promenade. [< Sp]

pa·sha (pə shä′, pash′ə, pä′shə), *n.* a title formerly borne by officials of high rank in Turkish dominions. Also, **pacha.** [< Turk; see BASHAW] —**pa·sha′dom,** *n.*

Pash·to (push′tō), *n.* an Indo-European, Iranian language that is the official language of Afghanistan and the chief vernacular of the eastern part of the nation. Also, **Pushtu.** Also called **Afghan.**

Pa·siph·a·ë (pə sif′ə ē′), *n.* *Class. Myth.* the wife of Minos, mother of Ariadne, and mother of the Minotaur by the Cretan bull.

pa·so do·ble (pä′sō dō′blā; *Sp.* pä′sô dô′vle), *pl.* **pa·so**

do·bles, *Sp.* **pa·sos do·bles** (pä′sôs dô′vles). **1.** a quick, light march often played at bullfights. **2.** a two-step, esp. one done to Latin-American rhythms. [< Sp: lit., double step]

pasque·flow·er (pask′flou′ər), *n.* **1.** an Old World, ranunculaceous plant, *Anemone Pulsatilla*, having purple flowers blooming about Easter. **2.** a related plant. *A. ludoviciana*, having similar flowers: the state flower of South Dakota. [*Pasque* (var. sp. of PASCH) + FLOWER (so named by the herbalist Gerarde in 1597); r. *passeflower* < MF *passefleur*]

pas·quil (pas′kwil), *n.* a pasquinade. [< NL *pasquill(us)* < It *pasquillo*, dim. of *Pasquino;* see PASQUINADE] —**pas·quil′ic, pas·quil′lic,** *adj.*

pas·quin·ade (pas′kwə nād′), *n.*, *v.*, **-ad·ed, -ad·ing.** —*n.* **1.** a satire or lampoon, esp. one posted in a public place. —*v.t.* **2.** to assail in a pasquinade. [*Pasquin* (< It *Pasquino*, name given an antique Roman statue (unearthed in 1501) which was annually decorated and posted with verses) + -ADE[1]; r. *pasquinata* < It] —**pas′quin·ad′er,** *n.*

pass (pas, päs), *v.t.* **1.** to move past; go by: *to pass someone on the road.* **2.** to let go without notice, remark, etc.; leave unconsidered; disregard; overlook. **3.** to cause or allow to go through or over a barrier, obstacle, etc.: *The guard passed the visitor.* **4.** to go across or over (a stream, threshold, etc.); cross. **5.** to undergo or complete successfully: *to pass an examination.* **6.** to cause or permit (a person) to complete a course of study, an examination, etc., successfully. **7.** to go beyond (a point, degree, stage, etc.); transcend; exceed; surpass. **8.** to cause to go or move onward: *to pass a rope through a hole.* **9.** to cause to go, move, or march by: *to pass troops in review.* **10.** to live during (a portion of time); spend. **11.** to cause to circulate or spread: *to pass rumors.* **12.** to cause to be accepted or received: *to pass a worthless check.* **13.** to convey, transfer, or transmit; deliver: *Pass the salt.* **14.** to pledge. **15.** to utter, pronounce, or speak. **16.** to discharge or void from the bowels. **17.** to sanction or approve, esp. by vote: *Congress passed the bill.* **18.** to obtain the approval or sanction of (a legislative body, committee, etc.), esp. by a vote: *The bill passed Congress.* **19.** to express or pronounce, as an opinion: *to pass judgment.* **20.** *Law.* to place legal title or interest in (another). **21.** to omit payment of (a dividend). **22.** (in feats of magic) to perform a pass on. **23.** *Baseball.* (of a pitcher) to give a base on balls to (a batter). **24.** *Sports.* to transfer (the ball or puck) to a teammate. —*v.i.* **25.** to go or move onward; proceed. **26.** to come to or toward, then go beyond: *to pass through town.* **27.** to go away; depart. **28.** to elapse or slip by, as time. **29.** to come to an end: *The crisis soon passed.* **30.** to die. **31.** to take place; happen; occur. **32.** to go about or circulate; be current. **33.** *U.S.* to serve as a marginally acceptable substitute. **34.** *U.S.* to live and be known as a white person although having some Negro ancestry. **35.** to be transferred or conveyed: *The crown passed to the king's nephew.* **36.** to be interchanged, as between two persons: *Sharp words passed between them.* **37.** to undergo transition or conversion: *to pass from a solid to a liquid state.* **38.** to go or get through a barrier, test, etc., successfully. **39.** to go uncensured or unchallenged: *Let the insult pass.* **40.** to express or pronounce an opinion, judgment, verdict, etc. (usually fol. by *on* or *upon*): *Will you pass on the authenticity of this drawing?* **41.** to be voided from the bowels. **42.** to obtain the approval or sanction of a legislative body, official committee, or the like: *The bill finally passed.* **43.** *Law.* **a.** (of a member of an inquest) to sit (usually fol. by *on* or *upon*): *to pass on a case.* **b.** to adjudicate. **c.** to vest legal title or interest in property in a new owner. **44.** *Sports.* to make a pass, as in football or ice hockey. **45.** *Cards.* **a.** to forgo one's opportunity to bid, play, etc. **b.** to throw in one's hand. **46.** *Fencing Obs.* to thrust or lunge. **47. bring to pass,** to cause to happen; bring about. **48. come to pass,** to occur; happen. **49. pass away, a.** to cease; end. **b.** to die. **50. pass for,** to be accepted as; be considered. **51. pass off, a.** to present or offer (something) under false pretenses; dispose of deceptively. **b.** to cause to be accepted or received under a false identity: *He passed himself off as a doctor.* **c.** to disregard; ignore. **52. pass on,** to die. **53. pass out,** *Informal.* to lose consciousness; faint. **54. pass over,** to disregard; ignore. **55. pass up,** *Informal.* to refuse or neglect to take advantage of; reject, as an opportunity. —*n.* **56.** a road, channel, or other means of passage through an obstructed region, as a narrow route across a depression in a mountain, a navigable channel, etc. **57.** a permission or license to pass, go, come, or enter. **58.** *Mil.* **a.** a document granting the right to cross lines or to enter or leave a military area. **b.** written authority given a soldier to leave a station or duty for a specified period of time. **59.** a free ticket or permit. **60.** *Sports.* the transfer of a ball or puck from one teammate to another. **61.** *Baseball.* See **base on balls.** **62.** *Fencing.* a thrust or lunge. **63.** a single movement, effort, etc.: *He made a pass at the enemy airfield.* **64.** *Informal.* a gesture or action that is intended to be sexually inviting. **65.** *Cards.* the act or statement of not bidding. **66.** (in feats of magic) **a.** a passing of the hand over, along, or before anything. **b.** the transference or changing of objects by or as by sleight of hand; a manipulation. **67.** a particular stage or state of affairs. **68.** an act of passing. **69.** one passage of work through a machine. **70.** *Archaic.* a witty sally or thrust. [ME *pass(en)* < OF *pass(er)* < LL **passāre* < L *pass(us)* step. See PACE[1]] —**pass′less,** *adj.*
—**Syn. 2.** ignore. **7.** excel. **18.** enact. **27.** leave.

pass., **1.** passenger. **2.** passim. **3.** passive.

pass·a·ble (pas′ə bəl, pä′sə-), *adj.* **1.** capable of being passed through or over, penetrated, crossed, etc. **2.** adequate; acceptable: *a passable knowledge of French.* **3.** capable of being circulated legally, as a coin. [late ME < MF] —**pass′a·ble·ness,** *n.*

pass·a·bly (pas′ə blē, pä′sə-), *adv.* fairly; moderately: *a passably good novel.*

pas·sa·ca·glia (pä′sə käl′yə, pas′ə-), *n.* **1.** a slow, dignified dance of Spanish origin. **2.** the music for this dance, based on an ostinato figure. **3.** a musical form based on continuous variations over a ground bass. [earlier *passacalle* < Sp *pasacalle*, lit., step (i.e., dance) in the street (*pasa-*, comb. form of *paso* step, PACE[1], + *calle* street < L *callem*, acc. of *callis* path); *-aglia* is a sp. change made to give word an Italian look]

pas·sade (pə sād′), *n.* *Manège.* a turn or course of a horse backward or forward on the same ground. [< F < It *passata*]

pas·sa·do (pə sä′dō), *n.*, *pl.* **-dos, -does.** *Fencing.* a forward thrust with the weapon while advancing with one foot. [alter. of Sp *pasada* or It *passata*]

pas·sage[1] (pas′ij), *n.*, *v.*, **-saged, -sag·ing.** —*n.* **1.** a portion or section of a written work; a paragraph, verse, etc.: *a passage of Scripture.* **2.** a phrase or other division of a musical work. **3.** *Fine Arts.* an area, section, or detail of a work, esp. with respect to its qualities of execution. **4.** the act or an instance of passing from one place, condition, etc., to another. **5.** the permission, right, or freedom to pass. **6.** the route or course by which a person or thing passes or travels. **7.** *Chiefly Brit.* a hall or corridor; passageway. **8.** an opening or entrance into, through, or out of something: *the nasal passages.* **9.** a voyage by water. **10.** the accommodation on a ship. **11.** the price charged for accommodation on a ship; fare. **12.** a lapse or passing, as of time. **13.** a progress or course, as of events. **14.** the enactment into law of a legislative measure. **15.** an interchange of communications, confidences, etc., between persons. **16.** an exchange of blows; altercation or dispute: *a passage at arms.* **17.** the act of causing something to pass; transference; transmission. **18.** an evacuation of the bowels. **19.** *Archaic.* an occurrence. —*v.i.* **20.** to make a passage; cross; voyage. [ME < OF]

pas·sage[2] (pas′ij, pə säzh′), *n.*, *v.*, **-saged, -sag·ing.** *Dressage.* —*n.* **1.** a slow, cadenced trot executed with great elevation of the feet and characterized by a moment of suspension before the feet strike the ground. —*v.i.* **2.** (of a horse) to execute such a movement. **3.** (of a rider) to cause a horse to execute such a movement. —*v.t.* **4.** to cause (a horse) to passage. [< F *passag(er)*, var. of *passéger* < It *passeggiare* to walk; see PACE[1]]

pas·sage·way (pas′ij wā′), *n.* a way affording passage, as a hall, corridor, etc.

Pas·sa·ic (pə sā′ik), *n.* a city in NE New Jersey. 55,124 (1970).

pass·a·long (pas′ə lông′, pas′ə long′), *n.* the act of passing something on to others in succession: *the high passalong of business magazines.*

Pas′sa·ma·quod′dy Bay′ (pas′ə mə kwod′ē, pas′-), an inlet of the Bay of Fundy, between Maine and New Brunswick, at the mouth of the St. Croix River.

pas·sant (pas′ənt), *adj.* *Heraldry.* (of a beast) represented as walking, with one forepaw raised, and as looking forward to the dexter side of the escutcheon unless specified as guardant. [< MF, prp. of *passer* to PASS; see -ANT]

pass·book (pas′bo͝ok′, päs′-), *n.* bankbook.

pass′ degree′, (in English universities) an ordinary bachelor's degree conferred without honors. Also called **poll, poll degree.**

pas·sé (pa sā′, pas′ā; *Fr.* PA sā′), *adj.* **1.** out-of-date; outmoded. **2.** past: *time passé.* **3.** past one's prime; aged. [< F, ptp. of *passer* to PASS]

passed′ ball′, *Baseball.* a pitched ball that the catcher can reasonably be expected to catch but misses, resulting in a base runner's or runners' advancing one or more bases or in the batter's reaching first base safely. Cf. **wild pitch.**

pas·sel (pas′əl), *n.* a group or lot of indeterminate number: *a passel of dignitaries.* [alter. of PARCEL]

passe·men·terie (pas men′trē; *Fr.* päs mäN trē′), *n.* trimming of braid, cord, etc. [< F]

pas·sen·ger (pas′ən jər), *n.* **1.** a person who is carried in an automobile, bus, train, airplane, or other conveyance. **2.** a wayfarer; traveler. [ME *passager* < MF, n. use of *passag(i)er* (adj.) passing, temporary; see PASSAGE, -AR[1]. For *-n-* cf. MESSENGER, HARBINGER, SCAVENGER, POPINJAY]

pas′senger pi′geon, an extinct, formerly abundant pigeon, *Ectopistes migratorius*, of North America.

passe-par·tout (pas′pär to͞o′; *Fr.* päs PAR to͞o′), *n.*, *pl.* **-touts** (-to͞oz′; *Fr.* -to͞o′). **1.** an ornamental mat for a picture. **2.** a method of framing in which a piece of glass is placed over a picture and is affixed to a backing by means of adhesive strips of paper or other material pasted over the edges. **3.** paper prepared for this purpose. **4.** something that passes or provides passage everywhere, as a master key. [< F: lit., pass everywhere]

passe·pied (päs pyā′), *n.*, *pl.* **-pieds** (-pyā′). **1.** a lively French dance of the 17th and 18th centuries. **2.** the music for this dance. [< F *passepied*, lit., pass (the) foot]

pass·er-by (pas′ər bī′, -bī′, pä′sər-), *n.*, *pl.* **pass·ers-by** (pas′ərz bī′, -bī′, pä′sərz-). a person passing by. Also, **pass′er·by′.**

pas·ser·ine (pas′ər in, -ə rīn′, -ə rēn′), *adj.* **1.** of, belonging, or pertaining to the order *Passeriformes*, comprising more than half of all birds and typically having the feet adapted for perching. **2.** oscine (def. 1). —*n.* **3.** any bird of the order *Passeriformes.* [< L *passerīn(us)* of a sparrow = *passer-* (s. of *passer*) sparrow + *-īnus* -INE[1]]

pas seul (*Fr.* pä sœl′), *pl.* **pas seuls** (*Fr.* pä sœl′). *Ballet.* a dance performed by one person; dance solo. [< F: lit., solo step]

pas·si·ble (pas′ə bəl), *adj.* capable of feeling; susceptible of sensation or emotion; impressionable. [ME < ML *passibil(is).* See PASSION, -IBLE] —**pas′si·bil′i·ty,** *n.*

pas·si·flo·ra·ceous (pas′ə flō rā′shəs, -flô-), *adj.* belonging to the *Passifloraceae*, or passionflower family of plants. [< NL *Passiflor(a)* the typical genus (see PASSION, FLORA) + -ACEOUS]

pas·sim (pä′sim; *Eng.* pas′im), *adv.* *Latin.* here and there: used to indicate the repetition of an idea, phrase, etc., in a book.

pass·ing (pas′ing, pä′sing), *adj.* **1.** going by or past; elapsing. **2.** fleeting; transitory: *a passing fancy.* **3.** done, given, etc., in passing; cursory: *a passing mention.* **4.** surpassing, preeminent, or extreme. **5.** indicating that a student has passed: *a passing grade.* —*adv.* **6.** *Archaic.* surpassingly; exceedingly; very. —*n.* **7.** the act of a person or thing that passes. **8.** a means or place of passage. **9.** death. **10. in passing,** by the way; incidentally. [ME] **—pass′ing·ly,** *adv.*

pass′ing bell′, **1.** a bell tolled to announce a death or funeral. **2.** a portent or sign of the passing away of anything.

pass′ing modula′tion, *Music.* See **transient modulation.**

pas·sion (pash′ən), *n.* **1.** any powerful or compelling emotion or feeling. **2.** strong affection; love. **3.** strong sexual desire; lust. **4.** an instance or experience of this. **5.** a person toward whom one feels strong love or sexual desire. **6.** a strong or extravagant fondness, enthusiasm, or desire for anything: *a passion for music.* **7.** the object of such a fondness or desire. **8.** an outburst of strong emotion or feeling. **9.** violent anger. **10.** the state of being acted upon or affected by something external (contrasted with *action*). **11.** (*often cap.*) *Theol.* **a.** the sufferings of Christ on the cross or His sufferings subsequent to the Last Supper. **b.** the narrative of Christ's sufferings as recorded in the Gospels. **12.** *Archaic.* the sufferings of a martyr. [ME, OE < eccl. L *passiōn-* (s. of *passiō*) Christ's sufferings on the cross, any of the Biblical accounts of these, special use of LL *passiō* suffering, submission < L *pass(us)* suffered, submitted, ptp. of *pati;* see -ION] **—Syn. 1.** See **feeling. 6.** fervor, zeal, ardor. **9.** ire, fury, wrath, rage. **—Ant. 1.** apathy.

pas·sion·al (pash′ə nᵊl), *adj.* **1.** of, pertaining to, or marked by passion: *a passional crime.* **—***n.* **2.** a book describing the sufferings of saints and martyrs. [< ML *passiōnāl(is)*]

pas·sion·ate (pash′ə nit), *adj.* **1.** influenced or dominated by intense emotion or strong feeling: *a passionate advocate of socialism.* **2.** expressing or revealing strong emotion. **3.** having or revealing intense enthusiasm. **4.** easily affected with or influenced by sexual desire. **5.** liable to or filled with anger. [< ML *passiōnāt(us)*] **—pas′sion·ate·ly,** *adv.* **—Syn. 1.** emotional, impulsive. **1–3.** ardent, impassioned, fervent. **5.** choleric, hot-headed. **—Ant. 2, 3.** cool.

pas·sion·flow·er (pash′ən flou′ər), *n.* any chiefly American climbing vine or shrub of the genus *Passiflora,* having showy flowers and a pulpy berry or fruit that in some species is edible. [trans. of NL *flōs passiōnis,* lit., flower of the Passion; so named because likened to Christ's wounds, crown of thorns, and other marks of suffering]

Passionflower, *Passiflora incarnata*

pas·sion·fruit (pash′ən fro͞ot′), *n.* any edible fruit of a passionflower, as the maypop.

pas·sion·less (pash′ən lis), *adj.* not feeling or moved by passion; cold or unemotional; calm or detached. **—pas′sion·less·ly,** *adv.* **—pas′sion·less·ness,** *n.*

pas′sion play′, a dramatic representation of the passion of Christ, such as that given every 10 years at the Bavarian village of Oberammergau. Also, **Pas′sion Play′.**

Pas′sion Sun′day, the fifth Sunday in Lent. [ME *Passioun Sonday*]

Pas′sion Week′, **1.** the week preceding Easter; Holy Week. **2.** the week before Holy Week, beginning with Passion Sunday. [ME *passion-woke*]

pas·sive (pas′iv), *adj.* **1.** not reacting visibly to something that might be expected to produce an emotion or feeling. **2.** not participating actively: *a passive member of a committee.* **3.** inactive; inert; quiescent. **4.** acted upon or affected by some external force rather than causing action (opposed to *active*). **5.** enduring or submitting without resistance: *a passive hypnotic subject.* **6.** *Gram.* noting a voice of verbal inflection indicating that the subject undergoes the action of the verb, as *carried* in *He is carried* (opposed to *active*). **7.** *Chem.* inactive, esp. under conditions in which chemical activity is to be expected. **8.** *Metall.* (of a metal) treated so as to be abnormally unresponsive to certain environments. **—***n. Gram.* **9.** the passive voice. **10.** a passive form or construction. [ME < L *passīv(us),* lit., submissive = *pass(us)* submitted (ptp. of *patī* to experience, undergo) + *-īvus* -IVE] **—pas′sive·ly,** *adv.* **—pas′sive·ness, pas·siv′i·ty,** *n.*

pas′sive immu′nity, *Immunol.* immunity resulting from the injection of antibodies from another organism or, in infants, from the transfer of antibodies through the placenta or from colostrum.

pas′sive resist′ance, opposition to a government or to specific laws by the use of noncooperation and other nonviolent methods. **—pas′sive resist′er.**

pas·siv·ism (pas′ə viz′əm), *n.* **1.** the quality of being passive. **2.** the principle or practice of passive resistance. **—pas′siv·ist,** *n.*

pass·key (pas′kē′, päs′-), *n., pl.* **-keys. 1.** See **master key. 2.** See **skeleton key. 3.** a private key. **4.** a latchkey.

Pas·so Fun·do (päs′so͞o fo͞onn′do͞o), a city in S Brazil. 50,559 (1960).

Pass·o·ver (pas′ō′vər, päs′-), *n.* **1.** Also called **Pesach, Pesah.** a Jewish festival, beginning on the eve of the 14th day of Nisan and celebrated for either seven or eight days, that commemorates the Exodus: marked chiefly by the Seder ritual and the observance of special dietary laws, as the eating of matzoth. **2.** (*l.c.*) See **paschal lamb** (def. 1).

pass·port (pas′pōrt, -pôrt, päs′-), *n.* **1.** an official document issued by the government of a country to one of its citizens, authorizing him to travel to foreign countries and authenticating his identity, citizenship, right to protection while abroad, and right to reenter his native country. **2.** any authorization to pass or go somewhere. **3.** anything that ensures admission or acceptance. [earlier *passeport* < MF = *passe-* (s. of *passer* to PASS) + *port* PORT[1]]

pass-through (pas′thro͞o′, päs′-), *n.* a windowlike opening in a wall, as one for passing food or dishes between a kitchen and a dining room.

pas·sus (pas′əs), *n., pl.* **-sus, -sus·es.** a section or division of a story, poem, etc.; canto. [< ML, L: step. See PACE[1]]

pass·word (pas′wûrd′, päs′-), *n.* a secret word or expression given to prove one's right to access, information, etc. Cf. **countersign.**

past (past, päst), *adj.* **1.** gone by or elapsed in time: *It was a bad time, but it's all past now.* **2.** having existed or occurred in a time previous to the present; bygone: *the past glories of Greece.* **3.** gone by just before the present time: *during the past year.* **4.** ago: *six days past.* **5.** having formerly been or served as; previous; earlier: *three past presidents of the club.* **6.** *Gram.* designating a tense or other verb formation that refers to events or states in time gone by. **—***n.* **7.** the time gone by. **8.** the history of a person, nation, etc. **9.** what has existed or has happened at some earlier time. **10.** an earlier period of a person's life, career, etc., that is characterized by imprudent or immoral conduct. **11.** *Gram.* **a.** the past tense, as *he ate, he smoked.* **b.** another verb formation or construction with past meaning. **c.** a form in the past tense. **—***adv.* **12.** so as to pass by or beyond. **—***prep.* **13.** beyond in time; after: *past noon.* **14.** beyond in space or position; farther on than. **15.** in a direction so as to pass by: *We went past the house.* **16.** beyond in amount, number, etc.: *past the maximum age.* **17.** beyond the reach or power of: *He is past recovery.* [ME; var. sp. of *passed,* ptp. of PASS]

pas·ta (pä′stə), *n.* any of various flour-and-egg food preparations of Italian origin, made of thin, unleavened dough. [< It < LL. See PASTE]

paste (pāst), *n., v.,* **past·ed, past·ing. —***n.* **1.** a mixture of flour and water, often with starch or the like, used as an adhesive. **2.** any material or preparation in a soft or plastic mass. **3.** dough, esp. when prepared with shortening. **4.** pasta. **5.** any of various soft food preparations: *almond paste.* **6.** a soft mixture used as a ceramic body. **7.** *Jewelry.* **a.** a brilliant, heavy glass, as strass, used for making imitation gems. **b.** an imitation gem of this material. **8.** *Slang.* a hard smack, blow, or punch. **—***v.t.* **9.** to fasten or stick with paste or the like. **10.** to cover with something applied by means of paste. **11.** *Slang.* to hit (a person) hard; esp. in the face. [ME < MF < LL *pasta* dough < Gk: barley porridge, n. use of neut. pl. of *pastós,* verbid of *pássein* to strew, sprinkle; a *pasta* was orig. a kind of gruel sprinkled with salt]

paste·board (pāst′bōrd′, -bôrd′), *n.* **1.** a stiff, firm board made of sheets of paper pasted or layers of paper pulp pressed together. **—***adj.* **2.** made of pasteboard. **3.** unsubstantial, flimsy, or sham.

pas·tel[1] (pa stel′, pas′tel), *n.* **1.** a color having a soft, subdued shade. **2.** a stick of dried paste made of pigments ground with chalk and compounded with gum water. **3.** the art of drawing with such sticks, or a drawing so made. **—***adj.* **4.** having a soft, subdued shade. **5.** drawn with pastels: *a pastel portrait.* [< F < It *pastell(o)* < LL *pastellus,* var. of L *pastillus* (see PASTILLE)]

pas·tel[2] (pas′tel), *n.* **1.** the woad plant. **2.** the dye made from it. [< MF < Pr < ML *pastell(um)* woad (orig. woad-paste), var. of LL *pastellus* PASTEL[1]; change of gender by influence of L *glastum* woad]

pas·tel·ist (pa stel′ist, pas′tel ist), *n.* an artist who draws with pastels. Also, *esp. Brit.,* **pas′tel·list.**

past·er (pā′stər), *n.* **1.** a slip of paper gummed on the back, to be pasted on or over something, as over a name on a ballot. **2.** a person or thing that pastes.

pas·tern (pas′tərn), *n.* **1.** the part of the foot of a horse, cow, etc., between the fetlock and the hoof. **2.** either of the two bones of this part, the upper, or first, phalanx **(great pastern bone)** and the lower, or second, phalanx **(small pastern bone),** between which is a joint **(pas′tern joint′).** [ME *pastron* shackle, prob. same word as MF *pasturon, pastern* < VL **pastōr(ia)* herding (see PASTOR, -IA) + ME, MF *-on* n. suffix]

Pas·ter·nak (pas′tər nak′), *n.* **Bo·ris Le·o·ni·do·vich** (bō rēs′ le o nē′do vich), 1890–1960, Russian poet and novelist: declined 1958 Nobel prize.

paste-up (pāst′up′), *n. Print.* a mechanical.

Pas·teur (pa stûr′; *Fr.* pä stœr′), *n.* **Louis** (lo͞o′ē; *Fr.* lwē), 1822–95, French chemist and bacteriologist.

pas·teur·ise (pas′chə rīz′, pas′tə-), *v.t.,* **-ised, -is·ing.** *Chiefly Brit.* pasteurize. **—pas′teur·i·sa′tion,** *n.*

pas·teur·ism (pas′chə riz′əm, pas′tə-), *n.* **1.** a treatment devised by Pasteur for preventing certain diseases, esp. hydrophobia, by inoculation with virus of gradually increasing strength. **2.** the act or process of pasteurizing milk, cheese, etc.

pas·teur·ize (pas′chə rīz′, pas′tə-), *v.t.,* **-ized, -iz·ing.** to expose (milk, cheese, etc.) to a high temperature to destroy certain microorganisms and prevent or arrest fermentation. Also, *esp. Brit.,* **pasteurise.** [PASTEUR + -IZE] **—pas′teur·i·za′tion,** *n.*

pas·tic·cio (pa stē′chō; *It.* päs tēt′chō), *n., pl.* **-ci** (-chē). a pastiche. [< It < ML *pasticius* a pie, pastry]

pas·tiche (pa stēsh′, pä-), *n.* a literary, musical, or artistic piece consisting wholly or chiefly of motifs or techniques borrowed from one or more sources. [< F < It *pasticcio* PASTICCIO]

pas·tille (pa stēl′, -stil′), *n.* **1.** a flavored lozenge, usually containing some medicine; troche. **2.** a roll or cone of paste containing aromatic substances, burned as a disinfectant or deodorant. Also, **pas·til** (pas′til). [< F < Sp *pastilla;* akin to L *pastillus* lump of meal, lozenge, pill, dim. of *panis* bread]

pas·time (pas′tīm′, päs′-), *n.* something that serves to make time pass agreeably. [late ME *pas(s)e tyme,* trans. of MF *passe-temps*] **—Syn.** entertainment.

past′ mas′ter, **1.** a person who is thoroughly expert in a profession, art, etc. **2.** a person who has held the office of master in a guild, lodge, etc.

Pas·to (päs′tō), *n.* **1.** a city in SW Colombia. 130,130 (est. 1964); ab. 8350 ft. high. **2.** a volcanic peak near this city. 13,990 ft.

pas·tor (pas′tər), *n.* a minister or priest in charge of a church. [< L: shepherd, lit., feeder = *pāst(us)* pastured (ptp. of *pāscere* to put to pasture) + *-or* -OR[2]; r. ME *pastour* < AF]

pas·to·ral (pas′tər əl, pä′stər-), *adj.* **1.** of, pertaining to, or consisting of shepherds. **2.** used for pasture, as land. **3.** having or suggesting the simplicity or serenity generally attributed to rural areas. **4.** pertaining to the country or to life in the country; rural; rustic. **5.** of or pertaining to a minister or clergyman or to his duties. **—***n.* **6.** a poem, play, or the like, dealing with the life of shepherds or with country life, commonly in a conventional or artificial manner. **7.** *Music.* pastorale. **8.** a treatise on the duties of a minister or clergyman. **9.** a letter from an ecclesiastic to his people. [ME < L *pāstōrāl(is)*] **—pas′to·ral·ly,** *adv.* **—Syn. 3.** rustic, rural, bucolic, idyllic. **6.** eclogue, idyl; georgic.

pas·to·rale (pas′tə räl′, -ral′, -rä′lē; *It.* päs′tô rä′le), *n.*, *pl.* **-rales,** *It.* **-ra·li** (-rä′lē). *Music.* **1.** an opera, cantata, or the like, with a pastoral subject. **2.** a piece of music suggestive of pastoral life. [< It, n. use of *pastorale* PASTORAL]

pas·to·ral·ism (pas′tər ə liz′əm, pä′stər-), *n.* the practice of herding as the primary economic activity of a society.

pas·tor·ate (pas′tər it, pä′stər-), *n.* **1.** the office or term of office of a pastor. **2.** a body of pastors. **3.** parsonage (def. 1). Also, **pas′tor·age.** [< ML *pāstōrāt(us)*]

pas·to·ri·um (pa stōr′ē əm, -stôr′-, pä-), *n. Southern U.S.* a parsonage. [< NL, n. use of L *pastōrius*]

past′ par′ticiple, *Gram.* a participle with past or perfect meaning; perfect participle, as *fallen, sung, defeated.*

past′ per′fect, *Gram.* pluperfect.

pas·tra·mi (pə strä′mē), *n.* a highly seasoned cut of smoked or pickled beef, usually from the shoulder section. [< Yiddish < Rum *pastramă* << Turk]

pas·try (pā′strē), *n.*, *pl.* **-tries. 1.** a sweet baked food made of paste, esp. the shortened paste used for pie crust and the like. **2.** any item of food of which such paste forms an essential part, as a pie, tart, etc.

pas·tur·age (pas′chər ij, päs′-), *n.* **1.** grass or herbage grown for grazing livestock. **2.** grazing ground. **3.** the activity or business of pasturing livestock.

pas·ture (pas′chər, päs′-), *n.*, *v.*, **-tured, -tur·ing.** —*n.* **1.** ground covered with grass or herbage, used for the grazing of livestock; grassland. **2.** a specific area or piece of such ground. **3.** grass or herbage for feeding livestock. —*v.t.* **4.** to feed (livestock) by putting them to graze on pasture. **5.** (of livestock) to graze upon. [ME < MF < LL *pāstūra.* See PASTOR, -URE] —**pas′tur·al,** *adj.* —**pas′tur·er,** *n.*

past·y (pā′stē), *adj.*, **past·i·er, past·i·est,** *n.*, *pl.* **past·ies.** —*adj.* **1.** of or like paste in consistency or appearance. —*n.* **2. pasties,** a pair of small, cuplike coverings for the nipples of a striptease dancer. —**past′i·ness,** *n.*

past·y-faced (pā′stē fāst′), *adj.* having a pale, unhealthy, pastelike complexion.

pat[1] (pat), *v.*, **pat·ted, pat·ting,** *n.* —*v.t.* **1.** to strike lightly or gently with something flat, usually in order to flatten, smooth, or shape. **2.** to stroke or tap gently with the palm or fingers as an expression of affection, approbation, etc. —*v.i.* **3.** to strike lightly or gently. **4.** to walk or run with light footsteps. **5. pat on the back,** *Informal.* to encourage, congratulate, or praise. —*n.* **6.** a light stroke, tap, or blow with the palm, fingers, or a flat object. **7.** the sound of this. **8.** a small piece or mass, usually flat and square, formed by patting, cutting, etc.: *a pat of butter.* **9. a pat on the back,** *Informal.* a word of encouragement or praise. [ME; perh. var. of PUTT]

pat[2] (pat), *adj.* **1.** exactly to the point or purpose. **2.** excessively glib. **3.** learned, known, or mastered perfectly or exactly: *to have something pat.* —*adv.* **4.** exactly or perfectly. **5.** aptly; opportunely. **6. stand pat,** to cling or hold firm to one's decision, policy, or beliefs. [? special use of PAT[1]]

pat., **1.** patent. **2.** patented.

pa·ta·ca (pə tä′kə), *n.* a silver coin and monetary unit of Macao, equal to 100 avos. [< Pg << Ar *abu taqa* a kind of coin]

pa·ta·gi·um (pə tā′jē əm), *n.*, *pl.* **-gi·a** (-jē ə). **1.** a wing membrane, as of a bat. **2.** the extensible fold of skin of certain insects and of a gliding mammal or reptile, as a flying squirrel. [< NL, special use of L *patagium* gold edging on a Roman tunic < Gk *patageîon* a gold tunic border]

Pat·a·go·ni·a (pat′ə gō′nē ə, -gōn′yə), *n.* **1.** the tableland region constituting the southern tip of Argentina. **2.** a region in S South America, in S Argentina and S Chile, extending from the Andes to the Atlantic. —**Pat′a·go′ni·an,** *adj.*, *n.*

patch (pach), *n.* **1.** a piece of material used to cover or reinforce a hole or worn place. **2.** a piece of material used to cover or protect an injured part. **3.** any of the pieces of cloth sewed together to form patchwork. **4.** a small piece or area: *a patch of ice.* **5.** a piece or tract of land, esp. a small one in which a specific type of plant grows or is cultivated. **6.** See **beauty spot** (def. 1). **7.** *Mil.* a cloth emblem worn on the upper uniform sleeve. —*v.t.* **8.** to mend, cover, or strengthen with or as with a patch or patches. **9.** to repair or restore, esp. in a hasty or makeshift way. **10.** to make by joining patches or pieces together: *to patch a quilt.* **11.** to settle or smooth over (a quarrel, difference, etc.) (often fol. by *up*): *to patch up a quarrel.* [ME *pacche;* ? akin to OPr *pedas* piece to cover a hole < VL **pedaceum,* lit., something measured; cf. ML *pedāre* to measure in feet; see PED-] —**patch′a·ble,** *adj.* —**patch′er,** *n.* —**patch′less,** *adj.*

Patch·en (pach′ən), *n.* **Kenneth,** 1911–72, U.S. poet and novelist.

patch·ou·li (pach′ŏŏ lē, pə chōō′lē), *n.* **1.** either of two East Indian, menthaceous plants, *Pogostemon Heyneanus* or *P. Cablin,* that yield a fragrant oil. **2.** a penetrating perfume derived from it. Also, **pachouli, patch′ou·ly.** [< Tamil *pacculi*]

patch′ pock′et, a pocket formed by sewing a piece of shaped material to the outside of a garment.

patch′ test′, a test for allergy in which an allergic condition is indicated by an inflammatory reaction to a patch of material impregnated with an allergen applied to the skin.

patch·work (pach′wûrk′), *n.* **1.** sewn work made of pieces of cloth or leather of various colors or shapes. **2.** something made up of an incongruous variety of pieces or parts.

patch·y (pach′ē), *adj.*, **patch·i·er, patch·i·est. 1.** characterized by or made up of patches. **2.** occurring in, forming, or like patches. **3.** of inconsistent or irregular quality, texture, etc. —**patch′i·ly,** *adv.* —**patch′i·ness,** *n.*

patd., patented.

pate (pāt), *n.* **1.** the head. **2.** the crown or top of the head. [ME]

pâte (pät), *n.* porcelain paste used in ceramic work. [< F; see PASTE]

pâ·té (pä tā′), *n.*, *pl.* **-tés** (-tāz′; *Fr.* -tā′). **1.** *French Cookery.* a paste or spread made of liver, meat, fish, game, etc., often baked in a pastry and served as an hors d'oeuvre. **2.** See **foie gras.** [< F; MF *pastee.* See PASTE, -EE]

pâ·té de foie gras (pä tā′ də fwä′ grä′; *Fr.* pä tā′ də fwä grä′), *pl.* **pâ·tés de foie gras** (pä tāz′ də fwä′ grä′; *Fr.* pä tā′ də fwä grä′). See under **foie gras.** [< F: goose-liver pâté]

pa·tel·la (pə tel′ə), *n.*, *pl.* **-tel·lae** (-tel′ē). **1.** *Anat.* the flat, movable bone at the front of the knee; kneecap. **2.** *Biol.* a panlike or cuplike formation. [< L, dim. of *patina, patena* pan, lit., something open. See PATENT] —**pa·tel′lar,** *adj.*

pa·tel·late (pə tel′it, -āt), *adj.* **1.** having a patella. **2.** patelliform.

pa·tel·li·form (pə tel′ə fôrm′), *adj.* having the form of a patella; saucer-shaped, like a kneecap or limpet shell.

pat·en (pat′ᵊn), *n.* a metal plate on which the bread is placed in the celebration of the Eucharist. [ME *pateyn(e)* < OF *patene* < ML *patena, patina* Eucharistic plate (L: pan); akin to Gk *patánē*]

pa·ten·cy (pāt′ᵊn sē), *n.* **1.** the state of being patent. **2.** *Med.* the condition of not being blocked or obstructed. **3.** *Phonet.* openness of articulation, found more or less in all phonemes except stops. [PATEN(T) + -CY]

pat·ent (pat′ᵊnt *or, esp. Brit.,* pāt′ᵊnt), *n.* **1.** a government grant to an inventor for a stated period of time, conferring the exclusive right to make, use, and vend an invention. **2.** an invention, process, etc., that has been patented. **3.** an official document conferring some right, privilege, or the like. **4.** the instrument by which the United States conveys the legal fee-simple title to public land. —*adj.* **5.** protected by a patent. **6.** pertaining to or dealing with patents, as upon inventions. **7.** conferred by a patent, as a right or privilege. **8.** appointed by a patent, as a person. **9.** open to notice or observation; evident; obvious. **10.** *Chiefly Bot.* expanded or spreading. —*v.t.* **11.** to take out a patent on. **12.** to grant (public land) by a patent. [ME < L *patent-* (s. of *patēns*) open, orig. prp. of *patēre* to stand wide open; as n., short for *letters patent,* trans. of ML *litterae patentēs* open letters] —**pat′ent·a·bil′i·ty,** *n.* —**pat′ent·a·ble,** *adj.* —**pat′ent·a·bly,** *adv.* —**pat′ent·ly,** *adv.* —**Syn. 9.** clear, apparent, conspicuous. See **apparent.** —**Ant. 9.** obscure.

pat·ent·ee (pat′ᵊn tē′), *n.* a person, group, or company granted a patent. [late ME]

pat′ent flour′, a fine grade of flour, consisting chiefly of the inner part of the endosperm.

pat′ent leath′er (pat′ᵊnt, pat′ᵊn *or, esp. Brit.,* pāt′ᵊnt), a hard, glossy, smooth leather, used in shoes, bags, etc.

pat′ent med′icine, **1.** a medicine sold without a prescription. **2.** a medicine that is patented.

pat′ent of′fice, a governmental agency that administers and regulates patents and trademarks, in the U.S. a division of the Department of Commerce.

pat·en·tor (pat′ᵊn tər), *n.* a person who grants patents.

pat′ent right′, the exclusive right granted by a patent, as on an invention.

pa·ter (pā′tər; *also for 2* pat′ər), *n.* **1.** *Brit. Informal.* father. **2.** (*often cap.*) paternoster. [< L: father]

Pa·ter (pā′tər), *n.* **Walter (Horatio)** 1839–94, English critic, essayist, and novelist.

pa·ter·fa·mil·i·as (pā′tər fə mil′ē əs, pä′-, pat′ər-), *n.*, *pl.* **pa·ter·fa·mil·i·as·es** for 1, **pa·tres·fa·mil·i·as** (pā′trēz-fə mil′ē əs, pä′-, pa′-) for 2. **1.** the male head of a household or family, usually the father. **2.** *Roman Law.* **a.** the head of a Roman family. **b.** a free male citizen. [< L: lit., father (i.e., master) of the household; see FAMILY] —**pa′ter·fa·mil′iar,** *adj.* —**pa′ter·fa·mil′iar·ly,** *adv.*

pa·ter·nal (pə tûr′nᵊl), *adj.* **1.** characteristic of or befitting a father; fatherly. **2.** of or pertaining to a father. **3.** related on the father's side. **4.** derived or inherited from a father. [< LL *paternāl(is)* = L *patern(us)* paternal (*pater* father + *-nus* adj. suffix) + *-ālis* -AL[1]] —**pa·ter′nal·ly,** *adv.*

pa·ter·nal·ism (pə tûr′nᵊliz′əm), *n.* the system, principle, or practice of managing or governing individuals, businesses, nations, etc., in the manner of a father dealing with his children. —**pa·ter′nal·ist,** *n.*, *adj.* —**pa·ter′nal·is′tic,** *adj.* —**pa·ter′nal·is′ti·cal·ly,** *adv.*

pa·ter·ni·ty (pə tûr′ni tē), *n.* **1.** the state of being a father; fatherhood. **2.** derivation or acquirement from a father. **3.** origin or authorship. —*adj.* **4.** of or pertaining to a legal dispute in which an unwed mother accuses a man of fathering her child: *a paternity suit.* **5.** of or pertaining to fatherhood. [late ME *paternite* < eccl. L *paternitās* quality of fatherhood in God (said of or to a monk or priest)]

pa·ter·nos·ter (pā′tər nos′tər, pat′ər-), *n.* **1.** (*often cap.*) Also, **Pa′ter Nos′ter.** the Lord's Prayer, esp. in the Latin form. **2.** a recitation of this prayer as an act of worship. **3.** one of certain large beads in a rosary, indicating that the Lord's Prayer is to be said. [ME, OE; named from L *pater noster* our father, first two words of the prayer in Vulgate version (Matt. 6:9)]

Pa·ter Pa·tri·ae (pä′ter pä′trē ī′; *Eng.* pā′tər pā′trē ē′), *Latin.* father of his country.

Pat·er·son (pat′ər sən), *n.* a city in NE New Jersey. 144,824 (1970).

path (path, päth), *n.*, *pl.* **paths** (pathz, päthz, paths, päths). **1.** a way beaten or trodden by the feet of men or animals. **2.** a narrow walk or way: *a garden path; a bicycle path.* **3.** a route along which something moves: *the path of a hurricane.* **4.** a course of action, conduct, or procedure: *the path of righteousness.* [ME; OE *pæth;* c. G *Pfad*]
—**Syn. 1.** footpath, pathway. PATH, LANE, TRAIL are passages or routes not as wide as a way or road. A PATH is a way for passing on foot; a track, beaten by feet, not specially constructed: *a path through a field.* A LANE is a narrow road or track, generally between fields, often enclosed with fences or trees; sometimes it is an alley or narrow road between buildings in towns: *a lane leading to a farmhouse; Drury Lane.* A TRAIL is a rough way made or worn through woods or across mountains, prairies, or other untraveled regions: *an Indian trail.*

-path, **1.** an element occurring in agent nouns corresponding to nouns with stems ending in **-pathy** (*homeopath*). **2.** var. of **patho-** as final element of compounds (*psychopath*). Cf. **-pathia, -pathic, -pathy.**

path., **1.** pathological. **2.** pathology.

Pa·than (pə tän′, pət hän′), *n.* an Afghan.

pa·thet·ic (pə thet′ik), *adj.* **1.** causing or evoking pity. **2.** affecting or moving the feelings. **3.** pertaining to or caused by the feelings. **4.** miserably inadequate. Also, **pa·thet′i·cal.** [< LL *pathētic(us)* < Gk *pathētikós* sensitive = *pathēt(ós)* made or prone to suffer (verbal of *páschein* to suffer) + *-ikos* -IC] —**pa·thet′i·cal·ly,** *adv.* —**pa·thet′i·cal·ness,** *n.* —**Syn. 1.** plaintive. **2.** touching, tender. **3.** emotional.

pathet′ic fal′lacy, the endowment of nature, inanimate objects, etc., with human traits and feelings, as in *the smiling skies.* [coined by John Ruskin in *Modern Painters,* Vol. III, Part IV (1856)]

path·find·er (path′fīn′dər, päth′-), *n.* a person who finds or makes a path, way, route, etc., esp. through a wilderness. —**path′find′ing,** *n.*

-pathia, an obsolete var. of **-pathy:** *psychopathia.* [< NL]

-pathic, an element used to form adjectives from nouns with stems in **-pathy:** *psychopathic.* [< NL]

path·less (path′lis, päth′-), *adj.* without paths; trackless.

patho-, a learned borrowing from Greek meaning "suffering," "disease," "feeling," used in the formation of compound words: *pathology.* Also, *esp. before a vowel,* **path-.** Cf. **-path, -pathia, -pathic, -pathy.** [comb. form repr. Gk *páthos;* see PATHOS]

path·o·gen (path′ə jən), *n.* any disease-producing organism. Also, **path·o·gene** (path′ə jēn′).

path·o·gen·e·sis (path′ə jen′i sis), *n.* the production and development of disease. Also, **pa·thog·e·ny** (pə thoj′ə nē). [< NL] —**path·o·ge·net·ic** (path′ō jə net′ik), *adj.*

path·o·gen·ic (path′ə jen′ik), *adj.* disease-producing.

path·o·ge·nic·i·ty (path′ō jə nis′i tē), *n.* the disease-producing capacity of a microorganism.

pa·thog·no·mon·ic (pə thog′nə mon′ik), *adj. Med.* characteristic or diagnostic of a specific disease: *a pathognomonic sign of pneumonia.* [< Gk *pathognōmonik(ós)* skilled in judging disease. See PATHO-, GNOMON, -IC] —**pa·thog′no·mon′i·cal·ly,** *adv.*

pathol., 1. pathological. **2.** pathology.

path·o·log·i·cal (path′ə loj′i kəl), *adj.* **1.** of or pertaining to pathology. **2.** caused by or involving disease; morbid. **3.** dealing with diseases: *a pathological casebook.* Also, **path′o·log′ic.** [*pathologic* (< Gk *pathologik(ós);* see PATHOLOGY, -IC) + -AL¹] —**path′o·log′i·cal·ly,** *adv.*

pa·thol·o·gy (pə thol′ə jē), *n., pl.* **-gies. 1.** the science or the study of the origin, nature, and course of diseases. **2.** the conditions and processes of a disease. **3.** any deviation from a healthy, normal, or efficient condition. [earlier *pathologia* < L < Gk] —**pa·thol′o·gist,** *n.*

pa·thos (pā′thos), *n.* **1.** the quality or power, in literature, music, speech, or other expressive forms, of evoking a feeling of pity or compassion. **2.** pity. **3.** *Obs.* suffering. [< Gk: suffering, sensation, verbal n. of *páschein* to suffer]

path·way (path′wā′, päth′-), *n.* a path, course, route, or way.

-pathy, a noun element occurring in loan words from Greek, where it meant "suffering" (*antipathy; sympathy*), "feeling" (*telepathy*); in compound words of modern formation, often used with the meaning "morbid affection," "disease" (*arthropathy; deuteropathy; neuropathy; psychopathy*), and hence used also in names of systems or methods of treating disease (*allopathy; homeopathy; hydropathy; osteopathy*). Cf. **-path, -pathia.** [comb. form repr. Gk *pátheia* suffering, feeling = *páth(os)* PATHOS + *-eia* -Y³]

Pat·i·a·la (put′ē ä′lə), *n.* **1.** an important state of the former Punjab States: now part of Punjab in NW India. **2.** a city in E Punjab, in N India. 125,200 (1961).

pa·tience (pā′shəns), *n.* **1.** the bearing of provocation, annoyance, misfortune, pain, etc., without complaint, loss of temper, or irritation. **2.** an ability or willingness to suppress annoyance when confronted with delay: *to have patience with a child who is a slow learner.* **3.** quiet perseverance; even-tempered care; diligence: *to work with patience.* **4.** *Cards.* solitaire (def. 1). **5.** *Obs.* sufferance; leave; permission. [ME *pacience* < OF < L *patientia.* See PATIENT, -ENCE] —**Syn. 1.** composure, self-possession; sufferance. PATIENCE, ENDURANCE, FORTITUDE, STOICISM imply qualities of calmness, stability, and persistent courage in trying circumstances. PATIENCE may denote calm, self-possessed, and unrepining bearing of pain, misfortune, annoyance, or delay; or painstaking and untiring industry or (less often) application in the doing of something: *to bear afflictions with patience.* ENDURANCE denotes the ability to bear exertion, hardship, or suffering (without implication of moral qualities required or shown): *Running in a marathon requires great endurance.* FORTITUDE implies not only patience but courage and strength of character in the midst of pain, affliction, or hardship: *to show fortitude in adversity.* STOICISM is calm fortitude, with such repression of emotion as to seem almost like indifference to pleasure or pain: *The American Indians were noted for stoicism under torture.* **3.** persistence, assiduity.

pa·tient (pā′shənt), *n.* **1.** a person who is under medical or surgical treatment. **2.** *Archaic.* a sufferer or victim. —*adj.* **3.** bearing annoyance, pain, etc., without complaint or anger. **4.** characterized by or expressing such a quality. **5.** persevering or diligent, esp. over details. [ME *pacient* < MF < L *patient-* (s. of *patiēns*), prp. of *patī* to undergo, suffer, bear; see -ENT] —**pa′tient·ly,** *adv.* —**Syn. 1.** invalid. **3.** uncomplaining, long-suffering, forbearing. **4.** unruffled, self-possessed, composed. **5.** sedulous, assiduous, untiring. —**Ant. 3.** impatient, agitated.

pat·i·na (pat′ᵊnə), *n.* **1.** a film or incrustation, usually green, produced by oxidation on the surface of old bronze. **2.** any incrustation or film appearing gradually on a surface. **3.** a sheen, glow, aura, etc., esp. as the result of age, use, or association: *the patina of fine old leather.* [< It: coating < L: pan. See PATEN]

pa·ti·o (pat′ē ō′, pä′tē ō′), *n., pl.* **-ti·os. 1.** a courtyard, esp. of a house, surrounded by low buildings or walls. **2.** an area, usually paved, adjoining a house and serving as an area for outdoor living. [< Sp, OSp: courtyard, perh. orig. open area; cf. ML *patium* meadow, pasturage ? < L **patitus,* ptp. of *patēre* to lie open. See PATENT]

pa·tis·se·rie (pə tis′ə rē; *Fr.* pä tēsᵊ rᴇ′), *n., pl.* **-ries** (-rēz; *Fr.* -rᴇ′). **1.** an establishment where pastry, esp. French pastry, is made and sold. **2.** See **French pastry.** [< F *pâtisserie,* OF *patiserie*]

Pat·more (pat′mōr, -môr), *n.* **Co·ven·try** (**Ker·sey Digh·ton**) (kov′ən trē kûr′zē dīt′ᵊn, kuv′ən-), 1823–96, English poet and essayist.

Pat·mos (pat′mos, -mōs, pät′môs), *n.* one of the Dodecanese Islands, off the SW coast of Asia Minor: St. John is supposed to have been exiled here. Rev. 1:9. 2564 (1961); 13 sq. mi. Italian, **Pat·mo** (pät′mō). —**Pat′mi·an,** *adj.*

Pat·na (pat′nə, put′nä′), *n.* a city in and the capital of Bihar, in NE India, on the Ganges. 363,700 (1961).

Pat. Off., Patent Office.

pat·ois (pat′wä; *Fr.* pᴀ twᴀ′), *n., pl.* **pat·ois** (pat′wäz; *Fr.* pᴀ twᴀ′). **1.** a rural or provincial form of speech, esp. of French. **2.** an ungrammatical mixture of two or more languages. [< F: lit., clumsy speech; akin to OF *patoier* to handle clumsily < *pate* paw; see -ESE]

Pa·ton (pāt′ᵊn), *n.* **Alan (Stewart),** born 1903, South African novelist.

pat. pend., patent pending.

Pa·tras (pə tras′, pa′trəs), *n.* **1.** Greek, **Pa·trai** (pä′tʀᴇ). a seaport in the Peloponnesus, in W Greece, on the Gulf of Patras. 95,364 (1961). **2. Gulf of,** an inlet of the Ionian Sea in the NW Peloponnesus. 10 mi. long; 25 mi. wide.

pa·tres·fa·mil·i·as (pā′trēz fə mil′ē əs, pä′-, pa′-), *n.* a pl. of **paterfamilias.**

patri-, an element meaning "father," occurring originally in loan words from Greek and Latin (*patriarch; patrician*) and used in the formation of new compounds (*patrilineal*). [comb. form repr. L *pater,* Gk *patēr* FATHER]

pa·tri·arch (pā′trē ärk′), *n.* **1.** any of the earlier Biblical personages regarded as the fathers of the human race, comprising those from Adam to Noah (**antediluvian patriarchs**) and those between the Deluge and the birth of Abraham. **2.** any of the three great progenitors of the Israelites: Abraham, Isaac, or Jacob. **3.** any of the sons of Jacob (the **twelve patriarchs**) from whom the tribes of Israel were descended. **4.** (in the early Christian church) any of the bishops of any of the ancient sees of Alexandria, Antioch, Constantinople, Jerusalem, or Rome having authority over other bishops. **5.** *Gk. Orth. Ch.* the head of any of the ancient sees of Alexandria, Antioch, Constantinople, or Jerusalem, and sometimes including sees of other chief cities. Cf. **ecumenical patriarch. 6.** the head of certain other churches in the East, as the Coptic, Nestorian, and Armenian churches. **7.** *Rom. Cath. Ch.* **a.** the pope as patriarch of the West. **b.** any of certain bishops of the Eastern rites, as a head of an Eastern rite or a bishop of one of the ancient sees. **8.** *Mormon Ch.* any of the high dignitaries who pronounce the blessing of the church; Evangelist. **9.** one of the elders or leading older members of a community. **10.** a venerable old man. **11.** the male head of a family or tribal line. **12.** a person regarded as the father or founder of an order, class, etc. [ME; OE *patriarcha* < LL < Gk *patriárchēs* high-ranking bishop (eccl.), family head = *patri(á)* family (< *patēr* father) + *-archēs* -ARCH] —**pa′tri·ar′chal, pa′tri·ar′chic, pa′tri·ar′chi·cal,** *adj.* —**pa′tri·ar′chal·ly, pa′tri·ar′chi·cal·ly,** *adv.*

pa′triar′chal cross′, a Latin cross having a shorter crosspiece above the customary one. See illus. at **cross.**

pa·tri·ar·chate (pā′trē är′kit), *n.* **1.** the office, dignity, jurisdiction, province, or residence of an ecclesiastical patriarch. **2.** a patriarchy. [< ML *patriarchāt(us)*]

pa·tri·ar·chy (pā′trē är′kē), *n., pl.* **-chies.** a form of community in which the father is the supreme authority in the family, clan, or tribe, descent being reckoned in the male line. [< Gk *patriarchía*]

pa·tri·cian (pə trish′ən), *n.* **1.** a member of the original senatorial aristocracy in ancient Rome. **2.** any person of noble or high rank; aristocrat. —*adj.* **3.** of or belonging to the patrician families of ancient Rome. **4.** of high social rank or noble family. [< L *patrici(us)* patrician (*pat(e)r* father + *-ic-* -IC + *-ius* adj. suffix) + -AN; r. late ME *patricion* (-ION for -IAN)]

pa·tri·ci·ate (pə trish′ē it, -āt′), *n.* **1.** the patrician class. **2.** patrician rank. [< ML *patriciāt(us)* = L *patrici(us)* (see PATRICIAN) + *-atus* -ATE¹]

pat·ri·cide (pa′tri sīd′, pā′-), *n.* **1.** the act of killing one's father. **2.** a person who kills his father. —**pat′ri·cid′al,** *adj.*

Pat·rick (pa′trik), *n.* **Saint,** A.D. 389?–461?, English missionary and bishop in Ireland: patron saint of Ireland.

pat·ri·lin·e·al (pa′trə lin′ē əl, pā′-), *adj.* inheriting or determining descent through the male line. Also, **pat′ri·lin′e·ar.** —**pat′ri·lin′e·al·ly, pat′ri·lin′e·ar·ly,** *adv.*

pat·ri·lo·cal (pa′trə lō′kəl, pā′-), *adj. Anthropol.* of or pertaining to residence with the family or tribe of one's husband. Cf. **matrilocal.** —**pat′ri·lo·cal′i·ty,** *n.*

pat·ri·mo·ny (pa′trə mō′nē), *n., pl.* **-nies. 1.** an estate inherited from one's father or ancestors. **2.** any quality, characteristic, etc., that is inherited; heritage. **3.** the estate or endowment of a church, religious house, etc. [ME *patrimonie* < MF < L *patrimoni(um)*] —**pat′ri·mo′ni·al,** *adj.* —**Syn. 1.** inheritance.

pa·tri·ot (pā′trē ət, -ot′ *or, esp. Brit.,* pa′trē ət), *n.* a person who loves, supports, and defends his country and its interests. [< MF *patriote* < LL *patriōta* fellow countryman < Gk *patriṓtēs* < *pátrio(s)* of one's fathers < *patrís* one's fatherland]

pa·tri·ot·ic (pā′trē ot′ik *or, esp. Brit.,* pa′-), *adj.* **1.** of, like, or characteristic of a patriot. **2.** expressing or inspired by patriotism: *a patriotic ode.* [< LL *patriōtic(us)* < Gk *patriōtikós*] —**pa′tri·ot′i·cal·ly,** *adv.*

pa·tri·ot·ism (pā′trē ə tiz′əm *or, esp. Brit.,* pa′-), *n.* devoted love, support, and defense of one's country; national loyalty.

Pa′triots′ Day′, April 19th, the anniversary of the battle of Lexington in 1775, observed as a legal holiday in Massachusetts and Maine.

pa·tris·tic (pə tris′tik), *adj.* of or pertaining to the fathers of the Christian church or their writings. Also, **pa·tris′ti·cal.** —**pa·tris′ti·cal·ly,** *adv.*

Pa·tro·clus (pə trō′kləs), *n. Class. Myth.* a friend of Achilles who was slain by Hector and whose death led Achilles to return to battle.

pa·trol (pə trōl′), *v.,* **-trolled, -trol·ling,** *n.* —*v.t.* **1.** to pass regularly along (a specified route) or through (a specified district) in order to maintain order and security. —*v.i.* **2.** to pass along or through such a route or district for this purpose. —*n.* **3.** a person, thing, or group that patrols. **4.** *Mil.* a detachment of two or more men, often a squad or platoon, detailed for reconnaissance or combat. **5.** the act of patrolling. **6.** (in the Boy Scouts and Girl Scouts) a subdivision of a troop, usually consisting of about eight members. [< F *patrouille* (n.), *patrouiller* (v.) patrol, orig. a pawing (n.), to paw (v.) in mud; < (with suffixal *-ouille*) *patte* paw; *-r-* unexplained] —**pa·trol′ler,** *n.*

pa·trol·man (pə trōl′mən), *n., pl.* **-men. 1.** a policeman who is assigned to patrol a specific district, route, etc. **2.** a man who patrols.

patrol′ wag′on, an enclosed truck or van used by the police to transport prisoners. Also called **police wagon.**

pa·tron (pā′trən), *n.* **1.** a person who is a customer, client, or paying guest, esp. a regular one, of a store, hotel, or the like. **2.** a person who supports with money, efforts, or endorsement an artist, museum, charity, etc.: *art patrons.* **3.** *Rom. Hist.* the former master of a freedman still retaining certain rights over him. **4.** *Eccles.* a person who has the right to present a clergyman to a benefice. Also, *referring to a woman,* **pa·tron·ess** (pā′trə nis, pa′-). [ME < ML, L *patrōn(us)* legal protector, advocate (ML: lord, master) < *pater* father. See PATTERN] —**pa′tron·ly,** *adj.*

pa·tron·age (pā′trə nij, pa′-), *n.* **1.** the financial support or business afforded a store, hotel, or the like, by customers, clients, or paying guests. **2.** the encouragement or support of a patron, as toward an artist, institution, etc. **3.** the control of or power to make appointments to government jobs, esp. on a basis other than merit alone. **4.** the jobs so controlled. **5.** the distribution of such jobs, esp. on a political basis. **6.** a condescending manner or attitude in granting favors. **7.** advowson. [ME < MF]

pa·tron·ise (pā′trə nīz′, pa′-), *v.t.,* **-ised, -is·ing.** *Chiefly Brit.* patronize. —**pa′tron·is′er,** *n.*

pa·tron·is·ing (pa′trə nī′zing), *adj.* *Chiefly Brit.* patronizing. —**pa′tron·is′ing·ly,** *adv.*

pa·tron·ize (pā′trə nīz′, pa′-), *v.t.,* **-ized, -iz·ing. 1.** to give (a commercial establishment) one's patronage. **2.** to behave in an offensively condescending manner toward. **3.** to act as a patron toward; support. Also, *esp. Brit.,* **patronise.** —**pa′tron·iz′er,** *n.*

pa·tron·iz·ing (pā′trə nī′zing, pa′-), *adj.* displaying or indicative of an unpleasantly condescending manner. Also, *esp. Brit.,* **patronising.** —**pa′tron·iz′ing·ly,** *adv.*

pa′tron saint′, a saint regarded as the special guardian of a person, group, trade, place, country, etc.

pat·ro·nym·ic (pa′trə nim′ik), *adj.* **1.** (of names) derived from the name of a father or ancestor, esp. by the addition of a suffix or prefix indicating descent. **2.** (of a suffix or prefix) indicating such descent. —*n.* **3.** a patronymic name, as *Williamson* (son of William) or *Macdonald* (son of Donald). **4.** a family name; surname. [< LL *patrōnymic(us)* < Gk *patrōnymikós* = *patrōnym(os)* (see PATRI-, -ONYM) + *-ikos* -IC] —**pat′ro·nym′i·cal·ly,** *adv.*

pa·troon (pə trōōn′), *n.* an owner of a landed estate with manorial privileges granted by the government of New Netherland. [< D < L *patrōn(us).* See PATRON] —**pa·troon′ship,** *n.*

pat·sy (pat′sē), *n., pl.* **-sies.** *Slang.* **1.** a person upon whom the blame for something falls. **2.** a person who is easily deceived, persuaded, etc. [?]

pat·tée (pa tā′, pat′ē), *adj.* paty.

pat·ten (pat′ən), *n.* a shoe with a thick wooden sole to protect the feet from mud or wetness. [ME *paten* < MF *patin* wooden shoe, perh. < *patte* paw]

pat·ter[1] (pat′ər), *v.i.* **1.** to make a succession of light, tapping sounds. **2.** to walk quickly and softly. —*v.t.* **3.** to cause to patter. —*n.* **4.** a rapid succession of light tapping sounds. **5.** the act of pattering. [PAT[1] + -ER[6]]

pat·ter[2] (pat′ər), *n.* **1.** glib and rapid speech used esp. to attract attention or entertain. **2.** meaningless, rapid talk; chatter. **3.** the jargon or cant of any class, group, etc. **4.** amusing lines delivered rapidly by an entertainer or performer. —*v.i.* **5.** to talk glibly or rapidly, esp. with little regard to meaning. —*v.t.* **6.** to repeat or say rapidly or glibly. [var. of PATER]

pat·ter[3] (pat′ər), *n.* a person or thing that pats. [PAT[1] + -ER[1]]

pat·tern (pat′ərn), *n.* **1.** a design, esp. for decorating a surface, composed of a number of elements or objects arranged in a regular or formal manner. **2.** any marking, configuration, or arrangement that suggests such a design: *patterns of frost on the window.* **3.** a distinctive style, model, or form: *a new pattern of army rifle.* **4.** a mode of behavior or combination of acts, qualities, etc., regarded as characteristic of persons or things. **5.** an original or model considered for or deserving of imitation. **6.** anything designed to serve as a model or guide. **7.** the path of flight established for an aircraft approaching an airport at which it is to land. **8.** an example, instance, sample, or specimen. —*v.t.* **9.** to make or fashion after or according to a pattern. **10.** to cover or mark with a pattern. [ME *patron* < ML *patrōn(us)* model, special use of L *patrōnus* PATRON] —**pat′tern·less,** *adj.* —**Syn. 1.** figure. **3.** kind, sort. **5.** example. **9.** copy, imitate.

Pat·ti (pat′ē; *It.* pät′tē), *n.* **A·de·li·na** (ä′de lē′nä), *(Adela Juana Maria Patti),* 1843–1919, Italian operatic soprano, born in Spain.

Pat·ton (pat′ən), *n.* **George Smith,** 1885–1945, U.S. general.

pat·ty (pat′ē), *n., pl.* **-ties. 1.** a little pie; pâté. **2.** any item of food covered with dough, batter, etc., and fried or baked. **3.** a thin, round piece of finely divided food, as of meat. **4.** a thin, round piece, as of candy. [alter. of PÂTÉ]

pat′ty pan′, a variety of summer squash having a fluted rind.

pat′ty shell′, a cup-shaped shell of light, flaky pastry, for serving vegetable, fish, or meat mixtures.

pat·u·lous (pach′ə ləs), *adj.* **1.** open; gaping; expanded. **2.** *Bot.* **a.** spreading, as a tree or its boughs. **b.** spreading slightly, as a calyx. **c.** bearing the flowers loose or dispersed, as a peduncle. [< L *patulus* standing wide-open] —**pat′u·lous·ly,** *adv.* —**pat′u·lous·ness,** *n.*

pat·y (pat′ē), *adj.* *Heraldry.* (of a cross) having arms of equal length, each expanding outward from the center; formée: *a cross paty.* Also, **pattée.** [< MF *pattee* = *patte* paw + *-ee;* see -EE, -ATE[1]]

Pau (pō), *n.* a city in SW France: winter resort. 61,468 (1962).

P.A.U., Pan American Union.

pau·cis ver·bis (pou′kis wer′bis; *Eng.* pô′sis vûr′bis), *Latin.* in few words; with or by few words.

pau·ci·ty (pô′si tē), *n.* smallness or insufficiency of number or amount. [late ME *paucite* < L *paucitās* fewness < *pauc(us)* few; see -ITY]

Paul (pôl *for 1;* poul *for 2*), *n.* **1. Saint,** died A.D. c67, one of the 12 apostles and missionary to the gentiles: author of several of the Epistles. Cf. **Saul** (def. 2). **2. Jean** (zhäN). See **Richter, Jean Paul Friedrich.**

Paul I, 1. Saint, died A.D. 767, pope 757–767. **2.** Russian, **Pavel Petrovich,** 1754–1801, emperor of Russia 1796–1801 (son of Peter III). **3.** 1901–64, king of Greece 1947–64.

Paul II, *(Pietro Barbo)* 1417–71, Italian ecclesiastic: pope 1464–71.

Paul III, *(Alessandro Farnese)* 1468–1549, Italian ecclesiastic: pope 1534–49.

Paul IV, *(Gian Pietro Caraffa)* 1476–1559, Italian ecclesiastic: pope 1555–59.

Paul V, *(Camillo Borghese)* 1552–1621, Italian ecclesiastic: pope 1605–21.

Paul VI, *(Giovanni Batista Montini)* 1897–1978, Italian ecclesiastic: pope 1963–78.

Paul′ Bun′yan, a legendary giant lumberjack, an American folk hero.

paul·dron (pôl′drən), *n.* *Armor.* a piece of plate armor for the shoulder and the uppermost part of the arm. [earlier *paleron, poleron* (late ME *polronds,* pl.) < MF *(es)palleron* shoulder. See EPAULET]

Pau·li (pô′lē; *Ger.* pou′lē), *n.* **Wolf·gang** (wŏŏlf′gang; *Ger.* vôlf′gäng′), 1900–1958, Austrian physicist in the U.S.: Nobel prize 1945.

Pau′li exclu′sion prin′ciple, *Physics.* See **exclusion principle.** [named after W. PAULI]

Paul·ine (pô′līn), *adj.* of or pertaining to the apostle Paul or to his doctrines or writings. [< ML *Paulīn(us)*]

Paul·ing (pô′ling), *n.* **Li·nus Carl** (lī′nəs), born 1901, U.S. chemist: Nobel prize in chemistry 1954, Nobel prize for peace 1963.

Paul·in·ism (pô′lə niz′əm), *n.* the body of theological doctrine taught by or attributed to the apostle Paul. —**Paul′in·ist,** *n.* —**Paul′in·is′tic,** *adj.*

Pau·li·nus (pô lī′nəs), *n.* **Saint,** died A.D. 644, Roman missionary in England: 1st archbishop of York 633–644.

Paul·ist (pô′list), *n.* *Rom. Cath. Ch.* a member of the "Missionary Society of St. Paul the Apostle," a community of priests founded in New York in 1858.

pau·low·ni·a (pô lō′nē ə), *n.* **1.** a tree, *Paulownia tomentosa,* of Japan, having showy, pale-violet or blue flowers blossoming in early spring. **2.** any other tree of the genus *Paulownia.* [< NL; named after Anna *Paulovna,* daughter of Paul I of Russia; see -IA]

Paul′ Pry′, an inquisitive, meddlesome person. [from name of title character of *Paul Pry* (1853) by John Poole (1786–1872), English playwright]

Pa·u·mo′tu Archipel′ago (pä′ōō mō′tōō). See **Tuamotu Archipelago.**

paunch (pônch, pänch), *n.* **1.** the belly or abdomen. **2.** a large and protruding belly; potbelly. **3.** the rumen. [ME *paunche* < AF = MF *pance* < L *pantices* (pl.) bowels] —**paunched,** *adj.*

paunch·y (pôn′chē, pän′-), *adj.,* **paunch·i·er, paunch·i·est.** having a large and protruding belly. —**paunch′i·ness,** *n.*

pau·per (pô′pər), *n.* **1.** a very poor person. **2.** a person without any personal means of support. [< L: poor] —**pau′per·age,** *n.* —**pau′per·ism,** *n.*

pau·per·ise (pô′pə rīz′), *v.t.,* **-ised, -is·ing.** *Chiefly Brit.* pauperize.

pau·per·ize (pô′pə rīz′), *v.t.,* **-ized, -iz·ing.** to make a pauper of.

Pau·sa·ni·as (pô sā′nē əs), *n.* fl. A.D. c175, Greek traveler, geographer, and author.

pause (pôz), *n., v.,* **paused, paus·ing.** —*n.* **1.** a temporary stop or rest, esp. in speech or action. **2.** a break or rest in speaking or writing, made for emphasis. **3.** *Pros.* a break or suspension, as a caesura, in a line of verse. **4. give pause,** to cause to hesitate, as from surprise or doubt. —*v.i.* **5.** to make a brief stop or delay. **6.** to dwell or linger briefly, as upon an idea. [ME < L *pausa* < Gk *paûsis* a halt = *paú(ein)* (to) stop + *-sis* -SIS] —**paus′al,** *adj.* —**pause′less,** *adj.* —**pause′less·ly,** *adv.* —**paus′ing·ly,** *adv.* —**Syn. 1.** suspension, interruption, break, halt. **5.** rest. **6.** tarry, delay.

pa·vane (pə vän′, -van′; *Fr.* PA VAN′), *n., pl.* **pa·vanes** (pə vänz′, -vanz′; *Fr.* PA VAN′). a stately dance dating from the 16th century. Also, **pav·an** (pav′ən). [< MF < It *pavana,* contr. of *padovana* (fem.) of Padua (It *Padova*)]

pave (pāv), *v.t.,* **paved, pav·ing. 1.** to cover (a road, walk, etc.) with stones, tiles, concrete, or the like, so as to make a firm, level surface. **2. pave the way for,** to prepare for; make possible; lead up to. [ME *pave(n)* < MF *pav(er)* < VL **pavare* for L *pavīre* to beat, ram, tread down] —**pav′er,** *n.*

pa·vé (pə vā′, pav′ā), *n., pl.* **pa·vés** (pə vāz′, pav′āz). *Jewelry.* a setting of stones placed close together so as to show no metal between them. [< F, ptp. of *paver* to PAVE]

Pa·vel Pe·tro·vich (*Russ.* pä′vəl pə trô′vich). See **Paul I** (def. 2).

pave·ment (pāv′mənt), *n.* **1.** a paved surface. **2.** a material used for paving. **3.** *Chiefly Brit.* sidewalk. [ME < OF < L *pavīment(um)*]

Pa·vi·a (pä vē′ä), *n.* a city in N Italy, S of Milan. 73,503

pa·vil·ion (pə vil′yən), *n.* **1.** a light, usually open building used for shelter, concerts, exhibits, etc. **2.** *Archit.* a major projecting element of a façade. **3.** any of a number of separate or attached buildings, as in a hospital. **4.** a tent, esp. a large and elaborate one. **5.** Also called **base.** *Jewelry.* the part of a cut gem below the girdle. [ME *pavilon* < OF *paveillon* < L *pāpiliōn-* (s. of *pāpiliō*) butterfly]

pa·vil·lon (*Fr.* PA VĒ YÔN′), *n., pl.* **-vil·lons** (*Fr.* -VĒ YÔN′). *Music.* the bell of a wind instrument. [< F: lit., pavilion]

pav·ing (pā′ving), *n.* **1.** a pavement. **2.** material for paving. [late ME]

pav·ior (pāv′yər), *n.* **1.** a paver. **2.** paving. Also, *esp. Brit.,* **pav′iour.** [alter. of late ME *pavier,* itself alter. of PAVER]

pav·is (pav′is), *n.* a large, oblong shield of the late 14th through the early 16th centuries, often covering the entire body, used esp. by archers and infantrymen. Also, **pav′ise.** [ME *paveys* < MF *pavais* < OIt *pavese,* lit., of PAVIA]

Pav·lo·dar (päv′lo däʀ′), *n.* a city in NE Kazakstan in the S Soviet Union in Asia. 259,000.

Pav·lov (pav′lov; *Russ.* päv′lof), *n.* **I·van Pe·tro·vich** (i vän′ pe tʀô′vich), 1849–1936, Russian physiologist. —**Pav·lov·i·an** (pav lō′vē ən, -lô′-, -lov′ē-), *adj.*

Pav·lo·va (päv lō′və; *Russ.* päv′lo vä), *n.* **An·na** (än′nä), 1885–1931, Russian ballet dancer.

pav·o·nine (pav′ə nīn′, -nin), *adj.* **1.** of or like the peacock. **2.** resembling the feathers of a peacock, as in coloring. [< L *pāvōnīn(us)* < *pāvō* (s. *pāvōn-*) peacock; see -INE[1]]

paw[1] (pô), *n.* **1.** the foot of an animal, esp. one having claws. —*v.t.* **2.** to strike or scrape with the paws. **3.** *Informal.* to handle clumsily, rudely, or with unwelcome familiarity. —*v.i.* **4.** to beat or scrape the floor, ground, etc., with the paws or feet. [ME *pawe,* var. of *powe* < MF *poue* (c. Pr *pauta*) < Gmc; cf. D *poot,* G *Pfote*]

paw[2] (pô), *n. Informal.* father; pa. [by alter.]

pawk·y (pô′kē), *adj.,* **pawk·i·er, pawk·i·est.** *Scot. and North Eng.* cunning; sly. [*pawk* trick (Scot) + -Y[1]] —**pawk′i·ly,** *adv.* —**pawk′i·ness,** *n.*

pawl (pôl), *n.* a pivoted object adapted to engage with the teeth of a ratchet wheel or the like so as to prevent movement or to impart motion. [? < D *pal;* see PALE[2]]

pawn[1] (pôn), *v.t.* **1.** to deposit as security, as for money borrowed, esp. with a pawnbroker. **2.** to pledge; stake; risk: *to pawn one's life.* —*n.* **3.** the state of being pawned: *jewels in pawn.* **4.** something that is pawned. **5.** a person serving as security; hostage. **6.** the act of pawning. [late ME (Scot) *paun* pledge (r. 12th-century *pand,* found in Latinized form) < MFlem *paen;* akin to D *pand,* G *Pfand* pledge; cf. OF *pan(d)* < Gmc] —**pawn′a·ble,** *adj.* —**pawn·er** (pô′nər), **paw·nor** (pô′nər, -nôr), *n.* —**Syn. 4.** pledge.

pawn[2] (pôn), *n.* **1.** *Chess.* one of eight men of one color and of the lowest value, usually moved one square at a time vertically and capturing diagonally. **2.** a person who is used or manipulated to further another's purposes. [ME *poun* < AF = MF *poon,* var. of *paon,* earlier *pe(h)on,* lit., walker; see PEON[1]]

pawn·bro·ker (pôn′brō′kər), *n.* a person whose business is lending money at interest on personal, movable property deposited with him until redeemed. —**pawn′bro′king, pawn′bro′ker·age, pawn′bro′ker·y,** *n.*

Paw·nee (pô nē′), *n., pl.* **-nees,** (*esp. collectively*) **-nee. 1.** a member of a confederacy of North American Plains Indians of Caddoan stock living in northern Oklahoma. **2.** the language of the Pawnee Indians, a Caddoan language.

pawn·shop (pôn′shop′), *n.* the shop of a pawnbroker.

pawn′ tick′et, a receipt given for goods left with a pawnbroker.

paw·paw (pô′pô′), *n.* papaw.

Paw·tuck·et (pô tuk′it), *n.* a city in NE Rhode Island. 76,984 (1970).

pax (paks), *n.* **1.** (*cap.*) a period in history marked by general peace, usually imposed by a dominant nation. **2.** *Eccles.* See **kiss of peace.** [< L: peace]

Pax (paks), *n.* the ancient Roman goddess of peace, identified with the Greek goddess Irene.

Pax Ro·ma·na (paks′ rō mā′nə; *Lat.* päks′ ʀō mä′nä), the peace imposed by ancient Rome on its dominions. [< L: Roman peace]

pax vo·bis·cum (päks′ wō bis′ko͝om; *Eng.* paks′ vō bis′kəm), *Latin.* peace be with you.

pay[1] (pā), *v.,* **paid** or (*Obs. except for def. 10*) **payed; pay·ing;** *n.; adj.* —*v.t.* **1.** to satisfy (a demand or obligation) by giving over money or the like, as in a business transaction: *to pay the rent.* **2.** to give over (money or the like), as in a business transaction: *to pay $100 a month for an apartment.* **3.** to give over money or the like to (a person or organization), as in order to do business or fulfill an obligation: *to pay the landlord.* **4.** to reward or give compensation for. **5.** to be profitable to. **6.** to yield as a return: *The stock pays four percent.* **7.** to retaliate upon or punish (usually fol. by *back, off,* or *out*): *He paid me back by not coming.* **8.** to give or render (attention, compliments, etc.) as if due or fitting. **9.** to make (a call, visit, etc.). **10.** *Naut.* **a.** to let (a vessel) fall off to leeward. **b.** to let out (a rope) by slackening. —*v.i.* **11.** to give over money or the like to acquire something or settle an obligation. **12.** to yield a return, profit, or advantage; be worthwhile: *It pays to be honest.* **13.** to undergo revenge or retribution. **14. pay off, a.** to pay someone everything that is due him, esp. as final wages. **b.** to pay a debt in full. **c.** *Slang.* to bribe. **d.** to retaliate upon or punish. **e.** *Naut.* to fall off to leeward. **15. pay one's way,** to pay one's portion of shared expenses. **16. pay up, a.** to pay fully. **b.** to pay upon demand. —*n.* **17.** wages, salary, or a stipend. **18.** paid employ: *in the pay of the enemy.* —*adj.* **19.** (of earth) containing a commercially valuable mineral deposit. **20.** operable or accessible on deposit of a coin: *a pay telephone; a pay toilet.* [ME *pay(en)* < OF *pai(er)* < L *pācāre* to pacify (by force of arms), ML: to satisfy, settle (a debt). See PEACE] —**pay·ee′,** *n.* —**Syn. 1.** settle, liquidate. **3.** compensate. **4.** reimburse, indemnify. **17.** income. PAY, WAGE or WAGES, SALARY, STIPEND are terms for amounts of money or equivalent benefits, usually given at a regular rate or at regular intervals, in return for services. PAY is the general term: *His pay went up every year.* WAGE usually designates the pay given at an hourly, daily, or weekly rate, often for manual or semiskilled work; WAGES usually means the cumulative amount paid at regular intervals for such work: *an hourly wage; weekly wages.* SALARY designates a fixed, periodic payment for regular work or services, usually computed on a monthly or yearly basis: *an annual salary paid in twelve equal monthly installments.* STIPEND designates a periodic payment, either as a professional salary or, more commonly, as a salary in return for special services or as a grant in support of creative or scholarly work: *an annual stipend for work as a consultant; a stipend to cover living expenses.*

pay[2] (pā), *v.t.,* **payed, pay·ing.** *Naut.* to coat or cover (seams, a ship's bottom, etc.) with pitch, tar, or the like. [< MF, OF *pei(er)* < L *picāre* to smear with pitch]

pay·a·ble (pā′ə bəl), *adj.* **1.** to be paid; due: *a loan payable in 30 days.* **2.** capable of or liable to being paid. [late ME]

pay·back (pā′bak′), *n.* the period of time required to recoup a capital investment. Also called **pay′back′ pe′riod.**

pay·check (pā′chek′), *n.* **1.** a bank check given as salary or wages. **2.** salary or wages. Also, **pay′ check′.**

pay·day (pā′dā′), *n.* the day on which wages are paid.

pay′ dirt′, 1. dirt, gravel, or ore that can be mined profitably. **2.** *Informal.* any source of success or wealth.

pay·er (pā′ər), *n.* **1.** a person who pays. **2.** the person named in a bill or note as having to pay the holder. [ME]

pay·load (pā′lōd′), *n.* **1.** *Com.* the part of a cargo producing revenue or income, usually expressed in weight. **2.** *Rocketry, Aeron.* the bomb load, warhead, cargo, or passenger load of an aircraft, a rocket, a missile, etc.

pay·mas·ter (pā′mas′tər, -mä′stər), *n.* a person authorized by a company, etc., to pay out wages or salaries.

pay·ment (pā′mənt), *n.* **1.** the act of paying. **2.** something that is paid. **3.** reward or punishment; requital. [ME, var. of *paiement* < MF]

pay·nim (pā′nim), *n. Archaic.* **1.** a pagan or heathen. **2.** a Muslim. [ME < OF < LL *paganism(us)* PAGANISM]

pay·off (pā′ôf′, -of′), *n.* **1.** the payment of a salary, debt, wager, etc. **2.** the time at which such payment is made. **3.** a settlement or reckoning, as in retribution or reward. **4.** *Informal.* the consequence, outcome, or final sequence in a series of events, actions, or circumstances.

pay·o·la (pā ō′lə), *n. Slang.* a secret or private payment in return for the promotion of a product, service, etc., through the abuse of one's position, influence, or facilities. [humorous coinage: PAY[1] + *-ola,* as in *Victrola*]

pay·out (pā′out′), *n.* **1.** the act or an instance of paying, expending, or disbursing. **2.** money paid, expended, or disbursed, as a dividend.

pay′ phone′, a coin-operated public telephone.

pay·roll (pā′rōl′), *n.* **1.** a list of persons to be paid, with the amount due to each. **2.** the sum total of these amounts. **3.** the money paid out. **4.** the total number of people employed by a business firm or organization. Also, **pay′ roll′.**

pay′ sta′tion. See **pay phone.**

Paz Es·tens·so·ro (päs′ es′tens sô′ʀô), **Vic·tor** (bēk′tôʀ), born 1907, Bolivian economist and statesman: president 1952–56 and 1960–64.

Pb, *Chem.* lead. [< L *plumbum*]

PBX, a telephone system for private use. [*P(rivate) B(ranch) E)x(change)*]

PC, 1. See **personal computer. 2.** professional corporation.

pc., 1. *pl.* **pcs.** piece. **2.** prices.

P/C, 1. petty cash. **2.** price current. Also, **p/c**

P.C., 1. Past Commander. **2.** *Brit.* Police Constable. **3.** Post Commander. **4.** *Brit.* Prince Consort.

p.c., 1. percent. **2.** petty cash. **3.** postal card. **4.** (in prescriptions) after eating; after meals. [< L *post cibōs*] **5.** price current.

PCB, *Chem.* polychlorinated biphenyl: any of a family of highly toxic compounds, now banned in the U.S., formerly used in industry and manufacturing and frequently discharged into rivers in chemical wastes: known to cause skin diseases in humans and suspected of causing birth defects and cancer in animals.

P-Celt·ic (pē′sel′tik, -kel′-), *n.* **1.** the subbranch of Celtic in which the Proto-Indo-European *kw*-sound became a *p*-sound. Welsh, Breton, Cornish, and Gaulish belong to P-Celtic. —*adj.* **2.** of or belonging to P-Celtic.

pcf, pounds per cubic foot.

pci, pounds per cubic inch.

PCP, *Slang.* a powerful illicit hallucinogenic drug made from phencyclidine. [*p(hen)c(yclidine)* + perh. *(peace) p(ill),* earlier designation]

pct., percent.

Pd, *Chem.* palladium.

pd., paid.

P.D., 1. per diem. **2.** Police Department.

p.d., 1. per diem. **2.** potential difference.

PDB, paradichlorobenzene.

pdl, poundal.

P.D.Q., *Slang.* immediately; at once: *You'd better get started P.D.Q.* [*p(retty) d(amn) q(uick)*]

pe (pā; *Heb.* pā), *n.* the 17th letter of the Hebrew alphabet. [< Heb]

P.E., 1. Presiding Elder. **2.** Also, **p.e.** printer's error. **3.** *Statistics.* probable error. **4.** Protestant Episcopal.

p/e, price-earnings: *the p/e ratio.* Also, **P/E**

pea[1] (pē), *n., pl.* **peas,** (*Archaic or Brit. Dial.*) **pease;** *adj.* —*n.* **1.** the round, highly nutritious seed of a leguminous plant, *Pisum sativum.* **2.** the plant itself. **3.** any of various related or similar plants or their seed, as the chickpea. **4.** something resembling a pea, esp. in being small and round. —*adj.* **5.** pertaining to, growing, containing, or cooked with peas. [back formation from PEASE, wrongly taken as pl.]

pea[2] (pē), *n. Naut.* bill[3] (def. 3). [short for PEAK[1]]

Pea·bod·y (pē′bod′ē, -bə dē), *n.* **1. Endicott,** 1857–1944, U.S. educator. **2. George,** 1795–1869, U.S. merchant, banker, and philanthropist in England. **3.** a city in NE Massachusetts. 48,080 (1970).

peace (pēs), *n., v.,* **peaced, peac·ing,** *interj.* —*n.* **1.** the normal, nonwarring condition of a nation, a group of nations, or the world. **2.** a historical period during which such a condition exists. **3.** (*often cap.*) an agreement or treaty that ends a war: *the Peace of Ryswick.* **4.** a state of harmony among people or groups. **5.** the freedom from disorder normal in a community: *a breach of the peace.* **6.** cessation of or freedom from any strife or dissension. **7.** freedom of the mind from annoyance, distraction, etc. **8.** a state or condition conducive to, proceeding from, or characterized by tranquillity. **9.** silence; stillness. **10. hold one's peace,** to refrain from or cease speaking. **11. keep the peace,** to maintain public order. **12. make one's peace with,** to become reconciled with. **13. make peace,** to ask for or arrange a cessation of hostilities or antagonism. —*v.i.* **14.** *Obs.* to be or become silent. —*interj.* **15.** keep still! silence! [ME *pes* < OF, var. of *pais* < L *pax* (s. *pāc-*); akin to PACT] —**peace′less,** *adj.* —**peace′like′,** *adj.* —**Syn. 3.** armistice, truce, pact. **4.** rapport, concord, amity. **8, 9.** calm, quiet. —**Ant. 7.** insecurity, disturbance.

peace·a·ble (pē′sə bəl), *adj.* **1.** inclined to avoid strife or dissension. **2.** peaceful. [ME *pesible* < MF *paisible*] —**peace′a·ble·ness,** *n.* —**peace′a·bly,** *adv.* —**Syn. 1.** friendly, amiable. See **pacific.** —**Ant. 1.** quarrelsome, hostile.

Peace′ Corps′, a civilian agency, sponsored by the U.S. government, that sends volunteers to instruct citizens of underdeveloped countries in the execution of industrial, agricultural, educational, and public-health programs.

peace′ dove′ (duv), dove[1] (def. 5).

peace·ful (pēs′fəl), *adj.* **1.** characterized by peace; free from strife or disorder. **2.** of, pertaining to, or characteristic of a state or time of peace. **3.** peaceable; not argumentative or quarrelsome. [ME *pesful*] —**peace′ful·ly,** *adv.* —**peace′ful·ness,** *n.*

—**Syn. 1.** PEACEFUL, PLACID, SERENE, TRANQUIL refer to what is characterized by lack of strife or agitation. PEACEFUL today is rarely applied to persons; it refers to situations, scenes, and activities free of disturbances or, occasionally, of warfare: *a peaceful life.* PLACID, SERENE, TRANQUIL are used mainly of persons; when used of things (usually elements of nature) there is a touch of personification. PLACID suggests an unruffled calm that verges on complacency: *a placid disposition; a placid stream.* SERENE is a somewhat nobler word; when used of persons it suggests dignity, composure, and graciousness: *a serene old woman;* when applied to nature there is a suggestion of mellowness: *the serene landscapes of autumn.* TRANQUIL implies a command of emotions, often because of strong faith, that keeps a person unagitated even in the midst of excitement or danger. See also **pacific.**

peace·keep·ing (pēs′kē′ping), *n.* **1.** the maintenance of international peace and security by the United Nations through military force, as by operations in a particular area. **2.** an instance of this. —*adj.* **3.** for or pertaining to peacekeeping: *peacekeeping operations; peacekeeping assessments.*

peace·mak·er (pēs′mā′kər), *n.* a person, group, or nation that tries to make peace. [ME] —**peace′mak′ing,** *n., adj.*

peace′ of′fering, 1. a sacrificial offering made in order to assure communion with God. Ex. 20:24; Lev. 7:11–18. **2.** any offering made to procure peace.

peace′ of′ficer, a civil officer appointed to preserve the public peace, as a sheriff or constable.

peace′ pipe′, calumet.

Peace′ Riv′er, a river in W Canada, flowing NE from the Rocky Mountains in E British Columbia through Alberta to the Slave River. 1050 mi. long.

peace·time (pēs′tīm′), *n.* **1.** a time, or period, of peace. —*adj.* **2.** of or for such a period.

peach[1] (pēch), *n.* **1.** the subacid, juicy, drupaceous fruit of a tree, *Prunus Persica.* **2.** the tree itself, cultivated in temperate climates. **3.** a light pinkish yellow, as of a peach. **4.** *Informal.* a person or thing that is especially admired or enjoyed. —*adj.* **5.** made or cooked with peaches or a flavor like that of a peach. [ME *peche* < MF < LL *persica,* fem. sing., L, neut. pl. of *Persicus* Persian; r. OE *persic* (masc.) < L *Persic(us)*] —**peach′like′,** *adj.*

peach[2] (pēch), *v.i. Slang.* to inform against an accomplice or associate. [late ME *peche,* aph. var. of ME *apeche* < AF *apech(er)* < LL *impedicāre* to hold up. See IMPEACH] —**peach′er,** *n.*

peach·blow (pēch′blō′), *n.* a delicate yellowish pink.

peach′ Mel′ba, a dessert consisting of half a cooked peach served with vanilla ice cream and Melba sauce. Also, **peach′ mel′ba.**

peach·y (pē′chē), *adj.,* **peach·i·er, peach·i·est. 1.** resembling a peach, as in color or appearance. **2.** *Informal.* excellent; wonderful.

pea·coat (pē′kōt′), *n.* See **pea jacket.** [*pea* (see PEA JACKET) + COAT]

pea·cock (pē′kok′), *n., pl.* **-cocks,** (*esp. collectively*) **-cock,** *v.* —*n.* **1.** the male of the peafowl, distinguished by its long, erectile, greenish, iridescent tail coverts that are brilliantly marked with ocellated spots. **2.** any peafowl. **3.** a vain, self-conscious person. —*v.i.* **4.** to make a vainglorious display; strut like a peacock. [ME *pecok* = *pe-* (OE *pēa* peafowl < L *pāvōn-,* s. of *pāvō* peacock) + *cok* COCK[1]] —**pea′cock′ish,** *adj.* —**pea′cock′ish·ly,** *adv.*

Peacock (Peafowl), *Pavo cristatus* (Length 6½ to 7½ ft.)

Pea·cock (pē′kok′), *n.* **Thomas Love,** 1785–1866, English poet and novelist.

pea′cock blue′, a lustrous greenish blue, as of certain peacock feathers.

pea′cock ore′, bornite.

pea′ crab′, any of several tiny crabs of the family *Pinnotheridae,* the female of which lives as a commensal in the shells of bivalve mollusks.

pea·fowl (pē′foul′), *n., pl.* **-fowls,** (*esp. collectively*) **-fowl.** any of several gallinaceous birds of the genera *Pavo,* of India, Ceylon, southeastern Asia, and the East Indies, and *Afropavo,* of Africa. Cf. **peacock, peahen.** [*pea* + FOWL; see PEACOCK]

pea′ green′, a medium or yellowish green.

pea·hen (pē′hen′), *n.* the female peafowl. [late ME *pehenne.* See PEACOCK, HEN]

pea′ jack′et, a sailor's double-breasted jacket of thick navy-blue wool. [*pea,* var. sp. of *pay, pee, pie* coat of coarse woolen cloth (late ME *pee, pey, pie;* akin to D *pij,* EFris *pey,* dial. Sw *paje*) + JACKET; ? modeled on NFris *pijekkat*]

peak[1] (pēk), *n.* **1.** the pointed top of a mountain or ridge. **2.** a mountain with a pointed summit. **3.** the pointed top of anything. **4.** the highest or most important point or level: *the peak of his career.* **5.** the maximum point, degree, or volume of anything. **6.** a projecting point. **7.** See **widow's peak. 8.** a projecting front piece, or visor, of a cap. **9.** *Naut.* **a.** the contracted part of a ship's hull at the bow or the stern. **b.** the upper after corner of a sail that is extended by a gaff. **c.** the outer extremity of a gaff. —*v.t.* **10.** *Naut.* to raise the after end of (a yard, gaff, etc.) to or toward an angle above the horizontal. —*v.i.* **11.** to project in a peak. [? < MLG *pēk* pick, pike] —**peak′less,** *adj.* —**peak′like′,** *adj.* —**Syn. 1, 2, 4.** pinnacle. **4.** acme, zenith. —**Ant. 4.** abyss, nadir.

peak[2] (pēk), *v.i.* to become weak, thin, and sickly. [?] —**peak′ish,** *adj.* —**peak′y,** *adj.*

peaked[1] (pēkt, pē′kid), *adj.* having a peak. [late ME *pekyd.* See PEAK[1], -ED[2]]

peak·ed[2] (pē′kid), *adj.* pale; sickly. [PEAK[2] + -ED[2]]

peal (pēl), *n.* **1.** a loud, prolonged ringing of bells. **2.** a set of bells tuned to one another. **3.** a series of changes rung on a set of bells. **4.** any loud, sustained sound or series of sounds. —*v.t.* **5.** to sound loudly and sonorously. **6.** *Obs.* to assail with loud sounds. —*v.i.* **7.** to sound forth in a peal; resound. [ME *pele,* akin to *peal* to beat, strike (now dial.)]

Peale (pēl), *n.* **1. Charles Will·son** (wil′sən), 1741–1827, U.S. painter (father of Raphaelle Peale and Rembrandt Peale). **2.** his brother **James,** 1749–1831, U.S. painter. **3. Raph·a·elle** (raf′ā el′, -ē el′, rā′fā-, -fē-), 1774–1825, U.S. painter. **4.** his brother **Rem·brandt** (rem′brant), 1778–1860, U.S. painter.

Pe·a·no (pē ä′nō; *It.* pe ä′nô), *n.* **Giu·sep·pe** (jo͞o zep′pe), 1858–1932, Italian mathematician.

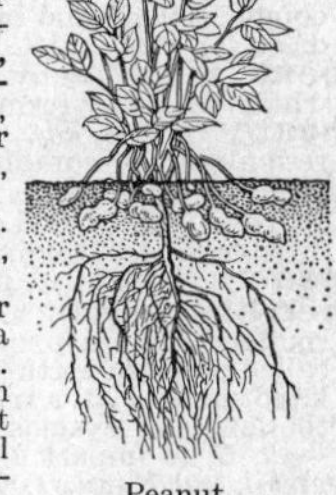

Peanut, *Arachis hypogaea*

pea·nut (pē′nut′), *n.* **1.** the pod or fruit or the enclosed edible seed of a leguminous plant, *Arachis hypogaea.* The pod is forced underground in growing, where it ripens. **2.** the plant itself. **3. peanuts,** *Slang.* a very small or trifling amount, esp. of money: *working for peanuts.* —*adj.* **4.** of or pertaining to the peanut or peanuts. **5.** made with or from peanuts.

pea′nut but′ter, a smooth paste made from finely ground roasted peanuts, used as a spread or in cookery.

pea′nut gal′lery, 1. *Informal.* the rearmost section of seats in the balcony of a theater. **2.** *Slang.* a source of insignificant criticism: *No remarks from the peanut gallery.*

pea′nut oil′, a yellow to greenish oil expressed or extracted from peanuts, used chiefly as a salad oil, as a vehicle for medicines, and in the manufacture of margarine and soap.

pear (pâr), *n.* the edible fruit, typically rounded but elongated and growing smaller toward the stem, of a rosaceous tree, *Pyrus communis.* [ME *pe(e)re,* OE *peru* < LL *pira,* fem. sing., L, pl. of *pirum* pear]

pearl[1] (pûrl), *n.* **1.** a smooth, rounded concretion formed within the shells of certain mollusks to enclose irritating foreign objects, and valued as a gem when lustrous and finely colored. **2.** an imitation of this. **3.** something similar in form, luster, etc., as a dewdrop. **4.** someone or something precious or choice. **5.** a very pale gray, commonly with a bluish tinge. **6.** mother-of-pearl (def. 1). **7.** *Print.* a 5-point type. **8. cast pearls before swine,** to offer or give something of value to those incapable of appreciating it. —*v.t.* **9.** to adorn or stud with or as with pearls. **10.** to make like pearls, as in form or color. —*v.i.* **11.** to dive, fish, or search for pearls. **12.** to assume a pearllike form or appearance. —*adj.* **13.** of the color or luster of pearl; nacreous. **14.** of or pertaining to pearls. **15.** set with a pearl or pearls. **16.** set or covered with mother-of-pearl. [ME *perle* < MF < It *perla* < VL **pernula,* dim. of L *perna* sea mussel] —**pearl′er,** *n.* —**pearl′like′,** *adj.*

pearl[2] (pûrl), *v.t., n.* purl[1].

pearl′ bar′ley, barley milled into small, round grains, used in cooking, esp. in soups.

pearl′ gray′, a very pale bluish gray.

Pearl′ Har′bor, a harbor near Honolulu, on S Oahu, in Hawaii: surprise attack by Japan on the U.S. naval base December 7, 1941, bringing the U.S. into World War II.

pearl·ite (pûr′līt), *n.* **1.** *Metall.* a microscopic lamellar structure found in iron or steel, composed of alternating layers of ferrite and cementite. **2.** *Petrog.* perlite. —**pearl·it·ic** (pûr lit′ik), *adj.*

pearl·ized (pûr′līzd), *adj.* resembling or made to resemble mother-of-pearl.

pearl′ mil′let, a tall grass, *Pennisetum glaucum,* cultivated in Africa, the Orient, and the southern U.S. for its edible seeds and as a forage plant.

pearl′ oys′ter, any of several marine bivalve mollusks of the family *Pteriidae,* some of which form pearls of great value: found in eastern Asia and off the coasts of Panama and Lower California.

Pearl′ Riv′er, 1. a river flowing from central Mississippi into the Gulf of Mexico. 485 mi. long. **2.** Chu-Kiang.

pearl·y (pûr′lē), *adj.,* **pearl·i·er, pearl·i·est. 1.** like a pearl, esp. in being white or lustrous; nacreous. **2.** adorned with or abounding in pearls, pearl, or mother-of-pearl. [late ME *peerly*] —**pearl′i·ness,** *n.*

Pearl′y Gates′, *Informal.* the entrance to heaven.

pearl′y nau′tilus, nautilus (def. 1). See illus. at **nautilus.**

pear-shaped (pâr′shāpt′), *adj.* **1.** having the shape of a pear; tapering near the top and bulging toward the base or bottom. **2.** (of a vocal tone) clear, resonant, and without harshness; full-bodied.

Pear·son (pēr′sən), *n.* **1. Karl,** 1857–1936, English statistician. **2. Lester Bowles** (bōlz), 1897–1972, Canadian diplomat and political leader: Nobel peace prize 1957; prime minister 1963–68.

peart (pērt, pyert), *adj. Dial.* lively; brisk; cheerful. [var. of PERT] —**peart′ly,** *adv.* —**peart′ness,** *n.*

Pea·ry (pēr′ē), *n.* **Robert Edwin,** 1856–1920, U.S. admiral and arctic explorer.

peas·ant (pez′ənt), *n.* **1.** one of a class of persons, as in European countries, of inferior social rank, usually engaged in farm labor. **2.** a rude, unsophisticated, usually uneducated person. **—***adj.* **3.** of, pertaining to, or characteristic of peasants or their traditions, way of life, crafts, etc. **4.** of or pertaining to rude, unsophisticated, or uneducated persons. [late ME *paissaunt* < AF, MF *paisant*, OF *paisenc* = *pais* country (< L *pāgus* country district) + *-enc* < Gmc; see -ING[1]]

peas·ant·ry (pez′ən trē), *n.* **1.** peasants collectively. **2.** the status or character of a peasant.

pease (pēz), *n., pl.* **pease.** *Archaic.* **1.** a pea. **2.** a pl. of **pea**[1]. [ME *pese*, OE *peose*, *pise* < LL *pisa*, fem. sing., L, pl. of *pisum* < Gk *píson* pea, pulse]

pease′ pud′ding, *Chiefly Brit.* a pudding of strained split peas mixed with egg.

pea·shoot·er (pē′sho͞o′tər), *n.* a tube through which dried peas, beans, etc., are blown, used as a toy.

pea′ soup′, 1. a thick soup made from split peas. **2.** *Informal.* dense, yellow fog.

peat (pēt), *n.* a highly organic soil, composed of partially decayed vegetable matter which is more than 50 percent combustible, found in marshy or damp regions: cut and then dried for use as fuel. [ME *pete* (AL *peta*) < ?]

peat′ moss′, any moss, esp. of the genus *Sphagnum*, from which peat may form.

peat·y (pē′tē), *adj.*, **peat·i·er, peat·i·est.** of, pertaining to, resembling, or containing peat.

pea·vey (pē′vē), *n., pl.* **-veys.** a cant hook having a sharply pointed end, used in handling logs. [named after Joseph *Peavey*, the inventor]

pea·vy (pē′vē), *n., pl.* **-vies.** peavey.

peb·ble (peb′əl), *n., v.,* **-bled, -bling.** **—***n.* **1.** a small rounded stone, esp. one worn by the action of water. **2.** Also called **peb′ble leath′er.** leather that has been given a granulated surface. **3.** a transparent, colorless rock crystal used for the lenses of eyeglasses. **4.** a lens made from this crystal. **—***v.t.* **5.** to impart a granulated surface to (leather). [ME *pibbil*, *puble*, etc., OE *pæbbel* (in place names)]

peb·bly (peb′lē), *adj.* **1.** having or covered with pebbles. **2.** (of a texture, design, etc.) having a granular surface.

pe·can (pi kän′, pi kan′, pē′kan), *n.* **1.** a hickory tree, *Carya illinoensis* (*C. Pecan*), indigenous to the lower Mississippi valley and grown in the southern U.S. for its oval, smooth-shelled nut having a sweet, oily, edible kernel: the state tree of Texas. **2.** the nut. [< Cree *pakan*]

pec·ca·ble (pek′ə bəl), *adj.* liable to sin or error. [< ML *peccābil(is)*. See PECCAVI, -BLE] **—pec′ca·bil′i·ty,** *n.*

pec·ca·dil·lo (pek′ə dil′ō), *n., pl.* **-loes, -los.** a petty sin or offense; trifling fault. [< Sp *pecadillo*, dim. of *pecado* sin < L *peccātum* transgression, n. use of neut. of ptp. of *peccāre* to err, offend]

pec·cant (pek′ənt), *adj.* **1.** sinning; guilty of moral offense. **2.** violating a rule; faulty; wrong. [< L *peccant-* (s. of *peccāns*, prp. of *peccāre*) = *pecc-* sin + *-ant-* -ANT] **—pec′can·cy,** *n.*

pec·ca·ry (pek′ə rē), *n., pl.* **-ries,** (*esp. collectively*) **-ry.** any of several piglike, artiodactylous, hoofed mammals of the genus *Tayassu*, of North and South America, ranging from Texas to Paraguay, as *T. angulatus* **(collared peccary),** having a dark gray coat with a white collar. [< Carib; akin to Apalai dial. *pakira*]

Collared peccary, *Tayassu angulatus* (About 2 ft. high at shoulder; length 3 ft.)

pec·ca·vi (pe kā′vē, -kä′vē), *n., pl.* **-vis.** any confession of guilt or sin. [< L, perf. 1st. pers. sing. of *peccāre* to go wrong]

Pe·chen·ga (pe cheng′gä), *n.* **1.** a region in NW RSFSR on the Finnish border: ceded by Finland 1944. 3860 sq. mi. **2.** an ice-free seaport in this region. Finnish, **Petsamo.**

Pe·cho·ra (pe chô′rä), *n.* a river in the NE Soviet Union in Europe, flowing from the Ural Mountains to the Arctic Ocean. 1110 mi. long.

peck[1] (pek), *n.* **1.** a dry measure of 8 quarts; the fourth part of a bushel, equal to 537.6 cubic inches. **2.** a container for measuring this quantity. *Abbr.*: pk, pk. [ME *pek* < OF < ?]

peck[2] (pek), *v.t.* **1.** to jab with the beak, as a bird does, or with something pointed, esp. with quick, repeated movements. **2.** to make (a hole) by such strokes. **—***v.i.* **3.** to make strokes with the beak or a pointed instrument. **4.** to pick or nibble at food. **—***n.* **5.** a quick stroke, as in pecking. **6.** a hole or mark made by pecking. [ME *pekk(en)* < MFlem; akin to PICK[1]]

peck·er (pek′ər), *n.* **1.** a person or thing that pecks. **2.** *Slang* (*vulgar*). penis. **3.** *Brit. Slang.* spirits or courage.

peck·er·wood (pek′ər wo͝od′), *n.* *Southern and Midland U.S.* woodpecker. [inversion of WOODPECKER]

peck′ing or′der, 1. a social relationship within a flock of poultry in which any one member may assert his dominance by pecking weaker members, but is in turn pecked by those stronger than he. **2.** a similar relationship within a human social group. Also, **peck′ or′der.**

Peck·sniff·i·an (pek snif′ē ən), *adj.* hypocritically affecting benevolence or high moral principles. [after Seth *Pecksniff*, character in *Martin Chuzzlewit*, a novel (1843) by Dickens; see -IAN] **—Peck′sniff·er·y,** *n.*

Pe·cos (pā′kəs, -kōs), *n.* a river flowing SE from N New Mexico through W Texas to the Rio Grande. 735 mi. long.

Pe′cos Bill′, a legendary cowboy who performed many fantastic feats including digging the Rio Grande River.

Pecs (pāch), *n.* a city in SW Hungary. 132,000 (est. 1964). German, **Fünfkirchen.**

pec·tase (pek′tās), *n.* *Biochem.* an enzyme found in various fruits and involved in the formation of pectic acid from pectin. [PECT(IN) + -ASE]

pec·tate (pek′tāt), *n.* *Chem.* a salt or ester of pectic acid. [PECT(IC) + -ATE[2]]

pec·ten (pek′tən), *n., pl.* **-tens, -ti·nes** (-tə nēz′). **1.** *Zool., Anat.* **a.** a comblike part or process. **b.** a pigmented vascular membrane with parallel folds suggesting the teeth of a comb, projecting into the vitreous humor of the eye in birds and reptiles. **2.** any bivalve mollusk of the genus *Pecten;* scallop. [< L: comb, akin to *pectere*, Gk *pékein* to comb, card]

pec·tic (pek′tik), *adj.* pertaining to pectin. [< Gk *pēktik(ós)* congealing = *pēkt(ós)* congealed (verbid of *pēgnýein* to make solid) + *-ikos* -IC]

pec′tic ac′id, *Chem.* any of several water-insoluble products of the hydrolysis of pectin esters.

pec·tin (pek′tin), *n.* *Biochem.* a white, amorphous, colloidal carbohydrate of high molecular weight, occurring in ripe fruits: used in fruit jellies, pharmaceuticals, and cosmetics because of its thickening and emulsifying properties and its ability to solidify to a gel. [< Gk *pēkt(ós)* fixed (see PECTIC) + -IN[2]] **—pec·ti·na·ceous** (pek′tə nā′shəs), *adj.*

pec·ti·nate (pek′tə nāt′), *adj.* formed into or having closely parallel, toothlike projections; comblike. Also, **pec′ti·nat′ed.** [< L *pectināt(us)*, ptp. of *pectināre*. See PECTEN, -ATE[1]] **—pec′ti·nate′ly,** *adv.* **—pec′ti·na′tion,** *n.*

pec·tize (pek′tīz), *v.t., v.i.,* **-tized, -tiz·ing.** to change into a jelly. [< Gk *pēkt(ós)* fixed (see PECTIC) + -IZE] **—pec′tiz·a·ble,** *adj.* **—pec′ti·za′tion,** *n.*

pec·to·ral (pek′tər əl), *adj.* **1.** of, in, on, or pertaining to the chest or breast; thoracic. **2.** worn on the breast or chest. **3.** of or for diseases of the lungs. **—***n.* **4.** something worn on the breast. **5.** See **pectoral fin. 6.** *Anat.* a pectoral part or organ, as a muscle. [late ME < L *pectorāl(is)* of the breast (*pector-*, s. of *pectus* breast, + *-ālis* -AL[1]); *pectorāle* breastplate (n. use of neut. of adj.)] **—pec′to·ral·ly,** *adv.*

pec′toral fin′, (in fishes) either of a pair of fins usually situated behind the head, one on each side, and corresponding to the forelimbs of higher vertebrates.

pec′toral gir′dle, 1. (in vertebrates) a bony or cartilaginous arch supporting the forelimbs. **2.** (in man) the bony arch, formed by the clavicle or collarbone and scapula or shoulder blade, that attaches the upper limb to the axial skeleton. Also called **pec′toral arch′.**

pec·u·late (pek′yə lāt′), *v.t., v.i.,* **-lat·ed, -lat·ing.** to steal or take dishonestly (money or property entrusted to one's care); embezzle. [v. use of obs. *peculate* embezzlement < L *pecūlāt(us)* (4th decl. n.) < ptp. s. of *pecūlārī* to embezzle, lit., to make public property private. See PECULIAR, -ATE[1]] **—pec′u·la′tion,** *n.* **—pec′u·la′tor,** *n.*

pe·cu·liar (pi kyo͞ol′yər), *adj.* **1.** strange; queer; odd. **2.** uncommon; unusual. **3.** distinguished in nature or character from others. **4.** belonging characteristically (usually fol. by *to*): *an expression peculiar to Canadians.* **5.** belonging exclusively to some person, group, or thing: *the peculiar properties of a drug.* **—***n.* **6.** a property or privilege belonging exclusively or characteristically to a person. **7.** *Brit.* a particular parish or church that is exempted from the jurisdiction of the ordinary or bishop in whose diocese it lies and is governed by another. [< L *pecūliār(is)* as one's own. See PECULIUM, -AR[1]] **—pe·cu′liar·ly,** *adv.* **—Syn. 1.** eccentric, bizarre. See **strange. 2.** extraordinary, singular. **3.** distinctive. **5.** individual, particular, special, unique. **—Ant. 2.** common.

pe·cu·li·ar·i·ty (pi kyo͞o′lē ar′i tē, -kyo͞ol yar′-), *n., pl.* **-ties. 1.** a characteristic or habit that is odd or unusual. **2.** something that is odd. **3.** the quality or condition of being peculiar. **4.** a distinguishing quality or characteristic. [< LL *pecūliāritās*] **—Syn. 1.** idiosyncrasy. **4.** See **feature.**

pe·cu·li·um (pi kyo͞o′lē əm), *n.* **1.** private property. **2.** *Roman Law.* property given by a paterfamilias to those subject to him, or by a master to his slave. [< L, dim. of *pecū* money, orig. flock of sheep, akin to *pecus* cattle. See FEE]

pe·cu·ni·ar·y (pi kyo͞o′nē er′ē), *adj.* **1.** pertaining to or consisting of money. **2.** (of a legal offense) involving a money penalty or fine. [< L *pecūniāri(us)* < *pecūnia* property, money (*pecū* flock of sheep + unexplained *-n-* + *-ia* -IA); see -ARY] **—pe·cu·ni·ar·i·ly** (pi kyo͞o′nē âr′i lē), *adv.* **—Syn. 1.** See **financial.**

ped-[1], var. of **pedo-**[1] before a vowel: *pedagogic.* Also, **paed-, paedo-.**

ped-[2], var. of **pedi-**[1] before a vowel.

ped-[3], var. of **pedo-**[2] before a vowel: *pedalfer.*

-ped, var. of **pedi-**[1], as final element of compound words: *pinnatiped.* Also, **-pede.** Cf. **-pod.**

ped., pedal.

ped·a·gog·ic (ped′ə goj′ik, -gō′jik), *adj.* of or pertaining to a pedagogue or pedagogy. Also, **ped′a·gog′i·cal, paedagogic.** [< Gk *paidagōgik(ós)* of a boy's tutor] **—ped′a·gog′i·cal·ly,** *adv.*

ped·a·gog·ics (ped′ə goj′iks, -gō′jiks), *n.* (*construed as sing.*) the science or art of teaching or education.

ped·a·gog·ism (ped′ə gog′iz əm, -gô′giz-), *n.* the manner, method, or characteristics of pedagogues. Also, **ped·a·gogu·ism** (ped′ə gog′iz əm, -gô′giz-).

ped·a·gogue (ped′ə gog′, -gôg′), *n.* **1.** a teacher; schoolteacher. **2.** a person who is pedantic, dogmatic, and formal. Also, **ped·a·gog.** [ME *pedagoge* < L *paedagōg(us)* < Gk *paidagōgós* a boy's tutor] **—ped′a·gogu′er·y, ped′a·gog′er·y,** *n.* **—ped′a·gogu′ish, ped′a·gog′ish,** *adj.*

ped·a·go·gy (ped′ə gō′jē, -goj′ē), *n.* **1.** the function or work of a teacher; teaching. **2.** the art or method of teaching. Also, **paedagogy.** [< Gk *paidagōgía* office of a boy's tutor]

ped·al (ped′əl *for 1–4;* pēd′əl *for 5–7*), *n., v.,* **-aled, -al·ing** or (*esp. Brit.*) **-alled, -al·ling,** *adj.* **—***n.* **1.** a foot-operated lever or part used to control, activate, or supply power for certain mechanisms. **2.** *Music.* **a.** a foot-operated keyboard, as on an organ. **b.** any of the keys of such a keyboard. **c.** See **pedal point. —***v.i.* **3.** to work or use a pedal or pedals. **—***v.t.* **4.** to work the pedals of. **—***adj.* **5.** of or pertaining to a foot or the feet. **6.** of or pertaining to a pedal or pedals. **7.** using pedals: *a pedal mechanism.* [< L *pedāl(is)* of the feet]

pe·dal·fer (pi dal′fər), *n.* a soil rich in alumina and iron, with few or no carbonates. [PED-[3] + L *al(ūmen)* ALUM + *fer(rum)* iron]

ped′al point′, *Music.* a tone sustained by one part, usually the bass, while other parts progress without reference to it.

ped′al push′ers, women's or girls' calf-length slacks.

ped·ant (ped′ənt), *n.* **1.** a person who makes an excessive or inappropriate show of learning. **2.** a person who overemphasizes rules or minor details. [< It *pedante* teacher, pedant < *ped-*, comb. form of *piede* foot (in meaning of servile follower); see -ANT] **—pe·dan·tic** (pə dan′tik), **pe·dan′ti·cal,** *adj.* **—pe·dan′ti·cal·ly,** *adv.*

pe·dan·ti·cism (pə dan′ti siz′əm), *n.* pedantry.

ped·ant·ry (ped′ən trē), *n., pl.* **-ries.** **1.** the character or practices of a pedant, as undue display of learning. **2.** slavish attention to rules, details, etc. **3.** an instance of being pedantic. [< It *pedanteria*]

ped·ate (ped′āt), *adj.* **1.** having a foot or feet. **2.** resembling a foot. **3.** having divisions like toes. **4.** *Bot.* (of a leaf) palmately parted or divided with the lateral lobes or divisions cleft or divided. [< L *pedāt(us)*] —**ped′ate·ly,** *adv.*

pedati-, a combining form meaning "pedate," used in the formation of compound words. [comb. form repr. L *pedāt(us)* PEDATE + -I-]

Pedate leaves
A, Bird's-foot violet, *Viola pedata;* B, Arum, genus *Arum*

ped·dle (ped′əl), *v.,* **-dled, -dling.** —*v.t.* **1.** to carry (goods, wares, etc.) from place to place for sale at retail; hawk. **2.** to deal out or dispense: *to peddle radical ideas.* —*v.i.* **3.** to travel from place to place with goods, wares, etc., for sale at retail. **4.** to occupy oneself with trifles; trifle. [appar. back formation from PEDDLER and confused with PIDDLE]

ped·dler (ped′lər), *n.* a person who peddles. Also, **pedlar, pedler.** [ME *pedlere,* unexplained var. of *peder* (ME *peoddare*) < *ped* basket (ME *pedde*)]

ped·dling (ped′liŋ), *adj.* trifling; paltry; piddling. —**ped′dling·ly,** *adv.*

-pede, var. of **-ped:** *centipede.*

ped·er·ast (ped′ə rast′, pē′də-), *n.* a man who engages in pederasty. Also, **paederast.** [< Gk *paiderast(ḗs)* lover of boys = *paid-* PED-¹ + *erastḗs* lover < *erân* to love]

ped·er·as·ty (ped′ə ras′tē, pē′də-), *n.* sexual relations between two males, esp. when one is a minor. Also, **paederasty.** [< NL *pederastia* < Gk *paiderastía* love of boys] —**ped′er·as′tic,** *adj.* —**ped′er·as′ti·cal·ly,** *adv.*

ped·es·tal (ped′i stəl), *n., v.,* **-taled, -tal·ing** or (*esp. Brit.*) **-talled, -tal·ling.** —*n.* **1.** an architectural support for a column, statue, vase, or the like. **2.** a supporting structure or piece; base. **3.** *Furniture.* a support for the top of a table or desk. **4. set** or **put on a pedestal,** to glorify; idealize. —*v.t.* **5.** to put on or supply with a pedestal. [alter. of MF *piedestal* < It *piedestallo,* var. of *piedistallo,* lit., foot of stall]

pe·des·tri·an (pə des′trē ən), *n.* **1.** a person who travels on foot. —*adj.* **2.** going or performed on foot. **3.** of or pertaining to walking. **4.** lacking in vitality, imagination, or distinction. [< L *pedestri-* (s. of *pedester* on foot < *pedes* one that goes on foot; see PEDI-¹) + -AN]

pe·des·tri·an·ism (pə des′trē ə niz′əm), *n.* **1.** the exercise or practice of walking. **2.** commonplace or prosaic manner, quality, etc.

pedi-¹, a learned borrowing from Latin meaning "foot," used in the formation of compound words: *pediform.* Also, **ped-², -ped.** [comb. form of L *ped-* (s. of *pēs*)]

pedi-², var. of **pedo-¹.**

pe·di·a·tri·cian (pē′dē ə trish′ən, ped′ē-), *n.* a physician who specializes in pediatrics. Also, *esp. Brit.,* **paediatrician.** Also, **pe·di·at·rist** (pē′dē a′trist, ped′ē-).

pe·di·at·rics (pē′dē a′triks, ped′ē-), *n.* (*construed as sing.*) the science dealing with the medical and hygienic care of children and with the diseases of children. Also, *esp. Brit.,* **paediatrics.** —**pe′di·at′ric,** *adj.*

ped·i·cab (ped′ə kab′), *n.* (esp. in Southeast Asia) a three-wheeled public conveyance operated by pedals, typically one having a hooded cab for two passengers mounted behind the driver.

ped·i·cel (ped′i səl, -sel′), *n.* **1.** *Bot.* **a.** a small stalk. **b.** an ultimate division of a common peduncle. **c.** one of the subordinate stalks in a branched inflorescence, bearing a single flower. **2.** *Zool.* a pedicle or peduncle. [< NL *pedicell(us),* dim. of L *pediculus* a little foot. See PEDICLE] —**ped·i·cel·lar** (ped′i sel′ər), *adj.*

A, Pedicel
B, Peduncle

ped·i·cel·late (ped′i sel′it, -āt, ped′i sə lit, -lāt′), *adj.* having a pedicel or pedicels. —**ped′i·cel·la′tion,** *n.*

ped·i·cle (ped′i kəl), *n.* *Zool.* a small stalk or stalklike support, as the connection between the cephalothorax and abdomen in certain arachnids. [< L *pedicul(us),* dim. of *pēs* foot]

pe·dic·u·lar (pə dik′yə lər), *adj.* of or pertaining to lice. [< L *pediculār(is)* < *pediculus,* dim. of *pedis* louse; see -CULE, -AR¹]

pe·dic·u·late (pə dik′yə lit, -lāt′), *adj.* **1.** of or related to the *Pediculati,* a group of teleost fishes characterized by the elongated base of their pectoral fins, simulating an arm or peduncle. —*n.* **2.** a pediculate fish. [< L *pedicul(us)* little foot (see PEDICLE) + -ATE¹]

pe·dic·u·li·cide (pə dik′yə li sīd′), *adj.* destructive to lice. Also, **pe·dic′u·li·ci′dal.** [< L *pedicul(us)* louse (see PEDICULAR) + -I- + -CIDE]

pe·dic·u·lo·sis (pə dik′yə lō′sis), *n.* *Pathol.* the state of being infested with lice. [< L *pedicul(us)* louse (see PEDICULAR) + -OSIS] —**pe·dic·u·lous** (pə dik′yə ləs), *adj.*

ped·i·cure (ped′ə kyŏŏr′), *n.* **1.** professional care or treatment of the feet. **2.** a person who makes a business of caring for the feet; chiropodist. [< F *pédicure*] —**ped′i·cur′ist,** *n.*

ped·i·form (ped′ə fôrm′), *adj.* in the form of a foot; footlike.

ped·i·gree (ped′ə grē′), *n.* **1.** an ancestral line; line of descent; lineage; ancestry. **2.** a genealogical record, esp. of animals. **3.** distinguished or pure ancestry, esp. of animals. **4.** derivation, origin, or history: *the pedigree of a word.* [late ME *pedegru* < AF = MF *pie de grue,* lit., foot of crane, a fanciful way of describing the appearance of the lines of a genealogical chart] —**ped′i·gree′less,** *adj.*

ped·i·greed (ped′ə grēd′), *adj.* having a pedigree; of purebred ancestry: *a pedigreed collie.*

ped·i·ment (ped′ə mənt), *n.* **1.** *Archit.* a low gable or gablelike feature, typically triangular and outlined with cornices. **2.** *Geol.* a gently sloping rock surface at the foot of a steep slope. [earlier *peremint,* illiterate mishearing and misapplication of PYRAMID; the word prob. intended was L *pedāmentum* vine prop] —**ped·i·men·tal** (ped′ə men′təl), *adj.*

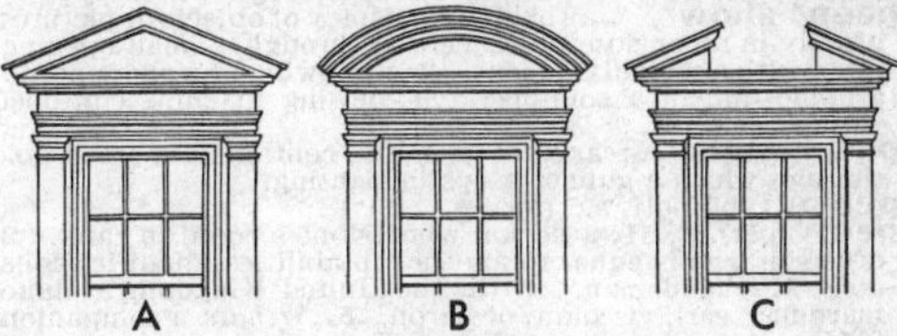

Pediments
A, Pointed; B, Curved; C, Broken

ped·lar (ped′lər), *n.* peddler. Also, **ped′ler.**

pedo-¹, a learned borrowing from Greek meaning "child," used in the formation of compound words: *pedology.* Also, **paed-, paedo-, ped-¹, pedi-².** [var. sp. of *paedo-,* Gk *paido-,* comb. form of *paid-* (s. of *paîs*) child]

pedo-², a learned borrowing from Greek meaning "soil," used in the formation of compound words: *pedology.* Also, *esp. before a vowel,* **ped-³.** [< Gk, comb. form of *pédon*]

pe·dol·o·gy¹ (pi dol′ə jē), *n.* the science that deals with the study of soils. —**pe·do·log·i·cal** (pēd′əloj′i kəl), *adj.* —**pe·dol′o·gist,** *n.*

pe·dol·o·gy² (pi dol′ə jē), *n.* **1.** the scientific study of the nature and development of children. **2.** pediatrics. [earlier *paidology, paedology*] —**pe·do·log·i·cal** (pēd′əloj′i kəl), *adj.* —**pe·dol′o·gist,** *n.*

pe·dom·e·ter (pi dom′i tər), *n.* an instrument that measures distance covered in walking by recording the number of steps taken. [< F *pédomètre*]

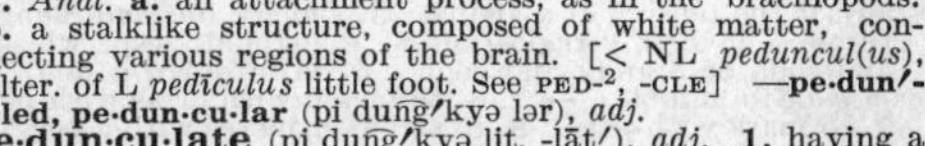

P, Peduncle

pe·dun·cle (pi duŋ′kəl), *n.* **1.** *Bot.* **a.** a flower stalk, supporting either a cluster or a solitary flower. **b.** the stalk bearing the fructification in fungi. **2.** *Zool.* a stalklike part or structure. **3.** *Anat.* **a.** an attachment process, as in the brachiopods. **b.** a stalklike structure, composed of white matter, connecting various regions of the brain. [< NL *peduncul(us),* alter. of L *pediculus* little foot. See PED-², -CLE] —**pe·dun′cled, pe·dun·cu·lar** (pi duŋ′kyə lər), *adj.*

pe·dun·cu·late (pi duŋ′kyə lit, -lāt′), *adj.* **1.** having a peduncle. **2.** growing on a peduncle. Also, **pe·dun′cu·lat′ed.** [< NL *pedunculāt(us)*] —**pe·dun′cu·la′tion,** *n.*

pee (pē), *v.,* **peed, pee·ing,** *n.* *Slang.* —*v.i.* **1.** to urinate. —*n.* **2.** urine. **3.** the act of urinating. [euphemism for *piss*]

Pee Dee (pē′ dē′), a river flowing through North and South Carolina into the Atlantic. 435 mi. long. Cf. **Yadkin.**

peek (pēk), *v.i.* **1.** to look or glance briefly or furtively, esp. through a small opening or from a concealed location; peep. —*n.* **2.** a brief or furtive look or glance. [ME *pike(n),* ? dissimilated var. of *kike* to peep < MD *kiken, kieken*]

peek·a·boo (pēk′ə bōō′), *n.* **1.** a game played with very young children, typically in which one covers his face or hides himself and then suddenly uncovers his face or reappears, calling "Peekaboo!" —*adj.* *Clothing.* **2.** decorated with openwork. **3.** made of a revealing material, as some blouses for women. [PEEK + *-a-* connective + BOO]

peel¹ (pēl), *v.t.* **1.** to strip (something) of its skin, bark, etc.: *to peel an orange.* **2.** to strip (the skin, bark, etc.) from something. **3.** *Croquet.* to cause (another player's ball) to go through a wicket. —*v.i.* **4.** (of skin, bark, etc.) to come off. **5.** to lose the skin, rind, bark, etc. **6. keep one's eyes peeled,** *Slang.* to watch closely or carefully. —*n.* **7.** the skin or rind of a fruit, vegetable, etc. [ME *pel(en),* OE *pilian* to strip, skin < L *pilāre* to remove hair < *pil(us)* hair. See PILL²] —**peel′a·ble,** *adj.* —**peel′er,** *n.*

—**Syn. 1.** PEEL, PARE agree in meaning to remove the skin or rind from something. PEEL means to pull or strip off the natural external covering or protection of something: *to peel an orange, a potato.* PARE is used of trimming off chips, flakes, or superficial parts from something, as well as of cutting off the skin or rind: *to pare the nails; to pare a potato.*

peel² (pēl), *n.* a shovellike implement for putting bread, pies, etc., into the oven or taking them out. [ME *pele* < MF < L *pāla* spade. See PALETTE]

Peel (pēl), *n.* **Sir Robert,** 1788–1850, British statesman: prime minister 1834–35, 1841–46; founder of the Irish constabulary.

Peele (pēl), *n.* **George,** 1558?–97?, English dramatist.

peel·ing (pē′liŋ), *n.* **1.** the act of a person or thing that peels. **2.** that which is peeled from something, as a piece of the skin or rind of a fruit; peel.

peen (pēn), *n.* **1.** a wedgelike, spherical, or other striking end of a hammer head opposite the face. —*v.t.* **2.** to enlarge, straighten, or smooth with a peen. Also, **pein.** [earlier *pen* < Scand; cf. Sw, Norw *pen* (n.) in same sense; akin to G *Pinne* peen. See PIN]

peep¹ (pēp), *v.i.* **1.** to look through a small opening or from a concealed location; peek. **2.** to look slyly or furtively. **3.** to look curiously or playfully. **4.** to come partially into view. —*n.* **5.** a quick or furtive look or glance. **6.** the first appearance, as of dawn. [late ME *pepe;* assimilated var. of PEEK]

peep² (pēp), *n.* **1.** a short, shrill little cry or sound, as of a young bird. **2.** any of various small sandpipers. —*v.i.* **3.** to utter a short, shrill little cry. **4.** to speak in a thin, weak voice. [ME *pepe(n), pipen;* cf. D, G *piepen,* OF *piper,* L *pipāre,* all imit.]

peep·er¹ (pē′pər), *n.* **1.** a person or thing that emits or utters a peeping sound. **2.** any of several frogs having a peeping call. [PEEP² + -ER¹]

peep·er² (pē′pər), *n.* a person who peeps, esp. in an abnormal prying manner. [PEEP¹ + -ER¹]

peep·hole (pēp′hōl′), *n.* a hole or opening through which to peer or look, as in a door.

Peep′ing Tom′, a person who secretly spies on others, esp. for sexual gratification; voyeur. [allusion to man who peeped at Lady Godiva as she rode through Coventry]

peep′ show′, **1.** an exhibited display of objects or pictures, usually in an enclosed box, viewed through a small opening, often with a magnifying lens. **2.** a showing of a short pornographic film in a coin-operated viewing machine equipped with a projector.

peep′ sight′, rear sight on a gun, containing a small hole through which a gunner peeps in sighting.

pee·pul (pē′pəl), *n.* pipal.

peer[1] (pēr), *n.* **1.** a person who is one's equal in rank. **2.** a person who is equal to another in abilities, qualifications, etc. **3.** a nobleman. **4.** (in the United Kingdom) a duke, marquess, earl, viscount, or baron. **5.** *Archaic.* a companion. [ME *per* < OF *per* < L *pār* equal]

peer[2] (pēr), *v.i.* **1.** to look narrowly or searchingly, as in the effort to discern clearly. **2.** to peep out or appear slightly. [< Flem *pier(en)* (to) look narrowly] **—peer′ing·ly,** *adv.*

peer·age (pēr′ij), *n.* **1.** the rank or dignity of a peer. **2.** the body of peers of a nation. **3.** a book listing these. [late ME *perage*]

peer·ess (pēr′is), *n.* **1.** the wife or widow of a peer. **2.** a woman having in her own right the rank of a peer.

peer·less (pēr′lis), *adj.* having no equal; matchless; unrivaled. [ME *pereles*] **—peer′less·ly,** *adv.* **—Syn.** unmatched, unequaled; unsurpassed.

peer′ of the realm′, *pl.* **peers of the realm.** any of a class of peers in Great Britain and Ireland entitled to sit in the House of Lords.

peeve (pēv), *v.,* **peeved, peev·ing,** *n.* **—***v.t.* **1.** to render peevish; annoy. **—***n.* **2.** a source of annoyance or irritation. [back formation from PEEVISH] **—Syn. 2.** gripe.

peeved (pēvd), *adj.* annoyed; irritated; vexed.

peev·ish (pē′vish), *adj.* cross, querulous, or fretful. [ME *pevysh* < ?] **—pee′vish·ly,** *adv.* **—pee′vish·ness,** *n.* **—Syn.** See **cross.**

pee·wee (pē′wē′), *n. Informal.* **1.** a person who is unusually small. **2.** an animal that is small for its kind; runt. [rhyming compound based on WEE]

pee·wit (pē′wit, pyōō′it), *n.* pewit.

peg (peg), *n., v.,* **pegged, peg·ging,** *adj.* **—***n.* **1.** a pin driven or fitted into something as a fastening, support, or marker. **2.** Also called **pin.** *Music.* a pin in the neck of a stringed instrument that may be turned in its socket to adjust the tension of a string. **3.** *Chiefly Baseball Slang.* a throw. **4.** *Brit., Anglo-Indian.* a highball, esp. whiskey and soda or brandy and soda. **5. take down a peg,** *Informal.* to humble. **—***v.t.* **6.** to fasten with or as with pegs. **7.** to mark with pegs. **8.** to strike or pierce with a peg. **9.** to keep (a commodity price, exchange rate, etc.) at a set level. **10.** *Chiefly Baseball Slang.* to throw (a ball). **11.** *Slang.* to identify, classify, or understand (someone): *She had him pegged as a big spender.* **—***v.i.* **12.** to work or continue persistently or energetically: *to peg away at homework.* **13.** *Chiefly Baseball Slang.* to throw a ball. **—***adj.* **14.** tapered toward the bottom of the leg: *peg trousers.* [ME *pegge* < MD *pegge* (n.), *peggen* (v.)] **—peg′less,** *adj.* **—peg′like′,** *adj.*

Pegasus

Peg·a·sus (peg′ə səs), *n., gen.* **-si** (-sī′) for 2. **1.** *Class. Myth.* a winged horse, created from the blood of Medusa, that opened the spring of Hippocrene with a stroke of its hoof and carried Bellerophon in his attack on the Chimera. **2.** *Astron.* the Winged Horse, a northern constellation between Cygnus and Aquarius.

peg·board (peg′bōrd′, -bôrd′), *n.* a board having holes into which pegs or hooks are placed.

peg·box (peg′boks′), *n.* the widened end of the neck of a stringed instrument, to which the tuning pegs are fixed.

peg′ leg′, **1.** a wooden leg. **2.** a person with a wooden leg. **—peg′legged′,** *adj.*

peg·ma·tite (peg′mə tīt′), *n.* **1.** a graphic intergrowth of quartz and feldspar; graphic granite. **2.** a coarsely crystalline granite or other high-silica rock occurring in veins or dikes. [< Gk *pēgmat-* (s. of *pêgma*) anything fastened together, a bond (cf. *pēgnýein* to stick) + -ITE[1]] **—peg·ma·tit·ic** (peg′mə tit′ik), *adj.*

peg-top (peg′top′), *adj.* (of clothing) wide at the hips and narrowing to the ankle: *peg-top trousers.*

Peh·le·vi (pā′lə vē′), *n.* the Pahlavi language.

P.E.I., Prince Edward Island.

Pei·ching (*Chin.* bā′jing′), *n.* Peking.

peign·oir (pān wär′, pen-, pān′wär, pen′-), *n.* a woman's dressing gown. [< F: lit., comber, i.e., something worn while one's hair is being combed = *peign(er)* (to) comb (< LL *pectināre;* see PECTEN) + *-oir* n. suffix]

pein (pēn), *n., v.t.* peen.

Pei·ping (bā′ping′), *n.* former name of **Peking.**

Pei·pus (pī′pəs), *n.* a lake in the W Soviet Union in Europe, on the E boundary of Estonia. 93 mi. long; 356 sq. mi. Russian, **Chudskoye Ozero.** Estonian, **Peip·si** (pāp′sē).

Pei·rae·us (pī rē′əs), *n.* Piraeus.

Pei·rai·evs (pē′RE efs′), *n.* Greek name of **Piraeus.**

Peirce (pûrs), *n.* **C(harles) S(an·ders)** (san′dərz), 1839–1914, U.S. philosopher and mathematician.

peise (pāz, pēz), *v.t.,* **peised, peis·ing.** *Brit. Dial.* **1.** to weigh, as in a balance. **2.** to weigh down; burden. [ME *peys, peis* < OF, ONF, AF (F *poids*) < L *pens(um)* weight < *pendere.* See POISE]

Pei·sis·tra·tus (pē sis′trə təs), *n.* Pisistratus.

pej·o·ra·tion (pej′ə rā′shən, pē′jə-), *n.* depreciation; a lessening in worth, quality, etc. [< ML *pējōrātiōn-* (s. of *pējōrātiō*) a making worse = LL *pējōrāt(us)* (ptp. of *pējōrāre* < *pējor* worse) + *-iōn-* -ION]

pe·jo·ra·tive (pi jôr′ə tiv, -jor′-, pej′ə rā′-, pē′jə-), *adj.* **1.** having a disparaging effect or force: *the pejorative affix -ling in princeling.* **—***n.* **2.** a pejorative form or word, as *poetaster.* [< L *pējōrāt(us)* made worse (see PEJORATION) + -IVE] **—pe·jo′ra·tive·ly,** *adv.* **—Syn. 1.** deprecatory.

pe·kin (pē′kin′), *n.* (*often cap.*) a silk fabric having broad stripes of equal width. [< F *pékin;* after PEKING]

Pe·kin (pē′kin′), *n.* one of a hardy breed of yellowish-white domestic ducks, raised originally in China. [after PEKING]

Pe·kin (pē′kin), *n.* a city in central Illinois. 31,375 (1970).

Pe·kin·ese (pē′kə nēz′, -nēs′), *n., pl.* **-ese.** Pekingese.

Pe·king (pē′king′; *Chin.* bā′jing′), *n.* a city in and the capital of the People's Republic of China, in the NE part, in central Hopeh province. 7,570,000. Also, **Pei-ching.** Formerly (1928–49), **Peiping.** Pinyin spelling, **Beijing.**

Pe·king·ese (pē′king ēz′, -ēs′, -kə nēz′, -nēs′), *n., pl.* **-ese** for 1, 4, *adj.* **—***n.* **1.** one of a Chinese breed of small dogs having a long, silky coat. **2.** the standard Chinese language. **3.** the dialect of Peking. **4.** a native or inhabitant of Peking. **—***adj.* **5.** of, pertaining to, or characteristic of Peking. Also, **Pekinese.**

Pekingese (6 in. high at shoulder)

Pe′king′ man′, a fossil man known from skeletal remains found in a Middle Pleistocene cave near Peking, China.

pe·koe (pē′kō *or, esp. Brit.,* pek′ō), *n.* a superior kind of black tea from Ceylon, India, and Java, made from leaves coarser than those used for orange pekoe. [< Chin (Amoy dial.) *pek-ho* white down]

pel·age (pel′ij), *n.* the hair, fur, wool, or other soft covering of a mammal. [< F < *poil* (OF *peil;* see POILU); see -AGE] **—pe·la·gi·al** (pə lā′jē əl), *adj.*

Pe·la·gi·an (pə lā′jē ən), *n.* **1.** a follower of Pelagius who denied original sin and maintained the freedom of the will. **—***adj.* **2.** of or pertaining to Pelagius or Pelagianism. [< LL *Pelagiān(us);* see -AN] **—Pe·la′gi·an·ism,** *n.*

pe·lag·ic (pə laj′ik), *adj.* **1.** of or pertaining to the seas or oceans. **2.** living or growing at or near the surface of the ocean, far from land, as certain animals or plants. [< L *pelagic(us)* < Gk *pelagikós* = *pélag(os)* the sea (c. L *pelagus*) + *-ikos* -IC]

Pe·la·gi·us (pə lā′jē əs), *n.* 360?–420?, English monk and theologian in Rome: teachings opposed by St. Augustine.

Pelagius I, died A.D. 561, pope 556–561.

Pelagius II, died A.D. 590, pope 579–590.

pel·ar·go·ni·um (pel′är gō′nē əm), *n.* any plant of the genus *Pelargonium,* the cultivated species of which are usually called geranium. Cf. **geranium** (def. 2). [< NL < Gk *pelargó(s)* stork + *(gerá)nion* GERANIUM]

Pe·las·gi (pə laz′jē), *n.pl.* the Pelasgians. [< L < Gk *Pelasgoí*]

Pe·las·gi·an (pə laz′jē ən), *adj.* **1.** of or pertaining to the Pelasgians. **—***n.* **2.** a member of a prehistoric people inhabiting Greece and the eastern Mediterranean area. [<< Gk *Pelásgi(os)* Pelasgian (< *Pelasg(oí)* PELASGI + *-ios* adj. suffix) + -AN]

Pe·las·gic (pə laz′jik), *adj.* Pelasgian (def. 1). [<< Gk *Pelasgik(ós).* See PELASGI, -IC]

pe·lec·y·pod (pə les′ə pod′), *n.* any mollusk of the class *Pelecypoda* (*Lamellibranchiata*), characterized by a bivalve shell enclosing the headless body and lamellate gills, comprising the oysters, clams, mussels, scallops, etc. [< NL *Pelecypod(a)* < Gk *péleky(s)* hatchet; see -POD]

Pe·lée (pə lā′), *n.* **Mount,** a volcano in the West Indies, on the island of Martinique: eruption 1902. 4428 ft.

pel·er·ine (pel′ə rēn′), *n.* a woman's short cape of fur or cloth, with long descending ends in front. [< F *pèlerine,* fem. of *pèlerin* pilgrim]

Pe′le's hair′ (pā′lāz, pē′lēz), volcanic glass thread, usually basaltic, caused by the solidification of exploding or ejected lava in the open air. [trans. of Hawaiian *ranoho o Pele* hair of Pele (goddess of the volcano Kilauea)]

Pe·le·us (pē′lē əs, pēl′yōōs), *n. Class. Myth.* a king of the Myrmidons, and father of Achilles.

Pe·lew′ Is′lands (pē lōō′). See **Palau Islands.**

pelf (pelf), *n. Disparaging.* money or riches. [ME, OF *pelfre* booty]

Pel·ham (pel′əm), *n.* a bit that is used with two pairs of reins, designed to serve the purpose of a full bridle. [after the proper name *Pelham*]

Pe·li·as (pē′lē əs, pel′ē-), *n. Class. Myth.* a son of Poseidon, who sent his nephew Jason to recover the Golden Fleece.

pel·i·can (pel′ə kən), *n.* any of several large, totipalmate, fish-eating birds of the family *Pelecanidae,* having a large bill with a distensible pouch. [ME, OE *pellican* < LL *pelicān(us),* var. of *pelecānus* < Gk *pelekân*]

Pelican, *Pelecanus erythrorhynchos* (Length 5 ft.)

Pel′ican State′, Louisiana (used as a nickname).

Pe·li·on (pē′lē ən; *Gk.* pē′lē ôn′), *n.* **Mount,** a mountain near the E coast of Greece, in Thessaly. 5252 ft.

pe·lisse (pə lēs′), *n.* **1.** an outer garment lined or trimmed with fur. **2.** a woman's long cloak with slits for the arms. [< F < LL *pellicia* mantle, n. use of fem. of *pellicius* of skin < *pellis* skin]

pe·lite (pē′līt), *n. Geol.* any clay rock. [< Gk *pēl(ós)* clay, earth + -ITE[1]] **—pe·lit·ic** (pi lit′ik), *adj.*

Pel·la (pel′ə), *n.* a ruined city in N Greece, NW of Salonika: the capital of ancient Macedonia; birthplace of Alexander the Great.

pel·la·gra (pə lā′grə, -lag′rə, -lä′grə), *n. Pathol.* a disease caused by a deficiency of niacin in the diet, characterized by skin changes, severe nerve dysfunction, and diarrhea. [< It < medical L: skin disease = *pell(is)* skin + *-agra* < Gk *ágra* seizure] **—pel·la·grose** (pə lā′grōs, -lag′rōs, -lä′grōs), **pel·la·grous** (pə lā′grəs, -lag′rəs, -lä′grəs), *adj.*

Pel·les (pel′ēz), *n.* **King,** *Arthurian Romance.* a character in the story of Lancelot's quest for the Holy Grail: father of Elaine.

pel·let (pel′it), *n.* **1.** a small, rounded or spherical body, as of food or medicine. **2.** a ball, usually of stone, formerly used as a missile. **3.** one of a charge of small shot, as for a shotgun. **4.** a bullet. **5.** a small wad or ball of wax, paper, etc., for throwing, shooting, or the like. **6.** *Ornith.* a small, roundish mass of matter regurgitated by certain predatory birds, consisting of the indigestible remains, as the fur, feathers, and bones, of the prey. —*v.t.* **7.** to form into pellets. **8.** to hit with pellets. [ME *pelet* < MF *pelote* < VL **pilotta*, dim. of L *pila* ball. See PILL[1], -ET]

pel·li·cle (pel′i kəl), *n.* a thin skin or membrane; film; scum. [< L *pellicul(a)* < *pellis* skin; see -CLE] —**pel·lic·u·lar** (pə lik′yə lər), **pel·lic·u·late** (pə lik′yə lit, -lāt′), *adj.*

pel·li·to·ry (pel′i tōr′ē, -tôr′ē), *n., pl.* **-ries.** an asteraceous plant, *Anacyclus Pyrethrum*, of Southern Europe, whose root is used as a local irritant. [alter. of ME *peletre* < AF, MF *piretre* < L *pyrethrum* < Gk *pýrethron*]

pell-mell (pel′mel′), *adv.* **1.** in a confused or hasty manner. —*adj.* **2.** hasty or confused: *a pell-mell rush to get to the station on time.* —*n.* **3.** a confused or jumbled mass or crowd. **4.** disorderly, headlong haste. Also, **pell′mell′.** [< MF *pelemele*, OF *pesle mesle*, rhyming compound based on *mesler* to mix. See MEDDLE]

pel·lu·cid (pə lo͞o′sid), *adj.* **1.** allowing the maximum passage of light. **2.** clear or limpid: *pellucid waters.* **3.** clear in meaning. [< L *pellūcid(us)*, var. of *perlūcidus*. See PER-, LUCID] —**pel·lu′cid·ly**, *adv.* —**Syn. 2.** transparent. —**Ant. 1, 2.** opaque. **3.** obscure.

Pe·lop·i·das (pə lop′i dəs), *n.* died 364 B.C., Greek general and statesman of Thebes.

Pel′oponne′sian War′, a war between Athens and Sparta, 431–404 B.C., resulting in a Spartan victory.

Pel·o·pon·ne·sus (pel′ə pə nē′səs), *n.* a peninsula forming the S part of Greece: site of the early Mycenaean civilization and of Sparta. 1,096,654 (1961); 8356 sq. mi. Also, **Pel·o·pon·nese** (pel′ə pə nēz′, -nēs′), **Pel·o·pon·ne·sos** (pel′ə pə nē′sos, -sôs, -sōs). Also called **Morea.** [< L < Gk *Peloponnēsos*, lit., island of PELOPS] —**Pel·o·pon·ne·sian** (pel′ə pə nē′zhən, -shən), *adj., n.*

Pe·lops (pē′lops), *n.* *Class. Myth.* a son of Tantalus and brother of Niobe, slain by Tantalus and served to the gods as food, but restored to life by Hermes.

pe·lo·ri·a (pə lōr′ē ə, -lôr′-), *n.* *Bot.* regularity of structure occurring abnormally in flowers normally irregular. [< NL < Gk *pélōr(os)* monstrous (*pélōr* monster + *-os* adj. suffix) + *-ia* -IA] —**pe·lor·ic** (pə lôr′ik, -lor′-), **pe·lo′ri·an, pe·lo·ri·ate** (pə lōr′ē it, -āt′, -lôr′-), *adj.*

pe·lo·rus (pə lōr′əs, -lôr′-), *n., pl.* **-rus·es.** *Navig.* a device for measuring in degrees the relative bearings of observed objects. [? < L *Pelōrus*, now Cape Faro in Sicily, the rounding of which requires skill in navigation]

pe·lo·ta (pə lō′tə; *Sp.* pe lô′tä), *n., pl.* **-tas** (-təz; *Sp.* -täs). **1.** a Basque and Spanish game from which jai alai was developed. **2.** the game of jai alai. **3.** the ball used in pelota and jai alai. [< Sp < MF *pelote*; see PELLET]

Pe·lo·tas (pə lô′təs), *n.* a city in S Brazil. 129,517 (1960).

pelt[1] (pelt), *v.t.* **1.** to attack with repeated blows or missiles. **2.** to throw (missiles). **3.** to drive by blows or missiles. **4.** to assail with abuse. **5.** to beat or rush against repeatedly. —*v.i.* **6.** to attack someone or something with repeated blows or missiles. **7.** to run. **8.** to beat or pound unrelentingly. **9.** *Rare.* to cast abuse. —*n.* **10.** a blow with a fist or missile. **11.** an unrelenting or repeated beating, as of rain, wind, etc. [?] —**pelt′er,** *n.*

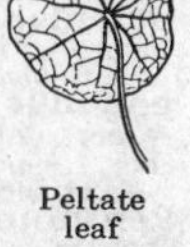

pelt[2] (pelt), *n.* the hide or skin of an animal. [late ME; ? back formation from PELTRY] —**Syn.** See **skin.**

pel·tate (pel′tāt), *adj.* *Bot.* having the stalk or support attached to the lower surface at a distance from the margin, as a leaf; shield-shaped. [< L *peltāt(us)* = *pelt(a)* shield + *-ātus* -ATE[1]] —**pel′tate·ly,** *adv.* —**pel·ta′tion,** *n.*

Peltate leaf

Pel′tier effect′ (pel′tyā), the change in temperature of either junction of a thermocouple when a current is maintained in the thermocouple and after allowance is made for a temperature change due to resistance. [named after Jean C. A. *Peltier* (1785–1845), French physicist who discovered it]

pelt·ing (pel′tiŋg), *adj.* *Archaic.* paltry; petty; mean. [? dial. *pelt* rags, rubbish (akin to Dan *pjalt* rag) + -ING[2]. See PALTRY]

Pel′ton wheel′ (pel′tᵊn), a high-pressure impulse water turbine in which one or more free jets of water are directed against the buckets of the rotor. [named after L. A. *Pelton* (d. 1908), American engineer, its inventor]

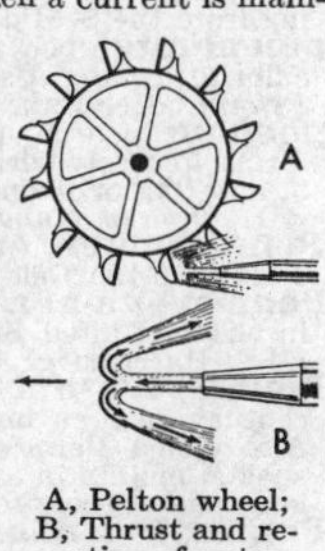

A, Pelton wheel; B, Thrust and reaction of water impinging on bucket

pelt·ry (pel′trē), *n., pl.* **-ries.** **1.** fur skins; pelts collectively. **2.** a pelt. [late ME < AF *pelterie*, OF *peleterie* furrier's wares = *peleter* furrier (< L *pilus* hair; see -ER[2]) + *-ie* -Y[3]]

pel·vic (pel′vik), *adj.* of or pertaining to the pelvis.

pel′vic fin′, (in fishes) either of a pair of fins on the lower surface of the body, corresponding to the hind limbs of a land vertebrate; ventral fin.

pel′vic gir′dle, **1.** (in vertebrates) a bony or cartilaginous arch supporting the hind limbs or analogous parts. **2.** (in man) the arch, formed by the innominate bones, that attaches the lower limb to the axial skeleton. Also called **pel′vic arch′.**

pel·vis (pel′vis), *n., pl.* **-vis·es, -ves** (-vēz). *Anat., Zool.* **1.** the basinlike cavity in the lower part of the trunk of many vertebrates, formed in man by the innominate bones, that sacrum, etc. **2.** the bones forming this cavity. **3.** the cavity of the kidney that receives the urine before it is passed into the ureter. [< L: basin; akin to Gk *pellís* bowl]

Pem·ba (pem′bə), *n.* an island near the E coast of equatorial Africa: formerly part of Zanzibar protectorate; now a part of Tanzania. 133,858 (1958); 380 sq. mi.

Pem·broke (pem′bro͝ok, -brōk), *n.* **1.** a municipal borough in and the county seat of Pembrokeshire, in SW Wales. 12,737 (1961). **2.** Pembrokeshire.

Pem·broke·shire (pem′bro͝ok shēr′, -shər, -brōk-), *n.* a county in SW Wales. 93,980 (1961); 614 sq. mi. *Co. seat:* Pembroke. Also called **Pembroke.**

pem·mi·can (pem′ə kən), *n.* a small, pressed cake of shredded dried meat mixed with fat and dried fruits or berries, originally prepared by North American Indians. Also, **pem′i·can.** [< Cree *pimikân*, akin to *pimii* grease, fat]

pem·phi·gus (pem′fə gəs, pem fī′-), *n.* *Pathol.* any of several similar diseases which are often fatal and are characterized by vesicles and bullae on the skin and mucous membranes. [< NL < Gk *pemphig-* (s. of *pémphix*) bubble + L *-us* n. suffix] —**pem·phi·goid** (pem′fə goid′), *n.* —**pem′phi·gous,** *adj.*

pen[1] (pen), *n. v.,* **penned, pen·ning.** —*n.* **1.** any of various instruments for writing or drawing with ink. **2.** such an instrument as a symbol of writing or of a writer or his style. **3.** a detachable metal penpoint. **4.** *Ornith.* **a.** a quill. **b.** a pinfeather. **5.** *Zool.* an internal, corneous or chitinous, feather-shaped structure in certain cephalopods, as the squid. —*v.t.* **6.** to write with or as with a pen. [ME *penne*, OE *pinn* < LL *penna* pen, feather, L: feather]

pen[2] (pen), *n., v.,* **penned** or **pent, pen·ning.** —*n.* **1.** a small enclosure for animals. **2.** animals so enclosed. **3.** an enclosure used for confinement or safekeeping. **4.** playpen. **5.** See **bull pen.** —*v.t.* **6.** to confine in or as in a pen. [ME *penne*, OE *penn* (in compounds); perh. akin to PIN]

pen[3] (pen), *n.* *Slang.* penitentiary. [shortened form]

pen[4] (pen), *n.* a female mute swan. [?]

pen-, var. of **pene-** before a vowel: *penumbra.*

Pen., peninsula. Also, **pen.**

pe·nal (pēn′ᵊl), *adj.* **1.** of, pertaining to, or involving legal punishment. **2.** prescribing punishment. **3.** used in or for punishment. **4.** subject to or incurring punishment: *a penal offense.* **5.** forfeitable as a penalty. [ME < L *poenāl(is)* = *poen(a)* penalty (< Gk *poinḗ* fine) + *-ālis* -AL[1]] —**pe·nal·i·ty** (pi nal′i tē), *n.* —**pe′nal·ly,** *adv.*

pe′nal code′, *Law.* the aggregate of statutory enactments dealing with crimes and their punishment.

pe·nal·ise (pēn′ᵊlīz′, pen′-), *v.t.,* **-ised, -is·ing.** *Chiefly Brit.* penalize. —**pe′nal·is′a·ble,** *adj.* —**pe′nal·i·sa′tion,** *n.*

pe·nal·ize (pēn′ᵊlīz′, pen′-), *v.t.,* **-ized, -iz·ing.** **1.** to subject to a penalty, as a person. **2.** to declare (an action, deed, etc.) punishable by law or rule. **3.** to put under a disadvantage or handicap. —**pe′nal·iz′a·ble,** *adj.* —**pe′nal·i·za′tion,** *n.*

pe′nal ser′vitude, *Eng. Crim. Law.* imprisonment together with hard labor.

pen·al·ty (pen′ᵊl tē), *n., pl.* **-ties.** **1.** a punishment imposed or incurred for a violation of law, rule, or agreement. **2.** something that is forfeited, as a sum of money. **3.** a disagreeable consequence of a person's actions or conduct. **4.** *Sports.* a disadvantage imposed for infraction of the rules. [<< ML *poenālitās*]

pen·ance (pen′əns), *n.* **1.** a punishment undergone in token of penitence for sin. **2.** a penitential discipline imposed by church authority. **3.** a sacrament, as in the Roman Catholic Church, consisting in a confession of sin followed by the forgiveness of the sin. [ME *penaunce* < AF; OF *peneance* < L *paenitentia* PENITENCE]

pe·nang (pə naŋg′), *n.* a heavyweight percale. [?]

Pe·nang (pē′naŋg′, -näŋg′, pi-), *n.* **1.** an island in SE Asia, off the W coast of the Malay Peninsula. 338,866 (1957); 110 sq. mi. **2.** a state including this island and parts of the adjacent mainland: now part of the federation of Malaysia; formerly one of the Straits Settlements and part of the former Federation of Malaya. 696,994 (est. 1964); 398 sq. mi. *Cap.:* George Town. **3.** See **George Town.**

pe·na·tes (pə nā′tēz), *n.pl.* *Rom. Religion.* gods who watched over a particular home or community. Also, **Pe·na′tes.** Cf. **lares.** [< L, akin to *penitus* inner, *penes* within]

pence (pens), *n.* *Brit.* a pl. of **penny:** used when the number of pennies is indicated (usually used in combination): *fourpence.*

pen·chant (pen′chənt; *Fr.* päɴ shäɴ′), *n.* a strong taste or liking for something. [< F, n. use of prp. of *pencher* to incline, lean < VL **pendicāre* << L *pendēre* to hang]

pen·cil (pen′səl), *n., v.,* **-ciled, -cil·ing** or (*esp. Brit.*) **-cilled, -cil·ling.** —*n.* **1.** a slender tube containing a core of a material that may be used for writing or drawing. **2.** any slender, pointed piece of a substance used for marking. **3.** a stick of cosmetic coloring material for use on the eyebrows, eyelids, etc. **4.** anything shaped or held like a pencil. **5.** a narrow set of lines, light rays, or the like, diverging from or converging to a point. —*v.t.* **6.** to use a pencil on. **7.** to write, draw, mark, or color with, or as with, a pencil. [ME *pencel* < MF *pincel* << L *pēnicill(us)* painter's brush or pencil, dim. of *pēniculus* little tail. See PENIS, -CULE]

pen·cil·i·form (pen sil′ə fôrm′, pen′sə lə-), *adj.* **1.** shaped like a pencil. **2.** (of a set of lines, rays, or the like) parallel or nearly parallel.

pen′cil push′er, *Informal.* a person who does routine office work involving writing, as a bookkeeper.

pen′cil sharp′ener, a rotary device for sharpening pencils or the like. —**pen′cil sharp′ening.**

pend (pend), *v.i.* **1.** to remain undecided or unsettled. **2.** to hang. **3.** *Obs.* to depend. [< L *pend(ēre)* (to) hang, depend]

pen·dant (pen′dənt), *n.* **1.** a hanging ornament, as an earring or the main piece in a necklace. **2.** a hanging ornament for an interior. **3.** a hanging electrical lighting fixture. **4.** a match, parallel, companion, or counterpart. **5.** Also, **pennant.** *Naut.* a hanging length of rope having a block or thimble secured to its free end. —*adj.* **6.** pendent. [ME *pendaunt* < MF *pendant*, n. use of prp. of *pendre* to hang < VL **pendere*, for L *pendēre*]

pen′dant cloud′, tuba (def. 2).

pen·dent (pen′dənt), *adj.* **1.** hanging or suspended. **2.** overhanging; jutting. **3.** undecided; pending. —*n.* **4.** pendant. [< L *pendent-* (s. of *pendēns*), prp. of *pendēre* to hang; r. *pendant* (adj.) < MF; see PENDANT] —**pen′den·cy,** *n* —**pen′dent·ly,** *adv.*

pen·den·te li·te (pen den′tē lī′tē), *Law.* during litigation. [< L: lit., with a lawsuit pending]

pen·den·tive (pen den′tiv), *n.* **1.** *Archit.* any of several spandrels, in the form of spherical triangles, forming a transition between the circular plan of a dome and the polygonal plan of the supporting masonry. —*adj.* **2. in pendentive,** *Print.* (of type) set in the form of a triangle resting on its apex. [PENDENT + -IVE, modeled on F *pendentif*]

P, Pendentive

pend·ing (pen′diŋ), *prep.* **1.** while awaiting; until. **2.** in the period during. —*adj.* **3.** awaiting decision or settlement. **4.** about to take place; impending. [PEND(ENT) + -ING[2]]

pen·drag·on (pen drag′ən), *n.* the supreme leader: the title of certain ancient British chiefs. [< Welsh: lit., head dragon] —**pen·drag′on·ship′,** *n.*

Pen·drag·on (pen drag′ən), *n.* either of two legendary kings of ancient Britain. Cf. **Arthur** (def. 2), **Uther.**

pen·du·lous (pen′jə ləs, pen′də-, -dyə-), *adj.* **1.** hanging down loosely. **2.** swinging freely; oscillating. **3.** vacillating; fluctuating. [< L *pendul(us)* hanging, swinging] —**pen′du·lous·ly,** *adv.*

pen·du·lum (pen′jə ləm, pen′də-, -dyə-), *n.* a long, suspended body, lever, etc., whose lower end moves to and fro in an arc when subjected to gravitational and other forces, used esp. in regulating the speed of a clock mechanism. [< NL, n. use of neut. of L *pendulus* PENDULOUS]

pene-, a prefix borrowed from Latin meaning "almost," used in the formation of compound words: *peneplain.* Also, *esp. before a vowel,* **pen-.** [< L *paene-,* comb. form of *paene*]

Pe·nei·os (pē′nē ôs′), *n.* modern Greek name of **Salambria.**

Pe·nel·o·pe (pə nel′ə pē), *n.* *Class. Myth.* the wife of Odysseus, who remained faithful to him during his absence at Troy in spite of having numerous suitors.

pe·ne·plain (pē′nə plān′, pē′nə plān′), *n.* *Geol.* an area reduced almost to a plain by erosion. Also, **pe′ne·plane′.** —**pe·ne·pla·na·tion** (pē′nə plə nā′shən), *n.*

pen·e·tra·ble (pen′i trə bəl), *adj.* capable of being penetrated. [< L *penetrābil(is)*] —**pen′e·tra·bil′i·ty,** *n.*

pen·e·tra·li·a (pen′i trā′lē ə), *n.pl.* the innermost parts or recesses of a place or thing. [< L, n. use of neut. pl. of *penetrālis* inner. See PENETRATE, -AL[1]] —**pen′e·tra′li·an,** *adj.*

pen·e·trance (pen′i trəns), *n.* *Genetics.* the frequency, expressed as a percentage, with which a particular gene produces its effect in a group of organisms.

pen·e·trant (pen′i trənt), *n.* **1.** a person or thing that penetrates. **2.** a substance that lowers the surface tension of water; wetting agent. **3.** a compound that penetrates the skin, as a cosmetic. —*adj.* **4.** penetrating. [< L *penetrant-* (s. of *penetrāns*) penetrating, prp. of *penetrāre*]

pen·e·trate (pen′i trāt′), *v.,* **-trat·ed, -trat·ing.** —*v.t.* **1.** to pierce or pass into or through. **2.** to enter the interior of. **3.** to enter and be diffused through; permeate. **4.** to affect or impress (the mind or feelings) deeply. **5.** to arrive at the truth or meaning of. —*v.i.* **6.** to go into, come to, or go through something after some difficulty. **7.** to be diffused through something. **8.** to understand the meaning or truth of something. **9.** to have a deep effect or impact on someone. [< L *penetrāt(us)* penetrated (ptp. of *penetrāre* = *penet-,* var. s. of *penit(us)* (see PENATES) + *-r-* (prob. after *(int)r(āre)* to ENTER + *-ātus* ptp. suffix] —**pen′e·tra′tor,** *n.* —**Syn. 1.** See **pierce. 4.** touch. **5.** fathom, discern.

pen·e·trat·ing (pen′i trā′tiŋ), *adj.* **1.** of a quality that penetrates, pierces, or pervades: *a penetrating shriek; a penetrating glance.* **2.** acute; discerning: *a penetrating observation.* Also, **penetrant.** —**pen′e·trat′ing·ly,** *adv.* —**Syn. 2.** keen, sharp. —**Ant. 2.** obtuse.

pen·e·tra·tion (pen′i trā′shən), *n.* **1.** the act or power of penetrating. **2.** permeation, as by an alien cultural influence. **3.** mental acuteness or discernment. [< L *penetrātiōn-* (s. of *penetrātiō*)] —**Syn. 3.** understanding, perception.

pen·e·tra·tive (pen′i trā′tiv), *adj.* **1.** tending to penetrate; piercing. **2.** acute; keen. [late ME < ML *penetrātīv(us)*]

pen·e·trom·e·ter (pen′i trom′i tər), *n.* a device for measuring the penetrability of a solid. [PENETR(ATE) + -O- + -METER]

Pe·ne·us (pə nē′əs), *n.* ancient name of **Salambria.**

Peng·hu (*Chin.* puŋ′ho͞o′), *n.* Pescadores. Also, **Peng·hu·tao** (*Chin.* puŋ′ho͞o′dou′).

pen·gö (pen′gœ′), *n., pl.* **-gö, -gös** (-gœz′). a silver coin and monetary unit of Hungary, replaced by the forint in 1946, equal to 100 fillér. [< Hung: lit., sounding; prp. of *pengeni* to sound, jingle]

pen·guin (pen′gwin, peŋ′-), *n.* *Ornith.* any of several flightless, aquatic birds of the family *Spheniscidae,* of the Southern Hemisphere, having webbed feet and wings reduced to flippers. [? named after *Penguin Island* (near Newfoundland), lit., white head island (i.e., one with a snow-capped height of land < Welsh *pen* head, peak + *gwyn* white), where many auks were found]

Emperor penguin, *Aptenodytes forsteri* (Length 4 ft.)

pen·hold·er (pen′hōl′dər), *n.* **1.** a holder in which a penpoint is placed. **2.** a rack for a pen or pens.

-penia, a combining form indicating deficiency: *leukopenia.* [< NL, comb. form repr. Gk *penía* poverty, need]

pen·i·cil (pen′i sil), *n.* a small, brushlike tuft of hairs, as on a caterpillar. [< L *pēnicill(us)* painter's brush or pencil. See PENCIL]

pen·i·cil·late (pen′i sil′it, -āt), *adj.* having a penicil or penicils. [< L *pēnicill(us)* (see PENCIL) + -ATE[1]] —**pen′i·cil′late·ly,** *adv.* —**pen′i·cil·la′tion,** *n.*

pen·i·cil·lin (pen′i sil′in), *n.* *Pharm.* an antibiotic, produced by molds of the genus *Penicillium,* having primarily a bacteriostatic rather than a bactericidal effect. [PENICILL(IUM) + -IN[2]]

pen·i·cil·li·um (pen′i sil′ē əm), *n., pl.* **-cil·li·ums, -cil·li·a** (-sil′ē ə). any fungus of the genus *Penicillium,* certain species of which are used in cheesemaking and as the source of penicillin. [< NL = L *pēnicill(us)* brush (see PENCIL) + *-ium* -IUM]

pen·in·su·la (pə nin′sə lə, -nins′yə lə), *n.* **1.** an area of land almost completely surrounded by water except for an isthmus connecting it with the mainland. **2. the Peninsula, a.** Iberia. **b.** a district in SE Virginia between the York and James rivers: Civil War battles. [< L *paenīnsula,* contr. of *paene īnsula* almost island] —**pen·in′su·lar,** *adj.* —**pen·in′su·lar·ism, pen·in·su·lar·i·ty** (pə nin′sə lar′i tē, -nins′yə-), *n.*

Penin′sular State′, Florida (used as a nickname).

pe·nis (pē′nis), *n., pl.* **-nes** (-nēz), **-nis·es.** the male organ of urination and copulation. [< L: a tail, the penis] —**pe·nile** (pēn′əl, pē′nīl), **pe·ni·al** (pē′nē əl), *adj.*

pen·i·tence (pen′i təns), *n.* the state of being penitent; regret for wrongdoing or sinning. [< eccl. L *pēnitentia,* var. sp. of L *paenitentia* a regretting. See PENITENT, -ENCE, PENANCE]

pen·i·tent (pen′i tənt), *adj.* **1.** feeling or expressing sorrow for sin or wrongdoing and intending atonement and amendment. —*n.* **2.** a penitent person. **3.** *Rom. Cath. Ch.* a person who confesses sin and submits to a penance. [ME < eccl. L *pēnitent-,* var. sp. of L *paenitent-* (s. of *paenitēns*) regretting, prp. of *paenitēre;* r. ME *penaunt* < AF] —**pen′i·tent·ly,** *adv.*

pen·i·ten·tial (pen′i ten′shəl), *adj.* of, pertaining to, proceeding from, or expressive of penitence or repentance. [< ML *poenitentiāl(is)*] —**pen′i·ten′tial·ly,** *adv.*

pen·i·ten·tia·ry (pen′i ten′shə rē), *n., pl.* **-ries,** *adj.* —*n.* **1.** a place for imprisonment, reformatory discipline, or punishment. **2.** *Rom. Cath. Ch.* a tribunal in the Curia Romana, presided over by a cardinal having jurisdiction over certain matters, as penance, confession, or dispensation. —*adj.* **3.** (of an offense) punishable by imprisonment in a penitentiary. **4.** of, pertaining to, or intended for imprisonment, reformatory discipline, or punishment. **5.** penitential. [ME < ML *poenitentiāri(us).* See PENITENCE, -ARY]

pen·knife (pen′nīf′), *n., pl.* **-knives.** a small pocketknife, formerly one used for making and repairing quill pens. [late ME *pen(ne)knif*]

pen·light (pen′līt′), *n.* a flashlight similar in size and shape to a fountain pen. Also, **pen′lite′.**

pen·man (pen′mən), *n., pl.* **-men. 1.** a person who writes or copies; scribe; copyist. **2.** an expert in penmanship.

pen·man·ship (pen′mən ship′), *n.* **1.** the art of writing with the pen. **2.** a person's style or manner of handwriting.

Penn (pen), *n.* **1. Sir William,** 1621–70, British admiral. **2.** his son, **William,** 1644–1718, English Quaker: founder of Pennsylvania 1682.

Penn., Pennsylvania. Also, **Penna.**

pen·na (pen′ə), *n., pl.* **pen·nae** (pen′ē). *Ornith.* a contour feather, as distinguished from a down feather, plume, etc. [< L: feather. See PEN[1]]

pen′ name′, a name used by an author instead of his real name; pseudonym; nom de plume.

pen·nant (pen′ənt), *n.* **1.** a long, tapering flag or burgee. **2.** a flag serving as an emblem of victory or championship. **3.** *Music.* hook (def. 10). **4.** *Naut.* pendant (def. 5). [b. PENNON and PENDANT]

pen·nate (pen′āt), *adj.* winged; feathered. Also, **pen′nat·ed.** [< L *pennāt(us)*]

Penn′ Hills′, a town in W Pennsylvania. 62,886 (1970).

pen·ni (pen′ē), *n., pl.* **pen·ni·a** (pen′ē ə), **pen·nis.** a copper coin of Finland, the 100th part of a markka. [< Finnish < LG *pennig* PENNY]

pen·ni·less (pen′ē lis), *adj.* without any money whatsoever; totally impoverished. [ME *peniles*] —**pen′ni·less·ly,** *adv.* —**pen′ni·less·ness,** *n.* —**Syn.** indigent. See **poor.** —**Ant.** rich.

Pen′nine Alps′ (pen′īn), a mountain range on the border between Switzerland and Italy: part of the Alps. Highest peak, Monte Rosa, 15,217 ft.

Pen′nine Chain′, a range of hills in N England, extending from the S Midlands to the Cheviot Hills.

pen·ni·nite (pen′ə nīt′), *n.* *Mineral.* a member of the chlorite group. Also called **pen·nine** (pen′in, -īn). [< G *Pennin* (after PENNINE ALPS) + -ITE[1]]

pen·non (pen′ən), *n.* **1.** a distinctive flag in any of various forms, formerly borne on the lance of a knight. **2.** a pennant. **3.** any flag or banner. [ME *penon* < MF, aug. of OF *pene* < L *penna* or *pinna* feather. See PEN[1]] —**pen′noned,** *adj.*

Penn·sau·ken (pen sô′kin), *n.* a township in W New Jersey, on the Delaware River. 36,394 (1970).

Penn·syl·va·ni·a (pen′səl vā′nē ə, -vān′yə), *n.* a state in the E United States. 11,793,909 (1970); 45,333 sq. mi. *Cap.:* Harrisburg. *Abbr.:* Pa., PA, Penn., Penna.

Penn′sylva′nia Dutch′, 1. the descendants of 18th-century settlers in Pennsylvania from SW Germany. **2.** Also called **Penn′sylva′nia Ger′man.** a German dialect spoken mainly in eastern Pennsylvania, developed from the language of these settlers.

Penn·syl·va·ni·an (pen′səl vā′nē ən, -vān′yən), *adj.* **1.** of or pertaining to the state of Pennsylvania. **2.** *Geol.* noting or pertaining to a period of the Paleozoic era, occurring from 270,000,000 to about 300,000,000 years ago and characterized by warm climates, swampy land areas, and the development of large reptiles and insects: sometimes considered as an epoch of the Carboniferous period. See table at **era.** —*n.* **3.** a native or inhabitant of Pennsylvania. **4.** *Geol.* the Pennsylvanian period or system.

pen·ny (pen′ē), *n., pl.* **pen·nies,** (*esp. collectively for 2*) **pence. 1.** a bronze coin of the U.S., the 100th part of a dollar; one cent. **2.** a bronze coin of Great Britain, the 12th part of a shilling: use phased out in 1971. *Abbr.:* d. **3.** Also called **new penny.** a bronze coin of the United Kingdom, the 100th part of a pound. *Abbr.:* p **4.** a bronze coin of Canada, the 100th part of a dollar. **5.** the 12th part of the shillings formerly used in various nations and territories. **6. a pretty penny,** *Informal.* a considerable sum of money: *Their car cost them a pretty penny.* [ME *peni,* OE *penig, pening, pending,* lit., something connected with *Penda,* 8th-century English (Mercian) king who coined the piece of money so named (see -ING[1]); D *penning,* G *Pfennig,* Icel *pen(n)ingr,* etc. < E]

-penny, a suffix forming adjectives that denote price or value (as used in *fourpenny nails, fivepenny nails,* etc., formerly meaning "nails costing fourpence, fivepence, etc., a hundred," but now nails of certain arbitrary sizes).

pen′ny an′te, 1. *Cards.* a game of poker in which the ante or limit is one cent. 2. *Informal.* any insignificant business transaction.

pen′ny arcade′, a hall or walk, as in an amusement park or carnival, that contains entertainment devices that can be operated for a penny or other small sum.

pen′ny dread′ful, a cheap, sensational novel of adventure, crime, or violence; dime novel.

pen′ny pinch′er, a miserly, niggardly, or stingy person. —**pen′ny-pinch′ing,** *n., adj.*

pen′ny post′, (formerly) any of various postal systems delivering mail for a penny a letter.

pen·ny·roy·al (pen′ē roi′əl), *n.* any herbaceous, labiate plant, as *Mentha Pulegium*, of the Old World, or *Hedeoma pulegioides*, of America, used medicinally and yielding a pungent aromatic oil. [< AF *puliol real* = MF *poliol* (< L **pulegiōl(um)*, dim. of *pulegium* pennyroyal) + *real*, earlier form of *royal*]

pen·ny·weight (pen′ē wāt′), *n.* (in troy weight) a unit of 24 grains or 1/20 of an ounce. *Abbr.:* dwt [ME *penyweight*, OE *penega gewihte*]

pen·ny·wort (pen′ē wûrt′), *n.* any of several plants having round or roundish leaves, as the navelwort. [late ME *penywort*]

pen·ny·worth (pen′ē wûrth′), *n.* 1. as much as may be bought for a penny. 2. a small quantity. 3. a bargain. [ME *penyworth*, OE *penigweorth*]

Pe·nob·scot (pə nob′skot, -skət), *n., pl.* **-scots,** (*esp. collectively*) **-scot** for 2. 1. a river flowing S from N Maine into Penobscot Bay. 350 mi. long. 2. a member of an Algonquian Indian tribe of the Abnaki confederacy, which occupied territory on both sides of the Penobscot Bay and River. 3. the dialect of the Abnaki language used by the Penobscot Indians.

Penob′scot Bay′, an inlet of the Atlantic in S Maine. 30 mi. long.

pe·nol·o·gy (pē nol′ə jē), *n.* 1. the science of the punishment of crime, in both its deterrent and its reformatory aspects. 2. the science of the management of prisons. [*peno-* (comb. form repr. Gk *poinḗ* penalty) + -LOGY] —**pe·no·log·i·cal** (pēn′əloj′i kəl), *adj.* —**pe·nol′o·gist,** *n.*

pen′ pal′, a person who keeps up an exchange of letters, usually with someone who is so far away that a personal meeting is unlikely.

pen·point (pen′point′), *n.* 1. the point or writing end of a pen, esp. a small, tapering, metallic device having a split tip for drawing up ink and for writing; nib. 2. the tip or point of a ball-point pen.

Pen·sa·co·la (pen′sə kō′lə), *n.* a seaport in NW Florida, on Pensacola Bay. 59,507 (1970).

Pen′saco′la Bay′, an inlet of the Gulf of Mexico, in NW Florida. ab. 30 mi. long.

pen·sée (päɴ sā′), *n., pl.* **-sées** (-sā′). *French.* a reflection or thought.

pen·sile (pen′sil), *adj.* 1. hanging, as the nests of certain birds. 2. building a hanging nest. [< L *pensil(is)* hanging down = *pens-*, a ptp. s. akin to *pendēre* to hang + *-ilis* -ILE] —**pen·sil′i·ty,** *n.*

pen·sion (pen′shən; *for 3 Fr.* päɴ syôɴ′), *n., pl.* **-sions** (-shənz; *for 3 Fr.* -syôɴ′), *v.* —*n.* 1. a fixed amount paid regularly by a former employer, a government, etc., to a retired, disabled, or deserving person or his dependents. 2. an allowance, annuity, or subsidy. 3. (in Europe) a. a boarding house. b. room and board. —*v.t.* 4. to grant a pension to. 5. to cause to retire on a pension (usually fol. by *off*): *They pensioned him off at 65.* [late ME < L *pensiōn-* (s. of *pensiō*) a weighing out, hence, a paying out, installment paying = *pens(us)* (ptp. of *pendere* to weigh out, pay by weight) + *-iōn-* -ION; r. ME *pensioun* < AF] —**pen′sion·a·ble,** *adj.* —**pen′sion·less,** *adj.*

pen·sion·ar·y (pen′shə ner′ē), *n., pl.* **-ar·ies,** *adj.* —*n.* 1. a pensioner. 2. a hireling. —*adj.* 3. of the nature of a pension. 4. receiving a pension. [< ML *pensionāri(us)*]

pen·sion·er (pen′shə nər), *n.* 1. a person who receives a pension. 2. a hireling. 3. *Obs.* a gentleman-at-arms. [late ME < AF]

pen·sive (pen′siv), *adj.* 1. dreamily or wistfully thoughtful. 2. expressing thoughtfulness or sadness. [< F (fem.); r. ME *pensif* < MF (masc.) < *penser* to think < L *pensāre* to weigh, consider. See PENSION, -IVE] —**pen′sive·ly,** *adv.* —**pen′sive·ness,** *n.*

—**Syn.** 1. PENSIVE, MEDITATIVE, REFLECTIVE suggest quiet modes of apparent or real thought. PENSIVE, the weakest of the three, suggests dreaminess or wistfulness, and may involve little or no thought to any purpose: *a pensive, faraway look.* MEDITATIVE involves thinking of certain facts or phenomena, perhaps in the religious sense of "contemplation," without necessarily having a goal of complete understanding or of action: *meditative but unjudicial.* REFLECTIVE has a strong implication of orderly, perhaps analytic, processes of thought, usually with a definite goal of understanding: *a careful and reflective critic.*

pen·ste·mon (pen stē′mən, pen′stə mən), *n.* pentstemon.

pen·stock (pen′stok′), *n.* a conduit for conveying water to a water wheel or turbine. [PEN² + STOCK]

pent (pent), *v.* 1. a pt. and pp. of **pen²**. —*adj.* 2. shut in; confined. [ptp. of late ME *pend* (now obs.), var. of PEN² (v.); cf. LEND]

Pent., Pentecost.

penta-, an element occurring in loan words from Greek, meaning "five" (*Pentateuch*); on this model, used in the formation of compound words (*pentavalent*). Also, *esp. before a vowel,* **pent-.** [< Gk *pent-, penta-*, comb. forms repr. *pénte* five]

pen·ta·bo·rane (pen′tə bōr′ān, -bôr′-), *n. Chem.* a liquid, B_5H_9, that ignites spontaneously in air: used as a rocket propellant. [PENTA- + BOR(ON) + -ANE]

pen·ta·chlo·ro·phe·nol (pen′tə klōr′ō fē′nōl, -nôl, -nol, -klôr′-), *n. Chem.* a white powder, C_6Cl_5OH, used chiefly in fungicides, disinfectants, and wood preservatives.

pen·ta·cle (pen′tə kəl), *n.* 1. pentagram. 2. a similar figure, as a hexagram. [< It *pentacolo* five-cornered object]

pen·tad (pen′tad), *n.* 1. a period of five years. 2. a group of five. 3. the number five. [< Gk *pentad-* (s. of *pentás*) group of five]

pen·ta·dac·tyl (pen′tə dak′təl, -til), *adj.* 1. having five digits on each hand or foot. 2. having five fingerlike projections or parts. [< L *pentadactyl(us)* < Gk *pentadáktylos*] —**pen′ta·dac′tyl·ism,** *n.*

pen·ta·dec·a·gon (pen′tə dek′ə gon′), *n. Geom.* a polygon having fifteen angles and fifteen sides.

108°

Pentagon (Regular)

pen·ta·gon (pen′tə gon′), *n.* 1. a polygon having five angles and five sides. 2. **the Pentagon,** a. a building in Arlington, Virginia, built in the form of a regular pentagon and containing most of the offices of the U.S. Department of Defense. b. the U.S. Department of Defense. [< LL *pentagōn(um)* < Gk *pentágōnon*, n. use of neut. of *pentágōnos* five-angled] —**pen·tag·o·nal** (pen tag′ə nəl), *adj.*

pen·ta·gram (pen′tə gram′), *n.* a regular, five-pointed, star-shaped figure, used as an occult symbolic figure. Also called **pentacle, pentangle.** [< Gk *pentágramm(on)*] —**pen·ta·gram·mat·ic** (pen′tə grə-mat′ik), *adj.*

Pentagram

pen·ta·he·dron (pen′tə hē′drən), *n., pl.* **-drons, -dra** (-drə). a solid figure having five faces. —**pen′ta·he′dral, pen′ta·he′dri·cal, pen′ta·he′drous,** *adj.*

pen·ta·hy·drate (pen′tə hī′drāt), *n. Chem.* a hydrate that contains five molecules of water, as potassium molybdate, $KMoO_4 \cdot 5H_2O$.

pen·tam·er·ous (pen tam′ər əs), *adj.* 1. consisting of or divided into five parts. 2. *Bot.* (of flowers) having five members in each whorl. [< NL *pentamerus*] —**pen·tam′er·ism, pen·tam′er·y,** *n.*

pen·tam·e·ter (pen tam′i tər), *Pros.* —*n.* 1. a verse of five feet. 2. Also called **elegiac pentameter.** *Class. Pros.* a verse consisting of two dactyls, one long syllable, two more dactyls, and another long syllable. 3. unrhymed verse of five iambic feet; heroic verse. —*adj.* 4. consisting of five metrical feet. [< L *pentameter* < Gk *pentámetros*]

pen·tane (pen′tān), *n. Chem., Pharm.* a hydrocarbon, C_5H_{12}, of the methane series, existing in three liquid isomeric forms.

pen·tan·gle (pen′tang gəl), *n.* pentagram.

pen·tan·gu·lar (pen tang′gyə lər), *adj.* having five angles and five sides; pentagonal.

pen·tap·o·dy (pen tap′ə dē), *n., pl.* **-dies.** *Pros.* a measure consisting of five feet. —**pen·ta·pod·ic** (pen′tə pod′ik), *adj.*

pen·tar·chy (pen′tär kē), *n., pl.* **-chies.** 1. a government or governing body consisting of five persons. 2. a union of five autonomous states. [< Gk *pentarchía*] —**pen′tarch,** *n.* —**pen·tar′chi·cal,** *adj.*

pen·ta·stich (pen′tə stik′), *n. Pros.* a strophe, stanza, or poem consisting of five lines or verses. [< NL *pentastich(us)* < Gk *pentástichos*]

pen·ta·syl·la·ble (pen′tə sil′ə bəl), *n.* a word or line of verse of five syllables. —**pen·ta·syl·lab·ic** (pen′tə si lab′ik), *adj.* —**pen′ta·syl′la·bism,** *n.*

Pen·ta·teuch (pen′tə to͞ok′, -tyo͞ok′), *n.* the first five books of the Old Testament. [< LL *Pentateuch(os)* < LGk *pentáteuchos (biblos)* = Gk *penta-* PENTA- + *teûch(os)* tool, implement > LGk: book] —**Pen′ta·teuch′al,** *adj.*

pen·tath·lon (pen tath′lən), *n.* an athletic contest comprising five different track and field events and won by the contestant gaining the highest total score. [< Gk *péntathlon* = *pent-* PENT- + *âthlon* contest]

pen′ta·ton′ic scale′ (pen′tə ton′ik, pen′-), *Music.* a scale having five tones to an octave, as the five black keys of a piano octave.

pen·ta·va·lent (pen′tə vā′lənt, pen tav′ə-), *adj. Chem.* 1. having a valence of 5: *pentavalent arsenic.* 2. quinquevalent (def. 2).

Pen·te·cost (pen′tə kôst′, -kost′), *n.* 1. a Christian festival celebrated on the seventh Sunday after Easter, commemorating the descent of the Holy Ghost upon the apostles; Whitsunday. 2. *Judaism.* Shabuoth. [ME *pentecoste*, OE *pentecosten* < LL *pentēcostē* < Gk *pentēkostḗ* fiftieth (day)]

Pen·te·cos·tal (pen′tə kô′stəl, -stəl, -kos′təl, -təl), *adj.* 1. of or pertaining to Pentecost. 2. noting or pertaining to any of the Christian groups, often fundamentalist, that emphasize the activity of the Holy Spirit, stress holiness of living, and express their religious feelings uninhibitedly, as by speaking in tongues. [< LL *pentēcostāl(is)*]

Pen·tel·i·cus (pen tel′ə kəs), *n.* a mountain in SE Greece, near Athens: noted for its fine marble. 3640 ft. Also, **Pen·tel·i·kon** (pen tel′ə kon′). —**Pen·tel′ic,** *adj.*

pent·house (pent′hous′), *n., pl.* **-hous·es** (-hou′ziz). 1. a separate apartment or dwelling on a roof. 2. a structure on a roof for housing elevator machinery, a water tank, etc. 3. a shelter with a sloping roof projecting from a wall. 4. See **shed roof.** [alter. (by folk etym.) of ME *pentis* < OF *apentis* annex; akin to APPENDIX]

pen·to·bar·bi·tal (pen′tə bär′bi tal′, -tôl′), *n. Pharm.* a barbiturate, $C_{11}H_{18}N_2O_3$, used chiefly in the form of its sodium or calcium salt as a hypnotic and as a sedative.

pen·tom·ic (pen tom′ik), *adj. Mil.* pertaining to or characterizing the organization of an army division into five groups for purposes of atomic warfare. [PENT- + (AT)OMIC]

pen·to·san (pen′tə san′), *n. Biochem.* any of a class of polysaccharides that occur in plants, humus, etc., and form pentoses upon hydrolysis. [PENTOSE + -AN]

pen·tose (pen′tōs), *n. Chem.* a monosaccharide containing five atoms of carbon, as xylose, $C_5H_{10}O_5$, or produced from pentosans by hydrolysis.

Pen·to·thal (pen′tə thôl′), *n. Pharm., Trademark.* thiopental.

pent·ste·mon (pent stē′mən), *n.* any of several North American plants of the genus *Pentstemon*, certain species of which are cultivated for their showy flowers. Also, **penstemon.** [< NL = *pent-* PENT- + Gk *stēmōn* warp, thread]

pent-up (pent′up′), *adj.* confined; restrained; curbed: *pent-up emotions.*

pen′tyl group′, *Chem.* any of the univalent, isomeric groups having the formula C_5H_{11}–.

pe·nu·che (pə no͞o′chē), *n.* **1.** Also, **panocha.** a candy made of brown sugar, butter, and milk, usually with nuts. **2.** panocha (def. 1). [var. of PANOCHA]

pe·nult (pē′nult, pi nult′), *n.* the next to the last syllable in a word. Also, **pe·nul·ti·ma** (pi nul′tə mə). [< L *paenultima* (*syllaba*), contr. of *paene ultima* almost the last; see ULTIMA]

pe·nul·ti·mate (pi nul′tə mit), *adj.* **1.** next to the last. **2.** of or pertaining to a penult or penults. —*n.* **3.** a penult.

pe·num·bra (pi num′brə), *n., pl.* **-brae** (-brē), **-bras. 1.** the partial or imperfect shadow surrounding the complete shadow of an opaque body. Cf. **umbra** (def. 3). **2.** the grayish marginal portion of a sunspot. Cf. **umbra** (def. 4). [< NL] —**pe·num′bral, pe·num′brous,** *adj.*

pe·nu·ri·ous (pə no͝or′ē əs, -nyo͝or′-), *adj.* **1.** extremely stingy. **2.** extremely poor; indigent. **3.** poorly or inadequately supplied. [< ML *pēnūriōs(us).* See PENURY, -OUS] —**pe·nu′ri·ous·ly,** *adv.* —**pe·nu′ri·ous·ness,** *n.* —**Syn. 1.** tight, close, niggardly. —**Ant. 1.** generous.

pen·u·ry (pen′yə rē), *n.* **1.** extreme poverty. **2.** scarcity; insufficiency. [late ME < L *pēnūria;* akin to Gk *peîna* hunger, *penía* poverty] —**Syn. 1.** indigence, need, want.

Pe·nu·ti·an (pə no͞o′tē ən, -shən), *n.* **1.** a North American Indian linguistic stock, tentatively established as being distributed from California northward through Oregon and British Columbia. —*adj.* **2.** of or pertaining to Penutian. [*Penuti* (learned coinage, combining *pen* two and *uti* two, taken from different languages of the stock) + -AN]

Pen·za (pen′zä), *n.* a city in the W RSFSR, in the central Soviet Union in Europe. 305,000 (1964).

Pen·zance (pen zans′), *n.* a seaport in SW Cornwall, in the SW extremity of England: resort. 19,433 (1961).

pe·on[1] (pē′ən, pē′on), *n.* **1.** (in Spanish America and southwestern U.S.) **a.** a person who tends a horse or mule. **b.** See **day laborer. 2.** (esp. in Mexico) a person held in servitude to work off debts or other obligations. [< Sp *peón* peasant, day laborer < VL **pedōn-* (s. of **pedō*) walker (> ML *pedōnes* infantry, OF *peon* pawn) < L *ped-* (s. of *pēs*) foot]

pe·on[2] (pē′ən, pē′on), *n.* (in India and Ceylon) **1.** a messenger or attendant. **2.** a native soldier. **3.** See **foot soldier.** [< Pg *peão,* F *pion* foot soldier, pedestrian, day laborer. See PEON[1]]

pe·on·age (pē′ə nij), *n.* **1.** the condition or service of a peon. **2.** the practice of holding persons in servitude or partial slavery, as to work off a debt or to serve a penal sentence.

pe·on·ism (pē′ə niz′əm), *n. Archaic.* peonage.

pe·o·ny (pē′ə nē), *n., pl.* **-nies. 1.** any ranunculaceous herb or shrub of the genus *Paeonia,* having large, showy flowers. **2.** the flower: the state flower of Indiana. [ME *pione* (< AF), OE *peonie* < LL *peōnia,* L *paeōnia* < Gk *paiōnía* peony, akin to *paiṓnios* healing]

peo·ple (pē′pəl), *n., pl.* **-ple, -ples** for 1, *v.,* **-pled, -pling.** —*n.* **1.** the whole body of persons constituting a community, tribe, race, or nation. **2.** the persons of any particular group or area. **3.** persons in relation to a ruler, leader, employer, etc. **4.** a person's family or relatives. **5.** the fellow members of one's group or community. **6.** the body of enfranchised citizens of a state. **7.** the ordinary persons of a community. **8.** persons indefinitely: *Won't people gossip?* **9.** human beings, as distinguished from animals. —*v.t.* **10.** to furnish with people; populate. **11.** to settle in or inhabit. [ME *peple* < AF *poeple,* OF *pueple* < L *popul(us).* See POPULAR] —**Syn. 1.** See **race**[2].

peo′ple mov′er, any of various experimental mass-transit systems whose general concept is the use of horizontal moving belts or unconventional vehicles to transport people around airports, shopping areas, etc.

peo′ple's com′mune, a usually rural, Communist Chinese social and administrative unit of from 2000 to 4000 families combined for collective farming, fishing, mining, or industrial projects. Also called **commune.**

Peo′ple's par′ty, *U.S. Politics.* a political party (1891–1904), advocating expansion of currency, state control of railroads, etc.

Pe·o·ri·a (pē ōr′ē ə, -ôr′-), *n.* a city in central Illinois, on the Illinois River. 126,963 (1970). —**Pe·o′ri·an,** *adj., n.*

pep (pep), *n., v.,* **pepped, pep·ping.** *Informal.* —*n.* **1.** spirit or animation; vigor; energy. —*v.t., v.i.* **2. pep up,** to make or become vigorous or lively. [short for PEPPER]

pep·er·o·ni (pep′ə rō′nē), *n.* a highly seasoned, hard sausage of beef and pork. Also, **pepperoni.** [< It, pl. of *peperone* Cayenne pepper plant, aug. of *pepe* PEPPER]

Pep·in (pep′in), *n.* ("*Pepin the Short*") died A.D. 768, king of the Franks 751–768 (father of Charlemagne).

pep·los (pep′ləs), *n., pl.* **-los·es.** a voluminous outer garment worn, draped in folds, by women in ancient Greece. Also, **peplus.** [< Gk]

pep·lum (pep′ləm), *n., pl.* **-lums, -la** (-lə). **1.** a short full flounce or an extension of a garment below the waist, covering the hips. **2.** a short skirt attached to a bodice or jacket. [< L < Gk **péplon* (only pl. *pépla* occurs). See PEPLOS]

pep·lus (pep′ləs), *n., pl.* **-lus·es.** peplos.

pe·po (pē′pō), *n., pl.* **-pos.** the characteristic fruit of cucurbitaceous plants, having a fleshy, many-seeded interior and a hard or firm rind, as the gourd, melon, cucumber, etc. [< L: large melon, pumpkin < Gk *pépōn,* short for *pépōn* (*síkyos*) a ripe (gourd)]

pep·per (pep′ər), *n.* **1.** a pungent condiment obtained from various plants of the genus *Piper,* esp. from the dried berries of the tropical, climbing shrub *P. nigrum.* **2.** any plant of the genus *Piper,* or the family *Piperaceae.* **3.** cayenne, or red pepper, prepared from species of Capsicum. **4.** any plant of the genus *Capsicum,* esp. the common garden pepper, *C. frutescens,* or its green or red, hot or sweet fruit. —*v.t.* **5.** to season with or as with pepper. **6.** to sprinkle with or as with pepper; dot; stud. **7.** to pelt with shot or missiles. [ME *peper, piper,* OE *piper* < L < Gk *péperi;* cf. D *peper,* G *Pfeffer,* Icel *piparr*]

pep·per-and-salt (pep′ər ən sôlt′), *adj.* composed of a fine mixture of black with white, as cloth.

pep·per·box (pep′ər boks′), *n.* a small box with perforations in the top, for sprinkling pepper. Also called **pepper pot.**

pep·per·corn (pep′ər kôrn′), *n.* **1.** the berry of the pepper plant, *Piper nigrum,* dried and used as a spice, often after being ground. **2.** anything very small, insignificant, or trifling. —*adj.* **3.** (of hair) growing in tightly spiraled clumps. [ME *pepercorn* < OE *piporcorn*] —**pep′per·corn′ish, pep′per·corn′y,** *adj.*

pep·per·grass (pep′ər gras′, -gräs′), *n.* any pungent plant of the genus *Lepidium,* used as a potherb or salad vegetable. Cf. **garden cress.**

pep·per·idge (pep′ər ij), *n.* the tupelo. [?]

pep′per mill′, a small hand mill for grinding peppercorns in the kitchen or at the table.

pep·per·mint (pep′ər mint′), *n.* **1.** a labiate herb, *Mentha piperita,* cultivated for its aromatic, pungent oil. **2.** Also called **pep′permint oil′.** this oil, or some preparation of it. **3.** a lozenge or confection flavored with it.

pep·per·o·ni (pep′ə rō′nē), *n.* peperoni.

pep′per pot′, 1. a West Indian stew, the principal flavoring of which is cassareep, with meat or fish and vegetables. **2.** a highly seasoned soup made of tripe and vegetables. **3.** pepperbox.

pep′per tree′, any of several chiefly South American, evergreen trees of the genus *Schinus,* cultivated in subtropical regions as an ornamental.

pep·per·y (pep′ə rē), *adj.* **1.** full of or tasting like pepper. **2.** of, pertaining to, or resembling pepper. **3.** sharp or stinging: *a peppery speech.* **4.** easily angered; irritable; irascible. —**pep′per·i·ly,** *adv.* —**pep′per·i·ness,** *n.* —**Syn. 1.** spicy. **3.** biting. **4.** hot-tempered, testy. —**Ant. 1.** mild, bland.

pep′ pill′, a pill, tablet, or capsule that consists typically of a form of the stimulant drug amphetamine.

pep·py (pep′ē), *adj.,* **-pi·er, -pi·est.** *Informal.* energetic; vigorous; lively. —**pep′pi·ly,** *adv.* —**pep′pi·ness,** *n.*

pep·sin (pep′sin), *n. Biochem.* **1.** an enzyme, produced in the stomach, that in the presence of hydrochloric acid splits proteins into proteoses and peptones. **2.** a commercial form of this substance, used as a digestive, as a ferment in the manufacture of cheese, etc. Also, **pep′sine.** [< Gk *pép(sis)* digestion (*pép(tein)* (to) digest + *-sis* -SIS) + -IN[2]]

pep·sin·ate (pep′sə nāt′), *v.t.,* **-at·ed, -at·ing.** to treat, prepare, or mix with pepsin.

pep·sin·o·gen (pep sin′ə jən), *n. Biochem.* a zymogen, occurring in the gastric glands, that during digestion is converted into pepsin. —**pep·si·no·gen·ic** (pep′sə nō jen′ik), **pep·si·nog·e·nous** (pep′sə noj′ə nəs), *adj.*

pep′ talk′, a vigorous talk, as to a person or group, calculated to arouse support for a cause, increase the determination to succeed, etc.

pep·tic (pep′tik), *adj.* **1.** pertaining to or associated with digestion; digestive. **2.** promoting digestion. **3.** of or pertaining to pepsin. —*n.* **4.** a substance promoting digestion. [< Gk *peptik(ós)* conducive to digestion = *pept(ós)* digested (verbid of *péptein*) + *-ikos* -IC]

pep′tic ul′cer, an erosion of the mucous membrane of the stomach or duodenum, caused in part by the corrosive action of the gastric juice. Cf. **gastric ulcer.**

pep·ti·dase (pep′ti dās′), *n. Biochem.* any of the class of enzymes that catalyze the hydrolysis of peptides or peptones to amino acids.

pep·tide (pep′tīd, -tid), *n. Biochem.* a compound containing two or more amino acids in which the carboxyl group of one acid is linked to the amino group of the other, as $H_2NCH_2CONHCH_2COOH$. [PEPT(IC) + -IDE]

pep·tize (pep′tīz), *v.t.,* **-tized, -tiz·ing.** to disperse (a substance) into colloidal form, usually in a liquid. [? < Gk *pépt(ein)* (to) digest + -IZE] —**pep·tiz′a·ble,** *adj.* —**pep′ti·za′tion,** *n.* —**pep′tiz·er,** *n.*

pep·tone (pep′tōn), *n. Biochem.* any of a class of diffusible, soluble substances into which proteins are converted by partial hydrolysis. [< G *Pepton* < Gk *peptón,* neut. of *peptós* cooked, digested, verbid of *péptein*] —**pep·ton·ic** (pep ton′ik), *adj.* —**pep·to·noid** (pep′tə noid′), *n.*

pep·to·nise (pep′tə nīz′), *v.t.,* **-nised, -nis·ing.** *Chiefly Brit.* peptonize. —**pep′to·ni·sa′tion,** *n.* —**pep′to·nis′er,** *n.*

pep·to·nize (pep′tə nīz′), *v.t.,* **-nized, -niz·ing.** to hydrolyze or dissolve by a proteolytic enzyme, as pepsin. —**pep′to·ni·za′tion,** *n.* —**pep′to·niz′er,** *n.*

Pepys (pēps, peps, pē′pis, pep′is), *n.* **Samuel,** 1633–1703, English diarist and naval official.

Pe·quot (pē′kwot), *n., pl.* **-quots,** (*esp. collectively*) **-quot.** a member of a former tribe of Algonquin Indians, in southern New England in the early 17th century. [? shortened var. of Narragansett *paquatanog* destroyers]

per (pûr; *unstressed* pər), *prep.* for each; through; by: *12 parts per thousand.* [< L, ML, OF: through, by, for, for each. See FOR]

—**Usage.** In commercial use A is preferred to PER by most stylists: *$40 a gross; 5 percent interest a year.*

per-, 1. a prefix meaning "through," "thoroughly," "utterly," "very": *pervert; pervade; perfect.* **2.** *Chem.* a prefix applied to inorganic acids and their salts to indicate that they possess an excess of the designated element: *percarbonic acid* ($H_2C_2O_5$); *permanganic acid* ($HMnO_4$); *potassium permanganate* ($KMnO_4$); *potassium persulfate* ($K_2S_2O_8$). [< L, comb. form of *per* PER, and used as an intensive]

Per., 1. Persia. **2.** Persian.

per., 1. period. **2.** person.

Pe·ra (pe′rä), *n.* a modern section of Istanbul, Turkey, N of the Golden Horn. 218,433 (1965). Also called **Beyoglu.**

per·ac·id (pər as′id), *n. Chem.* an oxyacid, the primary element of which is in its highest possible oxidation state, as perchloric acid, $HClO_4$, and permanganic acid, $HMnO_4$.

per·ad·ven·ture (pûr′əd ven′chər, per′-), *n.* **1.** chance or uncertainty. **2.** surmise. —*adv.* **3.** *Archaic.* it may be; maybe; possibly; perhaps. [ME *per aventure* < OF]

Pe·rae·a (pə rē′ə), *n.* a region in ancient Palestine, E of the Jordan and the Dead Sea.

Pe·rak (pā′rak, -räk, per′ə, pēr′ə), *n.* a state in Malaysia, on the SW Malay Peninsula. 1,384,321 (est. 1961); 7980 sq. mi. *Cap.:* Taiping.

per·am·bu·late (pər am′byə lāt′), *v.,* **-lat·ed, -lat·ing.** —*v.t.* **1.** to walk through, about, or over; travel through;

traverse. 2. to traverse in order to examine or inspect. —*v.i.* 3. to walk or travel about; stroll. [< L *perambulāt(us)* walked through, ptp. of *perambulāre*] —**per·am/bu·la/tion,** *n.* —**per·am·bu·la·to·ry** (pər am/byə lə tōr/ē, -tôr/ē), *adj.*

per·am·bu·la·tor (pər am/byə lā/tər), *n.* 1. *Chiefly Brit.* a baby carriage. 2. a person who makes a tour of inspection on foot. [< ML]

per an., per annum.

per an·num (pər an/əm), by the year; yearly. [< L]

per·bo·rate (pər bōr/āt, -bôr/-), *n.* *Chem.* a salt of perboric acid, as sodium perborate, $NABO_2 \cdot H_2O_2 \cdot 3H_2O$, used for bleaching, disinfecting, etc. Also called **peroxyborate.**

per·cale (pər kāl/), *n.* a closely woven, smooth-finished, plain or printed cambric. [< F < Pers *pargālah* rag; r. *percalla* < Pers]

per·ca·line (pûr/kə lēn/), *n.* a fine, lightweight cotton fabric used esp. for linings. [< F; see PERCALE, -INE[2]]

per cap·i·ta (pər kap/i tə), for each unit of population; by or for the individual person: *The income per capita of Southeast Asian countries is very low.* [< L: lit., by heads]

per·ceiv·a·ble (pər sē/və bəl), *adj.* capable of being perceived; perceptible. [ME *perceyvable*] —**per·ceiv/a·bil/i·ty, per·ceiv/a·ble·ness,** *n.* —**per·ceiv/a·bly,** *adv.*

per·ceive (pər sēv/), *v.t.*, **-ceived, -ceiv·ing.** 1. to become aware of, know, or identify by means of the senses: *They could dimly perceive the house through the mist.* 2. to apprehend, envision, or understand: *Can't you perceive the difference between right and wrong?* [ME *perceive(n)* < OF **perceivre, perçoivre* < L *percipere* to lay hold of, grasp = *per-* PER- + *-cipere*, comb. form of *capere* to take] —**per·ceiv·ed·ly** (pər sē/vid lē, -sēvd/-), *adv.* —**per·ceiv/er,** *n.* —**Syn. 1.** note, discover, observe. See **notice.**

per·cent (pər sent/), *n.* 1. Also called **per centum.** one one-hundredth part; [1]/100. 2. percentage (def. 1). 3. *Brit.* stocks, bonds, etc., that bear an indicated rate of interest. —*adj.* 4. reckoned on the basis of a rate or proportion per hundred (used in combination with a number in expressing rates of interest, proportions, etc.). *Symbol:* % Also, **per cent.** [short for ML *per centum* by the hundred] —**per·cent/al,** *adj.*

per·cent·age (pər sen/tij), *n.* 1. Also called **percent.** a rate or proportion per hundred. 2. an allowance, duty, commission, or rate of interest on a hundred items. 3. a proportion in general: *Only a small percentage of the class will graduate with honors.* —**per·cent/aged,** *adj.*

per·cen·tile (pər sen/tīl, -til), *Statistics.* —*n.* 1. one of the values of a variable that divides the distribution of the variable into 100 groups having equal frequencies. —*adj.* 2. of or pertaining to a percentile or a division of a distribution by percentiles.

per cent·um (pər sen/təm), percent (def. 1). [< L: lit., by the hundred]

per·cept (pûr/sept), *n.* 1. the mental result or product of perceiving, as distinguished from the act of perceiving. 2. that which is perceived; the object of perception. [< L *percept(um)* something perceived, n. use of neut. of *perceptus*, ptp. of *percipere* to PERCEIVE]

per·cep·ti·ble (pər sep/tə bəl), *adj.* capable of being perceived; recognizable; appreciable. [< LL *perceptibil(is)*] —**per·cep/ti·bil/i·ty, per·cep/ti·ble·ness,** *n.* —**per·cep/ti·bly,** *adv.* —**Syn.** discernible, apparent.

per·cep·tion (pər sep/shən), *n.* 1. the act or faculty of apprehending by means of the senses or of the mind; cognition; understanding. 2. immediate or intuitive recognition, as of moral or aesthetic qualities. 3. the result or product of perceiving; percept. 4. *Psychol.* a single unified awareness derived from sensory processes while a stimulus is present. 5. *Law.* the taking into possession of rents, crops, profits, etc. [late ME < L *perceptiōn-* (s. of *perceptiō*) comprehension, lit., a taking in] —**per·cep/tion·al,** *adj.*

per·cep·tive (pər sep/tiv), *adj.* 1. having the power or faculty of perceiving. 2. of, pertaining to, or showing perception. 3. having or showing keenness of insight, understanding, or intuition: *a perceptive analysis of the problems involved.* [< L *percept(us)* (see PERCEPT) + -IVE] —**per·cep/tive·ly,** *adv.* —**per/cep·tiv/i·ty, per·cep/tive·ness,** *n.*

per·cep·tu·al (pər sep/cho͞o əl), *adj.* of or pertaining to perception. [< L *perceptu(s)* (see PERCEPT) + -AL[1]] —**per·cep/tu·al·ly,** *adv.*

Per·ce·val (pûr/sə vəl), *n.* *Arthurian Romance.* Percival.

perch[1] (pûrch), *n.* 1. a pole or rod, usually fixed horizontally, serving as a roost for birds. 2. any place or object for a bird, animal, or person to alight or rest upon. 3. a high or elevated position, resting place, or the like. 4. a pole connecting the fore and hind running parts of a spring carriage or other vehicle. 5. a measure equivalent to a linear or square rod. 6. a solid measure for stone, commonly 16½ feet by 1½ feet by 1 foot. 7. *Textiles.* an apparatus for inspecting cloth. 8. *Obs.* any pole, rod, or the like. —*v.i.* 9. to alight or rest upon a perch, as a bird. 10. to settle or rest in some elevated position, as if on a perch. —*v.t.* 11. to set or place on or as on a perch. 12. to inspect (cloth) for defects and blemishes. [ME *perche* < OF < L *pertica* pole, staff, measuring rod] —**perch/er,** *n.*

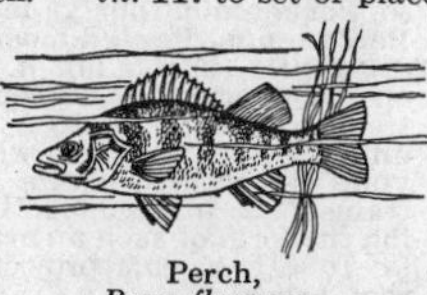
Perch, *Perca flavescens* (Length 1 ft.)

perch[2] (pûrch), *n., pl.* (*esp. collectively*) **perch,** (*esp. referring to two or more kinds or species*) **perch·es.** 1. any spiny-finned, fresh-water food fish of the genus *Perca*, as *P. flavescens*, found in the U.S., or *P. fluviatilis*, found in Europe. 2. any of various other spiny-finned, related fishes. 3. any of several embiotocid fishes, as *Hysterocarpus traski*, of California. [ME *perche* < MF < L *perca* < Gk *pérkē*]

per·chance (pər chans/, -chäns/), *adv.* *Literary.* 1. maybe; possibly. 2. by chance. [ME, var. of *par chance* by chance < AF]

Perche (pârsh; *Fr.* persh), *n.* a former division of N France.

Per·che·ron (pûr/chə ron/, -shə-), *n.* one of a French breed of draft horses, having a gray or black coat. [< F; named after *Perche*, French district where first bred]

per·chlo·rate (pər klōr/āt, -klôr/-), *n.* *Chem.* a salt or ester of perchloric acid, as potassium perchlorate, $KClO_4$.

perchlo/ric ac/id, *Chem.* a colorless, syrupy hygroscopic liquid, $HClO_4$, used chiefly as a reagent in analytical chemistry. —**per·chlor·ic** (pər klōr/ik, -klôr/-), *adj.*

perchloro-, a combination of **per-** and **chloro-**[2]: *perchloromethane.* Also, *esp. before a vowel,* **perchlor-.**

per·cip·i·ent (pər sip/ē ənt), *adj.* 1. perceiving. 2. having perception; discerning; discriminating. —*n.* 3. a person who perceives. [< L *percipient-* (s. of *percipiēns*) taking in, prp. of *percipere.* See PERCEIVE, -ENT] —**per·cip/i·ence, per·cip/i·en·cy,** *n.*

Per·ci·val (pûr/sə vəl), *n.* *Arthurian Romance.* a knight who sought the Holy Grail: comparable to Parzival or Parsifal in Teutonic legend. Also, **Perceval, Per/ci·vale.**

per·coid (pûr/koid), *adj.* 1. belonging to the *Percoidea*, a group of acanthopterygian fishes comprising the true perches and related families, and constituting one of the largest natural groups of fishes. 2. resembling a perch. Also, **per·coi·de·an** (pər koi/dē ən). [< L *perc(a)* PERCH[2] + -OID]

per·co·late (pûr/kə lāt/), **-lat·ed, -lat·ing.** —*v.t.* 1. to cause (a liquid) to pass through a porous body; filter. 2. (of a liquid) to filter through; permeate. 3. to brew (coffee) in a percolator. —*v.i.* 4. to pass through a porous substance; filter; ooze. 5. to become percolated. 6. to become active, lively, or spirited. [< L *percōlāt(us)* filtered, ptp. of *percōlāre.* See PER-, COLANDER, -ATE[1]] —**per/co·la·ble,** *adj.* —**per/co·la/tion,** *n.* —**per/co·la/tive,** *adj.*

per·co·la·tor (pûr/kə lā/tər), *n.* 1. a kind of coffee pot in which boiling water is forced up a hollow stem, filters through ground coffee, and returns to the pot below. 2. that which percolates.

per con·tra (pər kon/trə; *Lat.* per kōn/trä), on the other hand; on the contrary. [< L]

per·cuss (pər kus/), *v.t.* 1. to strike (something) so as to shake or cause a shock to. 2. *Med.* to strike or tap for diagnostic or therapeutic purposes. [< L *percuss(us)* struck hard, beaten, ptp. of *percutere* = *per-* PER- + *-cutere*, comb. form of *quatere* to shake. See QUASH[1]]

per·cus·sion (pər kush/ən), *n.* 1. the striking of one body against another with some sharpness; impact. 2. *Med.* the striking or tapping of a part of the body for diagnostic or therapeutic purposes. 3. percussion instruments collectively. 4. a sharp blow for detonating a percussion cap or the fuze of an artillery shell. 5. the act of percussing. [< L *percussiōn-* (s. of *percussiō*) a beating] —**per·cus/sion·al,** *adj.*

percus/sion cap/, a small metallic cap or cup containing fulminating powder, formerly exploded by percussion to fire the charge of small arms.

percus/sion in/strument, a musical instrument, as the drum, cymbal, piano, etc., that is struck to produce a sound.

per·cus·sion·ist (pər kush/ə nist), *n.* a musician who plays percussion instruments.

percus/sion lock/, a gunlock on a firearm that fires by striking a percussion cap. Cf. **flintlock.**

per·cus·sive (pər kus/iv), *adj.* of, pertaining to, or characterized by percussion. —**per·cus/sive·ly,** *adv.* —**per·cus/sive·ness,** *n.*

Per·cy (pûr/sē), *n.* 1. **Charles Hart·ing** (här/ting), born 1919, U.S. senator from Illinois since 1967. 2. **Sir Henry** ("*Hotspur*"), 1364–1403, English military and rebel leader. 3. **Thomas,** 1729–1811, English poet and antiquary: bishop of Dromore 1782–1811.

Per·di·do (*Sp.* per thē/thô), *n.* **Mon·te** (*Sp.* môn/te), a mountain in NE Spain, a peak of the Pyrenees. 10,994 ft. French, **Mont Perdu.**

per·die (pər dē/), *adv., interj.* *Archaic.* pardi.

per di·em (pər dē/əm, dī/əm), 1. by the day. 2. a daily allowance, usually for living expenses while traveling in connection with one's work. [< L]

per·di·tion (pər dish/ən), *n.* 1. a state of final spiritual ruin; loss of the soul; damnation. 2. the future state of the wicked. 3. hell. 4. utter destruction or ruin. [< L *perditiōn-* (s. of *perditiō*) destruction = *perdit(us)* ruined (ptp. of *perdere* to do for = *per-* PER- + *-dere*, comb. form of *dāre* to give) + *-iōn-* -ION; r. ME *perdicium* < OF]

per·du (pər do͞o/, -dyo͞o/, per-), *adj.* hidden; concealed; obscured. Also, **per·due/.** [< F: lost, ptp. of *perdre* < L *perdere* to lose. See PERDITION]

Per·du (per dy/), *n.* **Mont** (môn), French name of Monte Perdido.

per·dur·a·ble (pər do͝or/ə bəl, -dyo͝or/-), *adj.* permanent; everlasting; imperishable. [ME < LL *perdūrābil(is)*] —**per·dur/a·bil/i·ty, per·dur/a·ble·ness,** *n.* —**per·dur/a·bly,** *adv.*

père (per; *Eng.* pâr), *n., pl.* **pères** (per; *Eng.* pârz). *French.* 1. father. 2. senior: *Dumas père.*

per·e·gri·nate (per/ə grə nāt/), *v.*, **-nat·ed, -nat·ing.** —*v.i.* 1. to travel or journey, esp. on foot. —*v.t.* 2. to travel over; traverse. [< L *peregrīnāt(us)* traveled abroad (ptp.)] —**per/e·gri·na/tor,** *n.*

per·e·gri·na·tion (per/ə grə nā/shən), *n.* 1. travel from one place to another, esp. on foot. 2. a course of travel; journey. [< L *peregrīnātiōn-* (s. of *peregrīnātiō*) a traveling abroad]

per·e·grine (per/ə grin, -grēn/, -grīn/), *adj.* 1. foreign; alien; coming from abroad. —*n.* 2. See **peregrine falcon.** [< L *peregrīn(us)* foreign < *peregrē* abroad, lit., through (i.e., beyond the borders of) the (home) field = *per-* PER- + *-egr-*, comb. form of *ager* field + *-ē* adv. suffix; see -INE[1]] —**per·e·grin·i·ty** (per/ə grin/i tē), *n.*

per/egrine fal/con, a cosmopolitan falcon, *Falco peregrinus*, much used in falconry because of its swift flight. See illus. at **falcon.**

Pe·rei·ra (pe rä/rä), *n.* a city in W Colombia. 223,500 (est. 1964).

per·emp·to·ry (pə remp/tə rē, per/əmp tōr/ē, -tôr/ē), *adj.* 1. leaving no opportunity for denial or refusal; imperative: *a peremptory command.* 2. imperious or dictatorial. 3. *Law.* a. that precludes debate, question, etc. b. decisive or final. 4. positive or assertive in speech, tone, manner, etc. [< legal

L *peremptōri(us)* final, decisive, lit., deadly, destructive] —**per·emp′to·ri·ly,** *adv.* —**per·emp′to·ri·ness,** *n.*

per·en·ni·al (pə ren′ē əl), *adj.* **1.** lasting for an indefinitely long time; enduring. **2.** *Bot.* having a life cycle lasting more than two years. **3.** lasting or continuing throughout the year, as a stream. **4.** perpetual; everlasting; continuing; recurrent. —*n.* **5.** a perennial plant. **6.** something that is continuing or recurrent. [< L *perenni(s)* lasting the whole year through (*per-* PER- + *-enn-*, comb. form of *annus* year + *-is* adj. suffix) + -AL[1]] —**per·en·ni·al·i·ty** (pə ren′ē al′i tē), *n.* —**per·en′ni·al·ly,** *adv.* —**Syn. 1.** perdurable; constant, incessant, continual. **4.** undying, eternal, immortal.

peren′nial rye′grass. See under **ryegrass.**

Pé·rez de Cué·llar (pe′Res the kwe′yäR), *n.* **Ja·vier** (hä vyeR′), born 1920, Peruvian diplomat: secretary-general of the United Nations since 1982.

Pe·rez Es·qui·vel (pe′Res es′kē vel′), **A·dol·fo** (ä thôl′fô), born 1932, Argentine human rights activist: Nobel peace prize 1980.

perf., **1.** perfect. **2.** perforated.

perf·board (pûrf′bōrd′, -bôrd′), *n.* a panel of wood, plastic, etc., perforated closely with holes in which one can mount hooks, electronic or electrical components, etc. [PERF(ORATED) + BOARD]

per·fect (*adj., n.* pûr′fikt; *v.* pər fekt′, pûr′fikt), *adj.* **1.** conforming absolutely to the description or definition of the type: *a perfect sphere; a perfect gentleman.* **2.** excellent or complete beyond practical or theoretical improvement. **3.** exactly fitting the need in a certain situation or for a certain purpose. **4.** without any of the flaws or shortcomings that might be present: *a perfect apple.* **5.** correct in every detail: *a perfect copy.* **6.** thorough; complete; utter: *perfect strangers.* **7.** pure or unmixed: *perfect yellow.* **8.** unqualified; absolute. **9.** unmitigated; out-and-out. **10.** *Bot.* **a.** having all parts or members present. **b.** monoclinous. **11.** *Gram.* designating a tense or other verb formation noting a completed action or state. **12.** *Music.* **a.** applied to the consonances of unison, octave, and fifth, as distinguished from those of the third and sixth, which are called imperfect. **b.** applied to the intervals, harmonic or melodic, of an octave, fifth, and fourth in their normal form, as opposed to augmented and diminished. —*n. Gram.* **13.** the perfect tense. **14.** any verb formation or construction in the perfect tense. **15.** a form in the perfect, as *He had cooked the meal before six o'clock.* —*v.t.* **16.** to bring to completion; finish. **17.** to bring to perfection; make faultless. **18.** to bring nearer to perfection; improve. **19.** to make fully skilled. [< L *perfect(us)* done, finished, ptp. of *perficere* (*per-* PER- + *-ficere*, comb. form of *facere* to do); r. ME *parfit* < OF] —**per·fect′ed·ly,** *adv.* —**per·fect′er,** *n.* —**per′fect·ness,** *n.* —**Syn. 1, 2.** See **complete. 4.** unblemished. —**Ant. 2.** imperfect.

per·fec·ta (pûr fek′tə), *n.* exacta. [AmSp *perfecta quiniela*) perfect QUINIELA]

per·fect·i·ble (pər fek′tə bəl), *adj.* capable of becoming or of being made perfect. [< F < ML *perfectibil(is)*] —**per·fect′i·bil·ist,** *n.* —**per·fect′i·bil′i·ty,** *n.*

per·fec·tion (pər fek′shən), *n.* **1.** the state or quality of being or becoming perfect. **2.** the highest degree of proficiency, skill, or excellence, as in some art. **3.** a perfect embodiment of something. **4.** a quality, trait, or feature of the highest degree of excellence. **5.** the act or fact of perfecting. [< L *perfectiōn-* (s. of *perfectiō*) a finishing]

per·fec·tion·ism (pər fek′shə niz′əm), *n.* **1.** any of various doctrines holding that moral perfection is attainable. **2.** a personal standard or attitude that demands perfection.

per·fec·tion·ist (pər fek′shə nist), *n.* **1.** a person who adheres to or believes in perfectionism. **2.** a person who demands perfection of himself and his work. —*adj.* **3.** of, pertaining to, or distinguished by perfection or perfectionism. —**per·fec′tion·is′tic,** *adj.*

per·fec·tive (pər fek′tiv), *adj.* **1.** tending to make perfect; conducive to perfection. **2.** *Gram.* noting an aspect of verbal inflection, as in Russian, that indicates completion of the action or state denoted by the verb. —*n. Gram.* **3.** the perfective aspect. **4.** a form in the perfective. [< ML *perfectīv(us)*] —**per·fec′tive·ly,** *adv.* —**per·fec′tive·ness, per·fec·tiv·i·ty** (pûr′fek tiv′i tē), *n.*

per·fect·ly (pûr′fikt lē), *adv.* **1.** in a perfect manner or to a perfect degree. **2.** completely; adequately. [PERFECT + -LY; r. ME *parfitly*]

per·fec·to (pər fek′tō), *n., pl.* **-tos.** a rather thick, medium-sized cigar tapering toward both ends. [< Sp: lit., perfect]

per′fect par′ticiple. See **past participle.**

per′fect pitch′. See **absolute pitch** (def. 2).

per′fect ream′. See under **ream**[1] (def. 1).

per′fect rhyme′, **1.** See **rime riche. 2.** See **full rhyme.**

per′fect year′. See under **Jewish calendar.**

per·fer·vid (pər fûr′vid), *adj.* very fervid: *perfervid patriotism.* [< NL *perfervid(us)*] —**per′fer·vid′i·ty, per·fer′vid·ness,** *n.* —**per·fer′vid·ly,** *adv.*

per·fid·i·ous (pər fid′ē əs), *adj.* deliberately faithless; treacherous; deceitful: *a perfidious lover.* [< L *perfidiōs(us)* faithless, dishonest] —**per·fid′i·ous·ly,** *adv.* —**per·fid′i·ous·ness,** *n.* —**Syn.** false, disloyal; unfaithful, traitorous.

per·fi·dy (pûr′fi dē), *n., pl.* **-dies. 1.** deliberate breach of faith or trust; faithlessness; treachery. **2.** an act or instance of faithlessness or treachery. [< L *perfidia* faithlessness = *perfid(us)* faithless, lit., through (i.e., beyond the limits of) faith (*per-* PER- + *fid(ēs)* faith + *-us* adj. suffix) + *-ia* -Y[3]] —**Syn.** See **disloyalty.**

per·fo·li·ate (pər fō′lē it, -āt′), *adj. Bot.* having the stem apparently passing through the leaf, owing to congenital union of the basal edges of the leaf around the stem: *a perfoliate leaf.* [< NL *perfoliāt(us)* (see PER-, FOLIATE), the fem. of which, *perfoliāta*, was formerly used as the name of a plant with a stalk that seemed to grow through (pierce) its leafage] —**per·fo′li·a′tion,** *n.*

Perfoliate leaves

per·fo·rate (*v.* pûr′fə rāt′; *adj.* pûr′fə rit, -rāt′), *v.,* **-rat·ed, -rat·ing,** *adj.* —*v.t.* **1.** to make a hole or holes through by boring, punching, piercing, or the like. **2.** to pierce through or to the interior of; penetrate. —*v.i.* **3.** to make a way through or into something; penetrate. —*adj.* **4.** perforated. [< L *perforāt(us)* bored through, ptp. of *perforāre* to BORE[1] through; see PER-] —**per′fo·ra·ble,** *adj.* —**per′fo·ra′tive,** *adj.* —**per′fo·ra′tor,** *n.*

per·fo·rat·ed (pûr′fə rā′tid), *adj.* **1.** pierced with a hole or holes. **2.** *Philately.* (of a number of stamps joined together) having rows of closely spaced perforations dividing each stamp from the others. Also, **perforate.**

per·fo·ra·tion (pûr′fə rā′shən), *n.* **1.** a hole, or one of a number of holes, bored or punched through something, as those between individual postage stamps of a sheet to facilitate separation. **2.** the act of perforating. **3.** the state of being perforated. [late ME < ML *perforātiōn-* (s. of *perforātiō*) a boring through]

per·force (pər fōrs′, -fôrs′), *adv.* of necessity; by force of circumstance. [PER + FORCE; r. ME *par force* < MF]

per·form (pər fôrm′), *v.t.* **1.** to carry out; execute; do. **2.** to go through or execute in the proper or established manner. **3.** to carry into effect; fulfill. **4.** to act (a play, part, etc.), as on the stage. **5.** to render (music), as by playing or singing. **6.** to accomplish (any action involving skill or ability), as before an audience. —*v.i.* **7.** to fulfill a command, promise, or undertaking. **8.** to execute or do something. **9.** to act in a play. **10.** to perform music. **11.** to go through any performance. [ME *parform(en)* < AF *parforme(r)*, alter. (by assoc. with *forme* FORM) of OF, MF *parfournir* to accomplish. See PER-, FURNISH] —**per·form′a·ble,** *adj.* —**per·form′er,** *n.*

—**Syn. 1.** PERFORM, DISCHARGE, EXECUTE, TRANSACT mean to carry to completion a prescribed course of action. PERFORM is the general word, but usually implies regular, methodical, or prolonged application or work: *to perform an exacting task.* DISCHARGE implies carrying out an obligation, often a formal or legal one: *to discharge one's duties as a citizen.* EXECUTE means either to carry out an order or to carry through a plan or program: *to execute a maneuver.* TRANSACT, meaning to conduct or manage, has commercial connotations: *to transact business.* **3.** accomplish, achieve.

per·for·mance (pər fôr′məns), *n.* **1.** a musical, dramatic, or other entertainment. **2.** the act of performing. **3.** the execution or accomplishment of work, acts, feats, etc. **4.** a particular action, deed, or proceeding. **5.** the act of performing. **6.** the manner of performing or functioning.

perfor′mance test′, *Psychol.* a test designed to elicit manual or behavioral responses rather than verbal ones.

perform′ing arts′, arts or skills which require public performance, as acting, singing, dancing, etc.

perf. part., perfect participle.

per·fume (*n.* pûr′fyo͞om, pər fyo͞om′; *v.* pər fyo͞om′), *n., v.,* **-fumed, -fum·ing.** —*n.* **1.** a substance, extract, or preparation for diffusing or imparting an agreeable or attractive smell. **2.** the scent, odor, or volatile particles emitted by substances that smell agreeably. —*v.t.* **3.** (of substances, flowers, etc.) to impart a pleasant fragrance to. **4.** to impregnate with a sweet odor; scent. [earlier *parfume* (n.) < MF *parfum*, back formation from *parfumer* (v.)]

—**Syn. 1.** essence, attar, scent. **2.** PERFUME, AROMA, FRAGRANCE all refer to agreeable odors. PERFUME often indicates a strong, rich smell, natural or manufactured: *the perfume of flowers.* FRAGRANCE is best used of fresh, delicate, and delicious odors, esp. from growing things: *fragrance of new-mown hay.* AROMA is restricted to a somewhat spicy smell: *the aroma of coffee.* —**Ant. 2.** stench.

per·fum·er (pər fyo͞o′mər), *n.* **1.** a person or thing that perfumes. **2.** a person who makes or sells perfumes.

per·fum·er·y (pər fyo͞o′mə rē), *n., pl.* **-er·ies. 1.** perfumes collectively. **2.** the art or business of a perfumer. **3.** the place of business of a perfumer. **4.** the preparation of perfumes.

per·func·to·ry (pər fuŋk′tə rē), *adj.* **1.** performed merely as an uninteresting or routine duty; hasty and superficial. **2.** without interest, care, or enthusiasm; indifferent. [< LL *perfunctōr(ius)* negligent, lit., behaving like a *perfunctor*, one who is satisfied to get through = *perfunct(us)* experienced, undergone (ptp. of *perfungī*) + *-ōr-* -OR[2] + *-ius* adj. suffix. See PER-, FUNCTION] —**per·func′to·ri·ly,** *adv.* —**per·func′to·ri·ness,** *n.* —**Syn.** heedless, uninterested.

per·fuse (pər fyo͞oz′), *v.t.,* **-fused, -fus·ing. 1.** to overspread with moisture, color, etc. **2.** to diffuse (a liquid, color, etc.) through or over something. [< L *perfūs(us)* drenched, ptp. of *perfundere*] —**per·fu·sive** (pər fyo͞o′siv), *adj.*

per·fu·sion (pər fyo͞o′zhən), *n.* **1.** the act of perfusing. **2.** *Surg.* the pumping of a fluid through an organ or a tissue. [< L *perfūsiōn-* (s. of *perfūsiō*) a drenching]

Per·ga·mum (pûr′gə məm), *n.* **1.** an ancient Greek kingdom on the coast of Asia Minor: later a Roman province. **2.** the ancient capital of this kingdom: now the site of Bergama, in W Turkey. **3.** ancient name of **Bergama.** Also, **Per·ga·mon** (pûr′gə mən), **Per′ga·mus, Per′ga·mos.**

per·go·la (pûr′gə lə), *n.* **1.** an arbor formed of horizontal trelliswork supported on columns or posts, over which vines or other plants are trained. **2.** a colonnade having the form of such an arbor. [< It < L *pergula* projecting roof, arbor]

Pergola

Per·go·le·si (peR′gô le′zē), *n.* **Gio·van·ni Bat·tis·ta** (jô vän′nē bät tēs′tä), 1710–36, Italian composer.

perh., perhaps.

per·haps (pər haps′), *adv.* maybe; possibly. [earlier *per happes* by haps. See PER, HAP[1]]

pe·ri (pēr′ē), *n., pl.* **-ris. 1.** one of a race of beautiful, fairylike beings of Persian mythology. **2.** any lovely, graceful person. [< Pers *perī*, var. of *parī* fairy, MPers *parīk* < Avestan *pairikā* witch]

peri-, a prefix meaning "about," "around," "beyond," appearing in loan words from Greek (*peripeteia*); on this model, used in the formation of compound words (*perimorph*). [< Gk, comb. form of *perí* (adv. and prep.)]

Per·i·an·der (per′ē an′dər), *n.* died 585 B.C., tyrant of Corinth.

per·i·anth (per′ē anth′), *n.* *Bot.* the envelope of a flower, whether calyx or corolla or both. [earlier *perianth(ium)* < NL. See PERI-, ANTH-, -IUM] **—per′i·an′thi·al,** *adj.*

per·i·apt (per′ē apt′), *n.* an amulet. [< Gk *períapt(on)* amulet, n. use of neut. of *períaptos* hung around = *peri-* PERI- + *haptós,* verbid of *háptein* to fasten]

per·i·car·di·tis (per′ə kär dī′tis), *n.* *Pathol.* inflammation of the pericardium. **—per·i·car·dit·ic** (per′ə kär dit′ik), *adj.*

per·i·car·di·um (per′ə kär′dē əm), *n., pl.* **-di·a** (-dē ə). *Anat.* the membranous sac enclosing the heart. [< NL < Gk *perikárdion,* n. use of neut. of *perikárdios* heart-surrounding. See PERI-, CARDI-, -OUS] **—per′i·car′di·al,** *adj.*

per·i·carp (per′ə kärp′), *n.* **1.** *Bot.* the walls of a ripened ovary or fruit, sometimes consisting of three layers, the epicarp, mesocarp, and endocarp. **2.** a membranous envelope around the cystocarp of red algae. **3.** a seed vessel. [< NL *pericarp(ium)* < Gk *perikárpion* pod] **—per′i·car′pi·al, per′i·car′pic,** *adj.* **—per′i·car·poi′dal,** *adj.*

ABC, Pericarp of fruit of peach; A, Epicarp; B, Mesocarp; C, Endocarp

per·i·chon·dri·um (per′ə kon′drē əm), *n., pl.* **-dri·a** (-drē ə). *Anat.* the membrane of fibrous connective tissue covering the surface of cartilages except at the joints. [< NL; see PERI-, CHONDRI-] **—per′i·chon′dral, per′i·chon′dri·al,** *adj.*

Per·i·cle·an (per′ə klē′ən), *adj.* of or pertaining to Pericles or to 5th-century Athens.

Per·i·cles (per′ə klēz′), *n.* c490–429 B.C., Athenian statesman.

per·i·cline (per′ə klīn′), *n.* a mineral, a variety of albite, occurring in large white opaque crystals. [< Gk *periklinḗ(s)* sloping on all sides]

pe·ric·o·pe (pə rik′ə pē′), *n., pl.* **-pes, -pae** (-pē′). a selection or extract from a book. [< LL: section < Gk *perikopḗ* a cutting = *peri-* PERI- + *kopḗ* a cutting] **—pe·ric′o·pal, per·i·cop·ic** (per′ə kop′ik), *adj.*

per·i·cra·ni·um (per′ə krā′nē əm), *n., pl.* **-ni·a** (-nē ə). *Anat.* the external periosteum of the cranium. [< NL < Gk *perikránion,* n. use of neut. of *perikránios* skull-surrounding = *peri-* PERI- + *kraní(on)* CRANIUM + *-os* -OUS] **—per′i·cra′ni·al,** *adj.*

per·i·cy·cle (per′i sī′kəl), *n.* *Bot.* the outmost cell layer of the stele, frequently becoming a multilayered zone. [< Gk *períkykl(os)*]

per·i·derm (per′i dûrm′), *n.* *Bot.* the cork-producing tissue of stems together with the cork layers and other tissues derived from it. [short for NL *peridermis.* See PERI-, DERMIS] **—per′i·der′mal, per′i·der′mic,** *adj.*

pe·rid·i·um (pə rid′ē əm), *n., pl.* **-rid·e·a** (-rid′ē ə). *Bot.* the outer enveloping coat of the fruit body in many fungi, sometimes itself differentiated into outer and inner layers, exoperidium and endoperidium, respectively. [< NL < Gk *pēridion,* dim. of *pḗra* wallet] **—pe·rid′i·al,** *adj.* **—pe·rid·i·i·form** (pə rid′ē ə fôrm′), *adj.*

per·i·dot (per′i dot′), *n.* a transparent, usually green variety of olivine, used as a gem. [< F *péridot;* r. ME *peritot* < MF] **—per′i·dot′ic,** *adj.*

per·i·do·tite (per′i dō′tīt, pə rid′ə tīt′), *n.* any of a group of igneous rocks of granite texture, composed chiefly of olivine with an admixture of various other minerals, but nearly or wholly free of feldspar. [< F; see PERIDOT, -ITE¹] **—per·i·do·tit·ic** (per′i dō tit′ik, pə rid′ə-), *adj.*

per·i·gee (per′i jē′), *n.* *Astron.* the point in the orbit of a heavenly body, esp. the moon, or of an artificial satellite at which it is nearest to the earth. See diag. at **apogee.** [< NL *perigē(um),* var. of *perigaeum* < Gk *perígeion,* n. use of neut. of *perígeios* close to the earth = *peri-* PERI- + *gḗ(a)* earth + *-ios* -IOUS]

per·i·gon (per′ə gon′), *n.* an angle of 360°. Also called **round angle.**

Per·i·gor·di·an (per′ə gôr′dē ən), *adj.* of, pertaining to, or characteristic of an Upper Paleolithic cultural epoch in southern France. [after *Périgord,* France; see -IAN]

pe·rig·y·nous (pə rij′ə nəs), *adj.* *Bot.* **1.** situated around the pistil on the edge of a cuplike receptacle, as stamens, petals, etc. **2.** having stamens, petals, etc., so arranged. [< NL *perigynus*]

Perigynous flower (section)

pe·rig·y·ny (pə rij′ə nē), *n.* perigynous condition. [PERIGYN(OUS) + -Y³]

per·i·he·li·on (per′ə hē′lē ən, -hēl′yən), *n., pl.* **-he·li·a** (-hē′lē ə, -hēl′yə). *Astron.* the point in the orbit of a planet or comet at which it is nearest to the sun. Cf. **aphelion.** See diag. at **aphelion.** [< NL *perihēli(um)* < Gk *peri-* PERI- + *hḗli(os)* sun + *-on* neut. n. suffix] **—per′i·he′li·al,** *adj.*

per·il (per′əl), *n., v.,* **-iled, -il·ing** or (*esp. Brit.*) **-illed, -il·ling.** **—n. 1.** exposure to injury, loss, or destruction; risk; jeopardy; danger. **—v.t. 2.** to expose to danger; imperil; risk. [ME < OF < L *perīcul(um)* trial, test, danger] **—Syn. 1.** See **danger.**

per·il·ous (per′ə ləs), *adj.* involving or full of risk or peril; hazardous; dangerous: *a perilous undertaking.* [ME < AF *perillous* < L *perīculōs(us)*] **—per′il·ous·ly,** *adv.* **—per′il·ous·ness,** *n.* **—Syn.** risky. **—Ant.** safe.

per·i·lune (per′i lōōn′), *n.* the point in a lunar orbit that is nearest to the moon. [PERI- + *lune* < L *lūna* moon]

pe·rim·e·ter (pə rim′i tər), *n.* **1.** the circumference, border, or outer boundary of a two-dimensional figure. **2.** the length of such a boundary. [< F *périmètre* < L *perimetr(os)*] **—pe·rim′e·tral, per·i·met·ric** (per′ə me′trik), **per′i·met′ri·cal,** *adj.* **—per′i·met′ri·cal·ly,** *adv.* **—pe·rim′e·try,** *n.* **—Syn. 1.** periphery.

per·i·morph (per′ə môrf′), *n.* a mineral enclosing another mineral. Cf. **endomorph** (def. 1). **—per′i·mor′phic, per′i·mor′phous,** *adj.* **—per′i·mor′phism,** *n.*

per·i·ne·um (per′ə nē′əm), *n., pl.* **-ne·a** (-nē′ə). *Anat.* **1.** the area in front of the anus extending to the fourchette of the vulva in the female and to the scrotum in the male. **2.** the diamond-shaped area corresponding to the outlet of the pelvis, containing the anus and vulva or the roots of the penis. [< NL, var. of *perinaeum* < Gk *perínaion* (neut.), *perínaios* (masc.), var. of *períneos* = *peri-* PERI- + *iné(ein)* (to) discharge, evacuate + *-os* adj. suffix] **—per′i·ne′al,** *adj.*

per·i·neu·ri·tis (per′ə nōō rī′tis, -nyōō-), *n.* *Pathol.* inflammation of the perineurium.

per·i·neu·ri·um (per′ə nŏŏr′ē əm, -nyŏŏr′-), *n., pl.* **-neu·ri·a** (-nŏŏr′ē ə, -nyŏŏr′-). *Anat.* the sheath of connective tissue that encloses a bundle of nerve fibers. [< NL; see PERI-, NEUR-, -IUM] **—per′i·neu′ri·cal,** *adj.*

pe·ri·od (pēr′ē əd), *n.* **1.** a rather large interval of time that is meaningful in the life of a person, in history, etc., because of its particular characteristics. **2.** any specified division or portion of time. **3.** a definite, timed part of a game, school day, etc. **4.** *Music.* a division of a composition, consisting of two or more contrasted or complementary phrases. **5.** *Geol.* the basic unit of geological time, during which a standard rock system is formed, comprising several epochs and included with other periods in an era. **6.** *Physics.* the duration of one complete cycle of a wave or oscillation; the reciprocal of the frequency. **7.** *Astron.* **a.** Also called **period of rotation.** the time in which a body rotates once on its axis. **b.** Also called **period of revolution.** the time in which a planet or satellite revolves once about its primary. **8.** a round of time or series of years by which time is measured. **9.** a round of time marked by the recurrence of some phenomenon or occupied by some recurring process of action. **10.** the point of completion of a round of time or of the time during which something lasts or happens. **11.** a time of the month during which menstruation occurs. **12.** the time during which anything runs its course. **13.** the present time. **14.** the point or character (.) used to mark the end of a declarative sentence, indicate an abbreviation, etc. **15.** a full pause, as is made at the end of a complete sentence. **16.** See **periodic sentence. 17.** *Class. Pros.* a group of two or more cola. **—*adj.* 18.** noting, pertaining to, or characteristic of a historical period: *period piece; period costumes.* [late ME *peryod* < ML, L *period(us)* < Gk *períodos* circuit, period of time, period in rhetoric, lit., way around. See PERI-, -ODE²] **—Syn. 1.** interval. See **age. 2.** term.

pe·ri·od·ic¹ (pēr′ē od′ik), *adj.* **1.** recurring at intervals of time. **2.** occurring or appearing at regular intervals. **3.** repeated at irregular intervals; intermittent. **4.** *Physics.* recurring at equal intervals of time. **5.** *Astron.* **a.** characterized by a series of successive circuits or revolutions, as the motion of a planet or satellite. **b.** of or pertaining to a period, as of the revolution of a heavenly body. **6.** pertaining to or characterized by periodic sentences. [< L *periodic(us)* < Gk *periodikós*] **—pe′ri·od′i·cal·ly,** *adv.*

per·i·od·ic² (pûr′ī od′ik), *adj.* *Chem.* of or derived from a periodic acid. [PER- + IODIC]

per′i·od′ic ac′id (pûr′ī od′ik, pûr′-), *Chem.* any of a series of acids derived from I_2O_7 by the addition of water molecules, as HIO_4 or H_5IO_6.

pe·ri·od·i·cal (pēr′ē od′i kəl), *n.* **1.** a magazine or other publication that is issued at regularly recurring intervals. **—*adj.* 2.** published at regularly recurring intervals. **3.** of or pertaining to such publications. **4.** periodic. **—pe′ri·od′i·cal·ly,** *adv.*

period′ical cica′da. See **seventeen-year locust.**

pe·ri·o·dic·i·ty (pēr′ē ə dis′i tē), *n.* the character of being periodic; the tendency to recur at regular intervals. [< F *périodicité*]

pe′ri·od′ic law′ (pēr′ē od′ik, pēr′-), *Chem.* **1.** the law that the properties of the elements are periodic functions of their atomic numbers. **2.** (originally) the statement that the chemical and physical properties of the chemical elements recur periodically when the elements are arranged in the order of their atomic weights.

pe′ri·od′ic mo′tion (pēr′ē od′ik, pēr′-), *Physics.* any motion that recurs in identical forms at equal intervals of time.

pe′ri·od′ic sen′tence (pēr′ē od′ik, pēr′-), a sentence that, by leaving the completion of its main clause to the end, produces an effect of suspense. Cf. **loose sentence.**

pe′ri·od′ic sys′tem (pēr′ē od′ik, pēr′-), *Chem.* a system of classification of the elements based on the periodic law.

pe′ri·od′ic ta′ble (pēr′ē od′ik, pēr′-), *Chem.* a table in which the chemical elements, arranged according to their atomic numbers, are shown in related groups. See chart at **element.**

pe′riod of revolu′tion, *Astron.* period (def. 7b).

pe′riod of rota′tion, *Astron.* period (def. 7a).

per·i·o·don·tics (per′ē ə don′tiks), *n.* (*construed as sing.*) the branch of dentistry dealing with the study and treatment of diseases of the bone, connective tissue, and gum surrounding and supporting a tooth. Also, **per·i·o·don·tia** (per′ē ə don′shə, -shē ə). [< NL; see PERI-, -ODONT, -IUM, -ICS] **—per′i·o·don′tic,** *adj.*

pe′riod piece′, something, as a novel, painting, building, etc., of little interest or value aside from the fact that it evokes or epitomizes a particular period of history.

per·i·o·nych·i·a (per′ē ō nik′ē ə), *n.* *Pathol.* inflammation of the perionychium. [< NL < Gk *perí* PERI- + *onych-* (s. of *ónyx*) nail (see ONYX) + *-ia* -IA]

per·i·o·nych·i·um (per′ē ō nik′ē əm), *n., pl.* **-nych·i·a** (-nik′ē ə). *Anat.* the epidermis surrounding the base and sides of a fingernail or toenail. [< NL]

per·i·os·te·um (per′ē os′tē əm), *n., pl.* **-te·a** (-tē ə). *Anat.* the normal investment of bone, consisting of a dense, fibrous outer layer and a more delicate inner layer capable of forming bone. [< NL, var. of LL *periosteon* < Gk. See PERI-, OSTEO-] **—per′i·os′te·al, per′i·os′te·ous,** *adj.* **—per′i·os′te·al·ly,** *adv.*

per·i·os·ti·tis (per′ē o stī′tis), *n.* *Pathol.* inflammation of the periosteum. [PERIOST(EUM) + -ITIS] **—per·i·os·tit·ic** (per′ē o stit′ik), *adj.*

per·i·o·tic (per′ē ō′tik, -ot′ik), *adj.* *Anat.* **1.** surrounding the ear. **2.** noting or pertaining to certain bones or bony elements that form or help to form a protective capsule for the internal ear.

Per·i·pa·tet·ic (per′ə pə tet′ik), *adj.* **1.** of or pertaining to Aristotle, who taught philosophy while walking in the Lyceum of ancient Athens. **2.** of or pertaining to the Aristotelian school of philosophy. **3.** (*l.c.*) walking or traveling about; itinerant. —*n.* **4.** a member of the Aristotelian school. [late ME *perypatetik* < L *peripatēticus* < Gk *peripatētikós* of Aristotle and his school, lit., walking about = *peripatē-* (verbid s. of *peripateîn* to walk about) + *-tikos* -TIC] —**per′i·pa·tet′i·cal·ly,** *adv.* —**Per′i·pa·tet′i·cism,** *n.* —**Syn. 3.** wandering, roving; vagrant.

per·i·pe·tei·a (per′ə pi tī′ə), *n.* *Literature.* a sudden turn of events or reversal in the action, esp. of a dramatic work. Also, **per′i·pe·ti′a, pe·rip·e·ty** (pə rip′i tē). [< Gk: sudden change = *peripet(ḗs)*, lit., falling round (*peri-* PERI- + *pet-* fall, s. of *píptein* to fall) + *-eia* -Y[3]]

pe·riph·er·al (pə rif′ər əl), *adj.* Also, **per·i·pher·ic** (per′ə-fer′ik). **1.** pertaining to, situated in, or constituting the periphery. **2.** concerned with the comparatively superficial or not really essential aspects of the subject in question. **3.** *Anat.* outside of; external. **4.** of or pertaining to computer peripherals. —*n.* **5.** *Computer Technol.* a device or unit operating outside of the mainframe of a computer but connected to it, as a magnetic drum or tape unit. [< Gk *peripher(ḗs)* (see PERIPHERY) + -AL[1]] —**pe·riph′er·al·ly, per′i·pher′i·cally,** *adv.*

pe·riph·er·y (pə rif′ə rē), *n., pl.* **-er·ies. 1.** the external boundary of any surface or area. **2.** the external surface of a body. **3.** the relatively superficial or external aspects of the subject in question. **4.** *Anat.* the area in which nerves end. [ME *periferie* < ML *periferīa*, var. sp. of LL *peripherīa* < Gk *periphéreia* circumference, lit., a bearing round = *peri-* PERI- + *phér(ein)* to bear + *-eia* -Y[3]] —**Syn. 1.** circumference, perimeter. —**Ant. 1, 2.** center.

pe·riph·ra·sis (pə rif′rə sis), *n., pl.* **-ses** (-sēz′). **1.** a roundabout way of speaking; circumlocution. **2.** an expression phrased in such fashion. Also, **per·i·phrase** (per′ə-frāz′). [< L < Gk. See PERI-, PHRASE, -SIS]

per·i·phras·tic (per′ə fras′tik), *adj.* **1.** circumlocutory; roundabout. **2.** *Gram.* noting a construction of two or more words having the same syntactic function as an inflected word, as *of Mr. Smith* in *the son of Mr. Smith,* which is equivalent to *Mr. Smith's* in *Mr. Smith's son.* [< Gk *periphrastik(ós)* < *periphráz(ein)*. See PERI-, PHRASE, -TIC] —**per′i·phras′ti·cal·ly,** *adv.*

pe·rip·ter·al (pə rip′tər əl), *adj.* (of a classical temple) surrounded by a single row of columns. [< L *peripter(on)* (< Gk, n. use of neut. of *perípteros* encompassed round with columns; see PERI-, -PTEROUS) + -AL[1]]

pe·rique (pə rēk′), *n.* a rich-flavored tobacco produced in Louisiana. [said to have its name from *Périque,* nickname of Pierre Chenet, Louisiana grower who first developed it]

per·i·sarc (per′i särk′), *n.* *Zool.* the horny or chitinous outer case or covering with which the soft parts of hydrozoans are often protected. —**per′i·sar′cal, per′i·sar′cous,** *adj.*

per·i·scope (per′i skōp′), *n.* an optical instrument for viewing objects that are above the level of direct sight or in an otherwise obstructed field of vision. [back formation from PERISCOPIC]

per·i·scop·ic (per′i skop′ik), *adj.* **1.** *Optics.* (of certain lenses in special microscopes, cameras, etc.) giving distinct vision obliquely, or all around, as well as, or instead of, in a direct line. **2.** pertaining to periscopes or their use. Also, **per′i·scop′i·cal.** [< Gk *periskop(eîn)* (to) look about (see PERI-, -SCOPE) + -IC]

per·ish (per′ish), *v.i.* **1.** to die unseasonably through violence, privation, etc. **2.** to pass away; decay; disappear: *an age of elegance that perished.* [ME *periss(en)* < OF *periss-,* long s. of *perir* < L *perīre* to perish, lit., go through, spend fully = *per-* PER- + *īre* to go] —**Syn. 1.** expire. See **die**[1]. **2.** wither, shrivel, rot, vanish. —**Ant. 2.** appear.

per·ish·a·ble (per′i shə bəl), *adj.* **1.** subject to decay or destruction. —*n.* **2.** Usually, **perishables.** something perishable, esp. food. —**per′ish·a·bil′i·ty, per′ish·a·ble·ness,** *n.* —**per′ish·a·bly,** *adv.*

pe·ris·so·dac·tyl (pə ris′ō dak′t^{ə}l, -til), *adj.* **1.** having an uneven number of toes or digits on each foot. —*n.* **2.** any mammal of the order *Perissodactyla,* comprising the odd-toed hoofed quadrupeds and including the tapirs, rhinoceroses, and horses. Also, **pe·ris·so·dac·tyle** (pə ris′ō dak′t^{ə}l, -til, -tīl). Cf. **artiodactyl.** [< NL *perissodactyl(us)* < Gk *perissó(s)* uneven (< *perí* over; see PERI-) + *-daktylos* fingered, toed; see DACTYL, -OUS] —**pe·ris′so·dac′ty·lous,** *adj.*

per·i·stal·sis (per′i stôl′sis, -stal′-), *n., pl.* **-ses** (-sēz). *Physiol.* the progressive wave of contraction and relaxation of a tubular muscular system, as the alimentary canal, by which the contents are forced through the system. [< NL < Gk *peri-* PERI- + *stálsis* contraction = *stal-* (var. s. of *stéllein* to set, bring together, compress) + *-sis* -SIS] —**per′i·stal′tic,** *adj.* —**per′i·stal′ti·cal·ly,** *adv.*

per·i·stome (per′i stōm′), *n.* **1.** *Bot.* the one or two circles of small, pointed, toothlike appendages around the orifice of a capsule or urn of mosses, appearing when the lid is removed. **2.** *Zool.* any of various structures or sets of parts that surround or form the walls of a mouth or mouthlike opening. [< NL *peristom(a)*] —**per′i·sto′mi·al,** *adj.*

per·i·style (per′i stīl′), *n.* *Archit.* **1.** a colonnade surrounding a building or an open space. **2.** an open space, as a courtyard, surrounded by a colonnade. [< L *peristȳl(um)* < Gk *perístȳlon,* n. use of neut. of *perístȳlos* columned round = *peri-* PERI- + *stŷl(os)* column + *-os* -OUS] —**per′i·sty′lar,** *adj.*

per·i·the·ci·um (per′ə thē′shē əm, -sē əm), *n., pl.* **-ci·a** (-shē ə, -sē ə). *Bot.* the fructification of certain fungi, typically a minute, more or less completely closed, globose or flask-shaped body enclosing the asci. [< NL; see PERI-, THECA, -IUM] —**per′i·the′ci·al,** *adj.*

per·i·to·ne·um (per′i t^{ə}nē′əm), *n., pl.* **-to·ne·ums, -to·ne·a** (-t^{ə}nē′ə). *Anat.* the serous membrane lining the abdominal cavity and investing its viscera. [< LL, var. sp. of *peritonaeum* < Gk *peritónaion,* n. use of neut. of *peritónaios* < *perítonos* stretched round. See PERI-, TONE, -EOUS] —**per′i·to·ne′al,** *adj.*

per·i·to·ni·tis (per′i t^{ə}nī′tis), *n.* *Pathol.* inflammation of the peritoneum. —**per·i·to·nit·ic** (per′i t^{ə}nit′ik), **per′i·to·nit′al,** *adj.*

pe·rit·ri·chate (pə ri′trə kit, -kāt′), *adj.* (of bacteria) having flagella on the entire surface. Also, **per·i·trich·ic** (per′i trik′ik). —**per′i·trich, pe·rit·ri·chan** (pə ri′trə-kən), *n.*

per·i·wig (per′i wig′), *n.* a peruke or wig. [earlier *perwyke,* alter. of MF *perruque* PERUKE]

per·i·win·kle[1] (per′i wiŋ′kəl), *n.* **1.** any of various marine gastropods or sea snails, esp. *Littorina littorea,* used for food in Europe. **2.** the shell of any of these animals. [dissimilated var. of OE *pīnewincle* = *pīne* (< L *pīna* < Gk *pína,* var. of *pinna* kind of mollusk) + *wincle,* c. dial. Dan *vinkel* snail shell]

Periwinkle[1], *Littorina littorea* (Length to 1 in.)

per·i·win·kle[2] (per′i wiŋ′kəl), *n.* any trailing, evergreen, apocynaceous plant of the genus *Vinca,* as *V. minor,* having blue, white, or purple flowers, or *V. major,* having blue or variegated flowers. [late ME *perwinke,* earlier *pervinke,* OE *pervincae* < L *pervinca*]

per·jure (pûr′jər), *v.t.,* **-jured, -jur·ing.** to render (oneself) guilty of perjury. [late ME < L *perjūr(āre)* (to) swear falsely = *per-* through, i.e., beyond the limits + *jūrāre* to swear, lit., to be at law < *jūs* JUS; r. *parjure* < AF] —**per′jur·er,** *n.*

per·jured (pûr′jərd), *adj.* **1.** guilty of perjury. **2.** marked by or involving perjury. [late ME] —**per′jured·ly,** *adv.*

per·ju·ry (pûr′jə rē), *n., pl.* **-ries.** *Law.* the willful utterance of a false statement under oath or affirmation, before a competent tribunal, upon a point material to a legal inquiry. [ME < L *perjūri(um)* = *perjūr(us)* swearing falsely (see PERJURE) + *-ium* -Y[3]; r. *parjury* < AF] —**per·ju·ri·ous** (pər jŏŏr′ē əs), *adj.*

perk[1] (pûrk), *v.i.* **1.** to act, or carry oneself, in a jaunty manner. **2.** to become lively or vigorous, as after depression or sickness (usually fol. by *up*): *She began to perk up during dinner.* **3.** to put oneself forward briskly or presumptuously. —*v.t.* **4.** to raise smartly or briskly (often fol. by *up* or *out*): *to perk one's head up.* **5.** to dress smartly; make trim or jaunty (sometimes fol. by *up* or *out*): *to perk up a suit with a new blouse.* —*adj.* **6.** perky; jaunty. [ME *perke(n)*; ? akin to PEER[2]] —**perk′ing·ly,** *adv.* —**perk′ish,** *adj.*

perk[2] (pûrk), *v.i., v.t.* *Informal.* to percolate: *Is the coffee perking yet?* [by shortening]

perk·y (pûr′kē), *adj.,* **perk·i·er, perk·i·est.** jaunty; brisk; pert. —**perk′i·ly,** *adv.* —**perk′i·ness,** *n.*

Per·lis (pûr′lis), *n.* a state in Malaysia, on the SW Malay Peninsula. 101,357 (est. 1961); 310 sq. mi. *Cap.:* Kangar.

per·lite (pûr′līt), *n.* *Petrog.* a volcanic glass, usually appearing as a mass of enamellike globules, formed by concentric fractures. Also, **pearlite.** [< F; see PEARL[1], -ITE[1]] —**per·lit·ic** (pər lit′ik), *adj.*

Perm (perm), *n.* a city in the RSFSR, in the E Soviet Union in Europe. 763,000 (1965). Formerly, **Molotov.**

per·ma·frost (pûr′mə frôst′, -frost′), *n.* (in arctic or subarctic regions) perennially frozen subsoil. [PERMA(NENT) + FROST]

perm·al·loy (pûrm′al′oi, pûr′mə loi′), *n.* any of a class of alloys of high magnetic permeability, containing from 30 to 90 percent nickel. [PERM(ANENT) + ALLOY]

per·ma·nence (pûr′mə nəns), *n.* the condition or quality of being permanent; perpetual or continued existence. [late ME < ML *permanentia*]

per·ma·nen·cy (pûr′mə nən sē), *n., pl.* **-cies** for 2. **1.** permanence. **2.** something that is permanent. [< ML *permanentia*]

per·ma·nent (pûr′mə nənt), *adj.* **1.** existing perpetually; everlasting. **2.** intended to exist or function for a long, indefinite period without regard to unforeseeable conditions. **3.** long-lasting: *permanent pleating.* **4.** nonfading: *permanent ink.* —*n.* **5.** See **permanent wave.** [late ME < L *permanent-* (s. of *permanēns*) remaining, prp. of *permanēre.* See PER-, REMAIN, -ENT] —**per′ma·nent·ly,** *adv.* —**per′ma·nent·ness,** *n.* —**Syn. 1.** stable, invariable, constant.

per′manent mag′net, a magnet that retains its magnetism after being removed from an external magnetic field. —**per′manent mag′netism.**

per′manent press′, (of a fabric) wrinkle-resistant and requiring little or no ironing after washing.

per′manent wave′, a wave that is set into the hair by the application of a special chemical preparation and that remains for a number of months.

per·man·ga·nate (pər maŋ′gə nāt′), *n.* *Chem.* a salt of permanganic acid. Cf. **potassium permanganate.** [PERMANGAN(IC ACID) + -ATE[2]]

per′mangan′ic ac′id, *Chem.* an acid, $HMnO_4$, known only in solution. —**per·man·gan·ic** (pûr′man gan′ik), *adj.*

per·me·a·bil·i·ty (pûr′mē ə bil′i tē), *n.* **1.** the property or state of being permeable. **2.** the magnetic permeance of a substance compared with that of air.

per·me·a·ble (pûr′mē ə bəl), *adj.* capable of being permeated. [late ME < LL *permeābil(is).* See PERMEATE, -BLE] —**per′me·a·ble·ness,** *n.* —**per′me·a·bly,** *adv.*

per·me·ance (pûr′mē əns), *n.* **1.** the act of permeating. **2.** the conducting power of a magnetic circuit for magnetic flux; the reciprocal of magnetic reluctance.

per·me·ate (pûr′mē āt′), *v.,* **-at·ed, -at·ing.** —*v.t.* **1.** to pass through the substance or mass of. **2.** to penetrate through the pores, interstices, etc., of. **3.** to be diffused through; pervade; saturate. —*v.i.* **4.** to become diffused; penetrate. [< L *permeāt(us)* passed through, ptp. of *permeāre.* See PER-, MEATUS] —**per′me·a′tion,** *n.* —**per′me·a′tive,** *adj.* —**per′me·a′tor,** *n.*

per men·sem (per men′sem; *Eng.* pər men′səm), *Latin.* by the month.

Per·mi·an (pûr′mē ən), *adj.* **1.** *Geol.* noting or pertaining to a period of the Paleozoic era occurring from 220,000,000 to 270,000,000 years ago and characterized by the existence of many reptiles (formerly regarded as an epoch of the Carboniferous). See table at **era.** —*n.* **2.** *Geol.* the Permian period or system. **3.** a branch of Uralic, comprising certain Finno-Ugric languages, esp. Votyak and Zyrian, spoken in the northern Ural Mountains.

per mill (pər mil′), per thousand. Also, **per mil′.**

per·mil·lage (pər mil′ij), *n.* a rate or proportion per thousand. Cf. **percentage** (def. 1).

per·mis·si·ble (pər mis′ə bəl), *adj.* allowable; permitted. [late ME < ML *permissibil(is).* See PERMISSION, -IBLE] —**per·mis′si·bil′i·ty, per·mis′si·ble·ness,** *n.* —**per·mis′si·bly,** *adv.*

per·mis·sion (pər mish′ən), *n.* **1.** the act of permitting; formal or express allowance or consent. **2.** liberty or license granted to do something. [late ME < L *permissiōn-* (s. of *permissiō*) a yielding, giving leave = *permiss(us)* (ptp. of *permittere* to PERMIT) + *-iōn-* -ION]

per·mis·sive (pər mis′iv), *adj.* **1.** granting or denoting permission: *a permissive nod.* **2.** habitually or characteristically permitting or tolerating behavior that others might disapprove or forbid: *a permissive parent.* [PERMISS(ION) + -IVE; cf. F *permissif*] —**per·mis′sive·ly,** *adv.* —**per·mis′sive·ness,** *n.*

per·mit (*v.* pər mit′; *n.* pûr′mit, pər mit′), *v.,* **-mit·ted, -mit·ting,** *n.* —*v.t.* **1.** to allow to do something: *Permit me to explain.* **2.** to allow to be done or occur: *The law permits the sale of such drugs.* **3.** to tolerate; agree to. **4.** to afford opportunity for, or admit of: *vents to permit the escape of gases.* —*v.i.* **5.** to grant permission; allow liberty to do something. **6.** to afford opportunity or possibility. **7.** to allow or admit (usually fol. by *of*): *statements that permit of no denial.* —*n.* **8.** a written order granting special permission to do something. **9.** an authoritative or official certificate of permission; license. **10.** permission. [late ME < L *permitt(ere)* (to) let go through, give leave = *per-* PER- + *mittere* to let or make (someone) go] —**per·mit·tee** (pûr′mi tē′), *n.* —**per·mit′ter,** *n.* —**Syn. 1.** See **allow. 9.** franchise. —**Ant. 1.** refuse.

per·mit·tiv·i·ty (pûr′mi tiv′i tē), *n., pl.* **-ties.** See **dielectric constant.**

per·mu·tate (pûr′myə tāt′, pər myōō′tāt), *v.t.,* **-tat·ed, -tat·ing. 1.** to cause (something) to undergo permutation. **2.** to arrange (items) in a different sequence. [< L *permūtāt(us),* ptp. of *permūtāre* to PERMUTE; see -ATE[1]]

per·mu·ta·tion (pûr′myə tā′shən), *n.* **1.** *Math.* **a.** the act of changing the order of elements arranged in a particular order, as *abc* into *acb, bac,* etc., or of arranging a number of elements in groups made up of equal numbers of the elements in different orders, as *a* and *b* in *ab* and *ba;* a one-to-one transformation of a set with a finite number of elements. **b.** any of the resulting arrangements or groups. **2.** the act of permuting or permutating; alteration; transformation. [ME < L *permūtātiōn-* (s. of *permūtātiō*) thoroughgoing change] —**per′mu·ta′tion·al,** *adj.* —**per′mu·ta′tion·ist,** *n.* —**Syn. 2.** arrangement, change.

per·mute (pər myōōt′), *v.t.,* **-mut·ed, -mut·ing. 1.** to alter; change. **2.** *Math.* to subject to permutation. [< L *permūt(āre)* (to) change throughout] —**per·mut′a·bil′i·ty, per·mut′a·ble·ness,** *n.* —**per·mut′a·ble,** *adj.* —**per·mut′a·bly,** *adv.*

Per·nam·bu·co (pûr′nəm byōō′kō; *Port.* peʀ′nəm bōō′kōō), *n.* Recife.

per·ni·cious (pər nish′əs), *adj.* **1.** ruinous; injurious; hurtful: *a pernicious lie.* **2.** deadly; fatal: *a pernicious disease.* **3.** *Obs.* evil; wicked. [< L *perniciōs(us)* ruinous = *pernici(ēs)* ruin (*per-* PER- + *nici-,* var. of *neci-,* s. of *nex* death + *-ēs* n. suffix) + *-ōsus* -OUS] —**per·ni′cious·ly,** *adv.* —**per·ni′cious·ness,** *n.* —**Syn. 1.** harmful, detrimental, deleterious, destructive. **2.** lethal.

perni′cious ane′mia, *Pathol.* a severe anemia caused by the failure of the gastric mucosa to secrete the intrinsic factor necessary for the absorption of vitamin B_{12}, and characterized by a great reduction in the number of red blood cells, an increase in their size, and the presence in the blood of large primitive cells containing no hemoglobin.

per·nick·et·y (pər nik′i tē), *adj.* *Informal.* **1.** fastidious: fussy. **2.** requiring painstaking care. Also, **persnickety.** [orig. Scot] —**per·nick′et·i·ness,** *n.*

Per·nod (pâr nō′; *Fr.* peʀ nō′), *n.* *Trademark.* an anise- and licorice-flavored liqueur, originally from France.

Pe·rón (pə rōn′; *Sp.* pe ʀōn′), *n.* **1. E·va Duar·te de** (ē′və dwär′tā də; *Sp.* e′vä dwäʀ′te the), 1919–52, Argentine political figure (wife of Juan Perón). **2. Juan (Do·min·go)** (wän də ming′gō; *Sp.* hwän dô mēng′gô), 1895–1974, Argentine military and political leader: president 1946–55, 1973–74.

per·o·ne·al (per′ə nē′əl), *adj.* *Anat.* pertaining to or situated near the fibula. [< NL *peronē* the fibula (< Gk) + -AL[1]]

per·o·rate (per′ə rāt′), *v.i.,* **-rat·ed, -rat·ing. 1.** to speak at length; make a speech. **2.** to bring a speech to a close with a formal conclusion. [< L *perōrāt(us)* spoken fully or at the end, ptp. of *perōrāre*] —**per′o·ra′tor,** *n.*

per·o·ra·tion (per′ə rā′shən), *n.* *Rhet.* the concluding part of a speech or discourse, which recapitulates the principal points. [< L *perōrātiōn-* (s. of *perōrātiō*) the closing of a speech] —**per′o·ra′tion·al,** *adj.*

Pe·ro·vo (pe ʀô′vo), *n.* a city in the W RSFSR, in the central Soviet Union in Europe, near Moscow. 143,000 (1959).

per·ox·i·dase (pə rok′si dās′, -dāz′), *n.* *Biochem.* any of a class of oxidoreductase enzymes that catalyze the oxidation of a compound by the decomposition of hydrogen peroxide or of an organic peroxide.

per·ox·ide (pə rok′sīd), *n., v.,* **-id·ed, -id·ing.** —*n.* **1.** *Chem.* **a.** a compound containing the bivalent ion, –O–O–, derived from hydrogen peroxide, as sodium peroxide, NaOONa, or dimethyl peroxide, CH_3OOCH_3. **b.** that oxide of an element containing an unusually large amount of oxygen. **c.** hydrogen peroxide, H_2O_2 or H–O–O–H. —*v.t.* **2.** to use peroxide as a bleaching agent on (esp. the hair).

peroxy-, a combining form denoting the peroxy group: *peroxyborate.*

per·ox·y·bo·rate (pə rok′sē bōr′āt, -it, -bôr′-), *n.* *Chem.* perborate.

per·ox′y group′ (pə rok′sē), *Chem.* the bivalent group, $-O_2-$, derived from hydrogen peroxide. Also called **perox′y rad′ical.** [PER- + OXY-[2]]

per·ox′y·sul·fu′ric ac′id (pə rok′sē sul fyŏŏr′ik, -rok′-), *Chem.* See **persulfuric acid.**

per·pend[1] (pûr′pənd), *n.* a large stone passing through the entire thickness of a wall. [late ME < MF *perpain* < ?]

per·pend[2] (pər pend′), *Archaic.* —*v.t.* **1.** to consider. —*v.i.* **2.** to ponder; deliberate. [< L *perpend(ere)* (to) weigh carefully, ponder = *per-* PER- + *pendere* to weigh]

per·pen·dic·u·lar (pûr′pən dik′yə lər), *adj.* **1.** vertical; upright. **2.** *Geom.* meeting a given line or surface at right angles. **3.** (*cap.*) noting or pertaining to the last style of English Gothic architecture, prevailing from the late 14th through the early 16th century and characterized by the use of such features as the four-centered arch, the fan vault, and the hammer-beam roof. **4.** maintaining a standing or upright position; standing up. **5.** having a sharp pitch or slope; steep. —*n.* **6.** a perpendicular line or plane. **7.** an instrument for indicating the vertical line from any point. **8.** an upright position. **9.** *Rare.* moral uprightness; rectitude. **10.** *Naut.* either of two imaginary perpendicular lines, the forward one being taken through the fore part of the stem, and the after one usually through the after side of the sternpost. **11.** a sharply pitched or precipitously steep mountain face. [< L *perpendiculār(is)* vertical = *perpendicul(um)* plumb line (see PERPEND[2], -I-, -CULE) + *-āris* -AR[1]; r. ME *perpendiculer* < AF] —**per′pen·dic′u·lar′i·ty,** *n.* —**per′pen·dic′u·lar·ly,** *adv.* —**Syn. 1.** See **upright.** —**Ant. 1.** horizontal.

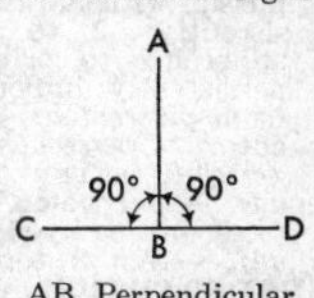

AB, Perpendicular to CD

per·pe·trate (pûr′pi trāt′), *v.t.,* **-trat·ed, -trat·ing. 1.** to perform, execute, or commit (a crime, wrong, etc.): *to perpetrate a murder.* **2.** to carry out or enact (a prank, deception, etc.). **3.** to present, execute, or do in a poor or tasteless manner: *who perpetrated this farce?* [< L *perpetrāt(us)* carried through (ptp. of *perpetrāre*) = *per-* PER- + *-petrā-* (var. s. of *patrāre* to father, bring about; see PATER) + *-tus* ptp. suffix] —**per′pe·tra′tion,** *n.* —**per′pe·tra′tor,** *n.*

per·pet·u·al (pər pech′ōō əl), *adj.* **1.** continuing or enduring forever. **2.** lasting an indefinitely long time: *perpetual snows.* **3.** continuing or continued without intermission or interruption: *a perpetual stream of visitors.* **4.** *Hort.* blooming more or less continuously throughout the season or the year. [late ME *perpetuall* < L *perpetuāl(is)* permanent = *perpetu(us)* uninterrupted (*per-* PER- + *petu-* (var. s. of *petere* to seek) + *-us* adj. suffix) + *-ālis* -AL[1]; r. ME *perpetuel* < MF] —**per·pet′u·al·ly,** *adv.* —**Syn. 1.** everlasting, permanent, enduring. See **eternal. 3.** continuous, unending, uninterrupted. —**Ant. 1.** temporary. **3.** discontinuous.

perpet′ual cal′endar, a calendar devised to be used for many years, as in determining the day of the week on which a given date falls.

perpet′ual mo′tion, *Mech.* the motion of a theoretical mechanism that, without any losses due to friction or other forms of dissipation of energy, would continue to operate indefinitely at the same rate without any external energy being applied to it.

per·pet·u·ate (pər pech′ōō āt′), *v.t.,* **-at·ed, -at·ing.** to make perpetual; preserve from extinction or oblivion. [< L *perpetuāt(us)* continued without interruption (ptp. of *perpetuāre*). See PERPETUAL, -ATE[1]] —**per·pet′u·a′tion,** *n.* —**per·pet′u·a′tor,** *n.*

per·pe·tu·i·ty (pûr′pi tōō′i tē, -tyōō′-), *n., pl.* **-ties. 1.** the state or character of being perpetual (often prec. by *in*). **2.** endless or indefinitely long duration or existence. **3.** something that is perpetual. **4.** an annuity paid for life. **5.** *Law.* a limitation or arrangement by which property is rendered not alienable for longer than the law allows. [late ME *perpetuite* < L *perpetuitās.* See PERPETUAL, -ITY]

Per·pi·gnan (peʀ pē nyäɴ′), *n.* a city in the S extremity of France. 86,156 (1962).

per·plex (pər pleks′), *v.t.* **1.** to cause to be puzzled or bewildered over what is not understood or certain. **2.** to make complicated or confused, as a matter, question, etc. **3.** to hamper with complications, confusion, or uncertainty. [back formation from PERPLEXED] —**per·plex′er,** *n.* —**per·plex′ing·ly,** *adv.* —**Syn. 1.** mystify, confound.

per·plexed (pər plekst′), *adj.* **1.** bewildered; puzzled. **2.** involved; entangled; complicated. [ME *perplex* intricate, confused (< L *perplex(us);* see PER-, COMPLEX) + -ED[2]] —**per·plex·ed·ly** (pər plek′sid lē), *adv.*

per·plex·i·ty (pər plek′si tē), *n., pl.* **-ties. 1.** the state of being perplexed; confusion; uncertainty. **2.** that which perplexes: *a case plagued with perplexities.* **3.** a tangled, involved, or confused condition or situation. [ME *perplexite* < OF < LL *perplexitāt-* (s. of *perplexitās*). See PERPLEXED, -ITY]

per·qui·site (pûr′kwi zit), *n.* **1.** an emolument over and above fixed income or salary. **2.** *Informal.* any bonus or fringe benefit granted an employee. **3.** something demanded or due as a particular privilege: *the perquisites of royalty.* [late ME < ML *perquīsīt(um)* something acquired, n. use of neut. of L *perquīsītus* diligently asked about or sought for (ptp. of *perquīrere*). See PER-, INQUISITIVE]

Per·rault (pe rō′; *Fr.* pe ʀō′), *n.* **Charles** (chärlz; *Fr.* shaʀl), 1628–1703, French poet, critic, and author of fairy tales.

per·ry (per′ē), *n., pl.* **-ries.** *Brit.* a fermented beverage, similar to cider, made from the juice of pears. [ME *pereye* < MF *perey,* var. of *pere* << VL **pirātum* (L *pir(a)* pear + *-ātum,* neut. of *-ātus* -ATE[1])]

Per·ry (per′ē), *n.* **1. Antoinette,** 1888–1946, U.S. actress, theatrical manager, and producer. **2. Matthew Cal·braith** (kal′brāth), 1794–1858, U.S. commodore. **3.** his brother, **Oliver Hazard,** 1785–1819, U.S. naval officer.

Pers, Persian (def. 4).

Pers., **1.** Persia. **2.** Persian.

pers., **1.** person. **2.** personal.

per·salt (pûr′sôlt′), *n.* *Chem.* **1.** (in a series of salts of a given metal or group) the salt in which the metal or group has a high, or the highest apparent, valence. **2.** (loosely) the salt of a peroxy acid.

per se (pər sē′, sā′), by, of, for, or in itself; intrinsically. [< L]

perse (pûrs), *adj.* of a very deep shade of blue or purple. [ME *pers* < ML *pers(us)*, perh. var. of *perseus* kind of blue, itself alter. of L *Persicus* Persian]

per′ sec′ond per′ sec′ond, a unit for expressing the rate of change of a rate of change, as of acceleration, which is the rate of change of velocity.

per·se·cute (pûr′sə kyo͞ot′), *v.t.*, **-cut·ed, -cut·ing. 1.** to pursue with harassing or oppressive treatment; harass persistently. **2.** to oppress with injury or punishment for adherence to principles or religious faith. **3.** to annoy persistently; importune; trouble. [late ME, back formation from *persecutour* << LL *persecūtor* persecutor, orig. prosecutor = *persecūt(us)* prosecuted, closely pursued (ptp. of *persequī*; see PER-, SEQUENCE) + *-or* -OR²] —**per′se·cu′tive,** *adj.* —**per′se·cu′tor,** *n.* —**per·se·cu·to·ry** (pûr′sə kyo͞o′tə rē, pûr′sə kyo͞o′-; pûr′sə kyə tôr′ē, -tôr′ē, pər sek′yə-), *adj.* —**Syn. 2.** torture, torment. **3.** badger, vex, pester.

per·se·cu·tion (pûr′sə kyo͞o′shən), *n.* **1.** the act of persecuting. **2.** the state of being persecuted. **3.** a program or campaign to exterminate, drive away, or subjugate a people because of their religious, ethical, or moral beliefs or practices. [ME *persecucio(u)n* < LL *persecūtiōn-* (s. of *persecūtiō*) persecution, L: prosecution] —**per′se·cu′tional,** *adj.*

Per·se·id (pûr′sē id), *n.* *Astron.* any of a shower of meteors appearing in August, and radiating from a point in the constellation Perseus. [< Gk, back formation from *Persēides* pl., taken to mean offspring of Perseus (constellation); see -ID¹]

Per·seph·o·ne (pər sef′ə nē), *n.* **1.** Also, **Proserpina, Proserpine.** *Class. Myth.* a daughter of Zeus and Demeter, abducted by Pluto to be queen of Hades, but allowed to return to the surface of the earth for part of the year. **2.** a personification of spring.

Per·sep·o·lis (pər sep′ə lis), *n.* an ancient capital of Persia: its imposing ruins are in S Iran, ab. 30 mi. NE of Shiraz. —**Per·se·pol·i·tan** (pûr′sə pol′i tᵊn), *adj., n.*

Per·se·us (pûr′sē əs, -so͞os), *n., gen.* **-se·i** (-sē ī′) for 2. **1.** *Class. Myth.* a hero, the son of Zeus and Danaë, who slew the Gorgon Medusa, and afterward saved Andromeda from a sea monster. **2.** *Astron.* a northern constellation between Cassiopeia and Taurus, containing the variable star Algol.

per·se·ver·ance (pûr′sə vēr′əns), *n.* steady persistence in a course of action, a purpose, a state, etc. [ME *perseveraunce* < AF, MF *perseverance* < L *persevērantia*] —**per′se·ver′ant,** *adj.*
—**Syn. 1.** doggedness, steadfastness. PERSEVERANCE, PERSISTENCE, TENACITY imply resolute and unyielding holding on, in following a course of action. PERSEVERANCE commonly suggests activity maintained in spite of difficulties; steadfast and long-continued application: *Endurance and perseverance combined to win in the end.* It is regularly used in a favorable sense. PERSISTENCE, which may be used in either a favorable or an unfavorable sense, implies unremitting (and sometimes annoying) perseverance: *persistence in a belief; persistence in talking when others wish to be quiet.* TENACITY, with the original meaning of adhesiveness, as of glue, is a dogged and determined holding on. Whether used literally or figuratively it has favorable implications: *a bulldog quality of tenacity; the tenacity of one's memory.*

per·se·vere (pûr′sə vēr′), *v.*, **-vered, -ver·ing.** —*v.i.* **1.** to persist in anything undertaken; maintain a purpose in spite of difficulty or obstacles; continue steadfastly. **2.** to persist in speech, interrogation, argument, etc.; insist. —*v.t.* **3.** to bolster, sustain, or uphold. [ME *persevere(n)* < MF *persever(er)* < L *persevērāre* to persist < *persevēr(us)* very strict] —**Syn. 1.** See **continue.**

per·se·ver·ing (pûr′sə vēr′ing), *adj.* displaying perseverance; persistent; steadfast: *a persevering student.* —**per′se·ver′ing·ly,** *adv.*

Per·shing (pûr′shing), *n.* **John Joseph** ("*Blackjack*"), 1860–1948, U.S. general: commander of the American Expeditionary Forces in World War I.

Per·sia (pûr′zhə, -shə), *n.* **1.** Also called **Per′sian Em′pire.** an ancient empire located in W and SW Asia: at its height it extended from Egypt and the Aegean to India; conquered by Alexander the Great 334–331 B.C. **2.** former official name (until 1935) of **Iran.** [< L, var. of *Persis* < Gk < OPers *Pārsa*]

Per·sian (pûr′zhən, -shən), *adj.* **1.** of or pertaining to Iran, its people, or their language. —*n.* **2.** a member of the native peoples of Iran, descended in part from the ancient Iranians. **3.** a citizen of ancient Persia. **4.** Farsi. *Abbr.:* Pers, Pers. **5. Persians.** See **Persian blinds.** [PERSI(A) + -AN; r. ME *Persien* < MF, r. OE *Persisc*; see PERSE, -ISH¹]

Per′sian blinds′, **1.** outside window shutters made of thin, movable horizontal slats. **2.** (loosely) Venetian blinds.

Per′sian car′pet, a handwoven carpet or rug produced in Iran and characterized by a usually tight, even pile and a variety of floral, foliate, animal, and avian designs woven in rich, harmonious colors. Also called **Per′sian rug′.**

Persian cat

Per′sian cat′, a long-haired variety of the domestic cat, originally raised in Persia and Afghanistan.

Per′sian Gulf′, an arm of the Arabian Sea, between SW Iran and Arabia. 600 mi. long.

Per′sian lamb′, **1.** the young lamb of the karakul sheep. **2.** the fur of this animal, used esp. for women's coats; caracul.

Per′sian mel′on, **1.** a round variety of muskmelon having a green, reticulate, unribbed rind and orange flesh. **2.** the plant bearing this fruit.

Per′sian wal′nut. See **English walnut.**

per·si·flage (pûr′sə fläzh′; *Fr.* per sē flȧzh′), *n.* **1.** light, bantering talk. **2.** a frivolous style of treating a subject. [< F < *persifl(er)* (to) banter = *per-* PER- + *siffler* to whistle, hiss << L *sībilāre*; see SIBILANT, -AGE]

per·sim·mon (pər sim′ən), *n.* **1.** any of several trees of the genus *Diospyros*, esp. *D. virginiana*, of North America, bearing astringent, plumlike fruit that is sweet and edible when ripe, and *D. Kaki*, of Japan and China, bearing soft, red or orange fruit. **2.** the fruit itself. [< Algonquian (Delaware) *pasimenan* (artificially) dried fruit]

per·sist (pər sist′, -zist′), *v.i.* **1.** to continue steadily or firmly in some state, purpose, course of action, or the like, esp. in spite of opposition, remonstrance, etc. **2.** to last or endure. **3.** to be insistent in a statement, request, question, etc. [< L *persist(ere)*, lit., to stand firm permanently = *per-* PER- + *-sistere*, a comb. form of *stāre* to stand] —**per·sist′er,** *n.* —**Syn. 1, 2.** See **continue. 3.** insist.

per·sist·ence (pər sis′təns, -zis′-), *n.* **1.** the act or fact of persisting. **2.** the quality of being persistent. **3.** continued existence or occurrence. **4.** the continuance of an effect after its cause is removed. Also, **per·sist′en·cy.** —**Syn. 1.** See **perseverance.**

persist′ence of vi′sion, the retention of a visual image for a short period of time after the removal of the stimulus that produced it.

per·sist·ent (pər sis′tənt, -zis′-), *adj.* **1.** persisting, esp. in spite of opposition; persevering. **2.** lasting or enduring. **3.** constantly repeated; continued: *persistent noise.* **4.** *Bot.* remaining beyond the normal time, as a leaf on a tree. **5.** *Zool.* holding to morphological character, or continuing in function or activity. [< L *persistent-* (s. of *persistēns*) persisting, prp. of *persistere*] —**per·sist′ent·ly,** *adv.* —**Syn. 1.** pertinacious, tenacious. See **stubborn.**

Per·sius (pûr′shəs, -shē əs), *n.* (*Aulus Persius Flaccus*) A.D. 34–62, Roman satirist.

per·snick·et·y (pər snik′i tē), *adj.* *Informal.* pernickety. —**per·snick′et·i·ness,** *n.*

per·son (pûr′sən), *n.* **1.** a human being. **2.** the actual self or individual personality of a human being. **3.** the body of a living human being, sometimes including the clothes being worn: *He had no money on his person.* **4.** the body in its external aspect. **5.** someone not entitled to social recognition or respect. **6.** *Law.* a human being, a group of human beings, a corporation, an estate, or other legal entity recognized by law as having rights and duties. **7.** *Gram.* a category used to distinguish between the speaker of an utterance and those to or about whom he is speaking. In English there are three persons in the pronouns, the first represented by *I* and *we*, the second by *you*, and the third by *he, she, it*, and *they.* Most verbs have distinct third person singular forms in the present tense, as *writes.* **8.** *Theol.* any of the three hypostases or modes of being in the Trinity, namely the Father, the Son, and the Holy Ghost. **9. in person,** in one's own bodily presence. [ME *persone* < L *persōna* role (in life, a play, a tale), LL: member (of the Trinity), orig. actor's mask, prob. < Etruscan *phersu*]
—**Syn. 1.** PERSON, INDIVIDUAL, PERSONAGE are terms applied to human beings. PERSON is the most general and common word: *the average person.* INDIVIDUAL views a person as standing alone or as a single member of a group: *the characteristics of the individual.* PERSONAGE is used of an outstanding or illustrious person: *a distinguished personage.*

-person, a suffix referring to the man or woman in a particular function, role, etc.: *salesperson; chairperson.*

per·so·na (pər sō′nə), *n., pl.* **-nae** (-nē), **-nas. 1.** a person, or the public role or character he assumes. **2. personae,** the characters in a play, novel, etc. [< L: mask, character]

per·son·a·ble (pûr′sə nə bəl), *adj.* of pleasing personal appearance; handsome or comely; attractive. [late ME] —**per′son·a·ble·ness,** *n.* —**per′son·a·bly,** *adv.*

per·son·age (pûr′sə nij), *n.* **1.** a person of distinction or importance. **2.** any person. **3.** a character in a play, story, etc. [late ME: body or image (statue, portrait) of a person (cf. ML *personagium*)] —**Syn. 1.** See **person.**

per·so·na gra·ta (per sō′nä grä′tä; *Eng.* pər sō′nə grä′tə, grā′tə, grat′ə), *pl.* **per·so·nae gra·tae** (per sō′nī grä′tī; *Eng.* pər sō′nē grä′tē, grā′-, grat′ē). *Latin.* an acceptable person, esp. a diplomatic representative acceptable to the government to which he is accredited.

per·son·al (pûr′sə nᵊl), *adj.* **1.** of, pertaining to, or coming as from a particular person; individual; private. **2.** relating to, directed to, or intended for a particular person: *a personal favor.* **3.** referring or directed to a particular person in a disparaging or offensive sense or manner: *personal remarks.* **4.** making personal remarks or attacks. **5.** done, effected, held, etc., in person: *a personal conference.* **6.** pertaining to or characteristic of a person, or self-conscious being. **7.** of the nature of an individual rational being. **8.** pertaining to one's person, or bodily aspect: *personal cleanliness.* **9.** *Gram.* noting person: *In Latin* portō "*I carry,*" *-ō is a personal ending.* **10.** of or pertaining to personal property. —*n.* **11.** *Journalism.* **a.** *U.S.* a short paragraph in a newspaper concerning a particular person, as one who is socially prominent. **b.** a brief, private notice in a newspaper or magazine. [ME < LL *persōnāl(is)*]

per′sonal comput′er, a microcomputer designed for individual use, as by a business person, student, or householder, for such applications as word processing, data management, financial analysis, computer games, etc. *Abbr.:* PC

per′sonal effects′, privately owned articles consisting chiefly of clothing, toilet items, etc., for intimate use by an individual. Cf. **household effects.**

per·son·al·ise (pûr′sə nᵊlīz′), *v.t.*, **-ised, -is·ing.** *Chiefly Brit.* personalize. —**per′son·al·i·sa′tion,** *n.*

per·son·al·ism (pûr′sə nᵊliz′əm), *n.* a modern philosophical movement locating ultimate value and reality in persons, human or divine. Also called **per′sonal ide′alism.** —**per′son·al·ist,** *n.* —**per′son·al·is′tic,** *adj.*

per·son·al·i·ty (pûr′sə nal′i tē), *n., pl.* **-ties. 1.** the visible aspect of one's character as it impresses others: *He has a pleasing personality.* **2.** a person as an embodiment of a collection of qualities. **3.** *Psychol.* **a.** the sum total of the physical, mental, emotional, and social characteristics of an individual. **b.** the organized pattern of behavioral characteristics of the individual. **4.** the quality of being a person; personal existence or identity. **5.** something apprehended as analogous to a distinctive human personality, as the atmosphere of a place or thing. **6.** Often, **personalities.** a disparaging or offensive statement referring to a particular person: *The argument deteriorated into personalities.* **7.** a famous, notable, or prominent person; celebrity. [ME *personalite* < LL *persōnālitās*] **—Syn. 1.** See **character.**

per·son·al·ize (pûr′sə n^{ə}līz′), *v.t.*, **-ized, -iz·ing. 1.** to make personal, as by applying a general statement to oneself. **2.** to personify. **3.** to have marked with one's initials or name, as stationery. Also, *esp. Brit.*, **personalise.** **—per′son·al·i·za′tion,** *n.*

per·son·al·ly (pûr′sə n^{ə}lē), *adv.* **1.** as regards oneself. **2.** as an individual: *to like someone personally, but not as an employee.* **3.** in person; directly. **4.** as if intended for or directed at one's own person: *to take someone's comments personally.* [ME]

per′sonal pro′noun, *Gram.* any of the pronouns indicating person in grammar, as, in English, *I, we, you, he, she, it, they.*

per′sonal prop′erty, *Law.* an estate or property consisting of movable articles both corporeal, as furniture or jewelry, or incorporeal, as stocks or bonds. **—Syn.** chattels, effects.

per·son·al·ty (pûr′sə n^{ə}l tē), *n., pl.* **-ties.** *Law.* personal estate or property. [< AF *personalte* < LL *persōnālitās* PERSONALITY]

per·so·na non gra·ta (per sō′nä nōn grä′tä; *Eng.* pər sō′nə non grä′tə, grā′-, grat′ə), *pl.* **per·so·nae non gra·tae** (per sō′nī nōn grä′tī; *Eng.* pər sō′nē non grä′tē, grā′-, grat′ē). *Latin.* an unwelcome or unacceptable person, esp. a diplomatic representative unacceptable to the government to which he is accredited.

per·son·ate[1] (pûr′sə nāt′), *v.*, **-at·ed, -at·ing.** **—*v.t.* 1.** to act or portray (a character in a play or the like). **2.** to impersonate, esp. with fraudulent intent. **3.** to personify. **—*v.i.* 4.** to act or play a part. [v. use of L *persōnātus* assumed, feigned, lit., masked. See PERSON, -ATE[1]] **—per′son·a′tion,** *n.* **—per′son·a′tive,** *adj.* **—per′son·a′tor,** *n.*

per·son·ate[2] (pûr′sə nit, -nāt′), *adj. Bot.* **1.** (of a bilabiate corolla) masklike. **2.** having the lower lip pushed upward so as to close the gap between the lips, as in the snapdragon. [< NL, L. See PERSONATE[1]]

per·son·hood (pûr′sən ho͝od′), *n.* **1.** the state or fact of being a person. **2.** the individual character of a human being.

per·son·i·fi·ca·tion (pər son′ə fə kā′shən), *n.* **1.** the attribution of personal nature or character to inanimate objects or abstract notions, esp. as a rhetorical figure. **2.** the representation of a thing or abstraction in the form of a person, as in art. **3.** the person or thing embodying a quality or the like; an embodiment: *He is the personification of tact.* **4.** an imaginary person or creature conceived of as representing a thing or abstraction. **5.** the act of personifying. [PERSONI(FY) + -FICATION] **—per·son′i·fi·ca′tor,** *n.*

per·son·i·fy (pər son′ə fī′), *v.t.*, **-fied, -fy·ing. 1.** to attribute personal nature or character to (an inanimate object or an abstraction), as in speech or writing. **2.** to represent (a thing or abstraction) in the form of a person, as in art. **3.** to be an embodiment of; typify. **4.** to personate. [cf. F *personnifier*, It *personificare*] **—per·son′i·fi′a·ble,** *adj.* **—per·son′i·fi′er,** *n.*

per·son·nel (pûr′sə nel′), *n.* the body of persons employed in any work, undertaking, or service. [< F, n. use of *personnel* (adj.) PERSONAL; r. *personal* (n.) = G *Personal*, var. of *Personale* < LL, neut. of *persōnālis* PERSONAL; cf. It, Dan *personale*]

per·son-to-per·son (pûr′sən tə pûr′sən), *adj.* **1.** (of a long-distance telephone call) chargeable only upon speaking with a specified person at the number called. Cf. **station-to-station.** **—*adv.* 2.** (in making a long-distance telephone call) to one specified person. Cf. **station-to-station. 3.** face-to-face; in person.

per·spec·tive (pər spek′tiv), *n.* **1.** a technique of depicting volumes and spacial relationships on a flat surface. Cf. **linear perspective. 2.** a picture employing this technique.

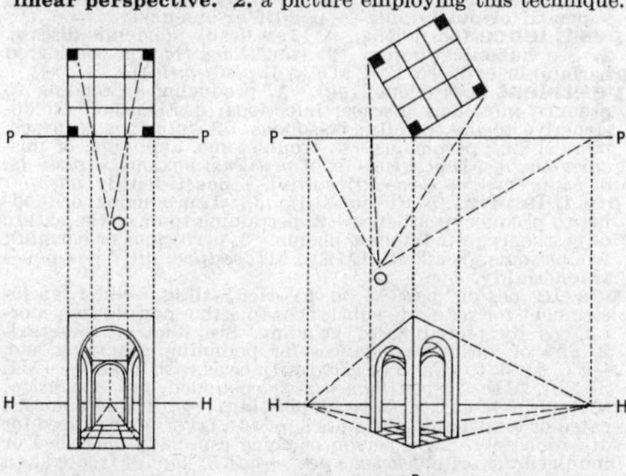

Perspective
A, One-point perspective; B, Two-point perspective; H, Horizon; O, Position of observer; P, Picture plane

3. a visible scene, esp. one extending to a distance; vista. **4.** the manner in which objects appear to the eye in respect to their relative positions and distance. **5.** one's mental view of facts, ideas, etc., and their interrelationships. **6.** the ability to see all the relevant data in a meaningful relationship. **7.** a mental view or prospect. **—*adj.* 8.** of or pertaining to the art of perspective, or represented according to its laws. [ME < ML *perspectīva (ars)* optical (science), *perspectīvum* optical glass, n. uses of fem. and neut. of *perspectīvus* optical < L *perspect(us)* seen through (see PER-, INSPECT) + *-īvus* -IVE] **—per·spec′tiv·al,** *adj.* **—per·spec′tived,** *adj.* **—per·spec′tive·less,** *adj.* **—per·spec′tive·ly,** *adv.*

per·spi·ca·cious (pûr′spə kā′shəs), *adj.* **1.** having keen mental perception; discerning. **2.** *Archaic.* having keen sight. [PERSPICACI(TY) + -OUS] **—per′spi·ca′cious·ly,** *adv.* **—per′spi·ca′cious·ness,** *n.* **—Syn. 1.** perceptive, acute.

per·spi·cac·i·ty (pûr′spə kas′i tē), *n.* keenness of mental perception; discernment; penetration. [earlier *perspicacite* < LL *perspicācitās* sharpness of sight = *perspicāci-* (s. of *perspicāx* sharp-sighted; see PERSPICUOUS) + *-tās* -TY[2]] **—Syn.** shrewdness, astuteness, acumen. See **perspicuity.**

per·spi·cu·i·ty (pûr′spə kyo͞o′i tē), *n.* **1.** clearness or lucidity, as of a statement. **2.** *Informal.* perspicacity. [< L *perspicuitās.* See PERSPICU(OUS), -ITY]
—Syn. 1. clarity, plainness, intelligibility. **2.** PERSPICUITY and PERSPICACITY are not properly synonyms. PERSPICACITY refers to the power of seeing clearly, to clearness of insight or judgment: *a man of acute perspicacity; the perspicacity of his judgment.* PERSPICUITY refers to that which can be seen through, i.e., to lucidity, clearness of style or exposition, freedom from obscurity: *the perspicuity of his argument.*

per·spic·u·ous (pər spik′yo͞o əs), *adj.* **1.** clear in expression or statement; lucid. **2.** perspicacious. [late ME < L *perspicuus* transparent = *perspicu-* (var. of *perspici-*, s. of *perspicere* to look or see through: *per-* PER- + *-spicere*, comb. form of *specere* to look) + *-us* -OUS] **—per·spic′u·ous·ly,** *adv.* **—per·spic′u·ous·ness,** *n.* **—Syn. 1.** intelligible, distinct, explicit. **—Ant. 1.** obscure.

per·spi·ra·tion (pûr′spə rā′shən), *n.* **1.** the act or process of perspiring. **2.** that which is perspired; sweat. [< medical NL *perspīrātiōn-* (s. of *perspīrātiō*) insensible sweating, lit., a breathing through]
—Syn. 2. PERSPIRATION, SWEAT refer primarily to moisture exuded by animals and people from the pores of the skin. PERSPIRATION is the more refined and elegant word, and is often used overfastidiously by those who consider SWEAT coarse. SWEAT is a strong word and in some cases is obviously more appropriate than PERSPIRATION: *a light perspiration; the sweat of his brow.* SWEAT is always used when referring to animals or objects: *Sweat drips from a horse's flanks.* It may also be used metaphorically of objects: *Sweat forms on apples after they are gathered.*

per·spir·a·to·ry (pər spī′rə tōr′ē, -tôr′ē), *adj.* of, pertaining to, or stimulating perspiration. [PERSPIRAT(ION) + -ORY[1]]

per·spire (pər spī^{ə}r′), *v.*, **-spired, -spir·ing.** **—*v.i.* 1.** to excrete watery fluid through the pores; sweat. **—*v.t.* 2.** to emit through pores; exude. [< L *perspīr(āre)* (to) blow constantly (said of the wind), lit., to breathe through; in NL: to sweat insensibly. See PER-, INSPIRE] **—per·spir′ing·ly,** *adv.* **—per·spir′y,** *adj.*

per·suade (pər swād′), *v.t.*, **-suad·ed, -suad·ing. 1.** to prevail on (a person) to do something. **2.** to induce to believe; convince. [< L *persuād(ēre).* See PER-, DISSUADE, SUASION] **—per·suad′a·bil′i·ty,** *n.* **—per·suad′a·ble,** *adj.* **—per·suad′er,** *n.* **—per·suad′a·bly,** *adv.* **—per·suad′ed·ly,** *adv.* **—per·suad′ing·ly,** *adv.*
—Syn. 1. urge, influence, entice, impel. PERSUADE, INDUCE, CONVINCE imply influencing someone's thoughts or actions. PERSUADE and INDUCE (followed by the infinitive) are used today mainly in the meaning of winning over a person to a certain course of action: *I persuaded him to call a doctor. I induced him to do it.* They differ in that PERSUADE suggests appealing more to the reason and understanding: *I persuaded him to go back to work* (although it is often lightly used: *Can't I persuade you to stay to supper?*); INDUCE emphasizes only the idea of successful influence, whether achieved by argument or by promise of reward: *What can I say that will induce you to work harder?* Owing to this idea of compensation, INDUCE may be used in reference to the influence of factors as well as of persons: *The prospect of a raise of salary induced him to stay.* CONVINCE means to satisfy the understanding of a person with regard to a truth or a statement: *to convince a person by quoting statistics.* Only when followed by a *that*-clause may CONVINCE refer to winning a person to a course of action: *I convinced her that she should go.* **—Ant. 1.** dissuade.

per·sua·si·ble (pər swā′sə bəl), *adj.* capable of being persuaded; open to or yielding to persuasion. [< L *persuāsibil(is)* convincing = *persuās(us)* (ptp. of *persuādēre* to PERSUADE) + *-ibil(is)* -IBLE] **—per·sua′si·bil′i·ty,** *n.*

per·sua·sion (pər swā′zhən), *n.* **1.** the act of persuading or seeking to persuade. **2.** power to persuade; persuasive force. **3.** the state or fact of being persuaded or convinced. **4.** a conviction or belief. **5.** a form or system of belief, esp. religious belief: *the Quaker persuasion.* **6.** a sect, group, or faction. [late ME < L *persuāsiōn-* (s. of *persuāsiō*); r. ME *persuacioun* < MF *persuacion*]

per·sua·sive (pər swā′siv), *adj.* **1.** able, fitted, or intended to persuade: *a very persuasive argument.* **—*n.* 2.** something that persuades; inducement. [ML *persuāsīv(us).* See PERSUASIBLE, -IVE] **—per·sua′sive·ly,** *adv.* **—per·sua′sive·ness,** *n.*

per′sul·fu′ric ac′id (pûr′sul fyo͝or′ik, pûr′-), *Chem.* a solid, H_2SO_5, used as an oxidizing agent for certain organic compounds. Also called **peroxysulfuric acid.**

pert (pûrt), *adj.* **1.** bold; forward; impertinent; saucy. **2.** lively; sprightly; in good health. **3.** *Obs.* clever. [ME, aph. var. of *apert* < L *apert(us)* open (ptp. of *aperīre*; see APERIENT) + OF *aspert* < L *expert(us)* EXPERT] **—pert′ly,** *adv.* **—pert′ness,** *n.* **—Syn. 1.** presumptuous, impudent.

pert., pertaining.

per·tain (pər tān′), *v.i.* **1.** to have reference or relation; relate. **2.** to belong or be connected as a part, adjunct, attribute, etc. **3.** to belong properly or fittingly; be appropriate. [ME *perte(i)ne, parte(i)ne* < MF *parten(ir)* < L *pertinēre* to be applicable, lit., to hold through, reach = *per-* PER- + *-tinēre*, comb. form of *tenēre* to hold]

Perth (pûrth), *n.* **1.** Also called **Perth·shire** (pûrth′shēr, -shər), a county in central Scotland. 127,018; 2493 sq. mi. **2.** its county seat: a port on the Tay River. 42,438. **3.** a city in and capital of Western Australia in SW Australia. 787,300.

Perth′ Am′boy (am′boi), a seaport in E New Jersey. 38,798 (1970).

per·ti·na·cious (pûr′tᵊnā′shəs), *adj.* **1.** holding tenaciously to a purpose; persevering. **2.** extremely or stubbornly persistent: *a pertinacious salesman.* —**per′ti·na′cious·ly,** *adv.* —**per′ti·na′cious·ness,** *n.*

per·ti·nac·i·ty (pûr′tᵊnas′i tē), *n.* the quality of being pertinacious; overinsistent tenacity or persistence: *the pertinacity of a social climber.* [< LL *pertinācitās* for L *pertinācia* stubbornness, perseverance = *pertināci-* (s. of *pertināx*) steadfast, stubborn + *-tās* -TY[2]] —**Syn.** determination.

per·ti·nent (pûr′tᵊnənt), *adj.* pertaining or relating to the matter at hand; relevant: *pertinent details.* [late ME < L *pertinent-* (s. of *pertinēns*) pertaining, prp. of *pertinēre.* See PERTAIN, -ENT] —**per′ti·nence, per′ti·nen·cy,** *n.* —**per′ti·nent·ly,** *adv.* —**Syn.** appropriate, fitting, fit. See **apt.**

per·turb (pər tûrb′), *v.t.* **1.** to disturb or disquiet greatly in mind; agitate. **2.** to throw into great disorder; derange. [ME *perturbe* < L *perturb(āre)* (to) throw into confusion = *per-* PER- + *turbāre* to disturb; see TURBID] —**per·turb′a·bil′i·ty,** *n.* —**per·turb′a·ble,** *adj.* —**per·turb′ing·ly,** *adv.*

per·tur·ba·tion (pûr′tər bā′shən), *n.* **1.** the act of perturbing. **2.** the state of being perturbed. **3.** mental disquiet or agitation. **4.** a cause of mental agitation. **5.** *Astron.* deviation of a celestial body from a regular orbit, caused by the presence of one or more other celestial bodies. [< L *perturbātiōn-* (s. of *perturbātiō*; see PERTURB, -ATION); r. ME *perturbacioun* < AF] —**per′tur·ba′tion·al,** *adj.*

per·tus·sis (pər tus′is), *n.* *Pathol.* See **whooping cough.** [< NL; see PER-, TUSSIS] —**per·tus′sal,** *adj.*

Pe·ru (pə ro͞o′), *n.* a republic in W South America. 15,500,000; 496,222 sq. mi. *Cap.:* Lima. Spanish, **Pe·rú** (pe ro͞o′). —**Pe·ru·vi·an** (pə ro͞o′vē ən), *adj., n.*

Peru′ Cur′rent, a cold Pacific Ocean current flowing N along the coasts of Chile and Peru. Also called **Humboldt Current.**

Pe·ru·gia (pe ro͞o′jä; *Eng.* pə ro͞o′jə), *n.* **1.** a city in central Umbria, in central Italy. 109,596 (1961). **2. Lake of,** Trasimeno. —**Pe·ru·gian** (pə ro͞o′jən, -jē ən), *adj., n.*

Pe·ru·gi·no (per′o͞o jē′nō; *It.* pe′ro͞o-jē′nô), (*Pietro Vannucci*) 1446–1524, Italian painter. —**Pe·ru·gin·esque** (pə ro͞o′jə-nesk′), *adj.*

pe·ruke (pə ro͞ok′), *n.* a wig, esp. of the kind worn by men in the 17th and 18th centuries; periwig. [< MF *perruque* < It *perrucca, parrucca* wig]

Peruke

pe·rus·al (pə ro͞o′zəl), *n.* **1.** a reading. **2.** the act of perusing; survey; scrutiny.

pe·ruse (pə ro͞oz′), *v.t.*, **-rused, -rus·ing. 1.** to read through, as with thoroughness or care. **2.** to read. **3.** to survey or examine in detail. [orig. sense, to use up. See PER-, USE] —**pe·rus′a·ble,** *adj.* —**pe·rus′er,** *n.*

Peru′vian bark′, cinchona (def. 2).

Peru′vian rhat′any. See under **rhatany** (def. 1).

Pe·ruz·zi (pe ro͞ot′tsē), *n.* **Bal·das·sa·re Tom·ma·so** (bäl′däs sä′re tôm mä′zô), 1481–1536, Italian architect and painter.

per·vade (pər vād′), *v.t.*, **-vad·ed, -vad·ing. 1.** to extend throughout; spread through every part of; permeate. **2.** *Rare.* to go everywhere throughout (a place), as a person. [< L *pervād(ere)* (to) pass through = *per-* PER- + *vādere* to go, walk] —**per·vad′er,** *n.* —**per·vad′ing·ly,** *adv.* —**per·va·sion** (pər vā′zhən), *n.* —**per·va·sive** (pər vā′siv), *adj.* —**per·va′sive·ly,** *adv.* —**per·va′sive·ness,** *n.*

per·verse (pər vûrs′), *adj.* **1.** willfully determined not to do what is expected or desired; contrary. **2.** characterized by or proceeding from such a determination: *a perverse mood.* **3.** petulant; cranky. **4.** persistent or obstinate in what is wrong. **5.** turned away from what is right, good, or proper; wicked. [ME *perverse* < L *pervers(us)* askew, orig. ptp. of *pervertere.* See PERVERT] —**per·verse′ly,** *adv.* —**per·verse′ness,** *n.* —**Syn. 1.** contumacious, disobedient. **4.** stubborn, headstrong. See **willful. 5.** evil, bad, sinful. —**Ant. 1.** agreeable. **4.** tractable.

per·ver·sion (pər vûr′zhən, -shən), *n.* **1.** the act of perverting. **2.** the state of being perverted. **3.** a perverted form of something. **4.** any of various means of attaining sexual gratification that are widely regarded as being abnormal. **5.** *Pathol.* a change to what is unnatural or abnormal: *a perversion of function or structure.* [ME < L *perversiōn-* (s. of *perversiō*)]

per·ver·si·ty (pər vûr′si tē), *n., pl.* **-ties** for 2. **1.** the state or quality of being perverse. **2.** an instance of this. [< L *perversitās*]

per·ver·sive (pər vûr′siv), *adj.* tending to pervert. [< L *pervers(us)* PERVERSE + -IVE]

per·vert (*v.* pər vûrt′; *n.* pûr′vərt), *v.t.* **1.** to turn away from the right course of action. **2.** to lead astray morally. **3.** to lead into mental error or false judgment. **4.** to turn to an improper use; misapply. **5.** to misconstrue or misinterpret, esp. deliberately; distort. **6.** to bring to a less excellent state; vitiate; debase. —*n.* **7.** a person who practices sexual perversion. **8.** *Pathol.* one affected with perversion. [ME *perverte* < L *pervert(ere)* (to) overturn, subvert = *per-* PER- + *vertere* to turn] —**per·vert′er,** *n.* —**per·vert′i·ble,** *adj.* —**Syn. 1.** divert. **2.** seduce, corrupt, demoralize. **3.** mislead, misguide. **6.** pollute, defile; impair, degrade.

per·vert·ed (pər vûr′tid), *adj.* **1.** turned from what is right; wicked; misguided; distorted. **2.** affected with or caused by perversion. —**per·vert′ed·ly,** *adv.* —**per·vert′ed·ness,** *n.*

per·vi·ous (pûr′vē əs), *adj.* **1.** admitting of passage or entrance; permeable: *pervious soil.* **2.** accessible to reason, feeling, argument, etc. [< L *pervius* passable = *per-* PER- + *vi(a)* way, road + *-us* -OUS] —**per′vi·ous·ness,** *n.*

Pe·sach (pā′säkh), *n.* *Judaism.* Passover (def. 1). Also, **Pe′sah.** [< Heb *pesaḥ*]

pe·sade (pə säd′, -zäd′, -zäd′), *n.* *Dressage.* a maneuver in which the horse is made to rear, keeping its hind legs stationary and its forelegs drawn in. [< F, earlier *posade* < It *posata* a halt (see POSE[1], -ADE[1]); *pes-* by assoc. with *peser* to weigh. See POISE]

Pe·sa·ro (pe′zä rô), *n.* a seaport in E Italy, on the Adriatic Sea. 66,519 (1961).

Pes·ca·do·res (pes′kə dôr′is, -ēz), *n.pl.* a group of small islands off the SE coast of China, in Formosa Strait: ceded to Japan 1895; returned to China 1945. 121,000 (est. 1971); ab. 50 sq. mi. Also called **Penghu, Penghutao.** Japanese, **Boko Gunto, Bokoto, Hoko Gunto, Hokoto.**

Pe·sca·ra (pes kä′rä), *n.* a city in E Italy, on the Adriatic Sea. 87,984 (1961).

pe·se·ta (pə sā′tə; *Sp.* pe se′tä), *n., pl.* **-tas** (-təz; *Sp.* -täs). **1.** a bronze coin and monetary unit of Spain and Spanish territories, equal to 100 centimos. *Abbr.:* P., Pta. **2.** a former silver coin of Spain and Spanish America, equal to two reals; pistareen. [< Sp, dim. of *pesa* a weight. See PESO]

Pe·sha·war (pe shä′wər), *n.* a city in N Pakistan, near the Khyber Pass: the capital of former North-West Frontier Province. 218,691 (1961).

Pe·shit·ta (pə shē′tə), *n.* the principal Syriac version of the Bible. Also, **Pe·shi·to** (pə shē′tō).

pes·ky (pes′kē), *adj.*, **-ki·er, -ki·est.** *Informal.* annoying; troublesome. [alter. of *pesty* (< PEST + -Y[1])] —**pesk′i·ness,** *n.*

pe·so (pā′sō; *Sp.* pe′sô), *n., pl.* **-sos** (-sōz; *Sp.* -sôs). **1.** a silver and copper coin and monetary unit of Mexico, equal to 100 centavos. *Abbr.:* P **2.** a silver coin and monetary unit of Cuba, equal to 100 centavos. *Abbr.:* P **3.** the monetary unit of Argentina, Colombia, the Dominican Republic, and Uruguay. **4.** a paper money and monetary unit of the Philippines, equal to 100 centavos. **5.** See **peso boliviano. 6.** a former silver coin of Spain and Spanish America, equal to eight reals; dollar; piece of eight; piaster. [< Sp: lit., weight < L *pēnsum* something weighed, n. use of neut. of *pēnsus*, ptp. of *pendere* to weigh]

pe′so bo·li·via′no, *pl.* **pe·sos bo·li·via·nos.** a paper money and monetary unit of Bolivia, equal to 100 centavos.

pes·sa·ry (pes′ə rē), *n., pl.* **-ries.** *Med.* **1.** an instrument worn in the vagina to remedy uterine displacement. **2.** a vaginal suppository. **3.** diaphragm (def. 4). [late ME *pessarie* < LL *pessāri(um)* a suppository = L *pess(um)* for *pessus* (< Gk *pessós* oval stone used in a game) + *-ārium* -ARY]

pes·si·mism (pes′ə miz′əm), *n.* **1.** the tendency to see or anticipate only what is disadvantageous, gloomy, or futile in life. **2.** the doctrine that the existing world and all things naturally tend to evil. **3.** the belief that the evil and pain in the world are not compensated for by goodness and happiness. [< L *pessim(us)* superl. of *malus* bad + -ISM; modeled on *optimism*]

pes·si·mist (pes′ə mist), *n.* **1.** a person who habitually sees or anticipates the worst, or is disposed to be gloomy. **2.** an adherent of the doctrine of pessimism.

pes·si·mis·tic (pes′ə mis′tik), *adj.* pertaining to or characterized by pessimism; gloomy. —**pes′si·mis′ti·cal·ly,** *adv.* —**Syn.** despairing, hopeless. See **cynical.**

pest (pest), *n.* **1.** a troublesome person, animal, or thing; nuisance. **2.** a destructive animal or thing. **3.** a deadly epidemic disease, esp. one produced by the plague bacillus. [< L *pest(is)* plague] —**Syn. 3.** plague, scourge, bane.

Pes·ta·loz·zi (pes′tᵊlot′sē; *It.* pes′tä lôt′tsē), *n.* **Jo·hann Hein·rich** (*Ger.* yō′hän hīn′rikh), 1746–1827, Swiss educational reformer.

pes·ter (pes′tər), *v.t.* to harass with petty annoyances; trouble; bother. [? aph. var. of *empester* < MF *empestrer* to hobble, entangle < VL **impāstōriāre* to hobble = *im-* IM-[1] + *pāstōria* a hobble, n. use of L *pāstōrius* of a herdsman or shepherd. See PASTOR, -IOUS] —**pes′ter·er,** *n.* —**Syn.** annoy, vex, tease, irritate, provoke, harry.

pest·hole (pest′hōl′), *n.* a location prone to epidemic disease.

pest·house (pest′hous′), *n., pl.* **-hous·es** (-hou′ziz). a house or hospital for persons infected with pestilential disease.

pes·ti·cide (pes′ti sīd′), *n.* a chemical preparation for destroying pests, as flies or mosquitoes. —**pes′ti·cid′al,** *adj.*

pes·tif·er·ous (pe stif′ər əs), *adj.* **1.** bringing or bearing disease; pestilential. **2.** pernicious; evil. [< L *pestiferus* plague-bringing = *pesti-* (s. of *pestis*) PEST + *-ferus* -FEROUS] —**pes·tif′er·ous·ly,** *adv.* —**pes·tif′er·ous·ness,** *n.*

pes·ti·lence (pes′tᵊləns), *n.* **1.** a deadly epidemic disease. **2.** See **bubonic plague. 3.** something that is considered harmful or evil. [ME < MF < L *pestilent(ia)*]

pes·ti·lent (pes′tᵊlənt), *adj.* **1.** producing or tending to produce infectious disease; infectious; pestilential. **2.** destructive to life; deadly; poisonous. **3.** injurious to peace, morals, etc.; pernicious. **4.** troublesome, annoying, or mischievous. [< L *pestilent-* (s. of *pestilēns*) noxious = *pesti-* (s. of *pestis*) PEST + *-lent-* adj. suffix] —**pes′ti·lent·ly,** *adv.*

pes·ti·len·tial (pes′tᵊlen′shəl), *adj.* **1.** producing, or tending to produce, pestilence. **2.** pertaining to or of the nature of pestilence, esp. bubonic plague. **3.** pernicious or harmful; troublesome; pestilent. [ME < ML *pestilentiāl(is)*] —**pes′ti·len′tial·ly,** *adv.*

pes·tle (pes′əl, pes′tᵊl), *n., v.*, **-tled, -tling.** —*n.* **1.** an instrument for reducing substances to a fine powder in a mortar, as by pounding or grinding. See illus. at **mortar**[1]. **2.** any of various appliances for pounding, stamping, etc. —*v.t., v.i.* **3.** to pound or grind with or as with a pestle. [ME *pestel* < MF < L *pīstillum* < *pīstus* pounded, ptp. of *pīnsere*]

pet[1] (pet), *n., adj., v.*, **pet·ted, pet·ting.** —*n.* **1.** any domesticated or tamed animal that is kept as a favorite and cared for affectionately. **2.** a person or thing especially cherished or indulged; favorite: *teacher's pet.* —*adj.* **3.** kept or treated as a pet: *a pet lamb.* **4.** cherished; favorite: *a pet theory.* **5.** showing affection: *a pet name.* —*v.t.* **6.** to treat as a pet; indulge. **7.** to fondle, caress, or stroke. —*v.i.* **8.** *Informal.* to make love by fondling and caressing. [? back formation from *pet lamb* cade lamb, ? syncopated var. of *petty lamb* little lamb; see PETTY] —**Syn. 6.** baby, humor, pamper.

pet[2] (pet), *n.* **1.** a fit of peevishness. —*v.i.* **2.** to be peevish; sulk. [appar. back formation from PETTISH] —**pet′ted·ly,** *adv.*

Pet., Peter.

Pé·tain (pā taN′), *n.* **Hen·ri Phi·lippe O·mer** (äN rē′ fē lēp′ ô mer′), 1856–1951, marshal of France: premier of the Vichy government 1940–44.

pet·al (pet′ᵊl), *n.* one of the segments of the corolla of a flower. [< NL *petal(um)* petal, L: metal plate < Gk *pétalon* a thin plate, leaf, n. use of neut. of *pétalos* spread out, akin to *petannýnai* to be open. See PATENT] —**pet′aled, pet′alled,** *adj.* —**pet′al·like′,** *adj.*

-petal, a combining form meaning "seeking," used in the formation of compound words: *centripetal.* [< NL *-pet(us),* repr. L *petere* to seek, + -AL[1]]
pet·al·if·er·ous (pet′əlif′ər əs), *adj.* bearing petals.
pet·al·ine (pet′əlin, -əlīn′), *adj.* pertaining to or resembling a petal. [< NL *petalin(us)*]
pet·a·lo·dy (pet′əlō′dē), *n. Bot.* a condition in flowers, in which certain organs, as the stamens in most double flowers, assume the appearance of or become metamorphosed into petals. [< Gk *petalṓd(ēs)* leaflike (see PETAL, -ODE[1]) + -Y[3]] —**pet·a·lod·ic** (pet′əlod′ik), *adj.*
pet·al·oid (pet′əloid′), *adj.* having the form or appearance of a petal.
pet·al·ous (pet′ələs), *adj.* having petals.
pe·tard (pi tärd′), *n.* **1.** an engine of war or an explosive device formerly used to blow in a door or gate, form a breach in a wall, etc. **2.** a kind of firecracker. **3. hoist by** or **with one's own petard,** caught in one's own trap. [< MF = *pet(er)* (to) break wind (< *pet* < L *pēdit(um)* a breaking wind, orig. neut. of ptp. of *pēdere* to break wind) + *-ard* -ARD]
pet·a·sus (pet′ə səs), *n., pl.* **-sus·es.** a broad-brimmed hat worn by ancient Greek travelers and hunters, often represented in art as a winged hat worn by Hermes or Mercury. Also, **pet·a·sos** (pet′ə səs, -sos′). [< L: hat with a broad brim < Gk *pétasos,* akin to *petannýnai* to spread out]
pet·cock (pet′kok′), *n.* a small valve or faucet, as for draining off excess or waste material from the cylinder of a steam engine or an internal-combustion engine. Also, **pet′ cock′.** [*pet,* perh. < F *pet* (see PETARD) + COCK[1]]
pe·ter[1] (pē′tər), *v.i. Informal.* to diminish gradually and then disappear or cease (usually fol. by *out*). [?]
pe·ter[2] (pē′tər), *n. Slang (vulgar).* penis. [from the name *Peter*]
Pe·ter (pē′tər), *n.* **1.** Also called **Simon Peter.** died A.D. 67?, one of the 12 apostles and the reputed author of two of the Epistles. **2.** either of these two Epistles in the New Testament, I Peter or II Peter. [ME; OE *Petrus* < L < Gk *Pétros* stone, trans. of Syriac *kēfā*]
Peter I, **1.** ("*the Great*") 1672–1725, czar of Russia 1682–1725. **2.** (*Peter Karageorgevich*) 1844–1921, king of Serbia 1903–21.
Peter III, 1728–62, czar of Russia 1762 (husband of Catherine II; father of Paul I).
Pe·ter·bor·ough (pē′tər bûr′ō, -bur′ō, -bər ə), *n.* **1.** a city in NE Northamptonshire, in central England. 62,031 (1961). **2.** a city in SE Ontario, in SE Canada. 47,185 (1961). **3. Soke of** (sōk), an administrative division in NE Northamptonshire, in central England. 74,442 (1961); 84 sq. mi.
Pe′ter·mann Peak′ (pā′tər män′), a mountain in E Greenland. 9645 ft.
Pe′ter Pan′ col′lar, a close-fitting flat collar with rounded corners set on a high, round neckline.
Pe′ter Prin′ciple, any of several satirical "laws" concerning organizational structure, especially one which holds that people tend to be promoted till they reach a level beyond their competence. [from the title of a book by Laurence J. *Peter* (b. 1919), Canadian educator]
Pe·ters·burg (pē′tərz bûrg′), *n.* a city in SE Virginia: besieged by Union forces 1864–65. 36,103 (1970).
pe·ter·sham (pē′tər s͟həm), *n.* a heavy woolen cloth for bulky outerwear. [after Viscount *Petersham* (1780–1851)]
Pe′ter's pence′, **1.** an annual tax, originally of a penny from each householder, formerly paid to the papal see. **2.** a voluntary contribution to the Pope, made by Roman Catholics everywhere. Also, **Pe′ter pence′.** [ME *Peteres peni*]
Pe′ter the Her′mit, c1050–1115, French monk: preacher of the first Crusade 1095–99. Also called **Pe′ter of Am′iens.**
pet·i·o·lar (pet′ē ə lər), *adj. Bot.* of, pertaining to, or growing from a petiole.
pet·i·o·late (pet′ē ə lāt′), *adj. Zool.* having a petiole or peduncle. Also, **pet′i·o·lat′ed.** [< NL *petiolāt(us)*]
pet·i·ole (pet′ē ōl′), *n.* **1.** *Bot.* the slender stalk by which a leaf is attached to the stem; leafstalk. **2.** *Zool.* a stalk or peduncle, as that connecting the abdomen and thorax in wasps. [< NL *petiol(us)* leafstalk, special use of L *petiolus,* scribal var. of *peciolus,* prob. for **pediciolus,* dim. of *pediculus* PEDICLE]
pet·it (pet′ē), *adj. Law.* small. [ME < MF; see PETTY]
pe·tit bour·geois (pə tē′ bo͝or z͟hwä′, pet′ē bo͝or′z͟hwä; *Fr.* pə tē bo͞or z͟hwä′), *pl.* **pe·tits bour·geois** (pə tē′ bo͝or z͟hwäz′, pet′ē bo͝or′z͟hwäz; *Fr.* pə tē bo͞or z͟hwä′). **1.** a person who belongs to the petite bourgeoisie. **2.** See **petite bourgeoisie.** [< F] —**pe·tit′-bour·geois′,** *adj.*
pe·tite (pə tēt′), *adj.* **1.** (of a woman) small in stature or figure; diminutive. —*n.* **2.** a dress size for a relatively short woman. [< F; fem. of PETIT] —**pe·tite′ness,** *n.*
pe·tite bour·geoi·sie (pə tēt′ bo͝or′z͟hwä zē′; *Fr.* pə tēt bo͞or z͟hwä zē′), the portion of the bourgeoisie having the least wealth and lowest social status; the lower middle class. [< F]
pet·it four (pet′ē fōr′, fôr′; *Fr.* pə tē fo͞or′), *pl.* **pet·its fours** (pet′ē fōrz′, fôrz′; *Fr.* pə tē fo͞or′). a small teacake, variously frosted and decorated. [< F: lit., small oven]
pe·ti·tion (pə tis͟h′ən), *n.* **1.** a formal request, often bearing the names of a number of petitioners, addressed to a person or body of persons in authority, soliciting some favor, right, mercy, or other benefit. **2.** a request, esp. a respectful or humble one; a supplication or prayer: *a petition for aid.* **3.** something sought by request or entreaty. —*v.t.* **4.** to beg for or request (something) by or as by petition. **5.** to address a formal petition to (someone). —*v.i.* **6.** to address or present a formal petition. **7.** to request or solicit, as by a petition. [ME *peticioun* < L *petītiōn-* (s. of *petītiō*) a seeking out = *petīt(us)* sought (ptp. of *petere*) + *-iōn-* -ION] —**pe·ti′tion·ar′y,** *adj.* —**pe·ti′tion·er,** *n.* —**Syn. 1.** suit. **2.** entreaty, solicitation, appeal. **6.** solicit, sue. See **appeal.**
pe·ti·ti·o prin·ci·pi·i (pi tis͟h′ē ō′ prin sip′ē ī′; *Lat.* pe tē′ti ō′ priŋ kip′i ē′), *Logic.* a fallacy in reasoning resulting from the assumption of that which in the beginning was set forth to be proved; begging the question. [< L, trans. of Gk *tò en archêi aitéisthai* an assumption at the outset]
pet′it ju′ry, *Law.* See **petty jury.** —**pet′it ju′ror.**
pet′it lar′ceny, *Law.* See **petty larceny.**
pe·tit mal (pə tē′ mal′; *Fr.* pə tē mal′), *Pathol.* a form of epilepsy characterized by unconsciousness for periods of short duration. Cf. **grand mal.** [< F: lit., small illness]
pet′it point′, **1.** a small stitch used in embroidery. Cf. **tent stitch. 2.** embroidery done on a canvas backing and resembling woven tapestry. [< F: lit., small stitch]
pet′ name′, a name or a term of address used to express affection for a person, thing, etc.: *His car's pet name is Betsy.*
petr-, var. of **petro-** before a vowel: *petrous.*
Pe·tra (pē′trə), *n.* an ancient city in SW Jordan: capital of the Nabataeans and the Edomites.
Pe·trarch (pē′trärk, pe′-), *n.* (*Francesco Petrarca*) 1304–1374, Italian poet. —**Pe·trar·chan** (pi trär′kən), *adj., n.*
Petrar′chan son′net, a sonnet form popularized by Petrarch, consisting of an octave with the rhyme scheme *abbaabba* and of a sestet with one of several rhyme schemes, as *cdecde* or *cdcdcd.* Also called **Italian sonnet.**
pet·rel (pe′trəl), *n.* **1.** any of numerous sea birds of the family *Procellariidae.* **2.** See **stormy petrel.** [earlier *pitteral;* present form by folk etym.: thought of as St. Peter's bird because it seems to walk on water. Matt. 14:29]
petri-, var. of **petro-** before elements of Latin origin: *petrifaction.*
pe′tri dish′ (pē′trē), a shallow, circular, glass or plastic dish with a loose-fitting cover over the top and sides, used for culturing bacteria and other microorganisms. [named after J. R. *Petri* (d. 1921), German bacteriologist]

Petri dish

Pe·trie (pē′trē), *n.* **Sir (William Matthew) Flin·ders** (flin′dərz), 1853–1942, English Egyptologist and archaeologist.
pet·ri·fac·tion (pe′trə fak′s͟hən), *n.* **1.** the act or process of petrifying. **2.** the state of being petrified. **3.** something petrified. Also, **pet·ri·fi·ca·tion** (pe′trə fə kā′s͟hən). [PETRI- + *-faction* < L *factiōn-* (s. of *factiō*) a making. See PETRIFY, FACTION] —**pet′ri·fac′tive,** *adj.*
Pet′rified For′est, a national park in E Arizona: fallen trees petrified by the action of mineral-laden water. 147 sq. mi.
pet·ri·fy (pe′trə fī′), *v.,* **-fied, -fy·ing.** —*v.t.* **1.** to convert into stone or a stony substance. **2.** to make rigid or inert; stiffen; benumb. **3.** to stupefy or paralyze with astonishment, horror, or other strong emotion. —*v.i.* **4.** to become petrified. [< MF *petrifier*] —**pet′ri·fi′a·ble,** *adj.* —**pe·trif·i·cant** (pi trif′ə kənt), *adj.* —**pet′ri·fi′er,** *n.*
Pe·trine (pē′trīn, -trin), *adj.* of the apostle Peter or Epistles bearing his name. [< LL *Petr(us)* (see PETER) + -INE[1]]
petro-, a combining form meaning "rock," "stone" (*petrology*) or "petroleum" (*petrochemical*). Also, **petr-, petri-.** [< Gk, comb. form of *pétra* rock, *pétros* stone]
pet·ro·chem·i·cal (pe′trō kem′i kəl), *n.* **1.** any substance obtained from petroleum, as gasoline, kerosene, or petrolatum. —*adj.* **2.** of or pertaining to petrochemistry or a petrochemical.
pet·ro·chem·is·try (pe′trō kem′i strē), *n.* **1.** the chemistry of rocks. **2.** the chemistry of petroleum or its products.
pet·ro·dol·lars (pe′trō dol′ərz), *n.pl.* huge surplus revenues accumulated by petroleum-exporting countries, esp. those of the Middle East.
petrog., petrography.
pet·ro·glyph (pe′trə glif′), *n.* a prehistoric drawing or carving on rock. [< F *pétroglyphe*] —**pet′ro·glyph′ic,** *adj.*
Pet·ro·grad (pe′trə grad′; *Russ.* pe tro grät′), *n.* former name (1914–24) of **Leningrad.**
pe·trog·ra·phy (pi trog′rə fē), *n.* the branch of petrology dealing with the description and classification of rocks. [< NL *petrographia*] —**pe·trog′ra·pher,** *n.* —**pet·ro·graph·ic** (pe′trə graf′ik), **pet′ro·graph′i·cal,** *adj.* —**pet′ro·graph′i·cal·ly,** *adv.*
pet·rol (pe′trəl), *n.* **1.** *Brit.* gasoline. **2.** *Archaic.* petroleum. [< MF *petrole* < ML *petroleum* PETROLEUM]
petrol., petrology.
pet·ro·la·tum (pe′trə lā′təm), *n.* a yellowish or whitish, translucent, semisolid, greaselike substance obtained from petroleum: used as a lubricant and in medicine as a protective dressing, emollient, and ointment base. Also called **petroleum jelly.** [< NL; see PETROLEUM, -ATE[2]]
pe·tro·le·um (pə trō′lē əm), *n.* an oily, thick, flammable, usually dark-colored liquid that is a form of bitumen or a mixture of various hydrocarbons, occurring naturally and commonly obtained by drilling: used as fuel or separated by distillation into gasoline, naphtha, benzene, kerosene, paraffin, etc. Cf. **crude oil.** [< ML: lit., rock oil = L *petr(a)* rock (< Gk) + *oleum* oil] —**pe·tro′le·ous,** *adj.*
petro′leum e′ther, a flammable, low-boiling hydrocarbon mixture produced by the fractional distillation of petroleum, used as a solvent.
petro′leum jel′ly, petrolatum.
pe·trol·ic (pi trol′ik), *adj.* of, pertaining to, or produced from petroleum. [PETRO(LEUM) + -IC]
pe·trol·o·gy (pi trol′ə jē), *n.* the scientific study of the origin, structure, composition, changes, and classification of rocks. —**pet·ro·log·ic** (pe′trə loj′ik), **pet′ro·log′i·cal,** *adj.* —**pet′ro·log′i·cal·ly,** *adv.* —**pe·trol′o·gist,** *n.*
pet·ro·nel (pe′trə nəl), *n.* a 15th-century firearm that was fired with the butt resting against the chest. [< MF *petrinal,* dial. var. of *poitrinal* = *poitrine* chest (VL **pectorīna,* n. use of fem. of *pectorīnus* of the breast; see PECTORAL, -INE[1]) + *-al* -AL[1]]
Pe·tro·ni·us (pi trō′nē əs), *n.* **Gai·us** (gā′əs), (*Gaius Petronius Arbiter*) ("*Arbiter Elegantiae*"), died A.D. 66?, Roman satirist.
Pe·tro·pav·lovsk (pe′tro päv′lofsk), *n.* a city in N Kazakstan, in the S Soviet Union in Asia. 156,000 (est. 1964).
Pe·tro·pav·lovsk-Kam·chat·ski (pe′tro päv′lofsk-käm c͟hät′skē), *n.* a city in SW Kamchatka, in the E Soviet Union in Asia. 110,000 (est. 1964).
pe·tro·sal (pi trō′səl), *adj.* **1.** petrous; hard. **2.** *Anat.* of or pertaining to the petrous portion of the temporal bone. [< L *petrōs(us)* rocky (see PETR-, -OSE[1]) + -AL[1]]
pet·rous (pe′trəs, pē′-), *adj.* **1.** *Anat.* noting or pertaining to the hard dense portion of the temporal bone, containing

the internal auditory organs; petrosal. **2.** like stone, esp. in hardness; stony; rocky. [< L *petrōs(us)* rocky]

Pe·tro·za·vodsk (pe′tRO zä vôtsk′), *n.* a city in the NW RSFSR, in the NW Soviet Union in Europe. 149,000.

pe·tsai (bā′tsī′), *n.* See **chinese cabbage.** [< Chin *pe ts'ai* white vegetable(s)]

Pet·sa·mo (*Fin.* pet′sä mô), *n.* Finnish name of **Pechenga.**

pet·ti·coat (pet′ē kōt′), *n.* **1.** an underskirt, esp. one of a decorative fabric, often trimmed and ruffled. **2.** any skirtlike part or covering. **3.** *Elect.* the skirt-shaped portion of an insulator. —*adj.* **4.** of women; female; feminine: *petticoat traits.* [late ME *petycote.* See PETTY, COAT]

pet·ti·fog (pet′ē fog′, -fôg′), *v.i.*, **-fogged, -fog·ging. 1.** to bicker or quibble over trifles. **2.** to carry on a petty or shifty law business. **3.** to practice chicanery of any sort. [back formation from *pettifogger* = PETTY + *fogger* < MLG *voger* or MD *voeger* one who arranges things; akin to OE *gefōg* a joining] —**pet′ti·fog′ger,** *n.* —**pet′ti·fog′ger·y,** *n.*

pet·tish (pet′ish), *adj.* peevish; petulant: *a pettish refusal.* [PET[1] + -ISH[1]; orig., like a spoiled child] —**pet′tish·ly,** *adv.* —**pet′tish·ness,** *n.*

pet·ti·toes (pet′ē tōz′), *n.pl.* **1.** the feet of a pig, esp. as food. **2.** the human toes or feet, esp. those of a child. [pl. of obs. *pettytoe* offal < MF *petite oye* giblets of a goose = *petite* PETITE + *oye* goose < LL *av(i)ca*]

pet·tle (pet′əl), *v.t.*, **-tled, -tling.** *Scot. and North Eng.* to fondle; pet. [PET[1] + -LE]

pet·to (pet′tô), *n., pl.* **-ti** (-tē). *Italian.* the chest or breast. Cf. **in petto.**

pet·ty (pet′ē), *adj.*, **-ti·er, -ti·est. 1.** of small importance or consequence; trifling; trivial: *petty grievances.* **2.** of secondary importance, rank, or merit: *a petty kingdom.* **3.** narrow in ideas, interests, etc.: *petty minds.* **4.** mean-spirited; spiteful: *a petty revenge.* [ME *pety* small, minor, var. of PETIT] —**pet′ti·ly,** *adv.* —**pet′ti·ness,** *n.*

—**Syn. 1.** negligible, inconsiderable, slight. PETTY, PALTRY, TRIFLING, TRIVIAL apply to that which is so insignificant as to be almost unworthy of notice. PETTY implies contemptible insignificance and littleness, inferiority and small worth: *petty quarrels.* PALTRY is applied to that which is beneath one's notice, even despicable: *a paltry amount.* That which is TRIFLING is so unimportant and inconsiderable as to be practically negligible: *a trifling error.* That which is TRIVIAL is slight, insignificant, and even in incongruous contrast to that which is significant: *a trivial remark.* **3.** small.

pet′ty cash′, a small cash fund for paying minor charges, as for office supplies, deliveries, etc.

pet′ty ju′ry, (in a civil or criminal proceeding) a jury, usually of 12 persons, impaneled to determine the facts and render a verdict. Also, **petit jury.** —**pet′ty ju′ror.**

pet′ty lar′ceny, *Law.* larceny in which the value of the goods taken is below a certain legally specified amount. Also, **petit larceny.** Cf. **grand larceny.**

pet′ty of′ficer, an enlisted man in the navy holding an official rank corresponding to that of a noncommissioned officer in the army.

pet·u·lance (pech′ə ləns), *n.* **1.** the state or quality of being petulant; peevishness. **2.** a petulant speech or action. [< L *petulantia* impudence]

pet·u·lant (pech′ə lənt), *adj.* moved to or showing sudden, impatient irritation, esp. over some trifling annoyance; ill-humored; fretful: *a petulant toss of the head.* [< L *petulant-* (s. of *petulāns*) impudent, akin to *petere* to attack] —**pet′u·lant·ly,** *adv.*

pe·tu·ni·a (pə to͞o′nē ə, -nyə, -tyo͞o′-), *n.* **1.** any solanaceous herb of the genus *Petunia,* native to tropical America, having funnel-shaped flowers of various colors. **2.** a deep, reddish purple. [< NL < obs. F *petun* tobacco < Tupi *petyn;* see -IA]

pe·tun·tse (pə to͝on′tsə; *Chin.* bô′dun′dzu′), *n.* a Chinese feldspathic mineral, pulverized and used in certain porcelains. Also, **pe·tun′tze.** [< Chin = *pe* white + *tun* mound + *tze* formative particle (akin to *tzu* offspring)]

peu à peu (PŒ A PŒ′), *French.* little by little.

peu de chose (pœdə shōz′), *French.* a trifling or unimportant matter.

Pevs·ner (*Russ.* pefs′neR), *n.* **An·toine** (*Fr.* äN TWAN′), 1886–1962, French sculptor and painter, born in Russia.

pew (pyo͞o), *n.* **1.** (in a church) one of a number of fixed benches with backs, accessible by aisles, for the use of the congregation. **2.** an enclosure with seats in a church, appropriated to the use of a family or other group of worshipers. [ME *puwe* < MF *puie* balcony < L *podia,* pl. (taken as sing.) of *podium* balcony. See PODIUM]

pe·wee (pē′wē), *n.* **1.** See **wood pewee. 2.** the phoebe. [imit.]

pe·wit (pē′wit, pyo͞o′it), *n.* the lapwing, *Vanellus vanellus.* Also, **peewit.** [imit.]

pew·ter (pyo͞o′tər), *n.* **1.** any of various alloys in which tin is the chief constituent, originally one of tin and lead. **2.** vessels or utensils made of such an alloy. —*adj.* **3.** consisting or made of pewter: *a pewter mug.* [ME *pewtre* < MF *peutre* << VL **piltrum* (> It *peltro*)]

pew·ter·er (pyo͞o′tər ər), *n.* a maker of pewter utensils or vessels. [ME *peuterer* < MF *peutrier*]

-pexy, a learned borrowing from Greek used, with the meaning "fixation," in the formation of compound words. [< Gk *-pēxia* = *pēx(is)* a fixing, solidity + *-ia* -Y[3]]

pe·yo·te (pā ō′tē, pē-; *Sp.* pe yô′te), *n., pl.* **-tes** (-tēz; *Sp.* -tes). **1.** a cactus, *Lophophora Williamsii,* one of the two species of mescal. **2.** a hallucinogenic drug obtained from this plant; mescaline: used esp. by the Indians of Mexico and certain regions of the southwest U.S. in religious ceremonies. **3.** (in Mexico) any of several related or unrelated cacti. [< MexSp < Nahuatl *peyotl*]

pey·tral (pā′trəl), *n.* *Armor.* a piece for the breast and shoulders of a horse. Also, **pey′trel, poitrel.** [ME *peytrel* < MF *peitral* < L *pectorāle* PECTORAL]

pF, picofarad; picofarads. Also, **pf**

pf, *Music.* fairly loud. [< It *poco forte*]

pf., **1.** pfennig. **2.** (of stock) preferred. **3.** proof.

Pfalz (pfälts), *n.* German name of The Palatinate.

Pfc., *Mil.* private first class.

pfd., (of stock) preferred.

pfen·nig (fen′ig; *Ger.* pfen′iKH), *n., pl.* **pfen·nigs, pfen·ni·ge** (*Ger.* pfen′i gə). **1.** a copper-coated iron coin of West Germany, the 100th part of a Deutsche mark. **2.** a minor coin of East Germany, 100th of ostmark. [< G: PENNY]

pfg., pfennig.

Pforz·heim (pfōrts′hīm′, pfôrts′-), *n.* a city in W Baden-Württemberg, in SW West Germany. 86,100 (1963).

PG, *U.S.* a designation by the motion-picture industry for films some of whose material may not be suitable for young children, with parental guidance suggested.

PG-13 (pē′jē′thûr′tēn′), *U.S.* a designation by the motion-picture industry for films with material unsuitable for children under age 13. Cf. **PG**

Pg, Portuguese (def. 3).

Pg., **1.** Portugal. **2.** Portuguese.

pg., page.

PGA, Professional Golfers' Association. Also, **P.G.A.**

Ph, *Chem.* phenyl.

pH, *Chem.* the symbol for the logarithm of the reciprocal of hydrogen ion concentration in gram atoms per liter. For example, a pH of 5 indicates a concentration of .00001 or 10^{-5} gram atoms of hydrogen ions in one liter of solution.

ph, phot; phots.

P.H., Public Health.

PHA, Public Housing Administration.

Phae·a·cia (fē ā′shə), *n.* *Class. Myth.* an island nation on the shores of which Odysseus was shipwrecked and discovered by Nausicaä. —**Phae·a′cian,** *n., adj.*

Phae·dra (fē′drə, fā′-, fed′rə), *n.* *Class. Myth.* a daughter of Minos and Pasiphaë, wife of Theseus, and stepmother of Hippolytus with whom she fell hopelessly in love, eventually hanging herself.

Phae·drus (fē′drəs), *n.* fl. A.D. c40, Roman fabulist.

Pha·ë·thon (fā′ə thən), *n.* *Class. Myth.* a son of Helios who borrowed the chariot of the sun for one day and drove it so dangerously close to earth that Zeus struck him down with a thunderbolt to save the world from catching fire. [< Gk: lit., shining]

pha·e·ton (fā′i tən *or, esp. Brit.,* fāt′ən), *n.* **1.** a light, four-wheeled carriage having one or two seats facing forward, and made in various forms. **2.** an automobile of the touring-car type. [special use of L *Phaetōn,* var. of *Phaethōn* PHAËTHON]

Phaeton

-phage, a learned borrowing from Greek meaning "eating," "devouring," used in biology to refer to phagocytes: *bacteriophage.* Also, **-phag.** Cf. **-phagia, phago-, -phagous, -phagy.** [< Gk *-phagos*]

-phagia, var. of **-phagy.** [< NL < Gk]

phago-, a learned borrowing from Greek referring to eating, used in the formation of compound words: *phagocyte.* Cf. **-phage, -phagous, -phagy.** [< Gk, comb. form akin to *phagein* to eat, devour]

phag·o·cyte (fag′ə sīt′), *n.* *Physiol.* a blood cell that ingests and destroys foreign particles, bacteria, and other cells. —**phag·o·cyt·ic** (fag′ə sit′ik), *adj.*

phag·o·cy·to·sis (fag′ə sī tō′sis), *n.* the ingestion and destruction of particlelike matter by cells.

-phagous, a word element meaning "eating," "feeding on," "devouring," used to form adjectives corresponding to nouns ending in *-phage: hylophagous.* [< Gk *-phagos*]

-phagy, a word element used as a noun termination meaning "eating," esp. as a practice or habit: *anthropophagy.* Also, **-phagia.** [< Gk *-phagia;* see -PHAGE, -Y[3]]

Phais·tos (fī′stəs), *n.* an ancient city in S central Crete: site of Minoan palace.

phal·ange (fal′ənj, fə lanj′), *n., pl.* **pha·lan·ges** (fə lan′jēz). *Anat., Zool.* a phalanx. [back formation from PHALANGES]

pha·lan·ge·al (fə lan′jē əl), *adj.* of or pertaining to a phalanx or the phalanges. [< NL *phalange(us)* + -AL[1]]

pha·lan·ger (fə lan′jər), *n.* any of numerous arboreal marsupials of the family *Phalangeridae,* of the Australian region, having foxlike ears and a long, bushy tail. [< L *phalang-* PHALANX + -ER[1]]

pha·lan·ges (fə lan′jēz), *n.* **1.** a pl. of **phalanx. 2.** pl. of **phalange.** [< L < Gk]

phal·an·ste·ri·an·ism (fal′ən stēr′ē ə niz′əm), *n.* Fourierism.

phal·an·ster·y (fal′ən ster′ē), *n., pl.* **-ster·ies. 1.** (in Fourierism) **a.** the buildings occupied by a phalanx. **b.** the community itself. **2.** any similar association, or the buildings they occupy. [< F *phalanstère,* b. *phalange* phalanx and *monastère* monastery]

pha·lanx (fā′langks, fal′angks), *n., pl.* **pha·lanx·es** or for 5, **pha·lang·es** (fə lan′jēz). **1.** (in ancient Greece) a formation of heavily-armed infantry in close ranks and files. **2.** any body of troops in close array. **3.** a compact or closely massed body of persons, animals, or things. **4.** (in Fourierism) a group of about 1800 persons, living together and holding their property in common. **5.** *Anat., Zool.* any of the bones of the fingers or toes. **6.** *Bot.* a bundle of stamens, joined by their filaments. [< L < Gk: military formation, bone of finger or toe, wooden roller, etc.]

phal·a·rope (fal′ə rōp′), *n.* any of three species of small, aquatic birds of the family *Phalaropodidae,* resembling sandpipers but having lobate toes. [< F < NL *Phalārop(ūs)* genus name < Gk *phalār(ís)* coot + *-o-* -o- + *poús* foot]

phal·lic (fal′ik), *adj.* of or pertaining to the phallus or phallicism. Also, **phal′li·cal.** [< Gk *phallik(ós)*]

phal·li·cism (fal′i siz′əm), *n.* worship of the phallus as symbolic of the creative power of nature. Also, **phal·lism** (fal′iz əm). —**phal′li·cist, phal′list,** *n.*

phal·lus (fal′əs), *n., pl.* **phal·li** (fal′ī), **phal·lus·es. 1.** an image of the male reproductive organ, symbolizing in certain religions the generative power in nature. **2.** *Anat.* the penis, the clitoris, or the sexually undifferentiated embryonic organ out of which either of these develops. [< L < Gk *phallós* penis]

-phane, a learned borrowing from Greek indicating resemblance (*cymophane*) or shining or transparent quality (*hydrophane*). Cf. **-phany.** [< Gk *phan-* (s. of *phaínein*) shine, appear (in pass.)]

phan·e·ro·crys·tal·line (fan′ə rō kris′t^{ə}lin, -t^{ə}līn′), *adj. Mineral.* (of a rock) having the principal constituents in the form of crystals visible to the naked eye. [< Gk *phanerό(s)* visible, manifest + CRYSTALLINE]

phan·er·o·gam (fan′ər ə gam′), *n. Bot.* any of the *Phanerogamia,* a former primary division of plants comprising those having reproductive organs; a flowering plant or seed plant (opposed to *cryptogam*). [< NL *phanerogam(us)* = Gk *phanerό(s)* visible (see -PHANE) + *-gamos* -GAMOUS] —**phan′er·o·gam′ic,** *adj.*

phan·tasm (fan′taz əm), *n.* **1.** an apparition or specter. **2.** a creation of the imagination or fancy. **3.** a mental image or representation of a real object. Also, **fantasm.** [< L *phantasm(a)* < Gk: image, vision, etc. (akin to *phantázein* to bring before the mind); r. ME *fantesme* < OF] —**Syn. 1.** ghost, vision. See **apparition. 2.** hallucination, illusion.

phan·tas·ma (fan taz′mə), *n., pl.* **-ma·ta** (-mə tə). phantasm (defs. 1, 2). [< L]

phan·tas·ma·go·ri·a (fan taz′mə gōr′ē ə, -gôr′-), *n.* **1.** a shifting series of phantasms or deceptive appearances, as in a dream. **2.** a changing scene made up of many elements. **3.** the optical illusion produced by a magic lantern or the like, in which figures increase or diminish in size, pass into each other, dissolve, etc. Also, **fantasmagoria.** [< NL < Gk *phántasm(a)* image, vision + (?) *agor(á)* an assembly + *-ia* -IA] —**phan·tas′ma·go′ri·al, phan·tas·ma·gor·ic** (fan-taz′mə gôr′ik, -gor′-), **phan·tas′ma·go′ri·an,** *adj.* —**phan-tas′ma·go′ri·al·ly, phan·tas′ma·gor′i·cal·ly,** *adv.*

phan·tas·ma·go·ry (fan taz′mə gōr′ē, -gôr′ē), *n., pl.* **-ries.** phantasmagoria.

phan·tas·mal (fan taz′məl), *adj.* pertaining to or of the nature of a phantasm; unreal; illusory; spectral. Also, **phan·tas′mic, phan·tas′mi·cal, phan·tas·mat·ic** (fan′taz-mat′ik).

phan·tast (fan′tast), *n.* fantast.

phan·ta·sy (fan′tə sē, -zē), *n., pl.* **-sies.** fantasy. —**phan-tas·tic** (fan tas′tik), **phan·tas′ti·cal,** *adj.*

phan·tom (fan′təm), *n.* **1.** an apparition or specter. **2.** an appearance or illusion without material substance, as a dream image, mirage, optical illusion, etc. **3.** a person or thing of merely illusory power, status, efficacy, etc.: *the phantom of fear.* —*adj.* **4.** of, pertaining to, or of the nature of a phantom; illusory: *a phantom ship.* Also, **fantom.** [ME *fantosme* < MF, OF < L *phantasma* PHANTASM] —**phan′tom·like′,** *adj.* —**Syn. 1, 2.** See **apparition. 4.** imaginary. —**Ant. 4.** real, material.

-phany, an element occurring in loan words from Greek, meaning "appearance," "manifestation" (*epiphany*); used in the formation of compound words. Cf. **-phane.** [< Gk *-phanía*]

Phar., **1.** pharmaceutical. **2.** pharmacology. **3.** pharmacopoeia. **4.** pharmacy. Also, **phar.**

Phar·aoh (fâr′ō, far′ō), *n.* a title of an ancient Egyptian king. [ME *Pharao,* OE *Pharaon* < L < Gk < Heb *par'ōh* < Egypt *pr-'o* great house] —**Phar·a·on·ic** (fâr′ā on′ik), **Phar′a·on′i·cal,** *adj.*

Phar′aoh ant′, a red or yellow ant, *Monomorium pharaonis,* commonly found as a household pest, esp. in the northern U.S. Also, **Phar′aoh's ant′.**

Phar·i·sa·ic (far′i sā′ik), *adj.* **1.** of or pertaining to the Pharisees. **2.** (*l.c.*) practicing or advocating strict observance of external forms and ceremonies of religion or conduct without regard to the spirit; self-righteous; sanctimonious. Also, **Phar′i·sa′i·cal.** [< LL *Pharisaic(us)* < Gk *Pharisaikós*] —**phar′i·sa′i·cal·ly,** *adv.* —**Phar′i·sa·ism, Phar·i·see·ism** (far′i sē iz′əm), *n.* —**Phar′i·sa·ist,** *adj.*

Phar·i·see (far′i sē′), *n.* **1.** *Judaism.* a member of an ancient Jewish sect that differed from the Sadducees chiefly in strictness of religious observance, interpreting the Scriptures liberally, adhering to oral laws and traditions, and in belief in an afterlife and the coming of a Messiah. **2.** (*l.c.*) a sanctimonious, self-righteous, or hypocritical person. [ME *Pharise, Farise,* OE *Farīsēus* < LL *Pharīsēus,* var. of *Pharīsaeus* < Gk *Pharīsaîos* < Aram *perīshāiyā,* pl. of *perīsh* separated]

Pharm., **1.** pharmaceutical. **2.** pharmacology. **3.** pharmacopoeia. **4.** pharmacy. Also, **pharm.**

phar·ma·ceu·ti·cal (fär′mə so͞o′ti kəl), *adj.* **1.** pertaining to pharmacy. —*n.* **2.** a pharmaceutical preparation; drug. Also, **phar′ma·ceu′tic.** [< LL *pharmaceutic(us)* (< Gk *pharmakeutikós;* see PHARMACO-) + -AL[1]] —**phar′-ma·ceu′ti·cal·ly,** *adv.*

phar·ma·ceu·tics (fär′mə so͞o′tiks), *n.* (*construed as sing.*) pharmacy (def. 1). [see PHARMACEUTICAL, -ICS]

phar·ma·cist (fär′mə sist), *n.* a person skilled in and having the authorization to engage in pharmacy; druggist; apothecary; pharmaceutical chemist. Also, *Rare,* **phar·ma·ceu·tist** (fär′mə so͞o′tist). —**Syn.** chemist.

pharmaco-, a learned borrowing from Greek meaning "drug," used in the formation of compound words: *pharmacology.* [comb. form repr. Gk *phármakon* drug]

phar·ma·co·dy·nam·ics (fär′mə kō dī nam′iks), *n.* (*construed as sing.*) the branch of pharmacology dealing with the action, effect, and breakdown of drugs within the body. —**phar′ma·co·dy·nam′ic, phar′ma·co·dy·nam′i·cal,** *adj.*

phar·ma·cog·no·sy (fär′mə kog′nə sē), *n.* See **materia medica** (def. 2). [PHARMACO- + -GNOS(IS) + -Y[3]] —**phar′-ma·cog′no·sist,** *n.* —**phar·ma·cog·nos·tic** (fär′mə kog-nos′tik), *adj.*

phar·ma·col·o·gy (fär′mə kol′ə jē), *n.* the science dealing with the preparation, uses, and esp. the effects, of drugs. [< NL *pharmacologia*] —**phar·ma·co·log·i·cal** (fär′mə kə-loj′i kəl), **phar′ma·co·log′ic,** *adj.* —**phar′ma·co·log′i-cal·ly,** *adv.* —**phar′ma·col′o·gist,** *n.*

phar·ma·co·poe·ia (fär′mə kə pē′ə), *n. Pharm.* **1.** a book published usually under governmental jurisdiction and containing a list of drugs, their formulas, methods for making medicinal preparations, and other related information. **2.** a stock of drugs. Also, **phar′ma·co·pe′ia.** [< NL < Gk *pharmakopoiía* drug maker's art = *phármako(n)* drug + *-poi(os)* maker, making (*poi(eîn)* (to) make + *-os* adj. suffix) + *-ia* -IA] —**phar′ma·co·poe′ial, phar′ma·co·poe′ic,** *adj.* —**phar′ma·co·poe′ist,** *n.*

phar·ma·cy (fär′mə sē), *n., pl.* **-cies.** **1.** the art and science of preparing and dispensing drugs. **2.** a drugstore. [earlier *pharmacia* < ML < Gk *pharmakeía* druggist's work. See PHARMACO-, -Y[3]]

Pha·ros (fâr′os), *n.* **1.** a small peninsula in the N United Arab Republic, near Alexandria: site of ancient lighthouse built by Ptolemy. **2.** the lighthouse on this peninsula. Cf. **Seven Wonders of the World.**

Phar·sa·lus (fär sā′ləs), *n.* an ancient city in central Greece, Thessaly: site of Caesar's victory over Pompey 48 B.C.

pharyng-, var. of **pharyngo-** before a vowel: *pharyngitis.*

pha·ryn·gal·ize (fə ring′gə līz′), *v.t.,* **-ized, -iz·ing.** *Phonet.* pharyngealize.

pha·ryn·ge·al (fə rin′jē əl, -jəl, far′in jē′əl), *adj.* **1.** of, pertaining to, or situated near the pharynx. **2.** *Phonet.* articulated with constriction of the pharynx. —*n.* **3.** *Phonet.* a pharyngeal sound. Also, **pha·ryn·gal** (fə ring′gəl). [< NL *pharynge(us)* pharyngeal (see PHARYNG-, -EOUS) + -AL[1]]

pha·ryn·ge·al·ize (fə rin′jē ə līz′, -jə līz′), *v.t.,* **-ized, -iz·ing.** *Phonet.* to pronounce with pharyngeal articulation.

phar·yn·gi·tis (far′in jī′tis), *n. Pathol.* inflammation of the mucous membrane of the pharynx.

pharyngo-, a learned borrowing from Greek, used as the combining form of **pharynx** in the formation of compound words: *pharyngology.* Also, *esp. before a vowel,* **pharyng-.** [< Gk, comb. form of *phárynx* throat]

phar·yn·gol·o·gy (far′ing gol′ə jē), *n.* the science of the pharynx and its diseases.

pha·ryn·go·scope (fə ring′gə skōp′), *n.* an instrument for inspecting the pharynx. —**phar·yn·gos·co·py** (far′ing-gos′kə pē), *n.*

phar·ynx (far′ingks), *n., pl.* **phar·yn·ges** (fə rin′jēz), **phar·ynx·es.** *Anat.* the tube or cavity, with its surrounding membrane and muscles, that connects the mouth and nasal passages with the esophagus. [< NL < Gk: throat, akin to *pháranx* gulf, chasm]

phase (fāz), *n., v.,* **phased, phas·ing.** —*n.* **1.** any of the major aspects in which a thing of varying forms or conditions manifests itself. **2.** a stage in a process of change or development. **3.** *Astron.* one of the recurring appearances or states of the moon or a planet in respect to the form, or the absence, of its illuminated disk. **4.** *Biol.* an aspect of or stage in meiosis or mitosis. **5.** *Zool.* See **color phase. 6.** *Chem.* a mechanically separate, homogeneous part of a heterogeneous system: *the solid, liquid, and gaseous phases of a system.* **7.** *Physics.* a particular stage or point of advancement in a cycle; the fractional part of the period through which the time has advanced, measured from some arbitrary origin. —*v.t.* **8.** to schedule or order so as to be available when or as needed. **9.** to put in phase; synchronize. **10. phase in,** to put into use or incorporate gradually or by degrees: *to phase in new machinery.* **11. phase out,** to ease out of service; withdraw gradually. [back formation from *phases,* pl. of NL *phasis* < Gk *phásis* appearance = *pha-* (root of *phaínein* to show) + *-sis* -SIS] —**phase′less,** *adj.* —**pha′sic, pha′-se·al,** *adj.* —**Syn. 1.** form, shape; facet, side.

phase-in (fāz′in′), *n.* the act or an instance of phasing in: *A phase-in of new machinery is scheduled.*

phase′ modula′tion, *Electronics.* radio transmission in which the carrier wave is modulated by changing its phase to transmit the amplitude and pitch of the signal.

phase-out (fāz′out′), *n.* the act or an instance of phasing out: *A phase-out of obsolete production methods is essential.*

phase′ rule′, *Physical Chem.* a law that the number of degrees of freedom in a system in equilibrium is equal to two plus the number of components less the number of phases. Thus, a system of ice, melted ice, and water vapor, being one component and three phases, has no degrees of freedom. Cf. **variance** (def. 4).

-phasia, a learned borrowing from Greek, used in the formation of compound words to refer to speech disorders: *aphasia.* Also, **-phasy.** [< Gk, comb. form akin to *phánai* to speak]

Ph.D., See **Doctor of Philosophy.** [< L *Philosophiae Doctor*]

pheas·ant (fez′ənt), *n.* **1.** any of numerous large, usually long-tailed, gallinaceous birds of the family *Phasianidae,* of the Old World. **2.** *Southern U.S.* the ruffed grouse. **3.** any of various other birds that resemble or suggest a pheasant. [ME *fesaunt* < AF, OF *fesan* < L *phāsiān(us)* < Gk *phāsiānós* (*órnis*) (bird) of the Phasis River]

Ring-necked pheasant, *Phasianus colchicus* (Length to 3 ft.)

Phei·dip·pi·des (fī dip′i dēz′), *n.* the Athenian runner who secured aid from Sparta in the struggle between the Athenians and the Persians 490 B.C.

phel·lem (fel′əm, -em), *n. Bot.* cork (def. 4). [< Gk *phell(ós)* cork + (PHLO)EM]

phel·lo·derm (fel′ə dûrm′), *n. Bot.* a layer of tissue in certain plants, formed from the inner cells of phellogen and consisting usually of parenchyma containing chlorophyll. [< Gk *phelló(s)* cork + -DERM] —**phel′lo·der′mal,** *adj.*

phel·lo·gen (fel′ə jən), *n. Bot.* cork cambium, a layer of tissue or secondary meristem external to the true cambium, giving rise to cork tissue on the outside and phelloderm on the inside. [< Gk *phelló(s)* cork + -GEN] —**phel·lo·ge·net·ic** (fel′ə jə net′ik), **phel·lo·gen·ic** (fel′ə jən′ik), *adj.*

phe·lo·ni·on (fe lō′nē ôn; *Eng.* fə lō′nē ən), *n., pl.* **-ni·a** (-nē ä; *Eng.* -nē ə), **-ni·ons.** *Gk. Orth. Ch.* a liturgical vestment resembling the chasuble, worn by priests. [< LGk: a kind of mantle, alter. of *phainólēs;* akin to *phaínein* to shine]

phen-, var. of **pheno-** esp. before a vowel: *phenazine.*

phe·na·caine (fē′nə kān′, fen′ə-), *n. Pharm.* a compound, $C_{18}H_{22}N_2O_2$, usually used in the form of its hydrochloride as a local anesthetic for the eye. [PHEN- + A(CET)- + (CO)CAINE]

phe·nac·e·tin (fə nas′i tin), *n. Pharm.* acetophenetidin. [PHEN(ETIDINE) + ACET(YL) + -IN²]

phen·a·cite (fen′ə sīt′), *n.* a rare vitreous mineral, beryllium silicate, Be_2SiO_4, occurring in crystals, sometimes used as a gem. [< Gk *phenak-* (s. of *phénax*) a cheat, quack + -ITE¹]

phe·nan·threne (fə nan′thrēn), *n. Chem.* a colorless isomer of anthracine, $C_{14}H_{10}$, derived from coal tar: used chiefly in dyestuffs and in the synthesis of drugs.

phen·a·zine (fen′ə zēn′, -zin), *n. Chem.* a yellow solid, $C_6H_4N_2C_6H_4$, used chiefly in the manufacture of dyes.

phen·cy·cli·dine (fen sī′kli dēn′, -sik′li-), *n.* an anesthetic drug, $C_{17}H_{25}N$, used as an animal tranquilizer: also widely used in several forms as an illicit hallucinogen. Cf. **angel dust, PCP.** [PHEN + CYCL(IC) + -ID³ + -INE¹]

phe·net·i·dine (fə net′i dēn′, -din), *n. Chem.* a colorless liquid, $H_2NC_6H_4OC_2H_5$, used chiefly in its para form in the synthesis of phenacetin, dyes, and other compounds. Also, **phe·net·i·din** (fə net′i din). [PHENET(OLE) + -ID³ + -INE²]

phen·e·tole (fen′i tōl′, -tol′), *n. Chem.* a colorless, volatile, aromatic liquid, $C_6H_5OC_2H_5$. [PHEN- + ET(HYL) + -OLE]

phen·for·min (fen fôr′min), *n. Pharm.* See **DBI.** [PHEN- + FORM(ALIN) + -IN²]

Phe·ni·cia (fə nish′ə, -nē′shə), *n.* Phoenicia.

phe·nix (fē′niks), *n.* phoenix.

Phe′nix Cit′y (fē′niks), a city in E Alabama, on the Chattahoochee River. 25,281 (1970).

pheno-, 1. a learned borrowing from Greek meaning "shining," used in the formation of compound words: *phenocryst.* **2.** *Chem.* a combining form indicating derivation from benzene, relationship to aromatic compounds, and referring to the phenyl group and sometimes phenol; used esp. before a consonant: *phenobarbital.* Also, *esp. before a vowel,* **phen-.** [< Gk *phaino-* shining, comb. form of *phaínein* to shine, appear; in chemical senses, used orig. with reference to products from the manufacture of illuminating gas]

phe·no·bar·bi·tal (fē′nō bär′bi tal′, -tôl′, -nə-), *n. Pharm.* a white powder, $C_{12}H_{12}N_2O_3$, available also as the sodium salt **(phenobar′bital so′dium)** for greater solubility: used as a sedative, a hypnotic, and as an antispasmodic in epilepsy. Also called **phenylethylmalonylurea.**

phe·no·cryst (fē′nə krist, fen′ə-), *n. Geol.* any of the conspicuous crystals in a porphyritic rock. [PHENO- + CRYST(AL)]

phe·nol (fē′nōl, -nol), *n. Chem.* **1.** Also called **carbolic acid.** a white, poisonous mass, C_6H_5OH, obtained from coal tar, or a hydroxyl derivative of benzene: used chiefly as a disinfectant, as an antiseptic, and in organic synthesis. **2.** any analogous hydroxyl derivative of benzene. —**phe·no·lic** (fi nō′lik, -nô′-, -nol′ik), *adj.*

phe·no·late (fēn′əlāt′), *n., v.,* **-lat·ed, -lat·ing.** —*n.* **1.** Also called **phenoxide.** a salt of phenol, as sodium phenolate, C_6H_5ONa. —*v.i.* **2.** to treat or impregnate with phenol.

phenol′ic res′in, *Chem.* any of a class of resins formed by the condensation of phenol, or a phenol derivative, with an aldehyde: used chiefly in the manufacture of paints and plastics, and as adhesives.

phe·nol·o·gy (fi nol′ə jē), *n.* the science dealing with the influence of climate on the recurrence of such annual phenomena of animal and plant life as bird migrations, budding, etc. [syncopated var. of PHENOMENOLOGY, with restriction to climatic phenomena] —**phe·no·log·i·cal** (fēn′əloj′i kəl), *adj.* —**phe′no·log′i·cal·ly,** *adv.* —**phe·nol′o·gist,** *n.*

phe·nol·phthal·ein (fē′nōl thal′ēn, -ē in, -fthal′-, -nol-), *n. Chem., Pharm.* a white, crystalline, water-insoluble compound, $C_{20}H_{14}O_4$, used as an indicator in acid-base titration and as a laxative.

phe·nom·e·na (fi nom′ə nə), *n.* a pl. of **phenomenon.**

phe·nom·e·nal (fi nom′ə nəl), *adj.* **1.** extraordinary or prodigious: *phenomenal speed.* **2.** of or pertaining to phenomena or to a phenomenon. **3.** of the nature of a phenomenon; perceivable by the senses. [PHENOMEN(ON) + -AL¹] —**phe·nom′e·nal·ly,** *adv.*

phe·nom·e·nal·ism (fi nom′ə nəliz′əm), *n. Philos.* **1.** the view that all things, including human beings, consist simply of the aggregate of their observable, sensory qualities. **2.** the doctrine that phenomena are the only objects of knowledge or the only form of reality. —**phe·nom′e·nal·ist,** *n.* —**phe·nom′e·nal·is′tic,** *adj.* —**phe·nom′e·nal·is′ti·cal·ly,** *adv.*

phe·nom·e·nol·o·gy (fi nom′ə nol′ə jē), *n. Philos.* **1.** a system based on the analysis of phenomena as intuitive essences of intentional character. **2.** (in Kant) the study of objects and events as they appear in experience. **3.** the descriptive study of phenomena. —**phe·nom·e·no·log·i·cal** (fi nom′ə nəloj′i kəl), **phe·nom′e·no·log′ic,** *adj.* —**phe·nom′e·no·log′i·cal·ly,** *adv.*

phe·nom·e·non (fi nom′ə non′), *n., pl.* **-na** (-nə) for 1, 3, **-nons** for 2. **1.** a fact, occurrence, or circumstance observed or observable: *the phenomena of nature.* **2.** something that impresses the observer as extraordinary; a remarkable thing or person. **3.** *Philos.* **a.** an appearance or immediate object of awareness in experience. **b.** *Kantianism.* a thing as it appears to the mind, as distinguished from a noumenon, or thing-in-itself. [< LL *phaenomenon* < Gk *phainómenon* appearance, n. use of neut. of *phainómenos,* prp. of *phaínesthai* to appear, pass. of *phaínein* to show] —**Syn. 1.** event, incident. **2.** prodigy, marvel, wonder.

phe·no·saf·ra·nine (fē′nə saf′rə nēn′, -nin), *n. Chem.* safranine (def. 2).

phe·no·thi·a·zine (fē′nə thī′ə -zēn′, -zin), *n. Chem.* a grayish-green to greenish-yellow solid, $C_{12}H_9NS$, used as an insecticide and vermifuge, and in the synthesis of pharmaceuticals.

phe·no·type (fē′nə tīp′), *n. Genetics.* **1.** the observable constitution of an organism. **2.** the appearance of an organism resulting from the interaction of the genotype and the environment. Cf. **genotype.** [PHENO(MENON) + TYPE; modeled on G *Phänotypus*] —**phe·no·typ·ic** (fē′nə tip′ik), **phe′no·typ′i·cal,** *adj.* —**phe′no·typ′i·cal·ly,** *adv.*

phe·nox·ide (fi nok′sīd), *n. Chem.* phenolate (def. 1).

phen·yl (fen′əl, fēn′əl), *adj. Chem.* containing the phenyl group.

phen′yl ac′etate, *Chem.* a colorless liquid, $CH_3COOC_6H_5$, having a phenolic odor: used chiefly as a solvent.

phen·yl·al·a·nine (fen′əlal′ə nēn′, fēn′əlal′-), *n. Biochem.* an amino acid, $C_6H_5CH_2CH(NH_2)COOH$, essential to the nutrition of man and most animals, obtained chiefly from egg white or skim milk. Also called **phen′yl·a·mi′no·pro·pi·on′ic ac′id** (fen′əl ə mē′nō prō prē on′ik, -am′ə nō-, fēn′-).

phen′ylene group′, *Chem.* any of three bivalent, isomeric groups having the formula $-C_6H_4-$, derived from benzene by the removal of two hydrogen atoms. Also called **phen′ylene rad′ical.** Cf. **meta, ortho, para².** —**phen·yl·ene** (fen′əlēn′, fēn′-), *adj.*

phen·yl·eth·yl·mal·o·nyl·u·re·a (fen′əl eth′əl mal′ə nil yōō rē′ə, fēn′-), *n. Pharm.* phenobarbital. [PHENYL + ETHYL + *malon(ic)* (of MALONIC ESTER) + -YL + UREA]

phen′yl group′, *Chem.* the univalent group, C_6H_5-, derived from benzene. Also called **phen′yl rad′ical.**

phen·yl·ke·to·nu·ri·a (fen′əl kēt′ənŏŏr′ē ə, -ənyŏŏr′-, fēn′-), *n. Pathol.* an inherited, abnormal condition characterized by phenylketones in the urine, due to faulty metabolism of phenylalanine, and usually first characterized by signs of mental retardation in infancy. [< NL; see PHENYL, KETONE, -URIA]

phen′yl meth′yl ke′tone, *Chem.* acetophenone.

phen′yl salic′ylate, *Chem.* salol.

pher·o·mone (fer′ə mōn′), *n. Biochem.* any of a class of hormonal substances secreted by an individual and stimulating a physiological or behavioral response from an individual of the same species. [< Gk *phér(ein)* (to) bear + -o- + (HOR)MONE]

phew (fyōō, pfyōō, whyōō), *interj.* (used as an exclamation to express exhaustion, relief, etc.): *Phew! It's hot!*

phi (fī, fē), *n., pl.* **phis.** the 21st letter of the Greek alphabet (Φ, φ).

phi·al (fī′əl), *n.* vial (def. 1).

Phi Be·ta Kap·pa (fī′ bā′tə kap′ə, bē′tə), **1.** a national honor society founded in 1776 whose members are chosen, for lifetime membership, from among college undergraduates of high academic distinction. **2.** a member of Phi Beta Kappa.

Phid·i·an (fid′ē ən), *adj.* of, associated with, or following the style of Phidias as exemplified in the Parthenon.

Phid·i·as (fid′ē əs), *n.* c500–432? B.C., Greek sculptor.

phil-, var. of **philo-** before a vowel: *philanthropy.*

-phil, var. of **-phile:** *eosinophil.*

Phil., 1. Philemon. **2.** Philippians. **3.** Philippine.

phil., 1. philosophical. **2.** philosophy.

Phila., Philadelphia.

Phil·a·del·phi·a (fil′ə del′fē ə), *n.* a city in SE Pennsylvania, on the Delaware River. 1,950,098 (1970). —**Phil′a·del′phi·an,** *adj., n.*

Phil′adel′phia law′yer, *Often Disparaging.* a lawyer noted for his ability in matters involving fine points and technicalities.

Phi·lae (fī′lē), *n.* an island in the Nile, in Upper Egypt: the site of ancient temples.

phi·lan·der (fi lan′dər), *v.i.* (of a man) to make love without serious intentions, esp. to carry on flirtations. [< Gk *philandr(os)* one who loves (of a woman, loving her husband); see PHIL-, ANDR-; later used in fiction as a proper name for a lover] —**phi·lan′der·er,** *n.* —**Syn.** trifle, dally.

phil·an·throp·ic (fil′ən throp′ik), *adj.* of, pertaining to, or characterized by philanthropy; benevolent. Also, **phil′an·throp′i·cal.** —**phil′an·throp′i·cal·ly,** *adv.*

phi·lan·thro·pist (fi lan′thrə pist), *n.* a person who practices philanthropy.

phi·lan·thro·py (fi lan′thrə pē), *n., pl.* **-pies** for 2, 3. **1.** affection for mankind, esp. as manifested in donations of money, property, or work to needy persons or to socially useful purposes: *works of philanthropy.* **2.** the activity of donating to such persons or purposes in this way. **3.** a philanthropic organization. [earlier *philanthropia* < LL < Gk: love for mankind]

phi·lat·e·ly (fi lat′əlē), *n.* the collection and study of postage stamps, revenue stamps, stamped envelopes, postmarks, postal cards, covers, and similar material relating to postal or fiscal history. [< F *philatélie* love of postage stamps < Gk *phil-* PHIL- + *atéleia* freedom from charges (taken to mean recipient's freedom from delivery charges by virtue of the stamp that sender affixed to the letter), lit., want of taxation = *a-* A-⁶ + *tél(os)* tax + *-eia* -Y³] —**phil·a·tel·ic** (fil′ə tel′ik), **phil′a·tel′i·cal,** *adj.* —**phil′a·tel′i·cal·ly,** *adv.* —**phi·lat′e·list,** *n.*

-phile, a word element meaning "loving," "friendly," or "lover," "friend," used in the formation of nouns and adjectives: *Anglophile; bibliophile.* Also, **-phil.** [< L *-philus, -phila* < Gk *-philos* dear, beloved (occurring in proper names). Cf. F *-phile*]

Philem., Philemon.

Phi·le·mon (fi lē′mən, fī-), *n.* **1.** *Class. Myth.* the husband of Baucis. **2.** an Epistle written by Paul. **3.** the person to whom this Epistle is addressed.

phil·har·mon·ic (fil′här mon′ik, fil′ər-), *adj.* **1.** fond of music; music-loving: used esp. in the name of certain musical societies and hence applied to their concerts. **2.** of or noting a musical group or organization. —*n.* **3.** such a group or organization; symphony orchestra. [modeled on F *philharmonique* or It *filarmonico*]

phil·hel·lene (fil hel′ēn), *n.* a friend or supporter of the Greeks. Also, **phil·hel·len·ist** (fil hel′ə nist, fil′he lē′nist). [< Gk *philéllēn* Greek-loving] —**phil·hel·len·ic** (fil′he len′ik, -lē′nik), *adj.* —**phil·hel·len·ism** (fil hel′ə niz′əm), *n.*

Phil. I., Philippine Islands.

-philia, a learned borrowing from Greek used esp. in pathological terminology to indicate an abnormal liking for or a tendency toward something: *hemophilia; necrophilia.* Cf. **-philous.** [< Gk *philía* loving. See -PHILE, -IA]

phil·i·beg (fil′ə beg′), *n.* filibeg.

Phil·ip (fil′ip), *n.* **1.** one of the 12 apostles. Mark 3:18; John 1:43–48; 6:5–7. **2.** one of the leaders of the Christian Hellenists in the early church in Jerusalem who afterwards became an evangelist and missionary. Acts 6; 8:26–40. **3. King,** died 1676, North American Indian chief: sachem of the Wampanoag tribe 1662–76; leader of the Indians in King Philip's War. **4. Prince, Duke of Edinburgh,** (*Philip Mountbatten*) born 1921, consort of Elizabeth II.

Philip I, **1.** 1052–1108, king of France 1060–1108. **2.** ("*the Handsome*") 1478–1506, king of Spain 1504–06 (son of Maximilian I).

Philip II, **1.** ("*Philip of Macedon*") 382–336 B.C., king of Macedonia 359–336 (father of Alexander the Great). **2.** ("*Philip Augustus*") 1165–1223, king of France 1180–1223. **3.** 1527–98, king of Spain 1556–98 (husband of Mary I).

Philip III, **1.** ("*Philip the Bold*") 1245–85, king of France 1270–85. **2.** 1578–1621, king of Spain 1598–1621.

Philip IV, **1.** ("*Philip the Fair*") 1268–1314, king of France 1285–1314. **2.** 1605–65, king of Spain 1621–65.

Philip V, **1.** ("*Philip the Tall*") 1294–1322, king of France 1316–22. **2.** 1683–1746, king of Spain 1700–46.

Philip VI, 1293–1350, king of France 1328–50.

Philip., Philippians.

Phi·lippe·ville (*Fr.* fē lēp vēl′; *Eng.* fil′ip vil′), *n.* former name of **Skikda.**

Phi·lip·pi (fi lip′ī), *n.* a ruined city in NE Greece, in Macedonia: Octavian and Mark Antony defeated Brutus and Cassius here, 42 B.C. —**Phi·lip·pi·an** (fi lip′ē ən), *adj., n.*

Phi·lip·pi·ans (fi lip′ē ənz), *n.* (*construed as sing.*) an Epistle written by Paul to the Christians in Philippi.

Phi·lip·pic (fi lip′ik), *n.* **1.** any of the orations delivered by Demosthenes against Philip II of Macedon. **2.** (*l.c.*) any discourse or speech of bitter denunciation.

Phil·ip·pine (fil′ə pēn′, fil′ə pēn′), *adj.* of or pertaining to the Philippines or their inhabitants.

Phil′ippine mahog′any, **1.** any of several Philippine trees yielding a wood that closely resembles mahogany. **2.** the wood of any of these trees.

Phil·ip·pines (fil′ə pēnz′, fil′ə pēnz′), *n.* (*construed as pl.*) an archipelago of 7083 islands in the Pacific, SE of China: formerly under the guardianship of the U.S.; now an independent republic. 43,940,000; 114,830 sq. mi. *Cap.:* Quezon City. Also, **Phil′ippine Is′lands.** Formerly, **Commonwealth of the Philippines** (1935–46). Official name, **Republic of the Philippines.**

Phil·ip·pop·o·lis (fil′ə pop′ə lis), *n.* Greek name of **Plovdiv.**

Phil·ips (fil′ips), *n.* **Ambrose,** 1675?–1749, English poet and dramatist.

Phil′ip the Good′, 1396–1467, duke of Burgundy 1419–1467.

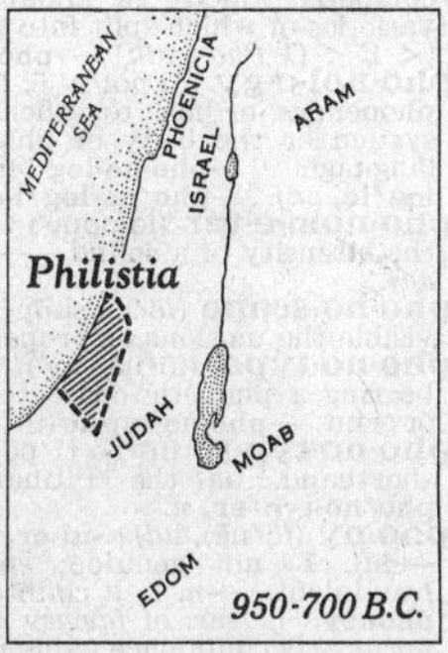

-philism, an element used to form abstract nouns from stems ending in **-phile:** *necrophilism.*

-philist, an element used to form personal nouns from stems ending in **-phile.**

Phi·lis·ti·a (fi lis′tē ə), *n.* an ancient country on the E coast of the Mediterranean. —**Phi·lis′ti·an,** *adj.*

Philistia

950-700 B.C.

Phil·is·tine (fil′i stēn′, -stīn′, fi lis′tin, -tēn), *n.* **1.** a native or inhabitant of Philistia. **2.** (*sometimes l.c.*) a person who is lacking in or smugly indifferent to culture, aesthetic refinement, etc., or is contentedly commonplace in ideas and tastes. —*adj.* **3.** (*sometimes l.c.*) lacking in or hostile to culture. **4.** of the ancient Philistines. [ME < LL *Philistīnī* (pl.) < LGk *Philistînoi* < Heb *p'lishtīm*] —**Phil·is·tin·ism** (fil′i stē niz′əm, -stī-, fi lis′tə niz′əm, -tē-), *n.*

Phil·lips (fil′ips), *n.* **1. Stephen,** 1868–1915, English poet and playwright. **2. Wen·dell** (wen′dᵊl), 1811–84, U.S. orator and reformer.

Phil′lips head′, a screw head having two partial slots crossed at right angles, driven by a special screwdriver. See illus. at **screw.** [after *Phillips Screws,* a trademark] —**Phil′lips-head′,** *adj.*

philo-, an element appearing in loan words from Greek, where it meant "loving" (*philology*); on this model, used in the formation of compound words (*philoprogenitive*). Also, *esp. before a vowel,* **phil-.** [< Gk, comb. form of *phílos* loving]

Phil·oc·te·tes (fil′ək tē′tēz), *n.* *Class. Myth.* the armor-bearer of Hercules, and the archer whose poisoned arrow caused the death of Paris in the Trojan War.

phil·o·den·dron (fil′ə den′drən), *n.* a tropical American climbing plant of the family *Araceae,* used as an ornamental. [< NL < Gk, n. use of neut. of *philódendros* fond of trees]

phi·log·y·ny (fi loj′ə nē), *n.* love of or liking for women. [< Gk *philogynía*] —**phi·log′y·nist,** *n.* —**phi·log′y·nous,** *adj.*

Phi·lo Ju·dae·us (fī′lō jo͞o dē′əs), c20 B.C.–A.D. c50, Alexandrian Jewish theologian and Hellenistic philosopher.

philol., **1.** philological. **2.** philology.

phi·lol·o·gy (fi lol′ə jē), *n.* **1.** the study of written records, their authenticity and original form, and the determination of their meaning. **2.** linguistics. [ME *philologie* < L *philologia* < Gk: love of learning and literature = *philólog(os)* literary, studious, argumentative, etc. + *-ia* -Y³] —**phil·o·log·i·cal** (fil′ə loj′i kəl), **phil′o·log′ic,** *adj.* —**phil′o·log′i·cal·ly,** *adv.* —**phi·lol′o·gist, phi·lol′o·ger,** *n.*

phil·o·mel (fil′ə mel′), *n.* *Poetic.* the nightingale. Also, **philomela.** [earlier *philomele, philomela* < L *philomēla* < Gk: nightingale; r. ME *philomene* < ML *philomēna,* dissimilated var. of *philomēla*]

Phil·o·me·la (fil′ə mē′lə), *n.* **1.** *Class. Myth.* an Athenian princess whose brother-in-law Tereus raped her and cut out her tongue. She was subsequently avenged and transformed into a nightingale. **2.** (*l.c.*) philomel.

phil·o·pro·gen·i·tive (fil′ō prō jen′i tiv), *adj.* **1.** producing offspring, esp. abundantly; prolific. **2.** of, pertaining to, or characterized by love for offspring, esp. one's own.

philos., **1.** philosopher. **2.** philosophical. **3.** philosophy.

phil·o·sophe (fil′ə sof′, fil′ə zof′; *Fr.* fē lô zôf′), *n., pl.* **-sophes** (-sofs′, -zofs′; *Fr.* -zôf′). a popular French intellectual or social philosopher of the 18th century, as Diderot, Rousseau, or Voltaire. [< F]

phi·los·o·pher (fi los′ə fər), *n.* **1.** a person who offers his views or theories on profound questions in ethics, metaphysics, logic, and other related fields. **2.** a person who is deeply versed in philosophy, as a professor of philosophy. **3.** a person who establishes the central ideas of some movement, cult, etc. **4.** a person who regulates his life by the light of reason. **5.** a philosophical, calm, or stoic person. [ME, var. of *philosophre* < AF (MF *philosophe*); r. OE *philosoph* < L *philosoph(us)* < Gk *philósophos* philosopher. See PHILO-, -SOPHY]

philos′ophers' stone′, *Alchemy.* an imaginary substance or preparation believed capable of transmuting baser metals into gold or silver and of prolonging life. Also, **philos′opher's stone′.**

phil·o·soph·i·cal (fil′ə sof′i kəl), *adj.* **1.** of or pertaining to philosophy: *philosophical studies.* **2.** versed in or occupied with philosophy. **3.** proper to or befitting a philosopher. **4.** rational and calm under trying circumstances. Also, **phil′o·soph′ic.** [< L *philosophic(us)* (< Gk *philosophikós;* see PHILOSOPHER, -IC) + -AL¹] —**phil′o·soph′i·cal·ly,** *adv.* —**phil′o·soph′i·cal·ness,** *n.*

phi·los·o·phise (fi los′ə fīz′), *v.i.,* **-phised, -phis·ing.** *Chiefly Brit.* philosophize. —**phi·los′o·phi·sa′tion,** *n.* —**phi·los′o·phis′er,** *n.*

phi·los·o·phism (fi los′ə fiz′əm), *n.* **1.** a false or contrived argument, esp. one designed to deceive. **2.** spurious or deceitful philosophy.

phi·los·o·phize (fi los′ə fīz′), *v.i.,* **-phized, -phiz·ing.** **1.** to speculate or theorize in a superficial or imprecise manner. **2.** to think or reason as a philosopher. Also, *esp. Brit.,* **philosophise.** —**phi·los′o·phi·za′tion,** *n.* —**phi·los′o·phiz′er,** *n.*

phi·los·o·phy (fi los′ə fē), *n., pl.* **-phies.** **1.** the rational investigation of the truths and principles of being, knowledge, or conduct. **2.** a system of philosophical doctrine: *the philosophy of Spinoza.* **3.** the critical study of the basic principles and concepts of a particular branch of knowledge: *the philosophy of science.* **4.** a system of principles for guidance in practical affairs: *a philosophy of life.* **5.** a philosophical, calm, or stoic attitude. [ME *philosophie* < L *philosophia* < Gk. See PHILO-, -SOPHY]

-philous, an element used to form adjectives from stems ending in **-phile:** *dendrophilous; heliophilous.* [< L *-philus* < Gk *-philos.* See -PHILE, -OUS]

phil·ter (fil′tər), *n.* **1.** a potion or drug that is supposed to induce a person to fall in love with someone. **2.** a magic potion for any purpose. Also, *esp. Brit.,* **phil′tre.** [16th-century *philter,* 17th-century *philtrum* < L; 17th-century *filtre* < L or F] —**phil′ter·er,** *n.*

Phit·sa·nu·lok (pit′sä no͞o lōk′), *n.* a city in central Thailand. 25,000 (est. 1961).

phle·bi·tis (flə bī′tis), *n.* *Pathol.* inflammation of a vein. [< NL] —**phle·bit·ic** (flə bit′ik), *adj.*

phlebo-, a learned borrowing from Greek meaning "vein," used in the formation of compound words: *phlebotomy.* Also, *esp. before a vowel,* **phleb-.** [< Gk, comb. form of *phléps*]

phle·bot·o·mise (flə bot′ə mīz′, flē-, fle-), *v.t.,* **-mised, -mis·ing.** *Chiefly Brit.* phlebotomize. —**phle·bot′o·mi·sa′tion,** *n.*

phle·bot·o·mize (flə bot′ə mīz′, flē-, fle-), *v.t.,* **-mized, -miz·ing.** to subject to phlebotomy; bleed. [< MF *phlebotomis(er)* (cf. ML *flebotomizāre*)] —**phle·bot′o·mi·za′tion,** *n.*

phle·bot·o·my (flə bot′ə mē), *n., pl.* **-mies.** *Med.* act or practice of opening a vein for letting blood; bleeding. [late ME *flebotomye,* etc. < LL *flebotomia,* var. of *phlebotomia* < Gk] —**phleb·o·tom·ic** (fleb′ə tom′ik), **phleb′o·tom′i·cal,** *adj.* —**phle·bot′o·mist,** *n.*

Phleg·e·thon (fleg′ə thon′, flej′-), *n.* *Class. Myth.* a river of fire, one of five rivers surrounding Hades. [< L < Gk < *phlegéthein* to blaze. See PHLEGM]

phlegm (flem), *n.* **1.** the thick mucus secreted in the respiratory passages and discharged through the mouth, esp. that occurring in the lungs and throat passages, as during a cold. **2.** *Old Physiol.* a humor regarded as causing sluggishness or apathy. **3.** sluggishness; apathy. **4.** self-possession; coolness. [ME *fleem* < MF *flemme* < LL *phlegma* < Gk: flame, phlegmatic humor = *phlég(ein)* (to) burn + *-ma* n. suffix] —**phlegm′less,** *adj.* —**Syn. 3.** indifference.

phleg·mat·ic (fleg mat′ik), *adj.* **1.** not easily excited to action or display of emotion; apathetic; sluggish. **2.** self-possessed; cool. **3.** of the nature of or abounding in the humor phlegm. Also, **phleg·mat′i·cal.** [< LL *phlegmatic(us)* < Gk *phlegmatikós* pertaining to phlegm = *phlegmat-* (s. of *phlégma*) + *-ikos* -IC] —**phleg·mat′i·cal·ly,** *adv.* —**phleg·mat′i·cal·ness, phleg·mat′ic·ness,** *n.* —**Syn. 1.** stolid, stoical, cold, uninterested. **2.** composed, collected, placid.

phlegm·y (flem′ē), *adj.,* **phlegm·i·er, phlegm·i·est.** of, pertaining to, or characterized by phlegm.

phlo·em (flō′em), *n.* the part of a vascular bundle consisting of sieve tubes, companion cells, parenchyma, and fibers and forming the food-conducting tissue of a plant. [< G < Gk *phló(os)* bark (var. of *phloiós*) + *-ēm(a)* -EME]

phlo·gis·tic (flō jis′tik), *adj.* **1.** *Pathol.* inflammatory. **2.** pertaining to or consisting of phlogiston. [< Gk *phlogist(ós)* inflammable (verbid of *phlogízein* to set on fire; akin to PHLOX, PHLEGM) + -IC]

phlo·gis·ton (flō jis′ton, -tən), *n.* a nonexistent chemical that, prior to the discovery of oxygen, was thought to be released during combustion. [< NL: inflammability, n. use of Gk neut. of *phlogistós* inflammable; see PHLOGISTIC]

phlog·o·pite (flog′ə pīt′), *n.* a mica, $KMg_3AlSi_3O_{10}(OH)_2$, usually yellowish-brown but sometimes reddish-brown. [< Gk *phlogōp(ós)* fiery-looking + -ITE[1]]

phlox (floks), *n.* **1.** any polemoniaceous herb of the genus *Phlox*, of North America, certain species of which are cultivated for their showy flowers of various colors. **2.** the flower of this plant. [< ML, special use of L *phlox* < Gk: a flame-colored plant, lit., a flame. See PHLEGM, PHLOGISTIC]

phlyc·tae·na (flik tē′nə), *n., pl.* **-nae** (-nē). *Pathol.* phlyctena.

phlyc·te·na (flik tē′nə), *n., pl.* **-nae** (-nē). *Pathol.* a small vesicle, blister, or pustule. [< NL, var. of *phlyctaena* < Gk *phlýktaina* a blister, akin to *phlýein, phlýzein* to swell, boil over]

Phnom Penh (nom′ pen′, pə nôm′ pen′), a city in and the capital of Cambodia, in the S part. 400,000. Also, **Pnom Penh, Pnom-penh, Pnompenh.**

-phobe, a suffix used to form personal nouns corresponding to nouns ending in **-phobia:** *Anglophobe.* [< Gk, comb. form of *phóbos* fearing]

pho·bi·a (fō′bē ə), *n.* an obsessive or irrational fear or anxiety. [abstracted from nouns ending in -PHOBIA] —**pho′bic,** *adj.* —**Syn.** aversion, hatred, dread.

-phobia, an element occurring in loan words from Greek (*hydrophobia*); on this model used in compound words with the meaning "fear," "dread," often implying abnormal fear or dread, or used with the implication of hatred or aversion (*agoraphobia*). [< L < Gk; see -PHOBE, -IA]

Pho·cae·a (fō sē′ə), *n.* an ancient seaport in Asia Minor: northernmost of the Ionian cities; later an important maritime state.

pho·cine (fō′sīn, -sin), *adj.* *Zool.* **1.** of or pertaining to seals. **2.** belonging to the subfamily *Phocinae,* comprising the earless or hair seals. [< L *phōc(a)* seal (< Gk *phṓkē*) + -INE[1]]

Pho·ci·on (fō′shē ən), *n.* 402?–317 B.C., Athenian statesman and general.

Pho·cis (fō′sis), *n.* an ancient district in central Greece, N of the Gulf of Corinth: site of Delphic oracle.

pho·co·me·li·a (fō′kō mē′lē ə, -mēl′yə), *n.* *Pathol.* a usually congenital deformity of the extremities in which the limbs are abnormally short. Also, **pho·com·e·ly** (fō kom′ə lē). [< NL < Gk *phṓkē* seal + *-melia* -MELIA]

phoe·be (fē′bē), *n.* any of several small, American flycatchers of the genus *Sayornis,* esp. *S. phoebe,* of eastern North America. [imit.; sp. by influence of PHOEBE]

Phoe·be (fē′bē), *n.* **1.** *Class. Myth.* a Titaness, daughter of Uranus and Gaea and mother of Leto: later identified with Artemis and with the Roman goddess Diana. **2.** *Literary.* the moon personified.

Phoe·bus (fē′bəs), *n.* **1.** *Class. Myth.* Apollo as the sun god. **2.** *Literary.* the sun personified. [< L < Gk *Phoîbos,* lit., bright, akin to *pháos* light; r. ME *Phebus* < ML] —**Phoe·be·an** (fi bē′ən, fē′bē-), *adj.*

Phoe·ni·cia (fi nish′ə, -nē′shə), *n.* an ancient kingdom on the Mediterranean, in the region of modern Syria, Lebanon, and Israel. Also, **Phenicia.** See map at **Tyre.**

Phoe·ni·cian (fi nish′ən, -nē′shən), *n.* **1.** a native or inhabitant of Phoenicia. **2.** the extinct Semitic language of the Phoenicians. —*adj.* **3.** of or pertaining to Phoenicia, its people, or their language. **4.** noting or pertaining to the script used for the writing of Phoenician from the 11th century B.C. or earlier and from which were derived the Greek, Roman, and all other western alphabets.

phoe·nix (fē′niks), *n.* **1.** (*sometimes cap.*) a unique mythical bird of great beauty fabled to live 500 or 600 years, to burn itself to death, and to rise from its ashes in the freshness of youth, and live through another life cycle. **2.** a person or thing of peerless beauty or excellence; paragon. Also, **phenix.** [< L < Gk *phoînix* a mythical bird, purple-red color, Phoenician; r. ME, OE *phēnix* < ML]

Phoe·nix (fē′niks), *n.* a city in and the capital of Arizona, in the central part. 581,562 (1970).

Phoe′nix Is′lands, a group of eight coral islands in the central Pacific: part of the British Gilbert and Ellice Islands; two of the group are under joint American and British control. 11 sq. mi.

phon-, var. of **phono-** before a vowel: *phonic.*

phon., phonetics.

pho·nate (fō′nāt), *v.t., v.i.,* **-nat·ed, -nat·ing.** **1.** *Phonet.* to provide (a sound source, and hence the pitch) for a given voiced continuant or vowel, through rapid, periodic glottal action. Cf. **voice** (def. 17). **2.** to vocalize. —**pho·na′tion,** *n.*

phone[1] (fōn), *n., v.t., v.i.,* **phoned, phon·ing.** *Informal.* telephone. [by shortening]

phone[2] (fōn), *n.* *Phonet.* a speech sound: *There are three phonetically different "t" phones in an utterance of "titillate" and two in an utterance of "tattletale."* Cf. **allophone, phoneme.** [< Gk; see PHON-] —**pho′nal,** *adj.*

-phone, var. of **phono-** as final element of compound words, esp. used in names of instruments: *megaphone; telephone; xylophone.*

phone′ book′. See **telephone book.** Also called **phone′ direc′tory.**

phone-in (fōn′in′), *n., adj.* call-in.

pho·ne·mat·ics (fō′nə mat′iks), *n.* (*construed as sing.*) phonemics. [< Gk *phōnēmat-* (s. of *phṓnēma;* see PHONEME) + -ICS]

pho·neme (fō′nēm), *n.* *Linguistics.* any of a small set of basic units of sound, different for each language, by which utterances are represented. In English the difference in sound and meaning between *pit* and *bit* is taken to indicate the existence of two labial phonemes, *p* and *b.* [< Gk *phṓnēma* sound]

pho·ne·mic (fə nē′mik, fō-), *adj.* **1.** of or pertaining to phonemes: *a phonemic system.* **2.** of or pertaining to phonemics. **3.** concerning or involving the discrimination of distinctive speech elements of a language: *a phonemic contrast.*

pho·ne·mics (fə nē′miks, fō-), *n.* (*construed as sing.*) **1.** the study of phonemes and phonemic systems. **2.** the phonemic system of a language. —**pho·ne·mi·cist** (fō nē′mi sist), *n.*

pho·nes·the·mic (fō′nis thē′mik), *adj.* *Linguistics.* (of a speech sound) shared in common by a set of echoic or symbolic words, as the *sn-* of *sneer, snarl, snatch, snide, snitch, snoop,* etc. [b. PHONEME and ESTHETIC]

phonet., phonetics.

pho·net·ic (fə net′ik, fō-), *adj.* **1.** of or pertaining to speech sounds, their production, or their transcription in written symbols. **2.** corresponding to pronunciation: *phonetic transcription; a phonetic alphabet.* **3.** agreeing with pronunciation: *phonetic spelling.* **4.** concerning or involving the discrimination of nondistinctive elements of a language. In English, certain phonological features, as length and aspiration, are phonetic but not phonemic. Also, *Rare,* **pho·net′i·cal.** [< NL *phōnētic(us)* < Gk *phōnētikós* vocal = *phōnēt(ós)* to be spoken (verbid of *phōneîn* to speak) + *-ikos* -IC] —**pho·net′i·cal·ly,** *adv.*

phonet′ic al′phabet, an alphabet containing a separate character for each distinguishable speech sound.

pho·ne·ti·cian (fō′ni tish′ən), *n.* a specialist in phonetics.

phonet′ic law′, *Historical Linguistics.* a statement of some regular pattern of sound change in a specific language, as Grimm's law.

pho·net·ics (fə net′iks, fō-), *n.* (*construed as sing.*) **1.** the science or study of speech sounds and their production, transmission, and reception, and their analysis, classification, and transcription. Cf. **acoustic phonetics, articulatory phonetics, auditory phonetics, physiological phonetics.** **2.** *Linguistics.* the science or study of speech sounds with respect to their role in distinguishing meanings among words (sometimes contrasted with *phonemics*). Cf. **phonology. 3.** the phonetic system of a particular language. [see PHONETIC, -ICS]

pho·ney (fō′nē), *adj.,* **-ni·er, -ni·est,** *n., pl.* **-neys.** phony. —**pho′ney·ness,** *n.*

phon·ic (fon′ik, fō′nik), *adj.* of or pertaining to speech sounds.

phon·ics (fon′iks, fō′niks), *n.* (*construed as sing.*) a method of teaching reading, pronunciation, and spelling based upon the phonetic interpretation of ordinary spelling.

phono-, a learned borrowing from Greek meaning "sound," "voice," used in the formation of compound words: *phonology.* Also, *esp. before a vowel,* **phon-.** Cf. **-phone, -phony.** [< Gk, comb. form repr. *phōnḗ*]

pho·no·gram (fō′nə gram′), *n.* a unit symbol of a phonetic writing system, standing for a speech sound, syllable, or other sequence of speech sounds without reference to meaning. —**pho′no·gram′ic, pho′no·gram′mic,** *adj.*

pho·no·graph (fō′nə graf′, -gräf′), *n.* any sound-reproducing machine using records, whether cylinders or disks.

pho·no·graph·ic (fō′nə graf′ik), *adj.* **1.** of, pertaining to, or characteristic of a phonograph. **2.** of, pertaining to, or noting phonography. Also, **pho′no·graph′i·cal.**

pho·nog·ra·phy (fō nog′rə fē), *n.* **1.** phonetic spelling, writing, or shorthand. **2.** a system of phonetic shorthand, as that invented by Sir Isaac Pitman in 1837. —**pho·nog′ra·pher, pho·nog′ra·phist,** *n.*

phonol., phonology.

pho·no·lite (fōn′ᵊlīt′), *n.* a fine-grained volcanic rock composed chiefly of alkali feldspar and nepheline, some varieties of which split into pieces that ring on being struck. [< F < G *Phonolith*] —**pho·no·lit·ic** (fōn′ᵊlit′ik), *adj.*

pho·nol·o·gy (fō nol′ə jē, fə-), *n., pl.* **-gies.** **1.** phonetics, phonemics, or both together. **2.** the phonetic and phonemic system or the body of phonetic and phonemic facts of a language. —**pho·no·log·i·cal** (fōn′ᵊloj′i kəl), **pho′no·log′ic,** *adj.* —**pho′no·log′i·cal·ly,** *adv.* —**pho·nol′o·gist,** *n.*

pho·nom·e·ter (fə nom′i tər), *n.* a device for measuring the intensity of a sound. —**pho·no·met·ric** (fō′nə me′trik), *adj.*

pho·no·scope (fō′nə skōp′), *n.* an instrument for making visible the motions or properties of a sounding body.

pho·no·type (fō′nə tīp′), *n.* *Print.* **1.** a piece of type bearing a phonetic character or symbol. **2.** phonetic type or print. —**pho·no·typ·ic** (fō′nə tip′ik), **pho′no·typ′i·cal,** *adj.*

pho·no·typ·y (fō′nə tī′pē), *n.* a system of phonetic shorthand, as the Pitman method. —**pho′no·typ′ist, pho′no·typ′er,** *n.*

pho·ny (fō′nē), *adj.,* **-ni·er, -ni·est,** *n., pl.* **-nies.** *Informal.* —*adj.* **1.** not genuine; spurious, counterfeit, or bogus; fraudulent. —*n.* **2.** a counterfeit or fake. **3.** a faker. Also, **phoney.** [? var. of *fawney* < Ir *fáinne* finger ring in phrase *fawney rig* confidence game in which a brass ring is sold as a gold one] —**pho′ni·ness,** *n.*

-phony, an element used in the formation of abstract nouns corresponding to nouns ending in **-phone:** *telephony.* [< Gk *-phōnia.* See -PHONE, -Y[3]]

phoo·ey (fo͞o′ē), *interj.* *Informal.* (an exclamation indicating rejection, contempt, or disgust): *Phooey on love!*

-phore, a learned borrowing from Greek meaning "bearer," "thing or part bearing (something)," used in the formation of compound words: *gonophore.* Cf. **-phorous.** [< NL *-phor(us)* < Gk *-phoros* bearing]

-phorous, an element used in the formation of adjectives corresponding to nouns with stems ending in **-phore:** *gonophorous.* [< NL *-phorus.* See -PHORE]

phos·gene (fos′jēn), *n.* *Chem.* a poisonous, colorless, very volatile liquid or suffocating gas, $COCl_2$, a chemical-warfare compound: used chiefly in organic synthesis. Also called **carbonyl chloride.** [< Gk *phôs* light (contr. of *pháos*) + *-genē(s)* -GEN]

phos·ge·nite (fos′jə nīt′), *n.* a mineral, lead chlorocarbonate, $Pb_2Cl_2CO_3$, occurring in crystals. [< G *Phosgenit*]

phosph-, var. of **phospho-** before a vowel: *phosphate.*

phos·pha·tase (fos′fə tās′), *n.* *Biochem.* an enzyme, found in body tissues, that breaks up compounds made of carbohydrates and phosphates.

phos·phate (fos′fāt), *n.* **1.** *Chem.* **a.** (loosely) a salt or ester of phosphoric acid, containing phosphorus. **b.** a tertiary salt of orthophosphoric acid, as sodium phosphate. **2.** *Agric.* a fertilizing material containing compounds of phosphorus. **3.** a carbonated drink of water and fruit syrup containing a little phosphoric acid. —**phos·phat·ic** (fos fat′ik), *adj.*

phos·pha·tide (fos′fə tīd′, -tid), *n.* *Biochem.* any of a group of fatty compounds, as lecithin, composed of phosphoric esters and occurring in cellular organisms. Also called **phospholipide, phospholipid, phospholipin.**

phos·pha·tise (fos′fə tīz′), *v.t.,* **-tised, -tis·ing.** *Chiefly Brit.* phosphatize. —**phos′pha·ti·sa′tion,** *n.*

phos·pha·tize (fos′fə tīz′), *v.t.,* **-tized, -tiz·ing.** **1.** to treat with phosphates. **2.** to change to phosphate. —**phos′pha·ti·za′tion, phos·pha·tion** (fos fā′shən), *n.*

phos·pha·tu·ri·a (fos′fə tŏŏr′ē ə, -tyŏŏr′-), *n. Pathol.* the presence of an excessive quantity of phosphates in the urine. —**phos′pha·tu′ric,** *adj.*

phos·phene (fos′fēn), *n. Physiol.* a luminous image produced by mechanical stimulation of the retina, as by pressure applied to the eyeball by the finger when the lid is closed. [< Gk *phôs* light (contr. of *pháos*) + *phaín(ein)* (to) show, shine]

phos·phide (fos′fīd, -fid), *n. Chem.* a binary compound of phosphorus with a basic element or group.

phos·phine (fos′fēn, -fin), *n. Chem.* **1.** a colorless, poisonous, ill-smelling, flammable gas, PH_3. **2.** any of certain organic derivatives of this compound.

phos·phite (fos′fīt), *n. Chem.* (loosely) a salt of phosphorous acid.

phospho-, a combining form representing **phosphorus:** *phosphoprotein.* Also, *esp. before a vowel,* **phosph-.** Cf. **phosphoro-.**

phos·pho·cre·a·tine (fos′fō krē′ə tēn′, -tin), *n. Biochem.* a compound, $C_4H_{10}O_5N_3P$, found chiefly in muscle, formed by the enzymatic interaction of an organic phosphate and creatine, the breakdown of which provides energy for muscle contraction.

phos·pho·lip·ide (fos′fō lip′īd, -id, -lī′pīd, -pid), *n. Biochem.* phosphatide. Also, **phos·pho·lip·id** (fos′fō lip′id, -lī′pid), **phos·pho·lip·in** (fos′fō lip′in, -lī′pin).

phos·pho·ni·um (fos fō′nē əm), *n. Chem.* the positively charged group, PH_4^+, analogous to ammonium, NH_4^+. [PHOSPH(ORUS + AMM)ONIUM]

phos·pho·nu·cle·ase (fos′fō nōō′klē ās′, -nyōō′-), *n. Biochem.* nucleotidase. [PHOSPHO- + NUCLE(IC ACID) + -ASE]

phos·pho·pro·tein (fos′fō prō′tēn, -tē in), *n. Biochem.* a protein composed of a molecule of protein linked with a substance other than nucleic acid or lecithin and containing phosphorous.

phos·phor (fos′fər), *n.* **1.** any of a number of substances that exhibit luminescence when struck by light of certain wavelengths, as by ultraviolet. **2.** *Literary.* a phosphorescent substance. —*adj.* **3.** *Archaic.* phosphorescent. [< F *phosphore* < NL *phosphor(us)* PHOSPHOROUS]

Phos·phor (fos′fər), *n.* the morning star, esp. Venus. Also, **Phos·phore** (fos′fōr, -fôr), **Phosphorus.** [< L *Phōsphor(us)* < Gk *Phōsphóros* the morning star, lit., the light-bringing one = *phôs* light + *-phoros* -PHORE]

phosphor-, var. of **phosphoro-** before a vowel: *phosphorate.*

phos·pho·rate (fos′fə rāt′), *v.t.,* **-rat·ed, -rat·ing. 1.** *Chem.* to combine or impregnate with phosphorus. **2.** to cause to have phosphorescence.

phos′phor bronze′, a bronze composed of about 80 percent copper, 10 percent tin, 9 percent antimony, and 1 percent phosphorus, and having great hardness and resistance to corrosion.

phos·pho·resce (fos′fə res′), *v.i.,* **-resced, -resc·ing.** to be luminous without sensible heat, as phosphorus.

phos·pho·res·cence (fos′fə res′əns), *n.* **1.** the property of being luminous at temperatures below incandescence, as from slow oxidation in the case of phosphorus or after exposure to light or other radiation. **2.** a luminous appearance resulting from this. **3.** any radiation emitted from a substance after the removal of the exciting agent. [PHOSPHORESC(ENT) + -ENCE]

phos·pho·res·cent (fos′fə res′ənt), *adj.* exhibiting phosphorescence. —**phos′pho·res′cent·ly,** *adv.*

phos·phor·ic (fos fôr′ik, -for′-), *adj. Chem.* of or containing phosphorus, esp. in the pentavalent state.

phosphor′ic ac′id, *Chem.* any of three acids, orthophosphoric acid, H_3PO_4, metaphosphoric acid, HPO_3, or pyrophosphoric acid, $H_4P_2O_7$, derived from phosphorus pentoxide, P_2O_5, and various amounts of water.

phosphor′ic anhy′dride, *Chem.* See **phosphorus pentoxide.**

phos·pho·rise (fos′fə rīz′), *v.t.,* **-rised, -ris·ing.** *Chiefly Brit.* phosphorize. —**phos′pho·ri·sa′tion,** *n.*

phos·pho·rism (fos′fə riz′əm), *n. Pathol.* condition of chronic phosphorus poisoning.

phos·pho·rite (fos′fə rīt′), *n.* **1.** a massive form of the mineral apatite: the principal source of phosphate for fertilizers. **2.** any of various compact or earthy, more or less impure varieties of calcium phosphate. —**phos·pho·rit·ic** (fos′fə rit′ik), *adj.*

phos·pho·rize (fos′fə rīz′), *v.t.,* **-rized, -riz·ing.** *Chem.* phosphorate. Also, *esp. Brit.,* **phosphorise.** —**phos′pho·ri·za′tion,** *n.*

phosphoro-, a combining form representing **phosphorus:** *phosphoroscope.* Also, *esp. before a vowel,* **phosphor-.** Cf. **phospho-.**

phos·phor·o·scope (fos fôr′ə skōp′, -for′-), *n.* an instrument for measuring the duration of evanescent phosphorescence in different substances.

phos·pho·rous (fos fōr′əs, -fôr′-, fos′fər əs), *adj. Chem.* containing trivalent phosphorus.

phos′phorous ac′id, *Chem.* an acid of phosphorus, H_3PO_3, from which phosphites are derived.

phos·pho·rus (fos′fər əs), *n., pl.* **-pho·ri** (-fə rī′). **1.** *Chem.* a solid, nonmetallic element existing in at least two allotropic forms, one that is yellow, poisonous, flammable, and luminous in the dark and another that is red, less poisonous, and less flammable. The element is a necessary constituent of bones, nerves, and embryos, and its compounds are used in matches and phosphate fertilizers. *Symbol:* P; *at. wt.:* 30.974; *at. no.:* 15; *sp. gr.:* (yellow) 1.82 at 20°C, (red) 2.20 at 20°C. **2.** any phosphorescent substance. **3.** phosphor. [< NL < L. See PHOSPHOR]

Phos·pho·rus (fos′fər əs), *n.* Phosphor.

phos′phorus pent·ox′ide (pen tok′sīd, -sid), *Chem.* a white, deliquescent powder, P_2O_5, that, in solution, forms orthophosphoric acid, metaphosphoric acid, or pyrophosphoric acid: used in the preparation of phosphoric acids, as a drying and dehydrating agent, and in organic synthesis. Also called **phosphoric anhydride.**

phos·pho·ryl·ase (fos′fər ə lās′, -lāz′, fos fôr′ə lās′, -for′-), *n. Biochem.* an enzyme, occurring widely in animal and plant tissue, that in the presence of an inorganic phosphate catalyzes the conversion of glycogen into sugar phosphate.

phot (fot, fōt), *n. Optics.* a unit of illumination, equal to 1 lumen per square centimeter. *Abbr.:* ph [< Gk *phōt-* (s. of *phôs*) light, contr. of *pháos*]

phot., **1.** photograph. **2.** photographer. **3.** photographic. **4.** photography.

pho·tic (fō′tik), *adj.* **1.** of or pertaining to light. **2.** pertaining to the generation of light by organisms or to their excitation by means of light.

pho·tics (fō′tiks), *n.* (*construed as sing.*) the science of light.

Pho·ti·us (fō′shē əs), *n.* A.D. c820–891, patriarch of Constantinople 858–867, 877–882.

pho·to (fō′tō), *n., pl.* **-tos.** *Informal.* photograph. [by shortening]

photo-, a learned borrowing from Greek meaning "light," sometimes used to represent "photographic" or "photograph" in the formation of compound words: *photoelectric.* [< Gk, comb. form of *phôs* (gen., *phōtós*)]

pho·to·ac·tin·ic (fō′tō ak tin′ik), *adj.* emitting radiation having the chemical effects of light and ultraviolet rays, as on a photographic film.

pho·to·bath·ic (fō′tə bath′ik), *adj.* in or relating to the stratum of ocean depth penetrated by sunlight.

pho·to·cath·ode (fō′tō kath′ōd), *n.* a cathode, typically of a cesium or sodium compound, that emits electrons when activated by light or other radiation.

pho·to·cell (fō′tō sel′), *n.* **1.** a phototube. **2.** See **photoelectric cell** (def. 1).

pho·to·chem·is·try (fō′tō kem′i strē), *n.* the branch of chemistry that deals with the chemical action of light. —**pho·to·chem·i·cal** (fō′tō kem′i kəl), **pho′to·chem′ic,** *adj.* —**pho′to·chem′i·cal·ly,** *adv.* —**pho′to·chem′ist,** *n.*

pho·to·chron·o·graph (fō′tə kron′ə graf′, -gräf′, -krō′nə-), *n.* **1.** an obsolete device for taking a series of instantaneous photographs of a rapidly moving object. **2.** a picture taken by such a device. **3.** an instrument for measuring small intervals of time by the photographic trace of a pencil of light. —**pho·to·chron·og·ra·phy** (fō′tə krə nog′rə fē), *n.*

pho·to·com·pose (fō′tō kəm pōz′), *v.t.,* **-posed, -pos·ing.** to set (type) on a photocomposer. —**pho·to·com·po·si·tion** (fō′tō kom′pi zish′ən), *n.*

pho·to·com·pos·er (fō′tō kəm pō′zər), *n.* a machine for setting type photographically.

pho·to·con·duc·tive (fō′tō kən duk′tiv), *adj.* **1.** *Physics.* of, pertaining to, or exhibiting photoconductivity. **2.** losing an electrical charge on exposure to light. —**pho′to·con·duc′tion,** *n.* —**pho′to·con·duc′tor,** *n.*

pho·to·con·duc·tiv·i·ty (fō′tō kon′duk tiv′i tē), *n. Physics.* the increase of the electric conductivity of a substance, often nonmetallic, caused by the absorption of electromagnetic radiation.

pho·to·cop·i·er (fō′tə kop′ē ər), *n.* copier (def. 2). Also called **pho′tocopying machine′.**

pho·to·cop·y (fō′tə kop′ē), *n., pl.* **-cop·ies,** *v.,* **-cop·ied, -cop·y·ing.** —*n.* **1.** a photographic copy of a document, print, or the like. —*v.t.* **2.** to copy (a document, print, or the like) photographically.

pho·to·cur·rent (fō′tō kûr′ənt, -kur′-), *n. Physics.* an electric current produced by a photoelectric effect. Also called **photoelectric current.**

pho·to·dis·in·te·gra·tion (fō′tō di sin′tə grā′shən), *n. Physics.* the disintegration of a nucleus, induced by its absorption of a photon.

pho·to·dy·nam·ics (fō′tō dī nam′iks, -di-), *n.* (*construed as sing.*) the science dealing with light in its relation to movement in plants. —**pho′to·dy·nam′ic, pho′to·dy·nam′i·cal,** *adj.*

pho·to·e·las·tic·i·ty (fō′tō i las tis′i tē, -ē la stis′-), *n. Physics.* the phenomenon of double refraction of polarized light by a transparent substance under elastic stress, used to measure strain in elastic, transparent materials. —**pho·to·e·las·tic** (fō′tō i las′tik), *adj.*

pho·to·e·lec·tric (fō′tō i lek′trik), *adj.* pertaining to the electronic or other electric effects produced by light. Also, **pho′to·e·lec′tri·cal.**

pho′toelec′tric cell′, *Electronics.* **1.** Also called **photocell.** a device incorporated in an electric circuit to make the resistance or electromotive force in part of the circuit variable in accordance with variations in the intensity of light or similar radiation falling upon it, thus making operations controlled by the circuit dependent on variations in illumination, a beam of radiation, or the like. **2.** a phototube.

pho′toelec′tric cur′rent, *Physics.* photocurrent.

pho′toelec′tric effect′, *Physics.* the phenomenon in which the absorption of electromagnetic radiation, as light, of sufficiently high frequency by a surface, usually metallic, induces the emission of electrons from the surface. Also called **photoemission.**

pho·to·e·lec·tric·i·ty (fō′tō i lek tris′i tē, -ē′lek-), *n. Physics.* **1.** electricity induced by electromagnetic radiation, as the photoelectric and photovoltaic effects, photoconductivity, and photoionization. **2.** the branch of physics that deals with these phenomena.

pho·to·e·lec·tron (fō′tō i lek′tron), *n. Physics.* an electron emitted from a system by a photoelectric effect.

pho·to·e·lec·tro·type (fō′tō i lek′trə tīp′), *n.* an electrotype made by photographic means.

pho·to·e·mis·sion (fō′tō i mish′ən), *n. Physics.* See **photoelectric effect.** —**pho·to·e·mis·sive** (fō′tō i mis′iv), *adj.*

photoeng., photoengraving.

pho·to·en·grave (fō′tō en grāv′), *v.t.,* **-graved, -grav·ing.** to make a photoengraving of. —**pho′to·en·grav′er,** *n.*

pho·to·en·grav·ing (fō′tō en grā′ving), *n.* **1.** a photographic process of preparing printing plates for letterpress printing. **2.** a process of photographic reproduction by which a relief printing surface is obtained for letterpress printing. **3.** a plate so produced. **4.** a print made from it.

pho′to fin′ish, *Sports.* a finish of a race in which two or more contestants are so close to being tied that the winner

must be determined by reference to a photograph of the finish. —**pho′to-fin′ish,** *adj.*
pho·to·fin·ish·ing (fō′tō fin′i shing), *n.* the act or occupation of developing films, printing photographs, etc.
pho′to·flash lamp′ (fō′tə flash′), a flash bulb.
pho′toflash photog′raphy. See **flash photography.**
pho′to·flood lamp′ (fō′tə flud′), an incandescent tungsten lamp in which high intensity is obtained by overloading voltage: used in photography, television, etc.
photog., 1. photographer. 2. photographic. 3. photography.
pho·to·gel·a·tin (fō′tə jel′ə tin), *adj.* pertaining to any photographic process in which gelatin is used to receive or transfer a print.
photogel′atin proc′ess, collotype (def. 1).
pho·to·gene (fō′tə jēn′), *n.* *Ophthalm.* an afterimage on the retina.
pho·to·gen·ic (fō′tə jen′ik), *adj.* **1.** being an attractive subject for photography or looking good in a photograph. **2.** *Biol.* producing or emitting light, as certain bacteria; luminiferous; phosphorescent. **3.** *Med.* produced or caused by light, as a skin condition. —**pho′to·gen′i·cal·ly,** *adv.*
pho·to·gram·me·try (fō′tə gram′i trē), *n.* the process of making surveys and maps through the use of photographs. —**pho·to·gram·met·ric** (fō′tō grə me′trik), **pho′to·gram·met′ri·cal,** *adj.* —**pho′to·gram′me·trist,** *n.*
pho·to·graph (fō′tə graf′, -gräf′), *n.* **1.** a picture produced by photography. —*v.t.* **2.** to take a photograph of. —*v.i.* **3.** to practice photography. **4.** to be photographed or suitable for being photographed, usually in some specified way: *The children photographed very attractively.* —**pho′to·graph′a·ble,** *adj.*
pho·tog·ra·pher (fə tog′rə fər), *n.* a person who takes photographs, esp. as an occupation.
pho·to·graph·ic (fō′tə graf′ik), *adj.* **1.** of or pertaining to photography. **2.** used in or produced by means of photography. **3.** suggestive of a photograph; extremely realistic and detailed, or remembering, reproducing, or functioning with the precision of a photograph: *photographic accuracy, a photographic memory.* Also, **pho′to·graph′i·cal.** —**pho′to·graph′i·cal·ly,** *adv.*
pho·tog·ra·phy (fə tog′rə fē), *n.* the process or art of producing images of objects on sensitized surfaces by the chemical action of light or of other forms of radiant energy, as x-rays or gamma rays.
pho·to·gra·vure (fō′tə grə vyŏŏr′, fō′tə grā′vyər), *n.* **1.** any of various processes, based on photography, by which an intaglio engraving is formed on a metal plate, from which reproductions are made. **2.** the plate. **3.** a print made from it.
pho·to·he·li·o·graph (fō′tə hē′lē ə graf′, -gräf′), *n.* *Astron.* an instrument for photographing the sun, consisting of a camera and a specially adapted telescope. Also called **heliograph.** —**pho·to·he·li·o·graph·ic** (fō′tə hē′lē ə graf′ik), *adj.* —**pho·to·he·li·og·ra·phy** (fō′tə hē′lē og′rə fē), *n.*
pho·to·jour·nal·ism (fō′tō jûr′nᵊliz′əm), *n.* journalism in which photography dominates written copy, as in certain magazines. —**pho′to·jour′nal·ist,** *n.*
pho·to·ki·ne·sis (fō′tō ki nē′sis, -kī-), *n.* *Physiol.* movement occurring upon exposure to light. [PHOTO- + Gk *kínēsis* movement; see KINETIC] —**pho·to·ki·net·ic** (fō′tō ki net′ik, -kī-), *adj.*
pho·to·lith·o (fō′tə lith′ō), *n., pl.* **-lith·os,** *adj.* —*n.* **1.** photolithography. **2.** photolithograph. —*adj.* **3.** photolithographic.
pho·to·lith·o·graph (fō′tə lith′ə graf′, -gräf′), *n.* **1.** a lithograph printed from a stone or the like upon which a picture or design has been formed by photography. —*v.t.* **2.** to make a photolithograph of.
pho·to·li·thog·ra·phy (fō′tō li thog′rə fē), *n.* the technique or art of making photolithographs. —**pho·to·lith·o·graph·ic** (fō′tə lith′ə graf′ik), *adj.* —**pho′to·li·thog′ra·pher,** *n.*
pho·to·lu·mi·nes·cence (fō′tə lōō′mə nes′əns), *n.* *Physics.* luminescence induced by the absorption of infrared radiation, visible light, or ultraviolet radiation. —**pho′to·lu′mi·nes′cent,** *adj.*
pho·tol·y·sis (fō tol′i sis), *n.* the breakdown of materials under the influence of light. —**pho·to·lyt·ic** (fōt′ᵊlit′ik), *adj.*
photom., photometry.
pho·to·map (fō′tə map′), *n., v.,* **-mapped, -map·ping.** —*n.* **1.** a mosaic of aerial photographs marked as a map, with grid lines, place-names, etc. —*v.t.* **2.** to map by means of aerial photography.
pho·to·me·chan·i·cal (fō′tō mə kan′i kəl), *adj.* noting or pertaining to any of various processes for printing from plates or other surfaces prepared by the aid of photography. —**pho′to·me·chan′i·cal·ly,** *adv.*
pho·tom·e·ter (fō tom′i tər), *n.* *Optics.* an instrument that measures luminous intensity or brightness, luminous flux, light distribution, color, etc. [< NL *photometr(um)*]
pho·tom·e·try (fō tom′i trē), *n.* the measurement of the intensity of light or of relative illuminating power. [< NL *photometria*] —**pho·to·met·ric** (fō′tə me′trik), **pho′to·met′ri·cal,** *adj.* —**pho′to·met′ri·cal·ly,** *adv.* —**pho·tom′e·trist, pho·to·me·tri·cian** (fō′tə me trish′ən), *n.*
pho·to·mi·cro·graph (fō′tə mī′krə graf′, -gräf′), *n.* a photograph taken through a microscope. —**pho·to·mi·crog·ra·pher** (fō′tə mī krog′rə fər), *n.* —**pho·to·mi·cro·graph·ic** (fō′tə mī′krə graf′ik), **pho′to·mi′cro·graph′i·cal,** *adj.* —**pho′to·mi′cro·graph′i·cal·ly,** *adv.* —**pho·to·mi·crog·ra·phy** (fō′tə mī krog′rə fē), *n.*
pho·to·mi·cro·scope (fō′tə mī′krə skōp′), *n.* a microscope having an illuminator and a camera mechanism for producing photomicrographs. —**pho·to·mi·cros·co·py** (fō′tə mī kros′kə pē), *n.*
pho·to·mon·tage (fō′tə mon täzh′, -môn-), *n.* *Photog.* See under **montage** (def. 1).
pho·to·mul·ti·pli·er (fō′tə mul′tə plī′ər), *n.* an extremely sensitive detector of light and of other radiation, consisting of a tube in which the electrons released by radiation striking a photocathode are accelerated to successive dynodes that release several electrons for each incident electron, greatly amplifying the signal produced by the incident radiation.
pho·to·mu·ral (fō′tə myŏŏr′əl), *n.* a wall decoration consisting of a very large photograph or photographs.
pho·ton (fō′ton), *n.* **1.** a quantum of electromagnetic radiation, usually considered as an elementary particle that is its own antiparticle and that has zero rest mass and charge, and a spin of one. *Symbol:* γ **2.** Also called **troland.** *Ophthalm.* a unit of measurement of retinal response to light.
pho·to-off·set (fō′tō ôf′set′, -of′-), *n., v.,* **-set, -set·ting.** —*n.* **1.** a method of printing, based on photolithography, in which the inked image is transferred from the metal plate to a rubber surface and then to the paper. —*v.t., v.i.* **2.** to print by photo-offset.
pho·to·pe·ri·od (fō′tə pēr′ē əd), *n.* *Biol.* the interval in a 24-hour period during which a plant or animal is exposed to light. —**pho·to·pe·ri·od·ic** (fō′tə pēr′ē od′ik), **pho′to·pe′ri·od′i·cal,** *adj.*
pho·to·pe·ri·od·ism (fō′tə pēr′ē ə diz′əm), *n.* *Biol.* the response, as affecting growth, reproduction, etc., of a plant or animal to the length of its photoperiod. Also called **pho·to·pe·ri·o·dic·i·ty** (fō′tō pēr′ē ə dis′i tē).
pho·toph·i·lous (fō tof′ə ləs), *adj.* thriving in strong light, as a plant. —**pho·toph′i·ly,** *n.*
pho·to·pho·bi·a (fō′tə fō′bē ə), *n.* *Pathol.* an abnormal dread or intolerance of light, as in iritis.
pho·to·phore (fō′tə fōr′, -fôr′), *n.* *Zool.* a luminous organ found in certain fishes and crustaceans.
pho·to·pi·a (fō tō′pē ə), *n.* *Ophthalm.* vision in bright light (opposed to *scotopia*). —**pho·top·ic** (fō top′ik, -tō′pik), *adj.*
pho·to·play (fō′tə plā′), *n.* a play presented or written to be presented as a motion picture; screenplay.
pho·to·print (fō′tə print′), *n.* **1.** a photographic print. **2.** a print made by a photomechanical process; a photocopy. —**pho′to·print′er,** *n.* —**pho′to·print′ing,** *n.*
pho·to·re·cep·tion (fō′tō ri sep′shən), *n.* the physiological perception of light. —**pho′to·re·cep′tive,** *adj.*
pho·to·re·con·nais·sance (fō′tō ri kon′i səns), *n.* reconnaissance for the purpose of aerial photography. Also, **pho′to-re·con′nais·sance.**
pho·to·sen·si·tive (fō′tə sen′si tiv), *adj.* sensitive to light or similar radiation. —**pho′to·sen′si·tiv′i·ty,** *n.*
pho·to·sphere (fō′tə sfēr′), *n.* **1.** a sphere of light or radiance. **2.** *Astron.* the luminous visible surface of the sun, being a shallow layer of strongly ionized gases. —**pho·to·spher·ic** (fō′tə sfer′ik), *adj.*
Pho·to·stat (fō′tə stat′), *n.* **1.** *Trademark.* a camera for making facsimile copies of documents, drawings, etc., in the form of paper negatives on which the positions of lines, objects, etc., in the originals are maintained. **2.** (*often l.c.*) a copy made with this camera. —*v.t., v.i.* **3.** (*l.c.*) to copy with this camera. —**pho′to·stat′ic,** *adj.*
pho·to·syn·the·sis (fō′tə sin′thi sis), *n.* *Biol., Biochem.* (esp. in plants) the synthesis of complex organic materials, esp. carbohydrates, from carbon dioxide, water, and inorganic salts, using sunlight as the source of energy and with the aid of a catalyst, as chlorophyll. —**pho·to·syn·thet·ic** (fō′tə sin thet′ik), *adj.* —**pho′to·syn·thet′i·cal·ly,** *adv.*
pho·to·tax·is (fō′tə tak′sis), *n.* *Biol.* movement of an organism toward or away from a source of light. Also, **pho′to·tax′y.** —**pho·to·tac·tic** (fō′tə tak′tik), *adj.*
pho·to·te·leg·ra·phy (fō′tō tə leg′rə fē), *n.* facsimile (def. 2).
pho·to·ther·mic (fō′tə thûr′mik), *adj.* **1.** pertaining to the thermal effects of light. **2.** pertaining to or involving both light and heat.
pho·to·to·pog·ra·phy (fō′tō tə pog′rə fē), *n.* topographical surveying employing photography. —**pho·to·top·o·graph·ic** (fō′tə top′ə graf′ik), **pho′to·top′o·graph′i·cal,** *adj.*
pho·to·trop·ic (fō′tə trop′ik), *adj.* *Bot.* **1.** taking a particular direction under the influence of light. **2.** growing toward or away from the light. —**pho′to·trop′i·cal·ly,** *adv.*
pho·tot·ro·pism (fō to′trə piz′əm), *n.* *Bot.* phototropic tendency or growth.
pho·to·tube (fō′tə tōōb′, -tyōōb′), *n.* *Electronics.* a diode in which light falling on the light-sensitive cathode causes electrons to be emitted, the electrons being collected by the plate.
pho·to·type (fō′tə tīp′), *n.* *Print.* **1.** a plate with a relief printing surface produced by photography. **2.** any process for making such a plate. **3.** a print made from it. —**pho·to·typ·ic** (fō′tə tip′ik), *adj.* —**pho′to·typ′i·cal·ly,** *adv.*
pho·to·ty·pog·ra·phy (fō′tō tī pog′rə fē), *n.* (not in current use) the art or technique of making printing surfaces by light or photography, by any of a large number of processes. —**pho·to·ty·po·graph·ic** (fō′tə tī′pə graf′ik), *adj.*
pho·to·typ·y (fō′tə tī′pē, fō tot′ə pē), *n.* (not in current use) the art or process of producing phototypes.
pho·to·vol·ta·ic (fō′tō vol tā′ik), *adj.* providing a source of electric current under the influence of light or similar radiation.
pho·to·zin·cog·ra·phy (fō′tō zing kog′rə fē), *n.* (not in current use) photoengraving using a sensitized zinc plate.
phpht (ft), *interj.* pht.
phr., phrase.
phras·al (frā′zəl), *adj.* of, consisting of, or of the nature of a phrase or phrases: *phrasal construction.*
phrase (frāz), *n., v.,* **phrased, phras·ing.** —*n.* **1.** *Gram.* a sequence of two or more words arranged grammatically and not having a subject and predicate, as a preposition and a noun or pronoun, an adjective and a noun, verb and an adverb, etc. **2.** *Rhet.* a word or group of spoken words that is perceived momentarily as a meaningful unit and that is preceded and followed by pauses. **3.** a mode of expression; phraseology: *a book written in the phrase of the West.* **4.** a characteristic, current, or proverbial expression: *a hackneyed phrase.* **5.** a brief utterance or remark. **6.** *Music.* a division of a composition, commonly a passage of four or eight measures, forming part of a period. —*v.t.* **7.** to express or word in a particular way; couch. **8.** to express in words: *to phrase one's thoughts.* **9.** *Music.* **a.** to mark off or bring out the phrases of (a piece), esp. in execution. **b.** to group (notes) into a phrase. [back formation from *phrases,* pl. of L *phrasis* < Gk: speech = *phrá(zein)* (to) speak + *-sis* -SIS]
phra·se·o·gram (frā′zē ə gram′), *n.* a written symbol or combination of written symbols, as in shorthand, used to represent a phrase.
phra·se·o·graph (frā′zē ə graf′, -gräf′), *n.* a phrase for which there is a phraseogram.

phra·se·ol·o·gist (frā′zē ol′ə jist), *n.* a person who affects a particular phraseology or is skilled in coining phrases.

phra·se·ol·o·gy (frā′zē ol′ə jē), *n.* **1.** manner or style of verbal expression; characteristic language: *legal phraseology.* **2.** expressions or phrases, taken collectively. [< NL *phraseologia*] —**phra·se·o·log·i·cal** (frā′zē ə loj′i kel), **phra′se·o·log′ic,** *adj.* —**Syn. 1.** See **diction.**

phras·ing (frā′zing), *n.* **1.** the act or a manner or method of forming phrases; phraseology. **2.** *Music.* the grouping of the notes of a musical line into distinct phrases.

phra·try (frā′trē), *n., pl.* **-tries. 1.** a grouping of clans or other social units within a tribe. **2.** (in ancient Greece) a subdivision of a phyle. [< Gk *phratría*] —**phra′tric, phra′tral, phra′tri·ac′, phra′tri·al,** *adj.*

phren-, var. of **phreno-** before a vowel: *phrenic.*

phren., 1. phrenological. **2.** phrenology.

phre·net·ic (fri net′ik), *adj.* Also, **phre·net′i·cal. 1.** frenetic. **2.** filled with extreme excitement, esp. in religious matters; fanatic. —*n.* **3.** a phrenetic person. [< L *phrenēticus* < LGk *phrenētikós,* Gk *phrenītikós* frenzied (see PHRENITIS, -IC); r. ME *frenetike* < AF] —**phre·net′i·cal·ly,** *adv.* —**phre·net′ic·ness,** *n.*

-phrenia, an element used in pathological terminology to indicate mental disorder: *schizophrenia.* [< NL < Gk *phren-* (s. of *phrḗn*) mind + *-ia* -IA]

phren·ic (fren′ik), *adj.* **1.** *Anat.* of or pertaining to the diaphragm. **2.** *Physiol.* relating to the mind or mental activity. [< NL *phrenic(us)*]

phre·ni·tis (fri nī′tis), *n.* *Pathol.* inflammation of the diaphragm. [< LL: delirium, frenzy < Gk] —**phre·nit·ic** (fri nit′ik), *adj.*

phreno-, a learned borrowing from Greek meaning "mind," "diaphragm," used in the formation of compound words: *phrenology.* Also, *esp. before a vowel,* **phren-.** [< Gk, comb. form repr. *phrḗn* mind, diaphragm]

phrenol., 1. phrenological. **2.** phrenology.

phre·nol·o·gy (fri nol′ə jē, fre-), *n.* a psychological theory or analytical method based on the idea that certain mental faculties and character traits are indicated by the configurations of a person's skull. —**phren·o·log·ic** (fren′ᵊloj′ik), **phren′o·log′i·cal,** *adj.* —**phre·nol′o·gist,** *n.*

phren·sy (fren′zē), *n., pl.* **-sies,** *v.t.,* **-sied, -sy·ing.** frenzy.

Phryg·i·a (frij′ē ə), *n.* an ancient country in central and NW Asia Minor.

Phryg·i·an (frij′ē ən), *n.* an Indo-European language that was the language of Phrygia.

Phryg′ian cap′, a soft, conical cap represented in ancient Greek art as part of Phrygian or oriental dress and associated, since the late 18th and early 19th centuries, with the liberty cap.

PHS, Public Health Service. Also, **P.H.S.**

pht (ft), *interj.* (used as an expression of mild anger or annoyance.) Also, **phpht.**

phthal·ein (thal′ēn, -ē in, fthal′-), *n.* *Chem.* any of a group of compounds formed by treating phthalic anhydride with phenols, from which certain important dyes are derived. [(NA)PHTHALE(NE) + -IN[2]]

phthal′ic ac′id, *Chem.* any of three isomeric acids having the formula $C_6H_4(COOH)_2$, esp. the ortho isomer, a solid used chiefly in the manufacture of dyes, medicine, and perfume. [(NA)PHTHAL(ENE) + -IC] —**phthal·ic** (thal′ik, fthal′-), *adj.*

phthal′ic anhy′dride, *Chem.* a white solid, $C_6H_4(CO)_2O$, used chiefly in manufacturing dyes, alkyd resins, and plasticizers.

phthal·o·cy·a·nine (thal′ə sī′ə nīn′, fthal′-), *n.* *Chem.* any of a group of blue or green pigments containing a metal, esp. copper. [(NA)PHTHAL(ENE) + -O- + CYANINE]

phthis·ic (tiz′ik), *Pathol.* —*n.* **1.** a wasting disease of the lungs; phthisis. **2.** asthma. —*adj.* **3.** pertaining to phthisis; phthisical. [< L *phthisic(us)* < Gk *phthisikós* (see PHTHISIS, -IC); r. ME *tisike* < ML *(p)tisic(us)*] —**phthis′i·cal, phthis′ick·y,** *adj.*

phthi·sis (thī′sis, fthī′-), *n.* *Pathol.* **1.** a wasting away. **2.** tuberculosis of the lungs; consumption. [< Gk: lung disease, lit., a wasting away = *phthí(ein)* (to) decay + *-sis* -SIS]

Phu·ket (po͞o′ket′), *n.* an island near the W coast of Thailand. 64,637 (est. 1956); 294 sq. mi.

-phyceae, a learned borrowing from Greek meaning "seaweed," used in the names of algae: *Schizophyceae.* [< NL (pl.); see PHYCO-]

-phyceous, an element used to form adjectives from nouns with stems ending in **-phyceae:** *schizophyceous.*

phyco-, a learned borrowing from Greek meaning "seaweed," "algae," used in the formation of compound words: *phycomycetous.* [< Gk *phŷko-,* comb. form repr. *phŷkos*]

phy·col·o·gy (fī kol′ə jē), *n.* the branch of botany dealing with algae. —**phy·co·log·i·cal** (fī′kə loj′i kəl), *adj.* —**phy·col′o·gist,** *n.*

phy·co·my·ce·tous (fī′kō mī sē′təs), *adj.* *Bot.* belonging or pertaining to the *Phycomycetes,* the lowest of the three primary subdivisions of the fungi, whose members more closely resemble algae than do the higher fungi. [< NL *Phycomycēt(ēs)* (see PHYCO-, -MYCETES) + -OUS]

Phyfe (fīf), *n.* **Dun·can** (dung′kən), 1768–1854, U.S. cabinetmaker, born in Scotland.

phyl-, var. of **phylo-** before a vowel: *phylic.*

-phyl, var. of **phyllo-** as final element of compound words: *chlorophyl.* Also, **-phyll.**

phy·la (fī′lə), *n.* pl. of **phylum.**

phy·lac·ter·y (fə lak′tə rē), *n., pl.* **-ter·ies. 1.** *Judaism.* either of two small, black, leather cubes, each containing a piece of parchment inscribed with specific Biblical verses: worn by men during the morning religious service on days other than the Sabbath and holy days, one strapped to the left arm, the other to the forehead. **2.** (in the early Christian church) a receptacle containing a holy relic. **3.** a reminder. **4.** an amulet, charm, or safeguard. [< LL *phylactēri(um)* < Gk *phylaktḗrion* outpost, safeguard, amulet; r. ME *philaterie* < ML *philatēri(um)*]

Phylacteries

phy·le (fī′lē), *n., pl.* **-lae** (-lē). (in ancient Greece) a tribe or clan, based on supposed kinship. [< Gk] —**phy′lic,** *adj.*

phy·let·ic (fī let′ik), *adj.* *Biol.* pertaining to race or species; phylogenic; racial. [< Gk *phyletik(ós).* See PHYLE, -TIC] —**phy·let′i·cal·ly,** *adv.*

phyll-, var. of **phyllo-** before a vowel: *phyllite.*

-phyll, var. of **-phyl.**

Phyl·lis (fil′is), *n.* a name used in pastoral literature for a country girl or sweetheart.

phyl·lite (fil′īt), *n.* a slaty rock with lustrous cleavage planes due to minute scales of mica. —**phyl·lit·ic** (fi lit′ik), *adj.*

phyllo-, a learned borrowing from Greek meaning "leaf," used in the formation of compound words: *phyllopod.* Also, **phyll-, -phyl, -phyll.** [< Gk, comb. form of *phýllon*]

phyl·lo·clade (fil′ə klād′), *n.* *Bot.* **1.** a flattened stem or branch having the function of a leaf. **2.** a cladophyll. [< NL *phylloclad(ium).* See PHYLLO-, CLAD-] —**phyl′lo·cla′di·oid′,** *adj.*

phyl·lode (fil′ōd), *n.* *Bot.* an expanded petiole resembling and having the function of a leaf. [< Gk *phyllṓdēs* leaflike] —**phyl·lo′di·al,** *adj.*

P, Phyllode

phyl·loid (fil′oid), *adj.* leaflike. [< NL *phylloid(es)*]

phyl·lome (fil′ōm), *n.* *Bot.* **1.** a leaf of a plant. **2.** a structure that corresponds to a leaf. [< NL *phyllōm(a)* < Gk: foliage] —**phyl·lom·ic** (fi lom′ik, -lō′mik), *adj.*

phyl·lo·pod (fil′ə pod′), *n.* **1.** any crustacean of the order *Phyllopoda,* having leaflike swimming appendages. —*adj.* **2.** belonging or pertaining to the *Phyllopoda.* Also, **phyl·lop·o·dan** (fi lop′ə dᵊn). [< NL *Phyllopod(a)*]

phyl·lo·tax·is (fil′ə tak′sis), *n., pl.* **-tax·es** (-tak′sēs). *Bot.* phyllotaxy.

phyl·lo·tax·y (fil′ə tak′sē), *n., pl.* **-tax·ies.** *Bot.* **1.** the arrangement of leaves on a stem or axis. **2.** the study of such arrangement. [PHYLLOTAX(IS) + -Y[3]] —**phyl·lo·tac·tic** (fil′ə tak′tik), **phyl′lo·tac′ti·cal, phyl′lo·tax′ic,** *adj.*

-phyllous, an element meaning "having leaves," "leaved," used in the formation of adjectives: *diphyllous; monophyllous.* [< Gk *-phyllos* pertaining to a leaf]

phyl·lox·e·ra (fil′ək sēr′ə, fi lok′sər ə), *n., pl.* **phyl·lox·e·rae** (fil′ək sēr′ē, fi lok′sə rē′), **phyl·lox·e·ras.** any of several plant lice of the genus *Phylloxera,* esp. *P. vitifoliae* of the U.S. and Europe, which attacks the leaves and roots of some grapevines. [< NL; see PHYLLO-, XER(O)-, -A]

phylo-, a learned borrowing from Greek meaning "race," "tribe," "kind": *phylogeny.* Also, *esp. before a vowel,* **phyl-.** [< Gk, comb. form of *phŷlon* PHYLON]

phy·log·e·ny (fī loj′ə nē), *n.* the development or evolution of a kind of animal or plant; racial history. Also, **phy·lo·gen·e·sis** (fī′lə jen′i sis). Cf. **ontogeny.** —**phy·lo·ge·net·ic** (fī′lə jə net′ik), **phy′lo·ge·net′i·cal, phy′lo·gen′ic,** *adj.* —**phy′lo·ge·net′i·cal·ly,** *adv.* —**phy·log′e·nist,** *n.*

phy·lon (fī′lon), *n., pl.* **-la** (-lə). a group that has genetic relationship, as a race. [< NL < Gk *phŷlon* race, tribe, class, akin to *phýein* to bring forth, produce]

phy·lum (fī′ləm), *n., pl.* **-la** (-lə). **1.** *Biol.* the major primary subdivision of the animal kingdom, consisting of one or more related classes. Cf. **division** (def. 13). **2.** *Linguistics.* a category consisting of language stocks that, because of cognates in vocabulary, are considered likely to be related by common origin. Cf. **stock** (def. 13). [< NL < Gk *phŷlon* PHYLON]

-phyre, a combining form of **porphyry:** *granophyre.* [< F, abstracted from *porphyre* PORPHYRY]

phys., 1. physical. **2.** physician. **3.** physics. **4.** physiological. **5.** physiology.

phys. chem., physical chemistry.

phys. ed. (fiz′ ed′), physical education.

phys. geog., physical geography.

physi-, var. of **physio-.**

phys·i·at·rics (fiz′ē a′triks), *n.* (*construed as sing.*) physiotherapy. —**phys′i·at′ric, phys′i·at′ri·cal,** *adj.*

phys·ic (fiz′ik), *n., v.,* **-icked, -ick·ing.** —*n.* **1.** a medicine that purges; cathartic; laxative. **2.** any medicine; a drug or medicament. **3.** *Archaic.* the medical art or profession. **4.** *Obs.* See **natural science.** —*v.t.* **5.** to treat with a physic or medicine. **6.** to treat with or act upon as a cathartic; purge. **7.** to work upon as a medicine does; relieve or cure. [ME *fisyke* < L *physica* natural science (ML: medical science) < Gk *physikḗ* science of nature, n. use of fem. adj.: pertaining to nature]

phys·i·cal (fiz′i kəl), *adj.* **1.** of or pertaining to the body: *physical exercise.* **2.** of or pertaining to that which is material: *the physical universe.* **3.** of or pertaining to the properties of matter and energy other than those peculiar to living matter: *physical science.* —*n.* **4.** See **physical examination.** [ME < ML *physicāl(is)* concerning medicine] —**phys′i·cal·ly,** *adv.* —**phys′i·cal·ness,** *n.*

—**Syn. 1.** somatic; carnal; fleshly. PHYSICAL, BODILY, CORPOREAL, CORPORAL agree in pertaining to the human body. PHYSICAL means connected with, or pertaining to, the body as a material organism: *physical strength, exercise.* BODILY means belonging to or concerned with the body as distinct from the mind or spirit: *bodily pain or suffering.* CORPOREAL, a more poetic and philosophical word than BODILY, refers esp. to the mortal substance of which the body is composed: *this corporeal habitation.* CORPORAL is now usually reserved for reference to punishments inflicted on the body. **2.** tangible; palpable. —**Ant. 1.** spiritual, mental.

phys′ical anthropol′ogy, the branch of anthropology dealing with the evolutionary changes in man's bodily structure and the classification of modern races, using mensurational and descriptive techniques. Cf. **cultural anthropology.**

phys′ical chem′istry, the branch of chemistry dealing with the relations between the physical properties of substances and their chemical composition and transformations.

phys′ical educa′tion, instruction in sports, exercises, and hygiene, esp. as part of a school or college program.

phys′ical examina′tion, an examination by a physician to determine a person's state of health or physical fitness, as for military service.

phys′ical geog′raphy, the branch of geography concerned with natural features and phenomena of the earth's surface, as land forms, ocean currents, vegetation, and animal life.

phys·i·cal·ism (fiz′i kə liz′əm), *n.* *Philos.* a doctrine associated with logical positivism and holding that every meaningful statement, other than the necessary statements of logic and mathematics, must refer directly or indirectly to observable properties of spatiotemporal things or events. [< G *Physikalism(us)*] —**phys′i·cal·ist,** *n., adj.*

phys·i·cal·is·tic (fiz′i kə lis′tik), *adj.* *Philos.* **1.** of or pertaining to physicalism. **2.** (of a statement) capable of being interpreted quantitatively in terms of space and time.

phys·i·cal·i·ty (fiz′i kal′i tē), *n., pl.* **-ties. 1.** the physical attributes of a person, esp. when overdeveloped or overemphasized. **2.** preoccupation with one's body, physical needs, or appetites.

phys′ical pen′dulum, *Physics.* any apparatus consisting of a body of possibly irregular shape allowed to rotate freely about a horizontal axis on which it is pivoted (distinguished from *simple pendulum*).

phys′ical sci′ence, the study of natural laws and processes other than those peculiar to living matter, as in physics, chemistry, and astronomy.

phys′ical ther′apy, physiotherapy. —**phys′ical ther′apist.**

phy·si·cian (fi zish′ən), *n.* **1.** a person who is legally qualified to practice medicine; doctor of medicine. **2.** a doctor of medicine other than a surgeon. [PHYSIC + -IAN (see -ICIAN); r. ME *fisicien* < OF]

phys·i·cist (fiz′i sist), *n.* a scientist who specializes in physics.

phys·i·co·chem·i·cal (fiz′ə kō kem′i kəl), *adj.* *Chem.* **1.** physical and chemical: *the physicochemical properties of an isomer.* **2.** pertaining to physical chemistry. [PHYSIC(AL) + -O- + CHEMICAL] —**phys′i·co·chem′i·cal·ly,** *adv.*

phys·ics (fiz′iks), *n.* (*construed as sing.*) the science that deals with matter, energy, motion, and force.

physio-, a word element representing **physical** and **physics:** *physiotherapy; physiognomy.* [< Gk *physio-,* comb. form of *phýsis.* See PHYSIC, -O-]

phys·i·o·crat (fiz′ē ə krat′), *n.* one of a school of political economists who followed Quesnay in regarding land as the basis of wealth and taxation and in advocating a laissez-faire economy. [< F *physiocrate*] —**phys′i·o·crat′ic,** *adj.*

phys·i·og·no·my (fiz′ē og′nə mē, -on′ə mē), *n., pl.* **-mies. 1.** the face or countenance, esp. when considered as an index to the character. **2.** the art of determining character or personal characteristics from the form or features of the body, esp. of the face. [< LL *physiognōmia < LGk, syncopated var. of Gk *physiognōmonía* art of judging a person by his features (see PHYSIO-, GNOMON, -Y³); r. ME *phisonomie,* etc. < ML *phisonomia*] —**phys·i·og·nom·ic** (fiz′ē og nom′ik, -ē ə nom′-), **phys′i·og·nom′i·cal, phys·i·og·no·mon·ic** (fiz′ē og′nə mon′ik, -on′ə-), **phys′i·og′no·mon′i·cal,** *adj.* —**phys′i·og′no·mist,** *n.*

phys·i·og·ra·phy (fiz′ē og′rə fē), *n.* **1.** the science of physical geography. **2.** *U.S.* geomorphology. **3.** the systematic description of nature in general. —**phys′i·og′ra·pher,** *n.* —**phys·i·o·graph·ic** (fiz′ē ə graf′ik), **phys′i·o·graph′i·cal,** *adj.*

physiol., 1. physiological. **2.** physiologist. **3.** physiology.

phys·i·o·log·i·cal (fiz′ē ə loj′i kəl), *adj.* **1.** of or pertaining to physiology. **2.** consistent with the normal functioning of an organism. Also, **phys′i·o·log′ic.** —**phys′i·o·log′i·cal·ly,** *adv.*

physiolog′ical phonet′ics, the branch of phonetics that deals with the motive processes, anatomical measurements, spirometric properties, muscle and membrane tone, and any or all kinetic and kinematic aspects of the production of speech.

phys·i·ol·o·gy (fiz′ē ol′ə jē), *n.* **1.** the science dealing with the functions of living organisms or their parts. **2.** the organic processes or functions of an organism or of any of its parts. [< L *physiologia* < Gk] —**phys′i·ol′o·gist,** *n.*

phys·i·o·ther·a·py (fiz′ē ō ther′ə pē), *n.* the treatment of disease or bodily weaknesses or defects by physical remedies, as massage, gymnastics, etc. —**phys′i·o·ther′a·pist,** *n.*

phy·sique (fi zēk′), *n.* **1.** physical or bodily structure, organization, or development. **2.** a person's body, esp. a man's body, with respect to its structure, musculature, etc. [< F < L *physic(us).* See PHYSIC]

phy·sis (fī′sis), *n., pl.* **-ses** (-sēz). **1.** the principle of growth or change in nature. **2.** nature as the source of growth or change. **3.** that which grows, becomes, or develops. [< Gk: origin, natural form of a thing]

physo-, a learned borrowing from Greek meaning "bladder," used in the formation of compound words: *physostigmine.* [comb. form repr. Gk *phŷsa* bladder, bellows]

phy·so·stig·mine (fī′sō stig′mēn, -min), *n.* *Pharm.* a colorless to pinkish, crystalline, slightly water-soluble alkaloid, $C_{15}H_{21}O_2N_3$, constituting the active principle of the Calabar bean: used chiefly as a miotic in glaucoma. [< NL *Phȳsostigm(a)* genus name; so called from the bladderlike apex of the style (see PHYSO-, STIGMA) + -INE²]

-phyte, var. of **phyto-** as final element of compound words: *lithophyte.*

phyto-, a learned borrowing from Greek meaning "plant," used in the formation of compound words: *phytogenesis.* Also, **-phyte.** [< Gk *phyt(ón)* a plant + -O-]

phy·to·gen·e·sis (fī′tə jen′i sis), *n.* the origin and development of plants. Also, **phy·tog·e·ny** (fī toj′ə nē). —**phy·to·ge·net·ic** (fī′tō jə net′ik), **phy′to·ge·net′i·cal,** *adj.* —**phy′to·ge·net′i·cal·ly,** *adv.*

phy·to·gen·ic (fī′tə jen′ik), *adj.* of plant origin.

phy·to·ge·og·ra·phy (fī′tō jē og′rə fē), *n.* the science dealing with the geographical relationships of plants. —**phy′to·ge·og′ra·pher,** *n.* —**phy·to·ge·o·graph·i·cal** (fī′tō jē′ə graf′i kəl), **phy′to·ge′o·graph′ic,** *adj.* —**phy′to·ge′o·graph′i·cal·ly,** *adv.*

phy·tog·ra·phy (fī tog′rə fē), *n.* the branch of botany dealing with the description of plants. [< NL *phytographia*] —**phy·tog′ra·pher, phy·tog′ra·phist,** *n.* —**phy·to·graph·ic** (fī′tə graf′ik), **phy′to·graph′i·cal,** *adj.*

phy·tol·o·gy (fī tol′ə jē), *n.* *Obs.* botany. [< NL *phytologia*] —**phy·to·log·ic** (fīt′ᵊloj′ik), **phy′to·log′i·cal,** *adj.*

phy·to·pa·thol·o·gy (fī′tō pə thol′ə jē), *n.* See **plant pathology.** —**phy·to·path·o·log·i·cal** (fī′tō path′ə loj′i kəl), **phy′to·path′o·log′ic,** *adj.* —**phy′to·pa·thol′o·gist,** *n.*

phy·toph·a·gous (fī tof′ə gəs), *adj.* herbivorous.

phy·to·plank·ton (fī′tə plaŋk′tən), *n.* the plant organisms in plankton. Cf. **zooplankton.**

phy·to·so·ci·ol·o·gy (fī′tō sō′sē ol′ə jē, -shē-), *n.* the branch of ecology dealing with the origin, composition, structure, and classification of plant communities. —**phy·to·so·ci·o·log·ic** (fī′tə sō′sē ə loj′ik, -sō′shē-), **phy′to·so′ci·o·log′i·cal,** *adj.* —**phy′to·so′ci·o·log′i·cal·ly,** *adv.* —**phy′to·so′ci·ol′o·gist,** *n.*

pi¹ (pī), *n., pl.* **pis. 1.** the 16th letter of the Greek alphabet (Π, π). **2.** *Math.* **a.** the letter π, used as the symbol for the ratio of the circumference of a circle to its diameter. **b.** the ratio itself; 3.141592+. [< Gk, used in mathematics to represent *periphérion* PERIPHERY]

pi² (pī), *n., v.,* **pied, pi·ing.** *U.S.* —*n.* **1.** printing types mixed together indiscriminately. —*v.t.* **2.** to reduce (printing types) to a state of confusion. Also, **pie.** [?]

Pi., piaster. Also, **pi.**

P.I., Philippine Islands.

Pia·cen·za (pyä chen′tsä), *n.* a city in N Italy, on the Po River. 87,930 (1961). Ancient, **Placentia.**

pi·ac·u·lar (pī ak′yə lər), *adj.* **1.** expiatory; atoning; reparatory. **2.** requiring expiation; sinful; wicked. [< L *piāculār(is)* atoning = *piācul(um)* a means of atoning (*piā(re)* (to) appease < *pius* PIOUS + *-culum* -CULE) + *-āris* -AR¹]

piaffe (pyaf), *n., v.,* **piaffed, piaff·ing.** *Dressage.* —*n.* **1.** a cadenced trot executed on one spot, with a well-elevated leg action. —*v.i.* **2.** (of a horse) to execute such a movement. —*v.t.* **3.** to cause (a horse) to piaffe. [< F *piaff(er)*; imit.]

pi·a ma·ter (pī′ə mā′tər), *Anat.* the delicate, fibrous, and highly vascular membrane forming the innermost of the three coverings of the brain and spinal cord. Cf. **arachnoid** (def. 2), **dura mater.** [ME < ML: lit., pious mother, imperfect trans. of Ar *umm raqīqah* tender mother]

pi·an (pē an′, -än′, pyän), *n.* *Pathol.* yaws. [< F < Tupi] —**pi·an′ic,** *adj.*

pi·a·nism (pē′ə niz′əm, pē an′iz-, pyan′-), *n.* performance by a pianist.

pi·a·nis·si·mo (pē′ə nis′ə mō′; *It.* pyä nēs′sē mô′), *adj., adv., n., pl.* **-mos.** *Music.* —*adj.* **1.** very soft. —*adv.* **2.** very softly. —*n.* **3.** a passage or movement played in this way. [< It, superl. of *piano* PIANO²]

pi·an·ist (pē an′ist, pyan′-, pē′ə nist), *n.* a person who plays the piano, esp. one who performs classical music professionally. [< F *pianiste* < It *pianista*]

pi·an·o¹ (pē an′ō, pyan′ō), *n., pl.* **-an·os.** a musical instrument in which hammers, operated from a keyboard, strike upon metal strings. Cf. **baby grand piano, grand piano, upright piano.** [short for PIANOFORTE]

Grand piano

pi·a·no² (pē ä′nō; *It.* pyä′nô), *Music.* —*adj.* **1.** soft; subdued. —*adv.* **2.** softly. *Abbr.:* p, p. [< It: soft, low (of sounds), plain, flat < L *plānus* PLAIN¹]

pian′o accor′dion, accordion (def. 1).

pi·an·o·for·te (pē an′ə fôr′tē, -tā, -fôr′-), *n.* piano¹. [< It (*gravecembalo col*) *piano e forte,* lit.: (harpsichord with) soft and loud. See PIANO², FORTE²]

pian′o roll′, a roll of paper containing perforations such that air passing through them actuates the keys of a player piano.

pian′o wire′, hard steel wire of high tensile strength.

pias., piaster.

pi·as·sa·va (pē′ə sä′və), *n.* **1.** a coarse, woody fiber obtained from either of two palms, *Leopoldinia Piassaba* or *Attalea funifera,* of South America, used in making brooms, mats, etc. **2.** either of these trees. Also, **pi′as·sa′ba.** [< Pg < Tupi *piaçaba*]

pi·as·ter (pē as′tər), *n.* *Numis.* **1.** the 100th part of the pound of Lebanon, Sudan, Syria, or the Arab Republic of Egypt. **2.** a paper money and monetary unit of Vietnam, equal to 100 cents. **3.** the former peso, or dollar, of Spain and Spanish America. Also, **pi·as′tre.** [< F *piastre* < It *piastra* thin sheet of metal, silver coin (short for *piastra d'argento,* lit., plate of silver), akin to *piastro* PLASTER]

Pia·ti·gor·sky (pyä′ti gôr′skē, pyat′i-), *n.* **Greg·or** (greg′ər), 1903–76, U.S. cellist, born in Russia.

Piau·í (pyou ē′), *n.* a state in NE Brazil. 1,263,368 (1960); 96,860 sq. mi. *Cap.:* Teresina.

Pia·ve (pyä′ve), *n.* a river in NE Italy, flowing S and SE into the Adriatic. 137 mi. long.

pi·az·za (pē az′ə, -ä′zə; *Brit.* pē at′sə, -ad′zə; *It.* pyät′tsä), *n., pl.* **pi·az·zas,** *It.* **piaz·ze** (pyät′tse). **1.** an open square or public place in a city or town, esp. in Italy. **2.** *Chiefly New Eng. and Southern U.S.* a porch on a house; veranda. **3.** *Chiefly Brit.* an arcade or covered walk or gallery. [< It < L *platēa* courtyard, orig., street < Gk *plateîa.* See PLACE]

pi·broch (pē′brokн), *n.* (in the Scottish Highlands) a musical piece performed on the bagpipe and consisting of a series of stylized variations on a ground theme. [< ScotGael *piobaireachd* piper music = *piob* PIPE¹ + *-air* -ER¹ + *-eachd,* n. suffix denoting quality or state]

pic (pik), *n., pl.* **pix** (piks), **pics.** *Slang.* **1.** a movie. **2.** a photograph. Also, **pix.** [short form of PICTURE]

pi·ca[1] (pī′kə), *n. Print.* **1.** a 12-point type of a size between small pica and English. **2.** the depth of this type size as a unit of linear measurement for type, pages containing type, etc.; one sixth of an inch. **3.** a 12-point type, widely used in typewriters, and having 10 characters to the inch. Cf. **elite** (def. 4). [< AL *pīca* a collection of church rules; appar. special (orig., jocular) use of L: magpie]

pi·ca[2] (pī′kə), *n. Pathol.* an appetite or a craving for unnatural food, as chalk or clay. [< medical L, special use of L: magpie, with reference to its omnivorous feeding]

pi·ca·dor (pik′ə dôr′; *Sp.* pē′kä t͟hôr′), *n., pl.* **-dors,** *Sp.* **-do·res** (-t͟hô′res). one of the mounted assistants to a matador, who opens the bullfight by jabbing the bull between the shoulders with a lance. [< Sp: lit., pricker = *pic(ar)* (to) prick (see PIQUE) + *-ador* < L *-ātor* -ATOR]

pic·a·nin·ny (pik′ə nin′ē), *n., pl.* **-nies.** pickaninny.

Pi·card (pē kar′), *n.* **Jean** (zhäN), 1620–82, French astronomer.

Pic·ar·dy (pik′ər dē), *n.* a region in N France: formerly a province.

pic·a·resque (pik′ə resk′), *adj.* **1.** pertaining to, characteristic of, or characterized by a form of prose fiction, originally developed in Spain, in which the adventures of an engagingly roguish hero are described in a series of usually humorous or satiric episodes that often depict, in realistic detail, the everyday life of the common people: *a picaresque novel; a picaresque hero; a picaresque element.* **2.** of, pertaining to, or resembling rogues. [< Sp *picaresco.* See PICARO, -ESQUE]

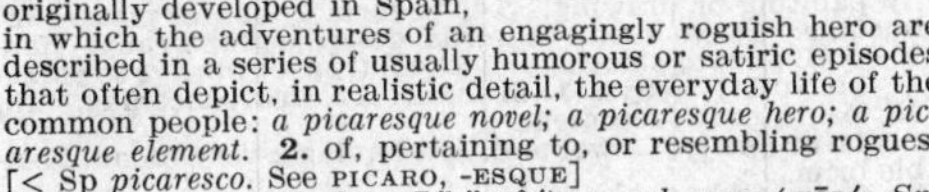

pic·a·ro (pik′ə rō′; *Sp.* pē′kä rō′), *n., pl.* **-ros** (-rōz′; *Sp.* -rôs′). a rogue or vagabond. [< Sp *pícaro* rogue]

pic·a·roon (pik′ə ro͞on′), *n.* **1.** a rogue, thief, or brigand. **2.** a pirate or corsair. —*v.i.* **3.** to act or operate as a pirate or brigand. [< Sp *picarón,* aug. of *pícaro* rogue] Also, **pickaroon.**

Pi·cas·so (pi kä′sō; *Sp.* pē käs′sô), *n.* **Pa·blo** (pä′blō; *Sp.* pä′vlô), 1881–1973, Spanish painter and sculptor in France.

pic·a·yune (pik′ē yo͞on′), *adj.* Also, **pic′a·yun′ish.** *Informal.* **1.** of little value or account; small; trifling: *a picayune amount; a picayune adjustment of the machine.* **2.** petty, carping, or prejudiced: *I didn't want to seem picayune by criticizing.* —*n.* **3.** (formerly, in Louisiana, Florida, etc.) a coin equal in value to half a Spanish real or six U.S. cents. [< F *picaillon* copper coin from Savoy and Piedmont < Pr *picaioun*] —**pic′a·yun′ish·ly,** *adv.* —**pic′a·yun′ish·ness,** *n.* —**Syn. 1.** trivial, insignificant. **2.** narrow-minded.

Pic·ca·dil·ly (pik′ə dil′ē), *n.* a street in London, England: noted for its fashionable shops, clubs, and residences. [named after *Pickadilly* Hall (early 17th century), which owed its name to some assoc. with *pickadilly* edging, ruff, var. of *pickedil* < D < Sp *picadillo, akin to *picado* slashed, pricked. See PICADOR]

Pic′cadilly Cir′cus, a traffic circle and open square in W London, England: theater and amusement center.

pic·ca·lil·li (pik′ə lil′ē), *n., pl.* **-lis.** a spiced pickle or relish of East Indian origin, made of chopped vegetables, usually green peppers and onions, often with cucumbers or green tomatoes. [earlier *piccalillo* Indian pickle; akin to PICKLE]

pic·ca·nin·ny (pik′ə nin′ē), *n., pl.* **-nies.** *Chiefly Brit.* pickaninny.

Pic·card (*Fr.* pē kar′), *n.* **1. Au·guste** (ō gyst′), 1884–1962, Swiss physicist, aeronaut, inventor, and deep-sea explorer: designer of bathyscaphes. **2.** his son **Jacques** (zhäk), born 1922, Swiss oceanographer and bathyscaphe designer, born in Belgium.

Pic·cin·ni (pēt chē′nē), *n.* **Nic·co·lò** (nēk′kô lô′) or **Ni·co·la** (nē kô′lä), 1728–1800, Italian composer, esp. of operas. Also, **Pic·ci′ni.**

pic·co·lo (pik′ə lō′), *n., pl.* **-los.** a small flute, sounding an octave higher than the ordinary flute. [< It: lit., small]

Piccolo

pic·co·lo·ist (pik′ə lō′ist), *n.* a person who plays the piccolo.

pice (pīs), *n., pl.* **pice. 1.** a former bronze coin of British India, one quarter of an anna. Cf. **pie**[4]. **2.** paisa (def. 2). [< Mahratti *paisā*]

pic·e·ous (pis′ē əs, pī′sē əs), *adj.* **1.** of, pertaining to, or resembling pitch. **2.** inflammable; combustible. **3.** *Zool.* black or nearly black as pitch. [< L *piceus* made of pitch = *pice-* (s. of *pix*) pitch + *-us* -OUS]

pich·i·ci·a·go (pich′i sē ä′gō, -ā′gō), *n., pl.* **-gos.** any of several small armadillos of the genera *Chlamydophorous* and *Burmeisteria,* of southern South America. [< AmerSp *pichiciego* < Guaraní *pichey* small armadillo + Sp *ciego* blind (< L *caecus*)]

pick[1] (pik), *v.t.* **1.** to choose or select, esp. with care. **2.** to provoke or bring on: *to pick a fight.* **3.** to attempt to find; seek out: *to pick flaws in an argument.* **4.** to steal the contents of, as a person's pocket. **5.** to open (a lock) with a device other than the key, as a sharp instrument, wire, etc., esp. for the purpose of burglarizing. **6.** to pierce, indent, dig into, or break up (something) with a pointed instrument: *to pick ore.* **7.** to form (a hole) by such action: *to pick a hole in asphalt.* **8.** to use a pointed instrument, the fingers, etc., on (a thing), in order to remove or loosen a part, other matter, etc. **9.** to clear or clean by such action: *to pick one's teeth.* **10.** to detach or remove piece by piece with the fingers: *She daintily picked the meat from the bones.* **11.** to pluck or gather one by one: *to pick flowers.* **12.** (of birds or other animals) to take up (small bits of food) with the bill or teeth. **13.** to separate, pull apart, or pull to pieces: *to

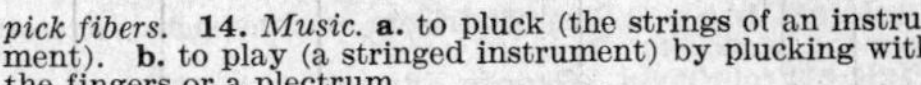

pick fibers.* **14.** *Music.* **a.** to pluck (the strings of an instrument). **b.** to play (a stringed instrument) by plucking with the fingers or a plectrum. —*v.i.* **15.** to use a pointed instrument or the like on something. **16.** (of birds or other animals) to take up small bits of food with the bill or teeth. **17.** to select carefully or fastidiously. **18. pick and choose,** to be very particular in choosing. **19. pick at, a.** *Informal.* to find fault with unnecessarily or persistently; nag. **b.** to eat (something) sparingly or daintily: *As he was ill, he only picked at his food.* **c.** to grasp at; touch; handle: *The baby loved to pick at her mother's necklace.* **20. pick off, a.** to remove by pulling or plucking off. **b.** to single out and shoot: *The hunter picked off a duck rising from the marsh.* **c.** *Baseball.* to put out (a base runner) in a pick-off play. **21. pick on,** *Informal.* to criticize or blame; tease; harass. **22. pick out, a.** to choose: designate: *to pick out one's successor.* **b.** to distinguish from that which surrounds or accompanies; recognize: *to pick out a well-known face in a crowd.* **c.** to discern (sense or meaning); discriminate. **d.** to play (a melody) by ear or work (it) out note by note. **e.** to extract by picking. **23. pick over,** to examine (an assortment of items) in order to make a selection: *Eager shoppers were picking over the shirts on the bargain tables.* **24. pick up, a.** to lift or take up: *to pick up a stone.* **b.** to recover (one's courage, health, etc.); regain. **c.** to gain by occasional opportunity; obtain casually: *to pick up a livelihood.* **d.** to take (a person or thing) into a car, ship, etc., or along with one. **e.** to bring into range of reception, observation, etc.: *to pick up Rome on one's radio.* **f.** to accelerate; speed up. **g.** to put in good order; tidy: *to pick up a room.* **h.** to make progress; improve: *Business is beginning to pick up.* **i.** *Informal.* to introduce oneself to and immediately take out socially or date: *He picked up a girl in the movies last night.* **j.** *Slang.* to take into custody; arrest: *They picked him up for vagrancy.* **k.** *Slang.* to obtain; find; purchase: *She picked up some nice shoes on sale.* **l.** *Informal.* to pay (a bill, as a restaurant check, for charges incurred by others as well as oneself). —*n.* **25.** act of choosing or selecting; choice; selection: *to take one's pick.* **26.** a person or thing selected: *He is our pick for president.* **27.** the choicest or most desirable part, example, or examples. **28.** priority in selection: *He gave me my pick of the litter.* **29.** the quantity of a crop picked, as from trees, bushes, etc., at a particular time. **30.** a stroke with something pointed. **31.** plectrum. [ME *pyke* (rhyming with *thyke* thick); c. D *pikken,* G *picken,* Icel *pikka* to pick; akin to PECK[2]] —**Syn. 1.** See **choose. 4.** rob, pilfer. **11.** reap, collect. **27.** best.

pick[2] (pik), *n.* **1.** a hand tool that consists of an iron or steel head, usually curved, tapering to a point at one or both ends, mounted on a wooden handle, and used for loosening and breaking up soil, rock, etc. **2.** any pointed or other tool or instrument for picking (often used in combination): *a toothpick.* [ME *pikk(e);* perh. var. of PIKE[4]] —**Syn. 1.** pickax.

pick[3] (pik), *Textiles.* —*v.t.* **1.** to cast (a shuttle). —*n.* **2.** (in a loom) one passage of the shuttle. **3.** filling (def. 4). [var. of PITCH[1]]

pick·a·back (pik′ə bak′), *adv., adj.* piggyback (defs. 1, 2). [earlier *a pickback*]

pick·a·nin·ny (pik′ə nin′ē), *n., pl.* **-nies.** *Usually Offensive.* a Negro child. Also, **picaninny;** *esp. Brit.,* **piccaninny.** [? < Pg *pequenino* very little one]

pick·a·roon (pik′ə ro͞on′), *n., v.* picaroon.

pick·ax (pik′aks′), *n., pl.* **-ax·es,** *v.,* **-axed, -ax·ing.** —*n.* **1.** a pick, esp. a mattock. —*v.t.* **2.** to cut or clear away with a pickax. Also, **pick′axe′.** [PICK[2] + AX; r. ME *picois* < MF, OF; akin to F *pic* PICK[2]. See PIQUE]

picked[1] (pikt), *adj.* **1.** specially chosen or selected. **2.** cleared or cleaned by or as by picking: *picked bones.* [PICK[1] + -ED[3]]

pick·ed[2] (pik′id, pikt), *adj. Brit. and New Eng.* pointed. [PICK[2] + -ED[2]]

Pick·ens (pik′ənz), *n.* **1. Andrew,** 1739–1817, American Revolutionary general. **2. Fort.** See **Fort Pickens.**

pick·er[1] (pik′ər), *n.* **1.** a person or thing that picks. **2.** a machine that loosens the fibers in material or yarn. [PICK[1] + -ER[1]]

pick·er[2] (pik′ər), *n. Textiles.* **1.** a tool or instrument for picking fibers. **2.** the piece that throws the shuttle of the loom through the warp. [PICK[3] + -ER[1]]

pick·er·el (pik′ər əl, pik′rəl), *n., pl.* (*esp. collectively*) **-el,** (*esp. referring to two or more kinds or species*) **-els. 1.** any of several small species of pike, as *Esox niger* and *E. americanus americanus,* found in eastern North America. **2.** the walleye or pikeperch, *Stizostedion vitreum.* **3.** *Brit.* a young pike. [ME *pickerel.* See PIKE[1], -EREL]

pick′erel frog′, a meadow frog, *Rana palustris,* common in eastern North America, similar to the leopard frog but with squarish dark spots on the back.

pick·er·el·weed (pik′ər əl wēd′, pik′rəl-), *n.* any American plant of the genus *Pontederia,* esp. *P. cordata,* a blue-flowered herb common in shallow fresh water.

Pick·er·ing (pik′ər ing, pik′ring), *n.* **1. Edward Charles,** 1846–1919, U.S. astronomer. **2.** his brother, **William Henry,** 1858–1938, U.S. astronomer.

pick·et (pik′it), *n.* **1.** a post, stake, or peg that is driven vertically into the ground for use in a fence, to fasten down a tent, etc. **2.** a person stationed before a business establishment in order to dissuade workers or shoppers from entering it during a strike. **3.** a person engaged in any similar demonstration, as against a government's policies or actions. **4.** *Mil.* a soldier or group of soldiers placed on a line forward of a position to warn against an enemy advance. —*v.t.* **5.** to enclose within a picket fence or stockade, as for protection, imprisonment, etc. **6.** to fasten or tether to a picket. **7.** to place pickets in front of or around (a factory, embassy, etc.), as during a strike or demonstration. **8.** *Mil.* **a.** to guard, as with pickets. **b.** to post as a picket. —*v.i.* **9.** to march, stand, sit, etc., as a picket. [< F *piquet.* See PIKE[2], -ET] —**pick′et·er,** *n.*

pick′et line′, a line of strikers or other demonstrators serving as pickets.
Pick·ett (pik′it), *n.* **George Edward,** 1825–75, Confederate general in the Civil War.
Pick·ford (pik′fərd), *n.* **Mary** (*Gladys Marie Smith*), 1893–1979, U.S. motion-picture actress, born in Canada.
pick·ing (pik′ing), *n.* **1.** the act of a person or thing that picks. **2.** something that is or may be picked or picked up. **3. pickings, a.** remains that are worth saving or appropriating. **b.** profits obtained by dishonest means. [ME]
pick·le (pik′əl), *n., v.,* **-led, -ling.** —*n.* **1.** a cucumber that has been preserved in brine, vinegar, or the like. **2.** something preserved in a brine or marinade. **3.** a liquid prepared with salt or vinegar for preserving or flavoring meat, vegetables, etc.; brine or marinade. **4.** *Metall.* an acid or other chemical solution in which metal objects are dipped to remove oxide scale or other adhering substances. **5.** *Informal.* a troublesome or awkward situation; predicament. —*v.t.* **6.** to preserve or steep in brine or other liquid. **7.** to antique (woodwork), as by bleaching. **8.** to treat with a chemical solution, as for the purpose of cleaning. [late ME *pikkyll, pekille* < MD *pekel;* akin to G *Pökel* brine, pickle] —**Syn. 5.** plight, quandary.
pick·led (pik′əld), *adj.* **1.** preserved or steeped in brine or other liquid: *pickled in formaldehyde.* **2.** *Slang.* drunk.
pick·lock (pik′lok′), *n.* **1.** a person who picks locks. **2.** an instrument for picking locks.
pick-me-up (pik′mē up′), *n.* *Informal.* **1.** an alcoholic drink taken to restore one's energy or good spirits. **2.** any restorative, as a snack or coffee.
pick-off (pik′ôf′, -of′), *n.* *Baseball.* a play in which a base runner, caught off base, is tagged out by an infielder on a quick throw, usually from the pitcher or catcher.
pick·pock·et (pik′pok′it), *n.* a person who steals from the pockets or purses of people in public places.
pick·thank (pik′thangk′), *n.* *Archaic.* a sycophant.
pick·up (pik′up′), *n.* **1.** *Informal.* a casual, usually unintroduced acquaintance, often one made in hope of a sexual relationship. **2.** *Auto.* **a.** capacity for rapid acceleration. **b.** Also called **pick′up truck′.** a small truck used for deliveries and light hauling. **3.** *Informal.* an improvement, as in business, health, etc. **4.** *Baseball.* the act of fielding a ball after it hits the ground. **5.** *Radio.* **a.** the act of receiving sound waves in the transmitting set in order to change them into electrical waves. **b.** a receiving or recording device. **c.** the place from which a broadcast is being transmitted. **6.** Also called **cartridge.** a device that generates electric impulses in accordance with the mechanical variations impressed upon a phonograph record. **7.** an instance of taking aboard passengers or freight, as by a truck. **8.** the person, freight, or shipment so taken aboard.
pick′up arm′. See **tone arm.**
pick-up-sticks (pik′up′stiks′), *n.* jackstraws played with sticks.
pick·wick (pik′wik), *n.* a picklike implement for catching up and raising the short wick of an oil lamp.
Pick·wick·i·an (pik wik′ē ən), *adj.* **1.** simple, kind, endearing, or otherwise like Mr. Pickwick, central character of Charles Dickens' novel *The Pickwick Papers* (1837). **2.** (of words or ideas) meant or understood in a sense different from the usual one. [def. 2: so called from Mr. Pickwick's attaching unusual meanings to words] —**Pick·wick′i·an·ly,** *adv.*
pick·y (pik′ē), *adj.,* **pick·i·er, pick·i·est.** extremely fussy or finicky, usually over trifles.
pic·nic (pik′nik), *n., v.,* **-nicked, -nick·ing.** —*n.* **1.** an outing or excursion, typically one in which food is eaten in the open air. **2.** *Informal.* an enjoyable experience, time, task, etc. —*v.i.* **3.** to hold or take part in a picnic. [< F *piquenique,* rhyming compound < ?] —**pic′nick·er,** *n.*
pico-, *Metric System.* a combining form meaning "one trillionth" (10^{-12}): *picometer.* [< Sp *pico* odd number, peak]
Pi·co del·la Mi·ran·do·la (pē′kō del′ə mə ran′dᵊlə; *It.* pē′kô del′lä mē rän′dô lä′), **Count Gio·van·ni** (jô vän′nē), 1463–94, Italian humanist and writer.
Pi·co de Tei·de (*Sp.* pē′kō t̶h̶e tā′t̶h̶e). See **Teide.**
pi·co·far·ad (pī′kō far′əd, -ad), *n.* *Elect.* one trillionth (10^{-12}) of a farad; one micromicrofarad. *Abbr.:* pF, pf
pic·o·line (pik′ə lēn′, -lin), *n.* *Chem.* any of three isomeric methyl derivatives of pyridine having the formula $CH_3C_5H_4N$, obtained from coal tar. [< L *pic-* (s. of *pix*) PITCH² + -OL² + -INE²] —**pic·o·lin·ic** (pik′ə lin′ik), *adj.*
Pi·co Ri·ve·ra (pē′kō ri vâr′ə), a city in SW California, near Los Angeles. 54,170 (1970).
pi·co·sec·ond (pī′kə sek′ənd), *n.* one trillionth (10^{-12}) of a second. *Abbr.:* ps, psec
pi·cot (pē′kō), *n.* one of a number of ornamental loops in embroidery, or along the edge of lace, ribbon, etc. [< F: a purl, lit., a splinter, dim. of *pic* pick < Gmc; see PIKE²]
picr-, var. of **picro-** before a vowel: *picrite.*
pic·rate (pik′rāt), *n.* *Chem.* a salt or ester of picric acid. —**pic′rat·ed,** *adj.*
pic′ric ac′id, *Chem.* a yellow, intensely bitter, poisonous acid, $C_6H_2(NO_2)_3OH$, used chiefly as an explosive. Also called **pi′cro·ni′tric ac′id** (pī′krō nī′trik, pī′krō-). —**pic·ric** (pik′rik), *adj.*
pic·rite (pik′rīt), *n.* an igneous rock composed chiefly of olivine and augite, but containing small amounts of feldspar.
picro-, a learned borrowing from Greek meaning "bitter" (*picrotoxin*), specialized in chemical terms as a combining form of **picric acid.** Also, *esp. before a vowel,* **picr-.** [comb. form repr. Gk *pikrós* bitter]
pic·ro·tox·in (pik′rə tok′sin), *n.* *Pharm.* a bitter, poisonous solid, $C_{30}H_{34}O_{13}$, obtained from the seeds of *Anamirta cocculus:* used chiefly in the treatment of barbiturate poisoning. —**pic′ro·tox′ic,** *adj.*
Pict (pikt), *n.* one of an ancient people of uncertain origin who inhabited parts of northern Britain. [back formation from ME *Pictes* (pl.) (< L *Pictī*); r. ME *Peghttes,* OE *Peohtas* < < L *Pictī,* lit., painted ones, pl. of *pictus,* ptp. of *pingere* to paint]
Pict·ish (pik′tish), *n.* **1.** the language of the Picts, apparently a Celtic language. —*adj.* **2.** of the Picts.
pic·to·graph (pik′tə graf′, -gräf′), *n.* **1.** a record consisting of pictorial symbols, as a prehistoric cave drawing or a graph or chart using symbolic pictures. **2.** a pictorial sign or symbol. [< L *pict(us)* painted (see PICTURE) + -o- + -GRAPH] —**pic·to·graph·ic** (pik′tə graf′ik), *adj.* —**pic′to·graph′i·cal·ly,** *adv.*
pic·tog·ra·phy (pik tog′rə fē), *n.* the use of pictographs; picture writing.
pic·to·ri·al (pik tōr′ē əl, -tôr′ē əl), *adj.* **1.** pertaining to, expressed in, or of the nature of a picture or pictures. **2.** illustrated by or containing pictures. **3.** of or pertaining to the art of painting and drawing pictures, the pictures themselves, or their makers. **4.** having or suggesting the visual appeal or imagery of a picture: *a pictorial description of the countryside.* —*n.* **5.** a periodical in which pictures constitute a leading feature. [< L *pictōri(us)* of a painter = *pictōri-* (s. of *pictor: pict(us)* ptp. of *pingere* to paint + *-or* -OR²) + -AL¹] —**pic·to′ri·al·ly,** *adv.* —**pic·to′ri·al·ness,** *n.* —**Syn. 4.** picturesque, vivid, striking.
pic·ture (pik′chər), *n., v.,* **-tured, -tur·ing.** —*n.* **1.** a representation of a person, object, or scene, as a painting or photograph. **2.** any visible image, however produced. **3.** a mental image. **4.** a graphic or vivid description or account. **5.** a tableau, as in theatrical representation. **6.** See **motion picture.** **7.** a person, thing, group, or scene regarded as resembling a work of pictorial art in beauty, fineness of appearance, etc. **8.** the image or counterpart of someone else. **9.** a visible or concrete embodiment of some quality or condition: *the picture of health.* **10.** a situation or set of circumstances. **11.** understanding of a situation: *Do you get the picture?* **12.** the viewing screen of a television set or a motion-picture theater. —*v.t.* **13.** to represent in a picture or pictorially, as by painting or drawing. **14.** to form a mental picture of; imagine. **15.** to depict in words; describe graphically. [late ME < L *pictūra* painting = *pict(us)* (ptp. of *pingere* to paint) + *-ūra* -URE] —**Syn. 1.** likeness. **11.** drift; meaning. **13, 15.** paint, draw, represent.
pic′ture hat′, a woman's hat having a very broad, flexible brim.
Pic·ture·phone (pik′chər fōn′), *n.* *Trademark.* a telephone equipped to receive and transmit a television image of those conversing.
pic′ture plane′, the plane of a painting, drawing, or the like, that is in the extreme foreground of a picture, is coextensive with but not the same as the material surface of the work, is the point of visual contact between the viewer and the picture, and is conceived as a major structural element in the production of abstract or illusionistic forms.
pic′ture post′ card′. See **post card** (def. 1).
pic·tur·esque (pik′chə resk′), *adj.* **1.** visually charming or quaint, as if resembling or suitable for a painting. **2.** (of writing, speech, etc.) strikingly graphic or vivid. **3.** having pleasing or interesting qualities; strikingly effective in appearance. [modeled (imperfectly) on F *pittoresque* < It *pittoresco* = *pittor(e)* painter + *-esco* -ESQUE] —**pic′tur·esque′ly,** *adv.* —**pic′tur·esque′ness,** *n.*
pic′ture tube′, a cathode-ray tube forming the screen on which televised images are reproduced.
pic′ture win′dow, a large window in a house, designed to frame the exterior view.
pic′ture writ′ing, **1.** the art of writing by using pictures or pictorial symbols. **2.** the pictures or symbols so used.
pic·ul (pik′əl), *n.* (in China and Southeast Asia) a weight equal to 100 catties, or from about 133 to about 143 pounds avoirdupois. [< Malay *pikul* full load (for a man), n. use of *pikul* (v.) to carry a full load]
pid·dle (pid′ᵊl), *v.,* **-dled, -dling.** —*v.i.* **1.** to waste time; dawdle; trifle. **2.** (often used of children and pets) to urinate. —*v.t.* **3.** to waste (time); fail to utilize (usually fol. by *away*): *We piddled away the afternoon.* [?] —**pid′dler,** *n.*
pid·dling (pid′ling), *adj.* trifling; petty; negligible.
pid·dock (pid′ək), *n.* any bivalve mollusk of the genus *Pholas* or the family *Pholadidae,* having long, ovate shells and burrowing in soft rock, wood, etc. [? akin to OE *puduc* wart]
pidg·in (pij′ən), *n.* an auxiliary language resulting from contact between two different languages that is primarily a simplified form of one of the languages, with considerable variation in pronunciation, and is an amalgam of the grammatical features common to both languages. Also, (*not in technical use*) **pigeon.** [perh. repr. Chin pronunciation of *business*]
pidg′in Eng′lish, **1.** an English jargon originally used in commerce in Chinese ports. **2.** any of several similar jargons used in other areas, as Melanesia or West Africa. Also, **Pidg′in Eng′lish.**
pie¹ (pī), *n.* **1.** a baked food having a sweet, savory, or meat filling, prepared in a pastry-lined pan or dish and often topped with a pastry crust. **2.** a layer cake with a filling of cream, jelly, or the like. [ME; special use of *pie* shallow pit < ONF *pi, pis,* dial. var. of OF *puis* < L *puteus* well, pit. See PIT¹]
pie² (pī), *n.* magpie. [ME < OF < L *pīca,* akin to *pīcus* woodpecker]
pie³ (pī), *n., v.t.,* **pied, pie·ing.** *U.S.* pi².
pie⁴ (pī), *n.* a former bronze coin of India, the 12th part of an anna. Cf. **pice.** [< Mahratti *pā′ī,* lit., a fourth]
pie·bald (pī′bôld′), *adj.* **1.** having patches of black and white or of other colors; parti-colored. —*n.* **2.** a piebald animal, esp. a horse. [PIE² (see PIED) + BALD]
pie′bald skin′, *Pathol.* vitiligo.
piece (pēs), *n., v.,* **pieced, piec·ing.** —*n.* **1.** a portion or quantity, as of some materials, forming a separate entity: *a piece of lumber.* **2.** a portion or quantity of a whole: *a piece of cake.* **3.** an individual thing of a particular class or kind: *a piece of furniture.* **4.** a part, fragment, or shred. **5.** a particular amount, as of work produced in a factory or cloth to be sold. **6.** an example of creativity or workmanship, as a picture or a literary composition. **7.** a short musical composition. **8.** one of the figures, counters, or the like, used in playing certain games on a board or table, esp. any chessman of superior rank, as distinguished from a pawn. **9.** an example, specimen, or instance of something. **10.** *Mil.* **a.** a soldier's rifle, pistol, etc. **b.** a cannon or other unit of ordnance: *field piece.* **11.** a coin: *a five-cent piece.* **12.** a distance: *down the road a piece.* **13.** *Slang* (*vulgar*). coitus or a woman as an object of coitus. **14. go to pieces,** to lose control of oneself; become emotionally or

physically upset. **15. of a piece,** of the same kind; harmonious; consistent. **16. speak one's piece,** *Informal.* to express one's opinion; reveal one's thoughts upon a subject. —*v.t.* **17.** to mend (a garment, article, etc.) by applying a piece or pieces; patch. **18.** to complete, enlarge, or extend by an added piece or something additional (often fol. by *out*): *to piece out a weak argument with additional data.* **19.** to make by or as if by joining pieces (often fol. by *together*). **20.** to join together, as pieces or parts. **21.** to join as a piece or addition to something. **22.** to assemble into a meaningful whole by combining available facts, information, details, etc. [ME *pece* < OF < Gaulish **pettia;* akin to Breton *pez* piece, Welsh, Cornish *peth* part] —**Syn. 2.** section, segment, fragment. See **part. 18.** augment.

pièce de ré·sis·tance (pyes də RĀ zē stäNs′; *Eng.* pē es′ də ri zē′stäns), *pl.* **pièces de ré·sis·tance** (pyes də RĀ zē-stäNs′; *Eng.* pē es′ də ri zē′stäns). *French.* **1.** the principal dish of a meal. **2.** the principal event, incident, article, etc., of a series or group.

piece-dyed (pēs′dīd′), *adj.* dyed after weaving (opposed to *yarn-dyed*).

piece′ goods′, goods, esp. fabrics, sold at retail by linear measure. Also called **yard goods.**

piece·meal (pēs′mēl′), *adv.* **1.** piece by piece: *to work piecemeal.* **2.** into pieces or fragments. —*adj.* **3.** done piece by piece. [ME *pecemele;* r. OE *styccemǣlum.* See PIECE, -MEAL]

piece′ of eight′, peso (def. 6).

piec·er (pē′sər), *n.* a person whose occupation is the joining together of pieces or threads, as in textile work.

piece·work (pēs′wûrk′), *n.* work done and paid for by the piece. Cf. **timework.** —**piece′work′er,** *n.*

pie′crust ta′ble (pī′krust′), *U.S. Furniture.* a table having a top, usually round, with a raised and intricately carved edge.

pied (pīd), *adj.* **1.** having patches of two or more colors: *a pied horse.* **2.** wearing pied clothing. [PIE[2] (with reference to the black and white plumage of the magpie) + -ED[3]]

pied-à-terre (pyā tA ter′), *n., pl.* **pied-à-terre** (pyā tA-ter′). *French.* a small dwelling for temporary use, as an apartment maintained in a foreign city. [lit., foot on ground]

Pied·mont (pēd′mont), *n.* **1.** a plateau between the coastal plain and the Appalachian Mountains, including parts of Virginia, North Carolina, South Carolina, Georgia, and Alabama. **2.** Italian, **Piemonte.** a region in NW Italy. 4,540,822; 11,335 sq. mi. **3.** (*l.c.*) a district lying along or near the foot of a mountain range. —*adj.* **4.** (*l.c.*) lying along or near the foot of a mountain range. [< It *Piemonte,* lit., foothill]

pied·mont·ite (pēd′mon tīt′), *n.* a mineral, similar to epidote but containing manganese. [< G]

Pied′ Pip′er, 1. the hero of a German folk legend, popularized in *The Pied Piper of Hamelin* (1842) by Robert Browning. **2.** (*sometimes l.c.*) a person who induces others to imitate his example, esp. by means of false or extravagant promises.

Pie·dras Ne·gras (pye′thräs ne′gräs), a city in N Mexico, on the Rio Grande. 65,883.

pie-eyed (pī′īd′), *adj. Slang.* drunk; intoxicated.

Pie·mon·te (pye môn′te), *n.* Italian name of **Piedmont.**

pie·plant (pī′plant′, -plänt′), *n. U.S.* the garden rhubarb: so called from its use in pies.

pier (pēr), *n.* **1.** a structure built to extend from land out over water, used as a landing place for ships, an entertainment or amusement area, etc. **2.** (in a bridge or the like) a support for the ends of adjacent spans. **3.** a portion of wall between doors, windows, etc. **4.** a pillar or post on which a gate or door is hung. **5.** a support of masonry or the like for sustaining vertical pressure. [ME *pere,* early ME *per* < AL *pera* pier of a bridge]

pierce (pērs), *v.,* **pierced, pierc·ing.** —*v.t.* **1.** to penetrate into or run through (something), as a sharp-pointed object or instrument does. **2.** to make a hole or opening in, as by boring into or through or perforating: *to pierce a piece o leather.* **3.** to make (a hole, opening, etc.) by or as by boring or perforating: *to pierce a hole in a piece of leather.* **4.** to force or make a way into or through: *a road that pierces the jungle.* **5.** to penetrate with the eye or mind; see into or through. **6.** to affect sharply with some sensation or emotion, as of cold, pain, or grief. **7.** to sound sharply through (the air, stillness, etc.), as a cry. —*v.i.* **8.** to force or make a way into or through something; penetrate. [ME *perce(n)* < OF *perc(er),* perh. < VL **pertiāre* < L *peritus* gone through (hence, pierced), ptp. of *perīre.* See PERISH] —**pierce′a·ble,** *adj.* —**pierc′er,** *n.*
—**Syn. 1.** enter, puncture. PIERCE, PENETRATE suggest the action of one object passing through another or making a way through and into another. The terms are used both concretely and figuratively. To PIERCE is to perforate quickly, as by stabbing; it suggests the use of a sharp-pointed instrument impelled by force: *to pierce the flesh with a knife; A scream pierces one's ears.* PENETRATE suggests a slow or difficult movement: *No ordinary bullet can penetrate an elephant's hide; to penetrate the depths of one's ignorance.*

Pierce (pērs), *n.* **Franklin,** 1804–69, 14th president of the U.S. 1853–57.

pierced (pērst), *adj.* **1.** punctured or perforated, as to form a decorative design. **2.** (of the ear) having the lobe punctured, as for earrings. **3.** *Heraldry.* (of a charge) open at the center to reveal the field: *a lozenge pierced.*

pierc·ing (pēr′sing), *adj.* **1.** loud or shrill, as the quality of a voice. **2.** extremely cold or bitter, as weather. **3.** appearing to gaze deeply into an object. **4.** perceptive or aware. **5.** sarcastic or caustic, as a remark; cutting. [ME] —**pierc′ing·ly,** *adv.* —**pierc′ing·ness,** *n.*

pier′ glass′, a tall mirror, often full-length, intended to be set between windows.

Pi·e·ri·a (pī ēr′ē ə), *n.* a coastal region in NE Greece, W of the Gulf of Salonika.

Pi·e·ri·an (pī ēr′ē ən), *adj.* **1.** of or pertaining to the Muses or to inspiration. **2.** of or pertaining to Pieria. **3.** of or pertaining to poetry or poetic inspiration. [< L *Pīeri(us)* of Pieria + -AN]

Pie′rian Spring′ (pī ēr′ē ən), *Class. Myth.* a fountain in Pieria, sacred to the Muses and supposedly conferring inspiration or learning on anyone who drank from it.

Pi·e·ri·des (pī ēr′i dēz′), *n.pl. Class. Myth.* **1.** the Muses. **2.** nine Thessalian maidens who lost a singing contest to the Muses, and were changed into magpies for insulting them.

Pie·ro del·la Fran·ce·sca (pyâr′ō del′ə fran ches′kə; frän-; *It.* pye′RŌ del′lä fRän ches′kä). See **Francesca, Piero della.** Also called **Pie′ro.**

Pierre (pēr), *n.* a city in and the capital of South Dakota, in the central part, on the Missouri River. 9,699 (1970).

Pi·er·rot (pē′ə rō′; *Fr.* pye RŌ′), *n., pl.* **-rots** (-rōz′; *Fr.* -RŌ′). a male character in certain French pantomime, having a whitened face and wearing a loose, white, fancy costume. [< F, dim. of *Pierre* Peter]

pier′ ta′ble, a low table or console intended to be set between two windows, often beneath a pier glass.

Pie·tà (pē′ā tä′, pyā tä′, pē ā′tə, pyā′-), *n.* (*sometimes l.c.*) *Fine Arts.* a representation of the Virgin Mary mourning the body of the dead Christ, usually shown held on her lap. [< It: lit., pity < L *pietās* PIETY]

Pie·ter·mar·itz·burg (pē′tər mar′its bûrg′), *n.* a city in and the capital of Natal province, in the E Republic of South Africa. 151,921.

Pi·e·tism (pī′i tiz′əm), *n.* **1.** a movement, originating in the Lutheran Church in Germany in the 17th century, that stressed personal piety over religious formality and orthodoxy. **2.** (*l.c.*) exaggeration or affectation of piety. [< G *Pietism(us)* < L *piet(ās)* PIETY + G *-ismus* -ISM] —**Pi′e·tist,** *n.* —**pi′e·tis′tic, pi′e·tis′ti·cal,** *adj.* —**pi′e·tis′ti·cal·ly,** *adv.*

pi·e·ty (pī′i tē), *n., pl.* **-ties** for 4. **1.** reverence for God or devout fulfillment of religious obligations. **2.** the quality or fact of being pious. **3.** dutiful respect or regard for parents, homeland, etc. **4.** a pious act, remark, belief, or the like. [ME *piete* < MF < L *pietās.* See PIOUS, -TY[2]] —**Syn. 1.** respect, veneration, awe. **2.** godliness, devoutness, holiness. —**Ant.** irreverence.

pi·e·zo·e·lec·tric·i·ty (pī ē′zō i lek tris′i tē, -ē′lek-), *n.* electricity, or electric polarity, produced by mechanical stress on a nonconducting crystal. [< Gk *piéz(ein)* (to) press + -o- + ELECTRICITY] —**pi·e·zo·e·lec·tric** (pī ē′zō i-lek′trik), *adj.* —**pi·e′zo·e·lec′tri·cal·ly,** *adv.*

pi·e·zom·e·ter (pī′i zom′i tər), *n.* any of several instruments for measuring the pressure of a fluid or the compressibility of a substance when subjected to such a pressure. [< Gk *piéz(ein)* (to) press + -o- + -METER] —**pi·e·zo·met·ric** (pī ē′zə me′trik), **pi·e′zo·met′ri·cal,** *adj.*

pi·e·zom·e·try (pī′i zom′i trē), *n.* the measurement of pressure or compressibility. [< Gk *piéz(ein)* (to) press + -o- + -METRY]

pif·fle (pif′əl), *n. Informal.* nonsense, as idle talk. [? akin to PUFF]

pig (pig), *n., v.,* **pigged, pig·ging.** —*n.* **1.** a young swine of either sex weighing less than 120 pounds. **2.** (loosely) any wild or domestic swine. **3.** the flesh of swine; pork. **4.** *Informal.* a person of piggish character or habits. **5.** *Metall.* **a.** an oblong mass of metal that has been run while still molten into a mold of sand or the like, esp. such a mass of iron from a blast furnace. **b.** one of the molds for such masses of metal. **c.** metal in the form of such masses. **d.** pig iron. **6.** *Offensive.* a policeman. —*v.i.* **7.** to bring forth pigs; farrow. **8. pig out,** *Slang.* to stuff oneself with food: *We pigged out on banana splits.* [ME *pigge* young pig, OE **pigga* (recorded from 11th century as nickname); ? akin to D *big* young pig]

pig′ bed′, *Metall.* a bed of sand into which molten metal is poured to mold pigs.

pig·boat (pig′bōt′), *n. Slang.* a submarine.

pi·geon[1] (pij′ən), *n.* **1.** any bird of the family *Columbidae,* having a compact body and short legs, esp. the larger species with square or rounded tails. Cf. **dove**[1] (def. 1). **2.** a domesticated member of this family, as one of the varieties of the rock dove. **3.** *Slang.* a person who is easily fooled; dupe. [ME *pejon* young dove < MF *pijon* < LL *pīpiōn-*]

pi·geon[2] (pij′ən), *n.* (not in technical use) pidgin.

pi′geon hawk′, a small American falcon, *Falco columbarius,* closely related to the European merlin.

pi·geon-heart·ed (pij′ən här′tid), *adj.* timid; meek.

pi·geon·hole (pij′ən hōl′), *n., v.,* **-holed, -hol·ing.** —*n.* **1.** a hole or recess, or one of a series of recesses, for pigeons to nest in. **2.** one of a series of small compartments in a desk, cabinet, or the like, used for filing papers, letters, etc. —*v.t.* **3.** to lay aside for future reference. **4.** to file away, as in a pigeonhole. **5.** to put aside and ignore. **6.** to put into categories. —**Syn. 3.** postpone. **5.** shelve. **6.** categorize; catalog.

pi·geon-liv·ered (pij′ən liv′ərd), *adj.* meek-tempered; spiritless; mild.

pi·geon-toed (pij′ən tōd′), *adj.* having the toes or feet turned inward.

pi·geon·wing (pij′ən wing′), *n. U.S.* **1.** a particular figure in skating, outlining the spread wing of a pigeon. **2.** a similar fancy step or evolution in dancing.

pig·fish (pig′fish′), *n., pl.* **-fish·es,** (*esp. collectively*) **-fish.** a grunt, *Orthopristis chrysopterus,* found off the Atlantic coast of the southern U.S.

pig·ger·y (pig′ə rē), *n., pl.* **-ger·ies.** *Chiefly Brit.* a pigpen.

pig·gin (pig′in), *n. Dial.* a small wooden pail or tub with a handle formed by continuing one of the staves above the rim. [? akin to Scot and north E *pig* crock, jar, potter's clay, late ME *pygg*]

pig·gish (pig′ish), *adj.* like a pig, esp. in being greedy or filthy. —**pig′gish·ly,** *adv.* —**pig′gish·ness,** *n.*

pig·gy (pig′ē), *n., pl.* **-gies.** a small or young pig.

pig·gy·back (pig′ē bak′), *adv.* **1.** on the back or shoulders like a pack: *The little girl rode piggyback on her father.* —*adj.* **2.** astride the back or shoulders: *a piggyback ride.* **3.** noting or pertaining to the carrying of one vehicle or the like by another, as the carrying of truck trailers on flatcars. —*v.t.* **4.** to carry (truck trailers) by railroad on flatcars. —*v.i.* **5.** to carry truck trailers by railroad on flatcars. Also, **pickaback** (for defs. 1, 2). [alter. of PICKABACK]

pig′gy bank′, a small bank, often having the shape of a pig, in which coins are saved.

pig·head·ed (pig′hed′id), *adj.* stupidly obstinate; stubborn. —**pig′head′ed·ly,** *adv.* —**pig′head′ed·ness,** *n.*

pig′ in a poke′, something purchased or acquired without a preliminary examination.

pig′ i′ron, 1. iron tapped from a blast furnace and cast into pigs in preparation for conversion into steel, cast iron, or wrought iron. **2.** iron in the chemical state in which it is when tapped from the blast furnace, without any subsequent alloying or refinement.

Pig′ Lat′in, a form of language derived from ordinary language by moving the first consonant or consonant cluster of each word to the end of the word and adding the sound (ā), as in *Eakspay igpay atinlay* meaning "Speak Pig Latin."

pig′ lead′ (led), lead molded in pigs.

pig·let (pig′lit), *n.* a little pig.

pig·ment (pig′mənt), *n.* **1.** a coloring matter or substance. **2.** a dry insoluble substance, usually pulverized, that when suspended in a liquid vehicle becomes a paint, ink, etc. **3.** *Biol.* any substance whose presence in the tissues or cells of animals or plants colors them. —*v.t.* **4.** to color; add pigment to. —*v.i.* **5.** to become pigmented; acquire color. [ME < L *pigment(um)* paint = *pig-* (r. of *pingere* to paint) + *-mentum* -MENT] —**pig′men·tar′y,** *adj.*

pig·men·ta·tion (pig′mən tā′shən), *n.* **1.** *Biol.* coloration with or deposition of pigment. **2.** coloration, esp. of the skin. [< LL *pigmentāt(us)* painted, colored (see PIGMENT, -ATE[1]) + -ION]

Pig·my (pig′mē), *n., pl.* **-mies,** *adj.* Pygmy.

pig·nus (pig′nəs), *n., pl.* **pig·no·ra** (pig′nər ə). *Roman and Civil Law.* **1.** property held as security for a debt. **2.** the contract containing such a pledge. [< L: lit., pledge]

pig·nut (pig′nut′), *n.* **1.** the nut of the brown hickory, *Carya glabra,* of North America. **2.** the tree itself. **3.** the tuber of a European plant, *Conopodium denudatum.*

pig·pen (pig′pen′), *n.* **1.** a pen for keeping pigs. **2.** a dirty or untidy place. Also called **pigsty.**

Pigs (pigz), *n.* **Bay of,** a bay of the Caribbean Sea in SW Cuba: attempted invasion of Cuba by anti-Castro forces April 1961.

pig·skin (pig′skin′), *n.* **1.** the skin of a pig. **2.** leather made from it. **3.** *Informal.* a football.

pig·stick (pig′stik′), *v.i.* to hunt for wild boar, usually on horseback and using a spear. —**pig′stick′ing,** *n.*

pig·stick·er (pig′stik′ər), *n.* **1.** a person who pigsticks. **2.** a slaughterer, esp. of hogs. **3.** *Slang.* a knife.

pig·sty (pig′stī′), *n., pl.* **-sties.** pigpen.

pig·tail (pig′tāl′), *n.* **1.** a braid of hair hanging down the back of the head. **2.** tobacco in a thin, twisted roll.

pig·weed (pig′wēd′), *n.* **1.** any goosefoot of the genus *Chenopodium,* esp. *C. album.* **2.** any of certain amaranths, as *Amaranthus retroflexus.*

pi·ka (pī′kə), *n.* any of several small mammals of the family *Ochotonidae,* closely related to the rabbits, inhabiting alpine regions of the Northern Hemisphere. [< Tungusic *piika*]

Pike, *Esox lucius* (Length to 4½ ft.)

pike[1] (pīk), *n., pl.* (*esp. collectively*) **pike,** (*esp. referring to two or more kinds or species*) **pikes. 1.** any of several large, slender, voracious, freshwater fishes of the genus *Esox,* having a long, flat snout. **2.** any of various superficially similar fishes, as the walleye or pikeperch. [ME, short for *pikefish,* so called from its pointed snout. See PIKE[4]]

pike[2] (pīk), *n., v.,* **piked, pik·ing.** —*n.* **1.** a shafted weapon having a sharp head, formerly used by the infantry. —*v.t.* **2.** to pierce, wound, or kill with or as with a pike. [< MF *pique,* fem. var. of *pic* pick < Gmc. See PIKE[4], PIQUE]

pike[3] (pīk), *n.* **1.** a toll road or highway; turnpike road. **2.** a turnpike or tollgate. **3.** the toll paid at a tollgate. [short for TURNPIKE]

pike[4] (pīk), *n.* **1.** a sharply pointed projection or spike. **2.** the pointed end of anything, as of an arrow or a spear. [ME *pīk* pick, spike, (pilgrim's) staff, OE *pīc* pointed tool. See PIKE[2]]

Pike (pīk), *n.* **1. James Albert,** 1913–69, U.S. Protestant Episcopal clergyman, lawyer, and author. **2. Zeb·u·lon Montgomery** (zeb′yŏŏ lən), 1779–1813, U.S. general and explorer.

pike·man (pīk′mən), *n., pl.* **-men.** a soldier armed with a pike.

pike·perch (pīk′pûrch′), *n., pl.* (*esp. collectively*) **-perch,** (*esp. referring to two or more kinds or species*) **-perch·es.** any of several pikelike fishes of the perch family, esp. the walleye, *Stizostedion vitreum.*

pik·er (pī′kər), *n.* *Informal.* a person who does anything in a contemptibly small or cheap way. [*pike,* var. of PICK[1] + -ER[1]]

Pikes′ Peak′, a mountain in central Colorado: a peak of the Rocky Mountains. 14,108 ft.

pike·staff (pīk′staf′, -stäf′), *n., pl.* **-staves** (-stāvz′). **1.** the shaft of a pike. **2.** a foot traveler's staff with a metal point or spike at the lower end. [ME *pykstaf*]

Pikes·ville (pīks′vil), *n.* a town in central Maryland, near Baltimore. 25,395 (1970).

pi·laf (pi läf′, pē′läf), *n.* **1.** rice cooked in a meat or poultry broth. **2.** a Middle Eastern dish consisting of sautéed rice steamed in bouillon, sometimes with poultry, meat, shellfish, etc., and flavored with herbs, spices, or the like. Also, **pilau.** [< Turk *pilāv* < Pers *pilāw*]

A, Pilasters on Renaissance wall surface; B, Detail of upper end of pilaster

pi·las·ter (pi las′tər), *n.* *Archit.* a shallow rectangular feature projecting from a wall, having a capital and base and usually imitating the form of a column. [PILE[1] (in obs. sense pillar) + -ASTER[1], modeled on It *pilastro* or ML *pīlastrum*] —**pi·las′tered,** *adj.*

Pi·late (pī′lət), *n.* **Pon·tius** (pon′shəs, -tē əs), fl. early 1st century A.D., Roman procurator of Judea A.D. 26–36?: the final authority concerned in the condemnation and execution of Jesus Christ.

Pi·la·tus (*Ger.* pē lä′tŏŏs), *n.* a mountain in central Switzerland, near Lucerne: a peak of the Alps; cable railway. 6998 ft.

pi·lau (pi läf′, pē′läf), *n.* pilaf.

pil·chard (pil′chərd), *n.* **1.** a small, southern European, marine fish, *Sardina pilchardus,* related to the herring but smaller and rounder. **2.** any of several related fishes, as *Sardinops caeruleus,* found off the California coast. [earlier *pilcher* < ?]

Pil·co·ma·yo (pēl′kô mä′yô), *n.* a river in S central South America, flowing SE from S Bolivia along the boundary between Paraguay and Argentina to the Paraguay River at Asunción. 1000 mi. long.

pile[1] (pīl), *n., v.,* **piled, pil·ing.** —*n.* **1.** an assemblage of things laid or lying one upon the other. **2.** a heap of wood on which something is burned. **3.** a lofty or large building or mass of buildings. **4.** *Informal.* a large accumulation of money. **5.** a bundle of pieces of iron ready to be welded and drawn out into bars; fagot. **6.** reactor (def. 4). —*v.t.* **7.** to lay or dispose in a pile (often fol. by *up*): *to pile up leaves.* **8.** to accumulate or store (often fol. by *up*): *to pile up money.* **9.** to cover or load with a pile or piles. —*v.i.* **10.** to accumulate, as money, debts, evidence, etc. (usually fol. by *up*): *The bills keep piling up.* **11.** *Informal.* to get somewhere in a more or less disorderly group. **12.** to gather or rise in a pile or piles (often fol. by *up*). [late ME < MF < L *pīla* pillar, mole of stone] —**Syn. 1.** collection, heap, mass, accumulation. **2.** pyre. **3.** edifice. **8.** amass, collect.

pile[2] (pīl), *n., v.,* **piled, pil·ing.** —*n.* **1.** a cylindrical or flat member of wood, steel, concrete, etc., often tapered or pointed at the lower end, hammered vertically into soil to form part of a foundation or retaining wall. **2.** *Heraldry.* an ordinary in the form of a wedge or triangle coming from one edge of the escutcheon, from the chief unless otherwise specified. **3. in pile,** *Heraldry.* (of a number of charges) arranged in the manner of a pile. —*v.t.* **4.** to furnish, strengthen, or support with piles. **5.** to drive piles into. [ME; OE *pīl* shaft < L *pīl(um)* javelin]

pile[3] (pīl), *n.* **1.** hair. **2.** soft, fine hair or down. **3.** wool, fur, or pelage. **4.** a fabric with a surface of upright yarns, cut or looped, as corduroy, Turkish toweling, velvet, and velveteen. **5.** such a surface. **6.** one of the strands in such a surface. [late ME < L *pil(us)* hair; *-i-* short in L but long in Anglicized school pronunciation]

pile[4] (pīl), *n.* Usually, **piles.** *Pathol.* **1.** hemorrhoid. **2.** the condition of having hemorrhoids. [late ME *pyles* (pl.) < L *pilae,* lit., balls. See PILL[1]]

pile[5] (pīl), *n.* the lower of two dies for coining by hand. [ME *pyl* < ML *pīla,* special use of L *pīla* PILE[1]]

pi·le·ate (pī′lē it, -āt′, pil′ē-), *adj.* *Bot., Zool.* having a pileus. [< L *pileāt(us)* capped. See PILEUS, -ATE[1]]

pi·le·at·ed (pī′lē ā′tid, pil′ē-), *adj.* *Ornith.* crested.

pi′leated wood′pecker, a large, black-and-white, American woodpecker, *Dryocopus pileatus,* having a prominent red crest.

pile′ driv′er, a machine for driving piles, usually composed of a tall framework in which either a weight is raised and dropped on a pile head or in which a steam hammer drives the pile.

pi·le·ous (pī′lē əs, pil′ē-), *adj.* hairy or furry.

pi·le·um (pī′lē əm, pil′ē-), *n., pl.* **pi·le·a** (pī′lē ə, pil′ē ə). the top of the head of a bird, from the base of the bill to the nape. [< NL, special use of L *pīleum,* var. of *pīleus* skullcap]

pile·up (pīl′up′), *n.* **1.** an accumulation, as of chores or bills. **2.** a massive collision of several or many moving vehicles.

pi·le·us (pī′lē əs, pil′ē-), *n., pl.* **pi·le·i** (pī′lē ī′, pil′ē ī′). **1.** *Bot.* the horizontal portion of a mushroom, bearing gills, tubes, etc., on its underside; a cap. **2.** *Zool.* **a.** the umbrella or bell of a jellyfish. **b.** pileum. **3.** a felt skullcap worn by the ancient Romans and Greeks. [< NL, special use of L *pīleus* skullcap; akin to Gk *pîlos* felt, felt cap]

pile·wort (pīl′wûrt′), *n.* **1.** fireweed. **2.** celandine (def. 2). [so called from its use in medicine]

pil·fer (pil′fər), *v.i., v.t.* to steal, esp. in small quantities; obtain (something) by petty theft. [v. use of late ME *pilfre* booty < MF *pelfre.* See PELF] —**pil′fer·er,** *n.* —**Syn.** take, filch, purloin.

pil·fer·age (pil′fər ij), *n.* **1.** the act or practice of pilfering; petty theft. **2.** that which is pilfered.

pil·gar·lic (pil gär′lik), *n.* **1.** *Dial.* a person regarded with facetious contempt or pity. **2.** *Obs.* a baldheaded man. [earlier *pyllyd garleke,* lit., peeled garlic, from fancied resemblance of a bald head to a peeled garlic bulb.] —**pil·gar′lick·y,** *adj.*

pil·grim (pil′grim, -grəm), *n.* **1.** a person who journeys, esp. a long distance, to some sacred place as an act of devotion. **2.** a traveler or wanderer. **3.** (*cap.*) one of the Pilgrim Fathers. [early ME *pilegrim, pelegrim;* c. OFris *pilegrim,* MLG *pelegrīm,* OHG *piligrīm,* Icel *pīlagrīmr,* all < ML *pelegrīnus,* dissimilated var. of L *peregrīnus* alien < *peregrē* abroad = *per-* PER- + *-egr-* (comb. form of *ager* field; see ACRE) + *-e* adv. suffix] —**Syn. 2.** wayfarer, sojourner.

pil·grim·age (pil′grə mij), *n.* **1.** a journey, esp. a long one, made to some sacred place as an act of devotion. **2.** any long journey, esp. one undertaken for a particular purpose, as to pay homage. [ME *pilegrimage* (see PILGRIM, -AGE); r. earlier *pelrimage,* alter. of OF *pelerinage*] —**Syn. 2.** See **trip.**

Pil′grim Fa′thers, the band of Puritans who founded the colony of Plymouth, Massachusetts in 1620.

pi·li (pē lē′), *n., pl.* **-lis. 1.** a Philippine, burseraceous tree, *Canarium ovatum,* the edible seeds of which taste like a sweet almond. **2.** Also called **pili′ nut′.** the seed of this tree. [< Tagalog]

pili-, a learned borrowing from Latin meaning "hair," used in the formation of compound words: *piliform.* [comb. form repr. L *pilus;* see -I-]

pi·lif·er·ous (pī lif′ər əs), *adj.* having or producing hair.

pil·i·form (pil′ə fôrm′), *adj.* having the form of a hair; resembling hair. [< NL *piliform(is)*]

pil·ing (pī′ling), *n.* **1.** a mass of building piles considered collectively. **2.** a structure composed of piles. [late ME *pylyng*]

pill[1] (pil), *n.* **1.** a small globular or rounded mass of medicinal substance that is to be swallowed whole. **2.** something unpleasant that has to be endured. **3. the pill,** (*sometimes caps.*) See **birth-control pill.** **4.** *Slang.* a tiresomely disagreeable person. **—*v.t.* 5.** to dose with pills. **6.** to form or make into pills. **—*v.i.* 7.** to form into small, pill-like balls, as the fuzz on a wool sweater. [late ME *pille* < MFlem *pille* < L *pilula*, dim. of *pila* ball; see -ULE]

pill[2] (pil), *v.t., v.i.* **1.** *Brit. Dial.* to peel. **2.** *Obs.* to cause to become or to become bald. [ME *pil(en)*, OE *pilian* to skin, peel < L *pil(āre)* (to) strip (of hair). See PILE[3]]

pill[3] (pil), *v.t.* *Archaic.* to rob, plunder, or pillage. [ME; metaphorical use of PILL[2]]

pil·lage (pil′ij), *v.*, **-laged, -lag·ing,** *n.* **—*v.t.* 1.** to strip of money or goods by open violence, as in war; plunder. **2.** to take as booty. **—*v.i.* 3.** to rob with open violence; take booty. **—*n.* 4.** act of plundering, esp. in war. **5.** booty or spoil. [ME *pilage* modeled on MF *pillage* < *piller* < LL **pīliāre* to take] **—pil′lag·er,** *n.* **—Syn. 1.** rob, sack, despoil, rape. **4.** rapine, depredation, spoliation. **5.** plunder.

pil·lar (pil′ər), *n.* **1.** an upright shaft or structure, of stone, brick, or other material, relatively slender in proportion to its height and of any shape in section, used as a building support or standing alone, as for a monument. **2.** a natural formation resembling such a construction. **3.** a person who is a chief supporter of a state, institution, etc. **4. from pillar to post,** from place to place, esp. aimlessly, or from one situation or predicament to another. **—*v.t.* 5.** to provide or support with pillars. [ME *pillare* < ML *pīlāre* (see PILE[1], -AR[2]); r. earlier *piler* < OF < ML, as above] **—pil′lared,** *adj.* **—pil′lar·like′,** *adj.* **—Syn. 1.** pilaster, pier. See **column.**

pil′lar box′, *Brit.* a pillarlike mailbox.

Pil′lars of Her′cules, the two promontories on either side of the eastern end of the Strait of Gibraltar: the Rock of Gibraltar in Europe and the Jebel Musa in Africa; fabled to have been raised by Hercules. Also called **Hercules' Pillars.**

pill·box (pil′boks′), *n.* **1.** a small box for holding pills. **2.** a small, low, concrete structure for enclosing machine guns and used as a minor fortress in warfare. **3.** a woman's low, round, brimless hat with straight sides and a flat top.

pill′ bug′, any of various small terrestrial isopods, esp. of the genus *Armadillo*, that can roll themselves up into a pill-shaped ball.

pil·lion (pil′yən), *n.* a pad or cushion attached behind the saddle of a horse or motorcycle for a second rider. [< Gael *pillean* cushion, pad, kind of saddle, dim. of *peall* skin, rug < L *pellis* skin]

pil·li·winks (pil′ə wiŋks′), *n.* (*construed as sing. or pl.*) an old instrument of torture similar to the thumbscrew. [Scot var. of late ME *pyrwykes, pyrewinkes*]

pil·lo·ry (pil′ə rē), *n., pl.* **-ries,** *v.,* **-ried, -ry·ing.** **—*n.* 1.** a wooden framework, with holes for securing the head and hands, formerly used to expose an offender to public derision. **—*v.t.* 2.** to set in the pillory. **3.** to expose to public ridicule or abuse. [ME *pyllory* < OF *pilori;* akin to Pr *espillori* pillory]

Pillory

pil·low (pil′ō), *n.* **1.** a bag or case made of cloth and filled with soft, resilient material, for cushioning a part of the body, as the head during sleep. **2.** a similar cushion, esp. a small one used for decoration, as on a sofa. **3.** any supporting piece or part, as the cushion or pad used in the making of bobbin lace. **—*v.t.* 4.** to rest on or as on a pillow. **5.** to support with pillows. **6.** to serve as a pillow for. **—*v.i.* 7.** to rest on or as on a pillow. [ME *pilwe*, OE *pylu* < L *pulvīnus* cushion, whence also G *Pfühl*] **—pil′low·less,** *adj.* **—pil′low·y, pil′low·like′,** *adj.*

pil′low block′, *Mach.* a cast-iron or steel block for supporting a journal or bearing.

pil·low·case (pil′ō kās′), *n.* a removable case, usually of cloth, for covering a pillow. Also called **pil·low·slip** (pil′ō-slip′).

pil′low lace′. See **bobbin lace.**

pil′low sham′, an ornamental cover laid over a bed pillow.

pilo-, a learned borrowing from Greek used, with the meaning "felt," in the formation of compound words: *pilocarpine.* [comb. form repr. Gk *pîlos* wool or hair made into felt]

pi·lo·car·pine (pī′lə kär′pēn, -pin, pil′ō-), *n.* *Pharm.* an alkaloid, $C_{11}H_{16}N_2O_2$, obtained from jaborandi: used in the form of its hydrochloride or nitrate chiefly to produce sweating, promote the flow of saliva, contract the pupil of the eye, and for glaucoma. [< NL *Pilocarp(us)* (see PILO-, -CARP) + -INE[1]]

Pi·los (pē′lôs), *n.* Greek name of **Navarino.**

pi·lose (pī′lōs), *adj.* covered with hair, esp. soft hair; furry. Also, **pilous.** [< L *pilōs(us)* shaggy. See PILE[3], -OSE[1]] **—pi·los·i·ty** (pī los′i tē), *n.*

pi·lot (pī′lət), *n.* **1.** *Aeron.* a person qualified to operate an aircraft. **2.** a person qualified to steer ships through certain difficult waters or into or out of a harbor. **3.** the steersman of a ship. **4.** a guide or leader. **5.** *Mach.* **a.** See **pilot light. b.** a guide for positioning two adjacent parts, often consisting of a projection on one part fitting into a recess in the other. **6.** *U.S. Informal.* cowcatcher. **7.** *Television.* See **pilot film.** **—*v.t.* 8.** to steer. **9.** to guide or conduct, as through unknown places or intricate affairs. **10.** to act as pilot on, in, or over. **—*adj.* 11.** serving as an experimental or trial undertaking prior to full-scale operation or use. [earlier *pylotte* < MF *pillotte* < It *pilota*, dissimilated var. of *pedota* < MGk **pēdótēs* steersman = *pēd(á)* rudder (pl. of *pēdón* oar) + *-ōtēs* agent suffix] **—pi′lot·less,** *adj.* **—Syn. 3.** helmsman. **10.** maneuver, manage.

pi·lot·age (pī′lə tij), *n.* **1.** the act, occupation, or skill of piloting. **2.** the fee paid to a pilot for his services. **3.** the process of directing the movement of a ship or aircraft by optical or electronic observations of landmarks. [< F]

pi′lot bis′cuit, hardtack. Also called **pi′lot bread′.**

pi′lot film′, a sample film intended to attract sponsors, esp. to a contemplated television series. Also called **pilot.**

pi·lot·fish (pī′lət fish′), *n., pl.* (*esp. collectively*) **-fish,** (*esp. referring to two or more kinds or species*) **-fish·es.** a small, marine fish, *Naucrates ductor*, often found around sharks.

pi·lot·house (pī′lət hous′), *n., pl.* **-hous·es** (-hou′ziz). *Naut.* an enclosed structure or space from which a vessel may be navigated. Also called **wheelhouse.**

pi′lot lamp′, an electric light that indicates whether a given motor, circuit, etc., is operating.

pi′lot light′, **1.** Also called **pilot′ burn′er.** a small flame kept burning, as in a gas stove, to light burners. **2.** See **pilot lamp.**

pi′lot whale′. See **black whale.**

pi·lous (pī′ləs), *adj.* pilose. [< L *pilōs(us)*. See PILOSE, -OUS]

Pil·sen (pil′zən), *n.* a city in Bohemia, in W Czechoslovakia. 141,736 (1963). Czech, **Plzeň.**

Pil·sner (pilz′nər, pils′-), *n.* (*sometimes l.c.*) **1.** a pale, light lager beer. **2.** Also called **Pil′sner glass′.** a tall glass that is tapered at the bottom, used esp. for beer. Also, **Pil·sen·er** (pil′zə nər, -sə-, pilz′nər, pils′-). [< G: lit., of PILSEN; see -ER[1]]

Pil·sud·ski (pil so͞ot′skē), *n.* **Jó·zef** (yo͞o′zef), 1867–1935, Polish marshal and statesman: president 1918–22; premier 1926–28, 1930.

Pilt′down man′ (pilt′doun′), a hypothetical early modern man whose existence, inferred from skull fragments found at Piltdown in SE England, in 1912, has now been completely discredited, the fragments being of modern origin.

pil·u·lar (pil′yə lər), *adj.* of, pertaining to, or resembling pills. [< L *pilul(a)* PILULE + -AR[1]]

pil·ule (pil′yo͞ol), *n.* a small pill. [< L *pilula*]

pil·y (pī′lē), *adj.* *Heraldry.* (of the field of an escutcheon, or an ordinary) divided into a number of piles: *pily of seven, or and gules.* [PILE[2] + -Y[1]]

Pi·ma (pē′mə), *n., pl.* **-mas,** (*esp. collectively*) **-ma. 1.** a member of an Indian people of southern Arizona and northern Mexico. **2.** See **Pima cotton.** **—Pi′man,** *adj.*

Pi′ma cot′ton, a variety of fine cotton developed from Egyptian cotton, produced in the southwestern U.S. Also called **Pima.**

pi·men·to (pi men′tō), *n., pl.* **-tos. 1.** the dried fruits of a tropical American myrtaceous tree, *Pimenta officinalis;* allspice. **2.** the pimiento. [alter. of Sp *pimiento* pepper plant, masc. of *pimienta* pepper fruit < LL *pigmenta* spice, pepper, pl. (taken as sing.) of L *pigmentum* PIGMENT]

pimen′to cheese′, a processed cheese made from Neufchâtel, cream cheese, Cheddar, or other cheese, combined with pimientos. Also, **pimien′to cheese′.**

pi′ me′son, *Physics.* a meson having a mass from approximately 264 to approximately 273 times that of an electron with positive, negative, or zero charge and spin of zero. Also called **pion.**

pi·mien·to (pi myen′tō, -men′-), *n., pl.* **-tos.** a garden pepper, used as a vegetable, a relish, etc. [see PIMENTO]

pimp (pimp), *n.* **1.** a man who solicits customers for a prostitute or a brothel, usually in return for a share of the proceeds; pander; procurer. **—*v.i.* 2.** to act as a pimp. [?]

pim·per·nel (pim′pər nel′, -nəl), *n.* a primulaceous herb of the genus *Anagallis*, esp. *A. arvensis* **(scarlet pimpernel),** having scarlet, purplish, or white flowers that close at the approach of bad weather. [late ME *pympernele* < MF *pimprenelle*, nasalized var. of OF *piprenelle* < LL **pipĕrīnella* = *piper* PEPPER + *-īn-* -INE[1] + *-ella* dim. suffix; r. OE *pipeneale* < LL *pipīnella*, syncopated var. of **piperinella*]

pimp·ing (pim′piŋ), *adj.* **1.** petty; insignificant; trivial. **2.** *Dial.* weak; sickly. [?]

pim·ple (pim′pəl), *n.* *Pathol.* a small, usually inflammatory swelling or elevation of the skin; a papule or pustule. [late ME *pinple*, nasalized var. of OE **pypel* (> *pyplian* to break out in pimples) < L *papula* pimple]

pim·ply (pim′plē), *adj.*, **-pli·er, -pli·est.** having many pimples. Also, **pim·pled** (pim′pəld).

pin (pin), *n., v.,* **pinned, pin·ning.** **—*n.* 1.** a short, slender piece of metal with a point at one end and a head at the other, for fastening things together. **2.** a small, slender, often pointed piece of wood, metal, etc., used to fasten, support, or attach things. **3.** any of various forms of fasteners, ornaments, or badges consisting essentially or partly of a pointed or penetrating wire or shaft (often used in combination): *a fraternity pin; a tiepin.* **4.** a short metal rod, as a linchpin, driven through the holes of adjacent parts, as a hub and an axle, to keep them together. **5.** a short cylindrical rod or tube, as a wristpin or crankpin, joining two parts so as to permit them to move in one plane relative to each other. **6.** the part of a cylindrical key stem that enters a lock. **7.** a clothespin. **8.** a hairpin. **9.** See **rolling pin. 10.** a peg, nail, or stud marking the center of a target. **11.** *Bowling.* one of the rounded wooden clubs set up as the target in tenpins, duckpins, etc. **12.** *Golf.* the flagstaff that identifies a hole. **13.** Usually, **pins.** *Informal.* the legs. **14.** *Music.* peg (def. 2). **15.** *Wrestling.* a fall. **16.** *Naut.* See **belaying pin. 17.** a very small amount; a trifle. **—*v.t.* 18.** to fasten or attach with or as with a pin or pins. **19.** to hold fast in a spot or position. **20.** to give one's fraternity pin to (a girl) as a pledge of one's fondness or attachment. **21.** *Wrestling.* to obtain a fall over one's opponent. **22. pin down, a.** to bind or hold to a course of action, a promise, etc. **b.** to define with clarity and precision: *to pin down a vague intuition.* **23. pin something on someone,** *Slang.* to blame someone for something on the basis of real or manufactured evidence. [ME *pinne*, OE *pinn* peg; c. D *pin*, G *Pinne*, Icel *pinni;* ? akin to MIr *benn* (for **bend*), now *beann* peak, steeple, gable, etc.]

pi·na·ceous (pi nā′shəs), *adj.* belonging to the *Pinaceae*, or pine family of trees and shrubs, comprising the pine, spruce, fir, etc. [< NL *Pīnāce(ae)* (see PINE[1], -ACEAE) + -OUS]

pi′ña cloth′ (pēn′yə), a fine, sheer fabric of pineapple-leaf fiber, used esp. for lingerie. [*piña* < Sp: pineapple]

pin·a·fore (pin′ə fōr′, -fôr′), *n.* a child's apron, usually one large enough to cover most of the dress.

pi·nas·ter (pī nas′tər, pi-), *n.* a pine, *Pinus Pinaster,* of southern Europe, having the cones arranged around the branches in radiating clusters. [< L: wild pine]

pi·ña·ta (pēn yä′tə, pin yä′-; *Sp.* pē nyä′tä), *n., pl.* **-tas** (-təz; *Sp.* -täs). (in Mexico and Central America) a gaily decorated crock or papier-mâché figure filled with toys, candy, etc., and suspended from above, esp. for birthday parties and Christmas festivities, so that blindfolded children may break it or knock it down with sticks and scramble for the contents. [< Sp: lit., pot]

pin·ball (pin′bôl′), *n.* any of various games in which a ball, driven by a spring to the top of a sloping board, rolls down against pins or bumpers and through channels which electrically record the score.

pin′ball machine′, the machine on which pinball is played.

pin′ boy′, a person stationed in the sunken area of a bowling alley behind the pins who arranges the pins and returns balls to the bowlers.

pince-nez (pans′nā′, pins′-; *Fr.* pans nā′), *n., pl.* **pince-nez** (pans′nāz′, pins′-; *Fr.* pans nā′). a pair of eyeglasses held on the face by a spring that pinches the nose. [< F: lit., pinch-nose]

pin·cers (pin′sərz), *n.* (*usually construed as pl.*) **1.** a gripping tool consisting of two pivoted limbs forming a pair of jaws and a pair of handles (usually used with *pair of*). **2.** *Zool.* a grasping organ or pair of organs resembling this. [ME *pinsers,* earlier *pynceours,* pl. of **pinceour* < AF *pince(r)* (to) PINCH + *-our* -OR²]

pinch (pinch), *v.t.* **1.** to compress between the finger and thumb, the teeth, the jaws of an instrument, or the like. **2.** to cramp within narrow bounds or quarters. **3.** to render (the face, body, etc.) unnaturally thin and drawn, as pain or distress does. **4.** to affect with discomfort, distress, or straitened circumstances, as cold, hunger, or need does. **5.** to stint (a person, family, etc.) in allowance of money, food, or the like. **6.** to hamper or inconvenience by lack of something specified. **7.** *Informal.* to stint the supply or amount of (a thing). **8.** to put a pinch or small quantity of (a powder, spice, etc.) into something. **9.** *Slang.* to steal. **10.** *Informal.* to arrest. **11.** *Naut.* to sail (a vessel) so close to the wind that her sails shake slightly and her speed is reduced. —*v.i.* **12.** to exert a sharp or painful compressing force: *This shoe pinches.* **13.** to cause sharp discomfort or distress. **14.** to economize unduly; stint oneself. **15. pinch pennies,** to stint on or be frugal with expenditures; economize. —*n.* **16.** the act of pinching; nip; squeeze. **17.** the amount of anything that can be taken up between the finger and thumb. **18.** a very small quantity of anything. **19.** sharp or painful stress, as of hunger, need, or any trying circumstances. **20.** a situation or time of special stress; an emergency. [ME *pinch(en)* < AF **pincher* (OF *pincier,* Sp *pinchar*) < LL **pīnctiāre,* b. **pīccāre* to prick and *punctiāre* to prick] —**pinch′a·ble,** *adj.*

pinch′ bar′, a kind of crowbar or lever with a projection that serves as a fulcrum. Also called **ripping bar, wrecking bar.**

pinch·beck (pinch′bek′), *n.* **1.** an alloy of copper and zinc, used in imitation of gold. **2.** something sham or counterfeit. —*adj.* **3.** made of pinchbeck. **4.** sham or counterfeit. [named after Christopher *Pinchbeck* (d. 1732), English watchmaker and its inventor]

pinch·bot·tle (pinch′bot′əl), *n.* a bottle with concave sides, as for containing liquor.

pinch·cock (pinch′kok′), *n.* a clamp for compressing a flexible pipe, as a rubber tube, in order to regulate or stop the flow of a fluid.

pin·check (pin′chek′), *n.* **1.** a very small check woven into fabric. **2.** a strong cotton cloth with a design of horizontal and vertical white dots on a blue ground, used esp. for workclothes.

pinch′ effect′, *Physics.* the tendency of an electric conductor or stream of charged particles to constrict, caused by the action of a magnetic field produced by a flow of electricity.

pinch·er (pin′chər), *n.* **1.** a person or thing that pinches. **2. pinchers,** pincers. [late ME *pynchar* niggard]

pinch-hit (pinch′hit′), *v.,* **-hit, -hit·ting.** —*v.i.* **1.** *Baseball.* to substitute at bat for a teammate. **2.** to substitute for someone. —*v.t.* **3.** to get, or make (a hit) in pinch-hitting. [back formation from PINCH HITTER] —**pinch′ hit′ter.**

Pin·chot (pin′shō), *n.* **Gifford,** 1863–1946, U.S. political leader, forester, and teacher.

pinch·pen·ny (pinch′pen′ē), *n., pl.* **-nies,** *adj.* —*n.* **1.** a miser or niggard. —*adj.* **2.** stingy; miserly. [ME]

Pinck·ney (pingk′nē), *n.* **1. Charles Cotes·worth** (kōts′-wûrth), 1746–1825, American patriot and statesman. **2.** his brother, **Thomas,** 1750–1828, American patriot and statesman.

pin′ curl′, a dampened curl secured by a clip or hairpin.

pin·cush·ion (pin′ko͝osh′ən), *n.* a small cushion into which pins are stuck until needed.

Pin·dar (pin′dər), *n.* 522?–443? B.C., Greek poet.

Pin·dar·ic (pin dar′ik), *adj.* **1.** of, pertaining to, or in the style of Pindar. **2.** of elaborate form and metrical structure, as an ode. —*n.* **3.** See **Pindaric ode.** [< L *Pindaric(us)* < Gk *Pindarikós*]

Pindar′ic ode′, *Pros.* an ode consisting of several triple units, each being composed of a strophe and an antistrophe of identical form followed by a contrasting epode. Also called **regular ode.**

pind·ling (pind′ling), *adj.* *Dial.* puny; sickly. [PINE² + -LING, modeled on *dwindling*]

Pin·dus (pin′dəs), *n.* a mountain range in central Greece. Highest peak, 7665 ft.

pine¹ (pīn), *n.* **1.** any evergreen, coniferous tree of the genus *Pinus,* having long, needle-shaped leaves, various species of which yield timber, turpentine, tar, pitch, etc. **2.** any of various similar coniferous trees. **3.** the wood of the pine tree. **4.** *Informal.* the pineapple. [ME; OE *pīn* < L *pīn(us)*] —**pine′like′,** *adj.*

pine² (pīn), *v.,* **pined, pin·ing,** *n.* —*v.i.* **1.** to yearn deeply; suffer with longing; long painfully (often fol. by *for*): *to pine for one's home and family.* **2.** to fail gradually in health or vitality from grief, regret, or longing (often fol. by *away*). **3.** *Archaic.* to be discontented; fret. —*v.t.* **4.** *Archaic.* to suffer grief or regret over. —*n.* **5.** *Archaic.* painful longing. [ME; OE *pīn(ian)* (to) torture < *pīn* torture < LL *pēna,* var. of L *poena* punishment. See PAIN] —**Syn. 2.** languish.

pin·e·al (pin′ē əl), *adj.* **1.** resembling a pine cone in shape. **2.** of or pertaining to the pineal body. [< medical L *pīneāl(is)* = L *pīne(a)* pine cone, n. use of fem. of *pīneus* of a pine tree (*pīn(us)* PINE¹ + *-eus* -EOUS) + *-ālis* -AL¹]

pin′eal appara′tus, a median outgrowth of the roof of the diencephalon in vertebrates which in some develops into the pineal eye and in others into the pineal body.

pin′eal bod′y, a body of unknown function present in the brain of all vertebrates having a cranium, believed to be a vestigial sense organ. Also called **pin′eal gland′.**

pin′eal eye′, an eyelike structure that develops from the pineal apparatus in certain cold-blooded vertebrates.

pine·ap·ple (pīn′ap′əl), *n.* **1.** the edible, juicy, collective fruit of a tropical, bromeliaceous plant, *Ananas comosus,* that develops from a spike or head of flowers and is surmounted by a crown of leaves. **2.** the plant itself, having a short stem and rigid, spiny-margined, recurved leaves. **3.** *Mil. Slang.* a fragmentation hand grenade. [ME *pinappel* pine cone]

Pineapple, *Ananas comosus*

Pine′ Bluff′, a city in central Arkansas, on the Arkansas River. 57,389 (1970).

pine′ cone′, the cone or strobile of a pine tree.

pine·drops (pīn′drops′), *n., pl.* **-drops. 1.** a slender, leafless, North American, ericaceous herb, *Pterospora andromedea,* having nodding white flowers, found growing under pines. **2.** beechdrops.

Pi·nel (pē nel′), *n.* **Phil·lippe** (fē lēp′), 1745–1826, French physician: reformer in treatment and care of mentally ill.

pi·nene (pī′nēn), *n.* *Chem.* a liquid terpene, $C_{10}H_{16}$, the principal constituent of oil of turpentine: used chiefly in the manufacture of camphor.

pine′ nee′dle, the needlelike leaf of a pine tree.

Pi·ne·ro (pə nēr′ō, -nâr′ō), *n.* **Sir Arthur Wing,** 1855–1934, English playwright and actor.

pin·er·y (pī′nə rē), *n., pl.* **-er·ies. 1.** a place in which pineapples are grown. **2.** a forest or grove of pine trees.

Pines (pīnz), *n.* **Isle of,** an island in the Caribbean, south of and belonging to Cuba. 1182 sq. mi.

pine·sap (pīn′sap′), *n.* either of two parasitic or saprophytic herbs of the genus *Monotropa* of eastern North America. Cf. **Indian pipe.**

pine′ sis′kin, a small, North American finch, *Spinus pinus,* found in coniferous forests, having yellow markings on the wings and tail.

pine′ tar′, a very viscid, blackish-brown liquid having an odor resembling that of turpentine, obtained by the destructive distillation of pine wood, used externally for skin infections and internally as an expectorant.

Pine′ Tree′ State′, Maine (used as a nickname).

pi·ne·tum (pī nē′təm), *n., pl.* **-ta** (-tə). an arboretum of pines and coniferous trees. [< L: a pine wood = *pīn(us)* PINE¹ + *-ētum* collective suffix of place]

pin·y (pī′nē), *adj.,* **pin·i·er, pin·i·est.** piny.

pin·feath·er (pin′feth′ər), *n.* *Ornith.* **1.** an undeveloped feather, before the web portions have expanded. **2.** a feather just coming through the skin.

pin·fish (pin′fish′), *n., pl.* **-fish·es,** (*esp. collectively*) **-fish.** a small fish, *Lagodon rhomboides,* of the porgy family, found in the bays of the South Atlantic and Gulf coasts of the U.S.

pin·fold (pin′fōld′), *n.* **1.** a pound for stray animals. **2.** a fold, as for sheep or cattle. **3.** a place of confinement or restraint. —*v.t.* **4.** to confine in or as in a pinfold. [late ME *pynfold* for **pindfold,* OE *pynd(an)* (to) impound (< *pund* POUND³) + *f(e)ald* FOLD²; r. ME *po(u)n(d)fold(e),* late OE *pundfald*]

ping (ping), *v.i.* **1.** to produce a sharp sound like that of a bullet striking a hard object, as a sheet of metal. —*n.* **2.** a pinging sound. [imit.]

Ping-Pong (ping′pong′), *n.* *Trademark.* See **table tennis.**

pin·guid (ping′gwid), *adj.* fat; oily; greasy. [< L *pingu(is)* fat (c. Gk *pīōn*) + -ID⁴] —**pin·guid′i·ty,** *n.*

pin·head (pin′hed′), *n.* **1.** the head of a pin. **2.** something small or insignificant. **3.** *Slang.* a stupid person.

pin·head·ed (pin′hed′id), *adj.* stupid or foolish. —**pin′-head′ed·ness,** *n.*

pin·hole (pin′hōl′), *n.* a small hole made by or as by a pin: *The print was marred by pinholes.*

pin·ion¹ (pin′yən), *n.* *Mach.* **1.** a gear with a small number of teeth, esp. one engaging with a rack or larger gear. **2.** a shaft or spindle cut with teeth engaging with a gear. [< F *pignon* cogwheel, MF *peignon* < *peigne* comb., var. of *pigne* < L *pectin-* (s. of *pecten*) comb; see PECTEN] —**pin′-ion·less,** *adj.* —**pin′ion·like′,** *adj.*

pin·ion² (pin′yən), *n.* **1.** the distal or terminal segment of the wing of a bird consisting of the carpus, metacarpus, and phalanges. **2.** the wing of a bird. **3.** a feather. **4.** the flight feathers collectively. —*v.t.* **5.** to cut off the pinion of (a wing) or bind (the wings), as in order to prevent a bird from flying. **6.** to disable or restrain (a bird) in such a manner. **7.** to bind (a person's arms or hands) so as to deprive him of the use of them. **8.** to disable (someone) in such a manner; shackle. **9.** to bind or hold fast, as to a thing. [late ME *pynyon* < MF *pignon* wing, pinion < VL **pinniōn* (s. of *pinniō*) < L *pinna* feather, wing, fin]

pin·ite (pin′īt, pī′nīt), *n.* a micalike mineral, essentially a hydrous silicate of aluminum and potassium. [< G *Pinit,* named after *Pini,* mine in Germany; see -ITE¹]

pink¹ (pingk), *n.* **1.** a color varying from light crimson to pale reddish purple. **2.** any of several caryophyllaceous plants of the genus *Dianthus,* as the clove pink or carnation. **3.** a carnation. **4.** the highest type or example of excellence. **5.** the highest form or degree: *in the pink of condition.* **6.** (*often cap.*) Also, **pinko.** *Disparaging.* a person with mildly left-wing political opinions. **7. pinks,** *Fox Hunting.* See **pink coat.** —*adj.* **8.** of the color pink: *pink marble.* **9.** *Disparaging.* holding leftist views, esp. in politics. [?] —**pink′ness,** *n.*

pink[2] (pingk), *v.t.* **1.** to pierce with a rapier or the like; stab. **2.** to finish at the edge with a scalloped, notched, or other ornamental pattern. **3.** to punch (cloth, leather, etc.) with small holes or figures for ornament. **4.** *Chiefly Brit. Dial.* to adorn or ornament, esp. with scalloped edges or a punched-out pattern. [ME *pynke(n)* (to) prick < OE *pinca* point < *pinn* PIN]

pink[3] (pingk), *n.* a kind of ship with a narrow overhanging stern. Also, **pinky.** [late ME *pynk* < MD *pinke* fishing boat]

pink′ boll′worm, the larva of a gelechiid moth, *Pectinophora gossypiella,* that feeds on the seeds of the bolls of cotton and was introduced into cotton-growing regions of the world from Asia. Also called **bollworm.**

pink′ coat′, *Fox Hunting.* the coat, usually scarlet, worn by male hunters. Also called **pinks.**

Pink·er·ton (ping′kər tən), *n.* **Allan,** 1819–84, U.S. detective, born in Scotland.

pink·eye (pingk′ī′), *n.* *Pathol.* a contagious, epidemic form of acute conjunctivitis occurring in man and certain animals: so called from the color of the inflamed eye.

Pin·kiang (*Chin.* bin′gyäng′), *n.* Harbin.

pink·ie (ping′kē), *n.* *Informal.* the little finger. Also, **pinky.** [< D *pinkje,* dim. of *pink* little finger]

pink′ing shears′, shears having notched blades, for pinking fabric.

pink·ish (ping′kish), *adj.* somewhat pink: *the pinkish glow of sunset.*

pink′ la′dy, a cocktail made with gin, grenadine, and egg white, shaken and strained before serving.

pink·o (ping′kō), *n., pl.* **-os, -oes.** pink[1] (def. 6).

pink′ rhododen′dron, a rhododendron, *Rhododendron macrophyllum,* of the western coast of the U.S.: the state flower of Washington. Also called **California rosebay.**

pink·root (pingk′ro͞ot′, -ro͝ot′), *n.* **1.** the root of any of various loganiaceous plants of the genus *Spigelia,* esp. that of *S. marilandica* of the U.S., which is used as a vermifuge. **2.** any of these plants.

Pink·ster (pingk′stər), *n.* *U.S. Dial.* Whitsuntide. Also, **Pinxter.** [< D: Easter << Gk (by alter.) *pentēkostē* PENTECOST]

pink′ster flow′er. See **pinxter flower.**

pink′ stern′, *Naut.* a sharp stern having a narrow, overhanging, raking transom. —**pink′-sterned′,** *adj.*

pink·y[1] (ping′kē), *n., pl.* **pink·ies.** pink[3]. [< D *pinkje,* dim. of *pink* PINK[3]]

pink·y[2] (ping′kē), *n., pl.* **pink·ies.** pinkie.

pin′ mark′, the circular indentation on the upper part of a type body, made by the pin that ejects the type from the caster.

pin′ mon′ey, **1.** any small sum set aside for minor expenditures. **2.** an allowance of money given by a husband to his wife for her personal expenditures.

pin·na (pin′ə), *n., pl.* **pin·nae** (pin′ē), **pin·nas.** **1.** *Bot.* one of the primary divisions of a pinnate leaf. **2.** *Zool.* **a.** a feather, wing, or winglike part. **b.** a fin or flipper. **3.** *Anat.* auricle (def. 1a). [< L: feather, wing, fin] —**pin′nal,** *adj.*

pin·nace (pin′is), *n.* **1.** a light sailing vessel, esp. one formerly used in attendance on a larger vessel. **2.** any of various kinds of ships' boats. [< MF *pinace* < OSp *pinaza,* lit., something made of *pino* PINE[1]]

pin·na·cle (pin′ə kəl), *n., v.,* **-cled, -cling.** —*n.* **1.** a lofty peak. **2.** the highest or culminating point, as of success, power, or fame. **3.** any pointed, towering part or formation, as of rock. **4.** *Archit.* a relatively small, upright structure, commonly terminating in a gable, a pyramid, or a cone, rising above the roof or coping of a building, or capping a tower, buttress, or other projecting architectural member. —*v.t.* **5.** to place on or as on a pinnacle. **6.** to form a pinnacle on; crown. [ME *pinacle* < MF < LL *pinnācul(um),* dim. of *pinna* battlement, pinnacle; see -CULE] —**Syn. 2.** apex, acme, summit, zenith. **3.** needle.

pin·nate (pin′āt, -it), *adj.* **1.** resembling a feather, as in construction or arrangement; having parts arranged on each side of a common axis. **2.** *Bot.* (of a leaf) having leaflets or primary divisions arranged on each side of a common petiole. Also, **pin′nat·ed.** [< L *pinnāt(us)* feathered, winged. See PINNA, -ATE[1]] —**pin′nate·ly, pin′nat·ed·ly,** *adv.*

Pinnate leaf

pinnati-, a combining form of **pinnate:** *pinnatipartite.* [repr. L *pinnātus;* see -I-]

pin·nat·i·fid (pi nat′ə fid), *adj.* *Bot.* (of a leaf) pinnately cleft, with clefts reaching halfway or more to the midrib. [< NL *pinnātifid(us)*]

pin·nat·i·lo·bate (pi nat′əlō′bāt), *adj.* *Bot.* (of a leaf) pinnately lobed, with the divisions extending less than halfway to the midrib.

pin·nat·i·ped (pi nat′ə ped′), *adj.* *Ornith.* having lobate feet. [< NL *pinnātiped-* (s. of *pinnātipēs*)]

pin·nat·i·sect (pi nat′i sekt′), *adj.* *Bot.* (of a leaf) divided in a pinnate manner.

pin·ner (pin′ər), *n.* **1.** a person or thing that pins. **2.** a headdress with a long hanging flap pinned on at each side.

pin·ni·grade (pin′ə grād′), *adj.* **1.** moving by means of finlike parts or flippers, as the seals and walruses. —*n.* **2.** a pinnigrade animal. [< NL *pinnigrad(us)*]

pin·ni·ped (pin′ə ped′), *adj.* **1.** belonging to the *Pinnipedia,* a suborder of carnivores with limbs adapted to an aquatic life, including the seals and walruses. —*n.* **2.** a pinniped animal. Also, **pin·ni·pe·di·an** (pin′ə pē′dē ən). [< NL *pinniped-* (s. of *pinnipēs*)]

pin·nu·la (pin′yə lə), *n., pl.* **-lae** (-lē′). **1.** a pinnule. **2.** a barb of a feather. [< L, dim. of *pinna* PINNA; see -ULE]

pin·nu·late (pin′yə lāt′), *adj.* having pinnules. Also, **pin′nu·lat′ed.**

pin·nule (pin′yo͞ol), *n.* **1.** *Zool.* **a.** a part or organ resembling a barb of a feather, a fin, or the like. **b.** a finlet. **2.** *Bot.* a secondary pinna, one of the pinnately disposed divisions of a bipinnate leaf. [see PINNULA] —**pin·nu·lar** (pin′yə lər), *adj.*

Pi·no·chet U·gar·te (pē′nô chet′ o͞o gär′te), **Au·gus·to** (ou go͞os′tô), born 1915, Chilean army general and political leader: president since 1973.

pi·noch·le (pē′nuk əl, -nok-), *n.* **1.** a card game played by two, three, or four persons, with a 48-card deck. **2.** a meld of the queen of spades and the jack of diamonds in this game. Also, **pi′noc·le.** [?]

pi·no·le (pi nō′lē; *Sp.* pē nô′le), *n.* corn or wheat, dried, ground, and sweetened, usually with the flour of mesquite beans. [< AmerSp < Nahuatl *pinolli*]

pi·ñon (pin′yən, pēn′yōn; *Sp.* pē nyôn′), *n., pl.* **pi·ñons,** *Sp.* **pi·ño·nes** (pē nyô′nes). any of various pines, esp. of the southern Rocky Mountain region, bearing large edible seeds. [< Sp < *piña* pine cone]

Pi·not (pē nō′), *n.* any of several varieties of purple or white vinifera grapes yielding a red (**Pinot noir**) or white (**Pinot blanc**) wine. [< F = *pine* pine cone + *-ot* n. suffix]

Pi·not blanc (pē′nō bläɴ′, pē nō′; *Fr.* pē nō bläɴ′). See under **Pinot.**

Pi·not noir (pē′nō nwär′, pē nō′; *Fr.* pē nō NWAR′). See under **Pinot.**

pin·point (pin′point′), *n.* **1.** the point of a pin. **2.** a trifle; pinhead. —*v.t.* **3.** to locate or describe exactly: *to pinpoint the problem.* —*adj.* **4.** exact; precise.

pin·prick (pin′prik′), *n.* any minute puncture made by or as by a pin.

pin′ rail′, *Naut.* a strong rail at the side of the deck of a vessel, for holding the pins to which some of the running rigging is belayed. Cf. **fife rail.**

pins′ and nee′dles, **1.** a tingly, prickly sensation in a limb that is recovering from numbness. **2. on pins and needles,** nervous or anxious, esp. in anticipation of something.

pin′ seal′, leather made of the skin of young seals.

pin·set·ter (pin′set′ər), *n.* *Bowling.* a mechanical apparatus that positions the pins and removes struck ones. Also called **pin·spot·ter** (pin′spot′ər).

Pinsk (pinsk; *Russ.* pēnsk), *n.* a city in SW Byelorussia, in the W Soviet Union in Europe: formerly in Poland. 39,000 (1959).

pin′ stripe′, **1.** a very thin stripe, esp. in fabrics. **2.** a fabric or garment having such stripes.

pint (pīnt), *n.* a liquid and also dry measure of capacity, equal to one half of a liquid and dry quart respectively. *Abbr.:* pt, pt. [ME *pynte* < MFlem: lit., plug; c. OFris, MLG *pint* penis. See PINTLE]

pin·ta (pin′tə; *Sp.* pēn′tä), *n.* *Pathol.* a nonvenereal treponematosis occurring chiefly in Central and South America, characterized by spots of various colors on the skin. [< AmerSp, special use of Sp *pinta* spot < VL **pincta,* fem. of **pinctus,* nasalized var. of L *pīctus,* ptp. of *pingere* to paint]

Pin·ta (pin′tə; *Sp.* pēn′tä), *n.* one of the three ships under charge of Columbus when he made his first voyage to America in 1492.

pin·ta·do (pin tä′dō), *n., pl.* **-dos, -does.** the cero, *Scomberomorus regalis.* Also, **pin·ta·da** (pin tä′də). [< Pg, ptp. of *pintar* to paint < VL **pinctus* painted. See PINTA]

pin·tail (pin′tāl′), *n., pl.* **-tails,** (*esp. collectively*) **-tail.** a long-necked river duck, *Anas acuta,* of the Old and New Worlds, having long narrow middle tail feathers.

pin-tailed (pin′tāld′), *adj.* *Ornith.* **1.** having a tapered tail with long, pointed central feathers. **2.** having the feathers of the tail stiff, narrow, and pointed.

Pintle

Pin·ter (pin′tər), *n.* **Harold,** born 1930, English playwright.

pin·tle (pin′təl), *n.* **1.** a pin or bolt, esp. one on which something turns, as the gudgeon of a hinge. **2.** a pin, bolt, or hook by which a gun or the like is attached to the rear of a towing vehicle. [ME, OE *pintel* penis; c. ODan *pintel;* see PINT]

pin·to (pin′tō, pēn′-), *adj., n., pl.* **-tos.** —*adj.* **1.** piebald; mottled; spotted: *a pinto horse.* —*n.* **2.** *Western U.S.* a pinto horse. **3.** See **pinto bean.** [< AmerSp (obs. Sp) < VL **pinctus* painted; see PINTA]

pin′to bean′, *Western U.S.* a variety of the common bean, *Phaseolus vulgaris,* having mottled or spotted seeds.

pint-size (pīnt′sīz′), *adj.* *Informal.* comparatively small in size. Also, **pint′-sized′.**

pin·up (pin′up′), *n.* *Informal.* **1.** a picture that may be pinned up on a wall, usually of an attractive girl. **2.** a girl in such a picture. —*adj.* **3.** of, pertaining to, or appearing in a pinup: *a pinup girl.* **4.** designed or suitable for hanging or fastening on a wall: *a pinup lamp.* Also, **pin′-up′.**

pin·weed (pin′wēd′), *n.* any cistaceous plant of the genus *Lechea,* having slender stems and narrow leaves.

pin·wheel (pin′hwēl′, -wēl′), *n.* **1.** a child's toy consisting of a wheel with vanes which is loosely attached by a pin to a stick, designed to revolve, and sometimes give off sparks, when turned or when blown by the wind. **2.** a kind of firework supported on a pin upon which it revolves when ignited, giving a dazzling display of light. Also, **pin′ wheel′.**

pin·work (pin′wûrk′), *n.* (in the embroidery of needlepoint lace) crescent-shaped stitches raised from the surface of the design.

pin·worm (pin′wûrm′), *n.* a small nematode worm, *Enterobius vermicularis,* infesting the intestine and migrating to the rectum and anus, esp. in children.

pin′ wrench′, a wrench having a pin for insertion into the heads of certain bolts to drive them. Cf. **spanner** (def. 2).

pinx., pinxit.

pinx·it (pingk′sit), *v.* *Latin.* he (or she) painted (it): formerly used on paintings as part of the artist's signature.

Pinx·ter (pingk′stər), *n.* Pinkster.

pinx′ter flow′er, a wild azalea, *Rhododendron nudiflorum* (*Azalea nudiflora*), of the U.S., having pink or purplish flowers. Also, **pinkster flower.**

pin·y (pī′nē), *adj.,* **pin·i·er, pin·i·est.** **1.** abounding in, covered with, or consisting of pine trees. **2.** pertaining to or suggestive of pine trees: *a piny fragrance.* Also, **piney.**

Pin·yin (pin′yin′), *n.* the official system for transliterating Chinese into the Roman alphabet, adopted by the People's Republic of China in 1979. Also called **Pin′yin′ sys′tem.** [< Chin *pinyin* lit., phonetic sound]

Pin·zón (pēn thôn′), *n.* **Mar·tín A·lon·zo** (mär tēn′ ä lôn′thô), c1440–93?, and his brother **Vi·cen·te Yá·ñez** (bē then′te yä′nyeth), c1460–1524?, Spanish navigators with Christopher Columbus.

pi·on (pī′on), *n. Physics.* See **pi meson.** [by shortening]

pi·o·neer (pī′ə nēr′), *n.* **1.** one of those who first enter or settle a region, thus opening it for occupation and development by others. **2.** one of those who are first or earliest in any field of inquiry, enterprise, or progress. **3.** one of a body of foot soldiers detailed to make roads, dig entrenchments, etc., in advance of the main body. **4.** *Ecol.* a plant or animal that successfully invades and becomes established in a bare area. **5.** (*cap.*) *U.S.* one of a series of unmanned lunar probes launched by a Delta booster. **—***v.i.* **6.** to act as a pioneer. **—***v.t.* **7.** to be the first to open or prepare (a way, settlement, etc.). **8.** to take part in the beginnings of; initiate: *to pioneer an aid program.* **9.** to lead the way for (a group); guide. **—***adj.* **10.** being the earliest, original, first of a particular kind, etc.: *a pioneer method of adult education.* **11.** of, pertaining to, or characteristic of a pioneer or pioneers. **12.** being a pioneer: *a pioneer fur trader.* [< MF *pionier,* OF *peonier* foot soldier. See PEON, -EER]

pi·ous (pī′əs), *adj.* **1.** having or showing a dutiful spirit of reverence for God, or an earnest wish to fulfill religious obligations. **2.** practiced or used with real or pretended religious motives, or for some ostensibly good object: *a pious deception.* **3.** characterized by a hypocritical concern with virtue; sanctimonious. **4.** sacred rather than secular: *pious literature.* **5.** *Archaic.* having or showing due respect or regard for parents or others. [< L *pius,* akin to *piāre* to propitiate] **—pi′ous·ly,** *adv.* **—pi′ous·ness,** *n.* **—Syn. 1.** devout, godly, reverent. See **religious.**

pip[1] (pip), *n.* **1.** one of the spots on dice, playing cards, or dominoes. **2.** one of the small segments on the surface of a pineapple. **3.** *Hort.* an individual rootstock of a plant, esp. of the lily of the valley. [earlier *peep* < ?]

pip[2] (pip), *n.* **1.** *Vet. Pathol.* a contagious disease of birds, esp. poultry, characterized by the secretion of a thick mucus in the mouth and throat. **2.** *Facetious.* any minor or unspecified ailment in a person. [ME *pippe* < MD < VL **pipita* for L *pītuīta* phlegm, pip]

pip[3] (pip), *n.* **1.** a small seed, esp. of a fleshy fruit, as an apple or orange. **2.** *Slang.* someone or something wonderful. [short for PIPPIN]

pip[4] (pip), *v.,* **pipped, pip·ping.** **—***v.i.* **1.** to peep or chirp. **2.** (of a young bird) to break out from the shell. **—***v.t.* **3.** to crack or chip a hole through (the shell), as a young bird. [var. of PEEP[2]]

pip[5] (pip), *n. Electronics.* an image, usually a spot of light, on a radarscope, produced by a radar wave reflected by an object. [imit.]

pi-pa (pē′pä′), *n.* a short-necked fretted lute of Chinese origin, formerly having four plucked strings but now usually six. Also, **p'i-p'a.** [< Chin]

pip·age (pī′pij), *n.* **1.** conveyance, as of water, gas, or oil, by means of pipes. **2.** the pipes so used. **3.** the sum charged for the conveyance.

pi·pal (pī′pəl), *n.* a fig tree, *Ficus religiosa,* of India, somewhat resembling the banyan. Also, **peepul.** [< Hindi *pīpal* < Skt *pippala*]

pipe[1] (pīp), *n., v.,* **piped, pip·ing.** **—***n.* **1.** a hollow cylinder of metal, wood, or other material, used for the conveyance of water, gas, steam, etc. **2.** any of various tubular or cylindrical formations, as an eruptive passage of a volcano or geyser. **3.** a tube of wood, clay, hard rubber, or other material, with a small bowl at one end, for smoking tobacco, opium, etc. **4.** a pipeful. **5.** *Music.* **a.** a musical wind instrument consisting of a single tube of wood or other material, as a flute, clarinet, or oboe. **b.** one of the tubes from which the tones of an organ are produced. **c.** a small end-blown flute played with one hand while the other beats a small drum. **6.** *Naut.* **a.** the sound of a boatswain's pipe. **b.** See **boatswain's pipe.** **7.** the call or utterance of a bird, frog, etc. **8. pipes,** *Informal.* the human vocal cords or the voice, esp. as used in singing. **9.** Usually, **pipes. a.** *Music.* bagpipe. **b.** a set of flutes, as panpipes. **c.** *Informal.* a tubular organ or passage of a human or animal body. **10.** *Mining.* a cylindrical vein or body of ore. **11.** *Bot.* the stem of a plant. **—***v.i.* **12.** to play on a pipe. **13.** *Naut.* to signal, as with a boatswain's pipe. **14.** to speak in a high-pitched or piercing tone. **15.** to make or utter a shrill sound like that of a pipe. **16.** *Mining.* to excavate a cylindrical hole. **17.** *Metall.* (of an ingot or the like) to acquire a cylindrical or conical depression at the top when cooling after being cast. **—***v.t.* **18.** to convey by or as by a pipe or pipes. **19.** to supply with pipes. **20.** to play (music) on a pipe or pipes. **21.** to summon, order, etc., by sounding the boatswain's pipe or whistle. **22.** to bring, lead, etc., by or as by playing on a pipe: *to pipe dancers.* **23.** to utter in a shrill tone: *to pipe a command.* **24.** to trim or finish with piping, as an article of clothing. **25. pipe down,** *Slang.* to stop talking; be quiet. **26. pipe up, a.** to begin to sing or to play (a musical instrument). **b.** to speak up; assert oneself. [ME *pipe(n),* OE *pīpian* (v.), ME, OE *pīpe* (n.) (c. D *pijp*) < VL **pīpa,* back formation from L *pīpāre* to chirp] **—pipe′less,** *adj.* **—pipe′like′,** *adj.*

pipe[2] (pīp), *n.* **1.** any large cask, esp. for wine or oil. **2.** such a cask as a measure of capacity for wine or other liquid, equal to 4 barrels, 2 hogsheads, or half a tun, and containing 126 wine gallons. **3.** such a cask with its contents. [ME < MF, ult. same as PIPE[1]]

pipe′ bomb′, a small homemade bomb, usually contained in a metal pipe.

pipe′ clay′, a fine, extremely plastic, white clay used for making tobacco pipes, whitening parts of military or other dress, and the like.

pipe′ dream′, *Informal.* a baseless fancy: *Her plans for a movie career had all been a pipe dream.*

pipe·fish (pīp′fish′), *n., pl.* (*esp. collectively*) **-fish,** (*esp. referring to two or more kinds or species*) **-fish·es.** any elongated, marine fish of the family *Syngnathidae,* having a tubular snout and covered with bony plates.

pipe·ful (pīp′fo͝ol), *n., pl.* **-fuls.** a quantity sufficient to fill the bowl of a pipe.

pipe′ line′, **1.** a conduit of pipe for the transportation of petroleum, petroleum products, natural gas, water, etc. **2.** a channel of information, esp. one which is direct, privileged, or confidential. Also, **pipe′line′,** *n.*

pipe′ of peace′, a calumet; peace pipe.

pipe′ or′gan, organ (def. 1).

pip·er (pī′pər), *n.* **1.** a person who plays on a pipe. **2.** a bagpiper. **3. pay the piper, a.** to pay the cost of or take responsibility for. **b.** to bear the unfavorable consequences of one's actions. [ME; OE *pīpere*]

pip·er·a·ceous (pip′ə rā′shəs, pī′pə-), *adj.* belonging to the *Piperaceae,* or pepper family of plants, which comprise the spice-bearing pepper, *Piper nigrum,* the betel and cubeb plants, etc. [< L *piper* pepper + -ACEOUS]

pipe-rack (pīp′rak′), *adj. Informal.* offering services or goods at low cost because of avoidance of expensive interior decoration: *a plain pipe-rack store for men's clothing.*

pi·per·a·zine (pi per′ə zēn′, -zin, pī-, pip′ər ə-), *n. Chem.* **1.** a ring compound, $C_4H_{10}N_2$, used chiefly in veterinary medicine as an anthelmintic, and as an insecticide. **2.** any derivative of this compound. [< L *piper* pepper + AZINE]

pi·per·i·dine (pi per′i dēn′, -din, pī-, pip′ər i-), *n. Chem.* a liquid, $C_5H_{11}N$, obtained from the alkaloid piperine or from pyridine: used chiefly as a solvent. [< L *piper* pepper + -ID[3] + -INE[1]]

pip·er·ine (pip′ə rēn′, -ər in), *n. Chem.* a white alkaloid, $C_{17}H_{19}NO_3$, obtained from pepper and other piperaceous plants and also prepared synthetically. [< L *piper* pepper + -INE[1]]

pi·per·o·nal (pi per′ ə nal′, pī-, pip′ər ə-), *n. Chem.* a white aldehyde, $CH_2(O_2)C_6H_3CHO$, which darkens on exposure to light: used chiefly in perfumery and organic synthesis. Also called **pi·per′o·nyl al′dehyde.** (pi per′ə nəl, pī-, pip′ər ə-). [PIPER(INE) + -ON(E) + -AL[3]]

pipe·stem (pīp′stem′), *n.* **1.** the stem of a tobacco pipe. **2.** something resembling this in slenderness, as an unusually thin arm or leg.

pi·pet (pī pet′, pi-), *n., v.t.,* **-pet·ted, -pet·ting.** pipette.

pi·pette (pī pet′, pi-), *n., v.,* **-pet·ted, -pet·ting.** **—***n.* **1.** a slender graduated tube for measuring and transferring liquids from one vessel to another. **—***v.t.* **2.** to measure or transfer a liquid with a pipette. [< F]

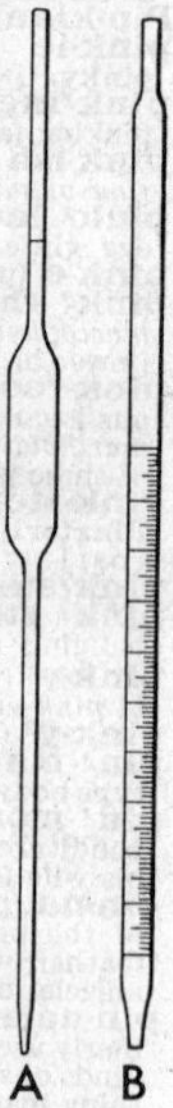

A B

Pipettes A, Transfer pipette; B, Measuring pipette

pip·ing (pī′ping), *n.* **1.** pipes collectively; a system or network of pipes. **2.** the act of a person or thing that pipes. **3.** a shrill sound. **4.** the sound or music of pipes. **5.** a tubular band of material for ornamentation, trimming garments and upholstery, etc., along edges and seams. **—***adj.* **6.** characterized by the music of the peaceful pipe rather than by that of the martial fife or trumpet. **7.** that pipes. **8.** emitting a shrill sound. **9. piping hot,** (of food or drink) very hot. [ME (n.); see PIPE[1], -ING[1], -ING[2]] **—pip′ing·ly,** *adv.*

pip·it (pip′it), *n.* any of several small songbirds of the genus *Anthus,* of the family *Motacillidae,* resembling the larks in coloration, structure, and habits. [imit.]

pip·kin (pip′kin), *n.* **1.** a small, earthen pot. **2.** *Dial.* piggin. [? PIPE[2] + -KIN]

pip·pin (pip′in), *n.* **1.** any of numerous, roundish, or oblate varieties of apple. **2.** *Bot.* a seed. [ME *pipin,* var. of *pepin* < OF]

pip·sis·se·wa (pip sis′ə wə), *n.* any evergreen, ericaceous herb of the genus *Chimaphila,* esp. *C. umbellata,* the leaves of which are used medicinally for their tonic, diuretic, and astringent properties. [< Cree *pipisisikweu,* lit., it breaks it up, i.e., fragments the stone in the bladder]

pip-squeak (pip′skwēk′), *n. Informal.* a small or unimportant person; twerp.

pip·y (pī′pē), *adj.,* **pip·i·er, pip·i·est.** **1.** pipelike; tubular. **2.** piping; shrill: *a pipy voice.* [PIPE[1] + -Y[1]]

pi·quant (pē′kənt, -känt), *adj.* **1.** agreeably pungent or sharp in taste or flavor; biting; tart: *a piquant aspic.* **2.** interesting, provocative, or lively: *a piquant wit.* **3.** *Archaic.* sharp or stinging, esp. to the feelings. [< F: lit., pricking (see PIQUE, -ANT); r. *pickante* < It *piccante*] **—pi′quan·cy, pi′quant·ness,** *n.* **—pi′quant·ly,** *adv.* **—Syn. 1.** spicy.

pique (pēk), *v.,* **piqued, piqu·ing,** *n.* **—***v.t.* **1.** to affect with sharp irritation and resentment, esp. by some wound to pride: *He piqued her by refusing her invitation.* **2.** to wound (the pride, vanity, etc.). **3.** to excite (interest, curiosity, etc.). **4.** to arouse an emotion or provoke to action: *to pique someone to answer a challenge.* **5.** *Archaic.* to pride (oneself) (usually fol. by *on* or *upon*). **—***v.i.* **6.** to cause anger, resentment, or sharp irritation in someone. **—***n.* **7.** a feeling of irritation or resentment, as from a wound to pride or self-esteem. [< MF *pique* (n.), *piquer* (v.) < VL **piccare;* see PICKAX, PIQUÉ, PIKE[2]]

pi·qué (pi kā′, pē-; *Fr.* pē kā′), *n.* a fabric of cotton, spun rayon, or silk, woven lengthwise with raised cords. [< F, ptp. of *piquer* to quilt, prick; see PIQUE[1]]

pi·quet (pi ket′, -kā′), *n.* a card game played by two persons with a pack of 32 cards, the cards from deuces to sixes being excluded. [< F; see PIC[1], -ET]

pi·ra·cy (pī′rə sē), *n., pl.* **-cies.** **1.** robbery or illegal violence at sea. **2.** the unauthorized appropriation or use of a copyrighted or patented work, idea, etc. [earlier *pyracie* < ML *pīrātīa* < LGk *peirāteía.* See PIRATE, -ACY]

Pi·rae·us (pī rē′əs, pi rā′əs), *n.* a seaport in SE Greece: the port of Athens. 186,223. Also, **Peiraeus.** Greek, **Peiraievs.**

pi·ra·gua (pi rä′gwə, -rag′wə), *n.* **1.** Also, **piroque.** a canoe made by hollowing out a tree trunk. **2.** a flat-bottomed sailing vessel having two masts. [< Sp < Carib: dugout]

Pi·ran·del·lo (pir′ən del′ō; *It.* pē′rän del′lô), *n.* **Lu·i·gi** (lo͞o ē′jē), 1867–1936, Italian dramatist, novelist, and poet.

Pi·ra·ne·si (pē′rä ne′zē), *n.* **Giam·bat·tis·ta** (jäm′bät-tēs′tä), or **Gio·van·ni Bat·tis·ta** (jō vän′nē bät tēs′tä), 1720–78, Italian architect and engraver.

pi·ra·nha (pi rän′yə, -ran′-), *n.* any of the small, extremely voracious, South American, characin fishes of the subfamily *Serrasalminae*, schools of which are known to attack and devour man and large animals. Also called **caribe.** [< Pg < Tupi]

Piranha, *Serrasalmus rhombeus* (Length to 1½ ft.)

pi·ra·ru·cu (pi rär′ə ko͞o′), *n.* the arapaima. [< Pg < Tupi *pirā-rucū*, lit., red fish]

pi·rate (pī′rət), *n., v.,* **-rat·ed, -rat·ing.** —*n.* **1.** a person who robs, or commits illegal violence, at sea or on the shores of the sea. **2.** a vessel employed by such persons. **3.** any plunderer, predator, etc.: *confidence men and other pirates.* **4.** a person who appropriates and reproduces the work or invention of another, without authorization, as for his own profit. —*v.t.* **5.** to commit piracy upon; plunder; rob. **6.** to take by piracy: *to pirate gold.* **7.** to appropriate and reproduce (a book, an invention, etc.) without authorization or legal right. —*v.i.* **8.** to commit or practice piracy. [late ME < L *pīrāta* < Gk *peirātḗs*, akin to *peirân* to attack] —**pi′rate·like′,** *adj.* —**pi·rat·i·cal** (pī rat′i kəl), **pi·rat′ic,** *adj.* —**pi·rat′i·cal·ly,** *adv.* —**Syn. 1.** freebooter, buccaneer, corsair, plunderer.

Pi′rate Coast′. See under **United Arab Emirates.**

Pi·rith·o·üs (pī rith′ō əs), *n. Class. Myth.* a prince of the Lapithae and friend of Theseus, in whose company he attempted to abduct Persephone from Hades.

pi·rogue (pi rōg′), *n.* piragua (def. 1). [< F < Sp]

pi·rosh·ki (pi rôsh′kē, -rosh′-), *n.* (*construed as pl.*) small turnovers or dumplings with a filling, as of meat or fruit. [< Russ *pirozhke* small pastries, dim. of *pirog* stuffed pastry]

pir·ou·ette (pir′o͞o et′), *n., v.,* **-et·ted, -et·ting.** —*n.* **1.** a whirling about on one foot or on the points of the toes, as in dancing. —*v.i.* **2.** to perform a pirouette; whirl, as on the toes. [< F: a whirl, top, etc., fem. of MF *pirouet* = *pirou-* (c. It *pirolo*, dim. of *piro* peg) + *-et* -ET]

Pi·sa (pē′zə; *It.* pē′zä), *n.* a city in NW Italy, on the Arno River: leaning tower. 91,108 (1961). —**Pi′san,** *adj., n.*

pis al·ler (pē ZA lā′), *French.* the last resort or resource.

Pi·sa·nel·lo (pē′zä nel′lô), *n.* **An·to·nio** (än tô′nyô), (*Antonio Pisano*), 1397–1455?, Italian painter and medalist.

Pi·sa·no (pē zä′nô), *n.* **Gio·van·ni** (jô vän′nē), c1245–c1320, and his father, **Ni·co·la** (nē kô′lä), c1220–78, Italian sculptors and architects.

pis·ca·ry (pis′kə rē), *n., pl.* **-ries. 1.** *Law.* the right or privilege of fishing in particular waters. **2.** a place for fishing. [late ME < ML *piscāria*, neut. pl. (fishing rights), fem. sing. (fishing place) of L *piscārius* of fishing or fish]

Pis·cat·a·way (pi skat′ə wā′), *n.* a township in central New Jersey, E of New Brunswick. 36,418 (1970).

pis·ca·tor (pi skā′tər, pis′kə-), *n.* fisherman. [< L = *piscāt(us)* a fishing (see PISCI-, -ATE[1]) + *-or* -OR[2]]

pis·ca·to·ry (pis′kə tōr′ē, -tôr′ē), *adj.* **1.** of or pertaining to fishermen or fishing: *piscatory rights.* **2.** devoted to or dependent upon fishing: *piscatory birds.* Also, **pis·ca·to·ri·al** (pis′kə tōr′ē əl, -tôr′-). [< L *piscātōri(us)* = *piscāt(us)* (see PISCATOR) + *-ōrius* -ORY[1]]

Pis·ces (pī′sēz, pis′ēz), *n., gen.* **Pis·ci·um** (pish′ē əm) for 1. **1.** *Astron.* the Fishes, a zodiacal constellation between Aries and Aquarius. **2.** *Astrol.* the twelfth sign of the zodiac. See illus. at **zodiac. 3.** (*italics*) the class of vertebrates comprising the fish and sometimes including, in certain classifications, the cyclostomes. [< L *piscēs*, pl. of *piscis* a fish]

pisci-, a learned borrowing from Latin meaning "fish," used in the formation of compound words: *piscivorous.* [comb. form repr. L *pisc(is)*]

pis·ci·cul·ture (pis′i kul′chər), *n.* the breeding, rearing, and transplantation of fish by artificial means. —**pis′ci·cul′tur·al,** *adj.* —**pis′ci·cul′tur·al·ly,** *adv.* —**pis′ci·cul′tur·ist,** *n.*

pis·ci·form (pis′ə fôrm′), *adj.* shaped like a fish.

pis·ci·na (pi sī′nə, pi sē′-), *n., pl.* **-nae** (-nē). *Eccles.* a basin with a drain used for certain ablutions, now generally in the sacristy. [< eccl. L, special use of L *piscīna* a fish pond, swimming pool = *pisci(s)* a fish + *-īna*, fem. of *-īnus* -INE[1]]

pis·cine (pis′in, -ēn, -in), *adj.* of, pertaining to, or resembling a fish or fishes. [< L *piscīn(us)* adj. See PISC(I)-, -INE[1]]

Pis·cis Aus·tri·nus (pī′sis ô strī′nəs, pis′is), *gen.* **Piscis Aus·tri·ni** (pī′sis ô strī′nī, pis′is). *Astron.* the Southern Fish, a southern constellation containing Fomalhaut.

pis·civ·o·rous (pi siv′ər əs), *adj.* fish-eating.

Pis·gah (piz′gə), *n.* **Mount,** a mountain ridge of ancient Palestine, now in Jordan, NE of the Dead Sea: from its summit (**Mt. Nebo**) Moses viewed the Promised Land. Deut. 34:1.

pish (psh; *spelling pron.* pish), *interj.* (used as an exclamation of contempt or impatience.) [imit.]

pi·si·form (pī′sə fôrm′), *adj.* **1.** having or resembling the form of a pea. **2.** *Anat., Zool.* pertaining to the pealike bone on the ulnar side of the carpus. [< NL *pisiform(is)* pea-shaped = *pisi-* (comb. form repr. L *pisum* pea < Gk *píson* pulse) + *-formis* -FORM]

Pi·sis·tra·tus (pī sis′trə təs, pi-), *n.* c605–527 B.C., tyrant of Athens 560–527 (father of Hipparchus and Hippias). Also, **Peisistratus.**

pis·mire (pis′mīər′), *n.* an ant. [ME *pissemyre*, lit., urinating ant = *pisse* to urinate + obs. *mire* ant < Scand (cf. Dan *myre*, Sw *myra*); c. D *mier;* pejorative name from stench of formic acid proper to ants]

pi·so·lite (pī′sə līt′, piz′ə-), *n.* limestone composed of rounded concretions about the size of a pea. [< NL *pisolith(us)* = Gk *píso(s)* pea + *líthos* -LITE] —**pis·o·lit·ic** (pis′ə lit′ik), *adj.*

piss (pis), *n., v.,* **pissed, piss·ing.** *Slang* (*vulgar*). —*n.* **1.** urine. —*v.i.* **2.** to urinate. —*v.t.* **3.** to urinate on or in. **4. pissed off,** angry, upset, or disgusted. [ME *pisse(n)* < OF *pissier* < VL **pisiare*, ultimately sound imit.]

Pis·sar·ro (pi sär′ō; *Fr.* pē SA RŌ′), *n.* **Ca·mille** (KA-mē′yə), 1830–1903, French painter.

pis·soir (pē SWAR′), *n., pl.* **-soirs** (-SWAR′). *French.* a street urinal for public use, enclosed by a low wall, screen, or the like.

pis·ta·chi·o (pi stash′ē ō′, -stä′shē ō′), *n., pl.* **-chi·os. 1.** the nut of an anacardiaceous tree, *Pistacia vera*, of southern Europe and Asia Minor, containing an edible, greenish kernel. **2.** the kernel itself. **3.** the tree itself. Also, **pis·tache** (pi stash′), **pista′chio nut′** (for defs. 1, 2). [< It *pistacchio* < L *pistācium* < Gk *pistákion* pistachio nut, dim. of *pistákē* pistachio tree < Pers *pistah;* r. late ME *pistace* < MF < L]

pis·ta·reen (pis′tə rēn′), *n.* **1.** peseta (def. 2). —*adj.* **2.** of little value or worth. [? < Sp *peseta*]

pis·til (pis′til), *n. Bot.* **1.** the ovule-bearing or seed-bearing organ of a flower, consisting when complete of ovary, style, and stigma. **2.** such organs collectively, where there are more than one in a flower. **3.** a gynoecium. [earlier *pistillum*, special use of L *pistillum* pestle]

pis·til·late (pis′tᵊlit, -tᵊlāt′), *adj. Bot.* **1.** having a pistil or pistils. **2.** having a pistil or pistils but no stamens.

Pis·to·ia (pē stô′yä), *n.* a city in N Tuscany, in N Italy. 82,401 (1961).

pis·tol (pis′tᵊl), *n., v.,* **-toled, -tol·ing** or (*esp. Brit.*) **-tolled, -tol·ling.** —*n.* **1.** a short firearm intended to be held and fired with one hand. —*v.t.* **2.** to shoot with a pistol. [< MF *pistole* (now obs.) < G *Pistole* < Czech *pišťal* pistol, pipe]

pis·tole (pi stōl′), *n.* **1.** a former gold coin of Spain, equal to two escudos. **2.** any of various former gold coins of Europe, as the louis d'or. [< MF, back formation from *pistolet* the coin]

pis·to·leer (pis′tᵊlēr′), *n. Obs.* a person, esp. a soldier, who uses or is armed with a pistol. Also, **pis′to·lier′.**

pis·tol-whip (pis′tᵊl hwip′, -wip′), *v.t.,* **-whipped, -whip·ping.** to hit (someone) repeatedly with a pistol, esp. in the head and shoulder area.

pis·ton (pis′tən), *n.* **1.** a disk or cylinder moving within a tube and exerting pressure on, or receiving pressure from, a fluid or gas within the tube. **2.** a pumplike valve used to change the pitch in a cornet or the like. [< F < It *pistone* piston, a learned alter. of *pestone* great pestle = *pest(are)* (to) pound (var. of ML *pistare* < L *pīstus*, ptp. of *pinsere* to pound) + *-one* aug. suffix]

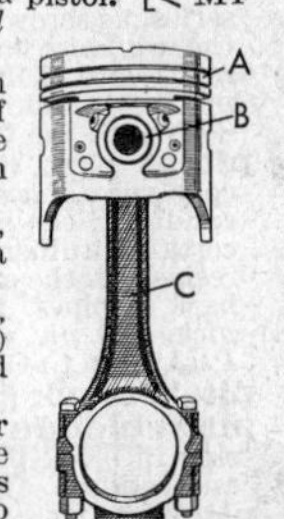

A, Piston of automobile engine; B, Wrist pin; C, Connecting rod

Pis·ton (pis′tən), *n.* **Walter,** 1894–1976, U.S. composer and teacher.

pis′ton ring′, a metallic ring, usually one of a series, and split so as to be expansible, placed around a piston in order to maintain a tight fit, as inside the cylinder of an engine.

pis′ton rod′, a rod communicating the rectilinear motion of a piston to the small end of a connecting rod or elsewhere.

pit[1] (pit), *n., v.,* **pit·ted, pit·ting.** —*n.* **1.** a naturally formed or excavated hole or cavity in the ground. **2.** a covered or concealed excavation in the ground, serving as a trap. **3.** *Mining.* **a.** an excavation made in digging for some mineral deposit. **b.** the shaft of a coal mine. **c.** the mine itself. **4.** the abode of evil spirits and lost souls; hell. **5.** a hollow or indentation in a surface: *glass flawed by pits.* **6.** a natural hollow or depression in the body: *the pit of the back.* **7.** a pockmark. **8.** an enclosure for combats, as of dogs or cocks. **9.** *U.S.* (in a commodity exchange) a part of the floor of the exchange where trading in a particular commodity takes place: *the corn pit.* **10.** *Archit.* **a.** all that part of the main floor of a theater behind the musicians. **b.** orchestra (def. 2a). —*v.t.* **11.** to mark with pits or depressions: *ground pitted by erosion.* **12.** to scar with pockmarks: *His forehead was pitted by chicken pox.* **13.** to place or bury in a pit, as for storage. **14.** to set in opposition or combat, as one against another. **15.** to set (animals) in a pit or enclosure, for fighting. —*v.i.* **16.** to become marked with pits or depressions. [ME; OE *pytt* < L *pute(us)* well, pit, shaft]

pit[2] (pit), *n., v.,* **pit·ted, pit·ting.** *U.S.* —*n.* **1.** the stone of a fruit, as of a cherry, peach, or plum. —*v.t.* **2.** to remove the pit from (a fruit or fruits). [< D: kernel; c. PITH]

pi·ta[1] (pē′tə), *n.* **1.** a fiber obtained from plants of the genera *Agave, Aechmea*, etc., used for cordage, mats, etc. **2.** any of these plants. [< Sp < Quechua]

pi·ta[2] (pē′tä), *n.* a flat, round, crusty Arab bread. [< Heb, dim. of *pat* loaf]

pit·a·pat (pit′ə pat′), *adv., n., v.,* **-pat·ted, -pat·ting.** —*adv.* **1.** with a quick succession of beats or taps: *Her heart beat pitapat with excitement.* —*n.* **2.** the movement or the sound of something going pitapat: *the pitapat of hail on a roof.* —*v.i.* **3.** to go pitapat. [imit. gradational compound]

Pit′cairn Is′land (pit′kârn), a small British island in the S Pacific, SE of Tuamotu Archipelago: settled 1790 by mutineers from *H.M.S. Bounty.* 107 (est. 1963); 2 sq. mi.

pitch[1] (pich), *v.t.* **1.** to erect or set up (a tent, camp, or the like). **2.** to put, set, or plant in a fixed or definite place or position. **3.** to throw, fling, hurl, or toss. **4.** *Baseball.* **a.** to deliver or serve (the ball) to the batter. **b.** to fill the position of pitcher in (a game). **5.** to set at a certain point, degree, level, etc.: *He pitched his hopes too high.* **6.** *Music.* to set at a particular pitch, or determine the key or keynote of (a melody). **7.** *Obs.* to set in order; to arrange, as a field of battle. **8.** *Obs.* to fix firmly, as in the ground; embed. —*v.i.* **9.** to plunge or fall forward or headlong. **10.** to lurch. **11.** to throw or toss. **12.** *Baseball.* **a.** to deliver or serve the ball to the batter. **b.** to fill the position of pitcher. **13.** to slope downward; dip. **14.** to plunge with alternate fall and rise of bow and stern. **15.** (of a rocket or guided missile) to deviate from a stable flight attitude by oscillations of the longitudinal axis in a vertical plane about the center of gravity. **16. pitch in,** *Informal.* **a.** to contribute; join in. **b.** to begin to work vigorously. **17. pitch into,** *Informal.* **a.** to attack verbally or physically. **b.** to begin to work on vigorously.

—*n.* **18.** relative point, position, or degree: *a high pitch of excitement.* **19.** degree of inclination or slope; angle: *the pitch of a roof.* **20.** the highest point or greatest height: *the pitch of success.* **21.** (in music, speech, etc.) degree of height or depth of a tone or of sound, depending upon the relative rapidity of the vibrations by which it is produced. **22.** a particular tonal standard with which given tones may be compared in respect to their relative level. **23.** *Acoustics.* the apparent predominant frequency sounded by an acoustical source. **24.** the act or manner of pitching. **25.** a throw or toss. **26.** *Baseball.* the serving of the ball to the batter by the pitcher. **27.** a pitching movement, as of a ship. **28.** a sloping part or place. **29.** a quantity of something pitched or placed somewhere. **30.** *Cricket.* the central part of the field; the area between the wickets. **31.** *Slang.* **a.** a high-pressure sales talk. **b.** a specific plan of action; angle: *to tackle a problem again, using a new pitch.* **32.** *Aeron.* **a.** the nosing of an airplane or spacecraft up or down about a transverse axis. **b.** the distance which a given propeller would advance in one revolution. **33.** (of a rocket or guided missile) **a.** the motion due to pitching. **b.** the extent of the rotation of the longitudinal axis involved in pitching. **34.** *Geol., Mining.* the inclination of the axis of a fold from the horizontal. **35.** *Mach.* **a.** the distance between the corresponding surfaces of two adjacent gear teeth. **b.** the distance between any two adjacent things in a series, as screw threads, rivets, etc. **36.** (in carpet weaving) the weftwise number of warp ends, usually determined in relation to 27 inches. **37.** *Cards.* See **all fours** (def. 2). [ME *picche(n)*; ? akin to PICK[1]]
—**Syn. 3.** See **throw.**

pitch[2] (pich), *n.* **1.** any of various dark, tenacious, and viscous substances for caulking and paving, consisting of the residue of the distillation of coal tar or wood tar. **2.** any of certain bitumens, as asphalt: *mineral pitch.* **3.** any of various resins. **4.** the sap or crude turpentine which exudes from the bark of pines. —*v.t.* **5.** to smear or cover with pitch. [ME *pich,* OE *pic* < L *pic-* (s. of *pix*), whence also D *pek,* G *Pech;* akin to Gk *píssa* (for **pikia*) pitch] —**pitch′like′,** *adj.*

pitch-black (pich′blak′), *adj.* extremely black, as pitch.

pitch·blende (pich′blend′), *n.* an impure uraninite, occurring in black pitchlike masses: the principal ore of uranium and radium. [half trans., half adoption of G *Pechblende*]

pitch-dark (pich′därk′), *adj.* extremely dark, as pitch: *The night was pitch-dark.* —**pitch′-dark′ness,** *n.*

pitched′ bat′tle, 1. a battle in which the orderly arrangement of forces and the location have been predetermined. **2.** an encounter in which the antagonists are completely and intensely engaged.

pitch·er[1] (pich′ər), *n.* **1.** a container, usually with a handle and spout or lip, for holding and pouring liquids. **2.** *Bot.* **a.** a pitcherlike modification of the leaf of certain plants. **b.** an ascidium. [ME *picher* < OF *pichier* < ML *picār(ium),* var. of *bicārium* BEAKER] —**pitch′er·like′,** *adj.*

pitch·er[2] (pich′ər), *n.* **1.** a person who pitches. **2.** *Baseball.* the player who delivers or serves the ball to the batter. **3.** *Golf.* a club with an iron head, the face of which has more slope than a mashie niblick but less slope than a pitching niblick. [PITCH[1] + -ER[1]]

pitch′er plant′, any of various plants having leaves modified into a pitcherlike receptacle, or ascidium, as the plants of the genera *Sarracenia* and *Darlingtonia.*

Pitcher plant, *Sarracenia pupurea*

pitch·fork (pich′fôrk′), *n.* **1.** a long-handled fork for pitching hay, stalks of grain, etc. —*v.t.* **2.** to pitch or throw with or as with a pitchfork.

pitch′ing nib′lick, *Golf.* a club with an iron head, the face of which has more slope than a pitcher but less slope than a niblick.

Pitch′ Lake′, a deposit of natural asphalt in SW Trinidad, West Indies. 114 acres.

pitch·man (pich′mən), *n., pl.* **-men. 1.** an itinerant salesman of small wares. **2.** any high-pressure salesman, as a concessionaire at a fair or carnival.

pitch·out (pich′out′), *n.* **1.** *Baseball.* a ball purposely thrown by a pitcher too far outside of the plate for the batter to hit, esp. in anticipation of an attempted steal by a base runner. **2.** *Football.* a lateral pass thrown behind the line of scrimmage by one back, esp. a T-formation quarterback, to another.

pitch′ pine′, any of several pines from which pitch or turpentine is obtained.

pitch′ pipe′, a small flute or reed pipe producing one or more pitches when blown into, used chiefly for establishing the proper pitch in singing or in tuning a musical instrument.

pitch′ shot′, *Golf.* a shot in which the ball is hit high into the air and with backspin to ensure little roll upon landing, used in approaching the green.

pitch·stone (pich′stōn′), *n.* a glassy igneous rock having a resinous luster and resembling hardened pitch. [trans. of G *Pechstein*]

pit·e·ous (pit′ē əs), *adj.* **1.** evoking or deserving pity; pathetic. **2.** *Archaic.* compassionate. [ME *pite* PITY + -OUS; r. ME *pitous* < OF < ML *pietōs(us)*] —**pit′e·ous·ly,** *adv.* —**pit′e·ous·ness,** *n.* —**Syn. 1.** moving, distressing, wretched, sorrowful. See **pitiful.**

pit·fall (pit′fôl′), *n.* **1.** a concealed pit prepared as a trap for men or animals. **2.** any trap or danger for the unwary. [ME *pittefalle* = OE *pytt* PIT[1] + *fealle* trap] —**Syn.** See **trap**[1].

pith (pith), *n.* **1.** *Bot.* the central cylinder of parenchymatous tissue in the stems of dicotyledonous plants. **2.** *Zool.* the soft inner part of a feather, a hair, etc. **3.** the important or essential part; essence; heart: *the pith of the matter.* **4.** weight; substance; solidity: *an argument without pith.* **5.** *Archaic.* spinal cord or bone marrow. **6.** *Archaic.* strength, force, or vigor; mettle: *men of pith.* —*v.t.* **7.** to remove the pith from (plants). **8.** to destroy the spinal cord or brain of. **9.** to slaughter, as cattle, by severing the spinal cord. [ME; OE *pitha;* c. D *pit.* See PIT[2]]

pit·head (pit′hed′), *n.* a mine entrance and the surrounding area.

pith·e·can·thro·poid (pith′ə kan′thrə poid′, -kən thrō′poid), *adj.* of, pertaining to, or resembling a *Pithecanthropus.*

pith·e·can·thro·pus (pith′ə kan′thrə pəs, -kən thrō′pəs), *n.* **1.** a member of the genus *Pithecanthropus.* **2.** (*cap., italics*) an extinct genus of apelike men, esp. *Pithecanthropus erectus* of the Pleistocene epoch of Java. [< NL < Gk *píthēk(os)* ape + *ánthrōpos* man]

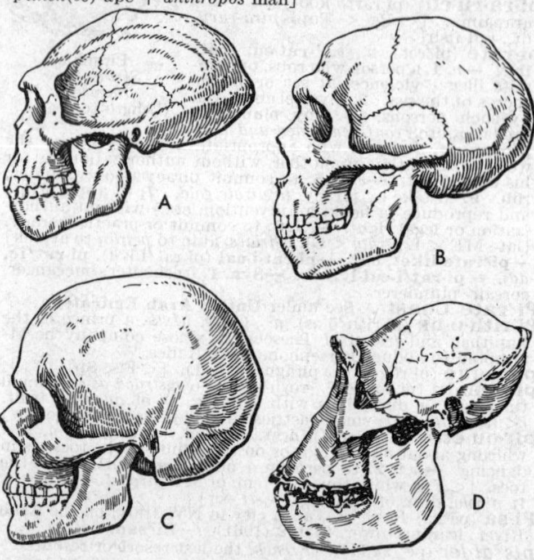

A, Pithecanthropus; B, Neanderthal man; C, Cro-Magnon; D, Gorilla

pith·y (pith′ē), *adj.,* **pith·i·er, pith·i·est. 1.** full of vigor, substance, or meaning; terse; forcible: *a pithy observation.* **2.** of, like, or abounding in pith. [ME] —**pith′i·ly,** *adv.* —**pith′i·ness,** *n.* —**Syn. 1.** succinct, pointed, meaty, concise.

pit·i·a·ble (pit′ē ə bəl), *adj.* **1.** evoking or deserving pity; lamentable. **2.** evoking or deserving contemptuous pity; miserable. [ME < OF *piteable* = *pite(er)* (to) PITY + *-able* -ABLE] —**pit′i·a·ble·ness,** *n.* —**pit′i·a·bly,** *adv.* —**Syn.** See **pitiful.**

pit·i·er (pit′ē ər), *n.* a person who pities.

pit·i·ful (pit′ə fəl), *adj.* **1.** such as to excite or deserve pity: *a pitiful fate.* **2.** such as to excite contempt by smallness, poor quality, etc.: *pitiful attempts.* **3.** *Rare.* full of pity or compassion; compassionate. [ME] —**pit′i·ful·ly,** *adv.* —**pit′i·ful·ness,** *n.*
—**Syn. 1.** lamentable, deplorable, pathetic. **1, 2.** PITIFUL, PITIABLE, PITEOUS apply to that which excites pity (with compassion or with contempt). That which is PITIFUL is touching and excites pity or is mean and contemptible: *a pitiful orphan; a pitiful exhibition of cowardice.* PITIABLE may mean lamentable, or wretched and paltry: *a pitiable hovel.* PITEOUS refers only to that which exhibits suffering and misery, and is therefore heartrending: *piteous poverty.* **2.** deplorable, mean, low, base, vile, despicable.

pit·i·less (pit′ē lis, pit′i-), *adj.* feeling or showing no pity; merciless: *pitiless criticism.* [ME *piteles*] —**pit′i·less·ly,** *adv.* —**pit′i·less·ness,** *n.* —**Syn.** unmerciful, implacable, relentless. See **cruel.** —**Ant.** merciful.

pit·man (pit′mən), *n., pl.* **-men** for 1, **-mans** for 2, 3. **1.** a person who works in a pit, as in coal mining. **2.** *Mach.* any of certain types of connecting rods. **3.** See **walking beam.**

Pit·man (pit′mən), *n.* **Sir Isaac,** 1813–97, English inventor of a system of shorthand. See illus. at **shorthand.**

pi·ton (pē′ton, -tōn; *Fr.* pē tôN′), *n., pl.* **-tons** (-tonz, -tōnz; *Fr.* -tôN′). *Mountain Climbing.* a metal spike with an eye through which a rope may be passed. [< F: ringbolt, peak (of a mountain)]

Pi′tot-stat′ic tube′ (pē′tō stat′ik, pē tō′-), *Aeron.* a device consisting of a modified Pitot tube for measuring velocity by means of the differential pressure between the impact and static openings, often connected to an airspeed indicator in aircraft. Also, **pi′tot-stat′ic tube′.** Also called **Pitot tube.** [see PITOT TUBE]

Pi′tot tube′ (pē′tō, pē tō′), **1.** an instrument for measuring fluid velocity by means of the differential pressure between the tip (dynamic) and side (static) openings. **2.** See **Pitot-static tube.** [named after Henri *Pitot* (1695–1771), French physicist, who invented it]

pits (pits), *n.pl.* *U.S. Slang.* an extremely unpleasant, boring, or depressing place, condition, person, etc.; the worst (usually prec. by *the*): *When you're alone, Christmas is the pits.*

Pitt (pit), *n.* **1. William, 1st Earl of Chatham,** 1708–78, British statesman. **2.** his son **William,** 1759–1806, British statesman: prime minister 1783–1801, 1804–06.

pit·tance (pit′ᵊns), *n.* **1.** a small allowance or sum for living expenses. **2.** a scanty income or remuneration. [ME *pitaunce* < OF *pitance,* var. of *pietance* piety, pity, allowance of food (in a monastery). See PITY, -ANCE]

pit·ter-pat·ter (pit′ər pat′ər), *n.* **1.** the sound of a rapid succession of light beats or taps, as of rain, footsteps, etc. —*v.i.* **2.** to produce this sound. —*adv.* **3.** with such a sound: *Mice ran pitter-patter through the deserted house.* [? imit.]

Pitts·burg (pits′bûrg), *n.* **1.** a city in W California. 20,651 (1970). **2.** a city in SE Kansas. 20,171 (1970).

Pitts·burgh (pits′bûrg), *n.* a port in SW Pennsylvania, at the confluence of the Allegheny and Monongahela rivers which forms the Ohio River: steel industry. 520,117 (1970).

Pitts′burg Land′ing, a village in SW Tennessee, on the Tennessee River: battle of Shiloh in 1862.

Pitts·field (pits′fēld′), *n.* a city in W Massachusetts. 57,020 (1970).

pi·tu·i·tar·y (pi to͞o′i ter′ē, -tyo͞o′-), *n., pl.* **-tar·ies,** *adj.* —*n.* **1.** See **pituitary gland. 2.** *Pharm.* the extract obtained from the lobes of the pituitaries of hogs, sheep, and other domestic animals: the posterior lobe constituent increases blood pressure, contracts stomach muscles, etc., and the anterior lobe constituent regulates growth of the skeleton. —*adj.* **3.** of, pertaining to, or involving the pituitary gland. **4.** noting a physical type of abnormal size with overgrown extremities that results from excessive pituitary secretion. [< L *pītuītāri(us)* pertaining to or secreting phlegm. See PIP[2], -ARY]

pitu′itary gland′, *Anat.* a small, oval endocrine gland attached to the base of the brain and situated in a depression of the sphenoid bone, which secretes several hormones. Also called **pitu′itary bod′y, hypophysis.**

pit′ vi′per, any of numerous venomous snakes of the family *Crotalidae,* as the rattlesnake, water moccasin, and copperhead, having a heat-sensitive pit on each side of the head between the eye and nostril.

pit·y (pit′ē), *n., pl.* **pit·ies,** *v.,* **pit·ied, pit·y·ing.** —*n.* **1.** sympathetic grief or sorrow excited by the suffering or misfortune of another, often leading one to give aid or to show mercy. **2.** a cause or reason for pity, sorrow, or regret: *What a pity you could not go!* **3. take** or **have pity on,** to show mercy for; be merciful to. —*v.t.* **4.** to feel pity or compassion for; be sorry for; commiserate. —*v.i.* **5.** to have compassion; feel pity. [ME *pite* < OF; early OF *pitet* < L *pietāt-* (s. of *pietās*) PIETY] —**pit′y·ing·ly,** *adv.* —**Syn. 1.** compassion.

pit·y·ri·a·sis (pit′ə rī′ə sis), *n.* **1.** *Pathol.* any of various skin diseases marked by the shedding of branlike scales of epidermis. **2.** *Vet. Pathol.* a skin disease in various domestic animals marked by dry scales. [< NL < Gk: branlike eruption = *pī́tyr(on)* bran, scale + *-iāsis* -IASIS]

più (pyo͞o), *adv. Music.* more: *più allegro.* [< It < L *plus*]

Pi·us I (pī′əs), **Saint,** pope A.D. 140–155?.

Pius II, (*Enea Silvio de Piccolomini*) 1405–64, Italian ecclesiastic: pope 1458–64. Literary name, **Aeneas Silvius.**

Pius III, (*Francesco Nanni Todeschini Piccolomini*) 1439–1503, Italian ecclesiastic: pope 1503.

Pius IV, (*Giovanni Angelo Medici*) 1499–1565, Italian ecclesiastic: pope 1559–65.

Pius V, Saint (*Michele Ghislieri*), 1504–72, Italian ecclesiastic: pope 1566–72.

Pius VI, (*Giovanni Angelo,* or *Giannangelo, Braschi*) 1717–1799, Italian ecclesiastic: pope 1775–99.

Pius VII, (*Luigi Barnaba Chiaramonti*) 1740–1823, Italian ecclesiastic: pope 1800–23.

Pius VIII, (*Francesco Saverio Castiglioni*) 1761–1830, Italian ecclesiastic: pope 1829–30.

Pius IX, (*Giovanni Maria Mastai-Ferretti*) 1792–1878, Italian ecclesiastic: pope 1846–78.

Pius X, Saint (*Giuseppe Sarto*), 1835–1914, Italian ecclesiastic: pope 1903–14.

Pius XI, (*Achille Ratti*) 1857–1939, Italian ecclesiastic: pope 1922–39.

Pius XII, (*Eugenio Pacelli*) 1876–1958, Italian ecclesiastic: pope 1939–58.

Pi·ute (pī o͞ot′), *n., pl.* **-utes,** (*esp. collectively*) **-ute.** Paiute.

piv·ot (piv′ət), *n.* **1.** a pin or short shaft on the end of which something rests and turns, or upon and around which something rotates or oscillates. **2.** the end of a shaft or arbor, resting and turning in a bearing. **3.** that on which something turns, hinges, or depends: *He is the pivot of her life.* **4.** the person in a line, as of troops on parade, whom the others use as a point around which to wheel or maneuver. **5.** a whirling around on one foot. —*v.i.* **6.** to turn on or as on a pivot. —*v.t.* **7.** to mount on, attach by, or provide with a pivot or pivots. [< F, OF < ?]

piv·ot·al (piv′ə tᵊl), *adj.* **1.** of, pertaining to, or serving as a pivot. **2.** of critical importance: *a pivotal event in his career.* —**piv′ot·al·ly,** *adv.*

pix[1] (piks), *n.* pyx.

pix[2] (piks), *n., pl.* **pix** for 2. **1.** a pl. of **pic. 2.** pic.

pix·i·lat·ed (pik′sə lā′tid), *adj.* amusingly eccentric. [PIXY + (TIT)ILLATED] —**pix′i·la′tion,** *n.*

pix·y (pik′sē), *n., pl.* **pix·ies,** *adj.* —*n.* **1.** a fairy or sprite, esp. a mischievous one. —*adj.* **2.** playfully impish or mischievous; prankish. Also, **pix′ie.** [?]

pix·y·ish (pik′sē ish), *adj.* pixy. Also, **pix′ie·ish.**

Pi·zar·ro (pi zär′ō; *Sp.* pē thär′rô, -sär′-), *n.* **Fran·cis·co** (fran sis′kō; *Sp.* fʀän thēs′kô, -sēs′-), c1470–1541, Spanish conqueror of Peru.

pi·zazz (pi zaz′), *n. Slang.* **1.** energy; vitality; vigor. **2.** attractive style; dash; flair. Also, **piz·zazz′.**

pizz., *Music.* pizzicato.

piz·za (pēt′sə), *n.* a flat, open-faced pie of Italian origin, consisting of a crust topped with tomato sauce and cheese, often garnished with anchovies, sausage, etc. [< It]

piz·ze·ri·a (pēt′sə rē′ə), *n. U.S.* a restaurant, bakery, or the like, where pizzas are made and sold. [< It = *pizz(a)* PIZZA + *-eria* -ERY]

piz·zi·ca·to (pit′sə kä′tō; *It.* pēt′tsē kä′tô), *adj., n., pl.* **-ti** (-tē). *Music.* —*adj.* **1.** played by plucking the strings with the finger instead of using the bow, as on a violin. —*n.* **2.** a note or passage so played. [< It, ptp. of *pizzicare* to pluck, pick, twang (a stringed instrument)]

p.j.'s (pē′jāz), *n.* (*construed as pl.*) *Informal.* pajamas. Also, **P.J.'s.**

pk, *pl.* **pks** (in dry measure) peck.

pk., *pl.* **pks. 1.** pack. **2.** park. **3.** peak. **4.** (in dry measure) peck.

pkg., *pl.* **pkgs.** package.

pkt., packet.

PKU test, a urine test for detecting phenylketonuria in infants.

pl., 1. place. **2.** plate. **3.** plural.

plac·a·ble (plak′ə bəl, plā′kə-), *adj.* capable of being placated or appeased; forgiving. [ME < OF < L *plācābil(is).* See PLACATE, -ABLE] —**plac′a·bil′i·ty, plac′a·ble·ness,** *n.*

plac·ard (plak′ärd, -ərd), *n.* **1.** a written or printed notice for posting in a public place; poster. —*v.t.* **2.** to post placards on or in. **3.** to publicize, or give notice of, by means of placards. **4.** to post as a placard. [late ME < MF]

pla·cate (plā′kāt, plak′āt), *v.t.,* **-cat·ed, -cat·ing.** to appease or pacify: *to placate an outraged citizenry.* [< L *plācāt(us),* ptp. of *plācāre* to quiet, calm, appease, akin to *placēre* to please; see -ATE[1]] —**pla′cat·er,** *n.* —**pla·ca·tion** (plā kā′shən), *n.* —**Syn.** conciliate, satisfy.

pla·ca·tive (plā′kə tiv, plak′ə-), *adj.* placatory.

pla·ca·to·ry (plā′kə tôr′ē, -tōr′ē, plak′ə-), *adj.* serving, tending, or intended to placate: *a placatory remark.* [< LL *plācātōri(us)*]

place (plās), *n., v.,* **placed, plac·ing.** —*n.* **1.** a particular portion of space, whether of definite or indefinite extent. **2.** space in general: *time and place.* **3.** the portion of space occupied by a person or thing. **4.** a space or spot set apart or used for a particular purpose: *The vase is in its place.* **5.** any part or spot in a body or surface: *a decayed place in a tooth.* **6.** a particular passage in a book or writing: *to find the place where one left off reading.* **7.** a space or seat for a person, as in a theater, train, etc.: *Please save my place for me.* **8.** position, situation, or circumstances: *if I were in your place.* **9.** a proper or appropriate location or position: *A restaurant is not the place for an argument.* **10.** a job, post, or office: *persons in high places in government.* **11.** a function or duty: *It is not your place to offer criticism.* **12.** high position or rank: *aristocrats of power and place.* **13.** official employment or position: *Several places have not been filled.* **14.** a region: *to travel to distant places.* **15.** an open space, or square, in a city or town. **16.** a short street, a court, etc. **17.** an area of habitation, as a city, town, or village. **18.** a building, location, etc., set aside for a specific purpose: *a place of worship.* **19.** a part of a building: *The kitchen is the sunniest place in the house.* **20.** a residence, dwelling, or house: *Have dinner at my place.* **21.** lieu; substitution (usually fol. by *of*): *Use water in place of milk.* **22.** a step or point in order of proceeding: *in the first place.* **23.** a fitting opportunity: *There's a place in this town for a man of his talents.* **24.** *Arith.* **a.** the position of a figure in a series, as in decimal notation. **b.** Usually, **places.** the figures of the series. **25.** *Drama.* one of the three unities. Cf. **unity** (def. 8). **26.** *Sports.* **a.** a position among the leading competitors, usually the first, second, or third at the finish line. **b.** *U.S.* the position of the competitor who comes in second in a horse race, harness race, etc. Cf. **show** (def. 28), **win** (def. 15). **27.** *Archaic.* room or space for entry or passage: *to make place for the gentry.* **28. give place to, a.** to give precedence or priority to: *Time passes and the old gives place to the new.* **b.** to be succeeded or replaced by: *Tears gave place to smiles.* **29. go places,** *Slang.* to become successful: *He'll never go places in that job.* **30. in place,** in the correct or usual position or order. **31. know** or **keep one's place,** to recognize and accept one's social rank, esp. if inferior. **32. out of place, a.** not in the correct or usual position or order. **b.** unsuitable to the circumstances or surroundings; inappropriate. **33. put someone in his place,** to lower someone's self-esteem; humble, esp. an arrogant person. **34. take place,** to happen; occur. —*v.t.* **35.** to put in the proper position or order; arrange; dispose: *Place the silverware on the table for dinner.* **36.** to put in a suitable place for some purpose: *to place an advertisement in the newspaper.* **37.** to put into particular or proper hands: *to place evidence with the district attorney.* **38.** to appoint (a person) to a post or office. **39.** to find a place, situation, etc., for (a person): *The agency had no trouble placing him with a good firm.* **40.** to determine or indicate the place of: *to place health among the greatest gifts of life.* **41.** to assign a certain position or rank to: *The army placed him in the infantry.* **42.** to put or set in a particular place, position, situation, or relation. **43.** to identify by connecting with the proper place, circumstances, etc.: *to place a face.* **44.** to employ (the voice) to sing or speak with consciousness of the bodily point of emphasis of resonance of each tone or register. —*v.i.* **45.** *Sports.* **a.** to finish among the first three competitors in a race. **b.** *U.S.* to finish second in a horse race, harness race, etc. **46.** to earn a specified standing with relation to others: *He placed fifth in a graduation class of 90.* **47.** to achieve any rank within a specified range signifying success in a competition. [ME; b. OE *plæce* and MF *place,* both < L *platea,* var. of *platēa* street, courtyard, area < Gk *plateîa* broad street, n. use of fem. of *platýs* broad; see PLATY-] —**Syn. 1.** location, locale, locality, site. **35.** See **put.**

pla·ce·bo (plə sē′bō), *n., pl.* **-bos, -boes. 1.** *Med., Pharm.* a substance having no pharmacological effect but given to a patient or subject of an experiment who supposes it to be a medicine. **2.** *Rom. Cath. Ch.* the vespers of the office for the dead. [ME < L: I shall be pleasing, acceptable]

place′ card′, a card with the name of a guest on it, placed on the table, indicating where he is to sit.

place′ kick′, *Football.* a kick in which the ball is held nearly upright on the ground as in a kickoff. Cf. **drop kick, punt**[1] (def. 1).

place-kick (plās′kik′), *Football.* —*v.t.* **1.** to make (a field goal or point after touchdown) by a place kick. **2.** to kick (the ball as held for a place kick). —*v.i.* **3.** to make a place kick. [v. use of PLACE KICK] —**place′-kick′er,** *n.*

place·man (plās′mən), *n., pl.* **-men.** *Brit.* a person who holds an office, esp. one appointed to a government office as a reward for political support of an elected officer. —**place′man·ship′,** *n.*

place′ mat′, a mat set on a dining table beneath a place setting.

place·ment (plās′mənt), *n.* **1.** act of placing. **2.** state of being placed. **3.** the act of an employment office or employer in filling a position. **4.** location or arrangement: *the placement of furniture.* **5.** *Football.* **a.** the placing of the ball on the ground in attempting a place kick. **b.** the position of the ball. **c.** a place kick.

place-name (plās′nām′), *n.* the name of a geographical location, as a town, city, village, etc.

pla·cen·ta (plə sen′tə), *n., pl.* **-tas, -tae** (-tē). **1.** *Anat., Zool.* the organ in most mammals, formed in the lining of the uterus by the union of the uterine mucous membrane with the membranes of the fetus, that provides for the nourishment of the fetus and the elimination of its waste products. **2.** *Bot.* **a.** the part of the ovary of flowering plants which bears the ovules. **b.** (in ferns and related plants) the tissue giving rise to sporangia. [< NL: something having a flat, circular form, L: a cake < Gk *plakóenta,* acc. of *plakóeis* (usu. contr. *plakoûnta, plakoûs*) flat cake < *pláx* (gen. *plakós*) flat] **—pla·cen′tal, plac·en·tar·y** (plas′ən ter′ē, plə-sen′tə rē), *adj.*

pla·cen·tate (plə sen′tāt), *adj.* having a placenta.

plac·en·ta·tion (plas′ən tā′shən), *n.* **1.** *Anat., Zool.* **a.** the formation of a placenta. **b.** the manner of the disposition or construction of a placenta. **2.** *Bot.* the disposition or arrangement of a placenta or placentas. [< F *placentation*]

Pla·cen·tia (plə sen′shə, -shē ə), *n.* ancient name of **Piacenza.**

plac·er[1] (plā′sər), *n.* **1.** a person who places or arranges things. **2.** a person or animal that is among the winners of a race or other contest. [PLACE + -ER[1]]

plac·er[2] (plas′ər), *n. Mining.* **1.** a superficial gravel or similar deposit containing particles of gold or the like. **2.** the site of a form of mining (**plac′er min′ing**) in which a placer deposit is washed to precipitate the gold. [< AmerSp: sandbank; akin to PLAZA. See PLACE]

place′ set′ting, the group of dishes and eating utensils, as knives, forks, etc., set at the place of each person at a meal.

pla·cet (plā′sit), *n.* an expression or vote of assent or sanction by the Latin word *placet* (*it pleases*).

plac·id (plas′id), *adj.* pleasantly calm or peaceful; tranquil. [< L *placid(us)* calm, quiet, akin to *placēre* to please (orig., to calm); see -ID[4]] **—pla·cid·i·ty** (plə sid′i tē), **plac′id·ness,** *n.* **—plac′id·ly,** *adv.* **—Syn.** quiet, undisturbed. See **peaceful.**

plack·et (plak′it), *n.* **1.** the opening or slit at the top of a garment that facilitates putting it on and taking it off. **2.** *Archaic.* a pocket, esp. one in a woman's skirt. **3.** *Archaic.* **a.** a petticoat. **b.** a woman. [< D, var. of MD *plackaet* breastplate = ML *placca* thin plate (see PLAQUE) + *-āta* -ATE[1]]

plac·oid (plak′oid), *adj.* platelike, as the scales or dermal investments of sharks. [< Gk *plak-* (s. of *pláx*) something flat, tablet + -OID]

pla·gal (plā′gəl), *adj. Music.* (of a Gregorian mode) having the final in the middle of the compass. Cf. **authentic** (def. 4a). [< ML *plagāl(is)* = *plag(a)* plagal mode (appar. back formation from *plagius* plagal; see PLAGIO-) + *-ālis* -AL[1]]

pla′gal ca′dence, *Music.* a cadence in which the chord of the tonic is preceded by that of the subdominant.

pla·gia·rise (plā′jə rīz′, -jē ə rīz′), *v.t., v.i.,* **-rised, -ris·ing.** *Chiefly Brit.* plagiarize. **—pla′gia·ris′er,** *n.*

pla·gia·rism (plā′jə riz′əm, -jē ə riz′-), *n.* **1.** the appropriation or imitation of the language, ideas, and thoughts of another author, and representation of them as one's original work. **2.** something appropriated and presented in this manner. **—pla′gia·rist,** *n.* **—pla′gia·ris′tic,** *adj.*

pla·gia·rize (plā′jə rīz′, -jē ə rīz′), *v.,* **-rized, -riz·ing.** **—***v.t.* **1.** to appropriate by plagiarism. **2.** to appropriate ideas, passages, etc., from (a work) by plagiarism. **—***v.i.* **3.** to commit plagiarism. Also, *esp. Brit.,* **plagiarise.** [PLAGIAR(ISM) + -IZE] **—pla′gia·riz′er,** *n.*

pla·gia·ry (plā′jə rē, -jē ə rē), *n., pl.* **-ries.** **1.** plagiarism. **2.** a plagiarist. [< L *plagiāri(us)* kidnapper = *plagi(um)* kidnapping (akin to *plagia* snare) + *-ārius* -ARY]

plagio-, a learned borrowing from Greek meaning "oblique," used in the formation of compound words: *plagioclase.* [comb. form repr. Gk *plágios* = *plág(os)* side + *-ios* adj. suffix]

pla·gi·o·ceph·a·ly (plā′jē ə sef′ə lē), *n. Med.* a deformity of the skull in which one side is more developed in the front and the other side is more developed in the rear. Also, **pla′gi·o·ceph′a·lism.** [PLAGIO- + CEPHAL- + -Y[3]]

pla·gi·o·clase (plā′jē ə klās′), *n.* any of the feldspar minerals varying in composition from acidic albite, $NaAlSi_3O_8$, to basic anorthite, $CaAl_2Si_2O_8$, found in most igneous rocks: shows twinning striations on good cleavage surfaces. [PLAGIO- + *-clase* < Gk *klásis* fracture] **—pla·gi·o·clas·tic** (plā′jē ə klas′tik), *adj.*

pla·gi·o·trop·ic (plā′jē ə trop′ik), *adj. Bot.* noting, pertaining to, or exhibiting a mode of growth which is more or less divergent from the vertical. **—pla′gi·o·trop′i·cal·ly,** *adv.*

pla·gi·ot·ro·pism (plā′jē o′trə piz′əm), *n. Bot.* plagiotropic tendency or growth. [PLAGIOTROP(IC) + -ISM]

plague (plāg), *n., v.,* **plagued, pla·guing.** **—***n.* **1.** an epidemic disease of high mortality; pestilence. **2.** an infectious, epidemic disease caused by a bacterium, *Pasteurella pestis,* characterized by fever, chills, and prostration, transmitted to man from rats by means of the bites of fleas. Cf. **bubonic plague.** **3.** any widespread affliction, calamity, or evil: *a plague of war.* **4.** any cause of trouble or vexation. **—***v.t.* **5.** to trouble or torment in any manner: *The question of his future plagues him with doubt.* **6.** to smite with a plague, pestilence, death, etc.; scourge: *those whom the gods had plagued.* **7.** to infect with a plague; cause an epidemic in or among. **8.** to afflict with any evil. [ME *plage* < L *plāga* stripe, wound, LL: pestilence; akin to Gk *plēgē* stroke] **—pla′guer,** *n.* **—Syn. 4.** nuisance, bother, annoyance. See **bother.**

plaice (plās), *n., pl.* (*esp. collectively*) **plaice,** (*esp. referring to two or more kinds or species*) **plaices.** **1.** a European flatfish, *Pleuronectes platessa,* used for food. **2.** any of various American flatfishes or flounders. [ME, var. of *plais* < OF < LL *platessa* flatfish < Gk *platýs* flat, broad]

plaid (plad), *n.* **1.** (loosely) a tartan pattern or a pattern suggesting one. **2.** a long, rectangular piece of cloth, usually with such a pattern and worn across the left shoulder by Scottish Highlanders. **—***adj.* **3.** (loosely) decorated with a tartan pattern or a pattern suggesting one. [< Gael *plaide*]

plain[1] (plān), *adj.* **1.** clear or distinct to the eye or ear: *in plain view.* **2.** clear to the mind; evident, manifest, or obvious: *to make one's meaning plain.* **3.** easily understood: *plain talk.* **4.** downright; sheer; utter: *plain folly.* **5.** free from ambiguity or evasion; candid; outspoken: *the plain truth.* **6.** without special pretensions, superiority, etc.; ordinary: *plain people.* **7.** not beautiful; physically unattractive or undistinguished: *a plain face.* **8.** without intricacies or difficulties: *a plain expository style.* **9.** with little or no embellishment or elaboration: *a plain blue suit.* **10.** without a pattern, figure, or device: *a plain fabric.* **11.** not rich, highly seasoned, or elaborately prepared, as food. **—***adv.* **12.** clearly and simply: *He's just plain stupid.* **—***n.* **13.** an area of land not significantly higher than adjacent areas and with relatively minor differences in elevation, commonly less than 500 feet, within the area. **14. The Plains.** See **Great Plains.** [ME < OF < L *plān(us)* flat, level, *plān(um)* flat country] **—plain′ly,** *adv.* **—plain′ness,** *n.* **—Syn. 2.** understandable, intelligible, unambiguous. **3.** direct. **5.** straightforward, frank, open. **6.** unpretentious. **9.** unadorned. See **simple.** **—Ant. 1.** indistinct.

plain[2] (plān), *v.i. Brit. Dial.* complain. [ME *plei(g)ne(n)* < OF *plaign-,* s. of *plaindre* < L *plangere* to beat (the breast, etc.), lament; akin to Gk *plēssein* to strike]

plain·chant (plān′chant′, -chänt′), *n.* plainsong (defs. 1, 2). [PLAIN[1] + CHANT, modeled on F *plain-chant*]

plain′-clothes′ man′ (plān′klōz′, -klōthz′), a police detective who wears mufti while on duty.

plain·clothes·man (plān′klōz′mən, -man′, -klōthz′-), *n., pl.* **-men** (-mən, -men′). See **plain-clothes man.**

Plain·field (plān′fēld′), *n.* a city in N New Jersey. 46,862 (1970).

plain′ knit′, the simplest knitted construction, consisting of vertical ribs visible on the right side and horizontal rows of stitches visible on the wrong side.

plain-laid (plān′lād′), *adj. Ropemaking.* noting a rope laid right-handed with three left-handed strands, without a heart.

plain′ lap′. See **lap joint** (def. 1).

Plain′ Peo′ple, members of the Amish, the Mennonites, or the Dunkers: so named because they wear plain dress and stress simple living.

plain′ sail′, **1.** any of the ordinary working sails of a vessel. **2.** all these sails, taken collectively.

Plains′ In′dian, a member of any of the American Indian tribes, as those of the Algonquian, Athabascan, Caddoan, Kiowa, Siouan, or Uto-Aztecan linguistic stocks, that formerly inhabited the Great Plains and were more or less nomadic, following the buffalo. Also called **Buffalo Indian.**

plains·man (plānz′mən), *n., pl.* **-men.** a man or inhabitant of the plains.

Plains′ of A′braham, a high plain adjoining the city of Quebec, Canada: English victory over the French in 1759.

plain·song (plān′sông′, -song′), *n.* **1.** the unisonous vocal music used in the Christian church from the earliest times. **2.** modal liturgical music; Gregorian chant. **3.** a cantus firmus or theme chosen for contrapuntal development. Also called **plainchant** (for defs. 1, 2). [trans. of ML *cantus plānus*]

plain-spo·ken (plān′spō′kən), *adj.* candid; blunt.

plaint (plānt), *n.* **1.** a complaint. **2.** *Law.* a statement of grievance. **3.** *Archaic.* a lament. [ME < MF < L *planct(us)* (4th decl. n.) a striking (the breast) in grief = *planct-* (ptp. s. of *plangere* to strike, etc.) + *-us,* u-stem suffix]

plain′ ta′ble. See **plane table.**

plain′ text′, the original message of a cryptogram expressed in ordinary language, as opposed to a coded or enciphered version. Cf. **cryptography.**

plain·tiff (plān′tif), *n. Law.* a person who brings suit in a court (opposed to *defendant*). [late ME *plaintif* complaining person, n. use of *plaintif,* early form of PLAINTIVE]

plain·tive (plān′tiv), *adj.* expressing sorrow or melancholy. [PLAINT + -IVE; r. ME *plaintif* < MF] **—plain′tive·ly,** *adv.* **—plain′tive·ness,** *n.* **—Syn.** wistful, sorrowful, sad. **—Ant.** happy, pleasant.

Plain·view (plān′vyōō′), *n.* a town on W Long Island, in SE New York. 31,695 (1970).

Plain weave

plain′ weave′, the tightest and most common of basic weave structures, the filling threads passing alternately over and under successive warp threads, producing a checkered surface. Cf. **satin weave, twill weave.**

plait (plāt, plat), *n.* **1.** a braid, as of hair or straw. **2.** a pleat or fold, as of cloth. **—***v.t.* **3.** to braid, as hair or straw. **4.** to make, as a mat, by braiding. **5.** pleat. [ME *pleyt* < MF *pleit* < VL **plict(um),* syncopated var. of L *plicitum,* n. use of neut. of *plicitus* folded, ptp. of *plicāre;* see PLY[2]]

plait·ing (plā′ting, plat′ing), *n.* that which is braided or pleated; plaits collectively. [ME *pleyting*]

plan (plan), *n., v.,* **planned, plan·ning.** **—***n.* **1.** a method of action or procedure. **2.** a design or scheme of arrangement: *an elaborate plan for seating guests.* **3.** a project or definite purpose: *plans for the future.* **4.** a drawing made to scale to represent the top view or a horizontal section of a structure or a machine. **5.** a map or diagram: *a plan of the dock area.* **6.** (in perspective drawing) one of several planes in front of a represented object, and perpendicular to the line between the object and the eye. **—***v.t.* **7.** to arrange or project a plan or scheme for (any work, enterprise, or proceeding): *to plan a new recreation center; to plan one's vacation.* **8.** to draw or make a plan of, as a building. **—***v.i.* **9.** to make a plan: *to plan for one's retirement.* [< F: plane, plan, groundwork, scheme < L *plān(us)* level, *plānum* level ground. See PLANE[1], PLAIN[1]]

—Syn. 1. plot, formula, system. PLAN, PROJECT, DESIGN, SCHEME imply a formulated method of doing something. PLAN refers to any method of thinking out acts and purposes beforehand: *What are your plans for today?* A PROJECT is a proposed or tentative plan, often elaborate or extensive: *an irrigation project.* DESIGN suggests art, dexterity, or craft (sometimes evil and selfish) in the elaboration or execution of a plan, and often tends to emphasize the purpose in view: *a disturbance brought about by design.* A SCHEME is apt to be either a speculative, possibly impractical, plan, or a selfish or dishonest one: *a scheme to swindle someone.* **4.** draft, diagram, chart. **7.** design, devise.

—Usage. Many teachers object to the phrase PLAN ON (followed by a gerund) considering it poor style for PLAN TO (followed by an infinitive): *I had planned to go to the movies tonight* (not *I had planned on going to the movies tonight*).

plan-, var. of **plano-**[1] before a vowel: *planate.*

pla·nar (plā′nər), *adj.* **1.** of or pertaining to a plane. **2.** flat. [< LL *plānār(is)* flat, on a level surface]

pla·nar·i·an (plə nâr′ē ən), *n.* *Zool.* a free-swimming flatworm having a trifid intestine. [< NL *Plānāri(a)* the typical genus (n. use of fem. of LL *plānārius* level, flat; see PLANE[1], -ARY) + -AN]

pla·nate (plā′nāt), *adj.* having a plane or flat surface. [< LL *plānāt(us)*, ptp. of *plānāre*]

Planarian, *Euplanaria tigrinum* (Length 1¼ in.)

pla·na·tion (plā nā′shən, plə-), *n.* the production of a flat or plane surface by erosion.

planch·et (plan′chit), *n.* a flat piece of metal for stamping as a coin; a coin blank. [< F *planche* PLANK + -ET]

plan·chette (plan chet′), *n.* a small, heart-shaped board supported by two castors and a pencil or stylus which, when moved across a surface by the light, unguided pressure of the fingertips, is supposed to trace meaningful patterns or written messages revealing subconscious thoughts, clairvoyant messages, etc. Cf. **ouija board.** [< F = *planche* PLANK + *-ette* -ETTE]

Planck (plängk), *n.* **Max Karl Ernst** (mäks kärl ernst), 1858–1947, German physicist: Nobel prize 1918.

Planck's′ con′stant, *Physics.* the fundamental constant of quantum mechanics, expressing the ratio of the energy of one quantum of radiation to the frequency of the radiation and approximately equal to 6.624×10^{-27} erg-seconds. *Symbol:* h [named after M. K. E. PLANCK]

Planck's′ radia′tion law′, *Physics.* the law that energy associated with electromagnetic radiation, as light, is composed of discrete quanta of energy, each quantum equal to Planck's constant times the corresponding frequency of the radiation: the fundamental law of quantum mechanics. Also called **Planck′ radia′tion for′mula, Planck's′ law′.** [named after M. K. E. PLANCK]

plane[1] (plān), *n., adj., v.,* **planed, plan·ing.** —*n.* **1.** a flat or level surface. **2.** *Math.* a surface generated by a line moving at a constant velocity with respect to a fixed point. **3.** *Fine Arts.* an area of a two-dimensional surface having determinate extension, and spatial direction or position: *horizontal plane.* **4.** a level of dignity, character, existence, development, or the like: *a high moral plane.* **5.** an airplane or a hydroplane. **6.** *Aeron.* a thin, flat or curved, extended section of an airplane or a hydroplane, affording a supporting surface. —*adj.* **7.** flat or level, as a surface. **8.** of or pertaining to planes or plane figures. —*v.i.* **9.** to glide. **10.** (of a boat) to lift partly out of water when running at high speed. [< L *plān(um)* level ground. See PLAIN[1]] —**plane′ness,** *n.* —**Syn. 4.** stratum, stage. **7.** smooth, even, flush.

plane[2] (plān), *n., v.,* **planed, plan·ing.** —*n.* **1.** *Carpentry.* any of various woodworking instruments for paring, truing, or smoothing, or for forming moldings, grooves, etc., by means of an inclined, adjustable blade pushed along and against the piece being worked. —*v.t.* **2.** to smooth or dress with or as with a plane or a planer. **3.** to remove by or as by means of a plane (usually fol. by *away* or *off*). —*v.i.* **4.** to work with a plane. **5.** to function as a plane. [late ME < MF < LL *plāna* (n.), *plānāre* (v.); akin to PLAIN[1], PLANE[1]]

A

B

Planes (def. 1)
A, Jack plane; B, Router

plane[3] (plān), *n.* See **plane tree.** [ME < MF < L *platan(us)* < Gk *plátanos* < *platýs* broad (with reference to the leaves)]

plane′ an′gle, *Math.* an angle between two intersecting lines.

plane′ geom′etry, *Math.* the geometry of figures whose parts all lie in one plane.

plan·er (plā′nər), *n.* **1.** *Carpentry.* a power machine for removing the rough or excess surface from a board. **2.** a machine for cutting flat surfaces on metal, having a cutting tool supported by an overhead frame beneath which the work slides on a bed with a reciprocating motion. Cf. **shaper** (def. 2).

plan′er tree′, a small, ulmaceous tree, *Planera aquatica,* growing in moist ground in the southern U.S., bearing a small, ovoid, nutlike fruit and yielding a compact light-brown wood. [named after I. J. *Planer,* 18th-century German botanist]

plan·et (plan′it), *n.* **1.** *Astron.* **a.** any of the nine large heavenly bodies revolving about the sun and shining by reflected light (Mercury, Venus, Earth, Mars, Jupiter, Saturn, Uranus, Neptune, or Pluto, in the order of their proximity to the sun). **b.** a similar body revolving about a star other than the sun. **c.** (formerly) a celestial body moving in the sky, as distinguished from a fixed star, formerly applied also to the sun and moon. **2.** *Astrol.* a heavenly body regarded as exerting an influence on mankind. [ME *planete* < ML *planēta,* pl. (taken as sing.) of LL *planētae* < Gk *planētai,* lit., wanderers]

plane′ ta′ble, *Surveying.* a drawing board mounted on a tripod, used in the field for obtaining and plotting survey data. Also, **plain table.**

plane-ta·ble (plān′tā′bəl), *v.t., v.i.,* **-bled, -bling.** to survey with a plane table.

plan·e·tar·i·um (plan′i târ′ē əm), *n., pl.* **-tar·i·ums, -tar·i·a** (-târ′ē ə). **1.** an apparatus or model representing the planetary system. **2.** a device that produces a representation of the heavens by the use of a number of moving projectors. **3.** the structure in which such a planetarium is housed. [< NL, neut. of L *planētārius* PLANETARY]

plan·e·tar·y (plan′i ter′ē), *adj., n., pl.* **-tar·ies.** —*adj.* **1.** of, pertaining to, or resembling a planet or the planets. **2.** wandering; erratic. **3.** terrestrial; global. **4.** *Mach.* noting or pertaining to an epicyclic gear train in which a sun gear is linked to one or more planet gears also engaging with an encircling ring gear. —*n.* **5.** *Mach.* a planetary gear train. [< L *planētāri(us)*]

plan′etary neb′ula, *Astron.* nebula (def. 1b).

plan·e·tes·i·mal (plan′i tes′ə məl), *Astron.* —*n.* **1.** one of the minute bodies that, hypothetically, was an original constituent of the solar system. —*adj.* **2.** of or pertaining to a planetesimal or planetesimals. [PLANET + (INFINI-T)ESIMAL]

planetes′imal hypoth′esis, *Astron.* the hypothesis that the solar system or a similar system originally consisted of the sun or another star and innumerable minute bodies revolving about it, and that these minute bodies gradually united to form the planets and satellites of the system.

plan′et gear′, *Mach.* any of the gears in an epicyclic train surrounding and engaging with the sun gear. Also called **planet wheel.**

plan·et·oid (plan′i toid′), *n.* *Astron.* an asteroid.

plane′ tree′, any tree of the genus *Platanus,* esp. *P. orientalis,* which is found wild from Italy to Persia and is grown in Europe as an ornamental, or *P. occidentalis,* the buttonwood or sycamore of North America.

plane′ trigonom′etry, *Math.* the branch of trigonometry dealing with plane triangles.

plan·et-struck (plan′it struk′), *adj.* **1.** stricken by the supposed astrological influence of a planet; blasted. **2.** panic-stricken. Also, **plan·et-strick·en** (plan′it strik′ən).

plan′et wheel′. See **planet gear.**

plan·gent (plan′jənt), *adj.* resounding loudly, esp. with a plaintive sound, as a bell. [< L *plangent-* (s. of *plangēns*) lamenting, prp. of *plangere.* See PLAIN[2], -ENT] —**plan′gen·cy,** *n.* —**plan′gent·ly,** *adv.*

plani-, var. of **plano-**[1]: *planimetry.*

pla·ni·form (plā′nə fôrm′, plan′ə-), *adj.* having a flattened shape, as an anatomical joint.

pla·nim·e·try (plə nim′i trē), *n.* the measurement of plane areas. —**plan·i·met·ric** (plan′ə me′trik), **plan′i·met′ri·cal,** *adj.*

plan′ing hull′, *Naut.* a hull that tends to rise from the water when under way so that no significant amount of water is displaced beyond a certain speed. Cf. **displacement hull.**

plan·ish (plan′ish), *v.t.* **1.** to give a smooth finish to (metal) by striking it lightly with a smoothly faced hammer or die. **2.** to give a smooth finish to (metal, paper, etc.) by passing it through rolls. [ME < OF *planiss-,* long s. of *planir* to smooth < *plan* level < L *plān(us)* PLAIN[1]] —**plan′ish·er,** *n.*

plan·i·sphere (plan′i sfēr′), *n.* **1.** a map of half or more of the celestial sphere with a device for indicating the part visible at a given time of a given location. **2.** a projection or representation of the whole or a part of a sphere on a plane. [PLANI- + SPHERE; r. ME *planisperie* < ML *plānisphaeri(um)*] —**plan·i·spher·i·cal** (plan′i sfer′i kəl), **plan′i·spher′ic,** *adj.*

plank (plangk), *n.* **1.** a long, flat piece of timber, thicker than a board. **2.** planking (def. 1). **3.** something to stand on or to cling to for support. **4.** one of the expressed principles or objectives comprising the political platform of a party campaigning for election. **5. walk the plank,** to be forced, as by pirates, to walk to one's death by stepping off a plank extending from the ship's side over the water. —*v.t.* **6.** to lay, cover, or furnish with planks. **7. plank** or **plunk down, a.** to lay or put down with force. **b.** *Informal.* to pay (money) immediately or speedily. [ME *planke* < ONF < L *planca* board, plank]

plank·ing (plang′king), *n.* **1.** planks collectively, as in a floor. **2.** act of laying or covering with planks.

plank·ton (plangk′tən), *n.* the aggregate of passively floating or drifting organisms in a body of water. [< G, special use of neut. of Gk *planktós* drifting < *plank-* (var. of *plang-,* s. of *plázesthai* to drift, roam, wander) + *-tos* verbid suffix; akin to L *planctus.* See PLAINT] —**plank·ton·ic** (plangk ton′ik), *adj.*

planned′ econ′omy, an economic system in which the government controls and regulates production, distribution, prices, etc. Cf. **free enterprise.**

planned′ par′enthood, the methods and practices by which parents may regulate the number and frequency of their children. Cf. **birth control.**

plan·ner (plan′ər), *n.* a person who plans.

plano-[1], a learned borrowing from Latin used, with the meaning "flat," "plane," in the formation of compound words: *planography.* Also, **plan-, plani-.** [comb. form repr. L *plānus* level, *plānum* level ground]

plano-[2], a learned borrowing from Greek used, with the meaning "moving," "capable of movement," in the formation of compound words. [comb. form repr. Gk *plános* wandering, roaming. See PLANET]

pla·no-con·cave (plā′nō kon′kāv), *adj.* *Optics.* pertaining to or noting a lens that is plane on one side and concave on the other. See diag. at **concave.**

pla·no-con·vex (plā′nō kon′veks), *adj.* *Optics.* pertaining to or noting a lens that is plane on one side and convex on the other. See diag. at **convex.**

plan·o·gam·ete (plan′ō gam′ēt, plan′ə gə mēt′), *n.* *Bot., Zool.* a motile gamete.

pla·no·graph (plā′nə graf′, -gräf′, plan′ə-), *Print.* —*v.t.* **1.** to print from a flat surface. —*n.* **2.** an impression so produced.

pla·nog·ra·phy (plə nog′rə fē), *n.* *Print.* the art or technique of printing from a flat surface directly or by offset. —**pla·no·graph·ic** (plā′nə graf′ik), *adj.* —**pla′no·graph′i·cal·ly,** *adv.*

plant (plant, plänt), *n.* **1.** any member of the vegetable group of living organisms: *A tree is a plant.* **2.** an herb or other small vegetable growth, in contrast with a tree or a shrub. **3.** a seedling or a growing slip, esp. one ready for transplanting. **4.** the equipment and often the buildings necessary to carry on any industrial business: *a manufacturing plant.* **5.** the complete equipment or apparatus for a particular mechanical process or operation: *the heating plant* *for a home.* **6.** the buildings, equipment, etc., of an institution: *the sprawling plant of the university.* **7.** a person, placed in an audience, whose rehearsed or prepared reactions, comments, etc., are meant to appear spontaneous. —*v.t.* **8.** to put or set in the ground for growth, as seeds, young trees, etc. **9.** to furnish or stock (land) with plants: *to plant ten acres with corn.* **10.** to establish or implant (ideas, principles, doctrines, etc.): *to plant a love for learning in growing children.* **11.** to introduce (a breed of animals) into a region or country. **12.** to deposit (young fish, or spawn) in a river, lake, etc. **13.** to bed (oysters). **14.** to insert or set firmly in or on the ground or some other body or surface: *to plant posts.* **15.** to place; put. **16.** *Informal.* to place with great force or firmness: *He planted his fist in the palm of his other hand.* **17.** to station or post: *to plant spies.* **18.** to locate; situate. **19.** to establish (a colony, city, etc.); found. **20.** to settle (persons), as in a colony. **21.** to say or place (something) in order to obtain a desired result, esp. one that will seem spontaneous. [(n.) ME, OE *plante* < L *planta* a shoot, sprig, scion (for planting), plant; (v.) ME *plante(n)*, OE *plantian* < L *plant(āre)* (to) plant] —**plant′like′,** *adj.*

Plan·tag·e·net (plan taj′ə nit), *n.* a member of the royal house that ruled England from the accession of Henry II in 1154 to the death of Richard III in 1485. [< F: lit., sprig of broom, nickname of the Angevin kings of England]

plan·tain[1] (plan′tin, -tᵊn), *n.* **1.** a tropical, herbaceous plant, *Musa paradisiaca,* resembling the banana. **2.** its fruit. [earlier *pla(n)tan* < Sp *plá(n)tano* plantain, also plane tree < ML *pla(n)tanus,* L *platanus* PLANE[3]]

plan·tain[2] (plan′tin, -tᵊn), *n.* any plant of the genus *Plantago,* esp. *P. major,* a weed with large, spreading leaves close to the ground and long, slender spikes of small flowers. [ME *plauntein* < OF *plantein* < L *plantāgin-* (s. of *plantāgō*) < *planta* sole of the foot, lit., something flat and spread out, like the broad leaf of the plantain; akin to Gk *platýs;* see PLATY-]

plan′tain lil′y, any liliaceous herb of the genus *Hosta,* of China and Japan, having large leaves and spikes or racemes of white, lilac, or blue flowers.

plan·tar (plan′tər), *adj.* *Anat., Zool.* of or pertaining to the sole of the foot. [< L *plantār(is)* = *plant(a)* sole of the foot + *-āris* -AR[1]]

plan·ta·tion (plan tā′shən), *n.* **1.** a farm or estate, esp. in a tropical or semitropical country, on which cotton, tobacco, coffee, or the like, is cultivated, usually by resident laborers. **2.** *Chiefly Brit.* a group of planted trees or plants. **3.** *Hist.* a colony or new settlement. **4.** *Rare.* the planting of seeds, young trees, etc. [late ME *plantacioune* < L *plantātiōn-* (s. of *plantātiō*) a planting] —**plan·ta′tion·like′,** *adj.*

plant·er (plan′tər, plän′-), *n.* **1.** a person who plants. **2.** an implement or machine for planting seeds in the ground. **3.** the owner or occupant of a plantation. **4.** *Hist.* a colonist or new settler. **5.** a decorative container for plants, ferns, etc. [ME *plaunter*]

plant′er's punch′, a punch made with rum, lime juice, sugar, and water or soda.

plant′ food′, nourishment, as fertilizer, for plants.

plan·ti·grade (plan′tə grād′), *adj.* **1.** walking on the whole sole of the foot, as man, the bears, etc. —*n.* **2.** a plantigrade animal. [< NL *plantigrad(us)* = L *plant(a)* sole + *-i-* -I- + *-gradus* -GRADE]

plant′ king′dom, plants collectively. Also called **vegetable kingdom.** Cf. **animal kingdom, mineral kingdom.**

plant′ louse′, **1.** aphid. **2.** any of various related insects.

plant′ pathol′ogy, the branch of botany dealing with diseases of plants.

plan·u·la (plan′yə lə), *n., pl.* **-lae** (-lē′). *Zool.* the ciliate, free-swimming larva of a coelenterate. [< NL, dim. of L *plānum* something flat] —**plan′u·lar, plan·u·late** (plan′yə lāt′), *adj.*

plaque (plak), *n.* **1.** a thin, flat plate or tablet of metal, porcelain, etc., intended for ornament, as on a wall. **2.** an inscribed commemorative tablet, usually of metal, placed on the side of a building, monument, or the like. **3.** a platelike brooch or ornament, esp. one worn as the badge of an honorary order. **4.** *Dentistry.* a gelatinous accumulation of bacteria and salivary mucin that forms on the teeth. [< F, back formation from *plaquier* to plate < MD *placken* to beat (metal) thin and flat. See PLACKET]

plash[1] (plash), *n.* **1.** a splash. **2.** a pool or puddle. —*v.t., v.i.* **3.** to splash. [ME *plasch,* OE *plæsc;* c. D, LG *plas,* prob. of imit. orig.] —**plash′ing·ly,** *adv.*

plash[2] (plash), *v.t.* pleach. [late ME < MF *plaiss(ier)* < *plais* hedge < VL **plaxum* < ?] —**plash′er,** *n.*

plash·y (plash′ē), *adj.,* **plash·i·er, plash·i·est. 1.** marshy; wet. **2.** splashing.

-plasia, an element of Greek origin used with the specialized meaning "plasmic growth": *hypoplasia.* Also, **-plasy.** [< NL < Gk *plás(is)* a molding + *-ia* -IA]

plasm (plaz′əm), *n.* plasma. (defs. 1–3).

plasm-, var. of **plasmo-** before a vowel: *plasmin.*

-plasm, an element meaning "something formed or molded," occurring as a noun termination in biological and other scientific terms: *protoplasm.* [comb. form repr. Gk *plásma.* See PLASMA]

plas·ma (plaz′mə), *n.* **1.** *Anat., Physiol.* the liquid part of blood or lymph, as distinguished from the suspended elements. **2.** *Biol.* protoplasm. **3.** whey. **4.** a green, faintly translucent chalcedony. **5.** *Physics.* a highly ionized gas containing an approximately equal number of positive ions and electrons. Also, **plasm** (for defs. 1–3). [< LL < Gk *plásma* something molded or formed, akin to *plássein* to form, mold. See PLASTIC] —**plas·mat·ic** (plaz mat′ik), **plas′mic,** *adj.*

plas′ma en′gine, an engine for space craft that produces reactive thrust by means of accelerating a stream of plasma.

plas·ma·gel (plaz′mə jel′), *n.* the gelatinous outer layer of cytoplasm of an amoeba, beneath the cell membrane.

plas′ma mem′brane, *Biol.* a cell membrane.

plas·ma·sol (plaz′mə sōl′, -sôl′, -sol′), *n.* the relatively fluid, inner cytoplasm of an amoeba.

plas·min (plaz′min), *n.* *Biochem.* fibrinolysin (def. 1).

plasmo-, a combining form of **plasma** or **protoplasm:** *plasmolysis.* Also, *esp. before a vowel,* **plasm-.** [comb. form, repr. Gk *plásma.* See PLASMA]

plas·mo·di·um (plaz mō′dē əm), *n., pl.* **-di·a** (-dē ə). **1.** *Biol.* an amoeboid, multinucleate mass or sheet of protoplasm characteristic of some stages of organisms, as a myxomycete or slime mold. **2.** any parasitic protozoan of the genus *Plasmodium,* causing malaria in man. [< NL; see PLASM-, -ODE[1]] —**plas·mo′di·al,** *adj.*

plas·mol·y·sis (plaz mol′i sis), *n.* *Bot.* contraction of the protoplasm in a living cell when water is removed by exosmosis. —**plas·mo·lyt·ic** (plaz′mə lit′ik), *adj.* —**plas′mo·lyt′i·cal·ly,** *adv.*

Plas·sey (plä′sē), *n.* a village in NE India, about 80 miles north of Calcutta: Clive's victory over a Bengal army here (1757) led to the establishment of British power in India.

-plast, a learned borrowing from Greek meaning "formed," "molded," used esp. in biological and botanical terms: *protoplast.* [comb. form, repr. Gk *plastós* formed, molded = *pláss(ein)* (to) form, mold + *-tos* verbid suffix. See PLASTIC]

plas·ter (plas′tər, plä′stər), *n.* **1.** a composition, as of lime or gypsum, sand, water, and sometimes hair, applied in a pasty form to walls, ceilings, etc., and allowed to harden and dry. **2.** powdered gypsum. **3.** See **plaster of Paris. 4.** a preparation for spreading upon cloth or the like and applying to the body for some healing purpose. —*v.t.* **5.** to cover (walls, ceilings, etc.) with plaster. **6.** to treat with gypsum or plaster of Paris. **7.** to lay flat like a layer of plaster. **8.** to daub or fill with plaster or something similar. **9.** to apply a plaster to (the body, a wound, etc.). **10.** to overspread with something, esp. thickly or excessively: *to plaster posters on a fence.* [ME, OE < ML *plastr(um)* plaster (both medical and building senses), aph. var. of L *emplastrum* < Gk *émplastron* salve = *em-* EM-[2] + *pláss(ein)* (to) mold, form + *-tron* -TRON] —**plas′ter·er,** *n.* —**plas′ter·y,** *adj.*

plas·ter·board (plas′tər bōrd′, -bôrd′, plä′stər-), *n.* paper-covered sheets of gypsum and felt for insulating or covering walls.

plas′ter cast′, any piece of sculpture reproduced in plaster of Paris.

plas·tered (plas′tərd, plä′stərd), *adj.* **1.** *Slang.* drunk. **2.** covered or treated with plaster. **3.** overspread, esp. thickly.

plas′ter of Par′is, calcined gypsum in white, powdery form, used as a base for gypsum plasters, as an additive of lime plasters, and as a material for making fine and ornamental casts. Also, **plas′ter of par′is.** [late ME; so called because prepared from the gypsum of *Paris,* France]

plas·ter·work (plas′tər wûrk′, plä′stər-), *n.* *Building Trades.* finish or ornamental work done in plaster.

plas·tic (plas′tik), *adj.* **1.** capable of being molded or of receiving form: *plastic substances.* **2.** produced by molding: *plastic figures.* **3.** having the power of molding or shaping formless or yielding material: *the plastic forces of nature.* **4.** being able to create, esp. within an art form; having the power of artistic expression: *the plastic imagination of great poets and composers.* **5.** *Fine Arts.* **a.** concerned with or pertaining to molding or modeling; sculptural. **b.** relating to three-dimensional form or space, esp. on a two-dimensional surface. **c.** pertaining to the tools or techniques of drawing, painting, or sculpture. **d.** characterized by an emphasis on formal structure. **6.** *Biol., Pathol.* formative. **7.** *Surg.* concerned with or pertaining to the remedying or restoring of malformed, injured, or lost parts. **8.** *Slang.* **a.** false, phony, or insincere: *plastic political speeches.* **b.** superficial, rootless, or inhuman: *a plastic society.* —*n.* **9.** Often, **plastics.** any of a group of synthetic or natural organic materials that may be shaped when soft and then hardened, including many types of resins, resinoids, polymers, cellulose derivatives, casein materials, and proteins: used in construction and decoration, and, drawn into filaments, for weaving. [< L *plastic(us)* that may be molded < Gk *plastikós*] —**plas′ti·cal·ly, plas′tic·ly,** *adv.*

-plastic, an element forming adjectives corresponding to nouns with stems ending in *-plasm, -plast,* and *-plasty: chloroplastic; protoplastic.* [see PLASTIC]

plas′tic art′, **1.** an art, as sculpture, in which forms are carved or modeled. **2.** an art, as painting or sculpture, in which forms are rendered in or as if in three dimensions.

plas′tic bomb′, an adhesive, puttylike substance composed of explosives, as nitroglycerine and nitrocellulose, detonated electrically or by fuse: used esp. in terrorist activities, guerrilla warfare, or the like.

plas′tic cred′it, *Informal.* credit granted to holders of credit cards, esp. by banks: so called because such cards are usually made of plastic.

plas·ti·cise (plas′ti sīz′), *v.t., v.i.,* **-cised, -cis·ing.** *Chiefly Brit.* plasticize. —**plas′ti·ci·sa′tion,** *n.*

plas·tic·i·ty (pla stis′i tē), *n.* **1.** the quality or state of being plastic. **2.** the capability of being molded, receiving shape, or being made to assume a desired form.

plas·ti·cize (plas′ti sīz′), *v.t., v.i.,* **-cized, -ciz·ing.** to render or become plastic. Also, *esp. Brit.,* **plasticise.** —**plas′ti·ci·za′tion,** *n.*

plas·ti·ciz·er (plas′ti sī′zər), *n.* any of a group of substances that are used in plastics or the like to impart viscosity, flexibility, softness, or other properties to the finished product. Also, *esp. Brit.,* **plas′ti·cis′er.**

plas′tic sur′gery, the branch of surgery dealing with the repair or replacement of malformed, injured, or lost organs or tissues. Also called **anaplasty.** —**plas′tic sur′geon.**

plas·tid (plas′tid), *n.* *Biol.* any of certain small specialized masses of protoplasm found in plant cells and certain protozoans. [< G *Plastide* < Gk *plastid-,* s. of *plástis,* fem. of *plástēs* modeler, creator = *pláss(ein)* (to) form + *-tēs* agent suffix]

plasto-, a learned borrowing from Greek meaning "formed," "molded," used in the formation of compound words: *plastometer.* Cf. **-plast.** [comb. form, repr. Gk *plastós*]

plas·tom·e·ter (pla stom′i tər), *n.* an instrument for measuring the plasticity of a substance. —**plas·to·met·ric** (plas′tə me′trik), *adj.* —**plas·tom′e·try,** *n.*

plas·tral (plas′trəl), *adj.* *Zool.* relating to the plastron. [PLASTR(ON) + -AL[1]]

plas·tron (plas′trən), *n.* **1.** a piece of plate armor for the upper part of the torso in front. **2.** *Fencing.* a quilted pad worn over part of the torso, for protection. **3.** an ornamental front piece of a woman's bodice. **4.** the starched front of a shirt. **5.** *Zool.* the ventral part of the shell of a turtle. [< MF < It *piastrone*, aug. of *piastra* metal plate, PIASTER. See PLASTER]

-plasty, an element meaning "formation," occurring in terms of the processes of plastic surgery (*dermoplasty; neoplasty*), and occasionally in other words (*galvanoplasty*). [< Gk *-plastia*. See -PLAST, -Y³]

-plasy, var. of **-plasia.**

plat¹ (plat), *n., v.,* **plat·ted, plat·ting.** —*n.* **1.** a plot of ground. **2.** *U.S.* a plan or map, as of land. —*v.t.* **3.** *U.S.* to make a plat of; plot. [ME (in place names); c. Goth *plat* patch; akin to PLOT²]

plat² (plat), *n., v.,* **plat·ted, plat·ting.** —*n.* **1.** a plait or braid. —*v.t.* **2.** to plait; braid. [var. of PLAIT]

plat-, var. of **platy-.**

plat., **1.** plateau. **2.** platoon.

Pla·ta (plä′tä), *n.* **Rí·o de la** (rē′ô t͟he lä), an estuary on the SE coast of South America between Argentina and Uruguay, formed by the Uruguay and Paraná rivers. 185 mi. long. Also, **La Plata, Pla′ta Riv′er;** *Brit.* **River Plate.**

Pla·tae·a (plə tē′ə), *n.* an ancient city in Greece, in Boeotia: Greeks defeated Persians here 479 B.C.

plat·an (plat′ən), *n.* See **plane tree.** [< L *platanus* < Gk *plátanos* plane tree]

plat du jour (plä′ də zhŏŏr′; *Fr.* plA dʏ zhōōr′), *pl.* **plats du jour** (pläz′ də zhŏŏr′; *Fr.* plA dʏ zhōōr′). the special dish of the day on a menu. [< F: dish of the day]

plate¹ (plāt), *n., v.,* **plat·ed, plat·ing.** —*n.* **1.** a shallow, usually circular dish, often of earthenware or porcelain, from which food is eaten or served. **2.** the contents of such a dish: *She had a vegetable plate for lunch.* **3.** the food and service for one person, as at a banquet: *The wedding breakfast cost $10 a plate.* **4.** an entire course on one dish. **5.** *Chiefly Brit.* domestic dishes, utensils, etc., of gold or silver. **6.** a dish used for collecting offerings, as in a church. **7.** a thin, flat sheet or piece of metal or other material, esp. of uniform thickness. **8.** metal in such sheets. **9.** a flat, polished piece of metal on which something may be or is engraved. **10.** a flat or curved sheet of metal, plastic, glass, or the like, on which a picture or text has been engraved, etched, molded, photographically developed, or drawn. It is inked, as in a press, for printing impressions on other surfaces. **11.** a printed impression from such a piece, as a woodcut. **12.** a full-page illustration in a book. **13.** plated metallic ware: *silver plate.* **14.** See **plate armor. 15.** *Dentistry.* **a.** the part of a denture that conforms to the mouth and contains the teeth. **b.** (loosely) the entire denture. **16.** *Baseball.* **a. the plate.** See **home plate. b.** rubber (def. 9). **17.** See **plate glass. 18.** *Photog.* a sheet of glass, metal, etc., coated with a sensitized emulsion, used for taking a photograph. **19.** *Anat., Zool., Biol.* a platelike part, structure, or organ. **20.** a thin piece or cut of beef from the lower end of the ribs. **21.** *Electronics.* one of the interior elements of a vacuum tube, toward which electrons are attracted by virtue of its positive charge; anode. **22.** *Carpentry.* any horizontal timber for supporting joists, rafters, or studs. **23.** a gold or silver cup or the like awarded as the prize in a horse race or some other contest. **24.** a horse race or some other contest for such a prize. —*v.t.* **25.** to coat (metal) with a thin film of gold, silver, nickel, etc., by mechanical or chemical means. **26.** to cover or overlay with metal plates for protection. **27.** *Metalworking.* **a.** to forge (a bloom or the like) into a broad piece. **b.** to hammer (cutlery) gently to produce an even surface. **28.** *Print.* to make a stereotype or electrotype plate from (type). **29.** *Papermaking.* to give a high gloss to (paper). [ME < OF: lit., something flat, n. use of fem. of *plat* flat < VL **platt(us)*, akin to Gk *platýs* broad, flat] —**plate′less,** *adj.* —**plate′like′,** *adj.*

plate² (plāt), *n.* *Obs.* a coin, esp. of silver. [ME < OF]

plate′ ar′mor, armor made of thin, flat, shaped pieces of wrought iron or steel.

pla·teau (pla tō′ *or, esp. Brit.,* plat′ō), *n., pl.* **-teaus, -teaux** (-tōz′, -tōz), *v.,* **-teaued, -teau·ing.** —*n.* **1.** a land area having a relatively level surface considerably raised above adjoining land on at least one side, and often cut by deep canyons. **2.** *Psychol.* a period of little or no apparent progress in an individual's learning, marked by an inability to increase speed, reduce number of errors, etc. **3.** any period of minimal growth or decline. —*v.i.* **4.** to reach a state or level of little growth or decline. [< F; OF *platel* flat object, dim. of *plat* PLATE¹]

plate·ful (plāt′fo͝ol), *n., pl.* **-fuls.** the amount that a plate will hold. [PLATE¹ + -FUL]

plate′ glass′, a soda-lime-silica glass formed by rolling the hot glass into a plate that is subsequently ground and polished, used in large windows, mirrors, etc.

plate·let (plāt′lit), *n.* a small platelike body, esp. a blood platelet.

plate′ mark′, hallmark.

plat·en (plat′ən), *n.* **1.** a flat plate in a printing press for pressing the paper against the inked type or plate to produce an impression. **2.** a rotating cylinder used for the same purpose. **3.** the roller of a typewriter. [earlier *platyne* < MF *platine.* See PLATE¹, -INE¹]

plat·er (plā′tər), *n.* **1.** a person or thing that plates. **2.** an inferior race horse.

plate′ tecton′ics, *Geol.* a theory that describes the earth's crust as being divided into a number of rigid plates that move independently of each other, giving rise to continental drift.

plate′ trac′ery, tracery formed of cut or pierced slabs of stone set on edge with the flat side outward.

plat·form (plat′fôrm), *n.* **1.** a raised flooring or structure, as in a hall or meeting place, for use by public speakers, performers, etc. **2.** a landing in a flight of stairs. **3.** the raised area between or alongside the tracks of a railroad station, from which the cars of the train are entered. **4.** *U.S.* the open entrance area, or vestibule, at the end of a railroad passenger car. **5.** *Mil.* **a.** solid ground on which artillery pieces are mounted. **b.** a metal stand or base attached to certain types of artillery pieces. **6.** *Naut.* flat (def. 33). **7.** a flat, elevated piece of ground. **8.** a body of principles on which a person or group, esp. a political candidate or party, takes a stand in appealing to the public; program. **9.** a set of principles; plan. [earlier *platte forme* < MF: lit., flat form, plane figure] —**Syn. 1.** stage, dais, rostrum, pulpit.

plat′form car′, flatcar.

plat·i·na (plat′ᵊnə, plə tē′nə), *n.* a native alloy of platinum with palladium, iridium, osmium, etc. [< Sp: lit., silverlike element = *plat(a)* silver (< Pr: lit., silver plate) + *-ina* -INE¹. See PLATINUM]

plat·ing (plā′ting), *n.* **1.** a thin coating of gold, silver, etc. **2.** an external layer of metal plates. **3.** the act of a person or thing that plates.

pla·tin·ic (plə tin′ik), *adj.* *Chem.* of or containing platinum, esp. in the tetravalent state.

plat·in·i·rid·i·um (plat′ᵊni rid′ē əm, -ᵊnī rid′-), *n.* a natural alloy composed chiefly of platinum and iridium.

plat·i·nize (plat′ᵊnīz′), *v.t.,* **-nized, -niz·ing.** to coat or plate with metallic platinum. —**plat′i·ni·za′tion,** *n.*

platino-, a combining form of **platinum:** *platinotype.* Also, *esp. before a vowel,* **platin-.**

plat·i·noid (plat′ᵊnoid′), *adj.* **1.** resembling platinum: *the platinoid elements.* —*n.* **2.** any of the metals, as palladium or iridium, with which platinum is commonly associated. **3.** an alloy of copper, zinc, and nickel, to which small quantities of such elements as tungsten or aluminum have been added.

plat·i·no·type (plat′ᵊnō tīp′), *n.* *Photog.* **1.** a process of printing positives in which a platinum salt is used, rather than the usual silver salts, in order to make a more permanent print. **2.** a print made by this process.

plat·i·nous (plat′ᵊnəs), *adj.* *Chem.* containing bivalent platinum.

plat·i·num (plat′ᵊnəm, plat′nəm), *n.* **1.** *Chem.* a heavy, grayish-white, highly malleable and ductile metallic element, resistant to most chemicals, and fusible only at extremely high temperatures: used for making chemical and scientific apparatus, as a catalyst, and in jewelry. *Symbol:* Pt; *at. wt.:* 195.09; *at. no.:* 78; *sp. gr.:* 21.5 at 20°C. **2.** a light, metallic gray, slightly more bluish than silver. [< NL, alter. of *platina* < Sp; see PLATINA]

plat′inum black′, *Chem.* a black powder consisting of very finely divided metallic platinum, used as a catalyst.

plat′inum blonde′, **1.** a girl or woman whose hair is of a pale blonde or silver color, often colored artificially by bleaching or dyeing. **2.** a pale blonde or silver color.

plat·i·tude (plat′i to͞od′, -tyo͞od′), *n.* **1.** a flat, dull, or trite remark, esp. one uttered as if it were fresh and profound. **2.** a quality or state of being flat, dull, or trite. [< F: lit., flatness = *plat* flat (see PLATE¹) + *-itude,* as in *latitude, altitude, magnitude,* etc.] —**Syn. 1.** cliché, truism.

plat·i·tu·di·nize (plat′i to͞od′ᵊnīz′, -tyo͞od′-), *v.i.,* **-nized, -niz·ing.** to utter platitudes. Also, *esp. Brit.,* **plat′i·tu′di·nise.** [PLATITUDIN(OUS) + -IZE]

plat·i·tu·di·nous (plat′i to͞od′ᵊnəs, -tyo͞od′-), *adj.* **1.** characterized by or given to platitudes. **2.** of the nature of or resembling a platitude. [PLATITUDE + (MULTITUD)INOUS] —**plat′i·tu′di·nous·ly,** *adv.* —**plat′i·tu′di·nous·ness,** *n.*

Pla·to (plā′tō), *n.* 427–347 B.C., Greek philosopher.

Pla·ton·ic (plə ton′ik, plā-), *adj.* **1.** of, pertaining to, or characteristic of Plato or his doctrines. **2.** pertaining to, involving, or characterized by Platonic love. **3.** (*usually l.c.*) purely spiritual; free from sensual desire, esp. in a relationship between a man and a woman. [< L *platōnic(us)* < Gk *platōnikós.* See PLATO, -IC] —**Pla·ton′i·cal·ly,** *adv.*

Platon′ic love′, **1.** *Platonism.* love of the idea of beauty, seen as terminating an evolution from physical desire for an individual through love of physical beauty and later of spiritual or ideal beauty. **2.** Also, **platon′ic love′.** an intimate relationship between a man and a woman that is characterized by the absence of sexual involvement.

Pla·to·nism (plāt′ᵊniz′əm), *n.* **1.** the philosophy or doctrines of Plato or his followers. **2.** a Platonic doctrine or saying. **3.** the belief that physical objects are impermanent representations of unchanging Ideas, and that the Ideas alone give true knowledge as they are known by the mind. **4.** (*sometimes l.c.*) the doctrine or practice of platonic love. [< NL *platōnism(us)*] —**Pla′to·nist,** *n., adj.*

pla·toon (plə to͞on′), *n.* **1.** a military unit consisting of two or more squads or sections and a headquarters. **2.** a small unit of a police force. **3.** a company or group of persons. **4.** *Football.* a group of players specially trained in one aspect of the game, as offense or defense, and used as a unit in their specialty. —*v.t.* **5.** to arrange into, or operate as, a platoon or platoons. [earlier *plotton* < F *peloton* little ball, group, platoon, dim. of *pelote* ball; see PELLET]

Platt·deutsch (plät′doich′), *n.* the informal German spoken in northern Germany. Also called **Low German.** [< G: lit., flat (i.e., lowland) German. See PLATE¹, DUTCH]

Platte (plat), *n.* a river flowing E from the junction of the North and South Platte rivers in central Nebraska to the Missouri River S of Omaha. 310 mi. long.

Plat·ten·see (plät′ᵊn zā′), *n.* German name of **Balaton.**

plat·ter (plat′ər), *n.* **1.** a large, shallow dish, usually elliptical in shape, from which food is served. **2.** *Slang.* a phonograph record. [ME *plater* < AF < *plat* dish. See PLATE¹, -ER²]

Platts·burgh (plats′bûrg), *n.* a city in NE New York, on Lake Champlain: battle, 1814. 18,715 (1970).

plat·y¹ (plā′tē), *adj.,* **plat·i·er, plat·i·est.** (of a rock) split into thin, flat pieces by uneven cooling. [PLATE¹ + -Y¹]

plat·y² (plat′ē), *n., pl.* (*esp. collectively*) **plat·y,** (*esp. referring to two or more kinds or species*) **plat·ys, plat·ies.** any of several fishes of the genus *Xiphophorus,* esp. *X. maculatus,* found in Mexico and often kept in aquariums. [< NL *Platy(poecilus)* genus name = *platy-* PLATY- + *-poecilus* < Gk *poikílos* mottled]

platy-, a learned borrowing from Greek meaning "flat," "broad," used in the formation of compound words: *platyhelminth.* Also, **plat-.** [comb. form repr. Gk *platýs*]

plat·y·ce·phal·ic (plat′ē sə fal′ik), *adj.* *Cephalom.* having a head whose cranial vault is broad or flat.

plat·y·hel·minth (plat′i hel′minth), *n.* any worm of the phylum *Platyhelminthes,* having bilateral symmetry and a soft, solid, usually flattened body, including the planarians, tapeworms, and trematodes; flatworm. [< NL *Platyhelminth(a)* flatworm] —**plat′y·hel·min′thic,** *adj.*

plat·y·pus (plat′i pəs), *n., pl.* **-pus·es, -pi** (-pī′). duckbill. [< NL < Gk *platýpous* broad-footed]

plat·yr·rhine (plat′i rīn′, -rin), *adj.* **1.** *Anthropol.* having a broad, flat-bridged nose. **2.** belonging or pertaining to the group *Platyrrhini,* comprising the New World monkeys, having a broad, flat nose and a usually long, prehensile tail. —*n.* **3.** a platyrrhine animal. Also, **plat·yr·rhin·i·an** (plat′i-rin′ē ən). [< NL *platyrrhīn(us)* = *platy-* PLATY- + Gk *rhin-* (s. of *rhīs*) nose]

plau·dit (plô′dit), *n.* Usually, **plaudits. 1.** a demonstration or round of applause, as for some approved or admired performance. **2.** any enthusiastic expression of approval: *Her cake won the plaudits of her guests.* [earlier *plaudite* (3 syllables) < L, 2nd pl. impv. of *plaudere* to APPLAUD]

Plau·en (plou′ən), *n.* a city in S central East Germany. 81,907.

plau·si·ble (plô′zə bəl), *adj.* **1.** having an appearance of truth or reason; seemingly worthy of approval or acceptance; credible; believable: *a plausible excuse; a plausible plot.* **2.** well-spoken and apparently worthy of confidence: *a plausible commentator.* [< L *plausibil(is)* deserving applause = *plaus(us)* (ptp. of *plaudere* to APPLAUD) + *-ibilis* -IBLE] —**plau′si·bil′i·ty, plau′si·ble·ness,** *n.* —**plau′si·bly,** *adv.*

plau·sive (plô′ziv, -siv), *adj.* **1.** *Rare.* applauding. **2.** *Obs.* plausible. [< L *plaus(us)* (ptp. of *plaudere* to APPLAUD) + -IVE]

Plau·tus (plô′təs), *n.* **Ti·tus Mac·ci·us** (tī′təs mak′sē əs), c254–c184 B.C., Roman dramatist.

play (plā), *n.* **1.** a dramatic composition or piece; drama. **2.** a dramatic performance, as on the stage. **3.** exercise or action by way of amusement or recreation. **4.** fun, jest, or trifling, as opposed to earnest: *He said it merely in play.* **5.** the playing or conduct of a game: *the fourth inning of play.* **6.** the manner or style of playing or of doing something: *We admired his fine play all last season.* **7.** an act or instance of playing or of doing something: *A stupid play cost him the match.* **8.** turn to play: *Whose play is it?* **9.** a playing for stakes; gambling. **10.** action, conduct, or dealing of a specified kind: *fair play; foul play.* **11.** action, activity, or operation: *the play of fancy.* **12.** brisk movement or action: *a fountain with a leaping play of water.* **13.** elusive change or movement, as of light or colors: *the play of a searchlight against the night sky.* **14.** a space in which something, as a part of a mechanism, can move. **15.** freedom of movement within a space. **16.** freedom for action, or scope for activity: *full play of the mind.* **17. bring into play,** to put into motion; introduce: *New evidence has been brought into play in this trial.* **18. make a play for,** *Slang.* **a.** to try to attract sexually: *He made a play for his buddy's girl.* **b.** to attempt to gain by impressing favorably: *This ad will make a play for new consumer markets.* —*v.t.* **19.** to act the part of (a person or character) in a dramatic performance; portray: *to play Lady Macbeth.* **20.** to perform (a drama, pantomime, etc.) on or as on the stage. **21.** to act or sustain (a part) in a dramatic performance or in real life: *to play the role of benefactor; to play the fool.* **22.** to give performances in: *to play the larger cities.* **23.** to engage in (a game, pastime, etc.). **24.** to contend against in a game. **25.** to function or perform as (a specified player) in a game or competition: *Jones will play left end.* **26.** to employ (a piece of equipment, a player, etc.) in a game: *He played his highest card. The coach played Jones at quarterback.* **27.** to use as if in playing a game, as for one's own advantage (often fol. by *off*): *He played one brother off against the other.* **28.** to stake or wager, as in a game. **29.** to lay a wager or wagers on (something); bet. **30.** to represent or imitate in jest or sport: *to play house.* **31.** to perform on (a musical instrument). **32.** to perform (music) on an instrument. **33.** to do, perform, or execute: *You shouldn't play tricks.* **34.** to act upon: *to play a hunch.* **35.** to cause to move or change lightly or quickly: *to play colored lights on a fountain.* **36.** to operate, or cause to operate, esp. continuously or with repeated action: *to play a hose on a fire.* **37.** to allow (a hooked fish) to exhaust itself by pulling on the line. —*v.i.* **38.** to exercise or employ oneself in diversion, amusement, or recreation. **39.** to do something in sport which is not to be taken seriously. **40.** to amuse oneself; toy; trifle (often fol. by *with*). **41.** to take part or engage in a game. **42.** to take part in a game for stakes; gamble. **43.** to conduct oneself or act in a specified way: *to play fair.* **44.** to act on or as on the stage; perform. **45.** to perform on a musical instrument. **46.** (of instruments, sound reproducing equipment, or music) to sound in performance: *Was the radio playing?* **47.** to be capable of or suitable for performance, as a dramatic script. **48.** to move freely within a space, as a part of a mechanism. **49.** to move about lightly or quickly: *The water of the fountain played in the air.* **50.** to present the effect of such motion, as light: *The lights played over the faces in the crowd.* **51.** to operate continuously or with repeated action, esp. upon something. **52. play both ends against the middle,** to maneuver opposing groups in order to benefit oneself. **53. play by ear,** to play music or a piece of music without having seen the printed sheet music, by memory from what one has heard. **54. play down,** to treat as of little importance; belittle. **55. played out, a.** exhausted; weary. **b.** out of fashion; hackneyed. **c.** used up; finished. **56. play fast and loose,** to act in an irresponsible or inconsiderate manner (often fol. by *with*): *He played fast and loose with her affections.* **57. play for time,** to prolong something in order to gain an advantage. **58. play into the hands of** or **into someone's hands,** to act in such a way as to give an advantage to one's opponent. **59. play it by ear,** to improvise, esp. in a challenging situation. **60. play off,** to play an extra game or round in order to settle a tie. **61. play one's cards.** See **card**[1] (def. 12). **62. play on** or **upon,** to exploit, as the feelings or weaknesses of another; take selfish advantage of: *to play on someone's good nature.* **63. play out, a.** to bring to an end; finish. **b.** to reel or pay out, as a rope or line. **64. play the game.** See **game**[1] (def. 15). **65. play up,** to magnify the importance of; publicize. **66. play up to,** *Informal.* to attempt to impress in order to gain someone's favor. **67. play with fire.** See **fire** (def. 22). [(n.) ME *pleye,* OE *plega;* (v.) ME *pleye(n),* OE *pleg(i)an* (c. MD *pleien* to leap for joy, dance, rejoice, be glad), gradational var. of *plagian,* akin to *plōg* PLOW] —**play′a·ble,** *adj.* —**play′less,** *adj.* —**play′like′,** *adj.*

—**Syn. 2.** show. **3.** diversion, pastime. PLAY, GAME, SPORT refer to forms of diverting activity. PLAY is the general word for any such form of activity, often undirected, spontaneous, or random: *Childhood is a time for play.* GAME refers to a recreational contest, mental or physical, usually governed by set rules: *a game of chess.* Besides referring to an individual contest, GAME may refer to a pastime as a whole: *Golf is a good game.* If, however, the pastime is one (usually an outdoor one) depending chiefly on physical strength, the word SPORT is applied: *Football is a vigorous sport.*

pla·ya (plī′ə; *Sp.* plä′yä), *n., pl.* **pla·yas** (plī′əz; *Sp.* plä′-yäs). *Western U.S.* the sandy, salty, or mud-caked flat floor of a desert basin having interior drainage, usually occupied by a shallow lake during or after prolonged, heavy rains. [< Sp: shore < LL *plagia,* n. use of fem. of *plagius*]

play·act (plā′akt′), *v.i.* **1.** to engage in make-believe. **2.** to perform in a play. —*v.t.* **3.** to dramatize. [back formation from PLAYACTING] —**play′act′ing,** *n.*

play·back (plā′bak′), *n.* **1.** the act of operating a phonograph, tape recorder, or the like, so as to hear a reproduction of the recording. **2.** the recording so played. **3.** (in a sound recording device) the equipment used in reproducing the sound on a recording so that it may be heard.

play·bill (plā′bil′), *n.* a program or announcement of a play.

play·boy (plā′boi′), *n.* a wealthy, carefree man who devotes most of his time to self-amusement, esp. to frequenting parties, night clubs, and sporting events, and often romancing a succession of attractive young women.

play-by-play (plā′bī plā′), *adj.* **1.** pertaining to or being a detailed account of each incident or act of an event. —*n.* **2.** such an account, as a broadcast of a sports event.

play·er (plā′ər), *n.* **1.** a person or thing that plays. **2.** a person who takes part or is skilled in some game. **3.** a person who plays parts on the stage; an actor. **4.** a performer on a musical instrument. **5.** See **record player. 6.** a gambler. [ME *pleyer,* OE *plegere*]

play′er pian′o, a piano that can play automatically when the keys are actuated by a pneumatic device controlled by a piano roll.

play·fel·low (plā′fel′ō), *n.* a playmate.

play·ful (plā′fəl), *adj.* **1.** full of play; sportive; frolicsome. **2.** pleasantly humorous or teasing: *a playful remark.* [ME *pleiful*] —**play′ful·ly,** *adv.* —**play′ful·ness,** *n.*

play·girl (plā′gûrl′), *n.* a girl or woman whose life is devoted to social activities for the sake of pleasure.

play·go·er (plā′gō′ər), *n.* a person who attends the theater often or habitually.

play·ground (plā′ground′), *n.* **1.** an outdoor area used specifically for recreation, esp. by children. **2.** any place of outdoor recreation, as a resort: *The Riviera is the playground of Europe.*

play·house (plā′hous′), *n., pl.* **-hous·es** (-hou′ziz). **1.** a theater. **2.** a small house for children to play in. **3.** a toy house. [ME; OE *pleghūs*]

play′ing card′, 1. one of the conventional set of 52 cards in four suits, as diamonds, hearts, spades, and clubs, used in playing various games of chance and skill. **2.** one of any set of cards used in playing games.

play′ing field′, *Chiefly Brit.* any official field or stadium for athletic contests.

play·let (plā′lit), *n.* a short play.

play·mate (plā′māt′), *n.* a child's companion in play.

play-off (plā′ôf′, -of′), *n.* **1.** (in competitive sports) the playing of an extra game, rounds, innings, etc., to settle a tie. **2.** a game or series of games, as between the leading teams of two leagues, to decide a championship.

play′ on words′, a pun.

play·pen (plā′pen′), *n.* a small enclosure in which an infant or young child can play safely by himself without constant supervision.

play·room (plā′ro͞om′, -ro͝om′), *n.* a room set aside for children's play or adult recreation.

play·suit (plā′so͞ot′), *n.* a sports costume for women and children, usually consisting of shorts and a shirt.

play·thing (plā′thing′), *n.* a thing to play with; toy.

play·time (plā′tīm′), *n.* time for play or recreation.

play·wright (plā′rīt′), *n.* a writer of plays; dramatist.

play·writ·ing (plā′rī′ting), *n.* the act of writing plays; work or profession of a playwright.

pla·za (plä′zə, plaz′ə), *n.* a public square or open space in a city or town. [< Sp < L *platea,* var. of *platēa* < Gk *plateîa* broad street. See PLACE]

plea (plē), *n.* **1.** something alleged, urged, or pleaded in defense or justification. **2.** an excuse or pretext. **3.** *Law.* **a.** an allegation made by, or on behalf of, a party to a legal suit, in support of his claim or defense. **b.** a defendant's answer to a legal declaration or charge. **c.** a suit or action. **4.** an appeal or entreaty: *a plea for mercy.* [ME *ple,* earlier *plaid* < OF < early ML *placit(um)* law court, suit, decision, decree, L: opinion (lit., that which is pleasing or agreeable)] —**Syn. 4.** request, petition, supplication.

plea-bar·gain (plē′bär′gin), *v.i.* to engage in plea-bargaining. —**plea′-bar′gain·er,** *n.*

plea-bar·gain·ing (plē′bär′gə ning), *n.* a practice in which a defendant in a criminal case is permitted to plead guilty to a lesser charge, thereby receiving a lighter sentence than if found guilty on the more serious charge and saving the state the effort and expense of a trial.

pleach (plēch), *v.t.* **1.** to interweave (branches, vines, etc.), as for a hedge or arbor. **2.** to braid (hair). [ME *pleche(n)*]

plead (plēd), *v.,* **plead·ed** or **plead** (pled) or **pled; plead·ing.** —*v.i.* **1.** to appeal or entreat earnestly: *to plead for time.* **2.** to use arguments or persuasions for or against something. **3.** *Law.* **a.** to make any allegation in an action at law. **b.** to put forward an answer on the part of a defendant to a legal declaration or charge. **c.** to address a court as an advocate. —*v.t.* **4.** to allege or urge in defense, justification, or excuse: *to plead ignorance.* **5.** *Law.* **a.** to maintain (a cause) by argument before a court. **b.** to allege or set forth (something) formally in an action at law. **c.** to allege or cite in legal defense: *to plead not guilty.* [ME *plaide(n)* < OF *plaid(i)e(r)* (to) go to law, plead < early

ML *placitāre* to litigate < L *placitum* opinion. See PLEA] —**plead′a·ble,** *adj.* —**plead′er,** *n.* —**Syn. 1.** beg, supplicate. **2.** reason. **4.** claim.

plead·ing (plē′ding), *n.* **1.** the act of a person who pleads. **2.** *Law.* **a.** the advocating of a cause in a court of law. **b.** the art or science of setting forth or drawing pleas in legal causes. **c.** a formal statement setting forth the cause of action or defense of a case. **d. pleadings,** the successive statements delivered alternately by plaintiff and defendant until issue is joined. [ME *pletynge*] —**plead′ing·ly,** *adv.* —**plead′ing·ness,** *n.*

pleas·ance (plez′əns), *n.* **1.** a place laid out as a pleasure garden or promenade. **2.** *Archaic.* pleasure. [ME *plesaunce* < MF *plaisance*]

pleas·ant (plez′ənt), *adj.* **1.** pleasing, agreeable, or enjoyable: *pleasant news; pleasant weather.* **2.** (of persons, manners, disposition, etc.) socially acceptable or adept; polite; amiable. **3.** *Archaic.* gay, sprightly, or merry. **4.** *Obs.* jocular or facetious. [ME *plesaunt* < MF *plaisant,* orig. prp. of *plaisir* to PLEASE; see -ANT] —**pleas′ant·ly,** *adv.* —**pleas′ant·ness,** *n.* —**Syn. 2.** congenial, friendly.

Pleas′ant Is′land, former name of **Nauru.**

pleas·ant·ry (plez′ən trē), *n., pl.* **-ries. 1.** good-humored teasing; banter. **2.** a humorous or jesting remark. **3.** a humorous action. [< F *plaisanterie,* OF *plesanterie*]

please (plēz), *v.,* **pleased, pleas·ing.** —*v.t.* **1.** to act to the pleasure or satisfaction of: *to please the public.* **2.** to be the pleasure or will of: *May it please your Majesty.* **3.** (used as a polite addition to requests, commands, etc.) if you would be so kind or obliging: *Please come here.* —*v.i.* **4.** to give pleasure or satisfaction; be agreeable: *manners that please.* **5.** to like, wish, or choose: *Go where you please.* **6. if you please, a.** if it be your pleasure; if you like or prefer. **b.** (used as an exclamation expressing astonishment, indignation, etc.): *The missing letter was in his pocket, if you please!* [ME *plese* < MF *plais(ir)* < L *placēre* to please, seem good. See PLACID] —**pleas′a·ble,** *adj.* —**pleas·ed·ly** (plē′zid lē, plēzd′-), *adv.* —**pleas′ed·ness,** *n.* —**pleas′er,** *n.*

pleas·ing (plē′zing), *adj.* affording pleasure; agreeable; gratifying. [ME *plesing*] —**pleas′ing·ly,** *adv.* —**pleas′ing·ness,** *n.* —**Syn.** pleasant, charming.

pleas·ur·a·ble (plezh′ər ə bəl), *adj.* such as to give pleasure; agreeable; pleasant: *a pleasurable experience.* —**pleas′ur·a·ble·ness,** *n.* —**pleas′ur·a·bly,** *adv.*

pleas·ure (plezh′ər), *n., v.,* **-ured, -ur·ing.** —*n.* **1.** the state or feeling of being pleased. **2.** enjoyment or satisfaction derived from what is to one's liking; gratification; delight. **3.** worldly or frivolous enjoyment: *the pursuit of pleasure.* **4.** sensual gratification. **5.** a cause or source of enjoyment or delight: *It was a pleasure to see you.* **6.** pleasurable quality: *the pleasure of his company.* **7.** a person's will, desire, or choice: *to make known one's pleasure.* —*v.t.* **8.** to give pleasure to; gratify; please. —*v.i.* **9.** to take pleasure; delight: *I pleasure in your company.* [late ME (see PLEASE, -URE); r. ME *plaisir* < MF < L *placēre* to please (n. use of inf.)] —**pleas′ure·less,** *adj.* —**pleas′ure·less·ly,** *adv.* —**pleas′ure·ful,** *adj.*
—**Syn. 1.** happiness, gladness, delectation. PLEASURE, ENJOYMENT, DELIGHT, JOY refer to the feeling of being pleased and happy. PLEASURE is the general term: *to take pleasure in beautiful scenery.* ENJOYMENT is a quiet sense of well-being and pleasurable satisfaction: *enjoyment at sitting in the shade on a warm day.* DELIGHT is a high degree of pleasure usually leading to active expression of it: *delight at receiving a hoped-for letter.* JOY is a feeling of delight so deep and lasting that a person radiates happiness and expresses it spontaneously: *joy at unexpected good news.* **4.** luxury, voluptuousness. **7.** preference, wish, inclination.

pleas′ure prin′ciple, (in Freudian theory) an instinct to avoid pain and obtain immediate pleasure without reference to other factors.

Pleas′ure Ridge′ Park′, a town in N Kentucky, S of Louisville. 28,566 (1970).

pleat (plēt), *n.* **1.** a fold of definite, even width made by doubling cloth or the like upon itself. —*v.t.* **2.** to fold or arrange in pleats. Also, **plait.** [var. of PLAIT] —**pleat′less,** *adj.*

pleb (pleb), *n.* a member of the plebs; a plebeian or commoner. [short for PLEBEIAN]

plebe (plēb), *n.* **1.** a member of the freshman class at the U.S. Military Academy or the U.S. Naval Academy. **2.** *Obs.* plebeian (def. 4). [short for PLEBEIAN]

ple·be·ian (plə bē′ən), *adj.* **1.** of, pertaining to, or belonging to the ancient Roman plebs. **2.** belonging or pertaining to the common people. **3.** common, commonplace, or vulgar. —*n.* **4.** a member of the ancient Roman plebs. **5.** a member of the common people. [< L *plēbēi(us)* of the plebs (*plēbē(s)* plebs + *-ius* adj. suffix) + -AN]

pleb·i·scite (pleb′i sīt′, -sit), *n.* **1.** a direct vote of the qualified electors of a state in regard to some important public question. **2.** the vote by which the people of a political unit determine autonomy or affiliation with another country. [< F < L *plēbiscīt(um)* decree of the plebs = *plēbī* (gen. sing. of *plēbēs* PLEBS) + *scītum,* n. use of neut. of *scītus,* ptp. of *scīscere* to enact, decree, orig., to seek to know, learn, inchoative of *scīre* to know]

plebs (plebz), *n., pl.* **ple·bes** (plē′bēz). **1.** the commons, as contrasted with the patricians, in ancient Rome. **2.** the common people; the populace. [< L]

plec·tog·nath (plek′tog nath′), *adj.* **1.** belonging to the *Plectognathi,* a group of teleost fishes having the jaws extensively ankylosed, and including the filefishes, globefishes, etc. —*n.* **2.** a plectognath fish. [< NL *plectognath(ī)* (pl.) < Gk *plektó(s)* plaited, twisted + *gnáthoi* jaws]

plec·tron (plek′tron), *n., pl.* **-tra** (-trə). plectrum.

plec·trum (plek′trəm), *n., pl.* **-tra** (-trə), **-trums.** a small piece of wood, metal, ivory, etc., for plucking the strings of a lyre, mandolin, etc. [< L < Gk *plēktron*]

pled (pled), *v.* a pt. and pp. of **plead.**

pledge (plej), *n., v.,* **pledged, pledg·ing.** —*n.* **1.** a solemn promise or agreement to do or refrain from doing something: *a pledge of aid; a pledge not to wage war.* **2.** something delivered or regarded as security for the payment of a debt or fulfillment of a promise. **3.** the state of being given or held as security: *to put a thing in pledge.* **4.** a person accepted for membership in a club, fraternity, etc., but not yet formally approved. **5.** an assurance of support or good will conveyed by drinking a person's health; a toast. **6.** *Obs.* **a.** a hostage. **b.** a person who becomes bail or surety for another. **7. take the pledge,** to make a solemn, formal vow to abstain from intoxicating drink. —*v.t.* **8.** to bind by or as by a pledge: *to pledge hearers to secrecy.* **9.** to promise solemnly to do, provide, etc.: *to pledge one's support.* **10.** to give or deposit as a pledge; pawn. **11.** to stake, as one's honor. **12.** to secure by a pledge; give a pledge for. **13.** to accept as a pledge for club or fraternity membership. **14.** to drink a health or toast to. —*v.i.* **15.** to make or give a pledge: *to pledge for someone.* [ME *plege* < AF < early ML *plev(ium), pleb(ium)* < *plebīre* to pledge < Gmc; cf. OE *plēon* to risk, G *pflegen* to look after. See PLIGHT²] —**pledge′a·ble,** *adj.* —**pledg′er,** *n.*

pledg·ee (plej ē′), *n.* a person to whom a pledge is made or with whom something is deposited as a pledge.

Pledge′ of Alle′giance, a solemn oath of allegiance or fidelity to the U.S., beginning, "I pledge allegiance to the flag," and forming part of many flag-saluting ceremonies.

pledg·et (plej′it), *n.* a pad of absorbent cotton, or the like, for use on a wound, sore, etc. [?]

-plegia, an element of Greek origin used in pathological terms denoting forms of paralysis: *paraplegia.* [< Gk = *plēg(ē)* blow, stroke + *-ia* -IA]

Ple·iad (plē′əd, plī′əd), *n.* **1.** any of the Pleiades. **2.** French, **Plé·iade** (plā yAd′). a group of seven French poets of the latter half of the 16th century. **3.** (*usually l.c.*) any group of eminent or brilliant persons or things, esp. when seven in number. [< Gk *Pleiad-* (s. of *Pleiás,* pl. *Pleiádes*), akin to *plein* to sail]

Ple·ia·des (plē′ə dēz′, plī′-), *n.pl.* **1.** *Class. Myth.* seven daughters of Atlas and half sisters of the Hyades, placed among the stars to save them from the pursuit of Orion. One of them (the **Lost Pleiad**) hides, either from grief or shame. **2.** *Astron.* a conspicuous group or cluster of stars in the constellation Taurus, commonly spoken of as seven, though only six are visible.

plein-air (plān′âr′; *Fr.* ple neR′), *adj.* **1.** noting or pertaining to a manner or style of painting developed chiefly in France in the mid-19th century, characterized by the representation of the luminous effects of natural light and atmosphere. **2.** designating a painting executed outdoors and representing a direct response to the scene or subject in front of the artist. [adj. use of F *plein air*: open (lit., full) air] —**plein′-air′ism, plein-air·isme** (*Fr.* ple ne Rēs′mᵊ), *n.*

pleio-, var. of **plio-.**

Plei·o·cene (plī′ə sēn′), *adj., n.* *Geol.* Pliocene.

Pleis·to·cene (plīs′tə sēn′), *Geol.* —*adj.* **1.** noting or pertaining to the epoch forming the earlier half of the Quaternary or one part of the Neocene period, originating about one million years ago, characterized by widespread glacial ice and by the appearance of man. See table at **era.** —*n.* **2.** the Pleistocene epoch or series. [< Gk *pleîsto(s)* (superl. of *polýs* much + -CENE]

ple·na·ry (plē′nə rē, plen′ə-), *adj.* **1.** full, complete, or absolute: *plenary powers.* **2.** attended by all qualified members; fully constituted: *a plenary session of Congress.* [< LL *plēnāri(us)* (see PLENUM, -ARY); r. ME *plener* < AF < LL *plēnār(is)*; see -AR¹]

ple′nary indul′gence, *Rom. Cath. Ch.* a remission of the total temporal punishment that is still due to sin after absolution. Cf. **indulgence** (def. 4).

ple·nip·o·tent (plə nip′ə tᵊnt), *adj.* plenipotentiary. [< ML *plēnipotent-* (s. of *plēnipotēns*). See PLENUM, -I-, POTENT]

plen·i·po·ten·ti·ar·y (plen′ē pə ten′shē er′ē, -shə rē), *n., pl.* **-ar·ies,** *adj.* —*n.* **1.** a person, esp. a diplomatic agent, invested with full authority to transact business on behalf of another. —*adj.* **2.** invested with full power or authority, as a diplomatic agent. **3.** conferring or bestowing full power, as a commission. **4.** absolute or full, as power. [< ML *plēnipotentiāri(us)*]

plen·ish (plen′ish), *v.t.* *Chiefly Scot.* to fill up; stock; furnish. [late ME *plenyss* < MF *pleniss-,* long s. of *plenir* to fill < L *plēnus* full. See PLENUM, -ISH²] —**plen′ish·er,** *n.* —**plen′ish·ment,** *n.*

plen·i·tude (plen′i to͞od′, -tyo͞od′), *n.* **1.** fullness or adequacy; abundance. **2.** the state of being full or complete: *With this work his artistry has reached its plenitude.* [< L *plēnitūdō.* See PLENUM, -I-, TUDE]

plen·te·ous (plen′tē əs), *adj.* **1.** plentiful or copious; abundant: *a plenteous supply of corn.* **2.** yielding abundantly; fruitful: *a plenteous harvest.* [ME *plenteus* (see PLENTY, -OUS); r. *plentivous* < OF = *plentif* abundant (*plent(e)* plenty + *-if* -IVE) + *-ous* -OUS]

plen·ti·ful (plen′ti fəl), *adj.* **1.** existing in great plenty. **2.** yielding abundantly. —**plen′ti·ful·ly,** *adv.* —**plen′ti·ful·ness,** *n.*
—**Syn. 1.** PLENTIFUL, AMPLE, ABUNDANT, BOUNTIFUL describe a more than adequate supply of something. PLENTIFUL suggests an over-adequate quantity: *a plentiful supply.* AMPLE suggests a more than adequate quality as well: *to give ample praise.* ABUNDANT implies a greater degree of plenty and BOUNTIFUL a still more ample quality as well: *an abundant, even a bountiful, harvest.* **2.** fruitful, bounteous, productive. —**Ant. 1.** sparse, scanty. **2.** barren, fruitless, sterile.

plen·ty (plen′tē), *n., pl.* **-ties,** *adj., adv.* —*n.* **1.** a full or abundant supply: *There is plenty of time.* **2.** the state or quality of being plentiful; abundance: *resources in plenty.* **3.** an abundance, as of goods or luxuries, or a time of such abundance: *peace and plenty.* —*adj.* **4.** *Informal.* plentiful or abundant. —*adv.* **5.** *Informal.* fully; quite: *plenty good enough.* [ME *plente* (< OF), later form of *plenteth* < OF *plented, plentet* < L *plēnitāt-* (s. of *plēnitās*) fullness. See PLENUM, -ITY]
—**Syn. 2.** copiousness, luxuriance, affluence. PLENTY, ABUNDANCE, PROFUSION refer to a large quantity or supply. PLENTY suggests a supply that is fully adequate to any demands: *plenty of money.* ABUNDANCE implies a great plenty,

an ample and generous oversupply: *an abundance of rain.* PROFUSION applies to such a lavish and excessive abundance as often suggests extravagance or prodigality: *luxuries in great profusion.*
—**Usage.** Note that the adjectival and adverbial uses of PLENTY are labeled *Informal.* In formal use PLENTY OF and PLENTIFUL are preferred for adjectives and AMPLY and QUITE are preferred for adverbs: *Food is never too plentiful in the area. That helping is quite enough for me.*

Plen′ty (plen′tē), *n.* **Sea of.** See **Mare Fecunditatis.**

ple·num (plē′nəm, plen′əm), *n., pl.* **ple·nums, ple·na** (plē′nə, plen′ə). **1.** the state or the space in which a gas, usually air, is contained at a pressure greater than atmospheric pressure. **2.** the whole of space regarded as being filled with matter (opposed to *vacuum*). **3.** a full assembly, as a joint legislative assembly. [< L, neut. of *plēnus* FULL]

pleo-, var. of **plio-.**

ple·och·ro·ism (plē ok′rō iz′əm), *n.* the property of certain crystals of exhibiting different colors when viewed from different directions under transmitted light. Cf. **dichroism** (def. 1), **trichroism.** [PLEO- + -CHRO(IC) + -ISM]

ple·o·mor·phism (plē′ə môr′fiz əm), *n. Zool., Bot.* existence of an animal or plant in two or more distinct forms during the life cycle; polymorphism. Also, **ple′o·mor′phy.**

ple·o·nasm (plē′ə naz′əm), *n.* **1.** the use of more words than are necessary to express an idea; redundancy. **2.** an instance of this, as *free gift* or *true fact.* **3.** a redundant word or expression. [< LL *pleonasm(us)* < Gk *pleonasmós* redundancy < *pleonázein* to be or have more than enough; cf. PLEO-, -ISM] —**ple′o·nas′tic,** *adj.* —**ple′o·nas′ti·cal·ly,** *adv.*

ple·o·pod (plē′ə pod′), *n. Zool.* a swimmeret. [< Gk *pléōn,* prp. of *plein* to swim, sail + -POD]

ple·si·o·saur (plē′sē ə sôr′), *n.* any marine reptile of the extinct genus *Plesiosaurus,* from the Jurassic and Cretaceous periods, having a small head, a long neck, four paddlelike limbs, and a short tail. [< NL *plēsiosaur(us)* < Gk *plēsío(s)* near + *saûros* -SAUR]

ples·sor (ples′ər), *n. Med.* plexor. [< Gk *plḗss(ein)* (to) strike + -OR²]

pleth·o·ra (pleth′ər ə), *n.* **1.** overfullness; superabundance: *a plethora of advice.* **2.** *Pathol. Obs.* a morbid condition due to excess of red corpuscles in the blood or increase in the quantity of blood. [< NL < Gk *plēthṓra* fullness]

ple·thor·ic (ple thôr′ik, -thor′-, pleth′ə rik), *adj.* **1.** overfull; turgid, inflated: *a plethoric, pompous speech.* **2.** of or pertaining to, or characterized by plethora. [PLETHOR(A) + -IC] —**ple·thor′i·cal·ly,** *adv.*

pleur-, var. of **pleuro-** before a vowel: *pleural.*

pleu·ra (plo͝or′ə), *n., pl.* **pleu·rae** (plo͝or′ē) for 1. **1.** *Anat., Zool.* a delicate serous membrane investing each lung in mammals and folded back as a lining of the corresponding side of the thorax. **2.** pl. of **pleuron.** [< NL < Gk: side, rib]

pleu·ral (plo͝or′əl), *adj.* of or pertaining to a pleura or pleuron.

pleu·ri·sy (plo͝or′i sē), *n. Pathol.* inflammation of the pleura, with or without a liquid effusion. [ME *pluresy* < OF *pleurisie* < LL *pleurisis,* alter. of L *pleurītis* < Gk; see PLEURA, -ITIS] —**pleu·rit·ic** (plo͝o rit′ik), *adj.*

pleu′risy root′, 1. a North American milkweed, *Asclepias tuberosa,* whose root formerly was used as a remedy for pleurisy. **2.** the root itself.

pleuro-, a learned borrowing from Greek meaning "side," "rib," "lateral," or "pleura," used in the formation of compound words: *pleuropneumonia.* Also, *esp. before a vowel,* **pleur-.** [see PLEURA, -O-]

pleu·ro·dont (plo͝or′ə dont′), *adj.* **1.** ankylosed or attached to the inner edge of the jaw, as a tooth. **2.** having teeth so ankylosed, as certain lizards. —*n.* **3.** a pleurodont animal.

pleu·ron (plo͝or′on), *n., pl.* **pleu·ra** (plo͝or′ə). *Entomol.* the lateral plate or plates of a thoracic segment of an insect. [< Gk: rib, pl. side]

pleu·ro·pneu·mo·ni·a (plo͝or′ō no͞o mōn′yə, -mō′nē ə, -nyo͞o-), *n. Pathol.* pleurisy conjoined with pneumonia.

Plev·en (plev′en), *n.* a city in N Bulgaria: siege of 143 days 1877. 80,179 (1964). Also, **Plev·na** (plev′nä).

plex·i·form (plek′sə fôrm′), *adj.* **1.** of, pertaining to, or resembling a plexus. **2.** intricate; complex.

Plex·i·glas (plek′sə glas′, -gläs′), *n. Trademark.* a lightweight thermoplastic polymer of methyl methacrylate, resistant to weathering: used for signs, windows, furniture, etc.

plex·or (plek′sər), *n. Med.* a small hammer with a soft rubber head or the like, used in percussion for diagnostic purposes. Also, **plessor.** [Gk *plêx(is)* stroke, percussion + -OR²]

plex·us (plek′səs), *n., pl.* **-us·es, -us. 1.** a network, as of nerves or blood vessels. **2.** any complex structure containing an intricate network of interrelated parts: *the plexus of international relations.* [< L: an interweaving, twining = *plex-* (ptp. s. of *plectere* to turn) + *-us* n. suffix (4th decl.), akin to *plicāre* to fold] —**plex′al,** *adj.*

plf., plaintiff. Also, **plff.**

pli·a·ble (plī′ə bəl), *adj.* **1.** easily bent; flexible; supple: *pliable leather.* **2.** easily influenced or persuaded; yielding. **3.** adaptable. [< F = *pli(er)* (to) PLY² + *-able* -ABLE] —**pli′a·bil′i·ty, pli′a·ble·ness,** *n.* —**pli′a·bly,** *adv.*

pli·ant (plī′ənt), *adj.* **1.** bending or yielding readily; flexible or supple: *pliant clay.* **2.** easily influenced; yielding; compliant. [ME < OF, prp. of *plier* to PLY²; see -ANT] —**pli′an·cy, pli′ant·ness,** *n.* —**pli′ant·ly,** *adv.* —**Syn. 1, 2.** pliable. See **flexible. 2.** tractable, docile.

pli·ca (plī′kə), *n., pl.* **pli·cae** (plī′sē). **1.** *Zool., Anat.* a fold or folding. **2.** Also called **pli′ca po·lon′i·ca** (pə lon′i kə). *Pathol.* a matted, filthy condition of the hair, caused by disease, vermin, etc. [< ML: a fold, back formation from L *plicāre* to PLY²] —**pli′cal,** *adj.*

Plicate leaf

pli·cate (plī′kāt, -kit), *adj.* folded like a fan; pleated. Also, **pli′cat·ed.** [< L *plicāt(us),* ptp. of *plicāre.* See PLY², -ATE¹] —**pli′cate·ly,** *adv.* —**pli′cate·ness,** *n.*

pli·ca·tion (plī kā′shən, pli-), *n.* **1.** the act or procedure of folding. **2.** the state or quality of being folded; a fold. Also, **plic·a·ture** (plik′ə chər). [late ME *plicacioun* < ML *plicātiōn-* (s. of *plicātiō*) a folding. See PLICATE, -ION]

pli·é (plē ā′), *n., pl.* **pli·és** (plē āz′; *Fr.* plē ā′). *Ballet.* a movement in which the legs are bent while the back is held straight. [< F, n. use of ptp. of *plier* to bend; see PLY²]

pli·er (plī′ər), *n.* **1. pliers,** (*sometimes construed as sing.*) small pincers with long jaws, for bending wire, holding small objects, etc. (usually used with *pair of*). **2.** a person or thing that plies. Also, *esp. Brit.,* **plyer.**

plight¹ (plīt), *n.* a condition, state, or situation, esp. an unfavorable one. [ME *plit* < AF (c. MF *pleit* PLAIT) fold, manner of folding, condition; meaning perh. influenced by PLIGHT² in archaic sense of danger] —**Syn.** See **predicament.**

plight² (plīt), *v.t.* **1.** to pledge (one's troth) in engagement to marry. **2.** to bind (someone) by a pledge, esp. of marriage. **3.** to give in pledge, as one's word, or to pledge, as one's honor. —*n.* **4.** *Archaic.* a pledge; engagement. [ME; OE *pliht* danger, risk; c. D *plicht,* G *Pflicht* duty, obligation]

plim·soll (plim′səl, -sôl, -sol), *n. Brit.* a canvas shoe with a rubber sole. Also, **plim′sol, plim′sole.** [? so called from fancied resemblance of the sole to a Plimsoll mark]

Plim′soll line′ (plim′səl, -sôl, -sol). *Naut.* See **load line.** [see PLIMSOLL MARK]

Plim′soll mark′, *Naut.* See **load-line mark.** Also called **Plim′soll.** [named after Samuel *Plimsoll* (1824–98), English M.P. and reformer who brought about its adoption]

plink (plingk), *v.i.* **1.** to shoot, as with a pistol, at targets selected at whim: *to plink at bottles tossed in the air.* **2.** to make a series of short, light, ringing sounds. —*v.t.* **3.** to shoot at for practice or amusement, as with a pistol: *to plink bottles set along a fence railing.* **4.** to cause to make a series of short, light, ringing sounds. —*n.* **5.** a plinking sound. [imit.] —**plink′er,** *n.*

plinth (plinth), *n. Archit.* **1.** a slablike member beneath the base of a column or pier. **2.** a square base or a lower block, as of a pedestal. **3.** (in joinery) a flat member at the bottom of an architrave, dado, baseboard, or the like. [earlier *plinthus* < L < Gk *plínthos* plinth, squared stone, brick, tile; see FLINT] —**plinth′like′,** *adj.*

Plin·y (plin′ē), *n.* **1.** (*Gaius Plinius Secundus*) ("*the Elder*") A.D. 23–79, Roman naturalist, encyclopedist, and writer. **2.** his nephew (*Gaius Plinius Caecilius Secundus*) ("*the Younger*") A.D. 62?–c113, Roman writer, statesman, and orator. —**Plin′i·an,** *adj.*

plio-, a learned borrowing from Greek meaning "more," and sometimes specialized to mean "Pliocene," used in the formation of compound words. Also, **pleio-, pleo-.** [comb. form repr. Gk *pleíōn* more (comp. of *polýs;* see POLY-)]

Pli·o·cene (plī′ə sēn′), *Geol.* —*adj.* **1.** noting or pertaining to an epoch either of the Tertiary or Neocene period, occurring from one million to ten million years ago, characterized by an increase in the size and numbers of mammals, by the growth of mountains, and by gradual cooling of the climate. See table at **era.** —*n.* **2.** the Pliocene epoch or series. Also, **Pleiocene.**

PLO, Palestine Liberation Organization.

plod (plod), *v.,* **plod·ded, plod·ding,** *n.* —*v.i.* **1.** to walk heavily or move laboriously; trudge. **2.** to work with constant and monotonous perseverance; drudge. —*v.t.* **3.** to walk heavily over or along. —*n.* **4.** the act or a course of plodding. **5.** a sound of or as of a heavy tread. [? imit.] —**plod′der,** *n.* —**plod′ding·ly,** *adv.* —**plod′ding·ness,** *n.* —**Syn. 1.** See **pace¹. 2.** toil, moil, labor.

Plo·eș·ti (plô yesht′), *n.* a city in S Rumania: the center of a rich oil-producing region. 133,711 (est. 1964).

-ploid, a combining form used in cytology and genetics to indicate the number of chromosomes: *haploid.* [orig. abstracted from HAPLOID, DIPLOID, etc.]

plop (plop), *v.,* **plopped, plop·ping,** *n., adv.* —*v.t.* **1.** to drop heavily: *She plopped her books on the desk.* —*v.i.* **2.** to make a sound like that of a flat object striking water without a splash. **3.** to drop or fall plump: *He plopped into a chair.* —*n.* **4.** a plopping sound or fall. **5.** the act of plopping. —*adv.* **6.** with a plop: *The stone fell plop into the water.* [imit.]

plo·sion (plō′zhən), *n. Phonet.* the forced release of the occlusive phase of a plosive, whether voiceless or unvoiced, either audible due to friction or inaudible due to a contiguous following consonant. Also called **explosion.** Cf. **implosion** (def. 2). [(EX)PLOSION]

plo·sive (plō′siv), *Phonet.* —*adj.* **1.** (of a stop consonant or occlusive) characterized by release in a plosion; explosive. —*n.* **2.** Also called **explosive.** a plosive speech sound. [(EX)PLOSIVE]

plot¹ (plot), *n., v.,* **plot·ted, plot·ting.** —*n.* **1.** a secret plan or scheme to accomplish some purpose, esp. a hostile, unlawful, or evil purpose: *a plot to overthrow the government.* **2.** the plan, scheme, or main story of a play, novel, poem, or short story. **3.** *Artillery.* a point or points located on a map or chart: *target plot.* —*v.t.* **4.** to plan secretly, esp. something hostile or evil: *to plot mutiny.* **5.** to mark on a plan, map, or chart, as a ship's course. **6.** to draw a plan or map of, as a tract of land or a building. **7.** to determine and mark (points), as on graph paper, by means of measurements or coordinates. **8.** to draw (a curve) by means of points so marked. **9.** to represent by means of such a curve. **10.** to devise or construct the plot of (a play, novel, etc.). **11.** to make (a calculation) by graph. —*v.i.* **12.** to form secret plans; conspire. [special use of PLOT²; pejorative use by assoc. with COMPLOT] —**plot′less,** *adj.* —**plot′less·ness,** *n.*
—**Syn. 1.** intrigue, conspiracy, cabal. **12.** PLOT, CONSPIRE, SCHEME imply secret, cunning, and often unscrupulous planning to gain one's own ends. To PLOT is to contrive a secret plan of a selfish and often treasonable kind: *to plot against someone's life.* To CONSPIRE is to unite with others in an illicit or illegal machination: *to conspire to seize a government.* To SCHEME is to plan ingeniously, subtly, and often craftily for one's own advantage: *to scheme how to gain power.*

plot² (plot), *n., v.,* **plot·ted, plot·ting.** —*n.* **1.** a small piece or area of ground: *a garden plot; burial plot.* —*v.t.* **2.** to divide (land) into plots. [ME, OE]

Plo·ti·nus (plō tī′nəs), *n.* A.D. 205?–270?, Roman philosopher, born in Egypt: founder of Neoplatonism.

plot·tage (plot′ij), *n.* the area within or comprising a plot of land.

plot·ter (plot′ər), *n.* **1.** a person or thing that plots. **2.** an instrument, as a protractor, for plotting lines and measuring angles on a chart.

plot′ting board′, *Mil.* a device based on a map or other representation of a region, for use in directing artillery fire.

plough (plou), *n., v.t., v.i.* *Chiefly Brit.* plow. —**plough′er,** *n.*

plough·boy (plou′boi′), *n.* *Chiefly Brit.* plowboy.

plough·man (plou′mən), *n., pl.* **-men.** *Chiefly Brit.* plowman.

plough·share (plou′shâr′), *n.* *Chiefly Brit.* plowshare.

Plov·div (plôv′dif), *n.* a city in S Bulgaria, on the Maritsa River. 206,069 (1964). Greek, **Philippopolis.**

plov·er (pluv′ər, plō′vər), *n.* **1.** any of various limicoline birds of the family *Charadriidae,* esp. those with a short tail and a bill like that of a pigeon. **2.** any of various shore birds, as the upland plover. [ME < AF; OF *plovier* rainbird < VL **pluviār(ius).* See PLUVIAL, -ER²]

plow (plou), *n.* **1.** an agricultural implement used for cutting, lifting, turning over, and partly pulverizing the soil. **2.** any of various implements resembling or suggesting this, as a contrivance for clearing away snow from a road, a device for trimming the edges of the leaves of a book, etc. **3.** (*cap.*) *Astron.* **a.** the constellation Ursa Major. **b.** the Big Dipper. —*v.t.* **4.** to turn up (the soil) with a plow. **5.** to make (a furrow) with a plow. **6.** to make a furrow, groove, etc., in (something) as with a plow (often fol. by *up*). **7.** to proceed through (a body of water) in the manner of a plow. **8.** to reinvest or reutilize (usually fol. by *back*): *to plow profits back into new plants and equipment.* —*v.i.* **9.** to till the soil or work with a plow. **10.** to take plowing in a specified way: *land that plows easily.* **11.** to move or proceed through something in a slow or forceful manner (often fol. by *through, into,* etc.): *I plowed through a stack of books. The car plowed into the house.* **12.** to move through water by cleaving the surface. Also, *esp. Brit.,* **plough.** [ME; OE *plōh* plowland; c. G *Pflug* plow] —**plow′a·ble,** *adj.* —**plow′er,** *n.*

plow·back (plou′bak′), *n.* **1.** a reinvestment of earnings or profits in a business enterprise instead of distributing them as dividends. **2.** the money thus reinvested.

plow·boy (plou′boi′), *n.* **1.** a boy who leads or guides a team drawing a plow. **2.** a country boy. Also, *esp. Brit.,* **ploughboy.**

plow·man (plou′mən), *n., pl.* **-men. 1.** a man who plows. **2.** a farm laborer or a rustic. Also, *esp. Brit.,* **ploughman.** [ME] —**plow′man·ship′,** *n.*

plow·share (plou′shâr′), *n.* the cutting part of the moldboard of a plow; share. Also, *esp. Brit.,* **ploughshare.** [ME *plowghschare*]

ploy¹ (ploi), *n.* **1.** a maneuver or stratagem, as in conversation, to gain the advantage. —*v.t.* **2.** *Mil. Archaic.* to move (troops) from a line into a column. Cf. **deploy.** —*v.i.* **3.** *Mil. Archaic.* to move from a line into a column. [late ME *ploye* to bend < MF *ploye(r),* c. *plier* < L *plicāre* to PLY²; see DEPLOY]

ploy² (ploi), *n.* *Chiefly Brit.* a personal and amusing escapade; revelry; carousal. [? aph. var. of EMPLOY]

PLSS (plis), *n.* *Aerospace.* portable life-support system.

plu., plural.

pluck (pluk), *v.t.* **1.** to pull off or out from the place of growth, as fruit, flowers, or feathers. **2.** to give a pull at: *to pluck someone's sleeve.* **3.** to pull with sudden force or with a jerk. **4.** to pull by force (often fol. by *away, off,* or *out*). **5.** to remove the feathers, hair, etc., from by pulling: *to pluck a chicken.* **6.** *Slang.* to rob, plunder, or fleece. **7.** to sound (the strings of a musical instrument) by pulling at them with the fingers or a plectrum. **8.** *Brit. Slang.* to reject (a candidate for a degree) in a university examination; fail or flunk (a student). —*v.i.* **9.** to pull or tug sharply (often fol. by *at*). **10.** to snatch (often fol. by *at*). **11. pluck up, a.** to eradicate; uproot. **b.** to summon up one's courage; rouse one's spirits. —*n.* **12.** the act of plucking; a tug. **13.** the heart, liver, and lungs, esp. of an animal used for food. **14.** courage or resolution in the face of difficulties. [ME *plukke(n),* OE *pluccian;* c. MLG *plucken;* akin to D *plukken,* G *pflücken*] —**pluck′er,** *n.* —**Syn. 2.** tug. **3.** yank, tear, rip. **14.** bravery, boldness, determination, mettle, nerve.

pluck·y (pluk′ē), *adj.,* **pluck·i·er, pluck·i·est.** having or showing pluck or courage; brave. —**pluck′i·ly,** *adv.* —**pluck′i·ness,** *n.* —**Syn.** courageous, determined; spunky.

plug (plug), *n., v.,* **plugged, plug·ging.** —*n.* **1.** a piece of wood or other material used to stop up a hole or aperture, to fill a gap, or to act as a wedge. **2.** *Elect.* a device to which the conductors of a cord may be attached and that establishes contact by insertion in a jack or being screwed into a receptacle. **3.** See **spark plug** (def. 1). **4.** a fireplug. **5.** a cake of pressed tobacco. **6.** *Chiefly U.S. Slang.* a worn-out or inferior horse. **7.** *Informal.* the favorable mention of a product, as in a radio or television program. **8.** *Angling.* an artificial lure fitted with one or more hooks, used chiefly in casting. —*v.t.* **9.** to stop or fill with or as with a plug (often fol. by *up*): *to plug up a leak; to plug a gap.* **10.** to insert or drive a plug into. **11.** to secure with or as with a plug. **12.** to insert (something) as a plug. **13.** *Informal.* to mention (a product) favorably, as in a radio or television program. **14.** *Slang.* to shoot. —*v.i.* **15.** *Informal.* to work steadily or doggedly (often fol. by *along*). **16. plug in,** to connect (an electrical device) with an outlet: *to plug in a toaster.* [< MD *plugge* (D *plug*) plug, peg; c. G *Pflock* plug, peg] —**plug′ga·ble,** *adj.* —**plug′ger,** *n.* —**plug′less,** *adj.*

plug-in (plug′in′), *adj.* **1.** that can be operated or connected simply by plugging in or inserting: *a plug-in hair-dryer; a plug-in transistor.* —*n.* **2. a.** plug (def. 2). **b.** jack¹ (def. 9). **3.** a plug-in appliance.

plug·ug·ly (plug′ug′lē), *n., pl.* **-lies.** *Informal.* a ruffian; rowdy; tough.

plum¹ (plum), *n.* **1.** the drupaceous fruit of any of several rosaceous trees of the genus *Prunus,* having an oblong stone. **2.** the tree itself. **3.** any of various other trees bearing a plumlike fruit. **4.** the fruit itself. **5.** a sugarplum. **6.** a raisin, as in a cake or pudding. **7.** a deep purple varying from bluish to reddish. **8.** *Slang.* an excellent or desirable thing, as a fine position, bonus, unexpected legacy, etc. [ME; OE *plūme* (c. G *Pflaume*) << Gk *proûmnon* plum, *proúmnē* plum tree] —**plum′like′,** *adj.*

plum² (plum), *adj., adv.* plumb (defs. 3–6).

plum·age (plo͞o′mij), *n.* **1.** the feathery covering of a bird. **2.** feathers collectively. [< MF] —**plum′aged,** *adj.*

plu·mate (plo͞o′māt, -mit), *adj.* *Zool.* resembling a feather, as a hair or bristle that bears smaller hairs. [< L *plūmāt(us)* feathered]

plumb (plum), *n.* **1.** a small mass of lead or other heavy material, as one suspended by a line and used to measure the depth of water or to ascertain a vertical line. **2. out of** or **off plumb,** not corresponding to the perpendicular; out of true. —*adj.* **3.** true according to a plumb line; perpendicular. —*adv.* **4.** in a perpendicular or vertical direction. **5.** exactly, precisely, or directly. **6.** *Informal.* completely or absolutely: *She was plumb mad.* —*v.t.* **7.** to test or adjust by a plumb line. **8.** to make vertical. **9.** to sound with or as with a plumb line. **10.** to measure (depth) by sounding. **11.** to examine closely in order to discover or understand: *to plumb someone's thoughts.* **12.** to seal with lead. **13.** to provide with plumbing. —*v.i.* **14.** to work as a plumber. Also, **plum** (for defs. 3–6). [ME *plumbe* < ML **plumba,* var. of L *plumbum* lead] —**plumb′less,** *adj.* —**Syn. 3.** vertical, straight, square.

plum·bag·i·na·ceous (plum baj′ə nā′shəs), *adj.* belonging to the *Plumbaginaceae,* or leadwort family of plants. [< L *plumbāgin-* (s. of *plumbāgō*) leadwort + -ACEOUS]

plum·ba·go (plum bā′gō), *n., pl.* **-gos. 1.** graphite. **2.** a drawing made by an instrument with a lead point. **3.** any plant of the genus *Plumbago,* comprising the leadworts. [< L, trans. of Gk *polýbdaina* lead ore < *pólybdos* lead]

plumb′ bob′, plummet (def. 1).

plum·be·ous (plum′bē əs), *adj.* resembling or containing lead; leaden. [< L *plumbeus* = *plumb(um)* lead + *-eus* -EOUS]

plumb·er (plum′ər), *n.* **1.** a person who installs and repairs piping, fixtures, etc., in connection with the water supply and drainage system. **2.** *Obs.* a worker in lead or similar metals. [late ME, sp. var. of ME *plomber* << LL *plumbār-(ius);* r. ME *plummer* < AF; OF *plummier*]

plumb·er·y (plum′ə rē), *n., pl.* **-er·ies. 1.** a plumber's workshop. **2.** plumbing (def. 2). [ME < OF *plommerie*]

plum·bic (plum′bik), *adj.* *Chem.* containing lead, esp. in the tetravalent state. [< L *plumb(um)* lead + -IC]

plum·bif·er·ous (plum bif′ər əs), *adj.* yielding or containing lead. [< L *plumb(um)* lead + -I- + -FEROUS]

plumb·ing (plum′ing), *n.* **1.** the system of pipes and other apparatus for conveying water, liquid wastes, etc., as in a building. **2.** the work or trade of a plumber. **3.** the act of a person who plumbs, as in measuring the depth of water or in ascertaining a vertical line.

plum·bism (plum′biz əm), *n.* *Pathol.* See **lead poisoning** (def. 1b). [< L *plumb(um)* lead + -ISM]

plumb′ line′, 1. a cord with a metal bob attached to one end, used to determine perpendicularity, the depth of water, etc. **2.** See **plumb rule.**

plum·bous (plum′bəs), *adj.* *Chem.* containing bivalent lead. [< L *plumbōs(us)*]

plumb′ rule′, a device for determining perpendicularity, consisting of a narrow board with a plumb line and bob suspended from an upper edge. [ME *plomreule*]

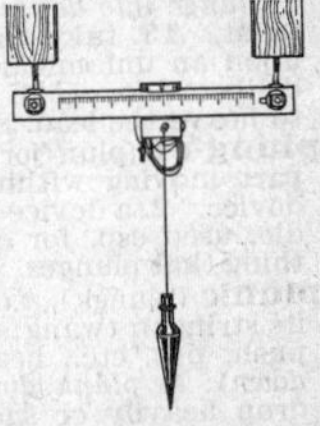
Plumb rule

plum·bum (plum′bəm), *n.* *Chem.* lead. *Abbr.:* Pb [< L]

plum′ duff′, a duff containing raisins.

plume (plo͞om), *n., v.,* **plumed, plum·ing.** —*n.* **1.** a feather. **2.** a large, long, or conspicuous feather: *the brilliant plume of a peacock.* **3.** a soft, fluffy feather: *the plume of an egret.* **4.** any plumose part or formation. **5.** a feather, a tuft of feathers, or some substitute, worn as an ornament, as on a hat, helmet, etc. **6.** a feather or featherlike token of honor or distinction, esp. one worn on a helmet. **7.** *Chiefly Literary.* plumage. —*v.t.* **8.** to furnish, cover, or adorn with plumes or feathers. **9.** (of a bird) to preen (itself or its feathers). **10.** to feel complacent satisfaction with (oneself); pride (oneself) (often fol. by *on* or *upon*). [earlier *plome, plume,* ME *plume,* OE *plūm* < L *plūma* soft feather (pl., down)] —**plume′less,** *adj.* —**plume′like′,** *adj.*

plum·met (plum′it), *n.* **1.** Also called **plumb bob.** a piece of lead or some other weight attached to a line, used for determining perpendicularity, for sounding, etc.; the bob of a plumb line. **2.** See **plumb rule. 3.** something that weighs down or depresses. —*v.i.* **4.** to plunge. [ME *plommet* < MF, dim. of *plomb* lead]

plum·my (plum′ē), *adj.,* **-mi·er, -mi·est. 1.** containing or resembling plums. **2.** *Brit. Informal.* good; desirable.

plu·mose (plo͞o′mōs), *adj.* **1.** having feathers or plumes; feathered. **2.** feathery or plumelike. [< L *plūmōs(us)*] —**plu′mose·ly,** *adv.*

plump¹ (plump), *adj.* **1.** well filled out or rounded in form; somewhat fleshy or fat. —*v.i.* **2.** to become plump (often fol. by *up* or *out*). —*v.t.* **3.** to make plump (often fol. by *up* or *out*): *to plump up the sofa pillows.* [late ME *plompe* dull, rude < MFlem; c. MLG *plump* blunt, thick, rude] —**plump′ly,** *adv.* —**plump′ness,** *n.* —**Syn. 1.** portly. See **stout. 2.** fatten. —**Ant. 1.** thin.

plump² (plump), *v.i.* **1.** to drop or fall heavily or suddenly; come down abruptly or with direct impact. **2.** *Chiefly Brit.* to vote exclusively for one candidate in an election, instead of distributing or splitting one's votes among a number. —*v.t.* **3.** to drop or throw heavily or suddenly (often fol. by *down*): *He plumped himself down and fell asleep.* **4.** to praise or extol. **5. plump for,** to support enthusiastically; be wholeheartedly in favor of. —*n.* **6.** a heavy or sudden fall. **7.** the sound resulting from such a fall. —*adv.* **8.** with a heavy or sudden fall or drop. **9.** directly or bluntly, as in speaking. **10.** in a vertical direction; straight down. **11.** with sudden encounter. **12.** with direct impact. —*adj.* **13.** direct; downright; blunt. [ME *plumpe(n)*; c. D *plompen*; prob. imit.]

plump[3] (plump), *n.* *Chiefly Brit. Dial.* a group or cluster. [late ME *plumpe* < ?]

plump·er[1] (plum′pər), *n.* **1.** an act of falling heavily; a plumping. **2.** *Chiefly Brit.* the vote of a person who plumps. [PLUMP[2] + -ER[1]]

plump·er[2] (plum′pər), *n.* something carried in the mouth to fill out hollow cheeks. [PLUMP[1] + -ER[1]]

plum′ pud′ding, a rich steamed or boiled pudding containing raisins, currants, citron, spices, etc.

plu·mule (plōōm′yōōl), *n.* **1.** *Bot.* the bud of the ascending axis of a plant while still in the embryo. **2.** *Ornith.* a down feather. [< NL, L *plūmula*] —**plu·mu·lar** (plōōm′yə-lər), *adj.*

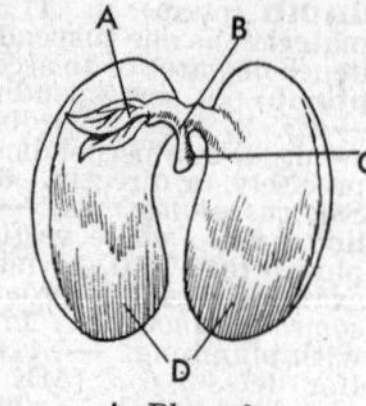

A, Plumule of a bean, *Vicia faba;* B, Hypocotyl; C, Radicle; D, Cotyledons

plum·y (plōō′mē), *adj.,* **plum·i·er, plum·i·est.** **1.** having plumes or feathers. **2.** adorned with a plume or plumes: *a plumy helmet.* **3.** plumelike or feathery.

plun·der (plun′dər), *v.t.* **1.** to rob of goods or valuables by open force, as in war, hostile raids, brigandage, etc.: *to plunder a town.* **2.** to rob, despoil, or fleece: *to plunder the public treasury.* **3.** to take wrongfully, as by pillage, robbery, or fraud: *to plunder a piece of property.* —*v.i.* **4.** to take plunder; pillage. —*n.* **5.** the act of plundering; pillage or spoliation. **6.** that which is taken in plundering; loot. **7.** anything taken by robbery, theft, or fraud. [< D *plunder(en)* (to) plunder, pillage, loot, sack] —**plun′der·er,** *n.* —**plun′der·ous,** *adj.*

plun·der·age (plun′dər ij), *n.* **1.** plunder (def. 5). **2.** *Law.* **a.** the embezzlement of goods on board a ship. **b.** the goods embezzled.

plunge (plunj), *v.,* **plunged, plung·ing,** *n.* —*v.t.* **1.** to cast or thrust forcibly or suddenly into a liquid, a penetrable substance, a place, etc.; immerse; submerge: *to plunge a dagger into one's heart.* **2.** to bring suddenly or forcibly into some condition, situation, etc.: *to plunge a country into war.* —*v.i.* **3.** to cast oneself, or fall as if cast, into water, a hole, etc. **4.** to rush or dash with headlong haste: *to plunge through a crowd.* **5.** *Informal.* to bet or speculate recklessly: *to plunge on the stock market.* **6.** to throw oneself impetuously or abruptly into some condition, situation, matter, etc.: *to plunge into debt.* **7.** to descend abruptly or precipitously, as a cliff or road. **8.** to pitch violently forward, as a horse, ship, etc. —*n.* **9.** the act of plunging. **10.** a leap or dive, as into water. **11.** a headlong or impetuous rush or dash: *a plunge into danger.* **12.** a sudden, violent pitching movement. **13. take the plunge,** to enter with sudden decision upon an unfamiliar course of action, as after hesitation or deliberation. [ME < MF *plung(i)e(r)* << VL **plumbicāre* to heave the lead. See PLUMB] —**Syn. 1.** See **dip.**

plung·er (plun′jər), *n.* **1.** *Mach.* a pistonlike reciprocating part moving within the cylinder of a pump or hydraulic device. **2.** a device consisting of a suction cup on a long handle, used esp. for clearing clogged drains. **3.** a person or thing that plunges. **4.** a reckless bettor or speculator.

plunk (plungk), *v.t.* **1.** to pluck (a stringed instrument or its strings); twang: *to plunk a guitar.* **2.** *Informal.* to throw, push, put, etc., heavily or suddenly; plump (often fol. by *down*): *to plunk down one's money.* —*v.i.* **3.** *Informal.* to drop heavily or suddenly; plump (often fol. by *down*): *to plunk down and take a nap.* —*adv.* **4.** *Informal.* squarely: *The ball landed plunk in the net.* [nasalized var. of PLUCK]

plu·per·fect (plōō pûr′fikt), *Gram.* —*adj.* **1.** designating a tense or other verb formation with perfect meaning in reference to past time, as *had done* in *He had done it when I came.* —*n.* **2.** the pluperfect tense, or other verb formation with such meaning. **3.** a form in the pluperfect. [< L *plū(s quam) perfect(um)* more than perfect]

plupf., pluperfect. Also, **plup.**

plur., **1.** plural. **2.** plurality.

plu·ral (plŏŏr′əl), *adj.* **1.** consisting of, containing, or pertaining to more than one. **2.** pertaining to or involving a plurality of persons or things: *plural marriage.* **3.** being one of such a plurality: *a plural wife.* **4.** *Gram.* noting or pertaining to a member of the category of number indicating that a word has more than one referent, as in English *men.* —*n.* *Gram.* **5.** the plural number. **6.** a form in the plural. [ME < L *plūrāl(is).* See PLUS, -AL[1]]

plu·ral·ism (plŏŏr′ə liz′əm), *n.* **1.** *Philos.* **a.** a theory that there is more than one basic substance or principle. Cf. **dualism** (def. 2a), **monism** (def. 1a). **b.** a theory that even if there is only one basic substance or principle many particular and distinct entities exist. Cf. **monism** (def. 1b). **2.** *Eccles.* **a.** the holding by one person of two or more offices at the same time. **b.** plurality (def. 7a). **3.** the state or quality of being plural. —**plu′ral·ist,** *n.* —**plu′ral·is′tic,** *adj.*

plu·ral·i·ty (plŏŏ ral′i tē), *n., pl.* **-ties.** **1.** the excess of votes received by the leading candidate, in an election in which there are three or more candidates, over those received by the next candidate (distinguished from *majority*). **2.** more than half of the whole; majority. **3.** a number greater than one. **4.** the fact of being numerous. **5.** a large number; multitude. **6.** the state or fact of being plural. **7.** *Eccles.* **a.** the holding by one person of two or more benefices at the same time; pluralism. **b.** any of the benefices so held. [ME *pluralite* < OF < LL *plūrālitās*]

plu·ral·ize (plŏŏr′ə līz′), *v.,* **-ized, -iz·ing.** —*v.t.* **1.** to express in the plural form; make plural: *to pluralize a noun.* —*v.i.* **2.** to receive or take a plural form. Also, *esp. Brit.,* **plu′ral·ise′.** —**plu′ral·i·za′tion,** *n.* —**plu′ral·iz′er,** *n.*

plu·ral·ly (plŏŏr′ə lē), *adv.* as a plural; in a plural sense. [ME *pluraliche.* See PLURAL, -LY]

pluri-, an element of Latin origin meaning "several," "many," used in the formation of compound words. [< L, comb. form repr. L *plūs* (s. *plūri-*) more (pl. many). See PLUS]

plus (plus), *prep.* **1.** more by the addition of; increased by: *ten plus two.* **2.** with the addition of; with: *He had wealth plus fame.* —*adj.* **3.** involving or noting addition. **4.** positive: *a plus quantity.* **5.** more (by a certain amount). **6.** *Elect.* pertaining to or characterized by positive electricity: *the plus terminal.* **7.** *Bot.* designating, in the absence of morphological difference, one of the two strains or mycelia in fungi which must unite in the sexual process. **8.** having a certain quality to an unusual degree: *He has personality plus.* —*n.* **9.** a plus quantity. **10.** See **plus sign.** **11.** something additional. **12.** a surplus or gain. —*conj.* **13.** also; and: *A bicycle is cheaper—plus, it's healthier.* [< L: more; akin to Gk *pleiōn,* Icel *fleiri* more, *fjöl* much, Goth *filu,* G *viel,* OE *feolu, fela,* Gk *polý,* OIr *il*]

plus′ fours′, baggy knickers, as for sports wear.

plush (plush), *n., adj.,* **plush·er, plush·est.** —*n.* **1.** a fabric, as of silk, cotton, or wool, whose pile is more than ⅛ inch high. —*adj.* **2.** connoting wealth or ease; luxurious: *a plush night club.* [< F *pluche,* syncopated var. of *peluche* << L *pilus* hair] —**plush′ness,** *n.*

plush·y (plush′ē), *adj.,* **plush·i·er, plush·i·est.** **1.** of, pertaining to, or resembling plush. **2.** characterized by luxury, wealth, or ease: *a plushy resort; a plushy new job.*

plus′ sign′, *Arith.* the symbol (+) indicating summation or a positive quality.

Plu·tarch (plōō′tärk), *n.* A.D. c46–c120, Greek biographer. —**Plu·tarch′i·an,** *adj.*

Plu·to (plōō′tō), *n.* **1.** *Class. Myth.* a name given to Hades, under which he is identified by the Romans with Orcus. **2.** *Astron.* the planet ninth in order from the sun, having a diameter that is probably somewhat less than that of the earth, a mean distance from the sun of 3,671,000,000 miles, and a period of revolution of 248.42 years: the outermost planet in the solar system.

plu·toc·ra·cy (plōō tok′rə sē), *n., pl.* **-cies.** **1.** the rule or power of wealth or of the wealthy. **2.** a class or group ruling or exercising power by virtue of its wealth. [< Gk *ploutokratía.* See PLUTUS, -CRACY]

plu·to·crat (plōō′tə krat′), *n.* a member of a plutocracy. [back formation from Gk *ploutokratía* PLUTOCRACY]

plu·to·crat·ic (plōō′tə krat′ik), *adj.* of, pertaining to, or characterized by a plutocracy or plutocrats. Also, **plu′to·crat′i·cal.** —**plu′to·crat′i·cal·ly,** *adv.*

plu·ton (plōō′ton), *n.* *Geol.* any body of igneous rock that solidified far below the earth's surface. [named after PLUTO] —**plu·ton′ic,** *adj.*

Plu·to·ni·an (plōō tō′nē ən), *adj.* **1.** Also, **Plu·ton·ic** (plōō ton′ik). of, pertaining to, or resembling Pluto or the lower world; infernal. **2.** (*often l.c.*) *Geol.* of or pertaining to the theory that the present condition of the earth's crust is mainly due to igneous action. [< L *Plūtōni(us)* (< Gk *Ploutṓnios* < *Ploútōn* PLUTO) + -AN]

plu·to·ni·um (plōō tō′nē əm), *n.* *Chem.* a radioactive element, capable of self-maintained explosive fission. It is formed by deuteron bombardment of neptunium, and has a fissionable isotope of major importance (Pu^{239}), that can be produced in chain-reacting units from uranium 238: used as fuel in some nuclear reactors. *Symbol:* Pu; *at. no.:* 94. [< Gk *Ploútōn* PLUTO + -IUM]

plu·vi·al (plōō′vē əl), *adj.* **1.** of or pertaining to rain, esp. much rain; rainy. **2.** *Geol.* occurring through the action of rain. [< L *pluviāl(is)* = *pluvi(a)* rain + *-ālis* -AL[1]]

plu·vi·om·e·ter (plōō′vē om′i tər), *n.* See **rain gauge.** [< L *pluvi(a)* rain + -o- + -METER] —**plu·vi·o·met·ric** (plōō′vē ə me′trik), **plu′vi·o·met′ri·cal,** *adj.* —**plu′vi·om′e·try,** *n.*

Plu·vi·ôse (plōō′vē ōs′; *Fr.* plʏ vyōz′), *n.* (in the French Revolutionary calendar) the fifth month of the year, extending from January 20 to February 18. [< F < L *pluviōs(us)* rainy]

plu·vi·ous (plōō′vē əs), *adj.* of or pertaining to rain; rainy. [< L *pluviōs(us)*]

ply[1] (plī), *v.,* **plied, ply·ing.** —*v.t.* **1.** to work with or at; employ busily; use: *to ply the needle.* **2.** to carry on, practice, or pursue: *to ply a trade.* **3.** to treat with or apply to (something) repeatedly (often fol. by *with*): *to ply a fire with fresh fuel.* **4.** to assail persistently: *to ply horses with a whip.* **5.** to supply with or offer something pressingly to: *to ply a person with drink.* **6.** to address (someone) persistently or importunately, as with questions; importune. **7.** to pass over or along (a river, stream, etc.) steadily or on a regular basis: *boats that ply the Ohio.* —*v.i.* **8.** to run or travel regularly over a fixed course or between certain places, as a boat, bus, etc. **9.** to perform one's work or office busily or steadily: *to ply with the oars; to ply at a trade.* [ME *plye,* aph. var. of *aplye* to APPLY] —**ply′ing·ly,** *adv.*

ply[2] (plī), *n., pl.* **plies.** **1.** one thickness or layer, as in certain wood products. **2.** a unit of yarn: *single ply.* **3.** bent, bias, or inclination. [ME *plie(n)* < MF *plier* to fold, bend, var. of *ployer,* OF *pleiier* < L *plicāre* to fold]

-ply, a combining form of **ply**[2]: *three-ply.*

ply·er (plī′ər), *n.* *Chiefly Brit.* plier.

Plym·outh (plim′əth), *n.* **1.** a seaport in SW Devonshire, in SW England, on the English Channel: naval base; the departing point of the *Mayflower* 1620. 204,279 (1961). **2.** a city in SE Massachusetts: the oldest town in New England, founded by the Pilgrims 1620. 18,606 (1970).

Plym′outh Breth′ren, a body of Christians founded in Plymouth, England, about 1830, having no ordained ministry, formal creed, or ritual, and accepting the Bible as the only guide.

Plym′outh Col′ony, *Amer. Hist.* the colony established in SE Massachusetts by the Pilgrim Fathers in 1620.

Plym′outh Rock′, **1.** a rock at Plymouth, Massachusetts, on which the Pilgrims who sailed on the *Mayflower* are said to have stepped ashore when they landed in 1620. **2.** one of an American breed of medium-sized chickens, raised for both meat and eggs.

ply·wood (plī′wŏŏd′), *n.* a building material consisting usually of an odd number of veneers glued over each other, usually at right angles.

Pl·zeň (pəl′zen′yə), *n.* Czech name of **Pilsen.**

Pm, *Chem.* promethium.

P.M., **1.** Past Master. **2.** Paymaster. **3.** See **p.m.** **4.** Police Magistrate. **5.** Postmaster. **6.** post-mortem. **7.** Prime Minister. **8.** Provost Marshal.

p.m., after noon; the period between 12 noon and 12 midnight. Cf. **a.m.** [< L *post merīdiem*]

P.M.G., 1. Paymaster General. 2. Postmaster General.

PMS, See **premenstrual syndrome.**

P/N, promissory note. Also, **p.n.**

pneu·ma (no͞o′mə, nyo͞o′-), *n.* **1.** the vital spirit; the soul. **2.** *Theol.* the Spirit of God; the Holy Ghost. [< Gk: lit., breath, wind, akin to *pnein* to blow, breathe]

pneu·mat·ic (no͝o mat′ik, nyo͝o-), *adj.* **1.** of or pertaining to air, gases, or wind. **2.** of or pertaining to pneumatics. **3.** operated by air or by the pressure or exhaustion of air: *a pneumatic drill.* **4.** filled with or containing compressed air, as a tire. **5.** of, by, or pertaining to a system of fast transmission of letters, packages, etc., by air pressure through a tube between two points, as in an office: *pneumatic dispatch.* **6.** *Theol.* of or pertaining to the spirit; spiritual. **7.** *Zool.* containing air or air cavities. —*n.* **8.** a pneumatic tire. [< L *pneumatic(us)* < Gk *pneumatikós* pertaining to air, breath or wind, spiritual = *pneumat-* (s. of *pneûma;* see PNEUMA) + *-ikos* -IC] —**pneu·mat′i·cal·ly,** *adv.*

pneu·mat·ics (no͝o mat′iks, nyo͝o-), *n.* (*construed as sing.*) the branch of physics that deals with the mechanical properties of air and other gases. Also called **pneumodynamics.** [see PNEUMATIC, -ICS]

pneumat′ic trough′, *Chem.* a trough filled with liquid for collecting gases in bell jars or bottles by displacement.

pneumato-, a learned borrowing from Greek meaning "air," "breath," "spirit," used in the formation of compound words: *pneumatology; pneumatophore.* [< Gk, comb. form of *pneûma*]

pneu·ma·tol·o·gy (no͞o′mə tol′ə jē, nyo͞o′-), *n.* **1.** *Theol.* doctrine concerning the Holy Spirit. **2.** the doctrine or study of spiritual beings. —**pneu·ma·to·log·ic** (no͞o′mə tᵊloj′ik, nyo͞o′-), **pneu′ma·to·log′i·cal,** *adj.* —**pneu′ma·tol′o·gist,** *n.*

pneu·ma·tol·y·sis (no͞o′mə tol′i sis, nyo͞o′-), *n.* *Geol.* the process by which minerals and ores are formed by the action of vapors given off from igneous magmas.

pneu·ma·to·lyt·ic (no͞o′mə tᵊlit′ik, nyo͞o′-), *adj.* pertaining to or formed by pneumatolysis.

pneu·ma·tom·e·ter (no͞o′mə tom′i tər, nyo͞o′-), *n.* an instrument for measuring either the quantity of air inhaled or exhaled during a single inspiration or expiration, or the force of inspiration or expiration.

pneu·ma·to·phore (no͞o′mə tə fōr′, -fôr′, nyo͞o′-; no͞omat′ə fōr′, -fôr′, nyo͞o-), *n.* **1.** *Bot.* a specialized structure developed from the root in certain plants growing in swamps and marshes, serving as a respiratory organ. **2.** *Zool.* the air sac of a siphonophore, serving as a float.

pneu·mec·to·my (no͞o mek′tə mē, nyo͞o-), *n., pl.* **-mies.** *Surg.* pneumonectomy.

pneumo-, an element of Greek origin, used to refer to air, respiration, or the lungs: *pneumococcus.* Cf. **pneumato-.** [repr. Gk *pneúmōn* lung, or *pneûma* wind, air, breath]

pneu·mo·ba·cil·lus (no͞o′mō bə sil′əs, nyo͞o′-), *n., pl.* **-cil·li** (-sil′ī). a bacterium, *Klebsiella pneumoniae,* causing a type of pneumonia and associated with other diseases, esp. of the respiratory tract. [< NL]

pneu·mo·coc·cus (no͞o′mə kok′əs, nyo͞o′-), *n., pl.* **-coc·ci** (-kok′sī). a bacterium, *Diplococcus pneumoniae,* causing lobar pneumonia and associated with other diseases, as pericarditis and meningitis. [< NL] —**pneu·mo·coc·cal** (no͞o′mə kok′əl, nyo͞o′-), **pneu·mo·coc·cic** (no͞o′mə kok′sik, nyo͞o′-), **pneu·mo·coc·cous** (no͞o′mə kok′əs, nyo͞o′-), *adj.*

pneu·mo·co·ni·o·sis (no͞o′mə kō′nē ō′sis, nyo͞o′-), *n.* *Pathol.* fibrous induration of the lungs due to irritation caused by the inhalation of dust, esp. in certain occupations, as coal mining. Also, **pneumonoconiosis, pneumonokoniosis.** [syncopated var. of PNEUMONOCONIOSIS]

pneu·mo·dy·nam·ics (no͞o′mə dī nam′iks, nyo͞o′-, -di-), *n.* (*construed as sing.*) pneumatics.

pneu·mo·gas·tric (no͞o′mə gas′trik, nyo͞o′-), *adj.* *Anat.* of or pertaining to the lungs and stomach.

pneu·mo·graph (no͞o′mə graf′, -gräf′, nyo͞o′-), *n.* *Med.* a device for recording graphically the respiratory movements of the thorax.

pneumon-, var. of **pneumono-** before a vowel: *pneumonectomy.*

pneu·mo·nec·to·my (no͞o′mə nek′tə mē, nyo͞o′-), *n., pl.* **-mies.** *Surg.* excision of part or all of a lung.

pneu·mo·nia (no͝o mōn′yə, -mō′nē ə, nyo͝o-), *n.* *Pathol.* **1.** inflammation of the lungs. **2.** an acute affection of the lungs, regarded as being caused by the pneumococcus. [< NL < Gk *pneumonía*]

pneu·mon·ic (no͝o mon′ik, nyo͝o-), *adj.* **1.** pulmonary. **2.** pertaining to or affected with pneumonia. [< NL *pneumonic(us)* < Gk *pneumonikós*]

pneumono-, a learned borrowing from Greek meaning "lung," used in the formation of compound words: *pneumonoconiosis.* Also, *esp. before a vowel,* **pneumon-.** [comb. form repr. Gk *pneúmōn* lung]

pneu·mo·no·co·ni·o·sis (no͞o′mə nō kō′nē ō′sis, nyo͞o′-), *n.* *Pathol.* pneumoconiosis. Also, **pneu′mo·no·ko′ni·o′sis.** [PNEUMONO- + Gk *kón(is)* dust + -OSIS]

pneu·mo·no·ul·tra·mi·cro·scop·ic·sil·i·co·vol·ca·no·co·ni·o·sis (no͞o′mə nō ul′trə mī′krə skop′ik sil′ə-kō′vol kā′nō kō′nē ō′sis, nyo͞o′-), *n.* *Pathol.* a disease of the lungs caused by breathing extremely fine siliceous dust. Also, **pneu′mo·no·ul′tra·mi′cro·scop′ic·sil′i·co′vol·ca′no·ko′ni·o′sis.** [< NL; see PNEUMONO-, ULTRAMICROSCOPIC, SILICO-, VOLCANO, CONIDIUM, -OSIS]

pneu·mo·tho·rax (no͞o′mə thōr′aks, -thôr′-, nyo͞o′-), *n.* the presence of air or gas in the pleural cavity. [< NL]

Pnom Penh (nom′ pen′, pə nôm′ pen′). See **Phnom Penh.** Also, **Pnom′-penh′, Pnom′penh′.**

pnxt., pinxit.

Pnyx (niks, pniks), *n.* a hill in Athens, Greece, near the Acropolis: the place of assembly in ancient Athens.

Po (pō), *n.* a river in Italy, flowing E from the Cottian Alps to the Adriatic. 418 mi. long. Ancient, **Padus.**

Po, *Chem.* polonium.

po., *Baseball.* put-out; put-outs.

P.O., 1. petty officer. 2. postal order. 3. post office.

po·a·ceous (pō ā′shəs), *adj.* belonging to the *Poaceae* (or *Gramineae*), the grass family of plants. [< NL *Po(a)* the typical genus (< Gk *póa* grass) + -ACEOUS]

poach[1] (pōch), *v.i.* **1.** *Chiefly Brit.* to trespass, esp. on another's game preserve, in order to steal animals or to hunt. **2.** to take game or fish illegally. **3.** (of land) to become broken up or slushy from being trampled. —*v.t.* **4.** to trespass on (private property), esp. in order to hunt game or to fish: *to poach a farm.* **5.** to steal (game or fish), as from another's preserve: *to poach deer.* **6.** to break or tear up by trampling. **7.** to mix with water and reduce to a uniform consistency, as clay. [< MF *poche(r)* (to) gouge < Gmc; akin to POKE[1]]

poach[2] (pōch), *v.t.* to cook (eggs, fish, fruits, etc.) in a hot liquid that is kept just below the boiling point. [var. of *potch,* late ME *pocche* < MF *pocher,* lit., to bag (the white of an egg being made to hold the yoke as a bag would) < *poche* bag, central F form of Picard *poque* < MD *poke* POKE[2]] —**poach′a·ble,** *adj.*

poach·er[1] (pō′chər), *n.* a person who trespasses on private property, esp. to catch fish or game illegally. [POACH[1] + -ER[1]]

poach·er[2] (pō′chər), *n.* a pan having a tight-fitting lid and metal cups for steaming or poaching eggs. [POACH[2] + -ER[1]]

POB, Post Office Box. Also, **P.O.B.**

Po·ca·hon·tas (pō′kə hon′təs), *n.* (*Rebecca Rolfe*) 1595?–1617, American Indian girl who is said to have prevented the execution of Captain John Smith.

Po·ca·tel·lo (pō′kə tel′ō), *n.* a city in SE Idaho. 40,036 (1970).

po·chard (pō′chərd, -kərd), *n., pl.* **-chards,** (*esp. collectively*) **-chard.** an Old World diving duck, *Aythya ferina,* having a chestnut-red head. [?]

pock (pok), *n.* **1.** a pustule on the body in an eruptive disease, as smallpox. **2.** a mark or spot left by or resembling such a pustule. **3.** a pit, hole, cavity, or the like: *The diggers left pocks in the field.* **4.** *Scot.* poke[2]. [ME *pokke,* OE *poc;* c. G *Pocke;* perh. akin to OE *pocca.* See POKE[2]]

pock·et (pok′it), *n.* **1.** a shaped piece of fabric attached inside or outside a garment and forming a pouch, used esp. for carrying small articles. **2.** a bag or pouch. **3.** any pouchlike receptacle, envelope, compartment, hollow, or cavity. **4.** a cavity in the earth, esp. one containing gold or other ore. **5.** a small ore body or mass of ore, frequently isolated. **6.** *Billiards, Pool.* any of the pouches at the corners and sides of the table. **7.** a position in which a competitor in a race is so hemmed in by others that his progress is impeded. **8.** *Naut.* a holder consisting of a strip of sailcloth sewed to a sail, and containing a thin wooden batten that stiffens the leech of the sail. **9.** *Anat.* any saclike cavity in the body: *a pus pocket.* **10.** any isolated group, area, element, etc., contrasted, as in status or condition, with a surrounding element or group: *pockets of resistance; a pocket of poverty.* **11. in one's pocket,** in one's possession; under one's influence: *He has the audience in his pocket.* **12. line one's pockets,** to profit, esp. at the expense of others. —*adj.* **13.** small enough or suitable for carrying in the pocket: *a pocket radio; a pocket dictionary.* **14.** relatively small. —*v.t.* **15.** to put into one's pocket. **16.** to take possession of as one's own, often dishonestly: *to pocket public funds.* **17.** to conceal or suppress: *to pocket one's pride.* **18.** to enclose or confine as in a pocket: *The town was pocketed in a small valley.* **19.** *Billiards, Pool.* to drive (a ball) into a pocket. **20.** *U.S.* to retain (a legislative bill) without action on it to prevent it from becoming a law. **21.** to hem in (a contestant) so as to impede progress, as in racing. [ME *poket* < MD < ONF (Picard) *poquet,* dim. of *poque* < MD *poke* POKE[2]; see -ET] —**pock′et·a·ble,** *adj.* —**pock′et·less,** *adj.* —**pock′et·like′,** *adj.*

pock′et bat′tleship, a small, heavily armed and armored warship serving as a battleship because of limitations imposed by treaty.

pock′et bil′liards, pool[2] (def. 7).

pock·et·book (pok′it bo͝ok′), *n.* **1.** a small bag or case, as of leather, for papers, money, etc., usually carried by a handle or in the pocket. **2.** pecuniary resources. **3.** Also, **pock′et book′.** a book, usually paperbound, that is small enough to fit into a pocket or purse.

pock′et bor′ough, (before the Reform Bill of 1832) any English borough whose representatives in Parliament were controlled by an individual or family.

pock·et·ful (pok′it fo͝ol′), *n., pl.* **-fuls.** the amount that a pocket will hold.

pock′et go′pher, any of numerous burrowing rodents of the family *Geomyidae,* of western and southern North America and Central America, having large, external cheek pouches. Also called **gopher.** See illus. at **gopher.**

pock·et·knife (pok′it nīf′), *n., pl.* **-knives.** a small knife with one or more blades that fold into the handle.

pock′et mon′ey, money for small current expenses.

pock′et mouse′, any of numerous burrowing rodents, esp. of the genus *Perognathus,* found chiefly in arid parts of the southwestern U.S. and northern Mexico, having fur-lined cheek pouches and usually long tails.

pock′et park′, a very small park, usually part of a city block containing tall buildings. Also called **minipark.**

pock·et-size (pok′it sīz′), *adj.* small enough to fit conveniently into one's pocket. Also, **pock′et-sized′.**

pock′et ve′to, **1.** a veto brought about by the failure of the President to sign a bill presented to him within ten days of the adjournment of Congress. **2.** a similar action on the part of any legislative executive.

pock·mark (pok′märk′), *n.* **1.** Usually, **pockmarks.** marks or pits left by a pustule in smallpox or the like. —*v.t.* **2.** to mark or scar with or as with pockmarks. —**pock′-marked′,** *adj.*

pock·y (pok′ē), *adj.,* **pock·i·er, pock·i·est.** of, characterized by, or covered with pocks. [ME *pokky*] —**pock′i·ly,** *adv.*

po·co (pō′kō; *It.* pô′kô), *adv.* *Music.* somewhat; rather: *poco presto.* [< It: little < L *paucus* few]

po·co a po·co (pō′kō ä pō′kō; *It.* pô′kô ä pô′kô), *Music.* gradually; little by little. [< It]

po·co·cu·ran·te (pō′kō ko͝o ran′tē, -rän′-; *It.* pô′kô-ko͞o rän′te), *n., pl.* **-ti** (-tē), *adj.* —*n.* **1.** a careless or indifferent person. —*adj.* **2.** caring little; indifferent; nondifferent person.

chalant. [< It: lit., caring little. See POCO, CURE, -ANT] —**po·co·cu·ran·tism** (pō′kō ko͞o ran′tiz əm, -rän′-), **po′co·cu·ran′te·ism,** *n.*

pod¹ (pod), *n., v.,* **pod·ded, pod·ding.** —*n.* **1.** a somewhat elongated, two-valved seed vessel, as that of the pea or bean. **2.** a dehiscent fruit or pericarp having several seeds. **3.** a streamlined compartment under the fuselage or wing of an airplane, for housing a jet engine, cargo, or weapons. —*v.i.* **4.** to produce pods. **5.** to swell out like a pod. [appar. back formation from *podder* peasecod gatherer. Cf. *podder,* var. of *podware,* unexplained var. of *codware* bagged vegetables (COD² pod, bag + *-ware* crops, vegetables)]

pod² (pod), *n.* a small herd or school, esp. of seals or whales. [? special (orig. facetious) use of POD¹]

pod³ (pod), *n.* the straight groove or channel in the body of certain augers or bits. [ME **pod* socket, special (technical) use of **pod,* OE *pād* covering, cloak, the socket being thought of as something that covers or hides what is thrust into it]

pod-, a learned borrowing from Greek meaning "foot," used in the formation of compound words: *podagra.* Also, *esp. before a consonant,* **podo-.** [comb. form repr. Gk *poûs* (gen. *podós*) FOOT]

-pod, a learned borrowing from Greek meaning "footed," used in the formation of compound words: *cephalopod.* [< Gk *-podos* = *pod-* (s. of *poûs*) foot + *-os* adj. suffix]

POD, port of debarkation.

P.O.D., **1.** pay on delivery. **2.** Post Office Department.

-poda, pl. of **-pod,** specialized in zoological terminology to denote the class of which the individual is a member: *Cephalopoda.*

po·dag·ra (pō dag′rə, pod′ə grə), *n. Pathol.* gout in the foot. [< L < Gk: lit., foot-trap = *pod-* POD- + *ágra* a catching, seizure] —**po·dag′ral, po·dag′ric, po·dag′ri·cal, pod·a·grous** (pod′ə grəs), *adj.*

-pode, var. of **-podium:** *megapode.*

po·des·ta (pō des′tə; *It.* pô′de stä′), *n.* any of certain magistrates in Italy, esp. a chief magistrate in a medieval community. [< It *podestà* power < L *potestās*]

Pod·go·ri·ca (*Serbo-Croatian.* pôd′gô RE′tsä), *n.* former name of **Titograd.** Also, **Pod′go·ri′tsa.**

Pod·gor·ny (pod gôR′ni), *n.* **Ni·ko·lai Vik·to·ro·vitch** (ni ko lī′ vēk′to RO vich), born 1903, Russian government official: member of the Presidium 1955–65; president of the Soviet Union 1965–77.

podg·y (poj′ē), *adj.,* **podg·i·er, podg·i·est.** *Chiefly Brit.* pudgy. —**podg′i·ly,** *adv.* —**podg′i·ness,** *n.*

po·di·a·try (pō dī′ə trē, pə-), *n. Med.* the treatment of minor foot ailments, as corns, bunions, etc. —**po·di′a·trist,** *n.*

po·di·um (pō′dē əm), *n., pl.* **-di·ums, -di·a** (-dē ə). **1.** a small platform for the conductor of an orchestra, for a public speaker, etc. **2.** *Archit.* **a.** a low wall forming a base for a construction, as a colonnade or dome. **b.** the masonry supporting a classical temple. **3.** *Zool., Anat.* a foot. **4.** *Bot.* a footstalk or stipe. [< L: elevated place, balcony < Gk *pódion* little foot = *pod-* POD- + *-ion* dim. suffix. See PEW]

-podium, an element meaning "footlike": *pseudopodium.* Also, **-pode.** [< NL; see PODIUM]

podo-, var. of **pod-** before a consonant: *podophyllin.*

Po·dolsk (po dôlsk′), *n.* a city in the W RSFSR, in the central Soviet Union in Europe, S of Moscow. 157,000 (est. 1965).

pod·o·mere (pod′ə mēr′), *n. Zool.* any segment of a limb of an arthropod.

pod·o·phyl·lin (pod′ə fil′in), *n.* a bitter irritant resin obtained from the rhizome of the May apple, used in medicine chiefly as a cathartic. Also called **pod′ophyl′lin res′in.** [< NL *Podophyll(um)* (see PODO-, -PHYLL) + -IN²] —**pod′o·phyl′lic,** *adj.*

-podous, a suffix used to form adjectives corresponding to nouns with stems in **-pod:** *cephalopodous.*

pod·sol (pod′sol), *n.* an infertile, acidic forest soil having an ash-colored upper layer, depleted of colloids and of iron and aluminum compounds, and a brownish lower layer in which these colloids and compounds have accumulated: found over large areas of N North America and Eurasia. Also, **pod·zol** (pod′zol). [< Russ *podzol,* lit., like ashes = *pod* near + *zola* ash] —**pod·sol′ic, pod·zol′ic,** *adj.*

pod·sol·ize (pod′sə līz′), *v.,* **-ized, -iz·ing.** —*v.t.* **1.** to make into podsol. —*v.i.* **2.** to become podsol. —**pod′sol·i·za′tion,** *n.*

Po·dunk (pō′duŋgk), *n.* any small and insignificant town. [special use of *Podunk,* near Hartford, Conn.]

pod·zol·ize (pod′zə līz′), *v.t., v.i.,* **-ized, -iz·ing.** podsolize. —**pod′zol·i·za′tion,** *n.*

Poe (pō), *n.* **Edgar Allan,** 1809–49, U.S. poet, short-story writer, and critic.

POE, **1.** port of embarkation. **2.** port of entry. Also, **P.O.E.**

po·em (pō′əm), *n.* **1.** a composition in verse, esp. a highly developed, imaginative one. **2.** a composition not in verse but characterized by great beauty of language or expression: *a prose poem from the Scriptures; a symphonic poem.* **3.** something having qualities that are suggestive of a poem. [< L *poēma* < Gk *póēma,* var. of *poíēma* poem, something made = *poi(eîn)* (to) make + *-ēma* -EME]

po·e·sy (pō′i sē, -zē), *n., pl.* **-sies.** **1.** *Archaic.* poetry in general. **2.** *Obs.* **a.** a poem or verse used as a motto. Cf. **posy** (def. 2). **b.** a poem. [ME *poesie* < MF < L *poēsis* < Gk *póēsis,* var. of *poíēsis* poetic art, poetry, lit., a making = *poiē-* (var. s. of *poieîn* to make) + *-sis* -SIS]

po·et (pō′it), *n.* **1.** a person who composes poetry. **2.** a person who has the gift of poetic thought, imagination, and creation, together with eloquence of expression. [ME *poete* < L *poēta* < Gk *poētḗs,* var. of *poiētḗs* poet, lit., maker = *poiē-* (var. s. of *poieîn* to make) + *-tēs* agent suffix] —**po′et·less,** *adj.* —**po′et·like′,** *adj.* —**Syn. 1.** versifier, bard.

poet., **1.** poetic. **2.** poetry.

po·et·as·ter (pō′it as′tər), *n.* an inferior poet; a writer of indifferent verse. [< ML or NL] —**po′et·as′ter·ing, po′et·as′ter·y,** *n.* —**Syn.** rhymester.

po·et·ess (pō′i tis), *n.* a female poet.

po·et·ic (pō et′ik), *adj.* Also, **po·et′i·cal.** **1.** possessing the qualities or charm of poetry. **2.** characteristic of or befitting a poet. **3.** endowed with the faculty or feeling of a poet: *a poetic eulogist.* **4.** having or showing the sensibility of a poet: *a poetic lover.* **5.** of or pertaining to poetry: *poetic literature.* **6.** expressed in or resembling poetry. **7.** celebrated in poetry, as a place. —*n.* **8.** poetics. [< L *poētic(us)* < Gk *po(i)ētikós*] —**po·et′i·cal·ly,** *adv.*

po·et·i·cise (pō et′i sīz′), *v.t., v.i.,* **-cised, -cis·ing.** *Chiefly Brit.* poeticize.

po·et·i·cize (pō et′i sīz′), *v.,* **-cized, -ciz·ing.** —*v.t.* **1.** to make (thoughts, feelings, etc.) poetic; express in poetry. —*v.i.* **2.** to speak or write poetry.

poet′ic jus′tice, an ideal distribution of rewards and punishments such as is common in some poetry and fiction.

poet′ic li′cense, license or liberty taken by a poet, prose writer, or other artist in deviating from rule, conventional form, logic, or fact, in order to produce a desired effect.

po·et·ics (pō et′iks), *n.* (*construed as sing.*) **1.** literary criticism treating of the nature and laws of poetry. **2.** the study of prosody. **3.** a treatise on poetry.

po·et·ise (pō′i tīz′), *v.i., v.t.,* **-ised, -is·ing.** *Chiefly Brit.* poetize. —**po′et·is′er,** *n.*

po·et·ize (pō′i tīz′), *v.,* **-ized, -iz·ing.** —*v.i.* **1.** to write poetry. **2.** to express oneself poetically. —*v.t.* **3.** to write about or express in poetic form. **4.** to make or treat as poetic; poeticize: *to poetize reality.* —**po′et·iz′er,** *n.*

po′et lau′reate, *pl.* **poets laureate.** **1.** (in Great Britain) a poet appointed for life as an officer of the royal household, formerly expected to write poems in celebration of court and national events. **2.** a poet recognized or acclaimed as the most eminent or representative of a country or locality.

po·et·ry (pō′i trē), *n.* **1.** the art of writing poems. **2.** literary work in metrical form; verse. **3.** prose with poetic qualities. **4.** poetic qualities however manifested. **5.** poetic spirit or feeling. [ME *poetrie* < ML *poētria* poetic art, L: poetess < Gk *poiḗtria,* var. of *poiētrís,* fem. of *poiētḗs* POET; see -Y³] —**po′et·ry·less,** *adj.*

—**Syn. 2.** POETRY, VERSE agree in referring to the work of a poet. The difference between POETRY and VERSE is usually the difference between substance and form. POETRY is lofty thought or impassioned feeling expressed in imaginative words: *Elizabethan poetry.* VERSE is any expression in words that conforms to accepted metrical rules and structure: *the differences between prose and verse.* —**Ant. 2.** prose.

po·gey (pō′gē), *n. Canadian.* **1.** any form of charity or government relief. Cf. **dole¹** (defs. 1, 3). **2.** unemployment insurance provided by the government. [earlier *pogie* workhouse < ?]

po·go·ni·a (pə gō′nē ə, -gōn′yə), *n.* a terrestrial orchid of the genus *Pogonia,* of North America. [< NL < Gk *pōgōnías* bearded (with reference to the lip which is frequently fringed)]

pog·o·nip (pog′ə nip), *n.* an ice fog that forms in the mountain valleys of the western U.S. [< Shoshone; said to mean white death]

po′go stick′ (pō′gō), a long stick having a pair of footrests attached to a powerful spring, so that, by standing on the footrests, a person can propel himself along in a series of leaps. Also, **po′go-stick′.** [*pogo* formerly trademark]

po·grom (pə grum′, -grom′, pō-), *n.* an organized massacre, esp. of Jews. [< Russ: devastation, destruction = *po-* perfective prefix + *-grom,* cf. *gromit′* to batter, hence wreck (< *grom* thunder)] —**Syn.** slaughter, butchery.

po·gy (pō′gē, pog′ē), *n., pl.* (*esp. collectively*) **-gy,** (*esp. referring to two or more kinds or species*) **-gies.** the menhaden. [? syncopated var. of Algonquian *pohegan* menhaden]

Po·hai (pō′hī′; *Chin.* bô′hī′), *n.* an arm of the Yellow Sea in NE China. Formerly, **Gulf of Chihli.**

poi (poi, pō′ē), *n.* a Hawaiian dish made of the root of the taro baked, pounded, moistened, and fermented. [< Hawaiian]

-poiesis, a combining form denoting production: *hematopoiesis.* [< Gk; see POESY, -SIS]

-poietic, a combining form meaning "producing": *hematopoietic.* [< Gk *poiētik(ós).* See POETIC]

poign·ant (poin′yənt, poin′ənt), *adj.* **1.** keenly distressing to the feelings: *poignant regret.* **2.** keen or strong in mental appeal. **3.** affecting or moving the emotions: *a poignant scene.* **4.** pungent to the smell. [ME *poynaunt* < MF *poignant,* prp. of *poindre* < L *pungere* to prick, pierce. See PUNGENT, -ANT] —**poign′an·cy,** *n.* —**poign′ant·ly,** *adv.* —**Syn. 1.** heartfelt. **4.** piquant, sharp.

poi·ki·lo·ther·mal (poi′kə lō thûr′məl, poi kil′ə-), *adj. Zool.* cold-blooded (def. 1). [< Gk *poikílo(s)* various + THERMAL] —**poi′ki·lo·ther′mism, poi′ki·lo·ther′my,** *n.*

poi·lu (pwä′lo͞o; *Fr.* PWA LY′), *n., pl.* **-lus** (-lo͞oz; *Fr.* -LY′). a French common soldier. [< F: lit., hairy, haired = *poil* hair (< L *pilus*) + *-u* ptp. suffix (< L *-utus*)]

Poin·ca·ré (PWAN KA RĀ′), *n.* **1. Jules Hen·ri** (zhYl äN-RĒ′), 1854–1912, French mathematician. **2.** his cousin, **Ray·mond** (RE MôN′), 1860–1934, French statesman: president of France 1913–20.

poin·ci·an·a (poin′sē an′ə, -ā′nə), *n.* **1.** any caesalpinaceous shrub or small tree of the genus *Poinciana,* esp. *P. pulcherrima,* having showy orange or scarlet flowers. **2.** a tree, *Delonix regia,* of Madagascar, having showy, scarlet flowers. [< NL; named after M. de *Poinci,* 17th-century governor of the French Antilles]

poin·set·ti·a (poin set′ē ə, -set′ə), *n.* a euphorbiaceous plant, *Euphorbia* (*Poinsettia*) *pulcherrima,* native to Mexico and Central America, having variously lobed leaves and brilliant scarlet, pink, or white bracts. [< NL; named after J. R. *Poinsett* (1799–1851), American minister to Mexico, who discovered the plant there in 1828]

point (point), *n* **1.** a sharp or tapering end, as of a dagger. **2.** a projecting part of anything: *a point of land.* **3.** something having a sharp or tapering end: *a pen point.* **4.** *Geom.* an element having position without extension, whose movement traces a line. **5.** a place or locality. **6.** a direction, esp. any of 32 compass directions 11° 15′ apart, used in navigation. **7.** a location on a scale, or the beginning of a phenomenon or process that this indicates: *the boiling point of water.* **8.** any specific moment or stage in an activity or process: *At this point, two new persons entered.* **9.** the moment or stage immediately preceding the appearance of a condition, the undertaking of an action, etc.: *on the point of hysteria.* **10.** a significant thing to be noted or understood. **11.** something that gives meaning or purpose to an argument, action, etc. **12.** an idea or objection that one advances for consideration, esp. when valid. **13.** a piece of advice or information; pointer. **14.** a quality or attribute to be taken into consideration. **15.** *Phonet.* a diacritic indicating a vowel or a modification of sound. **16.** an individual part or element of something. **17.** a distinguishing mark or quality, esp. one of an animal, used as a standard in stockbreeding, judging, etc. **18. points, a.** the extremities of an animal, esp. a horse or dog. **b.** *Railroads Brit.* a switch. **19.** a single unit, as in measurement or evaluation. **20.** (in craps) the number that must be thrown to win but not including 7 or 11 on the first roll: *Your point is 4.* **21.** *Cricket.* **a.** the position of the fielder who plays a short distance in front of and to the offside of the batsman. **b.** the fielder playing this position. **22.** *Hunting.* **a.** the action of a hunting dog in indicating the presence and location of game by pointing. **b.** the stance taken in pointing. **23.** a branch of a deer's antler. **24.** *Sports.* **a.** a cross-country run. **b.** a scoring unit in certain games and contests. **25.** *Educ.* one unit of credit. **26.** *Elect.* **a.** either of a pair of contacts tipped with tungsten or platinum that make or break current flow in a distributor, as in an automobile. **b.** *Brit.* an outlet or socket. **27.** *Com.* a unit of price quotation, as one dollar in stock tradings. **28.** *Jewelry.* a unit of weight equal to 1/100 of a carat. **29.** *Mil.* **a.** a patrol or reconnaissance unit that goes ahead of the advance party of an advance guard, or follows the rear party of the rear guard. **b.** the stroke in bayonet drill or combat. **30.** *Print. U.S.* a unit of type measurement equal to .013837 inch (1/72 inch), or 1/12 pica. **31.** a unit of measure of paper or card thickness, equal to .001 inch. **32.** See **point lace. 33.** the act of pointing. **34.** *Archaic.* a tagged ribbon or cord, formerly much used in dress, as for tying or fastening parts. **35. in point,** that is pertinent; applicable: *a case in point.* **36. in point of,** as regards; in reference to: *in point of fact.* **37. make a point of,** to regard as important. **38. stretch a point,** to depart from the usual procedure because of special circumstances. **39. to the point,** pertinent. —*v.t.* **40.** to direct (the finger, a weapon, etc.) at, to, or upon something. **41.** to indicate the presence or position of (usually fol. by *out*): *to point out an object in the sky.* **42.** to direct attention to (usually fol. by *out*): *to point out advantages.* **43.** to furnish with a point or points; sharpen. **44.** to mark with one or more points, dots, or the like. **45.** *Phonet.* to mark (letters) with points. **46.** to separate (figures) by dots or points (usually fol. by *off*): *Point off three figures in your answer.* **47.** to give greater or added force to, as an argument (often fol. by *up*): *to point up the necessity for caution.* **48.** *Hunting.* (of a hunting dog) to indicate the presence and location of (game) by standing rigid and facing toward it. **49.** *Masonry.* to fill the joints of (brickwork, stonework, etc.) with mortar or cement treated in various ways with tools after application. —*v.i.* **50.** to indicate position or direction, as with the finger. **51.** to direct the mind or thought in some direction; call attention to. **52.** to aim. **53.** to signify a tendency toward something: *conditions point to war.* **54.** to face in a particular direction. **55.** *Hunting.* (of a hunting dog) to point game. **56.** *Naut.* to sail close to the wind. [(n.) ME < OF *point* dot, mark, place, moment (< L *punctum*) + *pointe* sharp end (< L *puncta*); both L words ptp. forms of *pungere* to prick, stab; (v.) ME *poynte* < MF *point(er)* < *pointe* (n.)]

point-blank (point′blangk′), *adj.* **1.** aimed or fired straight at the mark, esp. from close range; direct. **2.** straightforward, plain, or explicit. —*adv.* **3.** with a direct aim; directly; straight. **4.** bluntly; frankly.

point′ count′, *Bridge.* **1.** a method of evaluating the strength of a hand by assigning a numerical value to high cards and to certain combinations and distributions of cards in the hand. **2.** the total number of points in a player's hand.

point cou·pé (*Fr.* pwan ko͞o pā′), **1.** Also called **cutwork.** a process for producing lace in which threads in the ground material are removed and ornamental patterns inserted. **2.** Also called **cutwork lace.** the lace produced by this process. [< F: cut point]

point d'Al·en·çon (*Fr.* pwan dȧ län sôn′). See **Alençon lace.** [< F: Alençon stitch]

point d'ap·pui (pwan dȧ pwē′), *pl.* **points d'ap·pui** (pwan dȧ pwē′). *French.* **1.** a prop; stay. **2.** *Mil.* a point of support for a battle line.

point-de-vice (point′di vīs′), *Archaic.* —*adv.* **1.** completely; perfectly; exactly. —*adj.* **2.** perfect; precise; scrupulously nice or neat. [ME *at point devis* arranged to a point, i.e., to a nicety, to perfection; see DEVICE]

point′ du′ty, *Brit.* the directing of traffic by a policeman, as at an intersection.

pointe (*Fr.* pwant), *n., pl.* **pointes** (*Fr.* pwant). *Ballet.* the tip of the toe. [< F: lit., point]

Pointe-à-Pi·tre (*Fr.* pwan tȧ pē′trᵊ), *n.* a seaport on central Guadeloupe, in the E West Indies. 45,000 (est. 1960).

point·ed (poin′tid), *adj.* **1.** having a point or points. **2.** sharp or piercing: *pointed wit.* **3.** having direct effect, significance, or force: *pointed criticism.* **4.** directed; aimed. **5.** directed particularly, as at a person, as a remark, look, etc. **6.** marked; emphasized: *a pointed indifference to other people.* [ME] —**point′ed·ly,** *adv.* —**point′ed·ness,** *n.* —**Syn. 2.** penetrating. —**Ant. 2.** blunt, dull.

point′ed arch′, an arch having a pointed apex.

Pointer (26 in. high at shoulder)

Pointe-Noire (*Fr.* pwant nwar′), *n.* a seaport in the S Republic of Congo. 56,865 (est. 1961).

point·er (poin′tər), *n.* **1.** a person or thing that points. **2.** a long, tapering stick used in pointing things out on a map, blackboard, etc. **3.** a hand on a watch dial or the like. **4.** the member of a gun crew who aims the weapon. **5.** one of a breed of short-haired hunting dogs trained to point game. **6.** a piece of advice, esp. on how to succeed in a specific area. **7. Pointers,** *Astron.* the two outer stars of the Big Dipper that lie on a line pointing to Polaris.

Point′ Four′, a program of U.S. aid providing scientific and technical assistance to underdeveloped countries: initiated in 1949 and subsequently absorbed into overall foreign-aid programs.

point′ group′, *Crystall.* a class of crystals determined by a combination of their symmetry elements, all crystals left unchanged by a given set of symmetry elements being placed in the same class.

Poin·til·lism (pwan′tᵊliz′əm, -tē iz′əm, poin′-), *n.* (*often l.c.*) *Painting.* a theory and technique developed by the Neo-Impressionists, based on the scientific theory that the juxtaposition of points or spots of pure colors, as blue and yellow, are optically mixed into the resulting hue, as green, by the viewer. Also called **Neo-Impressionism, Divisionism.** [< F *pointillisme* = *pointill(er)* (to) mark with points + *-isme* -ISM] —**poin′til·list,** *n.*

point′ lace′, lace made with a needle rather than with bobbins; needlepoint.

point·less (point′lis), *adj.* **1.** without a point. **2.** blunt, as an instrument. **3.** without force, meaning, or relevance. **4.** without a point scored, as in a game. [ME *point les*] —**point′less·ly,** *adv.* —**point′less·ness,** *n.*

point′ of hon′or, something that affects one's honor, reputation, etc.

point′ of or′der, *Parl. Proc.* a question raised as to whether proceedings are in order, or in conformity with parliamentary law.

point′ of view′, **1.** a specified or stated manner of consideration or appraisal; standpoint. **2.** an opinion or attitude.

point′ source′, *Physics, Optics.* a source of radiation sufficiently distant compared to its length and width that it can be considered as a point.

point′ sys′tem, **1.** *Print.* a system for grading the sizes of type bodies, leads, etc., that employs the point as a unit of measurement. Cf. **point** (def. 30). **2.** any of certain systems of writing and printing for the blind that employ embossed symbols for letters. **3.** a system of promoting students by an evaluation of their work on the basis of points representing quality of achievement.

point ti·ré (*Fr.* pwan tē rā′). See **drawn work.** [< F: drawn stitch]

point·y (poin′tē), *adj.,* **point·i·er, point·i·est.** having a comparatively sharp point.

poise[1] (poiz), *n., v.,* **poised, pois·ing.** —*n.* **1.** a state of balance or equilibrium, as from equality or equal distribution of weight; equipoise. **2.** dignified, self-confident manner or bearing; composure; self-possession. **3.** the way of being poised, held, or carried. **4.** the state or position of hovering. —*v.t.* **5.** to adjust, hold, or carry in equilibrium; balance evenly. **6.** to hold supported or raised, as in position for casting or using, etc. —*v.i.* **7.** to rest in equilibrium; be balanced. **8.** to hover, as a bird in the air. [late ME < MF; OF *peise,* 3rd pers. sing. pres. ind. of *peser* < L *pensāre,* freq. of *pendere* to weigh] —**pois′er,** *n.* —**Syn. 2.** self-control.

poise[2] (pwäz), *n.* *Physics.* a centimeter-gram-second unit of viscosity, equal to the viscosity of a fluid in which a stress of one dyne per square centimeter is required to maintain a difference of velocity of one centimeter per second between two parallel planes in the fluid that lie in the direction of flow and are separated by a distance of one centimeter. *Abbr.:* P, p [< F; named after Jean Louis Marie *Poiseuille* (1799–1869), French physician]

poised (poizd), *adj.* **1.** (of a person) composed, dignified, and self-assured. **2.** being in balance or equilibrium. **3.** teetering or wavering. **4.** hovering or suspended in midair.

poi·son (poi′zən), *n.* **1.** a substance that has an inherent tendency to destroy life or impair health. **2.** something that is harmful or pernicious, as to happiness or well-being. —*v.t.* **3.** to administer poison to. **4.** to kill or injure with or as with poison. **5.** to put poison into or upon. **6.** to ruin, vitiate, or corrupt. **7.** *Physical Chem.* to destroy or diminish the activity of (a catalyst or enzyme). —*adj.* **8.** causing poisoning; poisonous. [ME *puisun* < OF < L *pōtiōn-* (s. of *pōtiō*) drink, potion, poisonous draught] —**poi′son·er,** *n.* —**poi′son·less,** *adj.*

—**Syn. 1.** POISON, TOXIN, VENOM, VIRUS are terms for any substance that injures the health or destroys life when absorbed into the system, esp. of a higher animal. POISON is the general word: *a poison for insects.* A TOXIN is a poison produced in animal tissues by the action of microorganisms; it is a medical term for the albuminous secretion of microbes, which causes certain diseases: *A toxin produces diphtheria.* VENOM is used of the poisons secreted by certain animals and esp. of snakes, usually injected by bite or sting: *the venom of a cobra.* VIRUS is a medical term for the active organic element or poison which infects with and produces contagious disease: *the virus of scarlet fever.* **6.** contaminate, pollute, taint.

poi′son dog′wood. See **poison sumac.** Also called **poi′son el′der.**

poi′son gas′, any of various toxic gases, esp. those used in chemical warfare to kill or incapacitate on inhalation or contact, as phosgene, chlorine, etc.

Poison ivy, *Rhus radicans*

poi′son hem′lock, hemlock (defs. 1, 3).

poi·son·ing (poi′zə ning), *n.* *Pathol.* the condition produced by a poison or by a toxic substance. [ME *poisenynge*]

poi′son i′vy, any of several North American, anacardiaceous shrubs of the genus *Rhus,* having green flowers, white berries, and shiny, trifoliate leaves, poisonous to the touch, esp. a climbing species, *R. radicans,* growing on fences, rocks, trees, etc.

poi′son oak′, **1.** any of several shrubs of the genus *Rhus.* **2.** See **poison sumac. 3.** a poison ivy, *Rhus diversiloba,* of the Pacific coast of the U.S. and Canada.

poi·son·ous (poi′zə nəs), *adj.* **1.** full of or containing poison. **2.** malicious or harmful; vicious. —**poi′son·ous·ly,** *adv.* —**poi′son·ous·ness,** *n.*

poi·son-pen (poi′zən pen′), *adj.* composed or sent maliciously, as a letter, usually anonymously and for the purpose of damaging another's reputation or happiness.

poi′son su′mac, a highly poisonous shrub or small tree, *Rhus Vernix,* having pinnate leaves and whitish berries, growing in swamps.

Pois·son (pwä sōn′; *Fr.* PWA sôN′), *n.* **Si·mé·on De·nis** (sē mā ôN′ də nē′), 1781–1840, French mathematician.

Poisson′ distribu′tion, *Statistics.* a limiting form of the binomial probability distribution for small values of the probability of success and for large numbers of trials. [named after S. D. POISSON]

Poi·tiers (pwA tyā′), *n.* a city in W France: Roman ruins; battles A.D. 507, 732, 1356. 66,222 (1962).

Poi·tou (pwA to͞o′), *n.* **1.** a former province in W France. *Cap.:* Poitiers. See map at **Burgundy. 2. Gate of,** a wide pass near Poitiers.

poi·trel (poi′trəl), *n. Armor.* peytral.

poke[1] (pōk), *v.,* **poked, pok·ing,** *n.* —*v.t.* **1.** to prod or push, esp. with something narrow or pointed. **2.** to make (a hole, one's way, etc.) by or as by prodding or pushing. **3.** to thrust or push: *She poked her head out of the window.* **4.** to force, drive, or stir by or as by pushing or thrusting: *He poked the fire up.* —*v.i.* **5.** to make a pushing or thrusting movement with the finger, a stick, etc. **6.** to extend or project. **7.** to thrust oneself obtrusively. **8.** to search curiously; pry. **9.** to go or proceed in a slow or aimless way. **10. poke fun at,** to ridicule or mock, esp. covertly or slyly. —*n.* **11.** a thrust or push. [ME < MD, MLG *poken* to thrust. See POACH[1]]

poke[2] (pōk), *n.* **1.** *Midland U.S. and Scot.* a bag or sack. **2.** *Archaic.* a pocket. [ME < MD, whence also ONF *poque,* F *poche* bag, pocket. See POUCH]

poke[3] (pōk), *n.* **1.** a projecting brim at the front of a bonnet, framing the face. **2.** Also called **poke′ bon′net.** a bonnet or hat with such a brim. [appar. special use of POKE[1]]

Poke[3] (def. 2)

poke[4] (pōk), *n.* pokeweed. [short for Algonquian (Virginia) *puccoon* weed used for dyeing]

poke·ber·ry (pōk′ber′ē, -bə rē), *n., pl.* **-ries. 1.** the berry of the pokeweed. **2.** the plant.

pok·er[1] (pō′kər), *n.* **1.** a person or thing that pokes. **2.** a metal rod used for poking or stirring a fire.

pok·er[2] (pō′kər), *n.* a card game played by two or more persons, in which the players bet on the value of their hands, the winner taking the pool. [? orig. braggart, bluffer; cf. MLG *poken* to brag, play, MD *poken* to bluff, brag]

pok′er face′, a purposely expressionless face.

poke·weed (pōk′wēd′), *n.* a tall herb, *Phytolacca americana,* of North America, having juicy purple berries and a purple root used in medicine, and edible shoots resembling asparagus. Also called **poke·root** (pōk′ro͞ot′, -ro͝ot′).

pok·ey (pō′kē), *adj.,* **pok·i·er, pok·i·est,** *n., pl.* **pok·eys.** poky.

pok·y (pō′kē), *adj.,* **pok·i·er, pok·i·est,** *n., pl.* **pok·ies.** —*adj. Informal.* **1.** slow. **2.** (of a place) small and cramped. —*n.* **3.** *Slang.* a jail. —**pok′i·ly,** *adv.* —**pok′i·ness,** *n.*

POL, petroleum, oil, and lubricants.

Pol, Polish (def. 2).

Pol., **1.** Poland. **2.** Polish.

pol., **1.** political. **2.** politics.

Po·lack (pō′lak, -läk), *n. Offensive.* a person of Polish descent. [< Pol *Polak* a Pole]

Po·land (pō′lənd), *n.* a republic in central Europe. 34,362,000; ab. 121,000 sq. mi. (since 1946). *Cap.:* Warsaw. Polish, **Polska.**

Po′land Chi′na, one of an American breed of black hogs having white markings.

po·lar (pō′lər), *adj.* **1.** of or pertaining to a pole, as of the earth, a magnet, an electric cell, etc. **2.** opposite in character or action. **3.** capable of ionizing, as NaCl, HCl, or NaOH; electrolytic; heteropolar. **4.** central; pivotal. **5.** analogous to the polestar as a guide; guiding: *a polar precept.* [< ML *polār(is)*]

po′lar ax′is, *Math.* the fixed line, usually horizontal, from which the angle made by the radius vector is measured in a polar coordinates system.

po′lar bear′, a large white bear, *Thalarctos maritimus,* of the arctic regions.

Polar bear
(4 ft. high at shoulder; length 7½ ft.)

po′lar bod′y, *Biol.* one of the cells arising by the very unequal meiotic divisions of the ovum at or near the time of fertilization.

po′lar cir′cle, either the Arctic or the Antarctic circle.

po′lar coor′dinates, *Math.* a system of coordinates for locating a point in a plane by the length of its radius vector and the angle this vector makes with a fixed line.

po′lar dis′tance, *Astron.* codeclination.

po′lar front′, the transition region, or belt, between the cold polar easterly winds and the relatively warm southwesterly winds of the middle latitudes.

po·lar·im·e·ter (pō′lə rim′i tər), *n. Optics.* **1.** an instrument for measuring the extent of polarization in the light received from a given source. **2.** a form of polariscope for measuring the angular rotation of the plane of polarization. [< ML *polāri(s)* POLAR + -METER]

Po·lar·is (pō lâr′is, -lar′-), *n.* **1.** *Astron.* the polestar or North Star, a star of the second magnitude, close to the north pole of the heavens, in the constellation Ursa Minor: the outermost star in the handle of the Little Dipper. **2.** *U.S.* a two-stage ballistic missile, for firing from a submerged submarine. [short for ML *stella polāris* polar star]

po·lar·i·sa·tion (pō′lər i zā′shən *or, esp. Brit.,* -lə rī-), *n. Chiefly Brit.* polarization.

po·lar·ise (pō′lə rīz′), *v.t., v.i.,* **-ised, -is·ing.** *Chiefly Brit.* polarize. —**po′lar·is′a·ble,** *adj.* —**po′lar·is′er,** *n.*

po·lar·i·ty (pō lar′i tē, -pə-), *n.* **1.** *Physics.* **a.** the possession of a property or characteristic that produces unequal physical effects at different points in a body or system, as a magnet or storage battery. **b.** the positive or negative state in which a body reacts to a magnetic, electric, or other field. **2.** the presence or manifestation of two opposite or contrasting principles or tendencies.

po·lar·i·za·tion (pō′lər i zā′shən *or, esp. Brit.,* -lə rī-), *n.* **1.** *Optics.* a state, or the production of a state, in which rays of light or similar radiation exhibit different properties in different directions. **2.** *Elect.* the deposit of gases, produced during electrolysis, on the electrodes of a cell, increasing the resistance of the cell. **3.** the production or acquisition of polarity. Also, *esp. Brit.,* **polarisation.**

po·lar·ize (pō′lə rīz′), *v.,* **-ized, -iz·ing.** —*v.t.* **1.** to cause polarization in. **2.** to give polarity to. —*v.i.* **3.** to become polarized. Also, *esp. Brit.,* **polarise.** —**po′lar·iz′a·ble,** *adj.* —**po′lar·iz′er,** *n.*

po′lar lights′, the aurora borealis in the Northern Hemisphere or the aurora australis in the Southern Hemisphere.

Po·lar·oid (pō′lə roid′), *n. Trademark.* **1.** a material for producing polarized light from unpolarized light by dichroism. **2.** Also called **Po′laroid cam′era, Po′laroid Land′ cam′era.** a portable camera that produces a finished picture in seconds after each exposure.

Po′lar Re′gions, the regions within the Arctic and Antarctic circles.

pol·der (pōl′dər), *n.* a tract of low land, esp. in the Netherlands, reclaimed from the sea or other body of water and protected by dikes. [< D]

pole[1] (pōl), *n., v.,* **poled, pol·ing.** —*n.* **1.** a long, cylindrical, often slender piece of wood, metal, etc. **2.** a long, tapering piece of wood or other material that extends from the front axle of a vehicle between the animals drawing it. **3.** *Naut.* **a.** a light spar. **b.** the part of a mast between the uppermost standing rigging and the truck. **4.** a unit of length equal to 16½ feet; a rod. **5.** a square rod, 30¼ square yards. —*v.t.* **6.** to furnish with poles. **7.** to push, strike, or propel with a pole: *to pole a raft.* —*v.i.* **8.** to propel a boat, raft, etc., with a pole. [ME; OE *pāl* < L *pāl(us)* stake. See PALE[2]]

pole[2] (pōl), *n.* **1.** each of the extremities of the axis of the earth or of any spherical body. **2.** *Astron.* See **celestial pole. 3.** one of two opposite or contrasted principles or tendencies. **4.** a point of concentration of interest, attention, etc. **5.** *Physics.* either of the two regions or parts of an electric battery or the like, at which certain opposite forces are manifested or appear to be concentrated. **6.** *Biol.* **a.** either end of an ideal axis in a nucleus, cell, or ovum, about which parts are more or less symmetrically arranged. **b.** either end of a spindle-shaped figure formed in a cell during mitosis. **7. poles apart** or **asunder,** having widely divergent or completely opposite attitudes, interests, etc. [ME *po(o)l* < L *pol(us)* < Gk *pólos* pivot, axis, pole]

Pole (pōl), *n.* a native or inhabitant of Poland. [< G, sing. of *Polen,* MHG *Polanc* < *Poljane* Poles, lit., men of the field or plain]

Pole (pōl), *n.* **Reginald,** 1500–58, English cardinal and last Roman Catholic archbishop of Canterbury.

pole·ax (pōl′aks′), *n., pl.* **-ax·es** (-ak′siz), *v.,* **-axed, -ax·ing.** —*n.* **1.** a medieval shafted weapon with blade combining ax, hammer, and apical spike, used for fighting on foot. —*v.t.* **2.** to strike down or kill with or as with a poleax. [ME *pollax* battle-ax, lit., head-ax (see POLL[1], AX); akin to MLG *polexe*]

pole·axe (pōl′aks′), *n., pl.* **-ax·es** (-ak′siz), *v.t.,* **-axed, -ax·ing.** poleax.

pole′ bean′, any vinelike variety of bean that is trained to grow upright on a pole, trellis, fence, etc.

pole·cat (pōl′kat′), *n., pl.* **-cats,** (*esp. collectively*) **-cat. 1.** a European mammal, *Mustela putorius,* of the weasel family, having a blackish fur and ejecting a fetid fluid when attacked or disturbed. Cf. **ferret**[1] (def. 1). **2.** any of various North American skunks. [ME *polcat,* ? < MF *pol, poul* chicken (< L *pullus*); see CAT[1]]

pol. econ., political economy.

pole′ ham′mer, a shafted weapon having a spiked hammer head. Also called **war hammer.**

pole′ horse′, a horse harnessed beside the pole of a vehicle; poler; wheeler.

pole′ jump′. See **pole vault.**

pole-jump (pōl′jump′), *v.i.* pole-vault. —**pole′-jump′er,** *n.*

pole′ mast′, *Naut.* a mast on a sailing vessel, consisting of a single piece without separate upper masts.

po·lem·ic (pə lem′ik, pō-), *n.* **1.** a controversial argument, as one against some opinion, doctrine, etc. **2.** a person who argues in opposition to another; controversialist. —*adj.* **3.** Also, **po·lem′i·cal.** of or pertaining to disputation or controversy; controversial. [< Gk *polemik(ós)* of or for war = *pólem(os)* war + *-ikos* -IC] —**po·lem′i·cal·ly,** *adv.*

po·lem·ics (pə lem′iks, pō-), *n.* (*construed as sing.*) **1.** the art or practice of disputation or controversy. **2.** the branch of theology dealing with ecclesiastical disputation and controversy. Cf. **irenics.**

pol·e·mist (pol′ə mist), *n.* a person who is engaged or versed in polemics. Also, **po·lem·i·cist** (pə lem′i sist, pō-). [< Gk *polemist(ḗs)* warrior = *pólem(os)* war + *-istēs* -IST]

pol·e·mo·ni·a·ceous (pol′ə mō′nē ā′shəs), *adj.* belonging to the *Polemoniaceae,* a family of plants comprising the Jacob's-ladder, phlox, etc. [< NL *Polemōni(um)* the typical genus (< Gk *polemṓnion* kind of plant) + -ACEOUS]

po·len·ta (pō len′tə), *n.* (esp. in Italian cooking) a thick mush of corn meal. [< It < L: peeled or pearl barley]

pol·er (pō′lər), *n.* **1.** a person or thing that poles. **2.** See **pole horse.**

pole·star (pōl′stär′), *n.* **1.** Polaris. **2.** something that serves as a guiding principle.

pole′ vault′, *Track.* a field event in which a vault over a crossbar is performed with the aid of a long pole.

pole-vault (pōl′vôlt′), *v.i.* to perform a pole vault. —**pole′-vault′er,** *n.*

po·leyn (pō′lān), *n. Armor.* a piece of plate or leather protecting the knee. [ME *poleyn, polayne* < OF *po(u)lain*]

po·lice (pə lēs′), *n., v.,* **-liced, -lic·ing.** —*n.* **1.** an organized civil force for maintaining order, preventing and detecting crime, and enforcing the laws. **2.** (*construed as pl.*) members of such a force. **3.** the regulation and control of a community, esp. for the maintenance of public order, health, etc. **4.** the department of the government concerned with this, esp. with the maintenance of order. **—*v.t.* 5.** to regulate, control, or keep in order by or as by means of police. **6.** *Mil.* to clean or keep clean (a camp, post, etc.). [< MF: government, civil administration, police < LL *polītia*, var. of L *polītīa* POLITY]

police′ ac′tion, a relatively localized military action by regular armed forces, without a formal declaration of war, against guerrillas, insurgents, or others held to be violating international peace and order.

police′ court′, an inferior court with summary jurisdiction over certain minor offenses.

police′ dog′, 1. a dog trained to assist the police. **2.** See **German shepherd.**

po·lice·man (pə lēs′mən), *n., pl.* **-men.** a member of a police force or body.

police′ pow′er, the power of a nation to regulate the conduct of its citizens.

police′ state′, a nation in which the police, esp. a secret police, suppresses any act that conflicts with governmental policy.

police′ sta′tion, the police headquarters for a particular district. Also called **station house.**

police′ wag′on. See **patrol wagon.**

po·lice·wom·an (pə lēs′wo͝om′ən), *n., pl.* **-wom·en.** a female member of a police force.

pol·i·cli·nic (pol′ē klin′ik), *n.* a department of a hospital at which outpatients are treated. [< G *Poliklinik* = Gk *póli(s)* city + G *Klinik* CLINIC]

pol·i·cy[1] (pol′i sē), *n., pl.* **-cies. 1.** a definite course of action adopted for the sake of expediency, facility, etc. **2.** action or procedure conforming to or considered with reference to prudence or expediency. **3.** prudence, practical wisdom, or expediency. [ME *policie* government, civil administration < L *polītīa* POLITY] **—Syn. 1.** strategy, principle, rule. **3.** acumen, astuteness. **—Ant. 3.** naiveté.

pol·i·cy[2] (pol′i sē), *n., pl.* **-cies. 1.** a document embodying a contract of insurance. **2.** *U.S.* **a.** a method of gambling in which bets are made on numbers to be drawn by lottery. **b.** See **numbers game.** [< MF *police* (< It *polizza* < ML *apodīxa* receipt << Gk *apódeixis* a showing or setting forth; see APODICTIC, -SIS) + -Y[3]]

pol·i·cy·hold·er (pol′i sē hōl′dər), *n.* the individual or firm in whose name an insurance policy is written; an insured.

pol′icy loan′, *Insurance.* a loan made by a life-insurance company to a policyholder with the cash value of his policy serving as security.

po·li·o (pō′lē ō′), *n.* poliomyelitis. [shortened form]

po·li·o·en·ceph·a·li·tis (pō′lē ō en sef′ə lī′tis), *n. Pathol.* a disease characterized by inflammation of the gray matter of the brain; cerebral poliomyelitis. Also, **po·li·en·ceph·a·li·tis** (pō′lē en sef′ə lī′tis). [< NL < Gk *poliό(s)* gray + NL *encephalitis* ENCEPHALITIS]

po·li·o·my·e·li·tis (pō′lē ō mī′ə lī′tis), *n. Pathol.* an acute viral disease, most common in infants, characterized by inflammation of the nerve cells, mainly of the anterior horns of the spinal cord, and resulting in a motor paralysis, followed by muscular atrophy, and often by permanent deformities. Also called **infantile paralysis, polio.** [< NL < Gk *poliό(s)* gray + NL *myelitis* MYELITIS] **—po·li·o·my·e·lit·ic** (pō′lē ō mī′ə lit′ik), *adj.*

po·lis (pō′lis), *n., pl.* **-leis** (-līs). an ancient Greek city-state. [< Gk]

-polis, an element, meaning "city," appearing in loan words from Greek (*metropolis*), and used in the formation of place names (*Annapolis*). [comb. form repr. Gk *pólis* POLIS]

pol·ish (pol′ish), *v.t.* **1.** to make smooth and glossy, esp. by rubbing or friction. **2.** to render finished, refined, or elegant. **3.** to take or bring to a different state by polishing or refining (often fol. by *away, off,* or *out*). **—*v.i.* 4.** to become smooth and glossy through polishing. **5.** *Archaic.* to become refined or elegant. **6. polish off,** *Slang.* **a.** to finish or dispose of (something) quickly. **b.** to subdue or get rid of someone. **—*n.* 7.** a substance used to give smoothness or gloss. **8.** the act or an instance of polishing. **9.** the state of being polished. **10.** smoothness and a bright reflection of surface. **11.** superiority of manner or execution; refinement; elegance. [ME *polishe(n)* < MF *poliss-*, long s. of *polir* < L *polīre* to polish; see -ISH[2]] **—pol′ish·er,** *n.*
—Syn. 1. shine, brighten, burnish, buff, smooth. **10.** shine, gleam. POLISH, GLOSS, LUSTER, SHEEN refer to a smooth, shining, or bright surface from which light is reflected. POLISH suggests the smooth, bright reflection often produced by friction: *rubbed to a high polish.* GLOSS suggests a superficial, hard smoothness characteristic of lacquered, varnished, or enameled surfaces: *a gloss on oilcloth.* LUSTER denotes the characteristic quality of the light reflected from the surfaces of certain materials (pearls, silk, wax, freshly cut metals, etc.): *a pearly luster.* SHEEN suggests a glistening brightness such as that reflected from the surface of silk or velvet, or from furniture oiled and hand-polished: *a rich velvety sheen.*

Po·lish (pō′lish), *adj.* **1.** of, pertaining to, or characteristic of Poland, its inhabitants, or their language. **—*n.* 2.** a Slavic language, the principal language of Poland. *Abbr.:* Pol

Po′lish Cor′ridor, a strip of land near the mouth of the Vistula River: formerly separated Germany from East Prussia; given to Poland in the Treaty of Versailles 1919 to provide her with access to the Baltic.

pol·ished (pol′isht), *adj.* **1.** made smooth and glossy. **2.** naturally smooth and glossy. **3.** refined; elegant. **4.** flawless; skillful. [ME *polist*]

pol′ished rice′, white rice polished or buffed by leather-covered cylinders during processing.

polit., 1. political. **2.** politics.

Po·lit·bu·ro (pol′it byo͝or′ō, pə lit′-), *n.* a former committee in the Communist party of the Soviet Union: absorbed in 1952 into the Presidium. Also, **Po′lit·bu′reau.** [< Russ *Polit(icheskoye) Buro* political bureau]

po·lite (pə līt′), *adj.* **1.** showing good manners toward others, as in behavior, speech, etc.; courteous; civil: *a polite reply.* **2.** refined or cultured. [late ME < L *polīt(us)* polished, ptp. of *polīre*] **—po·lite′ly,** *adv.* **—po·lite′ness,** *n.* **—Syn. 1.** well-bred, gracious. See **civil. 2.** urbane, polished, poised, courtly, cultivated. **—Ant.** rude.

polit. econ., political economy.

pol·i·tesse (pol′i tes′; *Fr.* pô lē tes′), *n.* politeness. [< F: orig. clean or polished state < It *politezza*, var. of *pulitezza* (see POLITE); *-ess*, as in PROWESS]

Po·li·tian (pō lish′ən), *n.* (*Angelo Poliziano*) 1454–94, Italian classical scholar, teacher, and poet.

pol·i·tic (pol′i tik), *adj.* **1.** sagacious; prudent. **2.** shrewd; artful. **3.** expedient; judicious. **4.** political. Cf. **body politic.** [late ME *politik* < MF *politique* < L *polītic(us)* < Gk *polītikós* civic = *polī́t(ēs)* citizen (see POLITY) + *-ikos* -IC] **—pol′i·tic·ly,** *adv.* **—Syn. 1.** astute. **2.** sly, cunning, clever.

po·lit·i·cal (pə lit′i kəl), *adj.* **1.** of, pertaining to, or concerned with the science or art of politics. **2.** of, pertaining to, or connected with a political party. **3.** of or pertaining to the state or its government. **4.** having a definite policy or system of government. [< L *polītic(us)* civic (see POLITIC) + -AL[1]] **—po·lit′i·cal·ly,** *adv.*

polit′ical econ′omy, 1. a social science dealing with political policies and economic processes, their interrelations, and their mutual influence on social institutions. **2.** (in the 17th and 18th centuries) the art of management of communities, esp. as affecting the wealth of a government. **3.** (in the 19th century) a social science similar to modern economics, but dealing chiefly with governmental policies. **4.** economics (def. 1). **—polit′ical econ′omist.**

polit′ical sci′ence, the science of politics, or of the principles and conduct of government. **—polit′ical sci′entist.**

pol·i·ti·cian (pol′i tish′ən), *n.* **1.** a person who is active in party politics. **2.** a seeker or holder of public office, esp. one for whom politics is a career. **3.** an expert in political government or administration. **4.** a person who seeks advancement or power within an organization by dubious means. [< F *politicien*]
—Syn. 3. POLITICIAN, STATESMAN refer to a person skilled in politics. POLITICIAN is more often derogatory, and STATESMAN laudatory. POLITICIAN suggests the schemes and devices of a person who engages in politics for party ends or his own advantage: *a crafty politician.* STATESMAN suggests the eminent ability, foresight, and unselfish devotion to the interests of his country of a person dealing with (esp. important or great) affairs of state: *a distinguished statesman.*

po·lit·i·cise (pə lit′i sīz′), *v.t., v.i.,* **-cised, -cis·ing.** *Chiefly Brit.* politicize.

po·lit·i·cize (pə lit′i sīz′), *v.,* **-cized, -ciz·ing. —*v.t.* 1.** to give a political character or bias to. **—*v.i.* 2.** to engage in or discuss politics.

pol·i·tick (pol′i tik), *v.i.* to engage in politicking. [back formation from POLITICKING]

pol·i·tick·ing (pol′i tik′ing), *n.* activity undertaken for political reasons or ends, esp. to promote oneself or one's policies. [*politick*, var. of POLITIC + -ING[1]]

po·lit·i·co (pə lit′i kō′), *n., pl.* **-cos.** a politician. [< It or Sp]

politico-, a combining form of **political.**

pol·i·tics (pol′i tiks), *n.* (*construed as sing. or pl.*) **1.** the science or art of political government. **2.** the practice or profession of conducting political affairs. **3.** political affairs. **4.** political methods or maneuvers. **5.** political principles or opinions. **6.** use of intrigue or strategy in obtaining any position of power or control.

pol·i·ty (pol′i tē), *n., pl.* **-ties. 1.** a particular form or system of government. **2.** a state or other organized community or body. [< L *polītīa* < Gk *polīteía* citizenship, government, form of government, commonwealth = *polī́t(ēs)* citizen (see POLIS, -ITE[1]) + *-ia* -IA]

Polk (pōk), *n.* **James Knox,** 1795–1849, the 11th president of the U.S. 1845–49.

pol·ka (pōl′kə, pō′kə), *n., pl.* **-kas,** *v.,* **-kaed, -ka·ing. —*n.* 1.** a lively round dance of Bohemian origin, with music in duple meter. **2.** a piece of music for such a dance or in its rhythm. **—*v.i.* 3.** to dance the polka. [< Czech, var. of *pulka* half (step)]

pol′ka dot′ (pō′kə), *Textiles.* a dot or round spot repeated to form a pattern.

poll[1] (pōl), *n.* **1.** the act of voting at an election. **2.** the registration of such votes. **3.** Usually, **polls.** the place where votes are taken. **4.** an enumeration or a list of individuals, as for purposes of taxing or voting. **5.** a person or individual in a number or list. **6.** a sampling or collection of opinions on a subject, taken from either a selected or a random group of persons, as for the purpose of analysis. **7.** the head, esp. the part of it on which the hair grows. **8.** the back of the head. **9.** the rear portion of the head of a horse; the nape. **10.** the part of the head between the ears of certain animals, as the horse and cow. **11.** the broad end or face of a hammer. **—*v.t.* 12.** to receive at the polls, as votes. **13.** to enroll (someone), as for purposes of taxing or voting. **14.** to take or register the votes of (persons). **15.** to deposit or cast at the polls, as a vote. **16.** to bring to the polls, as voters. **17.** to take a sampling of the attitudes or opinions of. **18.** to cut short or cut off the hair, wool, etc., of (an animal); crop; clip; shear. **19.** to cut short or cut off (hair, wool, etc.). **20.** to cut off or cut short the horns of (cattle). **—*v.i.* 21.** to vote at the polls; give one's vote. [ME *polle* (hair of the) head < MLG: hair of the head, top of a tree or other plant; akin to Dan *puld*, Sw *pull* crown of the head]

poll[2] (pol), *n.* (esp. at Cambridge University, England) **1.** the body of students who read for or obtain a degree without honors. **2.** Also called **poll′ degree′.** See **pass degree.** [appar. < Gk *poll(oí)*, in *hoi polloí* the many; see POLY-]

pol·lack (pol′ək), *n., pl.* **-lacks,** (*esp. collectively*) **-lack.** a darkly-colored, North Atlantic food fish, *Pollachius virens*, of the cod family. Also, *esp. Brit.*, **pollock.** [assimilated var. of *podlok* (Scot); akin to Scot dial. *paddle* bumpfish; see -OCK]

Pol·lai·uo·lo (pō′lī wō′lō; *It.* pôl′lī wô′lô), *n.* **An·to·nio** (än tô′nyô), 1429–98, Italian sculptor, painter, engraver, and goldsmith. Also, **Pol·lai·o·lo** (pō′lī ō′lō; *It.* pôl′lī ô′lô), **Pol·laj·uo·lo** (pō′lī wō′lō; *It.* pôl′lī wô′lô).

pol·lard (pol′ərd), *n.* **1.** a tree cut back nearly to the trunk, so as to produce a dense mass of branches. **2.** an animal, as a stag, ox, or sheep, having no horns. —*v.t.* **3.** to convert into a pollard.

polled (pōld), *adj.* **1.** hornless, as the Aberdeen Angus. **2.** *Obs.* having the hair cut off.

poll·ee (pō lē′), *n.* a person who is asked questions in a poll. [POLL¹ + -EE]

pol·len (pol′ən), *n.* **1.** the fertilizing element of flowering plants, consisting of fine, powdery, yellowish grains or spores, sometimes in masses. —*v.t.* **2.** to pollinate. [< NL, special use of L: fine flour, mill dust] —**pol′lened,** *adj.* —**pol′len·less,** *adj.* —**pol′len·like′,** *adj.* —**pol·lin·ic** (pə lin′ik), **pol·lin′i·cal,** *adj.*

Pollen grains
A, Evening primrose, *Oenothera biennis;* B, Scotch pine, *Pinus sylvestris;* C, Chicory, *Chicorium intybus;* D, Hibiscus, *Hibiscus moscheutos;* E, Passionflower, *Passiflora caerulea*

pol′len count′, a count of the amount of pollen in the air for a given period of time.

pol·len·o·sis (pol′ə nō′sis), *n. Pathol.* See **hay fever.**

poll′ e′vil, *Vet. Pathol.* an acute swelling on the top of the head of a horse originating in an inflamed bursa that underlies the great neck ligament.

pol·lex (pol′eks), *n., pl.* **pol·li·ces** (pol′i sēz′). the innermost digit of the forelimb; thumb. [< L: thumb]

pol·li·nate (pol′ə nāt′), *v.t.,* **-nat·ed, -nat·ing.** *Bot.* to convey pollen to the stigma of (a flower). [< NL *pollin-* (s. of *pollen*) POLLEN + -ATE¹] —**pol′li·na′tor,** *n.*

pol·li·na·tion (pol′ə nā′shən), *n. Bot.* the transfer of pollen from the anther to the stigma.

pol·li·nif·er·ous (pol′ə nif′ər əs), *adj.* **1.** *Bot.* producing or bearing pollen. **2.** *Zool.* fitted for carrying pollen. [< NL *pollin-* (s. of *pollen*) POLLEN + -I- + -FEROUS]

pol·lin·i·um (pə lin′ē əm), *n., pl.* **-lin·i·a** (-lin′ē ə). *Bot.* an agglutinated mass or body of pollen grains, characteristic of orchidaceous and asclepiadaceous plants. [< NL = *pollin-* (s. of *pollen*) POLLEN + *-ium* -IUM]

pol·li·no·sis (pol′ə nō′sis), *n. Pathol.* See **hay fever.** [< NL = *pollin-* (s. of *pollen*) POLLEN + *-osis* -OSIS]

pol·li·wog (pol′ē wog′), *n.* a tadpole. Also, **pollywog.** [var. of *polliwig,* earlier *polwigge,* late ME *polwygle.* See POLL¹, WIGGLE]

pol·lock (pol′ək), *n., pl.* **-locks,** (*esp. collectively*) **-lock.** *Chiefly Brit.* pollack.

Pol·lock (pol′ək), *n.* **1. Channing,** 1880–1946, U.S. novelist and dramatist. **2. Jackson,** 1912–56, U.S. painter.

poll·ster (pōl′stər), *n.* a person whose occupation is the taking of public-opinion polls.

poll′ tax′, a capitation tax, sometimes levied as a prerequisite for voting.

pol·lu·tant (pə lo͞ot′ənt), *n.* **1.** something that pollutes. **2.** any chemical or waste product, as automobile exhaust or sewage, that contributes to the air or water pollution.

pol·lute (pə lo͞ot′), *v.t.,* **-lut·ed, -lut·ing.** **1.** to make foul or unclean; dirty: *to pollute the air with smoke.* **2.** to make impure or morally unclean; defile; desecrate. [ME *polute* < L *pollūt(us),* ptp. of *polluere* to soil, defile = *pol-* for *por-* intensive prefix (akin to PER-) + *-luere* to let loose (something bad), akin to LUES] —**pol·lut′er,** *n.* —**pol·lu′tion,** *n.* —**Syn. 1.** soil, befoul. **2.** taint, contaminate, corrupt, debase.

pol·lut·ed (pə lo͞o′tid), *adj.* **1.** made unclean or impure; contaminated; tainted: *polluted waters.* **2.** *Slang.* drunk. [late ME] —**pol·lut′ed·ness,** *n.*

Pol·lux (pol′əks), *n.* **1.** *Class. Myth.* the brother of Castor. Cf. **Castor and Pollux.** **2.** *Astron.* a first-magnitude star in the constellation Gemini.

poll′ watch′er, a representative of a political party who is assigned to the polls on Election Day to watch for violations of the laws that regulate voting, campaigning, etc.

Pol·ly·an·na (pol′ē an′ə), *n.* an excessively or blindly optimistic person. [from the name of the heroine created by Eleanor Porter (1868–1920), American writer]

pol·ly·wog (pol′ē wog′), *n.* polliwog.

po·lo (pō′lō), *n.* **1.** a game played on horseback between two teams of four players each, who score points by driving a wooden ball into the opponents' goal with a long-handled mallet. **2.** See **water polo.** [< Balti (Tibetan dial. of Kashmir): ball] —**po′lo·ist,** *n.*

Po·lo (pō′lō), *n.* **Mar·co** (mär′kō), c1254–1324, Venetian traveler.

po′lo coat′, a double-breasted, often belted, overcoat made of camel's hair or a similar fabric.

pol·o·naise (pol′ə nāz′, pō′lə-), *n.* **1.** a slow dance of Polish origin, in triple meter, consisting chiefly of a march or promenade in couples. **2.** a piece of music for, or in the rhythm of, such a dance. **3.** a coatlike outer dress of the 18th century, combining bodice and cutaway overskirt. [< F, fem. of *polonais* Polish = *Polon-* (< ML *Polonia* Poland) + *-ais* -ESE]

po·lo·ni·um (pə lō′nē əm), *n. Chem.* a radioactive element discovered by Pierre and Marie Curie in 1898; *Symbol:* Po; *at. no.:* 84; *at. wt.:* about 210. [< NL = *polon-* (< ML *Polonia* Poland) + *-ium* -IUM]

po′lo shirt′, a short-sleeved, pull-over sport shirt.

Pol·ska (pôl′skä), *n.* Polish name of **Poland.**

Pol·ta·va (pol tä′vä), *n.* a city in the E Ukraine, in the SW Soviet Union in Europe: Russian defeat of Swedes 1709. 278,000.

pol·ter·geist (pōl′tər gīst′), *n.* a ghost or spirit supposed to manifest its presence by noises, knockings, etc. [< G: lit., noise-ghost]

Pol·to·ratsk (*Russ.* pol to rätsk′), *n.* former name of **Ashkhabad.**

pol·troon (pol tro͞on′), *n.* a wretched coward; craven. [earlier *pultrowne,* etc. < MF *poultron* < OIt *poltrone* idler, coward, lit., one who lies abed (akin to *poltrire* to lie lazily in bed), appar. < obs. *poltro* bed < OHG *polstar* BOLSTER; see -OON] —**pol·troon′er·y,** *n.* —**Syn.** dastard.

poly-, an element, meaning "much," "many," occurring originally in loan words from Greek (*polyandrous; polychrome*), but now used freely as a general formative, esp. in scientific or technical words (*polyethylene*). [< Gk, comb. form repr. *polýs;* akin to OE *fela* many. See PLUS]

poly., polytechnic.

pol·y·an·drist (pol′ē an′drist), *n.* a woman who practices or favors polyandry.

pol·y·an·drous (pol′ē an′drəs), *adj.* **1.** of, pertaining to, characterized by, or practicing polyandry. **2.** *Bot.* having the stamens indefinitely numerous. [< Gk *polýandros* having many husbands]

pol·y·an·dry (pol′ē an′drē, pol′ē an′-), *n.* **1.** the practice or condition of having more than one husband at one time (distinguished from *monandry*). **2.** *Bot.* the state of being polyandrous. [< Gk *polyandría.* See POLY-, -ANDROUS, -Y³]

pol·y·an·gu·lar (pol′ē ang′gyə lər), *adj.* multangular; multiangular.

pol·y·an·thus (pol′ē an′thəs), *n., pl.* **-thus·es.** **1.** a hybrid primrose, *Primula polyantha.* **2.** a narcissus, *Narcissus Tazetta,* having small white or yellow flowers. [< NL < Gk *polýanthos* having many flowers]

pol·y·a·tom·ic (pol′ē ə tom′ik), *adj. Chem.* pertaining to a molecule containing more than two atoms.

pol·y·ba·sic (pol′ē bā′sik), *adj. Chem.* (of an acid) having two or more atoms of replaceable hydrogen. —**pol·y·ba·sic·i·ty** (pol′ē bə sis′i tē), *n.*

pol·y·ba·site (pol′ē bā′sīt, pə lib′ə sīt′), *n.* a mineral, Ag_9SbS_6: a minor ore of silver. [< G *Polybasit*]

Pol·y·carp (pol′ē kärp′), *n.* **Saint,** A.D. 69?–155, bishop of Smyrna and a Christian martyr.

pol·y·car·pic (pol′ē kär′pik), *adj. Bot.* **1.** producing fruit many times, as a perennial plant. **2.** having a gynoecium composed of two or more distinct ovaries. Also, **pol′y·car′pous.** [< NL *polycarpic(us)*] —**pol′y·car′py,** *n.*

pol·y·chaete (pol′ə kēt′), *n.* **1.** any annelid of the class *Polychaeta,* having unsegmented swimming appendages with many chaetae or bristles. —*adj.* **2.** Also, **pol′y·chae′tous.** belonging or pertaining to the *Polychaeta.* [< NL *Polychæta* < Gk *polychaítēs* having much hair]

pol·y·cha·sium (pol′ē kā′zhəm, -zhē əm, -zē əm), *n., pl.* **-sia** (-zhə, -zhē ə, -zē ə). *Bot.* a form of cymose inflorescence in which each axis produces more than two lateral axes. [< NL; see POLY-, DICHASIUM] —**pol′y·cha′si·al,** *adj.*

pol·y·chlo′rin·at·ed biphen′yl (pol′ē klôr′ə nā′tid, -klôr′-). See **PCB**

pol·y·chro·mat·ic (pol′ē krō mat′ik, -krə-), *adj.* having or exhibiting a variety of colors. Also, **pol·y·chro·mic** (pol′ē krō′mik). —**pol·y·chro·ma·tism** (pol′ē krō′mə tiz′əm), *n.*

pol·y·chrome (pol′ē krōm′), *adj., v.,* **-chromed, -chrom·ing.** —*adj.* **1.** being of many or various colors. **2.** decorated or executed in many colors, as a statue, vase, mural, etc. —*n.* **3.** a polychrome object or work. —*v.t.* **4.** to paint in many or various colors. [earlier *polychrom* < G < Gk *polýchrōmos* many-colored]

pol·y·chro·my (pol′ē krō′mē), *n.* the art of employing many colors in decoration, as in painting or architecture. —**pol′y·chro′mous,** *adj.*

pol·y·clin·ic (pol′ē klin′ik), *n.* a clinic or a hospital dealing with various diseases.

Pol·y·cli·tus (pol′ə klī′təs), *n.* fl. c450–c420 B.C., Greek sculptor. Also, **Pol′y·clei′tus, Pol·y·cle·tus** (pol′ə klē′təs).

pol·y·con·ic (pol′ē kon′ik), *adj.* pertaining to or utilizing two or more cones.

polycon′ic projec′tion, *Cartog.* a conic projection in which the parallels are arcs of circles that are not concentric but are equally spaced along the central straight meridian, all other meridians being curves equally spaced along the parallels.

pol·y·cot·y·le·don (pol′ē kot′əlēd′ən), *n.* a plant having more than two cotyledons, as certain gymnosperms. —**pol′y·cot′y·le′don·ous,** *adj.*

Po·lyc·ra·tes (pə lik′rə tēz′), *n.* died 522? B.C., Greek tyrant of Samos.

pol·y·crys·tal·line (pol′ē kris′təlēn′, -təlin), *adj.* **1.** (of a rock or metal) composed of more than one crystal. **2.** having or consisting of crystals that are variously oriented.

pol·y·dac·tyl (pol′ē dak′təl, -til), *adj.* **1.** having many or several digits. **2.** having more than the normal number of fingers or toes. —*n.* **3.** a polydactyl animal. [< Gk *polydáktyl(os)*] —**pol′y·dac′tyl·ism,** *n.*

pol·y·dip·si·a (pol′ē dip′sē ə), *n. Med.* excessive thirst. [< NL < Gk *polydíps(ios)* very thirsty (*poly-* POLY- + *díps(a)* thirst + *-ios* adj. suffix) + *-ia* -IA]

Pol·y·do·rus (pol′i dôr′əs, -dōr′-), *n.* **1.** fl. 1st century B.C., Greek sculptor who, with Agesander and Athenodorus, carved the Laocoön group. **2.** *Class. Myth.* a son of Cadmus and Harmonia who became king of Thebes.

pol·y·em·bry·o·ny (pol′ē em′brē ə nē, -ō′nē, -em brī′ə nē), *n. Embryol.* the production of more than one embryo from one egg. [POLY- + Gk *émbryon* EMBRYO + -Y³]

pol·y·es·ter (pol′ē es′tər, pol′ē es′tər), *n. Chem.* a polymer in which the monomer units are linked together by the group –COO–, usually formed by polymerizing a polyhydric alcohol with a polybasic acid: used chiefly in the manufacture of resins, plastics, and textile fibers.

pol·y·eth·yl·ene (pol′ē eth′ə lēn′), *n. Chem.* a plastic polymer of ethylene, $(–CH_2CH_2–)_n$, used chiefly for containers, electrical insulation, and packaging. Also called, *Brit.,* **polythene.**

po·lyg·a·la (pə lig′ə lə), *n.* any plant of the genus *Polygala,* comprising the milkworts. [< NL, genus name, special use of L *polygala* < Gk *polýgala,* pl. (taken as sing.) of *polýgalon* milkwort, lit., something very milky. See POLY-, GALAXY] —**pol·y·ga·la·ceous** (pol′ē gə lā′shəs), *adj.*

po·lyg·a·mous (pə lig′ə məs), *adj.* **1.** of, pertaining to, characterized by, or practicing polygamy. **2.** *Bot.* bearing both unisexual and hermaphrodite flowers on the same or on different plants. [< Gk *polýgamos*] —**po·lyg′a·mous·ly,** *adv.*

po·lyg·a·my (pə lig′ə mē), *n.* **1.** the practice or condition of having many or several spouses, esp. wives, at one time. Cf. **bigamy, monogamy** (def. 1). **2.** *Zool.* the habit of mating with more than one of the opposite sex. [< Gk *polygamía*] —**po·lyg′a·mist,** *n.*

pol·y·gen·e·sis (pol′ē jen′i sis), *n.* *Biol., Anthropol.* origin from more than one ancestral species or line. —**pol·y·ge·net·ic** (pol′ē je net′ik), *adj.* —**pol′y·ge·net′i·cal·ly,** *adv.*

pol·y·glot (pol′ē glot′), *adj.* **1.** knowing many or several languages; multilingual. **2.** containing, composed of, or in several languages. —*n.* **3.** a mixture or confusion of languages. **4.** a person who has a command of a number of languages. **5.** a book, esp. a Bible, containing the same text in several languages. [< ML *polyglōtt(us)* < Gk *polýglōttos* many-tongued]

Pol·yg·no·tus (pol′ig nō′təs), *n.* fl. c450 B.C., Greek painter.

pol·y·gon (pol′ē gon′), *n.* a figure, esp. a closed plane figure, having three or more usually straight sides. [< L *polygōn(um)* < Gk *polýgōnon*, neut. of *polýgōnos* many-angled] —**po·lyg·o·nal** (pə lig′ə nəl), *adj.* —**po·lyg′o·nal·ly,** *adv.*

pol·y·go·na·ceous (pol′ē gə nā′shəs), *adj.* belonging to the *Polygonaceae*, or buckwheat family of plants, comprising the knotgrass, jointweed, dock, etc. [POLYGON(UM) + -ACEOUS]

po·lyg·o·num (pə lig′ə nəm), *n.* any of several, chiefly herbaceous plants of the genus *Polygonum*, comprising the knotgrasses, bistorts, smartweeds, etc. [< NL < Gk *polýgonon* knotgrass, lit., something with many joints. See POLY-, KNEE]

pol·y·graph (pol′ē graf′, -gräf′), *n.* **1.** an apparatus for producing copies of a drawing or writing. **2.** a prolific or versatile author. **3.** a lie detector. [< Gk *polýgraph(os)* writing much] —**pol·y·graph·ic** (pol′ē graf′ik), *adj.* —**po·lyg·ra·phist** (pə lig′rə fist), **po·lyg′ra·pher,** *n.*

po·lyg·y·nous (pə lij′ə nəs), *adj.* **1.** of, pertaining to, characterized by, or practicing polygyny. **2.** *Bot.* having many pistils or styles.

po·lyg·y·ny (pə lij′ə nē), *n.* **1.** the practice or condition of having more than one wife at one time. Cf. **monogyny. 2.** (of a male animal) the condition of having two or more mates at a time. **3.** *Bot.* the state or condition of having many pistils or styles. [< Gk *polygýn(aios)* having many wives (see POLY-, -GYN) + -Y[3]] —**po·lyg′y·nist,** *n.*

pol·y·he·dral (pol′ē hē′drəl), *adj.* of, pertaining to, or having the shape of a polyhedron. [< Gk *polýedr(os)* many-based (see POLYHEDRON) + -AL[1]]

pol·y·he·dron (pol′ē hē′drən), *n., pl.* **-drons, -dra** (-drə). a solid figure having many faces. [< Gk *polýedron*, neut. of *polýedros* having many bases]

pol·y·hy·drox·y (pol′ē hī drok′sē), *adj.* *Chem.* containing two or more hydroxyl groups.

Pol·y·hym·ni·a (pol′ə him′nē ə), *n.* *Class. Myth.* the Muse of sacred music and dance. Also, **Polymnia.** [< L, alter. of Gk *Polýmnia*]

pol·y·math (pol′ē math′), *n.* a person learned in many fields. [< Gk *polymathḗs* knowing much = *poly-* POLY- + *-mathēs* (verbid of *manthánein* to learn)]

pol·y·mer (pol′ə mər), *n.* *Chem.* a compound of high molecular weight derived either by the addition of many smaller molecules, as polyethylene, or by the condensation of many smaller molecules with the elimination of water, alcohol, or the like, as nylon. [< Gk *polymer(ḗs)* having many parts]

pol·y·mer·ic (pol′ə mer′ik), *adj.* *Chem.* (of compounds) having the same elements combined in the same proportions by weight: recently extended to include substances of high molecular weight.

pol·y·mer·ise (pol′ə mə rīz′, pə lim′ə-), *v.t., v.i.,* **-ised, -is·ing.** *Chiefly Brit.* polymerize.

po·lym·er·ism (pə lim′ə riz′əm, pol′ə mə-), *n.* **1.** *Chem.* a polymeric state. **2.** *Biol., Bot.* a polymerous state.

po·lym·er·i·za·tion (pə lim′ər i zā′shən, pol′ə mər- *or, esp. Brit.,* pə lim′ə rī-, pol′ə mə rī-), *n.* *Chem.* the act or process of forming a polymer or polymeric compound. Also, *esp. Brit.,* **po·lym′er·i·sa′tion.**

po·lym·er·ize (pə lim′ə rīz′, pol′ə mə rīz′), *v.,* **-ized, -iz·ing.** *Chem.* —*v.t.* **1.** to subject to polymerization. —*v.i.* **2.** to undergo polymerization. Also, *esp. Brit.,* **polymerise.**

po·lym·er·ous (pə lim′ər əs), *adj.* **1.** *Biol.* composed of many parts. **2.** *Bot.* having numerous members in each whorl.

Pol·ym·nes·tor (pol′əm nes′tər), *n.* *Class. Myth.* a Thracian king who murdered Polydorus and stole the treasure that Priam had given him to guard during the Trojan War.

Po·lym·ni·a (pə lim′nē ə), *n.* Polyhymnia.

pol·y·morph (pol′ē môrf′), *n.* **1.** *Zool., Bot.* a polymorphous organism or substance. **2.** *Crystall.* any of the forms assumed by a polymorphous substance. [back formation from POLYMORPHOUS]

pol·y·mor·phism (pol′ē môr′fiz əm), *n.* **1.** the state or condition of being polymorphous. **2.** *Crystall.* crystallization into two or more chemically identical but crystallographically distinct forms. **3.** *Zool., Bot.* existence of an animal or plant in several form or color varieties. —**pol′y·mor·phis′tic,** *adj.*

pol·y·mor·pho·nu·cle·ar (pol′ē môr′fə no͞o′klē ər, -nyo͞o′-), *adj.* (of a leukocyte) having a lobulate nucleus.

pol·y·mor·phous (pol′ē môr′fəs), *adj.* having, assuming, or passing through many or various forms, stages, or the like. Also, **pol′y·mor′phic.** [< Gk *polýmorphos* multiform]

Pol·y·ne·sia (pol′ə nē′zhə, -shə), *n.* one of the three principal divisions of Oceania, comprising those island groups in the Pacific lying E of Melanesia and Micronesia and extending from the Hawaiian Islands S to New Zealand.

Pol·y·ne·sian (pol′ə nē′zhən, -shən), *adj.* **1.** of or pertaining to Polynesia, its inhabitants, or their languages. —*n.* **2.** a member of any of a number of brown-skinned peoples speaking closely related Austronesian languages, who inhabit Polynesia. **3.** the easternmost group of Malayo-Polynesian languages, including Maori, Tahitian, Samoan, Hawaiian, and the language of Easter Island.

Pol·y·ni·ces (pol′ə nī′sēz), *n.* *Class. Myth.* a son of Oedipus and Jocasta and brother of Eteocles and Antigone, on whose behalf the Seven against Thebes were organized. Also, **Pol′y·nei′ces.**

pol·y·no·mi·al (pol′ē nō′mē əl), *adj.* **1.** consisting of or characterized by many or several names or terms. —*n.* **2.** a polynomial name or term. **3.** *Algebra.* an expression consisting of two or more terms, as $2x^3 + 7x^2 + 4x + 2$. **4.** *Zool., Bot.* a species name containing more than two terms. [POLY- + (BI)NOMIAL]

pol·y·nu·cle·ar (pol′ē no͞o′klē ər, -nyo͞o′-), *adj.* having many nuclei. Also, **pol·y·nu·cle·ate** (pol′ē no͞o′klē it, -āt′, -nyo͞o′-).

pol·yp (pol′ip), *n.* **1.** *Zool.* **a.** a sedentary type of animal form characterized by a more or less fixed base, columnar body, and free end with mouth and tentacles, esp. as applied to coelenterates. **b.** an individual zooid of a compound or colonial organism. **2.** *Pathol.* a projecting growth from a mucous surface, as of the nose, being either a tumor or a hypertrophy of the mucous membrane. [ME *polip*, short for *polipus* nasal tumor (later, also cephalopod, now obs.) < ML, L *pōlypus* (in same senses) < Gk *pṓlypos*, *polýpous* many-footed. See POLY-, FOOT] —**pol′yp·ous,** *adj.*

pol·y·par·y (pol′ə per′ē), *n., pl.* **-par·ies.** the common supporting structure of a colony of polyps, as corals. [< NL *polypāri(um)*] —**pol·y·par·i·an** (pol′ə pâr′ē ən), *adj.*

pol·y·pep·tide (pol′ē pep′tīd), *n.* *Biochem.* one of a group of amides formed from amino acids, the simplest having the structure $H_2NCH_2CONHCH_2COOH$, with molecular weights up to about 10,000.

pol·y·pet·al·ous (pol′ē pet′əl əs), *adj.* *Bot.* having numerous or separate petals. —**pol′y·pet′al·y,** *n.*

pol·y·pha·gi·a (pol′ē fā′jē ə, -jə), *n.* *Pathol.* excessive desire to eat. [< NL < Gk] —**pol′y·pha′gi·an,** *adj.*

pol·y·phase (pol′ē fāz′), *adj.* *Elect.* having more than one phase.

Pol·y·phe·mus (pol′ə fē′məs), *n.* *Class. Myth.* a Cyclops who murdered Acis in jealousy over Galatea, and who was finally blinded by Odysseus.

Pol′yphe′mus moth′, a large, yellowish-brown silkworm moth, *Antheraea polyphemus*, having a prominent eyespot on each hind wing.

pol·y·phone (pol′ē fōn′), *n.* *Phonet.* a polyphonic letter or symbol. [< Gk *polýphōn(os)* having many tones]

pol·y·phon·ic (pol′ē fon′ik), *adj.* **1.** consisting of many voices or sounds. **2.** *Music.* **a.** having two or more voices or parts, each with an independent melody; contrapuntal. **b.** pertaining to music of this kind. **c.** capable of producing more than one tone at a time, as an organ or a harp. **3.** *Phonet.* having more than one phonetic value, as the letter *s*, which is voiced (z) in *nose* and unvoiced (s) in *salt.* —**pol′y·phon′i·cal·ly,** *adv.*

pol′yphon′ic prose′, prose characterized by the use of poetic devices, as alliteration, assonance, rhyme, etc., and esp. by rhythm not strictly metered.

po·lyph·o·ny (pə lif′ə nē), *n.* **1.** *Music.* polyphonic composition; counterpoint. **2.** *Phonet.* representation of different sounds by the same letter or symbol. [< Gk *polyphōnía* variety of tones or speech] —**po·lyph′o·nous,** *adj.*

pol·y·phy·let·ic (pol′ē fī let′ik), *adj.* developed from more than one ancestral type, as a group of animals. —**pol′y·phy·let′i·cal·ly,** *adv.*

pol·y·ploid (pol′ē ploid′), *adj., n.* *Biol.* —*adj.* **1.** having a chromosome number that is more than double the basic or haploid number. —*n.* **2.** a polyploid cell or organism. —**pol′y·ploi′dic,** *adj.* —**pol′y·ploi′dy,** *n.*

pol·y·po·dy (pol′ē pō′dē), *n., pl.* **-dies.** any fern of the genus *Polypodium*, as *P. vulgare*, having creeping rootstocks, deeply pinnatifid evergreen fronds, and round, naked sori. [< L *polypodi(um)* < Gk *polypódion* kind of fern, lit., something with many little feet. See POLY-, -PODIUM]

pol·yp·tych (pol′ip tik), *n.* a work of art composed of several connected panels. Cf. **diptych, triptych.** [special use of LL *polyptychum* < Gk *polýptychon* a register, roll, n. use of neut. of *polýptychos* having many folds]

pol·y·rhythm (pol′ē riṯẖ′əm), *n.* *Music.* the simultaneous occurrence of sharply contrasting rhythms within a composition. —**pol′y·rhyth′mic,** *adj.* —**pol′y·rhyth′mi·cal·ly,** *adv.*

pol·y·sac·cha·ride (pol′ē sak′ə rīd′, -rid), *n.* *Chem.* a carbohydrate, as starch, inulin, cellulose, etc., containing more than three monosaccharide units per molecule and capable of hydrolysis by acids or enzymes to monosaccharides. Also, **pol·y·sac·cha·rose** (pol′ē sak′ə rōs′, -rōz′).

pol·y·se·my (pol′ē sē′mē), *n.* diversity of meanings. [< NL *polysēmia* = LL *polysēm(us)* (< Gk *polýsēmos* with many significations = *poly-* POLY- + *sêm(a)* sign + *-os* adj. suffix) + *-ia* -Y[3]] —**pol′y·se′mous,** *adj.*

pol·y·sep·al·ous (pol′ē sep′ə ləs), *adj.* *Bot.* having the sepals separate or unconnected.

pol·y·sty·rene (pol′ē stī′rēn), *n.* *Chem.* a clear plastic or stiff foam, $[-CH(C_6H_5)CH_2-]_n$, a polymer of styrene, used chiefly as an insulator in refrigerators and air conditioners.

pol·y·syl·lab·ic (pol′ē si lab′ik), *adj.* **1.** consisting of three, four, or more syllables, as a word. **2.** characterized by such words, as a language, piece of writing, etc. Also, **pol′y·syl·lab′i·cal.** [< ML *polysyllab(us)* (< Gk *polysýllabos* of many syllables) + -IC] —**pol′y·syl·lab′i·cal·ly,** *adv.*

pol·y·syl·la·ble (pol′ē sil′ə bəl, pol′ē sil′-), *n.* a polysyllabic word.

pol·y·syn·de·ton (pol′ē sin′di ton′), *n.* *Rhet.* the use of a number of conjunctions in close succession. Cf. **asyndeton.** [< NL; see POLY-, ASYNDETON]

pol·y·syn·thet·ic (pol′ē sin thet′ik), *adj.* (of a language) characterized by a prevalence of relatively long words containing a large number of affixes to express syntactic relationships and meanings. Also, **pol′y·syn·thet′i·cal.** Cf. **analytic** (def. 3), **synthetic** (def. 3). [< LGk *polysýnthet(os)* much compounded]

pol·y·tech·nic (pol′ē tek′nik), *adj.* **1.** of, pertaining to, or offering instruction in industrial arts or scientific or technical subjects: *a polytechnic institute.* —*n.* **2.** a polytechnic school. [modeled on F *polytechnique*]

pol·y·tet·ra·flu·o·ro·eth·y·lene (pol′ē te′trə flo͞o′ə rō-eth′ə lēn′, -flo͝or′ō-, -flôr′-, -flōr′-), *n.* *Chem.* any polymer, plastic, or resin having the formula $(C_2F_4)_n$, noted for its slippery, nonsticking properties: used in the manufacture of gaskets, electrical insulation, frying-pan coatings, etc.

pol·y·the·ism (pol′ē thē iz′əm, pol′ē thē′iz əm), *n.* the doctrine of or belief in more than one god or in many gods. [cf. F *polythéisme*] —**pol′y·the′ist,** *n.* —**pol′y·the·is′tic, pol′y·the·is′ti·cal,** *adj.* —**pol′y·the·is′ti·cal·ly,** *adv.*

pol·y·thene (pol′ə thēn′), *n. Chem. Brit.* polyethylene.

pol·y·ton·al (pol′ē tōn′ᵊl), *adj. Music.* marked by or using polytonality. —**pol′y·ton′al·ly,** *adv.*

pol·y·to·nal·i·ty (pol′ē tō nal′i tē), *n. Music.* the use of more than one key at the same time. Also, **pol·y·ton·al·ism** (pol′ē tōn′ᵊliz′əm). —**pol·y·ton·al·ist** (pol′ē tōn′ᵊlist), *n.*

pol·y·typ·ic (pol′ē tip′ik), *adj.* having or involving many or several types. Also, **pol′y·typ′i·cal.**

pol·y·un·sat·u·rate (pol′ē un sach′ər it, -ə rāt′), *n.* a polyunsaturated substance. [back formation from POLYUNSATURATED]

pol·y·un·sat·u·rat·ed (pol′ē un sach′ə rā′tid), *adj.* of or noting a class of fats of animal or vegetable origin, esp. plant oils, whose molecules consist of carbon chains with many double bonds unsaturated by hydrogen atoms (associated with a low cholesterol content of the blood).

pol·y·u·re·thane (pol′ē yŏŏr′ə thān′), *n. Chem.* a light polymer whose foamed texture is produced by carbon dioxide, which evolves during its production and becomes trapped and forms pores: used for padding and insulation. Also, **pol·y·u·re·than** (pol′ē yŏŏr′ə than′).

pol·y·u·ri·a (pol′ē yŏŏr′ē ə), *n. Pathol.* the passing of an excessive quantity of urine. [< NL] —**pol′y·u′ric,** *adj.*

pol·y·va·lent (pol′ē vā′lənt, pə liv′ə lənt), *adj.* **1.** *Chem.* having more than one valence. **2.** *Bacteriol.* (of an immune serum) containing several antibodies, each capable of reacting with a specific antigen. —**pol′y·va′lence,** *n.*

pol·y·vi·nyl (pol′ē vī′nil, -vīn′ᵊl, -vin′il, -ᵊl), *adj. Chem.* pertaining to or derived from a vinyl polymer.

pol′yvi′nyl ac′etate, *Chem.* a nontoxic thermoplastic resin, $[-(H_2C\text{-}CHOOCCH_3)-]_n$, used as an adhesive in certain paints and as an intermediate in the synthesis of other polyvinyl compounds.

pol′yvi′nyl chlo′ride, a white, water-insoluble, thermoplastic resin, used chiefly on phonograph records and metal pipes, in floor coverings, and in fabrics, esp. rainwear.

pol·y·vi·nyl·i·dene (pol′ē vī nil′i dēn′), *adj. Chem.* pertaining to or derived from a polymer of a vinylidene compound.

pol′yvi′nyl res′in, *Chem.* any of the thermoplastic resins derived by the polymerization or copolymerization of a vinyl compound: used chiefly as adhesives, sizes, and coatings. Also called **vinyl resin.**

Po·lyx·e·na (pə lik′sə nə), *n. Class. Myth.* a daughter of Priam and Hecuba, loved by Achilles and sacrificed to appease his ghost.

pol·y·zo·an (pol′ē zō′ən), *adj., n.* bryozoan. [< NL *Polyzo(a)* name of the class (see POLY-, -ZOA) + -AN]

pol·y·zo·ar·i·um (pol′ē zō âr′ē əm), *n., pl.* **-ar·i·a** (-âr′ē-ə). *Zool.* a bryozoan colony, or its supporting skeleton. [< NL] —**pol′y·zo·ar′i·al,** *adj.*

pol·y·zo·ic (pol′ē zō′ik), *adj.* **1.** (of a bryozoan colony) composed of many zooids. **2.** (of a spore) producing many sporozoites.

pom·ace (pum′is), *n.* **1.** the pulpy residue of apples or similar fruit after crushing and pressing. **2.** any crushed or ground, pulpy substance. [? < ML *pōmāc(ium)* cider, n. use of L **pōmāceum,* neut. of **pōmāceus* of fruit. See POMACEOUS]

po·ma·ceous (pō mā′shəs), *adj.* of, pertaining to, or of the nature of pomes. [< NL *pōmāceus*]

po·made (pə mād′, -mäd′, pō-), *n., v.,* **-mad·ed, -mad·ing.** —*n.* **1.** a scented ointment, esp. for dressing the hair. —*v.t.* **2.** to apply pomade to. [earlier *pommade* < F < It *pomata* (so called because apples were orig. an ingredient) = *pom(a)* apple (< L, pl. of *pōmum* fruit) + *-ata* -ADE¹]

po·man·der (pō′man dər, pō man′dər), *n.* a mixture of aromatic substances, often in the form of a ball, formerly carried on the person as a supposed guard against infection but now placed in closets, dressers, etc. [late ME *pomandre,* dissimilated var. of **pomambre,* ML *pōmum ambrē* (i.e., *ambrae*), lit., pome of amber. See POME, AMBER]

po·ma·tum (pō mā′təm, -mä′-, pə-), *n.* pomade. [< NL, Latinization of POMADE; neut. (for fem.) to agree with L *pōmum* fruit]

pome (pōm), *n. Bot.* the characteristic fruit of the apple family, as an apple, pear, or quince, in which the edible flesh arises from the greatly swollen receptacle and not from the carpels. [late ME < MF << L *pōma,* pl. (taken as sing.) of *pōmum* fruit]

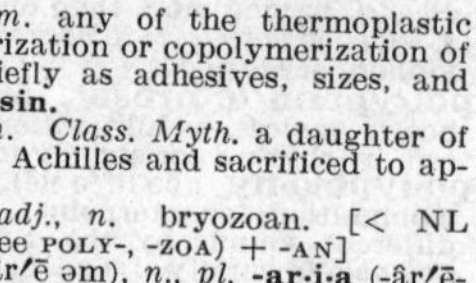

A, Pomegranate
B, Longitudinal section

pome·gran·ate (pom′-gran′it, pom′ə-, pum′-; pom′ə gran′it, pəm gran′-), *n.* **1.** a chambered, many-seeded, globose fruit, having a tough, usually red rind and surmounted by a crown of calyx lobes, the edible portion consisting of pleasantly acid flesh developed from the outer seed coat. **2.** the shrub or small tree, *Punica Granatum,* that bears it, widely cultivated in warm regions. [ME *poumgarnet,* etc. < MF *pome garnete,* etc. lit., seeded apple. See POME, GRENADE]

pom·e·lo (pom′ə lō′), *n., pl.* **-los. 1.** grapefruit (def. 1). **2.** shaddock (def. 1). Also, **pumelo.** [pseudo-Spanish alter. of *pamplemoose* < D *pompelmoes* shaddock, said to be a compound of *pomp(oen)* big + Pg *limões,* pl. of *limão* lemon]

Pomeranian
(7 in. high
at shoulder)

Pom·er·a·ni·a (pom′ə rā′nē ə, -rān′yə), *n.* a former province of NE Germany, now mostly in NW Poland. German, **Pommern.**

Pom·er·a·ni·an (pom′ə rā′nē ən, -rān′yən), *adj.* **1.** of, pertaining to, or characteristic of Pomerania. —*n.* **2.** one of a breed of small dogs having long, straight hair, erect ears, and a tail carried over the back.

po·mif·er·ous (pō mif′ər əs), *adj. Bot.* bearing pomes. [< L *pōmifer* fruit-bearing (see POME, -I-, -FER) + -OUS]

Pom·mard (pō märd′; *Fr.* pô MAR′), *n.* a dry red wine from Burgundy.

pom·mée (po mā′, pə-, pō-; *Fr.* pô mā′), *adj. Heraldry.* (of a cross) having arms with knoblike ends: *a cross pommée.* [< F: lit., balled = *pomme* apple, ball (see POME) + *-ée* -EE]

pom·mel (pum′əl, pom′əl), *n., v.,* (*esp. Brit.*) **-melled, -mel·ling.** —*n.* **1.** a knob, as on the hilt of a sword. **2.** the protuberant part at the front and top of a saddle. —*v.t.* **3.** to beat or strike with or as with the fists or a pommel. [ME *pomel* < MF (= ML *pomellus* ball, knob) < VL or LL **pōmellum,* dim. of L *pōmum* fruit]

Pom·mern (pôm′ərn), *n.* German name of **Pomerania.**

po·mol·o·gy (pō mol′ə jē), *n.* the science that deals with fruits and fruit growing. [< NL *pōmologia.* See POME, -O-, -LOGY] —**po·mo·log·i·cal** (pō′mə loj′i kəl), *adj.* —**po′mo·log′i·cal·ly,** *adv.* —**po·mol′o·gist,** *n.*

Po·mo·na (pə mō′nə), *n.* **1.** the ancient Roman goddess of fruit trees. **2.** a city in SW California, E of Los Angeles. 87,384 (1970). **3.** Also called **Mainland.** the largest of the Orkney Islands, N of Scotland. 13,352 (1951); 190 sq. mi.

pomp (pomp), *n.* **1.** stately or splendid display; splendor; magnificence. **2.** ostentatious or vain display. **3. pomps,** pompous displays, actions, or things. **4.** *Obs.* a stately or splendid procession; pageant. [ME < L *pompa* display, a parade, procession < Gk *pompḗ* in same senses, orig. a sending, akin to *pémpein* to send] —**Syn. 1.** See **show.**

pom·pa·dour (pom′pə dōr′, -dôr′, -dŏŏr′), *n.* **1.** an arrangement of a man's hair in which it is brushed up high from the forehead. **2.** an arrangement of a woman's hair in which it is raised over the forehead in a roll, sometimes over a pad. [named after the Marquise de POMPADOUR]

Pom·pa·dour (pom′pə dōr′, -dôr′, -dŏŏr′; *Fr.* pôN pA-dŏŏr′), *n.* **Marquise de** (*Jeanne Antoinette Poisson Le Normant d'Étioles*), 1721–64, mistress of Louis XV of France.

pom·pa·no (pom′pə nō′), *n., pl.* (*esp. collectively*) **-no,** (*esp. referring to two or more kinds or species*) **-nos. 1.** a deep-bodied food fish of the genus *Trachinotus.* **2.** a food fish, *Palometus simillimus,* of California. [< Sp *pámpano* kind of fish]

Pom′pano Beach′, a city in SE Florida. 38,544 (1970).

Pom·pe·ia (pom pē′ə), *n.* second wife of Julius Caesar, divorced in 62 B.C. Cf. **Calpurnia, Cornelia** (def. 2).

Pom·peii (pom pā′, -pā′ē), *n.* an ancient city in SW Italy, on the Bay of Naples: buried along with Herculaneum by an eruption of Mount Vesuvius in A.D. 79. —**Pom·pe·ian, Pom·pei·ian** (pom pā′ən, -pē′-), *adj., n.*

Pom·pey (pom′pē), *n.* (*Gnaeus Pompeius Magnus*) ("*the Great*") 106–48 B.C., Roman general and statesman: a member of the first triumvirate.

Pom·pi·dou (pôN pē dōō′), *n.* **Georges Jean Ray·mond** (zhôrzh zhäN RA môN′), 1911–74, French political leader and public official: president 1969–74.

pom·pom (pom′pom), *n.* an automatic antiaircraft cannon. Also, **pom′-pom.** [imit.]

pom·pon (pom′pon; *Fr.* pôN pôN′), *n., pl.* **-pons** (-ponz; *Fr.* -pôN′). **1.** an ornamental tuft or ball, as of feathers or wool. **2.** *Hort.* a form of small, globe-shaped flower head that characterizes a class or type of various flowering plants, esp. chrysanthemums and dahlias. [< F; repetitive formation, appar. based on *pompe* POMP]

pom·pos·i·ty (pom pos′i tē), *n., pl.* **-ties** for 3. **1.** the quality of being pompous. **2.** pompous parading of dignity or importance. **3.** an instance of this. Also, **pom·pous·ness** (pom′pəs nis) (for defs. 1, 2). [late ME *pomposite* < LL *pompōsitās*]

pomp·ous (pom′pəs), *adj.* **1.** characterized by an ostentatious display of dignity or importance. **2.** ostentatiously lofty or highflown: *a pompous speech.* **3.** characterized by pomp, stately splendor, or magnificence. [late ME < LL *pompōs(us)*] —**pomp′ous·ly,** *adv.* —**Syn. 1.** pretentious. **2.** inflated, turgid, bombastic.

Po·na·pe (pon′ə pā, pō′nä pe), *n.* an island in the W Pacific: under U.S. trusteeship. 18,536 including adjacent islands (1970); 134 sq. mi.

Pon·ca (poŋ′kə), *n., pl.* **-cas,** (*esp. collectively*) **-ca. 1.** a member of a Siouan people of northern Nebraska. **2.** the dialect of the Ponca Indians, reciprocally intelligible with Osage and belonging to the Siouan language family.

Pon′ca Cit′y (poŋ′kə), a city in N Oklahoma. 25,940 (1970).

ponce (pons), *n. Brit. Slang.* a pimp. [?]

Pon·ce (pôn′se), *n.* a seaport in S Puerto Rico. 128,233 (1970).

Ponce de Le·ón (pons′ də lē′ōn; *Sp.* pôn′the the le ôn′, pôn′se), **Juan** (hwän), c1460–1521, Spanish explorer.

Pon·chiel·li (pôŋ kyel′lē), *n.* **A·mil·ca·re** (ä mēl′kä re), 1834–86, Italian composer.

pon·cho (pon′chō), *n., pl.* **-chos.** a blanketlike cloak with a hole in the center to admit the head, often worn as a raincoat. [< AmerSp < Araucanian *pantho*]

pond (pond), *n.* a body of water smaller than a lake, sometimes artificially formed. [ME *ponde, pande,* OE *pond* pool, akin to *pynding* dam, *gepyndan* to impound. See POUND³]

pon·der (pon′dər), *v.i.* **1.** to consider something deeply and thoroughly; meditate. —*v.t.* **2.** to weigh carefully in the mind; consider thoughtfully. [ME *pondre(n)* < MF *ponderer* < L *ponderāre* to ponder, weigh] —**Syn. 1.** reflect, cogitate, deliberate, ruminate.

pon·der·a·ble (pon′dər ə bəl), *adj.* **1.** capable of being considered carefully or deeply. **2.** capable of being weighed. [< LL *ponderābil(is)*] —**pon′der·a·bil′i·ty,** *n.*

pon′der·o′sa pine′ (pon′də rō′sə, pon′-), **1.** a large pine, *Pinus ponderosa,* of western North America, having yellowish-brown bark: the state tree of Montana. **2.** its light, soft wood, used for making furniture and in the construction of houses, ships, etc. [< NL *Pinus ponderōsa* heavy pine]

pon·der·ous (pon′dər əs), *adj.* **1.** of great weight; heavy; massive. **2.** awkward or unwieldy. **3.** heavy; dull; labored: *a ponderous dissertation.* [late ME, var. of *ponderose* < L *ponderōs(us)*] —**pon′der·ous·ly,** *adv.* —**pon·der·os·i·ty** (pon′də ros′i tē), *n.*

Pon·di·cher·ry (pon′di cher′ē, -sher′ē), *n.* **1.** a former province of French India, on the Coromandel Coast; now a union territory of India. With Mahé, Karikal, and Yanaon,

369,079 (1961); 200 sq. mi. **2.** a seaport in and the capital of this territory. 58,600 (est. 1952). Also, **Pon·di·ché·ry** (pôN dē shā RĒ′). Cf. **French India.**

pond′ lil′y. See **water lily.**

pond′ scum′, any free-floating fresh-water alga that forms a green scum on water.

pond·weed (pond′wēd′), *n.* any aquatic plant of the genus *Potamogeton,* most species of which grow in ponds and quiet streams.

pone (pōn), *n.* *Southern U.S.* **1.** Also called **pone′ bread′.** a baked or fried bread made of corn meal. **2.** an oval-shaped loaf or cake of it. [< Algonquian (Va.); akin to Delaware *apân* baked]

pon·gee (pon jē′, pon′jē), *n.* **1.** silk of a slightly uneven weave made from filaments of wild silk woven in natural tan color. **2.** a cotton or rayon fabric imitating it. Cf. **Shantung** (def. 3), **tussah** (def. 1). [? < NChin *pun-chī,* lit., own loom (i.e. homemade) = Mandarin *pun-kī*]

pon·gid (pon′jid), *n.* any anthropoid ape of the family *Pongidae,* including the gibbon, gorilla, and chimpanzee. [back formation from NL *Pongidae* the family name = *Pong(o)* typical genus (< Congo *mpungu* ape) + *-idae* -IDAE]

pon·iard (pon′yərd), *n.* **1.** a dagger. —*v.t.* **2.** to stab with a poniard. [< F *poignard* < *poing* fist < L *pugn(us);* see -ARD]

pons (ponz), *n., pl.* **pon·tes** (pon′tēz). *Anat.* **1.** Also called **pons Varolii.** a band of nerve fibers in the brain connecting the lobes of the midbrain, medulla, and cerebrum. **2.** a connecting part. [< L *pōns* bridge (gen. *pontis*)]

Pons (ponz; *Fr.* pôNs), *n.* **Lil·y** (lil′ē; *Fr.* lē lē′), 1904–76, U.S. operatic soprano, born in France.

pons′ as·i·no′rum (as′ə nōr′əm, -nôr′-), the geometric proposition that if a triangle has two equal sides, the angles opposite are equal: so named from the difficulty beginners have in mastering it. [< L: bridge of asses]

Pon·selle (pon sel′), *n.* **Rosa (Mel·ba)** (mel′bə), born 1897, U.S. soprano.

pons′ Va·ro′li·i (və rō′lē ī), *pl.* **pon′tes Varo′lii.** pons (def. 1). [< NL: lit., Varoli's bridge; named after Costanzo Varoli, Italian anatomist (1543–75)]

Pon·ta Del·ga·da (*Port.* pôNN′tə del gä′də), a seaport on SW São Miguel island, in the E Azores. 24,491 (1960).

Pon·ta Gros·sa (pôNN′tə grô′sə), a city in S Brazil. 78,557 (1960).

Pont·char·train (pon′chər trān′), *n.* **Lake,** a shallow extension of the Gulf of Mexico in SE Louisiana, N of New Orleans. 41 mi. long; 25 mi. wide.

Pon·te·fract (pon′tə frakt′; *locally also* pum′frit, pom′-), *n.* a city in S Yorkshire, in N England, SE of Leeds: ruins of a 12th-century castle. 27,114 (1961).

Pon·ti·ac (pon′tē ak′), *n.* **1.** c1720–69, American Indian, chief of the Ottawa tribe. **2.** a city in SE Michigan. 85,279 (1970).

Pon·tian (pon′shən, -shē ən), *n.* pope A.D. 230–235. Also, **Pon·ti·a·nus** (pon′shē ā′nəs).

Pon·ti·a·nak (pon′tē ä′näk), *n.* a seaport on W Borneo, in central Indonesia. 146,547 (1961).

Pon·tic (pon′tik), *adj.* pertaining to the Pontus Euxinus or to Pontus.

pon·ti·fex (pon′tə feks′), *n., pl.* **pon·tif·i·ces** (pon tif′i sēz′). *Rom. Relig.* a member of the Pontifical College, which was presided over by a chief priest (**Pon′tifex Max′imus**). [< L: lit., bridgemaker = *ponti-* (s. of *pōns*) bridge + *-fec-* (var. s. of *facere* to make) + *-s* nom. sing. ending]

pon·tiff (pon′tif), *n.* **1.** any pontifex. **2.** any high or chief priest. **3.** *Eccles.* **a.** a bishop. **b.** the Pope. [earlier *pontife* < F, short for L *pontifex* PONTIFEX]

pon·tif·i·cal (pon tif′i kəl), *adj.* **1.** of, pertaining to, or characteristic of a pontiff; papal. **2.** pompous or dogmatic. —*n.* **3. pontificals,** the vestments and other insignia of a pontiff, esp. a bishop. [late ME < L *pontificāl(is)* = *pontific-* (s. of *pontifex*) PONTIFEX + *-ālis* -AL[1]] —**pon·tif′i·cal·ly,** *adv.*

Pontif′ical Col′lege, the chief body of priests in ancient Rome.

pon·tif·i·cate (*n.* pon tif′ə kit′, -kāt′; *v.* pon tif′ə kāt′), *n., v.,* **-cat·ed, -cat·ing.** —*n.* **1.** the office or term of office of a pontiff. —*v.i.* **2.** to speak in a pompous or dogmatic manner. **3.** to discharge the duties of a pontiff. [(n.) < L *pontificāt(us);* see PONTIFICAL, -ATE[1]; (v.) < ML *pontificāt(us)* ptp. of *pontificāre*]

pon·tif·i·ces (pon tif′i sēz′), *n.* pl. of **pontifex.**

pon·til (pon′til), *n.* punty. [< F; see POINT, -IL]

Pon·tine (pon′tēn, -tīn), *adj.* of the Pontine Marshes.

Pon′tine Marsh′es, an area in W Italy, SE of Rome: formerly marshy, now drained.

Pon′tius Pi′late (pon′shəs, -tē əs). See **Pilate, Pontius.**

pon·to·nier (pon′tᵊnēr′), *n.* *Mil.* an officer or soldier in charge of bridge equipment or the building of pontoon bridges. [< F *pontonnier.* See PONTOON, -IER]

pon·toon (pon to͞on′), *n.* **1.** *Mil.* a boat or some other floating structure used with others to support a temporary bridge. **2.** a float for a derrick, landing stage, etc. **3.** a seaplane float. Also, **pon·ton** (pon′tᵊn). [< F *ponton* < L *pontōn-* (s. of *pontō*) ferryboat, floating bridge. See PONS, -OON]

pon′toon bridge′, a bridge supported on pontoons.

Pon·tus (pon′təs), *n.* an ancient country in NE Asia Minor, bordering on the Black Sea: later a Roman province.

Pon′tus Eux·i′nus (yo͞ok sī′nəs), ancient name of the **Black Sea.**

po·ny (pō′nē), *n., pl.* **-nies,** *v.,* **-nied, -ny·ing.** **1.** a small horse of any of several breeds, usually not more than 14 hands high. **2.** a horse of any small type or breed. **3.** *Slang.* a literal translation or other text, used illicitly as an aid in schoolwork or while taking a test; crib. **4.** something small of its kind. **5.** a small glass for liquor, esp. cordials. —*v.t., v.i.* **6.** *Slang.* to prepare (lessons) by means of a pony. **7.** to pay (money), as in settling an account (fol. by *up*): *They made him pony up the money he owed.* [earlier *powney* < obs. F *poulenet,* dim. of *poulain* colt < ML *pullān(us)* (L *pull(us)* foal + *-ānus* -AN); see -ET]

po′ny express′, a system formerly used in the American West in which mail was carried by relays of mounted riders, esp. the system in use 1860–61.

po·ny·tail (pō′nē tāl′), *n.* an arrangement of a girl's or woman's hair in which the hair, usually long and straight, is drawn back tightly and fastened at the back of the head.

pooch (po͞och), *n.* *Slang.* a dog. [?]

pood (po͞od), *n.* a Russian weight equal to about 36 pounds avoirdupois. [< Russ *pud* < LG or Scand *pund* POUND[1]]

poo·dle (po͞od′ᵊl), *n.* one of a breed of active dogs having long, thick, frizzy or curly hair, usually trimmed in standard patterns, and occurring in three varieties differing only in size. [< G *Pudel,* short for *Pudelhund,* lit., splash-dog (i.e., water-dog) = *pudel(n)* (to) splash (see PUDDLE) + *Hund* HOUND[1]]

Poodle (miniature) (13 in. high at shoulder)

pooh (po͞o, pо̆о), *interj.* (used as an exclamation of disdain or contempt.)

Pooh Bah (po͞o′ bä′, bä′), (*often l.c.*) a person who holds several positions, esp. ones that give him importance. [after the character in Gilbert and Sullivan's operetta *The Mikado* (1885)]

pooh-pooh (po͞o′po͞o′), *v.t.* **1.** to express disdain or contempt for; dismiss lightly. —*v.i.* **2.** to express disdain or contempt. [v. use of redupl. of POOH]

pool[1] (po͞ol), *n.* **1.** a small body of standing water; pond. **2.** any small collection of liquid on a surface; puddle. **3.** a still, deep place in a stream. **4.** See **swimming pool.** **5.** a subterranean reservoir of oil or gas held in porous sedimentary rock. [ME; OE *pōl;* c. D *poel,* G *Pfuhl*]

pool[2] (po͞ol), *n.* **1.** an association of competitors who agree secretly to control the production, market, and price of a commodity for mutual benefit. **2.** *Finance.* a combination of persons or organizations for the purpose of manipulating the prices of securities. **3.** a combination of interests, funds, etc., formed for common advantage. **4.** a facility, resource, or service that is shared by a group of people: *a car pool.* **5.** the persons or parties involved. **6.** the stakes in certain games. **7.** Also called **pocket billiards.** any of various games played on a pool table with a cue ball and 15 other balls that are driven into the pockets. **8.** *Brit.* a billiard game. **9.** the total amount staked by a combination of bettors, as on a race. **10.** the combination of such bettors. **11.** *Fencing.* a match in which each teammate successively plays against each member of the opposing team. —*v.t.* **12.** to put (interests, money, etc.) into a pool, or common stock or fund. **13.** to form a pool of. **14.** to make a common interest of. —*v.i.* **15.** to enter into or form a pool or joint endeavor. [< F *poule* stakes, lit., hen. See PULLET] —**Syn. 1.** corner, monopoly.

pool′ hall′, *U.S.* poolroom (def. 1). Also, **pool′hall′.**

pool·room (po͞ol′ro͞om′, -ro͝om′), *n.* **1.** an establishment or room for the playing of pool or billiards. **2.** a place where betting is carried on, esp. illegally; a bookmaker's establishment.

pool′ ta′ble, a billiard table with six pockets, on which pool is played.

poon (po͞on), *n.* **1.** any of several East Indian trees of the genus *Calophyllum,* that yield a light, hard wood used for masts, spars, etc. **2.** the wood of these trees. [< Singhalese or Telugu *pūna*]

Poo·na (po͞o′nə), *n.* a city in W Maharashtra, W India, SE of Bombay. 597,600 (1961).

poop[1] (po͞op), *n.* **1.** a superstructure at the stern of a vessel. **2.** See **poop deck.** —*v.t.* **3.** (of a wave) to break over the stern of (a ship). **4.** to take (seas) over the stern. [late ME *pouppe* < MF << L *puppis* stern of a ship]

poop[2] (po͞op), *v.t.* *Slang.* **1.** to cause to become out of breath or fatigued; exhaust. **2. poop out,** to cease from or fail in something, as from fear or exhaustion. [ME *poupe(n)* (to) blow; imit.]

poop[3] (po͞op), *n.* *Slang.* information; low-down. [?]

poop′ deck′, a weather deck on top of a poop.

Po·o·pó (pô′ô pô′), *n.* a lake in SW Bolivia, in the Andes. 60 mi. long; 12,000 ft. above sea level.

poop-sheet (po͞op′shēt′), *n.* *Slang.* a circular, press release, etc., handed out to give the facts about a particular subject.

poor (po͝or), *adj.* **1.** lacking money or other means of support. **2.** *Law.* dependent on charity or public support. **3.** indicating or suggesting poverty: *a poor cottage.* **4.** wretchedly lacking; meager: *a country poor in natural resources.* **5.** unfortunate; unlucky: *Out of a job, poor fellow?* **6.** lacking in resources, capability, etc.: *poor soil; a poor memory.* **7.** not up to expectations: *poor workmanship; a poor turnout.* —*n.* **8.** (*construed as pl.*) poor persons collectively (usually prec. by *the*): *sympathy for the poor.* [ME *pov(e)re* < OF *povre* < L *pauper.* See PAUPER]

—**Syn. 1.** needy, indigent, destitute, penniless, poverty-stricken. POOR, IMPOVERISHED, PENNILESS refer to those lacking money. POOR is the simple term for the condition of lacking means to obtain the comforts of life: *a very poor family.* IMPOVERISHED often implies a former state of greater plenty, from which one has been reduced: *the impoverished aristocracy.* PENNILESS may mean destitute, or it may apply simply to a temporary condition of being without funds: *The widow was left penniless with three small children.* **6.** sterile, barren, unfruitful, unproductive. **7.** unsatisfactory. —**Ant. 1, 4, 6.** rich. **1.** wealthy.

poor′ boy′. See **hero sandwich.** Also called **poor′ boy′ sand′wich.**

poor′ farm′, a farm maintained at public expense for the housing and support of paupers.

poor·house (po͝or′hous′), *n., pl.* **-hous·es** (-hou′ziz). an institution in which paupers are maintained at public expense.

poor′ law′, a system of laws governing the public relief of the poor.

poor·ly (po͝or′lē), *adv.* **1.** in a poor manner or way. —*adj.* **2.** *Informal.* in poor health; somewhat ill. [ME *pourely*]

poor-spir·it·ed (po͝or′spir′i tid), *adj.* having or showing a cowardly or abject spirit.

poor′ white′, *Usually Derogatory.* a white person, esp. of the southern U.S., having low social and economic status.

poor′ white′ trash′, *Derogatory.* poor whites collectively.

pop[1] (pop), *v.*, **popped, pop·ping,** *n., adv.* —*v.i.* **1.** to make a quick, light, explosive sound. **2.** to burst open with such a sound. **3.** to come or go suddenly (usually fol. by *in* or *off*). **4.** to shoot with a firearm. **5.** *Baseball.* to hit a pop fly (often fol. by *up*). —*v.t.* **6.** to cause to burst open with a pop. **7.** to put or thrust quickly or suddenly: *Pop the rolls into the oven.* **8.** to shoot at (a target). **9.** *Slang.* to use (a drug in the form of pills), esp. excessively or habitually. **10. pop off, a.** to depart quickly. **b.** to die, esp. suddenly. **c.** to express oneself irately or indiscreetly. **11. pop the question,** *Informal.* to propose marriage. —*n.* **12.** a light, quick, explosive sound. **13.** an effervescent nonalcoholic beverage. **14.** a shot with a firearm. **15.** *Baseball.* See **pop fly.** —*adv.* **16.** with a popping noise. [late ME *poppe;* imit.]

pop[2] (pop), *Informal.* —*adj.* **1.** of or pertaining to popular songs: *pop music; pop singers.* **2.** of or pertaining to pop art. —*n.* **3.** popular music; a popular tune or recording. **4.** See **pop art.** [by shortening]

pop[3] (pop), *n.* *Informal.* father. [short form of POPPA]

pop., **1.** popular. **2.** popularly. **3.** population.

P.O.P., point of purchase.

pop′ art′, a style in the fine arts characterized chiefly by forms and images derived from comic strips and advertising posters. —**pop′ art′ist.**

Po·pa·yán (pō′pä yän′), *n.* a city in SW Colombia. 61,490 (est. 1961).

pop′ con′cert, a concert of popular and light classical music played by a symphony orchestra.

pop·corn (pop′kôrn′), *n.* **1.** any of several varieties of corn whose kernels burst open and puff out when subjected to dry heat. **2.** such corn when popped. [short for *popped corn*]

pope (pōp), *n.* **1.** (*often cap.*) the bishop of Rome as head of the Roman Catholic Church. **2.** a person considered as having or assuming authority or a position similar to that of the Roman Catholic pope. **3.** *Eastern Ch.* **a.** the Orthodox patriarch of Alexandria. **b.** (in certain churches) a parish priest. [ME; OE *pāpa* < eccl. L: bishop, pope < LGk *pápas* bishop, priest, var. of *páppas* father; see PAPA[1]]

Pope (pōp), *n.* **1. Alexander,** 1688–1744, English poet. **2. John,** 1822–92, Union general in the Civil War.

pop·er·y (pō′pə rē), *n.* *Disparaging.* Roman Catholicism.

pop-eyed (pop′īd′), *adj.* marked by bulging, staring eyes.

pop′ fly′, *Baseball.* a high fly ball hit to the infield or immediately beyond it that can easily be caught before reaching the ground. Also called **pop, pop-up.**

pop·gun (pop′gun′), *n.* a child's toy gun from which a pellet is shot by compressed air, producing a loud pop.

pop·in·jay (pop′in jā′), *n.* **1.** a person given to vain displays and empty chatter; coxcomb; fop. **2.** *Archaic.* a parrot. [ME *papejay, popingay,* etc. < MF *papegai, papingay* etc., parrot < Sp *papagayo* < Ar *bab(ba)ghā'*]

pop·ish (pō′pish), *adj.* *Usually Disparaging.* pertaining to or characteristic of the Roman Catholic Church. —**pop′ish·ly,** *adv.* —**pop′ish·ness,** *n.*

pop·lar (pop′lər), *n.* **1.** any of the rapidly growing, salicaceous trees of the genus *Populus,* usually characterized by the columnar or spirelike manner of growth of its branches. **2.** the light, soft wood of any of these trees, used for pulp. **3.** any of various similar trees, as the yellow poplar (**tulip tree**). **4.** the wood of any such tree. [ME *popler(e),* var. of *populer* = ME, OE *popul* (< L *pōpulus* poplar) + *-er* -ER[2]; suffix appar. added on model of MF *pouplier* = *pouple* poplar + *-ier* -ER[2]]

pop·lin (pop′lin), *n.* a finely corded fabric of cotton, rayon, silk, or wool, for dresses, draperies, etc. [< F *popeline,* earlier *papeline* < It *papalina,* fem. of *papalino* papal; so called from being made at the papal city of Avignon. See PAPAL, -INE[1]]

pop·lit·e·al (pop lit′ē əl, pop′li tē′əl), *adj.* *Anat.* of or pertaining to the ham, or the part of the leg back of the knee. [< NL *poplite(us)* the thin, flat, triangular muscle in back of the knee (= L *poplit-* (s. of *poples*) the ham + *-eus* -EOUS) + -AL[1]]

Po·po·cat·e·petl (pô′pô kä te′pet^əl, pō′pə kat′ə pet′^əl), *n.* a volcano in S central Mexico. 17,887 ft.

pop·o·ver (pop′ō′vər), *n.* a puffed muffin with a hollow center, made with a batter of flour, salt, egg, and milk.

pop·pa (pop′ə), *n.* *Informal.* father. [var. of PAPA[1]]

Pop·pae·a Sa·bi·na (po pē′ə sə bī′nə), died A.D. 65?, second wife of the Roman emperor Nero.

pop·per (pop′ər), *n.* **1.** a person or thing that pops. **2.** a utensil for popping corn.

pop·pet (pop′it), *n.* **1.** Also called **pop′pet valve′.** *Mach.* a rising and falling valve consisting of a disk at the end of a vertically set stem. **2.** *Brit. Dial.* a term of endearment for a girl or child. **3.** poppethead. [earlier form of PUPPET]

pop·pet·head (pop′it hed′), *n.* a tailstock or headstock of a lathe. Also called **poppet, puppet.**

pop·pied (pop′ēd), *adj.* **1.** covered or adorned with poppies: *poppied fields.* **2.** affected by or as if by opium; listless.

pop′ping crease′ (pop′ing), *Cricket.* a line parallel to and in advance of a bowling crease, marking the limit of a batsman's approach in hitting the ball.

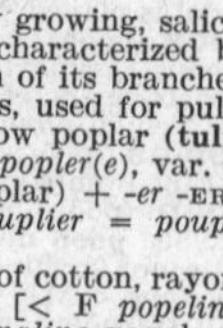

pop·ple (pop′əl), *v.*, **-pled, -pling,** *n.* —*v.i.* **1.** to move in a tumbling, irregular manner, as boiling water. —*n.* **2.** a poppling motion. [ME *pople(n);* imit.]

pop·py (pop′ē), *n., pl.* **-pies** for 1. **1.** any plant of the genus *Papaver,* having nodding red, violet, yellow, or white flowers. **2.** an extract, as opium, from such a plant. **3.** Also called **pop′py red′.** an orangeish red resembling scarlet. [ME; OE *popæg, papig* << VL **papāv(um)* for L *papāver*]

Poppy, *Papaver orientale*

pop·py·cock (pop′ē kok′), *n.* *Informal.* nonsense; bosh. [? < D *pappekak* (*pap* soft + *kak* dung)]

pop·py·head (pop′ē hed′), *n.* *Archit.* a finial or other ornament, often richly carved, as the top of the upright end of a bench or pew.

pop′py seed′, seed of the poppy plant, used as an ingredient or topping for breads, rolls, cakes, and cookies.

pops (pops), *adj.* of or pertaining to a symphony orchestra specializing in popular or light classical music. [see POP[2]]

Pop·si·cle (pop′si kəl, -sik′əl), *n.* *Trademark.* a flavored ice on a stick.

pop·u·lace (pop′yə ləs), *n.* **1.** the inhabitants of a place; population. **2.** the common people as distinguished from the higher classes. [< F < It *popolaccio* = *popol(o)* PEOPLE + *-accio* pejorative suffix]

pop·u·lar (pop′yə lər), *adj.* **1.** regarded with favor or affection by most persons. **2.** in favor with a single person or with a group of persons. **3.** pertaining to, originating in, or prevailing among the people as a whole: *a popular uprising; a popular belief.* **4.** appealing to or suitable for the tastes, means, etc., of ordinary persons: *popular music; popular prices.* [late ME *populer* < L *populār(is).* See PEOPLE, -AR[1]] —**Syn. 1.** favorite, approved, liked. **3.** common.

pop′ular etymol′ogy. See **folk etymology.**

pop·u·lar·ise (pop′yə lə rīz′), *v.t.,* **-ised, -is·ing.** *Chiefly Brit.* popularize. —**pop′u·lar·i·sa′tion,** *n.* —**pop′u·lar·is′er,** *n.*

pop·u·lar·i·ty (pop′yə lar′i tē), *n.* the quality or fact of being popular. [< L *populāritās* a courting of popular favor]

pop·u·lar·ize (pop′yə lə rīz′), *v.t.,* **-ized, -iz·ing.** to make popular; promote general understanding or acceptance of. Also, *esp. Brit.,* **popularise.** —**pop′u·lar·i·za′tion,** *n.* —**pop′u·lar·iz′er,** *n.*

pop·u·lar·ly (pop′yə lər lē), *adv.* **1.** by the people as a whole; generally; widely. **2.** in a popular manner.

pop′ular song′, a song written for its immediate commercial potential, intended for widespread dissemination through recordings, broadcasts, etc. Cf. **standard** (def. 9).

pop′ular sov′ereignty, 1. the doctrine that sovereign power is vested in the people. **2.** *Amer. Hist.* (before the Civil War) the doctrine that the people living in a Territory should be free of federal interference in determining domestic policy, esp. with respect to slavery.

pop′ular vote′, a vote made by qualified voters, as opposed to one made by the electoral college or by elected representatives. Cf. **electoral vote.**

pop·u·late (pop′yə lāt′), *v.t.,* **-lat·ed, -lat·ing. 1.** to inhabit; live in; be the inhabitants of. **2.** to furnish with inhabitants, as by colonization; people. [< ML *populāt(us),* ptp. of *populāre* to inhabit. See PEOPLE, -ATE[1]]

pop·u·la·tion (pop′yə lā′shən), *n.* **1.** the total number of persons inhabiting a country, city, or any district or area. **2.** the inhabitants of a place in general: *an uprising of the population.* **3.** the number or body of inhabitants of a specified kind in a place: *the native population.* **4.** *Statistics.* any finite or infinite aggregation of individuals, not necessarily animate, subject to a statistical study. **5.** *Ecol.* **a.** the assemblage of plants or animals living in a given area. **b.** all the individuals of a particular species in a given area. **6.** the act or process of populating. [< LL *populātiōn-* (s. of *populātiō*)] —**pop′u·la′tion·al,** *adj.*

Pop·u·list (pop′yə list), *n.* *U.S. Politics.* a member of the People's party. [< L *popul(us)* PEOPLE + -IST] —**Pop′u·lism,** *n.* —**Pop′u·lis′tic,** *adj.*

pop·u·lous (pop′yə ləs), *adj.* **1.** heavily populated. **2.** crowded with people. [late ME *populus* < L *populōs(us).* See PEOPLE, -OUS] —**pop′u·lous·ly,** *adv.* —**pop′u·lous·ness,** *n.*

pop-up (pop′up′), *adj.* **1.** of, pertaining to, or equipped with a device that pops up or causes something to pop up: *a pop-up electric toaster.* **2.** (of children's books) having additional pieces of artwork fastened to the pages so that, when opened, a three-dimensional object is formed or a mechanical movement, such as a door opening, can be activated by pulling a tab. —*n.* **3.** a pop-up book. **4.** *Baseball.* See **pop fly.**

por·bea·gle (pôr′bē′gəl), *n.* a shark of the genus *Lamna,* esp. *L. nasus,* a large, voracious species of the North Atlantic and North Pacific oceans. [orig. Cornish dial.]

por·ce·lain (pōr′sə lin, pôr′-; pōrs′lin, pôrs′-), *n.* **1.** a strong, vitreous, translucent ceramic material. **2.** ware made from this. [< F *porcelaine* < It *porcellana* (orig. a kind of shell) < *porcella* dim. of *porca* sow (see PORK); reason for name uncertain] —**por·ce·la·ne·ous, por·cel·la·ne·ous** (pōr′sə-lā′nē əs, pôr′-) *adj.*

por′celain enam′el, a glass coating made to adhere to a metal or another enamel by fusion.

por·ce·lain·ise (pōr′sə lə nīz′, pôr′-, pōrs′lə-, pôrs′-), *v.t.,* **-ised, -is·ing.** *Chiefly Brit.* porcelainize.

por·ce·lain·ize (pōr′sə lə nīz′, pôr′-, pōrs′lə- pôrs′-), *v.t.,* **-ized, -iz·ing.** to make into or coat with porcelain or something resembling porcelain. —**por′ce·lain·i·za′tion,** *n.*

porch (pōrch, pôrch), *n.* **1.** an exterior appendage to a building, forming a covered approach or vestibule to a doorway. **2.** *U.S.* a veranda. **3.** a portico. [ME *porche* < OF < L *portic(us)* porch, portico] —**porch′like′,** *adj.*

por·cine (pôr′sīn, -sin), *adj.* **1.** of or pertaining to swine. **2.** resembling swine; hoggish; piggish. [< L *porcīn(us)*]

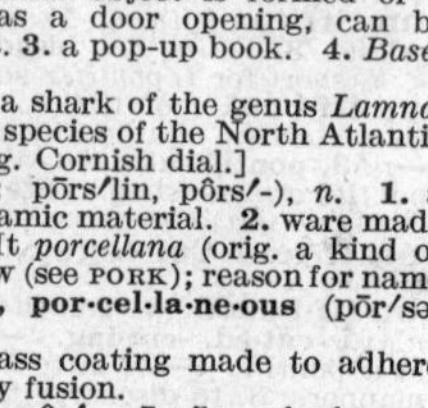

por·cu·pine (pôr′kyə pīn′), *n.* any of several rodents covered with stiff, sharp, erectile quills, or spines, as *Erethizon dorsatum,* of the U.S. and Canada, having short quills partially concealed by the hair. [late ME *porcupyne,* var. of *porcapyne;* r. *porke despyne* < MF *porc d'espine* thorny pig. See PORK, SPINE]

Porcupine, *Erethizon dorsatum* (Total length 3 ft.; tail 8 in.)

por′cupine ant′eater, an echidna.

pore[1] (pōr, pôr), *v.i.,* **pored, por·ing. 1.** to meditate or ponder intently. **2.** to read or study with steady attention or application. [ME *poure(n)* < ?]

pore[2] (pōr, pôr), *n.* **1.** a minute opening or orifice, as in the skin or a leaf, for perspiration, absorption, etc. **2.** a minute hole or interstice, as in a rock. [ME *poore* < LL *por(us)* < Gk *póros* passage]

por·gy (pôr′gē), *n., pl.* (*esp. collectively*) **-gy,** (*esp. referring to two or more kinds or species*) **-gies. 1.** a sparid food fish, *Pagrus pagrus,* found in the Mediterranean and off the Atlantic coasts of Europe and America. **2.** any of several other sparid fishes, as the scup. [*porg(o),* var. of *pargo* (< Sp or Pg < L *pag(a)rus* kind of fish < Gk *págros*, var. of *phágros*) + -Y²]

Po·ri (pô′Rē), *n.* a seaport in W Finland, on the Gulf of Bothnia. 59,543 (est. 1965).

Po·rif·er·a (pō rif′ər ə, pô-, pə-), *n.* the phylum comprising the sponges. [< NL: lit., the porous ones = L *por(us)* PORE² + *-i-* -I- + *-fera*, neut. pl. of *-fer* -FEROUS]

po·rif·er·an (pō rif′ər ən, pô-, pə-), *n.* **1.** any animal of the phylum *Porifera*, comprising the sponges. —*adj.* **2.** belonging or pertaining to the *Porifera*.

po·rif·er·ous (pō rif′ər əs, pô-, pə-), *adj.* bearing or having pores.

po·rism (pōr′iz əm, pôr′-), *n.* *Math.* a term used by the ancient Greeks, probably for a proposition affirming the possibility of finding such conditions as will render a certain problem indeterminate, or capable of innumerable solutions. [ME *porysme* < LL *porisma* < Gk: corollary, akin to *porízein* to bring about, deduce]

pork (pōrk, pôrk), *n.* **1.** the flesh of hogs used as food. **2.** *U.S. Slang.* appropriations, appointments, etc., made by the government for political reasons. [ME *porc* < OF < L *porc(us)* hog, pig; c. FARROW¹]

pork′ bar′rel, *U.S. Slang.* a government appropriation, bill, or policy that supplies funds for local improvements designed to ingratiate legislators with their constituents.

pork·er (pōr′kər, pôr′-), *n.* a pig, esp. one being fattened for its meat.

pork·pie (pōrk′pī′, pôrk′-), *n.* a snap-brimmed hat with a round, flat crown.

pork·y (pōr′kē, pôr′-), *adj.*, **pork·i·er, pork·i·est.** **1.** of, pertaining to, or resembling pork. **2.** fat; obese.

por·no (pôr′nō), *Slang.* —*adj.* **1.** Also, **por·ny** (pôr′nē). pornographic. —*n.* **2.** pornography. **3.** a pornographic film. Also, **porn** (pôrn). [by shortening]

por·nog·ra·phy (pôr nog′rə fē), *n.* obscene literature, art, or photography, esp. that having little or no artistic merit. [< Gk *pornográph(os)* writing or writer about harlots (*porno-*, comb. form of *pórnē* harlot, + *-graphos* -GRAPH) + -Y³] —**por·nog′ra·pher,** *n.* —**por·no·graph·ic** (pôr′nə graf′ik), *adj.* —**por′no·graph′i·cal·ly,** *adv.*

po·ros·i·ty (pō ros′i tē, pô-, pə-), *n.*, *pl.* **-ties** for 2. **1.** the state or quality of being porous. **2.** the ratio, expressed as a percentage, of the volume of the pores or interstices of a substance to the total volume of its mass. [ME *porosytee* < ML *porōsitās*. See POROUS, -ITY]

po·rous (pōr′əs, pôr′-), *adj.* **1.** full of pores. **2.** permeable by water, air, etc. [late ME, var. of *porose* < ML *porōs(us)*. See PORE², -OUS] —**po′rous·ly,** *adv.*

por·phy·rin (pôr′fə rin), *n.* *Biochem.* any of a group of iron-free or magnesium-free pyrrole derivatives, occurring in all plant and animal protoplasm, formed by the decomposition of hematin and chlorophyll. [< Gk *porphýr(a)* purple + -IN²]

por·phy·rit·ic (pôr′fə rit′ik), *adj.* **1.** of, pertaining to, containing, or resembling porphyry. **2.** noting, pertaining to, or resembling the texture or structure characteristic of porphyry. [late ME *porphiritike* < ML *porphyrītic(us)* < Gk *porphyrītikós* of PORPHYRY; see -IC]

por·phy·roid (pôr′fə roid′), *n.* **1.** a rock resembling porphyry. **2.** a sedimentary rock that has been metamorphosed so as to leave some original crystals in a fine-textured, layered matrix.

por·phy·rop·sin (pôr′fə rop′sin), *n.* a purple pigment resembling rhodopsin, found in the retina of certain freshwater fish.

por·phy·ry (pôr′fə rē), *n.*, *pl.* **-ries.** **1.** a very hard rock having a dark, purplish-red groundmass containing small crystals of feldspar. **2.** any rock containing coarse crystals in a finer-grained groundmass. [ME *porfurie, porfirie* < ML **porphyri(um)*, alter. of LL *porphyrītēs* < Gk, short for *porphyrītēs líthos* porphyritic (i.e., purplish) stone = *pórphyr(os)* purple + *-ītēs*; see -ITE¹]

Por·phy·ry (pôr′fə rē), *n.* (*Malchus*) A.D. c233–c304, Greek philosopher. —**Por·phyr·e·an, Por·phyr·i·an** (pôr fēr′ē ən), *adj.*

por·poise (pôr′pəs), *n.*, *pl.* (*esp. collectively*) **-poise,** (*esp. referring to two or more kinds or species*) **-pois·es.** **1.** any of several small, gregarious cetaceans of the genus *Phocaena*, usually blackish above and paler beneath, and having a blunt, rounded snout, esp. the common porpoise, *P. phocaena*, of both the North Atlantic and Pacific. **2.** any of several other small cetaceans, as the common dolphin, *Delphinus delphis.* [ME *porpoys* < MF *porpois* < LL **porcus piscis* hog fish, for L *porcus marīnus* sea hog]

Porpoise, *Phocaena phocaena* (Length 4 to 6 ft.)

por·ridge (pôr′ij, por′-), *n.* *Chiefly Brit.* a food made of oatmeal or some other meal or cereal, boiled to a thick consistency in water or milk. [var. of POTTAGE]

por·rin·ger (pôr′in jər, por′-), *n.* a low dish or cup, often with a handle, from which soup, porridge, or the like is eaten. [var. of late ME *potinger*, nasalized form of *potager* < MF. See POTTAGE, -ER²]

port¹ (pōrt, pôrt), *n.* **1.** a city, town, or other place where ships load or unload. **2.** a place along a coast in which ships may take refuge from storms; harbor. **3.** Also called **port of entry.** *Law.* any place at which customs officials are stationed and through which incoming passengers and cargo are allowed to enter a country. [ME, OE < L *port(us)* harbor, haven] —**port′less,** *adj.* —**Syn. 1.** See **harbor.**

port² (pōrt, pôrt), *n.* **1.** the left-hand side of a vessel or aircraft, facing forward. Cf. **starboard** (def. 1). —*adj.* **2.** of, pertaining to, or located to the port. **3.** *Naut.* (of a tack) with the wind striking the port side of a vessel. —*v.t., v.i.* **4.** to turn or shift to the port, or left, side. [special use of PORT⁴]

port³ (pōrt, pôrt), *n.* any of a class of very sweet wines, mostly dark-red, originally from Portugal. [after *Oporto* (Pg *o pôrto* the port). See OPORTO]

port⁴ (pōrt, pôrt), *n.* **1.** *Naut.* any of various readily sealed apertures in the side of a vessel or in a deckhouse, used as windows or as entrances to the vessel. **2.** *Mach.* an aperture in the surface of a cylinder, for the passage of steam, air, water, etc. **3.** a small aperture through which a gun can be fired or a camera directed. **4.** *Chiefly Scot.* a gate or portal, as a town or fortress. [ME, OE < L *porta* gate]

port⁵ (pōrt, pôrt), *v.t.* **1.** *Mil.* to carry (a rifle or other weapon) with both hands in a slanting direction across the front of the body with the barrel or like part near the left shoulder. —*n.* **2.** *Mil.* the position of a rifle or other weapon when ported. **3.** the manner of bearing oneself; carriage. [< F *port(er)* < L *portāre* to carry]

Port., **1.** Portugal. **2.** Portuguese.

port·a·bil·i·ty (pōr′tə bil′i tē), *n.* **1.** the state or quality of being portable. **2.** a plan or system under which employees may accumulate pension rights under any employer who is a participant in the plan negotiated with their union.

port·a·ble (pōr′tə bəl, pôr′-), *adj.* **1.** capable of being carried or conveyed. **2.** easily carried or conveyed by hand. **3.** *Obs.* endurable. —*n.* **4.** something that is portable, esp. as distinguished from a nonportable counterpart. [late ME < LL *portābil(is)*]

por·tage (pōr′tij, pôr′-), *n.*, *v.*, **-taged, -tag·ing.** —*n.* **1.** the act of carrying; carriage. **2.** the carrying of boats, goods, etc., overland from one navigable water to another. **3.** the place or course over which this is done. —*v.i.* **4.** to make a portage. —*v.t.* **5.** to carry on a portage. [late ME < MF]

Por·tage (pōr′tij, pôr′-), *n.* a city in SW Michigan, near Kalamazoo. 33,590 (1970).

por·tal¹ (pōr′tᵊl, pôr′-), *n.* **1.** a door, gate, or entrance, esp. one of imposing appearance. **2.** Also called **por′tal frame′.** an iron or steel bent for bracing a framed structure, having curved braces between the vertical members and a horizontal member at the top. **3.** an entrance to a tunnel or mine. [ME *portale* < ML, neut. of *portālis* of a gate. See PORTAL²] —**por′taled, por′talled,** *adj.*

por·tal² (pōr′tᵊl, pôr′-), *Anat.* —*adj.* **1.** noting or pertaining to the transverse fissure of the liver. —*n.* **2.** See **portal vein.** [< ML *portāl(is)* of a gate]

por′tal-to-por′tal pay′ (pōr′tᵊl tə pōr′tᵊl, pôr′tᵊl tə-pôr′tᵊl), payment, as to a miner or factory worker, that includes compensation for time spent on the employer's premises in preparation, in travel from the entrance to the assigned work area and back, etc.

por′tal vein′, *Anat.* the large vein conveying blood to the liver from the veins of the stomach, intestine, spleen, and pancreas.

por·ta·men·to (pōr′tə men′tō, pôr′-; *It.* pôR′tä men′tô), *n.*, *pl.* **-ti** (-tē), **-tos.** *Music.* a passing or gliding from one pitch or tone to another with a smooth progression. [< It: fingering, lit., a bearing, carrying. See PORT⁵, -MENT]

Port′ Ar′thur, **1.** Chinese, **Lü·shun** (lo͞o′sho͞on′). Japanese, **Ryojunko, Ryojun.** a seaport in S Liaoning province, in Manchuria, in NE China, on the Yellow Sea. 1,650,000. **2.** a seaport in SE Texas, on Sabine Lake. 57,371 (1970). **3.** a city in S Ontario, in S Canada, on Lake Superior. 108,411.

por·ta·tive (pōr′tə tiv, pôr′-), *adj.* **1.** capable of being carried; portable. **2.** having or pertaining to the power or function of carrying. [ME *portatif* < MF]

Port-au-Prince (pōrt′ō prins′, pôrt′-; *Fr.* pôR tō PRANS′), *n.* a seaport in and the capital of Haiti, in the S part. 550,000.

port′ author′ity, a government commission that manages bridges, tunnels, airports, and other such facilities of a port or city.

Port′ Blair′ (blâr), a seaport in and the capital of the Andaman and Nicobar Islands, on S Andaman. 26,212.

Port′ Ches′ter, a city in SE New York, on Long Island Sound. 25,803 (1970).

port·cul·lis (pōrt kul′is, pôrt-), *n.* (esp. in medieval castles) a strong grating, as of iron, made to slide along vertical grooves at the sides of a gateway of a fortified place and let down to prevent passage. [ME *portecolys* < MF *porte coleice* = *porte* PORT⁴ + *coleice*, fem. of *coleis* flowing, sliding < VL **cōlāticius*; see COULEE, -ITIOUS]

Portcullis

Port du Sa·lut (pōrt′ də sə lo͞o′, pôrt′; *Fr.* pôR dʏ sa lʏ′), Port-Salut.

Porte (pōrt, pôrt), *n.* the former Ottoman court or government in Turkey. Official name, **Sublime Porte.** [short for *Sublime Porte* High Gate, F trans. of Turkish *Babi Ali*, palace gate at which justice was administered]

porte-co·chere (pōrt′kō shâr′, -kə-, pôrt′-), *n.* **1.** a covered carriage entrance leading into a courtyard. **2.** a porch at the door of a building for sheltering persons entering and leaving carriages. Also, **porte′-co·chère′.** [< F: gate for coaches]

Port′ Eliz′abeth, a seaport in the SE Cape of Good Hope province, in the S Republic of South Africa. 406,000

porte-mon·naie (pôRt mô ne′; *Eng.* pōrt′mun′ē, pôrt′-), *n.*, *pl.* **-mon·naies** (-mô ne′; *Eng.* -mun′ēz). *French.* a small purse or pocketbook. [lit., money-carrier]

por·tend (pōr tend′, pôr-), *v.t.* **1.** to indicate in advance; foreshadow or presage, as an omen does. **2.** *Obs.* to signify; mean. [late ME < L *portend(ere)* (to) point out, indicate, portend, var. of *prōtendere* to extend. See PRO-¹, TEND¹]

por·tent (pōr′tent, pôr′-), *n.* **1.** an omen, esp. of something momentous. **2.** ominous significance: *an occurrence of dire portent.* **3.** a prodigy or marvel. [< L *portent(um)* sign, token, n. use of neut. of *portentus*, ptp. of *portendere* to PORTEND] —**Syn. 1.** augury, warning. See **sign. 2.** import.

por·ten·tous (pōr ten′təs, pôr-), *adj.* **1.** of the nature of a portent; momentous. **2.** ominous; threatening. **3.** amazing; prodigious. **4.** overinflated; pretentious; pompous. [< L *portentōs(us)*] —**por·ten′tous·ly,** *adv.*

por·ter[1] (pōr′tər, pôr′-), *n.* **1.** a person employed to carry baggage, as at a railroad station or a hotel. **2.** a person who does cleaning and maintenance work in a building, store, etc. **3.** *U.S.* an attendant in a railroad car, esp. a Pullman car. [ME, var. of *portour* < MF *porteour* < LL *portātōr-* (s. of *portātor*). See PORT[5], -OR[2]]

por·ter[2] (pōr′tər, pôr′-), *n. Chiefly Brit.* a person who has charge of a door or gate; doorkeeper. [ME < AF < LL *portār(ius)* gatekeeper. See PORT[4], -ER[2]]

por·ter[3] (pōr′tər, pôr′-), *n.* a heavy, dark-brown ale made with malt browned by drying at a high temperature. [short for *porter's ale,* appar. orig. brewed for porters]

Por·ter (pōr′tər, pôr′-), *n.* **1. Cole,** 1893–1964, U.S. composer. **2. David,** 1780–1843, U.S. naval officer. **3.** his son, **David Dix·on** (dik′sən), 1813–91, Union naval officer in the Civil War. **4. Katherine Anne,** 1890–1980, U.S. writer. **5. William Sydney.** See **O. Henry.**

por·ter·age (pōr′tər ij, pôr′-), *n.* **1.** the work of a porter or carrier. **2.** the charge for such work. [late ME]

por·ter·ess (pōr′tər is, pôr′-), *n.* portress.

por·ter·house (pōr′tər hous′, pôr′-), *n., pl.* **-hous·es** (-hou′ziz). **1.** Also called **por′terhouse steak′.** *U.S.* a choice cut of beef from between the prime ribs and the sirloin. **2.** *Archaic.* a place selling porter, ale, etc.

port·fo·li·o (pōrt fō′lē ō′, pôrt-), *n., pl.* **-li·os.** **1.** a portable case for carrying loose papers, prints, etc. **2.** such a case for carrying documents of a government department. **3.** the office or post of a minister of state or member of a cabinet. Cf. **minister without portfolio.** **4.** the securities owned by a person or company for investment purposes. [< It *portafoglio* = *porta-,* s. of *portare* to carry (< L) + *foglio* leaf, sheet (< L *folium*)]

Port Gen·til (*Fr.* pôʀ zhäɴ tē′), a seaport in W Gabon. 30,000 (est. 1969).

Port′ Har′court (här′kərt, -kōrt, -kôrt), a seaport in S Nigeria. 72,000 (est. 1963).

port·hole (pōrt′hōl′, pôrt′-), *n.* **1.** any of various relatively small ports in a vessel, as for light or ventilation. **2.** an opening in a wall, door, etc., as one through which to shoot.

Port′ Hud′son, village in SE Louisiana, on Mississippi, N of Baton Rouge: siege during Civil War 1863.

Port′ Hu′ron, a port in SE Michigan, on the St. Clair River, at the S end of Lake Huron. 35,794 (1970).

por·ti·co (pōr′tə kō′, pôr′-), *n., pl.* **-coes, -cos.** a structure consisting of a roof supported by columns or piers, usually attached to a building as a porch. [< It < L *porticus* porch, portico. See PORT[4]] —**por′ti·coed′,** *adj.*

Portico

por·tiere (pōr tyâr′, pôr-, pōr′tē âr′, pôr′-), *n.* a curtain hung in a doorway, either to replace the door or for decoration. [< F *portière* < ML *portāria,* n. use of fem. of LL *portārius;* see PORTER[2]] —**por·tiered′,** *adj.*

por·tière (pōr tyâr′, pôr-, pōr′tē âr′, pôr′-; *Fr.* pôʀ-tyeʀ′), *n., pl.* **-tières** (-tyârz′, -tē ârz′; *Fr.* -tyeʀ′). portiere.

por·tion (pōr′shən, pôr′-), *n.* **1.** a part of any whole. **2.** the part of a whole allotted to or belonging to a person or group; share. **3.** an amount of food served for one person; serving; helping. **4.** the part of an estate that goes to an heir or a next of kin. **5.** the money, goods, or estate that a woman brings to her husband at marriage; dowry. **6.** that which is allotted to a person by God or fate. —*v.t.* **7.** to divide into or distribute in portions or shares. **8.** to provide with or as with a portion. [ME *porcion* < OF < L *portiōn-* (s. of *portiō*) share, part, akin to *pars* PART] —**Syn. 1.** section, segment. See **part. 2.** allotment, quota, lot.

Port′ Jack′son, an inlet of the Pacific in SE Australia: the harbor of Sydney.

Port·land (pōrt′lənd, pôrt′-), *n.* **1.** a seaport in NW Oregon, at the confluence of the Willamette and Columbia rivers. 380,555 (1970). **2.** a seaport in SW Maine, on Casco Bay. 65,116 (1970).

Port′land cement′, a hydraulic cement usually made by burning a mixture of limestone and clay. Also, **port′land cement′.** [after the Isle of *Portland,* Dorsetshire, England]

Port′ Lou′is (lo͞o′is, lo͞o′ē), a seaport in and the capital of Mauritius, in the Indian Ocean. 136,000.

port·ly (pōrt′lē, pôrt′-), *adj.,* **-li·er, -li·est.** **1.** rather heavy or fat; stout. **2.** stately, dignified, or imposing. [PORT[5] (n.) + -LY] —**port′li·ness,** *n.*

port·man·teau (pōrt man′tō, pôrt-; pōrt′man tō′, pôrt′-), *n., pl.* **-teaus, -teaux** (-tōz, -tō; -tōz′, -tō′). *Chiefly Brit.* a case or bag to carry clothing in while traveling, esp. a leather trunk or suitcase that opens into two halves. [< F *portemanteau:* lit., cloak carrier. See PORT[5], MANTLE]

portman′teau word′, blend (def. 8).

Port′ Mores′by (mōrz′bē, môrz′-), a seaport in and the capital of Papua New Guinea: important Allied base in World War II. 76,507.

Pôr·to (pôʀ′to͝o), *n.* Portuguese name of **Oporto.**

Pôr·to A·le·gre (pôʀ′to͝o ä le′gʀə), a seaport in S Brazil. 625,957 (1960).

Pôr·to A·mé·lia (*Port.* pôʀ′to͝o ə me′lyə), a seaport in NE Mozambique. 52,148 (est. 1955).

Por·to·bel·lo (pōr′tō bel′ō, pôr′-), *n.* a small seaport on the Caribbean coast of Panama, NE of Colón: harbor discovered and named by Columbus 1502.

port′ of call′, a port visited briefly by a ship, usually to take on or discharge passengers and cargo or to undergo repairs.

port′ of en′try, port[1] (def. 3).

Port-of-Spain (pōrt′əv spān′, pôrt′-), *n.* a seaport on NW Trinidad, in the SE West Indies: the capital of Trinidad and Tobago. 67,867.

Por·to No·vo (pōr′tō nō′vō, pôr′-). a seaport in and the capital of Benin. 120,000.

Por·to Ri·co (pōr′tə rē′kō, pôr′-), former official name (until 1932) of **Puerto Rico.** —**Por′to Ri′can.**

Port′ Phil′lip Bay′, a bay in SE Australia: the harbor of Melbourne. 31 mi. long; 25 mi. wide.

por·trait (pōr′trit, -trāt, pôr′-), *n.* **1.** a likeness of a person, esp. of the face, as a painting, sculpture, or photograph. **2.** a verbal picture or description, usually of a person. [< MF: a drawing, image, etc., n. use of ptp. of *portraire* to PORTRAY]

por·trait·ist (pōr′tri tist, -trā-, pôr′-), *n.* a person who makes portraits.

por·trai·ture (pōr′tri chər, pôr′-), *n.* **1.** the art of portraying. **2.** a pictorial representation; portrait. **3.** a verbal picture. [ME < MF]

por·tray (pōr trā′, pôr-), *v.t.* **1.** to represent by a painting, sculpture, or the like. **2.** to represent (a person) dramatically, as on the stage. **3.** to depict in words; describe graphically. [ME *portraye* < MF *portraire* < LL *prōtrahere* to depict, L: to draw forth = *pro-* PRO-[1] + *trahere* to draw] —**por·tray′a·ble,** *adj.* —**por·tray′er,** *n.* —**Syn. 1, 3.** picture, delineate, limn. See **depict.**

por·tray·al (pōr trā′əl, pôr-), *n.* **1.** the act of portraying. **2.** a representation; portrait.

por·tress (pōr′tris, pôr′-), *n.* a female porter or doorkeeper. Also, **porteress.** [ME *porteresse*]

Port′ Roy′al, **1.** a village in S South Carolina, on Port Royal island: colonized by French Huguenots 1562. **2.** a historic town on SE Jamaica at the entrance to Kingston harbor: a former capital of Jamaica. **3.** former name of **Annapolis Royal.**

Port′ Sa·id′ (sä ēd′), a seaport in the NE Arab Republic of Egypt at the Mediterranean end of the Suez Canal. 256,100 (est. 1962). Also, **Port′ Sa·ïd′.**

Port-Sa·lut (pōr′sə lo͞o′, pôr′-; *Fr.* pôʀ sa lʏ′), *n.* a creamy, yellow, whole-milk cheese, esp. that made at the Trappist monastery of Port du Salut near the town of Laval, France. Also called **Port du Salut.**

Ports·mouth (pōrts′məth, pôrts′-), *n.* **1.** a seaport in S Hampshire, in S England, on the English Channel: chief British naval station. 215,198 (1961). **2.** a seaport in SE Virginia: navy yard. 110,963 (1970). **3.** a city in S Ohio, on the Ohio River. 27,633 (1970). **4.** a seaport in SE New Hampshire: naval base; Russian-Japanese peace treaty 1905. 25,717 (1970).

Port′ Sudan′, a seaport in the NE Sudan, on the Red Sea. 57,000 (est. 1964).

Por·tu·gal (pōr′chə gəl, pôr′-; *Port.* pôʀ′to͝o gäl′), *n.* a republic in SW Europe, on the Iberian Peninsula, W of Spain. (including the Azores and the Madeira Islands) 9,448,800; 35,414 sq. mi. *Cap.:* Lisbon.

Por·tu·guese (pōr′chə gēz′, -gēs′, pôr′-; pōr′chə gēz′, -gēs′, pôr′-), *adj., n., pl.* **-guese.** —*adj.* **1.** of, pertaining to, or characteristic of Portugal, its inhabitants, or their language. —*n.* **2.** a native or inhabitant of Portugal. **3.** a Romance language of Portugal and Brazil. *Abbr.:* Pg [< Pg *português,* Sp *portugués,* etc.]

Por′tuguese East′ Af′rica, former name of **Mozambique.**

Por′tuguese Guin′ea, a former Portuguese overseas province on the W coast of Africa between Guinea and Senegal: granted independence 1974. See **Guinea-Bissau.**

Por′tuguese In′dia, a former Portuguese overseas territory on the W coast of India, consisting of the districts of Gôa, Daman, and Diu: annexed by India 1961. *Cap.:* Gôa.

Por′tuguese man-of-war′, any of several large, oceanic hydrozoans of the genus *Physalia,* having a large, bladderlike structure by which they are buoyed up and from which are suspended numerous processes capable of severely injuring humans.

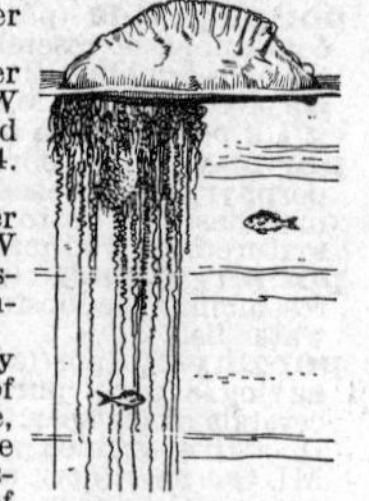

Portuguese man-of-war, *Physalia arethusa* (Float length about 8 in.; tentacles 40 to 60 ft.)

Por′tuguese Ti′mor, Timor (def. 3).

Por′tuguese West′ Af′rica, former name of **Angola.**

por·tu·lac·a (pōr′chə lak′ə, pôr′-), *n.* any plant of the genus *Portulaca,* comprising the purslanes. [< NL, genus name, L: PURSLANE]

por·tu·la·ca·ceous (pōr′chə lə kā′shəs, pôr′-), *adj.* belonging to the *Portulacaceae,* or purslane family of plants.

pos., **1.** position. **2.** positive. **3.** possession. **4.** possessive.

po·sa·da (pô sä′thä), *n., pl.* **-das** (-thäs). *Spanish.* an inn. [lit., halting place]

pose[1] (pōz), *v.,* **posed, pos·ing,** *n.* —*v.i.* **1.** to assume or hold a physical attitude, as for an artistic purpose. **2.** to make a pretense of being what one is not: *to pose as a friend.* **3.** to behave in an affected manner. —*v.t.* **4.** to cause to assume a fixed position in order to be depicted. **5.** to state or propound: *to pose a problem.* —*n.* **6.** a fixed position assumed in posing. **7.** an affected or false appearance or manner. [ME < MF *pose(r)* < LL *pausāre* to lay down (a sense due to confusion with L *pōnere* to place, put), L: to halt, stop < *pausa* a PAUSE] —**pos′ing·ly,** *adv.* —**Syn. 1.** sit, model. **6.** See **position.**

pose[2] (pōz), *v.t.,* **posed, pos·ing.** to embarrass or baffle, as by a difficult question or problem. [aph. var. of obs. *appose,* var. of OPPOSE, used in sense of L *appōnere* to put to]

Po·sei·don (pō sīd′ən, pə-), *n.* the ancient Greek god of the sea, identified by the Romans with Neptune.

Po·sen (pō′zən), *n.* a city in W Poland, on the Warta River. 455,500 (est. 1968). Polish, **Poznań.**

Poseidon

pos·er[1] (pō′zər), *n.* a person who poses. [POSE[1] + -ER[1]]

pos·er[2] (pō′zər), *n.* a question or problem that is puzzling or confusing. [POSE[2] + -ER[1]]

po·seur (pō zûr′; *Fr.* pô zœʀ′), *n., pl.* **-seurs** (-zûrz′; *Fr.* -zœʀ′). a person who attempts to impress others by assuming or affecting a manner, degree of elegance, etc. [< F; see POSE[1], -OR[2]]

posh (posh), *adj. Informal.* sumptuously comfortable or elegant; luxurious. [?]

pos·it (poz′it), *v.t.* **1.** to place, put, or set. **2.** to lay down or assume as a fact or principle; affirm; postulate. —*n.* **3.** something that is posited; assumption; postulate. [< L *posit(us)*, ptp. of *pōnere* to place, put]

po·si·tion (pə zish′ən), *n.* **1.** the location or place of a person or thing at a given moment. **2.** an arrangement or placement of one or more persons or things, or the parts thereof: *the position of two dancers; a sitting position.* **3.** a proper or customary location or arrangement: *out of position.* **4.** one's situation with regard to the advantage or disadvantage likely to result: *to be in an embarrassing position.* **5.** one's intentions, stated attitude, etc., on a matter in question. **6.** one's social standing. **7.** high social standing: *a man of position.* **8.** a post of employment; job. **9.** the act of positing. **10.** something that is posited. **11.** *Music.* **a.** the arrangement of tones in a chord, esp. with regard to the location of the root tone in a triad or to the distance of the tones from each other. **b.** any of the places along the neck of a stringed instrument where the hand is placed to finger a particular range of notes. **c.** any of the places to which the slide of a trombone is shifted to produce changes in pitch. **12.** *Classical Pros.* the situation of a short vowel before two or more consonants or their equivalent, making the syllable metrically long. —*v.t.* **13.** to put in a particular or appropriate position; place. **14.** to determine the position of; locate. [ME *posicioun* a positing < L *positiōn-* (s. of *positiō*) a placing, etc.] —**po·si′tion·al,** *adj.* —**Syn. 1.** station, place, locality, spot. **2.** disposition, array. POSITION, POSTURE, ATTITUDE, POSE refer to an arrangement or disposal of the body or its parts. POSITION is the general word for the arrangement of the body: *in a reclining position.* POSTURE is usually an assumed arrangement of the body, esp. when standing: *a relaxed posture.* ATTITUDE is often a posture assumed for imitative effect or the like, but may be one adopted for a purpose: *an attitude of prayer.* A POSE is an attitude assumed, in most cases, for artistic effect: *an attractive pose.* **6.** rank, place. **8.** POSITION, JOB, refer to a post of employment. POSITION is any employment, though usually above manual labor: *a position as clerk.* JOB is colloquial for POSITION, and applies to any work from lowest to highest in an organization: *a job as manager.*

posi′tion pa′per, a complete, usually published statement, as by an election candidate or a government agency, that sets forth the decisive stand taken on a specific current issue or issues.

pos·i·tive (poz′i tiv), *adj.* **1.** explicit; definite. **2.** determined by enactment or convention; arbitrarily laid down: *positive law.* **3.** admitting of no question: *positive proof.* **4.** confident in an opinion or assertion. **5.** without relation to or comparison with other things; not relative or comparative; absolute. **6.** *Informal.* downright; out-and-out: *She's a positive idiot.* **7.** possessing an actual force, being, existence, etc. **8.** *Philos.* **a.** constructive and sure, rather than skeptical. **b.** concerned with or based on matters of experience: *positive philosophy.* **9.** emphasizing what is laudable, hopeful, or to the good. **10.** consisting in or characterized by the presence or possession of distinguishing or marked qualities or features (opposed to *negative*): *Light is positive, darkness negative.* **11.** noting the presence of such qualities, as a term. **12.** measured or proceeding in a direction assumed as beneficial, progressive, or auspicious. **13.** (of government) assuming control or regulation of activities beyond those involved merely with the maintenance of law and order. **14.** *Elect.* indicating a point in a circuit that has a higher potential than that of another point, the current flowing from the point of higher potential to the point of lower potential. **15.** of, pertaining to, or noting the north pole of a magnet. **16.** *Chem.* (of an element or group) tending to lose electrons and become positively charged; basic. **17.** *Photog.* noting a print or transparency showing the brightness values as they are in the subject. **18.** *Gram.* being, noting, or pertaining to the initial degree of the comparison of adjectives and adverbs, as the positive form *good.* Cf. **comparative** (def. 4), **superlative** (def. 3). **19.** *Math.* noting a quantity greater than zero. **20.** *Biol.* oriented or moving toward the focus of excitation: *a positive tropism.* **21.** *Pathol.* (of a test) revealing the presence of the pathological condition tested for. **22.** *Biochem.* See **Rh factor.** —*n.* **23.** something positive. **24.** a positive quantity or symbol. **25.** *Photog.* a positive image, as on a print or transparency. **26.** *Gram.* **a.** the positive degree. **b.** a form in the positive degree, as *good, smooth.* [< L *positīv(us)*; r. ME *positif* < MF] —**pos′i·tive·ness,** **pos′i·tiv′i·ty,** *n.* —**Syn. 1.** unequivocal, clear, precise, sure.

pos·i·tive·ly (poz′i tiv lē; *esp. for 3* poz′i tiv′lē), *adv.* **1.** in a positive way or manner. **2.** decidedly; unquestionably; definitely. —*interj.* **3.** (used to express strong affirmation) yes, indeed!

pos′itive ray′, *Physics.* See **canal ray.**

pos·i·tiv·ism (poz′i tə viz′əm), *n.* **1.** the state or quality of being positive; definiteness; assurance. **2.** a philosophical system concerned with positive facts and phenomena and excluding speculation upon ultimate causes or origins. —**pos′i·tiv·ist,** *adj., n.* —**pos′i·tiv·is′tic,** *adj.* —**pos′i·tiv·is′ti·cal·ly,** *adv.*

pos·i·tron (poz′i tron′), *n. Physics.* an elementary particle having the same mass and spin as an electron but having a positive charge equal in magnitude to that of the electron; the antiparticle of the electron. [POSI(TIVE + ELEC)TRON]

pos·i·tro·ni·um (poz′i trō′nē əm), *n. Physics.* a short-lived atomic system consisting of a positron and an electron bound together.

poss., **1.** possession. **2.** possessive. **3.** possible. **4.** possibly.

pos·se (pos′ē), *n.* **1.** See **posse comitatus.** **2.** a body or force armed with legal authority. [< ML *posse* power, force, n. use of L inf.: to be able, have power = *pot-* (see POTENT) + *-se* inf. suffix]

pos′se co·mi·ta′tus (kom′i tä′təs, -tā′-), the body of men that a peace officer of a county is empowered to call to assist him in preserving the peace. [< ML: posse of the county]

pos·sess (pə zes′), *v.t.* **1.** to have as one's property; own. **2.** to have as a faculty, quality, or attribute. **3.** to have knowledge of: *to possess a language.* **4.** to make (someone) owner, holder, or master, as of property, information, etc.: *He possessed them of the facts.* **5.** to keep or maintain (oneself, one's mind, etc.) in a certain state, as of peace or patience. **6.** (of a spirit, esp. an evil one) to occupy, dominate, or control (a person) from within. **7.** (of a feeling, idea, etc.) to dominate or actuate in the manner of such a spirit. **8.** to cause to be dominated or influenced, as by an idea, feeling, etc. **9.** (of a man) to succeed in having sexual relations with. **10.** *Archaic.* to seize or take. **11.** *Archaic.* to gain or win. **12.** *Obs.* to occupy or hold. [ME *possesse(n)* < MF *possess(i)er*, back formation from *possession* POSSESSION] —**pos·ses′sor,** *n.* —**Syn. 1.** See **have.**

pos·sessed (pə zest′), *adj.* **1.** spurred or moved by a strong feeling, madness, or a supernatural power (often fol. by *by, of,* or *with*). **2.** self-possessed; poised. **3. possessed of,** having; possessing: *He is possessed of intelligence and ambition.* —**pos·sess·ed·ly** (pə zes′id lē, -zest′lē), *adv.*

pos·ses·sion (pə zesh′ən), *n.* **1.** the act or fact of possessing. **2.** the state of being possessed. **3.** ownership. **4.** *Law.* actual holding or occupancy, either with or without rights of ownership. **5.** a thing possessed or owned. **6.** a territorial dominion of a state or nation. **7.** *Sports.* **a.** physical control of the ball or puck by a player or team. **b.** the right of a team to put the ball into play. **8.** control, as over oneself. **9.** domination, actuation, or obsession by a feeling, idea, etc. **10.** the feeling or idea itself. [ME < L *possessiōn-* (s. of *possessiō*) a having or taking possession < (1) *possessus*, ptp. of *possidēre* to have and hold (opposed to *dominārī* to own absolutely); (2) *possessus*, ptp. of *possīdere* to take possession of; see -ION] —**Syn. 1, 3.** See **custody.**

pos·ses·sive (pə zes′iv), *adj.* **1.** of or pertaining to possession or ownership. **2.** desirous of possessing, esp. excessively and characteristically so. **3.** jealously opposed to the personal independence of or to any influence other than one's own upon a child, spouse, etc. **4.** *Gram.* indicating possession, ownership, origin, etc.: *a possessive adjective; a possessive pronoun; the possessive case.* —*n. Gram.* **5.** the possessive case, form, word, or construction. **6.** a form in the possessive case. [< L *possessīv(us)*] —**pos·ses′sive·ly,** *adv.* —**pos·ses′sive·ness,** *n.*

pos·ses·so·ry (pə zes′ə rē), *adj.* **1.** of or pertaining to a possessor or to possession. **2.** arising from possession: *a possessory interest.* **3.** having possession. [< LL *possessōri(us)* = L *possess(us)* (ptp. of *possidēre* to POSSESS) + *-ōrius* -ORY[1]]

pos·set (pos′it), *n.* a drink made of hot milk curdled with ale, wine, or the like, often sweetened and spiced. [late ME *poshote, possot,* ? OE *poswǣt drink good for cold = *pos* cold in the head + *wǣt* drink]

pos·si·bil·i·ty (pos′ə bil′i tē), *n., pl.* **-ties** for 2. **1.** the state or fact of being possible. **2.** something that is possible. [ME *possibilite* < LL *possibilitās*]

pos·si·ble (pos′ə bəl), *adj.* **1.** that may or can exist, happen, be done or be used, etc. **2.** that may be true or may be the case: *It is possible that he went.* [ME < L *possibil(is)* that may be done = *poss(e)* (to) be able (see POSSE) + *-ibilis* -IBLE] —**Syn. 1.** POSSIBLE, FEASIBLE, PRACTICABLE refer to that which may come about or take place without prevention by serious obstacles. That which is POSSIBLE is naturally able or even likely to happen, other circumstances being equal: *Discovery of a new source of plutonium is possible.* FEASIBLE refers to the ease with which something can be done and implies a high degree of desirability: *This plan is the most feasible.* PRACTICABLE applies to that which can be done with the means at hand and with conditions as they are: *We ascended the slope as far as was practicable.*

pos·si·bly (pos′ə blē), *adv.* **1.** perhaps; maybe. **2.** by any possibility; conceivably: *Could you possibly go?* [ME]

POSSLQ (pos′əl kyōō′), *n.* a person of the opposite sex who shares another's living quarters but is not related by blood, marriage, or adoption. [*p(artner of the) o(pposite) s(ex) s(haring) l(iving) q(uarters)*]

pos·sum (pos′əm), *n.* **1.** *U.S. Informal.* an opossum. **2.** *Australian.* any of various phalangers, esp. of the genus *Trichosurus.* **3. play possum,** *U.S. Informal.* to feign sleep or death. [short for OPOSSUM]

post[1] (pōst), *n.* **1.** a strong piece of timber, metal, or the like, set upright as a support, a point of attachment, a place for displaying notices, etc. **2.** *Furniture.* one of the principal uprights of a piece of furniture. **3.** *Horse Racing.* a pole on a race track indicating the point where a race begins or ends: *the starting post.* —*v.t.* **4.** to affix (a notice, bulletin, etc.) to a post, wall, or the like. **5.** to bring to public notice by or as by a placard: *to post a reward.* **6.** to denounce by a public notice or declaration. **7.** to enter the name of in a published list. [ME, OE < L *post(is)* a post, doorpost, whence also D, LG *post*, G *Pfosten*] —**Syn. 1.** column, pillar, pile, pole. **5.** announce, advertise, publicize.

post[2] (pōst), *n.* **1.** a position of duty, employment, or trust to which a person is assigned or appointed; assignment: *a diplomatic post.* **2.** the station or rounds of a person on duty. **3.** an installation at which military personnel are stationed or placed. **4.** *U.S.* a local unit of a veterans' organization. **5.** See **trading post** (def. 1). **6.** a place in the stock exchange where a particular stock is traded. **7.** (in the British military services) either of two bugle calls (**first post** and **last post**) giving notice of the time to retire for the night. —*v.t.* **8.** to place or station at a post. **9.** *Army, Navy.* (formerly) to appoint to a post of command. [< F *poste* < It *posto* < L *positum*, neut. of *positus*, ptp. of *pōnere* to place, put. See POSITION] —**Syn. 1.** See **appointment.**

post[3] (pōst), *n.* **1.** *Chiefly Brit.* **a.** a single dispatch or delivery of mail. **b.** the mail itself. **c.** an established mail system or service, esp. under government authority. **2.** *Brit.* **a.** See **post office** (def. 1). **b.** mailbox (def. 1). **3.** (formerly) one of a series of stations along a route, for furnishing relays of men and horses for carrying mail, currency, etc. **4.** (formerly) a person who travels express, esp. over a fixed route, carrying mail, currency, etc. **5.** any of various sizes of printing and writing papers and of books. —*v.t.* **6.** *Chiefly Brit.* to place in a mailbox for transmission; mail. **7.** *Bookkeep-*

ing. **a.** to transfer (an entry or item). **b.** to enter (an item) in due place and form. **c.** to make all the requisite entries in. **8.** to supply with up-to-date information; inform: *Keep me posted on his activities.* —*v.i.* **9.** *Manège.* (of a horseman) to rise from and descend to the saddle in accordance with the rhythm of a horse at a trot. **10.** to travel with speed. —*adv.* **11.** with speed or haste; posthaste. **12.** by post or courier. **13.** with post horses. [< F *poste* < It *posta* < L *posita,* fem. of *positus,* ptp., placed, put. See POST[2]]

Post (pōst), *n.* **Emily,** nee **Price,** 1873?–1960, U.S. writer on social etiquette.

post-, an element, meaning "behind," "after," "later," "subsequent to," "posterior to," occurring originally in loan words from Latin (*postscript*), but now used freely in the formation of compound words (*postfix; postgraduate; postorbital*). [< L, comb. form repr. *post* (adv. and prep.)]

post·age (pō′stij), *n.* the charge for the conveyance of a letter or other matter sent by mail, usually prepaid by means of a stamp or stamps.

post′age me′ter, an office machine that imprints postage of desired value and a dated postmark on an envelope, the postage having been prepaid at the post office by having the machine set for the lump sum purchased.

post′age stamp′, an official stamp used as evidence of prepayment of a designated postage or as an indication of postage due.

post·al (pōs′tᵊl), *adj.* of or pertaining to the post office or mail service: *postal delivery; postal employees.*

post′al card′, **1.** a card sold by the post office with a stamp already printed on it, usually mailable at a rate lower than that for letters in envelopes. **2.** See **post card** (def. 1).

post′al deliv′ery zone′, zone (def. 9).

post′al sav′ings bank′, any of the savings banks operated by the U.S. Post Office Department through local post offices and limited to small accounts: service established 1910 and terminated 1966.

post-ax·i·al (pōst ak′sē əl), *adj.* pertaining to or situated behind the axis of the body, esp. the posterior side of the axis of a limb.

post-bel·lum (pōst′bel′əm), *adj.* occurring after a war, esp. after the American Civil War: *post-bellum reforms.* Also, **post′bel′lum.** [< L *post bellum:* after the war]

post·box (pōst′boks′), *n.* *Brit.* mailbox (def. 1).

post·boy (pōst′boi′), *n.* **1.** a boy or man who rides post or carries mail. **2.** a postilion.

post′ card′, **1.** Also called **picture post card, postal card.** a small, commercially printed card, usually having a picture on one side and space for a short message: requires the affixing of a postage stamp for mailing. **2.** See **postal card** (def. 1). Also, **post′card′.**

post′ chaise′, (formerly) a four-wheeled coach for rapid transportation of passengers and mail.

post·date (pōst dāt′), *v.t.,* **-dat·ed, -dat·ing.** **1.** to give a date later than the true date to: *to postdate the termination of one's employment.* **2.** to date (a check, invoice, etc.) with a date later than the current date. **3.** to follow in time.

post·di·lu·vi·an (pōst′di lo͞o′vē ən), *adj.* **1.** existing or occurring after the Flood. —*n.* **2.** a person who lived after the Flood.

post·doc·tor·al (pōst dok′tər əl), *adj.* of or pertaining to study or professional work undertaken after the receipt of a doctorate: *postdoctoral courses.*

post·er (pō′stər), *n.* a placard or bill posted or intended for posting in a public place, as for advertising. [POST[1] (v.) + -ER[1]]

poste res·tante (pōst′ re stänt′ *or, esp. Brit.,* res′tänt; *Fr.* pôst RES TÄNT′), **1.** a direction written on mail intended for general delivery. **2.** *Chiefly Brit.* See **general delivery** (def. 2). [< F: lit., standing post]

pos·te·ri·or (po stēr′ē ər), *adj.* **1.** situated behind or at the rear of; hinder (opposed to *anterior*). **2.** coming after in order, as in a series. **3.** coming after in time; later; subsequent (sometimes fol. by *to*). **4.** pertaining to the caudal end of the body. **5.** *Anat.* of or pertaining to the dorsal side of man. **6.** *Bot.* (of an axillary flower) on the side next to the main axis. —*n.* **7.** Often, **posteriors.** the hinder parts of the body; buttocks. [< L, comp. of *posterus* coming after < *post* after] —**pos·te·ri·or·i·ty** (po stēr′ē ôr′i tē, -or′-), *n.* —**pos·te′ri·or·ly,** *adv.* —**Syn. 1.** See **back**[1].

pos·ter·i·ty (po ster′i tē), *n.* **1.** succeeding or future generations collectively. **2.** all descendants of one person. [ME *posterite* < L *posteritās.* See POSTERIOR, -ITY]

pos·tern (pō′stərn, pos′tərn), *n.* **1.** a back door or gate. **2.** a private entrance or any entrance other than the main one. —*adj.* **3.** of, pertaining to, or resembling a postern. [ME *posterne* < OF, var. of *posterle* < LL *posterula,* dim. of *postera* back door, n. use of fem. of *posterus* coming behind. See POSTERIOR, -ULE]

post′ exchange′, *U.S. Army.* a retail store on an army installation that sells goods and services to the servicemen and their dependents and certain authorized civilian personnel. *Abbr.:* PX

post·ex·il·i·an (pōst′eg zil′ē ən, -zil′yən, -ek sil′-), *adj.* *Judaism.* being or occurring subsequent to the Exile. Also, **post′ex·il′ic.**

post·fem·i·nist (pōst fem′ə nist), *adj.* **1.** pertaining to the period after the feminist movement of the 1970's. **2.** ideologically based on this movement: *postfeminist attitudes about motherhood.* —*n.* **3.** a supporter of a postfeminist ideology. —**post·fem′i·nism,** *n.*

post·fix (*v.* pōst fiks′; *n.* pōst′fiks′), *v.t.* **1.** to affix at the end of something; append; suffix. —*n.* **2.** something postfixed. **3.** a suffix added after closure of a set of suffixes. [modeled on *prefix*] —**post·fix′al, post·fix′i·al,** *adj.*

post-free (pōst′frē′), *adj.* **1.** that may be sent free of postal charges, as government mail. **2.** *Brit.* postpaid. —*adv.* **3.** *Brit.* postpaid.

post·gla·cial (pōst glā′shəl), *adj.* after a given glacial epoch, esp. the Pleistocene.

post·grad·u·ate (pōst graj′o͞o it, -āt′), *adj.* **1.** of, pertaining to, characteristic of, or consisting of advanced work done after graduation, as at a university: *a postgraduate seminar.* —*n.* **2.** a student doing postgraduate work.

post·haste (pōst′hāst′), *adv.* **1.** with the greatest possible speed or promptness. —*n.* **2.** *Archaic.* great haste.

post hoc, er·go prop·ter hoc (pōst hōk′ ER′gō PRŌP′-TER hōk′; *Eng.* pōst hok′ ûr′gō prop′tər hok′), *Latin.* after this, therefore because of it: a formula designating the fallacy of assuming something has caused an event merely because it preceded it.

post′ horse′, (formerly) a horse kept for the use of persons riding post or for hire by travelers.

post·hu·mous (pos′chə məs, -cho͞o-), *adj.* **1.** published after the death of the author: *a posthumous novel.* **2.** born after the death of the father. **3.** arising, occurring, or continuing after a person's death. [< L *posthumus,* erroneously (by assoc. with *humus* earth, ground, as if referring to burial) for *postumus* last, superl. of *posterus.* See POSTERIOR] —**post′hu·mous·ly,** *adv.*

post·hyp·not·ic (pōst′hip not′ik), *adj.* **1.** of or pertaining to the period after hypnosis. **2.** (of a suggestion) made during hypnosis so as to be effective after awakening. —**post′-hyp·not′i·cal·ly,** *adv.*

pos·tiche (pô stēsh′, po-), *adj.* **1.** superadded, esp. inappropriately, as a sculptural or architectural ornament. **2.** artificial, counterfeit, or false. —*n.* **3.** an imitation or substitute. **4.** pretense; sham. **5.** a false hairpiece. [< F < It (*ap*)*posticcio* < LL *appositīcius* put on, factitious, false. See APPOSITE, -ITIOUS]

pos·til·ion (pō stil′yən, po-), *n.* a person who rides the horse on the left of the leading pair when four or more horses are used to draw a carriage, or one who rides the horse on the left when only one pair is used. Also, *esp. Brit.,* **pos·til′lion.** [earlier *postillon* < MF < It *postiglione* < *posta* POST[3]]

Post-Im·pres·sion·ism (pōst′im presh′ə niz′əm), *n.* a varied development of Impressionism by a number of painters, chiefly between 1880 and 1900, stressing formal structure, as with Cézanne and Seurat, or the expressive possibilities of form and color, as with Van Gogh and Gauguin. Also, **post′im·pres′sion·ism.** —**Post′-Im·pres′sion·ist, post′-im·pres′sion·ist,** *n.* —**Post′-Im·pres′sion·is′tic, post′-im·pres′sion·is′tic,** *adj.*

post·lim·i·ny (pōst lim′ə nē), *n.* *Internat. Law.* the right by which persons and things taken in war are restored to their former status when coming again under the power of the nation to which they belonged. [< L *postlīmini(um),* lit., the state of being behind one's threshold, i.e., at home. See POST-, LIMINAL, -Y[3]]

post·lit·er·ate (pōst lit′ər it), *adj.* **1.** characterized by a rejection or neglect of traditional literary studies, interests, or values. **2.** concerned with means of communication, art forms, etc., that do not depend on printed matter or whose primary appeal is not literary or verbal.

post·lude (pōst′lo͞od), *n.* *Music.* **1.** a concluding piece or movement. **2.** a voluntary at the end of a church service. [POST- + L *lūd*(*us*) game, modeled on *prelude*]

post·man (pōst′mən), *n., pl.* **-men.** a mailman.

post·mark (pōst′märk′), *n.* **1.** an official mark stamped on mail, serving as a cancellation of the postage stamp and indicating the place and date of sending or receipt. —*v.t.* **2.** to stamp with a postmark.

post·mas·ter (pōst′mas′tər, -mä′stər), *n.* **1.** the official in charge of a post office. **2.** (formerly) the master of a station that furnishes post horses to travelers. —**post′mas′ter·ship′,** *n.*

post′master gen′eral, *pl.* **postmasters general.** the executive head of the postal system of a country.

post·me·rid·i·an (pōst′mə rid′ē ən), *adj.* of or pertaining to the afternoon.

post me·rid·i·em (pōst′ mə rid′ē əm). See **p.m.** [< L: after noon]

post·mil·len·ni·al (pōst′mi len′ē əl), *adj.* of or pertaining to the period following the millennium.

post·mil·len·ni·al·ism (pōst′mi len′ē ə liz′əm), *n.* the doctrine or belief that the second coming of Christ will follow the millennium. —**post′mil·len′ni·al·ist,** *n.*

post·mis·tress (pōst′mis′tris), *n.* a female official in charge of a post office.

post·mod·ern (pōst mod′ərn), *adj.* of or pertaining to architecture that consciously uses complex forms and allusions to historic styles.

post-mor·tem (pōst môr′təm), *adj.* **1.** of, pertaining to, or occurring in the time following death. **2.** of or pertaining to examination of the body after death. **3.** occurring after the end of something; after the event. —*n.* **4.** a post-mortem examination. **5.** an evaluation or discussion occurring after the end or fact of something. Also, **post·mor′tem.** [< L: after death]

post-mor′tem examina′tion, *Med.* an autopsy.

post·na·sal (pōst′nā′zəl), *adj.* located or occurring behind the nose or in the nasopharynx, as a flow of mucus.

post′nasal drip′, a trickling of mucus onto the pharyngeal surface from the posterior portion of the nasal cavity, usually caused by a cold or allergy.

post·na·tal (pōst nāt′ᵊl), *adj.* subsequent to childbirth: *postnatal infection.* —**post·na′tal·ly,** *adv.*

post-o·bit (pōst ō′bit, -ob′it), *adj.* effective after a particular person's death. [< L *post obit*(*um*) after death]

post-o′bit bond′, a bond paying a sum of money after the death of some specified person.

post′ of′fice, **1.** an office or station of a government postal system at which mail is received and sorted, from which it is dispatched and distributed, and at which stamps are sold or other services rendered. **2.** (*often caps.*) the depart-

---

post·a′nal, *adj.*
post′-Ar·is·to·te′lian, *adj.*
post′-Au·gus′tan, *adj.*
post-Cam′bri·an, *adj.*
post′-Car·bon·if′er·ous, *adj.*
post′-Car·o·lin′gi·an, *adj.*
post′-Car·te′sian, *adj.*
post-Chris′tian, *adj.*
post·clas′si·cal, *adj.*
post·con′so·nan′tal, *adj.*
post′con·va·les′cent, *adj.*
post′-Co·per′ni·can, *adj.*
post′-Dar·win′i·an, *adj.*
post′de·vel′op·men′tal, *adj.*
post′-De·vo′ni·an, *adj.*
post′di·ag·nos′tic, *adj.*
post′di·ges′tive, *adj.*
post′e·lec′tion, *adj.*
post-E′o·cene, *adj.*
post′gan·gli·on′ic, *adj.*
post′-Ju·ras′sic, *adj.*
post-Kant′i·an, *adj.*
post-Marx′i·an, *adj.*
post′men·o·pau′sal, *adj.*
post·men′stru·al, *adj.*
post′-Mes·o·zo′ic, *adj.*
post-Mi′o·cene′, *adj.*
post′-Mo·sa′ic, *adj.*
post′-My·ce·nae′an, *adj.*
post′-Na·po′le·on′ic, *adj.*
post′-New·to′ni·an, *adj.*
post·nup′tial, *adj.;* **-ly,** *adv.*

ment of a government charged with the transportation of mail. —**post′-of′fice,** *adj.*

Post′ Of′fice Depart′ment, *U.S.* the department of the federal government having responsibility for postal services.

post·op·er·a·tive (pōst op′ər ə tiv, -ə rā′tiv), *adj.* occurring after a surgical operation.

post·or·bit·al (pōst ôr′bi tᵊl), *adj.* *Anat., Zool.* located behind the orbit or socket of the eye.

post·paid (pōst′pād′), *adj., adv.* with the postage prepaid.

post′ par′tum (pär′təm), *Obstet.* of or pertaining to the period of time following childbirth; after delivery. Also, **post-par′tum, post·par′tum, post·par·tal** (pōst pär′tᵊl). Cf. **ante partum.** [< L: lit., after childbirth = *post* POST- + *partum,* acc. of *partus* a bringing forth (*part-,* ptp. s. of *parere* to bear + *-us* u-stem suffix)]

post·pone (pōst pōn′), *v.t.,* **-poned, -pon·ing. 1.** to put off to a later time; defer. **2.** to place after in order of importance or estimation; subordinate. [< L *postpōne(re)* (to) put after, lay aside = *post-* POST- + *pōnere* to put] —**post·pon′a·ble,** *adj.* —**post·pone′ment,** *n.* —**post·pon′er,** *n.*

post·po·si·tion (pōst′pə zish′ən, pōst′pə zish′ən), *n.* **1.** the act of placing after. **2.** the state of being so placed. **3.** *Gram.* **a.** the use of words, particles, or affixes following the elements they modify or govern, as the adjective *general* in *attorney general.* **b.** a word so used. —**post′po·si′tion·al,** *adj.*

post·pos·i·tive (pōst poz′i tiv), *Gram.* —*adj.* **1.** placed after. —*n.* **2.** a postposition. [< L *postposit(us)* (ptp. of *postponere;* see POSTPONE, POSITION) + -IVE] —**post·pos′i·tive·ly,** *adv.*

post·pran·di·al (pōst pran′dē əl), *adj.* after a meal, esp. after dinner. [POST- + L *prandi(um)* meal + -AL[1]] —**post·pran′di·al·ly,** *adv.*

post·rid·er (pōst′rī′dər), *n.* (formerly) a person who rides post; a mounted mail carrier.

post′ road′, 1. a road formerly having stations for furnishing horses for postriders, mail coaches, or travelers. **2.** a road or route over which mail is carried.

post·script (pōst′skript′, pōs′skript′), *n.* **1.** a paragraph, phrase, etc., added to a letter that has already been concluded and signed by the writer. **2.** any addition or supplement, as one appended by a writer to a book. [< L *postscript(um),* neut. of ptp. of *postscrībere* to write after]

pos·tu·lant (pos′chə lənt), *n.* **1.** a person who asks or applies for something. **2.** a candidate, esp. for admission into a religious order. [< F < L *postulant-* (s. of *postulāns*) asking for, prp. of *postulāre* to ask for, claim, require] —**pos′tu·lant·ship′,** *n.*

pos·tu·late (*v.* pos′chə lāt′; *n.* pos′chə lit, -lāt′), *v.,* **-lat·ed, -lat·ing,** *n.* —*v.t.* **1.** to ask, demand, or claim. **2.** to claim or assume the existence or truth of, esp. as a basis for reasoning. **3.** to assume without proof, or as self-evident; take for granted. **4.** *Math., Logic.* to assume as a postulate. —*n.* **5.** something taken as self-evident or assumed without proof as a basis for reasoning. **6.** *Math., Logic.* a proposition that requires no proof, being self-evident, or that is for a specific purpose assumed true, and that is used in the proof of other propositions; axiom. **7.** a fundamental principle. **8.** a necessary condition; prerequisite. [< L *postulāt(um)* thing requested, n. use of neut. of ptp. of *postulāre* to request, demand, akin to *pōscere* to request] —**pos′tu·la′tion,** *n.* —**pos′tu·la′tion·al,** *adj.* —**Syn. 3.** hypothesize, presuppose, conjecture. **5.** hypothesis, theory; axiom; assumption.

pos·tu·la·tor (pos′chə lā′tər), *n.* *Rom. Cath. Ch.* a priest who presents a plea for a beatification or canonization. Cf. **devil's advocate** (def. 2). [< L: claimant]

pos·ture (pos′chər), *n., v.,* **-tured, -tur·ing.** —*n.* **1.** the relative disposition of the parts of something. **2.** the position of the limbs or the carriage of the body as a whole. **3.** an affected or unnatural attitude. **4.** a mental or spiritual attitude. **5.** position, condition, or state, as of affairs. —*v.t.* **6.** to place in a particular posture or attitude. —*v.i.* **7.** to assume a particular posture. **8.** to assume affected or unnatural postures, as by bending or contorting the body. **9.** to pretend to have or affect a particular attitude: *to posture as a friend of the poor.* [< F < L *positūra.* See POSIT, -URE] —**pos′tur·al,** *adj.* —**pos′tur·er,** *n.* —**Syn. 2.** See **position.**

pos·tur·ise (pos′chə rīz′), *v.i.,* **-ised, -is·ing.** *Chiefly Brit.* posturize.

pos·tur·ize (pos′chə rīz′), *v.i.,* **-ized, -iz·ing.** to posture; pose.

post·war (pōst′wôr′), *adj.* of, pertaining to, or characteristic of a period following a war: *postwar problems.*

po·sy (pō′zē), *n., pl.* **-sies. 1.** a flower, nosegay, or bouquet. **2.** *Archaic.* a brief motto or the like, as one inscribed within a ring. [syncopated var. of POESY]

pot[1] (pot), *n., v.,* **pot·ted, pot·ting.** —*n.* **1.** a container of earthenware, metal, etc., usually round and deep and having a handle or handles and often a lid, used for cooking, serving, and other purposes. **2.** such a vessel with its contents: *a pot of stew.* **3.** the amount contained in or held by a pot; potful. **4.** a container of liquor or other drink: *a pot of ale.* **5.** *Brit.* See **chimney pot. 6.** all the money bet at a single time; pool. **7.** *Slang.* marijuana. **8.** a chamber pot. **9.** a lobster pot or any of various cagelike vessels for trapping crabs, eels, etc. **10. go to pot,** to become ruined; deteriorate. —*v.t.* **11.** to put or transplant into a pot. **12.** to preserve (food) in a pot. **13.** to cook in a pot. **14.** *Hunting.* **a.** to shoot (game birds) on the ground or water, or (game animals) at rest, instead of in flight or running. **b.** to shoot for food, not for sport. —*v.i.* **15.** *Slang.* to take a pot shot; shoot. [ME *pott* (see POTTER[1]); c. D, LG *pot* (? > F *pot*)] —**pot′like′,** *adj.*

pot[2] (pot), *n.* *Scot. and North Eng.* a deep hole; pit. [ME; ? same as POT[1]]

pot., potential.

po·ta·ble (pō′tə bəl), *adj.* **1.** fit or suitable for drinking: *potable water.* —*n.* **2.** Usually, **potables.** drinkable liquids; beverages. [< LL *pōtābil(is)* drinkable = L *pōtā(re)* (to) drink + *-bilis* -BLE] —**po′ta·bil′i·ty, po′ta·ble·ness,** *n.*

po·tage (pô tȦzh′; *Eng.* pō täzh′), *n.* *French.* a thick soup.

po·tam·ic (pō tam′ik, pə-), *adj.* of or pertaining to rivers. [< Gk *potam(ós)* river + -IC]

pot·ash (pot′ash′), *n.* **1.** potassium carbonate, esp. the crude impure form obtained from wood ashes. **2.** caustic potash. **3.** the oxide of potassium, K_2O. **4.** potassium, as carbonate of potash. [back formation from *pot-ashes* (pl.), trans. of early D *potasschen*]

po·tas·sic (pə tas′ik), *adj.* of, pertaining to, or containing potassium. [POTASS(IUM) + -IC]

po·tas·si·um (pə tas′ē əm), *n.* *Chem.* a silvery-white metallic element that oxidizes rapidly in the air and whose compounds are used as fertilizer and in special hard glasses. *Symbol:* K; *at. wt.:* 39.102; *at. no.:* 19; *sp. gr.:* 0.86 at 20°C. [< NL *potass(a)* (see POTASH) + *-ium*]

potas′sium ac′id tar′trate, *Chem.* See **cream of tartar.**

potas′sium an′timonyl tar′trate, *Chem.* See **tartar emetic.**

potas′sium ar′gon dat′ing, *Physics.* a method for estimating the age of a mineral by determining the ratio of argon to potassium in the mineral, based on the natural radioactive disintegration of potassium into argon.

potas′sium bitar′trate, *Chem.* See **cream of tartar.**

potas′sium bro′mide, *Chem.* a white powder, KBr, used chiefly in the manufacture of photographic papers and plates, in engraving, and as a sedative.

potas′sium car′bonate, *Chem.* a white powder, K_2CO_3, used chiefly in the manufacture of soap, glass, and potassium salts.

potas′sium chlo′rate, *Chem.* a white or colorless, poisonous solid, $KClO_3$, used chiefly as an oxidizing agent in the manufacture of explosives, fireworks, matches, bleaches, and disinfectants.

potas′sium cy′anide, *Chem.* a white, poisonous powder, KCN, having a faint almondlike odor, used chiefly in metallurgy and photography.

potas′sium dichro′mate, *Chem.* an orange-red, poisonous powder, $K_2Cr_2O_7$, used chiefly in dyeing, photography, and as a laboratory reagent.

potas′sium ferricy′anide, *Chem.* a bright-red, poisonous solid, $K_3Fe(CN)_6$, used chiefly in the manufacture of pigments, as Prussian blue, and of blueprint paper.

potas′sium ferrocy′anide, *Chem.* a lemon-yellow solid, $K_4Fe(CN)_6 \cdot 3H_2O$, used chiefly in casehardening and in dyeing.

potas′sium flu′oride, *Chem.* a white, poisonous powder, KF, used chiefly as an insecticide, a disinfectant, and in etching glass.

potas′sium hydrox′ide, *Chem.* a white, deliquescent solid, KOH, used chiefly in the manufacture of soap, as a laboratory reagent, and in medicine as a caustic. Also called **caustic potash, potas′sium hy′drate.**

potas′sium ni′trate, *Chem.* a compound, KNO_3, produced by nitrification in soil: used in gunpowders, fertilizers, and preservatives; saltpeter; niter.

potas′sium perman′ganate, *Chem.* a dark-purple solid, $KMnO_4$, used chiefly as an oxidizing agent, disinfectant, laboratory reagent, and as an astringent and antiseptic.

potas′sium so′dium tar′trate, *Chem.* See **Rochelle salt.**

potas′sium sul′fate, *Chem.* a solid, K_2SO_4, used chiefly in the manufacture of fertilizers, alums, and mineral water, and as a reagent in analytical chemistry.

po·ta·tion (pō tā′shən), *n.* **1.** the act of drinking. **2.** a drink or draft, esp. of an alcoholic beverage. [late ME *potacion* < L *pōtātiōn-* (s. of *pōtātiō*) a drinking = *pōtāt(us)* (ptp. of *pōtāre* to drink) + *-iōn-* -ION]

po·ta·to (pə tā′tō), *n., pl.* **-toes. 1.** Also called **Irish potato, white potato.** the edible tuber of a cultivated plant, *Solanum tuberosum.* **2.** the plant itself. **3.** See **sweet potato** (defs. 1, 2). [< Sp *patata* white potato, var. of *batata* sweet potato < Taino]

pota′to chip′, a thin slice of potato fried until crisp, usually salted and eaten cold. Also called **Saratoga chip.**

po·ta·to·ry (pō′tə tôr′ē, -tôr′ē), *adj.* of, pertaining to, or given to drinking. [< L *pōtātōri(us).* See POTATION, -ORY[1]]

pot-au-feu (pô tō fœ′), *n.* *French Cookery.* a clear soup containing meat and vegetables. [< F: lit., pot on the fire]

Pot·a·wat·o·mi (pot′ə wot′ə mē), *n. pl.* **-mis,** (*esp. collectively*) **-mi.** a member of an Algonquian Indian people originally of Michigan and Wisconsin.

pot·bel·ly (pot′bel′ē), *n., pl.* **-lies.** a distended or protuberant belly. —**pot′bel′lied,** *adj.*

pot·boil·er (pot′boi′lər), *n.* *Informal.* a mediocre work of literature or art produced merely for financial gain.

pot·boy (pot′boi′), *n.* *Brit.* a boy or man who serves customers in a tavern. Also called **potman.**

pot′ cheese′, a cheese similar to cottage cheese but with coarser curds and a drier consistency.

po·teen (pō tēn′), *n.* (in Ireland) illicitly distilled whiskey. Also, **potheen.** [< Ir *poitín* small pot, dim. of *pota* pot]

Po·tem·kin (pō tem′kin, pə-; *Russ.* po tyôm′kin), *n.* **Prince Gri·go·ri A·le·ksan·dro·vich** (gri gô′ri ä′le ksän′drо vich), 1739–91, Russian statesman and favorite of Catherine II.

po·tence (pōt′ᵊns), *n.* potency. [ME < OF < L *potentia* POTENCY]

po·ten·cy (pōt′ᵊn sē), *n., pl.* **-cies** for 4, 5. **1.** the state or quality of being potent. **2.** power; authority. **3.** efficacy; effectiveness; strength. **4.** capacity to be, become, or develop; potentiality. **5.** a person or thing exerting power or influence. [< L *potentia*] —**Syn. 1.** strength, force, energy, capacity, potential.

post-Ol′i·go·cene′, *adj.*
post·o′ral, *adj.*
post′-Or·do·vi′cian, *adj.*
post′-Pa·le·o·zo′ic, *adj.*
post-Paul′ine, *adj.*
post-Per′mi·an, *adj.*
post′pi·tu′i·tar′y, *adj.*
post-Pleis′to·cene′, *adj.*
post-Pli′o·cene′, *adj.*
post′-Ref·or·ma′tion, *n.*
post′-Rev·o·lu′tion·ar′y, *adj.*
post·sea′son, *adj.*
post·sea′son·al, *adj.*
post′-Si·lu′ri·an, *adj.*
post′-So·crat′ic, *adj.*
post′-Tal·mud′ic, *adj.*
post-Ter′ti·ar′y, *adj.*
post′-Tri·as′sic, *adj.*
post-Ve′dic, *adj.*
post′-Vic·to′ri·an, *adj.*

po·tent[1] (pōt′ənt), *adj.* **1.** powerful; mighty. **2.** cogent; persuasive. **3.** producing powerful physical or chemical effects: *a potent drug.* **4.** having or exercising great power or influence. **5.** (of a male) capable of sexual intercourse. [< L *potent-* (s. of *potēns*), prp. of *posse* to be able, have power; see -ENT] —**po′tent·ly,** *adv.* —**po′tent·ness,** *n.* —**Syn. 1.** strong, puissant. See **powerful. 4.** influential. —**Ant. 1.** weak. **4.** ineffectual.

po·tent[2] (pōt′ənt), *adj. Heraldry.* (of a cross) having a crosspiece at the extremity of each arm: *a cross potent.* [ME *potente* crutch; var. of *potence* < ML *potentia,* special use of L *potentia* POTENCY]

po·ten·tate (pōt′ən tāt′), *n.* a person who possesses great power; a sovereign, monarch, or ruler. [< LL *potentāt(us)* potentate, L: power, dominion]

po·ten·tial (pə ten′shəl), *adj.* **1.** possible, as opposed to actual: *the potential uses of nuclear energy.* **2.** capable of being or becoming: *a potential slum neighborhood.* **3.** *Gram.* expressing possibility. **4.** *Archaic.* potent[1]. —*n.* **5.** possibility; potentiality. **6.** a latent excellence or ability that may or may not be developed. **7.** *Gram.* **a.** a potential aspect, mood, construction, case, etc. **b.** a form in the potential. **8.** *Elect.* a quantity associated with a point near or within an electrified substance and represented either as the potential difference between the point and some reference point, as the ground nearby or the earth in general, assumed to have a zero potential, or as the work hypothetically necessary to bring a unit of positive charge from an infinite distance to the given point. **9.** *Math., Physics.* a type of function from which the intensity of a field may be derived, usually by differentiation. [< LL *potentiāl(is)*] —**Syn. 2.** See **latent. 5.** capacity, potency.

poten′tial en′ergy, *Physics.* the energy of a body or a system with respect to the position of the body or the arrangement of the particles of the system. Cf. **kinetic energy.**

po·ten·ti·al·i·ty (pə ten′shē al′i tē), *n., pl.* **-ties** for 2. **1.** the state or quality of being potential. **2.** something potential; a possibility: *Atomic destruction is a grim potentiality.* [< ML *potentiālitās*]

po·ten·tial·ly (pə ten′shə lē), *adv.* possibly but not yet actually: *potentially useful information.*

po·ten·ti·ate (pə ten′shē āt′), *v.t.,* **-at·ed, -at·ing. 1.** to cause to be potent; make powerful. **2.** to increase the effectiveness of; intensify. [< L *potenti(a)* power, POTENCY + -ATE[1]] —**po·ten′ti·a′tion,** *n.* —**po·ten′ti·a′tor,** *n.*

po·ten·til·la (pōt′ən til′ə), *n.* any rosaceous herb or small shrub of the genus *Potentilla,* of north temperate regions. [< NL, special use of ML *potentilla* garden valerian = *potent-* POTENT[1] + *-illa* dim. suffix]

po·ten·ti·om·e·ter (pə ten′shē om′i tər), *n. Elect.* a device for measuring electromotive force or potential difference by comparison with a known voltage. [POTENTI(AL) + -O- + -METER] —**po·ten·ti·o·met·ric** (pə ten′shē ə me′trik), *adj.*

pot·ful (pot′fo͝ol′), *n., pl.* **-fuls.** the amount that can be held by a pot.

pot·head (pot′hed′), *n. U.S. Slang.* a person who habitually uses marijuana.

poth·e·car·y (poth′ə ker′ē), *n., pl.* **-car·ies.** *Chiefly Dial.* apothecary. [ME *potecarie,* aph. var. of *apothecarie* APOTHECARY]

po·theen (pō thēn′), *n.* poteen.

poth·er (poth′ər), *n.* **1.** commotion; uproar. **2.** a disturbance; fuss. **3.** a choking or suffocating cloud, as of smoke or dust. —*v.t., v.i.* **4.** to worry; bother. [?]

pot·herb (pot′ûrb′, -hûrb′), *n.* **1.** any herbaceous vegetable prepared as food by cooking in a pot, as spinach. **2.** an herb added as seasoning in cookery, as thyme.

pot·hold·er (pot′hōl′dər), *n.* a thick piece of material, as a quilted or woven pad, used in handling hot pots and dishes to prevent burning the hands.

pot·hole (pot′hōl′), *n.* **1.** a deep hole, as in a road; pit. **2.** a hole formed in rock by the grinding action of the detrital material in eddying water. **3.** a cave opening vertically from the ground surface.

pot·hook (pot′ho͝ok′), *n.* **1.** a hook for suspending a pot or kettle over an open fire. **2.** an iron rod with a hook at the end, used to lift hot pots, irons, etc. **3.** an S-shaped stroke in writing. [late ME *pottehok*]

pot·house (pot′hous′), *n., pl.* **-hous·es** (-hou′ziz). *Brit.* a place where ale, beer, etc., are retailed; alehouse.

pot·hunt·er (pot′hun′tər), *n.* a person who hunts for food or profit, ignoring the rules of sport. —**pot′hunt′ing,** *n., adj.*

po·tiche (pō tēsh′; *Fr.* pô tēsh′), *n., pl.* **-tich·es** (-tē′shiz; *Fr.* -tēsh′). a vase or jar, as of porcelain, with a rounded or polygonal body narrowing at the top. [< F; akin to POT]

po·tion (pō′shən), *n.* a drink or draft, esp. one having or reputed to have medicinal, poisonous, or magical powers. [late ME *pocion* < L *pōtiōn-* (s. of *pōtiō*) a drinking = *pōt(us)* drunk (var. of *pōtātus,* ptp. of *pōtāre*) + *-iōn-* -ION; r. ME *pocioun* < AF]

Pot·i·phar (pot′ə fər), *n.* the Egyptian officer whose wife tried to seduce Joseph. Gen. 39:1–20.

pot·latch (pot′lach), *n.* (among American Indians of the northern Pacific coast, esp. the Kwakiutl) a ceremonial festival at which gifts are bestowed on the guests and property is destroyed by its owner in a show of wealth which the guests later attempt to surpass. [< Chinook, metathetic var. of Nootka *potshatl* gift]

pot′ liq′uor, the broth in which meat or vegetables, as salt pork or greens, have been cooked. Also, **pot′-liq′uor.**

pot·luck (pot′luk′, -luk′), *n.* food or a meal that happens to be available without special preparation or purchase: *to take potluck with a friend.*

pot·man (pot′mən), *n., pl.* **-men.** *Brit.* potboy.

pot′ mar′igold, the common marigold, *Calendula officinalis,* the flower heads of which are sometimes used in cookery for seasoning.

Po·to·mac (pə tō′mək), *n.* a river flowing SE from the Allegheny Mountains in West Virginia, along the boundary between Maryland and Virginia to the Chesapeake Bay. 287 mi. long.

Po·to·sí (pô′tô sē′), *n.* a city in S Bolivia: former silver-mining center. 57,000 (est. 1965); 13,022 ft. above sea level.

pot·pie (pot′pī′), *n.* **1.** a deep-dish pie containing meat, chicken, or the like, and often vegetables, topped with a pastry crust. **2.** a stew, as of chicken or veal, with dumplings, biscuits, or the like.

pot·pour·ri (pō′po͝o rē′, pō′po͝o rē′, pot po͝or′ē; *Fr.* pô po͞o RĒ′), *n., pl.* **-pour·ris** (-po͞o rēz′, -po͞o rēz′, -po͝or′ēz; *Fr.* -po͞o RĒ′). **1.** a mixture of dried petals of roses or other flowers with spices, kept in a jar for their fragrance. **2.** a musical medley. **3.** a collection of miscellaneous literary extracts. **4.** any mixture, esp. of unrelated objects, subjects, etc. [< F: lit., rotten pot, trans. of Sp *olla podrida;* see OLLA]

pot′ roast′, a dish of meat, usually of round or chuck steak, stewed in one piece and served in its own gravy.

Pots·dam (pots′dam; *Ger.* pôts′däm), *n.* a city in central East Germany, SW of Berlin: formerly the residence of German emperors. 109,867 (1964).

pot·sherd (pot′shûrd′), *n.* a broken pottery fragment, esp. one of archaeological value. [POT + *sherd,* var. of SHARD]

pot′ shot′, **1.** a shot fired at game with little regard to skill or the rules of sport. **2.** a shot at an animal or person within easy range, as from ambush. **3.** a casual or aimless shot. Also, **pot′shot′.**

pot·stone (pot′stōn′), *n.* a kind of soapstone, sometimes used for making pots and other household utensils.

pot·tage (pot′ij), *n.* a thick soup made of vegetables, with or without meat. [ME *potage* < OF: lit., something in or from a POT; see -AGE]

pot·ted (pot′id), *adj.* **1.** placed or enclosed in a pot. **2.** transplanted into or grown in a pot. **3.** preserved or cooked in a pot: *potted beef.* **4.** *Slang.* drunk.

pot·ter[1] (pot′ər), *n.* a person who makes pottery. [ME; late OE *pottere.* See POT, -ER[1]]

pot·ter[2] (pot′ər), *v.i., n. Chiefly Brit.* putter[1]. [freq. of obs. or dial. *pote* to push, poke, ME *poten,* OE *potian* to push, thrust. See PUT] —**pot′ter·er,** *n.* —**pot′ter·ing·ly,** *adv.*

Pot·ter (pot′ər), *n.* **Paul,** 1625–54, Dutch painter.

Pot·ter·ies, the (pot′ə rēz), a district in central England famous for the manufacture of pottery and china. Also called **Five Towns.** Cf. **Stoke-on-Trent.**

pot′ter's field′, a piece of ground reserved as a burial place for strangers and the friendless poor. Matt. 27:7.

pot′ter's wheel′, a device with a rotating horizontal disk upon which clay is molded by a potter.

pot·ter·y (pot′ə rē), *n., pl.* **-ter·ies. 1.** ceramic ware, esp. earthenware and stoneware. **2.** the art or business of a potter; ceramics. **3.** a place where earthen pots or vessels are made. [late ME: potter's workshop (cf. F *poterie*)]

pot·tle (pot′əl), *n.* **1.** a former liquid measure equal to two quarts. **2.** a pot or tankard of this capacity. **3.** the wine or other liquid in it. **4.** alcoholic beverages, as wine and liquor. [ME *potel* < MF, dim. of *pot* POT]

pot·to (pot′ō), *n., pl.* **-tos.** any of several lorislike, African lemurs of the genera *Perodicticus* and *Arctocebus,* esp. *P. potto,* having a short tail and vestigial index fingers. [< WAfr]

Pott's′ disease′ (pots), *Pathol.* caries of the bodies of the vertebrae, often resulting in marked curvature of the spine, and usually associated with a tuberculosis infection. [named after Percival *Pott* (1714–88), British surgeon, who described it]

Potts·town (pots′toun′), *n.* a borough in SE Pennsylvania. 25,355 (1970).

pot·ty[1] (pot′ē), *adj.,* **-ti·er, -ti·est. 1.** *Chiefly Brit. Informal.* eccentric. **2.** *Brit.* paltry; trifling; petty. [POT + -Y[1]]

pot·ty[2] (pot′ē), *n., pl.* **-ties. 1.** a seat of reduced size fitting over a toilet seat, for use by a small child. **2.** a small metal pot fitting under a potty-chair. [POT + -Y[2]]

pot·ty-chair (pot′ē châr′), *n.* a small chair with an open seat over a removable pot, for use by a child during toilet training.

pot-val·iant (pot′val′yənt), *adj.* brave only as a result of being drunk. —**pot′-val′iant·ly,** *adv.* —**pot-val·or** (pot′val′ər), **pot-val·ian·cy** (pot′val′yən sē), *n.*

pot·wal·lop·er (pot′wol′ə pər, pot wol′-), *n. Eng. Hist.* (in some boroughs before the Reform Bill of 1832) a man who qualified as a householder, and therefore a voter, by virtue of ownership of his own fireplace at which to boil pots. Also, **pot′-wal′lop·er.** Also called **pot·wal·ler** (pot′wol′ər). [POT[1] + WALLOPER; r. *potwaller,* lit., potboiler (POT[1] + *wall,* OE *weallan* to boil, + -ER[1])]

pouch (pouch), *n.* **1.** a bag, sack, or similar receptacle, esp. one for small articles or quantities: *a tobacco pouch.* **2.** a small moneybag. **3.** a bag for carrying mail. **4.** a bag or case of leather, used by soldiers to carry ammunition. **5.** a baggy fold of flesh under the eye. **6.** *Anat., Zool.* a baglike or pocketlike part; a sac or cyst, as of a marsupium, the sac beneath the bill of pelicans, or the saclike dilation of the cheeks of gophers. **7.** *Bot.* a baglike cavity. —*v.t.* **8.** to put into or enclose in a pouch, bag, or pocket; pocket. **9.** to arrange in the form of a pouch. **10.** (of a fish or bird) to swallow. —*v.i.* **11.** to form a pouch or a cavity resembling a pouch. [ME *pouche* < ONF, var. of OF *poche;* also *poke, poque* bag. See POKE[2]]

pouched (poucht), *adj.* having a pouch, as the pelicans, gophers, and marsupials.

pouch·y (pou′chē), *adj.,* **pouch·i·er, pouch·i·est.** possessing or resembling a pouch.

pouf (po͞of), *n.* **1.** a high headdress with the hair rolled in puffs, worn by women in the late 18th century. **2.** a puff of material as an ornament on a dress or headdress. **3.** *Chiefly Brit.* a hassock. [< F; see PUFF]

Pough·keep·sie (pə kip′sē), *n.* a city in SE New York, on the Hudson: regatta. 32,029 (1970).

Pouil·ly-Fuis·sé (po͞o yē fwē sā′), *n.* a dry white wine from Burgundy.

pou·lard (po͞o lärd′), *n.* a hen spayed to improve the flesh for use as food. Also, **pou·larde′.** [< F = *poule* hen (see PULLET) + *-ard* -ARD]

Pou·lenc (po͞o laNk′), *n.* **Fran·cis** (fRäN sēs′), 1899–1963, French composer and pianist.

poult (pōlt), *n.* the young of the domestic fowl, the turkey, the pheasant, or a similar bird. [late ME *pult(e)*; syncopated var. of PULLET]

poul·ter·er (pōl′tər ər), *n. Brit.* a poultryman. [obs. *poulter* poultry dealer (< F *pouletier;* see PULLET, -ER[2]) + -ER[1]]

poul·tice (pōl′tis), *n., v.,* **-ticed, -tic·ing.** —*n.* **1.** a soft, moist mass of meal, herbs, etc., spread on a cloth and applied as a medicament to the body. —*v.t.* **2.** to apply a poultice to. [earlier *pultes,* appar. pl. of L *puls* thick pap. See PULSE[2]]

poul·try (pōl′trē), *n.* domesticated fowl collectively, esp. those valued for their meat and eggs. [ME *pulletrie* < MF *pouleterie.* See PULLET, -ERY] —**poul′try·less,** *adj.* —**poul′try·like′** *adj.*

poul·try·man (pōl′trē mən), *n., pl.* **-men. 1.** a person who raises domestic fowls, esp. chickens, to sell as meat; a chicken farmer. **2.** a poultry dealer.

pounce[1] (pouns), *v.,* **pounced, pounc·ing,** *n.* —*v.i.* **1.** to swoop down suddenly, as a bird does in order to seize its prey. **2.** to spring, dash, or come suddenly. —*v.t.* **3.** to seize with or as with the talons. —*n.* **4.** the claw or talon of a bird of prey. **5.** a sudden swoop, as on an object of prey. [late ME; ? akin to PUNCH[2]] —**pounc′ing·ly,** *adv.*

pounce[2] (pouns), *v.t.,* **pounced, pounc·ing.** to emboss (metal) by hammering on an instrument applied to the reverse side. [? same as POUNCE[1]]

pounce[3] (pouns), *n., v.,* **pounced, pounc·ing.** —*n.* **1.** a fine powder, as of cuttlebone, formerly used to prevent ink from spreading in writing, as over an erasure or an unsized paper, or to prepare parchment for writing. **2.** a fine powder, often of charcoal, used in transferring a design through a perforated pattern. —*v.t.* **3.** to sprinkle, smooth, or prepare with pounce. **4.** to trace (a design) with pounce. **5.** to finish the surface of (hats) by rubbing with sandpaper or the like. [< F *ponce* << L *pūmic-,* of *pūmex* PUMICE] —**pounc′er,** *n.*

poun′cet box′ (poun′sit), a small perfume box with a perforated lid. [POUNCE[2] or POUNCE[3] + -ET]

pound[1] (pound), *v.t.* **1.** to strike repeatedly and with great force, as with an instrument, the fist, heavy missiles, etc. **2.** to produce or effect by striking or thumping, or in a manner resembling this (often fol. by *out*). **3.** to force (a way) by battering; batter (often fol. by *down*): *to pound a door down.* **4.** to crush by beating, as with an instrument; bray, pulverize, or triturate. —*v.i.* **5.** to strike heavy blows repeatedly: *to pound on a door.* **6.** to beat or throb violently, as the heart. **7.** to give forth a thumping sound. **8.** to walk or go with heavy steps; move along with force or vigor. —*n.* **9.** the act of pounding. **10.** a heavy or forcible blow. **11.** a thump. [ME *poune(n),* OE *pūnian;* akin to D *puin* rubbish] —**pound′er,** *n.* —**Syn. 1.** See **beat.**

pound[2] (pound), *n., pl.* **pounds,** (*collectively*) **pound. 1.** a unit of weight and of mass, varying in different periods and countries. **2.** *Weights and Measures.* **a.** (in English-speaking countries) an avoirdupois unit of weight equal to 7000 grains, divided into 16 ounces, used for ordinary commerce. **b.** (in the U.S.) a troy and apothecaries' unit of weight, equal to 5760 grains, divided into 12 ounces. **3.** Also called **pound sterling.** a paper money and monetary unit of the United Kingdom, equal to 20 shillings or 240 pence prior to February 1971, and after that date, consisting of 100 new pence. *Abbr.:* L; *Symbol:* £ **4.** any of the monetary units of various countries, as Cyprus, Ireland, Israel, Lebanon, Libya, Sudan, and Syria. [ME; OE *pund* (c. D *pond,* G *Pfund,* Goth, Icel *pund*) << L *pondō* pound (indeclinable n.), orig. abl. of *pondus* weight (2nd decl.)]

pound[3] (pound), *n.* **1.** an enclosure maintained by public authorities for confining stray or homeless animals. **2.** an enclosure for sheltering, keeping, confining, or trapping animals. **3.** an enclosure or trap for fish. **4.** a place of confinement or imprisonment. —*v.t.* **5.** to shut up in or as in a pound; impound, imprison. [late ME *poond,* late OE *pund-;* akin to POND]

Pound (pound), *n.* **Ezra (Loo·mis)** (lo͞o′mis), 1885–1972, U.S. poet and critic.

pound·age[1] (poun′dij), *n.* **1.** a tax, commission, rate, etc., of so much per pound sterling or per pound weight. **2.** weight in pounds. [ME; see POUND[2], -AGE]

pound·age[2] (poun′dij), *n.* **1.** confinement within an enclosure or within certain limits. **2.** the fee demanded to free animals from a pound. [POUND[3] + -AGE]

pound·al (poun′dᵊl), *n. Physics.* the foot-pound-second unit of force, equal to the force that produces an acceleration of one foot per second per second on a mass of one pound. *Abbr.:* pdl

pound′ cake′, a rich, sweet cake made with approximately a pound each of butter, sugar, and flour.

pound·er[1] (poun′dər), *n.* a person or thing that pounds, pulverizes, or beats. [POUND[1] + -ER[1]]

pound·er[2] (poun′dər), *n.* **1.** a person or thing having or associated with a weight or value of a pound or a specified number of pounds. **2.** a gun that discharges a missile of a specified weight in pounds (usually used in combination): *a ten-pounder.* [POUND[2] + -ER[1]]

pound-force (pound′fōrs′, -fôrs′), *n. Physics.* a foot-pound-second unit of force, equal to the force that produces an acceleration equal to the acceleration of gravity when acting on a mass of one pound. *Abbr.:* lbf

pound′ net′, *Angling.* a trap consisting of a system of nets staked upright in the water.

pound′ ster′ling, pound[2] (def. 3).

pour (pōr, pôr), *v.t.* **1.** to send (a liquid, fluid, or anything in loose particles) flowing or falling, as from one container to another, or into, over, or on something. **2.** to emit or propel, esp. continuously or rapidly. **3.** to produce or utter in or as in a stream or flood (often fol. by *out*): *to pour out one's troubles.* —*v.i.* **4.** to issue, move, or proceed in great quantity or number. **5.** to flow forth or along; stream. **6.** to rain heavily (often used impersonally with *it* as subject). —*n.* **7.** the act of pouring. **8.** an abundant or continuous flow or stream: *a pour of invective.* **9.** a heavy fall of rain. [ME *poure(n)*] —**pour′a·bil′i·ty,** *n.* —**pour′a·ble,** *adj.* —**pour′er,** *n.* —**pour′ing·ly,** *adv.*

pour·boire (po͞or bwar′), *n., pl.* **-boires** (-bwar′). *French.* a gratuity; tip. [lit., for drinking]

pour·par·ler (po͞or par lā′; *Eng.* po͝or′pär lā′), *n., pl.* **-lers** (-lā′; *Eng.* -lāz′). *French.* an informal preliminary conference. [lit., for talking]

pour·point (po͝or′point′, -pwant′), *n.* a stuffed and quilted doublet. [< F, n. use of ptp. of *pourpoindre* to quilt, perforate = *pour-,* for *par-* (< L *per*) through + *poindre* (< L *pungere* to prick, pierce); r. ME *purpont*]

pousse-ca·fé (po͞os′ka fā′; *Fr.* po͞os ka fā′), *n., pl.* **-fés** (-fāz′; *Fr.* -fā′). **1.** a small glass of liqueur served after coffee. **2.** a glass of various liqueurs arranged in layers. [< F: lit., coffee-pusher]

pous·sette (po͞o set′), *n.* a dance figure in which a couple or several couples dance around the ballroom, holding hands. [< F = *pouss(er)* (to) PUSH + *-ette* -ETTE]

Pous·sin (po͞o san′), *n.* **Ni·co·las** (nē kô lä′), 1594–1655, French painter.

pou sto (po͞o′ stō′; *Eng.* po͞o′ stō′, pou′), *Greek.* **1.** a place to stand on. **2.** a basis of operation. [lit., where I may stand]

pout[1] (pout), *v.i.* **1.** to thrust out the lips, esp. in displeasure or sullenness. **2.** to appear sullen. **3.** to swell out or protrude, as lips. —*v.t.* **4.** to protrude (the lips). **5.** to utter with a pout. —*n.* **6.** the act of pouting; a protrusion of the lips. **7.** a fit of sullenness: *to be in a pout.* [ME *poute(n);* c. Sw (dial.) *puta* to be inflated] —**pout′ing·ly,** *adv.*

pout[2] (pout), *n., pl.* (*esp. collectively*) **pout,** (*esp. referring to two or more kinds or species*) **pouts. 1.** See **horned pout. 2.** a northern, marine food fish, *Gadus luscus.* [OE *-pute,* in *ǣlepūte* eelpout; c. D *puit* frog]

pout·er (pou′tər), *n.* **1.** a person who pouts. **2.** one of a breed of long-legged domestic pigeons, characterized by the habit of puffing out the distensible crop.

pov·er·ty (pov′ər tē), *n.* **1.** the state or condition of having little or no money, goods, or means of support; condition of being poor; indigence. **2.** lack of something specified. **3.** deficiency of desirable ingredients, qualities, etc. **4.** scantiness; insufficiency. [ME *poverte* < OF < L *paupertāt-* (s. of *paupertās*) small means, moderate circumstances. See PAUPER, -TY[2]]
—**Syn. 1.** penury. POVERTY, DESTITUTION, NEED, WANT imply a state of privation and lack of necessities. POVERTY denotes serious lack of the means for proper existence: *living in a state of extreme poverty.* DESTITUTION, a somewhat more literary word, implies a state of having absolutely none of the necessities of life: *widespread destitution in countries at war.* NEED emphasizes the fact that help or relief is necessary: *Most of the people were in great need.* WANT emphasizes privations, esp. lack of food and clothing: *Families were suffering from want.* —**Ant. 1.** riches, wealth, plenty.

pov·er·ty-strick·en (pov′ər tē strik′ən), *adj.* suffering from poverty; extremely poor.

POW, prisoner of war. Also, **P.O.W.**

pow·der[1] (pou′dər), *n.* **1.** any solid substance reduced to a state of fine, loose particles by crushing, grinding, disintegration, etc. **2.** a preparation in this form, as gunpowder or face powder. —*v.t.* **3.** to reduce to powder; pulverize. **4.** to sprinkle or cover with powder. **5.** to apply powder to (the face, skin, etc.) as a cosmetic. **6.** to sprinkle or strew as if with powder. **7.** to ornament in this fashion, as with small objects scattered over a surface. —*v.i.* **8.** to use powder as a cosmetic. **9.** to become pulverized. [ME *poudre* < OF < L *pulver-* (s. of *pulvis*) dust, powder] —**pow′der·er,** *n.*

pow·der[2] (pou′dər), *n.* **1.** *Brit. Dial.* a sudden, frantic rush. **2. take a powder,** *Slang.* to leave in a hurry. [?]

pow′der blue′, a pale, grayish blue. —**pow′der-blue′,** *adj.*

pow′der boy′. See **powder monkey** (def. 1).

pow′der burn′, a skin burn caused by exploding gunpowder.

pow′der charge′, propellant (def. 2).

pow′dered milk′, dehydrated milk from which about 95 percent of the moisture has been evaporated. Also called **dry milk.**

pow′dered sug′ar, a sugar, less fine than confectioners' sugar, produced by pulverizing granulated sugar.

pow′der flask′, a small flask for gunpowder, formerly carried by soldiers and hunters.

pow′der horn′, a powder flask made from the horn of a cow or ox.

pow′der keg′, 1. a small, metal, barrellike container for gunpowder or blasting powder. **2.** a dangerous situation or thing, liable to explode or erupt.

pow′der met′allurgy, the art or science of manufacturing useful articles by compacting metal powders and other powders in a die, followed by sintering.

pow′der mon′key, 1. Also called **powder boy.** (formerly) a boy employed on warships to carry gunpowder from the magazine to the guns. **2.** a man in charge of explosives in any operation requiring their use.

pow′der puff′, a soft, feathery ball or pad, as of cotton or down, for applying powder to the skin.

pow′der room′, a room containing toilet and washing facilities for the use of female guests, as in a restaurant, night club, etc.; lavatory.

pow·der·y (pou′də rē), *adj.* **1.** consisting of or resembling powder. **2.** easily reduced to powder: *powdery plaster.* **3.** sprinkled or covered with or as with powder. [late ME *powdry*]

Pow·ell (pou′əl), *n.* **Lewis F(ranklin), Jr.,** born 1907, U.S. jurist: associate justice of the U.S. Supreme Court 1972–87.

pow·er (pou′ər), *n.* **1.** ability to do or act; capability of doing or accomplishing something. **2.** political or national strength. **3.** great or marked ability to do or act; strength; might; force. **4.** the possession of control or command over others; authority; ascendancy: *power over men's minds.* **5.** political ascendancy or control in the government of a country, state, etc. **6.** legal ability, capacity, or authority. **7.** delegated authority; authority granted to a person or persons in a particular office or capacity: *the powers of the president.* **8.** a document or written statement conferring legal authority. **9.** a person or thing that possesses or exercises authority or influence. **10.** a state or nation having international authority or influence: *The great powers held an international conference.* **11.** a military force. **12.** Often, **powers.** a deity; divinity: *the heavenly powers.* **13. powers,** *Theol.* an order of angels. Cf. **angel** (def. 1). **14.** *Dial.* a large number or amount: *There's a power of good eatin' at the church social.* **15.** *Physics.* **a.** work done or energy transferred per unit of time. *Symbol:* P **b.** the time rate of doing work. **16.** mechanical energy as distinguished from hand labor: *a loom driven by power.* **17.** a particular form of mechanical or physical energy: *hydroelectric power.* **18.** energy, force, or momentum: *The door slammed shut, seemingly under its own power.* **19.** *Math.* the product obtained by multiplying a quantity by itself one or more times: *The third power of 2 is 8.* **20.** *Optics.* **a.** the magnifying capacity of a microscope, telescope, etc., expressed as the ratio of the diameter of the image to the diameter of the object. **b.** the reciprocal of the focal length of a lens. —*v.t.* **21.** to supply with energy or other means of power. **22.** (of a fuel, engine, or any source able to do work) to supply force to operate (a machine). [ME *poër* < AF, orig. inf. < VL **potēre*, r. L *posse* to be able, have power. See POTENT[1]] —**Syn. 1.** capacity. **3.** energy. See **strength. 4, 5.** sway, rule, sovereignty. —**Ant. 1.** incapacity. **3.** weakness.

pow·er·boat (pou′ər bōt′), *n.* a boat propelled by mechanical power; motorboat.

pow′er brake′, *Auto.* a brake set by pressure from some power source, as a compressed-air reservoir, in proportion to a smaller amount of pressure on the brake pedal.

pow′er chain′, an endless chain for transmitting motion and power between sprockets on shafts with parallel axes.

pow′er dive′, *Aeron.* a dive, esp. a steep dive, by an aircraft in which the engine or engines are delivering thrust at or near full power.

pow·er·ful (pou′ər fəl), *adj.* **1.** having or exerting great power or force. **2.** physically strong, as a person. **3.** producing great physical effects, as a machine or a blow. **4.** potent; efficacious: *a powerful drug.* **5.** having great effectiveness, as a speech, speaker, reason, etc. **6.** having great power, authority, or influence; mighty. **7.** *Chiefly Dial.* great in number or amount. [late ME *powarfull*] —**pow′er·ful·ly,** *adv.* —**pow′er·ful·ness,** *n.*
—**Syn. 1.** forceful, strong. POWERFUL, MIGHTY, POTENT suggest great force or strength. POWERFUL suggests capability of exerting great force or overcoming strong resistance: *a powerful machine like a bulldozer.* MIGHTY, now chiefly rhetorical, implies an uncommon or overwhelming degree of power: *a mighty army.* POTENT implies great natural or inherent power: *a potent influence.* **5.** influential, convincing, forcible, cogent, effective. —**Ant. 1.** weak.

pow·er·house (pou′ər hous′), *n., pl.* **-hous·es** (-hou′ziz). **1.** *Elect.* a generating station. **2.** *Informal.* a person, group, team, or the like, having great energy, influence, strength, or potential for success.

pow·er·less (pou′ər lis), *adj.* **1.** unable to produce an effect. **2.** lacking power to act; helpless. —**pow′er·less·ly,** *adv.* —**pow′er·less·ness,** *n.*

pow′er line′, a line for conducting electric power.

pow′er of appoint′ment, *Law.* the right granted by a donor to a donee to dispose of the donor's property.

pow′er of attor′ney, *Law.* a written document given by one person or party to another authorizing the latter to act for the former.

pow′er pack′, *Electronics.* a device for converting the voltage from a power line or battery to the various voltages required by the components of an electronic circuit.

pow′er plant′, **1.** a plant, including engines, dynamos, etc., and the building or buildings necessary for the generation of power, as electric power. **2.** the machinery for supplying power for a particular mechanical process or operation.

pow′er pol′itics, international diplomacy based on the use or threatened use of military power.

pow′er se′ries, *Math.* an infinite series in which the terms are coefficients times successive powers of a given variable, or times products of powers of two or more variables.

pow′er sta′tion, *Elect.* a generating station.

pow′er steer′ing, *Auto.* a steering system in which the position of the steering wheel controls a power source that in its turn guides the wheels on which the vehicle turns.

pow′er struc′ture, **1.** the system of authority or influence in government, politics, education, etc.: *The state elections threatened to upset the existing power structure.* **2.** the people who participate in such a system.

Pow·ha·tan (pou′hə tan′, pou hat′ən), *n.* c1550–1618, Indian chief in Virginia, father of Pocahontas.

pow·wow (pou′wou′), *n.* **1.** (among North American Indians) a ceremony, esp. one accompanied by magic, feasting, and dancing, performed for the cure of disease, success in a hunt, etc. **2.** a council or conference of or with Indians. **3.** *Informal.* any conference or meeting. —*v.i.* **4.** to hold a powwow. [< Algonquian (Narragansett) *pow waw* or *po-wah*]

Pow·ys (pō′is), *n.* **John Cowper,** 1872–1963, and his brother, **Theodore Francis,** 1875–1953, English authors.

pox (poks), *n.* *Pathol.* **1.** a disease characterized by multiple skin pustules, as smallpox. **2.** *Informal.* syphilis. **3.** Also called **soil rot.** *Plant Pathol.* a disease of sweet potatoes, characterized by numerous pitlike lesions on the roots, caused by a fungus, *Streptomyces ipomoea.* **4.** *Archaic* (used interjectionally to express distaste, rejection, aversion, etc.): *A pox on your schemes!* [for *pocks,* pl. of POCK]

Po·yang (pô′yäng′), *n.* a lake in E China, in Kiangsi province. 90 mi. long.

Poz·nań (pôz′nän′yə), *n.* Polish name of **Posen.**

Po·zsony (pô′zhôn′yə), *n.* Hungarian name of **Bratislava.**

Poz·zuo·li (pot swô′lē; *It.* pôt tswô′lē), *n.* a seaport in SW Italy, near Naples: Roman ruins. 51,548 (1961).

pp, *Music.* pianissimo.

pp., **1.** pages. **2.** past participle. **3.** privately printed.

P.P., **1.** parcel post. **2.** parish priest. **3.** past participle. **4.** postpaid. **5.** prepaid.

p.p., **1.** parcel post. **2.** past participle. **3.** postpaid.

ppd., **1.** postpaid. **2.** prepaid.

ppl., participle.

ppm, **1.** parts per million. **2.** pulse per minute.

p.p.m., parts per million. Also, **P.P.M., ppm.**

ppr., present participle. Also, **p.pr.**

pps, pulse per second.

P.P.S., a second or additional postscript. Also, **p.p.s.** [< L *post postscriptum*]

ppt., *Chem.* precipitate.

P.Q., Province of Quebec.

PR, **1.** payroll. **2.** public relations. **3.** Puerto Rico (approved esp. for use with zip code).

Pr, Provençal.

Pr, *Chem.* praseodymium.

Pr., **1.** (of stock) preferred. **2.** Priest. **3.** Prince. **4.** Provençal.

pr., **1.** pair; pairs. **2.** power. **3.** (of stock) preferred. **4.** price. **5.** priest. **6.** printing. **7.** pronoun.

P.R., **1.** proportional representation. **2.** public relations. **3.** Puerto Rico.

prac·ti·ca·ble (prak′tə kə bəl), *adj.* **1.** capable of being done, effected, or put into practice, with the available means; feasible. **2.** capable of being used. [< ML *practic(āre)* (to) PRACTICE + -ABLE] —**prac′ti·ca·bil′i·ty, prac′ti·ca·ble·ness,** *n.* —**prac′ti·ca·bly,** *adv.*
—**Syn. 1.** workable, achievable, attainable. See **possible.** PRACTICABLE, PRACTICAL often cause confusion. PRACTICABLE means possible or feasible, able to be done, capable of being put into practice or of being used: *a practicable method of communication.* PRACTICAL (applied to persons) means sensible and businesslike, (applied to things) efficient and workable, as contrasted with theoretical: *practical measures.*

prac·ti·cal (prak′ti kəl), *adj.* **1.** of or pertaining to practice or action: *practical mathematics.* **2.** consisting of, involving, or resulting from practice or action: *a practical application of a rule.* **3.** of, pertaining to, or concerned with ordinary activities, business, or work: *practical affairs.* **4.** adapted or designed for actual use; useful. **5.** engaged or experienced in actual practice or work. **6.** inclined toward or fitted for actual work or useful activities: *a practical man.* **7.** mindful of the results, usefulness, advantages or disadvantages, etc., of action or procedure. **8.** matter-of-fact; prosaic. **9.** being such in practice or effect; virtual: *a practical certainty.* [ME *practik* (< LL *practic(us)* < Gk *praktikós: prak-* (verbid s. of *prássein* to do) + *-tikos* -TIC) + -AL[1]] —**prac′ti·cal′i·ty, prac′ti·cal·ness,** *n.*
—**Syn. 1.** See **practicable. 7.** PRACTICAL, JUDICIOUS, SENSIBLE refer to good judgment in action, conduct, and the handling of everyday matters. PRACTICAL suggests the ability to adopt means to an end or to turn what is at hand to account: *to adopt practical measures for settling problems.* JUDICIOUS implies the possession and use of discreet judgment and discrimination: *a judicious use of one's time.* SENSIBLE implies the possession and use of sound reason and common sense: *a sensible suggestion.* —**Ant. 7.** ill-advised, unwise, foolish.

prac′tical joke′, a playful trick, often involving some physical agent or means, in which the victim is placed in an embarrassing or disadvantageous position.

prac·ti·cal·ly (prak′tik lē), *adv.* **1.** in effect; virtually. **2.** in a practical manner: *to think practically.* **3.** from a practical point of view. **4.** almost; nearly.

prac′tical nurse′, a person who has not graduated from an accredited school of nursing but who is skilled in caring for the sick, usually under the direction of a licensed physician or registered nurse.

prac·tice (prak′tis), *n., v.,* **-ticed, -tic·ing.** —*n.* **1.** habitual or customary performance; operation: *office practice.* **2.** habit; custom. **3.** repeated performance or systematic exercise for the purpose of acquiring skill or proficiency: *Practice makes perfect.* **4.** skill gained by experience or exercise. **5.** the action or process of performing or doing something. **6.** the exercise or pursuit of a profession or occupation, esp. law or medicine. **7.** the business of a professional man. **8.** *Law.* the established method of conducting legal proceedings. **9.** *Archaic.* plotting; intrigue; trickery. **10.** Usually, **practices.** *Rare.* intrigues; plots. —*v.t.* **11.** to perform or do habitually or usually. **12.** to follow or observe habitually or customarily. **13.** to exercise or pursue as a profession, art, or occupation. **14.** to perform or do repeatedly in order to acquire skill or proficiency. **15.** to train or drill (a person, animal, etc.) in something in order to give proficiency. —*v.i.* **16.** to do something habitually or as a practice. **17.** to pursue a profession, esp. law or medicine. **18.** to exercise oneself by performance tending to give proficiency: *to practice at shooting.* **19.** *Archaic.* to plot or conspire. Also, **practise** (for defs. 11–19). [late ME *practize, practyse* < ML *practizāre,* alter. of *practicāre* < *practica* < Gk *praktikḗ* practical work, n. use of fem. of *praktikós;* see PRACTICAL, -IZE] —**prac′tic·er,** *n.* —**Syn. 2.** See **custom. 3.** application. See **exercise.**

prac·ticed (prak′tist), *adj.* **1.** experienced; expert; proficient. **2.** acquired or perfected through practice. Also, **prac′tised.**

prac′tice teach′er. See **student teacher.**

prac·tise (prak′tis), *v.t., v.i.,* **-tised, -tis·ing.** practice (defs. 11–19). —**prac′tis·er,** *n.*

prac·ti·tion·er (prak tish′ə nər), *n.* **1.** a person engaged in the practice of a profession, occupation, etc. **2.** *Christian Science.* a person authorized to practice healing. [alter. of *practician* (ME *practik* (see PRACTICAL) + -IAN) + -ER[1]]

prae-, var. of **pre-.**

prae·di·al (prē′dē əl), *adj.* **1.** of, pertaining to, or consisting of land or its products; real; landed. **2.** arising from or consequent upon the occupation of land. **3.** attached to land. Also, **predial.** [< ML *praediāl(is)* landed = *praedi(um)* farm, estate + *-ālis* -AL[1]] —**prae′di·al′i·ty,** *n.*

prae·fect (prē′fekt), *n.* prefect.

prae·lect (pri lekt′), *v.i.* prelect. —**prae·lec′tion,** *n.* —**prae·lec′tor,** *n.*

prae·mu·ni·re (prē′myōō nī′rē), *n.* *Eng. Law.* **1.** a writ charging the offense of resorting to a foreign court or authority, as that of the pope. **2.** the offense. [short for late ME *praemūnīre faciās* < ML (for L *praemonēre faciās* that you cause (someone) to be forewarned), the operative words of the writ < *praemūnīre* to warn (L: protect, lit., fortify). See PRAE-, MUNIMENT]

Prae·nes·te (prē nes′tē), *n.* ancient name of **Palestrina.**

prae·no·men (prē nō′mən), *n., pl.* **-nom·i·na** (-nom′ə nə, -nō′mə-), **-no·mens.** the first or personal name of a Roman citizen, as "Gaius" in "Gaius Julius Caesar." Also, **prenomen.** [< L; see PRAE-, NAME] —**prae·nom·i·nal** (prē nom′ə nəl), *adj.*

prae·tor (prē′tər), *n.* (in the ancient Roman republic) one of a number of elected magistrates charged chiefly with the administration of civil justice. Also, **pretor.** [late ME *pretor*

< L *praetor* leader, lit., one going before = *prae(i)t(us)* led (ptp. of *praeīre: prae-* PRAE- + *īre* to go) + *-or* -OR[2]] —**prae′-tor·ship′,** *n.*

prae·to·ri·an (prē tôr′ē ən, -tōr′-), *adj.* **1.** of or pertaining to a praetor. **2.** (*often cap.*) noting or pertaining to the Praetorian Guard. —*n.* **3.** a person having the rank of praetor or ex-praetor. **4.** (*often cap.*) a soldier of the Praetorian Guard. Also, **pretorian.** [< L *praetōriān(us)*]

Praeto′rian Guard′, *Rom. Hist.* the bodyguard of a military commander, esp. the imperial guard stationed in Rome.

Prag (prăk), *n.* German name of **Prague.**

prag·mat·ic (prag mat′ik), *adj.* Also, **prag·mat′i·cal** (for defs. 2, 3, 6, 7). **1.** treating historical phenomena with special reference to their causes, antecedent conditions, and results. **2.** *Philos.* of or pertaining to pragmatism. **3.** of or pertaining to the practical point of view or practical considerations. **4.** of or pertaining to the affairs of a state or community. **5.** busy; active. **6.** officious; meddlesome; interfering. **7.** dogmatic; opinionated. —*n.* **8.** See **pragmatic sanction. 9.** an officious or meddlesome person. [< L *pragmatic(us)* < Gk *pragmatikós* practical = *pragmat-* (s. of *prâgma*) deed, state business, etc. + *-ikos* -IC] —**prag·mat′i·cal′i·ty, prag·mat′i·cal·ness,** *n.* —**prag·mat′i·cal·ly,** *adv.*

prag·mat·i·cism (prag mat′i siz′əm), *n.* the pragmatic philosophy of C. S. Peirce, chiefly a theory of meaning: so called by him to distinguish it from the pragmatism of William James.

prag·mat·ics (prag mat′iks), *n.* (*construed as sing.*) *Logic, Philos.* the branch of semiotics dealing with causal and other relations between words, expressions, or symbols and their users.

pragmat′ic sanc′tion, any one of various imperial decrees with the effect of fundamental law.

prag·ma·tism (prag′mə tiz′əm), *n.* **1.** character or conduct that emphasizes practicality. **2.** a philosophical movement or system having various forms, but generally stressing practical consequences as constituting the essential criterion in determining meaning, truth, or value. Cf. **pragmaticism, instrumentalism. 3.** *Archaic.* **a.** officiousness; meddlesomeness. **b.** dogmatism; arrogance. [PRAGMAT(IC) + -ISM] —**prag′ma·tis′tic,** *adj.*

prag·ma·tist (prag′mə tist), *n.* **1.** a person who is oriented toward the success or failure of a particular line of action, thought, etc.; a practical person. **2.** an advocate or adherent of philosophical pragmatism. —*adj.* **3.** of, pertaining to, or characteristic of pragmatism. [PRAGMAT(IC) + -IST]

Prague (prăg), *n.* a city in and the capital of Czechoslovakia, in the W part, on the Moldau River: also the capital of Bohemia. 1,169,567. Czech, **Pra·ha** (PRÄ′hä). German, **Prag.**

Prai·ri·al (PRE RĒ AL′), *n.* (in the French Revolutionary calendar) the ninth month of the year, extending from May 20 to June 18. [< F]

prai·rie (prâr′ē), *n.* **1.** an extensive, level or slightly undulating, mostly treeless tract of land in the Mississippi valley, characterized by a highly fertile soil and originally covered with coarse grasses, and merging into drier plateaus in the west. **2.** a tract of grassland; meadow. [< F: meadow << L *prāt(um)* meadow + *-āria,* fem. of *-ārius* -ARY] —**prai′rie-like′,** *adj.*

prai′rie break′er, breaker[1](def.4).

prai′rie chick′en, either of two North American gallinaceous birds of western prairies, *Tympanuchus cupido* or *T. pallidicinctus,* having rufous, brown, black, and white plumage. Also called **prai′rie fowl′, prai′rie grouse′.**

prai′rie dog′, any of several gregarious, burrowing rodents of the genus *Cynomys,* of North American prairies, having a barklike cry.

Prairie dog, *Cynomys ludovicianus* (Total length 16 in.; tail 3½ in.)

prai′rie oys′ter, the testis of a calf, used as food. Cf. **mountain oyster.**

Prai′rie Prov′inces, the provinces of Manitoba, Saskatchewan, and Alberta, in W Canada.

prai′rie rose′, a climbing rose, *Rosa setigera,* of the central U.S., having pinkish to white flowers: the state flower of North Dakota.

prai′rie schoon′er, a covered wagon, similar to but smaller than the Conestoga wagon.

Prai′rie Vil′lage, a city in E Kansas, near Kansas City. 28,138 (1970).

prai′rie wolf′, coyote.

praise (prāz), *n., v.,* **praised, prais·ing.** —*n.* **1.** the act of expressing approval or admiration; commendation; laudation. **2.** the offering of grateful homage in words or song, as an act of worship. **3.** the state of being approved or admired. **4.** *Archaic.* a ground for praise, or a merit. —*v.t.* **5.** to express approval or admiration of; commend; extol. **6.** to offer grateful homage to (God or a deity), as in words or song. [ME *preise(n)* < OF *preisi(er)* (to) value, prize < LL *pretiāre* < L *pretium* price, worth, reward. See PRIZE[2]] —**praise′ful,** *adj.* —**praise′less,** *adj.* —**prais′er,** *n.* —**Syn. 1.** acclamation, plaudit, applause, approbation, compliment. **2.** encomium, eulogy, panegyric. **5.** laud, applaud, eulogize. **6.** glorify, magnify, exalt, honor. —**Ant. 1.** condemnation. **5.** depreciate.

praise·wor·thy (prāz′wûr′thē), *adj.* deserving of praise; laudable: *a praiseworthy motive.* —**praise′wor′thi·ly,** *adv.* —**praise′wor′thi·ness,** *n.*

Pra·krit (prä′krit, -krēt), *n.* any of the vernacular Indic languages of the ancient and medieval periods, as distinguished from Sanskrit. [< Skt *prākṛta* natural, common, vulgar = *pra-* before (c. PRE-) + *kṛ* to do, make + *-ta* ptp. suffix. See SANSKRIT] —**Pra·krit′ic,** *adj.*

pra·line (prä′lēn, prā′-, prä lēn′), *n.* any of various confections consisting of almonds, pecans, or other nuts, cooked in syrup, often prepared with brown sugar. [< F; named after Marshal du Plessis-*Praslin* (1598–1675), whose cook invented it]

prall·tril·ler (präl′tril′ər), *n. Music.* a mordent employing the upper musical tone. [< G: lit., rebounding trill]

pram[1] (pram), *n. Chiefly Brit. Informal.* perambulator. [by shortening]

pram[2] (präm), *n. Naut.* a flat-bottomed lighter used in Dutch and German ports. [< LG, D *praam;* c. G *Prahm* < Slav]

prance (prans, präns), *v.,* **pranced, pranc·ing,** *n.* —*v.i.* **1.** to spring from the hind legs; move by springing, as a horse. **2.** to ride on a horse doing this. **3.** to ride gaily, proudly, or insolently. **4.** to move or go in an elated manner; cavort. **5.** to dance or move in a lively or spirited manner; caper. —*v.t.* **6.** to cause to prance. —*n.* **7.** the act of prancing; a prancing movement. [ME *pra(u)nce;* akin to Dan (dial.) *prans(k)* spirited, said of a horse] —**pranc′er,** *n.* —**pranc′ing·ly,** *adv.*

prand., (in prescriptions) dinner. [< L *prandium*]

pran·di·al (pran′dē əl), *adj.* of or pertaining to a meal, esp. dinner. [< L *prandi(um)* luncheon, meal + -AL[1]] —**pran′di·al·ly,** *adv.*

prank[1] (prangk), *n.* **1.** a trick of an amusing or playful nature. **2.** *Rare.* a trick of a malicious nature. [?]

prank[2] (prangk), *v.t.* **1.** to dress or adorn in an ostentatious manner. —*v.i.* **2.** to make an ostentatious show or display. [akin to D *pronken* to show off, strut, *pronk* show, finery, MLG *prank* pomp]

prank·ish (prang′kish), *adj.* **1.** of the nature of a prank. **2.** full of pranks; playful. —**prank′ish·ly,** *adv.* —**prank′ish·ness,** *n.*

prank·ster (prangk′stər), *n.* a mischievous person who plays tricks, practical jokes, etc., at the expense of another.

prao (prou), *n., pl.* **praos.** proa (def. 2).

pra·se·o·dym·i·um (prā′zē ō dim′ē əm, prā′sē-), *n. Chem.* a rare-earth, metallic, trivalent element, named from its green salts. *Symbol:* Pr; *at. wt.:* 140.91; *at. no.:* 59; *sp. gr.:* 6.77 at 20°C. [< NL = *praseo-* (comb. form repr. Gk *prásios* leek-green) + (DI)DYMIUM]

prate (prāt), *v.,* **prat·ed, prat·ing,** *n.* —*v.i.* **1.** to talk excessively and pointlessly; babble. —*v.t.* **2.** to utter in empty or foolish talk. —*n.* **3.** the act of prating. **4.** empty or foolish talk. [late ME < MD *praete(n).* See PRATTLE] —**prat′er,** *n.* —**prat′ing·ly,** *adv.*

prat·fall (prat′fôl′), *n. Slang.* a fall in which a person lands on the buttocks. [*prat* the buttocks (< ?) + FALL]

prat·in·cole (prat′ing kōl′, prā′ting-), *n.* any of several limicoline birds of the genus *Glareola,* of the Eastern Hemisphere, having a short bill, long, narrow, pointed wings, and a forked tail. [< NL *Prātincol(a)* genus name = L *prāt(um)* meadow + *incola* inhabitant]

pra·tique (pra tēk′, prat′ik; *Fr.* PRA TĒK′), *n. Com.* license or permission to use a port, given to a ship after quarantine. [< F: practice < ML *practica.* See PRACTICE]

Pra·to (PRÄ′tô), *n.* a city in central Italy, near Florence. 111,634 (1961). Also called **Pra′to in To·sca′na** (ēn tô-skä′nä).

prat·tle (prat′əl), *v.,* **-tled, -tling,** *n.* —*v.i.* **1.** to talk in a foolish or simple-minded way; chatter; babble. —*v.t.* **2.** to utter by chattering or babbling. —*n.* **3.** the act of prattling. **4.** chatter; babble. **5.** a babbling sound. [< MLG *pratele(n)* (to) chatter, freq. of *praten* to PRATE; see -LE (def. 1)] —**prat′tler,** *n.* —**prat′tling·ly,** *adv.*

Prav·da (präv′də), *n.* the official newspaper of the Communist party in the U.S.S.R. Cf. **Izvestia.** [Russ: lit., truth]

prawn (prôn), *n.* **1.** any of various shrimplike decapod crustaceans of the genera *Palaemon, Penaeus,* etc., certain of which are used as food. —*v.t.* **2.** to catch prawns, as for food. [late ME *prane*] —**prawn′er,** *n.*

Prawn, *Palaemon serratus* (Length 3 to 4 in.)

prax·is (prak′sis), *n., pl.* **prax·is·es, prax·es** (prak′sēz). **1.** practice, as distinguished from theory; application or use, as of knowledge or skills. **2.** convention, habit, or custom. **3.** a set of examples for practice. [< ML < Gk *prâxis* deed, act, action]

Prax·it·e·les (prak sit′əlēz′), *n.* fl. c350 B.C., Greek sculptor. —**Prax·it′e·le′an,** *adj.*

pray (prā), *v.t.* **1.** to make earnest petition to (a person). **2.** to offer devout petition, praise, thanks, etc., to (God or an object of worship). **3.** to make petition or entreaty for; crave. **4.** to offer (a prayer). **5.** to bring, put, etc., by praying. —*v.i.* **6.** to make entreaty or supplication, as to a person or for a thing. **7.** to offer devout petition, praise, thanks, etc., to God or to an object of worship. **8.** to enter into spiritual communion with God or an object of worship through prayer. [ME *preie(n)* < OF *prei(er)* << L *precārī* to beg, pray < *prex* (s. *prec-*) prayer; akin to OE *fricgan,* D *vragen,* G *fragen,* Goth *fraihnan* to ask] —**pray′ing·ly,** *adv.* —**Syn. 1.** entreat, supplicate, beg, beseech, implore.

prayer[1] (prâr), *n.* **1.** a devout petition to, or any form of spiritual communion with, God or an object of worship. **2.** the act or practice of praying. **3.** a spiritual communion with God or an object of worship, as in supplication, thanksgiving, adoration, or confession. **4.** a formula or sequence of words used in or appointed for praying: *the Lord's Prayer.* **5.** a religious observance, either public or private, consisting wholly or mainly of prayer. **6.** that which is prayed for. **7.** a petition; entreaty. **8.** the section of a bill in equity, or of a petition, which sets forth the complaint or the action desired. [ME *preiere* < OF < ML *precāria,* orig. neut. pl. of L *precārius* obtained by entreaty = *prec-* (s. of *prex*) prayer + *-ārius* -ER[2]] —**prayer′less,** *adj.* —**prayer′less·ly,** *adv.*

pray·er[2] (prā′ər), *n.* a person who prays. [late ME *preyare.* See PRAY, -ER[1]]

prayer′ beads′ (prâr), a rosary.

prayer′ book′ (prâr), **1.** a book containing formal prayers to be used in public or private religious devotions. **2.** (*usually caps.*) See **Book of Common Prayer.**

prayer·ful (prâr′fəl), *adj.* given to, characterized by, or expressive of prayer; devout. —**prayer′ful·ly,** *adv.* —**prayer′ful·ness,** *n.*

prayer′ meet′ing (prâr), **1.** a meeting chiefly for prayer. **2.** (in certain Protestant churches) a meeting in midweek, chiefly for individual prayer and the offering of testimonies of faith. Also called **prayer′ serv′ice.**

prayer′ rug′ (prâr), a small rug upon which a Muslim kneels and prostrates himself during his devotions.

prayer′ shawl′ (prâr), *Judaism.* a tallith.

prayer′ wheel′ (prâr), a wheel or cylinder inscribed with or containing prayers, used chiefly by Buddhists of Tibet as a mechanical aid to continual praying, each revolution counting as an uttered prayer.

pray′ing man′tis, mantis. Also, **pray′ing man′tid.**

pre-, an element occurring originally in loan words from Latin, where it meant "before" (*preclude; prevent*); applied freely as a prefix, with the meanings "prior to," "in advance of," "early," "beforehand," "before," "in front of," and with other figurative meanings (*preschool; prewar; prepay; preaxial*). Also, **prae-.** [< L *prae-*, comb. form repr. *prae* (prep. and adv.); akin to FIRST, FORE[1]]

preach (prēch), *v.t.* **1.** to advocate or inculcate (religious or moral truth, right conduct, etc.) in speech or writing. **2.** to proclaim or make known (the gospel, good tidings, etc.) by sermon. **3.** to deliver (a sermon). —*v.i.* **4.** to deliver a sermon. **5.** to give earnest advice, as on religious or moral subjects. **6.** to do this in an obtrusive or tedious way. [ME *preche(n)* < OF *pre(ë)chie(r)* < eccl. L *praedicāre* to preach (L: to assert publicly, proclaim). See PREDICATE]

preach·er (prē′chər), *n.* **1.** a person whose occupation or function it is to preach the gospel. **2.** a person who preaches any doctrine, system of conduct, etc. [ME *precho(u)r* < OF *prech(e)or*, earlier *preëch(e)or* < eccl. L *praedicātor*]

preach·i·fy (prē′chə fī′), *v.i.*, **-fied, -fy·ing.** *Usually Disparaging.* to preach in an obtrusive or tedious way. —**preach′i·fi·ca′tion,** *n.*

preach·ment (prēch′mənt), *n.* **1.** the act of preaching. **2.** a sermon or other discourse, esp. when obtrusive or tedious. [ME *prechement* < OF *preë(s)chement* < ML *praedicāment(um)* speech (LL: PREDICAMENT)]

preach·y (prē′chē), *adj.*, **preach·i·er, preach·i·est.** *Informal.* tediously or pretentiously didactic.

pre·ad·am·ite (prē ad′ə mīt′), *n.* **1.** a person supposed to have existed before Adam. **2.** a person who believes that there were men in existence before Adam. —*adj.* Also, **pre·a·dam·ic** (prē′ə dam′ik). **3.** existing before Adam. **4.** of or pertaining to the preadamites.

pre·ad·o·les·cence (prē′adᵊles′əns), *n.* the period immediately preceding adolescence, usually designated as the years from 9 to 12. —**pre′ad·o·les′cent,** *adj., n.*

pre·am·ble (prē′am′bəl), *n.* **1.** an introductory statement; preface; introduction. **2.** the introductory part of a statute, deed, or the like, stating the reasons and intent of what follows. **3.** a preliminary or introductory fact or circumstance. **4.** (*cap.*) the introductory statement of the U.S. Constitution, setting forth the general principles of American government and beginning with the words, "We the people of the United States, in order to form a more perfect union, ..." [ME < ML *praeambul(um)*, n. use of neut. of LL *praeambulus* walking before] —**pre′am′bled,** *adj.* —**Syn. 1.** opening, beginning; foreword, prologue.

pre·am·pli·fi·er (prē am′plə fī′ər), *n.* a circuit or device that increases the strength of weak incoming signals, as in a radio or phonograph, esp. a separate component that also provides facilities for control and selection of inputs.

pre·ar·range (prē′ə rānj′), *v.t.*, **-ranged, -rang·ing.** to arrange in advance or beforehand. —**pre′ar·range′ment,** *n.*

pre·ax·i·al (prē ak′sē əl), *adj. Anat., Zool.* situated in front of the body axis. —**pre·ax′i·al·ly,** *adv.*

preb·end (preb′ənd), *n.* **1.** a stipend allotted from the revenues of a cathedral or a collegiate church to a canon or member of the chapter. **2.** the land yielding such a stipend. **3.** a prebendary. [ME *prebende* < ML *prēbenda*, var. of *praebenda* prebend, LL: allowance, neut. pl. ger. of L *prae(hi)bēre* to offer, furnish = *prae-* PRE- + *-hibēre*, comb. form of *habēre* to have, hold] —**pre·ben·dal** (pri ben′dᵊl), *adj.*

preb·en·dar·y (preb′ən der′ē), *n., pl.* **-dar·ies. 1.** a canon or clergyman who is entitled to a prebend. **2.** *Ch. of Eng.* an honorary canon having the title of a prebend but not receiving a stipend. [< ML *praebendāri(us)*]

prec., 1. preceded. 2. preceding.

Pre·cam·bri·an (prē kam′brē ən), *Geol.* —*adj.* **1.** noting or pertaining to the earliest era, ending 600,000,000 years ago, during which the earth's crust was formed and the first life appeared. —*n.* **2.** the Precambrian era. Also, **Pre-Cam′bri·an.**

pre·can·cel (prē kan′səl), *v.*, **-celed, -cel·ing** or (*esp. Brit.*) **-celled, -cel·ling,** *n. Philately.* —*v.t.* **1.** to cancel (a stamp) before placing it on a piece of postal matter. —*n.* **2.** a precanceled stamp. —**pre′can·cel·la′tion,** *n.*

pre·car·i·ous (pri kâr′ē əs), *adj.* **1.** dependent on circumstances beyond one's control; uncertain; unstable; insecure. **2.** dependent on the will or pleasure of another; liable to be withdrawn or lost at the will of another. **3.** exposed to or involving danger; dangerous; perilous; risky. **4.** having insufficient, little, or no foundation; based upon doubtful premises. [< L *precārius* obtained by entreaty or mere favor, hence uncertain. See PRAYER[1]] —**pre·car′i·ous·ly,** *adv.* —**pre·car′i·ous·ness,** *n.* —**Syn. 1.** unsteady, doubtful, dubious. **3.** hazardous. **4.** groundless, unfounded. —**Ant. 1.** secure. **3.** safe.

prec·a·to·ry (prek′ə tōr′ē, -tôr′ē), *adj.* characterized by or expressing entreaty or supplication: *precatory overtures.* Also, **prec·a·tive** (prek′ə tiv). [< LL *precātōri(us)* = L *precāt(us)* (ptp. of *precārī* to pray, entreat) + *-ōrius* -ORY[1]]

pre·cau·tion (pri kô′shən), *n.* **1.** a measure taken in advance to avert possible evil or to secure good results. **2.** caution employed beforehand; prudent foresight. —*v.t.* **3.** to forewarn; put on guard. [< LL *praecautiōn-* (s. of *praecautiō*)]

pre·cau·tion·ar·y (pri kô′shə ner′ē), *adj.* **1.** of, pertaining to, or characterized by precaution. **2.** expressing or advising precaution. Also, **pre·cau′tion·al.**

pre·cau·tious (pri kô′shəs), *adj.* using or displaying precaution.

pre·cede (pri sēd′), *v.*, **-ced·ed, -ced·ing.** —*v.t.* **1.** to go before, as in place, order, rank, importance, or time. **2.** to introduce by something preliminary; preface. —*v.i.* **3.** to go or come before. [ME *precede(n)* < L *praecēd(ere)*] —**pre·ced′a·ble,** *adj.*

prec·e·dence (pres′i dəns, pri sēd′ᵊns), *n.* **1.** the act or fact of preceding. **2.** priority in order, rank, importance, etc. **3.** priority in time. **4.** the right to precede others in ceremonies or social formalities. **5.** the order to be observed in ceremonies by persons of different ranks, as by diplomatic protocol. [PRECED(ENT)[2] + -ENCE]

prec·e·den·cy (pres′i dən sē, pri sēd′ᵊn sē), *n., pl.* **-cies.** precedence. [PRECED(ENCE) + -ENCY]

prec·e·dent[1] (pres′i dənt), *n.* **1.** a preceding instance or case that may serve as an example for or a justification in subsequent cases. **2.** *Law.* a legal decision serving as an authoritative rule in future similar cases. [late ME; n. use of PRECEDENT[2]] —**prec′e·dent·less,** *adj.*

pre·ced·ent[2] (pri sēd′ᵊnt, pres′i dənt), *adj.* preceding; anterior. [ME < L *praecēdent-* (s. of *praecēdēns*) going before, prp. of *praecēdere* to PRECEDE; see -ENT]

prec·e·den·tial (pres′i den′shəl), *adj.* **1.** of the nature of or constituting a precedent. **2.** having precedence.

pre·ced·ing (pri sē′ding), *adj.* that precedes; previous: *See the footnote on the preceding page.* —**Syn.** foregoing, prior, former, earlier. —**Ant.** succeeding, following.

pre·cent (pri sent′), *v.t.* **1.** to lead as a precentor in singing. —*v.i.* **2.** to act as a precentor. [back formation from PRECENTOR]

pre·cen·tor (pri sen′tər), *n.* a person who leads a church choir or congregation in singing. [< L *praecentor* leader in music = *praecent(us)* played before (ptp. of *praecinere*) + *-or* -OR[2]. See PRE-, CANTOR] —**pre·cen·to·ri·al** (prē′sen tōr′ē əl, -tôr′-), *adj.* —**pre·cen′tor·ship′,** *n.*

pre·cept (prē′sept), *n.* **1.** a commandment or direction given as a rule of action or conduct. **2.** an injunction as to moral conduct; maxim. **3.** a procedural directive or rule, as for the performance of some technical operation. **4.** *Law.* a written order issued pursuant to law. [ME < L *praecept(um)* maxim, n. use of neut. of *praeceptus* instructed, ptp. of *praecipere* to direct, lit., to take beforehand = *prae-* PRE- + *-cipere*, comb. form of *capere* to take] —**Syn. 1.** directive, order, guide, instruction.

pre·cep·tive (pri sep′tiv), *adj.* **1.** of the nature of or expressing a precept; mandatory. **2.** giving instructions; instructive. [late ME < L *praeceptīv(us)*] —**pre·cep′tive·ly,** *adv.*

pre·cep·tor (pri sep′tər, prē′sep-), *n.* **1.** an instructor; teacher; tutor. **2.** the head of a preceptory. Also, *referring to a woman,* **pre·cep′tress.** [late ME < L *praeceptor*] —**pre·cep·tor·ate** (pri sep′tər it), *n.* —**pre·cep·to·ri·al** (prē′sep tōr′ē əl, -tôr′-), **pre·cep′to·ral,** *adj.* —**pre′cep·to′ri·al·ly,** *adv.* —**pre·cep′tor·ship′,** *n.*

pre·cep·to·ry (pri sep′tə rē), *n., pl.* **-ries.** a subordinate house or community of the Knights Templars; commandery. [< ML *praeceptōria*]

pre·cess (prē ses′), *v.i. Mech.* to undergo precession. [back formation from PRECESSION]

pre·ces·sion (prē sesh′ən), *n.* **1.** the act or fact of preceding; precedence. **2.** *Astron.* **a.** See **precession of the equinoxes. b.** the related motion of the earth's axis of rotation. **3.** *Mech.* the motion of the rotation axis of a rigid body, as a spinning top, when a disturbing force is applied while the body is rotating: the rotation axis, moving in a direction perpendicular to the direction of the force, describes a cone with one end of the rotating body at its vertex. [< LL *praecessiōn-* (s. of *praecessiō*) a going before, advance = L *praecess(us)* (ptp. of *praecēdere* to PRECEDE) + *-iōn-* -ION]

pre·ces·sion·al (prē sesh′ə nᵊl), *adj.* **1.** pertaining to or resulting from the precession of the equinoxes. **2.** *Mech.* of, pertaining to, or characterized by precession.

preces′sion of the e′quinoxes, *Astron.* the earlier occurrence of the equinoxes in each successive sidereal year because of a slow retrograde motion of the equinoctial points along the ecliptic: caused by the gravitational force of the sun and the moon upon the earth.

pre′ab·sorb′, *v.*
pre·ab′stract, *adj.*
pre′ac·cept′, *v.*
pre′ac·cept′ance, *n.*
pre′ac·cus′tom, *v.t.*
pre′a·dapt′, *v.t.*
pre′ad·just′, *v.t.*
pre′ad·just′a·ble, *adj.*
pre′ad·just′ment, *n.*
pre′a·dult′, *adj.*
pre·ad′ver·tise′, *v.,* **-tised, -tis·ing.**
pre′af·firm′, *v.*
pre′af·fir·ma′tion, *n.*
pre′af·firm′a·tive, *adj.*
pre·aged′, *adj.*
pre′ag·ri·cul′tur·al, *adj.*
pre·al′ge·bra, *adj.*
pre′al·lot′, *v.t.,* **-lot·ted, -lot·ting.**
pre′al·pha·bet′i·cal, *adj.*
pre·a′nal, *adj.*
pre′an·nounce′, *v.t.,* **-nounced, -nounc·ing.**
pre′an·nounce′ment, *n.*
pre′an·tiq′ui·ty, *n.*
pre′ap·pear′ance, *n.*
pre′ap·per·cep′tion, *n.*
pre′ap·pli·ca′tion, *n.*
pre′ap·point′, *v.t.*
pre·arm′, *v.t.*
pre′-Ar·thu′ri·an, *adj.*
pre′ar·tic′u·late, *adj.*
pre-Ar′y·an, *adj.*
pre′as·cer·tain′, *v.t.*
pre′as·cer·tain′ment, *n.*
pre′as·sem′ble, *v.t.,* **-bled, -bling.**
pre′as·sem′bly, *n.*
pre′as·sign′, *v.t.*
pre′as·signed′, *adj.*
pre′as·sump′tion, *n.*
pre′as·sur′ance, *n.*
pre′-As·syr′i·an, *adj.*
pre′at·tune′, *v.t.,* **-tuned, -tun·ing.**
pre·au′di·to′ry, *adj.*
pre′-Au·gus′tan, *adj.*
pre′-Bab·y·lo′ni·an, *adj.*
pre′-Ba·co′ni·an, *adj.*
pre′bar·bar′ic, *adj.*
pre′bar·bar′i·cal·ly, *adv.*
pre·bar′bar·ous, *adj.*
pre·bill′, *v.t.*
pre·bless′, *v.t.*
pre·boil′, *v.t.*
pre-Brit′ish, *adj.*
pre-Bud′dhist, *adj.*
pre-Byz′an·tine′, *adj.*
pre·cal′cu·la·ble, *adj.*
pre·cal′cu·late′, *v.t.,* **-lat·ed, -lat·ing.**
pre′cal·cu·la′tion, *n.*
pre-Ca′naan·ite′, *n., adj.*
pre′-Ca·naan·it′ic, *adj.*
pre·can′cer·ous, *adj.*
pre′cap·i·tal·is′tic, *adj.*
pre′-Car·bon·if′er·ous, *adj.*
pre·car′di·ac′, *adj.*
pre′-Car·o·lin′gi·an, *adj.*
pre′cel·e·bra′tion, *n.*
pre-Celt′ic, *adj.*

pre·cinct (prē′siŋ̲kt), *n.* **1.** a district, as of a city, marked out for governmental, administrative, or other purposes: *a police precinct.* **2.** one of a fixed number of districts of a city, town, etc., divided for voting purposes. **3.** a space or place of definite or understood limits. **4.** Often, **precincts.** an enclosing boundary or limit. **5. precincts,** the parts or regions immediately surrounding a place; environs: *the precincts of a town.* **6.** *Chiefly Brit.* the ground immediately surrounding a church, temple, or the like. **7.** a walled or otherwise bounded or limited space within which a building or place is situated. [ME < ML *praecinct(um)*, neut. of L *praecinctus* girded about, surrounded (ptp. of *praecingere*) = *prae-* PRE- + *cing-* (s. of *cingere* to surround) + *-tus* ptp. suffix] **—Syn. 1, 2.** ward. **3.** territory. **6.** compound.

pre·ci·os·i·ty (presh′ē os′i tē), *n., pl.* **-ties.** fastidious or carefully affected refinement, as in language, style, or taste. [ME *preciousite* preciousness < MF *preciosite* < L *pretiōsitās*. See PRECIOUS, -ITY]

pre·cious (presh′əs), *adj.* **1.** of high price or great value; very valuable or costly. **2.** highly esteemed for some spiritual, nonmaterial, or moral quality. **3.** dear; beloved. **4.** flagrant; gross: *a precious fool.* **5.** affectedly or excessively delicate, refined, or nice: *precious manners.* **6.** highly important; irreplaceable or irretrievable. **—*n.* 7.** a dearly beloved person; darling. [ME *preciose* < L *pretiōs(us)* costly, valuable = *preti(um)* PRICE, value + *-ōsus* -OUS] **—pre′cious·ly,** *adv.* **—pre′cious·ness,** *n.* **—Syn. 1.** See **valuable.**

pre′cious met′al, a metal of the gold, silver, or platinum group.

pre′cious stone′ a gem, as a diamond, distinguished for its beauty and rarity, used in jewelry.

prec·i·pice (pres′ə pis), *n.* **1.** a cliff with a vertical, nearly vertical, or overhanging face. **2.** a situation of great peril: *on the precipice of war.* [< MF < L *praecipit(ium)* steep place = *praecipit-* (s. of *praeceps*) steep, lit., head before + *-ium* n. suffix. See PRE-, CAPUT] **—prec′i·piced,** *adj.*

pre·cip·i·tan·cy (pri sip′i tən sē), *n., pl.* **-cies. 1.** the quality or state of being precipitant. **2.** headlong or rash haste. **3. precipitancies,** hasty or rash acts. Also, **pre·cip′i·tance.** [PRECIPIT(ANT) + -ANCY]

pre·cip·i·tant (pri sip′i tᵊnt), *adj.* **1.** falling headlong. **2.** rushing headlong, rapidly, or hastily onward. **3.** hasty; rash. **4.** unduly sudden or abrupt. **—*n.* 5.** *Chem.* anything that causes precipitation. [< L *praecipitant-* (s. of *praecipitāns*), prp. of *praecipitāre* to cast down headlong] **—pre·cip′i·tant·ly,** *adv.*

pre·cip·i·tate (*v.* pri sip′i tāt′; *adj., n.* pri sip′i tit, -tāt′), *v.,* **-tat·ed, -tat·ing,** *adj., n.* **—*v.t.* 1.** to hasten the occurrence of; bring about prematurely, hastily, or suddenly. **2.** *Chem.* to separate (a substance) in solid form from a solution, as by means of a reagent. **3.** *Meteorol.* to condense (moisture) from a vaporous state into rain, snow, etc. **4.** to cast down headlong; fling or hurl down. **5.** to cast, plunge, or send, esp. violently or abruptly. **—*v.i.* 6.** to separate from a solution as a precipitate. **7.** to fall to the earth's surface as a condensed form of water; to rain, snow, hail, drizzle, etc. **8.** to be cast or thrown down headlong. **—*adj.* 9.** headlong. **10.** rushing headlong or rapidly onward. **11.** proceeding rapidly or with great haste: *a precipitate retreat.* **12.** exceedingly sudden or abrupt. **13.** done or made without sufficient deliberation; overhasty; rash. **—*n.* 14.** *Chem.* a substance precipitated from a solution. **15.** moisture condensed in the form of rain, snow, etc. [< L *praecipitāt(us)* (ptp. of *praecipitāre*) to cast down headlong = *praecipit-* (s. of *praeceps* steep; see PRECIPICE) + *-ātus* -ATE¹] **—pre·cip′i·tate·ly,** *adv.* **—pre·cip′i·tate·ness,** *n.* **—pre·cip′i·ta′tive,** *adj.* **—pre·cip′i·ta′tor,** *n.* **—Syn. 1.** accelerate; crystallize. **13.** reckless, indiscreet. **—Ant. 1.** retard. **13.** careful.

pre·cip·i·ta·tion (pri sip′i tā′shən), *n.* **1.** the act of precipitating. **2.** the state of being precipitated. **3.** a casting down or falling headlong. **4.** a hastening or hurrying in movement, procedure, or action. **5.** sudden haste. **6.** unwise or rash rapidity. **7.** *Chem., Physics.* the precipitating of a substance from a solution. **8.** *Meteorol.* **a.** falling products of condensation in the atmosphere, as rain, snow, or hail. **b.** the amount precipitated. [< L *praecipitātiōn-* (s. of *praecipitātiō*) a falling headlong. See PRECIPITATE, -ION]

pre·cip·i·tin (pri sip′i tin), *n.* *Immunol.* an antibody that reacts with its specific antigen to form an insoluble precipitate. [PRECIPIT(ATE) + -IN²]

pre·cip·i·tous (pri sip′i təs), *adj.* **1.** of the nature of or characterized by precipices: *a precipitous mountain.* **2.** extremely or impassably steep: *precipitous trails.* **3.** precipitate. [PRECIPIT(ATE) (adj.) + -OUS] **—pre·cip′i·tous·ly,** *adv.* **—pre·cip′i·tous·ness,** *n.* **—Syn. 2.** abrupt, sheer, perpendicular. **—Ant. 2.** flat, level.

pré·cis (prā sē′, prā′sē), *n., pl.* **-cis** (-sēz′, -sēz), *v.* **—*n.* 1.** an abstract or summary. **—*v.t.* 2.** to make a précis of. [< F, n. use of adj., lit., cut short. See PRECISE] **—Syn. 1.** digest, condensation.

pre·cise (pri sīs′), *adj.* **1.** definitely or strictly stated, defined, or fixed. **2.** being exactly that and neither more nor less: *a precise amount.* **3.** being just that and no other. **4.** definite or exact in statement, as a person. **5.** carefully distinct: *precise articulation.* **6.** exact in measuring, recording, etc. **7.** excessively or rigidly particular: *precise observance of rules.* [< L *praecīs(us)* lopped off, brief (ptp. of *praecīdere*) = *prae-* PRE- + *-cīsus*, comb. form of *caesus*, ptp. of *caedere* to cut] **—pre·cise′ly,** *adv.* **—pre·cise′ness,** *n.* **—Syn. 1.** explicit. See **correct. —Ant. 1.** indefinite.

pre·ci·sian (pri sizh′ən), *n.* **1.** a person who adheres punctiliously to the observance of rules or forms, esp. in matters of religion. **2.** one of the English Puritans of the 16th and 17th centuries. **—pre·ci′sian·ism,** *n.*

pre·ci·sion (pri sizh′ən), *n.* **1.** the state or quality of being precise. **2.** mechanical exactness. **3.** punctiliousness; strictness. **4.** *Math.* the degree to which the correctness of a quantity is expressed. Cf. **accuracy** (def. 3). **5.** *Chem., Physics.* the extent to which a given set of measurements of the same sample agree with their mean. Cf. **accuracy** (def. 2). **—*adj.* 6.** of, pertaining to, or characterized by precision: *precision instruments.* [< L *praecisiōn-* (s. of *praecisiō*) a cutting off] **—pre·ci′sion·al,** *adj.* **—pre·ci′sion·ism,** *n.* **—pre·ci′sion·ist,** *n.*

pre·ci·sive (pri sī′siv), *adj.* distinguishing (a person or thing) from another or others: *precisive imputation of guilt.* [< L *praecīs(us)* (see PRECISE) + -IVE]

pre·clin·i·cal (prē klin′i kəl), *adj.* *Med.* of or pertaining to the period prior to the appearance of symptoms.

pre·clude (pri klo͞od′), *v.t.,* **-clud·ed, -clud·ing. 1.** to prevent the presence, existence, or occurrence of; make impossible: *The slightness of the evidence precludes a conviction.* **2.** to exclude or debar from something. [< L *praeclūd(ere)* (to) shut off, close = *prae-* PRE- + *-clūdere*, comb. form of *claudere* to shut] **—pre·clud′a·ble,** *adj.* **—pre·clu·sion** (pri klo͞o′zhən), *n.* **—pre·clu·sive** (pri klo͞o′siv), *adj.* **—pre·clu′sive·ly,** *adv.*

pre·co·cial (pri kō′shəl), *adj.* (of birds) active, down-covered, and able to move about freely when hatched. [PRECOCI(OUS) + -AL¹]

pre·co·cious (pri kō′shəs), *adj.* **1.** forward in development, esp. mental development: *a precocious child.* **2.** prematurely developed, as the mind, faculties, etc. **3.** of or pertaining to premature development. **4.** *Bot.* **a.** flowering, fruiting, or ripening early, as plants or fruit. **b.** bearing blossoms before leaves, as plants. **c.** appearing before leaves, as flowers. [PRECOCI(TY) + -OUS] **—pre·co′cious·ly,** *adv.* **—pre·co′cious·ness,** *n.*

pre·coc·i·ty (pri kos′i tē), *n.* the state, condition, or tendency of being precocious. [< F *précocité* = *précoce* (< L *praecoci-*, s. of *praecox* early ripe) + *-ité* -ITY]

pre·cog·ni·tion (prē′kog nish′ən), *n.* knowledge of a future event or situation, esp. through extrasensory means. **—pre·cog·ni·tive** (prē kog′ni tiv), *adj.*

pre-Co·lum·bi·an (prē′kə lum′bē ən), *adj.* of or pertaining to the Americas before their discovery by Columbus: *pre-Columbian art.*

pre·con·ceive (prē′kən sēv′), *v.t.,* **-ceived, -ceiv·ing.** to form an idea or conception of in advance.

pre·con·cep·tion (prē′kən sep′shən), *n.* **1.** a conception or opinion formed beforehand. **2.** bias; predilection; prejudice. **—pre′con·cep′tion·al,** *adj.*

pre·con·cert (prē′kən sûrt′), *v.t.* to arrange in advance or beforehand, as by a previous agreement. **—pre′con·cert′ed·ly,** *adv.* **—pre′con·cert′ed·ness,** *n.*

pre·con·di·tion (prē′kən dish′ən), *v.t.* **1.** to subject (a person or thing) to a special treatment in preparation for something. **—*n.* 2.** a condition existing before or necessary to a subsequent result.

pre·co·nise (prē′kə nīz′), *v.t.,* **-nised, -nis·ing.** *Chiefly Brit.* preconize. **—pre′co·ni·sa′tion,** *n.* **—pre′co·nis′er,** *n.*

pre·co·nize (prē′kə nīz′), *v.t.,* **-nized, -niz·ing. 1.** to proclaim or commend publicly. **2.** to summon publicly. **3.** *Rom. Cath. Ch.* (of the pope) to declare solemnly in consistory the appointment of (a new bishop or other high ecclesiastic). [late ME < ML *praecōniz(āre)* (to) herald, announce = L *praecōn-* (s. of *praecō*) crier, herald + *-izāre* -IZE] **—pre′co·ni·za′tion,** *n.* **—pre′co·niz′er,** *n.*

pre·con·scious (prē kon′shəs), *adj.* **1.** *Psychoanal.* absent from but capable of being readily brought into consciousness; foreconscious. **2.** occurring prior to the development of consciousness. **—*n.* 3.** the preconscious portion of the mind. **—pre·con′scious·ly,** *adv.*

pre·con·tract (*n.* prē kon′trakt; *v.* prē′kən trakt′), *n.* **1.** a preexisting contract that legally prevents one from making a similar contract. **2.** (formerly) such an agreement constituting a legally binding betrothal. **—*v.t.* 3.** to bind by means of a precontract. **4.** to contract for or agree to do (something) in advance of beginning it. **—*v.i.* 5.** to make an advance contract or agreement. **—pre′con·trac′tive,** *adj.* **—pre·con·trac·tu·al** (prē′kən trak′cho͞o əl), *adj.*

pre·cook (prē ko͝ok′), *v.t.* to cook (food) partly or completely beforehand, so that it may be cooked or warmed quickly at a later time.

pre·crit·i·cal (prē krit′i kəl), *adj.* *Med.* anteceding a crisis.

pre·cur·sor (pri kûr′sər, prē′kûr-), *n.* **1.** a person or thing that precedes, as in a job, a method, etc.; a predecessor. **2.** a person or thing that goes before and indicates the approach of someone or something else; harbinger: *The first robin is a precursor of spring.* [< L *praecursor* forerunner. See PRE-, CURSIVE, -OR²] **—Syn. 1.** forerunner. **2.** herald.

pre·cur·so·ry (pri kûr′sə rē), *adj.* **1.** of the nature of a precursor; preliminary; introductory. **2.** indicative of something to follow. Also, **pre·cur·sive** (pri kûr′siv). [< L *praecursōri(us)*]

pred., predicate.

pre·da·cious (pri dā′shəs), *adj.* predatory; rapacious. Also,

pre′-Chau·ce′ri·an, *adj.*
pre·check′, *v.t.*
pre·chill′, *v.t.*
pre′-Chi·nese′, *adj.*
pre-Chris′tian, *adj., n.*
pre-Christ′mas, *adj.*
pre′civ·i·li·za′tion, *n.*
pre·clas′sic, *adj.*
pre·clas′si·cal, *adj.*
pre·clean′, *v.t.*
pre·clean′er, *n.*
pre·cog′i·tate′, *v.,* **-tat·ed, -tat·ing.**
pre′cog·i·ta′tion, *n.*
pre·col′lege, *adj.*
pre′col·le′giate, *adj.*
pre′com·bi·na′tion, *n.*
pre′con·ceal′, *v.t.*
pre′con·ceal′ment, *n.*
pre′con·ces′sion, *n.*
pre′con·demn′, *v.t.*
pre′con·dem·na′tion, *n.*
pre′con·jec′ture, *v.t.,* **-tured, -tur·ing.**
pre′con·nec′tion, *n.*
pre-Con′quest, *adj.*
pre′con·sid′er·a′tion, *n.*
pre′con·struct′, *v.t.*
pre′con·struc′tion, *n.*
pre′con·sul·ta′tion, *n.*
pre′con·trive′, *v.,* **-trived, -triv·ing.**
pre′con·vic′tion, *n.*
pre′-Co·per′ni·can, *adj.*
pre·coun′sel, *n., v.,* **-seled, -sel·ing** or (*esp. Brit.*) **-selled, -sel·ling.**
pre·cra′ni·al, *adj.*
pre′-Cru·sade′, *adj.*
pre·crys′tal·line, *adj.*
pre·cul′tur·al, *adj.*
pre·cure′, *v.t.,* **-cured, -cur·ing.**
pre·cur′rent, *adj.*

esp. Biol., **pre·da/ceous.** [PRED(ATORY) + -ACIOUS] **—pre·da/cious·ness, pre·dac·i·ty** (pri das/i tē); *esp. Biol.*, **pre·da/ceous·ness,** *n.*

pre·date (prē dāt/), *v.t.*, **-dat·ed, -dat·ing. 1.** to date before the actual time; antedate. **2.** to precede in date.

pre·da·tion (pri dā/shən), *n.* **1.** the act of plundering or robbing. **2.** predatory behavior. **3.** a relation between animals in which one organism captures and feeds on others. [< L *praedātiōn-* (s. of *praedātiō*) a taking of booty, plundering. See PREDATORY, -ION]

pred·a·tor (pred/ə tər), *n.* a predatory person, organism, or thing. [< L *praedātor* plunderer = *praedāt(us)* (ptp. of *praedārī* to plunder < *praeda* PREY) + *-or* -OR[2]]

pred·a·to·ry (pred/ə tōr/ē, -tôr/ē), *adj.* **1.** of, pertaining to, or characterized by plunder, exploitation, etc. **2.** living by plunder, exploitation, etc. **3.** *Zool.* habitually preying upon other animals. [< L *praedātōri(us)*] **—pred/a·to/ri·ly,** *adv.* **—pred/a·to/ri·ness,** *n.* **—Syn. 1, 2.** rapacious.

pre·dawn (prē dôn/, prē/-), *n.* **1.** the period immediately preceding dawn. **—***adj.* **2.** of or pertaining to the time immediately prior to dawn.

pre·de·cease (prē/di sēs/), *v.t.*, **-ceased -ceas·ing.** to die before (another person, an event, etc.).

pred·e·ces·sor (pred/i ses/ər, pred/i ses/ər *or, esp. Brit.*, prē/di ses/ər), *n.* **1.** a person who precedes another in an office, position, etc. **2.** something succeeded or replaced by something else. **3.** *Archaic.* an ancestor; forefather. [ME *predecessour* < AF < LL *praedēcessor* = L *prae-* PRE- + *dēcessor* retiring official (*dēcess(us)* retired (ptp. of *dēcēdere* to withdraw; see DE-, CEDE) + *-or* -OR[2])]

pre·des·ti·nar·i·an (pri des/tə nâr/ē ən), *adj.* **1.** of or pertaining to predestination. **2.** believing in predestination. **—***n.* **3.** a person who believes in predestination. [PREDESTIN(ATION) + -ARIAN] **—pre·des/ti·nar/i·an·ism,** *n.*

pre·des·ti·nate (*v.* pri des/tə nāt/; *adj.* pri des/tə nit, -nāt/), *v.*, **-nat·ed, -nat·ing,** *adj.* **—***v.t.* **1.** *Theol.* to foreordain or predestine by divine decree or purpose. **2.** *Obs.* to predetermine. **—***adj.* **3.** predestined; foreordained. [ME < L *praedestināt(us)*, ptp. of *praedestināre* to appoint beforehand] **—pre·des/ti·nate·ly,** *adv.*

pre·des·ti·na·tion (pri des/tə nā/shən, prē/des-), *n.* **1.** the act of predestinating or predestining. **2.** the state of being predestinated or predestined. **3.** fate; destiny. **4.** *Theol.* the foreordination by God of whatever comes to pass, esp. the salvation and damnation of souls. Cf. **election** (def. 4). [ME *predestinacioun* < LL *praedestinātiōn-* (s. of *praedestinātiō*)]

pre·des·tine (pri des/tin), *v.t.*, **-tined, -tin·ing.** to destine in advance; foreordain; predetermine: *He was predestined for success.* [ME *predestine(n)* < L *praedestin(āre)*] **—pre·des/ti·na·ble,** *adj.*

pre·de·ter·mi·nate (prē/di tûr/mə nit, -nāt/), *adj.* determined beforehand; predetermined. **—pre/de·ter/mi·nate·ly,** *adv.*

pre·de·ter·mine (prē/di tûr/min), *v.t.*, **-mined, -min·ing. 1.** to settle or decide in advance: *He had predetermined his answer to the offer.* **2.** to foreordain; predestine. **—pre/de·ter/mi·na/tion,** *n.* **—pre·de·ter·mi·na·tive** (prē/di tûr/mə-nā/tiv, -nə tiv), *adj.* **—pre/de·ter/min·er,** *n.*

pre·di·al (prē/dē əl), *adj.* praedial.

pred·i·ca·ble (pred/ə kə bəl), *adj.* **1.** that may be predicated. **—***n.* **2.** that which may be predicated; an attribute. **3.** *Logic.* any one of the various kinds of predicate that may be used of a subject. [< ML *praedicābil(is)* assertable, L: praiseworthy = *praedicā(re)* (to) declare publicly (see PREACH) + *-bilis* -BLE] **—pred/i·ca·bil/i·ty, pred/i·ca·ble·ness,** *n.* **—pred/i·ca·bly,** *adv.*

pre·dic·a·ment (pri dik/ə mənt), *n.* **1.** an unpleasantly difficult, perplexing, or dangerous situation. **2.** a class or category of logical or philosophical predication. **3.** *Archaic.* a particular state, condition, or situation. [ME < LL *praedicāment(um)* something predicated, asserted < *praedicāre.* See PREDICATE, -MENT] **—pre·dic·a·men·tal** (pri-dik/ə men/tᵊl), *adj.* **—pre·dic/a·men/tal·ly,** *adv.*
—Syn. 1. PREDICAMENT, PLIGHT, DILEMMA, QUANDARY refer to unpleasant or puzzling situations. PREDICAMENT and PLIGHT stress more the unpleasant nature, DILEMMA and QUANDARY the puzzling nature of the situation. PREDICAMENT and PLIGHT are sometimes interchangeable. PREDICAMENT, though capable of being used lightly, may also refer to a really crucial situation: *Stranded in a strange city without money, he was in a predicament.* PLIGHT, however, though originally meaning peril or danger, is seldom used today except lightly: *When his suit failed to come back from the cleaners, he was in a terrible plight.* DILEMMA means a position of doubt or perplexity in which a person is faced by two equally undesirable alternatives: *the dilemma of a person who must support one of two friends in an election.* QUANDARY is the state of mental perplexity of one faced with a difficult situation: *There seemed to be no way out of the quandary.*

pred·i·cant (pred/ə kənt), *adj.* **1.** preaching: *a predicant religious order.* **—***n.* **2.** a preacher. [< eccl. L *praedicant-* (s. of *praedicāns*) preaching. See PREACH, -ANT]

pred·i·cate (*v.* pred/ə kāt/; *adj., n.* pred/ə kit), *v.*, **-cat·ed, -cat·ing,** *adj., n.* **—***v.t.* **1.** to proclaim; declare; affirm; assert. **2.** *Logic.* **a.** to affirm or assert (something) of the subject of a proposition. **b.** to make (a term) the predicate of such a proposition. **3.** to connote; imply. **4.** to found (a statement, action, etc.); base (usually fol. by *on*): *He predicated his behavior on his faith in humanity.* **—***v.i.* **5.** to make an affirmation or assertion. **—***adj.* **6.** predicated. **7.** *Gram.* belonging to the predicate: *a predicate noun.* **—***n.* **8.** *Gram.* (in many languages, as English) a syntactic unit that functions as one of the two main constituents of a simple sentence, the other being the subject, and that consists of a verb and of all the words governed by the verb or modifying it, the whole often expressing the action performed by or the state attributed to the subject, as *is here* in *Larry is here.* **9.** *Logic.* that which is affirmed or denied concerning the subject of a proposition. [< L *praedicāt(us)* ptp. of *praedicāre* to declare publicly, assert = *prae-* PRE- + *-dicāre,* comb. form of *dīcere* to say, make known; see -ATE[1]] **—pred/i·ca/tion,** *n.* **—pred/i·ca/tion·al,** *adj.* **—pred/i·ca/tive,** *adj.* **—pred/i·ca/tive·ly,** *adv.*

pred/icate ad/jective, *Gram.* an adjective used in the predicate, esp. with a copulative verb and modifying the subject, as *dead* in *He is dead,* or the direct object, as *sick* in *It made him sick.*

pred/icate nom/inative, (in Latin, Greek, and certain other languages) a predicate noun or adjective in the nominative case.

pred/icate noun/, *Gram.* a noun used in the predicate with a copulative verb and having the same referent as the subject, as *king* in *He is the king.*

pred/icate objec/tive, *Gram.* See **objective complement.**

pred·i·ca·to·ry (pred/ə kə tōr/ē, -tôr/ē), *adj.* of or pertaining to preaching. [< eccl. L *praedicātōri(us)* of preaching. See PREACH, -ORY[1]]

pre·dict (pri dikt/), *v.t.* **1.** to tell in advance; prophesy. **—***v.i.* **2.** to foretell the future; make a prediction. [< L *praedict(us),* ptp. of *praedicere* to foretell = *prae-* PRE- + *dicere* to say; see DICTUM] **—pre·dict/a·bil/i·ty,** *n.* **—pre·dict/a·ble,** *adj.* **—pre·dict/a·bly,** *adv.* **—pre·dic/tor,** *n.*
—Syn. 1, 2. divine, augur, prognosticate, portend. PREDICT, PROPHESY, FORESEE, FORECAST mean to know or tell (usually correctly) beforehand what will happen. To PREDICT is usually to foretell with precision of calculation, knowledge, or shrewd inference from facts or experience: *Astronomers can predict an eclipse;* it may, however, be used quite lightly: *I predict she'll be a success at the party.* PROPHESY may have the solemn meaning of predicting future events by the aid of divine or supernatural inspiration: *The sibyl prophesied victory;* this verb, too, may be used loosely: *I prophesy he'll be back in the old job.* To FORESEE refers specifically not to the uttering of predictions but to the mental act of seeing ahead; there is often (but not always) a practical implication of preparing for what will happen: *He could foresee their objections.* FORECAST has much the same meaning as FORESEE, except that conjecture rather than real insight or knowledge may be involved, and that such conjecture is publicly announced. It has the same meaning as PREDICT when referring to the weather: *Rain and snow are forecast for tonight.*

pre·dic·tion (pri dik/shən), *n.* **1.** act of predicting. **2.** an instance of this; prophecy. [< L *praedictiōn-* (s. of *praedictiō*) a foretelling] **—Syn. 2.** forecast, augury, prognostication, divination.

pre·dic·tive (pri dik/tiv), *adj.* **1.** of or pertaining to prediction. **2.** being an indication of the future or of future conditions: *a cold wind predictive of snow.* [< LL *praedictīv(us)* foretelling] **—pre·dic/tive·ly,** *adv.* **—pre·dic/tive·ness,** *n.*

pre·dic·to·ry (pri dik/tə rē), *adj.* *Archaic.* predictive.

pre·di·gest (prē/di jest/, -dī-), *v.t.* to treat (food) by an artificial process analogous to digestion to facilitate digestion by the body. **—pre/di·ges/tion,** *n.*

pre·di·lec·tion (pred/ᵊl ek/shən, prēd/-), *n.* a tendency to think favorably of something; partiality. [< ML *praedīlect(us)* beloved, ptp. of *praedīligere* to prefer (see PRE-, DILIGENT) + -ION] **—Syn.** bias, inclination, liking.

pre·dis·pose (prē/di spōz/), *v.*, **-posed, -pos·ing. —***v.t.* **1.** to give an inclination or tendency to beforehand. **2.** to render subject, susceptible, or liable. **3.** to dispose beforehand. **4.** *Archaic.* to dispose of beforehand, as in a will, legacy, or the like. **—***v.i.* **5.** to give or furnish a tendency or inclination; *a job that predisposes to lung infection.* **—pre/dis·pos/al,** *n.* **—pre·dis·pos·ed·ly** (prē/di spō/zid lē, -spōzd/-), *adv.* **—pre/dis·pos/ed·ness,** *n.* **—Syn. 1.** prearrange, prepare. **3.** bias, incline.

pre·dis·po·si·tion (prē dis/pə zish/ən, prē/dis-), *n.* the condition of being predisposed: *a predisposition to think optimistically.* **—pre·dis/po·si/tion·al,** *adj.*

pre·dom·i·nance (pri dom/ə nəns), *n.* the state, condition, or quality of being predominant. Also, **pre·dom/i·nan·cy.** [PREDOMIN(ANT) + -ANCE]

pre·dom·i·nant (pri dom/ə nənt), *adj.* **1.** having ascendancy, power, or influence over others; ascendant. **2.** prevailing; prominent: *Green is the predominant color of leafage.* [< ML *praedominant-* (s. of *praedomināns*) predominating, prp. of *praedominārī*] **—pre·dom/i·nant·ly,** *adv.* **—Syn.** See **dominant.**

pre·dom·i·nate (pri dom/ə nāt/), *v.*, **-nat·ed, -nat·ing. —***v.i.* **1.** to be the stronger or leading element; preponderate; prevail: *The radicals might predominate in the government.* **2.** to have or exert controlling power (often fol. by *over*): *Good sense predominated over his fear.* **3.** to surpass others in authority or influence: *a poet who predominated.* **—***v.t.* **4.** to dominate or prevail over. [< ML *praedomināt(us),* ptp. of *praedominārī* to predominate] **—pre·dom·i·nate·ly** (pri dom/ə nit lē), *adv.* **—pre·dom/i·nat/ing·ly,** *adv.* **—pre·dom/i·na/tion,** *n.* **—pre·dom/i·na/tor,** *n.* **—Syn. 1.** outweigh. **2.** overrule, dominate.

pre·dy·nas·tic (prē/dī nas/tik), *adj.* of, pertaining to, or belonging to a time or period before the first dynasty of a nation, esp. the period in Egypt before c3200 B.C.

pree (PRĒ), *v.t.*, **preed, pree·ing. 1.** *Scot. and North Eng.* to try, test, or taste. **2. pree the mouth of,** *Scot.* to kiss. [shortened form of *preive,* collateral form of PROVE]

pre·e·lec·tion (prē/i lek/shən), *n.* **1.** a choice or selection made beforehand. **—***adj.* **2.** coming before an election: *preelection primaries.* Also, **pre/-e·lec/tion, pre/ë·lec/tion.**

pree·mie (prē/mē), *n.* *Informal.* a premature infant. Also, **premie.** [shortening and alter. of PREMATURE]

pre·em·i·nence (prē em/ə nəns), *n.* the state or character of being preeminent in quality, rank, influence, etc. Also, **pre-em/i·nence, pre·ëm/i·nence.** [ME < LL *praeēminentia*]

pre-Dan/te·an, *adj.*
pre/-Dar·win/i·an, *adj.*
pre/dem·o·crat/ic, *adj.*
pre/de·pres/sion, *adj.*
pre·des/ig·nate, *v.t.*, **-nat·ed, -nat·ing.**
pre/des·ig·na/tion, *n.*
pre/di·ag·nos/tic, *adj.*
pre/di·lu/vi·al, *adj.*
pre/di·rect/, *v.t.*
pre/dis·solve/, *v.t.*, **-solved, -solv·ing.**
pre/dis·tin/guish, *v.t.*
pre/dis·tress/, *n.*, *v.t.*
pre/di·vide/, *v.t.*, **-vid·ed, -vid·ing.**
pre/di·vi/sion, *n.*
pre-Do/ri·an, *adj.*
pre-Dor/ic, *adj.*
pre-East/er, *n.*
pre·ef/fort, *n.*
pre/e·lec/tric, *adj.*
pre/e·lec/tri·cal, *adj.*
pre/el·e·men/tal, *adj.*

pre·em·i·nent (prē em′ə nənt), *adj.* eminent above or before others; superior; surpassing. Also, **pre-em′i·nent, pre·ëm′i·nent.** [late ME < L *praeëminent-* (s. of *praeëminēns*), prp. of *praeēminēre* to project forward, be prominent] —**pre·em′i·nent·ly, pre-em′i·nent·ly, pre·ëm′i·nent·ly,** *adv.* —**Syn.** distinguished, peerless, supreme.

pre·empt (prē empt′), *v.t.* **1.** to occupy (land) in order to establish a prior right to buy. **2.** to acquire or appropriate before someone else: *to preempt the choicest cut of meat.* —*v.i.* **3.** *Bridge.* to make a preemptive bid. —*n.* **4.** *Bridge.* a preemptive bid. Also, **pre-empt′, pre·ëmpt′.** [back formation from PREEMPTION] —**pre·emp·tor, pre-emp·tor, pre·ëmp·tor** (prē emp′tôr), *n.* —**Syn. 1.** claim, appropriate, usurp.

pre·emp·tion (prē emp′shən), *n.* the act or right of claiming or purchasing before or in preference to others. Also, **pre-emp′tion, pre·ëmp′tion.** [< ML *praeëmpt(us)* bought beforehand (ptp. of *praeëmere*) + -ION. See PRE-, REDEEM]

pre·emp·tive (prē emp′tiv), *adj.* **1.** of or pertaining to preemption. **2.** *Bridge.* pertaining to a bid that is unnecessarily high, designed to prevent further bidding. Also, **pre-emp′tive, pre·ëmp′tive.** —**pre·emp′tive·ly, pre-emp′tive·ly, pre·ëmp′tive·ly,** *adv.*

preen[1] (prēn), *v.t.* **1.** (of animals, esp. birds) to trim or dress (feathers, fur, etc.) with the beak or tongue. **2.** to dress (oneself) carefully or smartly; primp. **3.** to pride (oneself) on something. —*v.i.* **4.** to make oneself appear elegant or smart. **5.** to be exultant or proud. [? b. PRUNE[3] and *preen* to pierce (late ME *prene,* v. use, now dial., of PREEN[2]), from the pricking action of a bird's beak in preening] —**preen′er,** *n.*

preen[2] (prēn), *n.* *Chiefly Brit. Dial.* a pin or brooch. [ME *prene,* OE *prēon* a pin; c. Icel *prjōnn* pin; akin to D *priem,* G *Pfriem* awl]

pre·en·gage (prē′en gāj′), *v.t., v.i.,* **-gaged, -gag·ing. 1.** to engage beforehand. **2.** to put under obligation, esp. to marry, by a prior engagement. **3.** to win the favor or attention of beforehand: *Other matters preengaged him.* Also, **pre′-en·gage′, pre′ën·gage′.**

pre·ex·il·i·an (prē′eg zil′ē ən, -zil′yən, -ek sil′-), *adj.* *Judaism.* being or occurring prior to the Exile. Also, **pre′-ex·il′i·an, pre′ëx·il′i·an, pre·ex·il′ic, pre′-ex·il′ic, pre′ëx·il′ic.** [PRE- + L *exili(um)* EXILE + -AN]

pre·ex·ist (prē′ig zist′), *v.i.* **1.** to exist beforehand. **2.** to exist in a previous state. —*v.t.* **3.** to exist prior to (something or someone else). Also, **pre′-ex·ist′, pre′ëx·ist′.** —**pre′ex·ist′ence, pre′-ex·ist′ence, pre′ëx·ist′ence,** *n.* —**pre′ex·ist′ent, pre′-ex·ist′ent, pre′ëx·ist′ent,** *adj.*

pref., 1. preface. **2.** prefaced. **3.** prefatory. **4.** preference. **5.** preferred. **6.** prefix. **7.** prefixed.

pre·fab (*adj., n.* prē′fab′; *v.* prē fab′), *adj., n., v.,* **-fabbed, -fab·bing.** —*adj.* **1.** prefabricated. —*n.* **2.** something prefabricated. —*v.t.* **3.** to prefabricate. [by shortening]

pre·fab·ri·cate (prē fab′rə kāt′), *v.t.,* **-cat·ed, -cat·ing. 1.** to fabricate or construct beforehand. **2.** to manufacture in standardized parts or sections ready for quick assembly and erection, as buildings. —**pre′fab·ri·ca′tion,** *n.* —**pre·fab′ri·ca′tor,** *n.*

pref·ace (pref′is), *n., v.,* **-aced, -ac·ing.** —*n.* **1.** a preliminary statement by the author or editor of a book, setting forth its purpose, expressing acknowledgment of assistance, etc. **2.** an introductory part, as of a speech. **3.** something preliminary or introductory. **4.** *Eccles.* a prayer of thanksgiving, the introduction to the canon of the Mass, ending with the *Sanctus.* —*v.t.* **5.** to provide with or introduce by a preface. **6.** to serve as a preface to. [ME < MF < ML *prēfātia* for L *praefātiō* a saying beforehand = *praefāt(us)* aforesaid (ptp. of *praefārī*) + *-iō(n)-* -ION] —**pref′ac·er,** *n.* —**Syn. 1.** See **introduction. 2, 3.** preamble, prologue.

pref·a·to·ry (pref′ə tōr′ē, -tôr′ē), *adj.* of, pertaining to, or of the nature of a preface: *prefatory explanations.* Also, **pref′a·to′ri·al.** [< L *praefāt(iō)* PREFACE + -ORY[1]] —**pref′a·to′ri·ly,** *adv.*

pre·fect (prē′fekt), *n.* **1.** a person appointed to any of various positions of command, authority, or superintendence, as the chief administrative official of a department of France or Italy. **2.** *Rom. Cath. Ch.* **a.** the dean of a Jesuit school or college. **b.** a cardinal in charge of a congregation in the Curia Romana. Also, **praefect.** [ME < L *praefect(us)* overseer, director (n. use of ptp. of *praeficere* to make before, i.e., put in charge) = *prae-* PRE- + *-fectus* (comb. form of *factus,* ptp. of *facere* to make); see FACT] —**pre·fec·to·ri·al** (prē′fek tōr′ē əl, -tôr′-), *adj.*

pre·fec·ture (prē′fek chər), *n.* the office, jurisdiction, territory, or official residence of a prefect. [< L *praefectūra*] —**pre·fec·tur·al** (pri fek′chər əl), *adj.*

pre·fer (pri fûr′), *v.t.,* **-ferred, -fer·ring. 1.** to set or hold before or above another or other persons or things in estimation. **2.** *Law.* to give priority, as to one creditor over another. **3.** to put forward or present (a statement, suit, etc.) for consideration or sanction. **4.** to put forward or advance, as in rank or office. [ME *preferre* < L *praeferre* to bear before, set before, prefer = *prae-* PRE- + *ferre* to BEAR[1]] —**pre·fer·red·ly** (pri fûr′id lē, -fûrd′-), *adv.* —**pre·fer′red·ness,** *n.* —**pre·fer′rer,** *n.* —**Syn. 1.** favor, fancy. See **choose. 3.** offer, proffer. —**Ant. 1.** reject. **3.** retract.

pref·er·a·ble (pref′ər ə bəl, pref′rə-), *adj.* **1.** worthy to be preferred. **2.** more desirable. [< F *préférable*] —**pref′er·a·bil′i·ty, pref′er·a·ble·ness,** *n.* —**pref′er·a·bly,** *adv.*

pref·er·ence (pref′ər əns, pref′rəns), *n.* **1.** the act of preferring. **2.** the state of being preferred. **3.** that which is preferred. **4.** a practical advantage given to one over others. **5.** a prior right or claim, as to payment of dividends or to assets upon dissolution. **6.** the favoring of one country or group of countries in international trade. [< ML *praeferentia*]

pref·er·en·tial (pref′ə ren′shəl), *adj.* **1.** of, pertaining to, or of the nature of preference. **2.** showing or giving preference. **3.** receiving preference, as a country in trade relations. [< ML *praeferenti(a)* PREFERENCE + -AL[1]] —**pref′er·en′tial·ism,** *n.* —**pref′er·en′tial·ist,** *n.* —**pref′er·en′tial·ly,** *adv.*

pre·fer·ment (pri fûr′mənt), *n.* **1.** the act of preferring. **2.** the state of being preferred **3.** advancement or promotion, as in rank. **4.** a position or office giving social or pecuniary advancement. [late ME]

preferred′ stock′, stock which has a superior claim to that of common stock with respect to dividends and often to assets in the event of liquidation.

pre·fig·u·ra·tion (prē fig′yə rā′shən, prē′fig-), *n.* **1.** the act of prefiguring. **2.** that in which something is prefigured. [ME *prefiguracioun* < LL *praefigūrātiōn-* (s. of *praefigūrātiō*) = *praefigūrāt(us)* (ptp. of *praefigūrāre* to PREFIGURE) + *-iōn-* -ION]

pre·fig·ure (prē fig′yər), *v.t.,* **-ured, -ur·ing. 1.** to represent beforehand; foreshadow. **2.** to represent to oneself beforehand; imagine. [late ME < LL *praefigūrāre*] —**pre·fig·ur·a·tive** (prē fig′yər ə tiv), *adj.* —**pre·fig′ur·a·tive·ly,** *adv.* —**pre·fig′ur·a·tive·ness,** *n.* —**pre·fig′ure·ment,** *n.*

pre·fix (*n.* prē′fiks; *v.* prē fiks′, prē′fiks), *n.* **1.** *Gram.* an affix placed before a base or another prefix, as *un-* in *unkind, un-* and *re-* in *unrewarding.* **2.** something prefixed, as a title before a person's name. —*v.t.* **3.** to fix or put before or in front. **4.** *Gram.* to add as a prefix. **5.** *Rare.* to fix, settle, or appoint beforehand. [(v.) late ME < MF *prefix(er)* < L *praefix(us),* ptp. of *praefīgere* to set up in front; (n.) < NL *praefix(um),* neut. of *praefixus*] —**pre·fix′a·ble,** *adj.* —**pre·fix·al** (prē′fik səl, prē fik′-), *adj.* —**pre′fix·al·ly,** *adv.* —**pre·fix·ion** (prē fik′shən), *n.*

pre·form (*v.* prē′fôrm′; *n.* prē′fôrm′), *v.t.* **1.** to form beforehand. **2.** to determine or decide beforehand: *to preform an opinion.* **3.** to shape or fashion beforehand: *to preform a mold.* —*n.* **4.** any of various uncompleted objects of manufacture after preliminary shaping. [< L *praeform(āre)*]

pre·for·ma·tion (prē′fôr mā′shən), *n.* **1.** previous formation. **2.** *Biol.* (formerly) the theory that the individual, with all its parts, preexists in the germ and grows from microscopic to normal proportions during embryogenesis. —**pre′for·ma′tion·ar·y,** *adj.*

pre·gla·cial (prē glā′shəl), *adj.* prior to a given glacial epoch, esp. the Pleistocene.

preg·na·ble (preg′nə bəl), *adj.* **1.** capable of being taken or won by force: *a pregnable fortress.* **2.** open to attack; assailable. [late ME *prenable* < MF = *pren-* (weak s. of *prendre* < L *pre(he)ndere* to seize, take) + *-able* -ABLE; *-g-* perh. from *expugnable* (now obs.). See IMPREGNABLE] —**preg′na·bil′i·ty,** *n.*

preg·nan·cy (preg′nən sē), *n., pl.* **-cies.** the state, condition, or quality of being pregnant.

preg·nant (preg′nənt), *adj.* **1.** having an offspring developing in the body; with child or young, as a woman or female mammal. **2.** fraught or abounding (usually fol. by *with*): *a silence pregnant with suspense.* **3.** fertile; rich (often fol. by *in*): *a mind pregnant in ideas.* **4.** full of meaning. **5.** full of possibilities; momentous. **6.** teeming with ideas or imagination. [late ME < L *praegnant-* (s. of *praegnāns*) heavy with young = *prae-* PRE- + *gn-* (as in *gnātus* born) + *-ant-* -ANT; see KIN] —**preg′nant·ly,** *adv.*

pre·heat (prē hēt′), *v.t.* to heat before using or before subjecting to some further process: *to preheat an oven before baking a cake.*

pre·hen·si·ble (pri hen′sə bəl), *adj.* able to be seized or grasped. [< L *prehens(us)* (see PREHENSION) + -IBLE]

pre·hen·sile (pri hen′sil, -sīl), *adj.* **1.** adapted for seizing or grasping something: *a prehensile limb.* **2.** fitted for grasping by wrapping around an object: *a prehensile tail.* [PREHENS(ION) + -ILE] —**pre·hen·sil·i·ty** (prē′hen sil′i tē), *n.*

pre·hen·sion (pri hen′shən), *n.* **1.** the act of seizing or grasping. **2.** mental apprehension. [< L *prehensiōn-* (s. of *prehensiō*) a taking hold = *prehens(us)* (ptp. of *prehendere* to seize = *pre-* PRE- + *-hendere* to grasp; akin to GET) + *-iōn-* -ION]

pre·his·tor·ic (prē′hi stôr′ik, -stor′-), *adj.* of or pertaining to a period prior to recorded history. Also, **pre′his·tor′i·cal.** —**pre′his·tor′i·cal·ly,** *adv.*

pre·his·to·ry (prē his′tə rē, -his′trē), *n., pl.* **-ries. 1.** the history of man in the period before recorded events, known mainly through archaeological research. **2.** a history of the events or incidents leading to a crisis, situation, or the like. —**pre·his·to·ri·an** (prē′hi stôr′ē ən, -stōr′-), *n.*

pre·hu·man (prē hyo͞o′mən *or, often,* -yo͞o′-), *adj.* **1.** preceding the appearance or existence of human beings. **2.** of or pertaining to a prototype of man. —*n.* **3.** a prehuman animal.

pre·ig·ni·tion (prē′ig nish′ən), *n.* ignition of the charge in an internal-combustion engine earlier in the cycle than is compatible with proper operation.

pre·judge (prē juj′), *v.t.,* **-judged, -judg·ing. 1.** to judge beforehand. **2.** to pass judgment on prematurely or without sufficient investigation. [< F *préjug(er)* < L *praejūdicāre*] —**pre·judg′er,** *n.* —**pre·judg′ment;** *esp. Brit.,* **pre·judge′ment,** *n.*

pre-Em′pire, *adj.*
pre′en·list′ment, *adj., n.*
pre′es·tab′lish, *v.t.*
pre·es′ti·mate′, *v.t.,* **-mat·ed, -mat·ing.**
pre′ex·am′i·na′tion, *n.*
pre′ex·am′ine, *v.t.,* **-ined, -in·ing.**
pre′ex·per′i·men′tal, *adj.*
pre′ex·pose′, *v.t.,* **-posed, -pos·ing.**
pre′ex·po′sure, *n.*
pre·fash′ion, *v.t., n.*
pre·feu′dal, *adj.*
pre·freeze′, *v.t.,* **-froze, -fro·zen, -freez·ing.**
pre·fur′nish, *v.t.*
pre·game′, *adj.*
pre·gen′i·tal, *adj.*
pre-Geor′gian, *adj.*
pre′-Ger·man′ic, *adj., n.*
pre-Goth′ic, *adj., n.*
pre-Greek′, *adj., n.*
pre·hard′en, *v.t.*
pre-He′brew, *adj., n.*
pre′-Hel·len′ic, *adj.*
pre′-His·pan′ic, *adj.*
pre′-Ho·mer′ic, *adj.*
pre′im·pe′ri·al, *adj.*
pre′in·au′gu·ral, *adj.*
pre·in′cli·na′tion, *n.*
pre′in·cline′, *v.t.,* **-clined, -clin·ing.**
pre·in′di·cate, *v.t.,* **-cat·ed, -cat·ing.**
pre·in′di·ca′tion, *n.*
pre′in·dus′tri·al, *adj.*
pre′in·form′, *v.t.*
pre′in·sert′, *v.t.*
pre′in·struct′, *v.t.*
pre′in·struc′tion, *n.*
pre′in·ti·ma′tion, *n.*
pre′-Is·lam′ic, *adj.*
pre-Jew′ish, *adj.*

prej·u·dice (prej′ə dis), *n., v.,* **-diced, -dic·ing.** —*n.* **1.** an unfavorable opinion or feeling formed beforehand or without knowledge, thought, or reason. **2.** any preconceived opinion or feeling, either favorable or unfavorable. **3.** unreasonable feelings, opinions, or attitudes, esp. of a hostile nature, directed against a racial, religious, or national group. **4.** such attitudes considered collectively. **5.** disadvantage, injury, or detriment to a person or persons resulting from some judgment or action of another or others. **6. without prejudice,** *Law.* without dismissing, damaging, or otherwise affecting a legal interest or demand. —*v.t.* **7.** to affect with a prejudice, either favorable or unfavorable. **8.** to affect to the disadvantage or detriment of; damage; injure. [ME < OF < L *praejūdic(ium)* prejudgment, orig. preliminary or previous judicial inquiry = *prae-* PRE- + *jūdicium* trial < *jūdex* (s. *jūdici-*) JUDGE] —**prej′u·diced·ly,** *adv.* —**Syn. 2.** preconception, predilection, predisposition. See **bias.**

prej·u·di·cial (prej′ə dish′əl), *adj.* causing prejudice or disadvantage; detrimental. [late ME < LL *praejūdiciālis* of a previous judgment] —**prej′u·di′cial·ly,** *adv.* —**prej′u·di′cial·ness,** *n.*

prel·a·cy (prel′ə sē), *n., pl.* **-cies. 1.** the office or dignity of a prelate. **2.** the order of prelates. **3.** the body of prelates collectively. **4.** *Often Derogatory.* the system of church government by prelates. [ME *prelacie* < AF < ML *praelātia.* See PRELATE, -Y³]

prel·ate (prel′it), *n.* an ecclesiastic of a high order, as an archbishop, bishop, etc. [ME *prelat* < ML *praelāt(us)* a civil or ecclesiastical dignitary, n. use of L *praelātus* (ptp. of *praeferre* to set before) = *prae-* PRE- + *lātus,* ptp. of *ferre* to bear] —**prel′ate·ship′,** *n.* —**pre·lat·ic** (pri lat′ik), *adj.*

prel·a·ture (prel′ə chər), *n.* prelacy (defs. 1–3). [< ML *praelātūra*]

pre·lect (pri lekt′), *v.i.* to lecture or discourse. Also, **praelect.** [< L *praelect(us),* ptp. of *praelegere* to lecture = *prae-* PRE- + *legere* to read aloud, choose] —**pre·lec·tion** (pri lek′shən), *n.* —**pre·lec′tor,** *n.*

pre·li·ba·tion (prē′lī bā′shən), *n.* a foretaste. [< L *praelībātiōn-* (s. of *praelībātiō*) a foretaste = *praelībāt(us)* (ptp. of *praelībāre* to taste beforehand) + *-iōn-* -ION]

pre·lim (prē′lim, prə lim′), *n. Slang.* preliminary (def. 3). [by shortening]

prelim., preliminary.

pre·lim·i·nar·y (pri lim′ə ner′ē), *adj., n., pl.* **-nar·ies.** —*adj.* **1.** preceding and leading up to the main part, matter, or business. —*n.* **2.** something preliminary, as an introductory or preparatory step. **3.** a boxing match or other athletic contest that takes place before the main event. **4.** a preliminary examination, as of a candidate for a degree. **5. preliminaries,** *Print.* See **front matter.** [< NL *praelīminār(is).* See PRE-, LIMINAL, -ARY] —**pre·lim′i·nar′i·ly,** *adv.* —**Syn. 1.** prefatory. PRELIMINARY, INTRODUCTORY both refer to that which comes before the principal subject of consideration. That which is PRELIMINARY is in the nature of preparation or of clearing away details that would encumber the main subject or problem; it often deals with arrangements and the like that have to do only incidentally with the principal subject: *preliminary negotiations.* That which is INTRODUCTORY leads with natural, logical, or close connection directly into the main subject of consideration: *introductory steps.* —**Ant. 1.** concluding.

pre·lit·er·ate (prē lit′ər it), *adj.* (of a culture) not leaving or having written records.

prel·ude (prel′yōōd, prāl′- prē′lōōd, prā′-) *n., v.,* **-ud·ed, -ud·ing.** —*n.* **1.** a preliminary to any major action, event, condition, or work. **2.** *Music.* **a.** a relatively short, independent instrumental composition, free in form and resembling an improvisation. **b.** a piece preceding a more important movement. **c.** the overture to an opera. **d.** an independent piece, of moderate length, sometimes used as an introduction to a fugue. **e.** music opening a church service; an introductory voluntary. —*v.t.* **3.** to serve as a prelude to. **4.** to introduce by a prelude. **5.** to play as a prelude. —*v.i.* **6.** to serve as a prelude. **7.** to give a prelude. **8.** to play a prelude. [(n.) earlier *preludy* < ML *praelūdi(um)* = *prae-* PRE- + *-lūdium* play, as in *hastilūdium* tournament (lit., spear-play); cf. L *lūdius* actor, lit., adj. of *lūdus* play, game; (v.) < L *praelūde(re)* (to) play beforehand] —**pre·lud·er** (pri lōō′dər, prel′yə dər), *n.* —**pre·lu′di·al,** *adj.*

pre·lu·sion (pri lōō′zhən), *n.* a prelude. [< L *praelūsiōn-* (s. of *praelūsiō*) a prelude = *praelūs(us)* (ptp. of *praelūdere;* see PRELUDE) + *-iōn-* -ION]

pre·lu·sive (pri lōō′siv), *adj.* introductory. Also, **pre·lu·so·ry** (pri lōō′sə rē). [< L *praelūs(us)* (see PRELUSION) + -IVE] —**pre·lu′sive·ly, pre·lu′so·ri·ly,** *adv.*

prem., premium.

pre·mar·i·tal (prē mar′i tᵊl), *adj.* preceding marriage.

pre·ma·ture (prē′mə tōōr′, -tyōōr′, -chōōr′, prē′mə-chōōr′), *adj.* **1.** occurring, coming, done, or born too soon or before the proper time. **2.** *Rare.* mature before the proper time. [< L *praemātūr(us)*] —**pre′ma·ture′ly,** *adv.* —**pre′ma·tu′ri·ty, pre′ma·ture′ness,** *n.*

pre·max·il·la (prē′mak sil′ə), *n., pl.* **-max·il·lae** (-mak-sil′ē). *Anat., Zool.* one of a pair of bones of the upper jaw of vertebrates, situated in front of and between the maxillary bones. [< NL *praemaxilla*] —**pre·max·il·lar·y** (prē mak′sə ler′ē), *adj.*

pre·med (prē med′), *Informal.* —*n.* Also, **pre·med′ic. 1.** a program of premedical study or training. **2.** a student enrolled in such a program. —*adj.* **3.** premedical.

pre·med·i·cal (prē med′i kəl), *adj.* of or pertaining to studies preparatory to the study of medicine.

pre·med·i·tate (pri med′i tāt′), *v.t., v.i.,* **-tat·ed, -tat·ing.** to meditate, consider, or plan beforehand. [< L *praemeditāt(us)* previously thought out, ptp. of *praemeditārī*] —**pre·med′i·tat′ed·ly,** *adv.* —**pre·med′i·tat′ed·ness,** *n.* —**pre·med′i·tat′ing·ly,** *adv.* —**pre·med′i·ta′tive,** *adj.* —**pre·med′i·ta′tor,** *n.* —**Syn.** See **deliberate.**

pre·med·i·ta·tion (pri med′i tā′shən), *n.* **1.** the act of premeditating. **2.** *Law.* sufficient forethought with intent to commit the act. [late ME *premeditacion* < L *praemeditātiōn-* (s. of *praemeditātiō*) a considering beforehand]

premen′strual syn′drome, *Pathol.* a complex of physical and emotional changes, including depression, irritability, altered appetite, bloating and water retention, and breast soreness, one or more of which may be experienced in the several days before the onset of menstrual flow. *Abbr.:* PMS

pre·mie (prē′mē), *n. Informal.* preemie.

pre·mier (pri mēr′, prim yēr′), *n.* **1.** See **prime minister. 2.** a chief officer. —*adj.* **3.** first in rank; chief; leading. **4.** first in time; earliest; oldest. [< F: lit., first < L *prīmār(ius)* of the first rank] —**pre·mier′ship,** *n.*

pre·miere (pri mēr′, -myâr′), *n., v.,* **-miered, -mier·ing,** *adj.* —*n.* **1.** a first public performance of a play, opera, etc. **2.** the leading woman, as in a drama. —*v.t.* **3.** to present publicly for the first time. —*v.i.* **4.** to have the first public showing. **5.** to perform publicly for the first time, as in a particular role. —*adj.* **6.** first; initial; principal: *a premiere performance.* [< F: lit., first; fem. of PREMIER]

pre·mière (pri mēr′, -myâr′; *Fr.* prə myeʀ′), *n., pl.* **-mières** (-mērs′, -myârs′; *Fr.* -myeʀ′), *v.t., v.i.,* **-miered, -mier·ing,** *adj.* premiere.

pre·mil·le·nar·i·an (prē′mil ə nâr′ē ən), *n.* **1.** a believer in premillennialism. —*adj.* **2.** of or pertaining to the doctrine of premillennialism or a believer in this doctrine. —**pre′mil·le·nar′i·an·ism,** *n.*

pre·mil·len·ni·al (prē′mi len′ē əl), *adj.* of or pertaining to the period preceding the millennium. —**pre′mil·len′ni·al·ly,** *adv.*

pre·mil·len·ni·al·ism (prē′mi len′ē ə liz′əm), *n.* the doctrine or belief that the Second Coming of Christ will precede the millennium. —**pre′mil·len′ni·al·ist,** *n.*

prem·ise (prem′is), *n., v.,* **-ised, -is·ing.** —*n.* **1.** Also, **prem′iss.** *Logic.* a proposition supporting or helping to support a conclusion. **2. premises, a.** a tract of land including its buildings. **b.** a building together with its grounds or other appurtenances. **c.** the property forming the subject of a conveyance or bequest. **3.** *Law.* **a.** a basis, stated or assumed, on which reasoning proceeds. **b.** (in a bill in equity) the statement of facts upon which the complaint is based. —*v.t.* **4.** to set forth beforehand, as by way of introduction or explanation. **5.** to assume, either explicitly or implicitly, (a proposition) as a premise for a conclusion; postulate. —*v.i.* **6.** to state or assume a premise. [ME *premiss* < ML *praemissa,* n. use of fem. of L *praemissus* sent before, ptp. of *praemittere* = *prae-* PRE- + *mittere* to send. See DISMISS, REMISS] —**Syn. 1.** assumption, postulate.

pre·mi·um (prē′mē əm), *n.* **1.** a prize, bonus, award, or reward given as an inducement, as to purchase products, enter competitions, etc. **2.** a bonus, gift, or sum additional to a price, wages, etc. **3.** *Insurance.* the amount paid or to be paid by the policyholder for coverage under the contract, usually in periodic installments. **4.** *Econ.* the excess value of one form of money over another of the same nominal value. **5.** a sum above the nominal or par value of a thing. **6.** the amount paid to the lender of stock by the borrower, typically a short seller. **7.** a fee paid for instruction in a trade or profession. **8.** a sum additional to the interest paid for the loan of money. **9. at a premium, a.** at an unusually high price. **b.** in short supply; in demand: *Housing is at a premium.* [< L *praemium* profit, reward] —**Syn. 2.** See **bonus.**

pre·mo·lar (prē mō′lər), *adj.* **1.** situated in front of the molar teeth. **2.** pertaining to a milk tooth which will later be supplanted by a permanent molar. —*n.* **3.** a premolar tooth. **4.** Also called **bicuspid.** (in man) any of eight teeth located in pairs on each side of the upper and lower jaws between the cuspids and molar teeth.

pre·mon·ish (pri mon′ish), *v.t., v.i. Rare.* to warn beforehand. [PRE- + *monish,* ME *mones,* back formation from *monest* (-*t* being taken as sign of ptp.) < OF *monester,* unexplained deriv. of L *monēre* to remind, warn. See ADMONISH]

pre·mo·ni·tion (prē′mə nish′ən, prem′ə-), *n.* **1.** a forewarning. **2.** an intuitive anticipation of a future event; presentiment. [< LL *praemonitiōn-* (s. of *praemonitiō*) forewarning]

pre·mon·i·to·ry (pri mon′i tōr′ē, -tôr′ē), *adj.* giving premonition; serving to warn beforehand. [< LL *praemonitōri(us)*]

pre·morse (pri môrs′), *adj. Biol.* having the end irregularly truncate, as if bitten or broken off. [< L *praemors(us)* bitten off in front (ptp. of *praemordēre*) = *prae-* PRE- + *morsus* bitten; see MORSEL]

pre·mun·dane (prē mun′dān, prē′mən dān′), *adj.* before the creation of the world; antemundane.

pre·na·tal (prē nāt′ᵊl), *adj.* previous to birth or to giving birth. —**pre·na′tal·ly,** *adv.*

Pren·der·gast (pren′dər gast′, -gäst′), *n.* **Maurice Braz·il** (braz′əl), 1859–1924, U.S. painter.

pre·no·men (prē nō′mən), *n., pl.* **-nom·i·na** (-nom′ə nə, -nō′mə-), **-no·mens.** praenomen.

pre·nom·i·nate (pri nom′ə nāt′, -nit), *adj. Obs.* mentioned beforehand. [< L *praenōmināt(us)* named before, ptp. of *praenōmināre*] —**pre·nom′i·na′tion,** *n.*

pre·no·tion (prē nō′shən), *n.* a preconception. [< L *praenōtiōn-* (s. of *praenōtiō*) an innate idea]

pre·oc·cu·pan·cy (prē ok′yə pən sē), *n.* **1.** the act, right, or instance of prior occupancy. **2.** the state of being absorbed in thought; preoccupation.

pre·oc·cu·pa·tion (prē ok′yə pā′shən, prē′ok-), *n.* **1.** the act of preoccupying. **2.** the state of being preoccupied. [< L *praeoccupātiōn-* (s. of *praeoccupātiō*) a taking possession beforehand]

pre·oc·cu·pied (prē ok′yə pīd′), *adj.* **1.** completely engrossed in thought; absorbed. **2.** previously occupied; taken; filled. **3.** *Biol.* already used as a name for some species, genus, etc. —**pre·oc′cu·pied′ly,** *adv.*

pre·oc·cu·py (prē ok′yə pī′), *v.t.,* **-pied, -py·ing. 1.** to

---

pre·Kant′i·an, *adj.*
pre·kin′der·gar′ten, *adj.*
pre·lim′it, *v.t.*
pre′-Lin·ne′an, *adj.*
pre·lo′cate, *v.,* **-cat·ed, -cat·ing.**
pre-Marx′i·an, *adj.*
pre′-Men·de′li·an, *adj.*
pre·men′stru·al, *adj.*
pre·mix′, *v.t.*
pre′mo·nar′chi·cal, *adj.*
pre·mon′e·tar′y, *adj.*
pre′-Mo·sa′ic, *adj.*
pre-Mus′lim, *adj.*
pre′-My·ce·nae′an, *adj.*
pre′-Na·po′le·on′ic, *adj.*
pre·na′tion·al, *adj.*
pre·nat′ur·al, *adj.*
pre′ne·o·lith′ic, *adj.*
pre′-New·to′ni·an, *adj.*
pre-Nor′man, *adj.*
pre-Norse′, *adj.*
pre·nup′tial, *adj.*
pre′ob·ser·va′tion, *n.*

engross to the exclusion of other things. **2.** to occupy beforehand or before others. —**pre·oc′cu·pi′er,** *n.*

prep (prep), *n., v.,* **prepped, prep·ping.** —*n. Informal.* **1.** See **preparatory school.** —*v.i.* **2.** to attend preparatory school. —*v.t.* **3.** to study (a subject), prepare (a person), etc., as for a course of study, operation, etc. [by shortening]

prep., **1.** preparation. **2.** preparatory. **3.** prepare. **4.** preposition.

pre·pack·age (prē pak′ij), *v.t.,* **-aged, -ag·ing.** to package (foodstuffs or manufactured goods) before retail distribution or sale. Also, **pre·pack′.**

prep·a·ra·tion (prep′ə rā′shən), *n.* **1.** a proceeding, measure, or provision by which one prepares for something: *preparations for a journey.* **2.** the act of preparing. **3.** the state of being prepared. **4.** something prepared, manufactured, or compounded: *a special preparation for treating sunburn.* **5.** a specimen, as an animal body, prepared for scientific examination, dissection, etc. **6.** *Music.* **a.** the preparing of a dissonance, by introducing the dissonant tone as a consonant tone in the preceding chord. **b.** the tone so introduced. **7.** *New Testament.* the day before the Sabbath or a feast day. **8. the Preparation,** the introductory prayers of the Mass or other divine service. [ME *preparacion* < L *praeparātiōn-* (s. of *praeparātiō*), a preparing = *praeparāt(us)* (ptp. of *praeparāre* to PREPARE) + *-iōn-* -ION]

pre·par·a·tive (pri par′ə tiv), *adj.* **1.** preparatory. —*n.* **2.** something that prepares. **3.** a preparation. [late ME *preparatif* < MF < ML *praeparātīv(us).* See PREPARATION, -IVE] —**pre·par′a·tive·ly,** *adv.*

pre·par·a·tor (pri par′ə tər), *n.* a person who prepares a specimen for scientific examination or exhibition. [< LL *praeparātor* preparer. See PREPARATION, -OR[2]]

pre·par·a·to·ry (pri pâr′ə tōr′ē, -tôr′ē, -par′-, prep′ər ə-), *adj.* **1.** serving or designed to prepare: *preparatory arrangements.* **2.** preliminary; introductory: *preparatory remarks.* **3.** of or pertaining to training that prepares for more advanced education. [< ML *praeparātōri(us).* See PREPARATION, -ORY[1]] —**pre·par′a·to′ri·ly,** *adv.*

prepar′atory school′, **1.** a private secondary school providing a college-preparatory education. **2.** *Brit.* a private elementary school.

pre·pare (pri pâr′), *v.,* **-pared, -par·ing.** —*v.t.* **1.** to put in proper condition or readiness: *to prepare a patient for surgery.* **2.** to provide with what is necessary; outfit: *to prepare an expedition.* **3.** to get (a meal) ready for eating. **4.** to manufacture, compound, or compose. **5.** *Music.* to lead up to (a discord, an embellishment, etc.) by some preliminary tone or tones. —*v.i.* **6.** to put things or oneself in readiness; get ready: *to prepare for war.* [late ME < L *praepar(āre)* (to) make ready beforehand = *prae-* PRE- + *parāre* to set, get ready] —**pre·par′er,** *n.*

pre·par·ed·ness (pri pâr′id nis, -pârd′nis), *n.* **1.** the state of being prepared; readiness. **2.** readiness for war.

pre·pay (prē pā′), *v.t.,* **-paid, -pay·ing.** to pay the charge upon in advance; pay beforehand. —**pre·pay′a·ble,** *adj.* —**pre·pay′ment,** *n.*

pre·pense (pri pens′), *adj.* planned or intended in advance; premeditated. [PRE- + *-pense* < L *pēns(us)* weighed, considered, ptp. of *pendere* to make (scales) hang down, hence, to weigh]

pre·pon·der·ance (pri pon′dər əns), *n.* superiority in weight, power, numbers, etc. Also, **pre·pon′der·an·cy.** [PREPONDER(ANT) + -ANCE]

pre·pon·der·ant (pri pon′dər ənt), *adj.* superior in weight, force, numbers, etc.; preponderating. [< L *praeponderant-* (s. of *praeponderāns*), prp. of *praeponderāre* to outweigh] —**pre·pon′der·ant·ly,** *adv.* —**Syn.** overpowering.

pre·pon·der·ate (pri pon′də rāt′), *v.i.,* **-at·ed, -at·ing.** **1.** to exceed something else in weight. **2.** to incline downward because of greater weight; be weighed down. **3.** to be superior in power, force, number, etc.; predominate. [< L *praeponderāt(us),* ptp. of *praeponderāre* to outweigh] —**pre·pon′der·at′ing·ly,** *adv.* —**pre·pon′der·a′tion,** *n.*

prep·o·si·tion (prep′ə zish′ən), *n. Gram.* any member of a class of words that are used before nouns or adjectives to form phrases functioning as modifiers of verbs, nouns, or adjectives, and that express a spatial, temporal, or other relationship, as *in, on, by, to, since.* [ME *preposicioun* < L *praepositiōn-* (s. of *praepositiō*) a putting before, a prefix, preposition] —**prep′o·si′tion·al,** *adj.* —**prep′o·si′tion·al·ly,** *adv.*

prep′osi′tional phrase′, *Gram.* a phrase consisting of a preposition, its object, which may be an adjective or a noun, and any modifiers of the object, as *in the gray desk I use.*

pre·pos·i·tive (prē poz′i tiv), *adj.* **1.** put before; prefixed: *a prepositive adjective.* **2.** *Gram.* (of a word) placed before another word to modify it. —*n.* **3.** *Gram.* a word used in a prepositive position. [< LL *praepositīv(us)* prefixed. See PREPOSITION, -IVE] —**pre·pos′i·tive·ly,** *adv.*

pre·pos·sess (prē′pə zes′), *v.t.* **1.** to possess or dominate mentally beforehand. **2.** to prejudice or bias, esp. favorably. **3.** to impress favorably at the outset.

pre·pos·sess·ing (prē′pə zes′ing), *adj.* that impresses favorably. —**pre′pos·sess′ing·ly,** *adv.* —**pre′pos·sess′ing·ness,** *n.*

pre·pos·ses·sion (prē′pə zesh′ən), *n.* **1.** the state of being prepossessed. **2.** a prejudice, esp. one in favor of a person or thing. —**pre′pos·ses′sion·ar′y,** *adj.*

pre·pos·ter·ous (pri pos′tər əs, -trəs), *adj.* completely contrary to nature, reason, or common sense; absurd; senseless; utterly foolish. [< L *praeposterus* with the hinder part foremost. See PRE-, POSTERIOR] —**pre·pos′ter·ous·ly,** *adv.* —**pre·pos′ter·ous·ness,** *n.* —**Syn.** unreasonable, excessive.

pre·po·ten·cy (pri pōt′ən sē), *n. Genetics.* the ability of one parent to impress its hereditary characters on its progeny because it possesses a greater number of homozygous, dominant, or epistatic genes. [< L *praepotentia*]

pre·po·tent (pri pōt′ənt), *adj.* **1.** preeminent in power, authority, or influence; predominant. **2.** *Genetics.* noting, pertaining to, or having prepotency. [< L *praepotent-,* prp. of *praeposse* to have greater power] —**pre·po′tent·ly,** *adv.*

prep·pie (prep′ē), *U.S. Informal.* —*n.* **1.** a person who attends or has recently graduated from a preparatory school. **2.** Also called **prep′pie look′.** a style of casual dress favored by preppies, typically consisting of slacks or skirts, button-down shirt, pullover sweater, and loafers. —*adj.* **3.** of or pertaining to preppies or the attitudes, habits, or esp. the style of dress associated with them. Also, **preppy.** [PREP + -IE]

prep·py (prep′ē), *n., pl.* **-pies,** *adj.* **-pi·er, -pi·est.** preppie.

pre·pran·di·al (prē pran′dē əl), *adj.* before a meal, esp. before dinner.

pre·puce (prē′pyo͞os), *n. Anat.* **1.** the fold of skin that covers the head of the penis; foreskin. **2.** a similar covering of the clitoris. [late ME < MF < L *praepūt(ium)* the foreskin = *prae-* PRE- + OL *pūt(os)* penis + *-ium* n. suffix]

Pre-Raph·a·el·ite (prē raf′ē ə līt′, -rā′fē-), *n.* **1.** one of a group of English artists **(Pre-Raph′aelite Broth′erhood)** formed in 1848 that aimed to revive the style and spirit of the Italian artists before the time of Raphael. —*adj.* **2.** of, pertaining to, or characteristic of the Pre-Raphaelites. —**Pre-Raph′a·el·it′ism,** *n.*

pre·re·cord (prē′ri kôrd′), *v.t.* to record (a radio show, television program, etc.) prior to an actual broadcast or showing.

pre·req·ui·site (pri rek′wi zit), *adj.* **1.** required beforehand. —*n.* **2.** something prerequisite.

pre·rog·a·tive (pri rog′ə tiv), *n.* **1.** an exclusive right, privilege, etc., exercised by virtue of rank, office, or the like. **2.** a right, privilege, etc., limited to a specific person, or to persons of a particular category: *Voting is the prerogative of adult citizens.* **3.** a power, immunity, or the like, restricted to a sovereign government or its representative. **4.** *Obs.* precedence. —*adj.* **5.** having or exercising a prerogative. [late ME < L *praerogātīv(us)* (adj.) voting first, *praerogātīva* (n. use of fem. of adj.) tribe or century with right to vote first] —**Syn. 1.** See **privilege.**

Pres., **1.** Presbyterian. **2.** President.

pres., **1.** present. **2.** presidency.

pre·sa (prā′sə; *It.* pʀe′sä), *n., pl.* **-se** (-sā; *It.* -se). a mark, as :S:, +, or ※, used in a canon, round, etc., to indicate where the successive voice parts are to take up the theme. [< It: lit., a taking up, fem. of *preso,* ptp. of *prendere* to take < L *prehendere* to seize]

pres·age (*n.* pres′ij; *v.* pres′ij, pri sāj′), *n., v.,* **-aged, -ag·ing.** —*n.* **1.** a presentiment or foreboding. **2.** something that portends or foreshadows a future event, as an omen. **3.** prophetic significance; augury. **4.** foresight; prescience. **5.** *Archaic.* a forecast or prediction. —*v.t.* **6.** to have a presentiment of. **7.** to portend, foreshow, or foreshadow. **8.** to forecast; predict. —*v.i.* **9.** to make a prediction. **10.** *Archaic.* to have a presentiment. [ME < L *praesāg(ium)* a foreboding < *praesāgus* divining, lit., perceiving beforehand = *prae-* PRE- + *-sāgus,* akin to *sāgīre* to perceive intuitively] —**pres′age·ful,** *adj.* —**pres′age·ful·ly,** *adv.* —**pres′ag·er,** *n.* —**Syn. 1.** foreshadowing, indication, premonition.

pre·sanc·ti·fied (prē sangk′tə fīd′), *adj.* (of the Eucharistic elements) consecrated at a previous Mass. [trans. of ML *praesanctificātus*] —**pre·sanc′ti·fi·ca′tion,** *n.*

Presb., Presbyterian.

pres·by·ope (prez′bē ōp′, pres′-), *n. Ophthalm.* a presbyopic person. [back formation from PRESBYOPIA]

pres·by·o·pi·a (prez′bē ō′pē ə, pres′-), *n. Ophthalm.* a defect of vision incident to advancing age, in which near objects are seen with difficulty; farsightedness. [< Gk *presby-* (comb. form of *présbys* old, old man) + -OPIA] —**pres·by·op·ic** (prez′bē op′ik, pres′-), *adj.*

pres·by·ter (prez′bi tər, pres′-), *n.* **1.** (in the early Christian church) an office bearer who exercised teaching, priestly, and administrative functions. **2.** (in hierarchical churches) a priest. **3.** an elder in a Presbyterian church. [< eccl. L < Gk *presbýter(os)* elder = *présby(s)* old + *-teros* comp. suffix] —**pres·byt·er·al** (prez bit′ər əl, pres-), *adj.*

pres·byt·er·ate (prez bit′ər it, -ə rāt′, pres-), *n.* **1.** the office of a presbyter or elder. **2.** a body of presbyters or elders. [< ML *presbyterāt(us)*]

pres·by·te·ri·al (prez′bi tēr′ē əl, pres′-), *adj.* **1.** of or pertaining to a presbytery. **2.** presbyterian (def. 1).

pres·by·te·ri·an (prez′bi tēr′ē ən, pres′-), *adj.* **1.** pertaining to or based on the principle of ecclesiastical government by presbyters or presbyteries. **2.** (*cap.*) designating or pertaining to various churches having this form of government and adhering to modified forms of Calvinism. —*n.* **3.** (*cap.*) a member of a Presbyterian church; an adherent of Presbyterianism.

Pres·by·te·ri·an·ism (prez′bi tēr′ē ə niz′əm, pres′-), *n.* **1.** church government by presbyters or elders. **2.** the doctrines of Presbyterian churches.

pres·by·ter·y (prez′bi ter′ē, pres′-), *n., pl.* **-ter·ies.** **1.** a body of presbyters or elders. **2.** (in Presbyterian churches) an ecclesiastical court consisting of all the ministers and one or two presbyters from each congregation in a district. **3.** the churches under the jurisdiction of a presbytery. **4.** the part of a church appropriated to the clergy. **5.** *Rom. Cath. Ch.* a rectory. [late ME *presbetory, -bitory* < LL *presbyteri(um)* < Gk *presbytérion.* See PRESBYTER, -IUM]

pre·school (*adj.* prē′sko͞ol′; *n.* prē′sko͞ol′), *adj.* **1.** of, pertaining to, or intended for a child between infancy and school age: *preschool education.* —*n.* **2.** a school or nursery for preschool children.

pre′or·dain′, *v.t.*
pre′or·di·na′tion, *n.*
pre′or·gan′ic, *adj.*
pre′or·gan·i·za′tion, *n.*
pre′pal′a·tal, *adj.*
pre′pa·le·o·lith′ic, *adj.*
pre′-Pa·le·o·zo′ic, *adj.*
pre-Per′mi·an, *adj.*
pre·place′, *v.t.,* **-placed, -plac·ing.**
pre·place′ment, *n.*
pre·plan′, *v.,* **-planned, -plan·ning.**
pre′-Pro·hi·bi′tion, *adj.*
pre·pur′chase, *n., v.t.,* **-chased, -chas·ing.**
pre′-Ref·or·ma′tion, *adj., n.*
pre·reg′is·ter, *v.*
pre′reg·is·tra′tion, *n.*
pre-Ren′ais·sance, *adj.*
pre′re·pub′li·can, *adj.*
pre′-Rev·o·lu′tion, *adj.*
pre′-Rev·o·lu′tion·ar′y, *adj.*
pre′rev·o·lu′tion·ar′y, *adj.*
pre-Ro′man, *adj.*
pre′ro·man′tic, *adj.*
pre-Sax′on, *adj.*
pre′scho·las′tic, *adj.*

pre·sci·ence (prē′shē əns, -shəns, presh′ē-, presh′əns), *n.* knowledge of things before they exist or happen; foreknowledge; foresight. [ME < LL *praescientia* foreknowledge] —**pre′sci·ent,** *adj.* —**pre′sci·ent·ly,** *adv.*

pre·scind (pri sind′), *v.t.* **1.** to separate in thought; abstract. **2.** to remove. —*v.i.* **3.** to withdraw the attention. [< L *praescind(ere)* (to) cut off in front. See PRE-, RESCIND]

pre·score (prē skōr′, -skôr′), *v.t.*, **-scored, -scor·ing. 1.** to score in advance, as for facilitating bending of cardboard. **2.** to record the sound of (a motion picture) before filming.

Pres·cott (pres′kət), *n.* **William Hick·ling** (hik′ling), 1796–1859, U.S. historian.

pre·scribe (pri skrīb′), *v.*, **-scribed, -scrib·ing.** —*v.t.* **1.** to lay down as a rule or a course to be followed. **2.** *Med.* to designate or order the use of (a remedy, treatment, etc.). **3.** *Law.* to render invalid by prescription. —*v.i.* **4.** to lay down rules; direct; dictate. **5.** *Med.* to designate remedies, treatment, etc., to be used. **6.** *Law.* **a.** to claim a right by virtue of prescription. **b.** to become invalid or outlawed by negative prescription. [late ME < legal L *praescrībe(re)* (to) hold (property) by legal prescription, lit., to write before or above = *prae-* PRE- + *scrībere* to write; see SCRIBE[1]] —**pre·scrib′a·ble,** *adj.* —**pre·scrib′er,** *n.* —**Syn. 1.** direct, dictate, decree, appoint, ordain.

pre·script (*adj.* pri skript′, prē′skript; *n.* prē′skript), *adj.* **1.** prescribed. —*n.* **2.** that which is prescribed or laid down, as a rule, precept, or order. [< L *praescript(um)* an order, rule, lit., something written before or above, n. use of neut. of ptp. of *praescrībere* to PRESCRIBE]

pre·scrip·ti·ble (pri skrip′tə bəl), *adj.* **1.** subject to or suitable for prescription. **2.** depending on or derived from prescription, as a claim or right. [< ML *prescriptibil(is).* See PRESCRIPTION, -IBLE] —**pre·scrip′ti·bil′i·ty,** *n.*

pre·scrip·tion (pri skrip′shən), *n.* **1.** *Med.* **a.** a direction, usually written, by the physician to the pharmacist for the preparation and use of a medicine or remedy. **b.** the medicine prescribed. **2.** the act of prescribing. **3.** that which is prescribed. **4.** *Law.* **a.** a long or immemorial use of some right so as to give a right to continue such use. **b.** the process of acquiring a right by uninterrupted assertion of the right over a long period of time. —*adj.* **5.** (of drugs) sold only upon medical prescription; ethical. [ME < legal L *praescriptiōn-* (s. of *praescrīptiō*) legal possession (of property), law, order, lit., a writing before, hence, a heading]

pre·scrip·tive (pri skrip′tiv), *adj.* **1.** that prescribes; giving directions or injunctions. **2.** depending on or arising from effective legal prescription, as a right or title established by a long unchallenged tenure. [modeled on *descriptive,* etc.] —**pre·scrip′tive·ly,** *adv.* —**pre·scrip′tive·ness,** *n.*

pres·ence (prez′əns), *n.* **1.** the state or fact of being present, as with others or in a place. **2.** attendance or company. **3.** immediate vicinity; close proximity. **4.** *Chiefly Brit.* the immediate personal vicinity of a great personage. **5.** the ability to project a sense of ease, poise, or self-assurance. **6.** personal appearance or bearing, esp. of a dignified or imposing kind. **7.** a person, esp. of dignified or fine appearance. **8.** a divine or supernatural spirit felt to be present. **9.** the military or economic power of a country as reflected abroad by the stationing of troops, the sale of its goods, etc.: *the American military presence in Greece; the Japanese presence in the U.S. consumer market.* [ME < MF < L *praesentia.* See PRESENT[1], -ENCE]

pres′ence cham′ber, the special room in which a great personage, as a sovereign, receives guests, etc.

pres′ence of mind′, a calm state of mind that allows one to act effectively in emergencies.

pres·ent[1] (prez′ənt), *adj.* **1.** being, existing, or occurring at this time or now. **2.** at this time: *articles for present use.* **3.** *Gram.* designating a tense or other verb formation, or noting an action or state occurring at the moment of speaking. *Knows* is a present form in *He knows that.* **4.** being with one or others, or in the specified or understood place (opposed to *absent*). **5.** being here or there, rather than elsewhere. **6.** existing in a place, thing, combination, or the like: *Carbon is present in many minerals.* **7.** being actually here or under consideration. **8.** being before the mind. **9.** *Obs.* mentally alert and calm. **10.** *Obs.* immediate or instant. —*n.* **11.** the present time. **12.** *Gram.* **a.** the present tense. **b.** a verb formation or construction with present meaning. **c.** a form in the present. **13. presents,** *Law.* the present writings, or this document, used in a deed, a lease, etc., to denote the document itself. **14.** *Obs.* the matter in hand. **15. at present,** at the present time or moment; now. **16. for the present,** for now; temporarily. [ME < L *praesent-* (s. of *praesēns*) there, here, special use of prp. of *praeēsse* to be before (others), i.e., to preside, be in charge. See PRE-, ESSE, -ENT] —**pres′ent·ness,** *n.* —**Syn. 1.** extant. See **current.** —**Ant. 1.** absent.

pre·sent[2] (*v.* pri zent′; *n.* prez′ənt), *v.t.* **1.** to furnish or endow with a gift or the like, esp. by formal act. **2.** to bring, offer, or give, often in a formal way: *to present one's card.* **3.** to afford or furnish, as an opportunity. **4.** to hand or send in, as a bill or a check, for payment. **5.** to introduce (a person) to another, esp. in a formal manner. **6.** to bring before or introduce to the public. **7.** to come to show (oneself) before a person, in or at a place, etc. **8.** to show or exhibit. **9.** to bring before the mind; offer for consideration. **10.** to set forth in words. **11.** to represent, impersonate, or act, as on the stage. **12.** to direct, point, or turn (something) to something or someone: *He presented his back to the audience.* **13.** to level or aim (a weapon, esp. a firearm). **14.** *Law.* **a.** to bring a formal charge or indictment against. **b.** to bring formally to the notice of the proper authority, as an offense. **15.** *Eccles. Brit.* to offer or recommend (a clergyman) to the bishop for institution to a benefice. —*n.* **16.** a thing presented as a gift; gift. [ME *presente(n)* < OF *presente(r)* < L *praesentāre* to make (someone or something) present, i.e., to exhibit, bring into the presence of (someone) (ML: to make as a gift). See PRESENT[1]] —**pre·sent′er,** *n.* —**Syn. 1.** bestow, donate. See **give. 2.** proffer. **3.** yield. **5.** See **introduce. 9.** introduce. **11.** enact. **16.** benefaction, grant, tip, gratuity. PRESENT, GIFT, DONATION, BONUS refer to something freely given. PRESENT and GIFT are both used of something given as an expression of affection, friendship, interest, or respect. PRESENT is the less formal; GIFT is generally used of something conferred (esp. with ceremony) on an individual, a group, or an institution: *a birthday present; a gift to a bride.* DONATION applies to an important gift, usually of considerable size, though the term is often used, to avoid the suggestion of charity, in speaking of small gifts to or for the needy: *a donation to an endowment fund, to the Red Cross.* BONUS applies to something given in addition to what is due, esp. to employees who have worked for a long time or particularly well: *a Christmas bonus.*

pre·sent·a·ble (pri zen′tə bəl), *adj.* **1.** that may be presented. **2.** suitable, as in appearance, dress, manners, etc., for being introduced into society or company. **3.** of sufficiently good appearance, or fit to be seen. —**pre·sent′a·bil′i·ty, pre·sent′a·ble·ness,** *n.* —**pre·sent′a·bly,** *adv.*

present′ arms′, *Mil.* **1.** a position of salute in the manual of arms in which the rifle is held in both hands vertically in front of the body, with the muzzle upward and the trigger side forward. **2.** (for troops in formation not under arms) the hand salute.

pres·en·ta·tion (prez′ən tā′shən, prē′zən-), *n.* **1.** the act of presenting. **2.** the state of being presented. **3.** introduction, as of a person at court. **4.** exhibition or representation, as of a play or film. **5.** offering, delivering, or bestowal, as of a gift. **6.** a gift. **7.** *Com.* presentment (def. 6). **8.** *Obstet.* the appearance of a particular part of the fetus at the mouth of the uterus during labor. **9.** *Eccles.* the act or the right of presenting a clergyman to the bishop for institution to a benefice. [ME < eccl. L *praesentātiōn-* (s. of *praesentātiō*) nomination (of a priest) to a benefice, religious dedication (of a person) by bringing him before God]

pres·en·ta·tion·al (prez′ən tā′shənəl, prē′zən-), *adj.* **1.** of or pertaining to presentation. **2.** notional (def. 6).

pres·en·ta·tion·ism (prez′ən tā′shə niz′əm, prē′zən-), *n.* *Epistemology.* the doctrine that in perception there is a direct awareness of the object of knowledge. Also called **present′ative re′alism.** —**pres′en·ta′tion·ist,** *n., adj.*

pre·sent·a·tive (pri zen′tə tiv), *adj.* **1.** (of an image, idea, etc.) presented, known, or capable of being known directly. **2.** *Eccles.* admitting of or pertaining to presentation. **3.** *Philos.* immediately knowable; capable of being known without thought or reflection.

pres·ent-day (prez′ənt dā′), *adj.* current; modern: *present-day techniques; present-day English.*

pres·en·tee (prez′ən tē′), *n.* **1.** a person to whom something is presented. **2.** a person who is presented, as to a benefice. [late ME < AF]

pre·sen·ti·ment (pri zen′tə mənt), *n.* a feeling or impression of something about to happen, esp. something evil; foreboding. [< F, obs. spelling of *pressentiment*] —**pre·sen′ti·ment′al,** *adj.*

pre·sen·tive (pri zen′tiv), *adj.* *Semantics.* notional (def. 6). —**pre·sen′tive·ly,** *adv.* —**pre·sen′tive·ness,** *n.*

pres·ent·ly (prez′ənt lē), *adv.* **1.** in a little while; soon: *They will be here presently.* **2.** *Informal.* at the present time. *He is presently out of the country.* **3.** *Archaic.* immediately: [ME] —**Syn. 1.** shortly, forthwith. See **immediately.** —**Usage.** Careful writers and speakers avoid the use of PRESENTLY to mean "at the present time."

pre·sent·ment (pri zent′mənt), *n.* **1.** the act of presenting, esp. to the mind, as an idea, view, etc. **2.** the state of being presented. **3.** a presentation. **4.** the manner or mode in which something is presented. **5.** a representation, picture, or likeness. **6.** *Com.* the presenting of a bill, note, or the like, as for acceptance or payment. **7.** *Law.* the written statement of an offense by a grand jury of their own knowledge when no indictment has been laid before them. **8.** a theatrical presentation. [ME *presentement* < MF]

pres′ent par′ticiple, a participle with present meaning, as *growing* in *a growing boy.*

pres′ent per′fect, 1. (in English) the tense form consisting of the present tense of *have* with a past participle and noting that the action of the verb was completed prior to the present, as *I have finished.* **2.** a tense of similar construction found in certain other languages. **3.** a form in this tense.

pres·er·va·tion·ist (prez′ər vā′shə nist), *n.* a person who advocates or promotes preservation, esp. of wildlife, natural areas, historical places, etc.

pre·serv·a·tive (pri zûr′və tiv), *n.* **1.** something that preserves or tends to preserve. **2.** a chemical substance used to preserve foods from decomposition or fermentation. —*adj.* **3.** tending to preserve. [ME < MF *preservatif* < ML *praeservātīv(us)*]

pre·serve (pri zûrv′), *v.*, **-served, -serv·ing,** *n.* —*v.t.* **1.** to keep alive or in existence; make lasting: *to preserve our liberties.* **2.** to keep safe from harm or injury; save. **3.** to keep up; maintain: *to preserve historical monuments.* **4.** to keep possession of; retain. **5.** to prepare (food or any perishable substance) so as to resist decomposition or fermentation. **6.** to prepare (fruit, vegetables, etc.) by cooking with sugar. **7.** to maintain and reserve (game, fish, etc.) for private use in hunting or fishing. —*v.i.* **8.** to preserve fruit, vegetables, etc.; make preserves. **9.** to maintain a preserve for game or fish, esp. for sport. —*n.* **10.** something that preserves. **11.** something that is preserved. **12.** Usually, **preserves.** fruit, vegetables, etc., prepared by cooking with sugar. **13.** a place set apart for the protection and propagation of game or fish, esp. for sport. [ME *preserve(n)* < ML *praeserv(āre)* (to) guard (LL: to observe), L *prae-* PRE- + *servāre* to watch over, keep, preserve, observe] —**pre·serv′a·bil′i·ty,** *n.* —**pre·serv′a·ble,** *adj.* —**pres·er·va·tion** (prez′ər vā′shən), *n.* —**pre·serv′er,** *n.* —**Syn. 1.** conserve. **2.** safeguard, shelter, shield. See **defend.** —**Ant. 1.** destroy.

pre·shrunk (prē shrungk′), *adj.* (of a fabric or garment) shrunk during manufacture to reduce the potential shrinkage in laundering. Also, **pre·shrunk′.**

pre·side (pri zīd′), *v.i.*, **-sid·ed, -sid·ing. 1.** to occupy the place of authority or control, as in an assembly, meeting, etc.; act as president or chairman. **2.** to exercise management or control (usually fol. by *over*): *The lawyer presided over the estate.* [< L *praesid(ēre)* (to) preside over, lit., sit

pre′sci·en·tif′ic, *adj.*
pre·sea′son, *adj.*
pre′se·lect′, *v.t.*
pre′-Se·mit′ic, *adj.*
pre·set′, *v.t.*, **-set, -set·ting.**
pre′-Shake·spear′i·an, *adj.*
pre·shape′, *v.t.*, **-shaped, -shap·ing.**

in front of = *prae-* PRE- + *-sidēre,* comb. form of *sedēre* to sit] —**pre·sid′er,** *n.*

pres·i·den·cy (prez′i dən sē), *n., pl.* **-cies. 1.** the office, function, or term of office of a president. **2.** (*often cap.*) the office of President of the United States. **3.** *Mormon Ch.* **a.** a local governing body consisting of a council of three. **b.** (*often cap.*) the highest administrative body, composed of the prophet and his two councilors. **4.** the former designation of any of the three original provinces of British India: Bengal, Bombay, and Madras. [< ML *praesidentia.* See PRESIDENT, -ENCY]

pres·i·dent (prez′i dənt), *n.* **1.** (*often cap.*) the highest executive officer of a modern republic, as the Chief Executive of the United States. **2.** an officer appointed or elected to preside over an organized body of persons. **3.** the chief officer of a college, university, society, corporation, etc. **4.** a person who presides. [ME < L *praesident-* (s. of *praesidēns*), n. use (in pl.) of prp. of *praesidēre* to PRESIDE, govern; see -ENT]

pres·i·dent-e·lect (prez′i dənt i lekt′), *n.* a president after election but before induction into office.

pres·i·den·tial (prez′i den′shəl), *adj.* **1.** of or pertaining to a president or presidency. **2.** of the nature of a president. [< ML *praesidentiāl(is)*] —**pres′i·den′tial·ly,** *adv.*

pre·sid·i·o (pri sid′ē ō′; *Sp.* pre sē′thyô), *n., pl.* **-sid·i·os** (-sid′ē ōz′; *Sp.* -sē′thyôs). **1.** a garrisoned fort; military post. **2.** a Spanish penal settlement. [< Sp < L *praesidium* guard, garrison, post, lit., defense, protection. See PRESIDIUM] —**pre·sid′i·al, pre·sid·i·ar·y** (pri sid′ē er′ē), *adj.*

pre·sid·i·um (pri sid′ē əm), *n.* (*often cap.*) (in the Soviet Union) an administrative committee, usually permanent and governmental, acting when its parent body is in recess but exercising full powers. [< L *praesidium* < *praes(es)* (s. *praesid-*), lit., sitting before, i.e., guarding (adj.), defender, ruler, leader (n.). See PRESIDE, PRESIDENT]

pre·sig·ni·fy (prē sig′nə fī′), *v.t.,* **-fied, -fy·ing.** to signify or indicate beforehand; foretell. [< L *praesignifi(cāre)* (to) show beforehand. See PRE-, SIGNIFY]

pre-So·crat·ic (prē′sə krat′ik, -sō-), *adj.* **1.** of or pertaining to the philosophers or philosophical systems of the period before Socrates. —*n.* **2.** any philosopher of this period.

pres. part., See **present participle.**

press[1] (pres), *v.t.* **1.** to act upon with steadily applied weight or force. **2.** to move by weight or force in a certain direction or into a certain position. **3.** to compress or squeeze, as to alter in shape or size. **4.** to weigh heavily upon; subject to pressure. **5.** to hold closely, as in an embrace; clasp. **6.** to flatten; make smooth. **7.** to extract juice, sugar, etc., from by pressure. **8.** to squeeze out or express, as juice. **9.** to beset or harass. **10.** to trouble or oppress, as by lack of something. **11.** to constrain or compel. **12.** to urge onward; hasten. **13.** to urge, importune, insist, or entreat. **14.** to emphasize or insist upon: *He pressed his own ideas on us.* **15.** to plead with insistence: *to press a claim.* **16.** to push forward.
—*v.i.* **17.** to exert weight, force, or pressure. **18.** to iron clothing, curtains, etc. **19.** to bear heavily, as upon the mind. **20.** to compel haste or attention. **21.** to use urgent entreaty: *to press for an answer.* **22.** to push forward or advance with force, eagerness, or haste. **23.** to crowd or throng.
—*n.* **24.** printed publications collectively, esp. newspapers and periodicals. **25.** all the media and agencies that print, broadcast, or gather and transmit news. **26.** their editorial employees, taken collectively. **27.** *Journalism.* the consensus of critical commentary or amount of coverage: *The play received a good press.* **28.** *Print.* **a.** a printing press. **b.** See **cylinder press. c.** See **rotary press. 29.** an establishment for printing books, magazines, etc. **30.** the process or art of printing. **31.** any of various devices or machines for exerting pressure. **32.** the act of pressing; pressure. **33.** a pressing or pushing forward. **34.** a crowding, thronging, or pressing together. **35.** a crowd, throng, or multitude. **36.** the state of being pressed. **37.** the desired smooth or creased effect caused by ironing or pressing: *His suit was out of press.* **38.** pressure or urgency, as of affairs or business. **39.** an upright case, or piece of furniture, for holding clothes, books, pamphlets, etc. **40. go to press,** to begin being printed. [ME *presse(n),* v. use of n. *presse* (but cf. OF *presser* < L *pressāre,* freq. of *premere,* ptp. *pressus,* to press) OE *press* clothespress < ML *pressa,* n. use of fem. ptp. of L *premere*] —**press′a·ble,** *adj.*
—**Syn. 9.** annoy, worry, torment, assail, besiege. **11.** push. **13.** induce, persuade, beg, implore. **34.** crush.

press[2] (pres), *v.t.* **1.** to force into service, esp. naval or military service; impress. **2.** to make use of in a manner different from that intended or desired: *French taxis were pressed into service as troop transports.* —*n.* **3.** impressment into service, esp. naval or military service. [back formation from *prest,* ptp. of obs. *prest* to take (men) for military service, v. use of PREST[2] in sense of enlistment money]

press′ a′gent, a person employed to promote the interests of an individual, organization, etc., by obtaining favorable publicity through advertisements, mentions in columns, and the like.

press·board (pres′bōrd′, -bôrd′), *n.* a kind of millboard or pasteboard.

press′ box′, a press section, esp. at a sports event.

Press·burg (pres′bŏŏrk′), *n.* German name of **Bratislava.**

press′ con′ference, a prearranged interview with newsmen, held to elicit publicity or to fulfill a request from the press.

pressed′ glass′, molded glass that has been shaped or given its pattern, while molten, by the action of a plunger thrust into the mold.

press·er (pres′ər), *n.* **1.** a person or thing that presses or applies pressure. **2.** a person whose occupation is pressing or ironing clothes.

press′ gal′lery, a press section, esp. in a legislative chamber.

press′ gang′, a body of men under the command of an officer, formerly employed to impress other men for service, esp. in the navy or army. Also, **press′gang′.**

press·ing (pres′ing), *adj.* urgent; demanding immediate attention. [ME *presing* (n.)] —**press′ing·ly,** *adv.* —**press′ing·ness,** *n.*

press·man (pres′mən), *n., pl.* **-men. 1.** a man who operates or has charge of a printing press. **2.** *Brit.* a writer or reporter for the press.

press·mark (pres′märk′), *n.* *Library Science Brit.* a class number for a book.

press′ of sail′, *Naut.* as much sail as the wind or other conditions will permit a ship to carry. Also called **press′ of can′vas.**

pres·sor (pres′ər), *adj.* *Physiol.* causing an increase in blood pressure; causing vasoconstriction. [attributive use of LL *pressor* presser = L *press(us)* (ptp. of *premere* to press) + *-or* -OR[2]]

press′ release′, *Journalism.* a statement prepared and distributed to the press, as by a public-relations firm. Also called **news release, release.**

press·room (pres′rōōm′, -rŏŏm′), *n.* the room in a printing or newspaper publishing establishment where the printing presses are installed.

pres·sure (presh′ər), *n., v.,* **-sured, -sur·ing.** —*n.* **1.** the exertion of force upon a surface by an object, fluid, etc., in contact with it. **2.** *Physics.* force per unit area. *Symbol:* P Cf. **stress** (def. 5). **3.** *Meteorol.* See **atmospheric pressure. 4.** the state of being pressed or compressed. **5.** harassment; oppression. **6.** a constraining or compelling force or influence: *social pressures.* **7.** urgency, as of affairs or business. **8.** *Obs.* that which is impressed. —*v.t.* **9.** to force (someone) toward a particular end. **10.** to make deliberate use of public opinion, personal ties, or the like, to create psychological pressure on; influence. **11.** pressurize. [ME < L *pressūr(a)*] —**pres′sure·less,** *adj.*

pres′sure cab′in, *Aeron.* a pressurized cabin.

pres′sure cen′ter, *Meteorol.* the central point of an atmospheric high or low. Cf. **high** (def. 38), **low**[1] (def. 45).

pres·sure-cook (presh′ər kŏŏk′), *v.t.* to cook in a pressure cooker.

pres′sure cook′er, a reinforced covered pot, in which soups, meats, vegetables, etc., may be cooked quickly in heat above boiling point by steam maintained under pressure.

pres′sure gauge′, an instrument for measuring the pressure of a gas or liquid.

pres′sure gra′dient, *Meteorol.* the change in atmospheric pressure per unit of horizontal distance in the direction in which pressure changes most rapidly.

pres′sure group′, a special-interest group that attempts to influence legislation.

pres′sure head′, *Physics.* head (def. 27).

pres′sure point′, a point on the body where relatively slight pressure serves to press an artery lying close to the surface against underlying bony tissue, so as to arrest the flow of blood into a part.

pres·su·rize (presh′ə rīz′), *v.t.,* **-rized, -riz·ing. 1.** to maintain normal air pressure in (the cockpit or cabin of) an airplane designed to fly at high altitudes. **2.** to apply pressure to (a gas or liquid). **3.** to pressure-cook. —**pres′sur·i·za′tion,** *n.*

pres′surized suit′, *Aeron.* an airtight suit that can be inflated to maintain approximately normal atmospheric pressure on a flyer at high altitudes.

press·work (pres′wûrk′), *n.* **1.** the working or management of a printing press. **2.** the work done by it.

prest[1] (prest), *adj.* *Obs.* ready. [ME < OF < LL *praest(us)* ready. See PRESTO]

prest[2] (prest), *n.* *Obs.* **1.** a loan. **2.** an advance payment on wages. [late ME *prestte* < MF *prest,* OF, back formation from *prester* to lend < L *praestāre* to perform, vouch for, excel (ML: to lend), lit., to stand in front. See PRE-, STAND]

Pres′ter John′ (pres′tər), a legendary Christian monk and ruler during the Middle Ages, associated with fabulous narratives of travel and thought to have ruled in Asia or Africa.

pres·ti·dig·i·ta·tion (pres′ti dij′i tā′shən), *n.* sleight of hand; legerdemain. [< F, lit., ready-fingerness, alter. of L *praestīgiae* (see PRESTIGE) juggler's tricks. See PREST[1], DIGIT, -ATION] —**pres′ti·dig′i·ta′tor,** *n.* —**pres·ti·dig·i·ta·to·ry** (pres′ti dij′i tə tōr′ē, -tôr′ē), **pres·ti·dig·i·ta·to·ri·al** (pres′ti dij′i tə tōr′ē əl, -tôr′-), *adj.*

pres·tige (pre stēzh′, -stēj′, pres′tij), *n.* **1.** high reputation or influence arising from success, achievement, rank, or the like. **2.** distinction or reputation attaching to a person or thing and dominating the mind of others. —*adj.* **3.** having or showing success, rank, wealth, etc. [< F, orig. pl. < L *praestīgiae* juggler's tricks, dissimilated var. of **praestrīgiae,* akin to *praestringere* to blunt (sight or mind), lit., to press in front. See PRE-, STRIGIL] —**Syn. 1.** weight, importance.

pres·tig·ious (pre stij′əs, -stij′ē əs, -stē′jəs, -stē′jē əs), *adj.* having a high reputation; honored; esteemed. [< L *praestīgiōs(us)* full of tricks, deceitful = *praestīgi(um)* (see PRESTIGE) + *-ōsus* -OUS]

pres·tis·si·mo (pre stis′ə mō′; *It.* pre stēs′sē mô′), *adv.* in the most rapid tempo (used as a musical direction). [< It: most quickly, superl. of *presto* PRESTO]

prest′ mon′ey, *Brit. Obs.* a sum of money advanced to men enlisting in the army or navy.

pres·to (pres′tō), *adv., adj., n., pl.* **-tos.** —*adv.* **1.** quickly or immediately. **2.** at a rapid tempo (used as a musical direction). —*adj.* **3.** quick or rapid. **4.** executed at a rapid tempo (used as a musical direction). —*n.* **5.** *Music.* a movement or piece in quick tempo. [< It: quick, quickly < LL *praestus* (adj.) ready, L *praestō* (adv.) at hand]

pres′to chan′go (chān′jō), change at once (usually used imperatively, as in a magician's command). [rhyming alter. of CHANGE]

Pres·ton (pres′tən), *n.* a seaport in W Lancashire, in NW England. 113,208 (1961).

Pres·ton·pans (pres′tən panz′), *n.* a seaside resort in SE Scotland, E of Edinburgh: battle 1745. 3183 (est. 1964).

pre·stress (prē stres′), *v.t.* **1.** (in certain concrete construction) to apply stress to (reinforcing strands) before they assume a load. **2.** to make (a concrete member) with prestressed reinforcing strands.

pre·sift′, *v.t.* **pre′-Si·lu′ri·an,** *adj.* **pre·slav′er·y,** *adj.* **pre′-So·lo′ni·an,** *adj.*

pre′stressed con′crete, concrete reinforced with wire strands, tensioned within their elastic limit to give an active resistance to loads.

pre·sum·a·ble (pri zo͞o′mə bəl), *adj.* capable of being taken for granted; probable. —**pre·sum′a·bly,** *adv.*

pre·sume (pri zo͞om′), *v.,* **-sumed, -sum·ing.** —*v.t.* **1.** to take for granted, assume, or suppose. **2.** *Law.* to assume as true in the absence of proof to the contrary. **3.** to undertake with unwarrantable boldness. **4.** to undertake or venture (to do something), as by taking a liberty: *to presume to speak for another.* —*v.i.* **5.** to take something for granted; suppose. **6.** to act or proceed with unwarrantable boldness. **7.** to rely in acting unwarrantably or in taking liberties (usually fol. by *on* or *upon*): *Do not presume upon his tolerance.* [ME < L *praesūme(re)* (to) take beforehand (LL: take for granted, assume, dare) = *prae-* PRE- + *sūmere* to take up, suppose (*su-* SUB- + *-(e)mere* to take)] —**pre·sum·ed·ly** (pri zo͞o′mid lē), *adv.* —**pre·sum′er,** *n.* —**pre·sum′ing·ly,** *adv.* —**Syn. 1.** presuppose. **6.** overstep.

pre·sump·tion (pri zump′shən), *n.* **1.** the act of presuming. **2.** assumption of something as true. **3.** belief on reasonable grounds or probable evidence. **4.** that which is presumed; an assumption. **5.** a ground or reason for presuming or believing. **6.** *Law.* an inference required or permitted by law as to the existence of one fact from proof of the existence of other facts. **7.** an assumption, often not fully established, that is taken for granted. **8.** unwarrantable boldness. [ME: effrontery, supposition < L *praesūmptiōn-* (s. of *praesūmptiō*) anticipation, supposition, LL: presumptuousness = *praesūmpt(us)* (ptp. of *praesūmere* to undertake beforehand; see PRESUME) + *-iōn-* -ION]

presump′tion of in′nocence, *Law.* the rebuttable presumption of the innocence of the defendant in a criminal action in Anglo-Saxon jurisprudence, placing upon the prosecution the burden of proof of his guilt.

pre·sump·tive (pri zump′tiv), *adj.* **1.** affording ground for presumption: *presumptive evidence.* **2.** based on presumption: *a presumptive title.* **3.** based on inference. [< LL *praesūmptīv(us).* See PRESUMPTION, -IVE] —**pre·sump′tive·ly,** *adv.*

pre·sump·tu·ous (pri zump′cho͞o əs), *adj.* **1.** characterized by or showing readiness to presume. **2.** unwarrantedly bold; forward. **3.** *Obs.* presumptive. [ME < LL *praesūmptuōs(us),* var. of L *praesūmptiōsus.* See PRESUMPTION, -OUS] —**pre·sump′tu·ous·ly,** *adv.* —**pre·sump′tu·ous·ness,** *n.* —**Syn. 1, 2.** impertinent, audacious; fresh; arrogant. See **bold.** —**Ant. 1, 2.** modest, unassuming.

pre·sup·pose (prē′sə pōz′), *v.t.,* **-posed, -pos·ing. 1.** to suppose or assume beforehand. **2.** (of a thing, condition, or state of affairs) to require or imply as an antecedent condition. [ME < MF *présuppose(r)*] —**pre·sup·po·si·tion** (prē′sup ə zish′ən), *n.* —**pre′sup·po·si′tion·less,** *adj.* —**Syn. 1.** presume.

pre·sur·mise (prē′sər mīz′), *n., v.,* **-mised, -mis·ing.** —*n.* **1.** a surmise previously formed. —*v.t.* **2.** to surmise beforehand.

pret., preterit.

pre·tence (pri tens′, prē′tens), *n.* *Chiefly Brit.* pretense. —**pre·tence′ful,** *adj.* —**pre·tence′less,** *adj.*

pre·tend (pri tend′), *v.t.* **1.** to cause or attempt to cause (what is not so) to seem so; feign: *to pretend illness.* **2.** to appear falsely so as to deceive: *to pretend to go to sleep.* **3.** to allege or profess falsely: *He pretended to have no knowledge of her whereabouts.* —*v.i.* **4.** to make believe. **5.** to lay claim to (usually fol. by *to*): *He pretended to the throne.* **6.** to make pretensions (usually fol. by *to*): *He pretends to great knowledge.* **7.** *Obs.* to aspire, as a suitor or candidate (fol. by *to*). [ME *pretende(n)* < L *praetendere* to stretch forth, put forward, pretend]
—**Syn. 1.** simulate, fake, sham, counterfeit. PRETEND, AFFECT, ASSUME, FEIGN imply an attempt to create a false appearance. To PRETEND is to create an imaginary characteristic or to play a part: *to pretend sorrow.* To AFFECT is to make a consciously artificial show of having qualities which one thinks would look well and impress others: *to affect shyness.* To ASSUME is to take on or put on a specific outward appearance, often (but not always) with intent to deceive: *to assume an air of indifference.* To FEIGN implies using ingenuity in pretense, and some degree of imitation of appearance or characteristics: *to feign surprise.*

pre·tend·ed (pri ten′did), *adj.* **1.** falsely professed: *a pretended interest in art.* **2.** feigned, fictitious, or counterfeit: *pretended wealth.* **3.** alleged or asserted; reputed. [late ME] —**pre·tend′ed·ly,** *adv.*

pre·tend·er (pri ten′dər), *n.* **1.** a person who pretends, esp. for a dishonest purpose. **2.** an aspirant or claimant (often fol. by *to*): *a pretender to the throne.* **3.** a person who makes unjustified or false claims, statements, etc.

pre·tense (pri tens′, prē′tens), *n.* **1.** pretending or feigning; make-believe. **2.** a false show of something: *a pretense of friendship.* **3.** a piece of make-believe. **4.** the act of pretending or alleging falsely. **5.** a false allegation or justification. **6.** insincere or false profession. **7.** the putting forth of an unwarranted claim. **8.** the claim itself. **9.** any allegation or claim. **10.** pretension (usually fol. by *to*): *destitute of any pretense to wit.* **11.** pretentiousness. Also, *esp. Brit.,* **pretence.** [late ME < LL *praetensa, n. use of fem. of *praetensus,* ptp. (r. L *praetentus*) of *praetendere* to PRETEND] —**pre·tense′ful,** *adj.* —**pre·tense′less,** *adj.* —**Syn. 1.** shamming, fabrication. **2.** semblance.

pre·ten·sion (pri ten′shən), *n.* **1.** laying of a claim to something. **2.** a claim or title to something. **3.** Often, **pretensions.** a claim made, esp. indirectly or by implication, to some quality, merit, or the like. **4.** a claim to dignity, importance, or merit. **5.** pretentiousness. **6.** the act of pretending or alleging. **7.** an allegation of doubtful veracity. **8.** a pretext. [< ML *praetensiōn-* (s. of *praetensiō*)]

pre·ten·tious (pri ten′shəs), *adj.* **1.** full of pretense or pretension. **2.** characterized by assumption of dignity or importance. **3.** ostentatious. [earlier *pretensious.* See PRETENSION, -OUS] —**pre·ten′tious·ly,** *adv.* —**pre·ten′tious·ness,** *n.* —**Syn. 2.** pompous. **3.** showy.

preter-, an element, meaning "beyond," "more than," "by," "past," occurring originally in loan words from Latin (*preterit*), and used in the formation of compound words (*preterhuman*). [< L *praeter-,* repr. *praeter* (adv. and prep.)]

pre·ter·hu·man (prē′tər hyo͞o′mən *or, often,* -yo͞o′-), *adj.* beyond what is human; *preterhuman experience.*

pret·er·it (pret′ər it), *n.* *Gram.* **1.** past (def. 12). **2.** a preterit tense. **3.** a verb form in this tense. —*adj.* **4.** *Gram.* noting a past action or state. **5.** *Archaic.* bygone; past. Also, **pret′er·ite.** [ME < L *praeterit(us)* past, ptp. of *praeterīre* to go by = *praeter-* PRETER- + *īre* to go]

pret·er·i·tion (pret′ə rish′ən), *n.* **1.** the act of passing by or over; omission; disregard. **2.** *Law.* the passing over by a testator of an heir. **3.** *Calvinistic Theol.* the passing over by God of those not elected to salvation or eternal life. [< LL *praeteritiōn-* (s. of *praeteritiō*) a passing by]

pre·ter·i·tive (pri ter′i tiv), *adj.* *Gram.* (of verbs) limited to past tenses.

pre·ter·mit (prē′tər mit′), *v.t.,* **-mit·ted, -mit·ting. 1.** to let pass without notice; disregard. **2.** to leave undone; neglect; omit. **3.** to suspend or interrupt. [< L *praetermitt(ere)* (to) let pass = *praeter-* PRETER- + *mittere* to let go] —**pre·ter·mis·sion** (prē′tər mish′ən), *n.* —**pre′ter·mit′ter,** *n.*

pre·ter·nat·u·ral (prē′tər nach′ər əl, -nach′rəl), *adj.* **1.** out of the ordinary course of nature; exceptional or abnormal. **2.** outside of nature; supernatural. [< ML *praeternātūrāl(is),* adj. for L phrase *praeter nātūram* beyond nature] —**pre′ter·nat′u·ral·ism, pre·ter·nat·u·ral·i·ty** (prē′tər nach′ə ral′i tē), **pre′ter·nat′u·ral·ness,** *n.* —**pre′ter·nat′u·ral·ly,** *adv.* —**Syn. 1.** unusual, extraordinary, unnatural. See **miraculous.** —**Ant. 1.** ordinary, usual.

pre·test (*n.* prē′test; *v.* prē test′), *n.* **1.** an advance or preliminary testing or trial, as of a new product. **2.** a test given to determine if a student is prepared to begin a new course of study. —*v.t.* **3.** to give a pretest to (a student, product, etc.). —*v.i.* **4.** to conduct a pretest.

pre·text (prē′tekst), *n.* **1.** something that is put forward to conceal a true purpose or object; an ostensible reason. **2.** the misleading appearance or behavior assumed with this intention. [< L *praetext(um)* pretext, ornament, n. use of neut. ptp. of *praetexere* to pretend, lit., to weave in front, hence, adorn. See PRE-, TEXTURE] —**Syn. 2.** subterfuge, evasion.

pre·tor (prē′tər), *n.* praetor. —**pre·to·ri·al** (prē tōr′ē əl, -tôr′-), *adj.* —**pre·to′ri·an,** *adj., n.*

Pre·to·ri·a (pri tōr′ē ə, -tôr′-), *n.* a city in and the administrative capital of the Republic of South Africa, in the NE part; also the capital of Transvaal. 595,000.

Pre·to·ri·us (pri tōr′ē əs, -tôr′-; *Du.* prä tō′rē o͝os′), *n.* **An·dries Wil·hel·mus Ja·co·bus** (än′drēs vil hel′mo͝os yä kō′bo͝os), 1799–1853, Boer soldier and statesman in South Africa.

pret·ti·fy (prit′ə fī′), *v.t.,* **-fied, -fy·ing. 1.** *Often Disparaging.* to make pretty: *to prettify a shopping center.* **2.** to minimize or gloss over (something unpleasant). —**pret′ti·fi·ca′tion,** *n.* —**pret′ti·fi′er,** *n.*

pret·ty (prit′ē), *adj.,* **-ti·er, -ti·est,** *n., pl.* **-ties,** *adv., v.,* **-tied, -ty·ing.** —*adj.* **1.** pleasing or attractive to the eye in a feminine or childlike way. **2.** (of things, places, etc.) pleasing to the eye. **3.** pleasing to the ear: *a pretty tune.* **4.** pleasing to the mind or aesthetic taste. **5.** (often used ironically) fine; grand; *This is a pretty mess!* **6.** *Informal.* considerable, fairly great; *a pretty sum.* **7.** *Archaic or Scot.* brave; hardy. —*n.* **8.** Usually, **pretties.** pretty ornaments, clothes, etc. **9.** (used in address) a pretty person. —*adv.* **10.** moderately: *Her work was pretty good.* **11.** quite; very: *The wind blew pretty hard.* **12.** *Chiefly Dial.* prettily. **13. sitting pretty,** *Slang.* **a.** in an advantageous position. **b.** well-to-do; successful. —*v.t.* **14.** to make pretty; improve the appearance of (sometimes fol. by *up*): *to pretty oneself for a party; to pretty up a room.* [ME *prety, praty,* OE *prættig,* cunning, wily < *prætt* a trick, wile; c. D *part* trick, prank, Icel *prettr* trick, *prettugr* tricky] —**pret′ti·ly,** *adv.* —**pret′ti·ness,** *n.* —**pret′ty·ish,** *adj.* —**Syn. 1.** See **beautiful. 2–4.** pleasant. **10.** fairly, somewhat. —**Ant. 1.** ugly.

pre·typ·i·fy (prē tip′ə fī′), *v.t.,* **-fied, -fy·ing.** to anticipate or prefigure the typical form of.

pret·zel (pret′səl), *n.* a crisp, dry biscuit, usually in the form of a knot or stick, salted on the outside. [< G *Pretzel,* var. of *Bretzel*; cf. ML *bracellus* bracelet]

Preus·sen (proi′sən), *n.* German name of **Prussia.**

pre·vail (pri vāl′), *v.i.* **1.** to exist everywhere or generally. **2.** to appear or occur as the most important or conspicuous feature or element. **3.** to be or prove superior in power or influence (usually fol. by *over*). **4.** to become dominant or win out. **5.** to use persuasion or inducement successfully (usually fol. by *on* or *upon*): *Can you prevail on him to go?* [ME *prevaylle(n)* (to) grow very strong < L *praevalē(re)* (to) be more able. See PRE-, -VALENT] —**pre·vail′er,** *n.* —**Syn. 2.** preponderate. **3.** overcome. —**Ant. 3.** lose.

pre·vail·ing (pri vā′ling), *adj.* **1.** predominant. **2.** generally current. **3.** having superior power or influence. **4.** effectual. —**pre·vail′ing·ly,** *adv.* —**Syn. 1.** preponderant, dominant; prevalent. **2.** common. See **current.**

prev·a·lent (prev′ə lənt), *adj.* **1.** of wide extent or occurrence. **2.** in general use or acceptance. [< L *praevalent-* (s. of *praevalēns*), prp. of *praevalēre* to PREVAIL; see -ENT] —**prev′a·lence, prev′a·lent·ness,** *n.* —**prev′a·lent·ly,** *adv.* —**Syn.** common, extensive. See **current.**

pre·var·i·cate (pri var′ə kāt′), *v.i.,* **-cat·ed, -cat·ing.** to speak falsely or misleadingly with deliberate intent; lie. [< L *praevāricāt(us),* ptp. of *praevāricārī* to walk as if straddling, (legal L: engage in collusion, eccl. L: transgress) = *prae-* PRE- + *vāricāre* to straddle < *vāric(us)* straddling (*vār(us)* crooked, bent + *-icus* -IC)] —**pre·var′i·ca′tion,** *n.* —**pre·var′i·ca′tive, pre·var·i·ca·to·ry** (pri var′ə kə tōr′ē, -tôr′ē), *adj.* —**pre·var′i·ca′tor,** *n.*

pre·ven·ient (pri vēn′yənt), *adj.* **1.** coming before; antecedent. **2.** anticipatory. [< L *praevenient-* (s. of *praeveniēns*) coming before, prp. of *praevenīre* to anticipate. See PREVENT] —**prev·e·nance** (prev′ə nəns), **pre·ven·ience** (pri vēn′yəns), *n.* —**pre·ven′ient·ly,** *adv.*

pre·vent (pri vent′), *v.t.* **1.** to keep from occurring. **2.** to hinder or stop from doing something: *There is nothing to prevent us from going.* **3.** *Archaic.* to act ahead of; forestall. **4.** *Archaic.* to precede. **5.** *Archaic.* to anticipate. —*v.i.* **6.**

pre·sur′gi·cal, *adj.* **pre-Ter′ti·ar′y,** *adj.* **pre-Tu′dor,** *adj.* **pre′un′ion,** *adj.*

to interpose a hindrance. [ME < L *praevent(us)* started beforehand, ptp. of *praevenīre* to anticipate = *prae-* PRE- + *venīre* to come] —**pre·vent′a·bil′i·ty,** *n.* —**pre·vent′a·ble, pre·vent′i·ble,** *adj.* —**pre·vent′er,** *n.*
—**Syn. 1.** obstruct, forestall, preclude, obviate, thwart. PREVENT, HAMPER, HINDER, IMPEDE refer to different degrees of stoppage of action or progress. To PREVENT is to stop something effectually by forestalling action and rendering it impossible: *to prevent the sending of a message.* To HAMPER is to clog, entangle, or put an embarrassing restraint upon: *to hamper preparations for a trip.* To HINDER is to keep back by delaying or stopping progress or action: *to hinder the progress of an expedition.* To IMPEDE is to make difficult the movement or progress of anything by interfering with its proper functioning: *to impede a discussion by demanding repeated explanations.* —**Ant. 1.** help, assist.

pre·ven·tion (pri ven′shən), *n.* **1.** the act of preventing. **2.** a preventive. [< LL *praeventiōn-* (s. of *praeventiō*)]

pre·ven·tive (pri ven′tiv), *adj.* **1.** *Med.* noting or pertaining to the prevention of disease. **2.** serving to prevent or hinder: *preventive medicine.* —*n.* **3.** *Med.* a drug or other substance for preventing disease. **4.** a preventive agent or measure. Also, **pre·vent·a·tive** (pri ven′tə tiv) (for defs. 2, 4). —**pre·ven′tive·ly,** *adv.* —**pre·ven′tive·ness,** *n.*

pre·view (prē′vyo͞o′), *n.* **1.** an earlier or previous view. **2.** an advance showing of a motion picture, play, etc., before its public opening. **3.** a showing of brief scenes in a motion picture, television show, etc., for purposes of advertisement. **4.** anything that gives an advance idea or impression of something to come. —*v.t.* **5.** to view or show beforehand or in advance. Also, **prevue.** —**pre′view′er,** *n.*

pre·vi·ous (prē′vē əs), *adj.* **1.** coming or occurring before another such one; prior. **2. previous to,** before; prior to. [< L *praevius* going before. See PRE-, VIA, -OUS] —**pre′vi·ous·ly,** *adv.* —**Syn. 1.** earlier, former, preceding.

pre′vious ques′tion, *Parl. Proc.* a move that a vote be taken at once on a main question, esp. as a means of cutting off further debate.

pre·vise (pri vīz′), *v.t.*, **-vised, -vis·ing. 1.** to foresee. **2.** to forewarn. [< L *praevīs(us)* foreseen, ptp. of *praevidēre*]

pre·vi·sion (pri vizh′ən), *n.* **1.** foresight, foreknowledge, or prescience. **2.** a prophetic or anticipatory vision or perception. —**pre·vi′sion·al,** *adj.*

pre·vo·cal·ic (prē′vō kal′ik), *adj.* *Phonet.* immediately preceding a vowel. —**pre′vo·cal′i·cal·ly,** *adv.*

pre·vo·ca·tion·al (prē′vō kā′shə nᵊl), *adj.* of, pertaining to, or constituting preliminary vocational training.

Pré·vost d'Ex·iles (prā vō′ deg zēl′), **An·toine Fran·çois** (äN twaN′ fräN swa′), ("*Abbé Prévost*"), 1697–1763, French novelist.

pre·vue (prē′vyo͞o′), *n.*, *v.t.*, **-vued, -vu·ing.** preview.

pre·war (prē′wôr′), *adj.* existing or prevailing before a war.

prex·y (prek′sē), *n.*, *pl.* **prex·ies.** *Slang.* a president, esp. of a college or university. Also, **prex.** [*prex* (by shortening and alter. of *president*) + -Y²]

prey (prā), *n.* **1.** an animal hunted or seized for food, esp. by a carnivorous animal. **2.** any victim. **3.** the action or habit of preying; *a beast of prey.* **4.** *Archaic.* booty or plunder. —*v.i.* **5.** to seize and devour prey, as an animal does. **6.** to make attacks for booty or plunder. **7.** (of thoughts and emotions) to exert a harmful and obsessive influence on the mind. **8.** to victimize another or others: *to prey upon the poor.* [ME *preye* < OF < L *praeda* booty, prey] —**prey′er,** *n.*

Pri·am (prī′əm), *n.* *Class. Myth.* a king of Troy, the husband of Hecuba and father of Paris, Cassandra, and Hector.

pri·a·pe·an (prī′ə pē′ən), *adj.* priapic. [< F *priapéen* < L *Priāpē(ius)* < Gk *Priápeios.* See PRIAPUS, -AN]

pri·ap·ic (prī ap′ik), *adj.* **1.** (*sometimes cap.*) of or pertaining to Priapus; phallic. **2.** exaggeratedly concerned with masculinity and male sexuality.

pri·a·pism (prī′ə piz′əm), *n.* **1.** *Pathol.* continuous erection of the penis, esp. due to disease. **2.** prurient behavior or display. —**pri′a·pis′mic,** *adj.*

Pri·a·pus (prī ā′pəs), *n.* *Class. Myth.* a god of male procreative power, the son of Dionysus and Aphrodite.

Prib′i·lof Is′lands (prib′ə lof′), a group of islands in the Bering Sea, SW of Alaska, and belonging to the U.S.: the breeding ground of fur seals.

price (prīs), *n.*, *v.*, **priced, pric·ing.** —*n.* **1.** the sum of money or its equivalent for which anything is bought, sold, or offered for sale. **2.** the disadvantage or sacrifice attending something chosen. **3.** a reward, as for a capture or killing: *a price on someone's head.* **4.** a reward for which a person will forsake his principles or obligations: *Has every man his price?* **5.** odds (def. 2). **6.** *Archaic.* value or worth. **7.** *Archaic.* great value or worth (usually prec. by *of*): *articles of price.* **8. at any price,** at any cost or sacrifice, no matter how great. **9. beyond** or **without price,** of incalculable value; priceless. —*v.t.* **10.** to fix the price of. **11.** to ask or ascertain the price of. [ME *pris* < OF < L *pret(ium)* price, value, worth] —**price′a·ble,** *adj.* —**pric′er,** *n.*
—**Syn. 1, 4.** PRICE, CHARGE, COST, EXPENSE refer to outlay or expenditure required in buying or maintaining something. PRICE is used mainly of single, concrete objects offered for sale; CHARGE, of services: *What is the price of that coat? There is a small charge for mailing packages.* COST is mainly a purely objective term, often used in financial calculations: *The cost of building a new annex was estimated at $10,000.* EXPENSE suggests cost plus incidental expenditure: *The expense of a journey was more than the contemplated cost.* Only CHARGE is not used figuratively. PRICE, COST, and sometimes EXPENSE may be used to refer to the expenditure of mental energy, what a person "pays" in anxiety, suffering, etc.

Price (prīs), *n.* **(Mary) Le·on·tyne** (lē′ən tēn′), born 1927, U.S. soprano.

price′-earn′ings ra′tio (prīs′ûr′ningz), the ratio of the market price of a share of common stock to the earnings per share, often used in security analysis and simply expressed as a numeral **(price′-earn′ings mul′tiple).**

price′ in′dex, an index of the changes in the prices of goods and services, based on the prices of the same goods and services at a period arbitrarily selected as a base, usually expressed as 100: *the consumer price index.*

price·less (prīs′lis), *adj.* **1.** beyond all price; invaluable. **2.** *Informal.* delightfully amusing: *That was a priceless anecdote!*—**price′less·ness,** *n.*

price′ support′, government maintenance of the price of a commodity, product, etc., esp. by means of a public subsidy or government purchase.

price′ war′, *Com.* a period of intensive competition, esp. among retailers, in which prices are repeatedly cut.

pric·ey (prī′sē), *adj.*, **pric·i·er, pric·i·est.** *Informal.* expensive or unduly expensive: *a pricey wine.* Also, **pricy.** [PRICE + -Y²] —**pric′i·ly,** *adv.* —**pric′i·ness,** *n.*

Prich·ard (prich′ərd), *n.* a city in S Alabama. 41,578 (1970).

prick (prik), *n.* **1.** a mark or puncture made by something small and sharp. **2.** the act of pricking, or the state or sensation of being pricked. **3.** the pointed end of a prickspur. **4.** *Slang* (*vulgar*) **a.** the penis. **b.** an obnoxious man; cad. **5.** *Obs.* any pointed instrument or weapon. **6. kick against the pricks,** to resist incontestable facts or authority. —*v.t.* **7.** to pierce with something small and sharp. **8.** to affect with sharp pain, as from piercing. **9.** to cause (someone) sharp mental pain. **10.** to urge on with or as with a goad or spur. **11.** to mark with a series of pricks. **12.** to cause to stand erect or point upward. **13.** to measure (distances or areas) on a chart with dividers. **14.** *Hort.* to transplant (a seedling) into a container that provides more room for growth. —*v.i.* **15.** to perform the action of jabbing or puncturing something. **16.** to have a sensation of being pricked. **17.** *Archaic.* to spur or urge a horse on; ride rapidly. **18. prick up one's ears,** to show sudden interest; listen attentively. [ME *prike* (n.), *prike(n)* (v.), OE *prica, price* dot, point, *prician* (v.); c. D, LG *prik* point] —**prick′er,** *n.*

prick·et (prik′it), *n.* **1.** a sharp metal point on which to stick a candle. **2.** a candlestick with one or more such points. **3.** a buck in his second year. [ME]

prick·le (prik′əl), *n.*, *v.*, **-led, -ling.** —*n.* **1.** a sharp point. **2.** a small, pointed process growing from the bark of a plant. **3.** a pricking sensation. —*v.t.* **4.** to prick lightly. **5.** to cause a mild pricking or tingling sensation in. —*v.i.* **6.** to tingle as if pricked. [ME *prykel,* OE *pricel*]

prick·ly (prik′lē), *adj.*, **-li·er, -li·est. 1.** full of or armed with prickles. **2.** full of troublesome aspects, as a problem. **3.** prickling; smarting: *a prickly sensation.* —**prick′li·ness,** *n.*

prick′ly ash′, a rutaceous shrub or small tree, *Zanthoxylum americanum,* having aromatic leaves and usually prickly branches. Also called **angelica tree.**

prick′ly heat′, *Pathol.* a cutaneous eruption accompanied by a prickling and itching sensation, caused by an inflammation of the sweat glands.

prick′ly pear′, 1. the pear-shaped or ovoid, often prickly and sometimes edible fruit of any cactus of the genus *Opuntia.* **2.** the plant itself.

prick′ly pop′py, any tropical American plant of the genus *Argemone,* esp. *A. mexicana,* having prickly pods and leaves and yellow or white, poppylike flowers.

prick′ song′, *Archaic.* **1.** written music. **2.** descant (def. 1a). [short for *pricked song*]

pric·y (prī′sē), *adj.*, **pric·i·er, pric·i·est.** *Informal.* pricey.

pride (prīd), *n.*, *v.*, **prid·ed, prid·ing.** —*n.* **1.** the state or quality of being proud. **2.** self-respect: *Show a little pride!* **3.** a feeling of self-esteem arising from one's accomplishments, possessions, etc. **4.** arrogant behavior or conduct. **5.** an exaggerated idea of one's dignity or importance. **6.** a feeling of gratification arising from association with something that is good or laudable: *civic pride.* **7.** something that causes a person or persons to be proud: *His art collection was the pride of the family.* **8.** the best one of a kind. **9.** the most flourishing state or period. **10.** mettle in a horse. **11.** *Literary.* splendor, magnificence, or pomp. **12.** a company or group of lions. —*v.t.* **13.** to indulge (oneself) in a feeling of pride (usually fol. by *on* or *upon*): *She prides herself on her cooking.* [ME; OE *prȳde* (c. Icel *prȳthi* pomp) < *prūd* PROUD] —**pride′ful,** *adj.* —**pride′ful·ly,** *adv.* —**pride′ful·ness,** *n.* —**pride′less,** *adj.* —**pride′less·ly,** *adv.*
—**Syn. 3, 4.** PRIDE, CONCEIT, SELF-ESTEEM, EGOTISM, VANITY, imply a favorable idea of one's own appearance, advantages, achievements, etc., and often apply to offensive characteristics. PRIDE is a lofty, and sometimes arrogant, assumption of superiority in some respect: *Pride must have a fall.* CONCEIT implies an exaggerated estimate of one's own abilities or attainments, together with pride: *blinded by conceit.* SELF-ESTEEM may imply an estimate of oneself that is higher than that held by others: *a ridiculous self-esteem.* EGOTISM implies an excessive preoccupation with oneself or with one's own concerns, usually but not always accompanied by pride or conceit: *His egotism blinded him to the suffering of others.* VANITY implies self-admiration and an excessive desire to be admired by others: *His vanity was easily flattered.* —**Ant. 3, 4.** humility, modesty.

prie-dieu (prē′dyo͝o′; *Fr.* prē dyœ′), *n.*, *pl.* **-dieus, -dieux** (-dyo͝oz′), *Fr.* **-dieu.** a piece of furniture for kneeling on during prayer, having a shelf above for a book. [< F: lit., pray God]

pri·er (prī′ər), *n.* a person who looks or searches curiously or inquisitively into something. Also, **pryer.**

priest (prēst), *n.* **1.** Also, *referring to a woman,* **priest′ess,** a person whose office it is to perform religious rites, and esp. to make sacrificial offerings. **2.** (in Christian use) **a.** a person ordained to the sacerdotal or pastoral office; clergyman; minister. **b.** (in hierarchical churches) a clergyman of the order next below that of bishop. **3.** a minister of any religion. [ME *preest,* OE *prēost,* alter. of PRESBYTER]

priest·craft (prēst′kraft′, -kräft′), *n.* the training, knowledge, and abilities necessary to a priest.

priest·hood (prēst′ho͝od), *n.* **1.** the condition or office of a priest. **2.** priests collectively. [ME, OE *prēosthād*]

Priest·ley (prēst′lē), *n.* **1. J(ohn) B(oyn·ton)** (boin′tən, -tᵊn), 1894–1984, English author and dramatist. **2. Joseph,** 1733–1804, English chemist, author, and clergyman.

priest·ly (prēst′lē), *adj.*, **-li·er, -li·est. 1.** of or pertaining to a priest. **2.** characteristic of or befitting a priest. [ME; OE *prēostlic*] —**priest′li·ness,** *n.*

pre′-Vic·to′ri·an, *adj.* **pre·warm′,** *v.t.* **pre·warn′,** *v.t.* **pre·wash′,** *n.*, *v.t.*

prig[1] (prig), *n.* a person who adheres smugly or unthinkingly to rigid standards of propriety or morality. [formerly, coxcomb; perh. akin to PRINK] —**prig′ger·y,** *n.* —**prig′gish,** *adj.* —**prig′gish·ly,** *adv.* —**prig′gish·ness,** *n.*

prig[2] (prig), *v.i.,* **prigged, prig·ging.** **1.** *Scot. and North Eng.* to haggle or argue over price. **2.** *Brit. Informal.* to beg or entreat; ask a favor. [orig. cant]

prim (prim), *adj.,* **prim·mer, prim·mest,** *v.,* **primmed, prim·ming.** —*adj.* **1.** formally precise or proper, as persons or their conduct. —*v.i.* **2.** to draw up the mouth in an affectedly nice or precise way. —*v.t.* **3.** to make prim, as in appearance. **4.** to draw (one's features) into a prim expression. [?] —**prim′ly,** *adv.* —**prim′ness,** *n.*

prim., **1.** primary. **2.** primitive.

pri′ma balleri′na (prē′mə), the principal ballerina in a ballet company. [< It]

pri·ma·cy (prī′mə sē), *n., pl.* **-cies** for 2, 3. **1.** the state of being first in order, rank, importance, etc. **2.** Also called **primateship.** *Eng. Eccles.* the office, rank, or dignity of a primate. **3.** *Rom. Cath. Ch.* the jurisdiction of a bishop, as a patriarch, over other bishoprics, or the supreme jurisdiction of the pope as supreme bishop. [ME *primacie* < ML *prīmātia,* alter. of L *prīmātus* (see PRIME, -ATE[1]); see -Y[3]]

pri·ma don·na (prē′mə don′ə, prim′ə; *It.* prē′mä dôn′nä), *pl.* **pri·ma don·nas,** *It.* **pri·me don·ne** (prē′me dôn′ne). **1.** a first or principal female singer of an operatic company; diva. **2.** a high-strung, vain, temperamental person. [< It: lit., first lady]

pri·mae·val (prī mē′vəl), *adj.* primeval.

pri·ma fa·ci·e (prī′mə fā′shē ē′, fā′shē, fā′shə), **1.** at first appearance, before investigation. **2.** immediately plain or clear. [< L]

pri′ma fa′cie ev′idence, *Law.* evidence sufficient to establish a fact, or to raise a presumption of fact, unless rebutted.

pri·mal (prī′məl), *adj.* **1.** first; original; primeval. **2.** of first importance; fundamental. [< ML *prīmāl(is)*]

pri·mar·i·ly (prī mâr′ə lē, prī′mer ə lē, -mər ə-), *adv.* **1.** essentially; mostly; chiefly; principally. **2.** in the first instance; at first; originally.

pri·ma·ry (prī′mer ē, -mə rē), *adj., n., pl.* **-ries.** —*adj.* **1.** most important or essential; chief; principal: *one's primary goals in life.* **2.** being the first or earliest in a series, sequence, order of development, etc. **3.** being of the simplest or most basic order of its or their kind: *a primary constituent; a primary classification.* **4.** not dependent on or derived from something else: *a primary cause.* **5.** of, pertaining to, or characteristic of primary school. **6.** *Ornith.* pertaining to any of the set of flight feathers situated on the distal segment of a bird's wing. **7.** *Elect.* noting or pertaining to the circuit, coil, winding, or current that induces current in secondary windings in an induction coil, transformer, or the like. **8.** *Chem.* **a.** involving or obtained by replacement of one atom or group. **b.** noting or containing a carbon atom united to no other or to only one other carbon atom in a molecule. **9.** (of Latin, Greek, Sanskrit tenses) having reference to present or future time. Cf. **secondary** (def. 9). —*n.* **10.** that which is first in order, rank, or importance. **11.** *U.S. Politics.* **a.** Also called **primary election.** a preliminary election in which voters of each party nominate candidates for office, party officers, etc. **b.** caucus. **12.** See **primary color.** **13.** *Ornith.* a primary feather. **14.** *Astron.* **a.** a body in relation to a smaller body or smaller bodies revolving around it. **b.** the brighter of the two stars comprising a double star. Cf. **companion**[1] (def. 6). [late ME < L *prīmāri(us)* of the first rank] —**pri′ma·ri·ness,** *n.* —**Syn.** **1.** main, prime. **2.** original; primeval; beginning. See **elementary.** —**Ant.** **1, 2.** last. **2.** final.

pri′mary ac′cent, the principal or strongest stress of a word.

pri′mary cell′, *Elect.* a cell designed to produce electric current through an electrochemical reaction that is not efficiently reversible, so that the cell when discharged cannot be efficiently recharged by an electric current.

pri′mary col′or, a color, as red, yellow, or blue, that in mixture yields other colors. Cf. **complementary color** (def. 1), **secondary color, tertiary color.**

pri′mary elec′tion, primary (def. 11a).

pri′mary inten′tion, intention (def. 4a).

pri′mary school′, **1.** See **elementary school.** **2.** a school covering the first three or four years of public school.

pri·mate (prī′māt *or, esp. for 1,* prī′mit), *n.* **1.** *Eccles.* an archbishop or bishop ranking first among the local bishops. **2.** any mammal of the order *Primates,* including man, the apes, monkeys, and lemurs. [ME *primat* < eccl. L *prīmāt-* (s. of *prīmās*) of first rank (adj.), archbishop (n.) < *prīm(us)* first. See PRIME] —**pri·ma′tal,** *adj., n.* —**pri·ma·tial** (prī mā′shəl), **pri·mat·i·cal** (prī mat′i kəl), *adj.*

pri·mate·ship (prī′mit ship′, -māt-), *n.* primacy (def. 2).

prime (prīm), *adj., n., v.,* **primed, prim·ing.** —*adj.* **1.** of the first importance. **2.** of the greatest relevance or significance. **3.** of the highest eminence or rank. **4.** of the greatest commercial value: *prime building lots.* **5.** first-rate. **6.** (of meat) of the first grade or best quality: *prime ribs of beef.* **7.** being the first in order of time, existence, or development. **8.** basic; fundamental. **9.** *Math.* **a.** not divisible without remainder by any number except itself and unity. **b.** having no common divisor except unity: *The number 2 is prime to 9.* **10.** *Banking.* chargeable as minimum interest on business loans to best-rated clients: *the prime rate.* —*n.* **11.** the most flourishing stage or state. **12.** the time of early manhood or womanhood. **13.** the choicest or best part of anything. **14.** a grade, classification, or designation indicating the highest quality. **15.** the beginning or earliest stage of something. **16.** the spring of the year. **17.** the first hour or period of the day, after sunrise. **18.** *Eccles.* the second of the seven canonical hours or the service for it, originally fixed for the first hour of the day. **19.** *Math.* **a.** a prime number. **b.** one of the equal parts into which a unit is primarily divided. **20.** the mark (′) often used to distinguish the designations of similar quantities: *a, a′.* **21.** *Fencing.* the first of eight defensive positions. **22.** *Music.* **a.** unison (def. 2). **b.** (in a scale) the tonic or keynote. **23.** *Banking.* the prime interest rate. —*v.t.* **24.** to prepare or make ready for a particular purpose or operation. **25.** to supply or fill with an explosive charge for firing. **26.** to pour or admit liquid into (a pump) to expel air and make it ready for action. **27.** to put fuel into (a carburetor) before starting an engine, in order to insure a sufficiently rich mixture at the start. **28.** to cover (a surface) with a preparatory coat or color, as in painting. **29.** to supply or equip with information, words, etc., for use. [(adj.) late ME < L *prīm(us)* first (superl. of *prior* PRIOR[1]); (n.) ME; OE *prīm* < L *prīma* (*hōra*) first (hour); (v.) ? special use of n.] —**prime′ness,** *n.*

prime′ cost′, that part of the cost of a commodity deriving from the labor and materials directly utilized in its manufacture.

prime′ merid′ian, a meridian from which longitude east and west is reckoned, usually that of Greenwich, England.

prime′ min′ister, the first or principal minister of certain governments; chief of the cabinet or ministry. —**prime-min·is·te·ri·al** (prīm′min′i stēr′ē əl), *adj.* —**prime′-min′is·ter·ship′,** *n.* —**prime′ min′istry.**

prime′ mov′er, **1.** *Mech.* **a.** the initial power source that puts a machine in motion. **b.** a machine, as a water wheel or steam engine, that receives and modifies energy as supplied by some natural source. **2.** Also called **unmoved mover.** *Aristotelianism.* that which is the first cause of all movement and does not itself move.

prim·er[1] (prim′ər *or, esp. Brit.,* prī′mər), *n.* **1.** an elementary book for teaching children to read. **2.** any book that teaches elementary principles. [ME < ML *prīmār(ium),* n. use of neut. of *prīmārius* PRIMARY]

prim·er[2] (prī′mər), *n.* **1.** a person or thing that primes. **2.** a cap, cylinder, etc., containing a compound that may be exploded by percussion or other means, used for firing a charge of powder. **3.** a first coat or layer of paint, size, etc., given to any surface as a base, sealer, or the like. [PRIME (v.) + -ER[1]]

prime′ time′, *Radio and Television.* the evening broadcasting hours, generally between 8 and 11 P.M., considered as drawing the largest available audience.

pri·me·val (prī mē′vəl), *adj.* of or pertaining to the first age or ages, esp. of the world. Also, **primaeval.** [< L *prīmaev(us)* young (see PRIME + AGE) + -AL[1]] —**pri·me′val·ly,** *adv.* —**Syn.** primary, primordial, pristine.

prim·ing (prī′ming), *n.* **1.** the powder or other material used to ignite a charge. **2.** the act of a person or thing that primes. **3.** material used as a primer, or first coat or layer of paint, size, etc.

pri·mip·a·ra (prī mip′ər ə), *n., pl.* **-a·rae** (-ə rē′). *Obstet.* a woman who has borne but one child or who is parturient for the first time. [< L *prīmi-* (comb. form of *prīmus;* see PRIME) + *-para,* fem. of *-parus* -PAROUS] —**pri·mi·par·i·ty** (prī′mi par′i tē), *n.* —**pri·mip′a·rous,** *adj.*

prim·i·tive (prim′i tiv), *adj.* **1.** being the first or earliest of the kind or in existence. **2.** early in the history of the world or of mankind. **3.** characteristic of early ages or of an early state of human development. **4.** *Anthropol.* of or pertaining to a race, group, etc., having cultural or physical similarities with their early ancestors. **5.** unaffected or little affected by civilizing influences. **6.** being in its or the earliest period. **7.** simple or crude. **8.** original or radical, as distinguished from derivative. **9.** primary, as distinguished from secondary. **10.** *Biol.* **a.** rudimentary; primordial. **b.** noting species, varieties, etc., only slightly evolved from early antecedent types. **c.** of early formation and temporary, as a part that subsequently disappears. —*n.* **11.** someone or something primitive. **12.** *Fine Arts.* **a.** a naïve or unschooled artist. **b.** an artist belonging to the early stage in the development of a style. **c.** a work of art by a primitive artist. **13.** *Math.* **a.** a geometric or algebraic form or expression from which another is derived. **b.** a function of which the derivative is a given function. **14.** the form from which a given word or other linguistic form has been derived. [< L *prīmitīv(us)* first of its kind; r. ME *primitif* < MF] —**prim′i·tive·ly,** *adv.* —**prim′i·tive·ness, prim′i·tiv′i·ty,** *n.* —**Syn.** **1, 2.** prehistoric, primal, primary, primordial.

prim′itive cell′, *Crystall.* a unit cell containing no points of the lattice except at the corners of the cell.

Prim′itive German′ic, Germanic (def. 5).

prim·i·tiv·ism (prim′i ti viz′əm), *n.* **1.** the belief that primitive or chronologically early civilizations are qualitatively superior to contemporary civilization. **2.** the state of being primitive, as a culture. **3.** the qualities collectively that characterize primitive art. —**prim′i·tiv·ist,** *n.* —**prim′i·tiv·is′tic,** *adj.*

pri·mo·gen·i·tor (prī′mə jen′i tər), *n.* **1.** a first parent or earliest ancestor. **2.** a forefather or ancestor. [< LL: lit., first begetter = L *prīmō* at first + *genitor* (*genit(us)* begotten, ptp. of *gignere* to beget + *-or* -OR[2])]

pri·mo·gen·i·ture (prī′mə jen′i chər), *n.* **1.** the state or fact of being the first-born of children of the same parents. **2.** *Law.* the system of inheritance or succession by the first-born, specifically the eldest son. [< LL *prīmōgenitūra* a first birth = L *prīmō* at first + *genitūra* (*genit(us)* begotten + *-ure* -URE)] —**pri′mo·gen′i·tar′y, pri′mo·gen′i·tal,** *adj.*

pri·mor·di·al (prī môr′dē əl), *adj.* **1.** constituting a beginning or source. **2.** *Biol.* primitive; initial; first formed. **3.** pertaining to or existing at or from the very beginning. [ME < LL *prīmōrdiāl(is)* of the beginning] —**pri·mor·di·al·i·ty** (prī môr′dē al′i tē), *n.* —**pri·mor′di·al·ly,** *adv.*

pri·mor·di·um (prī môr′dē əm), *n., pl.* **-di·a** (-dē ə). *Embryol.* the first recognizable, histologically differentiated stage in the development of an organ. [< L, n. use of neut. of *prīmōrdius* original = *prīm(us)* PRIME + *ōrdi-* (s. of *ōrdīrī* to begin) + *-us* adj. suffix]

primp (primp), *v.t.* **1.** to dress or adorn with care. —*v.i.* **2.** to groom oneself carefully. [akin to PRIM]

prim·rose (prim′rōz′), *n.* **1.** any perennial herb of the genus *Primula,* as *P. vulgaris,* of Europe, having yellow flowers, or *P. sinensis,* of China, having variously colored flowers. **2.** See **evening primrose.** **3.** pale yellow. —*adj.* **4.** of or pertaining to the primrose. **5.** Also, **prim′rosed′.** having primroses. [ME *primerose* < ML *prīma rosa* first rose]

prim′rose path′, **1.** a way of life devoted to irresponsible hedonism. **2.** a course of action that is easy or tempting but treacherous.

prim·u·la (prim′yə lə), *n.* primrose (def. 1). [< ML, short for *prīmula vēris,* lit., first (flower) of spring]

prim·u·la·ceous (prim′yə lā′shəs), *adj.* belonging to the *Primulaceae,* or primrose family of plants.

pri·mum mo·bi·le (prē′mo͝om mō′bi le′; *Eng.* prī′məm mob′ə lē′), *Latin.* See **prime mover.** [lit.: first moving (thing)]

pri·mus in·ter pa·res (prē′mo͝os in′ter pä′res; *Eng.* prī′məs in′tər pâ′rēz), *Latin.* first among equals.

prin., 1. principal. 2. principally. 3. principle.

prince (prins), *n.* **1.** a nonreigning male member of a royal family. **2.** *Hist.* a sovereign or monarch; king. **3.** (in Great Britain) a man or boy having the sovereign as a parent or paternal grandparent. **4.** the ruler of a principality or of a small state, as one actually or nominally subordinate to a suzerain. **5.** a person or thing that is chief or preeminent in any class, group, etc. **6.** a person possessing admirable characteristics. [ME < OF < L *princip-* (s. of *princeps*) first, principal (adj.), principal person, leader (n.) = *prīn-* PRIME + *-cep-* (comb. form of *capere* to take) + *-s* nom. sing. ending]

Prince′ Al′bert, 1. See **Albert, Prince. 2.** a city in central Saskatchewan, in S Canada. 28,631. **3.** a long, double-breasted frock coat.

Prince′ Al′bert Na′tional Park′, a national park in W Canada, in central Saskatchewan. 1869 sq. mi.

Prince′ Charm′ing, a man who embodies a woman's romantic ideal.

prince′ con′sort, a prince who is the husband of a reigning female sovereign.

prince·dom (prins′dəm), *n.* **1.** the position, rank, or dignity of a prince. **2.** the domain of a prince; principality. **3. princedoms,** (in medieval angelology) principalities.

Prince′ Ed′ward Is′land, an island in the Gulf of St. Lawrence, forming a province of Canada. 116,251; 2184 sq. mi. *Cap.:* Charlottetown.

prince·ling (prins′ling), *n.* **1.** a young prince. **2.** a subordinate, minor, or insignificant prince.

prince·ly (prins′lē), *adj.*, **-li·er, -li·est. 1.** lavish or magnificent: *a princely entertainment.* **2.** suitable to or befitting a prince. **3.** of or pertaining to a prince. **—prince′li·ness,** *n.*

Prince′ of Dark′ness, Satan.

Prince′ of Peace′, Jesus Christ, regarded by Christians as the Messiah. Isa. 9:6.

Prince′ of Wales′, 1. a title conferred on the male heir apparent to the British throne. **2. Cape,** a cape in W Alaska, on Bering Strait opposite the Soviet Union: the westernmost point of North America.

Prince′ of Wales′ Is′land, 1. the largest island in the Alexander Archipelago, in SE Alaska. 1500 sq. mi. **2.** an island in N Canada, in the Northwest Territories. ab. 14,000 sq. mi.

prince′ re′gent, a prince who is regent of a country.

prince′ roy′al, the eldest son of a king or queen.

Prince′ Ru′pert, 1. See **Rupert, Prince. 2.** a seaport and railway terminus in W British Columbia, in W Canada. 14,754.

prince's-feath·er (prin′siz feth′ər), *n.* a tall, showy plant, *Amaranthus hybridus hypochondriacus,* having reddish foliage and thick spikes of small, red flowers.

Prince′s Is′land, former name of **Principe.**

prin·cess (prin′sis, -ses), *n.* **1.** a nonreigning female member of a royal family. **2.** *Hist.* a female sovereign or monarch; queen. **3.** the consort of a prince. **4.** (in Great Britain) a woman or girl having the sovereign as a parent or paternal grandparent. **—*adj.* 5.** Also, **prin′cesse.** (of a woman's dress, coat, or the like) styled with a close-fitting bodice and flared skirt, cut in single pieces, as gores, from shoulder to hem. [ME *princesse* < MF] **—prin′cess·ly,** *adj.*

Prin·cess (prin′sis, -ses), *n. Trademark.* a compact, streamlined model of telephone available in several colors and offered to subscribers at an additional charge.

prin′cess re′gent, 1. a princess who is regent of a country. **2.** the wife of a prince regent.

prin′cess roy′al, 1. the eldest daughter of a king or queen. **2.** (in Great Britain and, formerly, Prussia) an eldest princess to whom this title has been granted for life by the sovereign.

Prince·ton (prins′tən), *n.* a borough in central New Jersey: battle 1777. 12,311 (1970).

prin·ci·pal (prin′sə pəl), *adj.* **1.** first or highest, as in rank, importance, or value. **2.** of or constituting principal or capital: *a principal investment.* **—*n.* 3.** a chief or head. **4.** the head or director of a school or, esp. in England, a college. **5.** a person who takes a leading part in any activity, as a play; chief actor or doer. **6.** the first player of a division of instruments in an orchestra, excepting the leader of the first violins. **7.** something of principal or chief importance. **8.** *Law.* **a.** a person who authorizes another, as an agent, to represent him. **b.** a person directly responsible for a crime, either as an actual perpetrator or as an abettor present at its commission. **9.** a person primarily liable for an obligation. **10.** the main body of an estate or the like, as distinguished from income. **11.** *Finance.* a capital sum, as distinguished from interest or profit. **12.** a principal framing member, as a major roof truss. **13.** each of the combatants in a duel, as distinguished from the seconds. [ME < L *prīncipāl(is)* first, chief] **—prin′ci·pal·ship′,** *n.*

prin′cipal clause′, the main clause.

prin·ci·pal·i·ty (prin′sə pal′i tē), *n., pl.* **-ties. 1.** a state ruled by a prince, duke, etc. **2.** the position or authority of a prince or chief ruler. **3.** the rule of a prince of a small or subordinate state. **4. principalities,** *Theol.* an order of angels. Cf. **angel** (def. 2). [ME *principalite* < OF < LL *prīncipālitāt-* (s. of *prīncipālitās*) first place, superiority (ML: authority or territory of a prince)]

prin·ci·pal·ly (prin′sə pə lē, -sip lē), *adv.* for the most part; mainly. [ME] **—Syn.** See **especially.**

prin′cipal parts′, *Gram.* a set of inflected forms of a form class from which all the other inflected forms can be derived, as *sing, sang, sung; smoke, smoked.*

Prin·ci·pe (prin′si pē; *Port.* prēnn′sē pə), *n.* an island in the independent country of St. Thomas and Principe: in the Gulf of Guinea, off the W coast of Africa. Formerly, **Prince's Island.**

prin·cip·i·um (prin sip′ē əm), *n., pl.* **-cip·i·a** (-sip′ē ə). a principle. [< L: lit., that which is first. See PRINCE, -IUM]

prin·ci·ple (prin′sə pəl), *n.* **1.** an accepted or professed rule of action or conduct. **2.** a basic law, axiom, or doctrine. **3. principles,** a personal or specific basis of conduct or operation. **4.** a guiding sense of the requirements and obligations of right conduct: *a man of principle.* **5.** a characteristic form of composition or organization, method of operation, etc.: *the principle of capillarity; a constitution on the British principle.* **6.** an originating or actuating agency or force: *the principles of Yin and Yang.* **7.** *Chem.* a constituent of a substance, esp. one giving to it some distinctive quality or effect. **8. in principle,** in theory, without regard to an actual situation. **9. on principle,** in support of, or as a demonstration of, one's principles. [ME, alter. of MF *principe* or L *prīncipium,* on analogy of *manciple*]

prin·ci·pled (prin′sə pəld), *adj.* imbued with or having principles (often used in combination): *high-principled.*

prink (pringk), *v.t.* **1.** to deck or dress for show. **—*v.i.* 2.** to deck oneself out. **3.** to fuss over one's dress, esp. before the mirror. [appar. akin to PRANK[2]] **—prink′er,** *n.*

print (print), *v.t.* **1.** to cause (a text, picture, or design) to be reproduced or represented on a surface or surfaces through the transfer by machinery of ink, dye, pigment, etc. **2.** to cause (a material or surface) to receive a text, picture, or design reproduced or represented by such means. **3.** to write in letters like those commonly used in print. **4.** *Computer Technol.* to produce (data) in legible alphanumeric form. **5.** to indent or mark by pressing. **6.** to produce or fix (an indentation or mark), as by pressure. **7.** to apply with pressure so as to leave an indentation or mark. **8.** *Photog.* to produce a positive picture from (a negative) by the transmission of light. **—*v.i.* 9.** to reproduce or represent a text, picture, or design by the transfer with machinery of ink, dye, pigment, etc. **10.** to write in characters such as are used in print. **11.** to follow the trade of a printer. **12. print out,** *Computer Technol.* to print (output), usually on paper moving continuously through a printer. **—*n.* 13.** the state of being printed. **14.** printed lettering. **15.** printed matter. **16.** a printed publication, as a newspaper or magazine. **17.** newsprint. **18.** a picture or design produced by printing. **19.** an indentation, mark, etc., made by the pressure of one thing on another. **20.** *Textiles.* **a.** a design or pattern on cloth made by dyeing, weaving, or printing, as with engraved rollers. **b.** a cloth so treated. **c.** an article made of this cloth. **21.** *Photog.* a picture, esp. a positive made from a negative. **22.** any photochemically reproduced image, as a blueprint. **23. in print, a.** in printed form; published. **b.** (of a book) still available for purchase from the publisher. **24. out of print,** (of a book) no longer available from the publisher. [ME *priente* < OF: impression, print, n. use of fem. ptp. of *preindre* < L *premere* to press]

print., printing.

print·a·ble (prin′tə bəl) *adj.* **1.** capable of being printed. **2.** suitable for publication; fit to print. **—print′a·bil′i·ty, print′a·ble·ness,** *n.*

print′ed cir′cuit, (in electronic equipment) a circuit in which the interconnecting wires have been replaced by conductive strips printed, etched, etc., onto a dielectric sheet.

print·er (prin′tər), *n.* **1.** a person or thing that prints, esp. one whose occupation is printing. **2.** *Computer Technol.* a mechanism or machine that produces an output of printed alphanumeric characters.

print′er's dev′il, devil (def. 4).

print′er's ream′. See under **ream**[1] (def. 1).

print·er·y (prin′tə rē), *n., pl.* **-er·ies. 1.** (formerly) an establishment for printing by means of type. **2.** an establishment where printing, as of books or newspapers, is done.

print·head (print′hed′), *n.* the printing element, as a daisy wheel or thimble, on a computer printer.

print·ing (prin′ting), *n.* **1.** the art, process, or business of producing printed texts. **2.** the act of a person or thing that prints. **3.** printed matter. **4.** the whole number of copies of a book, etc., printed at one time. **5.** writing in which the letters resemble printed ones. [ME]

print′ing press′, a machine for printing on paper or the like from type, plates, etc.

print·mak·er (print′mā′kər), *n.* a person who makes prints, esp. an artist working in one of the graphic mediums.

print·mak·ing (print′mā′king), *n.* the art or technique of making prints.

print-out (print′out′), *n. Computer Technol.* the printed output of a computer.

print′ shop′, 1. a shop where prints or graphics are sold. **2.** a shop where printing is done.

pri·or[1] (prī′ər), *adj.* **1.** preceding in time or in order; earlier or former; previous. **2. prior to,** before; until. [< L: former, elder, superior (adj.), before (adv.), comp. of OL *pri* before; akin to PRIME, PRE-]

pri·or[2] (prī′ər), *n.* an officer in a monastic order or religious house, sometimes next in rank below an abbot. [ME, OE < ML, LL: superior, head] **—pri′or·ship′,** *n.*

Pri·or (prī′ər), *n.* **Matthew,** 1664–1721, English poet.

pri·or·ate (prī′ər it), *n.* **1.** the office, rank, or term of office of a prior. **2.** a priory. [ME < LL *priōrāt(us)* priority, preference (ML: office of prior)]

pri·or·ess (prī′ər is), *n.* a woman holding a position corresponding to that of a prior. [ME *prioresse* < OF]

pri·or·i·tize (prī or′i tīz′, -ôr′-), *v.t.* **-tized, tiz·ing. 1.** to arrange or do according to priorities: *learning to prioritize our assignments.* **2.** to give a high priority to. **—pri·or′i·ti·za′tion,** *n.*

pri·or·i·ty (prī or′i tē, -ôr′-), *n., pl.* **-ties** for 2, 3. **1.** the state or quality of being earlier in time, occurrence, etc. **2.** precedence in order, rank, privilege, etc. **3.** the right to take precedence in obtaining certain supplies, services, facilities, etc., esp. during a shortage. [ME < MF *priorite* < ML *priōritās*]

pri·or·y (prī′ə rē), *n., pl.* **-ries.** a religious house governed by a prior or prioress. [ME *priorie* < ML *priōria*]

Pri·pet (prē′pet), *n.* a river in the W Soviet Union in Europe flowing E through the Pripet Marshes to the Dnieper River in NW Ukraine. 500 mi. long. Russian, **Pripyat** (*Russ.* prē pyät′yᵊ). Polish, **Prypeć.**

Pri′pet Marsh′es, an extensive wooded marshland in the W Soviet Union in Europe: dense network of rivers, lakes, and canals. 33,500 sq. mi.

Pris·ci·an (prish′ē ən, prish′ən), *n.* fl. A.D. c500, Latin grammarian.

prise (prīz), *v.t.*, **prised, pris·ing,** *n.* prize[3].

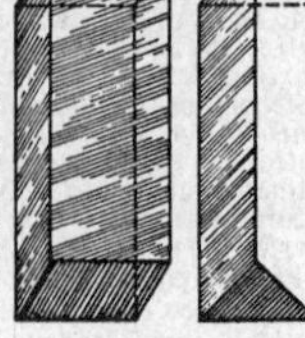
Prisms

prism (priz′əm), *n.* **1.** *Optics.* a transparent solid body, used for dispersing light into a spectrum or for reflecting rays of light. **2.** *Geom.* a solid having bases or ends that are parallel, congruent polygons and sides that are parallelograms. **3.** *Crystall.* a form having faces parallel to the vertical axis and intersecting the horizontal axes. [< LL *prism(a)* < Gk: lit., something sawed, akin to *prízein* to saw, *pristēs* sawyer]

pris·mat·ic (priz mat′ik), *adj.* **1.** of, pertaining to, or like a prism. **2.** formed by or as by a transparent prism. **3.** spectral in color. **4.** highly varied or faceted. Also, **pris·mat′i·cal.** [< Gk *prismat-* (s. of *prísma*) PRISM + -IC] **—pris·mat′i·cal·ly,** *adv.*

pris·ma·toid (priz′mə toid′), *n.* *Geom.* a polyhedron having its vertices lying on two parallel planes. [< Gk *prismat-* (s. of *prísma*) PRISM + -OID]

pris·moid (priz′moid), *n.* *Geom.* a solid having sides that are trapezoids and bases or ends that are parallel and similar but not congruent polygons. Cf. **prism** (def. 2). **—pris·moi′dal,** *adj.*

pris·on (priz′ən), *n.* **1.** a building for the confinement of persons accused or convicted of crimes. **2.** any place of confinement. **3.** imprisonment. [ME < OF, var. of *preson* < L *pre(he)nsiōn-* (s. of *prehensiō*) seizure, arrest. See PREHENSION]

pris·on·er (priz′ə nər, priz′nər), *n.* **1.** a person who is confined in prison or kept in custody, esp. as the result of legal process. **2.** Also called **pris′oner of war′.** a person who is captured and held by an enemy during war, esp. a member of the armed forces. *Abbr.:* POW **3.** a person or thing deprived of liberty or kept in restraint. [ME < MF *prisonier*]

pris·sy (pris′ē), *adj.*, **-si·er, -si·est.** excessively or affectedly proper. [b. PRIM and SISSY] **—pris′si·ly,** *adv.* **—pris′si·ness,** *n.*

pris·tine (pris′tēn, -tin, -tīn), *adj.* **1.** of or pertaining to the earliest period or state. **2.** having its original purity. [< L *pristin(us)* early; akin to PRIME]

prith·ee (prith′ē), *interj.* *Archaic.* (I) pray thee.

priv., **1.** private. **2.** privative.

pri·va·cy (prī′və sē; *also Brit.* priv′ə sē), *n.* **1.** the state of being private; retirement or seclusion. **2.** secrecy. [late ME *privace*]

pri·vat·do·cent (prē vät′dō tsent′), *n.* (esp. in German universities) a private teacher or lecturer paid directly by his students. Also, **pri·vat′do·zent′.** Also called **docent.** [< G; see PRIVATE, DOCENT]

pri·vate (prī′vit), *adj.* **1.** belonging to some particular person or persons. **2.** concerning or restricted to only one person or specific persons. **3.** not intended to be made publicly known. **4.** intimate; most personal. **5.** having nothing to do with public life. **6.** of one of the lowest military ranks: *a private soldier.* **—n. 7.** a soldier of one of the three lowest enlisted ranks. **8. privates.** Also called **pri′vate parts′.** the external genitals. **9. in private,** away from public notice; privately. [ME *pryvat* < L *prīvāt(us)* private, lit., taken away (from public affairs), special use of ptp. of *prīvāre* to rob. See DEPRIVE, -ATE[1]] **—pri′vate·ly,** *adv.* **—pri′vate·ness,** *n.* **—Syn. 1, 2.** particular. **5.** sequestered, retired. **—Ant. 1–4.** general, public.

pri·va·teer (prī′və tēr′), *n.* **1.** (formerly) a privately owned warship commissioned by a government to fight or harass enemy shipping. **2.** privateersman. **—v.i. 3.** to cruise as a privateer. [PRIVATE + -EER, modeled on *volunteer*]

pri·va·teers·man (prī′və tērz′mən), *n.*, *pl.* **-men.** an officer or seaman of a privateer.

pri′vate eye′, *Slang.* a private detective. [*eye*, phonetic rendering of *I*, abbr. of *investigator*]

pri′vate first′ class′, a soldier ranking just below a corporal and above a private in the Army, or just below a lance corporal and above a private in the Marine Corps.

pri′vate prac′tice, the practice of one's profession as an independent rather than as an employee.

pri′vate school′, a school founded, conducted, and maintained by a private group rather than by the government, usually charging tuition and often following a particular philosophy, viewpoint, etc.

pri′vate sec′retary, a person who attends to the personal or confidential correspondence, files, etc., of a business executive, official, or the like.

pri·va·tion (prī vā′shən), *n.* **1.** lack of the usual comforts or necessaries of life. **2.** an instance of this. **3.** the act of depriving. **4.** the state of being deprived. [< F < L *prīvātiōn-* (s. of *prīvātiō*) a taking away] **—Syn. 1.** deprivation, want, need. See **hardship.**

priv·a·tive (priv′ə tiv), *adj.* **1.** causing, or tending to cause, deprivation. **2.** consisting in or characterized by the taking away, loss, or lack of something. **3.** *Gram.* indicating negation or absence. **—n. 4.** *Gram.* a privative element, as *a-* in *asymmetric.* [< L *prīvātīv(us)*] **—priv′a·tive·ly,** *adv.*

priv·et (priv′it), *n.* **1.** a European, oleaceous shrub, *Ligustrum vulgare,* having evergreen leaves and small white flowers, used for hedges. **2.** any of various other plants of the genus *Ligustrum.* [?]

priv·i·lege (priv′ə lij, priv′lij), *n.*, *v.*, **-leged, -leg·ing.** **—n. 1.** a right, immunity, or benefit enjoyed by a particular person or a restricted group of persons. **2.** an official grant of a special right or immunity, under certain conditions. **3.** the principle or condition of enjoying special rights or immunities. **4.** an advantage or source of pleasure granted to a person. **5.** *Stock Exchange.* an option to buy or sell stock at a stipulated price for a limited period of time. **—v.t. 6.** to endow with a privilege. **7.** to exempt (usually fol. by *from*). **8.** to authorize or license (something otherwise forbidden). [ME *privileg(i)e* < L *prīvilēgi(um)*, orig., a law for or against an individual = *prīvi-* (comb. form of *prīvus* one's own) + *lēg-* (see LEGAL) + *-ium* -IUM] **—Syn. 1.** PRIVILEGE, PREROGATIVE refer to a special advantage or right possessed by an individual or group. A PRIVILEGE is a right or advantage gained by birth, social position, effort, or concession. It can have either legal or personal sanction: *the privilege of paying half fare; the privilege of calling whenever one wishes.* PREROGATIVE refers to an exclusive right claimed and granted, often officially or legally, on the basis of social status, heritage, sex, etc.: *the prerogatives of a king; the prerogatives of management.* **3.** license, freedom, liberty.

priv·i·leged (priv′ə lijd, priv′lijd), *adj.* **1.** belonging to a class that enjoys a special privilege or privileges. **2.** entitled to or exercising a privilege. **3.** restricted to a select group or individual. **4.** *Law.* (of utterances or communications) **a.** not actionable in view of the circumstances. **b.** not requiring any testimony concerning them to be presented in court. **5.** *Navig.* (of a vessel) having the right of way. Cf. **burdened.** [ME]

priv·i·ly (priv′ə lē), *adv.* in a privy manner; secretly. [ME]

priv·i·ty (priv′i tē), *n.*, *pl.* **-ties.** **1.** private or secret knowledge. **2.** participation in the knowledge of something private or secret, esp. as implying concurrence or consent. **3.** *Law.* the relation between privies. [ME *privete, privite* < OF]

priv. pr., privately printed.

priv·y (priv′ē), *adj.*, **priv·i·er, priv·i·est,** *n.*, *pl.* **priv·ies.** **—adj. 1.** participating in the knowledge of something private or secret (usually fol. by *to*): *to be privy to a plot.* **2.** private; assigned to private uses. **3.** belonging or pertaining to some particular person or persons, esp. a sovereign. **4.** *Archaic.* secret, concealed, hidden, or secluded. **—n. 5.** outhouse (def. 2). **6.** *Law.* a person participating directly in or having a derivative interest in a legal transaction. [ME *prive* < OF: private (adj.), close friend, private place (n.) < L *prīvāt(us)* PRIVATE]

priv′y cham′ber, a private apartment in a royal residence. [ME]

priv′y coun′cil, **1.** a board or select body of personal advisers, as of a sovereign. **2.** (*caps.*) (in Great Britain) a body of persons who advise the sovereign in matters of state, the majority of members being selected by the prime minister. [ME *prive counseil* privy counsel] **—priv′y coun′cilor.**

priv′y purse′, *Brit.* a sum from the public revenues allotted to the sovereign for personal expenses.

priv′y seal′, (in Great Britain) the seal affixed to grants, documents, etc., that are to pass the great seal, and to documents of less importance that do not require the great seal. [ME *prive seal*]

prix fixe (prē′ fiks′; *Fr.* prē fēks′), *pl.* **prix fixes** (prē′ fiks′; *Fr.* prē fēks′). a fixed price charged for any meal chosen from the variety listed on the menu. Cf. **à la carte, table d'hôte.** [< F]

Prix Gon·court (prē′ gon ko͝or′; *Fr.* prē gôN ko͞or′), Goncourt (def. 2).

prize[1] (prīz), *n.* **1.** a reward for victory or superiority, as in a contest or competition. **2.** something won in a lottery or the like. **3.** anything striven for or worth striving for. **4.** something seized or captured, esp. an enemy's ship and cargo captured at sea according to the laws of war. **5.** *Archaic.* a contest or match. **—adj. 6.** having won a prize. **7.** worthy of a prize. **8.** given or awarded as a prize. [ME *prise* < MF: a seizing, capturing < L *pre(he)nsa*, n. use of fem. ptp. of *pre(he)ndere* to take + ME *prise*, var. of *pris* reward. See PRICE] **—Syn. 1.** See **reward.**

prize[2] (prīz), *v.t.*, **prized, priz·ing.** to value or esteem highly. [ME *prise* < MF *pris(ier)*, var. of *preisier* to PRAISE] **—Syn.** See **appreciate.**

prize[3] (prīz), *v.*, **prized, priz·ing,** *n.* **—v.t. 1.** *Chiefly Brit. Dial.* pry[2]. **—n. 2.** leverage. **3.** a lever. Also, **prise.** [ME *prise* < MF: a hold, grasp < L *pre(he)nsa*]

prize′ fight′, a contest between boxers for a prize, a sum of money, etc.; a professional boxing match. Also, **prize′fight′.** **—prize′ fight′er.** **—prize′fight′er,** *n.* **—prize′ fight′ing.** **—prize′fight′ing,** *n.*

priz·er (prī′zər), *n.* *Archaic.* a competitor for a prize.

prize′ ring′, a ring where prize fights take place; boxing ring.

p.r.n., (in prescriptions) as occasion arises; as needed. [< L *prō rē nātā*]

pro[1] (prō), *adv.*, *n.*, *pl.* **pros.** **—adv. 1.** in favor of a proposition, opinion, etc. **—n. 2.** a person who upholds the affirmative in a debate. **3.** an argument, consideration, vote, etc., in favor of something. Cf. **con**[1]. [< L *prō*, prep., in favor of, FOR; akin to Gk *prō*, Skt *pra*]

pro[2] (prō), *n.*, *pl.* **pros,** *adj.* *Informal.* professional. [shortened form]

pro-[1], **1.** a prefix indicating favor for some party, system, idea, etc., without identity with the group (*pro-British; procommunist; proslavery*), having *anti-* as its opposite. **2.** a prefix of priority in space or time having esp. a meaning of advancing or projecting forward or outward, and also used to indicate substitution, attached widely to stems not used as words: *provision; prologue; proceed; produce; protract; procathedral; proconsul.* [comb. form repr. L *prō* PRO[1]]

pro-[2], a prefix identical in meaning with **pro-**[1], occurring in words borrowed from Greek (*prodrome*) or formed of Greek (and occasionally Latin) elements. [comb. form repr. Gk *pró* for, before, in favor of]

Proa (def. 1)

pro·a (prō′ə), *n.* **1.** any of various types of South Pacific boat. **2.** a swift Malay sailing boat built with the lee side flat and balanced by a single outrigger. Also, **prao.** [< Malay *prāu*, var. of *perahu* boat]

prob., 1. probable. 2. probably. 3. problem.
prob·a·bi·lism (prob′ə bə liz′əm), *n.* 1. *Philos.* the doctrine that certainty is impossible and that probability suffices to govern faith and practice. 2. *Rom. Cath. Theol.* a theory that in cases of moral doubt, a person may follow a soundly probable opinion concerning the morality of an action. [< F *probabilisme*] —**prob′a·bi·list,** *n., adj.* —**prob′a·bi·lis′tic,** *adj.*
prob·a·bil·i·ty (prob′ə bil′i tē), *n., pl.* **-ties.** 1. the quality or fact of being probable. 2. something that is probable. 3. *Statistics.* a. the likelihood of an occurrence, expressed by the ratio of the number of actual occurrences to that of possible occurrences. b. the relative frequency with which an event occurs or is likely to occur. 4. **in all probability,** very probably; quite likely. [< L *probābilitās*]
probabil′ity curve′, *Statistics.* a curve that describes the distribution of probability over the values of a variate.
prob·a·ble (prob′ə bəl), *adj.* 1. likely to occur or prove true. 2. supported generally but not conclusively by the evidence. 3. affording ground for belief. [late ME < L *probābil(is)* likely, lit., capable of standing a test. See PROBE, -BLE]
prob′able cause′, *Law.* reasonable ground for a belief, esp. one justifying legal proceedings against a person.
prob·a·bly (prob′ə blē), *adv.* in all likelihood; very likely.
pro·bang (prō′bang), *n.* *Surg.* a long, slender, elastic rod with a sponge, ball, or the like, at the end, to be introduced into the esophagus or larynx, as for removing foreign bodies, or for introducing medication. [alter. (by assoc. with PROBE) of *provang,* unexplained coinage of the inventor]
pro·bate (prō′bāt), *n., adj., v.,* **-bat·ed, -bat·ing.** —*n.* 1. *Law.* the official proving of a will as authentic or valid in a probate court. —*adj.* 2. of or pertaining to probate or a court of probate. —*v.t.* 3. to establish the authenticity or validity of (a will). [late ME *probat* < L *probāt(um)* a thing approved, neut. ptp. of *probāre* to test and find good; see -ATE[1]]
pro′bate court′, a special court with power over administration of estates, the probate of wills, etc.
pro·ba·tion (prō bā′shən), *n.* 1. the act of testing. 2. a process of evaluation for the conduct, qualifications, etc., of a person. 3. *Law.* a. a method of dealing with offenders that allows them to go at large under supervision, as that of a person (**proba′tion of′ficer**) appointed for such duty. b. the state of having been conditionally released. 4. *Educ.* the condition of a student who is being given a chance to redeem failures or misconduct in order to retain a certain academic classification. 5. the testing of a candidate for membership in a religious body for holy orders. 6. *Archaic.* proof. [late ME *probacion* < L *probātiōn-* (s. of *probātiō*). See PROBATE, -ION] —**pro·ba′tion·al, pro·ba·tion·ar·y** (prō bā′shə ner′ē), *adj.* —**pro·ba′tion·ship′,** *n.*
pro·ba·tion·er (prō bā′shə nər), *n.* a person undergoing probation or trial.
pro·ba·tive (prō′bə tiv, prob′ə-), *adj.* 1. serving or designed for testing or trial. 2. affording proof or evidence. Also, **pro·ba·to·ry** (prō′bə tōr′ē, -tôr′ē). [late ME *probatiffe* < L *probātīv(us)* of proof] —**pro′ba·tive·ly,** *adv.*
probe (prōb), *v.,* **probed, prob·ing,** *n.* —*v.t.* 1. to search into or examine thoroughly. 2. to examine or explore with a probe. —*v.i.* 3. to examine or explore with or as with a probe. —*n.* 4. the act of probing. 5. a slender surgical instrument for exploring the depth or direction of a wound, sinus, or the like. 6. *U.S.* an investigation of suspected illegal activity. [< ML *proba* examination, LL: test. See PROOF] —**probe′a·ble,** *adj.* —**prob′er,** *n.*
pro·bi·ty (prō′bi tē, prob′i-), *n.* integrity; uprightness; honesty. [< L *probitās* uprightness = *prob(us)* upright + *-itās* -ITY]
prob·lem (prob′ləm), *n.* 1. any question or matter involving doubt, uncertainty, or difficulty. 2. a question proposed for solution or discussion. 3. *Math.* a statement requiring a solution. —*adj.* 4. difficult to train or guide; unruly: *a problem child.* 5. *Literature.* dealing with difficult choices: *a problem play.* [ME *probleme* < L *problēma* < Gk, akin to *probállein* to lay before = *pro-* PRO-[2] + *bállein* to throw] —**Syn. 1, 2.** puzzle, riddle, enigma.
prob·lem·at·ic (prob′lə mat′ik), *adj.* presenting a problem; doubtful; questionable. Also, **prob′lem·at′i·cal.** [< LL *problēmatic(us)* < Gk *problēmatikós* = *problēmat-* (s. of *próblēma*) PROBLEM + *-ikos* -IC] —**prob′lem·at′i·cal·ly,** *adv.* —**Syn.** indeterminate, unsettled, dubious, ambiguous.
pro bo·no pu·bli·co (prō bō′nō po͞o′bli kō′; *Eng.* prō bō′nō pub′lə kō′), *Latin.* for the public good.
pro·bos·cid·e·an (prō′bə sid′ē ən, -bo-, prō bos′i dē′ən), *adj.* 1. pertaining to or resembling a proboscis. 2. having a proboscis. 3. belonging or pertaining to the mammals of the order *Proboscidea,* consisting of the elephants and extinct related animals. —*n.* 4. a proboscidean animal. Also, **pro′bos·cid′i·an.** [< NL *Proboscide(a)* (L *probosci̇d-* (s. of *proboscis*) + *-ea* neut. pl. suffix) + -AN]
pro·bos·cis (prō bos′is), *n., pl.* **-bos·cis·es, -bos·ci·des** (-bos′i dēz′). 1. the trunk of an elephant. 2. any long flexible snout, as of the tapir. 3. Also called **beak.** the elongate, protruding mouth parts of certain insects, adapted for sucking or piercing. 4. *Zool.* any of various elongate feeding, defensive, or sensory organs of the oral region, as in certain leeches and worms. [< L < Gk *proboskís* elephant's trunk, lit., feeder = *pro-* PRO- + *bósk(ein)* (to) feed + *-is* (s. *-id-*) n. suffix]
proc., 1. procedure. 2. proceedings. 3. process. 4. proclamation. 5. proctor.
pro·caine (prō kān′, prō′kān), *n.* *Pharm.* a compound, $C_6H_4NH_2COOCH_2CH_2N(C_2H_5)_2$, used in the form of its hydrochloride chiefly as a local and spinal anesthetic. [PRO-[1] + (CO)CAINE]
pro·cam·bi·um (prō kam′bē əm), *n.* *Bot.* the meristem from which vascular bundles are developed. [< NL] —**pro·cam′bi·al,** *adj.*
pro·ca·the·dral (prō′kə thē′drəl), *n.* a church used temporarily as a cathedral.
pro·ce·dure (prə sē′jər), *n.* 1. an act or a manner of proceeding in any action or process; conduct. 2. a particular course or mode of action. 3. any given mode of conducting legal, parliamentary, or similar business. [< F *procédure*] —**pro·ce′dur·al,** *adj.* —**Syn. 2.** operation, maneuver, transaction. See **process.**
pro·ceed (prə sēd′), *v.i.* 1. to move or go forward or onward, esp. after stopping. 2. to carry on or continue any action or process. 3. to go on to do something. 4. to continue one's discourse. 5. *Law.* to begin and carry on a legal action. 6. to be carried on, as an action, process, etc. 7. to go or come forth; issue. 8. to arise, originate, or result. [ME *procede* < L *prōcēd(ere).* See PRO-[1], CEDE] —**pro·ceed′er,** *n.* —**Syn. 1.** progress, continue. See **advance. 7.** emanate. **8.** spring, ensue. —**Ant. 1.** recede.
pro·ceed·ing (prə sē′ding), *n.* 1. a particular action, or course of action. 2. an action, or a course of action, or conduct. 3. the act of a person or thing that proceeds. 4. **proceedings,** an activity continuing for some time. 5. *Law.* a. the instituting or carrying on of an action at law. b. a legal step or measure. —**Syn. 1, 2, 4.** See **process.**
pro·ceeds (prō′sēdz), *n.* 1. something that results or accrues. 2. the total sum derived from a sale or other transaction. 3. the profits or returns from a sale, investment, etc.
proc·e·leus·mat·ic (pros′ə lo͞os mat′ik), *adj.* *Pros.* 1. noting a metrical foot of four short syllables. 2. pertaining to or consisting of feet of this kind. —*n.* 3. a proceleusmatic foot. [< LL *proceleusmatic(us)* < Gk *prokeleusmatikós,* lit., calling for incitement = *pro-* PRO-[2] + *keleusmat-* (s. of *kéleusma* summons, akin to *keleúein* to rouse to action) + *-ikos* -IC]
Pro·cel·la·rum (prō′sə lâr′əm), *n.* **Oceanus.** See **Oceanus Procellarum.**
proc·ess (pros′es *or, esp. Brit.,* prō′ses), *n.* 1. a systematic series of actions directed to some end. 2. a specific, continuous action, operation, or series of changes. 3. the act of proceeding. 4. the state of being submitted to a continuing action or series of actions. 5. the course or lapse, as of time. 6. *Law.* a. the writ by which a defendant is brought before court for litigation. b. the whole course of the proceedings in an action at law. 7. *Photog.* photomechanical or photoengraving methods collectively. 8. *Biol., Anat.* a natural outgrowth, projection, or appendage. —*v.t.* 9. to treat or prepare by some particular process, as in manufacturing. 10. to handle (persons or matters) in a routine, orderly manner. 11. to institute a legal process against. 12. to serve a process or summons on. —*adj.* 13. prepared or modified by an artificial process: *process cheese.* 14. noting, pertaining to, or involving photomechanical or photoengraving methods: *process printing.* [ME *proces* < MF < L *prōcess(us)* a going forward = ptp. s. of *prōcēdere* to proceed + *-us* 4th decl. suffix] —**proc′ess·or, proc′ess·er,** *n.*
—**Syn. 1.** operation. PROCESS, PROCEDURE, PROCEEDING apply to something that goes on or takes place. A PROCESS is a series of progressive and interdependent steps by which an end is attained: *a chemical process.* PROCEDURE usually implies a formal or set order of doing a thing, a method of conducting affairs: *parliamentary procedure.* PROCEEDING (usually pl.) applies to what goes on or takes place on a given occasion: *May I interrupt the proceedings for a moment?*
pro·ces·sion (prə sesh′ən), *n.* 1. the act of moving along or proceeding in orderly succession or in a formal and ceremonious manner. 2. the line or body of persons or things moving along in such a manner. 3. the act of coming forth from a source. —*v.i.* 4. to go in procession. [early ME < LL *prōcessiōn-* (s. of *prōcessiō*) a religious procession, lit., a marching on]
pro·ces·sion·al (prə sesh′ə nəl), *adj.* 1. of, pertaining to, or suggesting a procession or processions. 2. sung or played during a procession, as a hymn or march. —*n.* 3. a piece of music, suitable for accompanying a procession. 4. a book containing hymns, litanies, etc., for use in religious processions. [< ML *prōcessiōnāl(is)*] —**pro·ces′sion·al·ly,** *adv.*
proc′ess print′ing, a method of printing almost any color by using a limited number of separate color plates, as red, yellow, and blue, in combination.
proc′ess serv′er, *Law.* a person who serves legal documents, as subpoenas, writs, or warrants, esp. those requiring appearance in court.
pro·cès-ver·bal (prō sā′ver bäl′; *Fr.* PRÔ se VER BAL′), *n., pl.* **-baux** (-bō′). a report of proceedings, as of an assembly. [< F; see PROCESS, VERBAL]
pro·chro·nism (prō′krə niz′əm, prok′rə-), *n.* the assignment of a chronological date that is too early. Cf. **anachronism, parachronism.** [PRO-[2] + Gk *chrón(os)* time + -ISM. See ANACHRONISM]
pro·claim (prō klām′, prə-), *v.t.* 1. to announce or declare in an official or formal manner. 2. to announce or declare in an open or ostentatious way. 3. to indicate or make known publicly or openly. 4. to extol or praise publicly: *Let them proclaim the Lord.* [late ME *proclame(n)* < L *prōclāmā(re)* (to) cry out] —**pro·claim′er,** *n.* —**Syn. 1.** See **announce.**
proc·la·ma·tion (prok′lə mā′shən), *n.* 1. something that is proclaimed. 2. the act of proclaiming. [late ME *proclamacyon* < L *prōclāmātiōn-* (s. of *prōclāmātiō*) = *prōclāmāt(us)* (ptp. of *prōclāmāre* to PROCLAIM) + *-iōn-* -ION]
pro·clit·ic (prō klit′ik), *Gram.* —*adj.* 1. (of a word) closely connected with the following word and not having an independent accent. —*n.* 2. a proclitic word. [< NL *proclitic(us);* modeled on *enclitic;* see PRO-[2]]
pro·cliv·i·ty (prō kliv′i tē), *n., pl.* **-ties.** natural or habit-

pro′a·bo·li′tion, *adj.*
pro′ad·min′is·tra′tion, *adj.*
pro′ad·mis′sion, *adj.*
pro·a·dop′tion, *adj.*
pro′a·gree′ment, *adj.*
pro′al·li′ance, *adj.*
pro′a·mend′ment, *adj.*
pro′-A·mer′i·can, *adj., n.*
pro′an·nex·a′tion, *adj.*
pro′ap·point′ment, *adj.*
pro′ap·prov′al, *adj.*
pro′ar·bi·tra′tion, *adj.*
pro·au·to·ma′tion, *adj.*
pro-Bib′li·cal, *adj.*
pro-Bol′she·vik, *adj., n.*
pro·boy′cott, *adj.*
pro-Bud′dhist, *n., adj.*
pro·busi′ness, *adj.*
pro·cap′i·tal·ist, *n., adj.*
pro-Cath′o·lic, *adj., n.*
pro′-Ca·thol′i·cism, *n.*
pro′cen·tral·i·za′tion, *adj.*
pro·church′, *adj.*
pro·cler′i·cal, *adj.*

ual inclination or tendency. [< L *prōclīvitās* tendency, lit., a steep descent, steepness = *prōclīv(is)* sloping forward, steep (*prō-* PRO-^{1} + *clīv(us)* slope + *-is* adj. suffix) + *-itās* -ITY] —**Syn.** bent, leaning, disposition. —**Ant.** aversion.

Pro·clus (prō′kləs, prok′ləs), *n.* A.D. c411–485, Greek philosopher and theologian.

Proc·ne (prok′nē), *n.* *Class. Myth.* an Athenian princess, the sister of Philomela and wife of Tereus. She was transformed into a swallow after feeding the flesh of their son to Tereus to punish him for raping Philomela.

pro·con·sul (prō kon′səl), *n.* **1.** *Rom. Hist.* a governor or military commander of a province who had consular authority. **2.** any appointed administrator over a dependency or an occupied area. [ME < L] —**pro·con′su·lar,** *adj.* —**pro·con′su·lar·ly,** *adv.*

pro·con·su·late (prō kon′sə lit), *n.* *Hist.* the office or term of a proconsul. Also, **pro·con′sul·ship′.** [< L *prōconsulāt(us)*]

Pro·co·pi·us (prō kō′pē əs), *n.* A.D. c490–c562, Greek historian.

pro·cras·ti·nate (prō kras′tə nāt′, prə-), *v.,* **-nat·ed, -nat·ing.** —*v.i.* **1.** to defer action; delay: *to procrastinate until an opportunity is lost.* —*v.t.* **2.** to put off till another day or time; defer; delay. [< L *prōcrāstināt(us)* (ptp. of *prōcrāstināre* to put off till the morrow) = *prō-* PRO-^{1} + *crās* tomorrow + *-tin(us)* adj. suffix + *-ātus* -ATE^1] —**pro·cras′ti·na′tion,** *n.* —**pro·cras′ti·na′tive, pro·cras·ti·na·to·ry** (prō kras′tə nə tōr′ē, -tôr′ē, prə-), *adj.* —**pro·cras′ti·na′tor,** *n.* —**Syn. 2.** prolong, postpone.

pro·cre·ant (prō′krē ənt), *adj.* **1.** tending to procreate. **2.** pertaining to procreation. [< L *prōcreant-* (s. of *prōcreāns*), prp. of *prōcreāre* to breed]

pro·cre·ate (prō′krē āt′), *v.,* **-at·ed, -at·ing.** —*v.t.* **1.** to beget or generate (offspring). **2.** to produce; bring into being. —*v.i.* **3.** to beget offspring. **4.** to produce; bring into being. [< L *prōcreāt(us)*, ptp. of *prōcreāre* to breed] —**pro′cre·a′tion,** *n.* —**pro′cre·a′tive,** *adj.* —**pro′cre·a′tive·ness,** *n.* —**pro′cre·a′tor,** *n.*

Pro·cris (prō′kris, prok′ris), *n.* *Class. Myth.* a daughter of the Athenian king Erechtheus who was killed while spying on her husband who mistook her for a concealed animal and threw at her a spear fated never to miss.

Pro·crus·te·an (prō krus′tē ən), *adj.* **1.** pertaining to or suggestive of Procrustes. **2.** tending to produce conformity by violent or arbitrary means.

Pro·crus·tes (prō krus′tēz), *n.* *Class. Myth.* a robber who stretched or amputated the limbs of travelers to make them conform to the length of his bed. He was killed by Theseus.

procto-, a learned borrowing from Greek meaning "anus," "rectum," used in the formation of compound words: *proctoscope.* Also, *esp. before a vowel,* **proct-.** [< Gk *prōkto-*, comb. form of *prōktós*]

proc·tol·o·gy (prok tol′ə jē), *n.* the branch of medicine dealing with the rectum and anus. —**proc·to·log·ic** (prok′tᵊloj′ik), **proc′to·log′i·cal,** *adj.* —**proc·tol′o·gist,** *n.*

proc·tor (prok′tər), *n.* **1.** (in a university or college) **a.** a person appointed to supervise students during examinations. **b.** *Chiefly Brit.* an official charged with the maintenance of good order. **2.** *Law.* an attorney, esp. in admiralty and ecclesiastical courts. —*v.t., v.i.* **3.** to supervise or monitor. [contracted var. of PROCURATOR] —**proc·to·ri·al** (prok tōr′ē əl, -tôr′-), *adj.* —**proc·to′ri·al·ly,** *adv.* —**proc′tor·ship′,** *n.*

proc·to·scope (prok′tə skōp′), *n.* an instrument for visual examination of the interior of the rectum. —**proc·to·scop·ic** (prok′tə skop′ik), *adj.* —**proc·tos·co·py** (prok tos′kə pē), *n.*

pro·cum·bent (prō kum′bənt), *adj.* **1.** lying on the face; prone; prostrate. **2.** *Bot.* (of a plant or stem) lying along the ground, but not putting forth roots. [< L *prōcumbent-* (s. of *prōcumbēns*) bending forward, prp. of *prōcumbere.* See PRO-, INCUMBENT]

pro·cur·ance (prō kyo͝or′əns), *n.* the act of bringing about or getting something; agency; procurement.

proc·u·ra·tion (prok′yə rā′shən), *n.* **1.** the act of procuring or obtaining. **2.** the act of procuring women for purposes of prostitution. **3.** the office or authority of a procurator, agent, or attorney. **4.** *Archaic.* management for another; agency. [ME *procuracion* < L *prōcūrātiōn-* (s. of *prōcūrātiō*) management = *prōcūrāt(us)* (ptp. of *prōcūrāre* to take care of; see PROCURE) + *-iōn-* -ION]

proc·u·ra·tor (prok′yə rā′tər), *n.* **1.** *Rom. Hist.* an imperial official with fiscal or administrative powers. **2.** an agent, a deputy, or attorney. [ME *procurat(o)ur* < L *prōcūrātor* manager. See PROCURATION, -OR^2] —**proc′u·ra′tor·ate, proc′u·ra′tor·ship′,** *n.* —**proc·u·ra·to·ri·al** (prok′yər ə tōr′ē əl, -tôr′-), **proc′u·ra·to′ry,** *adj.*

pro·cure (prō kyo͝or′), *v.,* **-cured, -cur·ing.** —*v.t.* **1.** to obtain or get by effort. **2.** to cause to occur or be in effect. **3.** to obtain (women or girls) for the purpose of prostitution. —*v.i.* **4.** to act as a procurer or pimp. [ME *procure(n)* < L *prōcūr(āre)* (to) take care of] —**pro·cur′a·ble,** *adj.* —**pro·cure′ment,** *n.* —**Syn. 1.** gain, win. See **get. 2.** contrive. **4.** pander, pimp. —**Ant. 1.** lose.

pro·cur·er (prō kyo͝or′ər), *n.* a person who procures, esp. a pander or pimp. Also, *referring to a woman,* **pro·cur·ess** (prō kyo͝or′is). [late ME r. ME *procurour* < AF << L *prōcūrātōr-* (s. of *prōcūrātor*) PROCURATOR]

Pro·cy·on (prō′sē on′), *n.* *Astron.* a first-magnitude star in the constellation Canis Minor. [< L < Gk *Prokýōn* name of a star, lit., before (*pro-* PRO-^{2}) the dog (*kýōn*), so called because it rises just before the Dog Star]

prod (prod), *v.,* **prod·ded, prod·ding,** *n.* —*v.t.* **1.** to poke or jab with or as with something pointed. **2.** to rouse or incite as if by poking; nag; goad. —*n.* **3.** the act or an instance of prodding. **4.** any of various pointed instruments, as a goad. [?] —**prod′der,** *n.*

prod., **1.** produce. **2.** produced. **3.** product.

prod·i·gal (prod′ə gəl), *adj.* **1.** wastefully or recklessly extravagant. **2.** giving or yielding profusely; lavishly abundant (sometimes fol. by *of* or *with*): *prodigal of smiles; prodigal with money.* —*n.* **3.** a person who spends or has spent his money or substance with wasteful extravagance; spendthrift. [back formation from PRODIGALITY] —**prod′i·gal·ly,** *adv.* —**Syn. 1.** profligate. **2.** copious, bounteous. **3.** waster, wastrel.

prod·i·gal·i·ty (prod′ə gal′i tē), *n., pl.* **-ties** for 2, 3. **1.** the quality or fact of being prodigal. **2.** an instance of this. **3.** lavish abundance. [ME *prodigalite* < L *prōdigālitās* wastefulness = *prōdig(us)* wasteful + *-āl(is)* -AL^1 + *-itās* -ITY]

pro·di·gious (prə dij′əs), *adj.* **1.** extraordinary, as in size or amount. **2.** wonderful or marvelous: *a prodigious feat.* **3.** abnormal; monstrous. **4.** *Obs.* ominous. [< L *prōdigiōs(us)* marvelous] —**pro·di′gious·ly,** *adv.* —**pro·di′gious·ness,** *n.* —**Syn. 1.** enormous, immense, huge, gigantic, tremendous. **2.** amazing, stupendous, astounding, wondrous. —**Ant. 1.** tiny. **2.** ordinary.

prod·i·gy (prod′i jē), *n., pl.* **-gies. 1.** a person having extraordinary talent or ability. **2.** something wonderful or marvelous. **3.** something abnormal or monstrous. **4.** *Archaic.* something extraordinary regarded as of prophetic significance. [< L *prōdigi(um)* prophetic sign = *prōd-* PRO-^{1} + *-igium,* akin to *-agium* in *adagium* ADAGE]

pro·drome (prō′drōm), *n.* *Pathol.* a premonitory symptom. [< F < NL *prodrom(us)* < Gk *pródromos* running before. See PRO-^{2}, -DROME] —**prod·ro·mal** (prod′rə məl), *adj.*

pro·duce (*v.* prə do͞os′, -dyo͞os′; *n.* prod′o͞os, -yo͞os, prō′do͞os, -dyo͞os), *v.,* **-duced, -duc·ing,** *n.* —*v.t.* **1.** to bring into existence. **2.** *Econ.* to create (something having exchange value). **3.** to bring forth; give birth to. **4.** to provide, furnish, or supply: *a mine producing silver.* **5.** *Finance.* to cause to accrue, as income. **6.** to present to view or notice; exhibit. **7.** to act as the producer of (a dramatic entertainment). **8.** to extend or prolong, as a line. —*v.i.* **9.** to create, bring forth, or yield offspring, products, etc. —*n.* **10.** that which is produced. **11.** agricultural products collectively, esp. vegetables and fruits. **12.** offspring, esp. of a female animal. [ME < L *prōdūce(re)* (to) lead or bring forward, extend, prolong, bring forth, produce = *prō-* PRO-^{1} + *dūcere* to lead] —**pro·duc′i·bil′i·ty, pro·duct·i·bil·i·ty** (prə duk′tə bil′i tē), **pro·duc′i·ble·ness, pro·duce′a·ble·ness,** *n.* —**pro·duc′i·ble, pro·duce′a·ble, pro·duct′i·ble,** *adj.* —**Syn. 1.** generate, create. **2.** make, manufacture. **4.** afford, yield. **6.** show. —**Ant. 1.** destroy, ruin. **6.** conceal.

pro·duc·er (prə do͞o′sər, -dyo͞o′-), *n.* **1.** a person who produces. **2.** *Econ.* a person who creates economic value, or produces goods and services. **3.** a person responsible for the financial and administrative aspects of a dramatic entertainment. **4.** *Theat. Brit.* a stage director.

produc′er gas′, a gas composed of carbon monoxide, hydrogen, and nitrogen, used as an industrial fuel, in certain gas engines, and in the manufacture of ammonia.

produc′er goods′, *Econ.* goods, as machinery, raw materials, etc., that are used in the process of creating consumer goods.

prod·uct (prod′əkt, -ukt), *n.* **1.** a thing produced by labor or effort. **2.** a person or thing considered as reflecting environmental influences: *a product of one's time.* **3.** *Chem.* a substance obtained from another substance through chemical change. **4.** *Math.* the result obtained by multiplying two or more quantities together. [late ME < L *prōduct(um)* (thing) produced, neut. of ptp. of *prōdūcere* to PRODUCE]

pro·duc·tion (prə duk′shən), *n.* **1.** the act of producing. **2.** something that is produced. **3.** *Econ.* the act of producing articles having exchange value. **4.** an amount that is produced: *Production is up this month.* **5.** a work of literature or art. **6.** the act of presenting for examination: *the production of evidence.* **7.** the organization and presentation of a dramatic entertainment. **8.** the entertainment itself. [< L *prōductiōn-* (s. of *prōductiō*) a lengthening] —**pro·duc′tion·al,** *adj.*

produc′tion num′ber, *Theat.* a specialty number or routine, usually performed by the entire cast, as of a musical comedy.

pro·duc·tive (prə duk′tiv), *adj.* **1.** having the power of producing. **2.** producing readily or abundantly: *a productive vineyard.* **3.** causing; bringing about (usually fol. by *of*): *conditions productive of crime and sin.* **4.** *Econ.* producing or tending to produce goods and services having exchange value. [< ML *productīv(us)*] —**pro·duc′tive·ly,** *adv.* —**pro·duc·tiv·i·ty** (prō′duk tiv′i tē, prod′ək-), **pro·duc′tive·ness,** *n.* —**Syn. 2.** fecund. PRODUCTIVE, FERTILE, FRUITFUL, PROLIFIC apply to the generative aspect of something. PRODUCTIVE refers to a generative source of continuing activity: *productive soil; a productive influence.* FERTILE applies to that in which seeds, literal or figurative, take root easily: *fertile soil; a fertile imagination.* FRUITFUL refers to that which has already produced and is capable of further production: *fruitful soil, discovery, theory.* PROLIFIC means highly productive: *a prolific farm, writer.* —**Ant. 2.** sterile.

pro·em (prō′em), *n.* an introductory discourse; introduction; preface; preamble. [< L *prooem(ium)* < Gk *prooímion* prelude (*pro-* PRO-^{2} + *oím(ē)* song + *-ion* dim. suffix); r. ME *proheme* < MF] —**pro·e·mi·al** (prō ē′mē əl), *adj.*

prof (prof), *n.* (*often cap.*) *Informal.* professor. [by shortening]

Prof., Professor.

prof·a·na·tion (prof′ə nā′shən), *n.* the act of profaning; desecration; defilement; debasement. [< LL *profānātiōn-* (s. of *profānātiō*) = L *profānāt(us)* desecrated (ptp. of *profānāre*) + *-iōn-* -ION; r. *prophanation* < MF. See PROFANE] —**pro·fan·a·to·ry** (prə fan′ə tōr′ē, -tôr′ē, prō-), *adj.* —**Syn.** sacrilege, blasphemy.

pro·fane (prə fān′, prō-), *adj., v.,* **-faned, -fan·ing.** —*adj.* **1.** characterized by irreverence for God or sacred things. **2.** not devoted to religious purposes; secular (opposed to *sacred*). **3.** unholy; heathen; pagan: *profane rites.* **4.** not initiated into religious rites or mysteries. **5.** common or vulgar. —*v.t.* **6.** to misuse (anything revered or respected); defile. **7.** to treat (anything sacred) with irreverence; violate the sanctity of. [(adj.) < L *profān(us)*, lit., before (outside of) the temple; r. earlier *prophane* < ML *prophān(us)* desecrated; (v.) < L *profān(āre)* < *profān(us)*; r. ME *prophane(n)* < ML *profān(āre)* (to) desecrate] —**pro·fane′ly,**

pro·com′mu·nism, *n.*	**pro′-Con·fed′er·ate,** *adj.*	**pro′con·tin′u·a′tion,** *adj.*	**pro′dis·ar′ma·ment,** *adj.*
pro·com′mu·nist, *adj., n.*	**pro′con·scrip′tion,** *adj.*	**pro′-Dar·win′i·an,** *adj.*	**pro′dis·so·lu′tion,** *adj.*
pro·com′pro·mise′, *adj.*	**pro′con·ser·va′tion,** *adj.*	**pro′dem·o·crat′ic,** *adj.*	**pro′en·force′ment,** *adj.*

adv. —**pro·fane′ness,** *n.* —**pro·fan′er,** *n.* —**Syn. 1.** blasphemous, sacrilegious, impious. **2.** temporal. **5.** base. **7.** desecrate. —**Ant. 2.** spiritual. **3.** holy.

pro·fan·i·ty (prə fan′i tē, prō-), *n., pl.* **-ties** for 2. **1.** the quality of being profane. **2.** profane conduct or language; a profane act or utterance. [< LL *profānitās*] —**Syn. 1, 2.** blasphemy, sacrilege. **2.** swearing, malediction; curse.

pro·fess (prə fes′), *v.t.* **1.** to lay claim to, often insincerely: *He professed extreme regret.* **2.** to admit frankly; affirm; acknowledge. **3.** to affirm faith in or allegiance to (a religion, God, etc.). **4.** to claim proficiency in (one's profession or business). **5.** to receive or admit into a religious order. —*v.i.* **6.** to make an avowal or declaration. **7.** to take the vows of a religious order. [back formation from PROFESSED]

pro·fessed (prə fest′), *adj.* **1.** avowed; acknowledged. **2.** professing to be qualified; professional, rather than amateur. **3.** having taken the vows of, or been received into, a religious order. **4.** alleged; pretended. [ME (in religious sense) < ML *profess(us)* (special use of L *professus,* ptp. of *profitērī* to declare publicly = *pro-* PRO-[1] + *-fitērī,* comb. form of *fatērī* to acknowledge) + -ED[2]]

pro·fess·ed·ly (prə fes′id lē), *adv.* **1.** allegedly. **2.** avowedly; by frank admission.

pro·fes·sion (prə fesh′ən), *n.* **1.** an occupation, esp. one requiring extensive education in a branch of science or the liberal arts. Cf. **learned profession. 2.** the body of persons engaged in such an occupation. **3.** the act of professing; avowal; a declaration. **4.** the declaration of belief in or acceptance of religion or a faith. **5.** an avowed religion or faith. **6.** the declaration made on entering into membership of a church or religious order. [ME < ML *professiōn-* (s. of *professiō*) the taking of the vows of a religious order, L: public declaration] —**Syn. 1.** calling. See **occupation.**

pro·fes·sion·al (prə fesh′ə nəl), *adj.* **1.** engaged in an activity as a means of livelihood or for gain: *a professional golfer; a professional potter.* **2.** of, pertaining to, or connected with a profession: *professional studies.* **3.** appropriate to a profession or to professions: *professional attitudes.* **4.** engaged in one of the learned professions: *a professional man.* **5.** competent; expert. **6.** of or for a professional person or his place of business or work: *a professional apartment.* —*n.* **7.** a person who belongs to one of the professions, esp. one of the learned professions. **8.** a person who makes a business of an occupation or hobby in which amateurs frequently engage. **9.** an expert player, as of golf or tennis, serving as a teacher, consultant, performer, or contestant; pro. —**pro·fes′sion·al·ly,** *adv.*

pro·fes·sion·al·ism (prə fesh′ə nəliz′əm), *n.* **1.** professional character, spirit, or methods. **2.** the standing, practice, or methods of a professional, as distinguished from an amateur.

pro·fes·sor (prə fes′ər), *n.* **1.** a college or university teacher of the highest academic rank in a particular branch of learning; a full professor. **2.** any college or university teacher. **3.** a teacher of or above the rank of assistant professor, esp. in a college or university. **4.** an instructor in some art or skilled sport. **5.** a person who professes his sentiments, beliefs, etc. [ME < ML: one who has taken the vows of a religious order, L: a public lecturer] —**pro·fes·so·ri·al** (prō′fə sôr′ē əl, -sōr′-, prof′ə-), *adj.* —**pro′fes·so′ri·al·ly,** *adv.* —**pro·fes′sor·ship′, pro·fes′sor·ate, pro·fes·so·ri·ate** (prō′fi sôr′ē it, -sōr′-, prof′i-), *n.*

prof·fer (prof′ər), *v.t.* **1.** to put before a person for acceptance; offer. —*n.* **2.** the act of proffering. **3.** an offer. [ME *profre(n)* < AF *profre(r),* var. of OF *poroffrir.* See PRO-[1], OFFER] —**prof′fer·er,** *n.* —**Syn. 1.** volunteer, propose, suggest. See **offer.**

pro·fi·cien·cy (prə fish′ən sē), *n.* skill; ability; expertness. [< L *prōfici(ēns)* PROFICIENT + -ENCY]

pro·fi·cient (prə fish′ənt), *adj.* **1.** well-advanced or expert; skilled. —*n.* **2.** *Archaic.* an expert. [< L *prōficient-* (s. of *prōficiēns*), prp. of *prōficere* to advance, make progress = *prō-* PRO-[1] + *-ficere,* comb. form of *facere* to make, do; see EFFICIENT] —**pro·fi′cient·ly,** *adv.* —**pro·fi′cient·ness,** *n.* —**Syn. 1.** adept, competent, experienced, accomplished, able, finished. —**Ant. 1.** unskilled, inept.

pro·file (prō′fīl), *n., v.,* **-filed, -fil·ing.** —*n.* **1.** the outline of an object, esp. the human face or head as viewed from one side. **2.** a picture or representation of the human profile. **3.** *Archit.* **a.** an outline of an object, as a molding, formed on a vertical plane passed through the object at right angles to one of its principal horizontal dimensions. **b.** a drawing or the like representing this (opposed to *alignment*). **4.** a verbal, arithmetical, or graphic analysis of a process or relationship: *a profile of consumer spending.* **5.** a concise biographical sketch. —*v.t.* **6.** to draw or write a profile of. [< It *profilo* (n.), *profilare* (v.)] —**Syn. 1.** silhouette.

pro′file plan′, *Naval Archit.* See **sheer plan.**

prof·it (prof′it), *n.* **1.** Often, **profits.** *Econ.* **a.** financial gain resulting from the use of capital in a transaction. Cf. **gross profit, net profit. b.** the ratio of such gain to the amount of capital invested. **c.** returns, as from property or investments. **d.** the monetary surplus left to a producer or employer after deducting expenditures. **2.** advantage; benefit; gain. —*v.i.* **3.** to gain an advantage or benefit. **4.** to make profit. **5.** to take advantage. **6.** to be of service or benefit. —*v.t.* **7.** to be of advantage or profit to. [ME < MF < L *prōfect(us)* progress, profit = *prōfect-* (ptp. s. of *prōficere* to make headway) + *-us* 4th decl. suffix. See PROFICIENT] —**prof′it·er,** *n.* —**prof′it·less,** *adj.* —**Syn. 1.** return. **2.** advancement, improvement. See **advance. 3, 7.** advance, improve. —**Ant. 1.** loss. **4.** lose.

prof·it·a·ble (prof′i tə bəl), *adj.* **1.** yielding profit; remunerative: *a profitable deal.* **2.** beneficial or useful. [ME] —**prof′it·a·bil′i·ty, prof′it·a·ble·ness,** *n.* —**prof′it·a·bly,** *adv.* —**Syn. 2.** advantageous, valuable, helpful.

prof′it and loss′, (in bookkeeping) an account of the gain and loss arising from business transactions.

prof′it and loss′ account′. See **income account** (def. 2).

prof·it·eer (prof′i tēr′), *n.* **1.** a person who exacts exorbitant profits, esp. by selling scarce or rationed items. —*v.i.* **2.** to act as a profiteer.

prof′it shar′ing, a system or plan under which the employees share in the profits of a business.

prof·li·gate (prof′lə git, -gāt′), *adj.* **1.** utterly and shamelessly immoral; thoroughly dissolute. **2.** recklessly prodigal or extravagant. —*n.* **3.** a profligate person. [< L *prōflīgāt(us)* broken down in character, degraded, lit., struck down, overthrown, ptp. of *prōflīgāre* to shatter, debase = *prō-* PRO-[1] + *-flīgāre,* comb. form of *flīgere* to strike; see -ATE[1]] —**prof·li·ga·cy** (prof′lə gə sē), **prof′li·gate·ness,** *n.* —**Syn. 1.** abandoned, licentious.

prof·lu·ent (prof′lo͞o ənt), *adj.* flowing smoothly or abundantly forth. [ME < L *prōfluent-* (s. of *prōfluēns*), prp. of *prōfluere* to flow forth]

pro for·ma (prō fôr′mä; *Eng.* prō fôr′mə), *Latin.* according to form; as a matter of form.

pro·found (prə found′), *adj.* **1.** having deep insight; intellectually penetrating: *a profound theologian; a profound theory.* **2.** originating in or penetrating to the depths of one's being: *profound anxiety.* **3.** thorough; pervasive: *profound influence.* **4.** existing far beneath the surface: *the profound depths of the ocean.* **5.** low: *a profound bow.* —*n.* *Archaic.* **6.** the deep sea; ocean. **7.** depth; abyss. [< ME < AF < L *profund(us)* deep, vast. See PRO-[1], FUND] —**pro·found′ly,** *adv.* —**pro·found′ness,** *n.* —**Syn. 1.** deep, sagacious. —**Ant. 1.** shallow, superficial.

pro·fun·di·ty (prə fun′di tē), *n., pl.* **-ties** for 2, 3. **1.** the quality or state of being profound; depth. **2.** Usually, **profundities.** profound or deep matters. **3.** a profoundly deep place; abyss. [late ME *profundite* < LL *profunditās*]

pro·fuse (prə fyo͞os′), *adj.* **1.** extravagantly generous (often fol. by *in*): *He was profuse in his praise.* **2.** made or done freely and abundantly: *profuse apologies.* **3.** abundant; in great amount. [late ME < L *profūs(us),* ptp. of *profundere* to pour out or forth] —**pro·fuse′ly,** *adv.* —**pro·fuse′ness,** *n.* —**Syn. 1.** See **lavish. 3.** See **ample.**

pro·fu·sion (prə fyo͞o′zhən), *n.* **1.** a great quantity or amount; abundance. **2.** lavish spending; extravagance. [< L *profūsiōn-* (s. of *profūsiō*). See PROFUSE, FUSION] —**Syn. 1.** copiousness, bounty. See **plenty. 2.** prodigality, profligacy, excess, waste. —**Ant. 1.** scarcity.

pro·fu·sive (prə fyo͞o′siv), *adj.* profuse; lavish; prodigal: *profusive generosity.* —**pro·fu′sive·ly,** *adv.* —**pro·fu′sive·ness,** *n.*

prog (prog), *v.,* **progged, prog·ging,** *n.* *Brit. Slang.* —*v.i.* **1.** to search or prowl about, as for food; forage. —*n.* **2.** food or victuals. [perh. b. PROD and BEG]

Prog., Progressive.

prog., **1.** progress. **2.** progressive.

pro·gen·i·tive (prō jen′i tiv), *adj.* capable of having offspring; reproductive. [PROGENIT(OR) + -IVE] —**pro·gen′i·tive·ness,** *n.*

pro·gen·i·tor (prō jen′i tər), *n.* **1.** a biologically or nonbiologically related ancestor; forefather: *a progenitor of the race.* **2.** an original or model for later developments; predecessor; precursor. [ME *progenitour* < L *prōgenitor* the founder of a family. See PRO-[1], PRIMOGENITOR]

prog·e·ny (proj′ə nē), *n., pl.* **-ny,** for plants or animals **-nies. 1.** a descendant or offspring, as a child, plant, or animal. **2.** such descendants or offspring collectively. [ME *progenie* < MF < L *prōgeniēs* offspring. See PRO-[1], GENITIVE]

pro·ges·ta·tion·al (prō′je stā′shə nəl), *adj.* *Med.* **1.** prepared for pregnancy, as the lining of the uterus prior to menstruation. **2.** of, noting, or characteristic of the action of progesterone.

pro·ges·ter·one (prō jes′tə rōn′), *n.* **1.** *Biochem.* a hormone, $C_{21}H_{30}O_2$, that prepares the uterus for the fertilized ovum and maintains pregnancy. **2.** *Pharm.* a commercial form of this compound: used in the treatment of functional bleeding, dysmenorrhea, threatened or recurrent abortion, etc. [PRO-[1] + GE(STATION) + STER(OL) + -ONE]

pro·glot·tis (prō glot′is), *n., pl.* **-glot·ti·des** (-glot′i dēz′). *Zool.* one of the segments of a tapeworm, containing complete male and female reproductive systems. Also, **pro·glot·tid** (prō glot′id). [< NL, alter. of Gk *proglōssis* point of the tongue. See PRO-[2], GLOTTIS] —**pro·glot′tic, pro′glot·tid′e·an,** *adj.*

prog·na·thous (prog′nə thəs, prog nā′-), *adj.* *Craniom.* having protrusive jaws. Also, **prog·nath·ic** (prog nath′ik). See illus. at **facial angle.** —**prog·na·thism** (prog′nə thiz′əm), **prog′na·thy,** *n.*

prog·nose (prog nōs′, -nōz′), *v.t., v.i.,* **-nosed, -nos·ing.** *Med.* to subject to or make a prognosis. [back formation from PROGNOSIS]

prog·no·sis (prog nō′sis), *n., pl.* **-ses** (-sēz). **1.** *Med.* a forecast of the probable course of a disease, esp. of the possibility for recovery. **2.** a forecast or prognostication. [< LL < Gk: foreknowledge]

prog·nos·tic (prog nos′tik), *adj.* **1.** of or pertaining to prognosis. **2.** predictive. —*n.* **3.** a forecast or prediction. **4.** an omen or portent. [(adj.) < ML *prognōstic(us)* < Gk *prognōstikós* of foreknowledge = *pro(gi)gnṓs(kein)* to know beforehand + *-tikos* -TIC; (n.) < L *prognōstic(on)* < Gk *prognōstikón,* neut. of *prognōstikós*]

prog·nos·ti·cate (prog nos′tə kāt′), *v.,* **-cat·ed, -cat·ing.** —*v.t.* **1.** to forecast from present indications. **2.** to foretoken; presage. —*v.i.* **3.** to make a forecast; prophesy. [< ML *prognōsticāt(us),* ptp. of *prognōsticāre*] —**prog·nos′ti·ca′tive,** *adj.* —**prog·nos′ti·ca′tor,** *n.* —**Syn. 1.** foretell, foresee, project.

prog·nos·ti·ca·tion (prog nos′tə kā′shən), *n.* **1.** the act of prognosticating. **2.** a forecast or prediction. [late ME *pronosticacion* < ML *prognōsticātiōn-* (s. of *prognōsticātiō*)]

pro·gram (prō′gram, -grəm), *n., v.,* **-gramed, -gram·ing** or (*esp. Brit. and Computer Technol.*) **-grammed, -gram·ming.** —*n.* Also, *esp. Brit.,* **pro′gramme. 1.** a plan or schedule to be followed. **2.** a coordinated group of things to be done or performed. **3.** a list of items, pieces, performers, etc., in a musical, theatrical, or other entertainment, dis-

pro·fas′cist, *adj., n.*
pro′fed·er·a′tion, *adj.*
pro·fem′i·nist, *n., adj.*
pro·for′eign, *n.*
pro-Freud′i·an, *adj., n.*
pro·gam′bling, *adj.*
pro-Gen′tile, *adj., n.*
pro·gov′ern·ment, *adj.*

tributed to members of the audience. **4.** a performance or production, esp. on radio or television. **5.** *Computer Technol.* a systematic plan for the automatic solution of a problem by a computer. —*v.i.* **6.** to plan a program. —*v.t.* **7.** to schedule as part of a program. **8.** *Computer Technol.* to prepare a program for. [< LL *programm(a)* < Gk: public notice in writing] —**pro′gram·ma·ble, pro′gram·a·ble,** *adj.*

pro·gram·mat·ic (prō′grə mat′ik), *adj.* **1.** of, pertaining to, consisting of, or resembling program music. **2.** of, advocating, or following a policy or program. —**pro′gram·mat′i·cal·ly,** *adv.*

pro·gram·mer (prō′gram ər), *n.* a person who prepares a program, esp. for a computer. Also, **pro′gram·er.**

pro′gram′ming lan′guage, *Computer Technol.* a set of symbols together with rules for their combination and interpretation used to write programs, such as ALGOL, COBOL, etc.

pro′gram mu′sic, music intended to convey an impression of definite images, scenes, or events (distinguished from *absolute music*).

prog·ress (*n.* prog′res *or, esp. Brit.,* prō′gres; *v.* prə gres′), *n.* **1.** movement toward a specific goal or a further stage. **2.** development or cumulative improvement, as of an individual or a civilization. **3.** forward or onward movement in space or time. **4.** *Biol.* increasing differentiation and perfection in the course of ontogeny or phylogeny. **5.** a journey, esp. a royal tour. **6. in progress,** going on; under way. —*v.i.* **7.** to advance. **8.** to go forward or onward in space or time. [late ME *progresse* < L *prōgress(us)* a going forward = *prōgress-,* ptp. s. of *prōgredī* to step forward, advance (*prō-* PRO-[1] + *-gredī,* comb. form of *gradī* to step; see GRADE) + *-us* 4th decl. suffix] —**Syn. 1, 2.** advance, progression, betterment. **8.** proceed; develop. —**Ant. 1, 2.** regression. **8.** regress.

pro·gres·sion (prə gresh′ən), *n.* **1.** the act of progressing; forward or onward movement. **2.** a movement from one member of a series to the next; succession; sequence. **3.** *Astron.* direct motion. **4.** *Math.* a succession of quantities in which there is a constant relation between each member and the one succeeding it. Cf. **arithmetic progression, geometric progression, harmonic progression. 5.** *Music.* the manner in which chords or melodic tones follow one another. [late ME < L *prōgressiōn-* (s. of *prōgressiō*)] —**pro·gres′sion·al,** *adj.* —**pro·gres′sion·al·ly,** *adv.*

pro·gres·sion·ist (prə gresh′ə nist), *n.* a person who believes in the progress of mankind and society. —**pro·gres′sion·ism,** *n.*

prog·ress·ist (prog′res ist, prō′gres ist), *n.* **1.** progressionist. **2.** progressive. —**prog′ress·ism,** *n.*

pro·gres·sive (prə gres′iv), *adj.* **1.** of, pertaining to, or characterized by progress. **2.** advocating progress, as in technology or politics. **3.** progressing; advancing; improving: *a progressive community.* **4.** (*cap.*) of or pertaining to any of the Progressive parties in politics. **5.** of, pertaining to, or following methods of progressive education: *a progressive school.* **6.** passing successively from one member of a series to the next. **7.** *Govt.* noting or pertaining to a form of taxation in which the rate increases with certain increases in taxable income. **8.** *Gram.* noting a verb aspect or other verb category that indicates continuing action or state, as in *He is doing it,* or *He was doing it.* **9.** *Med.* continuously increasing in extent or severity, as a disease. —*n.* **10.** a person who favors progress or reform, esp. in politics. **11.** (*cap.*) a member of a Progressive party. —**pro·gres′sive·ly,** *adv.* —**pro·gres′sive·ness,** *n.* —**Syn. 2, 10.** liberal. **6.** successive.

progres′sive educa′tion, an educational movement emphasizing creative, experimental classroom work and the development of a sense of democratic community.

progres′sive jazz′. See **modern jazz.**

Progres′sive par′ty, 1. a party formed in 1912 under the leadership of Theodore Roosevelt, advocating popular control of government, direct primaries, woman suffrage, etc. **2.** a similar party formed in 1924 under the leadership of Robert M. La Follette. **3.** a left-wing political party formed in 1948 under the leadership of Henry A. Wallace.

pro·gres·siv·ism (prə gres′ə viz′əm), *n.* **1.** the principles and practices of progressives. **2.** *Educ.* the view that schoolwork should deal particularly with the problems arising from modern cultural and technological change, and that teaching should utilize modern technological and scientific devices and methods. **3.** (*cap.*) the doctrines and beliefs of a Progressive party. —**pro·gres′siv·ist,** *n.*

pro·hib·it (prō hib′it), *v.t.* **1.** to forbid (an action, activity, etc.) by authority: *Smoking is prohibited here.* **2.** to forbid the action of (a person). **3.** to prevent; hinder. [late ME *prohibite* < L *prohibit(us),* ptp. of *prohibēre* to hold before, hold back, restrain, hinder, forbid = *pro-* PRO-[1] + *-hibēre,* comb. form of *habēre* to have, hold] —**pro·hib′it·er, pro·hib′i·tor,** *n.* —**Syn. 1.** interdict. See **forbid. 3.** obstruct.

pro·hi·bi·tion (prō′ə bish′ən), *n.* **1.** the legal prohibiting of the manufacture and sale of alcoholic beverages. **2.** (*often cap.*) the period from 1920 to 1933, when the sale of alcoholic beverages in the U.S. was forbidden by an amendment to the Constitution. **3.** the act of prohibiting. **4.** a law or decree that forbids. [ME *prohibicion* < L *prohibitiōn-* (s. of *prohibitiō*)] —**pro′hi·bi′tion·ar′y,** *adj.* —**Syn. 4.** interdiction.

pro·hi·bi·tion·ist (prō′ə bish′ə nist), *n.* **1.** a person who favors or advocates prohibition. **2.** (*cap.*) a member of the Prohibition party.

Prohibi′tion par′ty, *U.S.* a party organized in 1869, advocating the prohibition of alcoholic beverages.

pro·hib·i·tive (prō hib′i tiv), *adj.* **1.** serving to prohibit. **2.** sufficing to prevent the use, purchase, etc., of something: *prohibitive cost.* —**pro·hib′i·tive·ly,** *adv.* —**pro·hib′i·tive·ness,** *n.*

pro·hib·i·to·ry (prō hib′i tōr′ē, -tôr′ē), *adj.* prohibitive. [< L *prohibitōri(us)* restraining] —**pro·hib′i·to′ri·ly,** *adv.*

proj·ect (*n.* proj′ekt; *v.* prə jekt′), *n.* **1.** something that is contemplated, devised, or planned. **2.** a large or major undertaking, esp. one involving considerable money, personnel, and equipment. **3.** a specific task of investigation, esp. in scholarship. **4.** Also called **housing project.** a group of residential structures, usually built as public housing. **5.** a supplementary and often long-term assignment given by a teacher to a student or group of students. —*v.t.* **6.** to propose, contemplate, or plan. **7.** to throw, cast, or impel forward or onward. **8.** to calculate (future costs, rates of growth, or the like). **9.** to cast (an image, light, shadow, etc.) onto a surface or into space. **10.** to regard or envision as an objective reality: *He projected a thrilling picture of the party's future.* **11.** to cause to jut out or protrude. **12.** *Geom.* **a.** to throw forward an image of (a figure or the like) by straight lines or rays that pass through all its points and reproduce it on another surface. **b.** to transform the points (of one figure) into those of another by a correspondence between points. **13.** *Theat.* to use (one's voice, gestures, etc.) forcefully enough to be understood by an entire audience. —*v.i.* **14.** to communicate clearly and forcefully, esp. in a theatrical performance. **15.** *Psychol.* to ascribe one's own feelings to others. **16.** to extend or protrude beyond something else. [(n.) < L *prōject(um),* neut. of *prōject(us),* ptp. of *prōicere* to throw forward, extend = *prō-* PRO-[1] + *-icere,* comb. form of *jacere* to throw] —**Syn. 1.** See **plan. 8.** predict, estimate. **16.** obtrude, overhang.

pro·jec·tile (prə jek′til, -tīl), *n.* **1.** *Mil.* a bullet, shell, grenade, etc., for firing from a gun or similar weapon. **2.** a body projected or impelled forward, as through the air. —*adj.* **3.** impelling or driving forward, as a force. **4.** caused by impulse, as motion. **5.** capable of being impelled forward, as a missile. **6.** *Zool.* protrusile, as the jaws of a fish. [< NL, neut of adj. *prōjectilis* projecting]

pro·jec·tion (prə jek′shən), *n.* **1.** a projecting or protruding part. **2.** the state, process, or act of projecting. **3.** the result of an act or process of projecting. **4.** *Cartog.* a group of lines systematically drawn through points on a plane surface to represent corresponding points on the curved surface of the earth or celestial sphere. **5.** *Photog.* **a.** the act of casting onto a screen or other surface an image on a film, slide, etc. **b.** an image so cast. **6.** calculation of future costs, rates of growth, or the like. **7.** *Psychol.* the act of ascribing to someone or something else one's own attitudes, thoughts, etc. **8.** a plan or scheme. [< L *prōjectiōn-* (s. of *prōjectiō*) a throwing forward] —**pro·jec·tion·al** (prə jek′shə nəl), *adj.* —**Syn. 1.** jut, overhang, protrusion. **6.** estimate, prediction.

projec′tion booth′, a compartment in a movie theater from which the picture is projected on the screen.

pro·jec·tion·ist (prə jek′shə nist), *n.* a person who operates a motion-picture or slide projector.

projec′tion print′, *Photog.* a print made by the projection of an image onto sensitized paper.

pro·jec·tive (prə jek′tiv), *adj.* **1.** of or pertaining to projection. **2.** produced, or capable of being produced, by projection. **3.** *Psychol.* of, pertaining to, or noting a test or technique for revealing the hidden motives or underlying personality of an individual by the use of test materials that allow him to express himself freely instead of restricting him to set responses. —**pro·jec′tive·ly,** *adv.*

projec′tive geom′etry, the study of geometric properties that are unchanged by projection.

pro·jec·tor (prə jek′tər), *n.* **1.** an apparatus for throwing an image on a screen, projecting a beam of light, etc. **2.** a person who forms projects or plans; schemer.

pro·jec·tu·al (prə jek′cho͞o əl), *n.* *Educ.* any visual material, used in teaching, that is prepared for projection, as a motion picture, filmstrip, slide, etc. [PROJECT (V.) + *-ual,* as in VISUAL]

pro·jet (prō zhā′; *Fr.* prô zhe′), *n., pl.* **-jets** (-zhāz′; *Fr.* -zhe′). **1.** a project. **2.** a draft of a proposed treaty or other instrument. [< F < L *prōject(um)*]

Pro·ko·fiev (prō kō′fē əf, -ef′, prə-; *Russ.* prо kô′fyef), *n.* **Ser·gei (Ser·ge·e·vich)** (seʀ gā′ seʀ ge′yə vich), 1891–1953, Russian composer.

Pro·ko·pyevsk (prо kô′pyefsk), *n.* a city in the S central RSFSR, in the S Soviet Union in Asia, SE of Novosibirsk. 291,000 (est. 1965).

pro·lac·tin (prō lak′tin), *n.* *Biochem.* luteotropin.

pro·lam·in (prō lam′in, prō′lə min), *n.* *Biochem.* any of the class of simple proteins, as gliadin, hordein, or zein, found in grains, soluble in dilute acids, alkalis, and alcohols, and insoluble in water, neutral salt solutions, and absolute alcohol. Also, **pro·lam·ine** (prō lam′in, -ēn, prō′lə min, -mēn′). [PROL(INE) + AM(MONIA) + -IN[2]]

pro·lan (prō′lan), *n.* *Biochem.* a sex hormone found in high concentration in pregnancy urine, making possible the early diagnosis of pregnancy. [contr. of PROLACTIN]

pro·lapse (prō laps′), *n., v.,* **-lapsed, -laps·ing.** —*n.* **1.** Also, **pro·lap·sus** (prō lap′səs). *Pathol.* a falling down of an organ or part, as the uterus, from its normal position. —*v.i.* **2.** to fall or slip down or out of place. [< LL *prōlāps(us)* a slipping forth]

A B

A, Prolate spheroid
B, Oblate spheroid

pro·late (prō′lāt), *adj.* elongated along the polar diameter, as a spheroid generated by the revolution of an ellipse about its longer axis (opposed to *oblate*). [< L *prōlāt(us),* ptp. of *prōferre* to bring forward, extend]

pro·leg (prō′leg′), *n.* one of the abdominal ambulatory processes of caterpillars and other larvae, as distinct from the true or thoracic legs.

pro·le·gom·e·non (prō′lə gom′ə non′, -nən), *n., pl.* **-na** (-nə). a preliminary discussion; introductory essay, as prefatory matter in a book; a prologue. [< NL < Gk: being said beforehand, neut. of pass. prp. of *prolégein* = *pro-* PRO-[2] + *légein* to say] —**pro′le·gom′e·nous,** *adj.*

P, Prolegs of larva of monarch butterfly, *Danaus plexippus*

pro·lep·sis (prō lep′sis), *n., pl.* **-ses** (-sēz). **1.** *Rhet.* the anticipation of possible objections in order to answer them in advance. **2.** the assigning of a person, event, etc., to a period earlier than the actual one; prochronism. [< L < Gk:

pro-Hin′du, *adj.*
pro-Hit′ler, *adj.*
pro′im·mi·gra′tion, *adj.*
pro′in·dus′tri·al·i·za′tion, *adj.*
pro·in′dus·try, *adj.*
pro′in·te·gra′tion, *adj.*
pro′in·ter·ven′tion, *adj.*
pro′in·vest′ment, *adj.*
pro′ir·ri·ga′tion, *adj.*
pro-Jew′ish, *adj.*
pro·la′bor, *adj.*

anticipation, preconception = *prolēp-*, verbid s. of *prolambánein* to anticipate (*pro-* PRO-[2] + *lambánein* to take) + *-sis* -SIS] —**pro·lep·tic** (prō lep′tik), **pro·lep′ti·cal,** *adj.* —**pro·lep′ti·cal·ly,** *adv.*

pro·le·tar·i·an (prō′li târ′ē ən), *adj.* **1.** pertaining or belonging to the proletariat. **2.** (in ancient Rome) belonging to the lowest or poorest class of the people. —*n.* **3.** a member of the proletariat. [< L *prōlētāri(us)* citizen contributing to the state only through his offspring (*prōlēt-*, akin to *prōlēs* offspring (see PRO-[1], ADULT) + *-ārius* -ARY) + -AN] —**pro′le·tar′i·an·ism,** *n.*

pro·le·tar·i·an·ise (prō′li târ′ē ə nīz′), *v.t.*, **-ised, -is·ing.** *Chiefly Brit.* proletarianize. —**pro′le·tar′i·an·i·sa′tion,** *n.*

pro·le·tar·i·an·ize (prō′li târ′ē ə nīz′), *v.t.*, **-ized, -iz·ing. 1.** to convert or transform into a proletarian. **2.** to make proletarian. —**pro′le·tar′i·an·i·za′tion,** *n.*

pro·le·tar·i·at (prō′li târ′ē ət), *n.* **1.** the working class, including esp. those who do not possess capital and must sell their labor to survive. **2.** (in ancient Rome) the unpropertied class. [< F *prolétariat*]

pro·li·cide (prō′li sīd′), *n.* the killing of one's child or children. [< ML *prōli-* (comb. form repr. L *prōlēs* offspring; see PROLETARIAN) + -CIDE] —**pro′li·cid′al,** *adj.*

pro-life (prō līf′), *adj.* of or supporting a movement that strongly opposes unnecessary abortions or euthanasia: *pro-life demonstrators.* —**pro-lif′er,** *n.*

pro·lif·er·ate (prō lif′ə rāt′), *v.i., v.t.*, **-at·ed, -at·ing. 1.** to grow or produce by multiplication of parts, as in budding or cell division, or by procreation. **2.** to spread excessively and rapidly. [PROLIFER(OUS) + -ATE[1]] —**pro·lif′er·a′tive,** *adj.*

pro·lif·er·a·tion (prō lif′ə rā′shən), *n.* **1.** the growth or production of cells by multiplication of parts. **2.** an excessive, rapid spread: *nuclear proliferation.* [< F *prolifération* = *prolifère* (< ML; see PROLIFEROUS) + *-ation* -ATION]

pro·lif·er·ous (prō lif′ər əs), *adj.* **1.** proliferating. **2.** *Bot.* **a.** producing new individuals by budding or the like. **b.** producing an organ or shoot from an organ that is itself normally the last, as a shoot or a new flower from the midst of a flower. [< ML *prōlifer* bearing offspring + -OUS. See PROLICIDE, -FEROUS]

pro·lif·ic (prō lif′ik), *adj.* **1.** producing offspring, young, fruit, etc., abundantly. **2.** characterized by abundant productivity. [< ML *prōlific(us)* fertile. See PROLICIDE, -FIC] —**pro·lif·i·ca·cy** (prō lif′ə kə sē), **pro·lif′ic·ness, pro·lif′i·cal·ness,** *n.* —**pro·lif′i·cal·ly, pro·lif′ic·ly,** *adv.* —**Syn.** See **productive.** —**Ant.** barren.

pro·line (prō′lēn, -lin), *n.* *Biochem.* an alcohol-soluble amino acid found in all proteins. [alter. of PYRROLIDINE]

pro·lix (prō liks′, prō′liks), *adj.* **1.** tediously long and wordy. **2.** (of a person) given to speaking or writing at great length. [late ME < L *prōlix(us)* extended, long = *prō-* PRO-[1] + *-lixus*, akin to *līquī* to flow; see LIQUOR] —**pro·lix·i·ty** (prō lik′si tē), **pro·lix′ness,** *n.* —**pro·lix′ly,** *adv.* —**Syn. 1.** prolonged, protracted, extended. **2.** verbose.

pro·loc·u·tor (prō lok′yə tər), *n.* a presiding officer of an assembly; chairman. [< L: one who speaks out = *prōlocūt(us)* (ptp. of *prōloquī* = *prō-* PRO-[1] + *loquī* to speak) + *-or* -OR[2]] —**pro·loc′u·tor·ship′,** *n.*

pro·log·ise (prō′lô gīz′, -lo-, prō′lə jīz′), *v.i.*, **-ised, -is·ing.** *Chiefly Brit.* prologize. —**pro′log·is′er,** *n.*

pro·log·ize (prō′lô gīz′, -lo-, prō′lə jīz′), *v.i.*, **-ized, -iz·ing.** prologuize. —**pro′log·iz′er,** *n.*

pro·logue (prō′lôg, -log), *n., v.*, **-logued, -logu·ing.** —*n.* **1.** a preface to or introductory part of a discourse, poem, play, or novel. **2.** any introductory proceeding, event, etc. —*v.t.* **3.** to introduce with or as with a prologue. Also, **pro′log.** [ME *prologe*, OE *prologa* (masc.) < L *prōlog(us)* < Gk *prólogos*] —**Syn. 2.** preamble; beginning; prelude.

pro·logu·ize (prō′lô gīz′, -lo-), *v.i.*, **-ized, -iz·ing.** to compose or deliver a prologue. Also, **prologize;** *esp. Brit.,* **pro′logu·ise′, prologise.** —**pro′logu·iz′er,** *n.*

pro·long (prə lông′, -long′), *v.t.* **1.** to lengthen out in time; extend the duration of. **2.** to make longer in spatial extent. [late ME *prolonge* < LL *prōlong(āre)* (to) lengthen] —**pro·long′er,** *n.* —**pro·long′ment,** *n.* —**Syn. 1.** See **lengthen.**

pro·lon·gate (prə lông′gāt, -long′-), *v.t.*, **-gat·ed, -gat·ing.** prolong. [< LL *prōlongāt(us)*, ptp. of *prōlongāre* to PROLONG; see -ATE[1]]

pro·lon·ga·tion (prō′lông gā′shən, -long-), *n.* **1.** the act of prolonging. **2.** the state of being prolonged. **3.** a prolonged or extended form. **4.** an added part. [< LL *prōlongātiōn-* (s. of *prōlongātiō*) extension]

pro·longe (prō lonj′; *Fr.* PRô lôNzh′), *n., pl.* **-long·es** (-lon′jiz; *Fr.* -lôNzh′). *Mil.* a rope having a hook at one end and a toggle at the other, used for various purposes, as to draw a gun carriage. [< F, back formation from *prolonger* to PROLONG]

prolonge′ knot′, a knot consisting of three overlapping loops formed by a single rope passed alternately over and under itself at crossings. See illus. at **knot.**

pro·lu·sion (prō lo͞o′zhən), *n.* an introductory essay, preliminary to a more profound work. [< L *prōlūsiōn-* (s. of *prōlūsiō*) preliminary exercise, prelude = *prōlūs(us)*, ptp. of *prōlūdere* (*prō-* PRO-[1] + *lūdere* to play) + *-iōn-* -ION] —**pro·lu·so·ry** (prō lo͞o′sə rē), *adj.*

prom (prom), *n.* *U.S. Informal.* a formal dance, esp. at a school or college. [short for PROMENADE]

prom., promontory.

prom·e·nade (prom′ə nād′, -näd′), *n., v.*, **-nad·ed, -nad·ing.** —*n.* **1.** a stroll or walk, esp. in a public place. **2.** an area used for leisurely walking. **3.** a prom. **4.** a march of guests opening a formal ball. **5.** a march of dancers in folk or square dancing. —*v.i.* **6.** to take or take part in a promenade. **7.** to do a promenade in a folk or square dance. —*v.t.* **8.** to take a promenade through or on. **9.** to display as in a promenade; parade: *He promenaded her before her suitors.* [< F < *promen(er)* (to) lead out, take for a walk or airing < L *prōmināre* to drive (beasts) forward (*prō-* PRO-[1] + *mināre* to drive); see -ADE[1]] —**prom′e·nad′er,** *n.*

promenade′ deck′, a deck used for strolling on a passenger vessel.

Pro·me·the·an (prə mē′thē ən), *adj.* **1.** of or suggestive of Prometheus. **2.** creative; boldly original. —*n.* **3.** a person who resembles Prometheus in spirit or action.

Pro·me·the·us (prə mē′thē əs, -tho͞os), *n.* *Class. Myth.* a Titan who stole fire from Olympus and gave it to mankind in defiance of Zeus. As punishment he was chained to a rock, where an eagle daily tore at his liver until he was finally released by Hercules.

pro·me·thi·um (prə mē′thē əm), *n.* *Chem.* a rare-earth, metallic, trivalent element. *Symbol:* Pm; *at. no.:* 61. [< NL; see PROMETHEUS, -IUM]

prom·i·nence (prom′ə nəns), *n.* **1.** the state of being prominent; conspicuousness. **2.** something that is prominent, as a projection. **3.** *Astron.* a cloud of gas that rises high above the surface of the sun, seen during an eclipse or by means of a helioscope. [< L *prōminentia* a jutting out, protuberance]

prom·i·nent (prom′ə nənt), *adj.* **1.** standing out so as to be seen easily; conspicuous. **2.** standing out beyond a surface or line; projecting. **3.** leading, important, or well-known. [< L *prōminent-* (s. of *prōminēns*), prp. of *prōminēre* to jut out, stand out = *prō-* PRO-[1] + *minēre* to project] —**Syn. 2.** protruding, jutting, protuberant. **3.** eminent, celebrated, distinguished. —**Ant. 2.** recessed. **3.** unknown.

prom·is·cu·i·ty (prom′i skyo͞o′i tē, prō′mi-), *n., pl.* **-ties** for 2, 3. **1.** the state or fact of being promiscuous. **2.** a promiscuous sexual union. **3.** an indiscriminate mixture. [PROMISCU(OUS) + -ITY; cf. F *promiscuité*]

pro·mis·cu·ous (prə mis′kyo͞o əs), *adj.* **1.** characterized by frequent and indiscriminate changes of one's sexual partners. **2.** composed of a disordered mixture of various kinds of elements. **3.** indiscriminate; without discrimination. [< L *prōmiscuus* mixed up = *prō-* PRO-[1] + *miscu-* (perf. s. of *miscēre* to mix) + *-us* -OUS] —**pro·mis′cu·ous·ly,** *adv.* —**pro·mis′cu·ous·ness,** *n.* —**Syn. 1.** unchaste. **2.** confused, mixed, jumbled. —**Ant. 1, 2.** pure. **3.** selective.

prom·ise (prom′is), *n., v.*, **-ised, -is·ing.** —*n.* **1.** a declaration or assurance that something specified will or will not happen, be done, etc. **2.** indication of future excellence or achievement: *a writer who shows promise.* **3.** that which is promised. —*v.t.* **4.** to pledge or undertake by promise (usually used with an infinitive or a clause as object): *She promised to go tomorrow.* **5.** to make a promise of (a specified act, gift, etc.): *to promise help.* **6.** to afford ground for expecting: *The sky promised a storm.* **7.** to pledge to marry. **8.** *Informal.* to assure (used in emphatic declarations): *I won't go there again, I promise you that!* —*v.i.* **9.** to afford ground for expectation (often fol. by *well* or *fair*): *His forthcoming novel promises well.* **10.** to make a promise. [late ME *promis(se)* < ML *prōmissa*, for L *prōmissum*, n. use of neut. ptp. of *prōmittere* to promise, lit., to send forth = *prō-* PRO-[1] + *mittere* to send] —**Syn. 1.** word, pledge.

Prom′ised Land′, 1. Heaven. **2.** Canaan, the land promised by God to Abraham and his descendants. Gen. 12:7. **3.** (often *l.c.*) a place believed to hold final happiness.

prom·is·ee (prom′i sē′), *n.* *Law.* a person to whom a promise is made.

prom·is·ing (prom′i sing), *adj.* giving favorable promise: *a promising young man.* —**prom′is·ing·ly,** *adv.*

prom·i·sor (prom′i sôr′, prom′i sôr′), *n.* *Law.* a person who makes a promise.

prom·is·so·ry (prom′i sōr′ē, -sôr′ē), *adj.* containing, implying, or of the nature of a promise. [< ML *prōmissōri(us)*]

prom′issory note′, a written promise to pay a specified sum of money, at a fixed time or on demand.

prom·on·to·ry (prom′ən tōr′ē, -tôr′ē), *n., pl.* **-ries. 1.** a high point of land or rock projecting into the sea or other body of water; a headland. **2.** a bluff overlooking a lowland. **3.** *Anat.* a prominent or protuberant part. [< ML *prōmontōri(um)*, L *prōmunturium*, akin to *prōminēre* (see PROMINENT)]

pro·mote (prə mōt′), *v.t.*, **-mot·ed, -mot·ing. 1.** to encourage the existence or progress of; further. **2.** to advance in rank, dignity, position, etc. (opposed to *demote*). **3.** *Educ.* to advance to the next higher grade. **4.** to advertise or aid in developing (a business, product, etc.). **5.** *Slang.* to obtain (something) by trickery. [ME < L *prōmōt(us)*, ptp. of *prōmovēre* to move forward, advance. See PRO-[1], MOTIVE] —**pro·mot′a·ble,** *adj.* —**Syn. 1.** abet, assist, help. **2.** elevate, raise. —**Ant. 1.** discourage, obstruct. **2.** demote.

pro·mot·er (prə mō′tər), *n.* **1.** a person who aids in developing a company, project, product, etc. **2.** a person or thing that promotes. **3.** *Chem.* any substance that in small amounts is capable of increasing the activity of a catalyst. [r. earlier *promotour* < AF]

pro·mo·tion (prə mō′shən), *n.* **1.** advancement in rank, grade, or position. **2.** furtherance or encouragement. **3.** the act of promoting. **4.** the state of being promoted. **5.** material issued in behalf of some product, cause, institution, etc. [late ME < LL *prōmōtiōn-* (s. of *prōmōtiō*)] —**pro·mo′tion·al,** *adj.* —**pro·mo′tive,** *adj.*

prompt (prompt), *adj.* **1.** done, delivered, etc., without delay: *a prompt reply.* **2.** quick to act or respond. —*v.t.* **3.** to induce (someone) to action. **4.** to occasion or inspire (an act). **5.** to supply (an actor or reciter) with his forgotten lines, lyrics, or the like. —*v.i.* **6.** to supply forgotten lines, lyrics, or the like to an actor, singer, etc. —*n.* **7.** *Com.* a time limit given for the payment of a debt. **8.** the act of prompting. **9.** something serving to suggest or remind. [(adj.) late ME < L *prompt(us)* ready, prompt, special use of ptp. of *prōmere*, (v.) ME < ML *prōmpt(āre)* (to) incite, L: to distribute, freq. of *prōmere* to bring out = *prō-* PRO-[1] + *(e)mere* to take] —**prompt′ly,** *adv.* —**prompt′ness,** *n.* —**Syn. 4.** urge, spur, instigate.

prompt·book (prompt′bo͝ok′), *n.* *Theat.* a copy of the script of a play, containing cues and notes.

prompt·er (promp′tər), *n.* **1.** *Theat.* a person offstage who repeats missed cues and supplies actors with forgotten lines. **2.** a person or thing that prompts.

promp·ti·tude (promp′ti to͞od′, -tyo͞od′), *n.* promptness. [late ME < LL *prōmptitūdō*]

---

pro·mil′i·tar′y, *adj.* **pro′mi·nor′i·ty,** *adj.* **pro·mod′ern,** *adj.* **pro·mon′ar·chist,** *n., adj.*

prom·ul·gate (prom′əl gāt′, prō mul′gāt), *v.t.*, **-gat·ed, -gat·ing.** **1.** to put into operation (a law, decree of a court, etc.) by formal proclamation. **2.** to set forth or teach publicly (a creed, doctrine, etc.). [< L *prōmulgāt(us)*, ptp. of *prōmulgāre* to PROMULGE; see -ATE¹] —**prom·ul·ga·tion** (prom′əl gā′shən, prō′məl-), *n.* —**prom′ul·ga′tor,** *n.* —**Syn. 1.** announce, issue, declare. **2.** advocate.

pro·mulge (prō mulj′), *v.t.*, **-mulged, -mulg·ing.** *Archaic.* to promulgate. [< L *prōmulg(āre)*, unexplained var. of *prōvulgāre* to make publicly known. See PRO-¹, DIVULGE] —**pro·mulg′er,** *n.*

pro·my·ce·li·um (prō′mī sē′lē əm), *n.*, *pl.* **-li·a** (-lē ə). *Bot.* a short filament produced in the germination of a spore, which bears small spores and then dies. [< NL] —**pro′my·ce′li·al,** *adj.*

pron., **1.** pronoun. **2.** pronunciation.

pro·nate (prō′nāt), *v.*, **-nat·ed, -nat·ing.** —*v.t.* **1.** to rotate (the hand or forearm) so that the surface of the palm is downward or toward the back. **2.** (in vertebrates) to rotate (any limb or joint) in a similar manner. —*v.i.* **3.** to become pronated. [< LL *prōnāt(us)*, ptp. of *prōnāre* to bend (forward)] —**pro·na′tion,** *n.*

pro·na·tor (prō nā′tər), *n.* *Zool.* any of several muscles that enable pronation of the hand, forelimb, or foot in vertebrates.

prone (prōn), *adj.* **1.** having a natural tendency or inclination; disposed; liable: *to be prone to anger.* **2.** having the front part, as the face, the abdomen, or the palm of the hand, downward. **3.** lying flat; prostrate. **4.** having a downward direction or slope. [ME < L *prōn(us)* turned or leaning forward, inclined downward, disposed, prone] —**prone′ly,** *adv.* —**prone′ness,** *n.* —**Syn. 1.** apt, subject, tending. **3.** recumbent.

pro·neph·ros (prō nef′ros), *n.*, *pl.* **-roi** (-roi), **-ra** (-rə). *Embryol.* one of the three embryonic excretory organs of vertebrates, which becomes the functional kidney of certain lower fishes and is vestigial in the embryos of higher vertebrates. Cf. **mesonephros, metanephros.** [< NL < Gk *pro-* PRO-² + *nephrós* kidney] —**pro·neph·ric** (prō nef′rik), *adj.*

prong (prông, prong), *n.* **1.** one of the pointed tines of a fork. **2.** any pointed, projecting part, as of an antler. **3.** a branch of a stream. —*v.t.* **4.** to pierce or stab with a prong. **5.** to supply with prongs. [late ME *pronge*, var. of *prange* kind of fork; akin to OSw *prang* gorge, narrow street, MLG *prange* stake, *prangen* to press, Goth *(ana)-prangan* to oppress, Gk *brónchos* windpipe]

Pronghorn
(3 ft. high at shoulder; horns 12 to 15 in.; length 5½ ft.)

prong·horn (prông′hôrn′, prong′-), *n.*, *pl.* **-horns,** (*esp. collectively*) **-horn.** a fleet, antelopelike ruminant, *Antilocapra americana*, of the plains of western North America. Also called **prong′horn an′telope.**

pro·nom·i·nal (prō nom′ə nᵊl), *adj.* **1.** *Gram.* pertaining to, having the nature of, similar in meaning to, or derived from a pronoun: *"His" in "his book" is a pronominal adjective. "There" is a pronominal adverb.* —*n.* **2.** *Gram.* a pronominal word. [< LL *prōnōminā l(is)*. See PRONOUN, -AL¹] —**pro·nom′i·nal·ly,** *adv.*

pro·no·tum (prō nō′təm), *n.*, *pl.* **-ta** (-tə). the dorsal sclerite of the prothorax of an insect. [< NL]

pro·noun (prō′noun′), *n.* *Gram.* any number of a small class of words used as replacements or substitutes for a wide variety of nouns and noun phrases, as *I, you, he, this, who, what.* [< F *pronom* < L *prōnōmen* (s. *prōnōmin-*)]

pro·nounce (prə nouns′), *v.*, **-nounced, -nounc·ing.** —*v.t.* **1.** to enunciate or articulate (words, phrases, sounds, etc.). **2.** to utter in a particular manner: *He pronounces his words clearly.* **3.** to declare (a person or thing) to be as specified: *I pronounce this a perfect dinner.* **4.** to utter or deliver formally or officially: *to pronounce the man dead.* **5.** to announce with authority: *The judge pronounced the sentence.* **6.** to indicate the pronunciation of by providing a phonetic transcription. —*v.i.* **7.** to pronounce words, phrases, etc. **8.** to make an authoritative statement. [ME < MF *prononc(ier)* < L *prōnuntiāre* to proclaim, announce, recite, utter. See PRO-¹, ANNOUNCE] —**pro·nounce′a·ble,** *adj.* —**pro·nounc′er,** *n.*

pro·nounced (prə nounst′), *adj.* strongly or clearly apparent; decided. —**pro·nounc·ed·ly** (prə noun′sid lē), *adv.*

pro·nounce·ment (prə nouns′mənt), *n.* **1.** a formal or authoritative statement. **2.** an opinion or decision. **3.** act of pronouncing.

pron·to (pron′tō), *adv.* *Slang.* promptly; quickly. [< Sp (adj. and adv.): quick < L *prōmptus* PROMPT]

pro·nu·cle·us (prō nōō′klē əs, -nyōō′-), *n.*, *pl.* **-cle·i** (-klē ī′). *Embryol.* either of the gametic nuclei that unite in fertilization to form the nucleus of the zygote. [< NL] —**pro·nu′cle·ar,** *adj.*

pro·nun·ci·a·men·to (prə nun′sē ə men′tō, -shē ə-), *n.*, *pl.* **-tos.** a proclamation; manifesto. [< Sp *pronunciamiento* < L *prōnuntiā(re)* (to) PRONOUNCE + *-mentum* -MENT]

pro·nun·ci·a·tion (prə nun′sē ā′shən), *n.* **1.** the act or result of pronouncing words, phrases, sounds, etc. **2.** an accepted standard of pronouncing a given syllable, word, etc. **3.** the conventional patterns of treatment of the sounds of a language: *the pronunciation of French.* **4.** a phonetic transcription of a given word, phoneme, etc. [late ME *pronunciacion* < L *prōnuntiātiōn-* (s. of *prōnuntiātiō*) delivery (of a speech) = *prōnuntiāt(us)* (ptp. of *prōnuntiāre* to PRONOUNCE) + *-iōn-* -ION] —**pro·nun′ci·a′tion·al, pro·nun·ci·a·to·ry** (prə nun′sē ə tôr′ē, -tōr′ē), **pro·nun′ci·a′tive,** *adj.*

proof (prōōf), *n.* **1.** evidence sufficient to establish a thing as true or believable. **2.** the act of testing for truth, efficacy, or believability: *to put a thing to the proof.* **3.** the establishment of a truth; demonstration. **4.** *Law.* (in judicial proceedings) evidence having probative weight. **5.** an arithmetical operation serving to check the correctness of a calculation. **6.** *Math., Logic.* a sequence of steps, statements, or demonstrations that leads to a valid conclusion. **7.** a test to determine the quality, durability, etc., of materials used in manufacture. **8.** the state of having been tested and approved. **9.** proved strength, as of armor. **10.** *Distilling.* **a.** the arbitrary standard strength of alcoholic liquor. **b.** strength with reference to this standard: "100 proof" signifies a proof spirit, usually 50% alcohol. **11.** *Photog.* a trial print from a negative. **12.** *Print., Engraving, Etching, Lithography.* **a.** a trial impression taken from composed type, a plate, etc. **b.** one of a number of early and superior impressions taken before the printing of the ordinary issue: *to pull a proof.* —*adj.* **13.** impenetrable, impervious, or invulnerable: *proof against attack.* **14.** of tested strength or quality: *proof armor.* **15.** used for testing or proving. **16.** of standard strength, as an alcoholic liquor. —*v.t.* **17.** to test; examine for flaws, errors, etc. **18.** *Print.* prove (def. 6). **19.** to proofread. **20.** to provide with resistance against damage, deterioration, etc. (often used in combination): *to shrink-proof a shirt.* [ME *prove*, etc., alter. (by assoc. with PROVE) of *preove* < OF *prueve* < LL *proba* a test, akin to L *probāre* to test and find good] —**Syn. 1.** confirmation, corroboration, support. See **evidence. 2.** examination.

-proof, a combining form of **proof:** *foolproof; waterproof.*

proof·read (prōōf′rēd′), *v.*, **-read** (-red′), **-read·ing.** —*v.t.* **1.** to read (printers' proofs, copy, etc.) to detect and mark errors to be corrected. —*v.i.* **2.** to read printers' proofs, copy, etc., to detect and mark errors, esp. as an employee in a typesetting firm, newspaper office, or publishing house. [back formation from *proofreader*] —**proof′read′er,** *n.*

proof′ spir′it, an alcoholic liquor, or mixture of alcohol and water, containing one half of its volume of alcohol of a specific gravity of .7939 at 60° F.

prop¹ (prop), *v.*, **propped, prop·ping,** *n.* —*v.t.* **1.** to support with a prop: *to prop an old fence.* **2.** to rest (a thing) against a support. **3.** to support or sustain. —*n.* **4.** a stick, beam, or other rigid support. **5.** a person or thing serving as a support or stay: *His father is his financial prop.* [ME *proppe;* c. MD *proppe* prop, support]

prop² (prop), *n.* *Theat.* property (def. 10a). [by shortening]

prop³ (prop), *n.* *Informal.* a propeller. [by shortening]

prop., **1.** properly. **2.** property. **3.** proposition.

pro·pae·deu·tic (prō′pi dōō′tik, -dyōō′-), *adj.* Also **pro′pae·deu′ti·cal.** **1.** pertaining to or of the nature of preliminary instruction. **2.** introductory to some art or science. —*n.* **3.** a propaedeutic subject or study. [PRO-² + Gk *paideutik(ós)* pertaining to teaching = *paideú(ein)* (to) teach + *-tikos* -TIC]

prop·a·ga·ble (prop′ə gə bəl), *adj.* capable of being propagated. [< ML *propāgābil(is)*] —**prop′a·ga·bil′i·ty, prop′a·ga·ble·ness,** *n.*

prop·a·gan·da (prop′ə gan′də), *n.* **1.** information or ideas methodically spread to promote or injure a cause, group, nation, etc. **2.** the deliberate spreading of such information or ideas. **3.** the doctrines or principles propagated by an organization or movement. **4.** *Rom. Cath. Ch.* a committee of cardinals, established in 1622 by Pope Gregory XV to supervise foreign missions and the training of their priests. [< NL, short for *congregātiō dē propāgandā fidē* congregation for propagating the faith]

prop·a·gan·dise (prop′ə gan′dīz), *v.t., v.i.*, **-dised, -dis·ing.** *Chiefly Brit.* propagandize.

prop·a·gan·dize (prop′ə gan′dīz), *v.*, **-dized, -diz·ing.** —*v.t.* **1.** to propagate (principles, dogma, etc.) by means of propaganda. **2.** to subject to propaganda. —*v.i.* **3.** to carry on or disseminate propaganda. —**prop·a·gan·dism** (prop′ə gan′diz əm), *n.* —**prop′a·gan′dist,** *n., adj.* —**prop′a·gan·dis′tic,** *adj.* —**prop′a·gan·dis′ti·cal·ly,** *adv.*

prop·a·gate (prop′ə gāt′), *v.*, **-gat·ed, -gat·ing.** —*v.t.* **1.** to cause (a plant or animal) to multiply by natural reproduction. **2.** to reproduce (itself, its kind, etc.), as a plant or an animal does. **3.** to transmit (hereditary features or elements) to or through offspring. **4.** to spread (information, behavior, etc.) from person to person; disseminate. **5.** to cause to increase. **6.** to transmit (light, sound, heat, etc.) through space or a physical medium. —*v.i.* **7.** to multiply by natural reproduction; breed. [< L *propāgāt(us)* propagated (ptp. of *propāgāre* to fasten (cuttings of plants) out, spread for sprouting, propagate) = *propāg(ēs)* something set out, scion, slip (*pro-* PRO-¹ + *pāg-*, base of *pangere* to fasten + *-ēs* n. suffix) + *-ātus* -ATE¹] —**prop′a·ga′tive,** *adj.* —**prop′a·ga′tor,** *n.*

prop·a·ga·tion (prop′ə gā′shən), *n.* **1.** the act of propagating. **2.** the state of being propagated. **3.** multiplication by natural reproduction. **4.** transmission or dissemination. [late ME *propagacyon* < L *propāgātiōn-* (s. of *propāgātiō*)] —**prop′a·ga′tion·al,** *adj.*

pro·pane (prō′pān), *n.* *Chem.* a flammable gas, $CH_3CH_2CH_3$, occurring in petroleum and natural gas: used chiefly as a fuel and in organic synthesis. [PROP(IONIC) + -ANE]

pro·par·ox·y·tone (prō′pa rok′si tōn′), *Class. Gk. Gram.* —*adj.* **1.** having an accent or heavy stress on the antepenultimate syllable. —*n.* **2.** a proparoxytone word. [< Gk *paroxýton(os)*]

pro pa·tri·a (prō pä′trē ä′; *Eng.* prō pā′trē ə), *Latin.* for one's country.

pro·pel (prə pel′), *v.t.*, **-pelled, -pel·ling.** to drive, or cause to move, forward or onward. [late ME *propelle(n)* (to) expel < L *prōpell(ere)* (to) drive forward = *prō-* PRO-¹ + *pellere* to drive] —**Syn.** compel, project, move. —**Ant.** repel.

pro·pel·lant (prə pel′ənt), *n.* **1.** a propelling agent. **2.** *Mil.* the explosive used to fire a projectile from a gun. **3.** the fuel for propelling a rocket.

pro·pel·lent (prə pel′ənt), *adj.* **1.** serving or tending to propel or drive forward. —*n.* **2.** a propellant. [< L *prōpellent-* (s. of *prōpellēns*), prp. of *prōpellere* to drive forward]

pro·pel·ler (prə pel′ər), *n.* **1.** a person or thing that propels. **2.** a device having a revolving hub with radiating blades, for propelling a steamship, an airplane, etc.

pro·pend (prō pend′), *v.i.* *Obs.* to incline or tend. [< L *prōpend(ēre)* (to) hang down, be inclined]

pro-Mus′lim, *adj., n.* **pro·na′tion·al·ist,** *adj.* **pro′na·tion·al·is′tic,** *adj.* **pro-Ne′gro,** *adj.*

pro·pene (prō′pēn), *n. Chem.* propylene. [PROP(IONIC) + -ENE]

pro·pe·nol (prō′pə nōl′, -nôl′, -nol′), *n. Chem.* See **allyl alcohol** [PROPENE + -OL[1]]

pro·pense (prō pens′), *adj. Archaic.* having a tendency toward; prone; inclined. [< L *propens(us)* inclined, ptp. of *prōpendēre* to PROPEND] —**pro·pense′ly,** *adv.* —**pro·pense′ness,** *n.*

pro·pen·si·ty (prə pen′si tē), *n., pl.* **-ties. 1.** a natural inclination or tendency. **2.** *Obs.* favorable disposition or partiality. —**Syn. 1.** bent, leaning, penchant, proclivity.

pro′pe·nyl group′ (prō′pə nil), *Chem.* the univalent group, $CH_3CH{=}CH{-}$, derived from propylene. Also called **pro′penyl rad′ical.** [PROPENE + -YL] —**pro′pe·nyl, pro′pe·nyl′ic,** *adj.*

prop·er (prop′ər), *adj.* **1.** adapted or appropriate to the purpose or circumstances; fit; suitable. **2.** conforming to established standards of behavior or manners; correct or decorous. **3.** belonging or pertaining to a particular person or thing. **4.** strict; accurate. **5.** in the strict sense of the word (usually used postpositively): *Shellfish are not among the fishes proper.* **6.** *Gram.* (of a name, noun, or adjective) designating a particular person or thing, written in English with an initial capital letter, as *John; Chicago, Monday, American.* **7.** normal or regular. **8.** *Heraldry.* (of a device) depicted in its natural colors: *an oak tree proper.* **9.** *Eccles.* used only on a particular day or festival. **10.** *Chiefly Brit. Informal.* complete or thorough: *a proper thrashing.* **11.** *Archaic.* of good character; virtuous. —*n.* **12.** *Eccles.* a special office or special parts of an office appointed for a particular day or time. [ME *propre* < OF < L *propr(ius)* one's own] —**prop′er·ness,** *n.* —**Syn. 1.** suited. **2.** befitting, becoming, decent, polite. **3.** individual, peculiar. **4.** precise, exact.

prop′er frac′tion, *Math.* a fraction having the numerator less, or lower in degree, than the denominator.

prop·er·ly (prop′ər lē), *adv.* **1.** in a proper manner. **2.** correctly. **3.** appropriately. **4.** decorously. **5.** accurately. **6.** justifiably. **7.** thoroughly; completely. [ME]

prop′er noun′, a noun that is not normally preceded by an article or other limiting modifier, that refers to only one person or thing, and is usually capitalized, as *Lincoln, Richard, Pittsburgh.* Cf. **common noun.**

prop·er·tied (prop′ər tēd), *adj.* owning property.

Pro·per·ti·us (prō pûr′shē əs, -shəs), *n.* **Sex·tus** (sek′stus), c50–c15 B.C., Roman poet.

prop·er·ty (prop′ər tē), *n., pl.* **-ties** for 4, 8–10. **1.** the sum total of one's possessions, tangible and intangible. Cf. **personal property, real property. 2.** an item considered as part of one's property. **3.** land or real estate or certain rights accruing to them; real property. **4.** a piece of land. **5.** ownership; right of possession or disposal of anything. **6.** something at the disposal of a person or group, the community, etc. **7.** certain legal, intangible rights, as in copyright. **8.** an essential or distinctive attribute of something: *the chemical properties of alcohol.* **9.** *Logic.* (in Aristotle) an attribute not essential to a species but always connected with it and with it alone. **10.** *Theat.* **a.** any movable item used on the set in a theatrical or other production. **b.** a written work, play, movie, etc., bought or optioned for commercial production or distribution. [ME *proprete* possession, attribute, what is one's own. See PROPER, -TY[2], PROPRIETY] —**prop′er·ty·less,** *n.*
—**Syn. 1, 2.** PROPERTY, CHATTELS, EFFECTS, ESTATE, GOODS refer to what is owned. PROPERTY is the general word: *He owns a great deal of property. He said that the umbrella was his property.* CHATTELS is a term for pieces of personal property or movable possessions; it may be applied to livestock, automobiles, etc.: *a mortgage on chattels.* EFFECTS is a term for any form of personal property, including even things of the least value: *All his effects were insured against fire.* ESTATE refers to property of any kind that has been, or is capable of being, handed down to descendants or otherwise disposed of in a will: *He left most of his estate to his nephew.* It may consist of personal estate (money, valuables, securities, chattels, etc.) or real estate (land and buildings). GOODS refers to household possessions or other movable property, esp. that comprising the stock in trade of a business: *A store arranges its goods conveniently.* **8.** See **quality.**

prop′erty man′, a person responsible for the stage properties used in a play, movie, etc. Also called **propman, prop man.**

pro·phase (prō′fāz′), *n. Biol.* the first stage in mitosis, in which the chromosomes contract and become more stainable and the nuclear membrane disappears.

proph·e·cy (prof′i sē), *n., pl.* **-cies. 1.** the foretelling or prediction of what is to come. **2.** something that is declared by a prophet, esp. divinely inspired prediction, instruction, or exhortation. **3.** a divinely inspired utterance or revelation. **4.** the action, function, or faculty of a prophet. [ME *prophecie* < OF < LL *prophētīa* < Gk *prophēteía.* See PROPHET, -Y[3]]

proph·e·sy (prof′i sī′), *v.,* **-sied, -sy·ing.** —*v.t.* **1.** to foretell or predict. **2.** to indicate beforehand. **3.** to foretell by or as by divine inspiration. **4.** to utter in prophecy or as a prophet. —*v.i.* **5.** to make predictions, esp. by divine inspiration. **6.** to speak as a mediator between God and man. **7.** *Rare.* to teach religious subjects. [v. use and var. of PROPHECY] —**proph′e·si′a·ble,** *adj.* —**proph′e·si′er,** *n.* —**Syn. 1.** augur, prognosticate. See **predict.**

proph·et (prof′it), *n.* **1.** a person who speaks for God or a deity, or by divine inspiration. **2.** (in the Old Testament) a person chosen to speak for God and to guide the people of Israel, as one of the Major or Minor Prophets. **3.** one of a class of persons in the early church, next in order after the apostles, recognized as inspired to utter special revelations and predictions. I Cor. 12:28. **4. the Prophet,** Muhammad. **5.** an inspired teacher or leader. **6.** a person who foretells or predicts. Also, *referring to a woman,* **proph′et·ess.** [early ME *prophete* < LL *prophēta* < Gk *prophḗtēs* = *pro-* PRO-[2] + *-phētēs* speaker, action n. of *phánai* to speak] —**proph′et·like′,** *adj.*

pro·phet·ic (prə fet′ik), *adj.* **1.** of or pertaining to a prophet: *prophetic inspiration.* **2.** of the nature of or containing prophecy: *prophetic writings.* **3.** having the function or powers of a prophet. **4.** predictive, esp. when ominous: *prophetic warnings.* Also, **pro·phet′i·cal.** [< LL *prophēticus*) < Gk *prophētikós*] —**pro·phet′i·cal·ly,** *adv.*

Proph·ets (prof′its), *n.* (*construed as sing.*) the canonical group of books forming the second of the three Jewish divisions of the Old Testament, comprising Joshua, Judges, I and II Samuel, I and II Kings, Isaiah, Jeremiah, Ezekiel, Hosea, Joel, Amos, Obadiah, Jonah, Micah, Nahum, Habakkuk, Zephaniah, Haggai, Zechariah, and Malachi. Cf. **Hagiographa, Law of Moses.**

pro·phy·lac·tic (prō′fə lak′tik, prof′ə-), *adj.* **1.** protecting from disease, as a drug. **2.** preventive or protective. —*n.* **3.** *Med.* a prophylactic medicine or measure. **4.** a preventive. **5.** a condom. [< Gk *prophylaktik(ós)* of guarding = *prophylak-* (verbid s. of *prophylássein* to guard beforehand) + *-tikos* -TIC. See PROPHYLAXIS] —**pro′phy·lac′ti·cal·ly,** *adv.*

pro·phy·lax·is (prō′fə lak′sis, prof′ə-), *n. Med.* the prevention of disease or a disease, as by treatment. [< NL < Gk *pro-* PRO-[2] + *phýlaxis* a watching, guarding = *phylak-* (verbid s. of *phylássein* to guard) + *-sis* -SIS]

pro·pine (prō pēn′), *v.t.,* **-pined, -pin·ing.** *Archaic.* to offer as a present. [late ME < MF *propine(r)* (to) give to drink, drink one's health < L *propīnāre* < Gk *propínein* to drink first = *pro-* PRO-[2] + *pínein* to drink]

pro·pin·qui·ty (prō piŋ′kwi tē), *n.* **1.** nearness in place; proximity. **2.** nearness of relation; kinship. **3.** affinity of nature; similarity. **4.** nearness in time. [ME *propinquite* < L *propinquitās* nearness = *propinqu(us)* near (*prop(e)* near + *-inquus* adj. suffix) + *-itās* -ITY]

pro·pi·o·nate (prō′pē ə nāt′), *n. Chem.* an ester or salt of propionic acid. [PROPION(IC) + -ATE[2]]

pro′pi·on′ic ac′id (prō′pē on′ik, -ō′nik, prō′-), *Chem., Pharm.* a colorless, oily, water-soluble liquid, CH_3CH_2COOH, having a pungent odor: used in making bread-mold-inhibiting propionates, in perfumery, etc., and in medicine as a topical fungicide. [PRO-[2] + Gk *pīon-* (s. of *pīōn*) fat + -IC]

pro·pi·ti·ate (prə pish′ē āt′), *v.t.,* **-at·ed, -at·ing.** to make favorably inclined; conciliate. [< L *propitiāt(us),* ptp. of *propitiāre* to appease. See PROPITIOUS, -ATE[1]] —**pro·pi·ti·a·ble** (prə pish′ē ə bəl), *adj.* —**pro·pi′ti·at′ing·ly,** *adv.* —**pro·pi′ti·a′tive,** *adj.* —**pro·pi′ti·a′tor,** *n.* —**pro·pi·ti·a·to·ry** (prə pish′ē ə tōr′ē, -tôr′ē), *adj.* —**Ant.** anger, arouse.

pro·pi·ti·a·tion (prə pish′ē ā′shən), *n.* **1.** the act of propitiating; conciliation. **2.** something that propitiates. [ME *propiciacioun* < LL *propitiātiōn-* (s. of *propitiātiō*) appeasement]

pro·pi·tious (prə pish′əs), *adj.* **1.** presenting favorable conditions: *propitious weather.* **2.** indicative of favor; auspicious: *propitious omens.* **3.** favorably disposed. [late ME *propicius* < L *propitius* favorable = *prop(e)* near + *-itius* -ITIOUS] —**pro·pi′tious·ly,** *adv.* —**pro·pi′tious·ness,** *n.*

prop·jet (prop′jet′), *n. Aeron.* an airplane equipped with turbo-propeller engines.

prop′jet en′gine. See **turbo-propeller engine.**

prop·man (prop′man′), *n., pl.* **-men.** *Theat.* See **property man.** Also, **prop′ man′.**

prop·o·lis (prop′ə lis), *n.* a reddish resinous cement collected and used by bees. [< L < Gk: suburb]

pro·po·nent (prə pō′nənt), *n.* **1.** a person who puts forward a proposition or proposal. **2.** *Law.* a person who propounds a legal instrument, as a will. **3.** a person who supports a cause or doctrine. [< L *prōpōnent-* (s. of *prōpōnēns*). See PROPOSE, -ENT]

pro·por·tion (prə pōr′shən, -pôr′-), *n.* **1.** the comparative relation between things or magnitudes; ratio. **2.** proper or significant relation between things or parts. **3.** relative size or extent. **4. proportions,** dimensions. **5.** any portion or part in its relation to the whole. **6.** symmetry, harmony, or balance. **7.** *Math.* **a.** a relation of four quantities such that the first divided by the second is equal to the third divided by the fourth; the equality of ratios. **b.** See **rule of three.** —*v.t.* **8.** to adjust the size, amount, or proportion of in proper relation. [ME *proporcio(u)n* < L *prōportiōn-* (s. of *prōportiō*) symmetry, analogy] —**pro·por′tion·ment,** *n.* —**Syn. 6.** See **symmetry. 8.** regulate, balance, harmonize.

pro·por·tion·a·ble (prə pōr′shə nə bəl, -pôr′-), *adj.* proportional. [ME *proporcionable* < LL *prōportiōnābil(is)*] —**pro·por′tion·a·bil′i·ty,** *n.* —**pro·por′tion·a·bly,** *adv.*

pro·por·tion·al (prə pōr′shə n^əl, -pôr′-), *adj.* **1.** having or being in proportion. **2.** of or pertaining to proportion; relative. **3.** *Math.* having the same or a constant ratio or relation. [ME *proporcional* < L *prōportiōnāl(is)*] —**pro·por′tion·al′i·ty,** *n.* —**pro·por′tion·al·ly,** *adv.* —**Syn. 1.** harmonious, accordant, consonant.

propor′tional representa′tion, a method of voting by which political parties are given legislative representation in proportion to their popular strength.

pro·por·tion·ate (*adj.* prə pōr′shə nit, -pôr′-; *v.* prə pōr′shə nāt′, -pôr′-), *adj., v.,* **-at·ed, -at·ing.** —*adj.* **1.** proportioned; proportional. —*v.t.* **2.** to make proportionate. [ME *proporcionate* < LL *prōportiōnāt(us)*] —**pro·por′tion·ate·ly,** *adv.* —**Syn. 1.** consonant, harmonious, balanced.

pro·pos·al (prə pō′zəl), *n.* **1.** the act of offering or suggesting something for acceptance, adoption, or performance. **2.** a plan or scheme proposed. **3.** an offer of marriage.
—**Syn. 1.** recommendation. **2.** suggestion, design. PROPOSAL, PROPOSITION refer to an offer. A PROPOSAL is a plan, a scheme, an offer to be accepted or rejected: *to make proposals for peace.* PROPOSITION, used in mathematics to refer to a formal statement of truth, and often including the proof or demonstration of the statement, has something of this same meaning when used nontechnically (particularly in business). A PROPOSITION is a PROPOSAL in which the terms are clearly stated and their advantageous nature emphasized: *His proposition involved a large discount to the retailer.*

pro·pose (prə pōz′), *v.,* **-posed, -pos·ing.** —*v.t.* **1.** to offer for consideration, acceptance, or action: *to propose a new method.* **2.** to suggest. **3.** to nominate (a person) for office, membership, etc. **4.** to plan; intend. **5.** to offer (a toast). —*v.i.* **6.** to make an offer or suggestion, esp. of marriage. **7.** to form or consider a purpose or design. [ME < MF *propose(r)* by assoc. with derivatives of L *prōpositus,* ptp. of *prōpōnere* to set forth. See PROPOSITION] —**pro·pos′a·ble,**

adj. —**pro·pos′er,** *n.* —**Syn. 1.** proffer, tender, suggest, recommend.

prop·o·si·tion (prop′ə zish′ən), *n.* **1.** a plan or scheme proposed. **2.** an offer of terms for a transaction. **3.** *Informal.* a thing, matter, or person considered as something to be dealt with: *a tough proposition.* **4.** anything stated for purposes of discussion. **5.** *Logic.* a statement affirming or denying something so that it can be characterized as true or false. **6.** *Math.* a formal statement of a truth to be demonstrated or an operation to be performed; theorem; problem. **7.** a proposal of illicit sexual relations. —*v.t.* **8.** to propose a plan, deal, etc., to. **9.** to propose illicit sexual relations to. [ME *proposicio(u)n* < L *prōpositiōn-* (s. of *prōpositiō*) a setting forth. See PROPOSITUS, -ION] —**prop′o·si′tion·al,** *adj.* —**Syn. 1.** See **proposal.**

pro·pos·i·tus (prə poz′i təs), *n., pl.* **-ti** (-tī′). *Law.* the person from whom a line of descent is derived. [< NL, special use of ptp. of L *prōpōnere* to set forth, PROPOUND]

pro·pound (prə pound′), *v.t.* to put forward for consideration or acceptance: *to propound a new procedure; to propound a will in probate.* [later var. of ME *propone* < L *prōpōn(ere)* (to) set forth = *prō-* PRO-[1] + *pōnere* to put, place, set. See COMPOUND[1], EXPOUND] —**pro·pound′er,** *n.*

propr., proprietor.

pro·prae·tor (prō prē′tər), *n.* *Rom. Hist.* an officer with praetorial authority in charge of a province. Also, **pro·pre′tor.** [< L]

pro·pri·e·tar·y (prə prī′i ter′ē), *adj., n., pl.* **-tar·ies.** —*adj.* **1.** pertaining to, belonging to, or being a proprietor. **2.** pertaining to property or ownership. **3.** manufactured and sold only by the owner of the patent, trademark, etc. —*n.* **4.** a proprietor or group of proprietors. **5.** ownership. **6.** something owned, esp. a piece of real estate. **7.** a proprietary medicine. [late ME < LL *proprietāri(us)* owner (n.), of an owner, of ownership (adj). See PROPRIETY, -ARY] —**pro·pri·e·tar·i·ly** (prə prī′i târ′i lē, -prī′i ter′-), *adv.*

propri′etary col′ony, *Amer. Hist.* a colony granted to an individual or group by the British crown with full rights of government. Cf. **charter colony, royal colony** (def. 2).

pro·pri·e·tor (prə prī′i tər), *n.* **1.** the owner of a business establishment, a hotel, etc. **2.** a person who has the exclusive right or title to something; an owner. **3.** a group of proprietors. Also, *referring to a woman,* **pro·pri′e·tress** (for defs. 1, 2). [PROPRIET(ARY) + -OR[2]] —**pro·pri′e·tor·ship′,** *n.*

pro·pri·e·ty (prə prī′i tē), *n., pl.* **-ties.** **1.** conformity to established standards of proper behavior or manners. **2.** appropriateness to the purpose or circumstances; suitability. **3.** rightness or justness. **4. the proprieties,** the conventional standards of behavior in polite society; manners: *to observe the proprieties.* **5.** *Obs.* a property. **6.** *Obs.* a peculiarity or characteristic of something. [ME *propriete* < L *proprietās* peculiarity, ownership = *propri(us)* PROPER + *-etās,* var. of *-itās* -ITY] —**Syn. 1.** decency, modesty. See **etiquette. 2.** aptness, fitness, seemliness. **3.** correctness.

proprio-, a learned borrowing from Latin, used in the formation of compound words: *proprioceptive.* [comb. form repr. L *proprius* one's own, special, particular, proper]

pro·pri·o·cep·tive (prō′prē ə sep′tiv), *adj.* *Physiol.* pertaining to proprioceptors, the stimuli acting upon them, or the nerve impulses initiated by them. [PROPRIO- + (RE)CEPTIVE]

pro·pri·o·cep·tor (prō′prē ə sep′tər), *n.* *Physiol.* a receptor located in subcutaneous tissues, as muscles, that responds to stimuli produced within the body. [PROPRIO- + (RE)CEPTOR]

prop′ root′, *Bot.* an adventitious root that supports the plant, as the aerial roots of the mangrove tree or of corn.

prop·to·sis (prop tō′sis), *n.* *Pathol.* **1.** the forward displacement of an organ. **2.** exophthalmos. [< NL < Gk: a fall forward]

pro·pul·sion (prə pul′shən), *n.* **1.** the act of propelling. **2.** the state of being propelled. **3.** a propelling force or impulse. [< L *prōpuls(us)* (ptp. of *prōpellere* to PROPEL) + -ION] —**pro·pul·sive** (prə pul′siv), **pro·pul′so·ry,** *adj.*

pro·pyl (prō′pil), *adj.* *Chem.* containing a propyl group. [PROP(IONIC) + -YL]

prop·y·lae·a (prop′ə lē′ə), *n.* **1.** pl. of **propylaeum. 2.** (*construed as sing.*) propylaeum.

prop·y·lae·um (prop′ə lē′əm), *n., pl.* **-lae·a** (-lē′ə). an elaborate vestibule or entrance to a temple area. Also, **prop·y·lon** (prop′ə lon′). [< L < Gk *propýlaion* gateway, neut. of *propýlaios* before the gate = *pro-* PRO-[2] + *pýl(ē)* gate + *-aios* adj. suffix]

pro′pyl al′cohol, *Chem.* a liquid, $CH_3CH_2CH_2OH$, used chiefly in organic synthesis and as a solvent.

pro·pyl·ene (prō′pə lēn′), *n.* *Chem.* a flammable gas, $CH_3CH{=}CH_2$, of the olefin series: used chiefly in organic synthesis. Also, **propene.**

pro′pylene gly′col, *Chem.* a viscous liquid, $CH_3CHOHCH_2OH$, used chiefly as a lubricant, as an antifreeze, and as a solvent for fats, oils, waxes, and resins.

pro′pylene group′, *Chem.* the bivalent group, $-CH(CH_3)CH_2-$, derived from propylene or propane. Also called **pro′pylene rad′ical.**

pro′pyl group′, *Chem.* any of two univalent, isomeric groups having the formula C_3H_7-. Also called **pro′pyl rad′ical.** Cf. **isopropyl group.** —**pro′pyl, pro·pyl′ic,** *adj.*

prop·y·lite (prop′ə līt′), *n.* *Petrog.* a hydrothermally altered andesite or allied rock containing secondary minerals, as calcite, chlorite, serpentine, or epidote.

pro ra·ta (prō rā′tə, rä′-), in proportion; according to a certain rate. [< ML] —**pro-ra′ta,** *adj.*

pro·rate (prō rāt′, prō′rāt′), *v.i., v.t.,* **-rat·ed, -rat·ing.** to divide or distribute proportionately. [back formation from PRO RATA] —**pro·rat′a·ble,** *adj.* —**pro·ra′tion,** *n.*

pro·rogue (prō rōg′), *v.t.,* **-rogued, -rogu·ing.** to discontinue a session of (the British Parliament or a similar body). [late ME *proroge* < L *prōrog(āre)* (to) prolong, protract, defer, lit., to ask publicly = *prō-* PRO-[1] + *rogāre* to ask, propose] —**pro·ro·ga·tion** (prō′rə gā′shən), *n.* —**Syn.** suspend.

pros., **1.** proscenium. **2.** prosody.

pro·sa·ic (prō zā′ik), *adj.* **1.** commonplace or dull; unimaginative. **2.** of or like prose. Also, **pro·sa′i·cal.** [LL *prōsaic(us).* See PROSE, -IC] —**pro·sa′i·cal·ly,** *adv.* —**pro·sa′ic·ness,** *n.* —**Syn. 1.** humdrum, tiresome.

pro·sa·ism (prō zā′iz əm), *n.* **1.** prosaic character or style. **2.** a prosaic expression. Also, **pro·sa·i·cism** (prō zā′i siz′əm). [< F *prosaïsme* < L *prōsa* PROSE; see -ISM]

Pros. Atty., See **prosecuting attorney.**

pro·sce·ni·um (prō sē′nē əm), *n., pl.* **-ni·a** (-nē ə). *Theat.* **1.** Also called **prosce′nium arch′.** the arch that separates a stage from the auditorium. *Abbr.:* pros. **2.** (formerly) the apron or, esp. in ancient theater, the stage itself. [< L < Gk *proskḗnion* (also) LGk: stage curtain). See PRO-[2], SCENE]

pro·sciut·to (prō shoo′tō; *It.* prô shōōt′tô), *n.* spiced ham, often smoked, that has been cured by drying. [< It: lit., predried = *pro-,* for *pre-* PRE- + *(a)sciutto* dried]

pro·scribe (prō skrīb′), *v.t.,* **-scribed, -scrib·ing. 1.** to denounce or condemn. **2.** to prohibit; outlaw. **3.** to banish or exile. **4.** (in ancient Rome) to announce the name of (a person) as condemned to death and subject to confiscation of property. [< L *prōscrīb(ere)* (to) publish in writing, confiscate, outlaw] —**pro·scrib′er,** *n.*

pro·scrip·tion (prō skrip′shən), *n.* **1.** the act of proscribing. **2.** the state of being proscribed. **3.** outlawry, interdiction, or prohibition. [ME *proscripcioun* < L *prōscriptiōn-* (s. of *prōscriptiō*) public notice of confiscation or outlawry = *prōscript(us)* (ptp. of *prōscrībere* to PROSCRIBE) + *-iōn-* -ION] —**pro·scrip·tive** (prō skrip′tiv), *adj.* —**pro·scrip′tive·ly,** *adv.*

prose (prōz), *n., adj., v.,* **prosed, pros·ing.** —*n.* **1.** spoken or written language without metrical structure, as distinguished from poetry or verse. **2.** commonplace or dull expression, discourse, etc. **3.** *Liturgy.* a hymn sung after the gradual. —*adj.* **4.** of, in, or pertaining to prose. **5.** prosaic. —*v.t.* **6.** to turn into or express in prose. —*v.i.* **7.** to write or talk in a dull, prosaic manner. [ME < MF < L *prōsa (ōrātiō),* lit., straightforward (speech), fem. of *prōsus* for *prōrsus,* var. of *prōversus,* ptp. of *prōvertere* to turn forward = *prō-* PRO-[1] + *vertere* to turn] —**prose′like′,** *adj.*

pro·sec·tor (prō sek′tər), *n.* **1.** a person who dissects cadavers for anatomical demonstration. **2.** a person who performs autopsies. [< LL: anatomist, lit., one who cuts in public (or beforehand) = L *prōsect(us)* (ptp. of *prōsecāre* to cut out (body organs) in public sacrifice; see PRO-[1], SECT) + *-or* -OR[2]] —**pro·sec·to·ri·al** (prō′sek tōr′ē əl, -tôr′-), *adj.*

pros·e·cute (pros′ə kyōōt′), *v.,* **-cut·ed, -cut·ing.** —*v.t.* **1.** *Law.* **a.** to institute legal proceedings against (a person). **b.** to seek to enforce or obtain by legal process. **c.** to conduct criminal proceedings in court against. **2.** to follow up and complete (something undertaken). **3.** to practice or engage in. —*v.i. Law.* **4.** to institute and carry on a legal prosecution. **5.** to act as prosecutor. [late ME: to follow up, go on with < L *prōsecūt(us),* ptp. of *prōsequī* to pursue, proceed with = *prō-* PRO-[1] + *sequī* to follow] —**pros′e·cut′a·ble,** *adj.*

pros′ecuting attor′ney, *U.S.* (*sometimes caps.*) the public officer in a county, district, or other jurisdiction charged with carrying on the prosecution in criminal proceedings.

pros·e·cu·tion (pros′ə kyōō′shən), *n.* **1.** *Law.* **a.** the institution and carrying on of legal proceedings against a person. **b.** the body of officials by whom such proceedings are instituted and carried on. **2.** the following up and completion of something undertaken. [< LL *prōsecutiōn-* (s. of *prōsecutiō*) a following up]

pros·e·cu·tor (pros′ə kyōō′tər), *n.* **1.** *Law.* **a.** See **prosecuting attorney. b.** a person, as a complainant or chief witness, instigating prosecution in a criminal proceeding. **2.** a person who prosecutes. [< ML, LL: pursuer]

pros·e·lyte (pros′ə līt′), *n., v.,* **-lyt·ed, -lyt·ing.** —*n.* **1.** a person who has changed from one opinion, religious belief, sect, or the like, to another; convert. —*v.i., v.t.* **2.** to proselytize. [ME < LL *prosēlyt(us)* < Gk *prosḗlytos* newcomer, proselyte = *prosēluth-* (s. of *prosérchesthai* to approach) + *-os* n. suffix] —**Syn. 1.** neophyte, disciple.

pros·e·lyt·ise (pros′ə li tīz′, -lī-), *v.t., v.i.,* **-ised, -is·ing.** *Chiefly Brit.* proselytize. —**pros′e·lyt·is′er,** *n.*

pros·e·lyt·ism (pros′ə li tiz′əm, -lī-), *n.* **1.** act or fact of becoming a proselyte; conversion. **2.** state or condition of a proselyte. **3.** the act or practice of making proselytes. —**pros·e·lyt·i·cal** (pros′ə lit′i kəl), *adj.*

pros·e·lyt·ize (pros′ə li tīz′, -lī-), *v.t., v.i.,* **-ized, -iz·ing.** to convert or attempt to convert as a proselyte. Also, *esp. Brit.,* **proselytise.** —**pros′e·lyt·iz′er,** *n.*

pros·en·ceph·a·lon (pros′en sef′ə lon′), *n., pl.* **-las, -la** (-lə). *Anat.* the forebrain. [< NL < Gk *prós(ō)* forward + *enképhalon* ENCEPHALON] —**pros·en·ce·phal·ic** (pros′ensə fal′ik), *adj.*

pros·en·chy·ma (pros eng′kə mə), *n.* *Bot.* the tissue characteristic of the woody and phloem portions of plants, consisting typically of long, narrow cells with pointed ends. [< NL < Gk *pros-* toward, to + *énchyma* infusion; modeled on *parenchyma*] —**pros·en·chym·a·tous** (pros′eng kim′ə təs), *adj.*

prose′ po′em, a composition written as prose but having the concentrated, rhythmic, figurative language characteristic of poetry.

pros·er (prō′zər), *n.* **1.** a person who talks or writes in prose. **2.** a person who talks or writes prosaically.

Pro·ser·pi·na (prō sûr′pə nə), *n.* Persephone (def. 1). Also, **Pro·ser·pi·ne** (prō sûr′pə nē).

pro·sit (prō′sit; *Eng.* prō′sit), *interj.* *Latin.* (used esp. by Germans and Austrians as a toast) may it do good.

pro·slav·er·y (prō slā′və rē), *adj.* **1.** favoring slavery. **2.** *U.S. Hist.* favoring the continuance of Negro slavery. —*n.* **3.** the favoring or support of slavery. —**pro·slav′er,** *n.*

pros·o·dist (pros′ə dist), *n.* an expert in prosody.

pros·o·dy (pros′ə dē), *n.* **1.** the science or study of poetic meters and versification. **2.** a particular or distinctive system of metrics and versification: *Milton's prosody.* **3.** *Linguistics.* the stress patterns of an utterance. [late ME < L *prosōdia* < Gk *prosōidía* tone or accent, modulation of voice, song sung to music = *prós* toward + *ōidḗ* ODE + *-ia* -Y[3]] —**pro·sod·ic** (prə sod′ik), **pro·sod′i·cal,** *adj.*

pro·so·po·poe·ia (prō sō′pə pē′ə), *n.* *Rhet.* **1.** personification. **2.** representation of an imaginary, absent, or deceased person as speaking or acting. Also, **pro·so′po·pe′ia.** [< L

pro-Prot′es·tant, *adj., n.*
pro′re·form′, *adj.*
pro′res·to·ra′tion, *adj.*
pro′re·vi′sion, *adj.*
pro′rev·o·lu′tion·ar′y, *adj.*
pro-South′, *adj.*
pro-South′ern, *adj.*
pro-So′vi·et, *adj.*

< Gk *prosōpopoiía* personification = *prósōpo(n)* face, person + *poi(ein)* (to) make + *-ia* -IA]

pros·pect (pros′pekt), *n.* **1.** Usually, **prospects.** the probability of success, profit, etc., in the future: *good business prospects.* **2.** expectation; a looking forward. **3.** something in view as a source of profit. **4.** a potential customer or client. **5.** a potential candidate. **6.** outlook or view over a region or in a particular direction. **7.** a mental view or survey, as of a subject or situation. **8.** *Mining.* **a.** an apparent indication of ore or native metal. **b.** a spot giving such indications. **c.** workings, or an excavation, in a mine. **9.** *Archaic.* sight; range of vision. **10. in prospect,** expected; in view. —*v.t., v.i.* **11.** to search or explore (a region), as for gold. **12.** to work (a mine or claim). [late ME *prospecte* < L *prōspect(us)* outlook, view. See PROSPECTUS] —**pros·pec·tor** (pros′pek tər, prə spek′tər), *n.* —**Syn. 6, 7.** perspective.

pro·spec·tive (prə spek′tiv), *adj.* **1.** of or in the future. **2.** potential, likely, or expected. [< LL *prōspectīv(us).* See PROSPECTUS, -IVE] —**pro·spec′tive·ly,** *adv.*

pro·spec·tus (prə spek′təs), *n., pl.* **-tus·es.** a report describing a forthcoming project. [< L: outlook, view < *prōspectus,* ptp. of *prōspicere* to look forward = *prō-* PRO-[1] + *-spicere,* comb. form of *specere* to look]

pros·per (pros′pər), *v.i.* **1.** to be successful or fortunate, esp. financially. —*v.t.* **2.** *Archaic.* to make successful or fortunate. [late ME < L *prosper(āre)* (to) make happy]

pros·per·i·ty (pro sper′i tē), *n.* the state or condition of flourishing or being successful, esp. financially. [ME *prosperite* < OF < L *prosperitās.* See PROSPEROUS, -ITY]

pros·per·ous (pros′pər əs), *adj.* **1.** having or characterized by good fortune, success, or wealth. **2.** favorable or propitious. [late ME < L *prosperus,* var. of *prosper* favorable, lit., according to hope = *pro-* PRO-[1] + *-sper,* akin to *spēs* hope] —**pros′per·ous·ly,** *adv.* —**pros′per·ous·ness,** *n.*

pros·pho·ron (*Gk.* PRÔS′fô RÔN; *Eng.* pros′fə ron′, -fər ən), *n.* *Eastern Ch.* an uncut loaf of altar bread before it is consecrated. [< Gk, n. use of neut. of *prósphoros* fitting, suitable = *pros-* toward + *-phor-* (s. of *phérein* to bring) + *-os* adj. suffix]

pros·ta·glan·din (pros′tə glan′din), *n.* a group of powerful, hormonelike chemicals found in human and animal tissue, used in the treatment of heart and kidney diseases, peptic ulcers, reproductive problems, etc. [PROSTA(TE) + GLAND[1] + -IN[2]]

pros·tate (pros′tāt), *Anat.* —*adj.* **1.** Also, **pro·stat·ic** (prō stat′ik). of or pertaining to the prostate gland. —*n.* **2.** See **prostate gland.** [< NL *prostata* < Gk *prostátēs* one standing before. See PRO-[2], -STAT]

pros·ta·tec·to·my (pros′tə tek′tə mē), *n., pl.* **-mies.** *Surg.* excision of part or all of the prostate gland.

pros′tate gland′, *Anat.* the muscular, glandular organ which surrounds the urethra of males at the base of the bladder.

pros·the·sis (pros′thi sis *or, for 1,* pros thē′sis), *n., pl.* **-ses** (-sēz′ *or, for 1,* -sēz). **1.** *Med.* **a.** the addition of an artificial part to supply a defect of the body. **b.** the artificial part added. **2.** *Gram., Prosody.* the addition of one or more sounds or syllables to a word or a line of verse, esp. at the beginning. [< LL < Gk: a putting to, addition = *prós* to + *thésis* a placing; see THESIS] —**pros·thet·ic** (pros thet′ik), *adj.* —**pros·thet′i·cal·ly,** *adv.*

pros·thet·ics (pros thet′iks), *n.* (*construed as sing. or pl.*) the branch of surgery or of dentistry that deals with the replacement of missing parts with artificial structures. Cf. **prosthodontics.**

pros·tho·don·tics (pros′thə don′tiks), *n.* (*construed as sing.*) the branch of dentistry that deals with the restoration and replacement of missing teeth and other oral structures by artificial devices. Also, **pros·tho·don·tia** (pros′thə don′shə, -shē ə). [PROSTH(ESIS) + -ODONT + -ICS]

pros·ti·tute (pros′ti to͞ot′, -tyo͞ot′), *n., v.,* **-tut·ed, -tut·ing.** —*n.* **1.** a person, usually a woman, who engages in sexual intercourse for money; whore; harlot. **2.** a person who willingly uses his talent or ability in a base and unworthy way. —*v.t.* **3.** to hire (oneself) out as a prostitute. **4.** to put (one's talent or ability) to unworthy use. [< L *prōstitūt(a)* harlot, n. use of fem. of *prōstitūtus,* ptp. of *prōstituere* to expose (for sale) = *prō-* PRO-[1] + *-stituere,* comb. form of *statuere* to cause to stand; see STATUS]

pros·ti·tu·tion (pros′ti to͞o′shən, -tyo͞o′-), *n.* **1.** the act or practice of engaging in sexual intercourse for money. **2.** base or unworthy use, as of talent or ability. [< LL *prōstitūtiōn-* (s. of *prōstitūtiō*)]

pro·sto·mi·um (prō stō′mē əm), *n., pl.* **-mi·a** (-mē ə). the unsegmented, preoral portion of the head of certain lower invertebrates. [< NL < Gk *prostómion* mouth. See PRO-[2], STOMA, -IUM] —**pro·sto′mi·al,** *adj.*

pros·trate (pros′trāt), *v.,* **-trat·ed, -trat·ing,** *adj.* —*v.t.* **1.** to cast (oneself) face down on the ground, as in humility. **2.** to lay flat, as on or level with the ground. **3.** to overthrow, overcome, or reduce to helplessness. **4.** to reduce to physical exhaustion. —*adj.* **5.** lying flat or at full length, as on the ground. **6.** lying face down on the ground, as in humility. **7.** overthrown, overcome, or helpless. **8.** physically exhausted. **9.** utterly dejected; disconsolate. **10.** *Bot.* (of a plant or stem) lying flat on the ground. [ME *prostrat* < L *prōstrāt(us),* ptp. of *prōsternere* to throw prone = *prō-* PRO-[1] + *sternere* to stretch out] —**Syn. 5.** prone, supine, recumbent.

pros·tra·tion (pro strā′shən), *n.* **1.** the act of prostrating. **2.** the state of being prostrated. **3.** extreme mental or emotional depression. **4.** extreme physical exhaustion. [< LL *prōstrātiōn-* (s. of *prōstrātiō*) a lying prone]

pro·style (prō′stīl), *adj.* *Archit.* **1.** (of a classical temple) having a portico on the front with the columns in front of the antae. —*n.* **2.** a prostyle building or portico. [< L < Gk *próstyl(os)* = *pro-* PRO-[2] + *stŷlos* pillar]

pros·y (prō′zē), *adj.,* **pros·i·er, pros·i·est.** **1.** of the nature of or resembling prose. **2.** prosaic; dull, tedious. —**pros′i·ly,** *adv.* —**pros′i·ness,** *n.*

prot-, var. of **proto-** before a vowel: *protamine.*

Prot., Protestant.

pro·tac·tin·i·um (prō′tak tin′ē əm), *n.* *Chem.* a radioactive, metallic element. *Symbol:* Pa; *at. no.:* 91. Also, **protoactinium.**

pro·tag·o·nist (prō tag′ə nist), *n.* **1.** the leading character or hero of a drama or other literary work. **2.** a leader of or spokesman for a movement, cause, etc. [< Gk *prōtagōnist(ḗs)* actor who plays the first part, lit., first combatant. See PROTO-, ANTAGONIST] —**pro·tag′o·nism,** *n.*

Pro·tag·o·ras (prō tag′ər əs), *n.* c480–c421 B.C., Greek Sophist philosopher. —**Pro·tag·o·re·an** (prō tag′ə rē′ən), *adj.* —**Pro·tag′o·re′an·ism,** *n.*

pro·ta·mine (prō′tə mēn′, -min), *n.* *Biochem.* any of a group of basic, simple proteins that do not coagulate by heat, are soluble in ammonia, and upon hydrolysis form amino acids.

prot·an·o·pi·a (prōt′ᵊnō′pē ə), *n.* *Ophthalm.* a defect of vision in which the retina fails to respond to red. [< NL; see PROT-, AN-[1], -OPIA] —**prot·a·nop·ic** (prōt′ᵊnop′ik), *adj.*

prot·a·sis (prot′ə sis), *n., pl.* **-ses** (-sēz′). **1.** the clause expressing the condition in a conditional sentence, in English usually beginning with *if.* Cf. **apodosis.** **2.** the first part of an ancient drama, in which the characters are introduced and the subject is proposed. Cf. **catastasis, catastrophe** (def. 4), **epitasis.** [< L < Gk: proposition, lit., a stretching forward = *pro-* PRO-[2] + *tásis* a stretching (*ta-,* verbid s. of *teínein* to stretch + *-sis* -SIS)]

pro·te·an (prō′tē ən, prō tē′-), *adj.* **1.** readily assuming different forms or characters; variable. **2.** (of an actor) versatile. **3.** (*cap.*) of, pertaining to, or suggestive of Proteus.

pro·te·ase (prō′tē ās′), *n.* *Biochem.* any enzyme that acts upon proteins. [PROTE(IN) + -ASE]

pro·tect (prə tekt′), *v.t.* **1.** to defend or guard from attack, loss, insult, etc.; cover or shield from injury or danger. **2.** *Econ.* to guard or promote the growth of (a native industry) by a protective tariff. **3.** *Com.* to provide funds for the payment of (a draft, note, etc.). —*v.i.* **4.** to provide, or be capable of providing, protection. [< L *prōtect(us),* ptp. of *prōtegere* to cover in front = *prō-* PRO-[1] + *tegere* to cover; akin to TOGA, THATCH] —**Syn. 1.** screen, shelter. See **defend.** —**Ant. 1.** attack.

pro·tect·ing (prə tek′ting), *adj.* providing protection or shelter. —**pro·tect′ing·ly,** *adv.* —**pro·tect′ing·ness,** *n.*

pro·tec·tion (prə tek′shən), *n.* **1.** the act of protecting. **2.** the state of being protected. **3.** a thing, person, or group that protects. **4.** patronage. **5.** *Insurance.* coverage (def. 1). **6.** *Informal.* bribe money paid to avoid violence or prosecution. **7.** *Econ.* **a.** the system of fostering or developing home industries through duties imposed on competitive imports. **b.** Also called **protectionism.** the theory or practice of this system. **8.** a document that assures safety from harm, delay, or the like, for the person, persons, or property specified in it. [ME *proteccio(u)n* < LL *prōtectiōn-* (s. of *prōtectiō*) a covering in front] —**pro·tec′tion·al,** *adj.* —**Syn. 2.** security, safety. **3.** guard, defense. **4.** aegis. **8.** pass, permit.

pro·tec·tion·ism (prə tek′shə niz′əm), *n.* protection (def. 7b). —**pro·tec′tion·ist,** *n.*

pro·tec·tive (prə tek′tiv), *adj.* **1.** having the quality or function of protecting. **2.** tending to protect. **3.** of, pertaining to, or designed for economic protection. —**pro·tec′tive·ly,** *adv.* —**pro·tec′tive·ness,** *n.*

protec′tive colora′tion, a coloration an organism assumes that makes it less visible to predators.

protec′tive tar′iff, a tariff for the protection of domestic production, rather than for revenue.

pro·tec·tor (prə tek′tər), *n.* **1.** a person or thing that protects; defender; guardian. **2.** *Eng. Hist.* **a.** (*cap.*) Also called **Lord Protector.** the title of the head of the government during the period of the Protectorate, held by Oliver Cromwell (1653–58) and by Richard Cromwell, his son (1658–59). **b.** regent (def. 1). Also, *referring to a woman,* **pro·tec·tress** (prə tek′tris). [< LL; r. ME *protectour* < MF] —**pro·tec′tor·al,** *adj.* —**pro·tec′tor·ship′,** *n.*

pro·tec·tor·ate (prə tek′tər it), *n.* **1.** the relation of a strong state toward a weaker state or territory that it protects and partly controls. **2.** a state or territory so protected. **3.** (*cap.*) the period (1653–59) during which England was governed by the Protector.

pro·tec·to·ry (prə tek′tə rē), *n., pl.* **-ries.** an institution for the care of homeless or delinquent children.

pro·té·gé (prō′tə zhā′, prō′tə zhā′), *n.* a person under the patronage or care of someone influential who can further his career. Also, *referring to a woman,* **pro′té·gée′.** [< F, n. use of ptp. of *protéger* to protect < L *prōtegere.* See PROTECT]

pro·tein (prō′tēn, -tē in), *n.* **1.** *Biochem.* any of a group of nitrogenous organic compounds of high molecular weight, synthesized by plants and animals, that upon hydrolysis by enzymes yield amino acids, and that are required for all life processes in animals. **2.** (formerly) a substance thought to be the essential nitrogenous component of all organic bodies. —*adj.* **3.** *Biochem.* of the nature of or containing protein. Also, **pro·teid** (prō′tēd, -tē id), **pro·tein·a·ceous** (prō′tē nā′shəs, -tē i nā′-), **pro·tein′ic, pro·tei′nous.** [< G *Protein* < Gk *prōteî(os)* primary + G *-in* -IN[2]; r. *proteine* < F]

pro·tein·ase (prō′tē nās′, -tē i-), *n.* *Biochem.* any of a group of enzymes that are capable of hydrolyzing proteins.

pro tem (prō tem′). See **pro tempore.**

pro tem·po·re (PRŌ tem′pō RE′; *Eng.* prō tem′pə rē′), *Latin.* **1.** temporarily; for the time being. **2.** temporary.

pro·te·ol·y·sis (prō′tē ol′i sis), *n.* *Biochem.* the hydrolysis, or breaking down, of proteins into simpler compounds, as in digestion. [*proteo-* (comb. form repr. PROTEIN) + -LYSIS] —**pro·te·o·lyt·ic** (prō′tē ə lit′ik), *adj.*

pro·te·ose (prō′tē ōs′), *n.* *Biochem.* any of a class of soluble compounds derived from proteins by the action of the gastric juices, pancreatic juices, etc. [PROTE(IN) + -OSE[2]]

protero-, a learned borrowing from Greek meaning "earlier," "before," "former," used in the formation of compound words: *Proterozoic.* Also, *esp. before a vowel,* **proter-.** Cf. **proto-.** [< Gk, comb. form repr. *próteros,* comp. formed from *pró;* see PRO-[2]]

Prot·er·o·zo·ic (prot′ər ə zō′ik, prō′tər-), *Geol.* —*adj.* **1.** noting or pertaining to a period of the Precambrian era, occurring from 600,000,000 to about 1,500,000,000 years ago, characterized by the appearance of bacteria and marine

pro·suf′frage, *adj.* **pro′su·per·vi′sion,** *adj.* **pro′sur·ren′der,** *adj.* **pro·syn′di·cal·ism,** *n.*

algae; Algonkian. See table at **era.** —*n.* **2.** the Proterozoic period or system; Algonkian.

pro·test (*n.* prō′test; *v.* prə test′), *n.* **1.** an expression or declaration of objection, disapproval, or dissent. **2.** *Com.* a formal notarial certificate attesting the fact that a check, note, or bill of exchange has been presented for acceptance or payment and has been refused. **3.** *Law.* **a.** a formal statement disputing the legality of a demand for tax money or the like, made upon payment. **b.** a declaration that damage suffered by a ship's cargo is due solely to perils of the sea. **4.** *Sports.* a formal objection or complaint made to an official. —*v.i.* **5.** to give manifest expression to objection or disapproval; remonstrate. **6.** to make solemn or earnest declaration. —*v.t.* **7.** to make a protest or remonstrance against. **8.** to say in protest or remonstrance. **9.** to declare solemnly or earnestly. **10.** to make a formal notarial protest of (a bill of exchange or note). **11.** *Obs.* to call to witness. [(n.) ME < MF (now *protêt*); (v.) late ME *protest(e)* < MF *protester* < L *prōtestārī* to declare publicly = *pro-* PRO-[1] + *testārī* to testify < *testis* a witness] —**pro·test′a·ble,** *adj.* —**pro·test′er,** *n.* —**pro·test′ing·ly,** *adv.* —**Syn. 5.** complain. **6.** avow, attest. See **declare.**

Prot·es·tant (prot′i stənt), *n.* **1.** any Western Christian not an adherent of the Roman Catholic Church. **2.** any of the German princes who protested against the decision of the Diet of Speyer in 1529, which had denounced the Reformation. **3.** (*l.c.*) a person who protests. —*adj.* **4.** belonging or pertaining to Protestants or their religion. **5.** (*l.c.*) protesting. [sing. of *protestants* for L *prōtestantēs,* pl. of prp. of *prōtestārī* to bear public witness]

Prot′estant Epis′copal Church′, a church in the U.S. descended from the Church of England.

Prot·es·tant·ism (prot′i stən tiz′əm), *n.* **1.** the religion of Protestants. **2.** the Protestant churches collectively. **3.** adherence to Protestant principles.

prot·es·ta·tion (prot′i stā′shən, prō′ti-), *n.* **1.** the act of protesting or affirming. **2.** a solemn or earnest declaration or affirmation. **3.** formal expression or declaration of objection, dissent, or disapproval; protest. [ME *protestacio(u)n* < LL *prōtestātiōn-* (s. of *prōtestātiō*) declaration]

Pro·te·us (prō′tē əs, -tyōōs), *n.* **1.** *Class. Myth.* a sea god, son of Oceanus and Tethys, noted for his ability to assume different forms and to prophesy. **2.** a person or thing that readily changes appearance, character, principles, etc.

pro·tha·la·mi·on (prō′thə lā′mē on′, -ən), *n., pl.* **-mi·a** (-mē ə). a song or poem written to celebrate a marriage. [PRO-[2] + (EPI)THALAMION; coined by Edmund Spenser]

pro·tha·la·mi·um (prō′thə lā′mē əm), *n., pl.* **-mi·a** (-mē ə). prothalamion.

pro·thal·li·um (prō thal′ē əm), *n., pl.* **-thal·li·a** (-thal′ē ə.) **1.** *Bot.* the gametophyte of ferns and related plants. **2.** the analogous rudimentary gametophyte of seed-bearing plants. [< NL < Gk *pro-* PRO-[2] + *thallion,* dim. of *thallós* young shoot] —**pro·thal′li·al, pro·thal′lic, pro·thal·line** (prō thal′ēn, -īn), *adj.* —**pro·thal′loid,** *adj.*

pro·thal·lus (prō thal′əs), *n., pl.* **-thal·li** (-thal′ī). *Bot.* prothallium. [< NL]

proth·e·sis (proth′i sis), *n.* **1.** the addition of a sound or syllable at the beginning of a word. **2.** *Eastern Ch.* the preparation and preliminary oblation of the Eucharistic elements. [< LL < Gk: a putting before] —**pro·thet·ic** (prə thet′ik), *adj.* —**pro·thet′i·cal·ly,** *adv.*

pro·thon·o·tar·y (prō thon′ə ter′ē, prō′thə nō′tə rē), *n., pl.* **-tar·ies. 1.** a chief clerk or official in certain courts of law. **2.** *Rom. Cath. Ch.* **a.** one of a body of officials in the papal curia assigned solemn clerical duties. **b.** an honorary title for certain prelates. **3.** *Gk. Orth. Ch.* the chief secretary of the patriarch of Constantinople. Also, **protonotary.** [< ML *prōthonotārius*), LL *prōtonotārius.* See PROTO-, NOTARY] —**pro·thon·o·tar·i·al** (prō thon′ə târ′ē əl), *adj.*

pro·tho·rax (prō thôr′aks, -thôr′-), *n., pl.* **-tho·rax·es, -tho·ra·ces** (-thôr′ə sēz′, -thôr′-). the anterior division of the thorax of an insect, bearing the first pair of legs. [< NL] —**pro·tho·rac·ic** (prō′thō ras′ik, -thō-), *adj.*

pro·throm·bin (prō throm′bin), *n.* *Biochem.* one of the clotting factors in the blood, believed to be the protein changed by the body into thrombin. Also called **thrombogen.**

pro·tist (prō′tist), *n.* any organism of the group Protista. [< NL *Protist(a)* (pl.) < Gk *prṓtist(os)* the very first, superl. of *prôtos* first] —**pro·tis·tan** (prō tis′tən), *adj., n.* —**pro·tis′tic,** *adj.*

Pro·tis·ta (prə tis′tə), *n.pl.* a group of organisms including all the unicellular animals and plants. [< NL; see PROTIST]

pro·ti·um (prō′tē əm, -shē əm), *n.* *Chem.* the common isotope of hydrogen, of atomic weight 1.008. *Symbol:* H^1

proto-, a learned borrowing from Greek meaning "first," "foremost," "earliest form of," used in the formation of compound words (*protomartyr; protoplasm*), specialized in chemical terminology to denote the first of a series of compounds, or the one containing the minimum amount of an element. Also, *esp. before a vowel,* **prot-.** [< Gk, comb. form repr. *prôtos,* superl. formed from *pró;* see PRO-[2]]

pro·to·ac·tin·i·um (prō′tō ak tin′ē əm), *n.* *Chem.* protactinium.

pro·to·chor·date (prō′tō kôr′dāt), *n.* *Zool.* any of the nonvertebrate chordates, as the tunicates, cephalochordates, and hemichordates. [< NL *Protochordata* (pl.)]

pro·to·col (prō′tə kôl′, -kol′, -kōl′), *n.* **1.** the customs and regulations dealing with diplomatic formality, precedence, and etiquette. **2.** an original draft, minute, or record from which a document, esp. a treaty, is prepared. **3.** a supplementary international agreement. **4.** Also called **pro′tocol state′ment, pro′tocol sen′tence, pro′tocol proposi′tion.** *Philos.* a statement reporting an observation or experience in the most fundamental terms without interpretation: sometimes taken as the basis of empirical verification, as of scientific laws. —*v.i.* **5.** to draft or issue a protocol. [earlier *protocoll* < ML *prōtocoll(um)* < LGk *prōtókollon,* orig., a first leaf glued to the front of a manuscript and containing notes as to contents. See PROTO-, COLLOID] —**pro·to·col·ar** (prō′tə kol′ər), **pro′to·col′a·ry, pro′to·col′ic,** *adj.*

Pro·to-Ger·man·ic (prō′tō jər man′ik), *n.* **1.** the hypothetical ancestral language of the Germanic languages. —*adj.* **2.** of or pertaining to Proto-Germanic.

pro·to·hu·man (prō′tō hyōō′mən *or, often,* -yōō′-), *adj.* **1.** of, pertaining to, or like the early primates that had some human characteristics. —*n.* **2.** a protohuman animal.

Pro·to-In·do-Eu·ro·pe·an (prō′tō in′dō yŏŏr′ə pē′ən), *n.* Indo-European (def. 2).

pro·to·lan·guage (prō′tō lang′gwij, -lang′-), *n.* *Linguistics.* the hypothetically reconstructed or postulated parent form of a language or a group of related languages.

pro·to·lith·ic (prōt′ᵊlith′ik), *adj.* *Anthropol.* noting or pertaining to stone implements selected according to suitability of the form to a particular purpose without definite shaping on the part of the user.

pro·to·mar·tyr (prō′tō mär′tər), *n.* the first martyr in any cause. [late ME *prothomartyr* < ML *prōtomartyr* < Gk]

pro·ton (prō′ton), *n.* *Physics, Chem.* an elementary particle that is a fundamental constituent of all atomic nuclei having a positive charge equal in magnitude to that of the electron. [< Gk, neut. of *prôtos* first] —**pro·ton′ic,** *adj.*

pro·to·ne·ma (prō′tə nē′mə), *n., pl.* **-ma·ta** (-mə tə). *Bot.* a primary, usually filamentous structure produced by the germination of the spore in mosses and certain related plants, and upon which the leafy plant that bears the sexual organs arises as a lateral or terminal shoot. [< NL < Gk *prōto-* PROTO- + *nêma* thread] —**pro′to·ne′mal, pro·to·nem·a·tal** (prō′tə nem′ə tᵊl), *adj.* —**pro′to·nem′a·toid′,** *adj.*

pro·ton·o·tar·y (prō ton′ə ter′ē, prōt′ᵊnō′tə rē), *n., pl.* **-tar·ies.** prothonotary. —**pro·ton′o·tar′y·ship′,** *n.*

pro·to·path·ic (prō′tə path′ik), *adj.* *Physiol.* noting or pertaining to a general, nondiscriminating responsiveness to pain or temperature stimuli (opposed to *epicritic*). —**pro·top·a·thy** (prə top′ə thē), *n.*

pro·to·plasm (prō′tə plaz′əm), *n.* *Biol.* **1.** a typically translucent, colorless, semifluid, complex substance regarded as the physical basis of life, having the ability to sense and conduct stimuli and to metabolize; the living matter of all cells and tissues. **2.** (formerly) cytoplasm. [< NL *prōtoplasma*] —**pro′to·plas′mic, pro′to·plas′mal, pro·to·plas·mat·ic** (prō′tō plaz mat′ik), *adj.*

pro·to·plast (prō′tə plast′), *n.* **1.** *Biol.* **a.** the protoplasm within a cell considered as a fundamental entity. **b.** the primordial living unit or cell. **2.** a person or thing that is formed first; original; prototype. [< LL *prōtoplast(us)* the first man < Gk *prōtóplastos* formed first] —**pro′to·plas′tic,** *adj.*

pro·top·o·dite (prō top′ə dīt′), *n.* *Zool.* the basal portion of a biramous crustacean appendage. Also, **pro·to·pod** (prō′tə pod′). Cf. **endopodite.** —**pro·top·o·dit·ic** (prə top′ə dit′ik), *adj.*

pro·to·ste·le (prō′tə stē′lē, -stēl′), *n.* *Bot.* the solid stele of most roots, having a central core of xylem enclosed by phloem. —**pro·to·ste·lic** (prō′tə stē′lik), *adj.*

pro·to·troph·ic (prō′tə trof′ik), *adj.* **1.** (esp. of certain bacteria) requiring only inorganic substances for growth. **2.** (of certain microorganisms) requiring no specific nutriments for growth.

pro·to·type (prō′tə tīp′), *n.* **1.** the original or model on which something is based or formed. **2.** someone or something that serves as an example of its kind. **3.** something analogous to another thing of a later period. **4.** *Biol.* an archetype; a primitive form regarded as the basis of a group. [< NL *prōtotyp(on)* < Gk, n. use of neut. of *prōtótypos* original] —**pro′to·ty′pal, pro·to·typ·i·cal** (prō′tə tip′i kəl), **pro′to·typ′ic,** *adj.* —**pro′to·typ′i·cal·ly,** *adv.*

pro·tox·ide (prō tok′sīd, -sid), *n.* *Chem.* the oxide in a series of oxides having the smallest proportion of oxygen. Also, **pro·tox·id** (prō tok′sid).

Pro·to·zo·a (prō′tə zō′ə), *n.* the phylum comprising the protozoans. [< NL]

pro·to·zo·an (prō′tə zō′ən), *adj.* **1.** Also, **pro′to·zo′ic.** belonging or pertaining to the phylum *Protozoa,* comprising animals consisting of one cell or of a colony of like or similar cells. —*n.* **2.** any animal of the phylum *Protozoa.* [< NL *Protozo(a)* (see PROTO-, -ZOA) + -AN] —**pro′to·zo′al,** *adj.*

pro·to·zo·ol·o·gy (prō′tō zō ol′ə jē), *n.* the branch of zoology dealing with the protozoa. Also, **pro′to·zo·öl′o·gy.** —**pro·to·zo·o·log·i·cal, pro·to·zo·ö·log·i·cal** (prō′tə zō′ə loj′i kəl), *adj.* —**pro′to·zo·ol′o·gist, pro′to·zo·öl′o·gist,** *n.*

pro·to·zo·on (prō′tə zō′on, -ən), *n., pl.* **-zo·a** (-zō′ə). protozoan. [< NL, sing. of *Protozoa;* see PROTOZOAN] —**pro′to·zo′on·al,** *adj.*

pro·tract (prō trakt′), *v.t.* **1.** to draw out or lengthen in time; prolong. **2.** *Anat.* to extend or protrude. **3.** (in surveying, mathematics, etc.) to plot and draw (lines) with a scale and a protractor. [< L *prōtract(us)* drawn forth, prolonged (ptp. of *prōtrahere*)] —**pro·tract′ed·ly,** *adv.* —**pro·tract′ed·ness,** *n.* —**pro·tract′i·ble,** *adj.* —**pro·trac′tive,** *adj.* —**Syn. 1.** continue. See **lengthen.** —**Ant. 1.** curtail.

pro·trac·tile (prō trak′til), *adj.* capable of being protracted, lengthened, or protruded. —**pro′trac·til′i·ty,** *n.*

pro·trac·tion (prō trak′shən), *n.* **1.** the act of protracting. **2.** the state of being protracted. **3.** protrusion. **4.** something that is protracted. [< LL *prōtractiōn-* (s. of *prōtractiō*) prolongation]

pro·trac·tor (prō trak′tər), *n.* **1.** a person or thing that protracts. **2.** (in surveying, mathematics, etc.) an instrument having a graduated arc for plotting or measuring angles. **3.** *Anat.* a muscle which causes a part to protrude. [< ML]

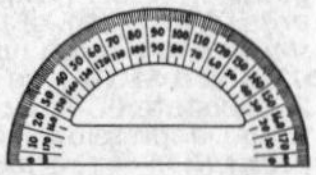

Protractor (def. 2)

pro·trude (prō trōōd′), *v.,* **-trud·ed, -trud·ing.** —*v.i.* **1.** to project. —*v.t.* **2.** to thrust forward; cause to project. [< L *prōtrūde(re)* (to) thrust forward = *prō-* PRO-[1] + *trūdere* to thrust] —**pro·trud′ent,** *adj.* —**pro·tru·si·ble** (prō trōō′sə bəl), **pro·trud′a·ble,** *adj.*

pro·tru·sile (prō trōō′sil), *adj.* capable of being thrust forth or extended, as the tongue of a hummingbird. [< L *prōtrūs(us)* (see PROTRUSION) + -ILE]

pro·tru·sion (prō trōō′zhən), *n.* **1.** the act of protruding. **2.** the state of being protruded. **3.** something that protrudes or projects. [< L *prōtrūs(us)* (ptp. of *prōtrūdere* to PROTRUDE) + -ION] —**Syn. 3.** projection, protuberance.

pro·tru·sive (prō trōō′siv), *adj.* **1.** projecting or protuberant. **2.** obtrusive. **3.** *Archaic.* pushing forward;

having propulsive force. [< L *prōtrūs(us)* (see PROTRUSION) + -IVE] —**pro·tru′sive·ly,** *adv.* —**pro·tru′sive·ness,** *n.*

pro·tu·ber·ance (prō to͞o′bər əns, -tyo͞o′-), *n.* **1.** the condition, state, or quality of being protuberant. **2.** a protuberant part or thing. [PROTUBER(ANT) + -ANCE] —**pro·tu·ber·an·tial** (prō to͞o′bə ran′shəl, -tyo͞o′-), *adj.* —**Syn. 2.** protrusion, swelling.

pro·tu·ber·an·cy (prō to͞o′bər ən sē, -tyo͞o′-), *n., pl.* **-cies.** protuberance. [PROTUBER(ANT) + -ANCY]

pro·tu·ber·ant (prō to͞o′bər ənt, -tyo͞o′-), *adj.* bulging out beyond the surrounding surface. [< LL *prōtūberant-* (s. of *prōtūberāns*), prp. of *prōtūberāre* to swell] —**pro·tu′ber·ant·ly,** *adv.*

pro·tyle (prō′tīl, -til), *n.* the hypothetical, primordial substance that supposedly differentiated into the chemical elements. Also, **pro·tyl** (prō′til). [irreg. < Gk *prōt-* PROT- + *hȳlē* material, matter]

proud (proud), *adj.* **1.** thinking well of oneself because of one's accomplishments, possessions, etc. **2.** feeling honored, as by a distinction conferred on one. **3.** governed in one's words or actions by self-respect. **4.** inclined to excessive self-esteem. **5.** promoting a feeling of pride: *a proud moment.* **6.** reflecting or suggesting pride. **7.** stately, majestic, or distinguished. **8.** *Obs.* brave. —*adv.* **9. do one proud, a.** to be a source of pride or credit to a person. **b.** to treat someone or oneself generously or lavishly. [ME; late OE *prūd* arrogant (c. Icel *prūthr* stately, fine), appar. < VL; cf. OF *prud, prod* gallant, LL *prōde* useful, L *prōdesse* to be of worth] —**proud′ly,** *adv.* —**proud′ness,** *n.*
—**Syn. 1.** contented, self-satisfied. **4.** overbearing, disdainful, imperious. PROUD, ARROGANT, HAUGHTY imply a consciousness of, or a belief in, one's superiority in some respect. PROUD implies sensitiveness, lofty self-respect, or jealous preservation of one's dignity, station, and the like. It may refer to an affectionate admiration of or a justifiable pride concerning someone else: *proud of his son.* ARROGANT applies to insolent or overbearing behavior, arising from an exaggerated belief in one's importance: *arrogant rudeness.* HAUGHTY implies lofty reserve and confident, often disdainful assumption of superiority over others: *the haughty manner of a debutante.* **7.** noble, splendid. —**Ant. 1.** dissatisfied. **4.** humble. **7.** mean; lowly.

proud′ flesh′, *Pathol.* See **granulation tissue.**

Prou·dhon (pro͞o dôN′), *n.* **Pierre Jo·seph** (pyer zhô-zef′), 1809–65, French socialist and writer.

Proust (pro͞ost), *n.* **Mar·cel** (MAR sel′), 1871–1922, French novelist. —**Proust′i·an,** *adj.*

proust·ite (pro͞o′stīt), *n.* *Mineral.* a mineral, silver arsenic sulfide, Ag_3AsS_3, occurring in crystals and masses: a minor ore of silver. [named after J. L. *Proust* (1754–1826), French chemist; see -ITE[1]]

Prov., **1.** Provençal. **2.** Provence. **3.** Proverbs. **4.** Province. **5.** Provost.

prov., **1.** province. **2.** provincial. **3.** provisional. **4.** provost.

prove (pro͞ov), *v.,* **proved, proved** or **prov·en, prov·ing.** —*v.t.* **1.** to establish the truth or genuineness of. **2.** to establish the quality of, as by a test or demonstration. **3.** *Law.* to establish the authenticity or validity of (a will); probate. **4.** to show (oneself) to have the character or ability expected of one. **5.** *Math.* to verify the correctness or validity of by mathematical demonstration or arithmetical proof. **6.** Also, **proof.** *Print.* to take a trial impression of (type, a cut, etc.). **7.** to cause (dough) to rise to the necessary lightness. **8.** *Archaic.* to experience. —*v.i.* **9.** to turn out: *The experiment proved to be successful.* **10.** to be found by trial or experience to be: *His story proved false.* [ME < OF *prove(r)* < L *probāre* to try, test, prove, approve < *prob(us)* good. See PROBITY] —**prov′a·bil′i·ty, prov′a·ble·ness,** *n.* —**prov′a·ble,** *adj.* —**prov′a·bly,** *adv.* —**prov′en·ly,** *adv.* —**Syn. 1.** demonstrate, confirm, substantiate, verify.

prov·e·nance (prov′ə nəns), *n.* a place of origin; source. [< F < *provenant,* prp. of *provenir* < L *prōvenīre* to come forth; see -ANCE, -ANT]

Pro·ven·çal (prō′vən säl′, prov′ən-; *Fr.* PRô väN SAL′), *adj.* **1.** of or pertaining to Provence, its people, or their language. —*n.* **2.** a native or inhabitant of Provence. **3.** a Romance language formerly widely spoken and written in southern France from the Alps to the Atlantic and still in use in some rural areas. *Abbr.:* Pr, Pr., Prov. Cf. **langue d'oc.** [< F < L *prōvinciāl(is)* PROVINCIAL]

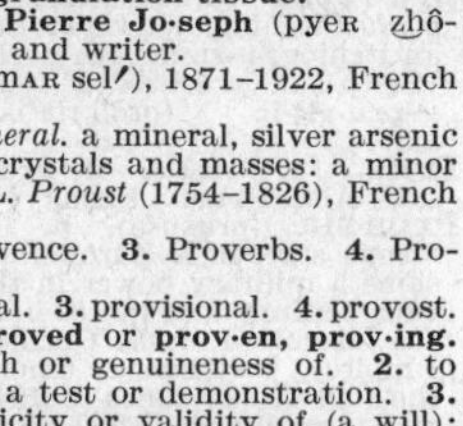

Pro·ven·çale (prō′vən säl′, prov′ən-; *Fr.* PRô väN SAL′), *adj.* *Cookery.* (*sometimes l.c.*) prepared with garlic or garlic and tomato. [< F; fem. of PROVENÇAL]

Pro·vence (PRô väNs′; *Eng.* prə väns′), *n.* a region in SE France, bordering on the Mediterranean: formerly a province; famous for medieval poetry and courtly traditions.

prov·en·der (prov′ən dər), *n.* **1.** dry food for livestock or other domestic animals. **2.** food; provisions. [ME *provendre* < OF, var. of *provende* prebend, provender < ML *prōbenda,* b. *praebenda* PREBEND and *prōvidēre* to look out for, PROVIDE] —**Syn. 1.** See **feed.**

pro·ve·ni·ence (prō vē′nē əns, -vēn′yəns), *n.* provenance; origin; source. [< L *prōveni(ent)-* (s. of *prōveniēns,* prp. of *prōvenīre* to come forth, arise) + -ENCE. See PROVENANCE]

pro·ven·tric·u·lus (prō′ven trik′yə ləs), *n., pl.* **-tric·u·li** (-trik′yə lī′). **1.** the glandular portion of the stomach of birds, in which food is partially digested before passing to the ventriculus or gizzard. **2.** a similar enlargement in the alimentary tract of several invertebrates. —**pro′ven·tric′u·lar,** *adj.*

prov·erb (prov′ərb), *n.* **1.** a short popular saying that expresses effectively some commonplace truth or useful thought. **2.** a person or thing that is commonly regarded as an embodiment or representation of some quality; byword. **3.** *Bible.* a profound saying, maxim, or oracular utterance requiring interpretation. —*v.t.* **4.** to make a byword of. [ME *proverbe* < MF < L *prōverb(ium)* adage = *prō-* PRO-[1] + *verb(um)* word + *-ium* collective suffix] —**Syn. 1.** aphorism, apothegm. PROVERB, MAXIM are terms for short, pithy sayings. A PROVERB is such a saying popularly known and repeated, usually expressing simply and concretely, though often metaphorically, a truth based on common sense or the practical experience of mankind: "*A stitch in time saves nine.*" A MAXIM is a brief statement of a general and practical truth, esp. one that serves as a rule of conduct or a precept: "*It is wise to risk no more than one can afford to lose.*"

pro·ver·bi·al (prə vûr′bē əl), *adj.* **1.** of, pertaining to, or characteristic of a proverb. **2.** expressed in or as in a proverb. **3.** being the subject of a proverb. **4.** well-known through frequent observation or mention: *poor as the proverbial church mouse.* [< L *prōverbiāl(is)*] —**pro·ver′bi·al·ly,** *adv.*

Prov·erbs (prov′ərbz), *n.* (*construed as sing.*) a book of the Bible, containing the sayings of sages.

pro·vide (prə vīd′), *v.,* **-vid·ed, -vid·ing.** —*v.t.* **1.** to furnish, supply, or equip. **2.** to afford or yield. **3.** *Law.* to arrange for or stipulate beforehand. **4.** *Archaic.* to prepare or procure beforehand. —*v.i.* **5.** to take measures with due foresight. **6.** to supply or allow means of sustenance (often fol. by *for*): *to provide for one's family.* [late ME *provide(n)* < L *prōvidē(re)* (to) foresee, look after, provide for = *prō-* PRO-[1] + *vidēre* to see] —**pro·vid′a·ble,** *adj.* —**pro·vid′er,** *n.*

pro·vid·ed (prə vī′did), *conj.* on the condition or understanding: *I'll go, provided he isn't there.* —**Syn.** granted. See **if.**

prov·i·dence (prov′i dəns), *n.* **1.** the foreseeing care and guardianship of God over His creatures. **2.** (*cap.*) God, esp. when conceived of as exercising this. **3.** a manifestation of divine care or direction. **4.** provident or prudent management of resources; prudence. [ME < L *prōvidentia* foresight, forethought. See PROVIDENT, -ENCE]

Prov·i·dence (prov′i dəns), *n.* a seaport in and the capital of Rhode Island, in the NE part, at the head of Narragansett Bay. 179,116 (1970).

prov·i·dent (prov′i dənt), *adj.* **1.** having or showing prudent foresight. **2.** characterized by or proceeding from foresight: *provident care.* **3.** mindful in making provision (usually fol. by *of*). **4.** economical; frugal; thrifty. [ME < L *prōvident-* (s. of *prōvidēns*), prp. of *prōvidēre.* See PROVIDE, -ENT] —**prov′i·dent·ly,** *adv.* —**prov′i·dent·ness,** *n.*

prov·i·den·tial (prov′i den′shəl), *adj.* of, pertaining to, or seeming to come from divine providence. [< L *prōvidenti(a)* PROVIDENCE + -AL[1]] —**prov′i·den′tial·ly,** *adv.*

pro·vid·ing (prə vī′ding), *conj.* on the condition or understanding; provided: *He can stay here providing he works.* [ME *provydyng*] —**Syn.** See **if.**

prov·ince (prov′ins), *n.* **1.** an administrative division or unit of a country. **2. the provinces,** the parts of a country outside of the capital or the largest cities. **3.** a country, territory, district, or region. **4.** *Geog.* an area lower in rank than a region. **5.** a particular sphere or field of activity or authority. **6.** an ecclesiastical territorial division. **7.** *Rom. Hist.* a country or territory administered by a governor sent from Rome. [ME < MF < L *prōvincia* province, official charge]

Prov·ince·town (prov′ins toun′), *n.* a resort town at the tip of Cape Cod, in SE Massachusetts: the first landing place of the Pilgrims in the New World 1620. 2836 (1970).

pro·vin·cial (prə vin′shəl), *adj.* **1.** belonging to a particular province. **2.** of or pertaining to the provinces. **3.** having or showing the manners, viewpoints, etc., considered characteristic of inhabitants of a province; unsophisticated; countrified; narrow or illiberal. **4.** (*cap.*) *Fine Arts.* noting or pertaining to the styles of architecture, furniture, etc., found in the provinces. —*n.* **5.** a person who lives in or comes from the provinces. **6.** a person who lacks urban sophistication or broad-mindedness. **7.** *Eccles.* **a.** the head of an ecclesiastical province. **b.** the presiding member of a religious order in a province. [ME < L *prōvinciāl(is)*] —**pro·vin′cial·ly,** *adv.*

pro·vin·cial·ism (prə vin′shə liz′əm), *n.* **1.** narrowness of mind, ignorance, or the like, considered as resulting from lack of exposure to cultural or intellectual activity. **2.** something, as a word or trait, that is characteristically provincial. **3.** devotion to the interests of one's own province rather than to the nation as a whole.

pro·vin·ci·al·i·ty (prə vin′shē al′i tē), *n., pl.* **-ties.** **1.** provincial character. **2.** a provincial characteristic.

prov′ing ground′, any place, context, or area for testing something, as scientific equipment or a theory.

pro·vi·sion (prə vizh′ən), *n.* **1.** the act of providing or supplying food or the like. **2. provisions,** a supply of food. **3.** an arrangement beforehand that provides for or against something. **4.** something that is provided. **5.** a formal or explicit statement of a condition demanded; proviso; stipulation. **6.** an appointment to an ecclesiastical office. —*v.t.* **7.** to supply with provisions. [ME < L *prōvisiōn-* (s. of *prōvisiō*) a foreseeing = *prōvīs(us)* (ptp. of *prōvidēre* to PROVIDE) + *-iōn-* -ION] —**pro·vi′sion·er,** *n.* —**pro·vi′sion·less,** *adj.* —**Syn. 1.** catering, purveying. **2.** store, stock.

pro·vi·sion·al (prə vizh′ə nəl), *adj.* Also, **pro·vi·sion·ar·y** (prə vizh′ə ner′ē). **1.** existing or serving only until permanently or properly replaced. **2.** accepted or adopted tentatively; conditional. —*n.* **3.** *Philately.* a stamp that is only valid temporarily. —**pro·vi′sion·al·ly,** *adv.*

pro·vi·so (prə vī′zō), *n., pl.* **-sos, -soes.** **1.** a clause in a statute, contract, or the like, by which a condition is introduced. **2.** a stipulation or condition. [late ME < ML *prōvīsō* (*quod*) it being provided (that), n. use of abl. neut. sing. of L *prōvīsus.* See PROVISION]

pro·vi·so·ry (prə vī′zə rē), *adj.* **1.** provisional. **2.** containing a proviso or condition; conditional. [< ML *prōvīsōri(us).* See PROVISION, -ORY[1]] —**pro·vi′so·ri·ly,** *adv.*

pro·vi·ta·min (prō vī′tə min), *n.* *Biochem.* a substance that an organism can transform into a vitamin, as carotene, which is converted to Vitamin A in the liver.

pro·un′ion, *adj.* **pro′-U·ni·tar′i·an,** *adj., n.* **pro′-U·nit′ed States′,** *adj.* **pro′u·ni·ver′si·ty,** *adj.*

Pro·vo (prō′vō), *n.* a city in central Utah. 53,131 (1970).

pro·vo·ca·teur (prō vok′ə to͝or′; *Fr.* prô vô ka tœr′), *n.* **1.** a person who provokes trouble, causes dissension, or the like; agitator. **2.** (*ital.*) See **agent provocateur.**

prov·o·ca·tion (prov′ə kā′shən), *n.* **1.** the act of provoking. **2.** something that incites, instigates, angers, or irritates. [ME < L *prōvocātiōn-* (s. of *prōvocātiō*) a calling forth = *prōvocāt(us)* (ptp. of *prōvocāre* to call forth) + *-iōn-* -ION] —**prov′o·ca′tion·al,** *adj.*

pro·voc·a·tive (prə vok′ə tiv), *adj.* tending or serving to provoke. [late ME < LL *prōvocātīv(us).* See PROVOCATION, -IVE] —**pro·voc′a·tive·ly,** *adv.* —**pro·voc′a·tive·ness,** *n.*

pro·voke (prə vōk′), *v.t.,* **-voked, -vok·ing. 1.** to anger, exasperate, or vex. **2.** to stir up, arouse, or call forth (feelings, desires, or activity). **3.** to incite or stimulate to action. **4.** to induce or bring about. **5.** *Obs.* to summon. [late ME < L *prōvoc(āre)* (to) call forth, challenge, provoke] —**pro·vok′er,** *n.* —**pro·vok′ing·ly,** *adv.* —**pro·vok′ing·ness,** *n.* —**Syn. 1.** annoy, aggravate, infuriate. See **irritate.** —**Ant. 1.** calm, propitiate.

pro·vo·lo·ne (prō′və lō′nē), *n.* a mellow, light-colored, Italian cheese, usually smoked after drying. Also called **pro′volo′ne cheese′.** [< It, aug. of *provola* kind of cheese]

prov·ost (prov′əst, prō′vōst *or, esp. in military usage,* prō′vō), *n.* **1.** a person appointed to superintend or preside. **2.** a high-ranking administrative officer of a college or university who has charge of the curriculum, faculty appointments, etc. **3.** *Eccles.* the chief dignitary of a cathedral or collegiate church. **4.** the steward or bailiff of a medieval manor. **5.** *Obs.* a prison keeper. [ME; OE *profost* < ML *prōposit(us),* lit., (one) placed before, president. See PRO-[1], POSIT] —**prov′ost·ship′,** *n.*

pro′vost court′ (prō′vō), a military court convened in occupied territory, empowered to try military personnel and civilians for minor offenses.

pro′vost guard′ (prō′vō), a detachment of soldiers assigned to police duties under the provost marshal. Cf. **military police.**

pro′vost mar′shal (prō′vō), **1.** *Army.* an officer on the staff of a commander, charged with police functions. **2.** *Navy.* an officer charged with the safekeeping of a prisoner pending trial by court-martial.

prow[1] (prou), *n.* the forepart of a ship or boat; bow. [< MF *proue* < dial. It (Genoese) *proa* < L *prōra* < Gk *prôira*]

prow[2] (prou), *adj.* *Archaic.* valiant. [ME < OF *prou* < LL **prōdis.* See PROUD]

prow·ess (prou′is), *n.* **1.** exceptional valor, bravery, or ability, in combat or battle. **2.** exceptional or superior ability. **3.** a valiant or daring deed. [ME *prowesse* < OF *proesse, proece* goodness, bravery = *prou,* earlier *prod* (see PROUD) + *-esse* < L *-itia* -ICE] —**prow′essed,** *adj.*

prowl (proul), *v.i.* **1.** to rove or go about stealthily, as in search of prey, plunder, etc. —*v.t.* **2.** to rove over or through (a place), as if seeking something. —*n.* **3.** the act of prowling. [ME *proll(en)* < ?] —**prowl′ing·ly,** *adv.* —**Syn. 1.** See **lurk.**

prowl′ car′. See **squad car.**

prowl·er (prou′lər), *n.* **1.** a person or animal that prowls. **2.** a person who goes stealthily about with some unlawful intention, as to commit a burglary or theft.

prox., proximo.

prox·i·mal (prok′sə məl), *adj.* situated toward the point of origin or attachment, as of a limb or bone. Cf. **distal.** [< L *proxim(us)* next (superl. of *prope* near) + -AL[1]] —**prox′i·mal·ly,** *adv.*

prox·i·mate (prok′sə mit), *adj.* **1.** immediately before or after in order. **2.** close; very near. **3.** approximate; fairly accurate. **4.** forthcoming; imminent. [< LL *proximāt(us),* ptp. of *proximāre* to near, approach. See PROXIMAL, -ATE[1]] —**prox′i·mate·ly,** *adv.* —**prox′i·mate·ness,** *n.* —**prox·i·ma·tion** (prok′sə mā′shən), *n.*

prox·im·i·ty (prok sim′i tē), *n.* nearness in place, time, order, occurrence, or relation. [late ME *proxymite* < L *proximitās* nearness, vicinity. See PROXIMAL, -ITY]

proxim′ity fuze′, a fuze for detonating a charge, as in a projectile, within a predesignated radius of a target.

prox·i·mo (prok′sə mō′), *adv.* in, of, or during the next month: *on the 10th proximo. Abbr:* prox. Cf. **instant** (def. 3), **ultimo.** [< L, abl. of *proximus* next. See PROXIMAL]

prox·y (prok′sē), *n., pl.* **prox·ies. 1.** the agency, function, or power of a person authorized to act as the deputy or substitute for another. **2.** the person so authorized. **3.** a written authorization empowering another person to vote or act for the signer. [ME *prokesye, procusie,* contr. of *procuracy* procuration. See PROCURE, -ACY]

prs., pairs.

prude (pro͞od), *n.* a person who is excessively proper or modest in speech, conduct, dress, etc. [< F: a prude (n.), prudish (adj.), short for *prudefemme,* OF *prodefeme* worthy or respectable woman. See PROUD, FEME]

pru·dence (pro͞od′ᵊns), *n.* **1.** the quality or fact of being prudent. **2.** caution with regard to practical matters. **3.** regard for one's own interests. **4.** provident care in the management of resources. [ME < MF < L *prūdentia*] —**Syn. 1.** PRUDENCE, FORESIGHT, FORETHOUGHT imply attempted provision against possible contingencies. PRUDENCE is care, caution, and good judgment, as well as wisdom in looking ahead: *sober prudence in handling one's affairs.* FORESIGHT implies a prudent looking ahead rather far into the future: *admirable foresight in planning.* FORETHOUGHT emphasizes the adequacy of preparation for the future: *Careful forethought prepared him for the emergency.* —**Ant. 1.** rashness.

pru·dent (pro͞od′ᵊnt), *adj.* **1.** judicious or wisely cautious in practical affairs. **2.** careful in providing for the future; provident. **3.** characterized by or proceeding from prudence. [ME < L *prūdent-* (s. of *prūdēns*), contr. of *prōvidēns* PROVIDENT] —**pru′dent·ly,** *adv.* —**Syn. 1.** sensible. **2.** economical, thrifty, saving. —**Ant. 1.** foolish. **2.** prodigal.

pru·den·tial (pro͞o den′shəl), *adj.* **1.** of, pertaining to, characterized by, or resulting from prudence. **2.** having discretionary or advisory authority, as in business matters. [< L *prūdenti(a)* PRUDENCE + -AL[1]] —**pru·den′tial·ly,** *adv.*

prud·er·y (pro͞o′də rē), *n.* **1.** excessive propriety or modesty in speech, conduct, etc. **2. pruderies,** prudish actions, phrases, or words. [< F *pruderie*]

Pru·d'hon (prʏ dôɴ′), *n.* **Pierre Paul** (pyer pôl), (*Pierre Prudon*), 1758–1823, French painter.

prud·ish (pro͞o′dish), *adj.* **1.** excessively proper or modest in speech, conduct, dress, etc. **2.** characteristic of a prude. —**prud′ish·ly,** *adv.* —**prud′ish·ness,** *n.* —**Syn. 1.** See **modest.**

pru·i·nose (pro͞o′ə nōs′), *adj.* *Bot., Zool.* covered with a frostlike bloom or powdery secretion, as a plant surface. [< L *pruīnōs(us)* frosty = *pruīn(a)* frost + *-ōsus* -OSE[1]]

prune[1] (pro͞on), *n.* **1.** a variety of plum that dries without spoiling. **2.** such a plum when dried. **3.** *Slang.* a dull, uninteresting person. [late ME < MF < L *prūna,* pl. (taken as sing.) of *prūnum* plum (*prūnus* plum tree) < Gk *proûnon,* var. of *proûmnon* PLUM[1]]

prune[2] (pro͞on), *v.t.,* **pruned, prun·ing. 1.** to cut or lop off (twigs, branches, or roots). **2.** to cut or lop superfluous or undesired twigs, branches, or roots from; trim. **3.** to rid or clear of (anything superfluous or undesirable). **4.** to remove (anything considered superfluous or undesirable). [late ME *prouyne(n)* < MF *proognie(r)* (to) prune (vines), var. of *provigner* < *provain* scion (< L *propāgin-,* s. of *propāgō;* see PROPAGATE) + *-er* inf. suffix] —**prun′a·ble,** *adj.*

prune[3] (pro͞on), *v.t.,* **pruned, prun·ing.** *Archaic.* to preen. [ME *prune(n), pruyne(n), proyne(n).* See PREEN[1]]

pru·nel·la (pro͞o nel′ə), *n.* a strong, lightweight worsted in a twill weave. Also, **prunelle, pru·nel·lo** (pro͞o nel′ō). [? special use of PRUNELLE, from the dark color of the cloth]

pru·nelle (pro͞o nel′), *n.* **1.** a plum-flavored liqueur. **2.** prunella. [< F, dim. of *prune* PRUNE[1]]

prun′ing hook′, an implement with a hooked blade, used for pruning vines, branches, etc.

prun′ing shears′, small, sturdy shears used for pruning shrubbery.

pru·ri·ent (pro͝or′ē ənt), *adj.* **1.** having or tending to have lascivious or lustful thoughts. **2.** causing lasciviousness or lust. [< L *prūrient-* (s. of *prūriēns*), prp. of *prūrīre* to itch] —**pru′ri·ence, pru′ri·en·cy,** *n.* —**pru′ri·ent·ly,** *adv.*

pru·rig·i·nous (pro͝o rij′ə nəs), *adj.* *Med.* itching. [< LL *prūrīginōs(us)* itchy, lascivious = *prūrīgin-* (s. of *prūrīgo*) PRURIGO + *-ōsus* -OUS]

pru·ri·go (pro͝o rī′gō), *n.* *Pathol.* a skin affection characterized by itching papules. [< L: an itching; see PRURIENT]

pru·ri·tus (pro͝o rī′təs), *n.* *Pathol.* itching. [< L *prūrītus* an itching, u-stem (4th decl), < ptp. of *prūrīre* to itch] —**pru·rit·ic** (pro͝o rit′ik), *adj.*

Prus., **1.** Prussia. **2.** Prussian. Also, **Pruss., Pruss**

Prus·sia (prush′ə), *n.* a former state in N Europe: became a military power in the 18th century and in 1871 led the formation of the German Empire; partitioned among the four Allied zones in 1945 and formally abolished as an administrative unit in 1947. German, **Preussen.** Cf. **East Prussia, West Prussia.**

Prus·sian (prush′ən), *adj.* **1.** of or pertaining to Prussia or its inhabitants. **2.** characterized by, exemplifying, or resembling Prussianism. —*n.* **3.** a native or inhabitant of Prussia. **4.** (originally) one of a Lettic people formerly inhabiting territory along and near the coast at the southeastern corner of the Baltic Sea. **5.** a Baltic language formerly spoken in Prussia; Old Prussian. *Abbr.:* Pruss

Prus′sian blue′, 1. a moderate to deep greenish blue. **2.** a dark-blue pigment, $Fe_4[Fe(CN)_6]_3$, used in painting, fabric printing, and laundry bluing.

prus·sian·ise (prush′ə nīz′), *v.t.,* **-ised, -is·ing.** (*sometimes cap.*) *Chiefly Brit.* prussianize. —**prus′sian·i·sa′tion,** *n.*

Prus·sian·ism (prush′ə niz′əm), *n.* the militaristic spirit, system, policies, or methods historically associated with the Prussians.

prus·sian·ize (prush′ə nīz′), *v.t.,* **-ized, -iz·ing.** (*sometimes cap.*) to make Prussian, as in character, method, or organization. Also, *esp. Brit.,* **prussianise.** —**prus′sian·i·za′tion,** *n.*

prus·si·ate (prush′ē āt′, -it, prus′-), *n.* *Chem.* **1.** a ferricyanide or ferrocyanide. **2.** a salt of prussic acid; a cyanide. [< F; see PRUSSI(C ACID), -ATE[2]]

prus′sic ac′id, *Chem.* See **hydrocyanic acid.** [< F *prussique,* lit., Prussian = *Prusse* PRUSSIA + *-ique* -IC] —**prus·sic** (prus′ik), *adj.*

Prut (pro͞ot), *n.* a river in E Europe, flowing SE from the Carpathian Mountains along the boundary between the Soviet Union and Rumania into the Danube. 500 mi. long. German, **Pruth** (pro͞ot).

pry[1] (prī), *v.i.,* **pried, pry·ing. 1.** to inquire impertinently into private matters. **2.** to look closely or curiously; peer. [ME *prye(n), prie(n)* < ?]

pry[2] (prī), *v.,* **pried, pry·ing.** *n., pl.* **pries.** —*v.t.* **1.** to raise, detach, or move by leverage. **2.** to obtain with difficulty, as information: *to pry a secret out of someone.* —*n.* **3.** a tool operating by means of leverage. **4.** the leverage exerted. [back formation from PRIZE[3], n. (taken as pl.)]

pry·er (prī′ər), *n.* prier.

pry·ing (prī′ing), *adj.* impertinently inquisitive; nosy. —**pry′ing·ly,** *adv.* —**pry′ing·ness,** *n.* —**Syn.** See **curious.**

Prynne (prin), *n.* **William,** 1600–69, English Puritan leader and pamphleteer.

Pry·peć′ (prĭ′pech), *n.* Polish name of the **Pripet.**

pryth·ee (prith′ē), *interj.* *Archaic.* prithee.

Prze·myśl (pshe′mishᵊl), *n.* a city in SE Poland: occupied by the Russians 1915. 49,000 (est. 1963).

ps, picosecond; picoseconds.

Ps., Psalm; Psalms. Also, **Psa.**

ps., **1.** pieces. **2.** pseudonym.

P.S., 1. permanent secretary. **2.** postscript. **3.** Privy Seal. **4.** Public School.

p.s., postscript.

psalm (säm), *n.* **1.** a sacred song or hymn. **2.** (*cap.*) any of the songs, hymns, or prayers contained in the Book of Psalms. **3.** a metric version or paraphrase of any of these. —*v.t.* **4.** to

pro·war′, *adj.* **pro-West′,** *adj.* **pro-West′ern,** *adj.* **pro-West′ern·er,** *n.*

sing, celebrate, or praise in psalms. [ME *psalme*, OE *ps(e)alm, sealm* < LL *psalm(us)* < Gk *psalmós* song sung to the harp, orig., a plucking as of strings, akin to *psállein* to twitch, play (the harp)] —**psalm′ic,** *adj.*

psalm·book (säm′bŏŏk′), *n.* a book containing psalms for liturgical or devotional use. [ME *salm boc*]

psalm·ist (sä′mist), *n.* **1.** the author of a psalm or psalms. **2. the Psalmist,** David, the traditional author of the Psalms. [< LL *psalmist(a)*]

psal·mo·dy (sä′mə dē, sal′mə-), *n., pl.* **-dies. 1.** psalms or hymns collectively. **2.** the act, practice, or art of singing these. [ME < LL *psalmōdia* < Rk *psalmōidía* singing to the harp] —**psal·mod·ic** (sä mod′ik, sal-), **psal·mod′i·cal, psal·mo·di·al** (sä mō′dē əl, sal-), *adj.* —**psal′mo·dist,** *n.*

Psalms (sämz), *n.* (*construed as sing.*) a book of the Bible, composed of 150 songs, hymns, and prayers.

Psal·ter (sôl′tər), *n.* **1.** the Book of Psalms. **2.** (*sometimes l.c.*) a book containing the Psalms for liturgical or devotional use. [< LL *psaltēr(ium)* the Psalter, L: a psaltery < Gk *psaltḗrion* stringed instrument; r. ME *sauter* (< AF) and OE *saltere* (< LL, as above)]

psal·te·ri·um (sôl tēr′ē əm, sal-), *n., pl.* **-te·ri·a** (-tēr′ē ə). *Zool.* the omasum. [< LL: the PSALTER, the folds of the omasum being likened to the leaves of a book] —**psal·te′ri·al,** *adj.*

psal·ter·y (sôl′tə rē), *n., pl.* **-ter·ies. 1.** an ancient musical instrument consisting of a flat sounding box with numerous strings which are plucked with the fingers or with a plectrum. **2.** (*cap.*) the Psalter. [< L *psaltērium* (see PSALTER); r. ME *sautrie* < OF]

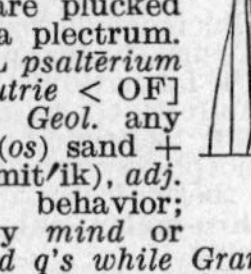

Psaltery

psam·mite (sam′īt), *n.* *Geol.* any sandstone. [< Gk *psámm(os)* sand + -ITE¹] —**psam·mit·ic** (sa mit′ik), *adj.*

p's and q's, manners; behavior; conduct (usually prec. by *mind* or *watch*): *Mind your p's and q's while Grandmother is here.* [? from children's difficulty in distinguishing the two letters]

PSAT, Preliminary Scholastic Aptitude Test.

PSC, Public Service Commission.

pschent (skent, pskent), *n.* the double crown of ancient Egyptian kings, symbolic of dominion over Upper and Lower Egypt. [< Egypt *p-shrenk*, lit., the double crown]

psec, picosecond; picoseconds.

pse·phite (sē′fīt, psē′-), *n.* *Geol.* any coarse rock, as breccia or conglomerate. [< Gk *psêph(os)* pebble + -ITE¹] —**pse·phit·ic** (sē fit′ik), *adj.*

pseud., pseudonym.

pseud·e·pig·ra·pha (sōō′də pig′rə fə), *n.* (*construed as pl.*) certain writings (other than the canonical books and the Apocrypha) professing to be Biblical in character. [< NL < Gk, neut. pl. of *pseudepígraphos* falsely inscribed, bearing a false title] —**pseud·ep·i·graph·ic** (sōō′dep ə graf′ik), **pseud′ep·i·graph′i·cal, pseud′e·pig′ra·phous,** *adj.*

pseu·do (sōō′dō), *adj.* false; counterfeit; spurious; sham; pretended. [ME: pretender; independent use of PSEUDO-]

pseudo-, a learned borrowing from Greek meaning "false," "pretended," "unreal," used in the formation of compound words (*pseudoclassic*): in scientific use, denoting deceptive resemblance to the following element (*pseudomorph*), and used often in chemical names of isomers. Also, *esp. before a vowel,* **pseud-.** [< Gk, comb. form of *pseudḗs* false]

pseu·do·a·quat·ic (sōō′dō ə kwat′ik, -kwot′-), *adj.* not aquatic but indigenous to moist regions.

pseu·do·carp (sōō′də kärp′), *n.* *Bot.* a fruit that includes parts in addition to the mature ovary and its contents, as the apple or pineapple. —**pseu′do·car′pous,** *adj.*

pseu·do-code (sōō′dō kōd′), *n.* *Computer Technol.* a program code unrelated to the hardware of a particular computer and requiring conversion to the code used by the computer before the program can be used.

pseu·do-in·tel·lec·tu·al (sōō′dō in′tᵊlek′chōō əl), *n.* **1.** a person exhibiting intellectual pretensions that have no basis in sound scholarship. **2.** a person who pretends an interest in intellectual matters for reasons of status.

pseu·do·morph (sōō′də môrf′), *n.* **1.** an irregular or unclassifiable form. **2.** a mineral having the outward appearance of another mineral that it has replaced by chemical action. —**pseu′do·mor′phic, pseu′do·mor′phous,** *adj.* —**pseu′do·mor′phism,** *n.*

pseu·do·nym (sōōd′ᵊnim), *n.* a fictitious name used by an author to conceal his identity; pen name. Cf. **allonym** (def. 1). [< Gk *pseudṓnym(on)* false name] —**Syn.** nom de plume.

pseu·do·nym·i·ty (sōōd′ᵊnim′i tē), *n.* **1.** pseudonymous character. **2.** the use of a pseudonym.

pseu·don·y·mous (sōō don′ə məs), *adj.* **1.** bearing a false or fictitious name. **2.** writing or written under a fictitious name. [< Gk *pseudṓnymos*] —**pseu·don′y·mous·ly,** *adv.*

pseu·do·po·di·um (sōō′də pō′dē əm), *n., pl.* **-di·a** (-dē ə). a temporary protrusion of the protoplasm of a protozoan, serving as an organ of locomotion, prehension, etc. Also, **pseu·do·pod** (sōō′də pod′), **pseu·do·pode** (sōō′də pōd′). [< NL] —**pseu·dop·o·dal** (sōō dop′ə dᵊl), **pseu′do·po′di·al, pseu·do·pod·ic** (sōō′də pod′ik), *adj.*

psf, pounds per square foot. Also, **p.s.f.**

pshaw (shô), *interj.* **1.** (used to express impatience, contempt, disbelief, etc.) —*n.* **2.** an exclamation of "pshaw!" —*v.i.* **3.** to say "pshaw." —*v.t.* **4.** to say "pshaw" at or to.

psi (sī, psē), *n., pl.* **psis.** the 23rd letter of the Greek alphabet (Ψ, ψ). [< Gk]

psi, pounds per square inch. Also, **p.s.i.**

psia, pounds per square inch, absolute.

psid, pounds per square inch, differential.

psig, pounds per square inch, gauge.

psil·o·cy·bin (sil′ə sī′bin, sī′lə-), *n.* *Pharm.* a crystalline solid, $C_{13}H_{18}O_3N_2P_2$, obtained from the mushroom *Psilocybe mexicana*, having a psychedelic effect. [< NL *Psilocyb(e)* kind of mushroom (< Gk *psīló(s)* bare + *kýbē* head) + -IN²]

psi·lom·e·lane (sī lom′ə lān′), *n.* a common mineral consisting of various impure manganese compounds: an ore of manganese. [< Gk *psīló(s)* bare, smooth + *mélan*, neut. of *mélas* black] —**psi·lo·me·lan·ic** (sī′lə mə lan′ik), *adj.*

Psi·lo·ri·ti (*Gk.* psē′lô rē′tē), *n.* **Mount,** modern name of Mount Ida.

psit·ta·co·sis (sit′ə kō′sis), *n.* *Pathol.* a severe infectious disease of birds and transmissible to man, characterized by high fever and pulmonary involvement; parrot fever. [< L *psittac(us)* parrot (< Gk *psittakós*) + -OSIS]

Pskov (pskôf), *n.* **1.** a lake in the W Soviet Union in Europe, forming the S part of Lake Peipus. **2.** a city near this lake. 105,000 (est. 1964).

pso·ra·le·a (sə rā′lē ə, sô-), *n.* any leguminous plant of the genus *Psoralea*, esp. the breadroot, *P. esculenta.* [< NL (genus name) < Gk, neut. pl. of *psōraléos* mangy, with reference to the glandular dots on the plant; see PSORIASIS]

pso·ri·a·sis (sə rī′ə sis), *n.* *Pathol.* a chronic skin disease characterized by scaly patches. [< NL < Gk *psōr(a)* itch + *-iasis* -IASIS] —**pso·ri·at·ic** (sôr′ē at′ik, sôr′-), *adj.*

P.SS., postscripts. Also, **p.ss.** [< L *postscripta*]

psst (pst), *interj.* (used to attract someone's attention.)

PST, Pacific Standard Time. Also, **P.S.T.**

psych (sīk), *v.t.*, **psyched, psych·ing.** *Slang.* to intimidate or frighten psychologically, or make nervous (often fol. by *out*): *to psych out the competition.* [shortened form of PSYCHOANALYZE]

psych-, var. of **psycho-** before some vowels: *psychasthenia.*

psych., **1.** psychological. **2.** psychology.

psy·chas·the·ni·a (sī′kəs thē′nē ə, -thə nī′ə), *n.* **1.** *Pathol.* mental weakness or exhaustion. **2.** *Psychiatry, Obs.* a neurosis marked by fear, anxiety, phobias, etc. [< NL] —**psy·chas·then·ic** (sī′kəs then′ik), *adj.*

Psy·che (sī′kē), *n.* **1.** *Class. Myth.* a personification of the soul in the form of a beautiful girl who was loved by Eros. **2.** (*l.c.*) the human soul, spirit, or mind. **3.** (*l.c.*) *Psychol., Psychoanal.* the mental or psychological structure of a person, esp. as a motive force. [< L < Gk: lit., breath < *psȳ́ch(ein)* (to) breathe, blow, hence, live]

psych·e·del·ic (sī′ki del′ik), *adj.* **1.** of or noting a mental state characterized by a profound sense of intensified sensory perception, sometimes accompanied by severe perceptual distortion and hallucinations and by extreme feelings of either euphoria or despair. **2.** of or noting any of various drugs producing this state, as LSD, mescaline, or psilocybin. **3.** resembling, characteristic of, or reproducing images, sounds, or the like experienced while in such a state: *a psychedelic painting.* —*n.* **4.** a psychedelic drug. Also, **psychodelic.** [PSYCHE + Gk *dêl(os)* visible, manifest, evident + -IC] —**psych′e·del′i·cal·ly,** *adv.*

psy·chi·a·trist (si kī′ə trist, sī-), *n.* a physician who practices psychiatry.

psy·chi·a·try (si kī′ə trē, sī-), *n.* the practice or the science of treating mental disorders. —**psy·chi·at·ric** (sī′kē a′trik), **psy′chi·at′ri·cal,** *adj.* —**psy′chi·at′ri·cal·ly,** *adv.*

psy·chic (sī′kik), *adj.* Also, **psy′chi·cal. 1.** of or pertaining to the human soul or mind; mental (opposed to *physical*). **2.** *Psychol.* pertaining to or noting mental phenomena originating outside of, or independently of, normal physiological processes. **3.** outside of natural or scientific knowledge; spiritual. **4.** of, pertaining to, associated with, attributed to, or caused by some nonphysical, apparently supernatural, force or agency. **5.** specially sensitive to the influence of such forces or agencies. —*n.* **6.** a person who is specially sensitive to psychic influences or forces; medium. [< Gk *psȳchik(ós)* of the soul. See PSYCHE, -IC] —**psy′chi·cal·ly,** *adv.*

psy′chic en′ergizer, *Med.* any of a class of drugs used in the treatment of mental depression; antidepressant.

psy·cho (sī′kō), *n., pl.* **-chos,** *adj.* *Slang.* —*n.* **1.** a psychopathic or neurotic person. —*adj.* **2.** psychopathic; psychoneurotic. [shortened form]

psycho-, a learned borrowing from Greek, used to represent **psyche** (*psychological*) and **psychological** (*psychoanalysis*) in compound words. Also, *esp. before a vowel,* **psych-.** [< Gk, comb. form of *psȳchḗ* breath, spirit, mind]

psychoanal., psychoanalysis.

psy·cho·a·nal·y·sis (sī′kō ə nal′i sis), *n.* **1.** a systematic structure of theories concerning the relation of conscious and unconscious psychological processes. **2.** a technical procedure for investigating unconscious mental processes and for treating psychoneuroses. [< G *Psychoanalyse*] —**psy·cho·an·a·lyt·ic** (sī′kō an′ᵊlit′ik), **psy′cho·an′a·lyt′i·cal,** *adj.* —**psy′cho·an′a·lyt′i·cal·ly,** *adv.*

pseu′do-A·mer′i·can, *adj.*
pseu′do·an·tique′, *adj.*
pseu′do·ar·cha′ic, *adj.*
pseu′do·a·ris′to·crat′ic, *adj.*
pseu′do·ar·tis′tic, *adj.*
pseu′do·bi′o·graph′i·cal, *adj.*
pseu′do-Bo·he′mi·an, *adj.*
pseu′do·clas′sic, *adj.*
pseu′do·clas′si·cal, *adj.*
pseu′do·clas′si·cism, *n.*
pseu′do·col·le′giate, *adj.*
pseu′do·con·serv′a·tive, *adj.*; **-ly,** *adv.*
pseu′do·cul′ti·vat′ed, *adj.*
pseu′do·cul′tur·al, *adj.*
pseu′do·dem′o·crat′ic, *adj.*
pseu′do-E·gyp′tian, *adj.*
pseu′do-E·liz′a·be′than, *adj.*
pseu′do-Eng′lish, *adj.*
pseu′do-French′, *adj.*
pseu′do·gen·teel′, *adj.*
pseu′do-Geor′gian, *adj.*
pseu′do-Ger′man, *adj.*
pseu′do-Goth′ic, *adj.*
pseu′do-Gre′cian, *adj.*
pseu′do-Greek′, *adj.*
pseu′do·gy′rate, *adj.*
pseu′do·he·ro′ic, *adj.*
pseu′do·his·tor′ic, *adj.*
pseu′do·his·tor′i·cal, *adj.*
pseu′do-I·tal′ian, *adj.*
pseu′do·leg′end·ar′y, *adj.*
pseu′do·lib′er·al, *adj.*
pseu′do·lit′er·ar′y, *adj.*
pseu′do·me′di·e′val, *adj.*
pseu′do·mod′ern, *adj.*
pseu′do·mod′est, *adj.*; **-ly,** *adv.*
pseu′do·myth′i·cal, *adj.*
pseu′do·o′ri·en′tal, *adj.*
pseu′do·or′tho·rhom′bic, *adj.*
pseu′do·pa′gan, *adj.*
pseu′do·pa′tri·ot′ic, *adj.*
pseu′do·phil′o·soph′i·cal, *adj.*
pseu′do·pro·fes′sion·al, *adj.*
pseu′do·psy′cho·log′i·cal, *adj.*
pseu′do-Ro′man, *adj.*
pseu′do·schol′ar·ly, *adj.*
pseu′do·sci′en·tif′ic, *adj.*
pseu′do·so′cial·is′tic, *adj.*
pseu′do-Span′ish, *adj.*
pseu′do-Vic·to′ri·an, *adj.*
pseu′do·vis′cous, *adj.*

psy·cho·an·a·lyst (sī′kō an′əlist), *n.* a person trained to practice psychoanalysis.
psy·cho·an·a·lyze (sī′kō an′əlīz′), *v.t.*, **-lyzed, -lyz·ing.** to investigate or treat by psychoanalysis.
psy·cho·bi·ol·o·gy (sī′kō bī ol′ə jē), *n.* the study of the relations or interactions between body and mind, esp. as exhibited in the nervous system. [< G *Psychobiologie*] —**psy·cho·bi·o·log·i·cal** (sī′kō bī′ə loj′i kəl), **psy′cho·bi′o·log′ic,** *adj.* —**psy′cho·bi·ol′o·gist,** *n.*
psy·cho·del·ic (sī′kō del′ik), *adj.* psychedelic.
psy·cho·dra·ma (sī′kō drä′mə, -dram′ə). a method of group psychotherapy in which patients take roles in improvisational dramatizations of emotionally charged situations.
psy·cho·dy·nam·ics (sī′kō dī nam′iks), *n.* (*construed as sing.*) *Psychol.* the systematic study of personality in terms of past and present experiences as related to motivation.
psy·cho·gen·e·sis (sī′kō jen′i sis), *n.* **1.** genesis of the psyche. **2.** *Psychol.* the origin of physical or psychological states out of the interplay of conscious and unconscious psychological forces. **3.** *Pathol.* the origin of symptoms as a result of emotional causes. [< NL] —**psy·cho·ge·net·ic** (sī′kō jə net′ik), *adj.* —**psy′cho·ge·net′i·cal·ly,** *adv.*
psy·cho·gen·ic (sī′kō jen′ik), *adj.* *Psychol.* originating in the mind or in a mental condition or process. [PSYCHOGEN(ESIS) + -IC]
psy·cho·graph (sī′kə graf′, -gräf′), *n.* **1.** *Psychol.* a graph indicating the relative strength of the personality traits of an individual. **2.** a psychologically oriented biography. —**psy·cho·graph·ic** (sī′kə graf′ik), *adj.* —**psy′cho·graph′i·cal·ly,** *adv.*
psychol., **1.** psychological. **2.** psychology.
psy·cho·lin·guis·tics (sī′kō ling gwis′tiks), *n.* (*construed as sing.*) the study of the relationships between language and the behavioral characteristics of the speaker. —**psy′cho·lin·guis′tic,** *adj.*
psy·cho·log·i·cal (sī′kə loj′i kəl), *adj.* **1.** of or pertaining to psychology. **2.** pertaining to the mind or to mental phenomena as the subject matter of psychology. **3.** of, pertaining to, dealing with, or affecting the mind, esp. as a function of awareness, feeling, or motivation. Also, **psy′cho·log′ic.** —**psy′cho·log′i·cal·ly,** *adv.*
psycholog′ical mo′ment, the proper or critical time for achieving a desired result.
psycholog′ical nov′el, a novel that focuses on the complex mental and emotional lives of its characters.
psy·chol·o·gise (sī kol′ə jīz′), *v.i.*, **-gised, -gis·ing.** *Chiefly Brit.* psychologize.
psy·chol·o·gism (sī kol′ə jiz′əm), *n.* *Usually Disparaging.* emphasis upon psychological factors in the development of a theory, as in history or philosophy.
psy·chol·o·gist (sī kol′ə jist), *n.* **1.** a specialist in psychology. —*adj.* **2.** Also, **psy·chol′o·gis′tic.** of or pertaining to psychologism.
psy·chol·o·gize (sī kol′ə jīz′), *v.i.*, **-gized, -giz·ing.** to make psychological investigations or speculations. Also, *esp. Brit.*, **psychologise.**
psy·chol·o·gy (sī kol′ə jē), *n.*, *pl.* **-gies.** **1.** the science of the mind or of mental states and processes. **2.** the science of human and animal behavior. **3.** the sum of the mental states and processes characteristic of a person or class of persons. [< NL *psȳchologia*]
psy·cho·met·rics (sī′kō me′triks), *n.* (*construed as sing.*) psychometry (def. 1).
psy·chom·e·try (sī kom′i trē), *n.* **1.** Also, **psychometrics.** *Psychol.* the measurement of mental traits, abilities, and processes. **2.** the alleged art or faculty of divining facts concerning an object or a person associated with it, by contact with or proximity to the object. —**psy′cho·met′ric, psy′cho·met′ri·cal,** *adj.* —**psy′cho·met′ri·cal·ly,** *adv.* —**psy·chom·e·tri·cian** (sī kom′i trish′ən), **psy·chom′e·trist,** *n.*
psy·cho·mo·tor (sī′kō mō′tər), *adj.* of or pertaining to a motor response caused by psychic processes.
psy·cho·neu·ro·sis (sī′kō nŏŏ rō′sis, -nyŏŏ-), *n.* an emotional disorder in which feelings of anxiety, obsessional thoughts, compulsive acts, and physical complaints without objective evidence of disease, in various patterns, dominate the personality. Also called **neurosis.** [< NL] —**psy·cho·neu·rot·ic** (sī′kō nŏŏ rot′ik, -nyŏŏ-), *adj.*, *n.*
psy·cho·path (sī′kə path′), *n.* **1.** a person who is mentally ill or unstable. **2.** See **psychopathic personality.**
psy·cho·path·ic (sī′kə path′ik), *adj.* of, pertaining to, or affected with psychopathy.
psychopath′ic personal′ity, *Psychiatry.* a type of personality characterized by amoral and antisocial behavior, lack of ability to establish meaningful personal relationships, extreme egocentricity, etc.
psy·cho·pa·thol·o·gy (sī′kō pə thol′ə jē), *n.* the science of diseases of the mind; mental pathology. —**psy·cho·path·o·log·i·cal** (sī′kō path′ə loj′i kəl), **psy′cho·path′o·log′ic,** *adj.* —**psy′cho·pa·thol′o·gist,** *n.*
psy·chop·a·thy (sī kop′ə thē), *n.* mental disease.
psy·cho·phar·ma·col·o·gy (sī′kō fär′mə kol′ə jē), *n.* the study of drugs that effect emotional and mental states.
psy·cho·phys·ics (sī′kō fiz′iks), *n.* (*construed as sing.*) the branch of psychology that deals with the relationships between physical stimuli and resulting sensations and mental states. [< G *Psychophysik*] —**psy·cho·phys·i·cal** (sī′kō fiz′i kəl), **psy′cho·phys′ic,** *adj.* —**psy′cho·phys′i·cal·ly,** *adv.* —**psy·cho·phys·i·cist** (sī′kō fiz′i sist), *n.*
psy·cho·phys·i·ol·o·gy (sī′kō fiz′ē ol′ə jē), *n.* the branch of physiology that deals with the interrelation of mental and physical phenomena. —**psy·cho·phys·i·o·log·i·cal** (sī′kō fiz′ē ə loj′i kəl), **psy′cho·phys′i·o·log′ic,** *adj.* —**psy′cho·phys′i·o·log′i·cal·ly,** *adv.* —**psy′cho·phys′i·ol′o·gist,** *n.*
psy·cho·pro·phy·lax·is (sī′kō prō′fə lak′sis, -prof′ə-), *n.* *Obstet.* a method by which an expectant mother is prepared for childbirth by psychological and physical conditioning, including education concerning labor and delivery, and breathing exercises. Also called **Lamaze′ technique′.** —**psy·cho·pro·phy·lac·tic** (sī′kō prō′fə lak′tik), *adj.*
psy·cho·sex·u·al (sī′kō sek′shŏŏ əl), *adj.* of or pertaining to the relationship of psychological and sexual phenomena. —**psy′cho·sex′u·al′i·ty,** *n.* —**psy′cho·sex′u·al·ly,** *adv.*
psy·cho·sis (sī kō′sis), *n.*, *pl.* **-ses** (-sēz). any major, severe form of mental disorder or disease affecting the total personality. [<LGk *psȳ́chōsis* animation, principle of life] —**psy·chot·ic** (sī kot′ik), *adj.*, *n.* —**Syn.** insanity.
psy·cho·so·cial (sī′kō sō′shəl), *adj.* of, pertaining to, or caused by both psychological and social factors.
psy·cho·so·mat·ic (sī′kō sō mat′ik, -sə-), *adj.* noting a physical disorder that is caused by or notably influenced by the emotional state of the patient.
psy′chosomat′ic med′icine, the application of psychology in the study and treatment of physical disorders.
psy·cho·so·mat·ics (sī′kō sō mat′iks, -sə-), *n.* (*construed as sing.*) See **psychosomatic medicine.**
psy·cho·sur·ger·y (sī′kō sûr′jə rē), *n.* treatment of mental diseases by means of brain surgery. Cf. **lobotomy.**
psy·cho·tech·nol·o·gy (sī′kō tek nol′ə jē), *n.* the body of knowledge, theories, and techniques developed for understanding and influencing individual, group, and societal behavior in specified situations. Also called **psy′cho·tech′nics.** —**psy·cho·tech·no·log·i·cal** (sī′kō tek′nəloj′i kəl), *adj.* —**psy′cho·tech·nol′o·gist,** *n.*
psy·cho·ther·a·peu·tics (sī′kō ther′ə pyŏŏ′tiks), *n.* (*construed as sing.*) psychotherapy. —**psy′cho·ther′a·peu′tic,** *adj.* —**psy′cho·ther′a·peu′ti·cal·ly,** *adv.* —**psy′cho·ther′a·peu′tist,** *n.*
psy·cho·ther·a·py (sī′kō ther′ə pē), *n.* the science or method of curing psychological abnormalities and disorders by psychological techniques, esp. by psychoanalysis, group therapy, or consultation. —**psy′cho·ther′a·pist,** *n.*
psy·chot·o·mi·met·ic (sī kot′ō mi met′ik), *adj.* (of a drug) tending to produce symptoms like those of a psychosis.
psy·cho·trop·ic (sī′kō trop′ik), *adj.* affecting mental activity, as a hallucinogenic drug.
psychro-, a learned borrowing from Greek meaning "cold," used in the formation of compound words: *psychrometer.* [comb. form repr. Gk *psȳchrós*]
psy·chrom·e·ter (sī krom′i tər), *n.* an instrument for determining atmospheric humidity consisting of a wet-bulb and a dry-bulb thermometer. —**psy·chro·met·ric** (sī′krə me′trik), **psy′chro·met′ri·cal,** *adj.*
Pt, *Chem.* platinum.
pt, pint; pints.
Pt., **1.** point. **2.** port.
pt., **1.** part. **2.** past tense. **3.** payment. **4.** pint; pints. **5.** point. **6.** port. **7.** preterit.
P.T., **1.** Pacific time. **2.** physical training.
p.t., **1.** Pacific time. **2.** past tense. **3.** pro tempore.
PTA, See **Parent-Teacher Association.** Also, **P.T.A.**
Pta., *pl.* **Ptas.** peseta.
Ptah (ptä, ptäкн), *n.* an ancient Egyptian deity, believed to be the creator of the universe and sometimes identified with other gods.
ptar·mi·gan (tär′mə gən), *n.*, *pl.* **-gans** (*esp. collectively*) **-gan.** any of several grouses of the genus *Lagopus,* of mountainous and cold northern regions, having feathered feet. [< Gael *tarmarchan,* appar. var. of Ir *tarmanach*]

Ptarmigan,
Lagopus lagopus
(Length 15 in.)

PT boat, *U.S.* a small, fast, lightly armed, unarmored, highly maneuverable boat used chiefly for torpedoing enemy shipping. Also called **mosquito boat.** [*p*(*atrol*) *t*(*orpedo*)]
pter-, var. of **ptero-** before a vowel.
-pter, var. of **ptero-** as final element of compound words: *hymenopter.*
pter·i·dol·o·gy (ter′i dol′ə jē), *n.* the branch of botany dealing with ferns and related plants, as horsetails and club mosses. [*pterido-* (comb. form repr. Gk *pterid-,* s. of *pterís* fern) + -LOGY] —**pter·i·do·log·i·cal** (ter′i dəloj′i kəl), *adj.* —**pter′i·dol′o·gist,** *n.*
pte·rid·o·phyte (tə rid′ə fīt′, ter′i dō fīt′), *n.* any plant of the division *Pteridophyta,* characterized by vascular tissue and differentiation into root, stem, and leaves, comprising the ferns, horsetails, and club mosses. [< NL *Pteridophyt*(*a*) = Gk *pterido-* (comb. form repr. Gk *pterís* fern) + *-phyta,* pl. of *-phyton* -PHYTE] —**pte·rid·o·phyt·ic** (tə rid′ə fit′ik, ter′i dō-), **pter·i·doph·y·tous** (ter′i dof′i təs), *adj.*
ptero-, a learned borrowing from Greek meaning "wing," "feather," used in the formation of compound words: *pterodactyl.* Also, **pter-, -pter.** [< NL, comb. form repr. Gk *pterón*]
pter·o·dac·tyl (ter′ə dak′til), *n.* any flying reptile of the extinct order *Pterosauria,* from the Jurassic and Cretaceous periods, having the outside digit of the forelimb greatly elongated and supporting a wing membrane. [< NL *Pterodactyl*(*us*), genus name] —**pter′o·dac·tyl′ic,** *adj.* —**pter′o·dac′tyl·id,** *adj.*, *n.* —**pter′o·dac′tyl·ous,** *adj.* —**pter′o·dac′tyl·oid′,** *adj.*

Pterodactyl,
genus *Pterodactylus*
(Wingspread 1 to 20 ft.)

pter·o·pod (ter′ə pod′), *adj.* **1.** belonging or pertaining to the *Pteropoda,* a group of mollusks which have the lateral portions of the foot expanded into winglike lobes. —*n.* **2.** a pteropod mollusk. [< NL *Pteropod*(*a*) (pl.) < Gk]
pter·o·saur (ter′ə sôr′), *n.* a pterodactyl. [< NL *Pterosaur*(*us*)]
-pterous, an element meaning "winged," used in the formation of adjectives: *dipterous.* [< Gk *-pteros,* comb. form akin to *pterón* wing]
pter·y·goid (ter′ə goid′), *adj.* **1.** winglike. **2.** *Anat.* of, pertaining to, or situated near the pterygoid process. —*n.* **3.** *Anat.* a pterygoid part, as a muscle or nerve. [< Gk *pterygoeid*(*ḗs*) = *pteryg-* (s. of *ptéryx*) wing, fin + *-oeidēs* -OID]
pter′ygoid proc′ess, *Anat.* a process on each side of the sphenoid bone, consisting of two plates separated by a notch.
pter·y·la (ter′ə lə), *n.*, *pl.* **-lae** (-lē′, -lī′). *Ornith.* one of the feathered areas on the skin of a bird. [< NL < Gk *pteró*(*n*) feather + *hýlē* wood]
ptg., printing.
P.T.O., please turn over (a page or leaf). Also, **p.t.o.**
Ptol·e·ma·ic (tol′ə mā′ik), *adj.* **1.** of or pertaining to Ptolemy or his system of astronomy. **2.** of or pertaining to

the Ptolemies or the period of their rule in Egypt. [< Gk *Ptolemaik(ós)*. See PTOLEMY, -IC]

Ptol′ema′ic sys′tem, *Astron.* a system elaborated by Ptolemy and subsequently modified by others, according to which the earth was the fixed center of the universe, with the heavenly bodies moving about it.

Ptol·e·my (tol′ə mē), *n., pl.* **-mies** for 2. **1.** (*Claudius Ptolemaeus*) fl. A.D. 127–151, Hellenistic mathematician, astronomer, and geographer in Alexandria. **2.** any of the kings or queens of the Macedonian dynasty which ruled Egypt 323–30 B.C.

Ptolemy I, (*Ptolemy Soter*) 367?–280 B.C., ruler of Egypt 323–285: founder of Macedonian dynasty in Egypt.

Ptolemy II, (*Ptolemy Philadelphus*) 309?–247? B.C., king of Egypt 285–247? (son of Ptolemy I).

pto·maine (tō′mān, tō mān′), *n.* any of a class of basic nitrogenous substances produced during putrefaction of animal or plant protein and that cause food poisoning. [< It *ptomaina* < Gk *ptôma* dead body + *-ina* -INE[2]] —**pto·main′ic,** *adj.*

pto′maine poi′soning, **1.** a toxic condition caused by the ingestion of a ptomaine. **2.** (erroneously) food poisoning.

pto·sis (tō′sis), *n. Pathol.* **1.** a drooping of the upper eyelid. **2.** prolapse or drooping of any organ. [< NL < Gk: a falling] —**pto·tic** (tō′tik), *adj.*

pts., **1.** parts. **2.** payments. **3.** pints. **4.** points. **5.** ports.

pty·a·lin (tī′ə lin), *n. Biochem.* an enzyme in the saliva of man and certain lower animals, possessing the property of converting starch into dextrin and maltose. [< Gk *ptýal(on)* spittle, saliva + -IN[2]]

pty·a·lism (tī′ə liz′əm), *n. Pathol.* excessive secretion of saliva. [< Gk *ptyalism(ós)* expectoration = *ptýal(on)* spittle + *-ismos* -ISM]

Pu, *Chem.* plutonium.

pub (pub), *n. Chiefly Brit. Informal.* a tavern. [short for PUBLIC HOUSE]

pub., **1.** public. **2.** publication. **3.** published. **4.** publisher. **5.** publishing.

pu·ber·ty (pyōō′bər tē), *n.* the period or age at which a person is first capable of sexual reproduction of offspring: in common law, presumed to be 14 years in the male and 12 years in the female. [ME *puberte* < L *pūbertās* adulthood = *pūber* grown-up + *-tās* -TY[2]]

pu·bes[1] (pyōō′bēz), *n., pl.* **pu·bes.** *Anat.* **1.** the lower part of the abdomen, esp. the region between the right and left iliac regions. **2.** the hair appearing on the lower part of the abdomen at puberty. [< L *pūbēs* pubic hair, groin]

pu·bes[2] (pyōō′bēz), *n.* pl. of **pubis.**

pu·bes·cent (pyōō bes′ənt), *adj.* **1.** arriving or arrived at puberty. **2.** *Bot., Zool.* covered with down or fine short hair. [< L *pūbescent-* (s. of *pūbescēns*), prp. of *pūbēscere* to attain puberty, reach puberty, become hairy or downy] —**pu·bes′cence, pu·bes′cen·cy,** *n.*

pu·bic (pyōō′bik), *adj.* of, pertaining to, or situated near the pubes or the pubis. [PUB(ES)[1] + -IC]

pu·bis (pyōō′bis), *n., pl.* **-bes** (-bēz). *Anat.* that part of either innominate bone that, with the corresponding part of the other, forms the front of the pelvis. [short for NL *os pūbis* bone of the PUBES[1]]

publ., **1.** published. **2.** publisher.

pub·lic (pub′lik), *adj.* **1.** of, pertaining to, or affecting a population or a community as a whole. **2.** open to all persons. **3.** owned by a community. **4.** performed on behalf of a community. **5.** serving a community, as an official. **6.** generally known, as a piece of information. **7.** familiar to the public, as a person; prominent. **8.** conducted in public: *to retire from public life.* **9.** intending good to the community: *public spirit.* **10.** *Rare.* of or pertaining to all mankind; universal. —*n.* **11.** the people constituting a community, state, or nation. **12.** a particular group of people having something in common: *the book-buying public.* **13. go public,** (of a corporation) to issue stock for sale to the public. **14. in public, a.** not in private; without concealment. **b.** so as to involve contact with the public. [< L *pūblic(us)* (earlier *pōblicus, pōplicus;* see PEOPLE, -IC); r. late ME *publique* < MF]

pub′lic account′ant, an accountant who offers his services to the public at large in contrast to one employed on a full-time basis by a company. —**pub′lic account′ing.**

pub′lic-ad·dress′ sys′tem (pub′lik ə dres′), a combination of electronic devices that makes sound audible, via loudspeakers, to many people, as in an auditorium or out of doors.

pub′lic affairs′, matters of general interest or concern, esp. those dealing with current social or political problems.

pub·li·can (pub′lə kən), *n.* **1.** *Brit. Informal.* a person who owns or manages a tavern; the keeper of a pub. **2.** *Rom. Hist.* a tax collector. [ME < L *pūblicān(us)*]

pub·li·ca·tion (pub′lə kā′shən), *n.* **1.** the act of publishing. **2.** the act of bringing to public notice. **3.** the state or fact of being published. **4.** something that is published, esp. a periodical. [ME *publicacioun* < L *pūblicātiōn-* (s. of *pūblicātiō*) a making public, confiscation = *pūblicāt(us)* made public, confiscated (ptp. of *pūblicāre*) + *-iōn-* -ION]

pub′lic charge′, a person who is in economic distress and is supported by government expense.

pub′lic conven′ience, *Chiefly Brit.* a rest room, esp. at a large public place, as at a railroad station.

pub′lic debt′. See **national debt.**

pub′lic defend′er, *U.S.* a lawyer employed by a city or county to represent indigents in criminal cases at public expense.

pub′lic domain′, *Law.* **1.** the status of a literary work or an invention whose copyright or patent has expired. **2.** land owned by the government.

pub′lic en′emy, **1.** a person who is a danger or menace to the public, usually as shown by his criminal record. **2.** a nation or government with which one's own is at war.

pub′lic house′, **1.** *Brit.* a tavern. **2.** an inn or hostelry.

pub·li·cist (pub′li sist), *n.* **1.** a press agent or public-relations man. **2.** a person who is expert in or writes on current public or political affairs. **3.** an expert in public or international law. [< G]

pub·lic·i·ty (pu blis′i tē), *n.* **1.** public notice resulting from mention through any means of communication, including word of mouth. **2.** the business or technique of attracting public attention to persons, products, etc. **3.** the material used for this purpose. **4.** the state of being open to general observation or knowledge. [< F *publicité* < ML *pūblicitās*]

pub·li·cize (pub′li sīz′), *v.t.,* **-cized, -ciz·ing.** to give publicity to; bring to public notice.

pub′lic law′, **1.** a law or statute of a general character that applies to the people of a whole state or nation. **2.** a branch of law dealing with the legal relationships between the state and individuals and with the relations among governmental agencies.

pub·lic·ly (pub′lik lē), *adv.* **1.** in a public or open manner. **2.** by the public. **3.** in the name of the community. **4.** by public action or consent.

pub·lic·ness (pub′lik nis), *n.* quality or state of being public or being owned by the public.

pub′lic opin′ion, the collective opinion of many people on some issue, problem, etc.

pub′lic-o·pin′ion poll′ (pub′lik ə pin′yən), a poll taken by sampling a cross section of the public, as to predict election results or to estimate public attitudes on issues.

pub′lic pros′ecutor, an officer charged with the conduct of criminal prosecution in the interest of the public.

pub′lic rela′tions, **1.** the efforts of a corporation to promote good will between itself and the public. **2.** the methods used to promote such good will.

pub′lic room′, (esp. in a hotel or ship) a lounge or other room that is open to all.

pub′lic school′, **1.** (in the U.S.) a school, usually for primary or secondary grades, that is maintained at public expense. **2.** (in England) any of a number of endowed boarding schools, esp. for boys, that prepare students for university study or public service. —**pub′lic-school′,** *adj.*

pub′lic serv′ant, a person holding a government office by election or appointment.

pub′lic serv′ice, **1.** the business of supplying an essential commodity or service to the general public. **2.** government employment, esp. in a branch of civil service. **3.** a service to the public rendered without charge by a profit-making organization.

pub′lic-serv′ice corpora′tion (pub′lik sûr′vis), a private or quasi-private corporation chartered to provide an essential commodity or service to the public.

pub·lic-spir·it·ed (pub′lik spir′i tid), *adj.* having or showing an unselfish interest in the public welfare.

pub′lic util′ity, a business enterprise performing an essential public service and regulated by the federal, state, or local government. —**pub′lic-u·til′i·ty,** *adj.*

pub′lic works′, structures, as roads, dams, or post offices, paid for by government funds for public use.

pub·lish (pub′lish), *v.t.* **1.** to issue (printed or otherwise reproduced textual or graphic material) for sale or distribution to the public. **2.** to issue publicly the work of (an author, artist, etc.). **3.** to announce formally or officially. **4.** to make publicly or generally known. —*v.i.* **5.** to engage in the publishing of textual or graphic material. **6.** (of an author) to have work published. [ME *publisshe* < AF *publiss-, long s. of *publir for MF *publier* < L *pūblicāre* to make PUBLIC] —**pub′lish·a·ble,** *adj.*

pub·lish·er (pub′li shər), *n.* **1.** a person or company whose business is the publishing of books, periodicals, engravings, or the like. **2.** the business head of a newspaper organization, commonly the owner or the representative of the owner.

pub·lish·ing (pub′li shing), *n.* the business or activity of a publisher. [ME *publyssynge*]

pub·lish·ment (pub′lish mənt), *n. Archaic.* publication.

Puc·ci·ni (pōō chē′nē; *It.* pōōt chē′nē), *n.* **Gia·co·mo** (jä′kô mô), 1858–1924, Italian operatic composer.

puc·coon (pə kōōn′), *n.* **1.** any of certain plants that yield a red dye, as the bloodroot and certain boraginaceous herbs of the genus *Lithospermum.* **2.** the dye itself. [< Algonquian (Va.); see POKE[4]]

puce (pyōōs), *n.* dark or brownish purple. [< F: lit., flea < L *pūlic-, s.* of *pūlex*]

puck (puk), *n. Ice Hockey.* a black disk of vulcanized rubber which is to be hit into the goal. [alter. of POKE[1]]

Puck (puk), *n.* a particularly mischievous sprite or fairy who appears as a character in Shakespeare's comedy, *A Midsummer Night's Dream.* Also called **Hobgoblin, Robin Goodfellow.** [ME *pouke,* OE *pūca;* c. Icel *pūki* a mischievous demon]

puck·er (puk′ər), *v.t., v.i.* **1.** to draw or gather into wrinkles or irregular folds, as material or a part of the face; constrict: *Worry puckered his brow.* —*n.* **2.** a wrinkle; an irregular fold. **3.** a puckered part, as of cloth tightly or crookedly sewn. **4.** *Archaic.* a state of agitation or perturbation. [appar. a freq. form connected with POKE[2]; see -ER[6] and for the meaning cf. PURSE] —**puck′er·er,** *n.* —**puck·er·y** (puk′ə rē), *adj.*

puck·ish (puk′ish), *adj.* (*often cap.*) mischievous; impish. [PUCK + -ISH[1]]

pud·ding (pŏŏd′ing), *n.* **1.** a thick, soft dessert, typically containing flour, milk, eggs, and sweetening, and sometimes garnished or mixed with fruit, preserves, etc. **2.** a similar dish, unsweetened and served as or with a main dish: *corn pudding.* [ME *poding* kind of sausage; cf. OE *puduc* wen, sore (? orig. swelling), LG *puddewurst* black pudding]

pud′ding stone′, *Geol.* conglomerate (def. 2).

pud·dle (pud′ᵊl), *n., v.,* **-dled, -dling.** —*n.* **1.** a small pool of water, esp. on the ground. **2.** a small pool of any liquid. **3.** an impervious mixture of clay and water. —*v.t.* **4.** to mark or scatter with puddles. **5.** to make (clay or the like) into puddle. **6.** *Metall.* to subject (molten iron) to the process of puddling. [ME *puddel, podel,* appar. dim. of OE *pudd* ditch, furrow; akin to LG *pudel* puddle] —**pud′dler,** *n.* —**pud′dly,** *adj.*

pud·dling (pud′ling), *n.* **1.** the act of a person or thing that puddles. **2.** *Metall.* the act or process of melting pig iron in a reverberatory furnace **(pud′dling fur′nace)** and refining it by ridding it of slag. **3.** the act or method of making puddle.

pu·den·cy (pyōōd′ᵊn sē), *n.* modesty; bashfulness;

shamefacedness. [< LL *pudentia* shame = L *pudent-* (s. of *pudēns*, prp. of *pudēre* to be ashamed) + *-ia* -Y[3]; see -ENCY]

pu·den·dum (pyo͞o den′dəm), *n., pl.* **-da** (-də). Usually, **pudenda.** *Anat.* the external genital organs, esp. those of the female; vulva. [< LL, special use of neut. of L *pudendus*, ger. of *pudēre* to be ashamed]

pudg·y (puj′ē), *adj.*, **pudg·i·er, pudg·i·est.** short and fat or thick. Also, *esp. Brit.*, **podgy.** [?] —**pudg′i·ly,** *adv.* —**pudg′i·ness,** *n.*

Pue·bla (pwe′blä), *n.* **1.** a state in S central Mexico. 2,094,546 (est. 1963); 13,124 sq. mi. **2.** the capital of this state, in the N part. 338,685 (est. 1965).

pueb·lo (pweb′lō; *for 4 also Sp.* pwe′blô), *n., pl.* **pueb·los** (pweb′lōz; *for 4 also Sp.* pwe′blôs). **1.** the adobe or stone communal house or group of houses of certain Indians of Arizona and New Mexico. **2.** (*cap.*) a member of an Indian people living in such houses. **3.** an Indian village. **4.** (in Spanish America) a town or village. [< Sp: town, people < L *populus* people]

Pueb·lo (pweb′lō), *n.* a city in central Colorado. 97,453 (1970).

pu·er·ile (pyo͞o′ər il, -ə rīl′, pyŏŏr′il, -īl), *adj.* **1.** of or pertaining to a child. **2.** childishly foolish. [< L *puerīl(is)* boyish = *puer* boy + *-īlis* -ILE] —**pu′er·ile·ly,** *adv.* —**Syn. 1.** boyish, youthful, juvenile. **2.** juvenile.

pu·er·il·ism (pyo͞o′ər ə liz′əm, pyŏŏr′ə-), *n. Psychiatry.* childishness in the behavior of an adult.

pu·er·il·i·ty (pyo͞o′ə ril′i tē), *n., pl.* **-ties** for 3. **1.** the state or quality of being a child. **2.** the quality of being childishly foolish. **3.** something, as an act, remark, etc., that is puerile. [earlier *puerilit(i)e* < L *puerīlitās*]

pu·er·per·al (pyo͞o ûr′pər əl), *adj.* **1.** of or pertaining to a woman in childbirth. **2.** pertaining to or connected with childbirth. [< NL *puerperāl(is)* of childbirth]

puer′peral fe′ver, *Pathol.* an infection occurring during the puerperium. Also called **childbed fever.**

pu·er·pe·ri·um (pyo͞o′ər pēr′ē əm), *n. Obstet.* the state of a woman during and just after childbirth. [< L: childbirth = *puerper(us)* of a woman in labor (*puer* boy, child + *-perus* bringing forth) + *-ium* n. suffix of result]

Puer·to Ri·co (pwer′tə rē′kō, pōr′-, pôr′-; *Sp.* pweʀ′tô ʀē′kô), an island in the central West Indies: a commonwealth associated with the U.S. 2,712,033 (1970); 3435 sq. mi. *Cap.:* San Juan. *Abbr.:* PR Formerly (until 1932), **Porto Rico.** —**Puer′to Ri′can,** *adj., n.*

Puer·to Val·lar·ta (pweʀ′tô vä yäʀ′tä), a seaport in W Mexico on the Pacific: resort. 15,462 (1960).

puff (puf), *n.* **1.** an abrupt blast or emission of air, breath, vapor, etc. **2.** the sound of this. **3.** that which is emitted. **4.** a shallow inhaling and exhaling, as of smoke in smoking. **5.** an inflated or distended part of a thing. **6.** a light pastry with a filling of cream or jam. **7.** a portion of material gathered and held down at the edges but left full in the middle, as in the sleeve of a dress. **8.** a cylindrical roll of hair. **9.** a quilted bed covering, usually filled with down. **10.** a commendation, esp. an exaggerated one made for commercial reasons. —*v.i.* **11.** to blow with short, quick blasts, as the wind. **12.** to be emitted in a puff. **13.** to breathe quick and hard, as after violent exertion. **14.** to emit puffs of air, smoke, etc. **15.** to move with such puffs. **16.** to take puffs in smoking. **17.** to become inflated, distended, or swollen. —*v.t.* **18.** to send forth (air, vapor, etc.) in short, quick blasts. **19.** to move by puffing. **20.** to extinguish by means of a puff. **21.** to smoke (a cigar, pipe, etc.). **22.** to inflate or swell. **23.** to inflate with pride, vanity, etc. **24.** to praise unduly or with exaggeration. **25.** to arrange in puffs, as the hair. [(n.) ME; OE *pyff;* (v.) ME *puffe(n)*, OE *pyffan;* imit.] —**puff′ing·ly,** *adv.*

puff′ ad′der, 1. a large, thick-bodied, African viper, *Bitis arientans*, that inflates its body and hisses when disturbed. **2.** See **hognose snake.**

puff·ball (puf′bôl′), *n.* any of various basidiomycetous fungi, esp. of the genus *Lycoperdon* and allied genera, characterized by a ball-like fruit body which emits a cloud of spores when broken.

puff·er (puf′ər), *n.* **1.** a person or thing that puffs. **2.** Also called **blowfish, globefish.** any of various fishes of the family *Tetraodontidae*, capable of inflating the body with water or air until it resembles a globe, the spines in the skin becoming erected.

puff·er·y (puf′ə rē), *n., pl.* **-er·ies.** undue or exaggerated praise, as in publicity.

puf·fin (puf′in), *n.* any of several sea birds of the genera *Fratercula* and *Lunda*, having a short neck and a large, compressed, grooved bill. [ME *poffin, poffyn* < ?]

Puffin, *Fratercula arctica* (Length 1 ft.)

puff′ paste′, a dough used in making very light, flaky, rich pastry for pies, tarts, and the like.

puff·y (puf′ē), *adj.*, **puff·i·er, puff·i·est. 1.** shortwinded; panting. **2.** inflated, distended, or swollen. **3.** conceited. —**puff′i·ly,** *adv.* —**puff′i·ness,** *n.*

pug[1] (pug), *n.* **1.** one of a breed of small, short-haired dogs having a tightly curled tail, a deeply wrinkled face, and a smooth coat that is black or silver and fawn with black markings. **2.** See **pug nose. 3.** a fox. [?] —**pug′gish, pug′gy,** *adj.*

pug[2] (pug), *v.t.*, **pugged, pug·ging.** to knead (clay or the like) with water to make it plastic. [?]

pug[3] (pug), *n. Slang.* a boxer; pugilist. [short for PUGILIST]

pug[4] (pug), *n. Anglo-Indian.* a footprint, esp. of a game animal. [< Hindi *pag*]

pug·a·ree (pug′ə rē), *n.* pugree. Also, **pug′ga·ree, pug·gree** (pug′rē).

Pug[1] (def. 1) (10 in. high at shoulder)

Pu′get Sound′ (pyo͞o′jit), an arm of the Pacific, in NW Washington.

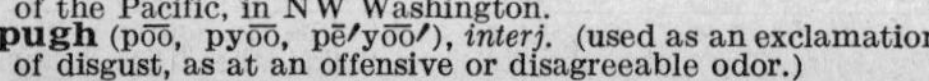

pugh (po͞o, pyo͞o, pē′yo͞o′), *interj.* (used as an exclamation of disgust, as at an offensive or disagreeable odor.)

pu·gil·ism (pyo͞o′jə liz′əm), *n.* the art or practice of fighting with the fists; boxing. [< L *pugil* boxer (akin to *pugnus* fist and *pugnāre* to fight) + -ISM]

pu·gil·ist (pyo͞o′jə list), *n.* a person who fights with his fists, esp. a professional. [< L *pugil* boxer + -IST] —**pu′gil·is′tic,** *adj.*

Pu·glia (po͞o′lyä), *n.* Italian name of **Apulia.**

pug·na·cious (pug nā′shəs), *adj.* excessively inclined to quarrel or fight; quarrelsome. [*pugnaci(ty)* (< L *pugnācitās* combativeness = *pugnāci-*, s. of *pugnāx* combative + *-tās* -TY[2]) + -OUS] —**pug·na′cious·ly,** *adv.* —**pug·nac·i·ty** (pug nas′i tē), **pug·na′cious·ness,** *n.* —**Syn.** argumentative, contentious. —**Ant.** agreeable.

pug′ nose′, a short, broad, somewhat turned-up nose. —**pug-nosed** (pug′nōzd′), *adj.*

pug·ree (pug′rē), *n.* **1.** a light turban worn by natives in India. **2.** a scarf of silk or cotton, wound round a hat or sun helmet. Also, **pugaree, puggaree, puggree.** [< Hindi *pagrī* turban]

P'u-i (*Chin.* po͞o′ē′), *n.* Pu-yi.

puis·ne (pyo͞o′nē), *adj.* **1.** *Law.* inferior in rank; junior. —*n.* **2.** an associate judge. [< AF = OF *puis* after (< L *posteā*) + *ne* born, ptp. of *naistre* to be born (< L *nascere*)]

pu·is·sance (pyo͞o′i səns, pyo͞o is′əns, pwis′əns), *n. Literary.* power, might, or force. [late ME < MF]

pu·is·sant (pyo͞o′i sənt, pyo͞o is′ənt, pwis′ənt), *adj. Literary.* powerful; mighty; potent. [late ME < MF << VL **possent-* (s. of **possēns*) for L *potent-* (s. of *potēns*), prp. of *posse* to be able, have power; see -ANT] —**pu′is·sant·ly,** *adv.*

puke (pyo͞ok), *n., v.i., v.t.*, **puked, puk·ing.** *Slang.* vomit. [?]

puk·ka (puk′ə), *adj. Anglo-Indian.* genuine, reliable, or good. [< Hindi *pakkā* cooked, ripe, mature]

puk′ka sa′hib, *Anglo-Indian.* a term of respectful address formerly used by natives of India to British colonial authorities. Cf. **pukka, sahib.**

pul (po͞ol), *n., pl.* **puls, pu·li** (po͞o′lē). a copper coin of Afghanistan, the 100th part of an afghani. [< Pers *pūl* < Turk *pul*]

Pu·las·ki (pŏŏ las′kē, -kī, pə-), *n.* **1. Count Cas·i·mir** (kaz′ə mir), 1748–79, Polish patriot; general in the American Revolutionary army. **2. Fort.** See **Fort Pulaski.**

pul·chri·tude (pul′kri to͞od′, -tyo͞od′), *n.* physical beauty; comeliness. [ME < L *pulchritūdō* beauty = *pulchri-* (comb. form of *pulcher* beautiful) + *-tūdō* -TUDE]

pul·chri·tu·di·nous (pul′kri to͞od′ənəs, -tyo͞od′-), *adj.* physically beautiful; comely. [< L *pulchritūdin-* (s. of *pulchritūdō*) + -OUS]

pule (pyo͞ol), *v.i.*, **puled, pul·ing.** to cry in a thin voice; whine; whimper. [? imit.] —**pul′er,** *n.*

pu·li (pŏŏl′ē, pyo͞o′lē), *n., pl.* **pu·lik** (pŏŏl′ēk, pyo͞o′lēk), **pu·lis.** one of a Hungarian breed of medium-sized sheep dogs having long, fine hair that often mats, giving the coat a corded appearance. [< Hung]

Pu·litz·er (pŏŏl′it sər, pyo͞o′lit-), *n.* **Joseph,** 1847–1911, U.S. journalist and publisher, born in Hungary.

Pu′litzer Prize′, *U.S.* one of a group of annual prizes in journalism, literature, music, etc., established by Joseph Pulitzer.

pull (pŏŏl), *v.t.* **1.** to take hold of and cause to move toward or after oneself or itself. **2.** to take hold of and attempt to bring toward or after oneself or itself. **3.** to rend or tear in the manner specified: *to pull cloth to pieces.* **4.** to dislodge with a pull, as a nail or tooth. **5.** to strip of feathers, hair, etc., as a bird or a hide. **6.** *Informal.* to draw out (a weapon) for ready use (usually fol. by *on*). **7.** *Informal.* to attempt or perform (something surprising or illegal): *to pull a robbery.* **8.** to put on, as a facial expression. **9.** to attract or win: *to pull votes.* **10.** *Print., Graphics.* to take (an impression or proof) from type, a cut or plate, etc. **11.** to propel by rowing, as a boat. **12.** to strain (a muscle, ligament, or tendon). **13.** to hold in or check (a race horse), esp. so as to prevent from winning. **14.** *Sports.* to hit (a ball) so that it travels in a direction opposite to the side from which it was struck, as when a right-handed batter hits into left field. —*v.i.* **15.** to grasp something and attempt to bring it toward or after oneself or itself (often fol. by *at*). **16.** to inhale through a pipe, cigarette, etc. **17.** to become or come as specified, by being pulled: *Wet paper pulls apart.* **18.** to row. **19. pull in,** to reach a place; arrive. **20. pull off,** *Slang.* to perform successfully, esp. something difficult. **21. pull oneself together,** to regain command of one's emotions. **22. pull out, a.** to leave; depart. **b.** to cease action or participation. **23. pull punches.** See **punch**[1] (def. 2). **24. pull someone's leg,** to chide or tease a person. **25. pull through,** to come safely through (a crisis, illness, etc.). —*n.* **26.** the act or an instance of pulling or drawing. **27.** a force used in pulling. **28.** a drawing in of a liquid or of smoke through the mouth. **29.** *Slang.* influence, as with persons able to grant favors. **30.** a handle or the like for pulling. **31.** a spell, or turn, at rowing. **32.** a stroke of an oar. **33.** *Sports.* a pulling of the ball, as in baseball or golf. [ME *pulle(n)*, OE *pullian* to pull, pluck; cf. MLG *pūlen* to strip off husks, pick, Icel *pūla* to work hard] —**Ant. 1.** push.

pull·back (pŏŏl′bak′), *n.* **1.** the act of pulling back. **2.** that which pulls something back or impedes its forward movement. **3.** pull-out (def. 2).

pul·let (pŏŏl′it), *n.* a young hen, less than one year old. [ME *polet* < MF *poulet*, dim. of *poul* cock < L *pull(us)* chicken, young of an animal; akin to FOAL]

pul·ley (pŏŏl′ē), *n., pl.* **-leys. 1.** a wheel for supporting, guiding, or transmitting force to or from a moving rope, chain, or belt passing over its edge. **2.** a combination of such wheels in one or more blocks, used with ropes or chains to form a tackle. [ME *poley, puly* < MF *po(u)lie* << Gk **polīdion* little pivot. See POLE[2], -IDION]

Pull·man (pŏŏl′mən), *n., pl.* **-mans** for 2. **1. George Mortimer,** 1831–97, U.S. inventor and railroad car designer. **2.** *Trademark.* a railroad sleeping car or parlor car.

pul·lo′rum disease′ (pə lōr′əm, -lôr′-), *Vet. Pathol.* a highly contagious disease caused by the bacterium *Salmonella pullorum*, transmitted esp. during egg production from a hen to her chicks, and characterized by lassitude, loss of appetite, and diarrhea. [< L *pullōrum*, gen. pl. of *pullus* cockerel, chicken]

pull-out (po͝ol′out′), *n.* **1.** the act of pulling out. **2.** Also called **pullback.** a planned or arranged withdrawal of military personnel, as for tactical reasons. **3.** a flight maneuver in which an aircraft levels into horizontal flight following a dive. Also, **pull′out′.**

pull·o·ver (po͝ol′ō′vər), *n.* **1.** a garment, esp. a sweater, that is put on by drawing over the head. —*adj.* **2.** designed to be put on by drawing over the head. Also called **slipover.**

pul·lu·late (pul′yə lāt′), *v.i.*, **-lat·ed, -lat·ing. 1.** to send forth sprouts, buds, etc. **2.** to breed, produce, or create rapidly. **3.** to increase rapidly; multiply. **4.** to exist abundantly; swarm; teem. **5.** to be produced as offspring. [< L *pullulāt(us)* (ptp. of *pullulāre* to sprout) < *pullul(us)* a sprout, young animal, dim. of *pullus;* see PULLET] —**pul′lu·la′tion,** *n.*

pul·mo·nar·y (pul′mə ner′ē, po͝ol′-), *adj.* **1.** of or pertaining to the lungs. **2.** of the nature of a lung; lunglike. **3.** affecting the lungs. **4.** having lungs or lunglike organs. [< L *pulmōnāri(us)* of the lungs = *pulmōn-* (s. of *pulmō* lung; akin to Gk *pleúmōn,* later *pneúmōn* lung) + *-ārius* -ARY]

pul′monary ar′tery, an artery conveying venous blood from the right ventricle of the heart to the lungs.

pul′monary valve′, *Anat.* a semilunar valve between the pulmonary artery and the right ventricle of the heart that prevents the blood from flowing back into the right ventricle.

pul′monary vein′, a vein conveying arterial blood from the lungs to the left atrium of the heart.

pul·mo·nate (pul′mə nāt′, -nit), *adj.* **1.** *Zool.* having lungs or lunglike organs. **2.** belonging to the *Pulmonata,* an order or group of gastropod mollusks usually breathing by means of a lunglike sac, and including most of the terrestrial snails and the slugs and certain aquatic snails. —*n.* **3.** a pulmonate gastropod. [< NL *pulmōnāt(us).* See PULMONARY, -ATE[1]]

pul·mon·ic (pul mon′ik), *adj.* **1.** pulmonary. **2.** pneumonic. [< F *pulmonique*]

Pul·mo·tor (pul′mō′tər, po͝ol′-), *n.* *Trademark.* a mechanical device for artificial respiration that forces oxygen into the lungs when respiration has ceased because of asphyxiation, drowning, etc.

pulp (pulp), *n.* **1.** the succulent part of a fruit. **2.** the pith of the stem of a plant. **3.** a soft or fleshy part of an animal body. **4.** the inner substance of the tooth, containing arteries, veins, and lymphatic and nerve tissue. **5.** any soft, moist, slightly cohering mass, as of linen or wood, used in the making of paper. **6.** a cheap magazine or book, usually containing sensational and lurid material. Cf. **slick**[1] (def. 8). **7.** *Mining.* crushed or pulverized ore. —*v.t.* **8.** to reduce to pulp. **9.** to remove the pulp from. —*v.i.* **10.** to become reduced to pulp. [earlier *pulpe* < L *pulpa* flesh, later pulp of fruit]

pulp′ cav′ity, *Dentistry.* the entire space occupied by pulp, composed of the root canal and pulp chamber.

pul·pit (po͝ol′pit, pul′-), *n.* **1.** a platform or raised structure in a church, from which the clergyman delivers the sermon or conducts the service. **2. the pulpit, a.** the clerical profession; the ministry. **b.** clergymen collectively. **3.** a guard rail at the bow or stern of a small boat. [ME < LL *pulpit(um)* pulpit, L: platform, stage] —**pul′pit·al,** *adj.*

pulp·wood (pulp′wo͝od′), *n.* spruce or other soft wood suitable for making paper.

pulp·y (pul′pē), *adj.*, **pulp·i·er, pulp·i·est.** of, characteristic of, or resembling pulp; fleshy or soft. —**pulp′i·ly,** *adv.*

pul·que (po͝ol′kē; *Sp.* po͞ol′ke), *n.* a fermented milkish drink made from the juice of certain species of agave in Mexico. [< MexSp << Nahuatl]

pul·sar (pul′sär), *n.* one of a number of sources of rapidly pulsating radio energy located within the Galaxy. [puls(ating radio source) + *-ar,* by analogy with QUASAR]

pul·sate (pul′sāt), *v.i.*, **-sat·ed, -sat·ing. 1.** to expand and contract rhythmically, as the heart. **2.** to vibrate; quiver. [< L *pulsāt(us),* ptp. of *pulsāre* to batter, strike, make (strings) vibrate. See PULSE[1]]
—**Syn. 1.** pulse. PULSATE, BEAT, PALPITATE, THROB refer to the recurrent vibratory movement of the heart, the pulse, etc. To PULSATE is to move in a definite rhythm, temporarily or for a longer duration: *Blood pulsates in the arteries.* To BEAT is to repeat a vibration or pulsation regularly for some time: *One's heart beats many times a minute.* To PALPITATE is to beat at a rapid rate, often producing a flutter: *to palpitate with excitement.* To THROB is to beat with an unusual force that is often associated with pain: *His heart throbbed with terror.*

pul·sa·tile (pul′sə til, -tīl′), *adj.* pulsating; throbbing. [< ML *pulsātil(is)*] —**pul·sa·til·i·ty** (pul′sə til′i tē), *n.*

pul·sa·tion (pul sā′shən), *n.* **1.** the act of pulsating; beating or throbbing. **2.** a beat or throb, as of the pulse. **3.** vibration or undulation. **4.** a single vibration. [< L *pulsātiōn-* (s. of *pulsātiō*)] —**pul·sa′tion·al,** *adj.*

pul·sa·tive (pul′sə tiv), *adj.* pulsating or throbbing. —**pul′sa·tive·ly,** *adv.*

pul·sa·tor (pul′sā tər, pul sā′-), *n.* **1.** something that pulsates, beats, or throbs. **2.** something that causes pulsations. [< L: a striker]

pul·sa·to·ry (pul′sə tōr′ē, -tôr′ē), *adj.* pulsating or throbbing. [PULSAT(ION) + -ORY[1]]

pulse[1] (puls), *n.*, *v.*, **pulsed, puls·ing.** —*n.* **1.** the regular throbbing of the arteries, caused by the successive contractions of the heart. **2.** a single pulsation, or beat or throb, of the arteries or heart. **3.** a stroke, vibration, or undulation, or a rhythmic series of these. **4.** *Elect.* a momentary, sudden fluctuation in an electrical quantity, as in voltage or current. **5.** a throb of life, emotion, etc. **6.** the prevailing attitudes or sentiments, as of the public. —*v.i.* **7.** to beat or throb; pulsate. **8.** to beat, vibrate, or undulate. [< L *puls(us)* a beat < *pulsus,* ptp. of *pellere* to set in motion by beating or striking; r. ME *pous* < MF] —**pulse′less,** *adj.*

pulse[2] (puls), *n.* **1.** the edible seeds of certain leguminous plants, as peas, beans, or lentils. **2.** a plant producing such seeds. [ME *puls* < L: thick pap of meal, pulse. See POULTICE]

pulse·beat (puls′bēt′), *n.* a hint or intimation of feeling, desires, etc.: *the pulsebeat of an audience.*

pulse′jet en′gine (puls′jet′), *Aeron.* a jet engine equipped with valves that open to admit air and close for combustion, giving a pulsating thrust. Also, **pulse′-jet en′gine.** Also called **pulse′jet′, pulse′-jet′, pul·so·jet** (pul′sō jet′).

pulse′ pres′sure, the pressure of the pulse; the difference between the systolic and diastolic pressures.

pulse′ rate′, *Med.* the rate of the pulse, stated in pulsations per minute.

pul·sim·e·ter (pul sim′i tər), *n.* an instrument for measuring the strength or quickness of the pulse. Also, **pul·som·e·ter** (pul som′i tər). [*pulsi-* (comb. form repr. PULSE[1]) + -METER]

pul·ver·a·ble (pul′vər ə bəl), *adj.* pulverizable. [obs. *pulver* (< L *pulverāre* to pulverize) + -ABLE; see PULVERIZE]

pul·ver·ise (pul′və rīz′), *v.t.*, *v.i.*, **-ised, -is·ing.** *Chiefly Brit.* pulverize. —**pul′ver·is′a·ble,** *adj.* —**pul′ver·i·sa′tion,** *n.* —**pul′ver·is′er,** *n.*

pul·ver·ize (pul′və rīz′), *v.*, **-ized, -iz·ing.** —*v.t.* **1.** to reduce to dust or powder, as by pounding or grinding. **2.** to demolish or crush completely. —*v.i.* **3.** to become reduced to dust. [< LL *pulveriz(āre)* (to) reduce to powder = L *pulver-* (s. of *pulvis*) dust + *-izāre* -IZE] —**pul′ver·iz′a·ble,** *adj.* —**pul′ver·i·za′tion,** *n.* —**pul′ver·iz′er,** *n.*

pul·ver·u·lent (pul ver′yə lənt, -ə lənt), *adj.* **1.** consisting of dust or fine powder. **2.** crumbling to dust or powder. **3.** covered with dust or powder. [< L *pulverulent(us)* dusty. See PULVERIZE, -ULENT] —**pul·ver′u·lence,** *n.*

pul·vil·lus (pul vil′əs), *n.*, *pl.* **-vil·li** (-vil′ī). *Entomol.* a soft, padlike structure located at the base of each claw on the feet of certain insects. [< L, dim. of *pulvīnus* cushion]

pul·vi·nate (pul′və nāt′), *adj.* **1.** cushion-shaped. **2.** having a pulvinus. Also, **pul′vi·nat′ed.** [< L *pulvīnāt(us)* cushioned. See PULVINUS, -ATE[1]] —**pul′vi·nate′ly,** *adv.*

pul·vi·nus (pul vī′nəs), *n.*, *pl.* **-ni** (-nī). *Bot.* a cushionlike swelling at the base of a leaf or leaflet, at the point of junction with the axis. [< L: cushion]

pu·ma (pyo͞o′mə), *n.* **1.** a cougar. **2.** its fur. [< Sp < Quechuan]

pum·e·lo (pum′ə lō′), *n.* pomelo.

pum·ice (pum′is), *n.*, *v.*, **-iced, -ic·ing.** —*n.* **1.** Also called **pum′ice stone′.** a porous or spongy form of volcanic glass, used as an abrasive. —*v.t.* **2.** to rub, smooth, clean, etc., with pumice. [< L *pūmic-,* s. of *pūmex* pumice stone; r. late ME *pomyce, pomeys,* etc. < MF *pomis* < L; r. OE *pūmic* < L] —**pu·mi·ceous** (pyo͞o mish′əs), *adj.*

pum·mel (pum′əl), *v.*, **-meled, -mel·ing** or (*esp. Brit.*) **-melled, -mel·ling,** *n.* —*v.t.* **1.** to beat or thrash with or as if with the fists. —*n.* **2.** pommel[1]. [alter. of POMMEL[1]]

pump[1] (pump), *n.* **1.** an apparatus or machine for moving or altering the pressure of fluids in confined spaces, as by suction or pressure. —*v.t.* **2.** to move (a fluid) with a pump. **3.** to empty of a fluid by means of a pump (often fol. by *out*). **4.** to inflate by pumping (often fol. by *up*): *to pump up a tire.* **5.** to operate or move by an up-and-down or back-and-forth action. **6.** to drive, force, etc., like a pump or as by using a pump: *The heart pumps blood. He pumped a feeling of hope into his listeners.* **7.** to question (someone) artfully or persistently to elicit information. **8.** to elicit (information) by questioning. —*v.i.* **9.** to work a pump. **10.** to move up and down like a pump handle. **11.** to come out in spurts. [late ME *pumpe;* c. G *Pumpe,* D *pomp*] —**pump′er,** *n.* —**pump′less,** *adj.* —**pump′like′,** *adj.*

pump[2] (pump), *n.* a lightweight, low-cut shoe without a fastening, worn esp. by women. [?]

pump-ac·tion (pump′ak′shən), *adj.* (of a shotgun or rifle) having an action that extracts the empty case, loads, and cocks the piece by means of a hand-operated lever that slides backward and forward; slide-action.

pum·per·nick·el (pum′pər nik′əl), *n.* a coarse, slightly sour bread made of unbolted rye. [< G]

pump′ gun′, a shotgun or rifle having a pump-action mechanism.

pump·kin (pump′kin *or, commonly,* pung′kin), *n.* **1.** a large, edible, orange-yellow fruit borne by a coarse, decumbent vine, *Cucurbita Pepo.* **2.** the vine itself. **3.** any of certain varieties of this plant. [alter. of *pumpion* (see -KIN), var. of *pompon* < MF, nasalized var. of *popon* melon, earlier *pepon* < L *pepōn-* (s. of *pepō*) < Gk *pépōn* kind of melon]

pump′kin head′, a slow or dim-witted person; dunce.

pump·kin·seed (pump′kin sēd′ *or, commonly,* pung′kin-), *n.* **1.** the seed of the pumpkin. **2.** a fresh-water sunfish, *Lepomis gibbosus,* found in eastern North America. **3.** a butterfish, *Poronotus triacanthus.*

pump′ prim′ing, *U.S.* the spending of government funds to stimulate the national economy.

pun (pun), *n.*, *v.*, **punned, pun·ning.** —*n.* **1.** the humorous use of a word or a combination of words so as to emphasize different meanings or applications, or the use of words that are alike or nearly alike in sound but different in meaning; a play on words. **2.** the word or phrase used in this way. —*v.i.* **3.** to make puns. [? special use of *pun,* var. (now dial.) of POUND[1]; i.e., to mistreat (words)]

pu·na (po͞o′nä), *n.* a high, cold, arid plateau, as in the Peruvian Andes. [< AmerSp < Quechuan]

punch[1] (punch), *n.* **1.** a thrusting blow, esp. with the fist. **2. pull punches, a.** to lessen deliberately the force of one's blows. **b.** *Informal.* to speak with restraint or tact. —*v.t.* **3.** to give a sharp thrust or blow to, esp. with the fist. **4.** *Western U.S. and Western Canada.* to drive (cattle). **5.** to poke or prod sharply. **6.** to strike or hit vigorously in operating. —*v.i.* **7.** to give sharp blows, as with the fist. [perh. var. of POUNCE[1]] —**punch′er,** *n.*

punch[2] (punch), *n.* **1.** a tool or machine for perforating or stamping materials, driving nails, etc. —*v.t.* **2.** to perforate, stamp, or drive with a punch. [short for *puncheon,* ME *ponson* < MF *ponçon* < L *punctiōn-* (s. of *punctiō*) a pricking, hence, pricking tool. See POINT, -ION]

punch[3] (punch), *n.* **1.** a beverage consisting of wine or spirits mixed with water, milk, etc., and flavored with sugar, lemon, spices, etc. **2.** a beverage of two or more fruit juices, sugar, and water, often carbonated. [perh. short for PUNCHEON[1]; if so, a metonymic use]

Punch (punch), *n.* **1.** the chief character in a Punch-and-Judy show. **2. pleased as Punch,** highly pleased; delighted. [short for PUNCHINELLO]

Punch′-and-Ju′dy show′ (punch′ən jo͞o′dē), a puppet show having a conventional plot consisting chiefly of slapstick humor and the tragicomic misadventures of a grotesque, hook-nosed, humpback buffoon, Punch, and his wife, Judy.

punch·ball (punch′bôl′), *n.* a form of baseball in which a rubber ball is batted with the fist.

punch·board (punch′bōrd′, -bôrd′), *n.* a small board, used for gambling, containing holes filled with slips of paper printed with concealed numbers that are punched out by a player in an attempt to win a prize.

punch′ bowl′, a large bowl from which a beverage, as punch, lemonade, or the like, is served by means of a ladle.

punch′ card′, a card having holes punched in specific positions and patterns so as to represent data to be stored or processed mechanically, electrically, or photoelectrically.

punch-drunk (punch′drungk′), *adj.* **1.** (esp. of a boxer) having cerebral concussion caused by repeated blows to the head and consequently exhibiting physical unsteadiness, slowness of movement, hesitant speech, and dulled mentality. **2.** *Informal.* befuddled; dazed.

punched′ tape′, *Computer Technol.* a paper tape for coding data by means of a row or a series of rows of holes punched across its width.

pun·cheon[1] (pun′chən), *n.* **1.** a large cask of varying capacity, but usually 80 gallons. **2.** its volume as a measure. [late ME *poncion* < MF *ponçon* < ?]

pun·cheon[2] (pun′chən), *n.* **1.** a heavy slab of timber, roughly dressed, for use as a floorboard. **2.** a short, upright framing timber. **3.** (in goldsmith work) **a.** any of various pointed instruments; a punch. **b.** a stamping tool. [ME *ponson* < MF *ponçon* < L *punctiōn-* (s. of *punctiō*) a pricking, hence, pricking tool]

Pun·chi·nel·lo (pun′chə nel′ō), *n.* the grotesque or absurd chief character in a puppet show of Italian origin: the prototype of Punch. [var. of *Polichinello* < It *Pollecenella* (Naples dial.), dim. of *pollecena* turkey-cock chick]

punch′ing bag′, an inflated or stuffed bag, usually suspended, punched with the fists as an exercise.

punch′ line′, a phrase or sentence that produces the desired effect in a speech, advertisement, or joke.

punch′ press′, *Mach.* a power-driven machine used to shape material under pressure or by heavy blows.

punch·y (pun′chē), *adj.*, **punch·i·er, punch·i·est.** *Informal.* punch-drunk.

punc·tate (pungk′tāt), *adj.* marked with points or dots; having minute spots or depressions. Also, **punc′tat·ed.** [< NL *punctāt(us)* dotted. See POINT, -ATE[1]]

punc·ta·tion (pungk tā′shən), *n.* **1.** punctate condition or marking. **2.** one of the marks or depressions in something that is punctate. [< ML *punctāt(us)* marked, punctuated]

punc·ti·form (pungk′tə fôrm′), *adj.* shaped like or of the nature of a point or dot. [< L *punct(um)* POINT]

punc·til·i·o (pungk til′ē ō′), *n.*, *pl.* **-til·i·os** for 1. **1.** a fine point, particular, or detail, as of conduct, ceremony, or procedure. **2.** strictness or exactness in the observance of formalities or amenities. [m. It *puntiglio* < Sp *puntillo,* dim. of *punto* < L *punctum* POINT]

punc·til·i·ous (pungk til′ē əs), *adj.* strict or exact in the observance of all formalities or amenities of conduct or actions. —**punc·til′i·ous·ly,** *adv.* —**punc·til′i·ous·ness,** *n.* —**Syn.** precise, careful, conscientious. —**Ant.** careless.

punc·tu·al (pungk′cho͞o əl), *adj.* **1.** arriving, acting, or happening at the time or times appointed; prompt. **2.** pertaining to or of the nature of a point. **3.** *Obs.* punctilious. [late ME < ML *punctuāl(is)* of a point. See POINT, -AL[1]] —**punc·tu·al·i·ty** (pungk′cho͞o al′i tē), *n.* —**punc′tu·al·ly,** *adv.* —**punc′tu·al·ness,** *n.*

punc·tu·ate (pungk′cho͞o āt′), *v.*, **-at·ed, -at·ing.** —*v.t.* **1.** to mark or divide with punctuation marks. **2.** to interrupt at intervals. **3.** to give emphasis or force to: *a design punctuated by brilliant colors.* —*v.i.* **4.** to insert or use marks of punctuation. [< ML *punctuāt(us)* (ptp. of *punctuāre* to point < L *punctum* POINT); see -ATE[1]] —**punc′tu·a′tor,** *n.*

punc·tu·a·tion (pungk′cho͞o ā′shən), *n.* **1.** the practice or system of using certain conventional marks or characters, as periods or commas, in writing or printing in order to make the meaning clear, as in ending a sentence, separating clauses, etc. **2.** See **punctuation mark.** [< ML *punctuātiōn-* (s. of *punctuātiō*) a marking, pointing] —**punc′tu·a′tive,** *adj.*

punctua′tion mark′, any of a group of conventional marks or characters used in punctuation, as the period, comma, semicolon, question mark, or dash.

punc·ture (pungk′chər), *n.*, *v.*, **-tured, -tur·ing.** —*n.* **1.** the act of piercing or perforating, as with a pointed object. **2.** a hole or mark so made. —*v.t.* **3.** to pierce or perforate, as with a pointed object. **4.** to make (a hole, perforation, etc.) by piercing or perforating. —*v.i.* **5.** to become punctured. [< L *punctūra* a pricking. See POINT, -URE] —**punc′tur·a·ble,** *adj.* —**punc′ture·less,** *adj.* —**punc′tur·er,** *n.*

pun·dit (pun′dit), *n.* **1.** (in India) a Brahman with profound knowledge of Sanskrit, Hindu law, etc. **2.** an expert or authority. **3.** a person who makes comments or judgments in a solemnly authoritative manner. [< Hindi *paṇḍit* < Skt *paṇḍita* learned man; as adj., learned] —**pun·dit′ic,** *adj.* **pun·dit′i·cal·ly,** *adv.*

pung (pung), *n.* *U.S. and Canada.* a sleigh with a boxlike body on runners. [short for *tom-pung,* alter. of TOBOGGAN]

pun·gent (pun′jənt), *adj.* **1.** sharply affecting the organs of taste or smell, as if by a penetrating power; biting; acrid. **2.** acutely distressing to the feelings or mind; poignant. **3.** caustic or sharply expressive: *pungent remarks.* **4.** mentally stimulating or appealing: *pungent wit.* **5.** *Biol.* piercing or sharp-pointed. [< L *pungent-* (s. of *pungēns*), prp. of *pungere* to prick. See POIGNANT, POINT, etc.] —**pun′gen·cy,** *n.* —**pun′gent·ly,** *adv.* —**Syn. 1.** hot, peppery, piquant, sharp. **4.** keen, sharp. —**Ant. 1.** mild, bland. **4.** dull.

Pu·nic (pyo͞o′nik), *adj.* **1.** of or pertaining to the ancient Carthaginians. —*n.* **2.** the language of ancient Carthage, a form of late Phoenician. [< L *Pūnic(us),* var. of *Poenicus* Carthaginian, orig. Phoenician < Gk *Phoînix*]

Pu′nic Wars′, the three wars waged by Rome against Carthage, 264–241, 218–201, and 149–146 B.C., resulting in the defeat and annexation of Carthage.

pun·ish (pun′ish), *v.t.* **1.** to subject (a person) to pain, confinement, death, etc., as a penalty for some offense. **2.** to inflict such a penalty for (an offense). **3.** to handle severely or roughly, as in a fight. **4.** to put to painful exertion. —*v.i.* **5.** to inflict punishment. [ME *punische(n)* < MF *puniss-,* long s. of *punir* < L *pūnīre*] —**pun′ish·er,** *n.* —**Syn. 1.** chastise, castigate. **1, 2.** penalize. —**Ant. 1.** reward.

pun·ish·a·ble (pun′i shə bəl), *adj.* (of a person or an offense) liable to punishment. —**pun′ish·a·bil′i·ty,** *n.*

pun·ish·ment (pun′ish mənt), *n.* **1.** the act of punishing. **2.** the fact of being punished. **3.** a penalty inflicted for an offense, fault, etc. **4.** severe handling or treatment. [ME *punysshement* < AF *punisement* = OF *punissement*]

pu·ni·tive (pyo͞o′ni tiv), *adj.* serving for, concerned with, or inflicting punishment. Also, **pu·ni·to·ry** (pyo͞o′ni tōr′ē, -tôr′ē). [< ML *pūnītīv(us)* of punishment = L *pūnīt(us)* (ptp. of *pūnīre* to punish) + *-īvus* -IVE] —**pu′ni·tive·ly,** *adv.* —**pu′ni·tive·ness,** *n.*

Pun·jab (pun jäb′, pun′jäb), *n.* **1.** a former province in NW India: now divided between Punjab (in India) and West Punjab (in Pakistan). **2.** a state in NW India. 15,230,000; 47,456 sq. mi. *Cap.:* Chandigarh.

Pun·ja·bi (pun jä′bē), *n.* **1.** a native of Punjab, India. **2.** Panjabi (def. 2). [< Hindi *Pañjābī* < Pers *Panjab*]

Pun′jab States′, a former group of states in NW India: amalgamated with Punjab state (in India) in 1956.

pun′ji stake′ (po͝on′jē), a sharp bamboo stake for concealing in grass at a 45-degree angle so as to gash the feet and legs of enemy soldiers. Also called **pun′ji stick′.** [?]

punk[1] (pungk), *n.* **1.** any prepared substance that will smolder and can be used to light fireworks, fuses, etc. **2.** dry, decayed wood that can be used as tinder. **3.** amadou; touchwood. [? sandhi var. of SPUNK]

punk[2] (pungk), *n.* **1.** *Slang.* **a.** something or someone worthless or unimportant. **b.** a petty criminal or hoodlum. **2.** See **punk rock. 3.** *Archaic.* a prostitute. —*adj.* **4.** *Informal.* poor in quality or condition. **5.** *Slang.* characteristic of punk rock or those who perform it. [?]

pun·kah (pung′kə), *n.* (esp. in India) a fan, esp. a large, swinging, screenlike fan hung from the ceiling and kept in motion by a servant or by machinery. Also, **pun′ka.** [< Hindi *pankhā* < Skt *pakshaka*]

punk·ie (pung′kē), *n.* any of the minute biting gnats of the family *Ceratopogonidae.* Also called **biting midge.** [< New York D *punki,* appar. < Delaware *punk* ashes, dust]

punk′ rock′, a type of rock-'n'-roll, culminating in the 1970's and characterized by loud, insistent music and abusive or violent protest lyrics, and whose performers and followers are distinguished by extremes of dress and socially defiant behavior. Also called **punk.** —**punk′ rock′er.**

pun·ster (pun′stər), *n.* a person who makes puns frequently.

punt[1] (punt), *n.* **1.** *Football.* a kick in which the ball is dropped and then kicked before it touches the ground. Cf. **drop kick, place kick. 2.** *Chiefly Brit.* a small, shallow boat, used for short outings on rivers or lakes and propelled by poling. —*v.t.* **3.** *Football.* to kick (a dropped ball) before it touches the ground. **4.** to pole (a small boat) along. **5.** to convey in or as in a punt. —*v.i.* **6.** to punt a football. **7.** *Chiefly Brit.* **a.** to pole a boat along. **b.** to travel or have an outing in a punt. [OE < L *pontō* punt, PONTOON[1]] —**punt′er,** *n.*

punt[2] (punt), *v.i.* **1.** *Cards.* to lay a stake against the bank, as at faro. **2.** *Brit.* to gamble; wager. [< F *pont(er)* < *ponte* punter, point in faro < Sp *punto* POINT] —**punt′er,** *n.*

Pun·ta A·re·nas (po͞on′tä ä RE′näs), a seaport in S Chile, on the Strait of Magellan: the southernmost city in the world. 64,456. Also called **Magallanes.**

pun·ty (pun′tē), *n.*, *pl.* **-ties.** an iron rod used in glassmaking for handling the hot glass. Also called **pontil.** [var. of PONTIL]

pu·ny (pyo͞o′nē), *adj.*, **-ni·er, -ni·est. 1.** of less than normal size and strength; weak. **2.** unimportant; insignificant. **3.** *Obs.* puisne. [sp. var. of PUISNE] —**pu′ni·ness,** *n.*

pup (pup), *n.*, *v.*, **pupped, pup·ping.** —*n.* **1.** a young dog; puppy. **2.** the young of certain other animals, as of foxes and seals. —*v.i.* **3.** to give birth to pups. [var. of PUPPY]

pu·pa (pyo͞o′pə), *n.*, *pl.* **-pae** (-pē), **-pas.** an insect in the nonfeeding, usually immobile, transformation stage between the larva and the imago. See illus. under **metamorphosis.** [< NL, special use of L *pūpa* girl, doll, puppet. See PUPIL[1], PUPPET] —**pu′pal,** *adj.*

pu·par·i·um (pyo͞o pâr′ē əm), *n.*, *pl.* **-par·i·a** (-pâr′ē ə). *Entomol.* a pupal case formed of the cuticula of a preceding larval instar. [< NL] —**pu·par′i·al,** *adj.*

pu·pate (pyo͞o′pāt), *v.i.*, **-pat·ed, -pat·ing.** to become a pupa. [PUP(A) + -ATE[1]] —**pu·pa′tion,** *n.*

pu·pil[1] (pyo͞o′pəl), *n.* **1.** a person, usually young, who studies in a school under the close supervision of a teacher. **2.** any person who takes lessons from someone, formally or informally; a student. **3.** *Civil Law.* an orphaned or emancipated minor under the care of a guardian. [ME *pupille* < MF < L *pūpillus* (masc.), *pūpilla* (fem.) orphan, ward, diminutives of *pūpus* boy, *pūpa* girl] —**pu′pil·less,** *adj.* —**Syn. 1.** apprentice, novice. PUPIL, DISCIPLE, SCHOLAR, STUDENT refer to a person who is studying or who has studied a great deal. A PUPIL is a person under the close supervision of a teacher, either because of his youth or of specialization in some branch of study: *a grade-school pupil; the pupil of a famous musician.* A DISCIPLE is a person who follows the teachings or doctrines of a person whom he considers to be a master or authority: *a disciple of Swedenborg.* SCHOLAR, once meaning the same as PUPIL, is today usually applied to a person who has acquired wide erudition in some field of learning: *a great Latin scholar.* A STUDENT is a person attending an educational institution or someone who has devoted much attention to a particular problem: *a college student; a student of politics.*

pu·pil[2] (pyo͞o′pəl), *n.* *Anat.* the expanding and contracting opening in the iris of the eye, through which light passes to the retina. [< L *pūpilla*, lit., little doll. See PUPA]

pu·pil·age (pyo͞o′pə lij), *n.* the state or period of being a pupil.

pu·pil·lar·y¹ (pyo͞o′pə ler′ē), *adj.* of or pertaining to a pupil or student. [< L *pūpillāri(s)*. See PUPIL¹, -ARY]

pu·pil·lar·y² (pyo͞o′pə ler′ē), *adj. Anat.* pertaining to the pupil of the eye. [< L *pūpill(a)* PUPIL² + -ARY]

pu′pil teach′er. See **student teacher.**

pu·pip·a·rous (pyo͞o pip′ər əs), *adj.* (of an insect) bearing fully developed larvae that are ready to pupate. [< NL *pūpiparus*. See PUPA, -I-, -PAROUS]

pup·pet (pup′it), *n.* **1.** an artificial figure representing a human being or an animal, manipulated by the hand, wires, etc., as on a miniature stage. Cf. **marionette. 2.** a person or thing whose actions are prompted and controlled by another or others. **3.** a small doll. **4.** *Mach.* poppethead. [earlier *poppet*, ME *popet*, appar. < MLG *poppe* doll < LL *puppa*, var. of L *pūpa* doll; see -ET] —**pup′pet·like′,** *adj.*

pup·pet·eer (pup′i tēr′), *n.* a person who manipulates puppets, esp. as an entertainment.

pup·pet·ry (pup′i trē), *n.* the art of making puppets and presenting puppet shows.

pup·py (pup′ē), *n., pl.* **-pies. 1.** a young dog, esp. one less than a year old. **2.** pup (def. 2). **3.** a presuming, conceited, or empty-headed young man. [late ME *popi*. See PUPPET, -Y²] —**pup′py·hood′, pup′py·dom,** *n.* —**pup′py·ish,** *adj.* —**pup′py·like′,** *adj.*

pup′py love′, temporary infatuation of a juvenile.

pup′ tent′. See **shelter tent.**

pur (pûr), *v.t., v.i.,* **purred, pur·ring.** purr.

Pu·ra·na (po͞o rä′nə), *n.* any of a large number of traditional collections of epics, myths, popular lore, etc., embodying the principles of popular Hindu religion and ethics. [< Skt: of old] —**Pu·ra′nic,** *adj.*

pur·blind (pûr′blīnd′), *adj.* **1.** nearly or partially blind; dim-sighted. **2.** slow or deficient in understanding, imagination, or vision. **3.** *Obs.* totally blind. [ME *pur blind* PURE (adv.) blind]

Pur·cell (pûr′səl), *n.* **Henry,** 1658?–95, English composer.

Purcell′ Moun′tains, a range in SE British Columbia and NW Montana. Highest peak, Mt. Farnham, 11,340 ft.

Pur·chas (pûr′chəs), *n.* **Samuel,** 1575?–1626, English writer and editor of travel books.

pur·chase (pûr′chəs), *v.,* **-chased, -chas·ing,** *n.* —*v.t.* **1.** to acquire by the payment of money or its equivalent; buy. **2.** to acquire by effort, sacrifice, etc. **3.** to be sufficient to buy: *One dollar purchases a subscription.* **4.** *Law.* to acquire land or other property other than by inheritance. **5.** to move, haul, or raise, esp. by applying mechanical power. **6.** to get a leverage on in order to move, haul, or raise. **7.** *Obs.* to procure, acquire, or obtain. —*n.* **8.** acquisition by the payment of money or its equivalent. **9.** something that is purchased. **10.** such a thing with relation to its worth at the price: *a good purchase.* **11.** *Law.* the acquisition of land or other property by other means than inheritance. **12.** acquisition by means of effort, labor, etc. **13.** a lever, tackle, or other device that provides mechanical advantage or power. **14.** an effective hold or position, as for applying power in moving or raising a heavy object; leverage. **15.** the annual return or rent from land. **16.** *Obs.* booty. [ME < AF *purchase(r)* (to) seek to obtain, procure = *pur-* (< L *prō* for) + *chacer* to CHASE¹] —**pur′chas·a·ble,** *adj.* —**pur′chas·er,** *n.* —**Syn. 1.** See **buy.**

pur′chase tax′, *Brit.* a sales tax on nonessential and luxury goods.

pur·dah (pûr′də), *n.* (in India, Pakistan, etc.) **1.** a screen, curtain, or veil, used for hiding women from the sight of men or strangers. **2.** seclusion in this manner or the practice of such seclusion. Also, **pur′da, pardah.** [< Hindi (Urdu) *pardah* curtain < Pers]

pure (pyo͝or), *adj.,* **pur·er, pur·est. 1.** free from anything of a different, inferior, or contaminating kind. **2.** of unmixed descent or ancestry. **3.** (of literary style) straightforward; unaffected. **4.** abstract or theoretical (opposed to *applied*): *pure science.* **5.** clear and true: *pure tones.* **6.** absolute; utter; sheer: *pure joy.* **7.** being that and nothing else; mere: *a pure accident.* **8.** clean, spotless, or unblemished. **9.** untainted with evil or guilt. **10.** physically chaste; virgin. **11.** ceremonially or ritually clean. **12.** independent of sense or experience: *pure knowledge.* **13.** *Biol., Genetics.* **a.** homozygous. **b.** containing only one characteristic for a trait. **14.** *Phonet.* monophthongal. [ME *pur* < OF < L *pūr(us)* clean, unmixed, plain, pure] —**pure′ness,** *n.* —**Syn. 1.** unmixed, unadulterated, uncontaminated, uncorrupted. **9.** virtuous, undefiled, guiltless.

pure·bred (*adj.* pyo͝or′bred′; *n.* pyo͝or′bred′), *adj.* **1.** of or pertaining to an animal, all the ancestors of which derive over many generations from a recognized breed. —*n.* **2.** a purebred animal, esp. one of registered pedigree.

pure′ cul′ture, the growth of only one microorganism in a culture.

pu·rée (pyo͝o rā′, -rē′, pyo͝or′ā; *Fr.* PY RA′), *n., v.* **-réed, -ré·ing.** —*n.* **1.** a cooked and sieved food, esp. a vegetable or fruit. **2.** a soup made with puréed ingredients. —*v.t.* **3.** to make a purée of. [< F, n. use of fem. ptp. of *purer* to strain, lit., make PURE]

pure·heart·ed (pyo͝or′här′tid), *adj.* (of a person) without malice, treachery, or evil intent.

pure′ line′, *Genetics.* a uniform strain of organisms that is relatively pure genetically because of continued inbreeding along with selection.

pure·ly (pyo͝or′lē), *adv.* **1.** in a pure manner; without admixture. **2.** merely; only; solely. **3.** entirely; completely. **4.** innocently, virtuously, or chastely. [ME *purliche*]

pure′ rea′son, *Kantianism.* reason based on a priori principles and providing a unifying ground for the perception of the phenomenal world.

pur·fle (pûr′fəl), *n., v.t.,* **-fled, -fling.** —*n.* **1.** Also called **pur′fling.** an ornamental border, esp. inlay on a stringed instrument. —*v.t.* **2.** to finish with an ornamental border. [ME *purfile(n)* < MF *porfile(r)* (to) make or adorn a border = *por-* PRO-¹ + *filer* to spin < *fil* thread, FILE¹. See PROFILE]

pur·ga·tion (pûr gā′shən), *n.* the act of purging. [ME *purgacioun* < L *pūrgātiōn-* (s. of *pūrgātiō*) a cleansing, purging = *pūrgāt(us)* (ptp. of *pūrgāre* to PURGE) + *-iōn-* -ION]

pur·ga·tive (pûr′gə tiv), *adj.* **1.** purging or cleansing, esp. by causing evacuation of the bowels. —*n.* **2.** a purgative medicine; cathartic. [< LL *pūrgātīv(us)* (see PURGATION, -IVE); r. late ME *purgatyf* < MF] —**pur′ga·tive·ly,** *adv.*

pur·ga·to·ri·al (pûr′gə tōr′ē əl, -tôr′-), *adj.* **1.** removing or purging sin; expiatory. **2.** of, pertaining to, or like purgatory.

pur·ga·to·ry (pûr′gə tōr′ē, -tôr′ē), *n., pl.* **-ries,** *adj.* —*n.* **1.** a condition or place in which, according to Roman Catholics and others, the souls of those dying penitent are purified from venial sins, or undergo the remaining temporal punishment for mortal sin forgiven on earth. **2.** any condition or place of temporary punishment, suffering, or expiation. —*adj.* **3.** serving to cleanse, purify, or expiate. [ME *purgatorie* < ML *pūrgātōri(um)*, n. use of neut. of LL *pūrgātōrius* purging. See PURGATION, -ORY¹]

purge (pûrj), *v.,* **purged, purg·ing,** *n.* —*v.t.* **1.** to rid of whatever is impure or undesirable. **2.** to rid, clear, or free (usually fol. by *of* or *from*): *to purge a political party of disloyal members.* **3.** to clear of imputed guilt or ritual uncleanliness. **4.** to atone for (an offense). **5.** to remove by cleansing or purifying. **6.** to clear or empty (the bowels) by causing evacuation. **7.** to cause evacuation of the bowels of (a person). **8.** to put to death or otherwise eliminate in the course of a political purge. —*v.i.* **9.** to become cleansed or purified. **10.** to undergo or cause purging of the bowels. —*n.* **11.** the act or process of purging. **12.** the killing or expulsion of persons for political reasons. **13.** something that purges, as a purgative medicine or dose. [ME <OF *purg(i)er* < L *pūrgāre* to cleanse] —**purge′a·ble,** *adj.* —**purg′er,** *n.*

Pu·ri (po͝or′ē, po͝o rē′), *n.* a seaport in E India, on the Bay of Bengal: Hindu pilgrimage center. 49,057 (1951).

pu·ri·fy (pyo͝or′ə fī′), *v.,* **-fied, -fy·ing.** —*v.t.* **1.** to make pure; free from anything that debases, pollutes, adulterates, or contaminates. **2.** to free from guilt or sin. **3.** to clear or purge (usually fol. by *of* or *from*): *to purify a text of errors.* **4.** to make clean for ceremonial or ritual use. —*v.i.* **5.** to become pure. [ME *purifie(n)* < MF *purifie(r)* < L *pūrificāre*] —**pu′ri·fi·ca′tion,** *n.* —**pu·rif·i·ca·to·ry** (pyo͝o rif′ə kə tōr′ē, -tôr′ē), *adj.* —**pu′ri·fi′er,** *n.*

Pu·rim (po͝or′im; *Heb.* po͞o REM′), *n.* a Jewish festival celebrated on the 14th day of Adar, that commemorates the deliverance of the Jews in Persia from destruction by Haman. [< Heb, pl. of *pūr* lot]

pu·rine (pyo͝or′ēn, -in), *n. Chem.* a compound, $C_5H_4N_4$, from which is derived a group of compounds including uric acid, xanthine, and caffeine. [alter. of G *Purin.* See PURE, URIC, -INE²]

pur·ism (pyo͝or′iz əm), *n.* **1.** strict observance of or insistence on purity in language, style, etc. **2.** an instance of this. —**pur′ist,** *n.* —**pu·ris′tic, pu·ris′ti·cal,** *adj.* —**pu·ris′ti·cal·ly,** *adv.*

Pu·ri·tan (pyo͝or′i tᵊn), *n.* **1.** a member of a sect of Protestant 16th-century England advocating simplicity in doctrine and worship, and strictness in religious discipline. **2.** (*l.c.*) a person who is strict in moral matters. —*adj.* **3.** of or pertaining to the Puritans. **4.** (*l.c.*) of, pertaining to, or characteristic of a moral puritan; puritanical. [< LL *pūrit(ās)* PURITY + -AN] —**Pu′ri·tan·ly,** *adv.*

pu·ri·tan·i·cal (pyo͝or′i tan′i kəl), *adj.* **1.** very strict in moral matters, often excessively so; rigidly austere. **2.** (*sometimes cap.*) of, pertaining to, or characteristic of Puritans or Puritanism. Also, **pu′ri·tan′ic.** —**pu′ri·tan′i·cal·ly,** *adv.*

Pu·ri·tan·ism (pyo͝or′i tᵊniz′əm), *n.* **1.** the principles and practices of the Puritans. **2.** (*l.c.*) extreme strictness in moral matters.

pu·ri·ty (pyo͝or′i tē), *n.* **1.** the condition or quality of being pure; freedom from anything that contaminates or adulterates. **2.** *Optics.* the chroma, saturation, or degree of freedom from white of a given color. **3.** ceremonial or ritual cleanness. **4.** freedom from guilt or sin. **5.** physical chastity; virginity. [< LL *pūritās*; r. ME *pur(e)te* < AF]

purl¹ (pûrl), *v.t., v.i.* **1.** to knit with inversion of the stitch. **2.** to finish with loops or a looped edging. —*n.* **3.** a stitch used in hand knitting to make a rib effect. **4.** thread made of twisted gold or silver wire. Also, **pearl.** [var. of obs. or dial. *pirl* to twist (threads, etc.) into a cord]

purl² (pûrl), *v.i.* **1.** to flow with rippling motion, as a shallow stream does over stones. **2.** to flow with a murmuring sound. —*n.* **3.** the action or sound of purling. **4.** a circle or curl made by the motion of water; ripple; eddy. [akin to Norw *purla* to bubble up, gush]

pur·lieu (pûr′lo͞o, pûrl′yo͞o), *n.* **1.** a piece of land on the border of a forest. **2.** an outlying district or region, as of a town or city. **3.** *Brit.* a piece of land from a royal forest, turned over to private uses subject to certain restrictions. **4. purlieus,** environs or neighborhood. **5.** a place where a person may range at large. **6.** a person's haunt or resort. [alter. (simulating F *lieu* place) of earlier *parlewe, parley, paraley* purlieu of a forest < AF *purale(e)* a going through = *pur* (< L *prō* for; confused with *per* through) + *aller* (see ALLEY)]

pur·lin (pûr′lin), *n.* a longitudinal member in a roof frame for supporting common rafters between the plate and the ridge. Also, **pur′line.** [?]

pur·loin (pər loin′, pûr′loin), *v.t.* **1.** to take dishonestly; steal; pilfer. —*v.i.* **2.** to commit theft; steal. [late ME *purloyne(n)* < AF *purloigne(r)* (to) put off, remove = *pur-* (< L *prō* for) + *loin* far off (< L *longē*)] —**pur·loin′er,** *n.*

pur·ple (pûr′pəl), *n., adj., v.,* **-pled, -pling.** —*n.* **1.** any color intermediate between red and blue. **2.** cloth or clothing of this hue, esp. as a symbol of imperial, royal, or other high rank. **3.** deep red; crimson. **4. born in** or **to the purple,** of royal or exalted birth. —*adj.* **5.** of the color purple. **6.** full of exaggerated literary devices and effects. —*v.t., v.i.* **7.** to make or become purple. [ME *purpel*, OE *purpl(e)*, var. of *purpur(e)* < L *purpura* < Gk *porphýra* kind of shellfish yielding purple dye]

Pur′ple Heart′, *U.S. Armed Forces.* a medal awarded

for wounds received in action against an enemy or as a direct result of an act of the enemy.
pur′ple mar′tin, a large, American swallow, *Progne subis*, the male of which is blue-black.
pur·plish (pûr′plish), *adj.* of or having a somewhat purple hue.
pur·port (*v.* pər pōrt′, -pôrt′, pûr′pōrt, -pôrt; *n.* pûr′pōrt, -pôrt), *v.t.* **1.** to profess or claim, often falsely. **2.** to convey to the mind as the meaning or thing intended; express or imply. —*n.* **3.** the meaning, import, or sense: *the main purport of his letter.* **4.** a purpose or intention. [late ME < AF *purport(er)* (to) convey = *pur-* PRO-[1] + *porter* to carry (< L *portāre*)] —**Syn. 2.** mean, intend, signify. **3.** implication, drift, trend, gist. See **meaning.**
pur·pose (pûr′pəs), *n.*, *v.*, **-posed, -pos·ing.** —*n.* **1.** the reason for which something exists or happens. **2.** an intended or desired result; end; aim; goal. **3.** determination; resoluteness. **4.** the subject or point under consideration. **5.** practical result, effect, or advantage: *to act to good purpose.* **6. of set purpose,** with intention; deliberately. **7. on purpose,** by design; intentionally. **8. to the purpose,** relevant; to the point. —*v.t.* **9.** to set as an aim, intention, or goal for oneself; purpose. **10.** to intend; design. **11.** to resolve (to do something). —*v.i.* **12.** to have a purpose. [ME *purpos* < OF < *purpos(er)*, var. of *proposer* to PROPOSE] —**pur′pose·less,** *adj.* —**pur′pose·less·ly,** *adv.* —**pur′pose·less·ness,** *n.* —**Syn. 1.** See **intention. 10.** mean.
pur·pose·ful (pûr′pəs fəl), *adj.* **1.** having a purpose. **2.** determined; resolute. **3.** full of meaning; significant. —**pur′pose·ful·ly,** *adv.* —**pur′pose·ful·ness,** *n.*
pur·pose·ly (pûr′pəs lē), *adv.* **1.** intentionally; deliberately. **2.** with a specified purpose; expressly.
pur·pos·ive (pûr′pə siv), *adj.* **1.** having, showing, or acting with a purpose. **2.** serving some purpose. **3.** determined; resolute. **4.** of or characteristic of purpose. —**pur′pos·ive·ly,** *adv.* —**pur′pos·ive·ness,** *n.*
pur·pure (pûr′pyo͝or), *Heraldry.* —*n.* **1.** the tincture or color purple. —*adj.* **2.** of the tincture or color purple. [ME, OE < L *purpura* PURPLE]
pur·pu·rin (pûr′pyə rin), *n.* *Chem.* a reddish, crystalline, anthraquinone dye, $C_{14}H_5O_2(OH)_3$, isomeric with flavopurpurin. [< L *purpur(a)* PURPLE + -IN[2]]
purr (pûr), *v.i.* **1.** to utter a low, continuous, murmuring sound, as a cat does when pleased. —*v.t.* **2.** to express by or as if by purring. —*n.* **3.** the act of purring. **4.** the sound of purring. Also, **pur.** [imit.] —**purr′ing·ly,** *adv.*
purse (pûrs), *n.*, *v.*, **pursed, purs·ing.** —*n.* **1.** a small bag, pouch, or case for carrying money. **2.** a woman's handbag or pocketbook. **3.** anything resembling a purse. **4.** a sum of money collected as a present or the like. **5.** a sum of money offered as a prize or reward. **6.** money available for spending. —*v.t.* **7.** to contract into folds or wrinkles; pucker: *to purse one's lips.* **8.** *Archaic.* to put into a purse. [ME, OE *purs*, b. *pusa* bag (c. Icel *posi*) and ML *bursa* bag (<< Gk *býrsa* hide, leather)] —**purse′like′,** *adj.*
purs·er (pûr′sər), *n.* an officer in charge of the accounts and documents of a ship and who keeps money and valuables for passengers. [late ME]
purse′ strings′, the right or power to manage the disposition of money: *to control the family purse strings.*
purs·lane (pûrs′lān, -lin), *n.* **1.** a low, trailing herb, *Portulaca oleracea*, having yellow flowers, used as a salad plant and potherb. **2.** any other portulacaceous plant. [ME *purcelan(e)* < MF *porcelaine* < LL *porcillāgin-* (s. of *porcillāgō*) for L *porcilāca*, var. of *portulāca*]
pur·su·ance (pər so͞o′əns), *n.* the following or carrying out of some plan, course, injunction, or the like.
pur·su·ant (pər so͞o′ənt), *adj.* **1.** pursuing. —*adv.* **2.** Also, **pur·su′ant·ly.** in agreement or conformity (usually fol. by *to*): *pursuant to local custom.* [r. ME *poursuivant* < MF]
pur·sue (pər so͞o′), *v.*, **-sued, -su·ing.** —*v.t.* **1.** to follow in order to overtake. **2.** to harass continually: *a man pursued by troubles.* **3.** to strive to gain or accomplish. **4.** to proceed in accordance with (a method, plan, etc.). **5.** to carry on or continue (a course of action or the like). **6.** to practice (an occupation or pastime). **7.** to continue to discuss (a topic). **8.** to follow: *He pursued the river to its source. He felt their eyes pursuing him.* —*v.i.* **9.** to follow in pursuit. **10.** to continue. [ME *pursue(n)* < AF *pursue(r)* << L *prōsequī* to pursue, follow, continue. See PRO-[1], SUE, PROSECUTE] —**pur·su′er,** *n.* —**Syn. 1.** trail, hunt. **2.** dog.
pur·suit (pər so͞ot′), *n.* **1.** the act of pursuing. **2.** an effort to secure or attain something: *the pursuit of happiness.* **3.** any regular occupation or pastime. [ME < AF *purseute* << VL **prōsequita* for L *prōsecūta*, fem. of *prōsecūtus*, ptp. of *prōsequī* to PURSUE] —**Syn. 1.** chase, hunt. **2.** search.
pur·sui·vant (pûr′swi vənt), *n.* a heraldic officer of the lowest class, ranking below a herald. [< F *poursuivant* (prp. of *poursuivre* to PURSUE); r. ME *pursevant* < MF *pursivant*]
pur·sy (pûr′sē), *adj.*, **-si·er, -si·est.** **1.** short-winded, esp. from corpulence or fatness. **2.** corpulent or fat. [late ME *purcy*, var. of ME *pursif* < AF *porsif*, var. of OF *polsif* < *pols(er)* (to) pant, heave, PUSH + *-if* -IVE] —**pur′si·ly,** *adv.* —**pur′si·ness,** *n.*
pur·te·nance (pûr′tᵊnəns), *n.* *Archaic.* the heart, liver, and lungs of an animal. [ME; aph. var. of APPURTENANCE]
pu·ru·lence (pyo͝or′ə ləns, pyo͝or′yə-), *n.* **1.** the condition of containing or forming pus. **2.** pus. Also, **pu′ru·len·cy.** [< LL *pūrulentia.* See PURULENT, -ENCE]
pu·ru·lent (pyo͝or′ə lənt, pyo͝or′yə-), *adj.* **1.** full of, containing, forming, or discharging pus. **2.** attended with suppuration. **3.** of the nature of or like pus. [< L *pūrulent(us)* = *pūr-* (comb. form of *pūs*) PUS + *-ulentus* -ULENT] —**pu′ru·lent·ly,** *adv.*
Pu·rús (*Sp.* po͞o ro͞os′; *Port.* po͝o ro͞os′), *n.* a river in NW central South America, flowing NE from E Peru through W Brazil to the Amazon. 2000 mi. long.
pur·vey (pər vā′), *v.t.* to provide, furnish, or supply (esp. food or provisions). [ME *purveie(n)* < AF *purveie(r)* < L *prōvidēre* to PROVIDE]
pur·vey·ance (pər vā′əns), *n.* **1.** the act of purveying. **2.** something that is purveyed, as provisions. [r. ME *purvea(u)nce*, *purvya(u)nce*, etc. < OF *purveance* < L *providentia.* See PROVIDENCE]
pur·vey·or (pər vā′ər), *n.* a person who purveys, provides, or supplies. [r. ME *pourveour* < AF]
pur·view (pûr′vyo͞o), *n.* **1.** the range of operation, authority, concern. **2.** the range of vision, insight, or understanding. **3.** *Law.* **a.** that which is provided or enacted in a statute, as distinguished from the preamble. **b.** the purpose or scope of a statute. **4.** the full scope or compass of any document, statement, subject, book, etc. [ME *purveu* < AF < VL **providutus* for L *prōvīsus*, ptp. of *prōvidēre* to PROVIDE]
pus (pus), *n.* a yellow-white, more or less viscid substance produced by suppuration and found in abscesses, sores, etc., consisting of a liquid plasma in which leukocytes are suspended. [< L; akin to Gk *pýon* pus. See PYO-] —**pus′like′,** *adj.*
Pu·san (po͞o′sän′), *n.* a seaport in SE South Korea. 1,419,808 (est. 1965). Japanese, **Fusan, Fuzan.**
Pu·sey (pyo͞o′zē), *n.* **1. Edward Bou·ve·rie** (bo͞o′və rē), 1800–82, English clergyman. **2. Nathan Marsh** (märsh), born 1907, U.S. educator: president of Harvard University 1953–71.
Pu·sey·ism (pyo͞o′zē iz′əm), *n.* Tractarianism. [E. B. PUSEY + -ISM] —**Pu′sey·is′ti·cal, Pu′sey·is′tic,** *adj.* —**Pu·sey·ite** (pyo͞o′zē īt′), *n.*
push (po͝osh), *v.t.* **1.** to press against in order to move away. **2.** to move in a specified way by pressing. **3.** to make (one's way, a path, etc.) by thrusting obstacles aside. **4.** to urge to some action or course. **5.** to carry toward a conclusion or extreme. **6.** to depend excessively upon: *to push one's luck.* **7.** to press the adoption, use, purchase, etc., of. **8.** to put into difficulties because of the lack of something specified (usually fol. by *for*): *to be pushed for time.* **9.** *Informal.* to be close to, esp. in age: *The maestro is pushing ninety-two.* —*v.i.* **10.** to move or attempt to move someone or something by pressing. **11.** to make one's way with effort or persistence, as against difficulty or opposition. **12.** to move on being pushed: *a swinging door that pushes easily.* **13.** *Slang.* to sell narcotics. **14. push off,** *Informal.* to go away; depart. —*n.* **15.** the act or an instance of pushing. **16.** a vigorous onset or effort. **17.** a determined advance against opposition, obstacles, etc. **18.** the pressure of circumstances, activities, etc. **19.** *Informal.* persevering energy; enterprise. [ME *posshe(n)* < MF *pousse(r)*, OF *po(u)lser* < L *pulsāre.* See PULSATE]
push·ball (po͝osh′bôl′), *n.* **1.** a game played with a large, heavy ball, usually about six feet in diameter, which two sides attempt to push to opposite goals. **2.** the ball used in this game.
push-bike (po͝osh′bīk′), *n.* *Brit.* a standard bicycle, operated by pedals rather than a motor. Also, **push′ bi′cycle, push′ cy′cle.**
push′ broom′, a wide broom with a long handle, pushed by hand and used for sweeping large areas.
push′ but′ton, a button or knob depressed to open or close an electric circuit. —**push′-but′ton,** *adj.*
push·cart (po͝osh′kärt′), *n.* a light cart to be pushed by hand, used esp. by street vendors.
push·er (po͝osh′ər), *n.* **1.** a person or thing that pushes. **2.** *Aeron.* an airplane whose propellers push rather than pull. **3.** *Slang.* a peddler of narcotics.
push·ing (po͝osh′ing), *adj.* **1.** that pushes. **2.** enterprising; energetic. **3.** tactlessly or officiously aggressive; forward; intrusive. —**push′ing·ly,** *adv.* —**push′ing·ness,** *n.*
Push·kin (po͝osh′kin), *n.* **A·le·xan·der Ser·ge·e·vich** (ä′le ksän′dər sɛʀ ge′yə vich), 1799–1837, Russian poet, short-story writer, and dramatist.
push·o·ver (po͝osh′ō′vər), *n.* *Slang.* **1.** anything done easily. **2.** an easily defeated person or team.
push-pull (po͝osh′po͝ol′), *n.* *Radio.* a two-tube symmetrical arrangement in which the grid excitation voltages are opposite in phase.
push′ shot′, *Basketball.* an overhand shot with one hand from a point relatively distant from the basket.
Push·tu (push′to͞o), *n.* Pashto. Also, **Push·to** (push′tō).
push-up (po͝osh′up′), *n.* an exercise in which a person, keeping the body and legs straight, alternately pushes himself up from the ground by straightening his arms and lets himself down by bending them.
push·y (po͝osh′ē), *adj.*, **push·i·er, push·i·est.** *Informal.* obnoxiously self-assertive. —**push′i·ness,** *n.*
pu·sil·la·nim·i·ty (pyo͞o′sə lə nim′i tē), *n.* timidity; cowardliness. [late ME < eccl. L *pusillanimitās*]
pu·sil·lan·i·mous (pyo͞o′sə lan′ə məs), *adj.* **1.** lacking courage or resolution. **2.** proceeding from or indicating a cowardly spirit. [< LL *pusillanim(is)* petty-spirited = L *pusill(us)* very small, petty + *-anim(is)* -spirited, -minded (*anim(us)* spirit + *-is* adj. suffix) + -OUS] —**pu′sil·lan′i·mous·ly,** *adv.* —**Syn. 1.** timorous, fearful.
puss[1] (po͝os), *n.* **1.** a cat. **2.** a girl or woman. [akin to D *poes*, LG *puus-katte*, dial. Sw *katte-pus*, Norw *puse(kat)*, etc.] —**puss′like′,** *adj.*
puss[2] (po͝os), *n.* *Slang.* the face. [< Ir *pus* lip, mouth]
puss·ley (pus′lē), *n.* *Informal.* purslane.
puss·y[1] (po͝os′ē), *n.*, *pl.* **puss·ies.** a cat, esp. a kitten. Also called **pussycat.** [PUSS[1] + -Y[2]]
pus·sy[2] (pus′ē), *adj.*, **-si·er, -si·est.** *Med.* puslike. [PUS + -Y[1]]
pus·sy[3] (po͝os′ē), *n.*, *pl.* **-sies.** *Slang* (*usually vulgar*). **1.** the vulva. **2.** sexual intercourse. **3.** the woman as an object of sex. [? perh. OE *pusa* bag (see PURSE), influenced by PUSS[1]]
puss·y·cat (po͝os′ē kat′), *n.* **1.** pussy[1]. **2.** *Slang.* a highly agreeable, well-liked person, thing, or situation.
puss·y·foot (po͝os′ē fo͝ot′), *v.*, *n.*, *pl.* **-foots.** —*v.i.* **1.** to go or move in a stealthy or cautious manner. **2.** to act cautiously or timidly, as if afraid to commit oneself on a point at issue. —*n.* **3.** a person with a catlike or soft and stealthy tread.
puss′y wil′low (po͝os′ē), **1.** a small, American willow, *Salix discolor*, having silky catkins. **2.** any of various similar willows.

Pussy willow, *Salix discolor*

pus·tu·lant (pus′chə lənt), *adj.* **1.** causing the formation of pustules. —*n.* **2.** a medicine or agent causing pustulation. [< LL *pūstulant-* (s. of *pūstulāns*), prp. of *pūstulāre* to blister. See PUSTULE, -ANT]

pus·tu·lar (pus′chə lər), *adj.* **1.** of, pertaining to, or of the nature of pustules. **2.** characterized by pustules. Also, **pus′tu·lous.** [< NL *pūstulār(is)*]

pus·tu·late (*v.* pus′chə lāt′; *adj.* pus′chə lit, -lāt′), *v.*, **-lat·ed, -lat·ing,** *adj. Pathol.* —*v.i.* **1.** to become pustular. —*adj.* **2.** covered with pustules. [< LL *pūstulāt(us)*, ptp. of *pūstulāre* to blister]

pus·tu·la·tion (pus′chə lā′shən), *n.* the formation or breaking out of pustules. [< LL *pūstulātiōn-* (s. of *pūstulātiō*) a blistering]

pus·tule (pus′chōōl), *n.* **1.** *Pathol.* a small elevation of the skin containing pus. **2.** any pimplelike or blisterlike swelling or elevation. [ME < L *pūstula* pimple, blister, appar. var. of *pūsula;* akin to Gk *phȳsallís* bladder, *phȳsaléos* inflated] —**pus′tuled,** *adj.*

put (pŏŏt), *v.*, **put, put·ting,** *n.* —*v.t.* **1.** to move or place (anything) so as to get it into or out of some place or position: *to put a book on the shelf.* **2.** to bring into some relation, state, etc.: *to put everything in order.* **3.** to place in the charge or power of a person, institution, etc.: *to put a child in a special school.* **4.** to subject to the endurance or suffering of something: *to put a person to trial.* **5.** to set to a duty, task, action, etc.: *I put her to setting the table.* **6.** to force or drive to some course or action: *to put an army to flight.* **7.** to render or translate, as into another language: *He put the novel into French.* **8.** to provide (words) with music as accompaniment; set: *to put a poem to music.* **9.** to assign or attribute: *He puts a political interpretation on anything social.* **10.** to set at a particular place, point, amount, etc., in a scale of estimation: *He puts the distance at five miles.* **11.** to bet or wager: *to put two dollars on a horse.* **12.** to express or state: *To put it honestly, I don't understand.* **13.** to apply, as to a use or purpose: *to put one's knowledge to practical use.* **14.** to set, give, or make: *to put an end to a practice.* **15.** to propose or submit for answer, consideration, deliberation, etc.: *to put a question before a committee.* **16.** to impose, as a burden, charge, or the like: *to put a tax on luxury articles.* **17.** to invest (often fol. by *in* or *into*): *to put one's money in real estate; to put one's savings into securities.* **18.** to throw or cast: *to put the shot.* —*v.i.* **19.** to go, move, or proceed: *to put out to sea.* **20. put about, a.** to disturb; worry. **b.** to turn in a different direction. **21. put across,** *Slang.* to cause to be understood or received favorably. **22. put aside,** to store up; save. **23. put down, a.** to write down; register; record. **b.** to suppress; check. **c.** *Slang.* to belittle or embarrass (a person). **24. put forth, a.** to propose; present. **b.** to exert; exercise. **c.** to grow shoots, buds, or leaves. **25. put forward,** to propose; present. **26. put in, a.** *Naut.* to enter a port or harbor. **b.** to interpose; intervene. **c.** to spend (time) as indicated. **27. put in for,** to apply for or request (something): *to put in for a transfer.* **28. put off, a.** to postpone; defer. **b.** to get rid of by delay or evasion. **c.** to launch (a boat). **29. put on, a.** to dress oneself with (an article or articles of clothing). **b.** to adopt, as an affectation. **c.** to cause to be performed, as a show. **30. put oneself out,** to go to trouble or expense. **31. put out, a.** to extinguish, as a fire. **b.** to disturb or annoy. **c.** to subject to inconvenience. **d.** *Baseball, Softball, Cricket.* to cause to be removed from an opportunity to reach base or score; retire. **e.** to manufacture or publish. **f.** *Slang* (*vulgar*). (of a woman) to indulge in coitus. **32. put over,** *Informal.* to accomplish successfully. **33. put someone on,** *Slang.* to tease a person, esp. with lies. **34. put something over on,** *Informal.* to take advantage of; deceive. **35. put through, a.** to accomplish or bring into effect. **b.** to make a telephone connection. **36. put to it,** to be confronted with difficulty. **37. put up, a.** to construct; erect. **b.** to provide (money); contribute. **c.** *Informal.* to lodge. **d.** to display; show. **e.** to propose as a candidate; nominate. **f.** *Archaic.* to sheathe one's sword; stop fighting. **38. put upon,** to take unfair advantage of. **39. put up to,** *Informal.* to provoke; prompt; incite. **40. put up with,** *Informal.* to endure; tolerate. **41. stay put,** *Informal.* to remain in the same place, rank, or position. —*n.* **42.** a throw or cast, esp. of a shot or stone from the shoulder. **43.** *Finance.* a contract that permits the holder to exercise an option to sell a certain amount of stock or a commodity at a set price within a given time. Cf. **call** (def. 57). [ME *putte(n)*, *puten* to push, thrust, put; akin to OE *putung* an impelling, inciting, *potian* to push, goad; c. Icel *pota* to thrust, poke]

—**Syn. 1.** PUT, PLACE, LAY, SET mean to bring or take an object (or cause it to go) to a certain location or position, there to leave it. PUT is the general word: *to put the dishes on the table; to put one's hair up.* PLACE is a more formal word, suggesting precision of movement or definiteness of location: *He placed his hand on the Bible.* LAY, meaning originally to cause to lie, and SET, meaning originally to cause to sit, are used particularly to stress the position in which an object is put: LAY usually suggests putting an object rather carefully into a horizontal position: *to lay a pattern out on the floor.* SET usually means to place upright: *to set a child on a horse.* **16.** levy, inflict.

pu·ta·men (pyōō tā′min), *n.*, *pl.* **-tam·i·na** (-tam′ə nə). *Bot.* a hard or stony endocarp, as a peach stone. [< L: that which is removed in pruning = *putā(re)* (to) trim + *-men* resultative suffix] —**pu·tam·i·nous** (pyōō tam′ə nəs), *adj.*

pu·ta·tive (pyōō′tə tiv), *adj.* commonly regarded as such; reputed; supposed. [late ME < LL *putātīv(us)* reputed = *putāt(us)* (ptp. of *putāre* to think, consider, reckon, orig. to cut, trim, prune, akin to *pavīre* to beat, ram down; see PAVE) + *-īvus* -IVE] —**pu′ta·tive·ly,** *adv.*

put-down (pŏŏt′doun′), *n.* **1.** a landing of an aircraft. **2.** *Slang.* a remark or act intended to humiliate, embarrass, or snub someone.

put·log (pŏŏt′lôg′, -log′, put′-), *n.* any of the short horizontal timbers supporting the floor of a builder's scaffold. [alter. (by assoc. with LOG[1]) of *putlock*, appar. PUT (ptp.) + LOCK]

Put·nam (put′nəm), *n.* **1. Israel,** 1718–90, American Revolutionary general. **2. Rufus,** 1738–1824, American Revolutionary officer: engineer and colonizer in Ohio.

put-on (*adj.* pŏŏt′on′, -ôn′; *n.* pŏŏt′on′, -ôn′), *adj.* **1.** assumed; feigned; pretended. —*n.* **2.** Also, **put′on′.** a teasing lie or prank, usually said or done with apparent seriousness.

put-out (pŏŏt′out′), *n. Baseball.* an instance of putting out a batter or base runner. [n. use of v. phrase *put out*]

put-put (put′put′, -put′ *for 1;* put′put′ *for 2*), *n.* **1.** the sound made by a small internal-combustion engine, motor scooter, etc. **2.** a small internal-combustion engine, or something, as a boat, model airplane, motor scooter, etc., equipped with one. Also, **putt′-putt′.** [imit.]

pu·tre·fac·tion (pyōō′trə fak′shən), *n.* the act or process of putrefying; the decomposition of organic matter by bacteria and fungi. [late ME < LL *putrefactiōn-* (s. of *putrefactiō*) a rotting = L *putrefact(us)* (ptp. of *putrefacere* to PUTREFY) + *-iōn-* -ION] —**pu′tre·fac′tive, pu·tre·fa·cient** (pyōō′trə fā′shənt), *adj.*

pu·tre·fy (pyōō′trə fī′), *v.*, **-fied, -fy·ing.** —*v.t.* **1.** to make putrid; cause to rot or decay. —*v.i.* **2.** to become putrid; rot. **3.** to become gangrenous. [late ME *putrefie(n)* < MF *putrefie(r)* < VL **putreficāre*, r. L *putrefacere* to make rotten] —**pu′tre·fi′a·ble,** *adj.* —**pu′tre·fi′er,** *n.*

pu·tres·cent (pyōō tres′ənt), *adj.* **1.** becoming putrid; in the process of putrefaction. **2.** of or pertaining to putrefaction. [< L *putrescent-* (s. of *putrescēns*), prp. of *putrescere* to grow rotten] —**pu·tres′cence,** *n.*

pu·tres·ci·ble (pyōō tres′ə bəl), *adj.* **1.** liable to become putrid. —*n.* **2.** a putrescible substance. [< L *putresc(ere)* (to) grow rotten (see PUTRESCENT) + -IBLE] —**pu·tres′ci·bil′i·ty,** *n.*

pu·tres·cine (pyōō tres′ēn, -in), *n. Biochem.* a liquid ptomaine, $NH_2(CH_2)_4NH_2$, having a disagreeable odor, usually produced by decayed animal tissue. [< L *putresc(ere)* (to) grow rotten (see PUTRESCENT) + -INE[2]]

pu·trid (pyōō′trid), *adj.* **1.** (of organic matter) in a state of foul decay or decomposition. **2.** of, pertaining to, or attended by putrefaction. **3.** having the odor of decaying flesh. **4.** of very low quality; rotten. [< L *putrid(us)* rotten = *putr(ēre)* (to) rot + *-idus* -ID[4]] —**pu·trid′i·ty, pu′trid·ness,** *n.* —**pu′trid·ly,** *adv.*

pu·tri·lage (pyōō′trə lij), *n.* putrid or putrescent matter. [< L *putrilāgin-* (s. of *putrilāgō*) putrefaction] —**pu·tri·lag·i·nous** (pyōō′trə laj′ə nəs), *adj.*

Putsch (pōōch), *n. German.* a revolt or uprising, esp. one that depends upon suddenness and speed.

putt (put), *Golf.* —*v.t., v.i.* **1.** to strike (the ball) so as to make it roll along the green into or near the hole. —*n.* **2.** an act of putting. **3.** a stroke made in putting. [var. of PUT]

put·tee (put′ē), *n.* **1.** a long strip of cloth wound spirally round the leg from ankle to knee. **2.** a gaiter or legging of leather or other material, as worn by soldiers, riders, etc. Also, **putty.** [< Hindi *paṭṭī* bandage; akin to Skt *paṭṭa* strip of cloth, bandage]

put·ter[1] (put′ər), *v.i.* to busy or occupy oneself in a leisurely or ineffective manner. Also, *esp. Brit.*, **potter.** [var. of POTTER[2]] —**put′ter·er,** *n.* —**put′ter·ing·ly,** *adv.*

putt·er[2] (put′ər), *n. Golf.* **1.** a person who putts. **2.** a club with a relatively short, stiff shaft and a wooden or iron head, used in putting. [PUTT + -ER[1]]

put·ter[3] (pŏŏt′ər), *n.* a person or thing that puts. [ME; see PUT, -ER[1]]

put·ti·er (put′ē ər), *n.* a person who putties, as a glazier.

putt′ing green′, *Golf.* green (def. 17b).

put·ty[1] (put′ē), *n.*, *pl.* **-ties,** *v.*, **-tied, -ty·ing.** —*n.* **1.** a compound, usually of whiting and linseed oil, used to secure window panes, patch woodwork defects, etc. **2.** any of various substances for sealing the joints of tubes or pipes. **3.** a fine mixture of lime and water with sand and plaster of Paris, used as a finish plaster coat. **4.** See **putty powder.** —*v.t.* **5.** to secure, cover, etc., with putty. [< F *potée*, lit., (something) potted. See POT[1], -EE]

put·ty[2] (put′ē), *n.*, *pl.* **-ties.** puttee.

put′ty knife′, a broad-bladed tool for puttying.

put′ty pow′der, an abrasive consisting chiefly of stannic oxide, used for polishing hard surfaces. Also called **putty, jeweler's putty.**

put·ty·root (put′ē rōōt′, -rŏŏt′), *n.* an American, orchidaceous plant, *Aplectrum hyemale*, having a slender naked rootstock that produces each spring a scape with a loose raceme of brownish flowers.

Pu·tu·ma·yo (pōō′tōō mä′yô), *n.* a river in NW South America, flowing SE from S Colombia into the Amazon in NW Brazil. 900 mi. long. Portuguese, **Iça.**

put-up (pŏŏt′up′), *adj. Informal.* planned beforehand in a secret or crafty manner: *a put-up job.*

put-up·on (pŏŏt′ə pon′), *adj.* ill-used; maltreated.

Puy-de-Dôme (pwē də dōm′), *n.* a mountain in central France. 4805 ft.

Pu-yi (pōō′yē′), *n.* **Henry,** 1906–67, as Hsüan T'ung, last emperor of China 1908–12; as K'ang Tê, puppet emperor of Manchukuo 1934–45. Also, **P'u-i.**

puz·zle (puz′əl), *n.*, *v.*, **-zled, -zling.** —*n.* **1.** a contrivance designed to amuse by presenting difficulties to be solved by ingenuity or patient effort. **2.** a puzzling question, matter, or person. **3.** a puzzled or perplexed condition. —*v.t.* **4.** to mystify; confuse; baffle. **5.** to exercise (onself or one's mind) over some problem or matter. —*v.i.* **6.** to ponder or study over some perplexing problem or matter. **7. puzzle out,** to solve by careful study or effort. [late ME *poselet* puzzled, confused] —**puz′zled·ly,** *adv.* —**puz′zling·ly,** *adv.*

—**Syn. 2.** PUZZLE, RIDDLE, ENIGMA refer to something baffling or confusing that is to be solved. A PUZZLE is a question or problem, intricate enough to be perplexing to the mind; it is sometimes a contrivance made purposely perplexing to test a person's ingenuity: *a crossword puzzle; The reason for their behavior remains a puzzle.* A RIDDLE is an intentionally obscure statement or question, the meaning of or answer to which is to be arrived at only by guessing: *the famous riddle of the Sphinx.* ENIGMA, originally meaning riddle, now refers to some baffling problem with connotations of mysteriousness: *He will always be an enigma to me.*

puz·zle·ment (puz′əl mənt), *n.* **1.** a puzzled state; perplexity. **2.** something puzzling.

puz·zler (puz′lər), *n.* **1.** a person who puzzles. **2.** a baffling thing or problem.
PVC, See **polyvinyl chloride.**
Pvt., Private.
PW, **1.** prisoner of war. **2.** public works.
PWA, Public Works Administration. Also, **P.W.A.**
P.W.D., Public Works Department. Also, **PWD**
pwr, power.
pwt., pennyweight. Also, **pwt**
PX, *pl.* **PXs.** *U.S. Army.* See **post exchange.**
pxt., pinxit.
py-, var. of **pyo-** before a vowel: *pyemia.*
pya (pyä, pē ä′), *n.* a copper coin of Burma, the 100th part of a kyat. [< Burmese]
py·ae·mi·a (pī ē′mē ə), *n.* *Pathol.* pyemia. —**py·ae′mic,** *adj.*
pycn-, var. of **pycno-** before a vowel: *pycnidium.*
pyc·nid·i·um (pik nid′ē əm), *n., pl.* **-nid·i·a** (-nid′ē ə). *Bot.* (in certain ascomycetes and *Fungi Imperfecti*) a globose or flask-shaped fruiting body bearing conidia on conidiophores. [< NL; see PYCN-, -IDIUM] —**pyc·nid′i·al,** *adj.*
pycno-, a learned borrowing from Greek meaning "dense," "close," "thick," used in the formation of compound words: *pycnometer.* Also, *esp. before a vowel,* **pycn-.** [< NL, comb. form repr. Gk *pyknós*]
pyc·nom·e·ter (pik nom′i tər), *n.* a container for determining the density of a liquid or solid.
Pyd·na (pid′nə), *n.* a town in ancient Macedonia, W of the Gulf of Salonika: decisive Roman victory over the Macedonians 186 B.C.
py·e·li·tis (pī′ə lī′tis), *n.* *Pathol.* inflammation of the pelvis or outlet of the kidney. [< NL] —**py·e·lit·ic** (pī′ə-lit′ik), *adj.*
pyelo-, a learned borrowing from Greek, used with the meaning "pelvis" in the formation of compound words. Also, *esp. before a vowel,* **pyel-.** [< NL, comb. form repr. Gk *pýelos* basin. See PELVIS]
py·e·mi·a (pī ē′mē ə), *n.* *Pathol.* a diseased condition in which pyogenic bacteria are circulating in the blood, characterized by the development of abscesses in various organs. Also, **pyaemia.** [< NL] —**py·e′mic,** *adj.*
py·gid·i·um (pī jid′ē əm), *n., pl.* **-gid·i·a** (-jid′ē ə). *Zool.* any of various structures or regions at the caudal end of the body in certain invertebrates. [< NL < Gk *pygḗ(ē)* rump + *-idion* dim. suffix] —**py·gid′i·al,** *adj.*
pyg·mae·an (pig mē′ən), *adj.* pygmy (defs. 5, 6). Also, **pyg·me′an.** [< L *pygmae(us)* dwarfish (see PYGMY) + -AN]
Pyg·ma·li·on (pig mā′lē ən, -māl′yən), *n.* *Class. Myth.* a sculptor and king of Cyprus who carved an ivory statue of a maiden and fell in love with it. It was brought to life, in response to his prayer, by Aphrodite, and was called Galatea.
Pyg·my (pig′mē), *n., pl.* **-mies,** *adj.* —*n.* **1.** *Anthropol.* **a.** a member of an equatorial African Negroid race of small stature. **b.** a Negrito of southeastern Asia, or of the Andaman or Philippine Islands. **2.** (*l.c.*) a tiny person or thing. **3.** (*l.c.*) a person or thing of small importance or that is badly lacking in some quality. **4.** one of a legendary race of dwarfs described by certain ancient historians. —*adj.* **5.** (*often l.c.*) of or pertaining to the Pygmies. **6.** (*l.c.*) of very small size, importance, power, etc. Also, **Pigmy.** [ME *pigmeis,* pl. of *pigmē* < L *Pygmae(us)* < Gk *pygmaîos* dwarfish (adj.), Pygmy (n.) = *pygm(ḗ)* distance from elbow to knuckles + *-aios* -EOUS] —**pyg′moid,** *adj.* —**pyg′my·ish,** *adj.* —**pyg′my·ism,** *n.* —**Syn. 1.** See **dwarf.**
py·in (pī′in), *n.* *Biochem.* an albuminous constituent of pus. —**py′ic,** *adj.*
py·jam·as (pə jä′məz, -jam′əz), *n.* (*construed as pl.*) *Chiefly Brit.* pajamas.
pyk·nic (pik′nik), *Psychol.* —*adj.* **1.** (of a physical type) having a fat, rounded build or body structure. Cf. **asthenic** (def. 2), **athletic** (def. 4). —*n.* **2.** a person of the pyknic type. [< Gk *pykn(ós)* thick + -IC]
py·lon (pī′lon), *n.* **1.** a marking post or tower for guiding aviators. **2.** a relatively tall structure flanking a gate or marking an entrance or approach, as to a bridge or avenue. **3.** a massive structure at the entrance to an ancient Egyptian temple, often consisting of two towers flanking a gate. **4.** a steel tower used as a support. [< Gk: gateway]
py·lo·rec·to·my (pī′lə rek′tə mē), *n., pl.* **-mies.** *Surg.* removal of the pylorus.
py·lo·rus (pī lōr′əs, -lôr′-, pi-), *n., pl.* **-lo·ri** (-lōr′ī, -lôr′ī). *Anat.* the opening between the stomach and the duodenum. [< LL < Gk *pylōrós,* lit., gatekeeper] —**py·lor·ic** (pī lôr′ik, -lor′-, pi-), *adj.*
Py·los (pē′lōs; *Eng.* pī′los, -lōs), *n.* Greek name of **Navarino.**
Pym (pim), *n.* **John,** 1584–1643, English statesman.
Pyn·chon (pin′chən), *n.* **William,** 1590?–1662, English colonist in America.
pyo-, a learned borrowing from Greek meaning "pus," used in the formation of compound words: *pyoderma.* Also, *esp. before a vowel,* **py-.** [< Gk, comb. form of *pýon*]
py·o·der·ma (pī′ō dûr′mə), *n.* *Pathol.* any disease of the skin characterized by the formation of pus. [< NL]
py·o·gen·ic (pī′ə jen′ik), *adj.* *Pathol.* **1.** producing or generating pus. **2.** attended with or pertaining to the formation of pus. —**py′o·gen′e·sis,** *n.*
py·oid (pī′oid), *adj.* *Pathol.* pertaining to pus; puslike. [< Gk *pyoeid(ēs)*]
Pyong·yang (pyung′yäng′), *n.* the capital of North Korea, in the SW part. 1,500,000. Japanese, **Heijo.**
py·or·rhe·a (pī′ə rē′ə), *n.* **1.** *Pathol.* a discharge of pus. **2.** Also called **pyorrhe′a al·ve·o·lar′is** (al vē′ə lar′is), **Riggs' disease.** *Dentistry.* a disease characterized in its severe forms by the formation of pus between the roots of the teeth and their surrounding tissues, and frequently accompanied by the loosening of the teeth. Also, **py′or·rhoe′a.** [< NL] —**py′or·rhe′al, py′or·rhoe′al, py′or·rhe′ic, py′or·rhoe′ic,** *adj.*
pyr-, var. of **pyro-,** often used before *h* or a vowel: *pyran.*
pyr·a·lid (pir′ə lid), *n.* **1.** any of numerous slender-bodied moths of the family *Pyralidae,* having elongated triangular forewings, the larvae of which include many crop pests. —*adj.* **2.** belonging or pertaining to the family *Pyralidae.* [< NL *Pyralid(ae)* = *Pyral(is)* type genus (< L *pyralis,* Gk *pyralís* an insect thought to live in fire; akin to *pŷr* fire) + *-idae* -ID[2]]
pyr·a·mid (pir′ə mid), *n.* **1.** *Geom.* a solid having a polygonal base with triangular sides that meet at an apex. **2.** any object in the form of such a solid. **3.** *Archit.* a massive masonry construction having a square or rectangular base and suggesting such a solid. **4.** a number of persons or things arranged or heaped up so as to suggest such a construction. **5.** *Crystall.* any form the planes of which intersect all three of the axes. **6.** *Stock Exchange.* the series of transactions involved in pyramiding. —*v.i.* **7.** to take, or become disposed in, the form of a pyramid. **8.** *Stock Exchange.* (in speculating on margin) to use profits of transactions not yet closed as margin for additional buying or selling in a new transaction. —*v.t.* **9.** to arrange in the form of a pyramid. **10.** to raise or increase (costs, wages, etc.) by adding amounts gradually. **11.** *Stock Exchange.* (in speculating on margin) to operate in, or employ in, pyramiding. [< L *pyramid-* (s. of *pyramis*) < Gk *pyramís* (gen. *pyramídos*) < Egypt; r. ME *pyramis* < L] —**pyr′a·mid·like′,** *adj.*

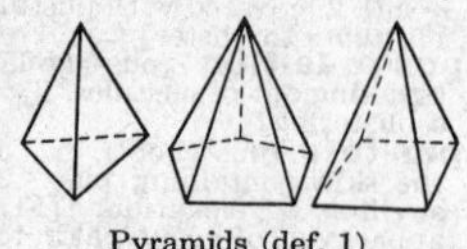
Pyramids (def. 1)

py·ram·i·dal (pi ram′i dᵊl), *adj.* **1.** of or pertaining to a pyramid: *the pyramidal form.* **2.** of the nature of a pyramid; pyramidlike. —**py·ram′i·dal·ly,** *adv.*
pyr·a·mid·i·cal (pir′ə mid′i kəl), *adj.* pyramidal. Also, **pyr′a·mid′ic.** [< Gk *pyramidik(ós)*] —**pyr′a·mid′i·cal·ly,** *adv.*
pyr′amid let′ter. See **chain letter.**
Pyr′a·mus and This′be (pir′ə məs), *Class. Myth.* two young lovers of Babylon who, in defiance of their parents, conducted their courtship clandestinely by talking through a crack in a wall. Each committed suicide, Pyramus on believing Thisbe dead, she on discovering his body.
py·ran (pī′ran, pī ran′), *n.* *Chem.* either of two compounds having the formula C_5H_6O, containing one oxygen and five carbon atoms arranged in a six-membered ring.
py·rar·gy·rite (pī rär′jə rīt′), *n.* a blackish mineral, silver antimony sulfide, $AgSbS_3$, showing, when transparent, a deep ruby-red color by transmitted light: an ore of silver; ruby silver. [PYR- + Gk *árgyr(on)* silver + -ITE[1]]
pyre (pīᵊr), *n.* a pile or heap of wood or other combustible material, used esp. for cremations. [< L *pyra* < Gk: hearth, funeral pile]
py·rene (pī′rēn), *n.* *Bot.* a putamen or stone, esp. when there are several in a single fruit; a nutlet. [< NL *pȳrēna* < Gk *pȳrēn* stone (of a fruit)]
Pyr·e·nees (pir′ə nēz′), *n.* a mountain range between Spain and France. Highest peak, Pic de Néthou, 11,165 ft. —**Pyr′e·ne′an,** *adj.*
py·re·thrin (pī rē′thrin), *n.* *Chem.* **1.** Also called **pyrethrin I.** a viscous, water-insoluble liquid, $C_{21}H_{28}O_3$, extracted from pyrethrum flowers, used as an insecticide. **2.** Also called **pyrethrin II.** a like compound, $C_{22}H_{28}O_5$, obtained and used similarly. [PYRETHR(UM) + -IN[2]]
py·re·thrum (pī rē′thrəm), *n.* **1.** any of several chrysanthemums, as *Chrysanthemum coccineum,* having finely divided leaves and showy red, pink, lilac, or white flowers, cultivated as an ornamental. **2.** any of several chrysanthemums, as *Chrysanthemum cinerariaefolium, C. coccineum,* or *C. Marschallii,* cultivated as a source of insecticides. **3.** *Pharm.* the dried flower heads of these plants, used chiefly as an insecticide and in treating certain skin disorders. [< L < Gk *pýrethron* feverfew, akin to *pyretós* fever]
py·ret·ic (pī ret′ik), *adj.* of, pertaining to, affected by, or producing fever. [< NL *pyretic(us)* = Gk *pyret(ós)* fever + L *-icus* -IC]
Py·rex (pī′reks), *n.* *Trademark.* any of a class of heat-resistant and chemical-resistant glassware used for cooking.
py·rex·i·a (pī rek′sē ə), *n.* *Pathol.* fever. [< NL < Gk *pýrex(is)* feverishness + *-ia* -IA] —**py·rex′i·al, py·rex′ic,** *adj.*
pyr·he·li·om·e·ter (pīᵊr′hē lē om′i tər, pir′-), *n.* *Astrophysics.* an instrument for measuring the total intensity of the sun's energy radiation. —**pyr·he·li·o·met·ric** (pīᵊr′hē lē ə-me′trik, pir′-), *adj.*
pyrid-, a combining form of **pyridine:** *pyridoxine.*
pyr·i·dine (pir′i dēn′, -din), *n.* *Chem.* a flammable, liquid organic base, C_5H_5N, having a disagreeable odor: used chiefly as a solvent and in organic synthesis. [PYR- + -ID[2] + -INE[2]] —**py·rid·ic** (pī rid′ik), *adj.*
pyr·i·dox·ine (pir′i dok′sēn, -sin), *n.* *Biochem.* a derivative of pyridine, $CH_3C_5N(CH_2OH)_2OH$, used for the formation of hemoglobin and in the prevention of pellagra; vitamin B_6. Also, **pyr·i·dox·in** (pir′i dok′sin). [PYRID(INE) + OX(YGEN) + -INE[2]]
pyr·i·form (pir′ə fôrm′), *adj.* pear-shaped. [< NL *pyriform(is)* = *pyri-* (for *piri-* pear) + *-formis* -FORM]
py·rim·i·dine (pī rim′i dēn′, pir′ə mi dēn′, -din), *n.* *Chem.* **1.** a heterocyclic ring compound, $C_4H_4N_2$, that is an important constituent of several biochemical substances, as thiamine. **2.** any of the group of compounds derived from this heterocyclic ring. [alter. of PYRIDINE]
py·rite (pī′rīt), *n.* a very common brass-yellow mineral, iron disulfide, FeS_2, with a metallic luster, burned to sulfur dioxide in the manufacture of sulfuric acid. Also, **pyrites.** Also called **iron pyrites.** [< L *pyrītē(s)* < Gk, orig. adj., of or in fire] —**py·rit·ic** (pī rit′ik, pə-), **py·rit′i·cal, py·ri·tous** (pə rī′təs, pī-), *adj.*
py·ri·tes (pī rī′tēz, pə-, pī′rīts), *n., pl.* **-tes.** *Mineral.* **1.** pyrite. **2.** marcasite. **3.** any of various other metallic sulfides, as of copper, tin, etc. [< L]
pyro-, **1.** a learned borrowing from Greek used, with the meaning "fire," "heat," "of, relating to, or concerned with fire or heat," in the formation of compound words: *pyrogen; pyrolysis.* **2.** *Chem.* a word element used before the name of an inorganic acid, indicating that its water content is intermediate between that of the corresponding ortho- (more water) and meta- (least water) acids: *pyrosulfuric acid* ($H_2S_2O_7$). **3.** *Geol.* used in the names of minerals, rocks, etc., indicating a quality produced by the action of fire: *pyrolusite.* Also, **pyr-.** [comb. form of Gk *pŷr* fire]

py·ro·cat·e·chol (pī′rō kat′ə chōl′, -chôl′, -chol′, -kōl′, -kôl′, -kol′, pir′ə-), *n.* *Chem.* catechol. Also, **py·ro·cat·e·chin** (pī′rə kat′ə chin, -kin, pir′ə-).

py·ro·chem·i·cal (pī′rə kem′i kəl), *adj.* pertaining to or producing chemical change at high temperatures. —**py′ro·chem′i·cal·ly,** *adv.*

py·ro·clas·tic (pī′rə klas′tik), *adj.* *Geol.* composed chiefly of fragments of volcanic origin, as agglomerate, tuff, and certain other rocks.

py·ro·crys·tal·line (pī′rə kris′tᵊlin, -tᵊlīn′, -tᵊlēn′), *adj.* *Petrog.* crystallized from a molten magma or highly heated solution.

py·ro·e·lec·tric (pī′rō i lek′trik), *adj.* **1.** pertaining to, subject to, or manifesting pyroelectricity. —*n.* **2.** a substance manifesting pyroelectricity. [back formation from PYRO-ELECTRICITY]

py·ro·e·lec·tric·i·ty (pī′rō i lek tris′i tē, -ē′lek-), *n.* electrification or electrical polarity produced in certain crystals by temperature changes.

py·ro·gal·late (pī′rə gal′āt), *n.* *Chem.* a salt or ether of pyrogallol. [PYROGALL(OL) + -ATE²]

py·ro·gal·lol (pī′rə gal′ōl, -ôl, -ol, -gə lōl′, -lôl′, -lol′), *n.* a white, poisonous, phenolic compound, $C_6H_3(OH)_3$, used as a developer in photography, a mordant for wool, in dyeing, and in the treatment of certain skin conditions. Also called **pyrogal′lic ac′id.** [PYRO- + GALL(IC)² + -OL¹] —**py′ro·gal′lic,** *adj.*

py·ro·gen (pī′rə jen′), *n.* a substance, as a thermostable bacterial toxin, that produces a rise in body temperature.

py·ro·gen·ic (pī′rə jen′ik), *adj.* **1.** producing or produced by heat or fever. **2.** produced by fire, as igneous rock.

py·rog·e·nous (pī roj′ə nəs), *adj.* *Geol.* produced by the action of heat, hot solutions, etc.

py·rog·nos·tics (pī′rəg nos′tiks), *n.pl.* those properties of a mineral that it exhibits when heated, alone or with fluxes, in the blowpipe flame, as the fusibility, intumescence, or other phenomena of fusion, flame coloration, etc.

py·rog·ra·phy (pī rog′rə fē), *n.* the process of burning designs on wood, leather, etc., with a heated tool. —**py·rog′ra·pher,** *n.* —**py·ro·graph·ic** (pī′rə graf′ik), *adj.*

py′ro·lig′ne·ous ac′id (pī′rə lig′nē əs), *Chem.* a yellowish, acidic, water-soluble liquid, containing about 10 percent acetic acid, obtained by the destructive distillation of wood: used for smoking meats. Also called **wood vinegar.**

py′rolig′neous al′cohol. See **methyl alcohol.** Also called **py′rolig′neous spir′it.**

py·ro·lu·site (pī′rə lo͞o′sīt, pī rol′yə sīt′), *n.* a common mineral, manganese dioxide, MnO_2, the principal ore of manganese. [PYRO- + Gk *loûs(is)* washing + -ITE¹]

py·rol·y·sis (pī rol′i sis), *n.* *Chem.* **1.** the subjection of organic compounds to very high temperatures. **2.** the resulting decomposition. —**py·ro·lyt·ic** (pī′rə lit′ik), *adj.*

py·ro·mag·net·ic (pī′rō mag net′ik), *adj.* *Physics.* (no longer current) thermomagnetic (def. 1).

py·ro·man·cy (pī′rə man′sē), *n.* divination by fire or by forms appearing in fire. [ME *piromancie* < ML *pyromantīa* < Gk *pyromanteía* divination by fire] —**py′ro·man′cer,** *n.* —**py′ro·man′tic,** *adj.*

py·ro·ma·ni·a (pī′rə mā′nē ə), *n.* a mania or compulsion to set things on fire. —**py′ro·ma′ni·ac,** *n.* —**py·ro·ma·ni·a·cal** (pī′rō mə nī′ə kəl), *adj.*

py·ro·met·al·lur·gy (pī′rə met′ᵊlûr′jē), *n.* the process or technique of refining ores with heat so as to accelerate chemical reactions or to melt the metallic or nonmetallic content.

py·rom·e·ter (pī rom′i tər), *n.* *Thermodynamics.* an apparatus for measuring high temperatures, esp. by the observation of the color produced by a substance upon heating or by thermoelectric means. —**py·ro·met·ric** (pī′rə me′trik), **py′ro·met′ri·cal,** *adj.* —**py′ro·met′ri·cal·ly,** *adv.* —**py·rom′e·try,** *n.*

py·ro·mor·phite (pī′rə môr′fīt), *n.* a mineral, lead chlorophosphate, $Pb_5P_3O_{12}Cl$: a minor ore of lead. [< G *Pyromorphit*]

py·rone (pī′rōn, pī rōn′), *n.* *Chem.* either of two heterocyclic ketones having the formula $C_5H_4O_2$.

py·rope (pī′rōp), *n.* a mineral, magnesium-aluminum garnet, $Mg_3Al_2Si_3O_{12}$, frequently used as a gem. [ME *pirope* < L *pyrōp(us)* gold-bronze < Gk *pyrōpós*, lit., fire-eyed = *pŷr* fire + *ōp-* (s. of *ṓps*) eye + *-os* adj. suffix]

py·ro·phor·ic (pī′rə fôr′ik, -for′-), *adj.* *Chem.* capable of igniting spontaneously in air. [< Gk *pyrophór(os)* fire-bearing (see PYRO-, -PHOROUS) + -IC]

py·ro·phos·phate (pī′rə fos′fāt), *n.* *Chem.* a salt or ester of pyrophosphoric acid. [PYROPHOSPH(ORIC ACID) + -ATE²]

py′ro·phos·phor′ic ac′id (pī′rō fos fôr′ik, -for′-, pī′-), *Chem.* a powder, $H_4P_2O_7$, formed by the union of one molecule of phosphorus pentoxide with two molecules of water.

py·ro·pho·tom·e·ter (pī′rō fō tom′i tər), *n.* *Physics.* a form of pyrometer that measures temperature by optical or photometric means.

py·ro·phyl·lite (pī′rə fil′īt), *n.* a micalike mineral, hydrous aluminum silicate, $AlSi_2O_2(OH)_4$. [< G *Pyrophyllit*; so called from its exfoliating when heated]

py·ro·sis (pī rō′sis), *n.* *Pathol.* heartburn (def. 1). [< NL < Gk; see PYR-, -OSIS]

py·ro·stat (pī′rə stat′), *n.* a thermostat for high temperatures.

py·ro·sul·fate (pī′rə sul′fāt), *n.* *Chem.* a salt of pyrosulfuric acid. [PYROSULF(URIC) + -ATE²]

py·ro·sul·fu·ric (pī′rō sul fyo͝or′ik), *adj.* *Chem.* of or derived from pyrosulfuric acid. Also, **py′ro·sul·phu′ric.** Also called **disulfuric, disulphuric.**

py′rosulfu′ric ac′id, *Chem.* a corrosive liquid, $H_2S_2O_7$: used chiefly as a dehydrating agent in the manufacture of explosives and as a sulfating or sulfonating agent in the manufacture of dyes.

py·ro·tech·nics (pī′rə tek′niks), *n.* (*construed as sing. or pl.*) **1.** the art of making fireworks. **2.** the use of fireworks for display, military purposes, etc. **3.** a display of fireworks. **4.** a brilliant or sensational display, as of rhetoric, musicianship, etc. **5.** *Mil.* ammunition containing chemicals for producing smoke or light, as for signaling, illuminating, or screening. Also, **py′ro·tech′ny** (for defs. 1, 2). —**py′ro·tech′nic, py′ro·tech′ni·cal,** *adj.* —**py′ro·tech′ni·cal·ly,** *adv.* —**py′ro·tech′nist,** *n.*

py·ro·tox·in (pī′rə tok′sin), *n.* pyrogen.

py·rox·ene (pī′rok sēn′), *n.* a very common group of minerals of many varieties, silicates of magnesium, iron, calcium, and other elements, occurring as important constituents of many kinds of rocks, esp. basic igneous rocks. [< F; see PYRO-, XENO-; orig. supposed to be a foreign substance when found in igneous rocks] —**py·rox·en·ic** (pī′rok sen′ik), *adj.*

py·rox·e·nite (pī rok′sə nīt′), *n.* any rock composed essentially, or in large part, of pyroxene of any kind.

py·rox·y·lin (pī rok′sə lin), *n.* a nitrocellulose compound containing fewer nitrate groups than guncotton, used in the manufacture of artificial silk, leather, oilcloth, etc. Also, **py·rox·y·line** (pī rok′sə lin, -lēn′). [PYRO- + XYL- + -IN²]

Pyr·rha (pir′ə), *n.* *Class. Myth.* a daughter of Epimetheus and the wife of Deucalion.

pyr·rhic¹ (pir′ik), *Pros.* —*adj.* **1.** consisting of two short or unaccented syllables. **2.** composed of or pertaining to pyrrhics. —*n.* **3.** a pyrrhic foot. [< L *pyrrhich(ius)* < Gk *pyrrhíchios* pertaining to the *pyrrhíchē* PYRRHIC²]

pyr·rhic² (pir′ik), *n.* **1.** an ancient Grecian warlike dance. —*adj.* **2.** of, pertaining to, or denoting this dance. [< L *pyrrhich(a)* < Gk *pyrrhíchē* a dance; said to be named after *Pyrrhichus*, the inventor]

Pyr·rhic (pir′ik), *adj.* of, pertaining to, or resembling Pyrrhus, king of Epirus, or his costly victory.

Pyr′rhic vic′tory, a victory or goal gained at too great a cost.

Pyr·rho (pir′ō), *n.* c365–c275 B.C., Greek philosopher.

Pyr·rho·nism (pir′ə niz′əm), *n.* extreme or absolute skepticism. [< Gk *Pýrrhōn* PYRRHO + -ISM] —**Pyr′rho·nist,** *n.* —**Pyr′rho·nis′tic,** *adj.*

pyr·rho·tite (pir′ə tīt′), *n.* a common mineral, iron sulfide, approximately FeS, having a bronze color and metallic luster and being slightly magnetic; iron pyrites. Also, **pyr·rho·tine** (pir′ə tēn′, -tin). [< Gk *pyrrhót(ēs)* redness + -ITE¹]

pyr·rhu·lox·i·a (pir′ə lok′sē ə), *n.* a cardinallike grosbeak, *Pyrrhuloxia sinuata*, of the southwestern U.S. and Mexico, having a bill superficially resembling that of a parrot. [< NL *Pyrrhu(la)* finch genus (< Gk *pyrrhoúlas* a red bird < *pyrrhós* red) + *Loxia* crossbill genus = Gk *lox(ós)* oblique + *-ia* -IA]

Pyr·rhus (pir′əs), *n.* **1.** c318–272 B.C., king of Epirus c300–272. **2.** *Class. Myth.* Neoptolemus.

pyr·role (pi rōl′, pir′ōl), *n.* *Chem.* a toxic, five-membered ring compound, C_4H_5N, that is a component of chlorophyll, hemin, and other important naturally occurring substances. [< Gk *pyrr(hós)* red + -OLE] —**pyr·rol·ic** (pi rol′ik), *adj.*

py·ru′vic ac′id (pī ro͞o′vik, pi-), *Chem., Biochem.* a pungent liquid, $CH_3COCOOH$, important in many metabolic and fermentative processes. [PYR- + L *ūv(a)* grape + -IC]

Py·thag·o·ras (pi thag′ər əs), *n.* c582–c500 B.C., Greek philosopher and mathematician.

Py·thag·o·re·an (pi thag′ə rē′ən), *adj.* **1.** of or pertaining to Pythagoras, to his school, or to his doctrines. —*n.* **2.** a follower of Pythagoras. [< L *Pȳthagorē(us)* (< Gk *Pȳthagóreios* of Pythagoras) + -AN]

Pythag′ore′an the′orem, *Geom.* the theorem that the square of the hypotenuse of a right triangle is equal to the sum of the squares of the other two sides.

Pyth·i·a (pith′ē ə), *n.* *Gk. Myth.* the priestess of Apollo at Delphi who delivered the oracles. [< L < Gk, fem. of *Pȳ́thios* Pythian]

Pyth·i·ad (pith′ē ad′), *n.* the four-year period between two celebrations of the Pythian Games. [< Gk *Pȳthiad-* (s. of *Pȳthiás*)]

Pyth·i·an (pith′ē ən), *adj.* Also, **Pyth′ic.** **1.** of or pertaining to Delphi, in ancient Greece. **2.** of or pertaining to Apollo, with reference to his oracle at Delphi. —*n.* **3.** a Pythian priestess. [< L *Pȳthi(us)* (< Gk *Pȳ́thios* of Delphi and the oracle) + -AN]

Pyth′ian Games′, a national festival of ancient Greece, held every four years at Delphi in honor of Apollo.

Pyth·i·as (pith′ē əs), *n.* See **Damon and Pythias.**

py·thon¹ (pī′thon, -thən), *n.* any of several Old World constrictors of the family *Boidae*, of the subfamily *Pythoninae*, often growing to a length of more than 20 feet. [< NL, special use of Gk *Pȳ́thōn* the dragon killed by Apollo at Delphi]

py·thon² (pī′thon, -thən), *n.* **1.** a spirit or demon. **2.** a person who is possessed by a spirit and prophesies with its aid. [< LGk; relation to PYTHON¹ not clear]

py·tho·ness (pī′thə nis, pith′ə-), *n.* **1.** a woman believed to be possessed by an oracle, as the priestess of Apollo at Delphi. **2.** a woman with power of divination; witch. [r. ME *phytonesse* < MF]

py·thon·ic (pī thon′ik, pi-), *adj.* prophetic; oracular. [< LL *pythōnic(us)* < Gk *pythōnikós* prophetic]

py·u·ri·a (pī yo͝or′ē ə), *n.* *Pathol.* the presence of pus in the urine.

Pyxidium of purslane

pyx (piks), *n.* **1.** *Eccles.* the box or vessel in which the reserved Eucharist or Host is kept. **2.** Also called **pyx′ chest′.** a box or chest at a mint, in which specimen coins are deposited and reserved for trial by weight and assay. Also, **pix.** [late ME *pyxe* < L *pyx(is)* < Gk: a box, orig. made of boxwood]

pyx·id·i·um (pik sid′ē əm), *n.*, *pl.* **pyx·id·i·a** (pik sid′ē ə). *Bot.* a seed vessel which dehisces transversely, the top part acting as a lid, as in the purslane. [< NL < Gk *pyxídion* a little box = *pyxid-* (s. of *pyxís*) a box + *-ion* dim. n. suffix]

pyx·ie (pik′sē), *n.* either of two trailing, shrubby, evergreen plants, *Pyxidanthera barbulata* or *P. brevifolia*, of the eastern U.S., having numerous small, starlike blossoms. [short for NL *Pyxidanthera*. See PYXIDIUM, ANTHER]

pyx·is (pik′sis), *n.*, *pl.* **pyx·i·des** (pik′si dēz′). **1.** *Gk. and Rom. Antiq.* a box of a usually cylindrical shape having a lid with a knob in the center, used for toilet articles. **2.** pyx (def. 1). **3.** *Bot.* a pyxidium. [ME < L: PYX]

DEVELOPMENT OF MAJUSCULE									
NORTH SEMITIC	GREEK		ETR.	LATIN		MODERN			
						GOTHIC	ITALIC	ROMAN	
							Q	Q	

DEVELOPMENT OF MINUSCULE						
ROMAN CURSIVE	ROMAN UNCIAL	CAROL. MIN.	MODERN			
			GOTHIC	ITALIC	ROMAN	
				q	q	

The seventeenth letter of the English alphabet developed in its present form from Latin. Its equivalent in Greek was *koppa* (ϙ), which became obsolete except as a numeral, and in North Semitic it was *qoph*, which represented a guttural *k*-like sound. When adopted from the Etruscans, the Latin alphabet contained three symbols for the *k*-sound (Q, C, K), and the use of Q was limited to the sound (k) when it was labialized and followed in spelling by U, a practice generally maintained today.

In Old English the Q does not appear, its labialized sound being written CW or, later, KW.

Q, q (kyo͞o), *n., pl.* **Q's** or **Qs, q's** or **qs.** **1.** the 17th letter of the English alphabet, a consonant. **2.** any spoken sound represented by the letter *Q* or *q*, as in *quick, torque*, or *Iraq.* **3.** a written or printed representation of the letter *Q* or *q.* **4.** a device, as a printer's type, for reproducing the letter *Q* or *q.*

Q, *Chess.* queen.

Q, 1. the 17th in order or in a series, or, when *I* is omitted, the 16th. **2.** *Physics.* heat. **3.** Also called **Q-factor.** *Electronics.* the ratio of the reactance to the resistance of an electric circuit or component.

Q., 1. quarto. **2.** Quebec. **3.** Queen. **4.** question. **5.** (in Guatemala) quetzal; quetzals.

q., 1. farthing. [< L *quadrans*] **2.** quart; quarts. **3.** query. **4.** question. **5.** quintal. **6.** quire.

Qa·dha·fi (kə dä′fē), *n.* **Mu·am·mar (Muhammad) al-** or **el-** (mo͞o ä′mär, al, el), born 1942, Libyan army colonel and political leader: chief of state since 1969. Also, **Qad·da′fi.**

qa·id (kä ēth′, kīth), *n.* caid.

Qa·ra Qum (kä rä′ ko͝om′). See **Kara Kum.**

Qa·tar (kä′tär), *n.* **1.** a peninsula in E Arabia, on the Persian Gulf. **2.** an independent state coextensive with this peninsula: formerly a British protectorate. 190,000; ab. 6000 sq. mi. *Cap.:* Doha. Also, **Katar.**

QB, *Chess.* queen's bishop.

Q.B., Queen's Bench.

q.b., *Football.* quarterback.

QBP, *Chess.* queen's bishop's pawn.

Q.C., 1. Quartermaster Corps. **2.** Queen's Counsel.

Q-Celt·ic (kyo͞o′sel′tik, -kel′-), *n.* **1.** the subbranch of Celtic in which the Proto-Indo-European *kw*-sound became a *k*-sound. Gaelic, Irish, and Manx belong to Q-Celtic. —*adj.* **2.** of or belonging to Q-Celtic.

Q.E.D., which was to be shown or demonstrated (used esp. in mathematical proofs). [< L *quod erat demonstrandum*]

Q-fac·tor (kyo͞o′fak′tər), *n.* Q (def. 3). [*q*(*uality*) *factor*]

Q-fe·ver (kyo͞o′fē′vər), *n.* *Pathol.* a fever exhibiting pneumonialike symptoms, caused by the rickettsia *Coxiella burnetti.* [*q*(*uery*)]

Q gauge. See **O gauge** (def. 2).

q.h., (in prescriptions) every hour. [< L *quāque hōrā*]

Qi·a·na (kē ä′nə), *n.* *Trademark.* a lightweight silklike man-made fiber chemically classed as nylon.

qin·tar (kin tär′), *n.* a money of account of Albania, the 100th part of a lek. Also, **qin·dar** (kin där′). [< Albanian]

Qishm (kish′əm), *n.* an island S of and belonging to Iran, in the Strait of Hormuz. ab. 25,000; 68 mi. long.; ab. 510 sq. mi.

Qi·zil Qum (ki zil′ ko͝om′). See **Kyzyl Kum.**

QKt, *Chess.* queen's knight.

QKtP, *Chess.* queen's knight's pawn.

QM, Quartermaster. Also, **Q.M.**

QMC, Quartermaster Corps. Also, **Q.M.C.**

QMG, Quartermaster General. Also, **Q.M.G., Q.M.Gen.**

QNP, *Chess.* queen's knight's pawn.

qoph (ko͝of; *Heb.* kôf), *n.* koph.

QP, *Chess.* queen's pawn.

Qq., quartos.

qq.v., (in formal writing) which (words, things, etc.) see. Cf. **q.v.** [< L *quae vide*]

QR, *Chess.* queen's rook.

qr., *pl.* **qrs. 1.** farthing. **2.** quarter. **3.** quire.

QRP, *Chess.* queen's rook's pawn.

q.s., 1. (in prescriptions) as much as is sufficient; enough. [< L *quantum sufficit*] **2.** See **quarter section.**

qt., 1. quantity. **2.** *pl.* **qt., qts.** quart.

q.t., *Slang.* **1.** quiet. **2. on the q.t.,** stealthily; secretly: *to meet someone on the q.t.* [*q*(*uie*)*t*]

qto., quarto.

qtr., 1. quarter. **2.** quarterly.

qty., quantity.

qu., 1. quart. **2.** quarter. **3.** quarterly. **4.** queen. **5.** query. **6.** question.

qua (kwā, kwä), *adv.* as; as being; in the character or capacity of: *art qua art.* [< L, fem. abl. sing. of *qui* WHO]

Quaa·lude (kwā′lo͞od′), *n.* *Trademark.* methaqualone.

quack[1] (kwak), *n.* **1.** the harsh, throaty cry of a duck or any similar sound. —*v.i.* **2.** to utter a quack. [imit. Cf. D *kwakken*, G *quacken*]

quack[2] (kwak), *n.* **1.** a fraudulent or ignorant pretender to medical skill. **2.** a pretender to any skill, knowledge, or qualifications; charlatan. —*adj.* **3.** being a quack: *a quack doctor.* **4.** presented falsely as having curative powers: *quack medicine.* **5.** involving quackery: *quack methods.* —*v.i.* **6.** to play the quack. [short for QUACKSALVER] —**quack′ish,** *adj.* —**quack′ish·ly,** *adv.* —**quack′ish·ness,** *n.*

quack·er·y (kwak′ə rē), *n.* the practice of a quack.

quack′ grass′, a couch grass, *Agropyron repens*, a pernicious weed in cultivated fields. [alter. of QUICK GRASS]

quack·sal·ver (kwak′sal′vər), *n.* a quack doctor. [< early D]

quad[1] (kwod), *n.* *Informal.* a quadrangle, as on a college campus. [shortened form]

quad[2] (kwod), *n., v.,* **quad·ded, quad·ding.** *Print.* —*n.* **1.** Also called **quadrat.** a piece of type metal of less height than the lettered types, used for spacing. —*v.t.* **2.** to space out (matter) by means of quads. [short for QUADRAT]

quad[3] (kwod), *n.* *Chiefly Brit. Slang.* quod.

quad[4] (kwod), *n.* *Informal.* a quadruplet. [shortened form]

quad[5] (kwod), *adj.* **1.** quadraphonic. —*n.* **2.** quadraphonic sound system. [by shortening]

quad., quadrangle.

quad·plex (kwod′pleks′), *adj.* **1.** fourfold; quadruple. —*n.* **2.** a building having four dwelling units. [shortened form of QUADRUPLEX]

quadr-, var. of **quadri-** before a vowel: *quadrennial.*

quad·ra·ge·nar·i·an (kwod′rə jə nâr′ē ən), *adj.* **1.** 40 years of age. **2.** between the ages of 40 and 50. —*n.* **3.** a person who is 40 years old or whose age falls between 40 and 50. [< L *quadrāgēnāri*(*us*) consisting of forty (*quādrāgēn*(*i*) forty each + *-ārius* -ARY) + -AN]

Quad·ra·ges·i·ma (kwod′rə jes′ə mə), *n.* **1.** Also called **Quadrages′ima Sun′day.** the first Sunday in Lent. **2.** *Obs.* the 40 days of Lent. [< ML, short for L *quadrāgēsima dies* fortieth day] —**Quad′ra·ges′i·mal,** *adj.*

quad·ran·gle (kwod′rang′gəl), *n.* **1.** a plane figure having four angles and four sides, as a square. **2.** a square or quadrangular space or court that is surrounded by a building or buildings, as on a college campus. **3.** the building or buildings around such a space or court. **4.** the area shown on one of the standard topographic sheets of the U.S. Geological Survey (approximately 17 miles north to south and from 11 to 15 miles east to west). [ME < LL *quadrangul*(*um*) (neut.), lit., four-cornered (thing)]

quad·rans (kwod′ranz), *n., pl.* **quad·ran·tes** (kwod-ran′tēz). a bronze coin of ancient Rome, the fourth part of an as. [< L: lit., fourth part]

quad·rant (kwod′rənt), *n.* **1.** a quarter of a circle; an arc of 90°. **2.** the area included between such an arc and two radii drawn one to each extremity. **3.** something shaped like a quarter of a circle. as a part of a machine. **4.** *Geom., Astron.* one of the four parts into which an area is divided by two perpendicular lines, numbered counterclockwise from upper right: *The first quadrant of the moon.* **5.** an instrument, usually containing a graduated arc of 90°, used in astronomy, navigation, etc., for measuring altitudes. [ME < L *quadrant-* (s. of *quadrāns*) 4th part] —**quad·ran·tal** (kwo dran′tᵊl), *adj.*

quadran′tal correc′tor, *Navig.* either of two soft iron spheres secured to the sides of a binnacle to compensate for compass deviation due to horizontol magnetic currents. See illus. at **binnacle.**

quad·ra·phon·ic (kwod′rə fon′ik), *adj.* of, noting, or pertaining to the recording and reproduction of sound over four separate transmission channels instead of the customary two of the stereo system: *quadraphonic records.* Also, **quad·ri·phon·ic** (kwod′rə fon′ik), **quad·ro·phon·ic** (kwod′rə fon′ik). [alter. QUADRI + PHONIC]

quad·rat (kwod′rət), *n.* **1.** *Print.* quad[2] (def. 1). **2.** *Ecol.* a square or rectangular plot of land marked off for the study of plants and animals. [var. of QUADRATE]

quad·rate (*n., adj.* kwod′rit, -rāt; *v.* kwod′rāt), *n., adj., v.,* **-rat·ed, -rat·ing.** —*n.* **1.** a square, or something square or rectangular. **2.** *Zool.* one of a pair of bones in the skulls of many lower vertebrates, to which the lower jaw is articulated. —*adj.* **3.** square or rectangular. **4.** *Zool.* of or pertaining to the quadrate. —*v.t.* **5.** to cause to conform or harmonize; adapt. —*v.i.* **6.** to agree or conform. [ME *quadrat* < L *quadrāt*(*us*) (ptp. of *quadrāre* to make square)]

quad·rat·ic (kwo drat′ik), *adj.* **1.** square. **2.** *Algebra.* involving the square and no higher power of the unknown quantity; of the second degree. —*n.* **3.** a quadratic polynomial or equation.

quadrat′ic equa′tion, *Math.* an equation containing the square and no higher power of the unknown quantity.

quadrat′ic for′mula, *Math.* the formula for determining the roots of a quadratic equation from its coefficients: $x = (-b \pm \sqrt{b^2-4ac})/2a$ for the equation $ax^2 + bx + c = 0$.

quad·rat·ics (kwo drat′iks), *n.* (*construed as sing.*) the branch of algebra that deals with quadratic equations.

quad·ra·ture (kwod′rə chər), *n.* **1.** the act of squaring. **2.** *Math.* **a.** the act or process of finding a square equal in area to a given surface, esp. a surface bounded by a curve. **b.** the act or process of finding an area or calculating an integral, esp. by numerical methods. **c.** a definite integral. **3.** *Astron.* **a.** the situation of two heavenly bodies when their longitudes differ by 90°. **b.** either of the two points in the orbit of a body, as the moon, midway between the syzygies. **c.** (of the moon) the points or moments at which a half moon is visible. [< L *quadrātūra* = *quadrāt*(*us*) (ptp. of *quadrāre*; see QUADRATE) + *-ūra* -URE]

quad·ren·ni·al (kwo dren′ē əl), *adj.* **1.** occurring every four years. **2.** of or lasting for four years. —*n.* **3.** an event occurring every four years. [earlier *quadriennial* < L *quadrienni(s)* + -AL[1]] —**quad·ren′ni·al·ly,** *adv.*

quad·ren·ni·um (kwo dren′ē əm), *n., pl.* **quad·ren·ni·ums, quad·ren·ni·a** (kwo dren′ē ə). a period of four years. [< NL, alter. of L *quadriennium*]

quadri-, a learned borrowing from Latin meaning "four," used in the formation of compound words: *quadrilateral.* Also, *esp. before a vowel,* **quadr-.** [< L; cf. *quattuor* four]

quad·ric (kwod′rik), *Math.* —*adj.* **1.** of the second degree (said esp. of functions with more than two variables). —*n.* **2.** a surface such as an ellipsoid or paraboloid as defined by a second-degree equation in three real variables.

quad·ri·cen·ten·ni·al (kwod′ri sen ten′ē əl), *adj.* **1.** of, pertaining to, or marking the completion of a period of four hundred years. —*n.* **2.** a quadricentennial anniversary or its celebration.

quad·ri·ceps (kwod′ri seps′), *n., pl.* **-ceps·es** (-sep′siz), **-ceps.** *Anat.* a large muscle in front of the thigh, the action of which extends the leg or bends the hip joint. [< NL = *quadri-* QUADRI- + *-ceps* (as in *biceps*)] —**quad·ri·cip·i·tal** (kwod′ri sip′i təl), *adj.*

quad·ri·fid (kwod′rə fid), *adj.* cleft into four parts or lobes. [< L *quadrifid(us)*]

quad·ri·ga (kwo drī′gə), *n., pl.* **-gae** (-jē). *Class. Antiq.* a two-wheeled chariot drawn by four horses harnessed abreast. [< L, earlier pl. *quadrīgae,* contr. of *quadrijugae* a team of four; cf. QUADRI-, YOKE]

quad·ri·lat·er·al (kwod′rə lat′ər əl), *adj.* **1.** having four sides. —*n.* **2.** a plane figure having four sides and four angles. **3.** something of this form. **4.** *Geom.* **a.** a polygon with four sides. **b.** a figure formed by four straight lines that have six points of intersection. **5.** the space enclosed between and defended by four fortresses. [< L *quadrilater(us)* four-sided + -AL[1]. See QUADRI-, LATERAL]

A B

Quadrilaterals
A, Simple (def. 2)
B, Complete (def. 4b)

qua·drille[1] (kwə dril′, kə-), *n.* **1.** a square dance for four couples, consisting of five parts or movements, each complete in itself. **2.** the music for such a dance. [< F < Sp *cuadrilla* company, troop, dim. of *cuadra* square < L *quadra*]

qua·drille[2] (kwə dril′, kə-), *n.* a card game played by four persons. [< F < Sp *cuartillo,* dim. of *cuarto* fourth < L *quartus*]

qua·drille[3] (kwə dril′, kə), *adj.* ruled in squares, as graph paper.

quad·ril·lion (kwo dril′yən), *n., pl.* **-lions,** (*as after a numeral*) **-lion,** *adj.* —*n.* **1.** a cardinal number represented in the U.S. and France by one followed by 15 zeros, and, in Great Britain and Germany, by one followed by 24 zeros. —*adj.* **2.** amounting to one quadrillion in number. [QUADR- + *-illion* (as in *million*)] —**quad·ril′lionth,** *n., adj.*

quad·ri·no·mi·al (kwod′rə nō′mē əl), *Algebra.* —*adj.* **1.** consisting of four terms. —*n.* **2.** a quadrinomial expression. [QUADRI- + (BI)NOMIAL]

quad·ri·par·tite (kwod′rə pär′tīt), *adj.* **1.** divided into or consisting of four parts. **2.** involving four participants: *a quadripartite treaty.* [ME < L *quadripartīt(us)*]

quad·ri·va·lent (kwod′rə vā′lənt, kwo driv′ə-), *adj.* *Chem.* **1.** having a valence of four; tetravalent. **2.** exercising four different valences, as antimony with valences of +5, +4, +3, and -3. —**quad′ri·va′lence, quad′ri·va′len·cy,** *n.*

quad·riv·i·al (kwo driv′ē əl), *adj.* **1.** having four ways or roads meeting in a point. **2.** of or pertaining to the quadrivium. [ME < ML *quadriviāl(is)* = LL *quadrivi(um)* QUADRIVIUM + *-ālis* -AL[1]]

quad·riv·i·um (kwo driv′ē əm), *n., pl.* **quad·riv·i·a** (kwo driv′ē ə). (during the Middle Ages) the more advanced division of the seven liberal arts, comprising arithmetic, geometry, astronomy, and music. Cf. **trivium.** [< LL, special use of L *quadrivium* place where four ways meet]

quad·roon (kwo dro͞on′), *n.* **1.** a person who is one-fourth Negro and three-fourths white. **2.** the offspring of a mulatto and a white person. [alter. of Sp *cuarterón* < *cuarto* fourth < L *quartus*]

quad·ru·mane (kwod′ro͝o mān′), *n.* a quadrumanous animal, as a monkey. [< NL *quadrumana* = *quadru-* (see QUADRI-) + *-mana* (< L *manus* hand)]

quad·ru·ma·nous (kwo dro͞o′mə nəs), *adj.* having all four feet adapted for use as hands, as monkeys. [< NL *quadrumanus*]

quad·ru·ped (kwod′ro͝o ped′), *adj.* **1.** four-footed. —*n.* **2.** an animal, esp. a mammal, having four feet. [< L *quadruped-* (s. of *quadrupēs*) = *quadru-* (see QUADRI-) + *-ped-* -PED] —**quad·ru·pe·dal** (kwo dro͞o′pi dəl, kwod′ro͝o ped′əl), *adj.*

quad·ru·ple (kwo dro͞o′pəl, kwod′ro͝o-), *adj., n., v.,* **-pled, -pling.** —*adj.* **1.** fourfold; consisting of four parts. **2.** four times as great. **3.** *Music.* having four beats to a measure. —*n.* **4.** a number, amount, etc., four times as great as another. —*v.t., v.i.* **5.** to make or become four times as great. [ME < L *quadrupl(us)*] —**quad·ru′ply,** *adv.*

quad·ru·plet (kwo drup′lit, -dro͞o′plit, kwod′ro͝o plit), *n.* **1.** any group or combination of four. **2. quadruplets,** four children born of one pregnancy. **3.** one of four such children or offspring. **4.** *Music.* a group of four notes of equal value performed in the time normally taken for three. [QUADRUPLE + -ET (modeled on *triplet*)]

quadru′ple time′, a measure consisting of four beats or pulses with accent on the first and third.

quad·ru·plex (kwod′ro͝o pleks′, kwo dro͞o′pleks), *adj.* **1.** fourfold; quadruple. **2.** noting or pertaining to a system of telegraphy by which four messages may be transmitted simultaneously over one wire. [< L] —**quad·ru·plic·i·ty** (kwod′ro͝o plis′i tē), *n.*

quad·ru·pli·cate (*n., adj.* kwo dro͞o′plə kit, -kāt′; *v.* kwo dro͞o′plə kāt′), *n., adj., v.,* **-cat·ed, -cat·ing.** —*n.* **1.** a group, series, or set of four identical copies (usually prec. by *in*). —*adj.* **2.** having or consisting of four identical parts; fourfold. **3.** noting the fourth copy or item. —*v.t.* **4.** to make four copies of something. **5.** to make four times as great, as by multiplying. [< L *quadruplicāt(us)* (ptp. of *quadruplicāre*) = *quadruplic-* (s. of *quadruplex* QUADRUPLEX) + *-ātus* -ATE[1]] —**quad·ru′pli·ca′tion,** *n.*

quae·re (kwēr′ē), *n.* a query or question. [< L, 2nd pers. sing. impv. of *quaerere* to seek, ask]

quaes·tor (kwes′tər, kwē′stər), *n.* *Rom. Hist.* **1.** one of two officials serving as public prosecutors. **2.** one of the public magistrates in charge of government funds. Also, **questor.** [ME *questor* < L *quaestor* = *quaest(us)* (ptp. of *quaerere* to seek) + *-or* -OR[2]] —**quaes·to·ri·al** (kwe stôr′ē-əl, -stōr′-, kwē-), *adj.* —**quaes′tor·ship′,** *n.*

quaff (kwäf, kwaf, kwôf), *v.i.* **1.** to drink a beverage, esp. an intoxicating one, copiously and with hearty enjoyment. —*v.t.* **2.** to drink (a beverage) copiously and heartily. —*n.* **3.** the beverage quaffed. [?] —**quaff′er,** *n.*

quag (kwag, kwog), *n.* a quagmire. [? akin to QUAKE]

quag·ga (kwag′ə), *n.* an extinct, equine mammal, *Equus quagga,* of southern Africa, related to and resembling the zebra, but striped only on the fore part of the body and the head. [< SAfrD (now obs.) < Zulu, ? < *quag* striped]

quag·gy (kwag′ē, kwog′ē), *adj.,* **-gi·er, -gi·est.** of the nature of or resembling a quagmire; marshy; boggy. —**quag′gi·ness,** *n.*

quag·mire (kwag′mīər′, kwog′-), *n.* **1.** an area of miry or boggy ground whose surface yields under the tread; a bog. **2.** a situation from which extrication is very difficult. —**quag′mir′y,** *adj.*

qua·hog (kwô′hog, -hôg, kwə hog′, -hôg′), *n.* an edible clam, *Venus mercenaria,* found along the Atlantic coast, having a relatively thick shell. Also, **qua′haug.** [< AmerInd (Narragansett), aph. var. of *poquauhock*]

Quai d'Or·say (ke dôr se′), the quay along the south bank of the Seine in Paris, on which are located the department of foreign affairs and other French government offices.

Quail (bobwhite),
Colinus virginianus
(Length 9 in.)

quail[1] (kwāl), *n., pl.* **quails,** (*esp. collectively*) **quail. 1.** a small, migratory, gallinaceous game bird, *Coturnix coturnix,* of the Old World. **2.** any of several other birds of the genus *Coturnix* and allied genera. **3.** any of various New World, gallinaceous game birds of the genus *Colinus* and allied genera, esp. the bobwhite. [ME *quaille* < OF < Gmc; cf. D *kwakkel* quail, MD, MLG *quackele;* akin to QUACK[1]]

quail[2] (kwāl), *v.i.* to lose heart or courage in difficulty or danger; shrink with fear. [ME: to fail] —**Syn.** recoil, flinch, blench, cower.

quaint (kwānt), *adj.* **1.** strange, peculiar, or unusual in an interesting, pleasing, or amusing way: *a quaint sense of humor.* **2.** having an old-fashioned attractiveness or charm; oddly picturesque: *a quaint old house.* **3.** skillfully or cleverly made. **4.** *Archaic.* wise; skilled. **5.** *Obs.* sly; crafty. [ME *queinte* < OF, var. of *cointe* clever, pleasing << L *cognitus* known (ptp. of *cognoscere*)] —**quaint′ly,** *adv.* —**quaint′ness,** *n.* —**Syn. 1.** curious, unusual, uncommon. **2.** antiquated, archaic. —**Ant. 1.** ordinary.

quake (kwāk), *v.,* **quaked, quak·ing,** *n.* —*v.i.* **1.** (of persons) to shake or tremble from cold, weakness, fear, anger, etc. **2.** (of things) to shake or tremble, as from shock, internal convulsion, or instability. —*n.* **3.** an earthquake. **4.** a trembling or tremulous agitation. [ME; OE *cwacian* to shake, tremble] —**quak′ing·ly,** *adv.* —**Syn. 1.** shudder, tremble. See **shiver**[1]. **2.** quiver.

Quak·er (kwā′kər), *n.* a popular name for a member of the Religious Society of Friends. Also, *referring to a woman,* **Quak·er·ess** (kwā′kər is). —**Quak′er·ish,** *adj.* —**Quak′er·ism,** *n.* —**Quak′er·ly,** *adj., adv.*

Quak′er gun′, a dummy gun, as on a ship or fort: so called in allusion to the Quakers' opposition to war.

Quak·er-la·dies (kwā′kər lā′dēz), *n.* (*construed as pl.*) bluet (def. 2).

quak′ing as′pen. See under **aspen** (def. 1).

quak·y (kwā′kē), *adj.,* **quak·i·er, quak·i·est.** tending to quake. —**quak′i·ly,** *adv.* —**quak′i·ness,** *n.*

qual·i·fi·ca·tion (kwol′ə fə kā′shən), *n.* **1.** a quality, accomplishment, etc., that fits a person for some function, office, or the like. **2.** a circumstance or condition required for exercising a right, holding an office, or the like. **3.** act of qualifying. **4.** the state of being qualified. **5.** a modification, limitation, or restriction: *He endorsed the plan without qualification.* **6.** an instance of this: *He protected his argument with several qualifications.* [< ML *quālificātiōn-* (s. of *quālificātiō*) = *quālificāt(us)* (ptp. of *quālificāre* to QUALIFY) + *-iōn-* -ION]

qual·i·fied (kwol′ə fīd′), *adj.* **1.** having the necessary qualities, accomplishments, etc., as for a job or office. **2.** having the qualifications required by law or custom for holding an office, voting, etc. **3.** modified, limited, or restricted in some way. —**qual′i·fied′ly,** *adv.* —**Syn. 1.** able, capable, competent, fitted.

qual·i·fi·er (kwol′ə fī′ər), *n.* **1.** a person or thing that qualifies. **2.** *Gram.* a word that qualifies the meaning of another, as an adjective or adverb; modifier.

qual·i·fy (kwol′ə fī′), *v.,* **-fied, -fy·ing.** —*v.t.* **1.** to provide with proper or necessary skills, knowledge, credentials, etc.; make competent: *to qualify oneself for a job.* **2.** to attribute some quality or qualities to; characterize, call, or name. **3.** to modify or limit in some way; make less strong or positive: *to qualify an endorsement.* **4.** *Gram.* to modify. **5.** to make less violent, severe, or unpleasant; moderate; mitigate. **6.** to modify or alter the flavor or strength of. —*v.i.* **7.** to be fitted or competent for something. **8.** to get authority, license, power, etc., by fulfilling required conditions. **9.** *Sports.* to demonstrate the required ability to compete in a contest in an initial or preliminary competition or trial. **10.** to fire a rifle or pistol on a target range for a score high enough to achieve a rating of marksman, sharpshooter, or expert.

11. *Mil.* to pass a practical test in gunnery. [< ML *quālificāre* = L *quāl(is)* of what sort + *-ificāre* -IFY] —**qual′i·fi′a·ble,** *adj.* —**qual·i·fi·ca·to·ry** (kwol′ə fə kā′tə rē, -kə-tôr′ē, -tōr′ē), *adj.* —**qual′i·fy′ing·ly,** *adv.* —**Syn. 1.** fit, suit, prepare, equip. **2.** designate, label. **4.** restrict. See **modify. 6.** meliorate, soften, temper, reduce, diminish.

qual·i·ta·tive (kwol′i tā′tiv), *adj.* pertaining to or concerned with quality or qualities. [< LL *quālitātīv(us)* = *quālitāt-* (s. of *quālitās*) QUALITY + *-īvus* -IVE] —**qual′i·ta′tive·ly,** *adv.*

qual′itative anal′ysis, *Chem.* the analysis of a substance in order to ascertain the nature of its constituents. Cf. **quantitative analysis.**

qual·i·ty (kwol′i tē), *n., pl.* **-ties,** *adj.* —*n.* **1.** a characteristic, property, or attribute. **2.** character or nature, as belonging to or distinguishing a thing: *the quality of a sound.* **3.** character with respect to fineness or grade of excellence: *food of poor quality.* **4.** high grade; great excellence. **5.** an accomplishment or attainment. **6.** high social position or status: *a man of quality.* **7.** *Acoustics.* the texture of a tone, dependent on its overtone content, which distinguishes it from others of the same pitch and loudness. **8.** *Phonet.* the tonal color, or timbre, that characterizes a particular vowel sound. **9.** *Logic.* the character of a proposition as affirmative or negative. —*adj.* **10.** of or having superior quality: *quality paper.* [ME *qualite* < OF < L *quālitās* = *quāl(is)* of what sort + *-itās* -ITY]
—**Syn. 1.** trait, character, feature. QUALITY, ATTRIBUTE, PROPERTY agree in meaning a particular characteristic (of a person or thing). A QUALITY is a characteristic, innate or acquired, which, in some particular, determines the nature and behavior of a person or thing: *naturalness as a quality; the quality of meat.* An ATTRIBUTE was originally a quality attributed, usually to a person or something personified; more recently it has meant a fundamental or innate characteristic: *an attribute of God; attributes of a logical mind.* PROPERTY applies only to things; it means a characteristic belonging specifically in the constitution of, or found (invariably) in, the behavior of a thing: *physical properties of uranium or of limestone.* **3.** nature, kind, grade, sort, condition.

qual′ity control′, a system for verifying and maintaining a desired level of quality in a product or process by careful planning, continued inspection, and corrective action where required.

qualm (kwäm, kwôm), *n.* **1.** a pang of conscience as to conduct; compunction: *He has no qualms about lying.* **2.** a sudden feeling of apprehensive uneasiness; misgiving. **3.** a sudden sensation or onset of faintness or illness, esp. of nausea. [?] —**qualm′ish,** *adj.* —**qualm′ish·ly,** *adv.* —**qualm′ish·ness,** *n.*

quam·ash (kwom′ash, kwə mash′), *n.* camass.

quan·da·ry (kwon′də rē, -drē), *n., pl.* **-ries.** a state of perplexity or uncertainty, esp. as to what to do; dilemma. [? < L *quand(ō)* when + *-āre* inf. suffix] —**Syn.** See **predicament.**

quan·dong (kwon′dong′), *n.* **1.** a santalaceous tree, *Fusanus acuminatus,* of Australia, bearing an edible drupaceous fruit whose seed has an edible kernel. **2.** the fruit, or the seed or nut. Also, **quan′dang′, quantong.** [< native Austral]

quant (kwant, kwont), *Brit.* —*n.* **1.** a pole having a flange near its tip, used for punting. —*v.t., v.i.* **2.** to punt. [late ME < L *cont(us)* < Gk *kontós* kind of pole]

quan·ta (kwon′tə), *n.* pl. of **quantum.**

quan·tic (kwon′tik), *n.* *Math.* a rational, integral, homogeneous function of two or more variables. [< L *quant(us)* how much + -IC]

quan·ti·fi·er (kwon′tə fī′ər), *n.* **1.** *Logic.* an expression, as "all" or "some," that indicates the quantity of a proposition. **2.** a word, esp. a modifier, that indicates the quantity of something.

quan·ti·fy (kwon′tə fī′), *v.t.,* **-fied, -fy·ing. 1.** to determine, indicate, or express the quantity of. **2.** *Logic.* to make explicit the quantity of (a proposition). [< ML *quantificāre* = *quant(us)* how much + *-ificāre* -IFY] —**quan′ti·fi′a·ble,** *adj.* —**quan′ti·fi·ca′tion,** *n.*

quan·ti·ta·tive (kwon′ti tā′tiv), *adj.* **1.** that is or may be estimated by quantity. **2.** of or pertaining to the describing or measuring of quantity. **3.** of or pertaining to a metrical system, as that of classical verse, based on the alternation of long and short, rather than accented and unaccented, syllables. **4.** of or pertaining to the length of a spoken vowel or consonant. [< ML *quantitātīv(us)* = L *quantitāt-* (s. of *quantitās*) QUANTITY + *-īvus* -IVE] —**quan′ti·ta′tive·ly,** *adv.* —**quan′ti·ta′tive·ness,** *n.*

quan′titative anal′ysis, *Chem.* the analysis of a substance to determine the amounts and proportions of its constituents. Cf. **qualitative analysis.**

quan·ti·ty (kwon′ti tē), *n., pl.* **-ties. 1.** a particular, indefinite, or considerable amount of anything: *a small quantity of milk.* **2.** an exact or specified amount or measure: *She mixed the ingredients in the quantities called for.* **3.** a considerable or great amount: *to extract ore in quantity.* **4.** *Math.* **a.** the property of magnitude involving comparability with other magnitudes. **b.** something having magnitude, or size, extent, amount, etc. **c.** magnitude or size, volume, area, length, etc. **5.** *Logic.* the character of a proposition as singular, universal, particular, or mixed. **6.** the amount, degree, etc., in terms of which another is greater or lesser. **7.** *Pros., Phonet.* the relative length or duration of a sound or a syllable. [ME *quantite* < OF < L *quantitās* = *quant(us)* how much + *-itās* -ITY]

quan·tize (kwon′tīz), *v.t.,* **-tized, -tiz·ing.** *Math., Physics.* to restrict (a variable) to discrete values, each of which is an integral multiple of the same quantity. [QUANT(UM) + -IZE] —**quan′ti·za′tion,** *n.*

quan·tong (kwon′tong′), *n.* quandong.

Quan·trill (kwon′tril), *n.* **William Clarke,** 1837–65, U.S. Confederate guerrilla leader.

quan·tum (kwon′təm), *n., pl.* **-ta** (-tə). **1.** quantity or amount: *the least quantum of evidence.* **2.** a particular amount. **3.** a share or portion. **4.** a large quantity; bulk. **5.** *Physics.* **a.** the smallest quantity of radiant energy, equal to Planck's constant times the frequency of the associated radiation. **b.** the fundamental unit of a quantized physical magnitude, as angular momentum. [< L, neut. of *quantus* how much]

quan′tum mechan′ics, *Physics.* **1.** the branch of mechanics that is applicable to systems at the atomic and nuclear level and that is composed of a theory (**nonrelativistic quantum mechanics**) for systems in which velocities are small compared to the speed of light, a theory (**relativistic quantum mechanics**) for systems in which velocities approach or equal the speed of light, and a theory (**quan′tum field′ the′ory**) for systems in which particles are created and destroyed (distinguished from *classical mechanics*). **2.** the mechanics of the phenomena described by these theories. —**quan′tum-me·chan′i·cal,** *adj.*

quan′tum num′ber, *Physics.* one of a set of integers or half-integers that describes an energy level of a particle or system of particles.

quan′tum statis′tics, *Physics.* statistics dealing with the distribution of similar kinds of elementary particles among their quantized energy levels.

quan′tum the′ory, *Physics.* the theory, based on Planck's radiation law, that changes of energy in atoms and molecules occur only in discrete quantities, each an integral multiple of a fundamental quantity, or quantum.

Quantz (kvänts), *n.* **Jo·hann Jo·a·chim** (yō′hän yō′ä-кнім), 1697–1773, German flutist; teacher of Frederick II of Prussia.

quar., **1.** quarter. **2.** quarterly.

quar·an·tine (kwôr′ən tēn′, kwor′-), *n., v.,* **-tined, -tin·ing.** —*n.* **1.** a strict isolation imposed to prevent the spread of disease. **2.** a period, originally forty days, of detention or isolation imposed upon ships, persons, etc., on arrival at a port or place, when suspected of carrying a contagious disease. **3.** a system of measures maintained by governmental authority at ports, on frontiers, etc., for preventing the spread of disease. **4.** the branch of the governmental service concerned with such measures. **5.** a place or station at which such measures are carried out, as a special port or dock where ships are detained. **6.** social or political isolation imposed as a punishment. **7.** a period of forty days. —*v.t.* **8.** to put in or subject to quarantine. **9.** to exclude, detain, or isolate, as for political, social, or hygienic reasons: *to quarantine aggressor nations.* [< It *quarantina* = *quarant(a)* forty (< L *quadrāgintā*) + *-ina* -INE[2]] —**quar′an·tin′a·ble,** *adj.*

quar′antine flag′, *Naut.* a yellow flag, designating the letter "Q" in the International Code of Signals: flown by itself to signify that a vessel has no disease on board and requests a pratique, flown with another flag to signify that there is disease on board ship.

quark (kwôrk), *n.* any of three types of elementary particles that are believed by some physicists to form the basis of all matter in the universe. [applied by M. GELL-MANN after a coinage in the novel *Finnegans Wake* by James Joyce]

Quarles (kwôrlz, kwärlz), *n.* **Francis,** 1592–1644, English poet.

Quar·ne·ro (kwär ne′rô), *n.* **Gulf of,** an arm of the Adriatic Sea, in NW Yugoslavia, E of the Istrian peninsula.

quar·rel[1] (kwôr′əl, kwor′-), *n., v.,* **-reled, -rel·ing** or (*esp. Brit.*) **-relled, -rel·ling.** —*n.* **1.** an angry dispute or altercation; a disagreement marked by a temporary or permanent break in friendly relations. **2.** a cause of dispute, complaint, or hostile feeling. —*v.i.* **3.** to disagree angrily; squabble; fall out. **4.** to dispute angrily; wrangle. **5.** to make a complaint; find fault. [ME *querele* < OF < L *querēl(l)a* complaint, akin to *querī* to complain] —**quar′rel·er;** *esp. Brit.,* **quar′rel·ler,** *n.* —**quar′rel·ing·ly;** *esp. Brit.,* **quar′rel·ling·ly,** *adv.*
—**Syn. 1.** argument, contention, difference. QUARREL, DISSENSION refer to disagreement and conflict. QUARREL applies chiefly to a verbal disagreement between individuals or groups, from a slight and petty difference of opinion to a violent altercation: *It was little more than a domestic quarrel. Their quarrel led to the barroom brawl.* DISSENSION usually implies a profound disagreement and bitter conflict. It also applies chiefly to conflict within a group or to members of the same group: *dissension within the union.* **3.** bicker, argue.

quar·rel[2] (kwôr′əl, kwor′-), *n.* **1.** a square-headed bolt or arrow, formerly used with a crossbow. **2.** Also, **quarry.** a small, square or diamond-shaped pane of glass, as used in latticed windows. [ME *quarel* < OF < ML *quadrellus,* dim. of L *quadrus* square]

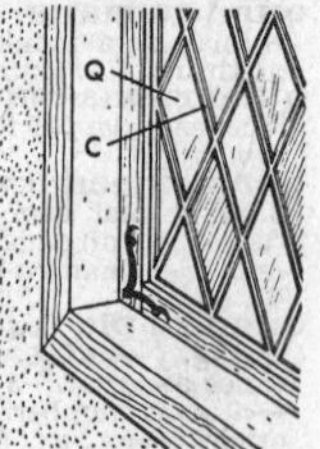

Q, Quarrel[2]
C, Came[2]

quar·rel·some (kwôr′əl səm, kwor′-), *adj.* inclined to quarrel; argumentative; contentious. —**quar′rel·some·ly,** *adv.* —**quar′rel·some·ness,** *n.*

quar·ri·er (kwôr′ē ər, kwor′-), *n.* a person who quarries stone. Also called **quarryman.** [ME *quaryer, quarriour* < OF *quarrier* = **quarre* QUARRY[1] + *-ier* -ER[1]]

quar·ry[1] (kwôr′ē, kwor′ē) *n., pl.* **-ries,** *v.,* **-ried, -ry·ing.** —*n.* **1.** an excavation or pit, usually open to the air, from which building stone, slate, or the like, is obtained by cutting, blasting, etc. —*v.t.* **2.** to obtain (stone) from or as from a quarry. **3.** to make a quarry in. [ME *quarey* < ML *quareia,* var. of *quareria* < VL **quadrāria* place where stone is squared < L *quadrāre* to square] —**quar′ri·a·ble, quar′ry·a·ble,** *adj.*

quar·ry[2] (kwôr′ē, kwor′ē), *n., pl.* **-ries. 1.** an animal or bird hunted or pursued. **2.** game, esp. game hunted with hounds or hawks. **3.** any object of search, pursuit, or attack. [ME *querre* < OF *cuiree* < *cuir* skin, hide < L *corium*]

quar·ry[3] (kwôr′ē, kwor′ē), *n., pl.* **-ries. 1.** a square stone or tile. **2.** quarrel[2] (def. 2). [n. use of obs. *quarry* (adj.) square < OF *quarre*]

quar·ry·man (kwôr′ē mən, kwor′-), *n., pl.* **-men.** quarrier.

quart (kwôrt), *n.* **1.** a unit of liquid measure of capacity, equal to one fourth of a gallon, or 57.749 cubic inches in the U.S. and 69.355 cubic inches in Great Britain. **2.** a unit of dry measure of capacity, equal to one eighth of a peck, or 67.201 cubic inches. **3.** a container holding, or capable of holding, a quart. [ME < OF *quarte* < ML *quarta* fourth (fem.)]

quart., **1.** quarter. **2.** quarterly.

quar·tan (kwôr′tᵊn), *adj.* **1.** (of a fever, ague, etc.) characterized by paroxysms that recur every fourth day, both days of consecutive occurrence being counted. **—*n.* 2.** a quartan fever or ague. [ME *quartaine* < OF < L (*febris*) *quartāna* (fever) of the fourth]

quar·ter (kwôr′tər), *n.* **1.** one of the four equal or equivalent parts into which anything is or may be divided: *a quarter of an apple.* **2.** a fourth part, esp. of one (¼). **3.** one fourth of a U.S. or Canadian dollar, equivalent to 25 cents. **4.** a silver coin of this value. **5.** a quarter-hour: *He stayed there for an hour and a quarter.* **6.** the moment marking this period: *The clock struck the quarter.* **7.** one fourth of a year: *The bank sends out a statement each quarter.* **8.** *Astron.* **a.** a fourth of the moon's period or monthly revolution, being the portion of its period or orbital course between a quadrature and a syzygy. **b.** either quadrature of the moon. Cf. **first quarter, last quarter. 9.** (in schools and colleges) one of the terms or periods into which instruction is organized, generally 10 to 12 weeks in length. **10.** *Sports.* any of the four periods that make up certain games, as football and basketball. Cf. **half** (def. 3). **11.** one fourth of a pound. **12.** one fourth of a mile; two furlongs. **13.** one fourth of a yard; 9 inches. **14.** a unit of weight: one fourth of a hundredweight. In the U.S. this equals 25 lbs., and in Britain 28 lbs. **15.** *Brit.* a measure of capacity, as for grain, equal to 8 bushels or, locally, to approximately this. **16.** the region of any of the four principal points of the compass or divisions of the horizon. **17.** such a point or division. **18.** any point or direction of the compass: *The wind is blowing in that quarter.* **19.** a region, district, or place. **20.** a particular district of a city or town, esp. one generally occupied by a particular class or group of people. **21.** Usually, **quarters. a.** housing accommodations, as a place of residence; lodgings. **b.** *Mil.* the buildings, houses, barracks, or rooms occupied by military personnel or their families. **22.** an unspecified part or member of a community, government, etc., that serves as a source of information, authority, etc.: *He received secret information from a high quarter.* **23.** mercy or indulgence, esp. as shown to a vanquished enemy: *to give quarter.* **24.** one of the four parts, each including a leg, of the body or carcass of a quadruped. **25.** *Vet. Med.* either side of a horse's hoof, between heel and toe. **26.** *Shoemaking.* the part of a shoe from the middle of the back to the vamp. **27.** *Naut.* **a.** the after part of a ship's side, usually from about the aftermost mast to the stern. **b.** the general horizontal direction 45° from the stern of a ship on either side. **c.** one of the stations to which crew members are called for battle, emergencies, or drills. **d.** the part of a yard between the slings and the yardarm. **28.** *Heraldry.* **a.** any of the four equal areas into which an escutcheon may be divided by a vertical and a horizontal line passing through the center. **b.** any of the variously numbered areas into which an escutcheon may be divided for the marshaling of different arms. **29.** each half of a cask, consisting of the portion from the bilge to the top chime and the portion from the bilge to the bottom chime. **—*v.t.* 30.** to divide into four equal or equivalent parts. **31.** to divide into parts fewer or more than four: *Quarter the pie into six pieces.* **32.** to cut the body of (a person) into quarters, esp. in executing for treason or the like. **33.** to furnish with lodging in a particular place. **34.** to impose (troops) on households, towns, etc., to be lodged and fed. **35.** to assign to a quarter or station, as on a battleship. **36.** to traverse (the ground) from left to right and right to left while advancing, as dogs in search of game. **37.** *Heraldry.* **a.** to divide (an escutcheon) into four or more parts. **b.** to place or bear quarterly on an escutcheon, as different coats of arms. **c.** to display (an additional coat of arms) on an escutcheon. **—*v.i.* 38.** to take up or be in quarters; lodge. **39.** to range to and fro, as dogs in search of game. **40.** *Naut.* to sail so as to have the wind or sea on the quarter. **—*adj.* 41.** being one of four equal or approximately equal parts into which anything is or may be divided. **42.** consisting of or equal to only about one fourth of the full measure. [ME < OF < L *quartār*(*ius*) = *quart*(*us*) fourth + *-ārius* -ARY] —**quar′ter·er,** *n.*

quar·ter·age (kwôr′tər ij), *n.* **1.** the act of providing troops with living accommodations. **2.** the cost of such accommodations. **3.** a shelter or lodging. **4.** a quarterly payment, charge, or allowance.

quar·ter·back (kwôr′tər bak′), *Football.* **—*n.* 1.** a back who usually lines up immediately behind the center and directs the offense of the team. **2.** the position played by this back. **—*v.t.* 3.** to direct the offense of (a team). **—*v.i.* 4.** to play the position of quarterback.

quar′terback sneak′, *Football.* a play in which the quarterback charges into the middle of the line, immediately after receiving the ball from the center.

quar′ter bind′ing, a style of bookbinding in which the spine is leather and the sides are cloth or paper. Cf. **half binding, three-quarter binding.** —**quar·ter-bound** (kwôr′tər bound′), *adj.*

quar·ter-breed (kwôr′tər brēd′), *n.* *U.S.* a person having only one white grandparent, esp. a person of American Indian ancestry.

quar′ter crack′, *Vet. Pathol.* See **sand crack.**

quar′ter day′, 1. (in England, Ireland, and Wales) one of the four days, Lady Day, Midsummer Day, Michaelmas, or Christmas, regarded as marking off the quarters of the year, on which quarterly payments are due, tenancies begin and end, etc. **2.** (in Scotland) one of the four days, Candlemas, Whitsunday, Lammas, or Martinmas, regarded as marking off the quarters of the year.

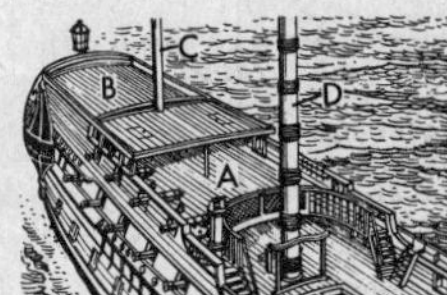

A, Quarter-deck; B, Poop deck; C, Mizzenmast; D, Mainmast

quar·ter-deck (kwôr′tər-dek′), *n.* *Naut.* the part of a weather deck that runs aft from the midship area or the main-mast to the stern or poop of a vessel. Also, **quar′ter deck′.**

quar·tered (kwôr′tərd), *adj.* **1.** divided into quarters. **2.** furnished with quarters or lodging. **3.** (of wood) quarter-sawed. **4.** *Heraldry.* (of an escutcheon) divided into four or more parts.

Quartered arms (def. 4)

quar·ter·fi·nal (kwôr′tər fīn′ᵊl), *Sports.* **—*adj.* 1.** of or pertaining to the contest or round preceding the semifinal one. **—*n.* 2.** a quarterfinal contest or round. —**quar′ter·fi′nal·ist,** *n.*

quar′ter grain′, the grain appearing in quartered wood.

quar′ter horse′, one of a breed of strong horses developed in the U.S. for short-distance races, usually a quarter of a mile.

quar·ter-hour (kwôr′tər our′, -ou′ər), *n.* **1.** a period of fifteen minutes. **2.** a point fifteen minutes after or before the hour.

quar·ter·ing (kwôr′tər ing), *n.* **1.** the act of a person or thing that quarters. **2.** the assignment of quarters or lodgings. **3.** *Heraldry.* **a.** the division of an escutcheon into quarters. **b.** the marshaling of various coats of arms on an escutcheon. **c.** any of the coats of arms so marshaled. **—*adj.* 4.** that quarters. **5.** lying at right angles. **6.** *Naut.* (of a wind) blowing on a ship's quarter.

quar·ter·ly (kwôr′tər lē), *adj., n., pl.* **-lies,** *adv.* **—*adj.* 1.** occurring, done, paid, issued, etc., at the end of every quarter of a year: *a quarterly report; quarterly interest.* **2.** pertaining to or consisting of a quarter. **—*n.* 3.** a periodical issued every three months. **—*adv.* 4.** by quarters; once each quarter of a year. **5.** *Heraldry.* **a.** with division into four quarters. **b.** in the four quarters of an escutcheon. [ME]

quar·ter·mas·ter (kwôr′tər mas′tər, -mä′stər), *n.* **1.** *Mil.* an officer charged with providing quarters, clothing, fuel, transportation, etc., for a body of troops. **2.** *Navy.* a petty officer having charge of signals, navigating apparatus, etc. [ME *quarter maister*]

Quar′termaster Corps′, *Mil.* the branch of the U.S. Army responsible for supplying food, clothing, fuel, and equipment and for the operation of commissaries, laundries, etc.

quar·tern (kwôr′tərn), *n.* *Chiefly Brit.* a quarter, or a fourth part, esp. of certain weights and measures, as of a pound, ounce, peck, or pint. [ME *quarteroun* < OF *quarteron* < *quart* fourth. See QUART[1]]

quar′ter nel′son, *Wrestling.* See under **nelson.**

quar′ter note′, *Music.* a note equivalent to one fourth of a whole note; crotchet. See illus. at **note.**

quar′ter rest′, *Music.* a rest equal in value to a quarter note. See illus. at **rest.**

quar′ter round′, a molding, as on an ovolo, whose section is a quarter circle.

quar·ter·saw (kwôr′tər sô′), *v.t.,* **-sawed, -sawed** or **-sawn, -saw·ing.** to saw (lumber) from quarter sections of logs so that the annual rings in any board form at least a 45° angle with the faces of the board.

quar′ter sec′tion, (in surveying and homesteading) a square tract of land, half a mile on each side, thus containing ¼ sq. mi. or 160 acres. *Abbr.:* q.s.

quar′ter ses′sions, *Law.* **1.** an English court of general criminal jurisdiction for crimes less than homicide, held quarterly. **2.** *U.S.* a court with limited criminal jurisdiction, having local administrative powers in some states.

quar·ter·staff (kwôr′tər staf′, -stäf′), *n., pl.* **-staves** (-stāvz′, -stavz′, -stävz′). a former English weapon consisting of a stout, iron-tipped pole six to eight feet long.

quar′ter tone′, *Music.* an interval equivalent to half of a semitone.

quar·tet (kwôr tet′), *n.* **1.** any group of four persons or things. **2.** an organized group of four singers or players. **3.** a musical composition for four voices or instruments. Also, *esp. Brit.,* **quar·tette′.** [< It *quartetto,* dim. of *quarto* fourth < L *quartus*]

quar·tic (kwôr′tik), *Algebra.* **—*adj.* 1.** of or pertaining to the fourth degree. **—*n.* 2.** Also called **biquadratic.** a quartic polynomial or equation. [< L *quart*(*us*) fourth + -IC]

quar·tile (kwôr′tīl, -til), *n.* **1.** *Statistics.* (in a frequency distribution) one of the values of a variable that divides the distribution of the variable into four groups having equal frequencies. **2.** *Astrol.* the aspect of two heavenly bodies when their longitudes differ by 90°. **—*adj.* 3.** *Astrol.* of or pertaining to a quartile aspect. [< ML *quartīl*(*is*) = L *quart*(*us*) fourth + *-īlis* -ILE]

quar·to (kwôr′tō), *n., pl.* **-tos,** *adj.* **—*n.* 1.** a book size of about 9½ × 12 inches, determined by folding printed sheets twice to form four leaves or eight pages. *Abbr.:* 4to, 4° **2.** a book of this size. **—*adj.* 3.** bound in quarto. [short for NL *in quartō* in fourth].

quartz (kwôrts), *n.* one of the commonest minerals, silicon dioxide, SiO_2, having many varieties that differ in color, luster, etc., and occurring either in masses (as agate, chalcedony, jasper, etc.) or in crystals (as rock crystal or amethyst); the chief constituent of sand and sandstone and an important constituent of many other rocks. [< G *Quarz,* prob. < Slavic, cf. Czech *tvrdý* quartz < *tvrdý* (adj.) hard]

quartz·if·er·ous (kwôrt sif′ər əs), *adj.* consisting of or containing quartz: *quartziferous rock.*

quartz·ite (kwôrt′sīt), *n.* a granular metamorphic rock consisting essentially of quartz in interlocking grains.

qua·sar (kwā′sär, -sər, -zər), *n.* *Astron.* one of a number of celestial objects, from four to ten billion light-years distant, that are powerful sources of radio energy. Also called **quasi-stellar radio source.** [*quas*(*i-stell*)*ar* (*radio source*)]

quash[1] (kwosh), *v.t.* to put down or suppress completely; quell; subdue: *to quash a rebellion.* [ME *quasche*(*n*) < OF *quasser* < L *quassāre* to shake (freq. of *quatere*)]

quash[2] (kwosh), *v.t.* to make void, annul, or set aside (a law, indictment, decision, etc.). [ME *quasche*(*n*) < OF *quasser* < L *quassāre* shake, but influenced by LL *cassāre* to annul < L *cassus* empty, void]

qua·si (kwā′zī, -sī, kwä′sē, -zē), *adj.* **1.** resembling; seeming: *a quasi liberal.* **—*adv.* 2.** seemingly but not actually (usually used in combination): *quasi-scientific.* [ME < L = *quam* as + *si* if]

quasi-, a combining form of **quasi:** *quasi-official, quasi-serious.*

qua/si con/tract, *Law.* an obligation imposed by law in the absence of a contract to prevent unjust enrichment.

qua·si-ju·di·cial (kwā/zī jo͞o dish/əl, kwā/sī-, kwä/sē-, -zē-), *adj.* having characteristics of a judicial act but performed by an administrative agency or official.

qua/si-stel/lar ra/dio source/ (kwā/sī stel/ər), quasar.

quass (kväs, kwäs), *n.* kvass.

quas·sia (kwosh/ə, -ē ə), *n.* **1.** any of several tropical, simaroubaceous trees or shrubs of the genera *Quassia* and *Picrasma.* **2.** Also called **bitter wood.** *Chem., Pharm.* a prepared form of the heartwood of any of these trees, used as an insecticide and as a tonic to dispel intestinal worms. [< NL, named after *Quassi,* 18th-century slave in Dutch Guiana who discovered its medicinal properties; see -IA]

qua·ter·nar·y (kwä/tər ner/ē, kwə tûr/nə rē), *adj., n., pl.* **-nar·ies.** —*adj.* **1.** consisting of four. **2.** arranged in fours. **3.** (*cap.*) *Geol.* noting or pertaining to the present period, forming the latter part of the Cenozoic era, beginning about 1,000,000 years ago and including the Recent and Pleistocene epochs. See table at **era.** —*n.* **4.** a group of four. **5.** the number four. **6.** (*cap.*) *Geol.* the Quaternary period. [ME < L *quaternāri(us)* = *quatern(ī)* four at a time + *-ārius* -ARY]

qua/ternary ammo/nium com/pound, *Chem.* any of a class of salts derived from ammonium in which the nitrogen atom is attached to four organic groups: many are cationic surface-active compounds used as antiseptics and disinfectants. Also called **qua/ternary ammo/nium salt/.**

qua·ter·nate (kwä/tər nāt/, kwə tûr/nit), *adj.* arranged in or consisting of four parts, as certain leaves. [<NL **quaternāt(us)* = L *quatern(ī)* four at a time + *-ātus* -ATE[1]]

qua·ter·ni·on (kwə tûr/nē ən), *n.* **1.** a group or set of four persons or things. **2.** *Math.* **a.** a quantity or operator expressed as the sum of a real number and three complex numbers, equivalent to the quotient of two vectors. The field of quaternions is not commutative under multiplication. **b. quaternions,** (*construed as sing.*) the calculus of such quantities. [ME *quaternioun* < LL *quaterniōn-* (s. of *quaterniō*) = L *quatern(ī)* four at a time + *-iōn-* -ION]

Quath·lam·ba (kwät läm/bä), *n.* Drakensberg.

qua·torze (kə tôrz/; *Fr.* KA tôRZ/), *n., pl.* **-torz·es** (-tôr/ziz; *Fr.* -tôRZ/). *Piquet.* a set of four cards of the same denomination, aces, kings, queens, jacks, or tens, scoring 14 points. [< F: fourteen << L *quattuordecim* = *quattuor* four + *-decim,* comb. form of *decem* ten]

quat·rain (kwo/trān), *n.* a stanza or poem of four lines, usually with alternate rhymes. [< F << L *quattuor* four]

qua·tre (kä/tər; *Fr.* KA/TRə), *n.* the four at cards, dice, or the like. [< F]

Qua·tre Bras (kä/trə brä/; *Fr.* KA-TRə BRÄ/), a village in central Belgium, near Brussels: a battle preliminary to the battle of Waterloo was fought here in 1815.

Quatrefoils

quat·re·foil (kat/ər foil/, ka/trə-), *n.* **1.** a leaf composed of four leaflets. **2.** *Archit.* a panellike ornament composed of four lobes, divided by cusps, radiating from a common center. [< OF *quatre* four + *-foil* (as in TREFOIL); r. ME *quaterfoil*] —**quat/re·foiled/,** *adj.*

quat·tro·cen·to (kwo/trō chen/tō; *It.* kwät/tRô chen/tô), *n.* (*often cap.*) the 15th century, used in reference to the Italian art of that time. [< It: lit., four hundred (short for fourteen hundred)] —**quat/tro·cen/tist,** *n.*

qua·ver (kwā/vər), *v.i.* **1.** to shake tremulously; quiver or tremble. **2.** to sound, speak, or sing tremulously. —*v.t.* **3.** to utter, say, or sing with a quavering or tremulous voice. —*n.* **4.** a quavering or tremulous shake, esp. in the voice. **5.** a quavering tone or utterance. **6.** *Music Chiefly Brit.* an eighth note. See illus. at **note.** [ME, b. QUAKE and WAVER] —**qua/ver·er,** *n.* —**qua/ver·ing·ly,** *adv.* —**qua/ver·y,** **qua/ver·ous,** *adj.*

quay (kē), *n.* a landing place, esp. one of solid masonry, constructed along the edge of a body of water; wharf. [sp. var. (after F *quai*) of earlier *kay,* also *key* (> the mod. pronunciation) < OF *kay, cay;* akin to Sp *cayo* shoal. See KEY[2]] —**quay/like/,** *adj.*

quay·age (kē/ij), *n.* **1.** a charge or fee for the use of a quay or quays. **2.** quays collectively. **3.** space appropriated to quays. [< F; see QUAY, -AGE]

Quayle (kwāl), *n.* **James Dan·forth** (dan/fôrth) (*Dan*), born 1947, 44th vice president of the U.S. since 1989.

Que., Quebec.

quean (kwēn), *n.* **1.** a bold, impudent woman; shrew; hussy. **2.** a prostitute. **3.** *Brit. Dial.* a girl or young woman, esp. a robust one. [ME *quene,* OE *cwene;* akin to OE *cwēn,* woman, queen]

quea·sy (kwē/zē), *adj.,* **-si·er, -si·est. 1.** inclined to or feeling nausea, as the stomach, a person, etc.; nauseous; nauseated. **2.** tending to cause nausea; nauseating. **3.** uneasy or uncomfortable, as feelings or the conscience. **4.** squeamish; excessively fastidious. [late ME < ?] —**quea/si·ly,** *adv.* —**quea/si·ness,** *n.*

Que·bec (kwi bek/), *n.* **1.** a province in E Canada. 5,657,000 (est. 1965); 594,860 sq. mi. **2.** a seaport in and the capital of this province, on the St. Lawrence: capital of New France 1663–1759, when it was taken by the English; wartime conferences 1943, 1944. 171,979 (1961). **3.** a word used in communications to represent the letter *Q.* French, **Qué·bec** (kā bek/) (for 1, 2).

Que·bec·er (kwi bek/ər), *n.* a native or inhabitant of Quebec, esp. the city of Quebec. Also **Que·beck/er.**

que·bra·cho (kā brä/chō; *Sp.* ke vRä/chô), *n., pl.* **-chos** (-chōz; *Sp.* -chôs). **1.** either of two anacardiaceous trees, *Schinopsis Lorentzii* or *S. Balansae,* the wood and bark of which are important in tanning and dyeing. **2.** an apocynaceous tree, *Aspidosperma quebrachoblanco,* yielding a medicinal bark. **3.** any of several hardwood South American trees. [< AmerSp, var. of *quiebracha* = Sp *quiebra* (s. of *quebrar* to break) + *hacha* ax, hatchet]

Quech·ua (kech/wä, -wə), *n., pl.* **-uas,** (*esp. collectively*) **-ua** for 2. **1.** a language spoken by about 4,000,000 people of the Andean plateaus from Quito, Ecuador, to Tucumán, Argentina. **2.** a member of an Indian people of Peru speaking Quechua. Also, **Kechua, Kechuan.**

Quech·uan (kech/wən), *adj., n., pl.* **-uans,** (*esp. collectively*) **-uan.** —*adj.* **1.** of or pertaining to the language of the Quechua. —*n.* **2.** Quechua.

queen (kwēn), *n.* **1.** the wife or consort of a king. **2.** a female sovereign or monarch. **3.** a woman, or something personified as a woman, that is foremost or preeminent in any respect: *a movie queen; a beauty queen.* **4.** a playing card bearing a picture of a queen. **5.** *Chess.* the most powerful piece of either color, privileged to move any unobstructed distance in any direction. **6.** *Slang.* a male homosexual. **7.** *Entomol.* a fertile female ant, bee, termite, or wasp. —*v.i.* **8.** to reign as queen. [ME *quene, quen,* OE *cwēn* woman, queen; akin to Gk *gyne* wife, Skt *jani*] —**queen/less,** *adj.* —**queen/like/,** *adj.*

Queen/ Anne/, noting or pertaining to the style of architecture, furnishings, and decoration prevailing in England in the early 18th century, characterized by simplicity and refinement of forms, with increasing attention to French and Italian models.

Queen/ Anne's/ lace/, an umbelliferous plant, *Daucus Carota,* having large, lacy umbels of minute, white flowers, the central one usually dark purple; the common, weedy form of the cultivated carrot.

Queen/ Anne's/ War/, the war (1702–13) in which England and its American colonies opposed France and its Indian allies.

Queen/ Char/lotte Is/lands, a group of islands in British Columbia off the W coast of Canada. 3014 (1961); 3970 sq. mi.

queen/ con/sort, the wife of a ruling king.

queen/ dow/ager, the widow of a king.

queen·ly (kwēn/lē), *adj.,* **-li·er, -li·est,** *adv.* —*adj.* **1.** belonging or proper to a queen: *queenly propriety.* **2.** befit-

qua/si-ab/so·lute/, *adj.*
qua/si-ac/a·dem/ic, *adj.*
qua/si-ac/ci·den/tal, *adj.*
qua/si-ac/tive, *adj.*
qua/si-a·dult/, *adj.*
qua/si-ad/van·ta/geous, *adj.*
qua/si-af·firm/a·tive, *adj.*
qua/si-al·ter/na·tive, *adj.*
qua/si-A·mer/i·can, *adj.*
qua/si-an/cient, *adj.*
qua/si-an·tique/, *adj.*
qua/si-ar·tis/tic, *adj.*
qua/si-au/to·mat/ic, *adj.*
qua/si-au/to·mat/i·cal·ly, *adv.*
qua/si-ben/e·fi/cial, *adj.*
qua/si-bi/o·graph/i·cal, *adj.*
qua/si-clas/sic, *adj.*
qua/si-col·le/giate, *adj.*
qua/si-com·mer/cial, *adj.;* **-ly,** *adv.*
qua/si-com·pet/i·tive, *adj.*
qua/si-com/pli·men/ta·ry, *adj.*
qua/si-com/pre·hen/sive, *adj.*
qua/si-com·pul/sive, *adj.*
qua/si-com·pul/so·ry, *adj.*
qua/si-con/fi·den/tial, *adj.;* **-ly,** *adv.*
qua/si-con/scious, *adj.;* **-ly,** *adv.*
qua/si-con·serv/a·tive, *adj.;* **-ly,** *adv.*
qua/si-con·tin/u·al, *adj.*
qua/si-con·tin/u·ous, *adj.*
qua/si-con·vinced/, *adj.*
qua/si-cor·rect/, *adj.;* **-ly,** *adv.*
qua/si-crim/i·nal, *adj.*
qua/si-def/i·nite, *adj.*
qua/si-de·lib/er·ate, *adj.;* **-ly,** *adv.*
qua/si-dem/o·crat/ic, *adj.*
qua/si-de·pend/ent, *adj.;* **-ly,** *adv.*
qua/si-de·vot/ed, *adj.;* **-ly,** *adv.*
qua/si-dip/lo·mat/ic, *adj.*
qua/si-e/co·nom/ic, *adj.*
qua/si-e·quiv/a·lent, *adj.*
qua/si-es·sen/tial, *adj.*
qua/si-ex·per/i·men/tal, *adj.;* **-ly,** *adv.*
qua/si-fa·mil/iar, *adj.;* **-ly,** *adv.*
qua/si-for/eign, *adj.*
qua/si-for·get/ful, *adj.*
qua/si-for/mal, *adj.*
qua/si-ha·bit/u·al, *adj.;* **-ly,** *adv.*
qua/si-he·red/i·tar/y, *adj.*
qua/si-he·ro/ic, *adj.*
qua/si-his·tor/ic, *adj.*
qua/si-hu/man, *adj.;* **-ly,** *adv.*
qua/si-hu/mor·ous, *adj.;* **-ly,** *adv.*
qua/si-in/de·pend/ent, *adj.;* **-ly,** *adv.*
qua/si-in·dus/tri·al, *adj.*
qua/si-in·her/it·ed, *adj.*
qua/si-in·nu/mer·a·ble, *adj.*
qua/si-in·tu/i·tive, *adj.;* **-ly,** *adv.*
qua/si-jo·cose/, *adj.;* **-ly,** *adv.*
qua/si-le/gal, *adj.;* **-ly,** *adv.*
qua/si-leg/end·ar/y, *adj.*
qua/si-leg/is·la/tive, *adj.;* **-ly,** *adv.*
qua/si-le·git/i·mate, *adj.*
qua/si-lib/er·al, *adj.;* **-ly,** *adv.*
qua/si-lit/er·ar/y, *adj.*
qua/si-log/i·cal, *adj.;* **-ly,** *adv.*
qua/si-mag/i·cal, *adj.;* **-ly,** *adv.*
qua/si-man/a·ge/ri·al, *adj.*
qua/si-ma·te/ri·al, *adj.;* **-ly,** *adv.*
qua/si-me·chan/i·cal, *adj.;* **-ly,** *adv.*
qua/si-mil/i·tar/y, *adj.*
qua/si-mi·rac/u·lous, *adj.;* **-ly,** *adv.*
qua/si-mod/ern, *adj.*
qua/si-myth/i·cal, *adj.;* **-ly,** *adv.*
qua/si-nat/u·ral, *adj.;* **-ly,** *adv.*
qua/si-nor/mal, *adj.;* **-ly,** *adv.*
qua/si-ob·jec/tive, *adj.;* **-ly,** *adv.*
qua/si-of·fi/cial, *adj.;* **-ly,** *adv.*
qua/si-or·gan/ic, *adj.*
qua/si-pa/tri·ar/chal, *adj.*
qua/si-pa/tri·ot/ic, *adj.*
qua/si-per/ma·nent, *adj.;* **-ly,** *adv.*
qua/si-per/son·al, *adj.*
qua/si-phil/o·soph/i·cal, *adj.;* **-ly,** *adv.*
qua/si-phys/i·cal, *adj.*
qua/si-po·lit/i·cal, *adj.;* **-ly,** *adv.*
qua/si-pri/vate, *adj.;* **-ly,** *adv.*
qua/si-pub/lic, *adj.;* **-ly,** *adv.*
qua/si-reg/u·lar, *adj.;* **-ly,** *adv.*
qua/si-re·li/gious, *adj.;* **-ly,** *adv.*
qua/si-ru/ral, *adj.*
qua/si-sci/en·tif/ic, *adj.*
qua/si-so/cial·is/tic, *adj.*
qua/si-spir/it·u·al, *adj.;* **-ly,** *adv.*
qua/si-stand/ard·ized/, *adj.*
qua/si-sys/tem·at/ic, *adj.*
qua/si-tan/gi·ble, *adj.*
qua/si-tech/ni·cal, *adj.;* **-ly,** *adv.*
qua/si-ter/ri·to/ri·al, *adj.*
qua/si-tra·di/tion·al, *adj.;* **-ly,** *adv.*
qua/si-u/ni·ver/sal, *adj.*

ting or suggestive of a queen: *queenly grace.* —*adv.* **3.** in a queenly manner.
Queen′ Mab′ (mab), *Irish and English Folklore.* a mischievous, tantalizing fairy who produces and governs the dreams of men.
Queen′ Maud′ Land′ (môd), a coastal region of Antarctica, S of Africa: Norwegian explorations.
Queen′ Maud′ Range′, a mountain range in Antarctica, in Ross Dependency, S of the Ross Sea. 500 mi. long.
queen′ moth′er, a queen dowager who is also mother of a reigning sovereign.
Queen′ of Heav′en, a designation of the Virgin Mary.
queen′ ol′ive, a large, meaty olive grown esp. in the area of Seville, Spain.
queen′ post′, either of a pair of timbers or posts extending vertically upward from the tie beam of a roof truss or the like, one on each side of the center.

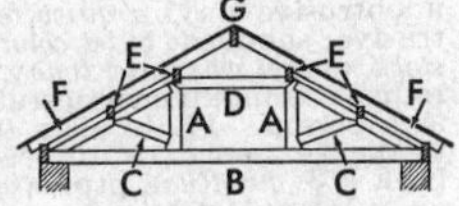

A, Queen post; B, Tie beam; C, Strut; D, Straining piece; E, Purlin; F, Common rafter; G, Ridgepole

queen′ re′gent, **1.** a queen who reigns in behalf of another. **2.** See **queen regnant.**
queen′ reg′nant, a queen who reigns in her own right. Also, **queen regent.**
Queens (kwēnz), *n.* a borough of E New York City, on Long Island. 1,986,473 (1970); 113.1 sq. mi.
Queen's′ Bench′. See **King's Bench.**
Queens′ber·ry rules′ (kwēnz′ber′ē, -bə rē). See **Marquis of Queensberry rules.**
Queen's′ Birth′day. See **King's Birthday.**
queen's′ col′our. See **king's colour.**
Queen's′ Coun′sel. See **King's Counsel.**
queen's′ Eng′lish. See **king's English.**
queen's′ ev′idence. See **king's evidence.**
queen's′ high′way. See **king's highway.**
queen-size (kwēn′sīz′), *adj.* **1.** (of a bed) larger than a double bed, but smaller than king-size, usually between 60 and 72 inches wide. **2.** pertaining to or made for a queen-size bed: *queen-size blankets.*
Queens·land (kwēnz′land′, -lənd), *n.* a state in NE Australia. 1,518,828 (1961); 670,500 sq. mi. *Cap.:* Brisbane.
queen's′-pawn o′penings (kwēnz′pôn′), (*construed as sing.*) a class of chess openings in which the pawn in front of the queen is advanced two squares on the first move.
Queens·town (kwēnz′toun′), *n.* former name of **Cóbh.**
queer (kwēr), *adj.* **1.** strange or odd from a conventional viewpoint; unusually different; singular: *a queer notion of justice.* **2.** of a questionable nature or character; suspicious; shady. **3.** not feeling physically right or well; giddy, faint, or qualmish: *to feel queer.* **4.** mentally unbalanced or deranged. **5.** *Slang.* homosexual. —*v.t.* **6.** to spoil; ruin. **7.** to jeopardize. —*n.* **8.** *Slang.* a homosexual. [? < G *quer* oblique, cross, adverse] —**queer′ly,** *adv.* —**queer′ness,** *n.* —**Syn. 1.** eccentric, weird. See **strange.**
Quel·i·ma·ne (kel′ə mä′nə), *n.* a seaport in E Mozambique. 151,618 (est. 1958).
quell (kwel), *v.t.* **1.** to suppress (a disorder, mutiny, or the like); put an end to; extinguish: *The troops quelled the rebellion.* **2.** to vanquish; subdue. **3.** to quiet or allay (emotions, anxieties, etc.). [ME *quelle(n),* OE *cwellan* to kill; akin to Icel *kvelja* to torment, G *quälen* to torture, vex] —**quell′a·ble,** *adj.* —**quell′er,** *n.* —**Syn. 1, 2.** crush, quash, defeat, conquer, quench. **3.** calm, pacify, compose.
Quel·part (kwel′pärt′), *n.* Cheju.
quel·que chose (kel′kə shōz′), kickshaw. [< F: something]
Que·moy (ki moi′), *n.* an island off the SE coast of China, in the Formosa Strait: remained with Nationalist China after the Communist conquest of the mainland. 45,347 (est. 1956); 50 sq. mi. Cf. **Matsu.**
quench (kwench), *v.t.* **1.** to slake, satisfy, or allay (thirst, desires, passion, etc.). **2.** to put out or extinguish (fire, flames, etc.). **3.** to cool suddenly by plunging into a liquid, as in tempering steel by immersion in water. **4.** to subdue or destroy; overcome; quell: *to quench an uprising.* [ME *quenche(n),* OE *-cwencan* (as in *acwencan* to quench), causative of *-cwincan* (as in *acwincan* to be extinguished)] —**quench′a·ble,** *adj.* —**quench′er,** *n.* —**quench′less,** *adj.*
que·nelle (kə nel′), *n.* a small ball of forcemeat mixture, usually boiled and served with a sauce or used as a garnish. [< F < G *Knödel* dumpling]
quer·ce·tin (kwûr′si tin), *n.* *Chem.* a yellow powder, $C_{15}H_{10}O_7$, obtained from the bark of quercitron, used as a dye; flavin. [< L *quercēt(um)* an oak wood + -IN[2]]
quer·cine (kwûr′sin, -sīn), *adj.* of or pertaining to an oak. [< L *querc(us)* oak + -INE[2]]
quer·ci·tron (kwûr′si′trən), *n.* **1.** an oak, *Quercus velutina,* the inner bark of which yields a yellow dye. **2.** the dye obtained from this bark. [< L *querc(us)* oak + CITRON]
Que·ré·ta·ro (ke re′tä rō′), *n.* **1.** a state in central Mexico. 355,045 (1960); 4432 sq. mi. **2.** a city in and the capital of this state, in the SW part: republican forces executed Emperor Maximilian here 1867. 66,225 (1960).
que·rist (kwēr′ist), *n.* a person who queries or questions.
quern (kwûrn), *n.* a primitive, hand-operated mill for grinding grain. [ME; OE *cweorn;* akin to Icel *kvern* hand mill]
quer·u·lous (kwer′ə ləs, kwer′yə-), *adj.* **1.** full of complaints; complaining. **2.** characterized by or uttered in complaint; peevish: *a querulous tone.* [late ME < L *querulus* = *quer(ī)* to complain + *-ulus* -ULOUS] —**quer′u·lous·ly,** *adv.* —**quer′u·lous·ness,** *n.* —**Syn.** petulant, testy.
que·ry (kwēr′ē), *n., pl.* **-ries,** *v.,* **-ried, -ry·ing.** —*n.* **1.** a question; inquiry. **2.** mental uncertainty or reservation; doubt. **3.** *Print.* a question mark (?), esp. as added to a manuscript, proof sheet, or the like, indicating doubt as to some point in the text. —*v.t.* **4.** to ask or inquire about. **5.** to question as doubtful or obscure: *to query a statement.* **6.** *Print.* to mark with a query. **7.** to ask questions of. [alter. of earlier *quere* < L *quaere,* impv. of *quaerere* to ask, seek; see -Y[3]] —**que′ry·ing·ly,** *adv.*
ques., question.
Ques·nay (ke ne′), *n.* **Fran·çois** (frän swa′), 1694–1774, French economist and physician.
quest (kwest), *n.* **1.** a search or pursuit made in order to find or obtain something: *a quest for uranium.* **2.** *Medieval Romance.* an adventurous expedition undertaken by a knight or knights to secure or achieve something. **3.** those engaged in such an expedition. **4.** *Brit. Dial.* inquest. —*v.i.* **5.** to search; seek (often fol. by *for* or *after*): *to quest after hidden treasure.* **6.** to go on a quest. **7.** *Hunting.* (of a dog) **a.** to search for game. **b.** to bay. —*v.t.* **8.** to search or seek for; pursue. [ME *queste* < MF << L *quaesita,* fem. ptp. of *quaerere* to seek] —**quest′er,** *n.* —**quest′ing·ly,** *adv.*
ques·tion (kwes′chən, kwesh′-), *n.* **1.** a sentence in an interrogative form, addressed to someone in order to get information in reply. **2.** a problem for discussion or under discussion; a matter for investigation. **3.** a matter of some uncertainty or difficulty; problem (usually fol. by *of*): *It was simply a question of time.* **4.** a subject of dispute or controversy. **5.** a proposal to be debated or voted on, as in a meeting or a deliberative assembly. **6.** the procedure of putting a proposal to vote. **7.** *Politics.* a problem of public policy submitted to the voters for an expression of opinion. **8.** the act of asking or inquiring; interrogation; query. **9.** inquiry into or discussion of some problem or doubtful matter. **10. beyond question,** beyond dispute; without doubt. Also, **beyond all question. 11. call in** or **into question, a.** to dispute; challenge. **b.** to cast doubt upon; question. **12. in question, a.** under consideration. **b.** in dispute. **13. out of the question,** not to be considered; unthinkable; impossible. —*v.t.* **14.** to ask (someone) a question; ask questions of; interrogate. **15.** to ask or inquire. **16.** to doubt: *He questioned her sincerity.* **17.** to challenge or dispute. —*v.i.* **18.** to ask a question or questions. [ME *questiun* < AF < L *quaestiōn-* (s. of *quaestiō*) = *quaest(us)* (ptp. of *quaerere* to ask) + *-iōn-* -ION] —**ques′tion·er,** *n.* —**Syn. 1.** inquiry, query, interrogation. **14.** query, examine. **15.** See **inquire.** —**Ant. 1, 14.** answer.
ques·tion·a·ble (kwes′chə nə bəl, kwesh′-), *adj.* **1.** of doubtful propriety, honesty, morality, respectability, etc.: *questionable activities; in questionable taste.* **2.** open to question or dispute; doubtful or uncertain: *a statement of questionable accuracy.* **3.** open to question as to being of the nature or value suggested: *a questionable privilege.* —**ques′tion·a·ble·ness, ques′tion·a·bil′i·ty,** *n.* —**ques′tion·a·bly,** *adv.* —**Syn. 2.** debatable, disputable, controvertible, dubitable, dubious. —**Ant. 1.** certain.
ques·tion·ing (kwes′chə ning, kwesh′-), *adj.* **1.** indicating or implying a question: *a questioning tone.* **2.** characterized by or indicating intellectual curiosity; inquiring: *an alert and questioning mind.* —*n.* **3.** an inquiry or interrogation. —**ques′tion·ing·ly,** *adv.*
ques·tion·less (kwes′chən lis, kwesh′-), *adj.* **1.** unquestionable; doubtless. **2.** unquestioning: *questionless faith in God.* —*adv.* **3.** without question; unquestionably. —**ques′tion·less·ly,** *adv.*
ques′tion mark′, **1.** Also called **interrogation point, interrogation mark.** a mark indicating a question: the mark (?) placed after a question. **2.** something unknown.
ques·tion·naire (kwes′chə nâr′, kwesh′-), *n.* a list of questions submitted for replies that can be analyzed for usable information. [< F = *questionn(er)* (to) question + *-aire;* see -ARY]
ques·tor (kwes′tər, kwē′stər), *n.* *Rom. Hist.* quaestor. —**ques·to·ri·al** (kwe stōr′ē əl, -stôr′-, kwē-), *adj.* —**ques′tor·ship′,** *n.*

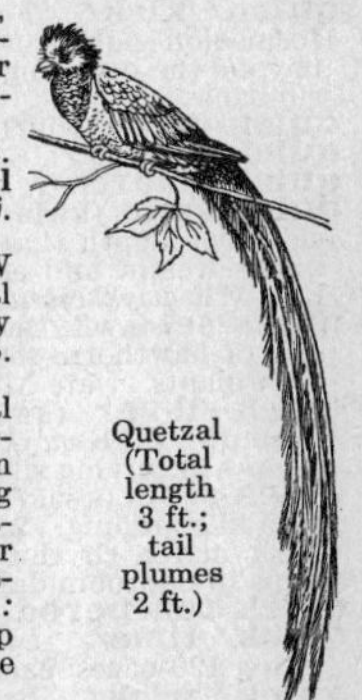
Quetzal (Total length 3 ft.; tail plumes 2 ft.)

Quet·ta (kwet′ä), *n.* a city in W central Pakistan: formerly the capital of British Baluchistan; almost totally destroyed by an earthquake 1935. 106,633 (1961).
quet·zal (ket säl′), *n.* **1.** a Central and South American bird, *Pharomachrus mocinna,* having golden-green and scarlet plumage, the male having long, flowing upper tail coverts: the national bird of Guatemala. **2.** a paper money and monetary unit of Guatemala, equal to 100 centavos. *Abbr.:* Q. Also, **que·zal** (ke säl′). [< AmerSp < Nahuatl *quetzalli* tailfeather of the bird *quetzaltototl*]
Quet·zal·co·a·tl (ket säl′kō ät′əl), *n.* the feathered serpent god of the Aztec and Toltec cultures.
queue (kyōō), *n., v.,* **queued, queu·ing.** —*n.* **1.** a braid of hair worn hanging down behind. **2.** a file or line, esp. of people waiting their turn. —*v.i., v.t.* **3.** to form in a line while waiting (often fol. by *up*). [< F << L *cōda* tail, r. *cauda*]
Que′zon Cit′y (kā′zon), a city on S Luzon Island, in the Philippines, NE of Manila; designated the national capital from 1948 through 1976 when Manila, the traditional capital, was made the official capital. 994,679.
Que·zon y Mo·li·na (kā′zon ē mō lē′nə; *Sp.* ke′sôn ē mô lē′nä, -thôn), **Ma·nuel Lu·is** (mä nwel′ lōō ēs′), 1878–1944, Philippine political leader; 1st president of the Philippine Commonwealth 1933–44.
quib·ble (kwib′əl), *n., v.,* **-bled, -bling.** —*n.* **1.** a use of ambiguous or irrelevant language or arguments to evade a point at issue. **2.** petty or carping criticism; a minor objection. —*v.i.* **3.** to equivocate. **4.** to carp; cavil. [? < *quib* gibe, appar. var. of QUIP] —**quib′bler,** *n.* —**Syn. 1.** evasion, equivocation, sophism, shift, ambiguity.
quib·bling (kwib′ling), *adj.* **1.** characterized by or consisting of quibbles; carping; niggling. —*n.* **2.** the act of a person who quibbles. **3.** an instance of quibbling. —**quib′bling·ly,** *adv.*
Qui·be·ron (kēbə rôn′), *n.* a peninsula in NW France, on the S coast of Brittany: British naval victory over the French 1759. 6 mi. long.

quiche (kēsh), *n.* *French Cookery.* a pielike dish consisting of an unsweetened pastry shell filled with a custard and usually flavored with cheese, onion, bacon, etc.: *quiche Lorraine.* [< F < G (dial.) *Küche,* dim. of *Kuche(n)* cake]
Qui·ché (kē chā′), *n.* a Mayan language of Guatemala.
quick (kwik), *adj.* **1.** done, proceeding, or occurring with promptness or rapidity, as an action, process, etc.; prompt; immediate: *a quick response.* **2.** finished or completed in a short time: *a quick shower.* **3.** moving, or able to move, with speed: *a quick fox; a quick train.* **4.** swift or rapid, as motion. **5.** hasty; impatient: *a quick temper.* **6.** lively or keen, as feelings. **7.** acting with swiftness or rapidity: *a quick worker.* **8.** prompt or swift to do something: *quick to respond.* **9.** prompt to perceive: *a quick eye.* **10.** prompt to understand, learn, etc.: *a quick student.* **11.** *Archaic.* endowed with life; living. —*n.* **12.** living persons collectively (usually prec. by *the*): *the quick and the dead.* **13.** the tender, sensitive flesh of the living body, esp. that under the nails. **14.** the vital or most important part. **15. cut to the quick,** to injure deeply; hurt the feelings of. —*adv.* **16.** quickly. [ME; OE *cwic, cwicu* living; c. OS *quik,* G *queck, keck,* Icel *kvikr;* akin to L *vīvus* living] —**quick′ness,** *n.*
—**Syn. 1.** fleet, expeditious. QUICK, FAST, SWIFT, RAPID describe speedy tempo. QUICK applies particularly to something practically instantaneous, an action or reaction, perhaps, of very brief duration: *to give a quick look around.* FAST and SWIFT refer to actions, movements, etc., that continue for a time, and usually to those that are uninterrupted; when used of communication, transportation, and the like, they suggest a definite goal and a continuous trip. SWIFT, the more formal word, suggests the greater speed: *a fast train; a swift message.* RAPID, less speedy than the others, applies to a rate of movement or action, and usually to a series of actions or movements, related or unrelated: *rapid calculation.* **5.** abrupt, curt. **6.** acute, sensitive, alert. **7.** nimble, agile, brisk. **10.** See **sharp.** —**Ant. 1, 6, 10.** slow.
quick′ as′sets, *Accounting.* liquid assets including cash, receivables, and marketable securities.
quick·en (kwik′ən), *v.t.* **1.** to make more rapid; accelerate; hasten: *She quickened her pace.* **2.** to give or restore vigor or activity to; rouse or stimulate: *to quicken the imagination.* **3.** to animate or revive; restore life to: *Spring rains quickened the earth.* —*v.i.* **4.** to become more active, sensitive, etc. **5.** to become alive; receive life. **6.** to enter that stage of pregnancy in which the child gives indications of life. **7.** (of a child in the womb) to begin to manifest signs of life. [ME *quiken(en)*] —**quick′en·er,** *n.* —**Syn. 2.** animate.
quick-fire (kwik′fīər′), *adj.* firing or equipped for firing rapidly, esp. at moving targets. Also, **quick′-fir′ing.**
quick-freeze (kwik′frēz′), *v.,* **-froze, -fro·zen, -freez·ing.** —*v.t.* **1.** to subject (food) to rapid refrigeration, permitting it to be stored almost indefinitely at freezing temperatures. —*v.i.* **2.** to quick-freeze food or become quick-frozen.
quick′ grass′, the couch grass, *Agropyron repens.*
quick·ie (kwik′ē), *Slang.* —*n.* **1.** a book, movie, etc., usually trivial in quality, requiring only a short time to produce. **2.** anything taking only a short time, esp. a quickly consumed alcoholic drink. —*adj.* **3.** done or made hurriedly, esp. as a temporary expedient.
quick′ kick′, *Football.* a punt made from an offensive formation not usually used for kicking, intended to go beyond the opposing safety men in order to prevent a possible runback.
quick·lime (kwik′līm′), *n.* lime[1] (def. 1).
quick·ly (kwik′lē), *adv.* with speed; very soon. [ME]
quick′ march′, a march in quick time.
quick·sand (kwik′sand′), *n.* a bed of loose sand of considerable depth that is so saturated with water as to yield under weight and engulf persons or animals entering upon it. [ME *qwykkesand*] —**quick′sand′y,** *adj.*
quick·set (kwik′set′), *n.* *Chiefly Brit.* **1.** a plant or cutting, esp. of hawthorn, set to grow, as in a hedge. **2.** a hedge of such plants. [late ME]
quick·sil·ver (kwik′sil′vər), *n.* the metallic element mercury. [ME *qwyksilver,* OE *cwicseolfor* (after L *argentum vīvum*) lit., living silver]
quick·step (kwik′step′), *n.* **1.** (formerly) a lively step used in marching. **2.** music adapted to such a march, or in a brisk march rhythm. **3.** a lively step or combination of steps in ballroom dancing.
quick-tem·pered (kwik′tem′pərd), *adj.* easily angered.
quick′ time′, *U.S. Mil.* a normal rate of marching in which 120 paces, each of 30 inches, are taken in a minute.
quick′ trick′, *Bridge.* a card or group of cards that will probably win the first or second trick in a suit, regardless of who plays it or at what declaration.
quick-wit·ted (kwik′wit′id), *adj.* having a nimble, alert mind. —**quick′-wit′ted·ly,** *adv.* —**quick′wit′ted·ness,** *n.*
quid[1] (kwid), *n.* a portion of something, esp. tobacco, that is to be chewed but not swallowed. [OE *cwidu* CUD]
quid[2] (kwid), *n., pl.* **quid.** *Brit. Slang.* one pound sterling. [?]
quid·di·ty (kwid′i tē), *n., pl.* **-ties. 1.** that which makes a thing what it is; the essential nature. **2.** a trifling nicety of subtle distinction, as in argument. [< ML *quidditās* = L *quid* what + *-itās* -ITY]
quid·nunc (kwid′nungk′), *n.* a person who is eager to know the latest news and gossip; a gossip or busybody. [< L *quid nunc* what now?]
quid pro quo (kwid′ prō kwō′), *pl.* **quid pro quos, quids pro quo** for 2. **1.** (*italics*) *Latin.* one thing in return for another. **2.** something that is given or taken in return for something else; substitute. [lit., something for something]
¿quién sa·be? (kyen sä′ve), *Spanish.* who knows?
qui·es·cent (kwē es′ənt), *adj.* resting; quiet, still, or inactive. [< L *quiescent-* (s. of *quiescēns,* prp. of *quiescere*) = *quiesc-* be quiet + *-ent-* -ENT] —**qui·es′cence, qui·es′cen·cy,** *n.* —**Syn.** dormant, latent.
qui·et[1] (kwī′it), *n.* **1.** freedom from noise, unwanted sound, etc. **2.** freedom from disturbance or tumult; tranquillity; calm. **3.** peace: *a time of quiet.* [ME < L *quiēt-* (s. of *quiēs*)] —**Syn. 1.** silence. **2.** stillness. —**Ant. 1.** noise.
qui·et[2] (kwī′it), *adj.* **1.** making no disturbance or trouble; not turbulent; peaceable. **2.** free from disturbance or tumult; tranquil; peaceful: *a quiet life.* **3.** free from disturbing thoughts, emotions, etc.: *a quiet conscience.* **4.** being at rest. **5.** refraining or free from activity, esp. busy or vigorous activity: *a quiet Sunday afternoon.* **6.** motionless or moving very gently: *quiet waters.* **7.** making no noise or sound, esp. no disturbing sound: *quiet neighbors.* **8.** free, or comparatively free, from noise: *a quiet street.* **9.** silent: *Be quiet!* **10.** restrained in speech, manner, etc.; saying little: *a quiet person.* **11.** said, expressed, done, etc., in a restrained or unobtrusive way: *a quiet reproach.* **12.** not showy or obtrusive; subdued: *quiet colors.* **13.** not busy or active: *The stock market was quiet today.* —*v.t.* **14.** to make quiet. **15.** to make tranquil or peaceful; pacify. **16.** to calm mentally, as a person. **17.** to allay (tumult, doubt, fear, etc.). **18.** to silence. —*v.i.* **19.** to become quiet (often fol. by *down*). [ME < L *quiēt(us),* ptp. of *quiescere* to be quiet] —**qui′et·er,** *n.* —**qui′et·ly,** *adv.* —**qui′et·ness,** *n.* —**Syn. 2.** calm, serene. **6.** unmoving. **8.** See **still**[1]. **14.** still, hush, silence. **15.** lull, soothe. —**Ant. 2.** perturbed. **6.** active. **8.** noisy.
qui·et·en (kwī′i tən), *v.t.* *Chiefly Brit.* to make quiet.
qui·et·ism (kwī′i tiz′əm), *n.* **1.** a form of religious mysticism of the 17th century, requiring extinction of the will and worldly interests, and passive meditation on the divine. **2.** some similar form of religious mysticism. **3.** mental or bodily repose or passivity. [< It *quietismo*] —**qui′et·ist,** *n., adj.* —**qui′et·is′tic,** *adj.*
qui·e·tude (kwī′i to͞od′, -tyo͞od′), *n.* the state of being quiet; tranquillity; calmness; stillness; quiet. [< ML *quiētūdō* < L *quiēt(us)* QUIET[2]; see -TUDE]
qui·e·tus (kwī ē′təs), *n., pl.* **-tus·es. 1.** a finishing stroke; anything that effectually ends or settles. **2.** discharge or release from life. **3.** a period of retirement or inactivity. [< ML: quit (in *quiētus est* he is quit, a formula of acquittance), L: he is quiet. See QUIET[2] (adj.); cf. QUIT[1] (adj.)]
quill (kwil), *n.* **1.** one of the large feathers of the wing or tail of a bird. **2.** the hard, hollow, basal part of a feather. **3.** a feather, as of a goose, formed into a pen for writing. **4.** one of the hollow spines on a porcupine or hedgehog. **5.** a plectrum of a harpsichord. **6.** a roll of bark, as of cinnamon, formed in drying. **7.** a reed or other hollow stem on which yarn is wound. **8.** a bobbin or spool. **9.** *Mach.* a hollow shaft or sleeve through which another independently rotating shaft may pass. —*v.t.* **10.** *Textiles.* **a.** to arrange (fabric) in flutes or cylindrical ridges, as along the edge of a garment. **b.** to wind on a quill, as yarn. **11.** to penetrate with or as with a quill or quills. **12.** to extract quills from. [ME *quil;* cf. LG *quiele,* G *Kiel*] —**quill′-like′,** *adj.*
Quill (kwil), *n.* **Michael Joseph,** 1905–66, U.S. labor leader, born in Ireland: president of the Transport Workers Union of America 1935–66.
quil·lai (ki lī′), *n.* soapbark (def. 1). [< AmerSp < Chilean (Araucanian)]
quillai′ bark′, soapbark (def. 2).
quill·back (kwil′bak′), *n., pl.* **-backs,** (*esp. collectively*) **-back.** a carpsucker, *Carpiodes cyprinus,* found in the central and eastern U.S., having one ray of the dorsal fin greatly elongated. Also called **quill′back carp′sucker.**
Quil·ler-Couch (kwil′ər ko͞och′), *n.* **Sir Arthur Thomas** ("Q"), 1863–1944, English novelist and critic.
quill·wort (kwil′wûrt′), *n.* any aquatic and paludal, pteridophytic plant of the genus *Isoëtes,* characterized by clustered, quill-like leaves bearing sporangia in their bases.
Quil·mes (kēl′mes), *n.* a city in E Argentina, near Buenos Aires. 318,144 (1960).
quilt (kwilt), *n.* **1.** a coverlet for a bed, made of two layers of fabric with some soft substance, as wool or down, between them and stitched in patterns to prevent the filling from shifting. **2.** anything quilted or resembling a quilt. **3.** a bedspread or counterpane, esp. a thick one. —*v.t.* **4.** to stitch together (two pieces of cloth and a soft interlining), usually in an ornamental pattern. **5.** to sew up between pieces of material. **6.** to pad or line with material. —*v.i.* **7.** to make quilts or quilted work. [ME *quilte* < OF *cuilte* < L *culcita* mattress, cushion] —**quilt′er,** *n.*
quilt·ed (kwil′tid), *adj.* **1.** resembling a quilt, as in texture, design, stitching, etc. **2.** padded, filled, or stitched in the manner of a quilt.
quilt·ing (kwil′ting), *n.* **1.** the act of a person who quilts. **2.** material for making quilts.
quilt′ing bee′, *U.S.* a social gathering where women make quilts.
quin·a·crine (kwin′ə krēn′), *n.* *Pharm.* an alkaloid, $C_{23}H_{30}ClN_3O$, used in the treatment of malaria. Also called **atebrin.** [QUIN(INE) + ACR(ID) + -INE[2]]
qui·na·ry (kwī′nə rē), *adj., n., pl.* **-ries.** —*adj.* **1.** pertaining to or consisting of five. **2.** arranged in fives. **3.** of, pertaining to, or noting a numerical system based on the number 5. —*n.* **4.** a number in a quinary system. [< L *quīnāri(us)* = *quīn(ī)* five each + *-ārius* -ARY]
qui·nate (kwī′nāt), *adj.* *Bot.* arranged in groups of five. [< L *quīn(ī)* five each + -ATE[1]]
quince (kwins), *n.* **1.** the hard, yellowish, acid fruit of a small, hardy, rosaceous tree, *Cydonia oblonga.* **2.** the tree itself. [ME *qwince,* appar. orig. pl. (taken as sing.) of *quyne, coyn* < MF *cooin* < L *cotōneum,* var. of *cydōnium* < Gk *kydṓnion* quince, lit., (apple) of Cydonia]
quin·cun·cial (kwin kun′shəl), *adj.* **1.** consisting of, arranged, or formed like a quincunx or quincunxes. **2.** *Bot.* noting a five-ranked arrangement of leaves. [< L *quincunciāl(is)* = *quincunci-* (s. of *quincunx*) + *-ālis* -AL[1]] —**quin·cun′cial·ly,** *adv.*
quin·cunx (kwing′kungks, kwin′-), *n.* **1.** an arrangement of five objects, as trees, in a square or rectangle, one at each corner and one in the middle. **2.** *Bot.* an imbricated arrangement of five petals or leaves, in which two are interior, two are exterior, and one is partly interior and partly exterior. [< L: five twelfths (*quinque-* QUINQUE- + *uncia* twelfth; see OUNCE[1]); orig. a Roman coin worth five twelfths of an as and marked with a quincunx of spots]
Quin·cy (kwin′zē *for 1, 2;* kwin′sē *for 3*), *n.* **1. Josiah,** 1744–75, American patriot and writer. **2.** a city in E Massachusetts, near Boston. 87,966 (1970). **3.** a city in W Illinois, on the Mississippi. 45,288 (1970).
quin·dec·a·gon (kwin dek′ə gon′), *n.* *Geom.* a polygon

having 15 angles and 15 sides. [< L *quindec(im)* fifteen + *-agon* (abstracted from *decagon*)]

quin·de·cen·ni·al (kwin′di sen′ē əl), *adj.* **1.** of or pertaining to a period of 15 years or the 15th occurrence of a series, as an anniversary. **—***n.* **2.** a 15th anniversary. [< L *quindec(im)* fifteen + *-ennial* (as in *decennial*)]

qui·nel·la (kwi nel′ə, kē-), *n.* a type of bet, esp. on horse races, in which the bettor must select the first- and second-place finishers without specifying their order of finishing. Also, **qui·ne′la.** Cf. **exacta.** [AmerSp *quiniela*]

quin·i·dine (kwin′i dēn′, -din), *n.* *Pharm.* an alkaloid isomeric with quinine, $C_{20}H_{24}N_2O_2$, obtained from the bark of certain species of cinchona trees or shrubs: used esp. as the sulfate, chiefly to regulate the heart rhythm and to treat malaria. [QUIN(INE) + -ID^3 + -INE^2]

qui·nine (kwī′nīn *or, esp. Brit.,* kwi nēn′), *n.* *Chem., Pharm.* **1.** a bitter alkaloid, $C_{20}H_{24}N_2O_2$, obtained from cinchona bark: used chiefly in the treatment of malaria. **2.** a salt of this alkaloid, esp. the sulfate. Also, **qui·ni·na** (kē nē′nə). [< Sp *quin(a)* < Quechua *kina* bark + -INE^2]

qui′nine wa′ter, tonic (def. 4).

quin′nat salm′on (kwin′at). See **chinook salmon.** [< AmerInd (Salishan) *t′ kwinnat*]

quin·oid (kwin′oid), *Chem.* **—***n.* **1.** a quinonoid substance. **—***adj.* **2.** quinonoid. [QUIN(ONE) + -OID] **—quinoi′dal,** *adj.*

qui·noi·dine (kwi noi′dēn, -din), *n.* *Pharm.* a mixture of alkaloids, obtained as a by-product in the manufacture of quinine and used as a cheap substitute for it. [QUIN(INE) + -OID + -INE^2]

quin·ol (kwin′ōl, -ôl, -ol), *n.* *Chem.* hydroquinone. [QUIN(INE) + -OL^1]

quin·o·line (kwin′^{ə}lēn′, -^{ə}lin), *n.* *Chem.* a nitrogenous base, C_9H_7N, used as a solvent and reagent and in the manufacture of dyes. Also, **chinoline.**

qui·none (kwi nōn′, kwin′ōn), *n.* *Chem.* **1.** a cyclic unsaturated diketone, $C_6H_4O_2$, used chiefly in photography and in tanning leather. **2.** any of a class of compounds of this type. Also, **chinone.** [QUIN(INE) + -ONE]

quinone′ di′i·mine (dī′ə mēn′), *Chem.* a solid, $HN{=}C_6H_4{=}NH$, the parent of the indamine dyes.

quin·o·noid (kwin′ə noid′, kwi nō′noid), *adj.* *Chem.* of or resembling quinone. Also, **quinoid.**

quin·qua·ge·nar·i·an (kwin̄g′kwə jə nâr′ē ən, kwin′-), *adj.* **1.** 50 years of age. **2.** between the ages of 50 and 60. **—***n.* **3.** a quinquagenarian person. [< L *quinquāgēnāri(us)* consisting of fifty + -AN]

Quin·qua·ges·i·ma (kwin̄g′kwə jes′ə mə, kwin′-), *n.* the Sunday before Lent; Shrove Sunday. Also called **Quinquages′ima Sun′day.** [ME < ML, short for L *quinquāgēsima diēs* fiftieth day] **—Quin′qua·ges′i·mal,** *adj.*

quinque-, an element meaning "five," occurring in loan words from Latin (*quinquennial*); on this model, used in the formation of compound words: *quinquevalent.* [< L, comb. form of *quinque*]

quin·quen·ni·al (kwin kwen′ē əl, kwin̄g-), *adj.* **1.** of or for five years. **2.** occurring every five years. **—***n.* **3.** something that occurs every five years. **4.** a fifth anniversary. **5.** a quinquennium. [late ME < L *quinquenni(s)* of five years + -AL^1] **—quin·quen′ni·al·ly,** *adv.*

quin·quen·ni·um (kwin kwen′ē əm, kwin̄g-), *n., pl.* **-quen·ni·ums, -quen·ni·a** (-kwen′ē ə). a period of five years. Also, **quin·quen·ni·ad** (kwin kwen′ē ad′, kwin̄g-). [< L]

quin·que·par·tite (kwin̄g′kwə pär′tīt, kwin′-), *adj.* divided into or consisting of five parts.

quin·que·va·lent (kwin̄g′kwə vā′lənt, kwin′-, kwin-kwev′ə lənt, kwin̄g-), *adj.* *Chem.* **1.** pentavalent (def. 1). **2.** exhibiting five different valences, as phosphorus with valences +5, +4, +3, +1, and −3. **—quin·que·va·lence** (kwin̄g′kwə vā′ləns, kwin′-, kwin kwev′ə ləns, kwin̄g-), **quin′que·va′len·cy,** *n.*

quin·sy (kwin′zē), *n.* *Pathol.* a suppurative inflammation of the tonsils; suppurative tonsillitis; tonsillar abscess. [ME *quin(e)sie* < ML *quinancia,* LL *cynanchē* < Gk *kynánchē* sore throat]

quint (kwint), *n.* *Informal.* a quintuplet. [shortened form]

quin·tain (kwin′t^{ə}n), *n.* an object mounted on a post or attached to a movable crossbar mounted on a post, used as a target in the medieval sport of tilting. [ME *quyntain* < MF *quintaine* < ML *quintāna* (L: street in a camp)]

Quintain

quin·tal (kwin′t^{ə}l), *n.* **1.** *Metric System.* a unit of weight equal to 100 kilograms and equivalent to 220.462 avoirdupois pounds. **2.** hundredweight. [late ME < L *quintāle* < Ar *qinṭār* weight of a hundred pounds, prob. << L *centēnārius.* Cf. CENTENARY]

quin·tes·sence (kwin tes′əns), *n.* **1.** the pure and concentrated essence of a substance. **2.** the most perfect embodiment of something. **3.** (in ancient and medieval philosophy) the fifth essence or element, ether, supposed to be the constituent matter of the heavenly bodies, the others being air, fire, earth, and water. [ME < ML *quinta essentia* fifth essence] **—quin·tes·sen·tial** (kwin′ti sen′shəl), *adj.* **—quin′tes·sen′tial·ly,** *adv.*

quin·tet (kwin tet′), *n.* **1.** any set or group of five persons or things. **2.** an organized group of five singers or players. **3.** a musical composition scored for five voices or instruments. Also, **quin·tette′.** [< F *quintette* < It *quintetto,* dim. of *quinto* fifth < L *quintus*]

quin·tic (kwin′tik), *Math.* **—***adj.* **1.** of the fifth degree. **—***n.* **2.** a quantity of the fifth degree. [< L *quint(us)* fifth + -IC]

quin·tile (kwin′til), *Astrol.* **—***adj.* **1.** of or pertaining to the aspect of two heavenly bodies that are one fifth of the zodiac, or 72°, apart. **—***n.* **2.** a quintile aspect. [< L, neut. of *quintilis* fifth]

Quin·til·ian (kwin til′yən, -ē ən), *n.* (*Marcus Fabius Quintilianus*) A.D. c35–c95, Roman rhetorician.

quin·til·lion (kwin til′yən), *n., pl.* **-lions,** (*as after a numeral*) **-lion,** *adj.* **—***n.* **1.** a cardinal number represented in the U.S. and France by 1 followed by 18 zeros, and, in Great Britain and Germany, by 1 followed by 30 zeros. **—***adj.* **2.** amounting to one quintillion in number. [< L *quint(us)* fifth + *-illion* (as in *million*)]

quin·tu·ple (kwin to͞o′pəl, -tyo͞o′-, -tup′əl, kwin′to͝o pəl, -tyo͝o-), *adj., n., v.,* **-pled, -pling.** **—***adj.* **1.** fivefold; consisting of five parts. **2.** five times as great or as much. **—***n.* **3.** a number, amount, etc., five times as great as another. **—***v.t., v.i.* **4.** to make or become five times as great. [< F = *quint* fifth + *-uple* (as in *quadruple*)]

quin·tu·plet (kwin tup′lit, -to͞o′plit, -tyo͞o′-, kwin′to͝o-plit, -tyo͝o-), *n.* **1.** any group or combination of five, esp. of the same kind. **2. quintuplets,** five children or offspring born of one pregnancy. **3.** one of five such children or offspring.

quin·tu·plex (kwin′to͝o pleks′, -tyo͝o-, kwin to͞o′pleks, -tyo͞o′-, -tup′lex), *adj.* fivefold; quintuple. [< LL = *quintu(s)* fifth + *-plex* -FOLD]

quin·tu·pli·cate (*n., adj.* kwin to͞o′plə kit, -tyo͞o′-; *v.* kwin-to͞o′plə kāt′, -tyo͞o′-), *n., adj., v.,* **-ca·ted, -cat·ing.** **—***n.* **1.** a group, series, or set of five identical copies (usually prec. by *in*). **—***adj.* **2.** having or consisting of five identical parts; fivefold. **3.** noting the fifth copy or item. **—***v.t.* **4.** to make five copies of something. **5.** to make five times as great, as by multiplying. [< LL *quintuplicāt(us)* (ptp. of *quintuplicāre*) = *quintuplic-* (s. of *quintuplex*) fivefold + *-ātus* -ATE^1] **—quin·tu′pli·ca′tion,** *n.*

quip (kwip), *n., v.,* **quipped, quip·ping.** **—***n.* **1.** a clever or witty remark or comment. **2.** a sarcastic remark; taunt; gibe. **3.** a quibble. **4.** an odd or fantastic action or thing. **—***v.i.* **5.** to utter quips. [back formation from *quippy* quip < L *quippe* indeed] **—quip′ster,** *n.* **—Syn. 1.** joke, witticism.

qui·pu (kē′po͞o, kwip′o͞o), *n.* a device consisting of a cord with knotted strings of various colors attached, used by the ancient Peruvians for recording events, keeping accounts, etc. [< Peruvian (Quechua): lit., knot]

quire^1 (kwī^{ə}r), *n.* **1.** a set of 24 uniform sheets of paper. **2.** *Bookbinding.* a section of printed leaves in proper sequence after folding; gathering. [ME *quayer* < MF *quaier* < VL **quaternum* set of four sheets, L *quarternī* four each]

quire^2 (kwī^{ə}r), *n., v.t., v.i.,* **quired, quir·ing.** *Archaic.* choir.

Quir·i·nal (kwir′ə n^{ə}l), *n.* **1.** one of the seven hills on which ancient Rome was built. **—***adj.* **2.** pertaining to or located on the Quirinal. [< L *Quirīnāl(is).* See QUIRINUS, -AL^1]

Qui·ri·nus (kwi rī′nəs), *n.* an ancient Roman god of war, identified with the deified Romulus; a personification of the Roman nation.

Qui·ri·tes (kwi rī′tēz), *n.pl.* the citizens of ancient Rome considered in their civil capacity. [< L, pl. of *Quirīs,* orig. an inhabitant of the Sabine town *Cures,* later a Roman citizen]

quirk (kwûrk), *n.* **1.** a peculiarity of action, behavior, or personality. **2.** a shift, subterfuge, or evasion; quibble. **3.** a sudden twist or turn: *a quirk of fate.* **4.** a flourish or showy stroke, as in writing. **5.** *Archit.* an acute angle or channel, as one dividing two parts of a molding or a flush bead from the adjoining surfaces. **6.** *Obs.* a quip. [?]

quirk·y (kwûr′kē), *adj.,* **quirk·i·er, quirk·i·est.** having or full of quirks. **—quirk′i·ly,** *adv.* **—quirk′i·ness,** *n.*

quirt (kwûrt), *n.* **1.** a riding whip consisting of a short, stout stock and a lash of braided leather. **—***v.t.* **2.** to strike with a quirt. [? < Sp *cuerda* cord]

quis·ling (kwiz′ling), *n.* a person who betrays his own country by aiding an invading enemy, often serving later in a puppet government; collaborationist. [after Vidkun *Quisling* (1887–1945), pro-Nazi Norwegian leader]

quit (kwit), *v.,* **quit** or **quit·ted, quit·ting,** *adj.* **—***v.t.* **1.** to stop, cease, or discontinue. **2.** to depart from; leave. **3.** to give up; let go; abandon; relinquish: *He quit his claim to the throne. He quit his job for a better position.* **4.** to release one's hold of (something grasped). **5.** *Archaic.* to acquit or conduct (oneself). **—***v.i.* **6.** to cease from doing something; stop. **7.** to give up or resign one's job or position. **8.** to stop trying, struggling, or the like; accept or acknowledge defeat. **—***adj.* **9.** released from obligation, penalty, etc.; free, clear, or rid (usually fol. by *of*): *quit of all debts.* [ME *quitte(n), quite(n)* < OF *quit(t)er* < ML *quittāre, quiētāre* to release, discharge, LL: QUIET^2] **—Syn. 3.** resign, surrender, release. **9.** acquitted, discharged.

quitch (kwich), *n.* See **couch grass.** Also called **quitch′ grass′.** [OE *cwice,* c. D *kweek,* Norw *kvike;* akin to QUICK (adj.)]

quit·claim (kwit′klām′), *Law.* **—***n.* **1.** a transfer of all one's interest, as in a parcel of real estate, esp. without a warranty of title. **—***v.t.* **2.** to quit or give up claim to (a possession, right, etc.). [ME *quitclayme* < AF *quiteclame* < *quiteclamer* to declare quit]

quit′claim deed′, *Law.* a deed that conveys to the grantee only such interests in property as the grantor may have, the grantee assuming responsibility for any claims brought against the property. Cf. **warranty** (def. 2b).

quite (kwīt), *adv.* **1.** completely, wholly, or entirely: *quite the reverse; not quite finished.* **2.** actually, really, or truly: *quite a sudden change.* **3.** to a considerable extent or degree: *quite objectionable.* [ME, adv. use of *quite* (adj.) QUIT]

Qui·to (kē′tô), *n.* a city in and the capital of Ecuador, in the N part. 599,828; 9348 ft. above sea level.

quit·rent (kwit′rent′), *n.* rent paid by a freeholder or copyholder in lieu of services.

quits (kwits), *adj.* **1.** on equal terms as a result of repayment or retaliation. **2. call it quits, a.** to end one's activity temporarily: *At 10 o'clock he decided to call it quits for the day.* **b.** to abandon an effort. [QUIT (adj.) + unexplained *-s*]

quit·tance (kwit′^{ə}ns), *n.* **1.** recompense or requital. **2.** discharge from a debt or obligation. **3.** a document certifying discharge from debt or obligation, as a receipt. [ME *quitaunce* < OF *quittance* = *quitt(er)* (to) QUIT + *-ance* -ANCE]

quit·ter (kwit′ər), *n.* *Informal.* a person who quits or gives up easily, esp. in the face of difficulty.

quit·tor (kwit′ər), *n.* *Vet. Pathol.* any of various infections of the foot in which tissues degenerate and form a slough. [ME *quittere* pus, quittor < OF *cuiture* a boiling < L *coctūra* a cooking = *coct(us)* (ptp. of *coquere* to cook) + *-ūra* -URE]

quiv·er[1] (kwiv′ər), *v.t., v.i.* **1.** to shake with a slight but rapid motion; vibrate tremulously; tremble. **—*n.* 2.** the act or state of quivering; a tremble or tremor. [ME; c. MD *quiveren* to tremble] **—quiv′er·er,** *n.* **—quiv′er·ing·ly,** *adv.* **—quiv′er·y,** *adj.* **—Syn. 2.** shudder, shiver. See **shake.**

quiv·er[2] (kwiv′ər), *n.* **1.** a case for holding or carrying arrows. **2.** the arrows in such a case. [ME < AF *quiveir*, var. of OF *quivre;* ? < Gmc; cf. OE *cocer* quiver]

quiv·er[3] (kwiv′ər), *adj. Archaic.* nimble; active. [ME *cwiver, quiver;* OE **cwifer* < ?]

qui vive (kē vēv′), **1.** (*italics*) *French.* who goes there? **2. on the qui vive,** on the alert; watchful. [lit., (long) live who? (i.e., on whose side are you?)]

quix·ot·ic (kwik sot′ik), *adj.* extravagantly chivalrous or romantic; visionary, impractical, or impracticable. Also, **quix·ot′i·cal.** [after *Don Quixote*, the hero so characterized in *Don Quixote de la Mancha* (1605, 1615), a novel by Cervantes; see -IC] **—quix·ot′i·cal·ly,** *adv.* **—Syn.** fanciful, fantastic, imaginary. **—Ant.** realistic, practical.

quix·ot·ism (kwik′sə tiz′əm), *n.* **1.** (*sometimes cap.*) quixotic character or practice. **2.** a quixotic idea or act. [see QUIXOTIC, -ISM]

quiz (kwiz), *v.,* **quizzed, quiz·zing,** *n., pl.* **quiz·zes.** **—*v.t.* 1.** to examine or test (a student or class) informally by questions. **2.** to question closely. **—*n.* 3.** an informal test or examination of a student or class. **4.** a questioning. **5.** a practical joke; hoax. [?] **—quiz′zer,** *n.*

quiz·mas·ter (kwiz′mas′tər, -mä′stər), *n.* a person who asks questions of contestants in a game, esp. as part of a quiz program.

quiz′ pro′gram, a radio or television program in which contestants compete, often for prizes, by answering questions. Also called **quiz′ show′.**

quiz·zi·cal (kwiz′i kəl), *adj.* **1.** questioning or puzzled: *a quizzical expression on her face.* **2.** odd, queer, or comical. **3.** derisively questioning, ridiculing, or chaffing. **—quiz′zi·cal′i·ty, quiz′zi·cal·ness,** *n.* **—quiz′zi·cal·ly,** *adv.*

Qum·ran (ko͝om′rän), *n.* See **Khirbet Qumran.** Also, **Qûm′ran.**

quo·ad hoc (kwō′äd hōk′; *Eng.* kwō′ad hok′), *Latin.* as much as this; to this extent.

quod (kwod), *n. Chiefly Brit. Slang.* jail. Also, **quad.** [?]

quod e·rat de·mon·stran·dum (kwōd e′rät dem′ōn strän′do͞om; *Eng.* kwod er′at dem′ən stran′dəm), *Latin.* which was to be shown or demonstrated.

quod e·rat fa·ci·en·dum (kwōd e′rät fä′kē en′do͞om; *Eng.* kwod er′at fā′shē en′dəm), *Latin.* which was to be done.

quod·li·bet (kwod′lə bet′), *n.* **1.** a subtle or elaborate argument or point of debate. **2.** *Music.* a humorous composition consisting of two or more complementary melodies played or sung together, usually to different texts. [ME << L *quod libet*, lit., what pleases, as you please] **—quod′li·bet′ic, quod′li·bet′i·cal,** *adj.* **—quod′li·bet′i·cal·ly,** *adv.*

quod vi·de (kwod vī′dē). See **q.v.** [< L: which see]

quoin (koin, kwoin), *n.* **1.** an external solid angle of a wall or the like. **2.** one of the stones forming it; cornerstone. **3.** a wedge-shaped piece of wood, stone, or other material, used for any of various purposes. **4.** *Print.* a wedge of wood or metal for securing type in a chase. **—*v.t.* 5.** to provide with quoins, as a corner of a wall. **6.** to secure or raise with a quoin or wedge. Also, **coign, coigne.** [var. of COIN]

quoit (kwoit), *n.* **1. quoits,** (*construed as sing.*) a game in which rings of rope or flattened metal are thrown at an upright peg, the object being to encircle it. **2.** a ring used in the game of quoits. **—*v.t.* 3.** to throw as or like a quoit. **—*v.i.* 4.** to play quoits. [ME *coyte* < ?]

quo ju·re? (kwō yo͞o′re; *Eng.* kwō jo͝or′ē), *Latin.* by what right?

quo mo·do (kwō mō′dō), *Latin.* **1.** in what way?; how? **2.** in the same manner that; as.

quon·dam (kwon′dam), *adj.* that formerly was or existed; former: *his quondam partner.* [< L]

Quon′set hut′ (kwon′sit), *Trademark.* a semicylindrical metal shelter having end walls, usually serving as a barracks, storage shed, etc.

quo·rum (kwōr′əm, kwôr′-), *n.* **1.** the number of members of a group or organization required to be present to transact business legally, usually a majority. **2.** a particularly chosen group. [< L *quōrum* of whom; from a use of the word in commissions written in Latin]

quot., quotation.

quo·ta (kwō′tə), *n.* **1.** the share or proportional part of a total which is required from, or is due or belongs to, a particular district, state, person, group, etc. **2.** a proportional part or share of a fixed total amount or quantity. **3.** the number of persons of a specified kind permitted to enroll in a college, join a club, immigrate to a country, etc. [< ML, short for L *quota pars* how great a part?]

quot·a·ble (kwō′tə bəl), *adj.* **1.** able to be quoted or easily quoted, as by reason of effectiveness, succinctness, or the like: *the most quotable book of the year.* **2.** suitable or appropriate for quotation: *His comments were hilarious but unfortunately not quotable.* **—quot′a·bil′i·ty, quot′a·ble·ness,** *n.* **—quot′a·bly,** *adv.*

quo·ta·tion (kwō tā′shən), *n.* **1.** something quoted; a passage quoted from a book, speech, etc. **2.** the act or practice of quoting. **3.** *Com.* the current or market price of a commodity or security. [< ML *quotātiōn-* (s. of *quotātiō*) = *quotāt(us)* (ptp. of *quotāre;* see QUOTE) + *-iōn-* -ION]

quota′tion mark′, one of the marks used to indicate the beginning and end of a quotation, usually shown as (") at the beginning and (") at the end or, for a quotation within a quotation, as single marks of this kind, as "*He said, 'I will go.'* " Also called **quote′ mark′.**

quote (kwōt), *v.,* **quot·ed, quot·ing,** *n.* **—*v.t.* 1.** to repeat (a passage, phrase, etc.) from a book, speech, or the like, as by way of authority or illustration. **2.** to repeat words from (a book, author, etc.). **3.** to cite, offer, or bring forward as evidence or support. **4.** to enclose (words) within quotation marks. **5.** *Com.* **a.** to state (a price). **b.** to state the current price of. **—*v.i.* 6.** to make a quotation or quotations, as from a book or author. **—*n.* 7.** a quotation. **8.** See **quotation mark.** [ME < ML *quotāre* to divide into chapters and verses < L *quot* how many] **—quot′er,** *n.*

quote·wor·thy (kwōt′wûr′t͟hē), *adj.* quotable. **—quote′wor′thi·ness,** *n.*

quoth (kwōth), *v. Archaic.* said (used with nouns and with first and third person pronouns and always placed before the subject): *Quoth the raven, "Nevermore."* [preterit of *quethe* (otherwise obs.), OE *cwethan* to say. Cf. BEQUEATH]

quoth·a (kwō′thə), *interj. Archaic.* indeed! (used ironically or contemptuously). [from *quoth a* quoth he]

quo·tid·i·an (kwō tid′ē ən), *adj.* **1.** daily: *a quotidian report.* **2.** everyday; ordinary. **3.** (of a fever, ague, etc.) characterized by paroxysms that recur daily. **—*n.* 4.** something recurring daily. **5.** a quotidian fever or ague. [< L *quotīdiān(us)* daily; r. ME *cotidien* < OF] **—quo·tid′i·an·ly,** *adv.* **—quo·tid′i·an·ness,** *n.*

quo·tient (kwō′shənt), *n. Math.* the result of division; the number of times one quantity is contained in another. [ME < L *quotiens* how many times]

quo war·ran·to (kwō wô ran′tō, wo-), *Law.* **1.** (in England and the U.S.) a trial, hearing, or other legal proceeding initiated to determine by what authority one has an office, franchise, or liberty. **2.** the pleading initiating such a proceeding. **3.** (formerly in England) a writ calling upon a person to show by what authority he claims an office, franchise, or liberty. [ME < ML: by what warrant]

Qu·ran (ko͝o rän′, -ran′), *n.* Koran.

q.v., (in formal writing) which see. Cf. **qq.v.** [< L *quod vide*]

Qy., query. Also, **qy.**

DEVELOPMENT OF MAJUSCULE								
NORTH SEMITIC	GREEK	ETR.	LATIN		MODERN			
					GOTHIC	ITALIC	ROMAN	
9	4	P	4	R	R	𝕽	*R*	R

DEVELOPMENT OF MINUSCULE					
ROMAN CURSIVE	ROMAN UNCIAL	CAROL. MIN.	MODERN		
			GOTHIC	ITALIC	ROMAN
r	R	r	𝔯	*r*	r

The eighteenth letter of the English alphabet developed from North Semitic. The Greek *rho* (ρ, P) is a later version of the same symbol. Its form in Latin (R) derives from a variant used in a local Greek script which added the short stroke at the right.

R, r (är), *n., pl.* **R's** or **Rs, r's** or **rs.** **1.** the 18th letter of the English alphabet, a consonant. **2.** any spoken sound represented by the letter *R* or *r*, as in *ran, carrot, star*, etc. **3.** a written or printed representation of the letter *R* or *r*. **4.** a device, as a printer's type, for reproducing the letter *R* or *r*.

R, 1. *Chem.* radical. **2.** *Elect.* resistance. **3.** *U.S.* a designation by the motion-picture industry for films to which those under 17 years of age will be admitted only when accompanied by a parent or adult guardian. **4.** *Theat.* stage right. **5.** *Physics.* roentgen. **6.** *Chess.* rook.

R, the 18th in order or in a series, or, when *I* is omitted, the 17th.

r, 1. *Physics.* roentgen. **2.** royal. **3.** ruble. **4.** *pl.* **rs,** rupee.

R., 1. rabbi. **2.** Radical. **3.** radius. **4.** railroad. **5.** railway. **6.** (in Lesotho, Botswana, etc.) rand; rands. **7.** Réaumur. **8.** rector. **9.** redactor. **10.** Regina. **11.** Republican. **12.** response. **13.** Rex. **14.** right. **15.** river. **16.** road. **17.** royal. **18.** ruble. **19.** rupee. **20.** *Theat.* stage right.

r., 1. rabbi. **2.** radius. **3.** railroad. **4.** railway. **5.** range. **6.** rare. **7.** *Com.* received. **8.** recipe. **9.** replacing. **10.** residence. **11.** right. **12.** rises. **13.** river. **14.** road. **15.** rod. **16.** royal. **17.** rubber. **18.** ruble. **19.** *Baseball.* run; runs. **20.** *pl.* **rs.** rupee.

Ra (rä), *n.* *Egyptian Religion.* a sun god of Heliopolis, a universal creator worshiped throughout Egypt (typically represented as a hawk-headed man bearing on his head the solar disk and the uraeus). Also, **Re.**

RA, regular army.

Ra, *Chem.* radium.

R.A., 1. rear admiral. **2.** *Astron.* right ascension. **3.** royal academician. **4.** Royal Academy.

R.A.A.F., Royal Australian Air Force.

Ra·bat (rä bät′), *n.* a seaport in and the capital of Morocco, in the NW part. 724,100.

ra·ba·to (rə bä′tō, -bā′-), *n., pl.* **-tos.** a wide stiff collar of the 17th century, worn flat over the shoulders or open in front and standing at the back. Also, **rebato.** [< F (obs.) *rabateau*, MF *rabat* < *rabattre* to beat back down, lessen; see REBATE[1]]

Ra·baul (rä boul′, rä′boul), *n.* a seaport on NE New Britain island, in the Bismarck Archipelago. 36,043 (est. 1963).

Rab·bath Am·mon (rab′əth am′ən, rä-bät′ äm mōn′), Amman.

rab·bet (rab′it), *n., v.,* **-bet·ed, -bet·ing.** —*n.* **1.** a deep notch formed in or near one edge of a board, timber, etc., to receive an edge of a board, door, etc. **2.** a joint made with a rabbet or rabbets. —*v.t.* **3.** to cut a rabbet in (a board or the like). **4.** to join (boards or the like) by means of a rabbet or rabbets. —*v.i.* **5.** to become joined by means of a rabbet. Also, **rebate.** [ME *rabet* < OF *rabat*; see REBATE[1]]

Rabbets

rab·bi (rab′ī), *n., pl.* **-bis. 1.** the spiritual leader of a Jewish congregation, who performs or supervises ritualistic, pastoral, educational, and other duties and activities. Cf. **cantor** (def. 2). **2.** a title of respect for a Jewish scholar or teacher. **3.** a Jewish scholar qualified to rule on questions of Jewish law. [< LL *rabbī* < Gk *rhabbí* < Heb *rabbī* my master (*rabh* master + *-i* my)]

rab·bin (rab′in), *n.* *Archaic.* rabbi. [< F << Aram *rabbīn* masters (pl. of *rab*)]

rab·bin·ate (rab′ə nit), *n.* **1.** the office or term of office of a rabbi. **2.** a group of rabbis: *the Orthodox rabbinate.*

Rab·bin·ic (rə bin′ik), *n.* the Hebrew language as used by rabbis in post-Biblical times.

rab·bin·i·cal (rə bin′i kəl), *adj.* **1.** of or pertaining to rabbis or their learning, writings, etc. **2.** for the rabbinate: *a rabbinical school.* Also, **rab·bin′ic.** [< ML *rabbīn(us)* of a RABBI + -ICAL]

rab·bin·ism (rab′ə niz′əm), *n.* the beliefs, practices, and precepts of the rabbis of the Talmudic period.

rab·bit (rab′it), *n., pl.* **-bits,** (*esp. collectively*) **-bit** for 1–3. **1.** any of several rodentlike lagomorph mammals of the genus *Sylvilagus*, esp. the cottontail. **2.** a small, long-eared, burrowing lagomorph, *Lepus cuniculus*, of the hare family. **3.** the fur of any member of the rabbit family. **4.** See **Welsh rabbit.** [ME *rabet*, prob. < ONF; cf. Walloon *robett*, Flem *robbe*]

rab′bit fe′ver, *Pathol., Vet. Pathol.* tularemia.

rab·bit·fish (rab′it fish′), *n., pl.* (*esp. collectively*) **-fish,** (*esp. referring to two or more kinds or species*) **-fish·es. 1.** a puffer, *Lagocephalus laevigatus*. **2.** a chimaera, *chimaera monstrosa*. [from the resemblance of its nose to a rabbit's]

rab′bit punch′, a short, sharp blow to the nape of the neck or the lower part of the skull.

rab·bit·ry (rab′i trē), *n., pl.* **-ries. 1.** a collection of rabbits. **2.** a place where rabbits are kept.

rab·ble[1] (rab′əl), *n., v.,* **-bled, -bling.** —*n.* **1.** a disorderly crowd; mob. **2. the rabble,** the lower classes; the common people. —*v.t.* **3.** to beset as a rabble does; mob. [ME *rabel*; ? akin to late ME *rablen* to chatter; ? imit.; see BABBLE]

rab·ble[2] (rab′əl), *n., v.,* **-bled, -bling.** *Metall.* —*n.* **1.** a tool or mechanically operated device used for stirring or mixing a charge in a roasting furnace. —*v.t.* **2.** to stir (a charge) in a roasting furnace. [< F *râble* fire shovel, tool, MF *roable* < L *rutābul(um)* fire rake = *rut(us)* (ptp. of *ruere* to upset, dig up) + *-ā-* thematic vowel + *-bulum* suffix of instrument] —**rab′bler,** *n.*

rab·ble·ment (rab′əl mənt), *n.* a tumult; disturbance.

rab·ble-rous·er (rab′əl rou′zər), *n.* a person who stirs up the passions or prejudices of the public, usually for his own interests; agitator. —**rab′ble-rous′ing,** *adj.*

Rab·e·lais (rab′ə lā′; *Fr.* RA ble′), *n.* **Fran·çois** (FRÄN-SWA′), c1490–1553, French satirist and humorist.

Rab·e·lai·si·an (rab′ə lā′zē ən, -zhən), *adj.* **1.** of, pertaining to, or suggesting François Rabelais or his broad, coarse humor. —*n.* **2.** a person who admires or studies the works of Rabelais. —**Rab′e·lai′si·an·ism,** *n.*

Ra·bi (rä′bē), *n.* **Is·a·dor Isaac** (iz′ə dôr′), born 1898, U.S. physicist: Nobel prize 1944.

Ra·bi·a (rə bē′ə), *n.* either of two successive months of the Islamic calendar, the third **(Rabia I)** or the fourth **(Rabia II).** [< Ar *rabī'* spring]

rab·id (rab′id), *adj.* **1.** irrationally extreme in opinion or practice. **2.** furious or raging; violently intense. **3.** affected with or pertaining to rabies; mad. [< L *rabid(us)* raving, furious, mad = *rab(ere)* (to) rave, be mad + *-idus* -ID[4]] —**rab·id′i·ty, rab′id·ness,** *n.* —**rab′id·ly,** *adv.*

ra·bies (rā′bēz, -bē ēz′), *n.* *Pathol.* an infectious disease of dogs, cats, bats, other animals, and man, usually fatal if prophylactic treatment is not administered, caused by the virus *Formido inexoribilis*, and usually transmitted to man by the bite of an infected animal; hydrophobia. [< L *rabiēs* rage, madness < *rabere* to be mad, rave] —**rab·ic** (rab′ik), *adj.*

Ra·bi·no·witz (rə bin′ə vits; *Yiddish.* RÄ′bi nô′vich), *n.* **Solomon.** See **Aleichem, Sholom.**

rac·coon (ra ko͞on′, rə-), *n., pl.* **-coons,** (*esp. collectively*) **-coon. 1.** a small nocturnal omnivorous animal, *Procyon lotor*, of North America, arboreal in habit, and having a sharp snout and a bushy ringed tail. **2.** the thick gray to brown underfur of the raccoon, with silver-gray guard hairs tipped with black. Also, **racoon.** [< AmerInd (Algonquian, Virginia) *ärähkunem* he scratches with the hands]

Raccoon
(Total length about 3 ft.; tail 1 ft.)

raccoon′ dog′, a small wild dog of the genus *Nycterentis* of eastern Asia, having dark marks around the eyes, resembling those of a raccoon.

race[1] (rās), *n., v.,* **raced, rac·ing.** —*n.* **1.** a contest of speed, as in running, driving, or sailing. **2. races,** a series of such contests, held at a certain place successively. **3.** any competitive activity in which speed is important: *an armaments race.* **4.** onward movement; an onward or regular course. **5.** *Geol.* **a.** a strong or rapid current of water, as in the sea or a river. **b.** the channel or bed of such a current or of any stream. **6.** an artificial channel leading water to or from a place where its energy is utilized. **7.** Also called **raceway.** *Mach.* a channel, groove, or the like, for sliding or rolling a part or parts, as the balls of a ball bearing. —*v.i.* **8.** to engage in a contest of speed; run a race. **9.** to run horses or dogs in races. **10.** to run, move, or go swiftly. **11.** (of an engine, wheel, etc.) to run with undue or uncontrolled speed when the load is diminished without corresponding diminution of fuel, force, etc. —*v.t.* **12.** to run a race against. **13.** to cause to run in a race or races. **14.** to cause to run, move, or go at high speed: *to race a motor.* [ME *ras(e)* < Scand; cf. OIcel *rās* a running, race, rush of liquid; c. OE *rǣs* a running]

race[2] (rās), *n.* **1.** a group of persons related by common descent, blood, or heredity. **2.** *Ethnol.* a subdivision of the human species, characterized by a more or less distinctive combination of physical traits that are transmitted in descent. **3.** a group of tribes or peoples forming an ethnic stock. **4.** the human race or family; mankind. **5.** *Zool.* a variety; a subspecies. **6.** a natural kind of living creature: *the race of fishes.* **7.** any group, class, or kind, esp. of persons. **8.** a characteristic taste or flavor, as of wine. [< F < It *razz(a)*, ? < Ar *ra's*]
—**Syn. 1.** tribe, clan, family, stock. RACE, NATION, PEOPLE are terms for a large body of persons thought of as a unit because of common characteristics. RACE refers to a large body of persons, animals, or plants characterized by similarity of descent: *the Mongoloid race.* NATION refers to a body of persons as living under an organized government, occupying a fixed area, and dealing as a unit in matters of peace and war with other similar groups: *the English nation.* PEOPLE has emotional connotations similar to those of *family.* PEOPLE refers to the persons composing a race, nation, tribe, etc., as members of a body with common interests and a unifying culture: *We are one people.* **4.** man.

race[3] (rās), *n.* a ginger root. [< MF *rais* < L *radic-* (s. of *radix*) root]

Race (rās), *n.* **Cape,** a cape at the SE extremity of Newfoundland.

race·a·bout (rās′ə bout′), *n.* a small, sloop-rigged racing yacht with a short bowsprit.
race·course (rās′kōrs′, -kôrs′), *n.* **1.** a race track. **2.** a current of water, as a millrace.
race′ horse′, a horse bred or kept for racing, esp. in flat races or steeplechases. Also, **race′-horse′, race′horse′.**
ra·ceme (rā sēm′, rə-), *n.* *Bot.* **1.** a simple indeterminate inflorescence in which the flowers are borne on short pedicels lying along a common axis, as in the lily of the valley. **2.** a compound inflorescence in which the short pedicels with single flowers of the simple raceme are replaced by racemes. [< L *racēm(us)* cluster of grapes] —**ra·cemed′,** *adj.*
ra·ce·mic (rā sē′mik, -sem′ik, rə-), *adj.* *Chem.* noting or pertaining to any of various organic compounds in which racemism occurs. [< F *racémique;* see RACEME, -IC]
race′mic ac′id, *Chem.* an isomeric modification of tartaric acid that is optically inactive but can be separated into dextrorotatory and levorotatory isomeric forms.
rac·e·mism (ras′ə miz′əm, rā sē′miz əm), *n.* *Chem.* the state of being optically inactive and separable into two substances of the same chemical composition as the original substance, one of which is dextrorotatory and the other levorotatory.
rac·e·mi·za·tion (ras′ə mi zā′shən *or, esp. Brit.,* -mī-), *n.* *Chem.* the conversion of an optically active substance into an optically inactive mixture of equal amounts of the dextrorotatory and levorotatory forms.
rac·e·mose (ras′ə mōs′), *adj.* **1.** *Bot.* **a.** having the form of a raceme. **b.** arranged in racemes. **2.** *Anat.* (of a gland) resembling a bunch of grapes; having branching ducts that end in acini. Also, **rac·e·mous** (ras′ə məs). [< L *racēmōs(us)* full of clusters] —**rac′e·mose·ly, rac′e·mous·ly,** *adv.*
rac·er (rā′sər), *n.* **1.** a person or thing that races or takes part in a race. **2.** anything having great speed. **3.** any of several slender, active snakes of the genera *Coluber* and *Masticophis.*
race′ ri′ot, a riot resulting from racial animosity.
race·run·ner (rās′run′ər), *n.* a lizard, *Cnemidophorus sexlineatus,* common in the eastern and central U.S., that runs with great speed.
race′ track′, **1.** a plot of ground, usually oval, laid out for horse racing. **2.** the course for any race. Also, **race′-track′, race′track′.**
race·way (rās′wā′), *n.* **1.** *Chiefly Brit.* a passage or channel for water, as a millrace. **2.** a race track on which harness races are held. **3.** *Mach.* race¹ (def. 7).
Ra·chel (rā′chəl *for 1;* RA shel′ *for 2*), *n.* **1.** Jacob's favorite wife, the mother of Joseph and Benjamin. Gen. 29–35. **2.** (*Elisa Félix*) c1820–58, French actress.
ra·chis (rā′kis), *n., pl.* **ra·chis·es, rach·i·des** (rak′i dēz′, rā′ki-). **1.** *Bot.* **a.** the axis of an inflorescence when somewhat elongated, as in a raceme. **b.** (in a pinnately compound leaf or frond) the prolongation of the petiole along which the leaflets are disposed. **c.** any of various axial structures. **2.** *Ornith.* the part of the shaft of a feather bearing the web. **3.** *Anat.* See **spinal column.** Also, **rhachis.** [< NL < Gk *rhāchis* spine, ridge] —**ra·chid·i·an** (rə kid′ē ən), **ra·chi·al** (rā′kē əl), **ra·chid′i·al,** *adj.*

R, Rachis (def. 1b)

ra·chi·tis (rə kī′tis), *n.* *Pathol.* rickets. [< NL < Gk *rhachîtis* inflammation of the spine. See RACHIS, -ITIS] —**ra·chit·ic** (rə kit′ik), *adj.*
Rach·ma·ni·noff (räk mä′nə nôf′; *Russ.* RÄKH mä′ni-nôf′), *n.* **Ser·gei (Was·si·lie·vitch)** (SER gā′ väs sē′lyə-vich), 1873–1943, Russian pianist and composer. Also, **Rach·ma′ni·nov′.**
ra·cial (rā′shəl), *adj.* of, pertaining to, or characteristic of one race, of races generally, or of relations between races: *racial conflict.* —**ra′cial·ly,** *adv.*
ra·cial·ism (rā′shə liz′əm), *n.* the belief in or the practice of racism. —**ra′cial·ist,** *n.* —**ra′cial·is′tic,** *adj.*
Ra·cine (RA sēn′ *for 1;* rə sēn′, rā- *for 2*), *n.* **1. Jean Bap·tiste** (zhäN BA tēst′), 1639–99, French dramatist. **2.** a city in SE Wisconsin. 95,162 (1970).
rac·ism (rā′siz əm), *n.* **1.** a doctrine that inherent differences among the various human races determine cultural or individual achievement, usually involving the idea that one's own race is superior. **2.** a policy, government, etc., based on such a doctrine. **3.** hatred or intolerance of another race or other races. [< F *racisme*] —**rac′ist,** *n., adj.*
rack¹ (rak), *n.* **1.** a framework on which articles or materials are arranged or deposited: *a clothes rack.* **2.** *Pool.* **a.** a wooden frame of triangular shape within which the balls are arranged before play. **b.** the balls so arranged. **3.** *Mach.* **a.** a bar, with teeth on one of its sides, adapted to engage with the teeth of a pinion or the like, as for converting circular into rectilinear motion or vice versa. **b.** a bar or rail having a series of notches for engaging with a pawl, cogwheel, or the like, as a middle rail on a cog railway. **4.** a former instrument of torture on which a victim was slowly stretched. **5.** a cause or state of intense suffering of body or mind. **6.** any violent strain. —*v.t.* **7.** to torture; distress acutely; torment. **8.** to strain in mental effort: *to rack one's brains.* **9.** to strain by physical force or violence. **10.** to stretch the body of (a person) in torture by means of a rack. **11.** *Naut.* to seize (two ropes) together side by side. **12.** *Pool.* to put (the balls) in a rack. [ME *rekke, rakke* < MD *rec* framework, *recken* to stretch]

R, Rack¹ (def. 3a)
P, Pinion

rack² (rak), *n.* **1.** *Obs.* wreck; destruction. **2. go to rack and ruin,** to decay, decline, or become destroyed. [var. of WRACK¹]
rack³ (rak), *n.* **1.** the fast pace of a horse in which the legs move in lateral pairs but not simultaneously. —*v.i.* **2.** (of horses) to move in a rack. [? var. of ROCK²]
rack⁴ (rak), *n.* **1.** Also called **cloud rack.** a group of drifting clouds. —*v.i.* **2.** to drive or move, esp. before the wind. Also, **wrack.** [ME *wrak,* OE *wræc* what is driven (by wind or wave); c. MD, MLG *wrak* wreckage, a wreck; akin to OE *wrecan,* Icel *reka* to drive. See WREAK]
rack⁵ (rak), *v.t.* to draw off (wine, cider, etc.) from the lees. [late ME < OF; cf. obs. F *raqué* (of wine) pressed from the dregs of grapes]
rack⁶ (rak), *n.* the neck or the rib section of mutton, pork, or veal. [ME; OE *hrace;* c. G *Rachen,* MD *rake*]
rack·et¹ (rak′it), *n.* **1.** a loud noise, esp. of a disturbing or confusing kind; din; uproar. **2.** social excitement, gaiety, or dissipation. **3.** an organized illegal activity, such as the extortion of money from legitimate businessmen. **4.** Usually, **rackets.** organized illegal activities (prec. by *the*). **5.** *Slang.* source of livelihood; business. —*v.i.* **6.** to make a racket or noise. **7.** to take part in social gaiety or dissipation. [metathetic var. of dial. *rattick;* see RATTLE¹] —**Syn. 1.** tumult, disturbance, outcry. See **noise.** —**Ant. 1, 2.** tranquillity.

Rackets²
A, Tennis; B, Court tennis; C, Squash; D, Squash tennis; E, Badminton; F, Paddle tennis; G, Table tennis

rack·et² (rak′it), *n.* **1.** any of various light bats having a netting stretched in a more or less oval frame, used in tennis, badminton, etc. **2.** the short-handled paddle used to strike the ball in table tennis. **3. rackets,** (*construed as sing.*) racquet (def. 1). **4.** a snowshoe made in the approximate form of a tennis racket. Also, **racquet** (for defs. 1, 2, 4). [< MF *raquette, rachette,* ? < Ar *rāhet,* var. of *rāhat* palm of the hand] —**rack′et·like′,** *adj.*
rack·et·eer (rak′i tēr′), *n.* a person engaged in an organized illegal activity, as extortion.
rack·e·ty (rak′i tē), *adj.* **1.** making or causing a racket; noisy. **2.** fond of excitement or dissipation.
rack·le (rak′əl), *adj.* *Chiefly Scot.* headstrong; rash.
rack′ rail′way. See **cog railway.**
rack-rent (rak′rent′), *n.* **1.** Also, **rack′ rent′.** rent equal to or nearly equal to the full annual value of a property. —*v.t.* **2.** to exact the highest possible rent for. **3.** to demand rack-rent from. —**rack′-rent′er,** *n.*
rac·on·teur (rak′on tûr′), *n.* a person who is skilled in relating anecdotes. [< F = *racont(er)* (OF *re-* RE- + *aconter* to tell, ACCOUNT) + *-eur* -OR²]
ra·coon (ra ko͞on′, rə-), *n., pl.* **-coons,** (*esp. collectively*) **-coon.** raccoon.
rac·quet (rak′it), *n.* **1. racquets,** (*construed as sing.*) a game played with rackets and a ball by two or four persons on a four-walled court. **2.** racket² (defs. 1, 2, 4). [var. of RACKET²]
rac·quet·ball (rak′it bôl′), *n.* an indoor game played on a handball court in which a rubber ball is hit against the front wall by two or four players using short-handled strung racquets.
rac·y (rā′sē), *adj.,* **rac·i·er, rac·i·est. 1.** suggestive; risqué: *a racy story.* **2.** vigorous; lively; spirited. **3.** sprightly; piquant; pungent: *a racy literary style.* **4.** having an agreeably peculiar taste or flavor, as wine or fruit. [RACE¹ + -Y¹] —**rac′i·ly,** *adv.* —**rac′i·ness,** *n.* —**Syn. 1.** off-color.
rad (rad), *n.* a unit of absorbed radiation dose, equal to the radiation that imparts 100 ergs of energy per gram of the absorbing material. [shortened form of RADIATION]
rad, *Math.* radian; radians.
rad., **1.** *Math.* radical. **2.** radix.
ra·dar (rā′där), *n.* *Electronics.* a device for determining the presence and location of an object by measuring the time for the echo of a radio wave to return from it and the direction from which it returns. [*ra(dio) d(etecting) a(nd) r(anging)*]
ra′dar bea′con, a radar device at a fixed location, used as a navigational aid.
ra·dar·scope (rā′där skōp′), *n.* the viewing screen of radar equipment.
rad·dle (rad′əl), *n., v.,* **-dled, -dling.** —*n.* **1.** ruddle. —*v.t.* **2.** ruddle. **3.** to color coarsely.
Ra·detz·ky (rä dets′kē), *n.* **Count Jo·seph** (yō′zef), 1766–1858, Austrian field marshal.
Rad·ford (rad′fərd), *n.* **Arthur William,** 1896–1973, U.S. admiral; chairman of Joint Chiefs of Staff 1953–57.
Ra·dha·krish·nan (rä də krish′nən), *n.* **Sar·ve·pal·li** (sär ve päl′lē), 1888–1975, president of India 1962–67.
ra·di·al (rā′dē əl), *adj.* **1.** arranged like radii or rays. **2.** having elements or parts arranged like radii. **3.** made or moving in the direction of a radius; going from the center outward or from the circumference inward along a radius: *a radial cut.* **4.** *Zool.* pertaining to structures that radiate from a central point, as the arms of a starfish. **5.** of, like, or pertaining to a radius or a ray. **6.** *Mach.* having pistons moving inward and outward from a central point or shaft: *a radial engine.* **7.** *Anat.* of, pertaining to, or situated near the radius. **8.** *Entomol.* pertaining to, involving, or situated near the radius. [< ML *radiāl(is)* = L *radi(us)* RADIUS + *-ālis* -AL¹] —**ra′di·al·ly,** *adv.*

Radial arrangement of lines; C, Center

ra′di·al-ply′ tire′ (rā′dē əl plī′), a motor-vehicle tire in which the rayon or nylon plies are put straight across at a right angle to the direction of travel. Also called **ra′dial tire′.** Cf. **belted-bias tire, bias-ply tire.**
ra·di·an (rā′dē ən), *n.* *Math.* an angle at the center of a circle, subtending an arc of the circle equal in length to the radius: equal to 57.2958°. *Abbr.:* rad [RADI(US) + -AN]
ra·di·ance (rā′dē əns), *n.* **1.** radiant brightness or light. **2.** warm, cheerful brightness. Also, **ra′di·an·cy.** [RADI(ANT) + -ANCE]
ra·di·ant (rā′dē ənt), *adj.* **1.** emitting rays of light; shining; bright. **2.** bright with joy, hope, etc. **3.** *Physics.* emitted or propagated by radiation. —*n.* **4.** a point or object from which rays proceed. **5.** *Astron.* the point in the heavens from which a shower of meteors appears to radiate. [ME < L *radiant-* (s. of *radiāns,* prp. of *radiāre*) emitting beams = *radi(us)* beam, ray (see RADIUS) + *-ant-* -ANT] —**ra′di·ant·ly,** *adv.* —**Syn. 1.** beaming, refulgent, resplendent.
ra′diant en′ergy, *Physics.* energy transmitted in wave motion, esp. electromagnetic wave motion.
ra′diant flux′, *Physics.* the time rate of flow of radiant energy.

ra′diant heat′, *Thermodynamics.* heat energy transmitted by electromagnetic waves in contrast to heat transmitted by conduction or convection.

ra′diant heat′ing, 1. the means of heating by radiation in which the intervening air is not heated. Cf. **convection** (def. 1). 2. a system for heating by radiation from a surface.

ra·di·ate (*v.* rā′dē āt′; *adj.* rā′dē it, -āt′), *v.*, **-at·ed, -at·ing,** *adj.* —*v.i.* 1. to spread or move like rays or radii from a center. 2. to emit rays, as of light or heat; irradiate. 3. to issue or proceed in rays. 4. (of persons) to project cheerfulness, joy, etc. —*v.t.* 5. to emit in rays; disseminate, as from a center. 6. to project (joy, good will, etc.), as cheerful persons. —*adj.* 7. radiating from a center. 8. having rays proceeding from a central point or part. 9. having radial symmetry. [< L *radiāt(us)* (ptp. of *radiāre*). See RADIANT, -ATE[1]] —**ra′di·a·bil′i·ty,** *n.* —**ra′di·a·ble,** *adj.*

ra·di·a·tion (rā′dē ā′shən), *n.* 1. *Physics.* a. the process in which energy is emitted as particles or waves. b. the complete process in which energy is emitted by one body, transmitted through an intervening medium or space, and absorbed by another body. c. the energy transferred by these processes. 2. the act or process of radiating. 3. something that is radiated. 4. radial arrangement of parts. [< L *radiātiōn-* (s. of *radiātiō*) a glittering, shining] —**ra′di·a′tion·al,** *adj.*

radia′tion belt′, *Physics.* See **Van Allen belt.**

radia′tion sick′ness, *Pathol.* sickness caused by irradiation with x-rays or radioactive materials, characterized by nausea, vomiting, headache, cramps, diarrhea, loss of hair and teeth, decrease in blood cells, and prolonged hemorrhage.

ra·di·a·tive (rā′dē ā′tiv), *adj.* giving off radiation. Also, **ra·di·a·to·ry** (rā′dē ə tôr′ē, -tōr′ē).

ra·di·a·tor (rā′dē ā′tər), *n.* 1. a person or thing that radiates. 2. any of various heating devices, as a series or coil of heated pipes for warming the air. 3. a device constructed from thin-walled tubes and metal fins, used for cooling a circulating fluid, as in an automobile engine.

rad·i·cal (rad′i kəl), *adj.* 1. of or pertaining to roots or origins; fundamental. 2. thoroughgoing or extreme: *a radical change of policy.* 3. (*often cap.*) favoring drastic political, economic, or social reforms. 4. existing inherently in a thing or person: *radical defects of character.* 5. *Math.* a. pertaining to or forming a root. b. denoting or pertaining to the radical sign. c. irrational (def. 4b). 6. *Gram.* of or pertaining to a root. 7. *Bot.* of or arising from the root or the base of the stem. —*n.* 8. a person who holds or follows extreme principles; extremist. 9. (*often cap.*) a person who advocates fundamental political, economic, and social reforms by direct and often uncompromising methods. 10. *Math.* a. a quantity expressed as a root of another quantity. b. See **radical sign.** 11. *Chem.* a. group (def. 3). b. See **free radical.** 12. *Gram.* root[1] (def. 11). [ME < LL *rādīcāl(is)* having roots = L *rādīc-* (s. of *rādīx*) root + *-ālis* -AL[1]] —**Syn.** 2. complete, thorough, drastic, excessive, immoderate, violent. RADICAL, EXTREME, FANATICAL denote that which goes beyond moderation or even to excess in opinion, belief, action, etc. RADICAL emphasizes the idea of going to the root of a matter, and this often seems immoderate in its thoroughness or completeness: *radical ideas; radical changes or reforms.* EXTREME applies to excessively biased ideas, intemperate conduct, or repressive legislation: *to use extreme measures.* FANATICAL is applied to a person who has extravagant views, esp. in matters of religion or morality, which render him incapable of sound judgments, and excessive zeal which leads him to take violent action against those who have differing views: *fanatical in persecuting others.* 4. basic, essential; innate, ingrained. —**Ant. 2, 4.** superficial.

rad′ical empir′icism, *Philos.* (in William James) the doctrine that the only proper subject matter of philosophy is that which can be defined in terms of experience, and that relations are a part of experience. —**rad′ical empir′icist.**

rad·i·cal·ism (rad′i kə liz′əm), *n.* 1. the holding or following of radical or extreme views or principles. 2. the principles or practices of radicals.

rad·i·cal·ly (rad′ik lē), *adv.* 1. with regard to origin or root. 2. in a complete or basic manner; thoroughly; fundamentally.

rad′ical sign′, *Math.* the symbol $\sqrt{}$ or $\sqrt{}$, indicating extraction of a root of the quantity that follows it, as $\sqrt{25} = 5$ or $\sqrt[3]{a^3b^3} = ab$.

rad·i·cand (rad′ə kand′), *n.* *Math.* the quantity under a radical sign. [< L *rādīcand(um),* neut. ger. of *rādīcāre* < *rādīc-* (s. of *rādīx*) root]

rad·i·cel (rad′i sel′), *n.* *Bot.* a minute root; a rootlet. [< NL *radicell(a)* small root, rootlet < L *rādīc-* (s. of *rādīx*) root + *-ella* dim. suffix]

rad·i·ces (rad′i sēz′, rā′di-), *n.* pl. of **radix.**

rad·i·cle (rad′i kəl), *n.* 1. *Bot.* a. the lower part of the axis of an embryo; the primary root. b. a rudimentary root; a radicel or rootlet. 2. *Anat.* a small rootlike part or structure, as the beginning of a nerve or vein. [< L *rādīcul(a)* small root < *rādīc-* (s. of *rādīx*) root + *-ula* -ULE]

ra·di·i (rā′dē ī′), *n.* a pl. of **radius.**

ra·di·o (rā′dē ō′), *n., pl.* **-di·os,** *adj., v.,* **-di·oed, -di·o·ing.** —*n.* 1. the medium of wireless communication. 2. an apparatus for such communication. 3. a message transmitted by such a medium. —*adj.* 4. pertaining to, used in, or sent by radio. 5. pertaining to or employing radiations, as of electrical energy. —*v.t.* 6. to transmit (a message) by radio. 7. to send a message to (a person) by radio. —*v.i.* 8. to transmit communications by radio. [short for *radiotelegraphic* (or *-telephonic*) *instrument, message,* or *transmission*]

radio-, 1. a combining form representing "radio," "radium," "radioactive," "radiant energy": *radiogram; radiotracer; radiometer.* 2. a combining form meaning "radial." [orig. < F, comb. form repr. L *radius* beam, ray, RADIUS]

ra·di·o·ac·ti·vate (rā′dē ō ak′tə vāt′), *v.t.,* **-vat·ed, -vat·ing.** *Physics.* to make (a substance) radioactive.

ra·di·o·ac·tive (rā′dē ō ak′tiv), *adj.* *Physics, Chem.* of, pertaining to, exhibiting, or caused by radioactivity. —**ra′di·o·ac′tive·ly,** *adv.*

ra′dioac′tive decay′, *Physics.* decay (def. 8).

ra′dioac′tive fall′out, fallout.

ra′dioac′tive se′ries, *Physics, Chem.* a succession of elements each of which decays into the next until a stable element, usually lead, is produced. Also called **decay series.**

ra·di·o·ac·tiv·i·ty (rā′dē ō ak tiv′i tē), *n.* *Physics, Chem.* the phenomenon exhibited by certain elements spontaneously emitting radiation as a result of changes in the nuclei of atoms of the element. Also called **activity.**

ra′dio astron′omy, the branch of astronomy that utilizes extraterrestrial radiation in radio wavelengths rather than visible light for the study of the universe.

ra·di·o·au·to·graph (rā′dē ō ô′tə graf′, -gräf′), *n.* autoradiograph.

ra′dio bea′con, a radio station that sends a characteristic signal so as to enable ships or airplanes to determine their position or bearing by means of a radio compass.

ra′dio beam′, beam (def. 8).

ra·di·o·bi·ol·o·gy (rā′dē ō bī ol′ə jē), *n.* the branch of biology dealing with the effects of radiation on living matter. —**ra·di·o·bi·o·log·i·cal** (rā′dē ō bī′ə loj′i kəl), **ra′di·o·bi′o·log′ic,** *adj.* —**ra′di·o·bi·ol′o·gist,** *n.*

ra·di·o·broad·cast (*n.* rā′dē ō brôd′kast, -käst; *v.* rā′dē ō brôd′kast′, -käst′), *n., v.,* **-cast** or **-cast·ed, -cast·ing.** —*n.* 1. a broadcast by radio. —*v.t., v.i.* 2. to broadcast by radio.

ra′dio car′, an automobile, esp. a police car, equipped with a two-way radio for communication.

ra·di·o·car·bon (rā′dē ō kär′bən), *n.* *Chem.* 1. Also called **carbon 14, carbon-14.** a radioactive isotope of carbon with mass number 14 and a half life of about 5,568 years: widely used in the dating of organic materials. 2. any radioactive isotope of carbon.

radiocar′bon dat′ing, the determination of the age of objects of plant or animal origin by measurement of the radioactivity of their carbon content. Also called **carbon-14 dating.**

ra·di·o·chem·is·try (rā′dē ō kem′i strē), *n.* the chemical study of radioactive elements, both natural and artificial, and their use in the study of chemical processes. —**ra′di·o·chem′i·cal,** *adj.* —**ra′di·o·chem′ist,** *n.*

ra′dio com′pass, a radio receiver with a directional antenna for determining the bearing of the receiver from a radio transmitter.

ra·di·o·el·e·ment (rā′dē ō el′ə mənt), *n.* *Chem.* a radioactive element.

ra·di·o·fre·quen·cy (rā′dē ō frē′kwən sē), *n., pl.* **-cies.** 1. the frequency of the transmitting waves of a given radio message or broadcast. 2. a frequency within the range of radio transmission, from about 15,000 to 10^{11} cycles per second. Also, **ra′dio fre′quency.**

ra·di·o·gen·ic (rā′dē ō jen′ik), *adj.* *Physics.* produced by radioactive decay.

ra·di·o·gram (rā′dē ō gram′), *n.* 1. a message transmitted by radiotelegraphy. 2. *Brit.* a. an x-ray. b. a telegram.

ra·di·o·graph (rā′dē ō graf′, -gräf′), *n.* 1. a photographic image produced by the action of x-rays or rays from radioactive substances. —*v.t.* 2. to make a radiograph of.

ra·di·og·ra·phy (rā′dē og′rə fē), *n.* the production of radiographs. —**ra′di·og′ra·pher,** *n.* —**ra·di·o·graph·ic** (rā′dē ō graf′ik), **ra′di·o·graph′i·cal,** *adj.*

ra·di·o·i·so·tope (rā′dē ō ī′sə tōp′), *n.* a radioactive isotope, usually artificially produced. —**ra·di·o·i·so·top·ic** (rā′dē ō ī′sə top′ik), *adj.*

ra·di·o·lar·i·an (rā′dē ō lâr′ē ən), *n.* any minute, marine protozoan of the group or order *Radiolaria,* having an amoebalike body with radiating, filamentous pseudopodia and a usually elaborate outer skeleton. [< NL *Radiolari(a)* name of the class (L *radiol(us)* a small sunbeam = *radi(us)* RADIUS + *-olus* dim. suffix + *-aria* -ARIA + -AN]

ra·di·o·lo·ca·tion (rā′dē ō lō kā′shən), *n.* determination of the position and velocity of an object by radar.

ra·di·o·log·i·cal (rā′dē ō loj′i kəl), *adj.* 1. of or pertaining to radiology. 2. involving radioactive materials: *radiological warfare.* Also, **ra′di·o·log′ic.**

ra·di·ol·o·gy (rā′dē ol′ə jē), *n.* 1. the science dealing with x-rays or rays from radioactive substances, esp. for medical uses. 2. the examination or photographing of organs, bones, etc., with such rays. —**ra′di·ol′o·gist,** *n.*

ra·di·o·lu·mi·nes·cence (rā′dē ō lo͞o′mə nes′əns), *n.* *Physics.* luminescence induced by radiation emitted by a radioactive substance. —**ra′di·o·lu′mi·nes′cent,** *adj.*

ra·di·o·man (rā′dē ō man′), *n., pl.* **-men.** a person who operates a radio or repairs radio equipment.

ra·di·o·me·te·or·o·graph (rā′dē ō mē′tē ər ə graf′, -gräf′), *n.* radiosonde.

ra·di·om·e·ter (rā′dē om′i tər), *n.* 1. an instrument for demonstrating the transformation of radiant energy into mechanical work, consisting of an evacuated glass vessel containing vanes that revolve about an axis when exposed to radiant energy. 2. an instrument for detecting and measuring radiant energy. —**ra·di·o·met·ric** (rā′dē ō me′trik), *adj.* —**ra′di·om′e·try,** *n.*

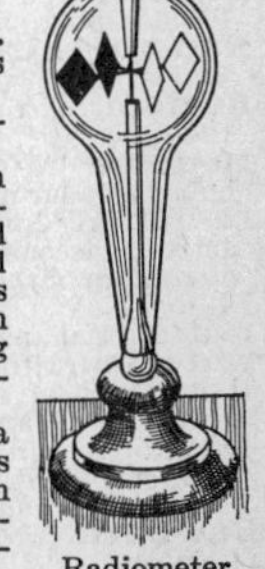
Radiometer

ra·di·o·phone (rā′dē ō fōn′), *n.* 1. a radiotelephone. 2. *Obs.* any of various devices for producing sound by the action of radiant energy. —*v.t., v.i.* 3. to radiotelephone. —**ra·di·o·phon·ic** (rā′dē ō fon′ik), *adj.* —**ra·di·oph·o·ny** (rā′dē of′ə nē), *n.*

ra·di·o·pho·to·graph (rā′dē ō fō′tə graf′, -gräf′), *n.* a photograph or other image transmitted by radio. Also called **ra′di·o·pho′to, ra·di·o·pho·to·gram** (rā′dē ō fō′tə gram′). —**ra·di·o·pho·tog·ra·phy** (rā′dē ō fə tog′rə fē), *n.*

ra·di·os·co·py (rā′dē os′kə pē), *n.* the examination of objects opaque to light by means of other radiation, usually x-rays. —**ra·di·o·scop·ic** (rā′dē ō skop′ik), *adj.*

ra·di·o·sen·si·tive (rā′dē ō sen′si tiv), *adj.* *Pathol.* (of certain tissues or organisms) sensitive to or destructible by various types of radiant energy, as x-rays, rays from radioactive material, or the like. —**ra′di·o·sen′si·tiv′i·ty,** *n.*

ra·di·o·sonde (rā′dē ō sond′), *n. Meteorol.* an instrument that is carried aloft by a balloon to radio back information on atmospheric temperature, pressure, and humidity. Also called **radiometeorograph.**

ra′dio spec′trum, the portion of the electromagnetic spectrum that includes radio waves.

ra′dio sta′tion, station (def. 9).

ra·di·o·stron·ti·um (rā′dē ō stron′shē əm, -tē əm), *n. Chem.* See **strontium 90.**

ra·di·o·sur·ger·y (rā′dē ō sûr′jə rē), *n.* therapeutic use of radioactive materials by surgical insertion.

ra·di·o·tel·e·gram (rā′dē ō tel′ə gram′), *n.* radiogram (def. 1).

ra·di·o·tel·e·graph (rā′dē ō tel′ə graf′, -gräf′), *n.* **1.** a telegraph in which messages or signals are sent by means of radio waves. —*v.t., v.i.* **2.** to transmit by radiotelegraph. —**ra′di·o·tel′e·graph′ic,** *adj.*

ra·di·o·te·leg·ra·phy (rā′dē ō tə leg′rə fē), *n.* the constructing or operating of radiotelegraphs.

ra·di·o·tel·e·phone (rā′dē ō tel′ə fōn′), *n.* **1.** a telephone in which sound or speech is transmitted by means of radio waves. —*v.t., v.i.* **2.** to telephone by radiotelephony. —**ra·di·o·tel·e·phon·ic** (rā′dē ō tel′ə fon′ik), *adj.*

ra·di·o·te·leph·o·ny (rā′dē ō tə lef′ə nē), *n.* the constructing or operating of radiotelephones.

ra′dio tel′escope, *Astron.* a concave reflector used to gather radio waves emitted by celestial sources and bring them to a receiver placed at the focus.

ra·di·o·ther·a·py (rā′dē ō ther′ə pē), *n.* treatment of disease by means of x-rays or of radioactive substances. —**ra′di·o·ther′a·pist,** *n.*

ra·di·o·ther·my (rā′dē ō thûr′mē), *n.* therapy that utilizes the heat from a short-wave radio apparatus or diathermy machine.

ra·di·o·tho·ri·um (rā′dē ō thôr′ē əm, -thōr′-), *n. Chem.* a disintegration product of thorium. [< NL]

ra·di·o·trac·er (rā′dē ō trā′sər), *n. Chem.* a radioactive isotope used as a tracer.

ra′dio tube′, a vacuum tube used in a radio receiving set.

ra′dio wave′, *Elect.* an electromagnetic wave having wavelength between 1 millimeter and 30,000 meters, or a frequency between 10 kilohertz and 300,000 megahertz.

rad·ish (rad′ish), *n.* **1.** the crisp, pungent, edible root of a cruciferous plant, *Raphanus sativus,* usually eaten raw. **2.** the plant itself. [late ME; OE *rǣdic* <* L *rādīc-* (s. of *rādīx*) root; cf. OHG *rātih,* G *Rettich*]

ra·di·um (rā′dē əm), *n. Chem.* a highly radioactive metallic element that upon disintegration produces the element radon and alpha particles: formerly widely used in the manufacture of luminescent paints, and in the treatment of disease. *Symbol:* Ra; *at. wt.:* 226; *at. no.:* 88. Cf. **Curie** (defs. 2, 3). [< NL = L *rad(ius)* RADIUS + *-ium* -IUM]

ra′dium ther′apy, treatment of disease by means of radium.

ra·di·us (rā′dē əs), *n., pl.* **-di·i** (-dē ī′), **-di·us·es. 1.** a straight line extending from the center of a circle or sphere to the circumference or surface. **2.** the length of such a line. **3.** any radial or radiating part. **4.** a circular area of an extent indicated by the length of the radius of its circumscribing circle. **5.** field or range of operation or influence. **6.** extent of possible operation, travel, etc., as under a single supply of fuel. **7.** *Anat.* the bone of the forearm on the thumb side. Cf. **ulna** (def. 1). **8.** *Zool.* a corresponding bone in the forelimb of other vertebrates. **9.** *Entomol.* one of the principal longitudinal veins in the anterior portion of the wing of an insect [< L: staff, rod, spoke, beam; see RAY[1]]

ra′dius vec′tor, *pl.* **radii vec·to·res** (vek tôr′ēz, -tōr′-), **radius vectors. 1.** *Math.* the length of the line segment joining a fixed point or origin to a given point. **2.** *Astron.* **a.** the straight line joining two bodies in relative orbital motion, as the line from the sun to a planet at any point in its orbit. **b.** the distance between two such bodies at any point in the orbit.

ra·dix (rā′diks), *n., pl.* **rad·i·ces** (rad′i sēz′, rā′di-), **ra·dix·es. 1.** *Math.* a number taken as the base of a system of numbers, logarithms, or the like. **2.** *Anat., Bot.* a root; a radical. **3.** *Gram.* root[1] (def. 11). [< L *rādīx* root; c. Gk *rhiza;* cf. Gk *rhádix* a shoot, twig]

RAdm, rear admiral.

Rad·nor (rad′nər), *n.* **1.** a town in SE Pennsylvania, near Philadelphia. 27,459 (1970). **2.** Radnorshire.

Rad·nor·shire (rad′nər shēr′, -shər), *n.* a county in E Wales. 18,431 (1961); 471 sq. mi. Also called **Radnor.**

Ra·dom (rä′dôm), *n.* a city in E Poland. 139,000 (est. 1963).

ra·dome (rā′dōm′), *n.* a dome-shaped device used to house a radar antenna. [RA(DAR) + DOME]

ra·don (rā′don), *n. Chem.* a rare, chemically inert, radioactive gaseous element produced by the disintegration of radium. *Symbol:* Rn; *at. no.:* 86; *at. wt.:* 222. [RAD(IUM) + -ON[2]]

rad/s, radians per second. Also, **rad/sec**

rad·u·la (raj′ŏŏ lə), *n., pl.* **-lae** (-lē′). a chitinous band in the mouth of most mollusks, set with numerous, minute, horny teeth and drawn backward and forward over the odontophore in the process of breaking up food. [< NL, L: scraper = *rād(ere)* (to) scrape, rub, scratch + *-ula* -ULE] —**rad′u·lar,** *adj.*

Rae·burn (rā′bərn), *n.* **Sir Henry,** 1756–1823, Scottish painter.

RAF, Royal Air Force. Also, **R.A.F.**

raff (raf), *n.* **1.** the riffraff; the rabble. **2.** *Brit. Dial.* trash; refuse. [ME *raf;* appar. abstracted from RIFFRAFF]

raf·fi·a (raf′ē ə), *n.* **1.** a palm, *Raphia pedunculata,* of Madagascar, having long, plumelike, pinnate leaves, the leafstalks of which yield an important fiber. **2.** the fiber of this palm, used for tying plants, small packages, etc., and for making matting, baskets, or the like. **3.** any other palm of the genus *Raphia.* [< Malagasy]

raf·fi·nose (raf′ə nōs′), *n. Chem.* a trisaccharide, $C_{18}H_{32}O_{16}\cdot 5H_2O$, occurring in the sugar beet, cottonseed, etc., that breaks down to fructose, glucose, and galactose on hydrolysis. [< F *raffin(er)* (to) refine + -OSE[2]]

raff·ish (raf′ish), *adj.* **1.** vulgar; low-class; tawdry. **2.** disreputable, rakish, or libertarian. —**raff′ish·ly,** *adv.* —**raff′ish·ness,** *n.*

raf·fle[1] (raf′əl), *n., v.,* **-fled, -fling.** —*n.* **1.** a form of lottery in which a number of persons buy one or more chances to win a prize. —*v.t.* **2.** to dispose of by a raffle. [ME *rafle* < MF < *rafler* to snatch; cf. RAFF]

raf·fle[2] (raf′əl), *n.* **1.** rubbish. **2.** *Naut.* a tangle, as of ropes or canvas. [RAFF + -LE]

raf·fles (raf′əlz), *n.* (*often cap.*) a gentlemanly burglar, amateur housebreaker, or the like. [after *Raffles,* hero of *The Amateur Cracksman,* by E. W. Hornung (1866–1921), English novelist]

raf·fle·sia (rə flē′zhə, -zhē ə, -zē ə, ra-), *n.* any stemless, leafless, parasitic plant of the genus *Rafflesia,* characterized by apetalous flowers, measuring three inches to three feet in diameter and exuding a putrid odor. [< NL, named after Sir T. Stamford *Raffles* (1781–1826), English governor in Sumatra who discovered it]

raft[1] (raft, räft), *n.* **1.** a more or less rigid floating platform made of buoyant materials: *an inflatable rubber raft.* **2.** a collection of logs, planks, etc., fastened together for floating on water. **3.** See **life raft. 4.** a slab of reinforced concrete providing a footing on yielding soil, usually for a whole building. —*v.t.* **5.** to transport on a raft. **6.** to form (logs or the like) into a raft. **7.** to travel or cross by raft. **8.** (of an ice floe) to transport (embedded organic or rock debris) from the shore out to sea. —*v.i.* **9.** to use a raft; go or travel on a raft. [ME *rafte* < Scand; cf. OIcel *raptr* RAFTER[1]]

raft[2] (raft, räft), *n. Informal.* a great quantity; a lot. [var. of RAFF in the sense of a large number (ME: abundance)]

raft·er[1] (raf′tər, räf′-), *n.* any of a series of timbers or the like, usually having a pronounced slope, for supporting the sheathing and covering of a roof. [ME; OE *rǣfter;* c. MLG *rafter,* OIcel *raptr.* See RAFT[1]]

raft·er[2] (raf′tər, räf′-), *n.* a flock, esp. of turkeys. [RAFT[2] + -ER[1]]

rafts·man (rafts′mən, räfts′-), *n., pl.* **-men.** a man who manages or is employed on a raft.

rag[1] (rag), *n.* **1.** a worthless piece of cloth, esp. one that is torn or worn. **2. rags,** ragged or tattered clothing. **3.** a shred, scrap, or fragmentary bit of anything. **4.** *Informal.* a newspaper or magazine regarded with contempt or distaste. **5.** *Bot.* the axis and carpellary walls of a citrus fruit. [ME *ragge* < Scand; cf. OIcel *rögg* tuft, shag]

rag[2] (rag), *v.,* **ragged, rag·ging,** *n. Informal.* —*v.t.* **1.** to scold. **2.** to subject to a teasing. **3.** *Brit.* to torment with jokes; play crude practical jokes on. —*n.* **4.** *Brit.* an act of ragging. [? special use of RAG[1]; but cf. OIcel *ragna* to curse]

rag[3] (rag), *n.* a musical composition in ragtime. [shortened form of RAGTIME]

ra·ga (rä′gə), *n.* one of the melodic formulas of Hindu music having the melodic shape, rhythm, and ornamentation prescribed by tradition. [< Skt *rāga* color, tone]

rag·a·muf·fin (rag′ə muf′in), *n.* **1.** a ragged, disreputable person; tatterdemalion. **2.** a child in ragged, ill-fitting, dirty clothes. [ME *Ragamoffyn,* name of a demon in the poem *Piers Plowman* (1393)]

rag′ doll′, a stuffed doll, esp. of cloth.

rage (rāj), *n., v.,* **raged, rag·ing.** —*n.* **1.** angry fury; violent anger. **2.** fury or violence of wind, waves, fire, disease, etc. **3.** violence of feeling, desire, or appetite. **4.** a violent desire or passion. **5.** ardor; fervor; enthusiasm. **6.** a fad or craze. **7.** *Obs.* insanity. —*v.i.* **8.** to act or speak with fury, show or feel violent anger. **9.** to move, rush, dash, or surge furiously. **10.** to proceed, continue, or prevail with great violence. [(n.) ME < OF < LL *rabia,* L *rabiēs* madness < *rabere* to rage; (v.) ME *rage(n)* < OF *ragie(r)* < *rage* (n.)] —**rag′ing·ly,** *adv.* —**Syn. 1.** wrath, ire. See **anger. 6.** vogue, fashion. **9.** rave, fume, storm. —**Ant. 1.** calm.

rag·ged (rag′id), *adj.* **1.** clothed in tattered garments. **2.** torn or worn to rags; tattered. **3.** shaggy, as an animal, its coat, etc. **4.** having loose or hanging shreds or fragmentary bits. **5.** full of rough or sharp projections; jagged: *ragged stones.* **6.** in a wild or neglected state. **7.** rough, imperfect, or faulty. **8.** harsh, as sound, the voice, etc. [ME *ragget*] —**rag′ged·ly,** *adv.* —**rag′ged·ness,** *n.* —**Syn. 1.** shabby. **2.** shredded, rent.

rag′ged edge′, 1. the brink, as of a cliff. **2.** any extreme edge; verge. **3. on the ragged edge,** in a dangerous or precarious position; on the verge of.

rag′ged rob′in, a caryophyllaceous plant, *Lychnis Floscuculi,* having flowers with dissected petals.

rag·ged·y (rag′i dē), *adj.* characterized by raggedness; somewhat ragged, tattered, or shaggy.

rag′ gourd′, luffa (def. 1).

rag·lan (rag′lən), *n.* a loose overcoat with raglan sleeves. [after Lord *Raglan* (1788–1855), British field marshal]

rag′lan sleeve′, a sleeve that begins at the neck and has a long, slanting seam line from the neck to the armhole.

rag·man (rag′man′, -mən), *n., pl.* **-men** (-men′, -mən). a man who gathers or deals in rags.

Rag·na·rok (räg′nə rok′), *n. Scand. Myth.* the destruction of the gods and of all things in a final battle with evil powers; Twilight of the Gods. Also, **Rag·na·rök** (räg′nə rœk′).

ra·gout (ra gōō′), *n., v.,* **-gouted** (-gōōd′), **-gout·ing** (-gōō′ing). —*n.* **1.** *French Cookery.* a highly seasoned stew of meat or fish. —*v.t.* **2.** to make into a ragout. [< F *ragoût* < *ragoûter* to restore the appetite of = *re-* RE- + *à* (< L *ad* to) + *goût* (< L *gustus* taste)]

rag′ pa′per, a high-quality paper made from cotton or linen pulp.

rag·pick·er (rag′pik′ər), *n.* a person who picks up rags and other waste material from the streets, refuse heaps, etc., for a livelihood.

rag′tag and bob′tail (rag′tag′), *Disparaging.* the riffraff or rabble. Also, **rag′, tag′, and bob′tail.**

rag·time (rag′tīm′), *n. Music.* **1.** rhythm in which the accompaniment is strict two-four time and the melody, with improvised embellishments, is in steady syncopation. **2.** music, esp. for piano, in this rhythm. [prob. RAG(GED) + TIME]

Ra·gu·sa (rä gōō′zä), *n.* **1.** a city in SE Sicily. 57,244 (1961). **2.** Italian name of **Dubrovnik.**

rag·weed (rag′wēd′), *n.* **1.** any of the composite herbs of the genus *Ambrosia*, the air-borne pollen of which is the most prevalent cause of autumnal hay fever. **2.** *U.S. Dial.* the marsh elder. **3.** *Brit.* the ragwort. [RAG[1] + WEED[1], so called from its ragged appearance]

rag·wort (rag′wûrt′), *n.* any of various composite plants of the genus *Senecio*, as *S. Jacobaea*, of the Old World, having yellow flowers and irregularly lobed leaves, or *S. aureus*, of North America, also having yellow flowers.

rah (rä), *interj.* (used as an exclamation of encouragement to a player or team.) [short for HURRAH]

Rah·way (rô′wā), *n.* a city in NE New Jersey. 29,114 (1970).

raid (rād), *n.* **1.** a sudden assault or attack, as on something to be seized or suppressed. **2.** *Mil.* a sudden attack on the enemy, as by air or by a small land force. **3.** *Finance.* a concerted attempt of speculators to force stock prices down. —*v.t.* **4.** to make a raid on. —*v.i.* **5.** to engage in a raid. [ME *raide* (north dial.), irreg. from OE *rād* expedition, lit., riding (whence ROAD); c. OIcel *reith*] —**raid′er,** *n.* —**Syn. 2.** incursion, invasion, inroad.

rail[1] (rāl), *n.* **1.** a bar of wood or metal fixed horizontally for any of various purposes, as for a support, barrier, fence, or railing. **2.** a fence; railing. **3.** one of a pair of steel bars that provide the running surfaces for the wheels of locomotives and railroad cars. **4.** the railroad as a means of transportation: *to travel by rail.* **5. rails,** stocks or bonds of railroad companies. **6.** *Naut.* a horizontal member capping a bulwark. **7.** *Carpentry, Furniture.* any of various horizontal framing members. Cf. **stile**[2]. —*v.t.* **8.** to furnish or enclose with a rail or rails. [ME *raile* < OF *raille* bar, beam < L *rēgula* bar, ruler, pattern]

rail[2] (rāl), *v.i.* **1.** to utter bitter complaint or vehement denunciation (often fol. by *at* or *against*): *to rail at fate.* —*v.t.* **2.** to bring, force, etc., by railing. [ME *rail(en)* < MF *raille(r)* (to) deride < Pr *ralhar* to chatter << LL *ragere* to shriek]

Rail,
Rallus limicola
(Length 9½ in.)

rail[3] (rāl), *n.* any of numerous birds of the subfamily *Rallinae*, of the family *Rallidae*, that have short wings, a narrow body, long toes, and a harsh cry and are found in grasslands, forests, and in marshes in most parts of the world. [ME *rale* < OF *raale* (c. Pr *rascla* < VL **rāsiculāre* freq. of L *rādere* (ptp. *rāsus*) to scratch]

rail·head (rāl′hed′), *n.* **1.** the farthest point to which the rails of a railroad have been laid. **2.** *Mil.* a railroad depot at which supplies are unloaded to be distributed or forwarded by truck or other means.

rail·ing (rā′ling), *n.* **1.** a fencelike barrier composed of one or more horizontal rails supported by widely spaced uprights; balustrade. **2.** banister. **3.** rails collectively.

rail·ler·y (rā′lə rē), *n., pl.* **-ler·ies. 1.** good-humored ridicule; banter. **2.** a bantering remark. [< F *raillerie* = MF *raill(er)* (to) RAIL[2] + *-erie* -ERY]

rail·road (rāl′rōd′), *n.* **1.** a permanent road laid with rails on which locomotives and cars are run. **2.** such a road together with its rolling stock, buildings, etc. **3.** the company of persons owning or operating such a plant. —*v.t.* **4.** to transport by means of a railroad. **5.** to supply with railroads. **6.** to send or push forward with great or undue speed: *to railroad a bill through a legislature.* **7.** *Informal.* to convict (a person) in a hasty manner by means of false charges or insufficient evidence.

rail·road·er (rāl′rō′dər), *n.* a person employed in the operation or management of a railroad.

rail′road flat′, an apartment with no corridor, so that one must pass through one room to enter the next.

rail·road·ing (rāl′rō′ding), *n.* the construction or operation of railroads.

rail-split·ter (rāl′split′ər), *n.* a person who splits logs into rails, esp. for fences.

rail·way (rāl′wā′), *n.* **1.** a railroad, esp. one using lightweight equipment or operating over short distances. **2.** any line or lines of rails forming a road for flanged-wheel equipment.

rai·ment (rā′mənt), *n.* *Chiefly Literary.* clothing; apparel; attire. [ME *rayment,* aph. var. of *arrayment.* See ARRAY, -MENT]

rain (rān), *n.* **1.** water that is condensed from the aqueous vapor in the atmosphere and falls in drops from the sky to the earth. **2.** a rainfall, rainstorm, or shower. **3. rains,** the rainy season; seasonal rainfall, as in India. **4.** weather marked by steady rainfall. **5.** a heavy and continuous descent of anything. —*v.i.* **6.** (of rain) to fall (usually used impersonally with *it* as subject): *It rained all night.* **7.** to fall like rain: *Tears rained from her eyes.* **8.** to send down rain. —*v.t.* **9.** to send down. **10.** to offer, bestow, or give abundantly. **11. rain cats and dogs,** *Informal.* to rain heavily or steadily. **12. rain out,** (of rain) to cause the cancellation or postponement of a contest, performance, or the like. [ME *rein,* OE *regn;* c. D, G *regen,* OIcel *regn*] —**rain′less,** *adj.* —**rain′less·ness,** *n.*

rain·bow (rān′bō′), *n.* **1.** a bow or arc of prismatic colors appearing in the heavens opposite the sun and caused by the refraction and reflection of the sun's rays in drops of rain. **2.** a similar bow of colors, esp. one appearing in the spray of a waterfall. **3.** any brightly multicolored arrangement or display. **4.** a wide variety or range; gamut. [ME *reinbowe,* OE *regnboga;* c. OIcel *regnbogi,* G *Regenbogen.* See RAIN, BOW[2]]

Rain′bow Bridge′, a natural stone bridge in S Utah: a national monument. 309 ft. high; 278-ft. span.

rain′bow trout′, a trout, *Salmo gairdnerii,* native in the coastal waters and streams from Lower California to Alaska.

rain′ check′, 1. a ticket for future use given to spectators at an outdoor event that has been postponed or interrupted by rain. **2.** an offered or requested postponement of an invitation.

rain·coat (rān′kōt′), *n.* a waterproof coat worn as protection against rain.

rain′ dance′, (esp. among American Indians) a ritualistic dance performed to bring rain.

rain·drop (rān′drop′), *n.* a drop of rain.

rain·fall (rān′fôl′), *n.* **1.** a fall or shower of rain. **2.** the amount of water falling in rain, snow, etc., within a given time and area, usually expressed as a hypothetical depth of coverage: *a rainfall of 70 inches a year.*

rain′ for′est, a tropical forest, usually of tall densely-growing evergreen trees, in an area of exceptionally high annual rainfall.

rain′ gauge′, an instrument for measuring rainfall.

Rai·nier (rā nēr′, rā′nēr, rə nēr′), *n.* **Mount,** a volcanic peak in W Washington, in the Cascade Range. 14,408 ft. Also called **Mount Tacoma.**

Rai·nier III (rā nēr′, re-, rə-; *Fr.* RE nyā′), *n.* **Rainier Louis Hen·ri Max·ence Ber·trand de Gri·mal·di** (lwē äN RĒ′ mAk säNs′ beR tRäN′ də grē mAl dē′), **Prince of Monaco,** born 1923, reigning prince of Monaco since 1949.

rain·mak·er (rān′mā′kər), *n.* **1.** (among American Indians) a medicine man who by various rituals and incantations seeks to cause rain. **2.** a person who induces rain to fall by using various scientific techniques. —**rain′mak′ing,** *n.*

rain·out (rān′out′), *n.* *Physics.* atomic fallout occurring in precipitation.

rain·proof (rān′prōōf′), *adj.* **1.** impervious to rain; keeping out or unaffected by rain: *a rainproof cover; a rainproof coat.* —*v.t.* **2.** to make impervious to rain.

Rains (rānz), *n.* **Sea of.** See **Mare Imbrium.**

rain·storm (rān′stôrm′), *n.* a storm of rain.

rain′ wa′ter, water fallen as rain.

rain·wear (rān′wâr′), *n.* waterproof or water-repellent clothing.

rain·y (rā′nē), *adj.,* **rain·i·er, rain·i·est. 1.** characterized by rain. **2.** wet with rain: *rainy streets.* **3.** bringing rain. [ME *reyny,* OE *rēnig*] —**rain′i·ly,** *adv.* —**rain′i·ness,** *n.*

rain′y day′, a time of need or emergency.

raise (rāz), *v.,* **raised, rais·ing,** *n.* —*v.t.* **1.** to move to a higher position; lift. **2.** to increase the height or vertical measurement of; heighten. **3.** to set upright. **4.** to build or erect (a structure). **5.** to promote the growth of (plants, animals, etc.), as for profit. **6.** to rear (a child). **7.** to activate or set in motion. **8.** to present for public consideration, as a question or objection. **9.** to assemble or gather: *to raise an army; to raise bail.* **10.** to awaken. **11.** to restore to life, as the dead. **12.** to invigorate, as one's spirits or hopes. **13.** to advance, as in rank or dignity. **14.** to increase, as in value, amount, or force. **15.** to make (one's voice) heard, as in the expression of an opinion. **16.** to utter (a shout, cry, etc.). **17.** to cause (dough or bread) to rise, as by the use of yeast. **18.** *Poker.* **a.** to increase (another player's bet). **b.** to bet at a higher level than (a preceding bettor). **19.** *Bridge.* to increase (the bid for a contract) by repeating one's partner's bid at a higher level. **20.** to increase the amount specified in (a check or the like) by fraudulent alteration. **21.** *Mil.* to end (a siege) by withdrawing the besieging forces or by compelling the besieging forces to withdraw. **22.** *Naut.* to cause to rise above the visible horizon by approaching nearer to it. **23.** to establish communication with by radio. **24.** *Phonet.* to alter the articulation of (a vowel) by placing the tongue in a higher position. The *a* of "man" is raised to *e* in the plural "men." Cf. **high** (def. 23). —*v.i.* **25.** *Dial.* to rise up; arise. **26. raise Cain.** See **Cain** (def. 2). —*n.* Also, *esp. Brit.,* **rise. 27.** an increase in amount, as of wages. **28.** the amount of such an increase. **29.** a raising, lifting, etc.; rise. **30.** a raised place. [ME *reise(n)* < Scand; cf. OIcel *reisa,* Goth *-raisjan* (causative of root in OE *rīsan* to RISE), OE *rǣran* to REAR[2]] —**rais′a·ble, raise′a·ble,** *adj.* —**rais′er,** *n.*
—**Syn. 1, 3.** RAISE, LIFT, HEAVE, HOIST imply bringing something up above its original position. RAISE, the most general word, may mean to bring something to or toward an upright position with one end resting on the ground; or it may be used in the sense of LIFT, moving an object a comparatively short distance upward but breaking completely its physical contact with the place where it had been: *to raise a ladder; to lift a package.* HEAVE implies lifting with effort or exertion: *to heave a huge box onto a truck.* HOIST implies lifting slowly and gradually something of considerable weight, usually with mechanical help, such as given by a crane or derrick: *to hoist steel beams to the top of the framework of a building.* See also **rise. 4.** construct, rear. **5.** cultivate, grow. **7.** originate, produce, effect. **12.** inspirit.

raised (rāzd), *adj.* **1.** fashioned or made as a surface design in relief. **2.** *Cookery.* made light by the use of yeast or other ferment but not with baking powder, soda, or the like.

rai·sin (rā′zin), *n.* a grape of any of various sweet varieties, dried in the sun or by artificial means, and often used in cookery. [ME *raisin, reisin* < OF < VL **racīm(us),* var. of L *racēmus*] —**rai′sin·y,** *adj.*

rai·son d'ê·tre (rā′zōn de′trə; *Fr.* RE zôN′ de′tRᵊ), *pl.* **rai·sons d'ê·tre** (rā′zōnz de′trə; *Fr.* RE zôN′ de′tRᵊ). reason or justification for being or existence.

raj (räj), *n.* (in India) rule; reign; dominion. [< Hindi *rāj* < Skt *rājya* < *rājati* he rules]

Ra·jab (rə jab′), *n.* the seventh month of the Islamic calendar. [< Ar]

ra·jah (rä′jə), *n.* **1.** a king or prince in India. **2.** a minor chief or dignitary. **3.** an honorary title conferred on Hindus in India. **4.** a title of rulers, princes, or chiefs in Java, Borneo, etc. Also, **ra′ja.** [< Hindi *rājā* < Skt *rājan;* c. L *rex* king]

Ra·ja·sthan (rä′jə stän′), *n.* a state in NW India; formerly Rajputana and a group of small states. 20,155,602 (1961); 132,078 sq. mi. *Cap.:* Jaipur. —**Ra·ja·stha·ni** (rä′jə-stä′nē), *adj.*

Raj·kot (räj′kōt), *n.* a city in S Gujarat, in W India. 193,500 (1961).

Raj·put (räj′pōōt), *n.* a member of a Hindu people noted for their military spirit. [< Hindi = Skt *rājan* king (see RAJ) + *putra* son]

Raj·pu·ta·na (räj′pōō tä′nə), *n.* a former region in NW India, now making up the principal part of Rajasthan.

rake[1] (rāk), *n., v.,* **raked, rak·ing.** —*n.* **1.** a shafted implement having a row of teeth for smoothing the surface of the ground, gathering fallen leaves, etc. **2.** any of various implements having a similar form and use. —*v.t.* **3.** to gather, draw, or remove with a rake. **4.** to clear, smooth, or prepare with a rake. **5.** to clear (a fire, embers, etc.) by stirring with a poker or the like. **6.** to gather or collect abundantly. **7.** to bring to light, usually for discreditable reasons. **8.** to search thoroughly through. **9.** to scrape; scratch. **10.** to fire guns along the length of (a position, body of troops, ship, etc.). **11.** to sweep with the eyes. —*v.i.* **12.** to use a rake. **13.** to search, as with a rake. **14.** to scrape; search. [ME; OE *raca;* c. G *Rechen,* OIcel *reka* shovel] —**rak′er,** *n.*

rake[2] (rāk), *n.* a dissolute or profligate person, esp. a man who is licentious; roué. [short for RAKEHELL]

rake[3] (rāk), *v.,* **raked, rak·ing,** *n.* —*v.i.* **1.** to incline from the vertical, as a mast, or from the horizontal. —*v.t.* **2.** to cause (something) to incline from the vertical or the horizontal. —*n.* **3.** inclination or slope away from the perpendicular or the horizontal. [? var. of OE *racian* to take a direction]

rake·hell (rāk′hel′), *n.* a licentious or dissolute man; rake. [interpreted as RAKE[2] + HELL, r. ME *rakel* (adj.) rash, rough, coarse, hasty; cf. ME *raken,* OE *racian* to take a course or direction, OIcel *reikall* wandering, unsettled]

rake-off (rāk′ôf′, -of′), *n. Informal.* **1.** a share or amount taken or received illicitly. **2.** a share, as of profits.

ra·ki (rä kē′, rak′ē), *n.* a liqueur of Greece and Turkey, having an anise flavor. Also, **ra·kee** (rə kē′, rak′ē). [< Turk]

rak·ish[1] (rā′kish), *adj.* like a rake; dissolute. [RAKE[2] + -ISH[1]] —**rak′ish·ly,** *adv.* —**rak′ish·ness,** *n.*

rak·ish[2] (rā′kish), *adj.* **1.** smart; jaunty; dashing: *a hat worn at a rakish angle.* **2.** (of a vessel) having an appearance suggesting speed. [RAKE[3] + -ISH[1]]

rale (ral, räl), *n. Pathol.* an abnormal crackling or rattling sound heard upon auscultation of the chest, caused by disease or congestion of the lungs. [< F *râle* < *râler* to make a rattling sound in the throat; cf. RAIL[3]]

Ra·leigh (rô′lē, rä′-), *n.* **1. Sir Walter.** Also, **Ra′legh.** 1552?–1618, English explorer and writer. **2.** a city in and the capital of North Carolina, in the central part. 123,793 (1970).

rall., rallentando.

ral·len·tan·do (rä′lən tän′dō; *It.* räl′len tän′dô), *adj. Music.* slackening; becoming slower. [< It, prp. of *rallentare* to abate]

ral·li·form (ral′ə fôrm′), *adj. Zool.* raillike in shape, anatomy, etc. [< NL *Rall(us)* name of genus (see RAIL[3]) + -I- + -FORM]

ral·ly[1] (ral′ē), *v.,* **-lied, -ly·ing,** *n., pl.* **-lies.** —*v.t.* **1.** to bring into order again; gather and organize anew. **2.** to draw or call (persons) together for a common action. **3.** to concentrate or revive, as one's strength or spirits. —*v.i.* **4.** to come together for common action. **5.** to come together or into order again. **6.** to come to the assistance of a person, party, or cause. **7.** to recover partially from illness. **8.** to acquire fresh strength or vigor. **9.** *Finance.* (of securities) to rise sharply in price after a drop. **10.** (in tennis, badminton, etc.) to engage in a rally. —*n.* **11.** a recovery from dispersion or disorder, as of troops. **12.** a renewal or recovery of strength, activity, etc. **13.** a drawing or coming together of persons, as for common action. **14.** *Finance.* a sharp rise in price or active trading after a declining market. **15.** (in tennis, badminton, etc.) **a.** an exchange of strokes between players before a point is scored. **b.** the hitting of the ball back and forth prior to the start of a match. **16.** *Boxing.* an exchange of blows. **17.** Also, **ral′lye.** a long-distance automobile race, esp. for sports cars, held on public roads with numerous checkpoints along the route. [< F *ralli(er),* OF = *re-* RE- + *alier* to join; see ALLY] —**ral′li·er,** *n.* —**Syn. 2, 4.** muster.

ral·ly[2] (ral′ē), *v.t.,* **-lied, -ly·ing.** to ridicule in a good-natured way; tease; chaff. [< F *raill(er)* (to) RAIL[2]]

ram (ram), *n., v.,* **rammed, ram·ming.** —*n.* **1.** a male sheep. **2.** (*cap.*) *Astron., Astrol.* the constellation or sign of Aries. **3.** any of various devices for battering, crushing, driving, or forcing something, esp. a battering ram. **4.** a heavy beak or spur projecting from the bow of a warship for penetrating the hull of an enemy's ship. **5.** a machine part that delivers pressure or a blow. **6.** See **hydraulic ram.** —*v.t.* **7.** to drive or force by heavy blows. **8.** to strike with great force; dash violently against. **9.** to cram; stuff. **10.** to push firmly. **11.** to force (a charge) into a firearm, as with a ramrod. [ME, OE; c. D, LG *ram,* G *Ramme*] —**ram′mer,** *n.*

RAM (ram), *n.* computer memory available to the user for creating, loading, or running programs and for the temporary storage and manipulation of data, any of which can be retrieved without reference to a fixed sequence. Cf. **ROM.** [*r(andom) a(ccess) m(emory)*]

ram-, an intensive prefix: *rambunctious.* [< Scand; cf. Icel *ram-* very, special use of *rammr* strong, sharp; akin to RAM]

Ra·ma (rä′mə), *n.* (in the *Ramayana*) any of the three avatars of Vishnu: Balarama, Parashurama, or Ramachandra.

Ra·ma·chan·dra (rä′mə chun′drə), *n.* the hero of the *Ramayana.*

Ram·a·dan (ram′ə dän′), *n. Islam.* **1.** the ninth month of the Islamic calendar. **2.** the daily fast that is rigidly enjoined from dawn until sunset during this month. [< Ar]

Ra·ma·krish·na (rä mə krish′nə), *n.* **Sri** (srē, shrē), 1834–86, Hindu religious reformer and mystic.

Ra·ma·ya·na (rä mä′yə nə), *n.* an epic of India concerned with the life and adventures of Ramachandra and his wife Sita.

Ram·a·zan (ram′ə zän′), *n.* (in India) Ramadan.

ram·ble (ram′bəl), *v.,* **-bled, -bling,** *n.* —*v.i.* **1.** to wander around in a leisurely, aimless manner. **2.** to take a course with many turns or windings, as a stream or path. **3.** to grow in a random, unsystematic fashion. **4.** to talk or write in a discursive, aimless way. —*v.t.* **5.** to walk aimlessly over or through. —*n.* **6.** a walk without a definite route, taken merely for pleasure. [? alter. of ME *romblen* = ROAM + -LE] —**Syn. 1.** stroll, saunter, amble. See **roam.**

ram·bler (ram′blər), *n.* **1.** a person or thing that rambles. **2.** any of several climbing roses having clusters of small flowers.

ram·bling (ram′bling), *adj.* **1.** aimlessly wandering. **2.** taking an irregular course; straggling. **3.** spread out irregularly in various directions: *a rambling house.* **4.** straying from one subject to another; discursive. [RAMBLE + -ING[2]]

Ram·bouil·let (ram′bo͝o lā′; *Fr.* RÄN bo͞o ye′), *n.* one of a breed of hardy sheep, developed from the Merino, that yield good mutton and a fine grade of wool. [named after *Rambouillet,* France, source of the breed]

ram·bunc·tious (ram bungk′shəs), *adj.* **1.** difficult to control or handle; wildly boisterous. **2.** turbulently active and noisy. [RAM- + var. of BUMPTIOUS]

ram·bu·tan (ram bo͞ot′ən), *n.* **1.** the bright-red, oval fruit of a Malayan sapindaceous tree, *Nephelium lappaceum,* covered with soft spines, or hairs, and having a subacid taste. **2.** the tree itself. [< Malay]

Ra·meau (RA mō′), *n.* **Jean Phi·lippe** (zhäN fē lēp′), 1683–1764, French composer and musical theorist.

Ra·mée (rə mā′), *n.* **Louise de la** (pen name: *Ouida*), 1839–1908, English novelist.

ram·e·kin (ram′ə kin), *n.* **1.** a small, separately cooked portion, esp. of a cheese mixture, baked in a small dish without a lid. **2.** a small dish in which food can be baked and served. Also, **ram′e·quin.** [< F *ramequin* < Gmc]

ra·men·tum (rə men′təm), *n., pl.* **-ta** (-tə). **1.** a scraping, shaving, or particle. **2.** *Bot.* one of the thin, chafflike scales covering the shoots or leaves of certain ferns. [< L = *rā(dere)* (to) scrape + *-mentum* -MENT]

Ram·e·ses I (ram′i sēz′). See **Ramses I.**

Rameses II. See **Ramses II.**

Rameses III. See **Ramses III.**

ra·mi (rā′mī), *n.* pl. of **ramus.**

ram·ie (ram′ē), *n.* **1.** an Asian, urticaceous shrub, *Boehmeria nivea,* yielding a fiber used esp. in making textiles. **2.** the fiber itself. [< Malay *rāmī*]

ram·i·fi·ca·tion (ram′ə fə kā′shən), *n.* **1.** the act or process of ramifying. **2.** a branch: *ramifications of a nerve.* **3.** a related or derived aspect, problem, etc., of something under consideration; outgrowth; consequence. **4.** *Bot.* **a.** a structure formed of branches. **b.** a configuration of branching parts. [< MF < ML *rāmificāt(us)* (ptp. of *rāmificāre* to RAMIFY) + MF *-ion* -ION]

ram·i·form (ram′ə fôrm′), *adj.* **1.** having the form of a branch; branchlike. **2.** branched. [< L *rām(us)* branch + -I- + -FORM]

ram·i·fy (ram′ə fī′), *v.t., v.i.,* **-fied, -fy·ing.** to divide or spread out into branches or branchlike parts; extend into subdivisions. [< MF *ramifi(er)* < ML *rāmificāre* = L *rām(us)* branch + *-ificāre* -IFY]

Ra·mil·lies (*Fr.* RA mē yē′), *n.* a village in central Belgium: Marlborough's defeat of the French 1706.

ram·jet (ram′jet′), *n.* a jet engine operated by the injection of fuel into a stream of air compressed by the forward speed of the aircraft. Also called **ram′jet en′gine.**

rammed′ earth′, a mixture of sand, loam, clay, and other ingredients rammed hard within forms as a building material.

ram·mish (ram′ish), *adj.* **1.** resembling a ram. **2.** having a disagreeable taste or smell; rank. [ME]

ra·mose (rā′mōs, rə mōs′), *adj.* **1.** having many branches. **2.** branching. [< L *rāmōs(us)* full of boughs = *rām(us)* branch + *-ōsus* -OSE[1]] —**ra′mose·ly,** *adv.* —**ra·mos·i·ty** (rə mos′i tē), *n.*

ra·mous (rā′məs), *adj.* **1.** ramose. **2.** resembling or pertaining to branches. [< L *rāmōs(us).* See RAMOSE, -OUS]

ramp (ramp), *n.* **1.** a sloping surface connecting two levels. **2.** a short concave slope or bend, as one connecting the higher and lower parts of a staircase railing at a landing. **3.** any extensive sloping walk or passageway. **4.** the act of ramping. **5.** *Aeron.* **a.** Also called **boarding ramp.** a movable staircase for entering or leaving the cabin door of an airplane. **b.** apron (def. 3). —*v.i.* **6.** to rise or stand on the hind legs, as a lion on a coat of arms. **7.** to rear as if to spring. **8.** to leap or dash with fury. **9.** to act violently; rage; storm. [(n.) < F *rampe;* (v.) ME *ramp(en)* < OF *ramp(er)* (to) creep, crawl, climb prob. < Gmc] —**ramp′ing·ly,** *adv.*

ram·page (*n.* ram′pāj; *v.* ram pāj′), *n., v.,* **-paged, -pag·ing.** —*n.* **1.** violent or excited behavior. **2.** a state of violent anger or agitation. —*v.i.* **3.** to rush, move, or act furiously or violently. [? < *ramp,* orig. Scot]

ram·pa·geous (ram pā′jəs), *adj.* violent; unruly; boisterous. —**ram·pa′geous·ly,** *adv.* —**ram·pa′geous·ness,** *n.*

ramp·an·cy (ram′pən sē), *n.* a rampant condition or position.

ramp·ant (ram′pənt), *adj.* **1.** violent in action or spirit; raging. **2.** in full sway; prevailing; unbridled. **3.** standing on the hind legs; ramping. **4.** *Heraldry.* (of a beast used as a charge) represented in profile facing the dexter side, with the body upraised and resting on the left hind leg, the tail and other legs elevated, the right foreleg highest, and the head in profile unless otherwise specified: *a lion rampant.* **5.** *Archit.* (of an arch or vault) springing at one side from one level of support and resting at the other on a higher level. [ME < OF, prp. of *ramper* to RAMP] —**ramp′ant·ly,** *adv.*

Rampant (Heraldic lion)

ram·part (ram′pärt, -pərt), *n.* **1.** *Fort.* **a.** a broad elevation or mound of earth raised as a fortification around a place and usually capped with a stone or earth parapet. **b.** such an elevation together with the parapet. **2.** anything serving as a bulwark or defense. —*v.t.* **3.** to furnish with or as if with a rampart. [< MF < *remparer* = *re-* RE- + *emparer* to take possession of < Pr *amparar* < L *ante-* ANTE- + *parāre* to PREPARE] —**Syn. 2.** fortification, breastwork, barricade.

ram·pi·on (ram′pē ən), *n.* **1.** a European campanula, *Campanula Rapunculus,* having an edible white tuberous root used in Europe for salad. **2.** any campanulaceous plant of the genus *Phyteuma,* having heads or spikes of blue flowers. [prob. alter. of MF *raiponce* < It *raponzo* < *rapa* turnip (< L)]

ram·rod (ram′rod′), *n.* **1.** a rod for ramming down the charge of a muzzle-loading firearm. **2.** a cleaning rod for the barrel of a firearm.

Ram·say (ram′zē), *n.* **1. Allan,** 1686–1758, Scottish poet. **2. George.** Dalhousie (def. 1). **3. James Andrew Broun.** Dalhousie (def. 2). **4. Sir William,** 1852–1916, English chemist: Nobel prize 1904.

Ram·ses I (ram′sēz), 1324?–1258 B.C., king of ancient Egypt. Also, **Rameses I.**

Ramses II, 1292–1225 B.C., king of ancient Egypt. Also, **Rameses II.**

Ramses III, 1198–1167 B.C., king of ancient Egypt. Also **Rameses III.**

Rams·gate (ramz′gāt′; *Brit.* ramz′git), *n.* a seaport in E Kent, in SE England: resort. 36,906 (1961).

ram·shack·le (ram′shak′əl), *adj.* loosely made or held together; rickety; shaky. [earlier *ramshackled* = RAM- + *shackled*, ptp. of *shackle* (var. of SHAKE); see -LE]

ram·son (ram′zən, -sən), *n.* **1.** a garlic, *Allium ursinum*, having broad leaves. **2.** Usually, **ramsons.** its bulbous root, used as a relish. [ME *ramsyn* (orig. pl., taken as sing.), OE *hramesan*, pl. of *hramsa* broadleafed garlic; c. Gk *krómmyon* onion]

ram·til (ram′til), *n.* See **Niger seed.** [< Bengali]

ram·u·lose (ram′yə lōs′), *adj.* *Bot., Zool.* having many small branches. Also, **ram·u·lous** (ram′yə ləs). [< L *rāmulōs(us)* full of branching veins = *rāmul(us)* little branch, twig (*rām(us)* branch + *-ul-* -ULE) + *-ōsus* -OSE[1]]

ra·mus (rā′məs), *n., pl.* **-mi** (-mī). *Bot., Zool., Anat.* a branch, as of a plant, vein, bone, etc. [< L: branch, bough]

ran (ran), *v.* pt. of **run.**

Ran (rän), *n.* *Scand. Myth.* a sea-goddess who drags down ships and drowns sailors: the wife of Aegir.

Ran·ca·gua (räng kä′gwä), *n.* a city in central Chile. 62,000 (est. 1966).

ranch (ranch), *n.* **1.** an establishment maintained for raising livestock under range conditions. **2.** the persons employed or living on it. **3.** *Chiefly Western U.S.* any farm or farming establishment. **4.** a dude ranch. **5.** See **ranch house** (def. 2). —*v.i.* **6.** to conduct or work on a ranch. [< AmerSp *ranch(o)* RANCHO]

ranch·er (ran′chər), *n.* a person who owns or works on a ranch.

ran·che·ro (ran châr′ō; *Sp.* rän che′rô), *n., pl.* **-che·ros** (-châr′ōz; *Sp.* -che′rôs). (in Spanish America and the southwestern U.S.) rancher. [< AmerSp]

ranch·ette (ranch et′), *n.* a small-scale ranch, typically of only a few acres.

ranch′ house′, **1.** the house of the owner of a ranch, usually of one story and with a low-pitched roof. **2.** any house of one story of the same general form, esp. one built in the suburbs.

Ran·chi (rän′chē), *n.* a city in S Bihar, in E India. 122,400 (1961).

ranch·man (ranch′mən), *n., pl.* **-men.** a rancher.

ran·cho (ran′chō, rän′-; *Sp.* rän′chô), *n., pl.* **-chos** (-chōz; *Sp.* -chôs). a ranch. [< AmerSp: small farm, camp (Sp: camp) < OSp *rancharse* to lodge, be billeted < MF *(se) ranger* to be arranged, be installed; see RANGE]

Ran·cho Cor·do·va (ran′chō kôr′də və), a town in central California. 30,451 (1970).

ran·cid (ran′sid), *adj.* **1.** having a rank, unpleasant, stale smell or taste, as through decomposition. **2.** (of an odor or taste) rank, unpleasant, and stale. [< L *rancid(us)* rank, stinking = **ranc(ēre)* (to) stink, be rancid + *-idus* -ID[4]] —**ran′cid·ness,** *n.*

ran·cid·i·ty (ran sid′i tē), *n.* **1.** a rancid state or quality. **2.** a rancid odor or taste.

ran·cor (rang′kər), *n.* bitter, rankling resentment or ill will; hatred; malice. Also, *esp. Brit.,* **ran′cour.** [ME *rancour* < MF < LL *rancōr-* (s. of *rancor*) rancidity = **ranc(ēre)* (see RANCID) + *-ōr-* -OR[1]] —**ran′cored;** *esp. Brit.,* **ran′coured,** *adj.* —**Syn.** bitterness, venom, animosity.

ran·cor·ous (rang′kər əs), *adj.* full of or showing rancor. —**ran′cor·ous·ly,** *adv.*

rand[1] (rand), *n.* (in shoemaking) a strip of leather set in a shoe at the heel before the lifts are attached. [ME, OE; c. D, G *rand* border, margin]

rand[2] (rand), *n.* the monetary unit of Botswana, Lesotho, the Republic of South Africa, South-West Africa, and Swaziland, equal to 100 cents. *Abbr.:* R. [< SAfrD: shield, monetary unit; special use of RAND[1]]

Rand, the (rand), Witwatersrand. —**Rand′ite,** *n.*

R&D, research and development.

Ran·dalls·town (ran′dəlz toun′), *n.* a town in central Maryland, near Baltimore. 33,683 (1970).

Rand·ers (rän′əRS), *n.* a seaport in E Jutland, in Denmark. 54,780 (1960).

Ran·dolph (ran′dolf, -dəlf), *n.* **1. A(sa) Philip** (ā′sə), 1889–1979, U.S. labor leader: president of the Brotherhood of Sleeping Car Porters 1925–1968. **2. Edmund Jen·nings** (jen′ingz), 1753–1813, U.S. statesman: first U.S. Attorney General 1789–94; Secretary of State 1794–95. **3. John,** 1773–1833, U.S. statesman and author. **4.** a town in E Massachusetts, S of Boston. 27,035 (1970).

ran·dom (ran′dəm), *adj.* **1.** proceeding, made, or occurring without definite aim, reason, or pattern. **2.** *Building Trades.* lacking uniformity of dimensions or pattern. See illus. at **ashlar.** —*adv.* **3.** *Building Trades.* without uniformity: *random-sized slates.* **4. at random,** in a random manner; haphazardly. [ME *raundon, random* < OF *randon* < *randir* to gallop < Gmc] —**ran′dom·ly,** *adv.* —**ran′dom·ness,** *n.* —**Syn. 1.** haphazard, chance, casual, stray, aimless.

ran′dom ac′cess mem′ory, *Computer Technol.* See **RAM.** Also, **ran′dom-ac′cess mem′ory.**

ran′dom sam′pling, *Statistics.* a method of selecting a sample from a statistical population in such a way that every possible sample that could be selected has the same probability of being selected.

ran′dom var′iable, *Statistics.* variate (def. 1).

R and R, **1.** rest and recuperation. **2.** rock-'n'-roll. Also, **R & R**

rand·y (ran′dē), *adj., n., pl.* **rand·ies.** —*adj.* **1.** *Scot.* rude and aggressive; obnoxious. **2.** sexually aroused; lustful. —*n.* **3.** *Scot.* a rude and aggressive person, esp. a surly beggar or a coarse woman. [*rand* (obs. var. of RANT) + -Y[1]]

ra·nee (rä′nē), *n.* (in India) **1.** the wife of a rajah. **2.** a reigning queen or princess. Also, **rani.** [< Hindi *rānī* < Skt *rājñī* queen (fem. of *rājan*)]

rang (rang), *v.* pt. of **ring**[2].

range (rānj), *n., adj., v.,* **ranged, rang·ing.** —*n.* **1.** the extent to which or the limits between which variation exists or is possible: *the range of steel prices.* **2.** the extent or scope of the operation or action of something: *within range of vision; the range of a pistol.* **3.** the distance of the target from a weapon. **4.** an area equipped with targets for practice in shooting weapons: *a rifle range.* **5.** an area used for flight-testing missiles. **6.** the distance of something to be located from some point of operation, as in sound ranging. **7.** the distance that can be covered by an aircraft, ship, or other vehicle, carrying a normal load without refueling. **8.** *Statistics.* the difference between the smallest and largest varieties in a statistical distribution. **9.** a continuous course of masonry of the same height from end to end. **10.** *Music.* compass (def. 4). **11.** *Survey.* **a.** the horizontal direction or extension of a survey line established by two or more marked points. **b.** a line established by markers or lights on shore for the location of soundings. **12.** (in U.S. public-land surveys) one of a series of divisions numbered east or west from the principal meridian of the survey and consisting of a row of townships, each six miles square, that are numbered north or south from a base line. **13.** a rank, class, or order: *in the higher ranges of society.* **14.** a row, line, or series, as of persons or things. **15.** an act of ranging or moving around, as over an area or region. **16.** a large, open region, esp. for the grazing of livestock. **17.** the region over which something is distributed: *the range of a weed.* **18.** a chain of mountains. **19.** a large stove equipped with burners and an oven. **20.** *Math.* the set of all values attained by a given function throughout its domain.
—*adj.* **21.** used or pastured on a range.
—*v.t.* **22.** to draw up or arrange (persons or things) in rows or lines or in a specific position, company, or group. **23.** to place or arrange systematically; set in order; dispose. **24.** to place in a particular class; classify: *They ranged themselves with the liberals.* **25.** to make straight, level, or even, as lines of type. **26.** to pass over or through (an area or region) in all directions, as in exploring or searching. **27.** to pasture (cattle) on a range. **28.** to direct or train, as a telescope, upon an object. **29.** to obtain the range of (something aimed at or to be located). **30.** *Naut.* to lay out (an anchor cable) so that the anchor may descend smoothly.
—*v.i.* **31.** to vary within specified limits: *prices ranging from $5 to $10; emotions ranging from smugness to despair.* **32.** to have range of operation, as specified. **33.** to find the range, as of something aimed at or to be located. **34.** to stretch out or extend in a line: *The shabby houses ranged along the road.* **35.** to extend, run, or go in a certain direction: *a boundary ranging east and west.* **36.** to lie or extend in the same line or plane, as one thing with another or others. **37.** to take up a position in a line or in order. **38.** to move around or through a region in all directions. **39.** to rove, roam, or wander: *The talk ranged over a variety of matters.* **40.** to extend, be found, or occur over an area or throughout a period, as animals or plants. [(n., adj.) ME < OF *renge* < *renc* line (see RANK[1]); (v.) ME *range(n)* < MF *rang(er)* < OF *rengier* < *renc* (n.)]
—**Syn. 1, 2.** sweep, reach. RANGE, COMPASS, LATITUDE, SCOPE refer to extent or breadth, with or without limits. RANGE emphasizes extent and diversity: *the range of one's interests.* COMPASS suggests definite limits: *within the compass of one's mind.* LATITUDE emphasizes the idea of freedom from narrow confines, thus breadth or extent: *granted latitude of action.* SCOPE suggests great freedom but a proper limit: *the scope of one's activities or of one's obligations.* **22, 24.** align, rank. **23.** array. **34.** lie. **38.** See **roam.**

range′ find′er, any of various instruments for determining the distance from the observer to a particular object, as for sighting a gun or adjusting the focus of a camera.

Range′ley Lakes′ (rānj′lē), a group of lakes in W Maine.

range′ light′, *Naut.* a light for indicating a channel. Also called **leading light.**

rang·er (rān′jər), *n.* **1.** See **forest ranger.** **2.** a member of a body of armed men who patrol a region as guards. **3.** a soldier specially trained for guerrilla warfare or making surprise raids. **4.** (*cap.*) *U.S.* one of a series of instrumented satellites for televising close-up pictures of the moon's surface. **5.** *Brit.* a keeper of a royal forest or park.

Ran·goon (rang gōōn′), *n.* a seaport in and the capital of Burma, in the S part. 1,530,434 (est. 1964).

rang·y (rān′jē), *adj.,* **rang·i·er, rang·i·est.** **1.** (of animals or persons) slender and long-limbed. **2.** given to or fitted for ranging or moving about, as animals. **3.** mountainous. —**rang′i·ness,** *n.*

ra·ni (rä′nē), *n., pl.* **-nis.** ranee.

Ran·jit Singh (run′jit sing′), ("*Lion of the Punjab*") 1780–1839, Indian maharaja: founder of the Sikh kingdom of Punjab.

rank[1] (rangk), *n.* **1.** a number of persons forming a distinct class in a social hierarchy or in any graded body. **2.** a social or official position or standing: *the rank of vice-president.* **3.** high position or station in the social scale. **4.** a class in any scale of comparison. **5.** relative position or standing: *a writer of the highest rank.* **6.** a row, line, or series of things or persons. **7.** Usually, **ranks.** the general body of any military or other organization apart from the officers or leaders. **8.** orderly arrangement; array. **9.** a line of persons, esp. soldiers, standing abreast in close-order formation (distinguished from *file*). **10.** a set of organ pipes of the same kind and tone quality. **11.** *Chess.* one of the horizontal lines of squares on a chessboard. **12. pull rank,** *Slang.* to make use unexpectedly of one's superior rank in demanding respect, obedience, etc. Also, **pull one's rank.** —*v.t.* **13.** to arrange in ranks or in regular formation. **14.** to assign to a particular position, station, class, group, etc. **15.** to outrank. —*v.i.* **16.** to form a rank or ranks. **17.** to occupy a place in a particular rank, class, etc. **18.** to have a specified rank or standing. **19.** to be the senior in rank: *The colonel ranks at this camp.* [< F *ranc* (obs.), OF *renc, ranc, rang* row, line < Gmc; cf. OE *hrinc* RING[1]] —**Syn. 3.** distinction, dignity. **6.** range, tier.

rank[2] (rangk), *adj.* **1.** growing with excessive luxuriance, as grass. **2.** producing an excessive and coarse growth, as land.

3. having an offensively strong smell or taste: *a rank cigar.* 4. offensively strong, as a smell or taste. 5. utter; absolute: *a rank outsider; rank treachery.* 6. highly offensive; disgusting. 7. grossly coarse, vulgar, or indecent: *rank language.* [ME; OE *ranc* bold, proud; c. Icel *rakkr* straight, bold] —**rank′ish,** *adj.* —**rank′ly,** *adv.* —**rank′ness,** *n.*

rank′ and file′, the general membership of an organization, nation, etc., exclusive of its leaders; ranks.

rank·er (rang′kər), *n. Brit.* a soldier in the ranks or a commissioned officer promoted from the ranks.

Ran·kine (rang′kin), *n.* **1. William John Mac·quorn** (mə kwôrn′), 1820–70, Scottish engineer and physicist. —*adj.* **2.** *Physics.* pertaining to an absolute scale of temperature (**Ran′kine scale′**) in which the degree intervals are equal to those of the Fahrenheit scale and in which 0° Rankine equals –459.7° Fahrenheit. Cf. **absolute scale, Kelvin** (def. 2).

rank·ing (rang′king), *adj.* **1.** senior or superior in rank, position, etc.: *a ranking diplomat.* **2.** prominent or highly regarded: *a ranking authority on Soviet affairs.* **3.** occupying a specified rank, position, etc. (often used in combination): *a low-ranking executive.*

ran·kle (rang′kəl), *v.,* **-kled, -kling.** —*v.i.* **1.** (of unpleasant feelings, experiences, etc.) to cause persistent keen irritation or bitter resentment; fester. —*v.t.* **2.** to cause keen irritation or bitter resentment in: *Her remark rankled him for days.* [ME *rancle(n)* < MF *rancler,* OF *(d)raoncler* to fester < *draoncle* a sore < VL **dracunculus,* dim. of L *dracō* serpent, DRAGON] —**ran′kling·ly,** *adv.*

ran·sack (ran′sak), *v.t.* **1.** to search thoroughly or vigorously through (a house, receptacle, etc.). **2.** to search through for plunder; pillage. [ME *ransake(n)* < Scand; cf. Icel *rannsaka* to search (a house) = *rann* house + *-saka,* akin to *sækja* to seek] —**ran′sack·er,** *n.*

ran·som (ran′səm), *n.* **1.** the redemption of a prisoner, slave, or kidnapped person, of captured goods, etc., for a price. **2.** the price paid or demanded. **3.** a means of deliverance or rescue from punishment for sin, esp. the payment of a redemptive fine. —*v.t.* **4.** to redeem from captivity, bondage, detention, etc., by paying a demanded price. **5.** to release or restore on receipt of a ransom. **6.** to deliver or redeem from punishment for sin. [(n.) ME *ransoun* < OF *rançon* < L *redemptiōn-* (s. of *redemptiō*) REDEMPTION; (v.) ME *ransoun(en)* < OF *rançonner* < n.] —**ran′som·er,** *n.*

Ran·som (ran′səm), *n.* **John Crowe** (krō), 1888–1974, U.S. poet, critic, and teacher.

rant (rant), *v.i.* **1.** to speak or declaim extravagantly or violently. —*v.t.* **2.** to utter or declaim in a ranting manner. —*n.* **3.** ranting, extravagant, or violent declamation. **4.** a ranting utterance. [< MD *rant(en)* (to) rave; c. G *ranzen* to frolic] —**rant′er,** *n.* —**rant′ing·ly,** *adv.*

Ran·toul (ran to͞ol′), *n.* a city in E Illinois. 25,562 (1970).

ra·nun·cu·la·ceous (rə nung′kyə lā′shəs), *adj.* belonging to the *Ranunculaceae,* the crowfoot or buttercup family of plants, including the marsh marigold, aconite, anemone, hepatica, clematis, columbine, larkspur, peony, etc. [< NL *Ranunculace(ae)* name of family. See RANUNCULUS, -ACEOUS]

ra·nun·cu·lus (rə nung′kyə ləs), *n., pl.* **-lus·es, -li** (-lī′). any plant of the genus *Ranunculus;* a buttercup or crowfoot. [< L *rānunculus* little frog, tadpole = *rān(a)* frog + *-unculus* double dim. suffix]

rap[1] (rap), *v.,* **rapped, rap·ping,** *n.* —*v.t.* **1.** to strike, esp. with a quick, smart, or light blow. **2.** to strike (an object, as a cane, pencil, etc.) against something with such a blow. **3.** to utter sharply or vigorously: *to rap out a command.* **4.** *Slang.* to sentence for a crime. —*v.i.* **5.** to knock smartly or lightly, esp. so as to make a noise: *to rap on a door.* **6.** *Slang.* **a.** to talk, chat, or converse. **b.** to discuss or argue. **c.** to achieve or maintain rapport. —*n.* **7.** a quick, smart, or light blow. **8.** the sound produced by such a blow. **9.** *Informal.* blame or punishment, esp. for a crime. **10.** *Slang.* **a.** a talk, chat, or conversation. **b.** a discussion or argument. **11. a bum rap,** *Slang.* a conviction for a crime that one did not commit. **12. beat the rap,** *Slang.* to succeed in evading the penalty for a crime; be acquitted. **13. take the rap,** *Slang.* to take the blame and punishment for a crime, error, etc., committed by another. [ME *rappe,* akin to Sw *rappa* to beat, drub, G *rappeln* to rattle] —**rap′per,** *n.*

rap[2] (rap), *n.* the least bit: *I don't care a rap.* [cf. G *Rappe* small coin]

rap[3] (rap), *v.t.,* **rapped** or **rapt, rap·ping. 1.** *Archaic.* **a.** to carry off; transport. **b.** to transport with rapture. **2.** *Obs.* to seize for oneself; snatch. [back formation from RAPT]

ra·pa·cious (rə pā′shəs), *adj.* **1.** given to seizing for plunder or the satisfaction of greed. **2.** inordinately greedy; predatory. **3.** (of animals) subsisting by the capture of living prey; predacious. [< L *rapāci-* (s. of *rapāx* greedy, akin to *rapere* to seize; see RAPE[1]) + -OUS] —**ra·pa′cious·ly,** *adv.* —**ra·pac·i·ty** (rə pas′i tē), **ra·pa′cious·ness,** *n.*

Ra·pal·lo (rä päl′lô), *n.* a seaport in NW Italy, on the Gulf of Genoa: treaties 1920, 1922. 20,762 (1961).

Ra·pa Nu·i (rä′pə no͞o′ē). See **Easter Island.**

rape[1] (rāp), *n., v.,* **raped, rap·ing.** —*n.* **1.** the act of physically forcing a woman to have sexual intercourse. **2.** any act of sexual intercourse that is forced upon a person. **3.** the act of seizing and carrying off by force. **4.** See **statutory rape.** —*v.t.* **5.** to force (a person, esp. a woman) to have sexual intercourse. **6.** to seize, take, or carry off by force. **7.** to plunder (a place). —*v.i.* **8.** to commit rape. [ME *rape(n)* < L *rapere* to seize, snatch] —**rap′ist,** *n.*

rape[2] (rāp), *n.* a brassicaceous plant, *Brassica Napus,* whose leaves are used for food for hogs, sheep, etc., and whose seeds yield rape oil. [ME < L *rāp-* (s. of *rāpum, rāpa*) turnip; c. Gk *rháphys*]

rape[3] (rāp), *n.* the residue of grapes, after the juice has been extracted, used as a filter in making vinegar. [< F *râpe* < Gmc; cf. OHG *raspōn* to scrape]

rape′ oil′, *Chem.* an oil expressed from rapeseed, used chiefly as a lubricant and an illuminant. Also called **rape′-seed oil′, colza oil.**

rape·seed (rāp′sēd′), *n.* **1.** the seed of the rape. **2.** the plant itself.

Raph·a·el (raf′ē əl, rā′fē-, rä′fī el′), *n.* **1.** (*Raffaello Santi* or *Sanzio*) 1483–1520, Italian painter. **2.** one of the archangels.

ra·phe (rā′ fē), *n., pl.* **-phae** (-fē). **1.** *Anat.* a seamlike union between two parts or halves of an organ or the like. **2.** *Bot.* **a.** (in certain ovules) a ridge connecting the hilum with the chalaza. **b.** a median line or slot on a cell wall of a diatom. [< NL < Gk *rhaphḗ* seam, suture, akin to *rháptein* to sew, stitch together]

raph·i·des (raf′i dēz′), *n.pl. Bot.* acicular crystals, usually composed of calcium oxalate, that occur in bundles in the cells of many plants. [< NL < Gk: pl. of *rhaphís* needle]

-raphy, var. of **-rrhaphy.**

rap·id (rap′id), *adj.* **1.** occurring within a short time; happening speedily: *rapid growth.* **2.** moving or acting with great speed; swift: *a rapid worker.* **3.** characterized by speed: *rapid motion.* —*n.* **4.** Usually, **rapids.** a part of a river where the current runs swiftly. [< L *rapid(us)* tearing away, seizing, swift. See RAPE[1], -ID[4]] —**rap′id·ly,** *adv.* —**Syn. 2.** See **quick.**

Rap·i·dan (rap′i dan′), *n.* a river in N Virginia, flowing E from the Blue Ridge Mountains into the Rappahannock River: Civil War battle 1862.

Rap′id Cit′y, a city in SW South Dakota. 43,836 (1970).

rap·id-fire (rap′id fīər′), *adj.* **1.** characterized by or delivered or occurring in rapid succession: *rapid-fire questions; rapid-fire events.* **2.** *Mil.* designating a rate of firing small arms that is intermediate between slow fire and quick fire.

ra·pid·i·ty (rə pid′i tē), *n.* a rapid state or quality; quickness; celerity. Also, **rap·id·ness** (rap′id nis). [< L *rapiditās*] —**Syn.** swiftness, fleetness. See **speed.**

rap′id trans′it, a means of rapid transportation in a metropolitan area, as a subway system.

ra·pi·er (rā′pē ər), *n.* **1.** a small sword, esp. of the 18th century, having a narrow blade and used for thrusting. **2.** a longer, heavier sword, esp. of the 16th and 17th centuries, having a double-edged blade and used for thrusting and slashing. [< MF *(espee) rapiere,* lit., rasping (sword); see RAPE[3]] —**ra′pi·ered,** *adj.*

Rapier and scabbard (17th century)

rap·ine (rap′in), *n.* the violent seizure and carrying off of another's property; plunder. [ME *rapine* < L *rapīna* robbery, pillage]

rap′ mu′sic, a style of popular music with a recurring background beat and an often rhyming chanted patter. Also called **rap.**

Rap·pa·han·nock (rap′ə han′ək), *n.* a river flowing SE from N Virginia into the Chesapeake Bay: battle 1863. 185 mi. long.

rap·pa·ree (rap′ə rē′), *n.* **1.** a 17th-century Irish plunderer. **2.** any freebooter or robber. [< Ir *rapaire*]

rap·pee (ra pē′), *n.* a strong snuff made from dark, rank tobacco leaves. [< F *râpé* grated (ptp. of *râper*); see RAPE[3]]

rap·pel (ra pel′, rə-), *n., v.,* **-pelled, -pel·ling.** —*n.* **1.** (in mountaineering) the act or method of moving down a steep incline or past an overhang by means of a double rope secured above and placed around the body and paid out gradually. —*v.i.* **2.** to descend by means of a rappel. [< F: lit., a recall. See REPEAL]

rap·per (rap′ər), *n.* **1.** the knocker of a door. **2.** a person or thing that raps or knocks.

rap·port (ra pôr′, -pôr′; *Fr.* RA PÔR′), *n.* a harmonious or sympathetic relation or connection: *to establish close rapport with one's students.* Cf. **en rapport.** [< F *rapporter* to bring back, produce, refer = *re-* RE- + *apporter,* OF *aporter* < L *apportāre* (*ap-* AP- + *portāre* to carry)]

rap·proche·ment (*Fr.* RA PRÔSH MÄN′), *n.* an establishment or reestablishment of harmonious relations, as between nations. [< F = *rapproche(r)* (to) bring near, bring together (*re-* RE- + *approcher;* see APPROACH) + *-ment* -MENT]

rap·scal·lion (rap skal′yən), *n.* a rascal; rogue; scamp. [earlier *rascallion,* based on RASCAL]

rap′ ses′sion, *Slang.* a group discussion, attended esp. by people with specific problems or complaints.

rap′ sheet′, *U.S. Slang.* a law-enforcement record of arrest or conviction.

rapt (rapt), *adj.* **1.** deeply engrossed or absorbed: *rapt in thought.* **2.** transported with emotion; enraptured: *rapt with joy.* **3.** showing or proceeding from rapture: *a rapt smile.* [ME (ptp.) < L *rapt(us)* seized, carried off (ptp. of *rapere*) = *rap-* (see RAPE[1]) + *-tus* ptp. suffix] —**rapt′ly,** *adv.* —**Syn. 2.** ecstatic.

rap·to·ri·al (rap tôr′ē əl, -tôr′-), *adj.* **1.** preying upon other animals; predatory. **2.** adapted for seizing prey, as claws. **3.** belonging or pertaining to the *Raptores,* a former order in which the falconiform and strigiform birds were erroneously grouped together. [< L *raptōr-* (s. of *raptor* one who seizes by force, robber: *rapt(us)* RAPT + *-or* -OR[2]) + -IAL]

Raptorial bird
Head and foot of golden eagle, *Aquila chrysaëtos*

rap·ture (rap′chər), *n.* **1.** ecstatic joy or delight; joyful ecstasy. **2.** Often, **raptures.** an utterance or expression of ecstatic delight. —*v.t.* **3.** *Literary.* to enrapture.

rap·tur·ous (rap′chər əs), *adj.* **1.** full of, feeling, or manifesting ecstatic joy or delight. **2.** characterized by, attended with, or expressive of such rapture: *rapturous surprise.* —**rap′tur·ous·ly,** *adv.* —**rap′tur·ous·ness,** *n.*

ra·ra a·vis (râr′ə ā′vis; *Lat.* RÄ′RÄ Ä′WIS), *pl.* **ra·rae a·ves** (râr′ē ā′vēz; *Lat.* RÄ′RĪ Ä′WES), a rare person or thing. [< L: rare bird]

rare[1] (râr), *adj.,* **rar·er, rar·est. 1.** coming or occurring infrequently; unusual; uncommon. **2.** thinly distributed over an area; few and widely separated. **3.** having the component parts relatively separated; thin: *rare gases.* **4.** unusually great: *sympathetic to a rare degree.* **5.** unusually excellent; admirable; fine: *She showed rare tact in inviting them.* [ME < L *rār(us)* loose, wide apart, thin] —**rare′ness,** *n.* —**Syn. 1.** exceptional, extraordinary, singular. **2.** sparse.

rare[2] (râr), *adj.,* **rar·er, rar·est.** (of meat) cooked just slightly. [ME *rere,* OE *hrēr* lightly boiled]

rare·bit (râr′bit), *n.* See **Welsh rabbit.**

rare′ earth′, *Chem.* the oxide of any of the rare-earth elements, contained in various minerals.

rare′-earth′ el′ement (râr′ûrth′), *Chem.* any of a group of closely related metallic elements of atomic number 57 to 71 inclusive, often divided into three subgroups: the cerium metals, lanthanum, cerium, praseodymium, neodymium, promethium, and samarium; the terbium metals, europium, gadolinium, and terbium; and the yttrium metals, dysprosium, holmium, erbium, thulium, yttrium, ytterbium, and lutetium. Also called **rare′-earth′ met′al.**

rar·e·fac·tion (râr′ə fak′shən), *n.* **1.** the act or process of rarefying. **2.** the state of being rarefied. [< ML *rārēfactiōn-* (s. of *rārēfactiō*) = L *rārēfact(us)* (ptp. of *rārēfacere;* see RAREFY) + *-iōn-* -ION] —**rar′e·fac′tion·al,** *adj.*

rar·e·fied (râr′ə fīd′), *adj.* **1.** extremely high or elevated; lofty; exalted: *rarefied thinking; rarefied art.* **2.** of, belonging to, or characterizing an exclusive group; select. **3.** not dense; rare; thin.

rar·e·fy (râr′ə fī′), *v.,* **-fied, -fy·ing.** —*v.t.* **1.** to make rare or rarer; make less dense: *to rarefy a gas.* **2.** to make less gross; refine: *to rarefy one's spiritual life.* —*v.i.* **3.** to become rare or less dense; become thinned: *Moisture rarefies when heated.* [ME *rarefie(n)* < MF *rarefie(r)* < L *rārēfacere* = *rār(us)* RARE[1] + *facere* to make; see -FY] —**rar′e·fi′a·ble,** *adj.* —**rar′e·fi′er,** *n.*

rare·ly (râr′lē), *adv.* **1.** on rare occasions; infrequently; seldom. **2.** exceptionally; in an unusual degree. **3.** unusually or remarkably well.

rare·ripe (râr′rīp′), *Bot.* —*adj.* **1.** ripening early. —*n.* **2.** a fruit or vegetable that ripens early. [*rare* early (obs. except dial.; var. of RATHE) + RIPE]

Rar·i·tan (rar′i tən, -tᵊn), *n.* former name of **Hazlet.**

rar·i·ty (râr′i tē), *n., pl.* **-ties** for 1. **1.** something rare, unusual, or uncommon, esp. something esteemed. **2.** the state or quality of being rare. **3.** unusual excellence. **4.** thinness, as of air or a gas. [< L *rāritās* thinness = *rār(us)* RARE[1] + *-itās* -ITY]

Ra·ro·tong·a (rar′ə tong′gə), *n.* one of the Cook Islands, in the S Pacific. 11,433; 26 sq. mi.

Ras Ad·dar (räs′ a där′). See **Bon, Cape.**

ras·bo·ra (raz bôr′ə, -bōr′ə, raz′bər ə), *n.* any of several minnows of the genus *Rasbora,* found in southeastern Asia and the Malay Archipelago, esp. the silvery *R. heteromorpha,* which has a black triangular marking near the tail and is often kept in aquariums. [< NL < EInd native name]

ras·cal (ras′kəl), *n.* **1.** a base, dishonest, or unscrupulous person. **2.** any mischievous person or animal. **3.** *Archaic.* a person belonging to the rabble. —*adj.* **4.** knavish; dishonest. [ME *rascaile, raskaille* < OF *rascaille* rabble; akin to RASH[2]] —**ras′cal·like′,** *adj.* —**Syn. 1.** rapscallion, scamp, villain.

ras·cal·i·ty (ra skal′i tē), *n., pl.* **-ties** for 2. **1.** rascally or knavish character or conduct. **2.** a rascally act.

ras·cal·ly (ras′kə lē), *adj.* **1.** characteristic of or befitting a rascal; dishonest; mean: *a rascally trick.* —*adv.* **2.** in a rascally manner.

rase (rāz), *v.t.,* **rased, ras·ing.** raze. —**ras′er,** *n.*

rash[1] (rash), *adj.* **1.** tending to act too hastily or without due consideration. **2.** characterized by or showing excessive haste or lack of consideration: *rash promises.* [ME; c. D, G *rasch* quick, brisk, OIcel *rǫskr* brave] —**rash′ly,** *adv.* —**rash′ness,** *n.* —**Syn. 1.** hasty, impetuous, reckless.

rash[2] (rash), *n.* **1.** an eruption or efflorescence on the skin. **2.** a flurry or epidemic of unpleasant occurrences: *a rash of robberies last month.* [< F *rache* (obs.), OF *rasche* skin eruption < *raschier* to scratch << L *rās(us),* ptp. of *rādere* to scratch] —**rash′like′,** *adj.*

rash·er (rash′ər), *n.* **1.** a thin slice of bacon or ham for frying or broiling. **2.** a portion or serving of such slices. [? akin to RASH[2]]

Ras·mus·sen (räs′mōō sən), *n.* **Knud Jo·han Vic·tor** (knōōth yō hän′ vēk′tôr), 1879–1933, Danish arctic explorer.

ra·so·ri·al (rə sôr′ē əl, -sōr′-), *adj.* given to scratching the ground for food, as poultry; gallinaceous. [< NL *Rasor(es)* name of an order of birds, LL, pl. of *rāsor* scratcher = L *rās(us)* (ptp. of *rādere* to scrape, scratch) + *-or* -OR[2] + -IAL]

Rasorial bird's foot

rasp (rasp, räsp), *v.t.* **1.** to scrape or abrade with a rough instrument. **2.** to scrape or rub roughly: *The glacier rasps the floor of the valley.* **3.** to grate upon or irritate: *The sound rasped his nerves.* **4.** to utter with a grating sound. —*v.i.* **5.** to scrape or grate. **6.** to make a grating sound. —*n.* **7.** an act of rasping. **8.** a rasping sound. **9.** a coarse file, used mainly on wood, having separate conical teeth. [ME *rasp(en)* < OF *rasp(er)* (to) scrape, grate < Gmc; see RAPE[3]] —**rasp′er,** *n.* —**rasp′ish,** *adj.*

rasp·ber·ry (raz′ber′ē, -bə rē, räz′-), *n., pl.* **-ries. 1.** the fruit of any of several rosaceous shrubs of the genus *Rubus,* consisting of small and juicy red, black, or pale-yellow drupelets forming a detachable cap about a convex receptacle. **2.** any shrub bearing this fruit. **3.** a dark reddish-purple color. **4.** *U.S.* See **Bronx cheer.** [earlier *rasp(is)* raspberry (< ?) + BERRY]

rasp·ing (ras′ping, rä′sping), *adj.* harsh; grating: *a rasping voice.* —**rasp′ing·ly,** *adv.* —**rasp′ing·ness,** *n.*

Ras·pu·tin (ra spyōō′tin, -spyōōt′ᵊn; *Russ.* räs pōō′tin), *n.* **Gri·go·ri E·fi·mo·vich** (gri gô′ri e fē′mo vich), 1871–1916, Siberian peasant monk who was influential at the court of Czar Nicholas II and Czarina Alexandra.

rasp·y (ras′pē, rä′spē), *adj.,* **rasp·i·er, rasp·i·est. 1.** harsh; grating; rasping. **2.** easily annoyed; irritable.

ras·sle (ras′əl), *v.i., v.t.,* **-sled, -sling,** *n. Dial.* wrestle.

Ras·ta (ras′tə), *n., adj.* Rastafarian.

Ras·ta·far·i·an (ras′tə fâr′ē ən), *n.* **1.** a follower of Rastafarianism. —*adj.* **2.** of or pertaining to Rastafarianism.

Ras·ta·far·i·an·ism (ras′tə fâr′ē ə niz′əm), *n.* a militant black religious cult, originally of Jamaica, that regards Africa as the Promised Land, to which all blacks will someday return, and the late Haile Selassie I, former emperor of Ethiopia, as the messiah. [< *Ras* prince *Tafari* (precoronation name of Haile Selassie I) + -AN + -ISM]

ras·ter (ras′tər), *n.* *Television.* a pattern of scanning lines covering the area upon which the image is projected in the cathode ray tube of a television set. [< G < L: toothed hoe, rake < *rādere* to scratch, scrape]

rat (rat), *n., interj., v.,* **rat·ted, rat·ting.** —*n.* **1.** any of several long-tailed rodents of the family *Muridae,* of the genus *Rattus* and related genera, distinguished from the mouse only in being larger. **2.** any of various similar or related animals. **3.** *Slang.* a scoundrel. **4.** *Slang.* **a.** a person who abandons his party or associates, esp. in a time of trouble. **b.** an informer. **5.** *U.S.* a pad with tapered ends used in women's hair styles to give the appearance of greater thickness. **6. smell a rat,** to suspect treachery; have suspicion. —*interj.* **7. rats,** *Slang.* (used as an exclamation of disappointment, disgust, etc.) —*v.i.* **8.** *Slang.* to turn informer; squeal. [ME *ratte,* OE *ræt;* c. G *Ratz, Ratte*] —**rat′like′,** *adj.*

rat·a·ble (rā′tə bəl), *adj.* **1.** capable of being rated, or appraised. **2.** proportional: *ratable distribution of wealth.* **3.** *Brit.* liable to local taxation. Also, **rateable.** —**rat′a·bil′i·ty, rat′a·ble·ness,** *n.* —**rat′a·bly,** *adv.*

rat·a·fi·a (rat′ə fē′ə), *n.* a liqueur flavored with almonds, fruit kernels, fruit, or the like. Also, **rat·a·fee** (rat′ə fē′). [< F (WInd Creole dial.)]

ratafi′a bis′cuit, *Brit.* a macaroon.

ra·tan (ra tan′), *n.* rattan.

rat·a·plan (rat′ə plan′), *n., v.,* **-planned, -plan·ning.** —*n.* **1.** a sound of beating or percussion; rub-a-dub. —*v.i.* **2.** to produce such a sound. [< F; imit.]

rat·a·tat (rat′ə tat′), *n.* a sound imitative of knocking or rapping. Also, **rat′-a-tat′-tat′.**

rat′bite fe′ver (rat′bīt′), *Pathol.* a relapsing fever, widely distributed geographically, caused by infection with a spirillum transmitted by rats. Also called **rat′bite disease′.**

ratch·et (rach′it), *n.* **1.** *Machinery.* a toothed bar with which a pawl engages. **2.** (not in technical use) a pawl or the like used with a ratchet or ratchet wheel. **3.** a mechanism consisting of such a bar or wheel with the pawl. **4.** See **ratchet wheel.** [alter. of F *rochet* < MF *rocquet* a blunt lance-head < Gmc]

ratch′et wheel′, a wheel, with teeth on the edge, into which a pawl drops or catches, as to prevent reversal of motion.

Ratchet wheel

rate[1] (rāt), *n., v.,* **rat·ed, rat·ing.** —*n.* **1.** the amount of a charge or payment with reference to some basis of calculation: *a high rate of interest.* **2.** a certain quantity or amount of something considered in relation to a unit of something else: *at the rate of 60 miles an hour.* **3.** a fixed charge per unit of quantity: *a rate of 10 cents a pound.* **4.** price; cost: *to cut rates on all household items.* **5.** degree of speed; pace, progress, etc.: *to work at a rapid rate.* **6.** degree or comparative extent of action or procedure: *the rate of increase in work output.* **7.** relative condition or quality; grade, class, or sort. **8.** assigned position in any of a series of graded classes; rating. **9.** *Insurance.* the premium charge per unit of insurance. **10.** a charge by a common carrier for transportation. **11.** a wage paid on a time basis. **12.** a charge or price established in accordance with a scale or standard. **13.** *Horol.* the relative adherence of a timepiece to perfect timekeeping, measured in terms of the amount of time gained or lost within a certain period. **14.** Usually, **rates.** *Brit.* **a.** a tax on property for some local purpose. **b.** any tax assessed and paid to a local government. **15. at any rate,** at all events; at least; still. —*v.t.* **16.** to estimate the value or worth of; appraise. **17.** to consider, regard, or account. **18.** to fix at a certain rate, as of charge or payment. **19.** to value, as for purposes of taxation. **20.** to make subject to a certain rate or tax. **21.** to place in a certain rank, class, etc., as a ship or a seaman. **22.** to arrange for the conveyance of (goods) at a certain rate. —*v.i.* **23.** to have value, standing, etc.: *Her performance didn't rate very high in the competition.* **24.** to have position in a certain class. **25.** to rank very high in estimation. [ME *rate(n)* < L phrase *prō ratā parte* according to a fixed part (i.e., proportionally), *rata* from *rērī* to judge]

rate[2] (rāt), *v.t., v.i.,* **rat·ed, rat·ing.** to chide vehemently; scold. [ME *(a)rate(n)* < Scand; cf. Sw *rata* to reject] —**rat′er,** *n.*

rate·a·ble (rā′tə bəl), *adj.* ratable. —**rate′a·bil′i·ty, rate′a·ble·ness,** *n.* —**rate′a·bly,** *adv.*

ra·tel (rāt′əl, rät′-), *n.* a badgerlike carnivore, *Mellivora capensis,* of Africa and India. [< SAfrD]

Ratel (11 in. high at shoulder; total length 3 ft.; tail 9 in.)

rate′ of exchange′, the ratio at which money of one country can be exchanged for money of another country. Also called **exchange rate.**

rate·pay·er (rāt′pā′ər), *n.* *Brit.* a person who pays rates, or local taxes. —**rate′pay′ing,** *adj., n.*

rat·er (rā′tər), *n.* **1.** a person who makes rates or ratings. **2.** a person or thing that is of a specific rating (usually used in combination): *The show's star is a first-rater.*

rat·fink (rat′fingk′), *n.* *Slang.* fink (def. 4).

Rat·haus (rät′hous′), *n., pl.* **-häu·ser** (-hoi′zər). *German.* a town hall. [lit., counsel house]

rathe (rāth), *adj.* **1.** Also, **rath** (rath). *Archaic.* growing, blooming, or ripening early in the year or season. —*adv.* **2.** *Brit. Dial.* early. [ME; OE *hræth, hræd* quick, active]

rath·er (*adv.* rath′ər, rä′thər; *interj.* rath′ûr′, rä′thûr′), *adv.* **1.** in a measure; to a certain extent; somewhat: *rather good.* **2.** in some degree: *I rather thought so.* **3.** more properly or justly; with better reason: *That is rather to be supposed.* **4.** more readily or willingly; sooner: *to die rather than yield; I would rather go today.* **5.** more properly or correctly: *He is a painter or, rather, a watercolorist.* **6.** on the contrary: *It's not generosity, rather self-interest.* **7. had rather.** See have (def. 27). —*interj.* **8.** *Chiefly Brit.* emphatically yes; assuredly. [ME; OE *hrather*, comp. of *hrathe* quickly, RATHE]

Rath′ke's pouch′ (rät′kəz), *Embryol.* an invagination of stomodeal ectoderm developing into the anterior lobe of the pituitary gland. [named after Martin Heinrich *Rathke* (1793–1860), German anatomist]

rat·hole (rat′hōl′), *n.* **1.** a hole made by a rat, as in a wall or floor: *The ratholes in the old barn must be plugged up.* **2.** the burrow or shelter of a rat. **3.** any small and uncomfortable room, office, apartment, etc.

raths·kel·ler (rät′skel′ər, rat′-, rath′-), *n.* **1.** (in Germany) the cellar of a town hall, often used as a beer hall or restaurant. **2.** a restaurant patterned on the German rathskeller, usually located below street level. [< G = *Rat(h)* counsel (abstracted from *Rathaus*) + *-s* 's[1] + *Keller* cellar]

rat·i·cide (rat′i sīd′), *n.* a substance or preparation for killing rats. —**rat′i·cid′al,** *adj.*

rat·i·fi·ca·tion (rat′ə fə kā′shən), *n.* **1.** the act or process of ratifying; confirmation; sanction. **2.** the state of being ratified. [< ML *ratificātiōn-* (s. of *ratificātiō*) = *ratificāt(us)* (ptp. of *ratificāre* to RATIFY) + *-iōn-* -ION]

rat·i·fy (rat′ə fī′), *v.t.*, **-fied, -fy·ing.** to confirm by expressing consent, approval, or formal sanction; validate: *It is doubtful that the new amendment to the constitution will be ratified.* [ME *ratifie(n)* < MF *ratifi(er)* < ML *ratific(āre)* = L *rat(us)* calculated (see RATE[1]) + *-ificāre* -IFY] —**rat′i·fi′er,** *n.* —**Syn.** corroborate, approve, establish. —**Ant.** veto, disapprove.

rat·i·né (rat′ənā′; *Fr.* RA tē nā′), *n.* a loosely woven fabric made with nubby or knotty yarns. Also, **ra·ti·ne** (rat′ənā′, ra tēn′). Also called **sponge cloth.** [< F, ptp. of *ratiner* to make a nap on cloth]

rat·ing[1] (rā′ting), *n.* **1.** classification according to grade or rank. **2.** *Naut.* **a.** assigned position in a particular class or grade, or relative standing, as of a ship or a seaman. **b. ratings,** crew members having certain ratings, esp. the enlisted personnel in the British Navy. **3.** the credit standing of a person or firm. **4.** *Radio, Television.* a percentage indicating the number of listeners to or viewers of a specific program. **5.** an amount fixed as a rate. **6.** *Brit.* apportioning of a tax. [RATE[1] + -ING[1]]

rat·ing[2] (rā′ting), *n.* an angry reprimand or rebuke; scolding. [RATE[2] + -ING[1]]

ra·tio (rā′shō, -shē ō′), *n., pl.* **-ti·os.** **1.** the relation between two similar magnitudes in respect to the number of times the first contains the second: *the ratio of 5 to 2, written 5:2 or 5/2.* **2.** proportional relation; rate: *the ratio between acceptances and rejections.* [< L *ratiō* a reckoning, account calculation; see REASON]

ra·ti·oc·i·nate (rash′ē os′ə nāt′), *v.i.*, **-nat·ed, -nat·ing.** to reason; carry on a process of reasoning. [< L *ratiōcināt(us)* reckoned, calculated, concluded (ptp. of *ratiōcinārī*) < *ratiō* reason] —**ra′ti·oc′i·na′tor,** *n.*

ra·ti·oc·i·na·tion (rash′ē os′ə nā′shən), *n.* the process of logical reasoning. [< L *ratiōcinātiōn-* (s. of *ratiōcinātiō*). See RATIOCINATE, -ION] —**ra′ti·oc′i·na′tive,** *adj.*

ra·tion (rash′ən, rā′shən), *n.* **1.** a fixed allowance of provisions or food, esp. for a soldier or sailor. **2.** an allotted amount of anything. **3. rations,** provisions. —*v.t.* **4.** to supply, apportion, or distribute as rations: *to ration food to an army.* **5.** to supply or provide with rations: *to ration an army with food.* **6.** to restrict the consumption of (a commodity, food, etc.): *to ration meat in wartime.* **7.** to restrict (a person) in the consumption or use of anything, as food: *to ration a person to a pound of meat a week.* [< F < L *ratiōn-* (s. of *ratiō*) REASON] —**Syn. 1.** portion, allotment. **4.** mete, dole, allot.

ra·tion·al (rash′ə nəl), *adj.* **1.** agreeable to or in accord with reason; reasonable; sensible. **2.** having or exercising reason, sound judgment, or good sense. **3.** being in full possession of one's reason; sane; lucid: *The patient appeared to be perfectly rational.* **4.** endowed with the faculty of reason; *Man is a rational animal.* **5.** of, pertaining to, or based on reasoning or reasoning powers: *the rational faculty; a rational explanation.* **6.** *Math.* **a.** of or pertaining to a rational number. **b.** (of a function) capable of being expressed exactly by a ratio of two polynomials. **7.** *Classical Pros.* capable of measurement in terms of the metrical unit or mora. —*n.* **8.** *Math.* See **rational number.** [ME *racional* < L *ratiōnāl(is)* = *ratiōn-* (s. of *ratiō*) reason + *-ālis* -AL[1]] —**ra′tion·al·ly,** *adv.* —**ra′tion·al·ness,** *n.* —**Syn. 2.** intelligent, wise, judicious. **5.** See **reasonable.** —**Ant. 2.** stupid. **3.** insane.

ra·tion·ale (rash′ə nal′), *n.* **1.** a statement of reasons. **2.** a reasoned exposition of principles. **3.** the fundamental body of reasons serving to account for something: *There seems to be no rationale to his behavior.* [< L *ratiōnāle*, neut. of *ratiōnālis* RATIONAL]

ra·tion·al·ise (rash′ə nəlīz′), *v.t., v.i.*, **-ised, -is·ing.** *Chiefly Brit.* rationalize. —**ra′tion·al·i·sa′tion,** *n.* —**ra′tion·al·is′er,** *n.*

ra·tion·al·ism (rash′ə nəliz′əm), *n.* **1.** the principle or habit of accepting reason as the supreme authority in matters of opinion, belief, or conduct. **2.** *Philos.* **a.** the doctrine that reason alone is a source of knowledge and is independent of experience. **b.** (in the philosophies of Descartes, Spinoza, etc.) the doctrine that all knowledge is expressible in self-evident propositions or their consequences. **3.** *Theol.* the doctrine that human reason, unaided by divine revelation, is an adequate or the sole guide to all attainable religious truth. —**ra′tion·al·ist,** *n.* —**ra′tion·al·is′tic, ra′tion·al·is′ti·cal,** *adj.* —**ra′tion·al·is′ti·cal·ly,** *adv.*

ra·tion·al·i·ty (rash′ə nal′i tē), *n., pl.* **-ties.** **1.** the state or quality of being rational. **2.** the possession of reason. **3.** agreeableness to reason; reasonableness. **4.** the exercise of reason. **5.** a reasonable view, practice, etc. [< LL *ratiōnālitās*. See RATIONAL, -ITY]

ra·tion·al·ize (rash′ə nəlīz′, rash′nəlīz′), *v.*, **-ized, -iz·ing.** —*v.t.* **1.** *Psychol.* to ascribe (one's acts, opinions, etc.) to causes that seem valid but actually are not the true, possibly unconscious causes. **2.** to remove unreasonable elements from. **3.** to make rational or conformable to reason. **4.** to treat or explain in a rational or rationalistic manner. **5.** *Math.* to eliminate radicals from (an equation or expression): *to rationalize the denominator of a fraction.* —*v.i.* **6.** to invent plausible explanations for acts, opinions, etc., that actually have other causes. **7.** to employ reason; think in a rational or rationalistic manner. Also, *esp. Brit.*, **rationalise.** —**ra′tion·al·i·za′tion,** *n.* —**ra′tion·al·iz′er,** *n.*

ra′tional num′ber, *Math.* a number that can be expressed exactly by a ratio of two integers.

Rat·is·bon (rat′is bon′, -iz-), *n.* Regensburg.

rat·ite (rat′īt), *adj.* *Ornithol.* **1.** having a flat, unkeeled sternum. —*n.* **2.** a bird having a ratite breastbone. [< L *rat(is)* raft, float + -ITE[2]]

rat·line (rat′lin), *n.* *Naut.* **1.** any of the small ropes or lines that traverse the shrouds horizontally and serve as steps for going aloft. **2.** Also, **rat′line stuff′,** three-stranded, right-laid, tarred hemp stuff of from 6 to 24 threads, used for ratlines, lashings, etc. Also, **rat′lin, rat′-lin, rattling.** [late ME *ratling, radelyng* < ?]

R, Ratline

ra·toon (ra to͞on′), *n.* **1.** a sprout or shoot from the root of a plant, esp. a sugarcane, after it has been cropped. —*v.i., v.t.* **2.** to put forth or cause to put forth ratoons. Also, **rattoon.** [< Sp *retoño* sprout < *retoñar* to sprout again in the fall = *re-* RE- + *(o)toñ(o)* AUTUMN + *-ar* inf. suffix] —**ra·toon·er,** *n.*

rat′ race′, *Informal.* any exhausting, unremitting activity or regular routine.

rats·bane (rats′bān′), *n.* **1.** rat poison. **2.** the trioxide of arsenic.

rat′ snake′, any of several New and Old World colubrid snakes, of the genus *Elaphe*, that feed chiefly on small mammals and birds. Also called **chicken snake.**

rat-tail (rat′tāl′), *n.* grenadier (def. 4). Also, **rat′tail′.**

rat′-tail file′, a slim file of circular cross section.

rat·tan (ra tan′), *n.* **1.** any of various climbing palms of the genus *Calamus* or allied genera. **2.** the tough stems of such palms, used for wickerwork, canes, etc. **3.** a stick or switch of this material. Also, **ratan.** [< Malay *rōtan*]

rat·ter (rat′ər), *n.* an animal used for catching rats, as a terrier or cat.

rat′ ter′rier, a terrier of any of several breeds developed esp. for catching rats, as the Manchester terrier.

rat·tle[1] (rat′əl), *v.*, **-tled, -tling,** *n.* —*v.i.* **1.** to give out or cause a rapid succession of short, sharp sounds, due to agitation, repeated concussions, or the like: *The windows rattled in their frames.* **2.** to move or go, esp. rapidly, with such sounds: *The car rattled along the highway.* **3.** to talk rapidly; chatter. —*v.t.* **4.** to cause to rattle. **5.** to drive, send, bring, etc., esp. rapidly, with rattling: *The wind rattled the metal can across the roadway.* **6.** to utter or perform in a rapid, lively, or facile manner (usually fol. by *off*): *to rattle off a speech.* **7.** to disconcert or confuse (a person). **8.** *Hunting.* to stir up (a cover). —*n.* **9.** a rapid succession of short, sharp sounds. **10.** a baby's toy, typically pellet-filled and producing a rattling noise when shaken. **11.** the series of horny, interlocking elements at the end of the tail of a rattlesnake, with which it produces a rattling sound. **12.** a rattling sound in the throat, as the death rattle. [ME *ratele(n)* (c. D *ratelen*, G *rasseln*); imit.] —**Syn. 1.** clatter.

rat·tle[2] (rat′əl), *v.t.*, **-tled, -tling.** *Naut.* to furnish with ratlines (usually fol. by *down*). [back formation from RATLINE (taken as verbal n.)]

rat·tle·brain (rat′əl brān′), *n.* a giddy, empty-headed, talkative person.

rat·tle·brained (rat′əl brānd′), *adj.* foolish; flighty; scatterbrained.

rat·tler (rat′lər), *n.* **1.** a rattlesnake. **2.** a person or thing that rattles. **3.** *Informal.* a fast freight train. [late ME]

rat·tle·snake (rat′əl snāk′), *n.* any of several New World pit vipers of the genera *Crotalus* and *Sistrurus*, having a rattle composed of a series of horny, interlocking elements at the end of the tail.

Rattlesnake, *Crotalus horridus* (Length 3½ to 6 ft.)

rat′tlesnake plan′tain, any of several low, terrestrial orchids, as *Goodyera repens*, of northern temperate regions.

rat′tlesnake root′, **1.** any of certain plants of the genus *Prenanthes* whose roots or tubers have been regarded as a remedy for snakebites, as *P. serpentaria* or *P. alba*. **2.** the snakeroot, *Polygala Senega*. **3.** the liliaceous plant, *Trillium cernuum*.

rat′tlesnake weed′, **1.** a hawkweed, *Hieracium venosum*, of eastern North America, whose leaves and root are thought to possess medicinal properties. **2.** a carrotlike weed, *Daucus pusillus*, of southern and western North America. **3.** any of certain other plants, as an umbelliferous plant, *Eryngium aquaticum*. **4.** See **rattlesnake plantain.**

rat·tle·trap (rat′əl trap′), *n.* a shaky, rattling object, as a rickety vehicle.

rat·tling[1] (rat′ling), *adj.* **1.** that rattles: *a rattling door.* **2.** remarkably good, lively, or fast: *a rattling party.* —*adv.* **3.** very: *a rattling good time.* [ME *rateling*]

rat·tling[2] (rat′lin), *n.* ratline.

rat·tly (rat′lē), *adj.* tending to rattle; making or having a rattling sound.

rat·ton (rat′ən), *n.* *Brit. Dial.* a rat. [ME *ratoun* < OF *raton*, dim. of *rat* RAT, ? < Gmc]

rat·toon (ra to͞on′), *n., v.i., v.t.* ratoon.

rat·trap (rat′trap′), *n.* **1.** a device for catching rats. **2.** a run-down, filthy, or dilapidated place.

rat·ty (rat′ē), *adj.*, **-ti·er, -ti·est.** **1.** full of rats. **2.** of or characteristic of a rat. **3.** wretched; shabby: *a ratty, old overcoat.*

rau·cous (rô′kəs), *adj.* harsh; strident; grating. [< L *rauc(us)* hoarse, harsh, rough + -OUS] —**rau′cous·ly,** *adv.* —**rau′cous·ness, rau·ci·ty** (rô′si tē), *n.*

raun·chy (rôn′chē, roun′-, rän′-), *adj.* *Slang.* **1.** being below standard; slovenly; careless. **2.** obscene; smutty: *a raunchy joke.* **3.** lecherous. [?]

Rausch·en·burg (roush′ən bûrg′), *n.* **Robert,** born 1925, U.S. artist.

rau·wol·fi·a (rô wo͝ol′fē ə), *n.* **1.** any tropical tree or shrub of the genus *Rauwolfia,* as *R. serpentina,* of India. **2.** an extract from the roots of *R. serpentina,* containing alkaloids the most important of which is reserpine: used in the treatment of hypertension and as a sedative. [< NL, named after L. *Rauwolf,* 16th-century German botanist; see -IA]

rav·age (rav′ij), *v.,* **-aged, -ag·ing,** *n.* —*v.t.* **1.** to work havoc upon; damage or mar by ravages. —*v.i.* **2.** to work havoc; do ruinous damage. —*n.* **3.** havoc; ruinous damage: *the ravages of war.* **4.** devastating or destructive action. [< F, MF = *rav(ir)* (to) RAVISH + *-age* -AGE] —**rav′age·ment,** *n.* —**rav′ag·er,** *n.*
—**Syn. 1.** ruin, despoil, plunder, pillage, sack. RAVAGE, DEVASTATE, LAY WASTE all refer, in their literal application, to the wholesale destruction of a countryside by an invading army (or something comparable). RAVAGE and DEVASTATE (the Latin equivalent of LAY WASTE) are also used in reference to other types of violent destruction and may have a purely figurative application. RAVAGE is often used of the results of epidemics: *The Black Plague ravaged Europe;* and even of the effect of disease or suffering on the human countenance: *a face ravaged by despair.* DEVASTATE, in addition to its concrete meaning (*vast areas devastated by bombs*), may also be used figuratively: *a devastating wit.* LAY WASTE has remained the closest to the original meaning of destruction of land: *The invading army laid waste the towns along the coast.* **3.** ruin, waste, desolation. —**Ant. 1.** build, repair. **4.** creation.

rave[1] (rāv), *v.,* **raved, rav·ing,** *n., adj.* —*v.i.* **1.** to talk wildly, as in delirium. **2.** (of a wind, water, storms, etc.) to make a wild or furious sound; rage. **3.** to express great or extravagant praise or admiration: *The critics raved over the play. She raved about her child's intelligence.* —*v.t.* **4.** to utter as if in madness. —*n.* **5.** an act of raving. **6.** an extravagantly enthusiastic appraisal or review of something, esp. a play. —*adj.* **7.** extravagantly enthusiastic in admiring or praising: *rave reviews of a new play.* [ME *rave(n),* prob. < MF *re(s)v(er)* (to) wander, be delirious] —**rav′er,** *n.*

rave[2] (rāv), *n.* a vertical sidepiece of the body of a wagon or sleigh. [alter. of dial. *rathe* (ME) < ?]

rav·el (rav′əl), *v.,* **-eled, -el·ing** or (*esp. Brit.*) **-elled, -el·ling,** *n.* —*v.t.* **1.** to disentangle or unravel the threads or fibers of (a woven or knitted fabric, rope, etc.). **2.** to tangle or entangle. **3.** to involve; confuse; perplex. **4.** to make clear; unravel. —*v.i.* **5.** to become disjoined thread by thread or fiber by fiber; fray. **6.** to become tangled. **7.** to become confused or perplexed. —*n.* **8.** a tangle or complication. [appar. < MD *ravel(en)* (to) entangle] —**rav′el·er;** *esp. Brit.,* **rav′el·ler,** *n.* —**rav′el·ly,** *adj.*

Ra·vel (rə vel′; *Fr.* RA vel′), *n.* **Mau·rice Jo·seph** (mō rēs′ zhô zef′), 1875–1937, French composer.

rave·lin (rav′lin), *n. Fort.* a V-shaped outwork outside the main ditch and covering the works between two bastions. [< MF, earlier *revelin* < It *rivellino,* dim. of *riva,* bank, rim]

rav·el·ing (rav′ə liṅg), *n.* something raveled out, as a thread drawn from a knitted or woven fabric. Also, *esp. Brit.,* **rav′el·ling.**

rav·el·ment (rav′əl mənt), *n.* entanglement; confusion.

ra·ven[1] (rā′vən), *n.* **1.** any of several large, corvine birds having lustrous, black plumage and a loud, harsh call, esp. *Corvus corax,* of the New and Old Worlds. —*adj.* **2.** of a lustrous black. [ME; OE *hrǣfn;* c. G *Rabe,* OIcel *hrafn*]

Raven, *Corvus corax* (Length 26 in.)

rav·en[2] (rav′ən), *v.i.* **1.** to seek plunder or prey. **2.** to eat or feed voraciously or greedily. **3.** to have a ravenous appetite. —*v.t.* **4.** to devour voraciously. **5.** *Obs.* to seize by force. —*n.* **6.** rapine; robbery. **7.** plunder or prey. Also, **ravin.** [ME *ravine* < MF < L *rapīn(a)* RAPINE]

rav·en·ing (rav′ə niṅg), *adj.* **1.** rapacious; voracious. —*n.* **2.** rapacity.

Ra·ven·na (rə ven′ə; *It.* RÄ ven′nä), *n.* a city in NE Italy: the capital of Italy in the period of the Byzantine Empire; tomb of Dante. 124,449 (1964).

rav·en·ous (rav′ə nəs), *adj.* **1.** extremely rapacious. **2.** extremely hungry; famished. **3.** extremely eager for satisfaction; desirous. [ME < OF *ravineus* = *ravin(er)* (to) RAVEN[2] + *-eus* -OUS] —**rav′en·ous·ly,** *adv.*
—**Syn. 1.** predatory. **2.** starved. RAVENOUS, VORACIOUS suggest a greediness for food and usually intense hunger. RAVENOUS implies extreme hunger, or a famished condition: *ravenous wild beasts.* VORACIOUS implies the eating of a great deal of food, or the disposition to eat a great deal, without reference to the degree of hunger: *a voracious small boy incessantly eating.* —**Ant. 1.** sated.

rav·in (rav′in), *v.i., v.t., n.* raven[2].

ra·vine (rə vēn′), *n.* a narrow, steep-sided valley, commonly one that has been eroded by running water. [ME < MF: torrent, OF: a violent rushing; see RAVEN]

rav·ing (rā′viṅg), *adj.* **1.** that raves; delirious; frenzied: *a raving maniac.* **2.** *Informal.* extraordinary or remarkable: *She's a raving beauty.* —*n.* **3.** irrational, incoherent talk. **4.** wildly extravagant or outrageous talk. —**rav′ing·ly,** *adv.*

ra·vi·o·li (rav′ē ō′lē, rä′vē-; *It.* RÄ vyô′lē), *n.* (*construed as sing. or pl.*) small, square envelopes of pasta filled with meat or cheese. [< It, pl. of dial. *raviolo* little turnip, dim. of *rava* < L *rāpa;* see RAPE[2]]

rav·ish (rav′ish), *v.t.* **1.** to seize and carry off by force. **2.** to carry off (a woman) by force. **3.** to rape (a woman). **4.** to fill with strong emotion, esp. joy. [ME *ravish(en)* < MF *raviss-* long s. of *ravir* to seize << L *rapere;* see RAPE[1]] —**rav′ish·er,** *n.* —**rav′ish·ment,** *n.*

rav·ish·ing (rav′i shiṅg), *adj.* entrancing; enchanting: *her ravishing beauty.* [ME; see RAVISH, -ING[2]]

raw (rô), *adj.* **1.** uncooked, as articles of food: *a raw carrot.* **2.** not having undergone processes of preparing, dressing, finishing, refining, or manufacture: *raw cotton.* **3.** unnaturally or painfully exposed, as flesh or a wound. **4.** crude in quality or character; not tempered or refined by art or taste. **5.** ignorant, inexperienced, or untrained: *a raw recruit.* **6.** brutally or grossly frank: *a raw portrayal of human passions.* **7.** brutally harsh or unfair: *a raw deal.* **8.** disagreeably damp and chilly, as the weather, air, etc. **9.** not diluted, as alcoholic spirits: *raw whiskey.* —*n.* **10.** a sore or irritated place, as an abrasion. **11. in the raw, a.** in the natural or unrefined state: *nature in the raw.* **b.** *Slang.* in the nude; naked. [ME; OE *hrēaw, hrǣw;* c. D *rauw,* G *roh;* akin to L *crūdus* raw, *cruor* blood, Gk *kréas* raw flesh] —**raw′ly,** *adv.* —**raw′ness,** *n.*
—**Syn. 1.** fresh. **2.** unprepared, rough. RAW, CRUDE RUDE refer to something not in a finished or highly refined state. RAW applies particularly to material not yet changed by a process, by manufacture, or by preparation for consumption: *raw cotton, leather.* CRUDE refers to that which still needs refining: *crude petroleum.* RUDE refers to what is still in a condition of rough simplicity or in a makeshift or roughly made form: *rude agricultural implements.* **5.** undisciplined, green, unskilled. **8.** cold, wet. **9.** straight, neat. —**Ant. 1.** prepared.

Ra·wal·pin·di (rä′wəl pin′de), *n.* a city in N Pakistan: its interim capital (1959–70). 343,000 (est. 1961).

raw·boned (rô′bōnd′), *adj.* having little flesh; gaunt.

raw′ fi′bers, textile fibers or filaments that have received no manipulation or treatment.

raw·hide (rô′hīd′), *n.* **1.** untanned skin of cattle or other animals. **2.** a rope or whip made of rawhide.

Raw·lings (rô′liṅgz), *n.* **Marjorie Kin·nan** (kin′ən), 1896–1953, U.S. novelist and journalist.

Raw·lin·son (rô′lin sən), *n.* **Sir Henry Cres·wicke** (krez′ik), 1810–95, English archaeologist, diplomat, and soldier.

raw′ mate′rial, material before being processed or manufactured into a final form: *Wool is a raw material of yarn.*

raw′ score′, the original score, as of a test, before it is statistically adjusted.

raw′ sien′na. See under **sienna** (def. 1).

raw′ silk′, reeled silk that has not had the sericin removed.

ray[1] (rā), *n.* **1.** a narrow beam of light. **2.** a slight manifestation; gleam: *a ray of hope.* **3.** a raylike line or stretch of something. **4.** a line of sight. **5.** *Physics, Optics.* **a.** any of the lines or streams in which light appears to radiate from a luminous body. **b.** the straight line normal to the wave front in the propagation of radiant energy. **c.** a stream of material particles all moving in the same straight line. **6.** *Math.* **a.** one of a system of straight lines emanating from a point. **b.** the part of a straight line considered as originating at a point on the line and as extending in one direction from that point. **7.** any part of a system of parts radially arranged. **8.** *Zool.* **a.** one of the branches or arms of a starfish or other radiate animal. **b.** one of the bony or cartilaginous rods in the fin of a fish. **9.** *Bot.* **a.** See **ray flower. b.** one of the branches of an umbel. **c.** See **vascular ray. d.** the marginal part of the flower head in certain composite plants. **10.** *Astron.* one of many long, bright streaks radiating from the large lunar craters. —*v.i.* **11.** to emit rays. **12.** to issue in rays. —*v.t.* **13.** to send forth in rays. **14.** to throw rays upon; irradiate. **15.** to subject to the action of rays, as in radiotherapy. **16.** to furnish with rays, or radiating lines. [ME *raie, raye* < OF *rai* < L *rad(ius)* RADIUS] —**Syn. 1.** See **gleam.**

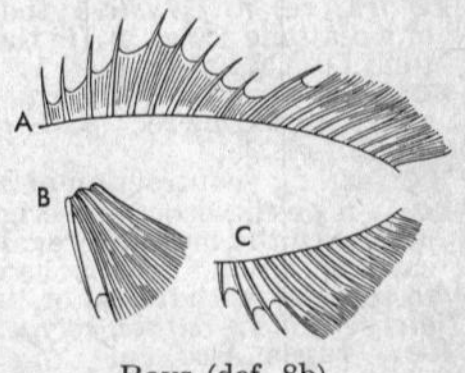

Rays (def. 8b)
A, Dorsal, with ten spines
B, Ventral, with one spine
C, Anal, with three spines

ray[2] (rā), *n.* any of numerous elasmobranch fishes having a flattened body adapted for life on the sea bottom and greatly enlarged pectoral fins with the gills on the undersides. [ME *raye* < L *rāia*]

Ray (rā), *n.* **Man** (man), 1890–1976, U.S. painter and photographer in France.

Ray·burn (rā′bûrn), *n.* **Sam(uel),** 1882–1961, U.S. lawyer and political leader: Speaker of the House 1940–47, 1949–53, 1955–61.

ray′ flow′er, *Bot.* one of the marginal florets surrounding the disk of tubular florets in the flower heads of certain composite plants. Also called **ray′ flo′ret.**

Ray·leigh (rā′lē), *n.* **John William Strutt** (strut), **3rd Baron,** 1842–1919, English physicist: Nobel prize 1904.

ray·less (rā′lis), *adj.* **1.** lacking rays or raylike parts. **2.** unlit, dark, or gloomy: *a rayless cave.*

ray·on (rā′on), *n.* **1.** a regenerated textile filament made from cellulose, cotton linters, etc., by passing a solution of any of these through spinnerets. **2.** fabric made of this filament. [< F = OF *rai* RAY[1] + *-on* dim. n. suffix]

Ray·town (rā′toun′), *n.* a city in W Missouri, near Kansas City. 33,306 (1970).

raze (rāz), *v.t.,* **razed, raz·ing.** to tear down; demolish; level to the ground. Also, **rase.** [ME *rase(n)* < MF *ras(er)* < *VL *rāsāre* to scrape, freq. of L *rādere*]

ra·zee (rā zē′), *n., v.,* **-zeed, -zee·ing.** —*n.* **1.** a sailing ship, esp. a warship, reduced in height by the removal of the upper deck. —*v.t.* **2.** to cut down (a ship) by removing the upper deck. [< F (*vaisseau*) *rasé* razed (ship), ptp. of *raser* to RAZE]

ra·zor (rā′zər), *n.* **1.** a sharp-edged instrument used esp. for shaving the face or trimming the hair. **2.** an electrically powered instrument used for the same purpose. —*v.t.* **3.** to shave, cut, or remove with or as with a razor. [ME *rasour* < OF *rasor* = *ras(er)* (to) RAZE + *-or* -OR[2]] —**ra′zor·less,** *adj.*

ra·zor·back (rā′zər bak′), *n.* **1.** a finback or rorqual. **2**

a wild or semiwild hog with a ridgelike back, common in the southern U.S.

ra′zor-billed auk′ (rā′zər bild′), a black and white auk, *Alca torda*, having a compressed black bill encircled by a white band. See illus. at **auk.** Also called **ra′zor·bill′.**

ra′zor clam′, any bivalve mollusk of the family *Solenidae*, esp. of the genus *Ensis*, as *E. directus* (**Atlan′tic ra′zor clam′**), having a long, rectangular, slightly curved shell.

razz (raz), *Slang.* —*v.t.* **1.** to deride; make fun of; tease. —*n.* **2.** raspberry (def. 4). [short for RASPBERRY]

raz·zle-daz·zle (raz′əl daz′əl), *n. Informal.* **1.** confusion, commotion, or riotous gaiety. **2.** *Chiefly Football.* deceptive action, esp. when flashily executed. **3.** showy and diverting but often meretricious activity. [rhyming compound based on DAZZLE]

razz·ma·tazz (raz′mə taz′), *n. Informal.* razzle-dazzle (def. 3). [by alter.]

Rb, *Chem.* rubidium.

RB-, *U.S. Mil.* (in designations of aircraft) reconnaissance bomber: *RB-57.*

R.B.I., *Baseball.* run batted in; runs batted in. Also, **RBI, rbi, r.b.i.**

R.C., **1.** Red Cross. **2.** Reserve Corps. **3.** Roman Catholic. Also, **RC**

R.C.A.F., Royal Canadian Air Force. Also, **RCAF**

R.C.Ch., Roman Catholic Church.

rcd., **1.** received. **2.** record.

R.C.M.P., Royal Canadian Mounted Police.

r-col·or (är′kul′ər), *n. Phonet.* a particular phonetic quality that results from a retroflex articulation. —**r′-col′ored,** *adj.*

rcpt., receipt.

Rct, **1.** receipt. **2.** *Mil.* recruit.

rd, rod; rods.

Rd., Road.

rd., **1.** rendered. **2.** road. **3.** rod; rods. **4.** round.

R.D., Rural Delivery.

RDA, **1.** (not in technical use) recommended daily allowance. **2.** recommended dietary allowance.

r-drop·ping (är′drop′ing), *adj. Phonet.* (of certain pronunciations of English) characterized by the absence of the sound *r* in postvocalic position in the same syllable, as often encountered in speech identified with the southern and eastern United States and with most of England; r-less.

Re (rā), *n. Egyptian Religion.* Ra.

Re, *Chem.* rhenium.

re[1] (rā, rē), *n. Music.* **1.** the syllable used for the second tone of a diatonic scale. **2.** (in the final system of solmization) the tone D. Cf. **sol-fa** (def. 1). [see GAMUT]

re[2] (rē), *prep. Chiefly Law and Com.* in the case of; with reference to; in re. [< L *rē* (in) the matter, affair, thing (abl. of *rēs*)]

're (ər, r), contraction of *are: How're you? They're here!*

re-, a prefix, occurring originally in loan words from Latin, used with the meaning "again" or "again and again" to indicate repetition, or with the meaning "back" or "backward" to indicate withdrawal or backward motion: *revert; regenerate; refurbish; retrace; retype.* Also, **red-.** [ME < L *re-, red-*]

Re., rupee. Also, **re.**

R.E., **1.** Reformed Episcopal. **2.** Right Excellent.

r.e., *Football.* right end.

REA, Rural Electrification Administration. Also, **R.E.A.**

reach (rēch), *v.t.* **1.** to get to or as far as; arrive at: *The boat reached the shore. His letter reached me.* **2.** to succeed in touching or seizing with an outstretched hand, a pole, etc.: *to reach a book on a high shelf.* **3.** to stretch or hold out; extend: *reaching out his hand in greeting.* **4.** to establish communication with: *I called but couldn't reach you. This program will reach a large audience.* **5.** to amount to, as in the sum or total: *The cost will reach millions.* **6.** to succeed in striking or hitting, as with a weapon or missile. —*v.i.* **7.** to make a stretch, as with the hand or arm. **8.** to become outstretched, as the hand or arm. **9.** to make a movement or effort as if to touch or seize something: *to reach for a gun.* **10.** to extend in operation or effect: *power that reaches throughout the land.* **11.** to stretch in space; extend in direction, length, distance, etc.: *a coat reaching to the knee.* **12.** to extend or continue in time. **13.** to get or come to a specified place, person, condition, etc. **14.** to amount (often fol. by *to*): *sums reaching to a considerable total.* **15.** to penetrate: *as far as the eye could reach.* **16.** *Naut.* **a.** to sail on a reach. **b.** to sail with the wind forward of the beam but so as not to require sailing close-hauled. —*n.* **17.** the act or an instance of reaching. **18.** the extent or distance of reaching: *within reach of his voice.* **19.** range of effective action, power, or capacity. **20.** a continuous stretch or extent of something: *a reach of woodland.* **21.** *Naut.* a point of sailing in which the wind is within a few points of the beam, either forward of the beam, directly abeam, or abaft the beam. **22.** the pole connecting the rear axle of a wagon to the transverse bar or bolster over the front axle supporting the wagon bed. **23.** a straight portion of a river between two bends. [ME *reche*, OE *rǣcan*; c. G *reichen*, D *reiken*] —**reach′a·ble,** *adj.* —**reach′er,** *n.* —**Syn. 1.** attain. **19.** area, sphere, scope.

reach-me-down (rēch′mē doun′), *n. Brit.* hand-me-down.

re-act (rē akt′, rē′-), *v.t.* to act or perform again. [RE- + ACT]

re·act (rē akt′), *v.i.* **1.** to act in response to an agent or influence. **2.** to act reciprocally upon each other, as two things. **3.** to act in a reverse direction or manner, esp. so as to return to a prior condition. **4.** to act in opposition, as against some force. **5.** to respond to a stimulus in a particular manner: *to react to a shock by jumping.* [RE- + ACT, prob. modeled on L *reagere*]

re·ac·tance (rē ak′təns), *n. Elect.* the opposition of inductance and capacitance to alternating current, equal to the product of the sine of the angular phase difference between current and voltage and the ratio of the effective voltage to the effective current. *Symbol:* X Cf. **capacitive reactance, inductive reactance.**

re·ac·tant (rē ak′tənt), *n.* **1.** a person or thing that reacts. **2.** *Chem.* any substance that undergoes a chemical change in a given reaction.

re·ac·tion (rē ak′shən), *n.* **1.** a reverse movement or tendency; an action in a reverse direction or manner. **2.** movement in the direction of extreme political conservatism or rightism. **3.** action in response to some influence, event, etc.: *the nation's reaction to the President's speech.* **4.** *Physiol.* action in response to a stimulus, as of the system or of a nerve or muscle. **5.** *Med.* **a.** the action caused by the resistance to another action. **b.** a return to the opposite physical condition, as after shock, exhaustion, or chill. **6.** *Bacteriol., Immunol.* the specific cellular effect produced by a foreign matter, as in testing for allergies. **7.** *Chem.* the reciprocal action of chemical agents upon each other; chemical change. **8.** Also called **nuclear reaction.** a process in which a nucleus that is bombarded by a photon, particle, or other nucleus, produces a nucleon, alpha particle, or the like, and a nucleus having approximately the same atomic weight as the original nucleus. **9.** *Mech.* the instantaneous response of a system to an applied force, manifested as the exertion of a force equal in magnitude but opposite in direction to the applied force. [RE- + ACTION, modeled on *react*] —**re·ac′tion·al,** *adj.* —**re·ac′tion·al·ly,** *adv.*

re·ac·tion·ar·y (rē ak′shə ner′ē), *adj., n., pl.* **-ar·ies.** —*adj.* **1.** of, pertaining to, marked by, or favoring reaction, as in politics. —*n.* **2.** a person who favors or inclines to reaction. Also, **re·ac′tion·ist.** [cf. F *réactionnaire*] —**re·ac′tion·ism, re·ac′tion·ar·ism,** *n.* —**Syn.** ultraconservative. —**Ant.** radical.

reac′tion en′gine, *Aeron., Rocketry.* any engine that produces power as a reaction to the momentum given to substances ejected from it, as a rocket or jet engine. Also called **reac′tion mo′tor.**

reac′tion forma′tion, *Psychoanal.* a behavioral tendency developed in direct opposition to a repressed impulse.

reac′tion time′, *Psychol.* the interval between stimulation and response.

re·ac·ti·vate (rē ak′tə vāt′), *v.,* **-vat·ed, -vat·ing.** —*v.t.* **1.** to render active again. —*v.i.* **2.** to be active again. —**re·ac′ti·va′tion,** *n.*

re·ac·tive (rē ak′tiv), *adj.* **1.** tending to react. **2.** pertaining to or characterized by reaction. **3.** *Elect.* pertaining to or characterized by reactance. —**re·ac′tive·ly,** *adv.* —**re′ac·tiv′i·ty, re·ac′tive·ness,** *n.*

re·ac·tor (rē ak′tər), *n.* **1.** a substance or person undergoing a reaction. **2.** *Elect.* a device whose primary purpose is to introduce reactance into a circuit. **3.** *Immunol., Vet. Med.* a patient or animal that reacts positively towards a foreign material. **4.** Also called **atomic pile, chain reactor, nuclear reactor, pile.** *Physics.* an apparatus in which a nuclear-fission chain reaction can be initiated, sustained, and controlled, for generating heat or producing useful radiation. **5.** *Chem.* (esp. in industry) a large container, as a vat, for processes in which the substances involved undergo a chemical reaction.

read[1] (rēd), *v.,* **read** (red), **read·ing** (rē′ding). —*v.t.* **1.** to look at carefully so as to understand the meaning of (something written, printed, etc.): *to read a book.* **2.** to utter aloud or render in speech (something written, printed, etc.): *reading a story to one's children.* **3.** to have such knowledge of (a language) as to be able to understand things written in it: *to read French.* **4.** to apprehend the meaning of (signs, characters, etc.) otherwise than with the eyes, as by means of the fingers: *to read Braille.* **5.** to recognize and understand the meaning of (signs, symbols, codes, or the like): *to read a semaphore.* **6.** to study the speech movements of (lips) so as to determine the words being spoken, as in total or partial deafness. **7.** to make out the significance of by scrutiny or observation: *to read the dark and cloudy sky.* **8.** to foresee, foretell, or predict: *to read a person's fortune in tea leaves.* **9.** to make out the character, motivations, desires, etc., of (a person or persons), as by the interpretation of outward signs. **10.** to infer (something not expressed) from what is read or considered (usually fol. by *into*): *He read sarcasm into her letter.* **11.** to adopt or give as a reading in a particular passage: *For "one thousand" another version reads "ten thousand."* **12.** to register or indicate, as a thermometer or clock. **13.** (in an electronic computer) **a.** to obtain (information), esp. from external units, as punch cards. **b.** to read (data) in or out. **14.** *Chiefly Brit.* to study, as at a university: *to read law.* **15.** to learn by or as by reading: *to read a person's thoughts.* **16.** to bring, put, etc., by reading: *to read oneself to sleep.* **17.** to give one (a lecture or lesson) by way of admonition or rebuke. **18.** to discover or explain the meaning of (a riddle, dream, etc.). —*v.i.* **19.** to read or peruse written or printed matter. **20.** to utter aloud or render in speech written or printed words that one is perusing: *to read to a person.* **21.** to give a public reading or recital. **22.** to inspect and apprehend the meaning of written or other signs or characters. **23.** to occupy oneself seriously with reading or study. **24.** to obtain knowledge or learn of some subject by reading. **25.** to admit of being read as specified: *His story reads well.* **26.** to have a certain wording. **27.** to admit of being interpreted: *a rule that reads two different ways.* **28.** (of an electronic computer) to read data. **29. read in,** to introduce formation into a computer. **30. read out, a.** to oust (a member of a political party or other group) by a public announcement of dismissal. **b.** to retrieve information from a computer. [ME *rede(n)*, OE *rǣdan* to counsel, read; c. D *raden*, G *raten*, OIcel *rādha;* akin to Skt *rādhnōti* achieves]

read[2] (red), *adj.* having knowledge gained by reading (usually used in combination): *a well-read person.* [ptp. of READ[1]]

Read (rēd), *n.* **1. George,** 1733–98, American political

re′a·ban′don, *v.t.*
re′ab·sorb′, *v.t.*
re′ab·sorp′tion, *n.*
re′ac·cede′, *v.t.,* **-ced·ed, -ced·ing.**
re·ac′cent, *v.t.*
re′ac·cept′, *v.t.*
re′ac·claim′, *v.t.*
re·ac′cli·mate′, *v.,* **-mat·ed, -mat·ing.**
re′ac·com′mo·date′, *v.,* **-dat·ed, -dat·ing.**
re′ac·com′pa·ny, *v.t.,* **-nied, -ny·ing.**
re′ac·cred′it, *v.t.*
re′ac·cuse′, *v.t.,* **-cused, -cus·ing.**
re′ac·cus′tom, *v.t.*
re′a·cid′i·fy′, *v.,* **-fied, -fy·ing.**
re′ac·quaint′, *v.t.*
re′ac·quaint′ance, *n.*
re′ac·quire′, *v.t.,* **-quired, -quir·ing.**
re′ac·qui·si′tion, *n.*

leader: president of the Continental Congress 1777–78. **2. Sir Herbert,** 1893–1968, English critic and poet.

read·a·ble (rē′də bəl), *adj.* **1.** easy or interesting to read. **2.** capable of being read; legible: *readable handwriting.* **—read′a·bil′i·ty, read′a·ble·ness,** *n.* **—read′a·bly,** *adv.*

Reade (rēd), *n.* **Charles,** 1814–84, English novelist.

read·er (rē′dər), *n.* **1.** a person who reads. **2.** a schoolbook for instruction and practice in reading. **3.** a person employed to read and evaluate manuscripts. **4.** a person who reads or recites before an audience; elocutionist. **5.** a person authorized to read the lessons, Bible, etc., in a church service. **6.** a lecturer or instructor, esp. in some British universities. **7.** an assistant to a professor, who grades examinations, papers, etc. [ME *redir(e), redar(e),* OE *rædere*]

read·er·ship (rē′dər ship′), *n.* **1.** the people who read a particular book, newspaper, magazine, etc. **2.** the duty, status, or profession of a reader.

read·i·ly (red′ᵊlē), *adv.* **1.** promptly; quickly; easily. **2.** in a ready manner; willingly. [ME *redily*]

read·i·ness (red′ē nis), *n.* **1.** the condition of being ready. **2.** ready action or movement; promptness; quickness; ease; facility. **3.** willingness; inclination; cheerful consent.

read·ing (rē′ding), *n.* **1.** the action or practice of a person who reads. **2.** *Speech.* the oral interpretation of written language. **3.** the interpretation given in the performance of a dramatic part, musical composition, etc.: *an interesting reading of the Beethoven 5th.* **4.** the extent to which a person has read; literary knowledge: *a man of wide reading.* **5.** matter read or for reading: *light reading.* **6.** the form or version of a given passage in a particular text: *the various readings of a line in Shakespeare.* **7.** an interpretation given to anything: *What is your reading of the situation?* **8.** the indication of a graduated instrument: *The thermometer reading is 101.2°.* **—***adj.* **9.** pertaining to or used for reading. **10.** given to reading: *the reading public.* [ME *redyng*]

Read·ing (red′ing), *n.* **1.** a city in and the county seat of Berkshire, in S England. 132,900. **2.** a city in SE Pennsylvania. 87,643 (1970).

read′ing desk′, a high desk for holding the text, notes, etc., of a speaker; lectern.

read′ing room′, a room set aside for reading, as in a library or club.

re·ad·just (rē′ə just′), *v.t.* to adjust again or anew; rearrange. **—re′ad·just′a·ble,** *adj.* **—re′ad·just′er,** *n.*

re·ad·just·ment (rē′ə just′mənt), *n.* **1.** an act of readjusting. **2.** the state of being readjusted. **3.** *Finance.* a rearrangement in the financial structure of a corporation, usually less drastic than a reorganization.

read′ on′ly mem′ory′ *Computer Technol.* See **ROM.** Also, **read′-on′ly mem′ory.**

read·out (rēd′out′), *n.* **1.** *Computer Technol.* the output of information from a computer in readable form, as on a video display unit or a printer. **2.** the information displayed on a graduated instrument.

read·y (red′ē), *adj.,* **read·i·er, read·i·est,** *v.,* **read·ied, read·y·ing,** *n., interj.* **—***adj.* **1.** completely prepared, in fit condition, or immediately available for action or use. **2.** willing or not hesitant: *ready to forgive.* **3.** prompt or quick in perceiving, comprehending, speaking, writing, etc. **4.** proceeding from or showing such quickness: *a ready reply.* **5.** prompt or quick in action, performance, manifestation, etc.: *a keen mind and ready wit.* **6.** inclined; disposed; apt: *too ready to criticize others.* **7.** in such a condition as to be imminent; likely at any moment: *a tree ready to fall.* **8.** immediately available for use: *ready money.* **9.** present or convenient. **10. make ready, a.** to bring to a state of readiness or completion; prepare. **b.** *Print.* to prepare and adjust a press for printing. **—***v.t.* **11.** to make ready; prepare. **12. ready about!** *Naut.* prepare to tack! **—***n.* **13. the ready, a.** *Informal.* ready money; cash. **b.** the condition or position of being ready for use: *to bring a rifle to the ready.* **—***interj.* **14.** (in calling the start of a race) be prepared to start: *Ready! Set! Go!* [ME *redy,* early ME *rædig,* OE *rǣde* prompt] **—Syn. 1.** fitted, fit, set. **2.** agreeable, glad, happy.

read·y-made (red′ē mād′), *adj.* **1.** made in advance for sale to any purchaser, rather than to order: *a ready-made coat.* **2.** made for immediate use. **3.** unoriginal; conventional. **—***n.* **4.** something that is ready-made, esp. a garment.

read·y-mix (red′ē miks′, -miks′), *n.* **1.** a commercial preparation already mixed for easy use: *a bride's reliance on ready-mixes.* **—***adj.* **2.** Also, **read′y-mixed′.** consisting of ingredients that are already mixed: *ready-mix pancakes.*

read′y room′, a room in which members of an aircrew await their orders for takeoff.

read·y-to-wear (red′ē tə wâr′), *n.* **1.** clothing made in standard sizes. **—***adj.* **2.** pertaining to or dealing in such clothing.

read·y-wit·ted (red′ē wit′id), *adj.* having a quick wit or intelligence.

Rea·gan (rā′gən), *n.* **Ronald (Wilson),** born 1911, 40th president of the U.S. 1981–89.

re·a·gent (rē ā′jənt), *n.* *Chem.* a substance that, because of the reactions it causes, is used in analysis and synthesis. [RE- + AGENT, modeled on REACT]

re·al[1] (rē′əl, rēl), *adj.* **1.** true; not merely ostensible or nominal. **2.** actual rather than imaginary, ideal, or fictitious. **3.** having actual, rather than imaginary, existence: *real events.* **4.** being actually such; not merely so-called: *a real victory.* **5.** genuine; authentic. **6.** unfeigned or sincere: *real sympathy; a real friend.* **7.** *Philos.* **a.** existent or pertaining to the existent as opposed to the nonexistent. **b.** actual as opposed to possible or potential. **c.** independent of experience as opposed to phenomenal or apparent. **8.** of or pertaining to real property. **9.** *Math.* **a.** of, pertaining to, or having the value of a real number. **b.** using real numbers: *real analysis; real vector space.* **—***adv.* **10.** *Informal.* very or extremely: *a real nice job.* **—***n.* **11.** *Math.* See **real number.** [ME < LL *reālis* = L *rē(s)* thing + *-ālis* -AL[1]] **—re′al·ness,** *n.*

re·al[2] (rē′əl, rēl; *Sp.* RE äl′), *n., pl.* **re·als** (rē′əlz, rēlz), *Sp.* **re·a·les** (RE ä′les). a former silver coin of Spain and Spanish America, the eighth part of a peso. [< Sp: royal < L *rēgāl(is)* REGAL]

re·al[3] (rā äl′; *Port.* RE äl′), *n.* sing. of **reis.**

re′al estate′ (rē′əl, rēl), **1.** property, esp. in land. **2.** See **real property.** **—re′al-es·tate′,** *adj.*

re·al·gar (rē al′gər), *n.* arsenic disulfide, As_2S_2, found native as an orange-red mineral and also produced artificially: used in pyrotechnics. [< ML *realger* < < Ar *rahj al-ghar* powder of the mine or cave]

re·a·li·a (rē ā′lē ə, rā ä′lē ə), *n.pl.* *Educ.* objects, as coins or tools, used by a teacher to illustrate everyday living. [< LL: real things (neut. pl.); see REAL[1]]

re′al in′come (rē′əl, rēl), the amount of goods and services that money income will buy.

re·al·ise (rē′ə līz′), *v.,* **-ised, -is·ing.** *Chiefly Brit.* realize.

re·al·ism (rē′ə liz′əm), *n.* **1.** interest in or concern for the actual or real, as distinguished from the abstract, speculative, etc. **2.** the tendency to view or represent things as they really are. **3.** *Fine Arts.* treatment of forms, colors, space, etc., as they appear in actuality or ordinary visual experience. Cf. **idealism** (def. 4). **4.** *Literature.* a theory of writing in which familiar aspects of life are represented in a straightforward or matter-of-fact manner. **5.** *Philos.* **a.** the doctrine that universals have a real objective existence. Cf. **conceptualism, nominalism. b.** the doctrine that objects of sense perception have an existence independent of the act of perception. Cf. **idealism** (def. 5). [REAL[1] + -ISM]

re·al·ist (rē′ə list), *n.* **1.** a person who tends to view or represent things as they really are. **2.** an artist or a writer whose work is characterized by realism. **3.** *Philos.* an adherent of realism. [REAL[1] + -IST; cf. F *réaliste*]

re·al·is·tic (rē′ə lis′tik), *adj.* **1.** concerned with or based on what is real or practical: *a realistic estimate of costs; a realistic planner.* **2.** characterized by or given to the representation in literature or art of things as they really are: *a realistic novel.* **3.** *Philos.* of or pertaining to realists or realism. **—re′al·is′ti·cal·ly,** *adv.*

re·al·i·ty (rē al′i tē), *n., pl.* **-ties** for 3, 4. **1.** the state or quality of being real. **2.** resemblance to what is real. **3.** a real thing or fact. **4.** *Philos.* **a.** something that exists independently of ideas concerning it. **b.** something that exists independently of all other things and from which all other things derive. **5. in reality,** in fact or truth; actually. [< ML *reālitāt-* (s. of *reālitās*)]

re·al·i·za·tion (rē′ə li zā′shən *or, esp. Brit.,* -lī-), *n.* **1.** the act of realizing. **2.** the state of being realized. **3.** an instance or result of realizing. **4.** *Music.* **a.** the act of realizing a figured bass. **b.** a printed score of a realized figured bass. Also, *esp. Brit.,* **realisation.** [< F *réalisation,* MF]

re·al·ize (rē′ə līz′), *v.,* **-ized, -iz·ing.** **—***v.t.* **1.** to grasp or understand clearly. **2.** to make real; give reality to (a hope, fear, plan, etc.). **3.** to convert into cash or money: *to realize securities.* **4.** to obtain as a profit or income for oneself. **5.** to bring as proceeds, as from a sale. **6.** *Music.* to sight-read or write out in notation the full harmony and ornamentation indicated by (a figured bass). **—***v.i.* **7.** to convert property or goods into cash or money. Also, *esp. Brit.,* **realise.** [< F *réalise(r),* MF; see REAL[1], -IZE] **—re′al·iz′a·ble,** *adj.* **—re′al·iz′a·bly,** *adv.* **—re′al·iz′er,** *n.* **—Syn. 1.** conceive.

re·al·iz·ing (rē′ə lī′zing), *adj.* showing clear perception: aware. Also, *esp. Brit.,* **realising.** **—re′al·iz′ing·ly,** *adv.*

re-al·ly (rē′ə lī′), *v.t., v.i.,* **-lied, -ly·ing.** to ally again or anew. [ME *realy*]

re·al·ly (rē′ə lē, rē′lē), *adv.* **1.** in reality; actually: *to see things as they really are.* **2.** genuinely or truly: *a really honest man.* **3.** indeed: *Really, this is too much.* **—***interj.* **4.** (used to express surprise, exasperation, etc.) [ME]

realm (relm), *n.* **1.** a royal domain; kingdom: *the realm of England.* **2.** the region, sphere, or domain within which anything occurs, prevails, or dominates: *the realm of dreams.* [ME *realme, reaume* < OF *reialme* < *reial* < L *rēgāl(is)* REGAL]

re′al num′ber (rē′əl, rēl), *Math.* a rational number or the limit of a sequence of rational numbers, as opposed to a complex number. Also called **real.**

re·al·po·li·tik (rē äl′pō′li tēk′), *n.* political realism, esp. policy based on power rather than on ideals. [< G]

re′al prop′erty (rē′əl, rēl), *Law.* an estate or property consisting of lands and all appurtenances to lands, as buildings, crops, or mineral rights.

re′al time′ (rē′əl, rēl), **1.** *Computer Technol.* the actual time elapsed in the performance of a computation by a computer, the result of the computation being required for the continuation of a physical process. **2. in real time,** *Informal.* at once; instantaneously. **—re′al-time′,** *adj.*

Re·al·tor (rē′əl tər, -tôr′), *n.* *Trademark.* a person in the real-estate business who is a member of the National Association of Realtors. [REALT(Y) + -OR[2]]

re·al·ty (rē′əl tē), *n.* real property or real estate. [ME]

re′al wag′es (rē′əl, rēl), wages estimated in purchasing power. Cf. **nominal wages.**

ream[1] (rēm), *n.* **1.** a standard quantity of paper, consisting of 20 quires or 500 sheets (formerly 480 sheets), or of 516 sheets (**printer's ream** or **perfect ream**). **2.** Usually, **reams.** a large quantity, as of writing. [ME *rem(e)* < MF *reime, rame* < Sp *rezma* < Ar *rizmah* bale]

ream[2] (rēm), *v.t.* to enlarge to desired size (a previously bored hole) by means of a reamer. [ME *reme,* OE *rēman* to open up (? var. of *rӯman* to widen); see ROOM]

re′a·dapt′, *v.t.*
re′ad·ap·ta′tion, *n.*
re·add′, *v.t.*
re′ad·dress′, *v.t.,* **-dressed** or **-drest, -dres·sing.**
re′ad·journ′, *v.*
re′ad·journ′ment, *n.*
re′ad·mis′sion, *n.*
re′ad·mit′, *v.,* **-mit·ted, -mit·ting.**
re′ad·mit′tance, *n.*
re′a·dopt′, *v.t.*
re′af·firm′, *v.t.*
re′af·fir·ma′tion, *n.*
re′a·lign′, *v.*
re′a·lign′ment, *n.*
re·al′lo·cate′, *v.t.,* **-cat·ed, -cat·ing.**
re′al·lo·ca′tion, *n.*
re′al·lot′, *v.t.,* **-lot·ted, -lot·ting.**
re′al·lot′ment, *n.*
re·al′ter, *v.*
re′al·ter·a′tion, *n.*

ream·er (rē′mər), *n.* any of various rotary tools, with helical or straight flutes, for finishing or enlarging holes drilled in metal.

re·an·i·mate (rē an′ə māt′), *v.t.,* **-mat·ed -mat·ing.** **1.** to give fresh vigor, spirit, or courage to. **2.** to restore to life; resuscitate. **—re·an′i·ma′tion,** *n.*

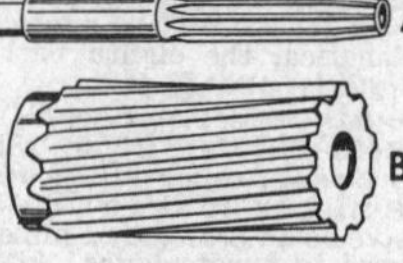

Reamers
A, Parallel hand reamer
B, Shell reamer

reap (rēp), *v.t.* **1.** to cut (wheat, rye, etc.) with a sickle or other implement or a machine, as in harvest. **2.** to gather or take (a crop, harvest, etc.). **3.** to get as a return, recompense, or result: *to reap large profits.* **—***v.i.* **4.** to reap a crop, harvest, etc. [ME *rep(en),* OE *repan, riopan;* c. MLG *repen* to ripple (flax); akin to RIPE] **—reap′a·ble,** *adj.*

reap·er (rē′pər), *n.* **1.** a machine for cutting standing grain; reaping machine. **2.** a person who reaps. **3. the Reaper.** Also called **Grim Reaper.** a personification of death as a human skeleton holding a scythe. [ME *reper,* OE *ripere*]

reap′ing machine′, any of various machines for reaping grain, often fitted with a device for bundling the cut grain.

re·ap·por·tion (rē′ə pōr′shən, -pôr′-), *v.t.* to apportion or distribute anew.

re·ap·por·tion·ment (rē′ə pōr′shən mənt, -pôr′-), *n.* **1.** the act of redistributing or changing the apportionment of something. **2.** the redistribution of representation in a legislative body.

rear[1] (rēr), *n.* **1.** the back of something, as distinguished from the front. **2.** the space or position at the back of something: *to move to the rear.* **3.** the buttocks; rump. **4.** the hindmost portion of an army, fleet, etc. **5. bring up the rear,** to be at the end; follow behind. **—***adj.* **6.** pertaining to or situated at the rear. [aph. var. of ARREAR] **—Syn. 6.** See **back**[1].

rear[2] (rēr), *v.t.* **1.** to take care of and support up to maturity: *to rear a child.* **2.** to raise by building; erect. **3.** to raise to an upright position: *to rear a ladder.* **—***v.i.* **4.** to rise on the hind legs, as a horse. **5.** to rise high, as a building or tower. [ME *rere(n),* OE *rǣran* to RAISE; c. Goth *-raisjan,* OIcel *reisa*] **—Syn. 1.** nurture, raise. **2.** construct.

Rear Adm., Rear Admiral.

rear′ ad′miral, a naval officer next in rank below a vice admiral.

rear′ ech′elon, (in a military operation) the troops, officers, etc., removed from the combat zone and responsible for administration, matériel, etc.

rear′ end′, **1.** the hindmost part of something. **2.** *Informal.* the buttocks; behind. Also called **tail end.**

rear′ guard′, a part of a military force detached from the main body to bring up and guard the rear from surprise attack, esp. in a retreat. [late ME *rier garde* < AF *reregard,* OF *rereguarde*]

re·arm (rē ärm′), *v.t.* **1.** to arm again, as a nation in preparation for war. **2.** to furnish with new or better weapons. **—re·ar·ma·ment** (rē är′mə mənt), *n.*

rear·most (rēr′mōst′), *adj.* farthest in the rear; last.

rear′ sight′, the sight nearest the breech of a gun.

rear·ward (rēr′wərd), *adj., adv.* **1.** Also, **rear′wards.** toward or in the rear. **—***n. Archaic.* **2.** a position at the rear. **3.** the rear division of a military unit. [ME *rerewarde* < AF]

Re′a Sil′via (rē′ə), *Rom. Legend.* See **Rhea Silvia.**

rea·son (rē′zən), *n.* **1.** a basis or circumstance explaining some belief, action, fact, or event. **2.** a statement presented in justification or explanation. **3.** the mental powers concerned with forming conclusions, judgments, or inferences. **4.** sound judgment; good sense. **5.** soundness of mind; sanity. **6.** *Logic.* a premise of an argument. **7.** *Philos.* **a.** the faculty or power of acquiring intellectual knowledge, either by direct understanding of first principles or by argument. **b.** the power of intelligent and dispassionate thought, or of conduct influenced by such thought. **8. by reason of,** because of. **9. in** or **within reason,** in accord with reason; proper. **10. stand to reason,** to be clear, obvious, or logical: *It stands to reason that we shall succeed.* **11. with reason,** with justification; properly. **—***v.i.* **12.** to think or argue in a logical manner. **13.** to form conclusions, judgments, or inferences from facts or premises. **—***v.t.* **14.** to think through logically, as a problem. **15.** to conclude or infer (usually fol. by *that*). **16.** to convince, persuade, etc., by reasoning. **17.** to support with reasons. [ME *resoun, reisun* < OF *reison, reson* < L *ratiōn-* (s. of *ratiō*) RATIO] **—rea′son·er,** *n.*
—Syn. 1. purpose, end, aim, object, objective. REASON, CAUSE, MOTIVE are terms for a circumstance (or circumstances) that brings about or explains certain results. A REASON is an explanation of a situation or circumstance that made certain results seem possible or appropriate: *The reason for the robbery was the victim's display of his money.* The CAUSE is the way in which the circumstances produce the effect, that is, make a specific action seem necessary or desirable: *The cause was the robber's extreme need of money.* A MOTIVE is the hope, desire, or other force that starts the action (or an action) in an attempt to produce specific results: *The motive was to get money to buy food for his family.* **2.** excuse, rationale, rationalization. **3.** understanding, intellect, mind, intelligence.
—Usage. Careful writers and speakers avoid the redundant expression "the reason is because." Instead, use "the reason is that": *He said that the reason he isn't coming is that* (not *because*) *his mother won't let him.*

rea·son·a·ble (rē′zə nə bəl, rēz′nə-), *adj.* **1.** agreeable to or in accord with reason or sound judgment; logical. **2.** not exceeding the limit prescribed by reason; not excessive: *reasonable terms.* **3.** moderate in price; not expensive. **4.** endowed with reason. **5.** capable of rational behavior, decision, etc. [ME *resonable* < MF *raisonnable* < L *ratiōnābil(is)*] **—rea′son·a·ble·ness, rea′son·a·bil′i·ty,** *n.* **—rea′son·a·bly,** *adv.*
—Syn. 1. sensible, intelligent, judicious, wise, equitable. REASONABLE, RATIONAL refer to the faculty of reasoning. REASONABLE has taken on more and more the pragmatic idea of simple common sense: *A reasonable supposition is one that appeals to our common sense.* RATIONAL is the more technical or more abstract term, concerned always with pure reason. It is applied to statements that reflect or satisfy highly logical thinking: *Her conclusions are always of a rational, never an emotional, nature.* **2.** equitable, fair, just.

rea·soned (rē′zənd), *adj.* **1.** based on reason. **2.** containing reasons: *a long, reasoned reply.* **—rea′soned·ly,** *adv.*

rea·son·ing (rē′zə ning), *n.* **1.** the act or process of a person who reasons. **2.** the process of forming conclusions, judgments, or inferences from facts or premises. **3.** the reasons, arguments, proofs, etc., resulting from this process. [ME *resoninge*] **—rea′son·ing·ly,** *adv.*

rea·son·less (rē′zən lis), *adj.* **1.** not having any reason or justification; senseless: *an utterly reasonless display of anger.* **2.** not having a natural capacity for reason. [ME *resonles*]

re·as·sure (rē′ə shŏŏr′), *v.t.,* **-sured, -sur·ing.** **1.** to restore to assurance or confidence: *His praise reassured me.* **2.** to assure again. **3.** to reinsure. **—re′as·sur′ance,** *n.* **—re·as·sur·ed·ly** (rē′ə shŏŏr′id lē), *adv.* **—re′as·sure′ment,** *n.* **—re′as·sur′ing·ly,** *adv.* **—Syn. 1.** encourage, hearten, comfort, inspirit.

re·a·ta (rē ä′tə), *n.* riata.

Réaum., Réaumur (temperature).

Ré·au·mur (rā′ə myŏŏr′; *Fr.* RA ō MYR′), *n.* **1. René Antoine Fer·chault de** (rə nā′ äN twan′ fer shō′ də), 1683–1757, French physicist and inventor. **—***adj.* **2.** Also, **Re′au·mur′.** noting or pertaining to a temperature scale (**Re′aumur scale′**) in which 0° represents the ice point and 80° represents the steam point. See illus. at **thermometer.**

reave[1] (rēv), *v.t.,* **reaved** or **reft, reav·ing.** *Archaic.* to take away by or as by force; plunder; rob. [ME *reve(n),* OE *rēafian;* c. G *rauben,* D *rooven* to ROB]

reave[2] (rēv), *v.t., v.i.,* **reaved** or **reft, reav·ing.** to rend; break; tear. [appar. special use of REAVE[1] (by assoc. with RIVE)]

reb (reb), *n. U.S. Informal.* a Confederate soldier. [shortened form of REBEL]

Reb (reb), *n. Yiddish.* Mister (used as a title of respect). [lit., rabbi]

re·bate[1] (rē′bāt, ri bāt′), *n., v.,* **-bat·ed, -bat·ing.** **—***n.* **1.** a refund of part of the original payment for some service or charge. **—***v.t.* **2.** to allow as a rebate. **3.** to deduct (a certain amount), as from a total. **4.** to return (part of an original payment). **5.** to blunt (an edged or pointed weapon). [ME *rebate(n)* < OF *rabat(re)* (to) beat, put down = *re-* RE- + *(a)batre;* see ABATE] **—re·bat′a·ble, re·bate′a·ble,** *adj.* **—re′bat·er,** *n.*

re·bate[2] (rē′bāt, rab′it), *n., v.,* **-bat·ed, -bat·ing.** rabbet.

re·ba·to (rə bä′tō), *n., pl.* **-tos.** rabato.

re·bec (rē′bek), *n.* a Renaissance fiddle with a pear-shaped body tapering into a neck that ends in a sickle-shaped or scroll-shaped pegbox. Also, **re′beck.** [< MF; r. ME *ribibe* < OF *rebebe* << Ar *rebāb*]

Rebec

Re·bek·ah (ri bek′ə), *n.* the sister of Laban, wife of Isaac, and mother of Esau and Jacob. Gen. 24–27.

reb·el (*n., adj.* reb′əl; *v.* ri bel′), *n., adj., v.,* **-belled, -bel·ling.** **—***n.* **1.** a person who refuses allegiance to, resists, or rises in arms against the government or ruler of his country. **2.** a person who resists any authority, control, or tradition. **—***adj.* **3.** rebellious; defiant. **4.** of or pertaining to rebels. **—***v.i.* **5.** to act as a rebel. **6.** to show or feel utter repugnance. [ME < OF *rebelle* < L *rebell(is)* renewing a war = *re-* RE- + *bell(um)* war + *-is* adj. suffix] **—Syn. 1.** insurrectionist, mutineer, traitor. **1, 3.** insurgent. **3.** mutinous. **5.** revolt, mutiny. **—Ant. 1.** patriot. **3.** loyal.

reb·el·dom (reb′əl dəm), *n.* **1.** a region or territory controlled by rebels. **2.** rebels collectively. **3.** rebellious conduct.

re·bel·lion (ri bel′yən), *n.* **1.** an open, armed resistance to one's government or ruler. **2.** resistance to or defiance of any authority, control, or tradition. [ME *rebellioun* < OF < L *rebelliōn-* (s. of *rebelliō*) = *rebell(āre)* (to) REBEL + *-iōn-* -ION] **—Syn. 1.** mutiny, sedition. See **revolt. 2.** insubordination, disobedience.

re·bel·lious (ri bel′yəs), *adj.* **1.** defying or resisting some established authority, tradition, etc.; insubordinate. **2.** pertaining to or characteristic of rebels or rebellion. **3.** (of things or animals) resisting treatment or management; refractory: *a rebellious horse; long, rebellious hair.* [ME < ML *rebelliōs(us)* = L *rebelli(ō)* REBELLION + *-ōsus* -OUS]

re′a·nal′y·sis, *n., pl.* **-ses.**
re·an′a·lyze′, *v.t.,* **-lyzed, -lyz·ing.**
re′ap·pear′, *v.i.*
re′ap·pear′ance, *n.*
re′ap·pli·ca′tion, *n.*
re′ap·ply′, *v.,* **-plied, -ply·ing.**
re′ap·point′, *v.t.*
re′ap·point′ment, *n.*
re′ap·prais′al, *n.*
re′ap·praise′, *v.t.,* **-praised, -prais·ing.**
re·ar′gue, *v.,* **-gued, -gu·ing.**
re′a·rous′al, *n.*
re′a·rouse′, *v.,* **-roused, -rous·ing.**
re′ar·range′, *v.,* **-ranged, -rang·ing.**
re′ar·range′ment, *n.*
re′ar·rest′, *v.t., n.*
re′as·cend′, *v.*
re′as·cent′, *n.*
re′as·sem′ble, *v.,* **-bled, -bling.**
re′as·sem′bly, *n., pl.* **-blies.**
re′as·sert′, *v.t.*
re′as·ser′tion, *n.*
re′as·sess′, *v.t.*
re′as·sess′ment, *n.*
re′as·sign′, *v.t.*
re′as·sign′ment, *n.*
re′as·sim′i·late′, *v.,* **-lat·ed, -lat·ing.**
re′as·sim′i·la′tion, *n.*
re′as·sort′, *v.*
re′as·sort′ment, *n.*
re′as·sume′, *v.t.,* **-sumed, -sum·ing.**
re′as·sump′tion, *n.*
re′at·tach′, *v.*
re′at·tach′ment, *n.*
re′at·tain′, *v.t.*
re′at·tain′ment, *n.*
re′at·tempt′, *v.t.*
re′a·vow′, *v.t.*
re′a·wake′, *v.,* **-woke** or **-waked, -wak·ing.**
re′a·wak′en, *v.*
re·bap′tism, *n.*
re′bap′tize, *v.,* **-tized, -tiz·ing.**

—**re·bel′lious·ly,** *adv.* —**re·bel′lious·ness,** *n.* —**Syn. 1.** defiant, mutinous, seditious, refractory, disobedient.

re·birth (rē bûrth′, rē′bûrth′), *n.* **1.** a new or second birth: *the rebirth of the soul.* **2.** a renewed existence, activity, or growth; renaissance; revival.

reb·o·ant (reb′ō ənt), *adj.* resounding or reverberating loudly. [< L *reboant-* (s. of *reboāns,* prp. of *reboāre*) = *re-* RE- + *bo(āre)* (to) cry aloud (c. Gk *boân*) + *-ant-* -ANT]

re·born (rē bôrn′), *adj.* having undergone rebirth.

re·bound (*v.* ri bound′; *n.* rē′bound′, ri bound′), *v.i.* **1.** to bound or spring back from force of impact. —*v.t.* **2.** to cause to bound back; cast back. —*n.* **3.** the act of rebounding; recoil. **4.** *Basketball.* **a.** a ball that bounces off the backboard or the rim of the basket. **b.** an instance of gaining hold of such a ball. **5. on the rebound, a.** after a bounce off the ground, a wall, etc.: *to hit a ball on the rebound.* **b.** *Informal.* after being rejected by another: *to marry someone on the rebound.* [ME *rebound(en)* < MF *rebond(ir)* = OF *re-* RE- + *bondir* to BOUND[2]]

re·bo·zo (ri bō′zō; *Sp.* re bô′thô, -sô), *n., pl.* **-zos** (-zōz; *Sp.* -thôs, -sôs). a long woven scarf, worn over the head and shoulders esp. by Mexican women. [< Sp: scarf, shawl = *re-* RE- + *bozo,* akin to *boca* mouth]

re·broad·cast (rē brôd′kast′, -käst′), *v.,* **-cast** or **-cast·ed, -cast·ing,** *n.* —*v.t.* **1.** to broadcast again from the same station. **2.** to relay from another station. —*n.* **3.** a program that is rebroadcast.

re·buff (*n.* ri buf′, rē′buf; *v.* ri buf′), *n.* **1.** a blunt or abrupt rejection, as of a person's advances. **2.** a peremptory refusal of a request, offer, etc. **3.** a check to action or progress. —*v.t.* **4.** to give a rebuff to; check; repel. [< MF *rebuff(er)* < It *ribuffare* to disturb, reprimand < *ribuffo* (n.) = *ri-* RE- + *buffo* puff]

re·build (rē bild′), *v.,* **-built** or (*Archaic*) **-build·ed; -build·ing.** —*v.t.* **1.** to repair, esp. by dismantling and reassembling with new parts. **2.** to revise, reshape, or reorganize. —*v.i.* **3.** to build again or afresh.

re·buke (ri byōōk′), *v.,* **-buked, -buk·ing,** *n.* —*v.t.* **1.** to express sternly one's disapproval to; reprove; reprimand. —*n.* **2.** stern disapproval; reproof; reprimand. [ME *rebuke(n)* < AF *rebuk(er)* (OF *rebuchier*) (to) beat back = *re-* RE- + *bucher* to beat, strike < Gmc] —**re·buk′ing·ly,** *adv.* —**Syn. 1.** censure, upbraid, chide. See **reproach.**

re·bus (rē′bəs), *n., pl.* **-bus·es.** a representation of a word or phrase by pictures, symbols, etc., that suggest that word or phrase or its syllables. [< L *rēbus* by things (abl. pl. of *rēs;* from *nōn verbīs sed rēbus* not by words but by things)]

re·but (ri but′), *v.,* **-but·ted, -but·ting.** —*v.t.* **1.** to refute by evidence or argument; disprove; confute. **2.** to oppose by contrary proof. —*v.i.* **3.** to provide some evidence or argument that refutes or opposes. [ME *reb(o)ut(en)* < OF *rebout(er)* = *re-* RE- + *bo(u)ter* to BUTT[3]] —**re·but′ta·ble,** *adj.*

re·but·tal (ri but′əl), *n.* act of rebutting, as in debate.

re·but·ter[1] (ri but′ər), *n.* a person who rebuts. [REBUT + -ER[1]]

re·but·ter[2] (ri but′ər), *n.* *Law.* a defendant's answer to a plaintiff's surrejoinder. [< AF *rebuter* REBUT (n. use of inf.)]

rec (rek), *n.* *Informal.* recreation. [by shortening]

rec., 1. receipt. **2.** recipe. **3.** record. **4.** recorder.

re·cal·ci·trant (ri kal′si trənt), *adj.* **1.** resisting authority or control; refractory. **2.** hard to deal with, manage, or operate. —*n.* **3.** a recalcitrant person. [< LL < L *recalcitrant-* (s. of *recalcitrāns,* prp. of *recalcitrāre*) = *re-* RE- + *calcitr(āre)* (to) strike with the heels, kick (*calc-,* s. of *calx* heel + *-i-* -I- + *-t-* freq. suffix) + *-ant-* -ANT] —**re·cal′ci·trance, re·cal′ci·tran·cy,** *n.* —**Syn. 1.** resistant, rebellious, opposed.

re·cal·ci·trate (ri kal′si trāt′), *v.i.,* **-trat·ed, -trat·ing.** to resist or oppose; show strong objection or repugnance. [< L *recalcitrāt(us)* (ptp. of *recalcitrāre;* see RECALCITRANT); see -ATE[1]] —**re·cal′ci·tra′tion,** *n.*

re·cal·cu·late (rē kal′kyə lāt′), *v.t.,* **-lat·ed, -lat·ing.** to calculate again, as to check a previous computation. —**re′-cal·cu·la′tion,** *n.*

re·ca·lesce (rē′kə les′), *v.i.,* **-lesced, -lesc·ing.** *Metall.* to become hot again (said esp. of cooling iron, which glows with increased brilliancy upon passing certain temperatures). [< L *recalēsc(ere)* (to) become warm again = *re-* RE- + *calesc-* grow warm (*cal(ēre)* (to) be warm + *-esc-* inceptive suffix)] —**re′ca·les′cence,** *n.* —**re′ca·les′cent,** *adj.*

re·call (*v.* ri kôl′; *n.* ri kôl′, rē′kôl′), *v.t.* **1.** to bring back to conscious memory; recollect; remember. **2.** to call back; summon to return. **3.** to bring (one's thoughts, attention, etc.) back to matters previously considered. **4.** to revoke or withdraw. **5.** (of a manufacturer) to call back (esp. an automobile) for inspection or repair of a defective part. —*n.* **6.** an act of recalling. **7.** recollection; remembrance. **8.** the act or possibility of revoking something. **9.** the removal or the right of removal of a public official from office by a vote of the people upon petition. **10.** the act of calling back (esp. of an automobile) for inspection or repair of a defective part. —**re·call′a·ble,** *adj.* —**Syn. 1.** See **remember. 4.** rescind, retract, recant, repeal; annul. **7.** memory. **8.** revocation, retraction, repeal; nullification. —**Ant. 1.** forget.

Ré·ca·mier (rā ka myā′), *n.* **Madame** (*Jeanne Françoise Julie Adélaïde Bernard*), 1777–1849, French social leader in the literary and political circles of Paris.

re·cant (ri kant′), *v.t.* **1.** to withdraw or disavow (a statement, opinion, etc.), esp. formally; retract. —*v.i.* **2.** to withdraw or disavow a statement, opinion, etc., esp. formally. [< L *recant(āre)* (to) sing back, sing again = *re-* RE- + *cant-* sing; see CHANT] —**re·can·ta·tion** (rē′kan tā′shən), *n.* —**re·cant′er,** *n.* —**Syn. 1.** recall, rescind, deny.

re·cap[1] (*v.* rē′kap′, rē kap′; *n.* rē′kap′), *v.,* **-capped, -cap·ping,** *n.* —*v.t.* **1.** to recondition (a worn automobile tire) by adding a new strip of prepared rubber and vulcanizing in a mold. —*n.* **2.** a recapped tire. —**re·cap′pa·ble,** *adj.*

re·cap[2] (rē′kap′), *n., v.,* **-capped, -cap·ping.** —*n.* **1.** a recapitulation. —*v.t., v.i.* **2.** to recapitulate. [by shortening]

re·cap·i·tal·i·za·tion (rē kap′i tᵊli zā′shən), *n.* a revision of a corporation's capital structure.

re·cap·i·tal·ize (rē kap′i tᵊlīz′), *v.t.,* **-ized, -iz·ing.** to renew or change the capital of.

re·ca·pit·u·late (rē′kə pich′ə lāt′), *v.,* **-lat·ed, -lat·ing.** —*v.t.* **1.** to review by a brief summary, as at the end of a speech or discussion; summarize. **2.** *Biol.* (of an organism) to repeat (ancestral evolutionary stages) in its development. —*v.i.* **3.** to sum up statements or matters. [< LL *recapitulāt(us)* (ptp. of *recapitulāre*) = *re-* RE- + *capitulātus;* see CAPITULATE] —**Syn. 1.** See **repeat.**

re·ca·pit·u·la·tion (rē′kə pich′ə lā′shən), *n.* **1.** the act of recapitulating. **2.** the state of being recapitulated. **3.** a brief review or summary, as of a speech. **4.** *Biol.* the theory that an organism during its embryonic development passes through stages in which certain ancestral structures are repeated. **5.** *Music.* the final restatement of the exposition in a sonata-form movement. [ME *recapitulacioun* < LL *recapitulātiōn-* (s. of *recapitulātiō*) = *recapitulāt(us)* (see RECAPITULATE) + *-iōn-* -ION] —**re′ca·pit′u·la′tive, re·ca·pit·u·la·to·ry** (rē′kə pich′ə lə tōr′ē, -tôr′ē), *adj.*

re·cap·ture (rē kap′chər), *v.,* **-tured, -tur·ing,** *n.* —*v.t.* **1.** to capture again. **2.** to recollect or reexperience vividly. **3.** (of a government) to take by recapture. —*n.* **4.** recovery or retaking by capture. **5.** the taking by the government of a fixed part of all earnings in excess of a certain percentage of property value. **6.** *Internat. Law.* the lawful reacquisition of a former possession. **7.** the state or fact of being recaptured.

re·cast (*v.* rē kast′, -käst′; *n.* rē′kast′, -käst′), *v.,* **-cast, -cast·ing,** *n.* —*v.t.* **1.** to cast again or anew. **2.** to form, fashion, or arrange again. —*n.* **3.** a recasting. **4.** a new form produced by recasting.

recd., received. Also, **rec'd.**

re·cede[1] (ri sēd′), *v.i.,* **-ced·ed, -ced·ing. 1.** to go to or toward a more distant point; withdraw. **2.** to become more distant. **3.** to slope backward: *a chin that recedes.* **4.** to withdraw from a viewpoint, promise, etc.; retreat. [< L *recēd(ere)* (to) go, fall back = *re-* RE- + *cēd-* go; see CEDE]

re·cede[2] (rē sēd′), *v.t.,* **-ced·ed, -ced·ing.** to cede back; yield or grant to a former possessor, as property, a possession, or a right. [RE- + CEDE]

re·ceipt (ri sēt′), *n.* **1.** a written acknowledgment of having received a specified amount of money, goods, etc. **2. receipts,** the amount or quantity received. **3.** the act of receiving. **4.** the state of being received. **5.** something that is received. **6.** a recipe. —*v.t.* **7.** to acknowledge in writing the payment of (a bill). **8.** to give a receipt for (money, goods, etc.). —*v.i.* **9.** to give a receipt, as for money or goods. [ME *receite* < AF (OF *recoite*) < L *recepta,* fem. ptp. of *recipere* to RECEIVE]

re·ceipt·or (ri sē′tər), *n.* **1.** a person who receipts. **2.** *Law.* a person to whom attached property is delivered for safekeeping.

re·ceiv·a·ble (ri sē′və bəl), *adj.* **1.** fit for acceptance; acceptable. **2.** awaiting receipt of payment. **3.** capable of being received. —*n.* **4. receivables,** business assets in the form of obligations due from others. [r. ME *recevable* < AF *receivable* (OF *recevable*)] —**re·ceiv′a·bil′i·ty,** *n.*

re·ceive (ri sēv′), *v.,* **-ceived, -ceiv·ing.** —*v.t.* **1.** to have (something) given or sent to one. **2.** to have (something) bestowed or conferred on one. **3.** to read or hear (a communication). **4.** to experience or undergo: *to receive bad treatment; to receive attention.* **5.** to bear or contain as a burden. **6.** to catch or be struck by (a blow, missile, etc.). **7.** to welcome or accept as a guest, member, etc. **8.** to react to (news, an occurrence, etc.) in a specified manner: *an idea received with enthusiasm.* **9.** to hold or bear (something applied, impressed, etc.). **10.** to accept as true or valid. —*v.i.* **11.** to get or accept something. **12.** to welcome guests. **13.** to pick up radio or television signals. [ME *receve* < ONF *receiv(re)* < L *recipere* = *re-* RE- + *-cipere,* comb. form of *capere* to take] —**Ant. 1.** give.

Received′ Stand′ard, the form of educated English spoken in the English public schools and at Oxford and Cambridge universities.

re·ceiv·er (ri sē′vər), *n.* **1.** a person or thing that receives. **2.** a device or apparatus that receives electric signals, waves, or the like, and renders them perceptible to the senses, as the part of a telephone held to the ear, a radio receiving set, etc. **3.** *Law.* a person appointed by a court to take charge of a business or property of others, pending litigation. **4.** *Com.* a person appointed to receive money due. **5.** a person who knowingly receives stolen goods. **6.** a device or apparatus for receiving or holding something; receptacle; container. **7.** (in a firearm) the basic metal unit housing the action and to which the barrel and other components are attached. **8.** *Chem.* a vessel for collecting and containing a distillate. See illus. at **alembic. 9.** *Football.* a player on the offensive team assigned to catch a forward pass. [r. ME *recevuere* < AF *receivour, recevour,* OF *recevere*]

re·ceiv·er·ship (ri sē′vər ship′), *n.* *Law.* **1.** the condition of being in the hands of a receiver. **2.** the position or function of being a receiver.

receiv′ing line′, a row formed by the hosts, guests of honor, or the like, for receiving guests formally at a ball, wedding, etc.

receiv′ing set′, an electrical apparatus for receiving radio or television signals.

re·cen·sion (ri sen′shən), *n.* an editorial revision of a literary work, esp. on the basis of critical examination of the text and the sources used. [< L *recensiōn-* (s. of *recensiō*) a reviewing = *recens(ēre)* (*re-* RE- + *censēre* to estimate, assess) + *-iōn-* -ION]

re·cent (rē′sənt), *adj.* **1.** of late occurrence, appearance, or origin; lately happening, done, made, etc. **2.** of or belonging to a time not long past. **3.** (*cap.*) *Geol.* noting or pertaining to the present epoch, originating at the end of the

re·bill′, *v.t.*
re·bind′, *v.,* **-bound, -bind·ing.**
re·boil′, *v.*
re·broad′en, *v.*
re·bur′i·al, *n.*
re·bur′y, *v.t.,* **-bur·ied, -bur·y·ing.**
re·but′ton, *v.t.*
re·cau′tion, *v.t.*
re·cel′e·brate′, *v.,* **-brat·ed, -brat·ing.**

glacial period and forming the latter half of the Quaternary or the latest part of the Neocene period; Holocene. See table at **era.** —*n.* **4.** (*cap.*) Also called **Holocene.** *Geol.* the Recent epoch or series. [< L *recent-* (s. of *recēns*) fresh, new] —**re′cent·ly,** *adv.* —**re′cent·ness,** *n.* —**Syn. 1.** fresh, new. —**Ant. 1.** early, old.

re·cep·ta·cle (ri sep′tə kəl), *n.* **1.** a container, device, etc., for receiving or holding something. **2.** *Bot.* the modified or expanded portion of an axis that bears the organs of a single flower or the florets of a flower head. [< L *receptācul(um)* reservoir = *receptā(re)* (to) take again, receive back (freq. of *recipere* to RECEIVE) + *-culum* -CLE]

R

R, Receptacle (Longitudinal section)

re·cep·tion (ri sep′shən), *n.* **1.** the act of receiving. **2.** the state of being received. **3.** a manner of being received. **4.** a function or occasion when persons are formally received: *a wedding reception.* **5.** the quality or fidelity attained in receiving radio or television broadcasts under given circumstances. [ME *recepcion* < L *receptiōn-* (s. of *receptiō*) = *recept(us)* (ptp. of *recipere* to RECEIVE) + *-iōn-* -ION]

re·cep·tion·ist (ri sep′shə nist), *n.* a person, usually a girl or woman, employed to receive callers, as in an office.

recep′tion room′, a room for receiving visitors, clients, patients, etc.

re·cep·tive (ri sep′tiv), *adj.* **1.** having the quality of receiving, taking in, or admitting. **2.** able or quick to receive knowledge, ideas, etc. **3.** willing or inclined to receive suggestions, offers, etc. **4.** of or pertaining to reception or receptors. [< ML *receptīv(us).* See RECEPTION, -IVE] —**re·cep′tive·ly,** *adv.* —**re·cep·tiv·i·ty** (rē′sep tiv′i tē), **re·cep′tive·ness,** *n.*

re·cep·tor (ri sep′tər), *n.* *Physiol.* an end organ or a group of end organs of sensory or afferent neurons, specialized to be sensitive to stimulating agents. [late ME *receptour* < OF < L *receptor.* See RECEPTION, -OR[2]]

re·cess (ri ses′, rē′ses), *n.* **1.** a temporary withdrawal or cessation from work or activity. **2.** a receding part or space, as a bay or alcove in a room. **3.** an indentation in a line or extent of coast, hills, forest, etc. **4. recesses,** a secluded or inner area or part. —*v.t.* **5.** to place or set in a recess. **6.** to set or form like a recess or with recesses. —*v.i.* **7.** to take a recess. [< L *recess(us)* n. use of ptp. of *recēdere* to RECEDE[1]]

re·ces·sion[1] (ri sesh′ən), *n.* **1.** the act of receding or withdrawing. **2.** a receding part of a wall, building, etc. **3.** a withdrawing procession, as at the end of a religious service. **4.** the short period centering on the peak of a business cycle; the start of business contraction. [< L *recessiōn-* (s. of *recessiō*). See RECESS, -ION]

re·ces·sion[2] (ri sesh′ən), *n.* a return of ownership to a former possessor. [RE- + CESSION]

re·ces·sion·al (ri sesh′ə nəl), *adj.* **1.** of or pertaining to a recession. **2.** of or pertaining to a recess, as of a legislative body. —*n.* **3.** a hymn or other piece of music played at the end of a service.

re·ces·sive (ri ses′iv), *adj.* **1.** tending to go, move, or slant back; receding. **2.** *Genetics.* of or pertaining to a recessive. —*n.* *Genetics.* **3.** either of a pair of alternative alleles whose effect is masked by the activity of the second when both are present in the same cell or organism. **4.** the trait or character determined by such an allele. Cf. **dominant** (def. 6). [< L *recess(us)* (see RECESS) + -IVE] —**re·ces′sive·ly,** *adv.* —**re·ces′sive·ness,** *n.*

re·charge·a·ble (rē chär′jə bəl), *adj.* (esp. of a lightweight storage battery) capable of being charged repeatedly from ordinary household electric current.

ré·chauf·fé (*Fr.* rā shō fā′), *n., pl.* **-fés** (*Fr.* -fā′). **1.** a warmed-up dish of food. **2.** anything old or stale brought into service again: *a réchauffé of outmoded ideas.* [< F, ptp. of *réchauffer* (*re-* RE- + *échauffer* to warm; see CHAFE)]

re·cher·ché (rə shâr′shā; *Fr.* rə sher shā′), *adj.* **1.** sought out with care. **2.** very rare, exotic, or choice. **3.** of studied refinement or elegance; precious. [< F: sought after, ptp. of *rechercher;* see RESEARCH]

re·cid·i·vism (ri sid′ə viz′əm), *n.* repeated or habitual relapse, as into crime. [< L *recidīv(us)* relapsing = *recid(ere)* (*re-* RE- + *cid-* fall, sp. var. of *cad-*) + *-īv(us)* -IVE + -ISM] —**re·cid′i·vist,** *n.* —**re·cid′i·vis′tic, re·cid′i·vous,** *adj.*

Re·ci·fe (re sē′fə), *n.* a seaport in E Brazil. 788,569 (1960). Also called **Pernambuco.**

rec·i·pe (res′ə pē′), *n.* **1.** a set of instructions for making or preparing something, esp. a food dish. **2.** a medical prescription. **3.** a method to attain a desired end: *a recipe for success.* [ME < L: take, impv. sing. of *recipere* to RECEIVE]

re·cip·i·ence (ri sip′ē əns), *n.* **1.** the act of receiving; reception. **2.** the state or quality of being receptive; receptiveness. Also, **re·cip′i·en·cy.** [RECIPI(ENT) + -ENCE]

re·cip·i·ent (ri sip′ē ənt), *n.* **1.** a person or thing that receives; receiver: *the recipient of a prize.* —*adj.* **2.** receiving or capable of receiving. [< L *recipient-* (s. of *recipiēns*) prp. of *recipere* to RECEIVE; see -ENT]

re·cip·ro·cal (ri sip′rə kəl), *adj.* **1.** given or felt by each toward the other; mutual. **2.** given, performed, felt, etc., in return. **3.** *Gram.* expressing mutual relation. **4.** *Math.* noting expressions, relations, etc., involving reciprocals: *a reciprocal function.* **5.** *Navig.* bearing in a direction 180° to a given direction; back. —*n.* **6.** something that is reciprocal to something else; equivalent; counterpart; complement. **7.** *Math.* the ratio of unity to a given quantity or expression; that by which the given quantity or expression is multiplied to produce unity: *The reciprocal of x is* $^1/_x$. [< L *reciproc(us)* returning, reciprocal + -AL[1]] —**re·cip′ro·cal′i·ty,** *n.* —**re·cip′ro·cal·ly,** *adv.* —**Syn. 1.** See **mutual.**

recip′rocal transloca′tion, *Genetics.* an exchange of segments between two nonhomologous chromosomes.

re·cip·ro·cate (ri sip′rə kāt′), *v.,* **-cat·ed, -cat·ing.** —*v.t.* **1.** to give, feel, etc., in return. **2.** to give and receive reciprocally; interchange. **3.** to cause to move alternately backward and forward. —*v.i.* **4.** to make a return, as for something given. **5.** to make interchange. **6.** to be correspondent. **7.** to move alternately backward and forward. [< L *reciprocāt(us)* moved back and forth (ptp. of *reciprocāre*). See RECIPROCAL, -ATE[1]] —**re·cip′ro·ca′tive, re·cip·ro·ca·to·ry** (ri sip′rə kə tôr′ē, -tōr′ē), *adj.* —**re·cip′ro·ca′tor,** *n.*

recip′rocating en′gine, any engine employing the rectilinear motion of one or more pistons in cylinders.

re·cip·ro·ca·tion (ri sip′rə kā′shən), *n.* **1.** an act or instance of reciprocating. **2.** a returning, usually for something given. **3.** a mutual giving and receiving. **4.** the state of being reciprocal or corresponding. [< L *reciprocātiōn-* (s. of *reciprocātiō*)]

rec·i·proc·i·ty (res′ə pros′i tē), *n.* **1.** a reciprocal state or relation. **2.** reciprocation; mutual exchange. **3.** the relation or policy in commercial dealings between countries by which corresponding advantages or privileges are granted by each country. [< L *reciproc(us)* (see RECIPROCAL) + -ITY]

re·ci·sion (ri sizh′ən), *n.* an act of canceling or voiding; cancellation. [< L *recīsiōn-* (s. of *recīsiō*) = *recīs(us)* (ptp. of *recīdere* to cut back; *re-* RE- + *-cīdere* to cut) + *-iōn-* -ION]

recit., *Music.* recitative.

re·cit·al (ri sīt′əl), *n.* **1.** a musical or similar entertainment given usually by a single performer or by a performer and one or more accompanists. **2.** an act or instance of reciting. **3.** a detailed statement. **4.** an account or description. —**Syn. 4.** See **narrative.**

rec·i·ta·tion (res′i tā′shən), *n.* **1.** an act of reciting. **2.** a recital or repetition of something from memory, esp. formally or publicly. **3.** oral response by a pupil or pupils to a teacher on a prepared lesson. **4.** a period of classroom instruction. [< L *recitātiōn-* (s. of *recitātiō*) = *recitāt(us)* (ptp. of *recitāre* to RECITE) + *-iōn-* -ION]

rec·i·ta·tive[1] (res′i tā′tiv, ri sī′tə-), *adj.* pertaining to or of the nature of recital. [RECITE + -ATIVE]

rec·i·ta·tive[2] (res′i tə tēv′), *Music.* —*adj.* **1.** of the nature of or resembling recitation or declamation. —*n.* **2.** a style of vocal music intermediate between speaking and singing. **3.** a passage, part, or piece in this style. [< It *recitativ(o)*]

rec·i·ta·ti·vo (res′i tə tē′vō; *It.* re′chē tä tē′vō), *n., pl.* **-vi** (*Eng., It.* -vē), **-vos.** *Music.* recitative[2].

re·cite (ri sīt′), *v.,* **-cit·ed, -cit·ing.** —*v.t.* **1.** to repeat the words of, as from memory, esp. in a formal manner. **2.** to give an account of. **3.** to enumerate. —*v.i.* **4.** to recite a lesson or part of a lesson for a teacher. **5.** to recite or repeat something from memory. [ME *recite(n)* < L *recit(āre)* (to) read aloud = *re-* RE- + *citāre* to summon, CITE] —**re·cit′a·ble,** *adj.* —**Syn. 2.** narrate, describe. See **relate. 3.** count, number, detail.

reck (rek), *v.i.* **1.** to have care, concern, or regard (often fol. by *of, with,* or a clause). **2.** to take heed. **3.** *Archaic.* to be of concern or importance; matter: *It recks not.* —*v.t.* **4.** to have regard for; mind; heed. [ME *rekk(en),* OE *reccan;* c. OE *rēcan,* OIcel *roekja* to have care, G (*ge*)*ruhen* to deign]

reck·less (rek′lis), *adj.* **1.** utterly unconcerned about the consequences of some action; without caution; careless (usually fol. by *of*): *to be reckless of danger.* **2.** characterized by or proceeding from such carelessness. [ME *rekles,* OE *recceleās* careless, var. of *rēceleās;* c. G *ruchlos*] —**reck′less·ly,** *adv.* —**reck′less·ness,** *n.* —**Syn. 1.** rash, heedless, incautious, negligent, imprudent. —**Ant. 1.** careful.

Reck·ling·hau·sen (rek′ling hou′zən), *n.* a city in NW West Germany. 129,350 (est. 1964).

reck·on (rek′ən), *v.t.* **1.** to count, compute, or calculate, as in number or amount. **2.** to esteem or consider; regard as. **3.** *Chiefly Midland and Southern U.S.* to think or suppose. —*v.i.* **4.** to count; make a computation or calculation. **5.** to settle accounts, as with a person (often fol. by *up*). **6.** to count, depend, or rely, as in expectation (often fol. by *on*). **7.** *Chiefly Midland and Southern U.S.* to think or suppose. **8. reckon with, a.** to include in consideration or planning; anticipate. **b.** to deal with. [ME *reken(en),* OE (*ge*)*recenian* to report, pay; c. G *rechnen* to compute] —**Syn. 1.** enumerate. **2.** account, deem, judge.

reck·on·er (rek′ə nər), *n.* a person or thing that reckons. [ME]

reck·on·ing (rek′ə ning), *n.* **1.** count; computation or calculation. **2.** the settlement of accounts, as between two businessmen. **3.** a statement of an amount due; bill. **4.** an accounting, as for things received or done. **5.** *Navig.* See **dead reckoning. 6.** See **day of reckoning** (def. 1). [ME]

re·claim (rē klām′), *v.t.* **1.** to claim or demand the return or restoration of, as a right, possession, etc. **2.** to claim again.

re·claim (ri klām′), *v.t.* **1.** to bring (wild, waste, or marshy land) into a condition for cultivation or other use. **2.** to recover (substances) in a pure or usable form from refuse, discarded articles, etc. **3.** to bring back to right conduct and thoughts; reform. —*n.* **4.** reclamation: *beyond reclaim.* [ME *recla(i)m(en)* < OF *reclam(er)* (tonic s. *reclaim-*) < L *reclāmāre* to cry out against = *re-* RE- + *clamāre* to CLAIM] —**re·claim′a·ble,** *adj.* —**re·claim′ant,** *n.* —**Syn. 2.** regain, restore. See **recover.**

rec·la·ma·tion (rek′lə mā′shən), *n.* **1.** the act or process of reclaiming. **2.** the state of being reclaimed. [< MF < L *reclāmātiōn-* (s. of *reclāmātiō*) crying out against = *reclāmāt(us)* (ptp. of *reclām(āre)*; see RECLAIM) + *-iōn-* -ION]

ré·clame (*Fr.* rā klȧm′), *n.* **1.** publicity. **2.** hunger for publicity. [< F < *réclamer;* see RECLAIM]

re·clas·si·fy (rē klas′ə fī′), *v.t.,* **-fied, -fy·ing. 1.** to classify anew. **2.** to change the Selective Service classification of. **3.** to change the security classification of (information, a document, etc.). —**re·clas′si·fi·ca′tion,** *n.*

re·cline (ri klīn′), *v.,* **-clined, -clin·ing.** —*v.i.* **1.** to lean or lie back; rest in a recumbent position. —*v.t.* **2.** to cause to lean back on something; place in a recumbent position. [ME *recline(n)* < L *reclīn(āre)* = *re-* RE- + *clīnare* to LEAN[1]] —**re·clin′a·ble,** *adj.* —**rec·li·na·tion** (rek′lə nā′shən), *n.* —**re·clin′er,** *n.*

reclin′ing chair′, an easy chair with the back and footrest adjustable to the comfort of the user.

rec·luse (*n.* rek′lo͞os, ri klo͞os′; *adj.* ri klo͞os′), *n.* **1.** a person who lives in seclusion or apart from society. —*adj.* **2.** shut off or apart from the world; living in seclu-

re·chal′lenge, *v.t.,* **-lenged, -leng·ing.**
re·chart′, *v.t.*
re·char′ter, *v.t.*
re·check′, *v.*
re′check, *n.*
re·chris′ten, *v.t.*
re·cir′cu·late′, *v.,* **-lat·ed, -lat·ing.**
re·clean′, *v.t.*
re·clothe′, *v.t.,* **-clothed** or **-clad, -cloth·ing.**

sion. [ME < OF *reclus* < L *reclūs(us)*, ptp. of *reclūdere* to shut up (earlier, to unclose) = *re-* RE- + *-clūd-*, var. of *claud-* CLOSE] —**re·clu′sive,** *adj.*

re·clu·sion (ri klo͞o′zhən), *n.* **1.** the condition or life of a recluse. **2.** a shutting up in seclusion. [ME < LL *reclūsiōn-* (s. of *reclūsiō*) a shutting off. See RECLUSE, -ION]

rec·og·nise (rek′əg nīz′), *v.t.*, **-nised, -nis·ing.** *Chiefly Brit.* recognize. —**rec′og·nis′a·ble,** *adj.*

rec·og·ni·tion (rek′əg nish′ən), *n.* **1.** the act of recognizing someone or something. **2.** the state of being recognized. **3.** the perception or acknowledgment of something as true or valid. **4.** appreciation of achievements, merit, services, etc., or an expression of this. **5.** formal acknowledgment conveying approval or sanction. **6.** formal acknowledgment of a person's right to speak at a particular time. **7.** *Internat. Law.* an official act by which one state acknowledges the existence of another state or government, or of belligerency or insurgency. [< L *recognitiōn-* (s. of *recognitiō*) = *recognit(us)* (ptp. of *recognoscere;* see RECOGNIZE) + *-iōn-* -ION] —**rec′og·ni′tion·al,** *adj.* —**re·cog·ni·tive** (ri kog′ni tiv), **re·cog·ni·to·ry** (ri kog′ni tōr′ē, -tôr′ē), *adj.*

re·cog·ni·zance (ri kog′ni zəns, -kon′i-), *n.* **1.** *Law.* **a.** a bond or obligation of record entered into before a court or magistrate, binding a person to do a particular act. **b.** the sum pledged as surety on such a bond. **2.** *Archaic.* recognition. [ME *reconissaunce, recognisance* < OF *reconuissance*]

rec·og·nize (rek′əg nīz′), *v.t.*, **-nized, -niz·ing.** **1.** to identify as something or someone previously seen, known, etc. **2.** to identify from knowledge of appearance or characteristics. **3.** to perceive as existing or true; realize. **4.** to acknowledge as the person entitled to speak at a particular time. **5.** to acknowledge formally as entitled to treatment as a political entity. **6.** to acknowledge or accept formally. **7.** to acknowledge or treat as valid: *to recognize a claim.* **8.** to acknowledge acquaintance with (someone that one meets). **9.** to show appreciation of (achievement, service, merit, etc.), as by some reward, public honor, or the like. **10.** *Law.* to acknowledge (an illegitimate child) as one's own. Also, *esp. Brit.*, **recognise.** [RECOGN(ITION) + -IZE; r. ME *racunnys, recognis* < OF *reconuiss-*, s. of *reconuistre* < L *recognoscere* = *re-* RE- + *cognoscere* to know; see COGNITION] —**rec′og·niz′a·bil′i·ty,** *n.* —**rec·og·niz·a·ble** (rek′əg nī′zə bəl, rek′əg nī′-), *adj.* —**rec′og·niz′a·bly,** *adv.*

re·coil (*v.* ri koil′; *n.* rē koil′, ri koil′), *v.i.* **1.** to draw back; start or shrink back, as in alarm, horror, or disgust. **2.** to spring or fly back, as in consequence of force of impact or the force of the discharge, as a firearm. **3.** to react against the originator or source (usually fol. by *on* or *upon*): *Plots frequently recoil upon the plotters.* **4.** *Physics.* (of an atom, a nucleus, or a particle) to undergo a change in momentum as a result either of a collision with an atom, a nucleus, or a particle or of the emission of a particle. —*n.* **5.** an act of recoiling. **6.** the distance through which a weapon moves backward after discharging. [ME *recoil(en), recul(en)* < OF *recul(er)* < L *re-* RE- + *cūlus* rump] —**re·coil′ing·ly,** *adv.*

re′coil escape′ment, *Horol.* See **anchor escapement.**

re·coil·less (ri koil′lis, rē′koil′-), *adj.* having little or no recoil: *a recoilless rifle.*

re-col·lect (rē′kə lekt′), *v.t.* **1.** to collect, gather, or assemble again. **2.** to rally (one's faculties, powers, spirits, etc.); recover or compose (oneself). [< L *recollect(us)*, taken as RE- + COLLECT]

rec·ol·lect (rek′ə lekt′), *v.t.* **1.** to recall to mind; recover knowledge of by memory; remember. —*v.i.* **2.** to have a recollection; remember. [< ML *recollect(us)* (n. use of ptp. of L *recolligere* to collect again) = L *re-* RE- + *collectus* COLLECT] —**rec′ol·lec′tive,** *adj.* —**rec′ol·lec′tive·ly,** *adv.*

rec·ol·lect·ed (rek′ə lek′tid), *adj.* **1.** calm; composed. **2.** remembered; recalled. **3.** characterized by or given to contemplation. —**rec′ol·lect′ed·ly,** *adv.*

re-col·lec·tion (rē′kə lek′shən), *n.* **1.** the act of re-collecting. **2.** the state of being re-collected. [RE-COLLECT + -ION]

rec·ol·lec·tion (rek′ə lek′shən), *n.* **1.** the act or power of recollecting, or recalling to mind; remembrance. **2.** something that is recollected. [< F *récollection* or ML *recollectiōn-* (s. of *recollectiō*) = *recollect(us)* (see RECOLLECT) + *-iōn-* -ION] —**Syn. 1.** recall. **1, 2.** memory. **2.** memoir.

re·com·bi·nant (rē kom′bə nənt), *adj.* of or resulting from new combinations of genetic material.

recom′binant DNA, *Biochem.* any of various techniques for inserting DNA fragments from the genes of one organism directly into the chromosomes of another so as to change genetic makeup: used in basic research and to produce vaccines, hormones, etc. Also called **gene-splicing.**

re·com·bi·na·tion (rē′kom bə nā′shən), *n.* *Genetics.* the formation of new combinations of genes either by crossing over at meiosis or by segregation.

rec·om·mend (rek′ə mend′), *v.t.* **1.** to present as worthy of confidence, acceptance, use, etc.; commend. **2.** to represent or urge as advisable or expedient. **3.** to suggest (a choice) as appropriate, beneficial, or the like. **4.** to cause to seem desirable or attractive: *a plan that has little to recommend it.* —*v.i.* **5.** to make a recommendation. [ME *recommend(en)* < ML *recommend(āre)* = L *re-* RE- + *commendāre* to COMMEND] —**rec·om·mend′a·ble,** *adj.* —**Syn. 1.** approve.

rec·om·men·da·tion (rek′ə men dā′shən), *n.* **1.** the act of recommending. **2.** something, as a letter, that serves to recommend. [ME *recommendacion* < ML *recommendātiōn-* (s. of *recommendātiō*) = *recommendāt(us)* (ptp. of *recommendāre* to RECOMMEND) + *-iōn-* -ION] —**Syn. 1.** See **advice.**

rec·om·mend·a·to·ry (rek′ə men′də tōr′ē, -tôr′ē), *adj.* serving to recommend; recommending. [< ML *recommendāt(us)* (see RECOMMENDATION) + -ORY[1]]

re·com·mit (rē′kə mit′), *v.t.*, **-mit·ted, -mit·ting.** **1.** to commit again. **2.** to refer again to a committee. —**re′com·mit′ment, re′com·mit′tal,** *n.*

rec·om·pense (rek′əm pens′), *v.*, **-pensed, -pens·ing,** *n.* —*v.t.* **1.** to repay or reward (someone), as for aid or service. **2.** to give compensation or requital for (loss, injury, or the like). —*v.i.* **3.** to repay or compensate someone. —*n.* **4.** a repayment or reward. **5.** a compensation or requital, as for loss or injury. [ME *recompense(n)* < MF *recompens(er)* < LL *recompens(āre)* = L *re-* RE- + *compensāre;* see COMPENSATE] —**rec′om·pen′sa·ble,** *adj.* —**rec′om·pens′er,** *n.* —**Syn. 1.** reimburse, recoup. **5.** payment, amends.

re·com·pose (rē′kəm pōz′), *v.t.*, **-posed, -pos·ing.** **1.** to compose again; rearrange. **2.** to restore to composure or calmness. —**re·com·po·si·tion** (rē′kom pə zish′ən), *n.*

re·con (ri kon′), *n.* *Informal.* reconnaissance. [by shortening]

rec·on·cil·a·ble (rek′ən sī′lə bəl, rek′ən sī′lə bəl), *adj.* capable of being reconciled. —**rec′on·cil′a·bil′i·ty,** *n.* —**rec′on·cil′a·bly,** *adv.*

rec·on·cile (rek′ən sīl′), *v.t.*, **-ciled, -cil·ing.** **1.** to cause to cease hostility or opposition. **2.** to cause (a person) to accept or be resigned to something not desired. **3.** to harmonize or settle (a quarrel, inconsistency, etc.) **4.** to restore (an excommunicate or penitent) to communion in a church. [ME *reconcile(n)* < L *reconcili(āre)* (to) make good again, repair. See RE-, CONCILIATE] —**rec′on·cil′er,** *n.* —**rec′on·cil′ing·ly,** *adv.* —**Syn. 1.** pacify, propitiate, placate.

rec·on·cil·i·a·tion (rek′ən sil′ē ā′shən), *n.* **1.** an act of reconciling. **2.** the state of being reconciled. **3.** the process of making consistent or compatible. [ME *reconsiliacion* < L *reconciliātiōn-* (s. of *reconciliātiō*)]

rec·on·cil·i·a·to·ry (rek′ən sil′ē ə tōr′ē, -tôr′ē), *adj.* tending to reconcile. [< L *reconciliāt(us)* (ptp. of *reconciliāre;* see RECONCILE, -ATE[1]) + -ORY[1]]

rec·on·dite (rek′ən dīt′, ri kon′dīt), *adj.* **1.** dealing with very profound, difficult, or abstruse subject matter. **2.** beyond ordinary knowledge or understanding; esoteric. **3.** little known; obscure. [earlier *recondit* < L *recondit(us)* hidden (ptp. of *recondere*) = *re-* RE- + *cond(ere)* to bring together (*con-* CON- + *-dere* put) + *-itus* -ITE[2]] —**rec′on·dite′ly,** *adv.* —**rec′on·dite′ness,** *n.* —**Syn. 2.** deep.

re·con·di·tion (rē′kən dish′ən), *v.t.* to restore to a good or satisfactory condition; repair; make over.

re·con·nais·sance (ri kon′i səns), *n.* **1.** the act of reconnoitering. **2.** *Mil.* a search made for useful military information in the field, esp. by examining the ground. **3.** *Survey, Civ. Eng.* a general examination or survey of a region, usually followed by a detailed survey. Also, **re·con′nois·sance.** [< F; MF *reconoissance* RECOGNIZANCE]

re·con·noi·ter (rē′kə noi′tər, rek′ə-), *v.t.* **1.** to inspect, observe, or survey (an enemy position, strength, etc.) in order to gain information for military purposes. **2.** to examine or survey (a region, area, etc.) for engineering, geological, or other purposes. —*v.i.* **3.** to make a reconnaissance. [< obs. F *reconnoître* to explore < MF *reconoistre.* See RECOGNIZE] —**re′con·noi′ter·er,** *n.*

re·con·noi·tre (rē′kə noi′tər, rek′ə-), *v.t.*, *v.i.*, **-tred, -tring.** *Chiefly Brit.* reconnoiter. —**re′con·noi′trer,** *n.*

re·con·sid·er (rē′kən sid′ər), *v.t.* **1.** to consider again, esp. with a view to change of decision or action. **2.** *Parl. Proc.* to take up for consideration a second time, as a prior decision. —*v.i.* **3.** to reconsider a matter. —**re′con·sid′er·a′tion,** *n.*

re·con·sti·tute (rē kon′sti to͞ot′, -tyo͞ot′), *v.t.*, **-tut·ed, -tut·ing.** to constitute again; reconstruct; recompose. —**re·con·sti·tu·ent** (rē′kən stich′o͞o ənt), *adj.*, *n.* —**re′con·sti·tu′tion,** *n.*

re·con·sti·tu·ted (ri kon′sti to͞o′tid, -tyo͞o′-), *adj.* constituted again, esp. of a liquid product made by adding water to dry solids from which the water has been evaporated.

re·con·struct (rē′kən strukt′), *v.t.* **1.** to construct again; rebuild; make over. **2.** to recreate in the mind from given or available information. **3.** *Historical Linguistics.* to arrive at (hypothetical earlier forms of words, phonemic systems, etc.) by comparison of data from a later language or group of related languages. —**re′con·struc′ti·ble,** *adj.* —**re′con·struc′tor,** *n.*

re·con·struct·ed (rē′kən struk′tid), *adj.* **1.** constructed again; rebuilt. **2.** noting a gem, esp. a ruby, made by an obsolete process from fused fragments of natural gems.

re·con·struc·tion (rē′kən struk′shən), *n.* **1.** the act of reconstructing. **2.** something that is reconstructed. **3.** (*cap.*) *U.S. Hist.* **a.** (after the Civil War) the reintegration of the former Confederate States into the Union. **b.** the period during which this took place, 1865–77. —**re′con·struc′tion·al,** *adj.*

Reconstruc′tion Acts′, *U.S. Hist.* the acts of Congress during the period from 1867 to 1877 providing for the reorganization of the former Confederate States.

Reconstruc′tion Finance′ Corpora′tion, a public corporation that was created by an act of Congress in 1932 to provide loans and other financial assistance to industrial, commercial, and banking organizations: abolished in 1957. *Abbr.:* RFC, R.F.C.

Re·con·struc·tion·ism (rē′kən struk′shə niz′əm), *n.* a religious and cultural movement originated in the U.S. that seeks to apply naturalism to Judaism and views Judaism as an evolving religious civilization, stressing the concept of Jewish values and culture and encouraging reinterpretation of tradition.

Re·con·struc·tion·ist (rē′kən struk′shə nist), *n.* an advocate or supporter of Reconstruction or Reconstructionism.

re·coin′, *v.t.*
re·coin′age, *n.*
re′col·o·ni·za′tion, *n.*
re·col′o·nize′, *v.t.*, **-nized, -niz·ing.**
re·col′or, *v.t.*
re·comb′, *v.*
re′com·mence′, *v.*, **-menced, -menc·ing.**
re′com·mence′ment, *n.*
re′com·par′i·son, *n.*
re′com·pound′, *v.*
re·con′cen·trate′, *v.*, **-trat·ed, -trat·ing.**
re′con·cen·tra′tion, *n.*
re′con·den·sa′tion, *n.*
re′con·dense′, *v.*, **-densed, -dens·ing.**
re′con·firm′, *v.t.*
re′con·fir·ma′tion, *n.*
re′con·nect′, *v.t.*
re·con′quer, *v.t.*
re·con′quest, *n.*
re·con′se·crate′, *v.t.*, **-crat·ed, -crat·ing.**
re′con·se·cra′tion, *n.*
re′con·sign′, *v.t.*
re′con·sign′ment, *n.*
re′con·sol′i·date′, *v.*, **-dat·ed, -dat·ing.**
re′con·sol′i·da′tion, *n.*
re′con·tend′, *v.i.*
re′con·test′, *v.*
re′con·tract′, *v.t.*
re′con·vene′, *v.*, **-vened, -ven·ing.**

re·con·vert (rē′kən vûrt′), *v.t.* **1.** to convert again. **2.** to change back to a previous form, opinion, character, function, etc. —**re′con·ver′sion,** *n.*

re·con·vey (rē′kən vā′), *v.t.* **1.** to convey again. **2.** to convey back to a previous position or place. —**re′con·vey′-ance,** *n.*

re·cord (*v.* ri kôrd′; *n., adj.* rek′ərd), *v.t.* **1.** to set down in writing or the like, as for the purpose of preserving evidence. **2.** to cause (one's opinion, vote, etc.) to be set down or registered. **3.** to register (sounds, signals, etc.) so that they can be reproduced by mechanical or electronic equipment. —*v.i.* **4.** to record something; make a record. —*n.* **5.** the act of recording. **6.** the state of being recorded, as in writing. **7.** a piece of writing, a chart, etc., that provides information or the like for ready reference. **8.** the information or the like provided. **9.** the impression made by one's past, esp. for good or bad. **10.** a disk or other object on which sounds are recorded for later reproduction. **11.** the greatest attainment of its kind, esp. in sports. **12.** *Law.* **a.** the commitment to writing, as authentic evidence, of something having legal importance. **b.** evidence preserved in this manner. **c.** an authentic or official written report of proceedings of a court of justice. **13.** a criminal record: *a suspect with a record.* **14. go on record,** to issue a public statement of one's opinion or stand. **15. off the record, a.** not for publication. **b.** not official. **c.** confidential. **16. on record, a.** existing as a matter of public knowledge; known. **b.** existing in a publication, document, file, etc. —*adj.* **17.** making or constituting a record. **18.** surpassing or superior to all others. [ME *record(en)* < OF *record(er)* < L *recordārī* to remember, recollect = *re-* RE- + *cord-* (s. of *cors*) heart] —**re·cord′a·ble,** *adj.* —**Syn. 1.** register, enroll, enter, note. **7.** chronicle, history, journal; note, memorandum.

rec′ord chang′er, a device that permits the playing of a stack of records automatically, one after another. Cf. **record player.**

re·cord·er (ri kôr′dər), *n.* **1.** a person who records, esp. as an official duty. **2.** *Eng. Law.* a judge in a city or borough court. **3.** a recording or registering apparatus or device. **4.** a device for recording sounds, esp. on tape or wire. **5.** an end-blown flute having a fipple mouthpiece. [r. ME: an official < AF *recordour,* OF *recorde-our*]

Recorder (def. 5)

re·cord·ing (ri kôr′ding), *n.* **1.** the act or practice of a person or thing that records. **2.** something that is recorded, as a musical work. [ME]

re·cord·ist (ri kôr′dist, -kôr′-), *n.* a technician who records sound, esp. on motion-picture film.

rec′ord play′er, 1. an electric machine for playing phonograph records, including a turntable, tone arm, amplifier, a built-in or detachable speaker or speakers, and a record changer. **2.** (loosely) any phonograph.

re·count (*v.* rē kount′; *n.* rē′kount′, rē kount′), *v.t.* **1.** to count again. —*n.* **2.** a second or additional count, as of votes in an election.

re·count (ri kount′), *v.t.* **1.** to relate or narrate in detail; describe. **2.** to tell one by one; enumerate. [ME *recount(en)* < MF *recont(er)* = *re-* RE- + *conter* to tell, COUNT[1]] —**Syn. 1.** See **relate.**

re·count·al (ri koun′tᵊl), *n.* an act of recounting.

re·coup (ri ko͞op′), *v.t.* **1.** to get back the equivalent of: *to recoup one's losses.* **2.** to regain or recover. **3.** to reimburse or indemnify; pay back. **4.** *Law.* to withhold (a portion of something due), having some rightful claim to do so. —*v.i.* **5.** to get back an equivalent, as of something lost. **6.** *Law.* to plead in defense a claim arising out of the same subject matter as the plaintiff's claim. —*n.* **7.** an act of recouping. [ME < MF *recoup(er)* (to) cut back, again = *re-* RE- + *couper* to cut; see COUP] —**re·coup′a·ble,** *adj.* —**re·coup′ment,** *n.* —**Syn. 1.** recover, restore, retrieve. **3.** recompense, remunerate.

re·course (rē′kōrs, -kôrs, ri kōrs′, -kôrs′), *n.* **1.** access or resort to a person or thing for help or protection. **2.** a person or thing resorted to for help or protection. **3.** the right to collect from a maker or endorser of a negotiable instrument. [ME *recours* < OF < LL *recurs(us),* L: return, retreat, n. use of ptp. of *recurrere* to run back; see RECUR]

re-cov·er (rē kuv′ər), *v.t.* to cover again or anew. [ME; see RE-, COVER]

re·cov·er (ri kuv′ər), *v.t.* **1.** to get back or regain (something lost or taken away). **2.** to make up for or make good (loss, injury, etc., to oneself). **3.** to regain the strength, composure, balance, etc., of (oneself). **4.** *Law.* **a.** to obtain by judgment in a court of law, or by legal proceedings. **b.** to acquire title to through judicial process. **5.** to reclaim from a bad state, practice, etc. **6.** to regain (a substance) in usable form, as from refuse material; reclaim. —*v.i.* **7.** to regain health after being sick, wounded, or the like (often fol. by *from*). **8.** to regain a former and better state or condition. **9.** *Law.* to obtain a favorable judgment in a suit for something. **10.** to make a recovery in fencing or rowing. [ME *recover(en)* < MF *recover(er)* < L *recuperāre* to regain, RECUPERATE] —**re·cov′er·a·ble,** *adj.*
—**Syn. 1.** restore. RECOVER, RECLAIM, RETRIEVE are to regain literally or figuratively something or someone. To RECOVER is to obtain again what one has lost possession of: *to recover a stolen jewel.* To RECLAIM is to bring back from error or wrongdoing, or from a rude or undeveloped state: *to reclaim desert land by irrigation.* To RETRIEVE is to bring back or restore, esp. something to its former, prosperous state: *to retrieve one's fortune.* **7.** heal, mend, recuperate.

re·cov·er·y (ri kuv′ə rē), *n., pl.* **-er·ies. 1.** the act of recovering. **2.** the possibility of recovering. **3.** the regaining of something lost or taken away. **4.** restoration or return to health or a normal condition, as after sickness or disaster. **5.** something gained in recovering. **6.** the reclamation of waste substances in usable form. **7.** *Law.* the obtaining of right to something by verdict or judgment of a court of law. **8.** *Fencing.* the movement to the position of guard after a lunge. **9.** *Rowing.* a return to a former position for making the next stroke. [ME < AF *recoverie*]

recov′ery room′, a hospital room for patients recovering from anesthesia.

recpt, receipt.

rec·re·ant (rek′rē ənt), *adj.* **1.** cowardly or craven. **2.** unfaithful, disloyal, or traitorous. —*n.* **3.** a coward. **4.** an apostate, traitor, or renegade. [ME < OF, prp. of *recreire* to yield in a contest = *re-* RE- + *creire* < L *crēdere* to believe] —**rec′re·ance, rec′re·an·cy,** *n.* —**rec′re·ant·ly,** *adv.* —**Syn. 1.** dastardly, pusillanimous, base. **2.** faithless, untrue. **3.** dastard. —**Ant. 1.** brave. **2.** loyal. **3.** hero.

re-cre·ate (rē′krē āt′), *v.t.,* **-at·ed, -at·ing.** to create anew. —**re′-cre·a′tor,** *n.* —**Syn.** reproduce, remake.

rec·re·ate (rek′rē āt′), *v.,* **-at·ed, -at·ing.** —*v.t.* **1.** to refresh by means of relaxation and enjoyment. **2.** to restore or refresh physically or mentally. —*v.i.* **3.** to take recreation. [< L *recreāt(us)* (ptp. of *recreāre* to create again, revive) = *re-* RE- + *creātus;* see CREATE] —**rec′re·a′tive,** *adj.* —**rec′re·a′tive·ly,** *adv.* —**rec′re·a′tor,** *n.*

re-cre·a·tion (rē′krē ā′shən), *n.* **1.** the act of creating anew. **2.** something created anew.

rec·re·a·tion (rek′rē ā′shən), *n.* **1.** refreshment by means of some pastime, agreeable exercise, or the like. **2.** a pastime, diversion, exercise, or other resource affording relaxation and enjoyment. **3.** the act of recreating. **4.** the state of being recreated. [ME *recreacion* < MF *recreation* or L *recreātiōn-* (s. of *recreātiō*) restoration, recovery = *recreāt(us)* (see RECREATE) + *-iōn-* -ION] —**rec′re·a′tion·al, rec·re·a·to·ry** (rek′rē ə tōr′ē, -tôr′ē), *adj.*

rec·re·ment (rek′rə mənt), *n.* **1.** *Physiol.* a secretion, as saliva, that is reabsorbed by the body. **2.** refuse separated from anything; dross. [< MF < L *recrēment(um)* dross, refuse = *re-* RE- + *crē-* separate (s. of *cernere;* see SHEAR) + *-mentum* -MENT] —**rec′re·men′tal,** *adj.*

re·crim·i·nate (ri krim′ə nāt′), *v.,* **-nat·ed, -nat·ing.** —*v.i.* **1.** to bring a countercharge against an accuser. —*v.t.* **2.** to accuse in return. [< ML *recrīmināt(us)* accused in turn (ptp. of *recrīmināri*) = *re-* RE- + *crīmin-* (s. of *crīmen*) CRIME + *-ātus* -ATE[1]] —**re·crim′i·na′tion,** *n.* —**re·crim′i·na′-tive, re·crim·i·na·to·ry** (ri krim′ə nə tōr′ē, -tôr′ē), *adj.* —**re·crim′i·na′tor,** *n.*

re·cru·desce (rē′kro͞o des′), *v.i.,* **-desced, -desc·ing.** to break out afresh, as a disease or an undesirable condition that has been quiescent. [< L *recrūdesc(ere)* (to) become raw again = *re-* RE- + *crūdescere* to grow harsh, worse (*crūd(us)* bloody (see CRUDE) + *-escere* inceptive suffix)]

re·cru·des·cence (rē′kro͞o des′əns), *n.* a fresh outbreak or spell of renewed activity, as of a disease or an undesirable condition; revival or reappearance in active existence. Also, **re′cru·des′cen·cy.** [< L *recrūdesc(ere)* (to) RECRUDESCE + -ENCE] —**re′cru·des′cent,** *adj.*

re·cruit (ri kro͞ot′), *n.* **1.** a newly enlisted or drafted member of the armed forces. **2.** a new member of a group, organization, or the like. —*v.t.* **3.** to enlist, as for service in one of the armed forces. **4.** to raise or increase (a force) by enlistment. **5.** to engage or hire (new employees, members, etc.). **6.** to furnish or replenish with a fresh supply; renew. **7.** to renew or restore (the health, strength, etc.). —*v.i.* **8.** to enlist men for service in one of the armed forces. **9.** to recover health, strength, etc. **10.** to gain new supplies of anything lost or wasted. [< F, s. of *recruter* < *recrue* new growth, ptp. of *recroître* (*re-* RE- + *croître* < L *crescere* to grow)] —**re·cruit′a·ble,** *adj.* —**re·cruit′er,** *n.*

re·cruit·ment (ri kro͞ot′mənt), *n.* the act or process of recruiting.

re·crys·tal·lise (rē kris′tᵊlīz′), *v.i., v.t.,* **-lised, -lis·ing.** *Chiefly Brit.* recrystallize. —**re′crys·tal·li·sa′tion,** *n.*

re·crys·tal·lize (rē kris′tᵊlīz′), *v.,* **-lized, -liz·ing.** —*v.i.* **1.** to become crystallized again. **2.** *Metall.* (of a metal) to acquire a new granular structure with new crystals because of plastic deformation. —*v.t.* **3.** to crystallize again. —**re′-crys·tal·li·za′tion,** *n.*

rect-, var. of **recti-** before a vowel: *rectangle.*

rect., 1. receipt. **2.** (in prescriptions) rectified. [< L *rectificātus*] **3.** rector. **4.** rectory.

rec·ta (rek′tə), *n.* a pl. of **rectum.**

rec·tal (rek′tᵊl), *adj.* of or pertaining to the rectum. [RECT(UM) + -AL[1]] —**rec′tal·ly,** *adv.*

rec·tan·gle (rek′tang′gəl), *n.* a parallelogram having four right angles. [< ML *rectangulum,* LL *rectangul(um)* right-angled triangle (neut. of *rectiangulus* having a right angle) = *recti-* RECT- + *angulum* ANGLE[1]]

Rectangle

rec·tan·gu·lar (rek tang′gyə lər), *adj.* **1.** shaped like a rectangle. **2.** having the base or section in the form of a rectangle: *a rectangular pyramid.* **3.** having one or more right angles. **4.** forming a right angle. [< ML *rectangul(um)* RECTANGLE + -AR[1]] —**rec·tan·gu·lar·i·ty** (rek tang′gyə lar′i tē), *n.* —**rec·tan′gu·lar·ly,** *adv.*

rectan′gular coor′dinates, *Math.* a coordinate system in which the axes meet at right angles.

rec·ti (rek′tī), *n.* pl. of **rectus.**

recti-, a learned borrowing from Latin meaning "right," "straight," used in the formation of compound words: *rectilinear.* Also, *esp. before a vowel,* **rect-.** [< L, comb. form of *rectus* RIGHT]

rec·ti·fi·er (rek′tə fī′ər), *n.* **1.** a person or thing that rectifies. **2.** *Elect.* an apparatus in which current more readily flows in one direction than in the reverse direction, used to change an alternating current into a direct current. **3.** the apparatus that in distillation separates the most volatile material by condensing it; condenser.

rec·ti·fy (rek′tə fī′), *v.t.,* **-fied, -fy·ing. 1.** to make, put, or set right; remedy; correct. **2.** to put right by adjustment or calculation. **3.** *Chem.* to purify (esp. a spirit or liquor) by repeated distillation. **4.** *Elect.* to change (an alternating current) into a direct current. **5.** to determine the length of (a curve). **6.** *Astron., Geog.* to adjust (a globe) for the solution of any proposed problem. [ME *rectifie(n)* < MF

re·cop′y, *v.t.,* **-cop·ied, -cop·y·ing.**
re·crate′, *v.t.,* **-crat·ed, -crat·ing.**
re·crit′i·cize′, *v.t.,* **-cized, -ciz·ing.**
re·cross′, *v.*
re·crown′, *v.t.*

rectifi(er) < ML *rectific(āre)* = L *rect(us)* RECT- + *-ificāre* -IFY] —**rec′ti·fi′a·ble,** *adj.* —**rec′ti·fi·ca′tion,** *n.* —**Syn. 1.** mend, emend, amend; ameliorate. **2.** adjust, regulate.

rec·ti·lin·e·ar (rek′tᵊlin′ē ər), *adj.* **1.** forming a straight line. **2.** formed by straight lines. **3.** characterized by straight lines. **4.** moving in a straight line. Also, **rec′ti·lin′e·al.** [< LL *rectilīne(us)* (*rect(us)* RECT- + *līnea* LINE[1]) + -AR[1]] —**rec′ti·lin′e·ar·ly,** *adv.*

rec·ti·tude (rek′ti to͞od′, -tyo͞od′), *n.* **1.** rightness of principle or practice; moral virtue. **2.** correctness. [ME < MF < LL *rectitūdin-* (s. of *rectitūdō*) straightness = L *rect(us)* RECTI- + *-tūdin-* -TUDE]

rec·to (rek′tō), *n., pl.* **-tos.** *Print.* a right-hand page of an open book or manuscript; the front of a leaf (opposed to *verso*). [< LL *rectō (foliō)* on the right-hand (leaf or page), abl. of L *rectus* right]

rec·tor (rek′tər), *n.* **1.** a clergyman in charge of a parish in the Protestant Episcopal Church. **2.** *Rom. Cath. Ch.* an ecclesiastic in charge of a college, religious house, or congregation. **3.** *Anglican Ch.* a clergyman who has charge of a parish with full possession of all its rights, tithes, etc. **4.** the head of certain universities, colleges, and schools. [ME *rectour* < L *rector* ruler, leader = *rect(us)* ruled (ptp. of *regere*) + *-or* -OR[2]] —**rec·to·ri·al** (rek tôr′ē əl, -tōr′-), *adj.*

rec·tor·ate (rek′tər it), *n.* the office, dignity, or term of a rector. [< ML *rectorāt(us)* office of rector = L *rectōr-* (s. of *rector*) RECTOR + *-ātus* -ATE[1]]

rec·to·ry (rek′tə rē), *n., pl.* **-ries. 1.** a rector's house; parsonage. **2.** *Brit.* a benefice held by a rector. [< ML *rectoria* = L *rectōr-* (s. of *rector*) RECTOR + *-ia* -Y[3]]

rec·tum (rek′təm), *n., pl.* **-tums, -ta** (-tə). *Anat.* the comparatively straight, terminal section of the intestine, ending in the anus. [< NL *rectum (intestinum)* the straight (intestine)]

rec·tus (rek′təs), *n., pl.* **-ti** (-tī). *Anat.* any of several straight muscles, as of the abdomen, thigh, eye, etc. [< NL *rectus (musculus)* the straight (muscle)]

re·cum·bent (ri kum′bənt), *adj.* **1.** lying down; reclining; leaning. **2.** at repose; idle. **3.** *Zool., Bot.* noting a part that leans or reposes upon anything. —*n.* **4.** a recumbent person, animal, plant, etc. [< L *recumbent-* (s. of *recumbēns*, prp. of *recumbere*) lying back = *re-* RE- + *cumb-* (cf. *cubāre* to lie down) + *-ent-* -ENT] —**re·cum′ben·cy, re·cum′bence,** *n.* —**re·cum′bent·ly,** *adv.* —**Syn. 1.** prone, supine; prostrate; inclined.

re·cu·per·ate (ri ko͞o′pə rāt′, -kyo͞o′-), *v.,* **-at·ed, -at·ing.** —*v.i.* **1.** to recover from sickness or exhaustion; regain health or strength. **2.** to recover from financial loss. —*v.t.* **3.** to restore to health, vigor, etc. [< L *recuperāt(us)* recovered (ptp. of *recuperāre*, sp. var. of *reciperāre*) = *re-* RE- + *cuper-* get, take + *-ātus* -ATE[1]] —**re·cu′per·a′tion,** *n.* —**re·cu′per·a′tor,** *n.* —**Syn. 1.** heal, mend.

re·cu·per·a·tive (ri ko͞o′pə rā′tiv, -pər ə tiv, -kyo͞o′-), *adj.* **1.** that recuperates. **2.** having the power of recuperating. **3.** pertaining to recuperation: *recuperative powers.* Also, **re·cu·per·a·to·ry** (ri ko͞o′pər ə tôr′ē, -tōr′ē, -kyo͞o′-). [< LL *recuperātīv(us)* that can be regained]

re·cur (ri kûr′), *v.i.,* **-curred, -cur·ring. 1.** to occur again, as an event or experience. **2.** to return to the mind: *The idea often recurs to me.* **3.** to come up again for consideration, as a question. **4.** to return, as in one's thoughts or actions. **5.** to have recourse. [< L *recurr(ere)* (to) run back = *re-* RE- + *currere* to run] —**re·cur′ring·ly,** *adv.*

re·cur·rence (ri kûr′əns, -kur′-), *n.* **1.** an act or instance of recurring. **2.** return to a previous condition, habit, subject, etc. **3.** recourse.

re·cur·rent (ri kûr′ənt, -kur′-), *adj.* **1.** that recurs; occurring or appearing again, esp. repeatedly. **2.** *Anat.* turned back so as to run in a reverse direction, as a nerve, artery, branch, etc. [< L *recurrent-* (s. of *recurrēns*, prp. of *recurrere*) running back. See RECUR, -ENT] —**re·cur′rent·ly,** *adv.* —**Syn. 1.** repeated; persistent, intermittent.

recur′rent fe′ver, *Pathol.* See **relapsing fever.**

recur′ring dec′imal. See **circulating decimal.**

re·cur·vate (ri kûr′vit, -vāt), *adj.* bent back or backward; recurved. [< L *recurvāt(us)* bent backward (ptp. of *recurvāre*). See RECURVE, -ATE[1]]

re·curve (ri kûrv′), *v.t., v.i.,* **-curved, -curv·ing.** to curve or bend back or backward. [< L *recurv(āre).* See RE-, CURVE]

rec·u·san·cy (rek′yə zən sē, ri kyo͞o′-), *n.* **1.** the state of being recusant. **2.** obstinate refusal or opposition. [RECUS(ANT) + -ANCY]

rec·u·sant (rek′yə zənt, ri kyo͞o′zənt), *adj.* **1.** refusing to submit, comply, etc. **2.** obstinate in refusal. **3.** *Eng. Hist.* (esp. of a Roman Catholic) refusing to attend services of the Church of England. —*n.* **4.** a person who is recusant. [< L *recūsant-* (s. of *recūsāns*, prp. of *recūsāre* to refuse, object) = *re-* RE- + *-cūs-* cause (var. of *causa*) + *-ant-* -ANT]

re·cuse (ri kyo͞oz′), *v.t.,* **-cused, -cus·ing.** *Rare.* to reject or challenge (a judge or juror) as disqualified to act, esp. because of interest or bias. [ME *recuse(n)* < MF *recus(er)* < L *recūs(āre)*; see RECUSANT] —**rec·u·sa·tion** (rek′yo͞o zā′shən), *n.*

re·cy·cle (rē sī′kəl), *v.t.,* **-cled, -cling. 1.** to cause to pass through or undergo further treatment, change, use, etc. **2.** to reuse (manufactured products) by breaking up, melting, cleaning, etc., and reprocessing the raw materials. —**re·cy·cla·bil·i·ty** (rē sī′klə bil′i tē), *n.* —**re·cy·cla·ble** (rē sī′klə bəl), *adj.*

red (red), *n., adj.,* **red·der, red·dest.** —*n.* **1.** any of various colors resembling the color of blood, toward one end of the visible spectrum. **2.** something red, as clothing. **3.** an animal with a reddish coat. **4.** an athlete who wears red as a team color. **5.** (*often cap.*) an ultraradical leftist in politics, esp. a communist. **6. in the red,** operating at a loss or being in debt. **7. see red,** *Informal.* to become enraged. —*adj.* **8.** of the color red. **9.** having distinctive areas or markings of red: *a red robin.* **10.** radically left politically. **11.** (*often cap.*) communist. [ME *red,* OE *rēad;* c. G *rot,* D *rood,* OIcel *raudhr,* L *rūfus, ruber,* Gk *erythrós;* see RUBELLA, RUFESCENT, ERYSIPELAS] —**red′ly,** *adv.* —**red′ness,** *n.*

red-, var. of **re-** before a vowel in some words: *redintegrate.*

-red, a native English suffix, denoting condition, formerly used in the formation of nouns: *hatred; kindred.* [ME *-rede,* OE *-rǣden*]

re·dact (ri dakt′), *v.t.* **1.** to put into suitable literary form; revise; edit. **2.** to draw up or frame (a statement, proclamation, etc.). [< L *redact(us)* led back (ptp. of *redigere*) = *red-* RED- + *actus* (see ACT)] —**re·dac′tion,** *n.* —**re·dac′tion·al,** *adj.* —**re·dac′tor,** *n.*

red′ alert′, (in military or civilian defense) the most urgent form of alert, signaling that an enemy attack is imminent.

red′ al′ga, an alga of the class *Rhodophyceae,* in which the chlorophyll is masked by a red or purplish pigment.

re·dan (ri dan′), *n.* *Fort.* a V-shaped work, usually projecting from a fortified line. [< F, var. of *redent* a double notching = *re-* RE- + *dent* tooth < L *dent-* (s. of *dēns*)]

red′ ant′, any of various reddish ants, esp. the Pharaoh ant.

red·bird (red′bûrd′), *n.* the cardinal, *Richmondena cardinalis.*

red′ blood′ cell′, an erythrocyte. Also called **red′ blood′ cor′puscle.**

red-blood·ed (red′blud′id), *adj.* vigorous; virile. —**red′-blood′ed·ness,** *n.*

red·breast (red′brest′), *n.* **1.** a robin. **2.** any of various other birds, as a dowitcher or knot. **3.** a fresh-water sunfish, *Lepomis auritus,* found in the eastern U.S.

red·bud (red′bud′), *n.* an American, leguminous tree *Cercis canadensis,* having small, budlike, pink flowers: the state tree of Oklahoma.

red·cap (red′kap′), *n.* *U.S.* a baggage porter in a railroad station.

red′ car′pet, 1. a red strip of carpet placed on the ground for high-ranking dignitaries to walk on when entering or leaving a building, vehicle, or the like. **2.** a display of courtesy or deference, as that shown to persons of high station. —**red′-car′pet,** *adj.*

red′ ce′dar, 1. Also called **eastern red cedar, savin.** an American, coniferous tree, *Juniperus virginiana,* yielding a fragrant, reddish wood used for making lead pencils, for interior finishing, etc. **2.** the western red cedar, *Thuja plicata.* **3.** the wood of these trees.

red′ cent′, *U.S. Informal.* a cent, as representative of triviality: *His promise isn't worth a red cent!*

Red′ Chi′na. See **China, People's Republic of.**

red′ clo′ver, a clover, *Trifolium pratense,* having red flowers, grown for forage: the state flower of Vermont.

red·coat (red′kōt′), *n.* (esp. during the American Revolution) a British soldier.

red′ cor′al, any of several corals of the genus *Corallium,* as *C. nobile,* of the Mediterranean Sea, having a red or pink skeleton, used for jewelry.

Red′ Cres′cent, an organization functioning as the Red Cross in Muslim countries.

Red′ Cross′, 1. an international philanthropic organization (**Red′ Cross′ Soci′ety**), formed in consequence of the Geneva Convention of 1864, to care for the sick and wounded in war, secure neutrality of nurses, hospitals, etc., and help relieve suffering caused by pestilence, floods, fires, and other calamities. **2.** a branch of this organization: *the American Red Cross.* **3.** Also, **red′ cross′.** See **Geneva cross.**

red′ deer′, 1. a deer, *Cervus elaphus,* of Europe and Asia, having a reddish-brown summer coat. **2.** the white-tailed deer, *Odocoileus virginianus,* in its summer coat.

red·den (red′ᵊn), *v.t.* **1.** to make or cause to become red. —*v.i.* **2.** to become red. **3.** to blush or flush, as from anger.

red·dish (red′ish), *adj.* somewhat red; tinged with red. [ME *redische.* See RED, -ISH[1]]

red·dle (red′ᵊl), *n., v.t.,* **-dled, -dling.** ruddle.

red-dog (red′dôg′, -dog′), *v.,* **-dogged, -dog·ging.** *Football.* (esp. of linebackers) —*v.t.* **1.** to charge directly for (the passer) as soon as the ball is snapped. —*v.i.* **2.** to red-dog the passer.

rede (rēd), *v.,* **red·ed, red·ing,** *n.* *Chiefly Brit. Dial.* —*v.t.* **1.** to counsel; advise. **2.** to explain. —*n.* **3.** counsel; advice. **4.** a plan; scheme. **5.** a tale; story. [ME *rede(n),* OE *rǣdan;* see READ[1]]

re·dec·o·rate (ri dek′ə rāt′), *v.t., v.i.,* **-rat·ed, -rat·ing.** to decorate again; change in appearance, as an apartment or office. —**re·dec′o·ra′tion,** *n.*

re·deem (ri dēm′), *v.t.* **1.** to buy or pay off; clear by payment: *to redeem a mortgage.* **2.** to buy back, as after a mortgage foreclosure. **3.** to recover (something pledged or mortgaged) by payment or other satisfaction. **4.** to convert (paper money) into specie. **5.** to exchange (bonds, coupons, trading stamps, etc.) for money or goods. **6.** to discharge or fulfill (a pledge, promise, etc.). **7.** to make up for; make amends for (some fault). **8.** to obtain the release or restoration of, as by paying a ransom. **9.** *Theol.* to deliver from sin and its consequences by means of a sacrifice offered for the sinner. [ME *redem(en)* < MF *redim(er)* < L *redimere* = *red-* RED- + *-imere* to buy, var. of *emere* to purchase] —**Syn. 1, 2, 8, 9.** free, rescue, save. —**Ant. 1.** abandon.

re·deem·a·ble (ri dē′mə bəl), *adj.* **1.** capable of being redeemed. **2.** that is to be redeemed. Also, **re·demp·ti·ble** (ri demp′tə bəl). —**re·deem′a·bil′i·ty,** *n.* —**re·deem′a·bly,** *adv.*

re·deem·er (ri dē′mər), *n.* **1.** a person who redeems. **2.** (*cap.*) Jesus Christ. [ME]

re·deem·ing (ri dē′ming), *adj.* offsetting or counterbalancing some fault.

red′ eft′. See under **eft**[1] (def. 1).

re·de·liv·er (rē′di liv′ər), *v.t.* **1.** to deliver again. **2.** to deliver back; return.

re·de·mand (rē′di mand′, -mänd′), *v.t.* **1.** to demand again. **2.** to demand back; demand the return of. —**re′de·mand′a·ble,** *adj.*

re′ded′i·cate′, *v.t.,* **-cat·ed, -cat·ing.**
re′de·fine′, *v.t.,* **-fined, -fin·ing.**
re′de·fy′, *v.t.,* **-fied, -fy·ing.**
re′de·lib′er·a′tion, *n.*
re·dem′on·strate′, *v.,* **-strat·ed, -strat·ing.**

re·demp·tion (ri demp′shən), *n.* **1.** the act of redeeming. **2.** the state of being redeemed. **3.** deliverance; rescue. **4.** *Theol.* deliverance from sin; salvation. **5.** atonement for guilt. **6.** repurchase, as of something sold. **7.** paying off, as of a mortgage, bond, or note. **8.** recovery by payment, as of something pledged. **9.** conversion or exchange, as of paper money for specie. [ME *redempcioun* < MF < LL *redemptiōn-* (s. of *redemptiō*) = L *redempt(us)* (ptp. of *redimere* to REDEEM) + *-iōn-* -ION] —**re·demp′tion·al,** *adj.*

re·demp·tion·er (ri demp′shə nər), *n.* *Amer. Hist.* (from 17th to early 19th centuries) an immigrant who obtained passage by becoming an indentured servant.

re·demp·tive (ri demp′tiv), *adj.* **1.** serving to redeem. **2.** of, pertaining to, or centering on redemption or salvation. [REDEMPT(ION) + -IVE] —**re·demp′tive·ly,** *adv.*

re·demp·to·ry (ri demp′tə rē), *adj.* **1.** of or pertaining to redemption; redemptive. **2.** redeeming; saving: *a redemptory act.* [REDEMPT(ION) + -ORY[1]]

re·de·ploy (rē′di ploi′), *Mil.* —*v.t.* **1.** to transfer (a unit, supplies, etc.) from one theater of war to another. —*v.i.* **2.** to execute a redeployment. —**re′de·ploy′ment,** *n.*

red·eye (red′ī′), *n.* *U.S. Slang.* cheap, strong whiskey.

red′-eyed vir′eo (red′īd′), an American vireo, *Vireo olivaceus,* having olive-green and white plumage and red irises. See illus. at **vireo.**

red-faced (red′fāst′), *adj.* **1.** having a red face. **2.** blushing or flushed with embarrassment, anger, resentment, or the like. —**red-fac·ed·ly** (red′fā′sid lē, -fāst′lē), *adv.*

red·fin (red′fin′), *n.* any of various small fresh-water minnows with red fins, esp. a shiner, *Notropis umbratilis,* found in eastern and central North America.

red′ fir′, **1.** any of several firs, as *Abies magnifica,* of the western U.S., having a reddish bark. **2.** the light, soft wood of these trees. **3.** See **Douglas fir.**

red·fish (red′fish′), *n., pl.* (*esp. collectively*) **-fish,** (*esp. referring to two or more kinds or species*) **-fish·es.** a North Atlantic rockfish, *sebastes marinus,* used for food. Also called **rosefish.**

red′ fox′, **1.** a fox, *Vulpes vulpes,* usually having orangish-red to reddish-brown fur. See illus. at **fox. 2.** any other animal of this genus, esp. *V. fulva,* of North America.

red′ gi′ant, *Astron.* a star in an intermediate stage of evolution, characterized by a large volume, low surface temperature, and reddish hue.

Red′ Guard′, a member of a Chinese Communist youth movement in the late 1960's, committed to the militant support of Mao Tse-tung.

red-hand·ed (red′han′did), *adj., adv.* in the very act of a crime, wrongdoing, etc., or in possession of self-incriminating evidence: *caught red-handed.* —**red′-hand′ed·ly,** *adv.*

red′ hat′, **1.** the broad-brimmed official hat of a Roman Catholic cardinal. **2.** a cardinal. Also called **scarlet hat.**

red·head (red′hed′), *n.* **1.** a person having red hair. **2.** an American diving duck, *Aythya americana,* the male of which has a bright chestnut-red head.

red·head·ed (red′hed′id), *adj.* **1.** having red hair, as a person. **2.** having a red head, as an animal, esp. a bird. Also, **red′head′ed.**

red′-headed wood′pecker, a black and white, North American woodpecker, *Melanerpes erythrocephalus,* having a red head and neck.

red′ heat′, **1.** the temperature of a red-hot body. **2.** the condition of being red-hot.

red′ her′ring, **1.** a smoked herring. **2.** something intended to divert attention from the real problem or matter at hand; a misleading clue.

red-hot (red′hot′), *adj.* **1.** red with heat. **2.** very excited or enthusiastic. **3.** violent; furious. **4.** fresh or new.

red·in·gote (red′ing gōt′), *n.* **1.** a dress or lightweight coat, usually belted, open along the entire front to reveal a dress or petticoat worn underneath it. **2.** a dress with a contrasting gore in front. [< F < E *riding coat*]

red·in·te·grate (red in′tə grāt′), *v.t.,* **-grat·ed, -grat·ing.** to make whole again; restore to a perfect state; renew; reestablish. [ME *redintegrate(n)* < L *redintegrāt(us)* made whole again (ptp. of *redintegrāre*) = *red-* RED- + *integr-* (s. of *integer*) whole + *-ātus* -ATE[1]] —**red·in′te·gra′tive,** *adj.*

red·in·te·gra·tion (red in′tə grā′shən), *n.* **1.** the act or process of redintegrating. **2.** *Psychol.* the tendency to repeat the response to a complex stimulus on later experiencing any part of the stimulus. [< L *redintegrātiōn-* (s. of *redintegrātiō* = *redintegrāt(us)* (see REDINTEGRATE] + *-iōn-* -ION]

re·di·rect (rē′də rekt′, -dī-), *v.t.* **1.** to direct again. —*adj.* **2.** *Law.* pertaining to the examination of a witness by the party calling him, after cross-examination. —**re′di·rec′tion,** *n.*

re·dis·count (rē dis′kount), *v.t.* **1.** to discount again. —*n.* **2.** an act of rediscounting. **3.** Usually, **rediscounts.** commercial paper discounted a second time.

re·dis·trict (rē dis′trikt), *v.t.* to divide anew into districts, as for electoral purposes.

red·i·vi·vus (red′ə vī′vəs), *adj.* living again; revived. [< LL: that lives again, L: renewed, renovated = *red-* RED- + *vīvus* alive]

Red·lands (red′ləndz), *n.* a city in SW California, near Los Angeles. 36,355 (1970).

red′ lead′ (led), *n.* an orange to red, heavy, earthy, poisonous powder, Pb_3O_4: used chiefly as a paint pigment, in the manufacture of glass and glazes, and in storage batteries. Also called **minium.** Cf. **litharge.**

red′ lead′ ore′ (led), crocoite.

red-let·ter (red′let′ər), *adj.* **1.** marked by red letters, as festival days in the church calendar. **2.** memorable; especially important or happy: *a red-letter day.*

red′ light′, **1.** a red lamp, used as a traffic signal to mean "stop." **2.** an order or directive to halt an action, project, etc. **3.** a signal of danger; warning.

red′-light′ dis′trict, an area or district in a city in which many houses of prostitution are located.

red·lin·ing (red′lī′ning), *n.* an arbitrary practice by which banks limit or refuse to grant mortgage loans for houses in blighted urban areas. [so called because such areas are said to be encircled by red pencil on maps]

red′ man′, a North American Indian.

red′ meat′, any meat that is dark-colored before cooking, as beef, lamb, venison, or mutton. Cf. **white meat** (def. 1).

Red·mond (red′mənd), *n.* **John Edward,** 1856–1918, Irish political leader.

red·neck (red′nek′), *n.* *Disparaging.* (in the southern U.S.) an uneducated, white farm laborer.

red′ oak′, **1.** any of several oak trees, as *Quercus velutina* or *Q. borealis,* of North America. **2.** the hard, cross-grained wood of these trees.

red′ o′cher, any of the red natural earths that are mixtures of hematites and are used as pigments.

red·o·lent (red′ələnt), *adj.* **1.** having a pleasant odor; fragrant. **2.** odorous or smelling (usually fol. by *of*): *a kitchen redolent of garlic.* **3.** suggestive; reminiscent (usually fol. by *of*). [ME < L *redolent-* (s. of *redolēns,* prp. of *redolēre* to emit odor) = *red-* RED- + *ol(ēre)* (to) smell + *-ent-* -ENT] —**red′o·lence, red′o·len·cy,** *n.* —**red′o·lent·ly,** *adv.*

Re·don (rə don′; *Fr.* RƏ dôN′), *n.* **O·di·lon** (ō′də lon; *Fr.* ô dē lôN′), 1840–1916, French painter and etcher.

Re·don′do Beach′ (rə don′dō), a city in SW California. 57,425 (1970).

red′ o′sier, **1.** a willow, *Salix purpurea,* having tough, flexible twigs or branches used for wickerwork. **2.** any willow having reddish branches. **3.** *U.S.* a dogwood, *Cornus stolonifera,* having red bark and sending up osierlike shoots.

re·dou·ble (rē dub′əl), *v.,* **-bled, -bling.** —*v.t.* **1.** to double; make twice as great. **2.** to echo or reecho. **3.** to go back over: *to redouble one's footsteps.* —*v.i.* **4.** to be doubled; become twice as great. **5.** to be echoed; resound. [late ME < MF *redoubl(er)*]

re·doubt (ri dout′), *n.* *Fort.* **1.** an isolated work forming a complete enclosure of any form, used to defend a prominent point. **2.** an independent earthwork built within a permanent fortification to reinforce it. [< F *redoute* < It *ridott(o)* < LL *reduct(us)* a refuge, n. use of ptp. of L *redūcere* to lead back; see REDUCE]

re·doubt·a·ble (ri dou′tə bəl), *adj.* **1.** that is to be feared; formidable. **2.** commanding or evoking respect, reverence, or the like. [ME *redoutable* < MF = *redout(er)* (to) fear (*re-* RE- + *douter* to fear, DOUBT) + *-able* -ABLE] —**re·doubt′a·bly,** *adv.*

re·dound (ri dound′), *v.i.* **1.** to have a good or bad effect or result, as to the advantage or credit of a person or thing. **2.** to result or acrue, as to a person. **3.** to come back or reflect upon a person to his honor or disgrace (usually fol. by *on* or *upon*). **4.** *Obs.* to proceed, issue, or arise. [ME *redound(en)* < MF *redond(er)* < L *redundāre* to overflow = *red-* RED- + *undāre* to surge (< *unda* wave)]

red-pen·cil (red′pen′səl), *v.t.,* **-ciled, -cil·ing** or (*esp. Brit.*) **-cilled, -cil·ling.** to delete, censor, correct, or abridge (written material) with or as with a pencil having a red lead: *The instructor red-penciled corrections on the exam papers.*

red′ pep′per, **1.** cayenne. **2.** a pepper, *Capsicum frutescens,* cultivated in many varieties, the yellow or red pods of which are used for flavoring, sauces, etc.

Red′ Poll′, one of a breed of red, hornless, dual-purpose cattle, raised originally in England. Also, **Red′ Polled′.**

red·poll (red′pōl′), *n.* any of various small fringilline birds of the genus *Acanthis,* the adults of which usually have a crimson crown patch.

re·draft (rē′draft′, -dräft′), *n.* **1.** a second draft or drawing. **2.** *Finance.* a draft on the drawer or endorsers of a protested bill of exchange for the amount of the bill plus the costs and charges. —*v.t.* **3.** to draft again.

re·dress (rē dres′), *v.t.* to dress again.

re·dress (*n.* rē′dres, ri dres′; *v.* ri dres′), *n.* **1.** the setting right of what is wrong. **2.** relief from wrong or injury. **3.** compensation or satisfaction for a wrong or injury. —*v.t.* **4.** to set right; remedy or correct (wrongs, injuries, etc.). [ME *redress(en)* < MF *redress(er),* OF *redrecier* = *re-* RE- + *drecier* to straighten; see DRESS] —**re·dress′a·ble, re·dress′i·ble,** *adj.* —**re·dress′er, re·dres′sor,** *n.*
—**Syn. 1.** indemnity, restoration, remedy, atonement. REDRESS, REPARATION, RESTITUTION suggest making amends or giving indemnification for a wrong. REDRESS may refer either to the act of setting right an unjust situation (as by some power), or to satisfaction sought or gained for a wrong suffered: *the redress of grievances.* REPARATION means compensation or satisfaction for a wrong or loss inflicted. The word may have the moral idea of amends: *to make reparation for one's neglect;* but more frequently it refers to financial compensation (which is asked for, rather than given): *the reparations demanded of the aggressor nations.* RESTITUTION means literally the restoration of what has been taken from the lawful owner, but may refer to restoring the equivalent of what has been taken, as in cash value: *He demanded restitution of his land or restitution for it.* **4.** amend.

Red′ Riv′er, **1.** a river flowing E from NW Texas along the S boundary of Oklahoma into the Mississippi River in Louisiana. ab. 1300 mi. long. **2.** Also called **Red′ Riv′er of the North′.** a river flowing N along the boundary between Minnesota and North Dakota to Lake Winnipeg in S Canada. 533 mi. long. **3.** Songka.

red·root (red′ro͞ot′, -ro͝ot′), *n.* **1.** a North American plant, *Lachnanthes tinctoria,* having sword-shaped leaves, woolly flowers, and a red root. **2.** any of various other plants having red roots, as the alkanet, *Alkanna tinctoria,* pigweed, *Amaranthus retroflexus,* etc.

red′ rose′, *Eng. Hist.* the emblem of the royal house of Lancaster. Cf. **Wars of the Roses, white rose.**

red′ sal′mon. See **sockeye salmon.**

re′de·pos′it, *v., n.*
re′de·scribe′, *v.t.,* **-scribed, -scrib·ing.**
re′de·sign′, *v.*
re′de·ter′mine, *v.,* **-mined, -min·ing.**
re′de·vel′op, *v.*
re′de·vel′op·er, *n.*
re′de·vel′op·ment, *n.*
re′di·gest′, *v.t.*
re′di·ges′tion, *n.*
re′dis·cov′er, *v.t.*
re′dis·cov′er·y, *n., pl.* **-er·ies.**
re′dis·solve′, *v.,* **-solved, -solv·ing.**
re′dis·trib′ute, *v.t.,* **-ut·ed, -ut·ing.**
re′dis·tri·bu′tion, *n.*
re′di·vide′, *v.,* **-vid·ed, -vid·ing.**
re·do′, *v.t.,* **-did, -done, -do·ing.**
re·dock′, *v.*
re·draw′, *v.,* **-drew, -drawn, -draw·ing;** *n.*
re·drill′, *v.*
re·dry′, *v.,* **-dried, -dry·ing.**

Red' Sea', an arm of the Indian Ocean, extending NW between Africa and Arabia: connected to the Mediterranean by the Suez Canal. 1450 mi. long; 170,000 sq. mi.; greatest depth, 7254 ft.

red' shift', *Physics, Astron.* the systematic shift toward longer wavelengths in the spectra of light from distant galaxies, assumed to be caused by the Doppler effect and indicating that the galaxies are receding.

red·skin (red'skin'), *n.* *Often Offensive.* a North American Indian.

red' snap'per, any of several snappers of the genus *Lutjanus,* esp. *L. blackfordi,* a large food fish found in the Gulf of Mexico.

red' squir'rel, a reddish squirrel, *Tamiasciurus hudsonius,* of North America. Also called **chickaree.**

red·start (red'stärt'), *n.* any of several small, Old World thrushes, usually with reddish-brown tails, esp. *Phoenicurus phoenicurus.* [RED + obs. *start* tail, ME *start, stert* tail, handle, OE *steort* tail]

red' tape', excessive formality and routine required before official action can be taken.

red' tide', a brownish-red discoloration of marine waters caused by the presence of enormous numbers of certain microscopic flagellates, esp. the dinoflagellates.

red·top (red'top'), *n.* a grass, *Agrostis alba,* certain forms of which have a reddish panicle.

re·duce (ri dōōs', -dyōōs'), *v.,* **-duced, -duc·ing.** —*v.t.* **1.** to cause to lessen in size, number, or amount. **2.** to act destructively upon (an object or substance) (often fol. by *to*): *a mansion reduced to ashes.* **3.** to lower in rank, dignity, or well-being: *a sergeant reduced to a corporal.* **4.** to treat analytically, as a complex idea. **5.** to lower in price. **6.** to bring under one's domination or control. **7.** *Photog.* to lessen the density of (an exposed negative). **8.** to adjust or correct by making allowances, as an astronomical observation. **9.** *Math.* to change the denomination or form of (a fraction, polynomial, etc.). **10.** *Chem.* **a.** to deoxidize. **b.** to add hydrogen to. **c.** to change (a compound) so that the valence of the positive element is lower. **11.** *Chem., Metall.* to bring into the metallic state by separating from nonmetallic constituents; smelt. **12.** to thin or dilute, as alcohol with water or paint with oil or turpentine. **13.** *Surg.* to restore to the normal place, relations, or condition, as a dislocated organ or a fractured bone with separation of the fragment ends. —*v.i.* **14.** to become reduced, esp. to lose weight, as by dieting. **15.** *Biol.* to undergo meiosis. [ME *reduce(n)* (to) lead back < L *rēdūc(ere)* (to) lead back, bring back = *re-* -RE- + *dūcere* to lead] —**re·duc'i·bil'i·ty,** *n.* —**re·duc'i·ble,** *adj.* —**re·duc'i·bly,** *adv.*

re·duced (ri dōōst', -dyōōst'), *adj.* **1.** that is or has been reduced. **2.** *Math.* noting a polynomial equation in which the second highest power is missing: *The cubic equation* $x^3 - 4x + 4 = 0$ *is reduced.*

reduced' he'moglobin, See under **hemoglobin.**

re·duc·er (ri dōō'sər, -dyōō'-), *n.* **1.** a person or thing that reduces. **2.** *Photog.* **a.** an oxidizing solution for lessening the density of an exposed negative. **b.** a developing agent.

reduc'ing a'gent, *Chem.* a substance that causes another substance to undergo reduction and that is oxidized in the process.

reduc'ing glass', a lens or mirror that produces a virtual image of an object smaller than the object itself.

re·duc·tase (ri duk'tās, -tāz), *n.* *Biochem.* any enzyme acting as a reducing agent. [REDUCT(ION) + -ASE]

re·duc·ti·o ad ab·sur·dum (RE dōōk'ti ō äd äb sōōr'dōōm; *Eng.* ri duk'shē ō' ad ab sûr'dəm), *Latin.* a reduction to an absurdity; the refutation of a proposition by showing its logical conclusion as absurd.

re·duc·tion (ri duk'shən), *n.* **1.** the act of reducing. **2.** the state of being reduced. **3.** the amount by which something is reduced or diminished. **4.** a form produced by reducing; a copy on a smaller scale. **5.** *Biol.* meiosis, esp. the first meiotic cell division in which the chromosome number is reduced. **6.** *Chem.* **a.** the removal of oxygen from an oxide. **b.** the addition of hydrogen to a compound. **c.** the lowering of the valence of a positive element in a compound. [late ME *reduccion* < MF *reduction* < L *rēductiōn-* (s. of *rēductiō*) a bringing back = *rēduct(us)* (ptp. of *rēdūcere;* see REDUCE) + *-iōn-* -ION] —**re·duc'tion·al,** *adj.*

re·duc·tive (ri duk'tiv), *adj.* **1.** of, pertaining to, characterized by, or producing reduction or abridgment. **2.** of or pertaining to change from one form to another. —*n.* **3.** something causing or inducing a reductive process. [REDUCT(ION) + -IVE] —**re·duc'tive·ly,** *adv.*

re·dun·dan·cy (ri dun'dən sē), *n., pl.* **-cies. 1.** the state of being redundant. **2.** superfluous repetition of words; verbosity. **3.** overabundance or excessive profusion or proliferation: *a redundancy of furniture.* **4.** something that is redundant. Also, **re·dun'dance.** [< L *redundantia* an overflowing, excess < *redundant-* (s. of prp.)]

re·dun·dant (ri dun'dənt), *adj.* **1.** characterized by verbosity or unnecessary repetition in expressing ideas; prolix. **2.** in excess of requirements; superfluous: *to shed redundant fat.* [< L *redundant-* (s. of *redundāns*), prp. of *redundāre.* See REDOUND, -ANT] —**re·dun'dant·ly,** *adv.*

redun'dant verb', *Gram.* a verb that has a variant for one or more of its inflected forms, as *light,* whose past can be *lit* or *lighted.*

redupl., reduplication.

re·du·pli·cate (*v.* ri dōō'plə kāt', -dyōō'-; *adj.* ri dōō'plə kit, -kāt', -dyōō'-), *v.,* **-cat·ed, -cat·ing,** *adj.* —*v.t.* **1.** to double; repeat. **2.** *Gram.* to form (a derivative or inflected form) by doubling a specified syllable or other portion of the primitive, sometimes with fixed modifications, as in Greek *léloipa* "I have left," *leípo* "I leave." —*v.i.* **3.** to become doubled. **4.** *Gram.* to become reduplicated. —*adj.* **5.** doubled. **6.** *Bot.* valvate, with the edges folded back so as to project outward. [< LL *reduplicāt(us)* (ptp. of *reduplicāre*) = L *re-* RE- + *duplic(āre)* (to) double + *-ātus* -ATE[1]]

re·du·pli·ca·tion (ri dōō'plə kā'shən, -dyōō'-), *n.* **1.** the act of reduplicating. **2.** the state of being reduplicated. **3.** something resulting from reduplicating. **4.** *Gram.* **a.** reduplicating as a grammatical pattern. **b.** the added element in a reduplicated form. **c.** a form containing a reduplicated element. [< LL *reduplicātiōn-* (s. of *reduplicātiō*)]

re·du·pli·ca·tive (ri dōō'plə kā'tiv, -dyōō'-), *adj.* **1.** tending to reduplicate. **2.** pertaining to or marked by reduplication. **3.** *Bot.* reduplicate (def. 6).

re·dux (ri duks'), *adj.* brought back, as following retirement, illness, or long inactivity; resurgent: *the Victorian era redux.* [< L, lit., leading back, led back = *re-* RE- + *duc-* (var. s. of *dūcere* to lead) + *-s* nom. sing. ending]

red·wing (red'wing'), *n.* a European thrush, *Turdus musicus,* having chestnut-red flank and axillary feathers.

red'-winged black'bird (red'wingd'), a North American blackbird, *Agelaius phoeniceus,* the male of which is black with scarlet patches on the wing.

red·wood (red'wŏŏd'), *n.* **1.** a coniferous tree, *Sequoia sempervirens,* of California, noted for its height of from 200 to over 300 feet: the state tree of California. **2.** the brownish-red timber of this tree. **3.** any of various trees yielding a reddish wood.

Red'wood Cit'y (red'wŏŏd'), a city in W California. 55,686 (1970).

ree (rē), *n.* reeve[3].

re·ech·o (rē ek'ō), *v.,* **-ech·oed, -ech·o·ing,** *n., pl.* **-ech·oes.** —*v.i.* **1.** to echo back, as a sound. **2.** to give back an echo; resound. —*v.t.* **3.** to echo back. **4.** to repeat like an echo. —*n.* **5.** a repeated echo. Also, **re-ech'o, re·ëch'o.**

reed (rēd), *n.* **1.** the straight stalk of any of various tall grasses, esp. of the genera *Phragmites* and *Arundo,* growing in marshy places. **2.** any of the plants themselves. **3.** *Music.* **a.** a musical pipe made from a reed or from the hollow stalk of some other plant. **b.** a small, flexible piece of cane or metal that is attached to the mouth of any of various wind instruments and vibrated by a stream of air. **c.** any instrument with such a device, as the oboe or clarinet. **4.** *Textiles.* the series of parallel strips of wires in a loom that force the weft up to the web and separate the threads of the warp. **5.** a unit of length, equal to 6 cubits. Ezek. 40:5. —*v.t.* **6.** to thatch with or as with reed. **7.** to make vertical grooves on (the edge of a coin, medal, etc.). [ME; OE *hrēod;* c. G, D *riet*]

Reed (rēd), *n.* **1. John,** 1887–1920, U.S. journalist and poet. **2. Walter C.,** 1851–1902, U.S. army surgeon who identified the mosquito that transmits the yellow-fever virus.

reed·bird (rēd'bûrd'), *n.* *Southern U.S.* bobolink.

reed·buck (rēd'buk'), *n., pl.* **-bucks,** (*esp. collectively*) **-buck.** any of several yellowish African antelopes of the genus *Redunca,* found near lakes and rivers, the male of which has short, forward-curving horns. [trans. of SAfrD *rietbok*]

reed·ing (rē'ding), *n.* *Archit.* **1.** a set of moldings, as on a column, resembling small convex fluting. **2.** a number of narrow, vertical grooves on the edge of a coin, medal, etc.

reed' mace', cattail (def. 1).

reed' or'gan, a musical keyboard instrument in which the sound is produced by vibrating metal reeds.

reed' pipe', an organ pipe having a reed that is vibrated by air to produce the sound.

reed' stop', a set of reed pipes in a pipe organ.

re·ed·u·cate (rē ej'ŏŏ kāt', -ed'yŏŏ-), *v.t.,* **-cat·ed, -cat·ing. 1.** to educate again, as for new purposes. **2.** to educate for resumption of normal activities, as a disabled person. Also, **re-ed'u·cate', re·ëd'u·cate'.** —**re·ed'u·ca'tion, re-ed'u·ca'tion, re·ëd'u·ca'tion,** *n.*

reed·y (rē'dē), *adj.,* **reed·i·er, reed·i·est. 1.** full of reeds: *a reedy marsh.* **2.** like a reed or reeds: *reedy grass.* **3.** having a sound like that of a reed instrument. [ME *reeddy*] —**reed'i·ness,** *n.*

reef[1] (rēf), *n.* **1.** a ridge of rocks or sand, often of coral debris, at or near the surface of the water. **2.** *Mining.* a lode or vein. [earlier *riff(e)* < D or LG *rif*]

reef[2] (rēf), *Naut.* —*n.* **1.** a part of a sail that is rolled and tied down to reduce the area exposed to the wind. —*v.t.* **2.** to shorten (sail) by tying in one or more reefs. **3.** to reduce the length of (a topmast, a bowsprit, etc.), as by lowering or sliding inboard. [ME *riff,* ? < MLG *rif,* or ? < Scand *rif*]

reef·er[1] (rē'fər), *n.* **1.** *Naut.* a person who reefs. **2.** *Clothing.* a short coat or jacket of thick cloth. **3.** *Slang.* a marijuana cigarette. [REEF[2] + -ER[1]; in def. 3, from the generalized sense of a rolled object]

ree·fer[2] (rē'fər), *n.* *Slang.* a refrigerated compartment, storeroom, car, or truck. [alter. and shortening of REFRIGERATOR]

reef' knot', *Naut.* a square knot used in tying reef points. Also called **flat knot.**

reef' point', *Naut.* a short piece of line fastened through a sail for tying in a reef.

reek (rēk), *n.* **1.** a strong, unpleasant smell. **2.** vapor or steam. —*v.i.* **3.** to smell strongly and unpleasantly. **4.** to be strongly pervaded with something offensive. **5.** to give off steam, smoke, etc. —*v.t.* **6.** to expose to or treat with smoke. **7.** to emit (smoke, fumes, etc.). [ME *rek(e),* OE *rēc;* c. G *rauch,* D *rook,* OIcel *reykr*] —**reek'ing·ly,** *adv.* —**reek'y,** *adj.*

reel[1] (rēl), *n.* **1.** a cylinder, frame, or other device that turns on an axis and is used to wind up or pay out something. **2.** *Chiefly Brit.* a spool of sewing thread. **3.** a quantity of something wound on a reel: *two reels of magnetic tape.* **4.** *Photog.* **a.** a spool on which film, esp. motion-picture film, is wound. **b.** a roll of motion-picture film. —*v.t.* **5.** to wind on a reel. **6.** to unwind (silk filaments) from a cocoon. **7.** to pull or draw in by winding a line on a reel. **8. reel off,** to say, write, or produce quickly and easily. [ME *rele,* OE *hrēol* c. OIcel *hræll* weaver's rod]

reel[2] (rēl), *v.i.* **1.** to sway or rock under a blow, shock, etc. **2.** to waver or fall back. **3.** to sway about in standing or walking, as from dizziness or intoxication; stagger. **4.** to turn round and round; whirl. **5.** to have a sensation of whirling: *His brain reeled.* —*v.t.* **6.** to cause to reel. —*n.* **7.** an act of reeling; a reeling or staggering movement. [ME *rel(en)* < *rele* REEL[1]] —**Syn. 3.** See **stagger.**

re·dye', *v.t.,* **-dyed, -dye·ing.** **re·earn',** *v.t.* **re·ed'it,** *v.t.* **re'e·ject',** *v.t.*

reel[3] (rēl), *n.* **1.** a lively dance popular in Scotland. **2.** See **Virginia reel.** [special use of REEL[2]]

reel′ and bead′. See **bead and reel.**

re·en·act (rē′ən akt′), *v.t.* to enact or perform again. —**re′en·act′ment,** *n.*

re·en·force (rē′en fōrs′, -fôrs′), *v.t.,* **-forced, -forc·ing.** reinforce. Also, **re′-en·force′, re′ën·force′.** —**re′en·force′ment, re′-en·force′ment, re′ën·force′ment,** *n.* —**re′en·forc′er, re′-en·forc′er, re′ën·forc′er,** *n.*

re·en·list (rē′ən list′), *v.i., v.t.* to enlist again: *The sergeant reenlisted for three years. They hoped to reenlist many of last year's volunteers.* Also, **re′-en·list′, re′ën·list′.**

re·en·list·ment (rē′ən list′mənt), *n.* **1.** an act of reenlisting. **2.** a person who reenlists. **3.** the period of service following a reenlistment: *His army reenlistment is three years.* Also, **re′-en·list′ment, re′ën·list′ment.**

re·en·ter (rē en′tər), *v.t.* **1.** to enter again. **2.** to record or enroll again. —*v.i.* **3.** to enter again. Also, **re-en′ter, re·ën′ter.** —**re·en·trance, re-en·trance, re·ën·trance** (rē en′trəns), *n.*

reen′tering an′gle, *Geom.* an interior angle of a polygon that is greater than 180°.

re·en·trant (rē en′trənt), *adj.* **1.** reentering: *a reentrant angle.* —*n.* **2.** a reentering angle or part.

re·en·try (rē en′trē), *n., pl.* **-tries. 1.** an act of reentering. **2.** the return into the earth's atmosphere of an artificial satellite, rocket, etc. **3.** *Law.* the retaking of possession under a right reserved in a prior conveyance. [late ME]

reeve[1] (rēv), *n.* **1.** an administrative officer of a town or district. **2.** *Brit.* an overseer or superintendent of workers, tenants, or an estate. **3.** *Canadian.* the presiding officer of a village or town council. [ME *(i)reve,* OE *gerēfa* high official, lit., head of a *rōf* array, number (of soldiers)]

reeve[2] (rēv), *v.t.,* **reeved** or **rove, reeved** or **rov·en, reev·ing.** *Naut.* **1.** to pass (a rope or the like) through a hole, ring, or the like. **2.** to fasten by placing through or around something. **3.** to pass a rope through (the swallow of a block). [? < D *reve(n)*; see REEF[2]]

reeve[3] (rēv), *n.* the female of the ruff, *Philomachus pugnax.* Also called **ree.** [?]

re·ex·am·ine (rē′ig zam′in), *v.t.,* **-ined, -in·ing. 1.** to examine again. **2.** *Law.* to examine (a witness) again after having questioned him previously. Also, **re′-ex·am′ine.** —**re′ex·am′in·a·ble, re′-ex·am′in·a·ble,** *adj.* —**re′ex·am′i·na′tion, re′-ex·am′i·na′tion,** *n.* —**re′ex·am′in·er, re′-ex·am′in·er,** *n.*

re·ex·port (*v.* rē′ik spōrt′, -spôrt′, rē eks′pōrt, -pôrt; *n.* rē eks′pōrt, -pôrt), *v.t.* **1.** to export again, as imported goods. —*n.* **2.** the act of reexporting. **3.** a commodity that is reexported. Also, **re′-ex·port′, re′ëx·port′.** —**re′ex·por·ta′tion, re′-ex·por·ta′tion, re′ëx·por·ta′tion,** *n.* —**re′ex·port′er, re′-ex·port′er, re′ëx·port′er,** *n.*

ref (ref), *n., v.t., v.i.,* **reffed, ref·fing.** *Sports Slang.* referee. [by shortening]

ref., 1. referee. **2.** reference. **3.** referred. **4.** reformation. **5.** reformed. **6.** refund.

re·face (rē fās′), *v.t.,* **-faced, -fac·ing.** to renew, restore, or repair the facing or outer surface of.

Ref. Ch., Reformed Church.

re·fect (ri fekt′), *v.t. Archaic.* to refresh, esp. with food or drink. [< L *refect(us)* made again, renewed (ptp. of *reficere*) = *re-* RE- + *fec-* make (comb. form of *facere* to make, do) + *-tus* ptp. suffix]

re·fec·tion (ri fek′shən), *n.* **1.** refreshment, esp. with food or drink. **2.** a portion of food or drink; repast. [ME *refeccioun* < L *refectiōn-* (s. of *refectiō*) restoration = *refect(us)* (see REFECT) + *-iōn-* -ION]

re·fec·to·ry (ri fek′tə rē), *n., pl.* **-ries.** a dining hall in a religious house, a college, or other institution. [< ML *refectōri(um)* = L *refect(us)* renewed, restored (see REFECT) + *-ōrium* -ORY[2]]

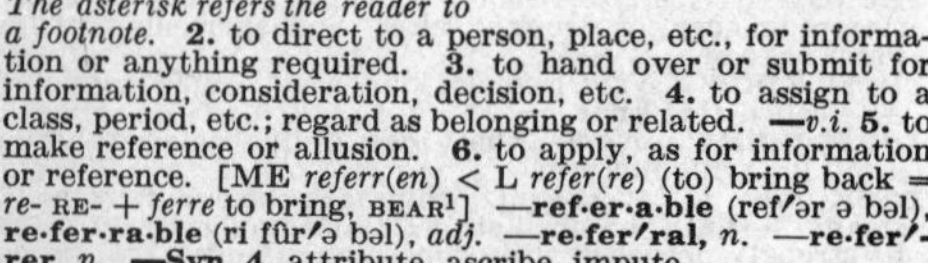
Refectory table (Italy, 16th century)

refec′tory ta′ble, 1. a long, narrow table having a single stretcher between trestlelike supports at the ends. **2.** a narrow dining table having extensible ends.

re·fer (ri fûr′), *v.,* **-ferred, -fer·ring.** —*v.t.* **1.** to direct the attention or thoughts of: *The asterisk refers the reader to a footnote.* **2.** to direct to a person, place, etc., for information or anything required. **3.** to hand over or submit for information, consideration, decision, etc. **4.** to assign to a class, period, etc.; regard as belonging or related. —*v.i.* **5.** to make reference or allusion. **6.** to apply, as for information or reference. [ME *referr(en)* < L *refer(re)* (to) bring back = *re-* RE- + *ferre* to bring, BEAR[1]] —**re·fer·a·ble** (ref′ər ə bəl), **re·fer·ra·ble** (ri fûr′ə bəl), *adj.* —**re·fer′ral,** *n.* —**re·fer′rer,** *n.* —**Syn. 4.** attribute, ascribe, impute.

ref·er·ee (ref′ə rē′), *n., v.,* **-eed, -ee·ing.** —*n.* **1.** a person to whom something is referred, esp. for decision or settlement; arbitrator; arbiter. **2.** (in certain games and sports) a judge having functions fixed by the rules of the game or sport; umpire. **3.** *Law.* a person selected by a court to take testimony in a case and return it to the court with recommendations. —*v.t.* **4.** to preside over as referee; act as referee in. —*v.i.* **5.** to act as referee. —**Syn. 1.** See **judge.**

ref·er·ence (ref′ər əns, ref′rəns), *n., v.,* **-enced, -enc·ing.** —*n.* **1.** an act or instance of referring. **2.** direction of the attention: *marks of reference.* **3.** a mention; allusion. **4.** direction or a direction to some source of information. **5.** use or recourse for purposes of information: *a library for public reference.* **6.** a person to whom one refers for testimony as to one's character, abilities, etc. **7.** a statement, usually written, made by this person. **8.** relation, regard, or respect: *all persons, without reference to age.* —*v.t.* **9.** to furnish (a book, dissertation, etc.) with references. **10.** to mention or arrange as a reference. —**Syn. 4.** note, citation. **7.** endorsement. **8.** consideration, concern.

ref′erence book′, a publication consulted for facts or background information, as an encyclopedia, dictionary, atlas, yearbook, etc.

ref′erence group′, *Sociol.* a group with which an individual identifies and whose values he accepts as guiding principles.

ref′erence mark′, *Survey.* a permanent mark set at a specific distance in a specific direction from a survey station so as to permit accurate reestablishment of the station.

ref·er·en·dum (ref′ə ren′dəm), *n., pl.* **-dums, -da** (-də). **1.** the principle or practice of referring measures proposed or passed by a legislative body to the vote of the electorate for approval or rejection. **2.** a vote on a measure thus referred. [< L: thing to be carried back (neut. ger. of *referre* to REFER)]

ref·er·ent (ref′ər ənt), *n.* **1.** the object or event to which a term or symbol refers. **2.** *Logic.* the first term in a proposition to which succeeding terms relate. [< L *referent-* (s. of *referēns*), prp. of *referre*]

ref·er·en·tial (ref′ə ren′shəl), *adj.* **1.** having reference: *referential to something.* **2.** containing a reference. **3.** used for reference. —**ref′er·en′tial·ly,** *adv.*

re·fer·ral (ri fûr′əl), *n.* **1.** an act of referring. **2.** the state of being referred. **3.** an instance of referring. **4.** a person recommended to someone or for something.

re·fill (*v.* rē fil′; *n.* rē′fil′), *v.t.* **1.** to fill again. —*n.* **2.** a material, supply, or the like, to replace something that has been used up. —**re·fill′a·ble,** *adj.*

re·fi·nance (rē fī′nans, rē′fī nans′), *v.t.,* **-nanced, -nanc·ing. 1.** to finance again. **2.** to obtain additional money or credit for. **3.** to supply additional money or credit to.

re·fine (ri fīn′), *v.,* **-fined, -fin·ing.** —*v.t.* **1.** to bring to a fine or a pure state. **2.** to purify from what is coarse, vulgar, or debasing. **3.** to bring to a finer state or form by purifying. **4.** to make more fine, elegant, or polished. —*v.i.* **5.** to become pure. **6.** to become more fine, elegant, or polished. **7.** to make fine distinctions in thought or language. —**re·fin′a·ble,** *adj.* —**re·fin′er,** *n.*

re·fined (ri fīnd′), *adj.* **1.** having or showing well-bred feeling, taste, etc. **2.** freed or free from coarseness, vulgarity, etc. **3.** freed from impurities. **4.** very subtle, precise, or exact. —**re·fin·ed·ly** (ri fī′nid lē, -fīnd′-), *adv.* —**re·fin′ed·ness,** *n.* —**Syn. 1.** cultivated, polished. **3.** clarified, distilled, purified. —**Ant. 1.** rude, coarse, crude.

re·fine·ment (ri fīn′mənt), *n.* **1.** fineness or elegance of feeling, taste, manners, language, etc. **2.** an instance of refined feeling, manners, etc. **3.** the act or process of refining. **4.** the quality or state of being refined. **5.** an improved form of something.

re·fin·er·y (ri fī′nə rē), *n., pl.* **-er·ies.** an establishment for refining something, as metal, sugar, or petroleum.

re·fin·ish (rē fin′ish), *v.t.* to give a new surface to (wood, furniture, etc.). —**re·fin′ish·er,** *n.*

re·fit (rē fit′), *v.,* **-fit·ted, -fit·ting,** *n.* —*v.t.* **1.** to fit, prepare, or equip again. —*v.i.* **2.** to renew supplies or equipment. **3.** to get refitted. —*n.* **4.** an act of refitting.

refl., 1. reflection. **2.** reflective. **3.** reflex. **4.** reflexive.

re·flate (ri flāt′), *v.,* **-flat·ed, -flat·ing.** —*v.i.* **1.** to increase again the amount of money and credit in circulation. —*v.t.* **2.** to increase (money and credit) again. [back formation from REFLATION]

re·fla·tion (ri flā′shən), *n.* the increasing of the amount of money and credit of a country in order to restore a price level. [RE- + (IN)FLATION]

re·flect (ri flekt′), *v.t.* **1.** to cast back (light, heat, sound, etc.) from a surface. **2.** to give back or show an image of; mirror. **3.** (of an act or its result) to serve to cast or bring (credit, discredit, etc.) on its performer. **4.** to happen as a result of: *The cost reflects the demand.* —*v.i.* **5.** to be turned or cast back, as light. **6.** to cast back light, heat, etc. **7.** to give back or show an image. **8.** to think, ponder, or meditate. **9.** to serve or tend to bring reproach or discredit by association. **10.** to serve to give a particular aspect or impression (usually fol. by *on*): *The test reflects well on your abilities.* [ME *reflect(en)* < L *reflect(ere)* (to) bend back = *re-* RE- + *flectere* to bend] —**re·flect′i·bil′i·ty,** *n.* —**re·flect′ing·ly,** *adv.* —**Syn. 8.** deliberate, contemplate. See **study.**

re·flect·ance (ri flek′təns), *n. Physics, Optics.* the ratio of the intensity of reflected radiation to that of the radiation incident on a surface. Cf. **albedo.**

reflect′ing tel′escope. See under **telescope** (def. 1). Also called **reflector.**

re·flec·tion (ri flek′shən), *n.* **1.** the act of reflecting. **2.** the state of being reflected. **3.** something that is reflected. **4.** the return of heat, light, images, etc., by a reflecting surface. **5.** serious thought upon a subject. **6.** a thought occurring in consideration or meditation. **7.** an imputation or reproach. **8.** *Anat.* the bending or folding back of a part upon itself. Also, *esp. Brit.,* **reflexion.** [ME < LL *reflexiōn-* (s. of *reflexiō*) a bending back = L *reflex(us)* (see REFLEX) + *-iōn-* -ION] —**re·flec′tion·al,** *adj.* —**re·flec′tion·less,** *adj.* —**Syn. 5.** meditation, rumination, deliberation, cogitation, study, thinking. **7.** aspersion.

re·flec·tive (ri flek′tiv), *adj.* **1.** that reflects; reflecting. **2.** of or pertaining to reflection. **3.** cast by reflection. **4.** giv-

re′e·lect′, *v.t.*
re′e·lec′tion, *n.*
re·el′i·gi·ble, *adj.*
re′em·bark′, *v.*
re′em·bod′y, *v.t.,* **-bod·ied, -bod·y·ing.**
re′e·merge′, *v.i.,* **-merged, -merg·ing.**
re′e·mer′gence, *n.*
re·em′pha·size′, *v.t.,* **-sized, -siz·ing.**
re′em·ploy′, *v.t.*
re′em·ploy′ment, *n.*
re′en·close′, *v.t.,* **-closed, -clos·ing.**
re′en·dow′, *v.t.*
re′en·gage′, *v.,* **-gaged, -gag·ing.**
re′en·joy′, *v.t.*
re′en·large′, *v.,* **-larged, -larg·ing.**
re′en·large′ment, *n.*
re′en·light′en, *v.t.*
re′en·slave′, *v.t.,* **-slaved, -slav·ing.**
re′e·nun′ci·a′tion, *n.*
re′e·quip′, *v.t.,* **-quipped, -quip·ping.**
re′e·rect′, *v.t.*
re′es·tab′lish, *v.t.*
re′es·tab′lish·ment, *n.*
re′e·val′u·ate′, *v.t.,* **-at·ed, -at·ing.**
re′e·val′u·a′tion, *n.*
re′ex·hib′it, *v.t.*
re′ex·pe′ri·ence, *v.,* **-enced, -enc·ing.**
re′ex·press′, *v.t.*
re·fash′ion, *v.t.*
re·fas′ten, *v.t.*
re·file′, *v.,* **-filed, -fil·ing.**
re·film′, *v.t.*
re·fil′ter, *v.t.*
re·fire′, *v.,* **-fired, -fir·ing.**

en to or concerned with meditation: *a reflective man.* —**re·flec′tive·ly,** *adv.* —**re·flec′tive·ness, re·flec·tiv·i·ty** (rē′flek tiv′i tē), *n.* —**Syn. 4.** thoughtful. See **pensive.**

re·flec·tor (ri flek′tər), *n.* **1.** a person or thing that reflects. **2.** a body, surface, or device that reflects light, heat, sound, or the like. **3.** a reflecting telescope. See under **telescope** (def. 1). **4.** *Physics.* a substance, as graphite or heavy water, used to prevent the escape of neutrons from the core of a reactor.

re·flex (*adj., n.* rē′fleks; *v.* ri fleks′), *adj.* **1.** *Physiol.* noting or pertaining to an involuntary response to a stimulus. **2.** occurring in reaction; responsive. **3.** cast back; reflected, as light or color. **4.** bent or turned back. —*n.* **5.** *Physiol.* **a.** Also called **re′flex act′.** movement caused by a reflex response. **b.** Also called **re′flex ac′tion.** the entire physiological process activating such movement. **6.** the reflected image of an object. —*v.t.* **7.** to subject to a reflex process. **8.** to bend, turn, or fold back. [< L *reflex(us)* bent back, ptp. of *reflectere* to REFLECT] —**re′flex·ly,** *adv.*

re′flex an′gle, *Geom.* an angle greater than 180°.

re′flex arc′, *Physiol.* the nerve pathways followed by an impulse in the production of a reflex.

re′flex cam′era, a camera in which the image is reflected by a mirror behind the lens onto a ground glass.

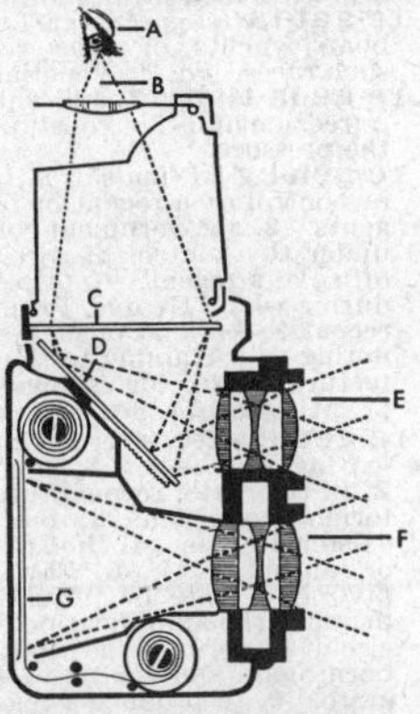

Reflex camera (twin-lens) A, Eye; B, Lens magnifying image on ground glass; C, Ground glass; D, Reflecting mirror; E, Focusing lens; F, Photographic lens; G, Film

re·flex·ion (ri flek′shən), *n.* *Chiefly Brit.* reflection. —**re·flex′ion·al,** *adj.*

re·flex·ive (ri flek′siv), *adj.* **1.** *Gram.* **a.** (of a verb) taking a subject and object with identical referents, as *shave* in *I shave myself.* **b.** (of a pronoun) used as an object to refer to the subject of a verb, as *myself* in *I shave myself.* **2.** reflex; responsive. **3.** able to reflect; reflective. —*n.* **4.** *Gram.* a reflexive verb or pronoun. [< ML *reflexīv(us)* turned back, reflected] —**re·flex′ive·ly,** *adv.* —**re·flex′ive·ness, re·flex·iv·i·ty** (rē′flek siv′i tē), *n.*

ref·lu·ent (ref′lo͞o ənt), *adj.* flowing back; ebbing, as the waters of a tide. [< L *refluent-* (s. of *refluēns*), prp. of *refluere*] —**ref′lu·ence,** *n.*

re·flux (rē′fluks′), *n.* a flowing back; ebb. [< ML *reflux(us)*]

re·for·est (rē fôr′ist, -for′-), *v.t.* to replant trees in a forest that has been affected by cutting, fire, or the like. —**re′for·est·a′tion,** *n.*

re-form (rē fôrm′, rē′-), *v.t., v.i.* to form again.

re·form (ri fôrm′), *n.* **1.** the improvement or amendment of what is wrong, corrupt, unsatisfactory, etc. **2.** an instance of this. **3.** the amendment of conduct, belief, etc. —*v.t.* **4.** to change to a better state, form, etc. **5.** to cause (a person) to abandon wrong or evil ways of life or conduct. **6.** to put an end to (abuses, disorders, etc.). —*v.i.* **7.** to abandon evil conduct or error. [(n.) < F *réforme* < *reformer;* (v.) ME *reform(en)* < MF, OF *reform(er)* < L *reformāre;* see RE-, FORM] —**re·form′a·ble,** *adj.* —**re·form′a·tive,** *adj.* —**re·form′er,** *n.* —**re·form′ing·ly,** *adv.* —**Syn. 1.** correction, reformation, betterment, amelioration. **4.** better, rectify, correct, amend, emend, ameliorate, repair, restore. —**Ant. 1.** deterioration. **4.** worsen.

ref·or·ma·tion (ref′ər mā′shən), *n.* **1.** the act of reforming. **2.** the state of being reformed. **3.** (*cap.*) the religious movement in the 16th century that led to the establishment of the Protestant churches. [ME *reformacion* < L *reformātiōn-* (s. of *reformātiō*) = *reformāt(us)* (ptp. of *reformāre* to REFORM) + *-iōn-* -ION] —**ref′or·ma′tion·al,** *adj.* —**Syn. 1.** improvement, betterment, correction, reform.

re·form·a·to·ry (ri fôr′mə tōr′ē, -tor′ē), *adj., n., pl.* **-ries.** —*adj.* **1.** serving or designed to reform. —*n.* **2.** Also called **reform′ school′.** a penal institution for reforming young offenders, esp. minors. [< L *reformāt(us)* (see REFORMATION) + -ORY[2]]

Reform′ Bill′, *Eng. Hist.* any of the bills passed by Parliament (1832, 1867, 1884) providing for an increase in the number of voters in elections for the House of Commons. esp. the bill of 1832 by which many boroughs with very few voters lost their individual representation in Parliament. Also called **Reform′ Act′.**

re·formed (ri fôrmd′), *adj.* **1.** amended by removal of faults, abuses, etc. **2.** improved in conduct, morals, etc. **3.** (*cap.*) noting or pertaining to Protestant churches, esp. Calvinist as distinguished from Lutheran. —**re·form·ed·ly** (ri fôr′mid lē), *adv.*

reformed′ spell′ing, a revised orthography intended to simplify the spelling of English words, esp. to eliminate unpronounced letters, as by substituting *thru* for *through, tho* for *though, slo* for *slow,* etc.

re·form·ist (ri fôr′mist), *n.* **1.** a person who advocates or practices reform; reformer. —*adj.* **2.** Also, **re·form·is·tic** (re′fər mis′tik). of or belonging to a movement for reform. —**re·form′ism,** *n.*

Reform′ Jew′, a Jew who adheres to a system of ethical monotheism and religious worship adapted from Orthodox Judaism to meet the demands of contemporary life, frequently subjecting religious law and custom to contemporary judgment. Cf. **Conservative Jew, Orthodox Jew.**

Reform′ Ju′daism, Judaism as observed by Reform Jews.

re·fract (ri frakt′), *v.t.* **1.** to subject to refraction. **2.** to determine the refractive condition of (an eye). [< L *refract(us)* broken up, weakened (ptp. of *refringere*) = *re-* RE- + *frac-* (perf. s. of *frangere* to BREAK)] —**re·fract′a·ble,** *adj.* —**re·fract′ed·ly,** *adv.*

refract′ing tel′escope. See under **telescope** (def. 1). Also called **refractor.**

re·frac·tion (ri frak′shən), *n.* **1.** *Physics.* the change of direction of a ray of light, sound, heat, or the like, in passing obliquely from one medium into another in which the speed of propagation differs. **2.** *Optics.* **a.** the ability of the eye to refract light so as to form an image on the retina. **b.** the determining of the refractive condition of the eye. **3.** *Astron.* **a.** the amount, in angular measure, by which the altitude of a celestial body is increased by the refraction of its light in the earth's atmosphere, being zero at the zenith and a maximum at the horizon. **b.** the observed altered location, as seen from the earth, of another planet or the like due to diffraction by the atmosphere. [< LL *refractiōn-* (s. of *refractiō*) a breaking up, open] —**re·frac′tion·al,** *adj.*

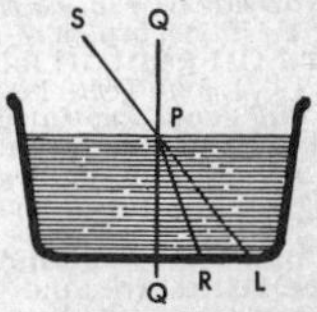

Refraction SP, Ray of light; SPL, Original direction of ray; SPR, Refracted ray; QQ, Perpendicular

re·frac·tive (ri frak′tiv), *adj.* **1.** of or pertaining to refraction. **2.** having power to refract. [< LL *refractīv(us)* breaking back] —**re·frac′tive·ly,** *adv.* —**re·frac·tiv·i·ty** (rē′frak tiv′i tē), *n.*

refrac′tive in′dex, *Optics.* See **index of refraction.**

re·frac·tom·e·ter (rē′frak tom′i tər), *n.* *Optics.* an instrument for determining the refractive index of a substance. —**re·frac·to·met·ric** (rē frak′tə me′trik), *adj.* —**re′frac·tom′e·try,** *n.*

re·frac·tor (ri frak′tər), *n.* **1.** a person or thing that refracts. **2.** a refracting telescope. See under **telescope** (def. 1).

re·frac·to·ry (ri frak′tə rē), *adj., n., pl.* **-ries.** —*adj.* **1.** hard or impossible to manage; stubbornly disobedient: *a refractory child.* **2.** resisting ordinary methods of treatment. **3.** difficult to fuse, reduce, or work, as an ore or metal. —*n.* **4.** a material having the ability to retain its physical shape and chemical identity when subjected to high temperatures. **5. refractories,** bricks of various shapes used in lining furnaces. **6.** *Physiol.* a momentary state of reduced irritability following a response. [var. of *refractary* (by analogy with adjectives in -ORY[1]) < L *refractāri(us)* stubborn, obstinate = *refract(us)* (see REFRACT) + *-ārius* -ARY] —**re·frac′to·ri·ly,** *adv.* —**Syn. 1.** obstinate, perverse, mulish, headstrong, intractable, unruly. —**Ant. 1.** obedient, tractable.

re·frain[1] (ri frān′), *v.i.* **1.** to keep oneself from doing, thinking, or saying something; abstain (often fol. by *from*). —*v.t.* **2.** *Archaic.* to curb. [ME *refrein(en)* < OF *refren(er)* < L *refrēn(āre)* (to) bridle = *re-* RE- + *frēn(um)* bridle] —**re·frain′ment,** *n.* —**Syn. 1.** cease, desist.

re·frain[2] (ri frān′), *n.* **1.** a phrase or verse recurring at intervals in a song or poem, esp. at the end of each stanza; chorus. **2.** *Music.* **a.** a musical setting for the refrain of a poem. **b.** any melody. **3.** the principal, recurrent section of a rondo. [ME *refreyne* < OF *refrain* < *refraindre* < VL **refrangere,* for L *refringere* to REFRACT]

re·fran·gi·ble (ri fran′jə bəl), *adj.* capable of being refracted, as rays of light. —**re·fran′gi·ble·ness, re·fran′gi·bil′i·ty,** *n.*

re·fresh (ri fresh′), *v.t.* Also, **re·fresh′en. 1.** to renew the well-being and vigor of (oneself or others), as with food, drink, or rest. **2.** to cheer or enliven (the mind or spirits). **3.** to stimulate (the memory). —*v.i.* **4.** to take refreshment, esp. food or drink. **5.** to become fresh or vigorous again; revive. [ME *refresch(en)* < MF, OF *refresch(ir)*] —**re·fresh′er,** *n.* —**re·fresh′ful,** *adj.* —**Syn. 1.** revive. **2.** freshen, reanimate. —**Ant. 2.** dispirit, discourage.

refresh′er course′, a study course serving as a review of previous education.

re·fresh·ing (ri fresh′ing), *adj.* **1.** having the power to restore well-being and vigor. **2.** cheering or enlivening the mind or spirits; stimulating. —**re·fresh′ing·ly,** *adv.*

re·fresh·ment (ri fresh′mənt), *n.* **1.** something that refreshes, esp. food or drink. **2.** the act of refreshing. **3.** the state of being refreshed. [ME *refresshement* < MF *refreschement*]

re·frig·er·ant (ri frij′ər ənt), *adj.* **1.** refrigerating; cooling. **2.** reducing bodily heat or fever. —*n.* **3.** a substance used as an agent in cooling or refrigeration. [< L *refrīgerant-* (s. of *refrīgerāns*), prp. of *refrīgerāre.* See REFRIGERATE, -ANT]

re·frig·er·ate (ri frij′ə rāt′), *v.t.,* **-at·ed, -at·ing.** to make or keep cold or cool, as for preservation. [< L *refrīgerāt(us)* made cool, ptp. of *refrīgerāre* = *re-* RE- + *frīgerāre* to make cool < *frīgor-* (s. of *frīgus*) cold; see -ATE[1]] —**re·frig′er·a′tive, re·frig·er·a·to·ry** (ri frij′ər ə tōr′ē, -tôr′ē), *adj.*

re·frig·er·a·tion (ri frij′ə rā′shən), *n.* **1.** the act or process of refrigerating. **2.** the state of being refrigerated. [ME *refrigeracion* < L *refrīgerātiōn-* (s. of *refrīgerātiō*)]

re·frig·er·a·tor (ri frij′ə rā′tər), *n.* **1.** a box, room, or cabinet in which foods, medications, chemicals, etc., are kept cool by means of ice or mechanical refrigeration. **2.** the part of a distilling apparatus that cools the volatile material, causing it to condense; condenser; rectifier.

re·frin·gent (ri frin′jənt), *adj.* refracting; refractive. [< L *refringent-* (s. of *refringēns*), prp. of *refringere* to break up. See REFRACT, -ENT] —**re·frin′gen·cy, re·frin′gence,** *n.*

reft (reft), *v.* a pt. and pp. of **reave.**

re′flow′, *v.*
re·flow′er, *v.i.*
re·fo′cus, *v.,* **-cused, -cus·ing** or (*esp. Brit.*) **-cussed, -cus·sing.**
re·fold′, *v.*
re·forge′, *v.t.,* **-forged, -forg·ing.**
re·for′mu·late′, *v.t.,* **-lat·ed, -lat·ing.**
re′for·mu·la′tion, *n.*
re·for′ti·fy′, *v.t.,* **-fied, -fy·ing.**
re·frac′ture, *v.,* **-tured, -tur·ing.**
re·frame′, *v.t.,* **-framed, -fram·ing.**
re·freeze′, *v.,* **-froze, -fro·zen, freez·ing.**
re·fry′, *v.,* **-fried, -fry·ing.**

re·fu·el (rē fyo͞o′əl), *v.*, **-eled, -el·ing** or (*esp. Brit.*) **-elled, -el·ling.** —*v.t.* **1.** to supply again with fuel: *to refuel an airplane.* —*v.i.* **2.** to take on a fresh supply of fuel.

ref·uge (ref′yo͞oj), *n.*, *v.*, **-uged, -ug·ing.** —*n.* **1.** shelter or protection from danger, trouble, etc.: *to take refuge from a storm.* **2.** a place of shelter, protection, or safety. **3.** anything to which one has recourse for aid, relief, or escape. —*v.t.* **4.** *Archaic.* to afford refuge to. —*v.i.* **5.** *Archaic.* to take refuge. [ME < MF < L *refug(ium)* < *refugere* to flee away (*re-* RE- + *fugere* to flee); see FUGITIVE] —**Syn. 1.** security, safety. **2.** asylum, retreat, sanctuary, haven, stronghold.

ref·u·gee (ref′yŏŏ jē′), *n.* a person who flees for refuge or safety, esp. to a foreign country, as in time of war. [< F *réfugié*, ptp. of *réfugier* to take refuge] —**ref′u·gee′ism,** *n.*

re·ful·gent (ri ful′jənt), *adj.* shining; radiant; glowing. [< L *refulgent-* (s. of *refulgēns*, prp. of *refulgēre*)] —**re·ful′gence, re·ful′gen·cy,** *n.* —**re·ful′gent·ly,** *adv.*

re·fund[1] (*v.* ri fund′; *n.* rē′fund), *v.t.* **1.** to give back or restore (esp. money); repay. —*v.i.* **2.** to make repayment. —*n.* **3.** a repayment. [ME *refund(en)* < L *refund(ere)* (to) pour back = *re-* RE- + *fund-* pour; see FOUND[3]] —**re·fund′a·ble,** *adj.* —**re·fund′er,** *n.* —**re·fund′ment,** *n.*

re·fund[2] (rē fund′), *v.t.* **1.** to fund anew. **2.** *Finance.* to replace (an old issue of bonds) with a new one. [RE- + FUND]

re·fur·bish (rē fûr′bish), *v.t.* to furbish again; renovate. —**re·fur′bish·ment,** *n.* —**Syn.** refurnish, redecorate.

re·fus·al (ri fyo͞o′zəl), *n.* **1.** an act or instance of refusing. **2.** priority in refusing or taking something; option. [ME *refusell*]

re·fuse[1] (ri fyo͞oz′), *v.*, **-fused, -fus·ing.** —*v.t.* **1.** to decline to accept (something offered): *to refuse the nomination for mayor.* **2.** to decline to give; deny (a request, demand, etc.): *to refuse permission.* **3.** to express a determination not to (do something): *to refuse to discuss the question.* **4.** to decline to submit to. **5.** (of a horse) to decline to leap over (a barrier). **6.** *Mil.* to bend or curve back (the flank units of a military force) so that they face generally to the flank rather than the front. **7.** *Obs.* to renounce. —*v.i.* **8.** to decline acceptance, consent, or compliance. [ME *refuse(n)* < MF, OF *refus(er)* << L *refūs(us)*, ptp. of *refundere* to pour back; see REFUND[1]] —**re·fus′a·ble,** *adj.* —**Syn. 1.** rebuff. REFUSE, DECLINE, REJECT, SPURN all imply nonacceptance of something. To DECLINE is milder and more courteous than to REFUSE, which is direct and often emphatic in expressing determination not to accept what is offered or proposed: *to refuse a bribe; to decline an invitation.* To REJECT is even more positive and definite than REFUSE: *to reject a suitor.* To SPURN is to reject with scorn: *to spurn a bribe.* —**Ant. 1.** accept, welcome.

ref·use[2] (ref′yo͞os), *n.* **1.** something that is discarded as worthless or useless; rubbish; trash; garbage. —*adj.* **2.** rejected as worthless; discarded: *refuse matter.* [ME < MF, OF *refus* denial, rejection < *refuser* to REFUSE[1]]

re·fuse·nik (ri fyo͞oz′nik), *n. Informal.* a Soviet citizen, usually Jewish, who has been denied permission to emigrate from the Soviet Union. Also, **re·fus′nik.** [REFUSE[1] + -NIK, perh. trans. of Russ *otkáznik*]

ref·u·ta·tion (ref′yŏŏ tā′shən), *n.* the act of refuting a statement, charge, etc.; disproof. Also, **re·fut·al** (ri fyo͞ot′əl). [< L *refūtātiōn-* (s. of *refūtātiō*) = *refūtāt(us)* checked, resisted (ptp. of *refūtāre* to REFUTE) + *-iōn-* -ION]

re·fut·a·tive (ri fyo͞o′tə tiv), *adj.* tending to refute; pertaining to refutation. [REFUTAT(ION) + -IVE]

re·fute (ri fyo͞ot′), *v.t.*, **-fut·ed, -fut·ing.** **1.** to prove to be false or erroneous, as an opinion, charge, etc. **2.** to prove (a person) to be in error. [< L *refūt(āre)* (to) check, rebut = *re-* RE- + *-fūtāre* to beat] —**re·fu·ta·bil·i·ty** (ri fyo͞o′tə bil′i tē, ref′yə-), *n.* —**re·fu·ta·ble** (ri fyo͞o′tə bəl, ref′yə tə-), *adj.* —**ref·u·ta·bly** (ref′yə tə blē), *adv.* —**re·fut′er,** *n.* —**Syn. 1.** disprove, rebut. **1, 2.** confute.

Reg., **1.** regiment. **2.** queen. [< L *rēgina*]

reg., **1.** regent. **2.** regiment. **3.** region. **4.** register. **5.** registered. **6.** registrar. **7.** registry. **8.** regular. **9.** regularly. **10.** regulation.

re·gain (ri gān′), *v.t.* **1.** to get again; recover. **2.** to succeed in reaching again; get back to: *to regain the shore.* —**re·gain′a·ble,** *adj.* —**re·gain′er,** *n.*

re·gal (rē′gəl), *adj.* **1.** of or pertaining to a king; royal: *the regal power.* **2.** befitting or resembling a king. **3.** stately; splendid. [ME < L *rēgāl(is)* ROYAL] —**re′gal·ly,** *adv.* —**Syn. 2.** See **kingly.** —**Ant. 3.** base.

re·gale (ri gāl′), *v.*, **-galed, -gal·ing,** *n.* —*v.t.* **1.** to give lavish pleasure to; delight. **2.** to entertain with choice food or drink. —*v.i.* **3.** to feast. —*n. Archaic.* **4.** a sumptuous feast. **5.** a choice article of food or drink. [< F *régal(er)* < OF *regale* feast, var. of *gale* pleasure < MD *wale* wealth]

re·ga·li·a (ri gā′lē ə, -gāl′yə), *n.pl.* **1.** the rights or privileges of a king. **2.** the ensigns or emblems of royalty, as the crown, scepter, etc. **3.** the decorations or insignia of any officer or order. **4.** rich clothing or finery. [< ML king's: prerogative, n. use of L neut. of *rēgālis* REGAL]

re·gal·i·ty (ri gal′i tē), *n.*, *pl.* **-ties.** **1.** royalty, sovereignty, or kingship. **2.** a right or privilege pertaining to a king. **3.** a kingdom. [ME *regalite* < MF < ML *rēgālitās*]

re·gard (ri gärd′), *v.t.* **1.** to look upon or think of with a particular feeling: *to regard a person with favor.* **2.** to have or show respect for: *to regard the law.* **3.** to think highly of; esteem. **4.** to take into account; consider. **5.** to look at; observe. **6.** to relate to; concern. **7.** to see, look at, or conceive of in a particular way; judge (usually fol. by *as*): *I regard every assignment as a challenge.* **8.** *Obs.* to show attention to; guard. —*v.i.* **9.** to pay attention. **10.** to look or gaze. **11. as regards.** See **as**[1] (def. 21). —*n.* **12.** reference; relation: *to err with regard to facts.* **13.** an aspect, point, or particular: *quite satisfactory in this regard.* **14.** thought; attention; concern. **15.** look; gaze. **16.** respect, esteem, or deference. **17.** kindly feeling; liking. **18. regards,** sentiments of esteem or affection: *Give them my regards.* **19.** *Obs.* aspect. [ME *regard* (n.) < MF *regard(er)* (to) look at] —**re·gard′a·ble,** *adj.* —**Syn. 3.** honor, revere, value.

re·gard·ant (ri gär′dᵊnt), *adj. Heraldry.* (of a beast) looking backward: *a stag regardant.* [ME < MF, prp. of *regarder* to REGARD]

re·gard·ful (ri gärd′fəl), *adj.* **1.** observant; heedful (often fol. by *of*): *a man regardful of the feelings of others.* **2.** showing or feeling regard or esteem; respectful.

re·gard·ing (ri gär′ding), *prep.* with regard to; respecting; concerning.

re·gard·less (ri gärd′lis), *adj.* **1.** having or showing no regard; heedless (often fol. by *of*): *regardless of the advice of his elders.* **2.** without regard to expense, danger, etc. —*adv.* **3.** without concern as to advice, warning, hardship, etc.; anyway: *I must make the decision regardless.* **4.** in spite of; without regard for: *We fought regardless of our injuries.* —**re·gard′less·ly,** *adv.* —**Syn. 1.** inattentive, negligent, neglectful, indifferent, unconcerned.

re·gat·ta (ri gat′ə, -gä′tə), *n.* **1.** a boat race, as of rowboats, yachts, or other vessels. **2.** an organized series of such races. [< It (Venetian) *regatta, regata*]

re·ge·la·tion (rē′jə lā′shən), *n. Physics.* the melting and refreezing of ice, at constant temperature, caused by varying the pressure.

re·gen·cy (rē′jən sē), *n.*, *pl.* **-cies,** *adj.* —*n.* **1.** the office or control of a regent or body of regents. **2.** a body of regents. **3.** a government consisting of regents. **4.** a territory under the control of a regent or regents. **5.** the term of office of a regent. **6.** (*cap.*) *Brit. Hist.* the period (1811–20) during which George, Prince of Wales, later George IV, was regent. —*adj.* **7.** of or pertaining to a regency. **8.** (*cap.*) noting or pertaining to the British Regency or to the architectural style, furnishings, manners, etc., then prevailing. [< ML *regentia.* See REGENT, -CY]

re·gen·er·ate (*v.* ri jen′ə rāt′; *adj.* ri jen′ər it), *v.*, **-at·ed, -at·ing,** *adj.* —*v.t.* **1.** to effect a complete moral reform in. **2.** to re-create, reconstitute, or make over, esp. in a better form or condition. **3.** to revive or produce anew; bring into existence again. **4.** *Biol.* to renew or restore (a lost, removed, or injured part). **5.** *Physics.* to restore (a substance) to a favorable state or physical condition. **6.** *Electronics.* to magnify the amplification of, by relaying part of the output circuit power into the input circuit. **7.** *Theol.* to cause to be born again spiritually. —*v.i.* **8.** to reform; become regenerate. **9.** to produce a regenerative effect. **10.** to undergo regeneration. —*adj.* **11.** reconstituted or made over in a better form. **12.** reformed. **13.** *Theol.* born again spiritually. [< L *regenerāt(us)* brought forth again (ptp. of *regenerāre*). See RE-, GENERATE] —**re·gen′er·a·ble,** *adj.* —**re·gen′er·a·cy,** *n.* —**re·gen′er·a′tor,** *n.*

re·gen·er·a·tion (ri jen′ə rā′shən), *n.* **1.** the act of regenerating. **2.** the state of being regenerated. **3.** *Electronics.* a feedback process in which energy from the output of an amplifier is fed back to the grid circuit to reinforce the input. **4.** *Biol.* the restoration or new growth by an organism of organs, tissues, etc., that have been lost, removed, or injured. **5.** *Theol.* spiritual rebirth; religious conversion. [ME *regeneracion* < LL *regenerātiō*]

re·gen·er·a·tive (ri jen′ə rā′tiv, -ər ə tiv), *adj.* **1.** of, pertaining to, or characterized by regeneration. **2.** tending to regenerate. [ME < ML *regenerātīv(us)*]

regen′erative feed′back, *Electronics.* See under **feedback** (def. 1).

re·gen·er·a·tor (ri jen′ə rā′tər), *n.* **1.** a person or thing that regenerates. **2.** (in a regenerative furnace) either of two chambers filled with a pile of loosely stacked bricks through which incoming air and hot exhaust gases pass alternately so that heat from the gases is stored in the bricks and given off to the air.

Re·gens·burg (rā′gəns bo͝ork′), *n.* a city in central Bavaria, in SE West Germany: battle 1809. 131,000. Also called **Ratisbon.**

re·gent (rē′jənt), *n.* **1.** a person who exercises the ruling power in a kingdom during the minority, absence, or disability of the sovereign. **2.** a member of the governing board of a state university or a state educational system. **3.** any of various officers of academic institutions. **4.** a ruler or governor. —*adj.* **5.** acting as regent of a country (usually used postpositively): *a prince regent.* **6.** *Archaic.* ruling; governing. [ME < L *regent-* (s. of *regēns*), prp. of *regere* to rule] —**re′gent·al,** *adj.* —**re′gent·ship′,** *n.*

Re·ger (rā′gər), *n.* **Max** (mäks), 1873–1916, German composer and pianist.

reg·gae (reg′ā, rā′gā), *n. Music.* a Jamaican blend of blues, calypso, and rock-'n'-roll, characterized by a strong rhythmic beat and lyrics of bitter social protest. [var. sp. of Jamaican E *rege* ragged; perh. influenced by RAG(TIME)]

Reg·gio Ca·la·bria (red′jô kä lä′bryä), a seaport in S Italy, on the Strait of Messina. 178,094. Also, **Reg·gio di Ca·la·bria** (red′jô dē′ kä lä′bryä).

Reg·gio E·mi·lia (red′jô e mē′lyä), a city in N Italy. 129,725. Also, **Reg·gio nel·l'E·mi·lia** (red′jô nel′le mē′lyä).

reg·i·cide (rej′i sīd′), *n.* **1.** the killing of a king. **2.** a person who kills a king. [< L *rēgi-* king (comb. form of *rēg-*, s. of *rēx*) + -CIDE] —**reg′i·cid′al,** *adj.*

re·gime (rə zhēm′, rā-), *n.* **1.** a mode or system of rule or government. **2.** a ruling or prevailing system. **3.** *Med.* regimen (def. 1). Also, **ré·gime′.** [< F *régime* < L *regimen* REGIMEN]

reg·i·men (rej′ə men′, -mən), *n.* **1.** *Med.* a regulated course of diet, exercise, or manner of living, intended to preserve or restore health or to attain some result. **2.** rule or government. **3.** a prevailing system. **4.** *Gram.* government (def. 7). [< L: rule, government, guidance = *reg(ere)* (to) rule + *-i-* -I- + *-men* act of, result of (n. suffix)]

reg·i·ment (*n.* rej′ə mənt; *v.* rej′ə ment′), *n.* **1.** *Mil.* a unit of ground forces, consisting of two or more battalions or battle groups, a headquarters unit, and certain supporting units. **2.** *Obs.* government. —*v.t.* **3.** to manage or treat (a person or group of persons) in an authoritarian manner with no regard for individual rights, differences, etc. **4.** to form into a regiment or regiments. **5.** to assign to a regiment or group. [ME < MF < LL *regiment(um)* = L *reg(ere)* (to) rule + *-i-* -I- + *-mentum* -MENT] —**reg′i·men·ta′tion,** *n.*

---

re·fur′nish, *v.t.*
re·gal′va·nize′, *v.t.*, **-nized, -niz·ing.**
re·gath′er, *v.*
re·gauge′, *v.t.*, **-gauged, -gaug·ing.**
re·gear′, *v.*
re·ger′mi·nate′, *v.*, **-nat·ed, -nat·ing.**
re′ger·mi·na′tion, *n.*
re·ger′mi·na′tive, *adj.*; **-ly,** *adv.*

reg·i·men·tal (rej′ə men′t^{ə}l), *adj.* **1.** of or pertaining to a regiment. —*n.* **2. regimentals,** the uniform of a regiment. —**reg′i·men′tal·ly,** *adv.*

Re·gin (rā′gin), *n.* (in the *Volsunga Saga*) a smith, the brother of Fafnir, who raises Sigurd and encourages him to kill Fafnir.

re·gi·na (ri jī′nə *for 1;* ri jē′nə, -jī′- *for 2*), *n.* **1.** queen. **2.** (*usually cap.*) the official title of a queen: *Elizabeth Regina.* [< L] —**re·gi′nal,** *adj.*

Re·gi·na (ri jī′nə), *n.* a city in and the capital of Saskatchewan, in the S part, in SW Canada: former capital of the Northwest Territories of Canada. 112,141 (1961).

Re·gi·o·mon·ta·nus (rē′jē ō mon tā′nəs, -tä′-, -tan′əs, rej′ē-; *Ger.* rā′gē ō mōn tä′no͞os), *n.* See **Müller, Johann.**

re·gion (rē′jən), *n.* **1.** an extensive, continuous part of a surface, space, or body: *a region of the earth.* **2.** Usually, **regions.** the vast or indefinite entirety of a space or area, or something compared to one: *the regions of the firmament; the regions of the mind.* **3.** a part of the earth's land surface having a generally homogeneous character with reference to history, economy, vegetation, etc. **4.** a large indefinite area or range of something specified; sphere: *a region of authority.* **5.** an area of interest; activity, pursuit, etc.; field. **6.** an administrative division of a city or territory. **7.** *Zoogeog.* a major faunal area of the earth's surface, sometimes one regarded as a division of a larger area. **8.** *Anat.* a place in or a division of the body or a part of the body: *the abdominal region.* [ME < AF *regiun* < L *regiōn-* (s. of *regiō*) direction, line, boundary = *reg(ere)* (to) rule + *-iōn-* -ION] —**Syn. 1.** area, section, portion.

re·gion·al (rē′jə n^{ə}l), *adj.* **1.** of or pertaining to a region, district, or area, as of a country. **2.** *Anat.* of, pertaining to, or localized in a particular area or part of the body. [< LL *regiōnāl(is)*] —**re′gion·al·ly,** *adv.*

re·gion·al·ism (rē′jə n^{ə}liz′əm), *n.* **1.** *Govt.* the principle or system of dividing a city, state, etc., into separate administrative regions. **2.** the advocacy of such a principle or system. **3.** a quality or characteristic peculiar to a certain area, as of an expression or speech pattern. **4.** devotion to the interests of one's own region. **5.** (*sometimes cap.*) the theory or practice of emphasizing regional characteristics in a work of literature or painting. —**re′gion·al·ist,** *n., adj.* —**re′gion·al·is′tic,** *adj.*

re·gion·al·ize (rē′jə n^{ə}līz′), *v.t.,* **-ized, -iz·ing.** to separate into or arrange by regions.

reg·is·ter (rej′i stər), *n.* **1.** a book in which records of acts, events, names, etc., are kept. **2.** a list or record of such acts, events, etc. **3.** an entry in such a book, record, or list. **4.** an official document issued to a merchant ship as evidence of its nationality. **5.** registration or registry. **6.** a mechanical device by which certain data are automatically recorded. **7.** See **cash register. 8.** *Music.* **a.** the compass or range of a voice or an instrument. **b.** (in an organ) a stop. **9.** a device for controlling the flow of warmed air or the like through an opening. **10.** *Print.* **a.** a precise adjustment or correspondence, as of lines or columns, esp. on the two sides of a leaf. **b.** correct relation or exact superimposition, as of colors in color printing. —*v.t.* **11.** to enter or cause to be entered in a register. **12.** to cause (mail) to be recorded upon delivery to a post office for safeguarding against loss, theft, damage, etc., during transmission. **13.** to enroll (a student, voter, etc.). **14.** to indicate by a record or scale, as instruments do. **15.** to indicate or show, as on a scale. **16.** *Print.* to cause to be in register. **17.** to show (surprise, joy, anger, etc.), as by facial expression or actions. **18.** to document (a merchant ship engaged in foreign trade). —*v.i.* **19.** to enter one's name or cause it to be entered in a register; enroll. **20.** *Print.* to be in register. **21.** to have some effect; make some impression. [(n.) ME *registre* < MF, OF < ML *registr(um),* alter. of LL *regesta* catalog (pl.), n. use of L neut. pl. of *regestus* carried back (ptp. of *regerere* = *re-* RE- + *gerere* to carry, bear); (v.) ME *registre(n)* << ML *registrāre* < *registrum*] —**reg′is·tra·ble, reg′is·ter·a·ble,** *adj.* —**Syn. 1.** record, ledger, archive. **2.** roll, roster, catalog, chronicle, schedule, annals. **11.** enroll, list, record, catalog, chronicle. **17.** demonstrate, evince.

reg·is·tered (rej′i stərd), *adj.* **1.** recorded, as in a register or book; enrolled. **2.** (of mail) recorded upon delivery to a post office for safeguarding against loss, theft, damage, etc. **3.** *Com.* officially listing the owner's name with the issuing corporation and suitably inscribing the certificate, as with bonds to evidence title. **4.** officially or legally certified by a government officer or board: *a registered patent.* **5.** noting cattle, horses, dogs, etc., having pedigrees verified and filed by authorized associations of breeders.

reg′istered nurse′, a graduate nurse who has passed a state board examination and been registered and licensed to practice nursing. *Abbr.:* R.N.

reg′ister ton′. See under **ton**^{1} (def. 6).

reg′ister ton′nage, *Naut.* the volume of a vessel, esp. the net tonnage as measured officially and registered for purposes of taxation.

reg·is·trant (rej′i strənt), *n.* a person who registers. [< ML *registrant-* (s. of *registrāns*), prp. of *registrāre.* See REGISTER, -ANT]

reg·is·trar (rej′i strär′, rej′i strär′), *n.* **1.** a person who keeps a record; an official recorder. **2.** an official at a school or college who maintains students' personal and academic records, issues reports of grades, mails out official publications, etc. [< ML *registrār(ius)*; r. ME *registrer* < AF < ML *registrātor* = *registrāt(us)* (see REGISTER, -ATE^1) + *-or* -OR^2] —**reg′is·trar·ship′,** *n.*

reg·is·tra·tion (rej′i strā′shən), *n.* **1.** the act of registering. **2.** an instance of this. **3.** an entry in a register. **4.** the group or number registered. **5.** a certificate attesting to the fact that someone or something has been registered: *a boat registration.* **6.** *Music.* the act or technique of selecting and combining organ stops. [< MF < ML *registrātiōn-* (s. of *registrātiō*). See REGISTER, -ATE^2, -ION] —**reg′is·tra′tion·al,** *adj.*

reg·is·try (rej′i strē), *n., pl.* **-tries. 1.** the act of registering; registration. **2.** a place where registers are kept; an office of registration. **3.** a register. **4.** the state of being registered. **5.** the nationality of a merchant ship as shown on its register. [REGIST(ER) + -RY]

reg′istry of′fice, *Brit.* **1.** a government office and depository in which records and civil registers are kept and civil marriages performed. **2.** an employment agency for domestic help, as maids, cooks, etc.

re·gi·us (rē′jē əs, -jis), *adj.* (of a professor in a British university) holding a chair founded by or dependent on the sovereign. [< L = *rēg-* (s. of *rēx*) king + *-ius* of, belonging to (adj. suffix)]

reg·let (reg′lit), *n.* **1.** *Archit.* a groove for guiding or holding a panel, window sash, etc. **2.** *Print.* **a.** a thin strip, usually of wood, less than type-high, used to produce a blank in or about a page of type. **b.** such strips collectively. [< F, dim. of *règle* RULE (< L *rēgula*)]

reg·nal (reg′n^{ə}l), *adj.* of or pertaining to a sovereign, sovereignty, or reign. [< ML *rēgnāl(is)* = L *rēgn(um)* rule, kingdom + *-ālis* -AL^1; see REIGN]

reg·nant (reg′nənt), *adj.* **1.** reigning; ruling (usually used following the noun it modifies): *a queen regnant.* **2.** exercising authority, rule, or influence. **3.** prevalent; widespread. [< L *rēgnant-* (s. of *rēgnāns,* prp. of *regnāre*). See REIGN, -ANT] —**reg·nan·cy** (reg′nən sē), *n.*

reg·nat po·pu·lus (reg′nät pō′po͝o lo͞os′; *Eng.* reg′nat pop′yə ləs), *Latin.* let the people rule: motto of Arkansas.

reg·o·lith (reg′ə lith), *n.* See **mantle rock.** [< Gk *rhêgo(s)* rug, blanket + -LITH]

re·gorge (ri gôrj′), *v.,* **-gorged, -gorg·ing.** —*v.t.* **1.** to disgorge; cast up again. —*v.i.* **2.** to rush back again; gush. [< F, MF *regorg(er)*]

regr., registrar.

re·gress (*v.* ri gres′; *n.* rē′gres), *v.i.* **1.** to move in a backward direction; go back. **2.** to revert to an earlier or less advanced state or form. —*n.* **3.** the act of going back; return. **4.** the right to go back. **5.** reversion to an earlier or less advanced state. [ME *regresse* (n.) < L *regress(us)* gone back, turned back, returned (ptp. of *regredī*) = *re-* RE- + *gressus,* ptp. of *gradī* to go, walk] —**re·gres′sor,** *n.*

re·gres·sion (ri gresh′ən), *n.* **1.** the act of going back to an earlier place or state; return; reversion. **2.** *Biol.* reversion to an earlier or less advanced state or form or to a common or general type. **3.** *Psychoanal.* the reversion to a chronologically earlier or less adapted pattern of behavior and feeling. **4.** a progressive subsidence of a disease. [< L *regressiōn-* (s. of *regressiō*). See REGRESS, -ION]

re·gres·sive (ri gres′iv), *adj.* **1.** regressing or tending to regress; retrogressive. **2.** (of a tax rate) decreasing proportionately with an increase in the tax base. —**re·gres′sive·ly,** *adv.*

re·gret (ri gret′), *v.,* **-gret·ted, -gret·ting,** *n.* —*v.t.* **1.** to feel sorrow or remorse for (an act, fault, disappointment, etc.). **2.** to think of with a sense of loss. —*n.* **3.** a sense of loss, disappointment, dissatisfaction, etc. **4.** a feeling of sorrow or remorse for a fault, act, loss, etc. **5. regrets,** a polite, usually formal refusal of an invitation. [ME *regret(en)* (v.) < MF, OF *regret(er)* = *re-* RE- + *-greter,* ? < Gmc] —**re·gret′ta·ble, re·gret′a·ble,** *adj.* —**re·gret′ta·bly, re·gret′a·bly,** *adv.* —**re·gret′ter,** *n.* —**re·gret′ting·ly,** *adv.* —**Syn. 1.** deplore, lament, bewail, bemoan, mourn, sorrow, grieve. **4.** REGRET, REMORSE imply a sense of sorrow about events in the past, usually wrongs committed or errors made. REGRET is distress of mind, sorrow for what has been done: *to have no regrets.* REMORSE implies pangs, qualms of conscience, a sense of guilt, regret, and repentance for sins committed, wrongs done, or duty not performed: *a deep sense of remorse.* —**Ant. 1.** rejoice. **4.** joy.

re·gret·ful (ri gret′fəl), *adj.* full of regret; sorrowful because of what is lost, gone, or done. —**re·gret′ful·ly,** *adv.* —**re·gret′ful·ness,** *n.*

Regt., 1. regent. **2.** regiment.

reg·u·la·ble (reg′yə lə bəl), *adj.* that can be regulated; controllable. [REGUL(ATE) + -ABLE]

reg·u·lar (reg′yə lər), *adj.* **1.** usual; normal; customary. **2.** evenly or uniformly arranged. **3.** characterized by fixed principle, uniform procedure, etc. **4.** recurring at fixed or uniform intervals. **5.** adhering to a rule or procedure; methodical. **6.** being consistently or habitually such: *a regular customer.* **7.** conforming to some accepted rule, principle, etc. **8.** *Informal.* real; genuine: *a regular fellow.* **9.** (of a flower) having the members of each of its floral circles or whorls normally alike in form and size. **10.** *Gram.* conforming to the most prevalent pattern of formation, inflection, construction, etc. **11.** *Math.* **a.** governed by one law throughout. **b.** (of a polygon) having all sides and angles equal. **c.** (of a polyhedron) having all faces congruent regular polygons, and all solid angles congruent. **d.** (of a function of a complex variable) analytic (def. 5). **12.** *Mil.* noting or belonging to the permanently organized, or standing, army of a state. **13.** *Internat. Law.* noting soldiers recognized as legitimate combatants in warfare. **14.** *Eccles.* subject to a religious rule, or belonging to a religious or monastic order (opposed to *secular*): *regular clergy.* **15.** *U.S. Politics.* of, pertaining to, or selected by the recognized agents of a political party. **16.** (of coffee) containing an average amount of milk or cream. —*n.* **17.** a habitual customer or client. **18.** *Eccles.* a member of a duly constituted religious order under a rule. **19.** *Mil.* a professional soldier. **20.** *U.S. Politics.* a party member who faithfully stands by his party. **21.** a size of garment designed for men of average build. **22.** an athlete who plays in most of the games, usually from the start. [ME *reguler* < MF < LL, L *rēgulār(is)* = *regula* ruler, pattern + *-āris* -AR^1] —**reg′u·lar′i·ty, reg′u·lar·ness,** *n.* —**Syn. 2.** even, formal, orderly, uniform. **4.** habitual, established, fixed. **5.** systematic. **6.** habitual.

re·glaze′, *v.t.,* **-glazed, -glaz·ing.**
re′glo·ri·fi·ca′tion, *n.*
re·glo′ri·fy′, *v.t.,* **-fied, -fy·ing.**
re·gloss′, *v.t.*
re·glue′, *v.t.,* **-glued, -glu·ing.**
re·grade′, *v.t.,* **-grad·ed, -grad·ing.**
re·grow′, *v.,* **-grew, -grown, -grow·ing.**
re·growth′, *n.*

Reg′ular Ar′my, *U.S.* the permanent, standing army maintained in peace as well as in war: a major component of the Army of the United States.

reg·u·lar·ise (reg′yə lə rīz′), *v.t.*, **-ised, -is·ing.** *Chiefly Brit.* regularize. —**reg′u·lar·i·sa′tion,** *n.*

reg·u·lar·ize (reg′yə lə rīz′), *v.t.*, **-ized, -iz·ing.** to make regular. —**reg′u·lar·i·za′tion,** *n.*

reg·u·lar·ly (reg′yər lē), *adv.* **1.** at regular times or intervals. **2.** according to plan, custom, etc.

reg′ular ode′, *Pros.* See **Pindaric ode.**

reg′ular year′. See under **Jewish calendar.**

reg·u·late (reg′yə lāt′), *v.t.*, **-lat·ed, -lat·ing. 1.** to control or direct by a rule, principle, method, etc. **2.** to adjust to some standard or requirement, as for amount, degree, etc. **3.** to adjust so as to ensure accuracy of operation. **4.** to put in good order. [< LL *rēgulāt(us)* (ptp. of *rēgulāre*) = *rēgul(a)* (see REGULAR) + *-ātus* -ATE[1]] —**reg·u·la·tive** (reg′yə lā′tiv, -yə lə tiv), **reg·u·la·to·ry** (reg′yə lə tôr′ē, -tôr′ē), *adj.* —**reg′u·la′tive·ly,** *adv.* —**Syn. 1.** manage, order, adjust, arrange, dispose, conduct. **2.** set.

reg·u·la·tion (reg′yə lā′shən), *n.* **1.** a rule or order prescribed by authority, as to regulate conduct; a governing direction or law. **2.** the act of regulating. **3.** the state of being regulated. —*adj.* **4.** prescribed by or conforming to regulation. **5.** usual; normal; customary.

reg·u·la·tor (reg′yə lā′tər), *n.* **1.** a person or thing that regulates. **2.** *Horol.* **a.** an adjustable device for regulating a timepiece. **b.** a master clock against which other clocks are checked. **3.** *Mach.* any of various valves or other devices for maintaining speed, pressure, etc., under changing conditions. **4.** *Elect.* a device for maintaining a designated characteristic, as voltage or current, at a predetermined value, or for varying it according to a predetermined plan.

reg·u·lus (reg′yə ləs), *n.*, *pl.* **-lus·es, -li** (-lī′). **1.** (*cap.*) *Astron.* a first-magnitude star in the constellation Leo. **2.** *Metall.* **a.** the metallic mass that forms beneath the slag at the bottom of the crucible or furnace in smelting ores. **b.** an impure intermediate product obtained in smelting ores. [< L: lit., little king (dim. of *rēx*); in early chemistry, antimony, so called because it readily combines with gold (the king of metals)]

Reg·u·lus (reg′yə ləs), *n.* **Marcus A·til·i·us** (ə til′ē əs), died 250? B.C., Roman general.

re·gur·gi·tate (ri gûr′ji tāt′), *v.*, **-tat·ed, -tat·ing.** —*v.i.* **1.** to surge or rush back, as liquids, gases, undigested food, etc. —*v.t.* **2.** to cause to surge or rush back. [< ML *regurgitāt(us)* (ptp. of *regurgitāre*) = *re-* RE- + *gurgit-* engulf, flood (< *gurgit-*, s. of *gurges* whirlpool) + *-ātus* -ATE[1]] —**re·gur·gi·tant** (ri gûr′ji tənt), *n.*

re·gur·gi·ta·tion (ri gûr′ji tā′shən), *n.* **1.** the act of regurgitating. **2.** *Med.* voluntary or involuntary return of partly digested food from the stomach to the mouth. **3.** *Physiol.* the reflux of blood through defective heart valves. [< ML *regurgitātiōn-* (s. of *regurgitātiō*)]

re·ha·bil·i·tate (rē′hə bil′i tāt′), *v.t.*, **-tat·ed, -tat·ing. 1.** to restore to a condition of good health, ability to work, or the like. **2.** to restore to good operation or management, as a bankrupt business. **3.** to reestablish the good reputation, rights, or standing of. [< ML *rehabilitāt(us)* restored (ptp. of *rehabilitāre*)] —**re′ha·bil′i·ta′tion,** *n.* —**re′ha·bil′i·ta′tive,** *adj.*

re·hash (*v.* rē hash′; *n.* rē′hash′), *v.t.* **1.** to work up (old material, as writing) in a new form. —*n.* **2.** the act of rehashing. **3.** something that has been rehashed.

re·hear (rē hēr′), *v.t.*, **-heard** (-hûrd′), **-hear·ing. 1.** to hear again. **2.** to reconsider officially, as a judge: *to rehear a case.*

re·hear·ing (rē hēr′ing), *n.* *Law.* a second presentation of the evidence and arguments of a case.

re·hears·al (ri hûr′səl), *n.* **1.** a session of exercise, drill, or practice, usually private, in preparation for a public performance, ceremony, etc. **2.** the act of rehearsing. **3.** a detailed relation or recital: *a rehearsal of woes.* [ME *rehersaille*]

re·hearse (ri hûrs′), *v.*, **-hearsed, -hears·ing.** —*v.t.* **1.** to practice (a performance, ceremony, etc.) before its public presentation or occurrence. **2.** to drill or train (an actor, musician, etc.) by rehearsal. **3.** to relate the facts or particulars of; recount. —*v.i.* **4.** to participate in a rehearsal. [ME *rehers(en), reherc(en)* < MF *reherc(ier)* (to) repeat = *re-* RE- + *hercier* to strike, harrow (< *herce, herse* a harrow); see HEARSE] —**re·hears′a·ble,** *adj.* —**re·hears′er,** *n.*

Rehn·quist (ren′kwist), *n.* **William H(ubbs),** born 1924, U.S. jurist: associate justice of the U.S. Supreme Court 1972–86; Chief Justice since 1986.

Reich (RĪKH), *n.* **Wil·helm** (vil′helm), 1897–1957, Austrian psychoanalyst.

Reich (rīk; *Ger.* RĪKH), *n.* (with reference to Germany) empire; realm; nation. Cf. **First Reich, Second Reich, Third Reich.** [< G: kingdom]

Rei·chen·berg (RĪ′KHən beRK′), *n.* German name of **Liberec.**

Reichs·füh·rer (RĪKHS′fY′RəR), *n.* *German.* the chief of the SS Troops. [lit., Reich leader]

reichs·mark (rīks′märk′; *Ger.* RĪKHS′märk′), *n.*, *pl.* **-marks, -mark.** the monetary unit of Germany between 1924 and 1948. Cf. **Deutsche mark, mark[2]** (def. 1), **ostmark.** [< G]

Reichs·tag (rīks′täg′; *Ger.* RĪKHS′täk′), *n.* *Ger. Hist.* the lower house of the German parliament from 1871 to 1945. Cf. **Bundestag.** [< G: Reich diet]

reichs·tha·ler (rīks′tä′lər; *Ger.* RĪKHS′tä′ləR), *n.*, *pl.* **-ler.** a silver thaler of Germany, originally issued in 1566. [< G]

Reichs·wehr (rīks′vär; *Ger.* RĪKHS′väR), *n.* the name of the German army from 1871 to 1945. [< G: Reich armed force]

Reid (rēd), *n.* **White·law** (hwīt′lô′, wīt′-), 1837–1912, U.S. diplomat and journalist.

re·i·fy (rē′ə fī′), *v.t.*, **-fied, -fy·ing.** to convert into or regard as a concrete thing: *to reify an abstract concept.* [< L *rē(s)* thing + -IFY] —**re′i·fi·ca′tion,** *n.*

reign (rān), *n.* **1.** the period during which a sovereign occupies the throne. **2.** royal rule or authority; sovereignty. **3.** dominating power or influence. —*v.i.* **4.** to have the power or title of a sovereign. **5.** to have supreme control, rule, or influence. **6.** to predominate; be prevalent. [ME *reine, regne* < OF *reigne* < L *rēgn(um)* realm, reign < *rēg-* (s. of *rēx*) king] —**Syn. 2.** dominion, suzerainty. **4.** rule, govern.

Reign′ of Ter′ror, a period of the French Revolution (1793–94) during which many persons, esp. of the nobility, were executed.

re·im·burse (rē′im bûrs′), *v.t.*, **-bursed, -burs·ing. 1.** to make repayment to (someone) for expense or loss incurred. **2.** to pay back; refund; repay. [RE- + obs. *imburse* < ML *imburs(āre)* = L *in-* IN-[2] + ML *bursa* purse, bag] —**re′im·burse′ment,** *n.* —**Syn. 1.** recompense, remunerate, indemnify, redress.

re·im·pres·sion (rē′im presh′ən), *n.* **1.** a second or repeated impression. **2.** a reprinting or a reprint.

Reims (rēmz; *Fr.* RANS), *n.* a city in NE France: cathedral; unconditional surrender of Germany May 7, 1945. 186,610. Also, **Rheims.**

rein (rān), *n.* **1.** a leather strap, fastened to each end of the bit of a bridle, by which the rider or driver controls a horse or other animal. **2.** any of certain other straps or thongs forming part of a harness. **3.** any means of curbing, controlling, or directing. —*v.t.* **4.** to check or guide (a horse or other animal) by exerting pressure on a bridle bit by means of the reins. **5.** to curb; restrain; control. —*v.i.* **6.** to obey the reins. **7.** to rein a horse or other animal. [ME *rene* < OF *re(s)ne* < VL **retina*; cf. L *retinēre* to hold back, RETAIN]

re·in·car·nate (*v.* rē′in kär′nāt; *adj.* rē′in kär′nit), *v.*, **-nat·ed, -nat·ing,** *adj.* —*v.t.* **1.** to given another body to; incarnate again. —*adj.* **2.** incarnate anew.

re·in·car·na·tion (rē′in kär nā′shən), *n.* **1.** the doctrine that the soul, upon death of the body, comes back to earth in another body or form. **2.** rebirth of the soul in a new body. **3.** a new incarnation or embodiment, as of a person.

rein·deer (rān′dēr′), *n.*, *pl.* **-deer,** (*occasionally*) **-deers.** any of several large deer of the genus *Rangifer*, of northern and arctic regions of Europe, Asia, and North America, both male and female of which have antlers. [ME *raynder(e)* < Scand; cf. OIcel *hreindȳri* = *hreinn* reindeer + *dȳr* animal, c. DEER]

Reindeer (European), *Rangifer tarandus* (4½ ft. high at shoulder; length 5½ ft.)

Rein′deer Lake′, a lake in central Canada, in NE Saskatchewan and NW Manitoba. 2444 sq. mi.

rein′deer moss′, any of several lichens of the genus *Cladonia*, esp. the gray, many-branched *C. rangiferina*, of arctic and subarctic regions, eaten by reindeer and caribou.

re·in·force (rē′in fōrs′, -fôrs′), *v.t.*, **-forced, -forc·ing. 1.** to strengthen with some added piece, support, or material. **2.** to strengthen (a military force) with additional men, ships, or aircraft. **3.** to make more forcible or effective. **4.** to augment; increase. **5.** *Psychol.* to strengthen the probability of (a response) to a given stimulus by giving or withholding a reward. Also, **reenforce, re-enforce, reënforce.** [RE- + *inforce*, alter. of ENFORCE]

re′inforced con′crete, concrete containing steel bars, strands, mesh, etc., to absorb tensile and shearing stresses.

re·in·force·ment (rē′in fōrs′mənt, -fôrs′-), *n.* **1.** the act of reinforcing. **2.** the state of being reinforced. **3.** something that reinforces or strengthens. **4.** Often, **reinforcements.** an additional supply of men, ships, aircraft, etc., for a military force.

Rein·hardt (RĪn′häRt), *n.* **Max** (mäks), (*Max Goldman*), 1873–1943, German theatrical director, producer, and actor; born in Austria.

reins[1] (rānz), pl. of **rein.**

reins[2] (rānz), *n.pl.* *Archaic.* **1.** the kidneys. **2.** the region of the kidneys, or the lower part of the back. **3.** the seat of the feelings or affections, formerly identified with the kidneys (esp. in Biblical use). [ME < OF; r. ME *reenes*, OE *rēnys* < L *rēnēs* kidneys, loins (pl.)]

re·in·state (rē′in stāt′), *v.t.*, **-stat·ed, -stat·ing.** to put back or establish again, as in a former position or state. —**re′in·state′ment, re′in·sta′tion,** *n.* —**re′in·sta′tor,** *n.*

re·in·sure (rē′in shŏŏr′), *v.t.*, **-sured, -sur·ing. 1.** to insure again. **2.** *Insurance.* to insure under a contract by which a first insurer relieves himself from a part or all of the risk and devolves it upon another insurer. —**re′in·sur′ance,** *n.* —**re′in·sur′er,** *n.*

re·han′dle, *v.t.*, **-dled, -dling.**
re·hang′, *v.t.*, **-hung, -hanged, -hang·ing.**
re·hard′en, *v.*
re·har′ness, *v.t.*
re·heat′, *v.t.*
re·heel′, *v.t.*
re·hem′, *v.t.*, **-hemmed, -hem·ming.**
re·hinge′, *v.t.*, **-hinged, -hing·ing.**
re·hire′, *v.t.*, **-hired, -hir·ing,** *n.*
re′ig·nite′, *v.t.*, **-nit·ed, -nit·ing.**
re′im·pose′, *v.*, **-posed, -pos·ing.**
re′im·pris′on, *v.t.*
re′in·cor′po·rate′, *v.*, **-rat·ed, -rat·ing.**
re′in·cor′po·rate, *adj.*
re′in·cur′, *v.t.*, **-curred, -cur·ring.**
re′in·duce′, *v.t.*, **-duced, -duc·ing.**
re′in·duct′, *v.t.*
re′in·duc′tion, *n.*
re′in·fect′, *v.t.*
re′in·fec′tion, *n.*
re′in·flame′, *v.*, **-flamed, -flam·ing.**
re′in·form′, *v.t.*
re′in·fuse′, *v.t.*, **-fused, -fus·ing.**
re′in·fu′sion, *n.*
re′in·oc′u·late′, *v.*, **-lat·ed, -lat·ing.**
re′in·oc′u·la′tion, *n.*
re′in·quire′, *v.*, **-quired, -quir·ing.**
re′in·quir′y, *n.*, *pl.* **-quir·ies.**
re′in·scribe′, *v.t.*, **-scribed, -scrib·ing.**
re′in·sert′, *v.t.*
re′in·ser′tion, *n.*
re′in·spect′, *v.t.*
re′in·stal·la′tion, *n.*
re′in·stall′ment, *n.*
re′in·struct′, *v.t.*

re·in·vest (rē′in vest′), *v.t.* to invest again, esp. to invest income derived from previous investments. —**re′in·vest′ment,** *n.*

reis (rās; *Port.* RĀS) *n.pl., sing.* **re·al** (rā äl′; *Port.* RE äl′). a former money of account of Portugal and Brazil. Cf. **milreis.** [< Pg, pl. of *real,* c. REAL[2]]

re·is·sue (rē ish′o͞o *or, esp. Brit.,* rē is′yo͞o), *n., v.,* **-sued, -su·ing.** —*n.* **1.** something that has been issued again: *This stamp is a reissue.* —*v.t.* **2.** to issue again. —**re·is′su·a·ble,** *adj.* —**re·is′su·er,** *n.*

re·it·er·ant (rē it′ər ənt), *adj.* reiterating or repeating, esp. to an intensified degree. [< L *reiterant-* (s. of *reiterāns*), prp. of *reiterāre*]

re·it·er·ate (rē it′ə rāt′), *v.t.,* **-at·ed, -at·ing.** to say or do again or repeatedly. [< L *reiterāt(us)* repeated, ptp. of *reiterāre* = *re-* RE- + *iterāre* to repeat < *iterum* again; see -ATE[1]] —**re·it′er·a·ble,** *adj.* —**re·it′er·a′tion,** *n.* —**re·it·er·a·tive** (rē it′ə rā′tiv, -ər ə tiv), *adj.* —**Syn.** See **repeat.**

reive (RĒV), *v.t., v.i.,* **reived, reiv·ing.** *Chiefly Scot.* to rob; plunder. [var. of REAVE[1]] —**reiv′er,** *n.*

re·ject (*v.* ri jekt′; *n.* rē′jekt), *v.t.* **1.** to refuse to have, take, act upon, etc. **2.** to refuse to grant (a request, demand, etc.). **3.** to refuse to accept (a person); rebuff. **4.** to throw away or discard as useless or unsatisfactory. **5.** to cast out or eject. —*n.* **6.** something rejected, as an imperfect article. [ME *reject(en)* (v.) < L *rejectus* thrown back (ptp. of *rejicere*) = *re-* RE- + *-jectus* var. of *jactus,* ptp. of *jacere* to throw] —**re·ject′a·ble,** *adj.* —**re·ject′er,** *n.* —**re·jec′tive,** *adj.* —**Syn. 1.** See **refuse**[1]. **1, 2.** repudiate, deny. **3.** repel, renounce. **4.** eliminate, jettison. **6.** second. —**Ant. 1.** accept.

re·jec·tion (ri jek′shən), *n.* **1.** the act of rejecting. **2.** the state of being rejected. **3.** something that is rejected. [< L *rejectiōn-* (s. of *rejectiō*) a throwing back. See REJECT, -ION]

rejec′tion slip′, a slip of paper, printed with a notification of rejection, attached by a publisher to a manuscript before returning it to its author or his agent.

re·joice (ri jois′), *v.,* **-joiced, -joic·ing.** —*v.i.* **1.** to be glad; take delight (often fol. by *in*): *to rejoice in another's happiness.* —*v.t.* **2.** to make joyful; gladden. [ME *rejoic(en)* < OF *rejouiss-,* long s. of *rejouir* = *re-* RE- + *jouir;* see JOY] —**re·joice′ful,** *adj.*

re·joic·ing (ri joi′sing), *n.* **1.** the act of a person who rejoices. **2.** Often, **rejoicings.** the feeling or the expression of joy. —**re·joic′ing·ly,** *adv.*

re·join[1] (rē join′), *v.t.* **1.** to come again into the company of. **2.** to join together again; reunite. —*v.i.* **3.** to become joined together again. [RE- + JOIN]

re·join[2] (ri join′), *v.t.* **1.** to say in answer; reply, esp. to counterreply. —*v.i.* **2.** to answer; reply, esp. to counterreply. **3.** *Law.* to answer a plaintiff's replication. [ME *rejoin(en)* < AF *rejoyn(er),* var. of MF *rejoindre* = *re-* RE- + *joindre* to JOIN] —**Syn. 2.** respond, retort.

re·join·der (ri join′dər), *n.* **1.** an answer to a reply; response. **2.** *Law.* a defendant's answer to a plaintiff's replication. [ME *rejoiner* < MF *rejoindre* (n. use of inf.); see REJOIN[2]] —**Syn. 1.** reply, riposte. See **answer.**

re·ju·ve·nate (ri jo͞o′və nāt′), *v.t.,* **-nat·ed, -nat·ing. 1.** to restore to youthful vigor, appearance, etc. **2.** *Phys. Geog.* **a.** to renew the activity, erosive power, etc., of (a stream) by the uplifting of the region it drains, or by removal of a barrier in the bed of the stream. **b.** to impress again the characters of youthful topography on (a region) by the action of rejuvenated streams. [RE- + L *juven(is)* young + -ATE[1]] —**re·ju′ve·na′tion,** *n.* —**re·ju′ve·na′tive,** *adj.* —**re·ju′ve·na′tor,** *n.* —**Syn. 1.** refresh, renew, freshen.

re·ju·ve·nes·cent (ri jo͞o′və nes′ənt), *adj.* **1.** becoming young again. **2.** making young again; rejuvenating. [< ML *rejuvenesc(ere)* (to) become young again (L *re-* RE- + *juven(is)* young + *-esc-* inceptive suffix) + -ENT] —**re·ju′ve·nes′cence,** *n.*

-rel, a noun suffix having a diminutive or pejorative force: *wastrel.* Also, **-erel.** [ME < OF *-erel, -erelle*]

rel., 1. relating. **2.** relative. **3.** relatively. **4.** religion. **5.** religious.

re-laid (rē lād′), *v.* pt. and pp. of **re-lay.**

re·lapse (*v.* ri laps′; *n.* ri laps′, rē′laps), *v.,* **-lapsed, -laps·ing,** *n.* —*v.i.* **1.** to fall or slip back into a former state, practice, etc. **2.** to fall back into illness after convalescence or apparent recovery. **3.** to fall back into vice, wrongdoing, or error. —*n.* **4.** the act of relapsing. **5.** a return of a disease or illness after partial recovery from it. [< L *relāps(us)* slid back, sunk back (ptp. of *relābī*). See RE-, LAPSE] —**re·laps′er,** *n.*

relaps′ing fe′ver, *Pathol.* one of a group of fevers characterized by relapses, occurring in many tropical countries, and caused by several species of spirochetes transmitted by several species of lice and ticks. Also called **recurrent fever.**

re·late (ri lāt′), *v.,* **-lat·ed, -lat·ing.** —*v.t.* **1.** to tell; give an account of (an event, circumstance, etc.). **2.** to bring into or establish in an association, connection, or relation. —*v.i.* **3.** to have reference or relation. **4.** to establish a social or sympathetic relationship with a person or thing. [< L *relāt(us)* carried back (ptp. of *referre*); see REFER] —**re·lat′a·bil′i·ty,** *n.* —**re·lat′a·ble,** *adj.* —**re·lat′er,** *n.*

—**Syn. 1.** narrate, delineate, detail, repeat. RELATE, RECITE, RECOUNT mean to tell, report, or describe in some detail an occurrence or circumstance. To RELATE is to give an account of happenings, events, circumstances, etc.: *to relate one's adventures.* To RECITE may mean to give details consecutively, but more often applies to the repetition from memory of something learned with verbal exactness: *to recite a poem.* To RECOUNT is usually to set forth consecutively the details of an occurrence, argument, experience, etc., to give an account in detail: *to recount an unpleasant experience.* —**Ant. 2.** dissociate.

re·lat·ed (ri lā′tid), *adj.* **1.** associated; connected. **2.** allied by nature, origin, kinship, marriage, etc. **3.** narrated. —**Syn. 1.** relevant, affiliated. **2.** linked, united, joined.

re·la·tion (ri lā′shən), *n.* **1.** an existing connection; a significant association between or among things. **2. relations, a.** the various forms of interaction between persons, peoples, countries, etc. **b.** sexual intercourse. **3.** the mode or kind of connection between one person and another, between man and God, etc. **4.** relationship (def. 2). **5.** a person who is related by blood or marriage; relative. **6.** reference; regard; respect: *to plan with relation to the future.* **7.** the act of relating or narrating. **8.** a narrative; account. **9.** *Law.* a principle whereby effect is given to an act done at one time as if it had been done at a previous time. **10.** *Math.* **a.** a property that associates two quantities in a definite order, as equality or inequality. **b.** a many-valued function. [ME *relacion* < L *relātiōn-* (s. of *relātiō*)] —**Syn. 1.** relationship; tie, link. **7.** recitation, recital, description. **8.** report, story, chronicle.

re·la·tion·al (ri lā′shə n[ə]l), *adj.* **1.** of or pertaining to relations. **2.** indicating or specifying some relation. **3.** *Gram.* serving to indicate relations between various elements in a sentence, as prepositions, conjunctions, etc. Cf. **notional** (def. 5).

re·la·tion·ship (ri lā′shən ship′), *n.* **1.** a connection, association, or involvement. **2.** connection between persons by blood or marriage. **3.** an emotional or other connection between people.

—**Syn. 1.** dependence, alliance, kinship. **2.** affinity, consanguinity. RELATIONSHIP, KINSHIP refer to connection with others by blood or by marriage. RELATIONSHIP can be applied to connection either by birth or by marriage: *relationship to a ruling family.* KINSHIP generally denotes common descent, and implies a more intimate connection than relationship: *the ties and obligations of kinship.*

rel·a·tive (rel′ə tiv), *n.* **1.** a person who is connected with another or others by blood or marriage. **2.** something having, or standing in, some relation to something else. **3.** something dependent upon external conditions for its specific nature, size, etc. (opposed to *absolute*). **4.** *Gram.* a relative pronoun, adjective, or adverb. —*adj.* **5.** considered in relation to something else; comparative. **6.** existing or having its significance only by relation to something else; not absolute or independent. **7.** having reference or regard; relevant; pertinent. **8.** *Gram.* noting or pertaining to a word or other element that constitutes or introduces a subordinate clause, as the relative pronoun *who* in *He's the man who saw you,* where *who saw you* is a relative clause. [< LL *relātīv(us)*]

rel′ative clause′, a clause that modifies an antecedent, as *who saw us* in the sentence *It was she who saw us.*

rel′ative den′sity, *Physics.* See **specific gravity.**

rel′ative fre′quency, *Statistics.* the ratio of the number of times an event occurs to the number of occasions on which it might occur in the same period.

rel′ative humid′ity, the amount of water vapor in the air, expressed as a percentage of the maximum amount that the air could hold at the given temperature. Also called **humidity.** Cf. **absolute humidity, dew point.**

rel·a·tive·ly (rel′ə tiv lē), *adv.* in a relative manner: *a relatively small difference.*

rel′ative pitch′, *Music.* **1.** the pitch of a tone as determined by its relationship to other tones in a scale. **2.** the ability to identify or sing a tone by mentally determining the distance of its pitch from that of a tone already sounded. Cf. **absolute pitch.**

rel′ative pro′noun, a pronoun that refers to an antecedent, as *who* in *It was I who told you.*

rel·a·tiv·ism (rel′ə ti viz′əm), *n.* *Philos.* any theory holding that criteria of judgment are relative, varying with individuals and their environments.

rel·a·tiv·ist (rel′ə ti vist), *n.* an adherent or advocate of relativism or of the principle of relativity.

rel·a·tiv·is·tic (rel′ə ti vis′tik), *adj.* **1.** of or pertaining to relativity or relativism. **2.** *Physics.* having a value that varies with velocity, in classical mechanics being equivalent to the value obtained when the velocity is appreciably smaller than the speed of light.

relativis′tic quan′tum mechan′ics, *Physics.* See under **quantum mechanics** (def. 1).

rel·a·tiv·i·ty (rel′ə tiv′i tē), *n.* **1.** the state or fact of being relative. **2.** *Physics.* a theory, formulated essentially by Albert Einstein, that all motion must be defined relative to a frame of reference and that space and time are relative, rather than absolute concepts: it consists of two principal parts. The theory dealing with uniform motion (**special theory of relativity**) is based on the two postulates that physical laws have the same mathematical form when expressed in any inertial system, and the velocity of light is independent of the motion of its source and will have the same value when measured by observers moving with constant velocity with respect to each other. The theory dealing with gravity (**general theory of relativity**) is based on the postulate that the local effects of a gravitational field and of acceleration of an inertial system are identical.

re·la·tor (ri lā′tər), *n.* a person who relates or tells; narrator.

re·lax (ri laks′), *v.t.* **1.** to make less tense, rigid, or firm; make lax. **2.** to diminish the force of (effort, attention, etc.). **3.** to make less strict or severe, as rules or discipline. **4.** to release or bring relief from the effects of tension, anxiety,

re·in′te·grate′, *v.,* **-grat·ed, -grat·ing.**
re′in·te·gra′tion, *n.*
re′in·ter′, *v.t.,* **-terred, -ter·ring.**
re′in·ter′pret, *v.*
re′in·ter′pre·ta′tion, *n.*
re′in·ter′ro·gate′, *v.,* **-gat·ed, -gat·ing.**
re′in·ter·ro·ga′tion, *n.*
re′in·trench′, *v.*
re′in·trench′ment, *n.*
re′in·tro·duce′, *v.t.,* **-duced, -duc·ing.**
re′in·tro·duc′tion, *n.*
re′in·ves′ti·gate′, *v.,* **-gat·ed, -gat·ing.**
re′in·ves·ti·ga′tion, *n.*
re′in·vig′or·ate′, *v.t.,* **-at·ed, -at·ing.**
re′in·vig′or·a′tion, *n.*
re′in·vite′, *v.,* **-vit·ed, -vit·ing.**
re′in·voke′, *v.t.,* **-voked, -vok·ing.**
re′in·volve′, *v.t.,* **-volved, -volv·ing.**
re′in·volve′ment, *n.*
re′ir·ri·ga′tion, *n.*
re·judge′, *v.,* **-judged, -judg·ing.**
re·kin′dle, *v.,* **-dled, -dling.**
re·la′bel, *v.t.,* **-beled, -bel·ing** *or (esp. Brit.)* **-belled, -bel·ling.**
re·laun′der, *v.t.*

etc. —*v.i.* **5.** to become less tense, rigid, or firm. **6.** to become less strict or severe; grow milder. **7.** to reduce or stop work or effort, esp. for the sake of rest or recreation. **8.** to release oneself from inhibition, worry, tension, etc. [ME *relax(en)* < L *relax(āre)* (to) stretch out again, loosen = *re-* RE- + *laxāre* to loosen < *laxus* slack, LAX] —**re·lax′a·tive, re·lax·a·to·ry** (ri lak′sə tōr′ē, -tôr′ē), *adj.* —**re·lax·ed·ly** (ri lak′sid lē), *adv.* —**Syn. 1, 5.** loosen, slacken. **3.** mitigate, weaken, ease. **6.** relent, soften. —**Ant. 1, 5.** tighten, tense.

re·lax·ant (ri lak′sənt), *adj.* **1.** of, pertaining to, or causing relaxation. —*n.* **2.** *Med.* a drug that relaxes, esp. one that lessens strain in muscle. [< L *relaxant-* (s. of *relaxāns*), prp. of *relaxāre*]

re·lax·a·tion (rē′lak sā′shən), *n.* **1.** abatement or relief from work, effort, etc. **2.** an activity or recreation that provides such relief; diversion. **3.** a loosening or slackening. **4.** diminution or remission of strictness or severity. [< L *relaxātiōn-* (s. of *relaxātiō*) = *relaxāt(us)* (ptp. of *relaxāre* to RELAX) + *-iōn-* -ION]

re-lay (rē lā′), *v.t.*, **-laid, -lay·ing.** to lay again. Also, **relay.**

re·lay[1] (*n.* rē′lā; *v.* rē′lā, ri lā′), *n.*, *v.*, **-layed, -lay·ing.** —*n.* **1.** a series of persons relieving one another or taking turns; shift. **2.** a fresh set of dogs or horses posted in readiness for use in a hunt, on a journey, etc. **3.** *Sports.* **a.** See **relay race. b.** a length or leg in a relay race. **4.** *Mach.* an automatic control device in which the settings of valves, switches, etc., are regulated by a powered element actuated by a smaller, sensitive element. **5.** *Elect.* a device, usually consisting of an electromagnet and an armature, by which a change of current or voltage in one circuit can be made to produce a change in the electric condition of another circuit or to affect the operation of other devices in the same or another electric circuit. —*v.t.* **6.** to carry forward by or as by relays: *to relay a message.* **7.** to provide with or replace by fresh relays. **8.** *Elect.* to retransmit (a signal, message, etc.) by or as by means of a telegraphic relay. —*v.i.* **9.** *Elect.* to relay a message. [ME *relai* (n.), *relai(en)* (v.) < MF *relais* (n.), *relai(er)* (v.), OF: to leave behind = *re-* RE- + *laier* to leave, alter. of *laissier* < L *laxāre*; see RELAX]

re·lay[2] (rē lā′), *v.t.*, **-laid, -lay·ing.** re-lay.

re′lay race′, *Sports.* a race between two or more teams of contestants, each contestant being relieved by a teammate after running part of the distance.

re-lease (rē lēs′), *v.t.*, **-leased, -leas·ing.** to lease again.

re·lease (ri lēs′), *v.*, **-leased, -leas·ing,** *n.* —*v.t.* **1.** to free from confinement, obligation, pain, etc.; let go. **2.** to free (anything) from that which fastens or restrains it. **3.** to allow to be known, published, done, or exhibited. **4.** *Law.* to give up, relinquish, or surrender (a right, claim, etc.). —*n.* **5.** liberation from confinement, obligation, pain, etc. **6.** liberation from anything that restrains or fastens. **7.** something that effects such liberation. **8.** a grant of permission, as to publish, use, or sell something. **9.** See **press release. 10.** the act of issuing this. **11.** *Law.* **a.** the surrender of a right or the like to another. **b.** a document embodying such a surrender. **12.** a control mechanism for starting or stopping a machine, esp. by removing some restrictive apparatus. [ME *reles(s)e(n)* (v.) < OF *relesser, relaissier* < L *relaxāre* to loosen; see RELAX]
—**Syn. 1.** loose, deliver. RELEASE, FREE, DISMISS, DISCHARGE, LIBERATE, EMANCIPATE may all mean to set at liberty, let loose, or let go. RELEASE and FREE, when applied to persons, suggest a helpful action. Both may be used (not always interchangeably) of delivering a person from confinement or obligation: *to free or release prisoners.* FREE (less often, RELEASE) is also used for delivering a person from pain, sorrow, etc.: *to free from fear.* DISMISS, meaning to send away, usually has the meaning of forcing to go unwillingly (*to dismiss a servant*), but may refer to giving permission to go: *The teacher dismissed the class early.* DISCHARGE, meaning originally to relieve of a burden (*to discharge a gun*), has come to refer to that which is sent away, and is often a close synonym to DISMISS; it is used in the meaning permit to go, in connection with courts and the armed forces: *The court discharged a man accused of robbery.* LIBERATE and EMANCIPATE, more formal synonyms for RELEASE and FREE, also suggest action intended to be helpful. LIBERATE suggests particularly the release from unjust punishment, oppression, and the like, and often means to set free through forcible action or military campaign: *They liberated the prisoners, the occupied territories, etc.* EMANCIPATE also suggests a release of some size and consequence, but one that is less overt, a more formal or legal freedom; and it sometimes connotes an inner liberation: *Lincoln emancipated the slaves. John emancipated himself.* **2.** loose, extricate, disengage. **3.** announce, publish. **5.** deliverance, emancipation. —**Ant. 1.** bind. **2.** fasten.

rel·e·gate (rel′ə gāt′), *v.t.*, **-gat·ed, -gat·ing. 1.** to send or consign to an inferior position, place, or condition. **2.** to consign or commit (a matter, task, etc.), as to a person. **3.** to assign or refer (something) to a particular class or kind. **4.** to send into exile; banish. [< L *relēgāt(us)* sent away, dispatched, ptp. of *relēgāre*] —**rel·e·ga·ble** (rel′ə gə bəl), *adj.* —**rel′e·ga′tion,** *n.* —**Syn. 2.** confide, entrust.

re·lent (ri lent′), *v.i.* **1.** to become more mild, compassionate, or forgiving. **2.** to become less severe; slacken. —*v.t.* **3.** *Obs.* to cause to soften in feeling, temper, or determination. [ME *relent(en)* ? << RE- + L *lent(us)* tough, viscous, slow] —**re·lent′ing·ly,** *adv.* —**Syn. 1.** bend, yield.

re·lent·less (ri lent′lis), *adj.* unyieldingly severe, strict, or harsh; unrelenting. —**re·lent′less·ly,** *adv.* —**re·lent′less·ness,** *n.* —**Syn.** rigid, stern, unforgiving, merciless, pitiless, hard. —**Ant.** merciful.

rel·e·vant (rel′ə vənt), *adj.* bearing upon or connected with the matter in hand; to the purpose; pertinent. [< ML *relevant-* (s. of *relevāns*), special use of L, prp. of *relevāre* to raise, lift up. See RELIEVE, -ANT] —**rel′e·vance, rel′e·van·cy,** *n.* —**rel′e·vant·ly,** *adv.* —**Syn.** applicable, germane, apposite, appropriate, suitable, fitting. See **apt.**

re·li·a·ble (ri lī′ə bəl), *adj.* that may be relied on; trustworthy. —**re·li′a·bil′i·ty,** *n.* —**re·li′a·bly,** *adv.*
—**Syn.** trusty, authentic, consistent. RELIABLE, INFALLIBLE, TRUSTWORTHY apply to persons, objects, ideas, or information that can be depended upon with confident certainty. RELIABLE suggests consistent dependability of judgment, character, performance, or result: *a reliable formula, judge, car, meteorologist.* INFALLIBLE suggests the complete absence of error, breakdown, or poor performance: *an infallible test, system, marksman.* TRUSTWORTHY emphasizes the steady and honest dependability that encourages one's confidence, belief, or trust: *trustworthy and accurate reports.* —**Ant.** undependable, questionable, deceitful.

re·li·ance (ri lī′əns), *n.* **1.** confident or trustful dependence. **2.** confidence. **3.** something or someone relied on.

re·li·ant (ri lī′ənt), *adj.* **1.** having or showing dependence. **2.** confident; trustful. —**re·li′ant·ly,** *adv.*

rel·ic (rel′ik), *n.* **1.** a surviving memorial of something past. **2.** an object having interest by reason of its age or its association with the past. **3.** a surviving trace of something. **4. relics, a.** remaining parts or fragments. **b.** the remains of a deceased person. **5.** something kept in remembrance; souvenir; memento. **6.** *Eccles.* the body, a part of the body, or some personal memorial of a saint, martyr, or other sacred person. Also, *Archaic,* **relique.** [ME *relik* < OF *relique* < L *reliquiae* (pl.) remains (> OE *reliquias*) = *reliqu(us)* remaining + *-iae* pl. n. suffix]

rel·ict (rel′ikt), *n.* **1.** *Ecol.* a plant or animal species living in an environment that has changed from that which is typical for it. **2.** a remnant or survivor. **3.** *Archaic.* a widow. [late ME < ML *relicta* widow (L *relictus,* ptp. of *relinquere* to RELINQUISH)]

re·lief[1] (ri lēf′), *n.* **1.** ease or deliverance through the removal of pain, distress, anxiety, etc. **2.** a means of such ease or deliverance. **3.** help given to those in poverty or need. **4.** something that provides a pleasing change, as from monotony. **5.** release from a post of duty, as by the arrival of a replacement. **6.** the person or persons acting as this replacement. **7.** the rescue of a besieged town, fort, etc., from an attacking force. **8.** *Feudal Law.* a payment made by an heir to his lord upon succeeding to the estate. **9.** *Literature.* a distinct or abrupt change in mood, scene, action, etc., resulting in a reduction of intensity, as in a play or novel. **10. on relief,** receiving financial assistance from a municipal, state, or federal government because of poverty or need. [ME *relef* < OF *relief* < *relever* to raise; see RELIEVE] —**Syn. 1.** mitigation, assuagement, comfort. **3.** succor, aid, redress, remedy. —**Ant. 1.** intensification.

Relief[2]
A, Bas-relief; B, High relief

re·lief[2] (ri lēf′), *n.* **1.** prominence, distinctness, or vividness due to contrast. **2.** the projection of a figure or part from the ground or plane on which it is formed, as in sculpture or similar work. **3.** a piece or work in such projection. **4.** an apparent projection of parts in a painting, drawing, etc., giving the appearance of the third dimension. **5.** *Phys. Geog.* a contour variation of the land surface in relation to the surrounding land. **6.** *Print.* any printing process by which the printing ink is transferred to paper or another printed surface from areas that are higher than the rest of the block. [< F *relief,* It *rilievo;* see RELIEF[1]]

relief′ map′, a map showing the relief of an area.

relief′ pitch′er, *Baseball.* **1.** a pitcher brought into a game to replace another pitcher, often in a critical situation. **2.** a pitcher regularly so used.

re·li·er (ri lī′ər), *n.* a person or thing that relies.

re·lieve (ri lēv′), *v.*, **-lieved, -liev·ing.** —*v.t.* **1.** to ease or alleviate (pain, distress, etc.). **2.** to free from anxiety, fear, pain, etc. **3.** to free from need, poverty, etc. **4.** to bring effective aid to (a besieged town, fort, etc.). **5.** to ease (a person) of any burden, as by legal means. **6.** to reduce (a pressure, load, weight, etc., on a device or object under stress). **7.** to break or vary the sameness of: *to relieve the tension of a drama with comic episodes.* **8.** to bring into relief or prominence. **9.** to release (a person on duty) by coming as or providing a substitute or replacement. **10. to relieve oneself,** to urinate or defecate. [ME *relev(en)* < MF *relever* to raise < L *relevāre* to lift, raise up again, lighten = *re-* RE- + *levāre* to raise] —**re·liev′a·ble,** *adj.* —**re·liev·ed·ly** (ri-lē′vid lē), *adv.* —**re·liev′er,** *n.* —**Syn. 1.** mitigate, lessen. **1–4.** aid, help, assist. **3.** support, sustain. **4.** succor. —**Ant. 1.** intensify.

re·lie·vo (ri lē′vō, -lyev′ō), *n.*, *pl.* **-vos.** *Obs.* relief[2] (defs. 2, 3). [< It RILIEVO]

relig., religion.

re·li·gion (ri lij′ən), *n.* **1.** a set of beliefs concerning the cause, nature, and purpose of the universe, esp. when considered as the creation of a superhuman agency or agencies, usually involving devotional and ritual observances and often having a moral code for the conduct of human affairs. **2.** a specific and institutionalized set of beliefs and practices generally agreed upon by a number of persons or sects: *the Christian religion; the Buddhist religion.* **3.** the body of persons or institutions adhering to a set of religious beliefs and practices: *a world council of religions.* **4.** a deep conviction of the validity of religious beliefs and practices: *to get religion.* **5.** the life or state of a monk, nun, etc.: *to enter religion.* **6.** the practice of religious beliefs; ritual observance of faith. **7.** a point or matter of ethics or conscience: *to make a religion*

re·learn′, *v.*, **-learned** or **-learnt, -learn·ing.**
re·let′, *v.*, **-let, -let·ting.**
re·let′ter, *v.t.*
re·li′cense, *v.t.*, **-censed, -cens·ing.**
re·light′, *v.*, **-light·ed** or **-lit, -light·ing.**

of fighting prejudice. **8. religions,** *Archaic.* religious rites. **9.** *Archaic.* strict faithfulness; devotion: *a religion to one's vow.* [ME *religioun* < L *religiōn-* (s. of *religiō*) conscientiousness, piety, ? = *relig(āre)* to tie, fasten (*re-* RE- + *lig-* bind, tie) + *-iōn-* -ION]

re·li·gion·ism (ri lij′ə niz′əm), *n.* exaggerated or pretended religious zeal. —**re·li′gion·ist,** *n.* —**re·li′gion·is′tic,** *adj.*

re·li·gi·ose (ri lij′ē ōs′), *adj.* characterized by religiosity. [< L *religiōsus;* see RELIGIOUS]

re·lig·i·os·i·ty (ri lij′ē os′i tē), *n.* **1.** the quality of being religious; devoutness. **2.** affected or excessive devotion to religion. [ME *religiosite* < L *religiōsitās* = *religiōs(us)* RELIGIOUS + *-itās* -ITY]

re·li·gious (ri lij′əs), *adj., n., pl.* **-gious.** —*adj.* **1.** of, pertaining to, or concerned with religion. **2.** imbued with or exhibiting religion. **3.** scrupulously faithful; conscientious: *religious care.* **4.** pertaining to or connected with a monastic or religious order. **5.** appropriate to religion or to sacred rites or observances. —*n.* **6.** a member of a religious order, congregation, etc. [ME < L *religiōs(us)* = *religi(ō)* RELIGION + *-ōsus* -OUS] —**re·li′gious·ly,** *adv.* —**re·li′gious·ness,** *n.*
—**Syn. 2.** reverent. RELIGIOUS, DEVOUT, PIOUS indicate a spirit of reverence toward God. RELIGIOUS is a general word, applying to whatever pertains to faith or worship: *a religious ceremony.* DEVOUT indicates a fervent spirit, usually genuine and often independent of outward observances: *a deeply devout though unorthodox church member.* PIOUS implies extreme conformity with outward observances and can suggest sham or hypocrisy: *a pious hypocrite.* —**Ant. 2.** impious.

Reli′gious Soci′ety of Friends′, the sect founded by George Fox in England about 1650, opposed to oath-taking and all war: its members are commonly called Quakers.

re·lin·quish (ri liŋ′kwish), *v.t.* **1.** to renounce or surrender (a possession, right, etc.). **2.** to put aside or desist from. **3.** to let go; release. [late ME < MF *relinquiss-*, extended s. of *relinquir* < L *relinquere* to leave behind = *re-* RE- + *linquere* to leave] —**re·lin′quish·er,** *n.* —**re·lin′quish·ment,** *n.* —**Syn. 2.** yield, forgo, resign. See **abandon**[1].

rel·i·quar·y (rel′ə kwer′ē), *n., pl.* **-quar·ies.** a repository or receptacle for a relic or relics. [< MF *reliquaire* < ML *reliquiār(ium)* = L *reliqui(ae)* remains (see RELIC) + *-ārium* -ARY]

rel·ique (rel′ik; *Fr.* rə lēk′), *n., pl.* **rel·iques** (rel′iks; *Fr.* rə lēk′). *Archaic.* relic.

re·liq·ui·ae (ri lik′wē ē′), *n.* (*construed as pl.*) remains, as those of fossil organisms. [< L; see RELIC]

rel·ish (rel′ish), *n.* **1.** liking or enjoyment of the taste of something. **2.** pleasurable appreciation of anything; liking. **3.** *Cookery.* something savory or appetizing, as a sweet pickle of minced vegetables. **4.** a pleasing or appetizing flavor. **5.** a pleasing or enjoyable quality. **6.** a taste or flavor. **7.** a smack, trace, or touch of something. —*v.t.* **8.** to take pleasure in; like; enjoy. **9.** to make pleasing to the taste. **10.** to like the taste or flavor of. —*v.i.* **11.** to have taste or flavor. **12.** to be agreeable or pleasant. [alter. of ME *reles* aftertaste, scent < OF, var. of *relais* remainder, that left behind; see RELEASE] —**rel′ish·a·ble,** *adj.* —**rel′ish·ing·ly,** *adv.* —**Syn. 1, 2.** gusto, zest. **2.** inclination, partiality, predilection, preference. **3.** condiment, appetizer. **6.** savor. **8.** appreciate. —**Ant. 1, 2.** distaste, disfavor.

re·live (ri liv′), *v.,* **-lived, -liv·ing.** —*v.t.* **1.** to experience again, as an emotion. **2.** to live (one's life) again. —*v.i.* **3.** to live again. —**re·liv′a·ble,** *adj.*

re·lo·cate (rē lō′kāt), *v.,* **-cat·ed, -cat·ing.** —*v.t.* **1.** to locate again. **2.** to locate in another place. **3.** *Chiefly U.S.* to move to another place, as one's business, residence, etc. —*v.i.* **4.** *Chiefly U.S.* to move one's business, home, etc., to another place. —**re′lo·ca′tion,** *n.*

rel. pron., relative pronoun.

re·luct (ri lukt′), *v.i. Archaic.* to show opposition; rebel. [< L *reluct(ārī)* = *re-* RE- + *luct(ārī)* (to) strive, struggle]

re·luc·tance (ri luk′təns), *n.* **1.** unwillingness; disinclination. **2.** *Elect.* the resistance to magnetic flux offered by a magnetic circuit. Also, **re·luc′tan·cy.** [RELUCT(ANT) + -ANCE]

re·luc·tant (ri luk′tənt), *adj.* **1.** unwilling; disinclined: *a reluctant presidential candidate.* **2.** struggling in opposition. [< L *reluctant-* (s. of *reluctāns*), prp. of *reluctārī*] —**re·luc′tant·ly,** *adv.*
—**Syn. 1.** RELUCTANT, LOATH, AVERSE describe disinclination toward something. RELUCTANT implies some sort of mental struggle, as between disinclination and sense of duty: *reluctant to expel students.* LOATH describes extreme disinclination: *loath to part from a friend.* AVERSE, used with *to* and a noun or a gerund, describes a long-held dislike or unwillingness, though not a particularly strong feeling: *averse to an idea; averse to getting up early.* —**Ant. 1.** willing.

re·lume (ri lo͞om′), *v.t.,* **-lumed, -lum·ing.** to light or illuminate again. [< LL *relūm(ināre*). See RELUMINE]

re·lu·mine (ri lo͞o′min), *v.t.,* **-mined, -min·ing.** to relume. [< LL *relūmin(āre)* = L *re-* RE- + *(il)lūmināre* to ILLUMINE]

re·ly (ri lī′), *v.i.,* **-lied, -ly·ing.** to depend confidently (usually fol. by *on* or *upon*): *to rely on another's help.* [ME *relie(n)* < MF *relie(r)* < L *religāre* to tie back. See RE-, LIGAMENT]

rem (rem), *n.* the quantity of ionizing radiation whose biological effect is equal to that produced by one roentgen of x-rays. Cf. **rep**[3]. [*r(oentgen) e(quivalent in) m(an)*]

re·main (ri mān′), *v.i.* **1.** to continue in the same state; continue to be as specified. **2.** to stay behind or in the same place. **3.** to be left after the removal, loss, etc., of all else. **4.** to be left to be done, told, shown, etc. **5.** to be reserved or in store. —*n.* **6.** Usually, **remains.** something that remains or is left. **7. remains, a.** writings unpublished at the time of the author's death. **b.** traces of some quality, condition, etc. **c.** a dead body; corpse. **d.** parts or substances remaining from animal or plant life: *fossil remains.* [ME *remain(en)* < AF *remain-*, stressed s. of MF *remanoir* < L *remanēre* = *re-* RE- + *manēre* to stay; see MANOR] —**Syn. 1.** abide, stay. See **continue. 2.** wait, tarry, rest. **3.** endure, abide. —**Ant. 2.** depart.

re·main·der (ri mān′dər), *n.* **1.** something that remains or is left; a remaining part. **2.** *Arith.* **a.** the quantity that remains after subtraction. **b.** the portion of the dividend that is not evenly divisible by the divisor. **3.** *Law.* a future interest so created as to take effect at the end of another estate, as when property is conveyed to one person for life and then to another. **4. remainders,** *Philately.* the quantities of stamps on hand after they have been demonetized or otherwise voided for postal use. **5.** a copy of a book remaining in the publisher's stock when its sale has practically ceased, frequently sold at a reduced price. —*adj.* **6.** remaining; leftover. —*v.t.* **7.** to dispose of or sell as a remainder. [ME < AF, n. use of MF *remaindre* to remain]
—**Syn. 1.** residuum, remnant, excess, rest, overage. REMAINDER, BALANCE, RESIDUE refer to a portion left over. REMAINDER is the general word (*the remainder of one's life*); it may refer in particular to the mathematical process of subtraction: *7 minus 5 leaves a remainder of 2.* BALANCE, originally a bookkeeper's term referring to the amount of money left to one's account (*a bank balance*), is often used colloquially as a synonym for REMAINDER: *the balance of the day.* RESIDUE is used particularly to designate what remains as the result of a process; this is usually a chemical process, but the word may also refer to a legal process concerning inheritance: *a residue of ash left from burning leaves.*

re·main·der·man (ri mān′dər mən), *n., pl.* **-men.** *Law.* a person who owns a remainder.

re·make (*v.* rē māk′; *n.* rē′māk′), *v.,* **-made, -mak·ing,** *n.* —*v.t.* **1.** to make again or anew. —*n.* **2.** something, as a motion picture, that is made again or anew.

re·man (rē man′), *v.t.,* **-manned, -man·ning. 1.** to furnish with a fresh supply of men. **2.** to restore the courage of.

re·mand (ri mand′, -mänd′), *v.t.* **1.** to send back or consign again. **2.** *Law.* **a.** to send back (a case) to a lower court, as for further proceedings. **b.** to send back (a prisoner or accused person) into custody, as to await further proceedings. —*n.* **3.** the act of remanding. **4.** the state of being remanded. **5.** a person remanded. [ME *remaund(en)* < OF *remand(er)* < LL *remandāre* to repeat a command, send back word = L *re-* RE- + *mandāre* to entrust, enjoin; see MANDATE]

remand′ home′, *Brit.* a detention home for juvenile offenders aged 8–16 years. Cf. **borstal.**

rem·a·nence (rem′ə nəns), *n. Elect.* the magnetic flux that remains in a magnetic circuit after an applied magnetomotive force has been removed. [REMAN(ENT) + -ENCE]

rem·a·nent (rem′ə nənt), *adj.* remaining; left behind. [< L *remanent-* (s. of *remanēns*), prp. of *remanēre.* See REMAIN, -ENT]

re·mark (ri märk′), *v.t.* **1.** to say casually, as in making a comment. **2.** to note; perceive; observe. **3.** *Obs.* to mark distinctively. —*v.i.* **4.** to make a remark or observation. —*n.* **5.** the act of remarking; notice. **6.** comment or mention. **7.** a casual or brief expression of thought or opinion. **8.** *Fine Arts.* remarque. [< F, MF *remarqu(er)* (to) note, heed = *re-* RE- + *marquer* to MARK[1]] —**re·mark′er,** *n.*
—**Syn. 2.** heed, regard, notice. **4.** comment. **5.** regard. **7.** REMARK, COMMENT, NOTE, OBSERVATION imply giving special attention, an opinion, or a judgment. A REMARK is usually a casual and passing expression of opinion: *a remark about a play.* A COMMENT expresses judgment or explains a particular point: *a comment on the author's scholarship.* A NOTE is a memorandum or explanation, as in the margin of a page: *a note explaining a passage.* OBSERVATION suggests a note based on judgment and experience: *an observation on usages.* —**Ant. 2.** ignore.

re·mark·a·ble (ri mär′kə bəl), *adj.* **1.** notably unusual; extraordinary. **2.** worthy of notice. [< F *remarquable*] —**re·mark′a·bil′i·ty, re·mark′a·ble·ness,** *n.* —**re·mark′a·bly,** *adv.* —**Syn. 2.** notable, noteworthy, striking, unusual, singular, uncommon. —**Ant. 1, 2.** common, ordinary.

re·marque (ri märk′), *n. Fine Arts.* **1.** a distinguishing mark or small sketch engraved in the margin of a plate to indicate a particular stage in its development. **2.** a plate so marked. Also, **remark.** [< F; see REMARK]

Re·marque (ri märk′; *Ger.* rə märk′), *n.* **E·rich Ma·ri·a** (er′ik mə rē′ə; *Ger.* ā′rikh mä rē′ä), 1898–1970, German novelist in the U.S.

re·match (*n.* rē′mach′; *v.* ri mach′), *n., v.* —*n.* **1.** a second contest between two opponents. —*v.t.* **2.** to match again.

Rem·brandt (rem′brant, -bränt; *Du.* rem′bränt), *n.* (*Rembrandt Harmenszoon van Rijn* or *van Ryn*) 1606–69, Dutch painter. —**Rem′brandt·esque′,** *adj.*

re·me·di·a·ble (ri mē′dē ə bəl), *adj.* capable of being remedied. [ME < MF < L *remediābil(is)* curable] —**re·me′di·a·ble·ness,** *n.* —**re·me′di·a·bly,** *adv.*

re·me·di·al (ri mē′dē əl), *adj.* **1.** affording remedy. **2.** intended to correct or improve one's skill in a specified field: *remedial math.* [< LL *remediāl(is).* See REMEDY, -AL[1]] —**re·me′di·al·ly,** *adv.*

reme′dial read′ing, instruction in reading aimed at increasing speed and comprehension by correcting poor reading habits.

rem·e·di·less (rem′i dē lis), *adj.* not admitting of remedy; unremediable. [ME]

rem·e·dy (rem′i dē), *n., pl.* **-dies,** *v.,* **-died, -dy·ing.** —*n.* **1.** something, as a medicine, that cures or relieves a disease or bodily disorder. **2.** something that corrects or removes an evil of any kind. **3.** *Law.* legal redress. —*v.t.* **4.** to cure, relieve, or heal. **5.** to restore to the natural or proper condition; put right: *to remedy a matter.* **6.** to counteract or remove: *to remedy an evil.* [ME *remedie* < AF < L *remedi(um)*

re·line′, *v.t.,* -lined, -lin·ing.
re·liq′ui·date′, *v.,* -dat·ed, -dat·ing.
re′liq·ui·da′tion, *n.*
re·list′, *v.t.*
re·load′, *v.*
re·loan′, *n., v.t.*
re·mail′, *v.t.*
re′man·u·fac′ture, *v.t.,* -tured, -tur·ing.
re·mar′riage, *n.*
re·mar′ry, *v.,* -ried, -ry·ing.
re·mar′shal, *v.t.,* -shaled, -shal·ing or (*esp. Brit.*) -shalled, -shal·ling.
re′ma·tric′u·late, *v.,* -lat·ed, -lat·ing.
re·meas′ure, *v.t.,* -ured, -ur·ing.
re·meas′ure·ment, *n.*

= *remed(ērī)* (*re-* RE- + *medērī* to heal) + *-ium* -Y[3]] **—Syn. 1.** cure, restorative, specific, medicament, medication. **2.** corrective, antidote. **5.** See **cure. 6.** repair, correct, redress, renew. **—Ant. 5.** worsen.

re·mem·ber (ri mem′bər), *v.t.* **1.** to recall to the mind by an act or effort of memory; think of again. **2.** to retain in the memory; keep in mind: *Remember your appointment.* **3.** to have (something) come into the mind again: *I just remembered his name.* **4.** to reward; tip. **5.** to mention (a person) to another as sending kindly greetings. **6.** *Archaic.* to remind. **—*v.i.* 7.** to possess or exercise the faculty of memory. [ME *remembre(n)* < OF *remembr(er)* < LL *rememor(ārī)* = *re-* RE- + L *memor* mindful; see MEMORY] **—re·mem′ber·er,** *n.*

—Syn. 1. REMEMBER, RECALL, RECOLLECT refer to bringing back before the conscious mind things that exist in the memory. REMEMBER implies that a thing exists in the memory, though not actually present in the thoughts at the moment: *to remember the days of one's childhood.* RECALL, a rather conversational word, implies a voluntary effort, though not a great one: *to recall the words of a song.* RECOLLECT implies an earnest voluntary effort to remember some definite, desired fact or thing: *I cannot recollect the exact circumstances.* **—Ant. 1, 2.** forget.

re·mem·brance (ri mem′brəns), *n.* **1.** a retained mental impression; memory. **2.** the act or fact of remembering. **3.** the ability to remember. **4.** the length of time over which recollection or memory extends. **5.** commemoration: *to hold someone's name in remembrance.* **6.** something that serves to bring to or keep in mind; memento. **7.** a gift given as a token of love or friendship. **8. remembrances,** greetings; respects. [ME < OF; see REMEMBER, -ANCE] **—Syn. 1.** recollection, reminiscence. **3.** memory. **6.** keepsake, trophy, souvenir, token, memorial.

Remem′brance Day′, November 11, observed as a legal holiday in Canada in memory of those who died in World Wars I and II, similar to Veterans Day in the U.S.

re·mem·branc·er (ri mem′brən sər), *n.* **1.** a person or thing that reminds another of something. **2.** a reminder; memento; souvenir. **3.** (*usually cap.*) (formerly) any of certain officials of the Court of Exchequer. [ME < AF]

re·mex (rē′meks), *n., pl.* **rem·i·ges** (rem′i jēz′). *Ornith.* one of the flight feathers of the wing. [< L: oarsman = *rēm(us)* oar + *-ex* agent suffix] **—re·mig·i·al** (ri mij′ē əl), *adj.*

re·mind (ri mīnd′), *v.t.* to cause (a person) to remember. **—re·mind′er,** *n.*

re·mind·ful (ri mīnd′fəl), *adj.* **1.** reviving memory of something. **2.** retaining memory of something.

Rem·ing·ton (rem′ing tən), *n.* **Frederic,** 1861–1909, U.S. painter and sculptor.

rem·i·nisce (rem′ə nis′), *v.i.,* **-nisced, -nisc·ing.** to recall past experiences, events, etc.; indulge in reminiscence. [back formation from REMINISCENCE] **—Syn.** remember, recollect, muse.

rem·i·nis·cence (rem′ə nis′əns), *n.* **1.** the act or process of recalling past experiences, events, etc. **2.** a mental impression retained and revived. **3.** Often, **reminiscences.** a recollection narrated or told. **4.** something that recalls or suggests something else. [< MF < LL *reminiscentia.* See REMINISCENT, -ENCE] **—Syn. 1.** recollection. **2.** memory. **3.** anecdote, tale, memoir. **4.** reminder.

rem·i·nis·cent (rem′ə nis′ənt), *adj.* **1.** awakening memories of something previously known; suggestive (usually fol. by *of*): *a style reminiscent of Hemingway's.* **2.** characterized by or of the nature of reminiscence or reminiscences. **3.** given to reminiscence. [< L *reminiscent-* (s. of *reminiscēns*) remembering, prp. of *reminiscī* = *re-* RE- + *-miniscī* (< *ment-*, s. of *mēns* mind) + *-ent-* -ENT] **—rem′i·nis′cent·ly,** *adv.*

re·mise (ri mīz′), *v.t.,* **-mised, -mis·ing.** *Law.* to give up a claim to. [ME < MF, ptp. (fem.) of *remettre* to put back, deliver < L *remittere* to REMIT]

re·miss (ri mis′), *adj.* **1.** negligent, careless, or slow, as in performing one's duty. **2.** characterized by negligence. **3.** lacking force or energy. [ME < L *remiss(us)* sent back, relaxed (ptp. of *remittere*); see REMIT] **—re·miss′ly,** *adv.* **—re·miss′ness,** *n.* **—Syn. 1, 2.** derelict, thoughtless, lax, slack, neglectful. **3.** dilatory, slothful, slow.

re·mis·si·ble (ri mis′ə bəl), *adj.* that may be remitted. [< MF < LL *remissibil(is)*] **—re·mis′si·bil′i·ty, re·mis′si·ble·ness,** *n.*

re·mis·sion (ri mish′ən), *n.* **1.** the act of remitting. **2.** pardon; forgiveness, as of sins or offenses. **3.** abatement or diminution, as of disease, labor, intensity, etc. **4.** the relinquishment of a payment, obligation, etc. [ME < OF < L *remissiōn-* (s. of *remissiō*). See REMISE, -ION] **—re·mis′sive,** *adj.* **—re·mis′sive·ly,** *adv.* **—re·mis′sive·ness,** *n.* **—Syn. 2.** absolution. **3.** lessening, relaxation. **4.** release. **—Ant. 2.** blame, censure. **3.** intensification.

re·mit (ri mit′), *v.,* **-mit·ted, -mit·ting,** *n.* **—*v.t.* 1.** to send (money), as in payment. **2.** to refrain from inflicting or enforcing, as a punishment. **3.** to refrain from exacting, as a payment or service. **4.** to pardon or forgive. **5.** to slacken; abate; relax. **6.** to give back. **7.** *Law.* to send back (a case) to an inferior court for further action. **8.** to put back into a previous position or condition. **9.** to postpone; defer. **10.** *Obs.* to set free; release. **11.** *Obs.* to send back to prison or custody. **12.** *Obs.* to give up; surrender. **—*v.i.* 13.** to send money, as in payment. **14.** to abate, as a fever. **—*n.* 15.** *Law.* a transfer of the record of an action from one jurisdiction to another. [ME *remitt(en)* < L *remitt(ere)* (to) send back, let go back, concede, allow = *re-* RE- + *mittere* to send] **—re·mit′ta·ble,** *adj.* **—Syn. 1.** forward. **4.** excuse, overlook. **5.** diminish. **6.** return, restore. **—Ant. 1.** retain. **4.** condemn.

re·mit·tal (ri mit′ᵊl), *n.* a remission.

re·mit·tance (ri mit′ᵊns), *n.* **1.** the sending of money, checks, etc., to a recipient. **2.** the money or its equivalent sent.

remit′tance man′, a person who is supported abroad chiefly by remittances from home.

re·mit·tent (ri mit′ᵊnt), *adj.* **1.** abating for a time or at intervals. **2.** of, pertaining to, or characterized by a remittent fever. **—*n.* 3.** a remittent fever. [< L *remittent-* (s. of *remittēns*) sending back (prp. of *remittere*)] **—re·mit′tence, re·mit′ten·cy,** *n.* **—re·mit′tent·ly,** *adv.*

rem·nant (rem′nənt), *n.* **1.** a remaining, usually small part, quantity, number, or the like. **2.** a fragment or scrap. **3.** a small, unsold or unused piece of cloth, lace, etc. **4.** a trace; vestige. **—*adj.* 5.** remaining; leftover. [ME *remna(u)nt*, contr. of *remenant* < OF, prp. of *remenoir* to REMAIN] **—rem′nant·al,** *adj.* **—Syn. 1.** remainder, residue, residuum, rest, remains.

re·mod·el (rē mod′ᵊl), *v.t.,* **-eled, -el·ing** or (*esp. Brit.*) **-elled, -el·ling.** to reconstruct; make over. **—re·mod′el·er;** *esp. Brit.,* **re·mod′el·ler,** *n.* **—Syn.** renew, renovate, recreate, repair.

re·mon·strance (ri mon′strəns), *n.* **1.** the act of remonstrating; expostulation. **2.** a protest. [< MF = *remonstr(er)* (< ML *remonstrāre* to point out; see REMONSTRATE) + *-ance* -ANCE]

re·mon·strant (ri mon′strənt), *adj.* **1.** remonstrating; expostulatory. **—*n.* 2.** a person who remonstrates. [< ML *remonstrant-* (s. of *remonstrāns*, prp. of *remonstrāre*). See REMONSTRATE, -ANT] **—re·mon′strant·ly,** *adv.*

re·mon·strate (ri mon′strāt), *v.,* **-strat·ed, -strat·ing.** **—*v.t.* 1.** to say or plead in protest, objection, or disapproval. **2.** *Obs.* to point out; show. **—*v.i.* 3.** to present reasons in complaint; plead in protest. [< ML *remonstrāt(us)* exhibited, demonstrated, ptp. of *remonstrāre* = *re-* RE- + *monstrāre* to show; see -ATE[1]] **—re·mon′strat·ing·ly,** *adv.* **—re·mon·stra·tion** (rē′mon strā′shən, rem′ən-), *n.* **—re·mon·stra·tive** (ri mon′strə tiv), *adj.* **—re·mon′stra·tive·ly,** *adv.* **—re·mon·stra·tor** (ri mon′strā tər), *n.* **—Syn. 3.** argue, object, expostulate.

rem·on·toire (rem′ən twär′), *n.* *Horol.* an escapement for giving a uniform impulse to a pendulum or balance. Also, **rem′on·toir′.** [< F: winder < *remonter* to raise, wind up, REMOUNT; see -ORY[2]]

rem·o·ra (rem′ər ə), *n.* **1.** any of several fishes of the family *Echeneididae,* having on the top of the head a sucking disk by which they can attach themselves to sharks, turtles, ships, and other moving objects. **2.** an obstacle, hindrance, or obstruction. [< L: lit., delay, hindrance = *re-* RE- + *mora* delay]

Remora, *Echeneis naucrates* (Length 3 ft.)

re·morse (ri môrs′), *n.* **1.** deep and painful regret for wrongdoing; compunction. **2.** *Obs.* pity; compassion. [ME < MF *remors* < LL *remors(us)*, L: bitten again, harassed (ptp. of *remordēre* = *re-* RE- + *mordēre* to bite, sting, attack; see MORDANT)] **—Syn. 1.** contrition. See **regret.**

re·morse·ful (ri môrs′fəl), *adj.* **1.** full of remorse. **2.** characterized by or due to remorse: *a remorseful mood.* **—re·morse′ful·ly,** *adv.* **—re·morse′ful·ness,** *n.* **—Syn.** contrite, regretful, penitent.

re·morse·less (ri môrs′lis), *adj.* without remorse; merciless; pitiless; relentless. **—re·morse′less·ly,** *adv.* **—re·morse′less·ness,** *n.* **—Syn.** ruthless, unrelenting, implacable, inexorable.

re·mote (ri mōt′), *adj.,* **-mot·er, -mot·est.** **1.** far apart; far distant in space. **2.** out-of-the-way; secluded. **3.** distant in time. **4.** distant in relationship or connection: *a remote ancestor.* **5.** far off; abstracted; removed: *principles remote from actions.* **6.** not directly involved or influential: *the remote causes of the war.* **7.** slight or faint: *a remote chance.* **8.** reserved and distant in manner; aloof; not warmly cordial. [< L *remōt(us)* moved back, ptp. of *removēre*; see REMOVE] **—re·mote′ly,** *adv.* **—re·mote′ness,** *n.* **—Syn. 2.** sequestered, isolated, removed, apart, solitary. **7.** inconsiderable. **8.** withdrawn. **—Ant. 1.** close, near.

remote′ control′, control of the operation of an apparatus from a distance, as of a guided missile by radio signals. **—re·mote′-con·trol′,** *adj.*

re·mo·tion (ri mō′shən), *n.* **1.** the act of removing; removal. **2.** *Obs.* departure. [ME *remosion* < L *remōtiōn-* (s. of *remōtiō*) a putting back, removing. See REMOTE, -ION]

ré·mou·lade (rā′mə läd′; *Fr.* RĀ mōō LAD′), *n.* a cold sauce made with mayonnaise and various condiments and herbs, as chopped pickles, capers, mustard, parsley, chervil, and tarragon. [< F < (dial.) *rémola,* alter. of L *armoracea* horseradish; see -ADE[1]]

re·mount (*v.* rē mount′; *n.* rē′mount′, rē mount′), *v.t., v.i.* **1.** to mount again; reascend. **—*n.* 2.** a fresh horse. [ME *remounten* < OF *remonter*]

re·mov·a·ble (ri mōō′və bəl), *adj.* **1.** that may be removed. **2.** made or attached with a zipper, buttons, screw-and-thread device, etc., for easy removal when desired: *a raincoat with a removable lining.* **—re·mov′a·bil′i·ty, re·mov′a·ble·ness,** *n.* **—re·mov′a·bly,** *adv.*

re·mov·al (ri mōō′vəl), *n.* **1.** the act of removing. **2.** change of residence, position, etc. **3.** dismissal, as from an office.

re·move (ri mōōv′), *v.,* **-moved, -mov·ing.** *n.* **—*v.t.* 1.** to move from a place or position; take away or off. **2.** to take off or shed (an article of clothing). **3.** to move or shift to another place or position; transfer. **4.** to put out; send away. **5.** to dismiss or force from a position or office; discharge. **6.** to take away or eliminate. **7.** to do away with; put an end to. **8.** to kill; assassinate. **—*v.i.* 9.** to move from one place, as of residence, to another. **10.** to go away; depart; disappear. **—*n.* 11.** the act of removing. **12.** a removal from one place, as of residence, to another. **13.** the distance by which one person, place, or thing is separated from another: *to see something at a remove.* **14.** a mental distance resulting from psychological detachment or lack

---

re·melt′, *v.t.*
re·mend′, *v.*
re·mi′grate, *v.i.,* **-grat·ed, -grat·ing.**
re′mil·i·ta·ri·za′tion, *n.*
re·mil′i·ta·rize′, *v.t.,* **-rized, -riz·ing.**
re·mix′, *v.,* **-mixed** or **-mixt, -mix·ing.**
re′mod·i·fi·ca′tion, *n.*
re·mod′i·fy, *v.,* **-fied, -fy·ing.**
re·mod′u·late′, *v.t.,* **-lat·ed, -lat·ing.**
re·mold′, *v.*
re·mon′e·ti·za′tion, *n.*
re·mon′e·tize, *v.t.,* **-tized, -tiz·ing.**
re·mort′gage, *v.t.,* **-gaged, -gag·ing.**

of experience: *to criticize something at a remove.* **15.** a degree of difference, as that due to descent, transmission, etc. **16.** a step or degree, as in a graded scale. [ME *remove(n)* < OF *remouv(oir)* < L *removēre*] —**re·mov′er,** *n.* —**Syn. 1.** dislodge. **3.** displace, transport. **6.** extract, abstract. —**Ant. 1.** leave. **9.** remain.

re·moved (ri mo͞ovd′), *adj.* **1.** remote; separate; distinct from. **2.** (of a cousin) distant by a given number of degrees of descent or kinship: *a first cousin twice removed.* —**re·mov·ed·ly** (ri mo͞o′vid lē, -mo͞ovd′-), *adv.* —**re·mov′ed·ness,** *n.* —**Syn. 1.** withdrawn, abstracted; isolated, solitary.

Rem·scheid (ʀem′shīt), *n.* a city in W West Germany, in the Ruhr region. 128,600 (1963).

re·mu·ner·ate (ri myo͞o′nə rāt′), *v.t.,* **-at·ed, -at·ing. 1.** to pay, recompense, or reward. **2.** to yield a recompense for. [< L *remūnerāt(us)* repaid, rewarded (ptp. of *remūnerārī*) = *re-* RE- + *mūner(āre)* (to) give, bestow (< *mūner-*, s. of *munus* gift) + *-ātus* -ATE[1]] —**re·mu′ner·a·bil′i·ty,** *n.* —**re·mu′ner·a·ble,** *adj.* —**re·mu′ner·a·bly,** *adv.* —**re·mu′ner·a′tor,** *n.* —**Syn. 1.** reimburse, requite, compensate.

re·mu·ner·a·tion (ri myo͞o′nə rā′shən), *n.* **1.** the act of remunerating. **2.** something that remunerates; reward; pay. [late ME *remuneracion* < L *remūnerātiōn-* (s. of *remūnerātiō*) = *remūnerāt(us)* (see REMUNERATE) + *-iōn-* -ION]

re·mu·ner·a·tive (ri myo͞o′nə rā′tiv, -nər ə tiv), *adj.* **1.** affording remuneration; profitable: *remunerative work.* **2.** that remunerates. —**re·mu·ner·a·tive·ly** (ri myo͞o′nə-rā′tiv lē, -nər ə tiv-), *adv.* —**re·mu′ner·a′tive·ness,** *n.*

Re·mus (rē′məs), *n. Rom. Legend.* See under **Romulus.**

Ren·ais·sance (ren′i säns′, -zäns′, ren′i säns′, -zäns′, ri nā′səns; *Fr.* rə ne säɴs′), *n.* Also, **Renascence. 1.** the intellectual and artistic movement beginning in 14th-century Florence and extending throughout Europe by the 17th century. **2.** the period of history during which this movement was effective. **3.** (*l.c.*) a renewal of life, vigor, interest, etc.; rebirth; revival: *a moral renaissance.* —*adj.* **4.** of, pertaining to, or suggestive of the European Renaissance of the 14th through the 17th centuries: *Renaissance attitudes.* **5.** noting or pertaining to the group of styles of architecture originated in Italy in the 15th and 16th centuries as adaptations of ancient Roman architectural details or compositional forms to contemporary uses. **6.** noting or pertaining to the furnishings or decorations of the Renaissance, in which motifs derived from classical antiquity frequently appear. [< F, MF: rebirth = *renaiss-* (s. of *renaistre* to be born again < L *renascī: re-* RE- + *nascī* to be born) + *-ance* -ANCE]

Ren′aissance man′, a person of broad intellectual and cultural interests encompassing the full spectrum of available knowledge; an ideal man possessing universal knowledge.

re·nal (rēn′ᵊl), *adj.* of or pertaining to the kidneys or the surrounding regions. [< LL *rēnāl(is)* = L *rēn(ēs)* kidneys (pl.) + *-ālis* -AL[1]]

Re·nan (ri nan′; *Fr.* rə näɴ′), *n.* **Er·nest** (ûr′nist; *Fr.* ᴇʀ nest′), 1823–92, French philologist, historian, and critic.

Ren·ard (ren′ərd), *n.* Reynard. —**Ren·ard·ine** (ren′ər-din), *adj.*

Re·nas·cence (ri nas′əns, -nā′səns-), *n.* (*sometimes l.c.*) Renaissance. [RENASC(ENT) + -ENCE]

re·nas·cent (ri nas′ənt, -nā′sənt-), *adj.* being reborn; springing again into being or vigor: *a renascent interest in Henry James.* [< L *renascent-* (s. of *renascēns*), prp. of *renascī.* See RENAISSANCE, -ENT]

ren·con·tre (ren kon′tər; *Fr.* räɴ kôɴ′tʀᵊ), *n., pl.* **-tres** (-tərz; *Fr.* -tʀᵊ). rencounter. [< F]

ren·coun·ter (ren koun′tər), *n.* **1.** a hostile meeting; battle. **2.** a contest of any kind. **3.** a casual meeting. [< MF *rencontr(er).* See RE-, ENCOUNTER]

rend (rend), *v.,* **rent, rend·ing.** —*v.t.* **1.** to separate into parts with force or violence. **2.** to tear apart, split, or divide. **3.** to pull or tear violently. **4.** to tear (one's garments or hair) in grief, rage, etc. **5.** to disturb (the air) sharply with loud noise. **6.** to distress (the heart) with painful feelings. —*v.i.* **7.** to render or tear something. **8.** to become torn, split, or divided. [ME *rende(n)*, OE *rendan;* c. OFris *renda*] —**rend′i·ble,** *adj.* —**Syn. 2.** sunder, sever, cleave. See **tear**[2].

ren·der (ren′dər), *v.t.* **1.** to cause to be or become; make. **2.** to do; perform. **3.** to furnish; provide: *to render aid.* **4.** to exhibit or show (obedience, attention, etc.). **5.** to present for consideration, approval, payment, etc. **6.** to pay as due (a tax, tribute, etc.). **7.** to deliver formally or officially; hand down: *to render a verdict.* **8.** to translate into another language. **9.** to represent; depict, as in painting. **10.** to represent (a perspective view of a projected building) in drawing. **11.** to interpret (a part in a drama, a piece of music, etc.). **12.** to give in return or requital. **13.** to give back; restore. **14.** to give up; surrender. **15.** *Building Trades.* to cover (masonry) with a first coat of plaster. **16.** to melt, as fat; try out: *to render lard.* —*v.i.* **17.** to provide due reward. **18.** to try out oil from fat, blubber, etc., by melting. —*n.* **19.** *Building Trades.* a first coat of plaster for a masonry surface. [ME *rendre(n)* < MF *rendre* < VL **rendere*, alter. (formed by analogy with *prendere* to take) of *reddere* to give back = *red-* RE- + *dare* to give] —**ren′der·a·ble,** *adj.* —**ren′der·er,** *n.* —**Syn. 3.** give, supply, contribute, afford. **4.** demonstrate. **14.** cede, yield.

ren·der·ing (ren′dər ing), *n.* **1.** an instance of interpretation, rendition, or depiction, as of a dramatic part, a musical composition, an idea, etc. **2.** a translation. **3.** a representation of a building, interior, etc., in perspective. [ME]

ren′dering works′, (*construed as sing.*) a factory or plant that renders and processes livestock carcasses into tallow, hides, fertilizer, etc. Also called **ren′dering plant′.**

ren·dez·vous (rän′də vo͞o′, -dā-; *Fr.* räɴ de vo͞o′), *n., pl.* **-vous** (-vo͞oz′; *Fr.* -vo͞o′), *v.,* **-voused** (vo͞od′), **-vous·ing** (-vo͞o′ing). —*n.* **1.** an agreement between two or more persons to meet at a certain time and place. **2.** a place for meeting or assembling, as of troops or ships. **3.** *Rocketry.* **a.** the meeting of two or more space vehicles in outer space at a prearranged time and point. **b.** the point where such a meeting is made. **c.** the time of such a meeting. —*v.i.* **4.** to assemble at an agreed time and place. **5.** to carry out a rendezvous in outer space. —*v.t.* **6.** *U.S.* to bring together (troops or ships) at a certain time and place. [< MF, n. use of v. phrase *rendez-vous* present or betake yourselves; see RENDER]

ren·di·tion (ren dish′ən), *n.* **1.** the act of rendering. **2.** a translation. **3.** an interpretation, as of a role or a piece of music. **4.** *Archaic.* surrender. [< obs. F, MF, alter. of *reddition* (> ME *reddicion*) < LL *redditiōn-* (s. of *redditiō*) = L *reddit(us)* (ptp. of *reddere;* see RENDER) + *-iōn-* -ION]

ren·e·gade (ren′ə gād′), *n.* **1.** a person who deserts a party or cause for another. **2.** an apostate from a religious faith. —*adj.* **3.** of or like a renegade; traitorous. [< Sp *renegad(o)* < ML *renegāt(us)* (ptp. of *renegāre*) = *re-* RE- + *negāre* to deny + *-ātus* -ADE[1]]

ren·e·ga·do (ren′ə gā′dō), *n., pl.* **-dos.** *Archaic.* a renegade.

re·nege (ri nig′, -nēg′, -neg′), *v.,* **-neged, -neg·ing.** —*v.i.* **1.** *Cards.* to play a card that is not of the suit led when one can follow suit; break a rule of play. **2.** to go back on one's word. —*v.t.* **3.** *Archaic.* to deny; disown; renounce. [< ML *reneg(āre)* = *re-* RE- + *negāre* to deny] —**re·neg′er,** *n.*

re·ne·go·ti·ate (rē′ni gō′shē āt′), *v.,* **-at·ed, -at·ing.** —*v.t.* **1.** to negotiate again, as a loan, treaty, etc. **2.** *U.S. Govt.* to reexamine (a contract) with a view to eliminating or modifying those provisions found to represent excessive profits to the contractor. —*v.i.* **3.** to negotiate anew. **4.** *U.S. Govt.* to reexamine the costs and profits involved in a contract for adjustment purposes. —**re·ne·go·ti·a·ble** (rē′ni gō′shē ə-bəl), *adj.* —**re′ne·go′ti·a′tion,** *n.*

re·new (ri no͞o′, -nyo͞o′), *v.t.* **1.** to begin or take up again; resume. **2.** to make effective for an additional period: *to renew a lease.* **3.** to restore or replenish. **4.** to make, say, or do again. **5.** to revive; reestablish. **6.** to recover (youth, strength, etc.). **7.** to restore to a former state; make new or as if new again. —*v.i.* **8.** to begin again; recommence. **9.** to renew a lease, note, etc. **10.** to be restored to a former state; become new or as if new again. [ME *renew(en)*] —**re·new′a·bil′i·ty,** *n.* —**re·new′a·ble,** *adj.* —**re·new′a·bly,** *adv.* —**re·new·ed·ly** (ri no͞o′id lē, -nyo͞o′-), *adv.* —**re·new′er,** *n.*

—**Syn. 3.** restock. **7.** recreate, rejuvenate, regenerate, reinstate, mend. RENEW, RENOVATE, REPAIR, RESTORE suggest making something the way it formerly was. To RENEW means to bring back to an original condition of freshness and vigor: *to renew one's enthusiasm.* RENOVATE means to do over or make good any dilapidation of something: *to renovate an old house.* To REPAIR is to put into good or sound condition; to make good any injury, damage, wear and tear, decay, etc.; to mend: *to repair the roof of a house.* To RESTORE is to bring back to its former place or position something that has faded, been lost, etc., or to reinstate a person in rank or position: *to restore a painting, a king to his throne.*

re·new·al (ri no͞o′əl, -nyo͞o′-), *n.* **1.** the act of renewing. **2.** the state of being renewed. **3.** an instance of this.

Ren·frew (ren′fro͞o), *n.* a county in SW Scotland. 338,815 (1961); 225 sq. mi. *Co. seat:* Renfrew. Also called **Ren·frew·shire** (ren′fro͞o shēr′, -shər).

Re·ni (ʀe′nē), *n.* **Gui·do** (gwē′dô), 1575–1642, Italian painter.

reni-, a learned borrowing from Latin meaning "kidney," used in the formation of compound words: *reniform.* [< L, comb. form of *rēnēs* kidneys]

ren·i·form (ren′ə fôrm′, rē′nə-), *adj.* kidney-shaped: *a reniform leaf; hematite in reniform masses.* [< NL *rēniform(is)*]

Reniform leaf

re·nin (rē′nin), *n. Biochem.* an enzyme found in ischemic kidneys. [REN(I)- + -IN[2]]

re·ni·tent (ri nīt′ᵊnt, ren′i tənt), *adj.* **1.** resisting pressure; resistant. **2.** stubbornly or persistently opposing; recalcitrant. [< L *renītent-* (s. of *renītēns*, prp. of *renītī*) = *re-* RE- + *nīt(ī)* (to) strive, make an effort + *-ent-* -ENT] —**re·ni′ten·cy, re·ni′tence,** *n.*

Rennes (ren), *n.* a city in NW France: former capital of Brittany. 157,692 (1962).

ren·net (ren′it), *n.* **1.** the lining membrane of the fourth stomach of a calf or of the stomach of certain other young animals. **2.** *Biochem.* the rennin-containing substance from the stomach of the calf. **3.** a preparation or extract of the rennet membrane, used to curdle milk, as in making cheese, junket, etc. [ME; cf. OE *(ge)rennan*, G *gerinnen* to coagulate; akin to RUN]

ren·nin (ren′in), *n. Biochem.* a coagulating enzyme forming the active principle of rennet and able to curdle milk. [RENN(ET) + -IN[2]]

Re·no (rē′nō), *n.* a city in W Nevada. 72,863 (1970).

Re·noir (ren′wär; *Fr.* rə nwaʀ′), *n.* **Pierre Au·guste** (pyeʀ ō gʏst′), 1841–1919, French painter.

re·nounce (ri nouns′), *v.,* **-nounced, -nounc·ing,** *n.* —*v.t.* **1.** to give up or put aside voluntarily. **2.** to give up by formal declaration: *to renounce a claim.* **3.** to repudiate; disown. —*v.i.* **4.** *Cards.* **a.** to play a card of a different suit from that led. **b.** to abandon or give up a suit led. **c.** to fail to follow the suit led. —*n.* **5.** *Cards.* an act or instance of renouncing. [ME *renounce(n)* < MF *renonc(er)* < L *renuntiāre* to bring back word, disclaim = *re-* RE- + *nuntiāre* to announce < *nuntius* messenger, news] —**re·nounce′able, re·nun·ci·a·ble** (rə nun′shē ə bəl, -sē-), *adj.* —**re·nounce′ment,** *n.* —**re·nounc′er,** *n.* —**Syn. 1.** forgo, forswear, leave, quit. See **abandon**[1]. **2.** resign, abdicate. **3.** disclaim, reject, disavow, deny. —**Ant. 1.** claim. **3.** accept.

ren·o·vate (ren′ə vāt′), *v.,* **-vat·ed, -vat·ing,** *adj.* —*v.t.* **1.** to make new or as if new again; repair. **2.** to reinvigorate; revive. —*adj.* **3.** *Archaic.* renovated. [< L *renovāt(us)* (ptp. of *renovāre*) = *re-* RE- + *nov(us)* NEW + *-ātus* -ATE[1]]

re·name′, *v.t.,* **-named, -nam·ing.**
re·nom′i·nate′, *v.t.,* **-nat·ed, -nat·ing.**
re′nom·i·na′tion, *n.*
re′no·ti·fi·ca′tion, *n.*
re·no′ti·fy′, *v.t.,* **-fied, -fy·ing.**

—ren′o·va′tion, n. —ren′o·va′tive, adj. —ren′o·va′tor, n. —Syn. 1. See renew.

re·nown (ri noun′), n. 1. widespread and high repute; fame. 2. Obs. report or rumor. [ME renoun < AF, OF renom < renomer to make famous < L re- RE- + nomināre to NAME] —Syn. 1. celebrity, eminence. —Ant. 1. disrepute.

re·nowned (ri nound′), adj. celebrated; famous. [ME] —re·nown·ed·ly (ri nou′nid lē, -nound′-), adv. —Syn. famed, distinguished, honored, notable.

rent[1] (rent), n. 1. a payment made periodically by a tenant to an owner or landlord in return for the use of land, a building, an apartment, etc. 2. a payment or series of payments made by a lessee to an owner in return for the use of machinery, equipment, etc. 3. Econ. the excess of the produce or return yielded by a given piece of cultivated land over the cost of production; the yield from a piece of land or real estate. 4. profit or return derived from any differential advantage in production. 5. Obs. revenue or income. 6. **for rent,** U.S. available for tenancy or use. —v.t. 7. to grant the use of (property) in return for periodical payments. 8. to take and hold (property) in return for such payments. —v.i. 9. to be leased or let for rent. [ME rente < OF < VL *rendita, fem. ptp. of *rendere; see RENDER] —rent′a·bil′i·ty, n. —rent′a·ble, adj. —Syn. 8. lease, let. See hire.

rent[2] (rent), n. 1. an opening made by rending or tearing; slit; fissure. 2. a breach of relations; schism. —v. 3. pt. and pp. of **rend.** [n. use of rent (v.), var. of REND] —Syn. 1. tear, split, rupture. 2. division, separation.

rent·al (ren′tᵊl), n. 1. an amount received or paid as rent. 2. an apartment, house, or other property offered or given for rent. 3. an income arising from rents received. —adj. 4. pertaining to rent. [ME < AL rentāle]

rent′al li′brary, U.S. See **lending library.**

rente (RäNt), n., pl. **rentes** (RäNt). French. 1. annual revenue or income. 2. **rentes,** perpetual bonds issued by the French government.

rent·er (ren′tər), n. 1. a person or organization that holds property by payment of rent. 2. the owner of rented property. [ME]

rent-free (rent′frē′), adv. 1. without payment of rent. —adj. 2. not subject to rent.

ren·tier (RäN tyā′), n., pl. **-tiers** (-tyā′). French. a person who has a fixed income, as from lands or bonds.

Ren·ton (ren′tᵊn), n. a city in W Washington, near Seattle. 26,229 (1970).

rent′ par′ty, a party given to raise money for the host's rent, by collecting a fee from each person who attends.

rent-roll (rent′rōl′), n. an account or schedule of rents, the amount due from each tenant, and the total received.

rent′ strike′, a temporary refusal by the tenants, as of an apartment building, to pay their rent, usually in protest over increases, inadequate facilities, etc.

re·nun·ci·a·tion (ri nun′sē ā′shən, -shē-), n. an act or instance of relinquishing, abandoning, repudiating, or sacrificing something, as a right, title, person, etc. [ME < L renunciātiōn- (s. of renunciātiō) proclamation = renunciāt(us) (ptp. of renuntiāre to RENOUNCE) + -iōn- -ION] —re·nun′ci·a′tive, re·nun·ci·a·to·ry (ri nun′sē ə tôr′ē, -tôr′ē, -shē ə-), adj.

ren·voi (ren voi′), n. 1. the expulsion by a government of an alien, esp. a foreign diplomat, from the country. 2. the referral of a case involving a jurisdictional dispute in international law to a law other than the local one. [< F: a sending back < renvoyer. See RE-, ENVOY]

re·o·pen (rē ō′pən), v.t., v.i. 1. to open again. 2. to start again; resume: *to reopen an argument; to reopen an attack.*

re·or·der (rē ôr′dər), n. 1. Com. a repeated order, as to replenish stock. —v.t. 2. to put in order again. 3. Com. to give a reorder for.

re·or·di·na·tion (rē′ôr dᵊnā′shən), n. 1. a second ordination. 2. Rom. Cath. Ch. the ordination of a priest whose first orders have been held invalid. 3. Eccles. the second ordination of a priest whose first orders were received from another church. [< ML reordinātiōn- (s. of reordinātiō)]

re·or·gan·ise (rē ôr′gə nīz′), v.t., v.i., **-ised, -is·ing.** Chiefly Brit. reorganize. —re·or′gan·is′er, n.

re·or·gan·i·za·tion (rē′ôr gə ni zā′shən or, esp. Brit., -nī-), n. 1. the act or process of reorganizing. 2. the state of being reorganized. 3. Finance. a thorough or drastic reconstruction of a business corporation.

re·or·gan·ize (rē ôr′gə nīz′), v.t., v.i., **-ized, -iz·ing.** to organize again. Also, esp. Brit., **reorganise.** —re·or′gan·iz′er, n.

rep[1] (rep), n. a transversely corded fabric of wook, silk, rayon, or cotton. Also, **repp.** [< F reps, ? < E ribs; see RIB[1]] —**repped,** adj.

rep[2] (rep), n. Slang. 1. repertory. 2. representative. 3. reputation. [by shortening]

rep[3] (rep), n. the quantity of ionizing radiation which, on absorption by living tissues, produces an energy gain equal to that produced by one roentgen of x-ray or of gamma radiation. Cf. **rem.** [r(oentgen) e(quivalent) p(hysical)]

Rep., 1. Representative. 2. Republic. 3. Republican.

rep., 1. repeat. 2. report. 3. reported. 4. reporter.

re·pair[1] (ri pâr′), v.t. 1. to restore to a good or sound condition after decay or damage; mend. 2. to restore or renew (one's strength, health, etc.). 3. to remedy; make good; make up for. 4. to make amends for; compensate. —n. 5. an act, process, or work of repairing. 6. Usually, **repairs. a.** an instance or operation of repairing: *to lay up a boat for repairs.* **b.** a repaired part or an addition made in repairing. 7. **repairs,** (in bookkeeping, accounting, etc.) the part of maintenance expense that has been paid out to keep fixed assets in usable condition. 8. the good condition resulting from continued maintenance and repairing: *to keep in repair.* [ME repair(en) < MF repar(er) < L reparāre = re- RE- + parāre to prepare; see PARE] —re·pair·a·bil·i·ty (ri pâr′ə bil′i tē), n. —re·pair′a·ble, adj. —re·pair′a·ble·ness, n. —re·pair′er, n. —Syn. 1. remodel, renovate. 2. patch, fix, amend. See **renew.**

re·pair[2] (ri pâr′), v.i. 1. to betake oneself; go, as to a place: *He repaired in haste to Washington.* 2. to go frequently or customarily. —n. 3. the act of going or going customarily; resort. [ME repaire(n) < OF repairier to return < LL repatriāre to return to one's fatherland; see REPATRIATE]

re·pair·man (ri pâr′man′, -mən), n., pl. **-men** (-men′, -mən). a man whose occupation is the making of repairs, readjustments, etc.

re·pand (ri pand′), adj. 1. Bot. having a wavy margin, as a leaf. 2. slightly wavy. [< L repand(us) bent backward, turned up = re- RE- + pandus bent, curved < pandere to spread out, extend] —re·pand′ly, adv.

Repand leaf

rep·a·ra·ble (rep′ər ə bəl), adj. capable of being repaired or remedied. [< L reparābil(is). See REPAIR[1], -ABLE] —rep′a·ra·bly, adv.

rep·a·ra·tion (rep′ə rā′shən), n. 1. the making of amends for wrong or injury done. 2. compensation or indemnity. 3. Usually, **reparations.** compensation payable by a defeated country to the victor or victors for damages or loss suffered during war. 4. restoration to good condition; repair. [ME reparacion < MF < LL reparātiōn- (s. of reparātiō) = L reparāt(us) (ptp. of reparāre to REPAIR[1]) + -iōn- -ION] —Syn. 1. indemnification, atonement, satisfaction, compensation. See **redress.** 3. renewal, renovation; repair.

rep·ar·tee (rep′ər tē′, -tā′), n. 1. a quick, witty reply. 2. conversation full of such replies; banter. 3. skill in making such replies. [< F repartie retort, n. use of fem. ptp. of repartir, MF = re- RE- + partir to PART]

re·par·ti·tion (rē′pär tish′ən, -pər-), n. 1. distribution. 2. reassignment; redistribution. —v.t. 3. to divide up.

re·pass (rē pas′, -päs′), v.t., v.i. to pass back or again. [ME repass(en) < MF, OF repass(er) = re- RE- + passer to PASS] —re·pas·sage (rē pas′ij), n.

re·past (ri past′, -päst′), n. 1. a quantity of food taken at a meal. 2. a meal. 3. mealtime. 4. Archaic. the taking of food. 5. Obs. food. —v.i. 6. to eat or feast. [ME < OF < LL repast(us), ptp. of repāscere to feed regularly = L re- RE- + pāscere to feed]

re·pa·tri·ate (v. rē pā′trē āt′; n. rē pā′trē it), v., **-at·ed, -at·ing,** n. —v.t. 1. to bring or send back (a person, esp. a prisoner of war, a refugee, etc.) to his own country. —n. 2. a person who has been repatriated. [< LL repatriāt(us) returned to one's fatherland (ptp. of repatriāre) = L re- RE- + patri(a) native country (n. use of fem. of patrius paternal < pater FATHER) + -ātus -ATE[1]] —re·pa·tri·a·ble (rē pā′trē ə bəl), adj. —re·pa′tri·a′tion, n.

re·pay (ri pā′), v., **-paid, -pay·ing.** —v.t. 1. to pay back or refund. 2. to make return for. 3. to make return to in any way. 4. to return: *to repay a visit.* —v.i. 5. to make return. [< MF repaier] —re·pay′a·ble, adj. —re·pay′ment, n. —Syn. 1. reimburse, indemnify.

re·peal (ri pēl′), v.t. 1. to revoke or withdraw formally or officially: *to repeal a grant.* 2. to revoke or annul (a law, tax, etc.) by express enactment. —n. 3. the act of repealing; revocation; abrogation. [ME repele(n) < AF repeler(er) = re- RE- + apeler to APPEAL] —re·peal′a·bil′i·ty, re·peal′a·ble·ness, n. —re·peal′a·ble, adj. —re·peal′er, n. —Syn. 2. nullify, abolish, rescind, invalidate.

re·peat (ri pēt′), v.t. 1. to say or utter again (something already said). 2. to say or utter in reproducing the words, inflections, etc., of another. 3. to reproduce (utterances, sounds, etc.) in the manner of an echo, a phonograph, or the like. 4. to tell (something heard) to another or others. 5. to do, make, or perform again. 6. to go through or undergo again. —v.i. 7. to do or say something again. 8. to cause a slight regurgitation. 9. U.S. to vote illegally by casting more than one vote in the same election. —n. 10. the act of repeating. 11. something repeated; repetition. 12. a duplicate or reproduction of something. 13. Music. **a.** a passage to be repeated. **b.** a sign, as a vertical arrangement of dots, calling for the repetition of a passage. [ME repete(n) < MF repet(er) < L repetere to attack again, demand return of = re- RE- + petere to reach towards, seek] —re·peat′a·bil′i·ty, n. —re·peat′a·ble, adj.

—Syn. 1. iterate, recite, rehearse. 1, 5. REPEAT, RECAPITULATE, REITERATE refer to saying a thing more than once. To REPEAT is to do or say something over again: *to repeat a question, an order.* To RECAPITULATE is to restate in brief form, to summarize, often by repeating the principal points in a discourse: *to recapitulate an argument.* To REITERATE is to do or say something over and over again, often for emphasis: *to reiterate a refusal, a demand.* 3. echo, reecho.

re·peat·ed (ri pē′tid), adj. done, made, or said again and again. —re·peat′ed·ly, adv.

re·peat·er (ri pē′tər), n. 1. a person or thing that repeats. 2. a repeating firearm. 3. Horol. a timepiece, esp. a watch, that may be made to strike the hour or part of the hour. Cf. **clock watch.** 4. Educ. a pupil who repeats a course or group of courses that he has failed. 5. U.S. a person who votes illegally by casting more than one vote in the same election. 6. a device capable of receiving one-way or two-way communications signals and delivering corresponding signals. 7. Also called **substitute.** Naut. any one of three distinctive signal flags raised in a hoist with letter or number flags to indicate that the first, second, or third letter or number from the top is being repeated. 8. U.S. a habitual criminal or law violator.

repeat′ing dec′imal, Math. See **circulating decimal.**

repeat′ing fire′arm, a firearm capable of discharging a number of shots without reloading.

re·pel (ri pel′), v., **-pelled, -pel·ling.** —v.t. 1. to drive or force back (an assailant, invader, etc.). 2. to thrust back or away: *He repelled the medicine.* 3. to resist effectively (an attack, onslaught, etc.): *to repel the army's assault.* 4. to keep off or out; fail to mix with: *Water and oil repel each*

re·num′ber, v.t.
re′ob·ject′, v.i.
re′ob·tain′, v.t.
re′ob·tain′a·ble, adj.
re′oc·cu·pa′tion, n.
re·oc′cu·py′, v.t., -pied, -py·ing.
re′oc·cur′, v.i., -curred, -cur·ring.
re′oc·cur′rence, n.
re·oil′, v.
re·or′i·ent, v.
re·or′i·en·ta′tion, n.
re·pac′i·fy′, v.t., -fied, -fy·ing.
re·pack′, v.
re·pack′age, v.t., -aged, -ag·ing.
re·pave′, v.t., -paved, -pav·ing.

other. **5.** to resist the absorption or passage of (water or other liquid). **6.** to resist involvement in: *to repel temptation*. **7.** to refuse to accept or admit; reject: *to repel a suggestion*. **8.** to discourage the advances of (a person). **9.** to cause distaste or aversion in: *Her untidy appearance repelled him*. **10.** to push back or away by a force, as one body acting upon another (opposed to *attract*). **—*v.i.*** **11.** to act with a force that drives or keeps away something. **12.** to cause distaste or aversion. [ME *repelle(n)* < L *repell(ere)* (to) drive back = *re-* RE- + *pellere* to drive, push; see REPULSE] **—re·pel′lence, re·pel′len·cy,** *n.* **—re·pel′ler,** *n.* **—re·pel′ling·ly,** *adv.* **—re·pel′ling·ness,** *n.* **—Syn. 1.** repulse, parry, ward off. **3.** withstand, oppose, rebuff. **7.** decline, rebuff. **—Ant. 1.** attract.

re·pel·lent (ri pel′ənt), *adj.* **1.** causing distaste or aversion; repulsive. **2.** repelling; driving back. **—*n.*** **3.** something that repels: *insect repellent*. **4.** *Textiles.* any of various solutions applied to increase resistance, as to water, moths, etc. Also, **re·pel′lant.** [< L *repellent-* (s. of *repellēns*, prp. of *repellere*) driving back] **—re·pel′lent·ly, re·pel′lant·ly,** *adv.*

re·pent[1] (ri pent′), *v.i.* **1.** to feel sorry, self-reproachful, or contrite for a past action, attitude, etc. (often fol. by *of*): *to repent of a thoughtless act*. **2.** to feel remorse for sin or fault; be penitent (often fol. by *of*). **—*v.t.*** **3.** to remember or regard with self-reproach or contrition. **4.** to feel sorry for; regret. [ME *repente(n)* < OF *repent(ir)* = *re-* RE- + *pentir* to feel sorrow (< L *paenitēre* to regret, be sorry); see PENITENT] **—re·pent′er,** *n.* **—re·pent′ing·ly,** *adv.*

re·pent[2] (rē′pənt), *adj.* **1.** *Bot.* creeping. **2.** *Zool.* reptant. [< L *rēpent-* (s. of *rēpēns*, prp. of *rēpere*) = *rēp(ere)* (to) creep, crawl + *-ent-* -ENT]

re·pent·ance (ri pen′tᵊns), *n.* remorse or contrition for a sin, wrongdoing, or the like; compunction. [ME *repentaunce* < OF *repentance*] **—Syn.** contriteness, penitence, sorrow, regret. **—Ant.** impenitence.

re·pent·ant (ri pen′tᵊnt, -pen′tənt), *adj.* **1.** experiencing repentance. **2.** characterized by or showing repentance. [ME *repentaunt* < OF *repentant* (prp. of *repentir*)] **—re·pent′ant·ly,** *adv.*

re·per·cus·sion (rē′pər kush′ən), *n.* **1.** an effect or result, often indirect or remote, of some event or action. **2.** the state of being driven back by a resisting body. **3.** a rebounding or recoil of something after impact. **4.** reverberation; echo. [< L *repercussiōn-* (s. of *repercussiō*) a rebounding = *repercussus* struck back (ptp. of *repercutere*) + *-iōn-* -ION]

re·per·cus·sive (rē′pər kus′iv), *adj.* **1.** causing repercussion; reverberating. **2.** reflected; reverberated. [ME *repercussif* < OF < L *repercuss(us)*. See REPERCUSSION, -IVE] **—re′per·cus′sive·ly,** *adv.* **—re′per·cus′sive·ness,** *n.*

rep·er·toire (rep′ər twär′, -twôr′), *n.* **1.** the list of dramas, operas, or the like, that a company, actor, singer, etc., is prepared to perform. **2.** the entire stock of works existing in a particular artistic field. Also, **rép′er·toire′.** [< F: REPERTORY]

rep·er·to·ry (rep′ər tōr′ē, -tôr′ē), *n.*, *pl.* **-ries. 1.** repertoire. **2.** a theatrical company that performs regularly and in alternate sequence several plays, operas, or the like. **3.** a store or stock of things available. **4.** storehouse. [< LL *repertōri(um)* inventory = L *repert(us)* found, ascertained, ptp. of *reperīre* (*re-* RE- + *parīre* to bring forth, sp. var. of *parere*) + *-ōrium* -ORY[2]] **—rep′er·to′ri·al,** *adj.*

rep·e·tend (rep′i tend′, rep′i tend′), *n.* **1.** *Math.* the part of a circulating decimal that is repeated, as 1234 in .123412341234 . . . . **2.** *Music.* a phrase or sound that is repeated. [< L *repetend(um)* that which is to be repeated, neut. ger. of *repetere* to REPEAT]

rep·e·ti·tion (rep′i tish′ən), *n.* **1.** the act of repeating; a repeated action, performance, etc. **2.** repeated utterance; reiteration. **3.** a reproduction, copy, or replica. [< L *repetītiōn-* (s. of *repetītiō*) = *repetīt(us)* (ptp. of *repetere* to REPEAT) + *-iōn-* -ION]

rep·e·ti·tious (rep′i tish′əs), *adj.* full of repetition, esp. of a tedious kind. [< L *repetīt(us)* (ptp. of *repetere* to REPEAT) + -IOUS] **—rep′e·ti′tious·ly,** *adv.* **—rep′e·ti′tious·ness,** *n.*

re·pet·i·tive (ri pet′i tiv), *adj.* pertaining to or characterized by repetition. [< L *repetīt(us)* (ptp. of *repetere* to REPEAT) + -IVE] **—re·pet′i·tive·ly,** *adv.* **—re·pet′i·tive·ness,** *n.*

re·phrase (rē frāz′), *v.t.*, **-phrased, -phras·ing.** to phrase again or differently, as to be more tactful, concise, etc.

re·pine (ri pīn′), *v.i.*, **-pined, -pin·ing.** to be fretfully discontented; fret; complain. **—re·pin′er,** *n.*

re·place (ri plās′), *v.t.*, **-placed, -plac·ing. 1.** to assume the former role, position, or function of; substitute for. **2.** to provide a substitute or equivalent in the place of. **3.** to restore; return; make good. **4.** to restore to a former or the proper place. **—re·place′a·bil′i·ty,** *n.* **—re·place′a·ble,** *adj.* **—re·plac′er,** *n.*

—Syn. 1. succeed. REPLACE, SUPERSEDE, SUPPLANT refer to putting one thing or person in place of another. To REPLACE is to take the place of, to succeed: *Mr. A. will replace Mr. B. as president.* SUPERSEDE implies that that which is replacing another is an improvement: *The typewriter has superseded the pen.* SUPPLANT implies that that which takes the other's place has ousted the former holder, esp. by usurping the position or function by art or fraud: *to supplant a former favorite.* **3.** refund, repay.

re·place·ment (ri plās′mənt), *n.* **1.** the act of replacing. **2.** a person or thing that serves to replace another. **3.** *Mil.* a member of the armed forces assigned to fill a vacancy in a military unit. **4.** Also called **metasomatism, metasomatosis.** *Geol.* the process of practically simultaneous removal and deposition by which a new mineral of partly or wholly differing chemical composition grows in the body of an old mineral or mineral aggregate. **5.** *Crystall.* substitution of one or more faces for an angle or edge.

re·plead·er (rē plē′dər), *n.* *Law.* **1.** a second pleading. **2.** the right or privilege of pleading again.

re·plen·ish (ri plen′ish), *v.t.* **1.** to make full or complete again: *to replenish one's stock of food*. **2.** to supply (a fire, stove, etc.) with fresh fuel. **3.** to fill again or anew. [ME *replenisshe(n)* < MF *repleniss-*, long s. of *replenir* to fill, OF = *re-* RE- + *plenir* to fill (< *plein* < L *plēnus* FULL[1])] **—re·plen′ish·er,** *n.* **—re·plen′ish·ment,** *n.*

re·plete (ri plēt′), *adj.* **1.** abundantly supplied or provided; filled (usually fol. by *with*): *a scholarly paper replete with classical allusions*. **2.** stuffed or gorged with food and drink. [ME *repleet* < MF *replet* < L *replēt(us)* filled up, ptp. of *replēre* (*re-* RE- + *plēre* to fill)] **—re·plete′ly,** *adv.* **—re·plete′ness,** *n.* **—re·ple′tive,** *adj.* **—re·ple′tive·ly,** *adv.* **—Syn. 2.** sated, satiated, glutted, surfeited.

re·ple·tion (ri plē′shən), *n.* **1.** the condition of being abundantly supplied or filled; fullness. **2.** overfullness resulting from excessive eating or drinking; surfeit. **3.** the fulfillment of a desire, need, etc. [ME *repleccioun* surfeit < MF < LL *replētiōn-* (s. of *replētiō*) = L *replēt(us)* filled up (see REPLETE) + *-iōn-* -ION]

re·plev·in (ri plev′in), *Law.* **—*n.*** **1.** an action for the recovery of goods or chattels wrongfully taken or detained. **2.** the common-law action or writ by which goods or chattels are replevied. **—*v.t.*** **3.** to replevy. [ME < AF < *replevir* to bail out, admit to bail, OF; see RE-, PLEDGE]

re·plev·i·sa·ble (ri plev′i sə bəl), *adj.* *Law.* capable of being replevied. Also, **re·plev·i·a·ble** (ri plev′ē ə bəl). [< AF = *repleviss-* (long s. of *replevir*; see REPLEVIN) + *-able* -ABLE]

re·plev·y (ri plev′ē), *v.*, **-plev·ied, -plev·y·ing,** *n.*, *pl.* **-plev·ies.** *Law.* **—*v.t.*** **1.** to recover possession of by replevin. **—*n.*** **2.** a seizure in replevin. [late ME < OF *replevi(r)*; see REPLEVIN]

rep·li·ca (rep′lə kə), *n.* **1.** a copy or reproduction of a work of art, esp. by the original artist. **2.** any close or exact copy or reproduction, esp. on a smaller scale. [< It: reply, repetition < *replicare* to repeat < LL *replicāre* to REPLY]

rep·li·cate (rep′lə kit), *adj.* folded; bent back on itself. Also, **rep·li·cat·ed** (rep′lə kā′tid). [< L *replicāt(us)* folded back, ptp. of *replicāre*. See RE-, PLY[2], -ATE[1]]

rep·li·ca·tion (rep′lə kā′shən), *n.* **1.** a reply; answer. **2.** a reply to an answer. **3.** *Law.* the reply of the plaintiff or complainant to the defendant's plea or answer. **4.** reverberation; echo. **5.** a copy. **6.** duplication of an experiment, esp. to expose or reduce error. [ME *replicacioun* < MF *replication* < L *replicātiōn-* (s. of *replicātiō*) a rolling back]

re·ply (ri plī′), *v.*, **-plied, -ply·ing,** *n.*, *pl.* **-plies. —*v.i.*** **1.** to make answer in words or writing; answer; respond. **2.** to respond by some action, performance, etc. **3.** to return a sound; echo; resound. **4.** *Law.* to answer a defendant's plea. **—*v.t.*** **5.** to return as an answer (usually used in negative constructions or fol. by a clause with *that*): *Not a syllable did he reply. He replied that no one would go.* **—*n.*** **6.** an answer or response in words or writing. **7.** a response made by some action, performance, etc. [ME *replie(n)* < MF *repli(er)* (to) fold back, reply < L *replicāre* to unroll, fold back; see REPLICATE] **—re·pli′er,** *n.* **—Syn. 1.** rejoin. **6.** rejoinder, riposte. See **answer.**

ré·pon·dez s'il vous plaît (rā pōn′dā sēl vo͞o plā′; *Fr.* rā pôN dā′ sēl vo͞o ple′). See **R.S.V.P.**

re·port (ri pōrt′, -pôrt′), *n.* **1.** an account or statement describing in detail an event, situation, or the like. **2.** a statement or announcement. **3.** a widely circulated statement or item of news; rumor; gossip. **4.** an account of a speech, debate, meeting, etc. **5.** a periodic statement of a student's grades, level of achievement, etc. **6.** a statement of a judicial opinion or decision. **7. reports,** *Law.* a collection of adjudications. **8.** repute; reputation; fame: *a man of bad report*. **9.** a loud noise, as from an explosion. **—*v.t.*** **10.** to carry and repeat, as an answer or message. **11.** to relate, as what has been learned by observation or investigation. **12.** to write an account of (an event, situation, etc.). **13.** to give or render a formal account or statement of. **14.** to make a formal report on (a bill, amendment, etc., officially referred). **15.** to make a charge against (a person), as to a superior. **16.** to make known the presence, condition, or whereabouts of. **17.** to present (oneself) to a person in authority. **18.** to write down (a speech, lecture, etc.). **19.** to relate or tell. **—*v.i.*** **20.** to prepare, make, or submit a report of something. **21.** to serve or work as a reporter, as for a newspaper. **22.** to make one's condition or whereabouts known. **23.** to present oneself duly, as at a place. [ME *report(en)* < MF, OF *report(er)* < L *reportāre* to carry back = *re-* RE- + *portāre* to carry] **—re·port′a·ble,** *adj.* **—Syn. 1.** description, story. **2.** bulletin, dispatch. **9.** shot, detonation. **10, 11.** relay. **15.** accuse. **19.** narrate, rehearse, recount, describe, detail, repeat.

re·port·age (ri pōr′tij, -pôr′-, rə pōr täzh′, -pôr-), *n.* **1.** the process of reporting news. **2.** reported news collectively. **3.** a written account of an act, event, history, etc., based on direct observation or on thorough research and documentation. [< F]

report′ card′, a periodic written report of a pupil's scholarship and behavior, sent to his parents or guardian.

re·port·ed·ly (ri pōr′tid lē), *adv.* according to report or rumor.

re·port·er (ri pōr′tər, -pôr′-), *n.* **1.** a person who reports. **2.** a person employed to gather and report news, as for a newspaper. **3.** a person who prepares official reports. [ME *reportour* < AF]

rep·or·to·ri·al (rep′ər tōr′ē əl, -tôr′-, rē′pōr-, -pôr-), *adj.* of or pertaining to a reporter or a report. [irreg. (-OR[2] r. -ER[1]) REPORTER + -IAL] **—rep′or·to′ri·al·ly,** *adv.*

re·pos·al (ri pō′zəl), *n.* *Obs.* the act of reposing.

re·pose[1] (ri pōz′), *n.*, *v.*, **-posed, -pos·ing. —*n.*** **1.** the state of reposing or being at rest; rest; sleep. **2.** peace; tranquillity; calm. **3.** dignified calmness; composure. **4.** absence of movement, animation, etc. **—*v.i.*** **5.** to lie or be at rest, as from work or activity. **6.** to lie dead. **7.** to be peace-

re·peo′ple, *v.t.*, **-pled, -pling.**
re·pin′, *v.t.*, **-pinned, -pin·ning.**
re·plan′, *v.t.*, **-planned, -plan·ning.**
re·plant′, *v.t.*
re·play′, *v.t.*
re·pop′u·late′, *v.t.*, **-lat·ed, -lat·ing.**

fully calm and quiet. **8.** to lie or rest on something. **9.** to depend or rely on a person or thing. —*v.t.* **10.** to rest; refresh by rest (often used reflexively). [ME *repose(n)* < MF, OF *repos(er)* < LL *repausāre* = L *re-* RE- + LL *pausāre* to rest (< L *pausa* PAUSE)] —**re·pos·ed·ly** (ri pō′zid lē), *adv.* —**re·pos′ed·ness,** *n.* —**re·pos′er,** *n.*

re·pose[2] (ri pōz′), *v.t.,* **-posed, -pos·ing. 1.** to put (confidence, trust, etc.) in a person or thing. **2.** to put at the disposal of a person or persons. **3.** *Archaic.* to deposit. [ME *repose(n)* (to) replace, irreg. (modeled after DISPOSE, etc.) < L *repos-,* perfect s. of *repōnere* to put back, replace]

re·pose·ful (ri pōz′fəl), *adj.* full of or suggesting repose; calm; quiet. —**re·pose′ful·ly,** *adv.* —**re·pose′ful·ness,** *n.* —**Syn.** restful, tranquil, peaceful, undisturbed.

re·pos·it (ri poz′it), *v.t.* **1.** to put back; replace. **2.** to lay up or store; deposit. [< L *reposit(us)* put back, replaced (ptp. of *repōnere*) = *re-* RE- + *posit(us)* placed (ptp. of *pōnere*); see POSIT]

re·po·si·tion (rē′pə zish′ən, rep′ə-), *n.* **1.** the act of depositing or storing. **2.** replacement, as of a bone. [< LL *repositiōn-* (s. of *repositiō*) a laying up. See REPOSIT, -ION]

re·pos·i·tor·y (ri poz′i tôr′ē, -tōr′ē), *n., pl.* **-tor·ies. 1.** a receptacle or place where things are stored. **2.** a burial place; sepulcher. **3.** a person to whom something is entrusted or confided. **4.** *Chiefly Brit.* warehouse (def. 1). [< L *repositōri(um)* that in which anything is placed. See REPOSIT, -ORY[2]]

re·pos·sess (rē′pə zes′), *v.t.* **1.** to possess again; regain possession of, esp. for nonpayment of money due. **2.** to put again in possession of something. —**re·pos·ses·sion** (rē′pə zesh′ən), *n.* —**re′pos·ses′sor,** *n.*

re·pous·sé (rə po͞o sā′), *adj.* **1.** decorated or raised in relief by hammering on the reverse side. —*n.* **2.** the art or process of producing repoussé designs. [< F, ptp. of *repousser.* See RE-, PUSH]

repp (rep), *n.* rep[1].

repr., 1. represented. **2.** representing. **3.** reprint. **4.** reprinted.

rep·re·hend (rep′ri hend′), *v.t.* to reprove or find fault with; rebuke; censure; blame. [ME *reprehend(en)* < L *reprehend(ere)* (to) hold back, restrain = *re-* RE- + *prehendere* to seize; see GET] —**rep′re·hend′a·ble,** *adj.* —**rep′re·hend′er,** *n.* —**Syn.** reproach, upbraid, chide, admonish.

rep·re·hen·si·ble (rep′ri hen′sə bəl), *adj.* deserving of reproof; blameworthy. [ME < LL *reprehensibil(is)* = L *reprehens(us)* (ptp. of *reprehendere* to REPREHEND) + *-ibilis* -IBLE] —**rep′re·hen′si·bil′i·ty, rep′re·hen′si·ble·ness,** *n.* —**rep′re·hen′si·bly,** *adv.* —**Syn.** culpable.

rep·re·hen·sion (rep′ri hen′shən), *n.* the act of reprehending; reproof. [ME < L *reprehensiōn-* (s. of *reprehensiō*) = *reprehens(us)* (ptp. of *reprehendere* to REPREHEND) + *-iōn-* -ION] —**rep·re·hen·sive** (rep′ri hen′siv), *adj.* —**rep′re·hen′sive·ly,** *adv.*

re-pre·sent (rē′pri zent′), *v.t.* to present again or anew.

rep·re·sent (rep′ri zent′), *v.t.* **1.** to serve to express, designate, stand for, or denote, as a word, symbol, or the like, does; symbolize. **2.** to express or designate by some term, character, symbol, or the like: *to represent musical sounds by notes.* **3.** to stand or act in the place of, as an agent does: *He represents the company in Ashtabula.* **4.** to speak and act for by delegated authority: *to represent one's government in a foreign country.* **5.** to act for or in behalf of (a constituency, state, etc.) by deputed right in exercising a voice in legislation or government: *He represents Chicago's third Congressional district.* **6.** to portray or depict; present the likeness of, as a picture does. **7.** to present or picture to the mind. **8.** to present in words; describe; state. **9.** to describe as having a particular character (usually fol. by *as, to be,* etc.): *The article represented the dictator as a benevolent despot.* **10.** to set forth so as to influence opinion or action. **11.** to present, produce, or perform, as on a stage. **12.** to impersonate, as in acting. **13.** to serve as an example or specimen of; exemplify. **14.** to be the equivalent of; correspond to. [ME *represent(en)* < MF *represent(er)* < L *repraesentāre* = *re-* RE- + *praesentāre* to PRESENT[2]] —**rep′re·sent′a·bil′i·ty,** *n.* —**rep′re·sent′a·ble,** *adj.*

rep·re·sen·ta·tion (rep′ri zen tā′shən), *n.* **1.** the act of representing. **2.** the state of being represented. **3.** a designation by some term, symbol, or the like. **4.** action or speech on behalf of a person, group, or the like, by an agent, deputy, or representative. **5.** the state or fact of being so represented. **6.** *Govt.* the state, fact, or right of being represented by legislative delegates. **7.** the body or number of representatives, as of a constituency. **8.** presentation to the mind, as of an idea or image. **9.** a mental image or idea so presented; concept. **10.** the act of rendering in visible form. **11.** a picture, figure, statue, etc. **12.** the production or a performance of a play or the like, as on the stage. **13.** Often, **representations.** a description or statement, as of things true or alleged. **14.** a statement of facts, reasons, etc., made in protest or remonstrance. **15.** *Law.* an implication or statement of fact to which legal liability may attach if material. [ME *representacion* < L *repraesentātiōn-* (s. of *repraesentātiō*) = *repraesentāt(us)* (ptp. of *repraesentāre* to REPRESENT) + *-iōn-* -ION] —**rep′re·sen·ta′tion·al,** *adj.*

rep·re·sen·ta·tion·al·ism (rep′ri zen tā′shə nᵊliz′əm), *n.* **1.** Also called **represen′tative re′alism.** *Epistemology.* the view that the objects of perception are ideas or sensa that represent external objects, esp. the Lockean doctrine that the perceived idea represents exactly the primary qualities of the external object. **2.** *Fine Arts.* the practice or principle of depicting an object in a recognizable manner. —**rep′re·sen·ta′tion·al·ist,** *n.* —**rep′re·sen·ta′tion·al·is′tic,** *adj.*

rep·re·sent·a·tive (rep′ri zen′tə tiv), *n.* **1.** a person or thing that represents another or others. **2.** an agent or deputy. **3.** a person who represents a constituency or community in a legislative body, esp. a member of the U.S. House of Representatives or a lower house in certain state legislatures. **4.** a typical example or specimen. —*adj.* **5.** serving to represent; representing. **6.** standing or acting for another or others. **7.** representing a constituency in legislation or government. **8.** characterized by, founded on, or pertaining to representation in government. **9.** exemplifying a group or kind; typical. **10.** corresponding to or replacing some other species or the like, as in a different locality. **11.** of, pertaining to, or characteristic of representationalism. **12.** pertaining to or of the nature of a mental image or representation. [ME < ML *repraesentātīv(us)* = *repraesentāt(us)* (see REPRESENTATION) + *-īvus* -IVE] —**rep′re·sent′a·tive·ly,** *adv.* —**rep′re·sent′a·tive·ness,** *n.*

re-press (rē′pres′), *v.t., v.i.* to press again or anew.

re·press (ri pres′), *v.t.* **1.** to keep under control; check or suppress. **2.** to put down or quell (sedition, disorder, etc.). **3.** to reduce (persons) to subjection. **4.** *Psychoanal.* to reject (painful or disagreeable ideas, memories, feelings, or impulses) from the conscious mind. [ME *repress(en)* < L *repress(us)* kept back, restrained (ptp. of *reprimere*) = *re-* RE- + *pressus;* see PRESS[1]] —**re·press′er, re·pres′sor,** *n.* —**re·press′i·ble,** *adj.* —**Syn. 1.** bridle, control. See **check. 2.** subdue, quash. —**Ant. 1, 2.** foster.

re·pres·sion (ri presh′ən), *n.* **1.** the act of repressing. **2.** the state of being repressed. **3.** *Psychoanal.* the rejection from consciousness of painful or disagreeable ideas, memories, feelings, or impulses. [ME *repressioun* < ML *repressiōn-* (s. of *repressiō*), LL; suppression. See REPRESS, -ION]

re·pres·sive (ri pres′iv), *adj.* tending or serving to repress. [< ML *repressīv(us).* See REPRESS, -IVE] —**re·pres′sive·ly,** *adv.* —**re·pres′sive·ness,** *n.*

re·prieve (ri prēv′), *v.,* **-prieved, -priev·ing,** *n.* —*v.t.* **1.** to respite (a person) from impending punishment. **2.** to relieve temporarily from any evil. —*n.* **3.** a respite from impending punishment. **4.** a warrant authorizing this. **5.** any respite or temporary relief. [b. ME *reprieven* to REPROVE, appar. taken in literal sense of to test again (involving postponement) and ME *repried* (ptp.) < OF *reprit* (see REPRISE)] —**re·priev′er,** *n.*

rep·ri·mand (rep′rə mand′, -mänd′), *n.* **1.** a severe, usually formal reproof or rebuke. —*v.t.* **2.** to reprove or rebuke severely, esp. in a formal way. [< F *réprimande,* MF *reprimend* < L *reprimenda* that is to be repressed (fem. ger. of *reprimere* = *re-* RE- + *primere* to PRESS[1])] —**rep′ri·mand′er,** *n.* —**rep′ri·mand′ing·ly,** *adv.* —**Syn. 1.** condemnation, reprehension. **1, 2.** censure. **2.** condemn, reprehend.

re·print (*v.* rē print′; *n.* rē′print′), *v.t.* **1.** to print again; print a new impression of. —*n.* **2.** a reproduction in print of matter already printed. **3.** a new impression, without alteration, of any printed work. —**re·print′er,** *n.*

re·pris·al (ri prī′zəl), *n.* **1.** (in warfare) retaliation against an enemy for injuries received. **2.** an act or an instance of retaliation. **3.** the action or practice of using force, short of war, against another nation, to secure redress of a grievance. **4.** the forcible seizure of property or subjects in retaliation. [ME *reprisail* < OF *reprisaille*] —**Syn. 1.** See **revenge.**

re·prise (ri prīz′ *for 1;* ri prīz′, rə prēz′ *for 2*), *n.* **1.** Usually, **reprises.** *Law.* an annual deduction, duty, or payment out of a manor or estate. **2.** *Music.* **a.** a repetition. **b.** a return to the first theme or subject. [ME < MF: a taking back, OF, n. use of fem. ptp. of *reprendre* to take back < L *reprehendere* to REPREHEND]

re·pro (rē′prō), *n., pl.* **-pros.** See **repro proof.**

re·proach (ri prōch′), *v.t.* **1.** to find fault with (a person, group, etc.); blame; censure. **2.** to upbraid or scold. **3.** to be a cause of blame or discredit to. —*n.* **4.** blame or censure conveyed in disapproval. **5.** an expression of upbraiding, censure, or reproof. **6.** disgrace, discredit, or blame. **7.** a cause or occasion of disgrace or discredit. **8.** an object of scorn or contempt. [ME *reproche* (n.) < OF *reprochier* < VL **repropiāre* = L *re-* RE- + LL *-propiāre* (< L *prope* near); see APPROACH] —**re·proach′a·ble,** *adj.* —**re·proach′a·ble·ness,** *n.* —**re·proach′a·bly,** *adv.* —**re·proach′er,** *n.* —**re·proach′ing·ly,** *adv.*

—**Syn. 1.** chide, abuse, reprimand, reprehend, condemn, criticize. REPROACH, REBUKE, REPROVE, SCOLD imply calling a person to account for something done or said. REPROACH is censure (often about personal matters, obligations, and the like) given with an attitude of faultfinding and some intention of shaming: *to reproach a person for neglect.* REBUKE suggests sharp or stern reproof given usually formally or officially and approaching *reprimand* in severity: *He rebuked him strongly for laxness in his accounts.* REPROVE is a word that suggests a milder or more kindly censure, often intended to correct the fault in question: *to reprove a person for inattention.* SCOLD suggests that censure is given at some length, harshly, and more or less abusively; it implies irritation, which may be with or without justification: *to scold a boy for jaywalking.* **4, 5.** rebuke, criticism, remonstrance. **6.** dishonor, shame. —**Ant. 1, 2, 4, 5.** praise. **6.** honor.

re·proach·ful (ri prōch′fəl), *adj.* **1.** full of or expressing reproach. **2.** *Obs.* deserving reproach; shameful. —**re·proach′ful·ly,** *adv.* —**re·proach′ful·ness,** *n.*

rep·ro·bate (rep′rə bāt′), *n., adj., v.,* **-bat·ed, -bat·ing.** —*n.* **1.** a depraved, unprincipled, or wicked person. **2.** a person rejected by God and beyond hope of salvation. —*adj.* **3.** morally depraved; unprincipled; bad. **4.** rejected by God and beyond hope of salvation. —*v.t.* **5.** to disapprove, condemn, or censure. **6.** (of God) to exclude (a person) from salvation. [ME *reprobate(n)* (v.) < L *reprobāt(us)* disapproved, rejected, ptp. of *reprobāre* to REPROVE] —**rep·ro·ba·cy** (rep′rə bə sē), **rep′ro·bate′ness,** *n.* —**rep′ro·bat′er,** *n.* —**Syn. 1.** miscreant, scoundrel, wretch. **2.** outcast, pariah. **3.** wicked, evil, corrupt. **5.** blame, rebuke, reprove.

rep·ro·ba·tion (rep′rə bā′shən), *n.* **1.** disapproval, condemnation, or censure. **2.** rejection. **3.** *Theol.* rejection by God. [ME *reprobacion* < LL *reprobātiōn-* (s. of *reprobātiō*) rejection. See REPROBATE, -ION] —**rep′ro·ba′tion·ar′y,** *adj.*

rep·ro·ba·tive (rep′rə bā′tiv), *adj.* reprobating; expressing reprobation. —**rep′ro·ba′tive·ly,** *adv.*

re·proc′essed wool′ (rē pros′est), unused wool fibers that have been unraveled, spun, and rewoven into fabric. Cf. **virgin wool.**

re·pro·duce (rē′prə do͞os′, -dyo͞os′), *v.,* **-duced, -duc·ing.** —*v.t.* **1.** to make a copy, representation, duplicate, or close

re·prac′tice, *v.t.,* **-ticed, -tic·ing.**
re·price′, *v.t.,* **-priced, -pric·ing.**
re·probe′, *v.,* **-probed, -prob·ing.**
re·proc′ess, *n.*
re′proc·la·ma′tion, *n.*

imitation of. **2.** to produce again or anew by natural process: *to reproduce a torn claw.* **3.** *Biol.* to produce by some process of generation or propagation, sexual or asexual. **4.** to cause or foster the reproduction of (animals or plants). **5.** to produce, form, make, or bring about again or anew in any manner. **6.** to recall to the mind or have a mental image of. **7.** to produce again, as a play. —*v.i.* **8.** to bear offspring; propagate. **9.** to turn out in a given manner when copied: *This picture will reproduce well.* —**re′pro·duc′er,** *n.* —**re′pro·duc′i·bil′i·ty,** *n.* —**re′pro·duc′i·ble,** *adj.* —**Syn. 3.** generate, propagate, beget. **5.** repeat. See **imitate.**

re·pro·duc·tion (rē′prə duk′shən), *n.* **1.** the act or process of reproducing. **2.** the state of being reproduced. **3.** something made by reproducing; copy; duplicate: *a photographic reproduction.* **4.** *Biol.* the natural process among animals and plants by which new individuals are generated. —**Syn. 3.** replica, facsimile. **4.** generation, propagation.

reproduc′tion proof′. See **repro proof.**

re·pro·duc·tive (rē′prə duk′tiv), *adj.* **1.** serving to reproduce. **2.** concerned with or pertaining to reproduction. —*n.* **3.** *Entomol.* a sexually mature male or female termite; a member of the reproductive caste. —**re′pro·duc′tive·ly,** *adv.* —**re′pro·duc′tive·ness,** *n.*

re·prog·ra·phy (ri prog′ra fē), *n.* the reproduction and duplication of documents, written materials, drawings, designs, etc., by any process making use of light rays or photographic means, including offset printing, microfilming, photography, office duplicating, etc. [REPRO(DUCTION) + (PHOTO)GRAPHY]

re·proof (ri pro͞of′), *n.* **1.** the act of reproving. **2.** an expression of censure or rebuke. [ME *reprof* < OF *reprove* < *reprover* to REPROVE] —**re·proof′less,** *adj.*

re′pro proof′, *Print.* a proof, usually on glossy paper, of a fidelity suitable for reproduction by photography for making a plate. Also called **reproduction proof, repro.**

re·prov·a·ble (ri pro͞o′və bəl), *adj.* deserving of reproof. [ME < MF] —**re·prov′a·ble·ness,** *n.*

re·prov·al (ri pro͞o′vəl), *n.* **1.** the act of reproving. **2.** a reproof.

re-prove (rē pro͞ov′), *v.t., v.i.,* **-proved, -proved** or **-prov·en, -prov·ing.** to prove again.

re·prove (ri pro͞ov′), *v.,* **-proved, -prov·ing.** —*v.t.* **1.** to address words of disapproval to; rebuke. **2.** to express disapproval of (actions, words, etc.). **3.** *Obs.* to disprove or refute. —*v.i.* **4.** to speak in reproof; administer a reproof. [ME *reprov(en)* < OF *reprov(er)* < LL *reprobāre* = L *re-* RE- + *probāre* to test, PROVE] —**re·prov′er,** *n.* —**re·prov′ing·ly,** *adv.* —**Syn. 1.** censure, reprimand, upbraid, chide, reprehend, admonish. See **reproach.** —**Ant. 1.** praise.

rept., report.

rep·tant (rep′tənt), *adj.* **1.** *Zool.* creeping. **2.** *Bot.* repent². [< L *reptant-* (s. of *reptāns,* prp. of *reptāre*) creeping = *rept-* (freq. s. of *rēpere* to creep) + *-ant-* -ANT]

rep·tile (rep′til, -tīl), *n.* **1.** any cold-blooded vertebrate of the class *Reptilia,* comprising the turtles, lizards, snakes, crocodilians, and the tuatara. **2.** (loosely) any of various animals that crawl or creep. **3.** a groveling, mean, or despicable person. —*adj.* **4.** creeping or crawling. **5.** groveling, mean, or despicable. [ME *reptil* < LL *reptile,* neut. of *reptilis* creeping = L *rept(us)* (ptp. of *rēpere* to creep) + *-ilis* -ILE] —**rep′tile·like′,** *adj.* —**rep·ti·loid** (rep′tᵊloid′), *adj.*

Rep·til·i·a (rep til′ē ə), *n.* the class comprising the reptiles. [< NL; see REPTILIAN]

rep·til·i·an (rep til′ē ən, -til′yən), *adj.* **1.** belonging or pertaining to the *Reptilia.* **2.** groveling, debased, or despicable; contemptible. **3.** mean; treacherous. —*n.* **4.** a reptile. [< NL *Reptili(a)* reptiles (pl. of *reptile,* neut. of LL *reptilis;* see REPTILE) + -AN]

Repub., **1.** Republic. **2.** Republican.

re·pub·lic (ri pub′lik), *n.* **1.** a state in which the supreme power rests in the body of citizens entitled to vote and is exercised by representatives chosen directly or indirectly by them. **2.** a state in which the head of government is an elected or nominated president, and not a monarch. **3.** (*cap.*) any of the five periods of republican government in France. Cf. **First Republic, Second Republic, Third Republic, Fourth Republic, Fifth Republic.** [< F *république,* MF < L *rēs publica* = *rēs* thing, matter + *publica* PUBLIC]

re·pub·li·can (ri pub′li kən), *adj.* **1.** of, pertaining to, or of the nature of a republic. **2.** favoring a republic. **3.** fitting or appropriate for the citizen of a republic. **4.** (*cap.*) of or pertaining to the Republican party. —*n.* **5.** a person who favors a republican form of government. **6.** (*cap.*) a member of the Republican party. [< F *républicain* < MF]

re·pub·li·can·ise (ri pub′li kə nīz′), *v.t.,* **-ised, -is·ing.** *Chiefly Brit.* republicanize. —**re·pub′li·can·i·sa′tion,** *n.*

re·pub·li·can·ism (ri pub′li kə niz′əm), *n.* **1.** republican government. **2.** republican principles or adherence to them. **3.** (*cap.*) the principles or policy of the Republican party.

re·pub·li·can·ize (ri pub′li kə nīz′), *v.t.,* **-ized, -iz·ing.** to make republican. [< F *républicanis(er)*] —**re·pub′li·can·i·za′tion,** *n.*

Repub′lican par′ty, 1. one of the two major political parties in the U.S.: originated 1854–56. **2.** *U.S. Hist.* See **Democratic-Republican party.**

Repub′lican Riv′er, a river flowing E from E Colorado through Nebraska and Kansas into the Kansas River. 422 mi. long.

re·pub·li·ca·tion (rē′pub lə kā′shən), *n.* **1.** publication anew. **2.** a book or the like published again.

re·pub·lish (rē pub′lish), *v.t.* **1.** to publish again. **2.** *Law.* to reexecute (a will). —**re·pub′lish·a·ble,** *adj.*

re·pu·di·ate (ri pyo͞o′dē āt′), *v.t.,* **-at·ed, -at·ing. 1.** to reject as having no authority or binding force: *to repudiate a claim.* **2.** to cast off or disown. **3.** to reject with disapproval or condemnation. **4.** to reject with denial. **5.** to refuse to acknowledge and pay (a debt), as a state or municipality. [< L *repudiāt(us)* cast off, put away (ptp. of *repudiāre*) = *repudi(um)* a casting off, divorce (*re-* RE- + *pud(ere)* (to) make ashamed, feel shame; see PUDENDUM) + *-ātus* -ATE¹] —**re·pu′di·a·ble,** *adj.* —**re·pu′di·a′tive,** *adj.* —**re·pu′di·a′tor,** *n.* —**Syn. 1.** disavow, renounce, discard, disclaim. **3.** condemn, disapprove. —**Ant. 1.** accept. **3.** approve, applaud.

re·pu·di·a·tion (ri pyo͞o′dē ā′shən), *n.* **1.** the act of repudiating. **2.** the state of being repudiated. **3.** refusal, as by a state or municipality, to pay a debt lawfully contracted. [< L *repudiātiōn-* (s. of *repudiātiō*)] —**re·pu·di·a·to·ry** (ri pyo͞o′dē ə tôr′ē, -tōr′ē), *adj.*

re·pugn (ri pyo͞on′), *v.t.* **1.** to oppose or refute. —*v.i.* **2.** *Archaic.* to resist. [ME *repugnen* < MF *repugn(er)* < L *repugnāre* to resist = *re-* RE- + *pugnāre* to fight]

re·pug·nance (ri pug′nəns), *n.* **1.** the state of being repugnant. **2.** strong distaste, aversion, or objection; antipathy. **3.** contradictoriness or inconsistency. Also, **re·pug′nan·cy.** [ME *repugnance* < MF < L *repugnantia* = *repugn(āre)* to REPUGN + *-antia* -ANCE] —**Syn. 2.** reluctance, hatred, hostility. See **dislike. 3.** contrariety, incompatibility, irreconcilability. —**Ant. 2.** attraction, liking. **3.** compatibility.

re·pug·nant (ri pug′nənt), *adj.* **1.** distasteful, objectionable, or offensive. **2.** objecting; averse. **3.** opposed or contrary, as in nature. [ME *repugnaunt* < MF < L *repugnant-* (s. of *repugnāns,* prp. of *repugnāre*) = *repugn-* REPUGN + *-ant-* -ANT] —**re·pug′nant·ly,** *adv.* —**Syn. 3.** antagonistic, adverse, hostile.

re·pulse (ri puls′), *v.,* **-pulsed, -puls·ing,** *n.* —*v.t.* **1.** to drive back; repel. **2.** to repel with denial, discourtesy, or the like. —*n.* **3.** the act of repelling. **4.** the fact of being repelled. **5.** a refusal or rejection. [< L *repuls(us),* ptp. of *repellere* to REPEL] —**re·puls′er,** *n.*

re·pul·sion (ri pul′shən), *n.* **1.** the act of repelling or driving back. **2.** the state of being repelled. **3.** the feeling of being repelled; distaste, repugnance, or aversion. **4.** *Physics.* the force that acts between bodies of like electric charge or magnetic polarity, tending to separate them. [< MF < ML *repulsiōn-* (s. of *repulsiō*]

re·pul·sive (ri pul′siv), *adj.* **1.** causing repugnance or aversion: *a repulsive mask.* **2.** tending to repel by denial, discourtesy, or the like. **3.** *Physics.* of the nature of or characterized by physical repulsion. —**re·pul′sive·ly,** *adv.* —**re·pul′sive·ness,** *n.*

re·pur·chase (rē pûr′chəs), *v.,* **-chased, -chas·ing,** *n.* —*v.t.* **1.** to buy again; regain by purchase. —*n.* **2.** the act of repurchasing. —**re·pur′chas·er,** *n.*

rep·u·ta·ble (rep′yə tə bəl), *adj.* **1.** held in good repute; honorable; respectable. **2.** considered to be good usage; standard: *reputable speech.* —**rep′u·ta·bil′i·ty, rep′u·ta·ble·ness,** *n.* —**rep′u·ta·bly,** *adv.*

rep·u·ta·tion (rep′yə tā′shən), *n.* **1.** the estimation in which a person or thing is generally held; repute. **2.** favorable repute; good name. **3.** a favorable and publicly recognized name or standing. **4.** the estimation or name of being, having, having done, etc., something specified. [ME *reputacioun* < L *reputātiōn-* (s. of *reputātiō*) computation, consideration = *reputāt(us)* (ptp. of *reputāre;* see REPUTE) + *-iōn-* -ION] —**rep′u·ta′tion·less,** *adj.*
—**Syn. 1.** regard, name. REPUTATION, CHARACTER are often confused. REPUTATION, however, is the word which refers to the position a person occupies or the standing that he has in the opinion of others, in respect to attainments, integrity, and the like: *a fine reputation; a reputation for honesty.* CHARACTER is the combination of moral and other traits which make one the kind of person he actually is (as contrasted with what others think of him): *Honesty is an outstanding trait of his character.* **2.** fame, distinction, renown, esteem, honor. —**Ant. 2.** disrepute.

re·pute (ri pyo͞ot′), *n., v.,* **-put·ed, -put·ing.** —*n.* **1.** reputation (defs. 1, 2). —*v.t.* **2.** to consider or esteem (a person or thing) to be as specified (usually used in the passive): *He was reputed to be a millionaire.* [ME *repute(n)* (v.) < MF *reput(er)* < L *reputāre* to compute, consider = *re-* RE- + *putāre* to think] —**Syn. 2.** hold, deem, reckon.

re·put·ed (ri pyo͞o′tid), *adj.* accounted or supposed to be such: *the reputed author of a book.*

re·put·ed·ly (ri pyo͞o′tid lē), *adv.* according to reputation or popular belief: *a reputedly honest man.*

req., **1.** request. **2.** required. **3.** requisition.

re·quest (ri kwest′), *n.* **1.** the act of asking for something to be given or done; solicitation or petition. **2.** an instance of this. **3.** a written statement of petition. **4.** something asked for. **5.** the state of being much asked for; demand. **6. at** or **by request,** in response or accession to a request. —*v.t.* **7.** to ask for, esp. politely or formally. **8.** to ask or beg (usually fol. by a clause or an infinitive): *to request that he leave; to request to be excused.* **9.** to ask or beg (someone) to do something. [ME *requeste* (n.) < OF < VL **requaesita* things asked for, n. use of neut. pl. ptp. of **requaerere* to seek, r. L *requīrere.* See REQUIRE, QUEST] —**re·quest′er,** *n.* —**Syn. 1.** entreaty, supplication, prayer. **7.** petition, supplicate. **9.** entreat, beseech.

Req·ui·em (rek′wē əm, rē′kwē-), *n.* **1.** *Rom. Cath. Ch.* **a.** Also called **Req′uiem Mass′.** the Mass celebrated for the repose of the souls of the dead. **b.** a celebration of this Mass. **c.** a plainsong setting for this Mass. **2.** any musical service, hymn, or dirge for the repose of the dead. Also, **req′ui·em.** [ME < L, acc. of *requiēs* rest (the first word of the introit of the mass for the dead)]

req·ui·es·cat (rek′wē es′kat), *n.* a wish or prayer for the repose of the dead. [< L: short for REQUIESCAT IN PACE]

re·qui·es·cat in pa·ce (re′kwē es′kät in pä′chā), *Latin.* may he (or she) rest in peace.

re·quire (ri kwīᵊr′), *v.,* **-quired, -quir·ing.** —*v.t.* **1.** to have need of; need. **2.** to order or enjoin to do something. **3.** to ask for authoritatively; demand. **4.** to impose need or occasion for. **5.** to call for or exact as obligatory. **6.** to place under an obligation or necessity. **7.** *Chiefly Brit.* to desire; wish to have. —*v.i.* **8.** to demand; impose obligation. [ME *require(n)* < L *requīr(ere)* = *re-* RE- + *-quīrere,* comb. form of *quaerere* to seek, search for] —**re·quir′a·ble,** *adj.* —**re·quir′er,** *n.* —**Syn. 3.** See **demand. 6.** obligate, necessitate. —**Ant. 3.** forgo.

re·quire·ment (ri kwīᵊr′mənt), *n.* **1.** a thing demanded or obligatory. **2.** an act or instance of requiring. **3.** a need or necessity. **—Syn. 1.** REQUIREMENT, REQUISITE refer to that which is necessary. A REQUIREMENT is some quality or performance demanded of a person in accordance with certain fixed regulations: *requirements for admission to college.* A REQUISITE is not imposed from outside; it is a factor that is judged necessary according to the nature of things, or to the circumstances of the case: *This system combines the two requisites of efficacy and economy.* REQUISITE may also refer to a concrete object judged necessary: *the requisites for perfect grooming.* **2.** order, command, injunction, directive, demand.

req·ui·site (rek′wi zit), *adj.* **1.** required or necessary for a particular purpose, position, etc.; indispensable. **—n. 2.** something requisite; a necessary quality, thing, etc. [ME < L *requīsīt(us)* sought again, demanded, ptp. of *requīrere;* see REQUIRE] **—req′ui·site·ly,** *adv.* **—req′ui·site·ness,** *n.* **—Syn. 1.** needed, needful. See **necessary. 2.** necessity. See **requirement. —Ant. 1.** dispensable. **2.** luxury.

req·ui·si·tion (rek′wi zish′ən), *n.* **1.** the act of requiring or demanding. **2.** a demand made. **3.** an authoritative or formal demand for something to be done, given, supplied, etc. **4.** a written request or order for something, as supplies. **5.** the form on which such an order is drawn up. **6.** an authoritative or official demand, as of one nation on another for extradition of a criminal. **7.** the state of being required for use or called into service. **8.** a requirement or essential condition. **—v.t. 9.** to require or take for use. **10.** to demand or take by authority, as for military purposes. [< L *requīsītiōn-* (s. of *requīsītiō*) a searching] **—req′ui·si′tion·ar′y,** *adj.* **—req′ui·si′tion·ist, req′ui·si′tion·er,** *n.*

re·quit·al (ri kwīt′ᵊl), *n.* **1.** the act of requiting. **2.** a return or reward for service, kindness, etc. **3.** a retaliation. **4.** something given or done as repayment, reward, punishment, etc.

re·quite (ri kwīt′), *v.t.,* **-quit·ed, -quit·ing. 1.** to make repayment or return for. **2.** to make retaliation for (a wrong, injury, etc.); avenge. **3.** to make return to (a person, group, etc.) for service, benefits, etc. **4.** to retaliate on (a person, group, etc.) for a wrong, injury, etc. **5.** to give or do in return. [RE- + obs. *quite,* var. of QUIT] **—re·quit′a·ble,** *adj.* **—re·quite′ment,** *n.* **—re·quit′er,** *n.* **—Syn. 1.** repay, recompense, compensate, reimburse. **2.** revenge.

re·ra·di·a·tion (rē′rā dē ā′shən), *n.* *Physics.* radiation emitted as a consequence of a previous absorption of radiation.

rere·dos (rēr′dos, rēr′i-, râr′i-), *n.* a screen or a decorated part of the wall behind an altar in a church. [ME, m. AF *areredos* < MF *arere* behind (see ARREAR) + *dos* back < L *dors(um)* DORSUM]

rere·mouse (rēr′mous′), *n., pl.* **-mice.** *Archaic.* a bat. [ME *reremous,* OE *hrēremūs,* prob. = *hrēr(an)* (to) move + *mūs* MOUSE]

re·run (*v.* rē run′; *n.* rē′run′), *v.,* **-ran, -run, -run·ning,** *n.* **—v.t. 1.** to run again. **—n. 2.** the act of rerunning. **3.** a reshowing of a film. **4.** the film itself.

res (rēz, rās), *n., pl.* **res.** *Chiefly Law.* an object or thing; matter. [< L]

res., 1. reserve. **2.** residence. **3.** resigned.

res ad·ju·di·ca·ta (rēz′ ə jo͞o′də kā′tə, rās), *Law.* See **res judicata.**

re·sal·a·ble (rē sā′lə bəl), *adj.* suitable for resale. Also, **re·sale′a·ble.**

re·sale (rē′sāl′, rē sāl′), *n.* **1.** the act of selling a second time. **2.** the act of selling something secondhand.

re·scind (ri sind′), *v.t.* **1.** to abrogate; annul; revoke; repeal. **2.** to invalidate (an act, measure, etc.) by a later action or a higher authority. [< L *rescind(ere)* (to) tear off again, cut away = *re-* RE- + *scindere* to tear, divide, destroy; see SCHISM] **—re·scind′a·ble,** *adj.* **—re·scind′er,** *n.* **—re·scind′ment,** *n.* **—Syn. 1.** nullify; retract, withdraw. **2.** countermand, repeal, veto.

re·scis·si·ble (ri sis′ə bəl), *adj.* able to be rescinded. [< L *resciss(us)* cut off, repealed (see RESCISSION) + -IBLE]

re·scis·sion (ri sizh′ən), *n.* the act of rescinding. [< LL *rescissiōn-* (s. of *rescissiō*) a making void, rescinding = *resciss(us)* (ptp. of *rescindere* to RESCIND) + *-iōn-* -ION]

re·scis·so·ry (ri sis′ə rē, -siz′-), *adj.* serving to rescind. [< LL *rescissōri(us)* pertaining to revoking or rescinding = L *resciss(us)* (see RESCISSION) + *-ōrius* -ORY[1]]

re·script (rē′skript′), *n.* **1.** a written answer, as of a Roman emperor or a pope, to a query or petition in writing. **2.** any edict, decree, or official announcement. **3.** the act of rewriting. **4.** something rewritten. [< L *rescript(um)* an imperial rescript (n. use of neut. ptp. of *rescrībere* to write back, reply)]

res·cue (res′kyo͞o), *v.,* **-cued, -cu·ing,** *n.* **—v.t. 1.** to free or deliver from confinement, violence, danger, or evil. **2.** *Law.* to take by forcible means from lawful custody. **—n. 3.** the act of rescuing. [ME *rescue(n)* (v.) < OF *rescour(re)* = *re-* RE- + *escourre* to shake, drive out, remove < L *excutere* (*ex-* EX-[1] + *-cutere,* comb. form of *quatere* to shake)] **—res′cu·a·ble,** *adj.* **—res′cu·er,** *n.* **—Syn. 1.** liberate, release, save, redeem, ransom, extricate, recover. **3.** liberation, deliverance, release.

re-search (rē sûrch′), *v.t., v.i.* to search again.

re·search (ri sûrch′, rē′sûrch), *n.* **1.** systematic inquiry into a subject in order to discover or revise facts, theories, etc. **2.** a particular instance or piece of research. **—v.i. 3.** to make researches. **—v.t. 4.** to make an extensive investigation into. [< MF *recerch(er)* (v.) (to) seek, OF = *re-* RE- + *cercher* to SEARCH] **—re·search′a·ble,** *adj.* **—re·search′er, re·search′ist,** *n.* **—Syn. 1.** scrutiny, study. See **investigation. 4.** study, inquire, examine, scrutinize.

re·seat (rē sēt′), *v.t.* **1.** to show to a new seat. **2.** to seat (someone) again, as in a legislative body, assembly, or the like. **3.** to make a new seat for, as a chair.

re·seau (rā zō′, rə-), *n., pl.* **-seaux** (-zōz′, -zō′), **-seaus. 1.** a network. **2.** a netted or meshed ground in lace. **3.** *Astron.* a network of fine lines on a glass plate, used in a photographic telescope to produce a corresponding network on photographs of the stars. **4.** *Meteorol.* a system of weather stations under the direction of a single agency or cooperating for common goals. Also, **ré·seau′.** [< F *réseau,* OF *resel,* dim. of *rais* net < L *rēte-* (s. of *rēte*)]

re·sect (ri sekt′), *v.t.* *Surg.* to do resection on. [< L *resect(us)* cut loose (ptp. of *resecāre*) = *re-* RE- + *secāre* to cut]

re·sec·tion (ri sek′shən), *n.* **1.** *Survey.* a technique of ascertaining the location of a point by taking bearings from the point on two other points of known location. **2.** *Surg.* the excision of part of an organ or tissue, esp. bone. [< L *resectiōn-* (s. of *resectiō*) a cutting off, trimming = *resect(us)* (ptp. of *resecāre* to cut off) + *-iōn-* -ION] **—re·sec′tion·al,** *adj.*

re·se·da (ri sē′də), *n.* **1.** any plant of the genus *Reseda,* esp. *R. odorata,* the garden mignonette. **2.** a grayish green. [< NL, L *resēdā,* lit., heal (impv. of *resedāre* to heal, assuage)]

res·e·da·ceous (res′i dā′shəs), *adj.* belonging to the *Resedaceae,* or mignonette family of plants. [< NL *Resedace(ae).* See RESEDA, -ACEOUS]

re·seed (rē sēd′), *v.t., v.i.* to seed again.

re·sem·blance (ri zem′bləns), *n.* **1.** the state or fact of resembling; similarity, esp. in appearance. **2.** a degree, kind, or point of likeness. **3.** a semblance of something. [ME < AF] **—Syn. 1.** RESEMBLANCE, SIMILARITY imply that there is a likeness between two or more people or things. RESEMBLANCE indicates primarily a likeness in appearance, either a striking one or one that merely serves as a reminder to the beholder: *The boy has a strong resemblance to his father.* SIMILARITY may imply a surface likeness, but usually suggests also a likeness in other characteristics: *There is a similarity in their tastes and behavior.* **2.** analogy, similitude. **3.** image. **—Ant. 1.** difference.

re·sem·blant (ri zem′blənt), *adj.* having a resemblance or similarity (sometimes fol. by *to*): *two persons with resemblant features; a mastery resemblant to that of Phidias.* [ME < OF; see RESEMBLE, -ANT]

re·sem·ble (ri zem′bəl), *v.t.,* **-bled, -bling. 1.** to be like or similar to. **2.** *Archaic.* to liken or compare. [ME *resemble(n)* < MF *resembl(er)* < OF = *re-* RE- + *sembler* to seem, be like < L *similāre* < *similis* like; see SIMILAR] **—re·sem′bling·ly,** *adv.*

re·send (rē send′), *v.t.,* **-sent, -send·ing. 1.** to send again. **2.** to send back.

re·sent (ri zent′), *v.t.* to feel or show displeasure or indignation at (a person, act, remark, etc.) from a sense of injury or insult. [< F *ressent(ir)* (to) be angry < OF *resentir* = *re-* RE- + *sentir* to feel < L *sentīre;* see SENSE] **—re·sent′ing·ly,** *adv.* **—re·sent′ive,** *adj.*

re·sent·ful (ri zent′fəl), *adj.* full of or marked by resentment. **—re·sent′ful·ly,** *adv.* **—re·sent′ful·ness,** *n.*

re·sent·ment (ri zent′mənt), *n.* the feeling of displeasure or indignation at some act, remark, person, etc., regarded as causing injury or insult. [< F *ressentiment* < MF; see RESENT, -MENT] **—Syn.** dudgeon, pique, envy, jealousy.

res·er·pine (res′ər pin, -pēn′, rə sûr′pin, -pēn), *n.* *Pharm.* an alkaloid, $C_{33}H_{40}N_2O_9$, obtained from the root of the rauwolfia, *Rauwolfia serpentina,* used to alleviate the symptoms of hypertension and as a tranquilizer. [< G *Reserpin* = *reserp-* (prob. irreg. < NL *Rauwolfia serpentina*) + *-in* -INE[2]]

res·er·va·tion (rez′ər vā′shən), *n.* **1.** the act of keeping back, withholding, or setting apart. **2.** the act of making an exception or qualification. **3.** an exception or qualification made expressly or tacitly. **4.** *U.S.* a tract of public land set apart, as for an Indian tribe. **5.** Often, **reservations.** the allotting or the securing of accommodations at a hotel, on a ship or airplane, etc., as for a traveler. **6.** the record or assurance of such an arrangement. [ME *reservacioun* < MF *reservation.* See RESERVE, -ATION]

re-serve (rē sûrv′), *v.t., v.i.,* **-served, -serv·ing.** to serve again.

re·serve (ri zûrv′), *v.,* **-served, -serv·ing,** *n., adj.* **—v.t. 1.** to keep back or save for future or special use, disposal, treatment, etc. **2.** to retain or secure by express stipulation. **—n. 3.** *Finance.* cash, or assets readily convertible into cash, held aside, as by a corporation, to meet expected or unexpected demands. **4.** something reserved, as for some purpose or need; a store or stock. **5.** a tract of public land set apart for a special purpose. **6.** an act of reserving; reservation, exception, or qualification. **7.** *Mil.* **a.** a fraction of a military force held in readiness. **b. reserves,** the enrolled but not regular components of the armed forces. **8.** formality and self-restraint in manner and relationship. **9.** reticence or silence. **10. in reserve,** put aside for a future need; reserved. **—adj. 11.** kept in reserve; forming a reserve. [ME *reserve(n)* (v.) < MF *reserv(er)* < L *reservāre* to keep back, retain = *re-* RE- + *servāre* to save] **—re·serv′a·ble,** *adj.* **—Syn. 1.** husband, hold, store. See **keep. 4.** supply. **9.** taciturnity, constraint, coldness. **—Ant. 1.** squander. **8, 9.** warmth.

reserve′ bank′, 1. any of the twelve U.S. Federal Reserve Banks. **2.** a bank authorized by a government to hold the reserves of other banks.

re·served (ri zûrvd′), *adj.* **1.** kept or set apart for some particular use or purpose. **2.** kept by special arrangement for some person or persons. **3.** formal or self-restrained in manner and relationship. **4.** characterized by reserve, as in disposition, manner, etc. [late ME] **—re·serv·ed·ly** (ri zûr′vid lē), *adv.* **—re·serv′ed·ness,** *n.* **—Syn. 3, 4.** composed, controlled, reticent, constrained, taciturn, withdrawn, distant, cold.

Reserve′ Of′ficers Train′ing Corps′, a body of male students at certain colleges and universities, who are given advance training toward becoming officers in the armed forces. *Abbr.:* R.O.T.C., ROTC

re·serv·ist (ri zûr′vist), *n.* a person who belongs to a reserve military force of a country.

res·er·voir (rez′ər vwär′, -vôr′, rez′ə-), *n.* **1.** a place where water is collected and stored for use, esp. water for supplying a community, irrigating land, etc. **2.** a receptacle or chamber for holding a liquid or fluid, as oil or gas. **3.** *Biol.* a cavity or part that holds some fluid or secretion. **4.** a place where anything is collected or accumulated in

re·read′, *v.,* **-read, -read·ing.**
re·roll′, *v.*
re·route′, *v.t.,* **-rout·ed, -rout·ing.**
re·sched′ule, *v.t.,* **-uled, -ul·ing.**
re·seal′a·ble, *adj.*
re·sell′, *v.,* **-sold, -sell·ing.**

great amount. **5.** a large or extra supply or stock; reserve. [< F *réservoir* = *réserv(er)* (to) RESERVE + *-oir* -ORY[2]]

re·set (*v.* rē set′; *n.* rē′set′), *v.*, **-set, -set·ting,** *n.* —*v.t.* **1.** to set again. —*n.* **2.** the act of resetting. **3.** that which is reset. **4.** a device used in resetting an instrument or control mechanism. —**re·set′ter,** *n.*

res ges·tae (rēz jes′tē, rās), **1.** things done; accomplishments; deeds. **2.** *Law.* the acts, circumstances, and statements that are incidental to the principal fact of a litigated matter. [< L]

resh (rāsh; *Heb.* RĀSH), *n.* the 20th letter of the Hebrew alphabet. [< Heb *rēsh*, lit., head]

re·shape (rē shāp′), *v.t.*, **-shaped, -shap·ing.** to shape again or into a different form.

re·ship (rē ship′), *v.*, **-shipped, -ship·ping.** —*v.t.* **1.** to ship again. **2.** to transfer from one ship to another. —*v.i.* **3.** to go on a ship again. **4.** (of a member of a ship's crew) to sign up for another voyage. —**re·ship′ment,** *n.*

Resht (resht), *n.* a city in NW Iran, near the Caspian Sea. 118,634 (est. 1963).

re·side (ri zīd′), *v.i.*, **-sid·ed, -sid·ing.** **1.** to dwell permanently or for a considerable time. **2.** (of things, qualities, etc.) to abide, lie, or be present habitually. **3.** to rest or be vested, as powers, rights, etc. [ME *reside(n)* < MF *resid(er)* < L *residēre* = *re-* RE- + *sid-* (var. of *sedēre* to sit)] —**re·sid′er,** *n.* —**Syn. 1.** live, abide, sojourn, stay, lodge, remain.

res·i·dence (rez′i dəns), *n.* **1.** the place, esp. the house, in which a person lives or resides; dwelling place; home. **2.** the act or fact of residing. **3.** the act of living or staying in a specified place while performing official duties, awaiting a divorce, etc. **4.** the time during which a person resides in a place. [ME < MF < ML *residentia* = L *resid(ēre)* (to) RESIDE + *-entia* -ENCE] —**Syn. 1.** habitation, domicile. See **house. 4.** stay, abode, sojourn.

res·i·den·cy (rez′i dən sē), *n.*, *pl.* **-cies. 1.** residence. **2.** the position or tenure of a medical resident. **3.** *Hist.* an administrative division of the Dutch East Indies. [RESI-D(ENT) + -ENCY]

res·i·dent (rez′i dənt), *n.* **1.** a person who resides in a place. **2.** a physician employed by a hospital while receiving specialized training. **3.** *Hist.* the governor of a residency in the Dutch East Indies. —*adj.* **4.** residing; dwelling in a place. **5.** living or staying at a place in discharge of duty. **6.** (of qualities) existing; intrinsic. **7.** (of birds) not migratory. [< L *resident-* (s. of *residēns*), prp. of *residēre* to RESIDE; see -ENT] —**res′i·dent·ship′,** *n.*

res′ident commis′sioner, *U.S.* a representative from a dependency who is entitled to speak, but not to vote, in the national House of Representatives.

res·i·den·tial (rez′i den′shəl), *adj.* **1.** of or pertaining to residence or residences. **2.** adapted or used for residence. —**res·i·den·ti·al·i·ty** (rez′i den′shē al′i tē), *n.* —**res′i·den′tial·ly,** *adv.*

res·i·den·ti·ar·y (rez′i den′shē er′ē, -shə rē), *adj.*, *n.*, *pl.* **-ar·ies.** —*adj.* **1.** residing; resident. **2.** bound to or involving official residence. —*n.* **3.** a resident. [< ML *residentiārius* = *residenti(a)* RESIDENCE + *-ārius* -ARY]

re·sid·u·al (ri zij′o͞o əl), *adj.* **1.** pertaining to or constituting a residue or remainder; remaining; leftover. **2.** *Math.* formed by the subtraction of one quantity from another: *a residual quantity.* **3.** of or pertaining to the payment of residuals. **4.** *Geol.* remaining after the soluble elements have been dissolved: *residual soil.* —*n.* **5.** a residual quantity; remainder. **6.** Often, **residuals.** something that remains to discomfort or disable a person following an illness, injury, operation, or the like; disability. **7.** *Math.* **a.** the deviation of one of a set of observations or numbers from the mean of the set. **b.** the deviation between an empirical and a theoretical result. **8.** Usually, **residuals.** additional pay given to a performer for repeated use of a film, radio or TV commercial, or the like, in which the performer appears. [< L *residu(um)* what is left over (neut. of *residuus*) = *re-* RE- + *sid-* (var. of *sedēre* to sit) + *-u(um)* adj. suffix + -AL[1]] —**re·sid′u·al·ly,** *adv.*

re·sid·u·ar·y (ri zij′o͞o er′ē), *adj.* pertaining to or of the nature of a residue, remainder, or residuum. [< L *residu(um)* what is left over (see RESIDUAL) + -ARY]

res·i·due (rez′i do͞o′, -dyo͞o′), *n.* **1.** that which remains after a part is taken, disposed of, or gone; remainder; rest. **2.** *Chem.* **a.** residuum. **b.** an atom or group of atoms considered as a group or part of a molecule. **c.** the part remaining as a solid on a filter paper after a liquid passes through in the filtration procedure. **3.** *Law.* the part of a testator's estate that remains after the payment of all debts, charges, special devises, and bequests. [ME < MF *residu* < L *residu(um)* what is left over; see RESIDUAL] —**Syn. 1.** remains, residuum. See **remainder.**

re·sid·u·um (ri zij′o͞o əm), *n.*, *pl.* **-sid·u·a** (-zij′o͞o ə). **1.** the residue, remainder, or rest of something. **2.** *Chem.* a quantity or body of matter remaining after evaporation, combustion, distillation, etc. **3.** any residual product. **4.** *Law.* the residue of an estate. [< L; see RESIDUAL]

re·sign (ri zīn′), *v.i.* **1.** to give up an office, position, etc., often formally (often fol. by *from*): *to resign from a committee.* **2.** to submit; yield. —*v.t.* **3.** to give up (an office, position, etc.), often formally. **4.** to relinquish (a right, claim, agreement, etc.). **5.** to submit (oneself, one's mind, etc.) without resistance. [ME *resign(en)* < MF *resign(er)* < L *resignāre* to open, release, cancel = *re-* RE- + *signāre* to mark, seal, SIGN] —**Syn. 1.** withdraw. **3.** abdicate, renounce; quit, leave. **4.** surrender, cede, forgo.

res·ig·na·tion (rez′ig nā′shən), *n.* **1.** the act of resigning. **2.** a formal statement, document, etc., stating that one gives up an office, position, etc. **3.** a submissive attitude, state, etc.; submission; unresisting acquiescence. [ME < MF < ML *resignātiōn-* (s. of *resignātiō*) a canceling, rescinding = L *resignāt(us)* (ptp. of *resignāre* to RESIGN) + *-iōn-* -ION] —**Syn. 1, 2.** abdication. **3.** meekness, patience, compliance, forbearance. —**Ant. 3.** recalcitrance.

re·signed (ri zīnd′), *adj.* **1.** submissive or acquiescent. **2.** characterized by or indicative of resignation. —**re·sign·ed·ly** (ri zī′nid lē), *adv.* —**re·sign′ed·ness,** *n.*

re·sile (ri zīl′), *v.i.*, **-siled, -sil·ing. 1.** to spring back; rebound; resume the original form or position, as an elastic body. **2.** to shrink back; recoil. [< MF *resil(ir)* < L *resilīre* to spring back; see RESILIENT] —**re·sile′ment,** *n.*

re·sil·ience (ri zil′yəns, -zil′ē əns), *n.* **1.** the power or ability to return to the original form or position after being bent, compressed, or stretched; elasticity. **2.** ability to recover readily from illness, depression, adversity, or the like; buoyancy. Also, **re·sil′ien·cy.** [< L *resil(īre)* (to) spring back, rebound + -ENCE]

re·sil·ient (ri zil′yənt, -zil′ē ənt), *adj.* **1.** springing back; rebounding. **2.** returning to the original form or position after being bent, compressed, or stretched. **3.** recovering readily from illness, depression, adversity, or the like; buoyant. [< L *resilient-* springing back (s. of *resiliēns*, prp. of *resilīre* = *re-* RE- + *sal(īre)* (to) leap, jump); see SALIENT] —**re·sil′ient·ly,** *adv.*

res·in (rez′in), *n.* **1.** any of a class of nonvolatile, solid or semisolid organic substances obtained directly from certain plants as exudations or prepared by polymerization of simple molecules: used in medicine and in the making of varnishes and plastics. **2.** a substance of this type obtained from certain pines; rosin. —*v.t.* **3.** to treat or rub with resin. [ME < MF *resine* < L *rēsīna* < Gk *rhētínē* pine resin] —**res′in·like′,** *adj.*

res·in·ate (rez′ə nāt′), *v.t.*, **-at·ed, -at·ing.** to treat with resin, as by impregnation.

res·in·if·er·ous (rez′ə nif′ər əs), *adj.* yielding resin.

res·in·oid (rez′ə noid′), *adj.* **1.** resinlike. —*n.* **2.** a resinoid substance. **3.** a gum resin.

res·in·ous (rez′ə nəs), *adj.* **1.** full of or containing resin. **2.** of the nature of or resembling resin. **3.** pertaining to or characteristic of resin. Also, **res·in·y** (rez′ə nē). [< L *rēsīnōs(us)*] —**res′in·ous·ly,** *adv.* —**res′in·ous·ness,** *n.*

re·sist (ri zist′), *v.t.* **1.** to withstand, strive against, or oppose. **2.** to withstand the action or effect of. **3.** to refrain or abstain from, esp. with difficulty or reluctance. —*v.i.* **4.** to make a stand or make efforts in opposition; act in opposition; offer resistance. —*n.* **5.** a substance that prevents or inhibits some action, as a coating that inhibits corrosion. [ME *resist(en)* < L *resist(ere)* (to) remain standing = *re-* RE- + *sistere* to cause to stand] —**re·sist′er,** *n.* —**re·sist′ing·ly,** *adv.* —**Syn. 1.** confront, counteract, rebuff. See **oppose.**

re·sist·ance (ri zis′təns), *n.* **1.** the act or power of resisting, opposing, or withstanding. **2.** the opposition offered by one thing, force, etc., to another. **3.** *Elect.* **a.** a property of a conductor by virtue of which the passage of current is opposed, causing electric energy to be transformed into heat. **b.** a conductor or coil offering such opposition; resistor. **4.** *Psychiatry.* opposition to an attempt to bring repressed thoughts or feelings into consciousness. **5.** (*usually cap.*) (esp. during World War II) an underground organization working to overthrow the occupying power, usually by acts of sabotage, guerrilla warfare, etc. [ME < MF]

re·sist·ant (ri zis′tənt), *adj.* **1.** resisting. —*n.* **2.** a person or thing that resists. [< MF *resistant* < L *resistent-* (s. of *resistēns*, prp. of *resistere*)] —**re·sist′ant·ly,** *adv.*

Re·sis·ten·cia (re′sēs ten′syä), *n.* a city in NE Argentina, on the Paraná River. 80,000 (est. 1965).

re·sist·i·ble (ri zis′tə bəl), *adj.* capable of being resisted. —**re·sist′i·bil′i·ty, re·sist′i·ble·ness,** *n.* —**re·sist′i·bly,** *adv.*

re·sis·tive (ri zis′tiv), *adj.* resisting; capable of or inclined to resistance. —**re·sis′tive·ly,** *adv.* —**re·sis′tive·ness,** *n.*

re·sis·tiv·i·ty (rē′zis tiv′i tē), *n.* **1.** the power or property of resistance. **2.** *Elect.* the resistance between opposite faces of a one-centimeter cube of a given material; ratio of electric intensity to cross-sectional area.

re·sist·less (ri zist′lis), *adj.* **1.** irresistible. **2.** not resisting. —**re·sist′less·ly,** *adv.* —**re·sist′less·ness,** *n.*

re·sis·tor (ri zis′tər), *n.* *Elect.* a device, the primary purpose of which is to introduce resistance into an electric circuit.

res ju·di·ca·ta (rēz′ jo͞o′ di kā′tə, rās), *Law.* a thing adjudicated; a case that has been decided. [< L]

res·na·tron (rez′nə tron′), *n.* *Electronics.* a tetrode with the grid connected to form a drift space for the electrons, for generating large power at very high frequency. [RES(O)NA(TOR) + -TRON]

re·sole (rē sōl′), *v.t.*, **-soled, -sol·ing.** to put a new sole on (a shoe, boot, etc.).

re·sol·u·ble[1] (ri zol′yə bəl, rez′əl-), *adj.* capable of being resolved. [< LL *resolubil(is)* = L *resolv(ere)* (to) RESOLVE + *-bilis* -BLE] —**re·sol′u·bil′i·ty, re·sol′u·ble·ness,** *n.*

re·sol·u·ble[2] (rē sol′yə bəl), *adj.* able to be redissolved.

res·o·lute (rez′ə lo͞ot′), *adj.* **1.** firmly resolved or determined. **2.** characterized by firmness and determination. [< L *resolut(us)*, ptp. of *resolvere* to RESOLVE] —**res′o·lute′ly,** *adv.* —**res′o·lute′ness,** *n.* —**Syn. 1.** firm, steadfast, fixed. See **earnest**[1]. **2.** unwavering, undaunted.

res·o·lu·tion (rez′ə lo͞o′shən), *n.* **1.** a formal expression of opinion or intention made, usually after voting, by a formal organization, a legislature, a club, or other group. Cf. **concurrent resolution, joint resolution. 2.** a resolve or determination. **3.** the act of resolving or determining, as upon an action or course of action, method, procedure, etc. **4.** the mental state or quality of being resolved or resolute; firmness of purpose. **5.** the act or process of resolving or separating into constituent or elementary parts. **6.** the resulting state. **7.** a solution or explanation, as of a problem, controversy, etc. **8.** *Music.* **a.** the progression of a voice part or of the harmony as a whole from a dissonance to a consonance. **b.** the tone or chord to which a dissonance is

Resolution (def. 8)
A, Dissonance
B, Consonance

re·set′tle, *v.*, **-tled, -tling.**	**re·sharp′en,** *v.*	**re·shuf′fle,** *v.*, **-fled, -fling;** *n.*	**re·sit′u·ate′,** *v.t.*, **-at·ed, -at·ing.**
re·set′tle·ment, *n.*	**re·shoe′,** *v.t.*, **-shod, -shoe·ing.**		

resolved. **9.** reduction to a simpler form; conversion. [ME < L *resolūtiōn-* (s. of *resolūtiō*) = *resolūt(us)* RESOLUTE + *-iōn-* -ION] **—Syn. 4.** resolve, determination, perseverance, tenacity.

re·solv·a·ble (ri zol′və bəl), *adj.* capable of being resolved. **—re·solv′a·bil′i·ty, re·solv′a·ble·ness,** *n.*

re·solve (ri zolv′), *v.,* **-solved, -solv·ing,** *n.* **—***v.t.* **1.** to fix or settle on by deliberate choice and will; determine (to do something). **2.** to separate into constituent or elementary parts; break up. **3.** to reduce or convert by or as by breaking up or disintegration. **4.** to convert or transform by any process (often used reflexively). **5.** to reduce by mental analysis (often fol. by *into*). **6.** to settle, determine, or state formally in a vote or resolution. **7.** to deal with (a question, matter, etc.) conclusively; solve. **8.** to clear away or dispel (doubts, fears, etc.). **9.** *Chem.* to separate (a racemic mixture) into its optically active components. **10.** *Music.* to cause (a voice part, etc.) to progress from a dissonance to a consonance. **11.** *Optics.* to separate and make visible the individual parts of (an image); distinguish between. **12.** *Med.* to cause (swellings, inflammation, etc.) to disappear without suppuration. **—***v.i.* **13.** to make up one's mind; determine. **14.** to break up or disintegrate. **15.** to be reduced or changed by breaking up or otherwise. **16.** *Music.* to progress from a dissonance to a consonance. **—***n.* **17.** a resolution or determination made, as to follow some course of action. **18.** determination; firmness of purpose. [ME < L *resolv(ere)* (to) unfasten, loosen, release = *re-* RE- + *solvere* to loosen; see SOLVE] **—re·solv′er,** *n.* **—Syn. 1.** confirm. See **decide. 2.** analyze, reduce. **8.** scatter, disperse. **17, 18.** decision.

re·solved (ri zolvd′), *adj.* determined; resolute. **—re·solv·ed·ly** (ri zol′vid lē), *adv.* **—re·solv′ed·ness,** *n.*

re·sol·vent (ri zol′vənt), *adj.* **1.** resolving; solvent. **—***n.* **2.** something resolvent. **3.** *Med.* a remedy that causes resolution of a swelling or inflammation. [< L *resolvent-* (s. of *resolvēns,* prp. of *resolvere*)]

resolv′ing pow′er, *Optics.* the ability of an optical device to produce separate images of close objects.

res·o·nance (rez′ə nəns), *n.* **1.** the state or quality of being resonant. **2.** the prolongation of sound by reflection; reverberation. **3.** *Phonet.* amplification of the range of audibility of any source of speech sounds, esp. of phonation, by various couplings of the cavities of the mouth, nose, sinuses, larynx, pharynx, and upper thorax, and, to some extent, by the skeletal structure of the head and upper chest. **4.** *Physics.* **a.** the state of a system in which an abnormally large vibration is produced in response to an external stimulus, occurring when the frequency of the stimulus is the same, or nearly the same, as a natural vibration frequency of the system. **b.** the vibration produced in such a state. **5.** *Elect.* the condition of a circuit with respect to a given frequency or the like in which the net reactance is a minimum and the current flow a maximum. **6.** *Chem.* the condition exhibited by a molecule when the actual arrangement of its valence electrons is intermediate between two or more arrangements having nearly the same energy, and the positions of the atomic nuclei are identical. [< MF < L *resonantia* echo = *reson(āre)* (to) RESOUND + *-antia* -ANCE]

res′onance radia′tion, *Physics.* radiation emitted by an atom or molecule, having the same frequency as that of an incident particle, as a photon, and usually involving a transition to the lowest energy level of the atom or molecule.

res·o·nant (rez′ə nənt), *adj.* **1.** resounding or reechoing, as sounds. **2.** deep and full of resonance. **3.** pertaining to resonance. **4.** producing resonance; causing amplification or sustention of sound. **5.** pertaining to a system in a state of resonance, esp. with respect to sound. **—***n.* **6.** *Phonet.* a vowel or a voiced consonant or semivowel that is neither a stop nor an affricate, as, in English, (m, n͡g, n, l, r, y, w). [< L *resonant-* (s. of *resonāns,* prp. of *resonāre*). See RESOUND, -ANT] **—res′o·nant·ly,** *adv.*

res·o·nate (rez′ə nāt′), *v.,* **-nat·ed, -nat·ing.** **—***v.i.* **1.** to resound. **2.** to act as a resonator; exhibit resonance. **3.** *Electronics.* to reinforce oscillations because the natural frequency of the device is the same as the frequency of the source. **4.** to amplify vocal sound by the sympathetic vibration of air in certain cavities and bony structures. **—***v.t.* **5.** to cause to resound. [< L *resonāt(us)* (ptp. of *resonāre*). See RESOUND, -ATE[1]] **—res′o·na′tion,** *n.*

res·o·na·tor (rez′ə nā′tər), *n.* **1.** anything that resonates. **2.** an appliance for increasing sound by resonance. **3.** an instrument for detecting the presence of a particular frequency by means of resonance. **4.** *Electronics.* **a.** a hollow enclosure made of conducting material of such dimensions that electromagnetic radiation of a certain frequency will resonate. **b.** any circuit having this frequency characteristic. [< NL = L *resonāt(us)* (see RESONATE) + *-or* -OR[2]]

re·sorb (ri sôrb′, -zôrb′), *v.t.* to absorb again, as an exudation. [< L *resorb(ēre)* = *re-* RE- + *sorbēre* to swallow, suck up] **—re·sorb′ence,** *n.* **—re·sorb′ent,** *adj.* **—re·sorp·tion** (ri sôrp′shən, -zôrp′-), *n.* **—re·sorp·tive** (ri sôrp′tiv, -zôrp′-), *adj.*

res·or·cin·ol (rez ôr′si nōl′, -nôl′, -nol′, ri zôr′-), *n. Chem., Pharm.* a solid, $C_6H_4(OH)_2$, used chiefly in making dyes, in tanning, in the synthesis of certain resins, and in treating certain skin conditions. Also, **res·or′cin.** [< NL; see RESIN, ORCINOL]

re-sort (rē sôrt′), *v.t.* to sort or arrange (cards, papers, etc.) again.

re·sort (ri zôrt′), *v.i.* **1.** to have recourse for use, service, or help, often as a final, available resource: *to resort to war.* **2.** to go, esp. frequently or customarily. **—***n.* **3.** a place to which people frequently or generally go, esp. one providing rest and recreation facilities for people on vacation. **4.** habitual or general going, as to a place or person. **5.** use of or appeal to some person or thing for aid, service, etc.; recourse: *to have resort to force; a court of last resort.* **6.** a person or thing resorted to for aid, service, etc. [ME *resort(en)* < OF *resort(ir)* = *re-* RE- + *sortir* to go out, leave, escape < ?] **—Syn. 1.** turn. **6.** resource.

re-sound (rē sound′), *v.i., v.t.* to sound again.

re·sound (ri zound′), *v.i.* **1.** to reecho or ring with sound, as a place. **2.** to make an echoing sound, or sound loudly, as a thing. **3.** to ring or be echoed, as sounds. **4.** to be famed or celebrated. **—***v.t.* **5.** to reecho (a sound). **6.** to give forth or utter loudly. **7.** to proclaim loudly (praise, disapproval, etc.). [ME *resounen* < MF *reson(er)* < L *resonāre* = *re-* RE- + *sonāre* to SOUND[1]] **—re·sound′ing·ly,** *adv.*

re·source (rē′sōrs, -sôrs, ri sōrs′, -sôrs′), *n.* **1.** a source of supply, support, or aid, esp. one held in reserve. **2. resources,** the collective wealth of a country or its means of producing wealth. **3.** Usually, **resources.** money or any property that can be converted into money; assets. **4.** Often, **resources.** an available means afforded by the mind or the personal capabilities. **5.** capability in dealing with a situation or in meeting difficulties. [< F *ressource* < OF *ressourse* < *resourdre* to rise up = *re-* RE- + *sourdre* < L *surgere* to rise up, lift] **—re·source′less,** *adj.* **—re·source′less·ness,** *n.* **—Syn. 1.** resort. **5.** inventiveness, adaptability, ingenuity, cleverness.

re·source·ful (ri sōrs′fəl, -sôrs′-), *adj.* able to deal skillfully and promptly with new situations, difficulties, etc. **—re·source′ful·ly,** *adv.* **—re·source′ful·ness,** *n.*

resp., 1. respective. **2.** respectively. **3.** respondent.

re·spect (ri spekt′), *n.* **1.** a particular, detail, or point (usually prec. by *in*): *to differ in some respect.* **2.** relation or reference: *inquiries with respect to a route.* **3.** admiration for or a sense of the worth or excellence of a person, a personal quality or trait, or something considered as a manifestation of a personal quality or trait. **4.** deference to a right, privilege, privileged position, or to someone or something considered as having certain rights or privileges. **5.** the condition of being esteemed or honored: *to be held in respect.* **6. respects,** a formal expression or gesture of esteem, deference, or friendship. **7.** discrimination or partiality in regard to persons or things. **—***v.t.* **8.** to hold in esteem or honor. **9.** to show regard or consideration for. **10.** to refrain from interfering with. **11.** to relate or have reference to. [< L *respect(us)* looked back on, looked at, ptp. of *respicere* = *re-* RE- + *specere* to look] **—re·spect′er,** *n.* **—Syn. 1.** regard, feature, matter. **2.** regard, connection. **3.** estimation, reverence, homage, honor. RESPECT, ESTEEM, VENERATION imply recognition of personal qualities by approbation and deference. RESPECT is commonly the result of admiration and approbation, together with deference: *to feel respect for a great scholar.* ESTEEM is deference combined with admiration and often with affection: *to hold a friend in great esteem.* VENERATION is an almost religious attitude of deep respect, reverence, and love, such as one feels for persons or things of outstanding superiority, endeared by long association: *veneration for one's grandparents, for noble traditions.* **7.** bias, preference. **8.** revere, venerate.

re·spect·a·bil·i·ty (ri spek′tə bil′i tē), *n., pl.* **-ties** for 4. **1.** the state or quality of being respectable. **2.** respectable social standing, character, or reputation. **3.** a respectable person or persons. **4. respectabilities,** things accepted as respectable.

re·spect·a·ble (ri spek′tə bəl), *adj.* **1.** worthy of respect or esteem; estimable; worthy. **2.** of good social standing, reputation, etc. **3.** pertaining or appropriate to such standing; proper or decent. **4.** of moderate excellence; fairly good; fair. **5.** considerable in size, number, or amount. **—re·spect′a·ble·ness,** *n.* **—re·spect′a·bly,** *adv.* **—Syn. 1.** honorable. **2.** respected, reputable. **4.** middling, passable, tolerable.

re·spect·ful (ri spekt′fəl), *adj.* full of, characterized by, or showing politeness or deference: *a respectful reply.* **—re·spect′ful·ly,** *adv.* **—re·spect′ful·ness,** *n.* **—Syn.** courteous, polite, decorous, civil, deferential. **—Ant.** discourteous, disrespectful.

re·spect·ing (ri spek′ting), *prep.* regarding; concerning.

re·spec·tive (ri spek′tiv), *adj.* pertaining individually or severally to each of a number of persons, things, etc.; particular: *the respective merits of the candidates.* [< ML *respectīv(us)*] **—re·spec′tive·ness,** *n.* **—Syn.** separate, individual; own.

re·spec·tive·ly (ri spek′tiv lē), *adv.* with respect to each of a number in the order given.

re·spell (rē spel′), *v.t.* to spell again or anew.

Re·spi·ghi (re spē′gē), *n.* **Ot·to·ri·no** (ôt′tô rē′nô), 1879–1936, Italian composer.

re·spir·a·ble (res′pər ə bəl, ri spīər′ə bəl), *adj.* **1.** capable of being respired. **2.** capable of respiring. [< LL *respīrābil(is)*] **—re·spir′a·bil′i·ty, re·spir′a·ble·ness,** *n.*

res·pi·ra·tion (res′pə rā′shən), *n.* **1.** the act of respiring; breathing. **2.** *Biol.* **a.** the sum total of the physical and chemical processes in an organism by which oxygen is conveyed to tissues and cells and the oxidation products, carbon dioxide and water, are given off. **b.** an analogous chemical process, as in muscle cells or in anaerobic bacteria, occurring in the absence of oxygen. [ME *respiracioun* < L *respīrātiōn-* (s. of *respīrātiō*) a breathing out = *respīrāt(us)* (ptp. of *respīrāre* to RESPIRE) + *-iōn-* -ION] **—res′pi·ra′tion·al,** *adj.*

res·pi·ra·tor (res′pə rā′tər), *n.* **1.** a device, usually of gauze, worn over the mouth, or nose and mouth, to prevent the inhalation of noxious substances, or the like. **2.** *Brit.* See **gas mask. 3.** an apparatus to produce or assist in artificial respiration. [< L *respīrāt(us)* (see RESPIRATION) + -OR[2]]

res·pi·ra·to·ry (res′pər ə tôr′ē, -tōr′ē, ri spīər′ə-), *adj.* pertaining to or serving for respiration: *the respiratory system of mammals.* [< LL *respīrātōri(us)* = L *respīrāt(us)* (see RESPIRATION) + *-ōrius* -ORY[1]]

re·spire (ri spīər′), *v.,* **-spired, -spir·ing.** **—***v.i.* **1.** to inhale and exhale air for the purpose of maintaining life; breathe. **2.** to breathe freely again, after anxiety, trouble, etc. **—***v.t.* **3.** to breathe; inhale and exhale. **4.** to exhale. [ME *respire(n)* < L *respīrāre* = *re-* RE- + *spīrāre* to breathe; see SPIRIT]

res·pite (res′pit), *n., v.,* **-pit·ed, -pit·ing.** **—***n.* **1.** a delay or cessation for a time, esp. of anything distressing or trying; an interval of relief. **2.** temporary suspension of the execution of a person condemned to death; reprieve. **—***v.t.* **3.** to relieve temporarily. **4.** to grant a delay in. [ME *respit* < OF < L *respect(us)*; see RESPECT] **—res′pite·less,** *adj.* **—Syn. 1.** hiatus, interval, rest, recess. **2.** postponement, stay. **3.** alleviate. **4.** postpone, suspend.

re·splend·ence (ri splen′dəns), *n.* a resplendent quality or state; splendor. Also, **re·splend′en·cy.** [ME < LL *resplendentia.* See RESPLENDENT, -ENCE]

re·splend·ent (ri splen′dənt), *adj.* shining brilliantly; gleaming; splendid. [< L *resplendent-* (s. of *resplendēns,* prp. of *resplendēre*) shining brightly = *re-* RE- + *splend(ēre)* (to) shine (see SPLENDOR) + *-ent-* -ENT] —**re·splend′ent·ly,** *adv.* —**Syn.** radiant, glistening, lustrous; dazzling.

re·spond (ri spond′), *v.i.* **1.** to reply or answer in words. **2.** to make a return by some action as if in answer. **3.** *Physiol.* to exhibit some action or effect as if in answer; react. **4.** to correspond. —*v.t.* **5.** to say in answer; reply. —*n.* **6.** *Archit.* a half pier, pilaster, or the like, projecting from a wall as a support for a lintel or an arch. **7.** *Eccles.* **a.** a short anthem chanted at intervals during the reading of a lection. **b.** responsory. **c.** response. [ME (n.) < eccl. L *respondēre* to sing a responsory (L: to promise in return, reply, answer) = *re-* RE- + *spondēre* to pledge, promise; see SPONSOR] —**Syn. 1.** rejoin. **2.** rise, react, reply. **4.** match.

re·spond·ence (ri spon′dəns), *n.* the act of responding; response: *respondence to a stimulus.* Also, **re·spond′en·cy.** [< obs. F]

re·spond·ent (ri spon′dənt), *adj.* **1.** answering; responsive. **2.** *Obs.* corresponding. —*n.* **3.** a person who responds or makes reply. **4.** *Law.* a defendant, esp. in appellate and divorce cases. [< L *respondent-* (s. of *respondēns*), prp. of *respondēre*]

re·spond·er (ri spon′dər), *n.* **1.** a person or thing that responds. **2.** *Electronics.* the part of a transponder that transmits the reply.

re·sponse (ri spons′), *n.* **1.** an answer or reply, as in words or in some action; rejoinder. **2.** *Biol.* any behavior of a living organism that results from stimulation. **3.** *Eccles.* **a.** a verse, sentence, phrase, or word said or sung by the choir or congregation in reply to the officiant. Cf. **versicle** (def. 2). **b.** responsory. [< L *respons(um),* n. use of neut. ptp. of *respondēre* to RESPOND; r. ME *respounse* < MF *respons*] —**re·sponse′less,** *adj.* —**Syn. 1.** See **answer.**

re·spon·si·bil·i·ty (ri spon′sə bil′i tē), *n., pl.* **-ties. 1.** the state or fact of being responsible. **2.** an instance of being responsible. **3.** a particular burden of obligation upon a person who is responsible. **4.** something for which a person is responsible. **5.** reliability or dependability, esp. in meeting debts or payments. —**Syn. 1.** answerability, accountability.

re·spon·si·ble (ri spon′sə bəl), *adj.* **1.** answerable or accountable, as for something within one's power or control. **2.** involving accountability or responsibility: *a responsible position.* **3.** chargeable with being the author, cause, or occasion of something (usually fol. by *for*). **4.** having a capacity for moral decisions and therefore accountable. **5.** able to discharge obligations or pay debts. [< L *respons(us)* (see RESPONSE) + -IBLE] —**re·spon′si·ble·ness,** *n.* —**re·spon′si·bly,** *adv.* —**Syn. 1.** liable. **4.** competent. **5.** solvent.

re·spon·sion (ri spon′shən), *n.* **1.** the act of responding or answering. **2. responsions,** the first examination for the Bachelor of Arts degree at Oxford University. [ME < L *responsiōn-* (s. of *responsiō*) an answer]

re·spon·sive (ri spon′siv), *adj.* **1.** making answer or reply, esp. responding or reacting readily to influences, appeals, efforts, etc. **2.** *Physiol.* acting in response, as to some stimulus. **3.** characterized by the use of responses: *responsive worship.* [< LL *responsīv(us)*] —**re·spon′sive·ly,** *adv.* —**re·spon′sive·ness,** *n.*

re·spon·sor (ri spon′sər), *n.* *Electronics.* the portion of an interrogator that receives and interprets the signals from a transponder.

re·spon·so·ry (ri spon′sə rē), *n., pl.* **-ries.** *Eccles.* an anthem sung after a lection by a soloist and choir alternately. [< LL *responsōri(um)*]

res pu·bli·ca (RES pōō′bli kä′; *Eng.* rēz pub′li kə, rās), *Latin.* the state; republic; commonwealth. [lit., public matter]

rest¹ (rest), *n.* **1.** the refreshing quiet or repose of sleep. **2.** refreshing ease or inactivity after exertion or labor. **3.** relief or freedom, esp. from troubles or exertion. **4.** a period or interval of inactivity, repose, or tranquillity. **5.** mental or spiritual calm; tranquillity. **6.** the repose of death: *eternal rest.* **7.** cessation or absence of motion. **8.** *Music.* **a.** an interval of silence between tones. **b.** a mark or sign indicating it. **9.** *Pros.* a short pause within a line; caesura. **10.** a place that provides shelter or lodging for travelers; abode. **11.** a piece or thing for something to rest on: *a chin rest.* **12.** a supporting device; support. **13. at rest, a.** in a state of repose, as in sleep. **b.** dead. **c.** quiescent; inactive; not in motion. **d.** free from worry; tranquil. **14. lay to rest,** to inter (a dead body); bury. —*v.i.* **15.** to refresh oneself, as by sleeping or relaxing. **16.** to relieve weariness by cessation of exertion or labor. **17.** to be at ease; have tranquillity or peace. **18.** to repose in death. **19.** to be quiet or still. **20.** to cease from motion; stop. **21.** to become or remain inactive. **22.** to remain without further action or notice: *to let a matter rest.* **23.** to lie, sit, lean, or be set: *His arm rested on the table.* **24.** *Agric.* to lie fallow. **25.** to be imposed as a burden or responsibility. **26.** to rely. **27.** to be based or founded. **28.** to be or be found where specified: *The blame rests with them.* **29.** to be present; dwell; linger (usually fol. by *on* or *upon*): *A sunbeam rests upon the altar.* **30.** to be fixed or directed on something, as the gaze, eyes, etc. **31.** *Law.* to terminate voluntarily the introduction of evidence in a case. —*v.t.* **32.** to give rest to; refresh with rest: *to rest oneself.* **33.** to lay or place for rest, ease, or support. **34.** to direct (as the eyes). **35.** to base, or let depend, as on some ground of reliance. **36.** to bring to rest; halt; stop. **37.** *Law.* to terminate voluntarily the introduction of evidence on. [(n.) ME, OE, akin to G *Rast;* (v.) ME *rest(en),* OE *restan;* akin to G *rasten*] —**rest′er,** *n.*

A B C D E F G H

Rests¹ (def. 8b)
A, Double whole;
B, Whole; C, Half;
D, Quarter; E, Eighth;
F, Sixteenth; G, Thirty-second; H, Sixty-fourth

rest² (rest), *n.* **1.** a remaining part; remainder. **2.** the others: *All the rest are going.* —*v.i.* **3.** to continue to be; remain as specified: *Rest assured that all is going well.* [ME < MF *rest(er)* (to) remain < L *restāre* to remain standing = *re-* RE- + *stāre* to STAND]

rest³ (rest), *n.* *Armor.* a support for a lance; lance rest. [ME; aph. var. of ARREST]

re·state (rē stāt′), *v.t.,* **-stat·ed, -stat·ing.** to state again or in a new way. —**re·state′ment,** *n.*

res·tau·rant (res′tər ənt, -tə ränt′), *n.* a place where meals are served to customers. [< F, n. use of prp. of *restaurer* < L *restaurāre* to RESTORE]

res·tau·ra·teur (res′tər ə tûr′; *Fr.* RES tô RA tœR′), *n., pl.* **-teurs** (-tûrz′; *Fr.* -tœR′). the owner or manager of a restaurant. [< F < LL *restaurātor* restorer = L *restaurāt(us)* (ptp. of *restaurāre* to RESTORE) + *-or* -OR²]

rest′ cure′, *Med.* a treatment for nervous disorders, consisting of a complete rest, usually combined with systematic diet, massage, and the like.

rest·ful (rest′fəl), *adj.* **1.** full of or giving rest. **2.** being at rest; quiet; tranquil; peaceful. [ME] —**rest′ful·ly,** *adv.* —**rest′ful·ness,** *n.* —**Syn. 2.** calm, serene. —**Ant. 2.** agitated.

rest′ home′, a residential establishment that provides special care for convalescents and aged or infirm persons.

rest·ing (res′ting), *adj.* **1.** being at rest; not active. **2.** *Bot.* dormant: applied esp. to spores or seeds that germinate after a period of dormancy.

res·ti·tu·tion (res′ti tōō′shən, -tyōō′-), *n.* **1.** reparation made by giving an equivalent or compensation for loss, damage, or injury caused; indemnification. **2.** the restoration of property or rights previously taken away, conveyed, or surrendered. **3.** restoration to the former or original state or position. **4.** *Physics.* the return to an original physical condition, esp. after elastic deformation. [ME < OF < L *restitūtiōn-* (s. of *restitūtiō*) a calling back again = *restitūt(us)* (ptp. of *restituere* to replace, restore: *re-* RE- + *statuere* to cause to stand; see STATUE) + *-iōn-* -ION] —**res′ti·tu′tive, res·ti·tu·to·ry** (res′ti tōō′tə rē, -tyōō′-), *adj.* —**Syn. 1.** recompense, amends, compensation, satisfaction, repayment. See **redress.**

res·tive (res′tiv), *adj.* **1.** restless; uneasy; impatient of control, restraint, or delay, as persons. **2.** refractory; stubborn. **3.** refusing to go forward; balky: *a restive horse.* [REST² + -IVE; r. ME *restif* stationary, balking < OF: inert] —**res′tive·ly,** *adv.* —**res′tive·ness,** *n.* —**Syn. 1.** nervous, unquiet. **2.** recalcitrant, disobedient, obstinate. —**Ant. 1.** patient, quiet. **2.** obedient, tractable.

rest·less (rest′lis), *adj.* **1.** characterized by or showing inability to remain at rest: *a restless mood.* **2.** unquiet or uneasy, as a person, the mind, the heart, etc. **3.** never at rest; perpetually agitated or in motion: *the restless sea.* **4.** without rest; without restful sleep: *a restless night.* **5.** unceasingly active; averse to quiet or inaction, as persons: *a restless crowd.* [ME *restles*] —**rest′less·ly,** *adv.* —**rest′less·ness,** *n.*

res·to·ra·tion (res′tə rā′shən), *n.* **1.** the act of restoring. **2.** the state or fact of being restored. **3.** a return of something to a former, original, normal, or unimpaired condition. **4.** restitution of something taken away or lost. **5.** something that is restored. **6.** a representation or reconstruction of an ancient building, extinct animal, etc., showing it in its original state. **7.** a putting back into a former position, dignity, etc. **8. the Restoration,** the period of the reign of Charles II (1660–85), sometimes extended to include the reign of James II (1685–88). [ME *restauracion* < LL *restaurātiōn-* (s. of *restaurātiō*) = L *restaurāt(us)* (ptp. of *restaurāre* to RESTORE) + *-iōn-* -ION]

re·stor·a·tive (ri stōr′ə tiv, -stôr′-), *adj.* **1.** serving to restore; pertaining to restoration. **2.** capable of renewing health or strength. —*n.* **3.** a restorative agent, means, or the like. **4.** a means of restoring a person to consciousness: *Smelling salts serve as a restorative.* [ME *restoratif* < MF *restauratif* < L *restaurāt(us)* (ptp. of *restaurāre* to RESTORE) + MF *-if* -IVE]

re·store (ri stōr′, -stôr′), *v.t.,* **-stored, -stor·ing. 1.** to bring back into existence, use, or the like; reestablish: *to restore order.* **2.** to bring back to a former, original, or normal condition, as a building, statue, or painting. **3.** to bring back to health, soundness, or vigor. **4.** to put back to a former place or position, rank, etc. **5.** to give back; make return or restitution of (anything taken away or lost). **6.** to reproduce, reconstruct, or represent (an ancient building, extinct animal, etc.) in the original state. [ME *restore(n)* < OF *restor(er)* < L *restaurāre* = *re-* RE- + **staurāre;* see STORE] —**re·stor′a·ble,** *adj.* —**re·stor′a·ble·ness,** *n.* —**re·stor′er,** *n.* —**Syn. 2.** mend. See **renew. 4.** replace, reinstate.

restr., restaurant.

re-strain (rē strān′), *v.t., v.i.* to strain again.

re·strain (ri strān′), *v.t.* **1.** to hold back from action; keep in check or under control; repress. **2.** to deprive of liberty, as by arrest or the like. **3.** to limit or hamper the activity, growth, or effect of: *to restrain trade with Cuba.* [ME *restreyn(en)* < MF *restreind(re)* < L *restringere* to bind back, bind fast = *re-* RE- + *stringere* to draw together; see STRAIN¹] —**re·strain′a·bil′i·ty,** *n.* —**re·strain′a·ble,** *adj.* —**re·strain·ed·ly** (ri strā′nid lē), *adv.* —**re·strain′ing·ly,** *adv.* —**Syn. 1.** bridle, suppress, constrain. See **check. 2.** restrict, circumscribe, confine, hinder, hamper. —**Ant. 1.** unbridle. **2.** free, liberate.

re·strain·er (ri strā′nər), *n.* **1.** a person or thing that restrains. **2.** *Photog.* a chemical added to a developer to retard its action.

re·straint (ri strānt′), *n.* **1.** a restraining action or influence. **2.** a means of restraining. **3.** the act of restraining,

re·stack′, *v.t.* **re·staff′,** *v.t.* **re·stage′,** *v.t.,* **-staged, -stag·ing.** **re·stamp′,** *v.* **re·start′,** *v., n.* **re·stock′,** *v.* **re·straight′en,** *v.*

or holding back, controlling, or checking. **4.** the state or fact of being restrained; deprivation of liberty; confinement. **5.** constraint or reserve in feelings, behavior, etc. [ME *restreinte* < MF *restrainte*, n. use of fem. ptp. of *restraindre* to RESTRAIN] —**Syn. 4.** restriction, imprisonment, incarceration. —**Ant. 4.** liberty.

restraint′ of trade′, action tending to interrupt the free flow of goods and services, as by price fixing and other practices that have the effect of reducing competition.

re·strict (ri strikt′), *v.t.* to confine or keep within limits, as of space, action, choice, quantity, etc. [< L *restrict(us)* drawn back, tightened, bound (ptp. of *restringere;* see RESTRAIN) = *re-* RE- + *strictus* STRICT] —**Syn.** curb, restrain.

re·strict·ed (ri strik′tid), *adj.* **1.** confined; limited. **2.** *U.S. Govt., Mil.* (of information, a document, etc.) limited to persons authorized to use such information, documents, etc. Cf. **classification** (def. 5). **3.** limited to or admitting only members of a particular group or class, esp. white gentiles. —**re·strict′ed·ly,** *adv.* —**re·strict′ed·ness,** *n.*

re·stric·tion (ri strik′shən), *n.* **1.** something that restricts; limitation. **2.** the act of restricting. **3.** the state of being restricted. [ME *restriccioun* < eccl. L *restrictiōn-* (s. of *restrictiō*). See RESTRICT, -ION] —**re·stric′tion·ist,** *n.*

re·stric·tive (ri strik′tiv), *adj.* **1.** serving to restrict. **2.** of the nature of a restriction. **3.** expressing or implying limitation of application, as terms or expressions. **4.** *Gram.* limiting the meaning of a modified element: *a restrictive adjective.* [ME < MF *restrictif* < L *restrict(us)* (see RESTRICT) + MF *-if* -IVE] —**re·stric′tive·ly,** *adv.* —**re·stric′tive·ness,** *n.*

restric′tive clause′, *Gram.* a relative clause that identifies the antecedent and that is usually not set off by commas in English. Cf. **descriptive clause.**

rest′ room′, *U.S.* a room or rooms, esp. in a public building, having washbowl, toilet, and other facilities.

re·struc·ture (ri struk′chər), *v.,* **-tured, -tur·ing.** —*v.t.* **1.** to effect a fundamental change in (an organization, system, etc.). —*v.i.* **2.** to restructure something.

re·sult (ri zult′), *v.i.* **1.** to arise or proceed as a consequence from actions, circumstances, premises, etc.; be the outcome. **2.** to terminate or end in a specified manner or thing. —*n.* **3.** that which results; outcome; consequence. **4.** *Math.* a quantity, expression, etc., obtained by calculation. [ME *result(en)* < L *result(āre)* (to) spring back, rebound = *resil(īre)* (to) spring back + *-t* freq. suffix; or *re-* RE- + *saltāre* to dance (*sal(īre)* (to) leap, spring + *-t* freq. suffix)] —**Syn. 1.** See **follow. 3.** end, product, fruit. See **effect.** —**Ant. 3.** cause.

re·sult·ant (ri zul′tənt), *adj.* **1.** that results; following as a result. **2.** resulting from the combination of two or more agents. —*n.* **3.** *Math., Physics.* a single vector, often representing a force or velocity, equivalent to two or more other such vectors, being their vector sum. **4.** that which results. [< L *resultant-* (s. of *resultāns*), prp. of *resultāre*]

re·sult·ing·ly (ri zul′ting lē), *adv.* as a result.

re·sume (ri zo͞om′), *v.,* **-sumed, -sum·ing.** —*v.t.* **1.** to take up or go on with again after interruption. **2.** to take or occupy again: *to resume one's seat.* **3.** to take or assume again. **4.** to take back. —*v.i.* **5.** to go on or continue after interruption. **6.** to begin again. [ME *resume(n)* < MF *resum(er)* or L *resūm(ere)* (to) take back, take again = *re-* RE- + *sūmere* to take (*sub-* SUB- + *emere* to acquire, obtain, take)] —**re·sum′a·ble,** *adj.* —**re·sum′er,** *n.*

ré·su·mé (rez′o͝o mā′, rez′o͝o mā′), *n.* **1.** a summing up; summary. **2.** a brief account of personal, educational, and professional qualifications and experience, as of an applicant for a job. Also, **re′su·me′.** [< F, n. use of ptp. of *résumer* to RESUME, sum up]

re·sump·tion (ri zump′shən), *n.* **1.** the act of resuming; a reassumption, as of something previously granted. **2.** the act or fact of taking up or going on with again, as of something interrupted. **3.** the act of taking again or recovering something given up or lost. [ME < MF < LL *resumptiōn-* (s. of *resumptiō*) = L *resumpt(us)* (ptp. of *resūmere* to RESUME) + *-iōn-* -ION]

re·sump·tive (ri zump′tiv), *adj.* **1.** that summarizes: *a resumptive statement of his business experience.* **2.** tending to resume or repeat. [RESUMPT(ION) + -IVE; r. ME: restorative < L *resumptīv(us)*] —**re·sump′tive·ly,** *adv.*

re·su·pi·nate (ri so͞o′pə nāt′), *adj.* **1.** bent backward. **2.** *Bot.* inverted; appearing as if upside down. [< L *resupīnāt(us)* bent backward, turned back (ptp. of *resupīnāre*) = *re-* RE- + *supīn-* (see SUPINE) + *-ātus* -ATE[1]]

re·su·pi·na·tion (ri so͞o′pə nā′shən), *n.* a resupinate condition. [< L *resupīnāt(us)* (see RESUPINATE) + -ION]

re·su·pine (rē′so͞o pīn′), *adj.* lying on the back; supine. [< L *resupīn(us)* bent back, lying back]

re·sur·face (rē sûr′fis), *v.t.,* **-faced, -fac·ing.** to give a new surface to.

re·sur·gam (re so͞or′gäm; *Eng.* ri sûr′gam), *Latin.* I shall rise again.

re·surge (ri sûrj′), *v.i.,* **-surged, -surg·ing.** to rise again, as from death or from virtual extinction. [< L *resurg(ere)* (to) rise again, appear again = *re-* RE- + *surgere* to lift up, raise, var. of *surrigere* (*sur-* SUR-[2] + *regere* to direct)]

re·sur·gent (ri sûr′jənt), *adj.* rising or tending to rise again; reviving. [< L *resurgent-* (s. of *resurgēns,* prp. of *resurgere*)] —**re·sur′gence,** *n.*

res·ur·rect (rez′ə rekt′), *v.t.* **1.** to raise from the dead; bring to life again. **2.** to bring back into use, practice, etc. —*v.i.* **3.** to rise from the dead. [back formation from RESURRECTION]

res·ur·rec·tion (rez′ə rek′shən), *n.* **1.** the act of rising again from the dead. **2.** (*cap.*) the rising again of Christ after His death and burial. **3.** (*cap.*) the rising again of men on the judgment day. **4.** the state of those risen from the dead. **5.** a rising again, as from decay or disuse; revival. [ME < eccl. L *resurrectiōn-* (s. of *resurrectiō*) the Easter church festival = *resurrect(us)* (ptp. of *resurgere* to rise again; see RESURGE) + *-iōn-* -ION] —**res′ur·rec′tion·al,** *adj.* —**res′ur·rec′tion·ar′y,** *adj.* —**res′ur·rec′tive,** *adj.*

res·ur·rec·tion·ist (rez′ə rek′shə nist), *n.* **1.** a person who brings something to life or view again. **2.** a believer in resurrection. **3.** Also called **resurrec′tion man′.** a person who exhumes and steals dead bodies, esp. for dissection; body snatcher.

re·sur·vey (*v.* rē′sər vā′; *n.* rē sûr′vā, rē′sər vā′), *v., n., pl.* **-veys.** —*v.t., v.i.* **1.** to survey again. —*n.* **2.** a new survey.

re·sus·ci·tate (ri sus′i tāt′), *v.t., v.i.,* **-tat·ed, -tat·ing.** to revive, esp. from apparent death or from unconsciousness. [< L *resuscitāt(us)* raised up again, revived (ptp. of *resuscitāre*) = *re-* RE- + *sus-* SUS- + *citāre* to move, arouse; see CITE[1]] —**re·sus·ci·ta·ble** (ri sus′i tə bəl), *adj.* —**re·sus′ci·ta′tion,** *n.* —**re·sus′ci·ta′tive,** *adj.*

re·sus·ci·ta·tor (ri sus′i tā′tər), *n.* **1.** a person or thing that resuscitates. **2.** a device used in the treatment of asphyxiation that, by forcing oxygen or a mixture of oxygen and carbon dioxide into the lungs, initiates respiration.

Resz·ke (res′kē; *Pol.* resh′ke), *n.* **1. É·douard de** (*Fr.* ā dwar′ də), 1855–1917, Polish operatic basso. **2.** his brother, **Jean de** (*Fr.* zhäɴ də), 1850–1925, Polish operatic tenor.

ret (ret), *v.t.,* **ret·ted, ret·ting.** to soak (flax or hemp) in order to remove the fiber from the woody tissue. [ME *ret(en), rett(en);* c. D *reten* (cf. D *roten,* G *rössen,* Sw *röta*)]

ret., **1.** retired. **2.** returned.

re·ta·ble (ri tā′bəl), *n.* a decorative structure raised above an altar at the back. [< F = OF *rere* at the back (< L *retrō*) + *table* TABLE]

re·tail (rē′tāl *for 1–4, 6;* ri tāl′ *for 5*), *n.* **1.** the sale of goods to ultimate consumers, usually in small quantities (opposed to *wholesale*). —*adj.* **2.** pertaining to, connected with, or engaged in sale at retail: *the retail price.* —*adv.* **3.** in a retail quantity or at a retail price. —*v.t.* **4.** to sell at retail; sell directly to the consumer. **5.** to relate or repeat in detail to others: *to retail scandal.* —*v.i.* **6.** to be sold at retail: *It retails at 50 cents.* [late ME < AF: a cutting < *retailler* to cut = *re-* RE- + *tailler* to cut; see TAIL[2]] —**re′tail·er,** *n.*

re·tain (ri tān′), *v.t.* **1.** to keep possession of. **2.** to continue to use, practice, etc. **3.** to continue to hold or have. **4.** to keep in mind; remember. **5.** to hold in place or position. **6.** to engage, esp. by payment of a preliminary fee: *to retain a lawyer.* [ME *retein(en)* < OF *reten(ir)* < L *retinēre* to hold back, hold fast = *re-* RE- + *tinēre* to hold] —**re·tain′a·bil′i·ty, re·tain′a·ble·ness,** *n.* —**re·tain′a·ble,** *adj.* —**re·tain′ment,** *n.* —**Syn. 1.** hold, preserve. See **keep.**

retained′ ob′ject, *Gram.* an object in a passive construction identical with the direct or indirect object in the active construction from which it is derived, as *me* in *the picture was shown me,* which is also the indirect object in the active construction *they showed me the picture.*

retained′ objec′tive com′plement, *Gram.* an objective complement that is kept in its predicative position following the verb when the verb is transformed into the passive voice, as *genius* in *He was considered a genius* from *(They) considered him a genius.*

re·tain·er[1] (ri tā′nər), *n.* **1.** a person or thing that retains. **2.** a servant, employee, or dependent. **3.** *Dentistry.* **a.** a device for holding the teeth in position: used in orthodontic correction. **b.** a part on a bridge or the like by which the bridge is attached to the natural teeth. [RETAIN + -ER[1]]

re·tain·er[2] (ri tā′nər), *n.* **1.** a fee paid to secure services, as of a lawyer. **2.** the act of retaining in one's service. **3.** the fact of being so retained. [ME *reteinir,* prob. n. use of MF *retenir* to RETAIN]

retain′ing wall′, a wall for holding in place a mass of earth or the like, as at the edge of a terrace or excavation.

re·take (*v.* rē tāk′; *n.* rē′tāk′), *v.,* **-took, -tak·en, -tak·ing,** *n.* —*v.t.* **1.** to take again; take back. **2.** to recapture. **3.** *Photog., Motion Pictures.* to photograph or film again. —*n.* **4.** the act of photographing or filming again. **5.** a picture, scene, sequence, etc., that is to be or has been photographed or filmed again. —**re·tak′er,** *n.*

re·tal·i·ate (ri tal′ē āt′), *v.,* **-at·ed, -at·ing.** —*v.i.* **1.** to return like for like, esp. evil for evil: *to retaliate for an injury.* —*v.t.* **2.** to requite or make return for (a wrong or injury) with the like. [< LL *retāliāt(us)* (ptp. of *retāliāre*) = *re-* RE- + *tāl-* (s. of *tālis*) such, of such a nature + *-i-* -I- + *-ātus* -ATE[1]] —**re·tal′i·a′tive, re·tal·i·a·to·ry** (ri tal′ē ə tōr′ē, -tôr′ē), *adj.* —**re·tal′i·a′tor,** *n.*

re·tal·i·a·tion (ri tal′ē ā′shən), *n.* the act of retaliating; return of like for like; reprisal.

re·tard (ri tärd′), *v.t.* **1.** to make slow; delay the progress of (an action, process, etc.); hinder or impede. —*v.i.* **2.** to be delayed. —*n.* **3.** retardation; delay. [< L *retard(āre)* (to) delay, protract = *re-* RE- + *tardāre* to loiter, be slow < *tardus* slow; see TARDY] —**re·tard′ing·ly,** *adv.*

re·tard·ant (ri tär′dənt), *n. Chem.* any substance capable of reducing the speed of a given reaction.

re·tard·ate (ri tär′dāt), *n., v.,* **-at·ed, -at·ing,** *adj.* —*n.* **1.** a person who is mentally retarded. —*v.t.* **2.** *Obs.* to retard. —*adj.* **3.** *Obs.* retarded. [< L *retardāt(us)* (ptp. of *retardāre*)]

re·tar·da·tion (rē′tär dā′shən), *n.* **1.** the act of retarding. **2.** the state of being retarded. **3.** something that retards; a hindrance. **4.** slowness or limitation in intellectual understanding and awareness, emotional development, academic progress, etc. Also, **re·tard·ment** (ri tärd′mənt). [ME *retardacion* < L *retardātiōn-* (s. of *retardātiō*). See RETARDATE, -ION] —**re·tard·a·tive** (ri tär′də tiv), **re·tard·a·to·ry** (ri tär′də tōr′ē, -tôr′ē), *adj.*

re·tard·ed (ri tär′did), *adj.* characterized by mental retardation: *a retarded child.*

re·tard·er (ri tär′dər), *n.* **1.** a person or thing that retards. **2.** *Chem.* **a.** any substance added to rubber to delay or prevent vulcanization. **b.** any substance added to cement or plaster to delay setting.

retch (rech), *v.i.* to make efforts to vomit. [OE *hrǣc(an)* (to) clear the throat < *hrāca* a clearing of the throat; cf. OIcel *hrǣkja* to hawk, spit]

retd., **1.** retained. **2.** returned.

re·string′, *v.,* **-strung, -string·ing.**
re·stud′y, *n., pl.* **-stud·ies;** *v.,* **-stud·ied, -stud·y·ing.**
re·stuff′, *v.t.*
re·style′, *v.,* **-styled, -sty·ling.**
re′sub·mis′sion, *n.*
re′sub·mit′, *v.,* **-mit·ted, -mit·ting.**
re′sub·scribe′, *v.,* **-scribed, -scrib·ing.**
re·sum′mon, *v.t.*
re′sup·ply′, *v.t.,* **-plied, -ply·ing;** *n., pl.* **-plies.**
re·swal′low, *v.*

re·te (rē′tē), *n., pl.* **re·ti·a** (rē′shē ə, -shə, -tē ə). a network, as of fibers, nerves, or blood vessels. [ME *riet* < L *rēte* net] —**re·ti·al** (rē′shē əl), *adj.*

re·tem (rē′tem), *n.* a shrub, *Genista raetam,* of Syria and Arabia, having white flowers: said to be the juniper of the Old Testament. [< Ar *ratam*]

re·tene (rē′tēn, ret′ēn), *n. Chem.* a crystalline hydrocarbon, $C_{18}H_{18}$, obtained chiefly from the tar of resinous woods and certain fossil resins. [< Gk *rhēt(inē)* resin + -ENE]

re·ten·tion (ri ten′shən), *n.* **1.** the act of retaining. **2.** the state of being retained. **3.** the power to retain; capacity for retaining. **4.** the act or power of remembering things; memory. [ME *retencion* < L *retentiōn-* (s. of *retentiō*) a keeping back = *retent(us)* (ptp. of *retinēre* to RETAIN) + *-iōn-* -ION]

re·ten·tive (ri ten′tiv), *adj.* **1.** tending or serving to retain something. **2.** having power or capacity to retain. **3.** having ability to remember; having a good memory. [ME *retentif* < MF < ML *retentīv(us)* = L *retent(us)* (see RETENTION) + *-īvus* -IVE] —**re·ten′tive·ly,** *adv.* —**re·ten′tive·ness,** *n.*

re·ten·tiv·i·ty (rē′ten tiv′i tē), *n.* the power to retain, esp. the ability to retain magnetization after the removal of the magnetizing force.

re·think (ri thingk′), *v.,* **-thought, -think·ing,** *n.* —*v.t.* **1.** to reconsider (a matter, problem, etc.), esp. profoundly. —*v.i.* **2.** to reconsider a matter, problem, etc., esp. profoundly. —*n.* **3.** the act of rethinking.

re·ti·ar·y (rē′shē er′ē), *adj.* **1.** using a net or any entangling device. **2.** netlike. **3.** making a net or web, as a spider. [< L *rēt-* (s. of *rēte*) net + -I- + -ARY]

ret·i·cent (ret′i sənt), *adj.* disposed to be silent; reserved. [< L *reticent-* (s. of *reticēns,* prp. of *reticere* to be silent) = *re-* RE- + *tac(ēre)* (to) be silent + *-ent-* -ENT] —**ret′i·cence, ret′i·cen·cy,** *n.* —**ret′i·cent·ly,** *adv.*

ret·i·cle (ret′i kəl), *n. Optics.* a network of fine lines, wires, or the like, placed in the focus of the objective of a telescope. [< L *rēticul(um)* little net = *rēt-* (s. of *rēte*) net + *-i-* -I- + *-culum* -CLE]

re·tic·u·lar (ri tik′yə lər), *adj.* **1.** having the form of a net; netlike. **2.** intricate or entangled. **3.** *Anat.* of or pertaining to a reticulum. [< NL *rēticulār(is)* = L *rēticul(um)* RETICLE + *-āris* -AR[1]] —**re·tic′u·lar·ly,** *adv.*

re·tic·u·late (*adj.* ri tik′yə lit, -lāt′; *v.* ri tik′yə lāt′), *adj., v.,* **-lat·ed, -lat·ing.** —*adj.* **1.** netted; covered with a network. **2.** netlike. **3.** *Bot.* having the veins or nerves disposed like the threads of a net. —*v.t.* **4.** to form into a network. **5.** to cover or mark with a network. —*v.i.* **6.** to form a network. [< L *rēticulāt(us)* netlike. See RETICLE, -ATE[1]] —**re·tic′u·late·ly,** *adv.*

retic′ulate py′thon, a python, *Python reticulatus,* of southeastern Asia and the East Indies, sometimes growing to a length of 32 feet: usually considered to be the largest snake in the world.

re·tic·u·la·tion (ri tik′yə lā′shən), *n.* a reticulated formation, arrangement, or appearance; network.

ret·i·cule (ret′ə kyōōl′), *n.* **1.** a small purse or bag, originally of network but later of silk, rayon, etc. **2.** *Optics.* a reticle. [< F *rēticule* < L *rēticul(um)* RETICLE]

re·tic·u·lo·en·do·the·li·al (ri tik′yə lō en′dō thē′lē əl, -thēl′yəl), *adj. Anat.* of or pertaining to the system of reticular and endothelial cells that are found in certain tissues and organs and that help maintain resistance and immunity to infection. [< L *rēticulo-* (comb. form of *rēticulum* RETICLE) + ENDOTHELIAL]

re·tic·u·lum (ri tik′yə ləm), *n., pl.* **-la** (-lə). **1.** a network; any reticulated system or structure. **2.** *Anat.* **a.** a network of intercellular fibers in certain tissues. **b.** a network of structures in the endoplasm or nucleus of certain cells. **3.** *Zool.* the second stomach of ruminating animals, between the rumen and the omasum. [< L: little net; see RETICLE]

re·ti·form (rē′tə fôrm′, ret′ə-), *adj.* netlike; reticulate. [< NL *rētiform(is)* = L *rēt-* (s. of *rēte*) net + *-i-* -I- + *-formis* -FORM]

ret·i·na (ret′ənə, ret′nə), *n., pl.* **ret·i·nas, ret·i·nae** (ret′ənē′). *Anat.* the innermost coat of the posterior part of the eyeball that receives the image produced by the crystalline lens, is continuous with the optic nerve, and contains the light-sensitive rods and cones. [ME *ret(h)ina* < ML *rētina,* prob. = L *rēt-* (s. of *rēte*) net + *-ina* -INE[1]] —**ret′i·nal,** *adj.*

ret·i·nene (ret′ənēn′), *n. Biochem.* either of the two carotenoids found in the vertebrate retina, the light-yellow crystalline compound, $C_{19}H_{27}CHO$, derived from rhodopsin or iodopsin by the action of light, or the orange-red crystalline compound, $C_{19}H_{25}CHO$, derived from porphyropsin by the action of light. [RETIN(A) + -ENE]

ret·i·ni·tis (ret′ənī′tis), *n. Pathol.* inflammation of the retina. [< NL; see RETINA, -ITIS]

ret·i·no·scope (ret′ənə skōp′), *n. Ophthalm.* skiascope.

ret·i·nos·co·py (ret′ənos′kə pē, ret′ənə skō′pē), *n. Ophthalm.* an objective method of determining the refractive error of an eye. —**ret·i·no·scop·ic** (ret′ənə skop′ik), *adj.* —**ret′i·no·scop′i·cal·ly,** *adv.* —**ret′i·nos′co·pist,** *n.*

ret·i·nue (ret′ənōō′, -ənyōō′), *n.* a body of retainers in attendance upon an important personage; suite. [ME *retinue* < MF, n. use of fem. ptp. of *retenir* to RETAIN] —**ret′i·nued′,** *adj.*

re·tire (ri tīər′), *v.,* **-tired, -tir·ing.** —*v.i.* **1.** to withdraw, or go away or apart, to a place of abode, shelter, or seclusion. **2.** to go to bed. **3.** to withdraw from office, business, or active life. **4.** to fall back or retreat according to plan, as from battle, an untenable position, danger, etc. **5.** to withdraw, leave, or remove oneself. —*v.t.* **6.** to withdraw from circulation by taking up and paying, as bonds, bills, etc. **7.** to withdraw or lead back (troops, ships, etc.), as from battle or danger; retreat. **8.** to remove from active service or the usual field of activity, as an officer in the armed forces. **9.** to withdraw (a machine, ship, etc.) permanently from its normal service, usually for scrapping. **10.** *Sports.* to put out (a batter, side, etc.). [< MF *retir(er)* (to) withdraw = *re-* RE- + *tirer* to draw] —**re·tir′er,** *n.* —**Syn. 5.** See **depart.**

re·tired (ri tīərd′), *adj.* **1.** withdrawn from or no longer occupied with one's business or profession. **2.** due or given a retired person: *retired pay.* **3.** withdrawn; secluded: *a retired little village.* —**re·tired′ly,** *adv.* —**re·tired′ness,** *n.*

re·tire·ment (ri tīər′mənt), *n.* **1.** the act of retiring. **2.** the state of being retired. **3.** removal or withdrawal from service, office, or business. **4.** the portion of a person's life during which he is retired. **5.** withdrawal into privacy or seclusion. **6.** privacy or seclusion. **7.** a private or secluded place. **8.** *Mil.* orderly withdrawal of a military force, according to plan, without pressure from the enemy. —*adj.* **9.** noting or pertaining to retirement. [< MF]

re·tir·ing (ri tīər′ing), *adj.* **1.** that retires. **2.** withdrawing from contact with others; shy. —**re·tir′ing·ly,** *adv.*

re·took (rē to͝ok′), *v.* pt. of **retake.**

re·tool (rē tōōl′), *v.t.* **1.** to replace or rearrange the tools and machinery of (a factory). **2.** to reorganize or rearrange, usually for the purpose of updating. —*v.i.* **3.** to replace or rearrange the tools or machinery of a factory.

re·tort[1] (ri tôrt′), *v.t.* **1.** to reply to, usually in a sharp or retaliatory way; reply in kind to. **2.** to return (an accusation, epithet, etc.) upon the person uttering it. **3.** to answer (an argument or the like) by another to the contrary. —*v.i.* **4.** to reply, esp. sharply. —*n.* **5.** a severe, incisive, or witty reply, esp. one that counters a first speaker's statement, argument, etc. **6.** the act of retorting. [< L *retort(us)* bent back (ptp. of *retorquēre*) = *re-* RE- + *torquēre* to twist, bend] —**re·tort′er,** *n.* —**Syn. 5.** See **answer.**

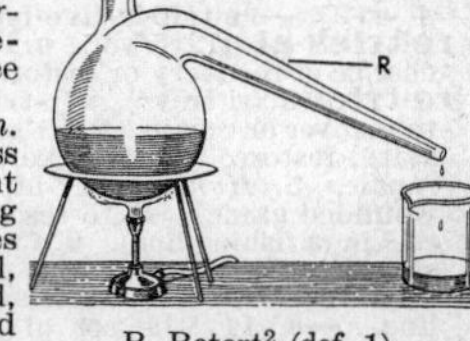

R, Retort[2] (def. 1)

re·tort[2] (ri tôrt′), *n.* **1.** *Chem.* a vessel, commonly a glass bulb with a long neck bent downward, used for distilling or decomposing substances by heat. **2.** *Metall.* a vessel, generally cylindrically shaped, within which an ore is heated so that the metal may be removed by distillation or sublimation. **3.** a vessel used in the manufacture of illuminating gas. [< MF *retorte* < ML *retorta,* fem. of *retortus* bent back (ptp. of L *retorquēre*); see RETORT[1]]

re·tor·tion (ri tôr′shən), *n.* the act of retorting. [< ML *retortiōn-* (s. of *retortiō*)]

re·touch (rē tuch′), *v.t.* **1.** to improve by new touches or the like; touch up or rework, as a painting, make-up, etc. **2.** *Photog.* to alter (a negative or positive) after development by adding or removing lines, lightening areas, etc. **3.** to dye, tint, or bleach (a new growth of hair) to match or blend with the color of an earlier and previously dyed growth. —*n.* **4.** an added touch to a picture, painting, etc., by way of improvement or alteration. **5.** an act or instance of dyeing the new growth of hair to blend with previously dyed growth. [< MF *retouch(er)*] —**re·touch′a·ble,** *adj.* —**re·touch′er,** *n.*

re-trace (rē trās′), *v.t.,* **-traced, -trac·ing.** to trace again, as lines in writing or drawing. Also, **retrace.**

re·trace (ri trās′), *v.t.,* **-traced, -trac·ing. 1.** to trace backward; go back over: *to retrace one's steps.* **2.** to go back over with the memory. **3.** to go over again with the sight or attention. **4.** re-trace. [< F *retrac(er),* MF *retracier*] —**re·trace′a·ble,** *adj.* —**re·trace′ment,** *n.*

re·tract[1] (ri trakt′), *v.t.* to draw back or in: *to retract fangs.* [ME *retract(en)* < L *retract(us)* drawn back (ptp. of *retrahere*) = *re-* RE- + *tractus;* see TRACT[1]]

re·tract[2] (ri trakt′), *v.t.* **1.** to withdraw (a statement, opinion, etc.) as inaccurate or unjustified. **2.** to withdraw or revoke (a decree, promise, etc.). —*v.i.* **3.** to draw or shrink back. **4.** to withdraw a promise, vow, etc. **5.** to make disavowal of a statement, opinion, etc.; recant. [< L *retract(āre)* (to) reconsider, withdraw = *re-* RE- + *tractāre* to drag, pull, take in hand (*trac-,* ptp. s. of *trahere* to pull + *-t-* freq. suffix)] —**re·tract′a·bil′i·ty, re·tract′i·bil′i·ty,** *n.* —**re·tract′a·ble, re·tract′i·ble,** *adj.*

re·trac·tile (ri trak′til), *adj. Zool.* capable of being drawn back or in, as the head of a tortoise; exhibiting the power of retraction. —**re′trac·til′i·ty,** *n.*

re·trac·tion (ri trak′shən), *n.* **1.** the act of retracting. **2.** the state of being retracted. **3.** withdrawal of a promise, statement, opinion, etc. **4.** retractile power. [ME *retraccioun* < L *retractiōn-* (s. of *retractiō*)]

re·trac·tive (ri trak′tiv), *adj.* tending or serving to retract. [ME *retractif* < ML **retractīv(us)*] —**re·trac′tive·ly,** *adv.* —**re·trac′tive·ness,** *n.*

re·trac·tor (ri trak′tər), *n.* **1.** a person or thing that retracts. **2.** *Anat.* a muscle that retracts an organ or protruded part. **3.** *Surg.* an instrument or appliance for drawing back an impeding part, as the edge of an incision.

re-tread (rē tred′), *v.t., v.i.,* **-trod, -trod·den** or **-trod, -tread·ing.** to tread again.

re·tread (*v.* rē tred′; *n.* rē′tred′), *v.,* **-tread·ed, -tread·ing,** *n.* —*v.t.* **1.** to put a new tread on (a worn pneumatic tire casing). —*n.* **2.** a retreaded tire.

re-treat (rē trēt′), *v.t., v.i.* to treat again.

re·treat (ri trēt′), *n.* **1.** the forced or strategic withdrawal of a military force before an enemy. **2.** the act of withdrawing, as into safety or privacy; retirement; seclusion. **3.** a place of refuge, seclusion, or privacy. **4.** an asylum, as for the insane. **5.** a retirement or a period of retirement for religious exercises and meditation. **6.** *Mil.* **a.** a flag-lowering ceremony held at sunset at a military installation. **b.** the bugle call or drumbeat played at this ceremony. **7. beat a**

re·teach′, *v.,* **-taught, -teach·ing.**
re·tell′, *v.,* **-told, -tell·ing.**
re·test′, *v.t.*
re·tes′ti·fy′, *v.,* **-fied, -fy·ing.**
re·thread′, *v.t.*
re·tie′, *v.t.,* **-tied, -ty·ing.**
re·tint′, *v.t.*
re·ti′tle, *v.t.,* **-tled, -tling.**
re·train′, *v.*
re′trans·fer′, *v.t.,* **-ferred, -fer·ring.**
re′trans·late′, *v.t.,* **-lat·ed, -lat·ing.**
re′trans·mit′, *v.t.,* **-mit·ted, -mit·ting.**

retreat, to withdraw or retreat, esp. hurriedly or in disgrace. —*v.i.* **8.** to withdraw, retire, or draw back, esp. for shelter or seclusion. **9.** to make a retreat. **10.** to slope backward; recede. **11.** to draw or lead back. [ME *retret* < OF, var. of *retrait,* n. use of ptp. of *retraire* to draw back < L *retrahere* (*re-* RE- + *trahere* to draw); see RETRACT[1]] —**re·treat′al,** *adj.* —**re·treat′ing·ness,** *n.* —**re·treat′ive,** *adj.* —**Syn. 2.** departure, withdrawal. **3.** shelter. **8.** leave. See **depart.** —**Ant. 1, 8, 9.** advance.

re·trench (ri trench′), *v.t.* **1.** to cut down, reduce, or diminish; curtail (expenses). **2.** to cut off or remove. **3.** *Mil.* to protect by a retrenchment. —*v.i.* **4.** to economize; reduce expenses. [< F *retrench(er)* (obs. var. of *retrancher*), MF *retrenchier* = *re-* RE- + *trenchier* to TRENCH] —**re·trench′a·ble,** *adj.* —**Syn. 1.** decrease, abridge, cut.

re·trench·ment (ri trench′mənt), *n.* **1.** the act of retrenching; a cutting down or off, as by the reduction of expenses. **2.** *Fort.* an interior work that cuts off a part of a fortification from the rest, and to which a garrison may retreat. [< F *retrenchement*]

re·tri·al (rē′trī′əl, -trīl′), *n.* a second judicial trial of a case that has been tried before.

ret·ri·bu·tion (re′trə byo͞o′shən), *n.* **1.** requital according to merits or deserts, esp. for evil. **2.** something given or inflicted in such requital. **3.** *Theol.* the distribution of rewards and punishments in a future life. [ME *retribucioun* < MF < eccl. L *retribūtiōn-* (s. of *retribūtiō*) = L *retribūt(us)* restored, given back (ptp. of *retribuere;* see RE-, TRIBUTE) + *-iōn-* -ION] —**Syn. 2.** See **revenge.**

re·trib·u·tive (ri trib′yə tiv), *adj.* characterized by retribution: *retributive justice.* Also, **re·trib·u·to·ry** (ri trib′yə tōr′ē, -tôr′ē). [*retribute* (< L *retribūt(us);* see RETRIBUTION) + -IVE] —**re·trib′u·tive·ly,** *adv.*

re·triev·al (ri trē′vəl), *n.* **1.** the act of retrieving. **2.** the chance of recovery or restoration: *lost beyond retrieval.*

re·trieve (ri trēv′), *v.,* **-trieved, -triev·ing,** *n.* —*v.t.* **1.** to recover or regain. **2.** to bring back to a former and better state; restore. **3.** to make amends for. **4.** to make good; repair. **5.** *Hunting.* (of hunting dogs) to fetch (killed or wounded game). **6.** to rescue or save. **7.** to draw back or reel in (a fishing line). **8.** *Computer Technol.* to obtain (data) stored in the memory of a computer. —*v.i.* **9.** *Hunting.* to retrieve game. **10.** to retrieve a fishing line. —*n.* **11.** the act of retrieving; recovery. **12.** the possibility of recovery. [ME *retrev(en)* < tonic s. of MF *retrouver* to find again = *re-* RE- + *trouver* to find; see TROVER] —**re·triev′a·ble,** *adj.* —**Syn. 1.** See **recover.**

Labrador retriever (2 ft. high at shoulder)

re·triev·er (ri trē′vər), *n.* **1.** a person or thing that retrieves. **2.** one of any of several breeds of dogs having a coarse, thick, oily coat, trained to retrieve game.

retro-, a prefix occurring in loan words from Latin meaning "backward" (*retrogress*); on this model, used in the formation of compound words (*retrorocket*). [< L, repr. *retrō* (adv.), backward, back, behind]

ret·ro·act (re′trō akt′), *v.i.* **1.** to act in opposition; react. **2.** to have reference to or influence on past occurrences.

ret·ro·ac·tion (re′trō ak′shən), *n.* action that is opposed or contrary to the preceding action.

ret·ro·ac·tive (re′trō ak′tiv), *adj.* **1.** operative with respect to past occurrences, as a statute; retrospective: *a retroactive law.* **2.** (of a pay raise) effective as of a past date. —**ret′ro·ac′tive·ly,** *adv.*

ret·ro·cede[1] (re′trə sēd′), *v.i.,* **-ced·ed, -ced·ing.** to go back; recede; retire. [< L *retrōcēd(ere)* (to) go back, retire = *retrō-* RETRO- + *cēdere* to go, move; see CEDE] —**ret·ro·ces·sion** (re′trə sesh′ən), **ret′ro·ced′ence,** *n.* —**ret′ro·ces′sive,** *adj.*

ret·ro·cede[2] (re′trə sēd′), *v.t.,* **-ced·ed, -ced·ing.** to cede back. —**ret·ro·ces·sion** (re′trə sesh′ən), **ret′ro·ced′ence,** *n.*

ret·ro·fire (re′trō fīər′), *v.,* **-fired, fir·ing.** —*v.t.* **1.** to ignite (a retrorocket). —*v.i.* **2.** (of a retrorocket) to become ignited.

ret·ro·fit (re′trō fit′, re′trō fit′), *v.,* **-fit·ted** or **-fit, -fit·ting,** *n.* —*v.t.* **1.** to modify equipment (in airplanes, automobiles, etc.) that is already in service using parts developed or made available after the time of original manufacture. —*n.* **2.** something that has been retrofitted. [RETRO- + FIT[1]]

ret·ro·flex (re′trə fleks′), *adj.* **1.** bent backward; exhibiting retroflexion. **2.** *Phonet.* articulated with the tip of the tongue curled upward and back against or near the juncture of the hard and soft palates; cacuminal; cerebral; coronal. Also, **ret·ro·flexed** (re′trō flekst′). [< L *retrōflex(us)* bent back (ptp. of *retrōflectere*)]

ret·ro·flex·ion (re′trə flek′shən), *n.* **1.** a bending backward. **2.** *Pathol.* a bending backward of the body of the uterus upon the cervix. **3.** *Phonet.* **a.** retroflex articulation. **b.** the acoustic quality resulting from retroflex articulation; r-color. Also, **ret′ro·flec′tion.** [< NL **retrōflexiōn-* (s. of **retrōflexiō*) = *retrōflex(us)* RETROFLEX + *-iōn-* -ION]

ret·ro·grade (re′trə grād′), *adj., v.,* **-grad·ed, -grad·ing.** —*adj.* **1.** moving backward; having a backward motion or direction; retiring or retreating. **2.** inverse or reversed, as order. **3.** *Chiefly Biol.* exhibiting degeneration or deterioration. **4.** *Astron.* **a.** moving in an orbit in the direction opposite to that of the earth in its revolution around the sun. **b.** appearing to move on the celestial sphere in the direction opposite to the natural order of the signs of the zodiac, or from east to west. Cf. **direct** (def. 25). **5.** *Music.* proceeding from the last note to the first. **6.** *Archaic.* contrary; opposed. —*v.i.* **7.** to move or go backward; retire or retreat. **8.** *Chiefly Biol.* to decline to a worse condition; degenerate. **9.** *Astron.* to have a retrograde motion. —*v.t.* **10.** *Archaic.* to turn back. [ME < L *retrōgrad(us)* going back < *retrōgradī* = *retrō-* RETRO- + *gradī* to step, go; see GRADE] —**ret·ro·gra·da·tion** (re′trō grā dā′shən), *n.* —**ret′ro·grade′ly,** *adv.* —**ret′ro·grad′ing·ly,** *adv.*

ret·ro·gress (re′trə gres′, re′trə gres′), *v.i.* **1.** to go backward into an earlier and usually worse or more primitive condition. **2.** to move backward. [< L *retrōgress(us)* having gone back or backward, ptp. of *retrōgradī,* collateral form of *retrogradāre;* see RETROGRADE] —**Syn. 1.** revert.

ret·ro·gres·sion (re′trə gresh′ən), *n.* **1.** the act of retrogressing; movement backward. **2.** *Biol.* degeneration; retrograde metamorphosis; passing from a more complex to a simpler structure. [< L *retrōgress(us)* (see RETROGRESS) + -ION]

ret·ro·gres·sive (re′trə gres′iv), *adj.* characterized by retrogression; degenerating. [< L *retrōgress(us)* (see RETROGRESS) + -IVE] —**ret′ro·gres′sive·ly,** *adv.*

ret·ro·len·tal (re′trō len′tᵊl), *adj.* of or pertaining to a position behind the lens of an eye. [RETRO- + *lental* < NL *lent-* (s. of *lens* < L; see LENS) + -AL[1]]

ret·ro·rock·et (re′trō rok′it), *n.* a small auxiliary rocket engine that has its exhaust nozzle pointed toward the direction of flight, for decelerating a larger rocket, separating one stage from another, etc. Also, **ret′ro-rock′et.**

re·trorse (ri trôrs′), *adj.* turned backward. [< L *retrōrs(us),* syncopated form of *retrōversus* bent backward = *retrō-* RETRO- + *versus* (ptp. of *vertere* to turn); see RETROVERSION] —**re·trorse′ly,** *adv.*

ret·ro·spect (re′trə spekt′), *n.* **1.** contemplation of the past; a survey of past time, events, etc. **2. in retrospect,** in looking back on past events. —*v.i.* **3.** to look back in thought; refer back (often fol. by *to*). —*v.t.* **4.** to look back upon; contemplate retrospectively. [< L *retrōspect(us)* having looked back at (ptp. of *retrōspicere*) = *retrō-* RETRO- + *spec(ere)* (to) look, behold + *-t(us)* ptp. suffix]

ret·ro·spec·tion (re′trə spek′shən), *n.* **1.** the act of looking back on things past. **2.** a survey of past events or experiences. [< L *retrōspect(us)* RETROSPECT + -ION]

ret·ro·spec·tive (re′trə spek′tiv), *adj.* **1.** directed to the past; contemplative of past events, experiences, etc. **2.** looking or directed backward. **3.** retroactive, as a statute. —*n.* **4.** an art exhibit showing an entire phase or representative examples of an artist's lifework. [< L *retrōspect(us)* RETROSPECT + -IVE] —**ret′ro·spec′tive·ly,** *adv.*

ret·rous·sé (re′tro͞o sā′; *Fr.* rə tro͞o sā′), *adj.* (esp. of the nose) turned up. [< F, ptp. of *retrousser,* MF = *re-* RE- + *trousser* to run, tuck up; see TRUSS]

ret·ro·ver·sion (re′trə vûr′zhən, -shən), *n.* **1.** a looking or turning back. **2.** the resulting state or condition. **3.** *Pathol.* a tilting or turning backward of an organ or part: *retroversion of the uterus.* [< L *retrōvers(us)* bent backward (*retrō-* RETRO- + *versus* turned, ptp. of *vertere*) + -ION]

ret·ro·vi·rus (re′trə vī′rəs, re′trə vī′-), *n., pl.* **-rus·es.** any of a family of single-stranded RNA viruses having a helical envelope and containing an enzyme that allows for a reversal of genetic transcription, from RNA to DNA rather than the usual DNA to RNA: the family includes the AIDS virus and certain viruses implicated in various cancers. —**ret′ro·vi′ral,** *adj.*

re·try (rē trī′), *v.t.,* **-tried, -try·ing.** to try again, as a judicial case.

re·turn (ri tûrn′), *v.i.* **1.** to go or come back, as to a former place, position, state, etc.: *to return from abroad.* **2.** to revert to a former owner. **3.** to revert or recur, as in thought or discourse: *He returned to his story.* **4.** to make a reply or retort. —*v.t.* **5.** to put, bring, take, give, or send back to the original place, position, etc.: *to return a book to a shelf.* **6.** to send or give back in reciprocation, recompense, or requital: *to return evil for good.* **7.** to reciprocate, repay, or requite (something sent, done, etc.) with something similar. **8.** *Law.* **a.** to give to a judge or official (a statement or a writ of actions done). **b.** to render (a verdict, decision, etc.). **9.** to reflect (light, sound, etc.). **10.** to yield (a profit, revenue, etc.), as in return for labor, expenditure, or investment. **11.** to report or announce officially: *to return a list of members.* **12.** to elect, as to a legislative body: *The voters returned him by a landslide.* **13.** *Cards.* to respond to (a suit led) by a similar lead: *She returned diamonds.* **14.** to turn back or in the reverse direction, as a served ball in tennis. **15.** *Chiefly Archit.* to turn away from or at an angle to the previous line of direction. **16.** *Mil.* to put (a weapon) back into an original holder. —*n.* **17.** the act or fact of returning as by going or coming back or bringing, sending, or giving back. **18.** a recurrence. **19.** reciprocation, repayment, or requital: *profits in return for outlay.* **20.** response or reply. **21.** a person or thing that is returned: *returns of mill goods.* **22.** the gain realized on an exchange of goods. **23.** a yield or profit, as from business or investment. **24.** Also called **tax return.** a statement on an officially prescribed form of income, exemptions, deductions, and tax due for purposes of tax payment or refund. **25.** Usually, **returns.** an official or unofficial report on a count of votes, candidates elected, etc.: *election returns.* **26.** *Brit.* See **return ticket** (def. 2). **27.** *Archit.* **a.** the continuation of a molding, projection, etc., in a different direction. **b.** a side or part that falls away from the front of any straight or flat member or area. **28.** *Sports.* **a.** the act of returning a ball. **b.** the ball so returned. **29.** *Football.* a runback. **30.** *Econ.* yield per unit as compared to the cost per unit involved in a specific industrial process. **31.** *Law.* **a.** the bringing back of a writ, summons, or subpoena, by a sheriff, to the court from which it is issued, with a brief report usually endorsed upon it. **b.** the report or certificate endorsed in such document. **32.** *Cards.* a lead which responds to a partner's lead. **33. returns, a.** merchandise shipped back to a supplier from a retailer or distributor as unsold or unsalable. **b.** merchandise returned to a retailer by a consumer. —*adj.* **34.** of or pertaining to return or returning: *a return trip.* **35.** sent, given, or done in return: *a return shot.* **36.** done or occurring again: *a return engagement of the opera.* **37.** noting a person or thing that is returned or returning to a place: *return cargo.* **38.** changing in direction, doubling or returning on itself: *a return bend in a road.* **39.** used for returning, recirculating, etc.: *the return road; a return pipe.* **40.** (of a game) played in order to provide the loser of an earlier game with the opportunity to win from the same opponent: *return match.* **41.** adequate, necessary, or provided to enable the return of a mailed package or letter to its sender: *return postage.* [ME *retorn(en)* < MF *retorn(er).* See RE-, TURN] —**Syn. 4.** rejoin. **5.** replace. **6.** exchange. **10.** pay, repay.

re·turn·a·ble (ri tûr′nə bəl), *adj.* **1.** that may be returned. **2.** requiring a return, as a writ to the court from which it is issued. [ME *retournable*] —**re·turn′a·bil′i·ty,** *n.*

re·turn′ tick′et, 1. *U.S.* a ticket for the return portion of a trip. 2. *Brit.* a round-trip ticket.

re·tuse (ri to͞os′, -tyo͞os′), *adj.* having an obtuse or rounded apex with a shallow notch, as leaves. [< L *retūs(us)* blunted, dull (ptp. of *retundere*) = *re-* RE- + *tund(ere)* (to) beat, strike (see STUTTER) + *-sus* ptp. suffix]

Retuse leaf

Reu·ben (ro͞o′bin), *n.* 1. the eldest son of Jacob and Leah. 2. one of the 12 tribes of Israel, traditionally descended from him.

Reu′ben sand′wich, a rye-bread sandwich filled, usually, with Swiss cheese, turkey, ham, coleslaw, and Russian dressing. [after Arnold *Reuben* (1883–1970), U.S. restaurateur who first created it]

Reuch·lin (ROIKH′lēn, ROIKH lēn′), *n.* **Jo·hann** (yō′hän), 1455–1522, German humanist scholar.

re·u·ni·fy (rē yo͞o′ni fī′), *v.t.,* **-fied, -fy·ing.** to unify again. —**re′u·ni·fi·ca′tion,** *n.*

re·un·ion (rē yo͞on′yən), *n.* 1. the act of uniting again. 2. the state of being united again. 3. a gathering of relatives, friends, or associates after separation.

Ré·u·nion (rē yo͞on′yən; *Fr.* RĀ Y NYÔN′), *n.* an island in the Indian Ocean, E of Madagascar: a department of France. 382,000 (est. 1964); 970 sq. mi. *Cap.:* St. Denis.

re·un·ion·ist (rē yo͞on′yə nist), *n.* a person who advocates the reunion of the Anglican Church with the Roman Catholic Church. —**re·un′ion·ism,** *n.* —**re·un′ion·is′tic,** *adj.*

re·u·nite (rē′yo͞o nīt′), *v.t., v.i.,* **-nit·ed, -nit·ing.** to unite again, as after separation. [< ML *reūnīt(us)* reunited (ptp. of *reūnīre*): (L *re-* RE- + *ūnītus* joined together; see UNITE[1])] —**re′u·nit′a·ble,** *adj.* —**re′u·nit′er,** *n.*

Reu·ther (ro͞o′thər), *n.* **Walter (Philip),** 1907–70, U.S. labor leader: president of the UAW 1946–70; president of the CIO 1952–55.

rev (rev), *n., v.,* **revved, rev·ving.** *Informal.* —*n.* 1. a revolution in an engine or the like. —*v.t.* 2. to accelerate sharply the speed of (an engine or the like) (often fol. by *up*). —*v.i.* 3. (of an engine or the like) to be revved. [short for REVOLUTION]

Rev., 1. Revelation; Revelations. 2. Reverend.

rev., 1. revenue. 2. reverse. 3. review. 4. revised. 5. revision. 6. revolution. 7. revolving.

Re·val (RĀ′väl), *n.* German name of **Tallinn.**

re·val·u·ate (ri val′yo͞o āt′), *v.t.,* **-at·ed, -at·ing.** to make a new valuation of. —**re·val′u·a′tion,** *n.*

re·val·ue (rē val′yo͞o), *v.t.,* **-ued, -u·ing.** to value again.

re·vamp (rē vamp′), *v.t.* to renovate, redo, or revise. —**re·vamp′er,** *n.* —**re·vamp′ment,** *n.*

re·vanche (ri vänch′), *n.* the policy of a state intent on regaining areas of its original territory that have been lost to other states. [< F: REVENGE] —**re·vanch′ism,** *n.* —**re·vanch′ist,** *n.*

re·veal (ri vēl′), *v.t.* 1. to make known; disclose; divulge: *to reveal a secret.* 2. to lay open to view; display; exhibit. —*n.* 3. an act or instance of revealing; revelation; disclosure. 4. *Archit.* **a.** the part of the jamb of a window or door opening between the outer wall surface and the window or door frame. **b.** the whole jamb of an opening between the outer and inner surfaces of a wall. [ME *revel(en)* < MF *revel(er)* < L *revēlāre* to unveil. See RE-, VEIL] —**re·veal′a·bil′i·ty, re·veal′a·ble·ness,** *n.* —**re·veal′a·ble,** *adj.* —**re·veal·ed·ly** (ri vē′lid lē, -vēld′-), *adv.* —**re·veal′er,** *n.* —**re·veal′ing·ly,** *adv.* —**re·veal′ing·ness,** *n.* —**re·vel·a·tive** (ri vel′ə tiv, rev′ə lā′-), *adj.* —**re·veal′ment,** *n.*

—**Syn. 1, 2.** unveil, announce. REVEAL, DISCLOSE, DIVULGE is to make known something previously concealed or secret. To REVEAL is to uncover as if by drawing away a veil: *The fog lifted and revealed the harbor.* To DISCLOSE is to lay open and thereby invite inspection: *to disclose the plans of a project.* To DIVULGE is to communicate, sometimes to a large number, what was at first intended to be confidential, or secret: *to divulge the terms of a contract.*

revealed′ relig′ion, Christianity based chiefly on the revelations of God to man, esp. as described in the Bible.

re·veal·ment (ri vēl′mənt), *n.* the act of revealing; revelation.

re·veg·e·tate (rē vej′i tāt′), *v.,* **-tat·ed, -tat·ing.** —*v.t.* 1. to provide with vegetation again. —*v.i.* 2. to grow again, as plants. —**re·veg′e·ta′tion,** *n.*

rev·eil·le (rev′ə lē; *Brit.* rə va′lē, -ve′-), *n.* a signal, as of a drum or bugle, sounded early in the morning to alert military personnel for assembly. [< F *réveillez,* pl. impv. of *réveiller* to awaken = *re-* RE- + *éveiller,* OF *esveillier* << L *ēvigilāre* to be vigilant (*ē-* EX-[1] + *vigilāre* to watch; see VIGIL)]

rev·el (rev′əl), *v.,* **-eled, -el·ing** or (*esp. Brit.*) **-elled, -el·ling,** *n.* —*v.i.* 1. to take great pleasure or delight (usually fol. by *in*). 2. to make merry; indulge in boisterous festivities. —*n.* 3. boisterous merrymaking or festivity; revelry. 4. Often, **revels.** an occasion of merrymaking or noisy festivity with dancing, masking, etc. [ME *revel(en)* < MF *revel(er)* (to) raise tumult, make merry < L *rebellāre* to REBEL] —**rev′el·er;** *esp. Brit.,* **rev′el·ler,** *n.* —**rev′el·ment,** *n.*

Re·vel (RE′vel yᵊ), *n.* Russian name of **Tallinn.**

rev·e·la·tion (rev′ə lā′shən), *n.* 1. the act of revealing or disclosing; disclosure. 2. something revealed or disclosed, esp. a striking disclosure, as of something not before realized. 3. *Theol.* **a.** God's disclosure of Himself and His will to His creatures. **b.** an instance of such communication or disclosure. **c.** that which is disclosed. **d.** that which contains such disclosure, as the Bible. 4. (*cap.*) Often, **Revelations.** See **Revelation of St. John the Divine.** [ME *revelacion* < MF < LL *revēlātiōn-* (s. of *revēlātiō*) = L *revēlāt(us)* (ptp. of *revēlāre* to REVEAL) + *-iōn-* -ION] —**rev′e·la′tion·al,** *adj.*

rev·e·la·tion·ist (rev′ə lā′shə nist), *n.* a person who believes in divine revelation.

Revela′tion of St. John′ the Divine′, The, the last book in the New Testament; the Apocalypse.

rev·e·la·tor (rev′ə lā′tər), *n.* a person who makes a revelation. [< LL = L *revēlāt(us)* (see REVELATION) + *-or* -OR[2]]

re·vel·a·to·ry (ri vel′ə tôr′ē, -tōr′ē, rev′ə lə-), *adj.* 1. having the characteristics of a revelation. 2. showing or disclosing (usually fol. by *of*): *a poem revelatory of personal sorrow.* [< L *revēlāt(us)* (see REVELATION) + -ORY[1]]

rev·el·ry (rev′əl rē), *n., pl.* **-ries.** reveling; boisterous festivity. [ME *revelrie*]

rev·e·nant (rev′ə nənt), *n.* 1. a person who returns. 2. a person who returns as a spirit after death; ghost. [< F: ghost, prp. of *revenir* to return = *re-* RE- + *venir* to come < L *venīre;* see -ANT]

re·venge (ri venj′), *v.,* **-venged, -veng·ing,** *n.* —*v.t.* 1. to exact punishment or expiation for a wrong on behalf of, esp. in a resentful or vindictive spirit: *He revenged his dead brother.* 2. to take vengeance for; inflict punishment for: *He revenged his brother's death.* —*v.i.* 3. *Obs.* to take revenge. —*n.* 4. the act of revenging; retaliation for injuries or wrongs. 5. something done in vengeance. 6. the desire to revenge; vindictiveness. 7. an opportunity of retaliation or satisfaction. [ME, *revenge(n)* < MF, OF *reveng(er)* = *re-* RE- + *vengier* to avenge < L *vindicāre;* see VINDICATE] —**re·venge′less,** *adj.* —**re·veng′er,** *n.*

—**Syn. 1.** See **avenge. 4.** requital. REVENGE, REPRISAL, RETRIBUTION, VENGEANCE suggest a punishment, or injury inflicted in return for one received. REVENGE is the carrying out of a bitter desire to injure another for a wrong done to oneself or to those who are felt to be like oneself: *to plot revenge.* REPRISAL, formerly any act of retaliation, is used specifically in warfare for retaliation upon the enemy for his actions: *to make a raid in reprisal for one by the enemy.* RETRIBUTION suggests just or deserved punishment, often without personal motives, for some evil done: *a just retribution for wickedness.* VENGEANCE is usually wrathful, vindictive, furious revenge: *implacable vengeance.*

re·venge·ful (ri venj′fəl), *adj.* full of revenge. —**re·venge′ful·ly,** *adv.* —**re·venge′ful·ness,** *n.* —**Syn.** malevolent, malicious, malignant. See **spiteful.**

rev·e·nue (rev′ən yo͞o′, -ə no͞o′), *n.* 1. the income of a government from taxation and other sources, appropriated for public expenses. 2. the government department charged with the collection of such income. 3. **revenues,** the collective items or amounts of income of a person, a state, etc. 4. the return or yield from any kind of property, service, etc.; income. 5. an amount of money regularly coming in. 6. a particular item or source of income. [ME < MF, n. use of fem. ptp. of *revenir* to come back < L *revenīre* = *re-* RE- + *venīre* to come] —**rev·e·nu·al** (rev′ən yo͞o′əl, -ə no͞o′-, ri ven′yo͞o-), *adj.* —**rev′e·nued′,** *adj.*

rev′enue cut′ter, cutter (def. 4).

rev·e·nu·er (rev′ə no͞o′ər, -nyo͞o′-), *n.* *U.S. Dial.* an agent of the Department of the Treasury whose responsibility is to discover and destroy illegal liquor stills and to arrest the operators.

rev′enue shar′ing, *U.S.* the system of disbursing part of federal tax revenues to state and local governments for their use. —**rev′e·nue-shar′ing,** *adj.*

rev′enue stamp′, a stamp for use as evidence that a governmental tax has been paid.

re·ver·ber·ant (ri vûr′bər ənt), *adj.* reverberating; reechoing. [< L *reverberant-* (s. of *reverberāns,* prp. of *reverberāre*) = *re-* RE- + *verber(āre)* (to) beat, lash (< *verber* whip) + *-ant-* -ANT] —**re·ver′ber·ant·ly,** *adv.*

re·ver·ber·ate (*v.* ri vûr′bə rāt′; *adj.* ri vûr′bə rit), *v.,* **-at·ed, -at·ing,** *adj.* —*v.i.* 1. to reecho or resound. 2. *Physics.* to be reflected many times, as sound waves from the walls of a confined space. 3. to rebound or recoil. —*v.t.* 4. to echo back or reecho (sound). 5. to cast back or reflect (light, heat, etc.). 6. to subject to reflected heat, as in a reverberatory furnace. —*adj.* 7. reverberant. [< L *reverberāt(us)* struck back (ptp. of *reverberāre*). See REVERBERANT, -ATE[1]] —**re·ver′ber·a·tive,** *adj.* —**re·ver′ber·a′tor,** *n.*

re·ver·ber·a·tion (ri vûr′bə rā′shən), *n.* 1. a reechoed sound. 2. the fact of being reverberated or reflected. 3. that which is reverberated. 4. the act or an instance of reverberating. 5. *Physics.* the persistence of a sound after its source has stopped, caused by multiple reflection of the sound within a closed space. 6. the act or process of subjecting something to reflected heat, as in a reverberatory furnace. [ME *reverberacioun* < ML *reverberātiōn-* (s. of *reverberātiō*)]

reverbera′tion time′, the time it takes for a sound made in a room to diminish by 60 decibels.

Reverberatory furnace (Section)

re·ver·ber·a·to·ry (ri vûr′bər ə tôr′ē, -tōr′ē), *adj., n., pl.* **-ries.** —*adj.* 1. characterized or produced by reverberation. 2. noting a furnace, kiln, or the like, in which the fuel is not in direct contact with the ore, metal, etc., to be heated, but furnishes a flame that plays over the material, esp. by being deflected downward from the roof. —*n.* 3. any device, as a furnace, embodying reverberation.

re·vere[1] (ri vēr′), *v.t.,* **-vered, -ver·ing.** to regard with respect tinged with awe; venerate. [< L *rever(ērī)* = *re-* RE- + *verērī* to stand in awe of, fear, feel reverence] —**re·ver′a·ble,** *adj.* —**re·ver′er,** *n.* —**Syn.** respect, honor, adore.

re·vere[2] (ri vēr′), *n.* revers.

Re·vere (ri vēr′), *n.* 1. **Paul,** 1735–1818, American silversmith and patriot, famous for his night horseback ride, April 18, 1775, to warn Massachusetts colonists of the coming of British troops. 2. a city on Massachusetts Bay, near Boston: seaside resort. 43,159 (1970).

rev·er·ence (rev′ər əns, rev′rəns), *n., v.,* **-enced, -enc·ing.** —*n.* 1. a feeling or attitude of deep respect tinged with awe; veneration. 2. the outward manifestation of this

re·twist, *v.*
re·type′, *v.t.,* -typed, -typ·ing.
re′up·hol′ster, *v.t.*
re′us·a·bil′i·ty, *n.*
re·us′a·ble, *adj.;* -ness, *n.*
re·use′, *v.,* -used, -us·ing, *n.*
re·use′a·ble, *adj.;* -ness, *n.*
re′u·ti·li·za′tion, *n.*
re·u′ti·lize′, *v.t.,* -lized, -liz·ing.
re·var′nish, *v.t.*

feeling: *to pay reverence.* **3.** a gesture indicative of deep respect; an obeisance, bow, or curtsy. **4.** the state of being revered. **5.** (*cap.*) a title used in addressing or mentioning a clergyman (usually prec. by *your* or *his*). **—*v.t.*** **6.** to regard or treat with reverence; venerate. [ME < L *reverentia* respect, fear, awe] **—rev′er·enc·er,** *n.* **—Syn. 1.** awe.

rev·er·end (rev′ər ənd, rev′rənd), *adj.* **1.** (*often cap.*) an epithet of respect applied to or prefixed to the name (of a clergyman). **2.** worthy to be revered; entitled to reverence. **3.** pertaining to or characteristic of the clergy. **—*n.*** **4.** a clergyman. [late ME < L *reverend(us)* worthy to be revered, ger. of *reverērī* to REVERE[1]] **—rev′er·end·ship′,** *n.*

rev·er·ent (rev′ər ənt, rev′rənt), *adj.* feeling, exhibiting, or characterized by reverence; deeply respectful: *a reverent greeting.* [ME < L *reverent-* (s. of *reverēns*), prp. of *reverērī* to REVERE[1]; see -ENT] **—rev′er·ent·ly,** *adv.*

rev·er·en·tial (rev′ə ren′shəl), *adj.* of the nature of or characterized by reverence; reverent: *reverential awe.* **—rev·er·en·ti·al·i·ty** (rev′ə ren′shē al′i tē), **rev′er·en′tial·ness,** *n.* **—rev′er·en′tial·ly,** *adv.*

rev·er·ie (rev′ə rē), *n.* **1.** a state of dreamy meditation or fanciful musing: *lost in reverie.* **2.** a daydream. **3.** a fantastic, visionary, or impractical idea. **4.** *Music.* an instrumental composition of a vague and dreamy character. Also, **revery.** [< F *rêverie* < *rêver* to speak wildly]

re·vers (ri vēr′, -vâr′), *n., pl.* **-vers** (-vērz′, -vârz′). **1.** a part of a garment turned back to show the lining or facing, as a lapel. **2.** a trimming simulating such a part. **3.** the facing used. Also, **revere.** [< F; see REVERSE]

re·ver·sal (ri vûr′səl), *n.* **1.** the act of reversing. **2.** an instance of this. **3.** the state of being reversed. **4.** *Law.* the overthrow of a decision.

re·verse (ri vûrs′), *adj., n., v.,* **-versed, -vers·ing.** **—*adj.*** **1.** opposite or contrary in position, direction, order, or character. **2.** acting in a manner opposite or contrary to that which is usual, as an appliance or apparatus. **3.** having the back or rear part toward the observer: *the reverse side of a fabric.* **4.** pertaining to or producing movement in a mechanism opposite to that made under ordinary running conditions. **5.** noting the printed matter in which the normally white page of a book appears black, and vice versa. **6.** noting or pertaining to an image like that seen in a mirror; backward; reversed. **—*n.*** **7.** the opposite or contrary of something. **8.** the back or rear of anything. **9.** *Numis.* **a.** the side of a coin, medal, etc., that does not bear the principal design (opposed to *obverse*). **b.** the side of an ancient coin that was struck by the upper die. **10.** an adverse change of fortune; a misfortune, check, or defeat: *to meet with an unexpected reverse.* **11.** *Mach.* **a.** the condition of being reversed: *to throw an engine into reverse.* **b.** a reversing mechanism. **—*v.t.*** **12.** to turn in an opposite position; transpose. **13.** to turn inside out or upside down. **14.** to turn in the opposite direction; send on the opposite course. **15.** to turn in the opposite order: *to reverse the process of evolution.* **16.** to alter to the opposite in character or tendency; change completely. **17.** to revoke or annul (a decree, judgment, etc.): *to reverse a verdict.* **18.** to change the direction of running of (a mechanism). **19.** to cause (a mechanism) to run in a direction opposite to that in which it commonly runs. **20.** *Print.* to print as a reverse. **—*v.i.*** **21.** to turn or move in the opposite or contrary direction, as in dancing. **22.** (of a mechanism) to be reversed. **23.** to shift into reverse gear. [(adj., n.) ME *revers* < MF < L *revers(us)*, ptp. of *revertere* to REVERT; (v.) ME *reverse(n)* < MF *revers(er)* < LL *reversāre,* freq. of *revertere,* as above] **—re·vers·ed·ly** (ri vûr′sid lē, -vûrst′lē), *adv.* **—re·verse′ly,** *adv.* **—re·vers′er,** *n.*
—Syn. 1. converse. See **opposite. 7.** converse, counterpart. **10.** mishap, misadventure, affliction. **12.** REVERSE, INVERT agree in meaning to change into a contrary position, order, or relation. To REVERSE is to place or move something so that it is facing in the opposite direction from the one faced previously: *to reverse from right to left; to reverse a decision.* To INVERT is to turn upside down: *to invert a stamp in printing; to invert a bowl over a plate.* **17.** repeal, rescind.

reverse′ discrimina′tion, the unfair treatment of majority groups (whites, men, etc.) resulting from preference, as in college admissions or employment practices, intended to remedy earlier discrimination against minorities (blacks, women, etc.).

re·vers·i·ble (ri vûr′sə bəl), *adj.* **1.** capable of being reversed or of reversing. **2.** capable of being changed back to a more desirable state; correctable. **3.** (of a fabric) woven or printed so that either side may be exposed. **4.** (of a garment) able to be worn with either side out. **—*n.*** **5.** a reversible fabric or garment. **—re·vers′i·bil′i·ty, re·vers′i·ble·ness,** *n.* **—re·vers′i·bly,** *adv.*

re·ver·sion (ri vûr′zhən, -shən), *n.* **1.** the act of reverting; return to a former practice, belief, condition, etc. **2.** the act of reversing. **3.** the state of being reversed. **4.** *Biol.* **a.** a reappearance of ancestral characters that have been absent in intervening generations. **b.** a return to an earlier or primitive type; atavism. **5.** *Law.* **a.** the returning of an estate to the grantor or his heirs after the interest granted expires. **b.** an estate that so returns. **c.** the right of succeeding to an estate. [ME < L *reversiōn-* (s. of *reversiō*) a turning back] **—re·ver′sion·al·ly,** *adv.*

re·ver·sion·ar·y (ri vûr′zhə ner′ē, -shə-), *adj.* of, pertaining to, or involving a reversion. Also, **re·ver′sion·al.**

re·ver·sion·er (ri vûr′zhə nər, -shə-), *n.* *Law.* a person who possesses a reversion.

re·vert (ri vûrt′), *n.* **1.** a person or thing that reverts. **—*v.i.*** **2.** to return to a former habit, practice, belief, condition, etc. **3.** to go back in thought or discussion. **4.** *Biol.* to return to an earlier or primitive type. **5.** *Law.* to go back to or return to the former owner or his heirs. [ME *revert(en)* < legal L *revertere* to turn back = *re-* RE- + *vertere* to turn] **—re·vert′i·bil′i·ty,** *n.* **—re·vert′i·ble,** *adj.* **—re·ver′tive,** *adj.* **—re·ver′tive·ly,** *adv.* **—Syn. 2, 4.** retrogress.

rev·er·y (rev′ə rē), *n., pl.* **-er·ies.** reverie.

re·vest (rē vest′), *v.t.* **1.** to vest (as a person) again, as with ownership or office; reinvest; reinstate. **2.** to vest (powers, office, etc.) again. **—*v.i.*** **3.** to become vested again in a person; go back again to a former owner. [ME *revest(en)* < eccl. L *revestīre* to reclothe]

re·vet (ri vet′), *v.t.,* **-vet·ted, -vet·ting.** to face, as an embankment, with masonry or other material. [< F *revêt(ir)*, lit., to reclothe. See REVEST]

re·vet·ment (ri vet′mənt), *n.* **1.** a facing of masonry or the like, esp. for protecting an embankment. **2.** an ornamental facing of marble, face brick, tiles, etc. [< F *revêtement*]

re·view (ri vyo͞o′), *n.* **1.** a critical article or report on a recent book, play, recital, or the like; critique; evaluation. **2.** a periodical publication containing articles on current events, books, art, etc.: *a literary review.* **3.** a second or repeated view of something. **4.** the process of going over a subject again in study or recitation in order to fix it in the memory or summarize the facts. **5.** an exercise designed or intended for study of this kind. **6.** an inspection, esp. a formal inspection of any military force, parade, or the like. **7.** a viewing of the past; contemplation or consideration of past events, circumstances, or facts. **8.** a general survey of something, esp. in words; a report or account of something. **9.** a judicial reexamination, as by a higher court, of the decision or proceedings in a case. **10.** *Theat.* revue. **—*v.t.*** **11.** to view, look at, or look over again. **12.** to go over (lessons, studies, work, etc.) in review. **13.** to inspect, esp. formally or officially. **14.** to look back upon; view retrospectively. **15.** to survey mentally: *to review the situation.* **16.** to present a survey of in speech or writing. **17.** to discuss (a book, play, etc.) in a critical review. **18.** *Law.* to reexamine judicially. **—*v.i.*** **19.** to write reviews. [< MF *revue,* n. use of fem. ptp. of *revoir* to see again < L *revidēre* = *re-* RE- + *vidēre;* see VIEW]
—Syn. 1. REVIEW, CRITICISM imply carefully examining something, making a judgment, and putting the judgment into (usually) written form. The words are freely interchanged when referring to motion pictures or theater, but REVIEW implies a somewhat less formal approach than CRITICISM in referring to literary works: *movie reviews; play reviews; book reviews.* Thus, one expects to find REVIEWS in newspapers and popular periodicals; CRITICISM is confined to more learned periodicals and books. **3.** reconsideration, reexamination. **17.** criticize.

re·view·al (ri vyo͞o′əl), *n.* the act of reviewing.

re·view·er (ri vyo͞o′ər), *n.* **1.** a person who reviews. **2.** a person who writes reviews of new books, plays, etc.

re·vile (ri vīl′), *v.,* **-viled, -vil·ing.** **—*v.t.*** **1.** to address or speak of abusively. **—*v.i.*** **2.** to speak abusively. [ME *revile(n)* < MF *reviler*] **—re·vile′ment,** *n.* **—re·vil′er,** *n.* **—re·vil′ing·ly,** *adv.* **—Syn. 1.** abuse, berate, disparage.

re·vis·al (ri vī′zəl), *n.* the act of revising; revision.

re·vise (ri vīz′), *v.,* **-vised, -vis·ing,** *n.* **—*v.t.*** **1.** to amend or alter. **2.** to alter after one or more typings or printings. **—*n.*** **3.** an act of revising. **4.** a revised form of something; revision. **5.** *Print.* a proof sheet taken after alterations have been made. [< L *revise(re)* (to) look back at, revisit, freq. of *revidēre* to see again; see REVIEW] **—re·vis′a·bil′i·ty,** *n.* **—re·vis′a·ble, re·vis′i·ble,** *adj.* **—re·vis′er, re·vi′sor,** *n.*
—Syn. 1. change; emend, correct.

Revised′ Stand′ard Ver′sion, a revision of the Bible, based on the American Standard Version and the King James Version, prepared by American scholars, published in its completed form in 1952. *Abbr.:* RSV

Revised′ Ver′sion of the Bi′ble, a recension of the Authorized Version, prepared by British and American scholars, the Old Testament being published in 1885, and the New Testament in 1881. Also called **Revised′ Ver′sion.**

re·vi·sion (ri vizh′ən), *n.* **1.** the act or work of revising. **2.** a process of revising. **3.** a revised form or version, as of a book. [< LL *revīsiōn-* (s. of *revīsiō*) = L *revīs(us)* (see REVISE) + *-iōn-* -ION] **—re·vi′sion·al, re·vi′sion·ar′y,** *adj.*

re·vi·sion·ism (ri vizh′ə niz′əm), *n.* **1.** (among Marxists) any departure from a Marxist doctrine, theory, or practice. **2.** the advocacy or approval of revision.

re·vi·sion·ist (ri vizh′ə nist), *n.* **1.** an advocate of revision, esp. of some political or religious doctrine. **2.** a reviser. **3.** a supporter of revisionism. **—*adj.*** **4.** of or pertaining to revisionists or their doctrines.

re·vi·so·ry (ri vī′zə rē), *adj.* pertaining to or for the purpose of revision.

re·vi·tal·ise (rē vīt′əlīz′), *v.t.,* **-ised, -is·ing.** *Chiefly Brit.* revitalize. **—re·vi′tal·i·sa′tion,** *n.*

re·vi·tal·ize (rē vīt′əlīz′), *v.t.,* **-ized, -iz·ing.** **1.** to give new life to. **2.** to give new vitality or vigor to. **—re·vi′tal·i·za′tion,** *n.*

re·viv·al (ri vī′vəl), *n.* **1.** the act of reviving. **2.** the state of being revived. **3.** restoration to life, consciousness, vigor, strength, etc. **4.** restoration to use, acceptance, or currency. **5.** a new production of an old play. **6.** a showing of an old motion picture. **7.** an awakening of interest in religion. **8.** an evangelistic service for the purpose of effecting a religious awakening. **9.** *Law.* the reestablishment of legal force and effect.

re·viv·al·ism (ri vī′və liz′əm), *n.* **1.** the tendency to revive what belongs to the past. **2.** the form of religious activity that manifests itself in revivals.

re·viv·al·ist (ri vī′və list), *n.* **1.** a person who revives former customs, methods, etc. **2.** a person who promotes or holds religious revivals. **—re·viv′al·is′tic,** *adj.*

Reviv′al of Learn′ing, the Renaissance in its relation to learning, esp. in literature **(Reviv′al of Lit′erature** or **Reviv′al of Let′ters).**

re·vive (ri vīv′), *v.,* **-vived, -viv·ing.** **—*v.t.*** **1.** to activate, set in motion, or take up again; renew. **2.** to make operative or valid again. **3.** to bring back into notice, use, or currency. **4.** to produce (an old play) again. **5.** to show (an old motion picture). **6.** to restore to life or consciousness. **7.** to quicken or renew in the mind; bring back. **—*v.i.*** **8.** to return to life, consciousness, vigor, strength, or a flourishing condition. **9.** to be quickened, restored, or renewed, as hope, memories, etc. **10.** to return to notice, use, or currency, as a subject, practice, doctrine, etc. **11.** to become operative or valid again. [ME *revive(n)* < L *revīvere* to live again = *re-* RE- +

re′ver·i·fi·ca′tion, *n.*
re·ver′i·fy′, *v.t.,* **-fied, -fy·ing.**
re·vict′ual, *v.,* **-ualed, -ual·ing** or (*esp. Brit.*) **-ualled, -ual·ling.**
re·vin′di·cate′, *v.t.,* **-cat·ed, -cat·ing.**
re′vin·di·ca′tion, *n.*
re·vi′o·late′, *v.t.* **-lat·ed, -lat·ing.**
re′vi·o·la′tion, *n.*

vīvere to live, be alive] —**re·viv′a·bil′i·ty,** *n.* —**re·viv′a·ble,** *adj.* —**re·viv′a·bly,** *adv.* —**re·viv′er,** *n.* —**re·viv′ing·ly,** *adv.* —**Syn. 1, 2.** reactivate. **6.** resuscitate.

re·viv·i·fy (ri viv′ə fī′), *v.t.*, **-fied, -fy·ing.** to restore to life; give new life to; revive; reanimate. [< F *révivifi(er)* < LL *revīvificāre.* See RE-, VIVIFY] —**re·viv·i·fi·ca·tion** (ri viv′ə fə kā′shən), *n.*

rev·i·vis·cence (rev′ə vis′əns), *n.* the act or state of being revived; revival; reanimation. Also, **rev′i·vis′cen·cy.** [< L *revīvisc(ere)* (to) come to life again (*re-* RE- + *vīviscere,* inceptive of *vīvere* to live) + -ENCE] —**rev′i·vis′cent,** *adj.*

rev·o·ca·ble (rev′ə kə bəl), *adj.* capable of being revoked. Also, **re·vok·a·ble** (ri vō′kə bəl). [late ME < L *revocābil(is)*] —**rev′o·ca·bil′i·ty, rev′o·ca·ble·ness,** *n.* —**rev′o·ca·bly,** *adv.*

rev·o·ca·tion (rev′ə kā′shən), *n.* **1.** the act of revoking; annulment. **2.** the state of being revoked. [ME *revocacion* < L *revocātiōn-* (s. of *revocātiō*) a calling back = *revocāt(us)* (ptp. of *revocāre* to REVOKE) + *-iōn-* -ION] —**rev·o·ca·tive** (rev′ə kā′tiv, ri vok′ə-), **rev·o·ca·to·ry** (rev′ə kə tôr′ē, -tōr′ē), *adj.*

re·voice (rē vois′), *v.t.*, **-voiced, -voic·ing.** to voice again or in return; echo.

re·voke (ri vōk′), *v.*, **-voked, -vok·ing,** *n.* —*v.t.* **1.** to take back or withdraw; annul, cancel, or reverse; rescind or repeal: *to revoke a decree.* **2.** *Archaic.* to bring or summon back. —*v.i.* **3.** *Cards.* to fail to follow suit when possible and required; renege. —*n.* **4.** *Cards.* an act or instance of revoking. [ME *revoke(n)* < L *revocāre* to call again = *re-* RE- + *vocāre* to call] —**re·vok′er,** *n.* —**re·vok′ing·ly,** *adv.*

re·volt (ri vōlt′), *v.i.* **1.** to break away from or rise against constituted authority, as by open rebellion; rebel; mutiny. **2.** to feel or demonstrate a rebellious attitude: *to revolt against parental authority.* **3.** to turn away in mental rebellion, utter disgust, or abhorrence: *He revolts from eating meat.* **4.** to feel horror or disgust: *I revolt at the sight of blood.* —*v.t.* **5.** to affect with disgust or abhorrence. —*n.* **6.** the act of revolting; an insurrection or rebellion. **7.** aversion, disgust, or loathing. **8.** the state of those revolting: *to be in revolt.* [< MF *revolt(er)* (v.) < It *rivoltare* to turn around < VL **revolvitāre,* freq. of L *revolvere* to roll back, unroll, REVOLVE] —**re·volt′er,** *n.*
—**Syn. 6.** REVOLT, INSURRECTION, REBELLION, REVOLUTION refer to risings in active resistance against civil or governmental authority. A REVOLT is a casting off of allegiance or subjection to rulers or authorities; it is usually a vigorous outbreak, whether brief or prolonged, and may arise from general turbulence or from opposition to tyranny or oppression: *a revolt because of unjust government.* An INSURRECTION may be local or general, and is often unorganized: *a popular insurrection in one province.* A REBELLION is on a larger scale than either of the foregoing, is generally better organized, and has for its object the securing of independence or the overthrow of government: *a widespread rebellion.* A REVOLUTION is a rebellion or any public movement (with or without actual fighting) that succeeds in overthrowing one government or political system and establishing another: *the American Revolution.* Accordingly, it may be used metaphorically of any development that upsets the established order: *the Industrial Revolution.*

re·volt·ing (ri vōl′ting), *adj.* **1.** disgusting; repulsive. **2.** rebellious. —**re·volt′ing·ly,** *adv.*

rev·o·lute (rev′ə lo͞ot′), *adj.* *Biol.* rolled backward or downward; rolled backward at the tip or margin, as a leaf. [< L *revolūt(us),* ptp. of *revolvere* to REVOLVE]

A, Revolute margined leaf; B, Transverse section

rev·o·lu·tion (rev′ə lo͞o′shən), *n.* **1.** a forcible overthrow of an established government or political system by the people governed. **2.** a complete, pervasive, usually radical change in something, often one made relatively quickly: *a revolution in architecture; a social revolution caused by automation.* **3.** a procedure or course, as if in a circuit, back to a starting point. **4.** a single turn of this kind. **5.** *Mech.* **a.** a turning around or rotating, as on an axis. **b.** a moving in a circular or curving course, as about a central point. **c.** a single cycle in such a course. **6.** *Astron.* **a.** (not in technical use) the turning of a heavenly body on its axis. **b.** the orbiting of one heavenly body around another. **c.** a single course of such movement. Cf. **rotation** (def. 2). **7.** a cycle of events in time or in a recurring period of time. **8.** *Geol.* a time of world-wide orogeny and mountain building. [ME *revolucion* < LL *revolūtiōn-* (s. of *revolūtiō*) = *revolūt(us)* (see REVOLUTE) + *-iōn-* -ION] —**Syn. 1.** insurrection, rebellion. See **revolt. 4.** cycle, circuit, round, rotation.

rev·o·lu·tion·ar·y (rev′ə lo͞o′shə ner′ē), *adj., n., pl.* **-ar·ies.** —*adj.* **1.** pertaining to, characterized by, or of the nature of a revolution, or a complete or marked change. **2.** productive of or furthering radical change: *a revolutionary discovery.* **3.** revolving. —*n.* **4.** a revolutionist. —**rev′o·lu′tion·ar′i·ly,** *adv.*

Revolu′tionary cal′endar, the calendar of the first French republic, adopted in 1793 and abandoned in 1805.

Revolu′tionary War′. See **American Revolution.**

rev·o·lu·tion·ise (rev′ə lo͞o′shə nīz′), *v.t.*, **-ised, -is·ing.** *Chiefly Brit.* revolutionize. —**rev′o·lu′tion·is′er,** *n.*

rev·o·lu·tion·ist (rev′ə lo͞o′shə nist), *n.* a person who advocates or takes part in a revolution.

rev·o·lu·tion·ize (rev′ə lo͞o′shə nīz′), *v.t.*, **-ized, -iz·ing.** **1.** to bring about a revolution in; effect a radical change in. **2.** to subject to a political revolution. Also, *esp. Brit.,* **revolutionise.** —**rev′o·lu′tion·iz′er,** *n.*

re·volve (ri volv′), *v.*, **-volved, -volv·ing.** —*v.i.* **1.** to turn around or rotate, as on an axis. **2.** to move in a circular or curving course or orbit. **3.** to proceed or occur in a round or cycle; recur. **4.** to be thought about or considered. —*v.t.* **5.** to cause to turn around, as on an axis. **6.** to cause to move in a circular or curving course, as about a central point. **7.** to think about; consider. [ME *revolve(n)* < L *revolv(ere)* (to) roll back = *re-* RE- + *volvere* to roll, turn round. See WALLOW] —**re·volv′a·ble,** *adj.* —**re·volv′a·bly,** *adv.*
—**Syn. 1.** See **turn. 2.** orbit, circle. **7.** ponder, study.

re·volv·er (ri vol′vər), *n.* **1.** a pistol having a revolving chambered cylinder for holding a number of cartridges that may be discharged in succession. **2.** a person or thing that revolves.

Revolver

re·volv·ing (ri vol′ving), *adj.* able to revolve: *a revolving table top; a revolving stage.* —**re·volv′ing·ly,** *adv.*

revolv′ing cred′it, credit automatically available up to a predetermined limit while payments are periodically made.

revolv′ing door′, an entrance door usually consisting of four rigid leaves set in the form of a cross and rotating about a central, vertical pivot.

revolv′ing fund′, any loan fund intended to be maintained by the repayment of past loans.

re·vue (ri vyo͞o′), *n.* **1.** a form of theatrical entertainment in which recent events, popular fads, etc., are parodied. **2.** any group of skits, dances, and songs. Also, **review.** [< F: REVIEW] —**re·vu′ist,** *n.*

re·vul·sion (ri vul′shən), *n.* **1.** a strong feeling of repugnance, distaste, or dislike. **2.** a sudden and violent change of feeling or response in sentiment, taste, etc. **3.** *Med.* the diminution of morbid action in one part of the body by irritation in another. **4.** the act of drawing something back or away. **5.** the fact of being so drawn. [< L *revulsiōn-* (s. of *revulsiō*) a tearing away = *revuls(us)* (ptp. of *revellere* to tear away = *re-* RE- + *vellere* to pluck) + *-iōn-* -ION] —**re·vul′sion·ar′y,** *adj.* —**Syn. 1.** disgust, loathing, aversion.

re·vul·sive (ri vul′siv), *adj.* **1.** causing or tending toward revulsion. —*n.* **2.** something that causes revulsion. [< L *revuls(us)* (see REVULSION) + -IVE] —**re·vul′sive·ly,** *adv.*

Rev. Ver., Revised Version (of the Bible).

re·ward (ri wôrd′), *n.* **1.** something given or received in return for service, merit, etc. **2.** a sum of money offered for the detection or capture of a criminal, the recovery of lost property, etc. —*v.t.* **3.** to recompense or requite (a person or animal) for service, merit, achievement, etc. **4.** to make return for or requite (service, merit, etc.); recompense. [ME *reward(en)* < ONF *reward(er)* (to) look at, var. of OF *regarder;* see REGARD] —**re·ward′a·ble,** *adj.* —**re·ward′a·ble·ness,** *n.* —**re·ward′a·bly,** *adv.* —**re·ward′er,** *n.* —**re·ward′less,** *adj.*
—**Syn. 1.** desert, pay, remuneration; premium, bonus. REWARD, PRIZE, RECOMPENSE imply something given or done in return for good or as compensation. A REWARD may refer to something abstract or concrete: *a 50-dollar reward; Her devotion was his reward.* PRIZE refers to something concrete offered as a reward of merit, or to be contested for and given to the winner: *to win a prize for an essay.* A RECOMPENSE is something given or done for acts performed, services rendered, etc.; or it may be something given in compensation for loss or injury suffered, etc.: *Renown was his principal recompense for years of hard work.* **3.** compensate, pay, remunerate.

re·wind (rē wīnd′), *v.t.*, **-wound** or (*Rare*) **-wind·ed; -wind·ing.** to wind again.

re·wire (rē wīər′), *v.t.*, **-wired, -wir·ing.** to provide with new wiring: *to rewire the electrical system in a house.* —**re·wir′a·ble,** *adj.*

re·word (rē wûrd′), *v.t.* **1.** to put into other words; paraphrase. **2.** to repeat.

re·write (*v.* rē rīt′; *n.* rē′rīt′), *v.*, **-wrote, -writ·ten, -writ·ing,** *n.* —*v.t.* **1.** to write in a different form or manner; revise. **2.** to write again. **3.** *U.S.* to write (news submitted by a reporter) for inclusion in a newspaper. —*n.* **4.** *U.S.* the news story written. **5.** something written in a different form or manner; revision. —**re·writ′er,** *n.*

rex (reks; *Eng.* reks), *n., pl.* **re·ges** (re′ges; *Eng.* rē′jēz). *Latin.* king.

Rey·kja·vik (rā′kyə vēk′), *n.* a seaport in and the capital of Iceland, in the SW part. 84,856.

Reyn·ard (ren′ərd, rā′närd), *n.* a name given to the fox, originally in the medieval beast epic, *Reynard the Fox.* Also, **Renard.**

Rey·naud (re nō′), *n.* **Paul** (pôl), 1898–1966, French statesman: premier 1940.

Reyn·olds (ren′əldz), *n.* **Sir Joshua,** 1723–92, English painter.

rf, *Music.* rinforzando. Also, **rfz**

rf., *Baseball.* right fielder.

r.f., **1.** radio frequency. **2.** range finder. **3.** *Baseball.* right field.

r.f.b., *Football.* right fullback. Also, **R.F.B.**

RFC, See **Reconstruction Finance Corporation.** Also, **R.F.C.**

RFD, See **rural free delivery.** Also, **R.F.D.**

r.g., *Football.* right guard.

Rh, *Chem.* rhodium.

Rh, *Biochem.* See **Rh factor.** Also, **Rh.**

R.H., Royal Highness.

r.h., right hand.

rhab·do·man·cy (rab′də man′sē), *n.* divination by means of a rod or wand, esp. in discovering ores, springs of

re·wake′, *v.,* **-waked** or **-woke, -wak·ing.**	**re·weave′,** *v.,* **-wove** or (*Rare*) **-weaved, -weav·ing.**	**re·win′,** *v.t.,* **-won** or (*Obs.*) **-wan; -won, -win·ning.**	**re·wound′,** *v.t.*
re·wak′en, *v.*	**re·weigh′,** *v.*	**re·work′,** *v.,* **-worked** or **-wrought, -work·ing.**	**re·wrap′,** *v.,* **-wrapped** or **-wrapt, -wrap·ping.**
re·warm′, *v.*	**re·weld′,** *v.*		**re·zone′,** *v.t.,* **-zoned, -zon·ing.**
re·wash′, *v.*	**re·wid′en,** *v.*		

water, etc. [< LGk *rhabdomanteía* = *rhábdo(s)* rod, wand + *manteía* -MANCY] —**rhab′do·man′tist,** *n.*

rha·chis (rā′kis), *n., pl.* **rha·chis·es, rha·chi·des** (rak′i-dēz′, rā′ki-). rachis.

Rhad·a·man·thys (rad′ə man′thəs), *n. Class. Myth.* a son of Zeus and Europa, rewarded for the justice he exemplified on earth by being made a judge in the lower world after his death. Also, **Rhad′a·man′thus.**

Rhae·ti·a (rē′shē ə), *n.* an ancient Roman province in S central Europe.

Rhae·tian (rē′shən), *adj.* **1.** of or pertaining to Rhaetia. **2.** Rhaeto-Romanic. **3.** *Geol.* Rhaetic. —*n.* **4.** Rhaeto-Romanic. Also, **Rhetian.**

Rhae′tian Alps′, a chain of the Alps in E Switzerland and W Austria. Highest peak, Mt. Bernina, 13,295 ft.

Rhae·tic (rē′tik), *adj. Geol.* of or pertaining to certain strata, extensively developed in the Rhaetian Alps, having features of the Triassic and Jurassic but generally classed as belonging to the former. Also, **Rhetic.** [< L *Rhaetic(us).* See RHAETIA, -IC]

Rhae·to-Ro·man·ic (rē′tō rō man′ik), *n.* **1.** a Romance language consisting of Friulian, Tyrolese Ladin, and the Romansh dialects. —*adj.* **2.** of or pertaining to Rhaeto-Romanic. Also, **Rhae′to-Ro·mance′, Rhaetian.** [*rhaeto-* (repr. L *rhaetus* Rhaetian) + ROMANIC (modeled on G *Rätoromanisch*)]

-rhagia, var. of **-rrhagia.** Also, **-rhage, -rhagy.**

rham·na·ceous (ram nā′shəs), *adj.* belonging to the *Rhamnaceae,* or buckthorn family of plants. [< Gk *rhámn(os)* thorn, prickly shrub + -ACEOUS]

rhap·sod·ic (rap sod′ik), *adj.* **1.** pertaining to, characteristic of, or of the nature or form of rhapsody. **2.** extravagantly enthusiastic; ecstatic. Also, **rhap·sod′i·cal.** [< Gk *rhapsōidik(ós)*] —**rhap·sod′i·cal·ly,** *adv.*

rhap·so·dise (rap′sə dīz′), *v.i., v.t.,* **-dised, -dis·ing.** *Chiefly Brit.* rhapsodize.

rhap·so·dist (rap′sə dist), *n.* **1.** a person who rhapsodizes. **2.** (in ancient Greece) a person who recited epic poetry, esp. professionally. [< Gk *rhapsōid(ós)* rhapsodist (*rhaps-,* var. s. of *rháptein* to stitch, + *-ōid(e)* ODE + *-os* n. suffix) + -IST] —**rhap′so·dis′tic,** *adj.*

rhap·so·dize (rap′sə dīz′), *v.,* **-dized, -diz·ing.** —*v.i.* **1.** to speak or write rhapsodies. **2.** to talk with extravagant enthusiasm. —*v.t.* **3.** to recite as a rhapsody. Also, *esp. Brit.,* **rhapsodise.**

rhap·so·dy (rap′sə dē), *n., pl.* **-dies. 1.** an exalted or exaggerated expression of feeling or enthusiasm. **2.** an epic poem, or a part of such a poem suitable for recitation at one time. **3.** a similar piece of modern literature. **4.** *Music.* an instrument composition irregular in form and suggestive of improvisation. [< L *rhapsōdia* < Gk *rhapsōidía* recital of epic poetry = *rhapsōid(ós)* RHAPSODIST + *-ia* -Y[3]]

rhat·a·ny (rat′ənē), *n., pl.* **-nies. 1.** either of two South American leguminous shrubs of the genus *Krameria, K. tiandra* (**knotty rhatany** or **Peruvian rhatany**), or *K. argentea* (**Brazilian rhatany** or **Pará rhatany**). **2.** the root of either of these plants, used esp. as an astringent and tonic. [< NL *rhatāni(a)* << Quechua *ratánya*]

Rhea, *Rhea americana* (Height 4 to 5 ft.; length 4¼ ft.)

r.h.b., *Football.* right halfback. Also, **R.H.B.**

Rhe·a (rē′ə), *n.* **1.** *Class. Myth.* a Titaness, the daughter of Uranus and Gaea, the wife and sister of Cronus, and the mother of Zeus, Poseidon, Hera, Hades, Demeter, and Hestia: identified with Cybele and, by the Romans, with Ops. **2.** (*l.c.*) either of two South American ratite birds, *Rhea americana* or *Pterocnemia pennata,* resembling the African ostrich but smaller and having three toes instead of two.

-rhea, var. of **-rrhea.** Cf. **rheo-.**

Rhe·a Sil·vi·a (rē′ə sil′vē ə), *Rom. Legend.* a vestal virgin who became the mother, by Mars, of Romulus and Remus. Also, **Rea Silvia.**

Rhee (rē), *n.* **Syng·man** (sing′mən), 1875–1965, president of South Korea 1948–60.

Rheims (rēmz; *Fr.* RANS), *n.* Reims.

Rhein (RĪN), *n.* German name of the **Rhine.**

Rhein·land (RĪN′länt′), *n.* German name of **Rhineland.**

Rhein·land-Pfalz (RĪN′länt′pfälts′), *n.* German name of **Rhineland-Palatinate.**

rhe·mat·ic (ri mat′ik), *adj.* **1.** pertaining to the formation of words. **2.** pertaining to or derived from a verb. [< Gk *rhēmatik(ós)* belonging to a word = *rhēmat-* (s. of *rhēma*) word + *-ikos* -IC]

Rhen·ish (ren′ish), *adj.* **1.** of the river Rhine or the regions bordering on it. —*n.* **2.** *Brit.* See **Rhine wine.** [< L *Rhēn(us)* RHINE + -ISH[1]; r. ME *Rhinisch* < OHG]

rhe·ni·um (rē′nē əm), *n. Chem.* a rare metallic element of the manganese subgroup. *Symbol:* Re; *at. no.:* 75; *at. wt.:* 186.2. [< NL = L *Rhēn(us)* RHINE + *-ium* -IUM]

rheo-, a learned borrowing from Greek meaning "flow," "current," "stream," used in the formation of compound words: *rheoscope.* Cf. **-rrhea.** [comb. form repr. Gk *rhéos* anything flowing]

rheo., rheostat; rheostats.

rhe·ol·o·gy (rē ol′ə jē), *n.* the study of the deformation and flow of matter. —**rhe·o·log·ic** (rē′ə loj′ik), **rhe′o·log′i·cal,** *adj.* —**rhe·ol′o·gist,** *n.*

rhe·om·e·ter (rē om′i tər), *n.* an instrument for measuring the flow of fluids, esp. blood. —**rhe·o·met·ric** (rē′ə me′trik), *adj.* —**rhe·om′e·try,** *n.*

rhe·o·scope (rē′ə skōp′), *n.* an instrument for detecting the presence of an electric current. —**rhe·o·scop·ic** (rē′ə-skop′ik), *adj.*

rhe·o·stat (rē′ə stat′), *n. Elect.* an adjustable resistor used for controlling the current in a circuit. —**rhe′o·stat′ic,** *adj.*

rhe·o·tax·is (rē′ə tak′sis), *n. Biol.* oriented movement of an organism in response to a current of fluid, esp. water. —**rhe·o·tac·tic** (rē′ə tak′tik), *adj.*

rhe·ot·ro·pism (rē o′trə piz′əm), *n.* the effect of a current of water upon the direction of plant growth. —**rhe·o·trop·ic** (rē′ə trop′ik), *adj.*

rhe·sus (rē′səs), *n.* a macaque, *Macaca mulatta,* of India, used in experimental medicine. Also called **rhe′sus mon′key.** See illus. at **monkey.** [< NL, arbitrary use of proper name << Gk *Rhêsos* mythical Thracian king]

Rhe′sus fac′tor (rē′səs). See **Rh factor.**

rhet., **1.** rhetoric. **2.** rhetorical.

Rhe·tian (rē′shən, -shē ən), *n., adj.* Rhaetian.

Rhe·tic (rē′tik), *adj. Geol.* Rhaetic.

rhe·tor (rē′tər), *n.* **1.** a master or teacher of rhetoric. **2.** an orator. [< L *rhētor* < Gk *rhḗtōr;* r. ME *rethor* < ML]

rhet·o·ric (ret′ər ik), *n.* **1.** the study of the effective use of language. **2.** the ability to use language effectively. **3.** the art or science of all specialized literary uses of language in prose or verse, including the figures of speech. **4.** the art of prose in general as opposed to verse. **5.** (in prose or verse) the undue use of exaggeration or display; bombast. **6.** (in classical oratory) the art of influencing the thought and conduct of an audience. [< L *rhētoric(a)* < Gk *rhētorikḗ* (*téchnē*) rhetorical (art); r. ME *rethorik* < ML *rēthorica*]

rhe·tor·i·cal (ri tôr′i kəl, -tor′-), *adj.* **1.** of, concerned with, or having the nature of rhetoric. **2.** used for, belonging to, or concerned with mere style or effect. **3.** marked by or tending to use bombast. [late ME < L *rhētoric(us)* (< Gk *rhētorikós*) + -AL[1]] —**rhe·tor′i·cal·ly,** *adv.* —**rhe·tor′i·cal·ness,** *n.*

rhetor′ical ques′tion, a question asked solely to produce an effect and not to elicit a reply, as, "What is so rare as a day in June?"

rhet·o·ri·cian (ret′ə rish′ən), *n.* **1.** an expert in the art of rhetoric. **2.** a person who writes or speaks in an elaborate or exaggerated style. **3.** a person who teaches rhetoric. [ME *rethoricien* < MF *rethorique* RHETORIC + *-ien* -IAN]

rheum (ro͞om), *n.* **1.** a thin, serous or catarrhal discharge. **2.** catarrh; cold. [ME *reume* < LL *rheuma* < Gk *rheûma* (*rhé(ein)* (to) flow + *-ma* n. suffix of result)] —**rheum′ic,** *adj.*

rheu·mat·ic (ro͞o mat′ik), *Pathol.* —*adj.* **1.** pertaining to or of the nature of rheumatism. **2.** affected with or subject to rheumatism. —*n.* **3.** a person affected with or subject to rheumatism. [ME *reumatik* < L *rheumatic(us)* < Gk *rheumatikós* = *rheumat-* (s. of *rheûma;* see RHEUM) + *-ikos* -IC] —**rheu·mat′i·cal·ly,** *adv.*

rheumat′ic fe′ver, *Pathol.* a serious disease, usually affecting children, characterized by fever, swelling and pain in the joints, sore throat, and cardiac involvement.

rheu·ma·tism (ro͞o′mə tiz′əm), *n. Pathol.* **1.** any disorder of the extremities or back, characterized by pain and stiffness. **2.** See **rheumatic fever.** [< L *rheumatism(us)* catarrh, rheum < Gk *rheumatismós* = *rheumat-* (s. of *rheûma;* see RHEUM) + *-ismos* -ISM]

rheu·ma·toid (ro͞o′mə toid′), *adj.* **1.** resembling rheumatism. **2.** rheumatic. Also, **rheu′ma·toi′dal.** [< Gk *rheumat-* (s. of *rheûma;* see RHEUM) + -OID] —**rheu′ma·toi′dal·ly,** *adv.*

rheu′matoid arthri′tis, *Pathol.* a chronic disease characterized by inflammation of the joints, frequently accompanied by marked deformities, and ordinarily associated with manifestations of a general or systemic affliction.

Rheydt (rīt), *n.* a city in W West Germany, adjacent to Mönchen-Gladbach. 96,000 (1963).

Rh factor, *Biochem.* any one of a group of inheritable antigens in the red blood cells of most persons, that on repeated transfusion into a person lacking such an antigen causes a severe reaction. The antigen may be transferred to a mother who lacks it by a fetus possessing it, and returned to subsequent fetuses to produce erythroblastosis. Also called **Rh, Rh., Rhesus factor.** [so called because first found in the blood of rhesus monkeys]

rhin-, var. of **rhino-** before a vowel: *rhinencephalon.*

rhi·nal (rīn′əl), *adj.* of or pertaining to the nose; nasal.

Rhine (rīn), *n.* a river flowing from SE Switzerland through West Germany and the Netherlands into the North Sea. 820 mi. long. German, **Rhein.** French, **Rhin** (RAN). Dutch, **Rijn.**

Rhine·land (rīn′land′, -lənd), *n.* **1.** German, **Rheinland.** that part of West Germany W of the Rhine. **2.** See **Rhine Province.**

Rhine·land-Pa·lat·i·nate (rīn′land pə lat′ənāt′, -ənit), *n.* a state in W West Germany: formerly part of Rhine Province. 3,493,000 (1963); 7655 sq. mi. *Cap.:* Mainz. German, **Rheinland-Pfalz.**

rhi·nen·ceph·a·lon (rī′nen sef′ə lon′), *n., pl.* **-lons, -la** (-lə). *Anat.* the part of the cerebrum containing the olfactory structures. —**rhi·nen·ce·phal·ic** (rī′nen sə fal′ik), **rhi′nen·ceph′a·lous,** *adj.*

Rhine′ Palat′inate, Palatinate (def. 1).

Rhine′ Prov′ince, a former province in W Germany, mostly W of the Rhine: now divided between Rhineland-Palatinate and North Rhine-Westphalia. Also called **Rhineland.** German, **Rheinland.**

rhine·stone (rīn′stōn′), *n.* an artificial gem of paste, often cut to resemble a diamond. [RHINE + STONE (trans. of F *caillou du Rhin*)]

Rhine′ wine′, **1.** any of numerous varieties of wine produced in the Rhine valley. **2.** any of a class of white wines, mostly light, still, and dry.

rhi·ni·tis (rī nī′tis), *n. Pathol.* inflammation of the nose or its mucous membrane.

rhi·no (rī′nō), *n., pl.* **-nos,** (*esp. collectively*) **-no.** a rhinoceros. [by shortening]

rhino-, a learned borrowing from Greek meaning "nose," used in the formation of compound words: *rhinology.* Also, *esp. before a vowel,* **rhin-.** [< Gk, comb. form of *rhís* (s. *rhin-*)]

Rhinoceros (Indian), *Rhinoceros unicornis* (5½ ft. high at shoulder; horn to 2 ft.; total length 13 ft.; tail 2 ft.)

rhi·noc·er·os (rī nos′ər əs), *n., pl.* **-os·es,** (*esp. collectively*) **-os.** any of several large, thick-skinned, odd-toed, hoofed mammals of the family *Rhinocerotidae,* of Africa and India, having one or two upright horns on the snout. [ME *rinoceros* < L *rhīnoceros* < Gk *rhīnókerōs* = *rhīno-* RHINO- + *kéras* horn (of an animal)]

rhi·nol·o·gy (rī nol′ə jē), *n.* the science dealing with the nose and its diseases. —**rhi·no·log·ic** (rin′ᵊloj′ik), **rhi′no·log′i·cal,** *adj.* —**rhi·nol′o·gist,** *n.*

rhi·no·plas·ty (rī′nō plas′tē), *n. Surg.* plastic surgery of the nose. —**rhi′no·plas′tic,** *adj.*

rhi·no·scope (rī′nə skōp′), *n. Med.* an instrument for examining the nasal passages.

rhi·nos·co·py (rī nos′kə pē), *n. Med.* the examination of the nasal passages. —**rhi·no·scop·ic** (rī′nə skop′ik), *adj.*

-rhiza, var. of **-rrhiza.**

rhizo-, a learned borrowing from Greek meaning "root," used in the formation of compound words: *rhizocarpous.* Also, *esp. before a vowel,* **rhiz-.** Cf. **-rhiza, -rrhiza.** [< Gk, comb. form of *rhíza*]

rhi·zo·bi·um (rī zō′bē əm), *n., pl.* **-bi·a** (-bē ə). *Bacteriol.* any of several rod-shaped bacteria of the genus *Rhizobium,* found as symbiotic nitrogen fixers in nodules on the roots of the bean, clover, etc. [< NL = *rhizo-* RHIZO- + Gk *bí(os)* life + L *-um* n. suffix]

rhi·zo·car·pous (rī′zō kär′pəs), *adj. Bot.* having the root perennial but the stem annual, as perennial herbs. Also, **rhi·zo·car·pic** (rī′zō kär′pik).

rhi·zo·ceph·a·lous (rī′zō sef′ə ləs), *adj. Zool.* belonging to the *Rhizocephala,* a group of degenerate hermaphrodite crustaceans that are parasitic chiefly on crabs.

rhi·zo·gen·ic (rī′zō jen′ik), *adj. Bot.* producing roots, as certain cells. Also, **rhi·zog·e·nous** (rī zoj′ə nəs).

rhi·zoid (rī′zoid), *adj.* **1.** rootlike. —*n.* **2.** (in mosses, ferns, etc.) one of the rootlike filaments by which the plant is attached to the substratum. —**rhi·zoi′dal,** *adj.*

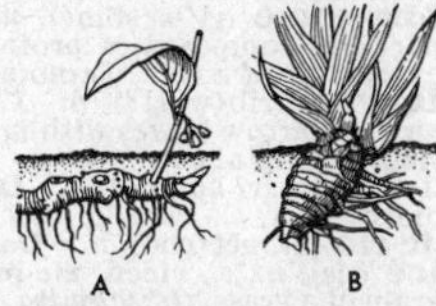

Rhizomes
A, Solomon's-seal, *Polygonatum commutatum;* B, Iris, *Iris versicolor*

rhi·zome (rī′zōm), *n. Bot.* a rootlike subterranean stem, commonly horizontal in position, which usually produces roots below and sends up shoots progressively from the upper surface. [< NL *rhizom(a)* < Gk *rhízōma* root, stem < *rhíza* root] —**rhi·zom·a·tous** (rī zom′ə təs, -zō′mə-), *adj.*

rhi·zo·mor·phous (rī′zō môr′fəs), *adj. Bot.* rootlike in form.

rhi·zo·pod (rī′zə pod′), *n.* any protozoan of the class *Rhizopoda,* having pseudopodia. [< NL *Rhizopod(a)* name of the class] —**rhi·zop·o·dan** (rī zop′ə dᵊn), *adj., n.* —**rhi·zop′o·dous,** *adj.*

Rhi·zo·pus (rī′zō pəs, -zə-), *n.* a genus of phycomycetous fungi including the bread mold *R. nigricans.* [< NL = *rhizo-* RHIZO- + Gk *poûs* foot]

rhi·zot·o·my (rī zot′ə mē), *n., pl.* **-mies.** *Surg.* the surgical section or cutting of the spinal nerve roots, usually posterior or sensory roots, to eliminate pain or paralysis.

Rh-neg·a·tive (är′āch′neg′ə tiv), *adj.* lacking the Rh factor.

rho (rō), *n., pl.* **rhos.** the 17th letter of the Greek alphabet (Ρ, ρ). [< Gk]

Rho., Rhodesia. Also, **Rhod.**

rhod-, var. of **rhodo-** before a vowel: *rhodamine.*

rho·da·mine (rō′də mēn′, -min), *n. Chem.* **1.** a red dye obtained by heating an amino derivative of phenol with phthalic anhydride. **2.** any of various related dyes.

Rhode′ Is′land (rōd), a state in the NE United States, on the Atlantic coast: the smallest state in the U.S. 949,723 (1970); 1214 sq. mi. *Cap.:* Providence. *Abbr.:* R.I., RI —**Rhode′ Is′lander.**

Rhode′ Is′land Red′, one of an American breed of chickens having dark reddish-brown feathers.

Rhodes (rōdz), *n.* **1. Cecil John,** 1853–1902, English colonial capitalist and government administrator in S Africa. **2.** a Greek island in the SE Aegean off the SW coast of Turkey: the largest of the Dodecanese Islands. 66,606; 542 sq. mi. **3.** a seaport on this island. 32,019; **4. Colossus of,** a huge bronze statue of Apollo that stood at the entrance to the harbor of Rhodes: completed 280 B.C. Cf. **Seven Wonders of the World.** Italian, **Rodi** (for defs. 2, 3). Greek, **Rhodos** (for defs. 2, 3).

Rho·de·sia (rō dē′zhə), *n.* **1.** Formerly, **Southern Rhodesia.** a former British colony in S Africa: unilaterally declared independence in 1965 and proclaimed a republic in 1970; name changed to **Zimbabwe** 1980. **2.** a region in S Africa, that comprised the British territories of Northern Rhodesia (now Zambia) and Southern Rhodesia (now Zimbabwe), forming part of the Federation of Rhodesia and Nyasaland. —**Rho·de′sian,** *adj., n.*

Rhode′sia and Nya′saland, Federa′tion of, a grouping of British territories in S Africa 1953–1963, comprising the present-day states of Zimbabwe, Zambia, and Malawi. Also called **Central African Federation.**

Rhode′sian man′, an extinct primitive man, *Homo rhodesiensis,* of the Late Pleistocene epoch, whose skeletal remains were found in Northern Rhodesia. —**Rho·de·soid** (rō dē′zoid), *adj.*

Rhodes′ schol′arship, one of a number of scholarships at Oxford University, established by the will of Cecil Rhodes, for selected students **(Rhodes′ schol′ars)** from the British Commonwealth and the United States.

Rho·di·an (rō′dē ən), *adj.* **1.** of or pertaining to the island Rhodes. —*n.* **2.** a native or inhabitant of Rhodes. [RHOD(ES) + -IAN]

rho·dic (rō′dik), *adj. Chem.* of or containing rhodium, esp. in the tetravalent state. [RHOD(IUM) + -IC]

rho·di·um (rō′dē əm), *n. Chem.* a metallic element of the platinum family, used to electroplate microscopes and instrument parts to prevent corrosion. *Symbol:* Rh; *at. wt.:* 102.905; *at. no.:* 45; *sp. gr.:* 12.5 at 20°C. [< NL]

rhodo-, a learned borrowing from Greek meaning "rose," used in the formation of compound words: *rhodolite.* Also, *esp. before a vowel,* **rhod-.** [< Gk, comb. form of *rhódon*]

rho·do·chro·site (rō′də krō′sīt), *n.* a mineral, manganese carbonate, $MnCO_3$, usually rose-red in color: a minor ore of manganese; manganese spar. [< Gk *rhodóchrōs* rose-colored (*rhódo(n)* RHODO- + *chrṓs* color) + -ITE[1]]

rho·do·den·dron (rō′də den′drən), *n.* any evergreen or deciduous, ericaceous shrub or tree of the genus *Rhododendron,* having showy, pink, purple, or white flowers. [< L < Gk *rhodódendron* (*rhódo(n)* RHODO- + *déndron* tree)]

rho·do·lite (rōd′ᵊlīt′), *n.* a rose or reddish-violet garnet used as a gem.

rho·do·nite (rōd′ᵊnīt′), *n.* a rose-red mineral, manganese silicate, $MnSiO_3$; manganese spar. [< G *Rhodonit* < Gk *rhódon* rose + G *-it* -ITE[1]]

Rhod·o·pe (rod′ə pē, ro dō′-), *n.* a mountain range in SW Bulgaria. Highest peak, Musala, 9597 ft.

rho·dop·sin (rō dop′sin), *n. Biochem.* a bright-red photosensitive pigment found in the rod-shaped cells of the retina of certain fishes and most higher vertebrates. Also called **visual purple.** [RHOD- + OPSIN]

rho·do·ra (rō dôr′ə, -dōr′ə, rə-), *n.* a low, ericaceous shrub, *Rhododendron canadensis,* of North America, having rose-colored flowers which appear before the leaves. [< L *rhodōra* name of a plant]

Rho·dos (RÔ′t͟hôs), *n.* Greek name of **Rhodes** (defs. 2, 3).

-rhoea, var. of **-rrhea.**

rhomb (rom, romb), *n.* rhombus. [< L *rhomb(us)*; cf. F *rhombe*]

rhom·ben·ceph·a·lon (rom′ben sef′ə lon′), *n., pl.* **-lons, -la** (-lə). *Anat.* the hindbrain.

rhom·bic (rom′bik), *adj.* **1.** having the form of a rhombus. **2.** having a rhombus as base or cross section. **3.** bounded by rhombuses, as a solid. **4.** *Crystall.* orthorhombic. Also, **rhom′bi·cal.**

rhom·bo·he·dron (rom′bə hē′drən), *n., pl.* **-drons, -dra** (-drə). a solid bounded by six rhombic planes. [< Gk *rhómbo(s)* RHOMBUS + -HEDRON] —**rhom′bo·he′dral,** *adj.*

rhom·boid (rom′boid), *n.* **1.** an oblique-angled parallelogram with only the opposite sides equal. —*adj.* **2.** Also, **rhom·boi′dal.** having a form like or similar to that of a rhombus; shaped like a rhomboid. [< LL *rhomboīd(es)* < Gk *rhomboeidḗs* (*schêma*) rhomboid (form, shape). See RHOMBUS, -OID] —**rhom·boi′dal·ly,** *adv.*

Rhomboid

rhom·bus (rom′bəs), *n., pl.* **-bus·es, -bi** (-bī). **1.** an oblique-angled equilateral parallelogram. **2.** a rhombohedron. [< L < Gk *rhómbos* anything that may be spun around < *rhémbein* to revolve]

rhon·chus (roŋ′kəs), *n., pl.* **-chi** (-kī). a coarse rattling noise in the bronchial tubes, caused by an accumulation of mucus or other material; rale. [< L: a snoring, croaking < Gk **rhónchos,* var. of *rhénchos*] —**rhon·chi·al** (roŋ′kē əl), **rhon·chal** (roŋ′kəl), *adj.*

Rhombus

Rhon·dda (ron′də), *n.* a city in S Wales. 86,400.

Rhone (rōn), *n.* **1.** a river flowing from the Alps in S Switzerland through the Lake of Geneva and SE France into the Mediterranean. 504 mi. long. **2.** a wine-growing region in E central France. French, **Rhône** (rōn).

rho·ta·cism (rō′tə siz′əm), *n. Phonet.* excessive use of the sound *r,* its misarticulation, or the substitution of another sound for it. [< NL *rhotacism(us)* < Gk **rhōtakismós* < *rhōtakízein* to use the letter rho too much] —**rho′ta·cis′tic,** *adj.*

Rh-pos·i·tive (är′āch′poz′i tiv), *adj.* possessing the Rh factor.

rhu·barb (ro͞o′bärb), *n.* **1.** any polygonaceous herb of the genus *Rheum,* as *R. officinale,* having a medicinal rhizome, and *R. Rhaponticum,* having edible leafstalks. **2.** the rhizome of any medicinal species of this plant, forming a combined cathartic and astringent. **3.** the edible fleshy leafstalks of any of the garden species. **4.** *U.S. Slang.* a quarrel or squabble. [ME *rubarb, reubarb* < OF *r(e)ubarbe* < ML *reubarb(arum)* < Gk *rhêon bárbaron* foreign rhubarb]

rhumb (rum, rumb), *n.* See **rhumb line.** [< Sp *rumb(o)* < L *rhombus* RHOMBUS]

rhum·ba (rum′bə, ro͝om′-), *n., pl.* **-bas** (-bəz), *v.i.,* **-baed** (-bəd), **-ba·ing** (-bə iŋ). rumba.

rhumb′ line′, a curve on the surface of a sphere that cuts all meridians at the same angle. It is the path taken by a vessel or aircraft that maintains a constant compass direction. Also called **loxodrome, rhumb.**

rhyme (rīm), *n., v.,* **rhymed, rhym·ing.** —*n.* **1.** identity in sound of some part, esp. the end, of words or lines of verse. **2.** a word agreeing with another in terminal sound: Find *is a rhyme for* mind *and* kind. **3.** verse or poetry having correspondence in the terminal sounds of the lines. **4.** a poem or piece of verse having such correspondence. **5.** verse (def. 4). **6. rhyme or reason,** logic, sense, or plan. —*v.t.* **7.** to treat in rhyme, as a subject; turn into rhyme, as something in prose. **8.** to compose (verse or the like) in metrical form with rhymes. **9.** to use (a word) as a rhyme to another word; use (words) as rhymes. —*v.i.* **10.** to make rhyme or verse; versify. **11.** to use rhyme in writing verse. **12.** to form a rhyme, as one word or line with another. **13.** to be composed in metrical form with rhymes, as verse. Also, **rime.** [ME *rime* < OF < *rimer* to rhyme < Gallo-Romance *rimāre* to put in a row < OHG *rīm* series, row; prob. not connected with L *rhythmus* rhythm] —**rhym′er,** *n.*

rhyme′ roy′al, *Pros.* a form of verse introduced into English by Chaucer, consisting of seven-line stanzas of iambic pentameter in which the first line rhymes with the third, the second with the fourth and fifth, and the sixth with the seventh.

rhyme′ scheme′, the pattern of rhymes in a poem, usually marked by letters to symbolize correspondences, as rhyme royal, *ababbcc.*

rhyme·ster (rīm′stər), *n.* a writer of inferior verse; poetaster. Also, **rimester.** —**Syn.** versifier.

rhyn·cho·ce·pha·lian (riŋ′kō sə fāl′yən), *adj.* **1.** belonging or pertaining to the *Rhynchocephalia,* an order of lizardlike reptiles that are extinct except for the tuatara. —*n.* **2.** a rhynchocephalian reptile. [< NL *Rhynchocephali(a)* name of the order < Gk *rhýncho(s)* snout; see CEPHAL-, -IAN]

rhy·o·lite (rī′ə līt′), *n.* a fine-grained igneous rock rich in silica: the volcanic equivalent of granite. [*rhyo-* (irreg. < Gk *rhýax* stream of lava) + -LITE] —**rhy·o·lit·ic** (rī′ə lit′ik), *adj.*

rhythm (rith′əm), *n.* **1.** movement or procedure with uniform or patterned recurrence of a beat, accent, or the like. **2.** *Music.* **a.** the pattern of regular or irregular pulses in music caused by the occurrence of strong and weak melodic and harmonic beats. **b.** a particular form of this: *duple rhythm; triple rhythm.* **3.** the pattern of recurrent strong and weak accents, vocalization and silence, and the distribution and combination of these elements in speech. **4.** *Pros.* **a.** metrical or rhythmical form; meter. **b.** a particular kind of metrical form. **c.** metrical movement. **5.** *Art, Literature.* a patterned repetition of a motif, formal element, etc., at regular or irregular intervals in the same or a modified form. **6.** procedure marked by the regular recurrence of particular elements, phases, etc. **7.** regular recurrence of elements in a system of motion. **8.** *Physiol.* the regular recurrence of an action or function, as of the beat of the heart, the menstrual cycle, etc. [< L *rhythm(us)* < Gk *rhythmós*, cf. *rhéein* to flow] —**rhythm′less,** *adj.*

rhythm-and-blues (rith′əm ən blo͞oz′), *n.* a folk-based but urbanized form of Negro popular music characterized by strong, repetitious rhythms and simple melodies.

rhyth·mic (rith′mik), *adj.* **1.** cadenced; rhythmical. —*n.* **2.** rhythmics. [< LL *rhythmic(us)* < Gk *rhythmikós*]

rhyth·mi·cal (rith′mi kəl), *adj.* **1.** periodic, as motion, a drumbeat, etc. **2.** having a flowing rhythm. **3.** of or pertaining to rhythm: *an excellent rhythmical sense.* —**ryth′mi·cal·ly,** *adv.* —**rhyth·mic·i·ty** (rith mis′i tē), *n.*

rhyth·mics (rith′miks), *n.* (*construed as sing.*) the science of rhythm and rhythmic forms. Also, **rhythmic.** [RHYTHM + -ICS]

rhyth·mist (rith′mist), *n.* **1.** a person versed in or having a fine sense of rhythm. **2.** a person who uses rhythm in a certain way: *a good rhythmist.*

rhythm′ meth′od, a method for preventing fertilization by abstaining from sexual intercourse on the days when conception is most likely to occur.

rhy·ton (rī′ton), *n., pl.* **-ta** (-tə). an ancient Greek drinking horn, having a base in the form of the head of a woman or animal. [< Gk *rhytón*, neut. of *rhytós* flowing, akin to *rhein* to flow]

R.I., 1. Queen and Empress. [< L *Regina et Imperātrix*] **2.** King and Emperor. [< L *Rēx et Imperātor*] **3.** Rhode Island.

RI, Rhode Island (approved esp. for use with zip code).

ri·al[1] (rē′ôl, -äl), *n.* a silver or cupronickel coin and monetary unit of Iran, equal to 100 dinars. [< Pers < Ar *riyāl* RIYAL]

ri·al[2] (rē ôl′, -äl′), *n.* riyal.

ri·al·to (rē al′tō), *n., pl.* **-tos.** an exchange or mart. [after the RIALTO in Venice]

Ri·al·to (rē al′tō; *also for 1, 2, It.* Rē äl′tô), *n.* **1.** a commercial center in Venice, Italy, consisting of an island and the surrounding district. **2.** a bridge spanning the Grand Canal in Venice, Italy: built in 1590. **3.** a city in SW California, near Los Angeles. 28,370 (1970). **4.** the theater district of New York City.

ri·ant (rī′ənt), *adj.* laughing or smiling; cheerful; gay. [< F, prp. of *rire* to laugh < L *rīdēre*] —**ri′ant·ly,** *adv.*

ri·a·ta (rē ä′tə), *n.* a lariat. Also, **reata.** [< Sp *reata* < *reatar* to tie again = *re-* RE- + *atar* < L *aptāre* to fit]

rib[1] (rib), *n., v.,* **ribbed, rib·bing.** —*n.* **1.** one of a series of curved bones that are articulated with the vertebrae and occur in pairs, 12 in man, on each side of the vertebrate body, certain pairs being connected with the sternum and forming the thoracic wall. **2.** a cut of meat, as beef, containing a rib. **3.** something resembling a rib in form, position, or use, as a supporting or strengthening part. **4.** *Archit.* **a.** any of several archlike members that support a vault at the groins. **b.** any of several molded members or moldings, including ridge ribs, on the surface of a vault, as those dividing the surface into panels. **5.** *Naut.* any of the curved framing members in a ship's hull that rise upward and outward from the keel; frame. **6.** a primary vein of a leaf. **7.** a vertical ridge in knitted fabrics. **8.** a ridge, as in poplin or rep, caused by heavy yarn. **9.** a wife, in humorous allusion to the creation of Eve. Gen. 2:21–22. —*v.t.* **10.** to furnish or strengthen with ribs. **11.** to enclose, as with ribs. **12.** to mark with riblike ridges or markings. [ME, OE *rib(b)*; c. G *Rippe*] —**rib′less,** *adj.* —**rib′like′,** *adj.*

rib[2] (rib), *v.t.,* **ribbed, rib·bing.** to tease; make fun of. [appar. short for *rib-tickle* (v.)]

rib·ald (rib′əld), *adj.* **1.** vulgar or indecent in speech, language, etc.; coarsely mocking, abusive, or irreverent. —*n.* **2.** a ribald person. [ME *ribald, ribaud* < OF *ribau(l)d* < *riber* to dissipate < MHG *rīben* to rub, be in heat, copulate] —**rib′ald·ly,** *adv.* —**Syn. 1.** low, obscene, gross.

rib·ald·ry (rib′əl drē), *n.* **1.** ribald character, as of language. **2.** ribald speech. [ME *ribaudrie* < OF]

rib·and (rib′ənd), *n.* *Archaic.* ribbon. [ME: RIBBON]

Rib·ben·trop (Rib′ən trōp′), *n.* **Jo·a·chim von** (yō′ä-khim fən), 1893–1946, German leader in the Nazi party: minister of foreign affairs 1938–45.

rib·bing[1] (rib′ing), *n.* **1.** ribs collectively. **2.** an assemblage or arrangement of ribs, as in cloth, a ship, etc. [RIB[1] + -ING[1]]

rib·bing[2] (rib′ing), *n.* the act or process of teasing. [RIB[2] + -ING[1]]

rib·bon (rib′ən), *n.* **1.** a woven strip or band of fine material, used for tying, etc. **2.** material in such strips. **3.** **ribbons,** torn or ragged strips; shreds: *clothes torn to ribbons.* **4.** a long, thin, flexible band of metal, as for a spring, a band saw, a tapeline, etc. **5.** a band of inked material used in a typewriter, adding machine, etc., that supplies ink for printing the figure on the striking typeface onto the paper beneath. **6.** *Carpentry.* a thin horizontal board framed into studding to support the ends of joists. **7.** a strip of material, as satin or rayon, being or representing a medal or similar decoration, esp. a military one: *an overseas ribbon.* —*v.t.* **8.** to adorn with ribbon. **9.** to streak or mark with something suggesting ribbon. **10.** to separate into or reduce to ribbonlike strips. —*v.i.* **11.** to form in ribbonlike strips. [ME *riban* < OF, var. of *r(e)uban*, ? < Gmc. See RUDDY, BAND[2]] —**rib′bon·like′, rib′bon·y,** *adj.*

rib·bon·fish (rib′ən fish′), *n., pl.* (*esp. collectively*) **-fish,** (*esp. referring to two or more kinds or species*) **-fish·es. 1.** any of several marine fishes of the family *Trachipteridae*, having a long, compressed, ribbonlike body. **2.** any of several related fishes, as the oarfish.

rib′bon worm′, a nemertean.

Ri·bei·rão Prê·to (Rē′bā Roun′ pRe′to͝o), a city in SE Brazil. 119,429 (1960).

Ri·be·ra (Rē ve′Rä; *Eng.* ri vâr′ə), *n.* **Jo·sé** (hô se′; *Eng.* hō zā′), ("*Lo Spagnoletto*"), 1588–1656, Spanish painter.

ri·bo·fla·vin (rī′bō flā′vin, rī′bō flā′-), *n.* *Biochem.* a compound derived from ribose, $C_{17}H_{22}N_4O_6$, a factor of the vitamin-B complex essential for growth, found in milk, fresh meat, eggs, leafy vegetables, etc., or made synthetically, and used in enriching flour, and in vitamin preparations. Also, **ri·bo·fla·vine** (rī′bō flā′vin, -vēn, rī′bō flā′-). Also called **lactoflavin, vitamin B$_2$, vitamin G.** [RIBO(SE) + FLAVIN]

ri·bo·nu·cle·ase (rī′bō no͞o′klē ās′, -nyo͞o′-), *n.* *Biochem.* any of the class of enzymes that catalyze the hydrolysis of RNA. [RIBONUCLE(IC ACID) + -ASE]

ri′bo·nu·cle′ic ac′id (rī′bō no͞o klē′ik, -nyo͞o-, rī′-), *Biochem.* See **RNA.** Also, **ri′bose nucle′ic ac′id.** [RIBO(SE) + NUCLEIC]

ri·bose (rī′bōs), *n.* *Chem.* a solid, $HOCH_2(CHOH)_3CHO$, a pentose sugar obtained by the hydrolysis of RNA. [alter. of ARABINOSE]

ri·bo·some (rī′bə sōm′), *n.* *Biol.* any of several minute particles composed of protein and RNA and found in the cytoplasm of a cell. [RIBO(SE) + -SOME[3]]

rib·wort (rib′wûrt′), *n.* **1.** a plantain, *Plantago lanceolata*, having narrow leaves with prominent ribs. **2.** any of various similar plantains.

Ri·car·do (ri kär′dō), *n.* **David,** 1772–1823, English economist.

Ric·cio (*It.* Rēt′chô), *n.* **Da·vid** (*It.* dä′vēd). See **Rizzio.**

rice (rīs), *n., v.,* **riced, ric·ing.** —*n.* **1.** the starchy seeds or grain of a grass, *Oryza sativa*, cultivated in warm climates and used for food. **2.** the plant itself. —*v.t.* **3.** to reduce to a form resembling rice: *to rice potatoes.* [ME *ris* < OF < It *riso* << Gk *óryzon*, var. of *óryza*; of Eastern orig.]

Rice (rīs), *n.* **Elmer,** 1892–1967, U.S. playwright.

rice·bird (rīs′bûrd′), *n.* *Southern U.S.* the bobolink.

rice′ pa′per, 1. a thin paper made from the straw of rice. **2.** a Chinese paper consisting of the pith of certain plants cut and pressed into thin sheets.

ric·er (rī′sər), *n.* an implement for ricing potatoes, squash, etc., by pressing them through small holes.

ri·cer·car (rē′chər kär′), *n.* *Music.* a chiefly polyphonic instrumental form of the 16th and 17th centuries closely resembling the vocal motet in structure and style. [apocopated var. and n. use of It *ricercare* to seek. See RESEARCH]

rich (rich), *adj.* **1.** having wealth or great possessions; abundantly supplied with resources, means, or funds: *a rich man; a rich nation.* **2.** abounding in natural resources: *a rich territory.* **3.** abounding (usually fol. by *in* or *with*): *a countryside rich in beauty; a design rich with colors.* **4.** of great value or worth; valuable: *a rich harvest.* **5.** (of food) delectably spicy, as a gravy, or sweet and abounding in butter or cream, as a pastry. **6.** costly, expensively elegant, or fine, as dress, jewels, etc. **7.** made of valuable materials or with elaborate workmanship, as buildings or furniture. **8.** (of wine) strong and finely flavored. **9.** (of color) deep, strong, or vivid: *rich purple.* **10.** full and mellow in tone. **11.** strongly fragrant; pungent: *a rich odor.* **12.** producing or yielding abundantly: *a rich soil.* **13.** abundant, plentiful, or ample. **14.** *Informal.* **a.** highly amusing. **b.** ridiculous; absurd. —*n.* **15.** (*construed as pl.*) rich persons collectively (usually prec. by *the*). [ME; OE *rīce* (adj.) < Gmc < Celt; c. G *reich* wealthy; akin to L *rēx*, Skt *rājan* king] —**rich′ly,** *adv.* —**rich′ness,** *n.* —**Syn. 1.** well-to-do, moneyed. RICH, WEALTHY, AFFLUENT, OPULENT agree in indicating abundance of possessions. RICH is the general word; it may imply that possessions are newly acquired: *a rich oilman.* WEALTHY suggests permanence, stability, and appropriate surroundings: *a wealthy banker.* AFFLUENT and OPULENT both suggest the possession of great wealth; AFFLUENT esp. connoting a handsome income and free expenditure of resources; OPULENT suggesting display or luxuriousness: *an affluent family; opulent circumstances.* **4.** valued. **6.** precious, high-priced, dear.

Rich·ard I (rich′ərd), ("*Richard the Lion-Hearted,*" "*Richard Coeur de Lion*") 1157–99, king of England 1189–99.

Richard II, 1367–1400, king of England 1377–99 (successor to and grandson of Edward III; son of Edward, Prince of Wales).

Richard III, (*Duke of Gloucester*) 1452–85, king of England 1483–85.

Rich′ard Roe′ (rō), a fictitious personage in legal proceedings, used esp. as the second such name when two persons whose real names cannot be ascertained are involved. Cf. **Jane Doe, John Doe.**

Rich·ards (rich′ərdz), *n.* **I(vor) A(rmstrong)** (ī′vər, ē′vər), 1893–1979, English literary critic in the U.S.

Rich·ard·son (rich′ərd sən), *n.* **1. Henry Handel** (*Henrietta Richardson Robertson*), 1870–1946, Australian novelist. **2. Henry Hob·son** (hob′sən), 1838–86, U.S. architect. **3. Samuel,** 1689–1761, English novelist. **4.** a city in NE Texas, near Dallas. 48,582 (1970).

Rich·e·lieu (rish′ə lo͞o′; *Fr.* Rēshə lyœ′), *n.* **1. Ar·mand Jean du Ples·sis** (ȧr mäN′ zhäN dy ple sē′), **Duc de,** 1585–1642, French cardinal and statesman. **2.** a river in S Quebec, flowing N from Lake Champlain to the St. Lawrence. 210 mi. long.

rich·es (rich′iz), *n.pl.* abundant and valuable possessions; wealth. [late ME, pl. of ME *riche* wealth, power (OE *rīce* power, rule; c. G *Reich* realm); confused with ME *richesse* wealth < OF = *riche* wealthy + *-esse* -ESS]

Rich·field (rich′fēld′), *n.* a city in E Minnesota, near Minneapolis. 47,231 (1970).

Rich·land (rich′lənd), *n.* a city in SE Washington, on the Columbia River. 26,290 (1970).

Rich·mond (rich′mənd), *n.* **1.** a port in and the capital of

Virginia, in the E part, on the James River: capital of the Confederacy 1861–65. 249,430 (est. 1970). **2.** a borough of SW New York City, comprising Staten Island. 295,443 (1970); 60.3 sq. mi. **3.** a seaport in W California, on San Francisco Bay. 79,043 (1970). **4.** a city in E Indiana. 43,999 (1970). **5.** a city in N Surrey, SE England, on the Thames, near London: site of Kew Gardens. 41,002 (1961).

rich′ rhyme′, *Pros.* See **rime riche.**

Rich·ter (rik′tər; *Ger.* riкн′tər), *n.* **Jean Paul Frie·drich** (zhäN poul frē′drikн), (pen name: *Jean Paul*), 1763–1825, German author.

Rich′ter scale′ (rik′ter), **a scale, ranging from 1 to 10, for indicating the intensity of an earthquake. [after Charles F. *Richter* (1900–85), U.S. seismologist]**

Richt·ho·fen (rikнt′hō′fən), *n.* **Baron Man·fred von** (män′fråt fən), 1892–1918, German aviator.

ri·cin (rī′sin, ris′in), *n.* *Chem.* a poisonous, protein powder from the bean of the castor-oil plant. [< NL *Ricin(us)* name of genus, L: castor-oil plant]

ric′in·o·le′ic ac′id (ris′ə nō lē′ik, -nō′lē-, ris′-), *Chem.* an unsaturated hydroxyl acid, $C_{17}H_{32}(OH)COOH$: used chiefly in soaps and textile finishing.

ric·in·o·le·in (ris′ə nō′lē in), *n.* *Chem.* the glyceride of ricinoleic acid, the chief constituent of castor oil. [RICIN-OLE(IC) + -IN[2]]

rick (rik), *n.* **1.** a large stack or pile of hay, straw, corn, or the like, in a field, esp. when thatched or covered by a tarpaulin; an outdoor or makeshift mow. **2.** a frame of horizontal bars and vertical supports, as used to hold barrels in a distillery, boxes in a warehouse, etc. —*v.t.* **3.** to form grain into a stack or pile. [ME *rek(e)*, *reek*, OE *hrēac;* akin to Icel *hraukr*, OFris *reak*, MD *rooc*, *roke*]

Rick·en·back·er (rik′ən bak′ər), *n.* **Edward Vernon** (*"Eddie"*), 1890–1973, U.S. aviator and aviation executive.

rick·ets (rik′its), *n.* *Pathol.* a disease of childhood, characterized by softening of the bones as a result of either malnutrition, ordinarily lack of Vitamin D, or of insufficient ingestion of calcium, or both, and often resulting in deformities. [?]

rick·ett·si·a (ri ket′sē ə), *n.*, *pl.* **-si·ae** (-sē ē′), **-si·as** (-sē əz). any of several bacterialike microorganisms of the genus *Rickettsia*, parasitic on arthropods and pathogenic for man and animals. [named after Howard T. *Ricketts* (1871–1910), American pathologist; see -IA] —**rick·ett′si·al,** *adj.*

rick·et·y (rik′i tē), *adj.* **1.** likely to fall or collapse; shaky: *a rickety chair.* **2.** feeble in the joints; tottering; infirm: *a rickety old man.* **3.** old, dilapidated, or in disrepair. **4.** irregular, as motion or action. **5.** affected with or suffering from rickets. **6.** pertaining to or of the nature of rickets. [RICKET(S) + -Y[1]] —**rick′et·i·ness,** *n.*

rick·ey (rik′ē), *n.*, *pl.* **-eys.** a drink made with lime juice, carbonated water, and a spirituous liquor, esp. gin. [after a Colonel *Rickey*]

Rick·o·ver (rik′ō vər), *n.* **Hyman George, 1900–86, vice admiral in U.S. Navy, born in Poland: helped develop the atomic submarine.**

rick·rack (rik′rak′), *n.* a narrow, zigzag braid or ribbon used as a trimming on clothing, linens, etc. Also, **ric′rac′.** [gradational redupl. of RACK[1]]

rick·shaw (rik′shô′), *n.* jinrikisha. Also, **rick′sha.** [by shortening and contr.]

ric·o·chet (rik′ə shā′ *or, esp. Brit.*, -shet′), *n.*, *v.*, **-cheted** (-shād′), **-chet·ing** (-shā′ing) or (*esp. Brit.*) **-chet·ted** (shet′id), **-chet·ting** (shet′ing). —*n.* **1.** the rebound or skip made by an object or a projectile after it hits a glancing blow against a surface. —*v.i.* **2.** to move in this way, as a projectile. [< F < ?] —**Syn. 2.** rebound, deflect, glance.

ri·cot·ta (ri kot′ə, -kô′tə; *It.* rē kôt′tä), *n.* a soft, Italian cottage cheese. [< It < L *recocta*, fem. of *recoctus*, ptp. of *recoquere* to re-cook. See RE-, COOK]

ric·tus (rik′təs), *n.*, *pl.* **-tus, -tus·es.** **1.** the gape of the mouth of a bird. **2.** the gaping or opening of the mouth. [< L: wide open mouth, ptp. of *ringī* to open the mouth wide] —**ric′tal,** *adj.*

rid[1] (rid), *v.t.*, **rid** or **rid·ded, rid·ding.** **1.** to clear, disencumber, or free of something objectionable (usually fol. by *of*): *I want to rid the house of mice.* **2.** to relieve or disembarrass (usually fol. by *of*): *to rid the mind of doubt.* **3.** *Archaic.* to deliver or rescue. [ME *ridd(en)*, OE *(ge)ryddan* to clear (land); c. OIcel *rhydhja* to clear, empty] —**rid′der,** *n.*

rid[2] (rid), *v.* *Archaic.* a pt. and pp. of **ride.**

rid·a·ble (rī′də bəl), *adj.* **1.** capable of being ridden, as a horse. **2.** capable of being ridden over, through, etc., as a road or a stream. —**rid′a·bil′i·ty,** *n.*

rid·dance (rid′ᵊns), *n.* **1.** the act or fact of clearing away or out, as anything undesirable. **2.** relief or deliverance from something. **3. good riddance,** (used interjectionally to express welcome relief at deliverance from something.)

rid·den (rid′ᵊn), *v.* a pp. of **ride.**

rid·dle[1] (rid′ᵊl), *n.*, *v.*, **-dled, -dling.** —*n.* **1.** a question stated so as to exercise one's ingenuity in answering it or discovering its meaning; conundrum. **2.** any puzzling question, problem, or matter. **3.** a puzzling or enigmatic thing or person. —*v.i.* **4.** to propound riddles; speak enigmatically. [ME *redele*, OE *rǣdelle*, var. of *rǣdels(e)* (*rǣd* counsel (see REDE) + *-sel*, with loss of *-s-* through confusion with -LE); c. G *Rätsel*, D *raadsel*] —**Syn. 1.** See **puzzle.**

rid·dle[2] (rid′ᵊl), *v.*, **-dled, -dling,** *n.* —*v.t.* **1.** to pierce with many holes suggesting those of a sieve. **2.** to sift through a riddle, as gravel; screen. **3.** to impair as if by puncturing: *a government riddled with graft.* —*n.* **4.** a coarse sieve, as one for sifting sand in a foundry. [ME *riddil*, OE *hriddel*, var. of *hridder*, *hrīder;* c. G *Reiter*, L *crībrum* sieve]

ride (rīd), *v.*, **rode** or (*Archaic*) **rid; rid·den** or (*Archaic*) **rid; rid·ing;** *n.* —*v.i.* **1.** to sit on and manage a horse or other animal in motion; be carried on the back of an animal. **2.** to be carried on something, as a litter, a person's shoulders, or the like. **3.** to be borne along on or in a vehicle. **4.** to move along in any way; be carried or supported: *riding on his friend's success.* **5.** to lie at anchor, as a ship. **6.** to appear to float in space, as a heavenly body. **7.** to turn or rest on something. **8.** to extend or project over something, as the edge of one thing over the edge of another thing. **9.** to move up from the proper place or position. **10.** to have a specified character for riding purposes: *The car rides smoothly.* **11.** to continue without interruption or interference. **12.** to be conditioned; depend (usually fol. by *on*): *Our hopes are riding on the merger.* —*v.t.* **13.** to sit on and manage (a horse, bicycle, etc.) so as to be carried along. **14.** to sit or move along on; be carried or borne along on. **15.** to rest on, esp. by overlapping. **16.** to control, dominate, or tyrannize over: *a country that is ridden by a power-mad dictator.* **17.** to ride over, along, or through (a road, region, etc.); traverse. **18.** to execute by riding: *to ride a race.* **19.** to cause to ride. **20.** to carry (a person) on something as if on a horse. **21.** to keep (a vessel) at anchor or moored. **22. ride down, a.** to trample or overturn by riding upon or against. **b.** to ride up to; overtake. **c.** *Naut.* to bear down upon (a rope of a tackle) with all one's weight. **23. ride out, a.** to sustain (a gale, storm, etc.) without damage, as while riding at anchor. **b.** to sustain or endure successfully. —*n.* **24.** a journey or excursion on a horse, camel, etc., or on or in a vehicle. **25.** a way, road, etc., made esp. for riding. **26.** a vehicle or device, as a ferris wheel, roller coaster, merry-go-round, or the like, on which people ride for amusement. **27. take for a ride,** *Slang.* **a.** to murder. **b.** to deceive; trick. [ME *ride(n)*, OE *rīdan;* c. OIcel *rītha*, G *reiten*. See ROAD]

ri·dent (rīd′ᵊnt), *adj.* laughing; smiling; cheerful. [< L *rīdent-* (s. of *rīdens*, prp. of *rīdēre*) = *rīd-* laugh + *-ent-* -ENT]

rid·er (rī′dər), *n.* **1.** a person who rides a horse or other animal, a bicycle, or the like. **2.** that which rides. **3.** any object or device that straddles, is mounted upon, or is attached to something else. **4.** a rail or stake used to brace the corners in a snake fence. **5.** an additional clause attached to a legislative bill in passing it. **6.** an addition or amendment to a document. [ME, OE *ridere*] —**rid′er·less,** *adj.*

rid·er·ship (rī′dər ship′), *n.* **1.** the people who ride a particular train, bus, subway, etc. **2.** the estimated number of such people.

ridge (rij), *n.*, *v.*, **ridged, ridg·ing.** —*n.* **1.** a long, narrow elevation of land; a chain of hills or mountains. **2.** the long and narrow upper edge, angle, or crest of something, as a hill, wave, vault, etc. **3.** the back of an animal. **4.** any raised, narrow strip, as on cloth. **5.** the horizontal line in which the tops of the rafters of a roof meet. **6.** (on a weather chart) a narrow, elongated area of high pressure. —*v.t.* **7.** to provide with or form into a ridge or ridges. **8.** to mark with or as with ridges. —*v.i.* **9.** to form ridges. [ME *rigge*, OE *hrycg* spine, crest, ridge; c. OIcel *hryggr*, D *rug*, G *Rücken*, L *crux*] —**ridge′like′,** *adj.*

ridge·ling (rij′ling), *n.* *Vet. Med.* a colt with undescended testicles. Also, **ridg′ling.** Also called **ridg·el, ridg·il** (rij′əl). [? RIDGE + -LING[2], from the belief that the undescended organs were in the animal's back]

ridge·pole (rij′pōl′), *n.* the horizontal timber or member at the top of a roof, to which the upper ends of the rafters are fastened. Also, **ridge′ pole′.** Also called **ridge·piece** (rij′pēs′), **ridge′ board′.** —**ridge′poled′,** *adj.*

Ridge·wood (rij′wŏŏd′), *n.* a city in NE New Jersey. 27,547 (1970).

Ridg·way (rij′wā), *n.* **Matthew (Bun·ker)** (bung′kər), born 1895, U.S. general: chief of staff 1953–55.

ridg·y (rij′ē), *adj.*, **ridg·i·er, ridg·i·est.** rising in ridges.

rid·i·cule (rid′ə kyōōl′), *n.*, *v.*, **-culed, -cul·ing.** —*n.* .1 speech or action intended to cause contemptuous laughter at a person or thing; derision. —*v.t.* **2.** to make fun of. [< L *rīdicul(um)* that excites laughter, a jest = *rīd(ēre)* (to) laugh + *-i-* -I- + *-culum* -CULE] —**rid′i·cul′er,** *n.*

—**Syn. 1.** mockery, raillery, sarcasm, satire, irony. **2.** chaff, twit, satirize, lampoon. RIDICULE, DERIDE, MOCK, TAUNT imply making game of a person, usually in an unkind, jeering way. To RIDICULE is to make fun of, either sportively and good-humoredly, or unkindly with the intention of humiliating: *to ridicule a pretentious person.* To DERIDE is to assail one with scornful laughter: *to deride a statement of belief.* To MOCK is sometimes playfully, sometimes insultingly, to imitate and caricature the appearance or actions of another: *She mocked the seriousness of his expression.* To TAUNT is maliciously and exultingly to press upon one's attention (and often on the notice of others) some annoying or humiliating fact: *to taunt a person defeated in a contest.* —**Ant. 1.** praise.

ri·dic·u·lous (ri dik′yə ləs), *adj.* causing or worthy of ridicule or derision; absurd; preposterous; laughable: *a ridiculous plan.* [< L *rīdiculōs(us)* laughable, droll = *rīdicul(us)* that excites laughter (see RIDICULE) + *-ōsus* -OUS] —**ri·dic′u·lous·ly,** *adv.* —**ri·dic′u·lous·ness,** *n.* —**Syn.** nonsensical, ludicrous, farcical. See **absurd.** —**Ant.** sensible.

rid·ing[1] (rī′ding), *n.* **1.** the act of a person or thing that rides. —*adj.* **2.** used in riding on horseback: *riding clothes.* [ME (n., adj.); OE *ridende* (adj.)]

rid·ing[2] (rī′ding), *n.* **1.** any of the three administrative divisions into which Yorkshire, England, is divided, namely, North Riding, East Riding, and West Riding. **2.** any similar administrative division elsewhere. [ME *triding*, OE **thriding* < Scand; cf. OIcel *thridjungr* third part; *t-* (of ME), var. of *th-* (of OE) lost by assimilation to *-t* in *east, west* which commonly preceded]

rid′ing breech′es, calf-length trousers, esp. of whipcord, flaring at the sides of the thighs and fitting snugly at the knees. Also called **breeches.** Cf. **jodhpur** (def. 1).

rid′ing crop′, crop (def. 7).

rid·ley (rid′lē), *n.*, *pl.* **-leys.** a sea turtle, *Lepidochelys olivacea kempi*, found chiefly in the Gulf of Mexico. [? after *Ridley*, proper name]

Rid·ley (rid′lē), *n.* **1. Nicholas,** c1500–55, English bishop, reformer, and martyr. **2.** a town in SE Pennsylvania, near Philadelphia. 39,085 (1970).

ri·dot·to (ri dot′ō), *n.*, *pl.* **-tos.** a public ball or dance with music and often in masquerade, popular in the 18th century. [< It: retreat, resort; see REDOUBT]

Rie·ka (rē ek′ə; *Serbo-Croatian.* rye′kä), *n.* Rijeka.

Rie·mann (rē′män; *Eng.* rē′män, -mən), *n.* **Ge·org Frie·drich Bern·hard** (gā ôrk′ frē′drikн bern′härt), 1826–66, German mathematician. —**Rie·mann′i·an,** *adj.*

Riemann′ian geom′etry, *Geom.* the branch of non-Euclidean geometry that replaces the parallel postulate of

Euclidean geometry with the postulate that in a plane every pair of lines intersects. Also called **elliptic geometry.**

Rie′mann in′tegral, *Math.* integral (def. 7a). [named after G. F. B. RIEMANN]

Ri·en·zi (rē en′zē; *It.* ryen′dzē), *n.* **Co·la di** (kô′lä dē), (*Nicholas Gabrini*), 1313?–54, Roman orator and tribune. Also, **Ri·en·zo** (rē en′zō; *It.* ryen′dzô).

Ries·ling (rēz′ling, rēs′-), *n.* **1.** a variety of grape grown in Europe and California. **2.** a fragrant white wine made from this grape. [< G]

Rif (rif), *n.* **Er** (er), a mountainous coastal region in N Morocco. Also, **Riff.**

rife (rīf), *adj.* **1.** of common or frequent occurrence; prevalent; in widespread existence, activity, or use: *Crime is rife in the slums.* **2.** current in speech or report: *Rumors about her are rife.* **3.** abundant, plentiful, or numerous. **4.** abounding. [ME; OE *rīfe;* c. OIcel *rīfr* abundant, MD *rijf*] —**rife′ly,** *adv.* —**rife′ness,** *n.* —**Syn. 3.** plenteous, multitudinous. —**Ant. 3.** scarce.

riff (rif), *n. Jazz.* a melodic phrase, often constantly repeated, forming an accompaniment or part of an accompaniment for a soloist. [alter. and shortening of REFRAIN[2]]

Riff (rif), *n., pl.* **Riffs, Riff·i** (rif′ē), (*esp. collectively*) **Riff. 1.** a member of a group of Berber-speaking tribes living in northern Morocco. **2.** Rif.

rif·fle (rif′əl), *n., v.,* **-fled, -fling.** —*n.* **1.** *U.S.* **a.** a rapid, as in a stream. **b.** a ripple, as upon the surface of water. **2.** *Mining.* **a.** the lining at the bottom of a sluice or the like, made of blocks or slats of wood, or stones, arranged in such a manner that grooves or openings are left between them for catching and collecting particles of gold. **b.** any of the slats of wood or the like so used. **c.** any of the grooves or openings formed. **3.** the method of riffling cards. —*v.t., v.i.* **4.** to cause or become a riffle. **5.** to turn hastily; flutter and shift. **6.** *Cards.* to shuffle by dividing the deck in two, raising the corners slightly, and allowing them to fall alternately together. [b. RIPPLE[1] and RUFFLE[1]]

riff·raff (rif′raf′), *n.* **1.** the worthless or disreputable element of society; rabble. **2.** worthless or low persons. [ME *rif and raf* every particle, things of small value < OF *rif et raf,* formed on *rifler* to spoil (see RIFLE[2]), *raffler* to ravage, snatch away]

ri·fle[1] (rī′fəl), *n., v.,* **-fled, -fling.** —*n.* **1.** a shoulder firearm with spiral grooves cut in the inner surface of the gun barrel to give the bullet a rotatory motion and thus render its flight more accurate. **2.** one of the grooves. **3.** a cannon with such grooves. **4. rifles,** (*often cap.*) any of certain military units or bodies equipped with rifles. —*v.t.* **5.** to cut spiral grooves within (a gun barrel, pipe, etc.). [< LG *rīfel(n)* (to) groove < *rīve, riefe* groove, flute, furrow; akin to OE *rifelede* wrinkled, *rīf* violent]

Rifle[1] (Garand)

ri·fle[2] (rī′fəl), *v.t.,* **-fled, -fling. 1.** to ransack and rob (a place, receptacle, etc.). **2.** to search and rob (a person). **3.** to steal or take away. [ME *rifel* < OF *rifl(er)* (to) scrape, graze, plunder < D *riffel(en)* (to) scrape; c. RIFLE[1]] —**ri′fler,** *n.* —**Syn. 1.** See **rob.**

ri·fle·man (rī′fəl mən), *n., pl.* **-men. 1.** a soldier armed with a rifle. **2.** an expert in the use of the rifle. —**ri′fle·man·ship′,** *n.*

ri′fle range′, a firing range for practice with rifles.

ri·fle·ry (rī′fəl rē), *n.* the art, practice, or sport of shooting at targets with rifles.

ri·fling[1] (rī′fling), *n.* **1.** the system of spiral grooves in a gun barrel, pipe, etc. **2.** the act or process of cutting such grooves. [RIFLE[1] + -ING[1]]

ri·fling[2] (rī′fling), *n.* the act or process of ransacking or robbing. [RIFLE[2] + -ING[1]]

rift[1] (rift), *n.* **1.** an opening made by splitting, cleaving, etc.; fissure; cleft; chink. **2.** an open space, as in a forest or cloud mass, or a clear interval. **3.** a break in friendly relations. **4.** a difference in opinion, belief, or interest, that causes such a break. **5.** *Geol.* **a.** a fault. **b.** a valley along the trace of a fault. **6.** the plane or direction along which a log or mass of granite can most easily be split. **7.** wood or a piece of wood that has been split radially from a log. —*v.t., v.i.* **8.** to burst open; split. [ME < Scand; cf. Dan *rift* cleft; akin to RIVE] —**rift′less,** *adj.*

rift[2] (rift), *v.i. Dial.* **1.** to belch. **2.** to break wind. [ME *rift(en)* < ON *rypta;* cf. Icel *ropa* to belch]

rig (rig), *v.,* **rigged, rig·ging,** *n.* —*v.t.* **1.** *Chiefly Naut.* **a.** to put in proper order for working or use. **b.** to fit (a vessel, a mast, etc.) with the necessary shrouds, stays, etc. **c.** to fit (shrouds, stays, sails, etc.) to the mast, yard, or the like. **2.** to furnish or provide with equipment, clothing, etc.; fit (usually fol. by *out* or *up*). **3.** to assemble, install, or prepare (often fol. by *up*). **4.** to manipulate fraudulently: *to rig prices.* **5. rig down,** *Naut.* to place in an inactive state, stowing all lines, tackles, and other removable parts. **6. rig up,** to equip or set up for use. —*n.* **7.** the arrangement of the masts, spars, sails, etc., on a boat or ship. **8.** apparatus for some purpose; equipment; outfit; gear: *a hi-fi rig; a fishing rig.* **9.** a carriage, buckboard, sulky, or wagon together with the horse or horses that draw it. **10.** the equipment used in drilling an oil well. **11.** *Informal.* costume or dress, esp. when odd or conspicuous, or when designated for a particular purpose: *That was quite a rig she wore to the party. He looks quite nifty in a butler's rig.* [ME *rigge(n)* ? < Scand; cf. Dan *rigge,* Sw *rigga* (*på*) to harness (up)]

Ri·ga (rē′gə), *n.* **1.** a seaport in and the capital of the Latvian Republic, in the W Soviet Union in Europe, on the Gulf of Riga. 657,000 (1965). **2. Gulf of,** an arm of the Baltic between the Latvian and Estonian republics of the Soviet Union. 90 mi. long.

rig·a·doon (rig′ə do͞on′), *n.* a lively dance for one couple, characterized by a peculiar jumping step and usually in quick duple meter. [< F *rigaudon,* perh. from name *Rigaud*]

rig·a·ma·role (rig′ə mə rōl′), *n.* rigmarole.

rig·a·to·ni (rig′ə tō′nē), *n. Italian Cookery.* a tubular pasta in short, ribbed pieces. [< It (n.pl.) = *rigat(o)* furrowed, lined, striped (ptp. of *rigare* < *riga* a line) + *-oni* pl. aug. suffix]

Ri·gel (rī′jəl, -gəl), *n. Astron.* a first-magnitude star in the constellation Orion. [< Ar *rijl* foot, so called from its position in the left foot of the figure of Orion]

rig·ger (rig′ər), *n.* **1.** a person who rigs. **2.** a person whose occupation is the fitting of the rigging of ships. **3.** a person who works with hoisting tackle, cranes, scaffolding, etc. **4.** *Aeron.* a mechanic skilled in the assembly, adjustment, and alignment of aircraft control surfaces, wings, and the like. **5.** a person who packs or folds parachutes.

rig·ging (rig′ing), *n.* **1.** the ropes, chains, etc., employed to support and work the masts, yards, sails, etc., on a ship. **2.** lifting or hauling tackle. **3.** *Informal.* clothing.

Riggs′′ disease′ (rigz), *Dentistry.* pyorrhea (def. 2). [named after John M. *Riggs* (1810–85), American dentist]

right (rīt), *adj.* **1.** in accordance with what is good, proper, or just: *right conduct.* **2.** in conformity with fact, reason, or some standard or principle; correct: *the right solution.* **3.** correct in judgment, opinion, or action. **4.** sound, normal, or sane, as a person or his mind. **5.** in good health or spirits. **6.** in a satisfactory state; in good order. **7.** principal, front, or upper: *the right side of cloth.* **8.** most convenient, desirable, or suitable. **9.** genuine; authentic: *the right owner.* **10.** noting, of, near, or pertaining to the side of a person or thing that is turned toward the east when the face is toward the north (opposed to *left*). **11.** (*often cap.*) noting or pertaining to political conservatives and their beliefs. **12.** straight: *a right line.* **13.** formed by or with reference to a perpendicular: *a right angle.* **14.** *Geom.* having an axis perpendicular to the base: *a right cone.* —*n.* **15.** a just claim or title, whether legal, prescriptive, or moral. **16.** Sometimes, **rights.** that which is due to anyone by just claim, legal guarantees, moral principles, etc. **17.** that which is morally, legally, or ethically proper. **18.** Sometimes, **rights.** the interest or ownership a person, group, or business has in property. **19.** the property itself or its value. **20.** *Finance.* **a.** the privilege that accrues to the stockholders to subscribe to additional shares of stock at an advantageous price. **b.** Often, **rights.** the document certifying this privilege. **21.** that which is in accord with fact, reason, etc. **22.** the state or quality or an instance of being correct. **23.** the side that is normally opposite to that where the heart is; the direction toward that side. **24.** a right-hand turn: *Make a right at the top of the hill.* **25.** the portion toward the right, as of troops in battle formation. **26.** (in a pair) the member that is shaped for, used by, or situated on the right side. **27.** the right hand: *Jab with your left and punch with your right.* **28.** (*usually cap.*) the part of a legislative assembly, esp. in continental Europe, that is situated on the right side of the presiding officer and that is customarily assigned to members of the legislature who hold more conservative or reactionary views than the rest of the members. **29.** the members of such an assembly who sit on the Right. **30. the Right,** those opposing any change in a liberal direction and usually advocating rigid maintenance of the established social, political, or economic order. Cf. **left**[1] (defs. 6a, b). **31.** *Boxing.* a blow delivered by the right hand. **32. by rights,** in fairness; justly. **33. in one's own right,** by reason of one's own ability, ownership, etc.; in or of oneself, as independent of others. **34. in the right,** having the support of reason or law; correct. **35. to rights,** into proper condition or order: *to set a room to rights.* —*adv.* **36.** in a straight line; straight; directly: *right to the bottom.* **37.** quite, or completely; all the way: *His hat was knocked right off.* **38.** immediately; promptly: *right after dinner.* **39.** exactly; precisely. **40.** uprightly or righteously. **41.** correctly or accurately: *to guess right.* **42.** properly or fittingly: *to act right.* **43.** advantageously, favorably, or well: *to turn out right.* **44.** toward the right hand; on or to the right. **45.** *Chiefly Dial.* extremely: *I was right glad to be there.* **46.** very (used in certain titles): *the right reverend.* **47. right and left,** on every side; in all directions. **48. right away** or **off,** without hesitation; immediately. **49. right on,** *Slang.* exactly right; precisely. —*v.t.* **50.** to put in or restore to an upright position: *to right a fallen lamp.* **51.** to put in proper order, condition, or relationship. **52.** to bring into conformity with fact; correct. **53.** to do justice to; avenge. **54.** to redress, as a wrong. —*v.i.* **55.** to resume an upright or the proper position. [ME; OE *reht, riht;* c. D, G *recht,* Icel *rett(r),* Goth *raiht(s);* akin to L *rectus*] —**Syn. 1.** equitable, fair, honest, lawful. **2.** accurate, true. **8.** proper. **40.** rightfully, rightly, justly, fairly. **42.** appropriately, suitably. —**Ant. 1–3, 7, 8, 17.** wrong.

right·a·bout (rīt′ə bout′), *n.* **1.** the position assumed by turning so as to face in the opposite direction. **2.** the act of so turning. —*adv.* **3.** facing or in the opposite direction: *Move that chair rightabout.* Also, **right′-a-bout′.**

right′ about′ face′, *Mil.* **1.** a command, given to a soldier or soldiers at attention, to turn the body about toward the right so as to face in the opposite direction. **2.** the act of so turning in a prescribed military manner.

right′ an′gle, the angle formed by two radii of a circle that are drawn to the extremities of an arc equal to one quarter of the circle; an angle of 90°. See diag. at **angle**[1]. —**right′-an′gled,** *adj.*

right′ ascen′sion, *Astron.* the arc of the celestial equator measured eastward from the vernal equinox to the foot of the great circle passing through the celestial poles and a given point on the celestial sphere, expressed in degrees or hours.

Right′ Bank′, a part of Paris, France, on the N bank of the Seine. Cf. **Left Bank.**

right·eous (rī′chəs), *adj.* **1.** characterized by uprightness or morality. **2.** morally right or justifiable: *righteous indignation.* **3.** acting in an upright, moral way; virtuous. [earlier *rightwos, rightwis* (remodeled with -OUS), OE *rihtwīs.* See RIGHT, WISE[2]] —**right′eous·ly,** *adv.* —**Syn. 3.** good, honest. —**Ant. 3.** evil, wicked.

right·eous·ness (rī′chəs nis), *n.* **1.** the quality or state of being righteous, just, or rightful. **2.** righteous conduct. [ME *rightwisnes(se),* OE *rihtwīsnes*]

right′ face′, *Mil.* **1.** a command, given to a soldier or soldiers at attention, to turn the body 90° toward the right. **2.** the act of so turning in a prescribed military manner.

right′ field′, *Baseball.* **1.** the area of the outfield to the right of center field as viewed from home plate. **2.** the position of the player covering this area.

right′ field′er, *Baseball.* the player whose position is right field.

right·ful (rīt′fəl), *adj.* **1.** having a valid or just claim, as to some property or position; legitimate. **2.** belonging or held by a valid or just claim. **3.** equitable or just, as actions, a cause, etc. [ME] —**right′ful·ly,** *adv.* —**right′ful·ness,** *n.*

right′ hand′, **1.** the hand that is on the right side, or the side opposite that where the heart is. **2.** the right side, as of a person, esp. this side considered as the side of precedence or courtesy. **3.** a position of honor or special trust. **4.** an extremely efficient or reliable person, esp. a person considered as one's assistant. [ME *riht hond,* OE *ryht handa*]

right-hand (rīt′hand′), *adj.* **1.** on the right. **2.** of, for, or with the right hand. **3.** most efficient or useful, as a helper or assistant. **4.** plain-laid.

right-hand·ed (rīt′han′did), *adj.* **1.** having the right hand or arm more serviceable than the left; using the right hand by preference. **2.** adapted to or performed by the right hand. **3.** *Mach.* **a.** rotating clockwise. **b.** noting a helical, or spiral, member, as a gear tooth or screw thread, that twists clockwise as it recedes from an observer. —*adv.* Also, **right′-hand′ed·ly.** **4.** in a right-handed manner. **5.** with the right hand. **6.** toward the right hand or in a clockwise direction. [ME] —**right′-hand′ed·ness,** *n.*

right-hand·er (rīt′han′dər), *n.* a person, esp. a baseball pitcher, who is right-handed.

right′-hand man′, an invaluable assistant.

right·ism (rī′tiz əm), *n.* conservatism, esp. in politics.

right·ist (rī′tist), *adj.* **1.** of, pertaining to, or noting conservative or reactionary views, esp. in politics. —*n.* **2.** a conservative or reactionary.

right-laid (rīt′lād′), *adj.* noting a rope, strand, etc., laid in a right-handed, or clockwise, direction.

right·ly (rīt′lē), *adv.* **1.** in accordance with truth or fact; correctly. **2.** in accordance with morality or equity; uprightly. **3.** properly, fitly, or suitably. [ME; OE *rihtlīce*]

right-mind·ed (rīt′mīn′did), *adj.* having correct, honest, or good opinions or principles. —**right′-mind′ed·ly,** *adv.* —**right′-mind′ed·ness,** *n.*

right·ness (rīt′nis), *n.* **1.** correctness or accuracy. **2.** propriety or fitness. **3.** moral integrity. **4.** *Obs.* straightness or directness. [ME; OE *rihtnes*]

right′ of way′, **1.** a common law or statutory right granted to a vehicle to proceed ahead of another. **2.** a path or route that may lawfully be used. **3.** a right of passage, as over another's land. **4.** the strip of land acquired for use by a railroad for tracks. **5.** land covered by a public road. **6.** land over which a power line passes.

right-of-way (rīt′əv wā′), *n., pl.* **rights-of-way.** See **right of way.**

right-oh (rīt′ō′, rīt′ō′; rī′tō′, -tō′), *interj.* *Chiefly Brit. Informal.* (used to express cheerful consent or understanding.) Also, **right′o′.**

rights (rīts), *Informal.* —*n.* **1.** See **civil rights.** —*adj.* **2.** civil-rights: *a rights worker.*

right′ sec′tion, a representation of an object as it would appear if cut by a plane perpendicular to its longest axis. Cf. **cross section.**

right-to-life (rīt′tə līf′), *adj.* pro-life: *right-to-life movement.* —**right′-to-lif′er,** *n.*

right′-to-work′ law′ (rīt′tə wûrk′), *U.S.* a state law that makes a closed shop illegal.

right′ tri′angle, a triangle having a right angle. See diag. at **triangle.**

right′ wing′, **1.** a conservative or reactionary political party, or a group of political parties. **2.** the conservative or reactionary element in a political or other organization. —**right′-wing′,** *adj.* —**right′-wing′er,** *n.*

right·y (rī′tē), *adv., n., pl.* **right·ies.** *Informal.* —*adv.* **1.** with the right hand. —*n.* **2.** a right-handed person.

rig·id (rij′id), *adj.* **1.** stiff or unyielding; not pliant or flexible; hard: *a rigid strip of metal.* **2.** firmly fixed or set. **3.** inflexible, strict, or severe: *rigid rules of social behavior.* **4.** exacting; rigorous: *a rigid examination.* **5.** so as to meet precise standards; stringent: *lenses ground to rigid specifications.* **6.** *Mech.* of, pertaining to, or noting a body in which the distance between any pair of points remains fixed under all forces. **7.** *Aeron.* **a.** (of an airship or dirigible) having a form maintained by a stiff, unyielding structure contained within the envelope. **b.** pertaining to a helicopter rotor that is held fixedly at its root. [< L *rigid(us)* = *rig(ēre)* (to) be stiff, stiffen + *-idus* -ID[4]] —**ri·gid′i·ty, rig′id·ness,** *n.* —**rig′id·ly,** *adv.* —**Syn. 1.** unbending, inflexible. **2.** immovable. **3.** austere, stern, unyielding. See **strict.**

ri·gid·i·fy (ri jid′ə fī′), *v.t., v.i.,* **-fied, -fy·ing.** to make or become rigid.

rig·ma·role (rig′mə rōl′), *n.* **1.** an elaborate or complicated procedure. **2.** meaningless talk. Also, **rigamarole.** [alter. of RAGMAN ROLL]

rig·or (rig′ər), *n.* **1.** strictness, severity, or harshness, as in dealing with persons. **2.** the full or extreme severity of laws, rules, etc. **3.** severity of living conditions; hardship; austerity. **4.** a severe or harsh act, circumstance, etc. **5.** scrupulous or inflexible accuracy or adherence: *the logical rigor of mathematics.* **6.** severity of weather or climate. **7.** an instance of this: *the rigors of winter.* **8.** *Pathol.* a sudden coldness, as that preceding certain fevers; chill. **9.** *Physiol.* a state of rigidity in muscle tissues during which they are unable to respond to stimuli due to the coagulation of muscle protein. **10.** *Obs.* stiffness or rigidity. Also, *esp. Brit.,* **rig′our.** [ME *rigour* < L *rigor* stiffness = *rig(ēre)* (to) be stiff + *-or* -OR[1]] —**Syn. 1.** inflexibility, stringency.

rig·or·ism (rig′ə riz′əm), *n.* extreme strictness, as in attitude. Also, *esp. Brit.,* **rig′our·ism.** [< F *rigorisme*]

rig·or mor·tis (rig′ər môr′tis, rī′gôr), the stiffening of the body after death. [< L: lit., stiffness of death]

rig·or·ous (rig′ər əs), *adj.* **1.** characterized by rigor; rigidly severe or harsh, as persons, rules, discipline, etc. **2.** severely exact or accurate; precise. **3.** (of weather or climate) uncomfortably severe or harsh, extremely inclement. **4.** *Logic, Math.* logically valid. [ME < ML *rigōrōs(us)*] —**rig′or·ous·ly,** *adv.* —**rig′or·ous·ness,** *n.* —**Syn. 1.** stern, austere, inflexible. See **strict.** —**Ant. 1.** flexible.

Rigs·dag (rigz′däg′), *n.* the former parliament of Denmark, consisting of an upper house and a lower house: replaced in 1953 by the unicameral Folketing. [< Dan = *rigs,* gen. of *rig* kingdom + *dag* diet, assembly. Cf. REICHSTAG]

Rig-Ve·da (rig vā′də, -vē′də), *n.* *Hinduism.* one of the Samhitas, a collection of 1028 hymns, dating from not later than the second millennium B.C. Also, **Rig-ve′da.** Cf. **Veda.** [< Skt = *ṛc* praise + *vēda* knowledge] —**Rig·ve·dic** (rig vā′dik, -vē′-), *adj.*

Riis (rēs), *n.* **Jacob August,** 1849–1914, U.S. journalist and social reformer, born in Denmark.

Ri·je·ka (rē ek′ə; *Serbo-Croatian.* RĒ ye′kä), *n.* a seaport in NW Yugoslavia, on the Gulf of Quarnero. 111,000 (1961). Also, **Rieka.** Formerly, **Fiume.**

rijks·daal·der (rīks′däl′dər), *n.* a silver coin of Holland, equal to 2½ gulden. [< D; see RIX-DOLLAR]

Rijn (RĪN), *n.* Dutch name of the **Rhine.**

Rijs·wijk (RĪS′vīk), *n.* Dutch name of **Ryswick.**

rik·i·sha (rik′shô), *n.* jinrikisha. Also, **rik′shaw.**

Riks·dag (riks′däg′), *n.* the bicameral parliament of Sweden. [see REICHSTAG]

Riks·mål (riks′môl; *Norw.* RĒKS′môl′), *n.* Bokmål. Formerly, **Riks′maal.**

rile (rīl), *v.t.,* **riled, ril·ing.** *Chiefly U.S.* **1.** to irritate or vex. **2.** to roil (water or the like). [var. of ROIL]

Ri·ley (rī′lē), *n.* **James Whit·comb** (hwit′kəm, wit′-), 1849–1916, U.S. poet.

ri·lie·vo (RĒ lye′vô; *Eng.* ril yev′ō), *n., pl.* **-lie·vi** (-lye′vē; *Eng.* -yev′ē). *Italian.* relief[2] (defs. 2, 3).

Ril·ke (ril′kə; *Ger.* RIL′kə), *n.* **Rai·ner Ma·ri·a** (rī′nər mə rē′ə; *Ger.* RĪ′nəR mä RĒ′ä), 1875–1926, Austrian poet, born in Prague.

rill[1] (ril), *n.* a small rivulet or brook. [< D or LG; cf. Fris *ril*]

rill[2] (ril), *n.* *Astron.* any of certain long, narrow trenches or valleys observed on the surface of the moon. Also, **rille.** [< G *Rille* channel < LG; see RILL[1]]

rim (rim), *n., v.,* **rimmed, rim·ming.** —*n.* **1.** the outer edge, border, or margin of something, esp. of a circular object. **2.** any edge, margin, or frame added to or around an object or area. **3.** the outer circle of a wheel, attached to the hub by spokes. **4.** a circular strip of metal forming the connection between an automobile wheel and tire. **5.** *Basketball.* the metal ring from which the net is suspended to form the basket. —*v.t.* **6.** to furnish with a rim, border, or margin. **7.** (of a ball) to roll around the edge of (a hole or basket) but not go in. [ME; OE *rima;* c. Icel *rimi* raised strip of land, ridge] —**Syn. 1.** lip, verge. —**Ant. 1.** center.

Rim·baud (ram bō′; *Fr.* RAN bō′), *n.* **(Jean Ni·co·las) Ar·thur** (zhäN nē kô lä′ AR tyR′), 1854–91, French poet.

rime[1] (rīm), *n., v.t., v.i.,* **rimed, rim·ing.** rhyme. —**rim′er,** *n.*

rime[2] (rīm), *n., v.,* **rimed, rim·ing.** —*n.* **1.** Also called **rime′ ice′.** an opaque coating of ice particles, caused by the rapid freezing of supercooled water droplets on impact with an object. Cf. **frost** (def. 2), **glaze** (def. 14). —*v.t.* **2.** to cover with rime or hoarfrost. [ME *rim,* OE *hrīm;* c. D *rijm,* OIcel *hrīm*]

rime riche (rēm rēsh′), *pl.* **rimes riches** (rēm rēsh′). *Pros.* rhyme created by the use of two different words, or groups of words, of which both the stressed syllables and any following syllables are identical, as in *lighted, delighted.* Also called **identical rhyme, perfect rhyme, rich rhyme.** [< F: lit., rich rhyme]

rime·ster (rīm′stər), *n.* rhymester.

rim·fire (rim′fīər′), *adj.* **1.** (of a cartridge) having the primer in a rim encircling the base. **2.** (of a firearm) designed for the use of such cartridges. Also, **rim′-fire′.**

Ri·mi·ni (rim′ə nē; *It.* RĒ′mē nē), *n.* **1. Fran·ces·ca da** (fran ches′kə də, frän-; *It.* fRän che′skä dä), 13th-century Italian noblewoman, a character in Dante's *The Divine Comedy:* killed by her husband in the act of adultery. **2.** a seaport in NE Italy, on the Adriatic. 94,075 (1961).

rim′ light′ing, backlighting.

ri·mose (rī′mōs, rī mōs′), *adj.* full of crevices, chinks, or cracks. Also, **ri·mous** (rī′məs). [< L *rīmōs(us)* full of cracks = *rīm(a)* cleft, crack, chink + *-ōsus* -OSE[1]]

rim·ple (rim′pəl), *n., v.,* **-pled, -pling.** —*n.* **1.** a wrinkle. —*v.t., v.i.* **2.** to wrinkle; crumple; crease. [ME; OE *hrympel;* see RUMPLE]

rim·rock (rim′rok′), *n.* *Geol.* **1.** rock forming the natural boundary of a plateau or other rise. **2.** bedrock forming the boundary of a placer or of a gravel deposit.

Rim·sky-Kor·sa·kov (rim′skē kôr′sə kôf′; *Russ.* RĒM′ski kôR sä kôf′), *n.* **Ni·co·lai An·dre·e·vich** (ni kô lī′ än dRe′yə vich), 1844–1908, Russian composer. Also, **Rim′ski-Kor′sa·kov′, Rim′sky-Kor′sa·koff′.**

rim·y (rī′mē), *adj.,* **rim·i·er, rim·i·est.** covered with rime ice. [OE *hrīmig*] —**rim′i·ness,** *n.*

rin (rin), *n., pl.* **rin.** a money of account of Japan, one tenth of a sen: removed from circulation in 1954. [< Jap]

rind (rīnd), *n.* a thick and firm outer coat or covering, as of fruits or cheeses. [ME, OE *rind(e);* c. G *Rinde*]

rin·der·pest (rin′dər pest′), *n.* *Vet. Pathol.* an acute, usually fatal, virus disease of cattle, sheep, etc., characterized by high fever, diarrhea, and lesions of the skin and mucous membranes. Also called **cattle plague.** [< G = *Rinder* cattle (pl. of *Rind*) + *Pest* pestilence]

rin·for·zan·do (*It.* RĒN′fôR tsän′dô), *adj., adv.* sforzando. [< It: reinforcing (prp. of *rinforzare* = *ri-* RE- + *inforzare* to ENFORCE)]

ring[1] (ring), *n., v.,* **ringed, ring·ing.** —*n.* **1.** a typically circular band of metal or other durable material, esp. one of precious metal, for wearing on the finger as an ornament, a token of betrothal or marriage, etc. **2.** anything having the form of such a band: *a ring of water; napkin ring.* **3.** a circular or surrounding line or mark: *dark rings around the eyes.* **4.** a circular course: *to dance in a ring.* **5.** the outside edge of a circular body, as a wheel; rim. **6.** a single turn in a spiral or helix or in a spiral course. **7.** *Geom.* the area or space between two concentric circles. **8.** *Bot.* See **annual ring.** **9.** a circle of bark cut from around a tree. **10.** a number of persons or things situated in a circle or in an ap-

proximately circular arrangement. **11.** an enclosed area, often circular, as for a sports contest or exhibition: *a circus ring.* **12.** a bullring. **13.** an enclosure for boxing and wrestling matches, usually consisting of a square, canvas-covered platform surrounded by ropes supported by posts. **14.** the sport of boxing; prize fighting. **15.** a group of persons cooperating for unethical or illegal purposes: *a ring of dope smugglers.* **16.** *Chem.* a number of atoms so united that they may be graphically represented in cyclic form. Cf. **chain** (def. 7). **17.** a bowlike or circular piece at the top of an anchor, to which the chain or cable is secured. **18.** *Astron.* See **ring formation.** **19.** Also called **spinning ring.** *Textiles.* (in the ring-spinning frame) a circular track of steel on which the traveler moves and that imparts twists to the yarn. **20. run rings around,** to surpass; outdo. **21. throw** or **toss one's hat in the ring.** See **hat** (def. 7). —*v.t.* **22.** to surround with a ring; encircle. **23.** to form into a ring. **24.** to insert a ring through the nose of (an animal). **25.** to hem in (animals) by riding or circling about them. **26.** to cut away the bark in a ring about (a tree, branch, etc.). —*v.i.* **27.** to form a ring or rings. **28.** to move or be arranged in a ring or a constantly curving course: *The road rings around the mountain.* [ME; OE *hring;* c. D, G *ring,* OIcel *hring(r).* See RANK[1]]
—**Syn. 2.** circle, circlet, hoop; annulus. **11.** arena, rink, circle. **15.** gang, mob, syndicate. RING, CLIQUE are terms applied with disapproving connotations to groups of persons. RING suggests a small and intimately related group, combined for selfish and often dishonest purposes: *a gambling ring.* A CLIQUE is a small group that prides itself on its congeniality and exclusiveness: *cliques in a school.*

ring[2] (ring), *v.,* **rang, rung, ring·ing,** *n.* —*v.i.* **1.** to give forth a clear resonant sound, as a doorbell, telephone bell, etc. **2.** to appear to the mind; seem: *His words rang false.* **3.** to cause a bell or bells to sound, esp. as a summons: *Just ring if you need anything.* **4.** to sound loudly; be loud or resonant; resound (often fol. by *out*): *His brave words rang out.* **5.** to be filled with sound; reecho with sound, as a place. **6.** (of the ears) to have the sensation of a continued humming sound. —*v.t.* **7.** to cause (a bell or device with a bell) to ring; sound by striking. **8.** to produce (sound) by or as by ringing. **9.** to announce or proclaim, usher in or out, summon, signal, etc., by or as by the sound of a bell. **10.** to test (a coin or other metal object) by the sound it produces when struck against something. **11.** *Chiefly Brit.* to telephone. **12. ring a bell.** See **bell**[1] (def. 7). **13. ring down the curtain, a.** to direct that the curtain of a theater be lowered or closed. **b.** to lower or close the curtain. **14. ring down the curtain on,** to bring to an end. **15. ring the changes.** See **change** (def. 33). **16. ring up, a.** *Chiefly Brit.* to telephone. **b.** to register (the amount of a sale) on a cash register. **17. ring up the curtain,** to raise or open the curtain in front of a stage. **18. ring up the curtain on,** to begin; inaugurate; initiate. —*n.* **19.** a ringing sound, as of a bell or bells. **20.** a sound or tone likened to the ringing of a bell: *rings of laughter.* **21.** any loud sound; sound continued, repeated, or reverberated. **22.** a set or peal of bells. **23.** a telephone call: *Give me a ring tomorrow.* **24.** the act or an instance of ringing a bell. **25.** a characteristic sound, as of a coin. **26.** the aspect or impression presented by a statement, an action, etc., taken as revealing a specified inherent quality: *a ring of assurance in his voice; the ring of truth; a false ring.* [ME *ring(en),* OE *hringan;* c. OIcel *hringja,* G *ringen*]

ring·bolt (ring′bōlt′), *n.* a bolt with a ring fitted in an eye at its head.

ring·bone (ring′bōn′), *n.* *Vet. Pathol.* a morbid bony growth on the pastern bones of a horse, often resulting in lameness. [RING[1] + BONE[1]]

ring·dove (ring′duv′), *n.* **1.** a European pigeon, *Columba palumbus,* having a whitish patch on each side of the neck. **2.** a small, Old World dove, *Streptopelia risoria,* having a black half circle around the neck.

ringed (ringd), *adj.* **1.** having or wearing a ring or rings. **2.** marked or decorated with or as with a ring or rings. **3.** surrounded by or as by a ring or rings. **4.** formed of or with rings; ringlike or annular: *a ringed growth.* [ME; see RING[1], -ED[3]]

ringed′ plain′. See **walled plain.**

ringed′ snake′. See **ring-neck snake.**

rin·gent (rin′jənt), *adj.* **1.** gaping. **2.** *Bot.* having widely spread lips, as some corollas. [< L *ringent-* (s. of *ringēns,* prp. of *ringī* to gape) = *ring-* open the mouth + *-ent-* -ENT]

ring·er[1] (ring′ər), *n.* **1.** a person or thing that encircles, rings, etc. **2.** a quoit or horseshoe so thrown as to encircle the peg. [RING[1] + -ER[1]]

ring·er[2] (ring′ər), *n.* **1.** a person or thing that rings or makes a ringing noise. **2.** *Slang.* a race horse, athlete, or the like entered in a competition under false representation. **3.** *Slang.* a person or thing that closely resembles another. [late ME; see RING[2], -ER[1]]

Ring′er's solu′tion (ring′ərz), *Pharm.* an aqueous solution of the chlorides of sodium, potassium, and calcium, isotonic with blood and tissue fluid, used chiefly for sustaining tissue in physiological experimentation. [named after Sydney *Ringer* (1835–1910), English physician]

ring′ fin′ger, the third finger, esp. of the left hand, on which an engagement ring, wedding band, etc., is traditionally worn. [ME *ringe finger,* OE *hring fingre*]

ring′ forma′tion, any circular or almost circular area of the moon completely or partially surrounded by elevations; ring; walled plain; crater.

ring′ frame′. See **ring-spinning frame.**

ring′ gear′, *Mach.* a gear in the form of a ring with internal teeth.

ring·hals (ring′hals), *n., pl.* **-hals, -hals·es.** an African cobra, *Hemachatus haemachatus,* that squirts or "spits" its venom at a victim. [< SAfrD = *ring* RING[1] + *hals* neck]

ring·lead·er (ring′lē′dər), *n.* a person who leads others, esp. in opposition to authority, law, etc. [RING[1] + LEADER]

ring·let (ring′lit), *n.* a curled lock of hair. —**ring′let·ed,** *adj.*

ring·mas·ter (ring′mas′tər, -mä′stər), *n.* a person in charge of the performances in a circus ring.

ring·neck (ring′nek′), *n.* a ring-necked bird.

ring-necked (ring′nekt′), *adj.* *Zool.* having a ring of distinctive color around the neck.

ring′-necked pheas′ant, a gallinaceous Asian bird, *Phasianus colchicus,* now introduced into Great Britain and the U.S. See illus. at **pheasant.**

ring′-neck snake′, any of several small, nonvenomous North American snakes of the genus *Diadophis,* usually having a conspicuous yellow or orange ring around the neck. Also, **ring′-necked snake′.** Also **ring snake, ringed snake.**

ring·side (ring′sīd′), *n.* **1.** the area immediately surrounding a ring, esp. the area occupied by the first row of seats on all sides of a boxing or wrestling ring. **2.** any place providing a close view. —*adj.* **3.** in or pertaining to a ringside area. **4.** having a close view.

ring·sid·er (ring′sīd′ər), *n.* a spectator at or near ringside, as of a boxing match or a nightclub performance.

ring′ snake′. See **ring-neck snake.**

ring′-spin·ning frame′ (ring′spin′ing), a machine containing the ring, traveler, and bobbin used in spinning yarn. Also called **ring frame, ring′ spin′ner.**

ring·tail (ring′tāl′), *n.* **1.** any phalanger of the genus *Pseudocheirus,* related by the structure of the molar teeth to the koala. **2.** cacomistle. [RING[1] + TAIL[1]]

ring-tailed (ring′tāld′), *adj.* having the tail ringed with alternating colors, as a raccoon.

ring·worm (ring′wûrm′), *n.* *Pathol.* any of a number of contagious skin diseases caused by certain parasitic fungi and characterized by the formation of ring-shaped eruptive patches. [ME]

rink (ringk), *n.* **1.** a smooth expanse of ice for ice skating, often artificially prepared and inside a building or arena. **2.** a smooth floor, usually of wood, for roller skating. **3.** a building or enclosure for ice skating or roller skating; skating arena. **4.** an area of ice marked off for the game of curling. **5.** a section of a bowling green where a match can be played. **6.** a set of players on one side in a lawn-bowling or curling match. [orig. Scot; ME *renk,* appar. < MF *renc* RANK[1]]

rink·y-dink (ring′kē dingk′), *Slang.* —*adj.* **1.** outmoded, shabby, or unsophisticated. —*n.* **2.** a person or thing that is outmoded, shabby, or unsophisticated. Also, **rink·y-tink** (ring′kē tingk′). [orig. unknown]

rinse (rins), *v.,* **rinsed, rins·ing,** *n.* —*v.t.* **1.** to douse or drench in clean water as a final stage in washing or as a light washing: *to rinse a cup.* **2.** to remove (soap, dirt, etc.) by such a process (often fol. by *off*): *to rinse the soap off.* —*n.* **3.** the act or an instance of rinsing. **4.** the water used for rinsing. **5.** any preparation that may be used on the hair after washing, as to remove all the soap or shampoo or to tint the hair. **6.** the act or an instance of using such a preparation on the hair. [ME *rynce(n)* < MF *rincer,* OF *recincier* < VL **recentiāre* to make new, refresh = L *recent-* fresh, RECENT + connective *-i-* + *-āre* inf. suffix] —**rins′a·ble, rins′i·ble,** *adj.*

rins·ing (rin′sing), *n.* **1.** the act of a person who rinses. **2.** an instance of rinsing. **3.** Usually, **rinsings.** the liquid with which anything has been rinsed. [ME *rinsynge*]

Rí·o Bra·vo (rē′ô brä′vô), Mexican name of **Rio Grande.**

Rí·o Cuar·to (rē′ô kwär′tô), a city in central Argentina. 59,900 (est. 1956).

Ri·o de Ja·nei·ro (rē′ō dā zhə nâr′ō, jə-, dē, də; *Port.* rē′o͝o də zhə ne′ro͝o), a seaport in SE Brazil: former capital. 3,223,408 (1960). Also called **Ri′o.**

Rí·o de la Pla·ta (*Sp.* rē′ô the lä plä′tä). See **Plata.**

Rí·o de O·ro (rē′ô the ô′rô), former name of **Villa Cisneros** (def. 1).

Ri·o Grande (rē′ō grand′, gran′dē, grän′dā *for 1; Port.* rē′o͝o gränn′də *for 2, 3*), **1.** Mexican, **Río Bravo.** a river flowing from SW Colorado through central New Mexico and along the boundary between Texas and Mexico into the Gulf of Mexico. 1800 mi. long. **2.** a river flowing W from SE Brazil into the Paraná River. 650 mi. long. **3.** Also, **Rio Grande do Sul.** See **São Pedro do Rio Grande do Sul.**

Ri·o Gran·de do Nor·te (rē′o͝o gränn′də do͝o nôr′tə), a state in E Brazil. 1,157,258 (1960); 20,464 sq. mi. *Cap.:* Natal.

Ri·o Gran·de do Sul (rē′o͝o gränn′də do͝o so͞ol′), **1.** a state in S Brazil. 5,448,823 (1960); 107,923 sq. mi. *Cap.:* Pôrto Alegre. **2.** See **São Pedro do Rio Grande do Sul.**

Rí·o Mu·ni (rē′ô mo͞o′nē), the mainland province of Equatorial Guinea, on the Guinea coast. 183,377 (1960); 10,040 sq. mi. *Cap.:* Bata.

Rí·o Ne·gro (rē′ō nā′grō; *Sp.* rē′ô ne′grô). See **Negro.**

Ri′on Strait′ (rē′on; *Gk.* rē′ôn), Lepanto (def. 3).

ri·ot (rī′ət), *n.* **1.** a noisy, violent public disorder caused by a group or crowd of persons. **2.** *Law.* a disturbance of the public peace by three or more persons acting together in a disrupting and tumultuous manner in carrying out their private purposes. **3.** violent or wild disorder or confusion. **4.** loose, wanton living; profligacy. **5.** unrestrained revelry. **6.** an unbridled outbreak, as of emotions or passions. **7.** a vivid display: *a riot of color.* **8.** *Informal.* something or someone hilariously funny. **9. run riot,** to act, grow, etc., without control or restraint. —*v.i.* **10.** to take part in a riot or disorderly public outbreak. **11.** to live in a loose, wanton manner, or indulge in unrestrained revelry. —*v.t.* **12.** to spend (money, time, etc.) in riotous living. [ME < OF *riote* debate, dispute, quarrel < *r(u)ihoter* to quarrel, dim. of *ruir* to make an uproar < L *rugīre* to roar] —**ri′ot·er,** *n.*
—**Syn. 1.** outbreak, brawl, fray, melee. **3.** uproar, tumult, disturbance. **10.** brawl, fight. **11.** carouse.

Ri′ot Act′, 1. an English statute of 1715 making it a felony for 12 or more persons to assemble unlawfully and riotously and to refuse to disperse upon proclamation. **2. read the riot act,** to reprimand or censure.

ri′ot gun′, a gun, esp. a shotgun with a short barrel, for quelling riots rather than inflicting serious injury.

ri·ot·ous (rī′ə təs), *adj.* **1.** (of an act) characterized by or of the nature of rioting or a disturbance of the peace. **2.** (of a person) inciting or taking part in a riot. **3.** given to or marked by unrestrained revelry; loose; wanton: *riotous living.* **4.** boisterous or uproarious: *riotous laughter.* **5.** *Informal.* hilariously funny. [ME] —**ri′ot·ous·ly,** *adv.*

ri′ot squad′, a group of police officers specially prepared for quelling public disturbances.

rip[1] (rip), *v.*, **ripped, rip·ping,** *n.* —*v.t.* **1.** to cut, tear apart, or tear away in a rough or vigorous manner. **2.** to saw (wood) in the direction of the grain. —*v.i.* **3.** to become torn apart or split open. **4. rip into,** *Informal.* to attack physically or verbally; assail. **5. rip off,** *Slang.* **a.** to steal or pilfer. **b.** to rob or steal from. **c.** to exploit or take advantage of. **6. rip out,** *Informal.* to utter angrily. —*n.* **7.** a rent made by ripping; tear. [late ME; c. Fris *rippe,* Flem *rippen;* cf. dial. E *ripple* to scratch] —**rip′pa·ble,** *adj.* —**Syn. 1.** See **tear**[2]. **7.** laceration, cut.

rip[2] (rip), *n.* a stretch of turbulent water at sea or in a river. [see RIP[1], RIPPLE[1]]

rip[3] (rip), *n.* *Informal.* a dissolute or worthless person. [prob. alter. of *rep,* shortened form of REPROBATE]

R.I.P., **1.** may he (or she) rest in peace. [< L *requiescat in pace*] **2.** may they rest in peace. [< L *requiescant in pace*] Also, **RIP**

ri·par·i·an (ri pâr′ē ən, rī-), *adj.* of, pertaining to, situated, or dwelling on the bank of a river or other body of water. [< L *rīpāri(us)* that frequents river banks (*rīp(a)* bank of a river + *-ārius* -ARY) + -AN]

ripar′ian right′, *Law.* a right, as use of water for irrigation, enjoyed by a person who owns riparian property.

rip′ cord′, **1.** *Aeron.* a cord on a parachute that, when pulled, opens the parachute for descent. **2.** a cord fastened in the bag of a passenger balloon or dirigible so that a sharp pull upon it will open the bag and let the gas escape, causing the balloon to descend rapidly.

ripe (rīp), *adj.*, **rip·er, rip·est.** **1.** having arrived at such a stage of growth or development as to be ready for reaping, gathering, eating, or use, as grain, fruit, cheese, beer, etc.; completely matured. **2.** resembling ripe fruit, as in ruddiness and fullness. **3.** arrived at the highest or a high point of development or excellence; mature. **4.** of mature judgment or knowledge. **5.** characterized by full development of body or mind: *of ripe years.* **6.** (of time) advanced: *a ripe old age.* **7.** (of ideas, plans, etc.) ready for action, execution, etc. **8.** (of people) fully prepared, ready, or mature enough to do or undergo something. **9.** ready for some operation or process: *a ripe abscess.* **10.** fully or sufficiently advanced; ready enough; auspicious: *The time is ripe for a new foreign policy.* [ME; OE *rīpe;* c. D *rijp,* G *reif;* akin to OE *rīpan* to REAP] —**ripe′ness,** *n.*
—**Syn. 1.** grown, aged. RIPE, MATURE, MELLOW refer to that which is no longer in an incomplete stage of development. RIPE implies completed growth beyond which the processes of decay begin: *a ripe harvest.* MATURE means fully grown and developed as used of living organisms: *a mature animal or tree.* MELLOW denotes complete absence of sharpness or asperity, with sweetness and richness such as characterize ripeness or age: *mellow fruit or flavor.*

rip·en (rī′pən), *v.t., v.i.* **1.** to make or become ripe. **2.** to bring or come to maturity, the proper condition, etc.; mature. —**rip′en·er,** *n.*

ri·pie·no (ri pyā′nō; *It.* RĒ pye′nô), *n., pl.* **-nos;** *It.* **-ni** (-nē), *adj.* *Music.* —*n.* **1.** tutti (defs. 3, 4). —*adj.* **2.** tutti (def. 2). [< It: full]

Rip·ley (rip′lē), *n.* **George,** 1802–80, U.S. literary critic, author, and social reformer: associated with the founding of Brook Farm.

rip·off (rip′ôf′, -of′), *n.* *Slang.* **1.** an act or instance of ripping off. **2.** exploitation, esp. of unfortunates. **3.** a person who rips off; thief.

ri·poste (ri pōst′), *n., v.,* **-post·ed, -post·ing.** —*n.* **1.** *Fencing.* a quick thrust given after parrying a lunge. **2.** a quick, sharp return in speech or action; counterstroke. —*v.i.* **3.** to make a riposte. Also, **ri·post′.** [< F, alter. of *risposte* < It *risposta* response < *rispondere* to RESPOND]

rip·per (rip′ər), *n.* **1.** a person or thing that rips. **2.** a killer, esp. a madman who mutilates his victims.

rip·ping (rip′ing), *adj.* **1.** of or pertaining to tearing. **2.** *Chiefly Brit. Slang.* excellent, splendid, or fine.

rip′ping bar′. See **pinch bar.**

rip·ple[1] (rip′əl), *v.,* **-pled, -pling,** *n.* —*v.i.* **1.** (of a liquid surface) to form small waves or undulations, as water agitated by a breeze. **2.** to flow with a light rise and fall or ruffling of the surface. **3.** (of a solid surface) to form or have small undulations, ruffles, or folds. **4.** (of sound) to undulate or rise and fall in tone, inflection, or magnitude. —*v.t.* **5.** to form small waves or undulations on; agitate lightly. **6.** to mark as if with ripples; give a wavy form to. —*n.* **7.** a small wave or undulation, as on water. **8.** any similar movement or appearance; a small undulation or wave, as in hair. **9.** *U.S.* a small rapid. **10.** a sound, as of water flowing in ripples: *a ripple of laughter.* [?] —**Syn. 1.** wave, undulate, purl. **5.** ruffle, curl, dimple. **7.** wavelet, ruffling.

rip·ple[2] (rip′əl), *n., v.,* **-pled, -pling.** —*n.* **1.** a toothed or comblike device for removing seeds or capsules from flax, hemp, etc. —*v.t.* **2.** to remove the seeds or capsules from (flax or hemp) with a ripple. [ME *ripel;* c. D *repel,* G *riffel*]

rip·pler (rip′lər), *n.* **1.** a person who ripples flax, hemp, etc. **2.** an instrument for rippling; ripple.

rip·plet (rip′lit), *n.* a small ripple.

rip·ply (rip′lē), *adj.* **1.** characterized by ripples; rippling. **2.** sounding like rippling water.

rip·rap (rip′rap′), *n.* **1.** a quantity of broken stone for foundations, revetments of embankments, etc. **2.** a foundation or wall of stones thrown together irregularly. [gradational redupl. of RAP[1]]

rip-roar·ing (rip′rōr′ing, -rôr′-), *adj.* *Informal.* boisterously wild and exciting; riotous. [RIP[1] + ROARING, alter. of *rip-roarious,* modeled on *uproarious*]

rip·saw (rip′sô′), *n.* a saw for cutting wood with the grain.

rip·snort·er (rip′snôr′tər), *n.* *Informal.* **1.** something or someone remarkably good or exciting. **2.** something or someone exceedingly strong or violent.

rip·tide (rip′tīd′), *n.* a tide that opposes another or other tides, causing a violent disturbance in the sea. [RIP[2] + TIDE[1]]

Rip·u·ar·i·an (rip′yo͞o âr′ē ən), *adj.* **1.** designating or pertaining to the group of Franks who dwelt along the Rhine near Cologne in the 4th century or their code of laws. —*n.* **2.** a Ripuarian Frank. [< ML *Ripuāri(us)* (sp. var. of *Ribuārius,* ? = L *rīp(a)* riverbank + *-ārius* -ARY) + -AN]

Rip Van Win·kle (rip′ van wing′kəl), a person who does not keep abreast of the times, after a man who sleeps for 20 years in a short story (1819–20) by Washington Irving.

rise (rīz), *v.,* **rose, ris·en** (riz′ən), **ris·ing,** *n.* —*v.i.* **1.** to get up from a lying, sitting, or kneeling posture; assume an upright position. **2.** to get up from bed, esp. to begin the day after a night's sleep. **3.** to become erect and stiff, as the hair in fright. **4.** to become active in opposition or resistance; revolt or rebel. **5.** to be built up, erected, or constructed. **6.** to spring up or grow, as plants. **7.** to become prominent on or project from a surface, as a blister. **8.** to come into existence; appear. **9.** to come into action, as a wind, storm, etc. **10.** to occur: *A quarrel rose between them.* **11.** to originate, issue, or be derived; to have a source. **12.** to move upward; ascend. **13.** to ascend above the horizon, as a celestial object. **14.** to extend directly upward; project vertically. **15.** to have an upward slant or curve. **16.** to attain higher rank, status, or importance or a higher economic level. **17.** *Angling.* (of fish) to come up toward the surface for food. **18.** to prove oneself equal to a demand, emergency, etc. (usually fol. by *to*): *to rise to the occasion.* **19.** to become animated, cheerful, or heartened, as the spirits. **20.** to become roused or stirred: *to feel one's temper rising.* **21.** to increase in height, as the level of a body of water. **22.** to swell or puff up, as dough from the action of yeast. **23.** to increase in amount, as prices. **24.** to increase in price or value, as commodities. **25.** to increase in degree, intensity, or force, as fever or color. **26.** to become louder or of higher pitch, as the voice. **27.** to adjourn or close a session, as a deliberative body or court. **28.** to return from the dead. —*v.t.* **29.** to cause to rise. **30.** *Naut.* to cause (something) to rise or appear above the visible horizon by approaching nearer to it; raise. **31. rise above,** to ignore or be indifferent to, as an insult.
—*n.* **32.** the act or an instance of rising. **33.** appearance above the horizon, as of the sun or moon. **34.** elevation or increase in rank, fortune, influence, power, etc. **35.** an increase in height, as of the level of water. **36.** the amount of such increase. **37.** an increase in amount, as of prices. **38.** an increase in price or value, as of commodities. **39.** *Chiefly Brit.* raise (defs. 27–30). **40.** an increase in degree or intensity, as of temperature. **41.** an increase in loudness or in pitch, as of the voice. **42.** *Archit., Building Trades.* the measured height of any of various things, as a roof or a flight of steps. **43.** origin, source, or beginning. **44.** a coming into existence or notice: *the rise of a new talent.* **45.** extension upward. **46.** the amount of such extension. **47.** upward slope, as of ground or a road. **48.** a piece of rising or high ground. **49.** *Angling.* the coming up of a fish for food or bait. **50. get a rise out of,** *Informal.* **a.** to provoke, as to action or anger. **b.** to evoke the expected or desired response. **51. give rise to,** to originate; produce; cause. [ME *rise(n),* OE *rīsan;* c. Goth *reisan,* OHG *rīsan,* D *rijzen.* See RAISE, REAR[2]]
—**Syn. 11.** arise, proceed. **12.** mount. **16.** succeed, advance. **29.** RISE, RAISE are not synonyms, although the forms of RAISE are commonly and mistakenly used as if they also meant RISE. RISE, the verb with irregular forms, seldom takes an object: *A person rises from a chair.* RAISE, with regular forms (*raised, have raised, raising*), originally meaning to cause something to rise, must have an object, either a concrete one or an abstract one: *He raised his hat. He had raised a question.* —**Ant. 12.** descend. **16.** fail.

ris·er (rī′zər), *n.* **1.** a person who rises, esp. from bed: *to be an early riser.* **2.** the vertical face of a stair step. [ME]

rish·i (rish′ē), *n.* *Hinduism.* an inspired sage or poet.

ris·i·bil·i·ty (riz′ə bil′i tē), *n., pl.* **-ties.** **1.** Often, **risibilities.** the ability or disposition to laugh; humorous awareness of the ridiculous and absurd. **2.** laughter. [< LL *rīsibil(itās)*]

ris·i·ble (riz′ə bəl), *adj.* **1.** having the ability, disposition, or readiness to laugh. **2.** causing or capable of causing laughter; laughable; comical. **3.** pertaining to or concerned with laughter. [LL *rīsibil(is)* that can laugh = L *rīs(us)* (ptp. of *rīdēre* to laugh) + *-ibilis* -IBLE]

ris·ing (rī′zing), *adj.* **1.** advancing, ascending, or mounting: *rising smoke.* **2.** growing or advancing to adult years: *the rising generation.* —*adv.* *U.S. Dial.* **3.** somewhat more than. **4.** in approach of; almost; well-nigh: *a lad rising sixteen.* —*n.* **5.** the act of a person or thing that rises. **6.** an insurrection; rebellion; revolt. **7.** something that rises; projection or prominence. [ME *riseng* (n.)]

ris′ing rhythm′, *Pros.* a rhythmic pattern created by a succession of metrical feet each of which is composed of one accented syllable preceded by one or more unaccented ones.

risk (risk), *n.* **1.** exposure to the chance of injury or loss; a hazard or dangerous chance. **2.** *Insurance.* **a.** the hazard or chance of loss. **b.** the degree of probability of such loss. **c.** the amount that the insurance company may lose. **d.** a person or thing with reference to the hazard involved in insuring him or it. **e.** the type of loss against which an insurance policy is drawn. —*v.t.* **3.** to expose to the chance of injury or loss; hazard: *to risk one's life to save another.* **4.** to venture upon; take or run the chance of. [< F *risque* < It *risc(hi)o* < *risicare* to dare, risk < Gk *rhíza* cliff, root (through meaning of to sail round a cliff)] —**Syn. 1.** venture, peril, jeopardy. **3.** imperil, endanger, jeopardize. **4.** dare.

risk′ cap′ital. See **venture capital.**

risk·y (ris′kē), *adj.,* **risk·i·er, risk·i·est.** attended with or involving risk; hazardous; perilous. —**risk′i·ly,** *adv.* —**risk′i·ness,** *n.*

Ri·sor·gi·men·to (RĒ sôR′jē men′tô), *n.* the period of or the movement for the liberation and unification of Italy 1750–1870. [< It = *risorg(ere)* (to) rise again (< L *resurgere*) + *-i-* -I- + *-mento* -MENT]

ri·sot·to (ri sô′tō, -sot′ō; *It.* RĒ zôt′tô), *n.* *Ital. Cookery.* a dish of rice cooked with broth and flavored with grated cheese and other seasonings. [< It]

ris·qué (ri skā′; *Fr.* RĒs kā′), *adj.* daringly close to indelicacy or impropriety; off-color: *a risqué story.* [< F, ptp. of *risquer* to RISK]

ri·tar·dan·do (rē′tär dän′dō; *It.* RĒ′täR dän′dô), *adj.* *Music.* becoming gradually slower. [< It, prp. of *ritardare;* see RETARD]

rite (rīt), *n.* **1.** a formal or ceremonial act or procedure prescribed or customary in religious or other solemn use. **2.** a particular form or system of religious or other ceremonial practice: *the Scottish rite in Freemasonry.* **3.** (*often cap.*) one of the historical versions of the Eucharistic service: *the Anglican Rite.* **4.** (*often cap.*) liturgy. **5.** (*sometimes cap.*) *Eastern Ch., Western Ch.* a division or differentiation of churches according to liturgy. **6.** any customary observance or practice: *the rite of the 10 a.m. coffee break.* [ME < L *rīt(us)*] **—Syn. 1.** observance, form. See **ceremony.**

rite′ of pas′sage, *Anthropol.* a ceremony marking an important period or change in a person's life, as puberty or marriage.

ri·tor·nel·lo (rit′ər nel′ō; *It.* rē′tôr nel′lô), *n., pl.* **-los,** *It.* **-li** (-lē). *Music.* **1.** an orchestral interlude between arias, scenes, or acts in 17th-century opera. **2.** a tutti section in a concerto grosso, aria, etc. [< It, dim. of *ritorno* RETURN]

rit·u·al (rich′o͞o əl), *n.* **1.** an established or prescribed procedure for a religious or other rite. **2.** a system or collection of religious or other rites. **3.** observance of set forms in public worship. **4.** any practice or pattern of behavior repeated in a prescribed manner reminiscent of religious ritual. **5.** a book of rites or ceremonies. **—*adj.* 6.** of the nature of or practiced as a rite or rites: *a ritual dance.* **7.** of or pertaining to rites: *ritual laws.* [< L *rītuāl(is).* See RITE, -AL[1]] —**rit′u·al·ly,** *adv.* **—Syn. 1.** See **ceremony. 6.** ceremonial, formal, sacramental. **—Ant. 6.** informal.

rit·u·al·ise (rich′o͞o ə līz′), *v.i., v.t.,* **-ised, -is·ing.** *Chiefly Brit.* ritualize.

rit·u·al·ism (rich′o͞o ə liz′əm), *n.* **1.** adherence to or insistence on ritual. **2.** the study of ritual practices.

rit·u·al·ist (rich′o͞o ə list), *n.* **1.** a student of or authority on ritual practices or religious rites. **2.** a person who practices or advocates observance of ritual, as in religious services. —**rit′u·al·is′tic,** *adj.* —**rit′u·al·is′ti·cal·ly,** *adv.*

rit·u·al·ize (rich′o͞o ə līz′), *v.,* **-ized, -iz·ing.** **—*v.i.* 1.** to practice ritualism. **—*v.t.* 2.** to make into a ritual. **3.** to convert (someone) to ritualism; impose ritualism upon. Also, *esp. Brit.,* **ritualise.**

rit′ual mur′der, a human sacrifice made to appease the gods or a god.

ritz (rits), *n. Slang.* **1.** ostentatious or pretentious display. **2. put on the ritz,** to live in elegance and luxury, esp. to make an ostentatious show of one's wealth. Also, **put on the Ritz.** [after the sumptuous hotels founded by César *Ritz* (d. 1918), Swiss entrepreneur]

ritz·y (rit′sē), *adj.,* **ritz·i·er, ritz·i·est.** *Slang.* swanky; elegant. —**ritz′i·ly,** *adv.* —**ritz′i·ness,** *n.*

riv., river.

riv·age (riv′ij, rī′vij), *n. Archaic.* a bank, shore, or coast. [ME < MF = *rive* river (< L *rīpa* river bank) + *-age* -AGE]

ri·val (rī′vəl), *n., adj., v.,* **-valed, -val·ing** or (*esp. Brit.*) **-valled, -val·ling.** **—*n.* 1.** a person who is competing for the same object or goal as another, or who tries to equal or outdo another; competitor. **2.** a person or thing that is in a position to dispute another's preeminence or superiority: *a stadium without a rival.* **3.** *Obs.* a companion in duty. **—*adj.* 4.** standing in rivalry; competing. **—*v.t.* 5.** to compete with in rivalry; strive to win from, equal, or outdo. **6.** to equal (something) as in some quality. **—*v.i.* 7.** *Archaic.* to engage in rivalry; compete. [< L *rīvāl(is),* orig. one who uses a stream in common with another = *rīv(us)* stream + *-ālis* -AL[1]] —**ri′val·less,** *adj.* **—Syn. 1.** See **opponent.**

ri·val·ry (rī′vəl rē), *n., pl.* **-ries. 1.** the action, position, or relation of a rival or rivals; competition; emulation. **2.** an instance of this. —**ri′val·rous,** *adj.* **—Syn. 1.** opposition, antagonism; jealousy.

rive (rīv), *v.,* **rived, rived** or **riv·en, riv·ing.** **—*v.t.* 1.** to tear or rend apart. **2.** to separate by striking; split; cleave. **3.** to rend, harrow, or distress (the feelings, heart, etc.). **4.** to split (wood) radially from a log. **—*v.i.* 5.** to become rent or split apart. [ME *rive(n)* < Scand; cf. OIcel *rīfa.* See RIFT[1]]

riv·en (riv′ən), *v.* **1.** a pp. of **rive.** **—*adj.* 2.** rent or split apart. **3.** split radially, as a log.

riv·er[1] (riv′ər), *n.* **1.** a natural stream of water of fairly large size flowing in a definite course or channel or series of diverging and converging channels. **2.** any stream or copious outpouring: *a river of lava; rivers of tears.* **3.** (*cap.*) *Astron.* the constellation Eridanus. **4. sell down the river,** to betray; desert; mislead. **5. up the river,** *Slang.* to or in prison. [ME < OF *rivere, riviere* < VL **rīpāria,* n. use of L fem. of *rīpārius* RIPARIAN]

riv·er[2] (rī′vər), *n.* a person who rives. [RIVE + -ER[1]]

Ri·ve·ra (ri vâr′ə; *Sp.* rē ve′rä), *n.* **1. Die·go** (dye′gô), 1886–1957, Mexican painter. **2. Mi·guel Pri·mo de** (mē gel′ prē′mô the), 1870–1930, Spanish general: dictator 1923–29.

riv·er·bank (riv′ər bangk′), *n.* the slopes bordering a riverbed.

riv′er ba′sin, *Phys. Geog.* the area of land drained by a river and its branches.

riv·er·bed (riv′ər bed′), *n.* the channel in which a river flows or formerly flowed.

riv′er carp′sucker, a carpsucker, *Carpiodes carpio,* found in silty rivers of the central and south central U.S.

riv·er·head (riv′ər hed′), *n.* the source or spring of a river.

riv′er horse′, a hippopotamus.

riv·er·ine (riv′ə rīn′, -ər in), *adj.* **1.** of or pertaining to a river. **2.** situated or dwelling beside a river.

Riv′er Plate′, *Brit.* See **Plata, Río de la.**

riv·er·side (riv′ər sīd′), *n.* **1.** a bank of a river. **—*adj.* 2.** on or near a bank of a river. [ME *river-syde*]

Riv·er·side (riv′ər sīd′), *n.* a city in SW California. 140,089 (1970).

riv·et (riv′it), *n., v.,* **-et·ed, -et·ing** or (*esp. Brit.*) **-et·ted, -et·ting.** **—*n.* 1.** a metal pin for passing through holes in two or more plates or pieces to hold them together, usually made with a head at one end, the other end being hammered into a head after insertion. **—*v.t.* 2.** to fasten with a rivet or rivets. **3.** to hammer or spread out the end of (a pin, bolt, etc.) in order to form a head and secure something; clinch. **4.** to fasten or fix firmly. **5.** to hold (the eye, attention, etc.) firmly. **6.** to hold the interest, attention, etc., of (a person). [ME *revette* < MF *river* to attach] —**riv′et·er,** *n.*

Riv·i·er·a (riv′ē âr′ə; *It.* rē vye′rä), *n.* a resort area along the Mediterranean coast, extending from Marseilles, in SE France, to La Spezia, in NW Italy. French, **Côte d'Azur.**

ri·vière (riv′ē âr′, ri vyâr′; *Fr.* rē vyer′), *n., pl.* **ri·vières** (riv′ē ârz′, ri vyârz′; *Fr.* rē vyer′). a necklace of diamonds or other gems. [< F: lit., river]

riv·u·let (riv′yə lit), *n.* a small stream; streamlet; brook. [earlier *rivolet* < It *rivolett(o),* dim. of *rivolo* < L *rīvulus* small stream]

rix-dol·lar (riks′dol′ər), *n.* any of various old silver coins, of Denmark, Holland, and Germany, having about equal value. [partial trans. of obs. D *rijksdaler;* c. G *Reichsthaler*]

Ri·yadh (rē yäd′), *n.* a city in Nejd, in central Saudi Arabia: the capital of Saudi Arabia. 450,000.

ri·yal (rē yôl′, -yäl′), *n.* the monetary unit of Saudi Arabia, equal to 20 qursh. Also, **rial.** [< Ar < Sp *real* REAL[2]]

Ri·zal (rē säl′), *n.* **Jo·sé** (hô se′), 1861–96, Philippine patriot, novelist, poet, and physician.

Riz·zio (rit′sē ō′, rēt′-; *It.* rēt′tsyô), *n.* **Da·vid** (dä′vēd), 1533?–66, Italian musician: private foreign secretary to Mary, Queen of Scots 1564–66. Also, **Riccio.**

RJ, *Mil.* road junction.

r-less (är′lis), *adj. Phonet.* r-dropping.

RM, reichsmark. Also, **r.m.**

rm., *pl.* **rms. 1.** ream. **2.** room.

R.M.A., *Brit.* **1.** Royal Marine Artillery. **2.** Royal Military Academy.

R.M.C., *Brit.* Royal Military College.

rms, (*often cap.*) See **root mean square.** Also, **r.m.s.**

R.M.S., **1.** Railway Mail Service. **2.** *Brit.* Royal Mail Service. **3.** *Brit.* Royal Mail Steamship.

Rn., *Chem.* radon.

R.N., **1.** See **registered nurse. 2.** *Brit.* Royal Navy.

RNA, *Biochem.* any of the class of nucleic acids that contains ribose, found chiefly in the cytoplasm of cells; pentose nucleic acid; PNA; yeast nucleic acid. Also called **ribonucleic acid, ribose nucleic acid.** Cf. **DNA.**

R.N.A.S., *Brit.* Royal Naval Air Service.

R.N.R., *Brit.* Royal Naval Reserve.

R.N.W.M.P., *Canadian.* Royal Northwest Mounted Police.

ro., **1.** recto. **2.** roan. **3.** rood.

R.O., **1.** Receiving Office. **2.** Receiving Officer. **3.** Regimental Order. **4.** *Brit.* Royal Observatory.

roach[1] (rōch), *n.* **1.** a cockroach. **2.** *Slang.* a cigarette butt, esp. a very short butt of a marijuana cigarette. [short form]

roach[2] (rōch), *n., pl.* **roach·es,** (*esp. collectively*) **roach. 1.** a European, fresh-water fish, *Rutilus rutilus,* of the carp family. **2.** any of various similar fishes found in eastern North America. **3.** a fresh-water sunfish of the genus *Lepomis,* found in E. North America. [ME *roche* < OF < ?]

roach[3] (rōch), *n.* **1.** the upward curve at the foot of a square sail. **—*v.t.* 2.** to clip or cut off (the mane of a horse). [?]

road (rōd), *n.* **1.** a long, narrow stretch with a smoothed or paved surface, made for traveling by motor vehicle, carriage, etc., between two or more points; street or highway. **2.** a way or course: *the road to peace.* **3.** Often, **roads.** Also called **roadstead.** *Naut.* a partly sheltered area of water near a shore in which vessels may ride at anchor. **4.** *Mining.* any tunnel in a mine used for hauling. **5. hit the road,** *Slang.* to begin or resume traveling. **6. one for the road,** a final alcoholic drink, taken just before departing from a party, tavern, or the like. **7. on the road, a.** traveling, esp. as a salesman. **b.** on tour, as a theatrical company. **8. take to the road,** to begin a journey or tour. Also, **take the road.** [ME *rod,* OE *rād* a riding, journey on horseback, akin to *rīdan* to RIDE]

road·a·bil·i·ty (rō′də bil′i tē), *n.* the ability of an automobile to ride smoothly and comfortably under adverse road conditions.

road′ a′gent, *U.S.* (formerly) a highwayman, esp. along stagecoach routes.

road·bed (rōd′bed′), *n.* **1.** the bed or foundation structure for the track of a railroad. **2.** the layer of ballast immediately beneath the ties of a railroad track. **3.** the material of which a road is composed.

road·block (rōd′blok′), *n.* **1.** an obstruction placed across a road for halting or hindering traffic, as by police to facilitate the capture of a pursued car or by the military to retard the advance of an enemy. **2.** any obstruction on a road, as a fallen tree. **3.** anything that obstructs progress toward an objective. **—*v.t.* 4.** to halt or obstruct with a roadblock.

road′ com′pany, a theatrical group that tours cities and towns, usually performing a single play.

road·e·o (rō′dē ō′), *n. U.S.* a competition, usually held annually, for professional truck drivers on their driving ability, skill, etc. [ROAD + (ROD)EO]

road′ gang′, **1.** a group of men employed to repair or build roads. **2.** (in the U.S.) a detail of prisoners set to repairing a road.

road′ hog′, a driver who obstructs traffic by occupying parts of two lanes.

road·house (rōd′hous′), *n., pl.* **-hous·es** (-hou′ziz). a tavern, night club, or the like, situated on a highway, usually beyond city limits.

road′ map′, a map for motorists, showing names and locations of places as well as route numbers, type of road improvement, and mileages of the highway network.

Roadrunner (Length 2 ft.)

road·run·ner (rōd′run′ər), *n.* a terrestrial cuckoo, *Geococcyx californianius,* of America. Also called **chaparral bird, chaparral cock.**

road′ show′, **1.** a show, as a play, musical comedy, etc., performed by a touring group of actors. **2.** an important motion picture, usually presented only twice daily on a reserved-seat basis. Also, **road′show′.**

road-show (rōd′shō′), *adj.* **1.** of or pertaining to road shows. **—*v.t.* 2.** to present as a road show.

road·side (rōd′sīd′), *n.* **1.** the side or border of the road; wayside. **—*adj.* 2.** on or near the side of a road.

road·stead (rōd′sted′), *n.* *Naut.* road (def. 3). [ME *radestede*]

road·ster (rōd′stər), *n.* **1.** an automobile having an open body, a single seat for two or three people, and a large trunk or a rumble seat. **2.** a horse for riding or driving on the road.

road′ test′, **1.** a check of an automobile's performance in actual operation on the road. **2.** an examination of a person's driving skill, conducted in normal traffic, esp. as a requirement for an automobile driver's license.

Road′ Town′, a town on SE Tortola, in the NE West Indies: capital of the British Virgin Islands. 3500.

road·way (rōd′wā′), *n.* **1.** the land over which a road is built; a road together with the land at its edge. **2.** the part of a road over which vehicles travel; road.

road·work (rōd′wûrk′), *n.* the exercise of running considerable distances, performed chiefly by boxers in training.

roam (rōm), *v.i.* **1.** to walk, go, or travel without a fixed purpose or direction; wander: *to roam about the world.* —*v.t.* **2.** to wander over or through: *to roam the countryside.* —*n.* **3.** the act or an instance of roaming; ramble. [ME *rome(n)* < ?] —**roam′er,** *n.*

—**Syn. 1.** stray, stroll, prowl. ROAM, RAMBLE, RANGE, ROVE imply wandering about, sometimes over a considerable amount of territory. ROAM implies a wandering or traveling over a large area, esp. as prompted by restlessness or curiosity: *to roam through a forest.* RAMBLE implies pleasant, carefree moving about, walking with no specific purpose and for a limited distance: *to ramble through fields near home.* RANGE usually implies wandering over a more or less defined but extensive area in search of something: *Cattle range over the plains.* ROVE sometimes implies wandering with specific incentive or aim, as an animal for prey: *Bandits rove through these mountains.*

roan (rōn), *adj.* **1.** (chiefly of horses) of the color sorrel, chestnut, or bay, sprinkled with gray or white. **2.** prepared from leather of this color. —*n.* **3.** a roan horse or other animal. **4.** a soft, flexible sheepskin leather, used in bookbinding, often made in imitation of morocco. [< MF < OSp *roano* < Gmc; cf. Goth *rauths* red]

Ro·a·noke (rō′ə nōk′), *n.* **1.** a city in SW Virginia. 92,115 (1970). **2.** a river flowing SE from western Virginia to Albemarle Sound in North Carolina. 380 mi. long.

Ro′anoke Is′land, an island off the NE coast of North Carolina, S of Albemarle Sound: site of unsuccessful colonizing attempts by Raleigh 1585, 1587.

roar (rōr, rôr), *v.i.* **1.** to utter a loud, deep cry or howl, as in distress or anger. **2.** to laugh loudly or boisterously: *to roar at a joke.* **3.** to make a loud sound or din, as thunder or cannon. **4.** to function or move with a loud, deep sound, as a vehicle: *The automobile roared away.* **5.** to make a loud noise in breathing, as a horse. —*v.t.* **6.** to utter or express in a roar: *to roar denials.* **7.** to bring, put, make, etc., by roaring: *to roar oneself hoarse.* —*n.* **8.** a loud, deep cry or howl, as of an animal or a person, esp. the characteristic sound of the lion. **9.** a loud, deep sound from an inanimate source: *the roar of the surf.* **10.** a loud outburst of laughter. [ME *rore(n),* OE *rārian;* c. OHG *rēren* to bellow] —**Syn. 1.** yell. See **cry. 3.** resound, boom.

roar·ing (rōr′ing, rôr′-), *n.* **1.** the act of a person or thing that roars. **2.** a loud, deep cry or sound or a series of such sounds. **3.** *Vet. Pathol.* a disease of horses causing them to make a loud noise in breathing under exertion. —*adj.* **4.** making or causing a roar, as an animal, thunder, etc. **5.** brisk or highly successful, as trade: *He did a roaring business selling souvenirs.* **6.** characterized by noisy, disorderly behavior: *roaring revelry.* —*adv.* **7.** very; extremely: *roaring drunk.* [ME *roryng* (n., adj.), OE *rarung* (n.)]

roar′ing for′ties, either of two areas in the ocean between 40° and 50° N or S latitude, noted for high winds and rough seas.

roast (rōst), *v.t.* **1.** to bake (meat or other food) by exposure to dry heat, esp. in an oven or on a spit. **2.** to brown, dry, or parch by exposure to heat, as coffee beans. **3.** to cook or heat by embedding in hot coals, embers, etc. **4.** to heat (any material) more or less violently. **5.** *Metall.* to heat (ore or the like) in such a way that it is exposed to air and oxidizes. **6.** to warm (one's hands, etc.) at a fire. **7.** *Informal.* to ridicule or criticize severely or mercilessly. —*v.i.* **8.** to roast meat or other food. **9.** to undergo the process of becoming roasted. —*n.* **10.** roasted meat or a piece of roasted meat, as a section of beef or veal. **11.** a piece of meat for roasting. **12.** anything that is roasted. **13.** the act or process of roasting. **14.** *Informal.* severe criticism. **15.** an outdoor get-together, as a picnic or barbecue, at which food is roasted and eaten: *a corn roast.* —*adj.* **16.** roasted: *roast beef.* [ME *rost(en)* < OF *rost(ir)* < Gmc; cf. D *roosten*]

roast·er (rō′stər), *n.* **1.** a pan or other utensil for roasting something. **2.** a chicken or other animal suitable for roasting. **3.** a person or thing that roasts. [ME]

roast·ing (rō′sting), *adj.* **1.** used or suitable to roast. **2.** exceedingly hot; scorching: *a roasting July.* —**roast′ing·ly,** *adv.*

rob (rob), *v.,* **robbed, rob·bing.** —*v.t.* **1.** to take something from (someone) by unlawful force or threat of violence; steal from. **2.** to deprive (someone) of some right or something legally due: *They robbed the family of the inheritance.* **3.** to plunder or rifle (a house, shop, etc.). **4.** to deprive of something unjustly or injuriously: *The umpire called the home run a foul ball and we lost the game—we were robbed!* —*v.i.* **5.** to commit or practice robbery. [ME *robb(en)* < OF *robb(er)* < Gmc; c. OHG *roubōn.* See REAVE]

—**Syn. 1.** ROB, RIFLE, SACK refer to seizing possessions that belong to others. ROB is the general word for taking possessions by unlawful force: *to rob a bank, a house.* A term with a more restricted meaning is RIFLE, to make a thorough search for what is valuable or worthwhile, usually within a small space: *to rifle a safe.* SACK is a term for robbery on a huge scale during war; it suggests destruction accompanying pillage and the massacre of civilians: *to sack a town.*

rob·a·lo (rob′ə lō′, rō′bə-), *n., pl.* **-los,** (*esp. collectively*) **-lo.** snook[1] (def. 1). [< Pg, m. Catalan *elobarro* << L *lupus* wolf]

rob·and (rob′ənd), *n.* *Naut.* a short piece of spun yarn or other material, used to secure a sail to a yard, gaff, or the like. Also, **robbin, robin.** [southern form answering to northern *raband* < D *rā* sailyard + *band* BAND[2]]

Robbe-Gril·let (RÔb gRē ye′), *n.* **A·lain** (A laN′), born 1922, French author.

rob·ber (rob′ər), *n.* a person who robs. [ME *robbere* < OF *robere*] —**Syn.** bandit, burglar. See **thief.**

rob′ber bar′on, *U.S.* a ruthlessly powerful and unscrupulous capitalist or industrialist of the late 19th century considered to have become wealthy by exploiting natural resources, corrupting legislators, or other unethical means.

rob′ber fly′, any of numerous swift-flying, often large, dipterous insects of the family *Asilidae* that are predaceous on other insects.

Robber fly, *Promachus vertebratus* (Length 1 in.)

rob·ber·y (rob′ə rē), *n., pl.* **-ber·ies. 1.** the act, the practice, or an instance of robbing. **2.** *Law.* the felonious taking of the property of another by violence or intimidation. Cf. **theft.** [ME *robberie* < OF] —**Syn. 1.** plunder, pillage; theft, burglary.

Rob·bia (rō′bē ə; *It.* RÔb′byä), *n.* **1. An·dre·a del·la** (än dRe′ä del′lä), 1435–1525, Italian sculptor. **2.** his uncle, **Lu·ca del·la** (lo͞o′kä del′lä), c1400–82, Italian sculptor.

Rob·bins·dale (rob′inz dāl′), *n.* a city in SE Minnesota, near Minneapolis. 16,845 (1970).

robe (rōb), *n., v.,* **robed, rob·ing.** —*n.* **1.** a long, loose or flowing gown or outer garment worn as ceremonial dress, an official vestment, etc. **2.** any long, loose garment, esp. one for wear while lounging or preparing to dress, as a bathrobe or dressing gown. **3.** a woman's gown or dress, esp. of a more elaborate kind. **4. robes,** apparel in general; dress; costume. **5.** a piece of fur, cloth, etc., used as a blanket, covering, or wrap: *a lap robe.* —*v.t.* **6.** to clothe or invest with a robe or robes; dress; array. —*v.i.* **7.** to put on a robe. [ME < OF: orig., spoil, booty < Gmc; cf. OHG *roub* < G *Raub*]

robe-de-cham·bre (RÔb də shäN′bRə), *n., pl.* **robes-de-cham·bre** (RÔb də shäN′bRə). *French.* a dressing gown.

Rob·ert I (rob′ərt), **1.** Also called **Robert the Bruce, Rob′ert Bruce′.** 1274–1329, king of Scotland 1306–29. **2.** ("*Robert the Devil*") died 1035, duke of Normandy 1028–1035 (father of William I of England).

Rob·ert·son (rob′ərt sən), *n.* **1. William,** 1721–93, Scottish historian. **2. Sir William Robert,** 1860–1933, British field marshal.

Rob′ert the Bruce′. See **Robert I.**

Robes·pierre (rōbz′pēr, -pē âr′; *Fr.* RÔ bes pyeR′), *n.* **Max·i·mi·lien Fran·çois Ma·rie I·si·dore de** (mAk sē mē lyaN′ fRäN swA′ mA Rē′ ē zē dôR′ də), 1758–94, French lawyer and revolutionary leader.

rob·in[1] (rob′in), *n.* **1.** any of several small, Old World birds having a red or reddish breast, esp. *Erithacus rubecula,* of Europe. **2.** a large, American thrush, *Turdus migratorius,* having a chestnut-red breast and abdomen. Also called **rob′in red′breast.** [ME *Robyn* < OF *Robin,* dim. of *Robert* Robert]

Robin, *Turdus migratorius* (Length 10 in.)

rob·in[2] (rob′in), *n.* *Naut.* roband.

Rob′in Good′fel·low (go͝od′fel′ō), Puck.

Rob′in Hood′, a legendary English outlaw of the 12th century who robbed the rich to give to the poor.

rob′in's-egg blue′ (rob′inz eg′), a pale green to a light greenish blue.

Rob·in·son (rob′in sən), *n.* **1. Edwin Arlington,** 1869–1935, U.S. poet. **2. Jack Roosevelt** ("*Jackie*"), 1919–72, U.S. baseball player.

ro·ble (rō′blā), *n.* **1.** a Californian white oak, *Quercus lobata.* **2.** any of several other trees, esp. of the oak and beech families. [< Sp, Pg << L *rōbur* oak tree]

ro·bot (rō′bət, -bot, rob′ət), *n.* **1.** a machine that resembles a man and does mechanical, routine tasks on command. **2.** a person who acts and responds in a mechanical, routine manner; automaton. **3.** any machine or mechanical device that operates automatically with humanlike skill. [first used in the play *R.U.R.* (by Capek), appar. back formation from Czech *robotnik* serf] —**ro′bot·ism,** *n.* —**ro·bot·is·tic** (rō′bə tis′tik, rob′ə-), *adj.* —**ro′bot·like′,** *adj.*

ro′bot bomb′, a rocket-propelled, gyroscopically steered, winged bomb, usually launched from the ground. Also called **buzz bomb.**

ro·bot·ics (rō bot′iks), *n.* (*construed as sing.*) the technology of using computer-controlled robots to perform industrial tasks, as on an assembly line. —**ro·bot′ic,** *adj.*

Rob·son (rob′sən), *n.* **Mount,** a mountain in SW Canada, in E British Columbia: highest peak in the Canadian Rockies, 12,972 ft.

ro·bust (rō bust′, rō′bust), *adj.* **1.** strong and healthy; hardy; vigorous. **2.** strongly or stoutly built: *his robust frame.* **3.** suited to or requiring bodily strength or endurance: *robust exercise.* **4.** rough, rude, or boisterous: *robust drinkers and dancers.* **5.** rich and full-bodied: *the robust flavor of freshly brewed coffee.* [< L *rūbust(us)* of oak, hard, strong < *rōbur* oak, strength] —**ro·bust′ly,** *adv.* —**ro·bust·ness,** *n.* —**Syn. 1.** powerful, sound. **4.** coarse.

ro·bus·tious (rō bus′chəs), *adj.* **1.** rough, rude, or boisterous. **2.** robust, strong, or stout. [ROBUST + -IOUS] —**ro·bus′tious·ly,** *adv.*

roc (rok), *n.* *Arabian Myth.* a fabulous bird of enormous size and strength. [< Ar *rukhkh,* prob. < Pers]

Ro·ca (rō′kə; *Port.* RÔ′kä), *n.* **Cape,** a cape in W Portugal, near Lisbon: the western extremity of continental Europe. Portuguese, **Cabo da Roca.**

roc·am·bole (rok′əm bōl′), *n.* a European, liliaceous plant, *Allium Scorodoprasum,* used like garlic. [< F < G *Rockenbolle,* lit., distaff bulb (from its shape)]

Ro·cham·beau (RÔ shäN bō′), *n.* **Jean Bap·tiste Do·na·tien de Vi·meur** (zhäN bA tēst′ dô nA syaN′ də vē mœʀ′), **Comte de,** 1725–1807, French general: marshal of France 1791–1807; commander of the French army in the American Revolution.

Ro·chelle (*Fr.* ʀô shel′), *n.* **La.** See **La Rochelle.**

Rochelle′ pow′ders, (not in technical use) See **Seidlitz powders.** [named after La Rochelle]

Rochelle′ salt′, *Chem., Pharm.* a solid, $KNaC_4H_4O_6 \cdot 4H_2O$, used in silvering mirrors, in the manufacture of Seidlitz powders and baking powder, and as a laxative. Also called **potassium sodium tartrate.** [named after La Rochelle]

roche mou·ton·née (ʀôsh moo tô nā′; *Eng.* rōsh′ mo͞ot′ᵊnā′), *pl.* **roches mou·ton·nées** (ʀôsh moo tô nā′; *Eng.* rōsh′ mo͞ot′ᵊnāz′). *French.* a knob or rock rounded and smoothed by glacial action. [lit., woolly rock]

Roch·es·ter (roch′es tər, -i stər), *n.* **1.** a city in W New York, on the Genesee River. 296,233 (1970). **2.** a city in SE Minnesota. 53,766 (1970). **3.** a city in N Kent, in SE England. 50,121 (1961).

roch·et (roch′it), *n.* a vestment of linen or lawn, resembling a surplice, worn esp. by bishops and abbots. [ME < OF *roc* outer garment < Gmc; cf. OE *rocc* outer garment]

rock[1] (rok), *n.* **1.** a large mass of stone forming a hill, cliff, promontory, or the like. **2.** *Geol.* **a.** mineral matter of various composition, consolidated or unconsolidated, assembled in masses or considerable quantities in nature, as by the action of heat or water. **b.** a particular kind of such matter: *igneous rock.* **3.** stone in the mass: *buildings that stand upon rock.* **4.** a stone of any size. **5.** something resembling or suggesting a rock. **6.** a firm foundation or support: *The Lord is my rock.* **7.** *Chiefly Brit.* a hard candy, variously flavored. **8.** *Slang.* **a.** a diamond. **b.** any gem. **9. on the rocks, a.** *Informal.* in or into a state of destruction or ruin: *Their marriage is on the rocks.* **b.** *Informal.* without funds; destitute; bankrupt. **c.** (of a beverage, esp. liquor or a cocktail) with ice cubes. [ME *rokk(e)* < OE *-rocc* < ML *rocca*] —**rock′less,** *adj.* —**rock′like′,** *adj.*

rock[2] (rok), *v.i.* **1.** to move or sway to and fro or from side to side. **2.** to be moved or swayed powerfully with excitement, emotion, etc. **3.** *Mining.* (of sand or gravel) to be washed in a cradle. **4.** rock-'n'-roll (def. 4). —*v.t.* **5.** to move or swing (someone or something) to and fro or from side to side, esp. gently. **6.** to lull in security, hope, etc. **7.** to affect deeply; stun; move or sway powerfully, as with emotion. **8.** to shake or disturb violently, as an explosion. **9.** *Graphic Arts.* to roughen the surface of (a copperplate) with a rocker preparatory to scraping a mezzotint. **10.** *Mining.* cradle (def. 14). —*n.* **11.** a rocking movement: *the gentle rock of the boat.* **12.** rock-'n'-roll (defs. 1, 2). —*adj.* **13.** rock-'n'-roll (def. 3). [ME *rock(en)* < OE *roccian;* c. MD *rocken;* akin to G *rücken;* OIcel *rykkja* to jerk] —**rock′ing·ly,** *adv.* —**Syn. 1.** See **swing**[1].

rock[3] (rok), *n.* See **striped bass.** [short for rockfish]

rock-and-roll (rok′ən rōl′), *n.* rock-'n'-roll. —**rock′-and-roll′er,** *n.*

rock′ and rye′, a bottled drink made with rye whiskey, rock candy, and fruit.

rock·a·way (rok′ə wā′), *n.* a light, fourwheeled carriage having two or three seats and a fixed top. [appar. named after *Rockaway,* New Jersey]

Rockaway

rock′ bar′nacle. See under **barnacle.**

rock′ bass′ (bas), **1.** a fresh-water game fish, *Ambloplites rupestris,* of the sunfish family, found in the eastern U.S. **2.** See **striped bass.**

rock′ bot′tom, the very lowest level.

rock-bot·tom (rok′bot′əm), *adj.* at the lowest possible limit or level; extremely low: *rock-bottom prices.*

rock-bound (rok′bound′), *adj.* hemmed in, enclosed, or covered by rocks; rocky: *a rock-bound coast.*

rock′ brake′, a fern of the genus *Pellaea.*

rock′ can′dy, sugar in large, hard, cohering crystals.

Rock′ Corn′ish, a hybrid chicken produced by mating Cornish and White Rock chickens.

rock′ crys′tal, transparent quartz, esp. when colorless.

rock′ dove′, a European pigeon, *Columba livia,* from which most domestic pigeons have been developed. Also called **rock pigeon.**

Rock·e·fel·ler (rok′ə fel′ər), *n.* **1. John D(a·vi·son)** (dā′vi sən), 1839–1937, and his son **John D(avison) Jr.,** 1874–1960, U.S. oil magnates and philanthropists. **2. Nelson A(ldrich),** 1908–79, governor of New York 1959–73; 41st vice president of the U.S. 1974–76 (son of John D. Rockefeller, Jr.).

rock·er (rok′ər), *n.* **1.** Also called **runner.** one of the curved pieces on which a cradle or a rocking chair rocks. **2.** See **rocking chair. 3.** any of various devices that operate with a rocking motion. **4.** *Graphic Arts.* a small steel plate with one curved and toothed edge for roughening a copperplate to make a mezzotint. **5.** *Mining.* cradle (def. 5). **6.** any of various things resembling a rocker in whole or in part, as an ice skate having a curved blade. **7. off one's rocker,** *Slang.* insane; crazy. [rock[2] + -er[1]]

rock′er arm′, *Mach.* a rocking or oscillating arm or lever rotating with a moving shaft or pivoted on a stationary shaft.

rock·et[1] (rok′it), *n.* **1.** any of various simple or complex tubelike devices containing combustibles that on being ignited liberate gases whose action propels the tube through the air: used for pyrotechnic effect, signaling, carrying a life line, hurling explosives at an enemy, putting a space capsule into orbit, etc. **2.** a space capsule or vehicle put into orbit by such devices. **3.** See **rocket engine.** —*v.t.* **4.** to move or transport by means of a rocket. —*v.i.* **5.** to move like a rocket. **6.** (of game birds) to fly straight up rapidly when flushed. [< F *roquet* < It *rocchetta,* appar. dim. of *rocca* distaff, with ref. to its shape] —**rock′et·like′,** *adj.*

rock·et[2] (rok′it), *n.* **1.** a European plant, *Eruca sativa,* used for making salads. **2.** any cruciferous plant of the genus *Hesperis,* having showy, purple or white, fragrant flowers. Cf. **dame's rocket. 3.** a noxious weed, *Barbarea vulgaris,* of the U.S. [< F *roquette* < It *rochetta* << L *ērūca* kind of colewort]

rock·e·teer (rok′i tēr′), *n.* **1.** a person who discharges, rides in, or pilots a rocket. **2.** a technician or scientist whose work pertains to rocketry. Also, **rock·et·er** (rok′i tər).

rock′et en′gine, a reaction engine supplied with its own solid or liquid fuel and oxidizer. Also called **rocket, rock′et mo′tor.**

rock′et gun′, any weapon that uses a rocket as a projectile, as a rocket launcher or bazooka.

rock′et launch′er, *Mil.* **1.** a tube used by infantrymen to fire rockets. **2.** a vehicle equipped with many such tubes for the simultaneous firing of rockets.

rock·et·ry (rok′i trē), *n.* the science of rocket design, development, and flight.

rock·et·sonde (rok′it sond′), *n.* *Meteorol.* a rocket-borne telemeter for gathering data on the atmosphere at very high altitudes. [rocket[1] + sonde]

rock·fish (rok′fish′), *n., pl.* (*esp. collectively*) **-fish,** (*esp. referring to two or more kinds or species*) **-fish·es. 1.** any of various fishes found around rocks. **2.** the striped bass, *Roccus saxatilis.* **3.** any of the North Pacific marine fishes of the genus *Sebastodes.* **4.** any other fish of the family *Scorpaenidae.*

rock′ flow′er, any shrub of the genus *Crossosoma,* native to the arid regions of the southwestern U.S.

Rock·ford (rok′fərd), *n.* a city in N Illinois. 147,370 (1970).

rock′ gar′den, 1. a garden on rocky ground or among rocks, for the growing of alpine or other plants. **2.** a garden decorated with rocks.

Rock·hamp·ton (rok hamp′tən, -ham′-), *n.* a city in E Queensland, in E Australia. 44,128 (1961).

Rock′ Hill′, a city in N South Carolina. 33,846 (1970).

Rock·ies, the (rok′ēz). See **Rocky Mountains.**

rock′ing chair′, a chair mounted on rockers or springs so as to permit a person to rock back and forth while sitting. Also called **rocker.**

rock′ing horse′, a toy horse, as of wood, mounted on rockers or springs, on which children may ride; hobbyhorse.

rock′ing rhythm′, *Pros.* a rhythmic pattern created by a succession of metrical feet each of which consists of one accented syllable between two unaccented ones.

Rock′ Is′land, a port in NW Illinois, on the Mississippi: government arsenal. 50,166 (1970).

rock·ling (rok′ling), *n., pl.* **-lings,** (*esp. collectively*) **-ling.** any of several small cods of the genera *Enchalyopus* and *Gaidropsarus,* found in the North Atlantic.

rock′ lob′ster. See **spiny lobster.**

rock′ ma′ple, the sugar maple, *Acer saccharum.*

rock′ milk′, glacial water carrying finely ground rock (**rock′ meal′**).

Rock·ne (rok′nē), *n.* **Knute (Kenneth)** (no͞ot), 1888–1931, U.S. football coach, born in Norway.

rock-'n'-roll, (rok′ən rōl′), *n.* **1.** a style of popular music marked by a heavily accented beat and a simple, repetitious phrase structure. **2.** a dance performed to this music, usually with vigorous, exaggerated movements. —*adj.* **3.** of or pertaining to this music. —*v.i.* **4.** to dance to or play rock-'n'-roll. Also, **rock-and-roll, rock′ 'n' roll′.** [contr. of phrase *rock and roll;* see rock[2]] —**rock′-'n'-roll′er, rock′ 'n' roll′er,** *n.*

rock′ pi′geon. See **rock dove.**

rock-ribbed (rok′ribd′), *adj.* **1.** having ribs or ridges of rock. **2.** unyielding; confirmed and uncompromising.

rock·rose (rok′rōz′), *n.* **1.** any plant of the genus *Cistus* or some allied genus, as *Helianthemum.* **2.** any cistaceous plant.

rock′ salt′, common salt occurring in extensive, irregular beds in rocklike masses.

Rock·ville (rok′vil), *n.* a city in central Maryland. 41,564 (1970).

Rock′ville Cen′tre, a city on W Long Island, in SE New York. 27,444 (1970).

rock·weed (rok′wēd′), *n.* a fucoid seaweed growing on rocks exposed at low tide.

Rock·well (rok′wel′, -wəl), *n.* **Norman,** 1894–1978, U.S. illustrator.

rock′ wool′. See **mineral wool.**

rock·y[1] (rok′ē), *adj.,* **rock·i·er, rock·i·est. 1.** full of or abounding in rocks. **2.** consisting of rock. **3.** rocklike. **4.** full of difficulties or hazards: *the rocky road to stardom.* **5.** firm; steadfast: *rocky endurance.* **6.** unfeeling; without sympathy or emotion. [rock[1] + -y[1]] —**rock′i·ness,** *n.*

rock·y[2] (rok′ē), *adj.,* **rock·i·er, rock·i·est. 1.** inclined or likely to rock; tottering; shaky; unsteady. **2.** uncertain. **3.** *Informal.* physically unsteady or weak, as from sickness. [rock[2] + -y[1]]

Rock′y Mount′, a city in NE North Carolina. 34,284 (1970).

Rock′y Moun′tain goat′, a long-haired, white, goatlike, bovid ruminant, *Oreamnos americanus,* of mountainous regions of western North America, having short, black horns.

Rocky Mountain goat (3½ ft. high at shoulder; length 5 ft.; horns 10 in.)

Rock′y Moun′tain Na′tional Park′, a national park in N Colorado. 405 sq. mi.

Rock′y Moun′tains, the chief mountain system in North America, extending from central New Mexico to N Alaska. Highest peak, Mount McKinley, 20,300 ft. Also called **Rockies.**

Rock′y Moun′tain sheep′, bighorn.

Rock′y Moun′tain spot′ted fe′ver, *Pathol.* a disease characterized by high fever, pains in the joints, bones, and muscles, and a cutaneous eruption, caused by rickettsia transmitted by ticks.

Rock′y Moun′tain States′, those states in the region of the Rocky Mountains, including Colorado, Idaho, Montana, Nevada, Utah, and Wyoming, and sometimes Arizona and New Mexico.

ro·co·co (rə kō′kō; *Fr.* RÔ kô kô′), *n.* **1.** a style of architecture and decoration, originating in France about 1720, evolved from Baroque types and distinguished by elegant refinement in using different materials (stucco, metal, wood, mirrors, tapestries) for a delicate overall effect and by its ornament of shellwork, foliage, etc. **2.** a homophonic musical style of the middle 18th century, marked by a generally superficial elegance and charm and by the use of elaborate ornamentation and stereotyped devices. —*adj.* **3.** (*cap.*) *Fine Arts.* noting or pertaining to a style of painting and sculpture developed simultaneously with the rococo in architecture and decoration, characterized chiefly by smallness of scale and playfulness of theme. **4.** of or resembling rococo architecture, decoration, or music or the general atmosphere and spirit of the rococo: *rococo charm.* **5.** ornate or florid in speech, literary style, etc. **6.** antiquated; outmoded: *old ladies with elegant, rococo manners.* [< F, irreg. < *rocaille* rock work, fancy decoration < *roc* ROCK[1]]

Rococo mirror

rod (rod), *n., v.,* **rod·ded, rod·ding.** —*n.* **1.** a stick, wand, staff, or the like, of wood, metal, or other material. **2.** a straight, slender shoot or stem of any woody plant, whether still growing or cut from the plant. **3.** See **fishing rod. 4.** a stick used for measuring. **5.** a unit of linear measure, 5½ yards or 16½ feet; linear perch or pole. **6.** a unit of square measure, 30¼ square yards; square perch or pole. **7.** a stick or a bundle of sticks or switches bound together for use as a whip, as an instrument of punishment. **8.** punishment or discipline. **9.** a wand, staff, or scepter carried as a symbol of office, authority, etc. **10.** authority, sway, or rule, esp. when tyrannical. **11.** See **lightning rod. 12.** a slender bar or tube for draping towels over, suspending curtains, etc. **13.** *Bible.* a branch of a family; tribe. **14.** *Slang.* a pistol or revolver. **15.** *Anat.* one of the rodlike cells in the retina of the eye, sensitive to low intensities of light. Cf. **cone** (def. 5). **16.** *Bacteriol.* a rod-shaped microorganism. **17.** *Survey.* Also called **leveling rod, stadia rod.** a light pole, conspicuously marked with graduations, held upright and read through a surveying instrument in leveling or stadia surveying. —*v.t.* **18.** to furnish or equip with a rod or rods, esp. lightning rods. **19.** to even (plaster or mortar) with a rod. [ME, OE *rodd;* akin. to OIcel *rudda* a kind of club] —**rod′like′,** *adj.*

rode (rōd), *v.* a pt. of **ride.**

ro·dent (rōd′ᵊnt), *adj.* **1.** belonging or pertaining to the order *Rodentia,* consisting of the gnawing or nibbling mammals, including the mice, squirrels, and beavers. **2.** (of such an animal) gnawing; biting; nibbling: *the rodent teeth of a rabbit.* —*n.* **3.** a rodent mammal. [< L *rōdent-* (s. of *rōdēns,* prp. of *rōdere* to eat away, gnaw) = *rōd-* gnaw + *-ent-* -ENT] —**ro′dent·like′,** *adj.*

ro·den·ti·cide (rō den′ti sīd′), *n.* a substance or preparation for killing rodents.

ro·de·o (rō′dē ō′, rō dā′ō), *n., pl.* **-de·os. 1.** a public exhibition of cowboy skills, as bronco riding and calf roping. **2.** a roundup of cattle. [< Sp: cattle ring < *rode(ar)* (to) go round < *rueda* wheel << L *rota*]

Rodg·ers (roj′ərz), *n.* **Richard,** 1902–79, U.S. composer of popular music.

Ro·di (RÔ′dē), *n.* Italian name of **Rhodes.** (defs. 2, 3).

Ro·din (rō dan′, -DAN′; *Fr.* RÔ DAN′), *n.* **(Fran·çois) Au·guste (Re·né)** (FRÄN SWA′ ō GYST′ Rə nā′), 1840–1917, French sculptor.

Rod·ney (rod′nē), *n.* **George Brydg·es** (brij′iz), **Baron,** 1718–92, British admiral.

rod·o·mon·tade (rod′ə mon tād′, -täd′, rō′də-, -mən-), *n., adj., v.,* **-tad·ed, -tad·ing.** —*n.* **1.** vainglorious boasting or bragging; pretentious, blustering talk. —*adj.* **2.** bragging. —*v.i.* **3.** to boast. [< MF < It *Rodomonte,* the boastful king of Algiers in epic poems of Boiardo and Ariosto + MF *-ade* -ADE[1]]

roe[1] (rō), *n.* **1.** the mass of eggs, or spawn, within the ovarian membrane of the female fish. **2.** the milt or sperm of the male fish. **3.** the eggs of any of various crustaceans, as the coral of the lobster. [ME *rowe;* c. OHG *rogo*]

roe[2] (rō), *n., pl.* **roes,** (*esp. collectively*) **roe.** See **roe deer.** [ME *roo* < OE *rā, rāha;* c. G *Reh*]

Roeb·ling (rō′bliŋ), *n.* **John Augustus,** 1806–69, U.S. engineer, born in Germany: designer of the Brooklyn Bridge.

roe·buck (rō′buk′), *n., pl.* **-bucks,** (*esp. collectively*) **-buck.** a male roe deer. [ME *robucke*]

roe′ deer′, a small, agile Old World deer, *Capreolus capreolus,* the male of which has three-pointed antlers. Also called **roe.** [OE *rāhdēor.* See ROE[2]]

Roent·gen (rent′gən, -jən, runt′-), *n.* **1. Wil·helm Kon·rad** (wil′helm kon′rad; *Ger.* vil′helm kôn′rät), 1845–1923, German physicist: discoverer of x-rays 1895; Nobel prize 1901. **2.** (*l.c.*) the unit of radiation equal to the amount of x- or gamma-radiation that will produce ions in air containing a quantity of positive or negative electricity equal to one electrostatic unit in 0.001293 gram of air. *Abbr.:* R, r —*adj.* **3.** (*sometimes l.c.*) of or pertaining to Wilhelm Roentgen, the Roentgen unit, or esp. to x-rays. Also, **Röntgen.**

roentgeno-, a combining form of **roentgen:** *roentgenogram.*

roent·gen·o·gram (rent′gə nə gram′, -jə-, runt′-), *n.* a photograph made with x-rays.

roent·gen·ol·o·gy (rent′gə nol′ə jē, -jə-, runt′-), *n.* the branch of medicine dealing with diagnosis and therapy through x-rays. —**roent·gen·o·log·ic** (rent′gə nᵊloj′ik, -jə-, runt′-), **roent′gen·o·log′i·cal,** *adj.* —**roent′gen·ol′o·gist,** *n.*

roent·gen·o·scope (rent′gə nə skōp′, -jə-, runt′-), *n. Physics.* a fluoroscope. —**roent·gen·o·scop·ic** (rent′gə nə-skop′ik, -jə-, runt′-), *adj.* —**roent·gen·os·co·py** (rent′gə-nos′kə pē, -jə-, runt′-), *n.*

roent·gen·o·ther·a·py (rent′gə nō ther′ə pē, -jə-, runt′-), *n.* treatment of disease by means of x-rays.

Roent′gen ray′, (*sometimes l.c.*) x-ray.

Roeth·ke (ret′kə), *n.* **Theodore,** 1908–63, U.S. poet.

ro·ga·tion (rō gā′shən), *n.* Usually, **rogations.** *Eccles.* solemn supplication, esp. as chanted during procession on the three days **(Roga′tion Days′)** before Ascension Day. [ME *rogacio(u)n* < L *rogātiōn-* (s. of *rogātiō*) = *rogāt(us)* (ptp. of *rogāre* to ask, beg) + *-iōn-* -ION]

rog·a·to·ry (rog′ə tôr′ē, -tōr′ē), *adj.* pertaining to asking or requesting. [< ML *rogātōri(us)* = L *rogāt(us)* (see ROGATION) + *-ōrius* -ORY[1]]

rog·er (roj′ər), *interj.* **1.** *Informal.* all right; O.K. **2.** message received and understood (a response to radio communications). **3.** (*often cap.*) See **Jolly Roger.** [from the name *Roger*]

Rog·ers (roj′ərz), *n.* **1. Will(iam Penn A·dair)** (ə dâr′), 1879–1935, U.S. actor and humorist. **2. William P(ierce),** born 1913, U.S. lawyer: Attorney General 1957–61; Secretary of State 1969–73.

Ro·get (rō zhā′, rō′zhā, rozh′ā), *n.* **Peter Mark,** 1779–1869, English lexicographer, educator, and physician.

rogue (rōg), *n., v.,* **rogued, ro·guing.** —*n.* **1.** a dishonest, knavish person; scoundrel. **2.** a playfully mischievous person; scamp. **3.** a tramp or vagabond. **4.** a rogue elephant or other animal of similar disposition. **5.** *Biol.* an organism varying markedly from the normal. —*v.i.* **6.** to live or act as a rogue. —*v.t.* **7.** to cheat. **8.** to uproot or destroy (inferior plants). **9.** to perform this operation upon: *to rogue a field.* [appar. short for obs. *roger* begging vagabond, b. ROA(MER + BEG)GAR] —**Syn. 1.** villain, swindler, cheat, mountebank. See **knave.**

rogue′ el′ephant, a vicious elephant that has been exiled from the herd.

ro·guer·y (rō′gə rē), *n.* **1.** roguish conduct; rascality. **2.** playful mischief.

rogues′ gal′lery, a collection of portraits of criminals and suspects maintained by the police for purposes of identification.

ro·guish (rō′gish), *adj.* **1.** knavish or rascally. **2.** playfully mischievous: *a roguish smile.* —**ro′guish·ly,** *adv.*

roil (roil), *v.t.* **1.** to render (water, wine, etc.) turbid by stirring up sediment. **2.** to disturb or disquiet; irritate. [?] —**Syn. 2.** annoy, fret, ruffle, exasperate, provoke.

roil·y (roi′lē), *adj.,* **roil·i·er, roil·i·est.** turbid; muddy.

roist·er (roi′stər), *v.i.* **1.** to act in a swaggering, boisterous, or uproarious manner. **2.** to revel noisily or without restraint. [v. use of *roister* (n.) < MF *ru(i)stre* ruffian, boor < *ru(i)ste* RUSTIC (n.)] —**roist′er·er,** *n.* —**roist′er·ous,** *n.* —**roist′er·ous·ly,** *adv.*

Ro·jas (rō′häs; *Sp.* RÔ′häs), *n.* **Fer·nan·do de** (feʀ nän′dô de), c1475–1541?, Spanish writer.

Rok (rok), *n.* a soldier in the army of the Republic of Korea. [after *R(epublic) o(f) K(orea)*]

ROK, Republic of Korea.

Ro·land (rō′lənd), *n.* a semilegendary paladin and a cousin of Charlemagne, renowned for his prowess and bravery; died in the battle of Roncesvalles (A.D. 778).

role (rōl), *n.* **1.** a part or character to be played by an actor. **2.** the proper or customary function of a person or thing. Also, **rôle.** [< F *rôle* ROLL (as of paper) containing the actor's part]

Rolf (rolf), *n.* Rollo. Also called **Rolf′ the Gang′er** (gaŋ′ər).

Rolfe (rolf), *n.* **John,** 1585–1622, English colonist in Virginia (husband of Pocahontas).

roll (rōl), *v.i.* **1.** to move along a surface by revolving or turning over and over, as a ball or a wheel. **2.** to move or be moved on wheels. **3.** to flow or advance with an undulating motion, as waves of water or billows of smoke. **4.** to extend in undulations, as land. **5.** to elapse, pass, or move, as time. **6.** to emit or have a deep, prolonged sound, as thunder, drums, etc. **7.** to trill, as a bird. **8.** to revolve or turn over, as a wheel on an axis or a person or animal lying down. **9.** (of the eyes) to turn in different directions. **10.** (of a vessel) **a.** to rock from side to side in open water. Cf. **heave** (def. 15b), **pitch**[1] (def. 14). **b.** to sail with a side-to-side rocking motion. **11.** to have a swinging or swaying gait. **12.** to curl up so as to form a tube or cylinder. **13.** to admit of being so curled. **14.** to be spread out after being curled up. **15.** to spread out as under a roller. **16.** (of a rocket or guided missile) to deviate from a stable flight attitude by rotation about its longitudinal axis. —*v.t.* **17.** to cause to move along a surface by revolving or turning over and over. **18.** to move along on wheels or rollers. **19.** to cause to flow onward with a sweeping or undulating motion. **20.** to utter or give forth with or cause to give forth a full, flowing, continuous sound. **21.** to trill: *to roll one's r's.* **22.** to cause to revolve or turn over, or over and over. **23.** to turn (the eyes) in different directions. **24.** to cause to sway or rock from side to side, as a ship. **25.** to wrap (something) around an axis, around upon itself, or into a rounded shape. **26.** to make by forming into a tube or cylinder: *to roll a cigarette.* **27.** to spread out flat (something curled up). **28.** to wrap, infold, or envelop, as in a covering. **29.** to spread out, level, etc., with a roller. **30.** to beat (a drum) with rapid, continuous strokes. **31.** (in certain games, as craps) to cast, or throw (dice). **32.** *Print.* to apply ink with a roller or series of rollers. **33.** *Slang.* to rob, esp. by going through the victim's pockets while he is drunk or sleeping. **34. roll around** or **round,** to arrive or come into being, often as part of a cycle: *when spring rolls around.* **35. roll in,** *Informal.* **a.** to luxuriate in; abound in: *rolling in money.* **b.** to go to bed; retire. **c.** to arrive, esp. in large numbers or quantity: *When do my dividends start rolling in?* **36. roll out, a.** to spread out or flatten: *to roll out dough.* **b.** *Slang.* to arise from bed; get up. **37. roll up, a.** to accumulate; collect. **b.** *Informal.* to arrive in a conveyance. —*n.* **38.** a document of paper, parchment, or the like, that is or may be rolled up. **39.** a list, register, or catalog, as of membership. **40.** anything rolled up in a ringlike or cylindrical form: *a roll of wire.* **41.** a cylindrical or rounded object or mass: *rolls of fat.* **42.** a cylinder serving as a core upon which something is rolled up. **43.** a roller. **44.** *Cookery.* **a.** thin cake spread with jelly or the like and rolled up. **b.** a small cake of bread, often rolled or doubled on itself before baking. **c.** meat rolled up and cooked. **45.** the act, process, or an instance of rolling. **46.** undulation, as of a surface. **47.** a sonorous or rhythmical flow of words. **48.** a deep, prolonged sound, as of thunder or drums. **49.** the trill of certain birds. **50.** a rolling motion or gait. **51.** *Aeron.* a single, complete rotation of an airplane about the axis of the fuselage with little loss of altitude or change of direction. **52.** *Slang.* **a.** paper currency carried folded or rolled up. **b.** bankroll; funds. **53.** (in various dice games) **a.** a single cast of or turn at casting the dice. **b.** the total number of pips or points made by a single cast; score or point. **54.** **strike off** or **from the rolls,** to remove from membership or practice, as to disbar. [ME *roll(en)* < OF *roll(er)* << L *rotula,* dim. of *rota* wheel] —**Syn. 1.** revolve. **4.** undulate. **39.** roster. See **list**[1].

Rol·land (rô läN′), *n.* **Ro·main** (rô maN′), 1866–1944, French novelist, music critic, and dramatist.

roll·a·way (rōl′ə wā′), *adj.* designed to be rolled out of the way when not in use: *rollaway bed.*

roll·back (rōl′bak′), *n.* a return to a lower level of prices, wages, etc., as by government order.

roll′ bar′, a very sturdy metal bar arching over an automobile from side to side to prevent injury to passengers in the event of rolling over.

roll′ call′, the calling of a list of names, as of soldiers or students, for checking attendance.

rolled′ gold′. See **filled gold.**

roll·er[1] (rō′lər), *n.* **1.** a person or thing that rolls. **2.** a cylinder, wheel, caster, or the like, upon which something is rolled along. **3.** a cylindrical object on which something is rolled up. **4.** a hollow, cylindrical object upon which hair is rolled up for setting in smooth waves. **5.** a cylindrical object for spreading, crushing, or flattening something. **6.** any of various other revolving cylindrical objects. **7.** a long, swelling wave advancing steadily. **8.** a rolled bandage. [ME]

roll·er[2] (rō′lər), *n.* *Ornith.* **1.** one of a variety of tumbler pigeons. **2.** any of several Old World birds of the family *Coraciidae* that tumble or roll over in flight. **3.** one of a variety of canaries having a warbling or trilling song. [< G *Roller* ROLLER[1]]

roll′er bear′ing, *Mach.* a bearing employing rollers to prevent friction.

roll′er coast′er, *U.S.* a small gravity railroad, esp. in an amusement park, having a train with open cars that moves along a high, sharply winding trestle built with steep inclines.

roll′er der′by, a contest between two teams on roller skates, held on a circular, usually banked board track, in which the teams race around the track in each unit of play, working to free a teammate or teammates for the opportunity to score by lapping one or more opponents.

roll′er skate′, a form of skate with four wheels or rollers, for use on a sidewalk or other surface offering traction.

roll·er-skate (rō′lər skāt′), *v.i.*, **-skat·ed, -skat·ing.** to glide about by means of roller skates. —**rol′ler skat′er.**

roll′er tow′el, a long towel sewn together at the ends and hung on a roller.

rol·lick (rol′ik), *v.i.* to move or act in a careless, frolicsome manner; behave in a free, hearty, gay, or jovial way. [b. RO(MP + FRO)LIC] —**rol′lick·er,** *n.*

rol·lick·ing (rol′i king), *adj.* swaggering and jolly: *a pair of rollicking drunken sailors.* —**rol′lick·ing·ly,** *adv.*

rol·lick·some (rol′ik səm), *adj.* rollicking; frolicsome.

roll·ing (rō′ling), *n.* **1.** the action, motion, or sound of anything that rolls. —*adj.* **2.** moving by revolving or turning over and over. **3.** rising and falling in gentle slopes, as land. **4.** moving in undulating billows, as clouds or waves. **5.** rocking or swaying from side to side. **6.** turning or folding over, as a collar. **7.** producing a deep, continuous sound. [late ME (n.)] —**roll′ing·ly,** *adv.*

roll′ing hitch′, a hitch on a spar or the like made to jam when stress is applied parallel to the object having the hitch.

roll′ing mill′, **1.** a mill where ingots, slabs, etc., of metal are passed between rolls to give them a certain thickness or cross-sectional form. **2.** a machine or set of rollers for rolling out or shaping metal.

roll′ing pin′, a cylinder of wood or other material, with a handle at each end, for rolling out dough.

roll′ing stock′, the wheeled vehicles of a railroad, including locomotives, cars, etc.

roll′ mold′ing, *Archit.* any molding of approximately cylindrical form.

roll·mop (rōl′mop′), *n.* a fillet of herring, rolled, usually around a pickle, and marinated in brine. [< G *Rollmops* = *roll(en)* (to) ROLL + *Mops* pug (dog)]

Rol·lo (rol′ō), *n.* A.D. c860–931?, Norse chieftain: 1st duke of Normandy 911?. Also called **Rolf, Rolf the Ganger, Roy, Hrolf.**

roll-on (rōl on′, -ôn′), *adj.* packaged in a container equipped with a roller that dispenses the content directly.

roll·o·ver (rōl′ō′vər), *n.* **1.** a rolling or turning over, esp. of an automobile. **2.** an extension, renewal, or deferral of a financial obligation, as a loan, investment, or tax.

roll′ top′, a flexible, sliding cover for the working area of a desk, rolling up beneath the top. —**roll′-top′, roll′top′,** *adj.*

roll·way (rōl′wā′), *n.* an incline for rolling or sliding logs.

Röl·vaag (rōl′väg), *n.* **O·le Ed·vart** (ō′lə ed′värt), 1876–1931, U.S. novelist and educator, born in Norway.

ro·ly-po·ly (rō′lē pō′lē, -pō′lē), *adj., n., pl.* **-lies.** —*adj.* **1.** short and plumply round, as a person. —*n.* **2.** a roly-poly person or thing. **3.** *Chiefly Brit.* a sheet of biscuit dough spread with jam, fruit, or the like, rolled up and steamed or baked. [earlier *rowle powle,* ? var. of *roll ye, poll ye.* See ROLL (v.), POLL[1] (v.)] —**Syn. 1.** fat, rotund, pudgy.

ROM (rom), *n.* computer memory in which program instructions, operating procedures, and other data are permanently stored, generally on electronic chips during manufacture, and which ordinarily cannot be changed by the user. Cf. **RAM** [*r(ead) o(nly) m(emory)*]

Rom., **1.** Roman. **2.** Romance. **3.** Romanic. **4.** Romans (New Testament). Also, **Rom** (for defs. 2, 3).

rom., roman type.

Ro·ma (rô′mä), *n.* Italian name of **Rome.**

Ro·ma·gna (rō män′yə; *It.* rô mä′nyä), *n.* a former province of the Papal States, in NE Italy. *Cap.:* Ravenna.

Ro·ma·ic (rō mā′ik), *n.* **1.** demotic (def. 3). —*adj.* **2.** of or pertaining to modern Greece, its inhabitants, or their language. [< Gk *Rhōmaïk(ós)* Roman = *Rhṓm(ē)* Rome + *-a-* connective vowel + *-ikos* -IC]

ro·maine (rō mān′, rə-), *n.* a variety of lettuce, *Lactuca sativa longifolia,* having a cylindrical head of long, relatively loose leaves. Also called **romaine′ let′tuce, cos, cos lettuce.** [< F, fem. of *romain* ROMAN]

Ro·mains (rô maN′), *n.* **Jules** (zhyl), (pen name of *Louis Farigoule*), 1885–1972, French novelist, poet, and dramatist.

ro·man (rô mäN′), *n., pl.* **-mans** (-mäN′). *French.* **1.** a metrical narrative, esp. in medieval literature. **2.** a novel.

Ro·man (rō′mən), *adj.* **1.** of or pertaining to the ancient or modern city of Rome, or to its inhabitants or their customs and culture. **2.** of or pertaining to the ancient kingdom, republic, and empire of Rome. **3.** of a kind or character regarded as typical of the ancient Romans: *Roman virtues.* **4.** (*usually l.c.*) noting or pertaining to the upright style of printing types most commonly used. **5.** of or pertaining to the Roman Catholic Church. **6.** noting, pertaining to, or resembling the architecture of ancient Rome, esp. characterized by such features as the semicircular arch, the dome, and groin and barrel vaults, and by the use of Greek orders as purely decorative motifs in adorning façades and interiors. **7.** pertaining to or consisting of Roman numerals. —*n.* **8.** a native, inhabitant, or citizen of ancient or modern Rome. **9.** the dialect of Italian spoken in Rome. **10.** (*usually l.c.*) roman type or lettering. [OE < L *Rōmān(us)* (see ROME, -AN); r. ME *Romain* < OF]

ro·man à clef (rô mä′ nA klā′), *pl.* **ro·mans à clef** (rô-mäN′ zA klā′). *French.* a novel that represents real events and characters under the guise of fiction. [lit., novel with (a) key]

Ro′man al′phabet. See **Latin alphabet.**

Ro′man arch′, a semicircular arch.

Ro′man cal′endar, the calendar used in ancient Rome prior to the Julian calendar.

Ro′man can′dle, a firework consisting of a tube that emits sparks and balls of fire.

Ro′man Cath′olic, **1.** of or pertaining to the Roman Catholic Church. **2.** a member of the Roman Catholic Church. Cf. **Catholic.**

Ro′man Cath′olic Church′, the Christian church of which the pope, or bishop of Rome, is the supreme head.

Ro′man Cathol′icism, the faith, practice, and system of government of the Roman Catholic Church.

ro·mance[1] (*n.* rō mans′, rō′mans; *v.* rō mans′; *adj.* rō′mans), *n., v.,* **-manced, -manc·ing,** *adj.* —*n.* **1.** a novel or other prose narrative typically characterized by heroic deeds, pageantry, romantic exploits, etc., usually in a historical or imaginary setting. **2.** the colorful world, life, or conditions depicted in such tales. **3.** a medieval narrative, originally one in verse and in some Romance dialect, treating of heroic, fantastic, or supernatural events, often in the form of an allegory. **4.** a baseless, fanciful story. **5.** romantic spirit, sentiment, emotion, or desire. **6.** romantic character or quality. **7.** a love affair. **8.** (*cap.*) Also, **Romanic.** Also called **Romance languages.** the group of Italic Indo-European languages descended since A.D. 800 from Latin, as French, Spanish, Italian, Portuguese, Rumanian, Provençal, Catalan, Rhaeto-Romantic, Sardinian, and Ladino. *Abbr.:* Rom —*v.i.* **9.** to indulge in fanciful stories or daydreams. **10.** to think or talk romantically. —*v.t.* **11.** *Informal.* to court; woo. —*adj.* **12.** (*cap.*) Also, **Romanic.** noting, of, or pertaining to Romance. [ME *romaunce* < OF < VL **Rōmānicē* (adv.) in a Romance language, L *Rōmānic(us)* ROMANIC] —**ro·manc′er,** *n.* —**Syn. 1.** story, fiction.

ro·mance[2] (rō mans′), *n.* **1.** *Music.* a short, simple melody, vocal or instrumental, of tender character. **2.** *Sp. Lit.* a short epic poem, esp. a historical ballad. [< F < Sp: kind of poem, ballad < OF *romanz* ROMANCE[1]]

Ro′mance lan′guages, romance[1] (def. 8).

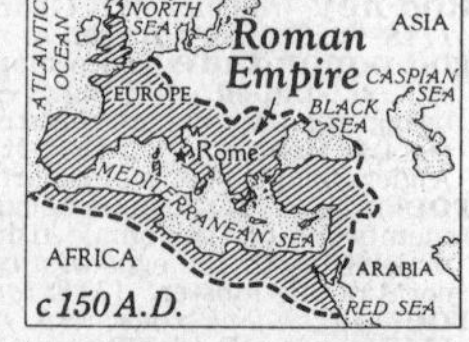

Ro′man col′lar. See **clerical collar.**

Ro′man Cu′ria. See **Curia Romana.**

Ro′man Em′pire, **1.** the lands and peoples subject to the authority of ancient Rome. **2.** the imperial form of Roman government established by Augustus in 27 B.C., and replacing the republic.

Ro·man·esque (rō′mə nesk′), *adj.* **1.** noting or pertaining to the style of architecture prevailing in western or southern Europe from the 9th through the 12th centuries, characterized by heavy masonry construction, using the round arch, the groin vault, and the barrel vault. **2.** pertaining to or designating the styles of sculpture, painting, or ornamentation of the corresponding period. **3.** (*l.c.*) of or pertaining to fanciful or extravagant literature, as romance or fable; fanciful. [ROMAN + -ESQUE; cf. F *romanesque* romantic]

ro·man-fleuve (rô mäN′flœv′), *n., pl.* **ro·mans-fleuves** (rô mäN′flœv′). *French.* saga (def. 3). [lit.: stream-novel]

Ro′man hol′iday, a public spectacle or controversy marked by barbarism, vindictiveness, or scandal.

Ro·ma·ni·a (rō mā′nē ə, -mān′yə), *n.* Rumania. —**Ro·ma′ni·an,** *n., adj.*

Ro·mâ·nia (rô mœ′nyä; *Eng.* rō mā′nē ə, -mān′yə), *n.* Rumanian name of **Rumania.**

Ro·man·ic (rō man′ik), *adj.* **1.** derived from the Romans. **2.** romance[1] (def. 12). —*n.* **3.** romance[1] (def. 8). [< L *Rōmānic(us)* Roman = *Rōmān(us)* ROMAN + *-icus* -IC]

Ro·man·ism (rō′mə niz′əm), *n.* *Usually Derogatory.* See **Roman Catholicism.**

Ro·man·ist (rō′mə nist), *n.* **1.** *Usually Derogatory.* a Roman Catholic. **2.** a person versed in Roman institutions, law, etc. **3.** Also, **Ro·man·i·cist** (rō man′i sist). a person versed in the Romance languages or literatures. [< NL *Romanist(a).* See ROMAN, -IST] —**Ro′man·is′tic,** *adj.*

Ro·man·ize (rō′mə nīz′), *v.,* **-ized, -iz·ing.** —*v.t.* **1.** to make Roman Catholic. **2.** to make Roman in character. —*v.i.* **3.** to conform to Roman Catholic doctrine and practices. **4.** to follow Roman practices. Also, *esp. Brit.,* **Ro′man·ise.** —**Ro′man·i·za′tion,** *n.* **Ro′man·iz′er,** *n.*

Ro′man law′, the system of jurisprudence elaborated by the ancient Romans.

Ro′man mile′, a unit of length used by the ancient Romans, equivalent to about 1620 yards.

Ro′man nose′, a nose having a prominent upper part or bridge. —**Ro′man-nosed′,** *adj.*

Ro′man nu′merals, the numerals in the ancient Roman system of notation, still used for certain limited purposes, as in some pagination, dates on buildings, etc. The common basic symbols are **I**(=1), **V**(=5), **X**(=10), **L**(=50), **C**(=100), **D**(=500), and **M**(=1000). The Roman numerals for one to nine are I, II, III, IV, V, VI, VII, VIII, IX. A bar over a letter multiplies it by 1000; thus, X̄ equals 10,000. Integers are written according to these two rules: If a letter is immediately followed by one of equal or lesser value, the two values are added; thus, XX equals 20, XV equals 15, VI equals 6. If a letter is immediately followed by one of greater value, however, the first is subtracted from the second; thus, IV equals 4, XL equals 40, CM equals 900. Examples: XLVII(=47), CXVI(=116), MCXX(=1120), MCMXIV (=1914). Roman numerals may be written in lower-case letters, though they appear more commonly in capitals.

Ro·ma·no (rō mä′nō), *n.* (*sometimes l.c.*) a hard, light-colored, sharp Italian cheese. [< It: ROMAN]

Ro·ma·nov (rō′mə nôf′, -nof′; *Russ.* RO mä′nof), *n.* **1.** a member of the imperial dynasty of Russia that ruled from 1613 to 1917. **2. Mi·kha·il Feo·do·ro·vich** (mi KHĪ ēl′ fyô′do RO vich), 1596–1645, emperor of Russia 1613–45: first ruler of the house of Romanov. Also, **Ro′ma·noff′.**

Ro·mans (rō′mənz), *n.* (*construed as sing.*) an Epistle of the New Testament, written by Paul to the Christian community in Rome.

Ro·mansh (rō mansh′, -mänsh′), *n.* **1.** a group of three Rhaeto-Romanic dialects spoken in E Switzerland. Cf. **Ladin** (def. 2). —*adj.* **2.** of or pertaining to Romansh. [< Rhaetian: ROMANIC]

ro·man·tic (rō man′tik), *adj.* **1.** of, pertaining to, or of the nature of romance. **2.** fanciful; impractical. **3.** imbued with or dominated by idealism, a desire for adventure, etc. **4.** characterized by a preoccupation with love or by the idealizing of love or one's beloved. **5.** displaying or expressing love. **6.** ardent; passionate; fervent. **7.** (*usually cap.*) of, pertaining to, or characteristic of a style of literature and art, esp. of the 19th century, that subordinates form to content, encourages freedom of treatment, emphasizes imagination, emotion, and introspection, and often celebrates nature, the common man, and freedom of the spirit (contrasted with *classical*). **8.** of or pertaining to a musical style, esp. of the 19th century, that is marked by the free expression of imagination and emotion, experimentation with form, and the increase in the size and range of the orchestra. **9.** imaginary, fictitious, or fabulous. **10.** noting, of, or pertaining to the dramatic role of a suitor or lover. —*n.* **11.** a romantic person. **12.** an adherent of Romanticism. **13. romantics,** romantic ideas, ways, etc. [< F *romantique* < *romant* earlier form of *roman* novel. See ROMANCE[1]] —**ro·man′ti·cal·ly,** *adv.* —**ro·man·ti·cist** (rō man′ti sist), *n.* —**Syn. 2.** extravagant, fantastic. **9.** improbable, unreal. —**Ant. 2.** practical, realistic.

ro·man·ti·cise (rō man′ti sīz′), *v.t., v.i.,* **-cised, -cis·ing.** *Chiefly Brit.* romanticize. —**ro·man′ti·ci·sa′tion,** *n.*

ro·man·ti·cism (rō man′ti siz′əm), *n.* **1.** romantic spirit or tendency. **2.** (*usually cap.*) the Romantic style or movement in literature and art, or adherence to its principles (contrasted with *classicism*).

ro·man·ti·cize (rō man′ti sīz′), *v.,* **-cized, -ciz·ing.** —*v.t.* **1.** to make romantic; invest with a romantic character. —*v.i.* **2.** to hold romantic notions, ideas, etc. Also, *esp. Brit.,* **romanticise.** —**ro·man′ti·ci·za′tion,** *n.*

Roman′tic Move′ment, the late 18th- and early 19th-century movement in France, Germany, England, and America to establish Romanticism in art and literature.

Ro·ma·nus (rō mā′nəs), *n.* died A.D. 897, Italian ecclesiastic: pope 897.

Rom·a·ny (rom′ə nē, rō′mə-), *n., pl.* **-nies** for 1, *adj.* —*n.* **1.** a Gypsy. **2.** Gypsies collectively. **3.** the Indic language of the Gypsies in its various local forms. —*adj.* **4.** pertaining to Gypsies, their language, or their customs. Also, **Rommany.** [< Gypsy *Romani,* fem. and pl. of *Romano* (adj.) < *Rom* a Gypsy man or boy, married man < Skt *ḍomba, ḍoma*]

ro·maunt (rō mänt′, -mônt′), *n. Archaic.* a romantic tale or poem. [< AF, var. of OF *romant* ROMANCE[1]]

Rom·berg (rom′bûrg), *n.* **Sig·mund** (sig′mənd), 1887–1951, Hungarian composer of light opera in the U.S.

Rom. Cath., Roman Catholic.

Rome (rōm), *n.* **1.** Italian, **Roma.** a city in and the capital of Italy, in the central part, on the Tiber: ancient capital of the Roman Empire; site of Vatican City, seat of authority of the Roman Catholic Church. 2,600,000. **2.** a city in central New York, E of Oneida Lake. 50,148 (1970). **3.** a city in NW Georgia. 30,759 (1970). **4.** the ancient Italian kingdom, republic, and empire whose capital was the city of Rome. **5.** the Roman Catholic Church. **6.** See **Roman Catholicism.**

Ro·me·o (rō′mē ō′), *n.* **1.** any male lover, after the romantic lover of Juliet in Shakespeare's tragedy *Romeo and Juliet.* **2.** (used in communications to represent the letter *R.*)

Rom·ish (rō′mish), *adj. Often Derogatory.* of or pertaining to the Roman Catholic Church.

Rom·ma·ny (rom′ə nē), *n., pl.* **-nies,** *adj.* Romany.

Rom·mel (rum′əl; *Ger.* RÔM′əl), *n.* **Er·win** (ûr′win; *Ger.* ER′vēn), ("*the Desert Fox*"), 1891–1944, German field marshal: commander of the German forces in North Africa in World War II.

Rom·ney (rom′nē, rum′-), *n.* **1. George,** 1734–1802, English painter. **2.** former name of **New Romney.**

Rom·ney (rom′nē, rum′-), *n.* one of an English breed of hardy sheep, having coarse, long wool. Also called **Rom′ney Marsh′.** [after the district in southwestern England]

romp (romp), *v.i.* **1.** to play or frolic in a lively or boisterous manner. **2.** to run or go rapidly and without effort, as in racing. —*n.* **3.** a lively or boisterous frolic. **4.** a quick or effortless pace. [var. of obs. *ramp* rough woman, lit., one who ramps; see RAMP (v.)] —**romp′er,** *n.* —**romp′ing·ly,** *adv.* —**Syn. 1, 3.** gambol.

romp·ers (rom′pərz), *n.* (*construed as pl.*) a loose outer garment combining a waist and short, bloused pants.

romp·ish (rom′pish), *adj.* given to romping; frolicsome. —**romp′ish·ly,** *adv.* —**romp′ish·ness,** *n.*

Ro·mu·lo (rom′yŏŏ lō′; *Sp.* RÔ′mōō lō′), *n.* **Car·los Pe·na** (kär′lôs pe′nä), 1901–85, Philippine diplomat, journalist, and educator.

Rom·u·lus (rom′yə ləs), *n. Rom. Legend.* the founder of Rome, in 753 B.C., and its first king: a son of Mars and Rhea Silvia, he and his twin brother, Remus, were abandoned as babies, suckled by a she-wolf, and brought up by a shepherd.

Ron·ces·valles (ron′sə valz′; *Sp.* RÔN′thes vä′lyes), *n.* a village in N Spain, in the Pyrenees: death of Roland A.D. 778. French, **Ronce·vaux** (RÔNS VŌ′).

ron·deau (ron′dō, ron dō′), *n., pl.* **-deaux** (-dōz, -dōz′). **1.** *Pros.* **a.** a short poem of fixed form, consisting of 13 or 10 lines on two rhymes and having the opening words or phrase used in two places as an unrhymed refrain. **b.** rondel (def. 1). **2.** a medieval monophonic or polyphonic song form consisting of two phrases, each repeated several times. [< MF: little circle; see RONDEL]

ron·del (ron′dᵊl), *n. Pros.* **1.** a short poem of fixed form, consisting usually of 14 lines on two rhymes, including a refrain made up of the initial couplet repeated in the middle and at the end, with the second line of the couplet sometimes being omitted at the end. **2.** rondeau (def. 1a). [ME < OF *rondel, rondeau,* dim. of *rond* ROUND[1]]

ron·de·let (ron′dᵊlet′, ron′dᵊlet′), *n.* a short poem of fixed form, consisting of five lines on two rhymes, and having the opening words or word used after the second and fifth lines as an unrhymed refrain. [< MF, dim. of *rondel* RONDEL]

ron·do (ron′dō, ron dō′), *n., pl.* **-dos.** *Music.* a work or movement, often the last movement of a sonata, having one principal subject which is stated at least three times in the same key and to which return is made after the introduction of each subordinate theme. [< It < F *rondeau;* see RONDEL]

Ron·dô·nia (RÔN dô′nyə), *n.* a state in W Brazil. 70,783 (1960); 93,815 sq. mi. *Cap.:* Pôrto Velho. Formerly, **Guaporé.**

ron·dure (ron′jər), *n.* **1.** a circle or sphere. **2.** a graceful curving or roundness. [< F *rondeur* < *rond* ROUND[1]]

Ron·sard (RÔN SAR′), *n.* **Pierre de** (pyer də), 1524–85, French poet.

Rönt·gen (rent′gən, -jən, runt′-; *Ger.* rœnt′gən), *n.* **Wil·helm Kon·rad** (vil′helm kôn′Rät). See **Roentgen.**

ron·yon (run′yən), *n. Obs.* a mangy creature. Also, **ronion.** [? < F *rogne* mange]

rood (rōōd), *n.* **1.** a crucifix, esp. a large one at the entrance to the choir or chancel of a church. **2.** a unit of length varying locally from 5½ to 8 yards. **3.** a unit of land measure equal to 40 square rods or ¼ acre. **4.** a unit of 1 square rod or thereabout. **5.** *Archaic.* the cross on which Christ died. [ME; OE *rōd;* c. G *Rute.* See ROD]

rood′ beam′, a beam extending across the entrance to the choir or chancel of a church to support the rood.

Roo·de·poort-Ma·rais·burg (rōō′də pōōrt′mä rä′bûrk), *n.* a city in S Transvaal, in the NE Republic of South Africa. 139,810.

rood′ screen′, a screen, often of elaborate design and properly surmounted by a rood, separating the nave from the choir or chancel of a church.

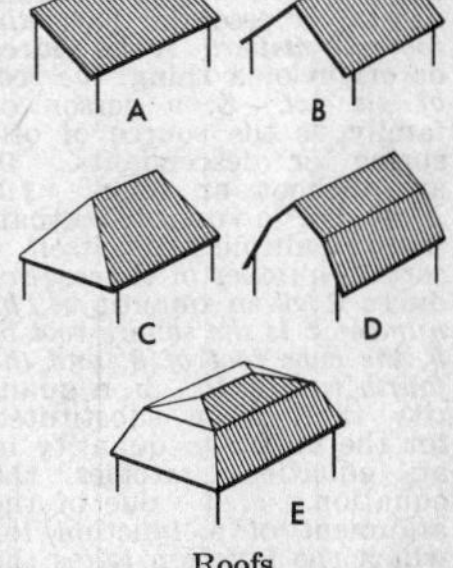

Roofs
A, Lean-to; B, Gable; C, Hip; D, Gambrel; E, Mansard

roof (rōōf, rŏŏf), *n., pl.* **roofs,** *v.* —*n.* **1.** the external upper covering of a house or other building. **2.** a frame for supporting this. **3.** something resembling the roof of a house, as the top of a car, the upper part of the mouth, etc. **4. raise the roof,** *Slang.* **a.** to create a loud noise. **b.** to complain or protest noisily. —*v.t.* **5.** to provide or cover with a roof. [ME; OE *hrōf;* c. D *roef* cover, cabin, OIcel *hrōf*]

roof·er (rōō′fər, rŏŏf′ər), *n.* a person who lays or repairs roofing.

roof′ gar′den, 1. a garden on the flat roof of a house or other building. **2.** the top or top story of a building, having a garden, restaurant, or the like.

roof·ing (rōō′fing, rŏŏf′ing), *n.* **1.** act of covering with a roof. **2.** material for roofs. **3.** a roof. [late ME *rovyng*]

roof′ing nail′, a short nail for nailing asphalt shingles or the like, having a broad head. See illus. at **nail.**

roof·top (rōōf′top′, rŏŏf′-), *n.* the roof of a building, esp. the outer surface.

roof·tree (rōōf′trē′, rŏŏf′-), *n.* **1.** the ridgepole of a roof. **2.** the roof itself. [late ME]

rook[1] (rŏŏk), *n.* **1.** a black, European crow, *Corvus frugilegus,* noted for its gregarious habits. **2.** a sharper or swindler. —*v.t.* **3.** to cheat; fleece; swindle. [ME *rōk,* OE *hrōc;* c. OIcel *hrōk(r),* OHG *hruoh*]

rook[2] (rŏŏk), *n. Chess.* one of two pieces of the same color, moved any unobstructed distance horizontally or vertically; castle. [ME *rok* < OF *roc* << Pers *rukh*]

rook·er·y (rŏŏk′ə rē), *n., pl.* **-er·ies. 1.** a colony of rooks. **2.** a breeding place of rooks. **3.** a breeding place or colony of other gregarious birds or animals.

rook·ie (rŏŏk′ē), *n.* **1.** an athlete playing his first season on a professional sports team. **2.** any raw recruit, as on a police force. [alter. of RECRUIT]

rook·y (rŏŏk′ē), *adj.,* **rook·i·er, rook·i·est.** full of or frequented by rooks.

room (rōōm, rŏŏm), *n.* **1.** a walled or partitioned portion of space within a building or other structure. **2. rooms,** a person's lodgings or quarters, as in a house or building. **3.** the persons present in a room. **4.** space or extent of space occupied by or available for something. **5.** opportunity or scope for something. —*v.i.* **6.** to occupy a room or rooms; lodge. [ME *roum,* OE *rūm;* c. D *ruim,* G *Raum*]

room′ and board′, lodging and meals.

room′ clerk′, a clerk at a hotel who keeps the guest register, sorts the incoming mail, etc.

room′ divid′er, an article of furniture, a freestanding bookcase, a screen, or the like, that separates one part of a room from another.

room·er (ro͞o′mər, ro͝om′ər), *n.* a lodger.

room·ette (ro͞o met′, ro͝o-), *n.* a small private compartment in a sleeping car of a train.

room·ful (ro͞om′fo͝ol, ro͝om′-), *n., pl.* **-fuls.** an amount or number sufficient to fill a room.

room·mate (ro͞om′māt′, ro͝om′-), *n.* a person who shares one's room or apartment.

room·y (ro͞o′mē, ro͝om′ē), *adj.,* **room·i·er, room·i·est.** affording ample room; spacious; large. —**room′i·ly,** *adv.* —**room′i·ness,** *n.*

roose (ro͞oz; *Scot.* rœz), *v.t., v.i.,* **roosed, roos·ing,** *n. Chiefly Scot.* praise. [< Scand; cf. OIcel *hrōsa* to praise]

Roo·se·velt (rō′zə velt′, -vəlt; *spelling pron.* ro͞o′zə velt′), *n.* **1. (Anna) Eleanor,** 1884–1962, U.S. diplomat, author, and lecturer (wife of Franklin Delano Roosevelt). **2. Franklin Del·a·no** (del′ə nō′), ("*FDR*"), 1882–1945, 32nd president of the U.S. 1933–45. **3. Theodore** (*Teddy,* "*T.R.*"), 1858–1919, 26th president of the U.S. 1901–09: Nobel peace prize 1906. **4. Río.** Formerly, **Río da Duvida.** a river flowing N from W Brazil to the Madeira River. ab. 400 mi. long.

roost (ro͞ost), *n.* **1.** a perch upon which birds or fowls rest at night. **2.** a large cage, house, or place for fowls or birds to roost in. **3.** a place for resting, lodging, or congregating, as an inn, club, etc. **4. rule the roost,** to be in charge or control; dominate. —*v.i.* **5.** to sit or rest on a roost, perch, etc. **6.** to settle or stay, esp. for the night. **7. come home to roost,** (of an action) to revert or react unfavorably to the doer; boomerang. [ME *roost,* OE *hrōst;* c. MD, Flem *roest*]

Rooster (Domestic)

roost·er (ro͞o′stər), *n.* the male of the domestic fowl; cock.

root[1] (ro͞ot, ro͝ot), *n.* **1.** a part of the body of a plant that develops, typically, from the radicle and grows downward into the soil, fixing the plant and absorbing nutriment and moisture. **2.** a similar organ developed from some other part of a plant, as one of those by which ivy clings to its support. **3.** any underground part of a plant, as a rhizome. **4.** something resembling or suggesting the root of a plant in position or function. **5.** the embedded or basal portion of a hair, tooth, nail, etc. **6.** the fundamental or essential part: *the root of a matter.* **7.** the source or origin of a thing: *the root of all evil.* **8.** a person or family as the source of offspring or descendants. **9.** an offshoot or scion. **10.** *Math.* **a.** a quantity that, when multiplied by itself a certain number of times, produces a given quantity: *The number 2 is the square root of 4, the cube root of 8, and the fourth root of 16.* **b.** a quantity that, when substituted for the unknown quantity in an equation, satisfies the equation. **c.** a value of the argument of a function for which the function takes the value zero. **11.** *Gram.* **a.** a morpheme that underlies an inflectional or derivational paradigm, as *dance,* the root in *danced, dancer,* or *ten-,* the root of Latin *tendere* "to stretch." **b.** such a form reconstructed for a parent language, as *sed-,* the hypothetical proto-Indo-European root meaning "sit." **12. roots,** the background provided by one's culture, religion, home, etc., often regarded as promoting the development of personal character or the stability of society as a whole. **13.** *Music.* **a.** the fundamental tone of a compound tone or of a series of harmonies. **b.** the lowest tone of a chord when arranged as a series of thirds; the fundamental. **14. root and branch,** utterly; entirely: *to destroy something root and branch.* **15. take root, a.** to send out roots; begin to grow. **b.** to become fixed or established. —*v.i.* **16.** to grow roots; take root. **17.** to become fixed or established. —*v.t.* **18.** to fix by or as by roots. **19.** to furnish with or as with roots. **20.** to implant or establish deeply. **21.** to pull, tear, or dig up by the roots. **22.** to extirpate; exterminate; remove completely (often fol. by *up* or *out*): *to root out crime.* [ME; late OE *rōt* < Scand; cf. Icel *rōt;* akin to OE *wyrt* plant, WORT[2], G *Wurzel,* L *rādix*] —**root′like′,** *adj.* —**Syn. 6.** basis. **7.** beginning, fountainhead. **8.** parent.

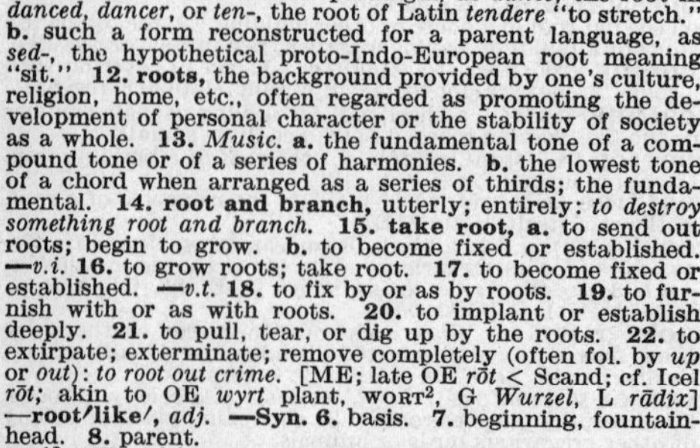

Roots
A, Tap (Ragweed, *Ambrosia trifida*); B, Fibrous (Plantain, *Plantago major*); C, Fleshy (Carrot, *Daucus carota*); D, Tuberous (Rue anemone, *Anemonella thalictroides*)

root[2] (ro͞ot, ro͝ot), *v.i.* **1.** to turn up the soil with the snout. **2.** to poke or pry, as if to find something. —*v.t.* **3.** to turn over with the snout (often fol. by *up*). **4.** to unearth; bring to light (often fol. by *up*). [var. of obs. *wroot,* OE *wrōt(an),* akin to *wrōt* a snout]

root[3] (ro͞ot, ro͝ot), *v.i.* **1.** to encourage by cheering. **2.** to lend moral support. [? var. of *rout* to make a loud noise < Scand; cf. Icel *rauta;* akin to L *rudere* to bellow]

Root (ro͞ot), *n.* **El·i·hu** (el′ə hyo͞o′), 1845–1937, U.S. lawyer and statesman: Nobel peace prize 1912.

root·age (ro͞o′tij, ro͝ot′ij), *n.* **1.** the act of taking root. **2.** a root system or firm fixture by means of roots.

root′ beer′, a fermented, carbonated soft drink flavored with the extracted juices of roots, barks, and herbs.

root′ canal′, *Dentistry.* the root portion of the pulp cavity.

root′ canal′ ther′apy, endodontics. Also called **root′ canal′ treat′ment.**

root′ cel′lar, a cellar, partially or wholly underground and usually covered with dirt, for storing root crops.

root′ crop′, a crop, as beets, turnips, sweet potatoes, etc., grown for its large and edible roots.

root·er[1] (ro͞o′tər), *n.* a person, thing, or animal that roots, as a pig with its snout. [ROOT[2] + -ER[1]]

root·er[2] (ro͞o′tər), *n.* **1.** a person who roots for, supports, or encourages a team or contestant. **2.** a loyal and enthusiastic helper, follower, or supporter. [ROOT[3] + -ER[1]]

root′ hair′, *Bot.* an elongated tubular extension of an epidermal cell of a root, serving to absorb water and minerals from the soil.

root·less (ro͞ot′lis, ro͝ot′-), *adj.* **1.** having no roots. **2.** having no basis of stability; unsteady. **3.** having no place or position in society; not in accord with the environment. [ME *rooteles*] —**root′less·ness,** *n.*

root·let (ro͞ot′lit, ro͝ot′-), *n. Bot.* **1.** a little root. **2.** a small or fine branch of a root.

root′ mean′ square′, *Math.* the square root of the arithmetic mean of the squares of the numbers in a given set of numbers. *Abbr.:* rms

root′ rot′, *Plant Pathol.* a symptom or phase of many diseases of plants, characterized by decay of the roots.

root·stalk (ro͞ot′stôk′, ro͝ot′-), *n. Bot.* a rhizome.

root·stock (ro͞ot′stok′, ro͝ot′-), *n.* **1.** *Hort.* a root and its associated growth buds, used as a stock in plant propagation. **2.** *Bot.* a rhizome.

root·y (ro͞o′tē, ro͝ot′ē), *adj.,* **root·i·er, root·i·est.** abounding in or consisting of roots. —**root′i·ness,** *n.*

rop·a·ble (rō′pə bəl), *adj.* **1.** capable of being roped. **2.** *Australian Informal.* angry.

rope (rōp), *n., v.,* **roped, rop·ing.** —*n.* **1.** a strong, thick line or cord, commonly one composed of twisted or braided strands of hemp, flax, wire, etc. **2.** a lasso. **3.** the sentence or punishment of death by hanging. **4.** a quantity of material or a number of things twisted or strung together in the form of a cord: *a rope of tobacco.* **5.** a stringy, viscid, or glutinous formation in a liquid: *ropes of slime.* **6. at the end of one's rope,** at the end of one's endurance or means. **7. know the ropes,** *Informal.* to be completely familiar with the operation or conduct of something. —*v.t.* **8.** to tie, bind, or fasten with a rope. **9.** to enclose, partition, or mark off with a rope or ropes (often fol. by *off*). **10.** to catch with a lasso; lasso. —*v.i.* **11.** to be drawn out into a filament of thread; become ropy. **12. rope in,** *Slang.* to lure or entice, esp. by deceiving. [ME; OE *rāp;* c. D *reep,* G *Reif*]

rope·danc·er (rōp′dan′sər, -dän′-), *n.* a person who walks across or performs acrobatics upon a rope stretched above the floor or ground. Also called **rope-walk·er** (rōp′wô′kər). —**rope′dance′,** *n.* —**rope′danc′ing,** *n.*

rop·er·y (rō′pə rē), *n., pl.* **-er·ies.** **1.** a place where ropes are made. **2.** *Archaic.* knavery; roguery. [ME *roperie*]

rope·walk (rōp′wôk′), *n.* a long, narrow path or building where ropes are made.

rope·way (rōp′wā′), *n.* tramway (def. 2).

rop·y (rō′pē), *adj.,* **rop·i·er, rop·i·est.** **1.** resembling a rope or ropes: *ropy muscles.* **2.** forming viscid or glutinous threads, as a liquid. —**rop′i·ly,** *adv.*

roque (rōk), *n.* a form of croquet played on a clay or hard-surface court surrounded by a low wall off which the balls may be played. [back formation from *roquet,* var. of CROQUET]

Roque·fort (rōk′fərt), *n.* a strong cheese, made of sheep's milk and veined with mold. Also called **Roque′fort cheese′.** [after *Roquefort,* a town in S France where it is made]

roq·ue·laure (rō′kə lōr′, -lôr′, -lōr′, -lôr′, rok′ə-; *Fr.* rôk[ə] lōr′), *n., pl.* **-laures** (-lōrz′, -lôrz′, -lōrz′, -lôrz′; *Fr.* -lōr′). a cloak reaching to the knees, worn by men during the 18th century. [named after the Duc de *Roquelaure* (1656–1738), French marshal]

Ror′schach test′ (rôr′shäk, rôr′-), *Psychol.* a test for revealing the underlying personality structure of an individual by associations evoked by a series of ink-blot designs. [named after Hermann *Rorschach* (1884–1922), Swiss psychiatrist]

Ro·sa (*It.* rô′zä; *Eng.* rō′zə), *n.* **1. Sal·va·tor** (säl′vä tôr′), 1615–73, Italian painter and poet. **2. Mon·te** (*It.* môn′te; *Eng.* mon′tē), a mountain between Switzerland and Italy, in the Pennine Alps: second highest peak of the Alps. 15,217 ft.

ro·sa·ceous (rō zā′shəs), *adj.* **1.** belonging to the *Rosaceae,* or rose family of plants, also comprising the blackberry, strawberry, agrimony, spiraea, etc. **2.** having a corolla of five broad petals, like that of a rose. **3.** like a rose; roselike: *rosaceous loveliness.* **4.** rose-colored; rosy. [< L *rosāceus* made of roses = *ros(a)* ROSE[1] + *-āceus* -ACEOUS]

ros·an·i·line (rō zan′[ə]lin, -[ə]lēn′), *n. Chem.* **1.** a red dye, $C_{20}H_{20}N_3Cl$, derived from aniline and orthotoluidine, a constituent of fuchsin. **2.** the base, $C_{20}H_{21}N_3O$, which, with hydrochloric acid, forms this dye. [ROSE[1] + ANILINE]

Ro·sa·rio (rō zä′rē ō′, -sä′-; *Sp.* rō sä′ryō), *n.* a port in E Argentina, on the Paraná River. 671,852 (1960).

ro·sar·i·um (rō zâr′ē əm), *n., pl.* **-i·ums, -i·a** (-ē ə). a rose garden. [< L; see ROSARY]

ro·sa·ry (rō′zə rē), *n., pl.* **-ries.** *Rom. Cath. Ch.* **1.** a series of prayers, usually consisting of 15 decades of aves, each decade being preceded by a paternoster and followed by a Gloria Patri, one of the mysteries or events in the life of Christ or the Virgin Mary being recalled at each decade. **2.** a string of beads used for counting these prayers during recitation. **3.** a similar string of beads consisting of five decades. [< ML *rosāri(um),* L: rose garden (n. use of neut. of *rosārius* of roses) = *ros(a)* ROSE[1] + *-ārium* -ARY]

Ros·ci·us (rosh′ē əs, rosh′əs), *n.* **Quin·tus** (kwin′təs), c126–c26 B.C., Roman actor.

Ros·com·mon (ros kom′ən), *n.* a county in Connaught, in the N Republic of Ireland. 59,217 (1961); 950 sq. mi. *Co. seat:* Roscommon.

rose[1] (rōz), *n., adj.* —*n.* **1.** any of the wild or cultivated, usually prickly-stemmed, showy-flowered shrubs of the genus

Rosa. **2.** any of various related or similar plants. **3.** the flower of any such shrub, of a red, pink, white, or yellow color. **4.** the traditional reddish color of this flower, variously a purplish red, pinkish red, or light crimson. **5.** an ornament shaped like or suggesting this flower. **6.** any of various diagrams showing directions radiating from a common center. **7.** *Jewelry.* an obsolete cut of gem, flat on the bottom and having an upper side with triangular facets. **1.** a perforated cap or plate, as at the end of a pipe, the spout of a watering pot, etc., to break a flow of water into a spray. **9. under the rose,** in secret; privately; stealthily. Cf. **sub rosa.** —*adj.* **10.** for, containing, or growing roses: *a rose garden.* **11.** scented like a rose or with roses. **12.** of the color rose. [ME, OE < L *rosa;* akin to Gk *rhódon*]

rose[2] (rōz), *v.* pt. of **rise.**

ro·sé (rō zā′), *n.* a pink table wine whose pale color is produced by removing the grape skins from the must before fermentation is completed. [< F: lit., pink]

rose′ aca′cia, a small tree, *Robina hispida,* of the southern Allegheny Mountains, having racemes of large, dark rose-colored flowers.

ro·se·ate (rō′zē it, -āt′), *adj.* **1.** tinged with rose; rosy. **2.** bright or promising. **3.** optimistic. [< L *rose(us)* rose-colored + -ATE[1]]

rose·bay (rōz′bā′), *n.* **1.** an oleander. **2.** a rhododendron.

rose·bud (rōz′bud′), *n.* the bud of a rose.

rose·bush (rōz′bo͝osh′), *n.* a shrub that bears roses.

rose′ chaf′er, a tan scarabaeid beetle, *Macrodactylus subspinosis,* that feeds on the flowers and foliage of roses, grapes, peach trees, etc. Also called **rose′ bee′tle.**

rose-col·ored (rōz′kul′ərd), *adj.* **1.** of rose color; rosy. **2.** (of an attitude, belief, etc.) optimistic.

rose′-colored glass′es, a cheerful or optimistic view of things.

Rose·crans (rōz′krans), *n.* **William Starke** (stärk), 1819–1898, U.S. general.

rose′ fe′ver, *Pathol.* a form of hay fever caused by the inhalation of rose pollen.

rose·fish (rōz′fish′), *n., pl.* (*esp. collectively*) **-fish,** (*esp. referring to two or more kinds or species*) **-fish·es.** redfish.

rose′ gera′nium, any of a class of geraniums of the genus *Pelargonium,* esp. *Pigraveolens,* cultivated for their fragrant leaves rather than for their small pink flowers.

rose′ hip′, hip[2].

rose′ mal′low, 1. any of several malvaceous plants of the genus *Hibiscus,* having rose-colored flowers. **2.** the hollyhock, *Althaea rosea.*

rose·mar·y (rōz′mâr′ē), *n., pl.* **-mar·ies.** an evergreen, menthaceous shrub, *Rosmarinus officinalis,* native to the Mediterranean region, used as a seasoning and in perfumery and medicine: a traditional symbol of remembrance. [ME *rose mary* (by folk etym., influenced by ROSE[1] and the name *Mary*) < L *rōs* dew + *marīnus* marine or *rōs maris* dew of the sea (in E the final *-s* mistaken for pl. sign)]

Rose·mead (rōz′mēd′), *n.* a city in SW California, near Los Angeles. 40,972 (1970).

rose′ moss′, a trailing purslane, *Portulaca grandiflora,* having showy, pink, purple, red, white, or yellow flowers.

Ro·sen·wald (rō′zən wôld′), *n.* **Julius,** 1862–1932, U.S. businessman and philanthropist.

rose′ of Jer′icho, an Asian, cruciferous plant, *Anastatica hierochuntica,* that curls up when dry and expands when moistened.

rose′ of Shar′on, 1. a shrub or small tree, *Hibiscus syriacus,* having showy pink, purple, or white bell-shaped flowers. **2.** a St.-John's-wort, *Hypericum calycinum.* **3.** a plant mentioned in the Bible. Song of Solomon 2:1.

ro·se·o·la (rō zē′ə lə), *n. Pathol.* **1.** a kind of rose-colored rash. **2.** measles; rubeola. [< NL = L *rose(us)* rose-colored + *-ola* fem. dim. suffix] —**ro·se′o·lar,** *adj.*

Ro·set·ta (rō zet′ə), *n.* a town in the N Arab Republic of Egypt, at a mouth of the Nile. 32,800 (est. 1957).

Roset′ta stone′, a stone slab, found in 1799 near Rosetta, bearing parallel inscriptions in Greek, Egyptian hieroglyphic, and demotic characters, making possible the decipherment of ancient Egyptian hieroglyphics.

ro·sette (rō zet′), *n.* **1.** any arrangement, part, object, or formation more or less resembling a rose. **2.** a rose-shaped arrangement of ribbon or other material, used as an ornament or badge. **3.** an architectural ornament resembling a rose or having a generally circular combination of parts. **4.** *Bot.* a circular cluster of leaves or other organs. **5.** one of the compound spots on a leopard. [< F: little rose, OF]

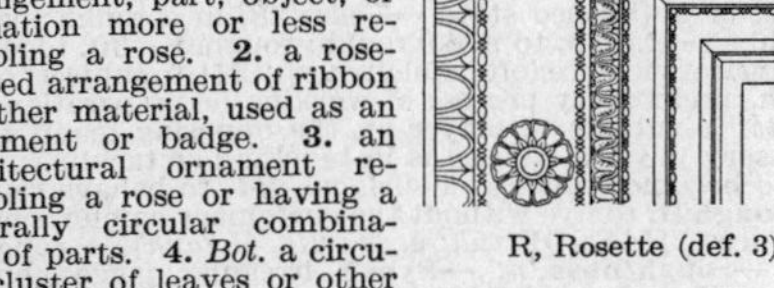

R, Rosette (def. 3)

Rose·ville (rōz′vil), *n.* **1.** a city in SE Michigan, near Detroit. 60,529 (1970). **2.** a city in SE Minnesota, near St. Paul. 34,518 (1970).

rose′ wa′ter, water tinctured with essential oil of roses.

rose′ win′dow, a circular window decorated with tracery symmetrical about the center.

rose·wood (rōz′wo͝od′), *n.* **1.** any of various reddish cabinet woods, sometimes with a roselike odor, yielded by certain tropical, fabaceous trees, esp. of the genus *Dalbergia.* **2.** a tree yielding such wood.

Rosh Ha·sha·nah (rōsh′ hə shä′nə, -shō′-, hä-, rôsh′; *Heb.* RÔSH′ hä shä nä′), *Judaism.* a high holy day, the Jewish New Year, celebrated on the first day or the first and second days of Tishri. Also, **Rosh′ Ha·sha′na, Rosh′ Ha·sho′noh, Rosh′ Ha·sho′no.** [< Heb *rōsh hashshānāh,* lit., beginning of the year]

Ro·si·cru·cian (rō′zə kro͞o′shən, roz′ə-), *n.* **1.** (in the 17th and 18th centuries) a person who belonged to a society professing esoteric principles of religion. **2.** a member of any of several later or modern bodies or societies professing principles derived from or attributed to the earlier Rosicrucians, esp. of an organization (**Rosicru′cian Or′der** or **Ancient Mystic Order Rosae Crucis**) that is active in America. —*adj.* **3.** of, pertaining to, or characteristic of the Rosicrucians. [< L *Rosicruc-* (Latinized form of (Christian) *Rosenkreuz,* name of the supposed 15th-century founder of the society = *ros(a)* rose + *-i-* -I- + *cruc-* (s. of *crux*) cross) + -IAN] —**Ro′si·cru′cian·ism,** *n.*

ros·i·ly (rō′zə lē), *adv.* **1.** with a rosy color. **2.** in a rosy manner; brightly, cheerfully, or optimistically.

ros·in (roz′in), *n.* **1.** *Chem.* the translucent, brittle, resin left after distilling the turpentine from the crude resin of the pine: used chiefly in making varnish, printing inks, etc., and for rubbing on the bows of such string instruments as the violin. **2.** resin. —*v.t.* **3.** to cover or rub with rosin. Also called **colophony.** [ME < OF, var. of *resine* RESIN]

ros·in·weed (roz′in wēd′), *n.* any coarse, North American, composite plant of the genus *Silphium,* having a resinous juice.

Ross (rôs, ros), *n.* **1. Betsy (Gris·com)** (gris′kəm), 1752–1836, maker of the first U.S. flag. **2. Sir James Clark,** 1800–62, English navigator: explorer of the Arctic and the Antarctic. **3.** his uncle, **Sir John,** 1777–1856, Scottish naval officer and arctic explorer. **4. Sir Ronald,** 1857–1932, English physician: Nobel prize 1902.

Ross′ and Crom′ar·ty (krom′ər tē, krum′-), a county in NW Scotland. 57,607 (1961); 3089 sq. mi. *Co. seat:* Dingwall.

Ross′ Depend′ency, a territory in Antarctica, including Ross Island, the coasts along the Ross Sea, and adjacent islands: a dependency of New Zealand. ab. 175,000 sq. mi.

Ros·set·ti (rō set′ē, -zet′ē, rə-), *n.* **1. Christina Georgina,** 1830–94, English poet. **2.** her brother, **Dante Gabriel,** (*Gabriel Charles Dante Rossetti*), 1828–82, English poet and painter.

Ross′ Ice′ Shelf′, an ice barrier filling the S part of the Ross Sea.

Ros·si·ni (rō sē′nē, rô-; *It.* RÔs sē′nē), *n.* **Gio·ac·chi·no An·to·nio** (jô′äk kē′nô än tô′nyô), 1792–1868, Italian composer.

Ross′ Is′land, an island in the W Ross Sea, off the coast of Victoria Land: part of the Ross Dependency; location of Mt. Erebus.

Ros·si ya (RO sē′yä), *n.* Russian name of **Russia.**

Ross′ Sea′, an arm of the Antarctic Ocean, S of New Zealand, extending into Antarctica.

Ros·tand (RÔ stäN′), *n.* **Ed·mond** (ed môN′), 1868–1918, French dramatist and poet.

ros·tel·late (ros′tᵊlāt′, -tᵊlit), *adj. Bot.* having a rostellum. [< NL **rostellāt(us)* = L *rostell(um)* ROSTELLUM + *-ātus* -ATE[1]]

ros·tel·lum (ro stel′əm), *n., pl.* **ros·tel·la** (ro stel′ə). **1.** *Bot.* any small, beaklike process. **2.** *Bot.* a beaklike modification of the stigma in many orchids. **3.** *Zool.* **a.** a projecting part of the scolex in certain tapeworms. **b.** a part of the mouth in many insects, designed for sucking. [< L: little beak, snout = *rōst(rum)* ROSTRUM + *-ellum* dim. suffix]

ros·ter (ros′tər), *n.* **1.** a list of persons or groups, as of military personnel with their turns of duty. **2.** any list, roll, or register. [< D *rooster* list, orig., gridiron (< *roosten* to roast); from the ruled paper used]

Ros·tock (ros′tok; *Ger.* RÔs′tôk), *n.* a seaport in N East Germany, on the Baltic. 179,352 (1964).

Ros·tov (rə stôf′; *Russ.* RO stôf′), *n.* a seaport in the SW RSFSR, in the S Soviet Union in Europe, on the Don River, near the Sea of Azov. 721,000 (1965). Also called **Ros·tov-on-Don** (rə stôf′on don′, -dôn′).

ros·tral (ros′trəl), *adj.* of or pertaining to a rostrum. [< LL *rōstrāl(is)* = L *rōstr(um)* ROSTRUM + *-ālis* -AL[1]] —**ros′tral·ly,** *adv.*

ros·trate (ros′trāt), *adj.* furnished with a rostrum. Also, **ros′trat·ed.** [< L *rōstrāt(us)* having a beak, curved at the end = *rōstr(um)* ROSTRUM + *-ātus* -ATE[1]]

ros·trum (ros′trəm), *n., pl.* **-tra** (-trə), **-trums. 1.** any platform, stage, or the like, for public speaking. **2.** a beaklike projection from the prow of a ship, esp. one on an ancient warship for ramming an enemy ship; beak; ram. **3.** Usually, **rostra.** (in ancient Rome) raised platform, adorned with the beaks of captured warships, from which an orator spoke. **4.** *Biol.* a beaklike process or extension of some part; rostellum. [< L *rōstrum* bill, beak of a bird, ship's prow (in pl., speaker's platform) = *rōs(us)* gnawed, eaten away (ptp. of *rōdere*) + *-trum* instrumental suffix]

Ros·well (roz′wel), *n.* a city in SE New Mexico. 33,908 (1970).

ros·y (rō′zē), *adj.* **ros·i·er, ros·i·est. 1.** pink or pinkish-red; roseate. **2.** (of a person, the complexion, etc.) having a fresh, healthy redness. **3.** cheerful or optimistic: *rosy anticipations.* **4.** made or consisting of roses: *a rosy bower.* [ME] —**ros′i·ness,** *n.* —**Syn. 2.** flushed, blooming, healthy. —**Ant. 2.** pale. **3.** unpromising; cheerless.

rot (rot), *v.,* **rot·ted, rot·ting,** *n., interj.* —*v.i.* **1.** to undergo decomposition; decay. **2.** to deteriorate, disintegrate, etc., as a result of decay (often fol. by *away, from, off,* etc.). **3.** to languish, as in confinement. **4.** to become morally corrupt. —*v.t.* **5.** to cause to rot. **6.** to cause to become morally corrupt. **7.** to ret (flax, hemp, etc.). —*n.* **8.** the process of rotting. **9.** decay; putrefaction. **10.** rotting or rotten matter. **11.** moral or social decay. **12.** *Pathol.* any disease characterized by malodorous decay. **13.** *Plant Pathol.* **a.** any of various forms of decay produced by fungi or bacteria. **b.** any disease so characterized. **14.** *Vet. Pathol.* a disease, esp. of sheep, characterized by decay of the hoofs. **15.** *Informal.* nonsense. —*interj.* **16.** (a mild exclamation of distaste or disgust.) [(n.) ME < Scand; cf. OIcel *rot;* (v.) ME *rot(en),* OE *rotian.* See RET] —**Syn. 1.** mold, molder, putrefy, spoil. See **decay. 9.** decomposition, mold. —**Ant. 6.** purify.

ro·ta (rō′tə), *n.* **1.** *Chiefly Brit.* **a.** a round or rotation of duties. **b.** an agenda or circuit of sporting events, played in different localities throughout the year. **2.** a roster. **3.** (*cap.*) Official name, **Sacred Roman Rota.** the ecclesiastical tribunal in Rome, constituting the court of final appeal. [< L: wheel]

Ro·tar·i·an (rō târ′ē ən), *n.* **1.** a member of a Rotary Club. —*adj.* **2.** of or pertaining to Rotarians or Rotary Clubs. [ROTARY (CLUB) + -AN] —**Ro·tar′i·an·ism,** *n.*

ro·ta·ry (rō′tə rē), *adj., n., pl.* **-ries.** —*adj.* **1.** turning or capable of turning around on an axis, as a wheel. **2.** taking place around an axis, as motion. **3.** having a part or parts that turn on an axis, as a machine. —*n.* **4.** See **traffic circle.** [< ML *rotāri(us)* = L *rot(a)* wheel + *-ārius* -ARY]

Ro′tary Club′, a local club of business and professional men that is a member of a world-wide organization (**Ro′tary Interna′tional**) devoted to serving the community and promoting world peace.

ro′tary en′gine, **1.** an engine, as a turbine, in which the impelling fluid produces torque directly rather than by acting upon reciprocating parts. **2.** a revolving radial engine.

ro′tary plow′, a series of swinging blades mounted on a horizontal power-driven shaft, for pulverizing unplowed soil. Also called **ro′tary till′er.**

ro′tary press′, *Print.* a printing press in which the type or plates are fitted to a rotating cylinder and impressed on a continuous roll of paper.

ro′tary wing′, *Aeron.* an airfoil that rotates about an approximately vertical axis, as that supporting a helicopter or autogiro in flight.

ro·tate[1] (rō′tāt, rō tāt′), *v.,* **-tat·ed, -tat·ing.** —*v.t.* **1.** to cause to turn around an axis or center point; revolve. **2.** to cause to go through a cycle of changes; cause to pass or follow in a fixed routine or succession: *to rotate farm crops.* **3.** to replace (a person, troops, etc.) by another or others, usually systematically. —*v.i.* **4.** to turn around on or as on an axis. **5.** to proceed in a fixed routine of succession. [< L *rotāt(us)* revolved (ptp. of *rotāre*) = *rot(a)* wheel + *-ātus* -ATE[1]] —**ro′tat·a·ble,** *adj.* —**Syn. 1.** wheel, whirl. See **turn.**

ro·tate[2] (rō′tāt), *adj.* wheel-shaped: applied esp. to a gamopetalous short-tubed corolla with a spreading limb. [< L *rot(a)* wheel + -ATE[1]]

ro·ta·tion (rō tā′shən), *n.* **1.** the act of rotating. **2.** *Astron.* **a.** the movement or path of the earth or a heavenly body turning on its axis. **b.** one complete turn of such a body. **3.** regularly recurring succession, as of officials. **4.** *Agric.* the act or process of varying the crops grown on the same ground. **5.** *Pool.* a game in which the balls are played in order by number. [< L *rotātiōn-* (s. of *rotātiō*) a wheeling about, rolling = *rotāt(us)* (see ROTATE[1]) + *-iōn-* -ION] —**ro·ta′tion·al,** *adj.*

ro·ta·tive (rō′tā tiv), *adj.* **1.** rotating or pertaining to rotation. **2.** producing rotation. **3.** happening in regular succession. [< L *rotāt(us)* (see ROTATE[1]) + -IVE] —**ro·ta·tive·ly** (rō′tə tiv lē), *adv.*

ro·ta·tor (rō′tā tər, rō tā′-), *n., pl.* **ro·ta·tors** for 1, **ro·ta·tor·es** (rō′tə tôr′ēz, -tōr′-) for 2. **1.** a person or thing that rotates. **2.** *Anat.* a muscle serving to rotate a part of the body. [< L *rotātor* = *rotāt(us)* (see ROTATE[1]) + *-or* -OR[2]]

ro·ta·to·ry (rō′tə tôr′ē, -tōr′ē), *adj.* **1.** pertaining to or of the nature of rotation. **2.** rotating, as an object. **3.** passing or following in rotation. **4.** causing rotation, as a muscle. [< NL *rotātōri(us)* = L *rotāt(us)* (see ROTATE[1]) + *-ōrius* -ORY[1]]

R.O.T.C. (är′ō tē sē′, rot′sē). See **Reserve Officers' Training Corps.** Also, **ROTC**

rote[1] (rōt), *n.* **1.** routine; a fixed, habitual, or mechanical course of procedure: *the rote of daily living.* **2. by rote,** from memory, without thought for meaning: *to learn a language by rote.* [ME < ?]

rote[2] (rōt), *n.* *Music.* crowd[2]. [ME < OF < Celt]

rote[3] (rōt), *n.* the sound of surf. [? < Scand]

ro·te·none (rōt′ənōn′), *n.* *Chem., Pharm.* a white, crystalline, water-insoluble, poisonous heterocyclic compound, $C_{23}H_{22}O_6$, obtained from derris root: used in certain insecticides and in the treatment of chiggers and scabies. [< Jap *rōten* derris plant + -ONE]

rot·gut (rot′gut′), *n.* *Slang.* cheap and inferior liquor.

Roth (rôth, roth), *n.* **Philip,** born 1933, U.S. short-story writer and novelist.

Roth·er·ham (roth′ər əm), *n.* a city in S Yorkshire, in N England. 85,346 (1961).

Roth·er·mere (roth′ər mēr′), *n.* **1st Viscount.** See **Harmsworth, Harold Sidney.**

Rothe·say (roth′sē, -sā), *n.* a town in and the county seat of Bute, on Bute island, in SW Scotland: resort; castle. 7656 (1961).

Roth·ko (roth′kō), *n.* **Mark,** 1903–70, U.S. painter, born in Russia.

Roth·schild (roth′chīld, roths′-, rôth′-, rôths′-; *for 1, 2, also Ger.* rōt′shilt), *n.* **1. Lionel Nathan, Baron de** ("*Lord Natty*"), 1809–79, English banker: member of Parliament (son of Nathan Meyer Rothschild). **2. May·er** (mī′ər, mā′ər; *Ger.* mī′ər) or **Mey·er** (mī′ər; *Ger.* mī′ər) **Am·schel** (am′shəl; *Ger.* äm′shəl) or **An·selm** (an′selm; *Ger.* än′zelm), 1743–1812, German banker: founder of international banking firm. **3.** his son, **Nathan Meyer, Baron de,** 1777–1836, English banker, born in Germany.

ro·ti·fer (rō′tə fər), *n.* any microscopic animal of the class *Rotifera,* found in fresh and salt waters, having a ciliary apparatus on the anterior end; a wheel animalcule. [< NL *Rotifer(a)* = L *rot(a)* wheel + *-i-* -I- + *-fer* -FER] —**ro·tif·er·al** (rō tif′ər əl), **ro·tif′er·ous,** *adj.*

ro·ti·form (rō′tə fôrm′), *adj.* shaped like a wheel. [< NL *rotiform(is)* = L *rot(a)* wheel + *-i-* -I- + *-formis* -FORM]

ro·tis·ser·ie (rō tis′ə rē), *n.* a small broiler with a motor-driven spit. [< F: roasting place]

rot·l (rot′əl), *n., pl.* **rotls, ar·tal** (är′täl). **1.** a unit of weight used in Islamic countries, varying widely in value, but of the order of the pound. **2.** a varying unit of dry measure used in Islamic countries. [< Ar *raṭl* ? < Gk *lítra* or L *lībra* pound]

ro·to (rō′tō), *n., pl.* **ro·tos.** rotogravure. [by shortening]

roto-, a combining form meaning "rotary," used in the formation of compound words: *rotogravure.* [< L *rot(a)* wheel + -o-]

ro·to·gra·vure (rō′tə grə vyŏŏr′, -grā′vyər), *n.* **1.** a photomechanical process by which pictures, typeset matter, etc., are printed from an intaglio copper cylinder. **2.** a print made by this process. **3.** *U.S.* a newspaper section printed by this process. [ROTO- + F *gravure* engraving]

ro·tor (rō′tər), *n.* **1.** a rotating part of a machine (opposed to *stator*). **2.** *Aeron.* a system of rotating airfoils, as the horizontal ones of a helicopter or of the compressor of a jet engine. [short for ROTATOR]

Ro·to·ru·a (rō′tə rōō′ə), *n.* a city on N central North Island, in New Zealand. 25,068 (1961).

rot·ten (rot′ən), *adj.* **1.** decomposing or decaying; putrid. **2.** morally corrupt. **3.** *Informal.* wretchedly bad, unpleasant, or unsatisfactory: *a rotten piece of work.* **4.** contemptible; despicable. **5.** (of soil, rocks, etc.) soft, yielding, or friable from decomposition. [ME *roten* < Scand; cf. Icel *rotinn* putrid] —**Syn. 1.** fetid, rank. **2.** immoral. **4.** disgusting, treacherous. —**Ant. 1.** sound. **2.** moral. **5.** hard, solid.

rot′ten bor′ough, **1.** (before the Reform Bill of 1832) any English borough that had very few voters yet was represented in Parliament. **2.** an election district that has more representatives in a legislative body than the number of its constituents would normally call for.

rot·ten·stone (rot′ən stōn′), *n.* a friable stone resulting from the decomposition of a siliceous limestone, used as a powder for polishing metals.

rot·ter (rot′ər), *n.* *Chiefly Brit. Slang.* a thoroughly worthless or objectionable person.

Rot·ter·dam (rot′ər dam′; *for 1 also Du.* rôt′ər däm′), *n.* **1.** a seaport in the SW Netherlands. 730,963 (1962). **2.** a town in E New York, on the Mohawk River. 25,214 (1970).

ro·tund (rō tund′), *adj.* **1.** round in shape; rounded: *ripe, rotund fruit.* **2.** plump; fat. **3.** full-toned or sonorous; orotund. [< L *rotund(us)* round, circular < *rota* wheel]

ro·tun·da (rō tun′də), *n.* a round building or hall, esp. one surmounted by a dome. [alter. of It *rotonda* < L *rotunda,* fem. of *rotundus* ROTUND]

ro·tun·di·ty (rō tun′di tē), *n., pl.* **-ties.** **1.** the condition or quality of roundness or plumpness, as of an object or person. **2.** fullness, as in tone or speech. **3.** a full or rounded tone, phrase, or the like. Also, **ro·tund′ness.** [< L *rotunditās*]

Rou·ault (rōō ō′; *Fr.* rwō), *n.* **Georges** (zhôrzh), 1871–1958, French painter.

Rou·baix (rōō be′), *n.* a city in N France, NE of Lille. 113,163 (1962).

rou·ble (rōō′bəl), *n.* ruble.

rou·é (rōō ā′, rōō′ā), *n.* a debauchee or rake; profligate. [< F, n. use of ptp. of *rouer* to break on the wheel < *roue* wheel < L *rota;* name first applied to the profligate companions of the Duc d'Orléans (c1720)]

Rou·en (rōō äN′, -än′; *Fr.* rwäN), *n.* a city in N France, on the Seine: cathedral. 123,474 (1962).

rouge (rōōzh), *n., v.,* **rouged, roug·ing.** —*n.* **1.** any of various red cosmetics for coloring the cheeks or lips. **2.** a reddish powder, chiefly ferric oxide, used for polishing metal, glass, etc. —*v.t.* **3.** to color with rouge. —*v.i.* **4.** to use rouge. [< F: red (adj.) < L *rube(us)*]

rouge et noir (rōōzh′ ā nwär′; *Fr.* rōōzh ā nwar′), a gambling game using cards, played at a table marked with two red and two black diamond-shaped spots on which the players place their stakes. [< F: red and black]

Rou·get de Lisle (rōō zhā′ də lēl′), **Claude Jo·seph** (klōd zhō zef′), 1760–1836, French army officer and composer of the French national anthem, *La Marseillaise.* Also, **Rou·get′ de l'Isle′.**

rough (ruf), *adj.* **1.** having a coarse or uneven surface. **2.** shaggy: *a dog with a rough coat.* **3.** steep, uneven, or wild: *rough country.* **4.** acting with or characterized by violence: *Boxing is a rough sport.* **5.** turbulent, as water or the air. **6.** uncomfortably or dangerously uneven: *The plane had a rough flight in the storm.* **7.** stormy or tempestuous, as wind, weather, etc. **8.** sharp or harsh: *a rough temper.* **9.** unmannerly or rude. **10.** disorderly or riotous: *a rough mob.* **11.** difficult or unpleasant: *to have a rough time of it.* **12.** harsh to the ear. **13.** harsh to the taste. **14.** coarse, as food. **15.** lacking culture or refinement. **16.** without ordinary comforts or conveniences: *rough camping.* **17.** requiring exertion or strength rather than intelligence or skill. **18.** unpolished, as language, verse, or style. **19.** approximate or tentative: *a rough guess.* **20.** crude, unwrought, nonprocessed, or unprepared: *rough rice.* **21.** *Phonet.* uttered with aspiration; having the sound of *h;* aspirated. —*n.* **22.** that which is rough, esp. rough ground. **23.** *Golf.* any part of the course bordering the fairway on which the grass, weeds, etc., are not trimmed. **24.** the unpleasant or difficult part of anything. **25.** anything in its crude or preliminary form, as a drawing. **26.** *Chiefly Brit.* a rowdy; ruffian. **27. in the rough,** in a rough, crude, or unfinished state. —*adv.* **28.** in a rough manner; roughly. —*v.t.* **29.** to make rough; roughen. **30.** to subject to physical violence (often fol. by *up*). **31.** to subject to some rough, preliminary process of working or preparation. **32.** *Sports.* to subject (a player on the opposing team) to unnecessary physical abuse, as in blocking or tackling. —*v.i.* **33.** to become rough, as a surface. **34.** to behave roughly. **35. rough it,** to live without the customary comforts or conveniences. [ME; OE *rūh;* c. D *ruig,* G *rauh*] —**rough′ly,** *adv.* —**rough′ness,** *n.* —**Syn. 1.** irregular, jagged, bumpy, craggy. **2.** hairy, bristly. **12.** noisy, cacophonous, raucous. **15.** impolite, uncivil, unpolished, rude. —**Ant. 1.** smooth, even, regular.

rough·age (ruf′ij), *n.* **1.** rough or coarse material. **2.** food, as green vegetables, bran, and certain fruits, containing a high proportion of indigestible cellulose.

rough-and-ready (ruf′ən red′ē), *adj.* **1.** rough or crude, but good enough for the purpose. **2.** exhibiting or showing rough vigor. —**rough′-and-read′i·ness,** *n.*

rough-and-tum·ble (ruf′ən tum′bəl), *adj.* **1.** characterized by violent, random, disorderly action and struggles, as a fight or mode of existence. **2.** given to such action.

rough′ breath′ing, **1.** the symbol (ʽ) used in the writing of Greek to indicate aspiration of the initial vowel or of the ρ over which it is placed. **2.** the aspirated sound indicated by this mark. Cf. **smooth breathing.** [trans. of L *spiritus asper*]

rough·cast (ruf′kast′, -käst′), *n., v.,* **-cast, -cast·ing.** —*n.* **1.** an exterior wall finish composed of mortar and fine pebbles mixed together and dashed against the wall. **2.** a crudely formed pattern or model. —*v.t.* **3.** to cover or coat with roughcast. **4.** to prepare in a rough form; rough-hew.

rough-dry (ruf′drī′), *v.,* **-dried, -dry·ing,** *adj.* —*v.t.* **1.** to dry (laundry) without smoothing or ironing. —*adj.* **2.** (of laundry) dried but not ironed. Also, **rough′dry′.**

rough·en (ruf′ən), *v.t., v.i.* to make or become rough or rougher.

rough·er (ruf′ər), *n.* a person or thing that roughs or roughs out something.

rough-hew (ruf′hyo͞o′), *v.t.*, **-hewed, -hewed** or **-hewn, -hew·ing. 1.** to hew (timber, stone, etc.) roughly or without smoothing or finishing. **2.** to shape roughly; give crude form to; roughcast. Also, **rough′hew′.**

rough·house (ruf′hous′), *n., pl.* **-hous·es** (-hou′ziz), *v.*, **-housed** (-houst′, -houzd′), **-hous·ing** (-houz′ing, -hous′-). —*n.* **1.** rough, disorderly playing, esp. indoors. —*v.i.* **2.** to engage in rough, disorderly play. —*v.t.* **3.** to handle roughly but with playful intent: *to roughhouse the cat.*

rough·neck (ruf′nek′), *n.* *Informal.* **1.** a rough, coarse person; a tough. **2.** *U.S.* any laborer working on an oil-drilling rig. Cf. **roustabout** (def. 3).

rough·rid·er (ruf′rī′dər), *n.* **1.** a person who breaks horses to the saddle. **2.** a person used to rough or hard riding.

Rough′ Rid′ers, the members of a volunteer regiment of U.S. cavalry, organized chiefly by Theodore Roosevelt for service in the Spanish-American War.

rough·shod (ruf′shod′), *adj.* **1.** shod with horseshoes having projecting nails or points. **2. ride roughshod over,** to treat harshly or domineeringly; override; crush.

rough-spo·ken (ruf′spō′kən), *adj.* coarse or vulgar in speech.

rough′ stuff′, *Slang.* unnecessary violence or infractions of the rules, as in sports.

rou·lade (ro͞o läd′), *n.* **1.** a musical embellishment consisting of a rapid succession of tones sung to a single syllable. **2.** a slice of meat rolled about a filling of minced meat and cooked. [< F: a rolling = *roul(er)* (to) roll + *-ade* -ADE[1]]

rou·leau (ro͞o lō′), *n., pl.* **-leaux, -leaus** (-lōz′). **1.** a roll or strip of something, as trimming on a hat brim. **2.** a stack or roll of coins put up in cylindrical form in a paper wrapping. [< F; MF *rolel,* dim. of *role* ROLL]

Rou·lers (ro͞o lârs′; *Fr.* ro͞o leʀ′), *n.* a city in NW Belgium: battles 1914, 1918. 35,957 (est. 1964).

rou·lette (ro͞o let′), *n., v.*, **-let·ted, -let·ting.** —*n.* **1.** a game of chance played at a table marked off with numbers from 1 to 36, one or two zeros, and several other sections affording the players a variety of betting opportunities, and having in the center a revolving, dishlike device (**roulette′ wheel′**) into which a small ball is spun to come to rest finally in one of the 37 or 38 compartments, indicating the winning number and its characteristics, as odd or even, red or black. **2.** a small wheel, esp. one with sharp teeth, mounted in a handle, for making lines of marks, dots, or perforations. **3.** *Geom.* a curve generated by the locus of a point on a closed curve that rolls without slipping on a fixed curve; cycloid, epicycloid, or hypocycloid. **4.** *Philately.* a row of short cuts, in which no paper is removed, made between individual stamps to permit their ready separation. —*v.t.* **5.** to mark, impress, or perforate with a roulette. [< F, dim. of *rouelle* wheel. See ROWEL]

Roum., **1.** Roumania. **2.** Roumanian.

Rou·ma·ni·a (ro͞o mā′nē ə, -mān′yə), *n.* Rumania. —**Rou·ma′ni·an,** *adj., n.*

Rou·me·li·a (ro͞o mē′lē ə, -mēl′yə), *n.* Rumelia.

round[1] (round), *adj.* **1.** having a flat, circular surface, as a disk. **2.** ring-shaped, as a hoop. **3.** curved like part of a circle, as an outline. **4.** having a circular cross section, as a cylinder; cylindrical. **5.** spherical or globular, as a ball. **6.** hemispherical. **7.** free from angularity; consisting of full, curved lines or shapes, as handwriting, parts of the body, etc. **8.** executed with or involving circular motion: *a round dance.* **9.** full, complete, or entire: *a round dozen.* **10.** noting, formed, or expressed by an integer or whole number with no fraction. **11.** expressed, given, or exact to the nearest multiple or power of ten; in tens, hundreds, thousands, or the like. **12.** considerable in amount; ample. **13.** full and sonorous, as sound. **14.** outspoken or unqualified: *a round assertion.* —*n.* **15.** any round shape or object. **16.** something circular in cross section, as a rung of a ladder. **17.** Sometimes, **rounds.** a completed course of time, series of events or operations, etc., ending at a point corresponding to that at the beginning. **18.** any complete course, series, or succession. **19.** Often, **rounds.** a going around from place to place, as in a habitual or definite circuit. **20.** a completed course or spell of activity, commonly one of a series, in some play or sport: *a round of bridge.* **21.** a single outburst, as of applause or cheers. **22.** a single discharge of shot by each of a number of guns, rifles, etc. **23.** a single discharge by one firearm. **24.** a charge of ammunition for a single shot. **25.** a single serving to everyone present: *a round of drinks.* **26.** a dance with the dancers arranged or moving in a circle or ring. **27.** movement in a circle or around an axis. **28.** Also called **round of beef.** the portion of the thigh of beef below the rump and above the leg. **29.** *Archery.* a specified number of arrows shot from a specified distance from the target in accordance with the rules. **30.** one of a series of three-minute periods making up a boxing match. **31.** *Music.* **a.** a short, rhythmical canon at the unison. **b. rounds,** the order followed in ringing a peal of bells in diatonic sequence from the highest to the lowest. **32.** *Golf.* a playing of the complete course. **33. in the round, a.** (of a theater) having a stage completely surrounded by seats for the audience. **b.** (of sculpture) not attached to a supporting background; freestanding. **34. make the rounds.** to go from one place to another, as in making deliveries, seeking employment, etc. —*adv.* Also, **'round. 35.** throughout a recurring period of time: *all year round.* **36.** around. —*prep.* **37.** throughout (a period of time): *a resort visited all round the year.* **38.** around: *It happened round noon.* —*v.t.* **39.** to make round. **40.** to free from angularity; fill out symmetrically. **41.** to bring to completeness or perfection; finish. **42.** to encircle or surround. **43.** to make a turn or partial circuit around or to the other side of: *to round a corner; to round a cape.* **44.** *Phonet.* **a.** to make the opening at (the lips) relatively round or pursed during an utterance. **b.** to pronounce (a speech sound, esp. a vowel) with rounded lips; labialize. **c.** to contract (the lips) laterally. Cf. **spread** (def. 8), **unround. 45.** *Math.* to replace by the nearest multiple of 10, with 5 being increased to the next highest multiple: *15,837 can be rounded to 15,840; then to 15,800; then to 16,000.* —*v.i.* **46.** to become round. **47.** to become free from angularity; become plump. **48.** to develop to completeness or perfection. **49.** to make a circuit; go the round, as a guard. **50.** to make a turn or partial circuit around something **51.** to turn around, as on an axis: *to round on one's heels.* **52. round down,** *Naut.* to separate the blocks of (a tackle) by pulling down on the lower one. **53. round in,** *Naut.* **a.** to haul in rope. **b.** to draw together the blocks of (a tackle). **54. round off, a.** to complete or perfect; finish. **b.** *Math.* round[1] (def. 45). **55. round out, a.** to complete or perfect. **b.** to fill out; become rounder. **56. round to,** *Naut.* to turn a sailing vessel in the direction from which the wind is blowing. **57. round up, a.** to drive or bring (cattle, sheep, etc.) together. **b.** to assemble; gather. **c.** *Naut.* to round in (a tackle). [ME < OF *rond* << L *rotund(us)* wheel-shaped; see ROTUND] —**round′ness,** *n.*

—**Syn. 9.** whole, unbroken. **16.** cylinder. **17.** cycle, revolution, period. —**Ant. 1.** angular.

round[2] (round), *v.t., v.i.* *Archaic.* to whisper. [ME *roun(en),* OE *rūnian,* cf. *rūn* a secret]

round·a·bout (round′ə bout′), *adj.* **1.** circuitous or indirect. **2.** (of clothing) cut circularly at the bottom. —*n.* **3.** a short, close-fitting coat or jacket, without skirts, for men or boys. **4.** *Chiefly Brit.* a merry-go-round. **5.** *Brit.* See **traffic circle.**

round′ an′gle, perigon.

round′ dance′, **1.** a dance characterized by circular or revolving movement, as the waltz. **2.** a dance in which the dancers are arranged in or move about in a circle.

round·ed (roun′did), *adj.* **1.** reduced to simple curves; made round. **2.** *Phonet.* pronounced with rounded lips; labialized: "*Boot*" *has a rounded vowel.* **3.** fully developed or characterized. **4.** round[1] (def. 11). [late ME] —**round′ed·ly,** *adv.* —**round′ed·ness,** *n.*

roun·del (roun′dᵊl), *n.* **1.** something round or circular. **2.** a decorative plate, panel, tablet, or the like, round in form. **3.** *Heraldry.* a small circular charge. **4.** *Pros.* **a.** a rondel or rondeau. **b.** a modification of the rondeau, consisting of nine lines with two refrains. **5.** a dance in a circle or ring; round dance. [ME *roundele* < OF *rondel* < *rond* ROUND[1] (adj.)]

roun·de·lay (roun′dᵊlā′), *n.* **1.** a song in which a phrase, line, or the like, is continually repeated. **2.** a dance in a circle; round dance. [m. (influenced by LAY[4]) MF *rondelet,* dim. of *rondel* ROUNDEL]

round·er (roun′dər), *n.* **1.** a person or thing that rounds something. **2.** a person who makes a round. **3.** a habitual drunkard or wastrel. **4. rounders,** (*construed as sing.*) a game somewhat resembling baseball, played in England.

round′ hand′, a style of handwriting in which the letters are round, full, and clearly separated.

Round·head (round′hed′), *n.* *Eng. Hist.* a member or supporter of the Parliamentarians during the English civil wars.

round·house (round′hous′), *n., pl.* **-hous·es** (-hou′ziz). **1.** a circular building for the servicing and repair of locomotives, built around a turntable. **2.** *Naut.* a cabin on the after part of a quarterdeck. **3.** *Slang.* a punch in which the fist describes a wide arc.

round·ish (roun′dish), *adj.* somewhat round. —**round′ish·ness,** *n.*

round·let (round′lit), *n.* a small circle or circular object. [ME *rondlet* < MF *rondelet;* see ROUNDELAY]

round·ly (round′lē), *adv.* **1.** in a round manner. **2.** vigorously or briskly. **3.** outspokenly, severely, or unsparingly. **4.** completely or fully.

round′ of beef′, round[1] (def. 28).

round′ rob′in, **1.** a sequence or series. **2.** a petition or the like having the signatures arranged in circular form so as to disguise the order of signing. **3.** a letter, notice, or the like, circulated from person to person in a group, often with individual comments being added by each. **4.** *Sports.* a tournament in which all of the entrants play each other at least once.

round-shoul·dered (round′shōl′dərd, -shōl′-), *adj.* having the shoulders bent forward, giving a rounded form to the upper part of the back.

rounds·man (roundz′mən), *n., pl.* **-men.** a person who makes rounds, as of inspection.

round′ steak′, a steak cut from directly above the hind leg of beef.

round′ ta′ble, **1.** a number of persons gathered together for a conference in which no order of rank is observed. **2.** the discussion, topic of discussion, or the conference itself. **3.** (*caps.*) *Arthurian Romance.* **a.** the table around which King Arthur and his knights sat. **b.** King Arthur and his knights as a body.

round-ta·ble (round′tā′bəl), *adj.* noting or pertaining to a conference, discussion, or deliberation in which each participant has equal status.

round′ trip′, a trip to a given place and back again. —**round′-trip′,** *adj.*

round·up (round′up′), *n.* **1.** the driving together of cattle, horses, etc., for inspection, branding, shipping to market, or the like, as in the West. **2.** the men who do this, with their horses. **3.** the gathering together of scattered items or groups of people. **4.** a summary, brief listing, or résumé of related facts, figures, or information.

round·worm (round′wûrm′), *n.* any nematode, esp. *Ascaris lumbricoides,* that infests the intestine of man and other mammals.

roup[1] (ro͞op), *n.* *Vet. Pathol.* any catarrhal inflammation of the eyes and nasal passages of poultry. [?]

roup[2] (ro͞op), *n.* hoarseness or huskiness. [prob. imit.]

roup·y[1] (ro͞o′pē), *adj.* affected with the disease roup. [ROUP[1] + -Y[1]] —**roup′i·ly,** *adv.*

roup·y[2] (ro͞o′pē), *adj.*, **roup·i·er, roup·i·est.** hoarse or husky. [ROUP[2] + -Y[1]]

rouse[1] (rouz), *v.*, **roused, rous·ing,** *n.* —*v.t.* **1.** to bring out of a state of sleep, inactivity, fancied security, apathy, depression, etc. **2.** to stir or incite to strong indignation or anger. **3.** to cause (game) to start from a covert or lair. **4.** *Naut.* to pull by main strength; haul. —*v.i.* **5.** to come out of a state of sleep, inactivity, etc. **6.** to start up from a covert or lair, as game. —*n.* **7.** a rousing. **8.** a signal for rousing; reveille. [late ME] —**rous·ed·ness** (rou′zid nis), *n.* —**rous′er,** *n.* —**Syn. 1.** arouse, stir, animate, stimulate.

rouse^2 (rouz), *n.* **1.** *Archaic.* a carouse. **2.** *Obs.* a bumper of liquor. [? var. of CAROUSE (*drink carouse* being wrongly analyzed as *drink a rouse*)]

rous·ing (rou′zing), *adj.* **1.** exciting; stirring: *a rousing song.* **2.** active or vigorous. **3.** brisk; lively: *a rousing trade.* —**rous′ing·ly,** *adv.*

Rous·seau (ro͞o sō′; *Fr.* ro͞o sō′), *n.* **1. Hen·ri** (äN rē′), ("*Le Douanier*"), 1844–1910, French painter. **2. Jean Jacques** (zhäN zhäk), 1712–78, French philosopher and author, born in Switzerland. **3. (Pierre É·tienne) The·o·dore** (pyeR ā tyen′ te ô dôR′), 1812–67, French painter.

roust (roust), *v.t.* to rout, as from a place: *to roust someone out of bed.* [perh. b. ROUSE^1 and ROUT^2]

roust·a·bout (rous′tə bout′), *n.* **1.** a wharf laborer or deck hand. **2.** a circus laborer. **3.** *Slang.* any unskilled laborer working in an oil field. Cf. **roughneck** (def. 2). [*roust* to rout out (? alter. of ROUSE^1) + ABOUT]

rout^1 (rout), *n.* **1.** a defeat attended with disorderly flight. **2.** a tumultuous or disorderly crowd of persons. **3.** *Law.* a disturbance of the public peace by three or more persons acting together in a manner that suggests an intention to riot. **4.** a large, formal evening party or social gathering. **5.** *Archaic.* a company or band of people. —*v.t.* **6.** to disperse in defeat and disorderly flight. [ME < AF *rute* << L *rupta* broken, fem. ptp. of *rumpere*]

rout^2 (rout), *v.i.* **1.** to root, as swine. **2.** to poke, search, or rummage. —*v.t.* **3.** to turn over or dig up (something) with the snout, as swine. **4.** to find or get by searching, rummaging, etc. (usually fol. by *out*). **5.** to cause to rise from bed. **6.** to force or drive out. **7.** to hollow out or furrow, as with a scoop, gouge, or machine. [alter. of ROOT^2; cf. MD *ruten* to root out]

rout^3 (rout, ro͞ot), *Chiefly Brit. Dial.* —*v.i., v.t.* **1.** to bellow; roar. —*n.* **2.** a bellow. [ME *rowt(en)* < Scand; see ROOT^3]

route (ro͞ot, rout), *n., v.,* **rout·ed, rout·ing.** —*n.* **1.** a course, way, or road for travel or shipping. **2.** a customary or regular line of travel or shipping: *air routes.* **3.** a specific territory, round, or number of stops regularly visited by a person in the performance of his work or duty, as by a vendor, deliveryman, or the like. —*v.t.* **4.** to fix the route of: *to route a tour.* **5.** to send or forward by a particular route. [ME < OF << L *rupta (via)* broken (road), fem. ptp. of *rumpere* to break] —**rout′er,** *n.*

rout·er (rou′tər), *n.* **1.** any of various tools or machines for routing, hollowing out, or furrowing. **2.** Also called **rout′er plane′.** *Carpentry.* a plane for cutting interior angles, as at the bottom of a groove. See illus. at **plane^2.**

rou·tine (ro͞o tēn′), *n.* **1.** a customary or regular course of procedure: *the routine of an office.* **2.** regular, unvarying, habitual, or unimaginative procedure. **3.** *Computer Technol.* **a.** a complete set of coded instructions directing a computer to perform a series of operations. **b.** a series of operations performed by the computer. **4.** a regularly given individual act, performance, or part of a performance, as a song or dance. —*adj.* **5.** of the nature of, proceeding by, or adhering to routine: *routine duties.* [< F < *route* ROUTE] —**rou·tine′ly,** *adv.*

rou·tin·ism (ro͞o tē′niz əm), *n.* adherence to routine. —**rou·tin·ist** (ro͞o tē′nist), *n.*

rou·tin·ize (ro͞o tē′nīz), *v.t.,* **-ized, -iz·ing. 1.** to develop into a regular procedure. **2.** to reduce to a customary procedure.

roux (ro͞o), *n.* a mixture of fat and flour used to thicken sauces. [< F: browned, reddish << L *russ(us),* akin to *ruber* RED]

rove^1 (rōv), *v.,* **roved, rov·ing,** *n.* —*v.i.* **1.** to wander about without definite destination. —*v.t.* **2.** to wander over or through; traverse: *to rove the woods.* —*n.* **3.** the act of roving. [ME *rove(n)* < Scand; cf. Icel *rāfa*] —**Syn. 1.** stroll, amble, stray. See **roam.**

rove^2 (rōv), *v.* a pt. and pp. of **reeve^2.**

rove^3 (rōv), *v.,* **roved, rov·ing,** *n.* —*v.t.* **1.** to form (slivers of wool, cotton, etc.) into slightly twisted strands in a preparatory process of spinning. **2.** to draw fibers or the like through an eye or other small opening. **3.** to attenuate, compress, and twist slightly in carding. —*n.* **4.** *Brit.* roving^2. [?]

rove′ bee′tle, any of numerous beetles of the family *Staphylinidae,* having a slender, elongated body and very short elytra, and capable of running swiftly.

rove-o·ver (rōv′ō′vər), *adj. Pros.* (in sprung rhythm) of or pertaining to the completion of a metrical foot, incomplete at the end of one line, with a syllable or syllables from the beginning of the next line.

rov·er^1 (rō′vər), *n.* **1.** a person who roves; wanderer. **2.** *Archery.* **a.** a mark selected at random. **b.** one of a group of fixed marks at a long distance. **c.** an archer who shoots from a distance. [ROVE^1 + -ER^1]

rov·er^2 (rō′vər), *n.* **1.** a pirate. **2.** *Obs.* a pirate ship. [ME < MD or MLG: robber = *rov(en)* (to) rob + *-er* -ER^1]

rov·ing^1 (rō′ving), *adj.* **1.** roaming or wandering. **2.** not restricted as to work or place of work: *a roving editor.* **3.** not assigned to any particular diplomatic post but appointed on a special mission: *a roving ambassador.* [ROVE^1 + -ING^2] —**rov′ing·ly,** *adv.* —**rov′ing·ness,** *n.*

rov·ing^2 (rō′ving), *n.* **1.** a soft strand of fiber that has been twisted, attenuated, and freed of foreign matter preparatory to its conversion into yarn. **2.** the final phase of carding in which this is done. [ROVE^3 + -ING^1]

row^1 (rō), *n.* **1.** a number of persons or things arranged in a line, esp. a straight line: *a row of apple trees.* **2.** a line of adjacent seats facing the same way, as in a theater. **3.** a street formed by two continuous lines of buildings. **4.** *Checkers.* one of the horizontal lines of squares on a checkerboard; rank. **5. hard** or **long row to hoe,** a difficult task or set of circumstances. —*v.t.* **6.** to put in a row. [ME *row(e),* OE *rāw;* akin to Lith *raiwe* stripe, L *rīma* cleft, fissure]

row^2 (rō), *v.i.* **1.** to propel a vessel by the leverage of an oar or the like. —*v.t.* **2.** to propel (a vessel) by the leverage of an oar or the like. **3.** to convey in a boat that is rowed. **4.** to employ, use, or be equipped with (a number of oars). **5.** to use (oarsmen) for rowing. **6.** to row against in a race. —*n.* **7.** the act or an instance or period of rowing. **8.** an excursion in a rowboat. [ME *row(en),* OE *rōwan;* c. OIcel *rōa;* akin to L *rēmus* oar. See RUDDER] —**row′a·ble,** *adj.* —**row′er,** *n.*

row^3 (rou), *n.* **1.** a noisy dispute or quarrel; commotion. **2.** *Informal.* noise or clamor. —*v.i.* **3.** to quarrel noisily. [?]

row·an (rō′ən, rou′-), *n.* **1.** the European mountain ash, *Sorbus Aucuparia,* having red berries. **2.** either of two American mountain ashes, *Sorbus americana* or *S. sambucifolia.* **3.** Also called **row·an·ber·ry** (rō′ən ber′ē, rou′-). the berry of any of these trees. [< Scand; cf. Norw *raun*]

row·boat (rō′bōt′), *n.* a small boat designed for rowing.

row·dy (rou′dē), *n., pl.* **-dies,** *adj.,* **-di·er, -di·est.** —*n.* **1.** a rough, disorderly person. —*adj.* **2.** rough and disorderly: *rowdy behavior at school.* [? irreg. from ROW^3] —**row′di·ly,** *adv.* —**row′di·ness,** *n.* —**row′dy·ish,** *adj.* —**row′dy·ish·ly,** *adv.* —**row′dy·ish·ness,** *n.* —**row′dy·ism,** *n.*

Rowe (rō), *n.* **Nicholas,** 1674–1718, British poet and dramatist: poet laureate 1715–18.

row·el (rou′əl), *n., v.,* **-eled, -el·ing** or (*esp. Brit.*) **-elled, -el·ling.** —*n.* **1.** a small wheel with radiating points, forming the extremity of a horseman's spur. See illus. at **spur^1. 2.** *Vet. Pathol.* a piece of leather or the like inserted beneath the skin of a horse or other animal to cause a discharge. —*v.t.* **3.** to prick or urge with a rowel. [ME *rowelle* < MF *ruelle,* OF *roel,* dim. of *roe, roue* wheel < L *rota*]

row·en (rou′ən), *n.* the second crop of grass or hay in a season; aftermath. [ME *reywayn* < ONF **rewain;* c. F *regain*]

row′ house′ (rō), one of a continuous group or row of houses having a uniform structure and appearance, often joined by common side walls.

row′ing boat′ (rō′ing), *Brit.* rowboat.

Rox·as (rō′häs; *Sp.* rô′häs), *n.* **Ma·nuel** (mä nwel′), 1892–1948, Philippine statesman: 1st president 1946–48.

Rox·burgh (roks′bûr′ō, -bur′ō *or, esp. Brit.,* -brə), *n.* a county in SE Scotland. 43,171 (1961); 666 sq. mi. *Co. seat:* Jedburgh. Also called **Rox·burgh·shire** (roks′bûr′ō shēr′, -shər, -bur′ō-, -brə-).

Roy (roi), *n.* Rollo.

roy·al (roi′əl), *adj.* **1.** of or pertaining to a king, queen, or other sovereign. **2.** descendent from or related to a king or line of kings: *a royal prince.* **3.** noting or having the rank of a king or queen. **4.** established or chartered by or existing under the patronage of a sovereign: *a royal society.* **5.** proceeding from or performed by a sovereign: *a royal warrant.* **6.** appropriate to or befitting a sovereign; kinglike or princely; magnificent; stately: *royal splendor.* **7.** (*usually cap.*) *Brit.* in the service of the monarch or of the Commonwealth. **8.** *Informal.* fine; excellent: *in royal spirits.* **9.** beyond the common or ordinary in size, quality, etc. —*n.* **10.** *Naut.* a sail set on a royal mast. See diag. at **ship. 11.** a size of printing paper, 19 × 24 to 20 × 25 inches. **12.** *Chiefly Brit.* a size of drawing or writing paper, 19 × 24 inches. [ME < MF < L *rēgāl(is)* kingly = *rēg-* (s. of *rēx*) king + *-ālis* -AL^1] —**roy′al·ly,** *adv.* —**Syn. 6.** majestic. See **kingly.**

Roy′al Acad′emy, a society founded in 1768 by George III of England for the establishment of an art school and an annual exhibition of works by living artists. Official name, **Roy′al Acad′emy of Arts′.**

roy′al ant′ler, the third prong from the base of a stag's antler. Also called **tres·tine, trez·tine.**

roy′al blue′, a deep blue, often with a faint reddish tinge.

roy′al col′ony, 1. a colony administered by officers of the crown. **2.** *Amer. Hist.* a colony administered by a royal governor and council and having a representative assembly. Cf. **charter colony.**

roy′al fern′, a fern, *Osmunda regalis,* having tall, upright fronds.

roy′al flush′, *Poker.* the five highest cards of a suit.

roy·al·ist (roi′ə list), *n.* **1.** a supporter or adherent of a king or royal government, esp. in times of rebellion or civil war. **2.** a loyalist in the American Revolution; Tory. —*adj.* **3.** of or pertaining to royalists. —**roy′al·ism,** *n.* —**roy′al·is′tic,** *adj.*

roy′al jel′ly, a viscous aliment secreted from the pharyngeal glands of worker honeybees, fed to all larvae during their first few days and afterward only to those larvae selected to be queens.

roy′al mast′, *Naut.* a mast situated immediately above, and generally formed as a single spar with, a topgallant mast.

Roy′al Oak′, a city in SE Michigan, near Detroit. 86,238 (1970).

roy′al palm′, any of several tall, showy feather palms of the genus *Roystonea,* as *R. regia.* See illus. at **palm^2.**

roy′al poincian′a, a showy, leguminous tree, *Delonix regia,* native to Madagascar, having racemes of brilliant scarlet or orange flowers and bearing a flat, woody pod which often grows to a length of two feet. Also called **flamboyant.**

roy′al pur′ple, a deep bluish purple.

roy′al road′, an easy way or means to achieve something: *There is no royal road to learning.*

Roy′al Soci′ety, a society through which the British government has supported scientific investigation since 1662: it awards four annual medals for scientific achievement and merit. Official name, **Roy′al Soci′ety of Lon′don for Improv′ing Nat′ural Knowl′edge.**

roy·al·ty (roi′əl tē), *n., pl.* **-ties. 1.** royal persons collectively. **2.** royal status, dignity, or power; sovereignty. **3.** a person of royal lineage; member of a royal family. **4.** a prerogative or right belonging to a king or other sovereign. **5.** a royal domain; kingdom; realm. **6.** character or quality proper to or befitting a sovereign; kingliness; nobility. **7.** a compensation or portion of the proceeds paid to the owner of a right, as a patent or oil or mineral right, for the use of it. **8.** an agreed portion of the income from a work paid to its author, composer, etc., usually a percentage of the retail price of each copy sold. **9.** a royal right, as over minerals, granted by a sovereign to a person or corporation. **10.** the payment made for such a right. [ME *roialte* < OF]

Roy′al Worces′ter. See **Worcester china.**

Royce (rois), *n.* **Josiah,** 1855–1916, U.S. philosopher and educator.

R.P., 1. Reformed Presbyterian. 2. Regius Professor.
rpm, revolutions per minute. Also, **r.p.m.**
rps, revolutions per second. Also, **r.p.s.**
rpt., report.
R.Q., respiratory quotient. Also, **RQ**
R.R., 1. Railroad. 2. Right Reverend.
-rrhagia, a learned borrowing from Greek meaning "bursting forth," used in the formation of compound words: *bronchorrhagia.* Also, **-rhagia, -rhage, -rrhage, -rhagy, -rrhagy.** [< Gk *-rrhagia,* comb. form akin to *rhēgnýnai* to break, burst, shatter]
-rrhaphy, a learned borrowing from Greek meaning "suture," used in the formation of compound words: *herniorrhaphy.* Also, **-rhaphy.** [< Gk *-rrhaphia* a sewing together]
-rrhea, a learned borrowing from Greek meaning "flow," "discharge," used in the formation of compound words: *gonorrhea.* Also, **-rhea.** Cf. **rheo-.** [< NL *-rrhoea* < Gk *-rrhoia,* comb. form repr. *rhoía* a flow]
-rrhexis, a learned borrowing from Greek meaning "rupture," used in the formation of compound words. [< NL < Gk *rhêxis* a breaking, bursting]
-rrhiza, var. of **rhizo-** as second element of compounds: *mycorrhiza.* Also, **-rhiza.** [< NL < Gk *rhíza* root]
-rrhoea, var. of **-rrhea.**
Rs., 1. reis. 2. rupees.
R.S., 1. Recording Secretary. 2. Reformed Spelling.
r.s., right side.
RSFSR, See **Russian Soviet Federated Socialist Republic.** Also, **R.S.F.S.R.**
RSV, See **Revised Standard Version.**
R.S.V.P., please reply. [< F *r(épondez) s('il) v(ous) p(lait)* reply, if you please] Also, **rsvp, r.s.v.p.**
rt., right.
r.t., *Football.* right tackle.
Rt. Hon., Right Honorable.
Rt. Rev., Right Reverend.
Ru, *Chem.* ruthenium.
Ru·an·da-U·run·di (ro͞o än′də o͝o ro͞on′dē), *n.* a former territory in central Africa, E of Zaïre: formerly a United Nations trust territory 1946–62; now divided into the independent states of Rwanda and Burundi.
rub (rub), *v.,* **rubbed, rub·bing,** *n.* **—***v.t.* **1.** to subject the surface of (something) to pressure and friction, as in cleaning, polishing, etc.; move one thing back and forth, or with a rotary motion along the surface of (something else). **2.** to move, spread, or apply (something) with pressure and friction over something else. **3.** to move (two things) with pressure and friction over or back and forth over each other (often fol. by *together*): *He rubbed his hands together.* **4.** to mark, polish, force, move, etc. (something) by pressure and friction (often fol. by *over, in,* or *into*). **5.** to remove by pressure and friction; erase (often fol. by *off* or *out*). **—***v.i.* **6.** to exert pressure and friction on something. **7.** to move with pressure against something. **8.** to admit of being rubbed in a specified manner: *Chalk rubs off easily.* **9. rub it in,** *Informal.* to emphasize or reiterate something unpleasant in order to tease or annoy. **10. rub off on,** *Informal.* to transfer or communicate by association: *Some of his good luck rubbed off on me.* **11. rub out, a.** to obliterate; erase. **b.** *Slang.* to murder. **12. rub the wrong way,** to irritate; offend; annoy. **—***n.* **13.** the act or an instance of rubbing: *an alcohol rub.* **14.** something that annoys or irritates one's feelings. **15.** an annoying experience or circumstance. **16.** an obstacle, impediment, or difficulty: *We like nice things, but the rub is we can't afford them.* **17.** a rough or abraded area caused by rubbing. [ME *rubbe(n)*; c. Fris *rubben,* Dan *rubbe,* Sw *rubba*]
Rub' al Kha·li (*Arab.* ro͝ob′ äl ᴋʜä′lē; *Eng.* ro͝ob′ al kä′lē), a desert in S Arabia, N of Hadhramaut and extending from Yemen to Oman. Also called **Ar Rimal, Dahna, Great Sandy Desert.**
ru·basse (ro͞o bas′, -bäs′), *n.* a variety of rock crystal containing minute flakes of iron ore which impart a bright-red color: used as a decorative stone, sometimes imitated with dyes in crackled quartz. [< F *rubace,* appar. < *rubis* RUBY]
ru·ba·to (ro͞o bä′tō; *It.* ʀo͞o bä′tô), *adj., n., pl.* **-tos,** *adv. Music.* **—***adj.* **1.** having certain notes arbitrarily lengthened while others are correspondingly shortened, or vice versa. **—***n.* **2.** a rubato phrase or passage. **—***adv.* **3.** in a rubato manner. [< It *(tempo) rubato* stolen (time), ptp. of *rubare* to steal < Gmc; see ROB]
rub·ber[1] (rub′ər), *n.* **1.** Also called **India rubber, natural rubber, gum elastic, caoutchouc.** a highly elastic substance polymerized by the drying and coagulation of the latex or milky juice of rubber trees and plants, esp. *Hevea* and *Ficus* species, containing the group, $[-CH_2C-(CH_3)-CHCH_2-]_n$. **2.** a material made synthetically or by chemically treating and toughening this substance, used in the manufacture of erasers, electrical insulation, elastic bands, tires, and many other products. **3.** any of various similar substances and materials made synthetically. Cf. **synthetic rubber. 4.** a low overshoe of this material. **5.** an instrument or tool used for rubbing, polishing, scraping, etc. **6.** a person who rubs something, as to smooth or polish it. **7.** a person who gives massages; masseur or masseuse. **8.** swipe (def. 2). **9.** *Baseball.* an oblong piece of whitened material embedded in the mound at the point from which the pitcher delivers the ball. **10.** a coarse file. **11.** an eraser. **12.** See **rubber band. 13.** *Slang.* a condom. **—***adj.* **14.** made of, containing, or coated with rubber: *a rubber bath mat.* **15.** pertaining to or producing rubber: *a rubber plantation.* [RUB + -ER[1]] **—rub′ber·less,** *adj.* **—rub′ber·like′,** *adj.*
rub·ber[2] (rub′ər), *n.* **1.** (in certain card games, as bridge and whist) a series or round played until one side reaches a specific score or wins a specific number of hands. **—***adj.* **2.** *Sports.* noting an extra game that is played to break a tie. [?]
rub′ber band′, a narrow, circular or oblong band of rubber, used for holding things together, as papers.
rub′ber cement′, a liquid adhesive consisting of unvulcanized rubber dispersed in a volatile solvent.
rub·ber·ise (rub′ə rīz′), *v.t.,* **-ised, -is·ing.** *Chiefly Brit.* rubberize.
rub·ber·ize (rub′ə rīz′), *v.t.,* **-ized, -iz·ing.** to coat or impregnate with rubber or some preparation of it.
rub·ber·neck (rub′ər nek′), *Informal.* **—***n.* **1.** an extremely curious person. **2.** a sightseer; tourist. **—***v.i.* **3.** to look about or stare with great curiosity, as by craning the neck or turning the head.
rub′ber plant′, **1.** a moraceous plant, *Ficus elastica,* having shining, leathery leaves, growing native as a tall tree in India, the Malay Archipelago, etc., used as a source of rubber and cultivated in Europe and America as a house plant. **2.** any plant yielding caoutchouc or India rubber.
rub′ber stamp′, a device with a rubber printing surface, used for manually imprinting names, notices, etc.
rub·ber-stamp (rub′ər stamp′), *v.t.* **1.** to imprint with a rubber stamp. **2.** *Informal.* to give approval automatically or without consideration.
rub′ber tree′. See **rubber plant.**
rub·ber·y (rub′ə rē), *adj.* like rubber; elastic; tough.
rub·bing (rub′ing), *n.* **1.** the act of a person or thing that rubs. **2.** a reproduction of an incised or sculptured surface made by laying paper or the like upon it and rubbing with some marking substance. [ME]
rub′bing al′cohol, an aqueous solution of about 70-percent isopropyl alcohol or of denatured ethyl alcohol, used chiefly as a rubefacient and antiseptic.
rub·bish (rub′ish), *n.* **1.** worthless, unwanted material that is rejected or thrown out; debris; litter; trash. **2.** nonsense, as in writing, art, etc.: *sentimental rubbish.* [ME *rubbes, rob(b)ous* < ?. Cf. RUBBLE] **—rub′bish·y,** *adj.*
rub·ble (rub′əl *or, for 1,* ro͞o′bəl), *n.* **1.** rough fragments of broken stone, sometimes used in masonry. **2.** broken bits and pieces of anything, as that which is demolished: *Bombing and artillery barrages reduced the town to rubble.* [ME *rubel, robil* < ?. Cf. RUBBISH]
rub·ble·work (rub′əl wûrk′, ro͞o′bəl-), *n.* masonry built of rubble or roughly dressed stones.
rub·bly (rub′lē), *adj.,* **-bli·er, -bli·est.** made or consisting of rubble.
rub·down (rub′doun′), *n.* a massage, esp. after exercise or a steam bath.
rube (ro͞ob), *n. Slang.* an unsophisticated countryman; hick. [short for *Reuben,* man's name]
ru·be·fa·cient (ro͞o′bə fā′shənt), *adj.* **1.** causing redness of the skin, as a medicinal application. **—***n.* **2.** *Med.* a rubefacient application, as a mustard plaster. [< L *rubefacient-* (s. of *rubefaciēns,* prp. of *rubefacere*) = *rube(us)* RED + *-facient-* -FACIENT]
ru·be·fac·tion (ro͞o′bə fak′shən), *n.* **1.** the act or process of making red, esp. with a rubefacient. **2.** redness of the skin caused by a rubefacient. [< L *rubefact(us)* made red (ptp. of *rubefacere;* see RUBEFACIENT) + -ION]
ru·bel·la (ro͞o bel′ə), *n. Pathol.* See **German measles.** [< NL < L: reddish (neut. pl. of *rubellus*) = *rub(er)* red + *-ella* fem. dim. suffix]
ru·bel·lite (ro͞o bel′īt, ro͞o′bə līt′), *n.* a deep-red variety of tourmaline, used as a gem. [< L *rubell(us)* reddish (see RUBELLA) + -ITE[1]]
Ru·bens (ro͞o′bənz; *Flem.* ʀʏ′bəns), *n.* **Pe·ter Paul** (pē′tər pôl; *Flem.* pā′təʀ poul), 1577–1640, Flemish painter.
ru·be·o·la (ro͞o bē′ə lə, ro͞o′bē ō′lə), *n. Pathol.* **1.** measles. **2.** See **German measles.** [< NL = L *rube(us)* reddish (< *ruber;* see RUBY) + *-ol-* dim. suffix + *-a* -A] **—ru·be′o·lar,** *adj.*
ru·bes·cent (ro͞o bes′ənt), *adj.* becoming red; blushing. [< L *rubescent-* (s. of *rubescēns,* prp. of *rubescere*) = *rub(ēre)* (to) be red (< *ruber* red; see RUBY) + *-esc-* inceptive suffix + *-ent-* -ENT] **—ru·bes′cence,** *n.*
ru·bi·a·ceous (ro͞o′bē ā′shəs), *adj.* belonging to the *Rubiaceae,* or madder family of plants, comprising the coffee, cinchona, and ipecac plants, the gardenia, partridgeberry, houstonia, bedstraw, etc. [< NL *Rubiace(ae)* name of family = *Rubi(a)* name of genus (L *rubia* madder < *rubeus* reddish) + *-aceae* -ACEAE + -OUS]
Ru·bi·con (ro͞o′bə kon′), *n.* **1.** a river in N Italy flowing E into the Adriatic. 15 mi. long: by crossing this boundary between Cisalpine Gaul and Italy, to march against Pompey in 49 B.C., Julius Caesar committed himself to conquer or perish. **2. cross** or **pass the Rubicon,** to take a decisive, irrevocable step.
ru·bi·cund (ro͞o′bə kund′), *adj.* red or reddish; ruddy: *a rubicund complexion.* [< L *rubicund(us),* akin to *rubeus* RED] **—ru′bi·cun′di·ty,** *n.*
ru·bid·i·um (ro͞o bid′ē əm), *n. Chem.* an active metallic element resembling potassium. *Symbol:* Rb; *at. wt.:* 85.47; *at. no.:* 37; *sp. gr.:* 1.53 at 20°C. [< NL = L *rubid(us)* red (in allusion to the two red lines in its spectrum) + *-ium* -IUM] **—ru·bid′ic,** *adj.*
ru·big·i·nous (ro͞o bij′ə nəs), *adj. Bot., Zool.* rusty; rust-colored; brownish-red. Also, **ru·big·i·nose** (ro͞o bij′ə nōs′). [< L *rūbīginōs(us)* (sp. var. of *rōbīginōsus*) = *rūbīgin-* (s. of *rūbīgō* rust < *ruber* red) + *-ōsus* -OUS]
Ru·bin·stein (ro͞o′bin stīn′; *Russ.* ʀo͝o bin shtīn′; *Pol.* ʀo͞o′ben stīn′), *n.* **1. An·ton** (än tôn′), 1829–94, Russian pianist and composer. **2. Ar·tur** (är′tər; *Pol.* äʀ′to͞oʀ), 1887–1982, U.S. pianist, born in Poland.
ru·bi·ous (ro͞o′bē əs), *adj.* ruby-colored.
ru·ble (ro͞o′bəl), *n.* a silver coin and monetary unit of the Soviet Union, equal to 100 kopecks. Also, **rouble.** [< Russ *rubl'* < ?]
rub·off (rub′ôf′, -of′), *n.* **1.** an act of rubbing off, as to remove something. **2.** a deep mark, effect, or impact produced, esp. through constant, close contact.
ru·bric (ro͞o′brik), *n.* **1.** a title, heading, direction, or the like, in a manuscript, book, statute, etc., written or printed in red or otherwise distinguished from the rest of the text. **2.** a direction for the conduct of divine service or the administration of the sacraments, inserted in liturgical books. **3.** any rule of conduct or procedure. **4.** *Archaic.* red ocher. **—***adj.* **5.** rubrical. **6.** *Archaic.* red; ruddy. [< L *rubrīca* red earth (< *ruber* RED); r. ME *rubriche, rubrike* < OF]
ru·bri·cal (ro͞o′bri kəl), *adj.* **1.** reddish; marked with red.

2. of, pertaining to, contained in, or prescribed by rubrics, esp. liturgical rubrics. —**ru′bri·cal·ly,** *adv.*

ru·bri·cate (ro͞o′brə kāt′), *v.t.,* **-cat·ed, -cat·ing.** **1.** to mark or color with red. **2.** to furnish with or regulate by rubrics. [< LL *rubrīcāt(us)* colored red (ptp. of *rubrīcāre*) = *rubric(a)* red earth (see RUBRIC) + *-ātus* -ATE¹] —**ru′bri·ca′tion,** *n.* —**ru′bri·ca′tor,** *n.*

ru·bri·cian (ro͞o brish′ən), *n.* an expert in or close adherent to liturgical rubrics.

ru·by (ro͞o′bē), *n., pl.* **-bies,** *adj.* —*n.* **1.** a red variety of corundum, used as a gem. **2.** something made of this stone or one of its imitations, as a bearing in a watch. **3.** a deep red; carmine. **4.** *Print. Brit.* a 5½-point type nearly corresponding in size to American agate. —*adj.* **5.** containing or set or adorned with a ruby or rubies. **6.** ruby-colored. [ME *rubi* < MF, OF < L *rube(us)* RED, akin to *ruber*] —**ru′by·like′,** *adj.*

ru′by sil′ver, pyrargyrite.

ru′by spinel′, *Mineral.* a red, transparent variety of spinel, used as a gem. Also called **spinel ruby.**

ruche (ro͞osh), *n.* a strip of pleated lace, net, muslin, or other material for trimming or finishing a dress, as at the collar or sleeves. [< F: lit., beehive << ML *rūsca* bark, ? < Celt]

ruch·ing (ro͞o′shing), *n.* **1.** material for making a ruche. **2.** ruches collectively.

ruck¹ (ruk), *n.* **1.** a large number or quantity; mass. **2.** the great mass of undistinguished or inferior persons or things. [ME *ruke,* ? < Scand; cf. Norw *ruka,* in same senses; akin to RICK]

ruck² (ruk), *n.* **1.** a fold or wrinkle; crease. —*v.t., v.i.* **2.** to make or become creased or wrinkled. [< Scand; cf. OIcel *hrukka* to wrinkle]

ruck·sack (ruk′sak′, ro͝ok′-), *n.* a type of knapsack carried by hikers, bicyclists, etc. [< G: lit., back sack]

ruck·us (ruk′əs), *n.* *Informal.* **1.** a noisy commotion; fracas; rumpus. **2.** a heated controversy. [prob. b. RUC(TION + RUMP)US]

ruc·tion (ruk′shən), *n.* *Informal.* ruckus. [?]

rud·beck·i·a (rud bek′ē ə), *n.* any plant of the genus *Rudbeckia,* comprising the coneflowers. [< NL; named after Olaus *Rudbeck* (1630–1702), Swedish botanist; see -IA]

rudd (rud), *n.* a European fresh-water fish, *Scardinius erythrophthalmus,* of the carp family. [appar. special use of *rud* (now dial.), ME *rude,* OE *rudu* redness; cf. RED, RUDDY]

rud·der (rud′ər), *n.* **1.** *Naut.* a vertical blade at the stern of a vessel for changing a vessel's direction when in motion. **2.** *Aeron.* a movable control surface attached to a vertical stabilizer, located at the rear of an airplane and used, along with the ailerons, to turn the airplane. **3.** any means of directing or guiding a course, as a leader, principle, etc. [ME *rodder, rōther, ruder,* OE *rōther;* c. G *Ruder* < Gmc **rō-;* see ROW²] —**rud′der·less,** *adj.*

rud·der·post (rud′ər pōst′), *n.* *Naut.* the vertical shaft of a rudder, attached to the helm or tiller. Also called **rud·der·stock** (rud′ər stok′).

rud·dle (rud′ᵊl), *n., v.,* **-dled, -dling.** —*n.* **1.** a red variety of ocher, used for marking sheep, coloring, etc. —*v.t.* **2.** to mark or color with ruddle. Also, **raddle, reddle.** [dial. *rud* (see RUDD) + -LE]

rud·dock (rud′ək), *n.* *Brit. Dial.* the European robin, *Erithacus rubecula.* [ME *ruddoc,* OE *rudduc.* See RUDD, -OCK]

rud·dy (rud′ē), *adj.,* **-di·er, -di·est,** *adv.* —*adj.* **1.** of or having a fresh, healthy red color. **2.** red or reddish. **3.** *Brit. Slang.* bloody (used as a euphemism). —*adv.* **4.** *Brit. Slang.* bloody (used as a euphemism). [ME *rudi,* OE *rudig*] —**rud′di·ly,** *adv.* —**rud′di·ness,** *n.*

rude (ro͞od), *adj.,* **rud·er, rud·est.** **1.** discourteous or impolite: *a rude reply.* **2.** without culture, learning, or refinement. **3.** rough in manners or behavior; unpolished; uncouth. **4.** rough, harsh, or ungentle: *rude hands.* **5.** roughly built or made; crude: *a rude cottage.* **6.** harsh to the ear: *rude sounds.* **7.** primitively simple or lacking elegance: *a rude design.* **8.** violent or tempestuous. **9.** robust, sturdy, or vigorous: *rude strength.* **10.** approximate or tentative: *a rude first calculation of costs.* [ME *rude, ruide* < OF *ru(i)de* or L *rudis*] —**rude′ly,** *adv.* —**rude′ness,** *n.* —**Syn. 1.** uncivil, unmannerly, curt, brusque, impertinent, impudent, fresh. **2.** uncivilized, coarse, vulgar.

rudes·by (ro͞odz′bē), *n.* *Archaic.* an ill-mannered, disorderly person. [RUDE + *-sby,* derisive or playful suffix, perh. in imit. of such surnames as *Ormsby*]

ru·di·ment (ro͞o′də mənt), *n.* **1.** Usually, **rudiments. a.** the elemental or first principles of a subject. **b.** a mere beginning, first slight appearance, or undeveloped or imperfect form of something. **2.** *Biol.* an incompletely developed organ or part, as one in an embryonic stage or a vestigial part without a function. [< L *rudiment(um)* beginning = *rudi(s)* unformed, rough (see RUDE) + *-mentum* -MENT]

ru·di·men·ta·ry (ro͞o′də men′tə rē, -trē), *adj.* **1.** pertaining to rudiments or first principles; elementary. **2.** of the nature of a rudiment; undeveloped or vestigial. **3.** primitive. Also, **ru′di·men′tal.** —**ru′di·men′ta·ri·ly,** *adv.* —**ru′di·men′ta·ri·ness,** *n.* —**Syn. 1.** fundamental, initial. See **elementary. 2.** embryonic. —**Ant. 1.** advanced. **2.** mature.

Ru·dolf (ro͞o′dolf), *n.* **Lake,** a lake in E Africa, in N Kenya. 185 mi. long; 3500 sq. mi.

Ru·dolf I (ro͞o′dolf; *Ger.* ro͞o′dôlf), 1218–91, king of Germany and emperor of the Holy Roman Empire 1273–91: founder of the Hapsburg dynasty. Also, **Rudolph I.** Also called **Rudolph I of Hapsburg.**

rue¹ (ro͞o), *v.,* **rued, ru·ing,** *n.* —*v.t.* **1.** to feel sorrow over; repent of; regret bitterly. —*v.i.* **2.** to feel sorrow, repentance, or regret. —*n.* **3.** sorrow; repentance or regret. [ME *rue(n), rewe(n),* OE *hrēowan;* c. G *reuen*] —**ru′er,** *n.*

rue² (ro͞o), *n.* any strongly scented plant of the genus *Ruta,* esp. *R. graveolens,* having yellow flowers and leaves formerly used in medicine. [ME < MF < L *rūta* < Gk *rhytḗ*]

rue′ anem′one, a small, ranunculaceous plant, *Anemonella thalictroides,* of North America, having white or pinkish flowers.

rue·ful (ro͞o′fəl), *adj.* **1.** causing sorrow or pity; pitiable; deplorable. **2.** feeling, showing, or expressing sorrow or pity; mournful; doleful. [ME *reowful*] —**rue′ful·ly,** *adv.* —**rue′ful·ness,** *n.*

ru·fes·cent (ro͞o fes′ənt), *adj.* somewhat reddish; tinged with red; rufous. [< L *rūfescent-* (s. of *rūfescēns,* prp. of *rūfescere*) = *rūf(us)* RED + *-esc-* inceptive suffix + *-ent-* -ENT] —**ru·fes′cence,** *n.*

ruff¹ (ruf), *n.* **1.** a neckpiece or collar of lace, lawn, or the like, gathered or drawn into deep, full, regular folds, worn in the 16th and 17th centuries. **2.** a collar, or set of lengthened or specially marked hairs or feathers, on the neck of an animal. **3.** an Old World shore bird, *Philomachus pugnax,* the male of which has a frill of neck feathers during the mating season. Cf. **reeve.** —*v.t.* **4.** tease (def. 3). [? back formation from RUFFLE¹] —**ruff′like′,** *adj.*

Ruff (16th century)

ruff² (ruf), *Cards.* —*n.* **1.** the act or an instance of trumping when one cannot follow suit. **2.** an old game of cards, resembling whist. —*v.t., v.i.* **3.** to trump when unable to follow suit. [prob. < F *ro(u)ffle;* c. It *ronfa* a card game, prob. < G *Trumpf* TRUMP¹]

ruff³ (ruf), *n.* a small European fresh-water fish, *Acerina cernua,* of the perch family. [ME *ruf, roffe;* ? special use of ROUGH]

ruffed (ruft), *adj.* displaying or wearing a ruff.

ruffed′ grouse′, a North American grouse, *Bonasa umbellus,* having a tuft of feathers on each side of the neck. See illus. at **grouse.**

ruf·fi·an (ruf′ē ən, ruf′yən), *n.* **1.** a tough, lawless person; a brutal bully. —*adj.* **2.** Also, **ruf′fi·an·ly.** tough; lawless or brutal. [< MF < It *ruffiano,* ? < Langobardic *hruf* scurf + It *-ano* -AN] —**ruf′fi·an·ism,** *n.*

ruf·fle¹ (ruf′əl), *v.,* **-fled, -fling,** *n.* —*v.t.* **1.** to destroy the smoothness or evenness of. **2.** to erect (the feathers), as a bird in anger. **3.** to disturb, vex, or irritate. **4.** to turn (the pages of a book) rapidly. **5.** to pass (cards) through the fingers rapidly in shuffling. **6.** to draw up (cloth, lace, etc.) into a ruffle by gathering along one edge. —*v.i.* **7.** to be or become ruffled; undulate; flutter. **8.** to be or become vexed or irritated. —*n.* **9.** a break in the smoothness or evenness of some surface; undulation. **10.** a strip of cloth, lace, etc., drawn up by gathering along one edge, and used as a trimming on a dress, blouse, etc. **11.** some object resembling this, as the ruff of a bird. **12.** disturbance or vexation; annoyance; irritation. [ME *ruffel(en)* (v.); c. LG *ruffelen* to crumple, rumple; cf. OIcel *hruffa* to scratch] —**ruf′fly,** *adj.* —**ruf′fler,** *n.* —**Syn. 1.** disarrange, disorder, wrinkle, rumple. **3.** upset, annoy. **10.** frill, ruff. —**Ant. 1.** smooth, arrange, order. **3.** soothe, compose.

ruf·fle² (ruf′əl), *n., v.,* **-fled, -fling.** —*n.* **1.** a low, continuous beating of a drum. —*v.t.* **2.** to beat (a drum) in this manner. [archaic *ruff* in same sense as above (? imit.) + -LE]

Ruf·fo (ro͞of′fô), *n.* **Tit·ta** (tēt′tä), 1878–1953, Italian operatic baritone.

ru·fous (ro͞o′fəs), *adj.* reddish; tinged with red; brownish-red. [< L *rūf(us)* RED + -OUS]

rug (rug), *n.* **1.** a thick fabric for covering part of a floor, often woven of wool and often having an oblong shape with a border design. Cf. **carpet** (def. 1). **2.** the treated skin of an animal, used as a floor covering: *a goatskin rug.* **3.** *Chiefly Brit.* a piece of thick, warm cloth, used as a coverlet, lap robe, etc. [< Scand; cf. dial. Norw *rugga* a coarse covering (for bed or body)] —**rug′like′,** *adj.*

ru·ga (ro͞o′gə), *n., pl.* **-gae** (-jē). Usually, **rugae.** *Biol., Anat.* a wrinkle, fold, or ridge. [< L]

ru·gate (ro͞o′gāt, -git), *adj.* wrinkled; rugose. [< L *rūgāt(us),* ptp. of *rūgāre.* See RUGA, -ATE¹]

Rug·by (rug′bē), *n.* **1.** a city in E Warwickshire, in central England: boys' school. 51,651 (1961). **2.** Also called **Rug′by foot′ball, rugger.** a form of football played between two teams of 13 to 15 men each for two 40-minute halves of continuous action with no substitution of players: the oval football-type ball may be kicked or dribbled with the feet, butted, carried, or laterally passed.

rug·ged (rug′id), *adj.* **1.** having a roughly broken, rocky, hilly, or jagged surface: *rugged ground.* **2.** (of a face) wrinkled or furrowed, as by experience, the endurance of hardship, etc. **3.** roughly irregular, heavy, or hard in outline or form. **4.** rough, harsh, or stern, as persons, nature, etc. **5.** tempestuous; stormy. **6.** harsh to the ear. **7.** rude, uncultivated, or unrefined. **8.** capable of enduring hardship, wear, etc. [ME < Scand; cf. Sw *rugga* to roughen. See RUG] —**rug′ged·ly,** *adv.* —**rug′ged·ness,** *n.* —**Syn. 1.** uneven, irregular, craggy. **5.** turbulent. **6.** grating, cacophonous. **7.** unpolished, crude. —**Ant. 1.** smooth.

rug·ger (rug′ər), *n.* *Brit.* Rugby (def. 2). [by alter.]

ru·gose (ro͞o′gōs, ro͞o gōs′), *adj.* **1.** having wrinkles; wrinkled; ridged. **2.** *Bot.* (of leaves) having a roughly veined surface. [< L *rūgōs(us)* wrinkled. See RUGA, -OSE¹] —**ru′gose·ly,** *adv.* —**ru·gos·i·ty** (ro͞o gos′i tē), *n.*

Ruhr (ro͝or), *n.* **1.** a river in W West Germany, flowing NW and W into the Rhine. 144 mi. long. **2.** a mining and industrial region centered in the valley of the Ruhr.

ru·in (ro͞o′in), *n.* **1. ruins,** the remains of a building, town, etc., that has been destroyed or that is decaying. **2.** a destroyed or decayed building, town, etc. **3.** a fallen and wrecked or decayed condition. **4.** the downfall, decay, or destruction of anything. **5.** the complete loss of health, means, position, hope, or the like. **6.** something that causes a downfall or destruction. **7.** the downfall of a person. **8.** the act of causing destruction or a downfall. —*v.t.* **9.** to reduce to ruin; devastate. **10.** to bring (a person, company, etc.) to financial ruin; bankrupt. **11.** to injure (a thing) irretrievably. **12.** to seduce (a woman). —*v.i.* **13.** to fall into ruins; fall to pieces. **14.** to come to ruin. [ME *ruine* < MF < L *ruīn(a)* overthrow, collapse = *ru(ere)* (to) fall + *-īna* -INE²] —**ru′in·a·ble,** *adj.* —**ru′in·er,** *n.*

—**Syn. 3.** RUIN, DESTRUCTION, HAVOC imply irrevocable and often widespread damage. RUIN, from the verb meaning to fall to pieces, suggests a state of decay or disintegration (or an object in that state) that is apt to be more the result of the natural processes of time and change than of sudden violent activity from without: *The house has fallen to ruins;* only in its figurative application is it apt to suggest the result of destruction from without: *the ruin of her hopes.* DESTRUCTION may be on a large or small scale (*destruction of tissue, of enemy vessels*); it emphasizes particularly the act of destroying, while RUIN and HAVOC emphasize the resultant state. HAVOC, originally a cry that served as the signal for pillaging, has changed its reference from that of spoilation to devastation, being used particularly of the destruction following in the wake of natural calamities: *the havoc wrought by flood and pestilence.* Today it is used figuratively to refer to the destruction of hopes and plans: *This sudden turn of events played havoc with her carefully laid plans.* **4.** fall, overthrow, defeat, wreck. **9.** demolish, destroy, damage.

ru·in·a·tion (ro͞o′ə nā′shən), *n.* **1.** the act of ruining. **2.** the state of being ruined. **3.** something that ruins.

ru·in·ous (ro͞o′ə nəs), *adj.* **1.** bringing or tending to bring ruin; destructive; disastrous. **2.** fallen into ruin; dilapidated. **3.** consisting of ruins. **4.** *Informal.* extremely expensive. [ME *ruynouse* < L *ruīnōs(us)* = *ruīn(a)* RUIN + *-ōsus* -OUS] —**ru′in·ous·ly,** *adv.* —**ru′in·ous·ness,** *n.*

Ruis·dael (rois′dāl, -dăl, rīz′-, rīs′-; *Du.* rœis′dāl), *n.* **Ja·cob van** (yä′kôp vän), 1628?–82, Dutch painter. Also, **Ruysdael.**

rule (ro͞ol), *n., v.,* **ruled, rul·ing.** —*n.* **1.** a principle or regulation governing conduct, procedure, etc. **2.** the code of regulations observed by a religious order or congregation. **3.** the customary or normal condition, occurrence, practice, etc. **4.** control, government, or dominion. **5.** tenure or conduct of reign or office. **6.** a prescribed mathematical method for performing a calculation or solving a problem. **7.** ruler (def. 2). **8.** *Print.* a thin, type-high strip of metal, for printing a solid or decorative line or lines. **9.** *Law.* a formal order or direction made by a court, as for governing the procedure of the court. **10.** *Obs.* behavior. **11. as a rule,** generally; usually. —*v.t.* **12.** to control or direct; exercise dominating power, authority, or influence over; govern. **13.** to decide or declare judicially or authoritatively; decree. **14.** to mark with lines, esp. parallel straight lines, with the aid of a ruler or the like: *to rule paper.* **15.** to mark out or form (a line) by this method. **16.** to be superior or preeminent in (a specific field or group); dominate by superiority. —*v.i.* **17.** to exercise dominating power or influence; predominate. **18.** to exercise authority, dominion, or sovereignty. **19.** to make a formal decision or ruling, as on a point at law. **20.** to be prevalent or current. **21. rule out,** to refuse to acknowledge or admit; eliminate; exclude. [ME *riule, reule* < OF *riule* < L *rēgul(a)* straight stick, pattern] —**Syn. 1.** standard, law, ruling, guide, precept, order. **4.** command, domination, sway, authority, direction. **12.** RULE, ADMINISTER, COMMAND, GOVERN, MANAGE mean to exercise authoritative guidance or direction. RULE implies the exercise of authority as by a sovereign: *to rule a kingdom.* ADMINISTER places emphasis on the planned and orderly procedures used: *to administer the finances of an institution.* COMMAND suggests military authority and the power to exact obedience; to be in command of: *to command a ship.* To GOVERN is authoritatively to guide or direct persons or things, esp. in the affairs of a large administrative unit: *to govern a state.* To MANAGE is to conduct affairs, i.e., to guide them in a unified way toward a definite goal, or to direct or control people, often by tact, address, or artifice: *to manage a business.* **13.** deem, judge, settle, order.

rule′ of three′, *Math.* the method of finding the fourth term in a proportion when three terms are given.

rule′ of thumb′, 1. a general or approximate principle, procedure, or rule based on experience rather than on scientific knowledge. **2.** a rough, practical method of procedure.

rul·er (ro͞o′lər), *n.* **1.** a person who rules or governs; sovereign. **2.** Also, **rule.** a strip of wood, metal, or other material, having a straight edge and often marked off in inches or centimeters. [ME]

rul·ing (ro͞o′ling), *n.* **1.** an authoritative decision, as one by a judge on a debated point of law. **2.** the act of drawing straight lines with a ruler. **3.** ruled lines. —*adj.* **4.** governing or dominating: *the ruling party.* **5.** controlling; predominating. **6.** widespread; prevalent. [ME]

rum[1] (rum), *n.* **1.** an alcoholic liquor or spirit distilled from molasses or some other fermented sugar-cane product. **2.** alcoholic drink in general; intoxicating liquor. [? short for obs. *rumbullion;* cf. F *rebouillir* to boil again]

rum[2] (rum), *adj. Slang.* **1.** odd, strange, or queer: *a rum fellow.* **2.** *Archaic.* good or fine. [earlier *rome, room* great, ? < Gypsy; see ROMANY]

rum[3] (rum), *n. Cards.* rummy[1].

Rum, Rumanian (def. 3).

Rum., 1. Rumania. **2.** Rumanian.

Ru·ma·ni·a (ro͞o mā′nē ə, -mān′yə), *n.* a republic in SE Europe, bordering on the Black Sea: one of the Balkan States. 21,250,000; 91,654 sq. mi. *Cap.:* Bucharest. Also, **Romania, Roumania.** Rumanian, **România.**

Ru·ma·ni·an (ro͞o mā′nē ən, -mān′yən), *adj.* **1.** of or pertaining to Rumania, its inhabitants, or their language. —*n.* **2.** a native or inhabitant of Rumania. **3.** the language of Rumania, a Romance language. *Abbr.:* Rum Also, **Romanian, Roumanian.**

rum·ba (rum′bə, ro͝om′-; *Sp.* ro͞om′bä), *n., pl.* **-bas** (-bəz; *Sp.* -bäs), *v.,* **-baed** (-bəd), **-ba·ing** (-bə ing). —*n.* **1.** a dance, Cuban Negro in origin and complex in rhythm. **2.** an imitation of this dance in the U.S. —*v.i.* **3.** to dance the rumba. Also, **rhumba.** [< Sp, prob. of Afr orig.]

rum·ble (rum′bəl), *v.,* **-bled, -bling,** *n.* —*v.i.* **1.** to make a deep, heavy, somewhat muffled, continuous sound, as thunder. **2.** to move or travel with such a sound. —*v.t.* **3.** to give forth or utter with a rumbling sound. **4.** to cause to make or move with a rumbling sound. **5.** to subject to the action of a rumble or tumbling barrel, as for the purpose of polishing. —*n.* **6.** a deep, heavy, somewhat muffled, continuous sound. **7.** a rear part of a carriage containing seating accommodations, as for servants, or space for baggage. **8.** See **tumbling barrel. 9.** *Slang.* a street fight between two or more rival teen-age gangs. [ME; cf. D *rommelen,* prob. of imit. orig.] —**rum′bler,** *n.* —**rum′bling·ly,** *adv.*

rum′ble seat′, a seat formerly recessed into the back of a coupe or roadster, covered by a hinged lid which opened to form the back of the seat when in use.

Rumble seat

rum·bly (rum′blē), *adj.* attended with, making, or causing a rumbling sound.

Ru·me·li·a (ro͞o mē′lē ə, -mēl′yə), *n.* **1.** a division of the former Turkish Empire, in the Balkan Peninsula: included Albania, Macedonia, and Thrace. **2. Eastern,** a former autonomous province within this division: later became S Bulgaria. Also, **Roumelia.**

ru·men (ro͞o′min), *n., pl.* **-mi·na** (-mə nə). **1.** the first stomach of ruminating animals, lying next to the reticulum. **2.** the cud of a ruminant. [< L: throat, gullet]

Rum·ford (rum′fərd), *n.* **Count.** See **Thompson, Benjamin.**

Ru·mi (*Pers.* ro͞o′mē), *n.* **Ja·lal ud-din** (*Pers.* jä läl′ o͞od dēn′, o͝od-, ja-). See **Jalal ud-din Rumi.**

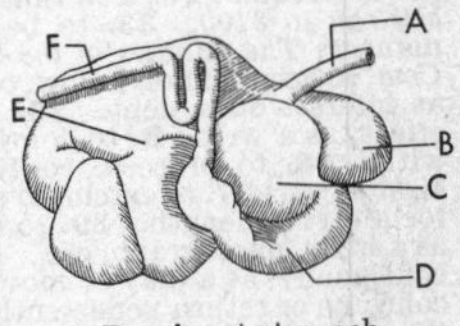

ru·mi·nant (ro͞o′mə nənt), *n.* **1.** any even-toed, hoofed mammal of the suborder *Ruminantia,* comprising cloven-hoofed, cud-chewing quadrupeds, and including the cattle, deer, camels, etc. —*adj.* **2.** ruminating; chewing the cud. **3.** contemplative; meditative. [< L *rūminant-* (s. of *rūmināns,* prp. of *rūminārī, rūmināre*) = *rūmin-* (s. of *rūmen*) RUMEN + *-ant-* -ANT] —**ru′mi·nant·ly,** *adv.*

Ruminant stomach
A, Esophagus; B, Reticulum; C, Omasum; D, Abomasum; E, Rumen; F, Small intestine

ru·mi·nate (ro͞o′mə nāt′), *v.,* **-nat·ed, -nat·ing.** —*v.i.* **1.** to chew the cud, as a ruminant. **2.** to meditate or muse; ponder. —*v.t.* **3.** to chew again or over and over. **4.** to meditate on; ponder. [< L *rūmināt(us)* chewed over again (ptp. of *rūminārī, rūmināre*). See RUMINANT, -ATE[1]] —**ru′mi·nat′ing·ly,** *adv.* —**ru′mi·na′tion,** *n.* —**ru′mi·na′tive,** *adj.* —**ru′mi·na′tive·ly,** *adv.* —**ru′mi·na′tor,** *n.* —**Syn. 2.** think, reflect.

rum·mage (rum′ij), *v.,* **-maged, -mag·ing,** *n.* —*v.t.* **1.** to search thoroughly or actively through (a place, receptacle, etc.), esp. by moving around, turning over, or looking through contents. **2.** to find, bring, or fetch by searching (often fol. by *out* or *up*). —*v.i.* **3.** to search actively, as in a place or receptacle, or among contents, goods, etc. —*n.* **4.** miscellaneous articles; odds and ends. **5.** a rummaging search. [aph. m. MF *arrumage* = *arrum(er)* (to) stow goods in the hold of a ship (< ?) + *-age* -AGE] —**rum′mag·er,** *n.*

rum′mage sale′, a sale of miscellaneous articles, esp. items contributed, to raise money for charity.

rum·mer (rum′ər), *n.* a large drinking glass or cup. [< D *roemer;* see ROEMER]

rum·my[1] (rum′ē), *n.* any of various card games for two, three, or four players, each usually being dealt seven, nine, or ten cards, in which the object is to match cards into sets and sequences. Also called **rum.** [? special use of *rummy* RUM[2]; see -Y[1]]

rum·my[2] (rum′ē), *n., pl.* **-mies,** *adj.* —*n.* **1.** *Slang.* a drunkard. —*adj.* **2.** of or like rum: *a rummy taste.* [RUM[1] + -Y[1]]

ru·mor (ro͞o′mər), *n.* **1.** a story or statement in general circulation without confirmation or certainty as to facts: *a rumor of war.* **2.** gossip; hearsay: *Don't listen to rumor.* **3.** *Archaic.* a continuous, confused noise; clamor; din. —*v.t.* **4.** to circulate, report, or assert by a rumor. Also, *esp. Brit.,* **ru′mour.** [ME *rumour* < MF < L *rūmor;* akin to Skt *rāuti, ravati* he cries]

rump (rump), *n.* **1.** the hind part of the body of an animal, as the hindquarters of a quadruped or sacrum of a bird. **2.** *Chiefly Brit.* a cut of beef from this part of the animal, behind the loin and above the round. **3.** the buttocks. **4.** the last, unimportant or inferior part: *a rump of territory.* **5.** the remnant of a legislature, council, etc., after a majority of the members have resigned or been expelled. **6. the Rump,** *Eng. Hist.* See **Rump Parliament.** [ME *rumpe* < Scand; cf. Dan *rumpe* rump; c. G *Rumpf* trunk] —**rump′less,** *adj.*

Rum·pel·stilts·kin (rum′pəl stilt′skin; *Ger.* ro͝om′pəl-shtilts′kin), *n.* a dwarf in a German folk tale who spins flax into gold for a maiden on the condition that she give him her first child or else guess his name.

rum·ple (rum′pəl), *v.,* **-pled, -pling,** *n.* —*v.t.* **1.** to crumple or crush into wrinkles. **2.** to ruffle; tousle. —*v.i.* **3.** to become wrinkled or crumpled. —*n.* **4.** a wrinkle or irregular fold; crease. [< MD *rompel* (n.) or MLG *rumpel*]

Rump′ Par′liament, *Eng. Hist.* the remnant of the Long Parliament after Pride's Purge, lasting intermittently until 1660.

rum·pus (rum′pəs), *n., pl.* **-pus·es.** a noisy or violent disturbance; commotion; uproar. [?]

rum′pus room′, a room in a house, for games, hobbies, parties, etc.

rum·run·ner (rum′run′ər), *n. U.S. Informal.* a person or ship engaged in smuggling liquor. —**rum′run′ning,** *n.*

run (run), *v.,* **ran, run, run·ning,** *n., adj.* —*v.i.* **1.** to go quickly by moving the legs more rapidly than at a walk and in such a manner that for an instant in each step all feet are off the ground. **2.** to move with haste; act quickly. **3.** to depart quickly; take to flight; flee or escape. **4.** to have recourse for aid, support, comfort, etc. **5.** to make a quick trip or informal visit for a short stay at a place. **6.** to go around, rove, or ramble without restraint. **7.** to move, roll, or progress from momentum or from being propelled. **8.** *Sports.* **a.** to take part in a race or contest. **b.** to finish in a race or contest in a certain numerical position: *The horse ran second.* **9.** to be or campaign as a candidate for election.

10. to migrate, as fish. **11.** to migrate upstream or inshore from deep water to spawn. **12.** to move under continuing power or force, as of the wind, a motor, etc. **13.** (of a ship, automobile, etc.) to be sailed or driven from a safe, proper, or given route. **14.** to ply between places, as a vessel or conveyance. **15.** to move, glide, turn, rotate, or pass easily, freely, or smoothly: *A rope runs in a pulley.* **16.** to creep, trail, or climb, as growing vines. **17.** to come undone or to unravel, as stitches or a fabric. **18.** to flow, as a liquid. **19.** to flow along, esp. strongly, as a stream, the sea, etc. **20.** to empty or transfer contents. **21.** to include a specific range of variations (usually fol. by *from*): *Your work runs from fair to bad.* **22.** to melt and flow. **23.** to spread on being applied to a surface, as a liquid. **24.** to undergo a spreading of colors: *materials that run when washed.* **25.** to flow forth as a discharge, as a liquid. **26.** to overflow or leak, as a vessel. **27.** to operate or function. **28.** to be in operation. **29.** to elapse; pass or go by, as time. **30.** to pass into or meet with a certain state or condition. **31.** to get or become: *The well ran dry.* **32.** to amount; total: *The bill ran to $100.* **33.** to be stated or worded in a certain manner: *The minutes of the last meeting run as follows.* **34.** *Com.* to accumulate, follow, or become payable in due course, as interest on a debt. **35.** *Law.* **a.** to have legal force or effect, as a writ. **b.** to continue to operate. **c.** to go along with. **36.** to proceed, continue, or go: *The story runs for eight pages.* **37.** to extend in a given direction. **38.** to extend for a certain length. **39.** to appear in print or be published as a story, photograph, etc. **40.** to be performed or be played continually, as a play or movie. **41.** to pass quickly. **42.** to continue or return persistently; recur: *a tune running through the head.* **43.** to have or tend to have or produce a specified character, quality, form, etc.: *This novel runs to long descriptions.* **44.** to be or continue to be of a certain or average size, number, etc. **45.** *Naut.* to sail before the wind. —*v.t.* **46.** to move or run along (a surface, way, path, etc.). **47.** to traverse (a distance) in running. **48.** to perform, compete in, or accomplish by or as by running. **49.** to compete against in a race. **50.** to ride or cause to gallop. **51.** to enter in a race. **52.** to bring into a specified state by running. **53.** to trace, track, pursue, or hunt, as game: *to run deer on foot.* **54.** to drive (an animal) or cause to go by pursuing. **55.** to cause to ply between places, as a vessel or conveyance. **56.** to carry or transport, as in a vessel or vehicle. **57.** to cause to pass quickly: *He ran his eyes over the letter.* **58.** to get past or through: *to run a blockade.* **59.** to smuggle (contraband goods). **60.** to work, operate, or drive. **61.** to publish, print, or make copies of. **62.** to process, refine, manufacture, or subject to an analysis or treatment. **63.** to keep operating or going, as a machine. **64.** to keep (a motor) idling for an indefinite period. **65.** to allow (a ship, automobile, etc.) to depart from a safe, proper, or given route, as by negligence or error. **66.** to sponsor, support, or nominate (a person) as a candidate for election. **67.** to manage or conduct: *to run a business; to run one's own life.* **68.** to expose oneself to or be exposed to (a chance, risk, etc.). **69.** to cause (a liquid) to flow: *to run the water for a bath.* **70.** to give forth or flow with (a liquid); pour forth or discharge. **71.** to cause to move easily, freely, or smoothly. **72.** to cause stitches in (a garment or fabric) to unravel or come undone: *to run a stocking on a protruding nail.* **73.** to bring or force into a certain condition. **74.** to drive, force, or thrust. **75.** to graze; pasture. **76.** to extend (something) in a particular direction or to a given point or place. **77.** to cause to fuse and flow, as metal for casting in a mold. **78.** to draw, trace, or mark out, as a line. **79.** to cost (an amount or approximate amount). **80.** to cost (a person) an amount or approximate amount: *That dress will run you $30.* **81. run across,** to meet or find accidentally. **82. run afoul of, a.** *Naut.* to collide with so as to damage and entangle. **b.** to incur or become subject to the wrath or ill will of. **83. run down, a.** to strike and fell or overturn, esp. to drive a vehicle into (someone). **b.** to pursue until captured; chase. **c.** to peruse; review. **d.** to cease operation; stop. **e.** to speak disparagingly of; criticize severely. **f.** to search out; trace; find: *to run down information.* **g.** *Baseball.* to tag out (a base runner) between bases. **84. run in, a.** to visit casually. **b.** *Slang.* to arrest; take to jail. **c.** *Print.* to insert (text) without indenting. **d.** to break in (new machinery). **85. run into, a.** to crash into; collide with. **b.** to meet accidentally. **c.** to amount to; total. **d.** to succeed; follow. **e.** to experience; encounter. **86. run in with,** *Naut.* to sail close to (a coast, vessel, etc.). **87. run off, a.** to leave quickly; depart. **b.** to create or perform rapidly or easily. **c.** to determine the winner (of a contest, race, etc.) by a runoff. **d.** to drive away; expel. **88. run on, a.** to continue without interruption. **b.** *Print.* to insert (text) without indenting. **c.** to add something, as at the end of a text. **89. run out, a.** to terminate; end. **b.** to become used up. **c.** to drive out; expel. **90. run out of,** to exhaust a quantity or supply of. **91. run out on,** *Informal.* to withdraw one's support from; abandon. **92. run over, a.** to hit and knock down, esp. with a vehicle. **b.** to go beyond; exceed. **c.** to repeat; review. **93. run through, a.** to pierce or stab, as with a sword. **b.** to consume or use up recklessly; squander. **c.** to rehearse quickly or informally. **94. run up, a.** to sew rapidly. **b.** to amass; incur: *running up huge debts.* **c.** to cause to increase; raise. **d.** to build, esp. hurriedly. —*n.* **95.** the act, an instance, or period of running. **96.** a fleeing, esp. in great haste; flight. **97.** a running pace: *The boys set out at a run.* **98.** distance covered, as by racing, running, during a trip, etc. **99.** the act, an instance, or a period of traveling or moving between two places; trip. **100.** a quick trip for a short stay at a place. **101.** *Mil.* **a.** See **bomb run. b.** any portion of a military flight during which the aircraft flies directly toward the target in order to begin its attack: *a strafing run.* **102.** *Aeron.* **a.** the rapid movement, under its own power, of an aircraft on a runway, water, or another surface. **b.** a routine flight from one place to another. **103.** an interval or period during which something, as a machine, operates or continues operating. **104.** the amount of anything produced in such a period. **105.** a line or place in knitted work where a series of stitches have slipped out or come undone: *a run in a stocking.* **106.** onward movement, development, progress, course, etc. **107.** the direction of something or of its component elements: *the run of the grain of wood.* **108.** the particular course, order, or tendency of something. **109.** freedom to move around in, pass through, or use something. **110.** any rapid or easy course of progress. **111.** a continuous series of performances, as of a play. **112.** an uninterrupted course of some state or condition; a spell. **113.** a continuous extent of something, as a vein of ore. **114.** an uninterrupted series or sequence of things, events, etc. **115.** a sequence of cards in a given suit: *a heart run.* **116.** any extensive continued demand, sale, or the like. **117.** a series of sudden and urgent demands for payment, as on a bank. **118.** a period during which liquid flows. **119.** the amount that flows during such a period: *a run of 500 barrels a day.* **120.** a small stream; brook; rivulet. **121.** a flow or rush, as of water. **122.** a kind or class, as of goods. **123.** an inclined course, as on a slope, designed or used for a specific purpose. **124.** a fairly large enclosure within which domestic animals may move about freely; runway: *a chicken run.* **125.** the movement of a number of fish upstream or inshore from deep water. **126.** large numbers of fish in motion, esp. inshore from deep water or up a river for spawning: *a run of salmon.* **127.** a number of animals moving together. **128.** *Music.* a rapid succession of tones; a roulade. **129.** *Baseball.* the score unit made by safely running around all the bases and reaching home plate. **130.** a series of successful shots, strokes, or the like, in a game. **131. a run for one's money, a.** close or keen competition. **b.** enjoyment or profit in return for one's expense. **132. in the long run,** in the course of long experience; in the end. **133. on the run,** *Informal.* **a.** moving quickly; hurrying about. **b.** while running or in a hurry. **c.** escaping or hiding from the police. —*adj.* **134.** melted or liquefied: *run butter.* **135.** poured in a melted state; run into and cast in a mold. [ME *rinne(n),* OE *rinnan;* c. G *rinnen,* Icel *rinna;* form. *run* orig. ptp., later extended to present tense]

run·a·bout (run′ə bout′), *n.* **1.** a small, light automobile or other vehicle, usually with an open top; roadster. **2.** a small pleasure motorboat. **3.** a person who roves around from place to place or group to group.

run·a·gate (run′ə gāt′), *n. Archaic.* **1.** a fugitive or runaway. **2.** a vagabond or wanderer. [RUN (v.) + obs. *agate* away; sense influenced by contamination with obs. *renegate* (ME *renegat* < ML *renegāt(us)* RENEGADE)]

run-a-round (run′ə round′), *n.* **1.** *Informal.* indecisive or evasive treatment, esp. in response to a request. **2.** *Print.* printed matter set on short lines beside an illustration in a column to make room for the illustration. Also, **run′a·round′.**

run·a·way (run′ə wā′), *n.* **1.** a person who runs away; fugitive; deserter. **2.** a horse or team that has broken away from control. **3.** the act of running away. —*adj.* **4.** having run away; escaped; fugitive. **5.** (of a horse or other animal) having escaped from the control of the rider or driver. **6.** pertaining to or accomplished by running away or eloping. **7.** easily won, as a contest. **8.** *Com.* characterized by a rapid, uncontrolled price rise: *runaway inflation.*

run·back (run′bak′), *n. Football.* a run that is made by a ball-carrying player toward the goal line of the opponent.

run′ci·ble spoon′ (run′sə bəl), a forklike utensil with two broad prongs and one sharp, curved prong, as used for serving hors d'oeuvres. [*runcible,* term coined in 1871 by Edward Lear]

run·ci·nate (run′sə nit, -nāt′), *adj. Bot.* pinnately incised, with the lobes or teeth curved backward, as of a leaf. [< L *runcinātus* planed off (ptp. of *runcināre*) = *runcin(a)* plane + *-ātus* -ATE[1]]

Runcinate leaf

run·dle (run′dᵊl), *n.* **1.** a rung of a ladder. **2.** a wheel or similar rotating object. **3.** *Dial.* runnel. [var. of ROUNDEL]

rund·let (rund′lit), *n.* **1.** an old British measure of capacity equal to about 18 wine gallons or 15 imperial gallons. **2.** a small cask. [ME *rondelet;* see ROUNDLET]

run-down (run′doun′), *adj.* **1.** fatigued; weary; exhausted. **2.** in a state of poor health. **3.** in neglected condition; fallen into disrepair. **4.** (of a clock, watch, etc.) not running because it is unwound.

run·down (run′doun′), *n.* a quick review or summary of main points of information, usually oral.

Rund·stedt (rŏŏnt′stet, rŏŏnd′-; *Ger.* rŏŏnt′shtet), *n.* **Karl Ru·dolf Gerd von** (kärl ro͞o′dôlf gerd fən), 1875–1953, German field marshal.

rune[1] (ro͞on), *n.* any of the characters of certain ancient alphabets, as of a script used for writing the Germanic languages, esp. of Scandinavia and Britain, from A.D. c200–c1200. [< Icel *rūn* a secret, writing, runic character; r. ME *runo, roun* a writing, counsel, speech, OE *rūn,* akin to *rūnian* to whisper. See ROUND[2]] —**rune′like′,** *adj.*

rune[2] (ro͞on), *n. Literary.* a poem, song, or verse. [< Finnish *runo* poem, canto < Scand; see RUNE[1]]

rung[1] (rung), *v.* pt. and pp. of **ring**[2].

rung[2] (rung), *n.* **1.** one of the crosspieces, usually rounded, forming the steps of a ladder. **2.** a rounded or shaped piece fixed horizontally, for strengthening purposes, as between the legs of a chair. [ME; OE *hrung;* c. Goth *hrunga* rod, G *Runge*] —**rung′less,** *adj.*

ru·nic[1] (ro͞o′nik), *adj.* **1.** consisting of or set down in runes: *runic inscriptions.* **2.** having some secret or mysterious meaning. [RUNE[1] + -IC]

ru·nic[2] (ro͞o′nik), *adj.* of the ancient Scandinavian class or type, as literature, poetry, etc. [RUNE[2] + -IC]

run-in (run′in′), *n.* **1.** *Informal.* a quarrel; argument. **2.** *Print.* matter that is added to a text, esp. without indenting for a new paragraph.

Run·jeet Singh (run′jit sing′). See **Ranjit Singh.**

run·kle (rung′kəl, ro͞ong′-), *n. Scot. and North Eng.* a wrinkle or crease. [< Scand; cf. OIcel *hrukka* to wrinkle]

run·nel (run′əl), *n.* **1.** a small stream; brook; rivulet. **2.** a small channel, as for water. [RUN (n.) + *-el* dim. suffix]

run·ner (run′ər), *n.* **1.** a person or thing that runs, esp. as a racer. **2.** a messenger, esp. of a bank or brokerage house. **3.** *Baseball.* See **base runner. 4.** a person whose business it is to solicit patronage or trade. **5.** something in or on which something else runs or moves. **6.** either of the long, bladelike strips of metal or wood on which a sled or sleigh slides. **7.**

the blade of an ice skate. **8.** a roller on which something moves along. **9.** *Furniture.* rocker (def. 1). **10.** an operator or manager, as of a machine. **11.** a long, narrow rug, suitable for a hall or passageway. **12.** a long, narrow strip of linen, embroidery, lace, or the like, placed across a table. **13.** *Bot.* **a.** a slender stolon that runs along the surface of the ground and sends out roots and leaves at the nodes, as in the strawberry. **b.** a plant that spreads by such stems. **14.** *Foundry.* any of the channels through which molten metal flows. **15.** a smuggler. **16.** a vessel engaged in smuggling. **17.** *Ichthyol.* a jurel, *Caranx crysos,* found from Cape Cod to Brazil. **18.** a tackle or part of a tackle consisting of a line rove through a single block and fixed at one end. See diag. at **tackle. 19.** any whip or fall used for hoisting. [ME]

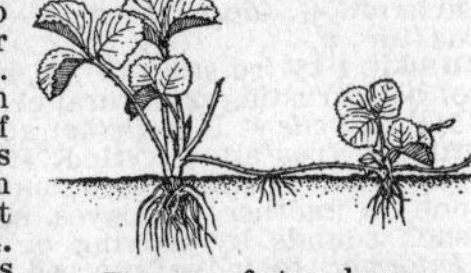
Runner of strawberry

run·ner-up (run′ər up′), *n., pl.* **run·ners-up. 1.** the competitor, player, or team finishing in second place, as in a race, contest, or tournament. **2.** any of those who place second, third, and fourth, or in the top ten.

run·ning (run′ing), *n.* **1.** the act of a person or thing that runs. **2.** managing or directing: *the running of a business.* **3.** the act or an instance of racing. **4.** the condition of a track or surface to be run or raced on; footing. **5.** the amount, quality, or type of a liquid flow. —*adj.* **6.** galloping, racing, moving, or passing rapidly. **7.** (of a horse) trained to proceed at a gallop. **8.** creeping or climbing, as plants: *a running vine.* **9.** moving or proceeding easily or smoothly. **10.** moving when pulled or hauled, as a rope. **11.** slipping or sliding easily, as a knot or a noose. **12.** operating or functioning, as a machine. **13.** (of measurement) linear; straight-line. **14.** cursive, as handwriting. **15.** liquid or fluid. **16.** present; current: *the running month.* **17.** prevalent, as a condition, state, etc.: *running prices.* **18.** going or carried on continuously; sustained. **19.** extending or repeated continuously: *a running pattern.* **20.** performed with or during a run: *a running leap.* **21.** discharging pus or other matter. —*adv.* **22.** in succession; consecutively. [ME]

run′ning board′, (formerly) a small footboard attached to each side of an automobile beneath the doors.

run′ning broad′ jump′. See under **broad jump.**

run′ning gear′, the working components of a vehicle that are not used to develop or transmit power.

run′ning head′, *Print.* a descriptive heading on each page of a book, periodical, etc. Also called **run′ning ti′tle.**

run′ning knot′, a slipknot.

run′ning light′, any of various lights displayed by a vessel or aircraft operating at night.

run′ning mar′tingale, martingale (def. 2).

run′ning mate′, 1. a horse entered in the same race as a more important horse from the same stable. **2.** a candidate for an office linked with another and more important office, as for the vice presidency.

run·ny (run′ē), *adj.,* **-ni·er, -ni·est. 1.** tending to run or drip: *a runny paste.* **2.** (of the nose) discharging mucus.

Run·ny·mede (run′i mēd′), *n.* a meadow on the S bank of the Thames, W of London, England: traditional site of the signing of the Magna Charta by King John, 1215.

run·off (run′ôf′, -of′), *n.* **1.** something that drains or flows off, as rain water. **2.** a final contest held to break a tie.

run-of-the-mill (run′əv *th*ə mil′), *adj.* merely average; commonplace; mediocre.

run-on (run′on′, -ôn′), *adj.* **1.** of or designating something that is added or run on: *a run-on entry in a dictionary.* **2.** *Pros.* (of a line of verse) having a thought that carries over to the next line, esp. without a syntactical break. —*n.* **3.** run-on matter.

run·o·ver (run′ō′vər), *adj.* (of a shoe) having the top above the heel twisted to one side through wear.

runt (runt), *n.* **1.** an animal that is small or stunted as compared with others of its kind. **2.** the smallest or weakest of a litter, esp. of pigs or puppies. **3.** a person who is small and contemptible. [< MD: ox, cow; akin to OHG *hrint,* G *Rind,* OE *hrīdher*] —**runt′ish,** *adj.* —**runt′ish·ly,** *adv.* —**runt′ish·ness,** *n.*

run-through (run′thrōō′), *n.* the performing of a sequence of designated actions, esp. as a trial prior to actual performance; rehearsal; practice.

runt·y (run′tē), *adj.,* **runt·i·er, runt·i·est.** stunted; dwarfish. —**runt′i·ness,** *n.*

run·way (run′wā′), *n.* **1.** a way along which something runs. **2.** Also called **airstrip.** a paved or cleared strip on which planes land and take off. **3.** a similar strip on which cars, trucks, etc., may park, load, or enter the stream of traffic. **4.** the beaten track or habitual path of deer or other wild animals. **5.** a fairly large enclosure in which domestic animals may range about: *a runway for dogs.* **6.** the bed of a stream. **7.** a narrow platform or ramp extending from a stage into the orchestra pit or into an aisle, as in a theater or night club. **8.** (in lumbering) a chute or incline for moving logs.

Run·yon (run′yən), *n.* **(Alfred) Da·mon** (dā′mən), 1884–1946, U.S. journalist and short-story writer.

ru·pee (rōō pē′, rōō′pē), *n.* **1.** a nickel coin and monetary unit of India, equal to 100 naye paise. *Abbr.:* R, Re. **2.** a nickel coin and monetary unit of Pakistan, equal to 100 pice. **3.** a paper money and monetary unit of Ceylon, equal to 100 cents. [< Hindi (Urdu) *rupīyā* < Skt *rūpya* wrought silver]

Ru·pert (rōō′pərt; *Ger.* RŌŌ′peRt), *n.* **Prince,** 1619–82, German Royalist general and admiral in the English Civil War.

ru·pi·ah (rōō pē′ə), *n., pl.* **-ah, -ahs.** a paper money and monetary unit of Indonesia, equal to 100 sen. [< Hindi *rupīyā* RUPEE]

rup·ture (rup′chər), *n., v.,* **-tured, -tur·ing.** —*n.* **1.** the act of breaking or bursting. **2.** the state of being broken or burst. **3.** a breach of harmonious, friendly, or peaceful relations. **4.** *Pathol.* hernia, esp. abdominal hernia. —*v.t.* **5.** to break or burst: *to rupture a blood vessel.* **6.** to cause a breach of: *to rupture friendly relations.* **7.** *Pathol.* to affect with hernia. —*v.i.* **8.** to suffer a break or rupture. [late ME *ruptur* < L *ruptūra* = *rupt(us)* (ptp. of *rumpere* to break) + *-ūra* -URE] —**rup′tur·a·ble,** *adj.*

ru·ral (rŏŏr′əl), *adj.* **1.** of, pertaining to, or characteristic of the country, country life, or country people; rustic. **2.** living in the country. **3.** of or pertaining to agriculture. [ME < MF < L *rūrāl(is)* = *rūr-* (s. of *rūs*) the country, as opposed to the city + *-ālis* -AL[1]] —**ru′ral·ism,** *n.* —**ru′ral·ist, ru′ral·ite′,** *n.* —**ru′ral·ly,** *adv.* —**ru′ral·ness,** *n.*
—**Syn. 1.** unsophisticated, rough. RURAL and RUSTIC are terms that refer to the country. RURAL is the official term: *rural education.* It may be used subjectively, and usually in a favorable sense: *the charm of rural life.* RUSTIC, however, may have either favorable or unfavorable connotations. In a derogatory sense, it means rough, boorish, or crude; in a favorable sense, it may suggest a homelike unsophistication or ruggedness: *rustic simplicity.* —**Ant. 1.** urban.

ru′ral dean′, a cleric ranking just below an archdeacon, in charge of an archdeaconry.

ru′ral free′ deliv′ery, free mail delivery in outlying country areas. *Abbr.:* RFD, R.F.D.

ru·ral·ise (rŏŏr′ə līz′), *v.t., v.i.,* **-ised, -is·ing.** *Chiefly Brit.* ruralize. —**ru′ral·i·sa′tion,** *n.*

ru·ral·i·ty (rŏŏ ral′i tē), *n., pl.* **-ties. 1.** rural character. **2.** a rural characteristic, matter, or scene.

ru·ral·ize (rŏŏr′ə līz′), *v.,* **-ized, -iz·ing.** —*v.t.* **1.** to make rural. —*v.i.* **2.** to spend time in the country; rusticate. Also, *esp. Brit.,* **ruralise.** —**ru′ral·i·za′tion,** *n.*

Ru·rik (rŏŏr′ik), *n.* died A.D. 879, Scandinavian prince: founder of the Russian monarchy. Russian, **Ryurik.**

Rus., 1. Russia. **2.** Russian. (def. 4).

ruse (rōōz), *n.* a trick, stratagem, or artifice. [ME (n. use of obs. *rusen* to detour) < MF < *ruser* to retreat. See RUSH[1]] —**Syn.** See **trick.**

Ru·se (rŏŏ′sā), *n.* a city in N Bulgaria, on the Danube. 126,792 (1964).

rush[1] (rush), *v.i.* **1.** to move, act, or progress with speed, impetuosity, or violence. **2.** to dash, esp. to dash forward for an attack or onslaught. **3.** to appear, go, pass, etc., rapidly or suddenly. —*v.t.* **4.** to perform, accomplish, or finish with speed, impetuosity, or violence: *He rushed the work.* **5.** to carry or convey with haste. **6.** to cause to move, act, or progress quickly; hurry. **7.** to attack suddenly and violently; charge. **8.** to overcome or capture (a person, place, etc.). **9.** *Informal.* to court intensively; woo. **10.** to entertain (a prospective fraternity or sorority member) before making bids for membership. **11.** *Football.* **a.** to carry (the ball) forward across the line of scrimmage: *The home team rushed the ball a total of 145 yards.* **b.** to carry the ball (a distance) forward from the line of scrimmage: *The home team rushed 145 yards.* **c.** (of a defensive team member) to attempt to force a way quickly into the backfield in pursuit of (the back in possession of the ball). —*n.* **12.** the act of rushing; a rapid, impetuous, or violent onward movement. **13.** a hostile attack. **14.** an eager rushing of numbers of persons to some region to be occupied or exploited: *the gold rush to California.* **15.** a sudden appearance or access: *a rush of blood to his face.* **16.** hurried activity; busy haste: *the rush of city life.* **17.** a hurried state, as from pressure of affairs. **18.** press of work, business, traffic, etc., requiring extraordinary effort or haste. **19.** *Football.* **a.** an attempt to carry or instance of carrying the ball across the line of scrimmage. **b.** the act or an instance of rushing the offensive back in possession of the ball. **20.** *U.S.* a scrimmage held as a form of sport between classes or bodies of students in colleges. **21.** Usually, **rushes.** *Motion Pictures.* the first prints made after shooting a scene or scenes. **22.** *Informal.* a series of lavish attentions paid a girl by a suitor. —*adj.* **23.** requiring or done in haste. **24.** characterized by excessive business, work, traffic, etc. [ME *rusche(n)* < AF *russh(er), russ(er),* c. OF *re(h)usser, re(h)user, ruser* << LL *recūsāre,* to push back < L: to refuse. See RECUSANT] —**rush′ing·ly,** *adv.*
—**Syn. 1.** hasten, run. RUSH, HURRY, SPEED imply swiftness of movement. RUSH implies haste and sometimes violence in motion through some distance: *to rush to the store.* HURRY suggests a sense of strain or agitation, a breathless rushing to get to a definite place by a certain time: *to hurry to an appointment.* SPEED means to go fast, usually by means of some type of transportation, and with some smoothness of motion: *to speed to a nearby city.* —**Ant. 16.** sloth, lethargy.

rush[2] (rush), *n.* **1.** any grasslike herb of the genus *Juncus,* having pithy or hollow stems, found in wet or marshy places. **2.** any plant of the family *Juncaceae.* **3.** a stem of such a plant, used for making chair bottoms, mats, baskets, etc. **4.** something of little or no value; trifle. [ME *rusch, risch,* OE *rysc, risc;* c. D, obs. G *Rusch*] —**rush′like′,** *adj.*

Rush (rush), *n.* **Benjamin,** 1745–1813, U.S. physician and political leader: author of medical treatises.

rush′ can′dle, 1. a candle made from a dried, partly peeled rush that has been dipped in grease. **2.** an insignificant person or thing. Also called **rush′light′.**

rush·ee (ru shē′), *n.* a college student who is rushed by a fraternity or sorority.

rush·er (rush′ər), *n.* **1.** a person or thing that rushes. **2.** *Football.* a player whose assignment is to rush or whose special skill is rushing.

rush′ hour′, a time of day in which large numbers of people are in transit, as going to or returning from work. —**rush′-hour′,** *adj.*

Rush·more (rush′mōr, -môr), *n.* **Mount,** a peak in the Black Hills of South Dakota that is a memorial **(Mount′ Rush′more Na′tional Memo′rial)** having 60-foot busts of Washington, Jefferson, Lincoln, and Theodore Roosevelt carved into its face by Gutzon Borglum. 6040 ft.

rush·y (rush′ē), *adj.,* **rush·i·er, rush·i·est. 1.** abounding with rushes or their stems. **2.** covered or strewn with rushes. **3.** consisting or made of rushes. **4.** rushlike. [ME] —**rush′i·ness,** *n.*

rusk (rusk), *n.* **1.** a slice of sweet raised bread dried and baked again in the oven; zwieback. **2.** light, soft, sweetened biscuit. [m. Sp or Pg *rosca* twist of bread, lit., screw]

Rusk (rusk), *n.* **(David) Dean,** born 1909, U.S. statesman: Secretary of State 1961–69.

Rus·kin (rus′kin), *n.* **John,** 1819–1900, English author, art critic, and social reformer.

Russ (rus), *n., pl.* **Russ, Russ·es,** *adj.* —*n.* **1.** a Russian. **2.** *Archaic.* the Russian language. —*adj.* **3.** Russian. [< Russ *Rus′*; cf. F, G *russe*, D *rus*]

Russ (rōōs), *n.* Niemen.

Russ, Russian (def. 4).

Russ., **1.** Russia. **2.** Russian (def. 4).

Rus·sell (rus′əl), *n.* **1. Bertrand (Arthur William), 3rd Earl,** (*Lord Russell*), 1872–1970, English philosopher and mathematician: Nobel prize for literature 1950. **2. George William** (pen name: *Æ*), 1867–1935, Irish poet and painter. **3. John Russell, 1st Earl,** (*Lord John Russell*), 1792–1878, British statesman: prime minister 1846–52, 1865–66 (grandfather of Bertrand Russell). **4. Lillian** (*Helen Louise Leonard*), 1861–1922, U.S. singer and actress.

rus·set (rus′it), *n.* **1.** yellowish brown, light brown, or reddish brown. **2.** a coarse brownish homespun cloth formerly used for clothing. **3.** any of various apples that have a rough brownish skin and ripen in the autumn. **4.** a brownish, roughened area on fruit, resulting from diseases, insects, or spraying. [ME < OF *rousset*, dim. of *rous* red << L *russ(us)*. See RED] —**rus′set·ish, rus′set·y,** *adj.* —**rus′set·like′,** *adj.*

Rus·sia (rush′ə), *n.* **1.** Also called **Russian Empire.** Russian, **Rossiya.** a former empire in E Europe and N Asia: overthrown by the Russian Revolution 1917. *Cap.:* St. Petersburg (1703–1917). **2.** See **Soviet Union.**

Rus′sia leath′er, a fine, smooth leather produced by careful tanning and dyeing, esp. in dark red.

Rus·sian (rush′ən), *adj.* **1.** of or pertaining to Russia, its people, or their language. —*n.* **2.** a native or inhabitant of Russia. **3.** a member of the dominant Slavic race of Russia. **4.** the principal Slavic language, the predominant language of Russia, written in a Cyrillic script. *Abbr.:* Russ, Russ., Rus. Cf. **Byelorussian, Great Russian** (def. 2), **Ukrainian** (def. 3). [< ML *Russiān(us)*]

Rus′sian dress′ing, mayonnaise mixed with chopped pickles, chili sauce, pimientos, etc.

Rus′sian Em′pire, Russia (def. 1).

Rus·sian·ise (rush′ə nīz′), *v.t.,* **-ised, -is·ing.** *Chiefly Brit.* Russianize. —**Rus′sian·i·sa′tion,** *n.*

Rus·sian·ize (rush′ə nīz′), *v.t.,* **-ized, -iz·ing.** to make Russian; impart Russian characteristics to. —**Rus′sian·i·za′tion,** *n.*

Rus′sian Or′thodox Church′, the autocephalous Eastern Church in Russia: the branch of the Orthodox Church that constituted the established church in Russia until 1917. Also called **Rus′sian Church′.**

Rus′sian Revolu′tion, 1. Also called **February Revolution.** the uprising in Russia in March, 1917 (February Old Style), in which the Czarist government collapsed and a provisional government was established. **2.** Also called **October Revolution.** the overthrow of this provisional government by a coup d'état on November 7, 1917 (October 25 Old Style), establishing the Soviet government.

Rus′sian roulette′, a game in which each participant in turn, using a revolver into which one bullet has been inserted, spins the cylinder, points the muzzle at his head, and pulls the trigger.

Rus′sian So′viet Fed′erated So′cialist Repub′lic, the largest of the constituent republics of the Soviet Union, comprising over three-fourths of the country's total area. 136,546,000; 6,593,391 sq. mi. *Cap.:* Moscow. *Abbr.:* RSFSR, R.S.F.S.R. Also called **Soviet Russia.**

Rus′sian Tur′kestan. See under **Turkestan.**

Rus′sian wolf′hound, borzoi.

Rus′sian Zone′, a zone in Germany controlled by the Soviet Union since 1945. Cf. **East Germany.**

Russo-, a combining form of **Russia** or **Russian:** *Russophobe.*

Rus′so-Jap′an·ese War′ (rus′ō jap′ə nēz′, -nēs′), the war (1904–1905) between Russia and Japan.

Rus·so·phile (rus′ə fīl′), *n.* a person who is friendly to, admires, or prefers Russia or Russian customs, institutions, etc.

Rus·so·phobe (rus′ə fōb′), *n.* a person who hates or fears Russia or the Russians. —**Rus′so·pho′bi·a,** *n.*

rust (rust), *n.* **1.** Also called **iron rust.** the red or orange coating that forms on the surface of iron when exposed to air and moisture, consisting chiefly of ferric hydroxide and ferric oxide formed by oxidation. **2.** any film or coating on metal caused by oxidation. **3.** any growth, habit, influence, or agency tending to injure, deteriorate, or impair the mind, character, etc. **4.** *Plant Pathol.* **a.** any of several diseases of plants, characterized by reddish, brownish, or black pustules on the leaves, stems, etc., caused by fungi of the order *Uredinales.* **b.** Also called **rust′ fun′gus.** a fungus causing this disease. **c.** any of several other diseases of unknown cause, characterized by reddish-brown spots or discolorations on the affected parts. **5.** reddish yellow, reddish brown, or yellowish red. —*v.i.* **6.** to become or grow rusty, as iron. **7.** to contract rust. **8.** to deteriorate or become impaired, as through inaction or disuse. **9.** to become rust-colored. —*v.t.* **10.** to affect with rust. **11.** to impair as if with rust. **12.** to make rust-colored. [ME; OE **rust*, var. of *rūst;* c. G *Rost;* akin to RED] —**Syn. 2.** corrosion. **8.** decay, decline.

rus·tic (rus′tik), *adj.* **1.** of, pertaining to, or living in the country, as distinguished from towns or cities; rural. **2.** simple, artless, or unsophisticated. **3.** uncouth, rude, or boorish. **4.** (of stonework) having the surfaces rough or irregular and the joints sunken or beveled. See illus. at **ashlar.** —*n.* **5.** a country person. **6.** an unsophisticated country person. [late ME < L *rūstic(us)* = *rūs* the country + *-t-* connective consonant + *-icus* -IC] —**rus′ti·cal,** *adj.* —**rus′ti·cal·ly, rus′tic·ly,** *adv.* —**rus′ti·cal·ness, rus′tic·ness,** *n.* —**Syn. 1.** See **rural.** —**Ant. 1.** urban.

rus·ti·cate (rus′tə kāt′), *v.,* **-cat·ed, -cat·ing.** —*v.i.* **1.** to go into the country for a sojourn or to live there. —*v.t.* **2.** to send to or domicile in the country. **3.** to make rustic, as persons, manners, etc. **4.** to finish (a wall surface) so as to produce a rustic appearance. **5.** *Brit.* to suspend (a student) from a university as punishment. [< L *rūsticāt(us)* (ptp. of *rūsticārī* to live in the country) = *rūstic(us)* RUSTIC + *-ātus* -ATE[1]] —**rus′ti·ca′tion,** *n.* —**rus′ti·ca′tor,** *n.*

rus·tic·i·ty (ru stis′i tē), *n., pl.* **-ties. 1.** the state or quality of being rustic. **2.** a rural characteristic or mannerism. [< MF *rusticite* < L *rustic(us)* RUSTIC + MF *-ite* -ITY]

rus·tle (rus′əl), *v.,* **-tled, -tling,** *n.* —*v.i.* **1.** to make a succession of slight, soft sounds, as of parts rubbing gently one on another, as leaves, silks, papers, etc. **2.** to cause such sounds by moving or stirring something. **3.** *U.S. Informal.* to move, proceed, or work energetically. —*v.t.* **4.** to move or stir so as to cause a rustling sound. **5.** *U.S. Informal.* to move, bring, or get by energetic action. **6.** *U.S. Informal.* to steal (livestock, esp. cattle). —*n.* **7.** the sound made by anything that rustles: *the rustle of leaves.* [ME; ? < OE **hruxl(an)*, var. of *hrūxl(an)* (to) make a noise; c. RUSH[1]] —**rus′tling·ly,** *adv.*

rus·tler (rus′lər), *n.* **1.** a person or thing that rustles. **2.** *U.S. Informal.* a cattle thief.

rust·proof (rust′prōōf′), *adj.* not subject to rusting.

rust·y[1] (rus′tē), *adj.,* **rust·i·er, rust·i·est. 1.** covered with or affected by rust. **2.** consisting of or produced by rust. **3.** of or tending toward the color rust. **4.** faded or shabby. **5.** impaired through disuse or neglect; out of practice. **6.** (of a sound) grating or harsh. [ME *rusti*, OE **rustig*, var. of *rūstig*] —**rust′i·ly,** *adv.* —**rust′i·ness,** *n.*

rust·y[2] (rus′tē), *adj.,* **rust·i·er, rust·i·est.** *Chiefly Dial.* ill-tempered; cross. [appar. special use of RUSTY[1] in the sense of rough, churlish; but cf. obs. *resty* RESTIVE]

rut[1] (rut), *n., v.,* **rut·ted, rut·ting.** —*n.* **1.** a furrow or track in the ground, esp. one made by the passage of a vehicle or vehicles. **2.** any furrow, groove, etc. **3.** a fixed and dull or unpromising way of life: *to fall into a rut.* —*v.t.* **4.** to make a rut or ruts in; furrow. [? var. of ROUTE]

rut[2] (rut), *n., v.,* **rut·ted, rut·ting.** —*n.* **1.** the periodically recurring sexual excitement of the deer, goat, sheep, etc. —*v.i.* **2.** to be in the condition of rut. [ME *rutte* < MF *rut, ruit* < LL *rugītus* a roaring, n. use of L ptp. of *rugīre* to roar]

ru·ta·ba·ga (rōō′tə bā′gə), *n.* **1.** a brassicaceous plant, *Brassica Napobrassica*, having a yellow- or white-fleshed, edible tuber. **2.** the edible tuber, a variety of turnip. Also called **Swedish turnip.** [< Sw (dial.) *rotabagge*]

ru·ta·ceous (rōō tā′shəs), *adj.* *Bot.* **1.** of or like rue. **2.** belonging to the *Rutaceae*, a family of plants comprising the rue, dittany, angostura-bark tree, orange, lemon, shaddock, kumquat, etc. [< NL *Rutace(ae)* name of the family (L *rūt(a)* RUE[2] + *-aceae* -ACEAE) + -OUS]

ruth (rōōth), *n.* **1.** pity or compassion. **2.** sorrow or grief. [ME *ruthe, reuthe.* See RUE[1], -TH[1]] —**Syn. 1.** mercy, sympathy. —**Ant. 1.** cruelty.

Ruth (rōōth), *n.* **1.** the wife of Boaz, the daughter-in-law of Naomi, and an ancestress of David. **2.** a book of the Bible bearing her name.

Ruth (rōōth), *n.* **George Herman** ("*Babe*"), 1895–1948, U.S. baseball player.

Ru·the·ni·a (rōō thē′nē ə), *n.* a former province in E Czechoslovakia. Cf. **Carpatho-Ukraine.**

Ru·the·ni·an (rōō thē′nē ən), *adj.* **1.** of or pertaining to the Little Russians, esp. a division of them dwelling in Galicia, Ruthenia, and neighboring regions. —*n.* **2.** one of the Ruthenian people. **3.** the dialect of Ukrainian spoken in Ruthenia.

ru·then·ic (rōō then′ik, -thē′nik), *adj.* *Chem.* containing ruthenium in a higher valence state than the corresponding ruthenious compound. [RUTHEN(IUM) + -IC]

ru·the·ni·ous (rōō thē′nē əs), *adj.* *Chem.* containing bivalent ruthenium. [RUTHEN(IUM) + -OUS]

ru·the·ni·um (rōō thē′nē əm), *n.* *Chem.* a rare metallic element, belonging to the platinum group of metals, and only slightly reactive with aqua regia. *Symbol:* Ru; *at. wt.:* 101.07; *at. no.:* 44; *sp. gr.:* 12.2 at 20°C. [< NL, named after RUTHENIA (because it was first found in ore from the region); see -IUM]

Ruth·er·ford (ruth′ər fərd), *n.* **1. Ernest** (*1st Baron Rutherford of Nelson*), 1871–1937, English physicist, born in New Zealand: Nobel prize for chemistry 1908. **2. Joseph Franklin,** 1869–1942, U.S. leader of Jehovah's Witnesses.

ruth·ful (rōōth′fəl), *adj.* **1.** compassionate or sorrowful. **2.** causing or tending to cause sorrow or pity. [ME] —**ruth′ful·ly,** *adv.* —**ruth′ful·ness,** *n.*

ruth·less (rōōth′lis), *adj.* without pity or compassion; cruel; merciless. [ME] —**ruth′less·ly,** *adv.* —**ruth′less·ness,** *n.* —**Syn.** See **cruel.** —**Ant.** merciful.

ru·ti·lant (rōōt′ᵊlənt), *adj.* glowing or glittering with ruddy or golden light. [< L *rutilant-* (s. of *rutilāns*, prp. of *rutilāre*) = *rutil(us)* red, reddish + *-ant-* -ANT]

ru·ti·lat·ed (rōōt′ᵊlā′tid), *adj.* *Mineral.* containing fine, embedded needles of rutile. [< L *rutilāt(us)* (ptp. of *rutilāre;* see RUTILANT) + -ED[2]]

ru·tile (rōō′tēl, -tīl), *n.* a common mineral, titanium dioxide, TiO_2, usually reddish brown in color with a brilliant metallic or adamantine luster, occurring in crystals: used to coat welding rods. [< F < G *Rutil* < L *rutil(is)* red]

Rut·land (rut′lənd), *n.* Rutlandshire.

Rut·land·shire (rut′lənd shēr′, -shər), *n.* a county in central England. 23,959 (1961); 152 sq. mi. *Co. seat:* Oakham. Also called **Rutland.**

Rut·ledge (rut′lij), *n.* **1. Ann,** 1816–35, fiancée of Abraham Lincoln. **2. Edward,** 1749–1800, U.S. lawyer and statesman. **3.** his brother, **John,** 1739–1800, U.S. jurist and statesman.

rut·tish (rut′ish), *adj.* salacious; lustful. —**rut′tish·ly,** *adv.* —**rut′tish·ness,** *n.*

rut·ty (rut′ē), *adj.,* **-ti·er, -ti·est.** full of or abounding in ruts, as a road. —**rut′ti·ly,** *adv.* —**rut′ti·ness,** *n.*

Ru·wen·zo·ri (rōō′wen zōr′ē, -zôr′ē), *n.* a mountain group in central Africa between Lake Albert and Lake Edward: Highest peak, Mt. Stanley, 16,790 ft.

Ruys·dael (rois′däl, -dāl, rīz′-, rīs′-; *Du.* rœis′däl), *n.* Ruisdael.

Ruy·ter (roi′tər; *Du.* rœi′tər), *n.* **Mi·chel A·dri·aans·soon de** (*Du.* mi′кнel ä′drē än′sōōn də), 1607–76, Dutch admiral.

RV, **1.** recreational vehicle. **2.** Revised Version (of the Bible).

R/W, right of way.

R.W., 1. Right Worshipful. **2.** Right Worthy.

Rwan·da (ro͞o än′də), *n.* a republic in central Africa, E of Zaïre: formerly comprising the northern part of the Belgian trust territory of Ruanda-Urundi; became independent July 1, 1962. 4,500,000; 10,169 sq. mi. *Cap.:* Kigali.

Rx, 1. prescription. **2.** (in prescriptions) take. [< L *recipe*] **3.** tens of rupees.

-ry, var. of **-ery:** *heraldry; husbandry; dentistry; tenantry; jewelry.* [ME *-rie* < OF; short form of -ERY]

Ry., Railway. Also, **Rwy.**

ry·a (rē′ə), *n.* a handwoven rug with a thick pile, usually with a strong, colorful design. [from *Rya*, city in Sweden, where orig. produced]

Rya·zan (RYÄ zän′yə), *n.* a city in the W RSFSR, SE of Moscow. 452,000.

Ry·binsk (*Russ.* RWĒ′binsk), *n.* former name of **Shcherbakov.**

Ry·der (rī′dər), *n.* **Albert Pink·ham** (piŋ′kəm), 1847–1917, U.S. painter.

rye[1] (rī), *n.* **1.** a widely cultivated cereal grass, *Secale cereale*, having one-nerved glumes and two- or three-flowered spikelets. **2.** the seeds or grain of this plant, used for making flour and whiskey, and as a livestock feed. **3.** a straight whiskey distilled from a mash containing 51 percent or more rye grain. **4.** *Eastern U.S. and Canada.* a blended whiskey. **5.** See **rye bread.** [ME; OE *ryge;* c. OIcel *rug(r);* akin to D *rogge,* G *Roggen*]

rye[2] (rī), *n.* a gentleman: *Romany rye.* [< Gypsy *rai* < Skt *rājan* king]

rye′ bread′, bread made either entirely or partly from rye flour, often with caraway seeds; rye.

rye·grass (rī′gras′, -gräs′), *n.* any of several European grasses of the genus *Lolium,* as *L. perenne* (**perennial ryegrass**), grown for forage in the U.S.

Ryo·jun·ko (RYÔ′jo͞on kô′), *n.* Japanese name of **Port Arthur.** Also called **Ryo·jun** (RYÔ′jo͞on′).

ry·ot (rī′ət), *n.* (in India) **1.** a peasant. **2.** a person who holds land as a cultivator of the soil. [< Urdu *ra'īyat, raiyat* < Pers < Ar *ra'īyah* flock or herd, peasantry]

Rys·wick (riz′wik), *n.* a village in the SW Netherlands, near The Hague: Treaty of Ryswick 1697. Dutch, **Rijswijk.**

Ryu·kyu (*Jap.* RYO͞O′kyo͞o; *Eng.* rē o͞o′kyo͞o′), *n.* a chain of 55 Japanese islands in the W Pacific between Kyushu island and Taiwan. 1,235,000; 2046 sq. mi.

Ryu·rik (RYO͞O′RIK), *n.* Russian name of **Rurik.**

S

DEVELOPMENT OF MAJUSCULE								
NORTH SEMITIC	GREEK		ETR.	LATIN		MODERN		
						GOTHIC	ITALIC	ROMAN
W	ϟ	Σ	ㄣ	ㄣ	S	𝔖	*S*	S

DEVELOPMENT OF MINUSCULE					
ROMAN CURSIVE	ROMAN UNCIAL	CAROL. MIN.	MODERN		
			GOTHIC	ITALIC	ROMAN
ʃ	S	S	ß	*s*	s

The nineteenth letter of the English alphabet developed from North Semitic, where its form was similar to that of the modern W. Descending through Greek *sigma* (ς), which itself exhibited some variety of use (ς, σ), it acquired its present form in Latin.

S, s (es), *n., pl.* **S's** or **Ss, s's** or **ss. 1.** the 19th letter of the English alphabet, a consonant. **2.** any spoken sound represented by the letter *S* or *s*, as in *saw, east,* or *gas.* **3.** something having the shape of an S. **4.** a written or printed representation of the letter *S* or *s.* **5.** a device, as a printer's type, for reproducing the letter *S* or *s.*

S, 1. satisfactory. **2.** Saxon. **3.** *Elect.* siemens. **4.** signature. **5.** small. **6.** soft. **7.** South. **8.** Southern.

S, 1. the 19th in order or in a series, or, when *I* is omitted, the 18th. **2.** *Chem.* sulfur. **3.** *Thermodynamics.* entropy.

s, 1. satisfactory. **2.** signature. **3.** small. **4.** soft. **5.** south.

's[1], an ending used in writing to represent the possessive morpheme after most singular and some plural nouns, noun phrases, and noun substitutes. [ME, OE *-es*]

's[2], **1.** contraction of *is: He's here.* **2.** contraction of *has: He's just gone.* **3.** *Informal.* contraction of *does: What's he do for a living now?*

's[3], *Archaic.* a contraction of *God's,* as in *'swounds; 'sdeath; 'sblood.*

's[4], a contraction of *us,* as in *Let's go.*

-s[1], a native English suffix used in the formation of adverbs: *always; betimes; needs; unawares.* Cf. **-ways.** [ME, OE *-es,* orig. gen. ending]

-s[2], an ending marking the third person sing. indicative present of verbs: *asks.* [ME (north), OE (north) *-(e)s* (orig. ending of 2nd pers. sing., as in L and Gk); r. ME, OE *-eth* -ETH[1]]

-s[3], an ending marking the regular plural of nouns: *boys.* Also, **-es.** [ME *-(e)s,* OE *-as,* pl. ending (nom. and acc.) of some masculine nouns]

-s[4], a quasi-plural ending, occurring in words for which there is no proper singular: *trousers; pants; shorts; scissors; shears.* [prob. abstracted from *trousers* and *scissors*]

S., 1. Sabbath. **2.** Saint. **3.** Saturday. **4.** Saxon. **5.** (in Austria) schilling; schillings. **6.** School. **7.** Sea. **8.** Senate. **9.** September. **10.** (in the United Kingdom) shilling; shillings. **11.** (in prescriptions) mark; write; label. [< L *signā*] **12.** Signor. **13.** Small. **14.** Socialist. **15.** Society. **16.** Fellow. [< L *socius*] **17.** (in Peru) sol; sols. **18.** South. **19.** Southern. **20.** (in Ecuador) sucre; sucres. **21.** Sunday.

s., 1. saint. **2.** school. **3.** second. **4.** section. **5.** see. **6.** series. **7.** (in the United Kingdom) shilling; shillings. **8.** sign. **9.** signed. **10.** silver. **11.** singular. **12.** sire. **13.** small. **14.** society. **15.** son. **16.** south. **17.** southern. **18.** steamer. **19.** stem. **20.** stem of. **21.** *Math.* steradian. **22.** *Metric System.* stere; steres. **23.** substantive.

Sa, *Chem. Obs.* samarium.

S/A, *Com.* See **société anonyme.**

S.A., 1. Salvation Army. **2.** South Africa. **3.** South America. **4.** South Australia. **5.** *Com.* See **société anonyme.**

Saa·di (sä dē′), *n.* (pen name of *Muslih-ud-Din*) 1184?–1291?, Persian poet. Also, **Sadi.**

Saar (zär, sär), *n.* **1.** Also called **Saar′ Ba′sin, Saarland.** a territory in W West Germany, in the Saar River valley: under French economic control following World War II until 1956. 1,102,000 (1963); 991 sq. mi. **2.** a river in W Europe, flowing N from the Vosges Mountains in NE France to the Moselle River in W West Germany. 150 mi. long. French, **Sarre.**

Saar·brück·en (zär bro͝ok′ən, sär-; *Ger.* zäʀ bʀʏk′ən), *n.* a city in the Saar in W West Germany. 133,100 (1963).

Saa·re·maa (sär′ə mä′), *n.* an island in the Baltic, at the mouth of the Gulf of Riga, forming part of Estonia in the Soviet Union in Europe. ab. 60,000; 1144 sq. mi. Also, **Saa·re** (sär′ā). German, **Oesel, Ösel.**

Saa·ri·nen (sär′ə nen′, -nən), *n.* **Ee·ro** (ā′rō), 1910–61, U.S. architect born in Finland.

Saar·land (zär′land′, sär′-; *Ger.* zär′länt′), *n.* Saar (def. 1). —**Saar′land′er,** *n.*

Sa·a·ve·dra La·mas (sä′ä ve′thrä lä′mäs), **Car·los** (käʀ′lôs), 1878?–1959, Argentine statesman and diplomat: Nobel peace prize 1936.

Sab., Sabbath.

Sa·ba (sä′bə), *n.* **1.** an island in the Netherlands Antilles, in the N Leeward Islands. 1094 (est. 1960); 5 sq. mi. **2.** Biblical name, **Sheba.** an ancient kingdom in SW Arabia.

Sa·ba·dell (sä′bä thel′), *n.* a city in NE Spain, N of Barcelona. 105,152 (1960).

sab·a·dil·la (sab′ə dil′ə), *n.* **1.** a liliaceous plant, *Schoenocaulon officinale,* of Mexico, having long, grasslike leaves and bitter seeds. **2.** the seeds of this plant, used medicinally and as a source of veratrine and veratridine. [< Sp *cebadilla* Indian caustic barley, dim. of *cebada* barley < L *cibāta,* fem. ptp. of *cibāre* to feed = *cib-* feed + *-āta* -ATE[1]]

Sa·bae·an (sə bē′ən), *adj., n.* Sabean.

Sa·bah (sä′bä), *n.* a part of the federation of Malaysia, on NE Borneo; formerly a British crown colony. 454,421 (est. 1960); 29,347 sq. mi. *Cap.:* Kota Kinabalu. Formerly, **North Borneo, British North Borneo.**

Sab·a·oth (sab′ē oth′, -ōth′, sab′ā-, sə bā′ōth), *n.* (*construed as pl.*) armies; hosts. Rom. 9:29; James 5:4. [<< Heb *ç'bāōth,* pl. of *çābā* army]

Sab·a·ti·ni (sab′ə tē′nē; *It.* sä′bä tē′nē), *n.* **Raf·a·el** (raf′ē əl), 1875–1950, English novelist and short-story writer, born in Italy.

sab·a·ton (sab′ə ton′), *n.* *Armor.* a piece of mail or plate for protecting the foot. Also called **solleret.** [ME < OPr aug. of *sabat(a)* shoe. See SABOT]

Sab·bat (sab′ət), *n.* (*sometimes l.c.*) *Demonology.* a secret rendezvous of witches and sorcerers for worshiping the Devil. Also, **Sabbath.** [< L *sabbat(um)* SABBATH]

Sab·ba·tar·i·an (sab′ə târ′ē ən), *n.* **1.** a person who observes the seventh day of the week, Saturday, as the Sabbath. **2.** a person who adheres to or favors a strict observance of the Sunday Sabbath. —*adj.* **3.** of or pertaining to the Sabbath and its observance. [< L *sabbatāri(us)* (see SABBATH, -ARY) + -AN] —**Sab′ba·tar′i·an·ism,** *n.*

Sab·bath (sab′əth), *n.* **1.** the seventh day of the week, Saturday, as the day of rest and religious observance among the Jews and in some Christian churches. Ex. 20:8–11; Deut. 5:13–15. **2.** the first day of the week, Sunday, similarly observed by most Christians in commemoration of the Resurrection of Christ. **3.** (*sometimes l.c.*) *Demonology.* Sabbat. [ME, var. of ME, OE *sabbat* < L *sabbat(um)* < Gk *sábbaton* < Heb *shabbat* rest] —**Syn. 2.** See **Sunday.**

Sab′bath School′, 1. See **Sunday School. 2.** (among Seventh-Day Adventists) such a school held on Saturday, their holy day.

Sab·bat·i·cal (sə bat′i kəl), *adj.* Also, **Sab·bat′ic. 1.** of or pertaining or appropriate to the Sabbath. **2.** (*l.c.*) bringing a period of rest: *a sabbatical leave.* —*n.* **3.** (*l.c.*) See **sabbatical year.** [< Gk *sabbatik(ós)* (see SABBATH, -IC) + -AL[1]]

sabbat′ical year′, 1. (in a school, college, or university) a year of release from normal teaching duties. **2.** *Chiefly Biblical.* a yearlong period to be observed by Jews once every seven years, during which all agricultural labors were to be suspended. Lev. 25. Cf. **jubilee** (def. 6).

Sa·be·an (sə bē′ən), *adj.* **1.** of or pertaining to ancient Saba. —*n.* **2.** an inhabitant of ancient Saba. Also, **Sabaean.** [< L *sabae(us)* (< Gk *sabaîos* of Saba or Sheba) + -AN]

Sa·bel·li·an (sə bel′ē ən), *n.* a member of a group of early Italian peoples including the Samnites and Sabines. [< L *Sabell(ī)* group of Italian tribes + -IAN]

sa·ber (sā′bər), *n.* **1.** a heavy, one-edged sword, usually slightly curved, used esp. by cavalry. **2.** *Fencing.* a sword having two cutting edges and a blunt point. —*v.t.* **3.** to strike, wound, or kill with a saber. Also, *Brit.,* **sabre.** [< F *sabre* < G *Sabel* (now *Säbel*) < Magyar *szablya* < Russ < ?]

sa′ber rat′tling, a threatening display of military force or a verbal threat to use such force.

sa′ber saw′, a portable electric jigsaw.

sa·ber-toothed (sā′bər to͞otht′), *adj.* having long, saberlike upper canine teeth, sometimes extending below the margin of the lower jaw. Also, *esp. Brit.,* **sabre-toothed.**

sa′ber-toothed ti′ger, any of several extinct catlike mammals from the Oligocene to Pleistocene epochs, having greatly elongated, saberlike upper canine teeth. Also, *esp. Brit.,* **sabre-toothed tiger.**

Saber-toothed tiger, *Smilodon californicus* (Length 6 ft.; teeth to 8 in.)

sa·bin (sā′bin), *n.* *Physics.* a unit of sound absorption, equal to one square foot of a perfectly absorptive surface. [named after W. C. *Sabine* (1868–1919), American physicist]

Sa·bin (sā′bin), *n.* **Albert Bruce,** born 1906, U.S. physician, born in Russia: developed Sabin vaccine.

Sa·bine (sə bēn′), *n.* a river flowing SE and S from NE Texas, forming the boundary between Texas and Louisiana and then through Sabine Lake to the Gulf of Mexico. ab. 500 mi. long.

Sa·bine (sā′bīn), *adj.* **1.** of or belonging to an ancient people of central Italy, subjugated by the Romans about 290 B.C. —*n.* **2.** one of the Sabine people. **3.** the Italic language of the Sabines. [< L *Sabīn(us)*]

Sabine′ Lake′, a shallow lake on the boundary between Texas and Louisiana. ab. 17 mi. long; 7 mi. wide.

Sa·bin·i·a·nus (sə bin′ē ā′nəs), *n.* died A.D. 606, pope 604–606.

Sa′bin vaccine′, an orally administered vaccine of live viruses for immunization against poliomyelitis. [named after A. B. SABIN]

sa·ble (sā′bəl), *n., pl.* **-bles,** (*esp. collectively for 1, 2*) **-ble,** *adj.* —*n.* **1.** an Old World weasellike mammal, *Mustela zibellina,* of cold regions, valued for its dark brown fur. **2.** a marten, esp. *Mustela americana.* **3.** the fur of the sable. **4.** the color black, esp. as one of the heraldic colors. —*adj.* **5.** of the color sable. **6.** made of the fur or hair of the sable. **7.** very dark; black. [ME < OF < MLG *sabel,* OHG *zobel* < Slav (cf. Pol *sobol*); meaning "black" is unexplained (sable fur is brown)]

Sable, *Mustela zibellina* (Total length 28 in.; tail 9½ in.)

Sa·ble (sā′bəl), *n.* **Cape, 1.** a cape on a small island at the SW tip of Nova Scotia, Canada: lighthouse. **2.** a cape at the S tip of Florida.

sa′ble an′telope, a large antelope, *Hippotragus niger,* of Africa, with long, saberlike horns.

Sable antelope (5 ft. high at shoulder; horns 2½ ft.; length 6½ ft.)

sa·ble·fish (sā′bəl fish′), *n., pl.* **-fish·es,** (*esp. collectively*) **-fish.** a large, blackish, food fish, *Anoplopoma fimbria,* found in the North Pacific.

sab·ot (sab′ō; *Fr.* SA bō′), *n., pl.* **sab·ots** (sab′ōz; *Fr.* SA bō′). **1.** a shoe made of a single block of wood hollowed out, worn by peasants in France, Belgium, etc., and as part of the Dutch peasant costume. **2.** a shoe with a thick wooden sole and sides and a top of coarse leather. **3.** *Mil.* a soft metal ring at the base of a projectile that makes the projectile conform to the rifling grooves of a gun. [< F, perh. MF, b. *savate* old shoe (c. OPr *sabata,* It *ciabatta,* Sp *zapato*) and *bot* BOOT[1]]

sab·o·tage (sab′ə täzh′, sab′ə täzh′), *n., v.,* **-taged, -tag·ing.** —*n.* **1.** any underhand interference with production, work, etc., in a plant, factory, etc., as by enemy agents during wartime or by employees during a trade dispute. **2.** any undermining of a cause. —*v.t.* **3.** to injure or attack by sabotage. [< F = *sabot-* (< *saboter* to botch) + *-age* -AGE]

sab·o·teur (sab′ə tûr′), *n.* a person who commits or practices sabotage. [< F; see SABOTAGE, -OR[2]]

sa·bra (sä′brə, -brä), *n.* a native of Israel. [< NHeb *sābrāh*]

sa·bre (sā′bər), *n., v.,* **-bred, -bring.** *Brit.* saber.

sa·bre·tache (sā′bər tash′, sab′ər-), *n.* a case, usually of leather, hanging from long straps beside the saber of a cavalryman. [< F < G *Säbeltasche* = *Säbel* SABER + *Tasche* pocket]

sa·bre-toothed (sā′bər to͞otht′), *adj. Chiefly Brit.* saber-toothed.

sa′bre-toothed ti′ger, *Chiefly Brit.* See **saber-toothed tiger.**

sac (sak), *n.* a baglike structure in an animal or plant, as one containing fluid. [< L *sacc(us)* SACK[1]] —**sac′like′,** *adj.*

Sac (sak, sôk), *n., pl.* **Sacs,** (*esp. collectively*) **Sac. 1.** a tribe of Algonquian-speaking Indians in Iowa and Oklahoma. **2.** a member of this tribe. Also, **Sauk.**

SAC, Strategic Air Command. Also, **S.A.C.**

sac·a·ton (sak′ə tōn′), *n.* a grass, *Sporobolus Wrightii,* used in semiarid regions for pasture or hay. [< AmerSp *zacatón,* aug. of *zacate* coarse grass < Nahuatl *zacatl*]

sac·but (sak′but′), *n.* sackbut (def. 1).

sac·cate (sak′it, -āt), *adj.* having a sac or the form of a sac. [< NL *saccāt(us).* See SACK[1], -ATE[1]]

sacchar-, a learned borrowing from Greek meaning "sugar," used in the formation of technical terms: *saccharoid.* Also, *esp. before a consonant,* **saccharo-.** [< Gk *sákchar*]

sac·cha·rate (sak′ə rāt′), *n. Chem.* **1.** a salt of saccharic acid. **2.** a compound formed by interaction of sucrose with a metallic oxide, usually lime, and useful in the purification of sugar.

sac·char′ic ac′id (sə kar′ik), *Chem.* a solid or syrup, $COOH(CHOH)_4COOH$, usually made by the oxidation of cane sugar, glucose, or starch by nitric acid.

sac·cha·ride (sak′ə rīd′, -rid), *n. Chem.* **1.** an organic compound containing a sugar or sugars. **2.** a simple sugar; monosaccharide. **3.** an ester of sucrose.

sac·char·i·fy (sə kar′ə fī′, sak′ər ə fī′), *v.t.,* **-fied, -fy·ing.** to convert (starch) into sugar. —**sac·char·i·fi·ca·tion** (sə-kar′ə fə kā′shən), *n.*

sac·cha·rim·e·ter (sak′ə rim′i tər), *n.* an optical instrument for determining the strength of sugar solutions by measuring the rotation of the plane of polarized light they produce.

sac·cha·rin (sak′ə rin), *n. Chem.* a powder, $C_6H_4COSO_2NH$, produced synthetically, which in dilute solution is 500 times as sweet as sugar: used as a noncaloric sugar substitute.

sac·cha·rine (sak′ə rin, -rīn′), *adj.* **1.** pertaining to, of the nature of, or containing sugar. **2.** sweet to excess: *a saccharine dessert.* **3.** cloyingly sweet in expression or sentiment: *a saccharine smile.* —**sac′cha·rine·ly,** *adv.* —**sac·cha·rin·i·ty** (sak′ə rin′i tē), *n.*

sac·cha·rise (sak′ə rīz′), *v.t.,* **-rised, -ris·ing.** *Chiefly Brit.* saccharize. —**sac′cha·ri·sa′tion,** *n.*

sac·cha·rize (sak′ə rīz′), *v.t.,* **-rized, -riz·ing.** to convert into sugar. —**sac′cha·ri·za′tion,** *n.*

saccharo-, var. of **sacchar-** before a consonant.

sac·cha·roid (sak′ə roid′), *adj. Geol.* having a granular texture like that of loaf sugar. Also, **sac′cha·roi′dal.**

sac·cha·rose (sak′ə rōs′), *n. Chem.* sucrose.

Sac·co (sak′ō; *It.* säk′kô), *n.* **Ni·co·la** (nē kô′lä), 1891–1927, Italian anarchist, in the U.S. after 1908: together with Bartolomeo Vanzetti, was found guilty of robbery and murder, 1921; executed 1927.

sac·cu·late (sak′yə lāt′), *adj.* formed into or having a saccule, sac, or saclike dilation. Also, **sac′cu·lat′ed.** [SACCUL(US) + -ATE[1]] —**sac′cu·la′tion,** *n.*

sac·cule (sak′yo͞ol), *n.* **1.** *Anat.* the smaller of two sacs in the membranous labyrinth of the internal ear. Cf. **utricle** (def. 3). **2.** a little sac. [< L *sacc(us)* SACK[1] + -ULE]

sac·cu·lus (sak′yə ləs), *n., pl.* **-li** (-lī′). a saccule. [< L. See SACK[1], -ULE]

sac·er·do·tal (sas′ər dōt′əl), *adj.* of priests; priestly. [late ME < L *sacerdōtāl(is)* = *sacerdōt-* (s. of *sacerdōs* priest) + *-ālis* -AL[1]] —**sac′er·do′tal·ly,** *adv.*

sac·er·do·tal·ism (sas′ər dōt′əliz′əm), *n.* the system, spirit, or methods of the priesthood. —**sac′er·do′tal·ist,** *n.*

SACEUR, Supreme Allied Commander, Europe.

sa·chem (sā′chəm), *n.* **1.** (among some tribes of American Indians) **a.** the chief of a tribe. **b.** the chief of a confederation. **2.** a member of the governing body of the League of the Iroquois. [< Narragansett *sachima*] —**sa·chem·ic** (sā-chem′ik, sā′chə mik), *adj.*

Sa·cher-Ma·soch (zä′KHƏR mä′zôKH), **Le·o·pold von** (lā′ō pōlt′ fən), 1836–95, Austrian novelist.

sa·chet (sa shā′ *or, esp. Brit.,* sash′ā), *n.* **1.** a small bag, case, or pad containing scented powder. **2.** Also called **sachet′ pow′der.** the powder contained in this. [late ME < MF = *sach-* (var. of *sac* SACK[1]) + *-et* -ET]

Sachs (saks; *Ger.* zäks), *n.* **Hans** (häns), 1494–1576, German Meistersinger: author of stories, songs and dramatic works.

Sach·sen (zäk′sən), *n.* German name of **Saxony.**

sack[1] (sak), *n.* **1.** a large bag of strong, coarsely woven material, as for grain, potatoes, coal, etc. **2.** the amount such a bag can hold. **3.** *U.S.* any bag: *a sack of candy.* **4.** Also, **sacque. a.** a loose-fitting dress, fashionable esp. in the early 18th century. **b.** a loose-fitting coat, jacket, or cape. **5.** *U.S. Slang.* bed: *I bet he's still in the sack.* **6.** *Slang.* dismissal or discharge, as from a job. **7.** *Baseball Slang.* a base. **8. hit the sack,** *U.S. Slang.* to go to bed. **9. hold the sack.** See **bag** (def. 12). —*v.t.* **10.** to put into a sack or sacks. **11.** *Slang.* to dismiss or discharge, as from a job. [ME *sak,* OE *sacc* < L *sacc(us)* bag, sackcloth < Gk *sákkos* < Sem (Heb *saq*); cf. Goth *sakkus* < Gk] —**sack′like′,** *adj.*

sack[2] (sak), *v.t.* **1.** to pillage or loot after capture. —*n.* **2.** the plundering of a captured place. [< MF phrase *mettre à sac* to put to pillage, lit., to put (the loot) in the bag; *sac,* in this sense < It *sacc(o)* looting, loot, special use of *sacco* SACK[1], bag] —**sack′er,** *n.* —**Syn. 1.** spoil, despoil. See **rob. 2.** looting.

sack[3] (sak), *n.* any of various strong light-colored wines formerly from Spain, the Canary Islands, etc. [< F (*vin*) *sec* dry (wine) < L *sicc(us)* dry]

sack·but (sak′but′), *n.* **1.** Also, **sacbut, sagbut.** a medieval form of the trombone. **2.** *Bible.* an ancient stringed musical instrument. Dan. 3. [< MF *saquebute,* var. of *saqueboute* = *saque(r)* (to) pull + *boute(r)* (to) push]

sack·cloth (sak′klôth′, -kloth′), *n.* **1.** sacking. **2.** coarse cloth worn as a sign of mourning or penitence. **3. in sackcloth and ashes,** in a state of repentance or sorrow; contrite. [ME]

sack′ coat′, a short coat or jacket with a straight back and no seam at the waist. —**sack′-coat′ed,** *adj.*

sack′ dress′, a loose, unbelted dress that hangs straight from the shoulder to the hemline.

sack·ful (sak′fo͝ol), *n., pl.* **-fuls.** the amount a sack holds. [late ME]

sack·ing (sak′ing), *n.* stout, coarse woven material of hemp, jute, or the like, chiefly for sacks. Also called **sackcloth.**

sack′ race′, a race in which each contestant jumps ahead while his legs are confined in a sack. —**sack′ rac′er.** —**sack′ rac′ing.**

Sack·ville (sak′vil), *n.* **Thomas, 1st Earl of Dorset,** 1536–1608, British statesman and poet.

Sack·ville-West (sak′vil west′), *n.* **Dame Victoria Mary** ("*V. Sackville-West*"), 1892–1962, English poet and novelist (wife of Harold Nicolson).

SACLANT, Supreme Allied Commander, Atlantic.

sacque (sak), *n.* sack[1] (def. 4).

sa·cral[1] (sā′krəl), *adj.* of or pertaining to sacred rites or observances. [< L *sacr(um)* sacred thing + -AL[1]]

sa·cral[2] (sā′krəl), *adj.* of or pertaining to the sacrum. [< NL *sacrāl(is)* pertaining to the SACRUM]

sac·ra·ment (sak′rə mənt), *n.* **1.** *Eccles.* **a.** a visible sign of an inward grace. **b.** a visible sign instituted by Jesus Christ to symbolize or confer grace. **2.** (*often cap.*) the Eucharist or Lord's Supper. **3.** the consecrated elements of the Eucharist, esp. the bread. **4.** something regarded as possessing a sacred character or mysterious significance. **5.** a sign, token, or symbol. **6.** an oath; solemn pledge. [ME < eccl. L *sacrāment(um)* obligation, oath. See SACRED, -MENT]

sac·ra·men·tal (sak′rə men′tᵊl), *adj.* **1.** of, pertaining to, or of the nature of a sacrament, esp. the sacrament of the Eucharist. **2.** powerfully binding: *a sacramental obligation.* —*n.* **3.** *Rom. Cath. Ch.* an action, as the sign of the cross, or a sacred object, resembling a sacrament but instituted by the Church rather than by Christ, regarded as a means of receiving sanctifying grace. [< LL *sacrāmentāl(is)*] —**sac′ra·men′tal·ly,** *adv.* —**sac′ra·men′tal·ness, sac′ra·men·tal′i·ty,** *n.*

sac·ra·men·tal·ist (sak′rə men′tᵊlist), *n.* a person who holds strong convictions about the importance and efficacy of the sacrament.

Sac·ra·men·tar·i·an (sak′rə men târ′ē ən), *n.* **1.** a person who maintains that the Eucharistic elements have only symbolic significance. **2.** (*l.c.*) a sacramentalist. —*adj.* **3.** of or pertaining to the Sacramentarians. **4.** (*l.c.*) of or pertaining to the sacraments. [< NL *sacrāmentāri(us)* (see SACRAMENT, -ARY) + -AN] —**Sac′ra·men·tar′i·an·ism,** *n.*

Sac·ra·men·to (sak′rə men′tō), *n.* **1.** a port in and the capital of California, in the central part, on the Sacramento River. 257,105 (1970). **2.** a river flowing S from N California to San Francisco Bay. 382 mi. long.

sa·cred (sā′krid), *adj.* **1.** devoted or dedicated to a deity or to some religious purpose; consecrated. **2.** entitled to veneration or religious respect by association with divinity or divine things; venerable. **3.** pertaining to or connected with religion, as literature, music, etc. (opposed to *profane* and *secular*). **4.** reverently dedicated to some person or object: *a monument sacred to St. Peter.* **5.** regarded with reverence; revered. **6.** secured against violation, infringement, etc., as by reverence or sense of right. **7.** properly immune from violence, interference, etc., as a person or his office. [ME < *sacr-* (s. of *sacren* to consecrate) < L *sacr(āre)* (to) devote = *sacer* holy + *-āre* inf. suffix; see -ED[2]] —**sa′cred·ly,** *adv.* —**sa′cred·ness,** *n.* —**Syn. 2.** See **holy. 4.** consecrated. **6.** sacrosanct. **7.** inviolate, inviolable. —**Ant. 2.** blasphemous.

Sa′cred Col′lege of Car′dinals, official name of the **College of Cardinals.**

sa′cred cow′, any individual, organization, or institution regarded as exempt from criticism.

Sa′cred Heart′, *Rom. Cath. Ch.* the physical heart of Jesus, to which special devotion is offered as a symbol of His love and redemptive sacrifice.

Sa′cred Ro′man Ro′ta, rota (def. 3).

sac·ri·fice (sak′rə fīs′), *n.*, *v.*, **-ficed, -fic·ing.** —*n.* **1.** the offering of animal, plant, or human life or of some material possession to a deity, as in propitiation or homage. **2.** someone or something that is so offered. **3.** the surrender or destruction of something prized or desirable for the sake of something considered as having a higher or more pressing claim. **4.** the thing so surrendered or destroyed. **5.** a loss incurred in selling something below its value. **6.** Also called **sac′rifice bunt′, sac′rifice hit′, sac′rifice fly′.** *Baseball.* a hit that enables a runner on base to advance while usually resulting in the batter's being put out at first base or by a caught fly. —*v.t.* **7.** to make a sacrifice or offering of. **8.** to surrender or allow to be harmed for the sake of something else. **9.** to dispose of (goods, property, etc.) regardless of profit. **10.** *Baseball.* to cause the advance of (a base runner) by a sacrifice. —*v.i.* **11.** *Baseball.* to make a sacrifice. **12.** to offer or make a sacrifice. [ME < OF < L *sacrific(ium)* = *sacri-* (comb. form of *sacer* holy) + *-fic-* -FIC + *-ium* n. suffix] —**sac′ri·fice′a·ble,** *adj.* —**sac′ri·fic′er,** *n.*

sac·ri·fi·cial (sak′rə fish′əl), *adj.* pertaining to or concerned with sacrifice. [< L *sacrifici(um)* SACRIFICE + -AL[1]] —**sac′ri·fi′cial·ly,** *adv.*

sac·ri·lege (sac′rə lij), *n.* **1.** the violation or profanation of anything sacred or held sacred. **2.** an instance of this. [ME < OF < L *sacrileg(ium)* = *sacri-* (comb. form of *sacrum* holy place) + *leg(ere)* (to) steal, gather + *-ium* n. suffix]

sac·ri·le·gious (sak′rə lij′əs, -lē′jəs), *adj.* **1.** guilty of sacrilege. **2.** involving sacrilege. [< L *sacrilegi(um)* SACRILEGE + -OUS] —**sac′ri·le′gious·ly,** *adv.*

sa′cring bell′ (sā′kriṅg), *Rom. Cath. Ch.* **1.** a small bell rung during Mass upon the Elevation. **2.** the occasion of tolling the church bell to signify the Elevation. [ME]

sac·ris·tan (sak′ri stən), *n.* an official in charge of the sacred vessels, vestments, etc., of a church or a religious house. Also called **sac·rist** (sak′rist, sā′krist). [ME < ML *sacristān(us)* = *sacrist(a)* custodian of sacred objects + *-ānus* -AN]

sac·ris·ty (sak′ri stē), *n.*, *pl.* **-ties.** a room in a church in which sacred vessels, vestments, etc., are kept. [< ML *sacristia.* See SACRISTAN, -Y[3]]

sacro-, a combining form of **sacrum:** *sacroiliac.*

sac·ro·il·i·ac (sak′rō il′ē ak′, sā′krō-), *Anat.* —*n.* **1.** the joint where the sacrum and ilium meet. —*adj.* **2.** of, pertaining to, or affecting this joint.

sac·ro·sanct (sak′rō saṅkt′), *adj.* sacred or inviolable. [< L *sacrō sānctus* made holy by sacred rite. See SACRED, SAINT] —**sac′ro·sanc′ti·ty, sac′ro·sanct′ness,** *n.*

sac·rum (sak′rəm, sā′krəm), *n.*, *pl.* **sac·ra** (sak′rə, sā′krə). *Anat.* a bone resulting from the ankylosis of two or more vertebrae between the lumbar and the coccygeal regions, in man forming the posterior wall of the pelvis. [< L (*os*) *sacrum* holy (bone): because used in sacrifices]

sad (sad), *adj.*, **sad·der, sad·dest. 1.** feeling unhappiness or grief: *to feel sad.* **2.** expressive of or characterized by sorrow: *a sad song.* **3.** causing sorrow. **4.** (of color) somber, dark, or dull; drab. **5.** deplorably bad; sorry: *a sad attempt.* [ME; OE *sæd;* c. G *satt,* Goth *saths* full, satisfied, L *satis* enough, *satur* sated. See SATIATE, SATURATE] —**sad′ly,** *adv.*
—**Syn. 1.** unhappy, despondent, gloomy, downcast, downhearted. SAD, DEPRESSED, DEJECTED, MELANCHOLY describe states of low spirits. SAD, the general term, varies in its suggestion from a slight, momentary unhappiness to deep-felt grief or to a continuous state of pensiveness, wistfulness, and resignation: *sorrowful and sad; sad and lonely.* DEPRESSED refers to a temporary lapse in natural buoyancy because of fatigue, a disagreeable experience, or the like: *depressed by a visit to the slums.* DEJECTED, though also referring to a temporary state of discouragement caused by some definite event or circumstance, implies lower spirits, being cast down by disappointment, frustration, or the like: *dejected over losing one's position.* MELANCHOLY describes a state caused rather by temperament and a chronically gloomy outlook than by any external reason: *habitually melancholy.* —**Ant. 1.** happy.

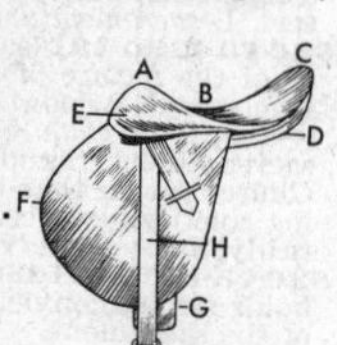

English saddle
A, Pommel; B, Seat; C, Cantle; D, Panel; E, Skirt; F, Flap; G, Girth; H, Stirrup leather; I, Stirrup

SAD, See **seasonal affective disorder.**

Sa·dat (sə dät′), *n.* **An·war el-** (än wär′ el), 1918–81, Egyptian political leader: president 1970–81; Nobel peace prize 1978.

sad·den (sad′ən), *v.t., v.i.* to make or become sad. —**sad′den·ing·ly,** *adv.*

sad·dle (sad′əl), *n.*, *v.*, **-dled, -dling.** —*n.* **1.** a seat for a rider on the back of a horse or other animal. **2.** a similar seat on a bicycle, tractor, etc. **3.** a part of a harness laid across the back of an animal and girded under the belly, to which the terrets and checkhook are attached. **4.** something resembling a saddle in shape or position. **5.** a cut of mutton, lamb, etc., comprising both loins. **6.** the posterior part of the back of poultry. **7.** a ridge connecting two higher elevations. **8. in the saddle,** in a position of authority. —*v.t.* **9.** to put a saddle on. **10.** to load or charge, as with a burden. —*v.i.* **11.** to put a saddle on a horse (often fol. by *up*). [ME *sadel,* OE *sadol;* c. G. *Sattel,* Icel *söthull;* akin to SIT]

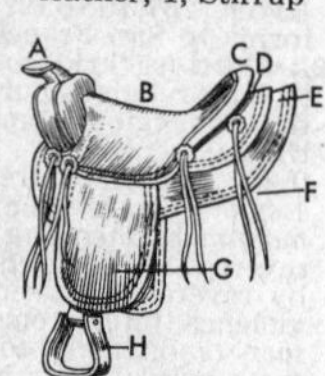

Western saddle
A, Pommel; B, Seat; C, Cantle; D, Back jockey; E, Skirt; F, Saddle strings; G, Flap; H, Stirrup

sad·dle-backed (sad′əl bakt′), *adj.* **1.** having the back or upper surface curved like a saddle. **2.** having a saddlelike marking on the back, as certain birds.

sad·dle·bag (sad′əl bag′), *n.* a large bag, usually one of a pair, hung from or laid over a saddle.

sad′dle blan′ket, a pad placed on a horse's back beneath a saddle.

sad·dle·bow (sad′əl bō′), *n.* the arched front part of a saddle or saddletree.

sad·dle·cloth (sad′əl klôth′, -kloth′), *n.*, *pl.* **-cloths** (-klôthz′, klo′thz, -klôths′, -kloths′). **1.** *Horse Racing.* a cloth placed over the saddle of a race horse bearing the horse's number. **2.** See **saddle blanket.**

sad′dle horse′. See **American saddle horse.**

sad′dle leath′er, hide, as from a cow or bull, that undergoes vegetable tanning and is used for saddlery.

sad·dler (sad′lər), *n.* a person who makes or deals in saddlery. [late ME *sadelere*]

sad·dler·y (sad′lə rē), *n.*, *pl.* **-dler·ies. 1.** saddles and other articles pertaining to the equipment of horses. **2.** the work, business, or shop of a saddler. [late ME *sadelerie*]

sad′dle shoe′, an oxford with a band of contrasting color across the instep. Also called **sad′dle ox′ford.**

sad′dle soap′, a soap, usually consisting chiefly of Castile, used for cleaning and preserving leather articles.

sad′dle sore′, an irritation or sore on a horse or rider caused by the rubbing of a saddle.

sad·dle·sore (sad′əl sōr′, -sôr′), *adj.* **1.** feeling sore or stiff from horseback riding. **2.** irritated or having sores produced by a saddle.

sad·dle·tree (sad′əl trē′), *n.* the frame of a saddle.

Sad·du·cee (saj′ə sē′, sad′yə-), *n.* *Judaism.* a member of an ancient Palestinian sect that differed from the Pharisees chiefly in interpreting the Bible literally, rejecting oral laws and traditions, and denying an afterlife and the coming of a Messiah. [back formation from ME *saddusees,* OE *sad-dūcēas* (pl.) < LL *saddūcaeī* < Gk *saddoukaîoi* < Heb *tsaddūqīm* offspring of Zadok] —**Sad′du·cee′ism,** *n.*

Sade (säd, sad; *Fr.* SAD), *n.* **Do·na·tien Al·phonse Fran·çois** (dô NA syaN′ al fôNs′ frän swa′), **Comte de** (*Marquis de Sade*), 1740–1814, French soldier and novelist, notorious for his perverted sexual activities.

sa·dhe (sä′dē, tsä′dē; *Heb.* tsä′dē), *n.* the 18th letter of the Hebrew alphabet. Also, **sa·di** (sä′dē), **tsadi.** [< Heb]

sa·dhu (sä′dōō), *n.* *Hinduism.* a holy man, esp. a monk. [< Skt, n. use of *sādhu* straight]

Sa·di (sä dē′), *n.* Saadi.

sad·i·ron (sad′ī′ərn), *n.* a solid flatiron. [SAD (in obs. sense, heavy, solid) + IRON]

sad·ism (sad′iz əm, sā′diz əm), *n.* *Psychiatry.* **1.** sexual gratification gained through causing physical pain or humiliation. **2.** any enjoyment in being cruel. Cf. **masochism.** [*sad-* (after Count D. A. F. de SADE) + -ISM. Cf. F *sadisme,* G *Sadismus,* etc.] —**sad′ist,** *n.*, *adj.* —**sa·dis·tic** (sə dis′tik, sa-, sā-), *adj.* —**sa·dis′ti·cal·ly,** *adv.*

sad·ness (sad′nis), *n.* the quality or state of being sad, unhappy, or melancholy. [ME *sadnesse*].

sad·o·mas·o·chism (sad′ō mas′ə kiz′əm, -maz′-, sā′dō-), *n.* sadism and masochism regarded as complementary aspects of a fundamental tendency that associates pleasure with the infliction of pain. [*sad-* (see SADISM) + *-o-* + MASOCHISM] —**sad′o·mas′o·chis′tic,** *adj.*

Sa·do·wa (sä′dô vä′), *n.* a village in NE Bohemia, in W Czechoslovakia: Prussian victory over Austrians 1866. Czech, **Sa·do·vá** (sä′dô vä).

sad′ sack′, *U.S. Informal.* a pathetically inept person.

Sa·far (sə fär′), *n.* the second month of the Islamic calendar. [< Ar]

sa·fa·ri (sə fär′ē), *n.*, *pl.* **-ris. 1.** an expedition for hunting, esp. in eastern Africa. **2.** any long or adventurous expedition. [< Swahili < Ar *safarī* pertaining to a journey, akin to *safara* to travel]

safe (sāf), *adj.*, **saf·er, saf·est,** *n.* —*adj.* **1.** free from hurt, injury, danger, or risk: *to arrive safe and sound.* **2.** secure from liability to harm, injury, danger, or risk: *a safe place.* **3.** involving little or no risk of mishap or error. **4.** dependable or trustworthy: *a safe guide.* **5.** avoiding danger or controversy. **6.** denied the chance to do harm; in secure custody: *a criminal safe in jail.* —*n.* **7.** a secure box, esp. of iron or steel, for storing valuable articles. **8.** any receptacle or structure for storage or preservation: *a meat safe.* **9.** *Slang.* a condom. [ME *sauf* < OF < L *salv(us)* intact, whole; see SAVE[2], SALVATION] —**safe′ly,** *adv.* —**safe′ness,** *n.*
—**Syn. 1.** protected, sound, guarded. SAFE, SECURE may both imply that something can be regarded as free from danger. These words are frequently interchangeable. SAFE, however, is applied more frequently to a person or thing that is out of or has passed beyond the reach of danger: *The ship is safe in port.* SECURE is applied more frequently to that about which there is no need to fear or worry: *to feel secure about the future; The foundation of the house does not seem very secure.* **4.** sure, reliable. **5.** wary, careful. **7.** strongbox.

safe-con·duct (sāf′kon′dukt), *n.* **1.** a document authorizing safe passage through a region, esp. in time of war. **2.** the privilege of such passage. **3.** the act of conducting in safety. [ME *sauf condut* < MF *sauf-conduit*]

safe-crack·er (sāf′krak′ər), *n.* a person who breaks open safes to rob them. —**safe′crack′ing,** *n.*

safe-de·pos·it (sāf′di poz′it), *adj.* providing safekeeping for valuables, as a vault or box in a bank. Also, **safety-deposit.**

safe·guard (sāf′gärd′), *n.* **1.** something that serves as a protection or defense or that ensures safety. **2.** a permit for safe passage. **3.** a guard or convoy. —*v.t.* **4.** to guard; protect; secure. [late ME *savegarde* < MF *salvegarde, sauvegarde*]

safe·keep·ing (sāf′kē′piṅg), *n.* **1.** the act of keeping in safety. **2.** protection or custody. [ME *safe kepyng*]

safe·ty (sāf′tē), *n.*, *pl.* **-ties** for 3–5. **1.** freedom from the occurrence or risk of injury or loss. **2.** the quality of averting or not causing injury or loss. **3.** a contrivance or device to prevent injury. **4.** *Football.* **a.** a play in which a player on the offensive team is tackled in his own end zone or downs the ball there, or in which the ball goes out of bounds on a fumble, having last been in bounds in or over the end zone and having last been in the possession of an offensive player. Cf. **touchback. b.** an award of two points to the opposing team on this play. **5.** *Baseball.* a base hit, esp. a single. **6.** *Slang.* a condom. [late ME *sauvete* < MF. See SAFE, -TY[2]]

safe′ty belt′, 1. See **seat belt. 2.** a belt or strap worn as a safety precaution by persons working at great heights.

safe·ty-de·pos·it (sāf′tē di poz′it), *adj.* safe-deposit.

safe′ty glass′, glass made by joining two plates or panes

of glass with a layer of plastic or artificial resin between to retain the fragments if the glass is broken.
safe′ty is′land, an area in the middle of a roadway for the safety of pedestrians. Also called **safe′ty zone′.**
Safe′ty Is′lands, a group of three islands in the Caribbean, off the coast of French Guiana, belonging to France. French, **Îles du Salut.**
safe′ty lamp′, a miner's lamp constructed to prevent immediate ignition of explosive gases.
safe′ty man′, *Football.* a player on defense who lines up farthest behind the line of scrimmage.
safe′ty match′, a match designed to ignite only when rubbed on a specially prepared surface.
safe′ty pin′, a pin bent back on itself to form a spring, with a guard to cover the point.
safe′ty ra′zor, a razor with a guard to prevent the blade from cutting the skin.
safe′ty valve′, **1.** a valve that opens to free confined gas or vapor exceeding a safe pressure. **2.** a harmless outlet for emotion, nervousness, etc.: *Tennis is his safety valve.*
saf·flow·er (saf′lou′ər), *n.* **1.** a thistlelike composite herb, *Carthamus tinctorius,* native to the Old World, having large, orange-red flower heads. **2.** its dried florets, used medicinally or as a red dyestuff. [< D *saffloer* < MF *saffleur* < It *saffiore* = *saf-* (< Ar *asf(ar)* yellow) + *fiore* FLOWER]
saf′flower oil′, an oil expressed or extracted from safflower seeds, used in cooking, as a salad oil, and as a vehicle for medicines, paints, varnishes, etc.
saf·fron (saf′rən), *n.* **1.** a crocus, *Crocus sativus,* having showy purple flowers. **2.** the dried, orange-colored stigmas of this, used to color confectionery and to color and flavor rolls, rice dishes, etc. **3.** Also called **saf′fron yel′low.** yellow orange. [ME *saffran, saffron* < ML *safrān(um)* (medical term) < Ar *zafarān,* akin to *asfar* yellow]
Sa·fid Rud (sa fēd′ rōōd′), a river flowing from NW Iran into the Caspian Sea. 450 mi. long.
S. Afr., **1.** South Africa. **2.** South African.
saf·ra·nine (saf′rə nēn′, -nin), *n.* *Chem.* **1.** any of a class of chiefly red organic dyes derived from phenazine, used for dyeing wool, silk, etc. **2.** Also called **phenosafranine.** a purplish-red dye, $C_{18}H_{14}N_4$. Also, **saf·ra·nin** (saf′rə nin). [< F or G *safran* SAFFRON + *-ine* -INE[2]]
SAfrD, South African Dutch (def. 1). Also, **S.Afr.D.**
saf·role (saf′rōl), *n.* *Chem.* a liquid, $C_3H_5C_6H_3O_2CH_2$, obtained from sassafras oil or the like: used in perfumery, for flavoring, and in the manufacture of soaps. Also, **saf·rol** (saf′rōl, -rôl, -rol). [(SAS)SAFR(AS) + -OLE]
sag (sag), *v.,* **sagged, sag·ging,** *n.* —*v.i.* **1.** to sink or bend downward by weight or pressure, esp. in the middle. **2.** to hang down unevenly. **3.** to droop; hang loosely. **4.** (of courage or the like) to weaken. **5.** to decline, as in price. **6.** *Naut.* **a.** (of a hull) to droop at the center or have excessive sheer. Cf. **hog** (def. 10). **b.** to be driven to leeward; make too much leeway. —*v.t.* **7.** to cause to sag. —*n.* **8.** an act or instance of sagging. **9.** the extent to which something sags. **10.** a place where something sags. **11.** a moderate decline in prices. **12.** *Naut.* **a.** deflection downward of a hull amidships, due to structural weakness. **b.** leeway (def. 1). [late ME *sagge(n),* prob. < Scand. Cf. D *zakken,* MLG *sacken,* Sw *sacka*]
sa·ga (sä′gə), *n.* **1.** a medieval Icelandic or Norse prose narrative of the achievements and events of a person or a family. **2.** any narrative of heroic exploits. **3.** Also called **sa′ga nov′el, roman-fleuve.** a form of the novel that chronicles the members or generations of a family or social group. [< Icel; c. SAW[3]] —**Syn. 2.** epic, tale, history.
sa·ga·cious (sə gā′shəs), *adj.* **1.** having or showing acute mental discernment and keen practical sense. **2.** *Obs.* keen of scent. [SAGACI(TY) + -OUS] —**sa·ga′cious·ly,** *adv.* —**sa·ga′cious·ness,** *n.* —**Syn. 1.** wise, sage, discerning.
sa·gac·i·ty (sə gas′i tē), *n.* acuteness of mental discernment and soundness of judgment. [< L *sagācitāt-* (s. of *sagācitās*) wisdom = *sagāci-* (s. of *sagāx*) wise + *-tāt-* -TY[2]]
sag·a·more (sag′ə mōr′, -môr′), *n.* a chief or great man among the American Indians of New England. [< Abnaki *sāgimo* one who overcomes]
sag·but (sag′but′), *n.* sackbut (def. 1).
sage[1] (sāj), *n., adj.,* **sag·er, sag·est.** —*n.* **1.** a profoundly wise man. —*adj.* **2.** wise, judicious, or prudent. **3.** *Archaic.* grave or solemn. [ME < OF < LL *sapidus* wise (L: tasty, tasteful) < *sapere* to know, be wise, orig. to taste; see SAPIENT] —**sage′ly,** *adv.* —**sage′ness,** *n.*
sage[2] (sāj), *n.* **1.** any menthaceous herb or shrub of the genus *Salvia.* **2.** a perennial herb, *Salvia officinalis,* whose grayish-green leaves are used in medicine and for seasoning in cookery. **3.** the leaves themselves. **4.** sagebrush. [ME *sa(u)ge* < MF *sauge, saulge* a plant < L *salvia* (so named from its supposed healing powers). See SAFE]
Sage (sāj), *n.* **Russell,** 1816–1906, U.S. financier.
sage·brush (sāj′brush′), *n.* any of several sagelike, bushy composite plants of the genus *Artemisia,* common on the dry plains of the western U.S.
Sa·ghal·ien (sä′gäl yen′), *n.* Sakhalin.
Sag·i·naw (sag′ə nô′), *n.* a port in E Michigan, on the Saginaw River. 91,849 (1970).
Sag′inaw Bay′, *n.* an arm of Lake Huron, off the E coast of Michigan. 60 mi. long.
sag·it·tal (saj′i t[ə]l), *adj.* **1.** *Anat.* **a.** of or pertaining to the suture between the parietal bones of the skull. **b.** (in direction or location) from front to back in the median plane or in a plane parallel to the median. **2.** pertaining to or resembling an arrow or arrowhead. [< NL *sagittāl(is)* = L *sagitt(a)* arrow + *-ālis* -AL[1]] —**sag′it·tal·ly,** *adv.*
Sag·it·ta·ri·us (saj′i târ′ē əs), *n., gen.* **-ta·ri·i** (-târ′ē ī′) for 1. **1.** *Astron.* the Archer, a zodiacal constellation between Scorpius and Capricorn. **2.** the ninth sign of the zodiac. See diag. at **zodiac.** [< L: archer. See SAGITTAL, -ARY]
sag·it·tate (saj′i tāt′), *adj.* shaped like an arrowhead. Also, **sa·git·i·form** (sə jit′ə fôrm′, saj′i tə-). [< NL *sagittāt(us).* See SAGITTAL, -ATE[1]]

Sagittate leaf

sa·go (sā′gō), *n.* **1.** a starchy foodstuff derived from the soft interior of the trunk of various palms and cycads, used in making puddings. **2.** See **sago palm.** [< Malay *sāgū*]
sa′go palm′, any of several Malayan feather palms of the genus *Metroxylon,* as *M. laeve* or *M. Rumphii,* that yield sago.
Sa·guache (sə wach′), *n.* Sawatch.
sa·gua·ro (sə gwä′rō, -wä′rō), *n., pl.* **-ros.** a tall cactus, *Carnegiea* (or *Cereus*) *gigantea,* of Arizona and neighboring regions, yielding a useful wood and bearing an edible fruit. See illus. at **cactus.** [< MexSp, var. of *sahuaro* < a native Ind name]
Sag·ue·nay (sag′ə nā′), *n.* a river in SE Canada, in Quebec, flowing SE from Lake St. John to the St. Lawrence. 125 mi. long.
Sa·gui·a el Ham·ra (sä′gē ə el ham′rə; *Sp.* sä′gyä el äm′rä), the former name of the N part of Spanish Sahara. 31,660 sq. mi. *Cap.:* El Aaiún.
Sa·hap·tin (sä hap′tən), *n., pl.* **-tins,** (*esp. collectively*) **-tin.** **1.** a member of an American Indian people of Oregon, Washington, and Idaho. **2.** a language used by several American Indian tribes, including the Nez Percés, of the Columbia River basin. Also, **Shahaptian.** [< Salish (NAmer) *Sahâptin(i)* (pl. of *Sáptini*)]
Sa·har·a (sə hâr′ə, -har′ə, -här′ə), *n.* a desert in N Africa, extending from the Atlantic to the Nile valley. ab. 3,500,000 sq. mi. [< Ar *çaḥra* desert] —**Sa·har′an, Sa·har′i·an,** *adj.*
Sa·ha·ran·pur (sə här′ən pŏŏr′), *n.* a city in NW Uttar Pradesh, in N India. 225,698.
sa·hib (sä′ib, -ēb, -hib, -hēb), *n.* (formerly in India) sir; master. [< Urdu < Ar *çāhib* master, lit., friend]
saice (sīs), *n.* syce.
said[1] (sed), *v.* **1.** pt. and pp. of **say.** —*adj.* **2.** *Chiefly Law.* named or mentioned before; aforesaid; aforementioned: *said witness; said sum.*
sa·id[2] (sä′id), *n.* *Islam.* sayyid.
Sa·i·da (sä′ē dä′), *n.* a seaport in SW Lebanon: the site of ancient Sidon. 24,740.
sai·ga (sī′gə), *n.* a goat antelope, *Saiga tartarica,* of western Asia and eastern Russia, having a greatly enlarged muzzle. [< Russ]
Sai·gon (sī gon′), *n.* a seaport in Vietnam, in the S part: capital of former South Vietnam 1954–76. 1,750,000. Official name, **Ho Chi Minh City.**

Saiga (2½ ft. high at shoulder; horns 9 in.; length 4½ ft.)

sail (sāl), *n.* **1.** an area of canvas or other fabric extended to the wind in such a way as to transmit the force of the wind to an assemblage of spars and rigging mounted firmly on a hull, raft, iceboat, etc., so as to drive it along. Cf. **fore-and-aft sail, square sail.** **2.** some similar piece or apparatus, as the part of an arm that catches the wind on a windmill. **3.** a voyage or excursion, esp. in a sailing vessel. **4.** sailing vessels collectively. **5.** sails for a vessel or vessels collectively. **6. make sail,** *Naut.* **a.** to set the sail or sails of a boat or increase the amount of sail already set. **b.** to set out on a voyage. **7. set sail,** to start a sea voyage. **8. under sail,** with sails set; in motion; sailing. —*v.i.* **9.** to move, as a ship. **10.** to travel by water. **11.** to manage a sailboat, esp. for sport. **12.** to begin a journey by water. **13.** to travel through the air, as a kite. **14.** to move along in a brisk, effortless way. —*v.t.* **15.** to sail upon, over, or through. **16.** to navigate (a vessel). **17. sail into,** *Informal.* **a.** to begin to act vigorously upon; take up or attack with enthusiasm. **b.** to attack verbally or physically; assail. [ME; OE *segl;* c. G *Segel,* Icel *segl;* ? = *seg-* cut (c. L *secāre,* etc.) + *-l* suffix; if so, basic meaning is piece, something cut off]

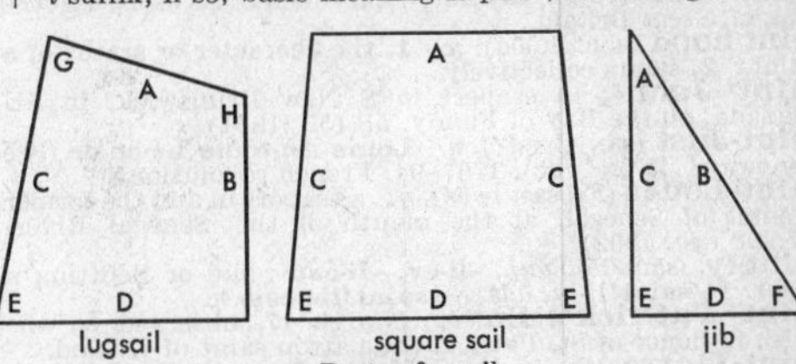

Parts of a sail
A, Head; B, Luff; C, Leech; D, Foot; E, Clew; F, Tack; G, Peak; H, Throat

sail·boat (sāl′bōt′), *n.* a boat having sails as its principal means of propulsion.
sail·cloth (sāl′klôth′, -kloth′), *n.* **1.** any of various fabrics for boat sails or tents. **2.** a lightweight canvas or canvaslike fabric used esp. for clothing and curtains.
sail·er (sā′lər), *n.* **1.** a vessel propelled by a sail or sails. **2.** a vessel with reference to its sailing qualities. [late ME]
sail·fish (sāl′fish′), *n., pl.* (*esp. collectively*) **-fish,** (*esp. referring to two or more kinds or species*) **-fish·es.** any of several large marine fishes of the genus *Istiophorus,* related to the swordfishes and having a very large, saillike dorsal fin, as *I. americanus,* found in the warmer parts of the Atlantic Ocean.

Sailfish, *Istiophorus orientalis* (Length to 11 ft.)

sail·ing (sā′ling), *n.* **1.** the activity of a person or thing that sails. **2.** any of various navigational methods for determining courses and distances. [ME *seiling,* OE *seglung*]
sail·mak·er (sāl′mā′kər), *n.* a person who makes or repairs sails.
sail′maker's palm′, palm[1] (def. 4).

sail·or (sā′lər), *n.* **1.** a person whose occupation is sailing or navigation. **2.** a seaman below the rank of officer. **3.** a flat-brimmed straw hat with a low, flat crown. [SAIL + -OR²(r. -ER¹)]
—Syn. 1. seafarer. SAILOR, SEAMAN, MARINER are terms for a person who leads a seafaring life. A SAILOR or SEAMAN is one whose occupation is on board a ship at sea, a member of a ship's crew below the rank of petty officer: *a sailor before the mast; an able-bodied seaman.* MARINER is a term now found only in certain technical expressions: *master mariner* (captain in merchant service); *mariner's compass* (ordinary compass as used on ships); formerly used much as "sailor" or "seafaring man," now the word seems high-flown or quaint: *Rime of the Ancient Mariner.*

sail·plane (sāl′plān′), *n., v.,* **-planed, -plan·ing.** **—***n.* **1.** a very light glider that can be lifted by an upward current of air. **—***v.i.* **2.** to soar in a sailplane.

sain (sān), *v.t. Archaic.* **1.** to make the sign of the cross on, as for protection against evil influences. **2.** to safeguard by prayer. **3.** to bless. [ME; OE *segn(ian)* (c. G *segnen* to bless) < eccl. L *sign(āre)* (to) SIGN with the cross]

sain·foin (sān′foin), *n.* a European fabaceous herb, *Onobrychis sativa viciae folia,* used for forage. [< F = MF *sain* (< L *sān(us)* healthy) + *foin* (< L *fēn(um), faen(um)* hay)]

saint (sānt), *n.* **1.** any of certain persons of exceptional holiness of life, formally recognized as such by the Christian church, esp. by canonization. **2.** (*usually cap.*) a designation in certain religious groups applied by the members to themselves. **3.** a person of great holiness, virtue, or benevolence. **—***v.t.* **4.** to canonize. **5.** to recognize or revere as a saint. [ME < OF < L *sanct(us)* sacred, adj. use of ptp. of *sancīre* to consecrate; r. OE *sanct* < L *sanct(us)*] **—saint′less,** *adj.*

Saint. For entries beginning with this word, see also **St., Ste.**

Saint′ Ag′nes's Eve′ (ag′ni siz), the night of January 20, superstitiously regarded as a time when a girl might see the image of her future husband.

Saint′ An′drew's cross′, an X-shaped cross; saltire. See illus. at **cross.**

Saint′ An′thony's cross′. See **tau cross.**

Saint′ An′thony's fire′, *Pathol.* any of certain skin conditions that are of an inflammatory or gangrenous nature, as erysipelas, ergotism, etc.

Saint′ Barthol′omew's Day′ Mas′sacre, *Fr. Hist.* a massacre of over 3000 Huguenots, instigated by Catherine de Médicis and begun in Paris on St. Bartholomew's Day, August 24, 1572.

Saint′ Bernard′, one of a breed of very large dogs having a massive head and long or medium-length hair, noted for their use in the Swiss Alps in rescuing travelers from the snow.

Saint Bernard
(28 in. high at shoulder)

Sainte-Beuve (saɴt bœv′), *n.* **Charles Au·gu·stin** (shärl ō gy staɴ′), 1804–69, French literary critic and poet.

saint·ed (sān′tid), *adj.* **1.** being among the saints. **2.** like a saint; saintly.

Saint-Ex·u·pé·ry (saɴ teg zy pā rā′), *n.* **An·toine de** (äɴ twaɴ′ də), 1900–45, French author and aviator.

Saint-Gau·dens (sānt gôd′ənz), *n.* **Augustus,** 1848–1907, U.S. sculptor, born in Ireland.

Saint′ George′'s cross′, the Greek cross as used in the flag of Great Britain.

saint·hood (sānt′ho͝od), *n.* **1.** the character or status of a saint. **2.** saints collectively.

Saint′ John′, a seaport in S New Brunswick, in SE Canada, on the Bay of Fundy. 55,153 (1961).

Saint-Just (saɴ zhyst′), *n.* **Louis An·toine Lé·on de** (lwē äɴ twaɴ′ lā ôɴ′ də), 1767–94, French revolutionist.

Saint-Lou·is (*Fr.* saɴ lwē′), *n.* a seaport in and the former capital of Senegal, at the mouth of the Senegal River. 47,900 (est. 1962).

saint·ly (sānt′lē), *adj.,* **-li·er, -li·est.** like or befitting a saint. **—saint′li·ly,** *adv.* **—saint′li·ness,** *n.*

Saint′ Pat′rick's Day′, March 17, observed by the Irish in honor of St. Patrick, the patron saint of Ireland.

Saint-Pierre (*Fr.* saɴ pyer′), *n.* **Jacques Hen·ri Ber·nar·din de** (zhäk äɴ rē′ ber nar daɴ′ də). See **Bernardin de Saint-Pierre, Jacques Henri.**

Saint-Saëns (saɴ säɴs′, -säɴ′), *n.* **Charles Ca·mille** (sharl ka mē′yᵊ), 1835–1921, French composer and pianist.

Saints·bur·y (sānts′bə rē), *n.* **George (Edward Bate·man)** (bāt′mən), 1845–1933, English literary critic and historian.

Saint-Si·mon (saɴ sē môɴ′), *n.* **1. Comte de,** 1760–1825, French philosopher and social scientist. **2. Louis de Rou·vroy** (lwē də ro͞o vrwa′), 1675–1755, French soldier, diplomat, and author.

Saint′ Val′en·tine's Day′ (val′ən tīnz′), February 14, observed in honor of St. Valentine as a day for the exchange of valentines and other tokens of affection.

Sai·pan (sī pan′), *n.* one of the Mariana Islands in the N Pacific, about 1350 mi. S of Japan: taken by U.S. forces June–July 1944. 7967 (1970); 71 sq. mi.

Sai·shu·to (sī′sho͞o tô′), *n.* Japanese name of **Cheju.**

saith (seth, sā′əth), *v. Archaic.* third pers. sing. pres. of **say.**

Sai·va (sī′və), *n. Hinduism.* a Bhakti sect devoted to Siva. [< Skt]

Sa·kai (sä′kī′), *n.* a seaport on S Honshu, in S Japan, near Osaka. 432,029 (1964).

sake¹ (sāk), *n.* **1.** benefit or well-being; interest; advantage: *for the sake of your soul.* **2.** purpose or end: *for the sake of appearances.* [ME; OE *sacu* lawsuit, cause; c. G *Sache* thing, Icel *sök* lawsuit; akin to Goth *sakjo* quarrel]

sa·ke² (sä′kē), *n.* a Japanese fermented alcoholic beverage made from rice. Also, **sa·ké, sa′ki.** [< Jap]

sa·ker (sā′kər), *n.* an Old World falcon, *Falco sacer cherrug,* used in falconry. Also called **sa′ker fal′con.** [ME *sagre, sacre* < MF *sacre* << Ar *ṣaqr*]

Sa·kha·lin (sak′ə lēn′; *Russ.* sä′khä lēn′), *n.* an island off the SE coast of the Soviet Union in Asia, N of Japan. 630,000 (est. 1965); 28,957 sq. mi. Also, **Saghalien.**

Sa·kha·rov (sä′kə rôf′, -rof′, sak′ə-; *Russ.* sä′khä rof), *n.* **An·drei (Dmi·tri·e·vich)** (än′drā di mē′trē ə vich; *Russ.* än drā′ dmē′tri ə vich), born 1921, Soviet nuclear physicist and human-rights advocate: Nobel peace prize 1975.

Sa·ki (sä′kē), *n.* See **Munro, H. H.**

Sak·ka·ra (sə kär′ə), *n.* Saqqara.

Sak·ta (shäk′tə), *n. Hinduism.* Shakta.

Sak·ti (shuk′tē), *n. Hinduism.* Shakti.

Sak·tism (shuk′tiz əm), *n. Hinduism.* Shaktism.

Sa·kya·mu·ni (sä′kyə mo͞on′ē), *n.* one of the names of Buddha. [< Skt: lit., hermit of the *Sākya* tribe or family]

sal (sal), *n. Chiefly Pharm.* salt. [< L]

sa·laam (sə läm′), *n.* **1.** a salutation meaning "peace," used esp. in Islamic countries. **2.** a very low bow or obeisance, esp. with the palm of the right hand placed on the forehead. **—***v.t., v.i.* **3.** to salute with a salaam. [< Ar: peace]

sal·a·ble (sā′lə bəl), *adj.* subject to or suitable for sale. Also, **saleable. —sal′a·bil′i·ty,** *n.* **—sal′a·bly,** *adv.*

sa·la·cious (sə lā′shəs), *adj.* **1.** lustful or lecherous. **2.** (of writings, pictures, etc.) obscene; grossly indecent. [< L *salāci-* (s. of *salāx*) lustful + -OUS] **—sa·la′cious·ly,** *adv.* **—sa·la′cious·ness, sa·lac·i·ty** (sə las′i tē), *n.* **—Syn. 1.** lewd, wanton, lascivious, libidinous. **2.** pornographic.

sal·ad (sal′əd), *n.* **1.** any of various usually cold dishes consisting of vegetables, as lettuce, tomatoes, cucumbers, etc., covered with a dressing and sometimes containing seafood, meat, or eggs. **2.** any herb or green vegetable, as lettuce, used for such a dish or eaten raw. [late ME *salad(e)* < MF *salade* < OPr *salad(a)* < VL **salāta* salted (fem. ptp. of **salāre* to salt). See SALT, -ATE¹]

sal′ad days′, a period of youthful inexperience.

sal′ad dress′ing, a sauce for a salad, usually with a base of oil and vinegar or of mayonnaise.

sal′ad fork′, a small, broad fork, for eating salad or dessert.

Sal·a·din (sal′ə din), *n.* (*Salāh-ed-Dīn Yūsuf ibn Ayyūb*) 1137–93, sultan of Egypt and Syria 1175–93.

Sa·la·do (sə lä′dō; *Sp.* sä lä′thō), *n.* **Rí·o** (rē′ō; *Sp.* rē′ô), a river in N Argentina, flowing SE to the Paraná River. ab. 1200 mi. long.

sal′ad oil′, an oil used in salad dressing, esp. olive oil or a vegetable oil, as from sesame, corn, or safflower.

Sal·a·man·ca (sal′ə mang′kə; *Sp.* sä′lä mäng′kä), *n.* a city in W Spain: Wellington's defeat of the French, 1812. 93,130 (est. 1963).

sal·a·man·der (sal′ə man′dər), *n.* **1.** any tailed amphibian of the order *Urodeles,* having a soft, moist, scaleless skin and typically an aquatic larval state, and living in a moist or aquatic habitat as an adult. **2.** a mythical being, esp. a lizard or other reptile, thought to be able to live in fire. [ME *salamandre* < L *salamandra* < Gk] **—sal′a·man′der·like′,** *adj.* **—sal·a·man·drine** (sal′ə man′drin), *adj.* **—sal′a·man′droid,** *adj.* **—Syn. 2.** See **sylph.**

Tiger salamander,
Ambystoma tigrinum
(Length 8 in.)

Sa·lam·bri·a (sə lam′brē ə, sä′läm brē′ə), *n.* a river in N Greece, in Thessaly, flowing E into the Gulf of Salonika. 125 mi. long. Ancient, **Peneus.** Modern Greek, **Peneios.**

sa·la·mi (sə lä′mē), *n.* a kind of sausage, originally Italian, often flavored with garlic. [< It, pl. of *salame* < VL **salāmen* = **salā(re)* (to) salt + *-men* n. suffix]

Sal·a·mis (sal′ə mis; *Gk.* sä′lä mēs′), *n.* an island off the SE coast of Greece, W of Athens, in the Gulf of Aegina: Greeks defeated Persians in a naval battle 480 B.C. 17,738 (1951); 39 sq. mi.

sal′ ammo′niac, *Chem.* See **ammonium chloride.**

sal·a·ried (sal′ə rēd), *adj.* **1.** receiving a salary: *a salaried employee.* **2.** yielding a salary: *a salaried job.*

sal·a·ry (sal′ə rē), *n., pl.* **-ries.** a fixed compensation periodically paid to a person for regular work or services. [ME *salarie* < AF < L *salāri(um)* salt money] **—Syn.** See **pay.**

Sa·la·zar (sal′ə zär′, säl′-; *Port.* sə lä zär′), *n.* **An·to·nio de O·li·vei·ra** (äɴ tô′nyo͝o də ô′lē vā′rə), 1889–1970, premier of Portugal 1933–70.

sale (sāl), *n.* **1.** the act of selling. **2.** a transfer of property for money or credit. **3.** a quantity sold. **4.** an opportunity to sell something; market. **5.** a disposal of goods at reduced prices. **6. for sale,** offered to be sold; made available to purchasers. [ME; late OE *sala;* c. Icel, OHG *sala.* Cf. SELL]

sale·a·ble (sā′lə bəl), *adj.* salable. **—sale′a·bil′i·ty,** *n.*

Sa·lem (sā′ləm), *n.* **1.** a seaport in NE Massachusetts: founded 1626; trials and executions of supposed witches 1692. 40,556 (1970). **2.** a city in and the capital of Oregon, in the NW part, on the Willamette River. 68,856 (1970). **3.** a city in central Madras, in S India. 249,100 (1961). **4.** an ancient city of Canaan, later identified with Jerusalem. Gen. 14:18; Psalms 76:2.

sal·ep (sal′ep), *n.* a starchy, demulcent drug or foodstuff consisting of the dried tubers of certain orchids. [< Turk *sālep* < dial. Ar *sa'leb,* Ar *tha'leb,* short for *khasyuth-tha'lab* fox's testicles]

sal·e·ra·tus (sal′ə rā′təs), *n.* sodium bicarbonate used in cookery; baking soda. [var. of L *sal aerātus.* See SAL, AERATE]

Sa·ler·no (sə lâr′nō, -lûr′-; *It.* sä ler′nô), *n.* a seaport in SW Italy: taken by U.S. forces September 1943. 118,171 (1961).

sales (sālz), *n.* **1.** pl. of **sale.** **—***adj.* **2.** of, pertaining to, or engaged in selling: *sales potential.*

sales·clerk (sālz′klûrk′), *n.* a salesperson in a store.

sales·girl (sālz′gûrl′), *n.* a girl who sells goods, esp. in a store.

sales·la·dy (sālz′lā′dē), *n., pl.* **-dies.** a saleswoman.

sales·man (sālz′mən), *n., pl.* **-men.** a man who sells goods, services, etc.

sales·man·ship (sālz′mən ship′), *n.* the technique of selling a product, creating interest in new ideas, etc.

sales·peo·ple (sālz′pē′pəl), *n.pl.* people engaged in selling, as the sales staff of a store.

sales·per·son (sālz′pûr′sən), *n.* a person who sells goods, esp. in a store.

sales′ promo′tion, the methods or techniques for creating public acceptance of or interest in a product.

sales·room (sālz′ro͞om′, -ro͝om′), *n.* **1.** a room in which goods are sold or displayed. **2.** an auction room.

sales′ talk′, a line of reasoning or argument intended to persuade someone to buy something.

sales′ tax′, a tax on sales or on receipts from sales, usually added to the selling price by the seller.

sales·wom·an (sālz′wo͝om′ən), *n., pl.* **-wom·en.** a woman who sells goods, esp. in a store.

Sal·ford (sôl′fərd, sô′-, sal′-), *n.* a city in SE Lancashire, in N England, near Manchester. 154,693 (1961).

Sa·li·an (sā′lē ən, sāl′yən), *adj.* of, pertaining to, or designating a Frankish people who lived in the region of the Rhine near the North Sea. [< L *Sali(ī)* tribal name + -AN]

Sal·ic (sal′ik, sā′lik), *adj.* of or pertaining to the Salian Franks. Also, **Salique.** [< ML *Salic(us).* See SALIAN, -IC]

sal·i·ca·ceous (sal′ə kā′shəs), *adj.* belonging to the *Salicaceae,* a family of trees and shrubs comprising the willows and poplars. [< NL *Salicāce(ae)* willow family (L *salic-,* s. of *salix* willow + *-āceae* -ACEAE) + -OUS]

sal·i·cin (sal′i sin), *n.* *Pharm.* a colorless, crystalline, water-soluble glucoside, $CH_2OHC_6H_4OC_6H_{11}O_5$, obtained from the bark of the American aspen: used in medicine chiefly as an antipyretic and analgesic. Also called **sal′i·cyl al′cohol glu′coside** (sal′i sil). [< F *salicine* < L *salic-* (s. of *salix*) willow + F *-ine* -INE[2]]

Sal′ic law′, **1.** a code of laws of the Salian Franks and other Germanic tribes. **2.** a law by which females were excluded from succession to the crown, as of the French monarchy.

sa·lic·y·late (sə lis′ə lāt′, -lit, sal′i sil′āt, sal′i sil′-), *n.* *Chem.* a salt or ester of salicylic acid.

sal′i·cyl′ic ac′id (sal′i sil′ik), *Chem., Pharm.* a powder, $C_6H_4(OH)(COOH)$, prepared from salicin or phenol: used as a food preservative, in the manufacture of aspirin, and as a remedy for rheumatic and gouty conditions. [SALICYL(ATE) + -IC]

sa·li·ence (sā′lē əns, sāl′yəns), *n.* **1.** the state or condition of being salient. **2.** a salient or projecting object, part, or feature. [see SALIENT, -ENCE]

sa·li·en·cy (sā′lē ən sē, sāl′yən-), *n., pl.* **-cies.** salience. [see SALIENT, -ENCY]

sa·li·ent (sā′lē ənt, sāl′yənt), *adj.* **1.** prominent or conspicuous. **2.** projecting or pointing outward. **3.** leaping or jumping. —*n.* **4.** a salient angle or part. **5.** *Mil.* **a.** the central projecting angle of a bastion. **b.** an outward projection in a battle line. [< L *salient-* (s. of *saliēns*), prp. of *salīre* to spring; see -ENT] —**sa′li·ent·ly,** *adv.* —**Syn. 1.** important, striking, remarkable. —**Ant. 1.** inconspicuous, unimportant.

sa·li·en·ti·an (sā′lē en′shē ən), *adj.* **1.** belonging or pertaining to the superorder *Salientia,* comprising the frogs and toads (order *Anura*) and extinct species. —*n.* **2.** a salientian amphibian. [< NL *Salienti(a)* leaping ones + -AN]

sa·lif·er·ous (sə lif′ər əs), *adj.* containing salt.

sal·i·fy (sal′ə fī′), *v.t.,* **-fied, -fy·ing.** **1.** to form into a salt, as by chemical combination. **2.** to mix or combine with a salt. —**sal′i·fi′a·ble,** *adj.* —**sal·i·fi·ca·tion** (sal′ə fə kā′shən), *n.*

sal·im·e·ter (sa lim′i tər), *n.* *Chem.* a salinometer.

sa·li·na (sə lī′nə), *n.* a saline marsh, spring, or the like. [< Sp < L *salīnae* saltworks]

Sa·li·na (sə lī′nə), *n.* a city in central Kansas. 37,714 (1970).

Sa·li·nas (sə lē′nəs), *n.* a city in W California. 58,896 (1970).

sa·line (sā′līn, -lēn), *adj.* **1.** of, containing, or resembling common table salt. **2.** of or pertaining to a chemical salt, esp. of sodium, potassium, magnesium, etc., as used as a cathartic. —*n.* **3.** a saline medicine. [< L *salīn(us)* salty. See SAL, -INE[1]] —**sa·lin·i·ty** (sə lin′i tē), *n.*

Sal·in·ger (sal′ən jər), *n.* **J(erome) D(avid),** born 1919, U.S. novelist and short-story writer.

sal·i·nom·e·ter (sal′ə nom′i tər), *n.* *Chem.* an instrument for measuring the amount of salt in a solution; salimeter. [*salino-* (comb. form of SALINE) + -METER] —**sal′i·nom′e·try,** *n.*

Sa·lique (sə lēk′, sal′ik, sā′lik), *adj.* Salic.

Salis·bur·y (sôlz′ber′ē, -bə rē), *n.* **1.** a city in and the county seat of Wiltshire, in S England: cathedral. 104,700. **2.** Official name, **Harare.** a city in and the capital of Zimbabwe, in the NE part. 513,000.

Salis′bury Plain′, a plateau in S England, N of Salisbury: the site of Stonehenge.

Salis′bury steak′, ground beef, shaped into a hamburger patty and broiled or fried [named after J. H. *Salisbury,* 19th-century English dietitian]

Sa·lish (sā′lish), *n.* a member of any of various American Indian peoples speaking a Salishan language. [< Salishan *sälst*]

Sa·lish·an (sā′lish ən, sal′ish-), *n.* **1.** a language family including Coeur d'Alêne and other languages of British Columbia and the northwestern U.S. —*adj.* **2.** of, pertaining to, or characteristic of this language family.

sa·li·va (sə lī′və), *n.* a viscid, colorless, watery fluid, secreted into the mouth by the salivary glands, that functions in the tasting, chewing, and swallowing of food, keeps the mouth moist, and starts the digestion of starches. [< L: spittle] —**sal·i·var·y** (sal′ə ver′ē), *adj.*

sal′ivary gland′, *Anat.* any of several glands, as the submaxillary glands, that secrete saliva.

sal·i·vate (sal′ə vāt′), *v.,* **-vat·ed, -vat·ing.** —*v.i.* **1.** to produce saliva. —*v.t.* **2.** to produce an excessive secretion of saliva in, as by the use of mercury. [< L *salīvāt(us)* (ptp. of *salīvāre* to spit). See SALIVA, -ATE[1]] —**sal′i·va′tion,** *n.*

Salk (sôlk, sôk), *n.* **Jonas E(dward),** born 1914, U.S. bacteriologist: developed Salk vaccine.

Salk′ vaccine′, a vaccine that contains three types of poliomyelitis viruses and induces immunity against the disease. [named after J. E. SALK]

salle à man·ger (SAL A mäN zhā′), *pl.* **salles à manger** (SAL A mäN zhā′). *French.* a dining room. [lit., hall for eating]

sal·let (sal′it), *n.* *Armor.* a light medieval helmet, usually with a vision slit or a movable visor. [ME, var. of *salade* < MF < Sp *celada* (or It *celata*) < L *caelāta* (*cassis*) engraved (helmet), fem. of *caelātus* (ptp. of *caelāre* to engrave); see -ATE[1]]

Sallet (15th century)

sal·low[1] (sal′ō), *adj.* **1.** of a pale, sickly, yellowish color. —*v.t.* **2.** to make sallow. [ME *sal(o)we,* OE *salo;* c. Icel *sölr* yellow, F *sale* dirty (< Gmc)] —**sal′low·ish,** *adj.* —**sal′low·ness,** *n.*

sal·low[2] (sal′ō), *n.* a willow, esp. *Salix caprea,* an Old World shrub or bushy tree used in making charcoal for gunpowder. [ME; OE *sealh;* c. OHG *salaha,* L *salix*]

Sal·lust (sal′əst), *n.* (*Caius Sallustius Crispus*) 86–34 B.C., Roman historian.

sal·ly (sal′ē), *n., pl.* **-lies,** *v.,* **-lied, -ly·ing.** —*n.* **1.** a sortie of troops from a besieged place upon an enemy. **2.** a sudden outward rush. **3.** an excursion or trip. **4.** an outburst or flight of passion, fancy, etc. **5.** a clever, witty, or fanciful remark. —*v.i.* **6.** to make a sally, as a body of troops from a besieged place. **7.** to set out on an excursion or trip. **8.** to set out briskly or energetically. **9.** (of things) to issue forth. [< MF *saillie* attack, n. use of fem. ptp. of *saillir* to rush forward < L *salīre* to leap] —**sal′li·er,** *n.*

sal′ly lunn′ (lun), a slightly sweetened teacake. Also, **Sal′ly Lunn′.** [named after a woman who sold them in Bath, England, at the end of the 18th century]

sal′ly port′, (in a fort or the like) **1.** a gateway permitting the passage of a large number of troops at a time. **2.** a postern.

Sal·ma·cis (sal′mə sis), *n.* *Class. Myth.* See under **Hermaphroditus.**

sal·ma·gun·di (sal′mə gun′dē), *n.* **1.** a mixed dish consisting of chopped meat, anchovies, eggs, onions, oil, etc., often served as a salad. **2.** a stew of meat and vegetables. **3.** any mixture or miscellany. [< F *salmigondis,* perh. < It *salami conditi* pickled SALAMI; see CONDIMENT]

sal·mi (sal′mē), *n.* a ragout of partially cooked game, as pheasant or woodcock, stewed in wine and butter. [< F, short for *salmigondis* SALMAGUNDI]

sal·mis (sal′mē; *Fr.* SAL mē′), *n., pl.* **-mis** (-mē; *Fr.* -mē′). salmi.

salm·on (sam′ən), *n., pl.* **-ons,** (*esp. collectively*) **-on.** **1.** a marine and fresh-water food fish, *Salmo salar,* of the family *Salmonidae,* having pink flesh, found off the North Atlantic coasts of Europe and North America, near the mouths of large rivers where it ascends to spawn. **2.** See **landlocked salmon.** **3.** any of several salmonoid food fishes of the genus *Oncorhynchus,* found in the North Pacific. **4.** light yellowish-pink. [ME *salmoun, samoun* < AF (c. OF *saumon*) < L *salmōn-,* s. of *salmō*]

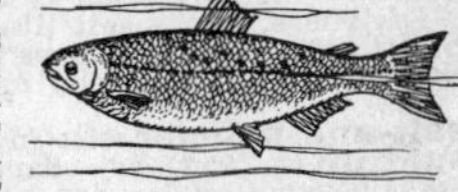

Chinook salmon,
Oncorhynchus tshawytscha
(Length to 6 ft.)

salm·on·ber·ry (sam′ən ber′ē), *n., pl.* **-ries.** **1.** the salmon-colored, edible fruit of a raspberry, *Rubus spectabilis,* of the Pacific coast of North America. **2.** the plant itself.

sal·mo·nel·la (sal′mə nel′ə), *n., pl.* **-nel·lae** (-nel′ē). *Bacteriol.* any of several rod-shaped, facultatively anaerobic bacteria of the genus *Salmonella,* as *S. typhosa,* that are pathogenic for man and warm-blooded animals. [< NL; named after Daniel E. *Salmon* (d. 1914), American veterinarian]

sal·mo·noid (sal′mə noid′), *adj.* **1.** resembling a salmon. **2.** belonging or pertaining to the suborder *Salmonoidea,* to which the salmon family belongs. —*n.* **3.** a salmonoid fish. [< NL *Salmōnoid(ea)* suborder of fishes. See SALMON -OID]

salm′on pink′, salmon (def. 4).

Sal′mon Riv′er Moun′tains, a range in central Idaho. Highest peak, 10,340 ft.

salm′on trout′, a European trout, *Salmo trutta.*

sal·ol (sal′ōl, -ôl, -ol), *n.* *Pharm.* a crystalline powder, $HOC_6H_4COOC_6H_5$: used as a preservative, an absorber of light in suntan preparations, as an antipyretic, antiseptic, and as a coating for pills in which the medicament is intended for enteric release. Also called **phenyl salicylate.** [formerly trademark]

Sa·lo·me (sə lō′mē, sə lō′mā), *n.* the daughter of Herodias, who danced for Herod Antipas and so pleased him that he granted her request for the head of John the Baptist. Matt. 14:6–10. Also, **Sa·lo′mé.**

Sal·o·mon (sal′ə mən), *n.* **Haym** (hīm), 1740?–85, American financier and patriot, born in Poland.

sa·lon (sə lon′; *Fr.* SA lôN′), *n., pl.* **-lons** (-lonz′; *Fr.* -lôN′). **1.** a drawing room or reception room in a large house. **2.** an assembly of guests in such a room, esp. the leaders in society, art, politics, etc. **3.** a hall used for the exhibition of works of art or the exhibition itself. **4.** a shop or business establishment for a product or service chiefly related to fashion or stylishness: *a dress salon; a shoe salon.* [< F < It *salone* aug. of *sala* hall < Gmc; cf. G *Saal,* OE *sæl,* etc.]

Sa·lo·ni·ka (sal′ə nē′kə, sə lon′ə kə), *n.* **1.** Also, **Sa·lon·i·ca** (sə lon′ə kə), **Sa·lo·ni·ki** (sä′lô nē′kē). Ancient, **Thessalonica, Therma.** Official name, **Thessaloníke.** a seaport in south-central Macedonia, in NE Greece, on the Gulf of Salonika. 250,920 (1961). **2. Gulf of,** an arm of the Aegean, in NE Greece. 70 mi. long.

sa·loon (sə lo͞on′), *n.* **1.** *U.S.* a place for the sale and consumption of alcoholic drinks. **2.** a room or place for general use for a specific purpose, as on a passenger ship. **3.** *Brit.* **a.** (in a tavern or pub) a section of a bar or barroom separated from the public bar and often having more comfortable furnishings and a quieter atmosphere. **b.** See **saloon car.** **4.** a drawing room or reception room. [var. of SALON]

saloon′ car′, *Brit.* **1.** Also called **saloon′ car′riage.** a railway sleeping, dining, or parlor car similar to a U.S. Pullman. **2.** sedan (def. 1).
sa·loop (sə lo͞op′), *n.* a hot drink of sassafras, milk, and sugar. [var. of SALEP]
Sal·op (sal′əp), *n.* Shropshire (def. 1). —**Sa·lo·pi·an** (sə-lō′pē ən), *adj., n.*
sal·pa (sal′pə), *n., pl.* **-pas, -pae** (-pē). any free-swimming oceanic tunicate of the genus *Salpa,* having a transparent, more or less fusiform body. [< NL, special use of L *salpa* < Gk *sálpē* kind of fish] —**sal·pi·form** (sal′pə fôrm′), *adj.*
sal·pin·gec·to·my (sal′pin jek′tə mē), *n., pl.* **-mies.** *Surg.* excision of the Fallopian tube. [< Gk *salping-* (s. of *sálpinx*) trumpet + -ECTOMY]
sal·pin·gi·tis (sal′pin jī′tis), *n. Pathol.* inflammation of a Fallopian tube or of a Eustachian tube. [< Gk *salping-* (see SALPINGECTOMY) + -ITIS] —**sal·pin·git·ic** (sal′pin jit′ik), *adj.*
sal·pinx (sal′piŋgks), *n., pl.* **sal·pin·ges** (sal pin′jēz). *Anat.* a trumpet-shaped tube, as a Fallopian or Eustachian tube. [< Gk: trumpet] —**sal·pin·gi·an** (sal pin′jē ən), *adj.*
sal·sa (säl′sə, sal′-; *Sp.* säl′sä), *n., pl.* **-sas** (-səz; *Sp.* -säs). **1.** a lively, vigorous type of contemporary Latin American popular music, blending predominantly Cuban rhythms with elements of jazz, rock, and soul music. **2.** a dance, similar to the mambo, performed to this music. [< Sp: lit., sauce, gravy]
sal·si·fy (sal′sə fē), *n., pl.* **-fies.** a purple-flowered plant, *Tragopogon porrifolius,* whose root has an oysterlike flavor and is used as a vegetable. Also called **oyster plant.** [< F *salsifi(s),* var. of *sassefy, sassef(f)ique* < It *sassef(r)ica* < ?]
sal′ so′da. See **sodium carbonate** (def. 2).
salt (sôlt), *n.* **1.** a crystalline compound, sodium chloride, NaCl, occurring as a mineral, a constituent of sea water, etc., and used for seasoning food, as a preservative, etc. **2.** *Chem.* any of a class of compounds that are formed by the replacement of one or more hydrogen atoms of an acid with elements or groups and that usually ionize in solution; a product formed by the neutralization of an acid by a base. **3. salts,** any of various salts used as purgatives, as Epsom salts. **4.** an element, as wit, that gives liveliness, piquancy, etc. **5.** a small, usually open dish used on the table for holding salt. **6.** *Informal.* a sailor, esp. an old or experienced one. **7. with a grain of salt,** with skepticism. **8. worth one's salt,** deserving of one's wages or salary. —*v.t.* **9.** to season, cure, preserve, or treat with salt. **10.** to furnish with salt: *to salt cattle.* **11.** to introduce rich ore or the like into (a mineral deposit) in order to give a false idea of its value. **12. salt away,** *Informal.* to keep in reserve. —*adj.* **13.** containing or having the taste of salt. **14.** producing one of the four basic taste sensations; not sweet, sour, or bitter. **15.** cured or preserved with salt. **16.** inundated by or growing in salt water: *salt marsh.* [ME; OE *sealt;* c. G *Salz,* Icel, Goth *salt,* L *sal*] —**salt′less,** *adj.* —**salt′like′,** *adj.* —**salt′ness,** *n.*
SALT (sôlt), Strategic Arms Limitation Talks.
Sal·ta (säl′tä), *n.* a city in NW Argentina. 121,491 (est. 1965).
salt-and-pep·per (sôlt′ᵊn pep′ər), *adj.* pepper-and-salt.
sal·tant (sal′tᵊnt), *adj.* dancing, leaping, or jumping. [< L *saltant-* (s. of *saltāns,* prp. of *saltāre* to jump about, dance, freq. of *salīre* to leap) = *sal-* jump + *-t-* freq. suffix + *-ant-* -ANT]
sal·ta·rel·lo (sal′tə rel′ō, sôl′-; *It.* säl′tä rel′lô), *n., pl.* **-los,** *It.* **-li** (-lē). a lively Italian dance for one person or a couple. [< It = *saltar(e)* < L *saltāre,* freq. of *salīre* to leap) + *-ello* dim. suffix]
sal·ta·tion (sal tā′shən), *n.* **1.** dancing; leaping. **2.** an abrupt movement or transition. **3.** *Biol.* a mutation. [< L *saltātiōn-* (s. of *saltātiō*) a dancing = *saltāt(us)* (ptp. of *saltāre;* see SALTARELLO) + *-iōn-* -ION]
sal·ta·to·ri·al (sal′tə tôr′ē əl, -tôr′-), *adj.* **1.** pertaining to saltation. **2.** *Zool.* characterized by or adapted for leaping. [SALTATORY + -AL[1]]
sal·ta·to·ry (sal′tə tôr′ē, -tôr′ē), *adj.* **1.** pertaining to or adapted for saltation. **2.** proceeding by abrupt movements. [< L *saltātōri(us)* = *saltātor* dancer + *-ius* adj. suffix]
salt·box (sôlt′boks′), *n.* **1.** a box in which salt is kept. **2.** a type of house found in New England, usually two stories high in front and having a gable roof continued downward to cover a low rear section. Also, **salt′box′.**
salt′ cake′, *Chem.* an impure form of sodium sulfate.
salt·cel·lar (sôlt′sel′ər), *n.* a shaker or dish for salt. [r. ME *saler* < OF *saliere* salt holder < L *salāria,* n. use of fem. of *salārius* (adj.) pertaining to salt. See SAL, -ARY]
salt·ed (sôl′tid), *adj.* seasoned, cured, or otherwise treated with salt. [ME]
salt·er (sôl′tər), *n.* **1.** a person who makes or sells salt. **2.** a person who salts meat, fish, etc. [ME; OE *sealtere* saltmaker]
salt·ern (sôl′tərn), *n.* **1.** a saltworks. **2.** a plot of land laid out in pools for the evaporation of sea water to produce salt. [OE *sealtærn* saltworks = *sealt* SALT + *ærn* house]
salt′ grass′, any of several grasses, as *Distichlis spicata,* that grow in salt marshes or meadows or in alkali soil.
salt·i·er[1] (sôl′tē ər), *adj.* comparative of **salty.**
sal·tier[2] (sal′tēr, -tiᵊr), *n.* saltire.
sal·ti·grade (sal′tə grād′), *adj.* **1.** moving by leaping. **2.** of or belonging to the family *Salticidae,* comprising the jumping spiders. [*salti-* comb. form of L *saltus* leap + -GRADE]
Sal·til·lo (säl tē′yō), *n.* a city in and the capital of Coahuila, in northern Mexico. 117,827 (est. 1965).
sal·tine (sôl tēn′), *n.* a crisp, salted cracker.
sal·tire (sal′tir, -tiᵊr, sôl′-), *n. Heraldry.* **1.** an ordinary in the form of a cross with arms running diagonally; Saint Andrew's cross. **2. in saltire,** (of charges) arranged in the form of a saltire. **3. per saltire,** diagonally in both directions: *party per saltire.* Also, **saltier.** [late ME *sawtire* < MF *sautoir* crossed jumping bar << L *saltātōr(ium)* something pertaining to jumping; see SALTATORY]
sal·tire·wise (sal′tir wīz′, -tiᵊr, sôl′-), *adv. Heraldry.* in the direction or manner of a saltire. Also, **sal·tire·ways** (sal′-tir wāz′, -tiᵊr-, sôl′-).
salt′ lake′, a body of water having no outlet to the sea and containing in solution a high concentration of salts, esp. sodium chloride.
Salt′ Lake′ Cit′y, a city in and the capital of Utah, in the N part, near the Great Salt Lake. 175,885 (1970).
salt′ lick′, **1.** a place to which wild animals go to lick natural salt deposits. **2.** a large block of salt placed in a field, barnyard, etc., for farm animals to lick.
salt′ marsh′, a marshy tract that is wet with salt water or flooded by the sea. [ME *saltmerche,* OE *sealtne mersc*]
Sal·to (säl′tô), *n.* a city in NW Uruguay, on the Uruguay River. 44,900 (est. 1954).
salt′ of the earth′, an individual or group considered as representative of the best or noblest elements of society.
Sal′ton Sea′ (sôl′tən, -tᵊn), a shallow saline lake in S California, in the Imperial Valley, formed by the diversion of water from the Colorado River into a salt-covered depression **(Sal′ton Sink′).** 236 ft. below sea level.
salt·pe·ter (sôlt′pē′tər), *n.* **1.** the form of potassium nitrate, KNO_3, that occurs naturally: used in the manufacture of fireworks, gunpowder, etc.; niter. **2.** See **Chile saltpeter.** Also, **salt′pe′tre.** [earlier *salt peter;* r. ME *sal peter, salpetre* < ML *salpetrē,* L *sal petrae* salt of rock]
salt′ pork′, pork cured with salt, esp. the fat pork taken from the back, sides, and belly.
salt′-ris·ing bread′ (sôlt′rī′ziŋ), a kind of bread leavened with a fermented mixture of salted milk, corn meal, flour, sugar, and soda.
Salt′ Riv′er, a river flowing W from E Arizona to the Gila River near Phoenix: Roosevelt Dam. 200 mi. long.
salt′ stick′, a crusty bread roll sprinkled with salt crystals, made in the shape of a cylinder tapered at the ends by rolling up a triangular piece of dough.
salt′ wa′ter, **1.** water containing a large amount of salt. **2.** ocean or sea water. [ME *saltwater,* OE *sealter wæter*]
salt·wa·ter (sôlt′wô′tər, -wot′ər), *adj.* **1.** of or pertaining to salt water. **2.** inhabiting salt water: *a saltwater fish.*
salt·works (sôlt′wûrks′), *n., pl.* **-works.** (*often construed as pl.*) a building or plant where salt is made.
salt·wort (sôlt′wûrt′), *n.* any of various plants of sea beaches, salt marshes, and alkaline regions, esp. of the genus *Salsola,* as *S. Kali,* a bushy plant having prickly leaves, or of the genus *Salicornia.* [trans. of D *zoutkruid.* See SALT, WORT[2]]
salt·y (sôl′tē), *adj.,* **salt·i·er, salt·i·est.** **1.** tasting of or containing salt; saline. **2** piquant or sharp; witty; racy. **3.** of the sea, sailing, or life at sea. [late ME] —**salt′i·ly,** *adv.* —**salt′i·ness,** *n.*
sa·lu·bri·ous (sə lo͞o′brē əs), *adj.* favorable to or promoting health; healthful. [< L *salūbr(is)* + -IOUS] —**sa·lu′bri·ous·ly,** *adv.* —**sa·lu′bri·ous·ness, sa·lu·bri·ty** (sə lo͞o′bri tē), *n.*
Sa·lu·ki (sə lo͞o′kē), *n.* (*sometimes l.c.*) one of a breed of black and tan, white, gold, or tricolor dogs resembling the greyhound and having fringes of long hair on the ears, legs, and thighs, raised originally in Egypt and southwestern Asia. [< Ar *salūqī,* lit., of *Salūq* old city in Arabia]

Saluki
(2 ft. high at shoulder)

sal·u·tar·y (sal′yə ter′ē), *adj.* **1.** favorable to or promoting health. **2.** promoting or conducive to some beneficial purpose. [< L *salūtāri(s).* See SALUTE, -ARY] —**sal·u·tar·i·ly** (sal′yə ter′ə lē, sal′yə târ′-), *adv.* —**sal′u·tar′i·ness,** *n.* —**Syn. 1.** See **healthy.**
sal·u·ta·tion (sal′yə tā′shən), *n.* **1.** the act of saluting. **2.** something uttered, written, or done by way of saluting. **3.** a word or phrase serving as the prefatory greeting in a letter or speech, as *Dear Sir* or *Ladies and Gentlemen.* [< L *salūtātiōn-* (s. of *salūtātiō*) greeting = *salūtāt(us)* (ptp. of *salūtāre* to greet; see SALUTE, -ATE[1]) + *-iōn-* -ION]
sa·lu·ta·to·ri·an (sə lo͞o′tə tôr′ē ən, -tôr′-), *n.* the student ranking second highest in a graduating class, who delivers the salutatory.
sa·lu·ta·to·ry (sə lo͞o′tə tôr′ē, -tôr′ē), *adj., n., pl.* **-ries.** —*adj.* **1.** pertaining to or of the nature of a salutation. —*n.* **2.** a welcoming address, esp. one given at a high-school or college commencement by the salutatorian. [< ML *salūtātōri(us).* See SALUTATION, -ORY[1]] —**sa·lu′ta·to′ri·ly,** *adv.*
sa·lute (sə lo͞ot′), *v.* **-lut·ed, -lut·ing,** *n.* —*v.t.* **1.** to address with expressions of good will, respect, etc.; greet. **2.** to make a bow or other gesture to, as in greeting, farewell, or respect. **3.** *Mil.* to pay respect to or honor by some formal act, as by raising the right hand to the head, presenting arms, firing cannon, dipping colors, etc. —*v.i.* **4.** to perform a salute or greeting. **5.** *Mil.* to give a salute. —*n.* **6.** an act of saluting or greeting. **7** *Mil.* **a.** the act of saluting. **b.** the position of the hand or rifle in saluting. [ME < L *salūt(āre)* (to) greet (lit., to hail) < *salūt-* (s. of *salūs*) health; r. *salue* < F *salue(r)* < L *salūtāre*] —**sa·lut′er,** *n.*
Salv., Salvador.
salv·a·ble (sal′və bəl), *adj.* fit for or capable of being saved or salvaged. [< LL *salv(āre)* (to) SAVE[1] + -ABLE] —**sal′va·bil′i·ty, sal′va·ble·ness,** *n.* —**sal′va·bly,** *adv.*
Sal·va·dor (sal′və dôr′; *for 1 also Sp.* säl′vä ᵺôr′; *for 2 also Port.* sal′və dôr′), *n.* **1.** See **El Salvador. 2.** official name of **São Salvador.**
sal·vage (sal′vij), *n., v.,* **-vaged, -vag·ing.** —*n.* **1.** the act of saving a ship or its cargo from perils of the seas. **2.** the act of saving any property from destruction. **3.** the property so saved. **4.** compensation given to those who voluntarily save a ship or its cargo. **5.** the value or proceeds upon sale of goods recovered from a fire. —*v.t.* **6.** to save from shipwreck, fire, etc. [< OF; see SAVE[1], -AGE]
sal·va·tion (sal vā′shən), *n.* **1.** the act of saving or protecting from harm or loss. **2.** the state of being thus saved or protected. **3.** a means of being thus saved or protected. **4.** *Theol.* deliverance from the power and penalty of sin; redemption. [ME *salvatio(u)n* < LL *salvātiōn-* (s. of *salvātiō*) = *salvāt(us)* (ptp. of *salvāre* to SAVE[1]; see ATE[1]) + *-iōn-* -ION; r. ME *sa(u)vaciun,* etc. < OF < L] —**sal·va′tion·al,** *adj*
Salva′tion Ar′my, an international charitable and evangelistic Christian organization founded in England in 1865 by William Booth and organized along quasi-military lines.
sal·va·tion·ist (sal vā′shə nist), *n.* **1.** a person who preaches salvation, deliverance from sin, etc. **2.** (*cap.*) a member of the Salvation Army. —**sal·va′tion·ism,** *n.*

salve[1] (sav, säv), *n., v.,* **salved, salv·ing.** —*n.* **1.** a medicinal ointment for healing or relieving wounds and sores. **2.** anything that soothes, mollifies, or relieves. —*v.t.* **3.** to soothe with or as with salve. [ME; OE *sealf;* c. G *Salbe* salve, Skt *sarpis* melted butter, etc.]

salve[2] (salv), *v.i., v.t.,* **salved, salv·ing.** to save from loss or destruction; salvage. [back formation from SALVAGE]

sal·ver (sal′vər), *n.* a tray, esp. one used for serving food, beverages, etc. [< Sp *salv(a)* kind of tray (orig. protective foretasting < *salvar* to save < L *salvāre*) + -ER[1]]

sal·ver·form (sal′vər fôrm′), *adj. Bot.* tubular with a flat, expanded limb, as certain gamopetalous corollas.

sal·vi·a (sal′vē ə), *n.* any plant of the genus *Salvia,* comprising the sages. [< NL, L: sage]

sal·vo[1] (sal′vō), *n., pl.* **-vos, -voes. 1.** a discharge of artillery or other firearms in regular succession, often performed as a salute. **2.** a round of cheers, applause, etc. [earlier *salva* < It < F *salve* < L *salvē* hail, greetings]

sal·vo[2] (sal′vō), *n., pl.* **-vos.** *Archaic.* **1.** an excuse or quibbling evasion. **2.** something to save a person's reputation or soothe his feelings. [< L *salvō,* abl. of *salvus* safe, found in legal phrases]

sal vol′atile, 1. See **ammonium carbonate. 2.** an aromatic alcoholic solution of ammonium carbonate. [< NL: volatile salt]

sal·vor (sal′vər), *n.* a person who salvages or helps to salvage a ship, cargo, etc. [SALV(AGE) + -OR[2]]

Sal·ween (sal′wēn′), *n.* a river in SE Asia, flowing S from SW China through Burma to Bay of Bengal. 1750 mi. long.

Salz·burg (sôlz′bûrg; *Ger.* zälts′bŏŏrk), *n.,* a city in W Austria: the birthplace of Mozart. 106,892 (1961).

SAM (sam), *n.* **1.** a special air service for sending parcels weighing up to 15 pounds to overseas servicemen: only the regular parcel-post rate to the U.S. port of shipment is charged. Cf. **PAL.** [*S(pace) A(vailable) M(ail)*] **2.** surface-to-air missile.

Sam., *Bible.* Samuel.

S.Am., 1. South America. **2.** South American.

A B C

Samara
A, White ash, *Fraxinus americana;* B, Ashleaf maple, *Acer negundo;* C, Hoptree, *Ptelea trifoliata*

Sa·ma′na Cay′ (sə mä′nə), a small, uninhabited island in central Bahamas: possibly first land in New World seen by Christopher Columbus 1492. 9 mi. long.

Sa·mar (sä′mär), *n.* an island in the E Philippines. 945,300; 5309 sq. mi.

sam·a·ra (sam′ər ə, sə mâr′ə), *n. Bot.* an indehiscent, usually one-seeded, winged fruit, as of the elm or maple. [< NL, special use of L: elm seed]

Sa·ma·ra (sə mär′ə; *Russ.* sä mä′rə), *n.* former name of **Kuibyshev.**

Sa·ma·rang (sə mä′räng), *n.* Semarang.

Sa·mar·i·a (sə mâr′ē ə), *n.* **1.** a district in ancient Palestine: later part of the Roman province of Syria; taken by Jordan 1948; occupied by Israeli forces 1967. **2.** the northern kingdom of the ancient Hebrews; Israel. **3.** the ancient capital of this kingdom.

Sa·mar·i·tan (sə mar′i tən), *n.* **1.** an inhabitant of Samaria. **2.** (*often l.c.*) See **good Samaritan.** —*adj.* **3.** of or pertaining to Samaria or Samaritans. [OE < LL *samarītān(us)* < Gk *samareī́t(ēs)* dweller in SAMARIA; see -AN]

sa·mar·i·um (sə mâr′ē əm), *n. Chem.* a rare-earth metallic element discovered in samarskite. *Symbol:* Sm; *at. wt.:* 150.35; *at. no.:* 62; *sp. gr.:* 7.49. [< NL; see SAMARSKITE, -IUM]

Sam·ar·kand (sam′ər kand′; *Russ.* sä′mär känt′), *n.* a city in E Uzbekistan in the SW Soviet Union in Asia, N of Afghanistan: taken by Alexander the Great 329 B.C.; Tamerlane's capital in the 14th century. 226,000 (est. 1964). Also, **Sam′ar·cand′.** Ancient, **Maracanda.**

Sa·mar·ra (sə mär′ə), *n.* a town in central Iraq, on the Tigris: seat of the early Abbasid caliphs.

sa·mar·skite (sə mär′skīt), *n.* a velvet-black mineral containing uranium, cerium, etc., occurring in masses: a minor source of uranium, thorium, and rare-earth oxides. [named after Col. von *Samarski,* 19th-century Russian army officer and inspector of mines; see -ITE[1]]

Sa·ma-Ve·da (sä′mə vā′də, -vē′də), *n. Hinduism.* one of the Samhitas, a collection of mantras and tunes used in connection with the Rig-Veda. Cf. **Veda.**

sam·ba (sam′bə, säm′-), *n., pl.* **-bas,** *v.,* **-baed, -ba·ing.** —*n.* **1.** a rhythmic Brazilian ballroom dance of African origin. —*v.i.* **2.** to dance the samba. [< Pg < Afr]

sam·bar (sam′bər, säm′-), *n.* a deer, *Rusa unicolor,* of India, Ceylon, Southeast Asia, and the East Indies, having three-pointed antlers. Also, **sam′bur, sam′bhar, sam′bhur.** [< Hindi < Skt *śambara*]

sam·bo (sam′bō), *n., pl.* **-bos. 1.** a Latin American of Negro and Indian or mulatto ancestry. **2.** *Offensive.* Negro. [< AmerSp *zambo* Negro, mulatto, perh. special use of Sp *zambo* bowlegged, supposedly < L *scamb(us)* < Gk *skambós* crooked]

Sam·bre (*Fr.* säɴ′brə), *n.* a river in W Europe, flowing NE through N France and S Belgium: battle 1918. 120 mi. long.

Sam′ Browne′ belt′, a belt having a supporting strap over the right shoulder, worn as part of a uniform. [named after its inventor, General Sir *Samuel Browne* (1824–1901)]

same (sām), *adj.* **1.** identical with what is about to be or has just been mentioned: *This street is the same one we were on yesterday.* **2.** being one or identical though having different names, aspects, etc.: *These are the same rules, though differently worded.* **3.** agreeing in kind, amount, etc.; corresponding: *two boxes of the same dimensions.* **4.** unchanged in character, condition, etc.: *It's the same town after all these years.* —*pron.* **5.** the person or thing just mentioned: *Sighted sub sank same.* **6. all the same, a.** even so; nevertheless. **b.** of no difference; immaterial. **7. just the same, a.** in the same manner. **b.** nevertheless. **8. the same,** in the same manner; in an identical or similar way: *I see the same through your glasses as I do through mine.* [ME; OE *same* (adv.); c. Icel *samr,* Gk *homós,* Skt *samá*]

sa·mekh (sä′mək; *Heb.* sä′mekh), *n.* the 15th letter of the Hebrew alphabet. Also, **sa′mech.** [< Heb: lit., a support]

same·ness (sām′nis), *n.* **1.** the state or quality of being the same; identity; uniformity. **2.** monotony; dullness.

S.Amer., 1. South America. **2.** South American.

Sam′ Hill′, *Slang.* hell: *Who in Sam Hill are you?* [*Sam* (orig. *salmon,* var. of *Sal(o)mon* an oath) + *hill,* euphemism for HELL]

Sam·hi·ta (sum′hi tä′), *n. Hinduism.* Veda (def. 2). [< Skt: a putting together]

sam·iel (sam yel′), *n.* simoom. [< Turk = *sam* poisonous + *yel* wind]

sam·i·sen (sam′i sen′), *n.* a guitarlike Japanese musical instrument having an extremely long neck and three strings, played with a plectrum. [< Jap < Chin *san-hsien* three-stringed (instrument)]

Samisen

sam·ite (sam′īt, sā′mīt), *n.* a heavy silk fabric, sometimes interwoven with gold, worn in the Middle Ages. [ME *samit* < OF < ML *(e)xamit(ium), samit(ium)* < Gk *hexámiton,* neut. of *hexámitos* having six threads. See HEXA-, MITOSIS]

sam·iz·dat (säm′iz dät′), *n.* **1.** a publishing system within the Soviet Union, by which dissenting manuscripts whose official publication is forbidden are reproduced, as by typewriter and carbons, and circulated privately. **2.** a work or periodical circulated by this system. [< Russ. = *samo-* self + *izdat (elstvo)* publishing house]

Saml., Samuel.

sam·let (sam′lit), *n.* a young salmon. [SALM(ON) + -LET]

Sam·ni·um (sam′nē əm), *n.* an ancient country in central Italy. —**Sam·nite** (sam′nīt), *adj., n.*

Sam·o (sam′ō), *n.* died A.D. 658, first ruler of the Slavs 623–658.

Sa·mo·a (sə mō′ə), *n.* a group of islands in the S Pacific, the islands W of 170° W longitude constituting an independent state and the rest belonging to the U.S. Formerly, **Navigators Islands.** Cf. **American Samoa, Western Samoa.**

Sa·mo·an (sə mō′ən), *adj.* **1.** of or pertaining to Samoa or its Polynesian people. —*n.* **2.** a native or inhabitant of Samoa. **3.** the Polynesian language of Samoa.

Sa·mos (sā′mos, sam′ōs; *Gk.* sä′môs), *n.* a Greek island in the E Aegean. 52,022 (1961); 194 sq. mi. —**Sa·mi·an** (sā′mē ən), *adj., n.*

Sam·o·thrace (sam′ə thrās′), *n.* a Greek island in the NE Aegean. Greek, **Sa·mo·thra·ke** (sä′mô thrä′kē). —**Sam·o·thra·cian** (sam′ə thrā′shən), *adj., n.*

sam·o·var (sam′ə vär′, sam′ə vär′), *n.* a metal urn, used esp. in the Soviet Union for heating water for making tea. [< Russ = *samo-* self (see SAME) + *-var* < *varit'* to boil]

Sam·o·yed (sam′ə yed′), *n.* **1.** a member of a Ural-Altaic people dwelling in NW Siberia and along the NE coast of the Soviet Union in Europe. **2.** Also, **Sam′o·yede′, Samoyedic.** a subfamily of Uralic languages spoken by the Samoyed people. **3.** one of a Russian breed of medium-sized dogs that have long, dense, white or cream hair and are used for herding reindeer and pulling sleds. [< Russ]

Sam·o·yed·ic (sam′ə yed′ik), *adj.* **1.** of or pertaining to the Samoyed people. —*n.* **2.** Samoyed (def. 2).

samp (samp), *n. U.S.* **1.** coarsely ground corn. **2.** a porridge made of it. [< Narragansett *(na)saump* mush]

sam·pan (sam′pan), *n.* any of various small boats of the Far East, as one propelled by a single scull over the stern and provided with a roofing of mats. [< Chin *san pan* kind of boat (lit., three boards)]

Sampan

sam·phire (sam′fīər), *n.* **1.** a succulent, apiaceous herb, *Crithmum maritimum,* of Europe, growing in clefts of rock near the sea. **2.** the glasswort. [earlier *samp(i)ere* < MF *(herbe de) Saint Pierre* (herb of) Saint Peter]

sam·ple (sam′pəl, säm′-), *n., adj., v.,* **-pled, -pling.** —*n.* **1.** a small part of anything or one of a number, intended to show the quality, style, or nature of the whole; specimen. —*adj.* **2.** serving as a specimen: *a sample piece of cloth.* —*v.t.* **3.** to take a sample or samples of; test or judge by a sample. [ME < OF *essample.* See EXAMPLE] —**Syn. 1.** See **example.**

sam·pler (sam′plər, säm′-), *n.* **1.** a person who samples. **2.** an embroidered cloth, serving to show a beginner's skill in needlework. **3.** a collection of samples or varied selections. [ME *samplere* < OF *(es)samplere, (e)xemplaire* < L *exemplār(ium)* EXEMPLAR]

sam·pling (sam′pling, säm′-), *n.* **1.** the act or process of selecting a sample for testing, analyzing, etc. **2.** the sample so selected.

sam·sa·ra (səm sär′ə), *n.* **1.** *Buddhism.* the process of coming into existence as a differentiated, mortal creature. Cf. **nirvana** (def. 1). **2.** *Hinduism.* the endless series of births, deaths, and rebirths to which all beings are subject. Cf. **nirvana** (def. 2). [< Skt *samsāra,* lit., running together]

sam·shu (sam′shōō, -syōō), *n.* a Chinese liqueur distilled from millet or rice. [< pidginE = *sam* (< ?) + *shu* (< Chin *chiu* spirits)]

Sam·son (sam′sən), *n.* a judge of Israel famous for his great strength. Judges 13–16.

Sam·u·el (sam′yōō əl), *n.* **1.** a judge and prophet of Israel. I Sam. 1–3; 8–15. **2.** either of two books of the Bible bearing his name.

sam·u·rai (sam′ŏŏ rī′), *n., pl.* **-rai.** *Japanese Hist.* **1.** a member of the hereditary warrior class in feudal Japan. **2.** a retainer of a daimyo. [< Jap]

San (sän), *n.* a river flowing from the Carpathian Mountains in the W Soviet Union through SE Poland into the Vistula: battles 1914–15. ab. 280 mi. long.

Sa·n'a (sä nä′), *n.* the capital of Yemen Arab Republic, in the SW Arabian Peninsula. 150,000. Also, **Sa·naa′.**

San An·ge·lo (san an′jə lō′), a city in W Texas. 63,884 (1970).

San An·to·ni·o (san′ an tō′nē ō′), a city in S Texas: site of the Alamo. 654,153 (1970). —**San′ Anto′nian.**

san·a·tive (san′ə tiv), *adj.* having the power to heal; curative. [< ML *sānātīv(us)* < LL *sānāt(us)* (ptp. of *sānāre* to heal) + *-īvus* -IVE; r. ME *sanatif* < MF]

san·a·to·ri·um (san′ə tōr′ē əm, -tôr′-), *n., pl.* **-ri·ums, -ri·a** (-rē ə). **1.** a hospital for the treatment of chronic diseases, as tuberculosis or various mental disorders. **2.** sanitarium. [< NL, neut. of LL *sānātōrius* healthful. See SANATIVE, -ORY[2]] —**Syn.** See **hospital.**

san·be·ni·to (san′bə nē′tō), *n., pl.* **-tos.** (under the Spanish Inquisition) **1.** a yellow garment worn by a condemned heretic at an auto-da-fé. **2.** a penitential garment worn by a confessed heretic. [< Sp, named after *San Benito* Saint Benedict, from its resemblance to the scapular believed to have been introduced by him]

San Ber·nar·di·no (san′ bûr′nər dē′nō), **1.** a city in S California. 104,783 (1970). **2. Mount,** a mountain in S California, a peak of the San Bernardino Mountains. 10,630 ft. **3.** a mountain pass in the Alps, in SE Switzerland. 6766 ft. high.

San′ Bernardi′no Moun′tains, a mountain range in S California. Highest peak, San Gorgonio, 11,485 ft.

San Ber·nar·do (san′ bər när′dō; *Sp.* sän′ beʀ när′thō), a city in central Chile, S of Santiago. 47,229.

San Blas (sän bläs′), **1. Gulf of,** a gulf of the Caribbean on the N coast of Panama. **2. Isthmus of,** the narrowest part of the Isthmus of Panama. 31 mi. wide.

San Bru·no (san bro͞o′nō), a city in W California, S of San Francisco. 36,254 (1970).

San Bue·na·ven·tu·ra (san bwā′nə ven to͝or′ə), a city in SW California. 57,964 (1970). Also called **Ventura.**

San Car·los (san kär′ləs), a city in W California, S of San Francisco. 25,924 (1970).

San·cho Pan·za (san′chō pan′zə; *Sp.* sän′chō pän′thä), a credulous follower or assistant. [from the squire in Cervantes' *Don Quixote de la Mancha* (1605 and 1615)]

San Cris·to·bal (sän′ kʀē stô′väl), a city in SW Venezuela. 122,047 (est. 1965).

sanc·ti·fied (sangk′tə fīd′), *adj.* **1.** made holy; consecrated. **2.** sanctimonious. —**sanc·ti·fi·ed·ly** (sangk′tə fī′id lē), *adj.*

sanc·ti·fy (sangk′tə fī′), *v.t.,* **-fied, -fy·ing. 1.** to make holy; consecrate. **2.** to purify or free from sin. **3.** to impart religious sanction to. **4.** to entitle to reverence or respect. **5.** to make productive of or conducive to spiritual blessing. [< eccl. L *sanctificāre* (see SANCTUS, -IFY); r. ME *seintefie(n)* < OF *saintifie(r)* < L] —**sanc′ti·fi′a·ble,** *adj.* —**sanc′ti·fi·ca′tion,** *n.* —**sanc′ti·fi′er,** *n.*

sanc·ti·mo·ni·ous (sangk′tə mō′nē əs), *adj.* **1.** making a hypocritical show of piety or righteousness. **2.** *Obs.* holy; sacred. —**sanc′ti·mo′ni·ous·ly,** *adv.* —**sanc′ti·mo′ni·ous·ness,** *n.*

sanc·ti·mo·ny (sangk′tə mō′nē), *n.* **1.** affected piety or righteousness. **2.** *Obs.* sanctity; sacredness. [< L *sanctimōnia* holiness. See SANCTUS, -MONY]

sanc·tion (sangk′shən), *n.* **1.** authoritative permission, as for an action. **2.** something that serves to support an action, condition, etc. **3.** something that gives binding force, as to an oath, rule of conduct, etc. **4.** *Law.* a provision of a law enacting a penalty for disobedience or a reward for obedience. **5.** *Internat. Law.* action by one or more states toward another state calculated to force it to comply with legal obligations. —*v.t.* **6.** to authorize, approve, or allow. **7.** to ratify or confirm. [< L *sanctiōn-* (s. of *sanctiō*). See SANCTUS, -ION] —**sanc′tion·a·ble,** *adj.* —**sanc′tion·er,** *n.*

sanc·ti·tude (sangk′ti to͞od′, -tyo͞od′), *n.* holiness; saintliness. [< L *sanctitūd(ō)*. See SANCTUS, -I-, -TUDE]

sanc·ti·ty (sangk′ti tē), *n., pl.* **-ties. 1.** holiness, saintliness, or godliness. **2.** sacred or hallowed character. **3.** a sacred thing. [< L *sanctitāt-* (s. of *sanctitās*) holiness = *sancti-* (see SANCTUS) + *-itāt* -ITY; r. ME *sauntite* < AF]

sanc·tu·ar·y (sangk′cho͞o er′ē), *n., pl.* **-ar·ies. 1.** a sacred or holy place. **2.** *Judaism.* **a.** the Biblical tabernacle or the Temple in Jerusalem. **b.** the holy of holies of these places of worship. **3.** an especially holy place in a temple or church. **4.** the part of a church around the altar; the chancel. **5.** a church or other sacred place formerly providing refuge or asylum. **6.** immunity, as to arrest, afforded by refuge in any place providing refuge or asylum. **7.** a tract of land where wildlife can breed and take refuge in safety from hunters. [ME < LL *sanctuāri(um)* = *sanctu-* (r. L *sanct-*) SANCTUS + *-ārium* -ARY] —**Syn. 1.** church, temple, altar, shrine.

sanc·tum (sangk′təm), *n., pl.* **-tums, -ta** (-tə). **1.** a sacred or holy place. **2.** an inviolably private place or retreat. [< L; neut. of SANCTUS]

sanc′tum sanc·to′rum (sangk tōr′əm, -tôr′-), **1.** the holy of holies of the Biblical tabernacle and the Temple in Jerusalem. **2.** sanctum (def. 2). [< L, trans. of Heb *qōdesh haqqodāshīm* holy of holies]

Sanc·tus (sangk′təs), *n.* the hymn with which the Eucharistic preface culminates. [< L: holy, n. use of ptp. of *sancīre* to hallow]

Sanc′tus bell′, a bell rung during the celebration of Mass to call attention to the more solemn parts.

sand (sand), *n.* **1.** small, loose grains or rock debris, esp. of quartz. **2.** Usually, **sands.** a tract or region composed principally of sand. **3. sands,** moments of time or of one's life. **4.** a dull reddish-yellow color. —*v.t.* **5.** to smooth or polish, as with sand or sandpaper. **6.** to sprinkle with or as with sand. **7.** to fill up with sand, as a harbor. **8.** to add sand to. [ME, OE; c. G *Sand,* Icel *sandr*]

Sand (sand; *Fr.* säɴ), *n.* **George** (jôrj; *Fr.* zhôʀzh), (pen name of *Lucie Aurore Dupin Dudevant*), 1804–76, French novelist.

san·dal[1] (san′dəl), *n., v.,* **-daled, -dal·ing** or (*esp. Brit.*) **-dalled, -dal·ling.** —*n.* **1.** a shoe consisting of a sole of leather or other material fastened to the foot by thongs or straps. **2.** any of various low shoes or slippers. **3.** a light, low rubber overshoe covering the front part of a woman's high-heeled shoe. **4.** a band or strap that fastens a low shoe or slipper. —*v.t.* **5.** to furnish with sandals. [< F *sandale;* r. ME *sandalie* < L *sandali(um)* < Gk *sandálion,* dim. of *sándalon*]

san·dal[2] (san′dəl), *n.* sandalwood. [ME *sandell* < ML *sandal(um)* < LGk *sántalon,* dissimilated var. of *sándanon* < Skt *candana*]

san·dal·wood (san′dəl wo͝od′), *n.* **1.** the fragrant heartwood of any of certain Asian trees of the genus *Santalum,* used for ornamental carving and burned as incense. **2.** any of these trees, esp. *S. album,* an evergreen of India. **3.** any of various related or similar trees or their woods, esp. a fabaceous tree, *Pterocarpus santalinus,* having a heavy dark-red wood that yields a dye.

San′dalwood Is′land, Sumba.

san·da·rac (san′də rak′), *n.* **1.** a brittle resin exuding from the bark of the sandarac tree, used chiefly as incense and in making varnish. **2.** See **sandarac tree.** [< ME *sandaracha* < L *sandarac(a)* < Gk *sandarákē* realgar]

san′darac tree′, a pinaceous tree, *Tetraclinis articulata* (*Callitris quadrivalvis*), yielding the resin sandarac and a hard, dark-colored wood much used in building.

sand·bag (sand′bag′), *n., v.,* **-bagged, -bag·ging.** —*n.* **1.** a bag filled with sand, used in fortification, as ballast, etc. **2.** such a bag used as a blackjack. —*v.t.* **3.** to furnish with sandbags. **4.** to hit with a sandbag. —**sand′bag′ger,** *n.*

sand·bank (sand′bangk′), *n.* a large mass of sand, as on a shoal or hillside.

sand′ bar′, a bar of sand formed in a river or sea by the action of tides or currents.

sand·blast (sand′blast′, -bläst′), *n.* **1.** a blast of air or steam laden with sand, used to clean, grind, cut, or decorate hard surfaces. **2.** the apparatus used to apply such a blast. —*v.t.* **3.** to clean, smooth, etc., with a sandblast. —**sand′blast′er,** *n.*

sand-blind (sand′blīnd′), *adj. Archaic.* partially blind; purblind. [ME; OE **sāmblind* = *sām-* SEMI- + *blind* BLIND] —**sand′-blind′ness,** *n.*

sand·box (sand′boks′), *n.* a box or receptacle for holding sand, esp. one for children to play in.

sand′box tree′, a euphorbiaceous tree, *Hura crepitans,* bearing a fruit that when ripe and dry bursts with a sharp report and scatters the seeds.

sand·bur (sand′bûr′), *n.* **1.** any of several bur-bearing weeds growing in sandy places, as a nightshade, *Solanum rostratum,* of the western U.S. **2.** a weed, *Franseria acanthicarpa,* related to the bristly ragweeds. **3.** any of several grasses of the genus *Cenchrus,* bearing prickly burs.

Sand·burg (sand′bûrg, san′-), *n.* **Carl,** 1878–1967, U.S. poet and biographer.

sand-cast (sand′kast′, -käst′), *v.t.,* **-cast, -cast·ing.** to produce (a casting) by pouring molten metal into sand molds. —**sand′ cast′ing.**

sand′ cher′ry, 1. any of several low, North American cherries that grow on dry or sandy soil, esp. *Prunus pumila,* of the Great Lakes region. **2.** the fruit of any of these shrubs.

sand′ crack′, *Vet. Pathol.* a crack or fissure in the hoof of a horse, extending from the coronet downward toward the sole. Also called **quarter crack.**

sand′ dol′lar, any of various flat, disklike sea urchins, esp. *Echinarachnius parma,* that live on sandy bottoms off the coasts of the U.S.

Sand dollar, *Mellita testudinata* (Width 3 in.)

sand′ eel′. See **sand lance.**

sand·er (san′dər), *n.* **1.** a person who sands. **2.** an apparatus for sanding or sandpapering.

sand·er·ling (san′dər ling), *n.* a small sandpiper, *Crocethia alba,* found on sandy beaches. [SAND + ME *urthling* plowman; see EARTH, -LING[1]]

sand·fish (sand′fish′), *n., pl.* (*esp. collectively*) **-fish,** (*esp. referring to two or more kinds or species*) **-fish·es.** either of two scaleless fishes of the family *Trichodontidae,* found in the North Pacific, which live in sand or mud.

sand′ flea′, 1. See **beach flea. 2.** chigoe.

sand·fly (sand′flī′), *n., pl.* **-flies.** any of several small, bloodsucking, dipterous insects of the genus *Phlebotomus* that are vectors of several diseases of man.

sand·glass (sand′glas′, -gläs′), *n.* an hourglass.

sand′ grouse′, any of several birds of the genus *Pteroclidae,* found in sandy areas of the Old World, resembling the related pigeons in shape and coloration.

san·dhi (san′dē, sän′-), *n., pl.* **-dhis.** *Linguistics.* morphophonemic alteration, esp. as determined by phonemic environment: *doncha* for *don't you.* [< Skt = *sam* together + *dhi* a putting; see DO[1]]

sand·hog (sand′hog′, -hôg′), *n.* a laborer who digs or works in sand, esp. one who digs underwater tunnels.

sand′ hop′per. See **beach flea.**

Sand·hurst (sand′hûrst), *n.* a village in SE Berkshire, in S England, near Reading: military college. 5144 (1951).

San Di·e·go (san′ dē ā′gō), a seaport in SW California: naval and marine base. 697,027 (1970).

sand·i·ness (san′dē nis), *n.* the state or quality of being sandy.

San·di·nis·ta (san′də nē′stə; *Sp.* sän′dē nēs′täs), *n., pl.* **-nis·tas** (-nē′stəz; *Sp.* -nēs′täs). a member of the revolutionary movement that took control of Nicaragua in 1979. [< AmerSp; Augusto *Sandino* (1893–1934), Nicaraguan guerrilla leader + *-ista* -IST]

S&L, *Banking.* savings and loan: *S&L associations.*

sand′ lance′, any slender, sand-inhabiting, marine fish of the family *Ammodytidae.* Also, **sand′ launce′.**

sand′ lil′y, a small, stemless plant, *Leucocrinum montanum,* of the western U.S., having lilylike flowers.

sand·lot (sand′lot′), *U.S.* —*n.* **1.** a vacant lot, esp. as used by boys for games or sports. —*adj.* **2.** Also, **sand′-lot′.** of, pertaining to, or played in such a lot. **3.** (of team sports) played by amateurs: *sandlot baseball.*

sand·man (sand′man′), *n., pl.* **-men.** the man who, in fairy tales or folklore, puts sand in the eyes of children to make them sleepy.

sand′ paint′ing, 1. a ceremony among Navaho, Hopi, and Pueblo Indians of creating flat symbolic designs with varicolored sand. **2.** a design so made.

sand·pa·per (sand′pā′pər), *n.* **1.** strong paper coated with a layer of sand or other abrasive, used for smoothing or polishing. —*v.t.* **2.** to smooth or polish with sandpaper.

sand·pi·per (sand′pī′pər), *n.* any of numerous shore-inhabiting birds of the family *Scolopacidae,* related to the plovers, typically having a slender bill and a piping call.

Spotted sandpiper, *Actitis macularia* (Length 7 in.)

sand·pit (sand′pit′), *n.* a deep pit in sandy soil from which sand is excavated.

San·dro·cot·tus (san′drō kot′əs), *n.* Greek name of **Chandragupta.** Also, **San·dra·kot·tos** (san′drō kot′əs; *Gk.* sän′drä kôt′tôs).

sand·stone (sand′stōn′), *n.* a rock formed of sand, usually quartz, cemented together by silica, calcium carbonate, iron oxide, and clay.

sand·storm (sand′stôrm′), *n.* a windstorm, esp. in a desert, that blows along great clouds of sand.

sand′ trap′, (on a golf course) a shallow pit partly filled with sand and designed to serve as a hazard.

San·dus·ky (sən dus′kē, san-), *n.* a port in N Ohio, on Lake Erie. 32,674 (1970).

sand′ verbe′na, any of several low, mostly trailing herbs of the genus *Abronia,* of the western U.S., having showy, verbenalike flowers.

sand′ vi′per, 1. See **hognose snake. 2.** See **horned viper.**

sand·wich (sand′wich, san′-), *n.* **1.** two or more slices of bread or the like with a layer of meat, fish, cheese, etc., between them. **2.** something that resembles or suggests a sandwich. —*v.t.* **3.** to put into a sandwich. **4.** to insert between two other things. [named after the fourth Earl of *Sandwich* (1718–92)]

Sand·wich (sand′wich), *n.* **1.** a town in E Kent, in SE England: one of the Cinque Ports. 4234 (1961).

sand′wich board′, two connected signboards that hang from the shoulders in front of and behind a person.

sand′wich coin′, a coin having a layer of one metal between layers of another, as a quarter with a layer of copper between layers of silver

Sand′wich Is′lands, former name of **Hawaii.**

sand′wich man′, a man who carries a sandwich board, usually for advertising or sometimes for picketing.

sand·worm (sand′wûrm′), *n.* any of several polychaetes that live in sand.

sand·wort (sand′wûrt′), *n.* any caryophyllaceous plant of the genus *Arenaria,* many of which grow in sandy soil.

sand·y (san′dē), *adj.,* **sand·i·er, sand·i·est. 1.** of the nature of or consisting of sand. **2.** containing or covered with sand. **3.** of a yellowish-red color: *sandy hair.* [ME; OE *sandig*]

Sand′y Hook′, a peninsula in E New Jersey, at the entrance to New York Bay: lighthouse. 6 mi. long.

sane (sān), *adj.,* **san·er, san·est. 1.** having a sound, healthy mind. **2.** having or showing reason, sound judgment, or good sense. **3.** sound; healthy. [< L *sān(us)* healthy] —**sane′ly,** *adv.* —**sane′ness,** *n.*

SANE (sān), *n.* a private nationwide organization in the U.S. established in 1957, that opposes nuclear testing and advocates international peace. [(*National Committee for a*) *Sane* (*Nuclear Policy*)]

San Fer·nan·do (sän fer nän′dô), a city in E Argentina, near Buenos Aires. 119,565.

San·ford (san′fərd), *n.* **Mount,** a mountain in SE Alaska. 16,208 ft.

San·for·ized (san′fə rīzd′), *adj. Trademark.* (of fabric) noting or undergoing a process for mechanical shrinking before tailoring.

San Fran·cis·co (san′ fran sis′kō), a seaport in W California, on San Francisco Bay: earthquake and fire 1906. 715,674 (1970). —**San′ Fran·cis′can.**

San′ Francis′co Bay′, a bay in W California: the harbor of San Francisco; connected with the Pacific by the Golden Gate strait. 50 mi. long; 3–12 mi. wide.

San′ Francis′co Peaks′, a mountain mass in N Arizona: highest point in the state, Humphrey's Peak, 12,611 ft. Also called **San′ Francis′co Moun′tain.**

sang (sang), *v.* pt. of **sing.**

San Ga·bri·el (san gā′brē əl), a city in SW California, near Los Angeles. 29,336 (1970).

San·gal·lo (säng gäl′lô), *n.* **1. An·to·nio Pic·co·ni da** (än tô′nyô pēk kô′nē dä) (*Antonio Cordiani*), 1484?–1546, Italian architect and engineer. **2.** his uncle, **Giu·lia·no da** (jo͞o lyä′nô dä), (*Giuliano Giamberti*), 1445–1516, Italian architect, sculptor, and engineer.

San Gen·na·ro (sän′ jen nä′rô), Italian name of **Januarius.** Also, **San Gen·nai·o** (jen nī′yô).

Sang·er (sang′ər), *n.* **Margaret Hig·gins** (hig′inz), 1883–1966, U.S. nurse and author: leader of birth-control movement.

sang-froid (*Fr.* sän frwa′), *n.* coolness of mind; calmness; composure. [< F: cold-bloodedness] —**Syn.** self-possession, poise, equanimity; self-control.

San Got·tar·do (sän′ gôt tär′dô), Italian name of **St. Gotthard.**

San·graal (sang grāl′), *n.* Grail. Also, **San·gre·al** (sang′-grē əl). [prob. < OF *Saint Graal*]

San·gre de Cris·to (sang′grē də kris′tō), a mountain range in S Colorado and N New Mexico: a part of the Rocky Mountains. Highest peak, Blanca Peak, 14,390 ft.

san·gri·a (sang grē′ə; *Sp.* säng grē′ä), *n.* an iced drink, usually of red wine that has been diluted, sweetened, and spiced. [< Sp: drink bloodlike in color = *sangr(e)* blood (see SANGUINE) + *-ia* n. suffix]

san·gui·nar·i·a (sang′gwə nâr′ē ə), *n.* **1.** the bloodroot, *Sanguinaria canadensis.* **2.** its medicinal rhizome. [< NL (*herba*) *sanguināria* bloody (herb). See SANGUINARY]

san·gui·nar·y (sang′gwə ner′ē), *adj.* **1.** full of or characterized by bloodshed. **2.** ready or eager to shed blood. **3.** composed of or marked with blood. [< L *sanguinār(us)* bloody] —**san′gui·nar′i·ly,** *adv.* —**san′gui·nar′i·ness,** *n.*

san·guine (sang′gwin), *adj.* **1.** cheerful, hopeful, or confident. **2.** reddish; ruddy: *a sanguine complexion.* **3.** (in old physiology) having blood as the predominating humor and consequently being cheerful. **4.** blood-red; red. [ME < L *sanguine(us)* bloody = *sanguin-* (s. of *sanguis*) blood + *-eus* -EOUS] —**san′guine·ly,** *adv.* —**san′guine·ness,** *n.*

san·guin·e·ous (sang gwin′ē əs), *adj.* **1.** Also, **san·gui·nous** (sang′gwə nəs). of, pertaining to, or containing blood. **2.** of the color of blood. **3.** involving much bloodshed. **4.** sanguine; confident. [< L *sanguineus* bloody. See SANGUINE] —**san·guin′e·ous·ness,** *n.*

san·guin·o·lent (sang gwin′ᵊlənt), *adj.* **1.** of or pertaining to blood. **2.** containing or tinged with blood; bloody. [< L *sanguinolent(us).* See SANGUINE, -OLENT] —**san·guin′o·len·cy,** *n.*

San·hed·rin (san hed′rin, -hē′drin, san′hi drin, san′i-), *n. Jewish Hist.* **1.** Also called **Great Sanhedrin.** the supreme legislative council and highest ecclesiastical and secular tribunal of the Jews, exercising its greatest authority from the 5th century B.C. to A.D. 70. **2.** Also called **Lesser Sanhedrin.** a lower tribunal of this period. Also, **San·he·drim** (san′hi drim, san′i-). [< LHeb < Gk *synédrion* = *syn-* SYN- + *hédr(a)* seat + *-ion* -IUM]

san·i·cle (san′i kəl), *n.* any umbelliferous herb of the genus *Sanicula,* as *S. marilandica,* of America, used in medicine. [ME < MF < ML *sānicul(a).* See SANE, -I-, -CLE]

sa·ni·es (sā′nē ēz′), *n. Pathol.* a thin, often greenish, serous fluid that is discharged from ulcers, wounds, etc. [< L: bloody matter] —**sa′ni·ous,** *adj.*

San Il·de·fon·so (sän ēl′de fôn′sô), a town in central Spain, near Segovia: 18th-century palace. 3245 (1950).

san·i·tar·i·an (san′i târ′ē ən), *adj.* **1.** sanitary; wholesome. —*n.* **2.** a specialist in public sanitation and health.

san·i·tar·i·um (san′i târ′ē əm), *n., pl.* **-tar·i·ums, -tar·i·a** (-târ′ē ə). an institution for the promotion of health; health resort. Also, **sanatorium.** [< L *sānit(ās)* health + -ARIUM] —**Syn.** See **hospital.**

san·i·tar·y (san′i ter′ē), *adj.* **1.** of or pertaining to health or the conditions affecting health, esp. with reference to cleanliness, precautions against disease, etc. **2.** favorable to health; free from dirt, bacteria, etc. **3.** promoting cleanliness. [< L *sānit(ās)* health + -ARY] —**san′i·tar′i·ly,** *adv.* —**Syn. 1, 2.** clean, unpolluted, antiseptic. SANITARY, HYGIENIC agree in being concerned with health. SANITARY refers more esp. to conditions affecting health or measures for guarding against infection or disease: *to insure sanitary conditions in preparing food.* HYGIENIC is applied to whatever concerns the care of the body and the promotion of health: *to live in hygienic surroundings with plenty of fresh air.* **2.** salutary.

san′itary belt′, a narrow belt, usually of elastic, for holding a sanitary napkin in place.

san′itary cor′don. See **cordon sanitaire.**

san′itary engineer′ing, a branch of civil engineering dealing with matters affecting public health, as water supply or sewage disposal. —**san′itary engineer′.**

san′itary nap′kin, an absorbent pad for wear by women during menstruation to absorb the uterine flow.

san·i·ta·tion (san′i tā′shən), *n.* the development and practical application of sanitary measures for the sake of cleanliness, protecting health, etc. [SANIT(ARY) + -ATION]

san·i·tise (san′i tīz′), *v.t.,* **-tised, -tis·ing.** *Chiefly Brit.* sanitize. —**san′i·ti·sa′tion,** *n.*

san·i·tize (san′i tīz′), *v.t.,* **-tized, -tiz·ing.** to free from dirt, germs, etc., as by cleaning or sterilizing. [SANIT(ARY) + -IZE] —**san′i·ti·za′tion,** *n.*

san·i·ty (san′i tē), *n.* **1.** the state of being sane; soundness of mind; mental normality. **2.** soundness of judgment. [ME *sanite* < L *sānitās*]

San Ja·cin·to (san′ jə sin′tō, hä-), a river in E Texas, flowing SE to Galveston Bay: Texans defeated Mexicans near the mouth of this river 1836.

San Joa·quin (san′ wô kēn′), a river in California, flowing NW from the Sierra Nevada Mountains to the Sacramento River. 350 mi. long.

San Jo·se (san′ hō zā′), a city in W California. 445,779 (1970).

San Jo·sé (sän′ hô se′), a city in and the capital of Costa Rica, in the central part. 228,302.

San′ Jo·se′ scale′, a scale insect, *Aspidiotus perniciosus,* that is highly destructive to fruit trees and shrubs. [named after SAN JOSE, where first found]

San Juan (san′ wän′, hwän′; *Sp.* sän hwän′), **1.** a seaport in and the capital of Puerto Rico, in the N part. 518,700. **2.** a city in W Argentina. 224,000.

San Juan de la Cruz (*Sp.* sän hwän′ de lä kro͞oth′). See **John of the Cross.**

San′ Juan′ Hill′, a hill in SE Cuba, near Santiago de Cuba: captured by U.S. forces in battle during the Spanish-American War in 1898.

San′ Juan′ Is′lands, a group of islands between NW Washington and SE Vancouver Island, Canada: a part of Washington.

San′ Juan′ Moun′tains, a mountain range in SW Colorado and N New Mexico: a part of the Rocky Mountains. Highest peak, Uncompahgre Peak, 14,306 ft.

sank (sangk), *v.* a pt. of **sink.**

San·khya (säng′kyə), *n.* a system of Hindu philosophy, stressing the reality and duality of spirit and matter. Also, **Samkhya.** [< Skt *sāmkhya* reckoning, number]

San Le·an·dro (san′ lē an′drō), a city in W California. 68,698 (1970).

San Lu·is O·bis·po (san lo͞o′is ə bis′pō), a city in W California. 28,036 (1970).

San Luis Po·to·sí (sän lwēs′ pô′tô sē′), **1.** a state in central Mexico. 1,115,342 (est. 1963); 24,415 sq. mi. **2.** the capital of this state. 180,881 (est. 1965).

San Ma·ri·no (san′ mə rē′nō; *It.* sän′ mä rē′nô), a small republic in E Italy: the oldest independent country in Europe. 19,621; 38 sq. mi. *Cap.:* San Marino.

San Mar·tín (san′ mär tēn′; *Sp.* sän′ mär tēn′), **José de** (hô se′ the), 1778–1850, South American general and statesman, born in Argentina.

San Ma·te·o (san′ mə tā′ō), a city in W California. 78,991 (1970).

San·mi·che·li (sän′mē ke′lē), *n.* **Mi·che·le** (mē ke′le), 1484–1559, Italian architect and military engineer.

san·nup (san′up), *n.* a married American Indian man. [< Narragansett *sannop*]

sann·ya·si (sun yä′sē), *n.* a Hindu monk. Also, **sann·ya·sin** (sun yä′sin); *referring to a woman,* **sann·ya·si·ni** (sun-yä′sē nē). [< Hindi: casting away]

San Pa′blo Bay′, the N part of San Francisco Bay, in W California.

San Ra·fael (san′ rə fel′), a city in W California, N of San Francisco. 38,977 (1970).

San Re·mo (san rē′mō, rā′-; *It.* sän re′mô), a seaport in NW Italy, on the Riviera: resort. 55,443 (1961).

sans (sanz; *Fr.* säɴ), *prep.* without. [ME < OF *sans,* earlier *sens* < L *sine* without, b. with *absentia* ABSENCE]

Sans., Sanskrit.

San Sal·va·dor (san sal′və dôr′; *Sp.* sän säl′vä ᵺôr′), **1.** Also called **Watling Island.** an island in the E Bahamas: first land in the New World seen by Christopher Columbus 1492. 776; 60 sq. mi. **2.** a city in and the capital of El Salvador. 368,313.

San·scrit (san′skrit), *n., adj.* Sanskrit. —**San′scrit·ist,** *n.*

San·scrit·ic (san skrit′ik), *adj.* Sanskrit (def. 2).

sans-cu·lotte (sanz′kyŏŏ lot′; *Fr.* säɴ ky lôt′), *n., pl.* **sans-cu·lottes** (sanz′kyŏŏ lots′; *Fr.* säɴ ky lôt′). **1.** (in the French Revolution) a revolutionary of the poorer class. **2.** any extreme republican or revolutionary. [< F: lit., without knee breeches]

sans-cu·lot·tide (sanz′kyŏŏ lot′id; *Fr.* säɴ ky lô tēd′), *n., pl.* **sans-cu·lot·tides** (sanz′kyŏŏ lot′idz; *Fr.* säɴ ky lô-tēd′). **1.** (in the French Revolutionary calendar) any of the five intercalary days (six in every fourth year) added at the end of the month of Fructidor. **2.** **sans-culottides,** the festivities held during these days. [< F; see SANS-CULOTTE; *-ide* (? < L *Idūs* IDES)]

sans doute (säɴ do͞ot′), *French.* without doubt; certainly.

San Se·bas·tián (san′ si bas′chən; *Sp.* sän′ se väs-tyän′), a seaport in N Spain: resort. 123,935 (est. 1960).

San·sei (sän′sā′), *n.* (*sometimes l.c.*) a grandchild of Japanese immigrants to the U.S. Cf. **Issei, Kibei, Nisei.** [< Jap: third generation]

san·se·vi·e·ri·a (san′sə vē ēr′ē ə, -sə vēr′ē ə), *n.* any plant of the genus *Sansevieria,* grown as a house plant for its stiff, sword-shaped leaves. [< NL; named after *San Seviero,* principality of Raimondo di Sangro (1710–71), learned Neapolitan; see -IA]

Sansk., Sanskrit.

San·skrit (san′skrit), *n.* **1.** an Indo-European, Indic language, in use since c1200 B.C. as the most important religious and literary language of India. *Abbr.:* Skt, Sans., Sansk. —*adj.* **2.** Also, **San·skrit′ic, Sanscritic.** of or pertaining to Sanskrit. Also, **Sanscrit.** [< Skt *saṁskṛta* well-made, perfected (lit., put together)] —**San′skrit·ist,** *n.*

San·so·vi·no (san′sō vē′nō; *It.* sän′sô vē′nô), *n.* **1.** **An·dre·a** (än dre′ä), (*Andrea Contucci*), 1460–1529, Italian sculptor and architect. **2.** his pupil, **Ja·co·po** (yä′kô pô), (*Jacopo Tatti*), 1486–1570, Italian sculptor and architect.

sans pa·reil (säɴ pa re′yᵊ), *French.* without equal.

sans peur et sans re·proche (säɴ pœr ā säɴ rə-prôsh′), *French.* without fear and without reproach.

sans′ ser′if (sanz), *Print.* a style of monotonal type without serifs. —**sans-ser·if** (sanz′ser′if), *adj.*

sans sou·ci (säɴ so͞o sē′), *French.* carefree.

San·ta (san′tə), *n.* See **Santa Claus.**

San·ta An·a (san′tə an′ə *or, for 1, 3, Sp.* sän′tä ä′nä), **1.** a city in NW El Salvador. 121,095 (1961). **2.** a city in SW California. 156,876 (1970). **3.** See **Santa Anna.**

San·ta An·na (sän′tä ä′nä; *Eng.* san′tə an′ə), **An·to·nio Ló·pez de** (än tô′nyô lô′pes ᵺe), 1795?–1876, Mexican general and revolutionist: dictator 1844–45; president 1833–35, 1853–55. Also, **Santa Ana.**

San·ta Bar·ba·ra (san′tə bär′bər ə, -brə), a city on the SW coast of California: Spanish mission. 70,215 (1970).

San′ta Bar′bara Is′lands, a group of islands off the SW coast of California.

San·ta Cat·a·li·na (san′tə kat′ᵊlē′nə), an island off the SW coast of California, opposite Long Beach: resort. 132 sq. mi. Also called **Catalina Island, Catalina.**

San·ta Cat·a·ri·na (san′tə kat′ə rē′nə; *Port.* säɴn′tə kä′tə rē′nə), a state in S Brazil. 3,351,400; 36,856 sq. mi. *Cap.:* Florianópolis.

San·ta Cla·ra (san′tə klar′ə; *for 1 also Sp.* sän′tä klä′rä), **1.** a city in central Cuba. 105,600 (est. 1962). **2.** a city in central California, S of San Francisco. 87,717 (1970).

San·ta Claus (san′tə klôz′), a benevolent figure of legend, associated with Saint Nicholaus, supposed to bring gifts to children on Christmas Eve. [< dial. D *Sante Klaas*]

San·ta Cruz (san′tə kro͞oz′; *Sp.* sän′tä kro͞os′), **1.** a city in central Bolivia. 83,000 (est. 1965). **2.** a city in W California. 32,076 (1970). **3.** an island in NW Santa Barbara Islands. **4.** See **St. Croix** (def. 1).

San′ta Cruz′ de Te·ne·rife′ (də ten′ə rif′; *Sp.* de te′ne rē′fe), a seaport on NE Tenerife island, in the W Canary Islands. 145,273 (est. 1960).

San·ta Fe (san′tə fā′), a city in and the capital of New Mexico, in the N part: founded c1605. 41,167 (1970). —**San′ta Fe′an.**

San·ta Fé (san′tə fā′; *Sp.* sän′tä fe′), a city in E Argentina. 259,560 (1965).

San′ta Fe′ Springs′, a city in SW California, near Los Angeles: oil wells. 14,750 (1970).

San′ta Fe′ Trail′, an important trade route going between Independence, Missouri, and Santa Fe, New Mexico, used from about 1821 to 1880.

San·ta Ger·tru·dis (san′tə gər tro͞o′dis), one of an American breed of beef cattle, developed from Shorthorn and Brahman stock and resistant to torrid temperatures. [named after a division of a ranch in Texas]

San·ta Is·a·bel (san′tə iz′ə bel′; *Sp.* sän′tä ē′sä bel′), former name of **Malabo.**

san·ta·la·ceous (san′tᵊlā′shəs), *adj.* belonging to the *Santalaceae,* or sandalwood family of plants. [< NL *santalā-ce(ae)* (< LGk *sántal(on)* sandalwood; see -ACEAE) + -OUS]

San·ta Ma·ri·a (san′tə mə rē′ə; *for 1, 2 also Sp.* sän′tä mä rē′ä), **1.** a city in W California. 32,749 (1970). **2.** an active volcano in W Guatemala. 12,300 ft. **3.** the flagship used by Columbus when he made his first voyage of discovery to America in 1492.

San·ta Mar·ta (san′tə mär′tə; *Sp.* sän′tä mär′tä), a seaport in NW Colombia. 62,650 (est. 1961).

San·ta Mau·ra (sän′tä mou′rä), Italian name of **Levkas.**

San·ta Mon·i·ca (san′tə mon′ə kə), a city in SW California, near Los Angeles, on Santa Monica Bay: resort. 88,289 (1970).

San·tan·der (sän′tän der′), *n.* a seaport in N Spain: Altamira cave drawings nearby. 103,108 (est. 1960).

San·ta Ro·sa (san′tə rō′zə), a city in W California, N of San Francisco. 50,006 (1970).

San·ta Ro·sa de Co·pán (sän′tä rô′sä ᵺe kô pän′), a town in W Honduras: site of extensive Mayan ruins. 7946 (1961). Also called **Copán.**

San·ta·ya·na (san′tē an′ə; *Sp.* sän′tä yä′nä), *n.* **George,** 1863–1952, Spanish philosopher and writer in the U.S.; in Europe after 1912.

San·tee (san tē′), *n.* a river flowing SE from central South Carolina to the Atlantic. 143 mi. long.

San·ti·a·go (san′tē ä′gō; *Sp.* sän tyä′gô), *n.* **1.** a city in and the capital of Chile, in the central part. 1,759,087. **2.** Also called **Santia′go de Com·po·ste′la** (ᵺe kôm′pô ste′lä). a city in NW Spain: pilgrimage center; cathedral. 70,893.

Santia′go de Cu′ba (də kyo͞o′bə; *Sp.* de ko͞o′vä), a seaport in SE Cuba: naval battle 1898. 219,800 (est. 1964).

San·tia·go del Es·te·ro (sän tyä′gô del e ste′rô), a city in N Argentina. 103,115 (est. 1965).

san·tims (sän′timz), *n., pl.* **-ti·mi** (-tə mē). a former coin of Latvia, the 100th part of a lat. [< Latvian < F *centime* CENTIME]

San·to An·dré (säɴn tŏŏ äɴn dre′), a city in E Brazil, near São Paulo. 415,025.

San·to Do·min·go (san′tō də miŋg′gō; *Sp.* sän′tô dô-mēŋg′gô), **1.** Formerly, **Ciudad Trujillo.** a city in and the capital of the Dominican Republic, on the S coast: first European settlement in America 1496. 980,000. **2.** former name of **Dominican Republic.**

san·ton·i·ca (san ton′ə kə), *n.* **1.** a wormwood, *Artemisia Cina.* **2.** the dried flower heads of this plant, used as a vermifuge. [< NL < LL (*herba*) *santonica* herb of the Santones, an Aquitanian tribe]

san·to·nin (san′tə nin), *n.* *Chem.* a crystalline compound, $C_{15}H_{18}O_3$, the active principle of santonica. [SANTON(ICA) + -IN[2]]

San·tos (san′təs; *Port.* säɴn′tŏŏs), *n.* a seaport in S Brazil: coffee port. 263,054 (1960).

San·tos-Du·mont (san′təs do͞o mont′, -dyo͞o-; *Port.* säɴn′-tŏŏz dŏŏ môɴnt′), *n.* **Al·ber·to** (äl ber′tô), 1873–1932, Brazilian aeronaut in France.

Sa·nu·si (sə no͞o′sē), *n., pl.* **-sis,** (*esp. collectively*) **-si.** a member of a fanatical, belligerent Muslim sect of North Africa. Also, **Senusi, Senussi.** [named after Muhammad ibn Ali as-*Sanūsi* (d. 1859), Algerian founder of the sect]

São Fran·cis·co (souɴ′ fräɴn sēs′kŏŏ), a river flowing E through E Brazil into the Atlantic. 1800 mi. long.

São Luiz do Ma·ra·nhão (souɴ′ lwēs′ dŏŏ mä′rə-nyouɴ′), a seaport on an island off the NE coast of Brazil: capital of Maranhão. 139,075 (1960). Also called **São′ Luiz′.**

São Mi·guel (*Port.* souɴ′ mē gel′), the largest island of the Azores. 150,000; 288 sq. mi.

Saône (sōn), *n.* a river flowing S from NE France to the Rhone. 270 mi. long.

São Pau·lo (souɴ′ pou′lŏŏ), a city in S Brazil. 3,300,218 (1960).

São′ Pau′lo de Lo·an′da (*Port.* də lŏŏ äɴn′də), Luanda.

São Pe·dro do Ri·o Gran·de do Sul (souɴ pe′drŏŏ dŏŏ rē′ŏŏ gräɴn′de dŏŏ so͞ol′), a seaport in SE Rio Grande do Sul, in SE Brazil. 87,528 (1960). Also called **Rio Grande, Rio Grande do Sul.**

Saor·stat Eir·eann (sâr′stät âr′ən; *Gaelic.* sār′stôt ā′rôn), Gaelic name of **Irish Free State.** Also called **Saor′stat′.**

São Sal·va·dor (souɴ′ säl′və dôr′), a seaport in E Brazil. 638,592 (1960). Also called **Bahia.** Official name, **Salvador.**

São To·mé (souɴ′ tō me′), Portuguese name of **St. Thomas.** Also, **São′ Tho·mé′.**

sap[1] (sap), *n., v.,* **sapped, sap·ping.** —*n.* **1.** the juice or vital circulating fluid of a plant, esp. of a woody plant. **2.** any vital body fluid. **3.** sapwood. **4.** *Slang.* a fool; dupe. **5.** *Slang.* a club, blackjack, etc., used as a bludgeon. —*v.t.* **6.** to drain the sap from. **7.** *Slang.* to strike with a sap. [ME; OE *sæp;* c. D *sap;* akin to G *Saft* juice, Icel *safi*]

sap[2] (sap), *n., v.,* **sapped, sap·ping.** —*n.* **1.** *Mil.* a deep, narrow trench leading to an enemy fortification or position. —*v.t.* **2.** *Mil.* **a.** to approach (an enemy fortification or position) by means of a sap or saps. **b.** to dig saps in (the ground). **3.** to undermine; weaken or destroy insidiously. —*v.i.* **4.** *Fort.* to dig a sap. [earlier *zappe* < It *zapp(a)* hoe, mattock; cf. ML *zapa* horseshoe] —**Syn. 3.** impair, enfeeble, deplete, exhaust, enervate.

s.ap., scruple (apothecary's weight).

sa·pan·wood (sə pan′wŏŏd′), *n.* sappanwood.

sap·head (sap′hed′), *n.* *Slang.* a simpleton; fool.

sap·head·ed (sap′hed′id), *adj.* *Slang.* silly; foolish. —**sap′head′ed·ness,** *n.*

sap·id (sap′id), *adj.* **1.** having taste or flavor. **2.** agreeable to the taste; palatable. **3.** agreeable to the mind. [< L *sapid(us)* flavored] —**sa·pid′i·ty, sap′id·ness,** *n.*

sa·pi·ent (sā′pē ənt), *adj.* wise or sage. [< L *sapient-* (s. of *sapiēns*, prp. of *sapere* to be wise) = *sapi-* taste, think + *-ent-* -ENT] —**sa′pi·ence, sa′pi·en·cy,** *n.* —**sa′pi·ent·ly,** *adv.* —**Syn.** sagacious. —**Ant.** stupid.

sap·in·da·ceous (sap′in dā′shəs), *adj.* belonging to the *Sapindaceae* or soapberry family of plants. [< NL *sāpindā-ce(ae)* soapberry family (*Sāpind(us)* (L *sāp(ō)* soap + *Indus* Indian) + *-āceae* -ACEAE) + -OUS]

Sa·pir (sə pēr′), *n.* **Edward,** 1884–1939, U.S. anthropologist and linguist, born in Germany.

sap·ling (sap′ling), *n.* a young tree.

sap·o·dil·la (sap′ə dil′ə), *n.* **1.** a large evergreen tree, *Achras Zapota*, of tropical America, bearing an edible fruit and yielding chicle. **2.** Also called **sap′odil′la plum′.** the fruit itself. [< Sp *zapotillo*, dim. of *zapote* < Nahuatl tsapotl]

sap·o·na·ceous (sap′ə nā′shəs), *adj.* soaplike; soapy. [< NL *sāpōnāceus* = L *sāpōn-* (s. of *sāpō*) SOAP + *-āceus* -ACEOUS] —**sap′o·na′ceous·ness,** *n.*

sa·pon·i·fy (sə pon′ə fī), *v.*, **-fied, -fy·ing.** *Chem.* —*v.t.* **1.** to convert (a fat) into soap by treating with an alkali. **2.** to decompose (any ester), forming the corresponding alcohol and acid or salt. —*v.i.* **3.** to become converted into soap. [< L *sāpōn-* (s. of *sāpō*) SOAP + -IFY] —**sa·pon′i·fi·ca′tion,** *n.* —**sa·pon′i·fi′er,** *n.*

sap·o·nin (sap′ə nin), *n.* any of a group of amorphous glucosidal compounds of steroid structure, characterized by an ability to form emulsions and to foam in aqueous solutions, and used as detergents. [< F *saponine* < L *sāpōn-* (s. of *sāpō*) SOAP + F *-ine* -IN[2]]

sa·por (sā′pər, -pôr), *n.* the quality in a substance that affects the sense of taste; savor; flavor. Also, *Brit.*, **sa′pour.** [ME *sapo(u)r* < L *sapor* SAVOR]

sap·o·rif·ic (sap′ə rif′ik), *adj.* producing or imparting flavor or taste. [< NL *sapōrific(us)*. See SAPOR, -I-, -FIC]

sap·o·rous (sap′ər əs), *adj.* full of flavor or taste; flavorful. [< LL *sapōrōs(us)*. See SAPOR, -OUS] —**sap·o·ros·i·ty** (sap′ə ros′i tē), *n.*

sap·o·ta·ceous (sap′ə tā′shəs), *adj.* belonging to the *Sapotaceae*, or sapodilla family of plants. [< NL *sapotāce(ae)* (see SAPOTA, -ACEAE) + -OUS]

sap·pan·wood (sə pan′wo͝od′), *n.* **1.** a dyewood yielding a red color, produced by a small, East Indian, caesalpiniaceous tree, *Caesalpinia Sappan*. **2.** the tree itself. Also, **sapanwood.** [< Malay *sapan(g)* + WOOD[1]]

sap·per (sap′ər), *n.* *Brit.* a soldier in a military unit of engineers, usually employed in the construction of trenches, fortifications, etc. [SAP[2] + -ER[1]]

Sap·phic (saf′ik), *adj.* **1.** pertaining to Sappho or to certain meters or a form of strophe or stanza used by or named after her. —*n.* **2.** a Sapphic verse. [< L *sapphic(us)* < Gk *sapphikós*. See SAPPHO, -IC]

Sap′phic ode′, *Pros.* See **Horatian ode.**

Sap·phi·ra (sə fī′rə), *n.* a woman who, with her husband, Ananias, was struck dead for lying. Acts 5.

sap·phire (saf′īər), *n.* **1.** any gem variety of corundum other than the ruby, esp. one of the blue varieties. **2.** a deep blue. [< L *sapphīr(us)* < Gk *sáppheiros* < Heb *sappīr* < ?; r. ME *safir* < OF]

sap·phir·ine (saf′ər in, -ə rēn′, -ə rīn′), *adj.* **1.** consisting of sapphire. **2.** having the color of a blue sapphire. —*n.* **3.** a pale-blue or greenish, usually granular mineral, a silicate of magnesium and aluminum. **4.** a blue variety of spinel. [< G *Saphirin*]

sap·phism (saf′iz əm), *n.* lesbianism. —**sap′phist,** *n.*

Sap·pho (saf′ō), *n.* c620–c565 B.C., Greek poetess, born in Lesbos.

Sap·po·ro (sä′pô rô′), *n.* a city on W Hokkaido, in N Japan. 704,182 (1964).

sap·py (sap′ē), *adj.*, **-pi·er, -pi·est. 1.** abounding in sap, as a plant. **2.** full of vitality and energy. **3.** *Slang.* silly or foolish. —**sap′pi·ness,** *n.*

sa·pre·mi·a (sə prē′mē ə), *n.* *Pathol.* a form of blood poisoning, esp. that caused by the toxins produced by certain microorganisms. —**sa·pre′mic,** *adj.*

sapro-, a learned borrowing from Greek meaning "rotten," used in the formation of technical terms: *saprogenic*. Also, *esp. before a vowel,* **sapr-.** [< Gk, comb. form of *saprós*]

sap·ro·gen·ic (sap′rō jen′ik), *adj.* **1.** producing putrefaction or decay, as certain bacteria. **2.** formed by putrefaction. Also, **sa·prog·e·nous** (sə proj′ə nəs).

sap·ro·lite (sap′rə līt′), *n.* *Petrog.* soft, disintegrated, usually more or less decomposed rock remaining in its original place. —**sap·ro·lit·ic** (sap′rə lit′ik), *adj.*

sa·proph·a·gous (sa prof′ə gəs), *adj.* *Biol.* (of a plant or animal) feeding on dead or decaying animal matter.

sap·ro·phyte (sap′rə fīt′), *n.* any organism that lives on dead organic matter, as certain fungi or bacteria. —**sap·ro·phyt·ic** (sap′rə fit′ik), *adj.* —**sap′ro·phyt′i·cal·ly,** *adv.*

sap·sa·go (sap′sə gō′), *n.* a strong, hard, usually green cheese of Swiss origin, made with sour skim milk and sweet clover. [alter. of G *Schabziger, Schabzieger* = *schab(en)* (to) grate + *Zi(e)ger* a kind of cheese]

sap·suck·er (sap′suk′ər), *n.* either of two American woodpeckers of the genus *Sphyrapicus* that drill holes in maple, apple, hemlock, etc., drinking the sap and eating the insects that gather there.

sap·wood (sap′wo͝od′), *n.* *Bot.* the softer part of the wood between the inner bark and the heartwood. Also called **alburnum.**

Saq·qa·ra (sə kär′ə), *n.* a village in the S Arab Republic of Egypt, S of Cairo: necropolis of ancient Memphis; step pyramids; mastabas. Also, **Sakkara.**

Sar., Sardinia.

S.A.R., Sons of the American Revolution.

Sa·ra (sär′ə), *n.*, *pl.* **-ras,** (*esp. collectively*) **-ra.** a member of a Negro people of the Central African Republic.

sar·a·band (sar′ə band′), *n.* **1.** a popular and vigorous Spanish castanet dance. **2.** a slow, stately Spanish dance in triple meter derived from this. **3.** a piece of music for or using the rhythm of this dance. Also, **sar′a·bande′.** [< F *sarabande* < Sp *zaraband(a)* < Ar, Pers *serbend* kind of dance]

Sar·a·cen (sar′ə sən), *n.* **1.** *Hist.* a member of any of the nomadic tribes on the Syrian borders of the Roman Empire. **2.** (in later use) an Arab. **3.** a Muslim, esp. one mentioned in connection with any of the Crusades. [OE < LL *Saracēn(us)* < LGk *Sarakēnós*] —**Sar·a·cen·ic** (sar′ə sen′ik), *adj.*

Sa·ra·gat (sä′rä gät′), *n.* **Giu·sep·pe** (jo͞o zep′pe), born 1898, Italian statesman: president 1964–71.

Sar·a·gos·sa (sar′ə gos′ə), *n.* a city in NE Spain, on the Ebro River. 291,181 (est. 1960). Spanish, **Zaragoza.**

Sar·ah (sâr′ə), *n.* the wife of Abraham and mother of Isaac. Gen. 17:15–22. Also, **Sa·rai** (sâr′ī, -ā ī′). [< Heb]

Sa·ra·je·vo (sar′ə yā′vō; *Serbo-Croatian.* sä′rä ye vô), *n.* a city in Bosnia, in central Yugoslavia: assassination of the Austrian Archduke Francis Ferdinand here June 28, 1914, precipitated World War I. 218,000 (1961). Also, **Serajevo.**

sa·ran (sə ran′), *n.* a thermoplastic copolymer of vinylidene chloride and usually small amounts of vinyl chloride or acrylonitrile: used as a fiber, for packaging, and for making acid-resistant pipe. [formerly trademark]

Sar′a·nac Lake′ (sar′ə nak′), a village in NE New York, near the Saranac Lakes: health resort. 6086 (1970).

Sar′anac Lakes′, a group of three lakes in NE New York, in the Adirondack Mountains.

Sa·ransk (sä ränsk′), *n.* a city in the W RSFSR, in the central Soviet Union in Europe. 132,000 (est. 1964).

sa·ra·pe (sə rä′pē; *Sp.* sä rä′pe), *n.*, *pl.* **-pes** (-pēz; *Sp.* -pes). serape.

Sar·a·so·ta (sar′ə sō′tə), *n.* a city in W Florida. 40,237 (1970).

Sar·a·to·ga (sar′ə tō′gə), *n.* **1.** former name of **Schuylerville. 2.** a city in W California, near San Jose. 27,110 (1970).

Sar′ato′ga chip′. See **potato chip.** Also called **Sarato′ga pota′to.**

Sar′ato′ga Springs′, a city in E New York: health resort; horse races. 18,845 (1970).

Sar′ato′ga trunk′, a type of large traveling trunk used mainly by women during the 19th century. [named after SARATOGA (SPRINGS)]

Sa·ra·tov (sä rä′tof), *n.* a city in the SW RSFSR, in the E Soviet Union in Europe, on the Volga. 684,000 (1965).

Sa·ra·wak (sə rä′wäk, -wä), *n.* a region in Malaysia, on NW Borneo: formerly a British crown colony 1946–63 and a British protectorate 1888–1946. 790,607 (est. 1962); ab. 50,000 sq. mi. *Cap.:* Kuching.

sarc-, var. of **sarco-,** esp. before a vowel: *sarcous*.

sar·casm (sär′kaz əm), *n.* **1.** harsh or bitter derision or irony. **2.** a sharply ironical taunt or gibe; a sneering or cutting remark. [< LL *sarcasm(us)* < Gk *sarkasmós* < *sarkáz(ein)* (to) rend (flesh), sneer; see SARCO-] —**Syn. 1.** bitterness, ridicule. See **irony. 2.** jeer.

sar·cas·tic (sär kas′tik), *adj.* **1.** characterized by, of the nature of, or pertaining to sarcasm. **2.** using or given to the use of sarcasm. Also, **sar·cas′ti·cal.** [SARC(ASM) + -ASTIC] —**sar·cas′ti·cal·ly,** *adv.* —**Syn. 2.** biting, cutting, mordant, bitter, derisive, ironic, sardonic. See **cynical.**

sarce·net (särs′nit), *n.* a very fine, soft, silk fabric, used esp. for linings. Also, **sarsenet.** [ME *sarsenet* < AF *sarzinet*, prob. = *sarzin-* SARACEN + *-et* -ET]

sarco-, a learned borrowing from Greek meaning "flesh," used in the formation of compound words: *sarcocarp*. Also, *esp. before a vowel,* **sarc-.** [< Gk *sark-* (s. of *sárx*) + -o-]

sar·co·carp (sär′kō kärp′), *n.* *Bot.* **1.** the fleshy mesocarp of certain fruits, as the peach. **2.** any fruit of fleshy consistency.

sar·coid (sär′koid), *Pathol.* —*n.* **1.** a growth resembling a sarcoma. —*adj.* **2.** resembling flesh; fleshy.

sar·co·ma (sär kō′mə), *n.*, *pl.* **-mas, -ma·ta** (-mə tə). *Pathol.* any of various malignant tumors originating in the connective tissue and attacking esp. the bones. [< NL < Gk *sárkōma* fleshy growth. See SARC-, -OMA] —**sar·co·ma·toid** (sär kō′mə toid′), **sar·co·ma·tous** (sär kō′mə təs, -kom′ə-), *adj.*

sar·co·ma·to·sis (sär kō′mə tō′sis), *n.* *Pathol.* the condition in which a sarcoma has become disseminated throughout the body. [*sarcomat-* (comb. form of SARCOMA) + -OSIS]

sar·coph·a·gus (sär kof′ə gəs), *n.*, *pl.* **-gi** (-jī′), **-gus·es.** a stone coffin, esp. one bearing sculpture, inscriptions, etc., often displayed as a monument. [< L < Gk *sarkophágos* flesh-eating (so called from the stone used, thought to consume the flesh of corpses)]

sar·cous (sär′kəs), *adj.* consisting of or pertaining to flesh or skeletal muscle.

sard (särd), *n.* a reddish-brown chalcedony, used as a gem. Also, **sardius, sardine.** [< L *sard(a)* < Gk *sárdios* SARDIUS]

Sar·da·na·pa·lus (sär′dənə pā′ləs, -dənap′ə ləs), *n.* a Greek name for **Ashurbanipal** or **Ashurnasirpal II.** Also **Sar·da·na·pal·los, Sar·da·na·pa·los** (sär′dənə pal′os, -ōs; *Gk.* sär′thä nä′pä lôs).

sar·dine[1] (sär dēn′), *n.*, *pl.* (*esp. collectively*) **-dine,** (*esp. referring to two or more kinds or species*) **-dines. 1.** the pilchard, *Sardina pilchardus*, often preserved in oil and used for food. **2.** any of various similar, closely related fishes. [ME *sardeine* < MF *sardine* < L *sardīn(a)*, dim. of *sarda* sardine]

sar·dine[2] (sär′dīn, -dən), *n.* sard. [late ME < LL *sardin(us)* < Gk *sárdinos* SARDIUS]

Sar·din·i·a (sär din′ē ə, -din′yə), *n.* **1.** a large island in the Mediterranean, W of Italy: with small nearby islands it comprises a department of Italy. 1,413,289 (1961); 9301 sq. mi. **2.** a former kingdom 1720–1860, including this island and Savoy, Piedmont, and Genoa (after 1815) in NW Italy: ruled by the House of Savoy. *Cap.:* Turin.

Sar·din·i·an (sär din′ē ən, -din′yən), *adj.* **1.** of or pertaining to Sardinia, its inhabitants, or their language. —*n.* **2.** a native or inhabitant of Sardinia. **3.** a Romance language spoken on Sardinia.

Sar·dis (sär′dis), *n.* an ancient city in W Asia Minor: the capital of ancient Lydia. Also, **Sar·des** (sär′dēz). —**Sar·di·an** (sär′dē ən), *n.*, *adj.*

sar·di·us (sär′dē əs), *n.* **1.** sard. **2.** the precious stone in the breastplate of the Jewish high priest. Ex. 28:17. [< L < Gk *sárdios* (stone) of SARDIS]

sar·don·ic (sär don′ik), *adj.* characterized by bitter or scornful derision. [alter. of earlier *sardonian* (influenced by F *sardonique*) < L *sardoni(us)* (< Gk *sardónios* of Sardinia) +

-AN; alluding to a Sardinian plant that when eaten was supposed to produce convulsive laughter ending in death] —**sar·don′i·cal·ly,** *adv.* —**sar·don′i·cism,** *n.* —**Syn.** biting, mordant, contemptuous.

sar·don·yx (sär don′iks, sär′dənikz), *n.* a chalcedony that is used for cameos and has sard and chalcedony of another color, usually white, arranged in straight parallel bands. [ME < L < Gk]

Sar·dou (sär do͞o′), *n.* **Vic·to·rien** (vēk tô ryen′), 1831–1908, French dramatist.

sar·gas·so (sär gas′ō), *n., pl.* **-sos.** a gulfweed. [< Pg, perh. special use of *sargaço* rockrose < L *salicastrum* = *salic-* (s. of *salix*) willow + *-astrum,* neut. of *-aster* -ASTER[1]]

Sargas′so Sea′, a relatively calm area of water in the N Atlantic, NE of the West Indies, noted for an abundance of seaweed.

sar·gas·sum (sär gas′əm), *n.* any seaweed of the genus *Sargassum,* widely distributed in the warmer waters of the globe, as *S. bacciferum,* the common gulfweed. [< NL; see SARGASSO]

Sar·gent (sär′jənt), *n.* **John Singer,** 1856–1925, U.S. painter.

Sar·gon II (sär′gon), died 705 B.C., king of Assyria 722–705.

sa·ri (sär′ē), *n., pl.* **-ris.** a long piece of cotton or silk, the principal outer garment of Hindu women, worn around the body with one end draped over the head or over one shoulder. [< Hindi *sārī* < Skt *śāṭī*]

sark (särk), *n. Scot. and North Eng.* any long, shirtlike garment worn next to the skin, as a chemise, nightshirt, or the like. [ME; OE *serc;* c. Icel *serkr*]

Sar·ma·ti·a (sär mā′shē ə, -shə), *n.* the ancient name of a region now in Poland and the W Soviet Union in Europe, between the Vistula and the Volga. —**Sar·ma′ti·an,** *adj., n.*

sar·men·tose (sär men′tōs), *adj. Bot.* having runners. Also, **sar·men·tous** (sär men′təs), **sar·men·ta·ceous** (sär′mən tā′shəs). [< L *sarmentōs(us)* = *sarment(um)* twig + *-ōsus* -OSE[1]]

Sar·nath (sär′nät), *n.* an ancient Buddhist pilgrimage center in N India, near Benares: Buddha's first sermon preached here.

Sar·nen (*Ger.* zär′nən), *n.* a town in and the capital of Obwalden, in central Switzerland, E of Bern.

Sar·noff (sär′nôf, -nof), *n.* **David,** 1891–1971, U.S. business leader and broadcasting executive, born in Russia.

sa·rong (sə rông′, -rong′), *n.* a loose-fitting, skirtlike garment formed by wrapping a strip of cloth around the lower part of the body, worn by men and women in the Malay Archipelago and certain islands of the Pacific Ocean. [< D < Malay]

Sa·ron′ic Gulf′ (sə ron′ik), an inlet of the Aegean, on the SE coast of Greece, between Attica and the Peloponnesus. 50 mi. long; 30 mi. wide. Also called **Gulf of Aegina.**

Sa·ros (sär′ōs, -ôs), *n.* **Gulf of,** an inlet of the Aegean, N of the Gallipoli Peninsula. 37 mi. long; 22 mi. wide.

Sa·roy·an (sə roi′ən), *n.* **William,** 1908–81, U.S. dramatist, short-story writer, and novelist.

Sar·pe·don (sär pēd′ən, -pē′don), *n. Class. Myth.* a Lycian prince, son of Zeus, killed by Patroclus in the Trojan War.

sar·ra·ce·ni·a (sar′ə sē′nē ə), *n.* any American marsh plant of the genus *Sarracenia,* having hollow leaves with a pitcherlike shape in which insects are trapped and digested, as *S. purpurea,* a common pitcher plant. [< NL = *Sarracen* (alter. of surname *Sarrazin*) + *-ia* -IA; named after a 17th-century physician and botanist of Quebec, the first to send specimens to Europe]

sar·ra·ce·ni·a·ceous (sar′ə sē′nē ā′shəs), *adj.* belonging to the *Sarraceniaceae,* the American pitcher-plant family. [< NL *Sarraceniaceae* (see SARRACENIA, -ACEAE) + -OUS]

Sarre (SAR), *n.* French name of **Saar.**

sar·sa·pa·ril·la (sär′sə pə ril′ə, sär′spə-, sas′pə-), *n.* **1.** any of various climbing or trailing tropical American plants of the genus *Smilax,* having a root that was formerly used as an alterative. **2.** the root. **3.** an extract or other preparation made of this root. **4.** a soft drink flavored with an extract of this root, as root beer. [< Sp *zarzaparrilla* = *zarza* bush + *parrilla,* dim. of *parra* vine]

sar·sen (sär′sən), *n.* any of numerous large sandstone blocks or fragments found in south central England, probably remnants of eroded Tertiary beds. Also called **Druid stone, graywether.** [syncopated var. of SARACEN, short for *Saracen boulder* Druid stone]

sarse·net (särs′nit), *n.* sarcenet.

Sar·to (sär′tō; *It.* sär′tô), *n.* **An·dre·a del** (än drā′ə del; *It.* än dre′ä del), (*Andrea Domenico d'Annolo di Francesco*), 1486–1531, Italian painter.

sar·to·ri·al (sär tôr′ē əl, -tōr′-), *adj.* **1.** of or pertaining to a tailor or to tailoring. **2.** *Anat.* pertaining to the sartorius. [< L *sartor* tailor + -IAL] —**sar·to′ri·al·ly,** *adv.*

sar·to·ri·us (sär tôr′ē əs, -tôr′-), *n., pl.* **-to·ri·i** (-tōr′ē ī′, -tôr′-). *Anat.* a long, flat, narrow muscle extending obliquely from the front of the hip to the inner side of the tibia, the action of which assists in bending the hip or knee joint and in rotating the thigh outward: the longest muscle in man. [< NL = L *sartor* tailor + *-ius* -IOUS]

Sar·tre (sär′trə, särt; *Fr.* SAR′trə), *n.* **Jean Paul** (zhäN pôl), 1905–80, French philosopher, novelist, and dramatist: declined 1964 Nobel prize for literature.

Sar·um (sâr′əm), *n.* ancient Roman name of Salisbury, England.

Sar′um use′, the liturgy or modified form of the Roman rite used in Salisbury before the Reformation.

Sa·se·bo (sä′sə bô′), *n.* a seaport on NW Kyushu, in SW Japan. 253,585 (1964).

Sa·se·no (sä′sə nô′), *n.* an island off the W coast of Albania, at the entrance to Valona Bay: belongs to Albania. 2 sq. mi.

sash[1] (sash), *n.* a long band or scarf of cloth worn over one shoulder or around the waist. [dissimilated var. of *shash* (turban of) muslin < Ar]

sash[2] (sash), *n.* **1.** a fixed or movable framework, as in a window or door, in which panes of glass are set. **2.** such frameworks collectively. —*v.t.* **3.** to furnish with sashes or with windows having sashes. [back formation from *sashes* (pl.), dissimilated var. of *shashes* CHASSIS]

sa·shay (sa shā′), *v.i. U.S. Informal.* **1.** to glide, move, or proceed easily or nonchalantly. **2.** to chassé in dancing. [metathetic var. of CHASSÉ]

Sask., Saskatchewan.

Sas·katch·e·wan (sas kach′ə won′), *n.* **1.** a province in W Canada. 951,000 (est. 1965); 251,700 sq. mi. *Cap.:* Regina. **2.** a river in SW Canada, flowing E to Lake Winnipeg: formed by the junction of the North Saskatchewan and South Saskatchewan rivers. 1205 mi. long.

sas·ka·toon (sas′kə to͞on′), *n.* any of several shad bushes, esp. the serviceberry, *Amelanchier canadensis.* [after SASKATOON]

Sas·ka·toon (sas′kə to͞on′), *n.* a city in S Saskatchewan, in SW Canada. 95,526 (1961).

sass[1] (sas), *n. Chiefly Midland U.S.* sauce.

sass[2] (sas), *Informal.* —*n.* **1.** impudent or disrespectful back talk. —*v.t.* **2.** to answer back in an impudent manner. [back formation from SASSY[1]]

sas·sa·fras (sas′ə fras′), *n.* **1.** an American, lauraceous tree, *Sassafras albidum.* **2.** the aromatic bark of its root, used esp. for flavoring beverages, confectionery, etc. [< Sp *sasafrás*]

sas′safras oil′, a volatile oil distilled from the root of the sassafras tree, used in flavoring, perfumery, and medicine.

sas′safras tea′, a tea made from the aromatic dried bark of the root of the sassafras tree, often used medicinally as a stimulant, diaphoretic, and diuretic.

Sas·sa·nid (sə sä′nid, -san′id), *n., pl.* **-sa·nids, -san·i·dae** (-sä′ni dē′, -san′i-). a member of a dynasty that ruled in Persia A.D. 226–651. Also, **Sas·sa·ni·an** (sə sā′nē ən), **Sassa·nide** (sas′ə nīd). [< NL = *Sassan* grandfather of first king of dynasty + *-idae* -ID[2]]

Sas·se·nach (sas′ə nakh, -nak), *n.* (in Gaelic-speaking areas) an English person or persons. [< Ir *sasanach* English = *sasan(a)* England (OE *seaxan* Saxons) + *-ach* adj. suffix]

Sas·soon (sa so͞on′), *n.* **Sieg·fried (Lo·raine)** (sēg′frēd lō rān′, lô-, sig′-), 1886–1967, English poet and novelist.

sas·sy[1] (sas′ē), *adj.,* **-si·er, -si·est.** *Informal.* saucy.

sas·sy[2] (sas′ē), *n.* See **sassy bark.** [< WAfr]

sas′sy bark′, **1.** the bark of a large, African, caesalpiniaceous tree, *Erythrophloeum guineense,* used by the natives as a poison in ordeals. **2.** Also called **sas·sy·wood** (sas′ē-wo͝od′). the tree itself.

sat (sat), *v.* a pt. and pp. of **sit.**

SAT, Scholastic Aptitude Test.

Sat., **1.** Saturday. **2.** Saturn.

Sa·tan (sāt′ən), *n.* the chief evil spirit; the great adversary of man; the devil. [OE < L < Gk < Heb: adversary]

sa·tang (sä tang′), *n., pl.* **-tang.** a money of account of Thailand, the 100th part of a baht. [< Siamese *satān*]

sa·tan·ic (sā tan′ik, sə-), *adj.* **1.** of Satan. **2.** characteristic of or befitting Satan. Also, **sa·tan′i·cal.** [< eccl. Gk *satanikós.* See SATAN, -IC] —**sa·tan′i·cal·ly,** *adv.* —**sa·tan′i·cal·ness,** *n.* —**Syn. 2.** evil, devilish, hellish, fiendish.

Sa·tan·ism (sāt′əniz′əm), *n.* **1.** the worship of Satan or the powers of evil. **2.** a travesty of Christian rites in which Satan is worshiped. **3.** diabolical or satanic disposition, behavior, or action. —**Sa′tan·ist,** *n.*

satch·el (sach′əl), *n.* a small bag, sometimes with a shoulder strap. [ME *sachel* < OF < L *saccell(us),* dim. of *saccus* SAC] —**satch′eled,** *adj.*

sate[1] (sāt), *v.t.,* **sat·ed, sat·ing.** **1.** to satisfy (any appetite or desire) fully. **2.** to surfeit; glut. [var. of obs. *sade* to satiate, OE *sad(ian),* perh. by contamination with L *sat* enough; see SAD] —**Syn. 1.** satiate, fill. **2.** gorge, stuff.

sate[2] (sat, sāt), *v. Archaic.* pt. and pp. of **sit.**

sa·teen (sa tēn′), *n.* a cotton or linen fabric simulating satin in weave and gloss. [var. of SATIN, by assoc. with *velveteen*]

sat·el·lite (sat′əlīt′), *n.* **1.** *Astron.* a body that revolves around a planet; moon. **2.** a person or thing that depends on, accompanies, or serves someone or something else. **3.** a country under the domination or influence of another. **4.** a man-made device launched from the earth into orbit around a planet or the sun. —*adj.* Also, **sat·el·lit·ic** (sat′əlit′ik). **5.** of, pertaining to, or constituting a satellite. **6.** subordinate to another authority. [< L *satellit-* (s. of *satelles*) attendant, member of bodyguard or retinue < Etruscan]

sa·tem (sä′təm), *adj.* belonging to or consisting of those branches of the Indo-European family in which alveolar or palatal fricatives, as the sounds (s) or (sh), developed in ancient times from Proto-Indo-European palatal stops: the satem branches are Indo-Iranian, Armenian, Slavic, Baltic, and Albanian. [< Avestan *satəm* hundred]

sa·tia·ble (sā′shə bəl, shē ə-), *adj.* capable of being satiated. [SATI(ATE) + -ABLE] —**sa′ti·a·bil′i·ty, sa′ti·a·ble·ness,** *n.* —**sa′ti·a·bly,** *adv.*

sa·ti·ate (*v.* sā′shē āt′; *adj.* sā′shē it, -āt′), *v.,* **-at·ed, -at·ing,** *adj.* —*v.t.* **1.** to supply with anything to excess, so as to disgust or weary; surfeit. **2.** to satisfy to the full; sate. —*adj.* **3.** *Archaic.* satiated. [< L *satiāt(us)* (ptp. of *satiāre* to satisfy) = *sati-* (see SAD) + *-ātus* -ATE[1]] —**sa′ti·a′tion,** *n.* —**Syn. 1.** glut, stuff, gorge.

sa·ti·at·ed (sā′shē ā′tid), *adj.* satisfied, as one's appetite or desire, to the point of boredom.

Sa·tie (sä tē′), *n.* **E·rik (Al·fred Les·lie)** (e rēk′ al fred′ les lē′), 1866–1925, French composer.

sa·ti·e·ty (sə tī′i tē), *n.* the state of being satiated; surfeit. [< L *satietāt-* (s. of *satietās*); r. *sacietie* < MF *sacieté*]

sat·in (sat′ən), *n.* **1.** See **satin weave. 2.** a fabric in a warp-effect or filling-effect satin weave. **3.** a dress or other garment of satin. —*adj.* **4.** of or like satin; smooth; glossy. **5.** made of or covered or decorated with satin. [ME *satyn,* etc. < MF *satin,* prob. < Ar *zaitūnī* of *Zaitūn* a city in China where the cloth was made, prob. Tsinkiang] —**sat′in·like′,** *adj.*

sat·i·net (sat′ənet′), *n.* **1.** a low-quality, satin-weave fabric containing cotton. **2.** *Obs.* a thin, light satin. Also, **sat′i·nette′.** [< F]

sat·in-flow·er (sat′ən flou′ər), *n.* an herb, *Godetia grandiflora,* of California, having short spikes of red flowers with deep red-blotched centers.

sat·in·pod (sat′ən pod′), *n.* either of two European,

cruciferous plants of the genus *Lunaria, L. annua,* or *L. rediviva,* cultivated for their shiny flowers and large, round, flat, satiny pods. [SATIN + POD[1]]

sat′in stitch′, a stitch used in making an embroidered pattern of closely placed, parallel stitches that resembles satin.

sat′in weave′, one of the basic weave structures in which the filling threads are interlaced with the warp at widely separated intervals, producing the effect of an unbroken surface. Also called **satin.** Cf. **plain weave, twill weave.**

Satin weave

sat·in·wood (sat′ᵊn wo͝od′), *n.* **1.** the satiny wood of an East Indian meliaceous tree, *Chloroxylon Swietenia,* used esp. for making furniture. **2.** the tree itself.

sat·in·y (sat′ᵊnē), *adj.* satinlike; smooth; glossy.

sat·ire (sat′īᵊr), *n.* **1.** the use of ridicule in exposing, denouncing, or deriding vice, folly, etc. **2.** a literary composition, in verse or prose, in which human folly, vice, etc., are held up to scorn, derision, or ridicule. **3.** a literary genre comprising such compositions. [< L *satir(a),* var. of *satura* medley < *satur* sated, var. of *satis* enough; see SAD] —**Syn. 1.** See **irony. 2, 3.** burlesque, caricature, parody, travesty. SATIRE, LAMPOON refer to literary forms in which vices or follies are ridiculed. SATIRE, the general term, often emphasizes the weakness more than the weak person, and usually implies moral judgment and corrective purpose: *Swift's satire of human pettiness and bestiality.* LAMPOON refers to a form of satire, often political or personal, characterized by the malice or virulence of its attack: *lampoons of the leading political figures.*

sa·tir·i·cal (sə tir′i kəl), *adj.* **1.** of, pertaining to, containing, or characterized by satire. **2.** indulging in or given to satire. Also, **sa·tir′ic.** [< LL *satiric(us)* (see SATIRE, -IC) + -AL[1]] —**sa·tir′i·cal·ly,** *adv.* —**sa·tir′i·cal·ness,** *n.* —**Syn. 1.** sardonic, ironical, cutting. See **cynical.**

sat·i·rise (sat′ə rīz′), *v.t.,* **-rised, -ris·ing.** *Chiefly Brit.* satirize. —**sat′i·ri·sa′tion,** *n.* —**sat′i·ris′er,** *n.*

sat·i·rist (sat′ər ist), *n.* **1.** a writer of satires. **2.** a person who indulges in satire.

sat·i·rize (sat′ə rīz′), *v.t.,* **-rized, -riz·ing.** to attack or ridicule with satire; subject to satire. Also, *esp. Brit.,* **satirise.** —**sat′i·ri·za′tion,** *n.* —**sat′i·riz′er,** *n.*

sat·is·fac·tion (sat′is fak′shən), *n.* **1.** the act of satisfying. **2.** the state of being satisfied. **3.** the cause or means of being satisfied. **4.** confident acceptance of something as satisfactory, dependable, true, etc. **5.** reparation or compensation, as for a wrong or injury. **6.** the opportunity of repairing a supposed wrong, as by a duel. **7.** payment or discharge, as of a debt or obligation. **8.** *Eccles.* **a.** the act of doing penance or making reparation for venial sin. **b.** the penance or reparation made. [< L *satisfactiōn-* (s. of *satisfactiō*) a doing enough = *satisfact(us)* (ptp. of *satisfacere* to SATISFY) + *-iōn-* -ION; r. ME *satisfaccioun* < AF] —**sat′is·fac′tion·al,** *adj.* —**Syn. 2.** gratification, enjoyment, pleasure. **5.** amends, indemnity, recompense.

sat·is·fac·to·ry (sat′is fak′tə rē), *adj.* **1.** giving or affording satisfaction. **2.** *Theol.* atoning or expiating. [< ML *satisfactōri(us).* See SATISFACTION, -ORY[1]] —**sat′is·fac′to·ri·ly,** *adv.*

sat·is·fied (sat′is fīd′), *adj.* **1.** content. **2.** completely paid, as a bill. **3.** convinced, as in an argument.

sat·is·fy (sat′is fī′), *v.,* **-fied, -fy·ing.** —*v.t.* **1.** to fulfill the desires, expectations, needs, or demands of (a person, the mind, etc.); give full contentment to. **2.** to put an end to (a desire, need, etc.) by sufficient or ample provision: *The meal satisfied his hunger.* **3.** to give assurance to; convince: *to satisfy oneself by investigation.* **4.** to solve or dispel, as a doubt. **5.** to discharge fully (a debt, obligation, etc.). **6.** to pay (a creditor). **7.** to make reparation to or for. **8.** *Math.* **a.** to fulfill the requirements or conditions of: *to satisfy a theorem.* **b.** (of a value of an unknown) to change (an equation) into an identity when substituted for the unknown: *x = 2 satisfies 3x = 6.* —*v.i.* **9.** to give satisfaction. [ME *satisfi(en)* < MF *satisfie(r)* < VL **satisficāre,* r. L *satisfacere* to do enough = *satis* enough + *facere* to do); see -FY] —**sat′is·fi′a·ble,** *adj.* —**sat′is·fi′er,** *n.* —**sat′is·fy′ing·ly,** *adv.* —**Syn. 1.** gratify, appease, pacify, please. SATISFY, CONTENT refer to meeting one's desires or wishes. To SATISFY is to meet to the full a person's wants, expectations, etc.: *to satisfy a desire to travel.* To CONTENT is to give enough to keep a person from being disposed to find fault or complain: *to content oneself with a moderate meal.*

Sa·to (sä′tô), *n.* **Ei·sa·ku** (ā′sä′ko͞o), born 1901, Japanese political leader: prime minister 1964–72.

sa·to·ri (sə tôr′ē, -tōr′ē), *n.* *Zen.* sudden enlightenment. [< Jap]

sa·trap (sā′trap, sa′-), *n.* **1.** a governor of a province under the ancient Persian monarchy. **2.** a subordinate ruler, often a despotic one. [ME < L *satrap(a)* < Gk *satrápēs* < OPers *xshathra-pāvan-* country-protector]

sa·trap·y (sā′trə pē, sa′-), *n., pl.* **-trap·ies.** the province or jurisdiction of a satrap. [< L *satrapia* < Gk *satrapeía*]

Sa·tsu·ma (sä′tso͞o mä′), *n.* a former province on S Kyushu, in SW Japan: famous for its porcelain ware.

sat·u·ra·ble (sach′ər ə bəl), *adj.* capable of being saturated. [< L *saturābil(is).* See SATURATE, -BLE] —**sat′u·ra·bil′i·ty,** *n.*

sat·u·rant (sach′ər ənt), *n.* **1.** something that causes saturation. —*adj.* **2.** that saturates; saturating. [< L *saturant-* (s. of *saturāns*) prp. of *saturāre* to SATURATE; see -ANT]

sat·u·rate (*v.* sach′ə rāt′; *adj.* sach′ər it, -ə rāt′), *v.,* **-rat·ed, -rat·ing** *adj.* —*v.t.* **1.** to cause (a substance) to unite with the greatest possible amount of another substance through solution, chemical combination, or the like. **2.** to charge to the utmost, as with magnetism. **3.** to soak, impregnate, or imbue thoroughly or completely. **4.** to destroy (a target) completely with many bombs or missiles. **5.** to furnish (a market) with goods to the point of oversupply. —*adj.* **6.** saturated. [< L *saturāt(us)* (ptp. of *saturāre* to fill) = *satur-* (see SAD) + *-ātus* -ATE[1]] —**sat′u·rat′er, sat′u·ra′tor,** *n.* —**Syn. 3.** See **wet.**

sat·u·rat·ed (sach′ə rā′tid), *adj.* **1.** soaked, impregnated, imbued, or charged thoroughly. **2.** (of colors) of maximum chroma or purity. **3.** *Chem.* **a.** (of a solution) containing the maximum amount of solute capable of being dissolved under given conditions. **b.** (of an organic compound) containing no double or triple bonds; having each single bond attached to an atom or group. **c.** (of an inorganic compound) having no free valence electrons.

sat·u·ra·tion (sach′ə rā′shən), *n.* **1.** the act or process of saturating. **2.** the state of being saturated. **3.** *Meteorol.* a condition in the atmosphere corresponding to 100 percent relative humidity. **4.** the degree of chroma or purity of a color; the degree of freedom from admixture with white. [< LL *saturātiōn-* (s. of *saturātiō*) a filling]

Sat·ur·day (sat′ər dē, -dā′), *n.* the seventh day of the week, following Friday. [OE *Sæter(nes)dæg,* trans. of L *Sāturnī diēs* Saturn's day; c. D *zaterdag,* LG *saterdag*]

Sat′urday-night′ spe′cial, *Slang.* a cheap, small-caliber handgun that is easily obtainable.

Sat·ur·days (sat′ər dēz, -dāz′), *adv.* on Saturdays.

Sat·urn (sat′ərn), *n.* **1.** an ancient Roman god of agriculture, identified with the Greek god Cronus. **2.** *Astron.* the planet sixth in order from the sun, having a diameter of 72,000 miles, a mean distance from the sun of 886,000,000 miles, a period of revolution of 29.5 years, and ten satellites, and is encompassed by a series of thin, flat rings. It is the second largest planet in the solar system. **3.** *Alchemy.* the metal lead. **4.** *U.S.* a space-vehicle launching booster developing up to 9,000,000 pounds of thrust.

Sat·ur·na·li·a (sat′ər nā′lē ə, -nāl′yə), *n., pl.* **-li·a, -li·as. 1.** (*sometimes construed as pl.*) the ancient Roman festival of Saturn, observed as a time of general feasting and unrestrained merrymaking. **2.** (*l.c.*) any period of unrestrained revelry. [< L = *Sāturn(us)* SATURN + *-ālia,* neut. pl. of *-ālis* -AL[1]] —**Sat′ur·na′li·an,** *adj.*

Sa·tur·ni·an (sə tûr′nē ən), *adj.* **1.** of or pertaining to the planet Saturn. **2.** of or pertaining to the god Saturn, or to the golden age when he reigned. **3.** prosperous, happy, or peaceful. [< L *sāturni(us)* of Saturn + -AN]

sa·tur·ni·id (sə tûr′nē id), *n.* **1.** any of several large, brightly colored moths of the family *Saturniidae,* comprising the giant silkworm moths. —*adj.* **2.** of or pertaining to the family *Saturniidae.* [< NL *Sāturniid(ae)* name of the family]

sat·ur·nine (sat′ər nīn′), *adj.* **1.** having or showing a sluggish, gloomy temperament. **2.** suffering from lead poisoning. **3.** due to absorption of lead, as bodily disorders. [ME < ML *sāturnīnus* (in astrol.)] —**sat′ur·nine′ly,** *adv.* —**sat′ur·nine′ness, sat·ur·nin·i·ty** (sat′ər nin′i tē), *n.*

sat·ur·nism (sat′ər niz′əm), *n.* *Pathol.* See **lead poisoning** (def. 1b). [< ML *Sāturn(us)* lead + -ISM; in alchemy the planet was thought to have leadlike properties]

Sat·ya·gra·ha (sut′yə grus′hə, ət yä′grə-), *n.* (in India) the policy of passive resistance inaugurated by Mohandas Gandhi. [< Hindi < Skt = *satya* truth + *graha* grasping]

sa·tyr (sā′tər, sat′ər), *n.* **1.** *Class. Myth.* one of a class of riotous, lascivious woodland deities, attendant on Bacchus, represented as part human and part goat. **2.** a lecher. **3.** a man who has satyriasis. **4.** Also, **sa′tyr but′terfly.** any of several butterflies of the family *Satyridae,* having gray or brown wings marked with eyespots. [ME < L *satyr(us)* < Gk *sátyros*] —**sa·tyr·ic** (sə tir′ik, sā tir′ik), **sa·tyr′i·cal,** *adj.*

sa·ty·ri·a·sis (sā′tə rī′ə sis, sat′ə-), *n.* *Pathol.* abnormal, uncontrollable sexual desire in men. Also called **sa·tyr·o·ma·ni·a** (sā′tə rō mā′nē ə, sat′ə-). [< NL < Gk]

sa′tyr play′, (in ancient Greek drama) a burlesque or ribald drama having a chorus of satyrs.

Sau (sou), *n.* German name of **Sava.**

sauce (sôs), *n., v.,* **sauced, sauc·ing.** —*n.* **1.** any preparation eaten as a gravy or as a liquid or semiliquid relish accompanying food. **2.** something that adds special piquance or zest. **3.** *U.S.* stewed fruit: *cranberry sauce.* **4.** *Dial.* garden vegetables eaten with meat. —*v.t.* **5.** to dress or prepare with sauce. [ME < MF < LL *salsa,* n. use of fem. of L *salsus* salted, ptp. of *sallere* to salt] —**sauce′less,** *adj.*

sauce·pan (sôs′pan′), *n.* a metal cooking pan of moderate depth, usually having a long handle and sometimes a cover.

sau·cer (sô′sər), *n.* a small, round, shallow dish, esp. one for holding a cup. [ME < OF *saussier.* See SAUCE, -ER[2]]

sau·cy (sô′sē), *adj.,* **-ci·er, -ci·est. 1.** impertinent; insolent. **2.** pert; boldly smart. —**sau′ci·ly,** *adv.* —**sau′ci·ness,** *n.* —**Syn. 1.** rude, impudent, fresh, brazen. **2.** jaunty.

Sa·ud (sä o͞od′), *n.* (*Saud ibn Abdul-Aziz*) 1901?–69, king of Saudi Arabia 1953–64 (son of ibn-Saud and brother of Faisal).

Sa·u′di Ara′bia (sä o͞o′dē, sou′dē, sô′-), a kingdom in N and central Arabia, including Hejaz, Nejd, and dependencies. 7,800,000; ab. 600,000 sq. mi. *Cap.:* Riyadh. Cf. **Jidda, Mecca.** —**Sau′di,** *adj., n.* —**Sau′di Ara′bian.**

sau·er·bra·ten (sour′brät′ᵊn, sou′ər-; *Ger.* zou′ər-brät′ᵊn), *n.* a pot roast of beef, marinated in a mixture of vinegar, sugar, and seasonings. [< G = *sauer* sour + *Braten* roast]

sauer·kraut (sour′krout′, sou′ər-), *n.* cabbage cut fine, salted, and allowed to ferment until sour. [< G = *sauer* sour + *Kraut* greens]

sau·ger (sô′gər), *n.* a fresh-water, North American pike-perch, *Stizostedion canadense.* [?]

Sau·gus (sô′gəs), *n.* a town in E Massachusetts, near Boston. 25,110 (1970).

Sauk (sôk), *n., pl.* **Sauks,** (*esp. collectively*) **Sauk.** Sac.

Saul (sôl), *n.* **1.** the first king of Israel. I Sam. 9. **2.** Also called **Saul′ of Tar′sus.** the original name of the apostle Paul. Acts 9:1–30; 22:3.

sault (so͞o), *n.* a waterfall or rapid. [ME *saut* < OF < L *salt(us)* leap]

Sault Ste. Ma·rie (so͞o′ sānt′ mə rē′), **1.** the rapids of the St. Marys River, between NE Michigan and Ontario, Canada. **2.** a city in S Ontario, in S Canada, near these rapids. 43,088 (1961). **3.** a city opposite it, in NE Michigan. 15,136 (1970). Also, **Sault′ Sainte′ Marie′.**

Sault Ste. Marie Canals, two ship canals, one in Canada and the other in Michigan, N and S of Sault Ste. Marie rapids and connecting Lakes Superior and Huron. 1½ mi. long. Also, **Sault′ Sainte′ Marie′ Canals′.** Also called **Soo Canals.**

sau·na (sou′nä, -nə, sô′-), *n.* a Finnish bath in which the bather is subjected to steam and to light strokings with switches made of birch branches. [< Finn]

saun·ter (sôn′tər, sän′-), *v.i.* **1.** to walk with a leisurely gait. —*n.* **2.** a leisurely walk; stroll. **3.** a leisurely gait. [late ME *santre* to muse] —**saun′ter·er,** *n.* —**Syn. 1–3.** amble, ramble.

-saur, var. of **sauro-,** occurring as final element in compound words: *dinosaur.*

sau·rel (sôr′əl), *n.* any of several marine carangid fishes of the genus *Trachurus.* [< F = *saur-* (< LL *saur(us)* horse mackerel < Gk *saûros* sea fish) + *-el* n. suffix]

sau·ri·an (sôr′ē ən), *adj.* **1.** belonging or pertaining to the *Sauria,* a group of reptiles originally including the lizards, crocodiles, and several extinct forms but now technically restricted to the lizards. **2.** resembling a lizard. —*n.* **3.** a saurian animal, as a dinosaur or lizard. [< NL *Sauri(a)* order of reptiles + -AN; see SAURO-]

-saurian, a combination of **-saur** and **-ian,** used in the formation of adjectives from nouns in **-saur:** *brontosaurian.*

saur·is·chi·an (sô ris′kē ən), *n.* **1.** any herbivorous or carnivorous dinosaur of the order *Saurischia,* having a three-pronged pelvis resembling that of a crocodile. Cf. **ornithischian.** —*adj.* **2.** belonging or pertaining to the *Saurischia.* [< NL *Saurischi(a)* name of the order (see SAURIAN, ISCHIUM) + -AN]

sauro-, a learned borrowing from Greek meaning "lizard," used in the formation of technical terms (*sauropod*); specialized in zoological terminology to mean a group of extinct reptiles. Also, **-saur, -saurus;** *esp. before a vowel,* **saur-.** Cf. **-saurian.** [comb. form of Gk *saûros*]

sau·ro·pod (sôr′ə pod′), *n.* any herbivorous dinosaur of the suborder *Sauropoda,* from the Jurassic and Cretaceous periods, having a small head, long neck and tail, and five-toed limbs, the species of which were the largest known land animals. [< NL *Sauropod(a)*]

-saurus, Latinized var. of **-saur:** *brontosaurus.*

sau·ry (sôr′ē), *n., pl.* **-ries. 1.** a sharp-snouted fish, *Scomberesox saurus,* found in the Atlantic Ocean. **2.** any of various related fishes. [< NL *saur(us)* (see SAUREL) + -Y²]

sau·sage (sô′sij), *n.* minced pork, beef, or other meats, together with added ingredients and seasonings, usually stuffed into a prepared intestine or other casing. [ME *sausige* < dial. OF *saussiche* < LL *salsīcia,* neut. pl. of *salsīcius* seasoned with salt < L *salsus* salted. See SAUCE, -ITIOUS] —**sau′sage·like′,** *adj.*

sau′sage curl′, a lock of hair formed into a curl resembling a sausage in shape.

Saus·sure (*Fr.* sō SYR′), *n.* **Fer·di·nand de** (*Fr.* fer dē-näN′ də), 1857–1913, Swiss linguist and Sanskrit scholar.

sau·té (sō tā′, sô-), *adj., v.,* **-téed** (-tād′), **-té·ing** (-tā′ing), *n.* —*adj.* **1.** cooked or browned in a pan with a small quantity of butter, oil, or other fat. —*v.t.* **2.** to cook in a small amount of fat; pan-fry. —*n.* **3.** a dish of sautéed food. [< F, ptp. of *sauter* < L *saltāre,* freq. of *salīre* to jump]

Sau·ternes (sō tûrn′, sô-; *Fr.* sō tern′), *n.* a sweet white table wine of France. Also, **sau·terne′.**

sauve qui peut (sōv kē pœ′), *French.* **1.** every man for himself. **2.** a rout or stampede. [lit: let him save (himself) who can]

Sa·va (sä′vä), *n.* a river flowing E from NW Yugoslavia to the Danube at Belgrade. 450 mi. long. German, **Sau.**

sav·age (sav′ij), *adj.* **1.** fierce or ferocious. **2.** uncivilized; barbarous. **3.** enraged or furiously angry, as a person. **4.** wild or rugged, as country or scenery. —*n.* **5.** an uncivilized human being. **6.** a fierce, brutal, or cruel person. **7.** a rude, boorish person. [ME *savage, sauvage* < MF *sauvage, salvage* < ML *salvāticus,* r. L *silvāticus* = *silv(a)* woods + *-āticus* adj. suffix] —**sav′age·ly,** *adv.* —**sav′age·ness,** *n.* —**Syn. 1.** wild; bloodthirsty. See **cruel. 3.** infuriated. **4.** rough. **7.** churl, oaf. —**Ant. 2.** cultured.

Sav·age (sav′ij), *n.* **Richard,** 1697?–1743, English poet.

Sav′age Is′land, Niue.

sav·age·ry (sav′ij rē), *n., pl.* **-ries. 1.** an uncivilized or barbaric state or condition; barbarity. **2.** savage nature, disposition, conduct, or act.

Sa·vai·i (sä vī′ē), *n.* an island in Western Samoa: largest of the Samoa group. 31,642 (1961); 703 sq. mi.

sa·van·na (sə van′ə), *n.* **1.** a plain characterized by coarse grasses and scattered tree growth, esp. on the margins of the tropics where rainfall is seasonal. **2.** grassland region with scattered trees, grading into either open plain or woodland, usually in subtropical or tropical regions. Also, **sa·van′nah.** [earlier *zavana* < Sp (now *sabana*) < Taino *zabana*]

Sa·van·nah (sə van′ə), *n.* **1.** a seaport in E Georgia, near the mouth of the Savannah River. 118,349 (1970). **2.** a river flowing SE from E Georgia along most of the boundary between Georgia and South Carolina and into the Atlantic. 314 mi. long.

sa·vant (sa vänt′, sav′ənt; *Fr.* SA VÄN′), *n., pl.* **sa·vants** (sa vänts′, sav′ənts; *Fr.* SA VÄN′). a man of profound or extensive learning. [< F: man of learning, scholar, old prp. of *savoir* to know < L *sapere* to be wise; see SAPIENT]

sa·vate (sə vat′), *n.* a sport resembling boxing but permitting blows with the feet. [< F: lit., old shoe. See SABOT]

save¹ (sāv), *v.,* **saved, sav·ing.** —*v.t.* **1.** to rescue from danger or possible harm, injury, or loss: *to save someone from drowning.* **2.** to keep safe, intact, or unhurt; safeguard: *God save the king.* **3.** to keep from being lost: *to save the game.* **4.** to avoid the spending, consumption, or waste of: *to save fuel with this new stove.* **5.** to set apart, reserve, or lay by: *to save money.* **6.** to treat carefully in order to reduce wear, fatigue, etc.: *to save one's eyes by reading under proper light.* **7.** to prevent the occurrence or necessity of; obviate: *A stitch in time saves nine.* **8.** *Theol.* to deliver from the power and consequences of sin. —*v.i.* **9.** to lay up money for reasons of economy or thrift. **10.** to be economical in expenditure. **11.** to preserve something from harm, injury, loss, etc. **12.** to bring about human salvation. [ME *sa(u)ve(n)* < OF *sauve(r)* < LL (esp. eccl.) *salvāre* to save; see SAFE] —**sav′a·ble, save′a·ble,** *adj.* —**sav′er,** *n.* —**Syn. 1.** salvage. **4.** store up, husband. **5, 9.** economize, hoard.

save² (sāv), *prep.* **1.** except; but: *All the guests had left save one.* —*conj.* **2.** except; but: *He would have gone, save that he had no means.* [ME; var. of SAFE] —**Syn. 1.** See **except**¹.

save-all (sāv′ôl′), *n.* **1.** a means, contrivance, or receptacle for preventing loss or waste. **2.** *Chiefly Dial.* overalls. **3.** *Naut.* **a.** a net secured between a pier and a ship, beneath cargo being transferred from one to the other. **b.** a sail for utilizing wind spilled from the regular sails of a vessel.

sav·e·loy (sav′ə loi′), *n. Chiefly Brit.* a highly seasoned, dried sausage. [prob. < F *cervelas,* MF *cervelat* < It *cervellat(o)* Milanese sausage, orig. containing pig's brains. See CEREBELLUM, -ATE¹]

sav·in (sav′in), *n.* **1.** a juniper, *Juniperus Sabina,* of Europe and Asia. **2.** a drug derived from the dried tops of this plant, formerly used in treating amenorrhea. **3.** See **red cedar** (def. 1). Also, **sav′ine.** [ME; OE *safine, savene* << L (*herba*) *Sabina* Sabine (herb)]

sav·ing (sā′ving), *adj.* **1.** tending or serving to save; rescuing; preserving. **2.** compensating; redeeming: *a saving sense of humor.* **3.** thrifty; economical. **4.** making a reservation: *a saving clause.* —*n.* **5.** economy in expenditure, use, etc. **6.** a reduction or lessening of expenditure or outlay. **7.** something saved. **8. savings,** sums of money saved by economy and laid away. —*prep.* **9.** except. **10.** with all due respect to or for: *saving your presence.* —*conj.* **11.** except. [ME]

sav′ing grace′, a quality that makes up for other generally negative characteristics.

sav′ings account′, a bank account on which interest is paid. Cf. **checking account.**

sav′ings and loan′ associa′tion, a cooperative savings institution that receives deposits in exchange for shares of ownership and invests its funds chiefly in mortgages on homes. Also called **building and loan association.**

sav′ings bank′, a bank that receives savings accounts only and pays interest to its depositors.

sav′ings bond′, a U.S. government bond with principal amounts up to $10,000.

sav·ior (sāv′yər), *n.* **1.** a person who saves or rescues. **2.** (*cap.*) a title of God or Christ. Also, *esp. Brit.,* **sav′iour.** [ME *saveour,* etc. < OF < eccl. L *Salvātor* Redeemer. See SALVATION, -OR²] —**sav′ior·hood′;** *esp. Brit.,* **sav′iour-hood′, sav′ior·ship′;** *esp. Brit.,* **sav′iour·ship′,** *n.*

Sa·voie (SA VWA′), *n.* French name of **Savoy.**

sa·voir-faire (sav′wär fâr′; *Fr.* SA VWAR FER′), *n.* knowledge of just what to do in any situation; tact. [< F: lit., knowing how to do] —**Syn.** adaptability, adroitness, diplomacy, discernment; skill, ability.

sa·voir-vi·vre (sav′wär vē′vrə, -vēv′; *Fr.* SA VWAR VĒ′-VRᵊ), *n.* knowledge of the world and the ways or usages of polite society. [< F: lit., knowing how to live]

Sa·vo·na (sä vô′nä), *n.* a city in N Italy on the Mediterranean. 72,047 (1961).

Sav·o·na·ro·la (sav′ə nə rō′lə; *It.* sä′vô nä RÔ′lä), *n.* **Gi·ro·la·mo** (ji rol′ə mō′; *It.* jē RÔ′lä mô), 1452–98, Italian monk, reformer, and martyr.

sa·vor (sā′vər), *n.* **1.** the quality in a substance that affects the sense of taste or of smell. **2.** a particular taste or smell. **3.** distinctive quality or property. **4.** power to excite or interest. **5.** *Archaic.* repute. —*v.i.* **6.** to have savor, taste, or odor. **7.** to hint, suggest, or smack (usually fol. by *of*): *His business practices savor of greed.* —*v.t.* **8.** to give a savor to; season; flavor. **9.** to enjoy, as by taste or smell. **10.** to give oneself to the enjoyment of. Also, *esp. Brit.,* **savour.** [ME *savo(u)r* < OF *savour* (n.), *savourer* (v.) < L *sapor* taste < *sap(ere)* (to) taste] —**sa′vor·er,** *n.* —**sa′vor·ing·ly,** *adv.* —**sa′vor·less,** *adj.* —**sa′vor·ous,** *adj.* —**Syn. 1.** relish; odor, fragrance. See **taste.**

sa·vor·y¹ (sā′və rē), *adj.,* **-vor·i·er, -vor·i·est,** *n.* —*adj.* **1.** pleasant or agreeable in taste or smell. **2.** piquant: *a savory jelly.* **3.** pleasing, attractive, or agreeable. —*n.* **4.** *Brit.* an aromatic, often spicy course or dish, served as an appetizer or as a dessert. Also, *esp. Brit.,* **savoury.** [ME *savori* (see SAVOR, -Y¹); r. ME *savure* < OF *savoure,* ptp. of *savourer* to savor] —**sa′vor·i·ly,** *adv.* —**sa′vor·i·ness,** *n.*

sa·vor·y² (sā′və rē), *n., pl.* **-vor·ies.** any aromatic, menthaceous herb of the genus *Satureia,* esp. *S. hortensis* **(summer savory)** and *S. montana* **(winter savory),** used in cookery. [ME *savery,* OE *sætherie, saturēge* < L *saturēia*]

sa·vour (sā′vər), *n., v.i., v.t. Chiefly Brit.* savor. —**sa′vour·er,** *n.* —**sa′vour·ing·ly,** *adv.* —**sa′vour·less,** *adj.* —**sa′vour·ous,** *adj.*

sa·vour·y (sā′və rē), *adj.,* **-vour·i·er, -vour·i·est,** *n. Chiefly Brit.* savory¹. —**sa′vour·i·ly,** *adv.* —**sa′vour·i·ness,** *n.*

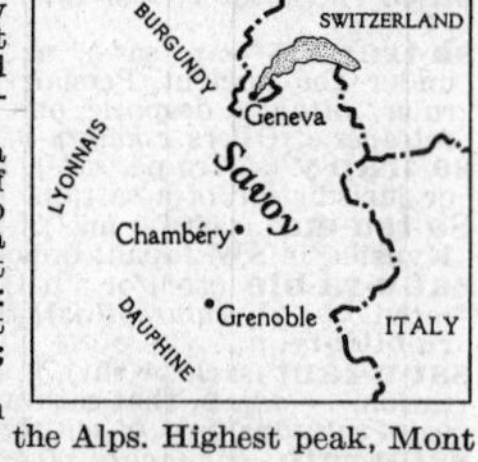

sa·voy (sə voi′), *n.* a variety of cabbage having a compact head of wrinkled, blistered leaves. [after SAVOY the region]

Sa·voy (sə voi′), *n.* **1.** a member of the royal house of Italy that ruled from 1861 to 1946. **2.** French, **Savoie.** a region in SE France, adjacent to the Swiss-Italian border: formerly a duchy; later a part of the kingdom of Sardinia; ceded to France, 1860.

Savoy′ Alps′, a mountain range in SE France: a part of the Alps. Highest peak, Mont Blanc, 15,781 ft.

Sa·voy·ard (sə voi′ərd, sav′oi ärd′; *Fr.* SA VWA YAR′), *n., pl.* **Sa·voy·ards** (sə voi′ərdz, sav′oi ärdz′; *Fr.* SA VWA-YAR′), *adj.* —*n.* **1.** a native or inhabitant of Savoy. **2.** the Franco-Provençal dialect spoken in Savoy. **3.** an enthusiast for or a performer in Gilbert and Sullivan operas: so called from the Savoy Theatre in London, where the operas were first given. —*adj.* **4.** of or pertaining to Savoy or the Savoyard dialect.

sav·vy (sav′ē), *v.,* **-vied, -vy·ing,** *n. Slang.* —*v.t., v.i.* **1.** to know; understand. —*n.* **2.** understanding; intelligence; sense. [< Sp *sabe,* pres. 3rd sing. of *saber* to know < L *sapere* to be wise; see SAPIENT]

saw[1] (sô), *n.*, *v.*, **sawed, sawed** or **sawn, saw·ing.** —*n.* **1.** a tool for cutting, typically a thin blade of metal with a series of sharp teeth. **2.** any similar tool or device, as a rotating disk, in which a sharp continuous edge replaces the teeth.

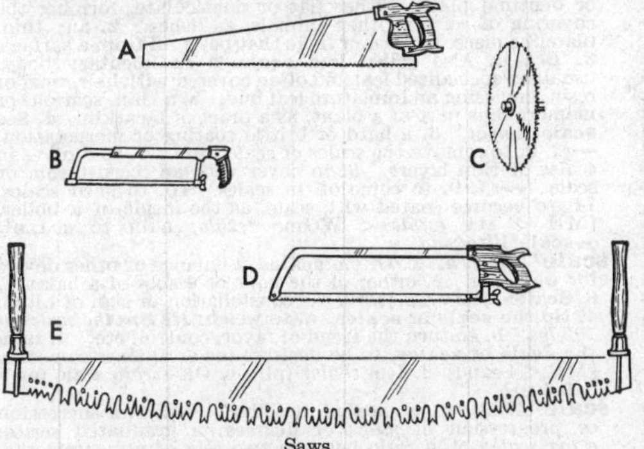

Saws
A, Handsaw; B, Hacksaw; C, Circular saw;
D, Butcher's saw; E, Lumberman's saw

—*v.t.* **3.** to cut or divide with a saw. **4.** to form by cutting with a saw. **5.** to cut as if using a saw: *to saw the air with one's hands.* **6.** to work (something) from side to side like a saw. —*v.i.* **7.** to use a saw. **8.** to cut with or as with a saw. **9.** to cut as a saw does. [ME *sawe*, OE *saga*, *sagu*; c. D *zaag*, Icel *sög*; akin to G *Säge* saw, L *secāre* to cut] —**saw′er,** *n.* —**saw′like′,** *adj.*

saw[2] (sô), *v.* a pt. of **see**[1].

saw[3] (sô), *n.* a maxim or proverb. [ME; OE *sagu*; c. G *Sage*, Icel *saga* SAGA; akin to SAY]

Sa·watch (sə wach′), *n.* a mountain range in central Colorado: part of the Rocky Mountains. Highest peak, Mount Elbert, 14,431 ft. Also, **Saguache.**

saw·bones (sô′bōnz′), *n.*, *pl.* **-bones, -bones·es.** (*construed as sing.*) *Slang.* a surgeon or physician.

saw·buck[1] (sô′buk′), *n.* a sawhorse. [cf. D *zaagbok*]

saw·buck[2] (sô′buk′), *n.* *Slang.* a ten-dollar bill. [so called from Roman numeral X and the crossbars of SAWBUCK[1]]

saw·dust (sô′dust′), *n.* small particles of wood produced in sawing.

sawed-off (sôd′ôf′, -of′), *adj.* **1.** sawed off at the end, as a shotgun or broomstick. **2.** *Slang.* of less than average size or stature.

saw·fish (sô′fish′), *n.*, *pl.* (*esp. collectively*) **-fish,** (*esp. referring to two or more kinds or species*) **-fish·es.** a large, elongated ray of the genus *Pristis*, found along tropical coasts and lowland rivers, with a bladelike snout bearing strong teeth on each side.

Sawfish, *Pristis pectinatus*
(Length 10 to 20 ft.)

saw·fly (sô′flī′), *n.*, *pl.* **-flies.** any of numerous hymenopterous insects of the family *Tenthredinidae*, the female of which has a sawlike ovipositor for inserting the eggs in the tissues of a host plant.

saw′ grass′, any of various cyperaceous plants, esp. of the genus *Cladium*, having sawtooth leaves.

saw·horse (sô′hôrs′), *n.* a movable frame or trestle for holding wood being sawed.

saw·mill (sô′mil′), *n.* a place or building in which timber is sawed into planks, boards, etc., by machinery; lumbermill.

sawn (sôn), *v.* a pp. of **saw**[1].

saw′ palmet′to, 1. a shrublike palmetto, *Serenoa repens*, of the southern U.S., having the leafstalks set with spiny teeth. **2.** a shrublike palmetto, *Paurotis Wrightii*, of Florida and the West Indies.

saw·tooth (sô′to͞oth′), *n.*, *pl.* **-teeth** (-tēth′), *adj.* —*n.* **1.** one of the cutting teeth of a saw. —*adj.* **2.** having a zigzag profile suggesting the cutting edge of a saw: *a sawtooth mountain.* **3.** serrate; saw-toothed.

saw-toothed (sô′to͞otht′), *adj.* serrate.

saw′-whet owl′ (sô′hwet′, -wet′), a very small, North American owl, *Aegolius acadicus*, having streaked brown plumage. [imit.]

saw·yer (sô′yər, soi′ər), *n.* **1.** a person who saws, esp. as an occupation. **2.** any of several long-horned beetles, esp. one of the genus *Monochamus*, the larvae of which bore in the wood of coniferous trees. [ME *sawier* = *sawe* SAW[1] + *-ier*, var. of -ER[1]]

sax (saks), *n.* *Informal.* saxophone. [by shortening]

Sax., 1. Saxon. **2.** Saxony.

sax·a·tile (sak′sə til), *adj.* living or growing on or among rocks. [< L *saxātilis* frequenting rocks = *sax(um)* rock + *-āt-* formative suffix + *-ilis* -ILE]

Saxe (saks), *n.* **1. Comte Her·mann Mau·rice de** (er män′ mō rēs′ də), 1696–1750, French military leader: marshal of France 1744. **2.** French name of **Saxony.**

Saxe-Al·ten·burg (saks′äl′tən bûrg′), *n.* a former duchy in Thuringia in central Germany.

Saxe-Co·burg-Go·tha (saks′kō′bûrg gō′thə), *n.* **1.** a member of the present British royal family, from the establishment of the house in 1901 until 1917 when the family name was changed to Windsor. **2. Albert Francis Charles Augustus Emanuel, Prince of.** See **Albert, Prince. 3.** a former duchy in central Germany.

Saxe-Mei·ning·en (saks′mī′ning ən), *n.* a former duchy in Thuringia in central Germany.

Saxe-Wei·mar-Ei·sen·ach (saks′vī′mär ī′zən äkн′), *n.* a former grand duchy in Thuringia in central Germany.

sax·horn (saks′hôrn′), *n.* any of a family of brass instruments close to the cornets and tubas. [named after A. *Sax* (1814–94), a Belgian who invented such instruments]

Saxhorn

sax·i·fra·ga·ceous (sak′sə frə gā′shəs), *adj.* belonging to the *Saxifragaceae*, or saxifrage family of plants.

sax·i·frage (sak′sə frij), *n.* any herb of the genus *Saxifraga*, certain species of which grow wild in the clefts of rocks, other species of which are cultivated for their flowers. [ME < L *saxifrag(a)* (*herba*) stone-breaking (herb) = *saxi-* stone + *-fraga*, fem. of *-fragus* brittle; see FRAGILE]

Sax·o Gram·mat·i·cus (sak′sō grə mat′ə kəs), c1150–1206?, Danish historian and poet.

Sax·on (sak′sən), *n.* **1.** an Englishman; Britisher. **2.** an Anglo-Saxon. **3.** (not in scholarly use) the Old English language. **4.** the Old English dialects of the regions settled by the Saxons. **5.** a native or inhabitant of Saxony. **6.** a member of a Germanic people in ancient times dwelling near the mouth of the Elbe, a portion of whom invaded and occupied parts of Britain in the 5th and 6th centuries. —*adj.* **7.** English (defs. 1, 2). **8.** of or pertaining to the early Saxons or their language. **9.** of or pertaining to Saxony. [ME, prob. < L *Saxo* (pl. *Saxonēs*) < Gmc; r. OE *Seaxan* (pl.)]

Sax·on·ism (sak′sə niz′əm), *n.* a word or idiom supposedly of Anglo-Saxon origin.

sax·o·ny (sak′sə nē), *n.* **1.** a fine, three-ply woolen yarn. **2.** a soft-finish, compact fabric for coats.

Sax·o·ny (sak′sə nē), *n.* **1.** a former state in S East Germany 1947–52. 6561 sq. mi. *Cap.:* Dresden. **2.** a former state of the Weimar Republic in E central Germany. 5788 sq. mi. *Cap.:* Dresden. **3.** a former province in N Germany. 9857 sq. mi. *Cap.:* Magdeburg. **4.** a medieval division of N Germany with varying boundaries: extended at its height from the Rhine to E of the Elbe. German, **Sachsen.** French, **Saxe.** —**Sax·o·ni·an** (sak sō′nē ən), *n.*, *adj.*

sax·o·phone (sak′sə fōn′), *n.* a musical wind instrument consisting of a conical, usually brass tube with keys or valves and a mouthpiece with one reed. [*sax* (see SAXHORN) + -o- + -PHONE] —**sax·o·phon·ic** (sak′sə fon′ik), *adj.* —**sax′o·phon′ist,** *n.*

sax·tu·ba (saks′to͞o′bə, -tyo͞o′-), *n.* a large bass saxhorn. [*sax* (see SAXHORN) + TUBA]

Saxophone

say (sā), *v.*, **said, say·ing,** *adv.*, *n.* —*v.t.* **1.** to utter or pronounce; speak: *What did he say? He said "Hello!"* **2.** to express in words; state; declare. **3.** to state as an opinion or judgment: *It is hard to say what is wrong.* **4.** to recite or repeat: *to say one's prayers.* **5.** to report or allege. **6.** to express (a message, viewpoint, etc.), as through a literary or other artistic medium. —*v.i.* **7.** to speak; declare; express an opinion. **8. that is to say,** in other words. —*adv.* **9.** approximately: *Come in, say, an hour.* **10.** for example. —*n.* **11.** what a person says or has to say. **12.** the right or opportunity to speak, decide, or exercise influence: *to have one's say in choosing the candidate.* **13.** a turn to say something. **14. have the say,** to have final authority. [ME *sey(en)*, *segg(en)*, OE *secgan*; c. D *zeggen*, G *sagen*, Icel *segja*; akin to SAW[3]] —**say′er,** *n.* —**Syn. 1.** remark, affirm. **5.** hold.

say·a·ble (sā′ə bəl), *adj.* **1.** of the sort that can be said or spoken. **2.** capable of being said clearly, eloquently, etc.

Sa·yan′ Moun′tains (sä yän′), a mountain range in the S Soviet Union in Asia. Highest peak, 11,447 ft.

say·est (sā′ist), *v.* *Archaic.* 2nd pers. sing. of **say.** Also, **sayst** (sāst).

say·ing (sā′ing), *n.* **1.** something said, esp. a proverb or apothegm. **2. go without saying,** to be completely self-evident. [ME] —**Syn. 1.** maxim, adage, aphorism.

sa·yo·na·ra (sī′ə när′ə; *Jap.* sä′yô nä′rä), *interj.*, *n.* farewell; good-by. [< Jap]

Sayre·ville (sâr′vil), *n.* a city in central New Jersey. 32,508 (1970).

says (sez), *v.* 3rd. pers. sing. pres. ind. of **say.**

say-so (sā′sō′), *n.*, *pl.* **say-sos. 1.** an individual's personal assertion. **2.** final authority; directing influence.

say·yid (sä′yid, sā′id), *n.* (in Islamic countries) a supposed descendant of Muhammad through his grandson Husain, the second son of his daughter Fatima. Also, **said, say′id.** [< Ar: lord]

Saz·e·rac (saz′ə rak′), *n.* a cocktail made with bourbon, bitters, absinthe or a substitute, and sugar, stirred or shaken with ice. [?]

Sb, *Chem.* antimony. [< L *stibium*]

sb., substantive.

S.B., 1. See **Bachelor of Science.** [< L *Scientiae Baccalaureus*] **2.** South Britain (England and Wales).

s.b., *Baseball.* stolen base; stolen bases.

SBA, Small Business Administration. Also, **S.B.A.**

SbE, See **south by east.**

'sblood (zblud), *interj.* *Obs.* (used as an oath.) [(*God*)'s *blood*]

SbW, See **south by west.**

SC, South Carolina (approved esp. for use with zip code).

Sc, *Chem.* scandium.

Sc., 1. Scotch. 2. Scotland. 3. Scots. 4. Scottish.

sc., 1. scale. 2. scene. 3. science. 4. scientific. 5. namely. [< L *scīlicet,* contr. of *scīre licet* it is permitted to know] 6. screw. 7. scruple. 8. sculpsit.

S.C., 1. Sanitary Corps. 2. Security Council (of the U.N.). 3. Signal Corps. 4. South Carolina. 5. Staff Corps. 6. Supreme Court.

s.c., small capitals.

scab (skab), *n., v.,* **scabbed, scab·bing.** —*n.* **1.** the incrustation that forms over a sore or wound during healing. **2.** *Vet. Pathol.* a mangy disease in animals, esp. sheep; scabies. Cf. **itch** (def. 8). **3.** *Plant Pathol.* **a.** a disease of plants characterized by crustlike lesions on the affected parts and caused by a fungus or bacterium. **b.** one of these crustlike lesions. **4.** a workman who refuses to join or act with a labor union or who takes a striker's place on the job. —*v.i.* **5.** to become covered with a scab. **6.** to act or work as a scab. [ME < Scand; cf. Sw *skabb,* c. dial. E *shab,* OE *sceabb;* cf. SHABBY, SHAVE] —**scab′like′,** *adj.*

scab·bard (skab′ərd), *n.* **1.** a sheath for a sword or the like. See illus. at **scimitar.** —*v.t.* **2.** to put into a scabbard; sheathe. [ME *scalburde, scauberge,* etc. (cf. AF *escauberz, escauberge,* ML *escauberca*) << dissimilated var. of OHG **skārberga* sword protection. See SHEARS, HARBOR]

scab·bed (skab′id, skabd), *adj.* **1.** covered with or affected by scabs. **2.** *Obs.* mean or petty. [ME]

scab·ble (skab′əl), *v.t.,* **-bled, -bling.** to shape or dress (stone) roughly. [var. of *scapple* < MF *escapel(er)* (to) dress (timber)]

scab·by (skab′ē), *adj.,* **-bi·er, -bi·est. 1.** covered with scabs; having many scabs. **2.** consisting of scabs. —**scab′bi·ly,** *adv.* —**scab′bi·ness,** *n.*

sca·bies (skā′bēz, -bē ēz′), *n.* (*construed as sing.*) *Pathol.* a contagious skin disease occurring esp. in sheep and cattle and also in man, caused by parasitic mites that burrow under the skin. Cf. **itch** (def. 8), **mange.** [< L: roughness, the itch < *scab(ere)* (to) scratch, scrape; c. SHAVE] —**sca·bi·et·ic** (skā′bē et′ik), *adj.*

sca·bi·ous[1] (skā′bē əs), *adj.* **1.** scabby. **2.** pertaining to or of the nature of scabies. [SCABI(ES) + -OUS]

sca·bi·ous[2] (skā′bē əs), *n.* any composite herb of the genus *Scabiosa,* having terminal heads of showy flowers, as *S. arvensis,* having purple flowers, or *S. atropurpurea,* having purple, pink, or white flowers. Also, **sca·bi·o·sa** (skā′bē ō′sə). [ME *scabiose* < ML *scabiōsa* (*herba*) scabies-curing (herb)]

scab·rous (skab′rəs), *adj.* **1.** having a rough surface because of minute points or projections. **2.** full of difficulties. **3.** indecent; obscene: *scabrous books.* [< L *scab(e)r* rough + -OUS] —**scab′rous·ly,** *adv.* —**scab′rous·ness,** *n.*

scad[1] (skad), *n., pl.* (*esp. collectively*) **scad,** (*esp. referring to two or more kinds or species*) **scads. 1.** any carangid fish of the genus *Decapterus,* found in tropical and subtropical shore waters. **2.** any of several related carangid fishes. [?]

scad[2] (skad), *n.* Often, **scads.** *Slang.* a great number or quantity. [dial. var. of *scalding* quantity. See SCALD[1]]

Scae·vo·la (sē′və lə, sev′ə-), *n.* **Ga·ius** (gā′əs) (or **Ca·ius**) (kā′əs) **Mu·ci·us** (myōō′ shē əs, -shəs), fl. 6th century B.C., Roman hero.

Sca′fell Pike′ (skô′fel′), a mountain in NW England, in Cumberland: highest peak in England. 3210 ft.

scaf·fold (skaf′əld, -ōld), *n.* **1.** a temporary structure for holding workmen and materials during the erection, repair, etc., of a building. **2.** an elevated platform on which a criminal is executed, usually by hanging. **3.** a raised platform or stage for exhibiting spectacles, seating spectators, etc. **4.** any raised framework. —*v.t.* **5.** to furnish with a scaffold or scaffolding. **6.** to support by or place on a scaffold. [ME < OF *escadafaut.* See E-, CATAFALQUE]

scaf·fold·ing (skaf′əl ding, -ōl-), *n.* **1.** a scaffold or system of scaffolds. **2.** materials for scaffolds.

scag (skag), *n. U.S. Slang.* heroin. Also, **skag.** [?]

scal·a·ble (skā′lə bəl), *adj.* capable of being scaled or climbed.

sca·lade (skə lād′), *n. Archaic.* escalade. [< OIt *scalada* a scaling. See SCALE[3], -ADE[1]]

scal·age (skā′lij), *n.* **1.** a percentage deduction granted in dealings with goods that are likely to shrink or leak. **2.** the amount of lumber estimated to be contained in a log being scaled.

sca·lar (skā′lər), *adj.* **1.** representable by position on a line; having only magnitude: *a scaler variable.* **2.** of, pertaining to, or utilizing a scalar. —*n.* **3.** *Math., Physics.* a quantity possessing only magnitude. Cf. **vector** (def. 1a). [< L *scālār(is)* of a ladder]

sca·lar·e (skə lâr′ē, -lär′ē), *n.* any of three deep-bodied, cichlid fishes, *Pterophyllum scalare, P. altum,* and *P. eimekei,* found in northern South American rivers, often kept in aquariums. [< L *scālāre,* neut. of *scālāris* (see SCALAR); from its ladderlike markings]

sca·lar·i·form (skə lar′ə fôrm′), *adj. Biol.* ladderlike. [< NL *scālāriform(is)*]

sca′lar prod′uct, *Math.* the quantity obtained by multiplying the corresponding coordinates of each of two vectors and adding the products, equal to the product of the magnitudes of the vectors and the cosine of the angle between them. Also called **dot product, inner product.** Cf. **vector product.**

scal·a·wag (skal′ə wag′), *n.* **1.** *Informal.* scamp; rascal. **2.** *U.S. Hist.* a native white Southern Republican during Reconstruction. Also, *esp. Brit.,* **scallawag.** [?] —**scal′a·wag′ger·y,** *n.* —**scal′a·wag′gy,** *adj.*

scald[1] (skôld), *v.t.* **1.** to burn with or as with hot liquid or steam. **2.** to subject to the action of boiling or hot liquid. **3.** to heat to a temperature just short of the boiling point: *to scald milk.* —*v.i.* **4.** to be or become scalded. —*n.* **5.** a burn caused by hot liquid or steam. **6.** any similar condition, esp. as the result of too much heat or sunlight. **7.** *Plant Pathol.* a blanching of the epidermis and adjacent tissues which turn brown, caused by improper growth or storage, as in apples, or by fungi, as in cranberries. [ME *scald(en)* < dial. OF *escalde(r)* < LL *excaldāre* to wash in hot water. See EX-[1], CALDARIUM]

scald[2] (skôld, skäld), *n.* skald. —**scald′ic,** *adj.*

scald[3] (skôld), *adj.* **1.** scabby; scurvy. —*n.* **2.** *Obs.* a scab. [SCALL + -ED[3]]

scale[1] (skāl), *n., v.,* **scaled, scal·ing.** —*n.* **1.** *Zool.* **a.** one of the thin, flat, horny plates forming the covering of certain animals, as snakes and lizards. **b.** one of the hard, bony or dentinal plates, either flat or denticulate, forming the covering of certain other animals, as fishes. **2.** any thin, platelike piece, lamina, or flake that peels off from a surface. **3.** *Bot.* **a.** Also called **bud scale.** a rudimentary body, usually a specialized leaf and often covered with hair, wax, or resin, enclosing an immature leaf bud. **b.** a thin, scarious or membranous part of a plant, as a bract of a catkin. **4.** See **scale insect. 5.** a hard or brittle coating or incrustation. —*v.t.* **6.** to remove the scales or scale from. **7.** to remove in scales or thin layers. **8.** to cover with an incrustation or scale. —*v.i.* **9.** to come off in scales. **10.** to shed scales. **11.** to become coated with scale, as the inside of a boiler. [ME < MF *escale* < WGmc **skāla;* akin to SCALE[2]] —**scale′like′,** *adj.*

scale[2] (skāl), *n.* **1.** Often, **scales.** a balance or other device for weighing. **2.** either of the pans or dishes of a balance. **3. Scales,** *Astron., Astrol.* the constellation or sign of Libra. **4. tip the scale** or **scales, a.** to weigh: *He tips the scales at 190 lbs.* **b.** to turn the trend of favor, control, etc. **5. turn the scale** or **scales,** to be decisive for or against someone. [ME < Scand; cf. Icel *skālar* (pl.), c. OE *scealu* scale (of a balance)]

scale[3] (skāl), *n., v.,* **scaled, scal·ing.** —*n.* **1.** a succession or progression of steps or degrees; a graduated series: *a tax scale.* **2.** a ratio between two sets of measurements, as on a map. **3.** a representation of either of these. **4.** an arrangement of things in order of importance, rank, etc.: *the social scale.* **5.** a series of marks used for measuring. **6.** an instrument, as a ruler, that bears such marks. **7.** the relative size of an object, scope of an activity, etc. **8.** any standard of measurement or estimation. **9.** *Arith.* a system of numerical notation: *the decimal scale.* **10.** *Music.* a succession of tones ascending or descending according to fixed intervals, esp. such a series beginning on a particular note: *the major scale of C.* **11.** *Educ., Psychol.* a graded series of tests or tasks for measuring intelligence, achievement, adjustment, etc. **12.** anything by which one may ascend. **13.** *Obs.* **a.** a ladder. **b.** a flight of stairs. —*v.t.* **14.** to climb by or as by a ladder; climb up or over. **15.** to make according to scale. **16.** to reduce in amount according to a fixed scale or proportion (often fol. by *down*). **17.** to measure by or as by a scale. **18.** *Lumbering.* **a.** to measure (logs). **b.** to estimate the amount of (standing timber). —*v.i.* **19.** to ascend or mount. **20.** to progress in a graduated series. [ME < L *scāl(ae)* ladder, stairs] —**scal′er,** *n.* —**Syn. 14.** See **climb.**

scale′ in′sect, any of numerous small, plant-sucking, homopterous insects of the superfamily *Coccoidea.*

scale′ moss′, any thalloid liverwort.

sca·lene (skā lēn′), *adj. Geom.* **1.** (of a cone or the like) having the axis inclined to the base. **2.** (of a triangle) having unequal sides. See diag. at **triangle.** [< LL *scalēn(us)* < Gk *skalēnós* unequal]

Sca·li·a (skə lē′ə), *n.* **An·to·nin** (an′tə nin), born 1936, associate justice of the U.S. Supreme Court since 1986.

Scal·i·ger (skal′i jər), *n.* **1. Joseph Jus·tus** (jus′təs), 1540–1609, French scholar and critic. **2.** his father, **Julius Caesar,** 1484–1558, Italian scholar, philosopher, and critic in France.

scal′ing lad′der, a ladder for climbing high walls.

scall (skôl), *n.* a scurf. [< Icel *skalli* bald head. Cf. SKULL]

scal·la·wag (skal′ə wag′), *n. Chiefly Brit.* scalawag. —**scal′la·wag′ger·y,** *n.* —**scal′la·wag′gy,** *adj.*

scal·lion (skal′yən), *n.* **1.** any onion that does not form a large bulb. **2.** a shallot. **3.** a leek. [ME < OF **escaloigne* < VL **escalonia,* var. of L *Ascalōnia* (*caepa*) onion of Ascalon, a seaport of Palestine; r. ME *scalone,* etc. < AF *scaloun* < VL, as above]

Scallop, *Pecten irradians* (Width 2 to 3 in.)

scal·lop (skol′əp, skal′-), *n.* **1.** any of the bivalve mollusks of the genus *Pecten* and related genera that swim by rapidly clapping the fluted shell valves together. **2.** the adductor muscle of certain species of such mollusks, esteemed as food. **3.** one of the shells of such a mollusk, usually having radial ribs and a wavy outer edge. **4.** *Cookery.* a thin slice of meat, usually further flattened by pounding. **5.** one of a series of rounded projections along the edge of a garment, cloth, etc. —*v.t.* **6.** to finish (an edge) with scallops. **7.** *Cookery.* to escallop. Also, **scollop.** [ME *scalop* < MF *escalope* shell < Gmc; cf. SCALP]

scal·ly·wag (skal′ē wag′), *n.* scalawag.

sca·lop·pi·ne (skä′lə pē′nē, skal′ə-), *n. Italian Cookery.* scallops, esp. of veal, flavored and sautéed, usually in a wine sauce: *scaloppine alla Marsala.* Also, **scal′lo·pi′ni.** [< It *scaloppine,* pl. of *scaloppina,* dim. of *scaloppa* thin slice of meat (perh. < MF *escalope* shell)]

scalp (skalp), *n.* **1.** the integument of the upper part of the head, usually including the associated subcutaneous structures. **2.** a part of this integument with the accompanying hair, taken by some North American Indians as a trophy of victory. —*v.t.* **3.** to cut or tear the scalp from. **4.** *Informal.* **a.** to buy and sell (stocks) so as to make quick profits. **b.** to sell (tickets) at higher than the official rates. —*v.i.* **5.** *Informal.* to scalp tickets, stocks, or the like. [ME (north) < Scand; cf. Icel *skālpr* leather sheath] —**scalp′er,** *n.*

scal·pel (skal′pəl), *n.* a small, light, usually straight knife used in surgical and anatomical operations and dissections. [< L *scalpell(um)* = *scalp-* (cf. *scalpere* to carve) + *-ellum* dim. suffix] —**scal·pel·lic** (skal pel′ik), *adj.*

scalp′ lock′, a long lock or tuft of hair left on the scalp by members of some North American Indian tribes as an implied challenge to their enemies.

scal·y (skā′lē), *adj.,* **scal·i·er, scal·i·est. 1.** covered with or abounding in scales or scale. **2.** characterized by or consisting of scales. **3.** peeling or flaking off in scales. —**scal′i·ness,** *n.*

scal′y ant′eater, pangolin.

scam (skam), *n. Slang.* a fraudulent scheme, esp. for making a quick, illegal profit. [orig. uncert.]

Sca·man·der (skə man′dər), *n.* an ancient name of the **Menderes.**

scam·mo·ny (skam′ə nē), *n., pl.* **-nies.** a twining, Asian convolvulus, *Convolvulus Scammonia.* [ME, OE *scamonie* < L *scammōnia* < Gk] —**scam·mo·ni·ate** (skə mō′nē it), *adj.*

scamp (skamp), *n.* **1.** a worthless and often mischievous person; rascal; rogue. —*v.t.* **2.** to do or perform in a hasty or careless manner. [obs. *scamp* to go (on highway) idly or for mischief, perh. < obs. D *schamp(en)* (to) be gone < OF *(e)scampe(r)* (to) DECAMP] —**scamp′ing·ly,** *adv.* —**scamp′ish,** *adj.* —**scamp′ish·ly,** *adv.* —**scamp′ish·ness,** *n.*

scamp·er (skam′pər), *v.i.* **1.** to run or go hastily. **2.** to run playfully about, as a child. —*n.* **3.** a scampering; a quick run. [obs. *scamp* to go (see SCAMP) + -ER[6]]

scam·pi (skam′pē), *n.* shrimp or prawns fried in oil and garlic. [< It, pl. of *scampo* shrimp]

scan (skan), *v.,* **scanned, scan·ning,** *n.* —*v.t.* **1.** to examine minutely; scrutinize carefully. **2.** to glance at or read hastily. **3.** to analyze (verse) for its prosodic or metrical structure. **4.** *Radar.* to traverse (a region) with a beam from a radar transmitter. —*v.i.* **5.** to examine the meter of verse. **6.** (of verse) to conform to the rules of meter. —*n.* **7.** an act or instance of scanning. [ME *scanne,* var. of **scanden* < LL *scand(ere)* scan verse, L: to climb] —**scan′na·ble,** *adj.* —**scan′ner,** *n.* —**Syn. 2.** skim.

Scan., Scandinavia.

Scand, Scandinavian (def. 3).

Scand., **1.** Scandinavia. **2.** Scandinavian.

scan·dal (skan′dᵊl), *n., v.,* **-daled, -dal·ing** or (*esp. Brit.*) **-dalled, -dal·ling.** —*n.* **1.** a disgraceful or discreditable action, circumstance, etc. **2.** public disgrace because of such an action. **3.** an offense caused by a fault or misdeed. **4.** malicious gossip. **5.** a person whose conduct brings disgrace or offense. —*v.t.* **6.** *Archaic.* to defame (someone) by spreading scandal. **7.** *Obs.* to disgrace. **8.** *Obs.* to scandalize. [< LL *scandal(um)* < eccl. Gk *skándalon* snare, cause of moral stumbling; r. ME *scandle* < OF (north) *(e)scandle* < LL, as above] —**Syn. 2.** dishonor, shame, ignominy, discredit. **4.** slander, calumny, aspersion.

scan·dal·ise (skan′dᵊlīz′), *v.t.,* **-ised, -is·ing.** *Chiefly Brit.* scandalize. —**scan′dal·i·sa′tion,** *n.* —**scan′dal·is′er,** *n.*

scan·dal·ize (skan′dᵊlīz′), *v.t.,* **-ized, -iz·ing.** to shock or horrify, as by immoral or improper conduct. [< eccl. L *scandaliz(āre)* < Gk *skandalízein*] —**scan′dal·i·za′tion,** *n.* —**scan′dal·iz′er,** *n.*

scan·dal·mon·ger (skan′dᵊl mung′gər, -mong′-), *n.* a person who spreads scandal or gossip.

scan·dal·ous (skan′dᵊləs), *adj.* **1.** disgraceful; shameful or shocking; improper: *scandalous behavior in public.* **2.** defamatory or libelous, as a speech or writing. [< ML *scandalōs(us)*] —**scan′dal·ous·ly,** *adv.* —**scan′dal·ous·ness,** *n.*

scan·dent (skan′dənt), *adj.* climbing, as a plant. [< L *scandent-* (s. of *scandēns,* prp. of *scandere* to climb); see -ENT]

Scan·der·beg (skan′dər beg′), *n.* (*George Castriota*) 1403?–68, Albanian chief and revolutionary leader. Turkish, **Iskander Bey.**

scan·di·a (skan′dē ə), *n. Chem.* oxide of scandium, Sc_2O_3. [< NL; see SCANDIUM, -IA]

Scan·di·a (skan′dē ə), *n.* ancient name of the S Scandinavian Peninsula.

Scan·di·an (skan′dē ən), *n.* a Scandinavian.

scan·dic (skan′dik), *adj. Chem.* of or pertaining to scandium: *scandic oxide.* [SCAND(IUM) + -IC]

Scan·di·na·vi·a (skan′də nā′vē ə), *n.* **1.** Norway, Sweden, Denmark, and sometimes Iceland and the Faeroe Islands: the former lands of the Norsemen. **2.** Also called **Scandinavian Peninsula.** the peninsula consisting of Norway and Sweden.

Scan·di·na·vi·an (skan′də nā′vē ən), *adj.* **1.** of or pertaining to Scandinavia, its inhabitants, or their languages. —*n.* **2.** a native or inhabitant of Scandinavia. **3.** the group of languages composed of Danish, Icelandic, Norwegian, Old Norse, Swedish, and the language of the Faeroe Islands; North Germanic. *Abbr.:* Scand, Scand.

Scandina′vian Penin′sula, Scandinavia (def. 2).

scan·di·um (skan′dē əm), *n. Chem.* a rare, trivalent, metallic element. *Symbol:* Sc; *at. wt.:* 44.956; *at. no.:* 21; *sp. gr.:* 3.0. [< NL; see SCANDIA, -IUM]

scan·sion (skan′shən), *n. Pros.* the metrical analysis of verse. [< LL *scānsiōn-* (s. of *scānsiō*), L: a climbing = *scāns(us)* (ptp. of *scandere* to climb) + *-iōn-* -ION]

scan·so·ri·al (skan sōr′ē əl, -sôr′-), *adj. Zool.* **1.** capable of or adapted for climbing, as the feet of certain birds, lizards, etc. **2.** habitually climbing, as a woodpecker. [< L *scānsōri(us)* for climbing (see SCANSION, -ORY[1]) + -AL[1]]

scant (skant), *adj.* **1.** barely sufficient in amount or quantity. **2.** barely amounting to as much as indicated: *a scant teaspoonful.* **3.** having an inadequate or limited supply (usually fol. by *of*): *scant of breath.* —*v.t.* **4.** to make scant; diminish. **5.** to stint the supply of. **6.** to treat slightly or inadequately. —*adv.* **7.** *Dial.* scarcely; barely; hardly. [ME < Scand; cf. Icel *skamt,* neut. of *skammr* short] —**scant′ly,** *adv.* —**scant′ness,** *n.* —**Syn. 2.** bare, mere. **3.** short, lacking, wanting, deficient. **4.** lessen, reduce, decrease, curtail. **5.** limit, restrict, skimp, scrimp. **6.** slight, neglect.

scant·ling (skant′ling), *n.* **1.** a timber of relatively small cross section. **2.** such timbers collectively. **3.** the width and thickness of a timber. **4.** a small quantity or amount. [SCANT + -LING[1]; r. ME *scantilon* < OF *(e)scantillon* gauge]

scant·y (skan′tē), *adj.,* **scant·i·er, scant·i·est.** **1.** scant in amount, quantity, etc. **2.** not adequate. **3.** lacking amplitude. —**scant′i·ly,** *adv.* —**scant′i·ness,** *n.*

—**Syn. 1, 2.** SCANTY, MEAGER, SPARSE refer to insufficiency or deficiency in quantity, number, etc. SCANTY denotes smallness or insufficiency of quantity, number, supply, etc.: *a scanty supply of food.* MEAGER indicates that something is poor, stinted, or inadequate: *meager fare; a meager income.* SPARSE applies particularly to that which grows thinly or is thinly strewn or sown, often over a wide area: *sparse vegetation; a sparse population.* —**Ant. 1, 2.** plentiful, ample.

Sca′pa Flow′ (skä′pə, skap′ə), an area of water off the N coast of Scotland, in the Orkney Islands: British naval base; German warships scuttled 1919.

scape[1] (skāp), *n.* **1.** *Bot.* a leafless peduncle rising from the ground. **2.** *Zool.* a stemlike part, as the shaft of a feather. **3.** *Entomol.* the stemlike basal segment of the antenna of certain insects. [< L *scāp(us)* stalk < Doric Gk *skâpos,* c. Attic *sképtron* staff, SCEPTER]

S—

S, Scape

scape[2] (skāp), *n., v.t., v.i.,* **scaped, scap·ing.** *Archaic.* escape. Also, **'scape.**

scape·goat (skāp′gōt′), *n.* **1.** a person made to bear the blame for others or to suffer in their place. **2.** *Chiefly Biblical.* a goat on whose head the high priest symbolically laid the sins of the people. Lev. 16:8–22.

scape·grace (skāp′grās′), *n.* a complete rogue or rascal; scamp.

scapho-, a learned borrowing from Greek meaning "boat," used in the formation of compound words. Also, *esp. before a vowel,* **scaph-.** [comb. form of Gk *skáphē*]

scaph·oid (skaf′oid), *adj.* **1.** boat-shaped; navicular. —*n.* **2.** *Anat.* a navicular. [< NL *scaphoīd(ēs)* < Gk *skaphoeidḗs* like a boat]

scaph·o·pod (skaf′ə pod′), *adj.* belonging or pertaining to the class *Scaphopoda,* comprising the tooth-shell mollusks. Also, **sca·phop·o·dous** (skə fop′ə dəs). [< NL *Scaphopod(a).* See SCAPHO-, -POD]

scap·o·lite (skap′ə līt′), *n.* **1.** any of a group of minerals of variable composition, essentially silicates of aluminum, calcium, and sodium. **2.** the member of the scapolite group intermediate in composition between meionite and marialite; wernerite. [< G *Skapolith.* See SCAPE[1], -O-, -LITE]

sca·pose (skā′pōs), *adj.* **1.** having scapes; consisting of a scape. **2.** resembling a scape.

s. caps., small capitals.

scap·u·la (skap′yə lə), *n., pl.* **-lae** (-lē′), **-las.** **1.** *Anat.* either of two flat, triangular bones, each forming the back part of a shoulder in man; shoulder blade. **2.** *Zool.* a dorsal bone of the pectoral girdle. [< L: shoulder]

scap·u·lar[1] (skap′yə lər), *adj.* of or pertaining to the shoulders or the scapula or scapulae. [< NL *scapulār(is).* See SCAPULA, -AR[1]]

scap·u·lar[2] (skap′yə lər), *n.* **1.** a loose, sleeveless monastic garment, hanging from the shoulders. **2.** two small pieces of woolen cloth, joined by strings passing over the shoulders, worn under the ordinary clothing as a badge of affiliation with a religious order, a token of devotion, etc. **3.** *Anat., Zool.* scapula. **4.** *Ornith.* one of the feathers of the scapular pteryla. [< ML *scapulāre.* See SCAPULA, -AR[2]]

scap·u·lar·y (skap′yə ler′ē), *adj.* scapular[1].

scar[1] (skär), *n., v.,* **scarred, scar·ring.** —*n.* **1.** the mark left by a healed wound, sore, or burn. **2.** any lasting aftereffect of trouble. **3.** *Bot.* a mark indicating a former point of attachment, as where a leaf has fallen from a stem. —*v.t.* **4.** to leave a scar upon. —*v.i.* **5.** to heal with a resulting scar. [aph. var. of ESCHAR]

scar[2] (skär), *n. Brit.* **1.** a precipitous, rocky place; cliff. **2.** a low or submerged rock in the sea. [ME *skerre* < Scand; cf. Icel *sker* SKERRY]

scar·ab (skar′əb), *n.* **1.** any scarabaeid beetle, esp. *Scarabaeus sacer,* regarded as sacred by the ancient Egyptians. **2.** a representation or image of a beetle, much used among the ancient Egyptians as a symbol, seal, amulet, or the like. **3.** a gem cut to resemble a beetle. Also, **scarabaeus** (for defs. 2, 3). [short for SCARABAEUS]

Scarab (def. 2)

scar·a·bae·id (skar′ə bē′id), *adj.* **1.** belonging or pertaining to the *Scarabaeidae,* a family of lamellicorn beetles, comprising the scarabs, dung beetles, June bugs, cockchafers, etc. —*n.* **2.** any scarabaeid beetle. Also, **scar′a·bae′an.** [< NL *scarabaeid(ae).* See SCARABAEUS, -ID[2]]

scar·a·bae·oid (skar′ə bē′oid), *adj.* Also, **scar·a·boid** (skar′ə boid′). **1.** resembling a scarab. **2.** of the nature of, or resembling, a scarabaeid. —*n.* **3.** an imitation or counterfeit scarab.

scar·a·bae·us (skar′ə bē′əs), *n., pl.* **-bae·us·es, -bae·i** (-bē′ī). scarab (defs. 2, 3). [< L; cf. Gk *kárabos* kind of beetle]

Scar·a·mouch (skar′ə mouch′, -mo͞osh′), *n.* a cowardly braggart: stock character in commedia dell'arte and farce. Also, **Scar′a·mouche′.** [< F *Scaramouche* < It *Scaramuccio* < *scaramuccia* skirmish, applied in jest]

Scar·bor·ough (skär′bûr′ō, -bur′ō, -bər ə), *n.* a seaport in E Yorkshire, in NE England: resort. 42,587 (1961).

scarce (skârs), *adj.,* **scarc·er, scarc·est,** *adv.* —*adj.* **1.** insufficient in number or amount to meet a demand readily. **2.** seldom found; rare. **3. make oneself scarce,** *Informal.* to depart, esp. suddenly. —*adv.* **4.** scarcely. [ME *scars* < OF (north) *(e)scars* < VL **excarps(us)* plucked out, var. of L *excerptus;* see EXCERPT] —**scarce′ness,** *n.* —**Syn. 2.** uncommon, infrequent. —**Ant. 1.** abundant.

scarce·ly (skârs′lē), *adv.* **1.** barely; hardly: *I can scarcely see.* **2.** definitely not: *This is scarcely the time for arguments!* **3.** probably not: *That is scarcely true.* [ME] —**Syn. 1.** See **hardly.**

scar·ci·ty (skâr′si tē), *n., pl.* **-ties.** **1.** insufficiency or smallness of supply; dearth. **2.** rarity; infrequency. [ME *scarsetee* < OF (north) *escarsete*]

scare (skâr), *v.,* **scared, scar·ing,** *n.* —*v.t.* **1.** to fill suddenly with fear or terror. —*v.i.* **2.** to become frightened: *That horse scares easily.* **3. scare up,** *Informal.* to obtain with effort. —*n.* **4.** a sudden fright or alarm, esp. with little or no reason. **5.** a time or condition of alarm or worry. [var. of

ME *skerre* < Scand; cf. Icel *skirra* < *skjarr* shy] **—scar′ing·ly,** *adv.* **—Syn. 1.** startle, intimidate. See **frighten.**

scare·crow (skâr′krō′), *n.* an object, traditionally a thin figure of a man in old clothes, set up to frighten crows or other birds away from crops.

scared·y-cat (skâr′dē kat′), *n. Informal.* a person who is easily frightened.

scare·head (skâr′hed′), *n. U.S. Informal.* a headline in exceptionally large type. Cf. **screamer** (def. 3).

scare·mon·ger (skâr′mung′gər, -mong′-), *n.* a person who spreads rumors of supposedly impending disasters. **—scare′mon′ger·ing,** *n.*

scarf[1] (skärf), *n., pl.* **scarfs,** (*esp. Brit.*) **scarves** (skärvz), *v.* **—n. 1.** a long, broad strip of cloth worn by a woman about the neck, shoulders, or head. **2.** a muffler. **3.** a necktie or cravat with hanging ends. **4.** a long cover or ornamental cloth for a bureau, table, etc. **—v.t. 5.** to cover or wrap with, or as with, a scarf. [? special use of SCARF[2]]

scarf[2] (skärf), *n., pl.* **scarfs,** *v.* **—n. 1.** a tapered or narrowed end on each of the pieces to be assembled with a scarf joint. **2.** *Whaling.* a strip of skin along the body of a whale. **—v.t. 3.** to assemble with a scarf joint. **4.** to form a scarf on (the end of a timber). **5.** *Whaling.* to make a groove in and remove the blubber and skin. [< Scand; cf. Sw *skarf* piece (of wood or cloth) for piecing out or together]

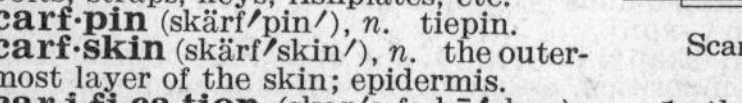
Scarf joints

scar-faced (skär′fāst′), *adj.* having a face marked by a scar or scars.

scarf′ joint′, a joint in which two timbers or other structural members are fitted together with long end laps of various forms and held in place with bolts, straps, keys, fishplates, etc.

scarf·pin (skärf′pin′), *n.* tiepin.

scarf·skin (skärf′skin′), *n.* the outermost layer of the skin; epidermis.

scar·i·fi·ca·tion (skar′ə fə kā′shən), *n.* **1.** the act or an instance of scarifying. **2.** the result of scarifying; scratch or scratches. [< LL *scarīficātiōn-* (s. of *scarīficātiō*)]

scar·i·fi·ca·tor (skar′ə fə kā′tər), *n.* a surgical instrument for scarifying. [< NL (coined by Ambroise Paré)]

scar·i·fy (skar′ə fī′), *v.t.,* **-fied, -fy·ing. 1.** to scratch or cut superficially. **2.** to wound by severe criticism. **3.** to loosen (the soil) with a type of cultivator. **4.** to hasten the sprouting of (hard-covered seeds) by making incisions in the seed coats. [< MF *scarifi(er)* < LL *scarīficāre,* alter. of L *scarīfāre* to make scratches < Gk *skariph(âsthai)* (to) sketch < *skárīph(os)* stylus; see -IFY] **—scar′i·fi′er,** *n.*

scar·i·ous (skâr′ē əs), *adj. Bot.* thin, dry, and membranous, as certain bracts. [alter. of *scariose* < NL *scariōs(us)* < ?; see -OUS]

scar·la·ti·na (skär′lə tē′nə), *n. Pathol.* See **scarlet fever.** [< NL < It *scarlattina* = *scarlatt(o)* SCARLET + *-ina* dim. suffix] **—scar′la·ti′nal, scar·la·ti·nous** (skär lat′ənəs), *adj.*

Scar·lat·ti (skär lät′ē; *It.* skär lät′tē), *n.* **1. A·les·san·dro** (ä′les sän′drô), 1659–1725, Italian composer. **2.** his son **Do·me·ni·co** (dô me′nē kô′), 1685–1757, Italian harpsichordist, organist, and composer.

scar·let (skär′lit), *n.* **1.** a bright red tending toward orange. **2.** a cloth or garments of this color. **—adj. 3.** of the color scarlet. [ME < ML *scarlett(um),* prob. < Pers *saqalāt* kind of cloth, usually bright red, rich and heavy]

scar′let fe′ver, *Pathol.* a contagious febrile disease caused by streptococci and characterized by a scarlet eruption.

scar′let hat′. See **red hat.**

scar′let let′ter, *U.S.* a scarlet letter "A," formerly worn by a person convicted of adultery.

scar′let lych′nis, a perennial lychnis, *Lychnis chalcedonica,* having scarlet or sometimes white flowers, the petals resembling a Maltese cross. Also called **Maltese cross.**

scar′let pim′pernel. See under **pimpernel.**

scar′let run′ner, a twining, South American bean plant, *Phaseolus coccineus,* having scarlet flowers.

scar′let tan′ager, an American tanager, *Piranga olivacea,* the male of which is bright red with black wings and tail during the breeding season. See illus. at **tanager.**

scar′let wom′an, an immoral woman, esp. an adulteress.

scarp (skärp), *n.* **1.** a line of cliffs formed by the faulting or fracturing of the earth's crust. **2.** *Fort.* an escarp. **—v.t. 3.** to form into a steep slope. [< It *scarp(a)* slope. See ESCARP]

scarp·er (skär′pər), *v.i. Brit.* to flee or depart suddenly, esp. without having paid one's bills. [?]

scarph (skärf), *n., v.t.* scarf[2] (defs. 1, 3, 4).

Scar·ron (ska rôN′), *n.* **Paul** (pôl), 1610–60, French novelist, dramatist, and poet.

scar′ tis′sue, connective tissue that has contracted and become dense and fibrous.

scarves (skärvz), *n. Chiefly Brit.* a pl. of **scarf**[1].

scar·y (skâr′ē), *adj.,* **scar·i·er, scar·i·est.** *Informal.* **1.** causing fright or alarm. **2.** easily frightened; timid.

scat (skat), *v.i.,* **scat·ted, scat·ting.** *Informal.* to go away or depart hastily (often used in the imperative). [a hiss + CAT]

scathe (skāth), *v.,* **scathed, scath·ing,** *n.* **—v.t. 1.** to attack with severe criticism. **2.** to hurt, harm, or injure, as by scorching. **—n. 3.** hurt, harm, or injury. [ME < Scand; cf. Icel *skathi* damage, harm; c. OE *sc(e)atha* malefactor, injury, G *Schade* shame] **—scathe′less, —scathe′less·ly,** *adv.*

scath·ing (skā′thing), *adj.* **1.** bitterly severe, as a remark. **2.** harmful, injurious, or searing. **—scath′ing·ly,** *adv.*

sca·tol·o·gy (skə tol′ə jē), *n.* **1.** obscenity, esp. words or humor referring to excrement. **2.** preoccupation with excrement or obscenity. **3.** the study of fossil excrement. Also called **coprology.** [< Gk *skato-* (comb. form of *skōr* dung) + -LOGY] **—scat·o·log·ic** (skat′əloj′ik), **scat′o·log′i·cal,** *adj.*

scat′ sing′ing, *Jazz.* singing in which improvised nonsense syllables are substituted for the words of a song, often in an attempt to approximate the sound and phrasing of a musical instrument.

scat·ter (skat′ər), *v.t.* **1.** to throw loosely about; distribute at irregular intervals: *to scatter seeds.* **2.** to send off in various directions. **3.** *Physics.* **a.** to refract or diffract (light or other electromagnetic radiation) irregularly so as to diffuse it in many directions. **b.** (of a medium) to diffuse or deflect (light or other waves) by collisions between the wave and particles of the medium. **—v.i. 4.** to separate and disperse in different directions. **—n. 5.** the act of scattering. **6.** that which is scattered. [ME *scatere;* cf. D *schateren* to burst out laughing] **—scat′ter·a·ble,** *adj.* **—scat′ter·er,** *n.* **—Syn. 1.** broadcast. **2.** SCATTER, DISPEL, DISPERSE imply separating and driving something away so that its form disappears. To SCATTER is to separate something tangible into parts at random, and drive these in different directions: *The wind scattered leaves all over the lawn.* To DISPEL is to drive away or scatter usually intangible things so that they vanish or cease to exist: *Photographs of the finish dispelled all doubts as to which horse won.* To DISPERSE is to cause (usually) a compact or organized tangible body to separate or scatter in different directions, to be reassembled if desired: *Tear gas dispersed the mob.*

scat·ter·brain (skat′ər brān′), *n.* a person incapable of serious, connected thought. Also, **scat′ter·brains′. —scat′ter·brained′,** *adj.*

scat·ter·ing (skat′ər ing), *adj.* **1.** distributed or occurring here and there at irregular intervals. **2.** distributing, dispersing, or separating. **—n. 3.** a small, scattered number or quantity. **4.** *Physics.* the process in which a wave or beam of particles is diffused or deflected by collisions with particles of the medium which it traverses. [ME]

scat′ter pin′, a woman's small ornamental pin, as worn with other similar pins on a dress, suit, etc.

scat′ter rug′, a small rug, placed in front of a chair, under a table, etc. Also called **throw rug.**

scat′ter-site′ hous′ing (skat′ər sīt′), *U.S.* a housing program designed to scatter minority or poverty groups throughout an urban area rather than concentrate them in one neighborhood.

scaup′ duck′ (skôp), any of several diving ducks of the genus *Aythya,* esp. *A. marila,* of the Northern Hemisphere. Also called **scaup.** [var. of *scalp duck* < ?]

scau·per (skô′pər), *n.* a graver with a flattened or hollowed blade, used in engraving. [var. of *scalper* < L *scalpr(um)* knife. See SCALPEL]

scav·enge (skav′inj), *v.,* **-enged, -eng·ing. —v.t. 1.** to cleanse from filth, as a street. **2.** to take or gather (something usable) from discarded material. **3.** to expel burnt gases from (the cylinder of an internal-combustion engine). **—v.i. 4.** to act as a scavenger. **5.** to search, esp. for food. [back formation from SCAVENGER]

scav·en·ger (skav′in jər), *n.* an organism, object, or person that scavenges, esp. an animal that feeds on dead organic matter. [nasalized var. of AF *scawager* = *scawage* (north OF *escawage* inspection) + *-er* -ER[2]; *escawage* = *escaw(er)* (to) inspect (< Flem *scauwen* to look at, c. SHOW) + *-age* -AGE]

Sc.B., See **Bachelor of Science.** [< L *Scientiae Baccalaureus*]

Sc.D., Doctor of Science. [< L *Scientiae Doctor*]

sce·nar·i·o (si nâr′ē ō′, -när′-), *n., pl.* **-nar·i·os. 1.** an outline of the plot of a dramatic work, giving particulars as to the scenes, characters, situations, etc. **2.** a screenplay or shooting script. **3.** an outline of a natural or expected course of events. [< It < L *scēnāri(um).* See SCENE, -ARY]

sce·nar·ist (si nâr′ist, -när′-), *n.* a writer of motion-picture scenarios. [SCENAR(IO) + -IST]

scend (send), *Naut.* **—v.i.** (of a vessel) **1.** to heave in a swell. **2.** to lurch forward from the motion of a heavy sea. **—n. 3.** the heaving motion of a vessel. **4.** the forward impulse imparted by the motion of a sea against a vessel. Also, **send.** [var. of SEND; cf. ASCEND]

scene (sēn), *n.* **1.** the place where some action or event occurs. **2.** any view or picture. **3.** an incident or situation in real life. **4.** an embarrassing display of emotion or bad manners. **5.** a division of a play, film, novel, etc., that represents a single episode. **6.** the place in which the action of a story, drama, or dramatic episode is supposed to occur. **7.** scenery (def. 2). **8. behind the scenes,** in secret or in private. [< L *scēn(a)* background (of the stage) < Gk *skēnḗ* booth (where actors dressed)] **—Syn. 1.** arena, stage, location. **2.** See **view. 3.** episode.

scen·er·y (sē′nə rē), *n., pl.* **-er·ies. 1.** the aggregate of features that give character to a landscape. **2.** a representation or illusion of a locale, as for a film or play.

sce·nic (sē′nik, sen′ik), *adj.* **1.** of or pertaining to natural scenery. **2.** having pleasing or beautiful scenery. **3.** of or pertaining to the stage or to stage scenery. **4.** representing a scene, action, or the like. Also, **sce′ni·cal.** [< L *scēnic(us)* < Gk *skēnikós* theatrical] **—sce′ni·cal·ly,** *adv.*

sce′nic rail′way, a miniature railroad for carrying passengers on a tour of an amusement park, resort, etc.

sce·nog·ra·phy (sē nog′rə fē), *n.* the art of representing objects in perspective. [< Gk *skēnographía.* See SCENE, -O-, -GRAPHY] **—sce·nog′raph·er,** *n.* **—sce·no·graph·ic** (sē′nə graf′ik, sen′ə-), **sce′no·graph′i·cal,** *adj.* **—sce′no·graph′i·cal·ly,** *adv.*

scent (sent), *n.* **1.** a distinctive odor, esp. when agreeable. **2.** an odor left in passing, by means of which an animal or person may be traced. **3.** small pieces of paper dropped by the hares in the game of hare and hounds. **4.** *Chiefly Brit.* perfume. **5.** a sense of smell. **—v.t. 6.** to perceive or recognize by or as by the sense of smell. **7.** to fill with an odor; perfume. **—v.i. 8.** to hunt by the sense of smell, as a hound. [ME *sent* < MF *sent(ir)* smell < L *sentīre* feel. Cf. SENSE]

scep·ter (sep′tər), *n.* **1.** a rod or wand borne in the hand as an emblem of regal or imperial power. **2.** royal or imperial power or authority; sovereignty. **—v.t. 3.** to give a scepter to; invest with authority. Also, *esp. Brit.,* **sceptre.** [ME *(s)ceptre* < OF < L *scēptr(um)* < Gk *skêptron* staff] **—scep·tral** (sep′trəl), *adj.*

scep·tic (skep′tik), *n., adj.* skeptic.

scep·ti·cal (skep′ti kəl), *adj.* skeptical. **—scep′ti·cal·ly,** *adv.*

scep·ti·cism (skep′ti siz′əm), *n.* skepticism.

scep·tre (sep′tər), *n., v.t.,* **-tred, -tring.** *Chiefly Brit.* scepter.

Sch., (in Austria) schilling; schillings.

sch., **1.** school. **2.** schooner.

Schaer·beek (*Flemish.* skHär′bāk), *n.* a city in central Belgium, near Brussels. 120,768 (est. 1964).

schap′pe silk′ (shä′pə), a yarn or fabric of or similar to spun silk. Also called **schap′pe.** [*schappe* < Swiss G: raw silk leavings; cf. F *échappement* leakage]

Scharn·horst (shärn′hôrst), *n.* **Ger·hard Jo·hann Da·vid von** (gâr′härt yō′hän dä′vēt fən), 1755–1813, Prussian general.

schat·chen (shät′khən), *n., pl.* **schat·cho·nim** (shät khô′-nim), **schat·chens.** *Yiddish.* shadchan.

Schaum·burg-Lip·pe (shoum′bo͝ork lip′ə), *n.* a former state in NW Germany.

Schech·ter (shek′tər), *n.* **Solomon,** 1847–1915, U.S. Hebraist, born in Rumania.

sched·ule (skej′o͞ol, -o͝ol, -o͞o əl; *Brit.* shed′yo͞ol, shej′o͞ol), *n., v.,* **-uled, -ul·ing.** —*n.* **1.** a number of duties, events, etc., listed usually in sequence with the time each will occur or will be allotted. **2.** a series of things to be done within a given period. **3.** a timetable. **4.** a written or printed statement of details, often in tabular form. **5.** *Obs.* a written paper. —*v.t.* **6.** to make a schedule of or enter in a schedule. **7.** to plan for a certain date. [< LL *schedul(a)* = L *sched(a)* leaf of paper + *-ula* -ULE; r. ME *cedule, sedule* < MF] —**sched′u·lar,** *adj.* —**Syn. 4.** table, register. See **list**[1].

scheel·ite (shā′līt, shē′-), *n.* *Mineral.* calcium tungstate, $CaWO_4$, an important ore of tungsten. [< G *Scheelit,* named after K. W. *Scheele,* (1742–86), Swedish chemist who first isolated tungstic acid; see -ITE[1]]

Sche·her·a·za·de (shə her′ə zä′də, -zäd′, -hēr′-), *n.* (in the 10th-century collection of Eastern folk tales *The Arabian Nights' Entertainments*) the wife of the sultan of India, who relates such interesting tales nightly that the sultan spares her life to hear the continuation.

Scheidt (shīt), *n.* **Sa·mu·el** (zä′mo͞o el′), 1587–1654, German organist and composer.

Schein (shīn), *n.* **Jo·hann Her·mann** (yō′hän her′män), 1586–1630, German composer.

Scheldt (skelt), *n.* a river in W Europe, flowing from N France through W Belgium and SW Netherlands into the North Sea. 270 mi. long. Flemish, **Schel·de** (skhel′də). French, **Escaut.**

Schel·ling (shel′ing), *n.* **Frie·drich Wil·helm Jo·seph von** (frē′drikh vil′helm yō′zef fən), 1775–1854, German philosopher.

sche·ma (skē′mə), *n., pl.* **-ma·ta** (-mə tə). **1.** a generalized diagram, plan, or scheme. **2.** (in Kantian epistemology) a concept, similar to a universal but limited to phenomenal knowledge, by which an object of knowledge or an idea of pure reason may be apprehended. [< Gk: form]

sche·mat·ic (skē mat′ik), *adj.* **1.** pertaining to or of the nature of a generalized diagram, plan, or scheme. —*n.* **2.** a generalized diagram or plan. [< NL *schēmatic(us)* < Gk *schēmatikós.* See SCHEME, -IC] —**sche·mat′i·cal·ly,** *adv.*

sche·ma·tise (skē′mə tīz′), *v.t.,* **-tised, -tis·ing.** *Chiefly Brit.* schematize. —**sche′ma·ti·sa′tion,** *n.*

sche·ma·tism (skē′mə tiz′əm), *n.* **1.** the particular form or disposition of a thing. **2.** a schematic arrangement. [< Gk *schēmatism(ós).* See SCHEMATIZE, -ISM]

sche·ma·tize (skē′mə tīz′), *v.t.,* **-tized, -tiz·ing.** to reduce to or arrange according to a scheme. Also, *esp. Brit.,* **schematise.** [< Gk *schēmatíz(ein)* (to) form. See SCHEME, -IZE] —**sche′ma·ti·za′tion,** *n.*

scheme (skēm), *n., v.,* **schemed, schem·ing.** —*n.* **1.** a plan, design, or program of action to be followed; project. **2.** an underhand plot; intrigue. **3.** a visionary or impractical project. **4.** any system of correlated things, or the manner of its arrangement. **5.** an analytical or tabular statement. **6.** a diagram, map, or the like. **7.** an astrological diagram of the heavens. —*v.t.* **8.** to devise as a scheme; plan; plot; contrive. —*v.i.* **9.** to lay schemes; devise plans; plot. [< ML *schēma, schēmat-* < Gk: form, figure] —**schem′er,** *n.* —**Syn. 1.** See **plan. 2.** cabal, conspiracy. **4.** pattern, schema, arrangement. **8.** project. See **plot**[1].

schem·ing (skē′ming), *adj.* given to making plans, esp. sly and underhand ones; crafty. —**schem′ing·ly,** *adv.*

Sche·nec·ta·dy (skə nek′tə dē), *n.* a city in E New York, on the Mohawk River. 77,958 (1970).

scher·zan·do (sker tsän′dō, -tsan′-), *adj.* (a musical direction) playful; sportive. [< It, prp. of *scherzare* to joke; see SCHERZO]

scher·zo (sker′tsō), *n., pl.* **-zos, -zi** (-tsē). *Music.* a movement or passage of light or playful character, esp. as the second or third movement of a sonata or a symphony. [< It: joke < G *Scherz* joke]

Sche·ven·ing·en (skhā′vən ing′ən), *n.* a town in the W Netherlands, near The Hague: seaside resort.

Schia·pa·rel·li (skyä′pə rel′ē, *It.* skyä′pä rel′lē), *n.* **Gio·van·ni Vir·gin·io** (jô vän′nē vēr jē′nyô), 1835–1910, Italian astronomer.

Schick′ test′, *Med.* a diphtheria-immunity test in which diphtheria toxoid is injected cutaneously, nonimmunity being characterized by an inflammation at the injection site. [named after Béla *Schick* (1877–1967), U.S. pediatrician]

Schie·dam (skhē däm′), *n.* a city in the SW Netherlands. 81,100 (est. 1962).

schil·ler (shil′ər), *n.* a bronzelike luster occurring on certain minerals. [< G: play of colors, glitter]

Schil·ler (shil′ər), *n.* **Jo·hann Chris·toph Frie·drich von** (yō′hän kris′tôf frē′drikh fən), 1759–1805, German poet, dramatist, and historian.

schil·ling (shil′ing), *n.* a copper and aluminum coin and monetary unit of Austria, equal to 100 groschen. *Abbr.:* S., Sch. [< G; c. SHILLING]

Schip·per·ke (skip′ər kē, -kə), *n.* one of a Belgian breed of small dogs having erect ears and a thick, black coat. [< D: little boatman; see SKIPPER[1]]

schism (siz′əm), *n.* **1.** division or disunion, esp. into opposing parties. **2.** the parties so formed. **3.** *Eccles.* **a.** a formal division within or separation from a church or religious body over some doctrinal difference. **b.** the state of a sect or body formed by such division. **c.** the offense of causing or seeking to cause such a division. [< eccl. L *schism(a), schismat-* < Gk *schísma* = *schíz(ein)* (to) split + *-ma, -mat-* n. suffix; r. ME *(s)cisme, sisme* < MF < L, as above]

schis·mat·ic (siz mat′ik), *adj.* **1.** Also, **schis·mat′i·cal.** of, pertaining to, or of the nature of schism; guilty of schism. —*n.* **2.** a person who promotes schism or is an adherent of a schismatic body. [< eccl. L *schismatic(us)* < Gk *schismatikós* (see SCHISM, -IC); r. ME *scismatik,* etc. < MF *scismatique* < L, as above]

schist (shist), *n.* any of a class of crystalline rocks whose constituent minerals have a more or less parallel or foliated arrangement, due mostly to metamorphic action. [< NL *schist(us)* < L *(lapis) schistos* < Gk: splittable = *schíz(ein)* (to) split + *-tos* adj. suffix]

schis·tose (shis′tōs), *adj.* of, resembling, or in the form of schist. Also, **schis·tous** (shis′təs). [SCHIST + -OSE[1]] —**schis·tos·i·ty** (shi stos′i tē), *n.*

schis·to·some (shis′tə sōm′), *n.* **1.** any elongated trematode of the genus *Schistosoma,* parasitic in the blood vessels of man and other mammals; a blood fluke. —*adj.* **2.** pertaining to or caused by schistosomes. [< NL *Schistosoma.* See SCHIST, -O-, -SOME[3]]

schis·to·so·mi·a·sis (shis′tə sō mī′ə sis), *n.* *Pathol.* infestation with schistosomes.

schizo-, a learned borrowing from Greek meaning "split," used in the formation of compound words: *schizogenesis.* Also, *esp. before a vowel,* **schiz-.** [< Gk, comb. form repr. *schízein* to part, split]

schiz·o·carp (skiz′ə kärp′), *n.* *Bot.* a dry fruit that at maturity splits into two or more one-seeded indehiscent carpels. —**schiz′o·car′pous, schiz′o·car′pic,** *adj.*

schiz·o·gen·e·sis (skiz′ə jen′i sis), *n.* *Biol.* reproduction by fission.

schi·zog·o·ny (ski zog′ə nē), *n.* *Biol.* (in the asexual reproduction of certain sporozoans) the multiple fission of a trophozoite or schizont into merozoites.

schiz·oid (skit′soid, skiz′oid), *adj.* *Psychol.* **1.** of or pertaining to a personality disorder marked by dissociation, passivity, withdrawal, depression, and autistic fantasies. **2.** of or pertaining to schizophrenia or multiple personality. —*n.* **3.** a schizoid person.

schiz·o·my·cete (skiz′ō mī sēt′), *n.* any of numerous organisms of the class *Schizomycetes,* comprising the bacteria. [SCHIZO- + -MYCETE(S)] —**schiz′o·my·ce′tic, schiz′o·my·ce′tous,** *adj.*

schi·zont (skī′zont, skiz′ont), *n.* *Biol.* (in the asexual reproduction of certain sporozoans) a cell that is developed from a trophozoite and undergoes multiple fission to form merozoites. [SCHIZ- + *-ont;* see ONTO-]

schiz·o·phre·ni·a (skit′sə frē′nē ə, -frēn′yə, skiz′ə-), *n.* a psychosis marked by withdrawn, bizarre, and sometimes delusional behavior and by intellectual and emotional deterioration. Also called **dementia praecox.** —**schiz·o·phrene** (skit′sə frēn′, skiz′ə-), *n.* —**schiz·o·phren·ic** (skit′sə fren′ik, skiz′ə-), *adj.*

schiz·o·phy·ceous (skiz′ə fī′shəs, -fish′əs), *adj.* *Bot.* belonging to the *Schizophyceae,* a class or group of unicellular and multicellular green or bluish-green algae that often cause pollution of drinking water.

schiz·o·phyte (skiz′ə fīt′), *n.* any of the *Schizophyta,* a group of plants comprising the schizomycetes and the schizophyceous algae, characterized by a simple structure and reproduction by simple fission or spores. —**schiz·o·phyt·ic** (skiz′ə fit′ik), *adj.*

schiz·o·pod (skiz′ə pod′), *n.* **1.** any crustacean of the former order or division *Schizopoda,* now divided into the orders *Mysidacea,* comprising the opossum shrimps, and *Euphausiacea.* —*adj.* **2.** Also, **schi·zop·o·dous** (ski zop′ə-dəs, skī-). belonging or pertaining to the *Schizopoda.*

schiz·o·thy·mi·a (skit′sə thī′mē ə, skiz′ə-), *n.* *Psychiatry.* an emotional state out of keeping with the ideational content. [SCHIZO- + NL *-thymia* < Gk *thȳm(ós)* soul, spirit, strength + *-ia* -IA] —**schiz′o·thy′mic,** *adj.*

schiz·y (skit′sē), *adj.* *U.S. Slang.* afflicted with schizophrenia; schizophrenic. [SCHIZ(OPHRENIC) + -Y[1]]

Schle·gel (shlā′gəl), *n.* **1. Au·gust Wil·helm von** (ou′go͝ost vil′helm fən), 1767–1845, German poet, critic, and translator. **2.** his brother, **Frie·drich von** (frē′drikh fən), 1772–1829, German critic, philosopher, and poet.

Schlei·er·ma·cher (shlī′ər mä′khər), *n.* **Frie·drich Ernst Da·ni·el** (frē′drikh ernst dä′nē el′), 1768–1834, German theologian and philosopher.

schle·miel (shlə mēl′), *n.* *Slang.* an awkward and unlucky person. Also, **schle·mihl′, shlemiel.** [< Yiddish < G, after Peter *Schlemihl,* title character of an 1814 novel by the German writer Adelbert von Chamisso (1781–1838)]

schlepp (shlep), *Slang.* —*v.t.* **1.** to carry; lug: *to schlepp an umbrella on a sunny day.* —*v.i.* **2.** to carry or lug something, esp. awkwardly. **3.** to go or move (often fol. by *around*). —*n.* **4.** a person of no importance. Also, **schlep.** [< Yiddish *shlep(en)* (to) drag < LG *schleppen;* c. HG *schleifen.* Cf. SLIP[1]]

Schle·si·en (shlā′zē ən), *n.* German name of **Silesia.**

Schles·wig (shles′wig; *Ger.* shlās′vikh), *n.* **1.** a seaport in N West Germany, on the Baltic. 33,600 (1963). **2.** a former duchy of Denmark: annexed by Prussia 1864; N part returned to Denmark 1920. Also, **Sleswick.** Danish, **Slesvig.**

Schles·wig-Hol·stein (shles′wig hōl′stīn; *Ger.* shlās′-vikh hôl′shtīn), *n.* **1.** two contiguous duchies of Denmark that were a center of international tension in the 19th century: Prussia annexed Schleswig 1864 and Holstein 1866. **2.** a state of N West Germany, including the former duchies of Holstein and Lauenburg and part of Schleswig. 2,364,000 (1963); 6055 sq. mi. *Cap.:* Kiel.

Schlie·mann (shlē′män′), *n.* **Hein·rich** (hīn′rikh), 1822–90, German archaeologist and expert on Homer.

schlie·ren (shlēr′ən), *n.* (*construed as pl.*) **1.** *Petrog.* streaks or irregularly shaped masses in an igneous rock that differ in texture or composition from the main mass. **2.** *Physics.* the visible streaks in a turbulent, transparent fluid, each streak being a region that has a density and index of refraction differing from that of the greater part of the fluid. [< G, pl. of *Schliere* streak]

schlock (shlok), *Slang.* —*adj.* **1.** Also, **schlock·y** (shlok′ē). grossly inferior in quality and taste. —*n.* **2.** something of cheap or inferior quality. [< Yiddish]

schmaltz (shmälts, shmôlts), *n.* *Informal.* exaggerated sentimentalism, as in music or soap operas. Also, **schmalz.** [< G, Yiddish; c. SMELT[1]; orig. meaning was grease, butter]

schmaltz·y (shmält′sē, shmôlt′-), *adj.* **schmaltz·i·er, schmaltz·i·est.** *Slang.* of, pertaining to, or characterized by schmaltz.

schmalz·y (shmält′sē, shmôlt′-), *adj.*, **schmalz·i·er, schmalz·i·est.** *Slang.* schmaltzy.

Schme·ling (shmel′ing; *Ger.* shmā′ling), *n.* **Max** (maks; *Ger.* mäks), born 1905, German boxer: world heavyweight champion 1930–32.

Schmidt (shmit), *n.* **Hel·mut** (hel′mo͝ot), born 1918, West German political leader: chancellor 1974–82.

Schmidt′ op′tics (shmit), optical systems, used in wide-field cameras and reflecting telescopes, in which spherical aberration and coma are reduced to a minimum by means of a spherical mirror with a corrector plate near its focus. [named after B. *Schmidt* (1879–1935), German inventor]

schmier·kase (shmēr′kāz′, -kā′zə), *n.* See **cottage cheese.** [< G: lit., smear-cheese]

schmo (shmō), *n., pl.* **schmoes.** *U.S. Slang.* a foolish, boring, or stupid person; a jerk. Also, **schmoe.** [< Yiddish; cf. *schmok* male member]

schmoose (shmo͞oz), *v.i.*, **schmoosed, schmoos·ing,** *n.* schmooze. Also, **schmoos.**

schmooze (shmo͞oz), *v.i.*, **schmoozed, schmooz·ing,** *n.* *Slang.* —*v.i.* **1.** to chat idly; gossip. —*n.* **2.** idle conversation; chatter. [< Yiddish, v. use of *schmues* < Heb *shemu'oth* reports, gossip < root *sm'* hear]

schmuck (shmuk), *n.* *Slang.* fool; oaf; jerk. [< Yiddish male member, lit., pendant; akin to OHG *smocko*, OE *smocc* SMOCK]

Schna·bel (shnä′bəl), *n.* **Ar·tur** (äʀ′to͞oʀ), 1882–1951, Austrian pianist.

schnapps (shnäps, shnaps), *n.* spirituous liquor, esp. Hollands or potato spirits. Also, **shnaps.** [< G < *schnap-p(er)* (to) nip]

schnau·zer (shnou′zər; *Ger.* shnou′-tsəʀ), *n.* (*sometimes cap.*) one of a German breed of dogs having a wiry, pepper-and-salt, black, or black-and-tan coat, occurring in three varieties differing only in size. [< G = *Schnauze* SNOUT + *-er* -ER[1]]

Schnauzer (Standard) (19 in. high at shoulder)

schneck·en (shnek′ən), *n.pl., sing.* **schneck·e** (shnek′ə). a sweet, spiral roll made from raised dough with chopped nuts, butter, and cinnamon. [< G: lit., snail, OHG *snecko.* See SNAIL]

schnei·der (shnī′dər), (in gin rummy) —*v.t.* **1.** to prevent (an opponent) from scoring a point in a game or match. —*n.* **2.** an act of schneidering or fact of being schneidered. [< G: tailor]

schnit·zel (shnit′səl), *n.* *German Cookery.* a veal cutlet. [< G: a shaving < *schnitzel(n)* (to) whittle]

Schnitz·ler (shnits′lər; *Ger.* shnits′ləʀ), *n.* **Ar·thur** (är′thər; *Ger.* äʀ′to͞oʀ), 1862–1931, Austrian dramatist and novelist.

schnook (shno͝ok), *n.* *Slang.* an unimportant or stupid person; dope. [< Yiddish; var. of *schmok* male member]

schnor·kle (shnôr′kəl), *n.* snorkel (def. 1). Also, **schnor′kel.**

schnor·rer (shnōr′ər, shnôr′-), *n.* *Slang.* a person who seeks aid from another without justification; sponger. [< Yiddish < G *Schnurrer* beggar]

scho·la can·to·rum (skō′lə kan tōr′əm, -tôr′-), *pl.* **scho·lae can·to·rum** (skō′lē kan tōr′əm, -tôr′-). **1.** an ecclesiastical choir or choir school. **2.** a section of a church, cathedral, or the like, for use by the choir. [< ML: school of singers]

schol·ar (skol′ər), *n.* **1.** a learned or erudite person, esp. one who has profound knowledge of a particular subject. **2.** a student; pupil. **3.** a student whose merit entitles him to money or other aid to pursue his studies. [< LL *scholār(is).* (See SCHOOL[1], -AR[2]); r. ME *scoler(e)*, OE *scolere* < LL, as above] —**schol′ar·less,** *adj.* —**Syn. 2.** See **pupil**[1].

schol·ar·ly (skol′ər lē), *adj.* **1.** of, suggesting, or befitting a scholar. —*adv.* **2.** like a scholar. —**schol′ar·li·ness,** *n.*

schol·ar·ship (skol′ər ship′), *n.* **1.** the qualities, skills, or attainments of a scholar. **2.** a gift made to a scholar to enable or assist him to pursue his studies. **3.** the accumulated knowledge of a group of scholars. —**Syn. 1.** See **learning.**

scho·las·tic (skə las′tik), *adj.* Also, **scho·las′ti·cal. 1.** of or pertaining to schools, scholars, or education. **2.** of or pertaining to scholasticism. **3.** pedantic. —*n.* **4.** (*sometimes cap.*) an adherent of scholasticism. **5.** a pedant. [< L *scholasticus* < Gk *scholastikós* studious, learned. See SCHOOL[1], -ISTIC] —**scho·las′ti·cal·ly,** *adv.*

scho·las·ti·cate (skə las′tə kāt′, -kit), *n.* *Rom. Cath. Ch.* a course of study for seminarians. [< NL *scholasticāt(us)*]

scho·las·ti·cism (skə las′ti siz′əm), *n.* **1.** (*sometimes cap.*) the system of theological and philosophical teaching predominant in the Middle Ages, based chiefly upon the authority of the church fathers and of Aristotle and his commentators. **2.** narrow adherence to traditional teachings, doctrines, or methods.

scho·li·ast (skō′lē ast′), *n.* **1.** an ancient commentator on the classics. **2.** a person who writes scholia. [< LGk *scholiast(ēs).* See SCHOLIUM, -IST] —**scho′li·as′tic,** *adj.*

scho·li·um (skō′lē əm), *n., pl.* **-li·a** (-lē ə). **1.** Often, **scholia.** an explanatory note or comment, as by an early grammarian on a classic text. **2.** a note added to illustrate or amplify, as in a mathematical work. [< ML < Gk *schólion,* dim. of *scholḗ* SCHOOL[1]]

Schön·berg (shœn′bûrg; *Ger.* shœn′berk), *n.* **Ar·nold** (är′nəld; *Ger.* äʀ′nəlt), 1874–1951, Austrian composer in the U.S.

Schon·gau·er (shōn′gou ər; *Ger.* shōn′gou əʀ), *n.* **Mar·tin** (mär′tᵊn; *Ger.* mäʀ′tēn), c1430–91, German engraver and painter.

school[1] (sko͞ol), *n.* **1.** an institution for teaching persons under college age. **2.** an institution or academic department for teaching in a particular field. **3.** a systematic program of studies: *a summer school.* **4.** the activity of teaching or of learning under instruction: *No school today!* **5.** the body of persons belonging to an educational institution: *The school rose and sang the Alma Mater.* **6.** a building, etc., housing an academic department or institution. **7.** any place, situation, etc., that instructs or indoctrinates. **8.** the body of pupils or followers of a master, system, method, etc. **9.** *Art.* **a.** a group of artists whose works reflect a common influence. **b.** the art and artists of a geographical location considered independently of stylistic similarity. **10.** any group of persons having common attitudes or beliefs. —*adj.* **11.** of or connected with school or schools. —*v.t.* **12.** to educate in or as in a school; teach; train. [ME *scole,* OE *scōl* < L *schol(a)* < Gk *scholḗ* leisure employed in learning]

school[2] (sko͞ol), *n.* **1.** a large number of fish, porpoises, whales, or the like, feeding or migrating together. —*v.i.* **2.** to form into, or go in, a school, as fish. [late ME *schol(e)* < D *school* troop, c. OE *scolu* SHOAL[2]]

school′ age′, 1. the age set by law for children to start school attendance. **2.** the period of school attendance required by law. —**school′-age′,** *adj.*

school·bag (sko͞ol′bag′), *n.* a bag for carrying school-books, school supplies, etc.

school′ board′, a local board or committee in charge of public education.

school·book (sko͞ol′bo͝ok′), *n.* a textbook.

school·boy (sko͞ol′boi′), *n.* a boy attending school.

school′ bus′, a vehicle used to transport students to and from school or used for other related purposes.

school·child (sko͞ol′chīld′), *n., pl.* **-chil·dren.** a child attending a school.

School·craft (sko͞ol′kraft′, -kräft′), *n.* **Henry Rowe** (rō), 1793–1864, U.S. explorer, ethnologist, and author.

school′ day′, 1. any day on which school is conducted. **2.** the daily hours during which school is conducted.

school·fel·low (sko͞ol′fel′ō), *n.* a schoolmate. [late ME]

school·girl (sko͞ol′gûrl′), *n.* a girl attending school.

school·house (sko͞ol′hous′), *n., pl.* **-hous·es** (-hou′ziz). a building in which a school is conducted. [late ME *scolehous*]

school·ing (sko͞o′ling), *n.* **1.** instruction, education, or training, esp. in a school. **2.** *Archaic.* reprimand. [late ME *scoling*]

school·man (sko͞ol′mən), *n., pl.* **-men. 1.** a person versed in scholastic learning or engaged in scholastic pursuits. **2.** (*sometimes cap.*) any of the medieval writers who dealt with theology and philosophy after the methods of scholasticism.

school·marm (sko͞ol′märm′), *n.* *Archaic.* a woman school-teacher. Also, **school·ma'am** (sko͞ol′mam′, -mäm′). [SCHOOL[1] + *marm,* var. of MA'AM]

school·mas·ter (sko͞ol′mas′tər, -mä′stər), *n.* **1.** a man who presides over or teaches in a school. —*v.t., v.i.* **2.** to teach in the capacity of schoolmaster. [ME *scolemaister*] —**school′mas′ter·ship′,** *n.*

school·mate (sko͞ol′māt′), *n.* a companion or associate at school.

school·mis·tress (sko͞ol′mis′tris), *n.* a woman who presides over or teaches in a school.

school·room (sko͞ol′ro͞om′, -ro͝om′), *n.* a room in which a class is conducted or pupils are taught.

school·teach·er (sko͞ol′tē′chər), *n.* a teacher in a school, esp. in one below the college level.

school·teach·ing (sko͞ol′tē′ching), *n.* the profession of a schoolteacher.

school′ tie′. See **old school tie.**

school·work (sko͞ol′wûrk′), *n.* the material studied in or for school, comprising homework and work done in class.

school·yard (sko͞ol′yärd′), *n.* **1.** the yard of a school. **2.** a playground or sports field near a school.

school′ year′, the months of the year during which school is open and attendance at school is required.

Schooner

schoon·er (sko͞o′nər), *n.* **1.** *Naut.* any of various types of sailing vessel having a foremast and mainmast, with or without other masts, and having fore-and-aft sails on all lower masts. Cf. **ketch, yawl**[1] (def. 2). **2.** *U.S. Informal.* a very tall glass, as for beer. [*scoon,* var. of dial. *scun* SCUD[1] (cf. dial. Sw *skunna,* OE *scyndan*) + -ER[1]]

schoon·er-rigged (sko͞o′nər rigd′), *adj.* rigged as a schooner, esp. with gaff sails and staysails only.

Scho·pen·hau·er (shō′pən hou′ər), *n.* **Ar·thur** (äʀ′-to͞oʀ), 1788–1860, German philosopher. —**Scho′pen·hau′-er·i·an,** *adj.* —**Scho′pen·hau′er·ism,** *n.*

schorl (shôrl), *n.* a black tourmaline. [< G *Schörl*] —**schor·la·ceous** (shôr lā′shəs), *adj.*

schot·tische (shot′ish), *n.* a round dance resembling the polka. [< G: Scottish (dance)]

Schrö·ding·er (shrœ′ding əʀ), *n.* **Er·win** (eʀ′vin), 1887–1961, German physicist: Nobel prize 1933.

Schrö′ding·er wave′ equa′tion (shrō′ding ər; *Ger.* shrœ′ding əʀ), *Physics.* the fundamental equation of quantum theory. Also called **Schrö′dinger equa′tion, Schrö′dinger wave′ equa′tion contain′ing the time′.** [named after E. SCHRÖDINGER]

Schu·bert (sho͞o′bərt; *Ger.* sho͞o′beʀt), *n.* **Franz** (fʀänts), 1797–1828, Austrian composer.

schul (sho͞ol, sho͝ol), *n., pl.* **schuln** (sho͞oln, sho͝oln). *Yiddish.* shul.

Schul·berg (sho͝ol′bərg), *n.* **Budd** (bud), born 1914, U.S. novelist and short-story writer.

Schu·man (sho͞o′mən *or, for 1, Fr.* sho͞o MAN′), *n.* **1. Ro·bert** (rob′ərt; *Fr.* rô beʀ′), 1886–1963, French political leader: premier of France 1947–48. **2. William (Howard),** born 1910, U.S. composer and teacher.

Schu·mann (sho͞o′män), *n.* **Ro·bert** (rob′ərt; *Ger.* ʀō′beʀt), 1810–56, German composer.

Schu·mann-Heink (sho͞o′män hīngk′), *n.* **Ernestine,** 1861–1936, U.S. contralto, born in Bohemia.

Schu′man Plan′, the plan for establishing the European Coal and Steel Community which was created in 1952, proposed by Robert Schuman in 1950.

Schum·pe·ter (sho͝om′pā tər), *n.* **Joseph A·lois** (ə lois′), 1883–1950, U.S. economist, born in Austria.
Schurz (shûrz, sho͝orts), *n.* **Carl,** 1829–1906, U.S. general, statesman, and newspaperman; born in Germany.
Schusch·nigg (sho͝osh′nik), *n.* **Kurt von** (kûrt von; *Ger.* ko͝ort fən), 1897–1977, Austrian statesman in the U.S.: Chancellor of Austria 1934–38.
schuss (sho͞os, sho͝os), *Skiing.* —*n.* **1.** a straight descent with no attempt to decrease speed. —*v.i.* **2.** to execute a schuss. [< G; c. SHOT[1]]
Schütz (shʏts), *n.* **Hein·rich** (hīn′rikh), 1585–1672, German composer.
Schutz·staf·fel (sho͝ots′shtä′fəl), *n. Ger.* See **SS Troops.**
Schuy·ler (skī′lər), *n.* **Philip John,** 1733–1804, American statesman and general in the Revolutionary War.
Schuy·ler·ville (skī′lər vil′), *n.* a village in E New York, on the Hudson: Battle of Saratoga 1777. 1402 (1970). Formerly, **Saratoga.**
Schuyl·kill (sko͞ol′kil, sko͞o′-), *n.* a river flowing SE from E Pennsylvania to the Delaware River at Philadelphia. 131 mi. long.
schwa (shwä, shvä), *n. Phonet.* **1.** the indeterminate vowel sound or sounds of most unstressed syllables of English, however represented; for example, the sound or sounds of *a* in *alone* and *sofa*, *e* in *system*, *i* in *easily*, *o* in *gallop*, *u* in *circus*. **2.** a mid-central, neutral vowel. **3.** the phonetic symbol ə. [< G < Heb *shewā*, name of a diacritic marking want of a vowel sound]
Schwa·ben (shvä′bən), *n.* German name of **Swabia.**
Schwartz (shwôrts), *n.* **Del·more** (del′mōr, -môr), 1913–66, U.S. poet, short-story writer, and critic.
Schwarz·wald (shvärts′vält′), *n.* German name of the **Black Forest.**
Schwein·furt (shvīn′fo͝ort), *n.* a city in N Bavaria, in West Germany, on the Main River. 57,800 (1963).
Schweit·zer (shwīt′sər, shvīt′-), *n.* **Albert,** 1875–1965, Alsatian missionary, doctor, and musician in Africa.
Schweiz (shvīts), *n.* German name of **Switzerland.**
Schwe·rin (shvā rēn′), *n.* **1.** a district in N East Germany: formerly part of Mecklenburg. 593,722 (1964). **2.** a city in this district. 100,000 (est. 1965).
Schwyz (shvēts), *n.* **1.** a canton in central Switzerland, bordering on the Lake of Lucerne. 78,048 (1960); 350 sq. mi. **2.** a city in and the capital of this canton, in the W part. 11,007 (1960).
sci., **1.** science. **2.** scientific.
sci·ae·noid (sī ē′noid), *adj.* **1.** belonging or pertaining to the *Sciaenidae*, a family of carnivorous acanthopterygian fishes including the drumfishes, certain kingfishes, etc. —*n.* **2.** a sciaenoid fish. Also, **sci·ae·nid** (sī ē′nid). [< L *sciaen(a)* a kind of fish (< Gk *skíaina*) + -OID]
sci·at·ic (sī at′ik), *adj.* **1.** *Anat.* of, pertaining to, situated near, or affecting the ischium or back of the hip. **2.** affecting the hip or the sciatic nerves. —*n.* **3.** *Anat.* a sciatic part, as a nerve, vein, or artery. [< ML *sciatic(us)*, alter. of Gk *ischiadikós* = *ischiad-* (s. of *ischiás*) hip pain + *-ikos* -IC]
sci·at·i·ca (sī at′i kə), *n. Pathol.* **1.** pain at some points of the sciatic nerve; sciatic neuralgia. **2.** any painful disorder extending from the hip down the back of the thigh and surrounding area. [< ML, n. use of fem. of *sciaticus* SCIATIC]
sci·ence (sī′əns), *n.* **1.** a branch of knowledge or study dealing with a body of facts or truths systematically arranged and showing the operation of general laws. **2.** systematic knowledge of the physical or material world. **3.** systematized knowledge of any kind. **4.** any skill that reflects a precise application of facts or principles. [ME < MF < L *scientia* knowledge = *sci-* (root of *scīre* to know) + *-entia* -ENCE]
sci′ence fic′tion, a form of fiction that draws imaginatively on scientific knowledge and speculation.
sci·en·tial (sī en′shəl), *adj.* **1.** having knowledge. **2.** of or pertaining to science or knowledge. [< ML *scientiāl(is)*. See SCIENCE, -AL[1]]
sci·en·tif·ic (sī′ən tif′ik), *adj.* **1.** of, pertaining to, or concerned with a science or the sciences. **2.** regulated by or conforming to the principles of exact science. **3.** systematic or accurate in the manner of an exact science. [< ML *scientific(us)*. See SCIENCE, -FIC] —**sci′en·tif′i·cal·ly,** *adv.*
sci′entific meth′od, a method of research in which a problem is identified, relevant data gathered, a hypothesis formulated, and the hypothesis empirically tested.
sci·en·tism (sī′ən tiz′əm), *n.* **1.** *Often Disparaging.* the attitudes, practices, etc., regarded as characteristics of scientists. **2.** advocacy of the application of principles derived from the natural sciences to other disciplines, including the humanities and the social sciences. **3.** scientific or pseudo-scientific language.
sci·en·tist (sī′ən tist), *n.* an expert in science, esp. one of the physical or natural sciences. [< L *scient(ia)* SCIENCE + -IST]
sci·en·tis·tic (sī′ən tis′tik), *adj.* **1.** characterized by or having an exaggerated belief in science. **2.** of, pertaining to, or characterized by scientism.
sci-fi (sī′fī′), *adj. Slang.* **1.** of or pertaining to science fiction: *an exciting new book for sci-fi fans.* —*n.* **2.** See **science fiction.**
scil·i·cet (sil′i set′), *adv.* to wit; namely. [< L: short for *scīre licet* it is permitted to know]
scil·la (sil′ə), *n.* a liliaceous plant of the genus *Scilla*, having bell-shaped flowers. [< L < Gk *skílla* sea onion]
Scil·la (sil′ə; *It.* shēl′lä), *n.* modern name of **Scylla.**
Scil′ly Isles′ (sil′ē), a group of about 140 small islands, belonging to Great Britain, SW of Land's End, England. 6½ sq. mi. *Cap.:* Hugh Town. Also, **Scil′ly Is′lands.** —**Scil·lo·ni·an** (si lō′nē ən), *adj., n.*
scim·i·tar (sim′i tər), *n.* a curved, single-edged sword of Oriental origin. Also, **scim′i·ter, simitar.** [< It *scimitar(ra)* << Pers *shamshīr*]

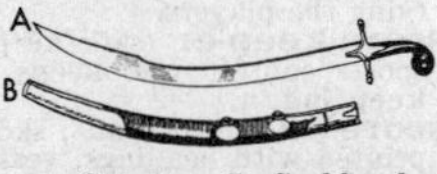

A, Scimitar; B, Scabbard

scin·coid (sing′koid), *adj.* **1.** of pertaining to, or resembling a skink. —*n.* **2.** a scincoid lizard. [< L *scinc(us)* SKINK + -OID]
scin·til·la (sin til′ə), *n.* a minute trace. [< L: spark]
scin·til·lant (sin′tᵊlənt), *adj.* scintillating; sparkling. [< L *scintillant-* (s. of *scintillāns*, prp. of *scintillāre* to flash)] —**scin′til·lant·ly,** *adv.*
scin·til·late (sin′tᵊlāt′), *v.,* **-lat·ed, -lat·ing.** —*v.i.* **1.** to emit sparks. **2.** to sparkle; flash: *a mind that scintillates with brilliance.* **3.** to twinkle, as the stars. —*v.t.* **4.** to emit as sparks; flash forth. [< L *scintillāt(us)* (ptp. of *scintillāre* to flash)] —**scin′til·lat′ing·ly,** *adv.*
scin·til·la·tion (sin′tᵊlā′shən), *n.* **1.** the act of scintillating. **2.** a spark or flash. **3.** *Astron.* the twinkling or tremulous effect of the light of the stars. **4.** *Meteorol.* any small-scale twinkling or shimmering of objects that are viewed through the atmosphere. **5.** *Physics.* a flash of light occurring as a result of the ionization of a phosphor when struck by an energetic photon or particle. [< L *scintillātiōn-* (s. of *scintillātiō*)]
scintilla′tion count′er, a device employing scintillation for detecting and measuring radioactivity.
sci·o·lism (sī′ə liz′əm), *n.* superficial knowledge. [< LL *sciol(us)* one who knows little + -ISM] —**sci′o·list,** *n.* —**sci′o·lis′tic,** *adj.*
sci·on (sī′ən), *n.* **1.** a descendant or child. **2.** Also, **cion.** a shoot or twig, esp. one cut for grafting or planting; a cutting. [ME < OF *cion* < Frankish **kīth* offshoot (c. OE *cīth* seed) + OF *-on* dim. suffix)]
Sci·o·to (sī ō′tə, -tō), *n.* a river in central Ohio, flowing S to the Ohio River. 237 mi. long.
Scip·i·o (sip′ē ō′), *n.* **1. Pub·li·us Cor·nel·ius Scip·i·o Af·ri·ca·nus Ma·jor** (pub′lē əs kôr nēl′yəs sip′ē ō′ af′ri kā′nəs mā′jər), ("*Scipio the Elder*"), 237–183 B.C., Roman general who defeated Hannibal. **2.** his adopted grandson, **Publius Cornelius Scipio Ae·mil·i·a·nus Af·ri·ca·nus Mi·nor** (ē mil′ē ā′nəs af′ri kā′nəs mī′nər), ("*Scipio the Younger*"), c185–129 B.C., Roman general: besieger and destroyer of Carthage.
sci·re fa·ci·as (sī′rē fā′shē as′; *Lat.* skē′re fä′kē äs′), *Law.* **1.** a writ requiring a party to show cause why a judgment, letters patent, etc., should not be executed, vacated, or annulled. **2.** such a judicial proceeding. [< L: lit., make (him) know]
scir·rhous (skir′əs, sir′-), *adj. Pathol.* **1.** of a hard, fibrous consistency. **2.** of, relating to, or constituting a scirrhus. [SCIRRH(US) + -OUS] —**scir·rhos·i·ty** (ski ros′i tē), *n.*
scir·rhus (skir′əs, sir′-), *n., pl.* **scir·rhi** (skir′ī, sir′ī), **scir·rhus·es.** *Pathol.* a hard, indolent tumor; a hard cancer. [< NL < L *scirros* < Gk *skírros*, var. of *skíros* hard covering < *skīrós* hard] —**scir′rhoid,** *adj.*
scis·sile (sis′il), *adj.* capable of being cut or divided; splitting easily. [< L *scissile*, neut. of *scissilis* = *sciss(us)* (ptp. of *scindere* to cut) + *-ilis* -ILE]
scis·sion (sizh′ən, sish′-), *n.* **1.** a cutting, dividing, or splitting; division; separation. **2.** *Chem.* cleavage (def. 5). [< LL *scissiōn-* (s. of *scissiō*) a cutting. See SCISSILE, -ION]
scis·sor (siz′ər), *v.t.* to cut or clip out with scissors. —**scis′sor·like,** *adj.*
scis·sors (siz′ərz), *n.* **1.** (*usually construed as pl.*) a cutting instrument for paper, cloth, etc., consisting of two blades so pivoted together that their sharp edges work one against the other (often used with *pair of*). **2.** (*construed as sing.*) *Gymnastics.* any of several feats in which the legs execute a scissorlike motion. **3.** (*construed as sing.*) *Wrestling.* a hold secured by clasping the legs around the body or head of the opponent. [ME *cisoures, sisoures* < MF *cisoires* < LL *cīsōria*, pl. of *cīsōrium* cutting tool. See CHISEL] —**scis′sor·like′,** *adj.*
scis′sors kick′, *Swimming.* a propelling motion of the legs in which they move somewhat like the blades of a pair of scissors, used in the sidestroke.
scis′sors truss′, a roof truss having tension members extending from the foot of each principal rafter to a point on the upper half of its opposite member.
scis·sor·tail (siz′ər tāl′), *n.* a flycatcher, *Muscivora forficata*, of the southern U.S., Mexico, and Central America, having a long, deeply forked tail.
scis·sure (sizh′ər, sish′-), *n. Archaic.* a longitudinal cleft or opening. [< L *scissūr(a)*. See SCISSILE, -URE]
sci·u·rine (sī′yo͞o rīn′, -rin), *adj.* of or pertaining to the squirrels and allied rodents of the family *Sciuridae*. [< L *sciūr(us)* (< Gk *skíouros* squirrel) + -INE[1]]
sci·u·roid (sī yo͝or′oid), *adj.* **1.** sciurine. **2.** *Bot.* resembling a squirrel's tail, as the spikes of certain grasses. [*sciur-* (see SCIURINE) + -OID]
sclaff (sklaf), *Golf.* —*v.t.* **1.** to scrape (the ground) with the head of the club just before impact with the ball. —*v.i.* **2.** to sclaff the ground with the club. —*n.* **3.** a sclaffing stroke. [special use of Scot *sclaf* to shuffle] —**sclaff′er,** *n.*
SCLC, Southern Christian Leadership Conference. Also, **S.C.L.C.**
scler-, *var. of* **sclero-** before a vowel: *sclerosis.*
scle·ra (sklēr′ə), *n. Anat.* a dense, white, fibrous membrane that, with the cornea, forms the external covering of the eyeball. [< Gk *sklērá* (fem.) hard]
scle·rec·to·my (skli rek′tə mē), *n., pl.* **-mies.** *Surg.* removal of the adhesions formed in the middle ear during chronic otitis media.
scle·ren·chy·ma (skli reng′kə mə), *n. Bot.* supporting or protective tissue composed of thickened and indurated cells from which the protoplasm has usually disappeared. [SCLER- + (PAR)ENCHYMA] —**scle·ren·chym·a·tous** (sklēr′eng-kim′ə təs, skler′-), *adj.*
scle·rite (sklēr′īt, skler′-), *n. Zool.* any chitinous, calcareous, or similar hard part, plate, spicule, or the like. —**scle·rit·ic** (skli rit′ik), *adj.*
sclero-, a learned borrowing from Greek meaning "hard," used with this meaning, and as a combining form of **sclera,** in the formation of compound words: *sclerometer.* Also, *esp. before a vowel,* **scler-.** [< Gk *sklērό(s)* hard]
scle·ro·der·ma (sklēr′ə dûr′mə, skler′-), *n. Pathol.* a disease in which all the layers of the skin become hardened and rigid. Also called **scle·ri·a·sis** (skli rī′ə sis).
scle·ro·der·ma·tous (sklēr′ə dûr′mə təs, skler′-), *adj. Zool.* covered with a hardened tissue, as scales.

scle·roid (sklēr′oid, skler′-), *adj.* *Biol.* hard or indurated.
scle·rom·e·ter (skli rom′i tər), *n.* any instrument for determining with precision the degree of hardness of a substance. —**scler·o·met·ric** (sklēr′ə me′trik, skler′-), *adj.*
scle·ro·pro·tein (sklēr′ō prō′tēn, -tē in), *n.* *Biochem.* protein that is fibrous and insoluble in water, serving a protective or supportive function in the body. Also called **albuminoid.**
scle·rosed (skli rōst′, sklēr′ōzd, skler′-), *adj.* *Pathol.* hardened or indurated, as by sclerosis. [SCLEROS(IS) + -ED[2]]
scle·ro·sis (skli rō′sis), *n., pl.* **-ses** (-sēz). **1.** *Pathol.* a hardening or induration of a tissue or part, or an increase of connective tissue or the like at the expense of more active tissue. **2.** *Bot.* a hardening of a tissue or cell wall by thickening or lignification. [< ML < Gk *sklḗrōsis* hardening] —**scle·ro′sal,** *adj.*
scle·rot·ic (skli rot′ik), *adj.* **1.** *Anat.* of or pertaining to the sclera. **2.** *Pathol., Bot.* pertaining to or affected with sclerosis. [< ML *sclērōtic(us)* < LGk *sklērōtikós* of hardening = Gk *sklērōt(ēs)* hardness (see SCLERO-) + *-ikos* -IC]
scle·ro·ti·um (skli rō′shē əm), *n., pl.* **-ti·a** (-shē ə). *Bot.* a vegetative, resting, food-storage body in certain higher fungi, composed of a compact mass of indurated mycelia. [< NL; see SCLEROTIC, -IUM] —**scle·ro·tial** (skli rō′shəl), *adj.*
scle·rot·o·my (skli rot′ə mē), *n., pl.* **-mies.** *Surg.* incision into the sclera, as to extract foreign bodies.
scle·rous (sklēr′əs, skler′-), *adj.* hard; firm; bony.
Sc.M., See **Master of Science.** [< L *Scientiae Magister*]
scoff (skôf, skof), *v.i.* **1.** to speak derisively; mock (often fol. by *at*). —*n.* **2.** an expression of mockery, derision, doubt, or derisive scorn. **3.** an object of mockery or derision. [ME *scof* < Scand; cf. obs. Dan *skof* mockery] —**scoff′er,** *n.* —**scoff′ing·ly,** *adv.*
—**Syn. 1.** gibe. SCOFF, JEER, SNEER imply behaving with scornful disapproval toward someone or about something. To SCOFF is to express insolent doubt or derision, openly and emphatically: *to scoff at a new invention.* To JEER is to shout in disapproval and scorn more coarsely and unintelligently than in scoffing: *The audience jeered at his singing.* To SNEER is to show by facial expression or tone of voice ill-natured contempt or disparagement: *He sneered unpleasantly in referring to his opponent's misfortunes.*
scoff·law (skôf′lô′, skof′-), *n.* *Informal.* a person who flouts the law, esp. one who fails to pay fines owed.
scold (skōld), *v.t.* **1.** to rebuke angrily; chide; reprimand. —*v.i.* **2.** to rebuke someone angrily. **3.** to use abusive language. —*n.* **4.** a person, esp. a woman, who is constantly scolding. [ME, var. of *scald* < Scand (cf. Icel *skald-stöng* libel-pole); akin to Ir *scéal* news] —**scold′a·ble,** *adj.* —**scold′er,** *n.* —**scold′ing·ly,** *adv.* —**Syn. 1.** reprove; censure. See **reproach. 4.** nag, shrew, virago.
scol·e·cite (skol′i sīt′, skō′li-), *n.* a zeolite mineral, a hydrous calcium aluminum silicate, $CaAl_2Si_3O_{10}·3H_2O$, occurring in masses and in needle-shaped, white crystals. [< Gk *skōlēk-* (s. of *skṓlēx*) SCOLEX + -ITE[1]]
sco·lex (skō′leks), *n., pl.* **sco·le·ces** (skō lē′sēz), **scol·i·ces** (skol′i sēz′, skō′li-). *Zool.* the anterior, headlike segment of a tapeworm, having suckers, hooks, or the like, for attachment. [< Gk *skṓlēx* worm]
sco·li·o·sis (skō′lē ō′sis, skol′ē-), *n.* *Pathol.* lateral curvature of the spine. [< Gk: a bending] —**sco·li·ot·ic** (skō′lē-ot′ik), *adj.*
scol·lop (skol′əp), *n., v.t.* scallop.
scol·o·pen·drid (skol′ə pen′drid), *n.* any myriapod of the order *Scolopendrida*, including many large, poisonous centipedes. [< NL *Scolopendrid(ae)* = *scolopendr(a)* (< Gk *skolópendra* multipede) + *-idae* -ID[2]] —**scol·o·pen·drine** (skol′ə pen′drīn, -drin), *adj.*
scom·broid (skom′broid), *adj.* **1.** resembling or related to the mackerel family *Scombridae.* —*n.* **2.** a mackerel or related scombroid fish. [< Gk *skómbr(os)* mackerel + -OID]
sconce[1] (skons), *n.* a bracket for candles or other lights, placed on a wall, mirror, etc. [ME *sconce, sconse* < monastic L *sconsa*, aph. var. of *absconsa*, n. use of fem. ptp. of *abscondere* to conceal; see ABSCOND]
sconce[2] (skons), *n., v.,* **sconced, sconc·ing.** —*n.* **1.** *Fort.* a small fort or defense work, as to defend a pass, bridge, etc. **2.** a protective screen or shelter. —*v.t.* **3.** *Fort.* to protect with a sconce. **4.** *Obs.* to protect; shelter. [< D *schans* < G *Schanze,* orig. bundle of wood]
sconce[3] (skons), *n.* **1.** the head or skull. **2.** sense or wit, [?]
scone (skōn, skon), *n.* **1.** a flat, round, leavened cake made of oatmeal, wheat flour, barley meal, or the like. **2.** one of the four quadrant-shaped pieces into which such a cake is often cut. **3.** Also called **dropped scone.** biscuit (def. 1). [< MD *schoon (brod)* fine (bread); c. SHEEN]
Scone (sko͞on, skōn), *n.* **1. Stone of,** a stone, formerly at Scone, Scotland, upon which Scottish kings sat at coronation, now placed beneath the coronation chair in Westminster Abbey. **2.** a village in SE Scotland. 2977 (1961).
S. Con. Res., Senate concurrent resolution.
scoop (sko͞op), *n.* **1.** a ladle or ladlelike utensil, esp. a small, deep-sided shovel with a short, horizontal handle, for taking up flour, sugar, etc. **2.** a utensil composed of a palm-sized, hollow hemisphere attached to a horizontal handle, for dishing out ice cream or other soft foods. **3.** the bucket of a dredge, steam shovel, etc. **4.** the quantity of material raised or held in such a utensil or bucket: *two scoops of chocolate ice cream.* **5.** a hollow or hollowed-out place. **6.** the act of ladling, dipping, dredging, etc. **7.** a news item revealed in one paper, magazine, newscast, etc., before any of its competitors can reveal it; beat. **8.** the act of gathering to oneself or lifting with the arms or hands. —*v.t.* **9.** to take up or out with or as with a scoop. **10.** to empty with a scoop. **11.** to form a hollow or hollows in. **12.** to form with or as if with a scoop. **13.** to reveal a news item before (one's competitors). **14.** to gather or put by a sweeping motion of one's arms or hands. —*v.i.* **15.** to remove or gather something with or as with a scoop. [ME *scope* < MD *schoepe*]
scoop·ful (sko͞op′fo͝ol′), *n., pl.* **-fuls.** the amount that a scoop can hold.
scoot (sko͞ot), *Informal.* —*v.i.* **1.** to go swiftly or hastily; dart. —*n.* **2.** a swift, darting movement or course. [< Scand; cf. Icel *skūta* to SHOOT]
scoot·er (sko͞o′tər), *n.* **1.** a child's vehicle that typically has one front and one rear wheel with a low footboard between, is steered by a handlebar, and is propelled by pushing one foot against the ground while resting the other on the footboard. **2.** Also called **motor scooter.** a similar but larger and heavier vehicle for adults, having a saddlelike seat mounted on the footboard and propelled by a motor. —*v.i.* **3.** to travel in or on a scooter.
scop (shop, skop), *n.* an Old English bard or poet. [OE; c. Icel *skop* mocking, OHG *skof* derision]
Sco·pas (skō′pəs), *n.* fl. 4th century B.C., Greek sculptor and architect.
scope (skōp), *n.* **1.** extent or range of view, outlook, application, operation, effectiveness, etc.: *an investigation of wide scope.* **2.** opportunity or freedom for movement or activity: *to give one's fancy full scope.* **3.** extent in space; a tract or area. **4.** length: *a scope of cable.* **5.** (used as a short form of *microscope, periscope, radarscope,* etc.) [< It *scop(o)* < Gk *skopó(s)* aim, mark to shoot at] —**Syn. 1.** See **range.**
-scope, a learned borrowing from Greek used, with the meaning "instrument for viewing," in the formation of compound words: *telescope.* Cf. **-scopy.** [< NL *-scop(ium)* < Gk *-skopion, -skopeion* = *skop(eîn)* (to) look at + *-ion, -eion* n. suffix]
Scopes (skōps), *n.* **John Thomas,** 1901–70, U.S. high-school biology teacher tried and nominally fined by the State of Tennessee in 1925 for teaching the Darwinian theory of evolution.
sco·pol·a·mine (skə pol′ə mēn′, -min, skō′pə lam′in), *n.* *Pharm.* a syrupy alkaloid, $C_{17}H_{21}NO_4$, used chiefly as a sedative, to augment the effect of narcotics in the production of twilight sleep, and as a mydriatic. Also called **hyoscine.** [*scopol-* (< NL *scopol(ia Japonica)* Japanese belladonna; genus named after G. A. *Scopoli* (1723–88), Italian naturalist) + AMINE]
scop·u·la (skop′yə lə), *n., pl.* **-las, -lae** (-lē′). *Zool.* a dense tuft of hairs, as on the feet of certain spiders. [< NL, L: a broom twig = *scōp(a)* broom + *-ula* -ULE]
scop·u·late (skop′yə lāt′, -lit), *adj.* *Zool.* broom-shaped; brushlike. [SCOPUL(A) + -ATE[1]]
-scopy, a suffix used to form abstract action nouns corresponding to nouns with stems ending in **-scope:** *telescopy.* [< Gk *skopía* watching. See -SCOPE, -Y[3]]
scor·bu·tic (skôr byo͞o′tik), *adj.* *Pathol.* pertaining to, of the nature of, or affected with scurvy. Also, **scor·bu′ti·cal.** [< NL *scorbūtic(us)* = ML *scorbūt(us)* scurvy (< MLG *scorbūk*) + *-icus* -IC] —**scor·bu′ti·cal·ly,** *adv.*
scorch (skôrch), *v.t.* **1.** to burn slightly so as to affect color, taste, etc. **2.** to parch or shrivel with heat. **3.** to criticize severely. —*v.i.* **4.** to become scorched: *Milk scorches easily.* —*n.* **5.** a superficial burn. [ME *scorche(n)*, b. *scorcnen* (< Scand; cf. Icel *skorpna* to shrivel) and TORCH] —**Syn. 1.** char, blister. **3.** excoriate, condemn. —**Ant. 3.** laud.
scorched′ earth′, a condition or policy in which all things useful to an invading army are destroyed, as by fire.
scorch·er (skôr′chər), *n.* **1.** a person or thing that scorches. **2.** *Informal.* a very hot day. **3.** something caustic or severe.
scorch·ing (skôr′ching), *adj.* **1.** burning; very hot. **2.** caustic or scathing: *a scorching denunciation.* —**scorch′ing·ly,** *adv.*
scor·da·tu·ra (skôr′də to͝or′ə; *It.* skôr′dä to͞o′rä), *n., pl.* **-tu·re** (-to͝or′ā; *It.* -to͞o′re), **-tu·ras.** *Music.* the tuning of a stringed instrument in other than the usual way to facilitate the playing of certain compositions. [< It = *scordat(o)*, ptp. of *scordare* to be out of tune (< L *(di)scordāre;* see DISCORD) + *-ura* n. suffix]
score (skōr, skôr), *n., pl.* **scores, score** for 11, *v.,* **scored, scor·ing.** —*n.* **1.** the record of points or strokes made by the competitors in a game or match. **2.** the total points or strokes made by one side, individual, play, game, etc. **3.** the act or an instance of making or earning a point or points. **4.** *Educ., Psychol.* the performance of an individual or group on an examination or test, expressed by a letter, number, or other symbol. **5.** a notch, scratch, or incision. **6.** a notch or mark for noting a single item. **7.** a reckoning or account made with these; tally. **8.** any account showing indebtedness. **9.** an amount recorded as due. **10.** a line drawn as a boundary or marker. **11.** a group or set of 20. **12.** a reason, ground, or cause: *to complain on the score of low pay.* **13.** *Informal.* the facts of a situation. **14.** *Music.* **a.** a written or printed piece of music containing all vocal and instrumental parts. **b.** a musical composition written to accompany a stage, film, or television presentation. **15. pay off** or **settle a score,** to avenge a wrong; retaliate. —*v.t.* **16.** to add to one's score. **17.** to make a specified score: *He scored 98 on the test.* **18.** to evaluate the results of (an examination or test). **19.** *Music.* **a.** to orchestrate. **b.** to compose a score for (a stage, film, or television presentation). **20.** to make notches, scratches, or incisions on, as meat before cooking or cardboard to facilitate bending. **21.** to record or keep a record of (points, items, etc.). **22.** to write down as a debt. **23.** to record as a debtor. **24.** to gain, achieve, or win: *The play scored a great success.* **25.** to berate or censure. —*v.i.* **26.** to make a point or points in a game or contest. **27.** to keep score, as of a game. **28.** to achieve an advantage or a success. **29.** to make notches, cuts, lines, etc. **30.** to run up a score or debt. [ME; late OE *scor(u)* < Scand; cf. Icel *skor* notch; akin to SHEAR] —**scor′er,** *n.*
score·board (skōr′bōrd′, skôr′bôrd′), *n.* *Sports.* a large board that shows the score of a contest and often other relevant information.
score·card (skōr′kärd′, skôr′-), *n.* a card for keeping score of a sports contest and, esp. in team sports, for identifying the players.
score·keep·er (skōr′kē′pər, skôr′-), *n.* an official of a sports contest who keeps record of the score. —**score′keep′ing,** *n.*
score·pad (skōr′pad′, skôr′-), *n.* a pad whose sheets are printed with headings, vertical or horizontal lines, symbols, or the like, to facilitate the recording of scores in a game.
sco·ri·a (skōr′ē ə, skôr′-), *n., pl.* **sco·ri·ae** (skōr′ē ē′, skôr′-). **1.** the refuse, dross, or slag left after melting or smelting metal; scum. **2.** a cinderlike basic cellular lava. [< L < Gk *skōría* < *skôr* dung] —**sco·ri·a·ceous** (skōr′ē-ā′shəs, skôr′-), *adj.*

sco·ri·fy (skōr′ə fī′, skôr′-), *v.t.*, **-fied, -fy·ing.** to reduce to scoria. —**sco′ri·fi·ca′tion,** *n.* —**sco′ri·fi′er,** *n.*

scorn (skôrn), *n.* **1.** open or unqualified contempt; disdain. **2.** an object of derision or contempt. **3.** *Archaic.* a derisive or contemptuous action or speech. **4. laugh to scorn,** to ridicule; deride. —*v.t.* **5.** to treat or regard with contempt or disdain. **6.** to reject contemptuously: *She scorned my help.* —*v.i.* **7.** to mock; jeer. [ME *scorn, scarn* < OF (*e*)*scarn* < Gmc; cf. obs. D *schern* mockery, trickery] —**scorn′er,** *n.* —**scorn′ing·ly,** *adv.* —**Syn. 1.** contumely. See **contempt. 5.** disdain, contemn, despise, detest. —**Ant. 3.** praise.

scorn·ful (skôrn′fəl), *adj.* full of scorn; derisive; contemptuous. [late ME] —**scorn′ful·ly,** *adv.* —**scorn′ful·ness,** *n.*

scor·pae·nid (skôr pē′nid), *n.* any of the *Scorpaenidae,* a family of marine fishes, including the rockfishes, scorpionfishes, etc. [< L *scorpaen*(*a*) (< Gk *skórpaina* kind of fish; see SCORPION) + -ID[2]] —**scor·pae′noid,** *adj., n.*

Scor·pi·o (skôr′pē ō′), *n.* **1.** the eighth sign of the zodiac. See illus. at **zodiac. 2.** *Astron.* Scorpius. [< L: SCORPION]

scor·pi·oid (skôr′pē oid′), *adj.* **1.** resembling a scorpion **2.** belonging or pertaining to the *Scorpionida,* the order of arachnids comprising the scorpions. **3.** curved at the end like the tail of a scorpion. [< L *scorpi*(*ō*) SCORPION + -OID]

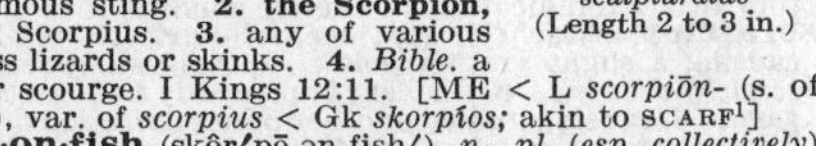

Scorpion, *Centruroides sculpturatus* (Length 2 to 3 in.)

scor·pi·on (skôr′pē ən), *n.* **1.** any of numerous arachnids of the order *Scorpionida,* widely distributed in warmer parts of the world, having a long, narrow, segmented tail that terminates in a venomous sting. **2. the Scorpion,** *Astron.* Scorpius. **3.** any of various harmless lizards or skinks. **4.** *Bible.* a whip or scourge. I Kings 12:11. [ME < L *scorpiōn-* (s. of *scorpiō*), var. of *scorpius* < Gk *skorpíos;* akin to SCARF[1]]

scor·pi·on·fish (skôr′pē ən fish′), *n., pl.* (*esp. collectively*) **-fish,** (*esp. referring to two or more kinds or species*) **-fish·es.** any of several marine scorpaenid fishes, esp. of the genus *Scorpaena,* having poisonous dorsal spines.

scor′pion spi′der. See **whip scorpion.**

Scor·pi·us (skôr′pē əs), *n., gen.* **-pi·i** (-pē ī′). *Astron.* the Scorpion, a zodiacal constellation between Sagittarius and Libra, containing the bright star Antares. Also, **Scorpio.** [< L < Gk *skorpíos* SCORPION]

scot (skot), *n. Hist.* **1.** a payment or charge. **2.** an assessment or tax. [ME < Scand; cf. Icel *skot,* c. OE *gescot*]

Scot (skot), *n.* **1.** a native or inhabitant of Scotland; Scotsman. **2.** one of an ancient Gaelic people who came from northern Ireland about the 6th century A.D. and settled in the northwestern part of Great Britain. [ME; OE *Scott*(*as*) (pl.) < LL *Scott*(*ī*) the Irish <?]

Scot, Scottish (def. 3).

Scot., 1. Scotch. **2.** Scotland. **3.** Scottish.

scotch (skoch), *v.t.* **1.** to injure so as to make harmless. **2.** to cut, gash, or score. **3.** to put a definite end to; crush; stamp out; foil: *to scotch a rumor; to scotch a plan.* **4.** to block or prop with a wedge or chock. —*n.* **5.** a cut, gash, or score. **6.** a block or wedge. [late ME *scocche;* prob. b. SCORE and NOTCH]

Scotch (skoch), *adj.* **1.** of or pertaining to Scotland, its inhabitants, or the dialect of English spoken in Scotland. **2.** (loosely) Scottish. **3.** *Informal.* provident; frugal. —*n.* **4.** the people of Scotland collectively. **5.** (*often l.c.*) See **Scotch whisky.** [syncopated var. of SCOTTISH]

Scotch′ broth′, a thick soup prepared from mutton, vegetables, and barley.

Scotch·gard (skoch′gärd′), *n. Trademark.* a fluorocarbon chemical used for the treatment of upholstery and other fabrics to render them water- and oil-repellent and stain-resistant.

Scotch-I·rish (skoch′ī′rish), *adj.* **1.** of or pertaining to the descendants of Scotch immigrants in northern Ireland. **2.** of mixed Scotch and Irish blood. —*n.* **3.** a person of Scotch and Irish descent.

Scotch·man (skoch′mən), *n., pl.* **-men.** Scotsman.

Scotch′ tape′, *Trademark.* a transparent or semi-transparent cellophane or cellulose acetate adhesive tape.

Scotch′ ter′rier. See **Scottish terrier.**

Scotch′ whis′ky, whiskey distilled in Scotland, esp. from malted barley in a pot still.

Scotch′ wood′cock, toast spread with anchovy paste and topped with loosely scrambled eggs.

sco·ter (skō′tər), *n., pl.* **-ters,** (*esp. collectively*) **-ter.** any of the large diving ducks of the genera *Melanitta* and *Oidemia,* found in northern parts of the Northern Hemisphere. [?]

scot-free (skot′frē′), *adj.* **1.** free from harm or penalty. **2.** free from payment of scot. [ME]

ScotGael, Scots Gaelic.

sco·tia (skō′shə), *n. Archit.* a deep concave molding between two fillets. See illus. at **molding.** [< L < Gk *skotía* darkness (from its shadow)]

Sco·tia (skō′shə), *n. Literary.* Scotland. [< L]

Scot·land (skot′lənd), *n.* a division of the United Kingdom in the N part of Great Britain. 5,205,000; 29,796 sq. mi. *Cap.:* Edinburgh.

Scot′land Yard′, the metropolitan police of London, England, esp. the branch engaged in crime detection.

Scoto-, a combining form of **Scotch:** *Scoto-Irish.* [comb. form of ML *Scōtus* SCOT]

sco·to·ma (skə tō′mə), *n., pl.* **-mas, -ma·ta** (-mə tə). *Pathol.* loss of vision in a part of the visual field; blind spot. [< ML < Gk *skótōma* dizziness = *skót*(*os*) darkness + *-ōma* -OMA] —**sco·tom·a·tous** (skō tom′ə təs), *adj.*

sco·to·pi·a (skə tō′pē ə, skō-), *n. Ophthalm.* vision in dim light (opposed to *photopia*). [< NL < Gk *skót*(*os*) darkness + *-opia* -OPIA] —**sco·top·ic** (skə top′ik, skō-), *adj.*

Scots (skots), *n.* **1.** Scottish (def. 3). —*adj.* **2.** Scottish (def. 1). **3.** Scotch. [syncopated form of *Scottis,* var. (north) of SCOTTISH]

Scots′ Gael′ic, the Gaelic of the Hebrides and the Highlands of Scotland, also spoken as a second language in Nova Scotia. *Abbr.:* ScotGael Also, **Scottish Gaelic.**

Scots·man (skots′mən), *n., pl.* **-men.** a Scot.

Scott (skot), *n.* **1. Dred** (dred), 1795?–1858, a Negro slave whose suit for freedom was denied by the U.S. Supreme Court. **2. Sir George Gilbert,** 1811–78, English architect. **3. Robert Fal·con** (fôl′kən, fal′-, fô′kən), 1868–1912, British naval officer and antarctic explorer. **4. Sir Walter,** 1771–1832, Scottish novelist and poet. **5. Win·field** (win′-fēld′), 1786–1866, U.S. general.

Scot·ti·cism (skot′i siz′əm), *n.* a word or idiom peculiar to or characteristic of Scottish. [< LL *scōtic*(*us*) (see SCOT, -IC) + -ISM]

Scot·tie (skot′ē), *n.* See **Scottish terrier.**

Scot·tish (skot′ish), *adj.* **1.** of or pertaining to the Scots, their country, or the dialect of English spoken there. —*n.* **2.** the people of Scotland. **3.** the dialect of English spoken in Scotland, marked by such pronunciation as a tongue-tip trill for the sound (r), a vowel ranging from (A) to (ä) for the sound (a), and the use of the sound (KH). *Abbr.:* Scot, Scot. Cf. **Scots Gaelic.** Also, **Scots** (for defs. 1, 3). [ME < LL *Scott*(*us*) SCOT + -ISH[1]]

Scot′tish Gael′ic. See **Scots Gaelic.**

Scottish terrier (10 in. high at shoulder)

Scot′tish rite′, one of the two advanced divisions of Masonic membership, leading to the 33rd degree. Cf. **York rite.**

Scot′tish ter′rier, one of a Scottish breed of small terriers having short legs and a wiry coat. Also called **Scotch terrier, Scottie, Scotty.**

Scotts·dale (skots′dāl′), *n.* a city in central Arizona, near Phoenix. 67,823 (1970).

Scot·ty (skot′ē), *n., pl.* **-ties. 1.** *Informal.* a Scot. **2.** See **Scottish terrier.**

Sco·tus (skō′təs), *n.* **John Duns.** See **Duns Scotus, John.**

scoun·drel (skoun′drəl), *n.* an unprincipled, dishonorable man; villain. [obs. *scoun*(*d*) (< ?) + -REL] —**Syn.** cad, bounder. See **knave.**

scoun·drel·ly (skoun′drə lē), *adj.* **1.** having the character of a scoundrel. **2.** of or like a scoundrel.

scour[1] (skour, skou′ər), *v.t.* **1.** to cleanse or polish by hard rubbing. **2.** to remove (dirt, grease, etc.) from something by hard rubbing. **3.** to clear or dig out (a channel, drain, etc.), as by the force of water, by removing debris, etc. **4.** to purge thoroughly, as an animal. **5.** to clear or rid of what is undesirable. **6.** to remove by or as by cleansing; get rid of. —*v.i.* **7.** to polish or clean a surface. **8.** to become clean when scoured. —*n.* **9.** the act of scouring. **10.** the place scoured. **11.** something that scours. **12.** the erosive force of moving water. **13.** Usually, **scours.** *Vet. Pathol.* diarrhea in horses and cattle caused by intestinal infection. [ME *scour*(*en*) < Scand; cf. Dan *skure* to rub, scour, Icel *skora* to rub]

scour[2] (skour, skou′ər), *v.i.* **1.** to move rapidly or energetically. **2.** to range about, as in search of something. —*v.t.* **3.** to run or pass quickly over or along. **4.** to range over, as in search: *They scoured the countryside for the lost child.* [ME *scour*(*en*) < obs. *scour* speed, ? < Scand; cf. Icel *skūr* storm (of wind, rain, battle); c. SHOWER]

scour·er[1] (skour′ər, skou′ər ər), *n.* **1.** a person who scours or cleans. **2.** an implement, device, or preparation for scouring. [SCOUR[1] + -ER[1]]

scour·er[2] (skour′ər, skou′ər ər), *n.* a person who scours or ranges about. [SCOUR[2] + -ER[1]]

scourge (skûrj), *n., v.,* **scourged, scourg·ing.** —*n.* **1.** a whip or lash, esp. one used on human beings. **2.** a person or thing that harasses or destroys. —*v.t.* **3.** to whip with a scourge; lash. **4.** to punish, chastise, or criticize severely. [ME < AF (*e*)*scorge* << LL *excoriāre* to EXCORIATE] —**scourg′er,** *n.* —**scourg′ing·ly,** *adv.* —**Syn. 2.** bane.

scour·ing (skour′ing, skou′ər-), *n.* **1.** the act of a person or thing that scours. **2. scourings,** (*construed as pl.*) **a.** dirt or refuse removed by scouring. **b.** refuse removed from grain. [ME]

scour′ing rush′, any of certain horsetails, esp. *Equisetum hyemale,* used for scouring and polishing.

scouse (skouz), *n. Brit. Naut.* a baked dish or stew made usually with meat and hardtack. [short for LOBSCOUSE]

scout[1] (skout), *n.* **1.** a soldier, warship, airplane, etc., employed in reconnoitering. **2.** a person sent out to obtain information. **3.** *Sports.* **a.** a person who observes and reports on the techniques, players, etc., of opposing teams. **b.** such a person who finds and recommends new talent for recruitment. **4.** a Boy Scout or Girl Scout. **5. a good scout,** a pleasant fellow. —*v.i.* **6.** to act as a scout; reconnoiter. —*v.t.* **7.** to examine, inspect, or observe for the purpose of obtaining information; reconnoiter. **8.** *Informal.* **a.** to seek; search for (usually fol. by *out* or *up*). **b.** to find by seeking, searching, or looking (usually fol. by *out* or *up*): *Scout out a good book for me to read.* [ME *scoute* < OF (*e*)*scoute,* back formation from *escolter, ascolter* (F *écouter* to listen) < LL *ascultāre,* var. of L *auscultāre* to AUSCULTATE]

scout[2] (skout), *v.t., v.i.* to reject with scorn; flout. [< Scand; cf. Icel *skūta* to scold] —**Syn.** disdain, contemn, despise.

scout′ car′, a fast, lightly armored military vehicle equipped with guns and used chiefly for reconnaissance.

scout·craft (skout′kraft′, -kräft′), *n.* **1.** practice of or skill at scouting. **2.** skill in the program of activities of the Boy Scouts or the Girl Scouts.

scout·er (skou′tər), *n.* **1.** a person who scouts. **2.** a Boy Scout who is 18 years of age or over.

scouth (skōōth), *n. Scot.* **1.** abundance; plenty. **2.** opportunity; scope. [?]

scout·ing (skou′ting), *n.* **1.** the act or an instance of reconnoitering; reconnaissance. **2.** the activities of a scout or scouts.

scout·mas·ter (skout′mas′tər, -mä′stər), *n.* the adult leader of a troop of Boy Scouts.

scow (skou), *n.* **1.** any of various vessels having a flat-bottomed rectangular hull with sloping ends. **2.** *Eastern U.S.* a barge carrying bulk material in an open hold. **3.** an old or clumsy boat; hulk; tub. —*v.t.* **4.** to transport by scow. [< D *schouw* ferryboat]

scowl (skoul), *v.i.* **1.** to draw down or contract the brows in a sullen, displeased, or angry manner. **2.** to have a gloomy or threatening look. —*v.t.* **3.** to express with a scowl. —*n.* **4.** a scowling expression. [ME *scoul* < Scand; cf. Dan *skule* to scowl] —**scowl′ing·ly,** *adv.* —**Syn. 1.** frown. **2.** glower.

scr., scruple.

scrab·ble (skrab′əl), *v.,* **-bled, -bling,** *n.* —*v.t.* **1.** to scratch or scrape, as with the claws or hands. **2.** to grapple or struggle with or as with the claws or hands. **3.** to scrawl; scribble. —*v.i.* **4.** to grab for or collect something in a disorderly way; scramble. —*n.* **5.** a scratching or scraping, as with the claws or hands. **6.** a scrawled or scribbled writing. **7.** a disorderly struggle for possession of something; scramble. [< D *schrabbel(en),* freq. of *schrabben* to scratch, perh. var. of *schrapen* to SCRAPE] —**scrab′bler,** *n.*

scrag (skrag), *n.* **1.** a lean or scrawny person or animal. **2.** the lean end of a neck of veal or mutton. [var. of dial. *crag,* late ME *cragge* < MFlem *krage* neck; see CRAW]

scrag·gly (skrag′lē), *adj.,* **-gli·er, -gli·est. 1.** irregular; uneven; jagged. **2.** shaggy; ragged; unkempt.

scrag·gy (skrag′ē), *adj.,* **-gi·er, -gi·est. 1.** lean or thin; scrawny. **2.** meager. **3.** irregular; craggy; jagged. —**scrag′gi·ly,** *adv.* —**scrag′gi·ness,** *n.*

scram (skram), *v.i.,* **scrammed, scram·ming.** *Informal.* to go away; get out. [var. of SCRAMBLE (by apocope)]

scram·ble (skram′bəl), *v.,* **-bled, -bling,** *n.* —*v.i.* **1.** to climb or move quickly using the hands and feet, as down a rough incline. **2.** to compete or struggle with others for possession or gain. **3.** to move in hasty urgency. **4.** *Mil.* to take off quickly to intercept enemy planes, as pilots or aircraft. —*v.t.* **5.** to collect or organize (things) in a hurried or disorderly manner. **6.** to mix confusedly. **7.** to cause to hurry or move hastily. **8.** to cook (eggs) in a pan, mixing whites and yolks together, usually with butter, milk, etc. **9.** to make (a radio or telephonic message) incomprehensible to interceptors by systematically changing the frequencies. —*n.* **10.** a quick climb or progression over rough, irregular ground, or the like. **11.** a struggle for possession or gain. **12.** any disorderly or hasty struggle or proceeding. **13.** *Mil.* a quick emergency takeoff of interceptors. [b. *scamble* to stumble along and SCRABBLE (in the same sense)]

scram·bler (skram′blər), *n.* **1.** a person or thing that scrambles. **2.** an electronic device that mixes and confuses telecommunications signals in order to make them unintelligible through certain circuits.

scran·nel (skran′əl), *adj. Archaic.* **1.** thin or slight. **2.** squeaky or unmelodious. [? back formation from *scranly < Norw *skran* lean + -LY; see SCRAWNY]

Scran·ton (skran′tən), *n.* a city in NE Pennsylvania. 103,564 (1970).

scrap[1] (skrap), *n., adj., v.,* **scrapped, scrap·ping.** —*n.* **1.** a small piece or portion; fragment. **2. scraps, a.** bits or pieces of food, esp. of leftover or discarded food. **b.** the remains of animal fat after the oil has been tried out. **3.** a detached piece of something written or printed: *scraps of poetry.* **4.** a worn or superfluous piece of material that can be reused in some way. **5.** an accumulation of such material. —*adj.* **6.** consisting of scraps or scrap. **7.** discarded or left over. —*v.t.* **8.** to make into scrap; break up. **9.** to discard as useless, worthless, or ineffective. [ME *scrappe* < Scand; cf. Icel *skrap*] —**scrap′ping·ly,** *adv.* —**Syn. 1.** morsel, crumb, bit.

scrap[2] (skrap), *n., v.i.,* **scrapped, scrap·ping.** *Informal.* —*n.* **1.** a fight or quarrel. —*v.i.* **2.** to engage in a fight or quarrel. [var. of SCRAPE]

scrap·book (skrap′bo͝ok′), *n.* an album in which pictures, newspaper clippings, etc., may be pasted or mounted.

scrape (skrāp), *v.,* **scraped, scrap·ing,** *n.* —*v.t.* **1.** to rub (a surface) with something rough or sharp, as to clean or smooth it. **2.** to remove (a thickness of material) by rubbing with something rough or sharp. **3.** to injure by brushing against something rough or sharp. **4.** to produce by scratching or scraping. **5.** to collect or gather laboriously or with difficulty (usually fol. by *up* or *together*). **6.** to rub roughly on or across (something). **7.** to draw or rub (a thing) roughly across something. **8.** to make a noise by or as by scraping (something). —*v.i.* **9.** to rub against something gratingly. **10.** to produce a grating and unmusical tone from a stringed instrument. **11.** to draw one's foot back noisily along the ground in making a bow. **12.** to manage or get by with difficulty or with only the barest margin. **13.** to economize or save by attention to even the slightest amounts. —*n.* **14.** an act or instance of scraping. **15.** a harsh, shrill, or scratching sound made by scraping. **16.** a scraped place. **17.** an embarrassing or distressing situation; predicament. **18.** a difference of opinion, fight, or quarrel; scrap. [ME < Scand; cf. Icel *skrapa*] —**scrap′a·ble,** *adj.*

scrap·er (skrā′pər), *n.* **1.** a person or thing that scrapes. **2.** any of various tools or utensils for scraping.

scrap·ing (skrā′ping), *n.* **1.** the act of a person or thing that scrapes. **2.** the sound of something being scraped. **3.** Usually, **scrapings.** something that is scraped off, up, or together. —**scrap′ing·ly,** *adv.*

scrap′ i′ron, old iron to be remelted or reworked.

scrap·page (skrap′ij), *n.* **1.** material broken into scrap. **2.** the conversion, esp. of automobiles, into scrap.

scrap·per (skrap′ər), *n. Informal.* a person who is always ready or eager for a fight, argument, or contest.

scrap·ple (skrap′əl), *n. U.S* a sausagelike preparation of ground pork, corn meal, and seasonings.

scrap·py[1] (skrap′ē), *adj.,* **-pi·er, -pi·est.** made up of scraps or of odds and ends; fragmentary; disconnected. [SCRAP[1] + -Y[1]] —**scrap′pi·ly,** *adv.* —**scrap′pi·ness,** *n.*

scrap·py[2] (skrap′ē), *adj.,* **-pi·er, -pi·est.** *Informal.* fond of fighting, arguing, or competing. [SCRAP[2] + -Y[1]]

scratch (skrach), *v.t.* **1.** to mark or mar the surface of by rubbing, scraping, or tearing with something sharp or rough: *to scratch one's hand on a nail.* **2.** to rub or draw along a rough, grating surface. **3.** to rub or scrape slightly, as with the fingernails, to relieve itching. **4.** to remove with a scraping or tearing action. **5.** to cancel (a written item) by or as by drawing a line through it (often fol. by *out*). **6.** to withdraw (an entry) from a race or competition. **7.** to write or draw by cutting into a surface. —*v.i.* **8.** to use the nails, claws, etc., for tearing, digging, etc. **9.** to relieve itching by scratching oneself. **10.** to make a slight grating noise; scrape. **11.** to earn a living or get along with great difficulty. **12.** to be withdrawn from a contest or competition. **13.** (in certain card games) to make no score; earn no points. **14.** *Billiards, Pool.* to make a shot that results in a penalty, esp. to pocket the cue ball without hitting the object ball. —*n.* **15.** a slight injury or mark, usually thin and shallow, caused by scratching. **16.** an act of scratching. **17.** a slight grating sound caused by scratching. **18.** the status of a competitor in a handicap who has no allowance and no penalty. **19.** the place or time at which such a competitor starts. **20.** *Billiards, Pool.* **a.** a shot in which a player scratches. **b.** a fluke or lucky shot. **21.** (in certain card games) a score of zero; nothing. **22.** *Slang.* money; cash. **23. from scratch, a.** from the very beginning or starting point. **b.** from nothing; without resources. **24. up to scratch,** up to standard; adequate; satisfactory. —*adj.* **25.** used for hasty writing, notes, etc.: *a scratch pad.* **26.** without any allowance, penalty, or handicap, as a competitor or contestant. **27.** *Informal.* gathered hastily and indiscriminately: *a scratch crew.* [b. obs. *scrat* to scratch (< ?) and obs. *cratch* (< MFlem *cratsen;* c. G *kratzen* to scratch)] —**scratch′er,** *n.*

Scratch (skrach), *n.* Old Scratch; Satan. [alter. of obs. *scrat* (OE **scratta* hermaphrodite); c. Icel *skratti* the devil, OHG *skraz* wood demon, etc.]

scratch′ pa′per, paper used for an informal note, jotting down an idea, or the like.

scratch′ sheet′, a racing publication giving the betting odds and other information on the horses entered at a race track or tracks during a racing day.

scratch′ test′, a test for allergy in which the skin is scratched and an allergen applied to the area, an inflammatory reaction indicating an allergic condition.

scratch·y (skrach′ē), *adj.,* **scratch·i·er, scratch·i·est. 1.** causing a slight grating noise. **2.** suggesting scratches: *a scratchy drawing.* **3.** uneven; haphazard: *He plays a scratchy game.* **4.** causing itching or other minor irritation of the skin: *a scratchy sweater.* —**scratch′i·ly,** *adv.* —**scratch′i·ness,** *n.*

scrawl (skrôl), *v.t.* **1.** to write or draw in a sprawling, awkward manner. —*n.* **2.** something scrawled, as handwriting. [late ME *scraule,* b. SPRAWL and CRAWL[1]; once said of movement of the limbs in general] —**scrawl′er,** *n.*

scrawl·y (skrô′lē), *adj.,* **scrawl·i·er, scrawl·i·est.** written or drawn awkwardly or carelessly. —**scrawl′i·ness,** *n.*

scrawn·y (skrô′nē), *adj.,* **scrawn·i·er, scrawn·i·est.** excessively thin; lean; scraggy: *a long, scrawny neck.* [var. of obs. *scranny* < Norw *skran* lean + -Y[1]] —**scrawn′i·ly,** *adv.* —**scrawn′i·ness,** *n.* —**Syn.** gaunt, emaciated.

screak (skrēk), *v.i.* **1.** to screech. **2.** to creak. —*n.* **3.** a screech. **4.** a creak. [< Scand; cf. Icel *skrækja*] —**screak′y,** *adj.*

scream (skrēm), *v.i.* **1.** to utter a loud, sharp, piercing cry. **2.** to emit a shrill, piercing sound. **3.** to laugh immoderately or uncontrollably. **4.** to shout or speak shrilly. —*v.t.* **5.** to utter with or as with a scream or screams. **6.** to make by screaming: *to scream oneself hoarse.* —*n.* **7.** a loud, sharp, piercing cry. **8.** a shrill, piercing sound. **9.** *Informal.* someone or something that is hilariously funny. [ME *scream(en),* OE **scrǣman;* akin to Icel *skraumi* chatterbox, braggart, *skruma* to jabber; *sc-* (for *sh-*) from obs. *scritch* to SCREECH] —**Syn. 1.** SCREAM, SHRIEK, SCREECH apply to crying out in a loud, piercing way. To SCREAM is to utter a loud, piercing cry, esp. of pain or fear: *to scream with terror.* SHRIEK usually refers to a sharper and briefer cry than SCREAM; when caused by fear or pain, it is indicative of more terror or distress. It is also used for the shrill half-suppressed cries of giddy women or girls: *to shriek with laughter.* SCREECH emphasizes the disagreeable shrillness and harshness of an outcry; the connotation is lack of dignity: *to screech like an old crone.* **7.** outcry, shriek, screech, screak.

scream·er (skrē′mər), *n.* **1.** a person or thing that screams. **2.** *Informal.* something or someone causing screams of excitement, laughter, or the like. **3.** *Journalism.* **a.** a sensational headline. **b.** banner (def. 6). Cf. **scarehead. 4.** *Ornith.* any of several South American birds of the family *Anhimidae,* having a harsh, trumpeting call.

scream·ing (skrē′ming), *adj.* **1.** uttering screams. **2.** boldly striking or startling: *screaming headlines.* **3.** *Informal.* causing hilarious laughter. —*n.* **4.** act or sound of a person or thing that screams. [late ME (n.)] —**scream′ing·ly,** *adv.*

scree (skrē), *n.* a steep mass of detritus on the side of a mountain. [< Scand; cf. Icel *skritha* landslide; akin to OE *scrīthan* to go, glide]

screech (skrēch), *v.i.* **1.** to utter or make a harsh, shrill cry or sound. —*v.t.* **2.** to utter with a screech. —*n.* **3.** a harsh, shrill cry or sound. [var. of obs. *scritch* to scream] —**screech′er,** *n.* —**Syn. 1.** See **scream.**

screech′ owl′, 1. any of numerous small, American owls of the genus *Otus,* having hornlike tufts of feathers, as *O. asio,* of North America. **2.** any owl having a harsh cry.

screech·y (skrē′chē), *adj.,* **screech·i·er, screech·i·est. 1.** like or suggesting a screech. **2.** producing screeches.

screed (skrēd), *n.* **1.** a long discourse or essay, esp. a diatribe. **2.** an informal letter, account, or other piece of writing. **3.** a guide used in surfacing plasterwork or cement work. **4.** *Brit. Dial.* a fragment or shred, as of cloth. **5.** *Scot.* **a.** a tear or rip, esp. in cloth. **b.** a drinking bout. [ME *screde* < Scand; cf. Icel *skrjōthr* shred, akin to OE *scrēade* SHRED]

screen (skrēn), *n.* **1.** a movable or fixed device, usually consisting of a covered frame, that provides shelter, serves as a partition, etc.: *a tall Oriental screen separating the living room from the dining room.* **2.** a permanent, usually ornamental partition, as around the choir of a church. **3.** anything that provides concealment, shelter, etc. **4.** a surface or area of material on which motion-picture, television, radar, or other images are projected or formed. **5.** the motion-picture medium or industry. **6.** a protective formation of troops, warships, etc. **7.** a frame holding a mesh of cloth, wire, or plastic, for placing in a window or doorway, around a porch, etc., to admit air but exclude insects. **8.** a sieve, riddle, or other meshlike device used to separate smaller particles or objects from larger ones, as for grain, sand, etc. **9.** *Photog.* a plate of ground glass or the like on which the image is brought into focus in a camera before being photographed. **10.** *Photoengraving.* a transparent plate containing two sets of fine parallel lines, one crossing the other, used in the halftone process. **11.** *Sports.* any of various offensive plays in which teammates form a protective formation around the ball carrier, pass receiver, shooter, etc. —*v.t.* **12.** to shelter, protect, or conceal with or as with a screen. **13.** to select, reject, consider, or group (people, objects, ideas, etc.) systematically. **14.** to sift or sort by passing through a screen. **15.** to project (a motion picture, slide, etc.) on a screen. **16.** to present, as a motion picture. **17.** to lighten (type or areas of a line engraving) by etching a regular pattern of dots or lines into the printing surface. [ME *screne* < AF; OF *escren* < MD *scherm;* c. G *Schirm* screen] —**screen′er,** *n.* —**screen′like′,** *adj.* —**Syn. 3.** guard, shield. **12.** veil, defend, shield, hide, mask.

screen·ing (skrē′ning), *n.* **1.** the act or work of a person who screens. **2.** a showing of a motion picture. **3. screenings,** (*construed as sing. or pl.*) coarse or rejected material left in a screen or sieve. **4.** meshed material.

screen·play (skrēn′plā′), *n.* **1.** a motion-picture scenario. **2.** See **motion picture.**

screen′ test′, a filmed audition to determine a person's suitability as a motion-picture actor.

screen·wri·ter (skrēn′rī′tər), *n.* a person who writes screenplays.

screw (skro͞o), *n.* **1.** a metal fastener having a tapered shank with a helical thread, driven into wood or the like by rotation. **2.** a threaded cylindrical rod, rotated to engage a threaded hole and used either as a fastener or as a device for applying power, as in a clamp or jack. Cf. **bolt**[1] (def. 3). **3.** something having a spiral form. **4.** See **screw propeller. 5.** a twist, turn, or twisting movement. **6.** *Chiefly Brit.* **a.** a little salt, sugar, tobacco, etc., carried in a twist of paper. **b.** *Slang.* a mean, old, or worn-out horse. **7.** *Brit. Informal.* salary; wages. **8.** *Slang.* a prison guard. **9.** *Slang* (*vulgar*). an act of coitus. **10. have a screw loose,** *Slang.* to be eccentric. **11. put the screws on,** to compel by exerting pressure on; use coercion on; force. —*v.t.* **12.** to attach or fasten with a screw or screws. **13.** to attach, detach, or adjust (an object having a screw or a helical thread) by a twisting motion. **14.** to contort (one's features) as by twisting; distort. **15.** to cause to become stronger or more intense (usually fol. by *up*): *to screw up one's courage.* **16.** to coerce or threaten. **17.** to extract or extort. **18.** *Slang* (*vulgar*). to have coitus with. —*v.i.* **19.** to turn as or like a screw. **20.** to be attached, detached, or adjusted by movement as a whole or in part in a helical path. **21.** *Slang* (*vulgar*). to have coitus. **22. screw up,** *Slang.* to ruin through bungling or stupidity. [ME *scrwe, screw(e);* cf. ME *escro(ue)* nut, MD *schrūve,* MHG *schrūbe* screw] —**screw′like′,** *adj.*

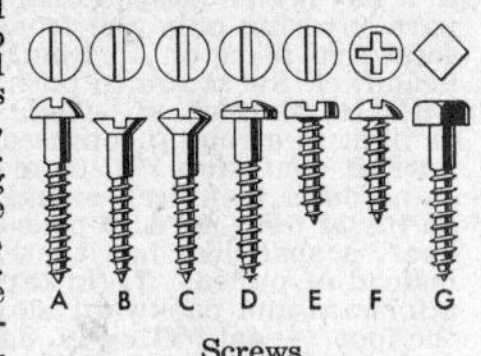

Screws
A, Round head; B, Flat head; C, Oval head; D, Fillister head; E, Sheet-metal screw; F, Phillips head; G, Lag screw

screw·ball (skro͞o′bôl′), *n.* **1.** *Slang.* an eccentric person; nut. **2.** *Baseball.* a pitched ball that curves toward the side of the plate from which it was thrown. —*adj.* **3.** *Slang.* eccentric, as ideas or conduct.

screw′ bean′, a mimosaceous tree, *Strombocarpa odorata* (*Prosopis pubescens*), of the southwestern U.S., bearing twisted pods used as fodder.

screw′ cap′, a cap designed to screw onto the threaded mouth of a bottle, jar, or the like.

screw·driv·er (skro͞o′drī′vər), *n.* **1.** a hand tool for turning a screw, consisting of a specially formed shank rotated by a handle at one end. **2.** a mixed drink made with vodka and orange juice. Also, **screw′ driv′er.**

screwed (skro͞od), *adj.* **1.** fastened with a screw or screws. **2.** having grooves like a screw; threaded. **3.** twisted; awry. **4.** *Chiefly Brit. Slang.* drunk; intoxicated.

screw′ eye′, a screw having a ring-shaped head.

screw·head (skro͞o′hed′), *n.* the head or top of a screw having a slot or slots for the end of a screwdriver.

screw′ nail′. See **drive screw.**

screw′ pine′, any tropical Asian tree or shrub of the genus *Pandanus,* having a long, narrow, rigid, spirally arranged leaves, aerial roots, and bearing an edible fruit.

screw′ propel′ler, a rotary propelling device, as for a ship or airplane, consisting of a number of blades so inclined as to tend to drive a helical path through the medium in which they rotate. —**screw′-pro·pelled′,** *adj.*

screw′ stock′, diestock.

screw·up (skro͞o′up′), *n.* *U.S. Slang.* **1.** a stupid mistake; blunder. **2.** a habitual blunderer.

screw·worm (skro͞o′wûrm′), *n.* the larva of any of certain flies of the genus *Callitroga,* which sometimes infests wounds, the nose, or navel of domestic animals and man.

screw·y (skro͞o′ē), *adj.,* **screw·i·er, screw·i·est.** *Slang.* **1.** crazy; nutty. **2.** disconcertingly strange: *There's something screwy about his story.*

Scria·bin (skrē ä′bin; *Russ.* skʀyä′bin), *n.* **A·le·ksan·dr Ni·ko·la·ie·vich** (ä′le ksän′dəʀ ni ko lä′yə vich), 1872–1915, Russian composer and pianist.

scrib·ble (skrib′əl), *v.,* **-bled, -bling,** *n.* —*v.t.* **1.** to write hastily or carelessly. —*v.i.* **2.** to write or draw in a hasty or careless way. **3.** to make meaningless marks with a pencil or pen. —*n.* **4.** a note or other writing that has little or no meaning. **5.** a hasty or careless drawing or piece of writing. **6.** handwriting, esp. when illegible. [late ME < ML *scrībill(āre)* (to) scribble, dim. of *scrībere* to write; see SHRIVE]

scrib·bler (skrib′lər), *n.* **1.** a writer whose work has little or no value. **2.** a person who scribbles.

scribe[1] (skrīb), *n.* **1.** a person who serves as a penman or copyist, esp. one who in former times made copies of manuscripts. **2.** a public clerk or writer, usually one having official status. **3.** *Judaism.* one of the scholars and teachers of Jewish law and tradition in ancient Palestine who transcribed, edited, and interpreted the Bible. **4.** a writer or author, esp. a newspaperman. [ME < L *scrīb(a)* clerk < *scrīb(ere)* (to) write] —**scrib′al,** *adj.*

scribe[2] (skrīb), *v.t.,* **scribed, scrib·ing.** to mark or score (wood or the like) with a pointed instrument as a guide to cutting or assembling. [? aph. var. of INSCRIBE]

Scribe (skʀēb), *n.* **(Au·gus·tin) Eu·gène** (ō gys taN′ œ zhen′), 1791–1861, French dramatist.

scrib·er (skrī′bər), *n.* a tool for scribing wood or the like.

scrim (skrim), *n.* **1.** a cotton or linen fabric of open weave used for bunting, curtains, etc. **2.** *Theat.* a piece of such fabric used for creating the illusion of a solid wall or backdrop under certain lighting conditions or creating a semi-transparent curtain when lit from behind. [?]

scrim·mage (skrim′ij), *n., v.,* **-maged, -mag·ing.** —*n.* **1.** a rough or vigorous struggle. **2.** *Football.* **a.** the action that takes place between the teams from the moment the ball is snapped until it is declared dead. **b.** a practice session or informal game played between two units of the same team. —*v.t., v.i.* **3.** to engage in a scrimmage. [var. of obs. *scrimish,* metathetic form of SKIRMISH] —**scrim′mag·er,** *n.*

scrimp (skrimp), *v.t.* **1.** to be sparing or restrictive of or in: *to scrimp food.* **2.** to provide sparingly for: *to scrimp his elderly parents.* —*v.i.* **3.** to be sparing or frugal; economize. [< Scand; cf. Sw *skrympa,* Norw, Dan *skrumpe* (orig. *skrimpa, strong v.) to shrivel, c. MHG *schrimpfen* to contract; see SHRIMP]

scrimp·y (skrim′pē), *adj.,* **scrimp·i·er, scrimp·i·est. 1.** scanty; meager; barely adequate. **2.** tending to scrimp; frugal. —**scrimp′i·ly,** *adv.* —**scrimp′i·ness,** *n.*

scrim·shaw (skrim′shô′), *n.* **1.** a carved or engraved article, esp. of whale ivory made by whalemen as a leisure occupation. **2.** such articles or work collectively. **3.** the art or technique of producing such work. —*v.i.* **4.** to produce scrimshaw. —*v.t.* **5.** to carve or engrave (whale ivory or whalebone) into scrimshaw. [?]

scrip[1] (skrip), *n.* **1.** a receipt, certificate, list, or similar brief piece of writing. **2.** a scrap of paper. **3.** *Finance.* **a.** a certificate representing a fraction of a share of stock. **b.** a certificate indicating the right of the holder to receive payment later in the form of cash, goods, or land. **4.** paper currency in denominations of less than one dollar, formerly issued in the United States. [? b. ME *scrit* SCRIPT and SCRAP[1]; in some senses, short for SUBSCRIPTION]

scrip[2] (skrip), *n.* *Archaic.* a bag or wallet carried by wayfarers. [ME *scrippe* < ML *scripp(um)* pilgrim's pack < ?]

Scripps (skrips), *n.* **Edward Wyl·lis** (wil′is), 1854–1926, U.S. newspaper publisher.

scrip·sit (skʀēp′sit; *Eng.* skrip′sit), *v.* *Latin.* he (or she) wrote (it).

script (skript), *n.* **1.** the letters or characters used in writing by hand; handwriting. **2.** a manuscript or document. **3.** the text of a manuscript or document. **4.** the written text of a play, motion picture, etc. **5.** any system of writing. **6.** *Print.* a type imitating handwriting. Cf. **cursive.** —*v.t.* **7.** to write a script for or on. [ME < L *scrīpt(um),* neut. ptp. of *scrībere* to write; r. ME *scrit* < OF *escrit* < L *scrīpt(um),* as above] —**script′er,** *n.*

Script., **1.** Scriptural. **2.** Scripture.

scrip·to·ri·um (skrip tōr′ē əm, -tôr′-), *n., pl.* **-to·ri·ums, -to·ri·a** (-tōr′ē ə, -tôr′-). a room in a monastery for writing or copying of manuscripts. [< ML]

scrip·tur·al (skrip′chər əl), *adj.* **1.** (*sometimes cap.*) of, pertaining to, or in accordance with sacred writings, esp. the Scriptures. **2.** rendered in or related to writing. [< NL *scrīptūrāl(is)*] —**scrip′tur·al·ly,** *adv.*

Scrip·ture (skrip′chər), *n.* **1.** Often, **Scriptures.** Also called **Holy Scripture, Holy Scriptures.** the sacred writings of the Old or New Testaments or both together. **2.** a short passage of the Bible; text. **3.** any writing or book, esp. when of a sacred or religious nature. **4.** (*sometimes l.c.*) a particular passage from the Bible. [< L *scrīptūr(a)* writing. See SCRIPT, -URE]

script·writ·er (skript′rī′tər), *n.* one who writes scripts, as for movies, radio, or television. —**script′writ′ing,** *n.*

scrive·ner (skriv′nər), *n.* **1.** scribe[1] (defs. 1, 2). **2.** a notary. [ME *scriveyner* = *scrivein* (< OF *(e)scrivein;* see SCRIBE[1], -AN) + *-er* -ER[1]]

scro·bic·u·late (skrō bik′yə lit, -lāt′), *adj.* *Bot., Zool.* furrowed or pitted. [< L *scrobicul(us)* (*scrobi(s)* ditch + *-culus* -CULE) + -ATE[1]]

scrod (skrod), *n.* *U.S.* young Atlantic cod or haddock. [?]

scrof·u·la (skrof′yə lə), *n.* *Pathol.* a form of tuberculosis characterized chiefly by swelling and degeneration of the lymphatic glands, esp. of the neck, and by inflammation of the joints. [< ML, sing. of LL *scrōfulae* (L *scrōf(a)* sow + *-ulae* -ULE); r. OE *scrofel* < LL]

scrof·u·lous (skrof′yə ləs), *adj.* **1.** of the nature of, resembling, or affected with scrofula. **2.** morally tainted. —**scrof′u·lous·ly,** *adv.* —**scrof′u·lous·ness,** *n.*

scroll (skrōl), *n.* **1.** a roll of parchment, paper, or other thin material, esp. one with writing on it. **2.** something, esp. an ornament, having a spiral or coiled form. **3.** a list, roll, roster, or schedule. **4.** (in Japanese and Chinese art) a painting or text on silk or paper that is either displayed on a wall or held by the viewer and is rolled up when not in use. [ME *scrowle;* b. ESCROW and ROLL]

Scroll (def. 2)

scroll′ saw′, a narrow saw mounted vertically in a frame, used for cutting curved ornamental designs.

scroll·work (skrōl′wûrk′), *n.* **1.** decorative work in which scroll forms figure prominently. **2.** ornamental work cut out with a scroll saw.

Scrooge (skro͞oj), *n.* (*often l.c.*) a miserly person, after a character in Dickens' story, *A Christmas Carol* (1843).

scroop (skro͞op), *v.i.* **1.** to emit a harsh, grating sound. —*n.* **2.** a scrooping sound. [b. SCRAPE and WHOOP]

scroph·u·lar·i·a·ceous (skrof′yə lâr′ē ā′shəs), *adj.* belonging to the *Scrophulariaceae,* or figwort family of plants, comprising the snapdragon, foxglove, etc. [< NL *scrophulari(a)* genus name (see SCROFULA, -ARIA) + -ACEOUS]

scro·tum (skrō′təm), *n., pl.* **-ta** (-tə), **-tums.** *Anat.* the pouch of skin that contains the testes and their coverings. [< L] —**scro′tal,** *adj.*

scrouge (skrouj, skro͞oj), *v.t., v.i.,* **scrouged, scroug·ing.** *Chiefly Dial.* to squeeze; crowd. [b. obs. *scruze* (itself b. SCREW and BRUISE) and GOUGE]

scrounge (skrounj), *v.,* **scrounged, scroung·ing,** *n.* —*v.t.* **1.** to borrow (a small item or amount) without any intention of returning or repaying it. **2.** to set or take without paying or at another's expense. **3.** to gather together by foraging; seek out. —*v.i.* **4.** to borrow, esp. a small item one is not expected to return or replace. **5. scrounge around,** to search or forage for something, esp. in a haphazard or disorganized fashion. —*n.* **6.** Also, **scroung′er.** a person who borrows habitually; sponger; moocher. [alter. of dial. *scringe* to glean]

scrub[1] (skrub), *v.,* **scrubbed, scrub·bing,** *n.* —*v.t.* **1.** to rub hard with a brush, cloth, etc., or against a rough surface in washing. **2.** to remove (dirt, grime, etc.) from something by hard rubbing while washing. **3.** to cleanse (a gas or vapor). **4.** *Rocketry.* to cancel or postpone (a missile flight). —*v.i.* **5.** to cleanse something by hard rubbing. —*n.* **6.** the act or an instance of scrubbing. [ME *scrobbe* < MD *scrobbe(n)*]

scrub[2] (skrub), *n.* **1.** low trees or shrubs collectively. **2.** a large area covered with such growth, as the Australian bush. **3.** a domestic animal of mixed or inferior breeding; mongrel. **4.** a small or insignificant person. **5.** anything undersized or inferior. **6.** *Sports.* a player not belonging to the varsity or regular team. —*adj.* **7.** small, undersized, or stunted. **8.** inferior or insignificant. **9.** abounding in or covered with low trees and shrubs: *scrub country.* [< Scand; cf. dial. Dan *skrub* brushwood, SHRUB[1]]

scrubbed[1] (skrubd), *adj.* cleaned by or as by scrubbing. [SCRUB[1] + -ED[2]]

scrub·bed[2] (skrub′id), *adj.* *Archaic.* stunted; scrubby. [SCRUB[2] + -ED[3]]

scrub·ber[1] (skrub′ər), *n.* a person or thing that scrubs. [SCRUB[1] + -ER[1]]

scrub·ber[2] (skrub′ər), *n.* **1.** a mongrel, esp. a mongrel steer. **2.** a thin or stunted steer. **3.** *Australian.* **a.** an inhabitant of the bush. **b.** any domestic animal that has run off into the bush and become wild, esp. a steer. [SCRUB[2] + -ER[1]]

scrub·board (skrub′bôrd′, -bōrd′), *n.* washboard (defs. 1, 2).

scrub·by (skrub′ē), *adj.,* **-bi·er, -bi·est. 1.** low or stunted, as trees. **2.** consisting of or covered with scrub, stunted trees, etc. **3.** undersized or inferior, as animals. —**scrub′bi·ness,** *n.*

scrub·land (skrub′land′), *n.* land on which the natural vegetation is chiefly scrub.

scrub′ nurse′, a nurse trained to serve as part of the surgically clean medical team handling instruments during an operation.

scrub′ oak′, any of several oaks, as *Quercus ilicifolia* and *Q. prinoides,* characterized by a shrubby manner of growth, usually found on dry, rocky soil.

scrub-up (skrub′up′), *n.* the act of washing or bathing thoroughly, esp. the aseptic washing by doctors and nurses before a surgical operation.

scrub·wom·an (skrub′wo͝om′ən), *n., pl.* **-wom·en.** a woman hired to clean a place; charwoman.

scruff (skruf), *n.* the nape or back of the neck. [var. of dial. *scuff, scuft* < D *schoft* horse's withers]

scruff·y (skruf′ē), *adj.,* **scruff·i·er, scruff·i·est.** untidy; shabby. [*scruff,* metathetic var. of SCURF + -Y[1]]

scrum·mage (skrum′ij), *n., v.,* **-maged, -mag·ing.** *Rugby.* —*n.* **1.** Also called **scrum** (skrum). a play in which the ball is rolled between the two opposing teams, the front-line players of which stand with arms around a teammate's waist, meet the opponent shoulder to shoulder, and attempt to kick the ball backward to a teammate. —*v.i.* **2.** to engage in a scrummage. [var. of SCRIMMAGE] —**scrum′mag·er,** *n.*

scrump·tious (skrump′shəs), *adj.* *Informal.* very pleasing, esp. to the senses; delectable; splendid: *a scrumptious casserole; a scrumptious satin gown.* [? alter. of SUMPTUOUS] —**scrump′tious·ly,** *adv.* —**scrump′tious·ness,** *n.*

scrunch (skrunch, skro͝onch), *v.t., v.i.* **1.** to crunch, crush, or crumple. —*n.* **2.** the act or sound of scrunching. [var. of CRUNCH]

scru·ple (skro͞o′pəl), *n., v.,* **-pled, -pling.** —*n.* **1.** a moral or ethical consideration or standard that acts as a restraining force. **2.** a very small portion or amount. **3.** a unit of weight equal to 20 grains or ⅓ of a dram, apothecaries' weight. —*v.i.* **4.** to have scruples. [< L *scrūpul(us)* = *scrūp(us)* rough pebble + *-ulus* -ULE] —**scru′ple·less,** *adj.* —**Syn. 1.** qualm, compunction.

scru·pu·lous (skro͞o′pyə ləs), *adj.* **1.** having or showing a strict regard for what one considers right. **2.** punctiliously or minutely careful, precise, or exact. [< L *scrūpulōs(us).* See SCRUPLE, -OSE[1], -OUS] —**scru·pu·los·i·ty** (skro͞o′pyə-los′i tē), **scru′pu·lous·ness,** *n.* —**scru′pu·lous·ly,** *adv.* —**Syn. 1.** conscientious, careful, circumspect. **2.** exacting.

scru·ta·ble (skro͞o′tə bəl), *adj.* capable of being understood by careful study or investigation. [< L *scrūt(ārī)* (to) scrutinize (see SCRUTINY) + -ABLE] —**scru′ta·bil′i·ty,** *n.*

scru·ti·nise (skro͞ot′ənīz′), *v.t., v.i.,* **-nised, -nis·ing.** *Chiefly Brit.* scrutinize. —**scru′ti·ni·sa′tion,** *n.* —**scru′ti·nis′er,** *n.* —**scru′ti·nis′ing·ly,** *adv.*

scru·ti·nize (skro͞ot′ənīz′), *v.,* **-nized, -niz·ing.** —*v.t.* **1.** to examine in detail with careful or critical attention. —*v.i.* **2.** to conduct a scrutiny. [SCRUTIN(Y) + -IZE] —**scru′ti·ni·za′tion,** *n.* —**scru′ti·niz′er,** *n.* —**scru′ti·niz′ing·ly,** *adv.*

scru·ti·ny (skro͞ot′ənē), *n., pl.* **-nies. 1.** a searching examination or investigation; minute inquiry. **2.** surveillance; close and continuous watching or guarding. **3.** a close and searching look. [< L *scrūtini(um)* the action of searching, of scrutinizing = *scrūt(ārī)* (to) search + *-inium* n. suffix] —**Syn. 1.** See **examination.**

scu·ba (sko͞o′bə), *n.* **1.** a portable breathing device for free-swimming divers, consisting of a mouthpiece joined by hoses to one or two tanks of compressed air which are strapped on the back. —*adj.* **2.** done by a free-swimming diver equipped with scuba: *scuba diving.* **3.** of or pertaining to a scuba device. [*s(elf)-c(ontained) u(nderwater) b(reathing) a(pparatus)*]

scud[1] (skud), *v.,* **scud·ded, scud·ding,** *n.* —*v.i.* **1.** to run or move quickly. **2.** *Naut.* to run before a gale with little or no sail set. **3.** *Archery.* (of an arrow) to fly too high and wide of the mark. —*n.* **4.** the act of scudding. **5.** clouds, spray, or the like, driven by the wind. **6.** low-drifting clouds appearing beneath a cloud from which precipitation is falling. [< Scand; cf. Norw *skudda* push]

scud[2] (skud), *v.,* **scud·ded, scud·ding,** *n.* —*v.t* **1.** to cleanse (a trimmed and roughly depilated skin or hide) of remaining hairs or dirt. —*n.* **2.** the hairs or dirt removed by scudding. [obs. *scud* dirt < ?]

Scu·dé·ry (skʏ dā rē′), *n.* **Mag·de·leine de** (mag də len′ də), 1607–1701, French novelist.

scu·do (sko͞o′dō), *n., pl.* **-di** (-dē). any of various gold or silver coins, of various Italian states, issued from the late 16th through the early 19th centuries. [< It < L *scūtum* shield]

scuff (skuf), *v.i.* **1.** to walk without raising the feet from the ground; shuffle. **2.** to scrape or rub one's foot back and forth over something. **3.** to be or become marred or scratched by scraping or wear. —*v.t.* **4.** to scrape (something) with one's foot or feet. **5.** to rub or scrape (one's foot or feet) over something. **6.** to mar by scraping or hard use, as shoes, furniture, etc. —*n.* **7.** the act or sound of scuffing. **8.** a flat-heeled slipper with a full-length sole and an upper part covering only the front of the foot. **9.** a marred or scratched place on an item, as from scraping or wear. [< Scand; cf. Sw *skuffa* to push]

scuf·fle (skuf′əl), *v.,* **-fled, -fling,** *n.* —*v.i.* **1.** to struggle or fight in a rough, confused manner. **2.** to go or move in hurried confusion. **3.** to move or go with a shuffle. —*n.* **4.** a rough, confused struggle or fight. **5.** a shuffling: *a scuffle of feet.* **6.** Also called **scuf′fle hoe′.** a spadelike hoe that is pushed instead of pulled. **7.** (in tap dancing) a forward and backward movement of the foot. —**scuf′fling·ly,** *adv.*

scul·dug·ger·y (skul dug′ə rē), *n.* skulduggery. Also, **scull·dug′ger·y.**

sculk (skulk), *v.i., n.* skulk. —**sculk′er,** *n.*

scull (skul), *n.* **1.** an oar mounted on a fulcrum at the stern of a small boat for moving from side to side to propel the boat. **2.** either of a pair of oars rowed by one oarsman. **3.** a boat propelled by an oar or oars. **4.** a light, narrow racing boat for one, two, or sometimes four oarsmen, each equipped with a pair of oars. **5. sculls,** a race involving such boats. —*v.t.* **6.** to propel or convey by means of a scull or sculls. —*v.i.* **7.** to propel a boat with a scull or sculls. [ME *sculle* < ?] —**scull′er,** *n.*

S

S, Scull (def. 1)

scul·ler·y (skul′ə rē), *n., pl.* **-ler·ies.** *Chiefly Brit.* **1.** a small room or section of a pantry in which food is cleaned, trimmed, and cut into cooking portions before being sent to the kitchen. **2.** a small room or section of a pantry or kitchen in which cooking utensils are cleaned and stored. [ME *squillerye* < MF *(e)scuelerie* = *escuele* dish (< L *scutella,* dim. of *scutra* pan) + *-rie* -RY]

scul·lion (skul′yən), *n.* **1.** a kitchen servant who does menial work. **2.** a low or contemptible person. [? < MF *(e)scou(v)illon* dishcloth = *escouve* broom (< L *scōpa*) + *-illon* dim. suffix]

sculp (skulp), *v.t.* to sculpture. [< L *sculp(ere)* (to) carve] —**Usage.** SCULP, like SCULPT, is often criticized as being a back formation from the verb SCULPTURE, but is actually from the Latin verb *sculpere.* SCULP is an older form than SCULPT, but less common in present-day writing. See also **sculpt.**

sculp., **1.** sculptor. **2.** sculptural. **3.** sculpture. Also, **sculpt.**

scul·pin (skul′pin), *n., pl.* (*esp. collectively*) **-pin,** (*esp. referring to two or more kinds or species*) **-pins. 1.** any small, fresh-water fish of the genus *Cottus,* of the family *Cottidae,* having a large head with one or more spines on each side; bull-head. **2.** any of numerous marine fishes of the same family. [?]

sculp·sit (sko͝olp′sit; *Eng.* skulp′sit), *Latin.* he (or she) engraved, carved, or sculptured (it). *Abbr.:* sc.

sculpt (skulpt), *v.t., v.i.* **1.** *Fine Arts.* to carve, model, or make by using the techniques of sculpture. **2.** to form, shape, or manipulate, as in the manner of sculpture: *Her hair was sculpted by a leading coiffeur.* [< F *sculpt(er)* < L *sculpt-* (ptp. s. of *sculpere* to carve)] —**Usage.** SCULPT is often criticized as being a nonstandard and irregular back formation from the verb SCULPTURE, but is actually from the French verb *sculpter.* SCULPT has been in use in serious writing for more than a century. See also **sculp.**

sculp·tor (skulp′tər), *n.* a person who practices the art of sculpture. [< L = *sculpt(us)* ptp. of *sculpere* to carve + *-or* -OR[2]]

sculp·tress (skulp′tris), *n.* a female sculptor. [SCULPT(O)R + -ESS]

sculp·ture (skulp′chər), *n., v.,* **-tured, -tur·ing.** —*n.* **1.** the art of carving, modeling, welding, or otherwise producing works of art in three dimensions, as in relief, intaglio, or in the round. **2.** such works of art collectively. **3.** an individual piece of such work. —*v.t.* **4.** to carve, model, weld, or otherwise produce (a piece of sculpture). **5.** to produce a portrait or image of in this way; represent in sculpture. **6.** *Phys. Geog.* to change the form of (the land surface) by erosion. —*v.i.* **7.** to work as a sculptor. [< L *sculptūr(a)* = *sculpt(us)* (ptp. of *sculpere* to carve) + *-ūra* -URE] —**sculp′tur·al,** *adj.* —**sculp′tur·al·ly,** *adv.*

sculp·tur·esque (skulp′chə resk′), *adj.* suggesting sculpture: *the sculpturesque beauty of her face.* —**sculp′tur·esque′ly,** *adv.* —**sculp′tur·esque′ness,** *n.*

scum (skum), *n., v.,* **scummed, scum·ming.** —*n.* **1.** a film of foul or extraneous matter that forms on the surface of a liquid. **2.** refuse or offscourings. **3.** a low, worthless, or evil person. **4.** such persons collectively; riffraff; rabble. **5.** scoria (def. 1). —*v.t.* **6.** to remove the scum from. **7.** to remove as scum. —*v.i.* **8.** to form scum; become covered with scum. [ME *scume* < MD *schūme;* c. G *Schaum* foam] —**scum′like′,** *adj.*

scum·my (skum′ē), *adj.*, **-mi·er, -mi·est.** 1. consisting of or having scum. 2. *Informal.* despicable; contemptible. —**scum′mi·ness,** *n.*

scun·ner (skun′ər), *n.* 1. an irrational dislike; loathing. —*v.i.* 2. *Scot. and North Eng.* to feel or show violent disgust, esp. to blanch or gag. —*v.t.* 3. *Scot. and North Eng.* to disgust; nauseate. [ME (Scot) *skunner* = *skurn* to flinch (akin to SCARE) + *-er* -ER[2], with loss of first *r* by dissimilation]

scup (skup), *n.* a sparid food fish, *Stenotomus versicolor,* found along the Atlantic coast of the U.S. [< Narragansett *mishcup* = *mishe* big + *kuppe* (having scales) close together]

scup·per (skup′ər), *n.* 1. *Naut.* a drain at the edge of a deck exposed to the weather, for allowing accumulated water to drain away into the sea or into the bilges. 2. a drain, closed by one or two flaps, for allowing water to run off the floor of a factory or other building to the exterior. 3. any opening in the side of a building, as in a parapet, for draining off rain water. [ME *skoper.* See SCOOP, -ER[1]]

scup·per·nong (skup′ər nông′, -nong′), *n.* 1. a silvery amber-green variety of muscadine grape. 2. the vine bearing this fruit, grown in the southern U.S. [short for *scuppernong grape,* named after a North Carolina river]

scurf (skûrf), *n.* 1. the scales or small shreds of epidermis that are continually exfoliated from the skin. 2. any scaly matter or incrustation on a surface. [ME, OE < Scand; cf. Dan *skurv,* akin to OE *sceorf*]

scurf·y (skûr′fē), *adj.*, **scurf·i·er, scurf·i·est.** resembling, producing, or covered with scurf. [ME] —**scurf′i·ness,** *n.*

scur·ril·i·ty (skə ril′i tē), *n., pl.* **-ties.** 1. a scurrilous quality or condition. 2. a scurrilous remark or attack. [< L *scurrīlitās*] —**Syn.** 2. vituperation, abuse, vilification.

scur·ril·ous (skûr′ə ləs), *adj.* 1. grossly or obscenely abusive: *a scurrilous attack on the mayor.* 2. characterized by or using low buffoonery; coarsely jocular or derisive: *a scurrilous jest.* [archaic *scurril(e)* (< L *scurrīlis* jeering = *scurr(a)* buffoon + *-īlis* -ILE[1]) + -OUS] —**scur′ril·ous·ly,** *adv.* —**scur′ril·ous·ness,** *n.* —**Syn.** 1. vituperative.

scur·ry (skûr′ē, skur′ē), *v.*, **-ried, -ry·ing,** *n., pl.* **-ries.** —*v.i.* 1. to go or move quickly or in haste. —*v.t.* 2. to send hurrying along. —*n.* 3. a scurrying rush: *the scurry of little feet on the stairs.* 4. a short run or race. [abstracted from HURRY-SCURRY]

S-curve (es′kûrv′), *n.* a curve shaped like an S.

scur·vy (skûr′vē), *n., adj.*, **-vi·er, -vi·est.** —*n.* 1. *Pathol.* a disease marked by swollen and bleeding gums, livid spots on the skin, prostration, etc., due to a diet lacking in vitamin C. —*adj.* 2. contemptible; despicable; mean. [SCURF + -Y[1]] —**scur′vi·ness,** *n.*

scur′vy grass′, a brassicaceous plant, *Cochlearia officinalis,* supposed to be a remedy for scurvy.

scut (skut), *n.* a short tail, esp. that of a hare, rabbit, or deer. [< Scand; cf. Icel *skott* tail]

scu·ta (skyo͞o′tə), *n.* pl. of **scutum.**

scu·tage (skyo͞o′tij), *n.* (in the feudal system) a payment exacted by a lord in lieu of military service due to him by the holder of a fee. [< ML *scūtāg(ium).* See SCUT(UM), -AGE]

Scu·ta·ri (sko͞o′tä rē′), *n.* 1. Also, **Skutari.** Turkish, **Usküder.** a section of Istanbul, Turkey, on the Asian shore of the Bosporus. 116,195 (1965). 2. **Lake,** a lake between NW Albania and S Yugoslavia. ab. 135 sq. mi.

scu·tate (skyo͞o′tāt), *adj.* 1. *Bot.* formed like a round buckler. 2. *Zool.* having scutes, shields, or large scales. [< L *scūtāt(us).* See SCUTUM, -ATE[1]]

scutch (skuch), *v.t.* 1. to dress (flax) by beating. —*n.* 2. Also called **scutch′er.** a device for scutching flax fiber. [< MF *(*e*)*scoucher* (F *écoucher*) to beat flax < VL **excuticāre,* r. L *excutere* (*ex-* EX-[1] + *quatere* to shatter)]

scutch·eon (skuch′ən), *n.* 1. escutcheon. 2. *Zool.* a scute. —**scut′cheon·less,** *adj.* —**scut′cheon·like′,** *adj.*

scute (skyo͞ot), *n.* *Zool.* 1. a dermal bony plate, as on an armadillo, or a large horny plate, as on a turtle. 2. a large scale. [< L *scūt(um)* shield]

scu·tel·late (skyo͞o tel′it, -āt, skyo͞ot′ᵊlāt′), *adj.* *Zool.* 1. having scutes. 2. formed into a scutellum. Also, **scu′tel·lat′ed.** [SCUTELL(UM) + -ATE[1]]

scu·tel·la·tion (skyo͞ot′ᵊlā′shən), *n.* *Zool.* a scutellate state or formation; a scaly covering, as on a bird's leg. [SCUTELL(UM) + -ATION]

scu·tel·lum (skyo͞o tel′əm), *n., pl.* **-tel·la** (-tel′ə). *Zool., Bot.* a small plate, scutum, or other shieldlike part. [< NL = L *scūt(um)* shield + *-ellum* dim. suffix]

scu·ti·form (skyo͞o′tə fôrm′), *adj.* shield-shaped. [< NL *scūtiform(is).* See SCUTUM, -I-, -FORM]

scut·tle[1] (skut′ᵊl), *n.* 1. a deep bucket for carrying coal. 2. *Brit. Dial.* a broad, shallow basket. [ME, orig. a dish or platter < L *scutell(a),* dim. of *scutra*]

scut·tle[2] (skut′ᵊl), *v.*, **-tled, -tling,** *n.* —*v.i.* 1. to run with quick, hasty steps; hurry. —*n.* 2. a quick pace. 3. a short, hurried run. [? var. of *scuddle,* freq. of SCUD[1]]

scut·tle[3] (skut′ᵊl), *v.*, **-tled, -tling,** *n.* —*v.t.* 1. to sink (a vessel) deliberately by opening seacocks or making openings in the bottom. 2. to abandon or destroy (as plans, hopes, etc.): *The lawyer scuttled his hopes of collecting the debt quickly.* —*n.* 3. *Naut.* **a.** a small hatch or port in the deck, side, or bottom of a vessel. **b.** a cover for this. 4. a small hatchlike opening in a roof or ceiling. [ME *skotel* < Sp (*e*)*scotill(a)* hatchway = *escot(e)* low neck (< Goth *skaut* seam) + *-illa* dim. suffix]

scut·tle·butt (skut′ᵊl but′), *n.* 1. *Naut.* **a.** an open cask containing drinking water. **b.** a drinking fountain for use by the crew of a vessel. 2. *Informal.* rumor; gossip.

scu·tum (skyo͞o′təm), *n., pl.* **-ta** (-tə). 1. *Zool.* scute (def. 1). 2. a large, oblong shield used by legionaries of ancient Rome. 3. (*cap.*) *Astron.* the Shield, a southern constellation north of Sagittarius and east of Aquila, containing a small, very bright star cloud. [< L: shield]

Scyl·la (sil′ə), *n.* 1. Modern, **Scilla.** a rock in the Strait of Messina off the S coast of Italy. 2. *Class. Myth.* a sea nymph who was transformed into a sea monster: later identified with the rock Scylla. Cf. **Charybdis** (def. 2). 3. **between Scylla and Charybdis,** between two equally perilous alternatives, neither of which can be passed without encountering and probably falling victim to the other.

scy·phate (sī′fāt), *adj.* cup-shaped. [< Gk *skýph(os)* bowl + -ATE[1]]

scy·phi·form (sī′fə fôrm′), *adj.* *Bot.* shaped like a cup or goblet. [< Gk *skýph(os)* bowl + -I- + -FORM]

Scy·pho·zo·a (sī′fə zō′ə), *n.* the class comprising the marine jellyfishes. [< NL = Gk *skýpho(s)* bowl + -ZOA]

scy·pho·zo·an (sī′fə zō′ən), *n.* 1. any coelenterate of the class *Scyphozoa,* comprising the true marine jellyfishes. —*adj.* 2. belonging or pertaining to the *Scyphozoa.*

Scy·ros (skī′ros, -rōs; *Gk.* skē′rôs), *n.* Skyros.

scythe (sīth), *n., v.*, **scythed, scyth·ing.** —*n.* 1. an implement consisting of a long, curving blade fastened at an angle to a handle, for cutting grass, grain, etc., by hand. —*v.t.* 2. to cut or mow with a scythe. [ME *sith,* OE *si(g)the;* c. Icel *sigth;* spelling *sc* by pseudo-etym. assoc. with L *scindere* to cut] —**scythe′like′,** *adj.*

Scyth·i·a (sith′ē ə), *n.* the ancient name of a region in SE Europe and Asia, lying N and E of the Black and Caspian seas: now part of the Soviet Union.

Scyth·i·an (sith′ē ən), *adj.* 1. pertaining to Scythia, its people, or their language. —*n.* 2. a native or inhabitant of Scythia. 3. an extinct Iranian language.

SD, South Dakota (approved esp. for use with zip code).

sd., sound.

S.D., 1. doctor of science. [< L *Scientiae Doctor*] 2. South Dakota. 3. *Statistics.* standard deviation.

s.d., 1. without naming a date. [< L *sine die* without a day] 2. *Statistics.* standard deviation.

S. Dak., South Dakota.

'sdeath (zdeth), *interj.* *Archaic.* (used as a mild oath.) [(*God*)'*s death*]

SDR, See **special drawing rights.** Also, **S.D.R.**

SE, 1. southeast. 2. southeastern. Also, **S.E.**

Se, *Chem.* selenium.

se-, a formal element occurring in loan words from Latin, where it meant "apart": *seduce; select.* [< L *sē(d)-* apart]

sea (sē), *n.* 1. the salt waters that cover the greater part of the earth's surface. 2. a division of these waters, of considerable extent, more or less definitely marked off by land boundaries: *the North Sea.* 3. one of the seven seas; ocean. 4. a large lake or landlocked body of water. 5. the degree or amount of turbulence of the ocean or other body of water, as caused by the wind. 6. the waves. 7. a large wave: *The heavy seas almost drowned us.* 8. a widely extended, copious, or overwhelming quantity: *a sea of faces.* 9. the work, travel, and shipboard life of a sailor: *The sea is a hard life for a man.* 10. **at sea, a.** on the ocean. **b.** perplexed; uncertain: *completely at sea as to how to answer the question.* 11. **put to sea,** to embark on a sea voyage: *The expedition is nearly ready to put to sea.* Also, **put out to sea.** —*adj.* 12. of, pertaining to, or adapted for use at sea. [ME *see,* OE *sǣ;* c. D *zee,* G *See,* Icel *sær* sea, Goth *saiws* marsh]

sea′ an′chor, *Naut.* any of various devices, as a drogue, dropped forward of a vessel at the end of a cable to hold the bow into the wind or sea during a storm.

Sea anemone, *Epiactis prolifera* (Width ¾ in.)

sea′ anem′one, any sedentary marine animal of the phylum *Coelenterata,* having a columnar body and one or more circles of tentacles surrounding the mouth.

sea′ bag′, a cylindrical canvas bag closed by a drawstring, used esp. by a sailor for his gear.

sea′ bass′ (bas), 1. any of numerous marine fishes of the family *Serranidae.* 2. any of numerous related or similar marine food fishes, as the croakers.

sea·bed (sē′bed′), *n.* the ocean floor, still mostly unexplored, that covers about three-quarters of the surface of the earth.

Sea·bee (sē′bē′), *n.* a member of the construction battalions of the U.S. Navy, established to build landing facilities, airfields, etc., in combat areas. [var. sp. of *CB, C(onstruction) B(attalion)*]

sea′ bird′, a bird frequenting the sea or coast. Also called **seafowl.**

sea′ bis′cuit, ship biscuit; hardtack.

sea·board (sē′bōrd′, -bôrd′), *n.* 1. the line where land and sea meet. 2. a region bordering a seacoast: *the Eastern seaboard.* —*adj.* 3. bordering on the sea. [late ME *seebord*]

Sea·borg (sē′bôrg), *n.* **Glenn T(he·o·dor)** (thē′ə dōr′, -dôr′), born 1912, U.S. chemist: codiscoverer of plutonium.

sea-born (sē′bôrn′), *adj.* 1. born in or of the sea, as naiads. 2. produced in or rising from the sea, as reefs.

sea·borne (sē′bōrn′, -bôrn′), *adj.* 1. transported by ship over the sea. 2. carried on or over the sea: *a seaborne fog.*

sea′ bread′, ship biscuit; hardtack.

sea′ bream′, 1. any of numerous marine sparid fishes, as *Pagellus centrodontus,* found off the coasts of Europe. 2. a porgy, *Archosargus rhomboidalis,* found in the Atlantic.

sea′ breeze′, a thermally produced wind blowing from a cool ocean surface onto adjoining warm land.

sea′ calf′. See **harbor seal.**

sea′ cap′tain, the master of a seagoing vessel.

sea′ change′, 1. a striking change, as in appearance, often for the better. 2. a transformation brought about by the sea.

sea′ chest′, a chest for a sailor's personal belongings.

sea·coast (sē′kōst′), *n.* the land immediately adjacent to the sea. [ME *see cost*]

sea·cock (sē′kok′), *n.* *Naut.* a valve in the hull of a vessel for admitting outside water into some part of the hull, as into a ballast tank. Also called **sea′ connec′tion, sea valve.**

sea′ cow′, 1. any sirenian, as the manatee or dugong. 2. *Obs.* the hippopotamus.

sea′ cra′dle, chiton (def. 2).

sea′ cu′cumber, any echinoderm of the class *Holothuroidea,* having a long, leathery body with tentacles around the anterior end.

sea′ dog′, 1. a sailor, esp. an old or experienced one. 2. See **harbor seal.**

sea·dog (sē′dôg′, -dog′), *n.* fogbow.
sea′ duck′, any of various diving ducks, esp. the eiders, found principally on seas.
sea′ ea′gle, any of several large eagles of the genus *Haliaetus*, that usually feed on fish.
sea′ ear′, abalone.
sea′ fan′, any of certain anthozoans, esp. *Gorgonia flabellum*, of the West Indies, in which the colony assumes a fanlike form.
sea·far·er (sē′fâr′ər), *n.* **1.** a sailor. **2.** a traveler on the sea.
sea·far·ing (sē′fâr′ing), *adj.* **1.** traveling by sea. **2.** following the sea as a business or calling. **3.** of, pertaining to, or occurring during a sea voyage. —*n.* **4.** the business or calling of a sailor.
sea′ foam′, **1.** the foam of the sea. **2.** meerschaum (def. 1). —**sea′-foam′,** *adj.*
sea·food (sē′fo͞od′), *n.* any salt-water fish or shellfish used for food.
sea·fowl (sē′foul′), *n., pl.* **-fowls,** (*esp. collectively*) **-fowl.** See **sea bird.**
sea′ front′, an area, including buildings, along the edge of the sea; waterfront.
sea·girt (sē′gûrt′), *n.* surrounded by the sea.
sea·go·ing (sē′gō′ing), *adj.* **1.** designed or fit for going to sea, as a vessel. **2.** going to sea; seafaring.
sea′ green′, a clear, light, bluish green. —**sea′-green′,** *adj.*
sea′ gull′, a gull, esp. any of the marine species.
sea′ hog′, a porpoise.
sea′ hol′ly, the eryngo, *Eryngium maritimum.*
sea′ horse′, **1.** any fish of the genus *Hippocampus*, of the pipefish family, having a prehensile tail, an elongated snout, and a head bent at right angles to the body. **2.** a fabled marine animal with the foreparts of a horse and the hind parts of a fish. **3.** a walrus. [ME *sehors* walrus; cf. G *Seepferd*]

Sea horse, *Hippocampus hudsonius* (Length 3 to 4 in.)

sea′-is·land cot′ton (sē′ī′lənd), a long-staple cotton, *Gossypium barbadense*, raised originally in the Sea Islands, now grown chiefly in the West Indies.
Sea′ Is′lands, a group of islands in the Atlantic, along the coasts of South Carolina, Georgia, and N Florida.
sea′ kale′, a broad-leaved, maritime, cruciferous plant, *Crambe maritima*, of Europe, used as a potherb.
sea′ king′, a Viking chief who ravaged the coasts of medieval Europe. [trans. of ON *sǣkonungr;* c. OE *sǣcyning*]
seal[1] (sēl), *n.* **1.** an embossed emblem, figure, symbol, word, letter, etc., used as attestation or evidence of authenticity. **2.** a stamp, medallion, ring, etc., engraved with such a device, for impressing paper, wax, lead, or the like: *The king applied the seal to the document.* **3.** the impression so obtained. **4.** a mark or symbol attached to a legal document and imparting a formal character to it, originally wax with an impression. **5.** a piece of wax or similar adhesive substance so attached to an envelope, folded document, etc., that it must be broken when the object is opened, insuring that the contents have not been tampered with or altered. **6.** anything that tightly or completely closes or secures a thing, as closures or fastenings for doors and railroad cars, adhesive stamps and tapes used to secure the flap of an envelope, etc. **7.** a decorative stamp, esp. as given to contributors to a charitable fund: *a Christmas seal.* **8.** that which serves as assurance, a confirmation, or bond: *His handshake was the only seal we needed to begin work.* **9.** *Plumbing.* a small amount of water held by a trap to exclude foul gases from a sewer or the like. —*v.t.* **10.** to affix a seal to in authorization, testimony, etc. **11.** to assure, confirm, or bind with or as with a seal: *They sealed the bargain with a handshake.* **12.** to close by any form of fastening that must be broken before access can be gained. **13.** to fasten or close tightly by or as if by a seal: *They tried to seal his lips.* **14.** to decide irrevocably: *to seal someone's fate.* **15.** to grant under one's seal or authority, as a pardon. **16.** *Mormon. Ch.* to make (a marriage or adoption) forever binding; solemnize. [ME *seel* < OF *seel* (> F *sceau*) < LL **sigell(um)*, L *sigillum*, dim. of *signum* SIGN; r. ME *seil*, OE (*in*)*segel* seal < LL, as above] —**seal′a·ble,** *adj.*

Great seal of the United States

seal[2] (sēl), *n., pl.* **seals,** (*esp. collectively for 1*) **seal,** *v.* —*n.* **1.** any of numerous marine carnivores of the suborder *Pinnipedia*, including the eared or fur seals, as the sea lion, and the earless or hair seals, as the harbor seal. **2.** the skin of such an animal. **3.** leather made from this skin. **4.** the fur of the fur seal; sealskin. —*v.i.* **5.** to hunt, kill, or capture seals. [ME *sele*, OE *seolh;* c. Icel *selr*] —**seal′like′,** *adj.*
seal·ant (sē′lənt), *n.* **1.** a substance used for sealing, as sealing wax, adhesives, etc. **2.** any of various liquids, paints, chemicals, or soft substances which may be applied to a surface or circulated through a system of pipes or the like, drying to form a hard, watertight coating. [SEAL[1] + -ANT, prob. by analogy with COOLANT]
sea′ lav′ender, any of several maritime, plumbaginaceous plants, of the genus *Limonium.*
sea′ law′yer, *Naut. Slang.* a seaman inclined to question or complain about the orders given.
sealed′ book′, something beyond understanding and therefore unknown.
sealed′ or′ders, orders that are given in sealed form to a commander of a vessel and are to be opened after the vessel is out of contact with the shore.
sea′ legs′, the ability to adjust one's sense of balance to the motion of a ship at sea: *On the third day of the cruise, he found his sea legs.*
seal·er[1] (sē′lər), *n.* **1.** a person or thing that seals. **2.** an officer appointed to examine and test weights and measures, and to set a stamp upon such as are true to the standard. **3.** a substance applied to a porous surface as base for varnish, paint, etc. [late ME *seler.* See SEAL[1], -ER[1]]
seal·er[2] (sē′lər), *n.* a person or vessel engaged in hunting seals. [SEAL[2] + -ER[1]]
seal·er·y (sē′lə rē), *n., pl.* **-er·ies.** **1.** the occupation of hunting seals. **2.** a place where seals are caught.
sea′ let′tuce, any seaweed of the genus *Ulva*, having large leaflike blades.
sea′ lev′el, the horizontal plane or level corresponding to the surface of the sea at mean level between high and low tide.
sea′ lil′y, a stalked, sessile crinoid.
seal′ing wax′, a resinous preparation, soft when heated, used for sealing letters, documents, etc. [ME *seling wax*]
sea′ li′on, any of several large, eared seals, as *Zalophus californicus* (**California sea lion**) of the Pacific coast of North America.

Sea lion, *Eumetopias jubata* (Length 10 ft.)

seal′ point′, a Siamese cat having a fawn-colored body and dark-brown points.
seal′ ring′, a finger ring bearing an incised design for embossing a wax seal.
seal·skin (sēl′skin′), *n.* **1.** the skin of a seal. **2.** the skin or fur of the fur seal when prepared for making garments or leather items. **3.** a garment or article made of this fur. —*adj.* **4.** made of sealskin: *a sealskin purse.* [ME *seleskin.* See SEAL[2], SKIN]
sea′ lung′wort, a boraginaceous herb, *Mertensia maritima*, growing on northern seacoasts.
Seal′y·ham ter′rier (sē′lē ham′, -lē əm), one of a Welsh breed of small terriers having short legs, a docked tail, and a wiry, mostly white coat. [named after *Sealyham*, Wales, where it was first bred]

Sealyham terrier (10½ in. high at shoulder)

seam (sēm), *n.* **1.** the line formed by sewing together pieces of cloth, leather, or the like. **2.** the stitches used to make such a line. **3.** any line formed by abutting edges. **4.** any linear indentation or mark, as a wrinkle or scar. **5.** *Knitting.* a line of stitches formed by purling. **6.** *Geol.* a comparatively thin stratum; a bed, as of coal. —*v.t.* **7.** to join with or as with stitches; make the seam or seams of. **8.** to furrow; mark with wrinkles, scars, etc. **9.** *Knitting.* to knit with or in a seam. —*v.i.* **10.** to become cracked, fissured, or furrowed. **11.** *Knitting.* to make a line of stitches by purling. [ME *seme*, OE *sēam;* c. G *Saum* hem; akin to SEW] —**seam′er,** *n.* —**seam′less,** *adj.*
sea-maid (sē′mād′), *n.* **1.** a mermaid. **2.** a goddess or nymph of the sea. Also, **sea-maid·en** (sē′mād′ən).
sea·man (sē′mən), *n., pl.* **-men.** **1.** a person skilled in seamanship. **2.** a man whose trade or occupation is assisting in the handling, sailing, and navigating of a ship during a voyage, esp. one below the rank of officer; sailor. **3.** *Navy.* an enlisted rating below petty officer. [ME *seeman*, OE *sǣmann*] —**sea′man·like′,** *adj.* —**Syn.** See **sailor.**
sea·man·ship (sē′mən ship′), *n.* the knowledge of and skill in all things pertaining to the operation, navigation, safety, and maintenance of a ship.
sea·mark (sē′märk′), *n.* a conspicuous object on land, visible from the sea, and serving to guide or warn mariners, as a beacon. [ME *see marke*]
sea′ mew′, a sea gull, esp. a common European species, *Larus canus.*
sea·mount (sē′mount′), *n.* a submarine mountain rising several hundred fathoms above the floor of the sea but having its summit well below the surface.
sea′ mouse′, any of several large, marine annelids of the genus *Aphrodite* and related genera, having a covering of long, fine, hairlike setae.
seam·stress (sēm′stris *or, esp. Brit.*, sem′-), *n.* a woman whose occupation is sewing. Also, **sempstress.** [< ME *sem(e)ster* (OE *sēamestre* = *sēam* SEAM + *-estre* -STER) + -ESS]
seam·y (sē′mē), *adj.*, **seam·i·er, seam·i·est.** **1.** unpleasant; disagreeable; sordid: *the seamy side of life.* **2.** having, showing, or of the nature of a seam. —**seam′i·ness,** *n.*
sé·ance (sā′äns), *n.* **1.** a meeting in which a spiritualist attempts to communicate with the spirits of the dead. **2.** a session or sitting, as of a class or organization. [< F: session = *sé-*, root of *seoir* to sit (< L *sedēre*) + *-ance* -ANCE]
sea′ on′ion, a liliaceous plant, *Urginea maritima*, of Mediterranean regions, yielding medicinal squill.
sea′ ot′ter, a marine otter, *Enhydra lutris*, of the shores of the northern Pacific.
sea′ pen′, any of several colonial coelenterates of the genus *Pennatula* and related genera, having the shape of a fleshy feather.
sea·plane (sē′plān′), *n.* an airplane provided with floats for taking off from and landing on water.

Sea otter (Total length 4 ft.; tail 1 ft.)

sea·port (sē′pōrt′, -pôrt′), *n.* **1.** a port or harbor on or accessible to a seacoast and providing accommodation for seagoing vessels. **2.** a town or city at such a place.

sea′ pow′er, 1. a nation that possesses formidable naval power. 2. naval strength.
sea′ purse′, the horny egg case of certain rays and sharks.
sea·quake (sē′kwāk′), *n.* an agitation of the sea caused by a submarine eruption or earthquake.
sear[1] (sēr), *v.t.* 1. to burn or char the surface of: *She seared the steak to seal in the juices.* 2. to mark with a branding iron. 3. to burn or scorch injuriously or painfully: *He seared his hand on a hot steam pipe.* 4. to make callous or unfeeling; harden. 5. to dry up or wither; parch. —*v.i.* 6. to become dry or withered, as vegetation. —*n.* 7. a mark or scar made by searing. —*adj.* 8. sere[1]. [ME *sere* (v., adj.), OE *sēarian* (v.) < *sēar* (adj.); c. D *zoor*]
sear[2] (sēr), *n.* a pivoted piece that holds the hammer at full cock or half cock in the firing mechanism of small arms. [< MF *serre* a grip < *serre(r)* (to) lock up, close < VL **serrāre* < LL *serāre* to bar (a door) < L *ser(a)* door bar; VL *-rr-* unexplained]
sea′ ra′ven, a large marine fish of the genus *Hemitripterus,* as *H. americanus,* common on the northern Atlantic coast of America.
search (sûrch), *v.t.* 1. to go or look through (a place, area, etc.) carefully in order to find something missing or lost. 2. to look at or examine (a person, object, etc.) carefully in order to find something concealed: *The police searched the suspect for the missing gems.* 3. to explore or examine in order to discover: *He searched the hills for gold.* 4. to look at, read, or examine (a record, writing, collection, repository, etc.) for information: *He searched the courthouse for a record of the deed to the land.* 5. to probe (a wound, sinus, etc.) with a surgical instrument. 6. to uncover or find by examination or exploration (often fol. by *out*): *to search out all the facts.* —*v.i.* 7. to inquire, investigate, examine, or seek; conduct an examination or investigation. 8. **search me,** *Slang.* (used as a negative response to a query): *Search me; I don't know who took your pen.* —*n.* 9. the act or an instance of searching; careful examination or investigation. 10. the practice, on the part of naval officers of a belligerent nation, of boarding and examining a suspected neutral vessel at sea in order to ascertain its true nationality and determine if it is carrying contraband. [late ME *serche(n), cerche(n)* < OF *cerchie(r)* < LL *circāre* to go around < *circ(us)* circle] —**search′a·ble,** *adj.* —**search′er,** *n.*
search·ing (sûr′ching), *adj.* 1. examining carefully or thoroughly. 2. acutely observant or penetrating: *a searching glance.* 3. piercing or sharp: *a searching wind.* —**search′ing·ly,** *adv.*
search·light (sûrch′līt′), *n.* 1. a device, usually consisting of a light and reflector, for throwing a strong beam of light in any direction. 2. a beam of light so thrown.
search′ par′ty, a group of persons conducting an organized search for someone or something lost or hidden.
search′ war′rant, *Law.* a court order authorizing the examination of a dwelling or other private premises by police officials, as for stolen goods.
sea′ rob′in, any of various gurnards, esp. certain American species of the genus *Prionotus.*
sea′ room′, unobstructed space at sea in which a vessel can be easily maneuvered or navigated.
sea′ rov′er, 1. a pirate. 2. a pirate ship.
sea·scape (sē′skāp′), *n.* a view, sketch, painting, or photograph of the sea. [SEA + *-scape,* modeled on *landscape*]
sea·scout·ing (sē′skou′ting), *n.* the branch of scouting that trains older boy scouts in boating and other water activities. —**sea′scout′,** *n.* —**sea′ scout′.**
sea′ ser′pent, an enormous, imaginary, snakelike or dragonlike marine animal.
sea′ shell′, the shell of any marine mollusk.
sea·shore (sē′shōr′, -shôr′), *n.* 1. land along the sea or ocean. 2. *Law.* the ground between the ordinary high-water and low-water marks.
sea·sick (sē′sik′), *adj.* afflicted with seasickness.
sea·sick·ness (sē′sik′nis), *n.* nausea and dizziness, sometimes accompanied by vomiting, resulting from the rocking or swaying motion of a vessel in which one is traveling at sea. Cf. **motion sickness.**
sea·side (sē′sīd′), *n.* 1. the land along the sea. —*adj.* 2. situated on or pertaining to the seaside. [ME *seeside*]
Sea·side (sē′sīd′), *n.* a city in W California, on Monterey Bay. 35,935 (1970).
sea′ slug′, a nudibranch.
sea′ snake′, any of several venomous, marine snakes of the family *Hydrophidae,* having a finlike tail.
sea·son (sē′zən), *n.* 1. one of the four periods of the year (spring, summer, autumn, and winter), beginning astronomically at an equinox or solstice, but geographically at different dates in different climates. 2. a period of the year characterized by particular conditions of weather, temperature, etc.: *the rainy season.* 3. a period of the year when something is best or available: *the oyster season.* 4. a period of the year marked by certain conditions, activities, etc.: *the baseball season.* 5. a period of the year immediately before and after a special holiday or occasion: *the Christmas season.* 6. any period or time: *in the season of my youth.* 7. a suitable, proper, or fitting time: *It's not the season for frivolity.* 8. **in season, a.** in the time or state for use, eating, etc.: *Asparagus is now in season.* **b.** in heat. 9. **out of season,** not in season: *The price is so high because lilacs are out of season now.* —*v.t.* 10. to heighten or improve the flavor of (food) by adding condiments, spices, herbs, or the like. 11. to give relish or a certain character to: *conversation seasoned with wit.* 12. to mature, accustom, harden, or condition by exposure to certain conditions or treatment: *troops seasoned by battle; a writer seasoned by experience.* 13. to dry or otherwise treat (lumber) so as to harden it and render it immune to shrinkage, warpage, etc. —*v.i.* 14. to become seasoned, matured, accustomed, or the like. [ME *sesoun, seson* < OF *se(i)son* < L *satiōn-* (s. of *satiō*) a sowing (VL: sowing time) = *sa-* (root of *serere* to sow) + *-t-* ptp. suffix + *-iōn-* -ION] —**sea′soned·ly,** *adv.* —**sea′son·er,** *n.* —**sea′son·less,** *adj.*
sea·son·a·ble (sē′zə nə bəl), *adj.* 1. suitable to or characteristic of the season: *seasonable weather.* 2. timely; opportune. [late ME *sesounable*] —**sea′son·a·ble·ness,** *n.* —**sea′son·a·bly,** *adv.* —**Syn.** 2. See **opportune.**
sea·son·al (sē′zə nəl), *adj.* pertaining to, dependent on, or accompanying the seasons of the year or some particular season; periodical: *seasonal work.* —**sea·son·al·i·ty** (sē′zə nal′i tē), *n.* —**sea′son·al·ly,** *adv.* —**sea′son·al·ness,** *n.*
sea′sonal affec′tive disor′der, recurrent winter depression characterized by oversleeping, overeating, and irritability, and relieved by longer hours of daylight or by light therapy. *Abbr.:* SAD
sea·son·ing (sē′zə ning), *n.* salt or an herb, spice, or the like, for heightening or improving the flavor of food.
sea′son tick′et, a ticket for a specified series or number of events or valid for unlimited use during a specified time, usually sold at a reduced rate, for athletic events, concerts, transportation, etc.
sea′ squirt′, any tunicate, esp. a sessile ascidian, so called from its habit of contracting its body and ejecting streams of water when disturbed.
seat (sēt), *n.* 1. something designed to support a person in a sitting position, as a chair or bench; a place on or in which one sits. 2. the part of a chair, sofa, or the like, on which one sits. 3. the part of the body on which one sits; the buttocks. 4. the part of the garment covering it: *the seat of one's pants.* 5. a manner of or posture used in sitting, as on a horse. 6. something on which the base of an object rests. 7. the base itself. 8. a place in which something belongs, occurs, or is established; site; location. 9. a place in which administrative power or the like is centered: *Washington is the seat of the U.S. government.* 10. a part of the body considered as the place in which an emotion or function is centered: *The heart is the seat of passion.* 11. the office or authority of a king, bishop, etc.: *the episcopal seat.* 12. a space in which a spectator or patron may sit; accommodation for sitting, as in a theater, stadium, etc. 13. right of admittance to such a space, esp. as indicated by a ticket. 14. a right to sit as a member in a legislative or similar body: *He was elected to a seat in the senate.* 15. a right to the privileges of membership in a stock exchange or the like. 16. *Carpentry.* an inwardly inclined surface on the bottom of a rafter providing a level resting place on the wall plate. —*v.t.* 17. to place on a seat or seats; cause to sit down. 18. to usher to a seat or find a seat for: *The usher seated us in the front row.* 19. to have seats for; accommodate with seats: *a theater that seats 1200 people.* 20. to put a seat on or into (a chair, garment, etc.). 21. to install in a position or office of authority, in a legislative body, etc. 22. to attach to or place firmly in or on something as a base: *Seat the telescope on the tripod.* [ME *sete* < Scand; cf. Icel *sæti;* c. D *gezeet,* G *Gesäss;* cf. OE *sǣt* house] —**seat′er,** *n.* —**seat′less,** *adj.*
sea′ tan′gle, any of various seaweeds, esp. of the genus *Laminaria.*
seat′ belt′, a webbed belt or strap secured to the seat of an automobile, airplane, etc., for fastening around the midsection of the passenger to keep him safely secured to his seat, as during a sudden stop. Also called **safety belt.**
seat·ing (sē′ting), *n.* 1. the act or an instance of furnishing with, assigning, or escorting to a seat or seats. 2. the arrangement of seats in a theater, stadium, etc. 3. material for seats, esp. upholstery. —*adj.* 4. of or pertaining to seats or those who are sitting: *the seating plan of a theater.*
SEATO (sē′tō), *n.* an organization formed in Manila (1954), comprising Australia, Great Britain, France, New Zealand, the Philippines, Thailand, and the United States, for collective defense against aggression in southeast Asia and the southwest Pacific: abolished in 1977. [*S(outh)e(ast) A(sia) T(reaty) O(rganization)*]
seat-of-the-pants (sēt′ əv thə pants′), *adj.* 1. done without the aid of aircraft instruments: *seat-of-the-pants flying.* 2. depending on instinct and experience rather than carefully organized or planned programs.
sea·train (sē′trān′), *n.* a ship for the transportation of loaded railroad cars.
sea′ trout′, 1. any of various species of trout found in salt water, as the salmon trout, *Salmo trutta.* 2. any of several fishes of the genus *Cynoscion.*
Se·at·tle (sē at′əl), *n.* a seaport in W Washington, on Puget Sound. 530,831 (1970).
seat·work (sēt′wûrk′), *n.* *Educ.* work that can be done by a child at his seat in school without supervision.
sea′ ur′chin, any echinoderm of the class *Echinoidea,* having a somewhat globular or discoid form, and a shell composed of many calcareous plates covered with projecting spines.

A B

Sea urchin, *Arbacia punctulata* A, With spines; B, Without spines

sea′ valve′, *Naut.* seacock.
sea′ wall′, a strong wall or embankment to prevent the encroachments of the sea, serve as a breakwater, etc. —**sea′-walled′,** *adj.*
sea′ wal′nut, a ctenophore, as of the genus *Mnemiopsis,* shaped like a walnut.
sea·ward (sē′wərd), *adv.* 1. Also, **sea′wards.** toward the sea: *a storm moving seaward.* —*adj.* 2. facing or tending toward the sea: *a seaward course.* 3. coming from the sea: *a seaward wind.* —*n.* 4. the direction toward the sea or away from the land.
sea·ware (sē′wâr′), *n.* seaweed, esp. coarse, large seaweed, used chiefly as a fertilizer. [OE *sǣwār* = *sǣ* SEA + *wār* seaweed]
sea·way (sē′wā′), *n.* 1. a way over the sea. 2. the progress of a ship through the waves. 3. a more or less rough sea: *a hard vessel to steer in a seaway.* 4. a canal, enlarged river, etc., giving access to a landlocked port by ocean-going vessels. [ME *seewey,* OE *sǣweg*]
sea·weed (sē′wēd′), *n.* 1. any plant or plants growing in the ocean. 2. a marine alga.
sea′ wolf′, 1. any of several large, voracious, marine fishes, as the wolffish or sea bass. 2. a pirate. [ME *seewolf*]
sea·wor·thy (sē′wûr′thē), *adj.* (of a vessel) made ready or being safe for a voyage at sea. —**sea′wor′thi·ness,** *n.*

sea′ wrack′, seaweed or a growth of seaweed, esp. of the larger kinds cast up on the shore.

seb-, var. of **sebi-** before a vowel: *sebaceous.*

se·ba·ceous (si bā′shəs), *adj. Physiol.* **1.** pertaining to, of the nature of, or resembling tallow or fat; fatty; greasy. **2.** secreting a fatty substance. [< NL *sēbāceus*]

seba′ceous gland′, any of the cutaneous glands which secrete oily matter for lubricating hair and skin.

se·bac·ic (si bas′ik, -bā′sik), *adj. Chem.* of or derived from sebacic acid. [SEBAC(EOUS) + -IC]

sebac′ic ac′id, *Chem.* a dibasic acid, $HOOC(CH_2)_8$-COOH, used in the manufacture of plasticizers and resins. [SEBAC(EOUS) + -IC] **—se·bas·ic** (si bas′ik, -bā′sik), *adj.*

Se·bas·tian (si bas′chən), *n.* **Saint,** died A.D. 288?, Roman martyr.

Se·bas·to·pol (si bas′tə pōl′), *n.* Sevastopol.

SEbE, See **southeast by east.**

sebi-, a combining form of **sebum:** *sebiferous.* Also, **sebo-;** *esp. before a vowel,* **seb-.**

se·bif·er·ous (si bif′ər əs), *adj. Biol.* sebaceous.

seb·or·rhe·a (seb′ə rē′ə), *n. Pathol.* an excessive and abnormal discharge from the sebaceous glands. Also, **seb′or·rhoe′a.** **—seb′or·rhe′al, seb′or·rhe′ic,** *adj.*

Se·bring (sē′bring), *n.* a town in central Florida: auto racing. 7223 (1970).

SEbS, See **southeast by south.**

se·bum (sē′bəm), *n. Physiol.* the fatty secretion of the sebaceous glands. [< L: tallow, grease]

sec[1] (sek), *adj.* (of wines) dry; not sweet. [< F]

sec[2] (sek), *n. Informal.* second[2] (def. 3). [by shortening]

sec[3] (sēk), *n. Trig.* secant. [by shortening]

SEC, *U.S. Govt.* Securities and Exchange Commission: a board charged with regulating the public offer and sale of securities. Also, **S.E.C.**

sec., **1.** second. **2.** secondary. **3.** secretary. **4.** sector.

se·cant (sē′kant, -kənt), *n.* **1.** *Geom.* an intersecting line, esp. one intersecting a curve at two or more points. **2.** *Trig.* **a.** (in a right triangle) the ratio of the hypotenuse to the side adjacent to a given angle. **b.** (originally) a line from the center of a circle through one extremity of an arc to the tangent from the other extremity. **c.** the ratio of the length of this line to that of the radius of the circle; the reciprocal of the cosine of a given angle or arc. *Abbr.:* sec **—*adj.*** **3.** cutting or intersecting, as one line or surface in relation to another. [< L *secant-* (s. of *secāns,* prp. of *secāre* to cut) = *sec-* (see SAW[1]) + *-ant-* -ANT] **—se′cant·ly,** *adv.*

Secant ACB being the angle, the ratio of BC to AC is the secant; or, AC being taken as unity, the secant is BC; BC secant of arc AD

se·cede (si sēd′), *v.i.,* **-ced·ed, -ced·ing.** to withdraw formally from an alliance, federation, or association, as from a political union or religious organization. [< L *sēcēd(ere)* (to) withdraw] **—se·ced′er,** *n.*

se·cern (si sûrn′), *v.t.* to discriminate or distinguish in thought. [< L *sēcern(ere)* = *sē-* SE- + *cernere* to sift] **—se·cern′ment,** *n.*

se·ces·sion (si sesh′ən), *n.* **1.** the act or an instance of seceding. **2.** (*often cap.*) *U.S. Hist.* the withdrawal from the Union of 11 Southern States in the period 1860–61, which brought on the Civil War. [< L *sēcessiōn-* (s. of *sēcessiō*) withdrawal = *sēcess(us)* (ptp. of *sēcēdere* to SECEDE) + *-iōn-* -ION] **—se·ces′sion·al,** *adj.*

se·ces·sion·ist (si sesh′ə nist), *n.* **1.** a person who secedes, advocates secession, or claims secession as a constitutional right. **—*adj.*** **2.** of or pertaining to secession or secessionists. **—se·ces′sion·ism,** *n.*

sech, hyperbolic secant. [SEC(ANT) + H(YPERBOLIC)]

sec. leg., according to law. [< L *secundum lēgem*]

se·clude (si klōōd′), *v.t.,* **-clud·ed, -clud·ing.** **1.** to place in or withdraw into solitude; remove from social contact and activity, etc. **2.** to isolate; shut off; keep apart. [< L *sēclūde(re)* = *sē-* SE- + *claudere* to bolt, bar]

se·clud·ed (si klōō′did), *adj.* **1.** sheltered or screened from general activity, view, etc.: *a secluded cottage.* **2.** withdrawn from or involving little human or social activity: *a secluded life.* **—se·clud′ed·ly,** *adv.* **—se·clud′ed·ness,** *n.* **—Syn.** **1.** isolated, sequestered. **2.** cloistered, private, secret.

se·clu·sion (si klōō′zhən), *n.* **1.** an act of secluding. **2.** the state of being secluded; retirement; solitude: *He sought seclusion in his study.* **3.** a secluded place. [< ML *sēclūsiōn-* (s. of *sēclūsiō*) = L *sēclūs(us)* (ptp. of *sēclūdere* to SECLUDE) + *-iōn-* -ION]

se·clu·sive (si klōō′siv), *adj.* **1.** tending to seclude, esp. oneself. **2.** causing or providing seclusion. [*secluse* (< L *sēclūs(us)* secluded) + -IVE] **—se·clu′sive·ness,** *n.*

sec·o·bar·bi·tal (sek′ō bär′bi tal′, -tôl′), *n. Pharm.* a white, odorless, slightly bitter powder, $C_{12}H_{18}N_2O_3$, used chiefly in the form of its sodium salt as a sedative and hypnotic. [SECO(NAL) + BARBITAL]

Sec·o·nal (sek′ə nôl′, -nal′, -nəl), *n. Pharm., Trademark.* secobarbital.

sec·ond[1] (sek′ənd), *adj.* **1.** next after the first; being the ordinal number for two. **2.** being one of two equal parts. **3.** next after the first in place, time, or value: *the second house from the corner.* **4.** next after the first in rank, grade, degree, status, or importance: *He was promoted from the second team before the next game.* **5.** alternate: *I have my hair cut every second week.* **6.** inferior. **7.** *Gram.* noting or pertaining to the second person. **8.** *Music.* being the lower of two parts for the same instrument or voice: *second horn; second alto.* **9.** other or another: *a second Solomon; We had beans and then a second vegetable.* **10.** *Auto.* of, pertaining to, or operating at the second lowest gear transmission ratio: *second gear.* **—*n.*** **11.** a second part, esp. of one (½). **12.** the second member of a series. **13.** a person who aids or supports another; assistant; backer. **14.** *Boxing.* a person who, between rounds of a prize fight, gives aid, advice, etc., to a boxer. **15.** a person who serves as a representative or attendant of a duelist. **16.** *Auto.* second gear: *He shifted into second.* **17.** a person who or thing that is next after the first in place, time, or value. **18.** a person who or thing that is next after the first in rank, grade, degree, status, or importance. **19.** Often, **seconds.** an additional helping of food: *He had seconds on the meat and potatoes.* **20.** (in parliamentary procedure) **a.** a person who expresses formal support of a motion so that it may be discussed or put to a vote. **b.** the act or an instance of doing this. **21.** (in certain British universities) a type or grade of college degree granted according to a student's performance on specific written and oral examinations. **22.** *Music.* **a.** a tone on the next degree from a given tone. **b.** the interval between such tones. **c.** the harmonic combination of such tones. **d.** the lower of two parts in a piece of concerted music. **e.** a voice or instrument performing such a part. **f.** an alto. **23.** Usually, **seconds.** *Com.* a product or goods below the first or highest quality, esp. containing visible flaws. **24.** *Baseball.* See **second base.** **—*v.t.*** **25.** to assist or support. **26.** to further or advance, as aims. **27.** (in parliamentary procedure) to express formal support of (a motion, proposal, etc.), as a necessary preliminary to further discussion or to voting. **28.** to act as second to (a boxer, duelist, etc.). **—*adv.*** **29.** in the second place; secondly: *The catcher is batting second in today's lineup.* [ME < OF < L *secund(us)* following, next, second = *sec-* (root of *sequī* to follow) + *-undus* adj. suffix] **—sec′ond·er,** *n.*

sec·ond[2] (sek′ənd), *n.* **1.** the sixtieth part of a minute of time. **2.** the sixtieth part of a minute of degree, often represented by the sign (″), as in 12° 10′ 30″, read as 12 degrees, 10 minutes, and 30 seconds. **3.** a moment or instant: *It takes only a second to phone.* [ME *seconde* < MF < ML *secund(a)* (*minūta*) second (minute); see SECOND[1]]

sec·ond·ar·y (sek′ən der′ē), *adj., n., pl.* **-ar·ies.** **—*adj.*** **1.** next after the first in order, place, time, importance, etc. **2.** belonging or pertaining to a second order, division, stage, period, rank, grade, etc. **3.** derived or derivative; not primary or original: *secondary sources of historical research.* **4.** of minor importance; subordinate; auxiliary. **5.** of or pertaining to secondary schools. **6.** *Chem.* **a.** involving or obtained by the replacement of two atoms or groups. **b.** noting or containing a carbon atom united to two other carbon atoms in a chain or ring molecule. **7.** *Elect.* noting or pertaining to the current induced by a primary winding or to the winding in which the current is induced in an induction coil, transformer, or the like. **8.** *Geol.* noting or pertaining to a mineral produced from another mineral by decay, alteration, or the like. **9.** *Gram.* **a.** derived. **b.** derived from a word which is itself a derived word: *a secondary derivative.* **c.** having reference to past time; noting or pertaining to a past tense: *the Latin, Greek, or Sanskrit secondary tenses.* Cf. **primary** (def. 9). **10.** *Ornith.* pertaining to any of a set of flight feathers on the second segment of a bird's wing. **11.** *Linguistics.* of, pertaining to, or characteristic of a secondary accent. **—*n.*** **12.** one who or that which is secondary. **13.** a subordinate, assistant, deputy, or agent. **14.** *Elect.* a winding in a transformer or the like in which a current is induced by a primary winding. **15.** *Football.* the defensive unit that lines up behind the linemen. [< L *secundāri(us).* See SECOND[1], -ARY] **—sec·ond·ar·i·ly** (sek′ən der′ə lē, sek′ən dâr′-), *adv.*

sec′ondary ac′cent, a stress accent weaker than a primary accent. Also called **sec′ondary stress′.**

sec′ondary cell′, *Elect.* See **storage cell.**

sec′ondary col′or, a color, as orange, green, or violet, produced by mixing two primary colors.

sec′ondary emis′sion, the emission of electrons (**sec′ondary elec′trons**) from a material that is bombarded with electrons or ions.

sec′ondary inten′tion. See under **intention** (def. 4b).

sec′ondary school′, a high school or a school of corresponding grade, ranking between a primary school and a college or university. **—sec′ond·ar′y-school′,** *adj.*

sec′ondary sex′ characteris′tic, *Med.* any of a number of manifestations specific to each sex and incipient at puberty but not essential to reproduction, as development of breasts or beard, muscularity, distribution of fat tissue, and change of pitch in voice. Also called **sec′ondary sex′ char′acter.**

sec′ondary syph′ilis, *Pathol.* the second stage of syphilis, characterized by eruptions of the skin and mucous membrane.

Sec′ond Bal′kan War′. See **Balkan War** (def. 2).

sec′ond base′, *Baseball.* **1.** the second in order of the bases from home plate. **2.** the position of the player covering the area of the infield between second and first bases.

sec′ond base′man, *Baseball.* the player whose position is second base.

sec′ond best′, **1.** the next to the best in performance, achievement, craftsmanship, etc. **2.** of or pertaining to the next to the best in performance, achievement, craftsmanship, etc. **—sec′ond-best′,** *adj.*

sec′ond child′hood, senility; dotage.

sec′ond class′, **1.** the class of accommodations, as on a train, that is less costly and luxurious than first class but more costly and luxurious than third class. Cf. **cabin class.** **2.** (in the U.S. postal system) the class of mail consisting of newspapers and periodicals not sealed against postal inspection. **3.** (in certain British universities) the group receiving next to highest distinction in an honors course.

sec·ond-class (sek′ənd klas′, -kläs′), *adj.* **1.** of a secondary class or quality. **2.** second-rate; inferior.

Sec′ond Com′ing, the coming of Christ on Judgment Day. Also called **Second Advent.**

sec′ond cous′in, a son or a daughter of a first cousin. Cf. **cousin** (def. 1).

sec′ond-de·gree′ burn′ (sek′ənd di grē′), *Pathol.* See under **burn**[1] (def. 31).

sec′ond deriv′ative, *Math.* the derivative of the derivative of a function: *Acceleration is the second derivative of distance with respect to time.*

Sec′ond Em′pire, the empire established in France (1852–70) by Louis Napoleon: the successor to the Second Republic; replaced by the Third Republic.

sec′ond estate′, the second of the three estates: the nobles in France; the lords temporal in England. Cf. **estate** (def. 5).

sec′ond fid′dle, 1. a secondary role: *to play second fiddle to another person.* 2. a person serving in a subsidiary capacity, esp. to one immediately superior.

sec′ond floor′, 1. the floor or story above the ground floor. 2. (in Britain and elsewhere outside the U.S.) the second story completely above ground level. Cf. **first floor.** Also called **second story.**

sec′ond growth′, the plant growth that follows the destruction of virgin forest.

sec·ond-guess (sek′ənd ges′), *v.t.* 1. to use hindsight in criticizing or correcting. 2. to predict (something) or outguess (someone): *We must try to second-guess what he'll do next.* —**sec′ond-guess′er,** *n.*

sec·ond hand (sek′ənd hand′ *for 1;* sek′ənd hand′ *for 2*), 1. the hand that indicates the seconds on a clock or watch. 2. an assistant or helper, as to a worker or foreman. 3. **at second hand,** from or through an intermediate source or means: *She got the information only at second hand.*

sec·ond·hand (sek′ənd hand′), *adj.* 1. not directly known or experienced; obtained from others or from books: *Most of his knowledge is secondhand.* 2. previously used or owned: *secondhand clothes.* 3. dealing in previously used goods: *a secondhand bookseller.* —*adv.* 4. when used or after being used or owned by another: *He bought the guitar secondhand.* 5. indirectly; by way of an intermediate source: *He heard the news secondhand.* —**sec′ond-hand′ed·ness,** *n.*

sec′ond inten′tion. See under **intention** (def. 4b).

Sec′ond Interna′tional, an international association formed in 1889 in Paris, uniting socialistic groups of various countries: in 1923 it joined with the Vienna International to form the Labor and Socialist International. Cf. **international** (def. 5).

sec′ond law′ of mo′tion, *Physics.* See under **law of motion.**

sec′ond law′ of thermodynam′ics. See under **law of thermodynamics.**

sec′ond lieuten′ant, *U.S. Mil.* an Army, Air Force, or Marine officer of the lowest commissioned rank. Cf. **ensign** (def. 4).

sec·ond·ly (sek′ənd lē), *adv.* in the second place; second.

sec′ond mate′, the officer of a merchant vessel next in command beneath the first mate. Also called **second officer.**

sec′ond mort′gage, a mortgage the lien of which is next in priority to a first mortgage.

sec′ond na′ture, an acquired habit or tendency that is so deeply ingrained as to appear automatic.

se·con·do (si kon′dō, -kōn′-; *It.* se kôn′dô), *n., pl.* **-di** (-dē). *Music.* the second or lower part in a duet, esp. in a piano duet. [< It; see SECOND[1]]

sec′ond of′ficer, *Naut.* See **second mate.**

sec′ond pa′per, *U.S. Informal.* (before 1952) an official petition for naturalization by a resident alien desiring to become a citizen, filed two years after his first paper and upon having lived in the U.S. for five years.

sec′ond per′son, *Gram.* the person used by a speaker in referring to the one or ones to whom he is speaking: in English *you* is a second person pronoun.

sec·ond-rate (sek′ənd rāt′), *adj.* 1. of lesser or minor quality, importance, worth, or the like: *a second-rate poet.* 2. inferior; mediocre: *a second-rate performance.* —**sec′ond-rate′ness,** *n.* —**sec′ond-rat′er,** *n.*

Sec′ond Reich′, the German Empire 1871–1919.

Sec′ond Repub′lic, the republic established in France in 1848 and replaced by the Second Empire in 1852.

sec′ond sheet′, 1. a sheet of blank stationery, used in a letter as the second and following pages to a sheet having a letterhead. 2. a sheet of lightweight paper, usually of inferior quality, on which a carbon copy is made.

sec′ond sight′, a supposed faculty of seeing future events; clairvoyance. —**sec′ond-sight′ed,** *adj.* —**sec′ond-sight′ed·ness,** *n.*

sec′ond sto′ry. See **second floor.**

sec·ond-sto·ry (sek′ənd stōr′ē, -stôr′ē), *adj.* 1. of or located on the second story or floor. 2. *Informal.* breaking in or carried out by breaking in through an upper-story window in order to burglarize an apartment or house: *The police said the theft was a second-story job.*

sec′ond-sto′ry man′, *Informal.* a burglar who enters through upstairs windows.

sec′ond thought′, 1. Often, **second thoughts.** reservation about a previous action, decision, judgment, or the like. 2. **on second thought,** after reconsideration: *On second thought, I don't think I'll go.*

sec′ond wind′ (wind), 1. the return of ease in breathing, due to restored normal operation of the heart, after exhaustion caused by continued physical exertion, as in running. 2. the energy for a renewed effort to continue an undertaking.

Sec′ond World′ War′. See **World War II.**

se·cre·cy (sē′kri sē), *n., pl.* **-cies.** 1. the state or condition of being secret, hidden, or concealed. 2. privacy; seclusion. 3. the habit or characteristic of being secretive; reticence. [obs. *secre* (< MF *secré* SECRET) + -CY; r. ME *secretee* = *secre* + *-tee* -TY[2]]

se·cret (sē′krit), *adj.* 1. done, made, or conducted without the knowledge of others: *secret negotiations between Germany and Italy.* 2. kept from the knowledge of any but the initiated or privileged: *a secret password.* 3. faithful in keeping a confidence; reticent. 4. designed or working to escape notice, knowledge, or observation: *a secret drawer; the secret police.* 5. secluded, sheltered, or withdrawn: *a secret hiding place.* 6. beyond ordinary human understanding; esoteric. 7. *U.S. Govt., Mil.* (of information, a document, etc.) **a.** bearing the classification *secret.* **b.** limited to persons authorized to use information, documents, etc., so classified. Cf. **classification** (def. 5). —*n.* 8. something that is or is kept secret, hidden, or concealed. 9. a mystery: *the secrets of nature.* 10. a reason or explanation not immediately or generally apparent. 11. a method, formula, plan, etc., known only to the initiated or the few: *the secret of happiness; a trade secret.* 12. *U.S. Govt., Mil.* a classification assigned to information, a document, etc., considered less vital to national security than top-secret but more vital than confidential, and limiting its use to persons who have been cleared by various government agencies as trustworthy to handle such material. Cf. **classification** (def. 5). 13. **in secret,** unknown to others; in private; secretly. [ME *secrette* < OF *secret* < L *sēcrēt(us)* hidden, orig. ptp. of *sēcernere* to SECERN] —**se′cret·ly,** *adv.* —**se′cret·ness,** *n.* —**Syn.** 1. clandestine, hidden, concealed, covert. 1, 2. private, confidential. 3. secretive. 6. occult.

se′cret a′gent, a person engaged in active espionage or counterespionage work for a secret service.

sec·re·tar·i·al (sek′ri târ′ē əl), *adj.* noting, of, or pertaining to a secretary or a secretary's skills and work.

sec·re·tar·i·at (sek′ri târ′ē ət), *n.* 1. the officials or office entrusted with administrative duties, maintaining records, and overseeing or performing secretarial duties, esp. for an international organization: *the secretariat of the United Nations.* 2. a group or department of secretaries. 3. the place where a secretary transacts business. Also, **sec′re·tar′i·ate.** [< F *secrétariat* < ML *sēcrētāriāt(us)*]

sec·re·tar·y (sek′ri ter′ē), *n., pl.* **-tar·ies.** 1. a person employed to handle correspondence and do routine work in a business office, usually involving taking dictation, typing, filing, and the like. 2. See **private secretary.** 3. a person, usually an official, who is in charge of the records, correspondence, minutes of meetings, and related affairs of an organization, company, association, etc. 4. (*often cap.*) an officer of state charged with the superintendence and management of a particular department of government, as a member of the president's cabinet in the U.S. 5. a piece of furniture for use as a writing desk. 6. Also called **sec′retary book′case.** a desk with bookshelves on top of it. [< ML *sēcrētāri(us)* < L *sēcrēt(um)* SECRET (n.) + *-ārius* -ARY] —**sec′re·tar′y·ship′,** *n.*

sec′retary bird′, a large, long-legged, raptorial bird, *Sagittarius serpentarius,* of Africa: so called from its crest which resembles quill pens stuck over the ear.

Secretary bird (Height 4 ft.)

sec·re·tar·y-gen·er·al (sek′ri ter′ē jen′ər əl), *n., pl.* **sec·re·tar·ies-gen·er·al.** the head or chief administrative officer of a secretariat.

sec′retary of state′, 1. the head and chief administrator of the U.S. Department of State. Cf. **foreign minister.** 2. any of several ministers in the British government: *the secretary of state for the Home Department.* 3. the appointed or elected official in a U.S. state government whose chief function is to distribute statutes, administer elections, keep archives, etc. Also, **Sec′retary of State′.**

se·crete[1] (si krēt′), *v.t.,* **-cret·ed, -cret·ing.** to discharge, generate, or release by the process of secretion. [back formation from SECRETION]

se·crete[2] (si krēt′), *v.t.,* **-cret·ed, -cret·ing.** to place out of sight; hide; conceal. [alter. of obs. *secret* (v. use of SECRET)] —**Syn.** See **hide**[1].

se·cre·tin (si krē′tin), *n. Biochem.* a hormone, produced in the small intestine, that activates the pancreas to secrete pancreatic juice.

se·cre·tion (si krē′shən), *n.* 1. (in a cell or gland) the act or process of separating, elaborating, and releasing a substance that fulfills some function within the organism or is excreted. 2. the product of this process. [< L *sēcrētiōn-* (s. of *sēcrētiō*) = *sēcrēt(us)* (ptp. of *sēcernere* to SECERN) + *-iōn-* -ION] —**se·cre·tion·ar·y** (si krē′shə ner′ē), *adj.*

se·cre·tive[1] (sē′kri tiv, si krē′-), *adj.* having a disposition to secrecy; reticent. [back formation from SECRETIVENESS (modeled on F *secrétivité*)] —**se′cre·tive·ly,** *adv.* —**se′cre·tive·ness,** *n.* —**Syn.** secret.

se·cre·tive[2] (si krē′tiv), *adj.* secretory. [SECRET(ION) + -IVE]

se·cre·to·ry (si krē′tə rē), *adj., n., pl.* **-ries.** —*adj.* 1. pertaining to secretion. 2. performing the process of secretion. —*n.* 3. a secretory organ, vessel, or the like.

se′cret serv′ice, 1. the branch of governmental service that conducts espionage and counterespionage activities. 2. (*caps.*) the branch of the U.S. Department of the Treasury charged chiefly with the discovery and apprehension of counterfeiters and of providing protection for the president and his immediate family. —**se′cret-serv′ice,** *adj.*

se′cret ser′vice man′, an agent of the Secret Service of the Department of the Treasury.

se′cret soci′ety, an organization, as a fraternal society, the members of which take secret initiation oaths, share secret passwords and rites, are bound to assist each other, etc.

Secs., 1. seconds. 2. sections.

sect (sekt), *n.* 1. a body of persons adhering to a particular religious faith; a religious denomination. 2. a group regarded as heretical or as deviating from a generally accepted religious tradition. 3. any group, party, or faction united by a specific doctrine or under a doctrinal leader. [ME *secte* < L *sect(a)* something to follow, pathway, course of conduct, school of thought, etc.; akin to *sequī* to follow]

-sect, a word element occurring in loan words from Latin, where it meant "cut": *intersect.* [< L *sect(us)* (ptp. of *secāre* to cut) = *sec-* (see SAW[1]) + *-tus* ptp. suffix]

sect., section.

sec·tar·i·an (sek târ′ē ən), *adj.* 1. of or pertaining to sectaries or sects. 2. narrowly confined or devoted to a particular sect. 3. narrowly confined or limited in interest, purpose, scope, etc. —*n.* 4. a member of a sect. [SECTARY + -AN] —**sec·tar′i·an·ly,** *adv.*

sec·tar·i·an·ise (sek târ′ē ə nīz′), *v.t.,* **-ised, -is·ing.** *Chiefly Brit.* sectarianize.

sec·tar·i·an·ism (sek târ′ē ə niz′əm), *n.* the spirit or tendencies of sectarians; adherence or excessive devotion to a particular sect, esp. in religion.

sec·tar·i·an·ize (sek târ′ē ə nīz′), *v.t.,* **-ized, -iz·ing.** to make sectarian. Also, *esp. Brit.,* **sectarianise.**

sec·ta·ry (sek′tə rē), *n., pl.* **-ries.** 1. a member of a particular sect, esp. of a heretical or schismatic religious sect. **2.** a Protestant of nonconformist denomination, esp. a minor one. **3.** a person zealously devoted to a particular sect. [< ML *sectārī(us).* See SECT, -ARY]

sec·tile (sek′til), *adj.* capable of being cut smoothly with a knife. [< L *sectilis* = *sect(us)* (ptp. of *secāre* to cut) + *-ilis* -ILE] —**sec·til′i·ty,** *n.*

sec·tion (sek′shən), *n.* **1.** a part that is cut off or separated. **2.** a distinct part or subdivision of anything, as an object, area, community, class, or the like: *the left section of a drawer; the poor section of town.* **3.** a distinct part or subdivision of a writing, as of a newspaper, legal code, chapter, etc.: *the financial section of a daily paper; section 2 of the bylaws.* **4.** one of a number of parts that can be fitted together to make a whole: *sections of a fishing rod.* **5.** (in most of the U.S. west of Ohio) one of the 36 numbered subdivisions, each one mile square, of a township. **6.** the act or an instance of cutting. **7.** *Surg.* **a.** the making of an incision. **b.** an incision. **8.** a thin slice of a tissue, mineral, or the like, as for microscopic examination. **9.** a representation of an object as it would appear if cut by a plane, showing its internal structure. **10.** *Mil.* **a.** a small unit consisting of two or more squads. **b.** Also called **staff section.** any of the subdivisions of a staff. **c.** a small tactical division in naval and air units. **11.** *Railroads.* **a.** a division of a sleeping car containing both an upper and a lower berth. **b.** a length of trackage, roadbed, signal equipment, etc., maintained by one crew. **12.** any of two or more trains, buses, or the like, running on the same route and scheduled at the same time, one right behind the other, and considered as one unit, as when a second is necessary to accommodate more passengers than the first can carry. **13.** a segment of a naturally segmented fruit, as of an orange or grapefruit. **14.** a division of an orchestra or of a band containing all the instruments of one class: *a record featuring Duke Ellington's rhythm section.* —*v.t.* **15.** to cut or divide into sections. **16.** to cut through so as to present a section. **17.** *Surg.* to make an incision. [< L *sectiōn-* (s. of *sectiō*) a cutting = *sect(us)* (ptp. of *secāre* to cut) + *-iōn-* -ION] —**Syn. 1.** See **part.**

sec·tion·al (sek′shə nᵊl), *adj.* **1.** pertaining or limited to a particular section; local or regional: *sectional politics.* **2.** composed of several independent sections: *a sectional sofa.* **3.** of or pertaining to a section. —*n.* **4.** a sofa composed of several independent sections that can be arranged individually or in various combinations. —**sec′tion·al·ly,** *adv.*

sec·tion·al·ise (sek′shə nᵊlīz′), *v.t.,* **-ised, -is·ing.** *Chiefly Brit.* sectionalize. —**sec′tion·al·i·sa′tion,** *n.*

sec·tion·al·ism (sek′shə nᵊliz′əm), *n.* excessive regard for sectional or local interests; regional or local spirit, prejudice, etc. —**sec′tion·al·ist,** *n.*

sec·tion·al·ize (sek′shə nᵊlīz′), *v.t.,* **-ized, -iz·ing. 1.** to render sectional. **2.** to divide into sections, esp. geographical sections. Also, *esp. Brit.,* **sectionalise.** —**sec′tion·al·i·za′tion,** *n.*

sec′tion gang′, *Railroads U.S.* a group of workmen who take care of a section of railroad track.

sec′tion hand′, *Railroads U.S.* a workman who works on a section gang. Also called **tracklayer.**

sec·tor (sek′tər), *n.* **1.** *Geom.* a plane figure bounded by two radii and the included arc of a circle. **2.** a mathematical instrument consisting of two flat rulers hinged together at one end and bearing various scales. **3.** *Mil.* a designated defense area, usually in a combat zone, for which a particular military unit is responsible. —*v.t.* **4.** to divide into sectors. [< L: cutter; LL: sector = *sect(us)* (ptp. of *secāre* to cut) + *-or* -OR[2]] —**sec′tor·al,** *adj.*

sec·to·ri·al (sek tōr′ē əl, -tôr′-), *adj.* **1.** of or pertaining to a sector. **2.** *Zool.* (of teeth) adapted for cutting; carnassial. [< NL *sectōri(us)* (see SECTOR, -ORY[1]) + -AL[1]]

sec·u·lar (sek′yə lər), *adj.* **1.** of or pertaining to worldly things or to things that are not regarded as religious, spiritual, or sacred; temporal. **2.** not pertaining to or connected with religion (opposed to *sacred*): *secular music.* **3.** (of education, a school, etc.) concerned with nonreligious subjects. **4.** (of members of the clergy) not belonging to a religious order; not bound by monastic vows (opposed to *regular*). **5.** occurring or celebrated once in an age or century: *the secular games of Rome.* **6.** going on from age to age; continuing through long ages. —*n.* **7.** a layman. **8.** one of the secular clergy. [< ML *sēculār(is)* < LL *saeculāris* worldly, temporal (opposed to eternal) L: of an age = *saecul(um)* long period of time + *-āris* -AR[1]; r. ME *seculer* < OF < L, as above] —**sec′u·lar·ly,** *adv.*

sec′ular hu′manism, any set of beliefs that promotes human values without specific allusion to religious doctrines. —**sec′ular hu′manist.**

sec·u·lar·ism (sek′yə lə riz′əm), *n.* **1.** secular spirit or tendency, esp. a system of political or social philosophy that rejects all forms of religious faith. **2.** the view that public education and other matters of civil policy should be conducted without the introduction of a religious element. —**sec′u·lar·ist,** *n.* —**sec′u·lar·is′tic,** *adj.*

sec·u·lar·i·ty (sek′yə lar′i tē), *n., pl.* **-ties. 1.** secular views or beliefs; secularism. **2.** the state of being devoted to the affairs of the world; worldliness. **3.** a secular matter.

sec·u·lar·ize (sek′yə lə rīz′), *v.t.,* **-ized, -iz·ing. 1.** to make secular; separate from religious or spiritual connection or influences; imbue with secularism. **2.** to change (clergy) from regular to secular. **3.** to transfer (property) from ecclesiastical to civil possession or use. Also, *esp. Brit.,* **sec′u·lar·ise′.** —**sec′u·lar·i·za′tion,** *n.* —**sec′u·lar·iz′er,** *n.*

se·cund (sē′kund, sek′und), *adj. Bot., Zool.* arranged on one side only; unilateral. [< L *secund(us)* following. See SECOND[1]] —**se′cund·ly,** *adv.*

Se·cun·der·a·bad (sə kun′dər ə bad′), *n.* a city in central India, part of Hyderabad.

se·cun·dum (se ko͝on′do͝om; *Eng.* sə kun′dəm), *prep. Latin.* according to.

se·cure (si kyo͝or′), *adj., v.,* **-cured, -cur·ing.** —*adj.* **1.** free from or not exposed to danger; safe. **2.** dependable; firm; not liable to fail, yield, become displaced, etc., as a support or a fastening: *The building was secure, even in an earthquake.* **3.** affording safety, as a place: *He needed a secure hideout.* **4.** in safe custody or keeping: *Here in the vault the necklace was secure.* **5.** free from care; without anxiety: *emotionally secure.* **6.** firmly established, as a relationship or reputation. **7.** sure; certain; assured: *to be secure of victory; He was secure in his religious belief.* **8.** *Archaic.* overconfident. —*v.t.* **9.** to get hold or possession of; procure; obtain: *to secure materials; to secure a high government position.* **10.** to free from danger or harm; make safe: *The sandbags secured the town during the flood.* **11.** to effect; make certain of; ensure: *The novel secured his reputation.* **12.** to make firm or fast, as by attaching: *to secure a rope.* **13.** to assure a creditor of payment by the pledge or mortgaging of property. **14.** to lock or fasten against intruders: *Did you secure the doors and windows?* **15.** to protect from attack by taking cover, by building fortifications, etc.: *The regiment secured its position while awaiting the enemy attack.* **16.** to capture (a person or animal): *No one is safe until the murderer is secured.* **17.** to tie up (a person), esp. by binding his arms or hands; pinion: *Secure the prisoner so that he won't escape again.* —*v.i.* **18.** to be or become safe; have or obtain security. **19.** *Naut.* to cover openings and make movable objects fast: *The crew was ordered to secure for sea.* [< L *sēcūr(us)* carefree = *sē-* SE- + *cūr(a)* care (see CURE) + *-us* adj. suffix] —**se·cur′a·ble,** *adj.* —**se·cure′ly,** *adv.* —**se·cure′ness,** *n.* —**se·cur′er,** *n.* —**Syn. 1.** See **safe. 2.** stable, fast. **9.** See **get. 10.** protect, guard.

Secu′rities and Exchange′ Commis′sion. See **SEC.**

se·cu·ri·ty (si kyo͝or′i tē), *n., pl.* **-ties,** *adj.* —*n.* **1.** freedom from danger, risk, etc.; safety. **2.** freedom from care, apprehension, or doubt. **3.** something that secures or makes safe; protection; defense. **4.** freedom from financial cares or from want: *The insurance policy gave the widow security.* **5.** precautions taken to guard against theft, sabotage, the stealing of military secrets, etc.: *The senator claimed security was lax and potential enemies know our plans.* **6.** an assurance; guarantee. **7.** *Law.* **a.** something given or deposited as surety for the fulfillment of a promise or an obligation, the payment of a debt, etc. **b.** a person who becomes surety for another. **c.** an evidence of debt or of property, as a bond or a certificate of stock. **8.** Usually, **securities.** stocks and bonds. **9.** *Archaic.* overconfidence; cockiness. —*adj.* **10.** of, pertaining to, or serving as security: *a security guard.* [< L *sēcūritās*]

secu′rity an′alyst, a person who specializes in evaluating information regarding stocks and bonds, as by measuring the ratio of their prices to their dividends and earnings. Also, **secu′rities an′alyst.** —**secu′rity anal′ysis.**

secu′rity blan′ket, 1. a blanket, pillow, or the like clung to by a baby for reassurance and comfort. **2.** something that gives one a sense of protection.

Secu′rity Coun′cil, the committee of the United Nations charged with maintaining international peace, composed of five permanent members (U.S., U.S.S.R., France, United Kingdom, and the People's Republic of China) and ten temporary members each serving for two years.

sec'y, secretary. Also, **secy.**

se·dan (si dan′), *n.* **1.** *U.S.* an enclosed automobile body having two or four doors and seating four or more persons on two full-width seats. **2.** See **sedan chair.** [perh. < L *sēd-(ēs)* seat + unexplained *-an*]

Sedan chair

Se·dan (si dan′; *Fr.* sə däN′), *n.* a city in NE France, on the Meuse River: defeat and capture of Napoleon III 1870. 21,766 (1962).

sedan′ chair′, an enclosed vehicle for one person, borne on poles by two bearers and common during the 17th and 18th centuries.

se·date (si dāt′), *adj., v.,* **-dat·ed, -dat·ing.** —*adj.* **1.** calm, quiet, or composed; undisturbed by passion or excitement: *a sedate social gathering; a sedate young lady.* —*v.t.* **2.** to put (a person) under sedation. [< L *sēdāt(us)* (ptp. of *sēdāre* to allay, quieten); akin to *sedēre* to SIT[1]] —**se·date′ly,** *adv.* —**se·date′ness,** *n.* —**Syn. 1.** collected, serene, unperturbed. See **staid.**

se·da·tion (si dā′shən), *n. Med.* **1.** the calming of mental excitement or abatement of physiological function, esp. by the administration of a drug. **2.** such an induced state. [< L *sēdātiōn-* (s. of *sēdātiō*). See SEDATE, -ION]

sed·a·tive (sed′ə tiv), *adj.* **1.** tending to calm or soothe. **2.** *Med.* allaying irritability or excitement; assuaging pain; lowering functional activity. —*n.* **3.** a sedative agent or remedy. [< ML *sēdātīv(us).* See SEDATE, -IVE]

sed·en·tar·y (sed′ᵊn ter′ē), *adj.* **1.** characterized by or requiring a sitting posture: *a sedentary occupation.* **2.** accustomed to sit or rest a great deal or to take little exercise. **3.** *Chiefly Zool.* **a.** abiding in one place; not migratory. **b.** pertaining to animals that move about little or are permanently attached to something, as a barnacle. [< L *sedentāri(us)* sitting = *sedent-* (*sed-* (see SIT[1]) + *-ent-* -ENT) + *-ārius* -ARY] —**sed·en·tar·i·ly** (sed′ən târ′ə lē, sed′ᵊn ter′-), *adj.* —**sed′en·tar′i·ness,** *n.*

Se·der (sā′dər), *n. Judaism.* a ceremonial dinner, held on the first night of Passover by Reform Jews and Jews in Israel or on both the first and second nights by Orthodox and Conservative Jews outside of Israel, that includes the reading of the Haggadah, the eating of specified foods symbolic of the Israelites' bondage in Egypt and of the Exodus. [< Heb: order, division]

sedge (sej), *n.* **1.** any rushlike or grasslike cyperaceous plant of the genus *Carex,* growing in wet places. **2.** any cyperaceous plant. **3.** siege (def. 5). [ME *segge,* OE *secg;* akin to SAW[1]; presumably so named from its sawlike edges]

Sedge·moor (sej′mo͝or′), *n.* a plain in SW England, in central Somerset: final defeat of Monmouth 1685.

sedg·y (sej′ē), *adj.,* **sedg·i·er, sedg·i·est. 1.** abounding in or bordered with sedge. **2.** of or like sedge.

se·di·le (se dī′lē), *n., pl.* **-dil·i·a** (-dil′ē ə). *Eccles.* one of the seats (usually three) on the south side of the chancel, often recessed, for the use of the officiating clergy. [< L *sedīle* sitting place = *sed(ēre)* (to) sit + *-īle* n. suffix]

sed·i·ment (sed′ə mənt), *n.* **1.** matter that settles to the bottom of a liquid; lees; dregs. **2.** *Geol.* mineral or organic matter deposited by water, air, or ice. [< L *sediment(um)* = *sedi-* (comb. form of *sedēre* to sit, settle) + *-mentum* -MENT] —**sed′i·men′tous,** *adj.*

sed·i·men·ta·ry (sed′ə men′tə rē), *adj.* **1.** of, pertaining to, or of the nature of sediment. **2.** *Geol.* formed by the deposition of sediment, as certain rocks. Also, **sed′i·men′tal.** —**sed·i·men·tar·i·ly** (sed′ə mən târ′ə lē, sed′ə mən ter′ə-lē), *adv.*

sed·i·men·ta·tion (sed′ə mən tā′shən), *n.* the deposition or accumulation of sediment.

se·di·tion (si dish′ən), *n.* **1.** incitement of public disorder or rebellion against a government. **2.** any action, esp. in speech or writing, promoting such disorder or rebellion. **3.** *Archaic.* rebellious disorder. [< L *sēditiōn-* (s. of *sēditiō*) = *sēd-* SE- + *-itiōn-* a going (*it(us)*, ptp. of *īre* to go + *-iōn-* -ION); r. ME *sedicioun* < AF < L] —**Syn. 1.** insurrection, mutiny. See **treason.**

se·di·tion·ar·y (si dish′ə ner′ē), *adj., n., pl.* **-ar·ies.** —*adj.* **1.** of or pertaining to sedition; seditious. —*n.* **2.** a person guilty of sedition.

se·di·tious (si dish′əs), *adj.* **1.** of, pertaining to, or of the nature of sedition. **2.** given to or guilty of sedition. [ME *sedicious* = *sedici(oun)* SEDITION + *-ous* -OUS; cf. L *sēditiōsus*] —**se·di′tious·ly,** *adv.* —**se·di′tious·ness,** *n.*

se·duce (si dōōs′, -dyōōs′), *v.t.,* **-duced, -duc·ing. 1.** to lead astray, as from duty, rectitude, or the like; corrupt. **2.** to persuade or induce to have sexual intercourse. **3.** to lead or draw away, as from principles, faith, or allegiance: *He was seduced by the prospect of gain.* **4.** to win over; attract; entice: *a supermarket seducing customers with special sales.* [< L *sēdūce(re)* (to) lead aside = *sē-* SE- + *dūcere* to lead; r. ME *seduise* < MF < L, as above] —**se·duc′er,** *n.* —**se·duc′i·ble, se·duce′a·ble,** *adj.* —**se·duc′ing·ly,** *adv.* —**se·duc′-ive,** *adj.* —**Syn. 1.** beguile, inveigle, lure.

se·duc·tion (si duk′shən), *n.* **1.** the act or an instance of seducing, esp. sexually. **2.** the condition of being seduced. **3.** a means of seducing; enticement. Also, **se·duce·ment** (si-dōōs′mənt, -dyōōs′-). [< L *sēductiōn-* (s. of *sēductiō*) a leading aside = *sēduct(us)* (ptp. of *sēdūcere* to SEDUCE) + *-iōn* -ION]

se·duc·tive (si duk′tiv), *adj.* enticing; beguiling; captivating: *a seductive smile.* [SEDUCT(ION) + -IVE] —**se·duc′tive·ly,** *adv.* —**se·duc′tive·ness,** *n.* —**Syn.** tempting, alluring. —**Ant.** repellent.

se·duc·tress (si duk′tris), *n.* a woman who seduces. [obs. *seduct(o)r* + -ESS]

se·du·li·ty (si dōō′li tē, -dyōō′-), *n.* sedulous quality. [< L *sēdulitās* = *sēdul(us)* SEDULOUS + *-itās* -ITY]

sed·u·lous (sej′ə ləs), *adj.* **1.** diligent in application or attention; persevering. **2.** persistently or carefully maintained: *sedulous flattery.* [< L *sēdulus* careful (OL *sē dolō* without guile); r. *sedulious.* See SEDULI(TY), -OUS] —**sed′u·lous·ly,** *adv.* —**sed′u·lous·ness,** *n.* —**Syn. 1.** assiduous, constant, untiring, tireless.

se·dum (sē′dəm), *n.* any fleshy, crassulaceous plant of the genus *Sedum,* usually having yellow, white, or pink flowers. [< NL < L: houseleek]

see[1] (sē), *v.,* **saw, seen, see·ing.** —*v.t.* **1.** to perceive with the eyes; look at. **2.** to view; visit or attend as a spectator: *to see a play.* **3.** to perceive mentally; discern; understand: *He could see the point of the argument.* **4.** to construct a mental image of: *He still saw his father as he was 25 years ago.* **5.** to accept or imagine as acceptable: *I can't see him as president.* **6.** to be cognizant of; recognize: *He was able to see charming traits in not-so-charming people.* **7.** to foresee: *He could see war ahead.* **8.** to ascertain, learn, or find out: *See who is at the door.* **9.** to have knowledge or experience of: *to see service in the diplomatic corps.* **10.** to make sure: *See that the work is done.* **11.** to visit or to meet and converse with: *I'll see you at your house tonight. He finally saw the ambassador.* **12.** to receive as a visitor: *The ambassador finally saw him.* **13.** to court, keep company with, or date frequently: *She's seeing too much of the same boy.* **14.** to provide aid or assistance to; provide money, sympathy, encouragement, etc., to: *He's seeing his brother through college.* **15.** to attend or escort: *to see someone home.* **16.** *Cards.* to match (a bet) or match the bet of (a bettor) by staking an equal sum: *I'll see your five and raise you five more.* **17.** to prefer (someone or something) to be as indicated (usually used as a mild oath): *I'll see you in hell before I sell you this house. He'll see the business fail before he admits he's wrong about advertising.* **18.** to read. —*v.i.* **19.** to have the power of sight. **20.** to understand intellectually or spiritually; have insight: *Philosophy teaches us to see.* **21.** to give attention or care: *See to it that the work is done.* **22.** to find out; make inquiry: *Go and see for yourself.* **23.** to consider; think; deliberate: *Let me see—how does that song go?* **24.** to look about; observe: *See—the sun is out!* **25. see about, a.** to investigate; inquire about. **b.** See **see**[1] (def. 29). **26. see off,** to take leave of (someone) setting out on a journey by going to the place of departure: *I went to the airport to see him off.* **27. see out,** to remain with (a task, project, etc.) until its completion. **28. see through, a.** to penetrate to the true nature of; comprehend; detect: *He could see through her lies.* **b.** to stay with to the end or until completion; persevere: *He saw the project through.* **29. see to,** to turn one's attention to; take care of. Also, **see about.** [ME < OE *sēon;* c. G *sehen,* Goth *saihwan,* D *zien,* Icel *sjá*] —**see′a·ble,** *adj.* —**see′a·ble·ness,** *n.* —**Syn. 1.** notice, discern, behold. See **watch. 3.** comprehend. **8.** determine. **15.** accompany.

see[2] (sē), *n.* *Eccles.* the seat, center of authority, office, or jurisdiction of a bishop. [ME *se(e)* < OF *se* (var. of *sie*) < L *sēd(ēs)* seat]

seed (sēd), *n., pl.* **seeds,** (*esp. collectively*) **seed,** *v.* —*n.* **1.** the fertilized, matured ovule of a flowering plant, containing an embryo or rudimentary plant. **2.** any propagative part of a plant, including tubers, bulbs, etc., esp. as preserved for growing a new crop. **3.** such parts collectively. **4.** any similar small part or fruit. **5.** the germ or propagative source of anything: *the seeds of discord.* **6.** offspring; progeny. **7.** sperm; semen. **8.** the ovum or ova of certain animals, as the lobster and the silkworm moth. **9.** a small air bubble in a glass object, caused by defective firing. **10. go** or **run to seed, a.** (of the flower of a plant) to pass to the stage of yielding seed. **b.** to lose vigor, power, or prosperity; deteriorate. **11. in seed, a.** (of certain plants) in the state of bearing ripened seeds. **b.** (of a field, a lawn, etc.) sewn with seed. —*v.t.* **12.** to sow (a field, lawn, etc.) with seed. **13.** to sow or scatter (seed). **14.** to sow or scatter (clouds) with crystals or particles of silver iodide, solid carbon dioxide, etc., to induce precipitation. **15.** to remove the seeds from (fruit). **16.** *Sports.* **a.** to arrange (the drawings for positions in a tournament) so that ranking players or teams will not meet in the early rounds of play. **b.** to distribute (ranking players or teams) in this manner. —*v.i.* **17.** to sow seed. **18.** to produce or shed seed. [ME; OE *sēd, sǣd;* c. G *Saat,* Icel *sāth,* Goth *-seths;* akin to sow[1]] —**seed′less,** *adj.* —**seed′less·ness,** *n.* —**seed′like′,** *adj.*

seed·bed (sēd′bed′), *n.* **1.** land prepared for seeding. **2.** a plot of ground where young plants are grown before transplanting.

seed·cake (sēd′kāk′), *n.* a sweet cake containing aromatic seeds, usually caraway.

seed′ cap′sule, *Bot.* the ripened walls of the ovary.

seed·case (sēd′kās′), *n.* a seed capsule; pericarp.

seed′ coat′, *Bot.* the outer integument of a seed.

seed′ corn′, ears or kernels of corn set apart as seed.

seed·er (sē′dər), *n.* **1.** a person or thing that seeds. **2.** any of various apparatus for sowing or planting seeds in the ground. **3.** a plant that produces many seeds, esp. one grown mainly to produce seeds for growing other plants. **4.** a device or utensil for removing seeds, as from grapefruit. [ME *sedere,* OE *sǣdere*]

seed′ leaf′, *Bot.* a cotyledon.

seed·ling (sēd′ling), *n.* **1.** a plant or tree grown from a seed. **2.** a tree not yet three feet high. **3.** any young plant, esp. one grown in a nursery for transplanting.

seed·man (sēd′mən), *n., pl.* **-men.** seedsman.

seed′ oy′ster, a very young oyster, esp. one used in the cultivating and transplanting of an oyster bed.

seed′ pearl′, a pearl weighing less than ¼ grain.

seed′ plant′, a seed-bearing plant; spermatophyte.

seeds·man (sēdz′mən), *n., pl.* **-men. 1.** a sower of seed. **2.** a dealer in seed. Also, **seedman.**

seed·time (sēd′tīm′), *n.* the season for sowing seed. [ME; OE *sǣdtīma*]

seed′ ves′sel, *Bot.* a pericarp.

seed·y (sē′dē), *adj.,* **seed·i·er, seed·i·est. 1.** abounding in seed. **2.** containing many seeds, as a piece of fruit. **3.** gone to seed; bearing seeds. **4.** poorly kept; run-down; shabby. **5.** shabbily dressed; unkempt: *a seedy old tramp.* **6.** physically run-down; under the weather: *He has felt a bit seedy since his operation.* —**seed′i·ly,** *adv.* —**seed′i·ness,** *n.*

See·ger (sē′gər), *n.* **1. Alan,** 1888–1916, U.S. poet. **2. Peter** ("*Pete*"), born 1919, U.S. folk singer and folklorist.

see·ing (sē′ing), *conj.* **1.** in view of the fact that; considering; inasmuch as. —*n.* **2.** the act of a person who sees. **3.** the sense of sight.

See′ing Eye′ dog′, a dog that has been especially trained to lead or guide a blind person in walking about. [named after the *Seeing Eye* organization in Morristown, New Jersey]

seek (sēk), *v.,* **sought, seek·ing.** —*v.t.* **1.** to go in search or quest of: *to seek the truth.* **2.** to try to find or discover by searching or questioning: *to seek the solution to a problem.* **3.** to try to obtain: *to seek fame.* **4.** to try or attempt (usually fol. by an infinitive): *to seek to convince a person.* **5.** to go to: *to seek a place to rest.* **6.** to ask for; request: *to seek advice.* **7.** *Archaic.* to search or explore. —*v.i.* **8.** to make inquiry. **9. be sought after,** to be desired or in demand. [ME *seke,* OE *sēca(n);* c. Icel *sækja,* G *suchen,* Goth *sōkjan,* L *sāgīre*] —**seek′er,** *n.*

seel (sēl), *v.t.* **1.** *Falconry.* to sew shut (the eyes of a falcon) during parts of its training. **2.** *Archaic.* **a.** to close (the eyes). **b.** to blind. [ME *sile(n)* < MF *sille(r), cille(r)* < *cil* eyelash < L *cil(ium)* eyelid, eyelash; see CILIA]

See·land (sē′lənd), *n.* Zealand.

seem (sēm), *v.i.* **1.** to appear to be, feel, do, etc.: *She seems better this morning.* **2.** to appear to one's own senses, mind, observation, judgment, etc.: *It seems to me that someone is calling.* **3.** to appear to exist: *There seems no need to go now.* **4.** to appear to be true, probable, or evident: *It seems likely to rain.* **5.** to give the outward appearance of being or to pretend to be: *He only seems friendly because he wants you to like him.* [ME *seme* < Scand; cf. Icel *sæma* (impersonal) befit] —**Syn. 4.** SEEM, APPEAR, LOOK refer to an outward aspect which may or may not be contrary to reality. SEEM is applied to that which has an aspect of truth and probability: *It seems warmer today.* APPEAR suggests the giving of an impression which may be superficial or illusory: *The house appears to be deserted.* LOOK more vividly suggests the use of the eye (literally or figuratively) or the aspect as perceived by the eye: *She looked very much frightened.*

seem·ing (sē′ming), *adj.* **1.** apparent; appearing, whether truly or falsely, to be as specified: *a seeming advantage.* —*n.* **2.** appearance, esp. outward or deceptive appearance. —**seem′ing·ly,** *adv.* —**seem′ing·ness,** *n.* —**Syn. 1.** ostensible. **2.** semblance, face.

seem·ly (sēm′lē), *adj.,* **-li·er, -li·est,** *adv.* —*adj.* **1.** fitting or becoming with respect to propriety or good taste; decent; decorous: *Her outburst of rage was hardly seemly.* **2.** suitable or appropriate; fitting: *Sending flowers would be a seemly gesture.* **3.** of pleasing appearance; handsome. —*adv.* **4.** in a seemly manner; fittingly; becomingly. [ME *semeli* < Scand; cf. Icel *sæmilega* becoming] —**seem′li·ness,** *n.* —**Syn. 1, 2.** right, proper, appropriate.

seen (sēn), *v.* pp. of **see**[1].

seep (sēp), *v.i.* **1.** to pass, flow, or ooze gradually through a porous substance: *Water seeps through cracks in the wall.* **2.** to become slowly diffused; permeate: *Fog seeped through the trees, obliterating everything.* —*n.* **3.** moisture that seeps out; seepage. **4.** a small spring, pool, or other place where liquid from the ground has oozed to the surface of the earth. [? var. of dial. *sipe* < OE *sīp(ian);* c. MLG *sīpen*]

seep·age (sē′pij), *n.* **1.** the act or process of seeping; leakage. **2.** something that seeps or leaks out. **3.** a quantity that has seeped out.

seep·y (sē′pē), *adj.*, **seep·i·er, seep·i·est.** (esp. of ground, a plot of land, or the like) soaked or oozing with water.

se·er (sē′ər *for 1;* sēr *for 2–4*), *n.* **1.** a person who sees; observer. **2.** a person who prophesies future events; prophet: *The industry seers predicted that sales would double.* **3.** a person who is endowed with profound moral and spiritual insight or knowledge; a wise man or sage with intuitive powers. **4.** a person who is reputed to have special powers of divination, as a crystal-gazer, palmist, etc.

seer·ess (sēr′is), *n.* a female seer.

seer·suck·er (sēr′suk′ər), *n.* a plainwoven cotton, rayon, or linen fabric, traditionally striped cotton with alternate stripes crinkled in the weaving. [< Hindi *sīrsakar* < Pers *shīr o shakkar,* lit., milk and sugar]

see·saw (sē′sô′), *n.* **1.** a recreation in which two children alternately ride up and down while seated at opposite ends of a plank balanced at the middle; teeterboard. **2.** a plank or apparatus for this recreation. **3.** an up-and-down or a back-and-forth movement or procedure. **—*adj.* 4.** moving up and down, back and forth, or alternately ahead and behind: *It was a seesaw game with the lead changing hands many times.* **—*v.i., v.t.* 5.** to move or cause to move in a seesaw manner: *The boat seesawed in the heavy sea.* [gradational compound based on SAW[1]]

seethe (sēth), *v.,* **seethed** or (*Obs.*) **sod; seethed** or (*Obs.*) **sod·den** or **sod; seeth·ing;** *n.* **—*v.i.* 1.** to surge or foam as if boiling. **2.** to be in a state of agitation or excitement. **3.** *Archaic.* to boil. **—*v.t.* 4.** to soak or steep. **5.** to cook by boiling or simmering; boil. **—*n.* 6.** the act of seething. **7.** the state of being agitated or excited. [ME; OE *sēothan;* c. G *sieden,* Sw *sjuda,* etc.] **—seeth′ing·ly,** *adv.* **—Syn. 5.** See **boil[1].**

see-through (sē′thro͞o′), *adj.* **1.** Also, **see-thru** (sē′-thro͞o′). transparent: *a see-through blouse.* **—*n.* 2.** transparency. **3.** a see-through item of clothing.

seg·ment (*n.* seg′mənt; *v.* seg ment′), *n.* **1.** one of the parts into which something naturally separates or is divided; a division or section: *a segment of an orange.* **2.** *Geom.* **a.** a part cut off from a figure, esp. a circular or spherical one, by a line or plane. **b.** a finite section of a line. **3.** *Zool.* **a.** any of the rings that compose the body of an annelid. **b.** any of the discrete parts of the body of an animal, esp. an arthropod. **c.** one of the sections of an arthropod appendage between the joints. **—*v.t., v.i.* 4.** to separate or divide into segments. [< L *segment(um)* = *seg-* (var. of *sec-,* root of *secāre* to cut) + *-mentum* -MENT] **—seg·men·tar·y** (seg′mən-ter′ē), *adj.* **—Syn. 1.** See **part.**

seg·men·tal (seg men′tᵊl), *adj.* **1.** of or pertaining to segments or segmentation. **2.** *Linguistics.* noting or pertaining to sequential speech: *segmental phonemes.* **—seg-men′tal·ly,** *adv.*

seg·men·tal·ize (seg men′tᵊlīz′), *v.t.,* **-ized, -iz·ing.** to separate into parts, elements, classes, etc. **—seg·men′tal·i-za′tion,** *n.*

seg·men·ta·tion (seg′mən tā′shən), *n.* **1.** division into segments. **2.** *Biol.* **a.** the subdivision of an organism or of an organ into more or less equivalent parts **b.** cell division.

segmenta′tion cav′ity, *Embryol.* blastocoele.

se·gno (sān′yō, sen′yō; *It.* se′nyô), *n., pl.* **se·gni** (sān′yē, sen′yē; *It.* se′nyē). *Music.* a sign, symbol, or mark at the beginning or end of a section to be repeated. [< It < L *sign-(um)* a sign]

se·go (sē′gō), *n., pl.* **-gos.** See **sego lily.** [< Paiute (*pa*)*sigo*]

se′go lil′y, 1. a liliaceous plant, *Calochortus Nuttallii,* of the western U.S., having showy, bell-shaped flowers: the state flower of Utah. **2.** its edible root.

Se·go·vi·a (sə gō′vē ə; *Sp.* se gô′vyä), *n.* **1. An·drés** (än drεs′), 1893–1987, Spanish guitarist. **2.** a city in central Spain: Roman aqueduct. 30,875 (1950).

seg·re·gate (*v.* seg′rə gāt′; *n.* seg′rə git, -gāt′), *v.,* **-gat·ed, -gat·ing,** *n.* **—*v.t.* 1.** to separate or set apart from others or from the main body or group; isolate. **2.** to require the separation of (a specific racial, religious, or other group) from the general body of society. **—*v.i* 3.** to separate, withdraw, or go apart from the main body and collect in one place. **4.** to practice, require, or enforce segregation. **5.** *Genetics.* (of allelic genes) to separate during meiosis. **—*n.* 6.** a segregated thing, person, or group. [ME *segregat* < L *sēgregāt(us)* (ptp. of *sēgregāre* to part from the flock) = *sē-* SE- + *greg-* (s. of *grex* flock) + *-ātus* -ATE[1]; see GREGARIOUS] **—seg·re·ga·ble** (seg′rə gə bəl), *adj.* **—seg′-re·ga′tive,** *adj.* **—seg′re·ga′tor,** *n.* **—Ant. 1.** integrate.

seg·re·gat·ed (seg′rə gā′tid), *adj.* **1.** characterized by or practicing racial segregation. **2.** restricted to one group, esp. exclusively on the basis of racial or ethnic membership. **3.** maintaining separate facilities for members of different, esp. racially different, groups. **—seg′re·gat′ed·ly,** *adv.* **—seg′re·gat′ed·ness,** *n.*

seg·re·ga·tion (seg′rə gā′shən), *n.* **1.** the act or practice of segregating. **2.** the state or condition of being segregated. **3.** *Genetics.* the separation of allelic genes in different gametes during meiosis, resulting in the separation of their characters in the progeny. [< LL *sēgregātiōn-* (s. of *sēgregātiō*)] **—seg′re·ga′tion·al,** *adj.*

seg·re·ga·tion·ist (seg′rə gā′shə nist), *n.* a person who favors, advocates, or practices segregation, esp. racial segregation.

se·gue (sā′gwā, seg′wā), *v.,* **-gued, -gue·ing,** *adj., adv.* *Music.* **—*v.i.* 1.** to continue at once with the next section or composition. **—*adj., adv.*** (of a musical section or composition) **2.** performed at once without a break. **3.** performed in the manner or style of the preceding section. [< It: (there) follows, 3rd pers. sing. pres. ind. of *seguire* < L *sequī* to follow. See SUE]

se·gui·dil·la (sā′gə dēl′yə, -dē′yə, seg′ə-; *Sp.* se′gē thē′-lyä), *n., pl.* **-dil·las** (-dēl′yəz, -dē′yəz; *Sp.* -thē′lyäs). **1.** *Pros.* a Spanish stanza of four to seven lines with a distinctive rhythmic pattern. **2.** a Spanish dance in triple meter for two persons. [< Sp = *seguid(a)* sequence + *-illa* dim. suffix; *seguida* = *segui-* (s. of *seguir* < L *sequī* to follow) + *-da* < L *-ta* fem. ptp. suffix]

sei·cen·to (sā chen′tō; *It.* se chen′tô), *n.* (*often cap.*) the 17th century, with reference to the Italian art or literature of that period. [< It: short for *mille seicento,* lit., a thousand six hundred]

seiche (sāsh), *n.* a sudden oscillation of the water of a lake, bay, etc., causing fluctuations in the water level and caused by wind, earthquakes, etc. [< SwissF]

sei·del (sīd′əl, zīd′-), *n.* a large beer mug, often having a hinged lid. [< G < MHG *sīdel* < L *situl(a)* bucket]

Seid′litz pow′ders (sed′lits), a mild laxative consisting of two powders, tartaric acid and a mixture of sodium bicarbonate and Rochelle salt, that are dissolved separately, mixed, and drunk after effervescence. [arbitrarily named after Bohemian village]

sei·gneur (sēn yûr′; *Fr.* se nyœr′), *n., pl.* **sei·gneurs** (sēn yûrz′; *Fr.* se nyœr′). (*sometimes cap.*) **1.** a lord, esp. a feudal lord. **2.** (in French Canada) a holder of a seigneury. [< F < VL *senior* lord. See SENIOR] **—sei·gneu·ri·al** (sēn-yûr′ē əl), *adj.*

sei·gneur·y (sēn′yə rē), *n.* (in French Canada) land originally held by grant from the king of France.

seign·ior (sēn′yər), *n.* (*sometimes cap.*) a lord, esp. a feudal lord; ruler. [ME *segnour* < AF; see SEIGNEUR]

seign·ior·age (sēn′yər ij), *n.* **1.** something claimed by a sovereign or superior as a prerogative. **2.** a charge on bullion brought to the mint to be coined. **3.** the difference between the cost of the bullion plus minting expenses and the value as money of the pieces coined, constituting a source of government revenue. Also, **seign′or·age.** [late ME *seigneurage* < MF]

seign·ior·y (sēn′yə rē), *n., pl.* **-ior·ies. 1.** the power or authority of a seignior. **2.** *Hist.* a lord's domain. Also, **signory.** [ME *seignorie* < OF; see SEIGNEUR, -Y[3]]

sei·gno·ri·al (sēn yōr′ē əl, -yôr′-), *adj.* of or pertaining to a seignior. Also, **seign·ior·al** (sēn′yər əl), **sei·gnio·ri·al** (sēn yōr′ē əl, -yôr′-), **seign·or·al** (sēn′yər əl). [*seignor* (var. of SEIGNIOR) + -IAL]

seine (sān), *n., v.,* **seined, sein·ing. —*n.* 1.** a fishing net that hangs vertically in the water, having floats at the upper edge and sinkers at the lower. **—*v.t.* 2.** to fish for or catch with a seine. **3.** to use a seine in (a body of water). **—*v.i.* 4.** to fish with a seine. [ME *seyne,* OE *segne* < WGmc **sagīna* < L *sagēna* < Gk *sagḗnē* fishing net] **—sein′er,** *n.*

Seine (sān; *Fr.* sen), *n.* a river in France, flowing NW through Paris to the English Channel. 480 mi. long.

seise (sēz), *v.,* **seised, seis·ing. —*v.t.* 1.** *Chiefly Brit.* seize. **2.** *Law.* seize (def. 6). **—*v.i.* 3.** *Chiefly Brit.* seize. **—seis′a·ble,** *adj.* **—seis′er,** *n.*

Sei·shin (sā shēn′), *n.* Japanese name of **Chongjin.**

sei·sin (sē′zin), *n.* *Law.* seizin.

seis·ing (sē′zing), *n.* *Chiefly Brit.* seizing.

seism (sī′zəm, -səm), *n.* an earthquake. [< Gk *seism(ós)* = *seí(ein)* (to) shake, quake + *-(i)smos* -ISM]

seis·mic (sīz′mik, sīs′-), *adj.* pertaining to, of the nature of, or caused by an earthquake. Also, **seis′mal, seis′mi·cal. —seis′mi·cal·ly,** *adv.*

seis·mic·i·ty (sīz mis′i tē, sīs-), *n., pl.* **-ties.** the frequency, intensity, and distribution of earthquakes in a given area.

seismo-, a combining form of **seism:** *seismograph.*

seis·mo·gram (sīz′mə gram′, sīs′-), *n.* a record made by a seismograph.

seis·mo·graph (sīz′mə graf′, -gräf′, sīs′-), *n.* any of various instruments for measuring and recording the vibrations of earthquakes. **—seis·mo·graph·ic** (sīz′mə-graf′ik, sīs′-), **seis′mo·graph′i·cal,** *adj.*

seis·mog·ra·phy (sīz mog′rə fē, sīs-), *n.* **1.** the scientific measuring and recording of the shock and vibrations of earthquakes. **2.** seismology. **—seis·mog′ra·pher,** *n.*

seismol., 1. seismological. **2.** seismology.

seis·mol·o·gy (sīz mol′ə jē, sīs-), *n.* the science or study of earthquakes and their phenomena. Also called **seismography. —seis·mo·log·ic** (sīz′mə loj′ik, sīs′-), **seis′mo·log′i·cal,** *adj.* **—seis′mo·log′i·cal·ly,** *adv.* **—seis·mol′o·gist,** *n.*

seis·mom·e·ter (sīz mom′i tər, sīs-), *n.* a seismograph equipped for measuring the actual movement of the ground. **—seis·mo·met·ric** (sīz′mə me′trik, sīs′-), **seis′mo·met′-ri·cal,** *adj.* **—seis·mom′et·ry,** *n.*

seis·mo·scope (sīz′mə skōp′, sīs′-), *n.* an instrument for recording the occurrence of an earthquake. **—seis·mo-scop·ic** (sīz′mə skop′ik, sīs′-), *adj.*

sei·sure (sē′zhər), *n.* *Chiefly Brit.* seizure.

seize (sēz), *v.,* **seized, seiz·ing. —*v.t.* 1.** to take hold of suddenly or forcibly; grasp: *to seize a weapon.* **2.** to grasp mentally; understand: *to seize an idea.* **3.** to take possession of by force or at will. **4.** to take possession or control of as if by suddenly laying hold: *Panic seized the crowd.* **5.** to take possession of legally; confiscate. **6.** Also, **seise.** *Law.* to put (someone) in seizin or legal possession of property (usually used in passive constructions): *She was seized of vast estates.* **7.** to capture; take into custody. **8.** to take advantage of promptly. **9.** *Naut.* to bind or fasten together with a seizing. **—*v.i.* 10.** to grab or take hold suddenly or forcibly (usually fol. by *on* or *upon*): *to seize on a rope.* **11.** to resort to a method, plan, etc., in desperation. Also, *esp. Brit.,* **seise.** [ME *saise(n), seise(n)* < OF *saisi(r)* < ML *sacīre* to place < Frankish cognate of Goth *satjan* to SET, put, place] **—seiz′-a·ble,** *adj.* **—seiz′er;** *Law.* **sei·zor** (sē′zər, -zôr), *n.* **—Syn. 7.** arrest, apprehend. See **catch. —Ant. 7.** release.

sei·zin (sē′zin), *n.* *Law.* **1.** (originally) possession of either land or chattel. **2.** the kind of possession or right to possession characteristic of estates of freehold. Also, **seisin.** [ME < OF *saisine* = *sais(ir)* (to) SEIZE + *-ine* -INE[2]]

seiz·ing (sē′zing), *n.* **1.** the act of a person or thing that seizes. **2.** *Naut.* a means of binding or fastening together two objects, as two ropes or parts of the same rope, by a number of longitudinal and transverse turns of marline, wire, or the like. Also, *esp. Brit.,* **seising.**

seiz′ing stuff′, *Naut.* tarred hemp small stuff, ordinarily right-laid from three strands of from two to four threads each.

Seizing (def. 2)

sei·zure (sē′zhər), *n.* **1.** the act or an instance of seizing. **2.** a taking possession of an item, property, or person legally or by force. **3.** a sudden attack, as of epilepsy or some other disease. Also, *esp. Brit.,* **seisure.**

se·jant (sē′jənt), *adj.* *Heraldry.* (of an animal) represented in a sitting posture: *a lion sejant.* Also, **se′jeant.** [var. of *seiante* < AF, MF *seant* = *se-* (root of *seoir* < L *sedēre* to sit) + *-ant* -ANT]

Se·ja·nus (si jā′nəs), *n.* **Lucius Ae·li·us** (ē′lē əs), died A.D. 31, Roman politician, commander of praetorian guard, and conspirator in the reign of Emperor Tiberius.

sel (sel), *n., adj., pron. Scot.* self.

sel., **1.** selected. **2.** selection; selections.

se·la·chi·an (si lā′kē ən), *adj.* **1.** belonging to the *Selachii,* a group of fishes comprising the sharks, skates, and rays. —*n.* **2.** a selachian fish. [< Gk *seláchē* shark + -AN]

sel·a·gi·nel·la (sel′ə ji nel′ə), *n.* any terrestrial, mosslike cryptogamic plant of the genus *Selaginella.* [< NL = *selāgin-* (s. of L *selāgō* a plant name) + *-ella* dim. suffix]

se·lah (sē′lə, sel′ə), *n.* an expression occurring frequently in the Psalms, thought to be a liturgical or musical direction. [< Heb]

se·lam·lik (si läm′lik), *n.* the portion of a Turkish palace or house reserved for men. [< Turk]

Se·lan·gor (sə läng′gôr, -gōr), *n.* a state in Malaysia, on the SW Malay Peninsula. 1,159,914 (est. 1961); 3160 sq. mi. *Cap.:* Kuala Lumpur.

Sel·den (sel′d^{ə}n), *n.* **John,** 1584–1654, English historian, Orientalist, and politician.

sel·dom (sel′dəm), *adv.* **1.** on only a few occasions; rarely; infrequently: *I seldom see them nowadays.* —*adj.* **2.** rare; infrequent. [ME; OE *seldum,* var. of *seldan;* c. G *selten,* Goth *silda-*] —**sel′dom·ness,** *n.*

se·lect (si lekt′), *v.t.* **1.** to choose in preference to another or others. —*adj.* **2.** chosen in preference to another or others; preferred. **3.** choice; of special excellence: *a select cut of meat.* **4.** careful in selecting; discriminating. **5.** carefully chosen; exclusive: *a select group of friends.* [< L *sēlect(us)* (ptp. of *sēligere* to gather apart) = *sē-* SE- + *lec-* (< *legere* to gather) + *-tus* ptp. suffix] —**se·lect′ly,** *adv.* —**se·lect′ness,** *n.* —**se·lec′tor,** *n.* —**Syn. 1.** See **choose.**

se·lect·ee (si lek tē′), *n.* a person selected by draft for service in the armed forces.

se·lec·tion (si lek′shən), *n.* **1.** the act or an instance of selecting. **2.** the state of being selected. **3.** a thing or a number of things selected. **4.** a group from which a choice may be made: *The store had a wide selection of bracelets.* **5.** *Biol.* a biological process resulting in the survival and perpetuation of only those forms of animal and plant life that are best adapted to the environment or have desirable inheritable characteristics. [< L *sēlectiōn-* (s. of *sēlectiō*) = *sēlect(us)* (see SELECT) + *-iōn-* -ION] —**Ant. 1.** rejection.

se·lec·tive (si lek′tiv), *adj.* **1.** having the function or power of selecting. **2.** characterized by selection, esp. fastidious selection. **3.** of or pertaining to selection. —**se·lec′tive·ly,** *adv.* —**se·lec′tive·ness,** *n.*

selec′tive serv′ice, **1.** compulsory military service. **2.** (*caps.*) **a.** of or pertaining to the Selective Service System. **b.** See **Selective Service System.**

Selec′tive Ser′vice Sys′tem, *U.S.* the federal agency charged with the administration of compulsory military service. Also called **Selective Service.**

se·lec·tiv·i·ty (si lek tiv′i tē), *n.* **1.** the state or quality of being selective. **2.** *Elect.* the property of a circuit, instrument, or the like, by virtue of which it can distinguish oscillations of a particular frequency. **3.** *Radio.* the ability of a receiving set to receive any one of a band of frequencies or waves to the exclusion of others.

se·lect·man (si lekt′mən), *n., pl.* **-men.** (in most New England states) one of a board of town officers chosen to manage certain public affairs.

sel·e·nate (sel′ə nāt′), *n. Chem.* a salt or ester of selenic acid. [SELEN(IC) + -ATE^2]

Se·le·ne (si lē′nē), *n. Class. Myth.* the moon goddess who loved Endymion: later identified with Artemis.

se·le·nic (si lē′nik, -len′ik), *adj. Chem.* of or containing selenium, esp. in the hexavalent state. [SELEN(IUM) + -IC]

sele′nic ac′id, *Chem.* a dibasic acid, H_2SeO_4, resembling sulfuric acid.

sel·e·nide (sel′ə nīd′, -nid), *n. Chem.* any compound in which bivalent selenium is combined with a positive element.

se·le·ni·ous (si lē′nē əs), *adj. Chem.* containing tetravalent or bivalent selenium. Also, **selenous.** [SELENI(UM) + -OUS]

sele′nious ac′id, a poisonous powder, H_2SeO_3, used chiefly as a reagent.

sel·e·nite (sel′ə nīt′, si lē′nīt), *n.* **1.** a variety of gypsum. **2.** *Chem.* a salt of selenious acid. [< L *selēnītē(s)* < Gk *selēnítēs líthos* moonstone] —**sel·e·nit·ic** (sel′ə nit′ik), **sel′e·nit′i·cal,** *adj.*

se·le·ni·um (si lē′nē əm), *n. Chem.* a nonmetallic element chemically resembling sulfur and tellurium, and having an electrical resistance that varies under the influence of light. *Symbol:* Se; *at. wt.:* 78.96; *at. no.:* 34; *sp. gr.:* (gray) 4.80 at 25°C, (red) 4.50 at 25°C. [< Gk *selḗn(ē)* moon + -IUM]

sele′nium cell′, *Elect.* a photovoltaic cell consisting of a thin strip of selenium placed between two metal electrodes.

seleno-, a learned borrowing from Greek meaning "moon," used in the formation of compound words: *selenography.* [comb. form repr. Gk *selḗnē*]

sel·e·nog·ra·phy (sel′ə nog′rə fē), *n.* the branch of astronomy that deals with the charting of the moon's surface. —**se·le·no·graph** (sə lē′nə graf′, -gräf′), *n.* —**sel′e·nog′ra·pher, sel′e·nog′ra·phist,** *n.* —**se·le·no·graph·ic** (si lē′nə graf′ik), **se·le′no·graph′i·cal,** *adj.* —**se·le′no·graph′i·cal·ly,** *adv.*

sel·e·nol·o·gy (sel′ə nol′ə jē), *n.* the branch of astronomy that deals with the physical characteristics of the moon, as with the nature and origin of its surface features. —**se·le·no·log·i·cal** (sə lēn′^{ə}loj′i kəl), *adj.* —**sel′e·nol′o·gist,** *n.*

se·le·nous (sə lē′nəs, sel′ə-), *adj. Chem.* selenious.

Se·leu·cia (si lo͞o′shə), *n.* **1.** an ancient city in Iraq, on the Tigris River: capital of the Seleucid empire. **2.** an ancient city in Asia Minor, near the mouth of the Orontes River: the port of Antioch.

Se·leu·cid (si lo͞o′sid), *n., pl.* **-ci·dae** (-si dē′), *adj.* —*n.* **1.** a member of a Macedonian dynasty 312–64 B.C., that ruled much of southwestern Asia. —*adj.* **2.** Also, **Se·leu·ci·dan** (si lo͞o′si d^{ə}n). of or pertaining to the Seleucids or their dynasty. [< NL *Seleucid(ēs)* < Gk *Seleukídēs* offspring of Seleucus]

Se·leu·cus I (si lo͞o′kəs), (*Seleucus Nicator*) 358?–281? B.C., Macedonian general under Alexander the Great: founder of the Seleucid dynasty.

self (self), *n., pl.* **selves,** *adj., pron., pl.* **selves.** —*n.* **1.** a person or thing considered with respect to complete individuality or separate identity: *one's own self.* **2.** a person's nature, character, etc.: *his better self.* **3.** personal interest. **4.** *Philos.* the subject of experience as contrasted with the object of experience; ego. —*adj.* **5.** being the same throughout; uniform. **6.** being of one piece or material with the rest. **7.** *Obs.* same. —*pron.* **8.** myself, himself, etc.: *to make a check payable to self.* [ME, OE; c. D *zelf,* G *selb-,* Icel *sjalfr,* Goth *silba*]

self-, a combining form of **self** and variously used with the meanings "of the self" (*self-analysis*) and "by oneself or itself" (*self-appointed*), and with the meanings "to, with, toward, for, on, in oneself" (*self-complacent*), "inherent in oneself or itself" (*self-explanatory*), "independent" (*self-government*), and "automatic" (*self-operating*).

self-a·base·ment (self′ə bās′mənt, self′-), *n.* humiliation of oneself, as from guilt or shame.

self-ab·ne·ga·tion (self′ab′nə gā′shən), *n.* self-denial or self-sacrifice

self-ab·sorbed (self′ab sôrbd′, -zôrbd′, self′-), *adj.* preoccupied with one's own thoughts, interests, etc. —**self-ab·sorp·tion** (self′ab sôrp′shən, -zôrp′-, self′-), *n.*

self-a·buse (self′ə byo͞os′, self′-), *n.* **1.** reproach of oneself. **2.** abuse of one's health. **3.** masturbation.

self-act·ing (self′ak′ting), *adj.* automatic. —**self′-ac′tion,** *n.*

self-ad·dressed (self′ə drest′), *adj.* addressed for return to the sender, as an envelope enclosed in a letter so as to expedite a reply.

self-ag·gran·dize·ment (self′ə gran′diz mənt, self′-), *n.* increase of one's own power, wealth, etc., esp. through aggressive acts. —**self-ag·gran·diz·ing** (self′ə gran′dī zing), *adj.*

self-a·nal·y·sis (self′ə nal′i sis, self′-), *n.* the application of psychoanalytic techniques and theories to an analysis of one's own personality and behavior. —**self-an·a·lyt·i·cal** (self′an′^{ə}lit′i kəl, self′-), *adj.*

self-an·ni·hi·la·tion (self′ə nī′ə lā′shən, self′-), *n.* **1.** self-destruction; suicide. **2.** immolation of the self in mystic contemplation of or in union with God.

self-ap·point·ed (self′ə poin′tid), *adj.* having undertaken by oneself, esp. officiously, to act in a specified capacity: *a self-appointed critic.*

self-as·ser·tion (self′ə sûr′shən, self′-), *n.* insistence on or expression of one's own importance, wishes, opinions, etc. —**self′-as·sert′ing,** *adj.* —**self′-as·sert′ing·ly,** *adv.* —**self′-as·ser′tive,** *adj.* —**self′-as·ser′tive·ly,** *adv.* —**self′-as·ser′tive·ness,** *n.* —**Syn.** assertiveness.

self-as·sur·ance (self′ə sho͝or′əns, self′-), *n.* self-confidence.

self-as·sured (self′ə sho͝ord′), *adj.* self-confident. —**self-as·sur·ed·ness** (self′ə sho͝or′id nis), *n.*

self-cen·tered (self′sen′tərd), *adj.* **1.** engrossed in self; selfish; egotistical. **2.** centered in oneself or itself. **3.** *Archaic.* fixed; unchanging. Also, *esp. Brit.,* **self′-cen·tred.** —**self′-cen′tered·ly;** *esp. Brit.,* **self′-cen′tred·ly,** *adv.* —**self′-cen′tered·ness;** *esp. Brit.,* **self′-cen′tred·ness,** *n.*

self-col·lect·ed (self′kə lek′tid, self′-), *adj.* having or showing self-control; composed; self-possessed.

self-com·mand (self′kə mand′, -mänd′, self′-), *n.* self-control.

self-com·pla·cent (self′kəm plā′sənt, self′-), *adj.* pleased with oneself; self-satisfied; smug. —**self′-com·pla′cence, self′-com·pla′cen·cy,** *n.* —**self′-com·pla′cent·ly,** *adv.*

self-com·posed (self′kəm pōzd′, self′-), *adj.* being or appearing to be composed; calm. —**self-com·pos·ed·ly** (self′kəm pō′zid lē, self′-), *adv.*

self-con·ceit (self′kən sēt′, self′-), *n.* an excessively favorable opinion of oneself. —**self′-con·ceit′ed,** *adj.*

self-con·fessed (self′kən fest′, self′-), *adj.* openly admitting to being a particular type of person.

self-con·fi·dence (self′kon′fi dəns, self′-), *n.* confidence in one's own judgment, ability, power, decisions, etc. —**self′-con′fi·dent,** *adj.* —**self′-con′fi·dent·ly,** *adv.* —**Syn.** assurance.

self-con·grat·u·la·tion (self′kən grach′ə lā′shən, self′-), *n.* the expression or feeling of uncritical satisfaction with oneself or one's own accomplishment, good fortune, etc.; complacency. —**self-con·grat·u·la·to·ry** (self′kən grach′ə lə tôr′ē, -tōr′ē, self′-), *adj.* —**self′-con·grat′u·lat′ing,** *adj.*

self-con·scious (self′kon′shəs, self′-), *adj.* **1.** excessively conscious of oneself as an object of observation by others. **2.** conscious of oneself or one's own thoughts, well-being, etc. —**self′-con′scious·ly,** *adv.* —**self′-con′scious·ness,** *n.*

self-con·tained (self′kən tānd′, self′-), *adj.* **1.** containing

self′-a·ban′don·ment, *n.*
self′-ab·hor′rence, *n.*
self′-ac′cu·sa′tion, *n.*
self′-ac·cused′, *adj.*
self′-ac·cus′ing, *adj.*
self′-ad·just′ing, *adj.*
self′-ad·min′is·tered, *adj.*
self′-ad′mi·ra′tion, *n.*
self′-ad·vance′ment, *n.*
self′-ad′ver·tise′ment, *n.*
self′-ad′ver·tis′ing, *adj., n.*
self′-a·lign′ing, *adj.*
self′-am′pu·ta′tion, *n.*
self′-ap·plaud′ing, *adj.*
self′-ap·plause′, *n.*
self′-ap·pre′ci·at′ing, *adj.*
self′-ap·pre′ci·a′tion, *n.*
self′-ap′pro·ba′tion, *n.*
self′-ap·prov′al, *n.*
self′-ap·prov′ing, *adj.*
self′-as·sumed′, *adj.*
self′-as·sum′ing, *adj.*
self′-as·sump′tion, *n.*
self′-a·ware′, *adj.;* **-ness,** *n.*
self′-be·tray′al, *n.*
self′-caused′, *adj.*
self′-clean′ing, *adj.*
self′-clos′ing, *adj.*
self′-cock′ing, *adj.*
self′-cog·ni′tion, *n.*
self′-com·mit′ment, *n.*
self′-con·cern′, *n.*
self′-con′dem·na′tion, *n.*
self′-con·demned′, *adj.*
self′-con·fine′ment, *n.*
self′-con·fin′ing, *adj.*
self′-con·sis′ten·cy, *n.*
self′-con·sis′tent, *adj.*
self′-con′sti·tut′ed, *adj.*
self′-con·sum′ing, *adj.*

in oneself or itself all that is necessary for independent action or existence. **2.** reserved or uncommunicative. **3.** self-controlled or self-possessed. **—self-con·tain·ed·ly** (self′kən tā′nid lē, self′-), *adv.* **—self′-con·tain′ed·ness,** *n.*

self-con·tra·dic·tion (self′kon′trə dik′shən, self′-), *n.* **1.** the act or an instance of contradicting oneself or itself. **2.** a statement containing contradictory elements. **—self′-con′tra·dict′ing,** *adj.* **—self′-con′tra·dic′to·ry,** *adj.*

self-con·trol (self′kən trōl′, self′-), *n.* control or restraint of oneself or one's actions, feelings, emotions, etc. **—self′-con·trolled′,** *adj.* **—self′-con·trol′ling,** *adj.*

self-crit·i·cal (self′krit′i kəl, self′-), *adj.* **1.** capable of criticizing oneself objectively. **2.** tending to find fault with one's own actions, motives, etc. **—self′-crit′i·cal·ly,** *adv.* **—self-crit·i·cism** (self′krit′i siz′əm, self′-), *n.*

self-de·ceit (self′di sēt′, self′-), *n.* self-deception.

self-de·ceived (self′di sēvd′, self′-), *adj.* **1.** holding an erroneous opinion of oneself, one's own effort, or the like. **2.** being mistaken, as from careless or wishful thinking.

self-de·ceiv·ing (self′di sē′ving, self′-), *adj.* **1.** tending to deceive or fool oneself. **2.** used in deceiving oneself, as in justifying one's actions, beliefs, etc.: *a self-deceiving argument.*

self-de·cep·tion (self′di sep′shən, self′-), *n.* the act or fact of deceiving oneself. Also called **self-deceit.** **—self′-de·cep′tive,** *adj.*

self-de·feat·ing (self′di fē′ting, self′-), *adj.* serving to frustrate, thwart, etc., one's own intention.

self-de·fense (self′di fens′, self′-), *n.* **1.** the act of defending one's person by physical force. **2.** a claim or plea that one's use of force was necessary to defend one's person. **3.** the act or an instance of defending one's own effort, opinion, plan, etc., as by argument. Also, *esp. Brit.,* **self′-de·fence′.** **—self′-de·fen′sive;** *esp. Brit.,* **self′-de·fen′cive,** *adj.*

self-de·lu·sion (self′di lo͞o′zhən, self′-), *n.* the act or fact of deluding oneself.

self-de·ni·al (self′di nī′əl, self′-), *n.* the denial of one's own wishes, desires, pleasures, etc. **—self′-de·ny′ing,** *adj.* **—self′-de·ny′ing·ly,** *adv.*

self-dep·re·cat·ing (self′dep′rə kā′ting, self′-), *adj.* representing oneself as having little or no value; excessively modest. **—self′-dep′re·cat′ing·ly,** *adv.* **—self′-dep′re·ca′tion,** *n.*

self-de·struct (self′di strukt′), *v.i.* **1.** to destroy oneself or itself. **—***adj.* **2.** causing something to self-destruct: *a self-destruct mechanism.* [back formation from SELF-DESTRUCTION]

self-de·struc·tive (self′di struk′tiv, self′-), *adj.* **1.** harmful, injurious, or destructive to oneself. **2.** exhibiting suicidal desires. **—self-de·struc·tion** (self′di struk′shən, self′-), *n.* **—self′-de·struc′tive·ly,** *adv.*

self-de·ter·mi·na·tion (self′di tûr′mə nā′shən, self′-), *n.* **1.** freedom from external control or influence. **2.** the right of a people to determine the way in which they shall be governed and whether they shall be self-governed or governed by another power. **—self′-de·ter′mined,** *adj.* **—self′-de·ter′min·ing,** *adj.*

self-de·vo·tion (self′di vō′shən, self′-), *n.* dedication of oneself to an activity, ideal, person, etc. **—self′-de·vot′ed,** *adj.* **—self′-de·vot′ed·ly,** *adv.* **—self′-de·vot′ed·ness,** *n.*

self-di·ges·tion (self′di jes′chən, self′-), *n.* autolysis.

self-dis·ci·pline (self′dis′ə plin, self′-), *n.* **1.** self-control. **2.** discipline and training of oneself, usually for improvement. **—self′-dis′ci·plined,** *adj.*

self-doubt (self′dout′), *n.* lack of confidence in the reliability of one's own motives, personality, thoughts, etc. **—self′-doubt′ing,** *adj.*

self-dram·a·tiz·ing (self′dram′ə tī′zing, self′-), *adj.* exaggerating one's own qualities, situation, etc., for the sake of attention. **—self′-dram′a·ti·za′tion,** *n.*

self-ed·u·cat·ed (self′ej′o͝o kā′tid, self′-), *adj.* educated by one's own efforts, esp. without formal instruction. **—self′-ed′u·ca′tion,** *n.*

self-ef·face·ment (self′i fās′mənt, self′-), *n.* the act or fact of keeping oneself in the background, as in humility. **—self′-ef·fac′ing,** *adj.* **—self′-ef·fac′ing·ly,** *adv.*

self-em·ployed (self′em ploid′, self′-), *adj.* earning one's living directly from one's own profession or business, as a free-lance writer or artist, rather than as an employee earning salary or commission from another. **—self′-em·ploy′ment,** *n.*

self-es·teem (self′e stēm′, self′-), *n.* respect for or a favorable impression of oneself. **—Syn.** See **pride.**

self-ev·i·dent (self′ev′i dənt, self′-), *adj.* evident in itself without proof or demonstration. **—self′-ev′i·dent·ly,** *adv.*

self-ex·am·i·na·tion (self′ig zam′ə nā′shən, self′-), *n.* examination of one's own conduct, motives, etc. **—self′-ex·am′in·ing,** *adj.*

self-ex·e·cut·ing (self′ek′sə kyo͞o′ting, self′-), *adj.* going into effect immediately without the need of supplementary legislation: *a self-executing treaty.*

self-ex·ist·ent (self′ig zis′tənt, self′-), *adj.* **1.** existing independently of any cause. **2.** having an independent existence. **—self′-ex·ist′ence,** *n.*

self-ex·plan·a·to·ry (self′ik splan′ə tôr′ē, -tōr′ē, self′-), *adj.* needing no explanation; obvious. Also, **self-ex·plain·ing** (self′ik splā′ning, self′-).

self-ex·pres·sion (self′ik spresh′ən, self′-), *n.* the expression or assertion of one's personality, as in conversation, behavior, poetry, painting, etc. **—self′-ex·press′ive,** *adj.*

self-feed (self′fēd′, self′-), *v.t.,* **-fed, -feed·ing.** *Agric.* to provide a supply of food to (animals) so as to allow them to eat as much and as often as they want. Cf. **hand-feed** (def. 1).

self-feed·er (self′fē′dər, self′-), *n.* an apparatus or machine that automatically discharges a supply of some material, esp. one for feeding livestock.

self-fer·ti·li·za·tion (self′fûr′tᵊli zā′shən, self′-), *n. Bot.* fertilization of a flower by a gamete from the same flower (opposed to *cross-fertilization*). **—self′-fer′ti·lized′,** *adj.*

self-for·get·ful (self′fər get′fəl, self′-), *adj.* disregarding one's own advantage, interest, etc. **—self′-for·get′ful·ly,** *adv.* **—self′-for·get′ful·ness,** *n.*

self-for·get·ting (self′fər get′ing, self′-), *adj.* self-forgetful. **—self′-for·get′ting·ly,** *adv.*

self-ful·fill·ment (self′fo͝ol fil′mənt, self′-), *n.* the act or fact of fulfilling one's ambitions, desires, etc., through one's own efforts. Also, *esp. Brit.,* **self′-ful·fil′ment.** **—self′-ful·fill′ing,** *adj.*

self-gov·erned (self′guv′ərnd, self′-), *adj.* **1.** governed by itself or having self-government; independent. **2.** self-regulating; self-determining. **3.** exercising self-control. **—self′-gov′ern·ing,** *adj.* **—Syn. 1.** autonomous.

self-gov·ern·ment (self′guv′ərn mənt, -ər mənt, self′-), *n.* **1.** control of the government of a state, community, or other body by its own members. **2.** the condition of being self-governed. **3.** self-control.

self-grat·i·fi·ca·tion (self′grat′ə fə kā′shən, self′-), *n.* the act of pleasing or satisfying oneself, esp. the gratification of one's impulses, needs, or desires.

self·heal (self′hēl′), *n.* **1.** a menthaceous plant, *Prunella vulgaris,* formerly believed to have healing properties. **2.** any of various other plants believed to have similar properties. [late ME *selfhele*]

self-help (self′help′, self′-), *n.* providing for or helping or the ability to provide for or help oneself without assistance from others. **—self′-help′ing,** *adj.*

self·hood (self′ho͝od), *n.* **1.** the state of being an individual person. **2.** one's personality. **3.** selfishness.

self-hyp·no·sis (self′hip nō′sis, self′-), *n.* autohypnosis. **—self-hyp·not·ic** (self′hip not′ik, self′-), *adj.* **—self′-hyp·not′i·cal·ly,** *adv.* **—self-hyp·no·tism** (self′hip′nə tiz′əm), *n.*

self-i·den·ti·fi·ca·tion (self′i den′tə fə kā′shən, self′-), *n.* identification of oneself with some other person or thing.

self-i·den·ti·ty (self′ī den′ti tē, self′-), *n.* the identity or consciousness of identity of a thing with itself.

self-im·age (self′im′ij), *n.* the idea, conception, or mental image one has of oneself.

self-im·por·tant (self′im pôr′tᵊnt, self′-), *adj.* having or showing an exaggerated opinion of one's own importance. **—self′-im·por′tance,** *n.* **—self′-im·por′tant·ly,** *adv.*

self-im·posed (self′im pōzd′, self′-), *adj.* imposed on one by oneself: *a self-imposed task.*

self-im·prove·ment (self′im pro͞ov′mənt, self′-), *n.* improvement of one's mind, character, etc., through one's own efforts. **—self′-im·prov′ing,** *adj.*

self-in·clu·sive (self′in klo͞o′siv, self′-), *adj.* including oneself or itself.

self-in·crim·i·nat·ing (self′in krim′ə nā′ting, self′-), *adj.* serving to incriminate oneself.

self-in·duced (self′in do͞ost′, -dyo͞ost′, self′-), *adj.* **1.** induced by oneself or itself. **2.** *Elect.* produced by self-induction.

self-in·duc·tion (self′in duk′shən), *n. Elect.* the process by which an electromotive force is induced in a circuit by a varying current in that circuit.

self-in·dul·gent (self′in dul′jənt, self′-), *adj.* **1.** indulging one's own desires, passions, whims, etc. **2.** showing such indulgence. **—self′-in·dul′gence,** *n.* **—self′-in·dul′gent·ly,** *adv.*

self-in·flict·ed (self′in flik′tid, self′-), *adj.* inflicted by oneself upon oneself: *a self-inflicted wound.* **—self′-in·flic′tion,** *n.*

self-in·sur·ance (self′in sho͝or′əns, self′-), *n.* a fund established by a person, business, etc., to cover the possible loss of property, etc.

self-in·ter·est (self′in′tər ist, -trist, self′-), *n.* **1.** regard for one's own interest or advantage, esp. with disregard for others. **2.** personal interest or advantage. **—self′-in′ter·est·ed,** *adj.* **—self′-in′ter·est·ed·ness,** *n.*

self·ish (sel′fish), *adj.* **1.** devoted to or caring only for oneself; concerned only with one's own interests. **2.** characterized by or revealing concern or care only for oneself. **—self′ish·ly,** *adv.* **—self′ish·ness,** *n.*

self-jus·ti·fi·ca·tion (self′jus′tə fə kā′shən, self′-), *n.* the act or fact of justifying oneself, esp. of offering excessive reasons, explanations, excuses, etc.

self-jus·ti·fy·ing (self′jus′tə fī′ing, self′-), *adj.* **1.** offering excuses for oneself. **2.** automatically adjusting printed or typed lines to fill a given space, esp. to conform to a rigid margin.

self-knowl·edge (self′nol′ij, self′-), *n.* knowledge or understanding of oneself, one's character, abilities, etc.

self·less (self′lis), *adj.* having little or no concern for oneself, esp. as regards fame, position, money, etc.; unselfish. **—self′less·ly,** *adv.* **—self′less·ness,** *n.*

self-lim·it·ed (self′lim′i tid, self′-), *adj.* (of a disease) running a definite and limited course.

---

self′-con·tempt′, *n.*
self′-con·tent′, *adj., n.*
self′-con·tent′ed·ly, *adv.*
self′-con·tent′ment, *n.*
self′-con·vict′ed, *adj.*
self′-cor·rect′ing, *adj.*
self′-cre·at′ed, *adj.*
self′-ded′i·ca′tion, *n.*
self′-de·fin′ing, *adj.*
self′-deg′ra·da′tion, *n.*
self′-de·jec′tion, *n.*
self′-de·light′, *n.*
self′-de·pend′ence, *n.*
self′-de·pend′ent, *adj.*
self′-de·pre′ci·a′tion, *n.*
self′-de·spair′, *n.*
self′-de·stroy′er, *n.*
self′-de·stroy′ing, *adj.*
self′-de·vel′op·ment, *n.*
self′-di·rect′ed, *adj.*
self′-di·rect′ing, *adj.*
self′-di·rec′tion, *n.*
self′-dis·sat′is·fac′tion, *n.*
self′-dis·trust′, *n.*
self′-dis·trust′ful, *adj.*
self′-dis·trust′ing, *adj.*
self′-doomed′, *adj.*
self′-driv′en, *adj.*
self′-e·lect′ed, *adj.*
self′-en·am′ored, *adj.*
self′-en·closed′, *adj.*
self′-en·joy′ment, *n.*
self′-en·rich′ment, *n.*
self′-e·vac′u·a′tion, *n.*
self′-e·volved′, *adj.*
self′-ex′al·ta′tion, *n.*
self′-ex·er′tion, *n.*
self′-ex·pand′ing, *adj.*
self′-flat′ter·y, *n.*
self′-fo′cused, *adj.*
self′-fo′cus·ing, *adj.*
self′-fo′cussed, *adj.*
self′-fo′cus·sing, *adj.*
self′-gen′er·at′ing, *adj.*
self′-giv′ing, *adj.*
self′-glo′ri·fi·ca′tion, *n.*
self′-glo′ri·fy′ing, *adj.*
self′-hate′, *n.*
self′-ha′tred, *n.*
self′-heal′ing, *adj.*
self′-hu·mil′i·at′ing, *adj.*
self′-hu·mil′i·a′tion, *n.*
self′-ig·nite′, *v.i.,* **-nit·ed, -nit·ing.**
self′-im′mo·la′tion, *n.*
self′-in′dig·na′tion, *n.*
self′-in·i′ti·at′ed, *adj.*
self′-in·i′ti·a·tive, *n.*
self′-in·struct′ed, *adj.*
self′-judg′ment, *n.*

self-liq·ui·dat·ing (self′lik′wi dā′ting, self′-), *adj.* **1.** capable of being sold and converted into cash within a short period of time or before the date on which the supplier must be paid. **2.** (of a property, loan, project, investment, etc.) used or operating in such a way as to repay the money needed to acquire it.

self-load·ing (self′lō′ding, self′-), *adj.* noting or pertaining to an automatic or semiautomatic firearm.

self-love (self′luv′), *n.* **1.** the tendency in man to promote his own welfare or well-being. **2.** self-respect. **3.** vanity. **4.** narcissism (def. 2).

self-made (self′mād′), *adj.* **1.** having succeeded in life unaided: *a self-made man.* **2.** made by oneself.

self-mor·ti·fi·ca·tion (self′môr′tə fə kā′shən), *n.* the inflicting of pain or privation on oneself.

self·ness (self′nis), *n.* selfhood.

self-o·pin·ion (self′ə pin′yən, self′-), *n.* opinion of oneself, esp. when unduly high.

self-o·pin·ion·at·ed (self′ə pin′yə nā′tid, self′-), *adj.* **1.** having an inordinately high regard for oneself, one's opinions, etc. **2.** stubborn or obstinate in holding to one's own opinions. Also, **self-o·pin·ioned** (self′ə pin′yənd).

self-per·pet·u·at·ing (self′pər pech′o͞o ā′ting, self′-), *adj.* **1.** continuing oneself in office, rank, etc., perpetually or beyond the normal limit. **2.** capable of indefinite continuation. —**self′-per·pet′u·a′tion,** *n.*

self-pit·y (self′pit′ē, self′-), *n.* pity for oneself, esp. a self-indulgent attitude concerning one's own difficulties. —**self′-pit′y·ing,** *adj.* —**self′-pit′y·ing·ly,** *adv.*

self-pol·li·na·tion (self′pol′ə nā′shən, self′-), *n.* *Bot.* the transfer of pollen from the anther to the stigma of the same flower, another flower on the same plant, or the flower of a plant of the same clone. Cf. **cross-pollination.** —**self-pol·li·nat·ed** (self′pol′ə nā′tid, self′-), *adj.*

self-por·trait (self′pōr′trit, -trāt, -pôr′-, self′-), *n.* **1.** a portrait of and by oneself, as a painting. **2.** any revelation by oneself of one's own personality and character, as in autobiography.

self-pos·sessed (self′pə zest′, self′-), *adj.* having or showing control of one's feelings, behavior, etc. —**self-pos·sess·ed·ly** (self′pə zes′id lē, -zest′lē, self′-), *adv.* —**Syn.** calm, collected, serene, cool.

self-pos·ses·sion (self′pə zesh′ən, self′-), *n.* the quality of being self-possessed.

self-pres·er·va·tion (self′prez′ər vā′shən, self′-), *n.* preservation of oneself from harm or destruction.

self-pro·nounc·ing (self′prə noun′sing), *adj.* having the pronunciation indicated directly on original spellings rather than separately in phonetic symbols.

self-pro·tec·tion (self′prə tek′shən, self′-), *n.* protection of oneself or itself. —**self′-pro·tect′ing,** *adj.* —**self′-pro·tec′tive,** *adj.*

self-ques·tion·ing (self′kwes′chə ning, self′-), *n.* review or scrutiny of one's own motives or behavior.

self-re·al·i·za·tion (self′rē′ə li zā′shən, self′-), *n.* the fulfillment of one's potential capacities.

self-re·gard (self′ri gärd′, self′-), *n.* **1.** consideration for oneself or one's own interests. **2.** self-respect. —**self′-re·gard′ing,** *adj.*

self-re·li·ance (self′ri lī′əns, self′-), *n.* reliance on oneself or one's own powers. —**self′-re·li′ant,** *adj.*

self-re·nun·ci·a·tion (self′ri nun′sē ā′shən, self′-), *n.* renunication of one's own will, interests, etc. —**self-re·nun·ci·a·to·ry** (self′ri nun′sē ə tōr′ē, -tôr′ē, -shē ə-, self′-), *adj.*

self-re·spect (self′ri spekt′, self′-), *n.* proper esteem or regard for the dignity of one's own character. —**self′-re·spect′ful, self′-re·spect′ing,** *adj.*

self-re·veal·ing (self′ri vē′ling, self′-), *adj.* displaying, exhibiting, or disclosing one's most private feelings, thoughts, etc. Also, **self-re·vel·a·to·ry** (self′ri vel′ə tōr′ē, -tôr′ē, -rev′ə lə-, self′-), **self-re·vel·a·tive** (self′ri vel′ə tiv, -rev′ə-lā′-, self′-). —**self-rev·e·la·tion** (self′rev′ə lā′shən, self′-), *n.*

self-right·eous (self′rī′chəs, self′-), *adj.* confident of one's own righteousness, esp. when smugly moralistic and intolerant of the opinions and behavior of others. —**self′-right′eous·ly,** *adv.* —**self′-right′eous·ness,** *n.*

self-ris·ing (self′rī′zing), *adj.* *Cookery.* (of flour) rising without the addition of leaven: *self-rising pancake flour.*

self-rule (self′ro͞ol′), *n.* self-government.

self-sac·ri·fice (self′sak′rə fīs′, self′-), *n.* sacrifice of one's interests, desires, pleasures, etc., as for duty or the good of another. —**self′-sac′ri·fic′ing,** *adj.* —**self′-sac′ri·fic′ing·ly,** *adv.* —**self′-sac′ri·fic′ing·ness,** *n.*

self·same (self′sām′), *adj.* being the very same; identical. [late ME *selve same;* see SELF, SAME; c. Dan *selvsamme,* OHG *selbsama*] —**self′same′ness,** *n.* —**Syn.** exact, very, same.

self-sat·is·fac·tion (self′sat′is fak′shən), *n.* satisfaction, usually smug, with oneself, one's achievements, etc.

self-sat·is·fied (self′sat′is fīd′, self′-), *adj.* feeling or showing self-satisfaction.

self-sat·is·fy·ing (self′sat′is fī′ing, self′-), *adj.* effecting satisfaction to oneself.

self-seek·er (self′sē′kər), *n.* a person who seeks his own interest or selfish ends.

self-seek·ing (self′sē′king), *n.* **1.** the seeking of one's own interest or selfish ends. —*adj.* **2.** given to or characterized by self-seeking; selfish. —**self′-seek′ing·ness,** *n.*

self-serv·ice (self′sûr′vis), *n.* **1.** unaided service of oneself, as in a shop or cafeteria. —*adj.* **2.** (of a shop, cafeteria, etc.) operated mainly by means of self-service.

self-serv·ing (self′sûr′ving), *adj.* **1.** preoccupied with one's own interests, often selfishly. **2.** serving to further one's own selfish interests.

self-sown (self′sōn′), *adj.* **1.** sown by itself, or without human or animal agency, as of a plant grown from seeds dropped from another plant. **2.** sown by any agency other than man, as of a plant grown from seeds scattered by birds or the wind.

self-start·er (self′stär′tər), *n.* **1.** a device that starts an internal-combustion engine without cranking by hand. **2.** *Informal.* a person who begins work or a project without needing to be told or encouraged to do so. —**self′-start′ing,** *adj.*

self-styled (self′stīld′), *adj.* styled, called, or considered by oneself as specified: *a self-styled leader.*

self-suf·fi·cient (self′sə fish′ənt, self′-), *adj.* **1.** able to supply one's own or its own needs without external assistance. **2.** having extreme confidence in one's own resources, powers, etc. Also, **self-suf·fic·ing** (self′sə fī′sing). —**self′-suf·fi′cien·cy,** *n.* —**self′-suf·fi′cient·ly,** *adv.*

self-sug·ges·tion (self′səg jes chən, -jesh′-, -sə-, self′-), *n.* autosuggestion.

self-sup·port (self′sə pōrt′, -pôrt′, self′-), *n.* the complete supporting or maintaining of oneself without relying on any outside aid. —**self′-sup·port′ed,** *adj.* —**self′-sup·port′ing,** *adj.* —**self′-sup·port′ing·ly,** *adv.*

self-sur·ren·der (self′sə ren′dər, self′-), *n.* the surrender or yielding up of oneself, one's will, affections, etc., as to another person, an influence, cause, etc.

self-sus·tain·ing (self′sə stā′ning, self′-), *adj.* self-supporting. —**self′-sus·tained′,** *adj.*

self-taught (self′tôt′), *adj.* **1.** having taught oneself to act in a specified capacity. **2.** learned by oneself.

self·ward (self′wərd), *adv.* Also, **self′wards. 1.** in the direction of or toward oneself. **2.** within oneself; inward: *She turned her thoughts selfward.* —*adj.* **3.** tending toward or directed at oneself. —**self′ward·ness,** *n.*

self-will (self′wil′, self′-), *n.* stubborn or obstinate willfulness, as in pursuing one's own wishes or aims. [ME, OE] —**self′-willed′,** *adj.* —**self′-willed′ly,** *adv.* —**self′-willed′ness,** *n.*

self-wind·ing (self′wīn′ding), *adj.* (of a timepiece) kept wound or wound periodically by a self-contained mechanism, as a system of weighted levers, etc.

Sel·juk (sel jo͝ok′), *adj.* **1.** noting or pertaining to several Turkish dynasties of the 11th to 13th centuries. —*n.* **2.** a member of a Seljuk dynasty or of a tribe ruled by them. Also, **Sel·juk·i·an** (sel jo͞o′kē ən).

Sel·kirk (sel′kûrk), *n.* **1. Alexander** (originally *Alexander Selcraig*), 1676–1721, Scottish sailor marooned on a Pacific island: supposed prototype of the hero of Defoe's novel *Robinson Crusoe* (1719). **2.** Also called **Sel·kirk·shire** (sel′kûrk shēr′, -shər). a county in SE Scotland. 21,055 (est. 1961); 268 sq. mi. *Co. seat:* Selkirk.

Sel′kirk Moun′tains, a mountain range in SW Canada. Highest peak, Mt. Sir Donald, 11,123 ft.

sell (sel), *v.,* **sold, sell·ing,** *n.* —*v.t.* **1.** to dispose of to a purchaser for a price: *He sold the car to me for $500.* **2.** to deal in; keep or offer for sale: *He sells insurance.* **3.** to make a sale or offer for sale to: *He'll sell me the car for $500.* **4.** to persuade or induce to buy. **5.** to cause to be accepted, esp. generally or widely: *to sell an idea to the public.* **6.** to cause or persuade to accept; convince: *to sell the voters on a candidate.* **7.** to accept a price for or make a profit of (something not a proper object for such action): *to sell one's soul.* **8.** to force or exact a price for: *The defenders of the fort sold their lives dearly.* —*v.i.* **9.** to make a sale of something. **10.** to offer something for sale: *I like his house—will he sell?* **11.** to be employed to persuade or induce others to buy, as a salesman or a clerk in a store. **12.** to have a specific price; be offered for sale at the price indicated (fol. by *at* or *for*): *Eggs sell at sixty cents a dozen.* **13.** to be in demand as a purchase. **14.** to win acceptance, approval, or adoption: *Here's an idea that'll sell.* **15. sell out, a.** to dispose of entirely by selling. **b.** *Informal.* to betray (an associate, a cause, etc.); turn traitor. **16. sell short.** See **short** (def. 20). **17. sell (someone) a bill of goods.** See **bill of goods** (def. 2). —*n.* **18.** the act or method of selling. [ME *selle(n),* OE *sellan;* c. Icel *selja,* LG *sellen,* Goth *saljan,* orig. to cause to take; gradational var. of Gk *heleîn* to take] —**Syn. 1.** See **trade.** —**Ant. 1.** buy.

sell·er (sel′ər), *n.* **1.** a person who sells; salesman or vendor. **2.** an article in the market, considered with reference to its sales: *This hat is one of the poorest sellers.*

sell′ers' mar′ket, a market in which goods and services are scarce and prices relatively high. Cf. **buyers' market.**

sell′ing race′, *Rare.* a claiming race at the end of which the winning horse is offered for sale.

sell·out (sel′out′), *n.* **1.** the act or an instance of selling out. **2.** an entertainment for which all the seats are sold.

Sel·ma (sel′mə), *n.* a city in central Alabama, on the Alabama River. 27,379 (1970).

Selt·zer (selt′sər), *n.* **1.** a naturally effervescent mineral water containing common salt and small quantities of

self′-loath′ing, *n., adj.*
self′-mas′ter·y, *n.*
self′-mo′tion, *n.*
self′-mov′ing, *adj.*
self′-mur′der, *n.*
self′-named′, *adj.*
self′-neg·lect′, *n., adj.*
self′-oc′cu·pied′, *adj.*
self′-op′er·at′ing, *adj.*
self′-or·dained′, *adj.*
self′-o·rig′i·nat′ed, *adj.*
self′-pow′ered, *adj.*
self′-praise′, *n.*
self′-pre·oc′cu·pa′tion, *n.*
self′-prep′a·ra′tion, *n.*
self′-pre·pared′, *adj.*
self′-pre·scribed′, *adj.*
self′-pro·claimed′, *adj.*
self′-pro·duced′, *adj.*
self′-pro·fessed′, *adj.*
self′-prof′it, *n.*
self′-pro·pelled′, *adj.*
self′-pro·pul′sion, *n.*
self′-pun′ish·ment, *n.*
self′-rec′ol·lec′tion, *n.*
self′-re·cord′ing, *adj.*
self′-re·flec′tion, *n.*
self′-ref′or·ma′tion, *n.*
self′-re′gis·ter·ing, *adj.*
self′-reg′u·lat′ing, *adj.*
self′-reg′u·la′tion, *n.*
self′-re·peat′ing, *adj.*
self′-re·pel′lent, *adj.*
self′-re·pose′, *n.*
self′-re·pres′sion, *n.*
self′-re·proach′, *n.*
self′-re·proof′, *n.*
self′-re·sent′ment, *n.*
self′-re·signed′, *adj.*
self′-re·straint′, *n.*
self′-re·strict′ed, *adj.*
self′-re·stric′tion, *n.*
self′-schooled′, *adj.*
self′-scru′ti·nized′, *adj.*
self′-scru′ti·niz′ing, *adj.*
self′-scru′ti·ny, *n.*
self′-seal′ing, *adj.*
self′-tor′ment, *n.*
self′-tor·ment′ing, *adj.*
self′-trained′, *adj.*
self′-trans′for·ma′tion, *n.*
self′-treat′ment, *n.*
self′-trust′, *n.*
self′-un′der·stand′ing, *n.*
self′-vin′di·ca′tion, *n.*
self′-wor′ship, *n.*

sodium, calcium, and magnesium carbonates. **2.** (*often l.c.*) a prepared water of similar composition. Also called **Selt′zer wa′ter.** [< G *Selterser* named after *Selters,* a village near Wiesbaden; see -ER¹]

sel·vage (sel′vij), *n.* **1.** the edge of woven fabric finished to prevent raveling. **2.** any similar strip or part, as at the side of wallpaper. **3.** a plate or surface through which a bolt of a lock passes. Also, **sel′vedge.** [SELF + EDGE, modeled on D *zelfegge*] —**sel′vaged,** *adj.*

selves (selvz), *n.* pl. of **self.**

Sem., **1.** Seminary. **2.** Semitic. Also, **Sem**

sem., semicolon.

se·man·tic (si man′tik), *adj.* **1.** of, pertaining to, or arising from the different meanings of words or other symbols. **2.** of or pertaining to semantics. [< Gk *sēmantik(ós)* having meaning = *sēmant(ós)* (*sēman-,* base of *sēmaínein* to show, mark + *-tos* verbal adj. suffix) + *-ikos* -IC] —**se·man′ti·cal·ly,** *adv.*

se·man·tics (si man′tiks), *n.* (*construed as sing.*) **1.** *Linguistics.* **a.** the study of meaning. **b.** the study of linguistic development by classifying and examining changes in meaning. **2.** *Logic, Philos.* the branch of semiotic dealing with the relations between signs and that which they denote. **3.** See **general semantics.** [see SEMANTIC, -ICS] —**se·man·ti·cist** (si man′ti sist), **se·man·ti·cian** (sē′man tish′ən), *n.*

sem·a·phore (sem′ə fōr′, -fôr′), *n., v.,* **-phored, -phor·ing.** —*n.* **1.** any of various devices for signaling or conveying information by changing the position of a light, flag, etc. **2.** a system of signaling by a person, by which a special flag is held in each hand and various positions of the arms indicate specific letters, numbers, etc. —*v.t., v.i.* **3.** to signal by semaphore or by some system of flags. [< Gk *sêma* sign + -PHORE] —**sem·a·phor·ic** (sem′ə fôr′ik, -for′-), **sem′a·phor′i·cal,** *adj.* —**sem′a·phor′i·cal·ly,** *adv.*

Semaphore (railroad)

Se·ma·rang (sə mär′äng), *n.* a seaport on N Java, in S Indonesia. 487,006 (est. 1961). Also, **Samarang.**

se·ma·si·ol·o·gy (si mā′sē ol′ə jē, -zē-), *n.* semantics, esp. the study of semantic change. [< Gk *sēmasí(a)* meaning + -O- + -LOGY] —**se·ma·si·o·log·i·cal** (si mā′sē ə loj′i kəl, -zē-), *adj.* —**se·ma′si·o·log′i·cal·ly,** *adv.* —**se·ma′si·ol′o·gist,** *n.*

se·mat·ic (si mat′ik), *adj.* *Biol.* serving as a sign or warning of danger, as the colors or markings of certain poisonous animals. [< Gk *sēmat-* (s. of *sêma*) sign + -IC]

sem·bla·ble (sem′blə bəl), *Archaic.* —*adj.* **1.** like or similar. **2.** seeming or apparent. —*n.* **3.** likeness; resemblance. [ME < MF = *sembl(er)* (to) seem + *-able* -ABLE. See SEMBLANCE] —**sem′bla·bly,** *adv.*

sem·blance (sem′bləns), *n.* **1.** outward aspect or appearance. **2.** an assumed or unreal appearance; show. **3.** a likeness, image, or copy. **4.** a spectral appearance; apparition. [ME < MF = *sembl(er)* (to) seem (see RESEMBLE) + *-ance* -ANCE]

se·mé (sə mā′), *adj.* *Heraldry.* covered with many small, identical figures. [< F: lit., sown, ptp. of *semer* < L *sēmināre* to sow = *sēmin-* (s. of *sēmen*) seed + *-āre* inf. suffix]

se·mei·ol·o·gy (sē′mī ol′ə jē), *n.* **1.** the science of signs. **2.** sign language. Also, **semiology.** [< Gk *sēmeîo(n)* sign + -LOGY] —**se·mei·o·log·ic** (sē′mī ə loj′ik), **se′mei·o·log′i·cal,** *adj.* —**se′mei·ol′o·gist,** *n.*

se·mei·ot·ic (sē′mī ot′ik, sē′mē-, sem′ī-, sem′ē-), *adj.* semiotic. Also, **se′mei·ot′i·cal.**

Sem·e·le (sem′ə lē′), *n.* *Class. Myth.* a daughter of Cadmus and mother, by Zeus, of Dionysus: she was destroyed when Zeus fulfilled her wish to see him as god of lightning.

sem·eme (sem′ēm), *n.* *Linguistics.* the meaning of a morpheme. [< Gk *sêm(a)* sign + -EME; coined by L. Bloomfield in 1933]

se·men (sē′mən), *n.* the viscid, whitish fluid produced in the male reproductive organs, containing spermatozoa. [< L: seed]

se·mes·ter (si mes′tər), *n.* **1.** an academic session constituting half of the academic year, lasting typically from 15 to 18 weeks. **2.** (in German universities) a session, lasting about six months. [< G < L *sēme(n)stris* = *sē* (comb. form of *sex* SIX) + *-menstris* monthly (*mens(is)* month + *-tris* adj. suffix)] —**se·mes′tral, se·mes·tri·al** (si mes′trē əl), *adj.*

semi-, an element borrowed from Latin meaning "half," freely prefixed to English words of any origin: *semifinal; semimonthly.* [ME < L; c. OE *sōm-, sām-* half (mod. dial. *sam-*), OHG *sāmi-,* Skt *sāmi-,* Gk *hēmi-*]

semi-ab·stract (sem′ē ab′strakt, -ab strakt′, sem′ī-), *adj.* pertaining to or designating a style of painting or sculpture in which the subject remains recognizable although the forms are highly stylized in a manner derived from abstract art. —**sem·i-ab·strac·tion** (sem′ē ab strak′shən, sem′ī-), *n.*

sem·i·an·nu·al (sem′ē an′yo͞o əl, sem′ī-), *adj.* **1.** occurring, done, or published every half year or twice a year. **2.** lasting for half a year: *a semiannual plant.* —**sem′i·an′nu·al·ly,** *adv.*

sem·i·a·quat·ic (sem′ē ə kwat′ik, -kwot′-, sem′ī-), *adj.* *Bot., Zool.* partly aquatic; growing or living close to water and sometimes found in water.

sem·i·ar·id (sem′ē ar′id, sem′ī-), *adj.* (of a region, land, etc.) characterized by very little annual rainfall, usually from 10 to 20 inches. —**sem·i·a·rid·i·ty** (sem′ē ə rid′i tē, sem′ī-), *n.*

sem·i·au·to·mat·ic (sem′ē ô′tə mat′ik, sem′ī-), *adj.* **1.** partly automatic. **2.** (of a firearm) automatically ejecting the cartridge case of a fired shot and loading the next cartridge from the magazine but requiring a squeeze of the trigger to fire each individual shot. —*n.* **3.** a self-loading rifle or other firearm. —**sem′i·au′to·mat′i·cal·ly,** *adv.*

sem·i·breve (sem′ē brēv′, sem′ī-), *n.* *Music Chiefly Brit.* a note half the length of a breve; whole note. See illus. at **note.**

sem·i·cen·te·nar·y (sem′ē sen′tᵊner′ē, sem′ī- *or, esp. Brit.,* -sen ten′ə rē, -tē′nə-), *adj., n., pl.* **-nar·ies.** semicentennial.

sem·i·cen·ten·ni·al (sem′ē sen ten′ē əl, sem′ī-), *adj.* **1.** of or pertaining to a 50th anniversary. —*n.* **2.** a 50th anniversary. **3.** the celebration of this anniversary.

sem·i·cir·cle (sem′i sûr′kəl), *n.* **1.** Also called **sem·i·cir·cum·fer·ence** (sem′ē sər kum′fər əns, -frəns, sem′ī-). half of a circle; the arc from one end of a diameter to the other. **2.** anything having or arranged in the form of a half of a circle. [< L *sēmicircul(us)*] —**sem·i·cir·cu·lar** (sem′i sûr′kyə lər), *adj.* —**sem′i·cir′cu·lar·ly,** *adv.*

semicir′cular canal′, *Anat.* any of the three curved tubular canals in the labyrinth of the ear, associated with the sense of equilibrium.

sem·i·co·lon (sem′i kō′lən), *n.* the punctuation mark (;) used to indicate a major division in a sentence where a more distinct separation is felt between clauses or items on a list than is indicated by a comma.

sem·i·con·duc·tor (sem′ē kən duk′tər, sem′ī-), *n.* a substance whose electric conductivity at normal temperature is intermediate between that of a metal and an insulator, esp. germanium and silicon. —**sem′i·con·duc′tion,** *n.*

sem·i·crys·tal·line (sem′ē kris′tᵊlin, -tᵊlīn′, sem′ī-), *adj.* partly or imperfectly crystalline.

sem·i·cyl·in·der (sem′ē sil′in dər, sem′ī-), *n.* half of a cylinder divided lengthwise. —**sem·i·cy·lin·dri·cal** (sem′ē si lin′dri kəl, sem′ī-), **sem′i·cy·lin′dric,** *adj.*

sem·i·des·ert (sem′ē dez′ərt, sem′ī-), *n.* an extremely dry area characterized by sparse vegetation.

sem·i·de·tached (sem′ē di tacht′, sem′ī-), *adj.* **1.** partly detached. **2.** noting or pertaining to a house joined by a party wall to another house.

sem·i·di·ur·nal (sem′ē dī ûr′nᵊl, sem′ī-), *adj.* **1.** pertaining to, consisting of, or accomplished in half a day. **2.** occurring every 12 hours or twice each day.

sem·i·dome (sem′ē dōm′, sem′ī-), *n.* a half dome, esp. as formed by a vertical section, as over a semicircular apse.

sem·i·el·lipse (sem′ē i lips′, sem′ī-), *n.* *Geom.* a half ellipse, usually one containing both ends of the major axis. —**sem·i·el·lip·tic** (sem′ē i lip′tik, sem′ī-), **sem′i·el·lip′ti·cal,** *adj.*

sem·i·fi·nal (sem′ē fīn′ᵊl, sem′ī-), *Sports.* —*adj.* **1.** of or pertaining to the penultimate round played in a tournament, the winners of which are qualified to play in the final round. **2.** (in boxing) of or pertaining to the second most important bout on a card, usually immediately preceding the main bout. —*n.* **3.** a semifinal contest or round. **4.** (in boxing) the second most important bout on a card.

sem·i·fi·nal·ist (sem′ē fīn′ᵊlist, sem′ī-), *n.* *Sports.* a person who participates or is qualified to participate in a semifinal contest.

sem·i·fit·ted (sem′ē fit′id, sem′ī-), *adj.* designed to fit closely but not snugly: *a semifitted jacket.*

sem·i·flu·id (sem′ē flo͞o′id, sem′ī-), *adj.* **1.** imperfectly fluid; having both fluid and solid characteristics. —*n.* **2.** a semifluid substance. Also called **semiliquid.** —**sem′i·flu·id′i·ty,** *n.*

sem·i·for·mal (sem′ē fôr′məl, sem′ī-), *adj.* partly formal; containing some formal elements: *a semiformal occasion; semiformal attire.*

sem·i·liq·uid (sem′ē lik′wid, sem′ī-), *adj., n.* semifluid. —**sem′i·li·quid′i·ty,** *n.*

sem·i·lit·er·ate (sem′ē lit′ər it, sem′ī-), *adj.* **1.** barely able to read and write. **2.** capable of reading but not writing.

sem·i·lu·nar (sem′ē lo͞o′nər, sem′ī-), *adj.* shaped like a half-moon; crescent.

sem′ilu′nar valve′, *Anat.* either of two valves consisting of a set of three crescent-shaped flaps of tissue in the aorta and in the pulmonary artery that prevents blood from flowing back into the heart after contraction. Cf. **aortic valve, pulmonary valve.**

sem·i·month·ly (sem′ē munth′lē, sem′ī-), *adj., n., pl.* **-lies,** *adv.* —*adj.* **1.** made, occurring, done, or published twice a month. —*n.* **2.** something occurring every half month or twice a month. **3.** a semimonthly publication. —*adv.* **4.** twice a month. —**Usage.** See **bimonthly.**

sem·i·nal (sem′ə nᵊl), *adj.* **1.** pertaining to, containing, or consisting of semen. **2.** *Bot.* of or pertaining to seed. **3.** having possibilities of future development. **4.** highly original and influencing future events or developments. [late ME < L *sēmināl(is)* = *sēmin-* (s. of *sēmen*) seed + *-ālis* -AL¹] —**sem′i·nal′i·ty,** *n.* —**sem′i·nal·ly,** *adv.*

sem·i·nar (sem′ə när′), *n.* **1.** a small group of students, as in a university, engaged in advanced study and original research under a member of the faculty and meeting regularly. **2.** a meeting of such a group. **3.** a course or subject of study for advanced students. **4.** any meeting for exchanging information and holding discussions. [< G < L *sēminār-(ium)* SEMINARY]

sem·i·nar·i·an (sem′ə nâr′ē ən), *n.* a student in a theological seminary.

sem·i·nar·y (sem′ə ner′ē), *n., pl.* **-nar·ies.** **1.** a special school providing education in theology, religious history, etc.: primarily intended to prepare students for the priesthood, ministry, or rabbinate. **2.** a school, esp. one of higher grade. **3.** a school of secondary or higher level for young

sem′i·ac′tive, *adj.*
sem′i·ag′ri·cul′tur·al, *adj.*
sem′i·au·ton′o·mous, *adj.*
sem′i·bi′o·graph′i·cal, *adj.;* **-ly,** *adv.*
sem′i·civ′i·li·za′tion, *n.*
sem′i·civ′i·lized, *adj.*
sem′i·clas′si·cal, *adj.;* **-ly,** *adv.*
sem′i·com′i·cal, *adj.*
sem′i·con′scious, *adj.*
sem′i·con′scious·ness, *n.*
sem′i·dai′ly, *adj., adv.*
sem′i·de·pend′ence, *n.*
sem′i·de·pend′ent, *adj.;* **-ly,** *adv.*
sem′i·di·vine′, *adj.*
sem′i·do·mes′ti·cat′ed, *adj.*
sem′i·do·mes′ti·ca′tion, *n.*
sem′i·dry′, *adj.*
sem′i·e·rect′, *adj.*
sem′i·fic′tion·al, *adj.;* **-ly,** *adv.*
sem′i·fic′tion·al·ized′, *adj.*
sem′i·fin′ished, *adj.*
sem′i·formed′, *adj.*
sem′i·glob′u·lar, *adj.*
sem′i·hard′, *adj.*
sem′i·il·lit′er·ate, *adj.*
sem′i·in·dus′tri·al, *adj.*
sem′i·in·dus′tri·al·ized′, *adj.*
sem′i·in·stinc′tive, *adj.;* **-ly,** *adv.*
sem′i·in·tox′i·cat′ed, *adj.*
sem′i·i·ron′i·cal, *adj.*
sem′i·leg′end·ar′y, *adj.*
sem′i·ma·ture′, *adj.*
sem′i·moun′tain·ous, *adj.*
sem′i·mys′ti·cal, *adj.*
sem′i·myth′i·cal, *adj.*

women. **4.** seminar (def. 1). [late ME < L *sēminări(um)* seed plot, nursery] —**sem/i·nar/i·al,** *adj.*

sem·i·na·tion (sem/ə nā/shən), *n.* a sowing or impregnating; dissemination. [< L *sēminātiōn-* (s. of *sēminātiō*) = *sēmināt(us)* (ptp. of *sēmināre* to sow; see SEMEN) + *-iōn-* -ION]

sem·i·nif·er·ous (sem/ə nif/ər əs), *adj.* **1.** *Anat.* conveying or containing semen. **2.** *Bot.* bearing or producing seed. [< L *sēmini-* seed (see SEMEN) + -FEROUS]

sem·i·niv·or·ous (sem/ə niv/ər əs), *adj.* feeding on seeds: *seminivorous birds.* [< L *sēmini-* seed (see SEMEN) + -VOROUS]

Sem·i·nole (sem/ə nōl/), *n., pl.* **-noles,** (*esp. collectively*) **-nole,** *adj.* —*n.* **1.** a member of a Muskogean tribe of American Indians, resident in Florida and in Oklahoma. —*adj.* **2.** of or pertaining to the Seminoles or their language. [< AmerInd (Creek) *Sim-a-nō-le* or *Iste siminōla* separatist, runaway]

se·mi·ol·o·gy (sē/mē ol/ə jē, sē/mī-, sem/ē-, sem/ī-), *n.* semeiology. —**se·mi·o·log·ic** (sē/mē ə loj/ik, sē/mī-, sem/ē-, sem/ī-), **se/mi·o·log/i·cal,** *adj.* —**se/mi·ol/o·gist,** *n.*

se·mi·ot·ic (sē/mē ot/ik, sē/mī-, sem/ē-, sem/ī-), *adj.* Also, **se/mi·ot/i·cal, semeiotic, semeiotical. 1.** pertaining to signs. **2.** *Med.* of or pertaining to symptoms; symptomatic. —*n.* **3.** Often, **semiotics.** *Logic, Philos.* a general theory of signs and symbolism, usually divided into the branches of pragmatics, semantics, and syntactics. [< Gk *sēmeî(on)* sign + -OTIC]

Se·mi·pa·la·tinsk (se/mi pä lä/tinsk), *n.* a city in NE Kazakstan, in the S Soviet Union in Asia, on the Irtish River. 191,000 (est. 1964).

Semipalmate foot

sem·i·pal·mate (sem/ē pal/māt, -mit, sem/ī-), *adj.* partially or imperfectly palmate, as a bird's foot; half-webbed. Also, **sem/i·pal/mat·ed.**

sem·i·par·a·sit·ic (sem/ē par/ə sit/ik, sem/ī-), *adj.* **1.** *Biol.* commonly parasitic but capable of living on dead or decaying animal matter. **2.** *Bot.* partly parasitic and partly photosynthetic. —**sem·i·par·a·site** (sem/ē par/ə sīt/, sem/ī-), *n.* —**sem·i·par·a·sit·ism** (sem/ē par/ə sī/tiz əm, sem/ī-), *n.*

sem·i·per·ma·nent (sem/ē pûr/mə nənt, sem/ī-), *adj.* not quite permanent.

sem·i·per·me·a·ble (sem/ē pûr/mē ə bəl, sem/ī-), *adj.* permeable to certain substances only: *a semipermeable membrane.* —**sem/i·per/me·a·bil/i·ty,** *n.*

sem·i·plas·tic (sem/ē plas/tik, sem/ī-), *adj.* imperfectly plastic; in a state between rigidity and plasticity.

sem·i·por·ce·lain (sem/ē pōr/sə lin, -pôr/-, -pōrs/lin, -pôrs/-, sem/ī-), *n.* any of several vitrified ceramic wares lacking the translucency or hardness of true porcelain but otherwise similar to it.

sem·i·post·al (sem/ē pōs/tᵊl, sem/ī-), *Philately.* —*n.* **1.** a postage stamp sold by a government at a premium above its face value, the excess being used for a nonpostal purpose, as a charity. —*adj.* **2.** noting or pertaining to such a stamp.

sem·i·pre·cious (sem/ē presh/əs, sem/ī-), *adj.* (of a stone) having commercial value as a gem but not classified as precious, as the amethyst or garnet.

sem·i·pri·vate (sem/ē prī/vit, sem/ī-), *adj.* having some degree of privacy but not fully private, as a hospital room with fewer beds than a ward. —**sem·i·pri·va·cy** (sem/ē-prī/və sē, sem/ī-), *n.*

sem·i·pro (sem/ē prō/, sem/ī-), *adj., n., pl.* **-pros.** *Informal.* semiprofessional.

sem·i·pro·fes·sion·al (sem/ē prə fesh/ə nᵊl, sem/ī-), *adj.* **1.** engaged in some field or sport for pay on a part-time basis. **2.** engaged in by paid, part-time people. **3.** having some features of professional work but requiring less knowledge, skill, or judgment. **4.** of, for, or pertaining to a semiprofessional person: *a semiprofessional apartment.* —*n.* **5.** a person who is active in some field or sport for pay on a part-time basis. —**sem/i·pro·fes/sion·al·ly,** *adv.*

sem·i·qua·ver (sem/ē kwā/vər), *n.* *Music Chiefly Brit.* a sixteenth note. See illus. at **note.** Also called **demiquaver.**

Se·mir·a·mis (si mir/ə mis), *n.* a legendary Assyrian queen, the founder of Babylon, noted for her beauty and strength.

sem·i·rig·id (sem/ē rij/id, sem/ī-), *adj.* **1.** not fully rigid; partly rigid. **2.** *Aeron.* noting or pertaining to a type of airship whose shape is maintained by means of a rigid keel-like structure and by internal gas pressure.

sem·i·round (sem/ē round/, sem/ī-), *adj.* having one surface that is round and another that is flat.

se·mis (sā/mis, sē/-), *n.* a copper coin of ancient Rome, the half part of an as. [< L; see SEMI-, AS²]

sem·i·skilled (sem/ē skild/, sem/ī-), *adj.* having or requiring more training and skill than unskilled labor but less than skilled labor.

sem·i·sol·id (sem/ē sol/id, sem/ī-), *adj.* **1.** having a somewhat firm consistency; more or less solid. —*n.* **2.** a semisolid substance.

sem·i·spher·ic (sem/ē sfer/ik, sem/ī-), *adj.* shaped like half a sphere; hemispheric. Also, **sem/i·spher/i·cal.** —**sem·i·sphere** (sem/i sfēr/), *n.*

Sem·ite (sem/īt *or, esp. Brit.,* sē/mīt), *n.* **1.** a member of any of various ancient and modern peoples originating in SW Asia, among whom are the Hebrews and Arabs. **2.** a Jew. **3.** a member of any of the peoples supposedly descended from Shem. [< NL *sēmīt(a)* < LL, Gk *Sēm* (< Heb *Shēm*) SHEM + *-īta* -ITE¹]

Se·mit·ic (sə mit/ik), *n.* **1.** an important subfamily of Afro-Asiatic languages, including Akkadian, Arabic, Aramaic, Hebrew, and Phoenician. *Abbr.:* Sem —*adj.* **2.** of or pertaining to the Semites or their languages, esp. of or pertaining to the Jews. [< NL *sēmītic(us)* = *sēmīt(a)* SEMITE + *-icus* -IC]

Se·mit·ics (sə mit/iks), *n.* (*construed as sing.*) the study of the Semitic languages, literature, etc. [see SEMITIC, -ICS] —**Sem·i·tist** (sem/i tist *or, esp. Brit.,* sē/mi-), *n.*

Sem·i·tism (sem/i tiz/əm *or, esp. Brit.,* sē/mi-), *n.* **1.** Semitic characteristics, esp. the ways, ideas, influence, etc., of the Jewish people. **2.** a word or idiom peculiar to, derived from, or characteristic of a Semitic language.

sem·i·tone (sem/ē tōn/), *n.* *Music.* a pitch interval halfway between two whole tones. Also called **half step, half tone.** —**sem·i·ton·ic** (sem/i ton/ik), **sem·i·ton·al** (sem/i-tōn/ᵊl), *adj.* —**sem/i·ton/al·ly,** *adv.*

sem·i·trail·er (sem/i trā/lər), *n.* a detachable trailer for hauling freight, having its forward end supported by the rear of its truck tractor.

sem·i·trop·i·cal (sem/ē trop/i kəl, sem/ī-), *adj.* subtropical. Also, **sem/i·trop/ic.** —**sem/i·trop/ics,** *n.pl.* —**sem/i-trop/i·cal·ly,** *adv.*

sem·i·vit·re·ous (sem/ē vi/trē əs, sem/ī-) *adj.* partially vitreous, as mineral constituents of volcanic rocks.

sem·i·vow·el (sem/ē vou/əl), *n.* **1.** *Phonet.* a speech sound of vowel quality used as a consonant, as (w) in *wet* or (y) in *yet.* **2.** a speech sound of consonantal quality used as a vowel, as (m, n, ng, r, l). [SEMI- + VOWEL; r. *semivocal* < L *sēmivocāl(is)* half vowel]

sem·i·week·ly (sem/ē wēk/lē, sem/ī-), *adj., n., pl.* **-lies,** *adv.* —*adj.* **1.** occurring, done, appearing, or published twice a week: *semiweekly visits.* —*n.* **2.** a semiweekly publication. —*adv.* **3.** twice a week. —**Usage.** See **biweekly.**

sem·i·year·ly (sem/ē yēr/lē, sem/ī-), *adj.* **1.** semiannual (def. 1). —*adv.* **2.** twice a year; semiannually.

Semmes (semz), *n.* **Raphael,** 1809–77, Confederate admiral in the American Civil War.

sem·o·li·na (sem/ə lē/nə), *n.* a granular, milled product of durum wheat, consisting almost entirely of endosperm particles. [m. It *semolino* = *semol(a)* bran (< L *simila* flour) + *-ino* dim. suffix]

Sem·pach (*Ger.* zem/päkн), *n.* a village in central Switzerland: Austrians defeated by Swiss 1386. 1345 (1960).

sem·per fi·de·lis (sem/pen fi dā/lis; *Eng.* sem/pər fi dā/-lis, -dē/-), *Latin.* always faithful: motto of the U.S. Marine Corps.

sem·per pa·ra·tus (sem/pen pä rä/to͝os; *Eng.* sem/pər pə rā/təs), *Latin.* always ready: motto of the U.S. Coast Guard.

sem·pi·ter·nal (sem/pi tûr/nᵊl), *adj.* *Literary.* everlasting; eternal. [late ME < LL *sempiternāl(is)* = L *sempitern(us)* everlasting (*semper* always + *eternus* (ETERNAL) + *-ālis* -AL¹] —**sem/pi·ter/nal·ly,** *adv.*

sem·pli·ce (sem/pli chā/; *It.* sem/plē che), *adj.* (used as a musical direction) simple; straightforward. [It: simple; see SIMPLICITY]

sem·pre (sem/prā; *It.* sem/pre), *adv.* (used in musical directions) throughout. [< It: always < L *semper*]

semp·stress (semp/stris, sem/tris), *n.* seamstress.

sen¹ (sen), *n., pl.* **sen.** a money of account of Japan, the 100th part of a yen, equal to 10 rin. [< Jap < Chin *ch'ien* coin]

sen² (sen), *n., pl.* **sen.** a money of account of Cambodia, the 100th part of a riel. [< native name in Cambodia]

sen³ (sen), *n., pl.* **sen.** an aluminum coin of Indonesia, the 100th part of a rupiah; cent. [< native name in Indonesia]

sen., 1. senate. **2.** senator. **3.** senior. Also, **sen**

sen·ar·mon·tite (sen/ər mon/tīt), *n.* a mineral, antimony trioxide, Sb_2O_3. [named after Henri de *Sénarmont* (d. 1862), French mineralogist; see -ITE¹]

sen·a·ry (sen/ə rē), *adj.* of or pertaining to the number six. [< L *sēnāri(us)* = *sēn(ī)* six each (*se(x)* SIX + *-nī* distributive suffix) + *-ārius* -ARY]

sen·ate (sen/it), *n.* **1.** an assembly or council having the highest deliberative functions. **2.** (*cap.*) the upper house of the legislature of certain countries, as the United States, France, etc. **3.** the room or building in which such a group meets. **4.** *Rom. Hist.* the supreme council of the Roman state. **5.** a governing, advisory, or disciplinary body, as in certain universities. [ME *senat* < L *senāt(us)* council of elders = *sen(ex)* old + *-ātus* -ATE³]

sen·a·tor (sen/ə tər), *n.* **1.** a member of a senate. **2.** (*cap.*) *U.S.* a title of respect accorded a person who is or has been a member of the Senate. [ME *senatour* < AF < L *senātor* = *senāt(us)* SENATE + *-or* -OR²] —**sen/a·tor·ship/,** *n.*

sen·a·to·ri·al (sen/ə tōr/ē əl, -tôr/-), *adj.* **1.** of, pertaining to, characteristic of, or befitting a senator or senate. **2.** consisting of senators. [< L *senātōri(us)* (see SENATOR, -IOUS) + -AL¹] —**sen/a·to/ri·al·ly,** *adv.*

senato/rial cour/tesy, *U.S.* the practice in the Senate of confirming only those presidential appointees approved by both senators from the state of the appointee, or by the senior senator of the president's party.

senato/rial dis/trict, *U.S.* one of a fixed number of districts into which a state is divided, each electing one member to the state senate. Cf. **assembly district, Congressional district.**

se·na·tus con·sul·tum (sə nä/to͝os kōn so͝ol/to͝om; *Eng.* sə nā/təs kən sul/təm), *pl.* **se·na·tus con·sul·ta** (sə nä/to͝os

sem/i·neu·rot/ic, *adj.*
sem/i·nor/mal, *adj.*
sem/i·nude/, *adj.*
sem/i·nu/di·ty, *n.*
sem/i·ob·liv/i·ous, *adj.*
sem/i·of·fi/cial, *adj.*
sem/i·o·paque/, *adj.*
sem/i·o/ri·en/tal, *adj.*
sem/i·pa/gan, *n., adj.*
sem/i·par/a·lyt/ic, *n., adj.*
sem/i·pet/ri·fied/, *adj.*
sem/i·po·lit/i·cal, *adj.*
sem/i·prim/i·tive, *adj.*
sem/i·pub/lic, *adj.*
sem/i·pur/pos·ive, *adj.*
sem/i·re·bel/lious, *adj.*
sem/i·re·fined/, *adj.*
sem/i·res/o·lute/, *adj.*
sem/i·re·spect/a·bil/i·ty, *n.*
sem/i·re·spect/a·ble, *adj.*
sem/i·re·tired/, *adj.*
sem/i·re·tire/ment, *n.*
sem/i·ru/ral, *adj.*
sem/i·sa/cred, *adj.*
sem/i·sa·tir/i·cal, *adj.*; -ly, *adv.*
sem/i·se/ri·ous, *adj.*
sem/i·so/cial·is/tic, *adj.*
sem/i·soft/, *adj.*
sem/i·spec/u·la/tive, *adj.*
sem/i·sub·ur/ban, *adj.*
sem/i·suc·cess/ful, *adj.*
sem/i·sweet/, *adj.*
sem/i·tra·di/tion·al, *adj.*
sem/i·trans·lu/cent, *adj.*
sem/i·trans·par/ent, *adj.*
sem/i·truth/ful, *adj.*
sem/i·ur/ban, *adj.*
sem/i·vol/un·tar/y, *adj.*
sem/i·wild/, *adj.*; -ly, *adv.*

kōn sŏŏl′tä; *Eng.* sə nā′təs kən sul′tə). *Latin.* a decree of the senate of ancient Rome.

send[1] (send), *v.,* **sent, send·ing.** —*v.t.* **1.** to cause, permit, or enable to go. **2.** to cause to be transmitted, as a letter. **3.** to order, direct, compel, or force to go. **4.** to direct, propel, or deliver to a particular point, position, condition, or direction: *to send a punch to the jaw.* **5.** to emit, discharge, or utter (usually fol. by *forth, off, out,* or *through*): *The flowers sent forth a sweet odor.* **6.** *Elect.* **a.** to transmit (a signal). **b.** to transmit (an electromagnetic wave or the like) in the form of pulses. **7.** *Slang.* to delight or excite. —*v.i.* **8.** to dispatch a messenger, agent, message, etc. **9.** *Elect.* to transmit a signal. **10. send down,** *Brit.* to expel, esp. from Oxford or Cambridge. **11. send for,** to request the coming or delivery of; summon. **12. send forth, a.** to produce; bear; yield. **b.** to export. **c.** to issue, as a publication. **13. send in,** to cause to be dispatched or delivered (to a destination). **14. send off,** to cause to depart or to be conveyed from oneself; dispatch; dismiss. **15. send out, a.** to distribute; issue. **b.** to send on the way; dispatch. **16. send packing,** to dismiss curtly; send away in disgrace. **17. send up, a.** to release or cause to go upward; let out. **b.** *Slang.* to sentence or send to prison. [ME *sende(n),* OE *sendan;* c. G *senden,* Goth *sandjan* (causative) < Gmc base **sinth-, *santh-* go, whence OE *sīth* journey] —**send′a·ble,** *adj.* —**send′er,** *n.* —**Syn. 2.** transmit, dispatch, forward. **4.** cast, hurl, fling, project. —**Ant. 1.** receive.

send[2] (send), *v.i.,* **sent, send·ing,** *n. Naut.* scend.

Sen·dai (sen′dī′), *n.* a city on NE Honshu, in central Japan. 472,954 (1964).

sen·dal (sen′dəl), *n.* a silk fabric in use during the Middle Ages or a garment made of it. [ME *cendal* < OF, prob. < dissimilated var. of Gk *sindōn* fine linen]

send-off (send′ôf′, -of′), *n. Informal.* **1.** a demonstration of good wishes for a person setting out on a trip, career, or other venture. **2.** a start given to a person or thing.

Sen·e·ca (sen′ə kə), *n., pl.* **-cas,** (*esp. collectively*) **-ca** for 1. **1.** a member of the largest tribe of the Iroquois Confederacy of North American Indians, located in western New York. **2.** an Iroquoian language of the Seneca, Onondaga, and Cayuga tribes. [< D *Sennecaas* (pl.) < Mohegan *A'sinnika,* trans. of Iroquoian *Oneniute'* (people of the) outstanding stone; see ONEIDA]

Sen·e·ca (sen′ə kə), *n.* **Lucius An·nae·us** (ə nē′əs), c4 B.C.–A.D. 65, Roman philosopher and writer of tragedies. —**Sen′e·can,** *adj.*

Sen′eca Lake′, a lake in W New York: one of the Finger Lakes. 35 mi. long.

sen·e·ga (sen′ə gə), *n.* **1.** the dried root of a milkwort, *Polygala Senega,* of the eastern U.S., used as an expectorant and diuretic. **2.** the plant itself. [var. of SENECA, from its use by this tribe]

Sen·e·gal (sen′ə gôl′), *n.* **1.** a republic in W Africa: independent member of the French Community; formerly part of French West Africa. 5,400,000; 76,084 sq. mi. *Cap.:* Dakar. **2.** a river in W Africa, flowing NW from E Mali to the Atlantic at St. Louis. ab. 1000 mi. long. French, **Sé·né·gal** (sā nā gal′).

Sen·e·ga·lese (sen′ə gô lēz′, -lēs′, -gə-), *adj., n., pl.* **-lese.** —*adj.* **1.** of or pertaining to the republic of Senegal. —*n.* **2.** a native or inhabitant of Senegal.

Sen·e·gam·bi·a (sen′ə gam′bē ə), *n.* a region in W Africa between the Senegal and Gambia rivers; now mostly in Senegal. —**Sen′e·gam′bi·an,** *adj.*

se·nes·cent (sə nes′ənt), *adj.* growing old; aging. [< L *senēscent-* (s. of *senēscēns,* prp. of *senēscere* to grow old) = *sen-* old + *-ēscent-* -ESCENT] —**se·nes′cence,** *n.*

sen·e·schal (sen′ə shəl), *n.* a steward in the household of a medieval prince. [ME < MF < Gmc; c. OHG *senescalh* (*sene-* old + *scalh* servant)]

Sen·ghor (*Fr.* saN gôr′), *n.* **Lé·o·pold Sé·dar** (*Fr.* lā ô pôld′ sā där′), born 1906, African poet, teacher, and statesman: president of the Republic of Senegal since 1960.

se·nhor (sin yōr′, -yôr′; *Port.* si nyôr′), *n., pl.* **se·nhors,** *Port.* **se·nho·res** (si nyô′rish). the Portuguese equivalent of *mister. Abbr.:* Sr. [< Pg < VL *senior* lord; see SENIOR]

se·nho·ra (sin yōr′ə, -yôr′ə; *Port.* si nyô′rə), *n., pl.* **se·nho·ras** (sin yōr′əz, -yôr′əz; *Port.* si nyô′rəsh). the Portuguese equivalent of *Mrs. Abbr.:* Sra. [< Pg, fem. of SENHOR]

se·nho·ri·ta (sēn′yə rē′tə, sān′-; *Port.* se′nyô rē′tə), *n., pl.* **-tas** (-təz; *Port.* -təsh). the Portuguese equivalent of *miss. Abbr.:* Srta. [< Pg, dim. of SENHORA]

se·nile (sē′nīl, -nil, sen′īl), *adj.* **1.** of, pertaining to, or characteristic of old age, esp. referring to a decline of the mental faculties. **2.** *Phys. Geog.* (of topographical features) eroded to the level of a featureless plain. —*n.* **3.** a senile person. [< L *senīlis* old = *sen(ex)* old man + *-īlis* -ILE]

se·nil·i·ty (si nil′i tē), *n.* the state of being senile, esp. the infirmity of old age.

sen·ior (sēn′yər), *adj.* **1.** older or elder (usually designating the older of two men bearing the same name, as a father whose son is named after him: often written as *Sr.* or *sr.* following the name). Cf. **junior** (def. 1). **2.** of earlier appointment or admission, as to an office, status, or rank: *a senior partner.* **3.** of higher or the highest rank or standing. **4.** (in American schools, colleges, and universities) of or pertaining to students in their final year or to their class. **5.** (in certain American colleges and universities) of or pertaining to the final two years of education. **6.** of earlier date; prior to. —*n.* **7.** a person who is older than another. **8.** a person of higher rank or standing than another, esp. by virtue of longer service. **9.** *U.S.* a student in his final year at a school, college, or university. **10.** a fellow holding senior rank in a college at an English university. [< L = *sen(ex)* old + *-ior* -ER[4]]

sen′ior cit′izen, an elderly or aged person, esp. one over 65 years of age.

sen′ior high′ school′. See under **high school** (def. 2).

sen·ior·i·ty (sēn yôr′i tē, -yor′-), *n., pl.* **-ties. 1.** the state of being senior. **2.** status obtained as the result of a person's length of service, as in a profession. [< ML *seniōritās* = L *senior* SENIOR + *-itās* -ITY]

sen′ior mas′ter ser′geant, *U.S. Air Force.* a noncommissioned officer of the second top grade, ranking below a chief master sergeant and above a master sergeant.

Sen·lac (sen′lak), *n.* a hill in SE England: site of the Battle of Hastings 1066.

sen·na (sen′ə), *n.* **1.** any caesalpiniaceous herb, shrub, or tree of the genus *Cassia.* **2.** any of various cathartic drugs consisting of the dried leaflets of certain of these plants. [< NL < Ar *sanā*]

Sen·nach·er·ib (sə nak′ər ib), *n.* died 681 B.C., king of Assyria 705–681.

Sen·nar (sen när′), *n.* a region in the E Sudan between the White and Blue Nile rivers, S of Khartoum: a former kingdom.

sen·net (sen′it), *n.* (in Elizabethan drama) a set of notes played on the trumpet or cornet to mark the entrance or exit of actors. [? var. of SIGNET]

Sen·nett (sen′it), *n.* **Mack** (*Michael Sinnott*), 1884–1960, U.S. motion-picture director and producer, esp. of comedies, born in Canada.

sen·night (sen′it, -it), *n. Archaic.* a week. Also, **se'n'-night.** [ME *sevenyht,* etc., OE *seofon nihta.* See SEVEN, NIGHT]

sen·nit (sen′it), *n.* **1.** a flat, braided cordage, formed by plaiting strands of rope yarn or other fiber, used as small stuff aboard ships. **2.** braided straw used in making hats. [?]

se·ñor (sān yōr′, -yôr′, sēn-; *Sp.* se nyôr′), *n., pl.* **se·ñors,** *Sp.* **se·ño·res** (se nyô′res). the Spanish equivalent of *mister. Abbr.:* Sr. [< Sp < VL *senior.* See SENIOR]

se·ño·ra (sān yōr′ə, -yôr′ə, sēn-; *Sp.* se nyô′rä), *n., pl.* **se·ño·ras** (sān yōr′əz, -yôr′-; *Sp.* se nyô′räs). the Spanish equivalent of *Mrs. Abbr.:* Sra. [< Sp, fem. of SEÑOR]

se·ño·ri·ta (sān′yə rē′tə, sēn′-; *Sp.* se nyô rē′tä), *n., pl.* **-tas** (-təz; *Sp.* -täs). the Spanish equivalent of *miss. Abbr.:* Srta. [< Sp, dim. of SEÑORA]

sen·sa (sen′sə), *n.* pl. of **sensum.**

sen·sate (sen′sāt), *adj.* **1.** perceived by the senses. **2.** *Obs.* endowed with sensation. [< LL *sensāt(us)*]

sen·sa·tion (sen sā′shən), *n.* **1.** the operation or function of the senses. **2.** a mental condition or physical feeling resulting from stimulation of a sense organ or internal bodily changes. **3.** *Physiol.* the faculty of perception of stimuli. **4.** a general, feeling not directly attributable to any given stimulus, as discomfort, anxiety, or doubt. **5.** mental excitement, esp. a state of excited feeling in an individual. **6.** a state of excited feeling or interest caused in a group, as by some rumor, occurrence, etc. **7.** a cause of such feeling or interest. [< ML *sensātiōn-* (s. of *sensātiō*). See SENSATE, -ION] —**sen·sa′tion·less,** *adj.* —**Syn. 2, 4.** See **sense.**

sen·sa·tion·al (sen sā′shə nəl), *adj.* **1.** of or pertaining to the senses or sensation. **2.** intended to produce or producing a startling effect, strong reaction, intense interest, etc., esp. by exaggerated, superficial, or lurid elements: *a sensational novel.* **3.** extraordinarily good. —**sen·sa′tion·al·ly,** *adv.* —**Syn. 2.** exciting, stimulating. —**Ant. 2.** prosaic, dull.

sen·sa·tion·al·ise (sen sā′shə nəlīz′), *v.t.,* **-ised, -is·ing.** *Chiefly Brit.* sensationalize.

sen·sa·tion·al·ism (sen sā′shə nəliz′əm), *n.* **1.** subject matter, language, or style designed to amaze or thrill. **2.** the use of or interest in this subject matter, language, or style. **3.** Also, **sensationism.** *Philos.* **a.** the doctrine that the good is to be judged only by the gratification of the senses. **b.** the doctrine that all ideas are derived from and are essentially reducible to sensations. **4.** *Psychol.* sensationism. —**sen·sa′tion·al·ist,** *n.* —**sen·sa′tion·al·is′tic,** *adj.*

sen·sa·tion·al·ize (sen sā′shə nəlīze′), *v.t.,* **-ized, -iz·ing.** to make sensational. Also, *esp. Brit.,* **sensationalise.**

sen·sa·tion·ism (sen sā′shə niz′əm), *n.* **1.** *Psychol.* a theory maintaining that experience consists solely of sensations. **2.** *Philos.* sensationalism (def. 3). —**sen·sa′tion·ist,** *n., adj.* —**sen·sa′tion·is′tic,** *adj.*

sense (sens), *n., v.,* **sensed, sens·ing.** —*n.* **1.** any of the faculties, as sight, hearing, smell, taste, or touch, by which man and animals perceive stimuli originating from outside or inside the body. **2.** these faculties collectively. **3.** their operation or function; sensation. **4.** a feeling or perception produced through the organs of touch, taste, etc., or resulting from a particular condition of some part of the body. **5.** a faculty or function of the mind analogous to sensation: *the moral sense.* **6.** any special capacity for perception, estimation, etc.: *a sense of humor.* **7.** Usually, **senses.** clear and sound mental faculties; good judgment: *Come to your senses.* **8.** a more or less vague perception or impression: *a sense of security.* **9.** discernment, realization, or recognition: *a sense of the worth of a thing.* **10.** the recognition of something as fitting: *a sense of duty.* **11.** sound, practical intelligence. **12.** something that is sensible or reasonable: *to talk sense.* **13.** the meaning, reason, or value of something: *you missed the sense of his statement.* **14.** the meaning of a word or group of words in a specific context. **15.** an opinion or judgment formed or held, esp. by an assemblage or body of persons: *the sense of a meeting.* **16.** *Math.* one of two opposite directions in which a vector may point. **17. in a sense,** according to one explanation or view; to a certain extent. **18. make sense,** to be reasonable or comprehensible. —*v.t.* **19.** to perceive (something) by the senses; become aware of. **20.** *Computer Technol.* **a.** to read (punched holes, tape, data, etc.) mechanically, electrically, or photoelectrically. **b.** to determine or locate the position or arrangement of (a computer part or parts). **21.** to grasp the meaning of; understand. **22.** to apprehend without or before manifest evidence: *to sense a person's hostility; to sense danger.* [< L *sēns(us)* sensation, feeling, understanding = *sēns-* (ptp. stem of *sentīre* to feel) + *-us* n. suffix (4th decl.)]
—**Syn. 4, 9.** SENSE, SENSATION refer to consciousness of stimulus or of a perception with an interpretation as pleasant or unpleasant. A SENSE is an awareness or recognition of something; the stimulus may be subjective and the entire process may be mental or intellectual: *a sense of failure.* A SENSATION is an impression derived from an objective (external) stimulus through any of the sense organs: *a sensation of heat.* The feeling is also applied to a general, indefinite physical or emotional feeling: *a sensation of weariness.* **14.** See **meaning. 15.** feeling, sentiment.

sense′ da′tum, 1. *Psychol.* a stimulus or an object of perception or sensation. **2.** *Epistemology.* datum (def 4).

sense·less (sens′lis), *adj.* **1.** destitute or deprived of sensation; unconscious. **2.** lacking mental perception, appreciation, or comprehension. **3.** stupid or foolish, as persons or actions. **4.** nonsensical or meaningless, as speech or writing.

—**sense′less·ly,** *adv.* —**sense′less·ness,** *n.* —**Syn. 1.** insensate, insensible. **2.** unperceiving. **3.** silly, idiotic.

sense′ or′gan, a specialized bodily structure that receives or is sensitive to stimuli; receptor.

sense′ percep′tion, perception by the senses rather than by the intellect.

sen·si·bil·i·ty (sen′sə bil′i tē), *n., pl.* **-ties. 1.** capacity for sensation or feeling. **2.** acuteness of apprehension or feeling. **3.** keen consciousness or appreciation. **4. sensibilities,** emotional capacities. **5.** Sometimes, **sensibilities.** liability to feel hurt or offended. **6.** Often, **sensibilities.** capacity for intellectual and aesthetic distinctions, feelings, tastes, etc. **7.** the property, as in plants or instruments, of being readily affected by external influences. [late ME *sensibilite* < MF < LL *sēnsibilitāt-* (s. of *sēnsibilitās*). See SENSIBLE, -ITY]
—**Syn. 1.** SENSIBILITY, SUSCEPTIBILITY, SENSITIVENESS, SENSITIVITY mean capacity to respond to or be affected by something. SENSIBILITY is, particularly, capacity to respond to aesthetic and emotional stimuli; delicacy of emotional or intellectual perception: *the sensibility of the artist.* SUSCEPTIBILITY is the state or quality of being impressionable and responsive, esp. to emotional stimuli; in the plural it has much the same meaning as SENSIBILITY: *a person of keen susceptibilities.* SENSITIVENESS is the state or quality of being sensitive, having a capacity of sensation and of responding to external stimuli: *sensitiveness to light.* SENSITIVITY is a special capability of being sensitive to physiological, chemical action: *the sensitivity of a nerve.*

sen·si·ble (sen′sə bəl), *adj.* **1.** having, using, or showing good sense or sound judgment: *a sensible young man.* **2.** cognizant; keenly aware (usually fol. by *of*): *sensible of his fault.* **3.** considerable in quantity, magnitude, etc. **4.** capable of being perceived by the senses; material: *the sensible universe.* **5.** capable of feeling or perceiving. **6.** perceptible to the mind. **7.** conscious. **8.** *Archaic.* sensitive. [late ME < OF < L *sēnsibil(is).* See SENSE, -IBLE] —**sen′si·ble·ness,** *n.* —**sen′si·bly,** *adv.* —**Syn. 1.** sagacious, rational, reasonable. See **practical. 2.** conscious, observant.

sen′sible hori′zon, *Astron.* See **horizon** (def. 2a).

sen·si·tise (sen′si tīz′), *v.t., v.i.,* **-tised, -tis·ing.** *Chiefly Brit.* sensitize. —**sen′si·ti·sa′tion,** *n.* —**sen′si·tis′er,** *n.*

sen·si·tive (sen′si tiv), *adj.* **1.** endowed with sensation. **2.** readily or excessively affected by external agencies or influences. **3.** having acute mental or emotional sensibility; easily affected, pained, annoyed, etc. **4.** pertaining to or connected with the senses or sensation. **5.** *Physiol.* having a low threshold of sensation or feeling. **6.** responding to stimuli, as leaves that move when touched. **7.** highly responsive to certain agents, as photographic paper. **8.** involving work, duties, or information of a highly secret or delicate nature. **9.** constructed to indicate, measure, or be affected by small amounts or changes, as a balance or thermometer. **10.** *Radio.* easily affected by external influences, esp. by radio waves. [< ML *sēnsitīv(us)* = L *sēnsi-* (see SENSIBLE) + *-tīvus* (irreg. for *-īvus* -IVE); r. ME *sensitif(e)* < MF < ML, as above] —**sen′si·tive·ly,** *adv.* —**sen′si·tive·ness,** *n.* —**Syn. 2, 3.** impressionable, susceptible.

sen′sitive plant′, 1. a tropical American plant, *Mimosa pudica,* having bipinnate leaves whose leaflets fold together when touched. **2.** any of various other plants that are sensitive to touch.

sen·si·tiv·i·ty (sen′si tiv′i tē), *n., pl.* **-ties. 1.** the state or quality of being sensitive. **2.** *Physiol.* **a.** the ability of an organism or part of an organism to react to stimuli; irritability. **b.** degree of susceptibility to stimulation. —**Syn. 1.** See **sensibility.**

sen′sitiv′ity train′ing, an educationally oriented, small group of persons who meet regularly, usually with a trained professional in charge, to improve their functioning as group members or leaders through increasing skills and awareness in a social context. Also called **sen′sitiv′ity ses′sion.**

sen·si·tize (sen′si tīz′), *v.,* **-tized, -tiz·ing.** —*v.t.* **1.** to render sensitive. **2.** *Photog.* to render (a film or the like) sensitive to light or other forms of radiant energy. **3.** *Immunol.* to render sensitive to a serum by a series of injections. —*v.i.* **4.** to become sensitized. Also, *esp. Brit.,* **sensitise.** [SENSIT(IVE) + -IZE] —**sen′si·ti·za′tion,** *n.* —**sen′si·tiz′er,** *n.*

sen·si·tom·e·ter (sen′si tom′i tər), *n. Photog.* an instrument for testing the sensitivity of various types of film. [SENSIT(IVE) + -O- + -METER] —**sen·si·to·met·ric** (sen′sə tō me′trik), *adj.* —**sen′si·to·met′ri·cal·ly,** *adv.* —**sen′si·tom′e·try,** *n.*

sen·sor (sen′sər), *n.* a device sensitive to light, temperature, radiation level, or the like, that transmits a signal to a measuring or control device. [< L *sēns(us)* (ptp. of *sentīre* to feel, perceive) + -OR[2]]

sen·so·ri·mo·tor (sen′sə rē mō′tər), *adj.* **1.** *Psychol.* of or pertaining to motor activity caused by sensory stimuli. Cf. **ideomotor. 2.** *Physiol.* both sensory and motor, as parts of the cerebral cortex. Also, **sen·so·mo·tor** (sen′sə mō′tər).

sen·so·ri·um (sen sôr′ē əm, -sōr′-), *n., pl.* **-so·ri·ums, -so·ri·a** (-sôr′ē ə, -sōr′-). **1.** a part of the brain or the brain itself regarded as the seat of sensation. **2.** the sensory apparatus of the body. [< LL = L *sēns(us)* (ptp. of *sentīre* to feel) + -ORIUM]

sen·so·ry (sen′sə rē), *adj.* **1.** of or pertaining to the senses or sensation. **2.** *Physiol.* noting a structure for conveying a sense impulse. Also, **sen·so·ri·al** (sen sôr′ē əl, -sōr′-). [SENSE + -ORY[1]]

sen·su·al (sen′shōō əl), *adj.* **1.** pertaining to, inclined to, or preoccupied with the gratification of the senses or appetites; carnal; voluptuous. **2.** lewd or unchaste. **3.** arousing or exciting the senses or appetites. **4.** worldly; materialistic; irreligious. **5.** of or pertaining to the senses or physical sensation; sensory. [late ME < L *sēnsuāl(is)* = *sēnsu(s)* SENSE + *-ālis* -AL[1]] —**sen′su·al·ly,** *adv.*
—**Syn. 1.** SENSUAL, SENSUOUS refer to experience through the senses. SENSUAL refers, often unfavorably, to the enjoyments derived from the senses, generally implying grossness or lewdness: *a sensual delight in eating; sensual excesses.* SENSUOUS refers, favorably or literally, to what is experienced through the senses: *sensuous impressions; sensuous poetry.*

sen·su·al·ise (sen′shōō ə līz′), *v.t.,* **-ised, -is·ing.** *Chiefly Brit.* sensualize. —**sen′su·al·i·sa′tion,** *n.*

sen·su·al·ism (sen′shōō ə liz′əm), *n.* **1.** sensuality. **2.** *Philos. Rare.* sensationalism (def. 3). **3.** *Aesthetics.* emphasis on sensuousness as the most important element in the beautiful.

sen·su·al·ist (sen′shōō ə list), *n.* **1.** a person given to indulging of his senses or appetites. **2.** a person who believes in a doctrine of sensationalism. —**sen′su·al·is′tic,** *adj.*

sen·su·al·i·ty (sen′shōō al′i tē), *n., pl.* **-ties. 1.** the quality or character of being sensual. **2.** unrestrained indulgence in sensual pleasures. **3.** lewdness; unchastity. Also called **sen′su·al·ness.** [ME *sensualite* < OF < LL *sēnsuālitāt-* (s. of *sēnsuālitās*)]

sen·su·al·ize (sen′shōō ə līz′), *v.t.,* **-ized, -iz·ing.** to render sensual. Also, *esp. Brit.,* **sensualise.** —**sen′su·al·i·za′tion,** *n.*

sen·sum (sen′səm), *n., pl.* **-sa** (-sə). See **sense datum.**

sen·su·ous (sen′shōō əs), *adj.* **1.** of or pertaining to sensible objects or to the senses. **2.** experienced through, perceived by, or affecting the senses. **3.** readily affected through the senses: *a sensuous temperament.* [< L *sēnsu-* (see SENSUAL) + -OUS] —**sen′su·ous·ly,** *adv.* —**sen′su·ous·ness, sen·su·os·i·ty** (sen′shōō os′i tē), *n.* —**Syn. 1.** sensible. See **sensual.**

sent (sent), *v.* pt. and pp. of **send.**

sen·tence (sen′t^{ə}ns), *n., v.,* **-tenced, -tenc·ing.** —*n.* **1.** *Gram.* a grammatical unit of one or more words, bearing minimal syntactic relation to the words that precede or follow it, often preceded and followed in speech by pauses, having one of a small number of characteristic intonation patterns, and typically expressing an independent statement, question, request, command, etc., as *Fire!* or *Summer is here.* **2.** *Law.* **a.** an authoritative decision, esp. the judicial determination of punishment. **b.** the punishment itself. **3.** *Music.* a period. **4.** *Archaic.* a saying, apothegm, or maxim. —*v.t.* **5.** to pronounce sentence upon. [ME < OF < L *sententia* opinion, decision = *sent-* (root of *sentīre* to feel) + *-entia* -ENCE] —**sen′tenc·er,** *n.*

sen′tence stress′, the stress pattern or patterns associated with words as arranged in sentences. Also called **sen′tence ac′cent.** Cf. **word stress.**

sen·ten·tious (sen ten′shəs), *adj.* **1.** abounding in pithy aphorisms or maxims, as a book. **2.** given to excessive moralizing; self-righteous. **3.** given to or using pithy sayings or maxims: *a sententious poet.* **4.** of the nature of a maxim. [late ME < L *sententiōs(us)* meaningful. See SENTENCE, -OUS] —**sen·ten′tious·ly,** *adv.* —**sen·ten′tious·ness,** *n.*

sen·tience (sen′shəns), *n.* sentient condition or character; capacity for sensation or feeling. Also, **sen′tien·cy.** [SENTI(ENT) + -ENCE]

sen·tient (sen′shənt), *adj.* **1.** having the power of perception by the senses. **2.** characterized by sensation. —*n.* **3.** a person or thing that is sentient. **4.** *Archaic.* the conscious mind. [< L *sentient-* (s. of *sentiēns,* prp. of *sentīre* to feel) = *senti-* feel + *-ent-* -ENT] —**sen′tient·ly,** *adv.*

sen·ti·ment (sen′tə mənt), *n.* **1.** an attitude toward something; opinion. **2.** a feeling or emotion: *a sentiment of pity.* **3.** refined or tender emotion or sensibility. **4.** exhibition or manifestation of feeling or sensibility in literature, art, or music. **5.** a thought influenced by or proceeding from feeling or emotion. [< ML *sentīment(um)* = L *sentī(re)* (to) feel + *-mentum* -MENT; r. ME *sentement* < OF < ML, as above]
—**Syn. 1.** See **opinion. 2.** See **feeling. 3.** SENTIMENT, SENTIMENTALITY are terms for sensitiveness to emotional feelings. SENTIMENT is a sincere and refined sensibility, a tendency to be influenced by emotion rather than reason or fact: *to appeal to sentiment.* SENTIMENTALITY implies affected, excessive, sometimes mawkish sentiment: *weak sentimentality.*

sen·ti·men·tal (sen′tə men′t^{ə}l), *adj.* **1.** expressive of or appealing to sentiment, esp. the tender emotions and feelings, as love, pity, nostalgia, etc.: *a sentimental song.* **2.** pertaining to or dependent on sentiment: *We kept the old photograph for purely sentimental reasons.* **3.** weakly emotional; mawkishly susceptible or tender: *a sentimental schoolgirl.* **4.** characterized by or showing sentiment or refined feeling. —**sen′ti·men′tal·ly,** *adv.* —**Syn. 1.** warm, sympathetic.

sen·ti·men·tal·ise (sen′tə men′t^{ə}līz′), *v.i., v.t.,* **-ised, -is·ing.** *Chiefly Brit.* sentimentalize. —**sen′ti·men′ta·li·sa′tion,** *n.*

sen·ti·men·tal·ism (sen′tə men′t^{ə}liz′əm), *n.* **1.** sentimental tendency or character. **2.** excessive indulgence in sentiment. **3.** a display of sentimentality.

sen·ti·men·tal·ist (sen′tə men′t^{ə}list), *n.* one given to sentiment or sentimentality.

sen·ti·men·tal·i·ty (sen′tə men tal′i tē), *n., pl.* **-ties** for 2, 3. **1.** the quality or state of being sentimental, esp. excessively sentimental. **2.** an instance of being sentimental. **3.** a sentimental act, gesture, etc. —**Syn.** See **sentiment.**

sen·ti·men·tal·ize (sen′tə men′t^{ə}līz′), *v.,* **-ized, -iz·ing.** —*v.i.* **1.** to indulge in sentiment. —*v.t.* **2.** to view (someone or something) sentimentally. Also, *esp. Brit.,* **sentimentalise.** —**sen′ti·men′ta·li·za′tion,** *n.*

sen·ti·nel (sen′t^{ə}n^{ə}l), *n., v.,* **-neled, -nel·ing** or (*esp. Brit.*) **-nelled, -nel·ling.** —*n.* **1.** a person or thing that watches or stands guard. **2.** a sentry. **3.** Also called **tag.** (in computer programming) a symbol, mark, or other labeling device indicating the beginning or end of a unit of information. —*v.t.* **4.** to watch over or guard as a sentinel. [MF *sentinelle* < It *sentinell(a)* < OIt *sentin(a)* vigilance (L *sent(īre)* (to) observe + *-īna* -INE[2])]

sen·try (sen′trē), *n., pl.* **-tries. 1.** a soldier stationed at a place to stand guard and prevent the passage of unauthorized persons, watch for fires, etc. **2.** a member of a guard or watch. [short for *sentrinel,* var. of SENTINEL]

sen′try box′, a small structure for sheltering a sentry from bad weather.

Se·nu·si (se nōō′sē), *n., pl.* **-sis.** *Islam.* Sanusi. Also, **Se·nus′si.** —**Se·nu′si·an, Se·nus′si·an,** *adj.* —**Se·nu·sism, Se·nus·sism** (sə nōō′siz əm), *n.*

Se·oul (sōl, sä′ŏŏl; *Kor.* syœ′ōōl′), *n.* a city in and the capital of South Korea, in the W part. 6,889,470. Japanese, **Keijo.**

Sep., **1.** September. **2.** Septuagint.

sep., **1.** sepal. **2.** separate.

se·pal (sē′pəl), *n.* *Bot.* one of the individual leaves or parts of the calyx of a flower. [< NL *sepal(um)* = *scep-* (< Gk *sképē* covering) + *(pet)alum* PETAL] —**se′paled, se′palled,** *adj.*

S, Sepal

-sepalous, a combining form of **sepal** and **-ous:** *polysepalous.*

sep·a·ra·ble (sep′ər ə bəl, sep′rə-), *adj.* capable of being separated, parted, or dissociated. [< L *sēparābil(is)* = *sēpar(āre)* (to) SEPARATE + *-ābilis* -ABLE] —**sep′a·ra·bil′i·ty, sep′a·ra·ble·ness,** *n.* —**sep′a·ra·bly,** *adv.*

sep·a·rate (*v.* sep′ə rāt′; *adj., n.* sep′ər it), *v.,* **-rat·ed, -rat·ing,** *adj., n.* —*v.t.* **1.** to keep apart, as by an intervening barrier or space: *to separate two fields by a fence.* **2.** to put, bring, or force apart; part. **3.** to set apart; disconnect; dissociate. **4.** to remove or sever from association, service, etc. **5.** to sort, part, divide, or disperse (an assemblage, mass, compound, etc.), as into individual units or elements. **6.** to take by parting or dividing; extract. —*v.i.* **7.** to part company; withdraw from personal association (often fol. by *from*). **8.** (of a married pair) to stop living together but without getting a divorce. **9.** to draw or come apart; become divided, disconnected, or detached. **10.** to become parted from a mass or compound. **11.** to take or go in different directions. —*adj.* **12.** detached, disconnected, or disjoined. **13.** unconnected; distinct; unique: *two separate questions.* **14.** being or standing apart; dispersed. **15.** existing or maintained independently: *separate organizations.* **16.** individual or particular: *each separate item.* **17.** (*sometimes cap.*) noting or pertaining to a church or other organization no longer associated with the original or parent organization. —*n.* **18.** something separate. **19.** offprint (def. 1). [late ME < L *sēparāt(us)* (ptp. of *sēparāre*) = *sē-* SE- + *par-* put (see PARE) + *-ātus* -ATE[1]] —**sep′a·rate·ly,** *adv.* —**sep′a·rate·ness,** *n.*
—**Syn. 1, 2.** sever, split. SEPARATE, DIVIDE imply a putting apart or keeping apart of things from each other. To SEPARATE is to remove from each other things previously associated: *to separate a mother from her children.* To DIVIDE is to split or break up carefully according to measurement, rule, or plan: *to divide a cake into equal parts.* **3.** disengage. **15.** independent. —**Ant. 1–3.** unite, connect.

sep·a·ra·tion (sep′ə rā′shən), *n.* **1.** the act, state, or an instance of separating. **2.** the state of being separated. **3.** a place, line, or point of parting. **4.** a gap, hole, rent, or the like. **5.** *Law.* cessation of conjugal cohabitation, as by mutual consent. **6.** *Rocketry.* the time or act of releasing a burned-out stage of a missile from the remainder. [late ME < L *sēparātiōn-* (s. of *sēparātiō*)]

separa′tion cen′ter, a place at which military personnel are processed for release from service.

sep·a·ra·tist (sep′ə rā′tist, -ər ə tist), *n.* a person who practices or advocates separation, esp. ecclesiastical or political separation. —**sep′a·ra·tism,** *n.*

sep·a·ra·tive (sep′ə rā′tiv, -ər ə tiv), *adj.* **1.** tending to separate. **2.** causing separation. [< LL *sēparātīv(us)*] —**sep′a·ra′tive·ly,** *adv.* —**sep′a·ra′tive·ness,** *n.*

sep·a·ra·tor (sep′ə rā′tər), *n.* **1.** a person or thing that separates. **2.** any of various apparatus for separating one thing from another, as cream from milk. [< LL *sēparātor*]

sep·a·ra·to·ry (sep′ər ə tōr′ē, -tôr′ē), *adj.* serving to separate. [< NL *sēparātōri(us)*]

Se·phar·dim (sə fär′dim, -fär dēm′), *n.pl., sing.* **-di** (-dē, -dē′). Jews of Spain and Portugal or their descendants. Cf. **Ashkenazim.** [pl. of ModHeb *sephardī* = Heb *sephārād* (region mentioned in Bible (Obadiah 20) and assumed to be Spain) + *-ī* suffix of appurtenance] —**Se·phar′dic,** *adj.*

Se·pher To·rah (sā fer′ tô rä′; *Eng.* sā′fər tōr′ə, tôr′ə), *pl.* **Si·phrei To·rah** (sē frā′ tô rä′), *Eng.* **Sepher Torahs.** *Hebrew.* a scroll of the Torah. [lit., book of law]

se·pi·a (sē′pē ə), *n.* **1.** a brown pigment obtained from the inklike secretion of various cuttlefish and used in drawing. **2.** a drawing made with this pigment. **3.** a cuttlefish of the genus *Sepia* or related genera. —*adj.* **4.** of a brown, grayish brown, or olive brown similar to that of sepia ink. [< L < Gk *sēpía* cuttlefish; akin to *sēpsis* SEPSIS] —**se′pi·a·like′,** *adj.* —**se·pic** (sē′pik, sep′ik), *adj.*

se·pi·o·lite (sē′pē ə līt′), *n.* meerschaum (def. 1). [< G *Sepiolit* < Gk *sēpio(n)* cuttlebone + G *-lit* -LITE]

se·poy (sē′poi), *n.* (in India) **1.** a native soldier trained in the British army. **2.** (formerly) such a soldier serving in the British Indian army. [var. of *sipahi* < Urdu < Pers *sipāhī* horseman, soldier < *sipāh* army]

Se′poy Rebel′lion, a revolt of the sepoy troops in British India (1857–59). Also called **Se′poy Mu′tiny, Indian Mutiny.**

sep·pu·ku (se pōō′kōō), *n.* (in Japan) hara-kiri. [< Jap]

sep·sis (sep′sis), *n.* *Pathol.* bacterial invasion of the body, esp. by pyogenic organisms: *wound sepsis.* [< Gk *sêpsis* decay; cf. *sēpein* to make rotten]

sept (sept), *n.* **1.** (in Scotland) a branch of a clan. **2.** a clan, esp. with reference to tribes or families in Ireland. **3.** *Anthropol.* a group believing itself derived from a common ancestor. [? < L *sēpt(um)* fold (in fig. use, e.g., *Sept of Christ*)]

sept-, a learned borrowing from Latin meaning "seven," used in the formation of compound words: *septet; septillion.* Also, *esp. before a consonant,* **septi-.** [< L *septem*]

Sept., **1.** September. **2.** Septuagint.

sep·ta (sep′tə), *n.* pl. of **septum.**

sep·tal (sep′tᵊl), *adj.* *Biol.* of or pertaining to a septum.

sep·tar·i·um (sep târ′ē əm), *n., pl.* **-tar·i·a** (-târ′ē ə). *Geol.* a concretionary nodule or mass, usually of calcium carbonate or of argillaceous carbonate of iron, traversed within by a network of cracks filled with calcite and other minerals. [< NL; see SEPT(UM), -ARIUM] —**sep·tar′i·an,** *adj.* —**sep·tar·i·ate** (sep târ′ē it), *adj.*

sep·tate (sep′tāt), *adj.* *Biol.* divided by a septum or septa.

sep·ta·va·lent (sep′tə vā′lənt), *adj.* *Chem.* septivalent. [b. SEPT(IVALENT) and (HEPT)AVALENT]

Sep·tem·ber (sep tem′bər), *n.* the ninth month of the year, containing 30 days. [OE < L: seventh (month) in the early Roman calendar; the *-re* of ME *Septembre* < OF *setembre*]

Septem′ber Mas′sacre, (in the French Revolution) the massacre of royalists and other inmates of the prisons of Paris, September 2–6, 1792.

Sep·tem·brist (sep tem′brist), *n.* a person who instigated or took part in the September Massacre. [SEPTEMBER + -IST, modeled on Pg *setembrista* (with reference to the revolution of September 1836 in Portugal); r. earlier *septembrizer* < F *septembriseur*]

sep·te·nar·y (sep′tə ner′ē), *adj., n., pl.* **-nar·ies.** —*adj.* **1.** of or pertaining to the number seven or forming a group of seven. **2.** septennial. —*n.* **3.** a group or set of seven. **4.** a period of seven years. **5.** the number seven. **6.** *Pros.* Also, **sep·te·nar·i·us** (sep′tə nâr′ē əs). a line of seven feet. [< L *septēnāri(us)* = *septēn(ī)* seven apiece (*septe(m)* seven + *-nī* distributive suffix) + *-ārius* -ARY]

sep·ten·de·cil·lion (sep′ten di sil′yən), *n., pl.* **-lions,** (*as after a numeral*) **-lion,** *adj.* —*n.* **1.** a cardinal number represented in the U.S. and France by one followed by 54 zeros and, in Great Britain and Germany, by one followed by 102 zeros. —*adj.* **2.** amounting to one septendecillion in number. [< L *septendec(im)* seventeen + *-illion,* as in *million*] —**sep·ten·de·cil′lionth,** *adj., n.*

sep·ten·ni·al (sep ten′ē əl), *adj.* **1.** occurring every seven years. **2.** of or for seven years. —*n.* **3.** something that occurs every seven years. [< L *septenni(s)* lasting seven years (*sept(em)* seven + *-ennis* lasting a year < *annus* year) + -AL[1]] —**sep·ten′ni·al·ly,** *adv.*

sep·ten·tri·o·nal (sep ten′trē ə nᵊl), *adj.* northern. [late ME < L *septentriōnāl(is)* = *septem triōn(ēs)* seven oxen (Great Bear constellation) + *-ālis* -AL[1]]

sep·tet (sep tet′), *n.* **1.** any group of seven persons or things. **2.** a company of seven singers or musicians. **3.** a musical composition for seven voices or instruments. Also, *esp. Brit.,* **sep·tette′.** [< G; see SEPT-, -ET]

septi-[1], var. of **sept-,** before a consonant: *septilateral.*

septi-[2], a combining form of **septum-:** *septicidal.*

sep·tic (sep′tik), *adj.* *Pathol.* **1.** infective, usually with a pus-forming microbe. **2.** pertaining to sepsis; infected. [< L *sēptic(us)* < Gk *sēptikós* = *sēpt(ós)* rotted + *-ikos* -IC] —**sep′ti·cal·ly,** *adv.* —**sep·tic·i·ty** (sep tis′i tē), *n.*

sep·ti·ce·mi·a (sep′ti sē′mē ə), *n.* *Pathol.* the invasion and persistence of pathogenic bacteria in the blood stream. Also, **sep′ti·cae′mi·a.** [< NL] —**sep′ti·ce′mic, sep′ti·cae′mic,** *adj.*

sep·ti·cid·al (sep′ti sīd′ᵊl), *adj.* *Bot.* characterized by splitting through the septa or dissepiments in dehiscence. —**sep′ti·ci′dal·ly,** *adv.*

sep′tic tank′, a tank in which solid organic sewage is decomposed and purified by anaerobic bacteria.

sep·tif·ra·gal (sep tif′rə gəl), *adj.* *Bot.* characterized by the breaking away of the valves from the septa or dissepiments in dehiscence. [SEPTI-[2] + L *frag-* (see FRAGILE) + -AL[1]] —**sep·tif′ra·gal·ly,** *adv.*

A, Septicidal dehiscence in capsule of a species of *Yucca;* B, Transverse section

sep·ti·lat·er·al (sep′tə lat′ər əl), *adj.* having seven sides.

sep·til·lion (sep til′yən), *n., pl.* **-lions,** (*as after a numeral*) **-lion,** *adj.* —*n.* **1.** a cardinal number represented in the U.S. and France by one followed by 24 zeros and, in Great Britain and Germany, by one followed by 42 zeros. —*adj.* **2.** amounting to one septillion in number. [< F = *sept* seven + *-illion,* as in *million*] —**sep·til′lionth,** *n., adj.*

sep·ti·va·lent (sep′tə vā′lənt), *adj.* *Chem.* having a valence of seven; heptavalent. Also, **septavalent.**

sep·tu·a·ge·nar·i·an (sep′cho͞o ə jə nâr′ē ən), *adj.* **1.** of the age of 70 years or between 70 and 80 years old. —*n.* **2.** a septuagenarian person. [< L *septuāgēnāri(us)*]

sep·tu·ag·e·nar·y (sep′cho͞o aj′ə ner′ē *or, esp. Brit.,* -ə jē′nə rē), *adj., n., pl.* **-nar·ies.** septuagenarian. [< L *septuāgēnāri(us)* = *septuāgēn(ī)* seventy each (distributive of *septuāgintā* seventy; see SEPTUAGINT) + *-ārius* -ARY]

Sep·tu·a·ges·i·ma (sep′to͞o ə jes′ə mə, -tyo͞o-, sep′cho͞o-), *n.* the third Sunday before Lent. Also called **Septuages′ima Sun′day.** [< eccl. L *septuāgēsima* (*diēs*) the seventieth (day); r. ME *septuages(i)me* < OF]

Sep·tu·a·gint (sep′to͞o ə jint′, -tyo͞o-, sep′cho͞o-), *n.* the oldest Greek version of the Old Testament, traditionally said to have been translated by 70 or 72 Jewish scholars at the request of Ptolemy II. [< L *septuāgint(ā)* seventy = var. of *septem* seven + *-gintā* decade] —**Sep′tu·a·gint′al,** *adj.*

sep·tum (sep′təm), *n., pl.* **-ta** (-tə). *Biol.* a dividing wall, membrane, or the like, in a plant or animal structure. [var. of L *saeptum* enclosure < neut. of *saeptus* (ptp. of *saepīre* to fence) = *saep-* fence + *-tus* ptp. suffix; akin to L *saepēs* hedge, fence]

sep·tu·ple (sep′to͞o pəl, -tyo͞o-, sep to͞o′pəl, -tyo͞o′-, -tup′əl), *adj., v.,* **-pled, -pling.** —*adj.* **1.** sevenfold; seven times as great. —*v.t.* **2.** to make seven times as great. [< LL *septupl(us)* = L *septu-* (see *Septuagint*) + *-plus* (see -FOLD)]

sep·tup·let (sep tup′lit, -to͞o′plit, -tyo͞o′-), *n.* **1.** any group or combination of seven. **2.** *Music.* a group of seven notes of equal value performed in the same amount of time normally taken to perform four or six.

sep·tu·plex (sep′to͞o pleks′, -tyo͞o-, sep to͞o′pleks, -tyo͞o′-, -tup′leks), *adj.* sevenfold; septuple. [< LL *septu-* (as in *septuplus* SEPTUPLE) + *-plex* -FOLD]

sep·tu·pli·cate (*n., adj.* sep to͞o′plə kit, -tyo͞o′-; *v.* sep-to͞o′plə kāt′, -tyo͞o′-), *n., adj., v.,* **-cat·ed, -cat·ing.** —*n.* **1.** a group, series, or set of seven identical copies (usually prec. by *in*). —*adj.* **2.** having or consisting of seven identical parts; sevenfold. **3.** noting the seventh copy or item. —*v.t.* **4.** to make seven copies of (something). **5.** to make seven times as great, as by multiplying. [< ML *septuplicāt(us)* (ptp. of *septuplicāre* to multiply by seven) = LL *septupl(us)* SEPTUPLE + *-plicātus,* as in *quadruplicātus;* see QUADRUPLICATE]

sep·ul·cher (sep′əl kər), *n.* **1.** a tomb, grave, or burial place. **2.** Also called **Easter sepulcher.** *Eccles.* **a.** a cavity in a mensa for containing relics of martyrs. **b.** a recess in some old churches in which the Eucharist was deposited on Good Friday and taken out at Easter. —*v.t.* **3.** to place in a sepulcher; bury. Also, *esp. Brit.*, **sepulchre.** [ME *sepulcre* < OF < L *sepulcr(um)* = *sepul-* (ptp. stem of *sepelīre* to bury) + *-crum* n. suffix of place]

se·pul·chral (sə pul′krəl), *adj.* **1.** of, pertaining to, or serving as a tomb. **2.** of or pertaining to burial. **3.** proper to or suggestive of a tomb; funereal or dismal. **4.** hollow and deep: *a sepulchral voice.* [< L *sepulcrāl(is).* See SEPULCHER, -AL[1]] —**se·pul′chral·ly,** *adv.*

sep·ul·chre (sep′əl kər), *n., v.t.*, **-chred, -chring.** *Chiefly Brit.* sepulcher.

sep·ul·ture (sep′əl chər), *n.* **1.** the act of placing in a sepulcher or tomb; burial. **2.** *Archaic.* sepulcher; tomb. [ME < OF < L *sepultūr(a)* = *sepult(us)* (ptp. of *sepelīre* to bury) + *-ūra* -URE] —**se·pul·tur·al** (sə pul′chər əl), *adj.*

seq., **1.** sequel. **2.** the following (one). [< L *sequens*]

seqq., the following (ones). [< L *sequentia*]

se·qua·cious (si kwā′shəs), *adj.* **1.** following with smooth or logical regularity. **2.** *Archaic.* following, imitating, or serving another person, esp. unreasoningly. [< L *sequāci-* (s. of *sequāx*) following (akin to *sequī* to follow) + -OUS] —**se·qua′cious·ly,** *adv.* —**se·quac·i·ty** (si kwas′i tē), **se·qua′cious·ness,** *n.*

se·quel (sē′kwəl), *n.* **1.** a literary work that is complete in itself but continues the narrative of a preceding work. **2.** an event or circumstance following something; subsequent course of affairs. **3.** a result, consequence, or inference. [late ME *sequel(e)* < L *sequēl(a)* what follows = *seq(uī)* to follow + *-ēla* n. suffix]

se·que·la (si kwē′lə), *n., pl.* **-lae** (-lē). *Pathol.* an abnormal condition resulting from a previous disease. [< L: SEQUEL]

se·quence (sē′kwəns), *n.* **1.** the following of one thing after another; succession. **2.** order of succession. **3.** a continuous or connected series: *a sonnet sequence.* **4.** something that follows; result; consequence. **5.** *Music.* a melodic or harmonic pattern repeated three or more times at different pitches. **6.** *Liturgy.* a hymn sometimes sung after the gradual and before the gospel; prose. **7.** *Motion Pictures.* a portion of a film story set in one place and time and without interruptions or breaks of any sort; episode. **8.** *Cards.* a series of three or more cards following one another in order of value, esp. of the same suit. [late ME < LL *sequentia* = *sequ-* (s. of *sequī* to follow) + *-entia* -ENCE] —**Syn. 1.** See **series. 2.** arrangement. **4.** outcome, sequel.

se·quent (sē′kwənt), *adj.* **1.** following; successive. **2.** following logically or naturally; consequent. **3.** characterized by continuous succession; consecutive. —*n.* **4.** something that follows in order or as a result. [< L *sequent-* (s. of *sequēns*, prp. of *sequī* to follow) = *sequ-* follow + *-ent-* -ENT] —**se′quent·ly,** *adv.*

se·quen·tial (si kwen′shəl), *adj.* **1.** characterized by regular sequence of parts. **2.** following; subsequent; consequent. —**se·quen·ti·al·i·ty** (si kwen′shē al′i tē), *n.* —**se·quen′tial·ly,** *adv.*

se·ques·ter (si kwes′tər), *v.t.* **1.** to remove or withdraw into solitude or retirement; seclude. **2.** to remove or separate. **3.** *Law.* to seize and hold, as the property of a debtor, until legal claims are satisfied. **4.** *Internat. Law.* to requisition, hold, and control (enemy property). [ME *sequestre* < legal L *sequestr(āre)* (to) put in hands of a trustee < *sequester* trustee, depositary] —**se·ques′tra·ble,** *adj.*

se·ques·tered (si kwes′tərd), *adj.* secluded; isolated.

se·ques·trate (si kwes′trāt), *v.t.*, **-trat·ed, -trat·ing. 1.** *Law.* **a.** to sequester (property). **b.** to confiscate. **2.** *Archaic.* to separate; seclude. [< L *sequestrāt(us)* (ptp. of *sequestrāre*) = *sequestr-* (see SEQUESTER) + *-ātus* -ATE[1]] —**se·ques·tra·tor** (sē′kwes trā′tər, si kwes′trā-), *n.*

se·ques·tra·tion (sē′kwes trā′shən, si kwes-), *n.* **1.** removal or separation; banishment or exile. **2.** a withdrawal into seclusion; retirement. [late ME *sequestracion* < LL *sequestrātiōn-* (s. of *sequestrātiō*) = *sequestrāt(us)* (ptp. of *sequestrāre* to SEQUESTER) + *-iōn-* -ION]

se·ques·trum (si kwes′trəm), *n., pl.* **-tra** (-trə). *Pathol.* a fragment of bone that has become necrotic as a result of disease or injury, and has separated from the normal bone structure. [< L: something set aside; see SEQUESTER] —**se·ques′tral,** *adj.*

se·quin (sē′kwin), *n.* **1.** a small shining disk or spangle used to ornament a dress, a woman's sweater, etc. **2.** a former gold coin, as of Venice or Turkey. [< F *sequin* < It *zecchin(o)* = *zecc(a)* mint (< Ar *sikkah* die, coin) + *-ino* -INE[2]] —**se′quined,** *adj.*

se·quoi·a (si kwoi′ə), *n.* either of two large coniferous trees of California, the big tree or the redwood, formerly included in the genus *Sequoia:* the big tree is now classified in the genus *Sequoiadendron.* [named after *Sequoya* (1770?–1843), Cherokee Indian scholar]

Sequoi′a Na′tional Park′, a national park in central California: giant sequoia trees. 604 sq. mi.

ser-, var. of **sero-** before a vowel: *serous.*

ser., **1.** series. **2.** sermon.

se·ra (sēr′ə), *n.* a pl. of **serum.**

sé·rac (si rak′; *Fr.* sā RAK′), *n., pl.* **-racs** (-raks′; *Fr.* -RAK′). a large irregularity of ice, as a pinnacle, found in glacial crevasses and formed by melting or movement of the ice. Also, **se·rac** (si rak′). [< F *sérac* kind of white cheese; cf. ML *serācium* < L *serum* whey]

se·ragl·io (si ral′yō, -räl′-), *n., pl.* **-ragl·ios. 1.** the part of a Muslim house or palace in which the wives and concubines are secluded; harem. **2.** a Turkish palace. Also called **se·rail** (sə rī′, -rīl′, -rāl′). [< It *serraglio* cage for wild beasts; cf. ML *serācula* little lock (< L *sera* bar, bolt), and cf. SEAR[2]; by assoc. with Turk *seray* palace, *serraglio* also came to mean harem]

se·ra·i (sə rä′ē, sə rī′), *n., pl.* **-ra·is.** (in Eastern countries) a caravansary. [< Turk *seray* < Pers *serāī* abode, palace. See CARAVANSARY]

Se·ra·je·vo (*Serbo-Croatian.* se′RÄ ye vô; *Eng.* ser′ə yā′vō), *n.* Sarajevo.

Se·rang (se räng′), *n.* Ceram.

se·ra·pe (sə rä′pē; *Sp.* se RÄ′pe), *n., pl.* **-pes** (-pēz; *Sp.* -pes). a blanketlike shawl or wrap, often of brightly-colored wool, as worn in Latin America. Also, **sarape.** [< MexSp *sarape*]

ser·aph (ser′əf), *n., pl.* **-aphs, -a·phim** (-ə fim). **1.** one of the celestial beings hovering above God's throne in Isaiah's vision. Isa. 6. **2.** a member of the highest order of angels. [back formation from SERAPHIM] —**ser′aph·like′,** *adj.*

se·raph·ic (si raf′ik), *adj.* of, like, or befitting a seraph. Also, **se·raph′i·cal.** [< eccl. L *seraphicus.* See SERAPHIM, -IC] —**se·raph′i·cal·ly,** *adv.* —**se·raph′i·cal·ness,** *n.*

ser·a·phim (ser′ə fim), *n.* a pl. of **seraph.** [< LL (Vulgate) < Heb *serāphīm*]

Se·ra·pis (si rā′pis), *n.* a Greco-Egyptian deity, combining the attributes of Osiris and Apis, identified in Egypt with the Ptolemies: later worshiped throughout the Greek and Roman empires.

Serb (sûrb), *n., adj.*, **1.** Serbian. **2.** Serbo-Croatian. [< Serbian *Srb*]

Serb., **1.** Serbia. **2.** Serbian.

Ser·bi·a (sûr′bē ə), *n.* a former kingdom in S Europe: now, with revised boundaries, a constituent republic of Yugoslavia, in the SE part. 7,571,000 (est. 1960); 34,116 sq. mi. *Cap.:* Belgrade. Formerly, **Servia.**

Ser·bi·an (sûr′bē ən), *adj.* **1.** of or pertaining to Serbia, its inhabitants, or their language. —*n.* **2.** a native or inhabitant of Serbia, esp. one of the Slavic peoples inhabiting it. **3.** Serbo-Croatian, esp. as spoken and written in Serbia. Also, **Serb.**

Serbo-, a combining form of **Serb:** *Serbo-Croatian.*

Ser·bo-Cro·a·tian (sûr′bō krō ā′shən, -shē ən), *n.* **1.** the principal Slavic language of Yugoslavia, usually written with Cyrillic letters in Serbia but with Roman letters in Croatia. —*adj.* **2.** of or pertaining to Serbo-Croatian. Also called **Serb.**

Serbs′, Cro′ats, and Slo′venes, Kingdom of, former name of **Yugoslavia.**

sere[1] (sēr), *adj.* dry; withered. Also, **sear.** [var. of SEAR[1]]

sere[2] (sēr), *n.* the series of stages in an ecological succession. [back formation from SERIES]

se·rein (sə ran′; *Fr.* sə RAN′), *n.* a very fine rain falling after sunset from a sky in which no clouds are visible. [< F; MF *serain* evening, nightfall < VL **sērān(um)* = L *sēr(um)* a late hour (neut. of *sērus* late) + *-ānum,* neut. of *-ānus* -AN]

ser·e·nade (ser′ə nād′), *n., v.*, **-nad·ed, -nad·ing.** —*n.* **1.** a complimentary performance of vocal or instrumental music in the open air at night, as by a lover under the window of his lady. **2.** a piece of music suitable for such performance. —*v.t.* **3.** to perform a serenade for. —*v.i.* **4.** to sing or play a serenade. [< F *sérénade* < It *serenat(a)*; see SERENATA] —**ser′e·nad′er,** *n.*

ser·e·na·ta (ser′ə nä′tə), *n., pl.* **-tas, -te** (-tā). *Music.* **1.** a form of secular cantata, often of a dramatic or imaginative character. **2.** an instrumental composition in several movements, intermediate between the suite and the symphony. [< It *serenata* evening song = *seren(o)* open air (n. use of adj. *sereno* SERENE) + *-ata* n. suffix]

Ser·en·dib (ser′ən dēb′), *n.* former name of **Ceylon.** Also, **Ser·en·dip** (ser′ən dip′).

ser·en·dip·i·ty (ser′ən dip′i tē), *n.* an aptitude for making desirable discoveries by accident. [SERENDIP + -ITY; Horace Walpole so named a faculty possessed by the heroes of a tale called *The Three Princes of Serendip*]

se·rene (sə rēn′), *adj.* **1.** calm, peaceful, or tranquil; unruffled. **2.** clear; fair: *serene weather.* **3.** (*usually cap.*) most high or august, used as a royal epithet (usually prec. by *his, your,* etc.): *his Serene Highness.* —*n.* **4.** *Archaic.* a clear or tranquil expanse of sea or sky. **5.** serenity; tranquillity. [< L *serēn(us)*] —**se·rene′ly,** *adv.* —**se·rene′ness,** *n.* —**Syn. 1.** unperturbed, composed. See **peaceful. 2.** unclouded. —**Ant. 1.** disturbed. **2.** clouded.

Se·ren·i·ta·tis (sə ren′i tā′tis), *n.* **Mare.** See **Mare Serenitatis.**

se·ren·i·ty (sə ren′i tē), *n., pl.* **-ties** for 2. **1.** the state or quality of being serene, calm, or tranquil. **2.** (*usually cap.*) a title of honor, respect, or reverence, used in speaking of or to certain members of royalty (usually prec. by *his, your,* etc.). [< L *serēnitās*] —**Syn. 1.** composure, calm, peacefulness.

Se·ren·i·ty (sə ren′i tē), *n.* **Sea of.** See **Mare Serenitatis.**

Se·reth (zā′Rət), *n.* German name of **Siret.**

serf (sûrf), *n.* **1.** a person in a condition of servitude, required to render services to his lord, commonly attached to the lord's land and transferred with it from one owner to another. **2.** a slave. [< MF < L *serv(us)* slave] —**serf′dom, serf′hood, serf′age,** *n.* —**serf′ish, serf′like′,** *adj.* —**serf′ish·ly,** *adv.* —**serf′ish·ness,** *n.*

Serg., Sergeant. Also, **Sergt.**

serge (sûrj), *n.* **1.** a twilled worsted or woolen fabric used esp. for clothing. **2.** cotton, rayon, or silk in a twill weave. [< F; r. ME *sarge* < MF < VL **sārica* for L *sērica* (*lāna*) Chinese (wool), i.e., silk; see SERIC-]

ser·geant (sär′jənt), *n.* **1.** a noncommissioned army officer of a rank above that of corporal. **2.** *U.S. Air Force.* any noncommissioned officer above the rank of airman first class. **3.** See **sergeant at arms. 4.** Also called **ser′geant at law′.** *Brit.* (formerly) a member of a superior order of barristers. Also, *esp. Brit.*, **serjeant.** [ME *sergant, serjant, serjaunt* < OF *sergent* << L *servient-* (s. of *serviēns*), prp. of *servīre.* See SERVE, -ENT] —**ser·gean·cy** (sär′jən sē), **ser′geant·ship′,** *n.*

ser′geant at arms′, an officer of a legislative body, whose main duty is to preserve order.

ser′geant first′ class′, *U.S. Army.* a noncommissioned officer ranking next above a staff sergeant and below a first or master sergeant.

ser·geant·fish (sär′jənt fish′), *n., pl.* **-fish·es,** (*esp. collectively*) **-fish. 1.** the cobia. **2.** any of several other marine fishes, as a snook, *Centropomus undecimalis.* [so called from the stripes on its fins]

ser′geant ma′jor, *Mil.* (in the U.S. Army and U.S.

Marine Corps) a noncommissioned officer of the highest enlisted rank.
ser·geant·y (sär′jən tē), *n.* *Medieval Eng. Law.* serjeanty.
Ser·gi·pe (sər zhē′pə), *n.* a state in E Brazil. 760,273 (1960); 8490 sq. mi. *Cap.:* Aracaju.
Ser·gi·us I (sûr′jē əs), died A.D. 701, Italian ecclesiastic: pope 687–701.
Sergius II, died A.D. 847, pope 844–847.
Sergius III, died A.D. 911, pope 904–911.
Sergius IV, died 1012, pope 1009–12.
se·ri·al (sēr′ē əl), *n.* **1.** anything published, broadcast, etc., in short installments at regular intervals. **2.** *Library Science.* a publication that is issued at regular intervals and is consecutively numbered. —*adj.* **3.** published in installments or successive parts. **4.** pertaining to such publication. **5.** of, pertaining to, or arranged in a series. [< NL *seriāl(is).* See SERIES, -AL[1]] —**se′ri·al·ly,** *adv.*
se·ri·al·ise (sēr′ē ə līz′), *v.t.*, **-ised, -is·ing.** *Chiefly Brit.* serialize. —**se′ri·al·i·sa′tion,** *n.*
se·ri·al·ize (sēr′ē ə līz′), *v.t.*, **-ized, -iz·ing. 1.** to publish in serial form. **2.** to broadcast, televise, or film in serial form. —**se′ri·al·ist,** *n.* —**se′ri·al·i·za′tion,** *n.*
se′rial num′ber, a number, usually one of a series, assigned for identification.
se·ri·ate (sēr′ē it, -āt′), *adj.* arranged or occurring in one or more series. [< L *seri(ēs)* SERIES + -ATE[1]] —**se′ri·ate·ly,** *adv.* —**se′ri·a′tion,** *n.*
se·ri·a·tim (sēr′ē ā′tim, ser′-), *adv., adj.* in a series; one after another. [< ML = L *seri(ēs)* SERIES + *-ātim* adv. suffix]
seric-, a learned borrowing from Latin meaning "silk," used in the formation of compound words: *sericin.* [comb. form of L *sēricum* < Gk *sērikón* silk, neut. of *sērikós* Chinese, silken = *sēr* silkworm + *-ikos* -IC]
se·ri·ceous (si rish′əs), *adj.* **1.** silky. **2.** covered with silky down, as a leaf. [< L *sēriceus*]
ser·i·cin (ser′i sin), *n.* *Chem.* a gelatinous organic compound obtained from silk.
ser·i·cul·ture (ser′ə kul′chər), *n.* the raising of silkworms for the production of raw silk. [< Gk *sēr* silkworm + -I- + CULTURE] —**ser′i·cul′tur·al,** *adj.* —**ser′i·cul′tur·ist,** *n.*
se·ries (sēr′ēz), *n., pl.* **-ries,** *adj.* —*n.* **1.** a group or a number of related or similar things, events, etc., arranged or occurring in temporal, spatial, or other order or succession. **2.** a set, as of coins, stamps, etc. **3.** *Math.* **a.** a sequence of terms combined by addition, as $1 + \frac{1}{2} + \frac{1}{4} + \frac{1}{8} + \frac{1}{2^n}$. **b.** See **infinite series. 4.** *Rhet.* a succession of coordinate sentence elements. **5.** *Elect.* an end-to-end arrangement of the components, as resistors, in a circuit so that the same current flows through each. Cf. **parallel** (def. 13). —*adj.* **6.** *Elect.* consisting of or having component parts connected in series. [< L *seriēs;* akin to *serere* to connect]
—**Syn. 1.** SERIES, SEQUENCE, SUCCESSION are terms for an orderly following of things one after another. SERIES is applied to a number of things of the same kind, usually related to each other, arranged or happening in order: *a series of baseball games.* SEQUENCE stresses the continuity in time, thought, cause and effect, etc.: *The scenes came in a definite sequence.* SUCCESSION implies that one thing is followed by another or others in turn, usually though not necessarily with a relation or connection between them: *succession to a throne.*
se·ries-wound (sēr′ēz wound′), *adj.* *Elect.* noting a commutator motor in which the field circuit and armature circuit are connected in series.
ser·if (ser′if), *n.* *Print.* a smaller line used to finish off a main stroke of a letter, as at the top and bottom of *M.* [? < D *schreef* stroke < MD *shriv(en)* (to) write]
ser·i·graph (ser′ə graf′, -gräf′), *n.* a print made by the silk-screen process. [*seri-* (as in SERICULTURE) + -GRAPH] —**se·rig·ra·pher** (si rig′rə fər), *n.* —**se·rig′ra·phy,** *n.*
ser·in (ser′in), *n.* a small finch, *Serinus serinus,* of Europe and northern Africa, closely related to the canary. [< MF *sere(i)n;* cf. OPr *serena, sirena* bee-eater (a green bird) < LL *sirēna,* L *sīrēn* SIREN]
ser·ine (ser′ēn, -in, sēr′-), *n.* *Biochem.* an amino acid, $HOCH_2CH(NH_2)COOH$, obtained by the hydrolysis of sericin. [SER(UM) + -INE[2]]
se·rin·ga (sə ring′gə), *n.* any of several Brazilian trees of the genus *Hevea,* yielding rubber. [< Pg, var. of SYRINGA]
Se·ring·a·pa·tam (sə ring′gə pə tam′), *n.* a town in S Mysore, in S India, former capital of Mysore: taken by the British 1799.
se·ri·o·com·ic (sēr′ē ō kom′ik), *adj.* partly serious and partly comic: *a seriocomic play.* Also, **se′ri·o·com′i·cal.** [*serio-* (comb. form of SERIOUS) + COMIC] —**se′ri·o·com′i·cal·ly,** *adv.*
se·ri·ous (sēr′ē əs), *adj.* **1.** of, showing, or characterized by deep thought. **2.** of grave or somber disposition, character, or manner: *a serious occasion; a serious man.* **3.** being in earnest; sincere; not trifling. **4.** requiring thought, concentration, or application. **5.** weighty or important: *Marriage is a serious matter.* **6.** giving cause for apprehension; critical: *a serious disease.* [< L *sērius* or LL *sēriōs(us);* see -OUS, -OSE[1]] —**se′ri·ous·ly,** *adv.* —**se′ri·ous·ness,** *n.*
—**Syn. 2.** sober, sedate, staid. See **earnest**[1]. **5.** momentous, grave. —**Ant. 5.** trivial.
ser·jeant (sär′jənt), *n.* *Chiefly Brit.* sergeant.
ser·jeant·y (sär′jən tē), *n.* *Medieval Eng. Law.* a form of land tenure in which a tenant holding of the king rendered services only to him. Also, **sergeanty.** [< OF *serjantie.* See SERGEANT, -Y[3]]
Ser·kin (sûr′kin; *Ger.* ser′kin), *n.* **Ru·dolf** (ro͞o′dolf; *Ger.* ro͞o′dôlf), born 1903, U.S. pianist, born in Bohemia.
ser·mon (sûr′mən), *n.* **1.** a discourse for the purpose of religious instruction or exhortation. **2.** any serious speech, discourse, or exhortation, esp. on a moral issue. **3.** a long, tedious speech. [ME < ML, L *sermōn-* (s. of *sermō;* ML: speech from pulpit; L: discourse) = *ser-* (root of *serere* to link up, organize) + *-mōn-* n. suffix] —**ser′mon·less,** *adj.*
ser·mon·ic (sər mon′ik), *adj.* of, pertaining to, or like a sermon. Also, **ser·mon′i·cal.** —**ser·mon′i·cal·ly,** *adv.*
ser·mon·ise (sûr′mə nīz′), *v.t., v.i.*, **-ised, -is·ing.** *Chiefly Brit.* sermonize. —**ser′mon·is′er,** *n.*
ser·mon·ize (sûr′mə nīz′), *v.*, **-ized, -iz·ing.** —*v.i.* **1.** to deliver or compose a sermon; preach. —*v.t.* **2.** to give exhortation to; lecture. Also, *esp. Brit.*, **sermonise.** —**ser′mon·iz′er,** *n.*
Ser′mon on the Mount′, a discourse delivered by Jesus to the disciples and others, containing the Beatitudes. Matt. 5–7; Luke 6:20–49.
sero-, a combining form of **serum:** *serology.* Also, *esp. before a vowel,* **ser-.**
se·rol·o·gy (si rol′ə jē), *n.* the science dealing with the properties and actions of the serum of the blood. —**se·ro·log·ic** (sēr′ə loj′ik), **se′ro·log′i·cal,** *adj.* —**se′ro·log′i·cal·ly,** *adv.* —**se·rol′o·gist,** *n.*
se·ro·sa (si rō′sə, -zə), *n., pl.* **-sas, -sae** (-sē, -zē). See **serous membrane.** [< NL, fem. of *serōsus* = L *ser(um)* SERUM + *-ōsus* -OSE[1]]
ser·o·tine (ser′ə tin, -tīn′), *adj.* late in occurring, developing, or flowering. Also, **se·rot·i·nous** (si rot′ᵊnəs). [< L *sērōtin(us)* = *sērō* (adv.) late + *-tinus* adj. suffix of time; cf. SEREIN]
ser·o·to·nin (ser′ə tō′nin), *n.* *Biochem.* a compound, $HOC_8H_5NCH_2CH_2NH_2$, occurring in the brain, intestines, and platelets, that induces vasoconstriction. [SERO- + TONE + -IN[2]]
se·rous (sēr′əs), *adj.* **1.** resembling serum; watery. **2.** containing or secreting serum. **3.** pertaining to or characterized by serum. [< L *serōs(us)*] —**se·ros·i·ty** (si ros′i tē), **se′rous·ness,** *n.*
se′rous flu′id, any of various fluids in the body resembling the serum of the blood.
se′rous mem′brane, *Anat., Zool.* any of various thin membranes, as the peritoneum, that line certain cavities of the body and exude a serous fluid. Also called **serosa.**
ser·ow (ser′ō), *n.* a goat antelope of the genus *Capricornis,* of eastern Asia, related to the goral. [m. *saro,* native (Tibeto-Burman) name in Sikkim]
ser·pent (sûr′pənt), *n.* **1.** a snake. **2.** a wily, treacherous, or malicious person. **3.** the Devil; Satan. Gen. 3:1–5. **4.** an obsolete wooden wind instrument with a serpentine shape and a deep, coarse tone. [ME (< MF) < L *serpent-,* s. of *serpēns,* n. use of prp. of *serpere* to creep, crawl; c. Gk *hérpein*]

Serpent (def. 4)

ser·pen·tine[1] (sûr′pən tēn′, -tīn′), *adj.* **1.** of, characteristic of, or resembling a serpent, as in form or movement. **2.** having a winding course, as a road; sinuous. **3.** shrewd, wily, or cunning; resembling a snake in treacherousness. [late ME < L *serpentīn(us)* snakelike = *serpent-* SERPENT + *-īnus* -INE[1]]
ser·pen·tine[2] (sûr′pən tēn′, -tīn′), *n.* a common mineral, hydrous magnesium silicate, $H_2Mg_3Si_2O_2$, usually oily green and sometimes spotted, occurring in many varieties: used for architectural and decorative purposes. [late ME *serpentyn* < ML *serpentīn(um)* < neut. of *serpentīnus* SERPENTINE[1]]
Ser·ra (ser′rä), *n.* **Ju·ní·pe·ro** (ho͞o nē′pe rô′), (*Miguel Jose Serra*), 1713–84, Spanish Roman Catholic missionary to the Indians in California and Mexico.
ser·ra·nid (sə rā′nid, -rä′-, -ran′id), *n.* **1.** any of numerous percoid fishes of the family *Serranidae,* found chiefly in warm seas, including the sea basses and groupers. —*adj.* **2.** belonging or pertaining to the family *Serranidae.* [< NL *Serranid(ae).* See SERRANOID]
ser·ra·noid (ser′ə noid′), *adj.* **1.** resembling or related to the sea bass family *Serranidae.* —*n.* **2.** a serranoid fish. [< NL *serrān(us)* genus of fishes (L *serr(a)* sawfish + *-ānus* -AN) + -OID]
ser·rate (*adj.* ser′it, -āt; *v.* ser′āt), *adj., v.,* **-rat·ed, -rat·ing.** —*adj.* **1.** *Bot., Anat.* notched on the edge like a saw: *a serrate leaf.* **2.** *Numis.* (of a coin) having a grooved edge. **3.** serrated. —*v.t.* **4.** to make serrate or serrated. [< L *serrāt(us)* = *serr(a)* saw + *-ātus* -ATE[1]]
ser·rat·ed (ser′ā tid), *adj.* having a notched edge or sawlike teeth: *the serrated blade of a bread knife.*

Serrate leaf

ser·ra·tion (se rā′shən), *n.* **1.** serrated condition or form. **2.** a serrated edge or formation. **3.** one of the notches or teeth of such an edge or formation. Also, **ser·ra·ture** (ser′ə chər). [< NL *serrātiōn-* (s. of *serrātiō*)]
ser·ri·form (ser′ə fôrm′), *adj.* resembling the notched edge of a saw; serrated. [*serri-* (comb. form of L *serra* saw) + -FORM]
ser·ru·late (ser′yə lit, -lāt′, ser′ə-), *adj.* finely or minutely serrate, as a leaf. Also, **ser′ru·lat′ed.** [< NL *serrulāt(us)* = L *serrul(a)* (dim. of *serra* saw) + *-ātus* -ATE[1]]
ser·ru·la·tion (ser′yə lā′shən, ser′ə-), *n.* **1.** serrulate condition or form. **2.** a fine or minute serration.
Ser·to·ri·us (sər tōr′ē əs, -tôr′-), *n.* **Quin·tus** (kwin′təs), died 72 B.C., Roman general and statesman.
ser·tu·lar·i·an (sûr′cho͞o lâr′ē ən), *n.* *Zool.* a type of hydroid that forms stiff, feathery colonies in which the cups holding the zooids are sessile. [< NL *Sertulāri(a)* genus name (L *sertul(a),* dim. of *serta* wreath + *-āria* -ARIA) + -AN]
se·rum (sēr′əm), *n., pl.* **se·rums, se·ra** (sēr′ə). **1.** the clear, pale-yellow liquid that separates from the clot in the coagulation of blood; blood serum. **2.** a fluid of this kind obtained from the blood of an animal that has been rendered immune to some disease by inoculation, used as an antitoxic or therapeutic agent. **3.** any watery animal fluid. **4.** the thin, clear part of the fluid of plants. **5.** (of milk) **a.** the portion left after butterfat, casein, and albumin have been removed. **b.** the portion left after the manufacture of cheese. [< L: whey] —**se′rum·al,** *adj.*
se′rum albu′min, 1. *Biochem.* the principal protein of the blood plasma. **2.** the commercial form of this substance, obtained from ox blood, used in textile printing, foods, and in the treatment of shock.

ser·val (sûr′vəl), *n., pl.* **-vals,** (*esp. collectively*) **-val.** a long-limbed African cat, *Felis serval,* having a tawny coat spotted with black, and about the size of a bobcat. [< NL < Pg (*lobo*) *cerval* lynx (lit., staglike wolf) < LL *cervāl(is)* deerlike = L *cerv(us)* stag + *-ālis* -AL¹]

Serval
(About 2 ft. high at shoulder; total length 5 ft.; tail 1 ft.)

serv·ant (sûr′vənt), *n.* **1.** a person employed by another, esp. one employed to perform domestic duties. **2.** a person in the service of another. **3.** a person employed by the government: *a public servant.* [ME < OF < *servant* serving = *serv-* (s. of *servir* to SERVE) + *-ant* -ANT] —**serv′ant·less,** *adj.* —**serv′ant·like′,** *adj.*

serve (sûrv), *v.,* **served, serv·ing,** *n.* —*v.i.* **1.** to act as a servant. **2.** to wait on table, as a waiter. **3.** to offer or have a meal or refreshments available, as for patrons or guests. **4.** to render assistance; be of use; help. **5.** to go through a term of service. **6.** to have definite use. **7.** to answer the purpose: *That will serve to explain my actions.* **8.** (in tennis, badminton, handball, etc.) to put the ball or shuttlecock in play. **9.** *Eccles.* to act as a server. —*v.t.* **10.** to be in the service of; work for. **11.** to render service to; help. **12.** to go through (a term of service, imprisonment, etc.). **13.** to render active service to (a king, commander, etc.). **14.** to render obedience or homage to (God, a sovereign, etc.). **15.** to perform the duties of (a position, an office, etc.): *to serve his mayoralty.* **16.** to answer the requirements of; suffice. **17.** to contribute to; promote: *to serve a cause.* **18.** to wait upon at table. **19.** to act as a host or hostess in offering (a person) a portion of food or drink. **20.** to offer or distribute (food or drink) to another. **21.** to provide with a regular or continuous supply of something. **22.** to treat in a specified manner: *That served him ill.* **23.** to gratify (desire, wants, needs, etc.). **24.** (of a male animal) to mate with; service. **25.** (in tennis, badminton, etc.) to put (the ball or shuttlecock) in play. **26.** *Law.* **a.** to make delivery of (a writ). **b.** to present (a person) with a writ. **27.** to operate or keep in action (a gun, artillery, etc.). **28.** *Naut.* to wrap (a rope) tightly with small stuff, keeping the turns as close together as possible, esp. after worming and parceling. **29. serve one right,** to treat one as he deserves, esp. to punish justly. —*n.* **30.** the act, manner, or right of serving, as in tennis. [ME *serve(n)* < OF *serv(ir)* < L *servīre* = *serv(us)* slave + *-īre* inf. suffix] —**serv′a·ble, serve′a·ble,** *adj.* —**Syn. 1, 2.** attend. **4, 11.** aid, succor.

serv·er (sûr′vər), *n.* **1.** a person who serves. **2.** something that serves or is used in serving, as a salver. **3.** a broad fork, spoon, or spatula for dishing out and serving individual portions of food, as vegetables, cake, pie, etc. **4.** *Eccles.* an attendant on the priest at Mass. **5.** (in tennis, badminton, handball, etc.) the player who puts the ball or shuttlecock in play.

Ser·ve·tus (sər vē′təs), *n.* **Michael,** 1511–53, Spanish physician and theologian, accused of heresy and burned at the stake. Spanish, **Mi·guel Ser·ve·to** (mē gel′ ser ve′tô). —**Ser·ve·tian** (sər vē′shən), *n.* —**Ser·ve′tian·ism,** *n.*

Ser·vi·a (sûr′vē ə), *n.* former name of **Serbia.** —**Ser′vi·an,** *adj., n.*

serv·ice¹ (sûr′vis), *n., adj., v.,* **-iced, -ic·ing.** —*n.* **1.** an act of assistance; help; aid. **2.** the supplying or supplier of utilities or commodities required or demanded by the public. **3.** the providing or a provider of accommodation and activities required by the public, as maintenance, repair, etc. **4.** the organized system of apparatus, appliances, employees, etc., for supplying some accommodation required by the public. **5.** the supplying or a supplier of public communication and transportation. **6.** the performance of duties or the duties performed, as by a waiter or servant. **7.** employment in any duties or work for a person, organization, government, etc. **8.** a department of public employment. **9.** the duty or work of public servants. **10.** the serving of a sovereign, state, or government in some official capacity. **11.** *Mil.* **a.** the armed forces: *in the service.* **b.** a branch of the armed forces, as the army or navy. **12.** *Ordn.* the actions required in loading and firing a cannon: *service of the piece.* **13.** Often, **services.** the performance of any duties or work for another; helpful or professional activity: *medical services.* **14.** something made or done by a commercial organization for the public benefit and without regard to direct profit. **15.** Also called **divine service.** public religious worship according to prescribed form and order. **16.** a ritual prescribed for some particular occasion: *the marriage service.* **17.** the serving of God by obedience, piety, etc. **18.** a musical setting of the sung parts of a liturgy. **19.** a set of dishes, utensils, etc., for general table use or for particular use. **20.** *Law.* the serving of a process or writ upon a person. **21.** *Naut.* tarred spun yarn or other small stuff for covering the exterior of a rope. **22.** (in tennis, badminton, etc.) **a.** act or manner of putting the ball or shuttlecock into play. **b.** the ball or shuttlecock as put into play. **23.** the mating of a female animal with the male. —*adj.* **24.** of service; useful. **25.** of, pertaining to, or used by servants, delivery men, etc., or in serving food. **26.** supplying maintenance and repair. **27.** of, for, or pertaining to the armed forces or one of them: *a service academy.* —*v.t.* **28.** to make fit for use; repair; restore to condition for service: *to service an automobile.* **29.** to supply with aid, information, or other incidental services. **30.** (of a male animal) to mate with (a female animal). [ME < OF < L *servit(ium)* servitude = *serv(us)* slave + *-itium* -ICE; r. ME *servise,* OE *serfise* < OF *servise* < L]

serv·ice² (sûr′vis), *n.* **1.** a service tree, esp. *Sorbus domestica.* **2.** the shadbush. [ME *serves,* pl. of *serve,* OE *syrfe* < VL **sorbea,* L *sorb(us)* SORB]

Ser·vice (sûr′vis), *n.* **Robert W(illiam),** 1874–1958, Canadian writer, born in England.

serv·ice·a·ble (sûr′vi sə bəl), *adj.* **1.** capable of or being of service; useful. **2.** wearing well; durable: *serviceable cloth.* **3.** capable of being used, worn, cleaned, repaired, etc., easily. **4.** *Archaic.* diligent or attentive in serving. [r. ME *servisable* < MF] —**serv′ice·a·bil′i·ty, serv′ice·a·ble·ness,** *n.* —**serv′ice·a·bly,** *adv.*

serv′ice ace′, ace (def. 2a).

serv·ice·ber·ry (sûr′vis ber′ē), *n., pl.* **-ries. 1.** the fruit of any service tree. **2.** a North American, rosaceous shrub or small tree, *Amelanchier canadensis,* bearing a berrylike fruit. **3.** any of various other plants of the genus *Amelanchier.*

serv′ice club′, a recreational center for members of the armed forces.

serv·ice·man (sûr′vis man′, -mən), *n., pl.* **-men** (-men′, -mən). **1.** a member of the armed forces of a country. **2.** a person whose occupation is to maintain or repair equipment.

serv′ice sta′tion, a place equipped for servicing automobiles, as by selling gasoline and oil, making repairs, etc.

serv′ice stripe′, *Mil.* a stripe worn on the left sleeve by an enlisted man to indicate a specific period of time served on active duty.

serv′ice tree′, 1. either of two European trees, *Sorbus domestica,* bearing a small, acid fruit that is edible when overripe, or *S. torminalis,* bearing a similar fruit. **2.** serviceberry (defs. 2, 3).

ser·vi·ette (sûr′vē et′), *n.* a table napkin. [late ME < MF = *servi(r)* (to) SERVE + *-ette* -ETTE; for the formation, cf. OUBLIETTE]

ser·vile (sûr′vil, -vīl), *adj.* **1.** slavishly submissive or obsequious; fawning: *servile flatterers.* **2.** characteristic of, proper to, or customary for slaves; abject: *servile obedience.* **3.** yielding slavishly (usually fol. by *to*). **4.** of, pertaining to, or characteristic of a slave or a servant. **5.** of or pertaining to a condition of servitude or property ownership in which a person is held as a slave or as partially enslaved. [late ME < L *servīlis* = *serv-* (s. of *servīre* to be a slave) + *-īlis* -ILE] —**ser′vile·ly,** *adv.* —**ser·vil′i·ty, ser′vile·ness,** *n.* —**Syn. 1, 2.** cringing, sycophantic. SERVILE, MENIAL, OBSEQUIOUS, SLAVISH characterize a person who behaves like a slave or an inferior. SERVILE suggests cringing, fawning, and abject submission: *servile responses to questions.* MENIAL applies to that which is considered undesirable drudgery: *the most menial tasks.* OBSEQUIOUS implies the ostentatious subordination of oneself to the wishes of another, either from fear or from hope of gain: *an obsequious waiter.* SLAVISH stresses the dependence and laborious toil of a person who follows or obeys without question: *slavish attentiveness to orders.*

serv·ing (sûr′viŋ), *n.* **1.** the act of a person or thing that serves. **2.** a single portion of food or drink; helping. —*adj.* **3.** for use in distributing food. [ME]

ser·vi·tor (sûr′vi tər), *n.* a person who is in or at the service of another; attendant. [ME *servitour* < AF < LL *servītor* = L *servīt(us)* (ptp. of *servīre* to SERVE) + *-or* -OR²]

ser·vi·tude (sûr′vi to͞od′, -tyo͞od′), *n.* **1.** slavery or bondage of any kind. **2.** compulsory service or labor as a punishment for criminals. **3.** *Law.* a right possessed by one person with respect to another's property for a limited purpose. [late ME < L *servitūdō.* See SERVICE, -TUDE] —**Syn. 1.** See **slavery.** —**Ant. 1.** liberty.

ser·vo (sûr′vō), *adj., n., pl.* **-vos.** —*adj.* **1.** acting as part of a servomechanism. **2.** pertaining to or having to do with servomechanisms. **3.** noting the action of certain mechanisms, as brakes, that are set in operation by other mechanisms but themselves augment the force of that action by the way in which they operate. —*n.* **4.** *Informal.* servomechanism. [short form of SERVOMECHANISM]

servo-, a learned borrowing from Latin, where it meant "slave" or "servant," used in the formation of compound words: *servomechanism.* [< L *serv(us)* + -o-]

Servo-, var. of **Serbo-.**

ser·vo·mech·an·ism (sûr′vō mek′ə niz′əm, sûr′vō-mek′-), *n.* an electronic control system in which a hydraulic, pneumatic, or other type of controlling mechanism is actuated and controlled by a low-energy signal. —**ser·vo·me·chan·i·cal** (sûr′vō mə kan′i kəl), *adj.* —**ser′vo·me·chan′i·cal·ly,** *adv.*

ser·vo·mo·tor (sûr′vō mō′tər), *n.* a motor or the like forming part of a servomechanism. [SERVO- + MOTOR, modeled on F *servo-moteur*]

ses·a·me (ses′ə mē), *n.* **1.** a tropical, herbaceous plant, *Sesamum indicum,* whose small oval seeds are edible and yield an oil. **2.** the seeds themselves, used to add flavor to bread, crackers, etc. **3.** See **open sesame.** Also called **benne** (for defs. 1, 2). [< Gk *sēsámē* < Sem; r. *sesam* < L *sēsam(um)* < Gk *sésamon*]

ses′ame oil′, a yellow oil expressed from the seeds of the sesame, used in cooking and in the manufacture of margarine, soap, and cosmetics.

ses·a·moid (ses′ə moid′), *adj. Anat.* shaped like a sesame seed, as certain small nodular bones. [< L *sēsamoīd(ēs)* < Gk *sēsamoeidḗs* like sesame seed]

sesqui-, a learned borrowing from Latin meaning "one and a half," used in the formation of compound words: *sesquicentennial.* [< L = *sē(mi)s* half-unit (*sēmi-* SEMI- + *as* AS²) + *-que* and (c. Gk *té,* Skt *ca,* Goth *-(u)h*)]

ses·qui·car·bon·ate (ses′kwi kär′bə nāt′, -nit), *n. Chem.* a salt intermediate between a carbonate and a bicarbonate or consisting of the two combined.

ses·qui·cen·ten·ni·al (ses′kwi sen ten′ē əl), *adj.* **1.** pertaining to or marking the completion of a period of 150 years. —*n.* **2.** a 150th anniversary or its celebration. —**ses′qui·cen·ten′ni·al·ly,** *adv.*

ses·qui·pe·da·li·an (ses′kwi pi dā′lē ən, -dāl′yən), *adj.* Also, **ses·quip·e·dal** (ses kwip′i dᵊl). **1.** given to using long words. **2.** (of words or expressions) very long. —*n.* **3.** a sesquipedalian word. [< L *sēsquipedāli(s)* of a foot and a half (see SESQUI-, PEDAL) + -AN] —**ses·qui·pe·dal·i·ty** (ses′kwi pi dal′i tē), **ses′qui·pe·da′li·an·ism, ses·quip·e·dal·ism** (ses kwip′i dᵊliz′əm, -kwi pēd′ᵊliz′-), *n.*

Ses·shu (ses shōō′), *n.* 1420?–1506, Japanese Zen Buddhist monk and painter.

ses·sile (ses′il, -īl), *adj. Biol.* **1.** attached by the base, or without any distinct projecting support, as a leaf issuing directly from the stem. **2.** permanently attached. [< L *sēssilis* fit for sitting on, low enough to sit on, dwarfish (said of plants) = *sēss(us)* (ptp. of *sedēre* to SIT) + *-ilis* -ILE] —**ses·sil·i·ty** (se sil′i tē), *n.*

Sessile plants
A, Flower; B, Leaves

ses·sion (sesh′ən), *n.* **1.** the sitting together of a court, council, legislature, or the like, for conference or the transaction of business. **2.** a single continuous sitting, or period of sitting, of persons so assembled. **3. sessions,** (in English law) the sittings or a sitting of justices in court, usually to deal with minor offenses, grant licenses, etc. **4.** a single continuous course or period of lessons, study, etc., in the work of a day at school: *two afternoon sessions a week.* **5.** a portion of the year into which instruction is organized at an educational institution. **6.** the governing body of a local Presbyterian church, composed of the pastor and the elders. **7.** a period of time during which a group of persons meets to pursue a particular activity. [late ME < ML, L *sēssiōn-* (s. of *sēssiō*, ML: law-court sitting, L: sitting) = *sēss(us)* (ptp. of *sedēre* to sit) + *-iōn-* -ION] —**ses′sion·al,** *adj.*

Ses·sions (sesh′ənz), *n.* **Roger Huntington,** 1896–1985, U.S. composer.

ses·terce (ses′tûrs), *n.* a silver coin of ancient Rome, the quarter of a denarius, equal to 2½ asses: introduced in the 3rd century B.C. [< L *sēstertius* = *sēs-* half-unit (see SES- QUI-) + *tertius* THIRD (i.e., 2 units and) half a 3rd one equal 2½ asses]

ses·ter·ti·um (se stûr′shē əm, -shəm), *n., pl.* **-ti·a** (-shē ə, -shə). a money of account of ancient Rome, equal to 1000 sesterces. [< L, gen. pl. of *sēstertius* SESTERCE, taken as neut. sing.]

ses·ter·tius (se stûr′shəs, -shē əs), *n., pl.* **-ti·i** (-shē ī′). sesterce. [< L]

ses·tet (se stet′, ses′tet), *n.* **1.** *Pros.* the last six lines of a sonnet in the Italian form, considered as a unit. Cf. **octave** (def. 3a). **2.** sextet (def. 2). [< It *sestett(o)* sextet = *sest(o)* (< L *sextus* SIXTH) + *-etto* -ET]

ses·ti·na (se stē′nə), *n., pl.* **-nas, -ne** (-nā). *Pros.* a poem of six six-line stanzas and a three-line envoy, originally without rhyme, in which each stanza repeats the end words of the lines of the first stanza, but in different order, the envoy using the six words again, three in the middle of the lines and three at the end. Also called **sextain.** [< It = *sest(o)* (< L *sextus* SIXTH) + *-ina* -INE[2]]

Ses·tos (ses′tos), *n.* an ancient Thracian town on the Hellespont: crossing point for Xerxes' invasion of Greece.

set (set), *v.,* **set, set·ting,** *n., adj.* —*v.t.* **1.** to put (something or someone) in a particular place. **2.** to place in a particular position or posture. **3.** to place in some relation to something or someone. **4.** to put into some condition: *to set a house on fire.* **5.** to put or apply: *to set fire to a house.* **6.** to put in the proper or desired order or condition for use. **7.** to distribute or arrange china, silver, etc., for use on (a table): *to set the table for dinner.* **8.** to arrange (the hair, esp. when wet) with rollers, clips, etc., so as to assume a particular style. **9.** to put (a price or value) upon something. **10.** to fix the value of at a certain amount or rate; value. **11.** to post, station, or appoint for the purpose of performing some duty: *to set spies on a person.* **12.** to determine or fix definitely: *to set a time limit.* **13.** to direct or settle resolutely or hopefully: *to set one's mind to a task; to set one's heart on a new dress.* **14.** to establish for others to follow. **15.** to prescribe or assign, as a task. **16.** to adjust (a mechanism) so as to control its performance. **17.** to adjust the hands of (a clock or watch) according to a certain standard. **18.** to fix or mount (a gem or the like) in a frame or setting. **19.** to ornament or stud with gems or the like: *a bracelet set with pearls.* **20.** to cause to sit; seat: *to set a child in a highchair.* **21.** to put (a hen) on eggs to hatch them. **22.** to place (eggs) under a hen or in an incubator for hatching. **23.** to place or plant firmly: *to set a flagpole in concrete.* **24.** to put into a fixed, rigid, or settled state, as the face, muscles, etc. **25.** to fix at a given point or calibration. **26.** to cause to take a particular direction. **27.** *Surg.* to put (a broken or dislocated bone) back in position. **28.** (of a hunting dog) to indicate the position of (game) by standing stiffly and pointing with the muzzle. **29.** *Music.* to fit, as words to music. **30.** *Theat.* to arrange the scenery, etc., on (a stage) for an act or scene. **31.** *Naut.* to spread and secure (a sail) so as to catch the wind. **32.** *Print.* **a.** to arrange (type) in the order required for printing. **b.** to put together types corresponding to (copy); compose in type: *to set an article.* **33.** *Cookery.* to put aside (a substance to which yeast has been added) in order that it may rise. **34.** to change into curd: *to set milk with rennet.* **35.** to cause (glue, mortar, or the like) to become fixed or hard. **36.** to urge, goad, or encourage to attack: *to set the hounds on a trespasser.* **37.** *Bridge.* to cause (the opposing partnership or their contract) to fall short. **38.** to affix or apply, as by stamping. —*v.i.* **39.** to pass below the horizon; sink: *The sun sets early in winter.* **40.** to decline; wane. **41.** to assume a fixed or rigid state, as the countenance, the muscles, etc. **42.** to become firm, solid, or permanent, as mortar. **43.** to sit on eggs to hatch them, as a hen. **44.** to hang or fit, as clothes. **45.** (of a flower's ovary) to develop into a fruit. **46.** (of a hunting dog) to indicate the position of game. **47.** to have a certain direction or course, as a wind, current, or the like. **48.** *Naut.* (of a sail) to be spread so as to catch the wind. **49. set about,** to begin on; start. **50. set aside, a.** to put to one side; reserve. **b.** to prevail over; discard; annul. **51. set back,** to hinder; impede. **52. set down, a.** to write or to copy or record in writing or printing. **b.** to land an airplane. **53. set forth, a.** to give account of; state; describe. **b.** to begin a journey; start. **54. set in,** to begin to prevail; arrive. **55. set off, a.** to cause to become ignited or to explode. **b.** to intensify or improve by contrast. **c.** to begin a journey or trip; depart. **56. set on,** to attack or cause to attack. Also, **set upon. 57. set out, a.** to begin a journey or course. **b.** to undertake; attempt. **c.** to define; describe. **d.** to plant. **58. set store by.** See **store** (def. 8). **59. set to, a.** to make a vigorous effort; apply oneself to work; begin. **b.** to begin to fight; contend. **60. set up, a.** to put upright; raise. **b.** to put into a high or powerful position. **c.** to construct; assemble; erect. **d.** to inaugurate; establish. **e.** to enable to begin in business; provide with means. —*n.* **61.** the act or state of setting. **62.** the state of being set. **63.** a collection of articles designed for use together: *a set of china; a chess set.* **64.** a series of volumes by one author, about one subject, etc. **65.** a number, company, or group of persons associated by common interests, occupations, conventions, or status. **66.** the fit, as of an article of clothing: *the set of his coat.* **67.** fixed direction, bent, or inclination. **68.** bearing or carriage: *the set of one's shoulders.* **69.** the assumption of a fixed, rigid, or hard state, as by mortar or glue. **70.** an apparatus for receiving radio or television programs; receiver. **71.** *Philately.* a group of stamps that form a complete series. **72.** *Tennis.* a unit of a match, consisting of a group of not fewer than six games with a margin of at least two games between the winner and loser. **73.** a construction representing a place or scene in which the action takes place in a stage or television production. **74.** *Mach.* **a.** the bending out of the points of alternate teeth of a saw in opposite directions. **b.** a permanent deformation or displacement of an object or part. **c.** a tool for giving a certain form to something, as a sawtooth. **75. a.** the number of couples required to execute a quadrille or the like. **b.** the formation of a quadrille or the like. **76.** *Hort.* a young plant, or a slip, tuber, or the like, suitable for planting. **77.** *Music.* a group of pieces played by a band, as in a night club, and followed by an intermission. **78.** *Naut.* **a.** the direction of a wind, current, etc. **b.** the form or arrangement of the sails, spars, etc., of a vessel. **79.** *Psychol.* a temporary state of an organism characterized by a readiness to respond to certain stimuli in a specific way. **80.** *Math.* a collection of objects or elements classed together. —*adj.* **81.** fixed or prescribed beforehand: *a set time; set rules.* **82.** specified; fixed. **83.** deliberately composed; customary: *set phrases.* **84.** fixed; rigid: *a set smile.* **85.** resolved or determined; habitually or stubbornly fixed. [ME *sette(n)*, OE *settan*; c. Icel *setja*, G *setzen*, Goth *satjan*, causative of *sitjan* to sit]

—**Syn. 1.** position, locate, situate, plant. See **put. 10.** estimate, evaluate. **42.** solidify, congeal, harden. **65.** clique. **67.** attitude. **68.** posture. **81.** predetermined.

Set (set), *n. Egyptian Religion.* the brother and murderer of Osiris, represented as having the head of a donkey or other mammal and personifying the desert. Also, **Seth.**

se·ta (sē′tə), *n., pl.* **-tae** (-tē). *Zool., Bot.* a stiff hair; bristle or bristlelike part. [< L, var. of *saeta* bristle] —**se′tal,** *adj.*

se·ta·ceous (si tā′shəs), *adj.* **1.** bristlelike; bristle-shaped. **2.** having bristles. [< NL *sētāceus.* See SETA, -ACEOUS] —**se·ta′ceous·ly,** *adv.*

set·back (set′bak′), *n.* **1.** a check to progress; a reverse or defeat. **2.** *Archit.* a recession of the upper part of a building from the building line, as to lighten the structure or to permit a desired amount of light and air to reach ground level at the foot of the building.

Seth (seth), *n.* the third son of Adam. Gen. 4:25

Seth (set), *n. Egyptian Religion.* Set.

seti-, a learned borrowing from Latin meaning "bristle," used in the formation of compound words: *setiform.* [< L, var. of *saeti-*; see SETA]

se·ti·form (sē′tə fôrm′), *adj.* bristle-shaped; setaceous.

set-in (set′in′), *adj.* made separately and placed within another unit.

set·off (set′ôf′, -of′), *n.* **1.** something that counterbalances or makes up for something else, as compensation for a loss. **2.** *Archit.* **a.** a reduction in the thickness of a wall. **b.** a flat or sloping projection on a wall, buttress, or the like, below a thinner part. **3.** something used to enhance the effect of another thing by contrasting it, as an ornament.

Se·ton (sēt′ən), *n.* **Ernest Thompson,** 1860–1946, English writer and illustrator in the U.S.

se·tose (sē′tōs, si tōs′), *adj.* covered with setae or bristles; bristly. [< L *sētōs(us).* See SETA, -OSE[1]]

set′ piece′, 1. *Theat.* a piece of stage scenery built to stand independently on the stage floor. **2.** a work of art, literature, music, etc., or a part of such a work having a conventionally prescribed thematic and formal structure.

set′ point′, *Tennis.* the point that if won would enable the scorer or his side to win the set.

set·screw (set′skrōō′), *n.* a screw passing through a threaded hole in a part to tighten the contact of that part with another.

set·tee (se tē′), *n.* a seat for two or more persons, having a back and usually arms, and often upholstered. [? var. of SETTLE[2]]

set·ter (set′ər), *n.* **1.** a person or thing that sets. **2.** one of any of several breeds of hunting dogs that originally had the habit of crouching when game was scented but are now trained to stand stiffly and point the muzzle toward the scented game. Cf. **English setter, Gordon setter, Irish setter.** [late ME]

set′ the′ory, the branch of mathematics that deals with relations between sets.

set·ting (set′ing), *n.* **1.** the act of a person or thing that sets. **2.** the surroundings or environment of anything. **3.** a frame or mounting for a jewel, etc. **4.** a group of all the articles required for setting a table or a single place at a table. **5.** the locale or period in which the action of a novel, play, film, etc., takes place. **6.** the scenery and other properties used in a dramatic performance. **7.** *Music.* **a.** a piece of music composed for certain words. **b.** a piece of music composed for a particular medium, or arranged for other than the original medium. [ME]

set·tle[1] (set′əl), *v.,* **-tled, -tling.** —*v.t.* **1.** to appoint, fix, or resolve definitely and conclusively; agree upon (as time, price, conditions, etc.). **2.** to place in a desired state or in order: *to settle one's affairs.* **3.** to pay, as a bill. **4.** to close (an account) by payment. **5.** to migrate to and organize (an area, territory, etc.); colonize. **6.** to cause to take up residence. **7.**

to furnish (a place) with inhabitants or settlers. **8.** to establish in a way of life, a business, etc. **9.** to quiet, calm, or bring to rest (the nerves, stomach, etc.). **10.** to stop from annoying or opposing. **11.** to make stable; place in a permanent position or on a permanent basis. **12.** to cause (a liquid) to become clear by depositing dregs. **13.** to cause (dregs, sediment, etc.) to sink or be deposited. **14.** to cause to sink down gradually; make firm or compact. **15.** to dispose of finally; close up: *to settle an estate.* **16.** *Law.* to secure (property) on or to a person by legal process. —*v.i.* **17.** to decide, arrange, or agree (often fol. by *on* or *upon*): *to settle on a plan of action.* **18.** to arrange matters in dispute; come to an agreement. **19.** to pay a bill; make a financial arrangement (often fol. by *up*). **20.** to take up residence in a new country or place. **21.** to come to rest, as from flight. **22.** to gather, collect, or become fixed in a particular place, direction, etc. **23.** to become calm or composed (often fol. by *down*). **24.** to come to rest. **25.** to sink down gradually; subside. **26.** to become clear by the sinking of suspended particles, as a liquid. **27.** to sink to the bottom, as sediment. **28.** to become firm or compact, as the ground. **29.** (of a female animal) to become pregnant; conceive. **30. settle down, a.** to become established in some routine, esp. upon marrying, after a period of independence or indecision. **b.** to become calm or quiet. **c.** to apply oneself to serious work. [ME; OE *setl(an)* < *setl* SETTLE[2]; c. D *zetelen*] —**set′tle·a·bil′i·ty,** *n.* —**set′tle·a·ble,** *adj.* —**set′tled·ly,** *adv.* —**set′tled·ness,** *n.* —**Syn. 1.** set, establish. **4.** liquidate. **6.** relocate. **7.** people, colonize. **9.** tranquilize, compose, still, pacify. **11.** stabilize, establish, confirm. **20.** locate, relocate. **25.** decline, fall, abate.

set·tle[2] (set′ᵊl), *n.* a long seat or bench, usually wooden, with arms and a high back. [ME; OE *setle;* c. G *Sessel* armchair, Goth *sitls* seat, L *sella* saddle]

Settle[2]

set·tle·ment (set′ᵊl mənt), *n.* **1.** the act or state of settling. **2.** the state of being settled. **3.** the act of making stable or putting on a permanent basis. **4.** an arrangement or adjustment, as of business affairs, a disagreement, etc. **5.** the establishment of a person in an employment, office, or charge. **6.** the settling of persons in a new country or place. **7.** a colony, esp. in its early stages. **8.** a small community, village, or group of houses in a thinly populated area. **9.** a community formed and populated by members of a particular religious or ideological group: *a Shaker settlement.* **10.** the satisfying of a claim or demand; a coming to terms. **11.** *Law.* **a.** the settling of property, title, etc., upon a person. **b.** the property so settled. **12.** *Brit.* legal residence in a specific place. **13.** *Social Work.* a welfare establishment in an underprivileged area providing facilities for the people in the area, including personnel to assist them. **14.** a subsidence or sinking of all or part of a structure.

set·tler (set′lər), *n.* **1.** a person or thing that settles. **2.** a person who settles in a new country or area.

set-to (set′to͞o′), *n., pl.* **-tos.** *Informal.* a usually brief, sharp fight or argument.

Se·tú·bal (si to͞o′bäl), *n.* **1. Bay of,** an inlet of the Atlantic, in W Portugal. 20 mi. long; 35 mi. wide. **2.** a seaport on this bay, near Lisbon. 50,966 (1960).

set·u·lose (sech′ə lōs′), *adj.* *Bot., Zool.* having or covered with setulae. Also, **set·u·lous** (sech′ə ləs). [< L *sētula* (dim. of SETA) + -OSE[1]]

set·up (set′up′), *n.* **1.** organization; arrangement. **2.** *Informal.* an undertaking or contest deliberately made easy. **3.** everything required for an alcoholic drink except the liquor. **4.** an arrangement of all the tools, parts, apparatus, etc., necessary for any of various specific jobs or purposes. **5.** a plan or projected course of action.

Seu·rat (sœ RA′), *n.* **Georges** (zhôrzh), 1859–91, French pointillist painter.

Seuss (so͞os), *n.* **Dr.** See **Geisel, Theodore Seuss.**

Se·vas·to·pol (sə vas′tə pōl′; *Russ.* se′väs tô′pol′yᵊ), *n.* a fortified seaport in the S Ukraine, in the SW Soviet Union in Europe: resort. 169,000 (est. 1962). Also, **Sebastopol.**

sev·en (sev′ən), *n.* **1.** a cardinal number, 6 plus 1. **2.** a symbol for this number, as 7 or VII. **3.** a set of this many persons or things. **4.** a playing card with seven pips. **5. sevens,** (*construed as sing.*) fan-tan (def. 1). —*adj.* **6.** amounting to seven in number. [ME; OE *seofan;* c. G *sieben,* Goth *sibun,* L *septem,* Gk *heptá,* Skt *saptá*]

Sev′en against′ Thebes′, *Class. Myth.* seven heroes, Adrastus, Amphiaraus, Capaneus, Hippomedon, Parthenopaeus, Polynices, and Tydeus, who led an expedition against Thebes to depose Eteocles in favor of his brother Polynices: the expedition failed, but the Epigoni, the sons of the Seven against Thebes, conquered the city ten years later.

sev′en-card stud′ (sev′ən kärd′), *Cards.* a variety of stud poker in which each player is dealt two cards down, four cards face up, and one card down. Cf. **stud poker** (def. 1).

sev′en dead′ly sins′. See **deadly sins.**

sev·en·fold (sev′ən fōld′), *adj.* **1.** comprising seven parts or members. **2.** seven times as great or as much. —*adv.* **3.** until seven times as many or as great: *multiplied sevenfold.* [ME; OE *seofonfeald*]

Sev′en Hills′ of Rome′, the seven hills on and about which the ancient city of Rome was built.

Sev′en Pines′. See **Fair Oaks.**

sev′en seas′, **1.** the navigable waters of the world. **2.** the seven oceans of the world: the Arctic, Antarctic, N and S Pacific, N and S Atlantic and Indian Oceans. Also, **Sev′en Seas′.**

sev·en·teen (sev′ən tēn′), *n.* **1.** a cardinal number, 10 plus 7. **2.** a symbol for this number, as 17 or XVII. **3.** a set of this many persons or things. —*adj.* **4.** amounting to 17 in number. [ME *seventene,* OE *seofontēne* (c. D *zeventien,* G *siebzehn*). See SEVEN, TEN]

sev·en·teenth (sev′ən tēnth′), *adj.* **1.** next after the sixteenth; being the ordinal number for 17. **2.** being one of 17 equal parts. —*n.* **3.** a seventeenth part, esp. of one (1/17). **4.** the seventeenth member of a series. [SEVENTEEN + -TH[2]; r. ME *seventethe,* OE *seofontēotha.* See SEVEN, TITHE]

sev′en·teen′-year lo′cust (sev′ən tēn′yēr′), a cicada, *Magicicada septendecim,* of the eastern U.S., having nymphs that live in the soil, usually emerging in great numbers after 17 years in the North or 13 years in the South. Also called **periodical cicada.**

sev·enth (sev′ənth), *adj.* **1.** next after the sixth; being the ordinal number for seven. **2.** being one of seven equal parts. —*n.* **3.** a seventh part, esp. of one (1/7). **4.** the seventh member of a series. **5.** *Music.* **a.** a tone on the seventh degree from a given tone (counted as the first). **b.** the interval between such tones. **c.** the harmonic combination of such tones. [ME; see SEVEN, -TH[2]; r. ME *sevethe,* OE *seofotha*] —**sev′enth·ly,** *adv.*

sev′enth chord′, *Music.* a chord formed by the superposition of three thirds.

sev·enth-day (sev′ənth dā′), *adj.* designating certain Christian denominations that make Saturday their chief day of rest and religious observance: *Seventh-Day Adventists.* Also, **Sev′enth-Day′.**

sev′enth heav′en, **1.** (esp. in Islam and the cabala) the highest heaven, where God and the most exalted angels dwell. **2.** a state of intense happiness; bliss.

sev·en·ti·eth (sev′ən tē ith), *adj.* **1.** next after the sixty-ninth; being the ordinal number for 70. **2.** being one of 70 equal parts. —*n.* **3.** a seventieth part, esp. of one (1/70). **4.** the seventieth member of a series. [ME *seventithe*]

sev·en·ty (sev′ən tē), *n., pl.* **-ties,** *adj.* —*n.* **1.** a cardinal number, 10 times 7. **2.** a symbol for this number, as 70 or LXX. **3.** a set of this many persons or things. **4. seventies,** the numbers, years, degrees, or the like, between 70 and 79, as in referring to numbered streets, indicating the years of a lifetime or of a century, or degrees of temperature. —*adj.* **5.** amounting to 70 in number. [ME; OE *seofontig*]

sev·en-up (sev′ən up′), *n.* See **all fours** (def. 2).

Sev′en Won′ders of the World′, the seven most remarkable structures of ancient times: the Egyptian pyramids, the Mausoleum erected by Artemisia at Halicarnassus, the Temple of Artemis at Ephesus, the Hanging Gardens of Babylon, the Colossus of Rhodes, the statue of Zeus by Phidias at Olympia, and the Pharos or lighthouse at Alexandria.

Sev′en Years′′ War′, the war (1756–63) in which England and Prussia defeated France, Austria, Russia, Sweden, and Saxony.

sev·er (sev′ər), *v.t.* **1.** to separate (a part) from the whole, as by cutting or the like. **2.** to divide into parts, esp. forcibly; cleave. **3.** to break off or dissolve (ties, relations, etc.). **4.** *Law.* to divide into parts; disunite (as an estate, titles of a statute, etc.). **5.** to distinguish; discriminate between. —*v.i.* **6.** to become separated, from each other or one from another; become divided into parts. [ME *sever(en)* < MF *sev(e)re(r)* (to) SEPARATE] —**sev′ered·ly,** *adv.* —**sev′er·ing·ly,** *adv.* —**sev′er·a·ble,** *adj.* —**Syn. 1.** sunder, disunite, disjoin. —**Ant. 1.** unite.

sev·er·al (sev′ər əl, sev′rəl), *adj.* **1.** being more than two but fewer than many in number or kind. **2.** respective; individual: *They went their several ways.* **3.** separate; different. **4.** single; particular. **5.** *Law.* binding two or more persons who may be sued separately on a common obligation. —*n.* **6.** several persons or things; a few; some. [ME < AF < ML *sēparāl(is)* = L *sēpar* SEPARATE + *-ālis* -AL[1]]

sev·er·al·ly (sev′ər ə lē, sev′rə-), *adv.* **1.** separately; singly. **2.** respectively. [ME]

sev·er·al·ty (sev′ər əl tē, sev′rəl-), *n., pl.* **-ties.** **1.** the state of being separate. **2.** *Law.* (of an estate, esp. land) the condition of being held or owned by separate and individual right. [< AF *severalte.* See SEVERAL, -TY[2]]

sev·er·ance (sev′ər əns, sev′rəns), *n.* **1.** the act of severing. **2.** the state of being severed. **3.** a breaking off, as of a friendship. **4.** *Law.* a division into parts, as of liabilities or provisions. [< AF]

se·vere (si vēr′), *adj.,* **-ver·er, -ver·est.** **1.** harsh; unnecessarily extreme. **2.** serious or stern in manner or appearance: *a severe face.* **3.** grave; critical. **4.** rigidly restrained in style, taste, manner, etc.; simple, plain, or austere. **5.** causing discomfort or distress by extreme character or conditions, as weather, cold, heat, etc.; unpleasantly violent, as rain or wind, a blow or shock, etc. **6.** difficult to endure, perform, fulfill, etc. **7.** rigidly exact, accurate, or methodical. [< L *sevēr(us),* or back formation from SEVERITY] —**se·vere′ly,** *adv.* —**se·vere′ness,** *n.* —**Syn. 2.** rigorous, strict, hard. See **stern**[1]. **4.** unadorned. **7.** demanding, exacting. —**Ant. 1.** lenient. **2.** gentle.

Sev·er·i·nus (sev′ə rī′nəs), *n.* died A.D. 640, pope 640.

se·ver·i·ty (si ver′i tē), *n., pl.* **-ties.** **1.** harshness, sternness, or rigor. **2.** austere simplicity, as of style or manner. **3.** violence or sharpness, as of cold or pain. **4.** grievousness; hard or trying character or effect. **5.** rigid exactness or accuracy. **6.** an instance of strict or severe behavior, punishment, etc. [late ME < L *sevēritāt-* (s. of *sevēritās*) = *sevēr-* SEVERE + *-itāt* -ITY]

Sev·ern (sev′ərn), *n.* a river in Great Britain, flowing from central Wales through W England into the Bristol Channel. 210 mi. long.

Se·ver·sky (sə ver′skē), *n.* **Alexander (Pro·co·fi·eff) de** (prə kō′fē ef′ də), 1894–1974, U.S. airplane designer, manufacturer, and writer; born in Russia.

Se·ve·rus (sə vēr′əs), *n.* **Lucius Sep·tim·i·us** (sep tim′ē əs), A.D. 146–211, Roman emperor 193–211.

Sé·vi·gné (sā vē nyā′), *n.* **Ma·rie de Ra·bu·tin-Chan·tal** (MA RĒ′ də RA BY TAN shän TAL′), **Marquise de,** 1626–96, French writer famed for her correspondence.

Se·ville (sə vil′, sev′il), *n.* a port in SW Spain, on the Guadalquivir River: site of the Alcazar; cathedral. 450,213 (est. 1960). Spanish, **Se·vil·la** (se vē′lyä).

Seville′ or′ange. See under **orange** (def. 2).

Sè·vres (se′vRᵊ; *Eng.* sev′rə, sev), *n.* **1.** a suburb of Paris in N France. 20,292 (1962). **2.** Also called **Sè′vres ware′.** the fine, elaborate porcelain made there since 1756.

sew (sō), *v.,* **sewed, sewn** or **sewed, sew·ing.** —*v.t.* **1.** to join or attach by stitches. **2.** to make, repair, etc., (a garment) by such means. **3.** to enclose or secure with stitches: *to sew flour in a bag.* **4.** to close (a hole, wound, etc.) by means of stitches (usually fol. by *up*). —*v.i.* **5.** to work with a needle and thread or with a sewing machine. **6. sew up,** *Slang.* to complete successfully. [ME *sewe(n)*, OE *siw(i)an;* c. OHG *siuwan*, Goth *siujan*, L *suere*]

sew·age (sōō′ij), *n.* the waste matter that passes through sewers. Also, **sewerage.** [SEWER[1], with -AGE for *-er*]

Sew·all (sōō′əl), *n.* **Samuel,** 1652–1730, American jurist, born in England.

Sew·ard (sōō′ərd), *n.* **William Henry,** 1801–72, U.S. statesman: Secretary of State 1861–69.

Sew′ard Penin′sula, a peninsula in W Alaska, on Bering Strait.

sew·er[1] (sōō′ər), *n.* an artificial conduit, usually underground, for carrying off waste water and refuse, as in a town or city. [ME *suer(e)* < OF *se(u)wiere* overflow channel (cf. OF *ess(e)ouer(e)* ditch) < L **exaquāria* drain for carrying water off. See EX-[1], AQUARIUM]

sew·er[2] (sō′ər), *n.* a person or thing that sews. [ME; see SEW, -ER[1]]

sew·er[3] (sōō′ər), *n.* (formerly) a household officer or head servant in charge of the service of the table. [ME, by aphesis < AF *asseour* seater = OF *asse(oir)* to seat (< L *adsidēre* to attend upon; see ASSIDUOUS) + *-our* -OR[2]]

sew·er·age (sōō′ər ij), *n.* **1.** the removal of waste water and refuse by means of sewers. **2.** a system of sewers. **3.** sewage.

sew·ing (sō′ing), *n.* **1.** the act or work of a person or thing that sews. **2.** something sewn or to be sewn. [ME]

sew′ing cir′cle, a group of women who meet regularly to sew, esp. for charitable purposes.

sew′ing machine′, any of various foot-operated or electric machines for sewing or making stitches, ranging from machines for sewing garments to industrial machines for sewing leather, book pages, or the like.

sewn (sōn), *v.* a pp. of **sew.**

sex (seks), *n.* **1.** either the male or female division of a species, esp. as differentiated with reference to the reproductive functions. **2.** the sum of the structural and functional differences by which the male and female are distinguished, or the phenomena or behavior dependent on these differences. **3.** the instinct or attraction drawing one sex toward another or its manifestation in life and conduct. **4.** coitus. —*v.t.* **5.** to ascertain the sex of, esp. of newly hatched chicks. [ME < L *sex(us)*, akin to *secus* < *secāre* to cut, divide; see SECTION]

sex-, an element, occurring in loan words from Latin, meaning "six" (*sexagenary*); on this model used in the formation of compound words: *sexpartite.* Also, **sexi-,** [< L, comb. form of *sex* SIX]

sex′ act′, sexual intercourse; copulation.

sex·a·ge·nar·i·an (sek′sə jə nâr′ē ən), *adj.* **1.** of the age of 60 years or between 60 and 70 years old. —*n.* **2.** a sexagenarian person. [< L *sexāgēnāri(us)* SEXAGENARY + -AN]

sex·ag·e·nar·y (sek saj′ə ner′ē), *adj., n., pl.* **-nar·ies.** —*adj.* **1.** of or pertaining to the number 60. **2.** composed of or proceeding by sixties. **3.** sexagenarian. —*n.* **4.** a sexagenarian. [< L *sexāgēnāri(us)* = *sexāgēn(ī)*, distributive of *sexāgintā* sixty + *-ārius* -ARY]

Sex·a·ges·i·ma (sek′sə jes′ə mə, -jā′zə-), *n.* the second Sunday before Lent. Also called **Sexages′ima Sun′day.** [< L *sexāgēsima (diēs)* sixtieth (day) < *sexāgintā* sixty = *sexā-* SIX + *-gntā* decade]

sex′ appeal′, a quality that charms and attracts members of the opposite sex.

sex·a·va·lent (sek′sə vā′lənt), *adj. Chem.* sexivalent.

sex·cen·te·nar·y (seks sen′tᵊner′ē, seks′sen ten′ə rē), *adj., n., pl.* **-nar·ies.** —*adj.* **1.** pertaining to 600 or 600 years. —*n.* **2.** a 600th anniversary or its celebration.

sex′ chro′mosome, *Genetics.* a chromosome that affects the determination of sex.

sex·de·cil·lion (seks′di sil′yən), *n., pl.* **-lions,** (*as after a numeral*) **-lion.** a cardinal number represented in the U.S. and France by one followed by 51 zeros and in Great Britain and Germany by one followed by 96 zeros.

sexed (sekst), *adj.* **1.** being of a particular sex or having sexual characteristics. **2.** characterized by sexuality.

sex·en·ni·al (sek sen′ē əl), *adj.* **1.** of or for six years. **2.** occurring every six years. [< L *sexenni(s)* six-year (*sex* six + *-ennis* yearly) + -AL[1]]

sex′ hor′mone, *Biochem.* any of a class of hormones that regulate the growth and function of the reproductive organs or stimulate the development of the secondary sexual characteristics.

sex′ hy′giene, a branch of hygiene concerned with sex and sexual behavior as they relate to individual and community well-being.

sexi-, var. of **sex-:** *sexivalent.*

sex·ism (sek′siz əm), *n.* discrimination against women, as in restricted career choices, job opportunities, etc.

sex·ist (sek′sist), *n.* a person who discriminates against women, as by thinking they are fit only for housework and child rearing, should be subservient to men, etc.

sex·i·va·lent (sek′sə vā′lənt), *adj. Chem.* having a valence of six. Also, **sexavalent.**

sex·less (seks′lis), *adj.* lacking in sex, sexual desires, or sex appeal.

sex-link·age (seks′ling′kij), *n. Genetics.* an association between genes in sex chromosomes that causes the characters determined by these genes to appear more frequently in one sex than in the other.

sex-linked (seks′lingkt′), *adj. Genetics.* **1.** (of a gene) located in a sex chromosome. **2.** (of a character) determined by a gene located in a sex chromosome.

sex·ol·o·gy (sek sol′ə jē), *n.* the study of sexual behavior. —**sex·ol′o·gist,** *n.*

sex·par·tite (seks pär′tīt), *adj.* **1.** divided into or consisting of six parts. **2.** *Archit.* (of a vault) divided into six compartments by two ogives and three transverse arches, one arch crossing the ogives at the point at which they cross each other. See illus. at **vault**[1].

sext (sekst), *n. Eccles.* the fourth of the seven canonical hours or the service for it, originally fixed for the sixth hour of the day taken as noon. [ME *sext(a)* < eccl. L *sexta (hōra)* sixth (hour)]

sex·tain (seks′tān), *n. Pros.* **1.** a stanza of six lines. **2.** sestina. [b. two obs. F words: *sixain* six-line stanza and *sestine* SESTINA]

sex·tant (seks′tənt), *n.* an astronomical instrument used for measuring angular distances of celestial bodies in determining latitude and longitude, esp. at sea. [< L *sextant-* (s. of *sextāns*) sixth part of a unit]

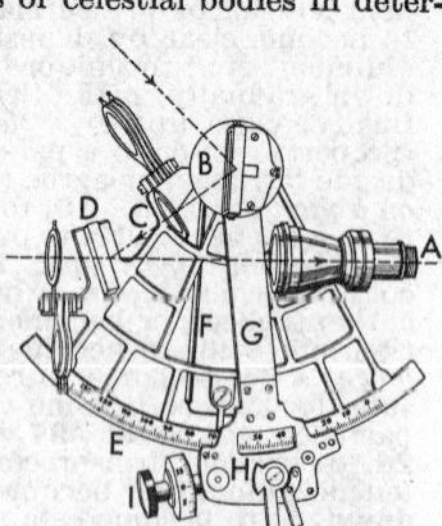

Sextant
A, Telescope; B, Mirror; C, Colored glass filter; D, Half mirror, half glass; E, Graduated arc; F, Handle; G, Movable index arm; H, Index; I, Vernier

sex·tet (seks tet′), *n.* **1.** any group or set of six. **2.** Also, **sestet.** *Music.* **a.** a company of six singers or players. **b.** a musical composition for six voices or instruments. Also, **sex·tette′.** [half-Latinized var. of SESTET; see SEX-]

sex·tile (seks′til), *adj.* **1.** *Astron.* noting or pertaining to the aspect or position of two heavenly bodies when 60° distant from each other. —*n.* **2.** *Astron.* a sextile position or aspect. [< L *sextīlis* = *sext(us)* sixth + *-īlis* -ILE]

sex·til·lion (seks til′yən), *n., pl.* **-lions,** (*as after a numeral*) **-lion,** *adj.* —*n.* **1.** a cardinal number represented in the U.S. and France by one followed by 21 zeros and in Great Britain and Germany by one followed by 36 zeros. —*adj.* **2.** amounting to one sextillion in number. [< F < L *sext(us)* sixth (power of) + *-illion*, as in *million*] —**sex·til′lionth,** *adj., n.*

sex·to·dec·i·mo (seks′tō des′ə mō′), *n., pl.* **-mos,** *adj.* sixteenmo (def. 1). [< L, abl. sing. of *sextusdecimus* sixteenth]

sex·ton (seks′tən), *n.* an official of a church charged with maintaining church property, ringing the bell, etc. [ME *sexteyn*, etc., syncopated var. of *segerstane*, etc. < AF *segerstaine* SACRISTAN]

sex·tu·ple (seks tōō′pəl, -tyōō′-, -tup′əl, seks′tŏŏ pəl, -tyŏŏ-), *adj., v.,* **-pled, -pling.** —*adj.* **1.** consisting of six parts; sexpartite. **2.** six times as great or as many. **3.** *Music.* characterized by six beats or pulses to the measure: *sextuple rhythm.* —*v.t., v.i.* **4.** to make or become six times as great. [< L *sext(us)* sixth + *-uple*, as in *quadruple, quintuple*]

sex·tu·plet (seks tup′lit, -tōō′plit, -tyōō′-, seks′tŏŏ plit, -tyŏŏ-), *n.* **1.** a group or combination of six things. **2.** one of six offspring born at one birth. **3. sextuplets,** six children or offspring born of one pregnancy. **4.** *Music.* a group of six notes of equal value performed in the time normally taken to perform four. [SEXTUPLE + -ET; cf. TRIPLET]

sex·tu·plex (seks′tŏŏ pleks′, -tyŏŏ-, seks tōō′pleks, -tyōō′-, -tup′leks), *adj.* sixfold; sextuple. [< L *sextu(s)* sixth + *-plex* -FOLD]

sex·tu·pli·cate (*n., adj.* seks tōō′plə kit, -kāt′, -tyōō′-, -tup′lə-; *v.* seks tōō′plə kāt′, -kit, -tyōō′-, -tup′lə-), *n., adj., v.,* **-cat·ed, -cat·ing.** —*n.* **1.** a group, series, or set of six identical copies (usually prec. by *in*). —*adj.* **2.** having or consisting of six identical parts; sixfold. **3.** noting the sixth copy or item. —*v.t.* **4.** to make six copies of (something). [SEXTUPL(E + DUPL)ICATE]

sex·u·al (sek′shōō əl), *adj.* **1.** of or pertaining to sex. **2.** occurring between or involving the two sexes: *sexual relations.* **3.** having sexual organs or reproducing by processes involving both sexes. [< LL *sexuāl(is).* See SEX, -AL[1]] —**sex′u·al·ly,** *adv.*

sex′ual in′tercourse, genital contact, esp. the insertion of the penis into the vagina followed by ejaculation; coitus; copulation.

sex·u·al·ise (sek′shōō ə līz′), *v.t.,* **-ised, -is·ing.** *Chiefly Brit.* sexualize. —**sex′u·al·i·sa′tion,** *n.*

sex·u·al·i·ty (sek′shōō al′i tē), *n.* **1.** sexual character; possession of the structural and functional differentia of sex. **2.** recognition of or emphasis upon sexual matters. **3.** involvement in sexual activity. **4.** an organism's readiness to engage in sexual activity.

sex·u·al·ize (sek′shōō ə līz′), *v.t.,* **-ized, -iz·ing.** to make sexual; endow with sexual characteristics. Also, *esp. Brit.,* **sexualise.** —**sex′u·al·i·za′tion,** *n.*

sex′ual reproduc′tion, *Biol.* reproduction involving the union of gametes.

sex′ual selec′tion, the Darwinian theory that mate selection is based on certain attractive characteristics, as coloration, behavior, song, etc.

sex·y (sek′sē), *adj.,* **sex·i·er, sex·i·est.** *Informal.* **1.** concerned predominantly or excessively with sex: *a sexy novel.* **2.** (of a person) sexually interesting or exciting; radiating sexuality. **3.** exciting or interesting: *a sexy car.*

Sey·chelles (sā shel′, -shelz′), *n.* (*construed as pl.*) a republic consisting of 92 islands in the Indian Ocean, NE of Madagascar: a former British colony. 59,000; 156 sq. mi. *Cap.:* Victoria.

Sey·han (sā hän′), *n.* Adana.

Sey·mour (sē′mōr, -môr), *n.* **Jane,** c1510–37, third wife of Henry VIII of England and mother of Edward VI.

sf, **1.** science fiction. **2.** *Music.* sforzando.

Sfax (sfäks), *n.* a seaport in E Tunisia, in N Africa. 75,000.

Sfc, *Mil.* sergeant first class.

sfm, surface feet per minute.

Sfor·za (sfôrt′sə; *It.* sfôʀ′tsä), *n.* **1. Count Car·lo** (kär′lô), 1873–1952, Italian statesman: anti-Fascist leader. **2. Fran·ces·co** (frän ches′kô), 1401–66, Italian condottiere: duke of Milan 1450–66. **3.** his son, **Lo·do·vi·co** (lô′dô vē′kô), ("*the Moor*"), 1451–1508, duke of Milan 1494–1500.

sfor·zan·do (sfôrt sän′dō; *It.* sfôʀ tsän′dô), *adj., adv. Music.* with force; emphatically. Also, **forzando, sfor·za·to** (sfôrt sä′tō; *It.* sfôʀ tsä′tô). [< It, ger. of *sforzare* = *s-* (< L *ex-*) EX-[1] + *forzare* (< VL **fortiāre*) to FORCE]

sfor·zan·do-pia·no (sfôrt sän′dō pē ä′nō; *It.* sfôʀ tsän′dô pyä′no), *adj., adv. Music.* accented, then soft.

sfp, sforzando-piano.

sfz, sforzando.

s.g., specific gravity.
sgd., signed.
sgraf·fi·to (skrä fē′tō; *It.* zgräf fē′tô), *n., pl.* **-ti** (-tē). **1.** a technique of ornamentation in which a surface layer of paint, plaster, slip, etc., is incised to reveal a ground of contrasting color. **2.** an object, esp. pottery, decorated by this technique. Cf. **graffito.** [< It; see EX-¹, GRAFFITO]
's Gra·ven·ha·ge (skhrä′vən hä′khə), Dutch name of The Hague.
Sgt., Sergeant.
Sgt. Maj., Sergeant Major.
sh (sh), *interj.* shh.
sh., **1.** share (def. 2). **2.** *Bookbinding.* sheet. **3.** shilling; shillings.
SHA, *Navig.* sidereal hour angle.
Sha·ban (shə bän′, shä-, shō-), *n.* the eighth month of the Islamic calendar. [< Ar *sha'bān*]
Shab·bas (shä′bəs), *n.* *Yiddish.* Sabbath (def. 1).
shab·by (shab′ē), *adj.,* **-bi·er, -bi·est. 1.** impaired by wear, use, etc.; worn. **2.** (of a room, house, etc.) showing signs of neglect. **3.** wearing worn clothes or having a slovenly or unkempt appearance. **4.** meanly ungenerous or unfair, as persons, actions, etc.; contemptible: *shabby behavior.* **5.** inferior; not up to par in quality, performance, etc. [*shab* (ME; OE *sceabb* SCAB) + -Y¹; c. G *schäbig*] **—shab′bi·ly,** *adv.* **—shab′bi·ness,** *n.*
Sha·bu·oth (shə vo͞o′əs, -ōs; *Heb.* shä vo͞o ôt′), *n.* *Judaism.* a festival, celebrated on the sixth day or on the sixth and seventh days of Sivan, that commemorates God's giving of the Ten Commandments to Moses. Also, **Shavuoth.** Also called **Pentecost.** [lit., weeks]
shack (shak), *n.* **1.** a rough cabin; shanty. **—***v.i.* **2. shack up,** *Slang.* **a.** to live together as husband and wife without being legally married. **b.** to have illicit sexual relations. **c.** to live at a place; reside. [short for *shackle* (shaky) hovel; see RAMSHACKLE] **—Syn. 1.** See **cottage.**
shack·le (shak′əl), *n., v.,* **-led, -ling. —***n.* **1.** a ring or other fastening, as of iron, for securing the wrist, ankle, etc.; fetter. **2.** a hobble or fetter for a horse or other animal. **3.** the U-shaped bar of a padlock. **4.** any of various fastening or coupling devices. **5.** Often, **shackles.** anything that serves to prevent freedom of movement, thought, etc. **—***v.t.* **6.** to confine or restrain by a shackle or shackles. **7.** to fasten or couple with a shackle. **8.** to restrict in action, thought, etc. [ME *shackle,* OE *sceacel* fetter; c. LG *schakel* hobble, Icel *skökull* wagon pole] **—shack′ler,** *n.* **—Syn. 1.** chain, manacle, handcuff, gyve, bilboes. **6.** fetter, chain, handcuff. **8.** restrain. **—Ant. 6, 8.** liberate, free.
Shack·le·ton (shak′əl tən), *n.* **Sir Ernest Henry,** 1874–1922, English explorer of the Antarctic.
shad (shad), *n., pl.* (*esp. collectively*) **shad,** (*esp. referring to two or more kinds or species*) **shads. 1.** a deep-bodied herring, *Alosa sapidissima,* a food fish that migrates up streams to spawn. **2.** any other fish of the genus *Alosa* or related genera. **3.** any of several unrelated fishes. [OE *sceadd;* c. LG *schade*]
shad·ber·ry (shad′ber′ē, -bə rē), *n., pl.* **-ries. 1.** the fruit of a shadbush. **2.** the plant itself. [*shad* (? dial. *shad* cool spot, OE *scead* SHADE, shelter) + BERRY]
shad·bush (shad′bo͝osh′), *n.* **1.** the serviceberry, *Amelanchier canadensis.* **2.** any of various other species of *Amelanchier.* Also called **shad·blow** (shad′blō′). [*shad* (see SHADBERRY) + BUSH¹]
shad·chan (shät′khən), *n., pl.* **shad·cha·nim** (shät khô′nim), **shad·chans.** *Yiddish.* a Jewish marriage broker; matchmaker. Also, **schatchen.** [< Heb *shadkhan*]
shad·dock (shad′ək), *n.* **1.** Also called **pomelo.** the large, roundish or pear-shaped, usually pale-yellow, orangelike, edible fruit of the rutaceous tree, *Citrus grandis,* grown in the Orient. **2.** the tree itself. [named after Captain *Shaddock,* 17th-century Englishman who brought the seed to the West Indies from the East Indies]
shade (shād), *n., v.,* **shad·ed, shad·ing. —***n.* **1.** a comparative darkness caused by the interception of rays of light. **2.** a place or an area of comparative darkness, as one sheltered from the sun: *Let's sit in the shade.* **3.** See **window shade. 4.** a lampshade. **5. shades, a.** gathering darkness: *shades of night.* **b.** *Slang.* sunglasses. **c.** a reminder of something: *shades of the Inquisition.* **6.** Usually, **shades.** a secluded or obscure place. **7.** comparative obscurity. **8.** a specter or ghost. **9.** *Gk. and Rom. Religion.* one of the spirits of the dead inhabiting Hades. **10.** a shadow. **11.** the degree of darkness of a color, determined by the quantity of black or by the lack of illumination. **12.** (in pictorial representation and photography) comparative darkness; a relatively dark area. **13.** a slight degree. **14.** a small amount; touch. **15.** anything used for protection against excessive light, heat, etc. **16. the shades,** Hades, as the abode of the spirits of the dead. **—***v.t.* **17.** to produce shade in or on. **18.** to obscure, dim, or darken. **19.** to screen or hide from view. **20.** to protect (something) from light, heat, etc., by or as by a screen. **21.** to cover or screen (a candle, light, etc.). **22.** *Fine Arts.* **a.** to introduce degrees of darkness into (a drawing or painting) in order to render light and shadow or give the effect of color. **b.** to render the values of light and dark on (a drawn figure, object, etc.), esp. in order to create an illusion of three-dimensionality. **23.** to change by imperceptible degrees. **24.** to reduce (the price of something) by way of a concession. **—***v.i.* **25.** to pass or change by slight gradations, as one color, quality, or thing into another. [ME; OE *sceadu;* see SHADOW; c. G *Schatten,* Goth *skadus,* Gk *skótos*] **—Syn. 1.** gloom, dusk. SHADE, SHADOW imply partial darkness or something less bright than the surroundings. SHADE indicates the lesser brightness and heat of an area where the direct rays of light do not fall: *the shade of a tree.* It differs from SHADOW in that it implies no particular form or definite limit, whereas SHADOW often refers to the form or outline of the object that intercepts the light: *the shadow of a dog.* **8.** apparition, phantom, spirit. **14.** trace, hint, suggestion. **15.** veil, screen. **18.** cloud, blur, obfuscate. **19.** conceal, shelter. **—Ant. 1.** light, glare.
shad·ing (shā′ding), *n.* **1.** a slight variation or difference of color, character, etc. **2.** the act of a person or thing that shades. **3.** the representation of values in a painting or drawing.
sha·doof (shä do͞of′), *n.* a water bucket suspended on a weighted rod, used in Egypt and other Eastern countries for raising water, esp. for irrigation. Also, **shaduf.** [Anglicized spelling of SHADUF]

Shadoof

shad·ow (shad′ō), *n.* **1.** a dark figure or image cast on a surface by a body intercepting light. **2.** shade or comparative darkness, as in an area. **3. shadows,** darkness, esp. that coming after sunset: *The place was now in shadows.* **4.** shelter; protection: *safe in the shadow of the church.* **5.** a slight suggestion; trace: *beyond the shadow of a doubt.* **6.** a specter or ghost: *pursued by shadows.* **7.** a hint or faint image or idea; intimation: *shadows of things to come.* **8.** a mere semblance: *the shadow of power.* **9.** a reflected image. **10.** (in painting, drawing, graphics, etc.) **a.** the representation of the absence of light on a form. **b.** the dark part of a picture, esp. as representing the absence of illumination. **11.** a period or instance of gloom, unhappiness, mistrust, doubt, dissension, or the like, as in friendship or one's life. **12.** a dominant, oppressive threat, influence, or atmosphere: *They lived under the shadow of war.* **13.** an inseparable companion: *The dog was his shadow.* **14.** a person who follows another surreptitiously in order to keep watch over him. **—***v.t.* **15.** to overspread with shadow; shade. **16.** to cast gloom over; cloud. **17.** to screen or protect from light, heat, etc.; shade. **18.** to follow (a person) about secretly in order to keep watch over his movements. **19.** to represent faintly, prophetically, etc. (often fol. by *forth*). **20.** *Archaic.* to shelter or protect. **21.** *Archaic.* to shade in painting, drawing, etc. [ME; OE *scead(u)we,* obl. case of *sceadu* SHADE; c. D *schaduw*] **—Syn. 1.** See **shade.**
shad′ow box′, a rectangular frame fronted with a glass panel for simultaneously displaying and protecting merchandise.
shad·ow·box (shad′ō boks′), *v.i.* **1.** to make the motions of attack and defense, as in boxing, in the absence of an opponent. **2.** to evade or avoid direct or decisive action.
shad′ow cab′inet, (in the British Parliament) a group of prominent members of the opposition who are expected to hold positions in the cabinet when their party assumes power.
shad·ow·graph (shad′ō graf′, -gräf′), *n.* **1.** a picture produced by throwing a shadow, as of the hands, on a lighted screen, wall, or the like. **2.** a radiograph.
shad·ow·land (shad′ō land′), *n.* a land or region of shadows, phantoms, unrealities, or uncertainties.
shad′ow play′, theatrical entertainment, often performed in pantomime, consisting of shadows projected onto a lighted screen. Also called **shad′ow pan′tomime, shad′ow show′, shad′ow the′ater.**
shad·ow·y (shad′ō ē), *adj.* **1.** resembling a shadow in faintness, slightness, etc.: *shadowy outlines.* **2.** unsubstantial, unreal, or illusory. **3.** abounding in shadow. **4.** enveloped in shadow. **5.** casting a shadow. [ME *shadewy*] **—shad′ow·i·ness,** *n.*
Shad·rach (shad′rak, shā′drak), *n.* a companion of Daniel who, with Meshach and Abednego, was thrown into the fiery furnace of Nebuchadnezzar and came out unharmed. Dan. 3:12–30.
sha·duf (shä do͞of′), *n.* shadoof. [< EgyptAr]
Shad·well (shad′wel′, -wəl), *n.* **Thomas,** 1642–92, English dramatist: poet laureate 1688–92.
shad·y (shā′dē), *adj.,* **shad·i·er, shad·i·est. 1.** abounding in shade; shaded: *shady paths.* **2.** giving shade: *a shady tree.* **3.** shadowy; indistinct; spectral. **4.** *Informal.* of dubious character; rather disreputable: *shady dealings.* **—shad′i·ly,** *adv.* **—shad′i·ness,** *n.*
SHAEF (shāf), Supreme Headquarters Allied Expeditionary Forces. Also, **Shaef.**
Shaf·i·i (shaf′ē ē), *n.* *Islam.* one of the four teachings of the Sunnah sect which is the most conservative in adopting new customs. Cf. **Hanafi, Hanbali, Maliki.**
shaft (shaft, shäft), *n.* **1.** a long pole forming the body of various weapons, as the lance or arrow, and used for handling or propelling. **2.** something directed at someone or something in sharp attack: *shafts of sarcasm.* **3.** a ray or beam: *a shaft of sunlight.* **4.** a long, comparatively straight handle serving as the grasping or balancing part of an implement or device, as of a hammer. **5.** *Mach.* a rotating or oscillating round, straight bar for transmitting motion and torque, usually supported on bearings and carrying gears, wheels, or the like, as a propeller shaft on a ship. **6.** a flagpole. **7.** *Archit.* **a.** the part of a column or pier between the base and capital. **b.** any distinct, slender, vertical masonry feature engaged in a wall or pier and usually supporting an arch or vault. **8.** a monument in the form of a column, obelisk, or the like. **9.** either of the parallel bars of wood between which the animal drawing a vehicle is hitched. **10.** any well-like passage or vertical enclosed space, as in a building: *an elevator shaft.* **11.** *Mining.* a vertical or sloping passageway leading to the surface. **12.** *Bot.* the trunk of a tree. **13.** *Zool.* the main stem or midrib of a feather. **14.** *Slang.* **a.** unfair treatment. **b.** a harsh remark. **—***v.t.* **15.** to push or propel with a pole. **16.** *Slang.* **a.** to treat unfairly. **b.** to take advantage of. [ME; OE *sceaft;* c. G *Schaft;* cf. L *scāpus* shaft, Gk *sképtron* SCEPTER]
Shaftes·bur·y (shafts′bə rē, shäfts′-), *n.* **1. Anthony Ash·ley Cooper** (ash′lē), **1st Earl of,** 1621–83, British statesman. **2.** his grandson, **Anthony Ashley Cooper, 3rd Earl of,** 1671–1713, British moral philosopher.
shaft·ing (shaf′ting, shäf′-), *n.* **1.** a number of shafts. **2.** *Mach.* a system of shafts. **3.** steel bar stock used for shafts. **4.** *Archit.* a system of shafts, as those in the reveals of an archway.

shag[1] (shag), *n.*, *v.*, **shagged, shag·ging.** —*n.* **1.** rough, matted hair, wool, or the like. **2.** a cloth with a nap, specifically one of silk but commonly a heavy wool. **3.** a coarse tobacco cut into fine shreds. —*v.t.* **4.** to make rough or shaggy, esp. with vegetation. **5.** to make rough or sharp. [OE *sceacga* (woolly) hair; c. Icel *skegg* beard; akin to SHAW]

shag[2] (shag), *n.* any of several small cormorants, esp. *Phalacrocorax aristotelis,* of Europe and northern Africa. [special use of SHAG[1], applied first to bird's crest]

shag[3] (shag), *v.t.*, **shagged,shag·ging. 1.** to chase or follow after; pursue. **2.** to fetch. **3.** *Baseball Slang.* to retrieve and throw back (balls) in batting practice. [?]

shag·bark (shag′bärk′), *n.* **1.** Also called **shag′bark hick′ory.** a hickory, *Carya ovata,* having rough bark and yielding a valuable wood. **2.** the nut of this tree. [SHAG(GY) + BARK[2]]

shag·gy (shag′ē), *adj.*, **-gi·er, -gi·est. 1.** covered with or having long, rough hair. **2.** untidy; unkempt. **3.** rough and matted, as a mane. **4.** having a rough nap, as cloth. —**shag′gi·ly,** *adv.* —**shag′gi·ness,** *n.*

shag′gy-dog′ sto′ry, a tediously prolonged joke with an absurd or irrelevant punch line.

shag·gy-mane (shag′ē mān′), *n.* an edible, inky-cap mushroom, *Coprinus comatus,* having a shaggy pileus.

sha·green (shə grēn′), *n.* **1.** an untanned leather with a granular surface, prepared from the hide of a horse, shark, seal, etc. **2.** the rough skin of certain sharks, used as an abrasive. —*adj.* **3.** Also, **sha·greened′.** resembling, covered with, or made of shagreen. [< F *chagrin,* var. of *sagrin* < Turk *sağri* rump]

shah (shä), *n.* (formerly, in Iran) king, sovereign. [< Pers: king] —**shah′dom,** *n.*

Shahansha (shä′än shä′), *n.* the title of the former ruler of Iran. [< Pers: king of kings. SEE SHAH]

Sha·hap·ti·an (shä hap′tē ən), *n.*, *pl.* **-ti·ans,** (*esp. collectively*) **-ti·an,** *adj.* Sahaptin.

Shah Ja·han (shä′ jə hän′), 1592?–1666, Mogul emperor in India 1628?–58: built the Taj Mahal. Also, **Shah′ Je·han′.**

Shah·ja·han·pur (shä′jə hän′po͝or′), *n.* a city in Uttar Pradesh, in N India. 110,400 (1961).

Shahn (shän), *n.* **Ben,** 1898–1969, U.S. painter, born in Lithuania.

shake (shāk), *v.*, **shook, shak·en, shak·ing,** *n.* —*v.i.* **1.** to move back and forth with short, quick, irregular motions. **2.** to tremble with emotion, cold, etc. **3.** to become dislodged and fall (usually fol. by *off* or *down*): *Sand shakes off easily.* **4.** to totter; become unsteady. **5.** to clasp another's hand in greeting, agreement, congratulations, etc. **6.** *Music.* to execute a trill. —*v.t.* **7.** to move (something or its support or container) to and fro or up and down with short, quick, forcible movements. **8.** to brandish or flourish: *to shake a stick at someone.* **9.** to grasp (someone or something) firmly in an attempt to move or rouse by vigorous movement to and fro. **10.** to dislodge or dispense (something) by short, quick, forcible movements of its support or container: *He took the bottle and shook two aspirin into his hand.* **11.** to cause to sway, rock, totter, etc.: *Don't shake the swing.* **12.** to agitate or disturb profoundly: *The experience shook him badly.* **13.** to cause to doubt or waver; weaken: *to shake one's faith.* **14.** *Music.* to trill (a note). **15.** to get rid of; elude. **16. shake down, a.** to cause to descend or settle by shaking; bring down. **b.** to condition; test: *to shake down a ship.* **c.** *Slang.* to extort money from. **17. shake off, a.** to rid oneself of; reject. **b.** to get away from; leave behind. **18. shake one's head, a.** to indicate disapproval, disagreement, or uncertainty by turning one's head slightly from side to side. **b.** to indicate approval, agreement, or acceptance by nodding one's head up and down. **19. shake up, a.** to shake in order to mix or loosen. **b.** to upset; jar. **c.** to agitate mentally or physically. —*n.* **20.** the act or an instance of shaking, rocking, swaying, etc. **21. shakes,** (*construed as sing.*) a state or spell of trembling, as caused by fear, fever, cold, etc. (usually prec. by *the*). **22.** a disturbing blow; shock. **23.** See **milk shake. 24.** the act or a manner of clasping another's hand in greeting, agreement, etc. **25.** *Informal.* treatment accorded one; deal: *a fair shake.* **26.** a cast of dice; roll. **27.** something resulting from shaking. **28.** a fissure in the earth or in timber. **29.** *Music.* trill[1] (def. 8). **30.** an instant: *I'll be with you in a shake.* **31.** *Carpentry.* a shingle or clapboard formed by splitting a short log into a number of tapered radial sections with a hatchet. **32. no great shakes,** not particularly able, important, or distinguished: *He's no great shakes as a draftsman.* **33. two shakes** or **two shakes of a lamb's tail,** a very short time; a moment. [ME; OE *sceac(an)*; c. LG *schacken,* OIcel *skaka*] —**shak′a·ble, shake′a·ble,** *adj.*

—**Syn. 1.** oscillate, waver. SHAKE, QUIVER, TREMBLE, VIBRATE refer to an agitated movement that, in living things, is often involuntary. To SHAKE is to agitate more or less quickly, abruptly, and often unevenly so as to disturb the poise, stability, or equilibrium of a person or thing: *a pole shaking under his weight.* To QUIVER is to exhibit a slight vibratory motion such as that resulting from disturbed or irregular (surface) tension: *The surface of the pool quivered in the breeze.* To TREMBLE (used more often of persons) is to be agitated by intermittent, involuntary movements of the muscles, much like shivering and caused by fear, cold, weakness, emotion, etc.: *Even stout hearts tremble with dismay.* To VIBRATE is to exhibit a rapid, rhythmical motion: *A violin string vibrates when a bow is drawn across it.*

shake·down (shāk′doun′), *n.* **1.** extortion, as by blackmail or threats of violence. **2.** a thorough search. **3.** a makeshift bed. **4.** the act or process of shaking down. —*adj.* **5.** (of a cruise or flight) intended to prepare a new vessel or aircraft for service by accustoming the crew to its peculiarities, breaking in its machinery, etc. Also, **shake′-down′.**

shak·er (shā′kər), *n.* **1.** a person or thing that shakes. **2.** a container with a perforated top from which a seasoning, a condiment, sugar, flour, or the like is shaken onto food. **3.** any of various containers for shaking beverages to mix the ingredients: *a cocktail shaker.* **4.** a dredger or caster. **5.** (*cap.*) a member of the Millennial Church, originating in England in the middle of the 18th century and now extant only in the U.S., practicing celibacy, common ownership of property, and a strict and simple way of life. [late ME]

Shak′er Heights′, a city in NE Ohio, near Cleveland. 36,306 (1970).

Shake·speare (shāk′spēr), *n.* **William,** 1564–1616, English poet and dramatist. Also, **Shakspere, Shake′spear.**

Shake·spear·e·an (shāk spēr′ē ən), *adj.* **1.** of, pertaining to, or suggestive of Shakespeare or his works. —*n.* **2.** a Shakespearean scholar. Also, **Shake·spear′i·an.** —**Shake·spear′e·an·ism, Shake·spear′i·an·ism,** *n.*

Shakespear′ean son′net, a sonnet form used by Shakespeare and having the rhyme scheme *abab, cdcd, efef, gg.* Also called **English sonnet.**

shake-up (shāk′up′), *n.* a thorough change in a business, department, or the like, as by dismissals and demotions.

Shakh·ty (shäKH′tē), *n.* a city in the SW RSFSR, in the S Soviet Union in Europe, in the Donets Basin. 201,000 (est. 1962).

shak′ing pal′sy, *Pathol.* See **Parkinson's disease.**

shak·o (shak′ō, shā′kō), *n.*, *pl.* **shak·os, shak·oes.** a military cap in the form of a cylinder or truncated cone, with a visor and a plume or pom-pon. [< F *schako* < Hung *csákó* < MHG *zacke* peak, point; see TACK[1]]

Shako

Shak·spere (shāk′spēr), *n.* **William.** See **Shakespeare.** —**Shak·sper′i·an,** *adj.*, *n.* —**Shak·sper′i·an·ism,** *n.*

Shak·ta (shäk′tə), *n.* *Hinduism.* a person who worships Shakti as the wife of Shiva. Also, **Sakta.** [< Skt *śākta* pertaining to Shakti]

Shak·ti (shuk′tē), *n.* *Hinduism.* **1.** the female principle or organ of generative power. **2.** the wife of a deity, esp. of Shiva. Also, **Sakti.** [< Skt *śakti*]

Shak·tism (shäk′tiz əm), *n.* *Hinduism.* the worship of Shakti as the wife of Shiva. Also, **Saktism.**

shak·y (shā′kē), *adj.*, **shak·i·er, shak·i·est. 1.** shaking **2.** trembling; tremulous. **3.** likely to break down or give way; insecure: *a shaky bridge.* **4.** wavering, as in allegiance: *shaky loyalty.* **5.** dubious; questionable: *shaky logic.* —**shak′i·ly,** *adv.* —**shak′i·ness,** *n.*

shale (shāl), *n.* a rock of fissile or laminated structure formed by the consolidation of clay or argillaceous material. [obs. *shale* to split (said of stone), to shell, ME *shale* SCALE[1], shell, husk, OE *sceal(u)* shell, husk, SCALE[2]]

shale′ oil′, petroleum distilled from bituminous shale.

shall (shal; *unstressed* shəl), *auxiliary v.*, *pres. sing. 1st pers.* **shall,** *2nd* **shall** or (*Archaic*) **shalt,** *3rd* **shall,** *pres. pl.* **shall;** *past sing. 1st pers.* **should,** *2nd* **should** or (*Archaic*) **shouldst** or **should·est,** *3rd* **should,** *past pl.* **should;** *imperative, infinitive, and participles lacking.* **1.** (generally used in the first person to denote simple future time) plan to, intend to, or expect to: *I shall go today.* **2.** (generally used in the second and third persons to denote authority or determination) will have to, is determined to, promises to, or definitely will: *You shall do it. He shall do it.* **3.** (used interrogatively in questions that admit of *shall* in the answer): *Shall he be told? He shall.* **4.** (used conditionally in all persons to indicate future time): *if he shall come.* [ME *shal,* OE *sceal;* c. OS *skal,* OHG *scal,* Icel *skal;* cf. G *soll,* D *zal*]

—**Usage.** In formal speech and writing, as well as in the informal speech of most educated speakers, SHALL is restricted to use with the first person, singular and plural: *I shall go, we shall be there.* WILL, in these contexts, is used with the second and third persons: *you, he, she, it, they will go, will be there.* Within this style, SHALL used with pronouns other than *I* and *we* denotes determination or command (*You shall go, even if you don't want to*); it sometimes carries the same force when used with *I* or *we: I shall return.*

shal·loon (sha lo͞on′), *n.* a light, twilled woolen fabric used chiefly for linings. [< F *chalon,* after *Châlons-sur-Marne,* where made]

shal·lop (shal′əp), *n.* any of various vessels formerly used for sailing or rowing in shallow waters. [< F *chaloupe* < G *Schaluppe* SLOOP]

shal·lot (shə lot′), *n.* **1.** a liliaceous plant, *Allium ascalonicum,* that resembles an onion and whose bulb forms bulblets used for flavoring in cookery and as a vegetable. **2.** the bulb or bulblet itself. **3.** a small onion. [< F *(é)chalote,* dim. of MF *eschaloigne* SCALLION]

shal·low (shal′ō), *adj.* **1.** of little depth; not deep: *shallow water; a shallow dish.* **2.** lacking depth; superficial: *a mind that is shallow.* —*n.* **3.** Usually, **shallows.** (*construed as sing. or pl.*) a shallow part of a body of water; shoal. —*v.t.*, *v.i.* **4.** to make or become shallow. [ME *schalowe;* akin to OE *sceald* shallow] —**shal′low·ly,** *adv.* —**shal′low·ness,** *n.*

sha·lom (shä lôm′; *Eng.* shə lōm′), *interj.* *Hebrew.* peace: a conventional Jewish greeting and farewell.

sha·lom a·lei·chem (shä lôm′ ä lā KHem′; *Eng.* shə lōm′ ə lā′KHəm, ä lā′KHəm, shō′ləm), *Hebrew.* peace to you: a conventional Jewish greeting.

shalt (shalt), *v.* *Archaic.* 2nd pers. sing. of **shall.**

sham (sham), *n.*, *adj.*, *v.*, **shammed, sham·ming.** —*n.* **1.** something that is not what it purports to be; a spurious imitation; fraud. **2.** a person who assumes a false character or identity; impostor. **3.** a cover or the like for giving a thing a different outward appearance: *a pillow sham.* **4.** *Obs.* hoax. —*adj.* **5.** pretended; counterfeit; feigned. **6.** designed, made, or used as a sham. —*v.t.* **7.** to produce an imitation of. **8.** to assume the appearance of; pretend to be: *to sham illness.* —*v.i.* **9.** to make a false show of something; pretend. [?] —**Syn. 1.** pretense. **5.** spurious, simulated. See **false.**

sha·man (shä′mən, shā′-, sham′ən), *n.* a medicine man; a person who works with the supernatural as both priest and doctor. [< Turkic, perh. < Chin *shamēn* < Pali *samana* Buddhist monk]

sha·man·ism (shä′mə niz′əm, shā′-, sham′ə-), *n.* **1.** the animistic religion of northern Asia, embracing a belief in powerful spirits who can be influenced only by shamans. **2.** any similar religion, as among the Indians of the American Northwest. —**sha′man·ist,** *n.*, *adj.* —**sha′man·is′tic,** *adj.*

Sha·mash (shä′mäsh), *n.* the Akkadian sun god who controls crops and represents righteousness: the counterpart of the Sumerian Utu.

sham·ble[1] (sham′bəl), *n.* **1. shambles,** (*construed as sing. or pl.*) **a.** a slaughterhouse. **b.** any place of carnage. **c.** any scene of destruction or disorder. **2.** *Brit. Dial.* a butcher's shop or stall. [ME *shamel,* OE *sc(e)amel* stool, table << LL *scamell(um),* dim. of L *scamnum* bench; cf. G *Schemel*]

sham·ble[2] (sham′bəl), *v.,* **-bled, -bling,** *n.* —*v.i.* **1.** to walk or go awkwardly; shuffle. —*n.* **2.** a shambling gait. [? *shamble-(legs)* one that walks wide (i.e., as if straddling) < obs. *shamble* table (see SHAMBLE[1]), so called because reminiscent of the legs of such a table]

shame (shām), *n., v.,* **shamed, sham·ing.** —*n.* **1.** the painful feeling arising from the consciousness of something dishonorable, improper, ridiculous, etc., done by oneself or another. **2.** susceptibility to this feeling: *to be without shame.* **3.** disgrace; ignominy. **4.** a fact or circumstance that is a cause for regret (often used with *it* as subject): *It's a shame you can't stay for dinner.* **5. for shame!** you should feel ashamed! **6. put to shame, a.** to cause to suffer shame or disgrace. **b.** to outdo; surpass. —*v.t.* **7.** to cause to feel shame; make ashamed. **8.** to drive, force, etc., through shame: *He shamed her into going.* **9.** to cover with ignominy or reproach; disgrace. [ME; OE *sc(e)amu;* c. G *Scham,* Icel *skömm*] —**sham′a·ble, shame′a·ble,** *adj.*
—**Syn. 1.** SHAME, EMBARRASSMENT, MORTIFICATION, HUMILIATION, CHAGRIN designate different kinds or degrees of painful feeling caused by injury to one's pride or self-respect. SHAME is a painful feeling caused by the consciousness or exposure of unworthy or indecent conduct or circumstances: *One feels shame at being caught in a lie.* It is similar to guilt in the nature and origin of the feeling. EMBARRASSMENT usually refers to a feeling less painful than that of SHAME, one associated with less serious situations, often of a social nature: *embarrassment over breaking a teacup at a party.* MORTIFICATION is a more painful feeling, akin to SHAME but also more likely to arise from social circumstances: *his mortification at being singled out for rebuke.* HUMILIATION is mortification at being humbled in the estimation of others: *Being ignored gives one a sense of humiliation.* CHAGRIN is humiliation mingled with vexation or anger: *He felt chagrin at his failure to remember his promise.* **7.** humiliate, mortify, humble.

shame·faced (shām′fāst′), *adj.* **1.** modest or bashful. **2.** showing shame: *shamefaced apologies.* [alter. of *shamefast,* OE *scamfæst* modest, bashful = *scam(u)* SHAME + *fæst* firmly fixed, FAST[1]] —**shame·fac·ed·ly** (shām′fā′sid lē, shām′fāst′lē), *adv.* —**shame′fac′ed·ness,** *n.*

shame·ful (shām′fəl), *adj.* **1.** causing shame. **2.** disgraceful; indecent: *shameful treatment.* [ME; OE *scamful*] —**shame′ful·ly,** *adv.* —**shame′ful·ness,** *n.* —**Syn. 1.** mortifying. **2.** dishonorable, ignominious, base.

shame·less (shām′lis), *adj.* **1.** lacking any sense of shame; immodest. **2.** insensible to disgrace. **3.** showing no shame. [ME; OE *sceamlēas*] —**shame′less·ly,** *adv.* —**shame′less·ness,** *n.* —**Syn. 1.** brazen, indecent, impudent. **2.** hardened, unprincipled, corrupt. —**Ant. 1.** modest.

Sha·mir (shä mēr′), *n.* **Yitz·hak** (yits′ KHäk), born 1915, Israeli political leader, born in Poland: prime minister 1983–84 and since 1986.

sham·mash (shä mäsh′; *Eng., Yiddish.* shä′məs), *n., pl.* **-ma·shim** (-mä shēm′; *Eng., Yiddish.* -mô′sim). *Hebrew., Judaism.* **1.** the custodian or sexton of a synagogue. **2.** the candle used on Hanukkah to kindle the other candle or candles in the menorah. [lit., servant]

sham·mer (sham′ər), *n.* a person who shams.

sham·my (sham′ē), *n., pl.* **-mies,** *v.,* **-mied, -my·ing.** chamois (defs. 2–6).

Sha·mo (shä′mô′), *n.* Chinese name of the **Gobi.**

sham·oy (sham′ē), *n., pl.* **-oys,** *v.,* **-oyed, -oy·ing.** chamois (defs. 2–6).

sham·poo (sham po͞o′), *v.,* **-pooed, -poo·ing,** *n.* —*v.t.* **1.** to wash (the head or hair), esp. with a shampoo. **2.** to clean (rugs, upholstery, or the like) with a special preparation. —*n.* **3.** the act of shampooing. **4.** a special preparation for washing the hair. [earlier *champo* < Hindi < *cāmpnā* to press] —**sham·poo′er,** *n.*

sham·rock (sham′rok), *n.* any of several trifoliate plants, usually a yellow-flowered trefoil, *Trifolium dubium:* the national emblem of Ireland. [< Ir *seamróg* shamrock, trefoil, clover, bunch of green grass = *seamar* trefoil, clover + *-óg* dim. suffix]

Shamrock, *Trifolium dubium*

sha·mus (shä′məs, shā′-), *n., pl.* **-mus·es.** *Slang.* **1.** a detective. **2.** a policeman. [b. *shāmus,* var. of SHAMMASH and *shāmus* Anglicized sp. of Ir *Séamas* James]

Shan (shän, shan), *n., pl.* **Shans,** (*esp. collectively*) **Shan. 1.** a group of Mongoloid tribes in the hills of Burma. **2.** a language spoken in the Shan State and belonging to the Thai group of languages.

shan·dy·gaff (shan′dē gaf′), *n.* *Chiefly Brit.* a mixed drink of beer with ginger beer. [?]

shang·hai (shang′hī, shang hī′), *v.t.,* **-haied, -hai·ing.** *Naut.* to enroll or obtain (a sailor) for the crew of a ship by unscrupulous means, as by force. [special use of SHANGHAI]

Shang·hai (shang hī′; *Chin.* shäng′hī′), *n.* **1.** a seaport in E China, near the mouth of the Yangtze. 10,000,000 (est. 1964). **2.** a type of long-legged chicken believed to be of Asian origin.

Shan·gri-la (shang′grə lä′, shang′grə lä′), *n.* **1.** a paradise on earth. **2.** an area whose name or location is unknown or kept secret. [after a hidden paradise in *Lost Horizon* (1933), a novel by James Hilton]

Shan·hai·kwan (shän′hī′gwän′), *n.* former name of **Linyu.**

shank (shangk), *n.* **1.** *Anat.* the part of the lower limb in man between the knee and the ankle; leg. **2.** a corresponding or analogous part in certain animals. **3.** the lower limb in man, including both the leg and the thigh. **4.** a cut of meat from the top of the front **(fore shank)** or back **(hind shank)** leg of an animal. **5.** a narrow, shaftlike part that connects two objects or two separated parts of the same object, as the shaft connecting the bit to the handle on a drill. **6.** a knob, small projection, or end of a device for attaching to another object, as a small knob on the back of a solid button. **7.** the long, straight part of an anchor connecting the crown and the ring. **8.** *Music.* crook (def. 7). **9.** *Informal.* the early or important part of a period of time. **10.** the narrow part of the sole of a shoe, lying beneath the instep. **11.** *Print.* the body of a type, between the shoulder and the foot. [ME; OE *sc(e)anca;* c. LG *schanke* leg, thigh; akin to G *Schenkel* thigh, *Schinken* ham]

Shan·kar (shän′kär), *n.* **Ra·vi** (rä′vē), born 1920?, Indian sitarist.

shanks′/ mare′, **1.** Also, **shank's′ mare′.** one's own legs, esp. as a means of locomotion. **2. ride shanks' mare,** to walk rather than ride.

Shan·non (shan′ən), *n.* a river flowing SW from N Ireland to the Atlantic: 240 mi. long.

Shan·si (shän′sē′), *n.* a province in N China. 15,960,000 (est. 1957); 60,656 sq. mi. *Cap.:* Taiyüan.

Shan′ State′ (shän, shan), a state in E Burma, along the Salween River. 1,987,000 (est. 1956); ab. 56,000 sq. mi. Cf. **Burma.**

shan't (shant, shänt), contraction of *shall not.*

shan·tey (shan′tē), *n., pl.* **-teys.** chantey.

shan·ti (shän′tē), *n.* *Hinduism.* peace. Also, **shan′tih.** [< Skt *śānti*]

Shan·tung (shan′tung′ *or, for* 3, shan′tung; *for 1, 2, also Chin.* shän′do͝ong′), *n.* **1.** a maritime province in NE China. 54,030,000 (est. 1957); 59,189 sq. mi. *Cap.:* Tsinan. **2.** a peninsula in the E part of this province, extending into the Yellow Sea. **3.** (*often l.c.*) *Textiles.* **a.** a heavy pongee. Cf. **tussah** (def. 1). **b.** a fabric imitating this, of rayon or cotton.

shan·ty[1] (shan′tē), *n., pl.* **-ties.** a crudely built hut, cabin, or house. [prob. < CanF *chantier* shed, workshop, log hut < L *canthēr(ius)* framework < Gk *kanthḗlios* pack ass] —**Syn.** See **cottage.**

shan·ty[2] (shan′tē), *n., pl.* **-ties.** chantey.

shan·ty·town (shan′tē toun′), *n.* an extremely poor section of a city or town where there are many shanties.

Shao·hing (shou′shing′), *n.* a city in NE Chekiang, in E China. 130,600 (est. 1953).

shape (shāp), *n., v.,* **shaped, shap·ing.** —*n.* **1.** the flat character of a form or object as defined by its contour or outline; the two-dimensional extent of a figure described by its boundary. **2.** something seen in silhouette: *A vague shape appeared through the mist.* **3.** an imaginary form; phantom. **4.** an assumed appearance; guise. **5.** organized form; orderly arrangement: *He could give no shape to his ideas.* **6.** condition or state of repair: *The old house was in bad shape.* **7.** the group of conditions forming a way of life or mode of existence: *What will the shape of the future be?* **8.** the figure or body of a person, esp. of a woman. **9.** something used to give form, as a mold or a pattern. **10.** *Building Trades, Metalworking.* a flanged metal beam or bar of uniform section. **11. take shape,** to assume a fixed form; become definite. —*v.t.* **12.** to give definite form, shape, organization, or character to; fashion or form. **13.** to couch or express in words. **14.** to adjust; adapt. **15.** to direct (one's course, future, etc.). —*v.i.* **16.** to come to a desired conclusion or take place in a specified way (often fol. by *up*): *If discussions shape up properly, the companies will merge.* [(n.) ME; OE *gesceapu* (pl.); r. ME *shap,* OE *(ge)sceap* (sing.); c. Icel *skap* state, mood; (v.) ME; OE *sceape(n)* (ptp.); r. ME *sheppe, shippe,* OE *sceppa(n), scyppan;* c. Icel *skepja,* Goth *-skapjan,* G *schaffen* to make] —**shap′a·ble, shape′a·ble,** *adj.* —**shape′less,** *adj.* —**shape′less·ly,** *adv.* —**shape′less·ness,** *n.* —**Syn. 1.** silhouette, appearance. See **form. 3.** specter, illusion. **5.** order, pattern.

Shapes (def. 10)
A, Angle iron; B, Channel iron; C, Z-bar; D, T-bar; E, H-beam; F, I-beam

SHAPE (shāp), *n.* Supreme Headquarters Allied Powers, Europe. Also, **Shape.**

shaped′ charge′, *Mil.* a warhead having a concave, hollow end and operating on the Munroe effect.

shape·ly (shāp′lē), *adj.,* **-li·er, -li·est.** having a pleasing shape, esp. with reference to a woman's figure. [SHAPE + -LY; r. ME *shaply, schaply;* cf. OE *gesceaplīce* (adv.) fitly] —**shape′li·ness,** *n.*

shap·er (shā′pər), *n.* **1.** a person or thing that shapes. **2.** a machine tool with a cutting part for forming flat surfaces. Cf. **planer** (def. 2).

shape-up (shāp′up′), *n.* a former method of hiring longshoremen in which the applicants appeared daily at the docks and a union hiring boss chose those who would be given work.

Sha·pi·ro (shə pēr′ō), *n.* **Karl (Jay),** born 1913, U.S. poet.

Shap·ley (shap′lē), *n.* **Har·low** (här′lō), 1885–1972, U.S. astronomer.

shard (shärd), *n.* **1.** a fragment, esp. of broken earthenware. **2.** *Zool.* **a.** a scale. **b.** a shell, as of an egg or snail. **3.** *Entomol.* an elytron of a beetle. Also, **sherd.** [ME; OE *sceard;* c. LG, D *schaard;* akin to SHEAR]

share[1] (shâr), *n., v.,* **shared, shar·ing.** —*n.* **1.** a part of a whole, esp. a portion allotted or assigned a member of a group. **2.** one of the equal fractional parts into which the capital stock of a joint-stock company or a corporation is divided. —*v.t.* **3.** to use, participate in, enjoy, receive, etc., jointly: *The two chemists shared the Nobel prize.* **4.** to divide and distribute in shares; apportion. —*v.i.* **5.** to give or receive a share or part; take part (often fol. by *in*). **6.** to receive equally. [ME; OE *scear(u)* cutting, division; c. D *schaar,* G *Schar* troop. See SHEAR] —**shar′a·ble, share′a·ble,** *adj.* —**shar′er,** *n.*
—**Syn. 1.** allotment, allocation; contribution; quota, lot. **4.** allot, dole, mete. **5.** SHARE, PARTAKE, PARTICIPATE

mean to join with others or to receive in common with others. To SHARE is to give or receive a part of something, or to enjoy or assume something in common: *to share in another's experiences.* To PARTAKE is to take for one's own personal use a portion of something: *to partake of food.* To PARTICIPATE is esp. to join with others in some thought, feeling, or, particularly, action: *to participate in a race, in a conversation.*

share[2] (shâr), *n.* a plowshare. [ME; OE *scear;* c. G *Schar.* See SHEAR]

share·crop (shâr′krop′), *v.t., v.i.,* **-cropped, -crop·ping.** to farm as a sharecropper. [back formation from SHARECROPPER]

share·crop·per (shâr′krop′ər), *n.* a tenant farmer who pays as rent a share of the crop.

share·hold·er (shâr′hōl′dər), *n.* a holder or owner of shares, esp. in a corporation.

Sha·ri (shä′rē), *n.* a river in N central Africa, flowing NW from the Central African Republic into Lake Chad. 1400 mi. long. Also, **Chari.**

sha·rif (shə rēf′), *n.* sherif.

shark[1] (shärk), *n.* any of a group of elongate, elasmobranch, mostly marine, fishes, certain species of which are large and ferocious. [?]

Shark[1], *Carcharodon carcharias* (Length 30 ft.)

shark[2] (shärk), *n.* **1.** a person who preys greedily on others, as by cheating or usury. **2.** *Slang.* a person who has unusual ability in a particular field. —*v.i.* **3.** to live by shifts and stratagems. —*v.t.* **4.** *Archaic.* to obtain by trickery or fraud; steal. [< G dial. *Schork,* var. of *Schurke* rascal]

shark·skin (shärk′skin′), *n.* **1.** a fine worsted fabric in twill weave, compact in texture and light to medium in weight, for suits. **2.** a smooth fabric of acetate or rayon with a dull or chalklike appearance, for apparel.

shark·suck·er (shärk′suk′ər), *n.* any of several remoras, as *Echeneis naucrates,* usually found attached to sharks.

Shar·on (shar′ən), *n.* a fertile coastal plain in ancient Palestine: now a coastal region N of Tel Aviv in Israel.

sharp (shärp), *adj.* **1.** having a thin cutting edge or a fine point; well-adapted for cutting or piercing: *a sharp knife.* **2.** terminating in an edge or point; not blunt or rounded: *The table had sharp corners.* **3.** involving a sudden or abrupt change in direction or course: *a sharp curve in the road.* **4.** clearly defined; distinct: *a sharp image; sharp differences of opinion.* **5.** pungent or biting in taste: *a sharp cheese.* **6.** piercing or shrill in sound: *a sharp cry.* **7.** keenly cold, as weather: *a sharp, biting wind.* **8.** felt acutely; intense: *sharp pain.* **9.** merciless, caustic, or harsh: *sharp words.* **10.** mentally acute, alert, or vigilant: *a sharp lad; a sharp watch for the enemy.* **11.** shrewd or astute: *a sharp bargainer.* **12.** shrewd to the point of dishonesty: *sharp practice.* **13.** *Music.* **a.** (of a tone) raised a chromatic half step in pitch: *F sharp.* **b.** above an intended pitch, as a note; too high (opposed to *flat*). **14.** *Slang.* very stylish: *a sharp dresser; a sharp jacket.* **15.** *Phonet.* fortis; voiceless. —*v.t.* **16.** *Music.* to raise in pitch, esp. by one chromatic half step. —*v.i.* **17.** *Music.* to sound above the true pitch. —*adv.* **18.** keenly or acutely. **19.** abruptly or suddenly. **20.** punctually: *Meet me at one o'clock sharp.* **21.** *Music.* above the true pitch. —*n.* **22.** *Music.* **a.** a tone one chromatic half step above a given tone. **b.** (in musical notation) the symbol (♯) indicating this. **23.** *Informal.* an expert; shark. [ME; OE *scearp;* c. G *scharf;* akin to Ir *cearb* a cut (n.), keen (adj.)] —**sharp′ly,** *adv.* —**sharp′ness,** *n.*

—**Syn. 1.** SHARP, KEEN refer to the edge or point of an instrument, tool, or the like. SHARP applies, in general, to a cutting edge or a point capable of piercing: *a sharp razor blade, a sharp point on a pencil.* KEEN is esp. applied to long edges, as of a saber: *a keen sword blade.* **5.** acrid, piquant. **7.** piercing, biting. **8.** severe. **9.** cutting, acid, pointed. **10.** attentive, clever, discriminating, discerning, perspicacious. As applied to mental qualities, SHARP, KEEN, INTELLIGENT, QUICK have varying implications. SHARP suggests an acute, sensitive, alert, penetrating quality: *a sharp mind.* KEEN implies observant, incisive, and vigorous: *a keen intellect.* INTELLIGENT means not only acute, alert, and active, but also able to reason and understand: *an intelligent reader.* QUICK suggests lively and rapid comprehension, prompt response to instruction, and the like: *quick at figures.* **12.** shady, deceitful. —**Ant. 1.** dull.

Sharp (shärp), *n.* **William** (pen name: *Fiona Macleod*), 1855?–1905, Scottish poet and critic.

sharp·en (shär′pən), *v.t., v.i.* to make or become sharp or sharper. —**sharp′en·er,** *n.*

sharp·er (shär′pər), *n.* **1.** a shrewd swindler. **2.** a professional gambler. Also, **sharpie.**

sharp-eyed (shärp′īd′), *adj.* sharp-sighted.

sharp·ie (shär′pē), *n.* **1.** a very alert person. **2.** *Slang.* an ostentatiously stylish person. **3.** sharper. **4.** (formerly) a long, flat-bottomed boat having a triangular sail on one or two masts. Also, **sharpy.**

Sharps·burg (shärps′bûrg), *n.* a town in NW Maryland: near the site of the battle of Antietam 1862.

sharp-set (shärp′set′), *adj.* **1.** eager in appetite or desire, esp. for food. **2.** set to present a sharply angled edge. —**sharp′-set′ness,** *n.*

sharp·shoot·er (shärp′sho͞o′tər), *n.* **1.** a person skilled in shooting, esp. with a rifle. **2.** *Mil.* **a.** (in rifle marksmanship) a rating below expert and above marksman. **b.** a person who has achieved this rating. **3.** *Slang.* an unscrupulous businessman who seeks quick profits. [SHARP (i.e., sharp-eyed) + SHOOTER; cf. G *Scharfschütz(e)* expert marksman] —**sharp′shoot′ing,** *n.*

sharp-sight·ed (shärp′sī′tid), *adj.* having keen sight or perception; sharp-eyed.

sharp-tongued (shärp′tungd′), *adj.* harsh or sarcastic in speech.

sharp-wit·ted (shärp′wit′id), *adj.* having or showing mental acuity. —**sharp′-wit′ted·ly,** *adv.* —**sharp′-wit′ted·ness,** *n.*

sharp·y (shär′pē), *n., pl.* **sharp·ies.** sharpie.

shash·lik (shäsh lik′, shäsh′lik), *n.* See **shish kebab.** Also, **shash·lick′, shas·lik′.** [< Russ < some Turkic dial.; see SHISH KEBAB]

Shas·ta (shas′tə), *n.* **Mount,** a volcanic peak in N California, in the Cascade Range. 14,161 ft.

Shas′ta dai′sy, any of several horticultural varieties of *Chrysanthemum maximum,* having large, daisylike flowers. [named after Mt. SHASTA]

Shas·tri (shäs′trē), *n.* **Lal Ba·ha·dur** (läl bä hä′do͝or), 1904–66, Indian statesman: prime minister 1964–66.

Shatt-al-A·rab (shat′al är′äb), *n.* a river in SE Iraq, formed by the junction of the Tigris and Euphrates rivers, flowing SE to the Persian Gulf. 123 mi. long.

shat·ter (shat′ər), *v.t.* **1.** to break (something) into pieces, as by a blow. **2.** to damage, as by breaking or crushing. **3.** to impair or destroy (health, nerves, etc.). **4.** to weaken, destroy, or refute (ideas, opinions, etc.). —*v.i.* **5.** to be broken into fragments or become weak or insubstantial. [ME *schater(en)* < ?; cf. SCATTER] —**shat′ter·er,** *n.* —**shat′ter·ing·ly,** *adv.* —**Syn. 1.** See **break.**

shat·ter·proof (shat′ər pro͞of′), *adj.* designed or made to resist shattering: *shatterproof glass.*

shave (shāv), *v.,* **shaved, shaved** or **shav·en, shav·ing,** *n.* —*v.i.* **1.** to remove a growth of beard with a razor. —*v.t.* **2.** to remove hair from (the face, legs, etc.) by cutting it off close to the skin with a razor. **3.** to cut off (hair, esp. the beard) close to the skin with a razor. **4.** to cut or scrape away the surface of with a sharp-edged tool. **5.** to reduce to shavings or thin slices. **6.** to cut or trim closely: *to shave a lawn.* **7.** to scrape, graze, or come very near to: *The car just shaved the garage door.* **8.** to reduce or deduct from (a price). —*n.* **9.** the act, process, or an instance of shaving or being shaved. **10.** a thin slice; shaving. **11.** any of various tools for shaving, scraping, removing thin slices, etc. [ME; OE *sceafan;* c. D *schaven* to plane (a plank), abrade (the skin), LG *schaven,* G *schaben,* Icel *skafa* to scrape, Goth *skaban* to shear, shave] —**shav′a·ble, shave′a·ble,** *adj.*

shave·ling (shāv′ling), *n.* **1.** young fellow; youngster. **2.** *Often Disparaging.* a head-shaven clergyman.

shav·en (shā′vən), *v.* **1.** a pp. of **shave.** —*adj.* **2.** closely trimmed.

shav·er (shā′vər), *n.* **1.** a person or thing that shaves. **2.** an electric razor. **3.** *Informal.* a small boy; youngster. **4.** a fellow. **5.** *Archaic.* a person who makes close bargains or is extortionate. [late ME]

shave·tail (shāv′tāl′), *n.* *Slang. U.S. Army.* a second lieutenant. [SHAVE + TAIL[1]; first said of unbroken army mules, whose tails were shaved to mark them as raw recruits]

Sha·vi·an (shā′vē ən), *adj.* **1.** of, pertaining to, or characteristic of George Bernard Shaw or his works: *Shavian humor.* —*n.* **2.** a specialist in the works of George Bernard Shaw. [*Shav-* (Latinization of SHAW) + -IAN]

shav·ie (shā′vē), *n.* *Scot.* a trick or prank. [special use of SHAVE swindle + -IE]

shav·ing (shā′ving), *n.* **1.** a very thin piece or slice, esp. of wood. **2.** the act of a person or thing that shaves. [ME]

Sha·vu·oth (shə vo͞o′ōs, -əs), *n.* *Judaism.* Shabuoth.

shaw (shô), *n.* *Dial.* a small wood or thicket. [ME *shawe,* OE *sceaga, scaga;* akin to SHAG[1]]

Shaw (shô), *n.* **1. George Bernard,** 1856–1950, Irish dramatist, critic, and novelist: Nobel prize 1925. **2. Henry Wheeler.** See **Billings, Josh. 3. Irwin,** 1913–84, U.S. dramatist and author. **4. Thomas Edward.** See **Lawrence, Thomas Edward.**

shawl (shôl), *n.* a piece of wool or other material worn for warmth, esp. by women, about the shoulders or the head and shoulders. [< Pers *shāl*]

shawm (shôm), *n.* an early musical woodwind instrument with a double reed: the forerunner of the modern oboe. [late ME *schalme* < MF *chaume* < L *calam(us)* stalk, reed < Gk *kálamos* reed; r. ME *schallemele* < MF *chalemel;* c. ML *calamella* flageolet, dim. of L *calamus* stalk, reed pipe]

Shaw·nee (shô nē′), *n., pl.* **-nees,** (*esp. collectively*) **-nee. 1.** a member of an Algonquian-speaking tribe formerly in the east-central U.S., now in Oklahoma. **2.** the Algonquian language of the Shawnee tribe. **3.** a city in central Oklahoma. 25,075 (1970). [back formation from *Shawanese* < Algonquian *shawun* south + -ESE]

Shaw·wal (shə wäl′), *n.* the tenth month of the Islamic calendar. [< Ar]

shay (shā), *n.* *Chiefly Dial.* a chaise. [back formation from CHAISE taken for plural]

Shays (shāz), *n.* **Daniel,** 1747–1825, American Revolutionary War soldier: leader of a popular insurrection **(Shays′ Rebel′lion)** in Massachusetts 1786–87.

Shcha·ran·sky (shə ran′skē, -rän′-), *n.* **(Na·tan) A·na·to·ly** (nä tän′ an′ə tō′lē), born 1948, Soviet mathematician and human-rights activist, in Israel since 1986.

Shcher·ba·kov (shcher bä kôf′), *n.* a city in the W RSFSR in the central Soviet Union in Europe, N of Moscow, on the Volga. 195,000. Formerly, **Rybinsk.**

she (shē), *pron., sing. nom.* **she,** *poss.* **her** or **hers,** *obj.* **her;** *pl. nom.* **they,** *poss.* **their** or **theirs,** *obj.* **them;** *n., pl.* **shes.** —*pron.* **1.** the female in question or last mentioned. **2.** the woman: *She who listens learns.* **3.** anything considered, as by personification, to be feminine: *spring, with all the memories she conjures up.* —*n.* **4.** a woman or female. **5.** an object or device considered as female or feminine. [ME, alter. of OE *sīe,* acc. of *sēo,* fem. demonstrative pronoun; r. OE *hīe,* acc. of *hēo,* fem. personal pronoun; see HE[1], HER]

she-, a combining form of **she:** *she-wolf.*

sheaf (shēf), *n., pl.* **sheaves. 1.** one of the bundles in which cereal plants, as wheat, are bound after reaping. **2.** any bundle, cluster, or collection: *a sheaf of papers.* [ME *shefe,* OE *scēaf;* c. D *schoof* sheaf, G *Schaub* wisp of straw, Icel *skauf* tail of a fox]

shear (shēr), *v.,* **sheared** or (*esp. Dial.*) **shore; sheared** or **shorn; shear·ing;** *n.* —*v.t.* **1.** to cut (something). **2.** to remove by or as by cutting or clipping: *to shear wool from sheep.* **3.** to cut or clip the hair, fleece, wool, etc., from: *to shear sheep.* **4.** to strip or deprive (usually fol. by *of*): *to shear someone of his power.* **5.** *Chiefly Scot.* to reap with a sickle. **6.** to travel through (air, water, etc.) by or as by cutting. **—***v.i.* **7.** to cut or cut through something with a sharp instrument. **8.** *Mech.* to become fractured along a plane as a result of forces acting parallel to the plane. **9.** *Chiefly Scot.* to reap crops with a sickle. **—***n.* **10.** Usually, **shears.** (*sometimes construed as sing.*) **a.** scissors of large size (usually used with *pair of*). **b.** any of various other cutting implements or machines having two blades that resemble or suggest those of scissors. **11.** the act or process of shearing or being sheared. **12.** a shearing of sheep (used in stating the age of sheep): *a sheep of one shear.* **13.** the quantity, esp. of fleece, cut off at one shearing. **14.** one blade of a pair of shears. **15.** Usually, **shears.** (*sometimes construed as sing.*) Also, **sheers.** Also called **shear legs.** a framework for hoisting heavy weights, consisting of two or more spars with their legs separated, fastened together near the top and steadied by guys, which support a tackle. **16.** a machine for cutting rigid material by moving the edge of a blade through it. **17.** *Mech.* the tendency of forces to deform or fracture a member in a direction parallel to the force, as by sliding one section of the member along another. **18.** *Physics.* the lateral deformation produced in a body by an external force, expressed as the ratio of the lateral displacement between two points lying in parallel planes to the vertical distance between the planes. [ME *shere(n),* OE *sceran;* c. D, G *scheren,* Icel *skera*] **—shear′er,** *n.*

shear′ legs′, shear (def. 15). Also, **sheerlegs.**

shear·ling (shēr′ling), *n.* **1.** *Chiefly Brit.* a yearling sheep that has been shorn once. **2.** short wool pulled from such a sheep. [ME *scherling*]

shear·wa·ter (shēr′wô′tər, -wot′ər), *n.* any of several long-winged sea birds, esp. of the genus *Puffinus,* allied to the petrels, that appear to shear the water with their wings when flying low.

sheat·fish (shēt′fish′), *n., pl.* **-fish·es,** (*esp. collectively*) **-fish.** a large, fresh-water catfish, *Silurus glanis,* of central and eastern Europe. [dissimilated var. of *sheath-fish;* see SHEATH (false trans. of G *Scheide* sheatfish), FISH]

sheath (shēth), *n., pl.* **sheaths** (shēthz), *v.* **—***n.* **1.** a case or covering for the blade of a sword, dagger, or the like. **2.** any similar close-fitting covering or case. **3** *Biol.* any of various closely enveloping parts or structures in an animal or plant organism, as the leaf base when it forms a vertical coating surrounding the stem. **4.** a close-fitting dress. **—***v.t.* **5.** to sheathe. [ME *sheth(e),* OE *scēath;* c. G *Scheide;* see SHED[2]]

sheath·bill (shēth′bil′), *n.* either of two white sea birds, *Chionis alba* or *C. minor,* of the colder parts of the Southern Hemisphere: so called from the horny sheath covering the base of the upper bill.

sheathe (shēth), *v.t.,* **sheathed, sheath·ing. 1.** to put (a sword, dagger, etc.) into a sheath. **2.** to plunge (a sword, dagger, etc.) into something as if into a sheath. **3.** to enclose in or as in a casing or covering. **4.** to cover or provide with a protective layer or sheathing. [ME *shethe.* See SHEATH] **—sheath′er,** *n.*

sheath·ing (shē′thing), *n.* **1.** the act of a person who sheathes. **2.** a covering or outer layer, as one of metal plates on a ship's bottom. **3.** material for forming any such covering.

sheath′ knife′, a knife carried in a sheath.

sheave[1] (shēv), *v.t.,* **sheaved, sheav·ing.** to gather, collect, or bind into a sheaf or sheaves. [from SHEAF]

sheave[2] (shiv, shēv), *n.* **1.** a pulley for hoisting or hauling, having a grooved rim for retaining a wire rope. **2.** a wheel with a grooved rim, for transmitting force to a cable or belt. [ME *schive;* akin to D *schijf* sheave, G *Scheibe* disk]

sheaves[1] (shēvz), *n.* pl. of **sheaf.**

sheaves[2] (shivz, shēvz), *n.* pl. of **sheave**[2].

She·ba (shē′bə), *n.* *Bible.* **1. Queen of,** the queen who visited Solomon to test his wisdom. I Kings 10:1–13. **2.** Biblical name of **Saba.**

she·bang (shə bang′), *n.* *Informal.* an organization, contrivance, affair, etc., considered in its total structure: *The whole shebang fell apart when the chairman quit.* [?]

She·bat (shə vät′), *n.* the fifth month of the Jewish calendar. Also, **Shevat.** Cf. **Jewish calendar.** [< Heb]

she·been (shə bēn′), *n.* *Scot., Irish Eng.* a tavern or house where liquor is sold illegally. Also, **she·bean′.** [< Ir *síbín,* cf. *séibín* small mug, hence (drink of) ale, very weak beer]

She·be·li (shi bā′lē), *n.* **We·bi** (wā′bi). See **Webi Shebeli.** Also, **Shibeli.**

She·boy·gan (shi boi′gən), *n.* a port in E Wisconsin, on Lake Michigan. 48,484 (1970).

She·chem (shē′kəm, -kem, shek′əm, -em), *n.* a town of ancient Palestine, near the site of Samaria; now in NW Israeli-occupied Jordan: first capital of the northern kingdom of Israel. 213,000 (est. 1968). Also, **Sichem, Sychem.** Modern name, **Nablus.**

She·chi·nah (shə kē′nə, -kī′-; *Heb.* shə khē nä′), *n.* *Theol.* Shekinah.

shed[1] (shed), *n.* **1.** a slight or rude structure built for shelter, storage, etc. **2.** a large, strongly built structure, often open at the sides or end. [OE *sced,* var. of *scead* SHADE, shelter]

shed[2] (shed), *v.,* **shed, shed·ding,** *n.* **—***v.t.* **1.** to pour forth (water or other liquid), as a fountain. **2.** to emit and let fall, as tears. **3.** to impart or release; give or send forth (light, sound, fragrance, influence, etc.). **4.** to resist being penetrated or affected by: *cloth that sheds water.* **5.** to cast off or let fall (leaves, hair, feathers, skin, shell, etc.) by natural process. **6.** *Textiles.* to separate (the warp) in forming a shed. **—***v.i.* **7.** to fall off, as leaves. **8.** to drop out, as hair, seed, or grain. **9.** to cast off hair, feathers, skin, or other covering or parts by natural process. **10. shed blood, a.** to cause blood to flow. **b.** to kill by violence; slaughter. **—***n.* **11.** *Textiles.* (on a loom) a triangular, transverse opening created between raised and lowered warp threads through which the shuttle passes in depositing the loose pick. [ME; OE *scēad(an),* var. of *scēadan;* c. G *scheiden* to divide] **—shed′a·ble, shed′da·ble,** *adj.* **—Syn. 3.** emit, radiate, spread. **4.** repel. **9.** molt.

she'd (shēd), **1.** contraction of *she had.* **2.** contraction of *she would.*

shed·der (shed′ər), *n.* **1.** a person or thing that sheds. **2.** a lobster, crab, etc., just before it molts. [ME]

she-dev·il (shē′dev′il, -dev′-), *n.* a woman who resembles a devil, as in extreme wickedness, cruelty, or bad temper.

shed′ roof′, a roof having a single slope. Also called **penthouse.**

Shee·ler (shē′lər), *n.* **Charles,** 1883–1965, U.S. painter.

sheen (shēn), *n.* **1.** luster; brightness; radiance. **2.** gleaming attire. **—***adj. Archaic.* **3.** shining. **4.** beautiful. [ME *sheene,* OE *scēne* beautiful; c. G *schön*] **—sheen′ful,** *adj.* **—Syn. 1.** See **polish.**

Sheen (shēn), *n.* **Fulton (John),** 1895–1979, U.S. Roman Catholic clergyman, writer, and teacher.

shee·ney (shē′nē), *n., pl.* **-neys.** *Offensive.* sheeny[2].

sheen·y[1] (shē′nē), *adj.,* **sheen·i·er, sheen·i·est.** shining; lustrous. [SHEEN + -Y[1]]

shee·ny[2] (shē′nē), *n., pl.* **shee·nies.** *Offensive.* a Jew. Also, **sheeney, shee′nie.** [?]

sheep (shēp), *n., pl.* **sheep. 1.** any of numerous ruminant mammals of the genus *Ovis,* of the family *Bovidae,* closely related to the goats, esp. *O. aries,* bred in a number of domesticated varieties. **2.** leather made from the skin of these animals. **3.** a meek, unimaginative, or easily led person. [ME; OE (north) *scēp;* c. D *schaap,* G *Schaf*]

sheep·ber·ry (shēp′ber′ē, -bə rē), *n., pl.* **-ries. 1.** a caprifoliaceous shrub or small tree, *Viburnum Lentago,* of North America, having cymes of small white flowers and edible, berrylike black drupes. **2.** the fruit itself.

sheep·cote (shēp′kōt′), *n.* *Chiefly Brit.* a pen or covered enclosure for sheep.

sheep-dip (shēp′dip′), *n.* *Vet. Med.* a lotion or wash applied to the fleece or skin of sheep to kill vermin.

sheep·dog (shēp′dôg′, -dog′), *n.* a dog trained to herd and guard sheep. Also, **sheep′ dog′.**

sheep·fold (shēp′fōld′), *n.* *Chiefly Brit.* an enclosure for sheep. [ME; OE *sceapa falde*]

sheep·head (shēp′hed′), *n., pl.* (*esp. collectively*) **-head,** (*esp. referring to two or more kinds or species*) **-heads.** a large California food fish, *Pimelometopon pulchrum,* of the wrasse family. [so called from the resemblance of its teeth to those of a sheep]

sheep·herd·er (shēp′hûr′dər), *n.* shepherd (def. 1). **—sheep′herd′ing,** *n., adj.*

sheep·ish (shē′pish), *adj.* **1.** embarrassed, as by having done something wrong or foolish. **2.** like sheep, as in meekness or docility. [ME *shepisshe*] **—sheep′ish·ly,** *adv.* **—sheep′ish·ness,** *n.*

sheep′ ked′ (ked). See **sheep tick.** [*ked,* earlier *cade* < ?]

sheep·man (shēp′mən, -man′), *n., pl.* **-men** (-mən, -men′). **1.** a man engaged in the tending or breeding of sheep, esp. the owner of a sheep ranch. **2.** a shepherd.

sheep's′ eyes′, shy, amorous, lovesick glances.

sheep·shank (shēp′shangk′), *n.* a kind of knot, hitch, or bend made on a rope to shorten it temporarily. [short for *sheepshank knot*]

sheeps·head (shēps′hed′), *n., pl.* (*esp. collectively*) **-head,** (*esp. referring to two or more kinds or species*) **-heads. 1.** a deep-bodied, black-banded food fish, *Archosargus probatocephalus,* found along the Atlantic coast of the U.S. **2.** a fresh-water drum, *Aplodinotus grunniens,* found in eastern North America. **3.** sheephead.

sheep·shear·ing (shēp′shēr′ing), *n.* **1.** the act of shearing sheep. **2.** the time or season of shearing sheep. **3.** a festival held at this time. **—sheep′shear′er,** *n.*

sheep·skin (shēp′skin′), *n.* **1.** the skin of a sheep, esp. such a skin dressed with the wool on, as for a garment. **2.** leather, parchment, or the like, made from the skin of sheep. **3.** *Informal.* a diploma. [ME *shepskinn*]

sheep′ sor′rel, a slender, polygonaceous weed, *Rumex Acetosella,* having hastate leaves with an acid taste.

sheep′ tick′, a wingless, bloodsucking dipterous insect, *Melophagus ovinus,* that is parasitic on sheep. Also called **sheep ked.** [late ME *scheptyke*]

sheer[1] (shēr), *adj.* **1.** transparently thin, as some fabrics; diaphanous: *sheer stockings.* **2.** unmixed with anything else: *We drilled a hundred feet through sheer rock.* **3.** unqualified; utter: *sheer nonsense.* **4.** very steep; almost completely vertical: *a sheer descent of rock.* **—***adv.* **5.** clear; completely; quite: *ran sheer into the thick of battle.* **6.** perpendicularly; vertically; very steeply. **—***n.* **7.** a thin, diaphanous material, as chiffon or voile. [ME *scere;* OE *scēr* clear, undisputed (in legal context); c. Icel *skǣrr;* akin to OE *scīr,* Icel *skīrr,* G *schier,* Goth *skeirs* clear] **—sheer′ly,** *adv.* **—sheer′ness,** *n.* **—Syn. 2.** unadulterated. **3.** absolute. **4.** abrupt, precipitous. **—Ant. 1.** opaque.

sheer[2] (shēr), *v.i.* **1.** to deviate from a course, as a ship; swerve. **—***v.t.* **2.** to cause to sheer. **—***n.* **3.** a deviation, or divergence, as of a ship from her course; swerve. **4.** the fore-and-aft upward curve of the hull of a vessel at the main deck or bulwarks. **5.** the position in which a ship at anchor is placed to keep her clear of the anchor. [from SHEER[1]; cf. sense development of CLEAR]

sheer·legs (shēr′legz′), *n.* (*usually construed as pl.*) See **shear legs.**

Sheer·ness (shēr′nis), *n.* a seaport in N Kent, in SE England, at the mouth of the Thames. 14,123 (1961).

sheer′ plan′, *Naval Archit.* a diagrammatic fore-and-aft elevation of the hull of a vessel. Also called **profile plan.** Cf. **body plan, half-breadth plan.**

sheers (shērs), *n.* shear (def. 15).

sheet[1] (shēt), *n.* **1.** a large rectangular piece of linen, cotton, or other material used as an article of bedding. **2.** a broad, relatively thin surface, layer, or covering: *a sheet of ice.* **3.** a relatively thin, usually rectangular form, piece, plate, or slab, as of photographic film, glass, or metal. **4.** material, as metal or glass, in the form of broad, relatively thin pieces. **5.** a sail, as on a ship or boat. **6.** a rectangular piece of paper or parchment. **7.** *Informal.* a newspaper or periodical. **8.** *Printing and Bookbinding.* a large, rectangular piece of printing paper, esp. one for printing a complete signature. **9.** *Philately.* the impression from a plate or the like on a single sheet of paper before any division of the paper into individual stamps. **10.** an extent, stretch, or expanse, as of fire, water, etc.: *sheets of flame.* **11.** *Geol.* a more or less horizontal mass of rock, esp. eruptive rock intruded between strata or spread over a surface. **—*v.t.* 12.** to furnish with a sheet or sheets. **13.** to wrap in a sheet. **14.** to cover with a sheet or layer of something. [ME *shete,* OE *scēte* (north), *sciete* < *scēat* corner, lap, sheet, etc.; c. D *schoot,* G *Schoss,* Icel *skaut*]

sheet[2] (shēt), *n.* **1.** *Naut.* **a.** a rope or chain for extending the clews of a square sail along a yard. **b.** a rope for trimming a fore-and-aft sail. **c.** a rope or chain for extending the lee clew of a course. **2. three sheets in** or **to the wind,** *Slang.* drunk. **—*v.t.* 3.** *Naut.* to trim, extend, or secure by means of a sheet or sheets. [ME *shete,* OE *scēatlīne* = *scēat(a)* lower corner of a sail (see SHEET[1]) + *līne* line, rope; c. LG *schote*]

sheet′ an′chor, **1.** *Naut.* a large anchor used only in cases of emergency. **2.** a final reliance or resource.

sheet′ bend′, a knot made between two ropes by forming a bight in one and passing the end of the other through the bight, around it, and under itself. Also called **weaver's hitch, weaver's knot.**

sheet′ glass′, glass in sheet form produced by drawing or by the cylinder-glass process.

sheet·ing (shē′ting), *n.* **1.** the act of covering with or forming into a sheet or sheets. **2.** wide muslin, chiefly for sheets.

sheet′ light′ning, lightning appearing merely as a general illumination over a broad surface, usually due to the reflection of the lightning of a distant thunderstorm.

sheet′ met′al, metal in sheets or thin plates.

sheet′ mu′sic, music, usually for popular songs, printed on unbound sheets of paper.

Shef·field (shef′ēld), *n.* a city in S Yorkshire, in N England. 493,954 (1961).

she·getz (shā′gits), *n., pl.* **shkotz·im** (shkôt′sim). *Yiddish.* a boy or man who is not Jewish. Cf. **shiksa.**

sheik (shēk), *n.* (in Arab and other Muslim use) **1.** chief or head; the head man of a village or tribe. **2.** the head of a religious body. Also, **sheikh.** [< Ar *shaikh* old man]

sheik·dom (shēk′dəm), *n.* the land or territory under the control of a sheik. Also, **sheikh′dom.**

shek·el (shek′əl), *n.* **1.** an ancient, originally Babylonian, unit of weight, of varying value, taken as equal to the fiftieth or the sixtieth part of a mina or to about a quarter to half an ounce. **2.** a coin of this weight, esp. the chief silver coin of the Hebrews. **3. shekels,** *Slang.* money; cash. [< Heb *sheqel*]

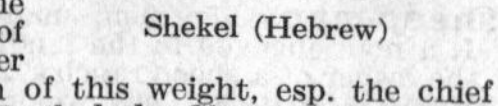
obverse reverse
Shekel (Hebrew)

She·ki·nah (shi kē′nə, -kī′-; *Heb.* shə KHē nä′), *n.* *Theol.* the presence of God on earth or a symbol or manifestation of His presence. Also, **Shechinah.** [< Heb]

shel·drake (shel′drāk′), *n., pl.* **-drakes,** (*esp. collectively*) **-drake. 1.** any of several Old World ducks of the genera *Tadorna* or *Casarca,* certain species of which have highly variegated plumage. **2.** any of various other ducks, esp. the merganser. [ME *sheldedrake* = *sheld* particolored (now obs.) + *drake* DRAKE[1]]

Sheldrake, *Tadorna tadorna* (Length 26 in.)

shelf (shelf), *n., pl.* **shelves** (shelvz). **1.** a thin slab of wood, metal, etc., fixed horizontally to a wall or in a frame, for supporting objects. **2.** the contents of this: *a shelf of books.* **3.** a surface or projection resembling this; ledge. **4.** a sandbank or submerged extent of rock in the sea or in a river. **5.** the bedrock underlying an alluvial deposit or the like. **6. on the shelf, a.** temporarily put aside; postponed. **b.** inactive; useless. [ME; OE *scylfe;* akin to LG *schelf* shelf, Icel *-skjalf* bench]

shelf′ ice′, ice forming part of or broken from an ice sheet.

shelf′ life′, the term or period during which a stored commodity remains effective, useful, or suitable for consumption.

shell (shel), *n.* **1.** a hard outer covering of an animal, as the hard case of a mollusk. **2.** any of various objects resembling such a covering, as in shape. **3.** the material constituting any of various coverings of this kind. **4.** the hard exterior of an egg. **5.** the usually hard, outer covering of a seed, fruit, etc. **6.** a hard, protecting or enclosing case or cover. **7.** (in a person) a reserved attitude or manner tending to conceal one's emotions, thoughts, etc.: *One could not penetrate his shell.* **8.** a hollow projectile for a cannon, mortar, etc., filled with an explosive charge designed to explode during flight, upon impact, or after penetration. **9.** a metallic cartridge used in small arms and small artillery pieces. **10.** a metal or paper cartridge, as for use in a shotgun. **11.** a cartridgelike pyrotechnic device that explodes in the air. **12.** *Cookery.* the lower pastry crust of a pie, tart, or the like, baked before the filling is added. **13.** *Physics.* **a.** any of several energy levels on which an electron may exist within an atom, the energies of the electrons on the same level being equal and on different levels being unequal. **b.** a group of nucleons of approximately the same energy. **14.** a light, long, narrow racing boat, for rowing by one or more persons. **15.** *Naut.* the plating, planking, or the like, covering the ribs and forming the exterior hull of a vessel. **16.** See **tortoise shell** (def. 1). **17.** a mollusk. **18.** an arena or stadium covered by a domed or arched roof. **19.** a saucer-shaped arena or stadium. **20.** the framework, external structure, or walls and roof of a building: *After the fire, only the shell of the school was left.* **21.** a small glass for beer. **22.** a woman's sleeveless blouse for wearing under a suit jacket. **—*v.t.* 23.** to take out of the shell, pod, etc.; remove the shell of. **24.** to separate (Indian corn, grain, etc.) from the ear, cob, or husk. **25.** to fire shells or explosive projectiles into, upon, or among; bombard. **—*v.i.* 26.** to fall or come out of the shell, husk, etc. **27.** to come away or fall off, as a shell or outer coat. **28. shell out,** *Slang.* to hand over (money); contribute; pay: *The people are being asked to shell out ten dollars for front-row seats.* [ME; OE *scell* (north), *sciell;* c. D *schil* peel, skin, rind, Icel *skel* shell, Goth *skalja* tile] **—shell′-less,** *adj.* **—shell′-like′,** *adj.*

Shell (def. 14)

she'll (shēl), **1.** contraction of *she will.* **2.** contraction of *she shall.*

shel·lac (shə lak′), *n., v.,* **-lacked, -lack·ing. —*n.* 1.** lac that has been purified and formed into thin sheets, used for making varnish. **2.** a varnish (**shellac′ var′nish**) made by dissolving this material in alcohol or a similar solvent. **3.** a phonograph record made of a breakable material containing shellac, esp. one to be played at 78 rpm. **—*v.t.* 4.** to coat or treat with shellac. **5.** *Slang.* **a.** to defeat; trounce. **b.** to thrash soundly. Also, **shel·lack′.** [SHELL + LAC[1], trans. of F *laque en écailles* lac in thin plates] **—shel·lack′er,** *n.*

shel·lack·ing (shə lak′ing), *n.* *Slang.* **1.** an utter defeat. **2.** a sound thrashing.

shell·back (shel′bak′), *n.* **1.** an old sailor. **2.** a person who has crossed the equator by boat.

shell·bark (shel′bärk′), *n.* the shagbark tree.

shell′ bean′, **1.** any of various kinds of bean grown for their unripe seeds, which are removed from the pods before cooking. **2.** the seed itself.

shell′ construc′tion, construction, esp. in reinforced concrete, formed of very thin, curved surfaces, most frequently in the form of vaults or symmetrical cantilevered constructions about columns.

shelled (sheld), *adj.* **1.** having the shell removed: *shelled pecans.* **2.** (esp. of field corn, grain, etc.) removed from the ear or husk: *shelled peas.* **3.** having or enclosed in a shell.

Shel·ley (shel′ē), *n.* **1. Mary Woll·stone·craft (Godwin)** (wŏŏl′stən kraft′, -kräft′), 1797–1851, English author (wife of Percy Bysshe Shelley). **2. Percy Bysshe** (bish), 1792–1822, English poet.

shell·fire (shel′fīər′), *n.* *Mil.* the firing of explosive shells or projectiles.

shell·fish (shel′fish′), *n., pl.* (*esp. collectively*) **-fish,** (*esp. referring to two or more kinds or species*) **-fish·es. 1.** an aquatic animal having a shell, as the oyster and other mollusks and the lobster and other crustaceans. **2.** a trunkfish. [ME; OE *scilfisc*]

shell′ game′, **1.** a sleight-of-hand swindling game resembling thimblerig but employing walnut shells or the like instead of cups. **2.** any deceit, swindle, fraud, or the like.

shell′ jack′et, a close-fitting, semiformal jacket, with a short back, worn in the tropics in place of a tuxedo.

shell′ shock′, *Psychiatry.* any of various nervous or mental disorders resulting from the cumulative emotional and psychological strain of warfare. **—shell′-shocked′, shell′shocked′,** *adj.*

shell·y (shel′ē), *adj.,* **shell·i·er, shell·i·est. 1.** abounding in shells: *a shelly surf.* **2.** consisting of a shell or shells. **3.** like a shell or shells.

shel·ter (shel′tər), *n.* **1.** something beneath, behind, or within which a person, animal, or thing is protected, as from storms, missiles, etc.; refuge. **2.** the protection or refuge afforded by such a thing: *He took shelter in a nearby barn.* **3.** a dwelling place or home considered as a refuge from the elements. **—*v.t.* 4.** to be a shelter for. **5.** to provide with a shelter; place under cover. **6.** to take under one's protection; shield. **—*v.i.* 7.** to take shelter; find a refuge. [? var. of obs. *sheltron* testudo, OE *scieldtruma* = *scield* SHIELD + *truma* body of fighting men; see TRIM] **—shel′ter·er,** *n.* **—shel′ter·less,** *adj.* **—Syn. 1.** retreat, asylum, sanctuary.

shel′ter tent′, a small, two-man, military tent consisting of two halves (**shel′ter halves′**) buttoned or tied together, held up by accessory ropes and poles. Also called **pup tent.**

Shel·ton (shel′tən), *n.* a city in SW Connecticut. 27,165 (1970).

shel·ty (shel′tē), *n., pl.* **-ties. 1.** See **Shetland pony. 2.** See **Shetland sheepdog.** Also, **shel′tie.** [*shelt* (< Scand; cf. Icel *hjaltr* native of SHETLAND) + -Y[2]]

shelve[1] (shelv), *v.t.,* **shelved, shelv·ing. 1.** to place (an object or objects) on a shelf or shelves. **2.** to put off or aside from consideration: *to shelve the question.* **3.** to remove from active use or service; dismiss. **4.** to furnish with shelves. [v. use of SHELVE(S)] **—shelv′er,** *n.*

shelve[2] (shelv), *v.i.,* **shelved, shelv·ing.** to slope gradually. [cf. WFris *skelf* not quite level]

shelves (shelvz), *n.* pl. of **shelf.**

shelv·ing (shel′ving), *n.* **1.** material for shelves. **2.** shelves collectively.

Shem (shem), *n.* the eldest of the three sons of Noah. Gen. 10:21.

Shem·ite (shem′īt), *n.* a Semite. **—Shem·it·ic** (she mit′ik), **Shem·it·ish** (shem′ī tish), *adj.*

Shen·an·do·ah (shen′ən dō′ə), *n.* **1.** a river flowing NE from N Virginia to the Potomac at Harpers Ferry, West Virginia. ab. 200 mi. long. **2.** a valley in N Virginia, between the Blue Ridge and Allegheny mountains: Civil War campaigns 1862–64.

Shen′ando′ah Na′tional Park′, a national park in N Virginia, including part of the Blue Ridge mountain range. 302 sq. mi.

she·nan·i·gan (shə nan′ə gən), *n.* *Informal.* **1.** nonsense; deceit; trickery. **2.** Usually, **shenanigans.** mischievous nonsense; prankishness. [?]

shend (shend), *v.t.,* **shent, shend·ing.** *Archaic.* **1.** to put to shame. **2.** to reproach or scold. **3.** to destroy or injure; damage. [ME; OE (*ge*)*scendan* (c. D *schenden,* G *schänden*) < *scand* shame, infamy]

Shen·si (shen′sē′; *Chin.* shun′shē′), *n.* a province in N China. 18,130,000 (est. 1957); 75,598 sq. mi. *Cap.:* Sian.

Shen·stone (shen′stən), *n.* **William,** 1714–63, English poet.

Shen·yang (shun′yäng′), *n.* Mukden.

She·ol (shē′ōl), *n.* (in Hebrew theology) **1.** the abode of the dead or of departed spirits. **2.** (*l.c.*) hell. [< Heb]

shep·herd (shep′ərd), *n.* **1.** a man who herds, tends, and guards sheep. **2.** a man who protects, guides, or watches over a person or group of people. **3.** a clergyman. **—***v.t.* **4.** to tend or guard as a shepherd: *to shepherd the flock.* **5.** to watch over carefully. **6.** to escort, guide, or direct. **7.** to counsel spiritually, as a clergyman. [ME *shepherde,* OE *scēphyrde.* See SHEEP, HERD[2]] **—shep′herd·less,** *adj.*

shep′herd dog′. See **sheep dog.**

shep·herd·ess (shep′ər dis), *n.* **1.** a girl or woman who herds sheep. **2.** a rural girl. [ME *shepherdesse*]

shep′herd's pie′, a baked dish of ground or diced meat with a crust of mashed potatoes.

shep·herd's-purse (shep′ərdz-pûrs′), *n.* a cruciferous weed, *Capsella Bursa-pastoris,* having white flowers and purselike pods.

Sher·a·ton (sher′ə tən, -tən), *n.* **1. Thomas,** 1751–1806, English cabinetmaker and furniture designer. **—***adj.* **2.** of the style of furniture designed by Sheraton.

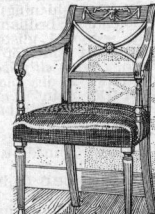

Sheraton chair

sher·bet (shûr′bit), *n.* **1.** a frozen fruit-flavored mixture, similar to an ice, but with milk, egg white, or gelatin added. **2.** *Brit.* a drink made of sweetened fruit juice diluted with water and ice. [< Turk < Pers *sherbat* < Ar *sharbah* a drink]

Sher·brooke (shûr′brŏŏk), *n.* a city in S Quebec, in SE Canada. 76,804.

sherd (shûrd), *n.* shard.

Sher·i·dan (sher′i dən, -dən), *n.* **1. Philip Henry,** 1831–88, Union general in the Civil War. **2. Richard Brins·ley** (brinz′lē), 1751–1816, Irish dramatist and political leader.

she·rif (she rēf′), *n.* **1.** a governor of Mecca descended from Muhammad. **2.** an Arab chief, prince, or ruler. Also, **sharif, shereef′.** [< Ar *sharīf* exalted (person)]

sher·iff (sher′if), *n.* **1.** *U.S.* the law-enforcement officer of a county or other civil subdivision of a state. **2.** (formerly) an important civil officer in an English shire. [ME *sher(r)ef,* OE *scīrgerēfa.* See SHIRE, REEVE[1]]

sher·lock (shûr′lok), *n.* *Informal.* **1.** a private detective. **2.** a person remarkably adept at solving mysteries, esp. by using logical deduction. Also, **Sher′lock.** [after *Sherlock* Holmes, fictitious detective in writings of Sir Arthur Conan Doyle]

Sher·man (shûr′mən), *n.* **1. James School·craft** (skōōl′kraft′, -kräft′), 1855–1912, vice president of the U.S. 1909–1912. **2. John,** 1823–1900, U.S. statesman (brother of William T.). **3. Roger,** 1721–93, American statesman. **4. William Tecumseh,** 1820–91, Union general in the Civil War. **5.** a city in NE Texas. 29,061 (1970).

Sher′man Antitrust′ Act′, an act of Congress (1890) prohibiting any contract, conspiracy, or combination of business interests in restraint of foreign or interstate trade. Cf. **Clayton Antitrust Act.** [named after John SHERMAN, its author]

Sher·pa (sher′pə, shûr′-), *n., pl.* **-pas,** (*esp. collectively*) **-pa.** a member of a people of Tibetan stock living in the Nepalese Himalayas, who often serve as porters on mountain-climbing expeditions.

sher·ry (sher′ē), *n., pl.* **-ries.** a fortified, amber-colored wine of southern Spain or any of various similar wines made elsewhere. [back formation from obs. *sherris* (the *-s* was mistaken for the plural sign) < Sp (*vino de*) *Xeres* (wine of) *Xeres* (now JEREZ)]

's Her·to·gen·bosch (ser′tō кнən bôs′), a city in the S Netherlands. 86,184. French, **Bois-le-Duc.**

Sher·wood (shûr′wŏŏd′), *n.* **Robert (Em·met)** (em′it), 1896–1955, U.S. dramatist.

Sher′wood For′est, an ancient royal forest in central England, chiefly in Nottinghamshire: the traditional home of Robin Hood.

she's (shēz), **1.** contraction of *she is.* **2.** contraction of *she has.*

Shet′land Is′lands (shet′lənd), an island group NE of the Orkney Islands, comprising a county of Scotland. 18,494 (1970); 550 sq. mi. *Co. seat:* Lerwick. Also called **Shetland, Zetland. —Shet′land Is′land·er.**

Shet′land po′ny, one of a breed of small but sturdy, rough-coated ponies, raised originally in the Shetland Islands. Also called **shelty.**

Shet′land sheep′dog (shēp′dôg′, -dog′), one of a breed of sheepdogs resembling a miniature collie, raised originally in the Shetland Islands. Also called **shelty.**

Shet′land wool′, **1.** the fine wool undercoat pulled by hand from Shetland sheep. **2.** thin, loosely twisted wool yarn for knitting or weaving.

Shetland pony (About 3 ft. high at shoulder)

sheugh (shŏŏкн), *n.* *Scot. and North Eng.* a furrow, ditch, or trench. Also, **sheuch** (shŏŏкн). [north var. of *sough* ditch, swamp, ME *sogh, sohn* < ?]

She·vat (shə vät′), *n.* Shebat.

shew (shō), *v.,* **shewed, shewn, shew·ing,** *n. Archaic.* show.

shew·bread (shō′bred′), *n.* *Judaism.* the bread placed in the holy of holies of the Biblical tabernacle and the Temple in Jerusalem by the priests as an offering to God. Ex. 25:30; Lev. 24:5–9. Also, **showbread.** [modeled on G *Schaubrot,* which renders Gk *ártoi enṓpioi,* trans. of Heb *lechem pānīm*]

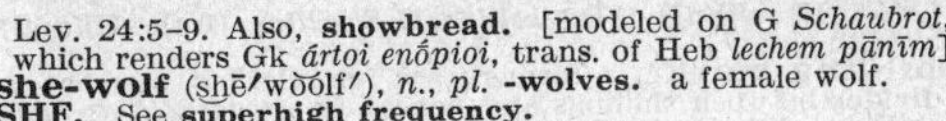

she-wolf (shē′wŏŏlf′), *n., pl.* **-wolves.** a female wolf.

SHF, See **superhigh frequency.**

shh (sh), *interj.* hush! be still! Also, **sh.**

Shi·ah (shē′ə), *n.* *Islam.* **1.** (*construed as pl.*) the Shiites. **2.** (*construed as sing.*) Shiite. [< Ar: lit., sect]

shi·at·su (shē ät′sōō), *n.* a method, originally Japanese, of treating bodily ills, fatigue, etc., by manual pressure applied at various points along the body. [< Japn *shi* finger + *atsu* pressure]

shi·bah (shē vä′; *Eng.* shiv′ə), *n.* *Hebrew, Judaism.* the mourning period, lasting traditionally for seven days, observed for a deceased parent or other close relative. Also, **shivah.** [lit., seven (days)]

shib·bo·leth (shib′ə lith, -leth′), *n.* **1.** a peculiarity of pronunciation, behavior, mode of dress, etc., which distinguishes a particular class or set of persons. **2.** a test word or pet phrase of a party, sect, etc. **3.** a word used by the Gileadites to distinguish the fleeing Ephraimites, who could not pronounce the sound *sh.* Judges 12:4–6. [< Heb: freshet]

shied (shīd), *v.* pt. and pp. of **shy.**

shield (shēld), *n.* **1.** a broad piece of armor, varying in form and size, carried apart from the body, usually on the left arm, as a defense against swords, lances, arrows, etc. **2.** something shaped like such a piece of armor, variously round, octagonal, triangular, or somewhat heart-shaped. **3.** a person or thing that protects. **4.** a policeman's, detective's, or sheriff's badge. **5.** *Ordn.* a steel screen attached to a gun to protect its crew, mechanism, etc **6.** a movable framework for protecting a miner at the place at which he is working. **7.** *Zool.* a protective plate or the like on the body of an animal, as a scute, enlarged scale, etc. **8.** See **dress shield. 9.** *Heraldry.* an escutcheon, esp. one broad at the top and pointed at the bottom, for displaying armorial bearings. **—***v.t.* **10.** to protect (someone or something) with or as with a shield. **11.** to hide or conceal; protect by hiding. **—***v.i.* **12.** to act or serve as a shield. [ME *shelde* OE *sceld*] **—shield′er,** *n.* **—shield′less,** *adj.* **—shield′like′,** *adj.*

Shield′ of Da′vid. See **Star of David.**

shiel·ing (shē′ling), *n.* *Scot.* a pasture or grazing ground. [Scot *shiel* pasture (ME *schele,* OE (north) **scēla;* c. Icel *skāli* hut, shed; akin to OE *scyr* hut, Icel *skūrr*]

shi·er[1] (shī′ər), *adj.* a comparative of **shy**[1].

shi·er[2] (shī′ər), *n.* a horse having a tendency to shy. Also, **shyer.** [SHY[1] + -ER[1]]

shi·est (shī′ist), *adj.* a superlative of **shy**[1].

shift (shift), *v.i.* **1.** to move from one place, position, direction, etc., to another. **2.** to manage by oneself (usually fol. by *for*). **3.** to get along by indirect methods. **4.** to change gears in driving an automobile. **5.** *Linguistics.* to undergo a systematic phonetic change. **—***v.t.* **6.** to put (something) aside and replace it by another or others; change or exchange. **7.** to transfer from one place, position, direction, person, etc., to another. **8.** *Auto.* to change (gears) from one ratio or arrangement to another. **9.** *Linguistics.* to change phonetically and in a systematic way. **—***n.* **10.** a change or transfer from one place, position, direction, person, etc., to another: *a shift in the wind.* **11.** a person's scheduled period of work: *the day shift.* **12.** a group of workers scheduled to work during such a period. **13.** *Auto.* a gearshift. **14.** *Clothing.* a straight, loose-fitting dress for women's wear with or without a belt. **15.** *Mining.* a dislocation of a seam or stratum; fault. **16.** *Music.* a change in hand position on the finger board of a stringed instrument. **17.** *Linguistics.* a change or system of parallel changes that affects the sound structure of a language. **18.** an expedient, evasion, artifice, or trick; ingenious device. **19.** change or substitution. **20.** *Archaic.* a woman's chemise or slip. [ME *shift(en),* OE *sciftan;* c. G *schichten* to arrange in order, Icel *skipta* to divide] **—shift′ing·ly,** *adv.* **—shift′ing·ness,** *n.* **—Syn. 18.** resort; wile, ruse, subterfuge, stratagem.

shift′ key′, a typewriter key that raises the carriage or lowers the typebar section, causing the character on the top half of the type face to print.

shift·less (shift′lis), *adj.* **1.** lacking in resourcefulness; inefficient. **2.** lacking in incentive, ambition, or aspiration; lazy. **—shift′less·ly,** *adv.* **—shift′less·ness,** *n.*

shift·y (shif′tē), *adj.,* **shift·i·er, shift·i·est. 1.** given to or full of evasions; tricky. **2.** suggesting a deceptive or evasive character: *a shifty look.* **3.** resourceful. **—shift′i·ly,** *adv.* **—shift′i·ness,** *n.*

Shi·ite (shē′īt), *n.* *Islam.* a member of one of the two great religious divisions of Islam, regarding Ali, the son-in-law of Muhammad, as the legitimate successor of Muhammad, and disregarding the three caliphs who actually did succeed him. Also, **Shiah, Shi·i** (shē ē′, shē′ē). Cf. **Sunnite.** [SHI(AH) + -ITE[1]] **—Shi·ism** (shē′iz əm), *n.* **—Shi·it·ic** (shē it′ik), *adj.*

shi·kar (shi kär′), *n., v.,* **-karred, -kar·ring.** (in India) **—***n.* **1.** the hunting of game for sport. **—***v.t., v.i.* **2.** to hunt. [< Urdu < Pers]

shi·ka·ri (shi kär′ē), *n., pl.* **-ris.** (in India) a person who hunts big game, esp. a professional guide or hunter. Also, **shi·ka′ree.** [< Urdu < Pers]

Shi·ko·ku (shē′kô kōō′), *n.* an island in SW Japan, S of Honshu: the smallest of the main islands of Japan. 3,904,014; 7249 sq. mi.

shik·sa (shik′sə), *n.* *Yiddish.* a girl or woman who is not Jewish.

shill[1] (shil), *n.* *Slang.* a person who poses as a customer in order to decoy others into participating, as at a gambling house, auction, etc. [?]

shill[2] (shil), *adj.* *Archaic.* shrill. [ME; OE *scyl* resonant]

shil·le·lagh (shə lā′lē, -lə), *n.* *Chiefly Irish Eng.* a cudgel, traditionally of blackthorn or oak. Also, **shil·la′la, shil·la′lah, shil·le′lah.** [after Irish town so named]

shil·ling (shil′ing), *n.* **1.** a cupronickel coin of the United Kingdom, the 20th part of a pound, equal to 12 pence: use phased out in 1971. *Abbr.:* s. **2.** a former fractional currency of various other nations and territories, as Ireland, Jamaica, Nigeria, etc., equal to one twentieth of a pound or 12 pence. **3.** the monetary unit of Kenya, Somalia, Tanzania, and Uganda.

[ME; OE *scilling;* c. D *schelling,* G *Schilling,* Goth *skillings;* akin to SHILL²]

shil′ling mark′, (formerly) a virgule, as used as a divider between shillings and pence: *One reads 2/6 as "two shillings and sixpence" or "two and six."*

Shil·long (shil lông′), *n.* a city in and the capital of Assam, in NE India: resort. 72,400 (1961).

shil·ly-shal·ly (shil′ē shal′ē), *v.,* **-lied, -ly·ing,** *n., pl.* **-shal·lies,** *adj., adv.* **—*v.i.*** **1.** to be irresolute; vacillate. **—*n.*** **2.** irresolution; indecision; vacillation. **—*adj.*** **3.** irresolute; undecided; vacillating. **—*adv.*** **4.** irresolutely. [orig. repeated question, *shall I? shall I?* later altered on the model of its synonym *dilly-dally*]

Shi·loh (shī′lō), *n.* **1.** a national park in SW Tennessee: Civil War battle 1862. **2.** an ancient town in central Palestine, in Israeli-occupied Jordan.

shil·pit (shil′pit), *adj. Scot.* **1.** (of a person) sickly; puny; feeble. **2.** (of liquor) weak; watery. [?]

shim (shim), *n., v.,* **shimmed, shim·ming.** **—*n.*** **1.** a thin slip or wedge of metal, wood, etc., for driving into crevices, as between machine parts to compensate for wear. **—*v.t.*** **2.** to fill out or bring to a level by inserting a shim or shims. [?]

shim·mer (shim′ər), *v.i.* **1.** to shine with or reflect a subdued, tremulous light; glimmer. **2.** to appear to quiver or vibrate in faint light or while reflecting heat waves. **—*n.*** **3.** a subdued, tremulous light or gleam. **4.** a quivering or vibrating motion or image as produced by reflecting faint light or heat waves. [ME *schimere,* OE *scimri(an);* c. D *schemeren,* G *schimmern* to glisten] **—shim′mer·ing·ly,** *adv.* **—Syn. 1.** See **glisten.**

shim·mer·y (shim′ə rē), *adj.* shimmering; shining softly.

shim·my (shim′ē), *n., pl.* **-mies,** *v.,* **-mied, -my·ing.** **—*n.*** **1.** an American ragtime dance marked by shaking of the hips and shoulders. **2.** wobbling in the front wheels of a motor vehicle. **3.** *Informal.* a chemise. **—*v.i.*** **4.** to dance the shimmy. **5.** to shake, wobble, or vibrate. [back formation from *shimmies* (var. of CHEMISE), mistaken for a plural]

Shi·mo·no·se·ki (shim′ə nə sä′kē; *Jap.* shē′mô nô se′kē), *n.* a seaport on SW Honshu, in SW Japan: treaty ending Sino-Japanese War signed 1895. 252,527 (1964).

shin¹ (shin), *n., v.,* **shinned, shin·ning.** **—*n.*** **1.** the front part of the leg from the knee to the ankle. **2.** the lower part of the foreleg in cattle; the metacarpal bone. **3.** the shinbone or tibia, esp. its sharp edge or front portion. **4.** *Chiefly Brit.* a cut of beef similar to the U.S. shank. **—*v.t., v.i.*** **5.** to climb by holding fast with the hands or arms and legs and drawing oneself up. [ME *shine,* OE *scin(u);* c. D *scheen,* G *Schien(bein)*]

shin² (shin; *Heb.* shēn), *n.* the 22nd letter of the Hebrew alphabet. [< Heb]

shin·bone (shin′bōn′), *n.* the tibia. [ME; OE *scinbān*]

shin·dig (shin′dig′), *n. Informal.* an elaborate or large dance, party, or other celebration. [? SHIN¹ + DIG; cf. slang *shinscraper* dance]

shin·dy (shin′dē), *n., pl.* **-dies.** *Informal.* **1.** a row; rumpus. **2.** *U.S.* a shindig. [var. of SHINDIG]

shine (shīn), *v.,* **shone** or, esp. for 7, 8, **shined; shin·ing;** *n.* **—*v.i.*** **1.** to give forth or glow with light; shed or cast light. **2.** to be bright with reflected light; glisten; sparkle. **3.** (of light) to appear brightly or strongly, esp. uncomfortably so. **4.** to appear with brightness or clearness, as feelings. **5.** to be or appear unusually animated, as the eyes or the face. **6.** to excel or be conspicuous. **—*v.t.*** **7.** to cause to shine. **8.** to direct the light of (a lamp, mirror, etc.). **9.** to put a gloss or polish on; polish. **10. shine up to,** *Slang.* to attempt to impress (a person), esp. for personal gain. **—*n.*** **11.** radiance or brightness caused by emitted or reflected light. **12.** luster; polish. **13.** sunshine; fair weather. **14.** a polish or gloss given to shoes. **15.** the act or an instance of polishing shoes. **16. take a shine to,** *U.S. Informal.* to take a liking or fancy to. [ME; OE *scīn(an);* c. D *schijnen,* G *scheinen,* Icel *skīna,* Goth *skeinan*] **—Syn. 1.** glimmer, shimmer. SHINE, BEAM, GLARE refer to the emitting or reflecting of light. SHINE refers to a steady glowing or reflecting of light: *to shine in the sun.* That which BEAMS gives forth a radiant or bright light: *to beam like a star.* GLARE refers to the shining of a light that is so strong as to be unpleasant and dazzling: *to glare like a headlight.* **9.** buff, burnish, brighten. **12.** gloss, sheen.

shin·er (shī′nər), *n.* **1.** a person or thing that shines. **2.** *Slang.* See **black eye** (def. 1). **3.** any of various small, American, fresh-water fishes having glistening scales, esp. a minnow. **4.** any of various silvery, marine fishes, as the menhaden or butterfish.

shin·gle¹ (shiŋ′gəl), *n., v.,* **-gled, -gling.** **—*n.*** **1.** a thin piece of wood, slate, metal, asbestos, or the like, usually oblong, laid in overlapping rows to cover the roofs and walls of buildings. **2.** a close-cropped haircut. **3.** *Informal.* a small signboard, esp. as hung before a doctor's or lawyer's office. **—*v.t.*** **4.** to cover with shingles, as a roof. **5.** to cut (hair) close to the head. [ME, var. of *shindle* < LL *scindula* alter. of L *scandula* = *scand-* split, scatter, c. Gk *skedánnȳnai,* E SCATTER, SHATTER + *-ula* -ULE] **—shin′gler,** *n.*

shin·gle² (shiŋ′gəl), *n. Chiefly Brit.* **1.** small, water-worn stones or pebbles such as lie in loose sheets or beds on the seashore. **2.** a beach, riverbank, or other area covered with such small stones or pebbles. [sandhi var. of earlier *chingle;* cf. Norw *singel* small stones]

shin·gle³ (shiŋ′gəl), *v.t.,* **-gled, -gling.** *Metalworking.* to hammer or squeeze (puddled iron) into a bloom or billet, eliminating as much slag as possible. [< F *cingle(r)* (to) whip, beat < G *zängeln* < *Zange* tongs]

shin·gles (shiŋ′gəlz), *n.* (*construed as sing. or pl.*) *Pathol.* a disease of the skin affecting the posterior roots of the peripheral nerves, caused by a virus, and characterized by clusters of blisters. Also called **herpes zoster, zoster.** [< medical L *cingul(um)* (lit., a girdle, belt) trans. of Gk *zōnē* ZONE in its medical sense; English form expresses plurality of eruptions (cf. MEASLES)]

shin·gly (shiŋ′glē), *adj.* consisting of or covered with shingle or small, loose stones or pebbles.

shin′ guard′, *Sports.* a padded protective covering for the shins and sometimes the knees, worn chiefly by catchers in baseball and goalkeepers in ice hockey.

shin·ing (shī′niŋ), *adj.* **1.** radiant; gleaming; bright. **2.** resplendent; brilliant. **3.** conspicuously fine. **—shin′ing·ly,** *adv.* **—Syn. 1.** glistening, effulgent. See **bright. 2.** lustrous.

shin·leaf (shin′lēf′), *n., pl.* **-leaves. 1.** a North American herb, *Pyrola elliptica,* having leaves used formerly for shinplasters. **2.** any plant of the genus *Pyrola.*

shin·ny¹ (shin′ē), *n., pl.* **-nies. 1.** a simple variety of hockey, played with a ball, block of wood, or the like, and clubs curved at one end. **2.** the club used in this game. [? var. of *shin ye,* cry used in the game]

shin·ny² (shin′ē), *v.i.,* **-nied, -ny·ing.** to shin. [SHIN¹ + *-y* of HURRY]

shin·plas·ter (shin′plas′tər, -plä′stər), *n.* **1.** a plaster for the shin or leg. **2.** *U.S.* (formerly) **a.** a piece of paper money of a denomination lower than one dollar. **b.** greatly depreciated currency; money of little value.

Shin·to (shin′tō), *n.* **1.** Also called **Shin′to·ism.** the native religion of Japan, primarily a system of nature and ancestor worship. **—*adj.*** **2.** Also, **Shin′to·is′tic.** of, pertaining to, or characteristic of Shinto. [< Jap < Chin *shên tao* way of the gods] **—Shin′to·ist,** *n., adj.*

shin·y (shī′nē), *adj.,* **shin·i·er, shin·i·est. 1.** bright or glossy in appearance. **2.** filled with light, as by sunshine. **3.** rubbed or worn to a glossy smoothness, as clothes. **—shin′i·ly,** *adv.* **—shin′i·ness,** *n.*

ship (ship), *n., v.,* **shipped, ship·ping.** **—*n.*** **1.** a vessel, esp. a large ocean-going one propelled by sails or engines. **2.** *Naut.* a sailing vessel square-rigged on all of three or more masts, having jibs, staysails, and a spanker. **3.** the crew of a vessel. **4.** an airship or airplane. **—*v.t.*** **5.** to put or take on board a ship or other means of transportation. **6.** to send or transport by ship, rail, truck, plane, etc. **7.** *Naut.* to take in (water) over the side. **8.** to bring (an object) into a ship or boat: *to ship oars.* **9.** to engage (someone) for service on a ship. **10.** to fix in a ship or boat in the proper place for use. **11.** *Informal.* to send away. **—*v.i.*** **12.** to go on board or travel by ship; embark. **13.** to engage to serve on a ship. **14. ship out, a.** to leave a country, esp. one's native country, by or as by ship. **b.** to send (someone) to another country, esp. from his native country, by or as by ship. **c.** *Informal.* to quit, resign, or be fired from a job. [ME, OE *scip;* c. D *schip,* G *Schiff,* Icel, Goth *skip*]

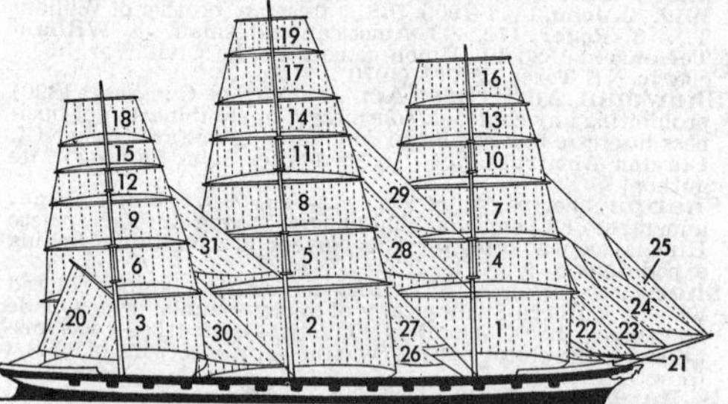

Ship (Full-rigged)
1, Foresail or forecourse; 2, Mainsail or main course; 3, Crossjack or mizzen course; 4, Fore lower topsail; 5, Main lower topsail; 6, Mizzen lower topsail; 7, Fore upper topsail; 8, Main upper topsail; 9, Mizzen upper topsail; 10, Fore lower topgallant; 11, Main lower topgallant; 12, Mizzen lower topgallant; 13, Fore upper topgallant; 14, Main upper topgallant; 15, Mizzen upper topgallant; 16, Fore royal; 17, Main royal; 18, Mizzen royal; 19, Skysail; 20, Spanker; 21, Fore staysail; 22, Jib; 23, Inner jib; 24, Outer jib; 25, Flying jib; 26, Main staysail; 27, Main topmast staysail; 28, Main topgallant staysail; 29, Main royal staysail; 30, Mizzen staysail; 31, Mizzen topgallant staysail

-ship, a native English suffix of nouns denoting condition, character, office, skill, etc.: *clerkship; friendship; statesmanship.* [ME, OE *-scipe;* akin to SHAPE; c. WFris, WFlem *schip*]

ship′ bis′cuit, hardtack. Also called **ship′ bread′.**

ship·board (ship′bōrd′, -bôrd′), *adj.* **1.** done, conducted, or designed for use aboard ship, esp. during an ocean voyage: *a shipboard telephone.* **—*n.*** **2.** *Archaic.* **a.** the deck or side of a ship. **b.** the situation of being on a ship. **3. on shipboard,** aboard a seagoing vessel. [late ME *shipbord* (see SHIP, BOARD); r. ME *shipesbord*]

ship·build·er (ship′bil′dər), *n.* **1.** a person whose occupation is the designing or constructing of ships. **2.** a commercial firm for building ships. **—ship′build′ing,** *n.*

ship′ canal′, a canal navigable by ships.

ship′ chan′dler, a person who deals in cordage, canvas, and other supplies for ships. **—ship′ chan′dlery.**

Ship′ka Pass′ (ship′kä), a mountain pass in central Bulgaria, in the Balkan Mountains. 4375 ft. high.

ship·lap (ship′lap′), *n. Carpentry.* **1.** an overlapping joint, as a rabbet, between two boards joined edge to edge. **2.** boarding joined with such joints. See illus. at **siding.**

ship·load (ship′lōd′), *n.* the cargo or load carried by a ship.

ship·man (ship′mən), *n., pl.* **-men.** *Archaic.* **1.** a sailor. **2.** the master of a ship. [ME, OE *scipman;* c. MD *schipman*]

ship·mas·ter (ship′mas′tər, -mä′stər), *n.* a person who commands a ship; master; captain. [ME *schipmaster;* c. G *Schiffmeister*]

ship·mate (ship′māt′), *n.* a person who serves with another on the same vessel.

ship·ment (ship′mənt), *n.* **1.** the act or an instance of shipping freight or cargo. **2.** a quantity of freight or cargo shipped at one time. **3.** that which is shipped.

ship′ mon′ey, *Early Eng. Law.* a tax levied on ports, maritime towns, etc., to provide support for the royal navy.

ship′ of the line′, (formerly) a sailing warship armed powerfully enough to serve in the line of battle, usually having cannons ranged along two or more decks; battleship.

ship·pa·ble (ship′ə bəl), *adj.* being in a suitable form or condition for shipping.

ship·per (ship′ər), *n.* a person who ships goods or makes shipments.

ship·ping (ship′ing), *n.* **1.** the act or business of a person or thing that ships. **2.** a number of ships, esp. merchant ships, taken as a whole; tonnage.

ship′ping clerk′, a clerk who attends to the packing, unpacking, receiving, sending out, and recording of shipments.

ship′ping room′, a place in a business concern where goods are packed and shipped.

ship′ping ton′. See under **ton**[1] (def. 5).

ship-rigged (ship′rigd′), *adj. Naut.* (of a sailing vessel) rigged as a ship; full-rigged.

ship's′ boy′, a male attendant, as a cabin boy, steward, etc., employed to wait on a ship's passengers or officers.

ship·shape (ship′shāp′), *adj.* **1.** in good order; well-arranged; trim or tidy. —*adv.* **2.** in a shipshape manner.

ship·side (ship′sīd′), *n.* the area alongside a ship, as on a pier. [ME]

ship's′ pa′pers, the documents legally required to be carried by an ocean-going vessel and usually consisting of a certificate of registry, logbook, cargo manifest, bills of lading, etc.

ship·way (ship′wā′), *n.* **1.** the structure that supports a ship being built. **2.** a ship canal.

ship·worm (ship′wûrm′), *n.* any of various marine bivalve mollusks that burrow into the timbers of ships, wharves, etc.

ship·wreck (ship′rek′), *n.* **1.** the destruction or loss of a ship, as by sinking. **2.** the remains of a wrecked ship. **3.** destruction or ruin. —*v.t.* **4.** to cause to suffer shipwreck. **5.** to destroy; ruin. —*v.i.* **6.** to suffer shipwreck. [r. ME *ship wrech,* OE *scipwræc]

ship·wright (ship′rīt′), *n. Shipbuilding.* a person who builds and launches wooden vessels or does carpentry work in connection with the building and launching of steel or iron vessels. [ME, OE *scipwyrhta*]

ship·yard (ship′yärd′), *n.* a yard or enclosure in which ships are built or repaired.

Shi·raz (shē räz′), *n.* a city in SW Iran. 269,278 (est. 1967).

shire (shīər), *n.* **1.** one of the counties of Great Britain. **2. the Shires,** the counties in the Midlands in which hunting is especially popular. [ME; OE *scīr* office of administration, jurisdiction of such an office, county]

Shi·ré (shē′rā), *n.* a river in SE Africa, flowing S from Lake Nyasa to the Zambezi River. 370 mi. long.

shire′ horse′, one of an English breed of large, strong draft horses, usually brown or bay with white markings.

shirk (shûrk), *v.t.* **1.** to evade (work, duty, responsibility, etc.). —*v.i.* **2.** to evade work, duty, etc. [var. of SHARK[2]]

shirk·er (shûr′kər), *n.* a person who evades work, duty, responsibility, etc.

Shir·ley (shûr′lē), *n.* **James,** 1596–1666, English dramatist.

shirr (shûr), *v.t.* **1.** to draw up or gather (cloth or the like) on three or more parallel threads. **2.** to bake (eggs removed from the shell) in a shallow dish or in individual dishes. —*n.* **3.** Also, **shirr′ing.** a shirred arrangement, as of cloth. [?]

shirt (shûrt), *n.* **1.** a long- or short-sleeved garment for the upper part of the body, typically having a collar and a front opening, worn chiefly by men. **2.** an undergarment of cotton or other material, for the upper part of the body. **3.** a shirtwaist. **4. keep one's shirt on,** *Slang.* to refrain from becoming angry or impatient; remain calm. **5. lose one's shirt,** *Slang.* to lose all that one possesses. [ME *schirte,* OE *scyrte;* c. G *Schürze,* D *schort* apron, Icel *skyrta* SKIRT]

shirt′ front′, dickey (def. 2).

shirt·ing (shûr′ting), *n.* any shirt fabric, as broadcloth or oxford.

shirt-sleeve (shûrt′slēv′), *adj.* **1.** not wearing a jacket; informally dressed: *a shirt-sleeve mob.* **2.** simple; plain; direct and straightforward in approach, manner, etc.: *shirt-sleeve diplomacy.* Also, **shirt′-sleeved′.**

shirt·tail (shûrt′tāl′), *n.* **1.** the part of a shirt below the waistline. **2.** *Journalism.* a brief item added at the end of a related newspaper story. —*adj.* **3.** *Slang.* of distant or uncertain relation.

shirt·waist (shûrt′wāst′), *n.* **1.** a tailored blouse or shirt worn by women. **2.** Also called **shirt′waist′ dress′.** a dress with a bodice and a front opening tailored like those of a dress shirt.

shish ke·bab (shish′ kə bob′), a dish consisting of kabobs broiled or roasted on a skewer. Also called **shashlik, shashlick, shaslick.** [< Turk; cf. SHASHLIK, KABOB]

shit (shit), *n.v.,* **shit, shit·ting,** *interj. Slang (vulgar).* —*n.* **1.** feces. **2.** an act of defecation. **3.** pretense, exaggeration, lies, or nonsense. —*v.i.* **4.** to defecate. —*interj.* **5.** (used to express disgust, contempt, disappointment, or the like.) [alter. of earlier shite (v.), ME *shiten,* OE **scītan;* n., deriv. of OE *scite* dung, *scitte* diarrhea]

shit′ list′, *U.S. Slang.* a list of people strongly disliked or in great disfavor.

shit·tah (shit′ə), *n., pl.* **shit·tim** (shit′im), **shit·tahs.** a tree, said to be acacia, probably *Acacia Seyal* or *A. tortilis,* that yielded the shittim wood of the Old Testament. [< Heb *shiṭṭāh*]

shit′tim wood′, the wood, probably acacia, of which the ark of the covenant and various parts of the tabernacle were made. Ex. 25, 26. Also called **shittim.** [< Heb *shiṭṭīm,* pl. of *shiṭṭāh* (see SHITTAH)]

shit·ty (shit′ē) *adj.,* **-ti·er, -ti·est.** *Slang (vulgar).* **1.** inferior or contemptible. **2.** inept or insignificant. [SHIT + -Y[1]]

shiv (shiv), *n. Slang.* a knife, esp. a switchblade. [? alter. of *chiv* blade < Gypsy]

Shi·va (shē′və), *n. Hinduism.* "the Destroyer," the third member of the Trimurti, along with Brahma the Creator and Vishnu the Preserver. Also, **Siva.** [< Skt: lit., the auspicious] —**Shi′va·ism,** *n.* —**Shi′va·ist,** *n.* —**Shi′va·is′tic,** *adj.*

Shiva

shi·vah (shē vä′; *Eng.* shiv′ə), *n. Hebrew.* shibah.

shiv·a·ree (shiv′ə rē′), *n., v.,* **-reed, -ree·ing.** —*n.* **1.** a mock serenade with kettles, pans, horns, and other noisemakers given for a newly married couple. —*v.t.* **2.** to serenade with a shivaree. Also, **charivaree, chivaree, chivari.** [alter. of CHARIVARI]

shive[1] (shīv), *n.* **1.** a sliver or fragment; splinter. **2.** a thin plug, as of wood or cork, for stopping the bunghole of a cask or the mouth of a bottle. [ME; c. G *Scheibe,* Icel *skīfa*]

shive[2] (shiv, shīv), *n.* a splinter or fragment of the husk of flax, hemp, etc. [late ME *scyfe;* c. Flem *schif,* MD *scheve,* G *Schebe*]

shiv·er[1] (shiv′ər), *v.i.* **1.** to shake or tremble with cold, fear, excitement, etc. **2.** *Naut.* **a.** (of a fore-and-aft sail) to shake when too close to the wind. **b.** (of a sailing vessel) to be headed so close to the wind that the sails shake. —*n.* **3.** a tremulous motion; a tremble or quiver. [ME *chivere* (n.); later *sh-* for sake of alliteration in phrase *chiver and shake*] —**shiv′er·er,** *n.* —**shiv′er·ing·ly,** *adv.*

—**Syn. 1.** SHIVER, QUAKE, SHUDDER refer to a vibratory muscular movement, a trembling, usually involuntary. We SHIVER with cold, or a sensation such as that of cold: *to shiver in thin clothing on a frosty day; to shiver with pleasant anticipation.* We QUAKE esp. with fear: *to quake with fright.* We SHUDDER with horror or abhorrence; the agitation is more powerful and deep-seated than shivering or trembling: *to shudder at pictures of a car accident.*

shiv·er[2] (shiv′ər), *v.t., v.i.* **1.** to break or split into fragments. —*n.* **2.** a fragment; splinter. [ME *schivere* fragment; c. G *Schiefer* schist]

shiv·er·y[1] (shiv′ə rē), *adj.* **1.** inclined to or characterized by shivers, quivers, or tremors. **2.** causing shivering. [SHIVER[1] + -Y[1]]

shiv·er·y[2] (shiv′ə rē), *adj.* readily breaking into shivers or fragments; brittle. [SHIVER[2] + -Y[1]]

Shi·zu·o·ka (shē′zo͞o ô′kä), *n.* a seaport on S Honshu, in central Japan. 361,502 (1964).

shlemiel (shlə mēl′), *n.* schlemiel.

shlock (shlok), *adj., n. Slang.* schlock.

shmo (shmō), *n., pl.* **shmoes.** schmo.

shnaps, (shnäps, shnaps), *n.* schnapps.

Sho·a (shō′ä), *n.* a former kingdom in E Africa: now a province of Ethiopia. 3,033,400 (1962); 25,290 sq. mi. *Cap.:* Addis Ababa.

shoal[1] (shōl), *n.* **1.** a place where a sea, river, or other body of water is shallow. **2.** a sandbank or sand bar in the bed of a body of water, esp. one that is exposed above the surface of the water at low tide. —*adj.* **3.** shallow. —*v.i.* **4.** to become shallow or more shallow. —*v.t.* **5.** to cause to become shallow. **6.** *Naut.* to sail (a vessel) into a shallow part of a body of water. [ME (Scot) *shald,* OE *sceald* shallow]

shoal[2] (shōl), *n.* **1.** any large number of persons or things. **2.** a school of fish. —*v.i.* **3.** to collect in a shoal; throng. [OE *scolu* shoal (of fish), multitude, troop; c. D *school;* see SCHOOL[2]]

shoal·y (shō′lē), *adj.,* **shoal·i·er, shoal·i·est.** full of shoals or shallows.

shoat (shōt), *n.* a young, weaned pig. Also, **shote.** [late ME *shote;* c. WFlem *schote*]

shock[1] (shok), *n.* **1.** a sudden and violent blow or impact; collision. **2.** a sudden and violent disturbance or commotion: *the shock of battle.* **3.** a sudden and violent disturbance of the mind, emotions, or sensibilities. **4.** the cause of such a disturbance: *The rebuke came as a shock.* **5.** *Pathol.* a collapse of circulatory function, caused by severe injury, blood loss, or disease, and characterized by pallor, sweating, weak pulse, and very low blood pressure. **6.** the physiological effect produced by the passage of an electric current through the body. **7.** (in a piece of metal) strong internal stresses, as from uneven heating. —*v.t.* **8.** to strike or jar with intense surprise, horror, disgust, etc. **9.** to strike against violently. **10.** to give an electric shock to. **11.** to create strong internal stresses in (a piece of metal), as by uneven heating. —*v.i.* **12.** to undergo a shock. [< MF *choc,* back formation from *choquer* to clash (in battle) < Gmc; cf. D *schokken* to shake, jolt, jerk] —**shock′a·bil′i·ty,** *n.* —**shock′a·ble,** *adj.*

—**Syn. 8.** stagger, astound, stupefy. SHOCK, STARTLE, STUN suggest a sudden, sharp surprise that affects a person somewhat like a blow. SHOCK suggests a strong blow, as it were, to one's nerves, sentiments, sense of decency, etc.: *The onlookers were shocked by the accident.* STARTLE implies the sharp surprise of sudden fright: *to be startled by a loud noise.* STUN implies such a shock as bewilders or stupefies: *stunned by the realization of an unpleasant truth.*

shock[2] (shok), *n.* **1.** a group of sheaves of grain placed on end and supporting one another in the field. **2.** a stack of cornstalks. —*v.t.* **3.** to make into shocks. [ME; c. LG *schok,* G *Schock* shock of grain, group of sixty]

shock[3] (shok), *n.* **1.** a thick, bushy mass, as of hair. —*adj.* **2.** shaggy, as hair. [special use of SHOCK[2], the hair being compared to a shock of wheat]

shock′ absorb′er, *Mach.* a device for damping sudden and rapid motion, as the recoil of a spring-mounted object from shock.

shock·er[1] (shok′ər), *n.* **1.** a person or thing that shocks. **2.** a sensational book, article, motion picture, or the like. [SHOCK[1] + -ER[1]]

shock·er[2] (shok′ər), *n.* a person or thing that bales grain into shocks. [SHOCK[2] + -ER[1]]

shock·ing (shok′ing), *adj.* **1.** causing intense surprise, disgust, etc. **2.** very bad: *shocking manners.* —**shock′ing·ly,** *adv.*

Shock·ley (shok′lē), *n.* **William Bradford,** born 1910, U.S. physicist: Nobel prize 1956.

shock·proof (shok′proof′), *adj.* **1.** Also, **shock′-proof′.** (of clockwork, machinery, etc.) protected against damage from shocks. —*v.t.* **2.** to protect (clockwork, machinery, etc.) against damage from shocks.

shock′ ther′apy, a method of treating certain psychotic disorders, as schizophrenia, by use of drugs or electricity (**electroconvulsive therapy**). Also called **shock′ treat′ment.**

shock′ troops′, *Mil.* troops especially selected, trained, and equipped for engaging in assault.

shock′ wave′, a region of abrupt change of pressure and density moving as a wave front at or above the velocity of sound, caused by an intense explosion, supersonic flow over a body, an earthquake, or the like.

shod (shod), *v.* a pt. and pp. of **shoe.**

shod·dy (shod′ē), *n., pl.* **-dies,** *adj.,* **-di·er, -di·est.** —*n.* **1.** a fibrous material obtained by shredding unfelted rags or waste. Cf. **mungo. 2.** anything inferior made to resemble what is of superior quality. **3.** pretense, as in art or manufacture. —*adj.* **4.** pretentious; sham. **5.** poorly made; of inferior quality. **6.** mean or reprehensible: *a shoddy trick.* **7.** made of or containing shoddy. [?] —**shod′di·ly,** *adv.* —**shod′di·ness,** *n.*

shoe (shoo), *n., pl.* **shoes,** (*esp. Dial.*) **shoon;** *v.,* **shod** or **shoed, shod** or **shoed** or **shod·den, shoe·ing.** —*n.* **1.** a covering for the human foot, usually of leather and consisting of a more or less stiff or heavy sole and a lighter upper part ending at or a short distance above or below the ankle. **2.** something resembling a shoe in form, position, or use. **3.** a horseshoe or a similar plate for the hoof of some other animal. **4.** the part of an automotive brake that applies friction to the wheel in stopping or slowing a car, truck, etc. **5.** the outer casing of a pneumatic automobile tire. **6.** a drag or skid for the wheel of a vehicle. **7.** the sliding contact by which an electric car or locomotive takes its current from the third rail. **8.** a band of iron on the bottom of the runner of a sleigh. —*v.t.* **9.** to provide or fit with a shoe or shoes. **10.** to protect or decorate with a ferrule, metal plate, etc. [ME *scho(o),* OE *sceō(h);* c. G *Schuh,* Icel *skōr,* Goth *skōhs*]

shoe·bill (shoo′bil′), *n.* a large, African, storklike bird, *Balaeniceps rex,* having a broad, flat bill shaped somewhat like a shoe.

Shoebill
(Height 5 ft.; length 3½ ft.)

shoe·black (shoo′blak′), *n.* *Chiefly Brit.* a bootblack.

shoe·horn (shoo′hôrn′), *n.* **1.** a shaped piece of horn, metal, or the like, for inserting into the heel of a shoe to make it slip on more easily. —*v.t.* **2.** to force into a limited space; squeeze.

shoe·lace (shoo′lās′), *n.* a string or lace for fastening a shoe.

shoe·mak·er (shoo′mā′kər), *n.* a person who makes or mends shoes. [ME] —**shoe′mak′ing,** *n.*

sho·er (shoo′ər), *n.* a person who shoes horses or other animals. [ME]

shoe·shine (shoo′shīn′), *n.* **1.** the act or an instance of cleaning and polishing a pair of shoes. **2.** the appearance of a polished shoe or shoes.

shoe·string (shoo′string′), *n.* **1.** a shoelace. **2.** *U.S. Informal.* a very small amount of money.

shoe′string catch′, a catch, as of a baseball, made close to the ground while running.

shoe′string pota′to, a long, sticklike slice of potato which is fried until crisp.

shoe′string tack′le, *Football Slang.* a tackle made around the ankles of the ball carrier.

shoe·tree (shoo′trē′), *n.* one of a pair of foot-shaped devices, usually of metal or wood, for placing in a shoe to maintain its shape when it is not worn.

sho·far (shō′fər; *Heb.* shô fäʀ′), *n., pl.* **-fars,** *Heb.* **-froth** (-frōt′). *Judaism.* a ram's horn made into a wind instrument, sounded at synagogue services on Rosh Hashanah and Yom Kippur. Also, **shophar.** [< Heb *shōphār*]

Shofar

sho·gun (shō′gun′, -goon′), *n.* *Japanese Hist.* the title of the chief military commanders from about the 8th to 12th centuries, applied to the hereditary officials who governed Japan, with the emperor as nominal ruler, until 1868. [< Jap < Chin *chiang chün* leader of an army] —**sho′gun′al,** *adj.*

sho·gun·ate (shō′gun′it, -āt, -goo′nit, -nāt), *n.* the office or rule of a shogun.

sho·ji (shō′zhē, -jē), *n., pl.* **-ji, -jis.** a light screen of translucent paper, used as a sliding door or room divider in Japanese homes. [< Jap]

Sho·la·pur (shō′lə po͝or′), *n.* a city in S Maharashtra in SW India. 337,600 (1961).

shone (shōn; *esp. Brit.* shon), *v.* a pt. and pp. of **shine.**

shoo (shoo), *interj., v.,* **shooed, shoo·ing.** —*interj.* **1.** (used to scare or drive away a cat, birds, etc.) —*v.t.* **2.** to drive away by saying or shouting "shoo." **3.** to request or force (a person) to leave. —*v.i.* **4.** to call out "shoo." [late ME *ssou* (interjection), imit.; cf. G *schu*]

shoo·fly (shoo′flī′), *n., pl.* **-flies.** *U.S.* a child's rocker having a seat supported between two boards cut and painted to resemble animals.

shoo′-fly pie′ (shoo′flī′), an open pie filled with a sweet crumb and molasses mixture and baked. [so called from the idea that flies, attracted by the molasses, will have to be shooed away]

shoo-in (shoo′in′), *n.* *Informal.* a candidate, competitor, etc., regarded as certain to win.

shook[1] (sho͝ok), *n.* **1.** a set of staves and headings sufficient for one hogshead, barrel, or the like. **2.** a set of the parts of a box, piece of furniture, or the like, ready to be put together. **3.** a shock of sheaves or the like. [short for *shook cask,* var. of *shaken cask* one dismounted for shipment]

shook[2] (sho͝ok), *v.* **1.** pt. of **shake.** —*adj.* **2.** Also, **shook′ up′.** *Slang.* strongly affected by an event, circumstance, etc.; emotionally unsettled.

shool (shool), *n., v.t., v.i.* *Dial.* shovel. [ME *schole,* etc., OE *scofl*]

shoon (shoon), *n.* *Chiefly Dial.* pl. of **shoe.**

shoot (shoot), *v.,* **shot, shoot·ing,** *n.* —*v.t.* **1.** to hit, wound, damage, kill, or destroy with a missile discharged from a weapon. **2.** to send forth or discharge (a missile) from a weapon: *to shoot a bullet.* **3.** to discharge (a weapon). **4.** to send forth (words, ideas, etc.) rapidly: *to shoot questions at someone.* **5.** to direct suddenly or swiftly: *He shot a smile at his wife.* **6.** to move suddenly; send swiftly along. **7.** to go over (country) in hunting game. **8.** to pass rapidly through, over, down, etc.: *to shoot a rapid.* **9.** to emit (a ray or rays, as of light) suddenly, briefly, or intermittently. **10.** to variegate by threads, streaks, etc., of another color. **11.** to cause to extend or project (often fol. by *out*): *He shot out his arm and grabbed the ball.* **12.** to discharge or empty, as down a chute. **13.** *Sports.* **a.** to throw, kick, or otherwise propel (a ball, puck, etc.), as at a goal or teammate. **b.** to score (a goal, points, etc.) by propelling the ball, puck, etc.: *to shoot a goal.* **14.** *Games.* to propel (a marble) from the crook or first knuckle of the forefinger by flicking with the thumb. **15.** (in dice games) **a.** to throw (the dice or a specific number). **b.** to wager or offer to bet (a sum of money): *I'll shoot ten bucks.* **16.** *Photog.* to photograph or film. **17.** to put forth (buds, branches, etc.), as a plant. **18.** to slide (a bolt or the like) into or out of its fastening. **19.** to pull (one's cuffs) abruptly toward one's hands. **20.** *Golf.* to make a final score of (so many strokes). **21.** to take the altitude of (a heavenly body): *to shoot the sun.* **22.** *Carpentry.* **a.** to plane or trim (an edge of a board or the like). **b.** to plane or trim (adjoining edges of two boards or the like) in order to make a close joint between them. **23.** to detonate; cause to explode. —*v.i.* **24.** to send forth missiles, from a bow, firearm, or the like. **25.** to be discharged, as a firearm. **26.** to hunt with a gun for sport. **27.** to move or pass suddenly or swiftly; spurt. **28.** to grow forth from the ground, as a stem. **29.** to put forth buds or shoots, as a plant; germinate. **30.** *Photog.* to photograph. **31.** *Motion Pictures.* to film or begin to film a scene or movie. **32.** to extend; jut: *a cape shooting out into the sea.* **33.** *Sports, Games.* to propel a ball, puck, etc., at a goal or in a particular way. **34.** to flow through or permeate the body, as a sensation: *Pain shot through his injured arm.* **35.** to carry by force of discharge or momentum: *The missile shot thousands of miles into space.* **36.** *Informal.* to begin, esp. to begin to talk. **37. shoot at** or **for,** *Informal.* to attempt to obtain or accomplish; strive toward. **38. shoot down,** to cause to fall by hitting with a shot. **39. shoot off one's mouth** or **face,** *Slang.* **a.** to talk indiscreetly, make thoughtless remarks, etc. **b.** to exaggerate. **40. shoot the breeze.** See **breeze**[1] (def. 3). **41. shoot the bull.** See **bull**[3] (def. 2). **42. shoot the works.** See **work** (def. 12). **43. shoot up, a.** to grow rapidly or suddenly. **b.** *Informal.* to damage or harass by reckless shooting. **c.** *Informal.* to wound by shooting. **d.** *Slang* to inject (an addictive drug) intravenously. —*n.* **44.** the act of shooting with a bow, firearm, etc. **45.** *Chiefly Brit.* a hunting trip or expedition. **46.** a match or contest at shooting. **47.** a growing or sprouting, as of a plant. **48.** a new or young growth that shoots off from some portion of a plant. **49.** the amount of such growth. **50.** a young branch, stem, twig, or the like. **51.** a sprout less than three feet high. **52.** a chute. **53.** *Rocketry.* the launching of a missile. **54.** *Rowing.* the interval between strokes. **55.** *Mining.* **a.** a small tunnel branching off from a larger tunnel. **b.** a narrow vein of ore. **c.** a hole or passage through which ore falls or slides to a lower level. [ME *shote(n),* OE *scēotan,* var. of *scēotan;* c. D *schieten,* G *schiessen,* Icel *skjōta*] —**shoot′er,** *n.* —**Syn. 2, 4.** project, hurl, throw. **15a.** roll. **27.** spring, start, dash. **32.** project, protrude.

shoot′ing box′, *Chiefly Brit.* a small house or lodge for use during the shooting season. Also called **shoot′ing lodge′.**

shoot′ing gal′lery, a place equipped with targets and used for practice in shooting.

shoot′ing i′ron, *U.S. Slang.* a firearm, esp. a pistol or revolver.

shoot′ing script′, a motion-picture scenario having the scenes arranged in the order in which they are to be photographed.

shoot′ing star′, **1.** a meteor as seen streaking across the sky at night. **2.** Also called **American cowslip.** a North American herb, *Dodecatheon meadia,* having bright, nodding flowers.

shoot′ing stick′, a device resembling a cane or walking stick, with a spike on one end and a folding seat on the other.

shop (shop), *n., v.,* **shopped, shop·ping.** —*n.* **1.** a retail store, esp. a small one. **2.** a small store or department in a large store selling a specific or select type of goods: *the ski shop at Smith's.* **3.** the workshop of a craftsman or artisan. **4.** any factory, office, or business. **5.** one's trade, profession, or business as a subject of conversation or preoccupation. **6. talk shop,** to discuss one's trade, profession, or business. —*v.i.* **7.** to visit shops and stores for purchasing or examining goods. [ME *shoppe,* OE *sceoppa* booth; akin to *scypen* stall (mod. dial. *shippon*), G *Schopf* leanto, *Schuppen* shed]

shop·boy (shop′boi′), *n.* *Brit.* a salesclerk.

shop′ chair′man. See **shop steward.**

shop·craft (shop′kraft′, -kräft′), *n.* **1.** any of various skilled trades engaged in repair and maintenance work, such as metalworking, boilermaking, etc., esp. in the railroad industry. **2.** the members of any such trade collectively.

shop·girl (shop′gûrl′), *n.* *Chiefly Brit.* a salesgirl.

sho·phar (shō′fər; *Heb.* shô fäʀ′), *n., pl.* **-phars,** *Heb.* **-phroth** (-frōt′). *Judaism.* shofar.

shop·keep·er (shop′kē′pər), *n.* a person who owns or operates a small store or shop. —**shop′keep′ing,** *n.*

shop·lift·er (shop′lif′tər), *n.* a person who steals goods from the shelves or displays of a retail store while posing as a customer. [obs. *shoplift* shoplifter (SHOP + LIFT) + -ER[1]] —**shop′lift′ing,** *n.*

shop·man (shop′mən), *n., pl.* **-men.** **1.** a salesman in a shop. **2.** *Chiefly Brit.* a shopkeeper.

shoppe (shop), *n.* a small shop (used chiefly on store signs).

shop·per (shop′ər), *n.* **1.** a person who shops. **2.** a retail buyer for another person or a business concern.

shop·ping (shop′ing), *n.* **1.** the act of a person who shops. **2.** the facilities or merchandise available to those who shop: *Chicago has good shopping.* **3.** the total of articles purchased: *The car trunk was full of shopping.* —*adj.* **4.** of, for, or pertaining to examining and buying merchandise.

shop′ping cen′ter, a group of stores within a single architectural plan, supplying most of the basic shopping needs, esp. in suburban areas.

shop′ stew′ard, a unionized employee elected to represent a shop, department, or the like, in dealings with his employer. Also called **shop chairman.**

shop·talk (shop′tôk′), *n.* conversation about one's trade, profession, or business.

shop·wom·an (shop′wo͝om′ən), *n., pl.* **-wom·en.** a saleswoman in a shop.

shop·worn (shop′wōrn′, -wôrn′), *adj.* worn or marred, as goods handled and exposed in a store.

shor·an (shōr′an, shôr′-), *n.* a system for aircraft navigation in which two signals sent from an aircraft are received and answered by two fixed transponders, the round-trip times of the signals enabling the navigator to determine his position. [*sho(rt) ra(nge) n(avigation)*]

shore[1] (shōr, shôr), *n.* **1.** the land along the edge of a sea, lake, broad river, etc. **2.** some particular country: *my native shore.* **3.** land, as opposed to sea or water: *a marine serving on shore.* **4.** *Law.* seashore (def. 2). —*adj.* **5.** of, pertaining to, or located on land, esp. land along the edge of a body of water: *a marine on shore duty.* [ME *schore,* OE *scora;* c. MD, MLG *schore;* see SHEAR]
—**Syn. 1.** strand, margin. SHORE, BANK, BEACH, COAST refer to an edge of land abutting on an ocean, lake, or other large body of water. SHORE is the general word: *The ship reached shore.* BANK denotes the land along a river or other watercourse, sometimes steep but often not: *The river flows between its banks.* BEACH refers to sandy or pebbly margins along a shore, esp. those made wider at ebb tide: *a private beach for bathers.* COAST applies only to land along an ocean: *the Pacific coast.*

shore[2] (shōr, shôr), *n., v.,* **shored, shor·ing.** *n.* **1.** a supporting post or beam with auxiliary members, esp. one placed obliquely against the side of a building, a ship in dock, or the like; prop; strut. —*v.t.* **2.** to support by a shore or shores; prop (usually fol. by *up*). [ME; c. MLG, MD *schore* prop]
—**Syn. 1.** brace, buttress, stay.

S, Shore[2]
P, Post supporting footing of wall

shore[3] (shōr, shôr), *v.* a pt. of **shear.**

shore′ bird′, a bird that frequents seashores, estuaries etc., as the sandpiper, plover, etc.; a limicoline bird.

shore′ leave′, **1.** permission to spend time ashore granted a ship's crew members or naval personnel. **2.** the time spent ashore during such leave.

shore·less (shōr′lis, shôr′-), *adj.* **1.** limitless; boundless. **2.** without a shore or beach suitable for landing.

shore·line (shōr′līn′, shôr′-), *n.* the line where shore and water meet.

shore′ patrol′, (*often caps.*) members of an organization in the U.S. Navy having police duties. *Abbr.:* SP

shore·ward (shōr′wərd, shôr′-), *adv.* **1.** Also, **shore′-wards.** toward the shore or land. —*adj.* **2.** facing, moving, or tending toward the shore or land: *a shoreward course.* **3.** coming from the shore, as a wind. —*n.* **4.** the direction toward the shore or away from the sea.

shor·ing (shōr′ing, shôr′-), *n.* **1.** a number or system of shores for steadying or supporting a wall, a ship in drydock, etc. **2.** the act of setting up shores.

shorn (shōrn, shôrn), *v.* a pp. of **shear.**

short (shôrt), *adj.* **1.** having little length; not long. **2.** having little height; not tall. **3.** extending or reaching only a little way: *a short path.* **4.** brief in duration; not extensive in time: *a short wait.* **5.** brief or concise, as writing. **6.** rudely brief; abrupt. **7.** low in amount; scanty: *short rations.* **8.** not reaching a point, mark, target, or the like. **9.** below the standard in extent, quantity, duration, etc. **10.** having a scanty or insufficient amount of (often fol. by *in* or *on*): *He was a bit short in experience.* **11.** *Cookery.* **a.** (of pastry and the like) crisp and flaky. **b.** (of dough) containing a relatively large amount of shortening. **12.** (of metals) deficient in tenacity; friable; brittle. **13.** *Finance.* **a.** not possessing at the time of sale commodities or securities that a person sells. **b.** noting or pertaining to a sale of commodities or securities that the seller does not possess, depending for profit on a decline in prices. **14.** *Phonet.* **a.** lasting a relatively short time. **b.** belonging to a class of sounds shorter in duration than another class, as the vowel of *but* as compared to that of *bought.* **c.** having the sound of the vowels in, conventionally, *bet, bit, put,* and *but,* and, popularly, in *hot* and *bat.* Cf. **long**[1] (def. 15). **15.** *Pros.* **a.** (of a syllable in quantitative verse) lasting a relatively shorter time than a long syllable. **b.** unstressed. **16. short of, a.** less than; inferior to. **b.** inadequately supplied with (money, food, etc.). **c.** without going to the length of; failing of; excluding. —*adv.* **17.** abruptly or suddenly: *to stop short.* **18.** briefly; curtly. **19.** on the near side of an intended or particular point: *The arrow landed short.* **20. sell short, a.** to sell commodities or securities without having them in one's actual possession at the time of the sale. **b.** *Informal.* to disparage or underestimate. —*n.* **21.** something that is short. **22.** that which is deficient or lacking. **23.** the gist of a matter (usually prec. by *the*). **24. shorts, a.** loose trousers, knee-length or shorter. **b.** short pants worn by men as an undergarment. **c.** *Finance.* short-term bonds. **d.** *Mining.* crushed ore failing to pass through a given screen, thus being of a larger given size than a specific grade. **e.** remnants, discards, or refuse of various cutting and manufacturing processes. **25.** *Elect.* See **short circuit.** **26.** *Pros.* a short sound or syllable. **27.** *Baseball.* shortstop. **28.** *Motion Pictures.* See **short subject.** **29.** *Finance.* a person who has sold short; a short seller. **30.** a deficiency or the amount of a deficiency. **31. for short,** by way of abbreviation: *Her name is Patricia, and she's called Pat for short.* **32. in short,** in brief. —*v.t.* **33.** *Elect.* to short-circuit. **34.** to sell (securities or commodities) short. —*v.i.* **35.** to make a short sale of securities or commodities. [ME; OE *sceort;* c. OHG *scurz* short, Icel *skortr* shortness, scarcity] —**short′ness,** *n.*
—**Syn. 1, 4.** SHORT, BRIEF are opposed to *long,* and indicate slight extent or duration. SHORT may imply duration but is also applied to physical distance and certain purely spatial relations: *a short journey.* BRIEF refers esp. to duration of time: *brief intervals.* **5.** terse, succinct. **6.** curt, sharp, testy.

short·age (shôr′tij), *n.* **1.** a deficiency in quantity: *a shortage of cash.* **2.** the amount of such deficiency.

short·bread (shôrt′bred′), *n.* a kind of butter cooky, commonly made in thick wheels or rolled and cut in fancy shapes.

short·cake (shôrt′kāk′), *n.* **1.** a cake made with a relatively large amount of butter or other shortening. **2.** a dessert made of short, baked biscuit dough, topped with strawberries or other fruit.

short-change (shôrt′chānj′), *v.t.,* **-changed, -chang·ing.** **1.** to give less than the correct change to. **2.** *Informal.* to cheat; defraud. Also, **short′ change′.** —**short′-chang′er,** *n.* **short′ chang′er.**

short′ cir′cuit, *Elect.* an abnormal condition of relatively low resistance between two points of different potential in a circuit, usually resulting in a flow of excess current.

short-cir·cuit (shôrt′sûr′kit), *v.t.* *Elect.* to make inoperable by establishing a short circuit in.

short·com·ing (shôrt′kum′ing), *n.* a failure, defect or deficiency in conduct, condition, thought, ability, etc.

short·cut (shôrt′kut′), *n.* **1.** Also, **short′ cut′.** a shorter or quicker way. —*adj.* **2.** comprising or providing a shorter or quicker way: *shortcut methods.*

short′ divi′sion, *Math.* division, esp. by a one-digit divisor, in which the steps of the process are performed mentally and are not written down.

short·en (shôr′tᵊn), *v.t.* **1.** to make short or shorter. **2.** to reduce, decrease, take in, etc.: *to shorten sail.* **3.** to make (pastry, bread, etc.) short, as with butter or other fat. —*v.i.* **4.** to become short or shorter. **5.** (of odds) to decrease. —**short′en·er,** *n.*
—**Syn. 1.** condense, lessen, limit, restrict. SHORTEN, ABBREVIATE, ABRIDGE, CURTAIL mean to make shorter or briefer. SHORTEN is a general word meaning to make less in extent or duration: *to shorten a dress, a prisoner's sentence.* The other three words suggest methods of shortening. To ABBREVIATE is to make shorter by omission or contraction: *to abbreviate a word.* To ABRIDGE is to reduce in length or size by condensing, summarizing, and the like: *to abridge a document.* CURTAIL suggests deprivation and lack of completeness because of cutting off part: *to curtail an explanation.* **4.** lessen.

short·en·ing (shôr′tᵊning, shôrt′ning), *n.* **1.** butter, lard, or other fat, used to shorten pastry, bread, etc. **2.** *Phonet.* the act, process, or an instance of making or becoming short. **3.** *Linguistics.* a word formed by dropping a part of a longer word or phrase.

Short′er Cat′echism, one of the two catechisms established by the Westminster Assembly in 1647, used chiefly in Presbyterian churches.

short·fall (shôrt′fôl′), *n.* **1.** the quantity or extent by which something falls short; deficiency; shortage. **2.** the act or fact of falling short.

short·hand (shôrt′hand′), *n.* **1.** a method of rapid handwriting using simple strokes, abbreviations, or symbols that designate letters, words, or phrases (distinguished from *longhand*). —*adj.* **2.** using or able to use shorthand. **3.** written in shorthand. **4.** of or pertaining to shorthand.

Shorthand
"This is an example of shorthand"
A, Gregg system
B, Pitman system

short-hand·ed (shôrt′han′did), *adj.* not having the usual or necessary number of workmen, helpers, etc. —**short′-hand′ed·ness,** *n.*

Short·horn (shôrt′hôrn′), *n.* one of an English breed of red, white, or roan beef cattle having short horns. Also called **Durham.**

shor·ti·a (shôr′tē ə), *n.* any plant of the genus *Shortia,* esp. *S. galacifolia,* of the mountains of North and South Carolina, having evergreen leaves and white, nodding flowers.

short·ie (shôr′tē), *n.* *Informal.* shorty.

short·ish (shôr′tish), *adj.* rather short.

short-lived (shôrt′līvd′, -livd′), *adj.* living or lasting only a little while.

short·ly (shôrt′lē), *adv.* **1.** in a short time; soon. **2.** briefly; concisely. **3.** curtly; rudely.

short′ or′der, an order for food that may be quickly prepared at a lunch counter, diner, or the like.

short-or·der (shôrt′ôr′dər), *adj.* of, pertaining to, or specializing in short orders: *a short-order cook.*

short-range (shôrt′rānj′), *adj.* having a limited extent, as in distance or time.

short′ shrift′, **1.** a brief time for confession or absolution given to a condemned prisoner before his execution. **2.** brief attention or minimal consideration in dealing with a person or matter.

short-sight·ed (shrôt′sī′tid), *adj.* **1.** unable to see far; near-sighted; myopic. **2.** lacking in foresight. Also, **short′sight′ed.** —**short′-sight′ed·ly,** *adv.* —**short′-sight′ed·ness,** *n.* —**Syn. 2.** unthinking, heedless.

short′ splice′, a splice made in instances where an increased thickness of the united rope is not objectionable, made by unlaying the ends of both ropes a certain distance, uniting them so that their strands overlap, then tucking each alternately over and under others several times. Cf. **long splice.** See illus. at **splice.**

short-spo·ken (shôrt′spō′kən), *adj.* speaking in a short, brief, or curt manner.

short·stop (shôrt′stop′), *n.* *Baseball.* **1.** the position of the player covering the area of the infield between second and third base. **2.** a fielder who covers this position.

short′ sto′ry, a piece of prose fiction, usually under 10,000 words. —**short′-sto′ry,** *adj.*

short′ sub′ject, *Motion Pictures.* a short film, as a documentary or travelogue, shown as part of a program with a feature-length film. Also called **short.**

short-tem·pered (shôrt′tem′pərd), *adj.* having a quick, hasty temper; irascible.

short-term (shôrt′tûrm′), *adj.* **1.** covering or applying to a relatively short period of time. **2.** *Finance.* maturing over a relatively short period of time: *a short-term loan.*

short′ ton′. See under **ton**[1] (def. 1). Also called **net ton.**

short-waist·ed (shôrt′wā′stid), *adj.* of less than average length between the shoulders and waistline; having a high waistline. Cf. **long-waisted.**

short·wave (shôrt′wāv′), *n., adj., v.,* **-waved, -wav·ing.** —*n.* **1.** *Elect.* an electromagnetic wave of 60 meters or less. **2.** See **shortwave radio.** —*adj.* **3.** of, pertaining to, or using shortwaves. —*v.i., v.t.* **4.** to transmit by shortwaves.

short′wave ra′dio, **1.** a radio transmitter that broadcasts shortwaves. **2.** a radio receiver that picks up shortwaves.

short-wind·ed (shôrt′win′did), *adj.* **1.** short of breath. **2.** brief or concise; to the point, as in speech, writing, etc.

short·y (shôr′tē), *n., pl.* **short·ies.** *Informal.* a person or thing that is exceptionally short, esp. a man of less than average height. Also, **shortie.**

Sho·sho·ne (shō shō′nē), *n., pl.* **-nes,** (*esp. collectively*) **-ne** for 3. **1.** a river in NW Wyoming, flowing NE into the Big Horn River. 120 mi. long. **2.** an American Indian language of the Shoshonean family. **3.** Shoshoni.

Sho·sho·ne·an (shō shō′nē ən, shō′shə nē′ən), *adj.* **1.** of or pertaining to a family of American Indian languages spoken in the western U.S. and including Shoshone, Comanche, Hopi, Paiute, and Ute. —*n.* **2.** the Shoshonean languages taken collectively.

Shosho′ne Cav′ern, a large cave in NW Wyoming: a national monument.

Shosho′ne Dam′, a dam on the Shoshone River. 328 ft. high.

Shosho′ne Falls′, falls of the Snake River, in S Idaho. 210 ft. high.

Sho·sho·ni (shō shō′nē), *n., pl.* **-nis,** (*esp. collectively*) **-ni.** a member of any of several American Indian peoples, ranging from Wyoming to California, who speak a Shoshonean language. Also, **Shoshone.**

Sho·sta·ko·vich (shos′tə kō′vich; *Russ.* sho stä kô′vich), *n.* **Di·mi·tri Di·mi·tri·e·vich** (di mē′trē di mē′trē ə vich; *Russ.* di mē′tri di mē′tri yə vich), 1906–75, Russian composer.

shot[1] (shot), *n., pl.* **shots** or, for 6, 8, **shot;** *v.,* **shot·ted, shot·ting.** —*n.* **1.** a discharge of a firearm, bow, etc. **2.** the range of or the distance traveled by a missile in its flight. **3.** an aimed discharge of a missile. **4.** an attempt to hit a target with a missile. **5.** the act or an instance of shooting a firearm, bow, etc. **6.** a small ball or pellet of lead, a number of which are loaded in a cartridge and used for one charge of a shotgun. **7.** such pellets collectively: *a charge of shot.* **8.** a projectile for discharge from a firearm or cannon. **9.** such projectiles collectively: *shot and shell.* **10.** a person who shoots; marksman. **11.** anything like a shot, esp. in being sudden and forceful. **12.** See under **shot put.** **13.** an aimed stroke, throw, or the like, as in certain games, esp. in an attempt to score. **14.** an attempt or try. **15.** a guess at something. **16.** *Informal.* a hypodermic injection, as of a serum or anaesthetic. **17.** *Informal.* a small quantity, esp. an ounce, of undiluted liquor. **18.** *Photog.* **a.** a photograph, esp. a snapshot. **b.** the act of making a photograph, esp. a snapshot. **19.** *Motion Pictures, Television.* a unit of action photographed without interruption and constituting a single camera view. **20.** *Foundry.* comparatively hard globules of metal in the body of a casting. **21.** *Naut.* a 90-foot length of anchor cable or chain. **22. by a long shot.** See **long shot** (def. 4). —*v.t.* **23.** to load or supply with shot. **24.** to weight with shot. [ME; OE *sc(e)ot, (ge)sceot;* c. G *Schoss, Geschoss;* akin to SHOOT]

shot[2] (shot), *v.* **1.** pt. and pp. of **shoot.** —*adj.* **2.** woven so as to have a changeable color; variegated, as silk. **3.** spread or streaked with color. **4.** *Slang.* in hopelessly bad condition; ruined.

shote (shōt), *n.* shoat.

shot·gun (shot′gun′), *n., adj., v.,* **-gunned, -gun·ning.** —*n.* **1.** a smoothbore gun for firing small shot to kill birds and small quadrupeds, though often used with buckshot to kill larger animals. —*adj.* **2.** of, pertaining to, used in, or carried out with a shotgun. —*v.t.* **3.** to fire a shotgun at. **4.** to use coercive methods.

shot′gun wed′ding, *U.S. Slang.* a wedding occasioned or precipitated by pregnancy.

shot′ put′, a field event in which a heavy metal ball (**shot**) is thrown for distance.

shot·ten (shot′ən), *adj.* **1.** (of fish, esp. herring) having recently ejected the spawn. **2.** *Obs.* (of a bone) dislocated. [old ptp. of SHOOT]

Shot·well (shot′wel′, -wəl), *n.* **James Thomson,** 1874–1965, U.S. diplomat, historian, and educator.

should (shood), *auxiliary v.* **1.** pt. of **shall.** **2.** (used with infinitive of a verb to form its subjunctive): *Were he to arrive, I should be pleased.* **3.** must; ought (used to indicate duty, propriety, or expediency): *You should not do that.* **4.** would (used to make a statement less direct or blunt): *I should hardly say that.* [ME *sholde,* OE *sc(e)olde;* see SHALL] —**Syn. 3.** See **must**[1].

shoul·der (shōl′dər), *n.* **1.** the part of each side of the body in man, at the top of the trunk, extending from each side of the base of the neck to the region where the arm articulates with the trunk. **2.** Usually, **shoulders.** these two parts together with the part of the back joining them. **3.** a corresponding part in animals. **4.** the upper foreleg and adjoining parts of a sheep, goat, etc. **5.** the joint connecting the arm or the foreleg with the trunk. **6.** a shoulderlike part or projection. **7.** a cut of meat that includes the upper joint of the foreleg. **8.** a steplike change in the contour of an object, as for opposing or limiting motion along it, for an abutment, etc. **9.** *Print.* the flat surface on a type body extending beyond the base of the letter or character. **10.** the part of a garment that covers, or fits over, the shoulder. **11.** either of the two edges or borders along a road, esp. that portion on which vehicles can be parked in emergencies. Cf. **soft shoulder.** —*v.t.* **12.** to push with or as with the shoulder, esp. roughly: *to shoulder someone aside.* **13.** to take upon, support, or carry on or as on the shoulder or shoulders. **14.** to assume as a responsibility: *to shoulder the expense.* —*v.i.* **15.** to push with or as with the shoulder. **16. shoulder arms,** *Mil.* **a.** to place a rifle muzzle upward on the right or left shoulder, with the buttstock in the corresponding hand. **b.** the command to shoulder arms. [ME *sholder,* OE *sculdor;* c. D *schouder,* G *Schulter*]

shoul′der blade′, the scapula.

shoul′der knot′, **1.** a knot of ribbon or lace worn on the shoulder in the 17th and 18th centuries. **2.** one of a pair of detachable ceremonial ornaments consisting of braided cord, worn on the shoulders by a commissioned officer.

shoul′der strap′, **1.** a strap worn over the shoulder, as to support a garment. **2.** a strip on the shoulder of a uniform to distinguish the rank of an officer.

should·na (shood′nə), *Scot.* contraction of *should not.*

should·n't (shood′ənt), contraction of *should not.*

shouldst (shoodst), *v.* *Archaic.* past 2nd pers. sing. of **shall.** Also, **should·est** (shood′ist).

shout (shout), *v.i.* **1.** to call or cry out loudly and vigorously. **2.** to speak or laugh noisily or unrestrainedly. —*v.t.* **3.** to utter or yell (something) loudly. —*n.* **4.** a loud call or cry. **5.** a sudden loud outburst, as of laughter. [ME *shoute;* c. Icel *skūta* to scold, chide, *skūti, skūta* a taunt; akin to SHOOT] —**shout′er,** *n.* —**Syn. 1.** yell, exclaim. See **cry.**

shove (shuv), *v.,* **shoved, shov·ing,** *n.* —*v.t.* **1.** to move along by force from behind; push. **2.** to push roughly or rudely; jostle. —*v.i.* **3.** to push. **4. shove off, a.** to push a boat from the shore. **b.** *Slang.* to go away; depart. —*n.* **5.** an act or instance of shoving. [ME *schouve(n),* OE *scūfan;* c. D *schuiven,* obs. G *schauben,* Icel *skūfa;* akin to Goth *-skiuban*] —**shov′er,** *n.*

shov·el (shuv′əl), *n., v.,* **-eled, -el·ing** or (*esp. Brit.*) **-elled, -el·ling.** —*n.* **1.** an implement consisting of a broad blade or scoop attached to a long handle, used for removing loose matter, as earth, snow, etc. **2.** any fairly large contrivance or machine with a broad blade or scoop for taking up or removing loose matter: *a steam shovel.* **3.** a shovelful. —*v.t.* **4.** to take up and cast or remove with a shovel: *to shovel coal.* **5.** to take up and move in large quantity roughly or carelessly as with a shovel. **6.** to dig or clear with or as with a shovel. —*v.i.* **7.** to work with a shovel. [ME *schovel,* OE *scofl;* c. D *schoffel* hoe; akin to G *Schaufel* shovel]

shov·el·er (shuv′ə lər, shuv′lər), *n.* **1.** a person or thing that shovels. **2.** *Ornith.* **a.** a cosmopolitan, fresh-water duck, *Anas clypeata,* having a broad, flat bill. **b.** any of several related, similar ducks. Also, *esp. Brit.,* **shov′el·ler.**

shov·el·ful (shuv′əl fool′), *n., pl.* **-fuls.** the amount that a shovel can hold.

shov′el hat′, a hat with a broad brim turned up at the sides and projecting with a shovellike curve in front and behind: worn by some ecclesiastics, chiefly in England. —**shov′el-hat′ted,** *adj.*

shov·el·nose (shuv′əl nōz′), *n.* any of various animals with a shovellike snout or head, as a shark, *Hexanchus corinus,* of the Pacific, or a guitarfish, *Rhinobatos productus,* of California.

shov·el-nosed (shuv′əl nōzd′), *adj.* having the head, snout, or beak broad and flat like the blade of a shovel.

show (shō), *v.,* **showed, shown** or **showed, show·ing,** *n.* —*v.t.* **1.** to cause or allow to be seen; exhibit; display. **2.** to present or perform as a public entertainment or spectacle: *to show a movie.* **3.** to guide, escort, or usher: *Show him in.* **4.** to explain or make clear; make known: *The president showed his intent in regard to foreign affairs.* **5.** to make known to; inform, instruct, or prove to: *I'll show you what I mean.* **6.** to prove or demonstrate. **7.** to indicate, register, or mark: *The thermometer showed 10 below zero.* **8.** to exhibit or offer for sale: *to show a house.* **9.** to allege, as in a legal document; plead, as a reason or cause. **10.** to express or make evident by one's behavior, speech, etc. **11.** to accord or grant (favor, kindness, etc.). —*v.i.* **12.** to be seen; be or become visible: *Did her slip show?* **13.** to be seen in a certain way: *to show to advantage.* **14.** *Informal.* **a.** to display one's goods or products. **b.** to keep an appointment; show up. **15.** to finish third in a horse race, harness race, etc. **16. show off, a.** to display ostentatiously. **b.** to seek to gain attention by displaying prominently one's abilities or accomplishments. **17. show up, a.** to make known, as faults; expose; reveal. **b.** to exhibit in a certain way; appear. **c.** *Informal.* to come to or arrive at a place. **d.** *Informal.* to outdo (another person). —*n.* **18.** a display, exhibition, or demonstration: *a true show of freedom.* **19.** pretentious display: *nothing but mere show.* **20.** any kind of public exhibition or exposition: *a show of Renoirs.* **21.** a radio or television program. **22.** a motion picture. **23.** the act or an instance of showing. **24.** appearance; impression: *to make a sorry show.* **25.** an unreal or deceptive appearance. **26.** an indication; trace. **27.** a theatrical production, performance, or company. **28.** the position of the competitor who comes in third in a horse race, harness race, etc. Cf. **place** (def. 26), **win**[1] (def. 15). **29. run the show,** to control a business, situation, etc. **30. steal the show, a.** to usurp the credit or get the applause for something: *He did all the work, but his wife stole the show.* **b.** to be the outstanding item or person in a group. **31. stop the show,** to win such enthusiastic applause that a theatrical performance is temporarily interrupted. [ME *showe(n)* (to) look at, show, OE *sceāwian,* var. of *scēawian* to look at; c. G *schauen,* D *schowen*] —**Syn. 3.** lead, conduct. **4.** interpret, clarify, elucidate; reveal, disclose, divulge. **9.** assert, affirm. **11.** bestow, confer. **18, 19.** SHOW, DISPLAY, OSTENTATION, POMP suggest the presentation of a more or less elaborate, often pretentious, appearance for the public to see. SHOW often indicates an external appearance that may or may not accord with actual facts: *a show of modesty.* DISPLAY applies to an intentionally conspicuous show: *a great display of wealth.* OSTENTATION is vain, ambitious, pretentious, or offensive display: *tasteless and vulgar ostentation.* POMP suggests such a show of dignity and authority as characterizes a ceremony of state: *The coronation was carried out with pomp and ceremony.* **20.** spectacle. **25.** deception.

show′ and tell′, a young children's activity, esp. in school, in which each participant produces an object of unusual interest and gives an account of it.

show′ bill′, an advertising poster.

show′ biz′ (biz), *U.S. Informal.* See **show business.**

show·boat (shō′bōt′), *n.* **1.** a boat, esp. a paddle-wheel steamer, used as a traveling theater. **2.** *Slang.* show-off (def. 1). —*v.i.* **3.** *Slang.* to show off.

show·bread (shō′bred′), *n. Judaism.* shewbread.

show′ busi′ness, the entertainment industry, comprising theater, motion pictures, television, radio, burlesque, etc.

show′ card′, an advertising placard or card.

show·case (shō′kās′), *n., v.,* **-cased, -cas·ing.** —*n.* **1.** a glass case for the display and protection of articles in shops, museums, etc. **2.** the setting, place, or vehicle for displaying something on a trial basis: *The club is a showcase for new comics.* —*v.t.* **3.** to exhibit or display.

show·down (shō′doun′), *n.* **1.** the laying down of one's cards, face upward, in a card game. **2.** a confrontation for the conclusive settlement of an issue.

show·er[1] (shou′ər), *n.* **1.** a brief fall of rain or, sometimes, of hail or snow. **2.** a fall of many objects, as tears, sparks, etc. **3.** a large supply or quantity: *a shower of wealth.* **4.** a party given for a bestowal of presents of a specific kind, as for a prospective bride. **5.** Also called **show′er bath′. a.** a bath in which water is sprayed on the body, usually from a perforated nozzle. **b.** the apparatus that does this, or the room in which it is done. —*v.t.* **6.** to wet, as with a shower of rain, water, etc. **7.** to pour down in a shower. **8.** to bestow liberally or lavishly. **9.** to bathe (oneself) in a shower. —*v.i.* **10.** to rain, hail, or snow in a shower. **13.** to take a shower bath. [ME *shour,* OE *scūr;* c. G *Schauer,* Icel *skūr,* Goth *skūra*] —**show′er·y,** *adj.*

show·er[2] (shō′ər), *n.* a person or thing that shows. [ME; see SHOW, -ER[1]]

Show·ers (shou′ərz), *n.* **Sea of.** See **Mare Imbrium.**

show′ girl′, a girl or woman who appears in the chorus of a show, night-club act, etc., mainly for decorative purposes.

show·i·ness (shō′ē nis), *n.* the property or characteristic of being showy.

show·ing (shō′ing), *n.* **1.** a show, display, or exhibition. **2.** the act of putting something on display. **3.** a performance or record considered for the impression it makes: *She made a good showing in college.* **4.** a setting forth or presentation, as of facts or conditions.

show·man (shō′mən), *n., pl.* **-men. 1.** a person who presents or produces a show, esp. of a theatrical nature. **2.** a person who is gifted in doing or presenting things theatrically.

show·man·ship (shō′mən ship′), *n.* the skill or ability of a showman.

shown (shōn), *v.* a pp. of **show.**

show-off (shō′ôf′, -of′), *n.* **1.** a person given to pretentious display. **2.** the act of showing off. —**show′-off′ish,** *adj.*

show·piece (shō′pēs′), *n.* **1.** something that is displayed or exhibited. **2.** something exhibited or worthy of exhibiting as a fine example of its kind.

show·place (shō′plās′), *n.* **1.** an estate, mansion, or the like, usually open to the public and renowned for its beauty, historical interest, etc. **2.** any home, building, office, etc., that is considered of flawless taste.

show·room (shō′ro͞om′, -ro͝om′), *n.* a room used for the display of merchandise or samples.

show-stop·per (shō′stop′ər), *n. Theat.* a line, act, performance, etc., that gains such enthusiastic applause that it temporarily interrupts a theatrical performance. Also, **show′ stop′per, show′stop′per.**

show′ win′dow, a display window in a store.

show·y (shō′ē), *adj.,* **show·i·er, show·i·est. 1.** making an imposing display: *showy flowers.* **2.** pompous; ostentatious; gaudy. —**Syn. 2.** See **gaudy**[1].

shr., share; shares.

shrank (shrangk), *v.* a pt. of **shrink.**

shrap·nel (shrap′nᵊl), *n.* **1.** *Mil.* **a.** a hollow projectile containing bullets or the like and a bursting charge, designed to explode before reaching the target, and to release a shower of missiles. **b.** such projectiles collectively. **2.** shell fragments. [named after H. *Shrapnel* (1761–1842), English army officer, its inventor]

shred (shred), *n., v.,* **shred·ded** or **shred, shred·ding.** —*n.* **1.** a piece cut or torn off, esp. in a narrow strip. **2.** a bit; scrap: *We haven't got a shred of evidence.* —*v.t.* **3.** to cut or tear into shreds. —*v.i.* **4.** to be cut up, torn, etc. [ME *schrede,* OE *scrēade;* c. Icel *skrjōthr* worn-out book, G *Schrot* chips] —**shred′der,** *n.*

Shreve·port (shrēv′pōrt′, -pôrt′), *n.* a city in NW Louisiana, on the Red River. 182,064 (1970).

shrew[1] (shro͞o), *n.* a woman of violent temper and speech; virago. [ME; special use of SHREW[2]] —**shrew′like′,** *adj.* —**Syn.** nag, scold.

shrew[2] (shro͞o), *n.* any of several small, mouselike insectivores of the genus *Sorex* and related genera, having a long, sharp snout. [ME; OE *scrēawa* < ?]

Shrew[2], *Blarina brevicauda* (Total length 5 in.; tail 1 in.)

shrewd (shro͞od), *adj.* **1.** astute or sharp in practical matters: *a shrewd politician.* **2.** *Archaic.* keen; piercing. **3.** *Archaic.* malicious. **4.** *Obs.* bad. **5.** *Obs.* shrewish. **6.** *Obs.* artful. [ME *shrewed,* ptp. of *shrew* to curse (now obs.), v. use of SHREW[1]] —**shrewd′ly,** *adv.* —**shrewd′ness,** *n.*

shrew·ish (shro͞o′ish), *adj.* having the disposition of a shrew; nagging. —**shrew′ish·ly,** *adv.* —**shrew′ish·ness,** *n.*

Shrews·bur·y (shro͞oz′ber′ē, -bə rē, shrōz′-), *n.* a city in and the county seat of Shropshire, in W England. 49,726 (1961).

shriek (shrēk), *n.* **1.** a sharp, shrill cry. **2.** a loud, high sound of laughter. **3.** any loud, shrill sound, as of a whistle. —*v.i.* **4.** to utter a sharp, shrill cry, as birds. **5.** to cry out sharply in a high voice. **6.** to utter loud, high-pitched sounds in laughing. **7.** (of a musical instrument, a whistle, etc.) to give forth a loud, shrill sound. —*v.t.* **8.** to utter in a shriek or shrieks. [earlier *shrick,* north var. of *shritch* (now dial.), ME *schriche(n),* back formation from OE *scriccettan;* akin to SHRIKE] —**shriek′er,** *n.* —**shriek′ing·ly,** *adv.* —**shriek′y,** *adj.* —**Syn.** See **scream.**

shriev·al (shrē′vəl), *adj.* of or pertaining to a sheriff. [SHRIEVE[1] + -AL[1]]

shriev·al·ty (shrē′vəl tē), *n., pl.* **-ties.** the office, term, or jurisdiction of a sheriff. [SHRIEVE[1] + *-alty,* as in *mayoralty*]

shrieve[1] (shrēv), *n. Archaic.* sheriff.

shrieve[2] (shrēv), *v.t., v.i.,* **shrieved, shriev·ing.** *Archaic.* shrive.

shrift (shrift), *n. Archaic.* **1.** absolution or remission of sins granted after confession and penance. **2.** confession to a priest. **3.** the act of shriving. Cf. **short shrift.** [ME; OE *scrift* penance; c. G, D *schrift* writing; see SHRIVE, SCRIPT]

shrike (shrīk), *n.* any of numerous predaceous, oscine birds of the family *Laniidae,* having a strong, hooked, and toothed bill, feeding on insects and sometimes on small birds and other animals. [OE *scrīc;* imit.; akin to Icel *-skrīkja* to twitter; see SHRIEK]

shrill (shril), *adj.* **1.** high-pitched and piercing in sound quality: *a shrill cry.* **2.** producing such a sound. **3.** full of or characterized by such a sound. **4.** betraying some strong emotion or attitude in an exaggerated amount. **5.** marked by great intensity, as a light, etc. —*v.t., v.i.* **6.** to cry shrilly. —*n.* **7.** a shrill sound. —*adv.* **8.** in a shrill manner; shrilly. [ME *shrille* (adj., v.); akin to OE *scrallettan* to sound loudly; c. G *schrill* (adj.), *schrillen* (v.); cf. Icel *skrīll* rabble] —**shrill′ness,** *n.* —**shril′ly,** *adv.*

shrimp (shrimp), *n., pl.* **shrimps,** (*esp. collectively for 1*) **shrimp,** *v., adj.* —*n.* **1.** any of several small, long-tailed, chiefly marine, decapod crustaceans of the genera *Crangon, Penaeus,* etc., certain species of which are used as food. **2.** *Slang.* a small or insignificant person. —*v.i.* **3.** to catch shrimps. —*adj.* **4.** (of food) made of or containing shrimp. **5.** of or pertaining to shrimp. [ME *shrimpe;* akin to MHG *schrimpfen* to contract, OE *scrimman* to shrink]

Shrimp, *Crangon vulgaris* (Length 2 in.)

shrimp·er (shrim′pər), *n.* **1.** a commercial shrimp fisherman. **2.** a small motor ship used for commercial shrimping.

shrine (shrīn), *n., v.,* **shrined, shrin·ing.** —*n.* **1.** a receptacle for sacred relics; a reliquary. **2.** a building enclosing the remains or relics of a saint. **3.** any structure or place consecrated or devoted to some saint, holy person, or deity. **4.** any place or object hallowed by its history or associations: *a historic shrine.* —*v.t.* **5.** to enshrine. [ME *schrine,* OE *scrīn;* c. G *Schrein,* D *schrijn* << L *scrīn(ium)* case for books and papers] —**shrine′like′,** *adj.*

Shrin·er (shrī′nər), *n.* a member of a fraternal order **(Ancient Arabic Order of Nobles of the Mystic Shrine)** that is an auxiliary of the Masonic order and is dedicated to good fellowship, health programs, charitable works, etc.

shrink (shringk), *v.* **shrank** or, often, **shrunk; shrunk** or **shrunk·en; shrink·ing;** *n.* —*v.i.* **1.** to draw back, as in retreat or avoidance. **2.** to contract or lessen in size, as from exposure to conditions of temperature or moisture. **3.** to become reduced in extent or scope. —*v.t.* **4.** to cause to shrink or contract; reduce. **5.** *Textiles.* to cause (a fabric) to contract during finishing, thus preventing later shrinkage. —*n.* **6.** the act or an instance of shrinking. **7.** a shrinking movement. **8.** shrinkage. **9.** *Slang.* See **head shrinker.** [ME *schrinke(n),* OE *scrincan;* c. MD *schrinken,* Sw *skrynka* to shrink, Norw *skrukka* old shrunken woman] —**shrink′a·ble,** *adj.* —**shrink′er,** *n.* —**shrink′ing·ly,** *adv.* —**Syn. 1.** withdraw, recoil, retire. **3.** See **decrease.**

shrink·age (shring′kij), *n.* **1.** the act or fact of shrinking. **2.** the amount or degree of shrinking. **3.** reduction or depreciation. **4.** contraction of a fabric in finishing or washing. **5.** the difference between the original weight of livestock and that after it has been prepared for marketing.

shrink′ing vi′olet, a shy, modest, or self-effacing person.

shrink-wrap (shringk′rap′), *v.,* **-wrapped, -wrap·ping,** *n.* —*v.t.* **1.** to wrap and seal (a book, a food product, etc.) in a flexible film that, when exposed to heat, shrinks to the contour of the merchandise. —*n.* **2.** a cover so wrapped. Also, **shrink-pack** (shringk′pak′).

shrive (shrīv), *v.,* **shrove** or **shrived, shriv·en** or **shrived, shriv·ing.** —*v.t.* **1.** to impose penance on (a sinner). **2.** to grant absolution to (a penitent). **3.** to hear the confession of (a person). —*v.i.* **4.** to hear confessions. **5.** to confess one's sins, as to a priest. [ME; OE *scrīfa(n)* (to) prescribe; c. G *schreiben* to write << L *scrībere;* see SCRIBE[1]]

shriv·el (shriv′əl), *v.t., v.i.,* **-eled, -el·ing** or (*esp. Brit.*) **-elled, -el·ling. 1.** to contract and wrinkle; shrink. **2.** to wither; make or become helpless or useless. [akin to Sw *skroflig* uneven, rough (? orig. wrinkled), dial. Sw *skryvla* wrinkle, OE *sceorfan* roughen] —**Syn. 1.** See **wither.**

shriv·en (shriv′ən), *v.* a pp. of **shrive.**

shroff (shrof), *n.* **1.** (in India) a banker or moneychanger. **2.** (in the Far East, esp. China) a native expert employed to test coins, esp. to detect those that are counterfeit. —*v.t.* **3.** to test the genuineness of (coins). [earlier *sharoffe* < Pg *xarrafo* < Urdu *ṣarrāf* moneychanger < Ar]

Shrop·shire (shrop′shēr, -shər), *n.* **1.** Also called **Salop.** a county in W England. 297,313 (1961); 134 sq. mi. *Co. seat:* Shrewsbury. **2.** one of an English breed of dark-faced sheep.

shroud (shroud), *n.* **1.** a cloth or sheet in which a corpse is wrapped for burial. **2.** something that covers or conceals like a garment: *a shroud of rain.* **3.** *Naut.* any of a number of taut ropes or wires converging from both sides on the head of a lower or upper mast to steady it against lateral sway: a part of the standing rigging. —*v.t.* **4.** to wrap or clothe for burial. **5.** to cover; hide from view. **6.** to veil in mystery. **7.** *Obs.* to shelter. —*v.i.* **8.** *Archaic.* to take shelter. [ME; OE *scrūd;* c. Icel *skrūth;* akin to SHRED] —**shroud′less,** *adj.* —**shroud′like′,** *adj.* —**Syn. 1.** winding sheet.

shroud-laid (shroud′lād′), *adj. Cordage.* noting a fiber rope of four strands laid right-handed with or without a core.

shrove (shrōv), *v.* a pt. of **shrive.** [ME *shroof,* OE *scrāf*]

Shrove·tide (shrōv′tīd′), *n.* the three days before Ash Wednesday. [ME *shroftyde.* See SHROVE, TIDE[1]]

Shrove′ Tues′day, the last day of Shrovetide; Mardi gras. [late ME *chroftetewesday*]

shrub[1] (shrub), *n.* a woody, perennial plant smaller than a tree, usually having permanent stems branching from or near the ground. [ME *shrubbe,* OE *scrybb* brushwood; c. Dan (dial.) *skrub*] —**shrub′less,** *adj.* —**shrub′like′,** *adj.*

shrub[2] (shrub), *n.* an acidulated beverage of fruit juice, sugar, and other ingredients, often including alcohol. [< Ar, metathetic var. of *shurb* drink; see SHERBET]

shrub·ber·y (shrub′ə rē), *n., pl.* **-ber·ies.** shrubs collectively.

shrub·by (shrub′ē), *adj.,* **-bi·er, -bi·est. 1.** consisting of or abounding in shrubs. **2.** resembling a shrub; shrublike. —**shrub′bi·ness,** *n.*

shrug (shrug), *v.,* **shrugged, shrug·ging,** *n.* —*v.t.* **1.** to raise and contract (the shoulders), expressing indifference, disdain, etc. —*v.i.* **2.** to raise and contract the shoulders. **3. shrug off, a.** to disregard; minimize. **b.** to rid oneself of. —*n.* **4.** the movement of raising and contracting the shoulders. **5.** a short sweater or jacket that ends above or at the waistline. [late ME *schrugge* to shudder, shrug]

shrunk (shrungk), *v.* a pp. and pt. of **shrink.**

shrunk·en (shrung′kən), *v.* a pp. of **shrink.**

shtick (shtik), *n. Slang.* **1.** (esp. in comic acting) a routine or piece of business inserted to gain a laugh or draw attention to oneself. **2.** one's special interest, talent, etc. Also, **shtik.** [< Yiddish *shtik* piece < Ger *Stück*]

shuck (shuk), *n.* **1.** a husk or pod. **2.** Usually, **shucks.** *Informal.* something useless or worthless: *Their idea isn't worth shucks.* **3.** the shell of an oyster or clam. —*v.t.* **4.** to remove the shucks from: *to shuck corn.* **5.** to peel off, as one's clothes. —*interj.* **6. shucks,** *Informal.* (used as a mild exclamation of disgust or regret.) [?] —**shuck′er,** *n.*

shud·der (shud′ər), *v.i.* **1.** to tremble convulsively, as from horror or cold. —*n.* **2.** a convulsive trembling, as from horror or cold. [ME *shodder* (c. G *schaudern* < LG), freq. of OE *scūdan* to tremble; see -ER[6]] —**Syn. 1.** quiver. See **shiver**[1].

shud·der·ing (shud′ər ing), *adj.* **1.** trembling or quivering with fear, dread, cold, etc. **2.** Also, **shud′der·y.** characterized by or causing a shudder. —**shud′der·ing·ly,** *adv.*

shuf·fle (shuf′əl), *v.,* **-fled, -fling,** *n.* —*v.i.* **1.** to walk clumsily or without lifting the feet. **2.** to scrape the feet over the floor in dancing. **3.** to move clumsily (usually fol. by *into*): *to shuffle into one's clothes.* **4.** to act evasively with respect to a stated situation (often fol. by *in, into,* or *out of*): *to shuffle out of one's responsibilities.* **5.** to intermix cards in a pack so as to change their relative positions. —*v.t.* **6.** to move (one's feet) along the ground or floor without lifting them. **7.** to perform (a dance) with such movements. **8.** to move (an object or objects) this way and that. **9.** to put, thrust, or bring evasively or haphazardly (usually fol. by *in, into, out,* etc.): *to shuffle one's way into favor.* **10.** to mix (cards in a pack) so as to change their relative positions. **11.** to jumble together, mix, or interchange the positions of (objects). **12. shuffle off, a.** to thrust aside; get rid of. **b.** to move away by, or as by, shuffling. —*n.* **13.** a scraping movement; dragging gait. **14.** an evasive trick; evasion. **15.** an act or instance of shuffling. **16.** *Cards.* **a.** a shuffling of cards in a pack. **b.** the right or turn to shuffle preparatory to dealing. **17.** a dance in which the feet are shuffled along the floor. [< LG *schuffeln* to walk clumsily or with dragging feet, mix (cards); akin to SHOVEL] —**shuf′fler,** *n.*

shuf·fle·board (shuf′əl bōrd′, -bôrd′), *n.* **1.** a game in which standing players shove or push disks with a long cue toward numbered scoring sections marked on a floor or deck. **2.** the marked surface on which this game is played. [alter. of earlier *shove board*]

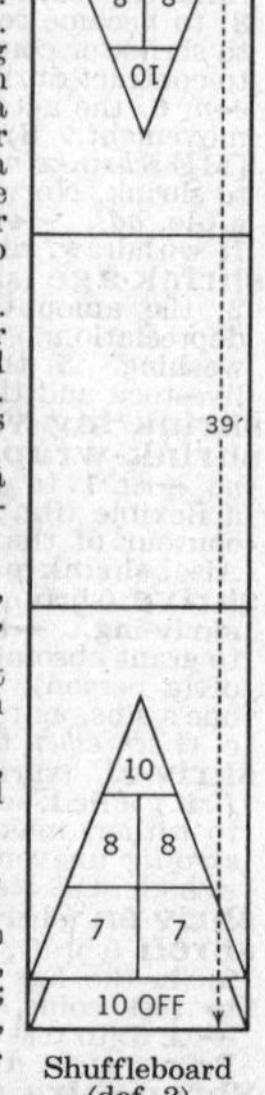

Shuffleboard (def. 2)

shuf·fling (shuf′ling), *adj.* **1.** moving in a dragging or clumsy manner. **2.** prevaricating; evasive. —**shuf′fling·ly,** *adv.*

Shu·fu (shōō′fōō′), *n.* Kashgar.

shul (shōōl, shŏŏl), *n., pl.* **shuln** (shōōln, shŏŏln). *Yiddish.* a synagogue. Also, **schul.**

Shu·lam·ite (shōō′lə mīt′), *n.* an epithet applied to the bride in the Song of Solomon 6:13.

Shul·han A·ruk (shōōl khän′ ä rōōkh′), a code of Jewish law and custom, published in 1565. Also, **Shulchan′ Aruch′.**

Shultz (shōōlts), *n.* **George,** born 1920, U.S. statesman: Secretary of State since 1982.

shun (shun), *v.t.,* **shunned, shun·ning.** to keep away from (a place, person, object, etc.), from motives of dislike, caution, etc.; avoid. [ME *shun(en),* OE *scunian* to avoid, fear] —**shun′na·ble,** *adj.* —**shun′ner,** *n.* —**Syn.** evade, eschew. —**Ant.** seek.

Shun (shōōn), *n.* See under **Yao.**

shunt (shunt), *v.t.* **1.** to shove or turn (someone or something) aside or out of the way. **2.** to sidetrack; get rid of. **3.** *Elect.* **a.** to divert (a part of a current) by connecting a circuit element in parallel with another. **b.** to place or furnish with a shunt. **4.** *Railroads.* to shift (rolling stock) from one track to another; switch. —*v.i.* **5.** to move or turn aside or out of the way. **6.** (of a locomotive with rolling stock) to move from track to track or from point to point, as in a railroad yard; switch. —*n.* **7.** the act of shunting; shift. **8.** *Elect.* a conducting element bridged across a circuit or a portion of a circuit, establishing a current path auxiliary to the main circuit. **9.** a railroad switch. **10.** *Anat., Surg.* a vascular channel through which blood is diverted from its normal path, esp. such a channel formed surgically. **11.** *Anat.* an anastomosis. —*adj.* **12.** *Elect.* being, having, or operating by means of a shunt: *a shunt circuit; a shunt generator.* [ME *schunt* to shy (said of horses); akin to SHUN] —**shunt′er,** *n.*

shunt-wound (shunt′wound′), *adj. Elect.* noting a motor or a generator that has the field circuit connected in parallel with the armature winding. —**shunt′ wind′ing.**

shush (shush), *interj.* **1.** hush (used as a command to be silent). —*v.t.* **2.** to silence (someone or something). [imit.]

shut (shut), *v.,* **shut, shut·ting,** *adj., n.* —*v.t.* **1.** to close (a door, cover, etc.). **2.** to close the doors of (often fol. by *up*): *to shut up a shop for the night.* **3.** to close (something) by bringing together or folding its parts: *Shut your book.* **4.** to confine; enclose: *to shut a bird into a cage.* **5.** to bar; exclude. **6.** to cause (a business, factory, store, etc.) to cease operations. **7.** *Obs.* to bolt; bar. —*v.i.* **8.** to become shut or closed; close. **9. shut down, a.** to settle over so as to envelop or darken, as fog. **b.** *Informal.* to close, esp. temporarily, as a factory. **c.** Also, **shut down on** or **upon,** *Informal.* to check or stop. **10. shut in, a.** to enclose. **b.** to confine, as from illness. **11. shut off, a.** to stop the passage of (water, traffic, electricity, etc.); close off. **b.** to isolate; separate. **12. shut out, a.** to exclude. **b.** to hide from view. **c.** to prevent the opposite side from scoring, as in baseball. **13. shut up, a.** to imprison; confine. **b.** to close entirely. **c.** *Informal.* to stop talking. **d.** *Informal.* to silence (someone). —*adj.* **14.** closed; fastened up: *a shut door.* —*n.* **15.** the act or time of shutting or closing. **16.** the line where two pieces of welded metal are united. [ME *schutte,* OE *scytta(n)* (to) bolt (a door); akin to SHOOT] —**Syn. 1.** See **close. 4.** imprison, cage. —**Ant. 1.** open.

shut·down (shut′doun′), *n.* a shutting down; a closing of a factory or the like for a time.

Shute (shōōt), *n.* **Nevil** (pen name of *Nevil Shute Norway*), 1899–1960, British novelist and aeronautical engineer.

shut-eye (shut′ī′), *n. Slang.* sleep.

shut-in (shut′in′), *adj.* **1.** confined to one's home, a hospital, etc., as from illness. **2.** *Psychiatry.* disposed to desire solitude. —*n.* **3.** a person confined by infirmity.

shut·off (shut′ôf′, -of′), *n.* **1.** an object or device that shuts something off. **2.** interruption; suspension.

shut·out (shut′out′), *n.* **1.** the act or an instance of shutting out. **2.** the state of being shut out. **3.** *Sports.* **a.** a preventing of the opposite side from scoring, as in baseball. **b.** any game in which one side does not score.

shut·ter (shut′ər), *n.* **1.** a solid or louvered cover for a window. **2.** a movable cover, slide, etc., for an opening. **3.** a person or thing that shuts. **4.** *Photog.* a mechanism for opening and closing the aperture of a camera lens to expose film or the like. —*v.t.* **5.** to close or provide with shutters.

shut·ter·bug (shut′ər bug′), *n. Photog. Slang.* an amateur photographer.

shut·tle (shut′əl), *n., v.,* **-tled, -tling,** *adj.* —*n.* **1.** a device in a loom for passing or shooting the filling yarn through the shed from one side of the web to the other. **2.** the sliding container that carries the lower thread in a sewing machine. **3.** a public conveyance, as a train, airplane, or bus, that travels back and forth at regular intervals over a short route. **4.** shuttlecock (def. 1). —*v.t.* **5.** to cause (someone or something) to move to and fro or back and forth by or as by a shuttle. —*v.i.* **6.** to move to and fro: *constantly shuttling between city and suburb.* —*adj.* **7.** of, noting, or pertaining to a shuttle as a transportation service: *a shuttle flight.* [ME *shotil,* OE *scytel* dart, arrow; c. Icel *skutill* harpoon]

shut·tle·cock (shut′əl kok′), *n.* **1.** Also called **shuttle.** the object that is struck back and forth in badminton and battledore, consisting of a feathered cork head and a plastic crown. **2.** the game of battledore. —*v.t.* **3.** to send or bandy to and fro. —*v.i.* **4.** to move or be bandied to and fro. —*adj.* **5.** of such a state or condition.

shy[1] (shī), *adj.,* **shy·er** or **shi·er, shy·est** or **shi·est,** *v.,* **shied, shy·ing,** *n., pl.* **shies.** —*adj.* **1.** bashful; retiring. **2.** easily frightened away; timid. **3.** suspicious; distrustful. **4.** reluctant; wary. **5.** deficient: *shy of funds.* **6.** short of a full amount or number: *We're still a few dollars shy of our goal.* **7.** not bearing or breeding freely, as plants or animals. **8. fight shy of,** to keep away from; avoid: *She fought shy of making the final decision.* —*v.i.* **9.** (esp. of a horse) to start back or aside, as in fear. **10.** to draw back; recoil. —*n.* **11.** a sudden start aside, as in fear. [late ME *schey,* early ME *scheowe,* OE *scēoh;* c. MHG *schiech;* akin to D *schuw,* G *scheu*] —**shy′er,** *n.* —**shy′ly,** *adv.* —**shy′ness,** *n.*
—**Syn. 1.** SLY, BASHFUL imply a manner that shows discomfort or lack of confidence in association with others. SHY implies a constitutional shrinking from contact or close association with others, together with a wish to escape notice: *shy and retiring.* BASHFUL suggests timidity about meeting others, and trepidation and awkward behavior when brought into prominence or notice: *a bashful child.* **4.** heedful, cautious, careful, chary. **10.** shrink. —**Ant. 1.** forward.

shy[2] (shī), *v.,* **shied, shy·ing,** *n., pl.* **shies.** —*v.t., v.i.* **1.** to throw with a swift, sudden movement: *to shy a stone.* —*n.* **2.** a quick, sudden throw. [? orig. causative use of SHY[1] (v.)] —**shy′er,** *n.* —**Syn. 1.** toss, pitch, fling, flip.

Shy·lock (shī′lok), *n.* **1.** a vengeful moneylender in Shakespeare's comedy *The Merchant of Venice* (1596 ?). **2.** a usurer.

shy·ster (shī′stər), *n. Informal.* a lawyer who uses unprofessional or questionable methods. [appar. SHY[1], in slang sense of shady, disreputable + -STER]

si (sē), *n. Music.* a syllable sometimes used for the seventh tone of a diatonic scale. Cf. **ti**[1]. [see GAMUT]

Si (sē; *Chin.* shē), *n.* a river in S China, flowing E from Yünnan province to the South China Sea near Canton. 1250 mi. long. Also called **Si-kiang.**

Si, *Chem.* silicon.
sí (sē), *adv., n. Spanish.* yes.
S.I., 1. Sandwich Islands. 2. Staten Island.
si·al·a·gog·ic (sī′ə lə goj′ik), *Med.* **—***adj.* **1.** encouraging salivary flow. **—***n.* **2.** sialagogue (def. 2). Also, **si′a·lo·gog′ic.** [SIALAGOG(UE) + -IC]
si·al·a·gogue (sī al′ə gôg′, -gog′), *Med.* **—***adj.* **1.** sialagogic (def. 1). **—***n.* **2.** a sialagogic agent or medicine. Also, **si·al′o·gogue′.** [< NL *sialagōg(us)* < Gk *sial(on)* saliva + *-agōgos* -AGOGUE]
Si·al·kot (sē äl′kōt′), *n.* a city in NE Pakistan: military station. 212,000.
Si·am (sī am′, sī′am), *n.* **1.** former name of **Thailand. 2. Gulf of,** an arm of the South China Sea, S of Thailand.
si·a·mang (sē′ə mang′), *n.* a large, black gibbon, *Hylobates syndactylus,* of Sumatra and the Malay Peninsula, having very long arms and the second and third digits partially united by a web of skin [< Malay]
Si·a·mese (sī′ə mēz′, -mēs′), *adj., n., pl.* **-mese. —***adj.* **1.** of or pertaining to Siam, its people, or their language. **2.** Thai (def. 5). **3.** twin; closely connected; similar. **—***n.* **4.** a native of Siam. **5.** Thai (def. 2). **6.** See **Siamese cat. 7.** (*usually l.c.*) a double inlet on the outside of a building by which fire engines can pump water to the standpipes and sprinkler system of the building.
Si′amese cat′, one of a breed of slender, short-haired cats, raised originally in Siam, having a fawn or grayish body with extremities of a darker shade of the same color.
Si′amese twins′, any twins who are born joined together in any manner.

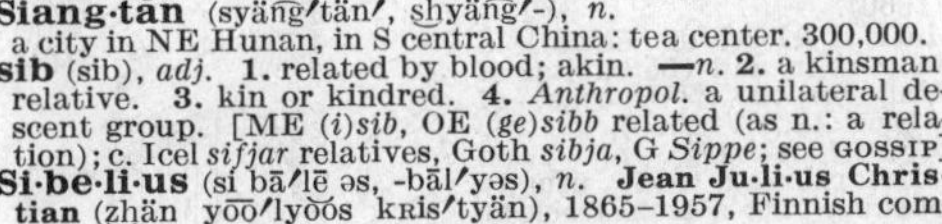
Siamese cat

Si·an (sē′än′, shē′-), *n.* a city in and the capital of Shensi province, in central China: capital of the ancient Chinese Empire. 1,600,000. Also, **Singan.**
Siang·tan (syäng′tän′, shyäng′-), *n.* a city in NE Hunan, in S central China: tea center. 300,000.
sib (sib), *adj.* **1.** related by blood; akin. **—***n.* **2.** a kinsman; relative. **3.** kin or kindred. **4.** *Anthropol.* a unilateral descent group. [ME *(i)sib,* OE *(ge)sibb* related (as n.: a relation); c. Icel *sifjar* relatives, Goth *sibja,* G *Sippe;* see GOSSIP]
Si·be·li·us (si bā′lē əs, -bāl′yəs), *n.* **Jean Ju·li·us Christian** (zhän yo͞o′lyo͞os kris′tyän), 1865–1957, Finnish composer.
Si·be·ri·a (sī bēr′ē ə), *n.* **1.** Russian, **Si·ber** (si bēr′yə). a part of the Soviet Union in N Asia, extending from the Ural Mountains to the Pacific. **2.** any undesirable or isolated locale, job, etc., to which a person is assigned as punishment, a mark of disfavor, or the like. **—Si·be′ri·an,** *adj., n.*
sib·i·lant (sib′ə lənt), *adj.* **1.** hissing. **2.** *Phonet.* characterized by a hissing sound; noting sounds like those spelled with *s* in *this* (this), *rose* (rōz), *pressure* (presh′ər), *pleasure* (plezh′ər), and certain similar uses of *ch, sh, z, zh,* etc. **—***n.* **3.** *Phonet.* a sibilant consonant. [< L *sībilant-* (s. of *sībilāns* hissing, whistling, prp. of *sībilāre*) = *sībil(us)* a hissing, whistling + *-ant-* -ANT] **—sib′i·lance, sib′i·lan·cy,** *n.* **—sib′i·lant·ly,** *adv.*
sib·i·late (sib′ə lāt′), *v.,* **-lat·ed, -lat·ing. —***v.i.* **1.** to hiss. **—***v.t.* **2.** to utter or pronounce with a hissing sound. [< L *sībilāt(us)* ptp. of *sībil(āre).* See SIBILANT, -ATE[1]] **—sib′i·la′tion,** *n.* **—sib′i·la′tor,** *n.*
sib·ling (sib′ling), *n.* **1.** a brother or sister. **2.** *Anthropol.* a comember of a sib. **—***adj.* **3.** of or pertaining to a brother or sister: *sibling rivalry.* [OE]
sib·yl (sib′il), *n.* **1.** any of certain women of antiquity reputed to possess powers of prophecy. **2.** a prophetess or witch. [< Gk *Síbyll(a)* prophetess, the sibyl; r. ME *Sibil* < ML *Sibill(a)*] **—si·byl·ic, si·byl·lic** (si bil′ik), **sib·yl·line** (sib′ə lēn′, -līn′, -lin), *adj.*
sic[1] (sik), *v.t.,* **sicked, sick·ing. 1.** to attack (used esp. as an imperative to a dog): *Sic 'em!* **2.** to incite to attack (usually fol. by *on*). Also, **sick.** [var. of SEEK]
sic[2] (sik), *adj. Chiefly Scot.* such.
sic (sēk; *Eng.* sik), *adv. Latin.* so; thus: usually written parenthetically to indicate that a word, phrase, passage, etc., which may appear incorrect has been quoted verbatim.
Sic., 1. Sicilian. 2. Sicily.
Si·ca·ni·an (si kā′nē ən), *adj.* Sicilian. [< L *Sīcani(us)* (*Sīcani(a)* Sicily + *-us* -OUS) + -AN]
sic·ca·tive (sik′ə tiv), *adj.* **1.** causing or promoting drying. **—***n.* **2.** a siccative substance, esp. in paint. [< LL *siccātīv(us)* = L *siccāt(us)* made dry, dried (ptp. of *siccāre;* see SACK[3], -ATE[1]) + *-īvus* -IVE]
sice (sīs), *n.* syce.
Si·chem (shē′kəm, -kem, shek′əm, -em), *n.* Shechem.
Si·ci·lia (sē chē′lyä *for 1;* si sil′yə, -sil′ē ə *for 2*), *n.* **1.** Italian name of **Sicily. 2.** an ancient name of **Sicily.**
Sic·i·lies, Two (sis′ə lēz). See **Two Sicilies.**
Sic·i·ly (sis′ə lē), *n.* an island in the Mediterranean, comprising a region of Italy, and separated from the SW tip of the mainland by the Strait of Messina: largest island in the Mediterranean. 4,909,996; 9924 sq. mi. *Cap.:* Palermo. Italian, **Sicilia.** Ancient, **Sicilia, Trinacria. —Si·cil·ian** (si sil′yən, -sil′ē ən), *adj., n.*
sick[1] (sik), *adj.* **1.** afflicted with ill health or disease; ill; ailing. **2.** nauseated. **3.** deeply affected with some unpleasant feeling, as of sorrow or disgust. **4.** mentally, morally, or emotionally deranged. **5.** characteristic of a sick mind. **6.** treating of or obsessed with that which is gruesome, sadistic, etc.: *sick jokes.* **7.** of, for, or pertaining to a sick person or persons: *He applied for sick benefits.* **8.** attended with or suggestive of sickness; sickly: *a sick pallor.* **9.** *Informal.* disgusted; chagrined. **10.** not in proper condition; impaired. **11.** *Agric.* **a.** failing to sustain adequate harvests of some crop (usually used in combination): *a wheat-sick soil.* **b.** containing harmful microorganisms: *a sick field.* **—***n.* **12.** (*construed as pl.*) sick persons collectively (usually prec. by *the*). [ME *sik, sek,* OE *sēoc;* c. D *ziek,* G *siech,* Icel *sjūyr,* Goth *siuks*]
—Syn. 1. infirm. SICK, AILING, INDISPOSED refer to any departure from a state of health. SICK is the general term, and may refer to any illness whether severe or mild. AILING implies a somewhat unhealthy condition, usually extending over some time. INDISPOSED applies to a slight, temporary illness. See also **ill. —Ant. 1.** well, hale, healthy.
sick[2] (sik), *v.t.* sic[1].
sick′ bay′, a hospital or dispensary, esp. aboard ship.
sick·bed (sik′bed′), *n.* the bed used by a sick person.
sick′ call′, *Mil.* **1.** a daily formation for those requiring medical attention. **2.** the period for this.
sick·en (sik′ən), *v.t., v.i.* to make or become sick. [ME *seknen, sicnen;* c. Icel *sjūkna*]
sick·en·ing (sik′ə ning), *adj.* causing or capable of causing sickness, esp. nausea, disgust, or loathing. **—sick′en·ing·ly,** *adv.*
sick′ head′ache, migraine.
sick·ish (sik′ish), *adj.* **1.** somewhat sickening or nauseating. **2.** somewhat sick or ill. **—sick′ish·ly,** *adv.* **—sick′ish·ness,** *n.*
sick·le (sik′əl), *n.* **1.** an implement for cutting grain, grass, etc., consisting of a curved, hooklike blade mounted in a short handle. **2.** (*cap.*) *Astron.* a group of stars in the constellation Leo, likened to this implement in formation. [ME *sikel,* OE *sicol;* c. D *zikkel,* G *Sichel,* all < L *secul(a);* akin to *secāre* to cut; see -ULE]

Sickle

sick·le·bill (sik′əl bil′), *n.* any of various birds having a long, curved bill, as the curlew or the thrasher.
sick′le cell′, *Pathol.* a shrunken, fragile erythrocyte having an abnormal shape owing to the loss of hemoglobin. [so called from the fact that the cells are often sickle-shaped] **—sick′le-cell′,** *adj.*
sick′le cell′ ane′mia, *Pathol.* a hereditary form of anemia occurring chiefly among blacks, and characterized by the presence of sickle cells and an abnormal type of hemoglobin in the blood, acute abdominal pains, and ulcerations on the legs; sicklemia. Also called **sick′le cell′ disease′.**
sick′le feath′er, one of the paired, elongated, sickle-shaped, middle feathers of the tail of the rooster.
sick·le·mi·a (sik′ə lē′mē ə, sik lē′-), *n. Pathol.* **1.** a hereditary trait occurring chiefly among blacks, characterized by the presence of deformed, generally crescent-shaped, erythrocytes and an abnormal form of hemoglobin, but often not resulting in anemia. **2.** See **sickle cell anemia. —sick·le·mic** (sik lē′mik, sik′ə-), *adj.*
sick·ly (sik′lē), *adj.,* **-li·er, -li·est,** *adv., v.,* **-lied, -ly·ing. —***adj.* **1.** not strong; unhealthy; ailing. **2.** of, connected with, or arising from ill health. **3.** marked by the prevalence of ill health, as a region. **4.** causing sickness. **5.** nauseating. **6.** maudlin and insipid. **7.** faint or feeble, as light or color. **—***adv.* **8.** in a sick or sickly manner. **—***v.t.* **9.** to cover with a sickly hue. [ME *siklich, sekly*] **—sick′li·ness,** *n.*
sick·ness (sik′nis), *n.* **1.** a particular disease or malady. **2.** the state or an instance of being sick. **3.** nausea; queasiness. [ME *siknesse, seknesse,* OE *sēocnesse*]
sick·out (sik′out′), *n.* a form of job action in which employees refuse to report for work, falsely claiming illness as the reason.
sick·room (sik′ro͞om′, -ro͝om′), *n.* a room in which a sick person is confined.
sic pas·sim (sēk päs′sim; *Eng.* sik pas′im), *Latin.* so throughout: used esp. as a footnote to indicate that a word, phrase, or idea recurs throughout the book being cited.
sic sem·per ty·ran·nis (sēk sem′per ty rän′nis; *Eng.* sik sem′pər ti ran′is), *Latin.* thus always to tyrants: motto of the state of Virginia.
sic tran·sit glo·ri·a mun·di (sēk trän′sit glō′re ä′ mo͞on′dē; *Eng.* sik tran′sit′ glōr′ē ə mo͞on′dī, glôr′-), *Latin.* thus passes away the glory of this world.
Si·cy·on (sish′ē on′, sis′-), *n.* an ancient city in S Greece, near Corinth. **—Sic·y·o·ni·an** (sis′ē ō′nē ən), *adj., n.*
Sid·dhart·ha (si där′tə, -thə), *n.* an epithet of Buddha meaning "he who has attained his goal."
Sid·dons (sid′ənz), *n.* **Sarah (Kemble),** 1755–1831, English actress.
sid·dur (sē do͞or′; *Eng.* sid′ər), *n., pl.* **-du·rim** (-do͞o rēm′), *Eng.* **-durs.** *Hebrew.* a Jewish prayer book used chiefly on days other than festivals and holy days. Cf. **mahzor.** [lit., order]
side (sīd), *n., adj., v.,* **sid·ed, sid·ing. —***n.* **1.** one of the surfaces forming the outside of or bounding a thing. **2.** either of the two broad surfaces of a thin, flat object, as a door. **3.** one of the lateral surfaces of an object. **4.** either of the two lateral parts or areas of a thing: *the right side and the left side.* **5.** either lateral half of a human or animal body. **6.** an aspect or phase: *to consider all sides of a problem.* **7.** region, direction, or position with reference to a central line, space, or point. **8.** a slope, as of a hill. **9.** one of two or more contesting teams, groups, parties, etc. **10.** the position, course, or part of a person or group opposing another: *I am on your side in this issue.* **11.** part or half of a family with reference to the line of descent through a parent. **12.** the space immediately adjacent to something or someone indicated. **13.** *Naut.* the hull portion that is normally out of the water, located between the stem and stern to port or starboard. **14.** *Billiards.* English (def. 5). **15. on the side,** *Informal.* **a.** separate from the main issue or point of interest. **b.** in addition to one's regular, or known work, interest, etc. **c.** as a side dish. **—***adj.* **16.** being at or on one side. **17.** coming from one side. **18.** directed toward one side: *a side blow.* **19.** subordinate or incidental: *a side issue.* **—***v.t.* **20.** to provide with sides or siding. **—***v.i.* **21.** to take or form sides. **22. side with** or **against,** to support or refuse to support one group, opinion, etc., against opposition: *He always sides with the underdog.* [ME, OE; c. D *zijde,* G *Seite,* Icel *sītha*]
side′ arm′, *Mil.* a weapon, as a pistol or sword, carried at the side or in the belt.
side·arm (sīd′ärm′), *adv.* **1.** with a swinging motion of the arm moving to the side of the body at shoulder level or below

and nearly parallel to the ground: *to pitch sidearm.* —*adj.* **2.** thrown or performed sidearm: *a sidearm curve ball.*

side′ band′, *Radio.* the band of frequencies at the sides of the carrier frequency of a modulated signal. Also, **side′band′.**

side·board (sīd′bōrd′, -bôrd′), *n.* **1.** a piece of furniture, as in a dining room, often with shelves, drawers, etc., for holding articles of table service. **2.** a board forming a side or a part of a side; sidepiece. [ME]

side·burns (sīd′bûrnz′), *n.pl.* **1.** the projections of the hairline forming a border on the face in front of each ear. **2.** short whiskers extending from the hairline to below the ears and worn with an unbearded chin. [alter. of BURNSIDES]

side·car (sīd′kär′), *n.* **1.** a small car attached on one side to a motorcycle and supported on the other side by a wheel of its own. **2.** a cocktail made with brandy, orange liqueur, and lemon juice.

side′ chain′, *Chem.* an open chain of atoms attached to an atom of a larger chain, or to a ring. Also called **lateral chain.**

side′ dish′, a serving of a portion of food in addition to the principal food.

side′ effect′, any secondary effect of a drug, chemical, or other medicine, esp. one that is harmful or unpleasant. Also, **side′-ef·fect′.**

side-glance (sīd′glans′, -gläns′), *n.* a glance directed to the side; an oblique or sideways look.

side·kick (sīd′kik′), *n.* *Informal.* **1.** a close friend. **2.** a confederate or assistant.

side·light (sīd′līt′), *n.* **1.** light coming from the side. **2.** an item of incidental information. **3.** *Naut.* either of two lights carried by a vessel under way at night, a red one on the port side and a green on the starboard.

side·line (sīd′līn′), *n., v.,* **-lined, -lin·ing.** —*n.* **1.** a line at the side of something. **2.** a business or activity pursued in addition to one's primary business. **3.** an auxiliary line of goods. **4.** *Sports.* **a.** either of the two lines defining the side boundaries of a playing field. **b. sidelines,** the area immediately beyond either sideline. —*v.t.* **5.** *Informal.* to render incapable of participation, esp. in a sport.

side·ling (sīd′ling), *adv.* **1.** sidelong or sideways; obliquely. —*adj.* **2.** having an oblique position; inclined or sloping. [ME; OE *sīdling*]

side·long (sīd′lông′, -long′), *adj.* **1.** directed to one side. **2.** inclined or slanting to one side. **3.** indirect; roundabout: *sidelong comments about his appearance.* —*adv.* **4.** toward the side; obliquely.

side·man (sīd′man′, -mən), *n., pl.* **-men** (-men′, -mən). an instrumentalist in a band or orchestra, esp. one supporting a soloist.

side′ meat′, *Chiefly Southern and Midland U.S.* salt pork and bacon taken from the sides of a hog.

side·piece (sīd′pēs′), *n.* a piece forming a side or a part of a side of something.

sider-[1], var. of **sidero-**[1] before a vowel: *siderite.*

sider-[2], var. of **sidero-**[2] before a vowel: *sidereal.*

si·de·re·al (sī dēr′ē əl), *adj.* **1.** determined by or from the stars: *sidereal time.* **2.** of or pertaining to the stars. [< L *sīdere(us)* of, belonging to the stars (*sīder-,* s. of *sīdus* constellation + *-eus* adj. suffix) + -AL[1]] —**si·de′re·al·ly,** *adv.*

side′real day′, the interval between two successive passages of the vernal equinox over the meridian, being about four minutes shorter than a mean solar day.

side′real hour′, one 24th part of a sidereal day.

side′real min′ute, *Astron.* the sixtieth part of a sidereal hour.

side′real month′. See under **month** (def. 5).

side′real sec′ond, *Astron.* the sixtieth part of a sidereal minute.

side′real year′, year (def. 3c).

sid·er·ite (sid′ə rīt′), *n.* **1.** a common mineral, iron carbonate, $FeCO_3$, a minor ore of iron. **2.** a meteorite consisting almost entirely of metallic minerals. [SIDER-[1] + -ITE[1]; in earlier (obs.) senses, var. of *siderites* < L < Gk *siderī́tēs* loadstone] —**sid·er·it·ic** (sid′ə rit′ik), *adj.*

sidero-[1], a learned borrowing from Greek meaning "iron," used in the formation of compound words: *siderolite.* Also, *esp. before a vowel,* **sider-.** [< Gk *sídēro(s)* iron]

sidero-[2], a learned borrowing from Latin meaning "star," "constellation," used in the formation of compound words. Also, *esp. before a vowel,* **sider-.** [< L *sīder-* (s. of *sīdus*) star group + -o-]

sid·er·og·ra·phy (sid′ə rog′rə fē), *n.* the art or technique of engraving on steel. —**sid′er·og′ra·pher,** *n.* —**sid·er·o·graph·ic** (sid′ər ə graf′ik), *adj.*

sid·er·o·lite (sid′ər ə līt′), *n.* a meteorite of roughly equal proportions of metallic iron and stony matter.

sid·er·o·sis (sid′ə rō′sis), *n.* *Pathol.* a disease of the lungs caused by inhaling iron or other metallic particles. [< NL < Gk *sidḗrōsis* ironwork] —**sid·er·ot·ic** (sid′ə rot′ik), *adj.*

side·sad·dle (sīd′sad′əl), *n.* **1.** a saddle for women on which the rider sits, facing forward, usually with both feet on the left side of the horse. —*adv.* **2.** seated on a sidesaddle. [late ME *syd saddyl*]

side′ show′, **1.** a minor show or exhibition in connection with a principal one, as at a circus. **2.** any subordinate event or matter.

side·slip (sīd′slip′), *v.,* **-slipped, -slip·ping,** *n.* —*v.i.* **1.** to slip to one side. **2.** (of an airplane) to slide sideways in a downward direction, toward the center of the curve described in turning. —*n.* **3.** the act or an instance of sideslipping.

side·split·ting (sīd′split′ing), *adj.* **1.** convulsively uproarious: *sidesplitting laughter.* **2.** producing uproarious laughter; extremely funny: *sidesplitting farce.* —**side′split′ting·ly,** *adv.*

side′ step′, a step to one side, as in dancing, boxing, etc.

side-step (sīd′step′), *v.,* **-stepped, -step·ping.** —*v.i.* **1.** to step to one side. **2.** to evade or avoid a decision, problem, etc. —*v.t.* **3.** to avoid or dodge (a person, issue, etc.), as by stepping aside.

side′ street′, a street leading away from a main street; an unimportant street or one carrying but little traffic.

side·stroke (sīd′strōk′), *n.* *Swimming.* a stroke in which the body is turned sideways in the water, the hands pull alternately, and the legs perform a scissors kick.

side·swipe (sīd′swīp′), *n., v.,* **-swiped, -swip·ing.** —*n.* **1.** a sweeping stroke or blow along the side. —*v.t.* **2.** to strike with such a blow. —**side′swip′er,** *n.*

side·track (sīd′trak′), *v.t., v.i.* **1.** to move from the main track to a siding, as a train. **2.** to move or distract from the main subject or course. —*n.* **3.** a short railroad track for loading, unloading, or storing cars. Cf. **siding.**

side·walk (sīd′wôk′), *n.* a walk, esp. a paved one, at the side of a street or road.

side′walk art′ist, **1.** an artist who draws pictures on the sidewalk, esp. with colored chalk, to solicit money from passers-by. **2.** an artist stationed on a sidewalk who draws portraits of passing individuals who sit for quick sketches.

side·wall (sīd′wôl′), *n.* the part of a pneumatic tire between the edge of the tread and the rim of the wheel.

side·ward (sīd′wərd), *adj.* **1.** directed or moving toward one side. —*adv.* **2.** Also, **side′wards.** toward one side. [ME]

side·way (sīd′wā′), *n.* **1.** a byway. —*adj., adv.* **2.** sideways.

side·ways (sīd′wāz′), *adv.* **1.** with a side foremost. **2.** facing to the side. **3.** toward or from one side; obliquely: *He glanced sideways at her.* —*adj.* **4.** moving, facing, or directed toward one side. **5.** indirect or evasive. Also, **sideway, side·wise** (sīd′wīz′).

side-wheel (sīd′hwēl′, -wēl′), *adj.* having sidewheels, as a steamboat. —**side′-wheel′er,** *n.*

side·wheel (sīd′hwēl′, -wēl′), *n.* *Naut.* either of a pair of paddle wheels on the sides of a vessel.

side′ whisk′ers, whiskers worn long and with the chin clean-shaven. —**side′-whisk′ered,** *adj.*

side·wind·er (sīd′wīn′dər), *n.* **1.** a severe swinging blow from the side. **2.** a rattlesnake, *Crotalus cerastes,* of the southwestern U.S. and northern Mexico, that moves in loose sand by throwing loops of the body forward. **3.** (*cap.*) *U.S.* an air-to-air, supersonic weapon that intercepts and destroys enemy aircraft, using an infrared homing system.

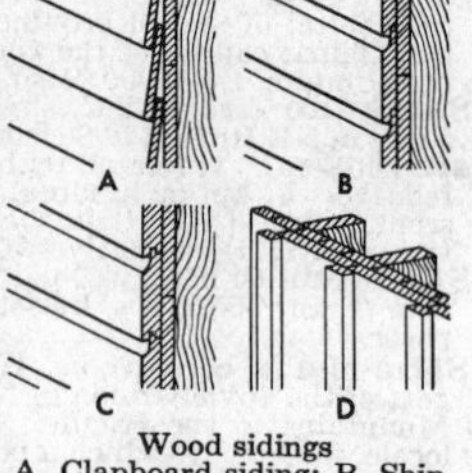

Wood sidings
A, Clapboard siding; B, Shiplap siding; C, Drop siding; D, Board and batten

Si·di-bel-Ab·bès (sē′dē bel-ə bes′), *n.* a city in NW Algeria. 105,357 with suburbs (1960).

Si·di If·ni (sē′dē ēf′nē), a seaport in and the capital of Ifni, on the NW coast of Africa. 12,751 (1960).

sid·ing (sī′ding), *n.* **1.** a short railroad track, usually opening onto a main track at both ends, onto which one of two meeting trains is switched until the other has passed. **2.** *U.S.* any of several varieties of weatherproof facing for frame buildings, composed of pieces attached separately as shingles, plain or shaped boards, or of various units of sheet metal or various types of composition materials.

si·dle (sīd′əl), *v.,* **-dled, -dling,** *n.* —*v.i.* **1.** to move sideways or obliquely. **2.** to edge along furtively. —*n.* **3.** a sidling movement. [back formation from SIDELING] —**si′dling·ly,** *adv.*

Sid·ney (sid′nē), *n.* **Sir Philip,** 1554–86, English poet, writer, statesman, and soldier. Also, **Sydney.**

Si·don (sīd′ən), *n.* a city of ancient Phoenicia: site of modern Saida. See map at **Tyre.** —**Si·do·ni·an** (sī dō′nē ən), *adj., n.*

Sid·ra (sid′rä), *n.* **Gulf of,** an inlet of the Mediterranean, on the N coast of Libya.

Sid·rah (sē drä′; *Eng.* sid′rə), *n., pl.* **Sid·roth** (sē drōt′), *Eng.* **Sid·rahs.** *Hebrew.* a Parashah chanted or read on the Sabbath. [lit., order]

siè·cle (sye′klə), *n., pl.* **-cles** (-klə). *French.* a century, age, or period.

siege (sēj), *n., v.,* **sieged, sieg·ing.** —*n.* **1.** the act or process of surrounding and attacking a fortified place in such a way as to isolate it from help and supplies, thereby making capture possible. **2.** any prolonged or persistent effort to overcome resistance. **3.** a series of illnesses, troubles, etc. **4.** a prolonged period of trouble or annoyance. **5.** Also, **sedge.** *Ornith.* **a.** a flock of herons. **b.** the station of a heron at prey. **6.** *Obs.* **a.** a seat of rank, as a throne. **b.** rank, class, or status. **7. lay siege to,** to besiege. —*v.t.* **8.** besiege. [ME *sege* < OF: seat, back formation from *siegier* < VL **sedicāre* to set < L *sedēre* to sit] —**siege′a·ble,** *adj.*

Siege′ Per′ilous, *Arthurian Romance.* a vacant seat at the Round Table that could be filled only by Sir Galahad, the predestined finder of the Holy Grail, and was fatal to pretenders.

Sieg·fried (sēg′frēd, sig′-; *Ger.* zēk′frēt), *n.* (in the *Nibelungenlied*) the son of Sigmund and Sieglinde and the husband of Kriemhild. He kills the dragon Fafnir, acquires the treasure of the Nibelungs, wins Brunhild for Gunther, and is finally killed by Hagen at the behest of Brunhild, whom he had once promised to marry: corresponds to Sigurd of the *Volsunga Saga.* Cf. **Brunhild.**

Sieg′fried line′, a zone of fortifications in W Germany facing the Maginot line, constructed before World War II. [named after SIEGFRIED]

Sieg Heil (zēk hīl′), *German.* hail to victory: a salute used by the Nazis.

Sieg·lin·de (sēg lin′də; *Ger.* zēkh lin′də), *n.* (in the *Nibelungenlied*) the wife of Sigmund and mother of Siegfried. Cf. **Signy.**

sie·mens (sē′mənz), *n.* (*construed as sing.*) a unit of conductance equal to one mho. *Abbr.:* S

Sie·mens (sē′mənz; *Ger.* zē′məns), *n.* **Sir William** (*Karl Wilhelm Siemens*), 1823–83, English inventor, born in Germany.

Sie·na (sē en′ə; *It.* sye′nä), *n.* a city in Tuscany, in central Italy, S of Florence: cathedral. 62,215 (1961).

Si·en·ese (sē′ə nēz′, -nēs′), *adj., n., pl.* **-ese.** —*adj.* **1.** of or pertaining to Siena or its people. —*n.* **2.** an inhabitant of Siena.

si·en·na (sē en′ə), *n.* **1.** a ferruginous earth used as a yellowish-brown pigment **(raw sienna)** or, after roasting in a furnace, as a reddish-brown pigment **(burnt sienna). 2.** the color of such a pigment. [< It (*terra di*) *Sien(n)a* (earth of) SIENA]

si·er·ra (sē er′ə), *n.* **1.** a chain of hills or mountains, the peaks of which suggest the teeth of a saw. **2.** any of several Spanish mackerels of the genus *Scomberomorus*, esp. *S. sierra*, found in western North America. **3.** a word used in communications to represent the letter *S*. [< Sp: lit., saw < L *serra*]

Si·er·ra Le·o·ne (sē er′ə lē ō′nē, lē ōn′), an independent country in W Africa: member of the British Commonwealth of Nations; formerly a British colony and protectorate. 3,000,000; 27,925 sq. mi. *Cap.:* Freetown.

Si·er·ra Ma·dre (sē er′ə mä′drā; *for 2 also Sp.* syeʀ′rä mä′thʀe), **1.** a mountain range extending from S Wyoming into N Colorado. **2.** two parallel mountain chains in Mexico, bordering the central plateau on the E and W, and extending SE into N Guatemala.

Si·er·ra Ne·vad·a (sē er′ə nə vad′ə, -vä′də *for 1; Sp.* syeʀ′rä ne vä′thä *for 2*), **1.** a mountain range in E California. Highest peak, Mt. Whitney, 14,495 ft. **2.** a mountain range in S Spain. Highest peak, Mulhacén, 11,420 ft.

si·es·ta (sē es′tə), *n.* a midday or afternoon rest or nap, esp. as taken in Spain and Latin America. [< Sp << L *sexta* (*hōra*) the sixth (hour), midday]

sieur (syœʀ), *n. French.* an old title of respect for a man.

sieve (siv), *n.*, *v.*, **sieved, siev·ing.** —*n.* **1.** an instrument with a meshed or perforated bottom, used for separating coarse from fine parts of loose matter, for straining liquids, etc. **2.** a person who cannot keep a secret. —*v.t., v.i.* **3.** to put or force through a sieve; sift. [ME *sive*, OE *sife;* c. D *zeef*, G *Sieb;* akin to SIFT] —**sieve′like′,** *adj.*

sieve′ cell′, *Bot.* an elongated cell whose walls contain perforations (**sieve′ pores′**) that are arranged in circumscribed areas (**sieve′ plates′**) and afford communication with similar adjacent cells.

sieve′ tube′, *Bot.* **1.** a vertical series of sieve cells in the phloem, specialized for the conduction of food materials. **2.** a single sieve cell.

Sie·yès (sye yes′), *n.* **Em·ma·nu·el Jo·seph** (e mᴀ ny el′ zhô zef′), ("*Abbé Sieyès*"), 1748–1836, French priest and revolutionist.

Sif·nos (sif′nos), *n.* Siphnos.

sift (sift), *v.t.* **1.** to separate and retain the coarse parts of (flour, ashes, etc.) with a sieve. **2.** to scatter by means of a sieve: *to sift sugar onto cake.* **3.** to separate by or as by a sieve. **4.** to examine closely: *The detectives are still sifting the evidence.* **5.** to question closely. —*v.i.* **6.** to sift something. **7.** to pass or fall through or as through a sieve. [ME *sift(en)*, OE *siftan;* c. D, MLG *siften;* see SIEVE] —**sift′er,** *n.*

sift·ings (sif′tiṅgz), *n.* (*construed as pl.*) **1.** something sifted: *siftings of flour.* **2.** that which is separated by sifting: *to discard the siftings.*

Sig., (in prescriptions) **1.** write; mark; label. [< L *signā*] **2.** *Med.* signature. **3.** let it be written. [< L *signētur*] **4.** signor. **5.** signore; signori.

sig., **1.** signature. **2.** signor. **3.** signore; signori.

si·gan·id (sə gan′id, -gā′nid), *n.* **1.** any fish of the family *Siganidae*, comprising the rabbitfishes. —*adj.* **2.** belonging or pertaining to the family *Siganidae*. [< NL *Siganid(ae)* = *Sigan(us)* genus name (< Ar *sijān* rabbitfish) + *-idae* -ID[2]]

Sig·geir (sig′gâr), *n.* (in the *Volsunga Saga*) the husband of Signy and killer of Volsung.

sigh (sī), *v.i.* **1.** to let out one's breath audibly, as from sorrow, weariness, relief, etc. **2.** to yearn or long; pine. **3.** to make a sound suggesting a sigh: *sighing wind.* —*v.t.* **4.** to express or utter with a sigh. **5.** to lament with sighing. —*n.* **6.** the act or sound of sighing. [ME *sighe(n)*, back formation from *sihte* sighed, past tense of ME *siken, sichen*, OE *sīcan*] —**sigh′er,** *n.* —**sigh′less,** *adj.* —**sigh′like′,** *adj.*

sight (sīt), *n.* **1.** the power or faculty of seeing; vision. **2.** the act, fact, or an instance of seeing. **3.** one's range of vision on some specific occasion: *Land is in sight.* **4.** a view; glimpse. **5.** mental perception or regard; judgment. **6.** something seen or worth seeing; spectacle. **7.** something shocking or distressing to see. **8.** *Chiefly Dial.* a multitude; great deal: *It's a sight better to work than to starve.* **9.** an observation taken with a surveying, navigating, or other instrument, to ascertain an exact position or direction. **10.** any of various mechanical or optical viewing devices, as on a firearm, for aiding the eye in aiming. **11.** *Obs.* skill; insight. **12.** **at first sight,** at the first glimpse; at once. **13.** **at sight, a.** immediately upon seeing, esp. without referring elsewhere for information: *to translate something at sight.* **b.** *Com.* on presentation: *a draft payable at sight.* **14.** **catch sight of,** to get a glimpse of; see. **15.** **know by sight,** to be able to identify by appearance only, as a person previously seen but not known by name. **16.** **not by a long sight,** *Informal.* **a.** probably not. **b.** definitely not. **17.** **on** or **upon sight,** immediately upon seeing: *Shoot him on sight.* —*v.t.* **18.** to see, glimpse, notice, or observe: *to sight a ship to the north.* **19.** to take a sight or observation of, esp. with surveying or navigating instruments. **20.** to direct or aim by a sight or sights, as a firearm. **21.** to provide with sights, or adjust the sights of, as a gun. —*v.i.* **22.** to aim or observe through a sight. **23.** to look carefully in a certain direction. [ME; OE (*ge*)*siht*, var. of (*ge*)*sihth* (c. G *Gesicht* face) < *sēon* to see[1]; see -TH[1]] —**sight′a·ble,** *adj.* —**sight′er,** *n.*

sight′ draft′, *Finance.* a draft payable upon presentation.

sight·hole (sīt′hōl′), *n.* a hole, as on a quadrant, through which to see or to sight.

sight·less (sīt′lis), *adj.* **1.** unable to see; blind. **2.** incapable of being seen; invisible. [ME] —**sight′less·ly,** *adv.* —**sight′less·ness,** *n.*

sight′ line′, any of the lines of vision between the spectators and the stage or area in a theater, stadium, etc.

sight·ly (sīt′lē), *adj.*, **-li·er, -li·est.** **1.** pleasing to the sight; attractive; comely. **2.** affording a fine view. —**sight′li·ness,** *n.*

sight-read (sīt′rēd′), *v.t., v.i.*, **-read, -read·ing.** to read, play, or sing without previous practice, rehearsal, or study of, the material to be treated. —**sight′-read′er,** *n.*

sight′ rhyme′, *Pros.* agreement in spelling, but not in sound, of the ends of words or of lines of verse, as in *have, grave*. Also called **eye rhyme.**

sight·see·ing (sīt′sē′iṅg), *n.* **1.** the act of visiting and seeing places and objects of interest. —*adj.* **2.** seeing, showing, or used for visiting sights: *a sightseeing bus.* Also, **sight′-see′ing.** —**sight′se′er, sight′-se′er,** *n.*

sig·il (sij′il), *n.* a seal or signet. [< L *sigill(um)*, dim. of *signum* SIGN; see SEAL[1]] —**sig·il·lar·y** (sij′ə ler′ē), *adj.* —**sig′il·is′tic,** *adj.*

Sig·is·mund (sij′is mənd, sig′is-; *Ger.* zē′gis mo͝ont′), *n.* 1368–1437, Holy Roman emperor 1411–37.

sig·los (sig′los), *n.*, *pl.* **-loi** (-loi). a silver coin of ancient Persia, the 20th part of a daric. [< Gk < Sem]

sig·ma (sig′mə), *n.* the 18th letter of the Greek alphabet Σ, σ, ς. [< L < Gk]

sig·mate (sig′mit, -māt), *adj.* having the form of the Greek sigma or the letter *S*. —**sig·ma·tion** (sig mā′shən), *n.*

sig·moid (sig′moid), *adj.* Also, **sig·moi′dal.** **1.** shaped like the letter *C*. **2.** shaped like the letter *S*. **3.** of, pertaining to, or situated near the sigmoid flexure of the large intestine. —*n.* **4.** *Anat.* a sigmoid part of the body, as the sigmoid flexure. [< Gk *sigmoeid(ēs)* shaped like a sigma] —**sig·moi′dal·ly,** *adv.*

sig′moid flex′ure, **1.** *Zool.* an S-shaped curve in a body part. **2.** *Anat.* an S-shaped curve of the large intestine between the descending colon and the rectum.

Sig·mund (sig′mənd, sēg′mo͝ont; *Ger.* zēᴋʜ′mo͝ont), *n.* **1.** (in the *Volsunga Saga*) the son of Volsung and Liod; the father, through his sister, Signy, of Sinfiotli; the husband first of Borghild, then of Hiordis; and the father of Sigurd. **2.** (in the *Nibelungenlied*) the king of the Netherlands and father of Siegfried.

sign (sīn), *n.* **1.** a token; indication. **2.** a conventional or arbitrary mark, figure, or symbol used technically as an abbreviation for the word or words it represents. **3.** an arbitrary or conventional symbol used in musical notation to indicate tonality, tempo, etc. **4.** a motion or gesture used to express or convey an idea, command, etc. **5.** a name, direction, warning, or advertisement, mounted on wood, metal, paper, or other material and permanently posted. **6.** *Med.* the objective indications of a disease. **7.** a trace; vestige. **8.** something that gives evidence of an event: *the first signs of spring.* **9.** Also called **sign of the zodiac.** *Astrol.* any of the 12 divisions of the zodiac. See diag. at **zodiac.** —*v.t.* **10.** to affix a signature to. **11.** to write as a signature. **12.** to engage by written agreement. **13.** to indicate; betoken. **14.** to mark with a sign, esp. the sign of the cross. **15.** to communicate by means of a sign; signal. —*v.i.* **16.** to write one's signature, as a token of agreement or obligation. **17.** to make a sign or signal. **18.** to obligate oneself by signature. **19.** **sign away** or **over,** to assign or dispose of by affixing one's signature to a document. **20.** **sign off, a.** to cease radio or television broadcasting, esp. at the end of the day. **b.** *Slang.* to become silent. **21.** **sign on, a.** to employ; hire. **b.** to bind oneself to work, as by signing a contract. **22.** **sign up, a.** to join an organization or group, esp. to enlist in the armed forces. **b.** to persuade to join an organization or to sign a contract. [ME *signe* < OF < L *sign(um)* mark, sign, token, ensign, signal, image]
—**Syn.** **1.** trace, hint, suggestion. **1, 4.** signal. **8.** indication, hint, augury. SIGN, OMEN, PORTENT name that which gives evidence of a future event. SIGN is a general word for whatever gives evidence of an event, past, present, or future: *Dark clouds are a sign of rain or snow.* An OMEN is an augury or warning of things to come; formerly depending upon religious practices or beliefs, it is used only of the future, in general, as good or bad: *birds of evil omen.* PORTENT, limited, like OMEN, to prophecy, may be used of a specific event, usually a misfortune: *portents of war.* **13.** signify, mean.

Si·gnac (sē nyᴀk′), *n.* **Paul** (pôl), 1863–1935, French painter.

sig·nal (sig′nəl), *n.*, *adj.*, *v.*, **-naled, -nal·ing** or (*esp. Brit.*) **-nalled, -nal·ling.** —*n.* **1.** anything that serves to warn, direct, command, or the like, as a light, a gesture, an act, etc. **2.** anything agreed upon or understood as the occasion for concerted action. **3.** an act, event, or the like, that causes or incites some action. **4.** a token; indication. **5.** *Elect., Radio.* an impulse, sound wave, etc., transmitted or received. **6.** *Cards.* a play that reveals to one's partner a wish that he continue or discontinue the suit led. —*adj.* **7.** serving as a signal. **8.** notable; outstanding. —*v.t.* **9.** to make a signal to. **10.** to communicate or make known by a signal. —*v.i.* **11.** to make communication by a signal or signals. [ME < ML, LL *signāle*, n. use of neut. of *signālis* of a sign] —**sig′nal·er;** *esp. Brit.* **sig′nal·ler,** *n.* —**Syn.** **1, 4.** sign.

Sig′nal Corps′, *U.S. Army.* a branch of the army responsible for military communications, meteorological studies, and related work.

sig·nal·ise (sig′nəlīz′), *v.t.*, **-ised, -is·ing.** *Chiefly Brit.* signalize.

sig·nal·ize (sig′nəlīz′), *v.t.*, **-ized, -iz·ing.** **1.** to make conspicuous. **2.** to point out or indicate particularly.

sig·nal·ly (sig′nəlē), *adv.* conspicuously; notably.

sig·nal·man (sig′nəl mən), *n.*, *pl.* **-men.** a person whose occupation or duty is signaling, as on a railroad or in the army.

sig·nal·ment (sig′nəl mənt), *n.* a detailed description of a person, usually for police identification. [< F *signalement* < *signaler* to signalize]

sig·na·to·ry (sig′nə tōr′ē, -tôr′ē), *adj.*, *n.*, *pl.* **-ries.** —*adj.* **1.** having signed or joined in signing a document: *the signatory powers to a treaty.* —*n.* **2.** a signer, or one of the signers, of a document. [< L *signātōri(us)* of, belonging to sealing = *signāt(us)* marked, sealed (ptp. of *signāre;* see SIGN, -ATE[1]) + *-ōrius* -ORY[1]]

sig·na·ture (sig′nə chər), *n.* **1.** a person's name, or a mark representing it, as signed or written by himself or by deputy, as in subscribing a letter or other document. **2.** the act of signing a document. **3.** *Music.* a sign or set of signs at the beginning of a staff to indicate the key or the time of a piece. **4.** *Radio.* a theme identifying a program. **5.** *Med.* the part of a prescription that gives the directions to be marked on the container of the medicine. *Abbr.:* S, Sig. **6.** *Bookbinding.* a printed sheet folded to page size for binding together, with other such sheets, to form a book, magazine, etc. **7.** *Print.* **a.** a letter or other symbol generally placed by the printer at the foot of the first page of every section to guide the binder in arranging the sections in sequence. **b.** a sheet so marked. [< ML *signātūra* a signing = L *signāt(us)* marked, sealed (see SIGNATORY) + *-ūra* -URE] —**sig′na·ture·less,** *adj.*

sign·board (sīn′bōrd′, -bôrd′), *n.* a board bearing a sign, as an advertisement, warning, etc.

sign·er (sī′nər), *n.* **1.** a person who signs. **2.** a person who writes his name, as in token of agreement.

sig·net (sig′nit), *n.* **1.** a small seal, as in a finger ring. **2.** a small official seal for legal documents, contracts, etc. **3.** an impression made by or as by a signet. —*v.t.* **4.** to stamp or mark with a signet. [ME < ML *signēt(um).* See SIGN, -ET]

sig′net ring′, a finger ring containing a small seal.

sig·nif·i·cance (sig nif′ə kəns), *n.* **1.** importance; consequence: *events of significance.* **2.** meaning; import. **3.** the quality of being significant or meaningful: *to give significance to the dullest of chores.* [late ME < L *significantia* force, meaning. See SIGNIFY, -ANCE] —**Syn. 1.** moment, weight. See **importance. 2.** See **meaning.** —**Ant. 1.** triviality.

sig·nif·i·can·cy (sig nif′ə kən sē), *n., pl.* **-cies.** significance. [< L *significantia*]

sig·nif·i·cant (sig nif′ə kənt), *adj.* **1.** important; of consequence. **2.** having or expressing a meaning. **3.** having a special, secret, or disguised meaning: *a significant wink.* —*n.* **4.** *Archaic.* something significant; a sign. [< L *significant-* (s. of *significāns*), prp. of *significāre* to SIGNIFY; see -ANT] —**sig·nif′i·cant·ly,** *adv.* —**Syn. 1.** momentous, weighty.

sig·ni·fi·ca·tion (sig′nə fə kā′shən), *n.* **1.** meaning; import; sense. **2.** the act or fact of signifying; indication. [ME *significacion* < L *significātiōn-* (s. of *significātiō*) signal, emphasis, meaning]

sig·nif·i·ca·tive (sig nif′ə kā′tiv), *adj.* **1.** serving to signify. **2.** significant; suggestive. [< LL *significātīv(us)* denoting = L *significāt(us)* meant (ptp. of *significāre;* see SIGNIFY, -ATE[1]) + *-īvus* -IVE] —**sig·nif′i·ca′tive·ly,** *adv.* —**sig·nif′i·ca′tive·ness,** *n.*

sig·ni·fy (sig′nə fī′), *v.,* **-fied, -fy·ing.** —*v.t.* **1.** to make known by signs, speech, or action. **2.** to be a sign of; mean; portend. —*v.i.* **3.** to be of importance. [ME *signifi(en)* < OF *signifie(r)* < L *significāre*] —**sig′ni·fi′a·ble,** *adj.* —**sig′ni·fi′er,** *n.* —**Syn. 1.** signal, express, indicate. **2.** represent, indicate, denote, betoken, imply.

si·gnior (sēn′yōr, -yôr, sin yōr′, -yôr′), *n.* signor.

sign′ lan′guage, a means of communication in which gestures, usually manual, substitute for spoken words, used by deaf-mutes, between speakers of different languages, etc.

sign′ man′ual, *pl.* **signs manual.** a personal signature, esp. that of a sovereign, on a public document.

sign′ of the cross′, (esp. in the Roman Catholic Church) a movement of the hand to indicate a cross, as from forehead to breast and left shoulder to right, or, in the Eastern Orthodox Church, from right shoulder to left.

sign′ of the zo′diac, sign (def. 9).

si·gnor (sēn′yōr, -yôr, sin yōr′, -yôr′; *It.* sē nyôʀ′), *n., pl.* **-gnors,** *It.* **-gno·ri** (-nyô′ʀē). a conventional Italian term of address or title of respect for a man. *Abbr.:* Sig., sig. Also, **signior.** [< It; see SIGNORE[1]]

si·gno·ra (sēn yōr′ə, -yôr′ə; *It.* sē nyô′ʀä), *n., pl.* **-ras,** *It.* **-re** (-ʀe). a conventional Italian term of address or title of respect for a married woman. [< It; fem. of SIGNORE[1]]

si·gno·re[1] (sin yōr′ā, -yôr′ā; *It.* sē nyô′ʀe), *n., pl.* **si·gno·ri** (sin yōr′ē, -yôr′ē; *It.* sē nyô′ʀē). a conventional Italian title of respect for a man, usually used separately; signor. [< It < VL *senior;* see SENIOR]

si·gno·re[2] (sin yōr′ā, -yôr′ā; *It.* sē nyô′ʀe), *n.* a pl. of **signora.**

Si·gno·rel·li (sē nyô ʀel′lē), *n.* **Lu·ca** (lo͞o′kä), c1445–1523, Italian painter.

si·gno·ri·na (sēn′yô rē′nə; *It.* sē′nyô ʀē′nä), *n., pl.* **-nas,** *It.* **-ne** (-ne). a conventional Italian term of address or title of respect for a girl or unmarried woman. [< It; dim. of SIGNORA; see -INE[1]]

si·gno·ri·no (sēn′yô rē′nō; *It.* sē′nyô ʀē′nô), *n., pl.* **-nos,** *It.* **-ni** (-nē). a conventional Italian title of respect for a young man. [< It; dim. of SIGNORE[1]; see -INE[1]]

si·gno·ry (sē′nyə rē), *n., pl.* **-ries.** seigniory.

sign·post (sīn′pōst′), *n.* **1.** a post bearing a sign that gives information or guidance. **2.** any immediate indication, obvious clue, etc.

Sig·ny (sig′nē, -ny), *n.* (in the *Volsunga Saga*) the daughter of Volsung and mother, by her brother, Sigmund, of Sinfiotli, with whose help she kills her husband, Siggeir, to avenge the murder of Volsung. Cf. **Sieglinde.**

Sig·urd (sig′ərd; *Ger.* zē′go͝oʀt), *n.* (in the *Volsunga Saga*) the son of Sigmund and Hiordis and the husband of Gudrun. He kills the dragon Fafnir, acquires the treasure of Andvari, wins Brynhild for Gunnar, and is finally killed at the behest of Brynhild, whom he had once promised to marry: corresponds to Siegfried of the *Nibelungenlied.*

Si·ha·nouk (sē′ä no͝ok′), *n.* See **Norodom Sihanouk.**

Si·kan·dar·a·bad (si kun′drä bäd′), *n.* Secunderabad.

Si·kang (shē′käng′), *n.* a former province in W China; now a part of Szechwan.

sike (sīk, sik), *n.* *Scot. and North Eng.* **1.** a small stream. **2.** a gully or ditch, esp. one that fills with water after a heavy rain. [ME < Scand; cf. Icel *sīk* ditch, c. OE *sīc* (now *sitch*) rill, MLG *sīk* puddle; akin to OHG *seih* urine, OE *sicerian* to ooze]

Sikh (sēk), *n.* **1.** a member of a Hindu religious sect, founded in the Punjab c1500 by the guru Nanak as a reformed offshoot of Hinduism, refusing to recognize the caste system or the supremacy of the Brahmanical priests and forbidding magic, idolatry, and pilgrimages. —*adj.* **2.** of or pertaining to the Sikhs or to Sikhism. [< Hindi: lit., disciple < Skt *śikṣati*]

Sikh·ism (sē′kiz əm), *n.* the religion and practices of the Sikhs.

Si·kiang (shē′kyäng′), *n.* Si.

Sik·kim (sik′im, si kēm′), *n.* a state in NE India, in the Himalayas between Nepal and Bhutan. 162,189 (1961); 2745 sq. mi. *Cap.:* Gangtok.

Sik·ki·mese (sik′ə mēz′, -mēs′) *n.pl.* **-mese,** *adj.* —*n.* **1.** a native or inhabitant of Sikkim. —*adj.* **2.** of or pertaining to Sikkim or its people.

Si·kor·sky (si kôr′skē), *n.* **I·gor** (ē′gôr), 1889–1972, U.S. aeronautical engineer, born in Russia.

si·lage (sī′lij), *n.* fodder preserved in a silo; ensilage.

si·lence (sī′ləns), *n., v.,* **-lenced, -lenc·ing,** *interj.* —*n.* **1.** absence of any sound; stillness. **2.** the state or fact of being silent. **3.** absence or omission of mention. **4.** the state of being forgotten; oblivion. **5.** concealment; secrecy. —*v.t.* **6.** to put or bring to silence; still. **7.** to put (doubts, fears, etc.) to rest; quiet. **8.** *Mil.* to still (enemy guns), as by a more effective fire. —*interj.* **9.** be silent! [ME < OF < L *silent(ium).* See SILENT, -ENCE]

si·lenc·er (sī′lən sər), *n.* **1.** a person or thing that silences. **2.** a device for deadening the report of a firearm. **3.** *Chiefly Brit.* the muffler on an internal-combustion engine.

si·lent (sī′lənt), *adj.* **1.** making no sound; quiet; still. **2.** refraining from speech. **3.** speechless; mute. **4.** not inclined to speak; taciturn; reticent. **5.** characterized by absence of speech or sound: *a silent prayer.* **6.** unspoken; tacit: *a silent assent.* **7.** omitting mention of something, as in a narrative. **8.** inactive or quiescent, as a volcano. **9.** not sounded or pronounced: *The "b" in "doubt" is a silent letter.* **10.** *Motion Pictures.* not having a sound track. —*n.* **11.** Usually, **silents.** silent films. [< L *silent-* (s. of *silēns*), prp. of *silēre* to be quiet; see -ENT] —**si′lent·ly,** *adv.* —**si′lent·ness,** *n.* —**Syn. 1.** See **still**[1]. —**Ant. 1.** noisy. **4.** talkative.

si′lent but′ler, a small receptacle having a handle and a hinged lid, used for collecting the contents of ashtrays, crumbs from a dinner table, etc., for disposal.

si′lent part′ner, *Com.* a partner taking no active part in the conduct of a business.

Si·le·nus (sī lē′nəs), *n., pl.* **-ni** (-nī) for 2. *Class. Myth.* **1.** a forest spirit, sometimes referred to as the oldest of the satyrs, and the foster father, teacher, and companion of Dionysus: often represented as a bearded old man. **2.** (*l.c.*) any of a group of forest spirits similar to satyrs: often represented as a drunken old man with the legs and ears of a horse.

si·le·sia (si lē′zhə, -shə, -sī-), *n.* a twilled fabric of acetate, rayon, or cotton, for garment linings. [after SILESIA]

Si·le·sia (si lē′zhə, -shə, sī-), *n.* a region in central Europe: formerly divided between Germany (which had the largest portion), Poland, and Czechoslovakia; by provision of the Potsdam agreement 1945 the greater part of German Silesia is now under Polish administration; rich deposits of coal, iron, and other minerals. German, **Schlesien.** Polish, **Slask.** Czech, **Slezsko.** —**Si·le′sian,** *adj., n.*

sil·hou·ette (sil′o͞o et′), *n., v.,* **-et·ted, -et·ting.** —*n.* **1.** a two-dimensional representation of the outline of an object, as an outline drawing, uniformly filled in with black. **2.** the outline or general shape of something. **3.** a dark image outlined against a lighter background. —*v.t.* **4.** to show in or as in a silhouette. [named after Étienne de *Silhouette* (1709–67), French finance minister]

Silhouette

silic-, a learned borrowing from Latin meaning "flint," "silica," "silicon," used in the formation of compound words: *silicide.* Also, **silici-, silico-.** [comb. form repr. L *silic-,* s. of *silex* flint]

sil·i·ca (sil′ə kə), *n.* the dioxide form of silicon, SiO_2, occurring esp. as quartz and agate: used usually in the form of its prepared white powder chiefly in the manufacture of glass, water glass, ceramics, and abrasives. Also called **silicon dioxide.** [< NL = *silic-* SILIC- + *-a* n. suffix]

sil′ica gel′, *Chem.* a highly adsorbent gelatinous form of silica, used chiefly as a dehumidifying and dehydrating agent.

sil·i·cate (sil′ə kit, -kāt′), *n.* *Chem.* any salt derived from the silicic acids or from silica. —**sil·i·ca·tion** (sil′ə kā′shən), *n.*

si·li·ceous (si lish′əs), *adj.* **1.** containing, consisting of, or resembling silica. **2.** growing in soil rich in silica. Also, **si·li′cious.** [< L *siliceus* of flint or limestone. See SILIC-, -EOUS]

silici-, var. of **silic-:** *siliciferous.*

si·lic·ic (si lis′ik), *adj.* *Chem.* **1.** containing silicon. **2.** of or pertaining to silica or acids derived from it.

silic′ic ac′id, *Chem.* any of certain amorphous gelatinous masses, formed when alkaline silicates are treated with acids, which dissociate into silica and water.

sil·i·cide (sil′i sīd′, -sid), *n.* *Chem.* a compound of two elements, one of which is silicon.

sil·i·cif·er·ous (sil′i sif′ər əs), *adj.* containing, combined with, or producing silica.

silic′ified wood′, wood that has been changed into quartz by a replacement of the cellular structure of the wood by siliceous waters.

si·lic·i·fy (si lis′ə fī′), *v.t., v.i.,* **-fied, -fy·ing.** to convert or be converted into silica. [SILIC- + -IFY] —**si·lic′i·fi·ca′tion.**

si·li·ci·um (si lish′ē əm, sə lis′-), *n.* silicon. [< NL]

sil·i·cle (sil′i kəl), *n.* *Bot.* a short silique. [< L *silicul(a)* little husk or pod. See SILIQUE, -ULE]

silico-, var. of **silic-.**

sil·i·con (sil′ə kən, -kon′), *n.* *Chem.* a nonmetallic element, having amorphous and crystalline forms, occurring in a combined state in minerals and rocks and constituting more than one fourth of the earth's crust: used in steel-making, alloys, etc. *Symbol:* Si; *at. wt.:* 28.086; *at. no.:* 14; *sp. gr.:* 2.4 at 20°C. [SILIC- + *-on,* modeled on *boron*]

sil′icon car′bide, *Chem.* a very hard crystalline compound, SiC, used as an abrasive and as an electrical resistor.

sil′icon diox′ide, *Chem.* silica.

sil·i·cone (sil′ə kōn′), *n.* *Chem.* any of a number of polymers containing alternate silicon and oxygen atoms, as $(-Si-O-Si-O-)_n$, whose properties are determined by the organic groups attached to the silicon atoms, and which are fluid, resinous, or rubbery, water-repellent and extremely stable in high temperatures: used as adhesives, lubricants, in electrical insulation, etc.

Sil′icon Val′ley, the area in northern California, in the Santa Clara valley region, where many of the design and manufacturing companies in the semiconductor industry are concentrated.

sil·i·co·sis (sil′ə kō′sis), *n. Pathol.* a disease of the lungs caused by the inhaling of siliceous particles. **—sil·i·cot·ic** (sil′ə kot′ik), *adj.*

si·lic·u·lose (si lik′yə lōs′), *adj. Bot.* **1.** bearing silicles. **2.** having the form or appearance of a silicle. [< NL *siliculōs(us).* See SILICLE, -OSE[1]]

si·lique (si lēk′, sil′ik), *n. Bot.* the long two-valved seed vessel or pod of cruciferous plants. [var. (< F) of L *siliqua,* lit., pod] **—sil·i·qua·ceous** (sil′ə kwā′shəs), *adj.*

Silique of plant, genus *Brassica*

silk (silk), *n.* **1.** the soft, lustrous fiber obtained as a filament from the cocoon of the silkworm. **2.** thread made from this fiber. **3.** cloth made from this fiber. **4.** a garment of this cloth. **5.** any fiber or filamentous matter resembling silk, as a filament produced by certain spiders. **6.** the hairlike styles on an ear of corn. **7. hit the silk,** *Slang.* to parachute from an aircraft; bail out. **—***adj.* **8.** made of silk. **9.** resembling silk; silky. **10.** of or pertaining to silk. [ME; OE *sioloc, seol(o)c* (c. Icel *silki*) < Baltic or Slav; cf. OPruss *silkas,* Russ *shëlk* << Gk *sērikón* silk, n. use of neut. of *sērikós* silken, lit., Chinese < *Sêres* the Chinese] **—silk′like′,** *adj.*

silk·a·line (sil′kə lēn′), *n.* a soft, thin cotton fabric with a smooth finish, for curtains, bedspreads, garment linings, etc. Also, **silk′o·line′, silk′o·lene′.** [SILK + *-aline,* var. of *-oline,* as in *crinoline*]

silk′ cot′ton, the silky covering of the seeds of certain tropical bombacaceous trees, used for stuffing cushions, pillows, etc.

silk′-cot·ton tree′ (silk′kot′ᵊn), any of several bombacaceous trees having seeds surrounded by silk cotton, esp. *Ceiba pentandra,* from which kapok is obtained.

silk·en (sil′kən), *adj.* **1.** made of silk. **2.** like silk in appearance or texture. **3.** clad in silk. **4.** smoothly ingratiating. **5.** elegant; luxurious. [ME; OE *seolcen*]

silk′ hat′, a tall, cylindrical, black hat covered with silk plush, worn by men as part of formal dress. Cf. **top hat.** **—silk′-hat′ted,** *adj.*

silk·screen (silk′skrēn′), *n.* **1.** a printmaking technique in which a mesh cloth is stretched over a heavy wooden frame and the design, painted on the screen by tusche or affixed by stencil, is printed by having a squeegee force color through the pores of the exposed areas. **2.** a print made by this technique. **—***v.t.* **3.** to print by silkscreen. **—***adj.* **4.** of, made by, or printed with silkscreen.

silk-stock·ing (silk′stok′ing), *adj.* **1.** rich or luxurious in dress. **2.** aristocratic or wealthy: *a silk-stocking neighborhood.* **—***n.* **3.** an aristocratic or wealthy person.

silk·weed (silk′wēd′), *n.* any milkweed of the family *Asclepiadaceae,* the pods of which contain a silky down.

silk·worm (silk′wûrm′), *n.* **1.** the larva of the Chinese silkworm moth, *Bombyx mori,* which spins a cocoon of commercially valuable silk. **2.** the larva of any of several moths of the family *Saturniidae,* which spins a silken cocoon. [ME *sylkewyrme,* OE *seolcwyrm*]

Silkworm, *Bombyx mori,* and cocoon

silk′worm moth′, any of several moths of the families *Bombycidae* and *Saturniidae,* the larvae of which are silkworms.

silk·y (sil′kē), *adj.,* **silk·i·er, silk·i·est. 1.** of or like silk; smooth, lustrous, soft, or delicate: *silky skin.* **2.** *Bot.* covered with fine, soft, closely set hairs, as a leaf. **—silk′i·ly,** *adv.* **—silk′i·ness,** *n.*

sill (sil), *n.* **1.** a horizontal timber, block, or the like, serving as a foundation of a wall, house, etc. **2.** the horizontal piece beneath a window, door, or other opening. **3.** *Geol.* a tabular body of intrusive igneous rock, ordinarily between beds of sedimentary rocks or layers of volcanic ejecta. [ME *sille,* OE *syl, sylle;* c. LG *süll,* Icel *syll;* akin to Icel *svill,* G *Schwelle*] **—sill′-like′,** *adj.*

sil·la·bub (sil′ə bub′), *n.* a drink or dish of sweetened milk or cream mixed with wine, cider, or the like. Also, **sil′li·bub′, syllabub.** [?]

sil·ly (sil′ē), *adj.,* **-li·er, -li·est,** *n., pl.* **-lies. —***adj.* **1.** weak-minded; stupid or foolish. **2.** absurd; ridiculous; irrational: *a silly idea.* **3.** *Informal.* stunned; dazed: *He knocked me silly.* **4.** *Obs.* rustic; plain; homely. **5.** *Obs.* lowly or humble. **—***n.* **6.** *Informal.* a silly or foolish person. [ME *sely, silly* happy, innocent, weak, OE (Anglian) *sēlig* = *sēl, sǣl* happiness + *-ig* -Y[1]; c. G *selig*] **—sil′li·ly,** *adv.* **—sil′li·ness,** *n.* **—Syn. 1.** witless, senseless. See **foolish.**

sil′ly bil′ly, *Informal.* a clownish person.

si·lo (sī′lō), *n., pl.* **-los,** *v.,* **-loed, -lo·ing. —***n.* **1.** a structure, typically cylindrical, in which fodder or forage is kept. **2.** a pit for storing grain, green feeds, etc. **3.** *Mil.* an underground installation of concrete and steel, housing a ballistic missile and the equipment for firing it. **—***v.t.* **4.** to put into or preserve in a silo. [< Sp, perh. < Celt; akin to OE *sāwan* to sow[1]]

Si·lo·am (si lō′əm, sī-), *n.* a spring and pool near Jerusalem. John 9:7.

Si·lo·ne (si lō′nē; *It.* sē lô′ne), *n.* **I·gna·zio** (ē nyä′tsyô), 1900–78, Italian author.

silt (silt), *n.* **1.** earthy matter, fine sand, or the like, carried by water and deposited as a sediment. **—***v.i.* **2.** to become filled or choked up with silt. **—***v.t.* **3.** to fill or choke up with silt. [late ME *cylte* gravel, ? orig. salty deposit; cf. OE *unsylt* unsalted, unseasoned, *sylting* seasoning, *syltan* to salt, season, Norw *sylt* salty swamp, *sylte,* G *Sülze* brine] **—sil·ta′tion,** *n.*

silt·y (sil′tē), *adj.,* **silt·i·er, silt·i·est.** of, pertaining to, or containing silt.

Sil·u·res (sil′yə rēz′), *n.pl.* an ancient British people who lived chiefly in southeastern Wales.

Si·lu·ri·an (si lo͝or′ē ən, sī-), *adj.* **1.** of or pertaining to the Silures or their country. **2.** *Geol.* noting or pertaining to a period of the Paleozoic era, occurring from 400,000,000 to 440,000,000 years ago and characterized by the appearance of air-breathing animals. See table at **era. —***n.* **3.** *Geol.* the Silurian period or system of rocks.

si·lu·rid (si lo͝or′id, sī-), *n.* **1.** any of numerous fishes of the family *Siluridae,* comprising the catfishes. **—***adj.* **2.** belonging or pertaining to the family *Siluridae.* [< NL *Silurid(ae)* name of the family < *Silūr(us)* genus name, special use of L *silūrus* < Gk *sílouros* a kind of fish; see -IDAE, -ID[2]]

sil·va (sil′və), *n.* **1.** the forest trees of a particular area. **2.** a descriptive flora of forest trees. Also, **sylva.** [< NL, special use of L *silva* woodland]

sil·van (sil′vən), *adj., n.* sylvan.

Sil·va·nus (sil vā′nəs), *n. Rom. Religion.* a god of woods and uncultivated land. Also, **Sylvanus.** [< L; see SYLVAN]

sil·ver (sil′vər), *n.* **1.** *Chem.* a white, ductile metallic element, used for making mirrors, coins, ornaments, table utensils, etc. *Symbol:* Ag; *at. wt.:* 107.870; *at. no.:* 47; *sp. gr.:* 10.5 at 20°C. **2.** coin made of this metal; money: *a handful of silver.* **3.** this metal as a commodity or considered as a currency standard. **4.** table articles made of or plated with silver. **5.** any flatware: *The kitchen silver is of stainless steel.* **6.** something resembling this metal in color, luster, etc. **7.** a color like that of the metal silver. **8.** *Photog. U.S.* any of the silver halides used for photographic purposes, as silver bromide. **—***adj.* **9.** consisting of, made of, or plated with silver. **10.** of or pertaining to silver. **11.** containing or yielding silver. **12.** resembling silver; silvery. **13.** eloquent; persuasive: *a silver tongue.* **14.** urging the use of silver as a currency standard: *silver economists.* **15.** indicating the 25th event of a series, as a wedding anniversary. **—***v.t.* **16.** to coat with silver or some silverlike substance. **17.** to give a silvery color to. **—***v.i.* **18.** to become a silvery color. [ME, OE *siolfor;* c. G *Silber,* Icel *silfr,* Goth *silubr*]

Sil·ver (sil′vər), *n.* **Ab·ba Hil·lel** (ab′ə), 1893–1963, U.S. rabbi, born in Lithuania.

sil′ver age′, *Class. Myth.* the second of the four ages of man: characterized by an increase of impiety and of human weakness.

sil′ver bell′, any North American shrub or small tree of the genus *Halesia,* having white, bell-shaped flowers. Also called **sil′ver-bell tree′.**

sil·ver·ber·ry (sil′vər ber′ē), *n., pl.* **-ries.** a shrub, *Elaeagnus argentea,* of north-central North America, having silvery leaves and flowers and silvery, drupelike, edible fruit.

sil′ver bro′mide, *Chem.* a yellowish powder, AgBr, that darkens on exposure to light: used chiefly in photographic emulsions.

sil′ver certif′icate. See under **certificate** (def. 4).

sil′ver chlo′ride, *Chem.* a white powder, AgCl, that darkens on exposure to light: used chiefly in photographic emulsions and in antiseptic silver preparations.

sil·ver·fish (sil′vər fish′), *n., pl.* (*esp. collectively*) **-fish,** (*esp. referring to two or more kinds or species*) **-fish·es. 1.** a white or silvery goldfish, *Carassius auratus.* **2.** any of various other silvery fishes, as the tarpon or shiner. **3.** a wingless, silvery-gray thysanuran insect, *Lepisma saccharina,* that feeds on starch and damages books, wallpaper, etc.

Silverfish, *Lepisma saccharina* (Length ⅓ in.)

sil′ver fox′, a red fox in the color phase in which the fur is black with silver-gray ends on the longer hairs.

sil′ver frost′, glaze (def. 14).

sil·ver·ing (sil′vər ing), *n.* **1.** the act or process of coating with silver or a substance resembling silver. **2.** the coating thus applied.

sil′ver i′odide, *Chem.* a pale-yellow solid, AgI, that darkens on exposure to light: used chiefly in medicine, photography, and artificial rainmaking.

Sil·ve·ri·us (sil vēr′ē əs), *n.* **Saint,** died A.D. 537, pope 536–537.

sil′ver ju′bilee. See under **jubilee** (def. 1).

sil·ver·ly (sil′vər lē), *adv.* with a silvery appearance or sound.

sil·vern (sil′vərn), *adj. Archaic.* made of or like silver. [ME *silver(e)n, selvern,* OE *seolfren, seolfern.* See SILVER, -EN[2]]

sil′ver ni′trate, *Chem., Pharm.* a corrosive, poisonous powder, $AgNO_3$, used chiefly in the manufacture of photographic emulsions and mirrors and as a laboratory reagent, antiseptic, and astringent.

sil′ver perch′, 1. *Ichthyol.* a drum, *Bairdiella chrysura,* found in the southern U.S. **2.** any of various silvery, perchlike fishes, as the white perch.

sil′ver plate′, 1. silver tableware. **2.** a coating of silver, esp. one electroplated on base metal.

sil·ver-plate (sil′vər plāt′), *v.t.,* **-plat·ed, -plat·ing.** to coat (base metal) with silver, esp. by electroplating.

sil′ver point′, the melting point of silver, equal to 960.8°C, used as a fixed point on the international temperature scale.

sil·ver·point (sil′vər point′), *n.* **1.** a technique of drawing with a silver stylus on specially prepared paper. **2.** a drawing made by this technique.

sil′ver screen′, motion pictures; the motion-picture industry: *a star of the silver screen.*

sil·ver·sides (sil′vər sīdz′), *n., pl.* **-sides.** any of several small fishes of the family *Atherinidae,* having a silvery stripe along each side, as *Menidia menidia,* found along the Atlantic coast of the U.S. Also, **sil′ver·side′.**

sil·ver·smith (sil′vər smith′), *n.* a person whose occupation is making and repairing articles of silver. [ME, OE *seolforsmith*] —**sil′ver·smith′ing,** *n.*

sil′ver spoon′, spoon (def. 4).

Sil′ver Spring′, a town in central Maryland, near Washington, D.C. 77,496 (1970).

sil′ver stand′ard, a monetary standard or system using silver of specified weight and fineness to define the basic unit of currency.

Sil′ver Star′, *U.S. Mil.* a medal consisting of a bronze star with a small silver star at the center, awarded for gallantry in action when the citation does not warrant the award of a Medal of Honor or the Distinguished Service Cross. Also called **Sil′ver Star′ Med′al.**

sil′ver thaw′, glaze (def. 14).

sil·ver-tongued (sil′vər tungd′), *adj.* persuasive; eloquent: *a silver-tongued orator.*

sil·ver·ware (sil′vər wâr′), *n.* articles, esp. eating and serving utensils, made of silver, stainless steel, or the like.

sil′ver wed′ding, the 25th anniversary of a wedding.

sil·ver·weed (sil′vər wēd′), *n.* **1.** a rosaceous plant, *Potentilla anserina,* the leaves of which have a silvery pubescence on the underside. **2.** a related short-stemmed plant, *P. argentea,* of Europe and North America, having similar leaves.

sil·ver·work (sil′vər wûrk′), *n.* fine or decorative work executed in silver.

sil·ver·y (sil′və rē), *adj.* **1.** resembling silver; of a lustrous grayish-white color: *the silvery moon.* **2.** having a clear, ringing sound like that of silver: *the silvery peal of bells.* **3.** containing or covered with silver: *silvery deposits.* —**sil′ver·i·ness,** *n.*

Sil·ves·ter I (sil ves′tər). See **Sylvester I.**

Silvester II. See **Sylvester II.**

sil·vi·cul·ture (sil′və kul′chər), *n.* the cultivation of forest trees; forestry. Also, **sylviculture.** [< L *silvi-* (comb. form of *silva* woodland) + CULTURE] —**sil′vi·cul′tur·al,** *adj.* —**sil′vi·cul′tur·ist,** *n.*

s'il vous plaît (sēl vōō ple′), *French.* if you please; please.

sim (sim), *n. Informal.* **1.** simulation. **2.** simulator.

sim., **1.** similar. **2.** simile.

si·mar (si mär′), *n.* a loose, lightweight jacket or robe for women, fashionable in the 17th and 18th centuries. [earlier *simarre* < F < It *zimarr(a)* gown < Sp *zamarra* sheepskin coat, *zamarro* sheepskin < Basque *zamar*]

sim·a·rou·ba (sim′ə rōō′bə), *n.* any tropical American, simaroubaceous tree of the genus *Simaruba,* having pinnate leaves, a drupaceous fruit, and a root whose bark contains an appetite stimulant. Also, **sim′a·ru′ba.** [< Carib *simaruba*]

sim·a·rou·ba·ceous (sim′ə rōō bā′shəs), *adj.* belonging to the *Simarubaceae,* a family of trees and shrubs, comprising the ailanthus, quassia, etc. Also, **sim′a·ru·ba′ceous.** [< NL *Simarub(a)* (see SIMAROUBA) + -ACEOUS]

Sim·e·on (sim′ē ən), *n.* **1.** a son of Jacob and Leah. Gen. 29:33. **2.** one of the 12 tribes of Israel, traditionally descended from him. **3.** a devout man of Jerusalem who praised God for letting him see the infant Jesus. Luke 2:25–35. Cf. **Nunc Dimittis.**

Sim′eon Sty·li′tes (stī lī′tēz), **Saint,** A.D. 390?–459, Syrian monk and stylite.

Sim·fe·ro·pol (sim fe rô′pol yᵊ), *n.* a city in the S Ukraine, in the SW Soviet Union in Europe, on the S Crimean Peninsula. 208,000 (est. 1964).

Sim·hath To·rah (sim′ḵhäs tōr′ə, tôr′ə; *Heb.* sēm ḵhät′ tô rä′), a Jewish festival, joyously celebrated on the 9th day of Sukkoth, that marks the completion and recommencement of the annual round of Torah readings in the synagogue. Also, **Sim′chath To′rah.** [< Heb: lit., celebration of the Torah]

sim·i·an (sim′ē ən), *adj.* **1.** of, pertaining to, or characteristic of apes or monkeys. —*n.* **2.** an ape or monkey. [< L *simi(a)* an ape (? < *sīmus* flat-nosed < Gk *sīmós*) + -AN] —**sim·i·an·i·ty** (sim′ē an′i tē), *n.*

sim·i·lar (sim′ə lər), *adj.* **1.** having likeness or resemblance, esp. in a general way: *two similar houses.* **2.** *Geom.* (of figures) having the same shape; having corresponding sides proportional and corresponding angles equal: *similar triangles.* [earlier *similary,* alter. of late ME *similable* similar < L *simil(is)* like + late ME *-able* -ABLE; see -ARY, -AR[1]] —**sim′i·lar·ly,** *adv.* —**Syn. 1.** like. —**Ant. 1.** different.

sim·i·lar·i·ty (sim′ə lar′i tē), *n., pl.* **-ties. 1.** the state of being similar; likeness; resemblance. **2.** a point or feature like or resembling another or another's: *a similarity of diction.* —**Syn. 1.** correspondence. See **resemblance.**

sim·i·le (sim′ə lē), *n.* **1.** a figure of speech in which two unlike things are explicitly compared, as in "she is like a rose." Cf. **metaphor. 2.** an instance of such a figure of speech or a use of words exemplifying it. [< L: likeness, comparison, n. use of neut. of *similis* like]

si·mil·i·tude (si mil′i tōōd′, -tyōōd′), *n.* **1.** likeness; resemblance. **2.** a person or thing that is like or the match or counterpart of another. **3.** a semblance: *a similitude of the truth.* **4.** a likening or comparison; parable or allegory. [< L *similitūdō* likeness = *simili(s)* like + *-tūdō* -TUDE]

sim·i·ous (sim′ē əs), *adj.* pertaining to or characteristic of apes or monkeys; simian. [< L *sīmi(a)* ape + -OUS] —**sim′i·ous·ness,** *n.*

sim·i·tar (sim′i tər), *n.* scimitar.

Simi′ Val′ley (si mē′), a city in SW California. 59,832 (1970).

Sim·la (sim′lə), *n.* a city in and the capital of Himachal Pradesh, in N India: the summer capital of India. 42,600 (1961).

Sim·mel (zim′əl), *n.* **Ge·org** (gā ôrk′), 1858–1918, German sociologist and philosopher.

sim·mer (sim′ər), *v.i.* **1.** to cook something in a liquid at or just below the boiling point. **2.** to make a gentle murmuring sound, as liquids cooking just below the boiling point. **3.** to be in a state of subdued or restrained activity, development, excitement, anger, etc. —*v.t.* **4.** to keep (liquid) in a state approaching boiling. **5.** to cook in a liquid kept at or just below the boiling point. **6. simmer down, a.** to reduce in volume by simmering. **b.** *Slang.* to become calm or quiet. —*n.* **7.** the state or process of simmering. [earlier *simber,* late ME *simper,* ? freq. of **sim,* imit. of sound made in simmering; see -ER[6]] —**sim′mer·ing·ly,** *adv.* —**Syn. 3.** See **boil[1].**

sim′nel cake′ (sim′nᵊl), *Chiefly Brit.* a rich, fruited cake covered with almond paste. [ME *simenel* < OF, unexplained alter. of L *simila* or Gk *semídālis* fine flour]

si·mo·le·on (sə mō′lē ən), *n. U.S. Slang.* a dollar. [?]

Si·mon (sī′mən), *n.* **1.** the original name of the apostle Peter. Cf. **Peter** (def. 1). **2. the Canaanite,** one of the 12 apostles. Matt. 10:4; Mark 3:18; Luke 6:15. **3.** a relative, perhaps a brother, of Jesus. Mark 6:3. **4.** ("*Simon Magus*") the Samaritan sorcerer converted by the apostle Philip. Acts 8:9–24. **5.** ("*Simon Magus*") fl. 2nd century A.D. ?, founder of a Gnostic sect and reputed prototype of the Faust legend: often identified with the Biblical Simon Magus.

si·mo·ni·ac (si mō′nē ak′), *n.* a person who practices simony. [ME < ML *simoniac(us)* (n., adj.). See SIMONY, -AC] —**si·mo·ni·a·cal** (sī′mə nī′ə kəl, sim′ə-), *adj.*

Si·mon·i·des (sī mon′i dēz′), *n.* 556?–468? B.C., Greek poet. Also called **Simon′ides of Ce′os** (sē′os).

Si′mon Le·gree′ (li grē′), a harsh, merciless master: named after the brutal overseer in Harriet Beecher Stowe's antislavery novel *Uncle Tom's Cabin* (1852).

Si′mon Pe′ter, Peter (def. 1).

si·mon-pure (sī′mən pyŏŏr′), *adj.* real; genuine: *a simon-pure accent.* [short for *the real Simon Pure,* alluding to the victim of impersonation in Mrs. S. Centlivre's play *A Bold Stroke for a Wife* (1718)]

si·mo·ny (sī′mə nē, sim′ə-), *n.* the sin of buying or selling ecclesiastical preferments, benefices, etc. [ME *simonie* < eccl. L *simonia;* so called from *Simon Magus,* who tried to purchase apostolic powers; see SIMON (def. 4), -Y[3]] —**si′mon·ist,** *n.*

si·moom (si mōōm′), *n.* a hot, suffocating, sand-laden wind of the deserts of Arabia, Syria, Africa, etc. Also, **si·moon** (si mōōn′). [< Ar *semūm,* akin to *samm* poisoning]

simp (simp), *n. Slang.* a fool; simpleton. [by shortening]

sim·pa·ti·co (sim pä′ti kō′, -pat′i-), *adj.* congenial; sympathetic. [< It: lit., sympathetic = *simpat(ia)* SYMPATHY + *-ico* -IC. Cf. Sp *simpático,* F *sympathique,* G *sympatisch*]

sim·per (sim′pər), *n.* **1.** a silly, self-conscious smile. —*v.i.* **2.** to smile in a silly, self-conscious way. —*v.t.* **3.** to say with a simper. [akin to MD *zimperlijc,* dial. Dan *simper* affected, Dan *sippe* affected woman, orig. one who sips (see SIP), a way of drinking thought to be affected] —**sim′per·ing·ly,** *adv.* —**Syn. 1, 2.** smirk.

sim·ple (sim′pəl), *adj.,* **-pler, -plest,** *n.* —*adj.* **1.** of a basic kind; not complicated or complex. **2.** readily understood or dealt with, as a problem. **3.** without superfluities, affectations, etc. **4.** in modest circumstances: *a simple laborer.* **5.** modest or candid in bearing or manner. **6.** being considered by itself; pure: *Simple common sense suggests it.* **7.** lacking in intelligence, knowledge, or experience. **8.** *Chem.* **a.** composed of only one substance or element: *a simple substance.* **b.** not mixed. **9.** *Bot.* not divided into parts: *a simple leaf; a simple stem.* **10.** *Zool.* not compound: *a simple ascidian.* **11.** *Math.* linear (def. 6). —*n.* **12.** an ignorant, foolish, or gullible person. **13.** something simple, unmixed, or uncompounded. **14.** *Archaic.* a person of humble origins; commoner. **15.** *Archaic.* an herb or other plant used for medicinal purposes: *country simples.* [ME < OF < L *simpl(us)* or *simplex.* See SIMPLEX] —**Syn. 2.** clear, lucid. **3.** plain, natural, unpretentious.

sim′ple equa′tion, an equation involving only the first power of the unknown quantity.

sim′ple frac′tion, a ratio of two integers.

sim′ple frac′ture, a fracture in which the bone does not pierce the skin. Also called **closed fracture.**

sim′ple fruit′, a fruit formed from one pistil.

sim·ple-heart·ed (sim′pəl här′tid), *adj.* free of deceit; artless; sincere. [late ME *symple herted*]

sim′ple in′terest, interest payable only on the principal; interest that is not compounded.

sim′ple machine′, *Mech.* machine (def. 4b).

sim·ple-mind·ed (sim′pəl mīn′did), *adj.* **1.** free of deceit or guile; unsophisticated. **2.** lacking in mental acuteness or sense. **3.** mentally deficient. Also, **sim′ple·mind′ed.** —**sim′ple-mind′ed·ly, sim′ple·mind′ed·ly,** *adv.* —**sim′ple-mind′ed·ness, sim′ple·mind′ed·ness,** *n.*

sim′ple pen′dulum, *Physics.* a hypothetical apparatus consisting of a point mass suspended from a weightless, frictionless thread, the motion of the body about the string being periodic and, if the amplitude is small, representing simple harmonic motion.

sim′ple sen′tence, a sentence having only one clause, as *I saw him the day before yesterday.* Cf. **complex sentence, compound-complex sentence, compound sentence.**

Sim′ple Si′mon, a simpleton: *He's a Simple Simon about politics.* [after the nursery-rhyme character]

sim′ple syr′up, *Pharm.* syrup (def. 3b).

sim′ple time′, *Music.* rhythm characterized by two or three beats or pulses to a measure.

sim·ple·ton (sim′pəl tən), *n.* a foolish or silly person.

sim·plex (sim′pleks), *adj.* **1.** simple; consisting of or characterized by a single element, action, or the like. **2.** pertaining to or noting a telegraphic or telephonic system in which communication between two stations takes place in only one direction at a time. —*n.* **3.** an apartment having all rooms on one floor. [< L: lit., one-fold = *sim-* one + *-plex* -FOLD]

sim·plic·i·ty (sim plis′i tē), *n., pl.* **-ties. 1.** the state, quality, or an instance of being simple. **2.** freedom from complexity or the possibility of confusing. **3.** absence of luxury, pretentiousness, etc.; plainness. **4.** freedom from deceit or guile; sincerity. **5.** lack of mental acuteness or shrewdness. [ME *simplicite* < L *simplicitās* simpleness = *simplici-* (s. of *simplex*) SIMPLEX + *-tās* -TY[2]]

Sim·pli·ci·us (sim plish′ē əs), *n.* **Saint,** died A.D. 483, pope 468–483.

sim·pli·fy (sim′plə fī′), *v.t.,* **-fied, -fy·ing.** to make less complex or complicated; make plainer or easier. [< F *simplifi(er)* < ML *simplificāre* to make simple = L *simpli-* (comb. form of *simplus* SIMPLE) + *-ficāre* -FY] —**sim′pli·fi·ca′tion,** *n.* —**sim′pli·fi·ca′tive,** *adj.* —**sim′pli·fi′er, sim′pli·fi·ca′tor,** *n.*

sim·plism (sim′pliz əm), *n.* oversimplification, as in the analysis of a problem.

sim·plis·tic (sim plis′tik), *adj.* characterized by extreme simplification; oversimplified. —**sim·plis′ti·cal·ly,** *adv.*

Sim·plon (sim′plon; *Fr.* san plôɴ′), *n.* a mountain pass in S Switzerland, in the Lepontine Alps. 6592 ft. high.

sim·ply (sim′plē), *adv.* **1.** in a simple manner; clearly and easily. **2.** plainly; unaffectedly. **3.** sincerely; artlessly. **4.** merely; only: *It is simply a cold.* **5.** unwisely; foolishly. **6.** wholly; absolutely: *simply irresistible.* [ME *simpleliche*]

sim·u·la·cre (sim′yə lā′kər), *n.* *Archaic.* simulacrum. [ME < MF < L *simulācr(um)*] —**sim·u·la·cral** (sim′yə lā′krəl), *adj.*

sim·u·la·crum (sim′yə lā′krəm), *n., pl.* **-cra** (-krə). **1.** a slight, unreal, or superficial likeness or semblance. **2.** an effigy, image, or representation. [< L: likeness, image = *simulā(re)* (to) SIMULATE + *-crum* instrumental suffix]

sim·u·lant (sim′yə lənt), *adj.* **1.** simulating; feigning; imitating. —*n.* **2.** a person or thing that simulates. [< L *simulant-* (s. of *simulāns*) imitating (prp. of *simulāre*). See SIMULATE, -ANT]

sim·u·lar (sim′yə lər), *Archaic.* —*n.* **1.** a person or thing that simulates; pretender. —*adj.* **2.** simulated; false; counterfeit. **3.** imitative; simulative. [< L *simul(āre)* (to) SIMULATE + -AR[1]]

sim·u·late (*v.* sim′yə lāt′; *adj.* sim′yə lit, -lāt′), *v.,* **-lat·ed, -lat·ing,** *adj.* —*v.t.* **1.** to make a pretense of; feign: *to simulate knowledge.* **2.** to assume or have the appearance or characteristics of; imitate. —*adj.* **3.** *Archaic.* simulated. [< L *simulāt(us)* imitated (ptp. of *simulāre* = *simul-* (var. of *simil-*; see SIMILAR) + *-ātus* -ATE[1]] —**sim′u·la′tive, sim·u·la·to·ry** (sim′yə lə tōr′ē, -tôr′ē), *adj.* —**Syn. 1.** pretend, counterfeit. **2.** affect.

sim·u·la·tion (sim′yə lā′shən), *n.* **1.** the act or process of pretending; feigning. **2.** an assumption or imitation of a particular appearance or form. [ME *simulacion* < L *simulātiōn-* (s. of *simulātiō*) a pretense]

sim·u·la·tor (sim′yə lā′tər), *n.* **1.** a person or thing that simulates. **2.** a machine for simulating certain environmental and other conditions for purposes of training or experimentation. [< L: imitator, counterfeiter]

si·mul·cast (sī′məl kast′, -käst′, sim′əl-), *n., v.,* **-cast, -cast·ing.** —*n.* **1.** a program broadcast simultaneously on radio and television. —*v.t.* **2.** to broadcast (a program) simultaneously on radio and television. [SIMUL(TANEOUS + BROAD)CAST]

si·mul·ta·ne·ous (sī′məl tā′nē əs, sim′əl-), *adj.* existing, occurring, or operating at the same time; concurrent: *simultaneous movements.* [< ML *simult(im)* at the same time (L *simul* together + *-tim* adv. suffix) + (CONTEMPOR)ANEOUS] —**si′mul·ta′ne·ous·ly,** *adv.* —**si′mul·ta′ne·ous·ness, si·mul·ta·ne·i·ty** (sī′məl tə nē′i tē, sim′əl-), *n.* —**Syn.** synchronous, coincident.

simulta′neous equa′tions, *Algebra.* a set of two or more equations, each containing two or more variables whose values can simultaneously satisfy both or all the equations in the set, the number of variables being equal to or less than the number of equations in the set.

sin[1] (sin), *n., v.,* **sinned, sin·ning.** —*n.* **1.** transgression of divine law: *the sin of Adam.* **2.** any act regarded as such a transgression, esp. a willful violation of some religious or moral principle. —*v.i.* **3.** to commit a sinful act. **4.** to offend against a tenaciously maintained principle, standard, etc. —*v.t.* **5.** to commit or perform sinfully. [ME; OE *syn(n)*; akin to G, D *sünde*, Icel *synd* sin, L *sons* guilty] —**sin′ning·ly,** *adv.* —**Syn. 1.** trespass, violation. **3.** transgress, trespass.

sin[2] (sēn), *n.* the 21st letter of the Hebrew alphabet.

sin, *Math.* sine.

Si·nai (sī′nī, sī′nē ī′), *n.* **1.** Also called **Si′nai Penin′sula.** a peninsula in NE Egypt, at the N end of the Red Sea between the Gulfs of Suez and Aqaba: occupied by Israel 1967. 230 mi. long. **2. Mount,** the mountain, of uncertain identity, on which Moses received the Law. Ex. 19. —**Si·na·it·ic** (sī′nē it′ik), **Si·na·ic** (si nā′ik), *adj.*

Si·na·lo·a (sēn′əlō′ə, sin′-; *Sp.* sē′nä lô′ä), *n.* a state in W Mexico, bordering on the Gulf of California. 1,714,000; 22,582 sq. mi. *Cap.:* Culiacán.

sin·a·pism (sin′ə piz′əm), *n.* *Med.* See **mustard plaster.** [< medical L *sināpism(us)* < Gk *sināpismós* application of mustard = *sināp(ízein)* (to) apply mustard + *-ismos* -ISM]

Sin·ar·quist (sin′är kist, -kwist), *n.* a member or advocate of an ultrareactionary movement organized in Mexico about 1937. [< AmerSp *sinarquist(a)* = *sin* (< L *sine* without) + *(an)arquista* ANARCHIST] —**Sin′ar·quism,** *n.* —**Sin′ar·quis′tic,** *adj.*

since (sins), *adv.* **1.** from then till now (often prec. by *ever*): *He was elected in June and has been chairman ever since.* **2.** between a particular past time and the present; subsequently: *He at first refused, but has since consented.* **3.** ago; before now: *long since.* —*prep.* **4.** continuously from or counting from: *It has been warm since noon.* **5.** between a past time or event and the present: *There have been many changes since the war.* —*conj.* **6.** in the period following the time when: *He has written once since he left.* **7.** continuously from or counting from the time when (often prec. by *ever*): *He has been busy ever since he came.* **8.** because; inasmuch as. [late ME *syn(ne)s*, ME *sithenes* = *sithen* (OE *siththan* since, orig. *sīth thām* after that; see SITH, THE[2]) + *-es* -S[1]] —**Syn. 9.** See **because.** —**Usage. 8.** See **as**[1].

sin·cere (sin sēr′), *adj.,* **-cer·er, -cer·est.** **1.** free from deceit, hypocrisy, or falseness; earnest: *a sincere letter of apology.* **2.** genuine; unfeigned. **3.** *Archaic.* pure; unmixed; unadulterated. **4.** *Obs.* sound; unimpaired. [< L *sincēr(us)* pure, clean, untainted] —**sin·cere′ly,** *adv.* —**Syn. 1.** frank, candid, open; unaffected. See **earnest**[1]. —**Ant. 1, 2.** false.

sin·cer·i·ty (sin ser′i tē), *n., pl.* **-ties.** freedom from deceit, hypocrisy, or falseness; earnestness. [< L *sincēritās*] —**Syn.** candor, frankness. See **honor.**

sin·ci·put (sin′sə put′), *n., pl.* **sin·ci·puts, sin·cip·i·ta** (sin sip′i tə). *Anat.* **1.** the forepart of the skull. **2.** the upper part of the skull. [< L: lit., half-head = *sin-* (var. of *sēmi-* SEMI-) + *-ciput*, comb. form of *caput* head] —**sin·cip·i·tal** (sin sip′i təl), *adj.*

Sin·clair (sin klâr′), *n.* **Up·ton (Beall)** (up′tən bel), 1878–1968, U.S. novelist, socialist, and reformer.

Sind (sind), *n.* a former province of Pakistan, in the lower Indus valley; now part of West Pakistan. 48,136 sq. mi. *Cap.:* Karachi.

Sind′bad the Sail′or (sind′bad, sin′-), (in the 10th-century collection of Eastern folk tales *The Arabian Nights' Entertainments*) a wealthy citizen of Baghdad who relates the adventures of his seven wonderful voyages. Also called **Sin′bad.**

Sin·dhi (sin′dē), *n.* a modern Indic language of the lower Indus valley. [< Ar *sindi* of SIND]

sine (sīn), *n.* *Trig.* **1.** (in a right triangle) the ratio of the side opposite a given angle to the hypotenuse. **2.** (of an angle) a trigonometric function equal to the ratio of the ordinate of the end point of the arc to the radius vector of this end point, the origin being at the center of the circle on which the arc lies and the initial point of the arc being on the x-axis. *Abbr.:* sin [< L *sin(us)* a curve, fold, pocket; used in NL to render Ar *jaib* curve, mistaken for *jiba* sine < Skt *jīva* chord of an arc, lit., bowstring]

Sine
ACB being the angle, the ratio of AB to BC is the sine; or, BC being taken as unity, the sine is AB

si·ne·cure (sī′nə kyŏŏr′, sin′ə-), *n.* **1.** an office or position requiring little or no work, esp. one yielding profitable returns. **2.** an ecclesiastical benefice without cure of souls. [< ML *(beneficium) sine cūrā* (benefice) without care; see CURE]

sine′ curve′, *Math.* a curve described by the equation $y = \sin x$, the ordinate being equal to the sine of the abscissa.

si·ne di·e (sī′ne dē′e; *Eng.* sī′nē dī′ē), *Latin.* without fixing a day for future action or meeting.

si·ne pro·le (sī′nē prō′lē), *Law.* without offspring or progeny. [< L]

si·ne qua non (si′ne kwä nōn′; *Eng.* sī′nē kwā non′), *Latin.* something essential; an indispensable condition. [lit., without which not]

sin·ew (sin′yōō), *n.* **1.** a tendon. **2.** Often, **sinews.** the source of strength, power, or vigor: *the sinews of the nation.* **3.** strength; power; vigor. —*v.t.* **4.** to furnish with sinews; strengthen, as by sinews. [ME; OE *sinu* (nom.), *sinuwe* (gen.); c. D *zenuw*, G *Sehne*, Icel *sin*; akin to Skt *snāva*]

sine′ wave′, *Physics.* a periodic oscillation, as simple harmonic motion, having the same geometric representation as a sine function.

sin·ew·y (sin′yōō ē), *adj.* **1.** having strong sinews: *a sinewy back.* **2.** of or like sinews; tough, firm, braided, or resilient: *a sinewy rope.* **3.** having conspicuous sinews; stringy: *tough, sinewy meat.* **4.** vigorous or forceful, as language, style, etc.: *a sinewy argument.* [ME] —**sin′ew·i·ness,** *n.*

Sin·fiot·li (sin′fyôt′lē), *n.* (in the *Volsunga Saga*) the son of Signy by her brother Sigmund. Also, **Sin′fjot′li.**

sin·fo·ni·a (sin′fō nē′ə; *It.* sēn′fô nē′ä), *n., pl.* **-ni·e** (-nē′ā; *It.* -nē′e). *Music.* a symphony. [< It]

sin·fo·niet·ta (sin′fən yet′ə, -fōn-), *n.* **1.** a short symphony. **2.** a small symphony orchestra, esp. one composed solely of stringed instruments. [< It; dim. of SINFONIA]

sin·ful (sin′fəl), *adj.* characterized by or full of sin; wicked: *a sinful life.* [ME; OE *synfull*] —**sin′ful·ly,** *adv.* —**sin′ful·ness,** *n.* —**Syn.** iniquitous, depraved, evil, immoral, corrupt.

sing (sing), *v.,* **sang** or, often, **sung; sung; sing·ing;** *n.* —*v.i.* **1.** to utter words or sounds in succession with musical modulations of the voice. **2.** to perform songs as a professional singer. **3.** to produce melodious sounds, as certain birds, insects, etc. **4.** to compose poetry. **5.** to tell about or praise someone or something in verse or song. **6.** to admit of being sung, as verses: *This lyric sings well.* **7.** to give out a continuous sound of musical quality. **8.** to make a short whistling, ringing, or whizzing sound: *The bullet sang past his ear.* **9.** to have the sensation of a ringing or humming sound, as the ears. **10.** *Slang.* to confess or act as an informer; squeal. —*v.t.* **11.** to utter with musical modulations of the voice, as a song. **12.** to escort or accompany with singing. **13.** to proclaim enthusiastically. **14.** to bring, send, put, etc., with or by singing: *She sang the baby to sleep.* **15.** to chant or intone: *to sing mass.* **16.** to tell or praise in verse or song. **17. sing out,** *Informal.* to call in a loud voice; shout. —*n.* **18.** the act or performance of singing. **19.** a gathering or meeting of persons for the purpose of singing. **20.** a singing, ringing, or whistling sound, as of a bullet. [ME; OE *sing(an)*; c. D *zingen*, G *singen*, Icel *syngva*, Goth *siggwan*] —**sing′a·ble,** *adj.* —**sing′ing·ly,** *adv.*

sing., singular.

Si·ngan (*Chin.* sē′ngän′), *n.* Sian.

Sin·ga·pore (sing′gə pōr′, -pôr′, sing′ə-), *n.* **1. Republic of,** an island republic in the South China Sea, S of the Malay Peninsula: formerly a British crown colony; an independent member of the Commonwealth of Nations since 1965. 2,300,000; 220 sq. mi. *Cap.:* Singapore. **2.** a seaport in and the capital of this republic. 1,400,000.

singe (sinj), *v.,* **singed, singe·ing,** *n.* —*v.t.* **1.** to burn superficially or slightly; scorch. **2.** to burn the ends, projections, nap, or the like, of (hair, cloth, etc.). **3.** to subject (the carcass of an animal or bird) to flame in order to remove hair, bristles, feathers, etc. —*n.* **4.** a superficial burn. **5.** the act of singeing. [ME *senge*, OE *sencgan*; c. G *sengen*, D *zengen*; akin to Icel *sangr* singed, burnt] —**singe′ing·ly,** *adv.*

sing·er[1] (sing′ər), *n.* **1.** a person who sings, esp. a trained or professional vocalist. **2.** a poet. **3.** a singing bird. [ME; see SING, -ER[1]]

sing·er[2] (sin′jər), *n.* a person or thing that singes. [SINGE + -ER[1]]

Sing·er (sing′ər), *n.* **1. Isaac Ba·she·vis** (bə shā′vis), born 1904, U.S. short-story writer (in Yiddish), born in Poland; Nobel prize 1978. **2. Isaac Mer·rit** (mer′it), 1811–75, U.S. inventor: improved the sewing machine.

Singh., Singhalese.

Sin·gha·lese (sing′gə lēz′, -lēs′), *adj., n., pl.* **-lese.** —*adj.*

1. pertaining to Ceylon (now Sri Lanka), its native people, or their language. —*n.* 2. a member of the Singhalese people. 3. an Indic language that is the language of most of Sri Lanka, including Colombo. Also, **Sinhalese.** [var. of *Sinhalese* < Skt *Sinhal(a)* Ceylon + -ESE]

sin·gle (sing′gəl), *adj., v.,* **-gled, -gling,** *n.* —*adj.* **1.** one only; only one in number; sole: *a single example.* **2.** of, pertaining to, or suitable for one person only: *a single bed.* **3.** unique; solitary: *He was the single survivor.* **4.** unmarried. **5.** pertaining to the unmarried state. **6.** of one against one, as combat or fight. **7.** consisting of only one part, element, or member: *a single lens.* **8.** sincere; honest; undivided: *single devotion.* **9.** separate; individual. **10.** uniform; applicable to all. **11.** (of a flower) having only one set of petals. **12.** *Brit.* of only moderate strength or body, as ale or beer. **13.** (of the eye) seeing rightly. —*v.t.* **14.** to pick or choose out from others (usually fol. by *out*): *to single out a fact for special mention.* **15.** *Baseball.* **a.** to cause the advance of (a base runner) by a one-base hit. **b.** to cause (a run) to be scored by a one-base hit (often fol. by *in*). —*v.i.* **16.** *Baseball.* to make a one-base hit. **17.** *Obs.* (of a horse) to go at single-foot. —*n.* **18.** one person or thing; a single one. **19.** an accommodation for one person, as a hotel room, cabin on a ship, etc. **20.** Also called **one-base hit.** *Baseball.* a base hit that enables a batter to reach first base safely. **21. singles,** (*construed as sing.*) a match with one player on each side. **22.** *Golf.* twosome (def. 4). **23.** *Cricket.* a hit for which one run is scored. **24.** *Informal.* a one-dollar bill: *a five and five singles.* **25.** Usually, **singles.** unmarried people collectively. [late ME; ME *sengle* < MF < L *singul(us)*; see SIMPLE] —**sin′gle·hood,** *n.* —**Syn. 1.** distinct, particular. **4.** unwed. **14.** select. **18.** individual.

sin·gle-act·ing (sing′gəl ak′ting), *adj.* (of a reciprocating engine, pump, etc.) having pistons accomplishing work only in one direction. Cf. **double-acting** (def. 1).

sin·gle-ac·tion (sing′gəl ak′shən), *adj.* (of a firearm) requiring the cocking of the hammer before firing each shot.

sin′gle bond′, *Chem.* a chemical linkage consisting of one covalent bond between two atoms of a molecule, represented in chemical formulas by one line or two vertical dots, as C–H or C:H.

sin·gle-breast·ed (sing′gəl bres′tid), *adj.* (of a garment, esp. a coat or jacket) having a single button or row of buttons in front for the center closing. Cf. **double-breasted.**

sin·gle-cross (sing′gəl krôs′, -kros′), *n. Genetics.* a cross between two inbred lines.

sin′gle cut′, *Jewelry.* a simple form of brilliant cut, having eight facets above and eight facets below the girdle. Also called **half-brilliant cut.**

sin·gle-cut (sing′gəl kut′), *adj.* noting a file having a series of parallel cutting ridges in one direction only.

sin′gle en′try, *Bookkeeping.* a simple accounting system noting only amounts owed by and due to a business. Cf. **double entry.** —**sin′gle-en′try,** *adj.*

sin′gle file′, a line of persons or things arranged one behind the other; Indian file.

sin·gle-foot (sing′gəl fo͝ot′), *n.* **1.** rack³. —*v.i.* **2.** (of a horse) to go at a rack.

sin·gle-hand·ed (sing′gəl han′did), *adj.* **1.** accomplished or done by one person alone; unaided. **2.** having, using, or requiring the use of only one hand or one person. —*adv.* **3.** by oneself; alone; without aid. —**sin′gle-hand′ed·ly,** *adv.* —**sin′gle-hand′ed·ness,** *n.*

sin·gle-heart·ed (sing′gəl här′tid), *adj.* sincere and undivided in feeling or spirit; dedicated.

sin·gle-knit (sing′gəl nit′), *n.* **1.** a fabric made on warp knit. **2.** a garment made of single-knit.

sin′gle-lens′ re′flex (sing′gəl lenz′), a type of reflex camera having only one lens, through which the photographer focuses the image and takes the picture. *Abbr.:* SLR

sin·gle-mind·ed (sing′gəl mīn′did), *adj.* **1.** having or showing a single aim or purpose: *a single-minded program.* **2.** dedicated; steadfast. —**sin′gle-mind′ed·ly,** *adv.* —**sin′gle-mind′ed·ness,** *n.*

sin·gle·ness (sing′gəl nis), *n.* the state or quality of being single.

sin·gle-phase (sing′gəl fāz′), *adj. Elect.* noting or pertaining to a circuit having an alternating current with one phase or with phases differing by 180°.

sin′gle quotes′, one pair of single quotation marks, written as (′ ′) and used esp. for a quotation within another quotation: *He said, "I told you to say 'Open sesame' when you want to enter the mountain."* Cf. **double quotes.**

sin·gle-shot (sing′gəl shot′), *adj.* (of a firearm) requiring loading before each shot; not having a cartridge magazine.

sin·gle-space (sing′gəl spās′), *v.,* **-spaced, -spac·ing.** —*v.t.* **1.** to type (copy) on each line space. —*v.i.* **2.** to type copy leaving no blank spaces between lines.

sin′gle Span′ish bur′ton, a tackle having a runner as well as the fall supporting the load. See diag. at **tackle.**

sin′gle stand′ard, **1.** a single set of principles or rules applying to everyone, as a single moral code applying to both men and women. Cf. **double standard. 2.** monometallism.

sin·gle·stick (sing′gəl stik′), *n.* **1.** a short, heavy stick. **2.** (formerly) **a.** a wooden stick held in one hand, used instead of a sword in fencing. **b.** fencing with such a stick.

sin·glet (sing′glit), *n. Chiefly Brit.* a man's undershirt or jersey.

sin′gle tape′. See under **magnetic tape.**

sin′gle tax′, *Econ.* a tax, as on land, that constitutes the sole source of public revenue. —**sin′gle-tax′,** *adj.*

sin·gle·ton (sing′gəl tən), *n.* **1.** something occurring singly. **2.** *Cards.* a card that is the only one of a suit in a hand.

sin·gle-track (sing′gəl trak′), *adj.* having a narrow scope; one-track: *a single-track mind.*

sin·gle·tree (sing′gəl trē′), *n.* whiffletree. [var. of SWINGLETREE]

sin′gle whip′. See under **whip** (def. 20). See **tackle.**

sin·gly (sing′glē), *adv.* **1.** apart from others; separately. **2.** one at a time; as single units. **3.** single-handed; alone. [ME *sengle*ly]

sing·song (sing′sông′, -song′), *n.* **1.** verse, or a piece of verse, of a jingling or monotonous character. **2.** monotonous rhythmical cadence, tone, or sound. **3.** *Brit.* a group sing. —*adj.* **4.** monotonous in rhythm.

sing·spiel (sing′spēl′; *Ger.* zing′shpēl′), *n.* a German opera, esp. of the 18th century, using spoken dialogue. [< G: lit., sing-play]

sin·gu·lar (sing′gyə lər), *adj.* **1.** extraordinary; remarkable; exceptional: *a singular success.* **2.** unusual or strange; odd; different: *singular behavior.* **3.** being the only one of its kind; unique: *a singular example.* **4.** separate; individual. **5.** *Gram.* noting or pertaining to a member of the category of number indicating that a word form has one referent or denotes one person, place, thing, or instance, as *boy,* a singular noun, or *goes,* a singular form of the verb. Cf. **dual** (def. 4), **plural** (def. 4). **6.** *Logic.* of or pertaining to something individual, specific, or not general. **7.** *Obs.* personal; private. **8.** *Obs.* single. —*n. Gram.* **9.** the singular number. **10.** a form in the singular. [ME < L *singulār(is).* See SINGLE, -AR¹] —**sin′gu·lar·ly,** *adv.* —**Syn. 1–4.** peculiar. **2.** bizarre.

sin·gu·lar·ise (sing′gyə lə rīz′), *v.t.,* **-ised, -is·ing.** *Chiefly Brit.* singularize. —**sin′gu·lar·i·sa′tion,** *n.*

sin·gu·lar·i·ty (sing′gyə lar′i tē), *n., pl.* **-ties** for 2. **1.** the state, fact, or quality of being singular. **2.** a singular, unusual, or unique quality. [ME *singularite* < LL *singulāritās*]

sin·gu·lar·ize (sing′gyə lə rīz′), *v.t.,* **-ized, -iz·ing.** to make singular. Also, *esp. Brit.,* **singularise.** —**sin′gu·lar·i·za′tion,** *n.*

sinh (sinch), *n. Math.* hyperbolic sine.

Sin·ha·lese (sin′hə lēz′, -lēs′), *adj., n., pl.* **-lese.** Singhalese.

Sin·i·cism (sin′i siz′əm), *n.* something characteristic of or peculiar to the Chinese. [*Sinic* Chinese (< ML *Sinic(us)* < MGk *Sinikós* = LGk *Sín(ai)* the Chinese + *-ikos* -IC) + -ISM]

Si·ning (shē′ning′), *n.* a city in and the capital of Chinghai, in W China. 250,000. Also, **Hsining.**

sin·is·ter (sin′i stər), *adj.* **1.** threatening or portending evil, harm, or trouble; ominous. **2.** malevolent; evilly intended. **3.** *Heraldry.* noting the side of an escutcheon or achievement of arms that is to the left of the hypothetical bearer (opposed to *dexter*). **4.** *Archaic.* of or on the left side; left. [late ME < L: on the left hand or side, hence unfavorable, injurious (from the Roman belief that unfavorable omens appear on one's left)] —**sin′is·ter·ly,** *adv.*

sinistr-, a learned borrowing from Latin meaning "left," "on the left," used in the formation of compound words: *sinistrous.* Also, *esp. before a consonant,* **sinistro-.** [< L *sinistr-,* s. of *sinister*]

sin·is·tral (sin′i strəl), *adj.* **1.** of, pertaining to, or on the left side; left (opposed to *dextral*). **2.** left-handed. [late ME < ML *sinistrāl(is)*] —**sin′is·tral·ly,** *adv.*

sin·is·tro·gy·ra·tion (sin′i strō′jī rā′shən, si nis′trō-), *n. Optics, Chem.* levorotation. —**sin′is·tro·gy′ric,** *adj.*

sin·is·trorse (sin′i strôrs′, si nis′trôrs, sin′i strôrs′), *adj. Bot.* (from a point of view at the center of the spiral) rising spirally from right to left, as a stem (opposed to *dextrorse*). [< L *sinistrōrs(us),* lit., turned leftwards, contr. of **sinistrōvorsus,* var. of **sinistrōversus.* See SINISTRO-, VERSUS]

sin·is·trous (sin′i strəs), *adj.* **1.** ill-omened; unlucky; disastrous. **2.** sinistral; left. —**sin′is·trous·ly,** *adv.*

Si·nit·ic (si nit′ik), *n.* **1.** a branch of Sino-Tibetan consisting of the various local languages and dialects whose speakers share literary Chinese as their standard language. —*adj.* **2.** of or pertaining to the Chinese, their language, or their culture. [< LL *Sīn(ae)* the Chinese (< LGk *Sínai*) + -ITIC]

sink (singk), *v.,* **sank** or, often, **sunk; sunk** or **sunk·en; sink·ing;** *n.* —*v.i.* **1.** to fall, drop, or descend gradually to a lower level. **2.** to go down toward or below the horizon. **3.** to slope downward; dip. **4.** to displace the volume of an underlying substance or object and become submerged or partially submerged (often fol. by *in* or *into*): *The battleship sank within two hours. His foot sank in the mud.* **5.** to fall or collapse slowly from weakness, fatigue, etc. **6.** to become absorbed in or gradually to enter a state or condition (usually fol. by *in* or *into*): *to sink into slumber.* **7.** to pass or fall into some lower state or condition. **8.** to fail in physical strength or health. **9.** to become lower in loudness, tone, or pitch. **10.** to enter or permeate the mind; become known or understood (usually fol. by *in* or *into*): *I repeated it till the words sank in.* **11.** to become hollow, as the cheeks. **12.** to sit, recline, or lie (usually fol. by *down, in, on,* etc.): *He sank down on the bench.*
—*v.t.* **13.** to cause to fall, drop, or descend gradually. **14.** to cause to become submerged. **15.** to lower or depress the level of. **16.** to bury, plant, or lay (a pipe, conduit, etc.) into or as into the ground. **17.** to bring to a worse or lower state or status. **18.** to reduce in amount, extent, intensity, etc. **19.** to lower in loudness, tone, or pitch. **20.** to invest in the hope of making a profit or gaining some other return. **21.** to dig, bore, or excavate (a hole, shaft, well, etc.).
—*n.* **22.** a basin or receptacle connected with a water supply, used for washing. **23.** a low-lying, poorly drained area where waters collect or disappear by sinking down into the ground or by evaporation. **24.** sinkhole (def. 2). **25.** a place of vice or corruption. **26.** a drain or sewer. **27.** any pond or pit for sewage or waste, as a cesspool or a pool for industrial wastes. [ME; OE *sinc(an);* c. D *zinken,* G *sinken*]

sink·age (sing′kij), *n.* the act, process, or an amount of sinking.

sink·er (sing′kər), *n.* **1.** a person or thing that sinks. **2.** a person employed in sinking, as one who sinks shafts. **3.** a weight, as of lead, for sinking a fishing line or net below the surface of the water. **4.** *Slang.* a doughnut.

sink·hole (singk′hōl′), *n.* **1.** a hole formed in soluble rock by the action of water, serving to conduct surface water to an underground passage. **2.** Also called **sink.** a depressed area in which waste or drainage collects. [ME]

Sin·kiang (sin′kyang′; *Chin.* shin′kyäng′), *n.* the westernmost division of China, bordering Tibet, India, the Soviet Union, and Mongolia: formerly a province. 7,270,000; 635,829 sq. mi. *Cap.:* Urumchi. Official name, **Sin′kiang-Ui′gur Auton′omous Re′gion** (sin′kyang′wē′gər, -go͝or; *Chin.* shin′kyäng′wē′go͝or′).

sink′ing fund′, a fund to extinguish an indebtedness, usually a bond issue.

sink′ing spell′, a temporary decline, as in health.

sin·less (sin′lis), *adj.* free from or without sin. [ME *sinles,* OE *synlēas*] —**sin′less·ly,** *adv.* —**sin′less·ness,** *n.*

sin·ner (sin′ər), *n.* a person who sins; transgressor. [ME]

Sinn Fein (shin′ fān′), **1.** a nationalist organization in Ireland founded about 1905. **2.** a member of this organization. [< Ir: we ourselves] —**Sinn′ Fein′er.** —**Sinn′ Fein′ism.**

sino-, a combining form of **sinus.**

Sino-, a combining form meaning "Chinese": *Sino-Tibetan; Sinology.* [< NL, comb. form repr. LL *Sīnae* the Chinese < LGk *Sînai* << Chin *Ch'in* CH'IN]

Si·nol·o·gist (sī nol′ə jist, si-), *n.* a person who specializes in Sinology. Also, **Si·no·logue** (sīn′ᵊ lôg′, -log′, sin′-). [SINOLOG(UE) (see SINO-, -LOGUE) + -IST]

Si·nol·o·gy (sī nol′ə jē, si-), *n.* the study of the language, literature, history, politics, customs, etc., of China. —**Si·no·log·i·cal** (sīn′ᵊloj′i kəl, sin′-), *adj.*

Si·no-Ti·bet·an (sī′nō ti bet′ᵊn, sin′ō-), *n.* **1.** a family of languages including esp. Burmese, Tibetan, and the various local languages and dialects whose speakers share literary Chinese as their standard language. —*adj.* **2.** of, belonging to, or pertaining to Sino-Tibetan.

sin·ter (sin′tər), *n.* **1.** siliceous or calcareous matter deposited by springs, as that formed around the vent of a geyser. **2.** *Metall.* the product of a sintering operation. —*v.t.* **3.** *Metall.* to bring about agglomeration in by heating. [< G: dross; see CINDER]

Sinuate leaf

sin·u·ate (*adj.* sin′yōō it, -āt′, *v.* sin′yōō āt′), *adj., v.,* **-at·ed, -at·ing.** —*adj.* Also, **sin′u·at′ed. 1.** bent in and out; winding; sinuous. **2.** *Bot.* having the margin strongly or distinctly wavy, as a leaf. —*v.i.* **3.** to curve or wind in and out; creep in a winding path. [< L *sinuāt(us)* bent, curved (ptp. of *sinuāre*). See SINUS, -ATE¹] —**sin′u·ate·ly,** *adv.*

sin·u·a·tion (sin′yōō ā′shən), *n.* a winding; sinuosity. [< LL *sinuātiōn-* (s. of *sinuātiō*)]

sin·u·os·i·ty (sin′yōō os′i tē), *n., pl.* **-ties** for 1. **1.** a curve, bend, or turn. **2.** the quality or state of being sinuous. [< ML *sinuōsitās*]

sin·u·ous (sin′yōō əs), *adj.* **1.** having many curves, bends, or turns; winding. **2.** indirect; devious. **3.** *Bot.* sinuate, as a leaf. [< L *sinuōs(us).* See SINUS, -OUS] —**sin′u·ous·ly,** *adv.* —**sin′u·ous·ness,** *n.* —**Syn. 1.** twisting, curved, serpentine, coiled, twining. **2.** roundabout. —**Ant. 1.** straight. **2.** direct.

si·nus (sī′nəs), *n., pl.* **-nus·es. 1.** a curve; bend. **2.** a curving part or recess. **3.** *Anat.* **a.** any of various cavities, recesses, or passages, as a hollow in a bone, or a reservoir or channel for venous blood. **b.** one of the hollow cavities in the skull connecting with the nasal cavities. **c.** an expanded area in a canal or tube. **4.** *Pathol.* a narrow, elongated abscess with a small orifice; a narrow passage leading to an abscess or the like. **5.** *Bot.* a small, rounded depression between two projecting lobes, as of a leaf. [< L: bent or curved surface, curve, fold, bay, hollow]

si·nus·i·tis (sī′nə sī′tis), *n.* *Pathol.* inflammation of a sinus or the sinuses. [< NL]

Si·nus Me·di·i (sē′nəs mā′dē ē′), a dark plain in the center of the face of the moon. ab. 13,000 sq. mi.

si·nus·oid (sī′nə soid′), *n.* *Math.* a curve described by the equation $y = a \sin x$, the ordinate being proportional to the sine of the abscissa.

si·nus·oi·dal (sī′nə soid′ᵊl), *adj.* **1.** *Math.* of or pertaining to a sinusoid. **2.** having a magnitude that varies as the sine of an independent variable: *a sinusoidal current.* —**si′nus·oi′dal·ly,** *adv.*

sinusoi′dal projec′tion, *Cartog.* an equal-area projection in which parallels are straight lines spaced at regular intervals, the central meridian is a straight line one-half the length of the equator, and the other meridians are curves symmetrical to the central meridian.

Si·nus Ro·ris (sē′nəs rōr′is, rôr′-), a dark plain in the second quadrant of the face of the moon, between Mare Frigoris and Oceanus Procellarum. Also called **Bay of Dew, Bay of Dews.**

Sion (*Fr.* SYÔN), *n.* a town in SW Switzerland: resort. 16,051 (1960).

Si·on (sī′ən), *n.* Zion.

-sion, a noun suffix appearing in loan words from Latin: *compulsion.* Cf. **-tion.** [< L = *-s(us),* var. of *-tus* ptp. suffix + *-iōn-* -ION]

Siou·an (sōō′ən), *n.* **1.** a language family formerly widespread from Saskatchewan to the lower Mississippi, also found in the Virginia and Carolina Piedmont, and including Catawba, Crow, Dakota, Hidatsa, Mandan, Osage, and Winnebago. **2.** Sioux (def. 1). —*adj.* **3.** of or pertaining to the Sioux or the Siouan languages.

Sioux (sōō), *n., pl.* **Sioux** (sōō, sōōz), *adj.* —*n.* **1.** a member of any of various American-Indian peoples, esp. of the Dakota tribe, speaking a Siouan language. —*adj.* **2.** of or pertaining to this tribe. [< F, short for *Nadowessioux* < Ojibwa *Nadoweisiu* enemy, lit., little snake]

Sioux′ Cit′y, a port in W Iowa, on the Missouri River. 85,925 (1970).

Sioux′ Falls′, a city in SE South Dakota. 72,488 (1970).

Sioux′ State′, North Dakota (used as a nickname).

sip (sip), *v.,* **sipped, sip·ping,** *n.* —*v.t.* **1.** to drink bit by bit; take small tastes of (a liquid). —*v.i.* **2.** to drink by sips. —*n.* **3.** an instance of sipping; a small taste of a liquid. **4.** a small quantity taken by sipping. [ME *sippe,* OE **sypþan* < *sopa* a sip]

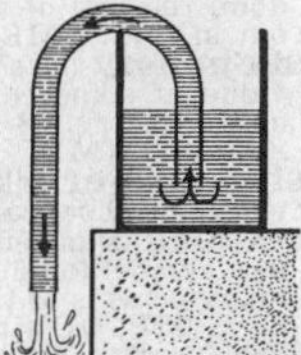

Siphon

Siph·nos (sif′nos), *n.* a Greek island in the SW Aegean Sea, in the Cyclades group: gold and silver mines. 28 sq. mi. Also, **Sifnos.**

si·phon (sī′fən), *n.* **1.** a tube or conduit bent into legs of unequal length, for use in transferring a liquid from an upper level to a lower one by means of suction created by the weight of the liquid in the longer leg. **2.** See **siphon bottle. 3.** a projecting tubular part of some animals, through which liquid enters or leaves the body. —*v.t., v.i.* **4.** to convey or pass through a siphon. Also, **syphon.** [< L *sīphōn-* (s. of *sīphō*) < Gk *síphōn* pipe, tube] —**si′phon·al, si·phon·ic** (sī fon′ik), *adj.*

si·phon·age (sī′fə nij), *n.* the action of a siphon.

si′phon bot′tle, a bottle for aerated water, fitted with a bent tube through the neck, the water being forced out, when a valve is opened, by the pressure on its surface of the gas accumulating within the bottle.

siphono-, a learned borrowing from Greek meaning "tube," "siphon," used in the formation of compound words: *siphonostele.* [< Gk *siphōno-,* comb. form of *síphōn* SIPHON]

si·pho·no·phore (sī′fə nə fōr′, -fôr′, sī fon′ə-), *n.* any pelagic hydrozoan of the order *Siphonophora,* being a floating or swimming colony composed of polyps. [< NL *Siphonophor(a)* = Gk *siphōnophór(os)* tube-carrying (see SIPHONO-, -PHORE) + L *-a* n. suffix] —**si·pho·noph·o·rous** (sī′fə nof′ər əs), *adj.*

si·phon·o·stele (sī fon′ə stēl′, sī′fə nō stēl′), *n.* *Bot.* a hollow tube of vascular tissue enclosing a pith and embedded in ground tissue. —**si·pho·no·ste·lic** (sī′fə nə stē′lik), *adj.*

Si·phrei To·rah (sē FRĀ′ tō RÄ′), *Hebrew.* a pl. of **Sepher Torah.**

Si·ple (sī′pəl), *n.* **Mount,** a mountain in Antarctica, on the E coast of Marie Byrd Land. 15,000 ft.

sip·per (sip′ər), *n.* **1.** a person who sips. **2.** a paper tube through which to sip; drinking straw.

sip·pet (sip′it), *n.* **1.** a small bit; fragment. **2.** a small piece of bread or the like for dipping in gravy, milk, etc.; a small sop. **3.** a crouton.

Si·quei·ros (sē kā′RÔS), *n.* **Da·vid Al·fa·ro** (dä vēth′ äl fä′RŌ), 1896–1974, Mexican painter.

sir (sûr), *n.* **1.** a respectful or formal term of address used to a man: *No, sir.* **2.** (*cap.*) the distinctive title of a knight or baronet: *Sir Walter Scott.* **3.** a lord or gentleman: *noble sirs and ladies.* **4.** *Archaic.* a title of respect used before a noun to designate profession, rank, etc.: *sir priest; sir clerk.* [weak var. of SIRE]

Si·rach (sī′rak), *n.* **Son of,** Jesus (def. 2).

Si·ra·cu·sa (sē′rä kōō′zä), *n.* Italian name of **Syracuse.**

Si·raj-ud-dau·la (si räj′ōōd dou′lə), *n.* 1728?–57, nawab of Bengal 1756–57. Also, **Surajah Dowlah.**

sir·dar (sər där′), *n.* **1.** (in India, Pakistan, and Afghanistan) a military chief or leader. **2.** (formerly) the British commander of the Egyptian army. [< Hindi *sardār* < Pers]

sire (sīᵊr), *n., v.,* **sired, sir·ing.** —*n.* **1.** the male parent of a quadruped. **2.** a respectful term of address, now used only to a male sovereign. **3.** *Archaic.* a father or forefather. **4.** *Archaic.* a person of importance or in a position of authority, as a lord. —*v.t.* **5.** to beget; procreate as the father. [ME < OF (nom. sing.) < VL **seior,* for L *senior* SENIOR]

si·ren (sī′rən), *n.* **1.** *Class. Myth.* one of several sea nymphs, part woman and part bird, supposed to lure mariners to destruction by their seductive singing. **2.** a seductively beautiful or charming woman, esp. one who beguiles and deceives men. **3.** an instrument for producing signals by the rapidly alternated interruption and release of a jet of air or steam. **4.** any of several aquatic, eellike salamanders of the family *Sirenidae,* having permanent external gills, small forelimbs, and no posterior limbs. —*adj.* **5.** of or like a siren. **6.** seductive, alluring, or tempting, esp. dangerously or harmfully. [ME *sereyn* < OF *sereine* < LL *Sīrēn(a)* for L *Sīrēn* < Gk *Seirḗn*] —**Syn. 2.** seductress, temptress, vamp.

si·re·ni·an (sī rē′nē ən), *n.* an aquatic, herbivorous mammal of the order *Sirenia,* including the manatee, dugong, etc. [< NL *Sireni(a)* (see SIREN, -IA) + -AN]

Si·ret (si ret′), *n.* a river in SE Europe, flowing SE from the Carpathian Mountains, in the SW Soviet Union in Europe, through E Rumania to the Danube. 270 mi. long. German, **Sereth.**

Si·ri·ci·us (si rish′ē əs), *n.* **Saint,** died A.D. 399, pope 384–399.

Sir·i·us (sir′ē əs), *n.* *Astron.* the Dog Star, the brightest star in the heavens, located in the constellation Canis Major. [< L *Sīrius* < Gk *Seírios*]

sir·loin (sûr′loin), *n.* the portion of the loin of beef in front of the rump. [late ME *surloyn.* See SUR-¹, LOIN]

si·roc·co (sə rok′ō), *n., pl.* **-cos. 1.** a hot, dry, dust-laden wind blowing from northern Africa and affecting parts of southern Europe. **2.** a warm, sultry south or southeast wind accompanied by rain, occurring in the same regions. [< It, var. of *scirocco* < Ar *sharq* east]

sir·rah (sir′ə), *n.* *Archaic.* a term of address used to inferiors or children to express impatience, contempt, etc. [unexplained var. of SIR]

sir·ree (sə rē′), *n.* (*sometimes cap.*) (used as an intensive with *no* or *yes*): *Will I go there again? No, sirree!* [alter. of SIR]

sir-rev·er·ence (sûr′rev′ər əns), *n.* *Obs.* (used as an expression of apology, as before unseemly or indelicate words.) [alter. of *save your reverence*]

sir·up (sir′əp, sûr′-), *n., v.t.* syrup.

sir·up·y (sir′ə pē, sûr′-), *adj.* syrupy.

sir·vente (sər vent′; *Fr.* SER VÄNT′), *n., pl.* **-ventes** (-vents′; *Fr.* -VÄNT′). a medieval poem or song of heroic or satirical character, as composed by a troubadour. Also, **sirventes′.** [back formation from Pr *sirventes,* lit., pertaining to a servant, i.e., lover (the *-s* being taken as pl. sign). See SERVANT, -ESE]

sis (sis), *n.* *Informal.* sister. [shortened form; cf. D *zus* for *zuster* SISTER]

-sis, a suffix appearing in loan words from Greek, where it was used to form abstract nouns of action, process, state, condition, etc.: *thesis; aphesis.* [< Gk, fem. n. suffix corresponding to adj. suffix *-tikos* -TIC]

si·sal (sī′səl, sis′əl), *n.* **1.** Also called **si′sal hemp′.** a fiber yielded by an agave, *Agave sisalana,* of Yucatán, used for making rope, rugs, etc. **2.** the plant itself. [short for *Sisal grass* or *hemp,* after *Sisal,* former seaport of Yucatán]

Sis·er·a (sis′ər ə), *n.* the commander of the Canaanite army: killed by Jael. Judges 4:17–22.

Si·sin·ni·us (si sin′ē əs), *n.* pope A.D. 708.

sis·kin (sis′kin), *n.* any of several small finches related to the goldfinch, esp. *Spinus spinus*, of Europe. Cf. **pine siskin.** [earlier *sysken* < MD *sijsyen* = *sijs* (? < MHG *zise;* cf. Pol *czyzik* siskin) + *-ken* -KIN]

Sis·ley (sis′lē; *Fr.* sēs lā′), *n.* **Al·fred** (al fred′), 1839–99, French painter.

sis·si·fied (sis′ə fīd′), *adj.* *Informal.* sissy.

sis·sy¹ (sis′ē), *n., pl.* **-sies. 1.** an effeminate boy or man. **2.** a timid or cowardly person. **3.** a little girl. [SIS + -Y²]

sis·sy² (sis′ē), *adj.* of, pertaining to, or characteristic of a sissy. [SIS + -Y¹] —**sis′si·ness, sis′sy·ness,** *n.*

sis′sy bar′, a tall looplike frame fitted to the rear of a bicycle saddle, functioning chiefly as a backrest.

sis·ter (sis′tər), *n.* **1.** a female offspring having both parents in common with another offspring; a female sibling. **2.** Also called **half sister.** a female offspring having only one parent in common with another offspring. **3.** stepsister. **4.** a thing regarded as feminine and associated as if by kinship with something else: *The ships are sisters.* **5.** a female fellow member, as of a church. **6.** a female member of a religious community; nun. **7.** *Brit.* a nurse in charge of a hospital ward; head nurse. **8.** *Informal.* a form of address used to a woman or girl, esp. jocularly or in contempt. —*adj.* **9.** being or considered a sister; related by, or as by, sisterhood: *sister ships.* —*v.t.* **10.** *Naut.* to strengthen (a broken or weakened member) by securing an auxiliary piece alongside it. [ME < Scand; cf. Icel *systir;* c. OE *sweoster,* D *zuster,* G *Schwester,* Goth *swistar,* Russ *sestra,* L *soror,* Skt *svasar*]

sis·ter·hood (sis′tər ho͝od′), *n.* **1.** the state of being a sister. **2.** a group of sisters, esp. of nuns or of female members of a church. **3.** an organization of women with a common interest or purpose, esp. a social or charitable one. [ME *sosterhode*]

sis·ter-in-law (sis′tər in lô′), *n., pl.* **sis·ters-in-law. 1.** the sister of one's husband or wife. **2.** the wife of one's brother. **3.** the wife of the brother of one's husband or wife. [ME *suster-in-lawe*]

sis·ter·ly (sis′tər lē), *adj.* of, like, or befitting a sister. —**sis′ter·li·ness,** *n.*

Sis·tine (sis′tēn, -tin, -tīn), *adj.* of or pertaining to any pope named Sixtus. Also, **Sixtine.** [< It *Sistin(o),* pertaining to *Sisto* man's name (< L *Sextus,* special use of *sextus* sixth); see -INE¹]

Sis′tine Chap′el, the chapel of the pope in the Vatican at Rome, built for Pope Sixtus IV and decorated with frescoes by Michelangelo and others.

sis·troid (sis′troid), *adj.* *Geom. Rare.* included between the convex sides of two intersecting curves (opposed to *cissoid*): *a sistroid angle.* [SISTR(UM) + -OID]

sis·trum (sis′trəm), *n., pl.* **-trums, -tra** (-trə). an ancient Egyptian percussion instrument consisting of a looped metal frame set in a handle and fitted with loose crossbars that rattle when shaken. [< L < Gk *seîstron* < *seíein* to shake]

Sistrum

Sis·y·phe·an (sis′ə fē′ən), *adj.* **1.** of or pertaining to Sisyphus. **2.** endless and unavailing, as labor or a task. [< L *Sīsyphē(ius)* of SISYPHUS (< Gk *Sīsýpheios* = *Sī-syph(os)* + *-eios* adj. suffix) + -AN]

Sis·y·phus (sis′ə fəs), *n.* *Class. Myth.* a son of Aeolus and ruler of Corinth, noted for his trickery: he was punished in Tartarus by being compelled to roll a stone to the top of a slope, the stone always escaping him near the top and rolling down again.

sit (sit), *v.,* **sat** or (*Archaic*) **sate; sat** or (*Archaic*) **sit·ten; sit·ting.** —*v.i.* **1.** to rest with the body supported by the buttocks or thighs; be seated. **2.** to be located or sited: *The house sits well up on the slope.* **3.** to rest or lie (usually fol. by *on* or *upon*): *An aura of greatness sits easily upon him.* **4.** to pose for an artist, photographer, etc. **5.** to remain quiet or inactive: *They let the matter sit.* **6.** (of a bird) to perch or roost. **7.** (of a hen) to cover eggs to hatch them; brood. **8.** to fit or be adjusted, as a garment. **9.** to occupy a place or have a seat in an official assembly or in an official capacity, as a legislator, judge, or bishop. **10.** to be convened or in session, as an assembly. **11.** to act as a baby-sitter. **12.** (of wind) to blow from the indicated direction. —*v.t.* **13.** to cause to sit; seat (often fol. by *down*): *Sit yourself down right here.* **14.** to sit astride or keep one's seat on (a horse or other animal). **15.** to provide seating accommodations or seating room for; seat. **16. sit in on,** to be a spectator, observer, or visitor at; participate in. **17. sit out, a.** to stay to the end of. **b.** to keep one's seat during (a dance, competition, etc.); fail to participate in. **18. sit pretty,** *Informal.* to succeed financially, socially, etc. **19. sit tight,** to bide one's time; take no action. [ME *sitte(n),* OE *sittan;* c. D *zitten,* G *sitzen,* Icel *sitja;* akin to Goth *sitan,* L *sedēre*]

si·tar (si tär′), *n.* a lute of India with a long, broad, fretted neck, two resonators made from gourds, and many sympathetic strings: played with a plectrum. [< Hindi *sitār*] —**si·tar′ist,** *n.*

sit·com (sit′kom′), *n.* *Informal.* See **situation comedy.** [by shortening]

sit′-down strike′ (sit′doun′), a strike during which workers occupy their place of employment and refuse to work until the strike is settled. Also called **sit′-down′.**

site (sīt), *n., v.,* **sit·ed, sit·ing.** —*n.* **1.** the position or location of a town, building, etc., esp. as to its environment. **2.** the area or plot of ground on which anything has been or is to be located. —*v.t.* **3.** to place in or provide with a site; locate. **4.** to put in position for operation, as artillery: *to site a cannon.* [ME < L *sit(us)* site, akin to *situs* founded, built, ptp. of *sinere* to set down]

sith (sith), *adv., prep., conj.* *Archaic.* since. [ME; OE *siththa,* dial. var. of *siththan,* orig. *sīth thām* after that = *sīth* later (than), comp. adv. (akin to Goth *seithus,* Icel *sīth-* late, G *seit* since) + *thām,* dat. of demonstrative pronoun; see THE², THAT]

sit-in (sit′in′), *n.* an organized passive protest, as against racial segregation, in which the demonstrators occupy an area prohibited to them, as in restaurants and other public places.

Sit·ka (sit′kə), *n.* a town in SE Alaska, on an island in the Alexander Archipelago: the capital of former Russian America. 3370 (1970). —**Sit′kan,** *n.*

sito-, a learned borrowing from Greek meaning "grain," "food," used in the formation of compound words: *sitosterol.* [< Gk, comb. form of *sîtos* grain]

si·tos·ter·ol (sī tos′tə rōl′, -rôl′, -rol′), *n.* *Chem.* any of five steroid alcohols having the formula $C_{22}H_{49}OH$, esp. the beta form, used in organic synthesis.

Si·tsang (sē′tsäng′), *n.* Chinese name of **Tibet.**

sit·ten (sit′ᵊn), *v.* *Archaic.* pp. of **sit.**

sit·ter (sit′ər), *n.* **1.** a person who sits. **2.** a person who stays with young children while the parents go out, usually for the evening; baby-sitter. [ME]

sit·ting (sit′ing), *n.* **1.** the act of a person or thing that sits. **2.** a period of being seated. **3.** the space in which to be seated. **4.** a brooding, as of a hen upon eggs; incubation. **5.** the number of eggs on which a bird sits during a single hatching; clutch. **6.** a session, as of a court or legislature. **7.** the time or space allotted to the serving of a meal to a group, as aboard a ship. [ME]

Sit′ting Bull′, 1834–90, Sioux warrior and tribal leader; defeated General Custer at battle of Little Bighorn, 1876.

sit′ting duck′, *Slang.* a helpless or open target or victim.

sit′ting room′, a small living room, often one that forms part of a suite in a hotel, private house, etc.

si·tu (sē′to͞o), *n.* *Latin.* See **in situ.**

sit·u·ate (*v.* sich′o͞o āt′; *adj.* sich′o͞o it, -āt′), *v.,* **-at·ed, -at·ing,** *adj.* —*v.t.* **1.** to put in or on a particular site or place; locate. —*adj.* **2.** *Archaic.* located; placed; situated. [< LL *situāt(us)* sited. See SITE, -ATE¹]

sit·u·at·ed (sich′o͞o ā′tid), *adj.* **1.** located; placed. **2.** placed in a particular position or condition, esp. with reference to financial resources.

sit·u·a·tion (sich′o͞o ā′shən), *n.* **1.** a manner of being situated; location or position with reference to environment. **2.** a place or locality. **3.** condition; case; plight. **4.** the state of affairs; combination of circumstances. **5.** a position or post of employment; job. **6.** a state of affairs of special or critical significance in the course of a play, novel, etc. [< ML *situātiōn-* (s. of *situātiō*)] —**sit′u·a′tion·al,** *adj.* —**Syn. 1.** site. **4.** See **state.**

sit′ua′tion com′edy, a comedy drama, esp. a television series, about characters who find themselves in complex, often ludicrous predicaments.

sit′ua′tion room′, a special room at a military or political headquarters, where the latest intelligence is gathered on any given military or political situation.

sit-up (sit′up′), *n.* an exercise in which a person, lying flat on the back and with the legs straight, lifts the torso to a sitting position without bending the legs.

si·tus (sī′təs), *n., pl.* **-tus. 1.** position; situation. **2.** the proper or original position, as of a part. [< L; see SITE]

Sit·well (sit′wəl, -wel), *n.* **1. Dame Edith,** 1887–1964, English poet and critic. **2.** her brother, **Sir Osbert,** 1892–1969, English poet and novelist. **3.** her brother, **Sir Sa·chev·er·ell** (sə shev′ər əl), born 1900, English poet and novelist.

sitz′ bath′ (sits, zits), **1.** a chairlike bathtub in which the thighs and hips are immersed in warm water. **2.** the bath so taken, usually as part of a therapeutic treatment. [half adoption, half trans. of G *Sitzbad,* lit., seat-bath]

sitz·mark (sits′märk′), *n.* *Skiing.* a sunken area in the snow marking a backward fall of a skier. [< G = *Sitz* seat + *Mark* mark]

Si·va (sē′və, shē′və), *n.* *Hinduism.* Shiva. —**Si′va·ism,** *n.* —**Si′va·ist,** *n.* —**Si′va·is′tic,** *adj.*

Si·van (siv′ən; *Heb.* sē vän′), *n.* the ninth month of the Jewish calendar. Cf. **Jewish calendar.**

Si·vas (sē väs′), *n.* a city in central Turkey. 109,165 (1965).

Si·wash (sī′wosh, -wôsh), *n.* *U.S. Informal.* any small, provincial college (often prec. by *old*). [< Chinook Jargon < F *sauvage* wild, SAVAGE; a disparaging name applied to American Indians]

six (siks), *n.* **1.** a cardinal number, five plus one. **2.** a symbol for this number, as 6 or VI. **3.** a set of this many persons or things. **4.** a playing card, die face, or half of a domino face with six pips. **5. at sixes and sevens, a.** in disorder or confusion. **b.** in disagreement or dispute. —*adj.* **6.** amounting to six in number. [ME, OE; c. D *zes,* LG *ses,* G *sechs,* Icel *sex,* Goth *saihs,* L *sex,* Gk *héx,* Skt *ṣaṣ*]

six·fold (siks′fōld′), *adj.* **1.** having six elements or parts. **2.** six times as great or as much. —*adv.* **3.** in sixfold measure. [ME *sexfold,* OE *sixfeald*]

six-foot·er (siks′fo͝ot′ər), *n.* *Informal.* a person who is roughly six feet tall.

six-gun (siks′gun′), *n.* a six-shooter.

Six′ Na′tions, the Five Nations of the Iroquois confederacy and the Tuscaroras.

606 (siks′ō siks′), *n.* arsphenamine. [so called from being the 606th compound tested by P. EHRLICH]

six-pack (siks′pak′), *n.* six bottles or cans of a beverage, esp. beer, packed in a cardboard carrying container.

six·pence (siks′pəns), *n., pl.* **-pence, -penc·es** for 2. **1.** (*construed as sing. or pl.*) *Brit.* a sum of six pennies. **2.** (*construed as sing.*) a cupronickel coin of the United Kingdom, the half of a shilling, equal to six pennies: use phased out in 1971. [ME *sexe pans*]

six·pen·ny (siks′pen′ē, -pə nē), *adj.* **1.** of the amount or value of sixpence; costing sixpence. **2.** of trifling value; cheap; paltry. **3.** *Carpentry.* noting a nail two inches long. *Abbr.:* 6d [ME]

six-shoot·er (siks′sho͞o′tər, -sho͞o′-), *n.* a revolver from which six shots can be fired without reloading.

six·teen (siks′tēn′), *n.* **1.** a cardinal number, ten plus six. **2.** a symbol for this number, as 16 or XVI. **3.** a set of this many persons or things. —*adj.* **4.** amounting to 16 in number. [ME, OE *sixtēne;* c. D *zestien,* G *sechzehn,* Icel *sextān.* See SIX, TEN, -TEEN]

16-gauge (siks′tēn′ gāj′), *adj.* **1.** of, pertaining to, or being a size of shotgun shell having a diameter of .662 inch. **2.** of, pertaining to, or being a shotgun using such a shell.

six·teen·mo (siks′tēn′mō), *n., pl.* **-mos,** *adj.* —*n.* **1.** Also called **sextodecimo.** a book size (about 4 × 6 inches) determined by printing on sheets folded to form 16 leaves or 32 pages. **2.** a book of this size. *Abbr.:* 16mo, 16° **—*adj.*** **3.** printed, folded, or bound in sixteenmo; sextodecimo.

six·teen·pen·ny (siks′tēn′pen′ē), *adj.* *Carpentry.* noting a nail 3½ inches long. *Abbr.:* 16d

six·teenth (siks′tēnth′), *adj.* **1.** next after the fifteenth; being the ordinal number for 16. **2.** being one of 16 equal parts. **—*n.*** **3.** a sixteenth part, esp. of one (1/16). **4.** the sixteenth member of a series. **5.** *Music.* See **sixteenth note.** [SIXTEEN + -TH[2]; r. ME *sixtenthe, sixtethe,* OE *sixtēotha.* See SIX, TITHE]

six′teenth′ note′, *Music.* a note having one sixteenth of the time value of a whole note; semiquaver. See **note.**

six′teenth′ rest′, a rest equal in value to a sixteenth note. See illus. at **rest[1].**

sixth (siksth), *adj.* **1.** next after the fifth; being the ordinal number for six. **2.** being one of six equal parts. **—*n.*** **3.** a sixth part, esp. of one (1/6). **4.** the sixth member of a series. **5.** *Music.* **a.** a tone on the sixth degree from a given tone (counted as a first). **b.** the interval between such tones. **c.** the harmonic combination of such tones. **—*adj.*** **6.** in the sixth place. [SIX + -TH[2]; r. *sixt,* ME *sixte,* OE *sixta*]

sixth′ chord′, *Music.* an inversion of a triad in which the second note (next above the root) is in the bass.

sixth′ sense′, a power of perception beyond the five senses; intuition.

six·ti·eth (siks′tē ith), *adj.* **1.** next after the fifty-ninth; being the ordinal number for 60. **2.** being one of 60 equal parts. **—*n.*** **3.** a sixtieth part, esp. of one (1/60). **4.** the sixtieth member of a series. [r. ME *sixtithe,* OE *sixtigetha.* See SIX, TITHE]

Six·tine (siks′tēn, -tin, -tīn), *adj.* Sistine.

Six·tus I (siks′təs), **Saint,** pope A.D. 116?–125?. Also, **Xystus I.**

Sixtus II, **Saint,** died A.D. 258, pope 257–258. Also, **Xystus II.**

Sixtus III, **Saint,** pope A.D. 432–440. Also, **Xystus III.**

Sixtus IV, (*Francesco della Rovere*) 1414–84, Italian ecclesiastic: pope 1471–84.

Sixtus V, (*Felice Peretti*) 1521–90, Italian ecclesiastic: pope 1585–90.

six·ty (siks′tē), *n., pl.* **-ties,** *adj.* **—*n.*** **1.** a cardinal number, 10 times 6. **2.** a symbol for this number, as 60 or LX. **3.** a set of this many persons or things. **4. sixties,** the numbers, years, degrees, or the like, between 60 and 69, as in referring to numbered streets, indicating the years of a lifetime or of a century, or degrees of temperature. **5. like sixty,** *Informal.* very easily or quickly. **—*adj.*** **6.** amounting to 60 in number. [ME, OE *sixtig;* c. D *zestig,* G *sechzig,* Icel *sextigir.* See SIX, -TY[1]]

six·ty-four·mo (siks′tē fōr′mō, -fôr′-), *n., pl.* **-mos,** *adj.* **—*n.*** **1.** a book size (about 2 × 3 inches) determined by printing on sheets folded to form 64 leaves or 128 pages. **2.** a book of this size. *Abbr.:* 64mo, 64° **—*adj.*** **3.** printed, folded, or bound in sixty-fourmo.

six·ty-fourth (siks′tē fōrth′, -fôrth′), *adj.* being one of 64 equal parts.

six′ty-fourth′ note′, *Music.* a note having one sixty-fourth of the time value of a whole note; hemidemisemiquaver. See illus. at **note.**

six′ty-fourth′ rest′, a rest equal in value to a sixty-fourth note. See illus. at **rest[1].**

six·ty-nine (siks′tē nīn′), *n.* **1.** a cardinal number, 60 plus 9. **2.** *Slang* (*usually vulgar*). simultaneous fellatio and cunnilingus by two partners.

six·ty·pen·ny (siks′tē pen′ē), *adj.* *Carpentry.* noting a nail six inches long. *Abbr.:* 60d

siz·a·ble (sī′zə bəl), *adj.* of considerable size; fairly large. Also, **sizeable.** **—siz′a·bly,** *adv.*

siz·ar (sī′zər), *n.* (at Cambridge University and at Trinity College, Dublin) an undergraduate who receives aid from the college for his maintenance. [SIZE[1] + -AR[3]] **—siz′ar·ship′,** *n.*

size[1] (sīz), *n., v.,* **sized, siz·ing.** **—*n.*** **1.** the spatial dimensions, proportions, or extent of anything: *the size of a farm.* **2.** considerable or great magnitude. **3.** any of a series of graduated measures for articles of manufacture or trade: *children's sizes of shoes.* **4.** extent; amount; range: *a fortune of great size.* **5.** actual condition, circumstance, or state of affairs: *That's about the size of it.* **6.** an expression of the magnitude of something in terms of the persons or things included: *the size of a town; the size of a shipment.* **7.** *Obs.* a fixed standard of quality or quantity, as for food, drink, or the like. **—*v.t.*** **8.** to separate or sort according to size. **9.** to make of a certain size. **10.** *Obs.* to regulate or control according to a fixed standard. **11. size up,** *Informal.* **a.** to form an estimate of (a situation, person, etc.); judge. **b.** to meet a certain standard. [ME *syse* < OF *sise,* aph. var. of *assise* ASSIZE; orig. control, regulation]
—Syn. 1. SIZE, VOLUME, MASS, BULK are terms referring to extent or dimensions of something that has magnitude and occupies space. SIZE is the general word: *of great size; small in size.* VOLUME often applies to something that has no fixed shape: *Smoke has volume.* MASS, also, does not suggest shape, but suggests a quantity of matter in a solid body: *a mass of concrete.* BULK suggests weight, and often a recognizable, though perhaps unwieldy, shape: *the huge bulk of an elephant.*

size[2] (sīz), *n., v.,* **sized, siz·ing.** **—*n.*** **1.** any of various gelatinous or glutinous preparations made from glue, starch, etc., used for filling the pores of cloth, paper, etc., or as an adhesive ground for gold leaf on books. **—*v.t.*** **2.** to coat or treat with size. [ME *sise, syse;* special use of SIZE[1]]

size·a·ble (sī′zə bəl), *adj.* sizable. **—size′a·ble·ness,** *n.* **—size′a·bly,** *adv.*

sized (sīzd), *adj.* having size as specified (often used in combination): *medium-sized; desk-sized.*

siz·ing (sī′zing), *n.* **1.** the act or process of applying size or preparing with size. **2.** size, as for glazing paper.

siz·y (sī′zē), *adj.,* **siz·i·er, siz·i·est.** *Archaic.* thick; viscous. **—siz′i·ness,** *n.*

siz·zle (siz′əl), *v.,* **-zled, -zling,** *n.* **—*v.i.*** **1.** to make a hissing sound, as in frying or burning. **2.** *Informal.* to be very hot: *It's sizzling out.* **—*n.*** **3.** a sizzling sound. [imit.]

S.J., Society of Jesus.

Sjael·land (shel′län), *n.* Danish name of **Zealand.**

S.J.D., Doctor of Juridical Science. [< L *Scientiae Juridicae Doctor*]

sk., sack.

skag (skag), *n.* *U.S. Slang.* scag.

Ska·gen (skä′gən), *n.* See **Skaw, the.**

Skag·er·rak (skag′ə rak′, skä′gə räk′), *n.* an arm of the North Sea, between Denmark and Norway. 150 mi. long; 80–90 mi. wide.

Skag·way (skag′wā′), *n.* a town in SE Alaska, near the famous White and Chilkoot passes to the Klondike gold fields: railroad terminus. 675 (1970).

skald (skôld, skäld), *n.* one of the ancient Scandinavian poets. Also, **scald.** [< Icel: poet] **—skald′ic,** *adj.* **—skald′ship,** *n.*

skat (skät), *n.* a card game for three players, using a pack of 32 playing cards, sevens through aces, the object being to fulfill any of various contracts, with scoring computed on strategy and on tricks won. [< It *scart(o)* a discard, back formation from *scartare* to discard = *s-* EX-[1] + *cart-* CARD[1] + *-o* masc. n. ending]

skate[1] (skāt), *n., v.,* **skat·ed, skat·ing.** **—*n.*** **1.** See **ice skate** (def. 1). **2.** See **roller skate.** **3.** the blade of an ice skate. **—*v.i.*** **4.** to glide or propel oneself over ice, the ground, etc., on skates. **5.** to glide or slide smoothly along. [back formation from D *schaats* skate, MD *schaetse* stilt (ML *scatia*) < ?]

skate[2] (skāt), *n., pl.* (*esp. collectively*) **skate,** (*esp. referring to two or more kinds or species*) **skates.** any of several rays of the genus *Raja,* usually having a pointed snout, as *R. binoculata,* found along the Pacific coast of the U.S., growing to a length of from less than two up to eight feet. [ME *scate* < Scand; cf. Icel *skata*]

Skate[2], *Raja erinacea* (Length to 2 ft.)

skate[3] (skāt), *n.* *Slang.* a person; fellow: *He's a good skate.* [? special use of SKATE[2]]

skate·board (skāt′bōrd′, -bôrd′), *n.* a device for riding upon, usually while standing, consisting of an oblong piece of wood mounted on skate wheels.

skat·er (skā′tər), *n.* **1.** a person who skates. **2.** See **water strider.**

skat·ole (skat′ōl, -ōl), *n.* a solid, C_9H_9N, having a fecal odor: used chiefly as a fixative in the manufacture of perfume. [< Gk *skat-* (s. of *skōr*) dung + -OLE]

Skaw, the (skô), a cape at the N tip of Denmark. Also called **Skagen.**

skean (shkēn, skēn), *n.* a knife or dagger formerly used in Ireland and in the Scottish Highlands. [< IrGael *sgian*]

ske·dad·dle (ski dad′əl), *v.,* **-dled, -dling,** *n.* *Informal.* **—*v.i.*** **1.** to run away hurriedly; flee. **—*n.*** **2.** a hasty flight. [?]

skeet (skēt), *n.* a form of trapshooting in which targets are hurled at varying elevations and speeds so as to simulate the angles of flight taken by game birds. Also called **skeet′ shoot′ing.** [? special use of dial. *skeet* to scatter, var. of SCOOT]

skeg (skeg), *n.* *Naut.* **1.** a knee reinforcing the junction between a keel and sternpost. **2.** any of various supporting members or areas of deadwood at the after end of a keel. [< D *scheg* cutwater < Scand; cf. Icel *skegg* cutwater, beard]

skein (skān), *n.* **1.** a length of yarn or thread wound on a reel or swift preparatory for use in manufacturing. **2.** anything wound in or resembling such a coil: *a skein of hair.* **3.** a flock of geese, ducks, or the like, in flight. [late ME *skeyne, skayne* < MF *(e)scaigne*]

skel·e·tal (skel′i təl), *adj.* of, pertaining to, or like a skeleton.

skel·e·ton (skel′i tən), *n.* **1.** *Anat., Zool.* **a.** the bones of a man or an animal considered as a whole, together forming the framework of the body. **b.** the bony or cartilaginous framework supporting and protecting the vertebrate body. **2.** any of various structures forming a rigid framework in an invertebrate. **3.** *Informal.* a very lean person or animal. **4.** a supporting framework, as of a leaf, building, or ship. **5.** an outline, as of a literary work: *the skeleton of the plot.* **6. skeleton in the closet,** a scandal that is concealed to avoid public disgrace; a shameful secret. **—*adj.*** **7.** of or pertaining to a skeleton. **8.** like a skeleton in being reduced to the essential parts or numbers: *a skeleton staff.* [< NL < Gk: mummy, n. use of neut. of *skeletós* dried up, verbal of *skéllein* to dry] **—skel′e·ton·like′,** *adj.*

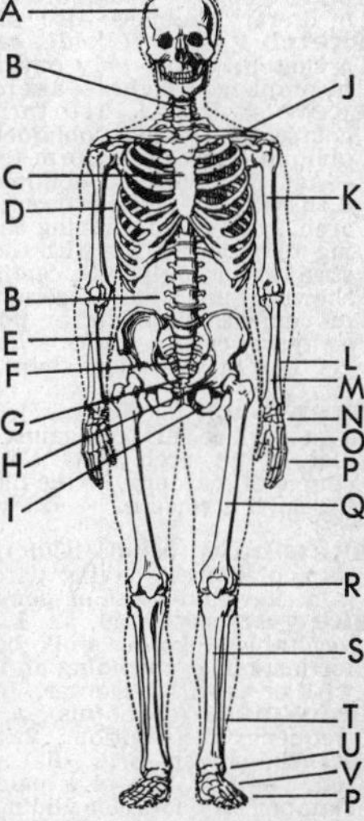

Skeleton (Human)
A, Cranium; B, Vertebrae; C, Sternum; D, Ribs; E, Ilium; F, Sacrum; G, Coccyx; H, Pubis; I, Ischium; J, Clavicle; K, Humerus; L, Ulna; M, Radius; N, Carpus; O, Metacarpus; P, Phalanx; Q, Femur; R, Patella; S, Tibia; T, Fibula; U, Tarsus; V, Metatarsus

skel·e·ton·ise (skel′i tᵊnīz′), *v.t.*, **-ised, -is·ing.** *Chiefly Brit.* skeletonize.

skel·e·ton·ize (skel′i tᵊnīz′), *v.t.*, **-ized, -iz·ing. 1.** to reduce to a skeleton, outline, or framework. **2.** to reduce in size or number, as a military unit. **3.** to construct in outline.

skel′eton key′, a key with nearly the whole substance of the bit filed away, so that it may open various locks. Also called **passkey.**

skel·lum (skel′əm), *n. Chiefly Scot.* a rascal. [< D *schelm* rogue, knave < MLG; c. G *Schelm* rogue, OHG *skelmo, scalmo* plague, corpse]

skelp[1] (skelp), *Scot. and North Eng.* **—*n.* 1.** a slap, smack, or blow, esp. one given with the open hand. **—*v.t.* 2.** to slap, smack, or strike (someone), esp. on the buttocks; spank. [late ME; prob. imit.]

skelp[2] (skelp), *n.* metal in strip form that is fed into various rolls and welded to form tubing. [? special use of SKELP[1]]

Skel·ton (skel′tᵊn), *n.* **John,** c1460–1529, English poet.

skep (skep), *n.* **1.** a round farm basket of wicker or wood. **2.** a beehive, esp. of straw. [ME *skeppe*, late OE *sceppe* < Scand; cf. Icel *skeppa* half-bushel; akin to G *Scheffel*]

skep·tic (skep′tik), *n.* **1.** a person who questions the validity or authenticity of something purporting to be factual. **2.** a person who maintains a doubting attitude, as toward values, plans, statements, or the character of others. **3.** a person who doubts the truth of a religion, esp. Christianity. **4.** (*cap.*) *Philos.* **a.** a member of a philosophical school of ancient Greece, who maintained that real knowledge of things is impossible. **b.** any thinker who doubts the possibility of real knowledge of any kind. **—*adj.* 5.** pertaining to skeptics or skepticism; skeptical. **6.** (*cap.*) pertaining to the Skeptics. Also, **sceptic.** [< L *sceptic(us)* < Gk *skeptikós* thoughtful, inquiring = *skept(esthai)* (to) consider + *-ikos* -IC] **—Syn. 3.** doubter. **—Ant. 3.** believer.

skep·ti·cal (skep′ti kəl), *adj.* **1.** inclined to skepticism; having doubt. **2.** showing doubt: *a skeptical smile.* **3.** denying or questioning the tenets of a religion. **4.** (*cap.*) of or pertaining to Skeptics or Skepticism. Also, **sceptical. —skep′ti·cal·ly,** *adv.* **—Syn. 1.** skeptic. **3.** unbelieving.

skep·ti·cism (skep′ti siz′əm), *n.* **1.** skeptical attitude or temper; doubt. **2.** doubt or unbelief with regard to a religion, esp. Christianity. **3.** (*cap.*) the doctrines or opinions of Skeptics. Also, **scepticism.** [< NL *scepticism(us)*] **—Syn. 1.** questioning. **2.** disbelief, atheism, agnosticism. **—Ant. 2.** faith.

sker·ry (sker′ē; *Scot.* skeʀ′ē), *n., pl.* **-ries.** *Chiefly Scot.* **1.** a small, rocky island. **2.** a coastline with such islands offshore. [Shetland *skerri* a rock in the sea < Scand; cf. Icel *sker* (*skerja*, gen. pl.) rock or reef (in the sea). See SCAR[2]]

sketch (skech), *n.* **1.** a simply or hastily executed drawing or painting, esp. a preliminary one, giving the essential features of the subject. **2.** a rough design, plan, or draft, as of a book. **3.** a brief or hasty outline of facts, occurrences, etc. **4.** a short piece of writing, usually descriptive. **5.** a short play or dramatic performance, as one forming part of a vaudeville program. **—*v.t.* 6.** to make a sketch of. **7.** to set forth in a brief or general account. **—*v.i.* 8.** to make a sketch or sketches. [< D *schets* << It *schizzo* < L *schedium* extemporaneous poem < Gk *schédion*, neut. of *schédios* extempore] **—sketch′er,** *n.* **—Syn. 2.** outline. **5.** skit, act, routine. **6.** draw, outline. See **depict.**

sketch·book (skech′bŏŏk′), *n.* **1.** Also called **sketch′ pad′.** a book or pad of drawing paper for sketches. **2.** a book of literary sketches. Also, **sketch′ book′.**

sketch·y (skech′ē), *adj.*, **sketch·i·er, sketch·i·est. 1.** like a sketch; giving only outlines or essentials. **2.** imperfect, incomplete or slight. **—sketch′i·ly,** *adv.* **—sketch′i·ness,** *n.*

skew (skyōō), *v.i.* **1.** to turn aside or swerve; take an oblique course. **2.** to look obliquely; squint. **—*v.t.* 3.** to give an oblique direction or form to. **4.** to misrepresent or distort. **—*adj.* 5.** having an oblique direction or position; slanting. **6.** having an oblique face or part: *skew gearing.* **7.** (of an arch, bridge, etc.) having the centerline of its opening forming an oblique angle with the direction in which its spanning structure is built. **8.** *Statistics.* (of a distribution) having skewness not equal to zero; asymmetric. **—*n.* 9.** an oblique movement, direction, or position. [late ME *skewe* to slip away, swerve < MD *schuwe(n)* (to) get out of the way, shun < *schu* to SHY[2]]

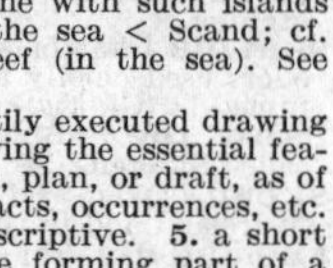

skew·back (skyōō′bak′), *n. Archit.* **1.** a sloping surface against which the end of an arch rests. **2.** a stone, course of masonry, or the like, presenting such a surface. **—skew′backed′,** *adj.*

S, Skewback

skew·bald (skyōō′bôld′), *adj.* **1.** (esp. of horses) having patches of brown and white. **—*n.* 2.** a skewbald horse or pony. [SKEW + (PIE)BALD]

skew·er (skyōō′ər), *n.* **1.** a long pin for holding meat or vegetables together while being cooked. **2.** any similar pin for fastening or holding an item in place. **—*v.t.* 3.** to fasten with or as with a skewer. [earlier *skiver* < ?]

skew·ness (skyōō′nis), *n. Statistics.* **1.** asymmetry in a frequency distribution. **2.** a measure of such asymmetry.

ski (skē *or, esp. Brit.,* shē), *n., pl.* **skis, ski,** *v.,* **skied, ski·ing. —*n.* 1.** one of a pair of long, slender runners worn clamped to boots, for gliding over snow. **2.** See **water ski. —*v.i.* 3.** to travel on skis, esp. for sport. **—*v.t.* 4.** to travel on skis over. [< Norw, var. of *skid;* c. Icel *skīth*, OE *scīd* thin slip of wood, G *Scheit* thin board] **—ski′a·ble,** *adj.*

ski·a·graph (skī′ə graf′, -gräf′), *n.* a radiograph made with x-rays. [back formation from *skiagraphy* < Gk *skiā-graphia* painting in light and shade = *skiā* shadow + *-graphia* -GRAPHY] **—ski·ag·ra·pher** (skī ag′rə fər), *n.* **—ski·a·graph·ic** (skī′ə graf′ik), **ski′a·graph′i·cal,** *adj.*

ski·a·scope (skī′ə skōp′), *n. Ophthalm.* an apparatus that determines the refractive power of the eye by observing the lights and shadows on the pupil when a mirror illumines the retina; retinoscope. [< Gk *skiā* a shadow, shade + -SCOPE] **—ski·as·co·py** (skī as′kə pē), *n.*

ski′ boot′, a heavy, thick-soled, ankle-high shoe for skiing, often having padding and extra supporting straps and laces around the ankle.

skid (skid), *n., v.,* **skid·ded, skid·ding. —*n.* 1.** a plank, bar, log, or the like, on which something heavy may be slid or rolled. **2.** a low, mobile platform on which goods are placed for ease in handling, moving, etc. **3.** a plank, low platform, etc., on or by which a load is supported. **4.** a choke or drag for preventing the wheel of a vehicle from rotating. **5.** a runner on the under part of some airplanes, enabling the aircraft to slide along the ground when landing. **6.** the act or an instance of skidding. **—*v.t.* 7.** to place on or slide along a skid or skids. **8.** to check or prevent motion with a skid, as of a wheel. **9.** to move or maneuver with a skidding motion: *to skid the car into a turn.* **—*v.i.* 10.** to slide along without rotating, as a wheel to which a brake has been applied. **11.** to slip or slide sideways relative to direction of wheel rotation, as an automobile in turning a corner rapidly. **12.** to slide forward under the force of momentum after forward motion has been braked, as a vehicle. **13.** (of an airplane when not banked sufficiently) to slide sideways, away from the center of the curve described in turning. Cf. **slip**[1] (def. 8). [appar. < Scand; cf. Icel *skīth*, c. OE *scīd* thin slip of wood; see SKI]

skid′ chain′. See **tire chain.**

skid·doo (ski dōō′), *v.i.*, **-dooed, -doo·ing.** *Informal.* to go away; get out. [? alter. of SKEDADDLE]

skid·proof (skid′prōōf′), *adj.* preventing or resistant to skidding, as certain road surfaces, vehicle tires, etc.

skid′ row′ (rō), a run-down urban area frequented by vagrants and consisting of flophouses, cheap barrooms, etc. Also called **Skid′ Road′.**

skid·way (skid′wā′), *n.* **1.** a road or path formed of logs, planks, etc., for sliding objects. **2.** a platform, usually inclined, for piling logs to be sawed or to be loaded onto a vehicle.

skied (skēd), *v.* pt. of **ski.**

Ski·en (shā′ən, shē′-), *n.* a city in S Norway. 45,440 (est. 1965).

ski·er (skē′ər), *n.* a person who skis.

skies (skīz), *n.* pl. of **sky.**

skiff (skif), *n.* any of various types of boats small enough for sailing or rowing by one person. [< early It *schif(o)* < OHG *scif* SHIP]

skif·fle (skif′əl), *n.* **1.** a jazz style of the 1920's played by bands made up of both standard and improvised instruments. **2.** a style of popular music deriving from hillbilly music and rock-'n'-roll, and played on a heterogeneous group of instruments, as guitar, washboard, and kazoo. [?]

ski·ing (skē′ing), *n.* the act or sport of gliding on skis.

ski·jor·ing (skē jôr′ing, -jōr′-, skē′jôr-, -jōr-), *n.* a sport in which a skier is pulled over snow or ice, generally by a horse. [< Norw *skikjøring* (*kj-* pronounced somewhat like E *j*), lit., ski-driving] **—ski·jor′er,** *n.*

ski′ jump′, 1. a snow-covered chute, as on the side of a hill, down which a skier glides to gain momentum for a leap from the horizontal ramp in which it terminates. **2.** a jump made by a skier. **—ski′ jump′er.**

Skik·da (skik′dä), *n.* a seaport in NE Algeria. 88,000 (1960). Formerly, **Philippeville.**

skil·ful (skil′fəl), *adj.* skillful. **—skil′ful·ly,** *adv.*

ski′ lift′, an apparatus for conveying skiers up the side of a slope, consisting typically of a series of chairs suspended from an endless cable driven by motors.

skill[1] (skil), *n.* **1.** the ability to do something well, arising from talent, training, or practice. **2.** competent excellence in performance. **3.** a craft, trade, or job requiring manual dexterity or special training. **4.** such a craft, trade, or job in which a person has competence and experience. **5.** *Obs.* understanding; discernment. **6.** *Obs.* reason; cause. [ME < Scand; cf. Icel *skil* distinction, difference; c. D *geschil* difference, quarrel. See SKILL[2]] **—skill′-less, skil′less,** *adj.*

skill[2] (skil), *v.i. Archaic.* **1.** to matter. **2.** to help; avail. [ME *skil(ien)* < Scand; cf. Icel *skilja* to distinguish, divide]

skilled (skild), *adj.* **1.** having skill; trained or experienced in work that requires skill. **2.** showing, involving, or requiring skill, as certain work. **—Syn. 1.** See **skillful.**

skil·let (skil′it), *n.* **1.** See **frying pan. 2.** *Chiefly Brit.* a long-handled saucepan. [late ME *skelet*, dim. of *skele* < Scand; cf. Icel *skjōla* pail, bucket; see -ET]

skill·ful (skil′fəl), *adj.* **1.** having or exercising skill, adroitness, or dexterity: *a skillful juggler.* **2.** showing or involving skill: *a skillful display of fancy diving.* Also, **skilful.** [ME] **—skill′ful·ly,** *adv.*

—Syn. 1. adroit, deft, adept, apt. SKILLFUL, SKILLED refer to readiness and adroitness in an occupation, craft, or art. SKILLFUL suggests esp. adroitness and dexterity: *a skillful watchmaker.* SKILLED implies having had long experience and thus having acquired a high degree of proficiency: *not an amateur but a skilled workman.* **—Ant. 1.** awkward, clumsy.

skim (skim), *v.,* **skimmed, skim·ming,** *n.* **—*v.t.* 1.** to take up or remove from the surface of a liquid, as with a spoon or ladle. **2.** to clear (liquid) thus: *to skim milk.* **3.** to move or glide lightly over or along (a surface, as of the ground or water): *The sailboat skimmed the lake.* **4.** to throw in a smooth gliding path over or near a surface, or so as to bounce or ricochet along the surface: *to skim a stone across the lake.* **5.** to read, study, consider, etc., in a cursory manner. **6.** to cover, as a liquid, with a thin layer: *Ice skimmed the lake at night.* **7.** *Slang.* to take off part of the winnings of a gambling casino or the like, illegally before recording the amount on which taxes are to be computed. **—*v.i.* 8.** to pass or glide lightly along over or near a surface. **9.** to read, study, consider, etc., something in a cursory way (usually fol. by *over*). **10.** to become covered with a thin layer. **—*n.* 11.** the act or an instance of skimming. **12.** something that is skimmed off. **13.** a thin layer of film formed on the surface of something, esp. a liquid, as the coagulated protein material formed on boiled milk. [late ME *skym*, var. of obs. *scum* to skim; see SCUM]

skim·ble-scam·ble (skim′bəl skam′bəl, skim′əl skam′-əl), *adj.* rambling; confused: *a skimble-scamble explanation.* Also, **skim′ble-skam′ble.** [gradational redupl. of dial. *scamble* to struggle, trample]

skim·mer (skim′ər), *n.* **1.** a person or thing that skims. **2.** a shallow utensil, usually perforated, used in skimming liquids. **3.** any of several gull-like birds of the family *Rynchopidae*, that skim the water with the elongated lower mandible immersed while in search of food. **4.** a stiff, wide-brimmed hat with a shallow, flat crown, usually made of straw. [SKIM + -ER[1]; r. ME *skemour, skymour,* var. of *schumour* < MF *(e)scumoir* ladle for skimming; see SCUM]

skim′ milk′, milk from which the cream has been skimmed. Also, **skimmed′ milk′.**

skim·mings (skim′ingz), *n.* that which is removed by skimming. [late ME *skemmyng*]

skimp (skimp), *v.t., v.i.* **1.** to scrimp. **2.** to scamp. **—***adj.* **3.** scrimpy; scanty. [?]

skimp·y (skim′pē), *adj.,* **skimp·i·er, skimp·i·est.** **1.** lacking in size, fullness, etc.; scanty: *a skimpy dinner.* **2.** too thrifty; stingy: *a skimpy housewife.* **—skimp′i·ly,** *adv.* **—skimp′i·ness,** *n.*

skin (skin), *n., v.,* **skinned, skin·ning.** **—***n.* **1.** the external covering or integument of an animal body, esp. when soft and flexible. **2.** such an integument stripped from the body of an animal, esp. a small animal; hide or pelt: *a beaver skin.* **3.** any of various thin, smooth coverings suggesting such an integument, as the rind or peel of fruit. **4.** any of various coatings or distinctive outer layers of material suggesting such an integument: *a skin of thin ice on the lake; the aluminum skin of an airplane.* **5.** a container made of animal skin, used for holding liquids, esp. wine. **6.** *Slang.* a dollar bill. **7. by the skin of one's teeth,** *Informal.* by an extremely narrow margin; just barely. **8. get under one's skin,** *Slang.* **a.** to irritate; bother. **b.** to affect deeply; impress. **9. have a thick skin,** to be insensitive to criticism or rebuffs. **10. have a thin skin,** to be extremely sensitive to criticism or rebuffs. **11. no skin off one's back** or **nose,** *Slang.* of no interest or concern, or involving no risk, to one. **12. save one's skin,** *Informal.* to avoid harm, esp. to escape death: *They betrayed their country to save their skins.* **—***v.t.* **13.** to strip or deprive of skin; flay; peel; husk. **14.** to remove or strip off (any covering, outer coating, surface layer, etc.). **15.** to scrape or rub a small piece of skin from (oneself), as in falling or scraping against something. **16.** *Informal.* to urge on, drive, or whip (a draft animal, as a mule or ox). **17.** to cover with or as with skin. **18.** *Slang.* to strip of money or belongings; fleece, as in gambling. [ME < Scand; cf. Icel *skinn;* c. G (dial.) *Schind(e)* skin of fruit] **—skin′like′,** *adj.*
—Syn. 2. fur. SKIN, HIDE, PELT are names for the outer covering stripped from animals. SKIN is the general word: *the skin of a muskrat.* HIDE applies to the untanned skin of large animals, as cattle, horses, elephants: *a buffalo hide.* PELT applies to the untanned skin of smaller animals: *a mink pelt.* **4.** hull, shell, husk, crust.

skin-deep (skin′dēp′), *adj.* **1.** superficial; not profound or substantial. **2.** of the depth of the skin.

skin-dive (skin′dīv′), *v.i.,* **-dived** or **-dove** (-dōv′), **-diving.** to engage in skin diving. **—skin′-div′er,** *n.*

skin′ div′ing, an underwater recreation in which the swimmer, equipped with a lightweight mask, foot fins, and either a snorkel or a portable air cylinder and breathing device, can move about quickly and easily underwater, as for exploring or spear fishing.

skin′ effect′, *Elect.* the phenomenon in which an alternating current tends to concentrate in the outer layer of a conductor.

skin′ flick′, *Slang.* a motion picture featuring nudity, scenes of sexual activity, etc.

skin·flint (skin′flint′), *n.* a mean, niggardly person; miser. **—skin′flint′y,** *adj.*

skin′ game′, any dishonest, cheating, or fraudulent scheme, business operation, or trick.

skin′ graft′, *Surg.* skin used for transplanting in skin grafting.

skin′ graft′ing, *Surg.* the transplanting of healthy skin from the patient's or another's body to a wound or burn, to form new skin. Also called **dermatoplasty.**

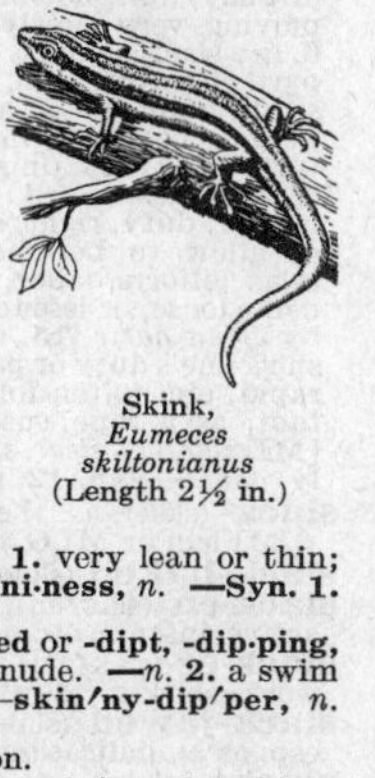

skink (skingk), *n.* any of numerous lizards of the family *Scincidae,* typically having flat, smooth, overlapping scales. [< L *scinc(us)* < Gk *skínkos* lizard]

Skink, *Eumeces skiltonianus* (Length 2½ in.)

skin·less (skin′lis), *adj.* **1.** deprived of skin. **2.** (of frankfurters or sausages) having no casing. [ME *skinles*]

skin·ner (skin′ər), *n.* **1.** a person who skins. **2.** a person who prepares or deals in skins or hides. **3.** *Informal.* a person who drives draft animals, as mules or oxen. [ME]

skin·ny (skin′ē), *adj.,* **-ni·er, -ni·est.** **1.** very lean or thin; emaciated. **2.** of or like skin. **—skin′ni·ness,** *n.* **—Syn. 1.** lank, gaunt, scrawny.

skin·ny-dip (skin′ē dip′), *v.i.,* **-dipped** or **-dipt, -dip·ping,** *n.* *Informal.* **—***v.i.* **1.** to swim in the nude. **—***n.* **2.** a swim in the nude. Also, **skin′ny dip′.** **—skin′ny-dip′per,** *n.* **—skin′ny dip′per.**

skin′ plan′ing, *Surg.* dermabrasion.

skin′ test′, a test in which a substance is introduced into the skin, as by application to a purposely abraded area or by injection, for the detection of allergic sensitivity to a specific pollen, protein, etc., or the presence of a disease.

skin·tight (skin′tīt′), *adj.* fitting almost as tightly as skin: *skintight trousers.*

skip[1] (skip), *v.,* **skipped, skip·ping,** *n.* **—***v.i.* **1.** to spring, jump, or leap lightly; gambol; move by nimble leaps and bounds. **2.** to pass from one point, thing, subject, etc., to another, disregarding or omitting what intervenes. **3.** *Informal.* to flee secretly. **4.** to ricochet or bounce along a surface; skim. **—***v.t.* **5.** to jump lightly over. **6.** to pass over without reading, noting, acting, etc.: *He skipped the description in the book.* **7.** to miss or omit (one or more of a series). **8.** *Informal.* to be absent from; avoid attendance at: *to skip a school class.* **9.** to cause to bounce or skim over a surface. **10.** *Informal.* to leave hastily and secretly or to flee from (a place): *He skipped town without paying his debts.* **—***n.* **11.** a skipping movement; a light jump or bounce. **12.** a gait marked by such jumps. **13.** the act or an instance of passing from one point or thing to another, with disregard of what intervenes. **14.** *Music.* a melodic interval greater than a second. [ME *skippe* < Scand; cf. Sw (obs.) *skuppa* to skip, Icel *skoppa* to spin (like a top), spring, run]
—Syn. 1. caper, hop. SKIP, BOUND refer to an elastic, springing movement. To SKIP is to give a series of light, quick leaps alternating the feet: *to skip about.* BOUND suggests a series of long, rather vigorous leaps; it is also applied to a springing or leaping type of walking or running rapidly and actively: *A dog came bounding up to meet him.* **2.** skim.

skip[2] (skip), *n., v.,* **skipped, skip·ping.** **—***n.* **1.** the captain of a curling or bowling team. **2.** *Informal.* skipper[1]. **—***v.t.* **3.** to serve as skip of. **4.** *Informal.* skipper[1]. [short for SKIPPER[1]]

ski′ pants′, pants worn for skiing, having the legs tapered to fit snugly at the ankles.

skip·jack (skip′jak′), *n., pl.* (*esp. collectively*) **-jack,** (*esp. referring to two or more kinds or species*) **-jacks.** any of various fishes that leap above the surface of the water, as a tuna, *Katsuwonus pelamis,* or the bonito.

ski·plane (skē′plān′), *n.* *Aeron.* an airplane equipped with skis to enable it to land on and take off from snow.

ski′ pole′, a slender pole, usually with a metal point at one end, a loop for the hand at the other, and a disk near the lower end to prevent its sinking into snow, used in skiing to gain momentum, maintain balance, etc.

skip·per[1] (skip′ər), *n.* **1.** the master or captain of a vessel, esp. of a small trading or fishing vessel. **2.** a captain or leader, as of a team. **—***v.t.* **3.** to act as skipper of. [ME < MD *schipper.* See SHIP, -ER[1]]

skip·per[2] (skip′ər), *n.* **1.** a person or thing that skips. **2.** any of various insects that hop or fly with jerky motions. **3.** any of numerous quick-flying, lepidopterous insects of the family *Hesperiidae,* closely related to the true butterflies. **4.** saury (def. 1). [SKIP[1] + -ER[1]]

skip·pet (skip′it), *n.* a small, round box for protecting an official or personal seal, as formerly stamped on a document. [ME *skipet* = *skip* alter. of SKEP + *-et* -ET]

skirl (skûrl), *v.i.* **1.** to play the bagpipe. **2.** *Scot. and North Eng.* to shriek. **—***n.* **3.** the sound of a bagpipe. [metathetic var. of late ME *scrille* < Scand]

skir·mish (skûr′mish), *n.* **1.** *Mil.* a fight between small bodies of troops, esp. advanced or outlying detachments of opposing forces. **2.** any brisk conflict or encounter. **—***v.i.* **3.** to engage in a skirmish. [ME *skirmysshe* < OF *(e)skirmiss-,* long s. of *eskirmir* < OHG *skirm(an);* r. ME *scarmouche* < OF *(e)scaramouche(r);* see SCARAMOUCH] **—skir′mish·er,** *n.* **—Syn. 1.** combat, brush. See **battle**[1].

skirr (skûr), *v.i.* **1.** to go rapidly; fly; scurry. **—***v.t.* **2.** to go rapidly over. **—***n.* **3.** a grating or whirring sound. [var. of SCOUR[2]]

skirt (skûrt), *n.* **1.** the part of a gown, dress, slip, or coat that extends downward from the waist. **2.** a one-piece garment extending downward from the waist and not joined between the legs, worn by women and girls. **3.** some part resembling or suggesting the skirt of a garment in shape or use, as an ornamental cloth strip covering the legs of furniture. **4.** a small leather flap on each side of a saddle, covering the metal bar from which the stirrup hangs. **5.** Also called **apron.** *Furniture.* **a.** a flat horizontal brace immediately beneath a chair seat, chest of drawers, etc. **b.** Also called **bed, frieze.** a flat brace or support immediately beneath a table top. **6.** Usually, **skirts.** the bordering, marginal, or outlying part of a place, group, etc.; the outskirts. **7.** *Slang.* a woman or girl. **—***v.t.* **8.** to border or edge with something. **9.** to pass or be situated along or around the border or edge of: *Traffic skirts the town.* **10.** to avoid, go around the edge of, or keep distant from (something that is controversial, risky, etc.): *The senator skirted the issue of higher taxes.* **—***v.i.* **11.** to pass or be situated on or along the border or edge of something. [ME *skirte* < Scand; cf. Icel *skyrta* SHIRT]

skirt·ing (skûr′ting), *n.* baseboard (def. 1).

ski′ run′, a trail, slope, course, or the like, used for skiing.

ski′ suit′, a warm, lightweight costume for skiing and other outdoor winter sports consisting of a short jacket and close-fitting trousers.

skit (skit), *n.* **1.** a short literary piece of a humorous or satirical character. **2.** a short, theatrical sketch or act, usually comical. **3.** a gibe or taunt. [ME: dirt, diarrhea; in 16th century, frivolous female < Scand; cf. Icel *skītr* filth, excrement, *skīta* diarrhea; akin to OE *scitte* purging]

ski′ tow′, a ski lift in which skiers are hauled up a slope while grasping a looped, endless rope driven by a motor.

skit·ter (skit′ər), *v.i.* **1.** to go, run, or glide lightly or rapidly. **2.** to skim along a surface. **3.** *Angling.* to draw a lure or a baited hook over the water with a skipping motion. **—***v.t.* **4.** to cause to skitter. [*skit* (var. of Scot and north E *skite* an oblique blow, joke, ? < Scand; cf. Icel *skȳt* 1st pers. sing. pres. indic. of *skjōta* to shoot) + -ER[6]]

skit·tish (skit′ish), *adj.* **1.** apt to start or shy: *a skittish horse.* **2.** restlessly or excessively lively: *a skittish mood.* **3.** fickle; uncertain. **4.** shy; coy. [late ME *skit* (see SKITTER) + *-ish* -ISH[1]] **—skit′tish·ly,** *adv.* **—skit′tish·ness,** *n.*

skit·tle (skit′ᵊl), *n.* *Chiefly Brit.* **1. skittles,** (*construed as sing.*) ninepins in which a wooden ball or disk is used to knock down the pins. **2.** one of the pins used in this game. [< Scand; cf. Dan *skyttel* SHUTTLE]

skive (skīv), *v.t.,* **skived, skiv·ing.** **1.** to split or cut, as leather, into layers or slices. **2.** to shave, as hides. [< Scand; cf. Icel *skīfa* slice, c. ME *schive* slice (of bread)]

skiv·er (skī′vər), *n.* **1.** a person or thing that skives. **2.** a thin sheepskin used for bookbinding.

skoal (skōl), *interj.* **1.** (used as a toast in drinking someone's health.) **—***n.* **2.** a toast. **—***v.i.* **3.** to drink a toast. [< Scand; cf. Dan *skaal* bowl, toast; c. G *Schale* SCALE[2]]

Sko·kie (skō′kē), *n.* a city in NE Illinois, near Chicago. 68,627 (1970).

skoo·kum (skōō′kəm), *adj. Northwest U.S., Canada.* **1.** large; powerful. **2.** excellent. [< Chinook Jargon]

Skop·lje (*Serbo-Croatian.* skôp′lye), *n.* a city in SE Yugoslavia: earthquake 1963. 212,000 (1961). Macedonian, **Skop·je** (skôp′ye). Turkish, **Üsküb, Üsküp.**

skreegh (skrēkh), *v.i., v.t., n. Scot.* screech. Also, **skreigh.**

Skt, Sanskrit (def. 1). Also, **Skt., Skr., Skrt.**

sku·a (skyōō′ə), *n.* **1.** Also called **great skua.** a large predatory bird, *Catharacta skua,* related to the jaegers, found in colder waters of both northern and southern seas. **2.** *Brit.* jaeger (def. 1). [< Faeroese *skū(g)vur;* c. Icel *skūfr* tassel, tuft, also skua (in poetry), akin to SHOVE[1]]

Skua, *Catharacta skua* (Length 2 ft.)

Skuld (skuld), *n. Scand. Myth.* a dwarf personifying the future: one of the three Norns that developed from Urdar. Cf. **Urd, Verdandi.**

skul·dug·ger·y (skul dug′ə rē), *n. Informal.* dishonorable proceedings; mean dishonesty or trickery. Also, **skullduggery, sculduggery, scullduggery.** [Amer var. of Scot *skulduddery* illicit sexual intercourse, obscenity, euphemistic alter. of ADULTERY]

skulk (skulk), *v.i.* **1.** to lie or keep in hiding, as for some evil purpose. **2.** to move or go in a stealthy manner; sneak; slink. **3.** *Brit.* to shirk duty; malinger. —*n.* **4.** a person who skulks. **5.** a pack or group of foxes. **6.** *Rare.* the act or an instance of skulking. Also, **sculk.** [ME < Scand; cf. Dan *skulke*] —**Syn. 1.** See **lurk.**

skull (skul), *n.* **1.** the bony framework of the head, enclosing the brain and supporting the face; the skeleton of the head. **2.** *Usually Disparaging.* the head as the seat of intelligence or knowledge. [ME *scolle* < Scand; cf. Sw (dial.) *skulle* skull, Norw (dial) *skol, skul* shell (of an egg or nut)]

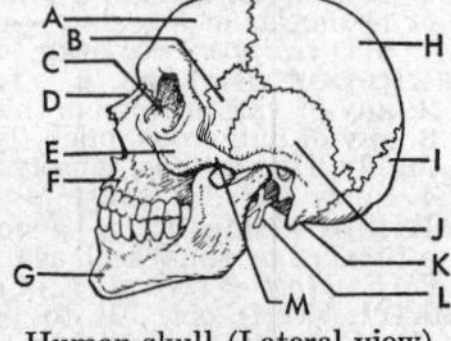
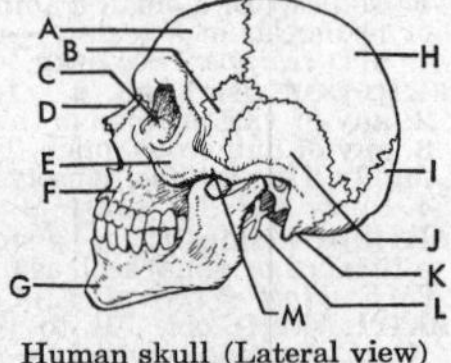

Human skull (Lateral view) A, Frontal bone; B, Sphenoid bone; C, Eye socket; D, Nasal bone; E, Zygomatic bone; F, Maxilla; G, Mandible; H, Parietal bone; I, Occipital bone; J, Temporal bone; K, Mastoid process; L, Styloid process; M, Zygomatic arch

skull′ and cross′bones, a representation of a front view of a human skull above two crossed bones, originally used on pirates' flags and now used as a warning sign, as in designating substances as poisons.

skull·cap (skul′kap′), *n.* **1.** a small, brimless, close-fitting cap, worn on the crown of the head. **2.** *Bot.* any of various labiate herbs of the genus *Scutellaria,* having a calyx resembling a helmet.

skull·dug·ger·y (skul dug′ə rē), *Informal. n.* skulduggery.

skunk (skuŋgk), *n., pl.* **skunks,** (*esp. collectively*) **skunk,** *v.* —*n.* **1.** a small, black, North American mammal, *Mephitis mephitis,* of the weasel family, having a longitudinal, white, V-shaped stripe on the back, and ejecting a fetid odor when alarmed or attacked. **2.** *Informal.* a thoroughly contemptible person. —*v.t.* **3.** *U.S. Slang.* to defeat thoroughly in a game. [< Algonquian; cf. Abnaki *segankw, segonkw*]

Skunk, *Mephitis mephitis* (Total length 2 ft.; tail 8 in.)

skunk′ cab′bage, 1. a low, fetid, broad-leaved, araceous plant, *Symplocarpus foetidus,* of North America. **2.** a similar araceous plant, *Lysichitum americanum,* found on the western coast of North America and in Siberia, Japan, etc. Also called **skunkweed.**

skunk·weed (skuŋgk′wēd′), *n.* **1.** a rank-smelling, perennial herb, *Polemonium confertum,* of the western U.S., having bluish-violet flowers. **2.** See **skunk cabbage.**

Sku·ta·ri (skōō′tä rē, -tə-), *n.* Scutari (def. 1).

sky (skī), *n., pl.* **skies.** Often, **skies** (for defs. 1–4). **1.** the region of the clouds or the upper air; the upper atmosphere of the earth. **2.** the heavens or firmament, appearing as a great vault. **3.** the supernal or celestial heaven. **4.** *Obs.* a cloud. **5. out of a clear sky,** without advance notice or warning; abruptly. Also, **out of a clear blue sky.** [ME < Scand; cf. Icel *sk͞y* cloud, c. OE *scēo* cloud; akin to Ir *cēo* fog, mist, smoke]

sky′ blue′, the color of the unclouded sky in daytime; azure. —**sky′-blue′,** *adj.*

sky·cap (skī′kap′), *n.* a porter who carries passenger baggage at an airport or air terminal. [SKY + (RED)CAP]

sky′ cav′alry. See **air cavalry.** Also, **sky′ cav′.**

sky·dive (skī′dīv′), *v.i.,* **-dived** or (*U.S. Informal and Brit. Dial.*) **-dove; -dived; -div·ing.** *Sports.* to make a parachute jump, delaying the opening of the parachute as long as possible. —**sky′div′er,** *n.*

Skye (skī), *n.* an island in the Hebrides, in NW Scotland. 7478 (1961); 670 sq. mi.

Skye′ ter′rier, one of a Scottish breed of small terriers having short legs and a dark or light blue-gray, gray, or fawn coat. [after SKYE]

Skye terrier (9 in. high at shoulder)

sky·ey (skī′ē), *adj. Chiefly Literary.* **1.** of or from the sky. **2.** skylike, esp. in color; sky-blue.

sky-high (skī′hī′), *adv., adj.* very high

sky·jack (skī′jak′), *v.t.* to hijack (an airliner), esp. to force it to fly to a country where one's own government forbids travelers to go or in order to hold the passengers and plane for ransom or for political reasons. [SKY + (HI)JACK] —**sky′jack′er,** *n.*

Sky·lab (skī′lab′), *n.* a space station, launched by the U.S. in 1973, to orbit the earth as a scientific laboratory to which three successive teams of astronauts were sent by ferry vehicles for extended periods of work.

sky·lark (skī′lärk′), *n.* **1.** either of two Eurasian larks, *Alauda arvensis* or *A. gulgula,* noted for their song in flight. —*v.i.* **2.** *Informal.* to frolic; sport; play. —**sky′lark′er,** *n.*

sky·light (skī′līt′), *n.* an opening in a roof or ceiling, fitted with glass, for admitting daylight.

sky·line (skī′līn′), *n.* **1.** the boundary line between earth and sky; the apparent horizon. **2.** the outline of the buildings of a city seen against the sky. Also, **sky′ line′.**

sky′ pi′lot, *Slang.* **1.** a clergyman, esp. a chaplain of the armed forces. **2.** an aviator.

sky·rock·et (skī′rok′it), *n.* **1.** a rocket firework that ascends into the air and explodes at a height, usually in a brilliant array of colored sparks. —*v.i.* **2.** to rise, succeed, or become famous rapidly or suddenly.

Skylark, *Alauda arvensis* (Length 7 in.)

Sky·ros (skī′ros, -rōs; *Gk.* skē′rôs), *n.* a Greek island in the W Aegean: the largest island of the N Sporades. 3500 (1965); 81 sq. mi. Also, **Scyros.**

sky·sail (skī′sāl′; *Naut.* skī′səl), *n. Naut.* (on a square-rigged vessel) a light square sail next above the royal. See diag. at **ship.**

sky·scrap·er (skī′skrā′pər), *n.* **1.** a tall building of many stories, esp. one for office or commercial use. **2.** *Archit.* a building completely supported by a framework of girders, as opposed to one supported by load-bearing walls.

sky′ train′, an airplane towing one or more gliders.

sky·ward (skī′wərd), *adv.* **1.** Also, **sky′wards.** toward the sky. —*adj.* **2.** directed toward the sky.

sky′ wave′, *Radio.* a radio wave propagated upward from the earth, whether reflected by the ionosphere or not.

sky·way (skī′wā′), *n.* **1.** *Informal.* See **air lane. 2.** an elevated highway, esp. one having the form of a tall viaduct.

sky·write (skī′rīt′), *v.,* **-wrote, -writ·ten, -writ·ing.** —*v.i.* **1.** to engage in skywriting. —*v.t.* **2.** to produce (a message, advertisement, etc.) by skywriting. —**sky′writ′er,** *n.*

sky·writ·ing (skī′rī′tiŋg), *n.* **1.** the act or technique of tracing words or designs against the sky with chemically produced smoke released from a maneuvering airplane. **2.** the words or designs so traced.

s.l., *Bibliog.* without place (of publication). [< L *sine loco*]

slab[1] (slab), *n., v.,* **slabbed, slab·bing.** —*n.* **1.** a broad, flat, somewhat thick piece of some solid material. **2.** a thick slice: *a slab of bread.* **3.** a rough outside piece cut from a log, as in making boards. —*v.t.* **4.** to make into a slab or slabs. **5.** to cover or lay with slabs. **6.** to cut the slabs or outside pieces from (a log). [ME *s(c)labbe*]

slab[2] (slab), *adj. Archaic.* thick, viscous. [appar. < Scand; cf. Dan *slab* slippery (adj.), mire (n.), Icel *slabb* slush]

slab·ber (slab′ər), *v.i., v.t., n.* slobber.

slab·ber·y (slab′ə rē), *adj.* slobbery.

slab-sid·ed (slab′sī′did), *adj. Informal.* **1.** having the sides long and flat, like slabs. **2.** tall and lank.

slack[1] (slak), *adj.* **1.** not tight, taut, or tense; loose: *a slack rope.* **2.** negligent; careless; remiss. **3.** slow, sluggish, or indolent: *He is slack in answering letters.* **4.** not active or busy; dull; not brisk: *the slack season in an industry.* **5.** moving very slowly, as the tide, wind, or water. —*adv.* **6.** in a slack manner. —*n.* **7.** a slack condition or part. **8.** the part of a rope, sail, or the like, that hangs loose, without strain upon it. **9.** a decrease in activity, as in work. **10.** *Geog.* a cessation in a strong flow, as of a current at its turn. **11.** *Pros.* (in sprung rhythm) the unaccented syllable or syllables. —*v.t.* **12.** to be remiss in respect to (some matter, duty, right, etc.); shirk; leave undone. **13.** to make or allow to become less active, vigorous, intense, etc.; relax (efforts, labor, speed, etc.) (often fol. by *up*). **14.** to make loose, or less tense or taut, as a rope; loosen (often fol. by *off* or *out*). **15.** to slake (lime). —*v.i.* **16.** to be remiss; shirk one's duty or part. **17.** to become less active, vigorous, rapid, etc. (often fol. by *up*). **18.** to become less tense or taut, as a rope; ease off. **19.** to become slaked, as lime. [ME *slac,* OE *slæc, slæc;* c. Icel *slakr,* OHG *slach*] —**slack′ly,** *adv.* —**Syn. 12.** neglect. **13.** reduce, slacken.

slack[2] (slak), *n.* the fine screenings of coal. [late ME *sleck* < MFlem or MLG *slecke*]

slack-baked (slak′bākt′), *adj.* improperly baked.

slack·en (slak′ən), *v.t., v.i.* **1.** to make or become less active, intense, etc. **2.** to make or become looser or less taut.

slack·er (slak′ər), *n.* **1.** a person who evades his duty or work; shirker. **2.** a person who evades military service.

slack-jawed (slak′jôd′), *adj.* having the mouth open, esp. as an indication of astonishment.

slacks (slaks), *n.* (*construed as pl.*) men's or women's trousers for informal wear.

slack′ suit′, 1. a man's suit for casual wear consisting of slacks and a matching shirt or loose-fitting jacket. **2.** Also called **pants suit.** a woman's suit for casual wear consisting of slacks and a matching jacket.

slack′ wa′ter, 1. a period when a body of water is between tides. **2.** water that is free of currents.

slag (slag), *n., v.,* **slagged, slag·ging.** —*n.* **1.** the more or less completely fused and vitrified matter separated during the reduction of a metal from its ore. **2.** the scoria from a volcano. —*v.t.* **3.** to convert into slag. —*v.i.* **4.** to form slag. [< MLG *slagge;* c. G *Schlacke* dross, slag; see SLACK[2]]

slain (slān), *v.* pp. of **slay.**

slake (slāk), *v.,* **slaked, slak·ing.** —*v.t.* **1.** to allay (thirst, desire, wrath, etc.) by satisfying. **2.** to cool or refresh. **3.** to make less active, vigorous, intense, etc. **4.** to cause disintegration of (lime) by treatment with water. Cf. **slaked lime. 5.** *Obs.* to make loose or less tense; slacken. —*v.i.* **6.** (of lime) to become slaked. **7.** *Archaic.* to become less active, intense, vigorous, etc.; abate. [ME; c. OE *slac(ian)* = *slæc* SLACK[1] + *-ian* v. suffix] —**slak′a·ble, slake′a·ble,** *adj.* —**slak′er,** *n.*

slaked′ lime′, a powder, $Ca(OH)_2$, obtained by the action of water on lime: used chiefly in mortars, plasters, and cements. Also called **calcium hydroxide, calcium hydrate, hydrated lime, lime hydrate.**

sla·lom (slä′ləm, -lōm), *n.* *Skiing.* a downhill race over a winding and zigzag course marked by poles or gates. [< Norw: lit., slope track]

slam[1] (slam), *v.,* **slammed, slam·ming,** *n.* —*v.t., v.i.* **1.** to shut with force and noise: *to slam the door.* **2.** to dash, strike, etc., with violent and noisy impact: *He slammed his books upon the table.* —*n.* **3.** a violent and noisy closing, dashing, or impact. **4.** the noise so made. [< Scand; cf. Icel *slambra,* Norw *slemma,* Sw (dial.) *slämma* to slam]

slam[2] (slam), *n.* *Cards.* **1.** the winning or bidding of all the tricks or all the tricks but one in a deal. Cf. **grand slam** (def. 1), **little slam. 2.** an old type of card game associated with ruff. [perh. special use of SLAM[1]]

slam-bang (slam′baŋ′), *adv.* *Informal.* **1.** with noisy violence. **2.** quickly and carelessly; slapdash.

slan·der (slan′dər), *n.* **1.** defamation; calumny. **2.** a malicious, false, and defamatory statement or report. **3.** *Law.* defamation by oral utterance rather than by writing, pictures, etc. —*v.t.* **4.** to utter slander concerning; defame. —*v.i.* **5.** to utter or circulate slander. [ME *sclaundre* < AF *(e)sclaundre,* c. OF *esclandre* < LL *scandal(um)* cause of offense, snare; see SCANDAL] —**slan′der·er,** *n.* —**slan′der·ous,** *adj.* —**slan′der·ous·ly,** *adv.*

slang[1] (slaŋ), *n.* **1.** very informal usage in vocabulary and idiom that is characteristically more metaphorical, playful, elliptical, vivid, and ephemeral than ordinary language. **2.** (in English and some other languages) speech and writing characterized by the use of vulgar and socially taboo vocabulary and idiomatic expressions. **3.** jargon. **4.** argot; cant. —*v.i.* **5.** to use slang or abusive language. —*v.t.* **6.** to assail with abusive language. [?]

slang[2] (slaŋ), *v.* *Chiefly Dial.* pt. of **sling**[1].

slang·y (slaŋ′ē), *adj.,* **slang·i·er, slang·i·est.** of, of the nature of, or containing slang: *a slangy expression.* —**slang′i·ly,** *adv.* —**slang′i·ness,** *n.*

slank (slaŋk), *v.* *Archaic.* pt. of **slink.**

slant (slant, slänt), *v.i.* **1.** to slope. **2.** to have or be influenced by a subjective point of view, personal feeling or inclination, etc. (usually fol. by *toward*). —*v.t.* **3.** to cause to slope. **4.** *Journalism.* **a.** (in writing) to render (information) unfaithfully or incompletely in order to reflect a particular viewpoint. **b.** to write, edit, or publish for the interest or amusement of a specific group of readers. —*n.* **5.** slanting or oblique direction; slope. **6.** a slanting line, surface, etc. **7.** virgule. **8.** a mental leaning, bias, or distortion. **9.** viewpoint; opinion; attitude. **10.** Also called **angle.** *Journalism.* the particular mood or vein in which something is written, edited, or published: *a humorous slant.* —*adj.* **11.** sloping; oblique. [aph. var. of ASLANT] —**Syn. 1, 5.** incline. **5.** pitch.

slant-eyed (slant′īd′, slänt′-), *adj.* (of a person) having eyes with epicanthic folds.

slant′ rhyme′, *Pros.* rhyme in which either the vowels or the consonants of stressed syllables are identical, as in *eyes, light; years, yours.* Also called **half rhyme, imperfect rhyme, near rhyme.**

slant·wise (slant′wīz′, slänt′-), *adv.* **1.** aslant; obliquely. —*adj.* **2.** slanting; oblique. Also, **slant·ways** (slant′wāz′, slänt′-).

slap (slap), *n., v.,* **slapped, slap·ping,** *adv.* —*n.* **1.** a sharp blow or smack, esp. with the open hand or with something flat. **2.** a sound made by or as if by such a blow. **3.** a sharply worded or sarcastic rebuke, censure, or comment. —*v.t.* **4.** to strike sharply, esp. with the open hand or with something flat. **5.** to bring (the hand, something flat, etc.) with a sharp blow against something. **6.** to dash or cast forcibly: *He slapped the package down.* **7.** *Informal.* to put or place promptly and sometimes haphazardly (often fol. by *on*). —*adv. Informal.* **8.** forcibly or suddenly. **9.** directly; straight: *The tug rammed slap into the side of the freighter.* [< LG *slapp, slappe;* imit.] —**slap′per,** *n.* —**Syn. 1.** See **blow**[1].

slap·dash (slap′dash′), *adv.* **1.** in a hasty, haphazard manner. —*adj.* **2.** hasty and careless; offhand. [SLAP (adv.) + DASH[1]]

slap·hap·py (slap′hap′ē), *adj.,* **-pi·er, -pi·est.** *Informal.* **1.** severely befuddled; punch-drunk: *a slaphappy boxer.* **2.** agreeably foolish.

slap·stick (slap′stik′), *n.* **1.** broad comedy characterized by violently boisterous action. **2.** a stick or lath used by harlequins, clowns, etc., as in pantomime, for striking other performers, esp. a combination of laths that make a loud, clapping noise without hurting the person struck.

slash (slash), *v.t.* **1.** to cut or mark with a violent sweeping stroke or by striking violently and at random, as with a knife, sword, or pen. **2.** to lash. **3.** to curtail, reduce, or alter. **4.** to make slits in (a garment) to show an underlying fabric. —*v.i.* **5.** to lay about one with sharp, sweeping strokes; make one's way by cutting. **6.** to make a sweeping, cutting stroke. —*n.* **7.** a sweeping stroke, as with a knife, sword, or pen. **8.** a cut, wound, or mark made with such a stroke. **9.** a curtailment, reduction, or alteration. **10.** an ornamental slit in a garment showing an underlying fabric. **11.** *U.S.* virgule. **12.** (in forest land) **a.** an open area strewn with debris of trees from felling or from wind or fire. **b.** the debris itself. [ME *slasch(en)* < ?]

slash·ing (slash′iŋ), *n.* **1.** a slash. —*adj.* **2.** sweeping; cutting. **3.** violent; severe. **4.** dashing; impetuous. —**slash′ing·ly,** *adv.*

slash′ pine′, **1.** a pine, *Pinus caribaea,* found in slashes and swamps in the southeastern U.S., yielding a hard, durable wood. **2.** the loblolly pine.

slash′ pock′et, a pocket set into a garment, to which easy access is provided by an exterior slit.

Śląsk (shlôNsk), *n.* Polish name of **Silesia.**

slat[1] (slat), *n., v.,* **slat·ted, slat·ting.** —*n.* **1.** a long, thin, narrow strip of wood, metal, etc., used as a support for a bed, as one of the horizontal laths of a Venetian blind, etc. **2. slats,** *Slang.* **a.** the ribs. **b.** the buttocks. —*v.t.* **3.** to furnish or make with slats. [ME *sclat, slatt* < MF *(e)sclat* splinter, fragment; see ÉCLAT]

slat[2] (slat), *v.,* **slat·ted, slat·ting,** *n.* *Chiefly Brit. Dial.* —*v.t.* **1.** to throw or dash with force. —*v.i.* **2.** to flap violently, as sails. —*n.* **3.** a slap; sharp blow. [ME *sleaten* < Scand; cf. Icel *sletta* to slap; akin to SLAY]

S. Lat., south latitude.

slate (slāt), *n., v.,* **slat·ed, slat·ing.** —*n.* **1.** a fine-grained rock that tends to split along parallel cleavage planes. **2.** a thin piece or plate of this rock or a similar material. **3.** a blackboard, esp. a small one. **4.** a dull, dark bluish gray. **5.** a list of candidates, officers, etc., to be considered for nomination, appointment, election, or the like. **6. clean slate,** a record marked by honorable or creditable conduct. —*v.t.* **7.** to cover with or as with slate. **8.** to write or set down for nomination or appointment. **9.** to place on a schedule. **10.** to censure or criticize harshly or violently; scold. [ME *sclate* < MF *(e)sclate,* fem. of *esclat;* see SLAT[1]]

slat·er (slā′tər), *n.* a person who lays slates, as for roofing. [ME *sclater*]

Sla·ter (slā′tər), *n.* **Samuel,** 1768–1835, U.S. industrialist, born in England.

slath·er (slath′ər), *Informal.* —*v.t.* **1.** to spread or apply thickly: *to slather butter on toast.* **2.** to spend or use lavishly. —*n.* **3.** Often, **slathers.** a generous amount: *They have slathers of money.* [?]

slat·ing (slā′tiŋ), *n.* **1.** the act or work of covering something with slates. **2.** materials for roofing with slates. **3.** a scolding.

slat·tern (slat′ərn), *n.* **1.** a slovenly, untidy woman or girl. **2.** a slut; harlot. [? akin to late ME *slatter* to slash or slit (clothes), freq. of SLAT[2]] —**slat′tern·ly,** *adj., adv.*

slat·y (slā′tē), *adj.,* **slat·i·er, slat·i·est. 1.** consisting of, resembling, or pertaining to slate. **2.** having the color of slate. —**slat′i·ness,** *n.*

slaugh·ter (slô′tər), *n.* **1.** the killing or butchering of cattle, sheep, etc., esp. for food. **2.** the brutal or violent killing of a person. **3.** the killing of great numbers of people or animals indiscriminately. **4.** *Informal.* a thorough defeat; trouncing. —*v.t.* **5.** to kill or butcher (animals), esp. for food. **6.** to kill in a brutal or violent manner. **7.** to slay in great numbers; massacre. **8.** *Informal.* to defeat thoroughly; trounce. [ME *slaghter* < Scand; cf. Icel *slātr* butcher's meat (earlier **slahtr*), *slātra* to butcher; akin to SLAY] —**slaugh′ter·er,** *n.* —**Syn. 2.** homicide, murder.

slaugh·ter·house (slô′tər hous′), *n., pl.* **-hous·es** (-hou′ziz). a building or place where animals are butchered for food; abattoir. [ME]

slaugh·ter·ous (slô′tər əs), *adj.* murderous; destructive. —**slaugh′ter·ous·ly,** *adv.*

Slav (släv, slav), *n.* **1.** one of a group of peoples in eastern, southeastern, and central Europe, including the Russians and Ruthenians (**Eastern Slavs**), the Bulgars, Serbs, Croats, Slavonians, Slovenes, etc. (**Southern Slavs**), and the Poles, Czechs, Moravians, Slovaks, etc. (**Western Slavs**). —*adj.* **2.** of, pertaining to, or characteristic of the Slavs; Slavic. [< ML *Slāv(us),* var. of *Sclāvus* (see SLAVE); r. ME *Sclave* < ML *Sclāv(us),* c. LGk *Sklābos*]

Slav, Slavic (def. 1).

Slav., Slavic.

slave (slāv), *n., v.,* **slaved, slav·ing.** —*n.* **1.** a person who is the property of another; a bond servant. **2.** a person entirely under the domination of some influence or person: *a slave to a drug.* **3.** a drudge: *a housekeeping slave.* **4.** *Mach.* a mechanism under control of and repeating the actions of a similar mechanism. Cf. **master** (def. 16). —*v.i.* **5.** to work like a slave; drudge. —*v.t.* **6.** to enslave. [ME *sclave* < ML *sclāv(us)* (masc.), *sclāv(a)* (fem.) slave, special use of *Sclāv(us)* Slav, so called because so many Slavs were enslaved in the early Middle Ages; see SLAV]

slave′ ant′, an ant enslaved by ants of another species.

slave′ brace′let, a braceletlike, ornamental circlet or chain worn around the ankle.

Slave′ Coast′, the coast of W equatorial Africa, between the Benin and Volta rivers: a center of slavery traffic 16th–19th centuries.

slave′ driv′er, **1.** an overseer of slaves. **2.** a hard taskmaster.

slave·hold·er (slāv′hōl′dər), *n.* a person who owns slaves. —**slave′hold′ing,** *n.*

slave′ la′bor, **1.** persons, esp. a large group, forced to perform labor under duress or threats, as political prisoners, prisoners in concentration camps, etc.; a labor force of slaves or slavelike prisoners. **2.** labor done by slaves.

slav·er[1] (slā′vər), *n.* a dealer in or an owner of slaves. [SLAVE + -ER[1]]

slav·er[2] (slav′ər, slā′vər, slä′-), *v.i.* **1.** to let saliva run from the mouth; slobber. **2.** to fawn. —*v.t.* **3.** to smear with saliva. —*n.* **4.** saliva coming from the mouth. [ME < Scand; cf. Icel *slafra.* See SLOBBER]

Slave′ Riv′er, a river in NE Alberta and Northwest Territories, in Canada: flowing from Lake Athabaska NW to Great Slave Lake. 258 mi. long.

slav·er·y (slā′və rē, slāv′rē), *n.* **1.** ownership of a person or persons by another or others. **2.** the condition of a slave. **3.** the keeping of slaves as a practice or institution. **4.** severe toil; drudgery.
—**Syn. 1.** thralldom, enthrallment. SLAVERY, BONDAGE, SERVITUDE refer to involuntary subjection to another or others. SLAVERY emphasizes the idea of complete ownership and control by a master: *to be sold into slavery.* BONDAGE indicates a state of subjugation or captivity often involving burdensome and degrading labor: *in bondage to a cruel master.* SERVITUDE is compulsory service, often such as is required as a legal penalty: *penal servitude.* **4.** moil, labor.

slave′ ship′, a ship for transporting slaves from their native homes to places of bondage.

Slave′ State′, *U.S. Hist.* any of the states where Negro slavery was legal until the Civil War.

slav·ey (slā′vē), *n., pl.* **-eys.** *Brit. Informal.* a female servant, esp. a maid of all work in a boardinghouse.

Slav·ic (slav′ik, slä′vik), *n.* **1.** a branch of the Indo-European family of languages, usually divided into East Slavic (Russian, Ukrainian, Byelorussian), West Slavic (Polish, Czech, Slovak, Sorbian), and South Slavic (Old Church Slavonic, Bulgarian, Serbo-Croatian, Slovene). *Abbr.:* Slav, Slav. —*adj.* **2.** of or pertaining to the Slavs or their languages. Also, **Slavonic.**

Slav·i·cist (slä′vi sist, slav′i-), *n.* a specialist in the study of the Slavic languages or literatures. Also, **Sla·vist** (slä′vist, slav′ist).

slav·ish (slā′vish), *adj.* **1.** of or befitting a slave: *slavish subjection.* **2.** being or resembling a slave; abjectly submissive. **3.** base; mean; ignoble: *slavish fears.* **4.** deliberately imitative; lacking originality. —**slav′ish·ly,** *adv.* —**slav′ish·ness,** *n.* —**Syn. 2.** groveling, sycophantic, fawning, cringing. See **servile.**

Slav·ism (slä′viz əm, slav′iz-), *n.* something that is native to, characteristic of, or associated with the Slavs or Slavic. Also, **Slav·i·cism** (slä′vi siz′əm, slav′i-).

Slavo-, a combining form of **Slav:** *Slavophile.*

slav·oc·ra·cy (slā vok′rə sē), *n., pl.* **-cies. 1.** the rule or domination of slaveholders. **2.** a dominating body of slaveholders.

Sla·vo·ni·a (slə vō′nē ə), *n.* a former region in N Yugoslavia. Cf. **Croatia.**

Sla·vo·ni·an (slə vō′nē ən), *adj.* **1.** of or pertaining to Slavonia or its inhabitants. **2.** Slavic. —*n.* **3.** a native or inhabitant of Slavonia. **4.** a Slav.

Sla·von·ic (slə von′ik), *adj.* **1.** Slavonian. **2.** Slavic. —*n.* **3.** Slavic. [< NL *slavonic(us)* = ML *Slavon(ia)* SLAVONIA + *-icus* -IC] —**Sla·von′i·cal·ly,** *adv.*

Slav·o·phile (slä′və fīl′, -fil, slav′ə-), *n.* **1.** a person who greatly admires the Slavs and Slavic ways. —*adj.* **2.** admiring or favoring the Slavs and Slavic interests, aims, customs, etc. Also, **Slav·o·phil** (slä′və fil, slav′ə-). —**Sla·voph·i·lism** (slə vof′ə liz′əm, slä′və fil iz′əm, slav′ə-), *n.*

Slav·o·phobe (slä′və fōb′, slav′ə-), *n.* a person who fears or hates the Slavs, their influence, or things Slavic. —**Slav′o·pho′bi·a,** *n.*

slaw (slô), *n.* coleslaw. [< D *sla*, short for *salade* SALAD]

slay (slā), *v.t.,* **slew, slain, slay·ing. 1.** to kill by violence. **2.** to destroy; extinguish. **3.** *Informal.* to affect or impress very strongly; overwhelm, esp. by means of amusement. **4.** *Obs.* to strike. [ME; OE *slēan;* c. D *slaan,* G *schlagen,* Icel *slā,* Goth *slahan* to strike, beat] —**slay′er,** *n.*

sleave (slēv), *v.,* **sleaved, sleav·ing,** *n.* —*v.t.* **1.** to divide or separate into filaments, as silk. —*n.* **2.** anything matted or raveled. **3.** a filament of silk obtained by separating a thicker thread. **4.** a silk in the form of such filaments. [OE *slǣfan,* c. *slīfan* to split; see SLIVER]

sleaze (slēz), *n. Slang.* **1.** a contemptible, vulgar, or slovenly person. **2.** sleazy quality, behavior, or material. [back formation from SLEAZY]

slea·zy (slē′zē, slā′zē), *adj.,* **-zi·er, -zi·est. 1.** thin or poor in texture, as a fabric; flimsy: *a sleazy dress.* **2.** contemptibly low or unimportant. [?] —**slea′zi·ly,** *adv.* —**slea′zi·ness,** *n.*

sled (sled), *n., v.,* **sled·ded, sled·ding.** —*n.* **1.** a small vehicle consisting of a platform mounted on runners for sliding over snow or ice. **2.** a sledge. —*v.i.* **3.** to coast, ride, or be carried on a sled. —*v.t.* **4.** to carry on a sled. [ME *sledde* < MFlem or MLG; akin to G *schlitten,* Icel *slethi.* See SLIDE]

sled·der (sled′ər), *n.* **1.** a person who rides on or steers a sled. **2.** a horse or other animal for drawing a sled.

sled·ding (sled′ing), *n.* **1.** the state of the ground permitting use of a sled: *The snow made a good sledding.* **2.** the conditions under which any task is accomplished. **3.** the act of riding or carrying on a sled.

sledge[1] (slej), *n., v.,* **sledged, sledg·ing.** —*n.* **1.** a vehicle mounted on runners and often drawn by draft animals, used for traveling or for carrying loads. **2.** a sled. **3.** *Brit.* a sleigh. —*v.t., v.i.* **4.** to travel or carry by sledge. [< D (dial.) *sleedse* < *slede,* var. of *sledde* SLED]

sledge[2] (slej), *n., v.,* **sledged, sledg·ing.** —*n.* **1.** See **sledge hammer.** —*v.t., v.i.* **2.** to sledge-hammer. [ME *slegge,* OE *slecg;* c. D *slegge,* Icel *sleggja;* akin to SLAY]

sledge′ ham′mer, a large, heavy hammer wielded with both hands.

sledge-ham·mer (slej′ham′ər), *v.t., v.i.* **1.** to strike, hammer, or beat with or as with a sledge hammer. —*adj.* **2.** like a sledge hammer; powerful; ruthless.

sleek[1] (slēk), *adj.* **1.** smooth or glossy, as hair, an animal, etc. **2.** well-fed or well-groomed. **3.** smooth in manners, speech, etc.; suave. [var. of SLICK[1]] —**sleek′ness,** *n.*

sleek[2] (slēk), *v.t.* to make sleek; smooth; slick. Also, **sleek′en.** [var. of SLICK[2]]

sleek·it (slē′kit), *adj.* **1.** *Scot.* sleek; smooth. **2.** *Chiefly Scot.* sly; sneaky. [< ptp. of SLEEK[2]]

sleep (slēp), *v.,* **slept, sleep·ing,** *n.* —*v.i.* **1.** to take the repose or rest afforded by a suspension of the voluntary exercise of the bodily functions and the natural suspension, complete or partial, of consciousness. **2.** *Bot.* to assume, esp. at night, a state similar to the sleep of animals, marked by closing of petals, leaves, etc. **3.** to be dormant, quiescent, or inactive, as faculties. **4.** to allow one's alertness, vigilance, or attentiveness to lie dormant. **5.** to lie in death: *They are sleeping in their tombs.* —*v.t.* **6.** to take rest in (a specified kind of sleep). **7.** to accommodate for sleeping; have sleeping accommodations for: *This trailer sleeps three people.* **8.** to spend or pass in sleep (usually fol. by *away* or *out*): *to sleep the day away.* **9.** to get rid of (a headache, hangover, etc.) by sleeping (usually fol. by *off* or *away*). **10. sleep in,** (of domestic help) to sleep at the place of one's employment. —*n.* **11.** the state of a person who or animal or plant that sleeps. **12.** a period of sleeping: *a brief sleep.* **13.** dormancy or inactivity. **14.** the repose of death. [(n.) ME; OE *slēp* (Anglian), *slǣp, slāp;* c. D *slaap,* G *Schlaf,* Goth *slēps;* (v.) ME *slepe,* OE *slēpan, slǣpan; slāpan;* c. D *slapen,* G *schlafen,* Goth *slēpan*] —**Syn. 11.** rest, repose.

Sleep (slēp), *n.* **Marsh of.** See **Palus Somni.**

sleep·er (slē′pər), *n.* **1.** a person or thing that sleeps. **2.** a heavy horizontal timber for distributing loads. **3.** *Brit.* a railway tie. **4.** a sleeping car. **5.** bunting[3]. **6.** *Informal.* something that or someone who becomes or may become successful or important after a period of being obscured or unimportant. [ME]

sleep-in (slēp′in′), *adj.* (of domestic help) sleeping at the place of one's employment: *a sleep-in maid.*

sleep·ing (slē′ping), *n.* **1.** the condition of being asleep. —*adj.* **2.** asleep. **3.** of, noting, pertaining to, or having accommodations for sleeping: *a sleeping compartment.* **4.** used to sleep in or on: *a sleeping jacket.* **5.** used to induce or aid sleep or while asleep: *a sleeping mask.* [ME]

sleep′ing bag′, a large bag, usually of warmly padded material and having a zipper in front, in which a person sleeps, as when camping out of doors.

sleep′ing car′, a railroad car fitted with sleeping accommodations.

sleep′ing pill′, a pill, tablet, or capsule, usually prescribed by a physician, for inducing sleep. Also called **sleep′ing tab′let.**

sleep′ing porch′, a porch enclosed with glass or screening or a room with open sides or a row of windows used for sleeping in the open air.

sleep′ing sick′ness, *Pathol.* **1.** Also called **African sleeping sickness, African trypanosomiasis.** a generally fatal disease, common in parts of Africa, characterized by fever, wasting, and progressive lethargy: caused by a parasitic protozoan, *Trypanosoma gambiense* or *T. rhodesiense,* which is carried by a tsetse fly, *Glossina palpalis.* **2.** Also called **epidemic encephalitis, lethargic encephalitis, nona.** a virus disease affecting the brain, characterized by apathy, sleepiness, extreme muscular weakness, and impairment of vision.

sleep·less (slēp′lis), *adj.* **1.** without sleep: *a sleepless night.* **2.** watchful; alert: *sleepless devotion to duty.* **3.** always active: *the sleepless ocean.* [ME] —**sleep′less·ly,** *adv.*

sleep·walk·ing (slēp′wô′king), *n.* **1.** the act of walking while asleep; somnambulism. —*adj.* **2.** of or pertaining to the act of walking while asleep; somnambulistic. —**sleep′walk′er,** *n.*

sleep·y (slē′pē), *adj.,* **sleep·i·er, sleep·i·est. 1.** ready or inclined to sleep; drowsy. **2.** of or showing drowsiness. **3.** lethargic; inactive: *a sleepy village.* **4.** inducing sleep; soporific: *sleepy warmth.* [ME] —**sleep′i·ly,** *adv.* —**sleep′i·ness,** *n.* —**Syn. 1.** tired, somnolent, slumberous.

sleep·y·head (slē′pē hed′), *n.* a sleepy person.

sleet (slēt), *n.* **1.** a frozen coating formed on the ground by the fall of freezing rain. **2.** precipitation in the form of frozen raindrops. **3.** *Chiefly Brit.* the precipitation of snow and rain simultaneously. —*v.i.* **4.** to send down sleet. **5.** to fall as or like sleet. [ME *slete;* akin to LG *slote,* G *Schlossen* hail]

sleet·y (slē′tē), *adj.,* **sleet·i·er, sleet·i·est.** of or pertaining to sleet. —**sleet′i·ness,** *n.*

sleeve (slēv), *n., v.,* **sleeved, sleev·ing.** —*n.* **1.** the part of a garment that covers the arm. **2.** an envelope, usually of paper, for protecting a phonograph record. **3.** *Mach.* a tubular piece, as of metal, fitting over a rod or the like. **4. laugh up** or **in one's sleeve,** to be secretly amused or contemptuous. **5. up one's sleeve,** kept secretly ready or close at hand. —*v.t.* **6.** to furnish with sleeves. [ME *sleve,* OE *slēfe* (Anglian); akin to D *sloof* apron]

sleeve·less (slēv′lis), *adj.* without a sleeve or sleeves. [ME, OE *slīefleas*]

sleeve·let (slēv′lit), *n.* a fitted sleeve or cover worn on the forearm for warmth or to protect a shirt sleeve.

sleigh (slā), *n.* **1.** a light vehicle on runners, that is usually open and generally horse-drawn, used esp. for transporting persons over snow or ice. —*v.i.* **2.** to travel or ride in a sleigh. [< D *slee,* short for *slede* SLED] —**sleigh′er,** *n.*

sleight (slīt), *n.* skill; dexterity. [ME; early ME *slēgth* < Scand; cf. Icel *slǣgth.* See SLY, -TH[1]]

sleight′ of hand′, 1. skill in feats requiring quick and clever movements of the hands, esp. for entertainment or deception, as jugglery or palming; legerdemain. **2.** the performance of such feats.

slen·der (slen′dər), *adj.* **1.** having a circumference that is small in proportion to the height or length: *a slender post.* **2.** attractively thin and well-formed: *the slender girls who work as models.* **3.** small in size, amount, extent, etc.; meager: *a slender income.* **4.** having little value, force, or justification: *slender prospects.* [ME *slendre, sclendre* < ?] —**slen′der·ly,** *adv.* —**slen′der·ness,** *n.*

—**Syn. 2.** SLENDER, SLIGHT, SLIM imply a tendency toward thinness. As applied to the human body, SLENDER implies a generally attractive and pleasing thinness: *slender hands.* SLIGHT often adds the idea of frailness to that of thinness: *a slight, almost fragile, figure.* SLIM implies a lithe or delicate thinness: *a slim and athletic figure.* —**Ant. 2.** fat, stocky.

slen·der·ize (slen′də rīz′), *v.,* **-ized, -iz·ing.** —*v.t.* **1.** to make slender or more slender. **2.** to cause to appear slender. —*v.i.* **3.** to become slender.

slept (slept), *v.* pt. and pp. of **sleep.**

Sles·vig (sles′vikh), *n.* Danish name of **Schleswig.**

Sles·wick (sles′wik), *n.* Schleswig.

sleuth (slo͞oth), *n.* **1.** *U.S. Informal.* a detective. **2.** a bloodhound. —*v.t., v.i.* **3.** to track or trail, as a detective. [short for SLEUTHHOUND]

sleuth·hound (slo͞oth′hound′), *n.* a bloodhound. [ME *slōth* track, trail (< Scand; cf. Icel *slōth*) + HOUND[1]]

slew[1] (slo͞o), *v.* pt. of **slay.**

slew[2] (slo͞o), *v.t., v.i., n.* slue[1]. [?]

slew[3] (slo͞o), *n. U.S., Canadian.* slough[1] (def. 3).

slew[4] (slo͞o), *n. Informal.* a great number; lot: *a whole slew of people.* [< Ir *sluagh* multitude, army]

Slezs·ko (sles′kô), *n.* Czech name of **Silesia.**

slice (slīs), *n., v.,* **sliced, slic·ing.** —*n.* **1.** a thin, broad, flat piece cut from something: *a slice of bread.* **2.** a part; portion of any kind: *a slice of land.* **3.** any of various implements with a thin, broad blade or part; spatula. **4.** *Sports.* **a.** the path described by a ball, as in baseball or golf, that curves in a direction corresponding to the side from which it was struck. **b.** a ball describing such a path. —*v.t.* **5.** to cut into slices. **6.** to cut through or cleave with or as with a knife. **7.** to separate in a slice or slices (sometimes fol. by *off, away, from,* etc.). **8.** *Sports.* to hit (a ball) so as to result in a slice. **—*v.i.*** *Sports.* **9.** (of a player) to slice the ball. **10.** (of a ball) to describe a slice in flight. [ME *s(c)lice* < OF *(e)sclice,* back formation from *esclicier* to split up < OHG *sclīzan;* c. OE *slītan,* Icel *slīta,* D *slijten;* see SLIT] **—slice′a·ble,** *adj.* **—slic′er,** *n.*

slick[1] (slik), *adj.* **1.** smooth and glossy; sleek. **2.** smooth in manners, speech, etc.; suave. **3.** sly; shrewdly adroit. **4.** ingenious; cleverly devised. **5.** slippery, esp. from being covered with or as with ice, water, or oil. **6.** *Slang.* wonderful; remarkable; first-rate. **—*n.* 7.** a smooth or slippery place or spot, or the substance causing it: *an oil slick.* **8.** *Informal.* a magazine printed on paper having a more or less glossy finish. Cf. **pulp** (def. 6). **9.** any of various paddlelike tools for smoothing a surface. **—*adv.* 10.** smoothly; cleverly. [ME *slike;* c. Flem *sleek* even, smooth; akin to SLICK[2]] **—slick′ly,** *adv.* **—slick′ness,** *n.*

slick[2] (slik), *v.t.* **1.** to make sleek or smooth. **2.** to use a slicker on (skins or hides). **3.** *Informal.* to make smart or fine; spruce up (usually fol. by *up*). **—*n.* 4.** any woodworking chisel having a blade more than two inches wide. [ME *slicke(n),* OE *slician;* akin to Icel *slīkja* to give a gloss to]

slick·en·side (slik′ən sīd′), *n.* *Geol.* a rock surface that has become polished and striated from the sliding or grinding motion of an adjacent rock mass. [SLICK[2] + -EN[3] + SIDE[1]]

slick·er[1] (slik′ər), *n.* *U.S.* **1.** a long, loose, oilskin raincoat. **2.** Also called **city slicker.** *Informal.* **a.** a swindler; a sly cheat. **b.** a sophisticated person from a large city. [SLICK[1] + -ER[1]] **—slick′ered,** *adj.*

slick·er[2] (slik′ər), *n.* a tool, usually of stone or glass, for scraping, smoothing, and working tanning agents into a skin or hide. [SLICK[2] + -ER[1]]

slide (slīd), *v.,* **slid, slid** or **slid·den, slid·ing,** *n.* **—*v.i.* 1.** to move along in continuous contact with a smooth or slippery surface: *to slide down a snow-covered hill.* **2.** to slip or skid. **3.** to pass or fall gradually into a specified state, character, practice, etc. **4.** *Baseball.* (of a base runner) to cast oneself, usually feet first, along the ground toward a base. **—*v.t.* 5.** to cause to slide, slip, or coast, as over a surface or with a smooth, gliding motion. **6.** to hand, pass along, or slip (something) easily or quietly (usually fol. by *in, into,* etc.). **7. let slide,** to allow to deteriorate, pursue a natural course, etc., without intervention on one's part. **—*n.* 8.** the act or an instance of sliding. **9.** a smooth surface for sliding on, as a type of chute in a playground. **10.** an object intended to slide. **11.** *Geol.* **a.** a landslide or the like. **b.** the mass of matter sliding down. **12.** a single transparency, as on a small positive film, for projection on a screen or for magnification through a viewer: *a color slide.* **13.** a usually rectangular plate of glass on which objects are placed for microscopic examination. **14.** *Music.* **a.** an embellishment or grace consisting of an upward or downward series of three or more tones, the last of which is the principal tone. **b.** a portamento. **c.** a U-shaped section of the tube of an instrument of the trumpet class, as the trombone, which can be pushed in or out to alter the length of the air column and change the pitch. **15.** (of a machine or mechanism) **a.** a moving part working on a track, channel, or guide rails. **b.** the surface, track, channel, or guide rails on which the part moves. [ME; OE *slīdan;* c. MLG *slīden,* MHG *slīten;* akin to SLED] **—slid′a·ble,** *adj.*
—Syn. 1. slither. SLIDE, GLIDE, SLIP suggest movement over a smooth surface. SLIDE suggests a rather brief movement of one surface over another in contact with it: *to slide downhill.* GLIDE suggests a continuous, smooth, easy, and (usually) noiseless motion: *A skater glides over the ice.* To SLIP is to slide smoothly, often in a sudden or accidental way: *to slip on the ice and fall.*

slide-ac·tion (slīd′ak′shən), *adj.* (of a rifle or shotgun) having a lever that when slid back and forth ejects the empty case and cocks and reloads the piece.

slide′ fas′tener, zipper (def. 2).

slide′ knot′, a knot formed by making two half hitches on the standing part of the rope, the second hitch being next to the loop, which can be tightened.

Slide′ Moun′tain, a mountain in SE New York: highest peak of the Catskill Mountains. 4204 ft.

slid·er (slī′dər), *n.* **1.** a person or thing that slides. **2.** *Baseball.* a fast pitch that curves slightly and sharply in front of a batter, away from the side from which it was thrown.

slide′ rule′, a device for rapid calculation, consisting essentially of a rule having a sliding section running along its middle, marked like the rule itself with graduated, usually logarithmic scales.

slide′ trombone′. See under **trombone.**

slid·ing (slī′ding), *adj.* **1.** rising or falling, increasing or decreasing, according to a standard or to a set of conditions. **2.** operated, adjusted, or moved by sliding: *a sliding door.* [ME; OE *slīdende*]

slid′ing scale′, **1.** a variable scale, esp. of industrial costs, as wages, which may be adapted to changes in demand. **2.** a wage scale varying with the selling price of goods produced, the cost of living, etc. **3.** a tariff scale varying according to the price of imports.

sli·er (slī′ər), *adj.* a comparative of **sly.**

sli·est (slī′ist), *adj.* a superlative of **sly.**

slight (slīt), *adj.* **1.** small in amount, degree, etc.: *a slight increase; a slight odor.* **2.** of little importance, influence, etc.; trivial: *a slight cut.* **3.** slender or slim; not heavily built. **4.** of little substance or strength. **—*v.t.* 5.** to treat as of little importance. **6.** to treat (someone) with indifference; ignore, esp. pointedly or contemptuously; snub. **7.** to give only superficial attention or effort to; scamp: *Students with spring fever slight their studies.* **—*n.* 8.** an instance of slighting treatment. **9.** a pointed and contemptuous discourtesy; affront. [ME; OE *sliht* (in *eorthslihtes* close to ground); c. Icel *slēttr,* G *schlicht,* Goth *slaihts* smooth] **—slight′ly,** *adv.* **—slight′ness,** *n.*
—Syn. 2. insignificant, trifling, paltry. **3.** See **slender. 4.** weak, feeble, fragile, unsubstantial. **7.** disdain, scorn. SLIGHT, DISREGARD, NEGLECT, OVERLOOK mean to pay no attention or too little attention to someone or something. To SLIGHT is irresponsibly to give only superficial attention to something important: *to slight one's work.* To DISREGARD is to pay no attention to a person or thing: *to disregard the rules;* in some circumstances, to DISREGARD may be admirable: *to disregard a handicap.* To NEGLECT is to shirk paying sufficient attention to a person or thing: *to neglect one's correspondence.* To OVERLOOK is to fail to see someone or something (possibly because of carelessness): *to overlook a bill that is due.* **9.** See **insult. —Ant. 1.** considerable.

slight·ing (slī′ting), *adj.* derogatory and disparaging; belittling. **—slight′ing·ly,** *adv.*

Sli·go (slī′gō), *n.* **1.** a county in Connaught province, in the NW Republic of Ireland. 53,561 (1961); 694 sq. mi. **2.** a seaport in and the county seat of Sligo. 13,145 (1961).

sli·ly (slī′lē), *adv.* slyly.

slim (slim), *adj.,* **slim·mer, slim·mest,** *v.,* **slimmed, slim·ming.** **—*adj.* 1.** slender, as in girth or form. **2.** meager: *a slim chance.* **3.** small or inconsiderable; scanty: *a slim income.* **—*v.t., v.i.* 4.** to make or become slim. [special use of obs. *slimme* lanky, despicable person < MD *slimme* crafty person, n. use of *slim* crafty; the dominant element in English usage came to be lankiness, whence thinness] **—slim′ly,** *adv.* **—slim′ness,** *n.* **—Syn. 1.** thin. See **slender. 3.** insignificant, trifling, paltry. **—Ant. 1.** fat.

slime (slīm), *n., v.,* **slimed, slim·ing.** **—*n.* 1.** thin, glutinous mud. **2.** any ropy or viscous liquid matter, esp. of a foul or offensive kind. **3.** a viscous secretion of animal or vegetable origin. **—*v.t.* 4.** to cover or smear with or as with slime. [ME *slyme,* OE *slīm;* c. D *slijm,* Icel *slīm,* G *Schleim*]

slime′ mold′, an organism usually considered to be a plant belonging to the class *Myxomycetes* or sometimes considered to be an animal belonging to the order *Mycetozoa,* characterized by a noncellular, multinucleate, creeping somatic phase and a propagative phase in which fruiting bodies are produced bearing spores that are covered by cell walls.

slim·y (slī′mē), *adj.,* **slim·i·er, slim·i·est.** **1.** of or like slime. **2.** abounding in or covered with slime. **3.** nasty and offensive. [ME] **—slim′i·ly,** *adv.*

sling[1] (sling), *n., v.,* **slung, sling·ing.** **—*n.* 1.** a flexible device for hurling a missile by hand, usually consisting of a strap with a string at each end that is whirled about to gain momentum before the missile is released. **2.** a slingshot. **3.** a bandage used to suspend or support an injured part of the body, as a bandage suspended from the neck to support an injured arm. **4.** a strap, band, or the like, forming a loop by which something is suspended or carried, as a strap attached to a rifle and passed over the shoulder. **5.** the act or an instance of slinging. **6.** a rope, chain, net, etc., used in hoisting freight. **—*v.t.* 7.** to throw, cast, or hurl; fling, as from the hand. **8.** to place in or move with a sling, as freight. **9.** to hang by a sling or place so as to swing loosely. [ME *slynge(n)* < Scand; cf. Icel *slyngva* to hurl, akin to OE *slingan* to wind, twist, c. G *schlingen*] **—Syn. 7.** pitch, toss.

sling[2] (sling), *n.* *U.S.* an iced alcoholic drink, containing gin or the like, water, sugar, and lemon or lime juice. [special use of *sling* a drinking, draught, lit., a flinging (into the throat); see SLING[1]]

sling′ chair′, any of several varieties of chairs having a seat and back formed from a single sheet of canvas, leather, or the like, hanging loosely in a frame.

sling·shot (sling′shot′), *n.* a Y-shaped stick with an elastic strip between the prongs for shooting stones and other small missiles.

slink (slingk), *v.,* **slunk** or (*Archaic*) **slank; slunk; slink·ing;** *n., adj.* **—*v.i.* 1.** to move or go in a furtive, abject manner, as from fear, cowardice, or shame. **2.** *Informal.* (of a woman) to walk or move in a slow, sinuous, provocative way. **—*v.t.* 3.** (esp. of cows) to bring forth (young) prematurely. **—*n.* 4.** a prematurely born calf or other animal. **—*adj.* 5.** born prematurely: *a slink calf.* [ME *slynke,* OE *slinca(n)* (to) creep, crawl; c. LG *slinken,* G *schlinken*] **—slink′ing·ly,** *adv.* **—Syn. 1.** skulk, sneak; lurk.

slink·y (sling′kē), *adj.,* **slink·i·er, slink·i·est.** **1.** characterized by or proceeding with slinking or stealthy movements. **2.** (esp. of women's clothing) made of soft, often clinging material and fitting the figure closely. **—slink′i·ly,** *adv.* **—slink′i·ness,** *n.*

slip[1] (slip), *v.,* **slipped** or (*Archaic*) **slipt; slipped; slip·ping;** *n.* **—*v.i.* 1.** to move smoothly or easily; glide; slide. **2.** to slide suddenly and accidentally: *He slipped on the icy ground. The cup slipped from her hand.* **3.** to allow something to evade one, as an opportunity. **4.** to elapse or pass quickly or imperceptibly (often fol. by *away* or *by*): *Money slips through his fingers.* **5.** to become involved or absorbed easily: *to slip into a new way of life.* **6.** to move or go quietly, cautiously, or unobtrusively: *to slip out of a room.* **7.** to make a mistake or error. **8.** *Aeron.* (of an aircraft when excessively banked) to slide sideways, toward the center of the curve described in turning. Cf. **skid** (def. 12). **9.** to fall below a standard or accustomed level of achievement: *His work slipped last year.* **10.** to deteriorate in health or mental power. **11.** to be said or revealed inadvertently (usually fol. by *out*): *The words slipped out before he could stop himself.*
—*v.t.* 12. to cause to move, pass, go, etc., with a smooth, easy, or sliding motion. **13.** to put, place, pass, insert, or take quickly or stealthily: *to slip a letter into a person's hand.* **14.** to put on or take off (a loose garment): *He slipped the shirt over his head.* **15.** to let or make (something) slide out of a fastening, the hold, etc.: *He slipped the lock, and the door creaked open.* **16.** to release from a leash, harness, etc., as a hound or a hawk. **17.** to get away or free oneself from; escape (a pursuer, restraint, leash, etc.): *The cow slipped its halter and ran out of the barn.* **18.** to untie or undo (a knot). **19.** *Naut.* to let go entirely, as an anchor cable or an anchor. **20.** to let pass unheeded; neglect or ignore. **21.** to pass from or escape (one's memory, attention, knowledge, etc.): *His name slips my mind.* **22.** to dislocate; put out of joint or position: *to slip a disk in the spine.* **23.** to shed or cast, as a

skin. **24.** (of animals) to bring forth (offspring) prematurely. **25. let slip,** to reveal unintentionally: *to let the truth slip.* **26. slip up,** to make an error; fail.
—*n.* **27.** the act or an instance of slipping. **28.** a sudden, accidental slide. **29.** a mistake in judgment; blunder. **30.** a mistake or oversight, as in speaking or writing, esp. a small one due to carelessness: *a slip in addition; a slip of the tongue.* **31.** an error in conduct; indiscretion. **32.** a decline or fall in quantity, quality, extent, etc., or from a standard or accustomed level. **33.** *Clothing.* **a.** a woman's underdress, sleeveless and usually having shoulder straps, extending from above the bust down to the hemline of the outer dress. **b.** an underskirt, as a half-slip or petticoat. **34.** a pillowcase. **35.** an inclined plane, sloping to the water, on which vessels are built or repaired. **36.** *Naut.* the difference between the speed at which a screw propeller or paddle wheel would move if it were working against a solid and the actual speed at which it advances through the water. **37.** *U.S.* a space between two wharves or in a dock for vessels to lie in. **38.** unintended movement or play between mechanical parts or the like. **39.** *Cricket.* **a.** the position of a fielder who stands behind and to the off side of the wicketkeeper. **b.** the fielder playing this position. **40.** *Geol.* **a.** the relative displacement of formerly adjacent points on opposite sides of a fault, measured along the fault plane. **b.** a small fault. **41.** Also called **glide.** *Metall.* plastic deformation of one part of a metallic crystal relative to the other part due to shearing action. **42. give someone the slip,** to elude a pursuer; escape from someone. [ME *slipp(e)* < MD *slippe(n)*; c. OHG *slipfan*] —**slip′less,** *adj.* —**slip′ping·ly,** *adv.*
—**Syn. 2.** slither. See **slide. 7.** err, blunder. **30.** error, fault.

slip[2] (slip), *n., v.,* **slipped, slip·ping.** —*n.* **1.** a piece suitable for propagation cut from a plant; scion or cutting. **2.** any long, narrow piece or strip, as of paper, land, etc. **3.** a young person, esp. one of slender form: *a mere slip of a girl.* **4.** a small piece of paper or office form on which information is noted: *a withdrawal slip.* **5.** a long seat or narrow pew in a church. —*v.t.* **6.** to take slips or cuttings from (a plant). **7.** to take (a part), as a slip from a plant. [late ME < MFlem *slippe* a cut, slip, strip]

slip[3] (slip), *n. Ceram.* a clay solution of creamy consistency for coating or decorating pottery biscuit. [ME, OE *slype;* see SLOP[1]]

slip·case (slip′kās′), *n.* a box for a book or set of books, open on one side to reveal the spine or spines.

slip·cov·er (slip′kuv′ər), *n.* **1.** an easily removed cloth cover for a piece of furniture. **2.** a book jacket. Also, **slip′ cov′er.**

slipe (slīp), *v.t.,* **sliped, slip·ing.** *Scot.* **1.** to peel or strip the outer coating from, esp. to peel bark from (a tree or twig). **2.** to slice. [ME *slype(n)* < ?]

slip·knot (slip′not′), *n.* a knot that slips easily along the cord or line around which it is made. Also, **slip′ knot′.** See illus. at **knot.**

slip·noose (slip′no͞os′), *n.* a noose with a slipknot, thus forming a noose that tightens as the rope is pulled. Also, **slip′ noose′.**

slip-on (slip′on′, -ôn′), *adj.* **1.** (of a garment) designed to be slipped on easily without opening or unfastening, as a loose sweater. —*n.* **2.** a slip-on article of dress.

slip·out (slip′out′), *adj.* **1.** designed to be easily slipped out or off without slitting, as a newspaper section. —*n.* **2.** a slipout section of a newspaper.

slip·o·ver (slip′ō′vər), *n., adj.* pullover.

slip·page (slip′ij), *n.* **1.** the act or an instance of slipping. **2.** an amount or extent of slipping. **3.** *Mach.* the amount of work dissipated by slipping of parts, excess play, etc.

slipped′ disk′, a displacement of an intervertebral cartilage resulting in severe back pain.

slip·per (slip′ər), *n.* any light, low-cut, slip-on shoe. [SLIP[1] + -ER[1]]

slip·per·wort (slip′ər wûrt′), *n.* any of several scrophulariaceous plants of the genus *Calceolaria,* of tropical America, having slipper-shaped flowers.

Slipperwort, *Calceolaria crenatiflora*

slip·per·y (slip′ə rē, slip′rē), *adj.,* **-per·i·er, -per·i·est.** **1.** tending or likely to cause slipping or sliding, as ice, oil, or a wet surface: *a slippery road.* **2.** tending to slip from the hold or grasp or from position: *a slippery rope.* **3.** likely to slip away or escape: *slippery prospects.* **4.** not to be depended on; shifty, tricky, or deceitful. **5.** unstable or insecure, as conditions: *a slippery situation.* [alter. of dial. *slipper* slippery (ME *sliper,* OE *slipor*); cf. LG *slipperig;* see -Y[1]] —**slip′per·i·ness,** *n.*

slip′pery elm′, **1.** an elm, *Ulmus fulva,* of eastern North America, having a mucilaginous inner bark. **2.** the bark of this elm, used as a demulcent.

slip·py (slip′ē), *adj.,* **-pi·er, -pi·est.** **1.** *Informal.* slippery. **2.** *Chiefly Brit.* quick; alert. —**slip′pi·ness,** *n.*

slip′ ring′, *Elect.* a metal ring mounted so that current may be conducted through stationary brushes into or out of a rotating member.

slip·sheet (slip′shēt′), *Print.* —*v.t., v.i.* **1.** to insert (blank sheets) between printed sheets as they come off the press to prevent offset. —*n.* **2.** a sheet so inserted.

slip·shod (slip′shod′), *adj.* **1.** careless, untidy, or slovenly: *slipshod work.* **2.** down-at-heel; seedy. —**slip′shod′di·ness, slip′shod′ness,** *n.*

slip·sole (slip′sōl′), *n.* an insole placed in a shoe for warmth or to adjust the size.

slip·stick (slip′stik′), *n. U.S. Slang.* See **slide rule.**

slip′ stitch′, *Sewing.* a loose stitch taken between two layers of fabric, as on a facing or hem, so as to be invisible on the right side or outside surface.

slip·stream (slip′strēm′), *n.* **1.** *Aeron.* the stream of air pushed back by a revolving aircraft propeller. Cf. **backwash** (def. 2). **2.** *Auto Racing.* the area of low air pressure behind a fast-moving car. Also, **slip′ stream′.**

slipt (slipt), *v. Archaic.* pt. of **slip**[1].

slip-up (slip′up′), *n. Informal.* a mistake, blunder, or oversight.

slip·ware (slip′wâr′), *n.* pottery decorated with slip.

slip·way (slip′wā′), *n. Naut.* (in a shipyard) the area sloping toward the water, in which the ways are located.

slit (slit), *v.,* **slit, slit·ting,** *n.* —*v.t.* **1.** to cut apart or open along a line; make a long cut, fissure, or opening in. **2.** to cut or rend into strips; split. —*n.* **3.** a straight, narrow cut, opening, or aperture. [ME *slitte* (n., v.), OE (north) *slitta* (v.); c. G *schlitzen* to split, slit; akin to OE *slite* a slit, *geslit* a bite, *slītan* to split; see SLICE]

slith·er (slith′ər), *v.i.* **1.** to slide down or along a surface from side to side. **2.** to go or walk with a sliding motion, as a snake. —*v.t.* **3.** to cause to slither. —*n.* **4.** a slithering movement; slide. [ME; var. of *sliddren,* OE *slid(e)rian,* freq. of *slīdan* to SLIDE; see -ER[6]] —**slith′er·y,** *adj.*

slit′ trench′, a narrow trench for one or more persons for protection against enemy fire and bombs.

sliv·er (sliv′ər), *n.* **1.** a small, slender piece, as of wood, split, broken, or cut off, usually lengthwise or with the grain; splinter. **2.** a strand of loose, untwisted fibers produced in carding. —*v.t.* **3.** to split or cut off a sliver from or to split or cut into slivers: *to sliver a log into kindling.* **4.** to form (textile fibers) into slivers. —*v.i.* **5.** to split. [ME *slivere* < *slive* to split, OE *-slīfan* (in *tōslīfan* to split up] —**sliv′er·like′,** *adj.*

sliv·o·vitz (sliv′ə vits, -wits, shliv′-), *n.* a dry, usually colorless, slightly bitter plum brandy from E Europe. Also, **sliv·o·vic, sliv·o·witz** (sliv′ə vits). [< Serbo-Croatian *sljivovic(a)* < *sljiva* plum]

Sloan (slōn), *n.* **John,** 1871–1951, U.S. painter.

slob (slob), *n. Slang.* a clumsy, slovenly, or boorish person. [< Ir *slab* mud << E, n. use of SLAB[2]]

slob·ber (slob′ər), *v.i.* **1.** to let saliva or liquid run from the mouth; slaver. **2.** to indulge in mawkish sentimentality. —*v.t.* **3.** to wet by slobbering: *Baby has slobbered his bib.* —*n.* **4.** saliva or liquid dribbling from the mouth; slaver. **5.** mawkishly sentimental speech or actions. Also, **slabber.** [var. of *slabber.* See SLAB[2], -ER[6]] —**slob′ber·er,** *n.*

slob·ber·y (slob′ə rē), *adj.* **1.** characterized by slobbering. **2.** disagreeably wet; sloppy. Also, **slabbery.** [ME]

Slo·cum (slō′kəm), *n.* **Joshua,** 1844–c1910, U.S. mariner, author, and lecturer; born in Nova Scotia.

sloe (slō), *n.* **1.** the small, sour, blackish fruit of the blackthorn, *Prunus spinosa.* **2.** blackthorn (def. 1). **3.** any of various other plants of the genus *Prunus,* as a shrub or small tree, *P. alleghaniensis,* bearing dark-purple fruit. [ME *slo,* OE *slā(h);* c. G *Schlehe,* D *slee*]

sloe-eyed (slō′īd′), *adj.* **1.** having very dark eyes; dark-eyed. **2.** having slanted eyes.

sloe′ gin′, a cordial or liqueur flavored with sloe.

slog (slog), *v.,* **slogged, slog·ging.** —*v.t.* **1.** to hit hard, as in boxing or cricket. **2.** to drive with blows. —*v.i.* **3.** to deal heavy blows. **4.** to walk or plod heavily. **5.** to toil. [var. of SLUG[2]] —**slog′ger,** *n.*

slo·gan (slō′gən), *n.* **1.** a distinctive phrase or motto of any party, group, manufacturer, or person; catchword or catch phrase. **2.** a war cry or gathering cry, as formerly used among the Scottish clans. [< Gael *sluagh-ghairm* army cry]

slo·gan·eer (slō′gə nēr′), *n.* **1.** a person who creates or uses slogans frequently. —*v.i.* **2.** to create or use slogans effectively so as to instill or change opinion.

sloop (slo͞op), *n.* a single-masted, fore-and-aft-rigged sailing vessel having a jib or gaff mainsail, the latter sometimes with a gaff topsail, and one or more headsails. Cf. **cutter** (def. 2), **knockabout** (def. 1). [< D *sloep;* c. G *Schlup;* akin to OE *slūpan* to glide]

sloop′ of war′, (formerly) a naval vessel having cannons on only one deck.

slop[1] (slop), *v.,* **slopped, slop·ping,** *n.* —*v.t.* **1.** to spill or splash (liquid). **2.** to spill liquid upon. **3.** to feed slop to (pigs or other livestock). —*v.i.* **4.** to spill or splash liquid (sometimes fol. by *about*): *She slopped about with her mop and bucket.* **5.** (of liquid) to spill or splash out of a container, as a bottle or glass (usually fol. by *over*): *The milk slopped over the table.* **6.** to walk or go through mud, slush, or water. **7.** *Informal.* to be unduly effusive or sentimental; gush. —*n.* **8.** a quantity of liquid carelessly spilled or splashed about. **9.** *Slang.* badly cooked or unappetizing food or drink. **10.** bran from bolted cornmeal mixed with an equal part of water and used as a feed for swine and other livestock. **11.** any similar watery feed; swill. **12.** Often, **slops.** the dirty water, liquid refuse, etc., of a household, restaurant, etc. **13.** kitchen refuse, often used as food for swine; swill. **14.** liquid mud. **15. slops,** *Distilling.* the mash remaining after distilling. [ME *sloppe,* OE *-sloppe* (in *cūsloppe* cowslip, lit., cow slime); akin to SLIP[3]]

slop[2] (slop), *n.* **1. slops, a.** clothing, bedding, etc., supplied to seamen from the ship's stores. **b.** cheap, ready-made clothing. **2.** a loose outer garment, as a jacket, tunic, or smock. [ME *sloppe,* OE *-slop* (in *overslop* overgarment); c. Icel *sloppr* gown]

slop′ ba′sin, *Brit.* a bowl into which the dregs, leaves, and grounds of teacups and coffee cups are emptied at the table. Also called **slop′ bowl′.**

slop′ chest′, a supply of clothing, boots, tobacco, and other personal goods for sale to seamen during a voyage.

slope (slōp), *v.,* **sloped, slop·ing,** *n.* —*v.i.* **1.** to have or take an inclined or oblique direction or angle considered with reference to a vertical or horizontal plane; slant. **2.** to fall obliquely or at an inclination: *The land sloped down to the sea.* —*v.t.* **3.** to direct at a slant or inclination; incline from the horizontal or vertical: *The sun sloped its beams.* **4.** to form with a slope or slant: *to slope an embankment.* —*n.* **5.** a portion of ground having a natural incline, as the side of a hill. **6.** inclination or slant, esp. downward or upward. **7.** the amount or degree of deviation from the horizontal or vertical. **8.** an inclined surface. **9.** Usually, **slopes.** hills, esp. foothills or bluffs. **10.** *Math.* **a.** the tangent of the angle between a given straight line and the x-axis of a system of Cartesian coordinates. **b.** the derivative of the function whose graph is a given curve evaluated at a designated point. [abstracted from ASLOPE]

slop·py (slop′ē), *adj.,* **-pi·er, -pi·est.** **1.** muddy, slushy, or very wet, as ground, footing, or weather. **2.** splashed or soiled with liquid. **3.** (of food or drink) prepared or served in an unappetizing way. **4.** overly emotional; gushy: *sloppy sentimentality.* **5.** careless; loose: *sloppy grammar.* **6.** untidy; slovenly. **7.** (of the surface of a race track) wet and containing puddles and mud still too thin and watery to be sticky. **—slop′pi·ly,** *adv.* **—slop′pi·ness,** *n.* **—Syn. 2, 6.** messy. **5.** slipshod. **6.** slatternly.

slop′ sink′, a deep sink for emptying scrub buckets.

slop·work (slop′wûrk′), *n.* **1.** the manufacture of cheap clothing. **2.** clothing of this kind. **—slop′work′er,** *n.*

slosh (slosh), *n.* **1.** watery mire or partly melted snow; slush. **2.** the lap or splash of liquid: *the slosh of waves against the shore.* **—*v.i.*** **3.** to splash in slush, mud, or water. **4.** (of a liquid) to move about actively within a container. **—*v.t.*** **5.** to stir or splash (something) around in a fluid. **6.** to splash (liquid) clumsily or haphazardly. [SLO(P[1] + SLU)SH]

slot[1] (slot), *n.*, *v.*, **slot·ted, slot·ting.** **—*n.*** **1.** a narrow, elongated depression, groove, notch, slit, or aperture, esp. a narrow opening for receiving or admitting something, as a coin or a letter. **2.** *Informal.* a place or position, as in a scheduled sequence or series. **—*v.t.*** **3.** to provide with a slot or slots. [ME < MF (*e*)*sclot* the hollow between the breasts <)]

slot[2] (slot), *n.* the track or trail of a deer or other animal, as shown by the marks of the feet. [< AF, MF (*e*)*sclot* the hoofprint of a horse, prob. < Scand; cf. Icel *slōth* track, trail; see SLEUTHHOUND]

slot′ car′, a plastic model of an automobile usually in the 1/32 or 1/87 scale, equipped with a tiny electric motor, for running on a slotted track through which electric current is provided for the motor by a power pack and a speed control: used chiefly as a miniature racing game.

Sloth, *Choloepus hoffmanni* (Length 2 ft.)

sloth (slôth *or, esp. for 3,* slōth), *n.* **1.** habitual disinclination to exertion; indolence; laziness. **2.** any of several sluggish, arboreal, tropical American edentates of the family *Bradypodidae*, having long, coarse hair and long, hooklike claws used for hanging from and moving upside down along the branches of trees. **3.** a pack or group of bears. [ME *slowth* (see SLOW, -TH[1]); r. OE *slǣwth* < *slǣw*, var. of *slāw* slow]

sloth′ bear′, a coarse-haired, long-snouted bear, *Melursus ursinus*, of India and Indochina.

Sloth bear (2½ ft. high at shoulder; length 5½ ft.)

sloth·ful (slôth′fəl, slōth′-), *adj.* sluggardly; indolent; lazy. [ME] **—sloth′ful·ly,** *adv.* **—sloth′ful·ness,** *n.* **—Syn.** See **idle.**

slot′ machine′, **1.** a box-like, metal gambling device operated by inserting a coin into a slot and pulling down a long handle attached at the side. **2.** any machine operated by inserting a coin into a slot, as a vending machine, a public laundry machine, a scale, or the like.

slouch (slouch), *v.i.* **1.** to sit or stand with an awkward, drooping posture. **2.** to move or walk with loosely drooping body and careless gait. **3.** to have a droop or downward bend, as a hat. **—*v.t.*** **4.** to cause to droop or bend down. **—*n.*** **5.** a drooping or bending forward of the head and shoulders; an awkward, drooping posture or carriage. **6.** an awkward, clumsy, or slovenly person. **7.** *Informal.* a lazy or inefficient person. [?] **—slouch′er,** *n.* **—slouch′ing·ly,** *adv.*

slouch·y (slou′chē), *adj.*, **slouch·i·er, slouch·i·est.** of or pertaining to a slouch, or to a slouching manner, posture, etc. **—slouch′i·ly,** *adv.* **—slouch′i·ness,** *n.*

slough[1] (slou *for 1, 2, 4;* slo͞o *for 3*), *n.* **1.** a swamp or swamplike region. **2.** a hole full of mire, as in a road. **3.** Also, **slew, slue.** *U.S., Canadian.* a marshy or reedy pool, pond, inlet, backwater, or the like. **4.** a condition of degradation, embarrassment, or helplessness. [ME; OE *slōh;* c. MLG *slōch*, MHG *sluoche* ditch]

slough[2] (sluf), *n.* **1.** the outer layer of the skin of a snake, which is cast off periodically. **2.** *Pathol.* a mass or layer of dead tissue separated from the surrounding or underlying tissue. **3.** *Cards.* a discard. **—*v.i.*** **4.** to be or become shed or cast off, as the slough of a snake. **5.** to cast off a slough. **6.** *Pathol.* to separate from the sound flesh, as a slough. **7.** *Cards.* to discard a card or cards. **—*v.t.*** **8.** to dispose or get rid of; cast (often fol. by *off*): *He managed to slough off his smoking habit.* **9.** to shed as or like a slough. **10.** *Cards.* to discard (a card or cards). Also, **sluff** (for defs. 3, 7, 10). [ME *slughe, slouh;* c. G *Schlauch* skin, bag] **—Syn. 5.** molt.

Slo·vak (slō′vak, -väk, slō vak′, -väk′), *n.* **1.** one of a Slavic people dwelling in Slovakia. **2.** the language of Slovakia, a Slavic language very similar to Czech. **—*adj.*** **3.** of or pertaining to the Slovaks or the Slovak language. [< Slovak *Slovāk* Slav]

Slo·va·ki·a (slō vä′kē ə, -vak′ē ə), *n.* a region in E Czechoslovakia: under German occupation 1939–45. 4,422,707; 18,921 sq. mi. *Cap.:* Bratislava. Czech, **Slo·ven·sko** (slô′ven skô′). **—Slo·va′ki·an,** *adj., n.*

slov·en (sluv′ən), *n.* a person who is habitually negligent, as in cleanliness, appearance, or work habits. [late ME < MFlem *sloovin* slattern; akin to SHUFFLE]

Slo·vene (slō vēn′, slō′vēn), *n.* **1.** one of a Slavic people dwelling in Slovenia. **2.** a South Slavic language spoken in Slovenia. **—*adj.*** **3.** of or pertaining to the Slovenes or the Slovene language. [< G < Slovenian << OSlav *Slověne;* cf. SLAV, SLOVAK]

Slo·ve·ni·a (slō vē′nē ə, -vēn′yə), *n.* a constituent republic of Yugoslavia, in the NW part: formerly in Austria. 1,727,000; 7819 sq. mi. *Cap.:* Ljubljana. **—Slo·ve′ni·an,** *adj., n.*

slov·en·ly (sluv′ən lē), *adj.*, **-li·er, -li·est,** *adv.* **—*adj.*** **1.** habitually untidy or unclean; not neat in appearance. **2.** careless; slipshod: *slovenly work.* **—*adv.*** **3.** in an untidy, careless, or slipshod manner. **—slov′en·li·ness,** *n.* **—Syn. 1.** slatternly. **—Ant. 1.** neat. **2.** careful.

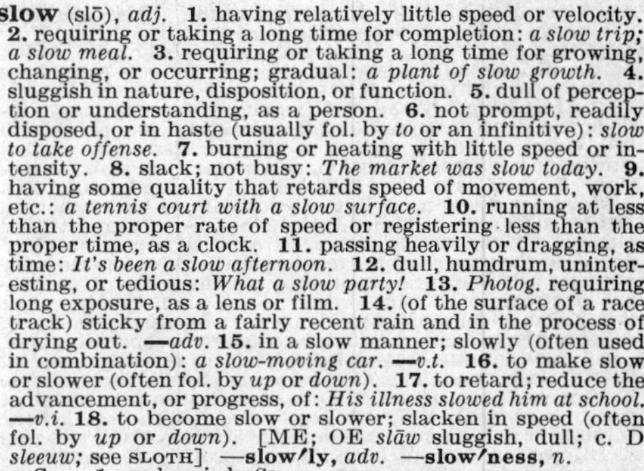

slow (slō), *adj.* **1.** having relatively little speed or velocity. **2.** requiring or taking a long time for completion: *a slow trip; a slow meal.* **3.** requiring or taking a long time for growing, changing, or occurring; gradual: *a plant of slow growth.* **4.** sluggish in nature, disposition, or function. **5.** dull of perception or understanding, as a person. **6.** not prompt, readily disposed, or in haste (usually fol. by *to* or an infinitive): *slow to take offense.* **7.** burning or heating with little speed or intensity. **8.** slack; not busy: *The market was slow today.* **9.** having some quality that retards speed of movement, work, etc.: *a tennis court with a slow surface.* **10.** running at less than the proper rate of speed or registering less than the proper time, as a clock. **11.** passing heavily or dragging, as time: *It's been a slow afternoon.* **12.** dull, humdrum, uninteresting, or tedious: *What a slow party!* **13.** *Photog.* requiring long exposure, as a lens or film. **14.** (of the surface of a race track) sticky from a fairly recent rain and in the process of drying out. **—*adv.*** **15.** in a slow manner; slowly (often used in combination): *a slow-moving car.* **—*v.t.*** **16.** to make slow or slower (often fol. by *up* or *down*). **17.** to retard; reduce the advancement, or progress, of: *His illness slowed him at school.* **—*v.i.*** **18.** to become slow or slower; slacken in speed (often fol. by *up* or *down*). [ME; OE *slāw* sluggish, dull; c. D *sleeuw;* see SLOTH] **—slow′ly,** *adv.* **—slow′ness,** *n.*
—Syn. 1. unhurried. SLOW, DELIBERATE, GRADUAL, LEISURELY mean unhurried and not happening rapidly. That which is SLOW acts or moves without haste: *a slow procession of cars.* DELIBERATE implies the slowness which marks careful consideration: *a deliberate and calculating manner.* GRADUAL suggests the slowness of that which advances one step at a time: *a gradual improvement.* That which is LEISURELY moves with the slowness allowed by ample time or the absence of pressure: *an unhurried and leisurely stroll.* **5.** dense. See **dull. 17.** hinder, impede. **—Ant. 1.** fast.

slow·down (slō′doun′), *n.* a slowing down, esp. a slowing of pace by workers to win demands from their employer.

slow′ fire′, a rate of firing small arms that allows time to aim before each firing. **—slow′-fire′,** *adj.*

slow′ gait′, a slow rack.

slow′ match′, a slow-burning match or fuse, often a rope or cord soaked in a solution of saltpeter.

slow-mo·tion (slō′mō′shən), *adj.* noting or pertaining to motion pictures in which the images on the screen appear to move more slowly than in nature, accomplished either by operating the camera at a higher rate of speed than is usual or by causing the projector to project a relatively smaller number of frames per second: *a slow-motion scene.*

slow·poke (slō′pōk′), *n.* *Informal.* a person who makes slow progress.

slow-wit·ted (slō′wit′id), *adj.* mentally slow or dull.

slow·worm (slō′wûrm′), *n.* a blindworm. [SLOW + WORM; r. ME *slowerm, slowurme,* OE *slāwerm, slāwyrm* = *slā-* (cf. dial. Sw *slo,* Norw *slo* slowworm) + *wyrm* worm]

S.L.P., Socialist Labor Party.

SLR, See **single-lens reflex.**

slub (slub), *v.*, **slubbed, slub·bing,** *n.* **—*v.t.*** **1.** to extend (slivers) and twist slightly in carding. **—*n.*** **2.** the fibers produced by slubbing. **3.** a slight irregularity in yarn. [?]

sludge (sluj), *n.* **1.** mud, mire, or ooze. **2.** a deposit of mud, ooze, or sediment, as at the bottom of a body of water, in a steam boiler or water tank, etc. **3.** broken ice, as on the sea. **4.** a mixture of some finely powdered substance and water. **5.** Also called **activated sludge.** *Bacteriol.* sewage sediment that contains a heavy growth of microorganisms, resulting from vigorous aeration. [var. of dial. *slutch, slitch,* ME *slich* slime, wet mud, whence *slucched* muddy]

sludg·y (sluj′ē), *adj.*, **sludg·i·er, sludg·i·est.** **1.** of or pertaining to sludge. **2.** covered with or containing sludge.

slue[1] (slo͞o), *v.*, **slued, slu·ing,** *n.* **—*v.t.*** **1.** to turn (a mast or other spar) around on its own axis, or without removing it from its place. **2.** to swing around. **—*v.i.*** **3.** to turn about; swing around. **—*n.*** **4.** the act of sluing. **5.** a position slued to. Also, **slew.** [?]

slue[2] (slo͞o), *n.* slough[1] (def. 3).

sluff (sluf), *n.*, *v.i.*, *v.t.* *Cards.* slough[2] (defs. 3, 7, 10).

slug[1] (slug), *n.*, *v.*, **slugged, slug·ging.** **—*n.*** **1.** any of various slimy, elongated, terrestrial gastropods related to the terrestrial snails, but having no shell or only a rudimentary one. **2.** a nudibranch. **3.** any heavy piece of crude metal. **4.** a piece of lead or other metal for firing from a gun. **5.** *Informal.* a rifle or pistol bullet or a shotgun shell. **6.** any metal disk used as a coin, generally counterfeit. **7.** *Slang.* a shot of liquor taken neat. **8.** *Print.* **a.** a thick strip of type metal less than type-high. **b.** such a strip containing a type-high number or other character for temporary use. **c.** a line of type in one piece, as produced by a Linotype. **9.** *Journalism.* a short phrase or title used to indicate the content of copy. **10.** *Physics.* a unit of mass, equivalent to approximately 32.2 pounds and having the property that a force of one pound acting upon a mass of this unit produces an acceleration of one foot per second per second. **—*v.t.*** **11.** *Print. Informal.* **a.** to make corrections by replacing entire lines of type, esp. as set by a Linotype. **b.** to read the first and last words of (lines of copy) against copy of the previous typesetting stage to detect errors made in setting the lines. **12.** *Journalism.* to furnish (copy) with a slug. [ME *slugge* sluggard < Scand; cf. Norw (dial.) *sluggje* heavy, slow person]

Slug[1] (def. 1), *Limax maximus* (Length 4 in.)

slug[2] (slug), *v.*, **slugged, slug·ging.** *Informal.* **—*v.t.*** **1.** to strike heavily; hit hard, esp. with the fist. **2.** to hit (a baseball) very hard or a great distance. **—*v.i.*** **3.** to hit or be capable of hitting hard. **4.** to trudge, fight, or push onward, as against obstacles or through mud or snow. [orig. from phrase *hit with a slug;* see SLUG[1]]

slug·fest (slug′fest′), *n.* *Informal.* **1.** a baseball game in which both teams make many extra-base hits. **2.** a boxing bout in which the boxers exchange many powerful blows.

slug·gard (slug′ərd), *n.* **1.** a person who is habitually inactive or lazy. —*adj.* 2. lazy; slothful. [ME *slogarde*] —**slug′gard·li·ness**, *n.* —**slug′gard·ly**, *adj.*

slug′ger (slug′ər), *n.* 1. a person, esp. a boxer, who strikes hard. 2. *Baseball.* a player who frequently gets extra-base hits; a strong hitter.

slug·gish (slug′ish), *adj.* 1. lacking in energy; lazy; indolent: *a sluggish disposition.* 2. not acting or working with full vigor, as bodily organs: *a sluggish liver.* 3. moving slowly, or having little motion, as a stream. 4. slow, as motion. 5. slack, as trade. [ME *slugissh*] —**slug′gish·ly**, *adv.* —**slug′gish·ness**, *n.* —**Syn.** 1. slothful. —**Ant.** 1. active.

sluice (slo͞os), *n.*, *v.*, **sluiced, sluic·ing.** —*n.* 1. an artificial channel for conducting water, fitted with a gate (**sluice′ gate′**) at the upper end for regulating the flow. 2. the body of water held back or controlled by a sluice gate. 3. a channel or stream of surplus water. 4. an artificial stream or water channel for moving solid matter: *a lumbering sluice.* 5. *Mining.* a long, inclined trough for washing or separating ores. —*v.t.* 6. to let out (water) by or as if by opening a sluice. 7. to drain (a pond, lake, etc.) by or as if by opening a sluice. 8. to open a sluice upon. 9. to flush or cleanse with a rush of water: *to sluice the decks of a boat.* —*v.i.* 10. to flow or pour through or as if through a sluice. [ME *scluse* < OF (*e*)*scluse* < LL *exclusa*, fem. of L *exclūsus*, ptp. of *exclūdere* to EXCLUDE] —**sluice′like′**, *adj.*

sluice·way (slo͞os′wā′), *n.* 1. a channel controlled by a sluice gate. 2. any artificial channel for water.

slum (slum), *n.*, *v.*, **slummed, slum·ming.** —*n.* 1. Often, **slums.** a thickly populated, squalid part of a city, inhabited by the poorest people. —*v.i.* 2. to visit slums, esp. out of curiosity. 3. to visit or frequent a place, group, or amusement spot considered to be low in social status. [orig. slang for room; < ?]

slum·ber (slum′bər), *v.i.* 1. to sleep, esp. lightly; doze. 2. to be in a state of inactivity, quiescence, or calm: *Vesuvius is slumbering.* —*v.t.* 3. to spend or pass (time) in slumbering (often fol. by *away, out,* or *through*): *to slumber the afternoon away.* 4. to dispel by slumbering (often fol. by *away*): *to slumber cares away.* —*n.* 5. Sometimes, **slumbers.** sleep, esp. light sleep. 6. a period of sleep, esp. light sleep. 7. a state of inactivity, quiescence, or calm. [ME *slumer(en)* (with epenthetic *b*), freq. of *slumen* to doze < OE *slūma* sleep; cf. G *schlummern*] —**slum′ber·er**, *n.* —**slum′ber·less**, *adj.*

slum·ber·land (slum′bər land′), *n.* an imaginary land described to children as the place they enter during sleep.

slum·ber·ous (slum′bər əs), *adj.* 1. sleepy; heavy with drowsiness, as the eyelids. 2. causing or inducing sleep. 3. pertaining to, characterized by, or suggestive of slumber. 4. inactive or sluggish; calm or quiet. Also, **slum′ber·y, slum′brous.** [ME]

slum′ber par′ty. See **pajama party.**

slum·gul·lion (slum gul′yən, slum′gul′-), *n.* a stew of meat, vegetables, potatoes, etc. [SLUM + *gullion*, prob. alter. of CULLION]

slum·ism (slum′iz əm), *n.* the prevalence and increase of urban slums and blighted areas.

slum·lord (slum′lôrd′), *n.* a landlord of slum buildings who refuses to improve them and charges exorbitant rents.

slump (slump), *v.i.* 1. to drop or fall heavily; collapse: *Suddenly she slumped to the floor.* 2. to assume a slouching, bowed, or bent position or posture. 3. to sink into a bog, muddy place, etc., or through ice or snow. 4. to decrease or fall suddenly and markedly, as prices. 5. to decline or deteriorate, as health, business, or quality. 6. to sink heavily, as the spirits. —*n.* 7. the act or an instance of slumping. 8. a decrease, decline, or deterioration. 9. a period of decline or deterioration. 10. a period in which the prices of stocks fall or are low, esp. a minor or short depression. 11. a period during which a person performs slowly, inefficiently, or ineffectively. 12. a slouching, bowed, or bent position or posture, esp. of the shoulders. [special use of *slump* bog; c. LG *schlump*]

slung (slung), *v.* pt. and pp. of **sling.**

slung′ shot′, a hand weapon consisting of a weight fastened to a short strap or the like.

slunk (slungk), *v.* a pt. and the pp. of **slink.**

slur (slûr), *v.*, **slurred, slur·ring,** *n.* —*v.t.* 1. to pass over lightly or without due mention or consideration (often fol. by *over*): *The report slurred over his contribution to the enterprise.* 2. to pronounce (a syllable, word, etc.) indistinctly. 3. to cast aspersions on; disparage; depreciate. 4. *Music.* **a.** to sing to a single syllable or play without a break (two or more tones of different pitch). **b.** to mark with a slur. —*v.i.* 5. to read, speak, or sing hurriedly and carelessly. —*n.* 6. a slurred utterance or sound. 7. a disparaging remark or a slight. 8. a blot or stain, as upon one's reputation. 9. *Music.* **a.** the combination of two or more tones of different pitch, sung to a single syllable or played without a break. **b.** a curved mark indicating this. [? dial. *slur* mud; akin to Icel *slor* offal (of fish)] —**Syn.** 1. slight. 3. slander, asperse. 7. innuendo, insult, affront. —**Ant.** 7. compliment.

slurb (slûrb), *n.* *U.S.* a sloppy, ill-planned suburban area. [SL(UM) + (SUB)URB] —**slurb′an**, *adj.*

slurp (slûrp), *Slang.* —*v.t., v.i.* 1. to eat or drink with loud sucking noises. —*n.* 2. a noisy intake of food or drink: *He drank his milk in three slurps.* [< D *slurp(en)*, MD *slorpen*]

slur·ry (slûr′ē), *n.*, *pl.* **-ries,** *v.*, **-ried, -ry·ing.** —*n.* 1. a suspension of a solid in a liquid. 2. *Ceram.* a thin slip. —*v.t.* 3. to prepare a suspension of (a solid in a liquid). [late ME *slory*; akin to SLUR]

slush (slush), *n.* 1. partly melted snow. 2. liquid mud; watery mire. 3. waste from the galley of a ship. 4. a mixture of grease and other materials for lubricating. 5. silly, sentimental, or weakly emotional talk or writing. —*v.t.* 6. to splash with slush. 7. to grease, polish, or cover with slush. 8. to fill or cover with mortar or cement. 9. to wash by splashing large amounts of water: *The crew slushed the deck of the ship.* [appar. c. Norw *slusk* slops, Sw *slask* mud, slops]

slush′ fund′, *U.S.* 1. a sum of money used for illicit or corrupt political purposes, as for buying influence. 2. *Naut.* a fund from the sale of slush, refuse fat, etc., spent for any small luxuries.

slush·y (slush′ē), *adj.*, **slush·i·er, slush·i·est.** 1. of or pertaining to slush. 2. *Informal.* tritely sentimental. —**slush′i·ly**, *adv.* —**slush′i·ness**, *n.*

slut (slut), *n.* 1. a dirty, slovenly woman. 2. an immoral or dissolute woman. [ME *slutte;* cf. dial. *slut* mud, Norw (dial.) *slutr* sleet, impure liquid] —**slut′tish**, *adj.* —**slut′tish·ly**, *adv.* —**slut′tish·ness**, *n.*

sly (slī) *adj.*, **sly·er** or **sli·er, sly·est** or **sli·est,** *n.* —*adj.* 1. cunning or wily: *sly as a fox.* 2. stealthy, insidious, or secret. 3. playfully artful, mischievous, or roguish: *sly humor.* —*n.* 4. **on the sly,** secretly; furtively. [ME *sly, sley* < Scand; cf. Icel *slægur*, Sw *slög* dexterous] —**sly′ly**, *adv.* —**sly′ness**, *n.* —**Syn.** 1. foxy, crafty. 2. surreptitious, furtive.

Sm, *Chem.* samarium.

S.M., 1. See **Master of Science.** [< L *Scientiae Magister*] 2. sergeant major. 3. State Militia.

smack[1] (smak), *n.* 1. a flavor, trace, touch of, or suggestion of something: *The chicken had just a smack of garlic.* 2. a taste, mouthful, or small quantity. —*v.i.* 3. to have a taste, flavor, trace, or suggestion (often fol. by *of*): *Your politeness smacks of condescension.* [ME *smacke*, OE *smæc*; c. MLG *smak*, G (*Ge*)*schmack* taste] —**Syn.** 1. hint. 3. suggest.

smack[2] (smak), *v.t.* 1. to strike sharply, esp. with the open hand or a flat object. 2. to drive or send with a sharp, resounding blow or stroke. 3. to close and open (the lips) smartly so as to produce a sharp sound, often as a sign of relish, as in eating. —*v.i.* 4. to smack the lips. 5. to collide, come together, or strike something forcibly. 6. to make a sharp sound as of striking against something. —*n.* 7. a sharp, resounding blow, esp. with something flat. 8. a smacking of the lips, as in relish or anticipation. 9. *Informal.* a resounding or loud kiss. —*adv.* *Informal.* 10. suddenly and violently: *He rode smack up against the side of the house.* 11. directly; straight: *The street runs smack along the river.* [cf. D, LG *smakken*, G (dial.) *schmacken;* imit.]

smack[3] (smak), *n.* *Eastern U.S.* a fishing vessel, esp. one having a well for keeping the catch alive. [prob. < D *smak;* c. MLG *smacke*]

smack[4] (smak), *n.* *U.S. Slang.* heroin. [?]

smack-dab (smak′dab′), *adv.* *Informal.* directly; squarely: *He fell smack-dab in the middle of the street.*

smack·ing (smak′ing), *adj.* 1. smart, brisk, or strong, as a breeze. 2. *Chiefly Brit. Slang.* smashing. —**smack′ing·ly**, *adv.*

small (smôl), *adj.* 1. of limited size; of comparatively restricted dimensions; not big; little. 2. slender, thin, or narrow: *a small waist.* 3. not great in amount, degree, number, duration, value, etc.: *a small salary; a small army.* 4. of low numerical value; denoted by a low number. 5. having but little land, capital, power, influence, etc., or carrying on business or some activity on a limited scale: *a small enterprise; a small businessman.* 6. of minor importance: *a small problem.* 7. humble, modest, or unpretentious: *small circumstances.* 8. mean or petty: *a small, miserly man.* 9. of little strength or force; slight: *A small effort is often worse than none.* 10. (of sound or the voice) gentle; with little volume. 11. young, esp. very young: *when I was a small boy.* 12. (of letters of the alphabet) lower-case (def. 1). 13. **feel small,** to be ashamed or mortified. —*adv.* 14. in a small manner: *They talked big but lived small.* 15. into small pieces: *Slice the cake small.* 16. in low tones; softly. —*n.* 17. that which is small: *Do you prefer the small or the large?* 18. a small or narrow part, as of the back. [ME *smale*, OE *smæl;* c. D *smal*, G *schmal*] —**small′ness**, *n.*

—**Syn.** 1. See **little.** 1, 3. SMALLER, LESS indicate a diminution, or not so large a size or quantity in some respect. SMALLER, as applied to concrete objects, is used with reference to size: *smaller apples.* LESS is used of material in bulk, with reference to amount, and in cases where attributes such as value and degree are in question: *A nickel is less than a dime* (in value). *A sergeant is less than a lieutenant* (in rank). As an abstraction, amount may be either SMALLER or LESS, though SMALLER is usually used when the idea of size is suggested: *a smaller opportunity.* LESS is used when the idea of quantity is present: *less courage.* 6. trifling, petty, unimportant, minor, paltry, insignificant. 8. stingy, selfish.

small′ arm′, Usually, **small arms.** a firearm designed to be held in one or both hands while being fired.

small′ beer′, 1. weak beer. 2. *Chiefly Brit. Slang.* matters or persons of little or no importance.

small-bore (smôl′bōr′, -bôr′), *adj.* of, noting, or relating to a .22-caliber firearm.

small′ cal′orie, calorie (def. 1b).

small′ cap′ital, an x-high capital letter. Also called **small′ cap′.**

small′ change′, coins of small denomination.

small′ cir′cle, a circle on a sphere, the plane of which does not pass through the center of the sphere. Cf. **great circle** (def. 1).

small·clothes (smôl′klōz′, -klōt͟hz′), *n.pl.* 1. *Brit.* small, personal items of clothing, as underwear, handkerchiefs, etc. 2. knee breeches, esp. the close-fitting ones worn in the 17th, 18th, and early 19th centuries.

small′ fry′, 1. small or young fish. 2. children. 3. unimportant persons or objects.

small′ game′, small, nonferocious wild animals and game birds hunted for sport, as rabbits or doves.

small′ hold′er, *Brit.* the tenant or owner of a small holding.

small′ hold′ing, *Brit.* a piece of land, usually from one to fifty acres, rented or sold to a farmer by county authorities for purposes of cultivation.

small′ hours′, the hours after midnight; early morning hours: *The party went on into the small hours.*

small′ intes′tine, intestine (def. 2).

small·ish (smô′lish), *adj.* rather small. [ME]

small-mind·ed (smôl′mīn′did), *adj.* selfish, petty, or narrow-minded. —**small′-mind′ed·ly**, *adv.* —**small′-mind′ed·ness**, *n.*

small·mouth bass (smôl′mouth′ bas′), a North American, fresh-water game fish, *Micropterus dolomieu*, yellowish-green above and lighter below, having the lower jaw extending up to the eye. Cf. **largemouth bass.**

small′ pas′tern bone′. See under **pastern** (def. 2).

small′ pota′toes, *Informal.* a person or thing of little significance, importance, or value.

small·pox (smôl′poks′), *n.* *Pathol.* an acute, highly contagious, febrile disease, caused by a virus, and characterized by a pustular eruption that often leaves permanent pits or scars on the skin.

small′ print′. See **fine print.**

small-scale (smôl′skāl′), *adj.* **1.** of limited extent; of small scope: *a small-scale enterprise.* **2.** being a relatively small map, model, etc., of the original.

small′-scale′ in′tegra′tion. See **SSI.**

small′ slam′, *Bridge.* See **little slam.**

small′ stores′, *Navy.* personal articles of regulation issue sold to sailors by a supply officer and charged to their pay, as extra clothing.

small′ stuff′, *Naut.* small cordage, as marlines, yarns, etc.

small·sword (smôl′sōrd′, -sôrd′), *n.* a light, tapering sword for thrusting, formerly used in fencing or dueling.

small′ talk′, light, unimportant conversation; chitchat.

small-time (smôl′tīm′), *adj.* of modest or insignificant importance or influence: *a small-time politician.* **—small′-tim′er,** *n.*

small-town (smôl′toun′), *adj.* **1.** of, pertaining to, or characteristic of a town or village. **2.** provincial or unsophisticated. **—small′-town′er,** *n.*

smalt (smôlt), *n.* powdered blue glass used to color vitreous materials. [< MF < It *smalt(o)* SMALTO]

smal·to (smäl′tō; *It.* zmäl′tô), *n., pl.* **-tos, -ti** (-tē). colored glass or similar vitreous material, or pieces of such material, used in mosaic. [< It < Gmc; akin to SMELT[1]]

smar·agd (smar′agd), *n.* *Rare.* emerald (def. 1). [ME *smaragde* < OF *smaragde, esmaragde;* see EMERALD]

sma·rag·dine (smə rag′din), *adj.* **1.** of or pertaining to emeralds. **2.** emerald-green in color. [< L *smaragdīn(us)* < Gk *smarágdinos* = *smáragd(os)* EMERALD + *-inos* -INE[1]]

sma·rag·dite (smə rag′dīt), *n.* *Mineral.* a green, foliated member of the amphibole group. [< F < Gk *smáragd(os)* EMERALD + F *-ite* -ITE[1]]

smarm (smärm), *n.* *Brit. Informal.* trite, cloying sentimentality. [?]

smarm·y (smär′mē), *adj.,* **smarm·i·er, smarm·i·est.** *Brit. Informal.* excessively or unctuously flattering, ingratiating, servile, affectionate, etc.

smart (smärt), *v.i.* **1.** to be a source of sharp, local, and usually superficial pain, as a wound. **2.** to be the cause of a sharp, stinging pain, as an irritating application, a blow, etc. **3.** to wound the feelings, as with words. **4.** to feel a sharp, stinging pain, as in a wound. **5.** to suffer keenly from wounded feelings: *She smarted under their criticism.* **6.** to feel shame or remorse or to suffer in punishment or in return for something. *—v.t.* **7.** to cause a sharp pain to or in. *—adj.* **8.** having or showing quick intelligence or ready mental capability. **9.** shrewd or sharp, as a person in dealing with others. **10.** clever, witty, or readily effective, as a speaker, speech, rejoinder, etc. **11.** dashingly or impressively neat or trim in appearance, as a person or garment. **12.** socially elegant; sophisticated or fashionable: *the smart crowd.* **13.** saucy; pert: *Let's not have any of your smart remarks.* **14.** quick or prompt in action, as a person. **15.** sharply brisk, vigorous, or active: *to walk with smart steps.* **16.** sharply severe: *a smart blow.* **17.** sharp or keen: *a smart pain.* *—adv.* **18.** in a smart manner; smartly. *—n.* **19.** a sharp local pain, usually superficial, as from a wound, blow, or sting. **20.** keen mental suffering, as from wounded feelings, affliction or grievous loss. [(v.) ME *smert(en),* OE *smeortan;* c. G *schmerzen* to smart, L *mordēre* to bite; (adj.) ME; OE *smeart;* (adv.) ME *smerte;* (n.) ME *smerte;* c. G *Schmerz*] **—smart′ing·ly,** *adv.* **—smart′ly,** *adv.* **—smart′ness,** *n.* **—Syn. 8.** bright, sharp. **12.** chic.

smart-al·ec (smärt′al′ik), *n.* **1.** See **smart aleck.** *—adj.* **2.** smart-alecky.

smart′ al′eck (al′ik), an obnoxiously conceited and impertinent person. [special use of *Aleck,* nickname for *Alexander*] **—smart′-al′eck·y, smart′-al′eck,** *adj.*

smart′ ass′, *U.S. Slang.* **1.** a clever, educated, or mentally superior person. **2.** See **wise guy.**

smart′ bomb′, *U.S. Mil. Slang.* an air-to-surface bomb that is guided to its target by either television or a laser beam.

smart·en (smär′tᵊn), *v.t.* **1.** to make more trim or spruce; improve in appearance (usually fol. by *up*). **2.** to make brisker, as a pace. **3.** to sharpen the judgment or broaden the experience of (usually fol. by *up*).

smart′ mon′ey, 1. money invested or wagered by experienced investors or bettors. **2.** such investors or bettors. **3.** *Law.* punitive or exemplary damages.

smart′ set′, sophisticated, fashionable people as a group.

smart·weed (smärt′wēd′), *n.* any of several weeds of the genus *Polygonum,* having a smarting, acrid juice.

smart·y (smär′tē), *n., pl.* **smart·ies.** *Informal.* See **smart aleck.** [SMART + -Y[2]]

smart·y-pants (smär′tē pants′), *n.* (*construed as sing.*) *Slang.* See **smart aleck.**

smash (smash), *v.t.* **1.** to break to pieces with violence and often with a crashing sound, as by striking, letting fall, or dashing against something; shatter: *He smashed the vase against the wall.* **2.** to destroy completely; ruin: *They smashed his hopes.* **3.** to hit or strike (someone or something) with force. **4.** *Tennis, Badminton, Table Tennis.* to hit (a ball or shuttlecock) overhead or overhand, causing the shot to move swiftly and to hit the ground or table usually at a sharp angle. *—v.i.* **5.** to break to pieces from a violent blow or collision. **6.** to dash with a shattering or crushing force or with great violence; crash (usually fol. by *against, into, through,* etc.). *—n.* **7.** the act or an instance of smashing or shattering. **8.** the sound of such a smash. **9.** a blow, hit, or slap. **10.** a destructive collision, as between automobiles. **11.** a smashed or shattered condition. **12.** a process or state of collapse, ruin, or destruction. **13.** financial failure or ruin. **14.** *Informal.* something achieving great success; hit. **15.** a drink made of brandy or other liquor with sugar, water, mint, and ice. **16.** *Tennis, Badminton, Table Tennis.* **a.** an overhead or overhand stroke causing the ball or shuttlecock to move swiftly and to hit the ground or table usually at a sharp angle. **b.** a ball hit with such a stroke. *—adj.* **17.** *Informal.* of, relating to, or constituting a great success: *He wrote many smash tunes.* [? b. SMACK[2] and MASH] **—smash′a·ble,** *adj.* **—Syn. 1.** See **break. 10.** crash.

smash·er (smash′ər), *n.* **1.** a person or thing that smashes. **2.** *Informal.* someone or something that is excellent, impressive, extraordinary, or the like.

smash·ing (smash′ing), *adj.* *Informal.* terribly good; marvelous.

smash-up (smash′up′), *n.* a complete smash, esp. a wreck of one or more vehicles.

smat·ter (smat′ər), *v.t.* **1.** to speak (a language, words, etc.) with superficial knowledge or understanding. **2.** to dabble in. *—n.* **3.** smattering. [ME < Scand; cf. Sw *smattra* to patter, rattle] **—smat′ter·er,** *n.*

smat·ter·ing (smat′ər ing), *n.* **1.** a slight, superficial, or introductory knowledge of something: *a smattering of Latin.* *—adj.* **2.** slight or superficial. **—smat′ter·ing·ly,** *adv.*

smaze (smāz), *n.* a mixture of haze and smoke. [SM(OKE + H)AZE[1]]

sm. c., *Print.* small capital; small capitals.

sm. cap., *pl.* **sm. caps.** *Print.* small capital.

smear (smēr), *v.t.* **1.** to spread or daub (an oily, greasy, viscous, or wet substance) on or over something: *to smear butter on bread.* **2.** to spread or daub an oily, greasy, viscous, or wet substance on: *to smear bread with butter.* **3.** to stain, spot, or make dirty with something oily, greasy, viscous, or wet. **4.** to sully, vilify, or soil (a reputation). **5.** *Slang.* to defeat decisively; overwhelm. *—n.* **6.** an oily, greasy, viscous, or wet substance, esp. a dab of such a substance. **7.** a stain, spot, or mark made by such a substance. **8.** a smudge. **9.** something smeared or to be smeared on a thing, as a glaze for pottery. **10.** a small quantity of something smeared on a slide for examination under a microscope. **11.** vilification; defamation. [ME *smere,* OE *smeoru;* c. D *smear,* G *Schmer* grease] **—smear′er,** *n.*

smear·case (smēr′kās′), *n.* *Dial.* any soft cheese suitable for spreading, esp. cream cheese. Also, **smiercase.** [half trans., half adoption of G *Schmierkäse,* lit., smear-cheese]

smear-sheet (smēr′shēt′), *n.* *Informal.* a newspaper or magazine specializing in gossip, scandal, etc.

smear·y (smēr′ē), *adj.,* **smear·i·er, smear·i·est. 1.** showing smears; smeared; bedaubed. **2.** tending to smear or soil. **—smear′i·ness,** *n.*

smeg·ma (smeg′mə), *n.* a thick, sebaceous secretion, consisting chiefly of desquamated epithelial cells, that collects beneath the foreskin or around the clitoris. [< L < Gk *smēgma* detergent, cleansing medicine]

smell (smel), *v.,* **smelled** or **smelt; smell·ing,** *n.* *—v.t.* **1.** to perceive the odor or scent of through the nose by means of the olfactory nerves; inhale the odor of: *I smell something burning.* **2.** to test by the sense of smell: *She smelled the meat to see if it was fresh.* **3.** to perceive, detect, or discover by shrewdness or sagacity: *The detective smelled foul play.* *—v.i.* **4.** to perceive something by its odor or scent (usually fol. by *at*). **5.** to search or investigate (usually fol. by *about*). **6.** to give off or have an odor or scent: *Do the purple flowers smell?* **7.** to have an odor or scent, as specified: *to smell delicious; to smell of fish.* **8.** to give out an offensive odor; stink. **9.** to have a trace or suggestion (usually fol. by *of*). **10. smell a rat.** See **rat** (def. 6). *—n.* **11.** the sense of smell; faculty of smelling. **12.** that quality of a thing which is or may be smelled; odor; scent. **13.** the act or an instance of smelling. **14.** a pervading appearance, character, quality, or influence: *the smell of money.* [early ME *smell(en), smull(en)* < ?] **—smell′er,** *n.*

smell′ing salts′, a preparation for smelling, consisting essentially of ammonium carbonate with some agreeable scent, used as a stimulant and restorative in cases of faintness, headache, and nausea.

smell·y (smel′ē), *adj.,* **smell·i·er, smell·i·est.** emitting a strong or unpleasant odor; reeking. **—smell′i·ness,** *n.*

smelt[1] (smelt), *v.t.* **1.** to fuse or melt (ore) in order to separate the metal contained. **2.** to obtain or refine (metal) in this way. [prob. < MD or MLG *smelt(en*); c. G *schmelzen* to MELT, smelt]

smelt[2] (smelt), *n., pl.* (*esp. collectively*) **smelt,** (*esp. referring to two or more kinds or species*) **smelts. 1.** a small, silvery food fish, *Osmerus eperlanus,* found in Europe. **2.** any other fish of the family *Osmeridae,* as the American smelt, *Osmerus mordax.* **3.** any of several superficially similar but unrelated fishes, esp. certain silversides, found in California. [ME, OE; cf. Norw *smelta* whiting]

smelt[3] (smelt), *v.* a pt. and pp. of **smell.**

smelt·er (smel′tər), *n.* **1.** a person or thing that smelts. **2.** a person who owns or works in a place where ores are smelted. **3.** a place where ores are smelted.

smelt·er·y (smel′tə rē), *n., pl.* **-er·ies.** smelter (def. 3).

Sme·ta·na (sme′tä nä; *Eng.* smet′ᵊnə), *n.* **Be·dřich** (*Czech.* be′drzhikн) or **Frederick,** 1824–84, Czech composer.

Smeth·wick (smeth′ik), *n.* a city in S Staffordshire in central England, near Birmingham. 68,372 (1961).

smew (smyōō), *n.* a merganser, *Mergus albellus,* of the northern parts of the Eastern Hemisphere, the male of which is white marked with black and gray. [?]

smid·gen (smij′ən), *n.* *Informal.* a very small amount. Also, **smid′gin.** [?]

smier·case (smēr′kās′), *n.* smearcase.

smi·la·ca·ceous (smī′lə kā′shəs), *adj.* belonging to the *Smilacaceae,* the smilax or greenbrier family of plants. [< NL *Smilacace(ae)* name of the family (L *smīlac-,* s. of *smīlax* bindweed (see SMILAX) + *-aceae* -ACEAE) + -OUS]

smi·lax (smī′laks), *n.* **1.** any plant of the genus *Smilax,* of the tropical and temperate zones, consisting mostly of vines having woody stems. **2.** a delicate, twining, liliaceous plant, *Asparagus medeoloides,* having glossy, bright-green leaves. [< L *smīlax* bindweed < Gk *smîlax* bindweed, yew]

smile (smīl), *v.,* **smiled, smil·ing,** *n.* *—v.i.* **1.** to assume a facial expression indicating usually pleasure, favor, or amusement, but sometimes derision or scorn, characterized by an upturning of the corners of the mouth and usually accompanied, esp. in indicating pleasure, by a brightening of the face and eyes. **2.** to regard with favor (often fol. by *on* or *upon*): *Luck smiled on us that night.* *—v.t.* **3.** to assume or give (a smile, esp. of a given kind): *She smiled a warm and friendly smile.* **4.** to express by a smile: *to smile approval.* **5.** to bring, put, drive, etc., by or as by smiling: *to smile one's tears away.* *—n.* **6.** the act or an instance of smiling; a smiling expression of the face. **7.** favor or kindly regard:

fortune's smile. **8.** a pleasant or agreeable appearance, look, or aspect. [ME *smylle;* c. OHG *smīlan,* Dan *smile*] —**smile′less,** *adj.* —**smil′er,** *n.* —**smil′ing·ly,** *adv.* —**Ant. 1, 6.** frown.

smirch (smûrch), *v.t.* **1.** to discolor or soil; spot or smudge with or as if with soot, dust, dirt, etc. **2.** to sully or tarnish (a reputation, character, etc.); disgrace; discredit. —*n.* **3.** a dirty mark or smear. **4.** a stain or blot, as on reputation. [ME *smorche;* b. SMEAR and SMUTCH] —**smirch′less,** *adj.* —**Syn. 1.** smear, dirty. **2.** taint, blot. **3.** smudge, smutch. **4.** taint. —**Ant. 1.** clean.

smirk (smûrk), *v.i.* **1.** to smile in an affected or offensively familiar way. —*v.t.* **2.** to express by a smirk: *He smirked his lewd delight at the joke.* —*n.* **3.** the smile or the facial expression of a person who smirks. [ME; OE *smearc(ian)*] —**smirk′er,** *n.* —**smirk′ing·ly,** *adv.* —**Syn. 1, 3.** simper.

smite (smīt), *v.,* **smote** or (*Obs.*) **smit** (smit); **smit·ten** or **smit; smit·ing.** —*v.t.* **1.** to strike or hit hard, with or as if with the hand, a stick or other weapon. **2.** to deliver or deal (a blow) by striking hard. **3.** to strike down, injure, or slay: *His sword had smitten thousands.* **4.** to afflict or attack with deadly or disastrous effect, as disease. **5.** to affect mentally, morally, or emotionally with a strong and sudden feeling: *His conscience smote him. They were smitten with terror.* **6.** to cause to fall in love; charm (usually used passively). —*v.i.* **7.** to strike; deal a blow or blows. **8.** to appear, fall, etc., with or as if with the force of a blow. **9. smite hip and thigh.** See **hip**[1] (def. 5). [ME; OE *smīt(an);* c. G *schmeissen* to throw, D *smijten*] —**smit′er,** *n.* —**Syn. 1.** knock, cuff, buffet, slap.

smith (smith), *n.* **1.** a worker in metal. **2.** a blacksmith. [ME, OE; c. G *Schmied,* OIcel *smidhr,* Goth *-smitha*]

Smith (smith), *n.* **1. Adam,** 1723–90, Scottish economist. **2. Alfred E(manuel),** 1873–1944, U.S. political leader. **3. Edmond Kir·by** (kûr′bē), 1824–93, Confederate general in the Civil War. **4. Ian Douglas,** born 1919, Rhodesian political leader: prime minister 1964–80. **5. John,** 1580–1631, English adventurer and colonist in Virginia. **6. Joseph,** 1805–44, U.S. religious leader: founded the Mormon Church. **7. Lo·gan Pear·sall** (lō′gən pēr′sôl), 1865–1946, U.S. essayist in England. **8. Margaret Chase,** born 1897, U.S. politician. **9. Sydney,** 1771–1845, English clergyman, writer, and wit.

smith·er·eens (smith′ə rēnz′), *n.pl. Informal.* small fragments; bits: *The vase broke into smithereens.* Also, **smithers** (smith′ərz). [*smithers* (< ?) + Ir dim. suffix *-een*]

smith·er·y (smith′ə rē), *n., pl.* **-er·ies. 1.** the work or craft of a smith. **2.** a smithy.

Smith·son (smith′sən), *n.* **James,** 1765–1829, English chemist and mineralogist: his bequest was used to found the Smithsonian Institution.

Smith·so′ni·an Institu′tion (smith sō′nē ən), an institution in Washington, D.C., founded 1846 with a grant left by James Smithson, for the increase and diffusion of knowledge: U.S. national museum and repository.

smith·son·ite (smith′sə nīt′), *n.* **1.** a native carbonate of zinc, $ZnCO_3$, that is an important ore of the metal. **2.** *Obs.* hemimorphite. [named after J. SMITHSON (who distinguished it from calamine); see -ITE[1]]

smith·y (smith′ē, smith′ē), *n., pl.* **smith·ies. 1.** the workshop of a smith, esp. a blacksmith. **2.** a blacksmith. [ME *smithi* < OIcel *smithja;* akin to OE *smiththe*]

smit·ten (smit′ən), *v.* a pp. of **smite.**

smock (smok), *n.* **1.** a loose, lightweight overgarment worn to protect the clothing while working, as by artists, salesgirls, etc. —*v.t.* **2.** to clothe in a smock. **3.** to draw (a fabric) by needlework into a honeycomb pattern with diamond-shaped recesses. [ME; OE *smocc;* orig. name for a garment with a hole for the head; cf. OIcel *smjūga* to put on (a garment) over the head] —**smock′like′,** *adj.*

smock·ing (smok′ing), *n.* **1.** smocked needlework. **2.** embroidery stitches used to hold gathered cloth in even folds.

smog (smog, smôg), *n.* a mixture of fog and smoke. [SM(OKE + F)OG[1]] —**Syn.** haze.

smoke (smōk), *n., v.,* **smoked, smok·ing.** —*n.* **1.** the visible vapor and gases given off by a burning or smoldering substance, esp. the gray, brown, or blackish mixture of gases and suspended carbon particles resulting from the combustion of wood, peat, coal, or other organic matter. **2.** something resembling this, as vapor or mist. **3.** something unsubstantial, evanescent, or without result: *Their hopes and dreams proved to be smoke.* **4.** an obscuring condition: *When the smoke of controversy has cleared, you will recognize him for the great man he is.* **5.** an act or period of smoking, esp. tobacco: *They had a smoke during the intermission.* **6.** something for smoking, as a cigar or cigarette. **7.** *Physics, Chem.* a system of solid particles suspended in a gaseous medium. **8. go up in smoke,** to terminate without producing a result; be unsuccessful. —*v.i.* **9.** to give off or emit smoke, as in burning. **10.** to give out smoke offensively or improperly, as a stove. **11.** to send forth steam or vapor, dust, or the like. **12.** to draw into the mouth and puff out the smoke of tobacco or the like, as from a pipe, cigar, or cigarette. —*v.t.* **13.** to draw into the mouth and puff out the smoke of: *to smoke tobacco.* **14.** to use (a pipe, cigarette, etc.) in this process. **15.** to expose to smoke. **16.** to fumigate (rooms, furniture, etc.). **17.** to cure (meat, fish, etc.) by exposure to smoke. **18.** to color or darken by smoke. **19. smoke out, a.** to drive from a refuge by means of smoke. **b.** to force into public view or knowledge; expose. [ME; OE *smoca;* c. Scot and north E *smeek* smoke, ME *smeke,* OE *smēoc(an)*] —**smok′a·ble, smoke′a·ble,** *adj.*

smoke′ bomb′, a bomb that upon detonation produces a continuous discharge of smoke rather than an explosion, used to mark an enemy target for attack, indicate wind direction, produce a smoke screen, etc.

smoke-dry (smōk′drī′), *v.,* **-dried, -dry·ing.** —*v.t.* **1.** to dry or cure (meat or other food) using smoke. —*v.i.* **2.** to become dried by smoke.

smoke-eat·er (smōk′ē′tər), *n. Slang.* a fire fighter.

smoke·house (smōk′hous′), *n., pl.* **-hous·es** (-hou′ziz). a building or place in which meat, fish, etc., are treated with smoke.

smoke·jack (smōk′jak′), *n.* an apparatus for turning a roasting spit, set in motion by the current of ascending gases in a chimney.

smoke·less (smōk′lis), *adj.* emitting, producing, or having little or no smoke.

smoke′less pow′der, any of various gunpowders, esp. nitrocellulose, which gives off little or no smoke.

smoke′ pot′, a can containing a chemical mixture that on being ignited produces a great quantity of smoke.

smoke·proof (smōk′proof′), *adj.* that cannot be penetrated by smoke, as a door or room.

smok·er (smō′kər), *n.* **1.** a person or thing that smokes. **2.** *Railroads.* Also called **smok′ing car′.** a passenger car for those who wish to smoke. **3.** an informal gathering, esp. of men, for smoking and entertainment, discussion, or the like.

smoke′ screen′, 1. a mass of dense smoke produced to conceal an area, vessel, or plane from the enemy. **2.** anything, as a statement, intended to disguise, conceal, or deceive.

smoke·stack (smōk′stak′), *n.* a tall pipe for the escape of the smoke or gases of combustion, as on a steamboat, locomotive, or factory. Also called **stack.**

smok′ing jack′et, a loose-fitting man's lounging jacket, worn indoors.

smok′ing stand′, an ashtray mounted on a low pedestal, often placed next to an armchair, sofa, etc.

smok·y (smō′kē), *adj.,* **smok·i·er, smok·i·est. 1.** emitting smoke, as a fire or torch, esp. in large amounts. **2.** hazy; darkened or begrimed with smoke. **3.** having the character or appearance of smoke: *smoky colors.* **4.** pertaining to or suggestive of smoke: *a smoky haze.* [ME] —**smok′i·ly,** *adv.* —**smok′i·ness,** *n.*

Smok′y Hill′, a river flowing E from E Colorado to the Republican River in central Kansas. 540 mi. long.

Smok′y Moun′tains. See **Great Smoky Mountains.**

smok′y quartz′, a crystallized variety of quartz, smoky-yellow to dark brown or black, used as a gem. Also called **cairngorm, Cairngorm stone.**

smol·der (smōl′dər), *v.i.* **1.** to burn or smoke without flame; undergo slow or suppressed combustion. **2.** to exist or continue in a suppressed state or without outward demonstration: *Hatred smoldered beneath his smile.* **3.** to display repressed feelings, as of indignation, anger, or the like: *His eyes smoldered with rage.* —*n.* **4.** dense smoke resulting from slow or suppressed combustion. **5.** a smoldering fire. Also, **smoulder.** [ME *smoulder(en)* < *smolder* smoky vapor, dissimilated var. of *smorther* SMOTHER]

Smo·lensk (smo lensk′), *n.* a city in the W RSFSR, in the W Soviet Union in Europe, SW of Moscow: Russians defeated by Napoleon 1812. 271,000.

Smol·lett (smol′it), *n.* **Tobias George,** 1721–71, English novelist.

smolt (smōlt), *n.* a young, silvery salmon migrating to the sea. [late ME; ? akin to SMELT[2]]

smooch[1] (smōōch), *v.t., n.* smutch.

smooch[2] (smōōch), *v.i. Informal.* **1.** to kiss. **2.** to pet. [?]

smooth (smōōth), *adj.* **1.** free from projections or unevenness of surface; not rough: *a smooth piece of wood; a smooth road.* **2.** generally flat or unruffled, as a calm sea. **3.** free from hairs or a hairy growth: *a smooth cheek.* **4.** of uniform consistency; free from lumps, as a batter, sauce, etc. **5.** allowing or having an even, uninterrupted movement or flow: *smooth driving.* **6.** easy and uniform, as motion or the working of a machine. **7.** having projections worn away: *a smooth tire casing.* **8.** free from hindrances or difficulties: *a smooth day at the office.* **9.** undisturbed, tranquil, or equable, as the feelings, temper, etc.; serene: *a smooth disposition.* **10.** elegant, easy, or polished, as a speech, manner, or person. **11.** free from harshness; bland or mellow. —*adv.* **12.** in a smooth manner; smoothly. —*v.t.* **13.** to make smooth of surface, as by scraping, planing, or pressing. **14.** to free from difficulties. **15.** to remove (obstacles) from the path of something or someone (often fol. by *away*). **16.** to make more polished, elegant, or agreeable, as wording or manners. **17.** to tranquilize, calm, or soothe (a person, the feelings, etc.). **18.** to gloss over, as something unpleasant or wrong (usually fol. by *over, out,* or *away*). —*n.* **19.** the act of smoothing. **20.** that which is smooth; a smooth part or place: *through the rough and the smooth.* [ME *smothe,* OE *smōth;* cf. OE *smēthe* smooth; c. OS *smōthi*] —**smooth′a·ble,** *adj.* —**smooth′er,** *n.* —**smooth′ly,** *adv.* —**smooth′ness,** *n.* —**Syn. 1.** polished; even, flat. See **level. 3.** bald, hairless. **9.** calm, peaceful. **13.** level. **17.** assuage, mollify. —**Ant. 1.** rough.

smooth·bore (smōōth′bōr′, -bôr′), *adj.* **1.** (of firearms) having a bore that is smooth; not rifled. —*n.* **2.** a smoothbore gun.

smooth′ breath′ing, a symbol (') used in the writing of Greek to indicate that the initial vowel over which it is placed is unaspirated. Cf. **rough breathing.**

smooth·en (smōō′thən), *v.t., v.i.* to make or become smooth.

smooth-faced (smōōth′fāst′), *adj.* **1.** beardless; clean-shaven; smooth-shaven. **2.** having a smooth, satinlike, or polished surface: *smooth-faced stone.*

smooth·ie (smōō′thē), *n. Informal.* a man who has a winningly polished manner, esp. in dealing with women. Also, **smoothy.**

smooth′ mus′cle, involuntary muscle in the walls of viscera and blood vessels, consisting of nonstriated, spindle-shaped fibers, each with a central nucleus.

smooth-shav·en (smōōth′shā′vən), *adj.* having the beard and mustache shaved off.

smooth-spo·ken (smōōth′spō′kən), *adj.* speaking or spoken easily and softly; gentle and persuasive.

smooth-tongued (smōōth′tungd′), *adj.* fluent or glib in speech.

smooth·y (smōō′thē), *n., pl.* **smooth·ies.** smoothie.

smor·gas·bord (smôr′gəs bōrd′, -bôrd′), *n.* a buffet meal of various hot and cold hors d'oeuvres, salads, casserole dishes, meats, cheeses, etc. Also, **smör·gås·bord** (*Swed.* smœʀ′gôs bōōd′). [< Sw *smörgåsbord* = *smörgås* sandwich + *bord* table]

smote (smōt), *v.* a pt. of **smite.**

smoth·er (smuth′ər), *v.t.* **1.** to stifle or suffocate, as by smoke or other means of preventing free breathing. **2.** to extinguish or deaden (fire, coals, etc.) by covering so as to exclude air. **3.** to cover closely or thickly; envelop: *to* *smother a steak with mushrooms.* **4.** to suppress or repress: *to smother a scandal; to smother one's grief.* **5.** *Cookery.* to cook in a closed vessel. **—*v.i.* 6.** to become stifled or suffocated; be prevented from breathing freely, as by smoke. **7.** to be stifled; be suppressed or concealed. **—*n.* 8.** dense, stifling smoke. **9.** a smoking or smoldering state, as of burning matter. **10.** a dense or enveloping cloud of fog, dust, etc. **11.** an overspreading profusion of anything: *a smother of papers.* [ME *smorther,* OE *smor(ian)* (to) suffocate + *-ther* agent suffix]

smoth·er·y (smuth′ə rē), *adj.* stifling; close: *a smothery atmosphere.*

smoul·der (smōl′dər), *v.i., n.* smolder.

smudge (smuj), *n., v.,* **smudged, smudg·ing. —*n.* 1.** a dirty mark or smear. **2.** a smeary condition. **3.** a stifling smoke. **4.** a smoky fire, esp. one made for driving away mosquitoes or safeguarding fruit trees from frost. **—*v.t.* 5.** to mark with dirty streaks or smears. **6.** to fill with smudge, as to drive away insects or protect fruit trees from frost. **—*v.i.* 7.** to form a smudge on something. **8.** to become smudged: *White shoes smudge easily.* **9.** to smolder or smoke; emit smoke, as a smudge pot. [ME *smoge* < ?] **—smudg′ed·ly,** *adv.* **—smudge′less,** *adj.*

smudge′ pot′, a container for burning a fuel to produce smudge, as for protecting fruit trees from frost.

smudg·y (smuj′ē), *adj.,* **smudg·i·er, smudg·i·est. 1.** marked with smudges; smeared; smeary. **2.** emitting a stifling smoke; smoky.

smug (smug), *adj.,* **smug·ger, smug·gest. 1.** contentedly confident of one's own respectability, ability, superiority, or correctness. **2.** trim; spruce; smooth; sleek. [perh. < D *smuk* neat; c. G *schmuck*] **—smug′ly,** *adv.* **—smug′ness,** *n.* **—Syn. 1.** conceited.

smug·gle (smug′əl), *v.,* **-gled, -gling. —*v.t.* 1.** to import or export (goods) secretly, in violation of the law, esp. without payment of legal duty. **2.** to bring, take, put, etc., surreptitiously: *She smuggled the gun into the jail inside a cake.* **—*v.i.* 3.** to import, export, or convey goods surreptitiously or in violation of the law. [< LG *smuggel(n)*; c. G *schmuggeln*] **—smug′gler,** *n.*

smut (smut), *n., v.,* **smut·ted, smut·ting. —*n.* 1.** a particle of soot; sooty matter. **2.** a black or dirty mark; smudge. **3.** indecent language or an obscene publication. **4.** *Plant Pathol.* **a.** a disease of plants, esp. cereal grasses, characterized by the conversion of affected parts into black, powdery masses of spores, caused by fungi of the order *Ustilaginales.* **b.** a fungus causing this disease. **—*v.t.* 5.** to soil or smudge. **—*v.i.* 6.** to become affected with smut, as a plant. [alter. of earlier *smit* (OE *smitte*), by assoc. with SMUDGE, SMUTCH]

smutch (smuch), *v.t.* **1.** to smudge or soil. **—*n.* 2.** a smudge or stain. **3.** dirt, grime, or smut. Also, **smooch.** [? < MHG *smutz(en)* (to) smear; c. G *Schmutz,* SMUT]

smutch·y (smuch′ē), *adj.,* **smutch·i·er, smutch·i·est.** of or pertaining to smutch; soiled; smudged.

Smuts (*Du.* smʏts; *Eng.* smuts), *n.* **Jan Chris·ti·aan** (*Du.* yän kʀis′tē än′), 1870–1950, South African statesman and general: prime minister 1919–24, 1939–48.

smut·ty (smut′ē), *adj.,* **-ti·er, -ti·est. 1.** soiled with smut, soot, or the like. **2.** indecent or obscene, as talk, writing, etc. **3.** given to indecent or obscene talk, writing, etc. **4.** (of plants) affected with the disease smut. **—smut′ti·ly,** *adv.* **—smut′ti·ness,** *n.*

Smyr·na (smûr′nə), *n.* **1.** former name of **Izmir. 2. Gulf of,** former name of the Gulf of Izmir. **3.** *Class. Myth.* Myrrha.

Smyr′na fig′, a fig, *Ficus Carica smyrniaca,* that requires caprification in order to produce fruit.

Sn, *Chem.* tin. [< L *stannum*]

snack (snak), *n.* **1.** a small portion of food or drink or a light meal, esp. one eaten between regular meals. **2.** anything that can be eaten quickly and without formality to appease the appetite, as potato chips, crackers, or the like. **3.** a share or portion. **—*v.i.* 4.** to have a snack or light meal, esp. between regular meals. [orig. n. use of *snack* to snap; cf. MD *snacken* to snap]

snack′ bar′, a lunchroom or restaurant where snacks or light meals are served.

Snaffle

snaf·fle (snaf′əl), *n., v.,* **-fled, -fling. —*n.* 1.** Also called **snaf′fle bit′.** a bit, usually jointed in the middle and without a curb, having a large ring at each end to which a rein and cheek strap are attached. **—*v.t.* 2.** to put a snaffle on (a horse). **3.** to control with a snaffle. [cf. D *snavel,* G *Schnabel* beak, mouth]

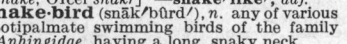

sna·fu (sna fo͞o′, snaf′o͞o), *n., adj., v.,* **-fued, -fu·ing. —*n.* 1.** a badly confused or ridiculously muddled situation. **—*adj.* 2.** in disorder; out of control; chaotic. **—*v.t.* 3.** to throw into disorder; muddle. [*s(ituation) n(ormal): a(ll) f(ouled) u(p)*]

snag (snag), *n., v.,* **snagged, snag·ging. —*n.* 1.** a tree or part of a tree held fast in the bottom of a river, lake, etc., and forming an impediment or danger to navigation. **2.** a short, projecting stump, as of a branch broken or cut off. **3.** any sharp or rough projection. **4.** a small, jagged hole or run as made from catching or tearing on a sharp projection. **5.** any obstacle or impediment: *to strike a snag in carrying out plans.* **—*v.t.* 6.** to run or catch up on a snag. **7.** to damage by so doing. **8.** to obstruct or impede, as a snag does: *His hostility snagged all my efforts.* **—*v.i.* 9.** to become entangled with some obstacle or hindrance. **10.** to become tangled, as twine, hair, etc.: *This line snags every time I cast.* **11.** (of a boat) to strike a snag. [< Scand; cf. Norw (dial.) *snag* stump, OIcel *snagi* clothespin] **—snag′like′,** *adj.*

snag·gle·tooth (snag′əl to͞oth′), *n., pl.* **-teeth.** a tooth growing out beyond or apart from others. [appar. SNAG + -LE + TOOTH] **—snag·gle-toothed** (snag′əl to͞otht′, -to͞othd′), *adj.*

snag·gy (snag′ē), *adj.,* **-gi·er, -gi·est. 1.** having snags or sharp projections, as a tree. **2.** abounding in snags or obstructions, as a river. **3.** snaglike; projecting sharply or roughly.

snail (snāl), *n.* **1.** any mollusk of the class *Gastropoda,* having a spirally coiled shell of a single valve and a ventral muscular foot on which it slowly glides about. **2.** a slow or lazy person. [ME; OE *snegel;* c. LG *snagel,* G (dial.) *Schnegel*] **—snail′like′,** *adj.*

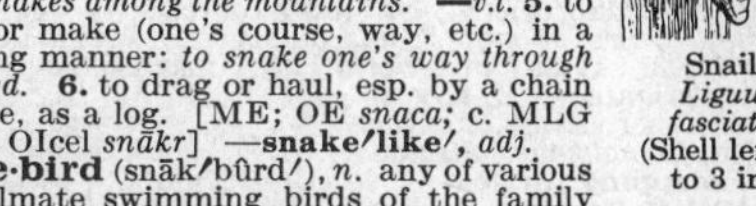

Snail, *Liguus fasciatus* (Shell length to 3 in.)

snail's′ pace′, an extremely slow rate of progress. **—snail-paced** (snāl′pāst′), *adj.*

snake (snāk), *n., v.,* **snaked, snak·ing. —*n.* 1.** any of numerous limbless, scaly, elongated reptiles of the suborder *Ophidia* (*Serpentes*). **2.** a treacherous person; an insidious enemy. **3.** (in plumbing) a device for dislodging obstructions in curved pipes, having a head fed into the pipe at the end of a flexible metal band. **—*v.i.* 4.** to move, twist, or wind in the manner of a snake: *The road snakes among the mountains.* **—*v.t.* 5.** to wind or make (one's course, way, etc.) in a twisting manner: *to snake one's way through a crowd.* **6.** to drag or haul, esp. by a chain or rope, as a log. [ME; OE *snaca;* c. MLG *snake,* OIcel *snākr*] **—snake′like′,** *adj.*

snake·bird (snāk′bûrd′), *n.* any of various totipalmate swimming birds of the family *Anhingidae,* having a long, snaky neck.

snake·bite (snāk′bīt′), *n.* **1.** the bite of a snake, esp. of one that is venomous. **2.** the resulting painful, toxic condition.

snake′ charm′er, an entertainer who seems to charm venomous snakes, usually by music.

snake′ dance′, 1. a ceremonial dance of the American Indian in which snakes are handled or imitated by the dancers. **2.** a parade or procession, esp. in celebration of a sports victory, in which the participants weave in single file in a serpentine course.

snake′ doc′tor, 1. a dragonfly. **2.** a hellgrammite.

snake′ eyes′, *Craps.* a cast of two; two aces.

snake′ fence′, a fence, zigzag in plan, made of rails resting across one another at an angle. Also called **worm fence.**

snake·head (snāk′hed′), *n.* a turtlehead plant.

snake-hipped (snāk′hipt′), *adj.* having thin, sinuous hips.

snake′ in the grass′, a treacherous person, esp. one who pretends friendship.

snake′ oil′, *Slang.* any of various liquid concoctions of questionable medical value sold as an all-purpose curative, esp. by traveling hucksters.

snake′ pit′, *Informal.* **1.** a mental hospital marked by squalor and inhumane or indifferent care of the patients. **2.** an intensely chaotic or disagreeable place or situation.

Snake′ Riv′er, a river flowing from NW Wyoming through S Idaho into the Columbia River in SE Washington: Shoshone Falls. 1038 mi. long.

snake·root (snāk′ro͞ot′, -ro͝ot′), *n.* **1.** any of various plants whose roots have been regarded as a remedy for snakebites, as an herb, *Aristolochia Serpentaria,* having a medicinal rhizome and rootlets, and a white-flowered plant, *Polygala Senega,* having a medicinal root. **2.** the North American bugbane.

snake·skin (snāk′skin′), *n.* **1.** the skin of a snake. **2.** leather made from the skin of a snake.

snake·weed (snāk′wēd′), *n.* bistort (def. 1).

snak·y (snā′kē), *adj.,* **snak·i·er, snak·i·est. 1.** of or pertaining to snakes. **2.** abounding in snakes, as a place. **3.** serpentine or sinuous. **4.** venomous; treacherous or insidious. **—snak′i·ly,** *adv.* **—snak′i·ness,** *n.*

snap (snap), *v.,* **snapped, snap·ping,** *n., adj., adv.* **—*v.i.* 1.** to make a sudden, sharp, distinct sound; crack, as a whip. **2.** to click, as a mechanism or the jaws or teeth coming together. **3.** to move, strike, shut, catch, etc., with a sharp sound, as a door, lid, or lock. **4.** to break suddenly, esp. with a sharp, cracking sound, as something slender and brittle: *The branch snapped during the storm.* **5.** to be radiant; sparkle or flash, as the eyes. **6.** to act or move with quick or abrupt motions of the body: *to snap to attention.* **7.** *Photog.* to take a photograph, esp. without formal posing of the subject. **8.** to make a quick or sudden bite or grab (often fol. by *at*). **9.** to utter a quick, sharp sentence or speech, esp. a command, reproof, retort, etc. (often fol. by *at*). **—*v.t.* 10.** to seize or obtain with or as with a quick bite or grab (often fol. by *up*): *The bargains were snapped up immediately.* **11.** to gain, judge, vote, etc., hastily: *They snapped the bill through Congress.* **12.** to cause to make a sudden, sharp sound: *to snap one's fingers.* **13.** to crack (a whip). **14.** to bring, strike, shut, open, operate, etc., with a sharp sound or movement: *to snap a lid down.* **15.** to address or interrupt (a person) quickly and sharply (usually fol. by *at*). **16.** to say or utter (words, a command, a retort, etc.) in a quick, sharp manner (sometimes fol. by *out*): *The irate customer snapped out his complaints.* **17.** to break suddenly, esp. with a cracking sound: *to snap a stick in half.* **18.** to take a photograph of, esp. quickly. **19.** *Football.* (of the center) to put (the ball) into play by passing it back to the quarterback or other member of the offensive backfield, esp. from between the legs when bent over double and facing the line of scrimmage. **20.** *Hunting.* to fire (a shot) quickly. **21. snap one's fingers at,** to be indifferent to or contemptuous of. **22. snap out of it,** *Informal.* to regain one's usual or normal composure, health, energy, or good spirits; recover.
—*n.* 23. a quick, sudden action or movement, as the flick of a whip or the breaking of a twig. **24.** a short, sharp sound, as that caused by breaking a twig. **25.** See **snap fastener. 26.** a quick, sharp manner of speaking. **27.** a quick or sudden bite or grab, as at something. **28.** something obtained by or as by biting or grabbing: *a snap of food.* **29.** a short spell or period, as of cold weather: *an unexpected cold snap.* **30.** *Photog.* a snapshot. **31.** *Informal.* an easy, profitable, or agreeable position, piece of work, or the like: *This job is a snap.* **32.** *Football.* the act or an instance of snapping the ball.

—*adj.* **33.** made, done, taken, etc., suddenly or offhand: *a snap judgment.* **34.** easy: *a snap course at college.* **35.** noting devices closing by pressure on a spring catch, or articles using such devices.
—*adv.* **36.** in a brisk, sudden manner. [< D or LG *snapp(en)*] —**snap′less,** *adj.* —**snap′pa·ble,** *adj.* —**snap′ping·ly,** *adv.*

snap·back (snap′bak′), *n.* **1.** a sudden rebound or recovery. **2.** *Football.* snap (def. 32).

snap′ bean′, *Bot.* See **string bean.**

snap′ brim′, **1.** a hat brim that can be turned up or down. **2.** Also called **snap′-brim hat′.** a man's felt hat, typically worn with the brim turned up in back and down in front. —**snap′-brim′, snap′-brimmed′,** *adj.*

snap·drag·on (snap′drag′ən), *n.* a plant, *Antirrhinum majus*, cultivated for its spikes of showy flowers, each having a corolla supposed to resemble the mouth of a dragon.

snap′ fas′tener, a fastening device in two pieces having a projection on one piece that snaps into a hole in the other, used esp. for holding parts of a garment together.

snap·per (snap′ər), *n., pl.* (*esp. collectively*) **-per,** (*esp. referring to two or more kinds or species*) **-pers** for 1, 2; **-pers** for 3. **1.** any of several large, marine fishes of the family *Lutjanidae.* **2.** any of various other fishes, as the bluefish, *Pomatomus saltratix.* **3.** See **snapping turtle.**

Snapping turtle, *Chelydra serpentina* (Length of carapace to 1 ft.; tail to 11 in.)

snap′ping bee′tle. See **click beetle.**

snap′ping tur′tle, any of several large, predaceous fresh-water turtles belonging to the family *Chelydridae,* esp. the edible *Chelydra serpentina,* having powerful jaws with which it bites viciously.

snap·pish (snap′ish), *adj.* **1.** disposed to speak or reply in an impatient or irritable manner. **2.** impatiently or irritably sharp; curt: *a snappish reply.* **3.** apt to snap or bite, as a dog. —**snap′pish·ly,** *adv.* —**snap′pish·ness,** *n.*

snap·py (snap′ē), *adj.,* **-pi·er, -pi·est.** **1.** snappish. **2.** snapping or crackling in sound, as a fire. **3.** quick or sudden in action or performance. **4.** *Informal.* crisp, smart, lively, brisk, etc. **5. make it snappy,** *Slang.* make haste; hurry. —**snap′pi·ly,** *adv.* —**snap′pi·ness,** *n.*

snap′ roll′, *Aeron.* a maneuver in which an airplane makes a rapid and complete revolution about its longitudinal axis while maintaining approximately level flight.

snap·shot (snap′shot′), *n., v.,* **-shot·ted, -shot·ting.** —*n.* **1.** an informal photograph, esp. one taken quickly by a simple hand-held camera. **2.** *Hunting.* a quick shot taken without deliberate aim. —*v.t., v.i.* **3.** to photograph informally and quickly.

snare[1] (snâr), *n., v.,* **snared, snar·ing.** —*n.* **1.** a device, usually consisting of a noose, for capturing birds or small animals. **2.** anything serving to entrap, entangle, or catch unawares; trap. **3.** *Surg.* a wire noose for removing tumors or the like by the roots or at the base. —*v.t.* **4.** to catch with a snare; entrap; entangle. **5.** to catch or involve by trickery or wile: *She snared me into going by using flattery.* [ME < Scand; cf. OIcel *snara;* r. OE *snearu;* c. OHG *snarahha*] —**snare′less,** *adj.* —**snar′er,** *n.* —**snar′ing·ly,** *adv.* —**Syn. 1.** See **trap**[1].

snare[2] (snâr), *n.* one of the strings of gut or of tightly spiraled metal stretched across the skin of a snare drum. [< MLG *snare* or MD *snaer* string; r. OE *snēr* string of a musical instrument]

snare′ drum′, a small double-headed drum, carried at the side or placed on a stationary stand, having snares across the lower head to produce a rattling or reverberating effect.

Snare drum

snark (snärk), *n.* a mysterious imaginary animal. [SN(AIL + SH)ARK; coined by Lewis Carroll]

snarl[1] (snärl), *v.i.* **1.** to growl angrily or viciously, as a dog. **2.** to speak in a savagely sharp, angry, or quarrelsome manner. —*v.t.* **3.** to say by snarling: *to snarl a threat.* —*n.* **4.** the act of snarling. **5.** a snarling sound or utterance. [obs. *snar* to snarl (c. D, LG *snarren,* G *schnarren*) + -LE] —**snarl′er,** *n.* —**snarl′ing·ly,** *adv.* —**snarl′y,** *adj.*

snarl[2] (snärl), *n.* **1.** a tangle, as of thread or hair. **2.** a complicated or confused condition or matter: *a traffic snarl.* **3.** a knot in wood. —*v.t.* **4.** to bring into a tangled condition, as thread, hair, etc.; tangle. **5.** to render complicated or confused (often fol. by *up*): *Your stupid questions snarl me up.* **6.** to raise or emboss, as parts of a thin metal vessel, by hammering on a tool **(snarl′ing i′ron)** held against the inner surface of the vessel. —*v.i.* **7.** to become tangled; get into a tangle. [ME < Scand; cf. OSw *snarel* noose = *snar(a)* SNARE[1] + *-el* -LE]

snatch (snach), *v.i.* **1.** to make a sudden effort to seize something, as with the hand; grab (usually fol. by *at*). —*v.t.* **2.** to seize by a sudden or hasty grasp: *He snatched the old lady's purse and ran.* **3.** to take, get, pull, etc., suddenly or hastily. **4.** *Slang.* to kidnap. —*n.* **5.** the act or an instance of snatching. **6.** a sudden motion to seize something; grab. **7.** a bit, scrap, or fragment of something: *snatches of conversation.* **8.** a brief period of effort, activity, or any experience: *to sleep in snatches throughout the night.* **9.** *Slang.* an act of kidnaping. **10.** *Slang* (*usually vulgar*). the vagina. [ME *snacche(n)* < ?; c. MD *snacken*] —**snatch′er,** *n.*

snatch′ block′, *n. Naut.* a fairlead having the form of a block that can be opened to receive the bight of a rope at any point along its length.

snatch·y (snach′ē), *adj.,* **snatch·i·er, snatch·i·est.** consisting of, occurring in, or characterized by snatches; spasmodic; irregular. —**snatch′i·ly,** *adv.*

snath (snath), *n.* the shaft or handle of a scythe. Also, **snathe** (snāth). [unexplained var. of *snead* (ME *snede,* OE *snǣd* < ?)]

snaz·zy (snaz′ē), *adj.,* **-zi·er, -zi·est.** *Slang.* extremely attractive or stylish; flashy: *a snazzy dresser.* [?] —**snaz′zi·ness,** *n.*

SNCC (snik), *n.* a U.S. civil-rights organization, established in 1960, to achieve political and economic power for Negroes through local and regional action groups. [*S(tudent) N(onviolent) C(oordinating) C(ommittee)*]

Snead (snēd), *n.* **Sam(uel Jackson)** (*"Slamming Sammy"*), born 1912, U.S. golfer.

sneak (snēk), *v.,* **sneaked** or (*esp. Dial.*) **snuck; sneak·ing;** *n.* —*v.i.* **1.** to go in a stealthy or furtive manner; slink; skulk. —*v.t.* **2.** to move, put, pass, etc., in a stealthy or furtive manner: *He sneaked the gun into his pocket.* **3.** *Informal.* to take or have surreptitiously; steal: *to sneak a smoke.* —*n.* **4.** a sneaking, underhand, or contemptible person. **5.** *Slang.* a tattletale; informer. [var. of ME *snik(an),* OE *snīcan* to creep; c. OIcel *snīkja* to hanker after] —**Syn. 1.** See **lurk.**

sneak·er (snē′kər), *n.* a shoe, usually of canvas, with a rubber or similar synthetic sole.

sneak·ing (snē′king), *adj.* **1.** acting in a furtive way. **2.** deceitfully underhand, as actions; contemptible. **3.** secret; not generally avowed. **4.** nagging or persistent: *a sneaking suspicion.* —**sneak′ing·ly,** *adv.* —**sneak′ing·ness,** *n.*

sneak′ pre′view, an advance screening of a motion picture, made in order to observe the reactions of the audience.

sneak′ thief′, a burglar who steals by sneaking into houses through open doors, windows, etc.

sneak·y (snē′kē), *adj.,* **sneak·i·er, sneak·i·est.** like or suggestive of a sneak; furtive; deceitful; sneaking. —**sneak′i·ly,** *adv.* —**sneak′i·ness,** *n.*

sneak′y pete′, *Slang.* inferior or homemade liquor or wine.

sneer (snēr), *v.i.* **1.** to smile scornfully or curl the lip in contempt. **2.** to speak or write in a manner expressive of derision, scorn, or contempt. —*v.t.* **3.** to utter or say in a sneering manner. —*n.* **4.** a look or expression suggestive of derision, scorn, or contempt. **5.** a derisive or scornful utterance or remark. **6.** an act of sneering. [ME *snere;* c. NFris *sneere* scorn, perh. also SNARL[1]] —**sneer′er,** *n.* —**sneer′ing·ly,** *adv.* —**Syn. 2.** gibe. See **scoff. 5.** scoff, gibe, jeer.

sneeze (snēz), *v.,* **sneezed, sneez·ing,** *n.* —*v.i.* **1.** to emit air or breath suddenly, forcibly, and audibly through the nose and mouth by involuntary, spasmodic action. **2. sneeze at,** *Informal.* to treat with contempt; scorn (usually in negative constructions): *That sum of money is nothing to sneeze at.* —*n.* **3.** an act or sound of sneezing. [late ME *snese;* r. earlier *fnese,* OE *fnēosan;* c. D *fniezen,* OIcel *fnȳsa*] —**sneeze′less,** *adj.* —**sneez′er,** *n.* —**sneez′y,** *adj.*

sneeze·wort (snēz′wûrt′), *n.* an asteraceous plant, *Achillea Ptarmica,* of Europe, the powdered leaves of which cause sneezing.

snell (snel), *n.* a short piece of nylon, gut, or the like, by which a fishhook is attached to a line. [?]

snick (snik), *v.t.* **1.** to cut, snip, or nick. **2.** to strike sharply. **3.** to snap or click (a gun, trigger, etc.). —*v.i.* **4.** to click. —*n.* **5.** a small cut; nick. **6.** a click. [? cf. Scot *sneck* to cut (off), OIcel *snikka* to whittle]

snick·er (snik′ər), *v.i.* **1.** to laugh in a half-suppressed often indecorous or disrespectful manner. —*v.t.* **2.** to utter with a snicker. —*n.* **3.** a snickering laugh. Also, **snigger.** [imit.] —**snick′er·ing·ly,** *adv.*

snick·er·snee (snik′ər snē′), *n.* a large knife. [var. (by alliterative assimilation) of earlier *stick or snee* thrust or cut < D *steken* to STICK[2] + *snijen* to cut]

snide (snīd), *adj.,* **snid·er, snid·est.** derogatory in a nasty, insinuating manner. [?] —**snide′ness,** *n.*

sniff (snif), *v.i.* **1.** to draw air through the nose in short, audible inhalations. **2.** to clear the nose by so doing; sniffle, as with emotion. **3.** to smell by short inhalations. **4.** to show disdain or contempt, esp. by a low snort (usually fol. by *at*). —*v.t.* **5.** to draw in or up through the nose by sniffing, as air, powder, etc.; inhale through the nose. **6.** to perceive by or as by smelling. —*n.* **7.** act of sniffing; a single, short, audible inhalation. **8.** the sound made by such an act. **9.** a barely perceptible scent or odor. [ME; back formation from SNIVEL] —**sniff′er,** *n.* —**sniff′ing·ly,** *adv.*

snif·fle (snif′əl), *v.,* **-fled, -fling,** *n.* —*v.i.* **1.** to sniff repeatedly, as from a head cold or in repressing tearful emotion: *She sniffled woefully.* —*n.* **2.** an act or sound of sniffling. **3. sniffles,** a condition, as a cold, marked by sniffling (usually prec. by *the*); snuffles. —**snif′fler,** *n.*

snif·fy (snif′ē), *adj.,* **-fi·er, -fi·est.** *Informal.* inclined to sniff, as in scorn; disdainful; supercilious.

snif·ter (snif′tər), *n.* **1.** Also called **inhaler.** a pear-shaped glass, narrowing at the top to intensify the aroma of brandy, liqueur, etc. **2.** *U.S. Slang.* a very small drink of liquor. [ME *snyfter* to sniff; imit.]

snig·ger (snig′ər), *v.i. v.t., n.* snicker. —**snig′ger·er,** *n.* —**snig′ger·ing·ly,** *adv.*

snig·gle (snig′əl), *v.,* **-gled, -gling.** —*v.i.* **1.** to fish for eels by thrusting a baited hook into their hiding places. —*v.t.* **2.** to catch by sniggling. [*snig* eel (late ME *snigge*) + -LE] —**snig·gler** (snig′lər), *n.*

snip (snip), *v.,* **snipped, snip·ping,** *n.* —*v.t.* **1.** to cut with a small, quick stroke, or a succession of such strokes, with scissors or the like. **2.** to remove or cut off (something) by or as by cutting in this manner: *to snip a rose.* —*v.i.* **3.** to cut with small, quick strokes. —*n.* **4.** the act of snipping, as with scissors. **5.** a small cut made by snipping. **6.** a small piece snipped off. **7.** a small piece, bit, or amount of anything: *a snip of food.* **8.** *Informal.* **a.** a small or insignificant person. **b.** a haughty or rude person. [?; cf. D, LG *snippen* to snip, catch, clip]

snipe (snīp), *n., pl.* **snipes,** (*esp. collectively*) **snipe** for 1, 2; *v.* **sniped, snip·ing.** —*n.* **1.** any of several long-billed, limicoline game birds of the genera *Gallinago* or *Limnocryptes,* found in marshy areas, as *G. gallinago* **(common snipe),** of Eurasia and America, having brownish, black, or white plumage. **2.** any of several related or unrelated, long-billed birds. **3.** a shot, usually from a hidden position. —*v.i.* **4.** to shoot or hunt snipe. **5.** to shoot at individuals, esp. enemy soldiers, from a concealed or distant position. **6.** to attack a person or his work with petulant or snide criticism, esp. anonymously or from a safe distance. [ME *snype* < Scand; cf. OIcel *snīpa*] —**snip′er,** *n.*

snipe·fish (snīp′fish′), *n., pl.* (*esp. collectively*) **-fish,** (*esp. referring to two or more kinds or species*) **-fish·es.** any of several fishes of the genus *Macroramphosus,* found in tropical and temperate seas, having a long, tubular snout and a compressed body.

snip·er·scope (snī′pər skōp′), *n.* a snooperscope designed for attaching to a rifle or carbine.

Wilson's snipe, *Capella delicata* (Length 11 in.)

snip·pet (snip′it), *n.* **1.** a small piece snipped off; a small bit, scrap, or fragment: *an anthology of snippets.* **2.** *Informal.* a small or insignificant person.

snip·py (snip′ē), *adj.,* **-pi·er, -pi·est.** **1.** *Informal.* sharp or curt, esp. in a contemptuous or haughty way. **2.** scrappy or fragmentary. Also, **snip·pe·ty** (snip′i tē). —**snip′pi·ly,** *adv.* —**snip′pi·ness, snip′pet·i·ness,** *n.*

snitch[1] (snich), *v.t. Informal.* to snatch or steal; pilfer. [? var. of SNATCH]

snitch[2] (snich), *Informal.* —*v.i.* **1.** to inform; tattle. —*n.* **2.** Also called **snitch′er.** an informer. [?]

sniv·el (sniv′əl), *v.,* **-eled, -el·ing** or (*esp. Brit.*) **-elled, -el·ling,** *n.* —*v.i.* **1.** to weep or cry with sniffling. **2.** to affect a tearful state; whine. **3.** to run at the nose; have a runny nose. **4.** to draw up mucus audibly through the nose. —*v.t.* **5.** to utter with sniveling or sniffling. —*n.* **6.** weak, whining, or pretended weeping. **7.** a light sniff or sniffle, as in weeping. **8.** a hypocritical show of feeling. **9.** mucus running from the nose. **10.** **snivels,** a sniveling condition; a slight head cold (usually prec. by *the*). [ME *snyvele;* cf. OE *snyflung* < *snofl* mucus; c. LG *snüfeln*] —**sniv′el·er;** *esp. Brit.,* **sniv′el·ler,** *n.*

snob (snob), *n.* **1.** a person who imitates, cultivates, or slavishly admires those with social rank, wealth, etc., and is condescending to others. **2.** a person who pretends to have social importance, intellectual superiority, etc. [orig. nickname for cobbler or cobbler's apprentice < ?]

snob·ber·y (snob′ə rē), *n., pl.* **-ber·ies.** snobbish character, conduct, trait, or act.

snob·bish (snob′ish), *adj.* **1.** of, pertaining to, or characteristic of a snob. **2.** having the character of a snob. —**snob′bish·ly,** *adv.* —**snob′bish·ness,** *n.*

snob·by (snob′ē), *adj.,* **-bi·er, -bi·est.** condescending, patronizing, or socially exclusive; snobbish. —**snob′bi·ly,** *adv.* —**snob′bi·ness, snob′bism,** *n.*

snood (snōōd), *n.* **1.** the distinctive headband formerly worn by young unmarried women in Scotland and northern England. **2.** a fillet for the hair. **3.** a netlike hat or part of a hat or fabric that holds or covers the back of a woman's hair. —*v.t.* **4.** to bind or confine (the hair) with a snood. [ME, OE *snōd;* c. NEEDLE]

snook (snōōk, snŏŏk), *n., pl.* (*esp. collectively*) **snook,** (*esp. referring to two or more kinds or species*) **snooks.** **1.** any basslike fish of the genus *Centropomus,* esp. *C. unidecimalis,* found in tropical Atlantic waters, valued as food and game. **2.** any of several related marine fishes. [< D *snoek*]

snook·er (snŏŏk′ər), *n.* a variety of pool played with 15 red balls and 6 balls of other colors. [?]

snoop (snōōp), *Informal.* —*v.i.* **1.** to go about in a sneaking, prying way; pry in a sly manner. —*n.* **2.** Also, **snoop′er.** a person who snoops. [< D *snoep(en)* (to) take and eat (food) on the sly]

snoop·er·scope (snōō′pər skōp′), *n.* a device that transmits infrared radiations and receives those reflected back from solid objects, producing an image on a fluorescent screen, enabling the user to see objects obscured by darkness.

snoop·y (snōō′pē), *adj.,* **snoop·i·er, snoop·i·est.** *Informal.* characterized by meddlesome curiosity; prying.

snoot (snōōt), *n.* **1.** *Slang.* the nose. **2.** *Informal.* a snob. [var. of SNOUT]

snoot·y (snōō′tē), *adj.,* **snoot·i·er, snoot·i·est.** *Informal.* snobbish. —**snoot′i·ly,** *adv.* —**snoot′i·ness,** *n.*

snooze (snōōz), *v.,* **snoozed, snooz·ing,** *n. Informal.* —*v.i.* **1.** to sleep; slumber; doze; nap. —*n.* **2.** a short sleep; nap. [?] —**snooz′er,** *n.* —**snooz′y,** *adj.*

Sno·qual′mie Falls′ (snō kwol′mē), falls of the Snoqualmie River, in W Washington. 270 ft. high.

snore (snôr, snōr), *v.,* **snored, snor·ing,** *n.* —*v.i.* **1.** to breathe during sleep with hoarse or harsh sounds, as caused by the vibrating of the soft palate. —*n.* **2.** the act, instance, or sound of snoring. [ME *snore(n);* c. MLG, MD *snorren*] —**snor′er,** *n.*

snor·kel (snôr′kəl), *n.* **1.** Also, **schnorkle, schnorkel.** a device permitting a submarine to remain submerged for prolonged periods, consisting of tubes extended above the surface of the water to take in air and to discharge exhaust gases and foul air. **2.** a tube through which a person may breathe while swimming face down in the water on or close to the surface. —*v.i.* **3.** to swim while breathing by means of such a tube. [< G *Schnorchel* air intake]

Snor·ri Stur·lu·son (snor′rē stœr′lə son; *Eng.* snôr′ē stûr′lə sən), 1179–1241, Icelandic historian and poet.

snort (snôrt), *v.i.* **1.** (of animals) to force the breath violently through the nostrils with a loud, harsh sound. **2.** (of persons) to express contempt, indignation, etc., by a similar sound. —*v.t.* **3.** to utter with a snort. **4.** to expel (air, sound, etc.) by or as by snorting. —*n.* **5.** the act or sound of snorting. **6.** *Slang.* a quick drink of liquor; shot. [ME *snort(en);* prob. akin to SNORE] —**snort′er,** *n.* —**snort′ing·ly,** *adv.*

snot (snot), *n. Informal.* mucus from the nose. [ME; OE *(ge)snot;* c. Dan *snot*]

snot·ty (snot′ē), *adj.,* **-ti·er, -ti·est.** *Informal.* snobbish; arrogant; supercilious. —**snot′ti·ly,** *adv.* —**snot′ti·ness,** *n.*

snout (snout), *n.* **1.** the part of an animal's head projecting forward and containing the nose and jaws; muzzle. **2.** *Entomol.* an anterior prolongation of the head bearing the mouth parts, as in snout beetles. **3.** anything that resembles or suggests an animal's snout in shape, function, etc. **4.** a nozzle or spout. **5.** *Usually Disparaging.* a person's nose, esp. when large or prominent. [ME *snute;* c. D *snuite,* G *Schnauze*] —**snout′ed,** *adj.* —**snout′less,** *adj.* —**snout′like′,** *adj.*

snout′ bee′tle, weevil (def. 1).

snow (snō), *n.* **1.** *Meteorol.* precipitation in the form of ice crystals, mainly of intricately branched, hexagonal form and often agglomerated into snowflakes, formed directly from the freezing of the water vapor in the air. Cf. **ice crystals, snow pellets.** **2.** these flakes as forming a layer on the ground or other surface. **3.** the fall of these flakes or a storm during which these flakes fall. **4.** something resembling a layer of these flakes in whiteness, softness, or the like. **5.** *Chem.* See **dry ice** (def. 1). **6.** *Slang.* cocaine or heroin. **7.** white spots on a television screen caused by a weak signal. —*v.i.* **8.** to fall as snow. —*v.t.* **9.** to let fall as or like snow. **10.** to cover, obstruct, etc., with snow (usually fol. by *over, under,* etc.). **11.** *Slang.* to persuade or deceive. [ME; OE *snāw;* c. D *sneeuw,* G *Schnee,* OIcel *snǣr,* Goth *snaiws,* L *nix* (gen. *nivis*), Gk *nīpha* (acc.), OCS *snĕgŭ*] —**snow′less,** *adj.* —**snow′like′,** *adj.*

snow·ball (snō′bôl′), *n.* **1.** a ball of snow pressed or rolled together, as for throwing. **2.** any of several shrubs of the genus *Viburnum,* having large clusters of white, sterile flowers. —*v.t.* **3.** to throw snowballs at. —*v.i.* **4.** to grow or become larger, greater, more intense, etc., at an accelerating rate. [ME]

snow·bank (snō′bangk′), *n.* a mound or heap of snow.

snow·bell (snō′bel′), *n.* a small, styracaceous tree of the genus *Styrax,* having white flowers.

snow·ber·ry (snō′ber′ē, -bə rē), *n., pl.* **-ries.** **1.** a caprifoliaceous shrub, *Symphoricarpos albus,* of North America, cultivated for its ornamental white berries. **2.** any of certain other white-berried plants.

snow·bird (snō′bûrd′), *n.* junco.

snow-blind (snō′blīnd′), *adj.* affected with snow blindness.

snow′ blind′ness, the usually temporary dimming of the sight caused by the glare of reflected sunlight on snow.

snow·bound (snō′bound′), *adj.* shut in or immobilized by snow.

snow·bush (snō′bŏŏsh′), *n.* any of several ornamental shrubs having a profusion of white flowers, as *Ceanothus velutinus,* of western North America.

snow·cap (snō′kap′), *n.* a layer of snow forming a cap on or covering the top of something, as a mountain peak or ridge. —**snow′capped′, snow′-capped′,** *adj.*

snow-clad (snō′klad′), *adj.* covered with snow.

Snow·don (snōd′ᵊn), *n.* a mountain in NW Wales: highest peak in Wales. 3560 ft.

snow·drift (snō′drift′), *n.* **1.** a mound or bank of snow driven together by the wind. **2.** snow driven before the wind.

snow·drop (snō′drop′), *n.* **1.** a low, spring-blooming herb, *Galanthus nivalis,* having drooping, white flowers. **2.** its bulbous root or flower. **3.** the woodland anemone.

snow·fall (snō′fôl′), *n.* **1.** a fall of snow. **2.** the amount of snow at a particular place or in a given time.

snow′ fence′, a barrier erected on the windward side of a road, house, barn, etc., serving as a protection from drifting snow.

snow·field (snō′fēld′), *n. Geol.* a large and relatively permanent expanse of snow.

snow·flake (snō′flāk′), *n.* **1.** one of the small, feathery masses or flakes in which snow falls. **2.** *Meteorol.* **a.** an agglomeration of snow crystals falling as a unit. **b.** any snow particle. **3.** any of certain European, amaryllidaceous plants of the genus *Leucojum,* resembling the snowdrop.

snow′ job′, *Slang.* an attempt to deceive or persuade through the use of exaggeration or flattery.

snow′ leop′ard, ounce[2].

snow′ line′, **1.** the line, as on mountains, above which there is perpetual snow. **2.** the latitudinal line marking the limit of the fall of snow at sea level.

snow·man (snō′man′), *n., pl.* **-men.** a figure, resembling that of a man, made out of packed snow.

snow′ mist′. See **ice crystals.**

snow·mo·bile (snō′mə bēl′), *n.* a vehicle adapted for traveling on or through snow. [SNOW + (AUTO)MOBILE]

snow·pack (snō′pak′), *n.* an extensive upland field of packed snow that melts slowly.

snow′ pel′lets, precipitation, usually of brief duration, consisting of crisp, white, opaque ice particles about two to five millimeters in diameter. Also called **graupel, tapioca snow.**

snow′ plant′, a leafless, parasitic plant, *Sarcodes sanguinea,* of the pine forests of the Sierra Nevada in California, having numerous erect flowers, a thickly scaled stem, and a corallike mass of roots.

snow·plow (snō′plou′), *n.* **1.** an implement or machine for clearing away snow from highways, railroad tracks, etc. **2.** *Skiing.* a maneuver, for decelerating or stopping, in which the heels of both skis are pushed outward.

snow·shed (snō′shed′), *n.* a structure, as over an extent of railroad track on a mountainside, for protection against snow.

snow·shoe (snō′shōō′), *n., v.,* **-shoed, -shoe·ing.** —*n.* **1.** a racket-shaped contrivance that may be attached to the foot to enable the wearer to walk on deep snow without sinking. —*v.i.* **2.** to walk or travel on snowshoes.

Snowshoes

snow·slide (snō′slīd′), *n.* an avalanche consisting largely or entirely of snow. Also, *esp. Brit.,* **snow-slip** (snō′slip′).

snow·storm (snō′stôrm′), *n.* a storm accompanied by a heavy fall of snow.

snow·suit (snō′sōōt′), *n.* a child's one- or two-piece outer garment for cold weather, typically consisting of heavily lined pants and jacket, often with a hood.

snow′ tire′, an automobile tire with a deep tread or protruding studs to give increased traction on snow or ice.

snow-white (snō′hwīt′, -wīt′), *adj.* white as snow.
snow·y (snō′ē), *adj.*, **snow·i·er, snow·i·est. 1.** abounding in or covered with snow: *snowy fields.* **2.** pertaining to, consisting of, or resembling snow. **3.** of the color of snow; snow-white: *snowy skin.* **4.** immaculate; unsullied. [ME *snawy,* OE *snāwig*] —**snow′i·ly,** *adv.* —**snow′i·ness,** *n.*
snow′y e′gret, a white egret, *Egretta thula,* of the warmer parts of the Western Hemisphere, formerly hunted in great numbers for its plumes or aigrettes.
snub (snub), *v.*, **snubbed, snub·bing,** *n.*, *adj.* —*v.t.* **1.** to treat with disdain or contempt, esp. by ignoring. **2.** to stop, check, or reject with a sharp rebuke or cutting remark. **3.** to check or stop suddenly (a rope or cable that is running out.) **4.** to check (a boat, an unbroken horse, etc.) by means of a rope or line made fast to a post or other fixed object. —*n.* **5.** the act or an instance of snubbing. **6.** a disdainful affront, slight, or insult. —*adj.* **7.** (of the nose) short and turned up at the tip. **8.** blunt. [ME < Scand; cf. OIcel *snubba* a rebuke] —**snub′ber,** *n.* —**snub′bing·ly,** *adv.* —**Syn. 1.** slight. **2.** reprove, reprimand.
snub·by (snub′ē), *adj.*, **-bi·er, -bi·est. 1.** somewhat snub, as the nose. **2.** short and thick or wide; stubby: *snubby fingers.* **3.** tending to snub people. —**snub′bi·ness,** *n.*
snub-nosed (snub′nōzd′), *adj.* **1.** having a snub nose: *a snub-nosed kid.* **2.** having a blunt end: *snub-nosed pliers.*
snuck (snuk), *v.* *Chiefly Dial.* pp. and pt. of **sneak.**
snuff[1] (snuf), *v.t.* **1.** to draw in through the nose by inhaling. **2.** to perceive by or as by smelling; sniff. **3.** to examine by smelling, as an animal does. —*v.i.* **4.** to sniff, as in order to smell something; snuffle. **5.** to draw powdered tobacco into the nostrils; take snuff. **6.** *Obs.* to express contempt or displeasure by sniffing (often fol. by *at*). —*n.* **7.** an act of snuffing; an inhalation through the nose; a sniff. **8.** smell, scent, or odor. **9.** a preparation of powdered tobacco, usually taken into the nostrils by inhalation. **10.** a pinch of such tobacco. **11. up to snuff,** *Informal.* **a.** *Brit.* not easily imposed upon; shrewd; sharp. **b.** up to a certain standard, as of health, performance, etc.; satisfactory. [< MD *snuff(en)* (to) snuffle] —**snuff′ing·ly,** *adv.*
snuff[2] (snuf), *n.* **1.** the charred or partly consumed portion of a candlewick. —*v.t.* **2.** to cut off or remove the snuff of (candles, tapers, etc.). **3.** to extinguish (often fol. by *out*). **4. snuff out, a.** to extinguish. **b.** to suppress; crush. [ME *snoffe* < ?]
snuff·box (snuf′boks′), *n.* a box for holding snuff, esp. one small enough to be carried in the pocket.
snuff·er[1] (snuf′ər), *n.* **1.** a person who snuffs or sniffs. **2.** a person who takes snuff. [SNUFF[1] + -ER[1]]
snuff·er[2] (snuf′ər), *n.* **1.** Usually, **snuffers.** a scissorlike instrument for removing the snuff of candles, tapers, etc. **2.** a simple device, usually a small cup or cone with a handle, for extinguishing a candle by momentarily closing off the burning wick from the air. **3.** a person who snuffs candles. [SNUFF[2] + -ER[1]]

Snuffers

snuf·fle (snuf′əl), *v.*, **-fled, -fling,** *n.* —*v.i.* **1.** to sniff or snuff. **2.** to draw the breath or mucus through the nostrils in an audible or noisy manner; sniffle; snivel. **3.** to speak through the nose or with a nasal twang. **4.** to whine; snivel. —*v.t.* **5.** to utter in a snuffling or nasal tone. —*n.* **6.** an act of snuffling. **7. snuffles,** the sniffles. **8.** a nasal tone of voice. [< Flem *snuffel(en)* = *snuff(en)* (to) SNUFF[1] + *-el-* -LE] —**snuf′fler,** *n.* —**snuf′fly,** *adj.*
snuff·y (snuf′ē), *adj.*, **snuff·i·er, snuff·i·est. 1.** resembling snuff. **2.** soiled with snuff. **3.** given to the use of snuff. **4.** having an unpleasant appearance.
snug (snug), *adj.*, **snug·ger, snug·gest,** *v.*, **snugged, snug·ging,** *adv.* —*adj.* **1.** warmly comfortable or cozy, as a place, accommodations, etc.: *a snug little house.* **2.** trim, neat, or compactly arranged, as a ship or its parts. **3.** fitting closely, as a garment: *a snug jacket.* **4.** more or less compact or limited in size, and sheltered or warm: *a snug harbor.* **5.** enabling one to live in comfort. **6.** secret; concealed; well-hidden. —*v.i.* **7.** to lie closely or comfortably; nestle. —*v.t.* **8.** to make snug. **9.** *Naut.* to prepare for a storm by taking in sail, lashing deck gear, etc. (usually fol. by *down*). —*adv.* **10.** in a snug manner. [< Scand; cf. OIcel *snöggr* short-haired, etc.] —**snug′ly,** *adv.* —**snug′ness,** *n.* —**Syn. 2.** tidy, ordered, orderly. **7.** cuddle, snuggle. **8.** settle, arrange. **9.** secure.
snug·ger·y (snug′ə rē), *n.*, *pl.* **-ger·ies.** *Brit.* **1.** a snug place or position. **2.** a comfortable or cozy room. Also, **snug′ger·ie.**
snug·gle (snug′əl), *v.*, **-gled, -gling.** —*v.i.* **1.** to lie or press closely, as for comfort or from affection; nestle; cuddle. —*v.t.* **2.** to draw or press closely against, as for comfort or from affection.
so[1] (sō), *adv.* **1.** in the way or manner indicated: *Do it so.* **2.** in that or this manner or fashion; thus: *So it turned out.* **3.** in the aforesaid state or condition: *It is broken and has long been so.* **4.** to the extent or degree indicated: *Do not walk so fast.* **5.** very or extremely: *I'm so sad.* **6.** very greatly: *My head aches so!* **7.** (used before an adverb or an adverbial clause and fol. by *as*) to such a degree or extent: *so far as I know.* **8.** having the purpose of: *a speech so commemorating the victory.* **9.** hence; therefore: *She is ill, and so cannot come to the party.* **10.** (used to emphasize or confirm a previous statement) most certainly: *I said I would come, and so I will.* **11.** (used to contradict a previous statement) indeed; truly; too: *I was so at the party!* **12.** likewise or correspondingly; also; too: *I did it, and so did he.* **13.** in such manner as to follow or result from: *As he learned, so did he teach.* **14.** in the way that follows; in this way. **15.** in the way that precedes; in that way. **16.** in such way as to end in: *So live your life that old age will bring you no regrets.* **17.** then; subsequently: *and so to bed.* **18. so to speak.** See **speak** (def. 15). **19. so what?** what significance does that have? Why should I care? *He hates me—so what?* —*conj.* **20.** in order that (often fol. by *that*): *Check carefully, so any mistakes will be caught.* **21.** with the result that (often fol. by *that*). **22.** on the condition that; if. —*pron.* **23.** such as has been stated: *to be good and stay so.* **24.** something that is about or near the persons or things in question, as in number or amount: *Of the original twelve, five or so remain.* —*interj.* **25.** (used as an exclamation of surprise, shock, indifference, etc., according to the manner of utterance.) **26.** that will do! stop! —*adj.* **27.** true as stated or reported: *Say it isn't so.* [ME; OE *swā;* c. D *zoo,* G *so,* Goth *swa*] —**Syn. 9.** See **therefore.**
—**Usage. 5.** Although many object to the use of so to mean "very," it is inoffensive enough to be so used in all but the most formal context. **20.** In ordinary speech and writing, THAT is frequently dropped after so, even though careful stylists usually include it.
so[2] (sō), *n.* *Music.* sol[1].
So., 1. South. **2.** southern.
s.o., shipping order.
soak (sōk), *v.i.* **1.** to lie in and become saturated or permeated with water or some other liquid. **2.** to pass, as a liquid, through pores, holes, or the like (usually fol. by *in, through, out,* etc.). **3.** to be thoroughly wet. **4.** to penetrate or become known to the mind or feelings (usually fol. by *in*): *The lesson didn't soak in.* —*v.t.* **5.** to place or keep in liquid in order to saturate thoroughly; steep. **6.** to wet thoroughly; saturate or drench. **7.** *Metall.* to heat (a piece) for reworking. **8.** to absorb or take in or up by absorption (often fol. by *up*). **9.** to extract or remove by or as by soaking (often fol. by *out*). **10.** *Slang.* to overcharge. —*n.* **11.** the act of soaking. **12.** the state of soaking or of being soaked. **13.** the liquid in which anything is soaked. **14.** *Slang.* a heavy drinker. [ME *soke,* OE *sōcia(n);* c. SUCK] —**soak′er,** *n.* —**soak′ing·ly,** *adv.* —**Syn. 2, 4.** seep. **6.** steep. See **wet.**
soak·age (sō′kij), *n.* **1.** the act of soaking. **2.** liquid that has seeped out or been absorbed.
soak·ers (sō′kərz), *n.* (*construed as pl.*) absorbent, knitted briefs or shorts, often of wool, used as a diaper cover on infants.
so-and-so (sō′ən sō′), *n.*, *pl.* **so-and-sos. 1.** someone or something not definitely named: *Mr. So-and-so.* **2.** a vicious or disliked person (used as a euphemism).
soap (sōp), *n.* **1.** a substance used for washing and cleansing purposes, usually made by treating a fat with an alkali. **2.** any metallic salt of an acid derived from a fat. **3. no soap,** *Slang.* the proposal, plan, etc., is rejected; to no effect: *He wanted me to vote for him, but I told him no soap.* —*v.t.* **4.** to rub, cover, lather, or treat with soap. [ME *sope,* OE *sāpe;* c. G *Seife,* D *zeep*] —**soap′less,** *adj.* —**soap′like′,** *adj.*
soap·bark (sōp′bärk′), *n.* **1.** a Chilean rosaceous tree, *Quillaja Saponaria.* **2.** the inner bark of this tree, used as a substitute for soap. **3.** any of various other saponaceous barks, as of mimosaceous shrubs of the genus *Pithecolobium.* **4.** a plant yielding such bark.
soap·ber·ry (sōp′ber′ē, -bə rē), *n.*, *pl.* **-ries. 1.** the fruit of any of certain tropical and subtropical trees of the genus *Sapindus,* esp. *S. Saponaria,* used as a substitute for soap. **2.** a tree bearing such fruit.
soap·box (sōp′boks′), *n.* **1.** a box, crate, or other container for soap. **2.** any place, platform, etc., used by a person to make an impassioned speech, appeal, or harangue.
soap′ bub′ble, 1. a bubble of soapsuds. **2.** something that lacks substance or permanence.
soap′ op′era (op′ər ə, op′rə), *Radio, Television. Informal.* a serialized melodramatic program presented during the daytime. [so called from the fact that many such programs were sponsored by soap companies]
soap′ plant′, a liliaceous herb, *Chlorogalum pomeridianum,* of California, the bulb of which was used by the Indians as a soap.
soap·stone (sōp′stōn′), *n.* a massive variety of talc with a soapy or greasy feel, used for hearths, washtubs, etc. Also called **soap′ earth′, steatite.**
soap·suds (sōp′sudz′), *n.* (*construed as pl.*) suds made with water and soap. —**soap′suds′y,** *adj.*
soap·wort (sōp′wûrt′), *n.* an herb, *Saponaria officinalis,* whose leaves are used for cleansing. [SOAP + WORT[2]]
soap·y (sō′pē), *adj.*, **soap·i·er, soap·i·est. 1.** containing or impregnated with soap: *soapy water.* **2.** covered with soap or lather: *soapy dishes.* **3.** of the nature of soap; resembling soap: *a soft, soapy fiber.* **4.** pertaining to or characteristic of soap: *a clean, soapy smell.* —**soap′i·ly,** *adv.* —**soap′i·ness,** *n.*
soar (sōr, sôr), *v.i.* **1.** to fly upward, as a bird. **2.** to fly at a great height, without visible movements of the pinions, as a bird. **3.** to glide along at a height, as an airplane. **4.** to rise or ascend to a height, as a mountain. **5.** to rise or aspire to a higher or more exalted level: *His hopes soared.* —*n.* **6.** the act or an instance of soaring. **7.** the height attained in soaring. [ME *sore* < MF *(e)ssor(er)* < VL **exaurāre* = *ex-* EX-[1] + *aur(a)* air + *-āre* inf. suffix] —**soar′er,** *n.* —**soar′ing·ly,** *adv.* —**Syn. 1.** See **fly**[1]. **4.** tower.
sob (sob), *v.*, **sobbed, sob·bing,** *n.* —*v.i.* **1.** to weep with a sound caused by a convulsive catching of the breath. **2.** to make a sound resembling this. —*v.t.* **3.** to utter with sobs. **4.** to put, send, etc., by sobbing or with sobs: *to sob oneself to sleep.* —*n.* **5.** the act of sobbing. **6.** any sound suggesting this. [ME *sobb(en),* appar. imit.] —**sob′ber,** *n.* —**sob′bing·ly,** *adv.* —**sob′ful,** *adj.* —**Syn. 1.** cry; blubber.
S.O.B., (*sometimes l.c.*) *Slang.* See **son of a bitch.** Also, **SOB**
so·be·it (sō bē′it), *conj.* *Archaic.* if it be so that; provided that.
so·ber (sō′bər), *adj.* **1.** not intoxicated or drunk. **2.** habitually temperate, esp. in the use of liquor. **3.** quiet or sedate in demeanor, as persons. **4.** marked by seriousness, gravity, solemnity, etc., as an occasion, speech, etc. **5.** subdued in tone, as color; not gay or showy, as clothes. **6.** free from excess, extravagance, or exaggeration: *sober facts.* **7.** showing self-control: *sober restraint.* **8.** sane or rational. —*v.t., v.i.* **9.** to make or become sober. [ME *sobre* < OF < L *sōbr(ius)*] —**so′ber·ing·ly,** *adv.* —**so′ber·ly,** *adv.* —**so′ber·ness,** *n.* —**Syn. 2.** abstinent, abstemious. **4.** serious, subdued. See **grave**[2]. **5.** somber, dull.
so·ber-mind·ed (sō′bər mīn′did), *adj.* self-controlled; sensible. —**so′ber-mind′ed·ness,** *n.*
So·bies·ki (sô byes′kē), *n.* **John.** See **John III** (def. 2).
so·bri·e·ty (sə brī′i tē, sō-), *n.* **1.** the state or quality of being sober. **2.** temperance or moderation, esp. in the use of alcoholic beverages. **3.** seriousness, gravity, or solemnity. [ME

sobrietie < L sōbrietās = sōbri(us) SOBER + -etās, var. of -itās -ITY]

so·bri·quet (sō′brə kā′, -ket′, sō′brə kā′, -ket′; *Fr.* sô brē ke′), *n., pl.* **-quets** (-kāz′, -kets′, -kāz′, -kets′; *Fr.* -ke′). a nickname. Also, **soubriquet.** [< F < ?]

sob′ sis′ter, a journalist, esp. a woman, who writes newspaper or magazine articles devoted chiefly to human-interest stories described with sentimental pathos.

sob′ sto′ry, 1. an excessively sentimental human-interest story. 2. an alibi or excuse, esp. one designed to arouse sympathy.

Soc., 1. socialist. 2. (*often l.c.*) society. 3. sociology.

soc·age (sok′ij), *n. Medieval Eng. Law.* a tenure of land held by the tenant in performance of specified services or by payment of rent, and not requiring military service. Also, **soc′cage.** [ME *sokage* < AF *socage* = *soc* SOKE + *-age* -AGE]

so-called (sō′kôld′), *adj.* 1. called or designated thus: *the so-called Southern bloc.* 2. incorrectly called or styled thus: *our so-called intellectual leaders.*

soc·cer (sok′ər), *n.* a type of football game played between two teams of 11 players, in which the ball is advanced only by kicking or by bouncing it off a part of the body other than the arms and hands: only the goalkeepers may use their hands to catch, carry, throw, or stop the ball. [(AS)SOC(IATION) + -ER¹]

So·che (sô′che′), *n.* a city in W Sinkiang, in W China, in a large oasis of the Tarim Basin. 80,000 (est. 1957). Also called **Yarkand.**

so·cia·bil·i·ty (sō′shə bil′i tē), *n.* 1. the act or an instance of being sociable. 2. the quality or state of being, or the disposition or inclination to be, sociable.

so·cia·ble (sō′shə bəl), *adj.* 1. inclined to associate with or be in the company of others. 2. friendly or agreeable in company; companionable. 3. characterized by or pertaining to companionship with others. [< L *sociābil(is)* = *soci(āre)* (to) unite (*socius* comrade) + *-ābilis* -ABLE] —**so′cia·ble·ness,** *n.* —**so′cia·bly,** *adv.* —**Syn.** 1, 2. See **social.**

so·cial (sō′shəl), *adj.* 1. pertaining to, devoted to, or characterized by friendly companionship or relations: *a social club.* 2. friendly or sociable, as persons or the disposition. 3. of, pertaining to, connected with, or suited to polite or fashionable society: *a social event.* 4. living or disposed to live in companionship with others or in a community, rather than in isolation: *Man is a social being.* 5. of or pertaining to human society, esp. as a body divided into classes according to worldly status: *social rank.* 6. of or pertaining to the life, welfare, and relations of human beings in a community: *social problems.* 7. pertaining to or advocating socialism. 8. *Zool.* living habitually together in communities, as bees or ants. Cf. **solitary** (def. 7). 9. *Bot.* growing in patches or clumps. 10. occurring between allies or confederates. —*n.* 11. a social gathering, esp. of or as given by an organized group: *a church social.* [< L *sociāl(is)* = *soci(us)* comrade + *-ālis* -AL¹] —**so′cial·ly,** *adv.* —**so′cial·ness** *n.*
—**Syn.** 1. amiable, companionable, genial, affable. SOCIAL, SOCIABLE agree in being concerned with mutual relations among people. SOCIAL is a general word and may refer to organized society as a whole: *social laws, equals, advancement.* SOCIABLE is more restricted in application and means fond of company and society, and good at "mixing": *a friendly and sociable sort of person.* —**Ant.** 2. introverted, withdrawn.

so′cial anthropol′ogy. See **cultural anthropology.** —**so′cial anthropol′ogist.**

so′cial bee′, any of several bees, as the honeybees or bumblebees, that live together in communities.

so′cial climb′er, a person who attempts to gain admission into a group with a higher social standing. —**so′cial climb′ing.**

so′cial con′tract, the voluntary agreement among individuals by which, according to any of various theories, as of Hobbes, Locke, or Rousseau, organized society is brought into being and invested with the right to secure mutual protection and welfare or to regulate the relations among its members. Also called **so′cial com′pact.**

So′cial Democ′racy, the principles and policies of a Social Democratic party.

So′cial Dem′ocrat, (esp. in Europe) a member of any of certain Social Democratic parties.

So′cial Democrat′ic par′ty, 1. *Hist.* a political party in Germany based on the economic and political ideology of Karl Marx. 2. any of several European political parties advocating a gradual transition to socialism or a modified form of socialism by and under democratic processes. 3. *U.S.* a political party, organized about 1897, that joined former members of the Socialist Labor party to form the Socialist party.

so′cial disease′, a disease ordinarily spread by social contact, esp. a venereal disease.

so′cial evolu′tion, *Sociol.* the gradual development of society and social forms, institutions, etc., usually through a series of peaceful stages.

so·cial·ise (sō′shə līz′), *v.t., v.i.,* **-ised, -is·ing.** *Chiefly Brit.* socialize. —**so′cial·i·sa′tion,** *n.*

so·cial·ism (sō′shə liz′əm), *n.* 1. a theory or system of social organization that advocates the ownership and control of industry, capital, land, etc., by the community as a whole. 2. procedure or practice in accordance with this theory. 3. (in Marxist theory) the stage following capitalism in the transition of a society to communism. Cf. **utopian socialism.**

so·cial·ist (sō′shə list), *n.* 1. an advocate or supporter of socialism. 2. (*cap.*) *U.S.* a member of the Socialist party. —*adj.* 3. socialistic. [SOCIAL(ISM) + -IST]

so·cial·is·tic (sō′shə lis′tik), *adj.* 1. of or pertaining to socialists or socialism. 2. in accordance with socialism. 3. advocating or supporting socialism. [SOCIAL(ISM) + -ISTIC] —**so′cial·is′ti·cal·ly,** *adv.*

So′cialist La′bor par′ty, *U.S.* a political party, organized in 1874, advocating the peaceful introduction of socialism.

So′cialist par′ty, *U.S.* a political party advocating socialism, formed about 1900, under the leadership of Eugene Debs, by former members of the Social Democratic party and the Socialist Labor party.

so·cial·ite (sō′shə līt′), *n.* a socially prominent person.

so·ci·al·i·ty (sō′shē al′i tē), *n.* 1. social nature or tendencies as shown in the assembling of individuals in communities. 2. the action on the part of individuals of associating together in communities. 3. the state or quality of being social. [< L *sociālitāt-* (s. of *sociālitās*)]

so·cial·ize (sō′shə līz′), *v.,* **-ized, -iz·ing.** —*v.t.* 1. to make social; make fit for life in companionship with others. 2. to make socialistic; establish or regulate according to the theories of socialism. 3. *Educ.* to treat as a group activity. —*v.i.* 4. to associate or mingle sociably with others. Also, *esp. Brit.,* **socialise.** —**so′cial·iz′a·ble,** *adj.* —**so′cial·i·za′tion,** *n.* —**so′cial·iz′er,** *n.*

so′cialized med′icine, any of various systems for providing the entire population with complete medical care through government subsidization of medical and health services.

so′cial organiza′tion, *Sociol.* the structure of social relations within a group, usually the relations between its subgroups and institutions.

so′cial psychol′ogy, the psychological study of social behavior, esp. of the reciprocal influence of the individual and the group with which he interacts.

So′cial Reg′ister, *Trademark.* the book listing the names, addresses, clubs, etc., of the principal members of fashionable society in a given city or area.

so′cial sci′ence, 1. the study of society and social behavior. 2. a science or field of study, as history, economics, etc., dealing with an aspect of society or forms of social activity. —**so′cial sci′entist.**

so′cial sec′retary, a personal secretary employed to make a person's social appointments and handle personal correspondence.

so′cial secu′rity, 1. (*usually caps.*) *U.S.* a life-insurance and old-age pension plan maintained by the federal government through compulsory payments by specific employer and employee groups. 2. the theory or practice of providing economic security and social welfare for the individual through government programs maintained by moneys from public taxation.

so′cial serv′ice, organized welfare efforts carried on under professional auspices. —**so′cial-serv′ice,** *adj.*

so′cial stud′ies, a course of instruction in an elementary or secondary school comprising such subjects as history, geography, civics, etc.

so′cial wel′fare, the services provided by a government for the benefit of the citizens.

so′cial work′, work designed to improve the social conditions in a community, as by seeking to relieve poverty or to promote the welfare of children. —**so′cial work′er.**

so·ci·e·tal (sə sī′i tᵊl), *adj.* noting or pertaining to large social groups, or to their activities, customs, etc. [SOCIET(Y) + -AL¹] —**so·ci′e·tal·ly,** *adv.*

so·cié·té a·no·nyme (sô syā tā′ A nô nēm′), *French.* a firm or corporation whose partners or stockholders have liability limited to their total investment. *Abbr.:* S.A., S/A [lit., anonymous society]

so·ci·e·ty (sə sī′i tē), *n., pl.* **-ties,** *adj.* —*n.* 1. an organized group of persons associated together for religious, benevolent, cultural, scientific, political, patriotic, or other purposes. 2. a body of individuals living as members of a community. 3. human beings collectively, associated or viewed as members of a community: *the evolution of human society.* 4. a highly structured system of human organization for large-scale community living that normally furnishes protection, continuity, security, and a national identity: *our American society.* 5. such a system characterized by its dominant economic class or form: *a middle-class society; an industrial society.* 6. a social group characterized by its economic or social status: *lower-class society; provincial society.* 7. companionship; company: *to enjoy someone's society.* 8. the social life of wealthy, prominent, or fashionable persons. 9. the social class that comprises such persons. 10. the condition of those living in companionship with others or in a community, rather than in isolation. 11. a community. 12. *Ecol.* a closely integrated group of social organisms of the same species held together by mutual dependence and exhibiting division of labor. —*adj.* 13. of, pertaining to, or characteristic of elegant society. [< MF *societe* < L *societāt-* (s. of *societās*) = *soci(us)* a companion + *-etāt-*, var. of *-itāt-* -ITY] —**Syn.** 1. association, brotherhood.

Soci′ety Is′lands, a group of islands in the S Pacific: a part of French Polynesia; largest island, Tahiti. (Excluding minor islands) 68,245 (est. 1962); 453 sq. mi. *Cap.:* Papeete.

Soci′ety of Friends′. See **Religious Society of Friends.**

Soci′ety of Je′sus. See under **Jesuit** (def. 1).

So·cin·i·an (sō sin′ē ən), *n.* 1. a follower of Faustus and Laelius Socinus who rejected the Trinity, the divinity of Christ, and original sin. —*adj.* 2. of or pertaining to the Socinians or their doctrines. [< NL *Sociniān(us)* of, pertaining to SOCINUS; see -IAN] —**So·cin′i·an·ism,** *n.*

So·ci·nus (sō sī′nəs), *n.* 1. **Faus·tus** (fô′stəs), (*Fausto Sozzini*), 1539–1604, Italian Protestant theologian and reformer. 2. his uncle, **Lae·li·us** (lē′lē əs), (*Lelio Sozzini*), 1525–62, Italian Protestant theologian and reformer.

socio-, a word element used, with the meaning "social," "sociological," or "society," in the formation of compound words: *sociometry; sociopath; socioeconomic.* [comb. form of L *socius* a fellow, companion, comrade; see -O-]

so·ci·o·ec·o·nom·ic (sō′sē ō ek′ə nom′ik, sō′shē-), *adj.* of, pertaining to, or signifying the combination or interaction of social and economic factors. —**so′ci·o·ec′o·nom′i·cal·ly,** *adv.*

sociol., 1. sociological. 2. sociology.

so·ci·o·log·i·cal (sō′sē ə loj′i kəl, sō′shē-), *adj.* 1. of, pertaining to, or characteristic of sociology. 2. dealing with social questions, esp. focusing on cultural and environmental factors rather than on personal characteristics. 3. organized and structured into a society; social. Also, **so′ci·o·log′ic.** [SOCIOLOG(Y) + -IC + -AL¹] —**so′ci·o·log′i·cal·ly,** *adv.*

so·ci·ol·o·gy (sō′sē ol′ə jē, sō′shē-), *n.* the science or study of the origin, development, organization, and functioning of human society; the science of fundamental laws of social relations, institutions, etc. [< F *sociologie*] —**so′ci·ol′o·gist,** *n.*

so·ci·om·e·try (sō′sē om′i trē, sō′shē-), *n.* the measurement of attitudes of social acceptance or rejection through expressed preferences among members of a social grouping. —**so·ci·o·met·ric** (sō′sē ə me′trik, sō′shē-), *adj.* —**so′ci·om′e·trist,** *n.*

so·ci·o·path (sō′sē ə path′, sō′shē-), *n. Psychiatry.* a person, as a psychopathic personality, whose behavior is antisocial or sexually deviant. —**so′ci·o·path′ic,** *adj.* —**so·ci·op·a·thy** (sō′sē op′ə thē, sō′shē-), *n.*

sock[1] (sok), *n., pl.* **socks** or, for 1, also **sox.** **1.** a short stocking usually reaching to the calf or just above the ankle. **2.** a lightweight shoe worn by ancient Greek and Roman comic actors. **3.** comedy; comic drama. Cf. **buskin** (def. 4). [ME *socke,* OE *socc* << L *socc(us)*]

sock[2] (sok), *Slang.* —*v.t.* **1.** to strike or hit hard. **2. sock away,** to put into savings or reserve. **3. sock in,** to be unable to fly because of adverse weather conditions. —*n.* **4.** a hard blow. —*adj.* **5.** extremely successful: *a sock show.* [?]

sock·dol·a·ger (sok dol′ə jər), *n. Slang.* **1.** something unusually large, heavy, etc. **2.** a heavy, finishing blow. [coinage based on SOCK[2] + DOXOLOGY (in slang sense of finish) + -ER[1]]

sock·et (sok′it), *n.* **1.** a hollow part or piece for receiving and holding some part or thing. **2.** *Elect.* **a.** a device intended to hold an electric light bulb mechanically and connect it electrically to circuit wires. **b.** Also called **wall socket.** a socket placed in a wall to receive a plug that makes an electrical connection with supply wiring. **3.** *Anat.* **a.** a hollow in one part for receiving another part: *the socket of the eye.* **b.** the concavity of a joint: *the socket of the hip.* —*v.t.* **5.** to place in or fit with a socket. [ME *soket* < AF; OF *soc* plowshare < Celt; see -ET]

sock′et wrench′, a box wrench with a socket that is an extension of the shank. See illus. at **wrench.**

sock′eye salm′on (sok′ī′), an important food fish, *Oncorhynchus nerka,* found in the North Pacific. Also called **red salmon, sock′eye′.** [< AmerInd (Salishan) *sukkegh* (by folk etymology)]

sock′ suspend′er, *Brit.* garter (def. 1).

so·cle (sok′əl, sō′kəl), *n. Archit.* a low, plain part forming a base for a column, pedestal, or the like; plinth. [< F < It *zoccol(o)* wooden shoe, base of a pedestal < L *soccul(us)* = *socc(us)* SOCK[1] + *-ulus;* see -CLE]

soc·man (sok′mən, sōk′-), *n., pl.* **-men.** sokeman. [< AL *socmann(us),* var. of *sokemannus* SOKEMAN]

So·co·tra (sō kō′trə, sok′ə trə), *n.* an island off the E coast of South Yemen, in the Indian Ocean, part of South Yemen. ab. 12,000; 1382 sq. mi. Also, **Sokotra.** —**So·co′tran,** *n., adj.*

Soc·ra·tes (sok′rə tēz′), *n.* 469?–399 B.C., Athenian philosopher. —**So·crat·ic** (sə krat′ik, sō-), *adj.*

Socrat′ic i′rony, pretended ignorance in discussion.

Socrat′ic meth′od, the dialectical method employed by Socrates to develop a latent idea or to elicit admissions from an opponent.

sod[1] (sod), *n., v.,* **sod·ded, sod·ding.** —*n.* **1.** a section cut or torn from the surface of grassland, containing the matted roots of grass. **2.** the surface of the ground, esp. when covered with grass; turf; sward. —*v.t.* **3.** to cover with sods or sod. [ME < MD or MLG *sode* turf]

sod[2] (sod), *n. Chiefly Brit. Slang.* **1.** sodomite. **2.** fellow; guy. [by shortening]

sod[3] (sod), *v. Archaic.* pt. of **seethe.**

so·da (sō′də), *n.* **1.** See **sodium hydroxide.** **2.** See **sodium carbonate** (def. 2). **3.** sodium, as in carbonate of soda. **4.** See **soda water.** **5.** a drink made with soda water, flavoring, such as fruit or other syrups, and often ice cream, milk, etc. **6.** (in faro) the card turned up in the dealing box before one begins to play. [perh. < It < ML < Ar *suwwād* kind of plant; cf. MF *soulde, soude*] —**so′da·less,** *adj.*

so′da ash′, *Chem.* See **sodium carbonate** (def. 1).

so′da bis′cuit, a biscuit having soda and sour milk or buttermilk as leavening agents.

so′da crack′er, a thin, crisp cracker prepared from a yeast dough that has been neutralized by baking soda.

so′da foun′tain, **1.** a counter, as in a restaurant or drug store, at which sodas, light meals, etc., are served. **2.** a container from which soda water is dispensed, usually through faucets.

so′da jerk′, *Informal.* a person who prepares and serves sodas, etc., at a soda fountain. Also, **so′da jerk′er.** [shortened form of *soda jerker*]

so′da lime′, a mixture of sodium hydroxide and calcium hydroxide. —**so′da-lime′,** *adj.*

so·da·lite (sō′dᵊlīt′), *n.* a mineral, sodium aluminum silicate with sodium chloride, $3NaAlSiO_4 \cdot NaCl$.

so·dal·i·ty (sō dal′i tē, sə-), *n., pl.* **-ties.** **1.** fellowship; comradeship. **2.** an association or society. **3.** *Rom. Cath. Ch.* a lay society for religious and charitable purposes. [< L *sodālitāt-* (s. of *sodālitās*) companionship = *sodāl(is)* companion + *-itāt-* -ITY]

so·da·mide (sō′də mīd′), *n. Chem.* See **sodium amide.** [SOD(IUM) + AMIDE]

so′da pop′, a carbonated and artifically flavored soft drink.

so′da wa′ter, **1.** an effervescent beverage consisting of water charged with carbon dioxide and often flavored. **2.** See **soda pop.** **3.** a weak solution of sodium bicarbonate, taken as a stomachic.

sod·bust·er (sod′bus′tər), *n. Informal.* a farmer who works the soil.

sod·den (sod′ᵊn), *adj.* **1.** soaked with liquid or moisture; saturated. **2.** heavy, lumpy, or soggy, as food that is poorly cooked. **3.** having a soaked appearance. **4.** bloated, as the face. **5.** expressionless, dull, or stupid. **6.** torpid; listless. **7.** *Archaic.* boiled. —*v.t., v.i.* **8.** to make or become sodden. **9.** *Archaic.* pp. of **seethe.** [ME *soden,* ptp. of to SEETHE] —**sod′den·ly,** *adv.* —**sod′den·ness,** *n.*

sodio-, (in organic chemistry) a combining form of **sodium.**

so·di·um (sō′dē əm), *n. Chem.* a metallic element that oxidizes rapidly in moist air, occurring in nature only in the combined state. *Symbol:* Na; *at. wt.:* 22.9898; *at. no.:* 11; *sp. gr.:* 0.97 at 20°C. [< NL; see SOD(A), -IUM]

so′dium am′ide, *Chem.* a flammable powder, $NaNH_2$, used chiefly in the manufacture of sodium cyanide and in organic synthesis. Also called **sodamide.**

so′dium ben′zoate, *Chem., Pharm.* a powder, C_6H_5COONa, used chiefly as a food preservative and as an antiseptic. Also called **benzoate of soda.**

so′dium bicar′bonate, *Chem., Pharm.* a water-soluble powder, $NaHCO_3$, used chiefly in the manufacture of sodium salts, baking powder, and beverages, as a laboratory reagent, as a fire extinguisher, and in medicine as an antacid. Also called **bicarbonate of soda, baking soda.**

so′dium car′bonate, *Chem.* **1.** Also called **soda ash.** a grayish-white powder, Na_2CO_3, used in the manufacture of glass, ceramics, soaps, paper, petroleum, sodium salts, as a cleanser, for bleaching, and in water treatment. **2.** Also called **sal soda, washing soda.** the decahydrated form of this salt, $Na_2CO_3 \cdot 10H_2O$, used similarly. **3.** the monohydrated form of this salt, $Na_2CO_3 \cdot H_2O$, used similarly, esp. in photography.

so′dium chlo′rate, *Chem.* a colorless solid, $NaClO_3$, used chiefly in the manufacture of explosives and matches, as a textile mordant, an oxidizing and bleaching agent, and as a weak antiseptic for the skin.

so′dium chlo′ride, *Chem.* salt (def. 1).

so′dium cy′anide, *Chem.* a poisonous powder, NaCN, used chiefly in casehardening alloys, in the leaching and flotation of ore, and in electroplating.

so′dium cyc′la·mate (sik′lə māt′, sī′klə-), *Chem.* a crystalline powder, $C_6H_{11}NHSO_3Na$, used chiefly as a sweetening agent, as in soft drinks, for low-calorie or diabetic diets. Cf. **calcium cyclamate.** [CYCL- + AM(IDE) + -ATE[2]]

so′dium dichro′mate, *Chem.* a red or orange solid, $Na_2Cr_2O_7 \cdot 2H_2O$, used as an oxidizing agent in the manufacture of dyes and inks, as a corrosion inhibitor, a mordant, in the tanning of leather, and in electroplating.

so′dium eth·yl·mer·cu·ri·thi·o·sa·lic′y·late (eth′əl-mər kyŏŏr′ə thī′ō sə lis′ə lāt′), *Pharm.* thimerosal.

so′dium flu′oride, a colorless poisonous solid, NaF, used chiefly in the fluoridation of water, as an insecticide, and as a rodenticide.

so′dium flu·o·ro·ac′e·tate (flōō′ə rō as′i tāt′, flŏŏr′ō-, flōr′ō-, flôr′ō-), *Chem.* a poisonous powder, FCH_2COONa, used for killing rodents.

so′dium glu′tamate, *Chem.* See **monosodium glutamate.**

so′dium hydrox′ide, *Chem.* a solid, NaOH: used chiefly in the manufacture of other chemicals, rayon, film, soap, as a laboratory reagent, and as a caustic. Also called **caustic soda.**

so′dium hyposul′fite, *Chem.* See **sodium thiosulfate.**

so′dium ni′trate, *Chem.* a crystalline compound, $NaNO_3$, that occurs naturally as Chile saltpeter: used in fertilizers, explosives, and glass.

So′dium Pen′tothal, *Pharm., Trademark.* the sodium salt of thiopental.

so′dium perbo′rate, *Chem.* a white, crystalline solid, $NaBO_2 \cdot H_2O_2 \cdot 3H_2O$ or $NaBO_3 \cdot 4H_2O$, used as a bleaching agent and disinfectant.

so′dium phos′phate, *Chem.* **1.** a slightly hygroscopic powder, NaH_2PO_4, used chiefly in dyeing and in electroplating. **2.** a compound that in its anhydrous form, Na_2HPO_4, is used in the manufacture of ceramic glazes, enamels, baking powder, and cheeses, and in its hydrated form, $Na_2HPO_4 \cdot xH_2O$, is used in the manufacture of dyes, fertilizers, detergents, and pharmaceuticals. **3.** a crystalline compound, $Na_3PO_4 \cdot 12H_2O$, used chiefly in the manufacture of water-softening agents, detergents, paper, and textiles.

so′dium pro′pionate, *Chem.* a powder, CH_3CH_2COONa, used in foods to prevent mold growth, and in medicine as a fungicide.

so′dium sil′icate, *Chem.* any of several compounds of formulas varying in ratio from $Na_2O \cdot 3.75SiO_2$ to $2Na_2O \cdot SiO_2$, and occurring as solids and liquids: used chiefly in dyeing, printing, and fireproofing textiles and in the manufacture of paper products and cement. Also called **water glass.**

so′dium sul′fate, *Chem.* a crystalline solid, Na_2SO_4, used in the manufacture of dyes, soaps, detergents, glass, and ceramic glazes.

so′dium thiosul′fate, *Chem.* a powder, $Na_2S_2O_3 \cdot 5H_2O$, used as an antichlor, bleach, and in photography as a fixing agent. Also called **hypo, hyposulfite, sodium hyposulfite.**

so′dium-va·por lamp′ (sō′dē əm vā′pər), *Elect.* an electric lamp in which sodium vapor is activated by current passing between two electrodes, producing a yellow, glareless light: used on streets and highways.

Sod·om (sod′əm), *n.* **1.** an ancient city destroyed, with Gomorrah, because of its wickedness. Gen. 18–19. **2.** any very sinful, corrupt, vice-ridden place.

So·do·ma, Il (ēl sô′dô mä), **Gio·van·ni An·to·nio de Baz·zi** (jô vän′nē än tô′nyô de bät′tsē), 1477–1549, Italian painter.

Sod·om·ite (sod′ə mīt′), *n.* **1.** an inhabitant of Sodom. **2.** (*l.c.*) a person who practices sodomy. [ME < MF < LL *Sodomīt(a)* < Gk *Sodomī́tēs*]

sod·om·y (sod′ə mē), *n.* **1.** unnatural, esp. anal, copulation. **2.** copulation of a human with an animal; bestiality. [ME *sodomie* < OF] —**sod·o·mit·i·cal** (sod′ə mit′i kəl), **sod′o·mit′ic,** *adj.* —**sod′o·mit′i·cal·ly,** *adv.*

Soe·kar·no (sōō kär′nō), *n.* See **Sukarno, Achmed.**

Soem·ba (sōōm′bä), *n.* Dutch name of **Sumba.**

Soem·ba·wa (sōōm bä′wä), *n.* Dutch name of **Sumbawa.**

Soen′da Is′lands (sōōn′dä). See **Sunda Islands.**

Soe·ra·ba·ja (sōō′rä bä′yä), *n.* Dutch name of **Surabaya.**

so·ev·er (sō ev′ər), *adv.* at all; in any case; of any kind; in any way (used with generalizing force after *who, what,* etc., sometimes separated by intervening words): *Choose what thing soever you please.*

-soever, a combining form of **soever:** *whatsoever.*

so·fa (sō′fə), *n.* a long, upholstered couch with a back and

two arms or raised ends. [< Ar *ṣuffah* platform used as a seat or Turk *sofa*]
so′fa bed′, a sofa that can be converted into a bed, as by lowering the back. Also, **so′fa-bed′.**
sof·fit (sof′it), *n. Archit.* the underside of an architectural feature, as a beam, arch, ceiling, vault, or cornice. [< F *soffite* < It *soffitt(o)* < LL **suffīct(us)*, L *suffixus* = *suf-* SUF- + *fig-* fasten + *-tus* ptp. suffix]
So·fi·a (sō′fē ə, sō fē′ə), *n.* a city in and the capital of Bulgaria, in the W part. 747,272 (1964). Also, **So·fi·ya.**
S. of Sol., Song of Solomon.
soft (sôft, soft), *adj.* **1.** yielding readily to touch or pressure; easily penetrated, divided, or changed in shape; not hard or stiff: *a soft pillow.* **2.** relatively deficient in hardness, as metal or wood. **3.** smooth and agreeable to the touch; not rough or coarse: *a soft fabric; soft skin.* **4.** producing agreeable sensations; pleasant or comfortable: *soft slumber.* **5.** low or subdued in sound: *soft music; a soft voice.* **6.** not harsh or unpleasant to the eye; not glaring: *soft light; a soft color.* **7.** gentle or mild, as wind or rain: *soft breezes.* **8.** gentle, mild, warm-hearted, or compassionate. **9.** smooth, soothing, or ingratiating: *soft words.* **10.** not harsh or severe, as a penalty or demand. **11.** responsive or sympathetic to the feelings, needs, etc., of others; tender-hearted. **12.** not strong or robust; delicate. **13.** *Informal.* easy; not difficult, laborious, trying, or severe: *a soft job.* **14.** *Informal.* easily influenced or swayed; easily imposed upon; impressionable. **15.** (of water) relatively free from mineral salts that interfere with the action of soap. **16.** *Rocketry.* (of a landing of a space vehicle) gentle; not harmful to the vehicle or its contents. **17.** *Photog.* **a.** (of a photographic image) having delicate gradations of tone. **b.** (of a focus) lacking in sharpness. **c.** (of a lens) unable to be focused sharply. **18.** *Phonet.* **a.** (of consonants) lenis, esp. lenis and voiced. **b.** (of *c* and *g*) pronounced as in *cent* and *gem.* **c.** (of consonants in Slavic languages) palatalized. Cf. **hard** (def. 30). **19.** foolish or stupid. **20.** (of a drug) not physically addictive, such as marijuana. **21. be soft on someone,** *Informal.* to be amorously inclined toward a person; have an affection for someone. —*n.* **22.** something soft or yielding; the soft part. **23.** softness. —*adv.* **24.** in a soft manner. —*interj. Archaic.* **25.** be quiet! hush! **26.** not so fast! stop! [ME *softe*, OE *sōfte*; c. G *sanft*] —**soft′ly,** *adv.* —**soft′ness,** *n.* —**Syn. 1.** pliable, malleable. **5.** dulcet, sweet. **8.** tender, sympathetic. **9.** mollifying. **12.** weak, feeble.
soft·ball (sôft′bôl′, soft′-), *n.* **1.** a form of baseball played on a smaller diamond with a larger and softer ball. **2.** the ball itself.
soft-boiled (sôft′boild′, soft′-), *adj. Cookery.* (of an egg) boiled in the shell not long enough to cause the yolk or white to solidify, usually less than five minutes (distinguished from *hard-boiled*).
soft′ chan′cre, *Pathol.* chancroid.
soft′ clam′. See **soft-shell clam.**
soft′ coal′. See **bituminous coal.**
soft-core (sôft′kōr′, soft′kôr′), *adj.* suggestive rather than explicit; involving only simulated or implied sexual acts: *soft-core pornography.* Cf. **hard-core** (def. 2).
soft-cov·er (sôft′kuv′ər, soft′-), *n., adj.* paperback.
soft′ drink′, a beverage that is not alcoholic or intoxicating and is usually carbonated, as root beer, ginger ale, etc.
sof·ten (sô′fən, sof′ən), *v.t.* **1.** to make soft or softer. —*v.i.* **2.** to become soft or softer. [ME]
sof·ten·er (sô′fə nər, sof′ə-), *n.* **1.** a person or thing that softens. **2.** *Chem.* any admixture to a substance for promoting or increasing its softness, smoothness, or plasticity.
sof′tening of the brain′, *Pathol.* a softening of the cerebrum, caused by impairment of the blood supply; encephalomalacia.
soft-finned (sôft′find′, soft′-), *adj. Ichthyol.* having fins supported by articulated rays rather than by spines, as a malacopterygian.
soft′ goods′, merchandise of limited durability, as textiles, carpets, clothing, etc. Cf. **hard goods.**
soft-head·ed (sôft′hed′id, soft′-), *adj.* foolish; stupid. —**soft′head′,** *n.* —**soft′-head′ed·ness,** *n.*
soft-heart·ed (sôft′här′tid, soft′-), *adj.* very sympathetic or responsive; generous in spirit. —**soft′-heart′ed·ly,** *adv.* —**soft′-heart′ed·ness,** *n.*
soft·ie (sôf′tē, sof′-), *n.* softy.
soft′ line′, a conciliatory or accommodative stand. —**soft′-line′,** *adj.*
soft-lin·er (sôft′lī′nər, soft′-), *n.* a person who takes a conciliatory or accommodative stand.
soft′ pal′ate. See under **palate** (def. 1).
soft′ ped′al, a pedal, as in a piano, for reducing tonal volume.
soft-ped·al (sôft′ped′ᵊl, soft′-), *v.,* **-aled, -al·ing** or (*esp. Brit.*) **-alled, -al·ling.** —*v.i.* **1.** to use the soft pedal. —*v.t.* **2.** to soften the sound of by using the soft pedal. **3.** *Informal.* to obscure or attempt to obscure the importance of, as an idea, fact, or the like.
soft′ rock′, an easy-listening, modified type of rock-'n'-roll in which the lyrics are usually more important and meaningful than the music. Cf. **hard rock.**
soft′ rot′, *Plant Pathol.* a disease of fruits and vegetables, characterized by a soft, watery decay of affected parts, caused by any of several bacteria or fungi.
soft′ sell′, a method of advertising or selling that is quietly persuasive, subtle, and indirect (opposed to *hard sell*).
soft-shell (sôft′shel′, soft′-), *adj.* **1.** Also, **soft′-shelled′.** having a soft, flexible, or fragile shell, as a crab having recently molted. —*n.* **2.** a soft-shell animal, esp. a soft-shell crab.
soft′-shell clam′, an edible clam, *Mya arenaria*, found on both coasts of North America, having an oval, relatively thin, whitish shell. Also called **soft clam.**
soft′-shell crab′, a crab, esp. the blue crab, that has recently molted, therefore having a soft, edible shell.
soft′-shelled tur′tle, any of numerous aquatic turtles of the family *Trionychidae*, found in North America, Asia, and Africa, having the shell covered with flexible, leathery skin instead of horny plates.
soft-shoe (sôft′sho͞o′, soft′-), *adj.* of, pertaining to, or characteristic of tap dancing done in soft-soled shoes, without taps.
soft′ shoul′der, the unpaved edge of a road.
soft′ soap′, **1.** the semifluid soap produced when potassium hydroxide is used in the saponification of a fat or an oil. **2.** *Informal.* flattery.
soft-soap (sôft′sōp′, soft′-), *v.t.* **1.** to apply soft soap to. **2.** *Informal.* to cajole; flatter.
soft-spo·ken (sôft′spō′kən, soft′-), *adj.* **1.** (of persons) speaking with a soft or gentle voice; mild. **2.** (of words) softly or mildly spoken; persuasive.
soft′ spot′, **1.** a weak or vulnerable position, place, condition, etc. **2.** emotional susceptibility.
soft′ touch′, *Slang.* **1.** a person who is easily influenced, imposed upon, duped, or convinced, esp. to give or lend money. **2.** a contestant, team, etc., that is easily defeated.
soft·ware (sôft′wâr′, soft′-), *n. Computer Technol.* any of the written programs, flow charts, etc., that may be inserted in computer programs. Cf. **hardware** (def. 4).
soft·wood (sôft′wo͝od′, soft′-), *n.* **1.** any wood that is relatively soft or easily cut. **2.** a tree yielding such a wood. **3.** *Forestry.* a coniferous tree or its wood. —*adj.* **4.** of, pertaining to, or made of softwood.
soft·y (sôf′tē, sof′-), *n., pl.* **-ties.** *Informal.* **1.** a person easily stirred to sentiment or tender emotion. **2.** a weak, silly, or foolish person. Also, **softie.**
Sog·di·an (sog′dē ən), *n.* **1.** a native or inhabitant of Sogdiana. **2.** the extinct Iranian language of Sogdiana. [< L *Sogdiān(us)*. See SOGDIANA, -IAN]
Sog·di·a·na (sog′dē ā′nə, -an′ə), *n.* a province of the ancient Persian Empire. *Cap.:* Samarkand.
sog·gy (sog′ē), *adj.,* **-gi·er, -gi·est.** **1.** soaked; thoroughly wet; sodden. **2.** damp and heavy, as poorly baked bread. **3.** spiritless, heavy, dull, or stupid: *a soggy novel.* [dial. *sog* bog + -Y[1]; cf. Norw (dial.) *soggjast* to get soaked] —**sog′gi·ly,** *adv.* —**sog′gi·ness,** *n.*
So·ho (sō′hō, sō hō′), *n.* a district in London, England, predominantly foreign since 1685: noted for its restaurants.
soi-di·sant (swa dē zäN′), *adj. French.* **1.** calling oneself thus; self-styled. **2.** so-called or pretended.
soi·gné (swän yā′; *Fr.* swa nyā′), *adj.* **1.** carefully or elegantly done, operated, or designed. **2.** well-groomed. Also, **soi·gnée′.** [< F, adj. use of ptp. of *soigner* to take care of < Gmc (cf. OS *sunnea* care, concern)]
soil[1] (soil), *n.* **1.** the portion of the earth's surface consisting of disintegrated rock and humus. **2.** a particular kind of earth: *sandy soil.* **3.** a country, land, or region. **4.** any place or condition providing the opportunity for growth or development. [ME *soile* < AF *soyl* < L *sol(ium)* seat, confused with *solum* ground] —**soil′less,** *adj.*
soil[2] (soil), *v.t.* **1.** to make unclean, dirty, or filthy, esp. on the surface. **2.** to smirch, smudge, or stain. **3.** to sully or tarnish, as with disgrace; defile morally, as with sin. —*v.i.* **4.** to become soiled. —*n.* **5.** the act or fact of soiling. **6.** the state of being soiled. **7.** a spot, mark, or stain. **8.** filth; sewage. **9.** ordure; manure. [ME *soil(en)* < OF *souill(er)*, *soill(ier)* (to) dirty < VL **suculāre* = *sus* pig + *-culus* -CLE + *-āre* inf. ending]
soil[3] (soil), *v.t.* **1.** to feed (cattle, horses, etc.) freshly cut green fodder in order to fatten them. **2.** to purge (horses, cattle, etc.) by feeding them green food. [?]
soil·age (soi′lij), *n.* grass or leafy plants raised as feed for fenced-in livestock.
soil′ bank′, a plan providing cash payments to farmers who cut production of certain surplus crops in favor of soil-enriching ones. —**soil′-bank′,** *adj.*
soil′ conserva′tion, any method to achieve the maximum utilization of the land and preservation of its resources.
soil′ rot′, *Plant Pathol.* pox (def. 3).
soil·ure (soil′yər), *n. Archaic.* a stain. [ME *soylure* < OF *soilleure* = *soill(ier)* (see SOIL[2]) + *-eure* -URE]
soi·ree (swä rā′), *n.* an evening party or social gathering, esp. one held for a particular purpose: *a musical soiree.* [< F < OF *soir* evening (< L *serum* late) + *-ée* ptp. suffix (as if < L *-āta*)]
soi·rée (swä rā′; *Fr.* swa rā′), *n., pl.* **-rées** (-rāz′; *Fr.* -rā′). soiree.
Sois·sons (swa sôN′), *n.* a city in N France, on the Aisne River: battles A.D. 486, 1918, 1944. 24,359 (1962).
so·journ (*v.* sō′jûrn, sō jûrn′; *n.* sō′jûrn), *v.i.* **1.** to stay for a time in a place; live temporarily. —*n.* **2.** a temporary stay. [ME *sojurne* < OF *sojorn* < *sojorn(er)* (to) rest, stay < VL **subdiurnāre* = L *sub-* SUB- + *diurn(us)* of a day; see JOURNEY] —**so′journ·er,** *n.*
soke (sōk), *n. Early Eng. Law.* **1.** the privilege of holding court, usually connected with the feudal rights of lordship. **2.** a district over which local jurisdiction was exercised. [late ME < ML *soc(a)* << OE *sōcn* seeking; c. SEEK]
soke·man (sōk′mən), *n., pl.* **-men.** a tenant holding land in socage. Also, **socman.** [ME < ML *sokemann(us)* < OE *sōcn* SOKE + *man* MAN[1]]
So·ko·to (sō′kō tō′, sō′kō tō′, sə kō′tō), *n.* a province in NW Nigeria: center of a Fulah empire in the 19th century. 3,193,019 (1963); 36,477 sq. mi.
So·ko·tra (sō kō′trə, sok′ə trə), *n.* Socotra.
sol[1] (sōl, sol), *n. Music.* **1.** the syllable used for the fifth tone of a diatonic scale. **2.** (in the fixed system of solmization) the tone G. Also, **so.** Cf. **sol-fa.** [see GAMUT]
sol[2] (sōl, sol), *n.* a former coin and money of account of France, the 20th part of a livre: discontinued in 1794. Also, **sou.** Cf. **solidus** (def. 2). [< OF *sol* < LL *sol(idus)* SOLIDUS; cf. It *soldo*, Sp *sueldo*]
sol[3] (sōl, sol; *Sp.* sôl), *n., pl.* **sols,** *Sp.* **so·les** (sô′les). a bronze coin and monetary unit of Peru, equal to 100 centavos. *Abbr.:* S. [< AmerSp, Sp: sun < L *sōl*]
sol[4] (sol, sōl), *n. Physical Chem.* a colloidal solution having the consistency of a liquid, as egg white (opposed to *gel*). [shortened form of HYDROSOL]
Sol (sol), *n.* **1.** an ancient Roman god personifying the sun, variously identified with the Greek Helios or the Indo-

Iranian god Mithras. **2.** the sun, personified by the Romans as a god.

Sol., **1.** Solicitor. **2.** Solomon.

sol., **1.** soluble. **2.** solution.

so·la (sō′lä; *Eng.* sō′lə), *adj. Latin.* (referring to a woman) alone (used formerly in stage directions). Cf. **solus.**

sol·ace (sol′is), *n., v.,* **-aced, -ac·ing.** —*n.* Also called **sol′ace·ment. 1.** comfort in sorrow, misfortune, or trouble; alleviation of distress or discomfort. **2.** something that gives comfort, consolation, or relief. —*v.t.* **3.** to comfort, console, or cheer (a person, oneself, the heart, etc.). **4.** to alleviate or relieve (sorrow, distress, etc.). [ME *solas* < OF < L *sōlāc(ium), sōlāt(ium)* = *sōlāt(us)* (ptp. of *sōlārī* to comfort; see -ATE[1]) + *-ium* n. suffix] —**sol′ac·er,** *n.* —**Syn. 1.** consolation, relief. **4.** soothe, mitigate, assuage, allay.

so·lan (sō′lən), *n.* a gannet. Also called **so′lan goose′.** [ME *soland* < Scand; cf. OIcel *sūla* gannet, Dan *and* goose]

sol·a·na·ceous (sol′ə nā′shəs), *adj.* belonging to the *Solanaceae,* or nightshade family of plants, comprising the solanums, belladonna, henbane, mandrake, tobacco, pepper, tomato, etc. [< NL *Sōlānāce(ae)* name of the family = L *sōlān(um)* nightshade + *-āceae;* see -ACEOUS]

so·la·num (sō lā′nəm), *n.* any gametopetalous herb, shrub, or small tree of the genus *Solanum,* comprising the nightshade, eggplant, potato, etc. [< L: nightshade]

so·lar (sō′lər), *adj.* **1.** of or pertaining to the sun: *solar phenomena.* **2.** determined by the sun: *solar hour.* **3.** proceeding from the sun, as light or heat. **4.** operating by the light or heat of the sun, as a mechanism: *a solar stove.* **5.** indicating time by means of or with reference to the sun: *a solar chronometer.* **6.** *Astrol.* subject to the influence of the sun. [< L *sōlār(is)* = *sōl-* (s. of *sōl*) the sun + *-āris* -AR[1]]

so′lar a′pex, *Astron.* the point on the celestial sphere, near Vega, toward which the solar system is moving relative to the visible stars.

so′lar bat′tery, a device for converting solar energy into electricity by means of photovoltaic cells.

so′lar con′stant, the average rate at which radiant energy is received from the sun by the earth, equal to 1.94 small calories per minute per square centimeter of area perpendicular to the sun's rays.

so′lar day′, *Astron.* the time interval between two successive transits by the sun of the meridian directly opposite that of the observer; the 24-hour interval from one midnight to the following midnight.

so′lar eclipse′. See under **eclipse** (def. 1a). —**so′lar eclip′tic.**

so·lar·ise (sō′lə rīz′), *v.t., v.i.,* **-ised, -is·ing.** *Chiefly Brit.* solarize. —**so′lar·i·sa′tion,** *n.*

so·lar·i·um (sō lâr′ē əm, sə-), *n., pl.* **-lar·i·ums, -lar·i·a** (-lâr′ē ə). a glass-enclosed room, porch, or the like, exposed to the sun's rays, as at a seaside hotel or for convalescents in a hospital. [< L: sundial, balcony, terrace = *sōl* the sun + *-ārium* -ARY]

so·lar·ize (sō′lə rīz′), *v.,* **-ized, -iz·ing.** —*v.t.* **1.** *Photog.* to reverse (an image) partially, as from negative to positive, by exposure to light during development. **2.** to affect by sunlight. —*v.i.* **3.** *Photog.* (of material) to become injured by overexposure. Also, *esp. Brit.,* **solarise.** —**so′lar·i·za′tion,** *n.*

so′lar month′, month (def. 1).

so′lar plex′us, 1. *Anat.* a network of nerves situated at the upper part of the abdomen, behind the stomach and in front of the aorta. **2.** *Informal.* a point on the stomach wall, just below the sternum, where a blow will affect this nerve center. [so called from the raylike pattern of the nerve fibers]

so′lar sys′tem, the sun together with all the planets and other bodies that revolve around it.

so′lar wind′ (wind), a cloud of protons, produced by solar storms, moving outward from the sun.

so′lar year′, year (def. 3b).

so·la·ti·um (sō lā′shē əm), *n., pl.* **-ti·a** (-shē ə). **1.** something given in compensation for inconvenience, loss, injury, or the like; recompense. **2.** *Law.* damages awarded to a plaintiff to compensate him for personal suffering or grief arising from an injury. [< L: comfort, relief. See SOLACE]

sold (sōld), *v.* pt. and pp. of **sell.**

Sol·dan (sol′dən, sōl′-, sōd′ən), *n.* **1.** the ruler of a Muslim country. **2.** *Archaic.* a sultan, esp. the sultan of Egypt. [ME < MF < Ar. See SULTAN]

sol·der (sod′ər), *n.* **1.** any of various alloys fused and applied to the joint between metal objects to unite them without heating the objects to the melting point. **2.** anything that joins or unites. —*v.t.* **3.** to join with solder. **4.** to join closely and intimately. **5.** to mend; repair; patch up. —*v.i.* **6.** to unite things with solder. **7.** to become soldered or united; grow together. [ME *sondur* < OF *soldure* < *sold(er)* (to) solder < L *solidāre* to make solid = *solid(us)* SOLID + *-āre* inf. suffix] —**sol′der·a·ble,** *adj.* —**sol′der·er,** *n.* —**sol′der·less,** *adj.*

sol′dering i′ron, an instrument for melting and applying solder.

sol·dier (sōl′jər), *n.* **1.** a person who serves in an army. **2.** an enlisted man in the army. **3.** a man of military skill or experience. **4.** a person who serves in any cause: *a soldier of the Lord.* **5.** *Entomol.* an ant or termite with powerful jaws or other device for protection. —*v.i.* **6.** to act or serve as a soldier. **7.** *Slang.* to loaf while pretending to work. [ME *souldiour* < OF = *soulde* pay (< L *solidus;* see SOL[2]) + *-ier* -IER]

sol·dier·ly (sōl′jər lē) *adj.* of, like, or befitting a soldier. —**sol′dier·li·ness,** *n.*

sol′dier of for′tune, 1. a military adventurer ready to serve anywhere for pay or for pleasure. **2.** a courageous person who seeks adventurous exploits.

Sol′dier's Med′al, a medal awarded to any member of the Army of the United States, or of any military organization serving with it, who distinguishes himself by heroism not involving conflict with an enemy.

sol·dier·y (sōl′jə rē) *n., pl.* **-dier·ies** for 2. **1.** soldiers collectively. **2.** a body of soldiers. **3.** military training or skill.

sol·do (sol′dō; *It.* sôl′dô) *n., pl.* **-di** (-dē). a former copper coin of Italy, the twentieth part of a lira. [< It < L *solid(um);* see SOL[2]]

sole[1] (sōl), *adj.* **1.** being the only one or ones; only: *the sole living relative.* **2.** being the only one of the kind; unique; unsurpassed. **3.** belonging or pertaining to one individual or group to the exclusion of all others; exclusive: *He has the sole right to the estate.* **4.** *Chiefly Law.* unmarried. [< L *sōlus* alone; r. ME *soule* alone < OF *sol* < L *sōl(us)*] —**sole′ness,** *n.* —**Syn. 1.** solitary. **3.** individual.

sole[2] (sōl), *n., v.,* **soled, sol·ing.** —*n.* **1.** the bottom or undersurface of the foot. **2.** the corresponding underpart of a shoe, boot, or the like, or this part exclusive of the heel. **3.** the bottom, undersurface, or lower part of anything. **4.** *Golf.* the part of the head of the club that touches the ground. —*v.t.* **5.** to furnish with a sole, as a shoe. **6.** *Golf.* to place the sole of (a club) on the ground, as in preparation for a stroke. [ME < OE < VL **sol(a),* for L *solea* sandal, sole; cf. Sp *suela*] —**sole′less,** *adj.*

sole[3] (sōl), *n., pl.* (*esp. collectively*) **sole,** (*esp. referring to two or more kinds or species*) **soles. 1.** a European flatfish, *Solea solea,* used for food. **2.** any other flatfish of the families *Soleidae, Achiridae,* and *Cynoglossidae,* having a hooklike snout. [ME < MF < VL **sola* (see SOLE[2]), so called from the flat shape of the fish; cf. Sp *suela,* It *soglia,* Pg *solha*]

sol·e·cism (sol′i siz′əm), *n.* **1.** a substandard or ungrammatical usage. **2.** a breach of good manners or etiquette. **3.** any error, impropriety, or inconsistency. [< L *soloecism(us)* < Gk *soloikismós* = *sóloik(os)* (*Sólo(i)* a city in Cilicia where incorrect Greek was spoken + *-ikos* -IC) + *-ismos* -ISM] —**sol′e·cist,** *n.* —**sol′e·cis′tic, sol′e·cis′ti·cal,** *adj.* —**sol′e·cis′ti·cal·ly,** *adv.*

sole·ly (sōl′lē), *adv.* **1.** as the only one or ones: *solely responsible.* **2.** exclusively or only: *plants found solely in the tropics.* **3.** merely.

sol·emn (sol′əm), *adj.* **1.** grave, sober, or mirthless, as a person, the face, mood, etc. **2.** gravely or somberly impressive. **3.** serious or earnest: *solemn assurances.* **4.** characterized by dignified or serious formality, as proceedings; of a formal or ceremonious character: *a solemn occasion.* **5.** made in due legal or other express form. **6.** marked or observed with religious rites; having a religious character: *a solemn holy day.* **7.** uttered, prescribed, or made according to religious forms. [ME *solempne* < LL *sōlennis, sōlempnis,* L *sōlemnis* consecrated, holy] —**sol′emn·ly,** *adv.* —**sol′emn·ness,** *n.* —**Syn. 1.** unsmiling, serious. See **grave**[2]. **2.** awe-inspiring, august. **6.** reverential, devotional, sacred.

sol·em·nise (sol′əm nīz′), *v.t., v.i.,* **-nised, -nis·ing.** *Chiefly Brit.* solemnize. —**sol′em·ni·sa′tion,** *n.* —**sol′em·nis′er,** *n.*

so·lem·ni·ty (sə lem′ni tē), *n., pl.* **-ties. 1.** the state or character of being solemn; earnestness. **2.** observance of rites or ceremonies, esp. a formal, solemn, ecclesiastical observance, as of a feast day. [ME *solempnete* < OF < L *sollemnitāt-* (s. of *sollemnitās*) = *sōlemn(is)* SOLEMN + *-itāt-* -ITY]

sol·em·nize (sol′əm nīz′), *v.,* **-nized, -niz·ing.** —*v.t.* **1.** to observe or commemorate with rites or ceremonies. **2.** to hold or perform (ceremonies, rites etc.) in due manner. **3.** to perform the ceremony of (marriage). **4.** to go through with ceremony or formality. **5.** to render solemn, serious, or grave; dignify. —*v.i.* **6.** to become solemn; conduct oneself with solemnity. Also, *esp. Brit.,* **solemnise.** [ME *solempnise* < ML *solemniz(āre)* = L *sōlemn(is)* SOLEMN + *-izāre* -IZE] —**sol′em·ni·za′tion,** *n.* —**sol′em·niz′er,** *n.*

so·le·no·don (sō lē′nə don′, -len′ə-), *n.* an insectivore of the family *Solenodontidae,* resembling a large shrew and having an elongate snout and a hairless, scaly tail. [< NL = *sōlēn* (L: razor clam < Gk *sōlḗn* channel, pipe, syringe, etc.) + Gk *odṓn* tooth]

Solenodon,
Solenodon paradoxus
(Total length about 2 ft.; tail 10 in.)

so·le·noid (sō′lə noid′), *n. Elect.* an electric conductor wound as a helix with small pitch, or as two or more coaxial helices, so that current through the conductor establishes a magnetic field within the helix. [< F *solénoïde* < Gk *sōlḗn* pipe, channel; see -OID] —**so′le·noi′dal,** *adj.*

So·lent (sō′lənt), *n.* **the,** a channel between the Isle of Wight and the mainland of S England. 2–5 mi. wide.

sol-fa (sōl′fä′, sol′-; sōl′fä′, sol′-), *n., v.,* **-faed, -fa·ing.** —*n.* **1.** *Music.* the set of syllables, *do, re, mi, fa, sol, la,* and *ti,* sung to the respective tones of the scale. **2.** the system of singing tones to these syllables. —*v.t.* **3.** to sing to the sol-fa syllables, as a tune. [see GAMUT] —**sol′-fa′ist,** *n.*

sol·fa·ta·ra (sōl′fə tär′ə, sol′-), *n.* a volcanic vent or area that gives off only sulfurous gases, steam, and the like. [< It (Neapolitan) *solfatara* < *solf(o)* < L *sulfur;* see SULFUR] —**sol′fa·ta′ric,** *adj.*

sol·fège (sol fezh′), *n. Music.* solfeggio. [< F < It]

sol·feg·gio (sol fej′ō, -fej′ē ō′), *n., pl.* **-feg·gi** (-fej′ē), **-feg·gios.** *Music.* **1.** a vocal exercise in which the sol-fa syllables are used. **2.** the use of the sol-fa syllables; solmization. [< It < *solfeggi(are)* = *solf(a)* GAMUT + *-eggiare* v. suffix]

Sol·fe·ri·no (sôl′fe rē′nô), *n.* a village in SE Lombardy, in N Italy: battle 1859. 1810 (1961).

soli-[1], a learned borrowing from Latin meaning "alone," "solitary," used in the formation of compound words: *solipsism.* [< L, comb. form of *sōlus.* See SOLE[1]]

soli-[2], a learned borrowing from Latin meaning "sun," used in the formation of compound words. [comb. form repr. L *sōl* sun + -I-]

so·lic·it (sə lis′it) *v.t.* **1.** to seek for by entreaty, earnest or respectful request, formal application, etc. **2.** to entreat or petition for something or for someone to do something; urge; importune. **3.** to seek to influence or incite to action, esp. unlawful or wrong action. **4.** to accost or lure (someone) with immoral intentions, as by or on behalf of a prostitute. —*v.i.* **5.** to make a petition or request, as for something desired. **6.** to solicit orders or trade, as for a business house. **7.** to accost someone with immoral intentions, esp. as a prostitute. [ME *solicit(en)* < MF *solliciter* < L *sollicitāre* to excite, agitate < *sollicitus* troubled (*soll(us)* whole +

citus, ptp. of *ciēre* to arouse)] **—Syn. 2.** beseech, beg, sue. **3.** excite, arouse, provoke.

so·lic·i·ta·tion (sə lis′i tā′shən), *n.* **1.** the act of soliciting. **2.** entreaty, urging, or importunity; a petition or request. **3.** enticement or allurement. [< L *sollicitātiōn-* (s. of *sollicitātiō*) = *sollicitāt(us)* (ptp. of *sollicitāre;* see SOLICIT, -ATE[1]) + *-iōn-* -ION]

so·lic·i·tor (sə lis′i tər), *n.* **1.** a person who solicits. **2.** a person whose business it is to solicit business, trade, etc. **3.** *U.S.* an officer having charge of the legal business of a city, town, etc. **4.** (in England and Wales) a member of that branch of the legal profession whose services consist of advising clients, representing them before the lower courts, and preparing cases for barristers to try in the higher courts. Cf. **barrister** (def. 1). [ME *solicitour* < MF *soliciteur*] **—so·lic′i·tor·ship′,** *n.* **—Syn. 4.** lawyer, attorney, counselor.

solic′itor gen′eral, *pl.* **solicitors general. 1.** a law officer who maintains the rights of the state in suits affecting the public interest, next in rank to the attorney general. **2.** *U.S.* **a.** (*caps.*) the law officer of the U.S. government next below the Attorney General having charge of appeals, as to the Supreme Court. **b.** the chief legal officer in some states.

so·lic·i·tous (sə lis′i təs) *adj.* **1.** anxious or concerned (usually fol. by *about, for,* etc. or a clause): *solicitous about a person's health.* **2.** anxiously desirous: *solicitous of the esteem of others.* **3.** eager (usually fol. by an infinitive): *solicitous to please.* **4.** careful or particular. [< L *sollicitus* agitated. See SOLICIT, -OUS] **—so·lic′i·tous·ly,** *adv.* **—so·lic′i·tous·ness,** *n.* **—Ant. 1.** unconcerned, careless.

so·lic·i·tude (sə lis′i to͞od′ -tyo͞od′) *n.* **1.** the state of being solicitous; anxiety or concern. **2. solicitudes,** causes of anxiety or care. **3.** excessive anxiety or assistance. [< L *sollicitūdō* uneasiness of mind < *sollicitus* agitated. See SOLICIT, -TUDE]

sol·id (sol′id) *adj.* **1.** having three dimensions (length, breadth, and thickness), as a geometrical body or figure. **2.** of or pertaining to bodies or figures of three dimensions. **3.** having the interior completely filled up; not hollow. **4.** without openings or breaks: *a solid wall.* **5.** firm, hard, or compact in substance: *solid ground.* **6.** having relative firmness, coherence of particles, or persistence of form, as matter that is not liquid or gaseous. **7.** pertaining to such matter: *Water in a solid state is ice.* **8.** dense, thick, or heavy in nature or appearance. **9.** not flimsy, slight, or light, as buildings, furniture, fabrics, food, etc.; substantial. **10.** of a substantial character; not superficial, trifling, or frivolous: *a solid work of scientific scholarship.* **11.** without separation or division; continuous: *a solid row of buildings.* **12.** whole or entire: *one solid hour.* **13.** consisting entirely of one substance or material: *solid gold.* **14.** uniform in tone or shades, as a color: *a solid blue dress.* **15.** real or genuine: *solid comfort.* **16.** sound or good, as reasons, arguments, etc.: *a solid basis.* **17.** sober-minded; fully reliable or sensible: *a solid citizen.* **18.** financially sound or strong. **19.** cubic: *A solid foot contains 1728 solid inches.* **20.** written without a hyphen, as a compound word. **21.** having the lines not separated by leads, or having few open spaces, as type or printing. **22.** thorough, vigorous, etc. (with emphatic force, often after *good*): *a good solid blow.* **23.** firmly united or consolidated: *a solid combination.* **24.** united or unanimous in opinion, policy, etc. **25.** *Informal.* on a friendly, favorable, or advantageous footing (often prec. by *in*): *He was in solid with her parents.* **26.** *Slang.* excellent, esp. musically. **—***n.* **27.** a body or object having three dimensions (length, breadth, and thickness). **28.** a solid substance or body; a substance exhibiting rigidity. [ME < L *solidus*] **—sol′id·ly,** *adv.* **—sol′id·ness,** *n.* **—Syn. 1.** cubic. **5.** dense. See **firm**[1]. **6.** cohesive, firm. **9.** sound, stable, stout. **11.** unbroken. **18.** solvent, safe. **22.** strong, stout. **—Ant. 1.** flat. **6.** loose. **11, 24.** divided.

sol·i·da·go (sol′i dā′gō), *n., pl.* **-gos.** any plant of the genus *Solidago,* which comprises the goldenrods. [< NL *Solidago* name of genus < ML *solidago* comfrey < L *solidāre* to heal, make whole < *solidus* SOLID]

sol′id an′gle, *Geom.* an angle formed by three or more planes intersecting in a common point or formed at the vertex of a cone.

sol·i·dar·i·ty (sol′i dar′i tē), *n., pl.* **-ties.** union or fellowship arising from common responsibilities and interests, as between members of a group. [< F *solidarité* = *solidaire* SOLIDARY + *-ité* -ITY] **—Syn.** stability, soundness, reliability.

sol·i·dar·y (sol′i der′ē) *adj.* characterized by or involving community of responsibilities and interests. [< F *solidaire* < MF]

sol′id geom′etry, the geometry of solid figures; geometry of three dimensions.

so·lid·i·fy (sə lid′ə fī′), *v.t., v.i.,* **-fied, -fy·ing. 1.** to make or become solid, esp. to change from a liquid or gaseous to a solid form. **2.** to unite firmly or consolidate: *to solidify one's ideas; that public opinion may solidify.* **3.** to form into crystals. [< F *solidifier*] **—so·lid′i·fi′a·ble,** *adj.* **—so·lid′i·fi·ca′tion,** *n.* **—so·lid′i·fi′er,** *n.*

so·lid·i·ty (sə lid′i tē), *n.* **1.** the state, property, or quality of being solid. **2.** firmness and strength; substantialness. **3.** strength of mind, character, finances, etc. [< L *soliditāt-* (s. of *soliditās*) = *solid(us)* SOLID + *-itāt-* -ITY]

Sol′id South′, *U.S.* those Southern states that traditionally support the programs and candidates of the Democratic party.

sol·id-state (sol′id stāt′), *adj.* *Electronics.* designating or pertaining to electronic devices, as transistors or crystals, that can control current without the use of moving parts, heated filaments, or vacuum gaps.

sol·i·dus (sol′i dəs), *n., pl.* **-di** (-dī′). **1.** a gold coin of Rome, introduced by Constantine and continued in the Byzantine Empire; bezant. **2.** (in medieval Europe) a money of account equal to 12 denarii. Cf. **sol**[2]. **3.** virgule. [< LL *solidus (nummus)* a solid (coin), a gold (coin), later, shilling, represented by a long s, whence the shilling mark (virgule)]

so·lil·o·quise (sə lil′ə kwīz′), *v.i., v.t.,* **-quised, -quis·ing.** *Chiefly Brit.* soliloquize. **—so·lil′o·quis′er,** *n.* **—so·lil′o·quis′ing·ly,** *adv.*

so·lil·o·quize (sə lil′ə kwīz′), *v.,* **-quized, -quiz·ing. —***v.i.* **1.** to utter a soliloquy; talk to oneself. **—***v.t.* **2.** to utter in a soliloquy; say to oneself. [SOLILOQU(Y) + -IZE] **—so·lil·o·quist** (sə lil′ə kwist), **so·lil′o·quiz′er,** *n.* **—so·lil′o·quiz′ing·ly,** *adv.*

so·lil·o·quy (sə lil′ə kwē), *n., pl.* **-quies. 1.** the act of talking while or as if alone. **2.** an utterance or discourse by a person who is talking to himself or is disregardful of or oblivious to any hearers present (often used as a device in drama to disclose a character's innermost thoughts). [< LL *sōliloquium* a talking to oneself, soliloquy = *soli-* SOLI-[1] + *loqu(ī)* (to) speak + *-ium;* see -Y[3]]

Sol·i·man I (sol′ə mən). See **Suleiman I.**

So·li·mões (sô′li moins′), *n.* Brazilian name of the Amazon from the Peruvian border to its junction with the Río Negro.

So·ling·en (zō′ling ən), *n.* a city in W West Germany, in the Ruhr region. 172,902 (est. 1964).

sol·ip·sism (sol′ip siz′əm), *n.* *Philos.* the theory that only the self exists or can be proved to exist. [SOLI-[1] + L *ips(e)* self + -ISM] **—sol′ip·sis′mal,** *adj.* **—sol′ip·sist,** *n., adj.* **—sol′ip·sis′tic,** *adj.*

sol·i·taire (sol′i târ′), *n.* **1.** Also called **patience.** any of various games played by one person with one or more regular 52-card packs. **2.** a precious stone, esp. a diamond, set by itself, as in a ring. [< F < L *sōlitārius* SOLITARY]

sol·i·tar·y (sol′i ter′ē), *adj., n., pl.* **-tar·ies. —***adj.* **1.** being alone or without companions; unattended. **2.** living alone: *a solitary man.* **3.** tending to avoid the society of others: *a solitary existence.* **4.** characterized by the absence of companions: *a solitary journey.* **5.** being the only one or ones: *a solitary exception.* **6.** characterized by solitude, as a place; unfrequented, secluded, or lonely. **7.** *Zool.* living habitually alone or in pairs, as certain wasps. Cf. **social** (def. 8). **—***n.* **8.** a person who lives alone or in solitude, as from religious motives. **9.** See **solitary confinement.** [ME < L *sōlitārius* alone, by itself, solitary = *sōlit(ās)* soleness (*sōlus* SOLE[1]; see -ITY) + *-ārius* -ARY] **—sol′i·tar′i·ly,** *adv.* **—sol′i·tar′i·ness,** *n.* **—Syn. 1.** lone. **6.** isolated, retired, sequestered, remote. **8.** hermit, recluse.

sol′itary confine′ment, the confinement of a prisoner in a cell or other place in which he is completely isolated from others.

sol·i·tude (sol′i to͞od′, -tyo͞od′), *n.* **1.** the state of being or living alone; lonely seclusion. **2.** remoteness from habitations, as of a place. **3.** a lonely, unfrequented place. [ME < MF < L *sōlitūdō*] **—sol·i·tu·di·nous** (sol′i to͞od′ənəs, -tyo͞od′-), *adj.*
—Syn. 1. retirement, privacy. SOLITUDE, ISOLATION refer to a state of being or living alone. SOLITUDE emphasizes the quality of being or feeling lonely and deserted: *to live in solitude.* ISOLATION may mean merely a detachment and separation from others: *to be put in isolation with an infectious disease.* **3.** desert, waste, wilderness.

sol·ler·et (sol′ə ret′, sol′ə ret′), *n.* *Armor.* sabaton. [< F, dim. of OF *soller* shoe << LL *subtēl* hollow under the sole of a shoe = *sub-* SUB- + *-tēl* (< *talus* ankle)]

sol·mi·za·tion (sol′mi zā′shən), *n.* *Music.* the act, process, or system of using certain syllables, esp. the sol-fa syllables, to represent the tones of the scale. [< F *solmisation* = *solmis(er)* (*sol* SOL[1] + *mi* MI + *-iser* -IZE) + *-ation* -ATION]

so·lo (sō′lō), *n., pl.* **-los, -li** (-lē), *adj., adv., v.* **—***n.* **1.** a musical composition, or a passage or section in a musical composition, written for performance by one singer or instrumentalist, with or without accompaniment. **2.** any performance by one person. **3.** a flight in an airplane by an unaccompanied pilot. **4.** *Cards.* any of certain games in which one person plays alone against others. **—***adj.* **5.** *Music.* performing or performed alone. **6.** alone; without a companion or partner: *a solo flight.* **—***adv.* **7.** on one's own; alone or unaccompanied. **—***v.i.* **8.** to perform or do a solo. [< It < L *sōlus* alone]

So·lo (sō′lō), *n.* former name of **Surakarta.**

so·lo·ist (sō′lō ist), *n.* a person who performs a solo or solos.

So′lo man′, an early man of the Upper Pleistocene, known from skull fragments found in Java. [named after the *Solo* River, central Java, near which remains were found]

Sol·o·mon (sol′ə mən), *n.* **1.** fl. 10th century B.C., king of Israel (son of David). **2.** an extraordinarily wise man; a sage. **—Sol·o·mon·ic** (sol′ə mon′ik), **Sol·o·mo·ni·an** (sol′ə mō′nē ən), *adj.*

Sol′omon Is′lands, 1. an archipelago in the W Pacific, E of New Guinea; politically divided between Papua New Guinea and the new country of the Solomon Islands: important WW II battles. **2.** an independent country comprising the larger, SE part of this archipelago: a former British protectorate; independent since 1978. 152,000; 11,458 sq. mi. *Cap.:* Honiara (on Guadalcanal).

Sol′omon's seal′, a mystic or talismanic symbol in the form of an interlaced outline of either a five-pointed or six-pointed star.

Solomon's seal

Sol·o·mon's-seal (sol′ə mənz sēl′), *n.* any of several liliaceous plants of the genus *Polygonatum,* having a thick rootstock bearing seallike scars. [trans. of ML *sigillum Solomōnis*]

So·lon (sō′lən), *n.* **1.** c638–c558 B.C., Athenian statesman. **2.** (*often l.c.*) a wise lawgiver. **—So·lo·ni·an** (sō lō′nē ən), **So·lon·ic** (sō lon′ik), *adj.*

so′ long′, *Informal.* good-by: *I said so long and left.*

sol·stice (sol′stis, sōl′-), *n.* **1.** *Astron.* either of the two times a year when the sun is at its greatest distance from the celestial equator: about June 21 and about December 22. Cf. **summer solstice, winter solstice. 2.** either of the two points in the ecliptic farthest from the equator. **3.**

a furthest or culminating point; a turning point. [< ME < OF < L *sōlstitium* = *sol-* sun + *-stitium* (*stat(us)* ptp. of *sistere* to stand still + *-ium;* see -ICE)]

sol·sti·tial (sol stish/əl, sōl-), *adj.* **1.** of or pertaining to a solstice or the solstices. **2.** occurring at or about the time of a solstice. **3.** characteristic of the summer solstice. [< L *sōlstitiālis* = *sōlstiti(um)* SOLSTICE + *-ālis* -AL[1]] —**sol·sti/tial·ly,** *adv.*

sol·u·bil·i·ty (sol/yə bil/i tē), *n.* the quality or property of being capable of being dissolved; relative capability of being dissolved.

sol·u·ble (sol/yə bəl), *adj.* **1.** capable of being dissolved or liquefied. **2.** capable of being solved or explained. —*n.* **3.** something soluble. [ME < LL *solūbilis* = L *solū(ere)* (to) dissolve + *-bilis* -BLE] —**sol/u·ble·ness,** *n.* —**sol/u·bly,** *adv.*

sol/uble glass/. See **sodium silicate.**

so·lus (sō/lōōs; *Eng.* sō/ləs), *adj. Latin.* (referring to a man) alone; by oneself (used formerly in stage directions). Cf. **sola.**

sol·ute (sol/yōōt, sō/lōōt), *n.* **1.** the substance dissolved in a given solution. —*adj.* **2.** *Bot.* not adhering; free. [< L *solūt(us)* loosened, freed (ptp. of *solvere*). See SOLVE]

so·lu·tion (sə lōō/shən), *n.* **1.** the act of solving a problem, question, etc. **2.** the state of being solved. **3.** a particular method of solving a problem. **4.** an explanation or answer. **5.** *Chem.* **a.** the act by which a gas, liquid, or solid is dispersed homogeneously in a gas, liquid, or solid without chemical change. **b.** such a substance, as dissolved sugar or salt in solution. **c.** a homogeneous, molecular mixture of two or more substances. [ME < L *solūtiōn-* (s. of *solūtiō*). See SOLUTE, -ION]

So·lu·tre·an (sə lōō/trē ən), *adj.* of, pertaining to, or characteristic of an Upper Paleolithic culture of Europe, characterized by the manufacture of bifacial blades. [named after *Solutré*, village in central France where the archeological relics were found; see -AN]

solv·a·ble (sol/və bəl), *adj.* **1.** capable of being solved, as a problem. **2.** *Archaic.* soluble (def. 1). —**solv/a·bil/i·ty, solv/a·ble·ness,** *n.*

solv·ate (sol/vāt), *n., v.,* **-at·ed, -at·ing.** *Chem.* —*n.* **1.** a compound formed by the interaction of a solvent and a solute. —*v.t.* **2.** to convert into a solvate. [SOLV(ENT) + -ATE[2]] —**solv·a/tion,** *n.*

Sol/vay proc/ess, a process for manufacturing sodium carbonate by saturating a concentrated solution of sodium chloride with ammonia, passing carbon dioxide through it, and calcining the product, sodium bicarbonate. [named after Ernest *Solvay* (1838–1922), Belgian chemist]

solve (solv), *v.t.,* **solved, solv·ing. 1.** to find the answer or explanation for. **2.** to work out the answer or solution to (a mathematical problem). [ME < L *solvere* to loosen, free, release, dissolve] —**solv/er,** *n.*

sol·ven·cy (sol/vən sē), *n.* a solvent condition; ability to pay all just debts.

sol·vent (sol/vənt), *adj.* **1.** able to pay all just debts. **2.** having the power of dissolving; causing solution. —*n.* **3.** a substance that dissolves another to form a solution. **4.** something that solves or explains. [< L *solvent-* (s. of *solvēns*), prp. of *solv(ere)*. See SOLVE, -ENT] —**sol/vent·ly,** *adv.*

Sol/way Firth/ (sol/wā), an arm of the Irish Sea between SW Scotland and NW England. 38 mi. long.

Sol·y·man I (sol/ə mən). See **Suleiman I.**

Sol·zhe·ni·tsyn (sōl/zhə ni/tsin), *n.* **Al·ex·an·dr** (al/ig zan/dər) **(Isayevich),** born 1918, Russian novelist: Nobel prize 1970; in exile since 1974, first in Switzerland, then in U.S.

so·ma (sō/mə), *n., pl.* **-ma·ta** (-mə tə), **-mas.** *Biol.* the body of an organism as contrasted with its germ cells. [< NL < Gk *sôma* the body, body as opposed to soul]

-soma, a learned borrowing from Greek meaning "body," used esp. in the formation of names of zoological genera: *Schistosoma.* Also, **-some.** [< NL < Gk *sôma*]

So·ma·li (sō mä/lē, sə-), *n., pl.* **-lis,** (*esp. collectively*) **-li. 1.** a member of a Hamitic race showing an admixture of Arab, Negro, and other ancestry, and dwelling in Somaliland and adjacent regions. **2.** the Cushitic language of the Somali.

So·ma·li·a (sō mä/lē ə, -mäl/yə), *n.* an independent republic on the E coast of Africa, formed from the former British Somaliland and the former Italian Somaliland. 3,400,000; 246,198 sq. mi. *Cap.:* Mogadiscio. Official name, **Soma/li Democrat/ic Repub/lic.** —**So·ma/li·an,** *adj., n.*

So·ma·li·land (sō mä/lē land/, sə-), *n.* a coastal region in E Africa, including Djibouti, Somalia, and part of Ethiopia.

Soma/liland Protec/torate, official name of the former **British Somaliland.**

somat-, var. of **somato-** before a vowel: *somatic.*

so·mat·ic (sō mat/ik, sə-), *adj.* **1.** *Anat., Zool.* pertaining to the cavity of the body of an animal or, more especially, to its walls. **2.** *Biol.* pertaining to or affecting the somatic cells, as distinguished from the germ cells. **3.** of the body; bodily; physical. [< Gk *sōmatikós* of, pertaining to the body] —**so·mat/i·cal·ly,** *adv.* —**Syn. 3.** corporal.

somat/ic cell/, *Biol.* **1.** one of the cells that take part in the formation of the body, becoming differentiated into the various tissues, organs, etc. **2.** any cell other than a germ cell.

somato-, a learned borrowing from Greek meaning "body," used in the formation of compound words: *somatoplasm.* Also, *esp. before a vowel,* **somat-.** [< Gk *sōmato-*, comb. form = *sōmat-* (s. of *sôma* body) + *-o-* -o-]

so·ma·tol·o·gy (sō/mə tol/ə jē), *n.* the branch of anthropology that deals with man's physical characteristics. —**so·ma·to·log·ic** (sō/mə tᵊloj/ik, sə mat/ᵊloj/-), **so/ma·to·log/i·cal,** *adj.* —**so/ma·to·log/i·cal·ly,** *adv.* —**so/ma·tol/o·gist,** *n.*

so·ma·to·plasm (sō/mə tə plaz/əm, sə mat/ə-), *n. Biol.* the protoplasm of a somatic cell, esp. as distinguished from germ plasm. —**so/ma·to·plas/tic,** *adj.*

so·ma·to·pleure (sō/mə tə plŏŏr/, sə mat/ə-), *n. Embryol.* the double layer formed by the association of the upper layer of the lateral plate of mesoderm with the overlying ectoderm, functioning in the formation of the body wall and amnion. [alter. of NL *somatopleura*. See SOMATO-, PLEURA] —**so/ma·to·pleu/ral, so/ma·to·pleu/ric,** *adj.*

so·ma·to·type (sō mat/ə tīp/), *n.* the type of human physique. [SOMATO- + -TYPE]

som·ber (som/bər), *adj.* **1.** gloomily dark; shadowy; dimly lighted: *a somber passageway.* **2.** dark and dull, as color, or as things in respect to color: *a somber dress.* **3.** gloomy, depressing, or dismal: *a somber mood.* **4.** extremely serious; grave. Also, *esp. Brit.,* **som/bre.** [< F *sombre* perh. << L *umbra* shade] —**som/ber·ly;** *esp. Brit.,* **som/bre·ly,** *adv.* —**som/ber·ness;** *esp. Brit.,* **som/bre·ness,** *n.* —**Syn. 1.** dusky, murky, sunless, dismal. **3.** melancholy. —**Ant. 1.** bright. **3.** cheerful.

som·bre·ro (som brâr/ō; *Sp.* sôm bre/rô), *n., pl.* **-bre·ros** (-brâr/ōz; *Sp.* -bre/rôs). a man's broad-brimmed hat, usually tall-crowned, worn in Spain and Mexico. [< Sp < *sombra* shade] —**som·bre/roed,** *adj.*

Sombrero

some (sum; *unstressed* səm), *adj.* **1.** being an undetermined or unspecified one: *Some person may object.* **2.** (used with plural nouns) certain: *Some days I stay home.* **3.** of a certain unspecified number, amount, degree, etc.: *to some extent.* **4.** unspecified but considerable in number, amount, degree, etc.: *We talked for some time. He was here some weeks* **5.** *Informal.* of considerable worth or consequence. —*pron.* **6.** certain persons, individuals, instances, etc., not specified. **7.** an unspecified number, amount, etc., as distinguished from the rest or in addition: *a thousand dollars and then some.* —*adv.* **8.** (used with numerals and with words expressing degree, extent, etc.) approximately; about: *Some 300 were present.* **9.** *Informal.* to some degree or extent; somewhat: *I like baseball some.* **10.** *Informal.* to a great degree or extent; considerably: *That's going some!* [ME; OE *sum,* c. MLG, MHG *sum,* Icel *sumr,* Goth *sums*]
—**Syn. 1.** SOME, ANY refer to an appreciable amount or number, and often to a portion of a larger amount. SOME suggests that no specified quantity is meant. ANY suggests that no particular amount is being distinguished from any other or from the remainder; it is any at all (or none). Both SOME and ANY may be used in affirmative or negative questions: *Will you (won't you) have some? Do you (don't you) have any?* But SOME must be used in affirmative statements and answers: *You may have some. Yes, I'd like some.* And ANY may be used only in negative statements and answers: *I don't care for any. No, I can't take any.* —**Ant. 1.** none.

-some[1], a native English suffix formerly used in the formation of adjectives: *quarrelsome; burdensome.* [ME, OE *-sum;* akin to Goth *-sama,* G *-sam;* see SAME]

-some[2], a collective suffix used with numerals: *twosome; threesome.* [ME *-sum,* OE *sum;* special use of SAME (pronoun)]

-some[3], a learned borrowing from Greek meaning "body," used in the formation of compound words: *chromosome.* Also, **-soma.** [< Gk; see SOMA]

some·bod·y (sum/bod/ē, -bud/ē, -bə dē), *pron., n., pl.* **-bod·ies.** —*pron.* **1.** some person. —*n.* **2.** a person of some note or importance. [ME]

some·day (sum/dā/), *adv.* at an indefinite future time. [ME]

some·deal (sum/dēl/), *adv. Archaic.* somewhat. [ME *somdel,* OE *sume dǣle,* dat. of *sum dǣl* some portion]

some·how (sum/hou/), *adv.* in some way not specified, apparent, or known.

some·one (sum/wun/, -wən), *pron.* some person; somebody. [ME] —**Usage.** See **anyone.**

some·place (sum/plās/), *adv.* somewhere. —**Usage.** See **anyplace.**

som·er·sault (sum/ər sôlt/), *n.* **1.** an acrobatic movement in which the body turns end over end, making a complete revolution. **2.** a complete overturn or reversal, as of opinion. —*v.i.* **3.** to perform a somersault. Also, **som·er·set** (sum/ər-set/), **summersault, summerset.** [< OF *sombresaut,* alter. of *sobresault;* cf. OPr *sobre* over (< L *super*), *saut* a leap (< L *saltus*)]

Som·er·set·shire (sum/ər set shēr/, -shər, -sit-), *n.* a county in SW England. 598,556 (1961); 1616 sq. mi. *Co. seat:* Taunton. Also called **Som/er·set.**

Som·er·ville (sum/ər vil/), *n.* a city in E Massachusetts, near Boston. 88,779 (1970).

some·thing (sum/thing), *pron.* **1.** some thing; a certain undetermined or unspecified thing. **2.** an additional amount, as of cents, minutes, etc., that is unknown, unspecified, or forgotten: *Our train gets in at two something.* —*n.* **3.** *Informal.* a thing or person of some value or consequence. —*adv.* **4.** in some degree; to some extent; somewhat. [ME, OE *sum thing*]

some·time (sum/tīm/), *adv.* **1.** at some indefinite or indeterminate point of time. **2.** at an indefinite future time: *Come to see me sometime.* —*adj.* **3.** having been formerly; former. [ME]

some·times (sum/tīmz/), *adv.* **1.** on some occasions; at times; now and then. **2.** *Obs.* once; formerly.

some·way (sum/wā/), *adv.* in some way; somehow. Also, **some/ way/, some/ways/.** [ME]

some·what (sum/hwut/, -hwot/, -hwət, -wut/, -wot/, -wət), *adv.* **1.** in some measure or degree; to some extent: *not angry but somewhat disturbed.* —*n.* **2.** some part, portion, amount, etc. [ME]

some·where (sum/hwâr/, -wâr/), *adv.* **1.** in or at some place not specified, determined, or known: *They live somewhere in Michigan.* **2.** to some place not specified or known: *They went out somewhere.* **3.** at or to some point in amount, degree, etc. (usually fol. by *about, around,* etc.). **4.** at some point of time (usually fol. by *about, between, in,* etc.): *somewhere about 1930; somewhere between 1930 and 1940; somewhere in the 1930's.* —*n.* **5.** an unspecified or uncertain place. [ME] —**Usage.** See **anyplace.**

some·wheres (sum/hwârz/, -wârz/), *adv. Chiefly Dial.* somewhere.

some·whith·er (sum/hwith/ər, -with/-), *adv.* **1.** to some unspecified place; somewhere. **2.** in some direction. [ME]

some·wise (sum/wīz/), *adv. Archaic.* somehow. [ME]

so·mite (sō/mīt), *n.* any of the longitudinal series of segments or parts into which the body of certain animals is divided; metamere. [SOM(A) + -ITE[1]] —**so·mi·tal** (sō/mitᵊl), **so·mit·ic** (sō mit/ik), *adj.*

Somme (sôm), *n.* a river in N France, flowing NW to the English Channel: battles, World War I, 1916, 1918; World War II, 1944. 150 mi. long.
som·me·lier (sum′əl yā′; *Fr.* sô mə lyā′), *n., pl.* **som·me·liers** (sum′əl yāz′; *Fr.* sô mə lyā′). a wine steward, as in a club or restaurant. [< F < MF, m. *sommier* one charged with arranging transportation = *somme* burden (<< LL *sagma* horse load < Gk: covering, pack saddle) + *-ier* -IER]
som·nam·bu·late (som nam′byə lāt′, səm-), *v.i.*, **-lat·ed, -lat·ing.** to walk during sleep, as a somnambulist does. [< L *somn(us)* sleep + *ambulātus*; see AMBULATE] —**som·nam·bu·lance** (som nam′byə ləns, səm-), *n.* —**som·nam′bu·lant,** *adj., n.* —**som·nam′bu·la′tion,** *n.* —**som·nam′bu·la′tor,** *n.*
som·nam·bu·lism (som nam′byə liz′əm, səm-), *n.* the act or habit of walking about, and often performing various other acts, while asleep; sleepwalking. [< NL *somnambulismus.* See SOMNAMBULATE, -ISM] —**som·nam′bu·list,** *n.* —**som·nam′bu·lis′tic,** *adj.*
Som·ni (som′nē), *n.* **Palus.** See **Palus Somni.**
som·nif·er·ous (som nif′ər əs, səm-), *adj.* bringing or inducing sleep, as drugs, influences, etc. [< L *somnifer* sleep-bringing (*somni-* sleep (comb. form of *somnus*) + *-fer*); see -FEROUS] —**som·nif′er·ous·ly,** *adv.*
som·nif·ic (som nif′ik, səm-), *adj.* causing sleep; soporific; somniferous. [< L *somnificus* causing sleep = *somni-* sleep (comb. form of *somnus*) + *-ficus* -FIC]
som·nil·o·quy (som nil′ə kwē, səm-), *n.* the act or habit of talking while asleep. [< L *somni-* (comb. form of *somnus*) sleep + *-loquy;* cf. COLLOQUY, SOLILOQUY] —**som·nil′o·quist,** *n.* —**som·nil′o·quous,** *adj.*
som·no·lent (som′nə lənt), *adj.* **1.** sleepy; drowsy. **2.** tending to cause sleep. [late ME *sompnolent* < OF < L *somnolentus* < *somn(us)* sleep] —**som′no·lence, som′no·len·cy,** *n.* —**som′no·lent·ly,** *adv.* —**Syn. 1.** slumberous. **2.** somniferous, soporific.
Som·nus (som′nəs), *n.* the ancient Roman god of sleep, identified with the Greek god Hypnos.
So·mo·za (sô mô′sä), *n.* **Luis** (lwēs), born 1922, Nicaraguan statesman: president 1956–63.
son (sun), *n.* **1.** a male child or person in relation to his parents. **2.** a male child or person adopted as a son. **3.** any male descendant: *a son of the Aztecs.* **4.** a male person regarded as the product of particular forces or influences: *a son of the soil.* **5.** a familiar term of address to a man or boy from an older person, an ecclesiastic, etc. **6. the Son,** the second person of the Trinity; Jesus Christ. [ME *sone,* OE *sunu;* c. D *zoon,* G *Sohn,* Icel *sunr, sonr,* Goth *sunus,* Lith *sūnùs,* Skt *sūnús*] —**son′less,** *adj.* —**son′like′,** *adj.*
son-, var. of **soni-** before a vowel: *sonance.*
so·nance (sō′nəns), *n.* **1.** the condition or quality of being sonant. **2.** *Obs.* a sound; a tune. —**Syn. 1.** voice, sound, noise.
so·nant (sō′nənt), *adj.* **1.** sounding; having sound. **2.** *Phonet.* voiced (opposed to *surd*). —*n. Phonet.* **3.** a speech sound that by itself makes a syllable or subordinates to itself the other sounds in the syllable; a syllabic sound. **4.** a voiced sound (opposed to *surd*). **5.** (in Indo-European) a sonorant. [< L *sonant-* (s. of *sonāns,* prp. of *sonāre*) sounding. See SON-, -ANT] —**so·nan·tal** (sō nan′tᵊl), **so·nan·tic** (sō nan′tik), *adj.*
so·nar (sō′när), *n.* **1.** a method for detecting and locating objects submerged in water by means of the sound waves they reflect or produce. **2.** the apparatus used in sonar. [*so(und) na(vigation) r(anging)*]
so·na·ta (sə nä′tə), *n. Music.* a composition for one or two instruments, typically in three or four contrasting movements. [< It < L *sonāta,* fem. of *sonātus* (ptp. of *sonāre*). See SONANT, -ATE¹]
sona′ta form′, a musical form comprising an exposition, in which the main themes are stated, a development section, a recapitulation of the material in the exposition, and, usually, a coda.
son·a·ti·na (son′ə tē′nə; *It.* sô′nä tē′nä), *n., pl.* **-nas,** *It.* **-ne** (-ne). *Music.* a short or simplified sonata. [< It, dim. of SONATA]
sonde (sond), *n. Rocketry.* a rocket or balloon used as a probe for observing phenomena in the atmosphere. [< F: plumb line; see SOUND³]
song (sông, song), *n.* **1.** a short metrical composition intended or adapted for singing, esp. one in rhymed stanzas; a lyric; a ballad. **2.** a musical piece adapted for singing or simulating a piece to be sung. **3.** poetical composition; poetry. **4.** the art or act of singing; vocal music. **5.** something that is sung. **6.** the musical or tuneful sounds produced by certain birds, insects, etc. **7. for a song,** at a very low price; as a bargain. [ME, OE; c. G *Sang,* OIcel *söngr,* Goth *saggws*] —**song′like′,** *adj.*
song′ and dance′, *Informal.* an explanatory story or statement, esp. a misleading, evasive, and complicated one.
song·bird (sông′bûrd′, song′-), *n.* **1.** a bird that sings. **2.** any passerine bird of the suborder *Oscines* or *Passeres.*
song′ cy′cle, a group of art songs that are usually all by the same poet and composer and have a unifying subject or idea.
song·fest (sông′fest′, song′-), *n.* an informal, often spontaneous gathering at which people sing folk songs, popular ballads, etc.
song·ful (sông′fəl, song′-), *adj.* abounding in song; melodious. —**song′ful·ly,** *adv.* —**song′ful·ness,** *n.*
Song·ka (song′kä′), *n.* a river in SE Asia, flowing SE from SW China through Indochina to the Gulf of Tonkin. 500 mi. long. Also called **Red River.**
song·less (sông′lis, song′-), *adj.* devoid of song; lacking the power of song, as a bird. —**song′less·ly,** *adv.* —**song′less·ness,** *n.*
Song′ of Sol′omon, The, a book of the Bible. Also called **Song′ of Songs′;** *Douay Bible,* **Canticle of Canticles.**
song·ster (sông′stər, song′-), *n.* **1.** a person who sings; a singer. **2.** a writer of songs or verses. [ME; OE *sangestre* woman singer]
song·stress (sông′stris, song′-), *n.* a female singer, esp. one who specializes in popular songs.
song·writ·er (sông′rī′tər, song′-), *n.* a person who writes the words or music, or both, for popular songs.
soni-, a learned borrowing from Latin meaning "sound," used in the formation of compound words: *soniferous.* Also, *esp. before a vowel,* **son-.** [< L *soni-,* comb. form of *sonus* sound]
son·ic (son′ik), *adj.* **1.** of or pertaining to sound. **2.** noting or pertaining to a speed equal to that of sound in air at the same height above sea level.
son′ic bar′rier. See **sound barrier.**
son′ic boom′, a loud noise caused by the shock wave generated by an object, as an aircraft, moving at supersonic speed.
son′ic depth′ find′er, a sonar instrument used to measure depths under water. Also called **fathometer.**
son·ics (son′iks), *n.* (*construed as sing.*) the branch of science that deals with the practical applications of sound. [see SONIC, -ICS]
so·nif·er·ous (sə nif′ər əs, sō-), *adj.* conveying or producing sound.
son-in-law (sun′in lô′), *n., pl.* **sons-in-law.** the husband of one's daughter. [ME]
son·net (son′it), *n.* **1.** *Pros.* a poem, properly expressive of a single, complete thought, idea, or sentiment, of 14 lines, usually in iambic pentameter, with rhymes arranged according to one of certain definite schemes, being in the strict or Italian form divided into a major group of 8 lines (the octave) followed by a minor group of 6 lines (the sestet), and in a common English form into 3 quatrains followed by a couplet. —*v.i.* **2.** to compose sonnets. —*v.t.* **3.** to celebrate in a sonnet or sonnets. [< It *sonett(o)* < OPr *sonet* = *son* poem (< L *sonus* sound) + *-et* -ET] —**son′net·like′,** *adj.*
son·net·eer (son′i tēr′), *n.* **1.** a composer of sonnets. —*v.i.* **2.** to compose sonnets; sonnetize. [r. earlier *sonnetier* < It *sonnettiere*]
son·net·ise (son′i tīz′), *v.i., v.t.,* **-ised, -is·ing.** *Chiefly Brit.* sonnetize. —**son′net·i·sa′tion,** *n.*
son·net·ize (son′i tīz′), *v.,* **-ized, -iz·ing.** —*v.i.* **1.** to write or compose sonnets. —*v.t.* **2.** to write sonnets on or to. —**son′net·i·za′tion,** *n.*
son′net se′quence, a group of sonnets composed by one poet and having a unifying theme or subject.
son·ny (sun′ē), *n.* little son (often used as a familiar term of address to a boy).
son′ of a bitch′, *pl.* **sons of bitches.** *Slang.* a contemptible or thoroughly disagreeable person; scoundrel.
son′ of a gun′, *pl.* **sons of guns.** *Slang.* **1.** rogue; rascal; scoundrel. **2.** (used as an affectionate greeting, term of address, etc.)
Son′ of God′, Jesus Christ, esp. as the Messiah.
Son′ of Man′, Jesus Christ, esp. as at the Last Judgment. [ME]
So·no·ra (sô nô′rä), *n.* a state in NW Mexico. 783,378 (1960); 70,484 sq. mi. *Cap.:* Hermosillo.
so·no·rant (sə nōr′ənt, -nôr′-, sō-), *Phonet.* —*n.* **1.** a voiced sound less sonorous than a vowel but more sonorous than a stop or fricative, as *l, r, m, n, y, w.* —*adj.* **2.** having the properties of a sonorant. [< L *sonōr-* (s. of *sonor*) sound, noise + -ANT; see SONOROUS]
so·nor·i·ty (sə nōr′i tē, -nor′-), *n., pl.* **-ties.** the condition or quality of being resonant or sonorous. [< ML *sonōritāt-* (s. of *sonōritās*) < LL: melodiousness = L *sonōr(us)* (see SONOROUS) + *-itāt-* -ITY]
so·no·rous (sə nōr′əs, -nôr′-, son′ər əs), *adj.* **1.** emitting or capable of emitting a sound, esp. a deep, resonant sound, as a thing or place. **2.** loud, deep, or resonant, as a sound. **3.** rich and full in sound, as language, verse, etc. **4.** high-flown; grandiloquent. [< L *sonōrus* noisy, sounding = *sonōr-* (s. of *sonor*) sound + *-us* -OUS] —**so·no′rous·ly,** *adv.* —**so·no′rous·ness,** *n.*
-sonous, a combination of **soni-** and **-ous,** as final element of compound words: *dissonous.*
son·ship (sun′ship), *n.* the state, fact, or relation of being a son.
Sons′ of Lib′erty, *Amer. Hist.* any of several patriotic societies that opposed the British colonial rule.
Soo′ Canals′ (so͞o). See **Sault Ste. Marie Canals.**
Soo·chow (so͞o′chou′; *Chin.* so͞o′jō′), *n.* former name of **Wuhsien.**
soo·ey (so͞o′ē), *interj.* (a shout used in calling pigs.) [? alter. of sow²]
soon (so͞on), *adv.* **1.** within a short period after a specified time, event, etc. **2.** before long; in the near future. **3.** promptly or quickly. **4.** readily or willingly: *I would as soon walk as ride.* **5.** *Obs.* immediately; at once; forthwith. **6. had sooner.** See **have** (def. 27). **7. sooner or later,** in the future; eventually. [ME; OE *sōna* at once; c. OHG *sān,* Goth *suns*]
soon·er (so͞o′nər), *n.* a person who settles on government land before it is legally opened to settlers in order to gain the choice of location.
Soon·er (so͞o′nər), *n.* a native or inhabitant of Oklahoma (the **Sooner State**) (used as a nickname).
Soon′er State′, Oklahoma (used as a nickname).
soot (so͝ot, so͞ot), *n.* **1.** a black, carbonaceous substance produced during imperfect combustion of fuel, rising in fine particles and adhering to the sides of the chimney conveying the smoke or carried in the atmosphere. —*v.t.* **2.** to mark, cover, or treat with soot. [ME; OE *sōt;* c. OIcel *sōt*]
sooth (so͞oth), *Archaic.* —*n.* **1.** truth, reality, or fact. —*adj.* **2.** soothing, soft, or sweet. **3.** true or real. [ME; OE *sōth* (n., adj.); c. OS *sōth,* OIcel *sannr,* Goth *sunjis* true, Skt *sat, sant,* based on a root meaning *be,* as in IS] —**sooth′ly,** *adv.*
soothe (so͞oth), *v.,* **soothed, sooth·ing.** —*v.t.* **1.** to tranquilize or calm, as a person, the feelings, etc.; relieve, comfort, or refresh. **2.** to mitigate, assuage, or allay, as pain, sorrow, doubt, etc. —*v.i.* **3.** to exert a soothing influence; bring tranquillity, calm, ease, or comfort. [ME *sothe,* OE *sōth(ian)* = *sōth* SOOTH + *-ian* inf. suffix] —**sooth′er,** *n.* —**sooth′ing·ly,** *adv.* —**sooth′ing·ness,** *n.* —**Syn. 2.** alleviate, soften. —**Ant. 1.** upset.
sooth·fast (so͞oth′fast′, -fäst′), *adj. Archaic.* **1.** true. **2.**

truthful. [ME *sothfast*, OE *sōthfæst*] —**sooth′fast′ly,** *adv.* —**sooth′fast′ness,** *n.*

sooth·say (so͞oth′sā′), *v.i.*, **-said, -say·ing.** to foretell events; predict. [back formation from SOOTHSAYER]

sooth·say·er (so͞oth′sā′ər), *n.* a person who professes to foretell events. [ME *sothseyere, sothseyer*]

soot·y (so͝ot′ē, so͞ot′ē), *adj.*, **soot·i·er, soot·i·est. 1.** covered, blackened, or smirched with soot. **2.** consisting of or resembling soot. [ME] —**soot′i·ly,** *adv.* —**soot′i·ness,** *n.*

soot′y mold′, 1. *Plant Pathol.* a disease of plants, characterized by a black, sooty growth covering the affected parts, caused by any of several fungi. **2.** any fungus, esp. of the family *Capnodiaceae*, causing this disease.

sop (sop), *n.*, *v.*, **sopped, sop·ping.** —*n.* **1.** a piece of solid food, as bread, for dipping in liquid food. **2.** anything thoroughly soaked. **3.** something given to pacify or quiet, or as a bribe. —*v.t.* **4.** to dip or soak in liquid food. **5.** to drench. **6.** to take up (liquid) by absorption (usually fol. by *up*): *to sop up gravy.* —*v.i.* **7.** to become or be soaking wet. **8.** (of a liquid) to soak (usually fol. by *in*). [ME; OE *sopp;* c. OIcel *soppa.* See SUP[2]]

SOP, Standard Operating Procedure. Also, **S.O.P.**

sop., soprano.

soph (sof), *n.* a sophomore. [by shortening]

soph·ism (sof′iz əm), *n.* **1.** a specious argument for displaying ingenuity in reasoning or for deceiving or defeating someone. **2.** any false argument; fallacy. [< L *sophism(a)* < Gk < *sophíz(esthai)* (to) act the sophist, become wise; r. *sophim* < ME < MF *sophime* < L, as above]

soph·ist (sof′ist), *n.* (*often cap.*) *Gk. Hist.* (in ancient Greece) any of a class of professional teachers of philosophy, rhetoric, etc., noted esp. for their ingenuity and speciousness in argumentation. [< L *sophist(a)* < Gk *sophistēs* sage = *sophíz(esthai)* (see SOPHISM) + *-istēs* -IST]

soph·ist·er (sof′i stər), *n.* **1.** a second- or third-year student at a university, esp. a British university. **2.** a specious, unsound, or fallacious reasoner. [ME < MF < L *sophista.* See SOPHIST]

so·phis·tic (sə fis′tik), *adj.* **1.** of the nature of sophistry; fallacious. **2.** characteristic or suggestive of sophistry. **3.** given to the use of sophistry. **4.** of or pertaining to sophists or sophistry. Also, **so·phis′ti·cal.** [< L *sophistic(us)* < Gk *sophistikós* = *sophist(ḗs)* (see SOPHIST) + *-ikos* -IC] —**so·phis′ti·cal·ly,** *adv.* —**so·phis′ti·cal·ness,** *n.*

so·phis·ti·cate (*n.*, *adj.* sə fis′tə kit, -kāt′; *v.* sə fis′tə-kāt′), *n.*, *adj.*, *v.*, **-cat·ed, -cat·ing.** —*n.* **1.** a sophisticated person. —*adj.* **2.** sophisticated. —*v.t.* **3.** to make less natural, simple, or ingenuous; make worldly-wise. **4.** to change (something) so as to deceive. —*v.i.* **5.** to use sophistry; quibble. [< ML *sophisticāt(us)* (ptp. of *sophisticāre*) = L *sophistic(us)* (see SOPHISTIC) + *-ātus* -ATE[1]]

so·phis·ti·cat·ed (sə fis′tə kā′tid), *adj.* **1.** (of a person, ideas, etc.) altered by education, experience, etc., so as to be worldly-wise; not naïve. **2.** pleasing or satisfactory to the tastes of sophisticates: *sophisticated clothes.* **3.** deceptive; misleading. **4.** complex or intricate, as a system, process, piece of machinery, or the like. Also, **sophisticate.** [< ML *sophisticāt(us)*] —**so·phis′ti·cat′ed·ly,** *adv.* —**Syn. 1.** worldly. —**Ant. 1.** naïve.

so·phis·ti·ca·tion (sə fis′tə kā′shən), *n.* **1.** sophisticated character, ideas, etc., as the result of education, worldly experience, etc. **2.** change from the natural character or simplicity, or the resulting condition. **3.** impairment or debasement, as of purity or genuineness. **4.** the use of sophistry, as a quibble or a fallacious argument. [< ML *sophisticātiōn-* (s. of *sophisticātiō*)]

soph·ist·ry (sof′i strē), *n.*, *pl.* **-ries. 1.** a subtle, tricky, superficially plausible, but generally fallacious method of reasoning. **2.** a false argument; sophism. [ME *sophistrie* < MF = *sophistre* SOPHIST + *-ie* -Y[3]]

Soph·o·cles (sof′ə klēz′), *n.* 495?–406? B.C., Greek dramatist. —**Soph·o·cle·an** (sof′ə klē′ən), *adj.*

soph·o·more (sof′ə mōr′, -môr′; sof′mōr, -môr), *n.* a student in his second year at a high school, college, or university. [< Gk *soph(ós)* wise, clever + *-o-* -O- + *mōr(ós)* foolish, silly]

soph·o·mor·ic (sof′ə môr′ik, -mor′-), *adj.* **1.** of or pertaining to a sophomore or sophomores. **2.** intellectually pretentious; immature. Also, **soph′o·mor′i·cal.** —**soph′o·mor′i·cal·ly,** *adv.*

-sophy, an element occurring in loan words from Greek (*philosophy; theosophy*); on this model used with the meaning "science of" in the formation of compound words (*anthroposophy*). [< Gk *-sophia*, comb. form of *sophía* skill, wisdom; see -Y[3]]

so·por (sō′pər), *n.* *Pathol.* a deep, unnatural sleep; lethargy. [< L]

sop·o·rif·er·ous (sop′ə rif′ər əs, sō′pə-), *adj.* bringing sleep; soporific. [< L *sopōrifer* = *sopōr-* (s. of *sopor*) sleep + *-i-* -I- + *-fer;* see -FEROUS] —**sop′o·rif′er·ous·ly,** *adv.* —**sop′o·rif′er·ous·ness,** *n.*

sop·o·rif·ic (sop′ə rif′ik, sō′pə-), *adj.* **1.** causing or tending to cause sleep. **2.** pertaining to or characterized by sleep or sleepiness; sleepy; drowsy. —*n.* **3.** something that causes sleep, as a medicine or drug. [< L *sopor* sleep + -I- + -FIC; cf. F *soporifique*] —**sop′o·rif′i·cal·ly,** *adv.*

sop·ping (sop′ing), *adj.* soaked; drenched: *Her clothes were sopping from the rain.*

sop·py (sop′ē), *adj.*, **-pi·er, -pi·est. 1.** soaked, drenched, or very wet, as ground. **2.** rainy, as weather. **3.** *Brit. Slang.* excessively sentimental; mawkish. —**sop′pi·ness,** *n.*

so·pran·o (sə pran′ō, -prä′nō), *n.*, *pl.* **-pran·os,** *adj.* *Music.* —*n.* **1.** the uppermost part or voice. **2.** the highest singing voice in women and boys. **3.** a part for such a voice. **4.** a singer with such a voice. —*adj.* **5.** of or pertaining to soprano; having the compass of a soprano. [< It: lit., what is above, high = *sopra* (< L *suprā* above) + *-ano* adj. suffix]

sopran′o clef′, *Music.* a sign locating middle C on the bottom line of the staff. See illus. at **C clef.**

so·ra (sōr′ə, sôr′ə), *n.* a small, short-billed rail, *Porzana carolina,* of North America. Also called **so′ra rail′.** [?]

So·ra·ta (sô rä′tə), *n.* **Mount,** a mountain in W Bolivia, in the Andes, near Lake Titicaca: two peaks, Ancohuma, 21,490 ft., and Illampu, 21,276 ft.

sorb (sôrb), *n.* **1.** a European tree, *Sorbus domestica.* **2.** Also called **sorb′ ap′ple.** the fruit of this tree, related to both the apple and the pear. [< L *sorb(um)* serviceberry, or *sorb(us)* service tree] —**sorb′ic,** *adj.*

Sorb (sôrb), *n.* a Wend. [< G *Sorbe*, var. of *Serbe* SERB]

Sorb·i·an (sôr′bē ən), *adj.* **1.** of or pertaining to the Wends or their language. —*n.* **2.** Also called **Wendish.** a Slavic language spoken by an isolated group in SE East Germany. **3.** a Wend.

sor·bose (sôr′bōs), *n.* *Biochem.* a ketohexose, $C_6H_{12}O_6$, used in the synthesis of vitamin C. [SORB + -OSE[2]]

sor·cer·er (sôr′sər ər), *n.* a person who is supposed to exercise supernatural powers through the aid of evil spirits; black magician; wizard. Also, *referring to a woman,* **sor·cer·ess** (sôr′sər is). [< MF *sorcier*, perh. < VL **sortiār(ius)* one who casts lots = L *sort-* (s. of *sors*) lot, fate + *-i-* -I- + *-ārius* -AR[2]]

sor·cer·y (sôr′sə rē), *n.*, *pl.* **-cer·ies.** the art, practices, or spells of a person who is supposed to exercise supernatural powers through the aid of evil spirits; black magic; witchery. [ME *sorcerie* < MF; see SORCERER, -Y[3]] —**sor′cer·ous,** *adj.* —**sor′cer·ous·ly,** *adv.*

Sor·del·lo (sôr del′ō; *It.* sôr del′lô), *n.* 13th-century Italian troubadour.

sor·did (sôr′did), *adj.* **1.** dirty or filthy. **2.** morally ignoble or base; vile: *sordid methods.* **3.** meanly selfish, self-seeking, or mercenary. [< L *sordid(us)* = *sord(ēs)* dirt + *-idus* -ID[4]] —**sor′did·ly,** *adv.* —**sor′did·ness,** *n.* —**Syn. 1.** soiled, unclean, foul. **2.** degraded, depraved. **3.** avaricious, tight, close, stingy. —**Ant. 1.** clean. **2.** honorable. **3.** generous.

sor·di·no (sôr dē′nō; *It.* sôr dē′nô), *n.*, *pl.* **-ni** (-nē). *Music.* mute (def. 8). [< It: a mute < L *surd(us)* deaf + *-īnus* -INE[1]]

sore (sōr, sôr), *adj.*, **sor·er, sor·est,** *n.*, *adv.* —*adj.* **1.** physically painful or sensitive, as a wound, diseased part, etc.: *a sore arm.* **2.** suffering bodily pain from wounds, bruises, etc., as a person: *He is sore from all that exercise.* **3.** suffering mental pain; grieved, distressed, or sorrowful. **4.** causing great mental distress or sorrow. **5.** *Informal.* annoyed; angered. **6.** causing annoyance or irritation: *a sore subject.* —*n.* **7.** a sore spot or place on the body. **8.** a source of grief, distress, irritation, etc. —*adv.* **9.** *Archaic.* sorely. [ME; OE *sār;* c. D *zeer*, OIcel *sārr*, G *sehr*] —**sore′ly,** *adv.* —**sore′ness,** *n.* —**Syn. 1.** tender. **3.** aggrieved, hurt, vexed. **4.** grievous, distressing. **7.** infection, abscess, ulcer, wound.

sore·head (sōr′hed′, sôr′-), *n.* *Informal.* a disgruntled or vindictive person, esp. an unsportsmanlike loser. [prob. < Scot *sorehead* a headache] —**sore′head′ed·ly,** *adv.* —**sore′head′ed·ness,** *n.*

So·rel (sô rel′), *n.* **Georges** (zhôrzh), 1847–1922, French engineer and social philosopher.

sore′ throat′, *Pathol.* a painful or sensitive condition of the throat exaggerated by swallowing or talking, usually caused by bacteria or viruses.

sor·gho (sôr′gō), *n.*, *pl.* **-ghos.** sorgo.

sor·ghum (sôr′gəm), *n.* **1.** a cereal grass, *Sorghum vulgare,* having broad, cornlike leaves and a tall, pithy stem bearing the grain in a dense terminal cluster. **2.** the syrup made from sorgo. [< NL < It *sorgo* SORGO]

sor·go (sôr′gō), *n.*, *pl.* **-gos.** any of several varieties of sorghum grown chiefly for the sweet juice yielded by the stems, used in making sugar and syrup and also for fodder. Also, **sorgho.** [< It, perh. < VL **Syricum (grano)* Syrian (grain), neut. of L *Syricus* of Syria]

so·ri (sōr′ī, sôr′ī), *n.* pl. of **sorus.**

sor·i·cine (sôr′i sin′, -sin, sor′i-), *adj.* *Zool.* of or resembling the shrews. [< L *sōricīn(us)* = *sōric-* (s. of *sōrex*) + *-īnus* -INE[1]]

so·ri·tes (sō rī′tēz, sô-), *n.* *Logic.* a form of argument having several premises and one conclusion, capable of being resolved into a chain of syllogisms, the conclusion of each of which is a premise of the next. [< L < Gk *sōreítēs*, lit., heaped, piled up < *sōr(ós)* a heap] —**so·rit·i·cal** (sō rit′i kəl, sô-), **so·rit′ic,** *adj.*

sorn (sôrn), *v.i.* *Scot.* to impose on another's hospitality; obtain free food, drink, or lodging by making demands on the friendship or generosity of others. [?] —**sorn′er,** *n.*

So·ro·kin (sə rō′kin, sô-; *Russ.* sô′ro kin), *n.* **Pi·ti·rim A·le·xan·dro·vitch** (pi ti rēm′ al′ig zan′drə vich; *Russ.* pi ti rem′ ä′le ksän′dro vich), 1889–1968, U.S. sociologist, born in Russia.

so·ror·ate (sōr′ə rāt′, sôr′-), *n.* subsequent or concurrent marriage with a wife's sister. [< L *sorōr-* (s. of *soror*) sister + -ATE[3]]

so·ror·i·cide (sə rôr′i sīd′, -ror′-), *n.* **1.** a person who kills his or her sister. **2.** the act of killing one's own sister. [< L *sorōricīd(a)* one who kills his sister, *-cīd(ium)* the act of killing one's sister = *sorōr-* (s. of *soror*) sister + *-cīda, -cīdium,* -CIDE] —**so·ror′i·cid′al,** *adj.*

so·ror·i·ty (sə rôr′i tē, -ror′-), *n.*, *pl.* **-ties.** a society or club of women or girls, esp. in a college. [< ML *sorōritās* = L *sorōr-* (s. of *soror*) sister + *-itās* -ITY]

soror′ity house′, a house occupied by a college or university sorority.

so·ro·sis[1] (sə rō′sis), *n.*, *pl.* **-ses** (-sēz). *Bot.* a fleshy multiple fruit composed of many flowers, seed vessels, and receptacles consolidated, as in the pineapple and mulberry. [< NL < Gk *sōrós* heap + NL *-ōsis* -OSIS]

so·ro·sis[2] (sə rō′sis), *n.*, *pl.* **-ses** (-sēz), **-sis·es.** a women's society or club. [after the name of a club established in 1869; based on L *soror* sister]

sorp·tion (sôrp′shən), *n.* *Physical Chem.* the binding of one substance by another by any mechanism, such as absorption, adsorption, or persorption. [back formation from ABSORPTION, ADSORPTION, etc.]

sor·rel[1] (sôr′əl, sor′-), *n.* **1.** light reddish-brown. **2.** a horse of this color, often with a light-colored mane and tail. [ME *sorrelle* < OF *sorel* = *sor* brown (< Gmc) + *-el* dim. suffix]

sor·rel[2] (sôr′əl, sor′-), *n.* **1.** any of various plants of the genus *Rumex,* having succulent acid leaves used in salads, sauces, etc. **2.** any of various sour-juiced plants of the genus *Oxalis.* Cf. **wood sorrel. 3.** any of various similar plants. [ME *sorell* < OF *surele* = *sur* sour (+ *-el* dim. suffix) < Gmc; akin to OHG *sūr* sour]

sor′rel tree′, a North American, ericaceous tree, *Oxydendrum arboreum,* having leaves with an acid flavor and racemes of white flowers. Also called **sourwood.**

Sor·ren·to (sə ren′tō; *It.* sôr ren′tô), *n.* a seaport in SW

Italy, on the Bay of Naples: resort; cathedral; ancient ruins. 11,837 (1961). —**Sor·ren·tine** (sôr′ən tēn′, sə ren′tēn), *adj.*

sor·row (sor′ō, sôr′ō), *n.* **1.** distress caused by loss, affliction, disappointment, etc.; grief, sadness, or regret. **2.** a cause or occasion of grief or regret, as an affliction, a misfortune, or trouble. **3.** the expression of grief, sadness, disappointment, or the like: *muffled sorrow.* —*v.i.* **4.** to feel sorrow; grieve. [ME; OE *sorg;* c. G *Sorge,* D *zorg,* OIcel *sorg,* Goth *saurga*] —**sor′row·er,** *n.* —**sor′row·less,** *adj.* —**Syn. 2.** adversity. **4.** mourn, lament. —**Ant. 1.** joy.

sor·row·ful (sor′ə fəl, sôr′-), *adj.* **1.** full of or feeling sorrow; grieved; sad. **2.** expressing sorrow; mournful; plaintive: *a sorrowful song.* **3.** involving or causing sorrow; distressing: *a sorrowful event.* [ME *sorowful,* OE *sorgful*] —**sor′row·ful·ly,** *adv.* —**sor′row·ful·ness,** *n.* —**Syn. 1.** unhappy, grieving. **2.** melancholy. **3.** dismal, doleful. —**Ant. 1.** happy.

sor·ry (sor′ē, sôr′ē), *adj.*, **-ri·er, -ri·est. 1.** feeling regret, compunction, sympathy, pity, etc. **2.** of a deplorable, pitiable, or miserable kind: *to come to a sorry end.* **3.** sorrowful, grieved, or sad. **4.** associated with sorrow; suggestive of grief or suffering; melancholy; dismal. **5.** wretched, poor, useless, or pitiful: *a sorry horse.* **6.** (used interjectionally as a conventional apology or expression of regret). [ME; OE *sārig;* c. LG *sērig,* OHG *sērag.* See SORE, -Y[1]] —**sor′ri·ly,** *adv.* —**sor′ri·ness,** *n.* —**Syn. 1.** regretful, sympathetic. **3.** unhappy, melancholy. **4.** grievous, painful. **5.** contemptible, worthless, shabby. —**Ant. 1.** happy.

sort (sôrt), *n.* **1.** a particular kind, species, variety, class, or group, distinguished by a common character or nature. **2.** character, quality, or nature: *girls of a nice sort.* **3.** an example of something undistinguished or barely adequate: *a sort of poet.* **4.** manner, fashion, or way: *We spoke in this sort for several minutes.* **5.** *Print.* any of the individual characters making up a font of type. **6. of sorts, a.** of a mediocre or poor kind: *a tennis player of sorts.* **b.** of one sort or another; of an indefinite kind. Also, **of a sort. 7. out of sorts, a.** in a bad temper; irritable. **b.** *Print.* short of certain characters of a font of type. **8. sort of,** *Informal.* in a way; quite; rather. —*v.t.* **9.** to arrange according to kind or class; separate into sorts; classify: *to sort socks; to sort eggs by grade.* **10.** to separate or take from other sorts or from others (often fol. by *out*): *to sort out the children's socks.* **11.** to assign to a particular class, group, or place (often fol. by *with, together,* etc.): *to sort people together indiscriminately.* —*v.i.* **12.** *Brit. Dial.* to associate, mingle, or be friendly. **13.** *Archaic.* to suit; agree; fit. [ME < MF < ML *sort-* (s. of *sors*) kind, in L: chance, lot] —**sort′a·ble,** *adj.* —**sort′a·bly,** *adv.* —**sort′er,** *n.* —**Syn. 1.** family, order, race, type. **4.** method, style. **9.** order, class, assort. —**Usage. 8.** See **kind**[2].

sor·tie (sôr′tē), *n., v.,* **-tied, -tie·ing.** —*n.* **1.** a rapid movement of troops from a besieged place to attack the besiegers. **2.** a body of troops involved in such a movement. **3.** the flying of an airplane on a combat mission. —*v.i.* **4.** to go on a sortie; sally forth. [< F, n. use of fem. ptp. of *sortir* to go out]

sor·ti·lege (sôr′tᵊlij), *n.* **1.** the drawing of lots for divination; divination by lot. **2.** sorcery; magic. [ME < ML *sortileg(ium)* < L *sortileg(us)* prophetic = *sorti-* (s. of *sors*) lot, chance + *-i-* -I- + *-legus* (< *legere* to read, choose out)]

so·rus (sôr′əs, sōr′-), *n., pl.* **so·ri** (sôr′ī, sōr′ī). *Bot.* one of the clusters of sporangia on the back of the fronds of ferns. [< NL < Gk *sōrós* heap]

SOS, 1. the letters represented by the radio telegraphic signal (··· – – – ···) used, esp. by ships in distress, as an internationally recognized call for help. **2.** any call for help.

Sos·no·wiec (sôs nô′vyets), *n.* a city in S Poland. 137,900 (est. 1964).

so-so (sō′sō′), *adj.* **1.** indifferent; neither very good nor very bad. —*adv.* **2.** in an indifferent or passable manner; indifferently; tolerably.

sos·te·nu·to (sos′tə no͞o′tō, sō′stə-; *It.* sôs′te no͞o′tô), *adj., n., pl.* **-tos,** *It.* **-ti** (-tē). *Music.* —*adj.* **1.** sustained or prolonged in the time value of the tones. —*n.* **2.** a movement or passage played in this manner. [< It, ptp. of *sostenere* to SUSTAIN]

sot (sot), *n.* a person who is habitually drunk; a chronic drunkard. [ME < OE *sott* fool]

So·ter (sō′tər), *n.* **Saint,** pope A.D. 166?–175?.

so·te·ri·ol·o·gy (sə tēr′ē ol′ə jē), *n. Theol.* the doctrine of salvation through Jesus Christ. [< Gk *sōtērí(a)* salvation, deliverance (*sōtēr-* (s. of *sōtḗr*) deliverer + *-ia* n. suffix) + -o- + -LOGY] —**so·te·re·o·log·ic** (sə tēr′ē ə loj′ik), **so·te′re·o·log′i·cal,** *adj.*

Soth·ern (suth′ərn), n. **E(dward) H(ugh),** 1859–1933, U.S. actor, born in England (husband of Julia Marlowe).

So·thic (sō′thik, soth′ik), *adj.* of Sirius, the Dog Star. [< Gk *Sōth(is)* Egyptian name for Sirius + -IC]

So′thic cy′cle, a period of 1460 Sothic years. Also called **So′thic pe′riod.**

So′thic year′, the fixed year of the ancient Egyptians, equivalent to 365¼ days.

so·tol (sō′tōl, sō tōl′), *n.* any liliaceous plant of the genus *Dasylirion,* of the southwestern U.S. and northern Mexico, resembling the yucca. [< MexSp < Nahuatl *tzotolli*]

sot·tish (sot′ish), *adj.* **1.** stupefied with or as with drink; drunken. **2.** given to excessive drinking. **3.** pertaining to or befitting a sot. —**sot′tish·ly,** *adv.* —**sot′tish·ness,** *n.*

sot·to vo·ce (sot′ō vō′chē; *It.* sôt′tô vô′che), in a low, soft voice so as not to be overheard. [< It: lit., under (the) voice]

sou (so͞o), *n.* **1.** (formerly) either of two bronze coins of France, equal to 5 centimes and 10 centimes. **2.** sol[2]. [< F< MF < OF *sol* SOL[2]]

sou., 1. south. **2.** southern.

sou·a′ri nut′ (so͞o är′ē), the large, edible, oily nut of a tall tree, *Caryocar nuciferum,* of tropical South America. Also called **butternut.** [< F *saouari* < Galibi *sawarra*]

sou·bise (so͞o bēz′), *n.* a brown or white sauce containing onions. Also called **soubise′ sauce′.** [< F, named after Prince Charles *Soubise* (1715–87), marshal of France]

sou·brette (so͞o bret′), *n.* **1.** a maidservant or lady's maid in a play, opera, or the like, esp. one displaying coquetry, pertness, and a tendency to engage in intrigue. **2.** an actress playing such a role. **3.** any lively or pert young woman. [< F: lady's maid < Pr *soubret(o)* < *soubret* affected < OPr *sobrar* < L *superāre* to be above] —**sou·bret′tish,** *adj.*

sou·bri·quet (so͞o′brə kā′, -ket′, so͞o′brə kā′, -ket′), *n.* sobriquet.

sou·car (sou kär′), *n.* a Hindu banker. Also, **sowcar.** [< Urdu *sāhūkār* great merchant]

Sou·chong (so͞o′shong′, -chong′), *n.* a variety of black tea grown in India and Ceylon. [< Chin (Cantonese) *sin-chung* small sort]

Sou·dan (so͞o däN′), *n.* French name of **Sudan.**

Sou·da·nese (so͞od′ᵊnēz′, -ᵊnēs′), *n., pl.* **-nese,** *adj.* Sudanese.

souf·fle (so͞o′fəl), *n. Pathol.* a murmuring or blowing sound. [< F; see SOUFFLÉ]

souf·flé (so͞o flā′, so͞o′flā), *adj.* **1.** Also, **souf·fléed′,** puffed up; made light, as by whipping or beating and cooking. —*n.* **2.** a light baked dish made fluffy with beaten egg whites combined with egg yolks, white sauce, and fish, cheese, or other ingredients. **3.** a similar dish made with fruit juices, chocolate, vanilla, or the like, and served as dessert. [< F, n. use of ptp. of *souffler* to blow, puff < L *sufflāre* to breathe on, blow on]

Sou·frière (so͞o fRYeR′), *n.* **1.** a volcano in the British West Indies, on St. Vincent island. 4048 ft. **2.** a volcano in the French West Indies, on Guadeloupe. 4869 ft.

sough (sou, suf), *v.i.* **1.** to make a rushing, rustling, or murmuring sound. —*n.* **2.** a sighing, rustling, or murmuring sound. [ME *swoghe,* OE *swōg(an)* (to) make a noise; c. OS *swōgan,* OE *swēgan,* Goth *-swōgjan*] —**sough′ful·ly,** *adv.* —**sough′less,** *adj.*

sought (sôt), *v.* pt. and pp. of **seek.**

soul (sōl), *n.* **1.** the principle of life, feeling, thought, and action in man, regarded as a distinct entity separate from the body; the spiritual part of man as distinct from the physical part. **2.** the spiritual part of man regarded in its moral aspect, or as capable of surviving death and subject to happiness or misery in a life to come. **3.** a disembodied spirit of a deceased person. **4.** the emotional part of man's nature; the seat of the feelings or sentiments. **5.** a human being; person. **6.** the animating principle; the essential element or part of something. **7.** the embodiment of some quality: *He was the very soul of tact.* **8.** (*cap.*) *Christian Science.* God. —*adj. Slang.* **9.** of or pertaining to Negroes; characteristic of or associated with Negroes: *soul music.* **10.** familiar with or sympathetic to Negroes, their culture, feelings, etc. [ME; OE *sawl;* c. D *ziel,* G *Seele,* OIcel *sāl,* Goth *saiwala,* ult. related to SEA, fancied habitation of the soul] —**soul′like′,** *adj.* —**Syn. 1.** spirit. **4.** heart. **6.** essence, core, heart.

soul·ful (sōl′fəl), *adj.* of or expressive of deep feeling or emotion: *soulful eyes.* —**soul′ful·ly,** *adv.* —**soul′ful·ness,** *n.*

soul′ kiss′, an open-mouthed kiss in which the tongue of one partner is manipulated in the mouth of the other. Also called **French kiss.**

soul·less (sōl′lis), *adj.* **1.** without a soul. **2.** lacking in nobility of soul, as persons; without spirit or courage. —**soul′less·ly,** *adv.* —**soul′ness·ness,** *n.*

soul′ mate′, a person with whom one has a strong affinity, esp. a person of the opposite sex.

soul-search·ing (sōl′sûr′ching), *n.* the act or process of close and penetrating analysis of oneself, to determine one's true motives and sentiments.

Soult (so͞olt), *n.* **Ni·co·las Jean de Dieu** (nē kô lä′ zhäN də dyœ), (*Duke of Dalmatia*), 1769–1851, French marshal.

sou mar·qué (so͞o′ mär kā′ *or, for 2,* -kē′; *Fr.* so͞o MAR-kā′), *n., pl.* **sous mar·qués** (so͞o′ mär kā′ *or, for 2,* -kē′; *Fr.* so͞o MAR kā′). **1.** a billon coin of France, issued in the 18th century for circulation in the colonies. **2.** something of little or no value. Also, **sou mar·kee** (so͞o′ mär′kē). [< F: marked sou]

sound[1] (sound), *n.* **1.** the sensation produced by stimulation of the organs of hearing by vibrations transmitted through the air or another medium. **2.** mechanical vibrations transmitted through an elastic medium, traveling in air at a speed of approximately 1100 feet per second at sea level. **3.** the particular auditory effect produced by a given cause: *the sound of music.* **4.** any auditory effect or audible vibrational disturbance: *all kinds of sounds.* **5.** *Phonet.* **a.** See **speech sound. b.** the audible result of an utterance or portion of an utterance: *the s-sound in "slight"; the sound of* m *in "mere."* **6.** the auditory effect of sound waves as transmitted or recorded by a particular system of sound reproduction: *the sound of a stereophonic recording.* **7.** the quality of an event, letter, etc., as it affects a person: *This report has a bad sound.* —*v.i.* **8.** to make or emit a sound. **9.** to be heard, as a sound. **10.** to convey a certain impression when heard or read: *to sound strange.* **11.** to give a specific kind of sound: *to sound loud.* **12.** to give the appearance of being: *The report sounds true.* —*v.t.* **13.** to cause to make or emit a sound: *to sound a bell.* **14.** to give forth (a sound): *The oboe sounded an A.* **15.** to announce, order, or direct by or as by a sound: *to sound a warning.* **16.** to utter audibly, pronounce, or express: *to sound each letter.* **17.** to examine by percussion or auscultation: *to sound a patient's chest.* **18. sound off,** *Slang.* **a.** to call out one's name, sequence number, etc. **b.** to complain freely or frankly. **c.** to exaggerate; boast. [(n.) ME *soun* < AF (OF *son*) < L *son(us);* (v.) ME *soun(en)* < OF *sun(er)* < L *sonāre* < *son(us),* as above] —**sound′a·ble,** *adj.* —**Syn. 1.** SOUND, NOISE, TONE refer to something heard. SOUND and NOISE are often used interchangeably for anything perceived by means of hearing. SOUND, however, is more general in application, being used for anything within earshot: *the sound of running water.* NOISE, caused by irregular vibrations, is more properly applied to a loud, discordant, or unpleasant sound: *the noise of shouting.* TONE is applied to a musical sound having a certain quality, resonance, and pitch.

sound[2] (sound), *adj.* **1.** free from injury, damage, defect, disease, etc.; healthy; robust. **2.** financially strong, secure, or reliable. **3.** competent, sensible, or valid: *sound judgment.* **4.** having no defect as to truth, justice, wisdom, or reason:

sound advice. **5.** of substantial or enduring character: *sound moral values.* **6.** following in a systematic pattern without any apparent defect in logic: *sound reasoning.* **7.** having no legal defect: *a sound title to property.* **8.** uninterrupted and untroubled; deep: *sound sleep.* **9.** vigorous, thorough, or severe: *a sound thrashing.* [ME *sund,* OE *(ge)sund;* c. D *gezond,* G *gesund*] —**sound′ly,** *adv.* —**sound′ness,** *n.* —**Syn. 1.** unharmed, whole, hale, unbroken, hardy. **2.** solvent. **4, 6.** valid, rational, logical.

sound[3] (sound), *v.t.* **1.** to measure or try the depth of (water, a deep hole, etc.) by letting down a lead or plummet at the end of a line, or by some equivalent means. **2.** to measure (depth) in such a manner, as at sea. **3.** to examine or test (the bottom, as of a lake, sea, etc.) with a lead that brings up adhering bits of matter. **4.** to examine or investigate; seek to fathom or ascertain: *to sound a person's views.* **5.** to seek to elicit the views or sentiments of (a person) by indirect inquiries, etc. (often fol. by *out*): *Why not sound him out about working for us?* **6.** *Surg.* to examine, as the urinary bladder, with a sound. —*v.i.* **7.** to use the lead and line or some other device for measuring depth, as at sea. **8.** to go down or touch bottom, as a lead. **9.** to plunge downward or dive, as a whale. **10.** to make investigation; seek information, esp. by indirect inquiries. —*n.* **11.** *Surg.* a long, solid, slender instrument for sounding or exploring body cavities or canals. [ME; OE *sund-* channel (in *sundgyrd* sounding pole, lit., channel pole) < Scand; cf. OIcel *sund* channel; c. OE *sund* sea (ult. related to SWIM)]

sound[4] (sound), *n.* **1.** a relatively narrow passage of water between larger bodies of water or between the mainland and an island. **2.** an inlet, arm, or recessed portion of the sea. **3.** the air bladder of a fish. [ME; OE *sund* swimming, channel, sea; see SOUND[3]]

Sound, the (sound), a strait between SW Sweden and Zealand, connecting the Kattegat and the Baltic. 87 mi. long; 3–30 mi. wide. Swedish and Danish, **Öresund.**

sound′ bar′rier, (not in technical use) a hypothetical barrier to flight beyond the speed of sound, so postulated because aircraft undergo an abruptly increasing drag force when traveling near the speed of sound. Also called **sonic barrier, transonic barrier.**

sound·board (sound′bōrd′, -bôrd′), *n.* See **sounding board.**

sound·box (sound′boks′), *n.* a chamber in a musical instrument, as the body of a violin, for increasing the sonority of its tone.

sound′ effect′, any sound, other than music or speech, artificially reproduced to create an effect in a dramatic presentation, as the sound of a storm, a creaking door, etc.

sound·er[1] (soun′dər), *n.* **1.** a person or thing that makes a sound or noise, or sounds something. **2.** *Telegraphy.* an instrument for receiving telegraphic impulses and converting them into sounds. [SOUND[1] + -ER[1]]

sound·er[2] (soun′dər), *n.* a person or thing that sounds depth, as of water. [SOUND[3] + -ER[1]]

sound·ing[1] (soun′ding), *adj.* **1.** emitting or producing a sound or sounds. **2.** resounding or sonorous. **3.** having an imposing sound; high-sounding; pompous. [SOUND[1] + -ING[2]] —**sound′ing·ly,** *adv.* —**sound′ing·ness,** *n.*

sound·ing[2] (soun′ding), *n.* **1.** Often, **soundings.** the act of sounding an area of water or examining the bottom with or as with a lead and line. **2. soundings, a.** an area of water able to be sounded with an ordinary lead and line. **b.** the results or measurement obtained by sounding with a lead and line. [SOUND[3] + -ING[1]]

sound′ing board′, **1.** a thin, resonant plate of wood forming part of a musical instrument, as a piano, that enhances the power and quality of the tone. **2.** a structure over or behind and above a speaker, orchestra, etc., to reflect the sound toward the audience. **3.** a person or group of persons whose reactions reveal the effectiveness of ideas put forth by someone else. Also called **soundboard.**

sound′ing lead′ (led). See under **sounding line.**

sound′ing line′, a line weighted with a lead or plummet **(sounding lead)** and bearing marks to show the length paid out, used for sounding, as at sea.

sound·less[1] (sound′lis), *adj.* without sound; silent; quiet. [SOUND[1] + -LESS] —**sound′less·ly,** *adv.* —**sound′less·ness,** *n.*

sound·less[2] (sound′lis), *adj.* unfathomable; very deep. [SOUND[3] + -LESS] —**sound′less·ly,** *adv.* —**sound′less·ness,** *n.*

sound·proof[1] (sound′pro͞of′), *adj.* impervious to sound. [SOUND[1] + PROOF] —**sound′proof′ing,** *n.*

sound·proof[2] (sound′pro͞of′), *v.t.* to cause to be soundproof. [back formation from *soundproofing*]

sound′ rang′ing, a method for determining the distance between a point and the position of a sound source by measuring the time lapse between the origin of the sound and its arrival at the point.

sound′ spec′trogram, a graphic representation, produced by a sound spectrograph, of the frequency, intensity, duration, and variation with time of the resonance of a sound or series of sounds. Also called **voiceprint.**

sound′ spec′trograph, an electronic device for recording sound spectrograms.

sound′ track′, a sound record on a motion-picture film.

sound′ truck′, a truck carrying a loudspeaker from which speeches, music, etc., are broadcast, as for advertising, campaigning, or the like.

sound′ wave′, *Physics.* a longitudinal wave in an elastic medium, esp. a wave producing an audible sensation.

soup (so͞op), *n.* **1.** a liquid food made by boiling or simmering meat, fish, or vegetables with various added ingredients. **2.** *Informal.* a thick fog. **3.** *Slang.* added power, esp. horsepower. **4.** *Slang.* nitroglycerine. **5. in the soup,** *Slang.* in trouble. —*v.t.* **6. soup up,** *U.S. Slang.* to improve the capacity for speed of (a motor or engine). [< F *soupe* < OF < Gmc; cf. D *sopen* to dunk. See SOP] —**Syn. 1.** broth, potage.

soup-and-fish (so͞op′ən fish′), *n. Informal.* a man's formal evening clothes. [alluding to the early courses of a formal dinner]

soup·çon (so͞op sôN′, so͞op′sôN), *n.* **1.** a slight trace or flavor; suspicion. **2.** a very small amount. [< F: a suspicion < MF *sospecon* < LL *suspectiōn-* (s. of *suspectiō*), r. *suspiciō* SUSPICION]

soup′ kitch′en, a place where food, usually soup, is served, at little or no charge, to the needy.

soup·spoon (so͞op′spo͞on′), *n.* a large spoon, designed for use in eating soup.

soup·y (so͞o′pē), *adj.,* **soup·i·er, soup·i·est. 1.** resembling soup in consistency. **2.** very thick; dense: *a soupy fog.* **3.** overly sentimental; mawkish.

sour (sour, sou′ər), *adj.* **1.** having an acid taste, resembling that of vinegar, lemon juice, etc.; tart. **2.** rendered acid or affected by fermentation; fermented. **3.** producing one of the four basic taste sensations; not bitter, salt, or sweet. **4.** characteristic of something fermented: *a sour smell.* **5.** distasteful or disagreeable; unpleasant. **6.** below standard; poor. **7.** bitter in spirit or temper; cross; peevish. **8.** (of gasoline or the like) contaminated by sulfur compounds. **9.** *Music, Informal.* off-pitch; badly produced: *a sour note.* —*n.* **10.** something that is sour. **11.** a cocktail made of whiskey or gin with lemon or lime juice and sugar. **12.** an acid or an acidic substance used in laundering and bleaching, as to decompose residual soap or bleach. —*v.i.* **13.** to become sour, rancid, mildewed, etc.; spoil. **14.** to become bitter, disillusioned, or uninterested. **15.** *Agric.* (of soil) to develop excessive acidity. —*v.t.* **16.** to make sour; cause sourness in: *What do they use to sour the mash?* **17.** to cause spoilage in; rot. **18.** to make bitter, disillusioned, or disagreeable. [ME; OE *sūr;* c. G *sauer,* D *zuur,* OIcel *sūrr*] —**sour′ish,** *adj.* —**sour′ly,** *adv.* —**sour′ness,** *n.* —**Ant. 1.** sweet.

sour·ball (sour′bôl′, sou′ər-), *n.* a round piece of hard candy with a tart or acid fruit flavoring.

source (sōrs, sôrs), *n.* **1.** any thing or place from which something comes, arises, or is obtained; origin. **2.** the beginning or place of origin of a stream or river. **3.** a book, statement, person, etc., supplying information. **4.** the person or business making interest or dividend payments. [ME *sours* < OF *sors,* ptp. of *sourdre* < L *surgere* to spring forth] —**source′less,** *adj.* —**Syn. 1.** originator. **3.** authority.

source′ mate′rial, original, authoritative, or basic materials utilized in research, as diaries, manuscripts, etc.

sour′ cher′ry, 1. a cherry, *Prunus Cerasus,* characterized by gray bark and the spreading habit of its branches. **2.** the red, tart fruit of this tree, used in making pies and preserves.

sour′ cream′, cream soured by the lactic acid produced by a ferment.

sour·dine (so͝or dēn′), *n. Music.* **1.** sordino. **2.** kit[2]. [< F: damper, mute < It *sordina* (fem.); see SORDINO]

sour·dough (sour′dō′, sou′ər-), *n.* **1.** *Western U.S. and Canada, Alaska, Brit. Dial.* leaven, esp. fermented dough kept from one baking to start the next instead of beginning each time with fresh yeast. **2.** a prospector or pioneer, esp. in Alaska or Canada. [ME]

sour′ grapes′, pretended disdain for something one does not or cannot have. [in allusion to Aesop's fable concerning the fox who, in an effort to save face, described as sour those grapes he could not reach]

sour′ gum′, the tupelo, *Nyssa sylvatica.*

sour′ mash′, a blended grain mash used in the distilling of some whiskeys, consisting of new mash and a portion of mash from a preceding run.

sour′ or′ange. See under **orange** (def. 2).

sour·puss (sour′po͝os′, sou′ər-), *n. Informal.* a person having a grouchy disposition that is often accompanied by a scowling facial expression.

sour′ salt′, crystals of citric acid used as a flavoring in foods, carbonated beverages, and pharmaceuticals.

sour·sop (sour′sop′, sou′ər-), *n.* **1.** the large, slightly acid, pulpy fruit of a small tree, *Annona muricata,* of the West Indies. **2.** the tree.

sour·wood (sour′wo͝od′, sou′ər-), *n.* See **sorrel tree.**

Sou·sa (so͞o′zə), *n.* **John Philip,** 1854–1932, U.S. band conductor and composer of marches.

sou·sa·phone (so͞o′zə fōn′, -sə-), *n.* a form of bass tuba, similar to the helicon, used in brass bands. [named after J. P. SOUSA + -PHONE] —**sou′sa·phon′ist,** *n.*

souse[1] (sous), *v.,* **soused, sous·ing,** *n.* —*v.t.* **1.** to plunge into water or other liquid; immerse. **2.** to steep in pickling brine; pickle. **3.** *Slang.* to intoxicate; make drunk. —*v.i.* **4.** to plunge into water or other liquid; fall with a splash. **5.** to be steeping or soaking in something. —*n.* **6.** an act of sousing. **7.** something kept or steeped in pickle. **8.** a liquid used as a pickle. **9.** *Slang.* a drunkard. [ME *sows* < MF *souce* pickled < Gmc]

souse[2] (sous), *v.,* **soused, sous·ing,** *n. Archaic.* —*v.i.* **1.** to swoop down. —*v.t.* **2.** to swoop or pounce upon. —*n.* *Falconry.* **3.** a rising while in flight. **4.** a swooping or pouncing. [see SOURCE in obs. sense of rise]

sou·tache (so͞o tash′; *Fr.* so͞o TASH′), *n.* a narrow braid used for trimming. [< F: braid of a hussar's shako < Hung *sujtas* flat braid for trimming]

sou·tane (so͞o tän′), *n. Eccles.* a cassock. [< F < It *sottan(a)* = *sott(o)* under (< L *subtus*) + *-ana* fem. adj. suffix]

south (*n., adj., adv.* south; *v.* south, south), *n.* **1.** a cardinal point of the compass directly opposite to the north. *Abbr.:* S **2.** the direction in which this point lies. **3.** (*often cap.*) a quarter or territory situated in this direction. **4.** (*cap.*) the general area south of Pennsylvania and the Ohio River and east of the Mississippi, consisting mainly of those states that formed the Confederacy. —*adj.* **5.** lying toward or situated in the south: *the south end of town.* **6.** in the direction of or toward the south. **7.** coming from the south, as a wind. —*adv.* **8.** toward the south: *heading south.* **9.** from the south. —*v.i.* **10.** to turn or move in a southerly direction. [ME; OE *sūth;* c. OHG *sund-,* G *süd*]

South′ Af′rica, Repub′lic of, a country in S Africa; member of the British Commonwealth until 1961. 25,000,000; 472,000 sq. mi. *Capitals:* Pretoria *and* Cape Town. Formerly, **Union of South Africa.**

South′ Af′rican, 1. of southern Africa. **2.** of the Republic of South Africa. **3.** a native or inhabitant of the Republic of South Africa, esp. one of European descent.

South′ Af′rican Dutch′, 1. Afrikaans. *Abbr.:* SAfrD **2.** the Boers.

South′ Af′rican Repub′lic, former name of **Transvaal.**

South′ Amer′ica, a continent in the S part of the Western Hemisphere. 219,000,000; ab. 6,900,000 sq. mi. —**South′ Amer′ican.**

South·amp·ton (south amp′tən, -hamp′-), *n.* a seaport in Hampshire, in S England. 208,710 (est. 1964).
Southamp′ton Insurrec′tion, an uprising by a group of slaves in Virginia in 1831, led by Nat Turner. Also called **Nat Turner's Rebellion.** [after *Southampton* County, Virginia, where it occurred]
Southamp′ton Is′land, an island in N Canada, at the entrance to Hudson Bay. 19,100 sq. mi.
South′ Ara′bia, **1. Protectorate of.** Formerly, **Aden Protectorate.** a former protectorate of Great Britain in S Arabia, divided into the Federation of South Arabia and the Eastern Aden Protectorate in 1962 and reunited to form Southern Yemen in 1967. **2. Federation of,** a former federation in S Arabia; now part of Southern Yemen.
South′ A′sia, the countries and land area of Afghanistan, Bangladesh, Bhutan, India, the Maldives, Nepal, Pakistan, Sikkim, and Sri Lanka.
South′ Austral′ia, a state in S Australia. 969,340 (1961); 380,070 sq. mi. *Cap.:* Adelaide.
South′ Bend′, a city in N Indiana. 125,580 (1970).
south·bound (south′bound′), *adj.* **1.** traveling southward. **2.** pertaining to southward travel.
south′ by east′, *Navig., Survey.* a point on the compass 11°15′ east of south. *Abbr.:* SbE
south′ by west′, *Navig., Survey.* a point on the compass 11°15′ west of south. *Abbr.:* SbW
South′ Caroli′na, a state in the SE United States, on the Atlantic coast. 2,590,516 (1970); 31,055 sq. mi. *Cap.:* Columbia. *Abbr.:* S.C., SC —**South′ Carolin′ian.**
South′ Cauca′sian, **1.** a family of languages including Georgian and others that are spoken on the south slopes of the Caucasus. **2.** of or pertaining to South Caucasian.
South′ Chi′na Sea′, a part of the W Pacific, bounded by SE China, Vietnam, the Malay Peninsula, Borneo, and the Philippines.
South′ Dako′ta, a state in the N central United States: a part of the Midwest. 666,257 (1970); 77,047 sq. mi. *Cap.:* Pierre. *Abbr.:* SD, S. Dak. —**South′ Dako′tan.**
South·down (south′doun′), *n.* one of an English breed of sheep, yielding mutton of high quality. [after SOUTH DOWN(S) where the breed was developed]
South′ Downs′, a range of low hills in S England.
south·east (south′ēst′; *Naut.* sou′ēst′), *n.* **1.** the point or direction midway between south and east. *Abbr.:* SE **2.** a region in this direction. **3.** (*cap.*) the southeast region of the United States. —*adj.* **4.** lying toward or situated in the southeast: *the southeast end of town.* **5.** in the direction of or toward the southeast. **6.** coming from the southeast, as a wind. —*adv.* **7.** toward the southeast. **8.** from the southeast. [ME *southest,* OE *sūthēast*] —**south′east′ern,** *adj.* —**south·east·ern·most** (south′ē′stərn mōst′ *or, esp. Brit.,* -məst), *adj.*
South′east A′sia, the countries and land area of Brunei, Burma, Cambodia, Indonesia, Laos, Malaysia, the Philippines, Portuguese Timor, Singapore, Thailand, and Vietnam. —**South′east A′sian.**
South′east A′sia Trea′ty Organiza′tion. See **SEATO.**
southeast′ by east′, *Navig., Survey.* a point on the compass 11°15′ east of southeast. *Abbr.:* SEbE
southeast′ by south′, *Navig., Survey.* a point on the compass 11°15′ south of southeast. *Abbr.:* SEbS
south·east·er (south′ē′stər; *Naut.* sou′ē′stər), *n.* a wind, gale, or storm from the southeast.
south·east·er·ly (south′ē′stər lē; *Naut.* sou′ē′stər lē), *adj.* **1.** of, pertaining to, or situated in the southeast. **2.** in the direction of or toward the southeast. **3.** coming from the southeast, as a wind. —*adv.* **4.** toward the southeast. **5.** from the southeast, as a wind.
south·east·ern·er (south′ē′stər nər), *n.* **1.** a native or inhabitant of the southeast. **2.** (*cap.*) a native or inhabitant of the southeastern U.S.
south·east·ward (south′ēst′wərd; *Naut.* sou′ēst′wərd), *adj.* **1.** moving, facing, or situated toward the southeast. —*adv.* **2.** Also, **south′east′wards.** toward the southeast. —*n.* **3.** the southeast.
south·east·ward·ly (south′ēst′wərd lē; *Naut.* sou′ēst′wərd lē), *adj., adv.* toward the southeast.
South·end-on-Sea (south′end′on sē′, -ôn-), *n.* a seaport in SE England, on Thames estuary. 164,976 (1961).
south·er (sou′thər), *n.* a wind or storm from the south, esp. a strong wind or a long or severe storm.
south·er·ly (suth′ər lē), *adj., adv., n., pl.* **-lies.** —*adj.* **1.** of, pertaining to, or situated in the south. **2.** in the direction of or toward the south. **3.** coming from the south, as a wind. —*adv.* **4.** toward the south, as a wind. **5.** from the south. —*n.* **6.** a southerly wind. [SOUTH + *-erly,* modeled on *easterly*] —**south′er·li·ness,** *n.*
south′erly burst′er, buster (def. 5). Also, **south′erly bust′er.**
south·ern (suth′ərn), *adj.* **1.** lying toward, situated in, or directed toward the south. **2.** coming from the south, as a wind. **3.** of or pertaining to the south. **4.** (*cap.*) of or pertaining to the South of the United States. **5.** *Astron.* being or located south of the celestial equator or of the zodiac. —*n.* **6.** *Chiefly Dial.* southerner (def. 2). **7.** (*cap.*) the dialect of English spoken in the eastern parts of Maryland, Virginia, and the Carolinas, in Florida, in the southern parts of Georgia, Alabama, Mississippi, and Louisiana, and in southeastern Texas. [ME; OE *sūtherne*]
South′ern Alps′, a mountain range in New Zealand, on South Island. Highest peak, Mt. Cook, 12,349 ft.
South′ern Cameroons′. See under **Cameroons** (def. 2).
South′ern Coal′sack, *Astron.* See under **Coalsack.**
South′ern Cross′, *Astron.* a southern constellation between Centaurus and Musca. Also called **Cross.**
South′ern Crown′, *Astron.* the constellation Corona Australis.
south·ern·er (suth′ər nər), *n.* **1.** a native or inhabitant of the south. **2.** (*cap.*) a native or inhabitant of the southern U.S.
South′ern Fish′, *Astron.* the constellation Piscis Austrinus.
South′ern Hem′isphere, the half of the earth between the South Pole and the equator.
south·ern·ism (suth′ər niz′əm). *n.* a pronunciation, figure of speech, or behavioral trait characteristic of the U.S. South.
south′ern lights′, *Astron.* See **aurora australis.**
south·ern·ly (suth′ərn lē), *adj.* southerly. —**south′ern·li·ness,** *n.*
south·ern·most (suth′ərn mōst′ *or, esp. Brit.,* -məst), *adj.* farthest south.
South′ern Rhode′sia, former name of **Zimbabwe** (def. 1). —**South′ern Rhode′sian.**
South′ern Slavs′. See under **Slav** (def. 1).
South′ern strat′egy. *U.S.* a political strategy which considers that the Democrats and Republicans are about equal in number in the Northeast, Midwest, and Far West, so that the winner of a national election will actually be determined by the vote of white Southerners.
south·ern·wood (suth′ərn wo͝od′), *n.* a woody-stemmed wormwood, *Artemisia Abrotanum,* of southern Europe, having aromatic, finely dissected leaves. Also called **old man.** [ME *southernwode,* OE *sūtherne wudu*]
South′ern Yem′en, a former name of **Yemen** (def. 1).
South′ Eu′clid, a city in NE Ohio, near Cleveland. 29,579 (1970).
Sou·they (sou′thē, suth′ē), *n.* **Robert,** 1774–1843, English poet and prose writer: poet laureate 1813–43.
South′ Farm′ingdale, a town on central Long Island, in SE New York. 20,464 (1970).
South·field (south′fēld′), *n.* a city in SE Michigan, W of Detroit. 69,285 (1970).
South′ Frig′id Zone′, the part of the earth's surface between the Antarctic Circle and the South Pole.
South′ Gate′, a city in SW California, near Los Angeles. 56,909 (1970).
South·gate (south′git, -gāt′), *n.* a city in SE Michigan, near Detroit. 33,909 (1970).
South′ Geor′gia, a British island in the S Atlantic, about 800 mi. SE of the Falkland Islands. 22; ab. 1000 sq. mi. —**South′ Geor′gian.**
South′ Hol′land, a province in the SW Netherlands. 2,697,894 (est. 1960); 1086 sq. mi. *Cap.:* The Hague.
south·ing (sou′thing), *n.* **1.** *Astron.* **a.** the transit of a heavenly body across the celestial meridian. **b.** *Obs.* south declination. **2.** movement or deviation toward the south. **3.** distance due south made by a vessel.
South·ing·ton (suth′ing tən), *n.* a town in central Connecticut. 30,946 (1970).
South′ Is′land, the largest island of New Zealand. 729,925 (est. 1961); 58,093 sq. mi.
South′ Kore′a, a country in E Asia: formed 1948 after the division of the former country of Korea at 38° N. 37,708,542; 36,600 sq. mi. *Cap.:* Seoul. Cf. **Korea** (def. 1). Official name, **Repub′lic of Kore′a.**
south·land (south′lənd, -land′), *n.* **1.** a southern area. **2.** the southern part of a country. —**south′land′er,** *n.*
South′ Ork′ney Is′lands, a group of islands in the British Antarctic Territory, N of the Antarctic Peninsula: formerly a dependency of the Falkland Islands; claimed by Argentina.
south·paw (south′pô′), *Informal.* —*n.* **1.** a person who is left-handed. **2.** *Sports.* a player who throws with his left hand, esp. a pitcher. —*adj.* **3.** left-handed.
South′ Plain′field, a city in N New Jersey. 21,142 (1970).
South′ Platte′, a river flowing NE from central Colorado to the Platte River in W Nebraska. 424 mi. long.
South′ Pole′, **1.** *Geog.* the end of the earth's axis of rotation marking the southernmost point of the earth. **2.** *Astron.* the point at which the axis of the earth extended cuts the southern half of the celestial sphere; the south celestial pole. **3.** (*l.c.*) See under **magnetic pole.**
South·port (south′pōrt, -pôrt′), *n.* a seaport in W Lancashire, in NW England: resort. 81,976 (1961).
South′ San′ Francis′co, a city in central California. 46,646 (1970).
South′ Sea′ Is′lands, the islands in the S Pacific Ocean. Cf. **Oceania.** —**South′ Sea′ Is′lander.**
South′ Seas′, the seas south of the equator.
South′ Shet′land Is′lands, a group of islands in the British Antarctic Territory, N of the Antarctic Peninsula: formerly a dependency of the Falkland Islands; claimed by Argentina and Chile.
South′ Shields′, a seaport in NE Durham, in NE England, at the mouth of the Tyne River. 109,533 (1961).
south-south·east (south′south′ēst′; *Naut.* sou′sou′ēst′), *n.* **1.** the point on the compass midway between south and southeast. —*adj.* **2.** in the direction of or toward this point. **3.** from this point, as a wind. —*adv.* **4.** toward this point. **5.** from this point. *Abbr.:* SSE [ME *south south est*]
south-south·west (south′south′west′; *Naut.* sou′sou′-west′), *n.* **1.** the point on the compass midway between south and southwest. —*adj.* **2.** in the direction of or toward this point. **3.** from this point, as a wind. —*adv.* **4.** toward this point. **5.** from this point. *Abbr.:* SSW
South′ Stick′ney (stik′nē), a town in NE Illinois, near Chicago. 29,900 (1970).
South St. Paul, a city in SE Minnesota. 25,016 (1970).
South′ Tem′perate Zone′, the part of the earth's surface between the tropic of Capricorn and the Antarctic Circle.
South′ Val′ley, a town in central New Mexico, near Albuquerque. 29,389 (1970).
South′ Vietnam′, a former country in SE Asia, that comprised Vietnam below 17°N: now part of reunified Vietnam. Cf. **North Vietnam, Vietnam.**
south·ward (south′wərd; *Naut.* suth′ərd), *adj.* **1.** moving, facing, or situated toward the south. —*adv.* **2.** Also, **south′wards.** toward the south. —*n.* **3.** the south. [ME; OE *sūth weard*]

south·ward·ly (south/wərd lē; *Naut.* suth/ərd lē), *adj.*, *adv.* toward the south.

South·wark (suth/ərk), *n.* a borough of central London, England, S of the Thames. 235,500.

south·west (south/west/; *Naut.* sou/west/), *n.* **1.** the point or direction midway between south and west. *Abbr.:* SW **2.** a region in this direction. **3.** (*cap.*) the southwest region of the United States. **—***adj.* **4.** lying toward or situated in the southwest: *the southwest end of town.* **5.** in the direction of or toward the southwest. **6.** coming from the southwest, as a wind. **—***adv.* **7.** toward the southwest: *heading southwest.* [ME; OE *sūthwest*] **—south/west/ern,** *adj.* **—south/west/ern·er,** *n.*

South/-West A/frica (south/west/), a territory in SW Africa: a former German protectorate; a mandate of the Republic of South Africa 1919–66; status in dispute since 1966 when the UN terminated the mandate and proclaimed UN administration pending independence. 1,027,000; 317,725 sq. mi. *Cap.:* Windhoek. Formerly, **German Southwest Africa.** Official (UN) name, **Namibia.** **—South/-West Af/rican.**

southwest/ by south/, *Navig., Survey.* a point on the compass 11°15′ south of southwest. *Abbr.:* SWbS

southwest/ by west/, *Navig., Survey.* a point on the compass 11°15′ west of southwest. *Abbr.:* SWbW

south·west·er (south/wes/tər; *Naut.* sou/wes/tər), *n.* **1.** a wind, gale, or storm from the southwest. **2.** a waterproof hat, usually of oilskin, having the brim very broad behind. **3.** Also called **nor'wester.** a slicker, fastening with buckles. Also, **sou'-west·er** (sou/wes/tər).

south·west·er·ly (south/wes/tər lē; *Naut.* sou/wes/tər lē), *adj.* **1.** of, pertaining to, or situated in the southwest. **2.** in the direction of or toward the southwest. **3.** coming from the southwest, as a wind. **—***adv.* **4.** toward the southwest. **5.** from the southwest, as a wind. [SOUTHWEST + *-erly*]

south·west·ward (south/west/wərd; *Naut.* sou/west/wərd), *adj.* **1.** moving, facing, or situated toward the southwest. **—***adv.* **2.** Also, **south/west/wards.** toward the southwest. **—***n.* **3.** the southwest.

south·west·ward·ly (south/west/wərd lē; *Naut.* sou/west/wərd lē), *adj., adv.* toward the southwest.

South/ Whit/tier, a town in SW California. 46,641 (1970).

South/ Yem/en, a former name of **Yemen** (def. 1).

Sou·tine (sōō tēn/), *n.* **Cha·im** (ᴋʜī im/, ᴋʜī/im), 1894–1943, Lithuanian painter in France.

Sou·van·na Phou·ma (sōō vän/nä pōō/mä), **Prince,** 1901–84, Laotian statesman: premier 1962–75.

sou·ve·nir (sōō/və nēr/, sōō/və nēr/), *n.* **1.** something given or kept as a reminder of a place visited, an incident, etc.; memento. **2.** a memory. [< F, n. use of (*se*) *souvenir* to remember < L *subvenīre* = *sub-* SUB- + *venīre* to come (to one's mind)]

sov·er·eign (sov/rin, sov/ər in, suv/-), *n.* **1.** a monarch or other supreme ruler. **2.** a person who has sovereign power. **3.** a body of persons or a state having sovereignty. **4.** a gold coin of the United Kingdom, equal to one pound sterling: went out of circulation after 1914. **—***adj.* **5.** belonging to or characteristic of a sovereign or sovereignty; royal. **6.** having supreme rank or power. **7.** supreme, as power. **8.** greatest in degree. **9.** being superior to all others. **10.** having independent and self-governing power, status, or authority: *a sovereign state.* **11.** potent, as a remedy. [ME *soverain* (alter. by influence of REIGN) < OF *soverain* < VL **superān(us)* = L *super-* SUPER- + *-ānus* -AN] **—sov/er·eign·ly,** *adv.* **—Syn. 1.** emperor, empress. **3.** government. **5.** regal, majestic, imperial. **7.** chief, paramount.

sov·er·eign·ty (sov/rin tē, suv/-), *n., pl.* **-ties. 1.** the quality or state of being sovereign. **2.** the status, dominion, power, or authority of a sovereign; royalty. **3.** supreme and independent power or authority in a state. **4.** a sovereign state, community, or political unit. [ME *soverainte* < AF *sovereynete* (OF *soverainete*)]

So·vetsk (so vyetsk/), *n.* a city in the W RSFSR, on the Memel River: formerly in East Prussia; peace treaty (1807) between France, Prussia, and Russia. 40,000. Formerly (until 1945), **Tilsit.**

so·vi·et (sō/vē et/, -it, sō/vē et/), *n.* **1.** (in the Soviet Union) an elected legislative council on the local, regional, and national levels culminating in the Supreme Soviet. **2.** any similar council or assembly elsewhere. **3. Soviets,** the governing officials or the people of the Soviet Union. **—***adj.* **4.** of or pertaining to a soviet. **5.** (*cap.*) of the Soviet Union. [< Russ *sovyet* council < ORuss *sŭvětŭ*] **—so·vi·et·dom** (sō/vē et/dəm, -it-, sō/vē et/-), *n.*

So·vi·et·ise (sō/vē i tīz/), *v.t.*, **-ised, -is·ing.** *Chiefly Brit.* Sovietize. **—So/vi·et·i·sa/tion,** *n.*

So·vi·et·ism (sō/vē i tiz/əm), *n.* **1.** (*sometimes l.c.*) a soviet system of government. **2.** (*often l.c.*) the practices and principles of a soviet government. **3.** a characteristic, mannerism, etc., expressive of the ideology of the Soviet Union. **—So/vi·et·ist,** *n., adj.*

So·vi·et·ize (sō/vē i tīz/), *v.t.*, **-ized, -iz·ing. 1.** (*sometimes l.c.*) to bring under the influence or domination of the Soviet Union. **2.** (*often l.c.*) to impose or institute a soviet system of government similar to that of the Soviet Union. Also, *esp. Brit.,* **Sovietise.** **—So/vi·et·i·za/tion,** *n.*

So/viet Moun/tains, a mountain range in the averted hemisphere or far side of the moon. ab. 1250 mi. long. Also called **So/viet Range/, So/viet Ridge/.**

So/viet of National/ities. See under **Supreme Soviet.**

So/viet of the Un/ion. See under **Supreme Soviet.**

So/viet Rus/sia, 1. the Soviet Union. **2.** See **Russian Soviet Federated Socialist Republic.**

So/viet Un/ion, a federal union of fifteen constituent republics, in E Europe and W and N Asia, comprising the larger part of the former Russian Empire. 260,040,000; 8,650,069 sq. mi. *Cap.:* Moscow. Also called **Russia.** Official name, **Union of Soviet Socialist Republics.**

sow[1] (sō), *v.*, **sowed, sown** or **sowed, sow·ing.** **—***v.t.* **1.** to scatter (seed) over land, earth, etc., for growth; plant. **2.** to plant seed so as to grow: *to sow a crop.* **3.** to scatter seed over (land, earth, etc.). **4.** to introduce, propagate, or spread; disseminate: *to sow distrust.* **5.** to strew with anything. **—***v.i.* **6.** to sow seed, as for a crop. [ME *sow(en),* OE *sāwan*] **—sow/a·ble,** *adj.* **—sow/er,** *n.*

sow[2] (sou), *n.* **1.** an adult female swine. **2.** *Metall.* **a.** a large mass of iron that has solidified in the common channel through which the molten metal flows to the smaller ones in which the pigs solidify. **b.** the common channel itself. [ME *sowe* < OE *sugu;* c. G *Sau,* OIcel *sȳr,* L *sūs,* Gk *hŷs,* Tocharian *suwo*]

so·war (sə wär/, -wôr/), *n.* (in India) a mounted native soldier. [< Urdu < Pers *sawār* horseman, MPers *asbār,* OPers *asabāra* = *asa-* horse + *-bāra* borne by]

sow·bel·ly (sou/bel/ē), *n.* See **side meat.**

sow/ bug/ (sou), any of several small, terrestrial isopods, esp. of the genus *Oniscus;* wood louse.

sow·car (sou kär/), *n.* soucar.

sow·ens (sō/ənz, sōō/-), *n.* (*construed as sing.*) *Scot., Irish Eng.* porridge made from oat bran or husks. Also, **so/wans.** [< ScotGael *sūghan* < *sūgh* sap]

So·we·to (sə wē/tō, -wā/-), *n.* a black township in South Africa, SW of Johannesburg: largest black urban settlement in southern Africa; racial riots 1976. 550,000.

sown (sōn), *v.* a pp. of **sow**[1].

sow/ this/tle (sou), any cichoriaceous plant of the genus *Sonchus,* esp. *S. oleraceus,* a weed having thistlelike leaves and yellow flowers. [ME *sowethistel,* var. of *sugethistel* < OE]

sox (soks), *n.* a pl. of **sock**[1].

soy (soi), *n.* **1.** Also called **soy/ sauce/, soy/a sauce/** (soi/ə). a salty, fermented sauce made from soybeans. **2.** the soybean. [< Jap *shoy* < *shōyū* < Chin (Peking) *chiang-yu* = *chiang* bean paste, sauce + *yu* oil]

soy·bean (soi/bēn/), *n.* **1.** a bushy, leguminous plant, *Glycine Soja,* of the Old World, grown in the eastern half of the U.S. chiefly for forage and soil improvement. **2.** its seed, processed as oil and livestock feed. Also called **soy·a** (soi/ə).

soy/bean oil/, a pale-yellow oil derived from soybeans: used in margarine, vegetable shortening, and salad oil, and in the manufacture of paints, soap, glycerine, etc.

so·zin (sō/zin), *n.* *Biochem.* any protein normally present in the animal body and serving as a defense against disease. [< Gk *sôz(ein)* (to) save, keep, preserve + -IN[2]]

SP, 1. Shore Patrol. **2.** Submarine Patrol.

Sp, Spanish (def. 3).

Sp., 1. Spain. **2.** Spaniard. **3.** Spanish.

sp., 1. special. **2.** species. **3.** specific. **4.** spelling.

S.P., 1. Shore Patrol. **2.** Socialist party. **3.** Submarine Patrol.

s.p., without issue. [< L *sine prole*]

spa (spä), *n.* **1.** a mineral spring, or a locality in which such springs exist. **2.** a resort hotel, esp. one situated near mineral springs. [generalized use of SPA]

Spa (spä), *n.* a resort town in E Belgium, SE of Liège: famous mineral springs. 9391.

space (spās), *n., v.*, **spaced, spac·ing,** *adj.* **—***n.* **1.** the unlimited or indefinitely great three-dimensional expanse in which all material objects are located and all events occur. **2.** the portion or extent of this in a given instance. **3.** extent or area in two dimensions; a particular extent of surface. **4.** *Fine Arts.* **a.** the designed and structured surface of a picture. **b.** the illusion of depth on a two-dimensional surface. **5.** the region beyond the earth's atmosphere containing the rest of the cosmos. **6.** a seat, berth, or room on a train, airplane, etc. **7.** a particular linear distance. **8.** *Math.* a system of objects with relations between the objects defined. **9.** extent, or a particular extent, of time. **10.** an interval of time; a while. **11.** an area or interval allowed for or taken by advertising, as in a periodical. **12.** *Music.* the interval between two adjacent lines of the staff. **13.** *Print.* a blank piece of metal used to separate words, sentences, etc. **14.** *Telegraphy.* an interval during the transmitting of a message when the key is not in contact. **—***v.t.* **15.** to fix the space or spaces of; divide into spaces. **16.** to set some distance apart. **17.** *Print., Writing.* **a.** to separate (words, letters, or lines) by spaces. **b.** to extend by inserting more space or spaces (usually fol. by *out*). **—***adj.* **18.** of or pertaining to space or spaces: *space design.* **19.** of, in, or pertaining to the region beyond the earth's atmosphere: *a space shot.* [ME < OF (*e*)*space* < L *spatium*] **—spac/er,** *n.*

space/ bar/, a horizontal bar on a typewriter keyboard that is depressed to move the carriage one space to the left.

space/ cap/sule, a container or vehicle for launching into space and designed to be recovered on its return, containing experimental animals and instruments or people.

space·craft (spās/kraft/, -kräft/), *n., pl.* **-craft.** any vehicle capable of traveling through space outside the earth's atmosphere.

spaced-out (spāst/out/), *adj.* *U.S. Slang.* dazed by the use of alcohol or narcotic drugs.

space/ heat/er, a small furnace for heating the air of the room in which it is situated.

space/ lat/tice, lattice (def. 4).

space·less (spās/lis), *adj.* **1.** having no limits or dimensions in space; limitless; unbounded. **2.** occupying no space.

space·man (spās/man/, -mən), *n., pl.* **-men** (-men/, -mən). an astronaut.

space/ med/icine, the branch of aviation medicine dealing with the effects on man of flying in space.

space·port (spās/pōrt/, -pôrt/), *n.* a site at which spacecraft are tested, launched, sheltered, maintained, etc.

space·ship (spās/ship/), *n.* a rocket-propelled vehicle designed to carry man and cargo to the moon or planets.

space/ shut/tle, a spacecraft designed for orbital missions, consisting of a reusable manned vehicle, two reusable solid rocket boosters that drop off after initial ascent, and an expendable external tank.

space/ sta/tion, a large artificial satellite in orbit around the earth: proposed esp. for the assembly and launching of spaceships.

space·suit (spās/sōōt/), *n.* a sealed and pressurized suit allowing the wearer to survive in outer space.

space-time (spās/tīm/), *n.* **1.** Also called **space/-time/ contin/uum.** the four-dimensional continuum, having three spatial coordinates and one temporal coordinate. **2.** the physical reality that exists within this four-dimensional continuum. **—***adj.* **3.** of, pertaining to, or noting a system with three spatial coordinates and one temporal coordinate. **4.** noting, pertaining to, or involving both space and time.

spa·cial (spā/shəl), *adj.* spatial. **—spa·ci·al·i·ty** (spā/shē al/i tē), *n.* **—spa/cial·ly,** *adv.*

spac·ing (spā/sing), *n.* **1.** the act of a person or thing that spaces. **2.** the arranging of spaces or objects in a space.

spa·cious (spā′shəs), *adj.* **1.** containing much space, as a house, street, etc.; amply large. **2.** occupying much space; vast. **3.** of a great extent or area. **4.** broad in scope, range, inclusiveness, etc. [ME < L *spatiōsus*] —**spa′cious·ly,** *adv.* —**spa′cious·ness,** *n.* —**Syn. 1.** roomy, capacious. **2.** extensive, huge. **3.** broad, large, great. —**Ant. 1.** small.

spade[1] (spād), *n., v.,* **spad·ed, spad·ing.** —*n.* **1.** a tool for digging, having a long handle and an iron blade that is adapted for pressing into the ground with the foot. **2.** an implement, piece, or part resembling this. **3.** a sharp projection on the bottom of a gun trail, designed to restrict backward movement of the carriage during recoil. **4. call a spade a spade,** to call something by its right name; speak plainly or bluntly. —*v.t.* **5.** to dig, cut, or remove with a spade. [ME; OE *spadu;* c. G *Spaten,* Icel *spathi* spade, D *spade,* Gk *spáthē* broad, flat piece of wood] —**spade′like′,** *adj.* —**spad′er,** *n.*

spade[2] (spād), *n.* **1.** a black figure shaped like an inverted heart with a short stem at the cusp opposite the point, used on playing cards. **2.** a card of the suit bearing such figures. **3. spades, a.** (*construed as sing. or pl.*) the suit so marked. **b.** (*construed as pl.*) *Casino.* the winning of seven spades or more. **4.** *Offensive.* a Negro. **5. in spades,** *Slang.* **a.** in the extreme; positively. **b.** without restraint; outspokenly. [< It *spada,* orig. sword, later mark on cards < L *spatha* < Gk *spáthē;* see SPADE[1]]

spade·fish (spād′fish′), *n., pl.* (*esp. collectively*) **-fish,** (*esp. referring to two or more kinds or species*) **-fish·es.** a deep-bodied, marine fish of the genus *Chaetodipterus,* esp. *C. faber,* found along the Atlantic coast of North America. [prob. SPADE[2] + FISH, in allusion to its shape]

spade·work (spād′wûrk′), *n.* preliminary work on which further activity is to be based.

spa·di·ceous (spā dish′əs), *adj. Bot.* **1.** of the nature of a spadix. **2.** bearing a spadix. [< NL *spādīceus* < L *spādīc-* (s. of *spādīx*). See SPADIX, -EOUS]

spa·dix (spā′diks), *n., pl.* **spa·di·ces** (spā dī′sēz). *Bot.* an inflorescence consisting of a spike with a fleshy or thickened axis, usually enclosed in a spathe. [< L: a broken palm branch and its fruit < Gk: a (torn-off) palm bough, akin to *spân* to tear off]

spa·do (spā′dō), *n., pl.* **spa·do·nes** (spā dō′nāz, spə-). **1.** *Civil Law.* an impotent person; one unable to procreate. **2.** a castrated man or animal. [late ME < L < Gk *spádōn* eunuch; see SPADIX]

Spa·do·li·ni (spä′dô lē′nē), *n.* **Gio·van·ni** (jô vän′nē), born 1925, Italian statesman: prime minister since 1981.

spae·ing (spā′ing), *n. Scot. and North Eng.* the act of prophesying; predicting. [Scot and north E *spae* to prophesy (ME *spa(n)* < ON *spā*) + -ING[1]]

spa·ghet·ti (spə get′ē), *n.* **1.** a pasta made in the form of long strings, boiled and served with any of a variety of meat, tomato, or other sauces. **2.** *Elect.* small tubing for insulating bare wire. [< It, pl. of *spaghetto,* dim. of *spago* cord]

spa·gyr·ic (spə jēr′ik), *Archaic.* —*adj.* **1.** pertaining to alchemy. —*n.* **2.** an alchemist. [< NL *spagyric(us),* prob. coined by Paracelsus] —**spa·gyr′i·cal·ly,** *adv.*

spa·hi (spä′hē), *n., pl.* **-his. 1.** one of a body of native Algerian cavalry in the French service. **2.** (formerly) a cavalryman in the Turkish army. Also, **spa′hee.** [< MF < Turk *sipahi* < Pers *sipāhī.* See SEPOY]

Spain (spān), *n.* a kingdom in SW Europe. Including the Balearic and Canary islands, 36,400,000; 194,988 sq. mi. *Cap.:* Madrid. Spanish, **España.**

spake (spāk), *v. Archaic.* a pt. of **speak.**

Spa·la·to (spä′lä tô), *n.* Italian name of **Split.**

spale (spāl), *n. Brit. Dial.* a splinter; chip. [perh. < Scand]

spall (spôl), *n.* **1.** a chip or splinter, as of stone or ore. —*v.t.* **2.** to break into smaller pieces, as ore. —*v.i.* **3.** to chip or splinter. [ME *spalle* chip] —**spall′er,** *n.*

spall·a·tion (spô lā′shən), *n. Physics.* a nuclear reaction in which several nucleons are released from the nucleus of an atom. [SPALL + -ATION]

Sp. Am., **1.** Spanish America. **2.** Spanish American.

span[1] (span), *n., v.,* **spanned, span·ning.** —*n.* **1.** the distance between the tip of the thumb and the tip of the little finger when the hand is fully extended. **2.** a unit of length corresponding to this distance, commonly taken as nine inches. **3.** a distance, amount, piece, etc., of this length or of some small extent: *a span of lace.* **4.** the distance or space between two supports of a bridge. **5.** the full extent, stretch, or reach of anything. **6.** *Aeron.* the distance between the wing tips of an airplane. **7.** a short space of time. —*v.t.* **8.** to measure by or as by the hand with the thumb and little finger extended. **9.** to encircle with the hand or hands, as the waist. **10.** to extend over or across (a section of land, a river, etc.). **11.** to provide with something that extends over. **12.** to extend, reach, or pass over (space or time). [ME, OE; c. G *Spanne,* D *span,* OIcel *spönn*]

span[2] (span), *n.* a pair of horses or other animals harnessed and driven together. [< Flem, D or LG *spann(en)* (to) fasten, unite] —**Syn.** team. See **pair.**

span[3] (span), *v.* a pt. of **spin.**

Span., **1.** Spaniard. **2.** Spanish.

span·cel (span′səl), *n., v.,* **-celed, -cel·ing** or (*esp. Brit.*) **-celled, -cel·ling.** —*n.* **1.** a noosed rope with which to hobble an animal, esp. a horse or cow. —*v.t.* **2.** to fetter with or as with a spancel. [< LG *spansel* < *spann(en)* (to) stretch; see SPAN[2]]

span·drel (span′drəl), *n.* **1.** *Archit.* an area between the extradoses, or exterior curves, of two adjoining arches, or between the extrados of an arch and a perpendicular through the extrados at the springing line. **2.** (in a steel-framed building) a panellike area between the head of a window on one level and the sill of a window immediately above. [ME *spaundrell,* prob. < AF *spaunder,* perh. c. OF *espandre* to EXPAND]

S, Spandrel

spang (spang), *adv. Informal.* directly; exactly: *The bullet landed spang on target.* [?]

span·gle (spang′gəl), *n., v.,* **-gled, -gling.** —*n.* **1.** a small, thin, often circular piece of glittering metal or other material, used esp. for decorating garments. **2.** any small, bright drop, object, spot, or the like. —*v.t.* **3.** to decorate with spangles. —*v.i.* **4.** to glitter with or like spangles. [ME *spangele* = *spange* spangle (perh. < MD) + -le -LE] —**span′gly,** *adj.*

Span·iard (span′yərd), *n.* a native or inhabitant of Spain. [ME *Spaignarde* < OF *(e)spaignart* = *Espaigne* SPAIN + *-art* -ARD]

span·iel (span′yəl), *n.* **1.** one of any of several breeds of small or medium-sized dogs, usually having a long, silky coat and long, drooping ears. **2.** a submissive person. [ME *spaynel* < OF *espaignol* Spanish dog < L *Hispāniol(us)* of Spain = *Hispani(a)* SPAIN + *-olus* dim. suffix] —**span′iel-like′,** *adj.*

Span·ish (span′ish), *adj.* **1.** of or pertaining to Spain, its people, or their language. —*n.* **2.** the Spanish people collectively. **3.** a Romance language, the language of Spain and Spanish America. *Abbr.:* Sp [ME]

Span′ish A·mer′ica, the Spanish-speaking countries south of the U.S.: Mexico, Central America (with the exception of Belize), South America (with the exceptions of Brazil, French Guiana, Guyana, and Suriname), and most of the West Indies.

Span·ish-A·mer·i·can (span′ish ə mer′i kən), *adj.* **1.** noting or pertaining to the parts of America where Spanish is the prevailing language. **2.** pertaining to Spain and America, sometimes to Spain and the United States. —*n.* **3.** a native or inhabitant of a Spanish-American country, esp. a person of Spanish descent.

Span′ish-Amer′ican War′, the war between the U.S. and Spain in 1898.

Span′ish Ar′abic, the Arabic language as used in Spain during the period of Moorish domination and influence, c900–1500. *Abbr.:* SpAr

Span′ish Arma′da, Armada (def. 1).

Span′ish bayonet′, any of certain liliaceous plants of the genus *Yucca,* having narrow, spine-tipped leaves. [alluding to its tropical American origin]

Span′ish bur′ton, *Naut.* any of several tackles employing a runner in addition to the fall. Cf. **single Spanish burton.**

Span′ish ce′dar, **1.** a tropical American meliaceous tree, *Cedrela odorata.* **2.** the fragrant, mahoganylike wood of this tree, formerly much used for making cigar boxes.

Span′ish Civ′il War′, the civil war in Spain 1936–39.

Span′ish fly′, **1.** Also called **cantharides.** a preparation of powdered blister beetles used medicinally as a skin irritant, diuretic, and aphrodisiac. **2.** Also called **cantharis.** a blister beetle, *Lytta vesicatoria,* used in this preparation. [so called from the fact that the beetles are found in abundance in Spain]

Span′ish Guin′ea, former name of **Equatorial Guinea.**

Span′ish influen′za, *Pathol.* **1.** an acute, highly infectious respiratory disease, caused by a virus, characterized by fever, cough, and generalized body aches. **2.** the pandemic respiratory infection that spread throughout the world during 1917–1918.

Span′ish Inquisi′tion, the Inquisition in Spain, 1480–1834.

Span′ish Main′, **1.** (formerly) the mainland of America adjacent to the Caribbean Sea, esp. the area between the mouth of the Orinoco River and the Isthmus of Panama. **2.** the Caribbean Sea: the route of the Spanish treasure galleons and a former haunt of pirates.

Span′ish Moroc′co. See under **Morocco** (def. 1).

Span′ish moss′, an epiphytic, bromeliaceous plant, *Tillandsia usneoides,* of the southern U.S., growing in long festoons that drape the branches of trees.

Span′ish nee′dles, **1.** a composite plant. *Bidens bipinnata,* having achenes with downwardly barbed awns. **2.** the achenes of this plant.

Span′ish om′elet, an omelet served with a sauce of tomatoes, onions, green peppers, and seasonings.

Span′ish on′ion, a large, mild, succulent onion.

Span′ish Sahar′a, a former Spanish province in NW Africa, comprising Río de Oro and Saguia el Hamra: status in dispute.

spank[1] (spangk), *v.t.* **1.** to strike (a person, usually a child), esp. on the buttocks with the hand, as in punishment. —*n.* **2.** a blow given in spanking. [imit.]

spank[2] (spangk), *v.i.* to move rapidly, smartly, or briskly. [back formation from SPANKING]

spank·er (spang′kər), *n.* **1.** *Naut.* **a.** a fore-and-aft sail on the aftermost lower mast of a sailing vessel having three or more masts. See diag. at **ship. b.** a designation given to the mast abaft the mizzenmast, usually the aftermost mast in any vessel. **2.** *Dial.* something remarkably fine. —*adj.* **3.** *Naut.* of or pertaining to a spanker mast. [?]

spank·ing[1] (spang′king), *adj.* **1.** moving rapidly and smartly. **2.** quick and vigorous. **3.** blowing briskly. **4.** *Informal.* unusually fine, great, large, etc. —*adv.* **5.** *Informal.* extremely, unusually, or remarkably; very: *The house was spanking clean.* [? < Scand; cf. Dan *spank* to strut] —**spank′ing·ly,** *adv.*

spank·ing[2] (spang′king), *n.* a series of blows, esp. on the buttocks with the hand, as in punishment. [SPANK[1] + -ING[1]]

span·ner (span′ər), *n.* **1.** a person or thing that spans. **2.** Also called **span′ner wrench′.** a wrench having a curved head with a hook or pin at one end for engaging notches or holes in collars, certain kinds of nuts, etc. Cf. **pin wrench. 3.** *Chiefly Brit.* a wrench, esp. one with fixed jaws.

span·worm (span′wûrm′), *n.* measuringworm.

spar[1] (spär), *n., v.,* **sparred, spar·ring.** —*n.* **1.** *Naut.* a stout pole forming a mast, yard, boom, gaff, or the like. **2.** *Aeron.* a principal lateral member of the framework of a wing of an airplane. —*v.t.* **3.** to provide or make with spars. [ME *sparre;* c. G *Sparren,* D *spar,* OIcel *sparri*] —**spar′like′,** *adj.*

spar[2] (spär), *v.,* **sparred, spar·ring,** *n.* —*v.i.* **1.** (of boxers) to make the motions of attack and defense with the arms and fists, esp. as a part of training. **2.** to box, esp. with light blows. **3.** to fight with the feet or spurs, as cocks do. **4.** to bandy words; dispute. —*n.* **5.** a motion of sparring. **6.** a boxing match. **7.** a dispute. [ME: orig., thrust (n. and v.); perh. c. SPUR]

spar[3] (spär), *n.* any of various more or less lustrous crystalline minerals (often used in combination): *calc-spar.* [back formation from *sparstone* spar, OE *spærstān* gypsum; cf. MLG *spar*] **—spar′like′,** *adj.*

Spar (spär), *n.* a woman enlisted in the women's reserve of the U.S. Coast Guard. Also, **SPAR.** [*s(emper) p(aratus) a(lways) r(eady)*]

SpAr, Spanish Arabic.

spar·able (spar′ə bəl), *n.* a small headless nail used by shoemakers. [var. of *sparrow bill*]

spar′ buoy′, *Naut.* a buoy shaped like a log or spar, anchored vertically.

spar′ deck′, *Naut.* the upper deck of a vessel, extending from stem to stern.

spare (spâr), *v.*, **spared, spar·ing,** *adj.*, **spar·er, spar·est,** *n.* **—***v.t.* **1.** to refrain from harming, punishing, or destroying. **2.** to deal gently or leniently with; show consideration for. **3.** to save from strain, discomfort, annoyance, or the like, or from a particular cause of it. **4.** to refrain from, forbear, omit, or withhold: *Spare us the gory details.* **5.** to refrain from employing, as some instrument, means, aid, etc. **6.** to set aside for a particular purpose. **7.** to give or lend, esp. without inconvenience or loss. **8.** to dispense with or do without. **9.** to use economically or frugally: *A walnut sundae, and don't spare the whipped cream!* **10.** to have remaining as excess or surplus. **—***v.i.* **11.** to use economy; be frugal. **12.** to refrain from inflicting injury or punishment. **13.** *Obs.* to refrain from action; forbear. **—***adj.* **14.** kept in reserve: *a spare tire.* **15.** being in excess of present need: *spare time.* **16.** frugally restricted; meager, as living, diet, etc. **17.** lean or thin, as a person. **18.** scanty or scant, as in amount, fullness, etc. **19.** sparing, economical, or temperate, as persons. **—***n.* **20.** a spare thing, part, etc. **21.** *Bowling.* **a.** the knocking down of all the pins with two bowls. **b.** a score so made. Cf. **strike** (def. 66). [ME; OE *spar(ian)*; c. D, G *sparen,* OIcel *spara*] **—spare′a·ble,** *adj.* **—spare′ly,** *adv.* **—spare′ness,** *n.* **—spar′er,** *n.* **—Syn. 6.** reserve.

spare·rib (spâr′rib′), *n.* a cut of pork containing ribs from the fore end of the row, where there is little meat adhering. [transposed var. of earlier *ribspare* < MLG *ribbespēr* rib cut; cf. *spare* (obs.) a cut, slice]

sparge (spärj), *v.*, **sparged, sparg·ing,** *n.* **—***v.t., v.i.* **1.** to scatter or sprinkle. **—***n.* **2.** a sprinkling. [< L *sparg(ere)* (to) sprinkle, scatter] **—sparg′er,** *n.*

spar·id (spar′id), *n.* **1.** any of numerous fishes of the family *Sparidae,* found chiefly in tropical and subtropical seas, including the porgies, the scups, etc. **—***adj.* **2.** belonging or pertaining to the *Sparidae.* [< NL *Sparid(ae)* < *Spar(us)* name of the genus < L < Gk *spáros* sea bream]

spar·ing (spâr′ing), *adj.* **1.** that spares. **2.** economical; chary (often fol. by *in* or *of*). **3.** lenient or merciful. **4.** frugally restricted. **5.** scanty; limited. [ME] **—spar′ing·ly,** *adv.* **—spar′ing·ness,** *n.* **—Syn. 2.** frugal, saving, penurious. **5.** meager, sparse.

spark[1] (spärk), *n.* **1.** a small ignited or fiery particle such as is thrown off by burning wood. **2.** *Elect.* **a.** the light produced by a sudden discontinuous discharge of electricity through air or another dielectric. **b.** the discharge itself. **c.** any electric arc of relatively small energy content. **d.** the electric discharge produced by a spark plug in an internal-combustion engine. **3.** a small amount or trace of something. **4.** a trace of life or vitality. **5. sparks,** (*construed as sing.*) *Slang.* a term of address for a radio operator on a ship or aircraft. **—***v.i.* **6.** to emit or produce sparks. **7.** to issue as or like sparks. **8.** to send forth gleams or flashes. **9.** (of the ignition of an internal-combustion engine) to function by producing sparks. **—***v.t.* **10.** *Informal.* to kindle, animate, or stimulate (interest, activity, spirit, etc.). [ME; OE *spearca;* c. MD, MLG *sparke*] **—spark′less,** *adj.* **—spark′less·ly,** *adv.* **—spark′like′,** *adj.*

spark[2] (spärk), *n.* **1.** an elegant or foppish young man. **2.** a beau, lover, or suitor. **3.** a woman of beauty, charm, or wit. **—***v.t.* **4.** *Informal.* to woo; court. **—***v.i.* **5.** *Informal.* to engage in courtship. [fig. use of SPARK[1], or metathetic var. of *sprack* lively < Scand; cf. OIcel *sprækr* sprightly] **—spark′ish,** *adj.* **—spark′ish·ly,** *adv.* **—spark′ish·ness,** *n.*

spark′ coil′, *Elect.* See **induction coil.**

spark·er (spär′kər), *n.* something that produces sparks.

spark′ gap′, *Elect.* **1.** a space between two electrodes, across which a discharge of electricity may take place. **2.** the electrodes and the space between, considered as a unit: used in ignition systems.

spark′ gen′erator, an alternating-current power source with a condenser discharging across a spark gap.

spar·kle (spär′kəl), *v.*, **-kled, -kling,** *n.* **—***v.i.* **1.** to shine with little gleams of light, as a brilliant gem. **2.** to emit sparks, as fire or burning matter. **3.** to effervesce, as wine. **4.** to be brilliant, lively, or vivacious. **—***v.t.* **5.** to cause to sparkle. **—***n.* **6.** a little spark or fiery particle. **7.** a luster or play of light. **8.** brilliance, liveliness, or vivacity. **—Syn. 1.** See **glisten. 7.** glitter.

spar·kler (spär′klər), *n.* **1.** a person or thing that sparkles. **2.** a firework that emits little sparks. **3.** a sparkling gem, esp. a diamond.

spar′kling wine′, a wine that is naturally carbonated by a second fermentation.

spark′ plug′, **1.** a device inserted in the cylinder of an internal-combustion engine, containing two terminals between which passes the electric spark that ignites the explosive gases. **2.** *Informal.* a person who leads, inspires, or animates a group.

spark·plug (spärk′plug′), *v.t.*, **-plugged, -plug·ging.** *Informal.* to lead, inspire, or animate. [v. use of SPARK PLUG]

spark′ transmit′ter, *Radio.* a transmitting set that generates electromagnetic waves by the oscillatory discharge from a capacitor through an inductor and a spark gap.

spar·ling (spär′ling), *n.*, *pl.* **-lings,** (*esp. collectively*) **-ling.** the European smelt, *Osmerus eperlanus.* [ME *sperlynge* < OF *(e)sperlinge* < Gmc; cf. G *Spierling*]

spar·oid (spâr′oid, spar′-), *adj.* **1.** resembling or pertaining to the porgy family, *Sparidae.* **—***n.* **2.** a sparoid fish. [< NL *Sparoīd(ēs)* = *Spar(us)* (see SPARID) + *-oīdēs* -OID]

spar·row (spar′ō), *n.* **1.** any of numerous American finches of the family *Fringillidae.* **2.** *Brit.* a house sparrow. **3.** any of several weaverbirds of the family *Ploceidae.* [ME *sparowe,* OE *spearwa;* c. Goth *sparwa,* OIcel *spörr*] **—spar′row·less,** *adj.* **—spar′row·like′,** *adj.*

spar·row·grass (spar′ō gras′, -gräs′), *n.* *Informal.* asparagus. [by folk etym.]

spar′row hawk′, **1.** a small, short-winged European hawk, *Accipiter nisus,* that preys on smaller birds. **2.** a small American falcon, *Falco sparverius.*

spar·ry (spär′ē), *adj.* of or pertaining to mineral spar.

sparse (spärs), *adj.*, **spars·er, spars·est.** **1.** thinly scattered or distributed. **2.** thin; not thick or dense. **3.** scanty; meager. [< L *spars(us)* scattered, ptp. of *spargere* to SPARGE] **—sparse·ly,** *adv.* **—sparse′ness, spar·si·ty** (spär′si tē), *n.* **—Syn.** See **scanty. —Ant.** abundant.

Spar·ta (spär′tə), *n.* an ancient city in S Greece; the capital of Laconia and the chief city of the Peloponnesus; at one time the dominant city of Greece; famous for strict discipline and training of soldiers. Also called **Lacedaemon.**

Spar·ta·cus (spär′tə kəs), *n.* died 71 B.C., Thracian slave, gladiator, and insurrectionist.

Spar·tan (spär′tᵊn), *adj.* Also, **Spar·tan·ic** (spär tan′ik). **1.** of or pertaining to Sparta or its people. **2.** like the Spartans; disciplined and austere. **3.** brave; undaunted. **—***n.* **4.** a native or inhabitant of Sparta. **5.** a person of Spartan characteristics. [< L *Spartān(us)* = *Spart(a)* SPARTA (< Gk) + *-ānus* -AN] **—Spar′tan·ism,** *n.* **—Spar′tan·ly, Spar·tan′i·cal·ly,** *adv.*

Spar·tan·burg (spär′tᵊn bûrg′), *n.* a city in NW South Carolina. 44,546 (1970).

spar·te·ine (spär′tē ēn′, -in), *n.* a bitter, poisonous, liquid alkaloid obtained from the common broom, *Cytisus scoparius,* used in medicine. [< NL *Sparti(um)* name of a genus (< Gk *spárt(os)* a kind of broom + L *-ium* n. suffix) + -INE[1]]

Spar·ti (spär′tī), *n.pl.* *Class. Myth.* a group of warriors who sprang fully armed from the dragon's teeth that Cadmus had planted in the ground. The warriors immediately fought among themselves until there were left only the five survivors who were to become the ancestors of the Theban nobility.

spasm (spaz′əm), *n.* **1.** *Med.* a sudden, abnormal, involuntary muscular contraction; an affection consisting of a continued muscular contraction **(tonic spasm),** or of a series of alternating muscular contractions and relaxations **(clonic spasm). 2.** any sudden, brief spell of energy, feeling, etc. [ME *spasme* < L *spasm(us)* < Gk *spasmós* convulsion < *spâ(n)* (to) pull, tug]

spas·mod·ic (spaz mod′ik), *adj.* **1.** pertaining to or of the nature of a spasm; characterized by spasms. **2.** resembling a spasm or spasms; sudden but brief: *spasmodic efforts at reform.* Also, **spas·mod′i·cal.** [< ML *spasmodic(us)* < Gk *spasmōd(ēs)* < *spasmós* SPASM; see -IC] **—spas·mod′i·cal·ly,** *adv.*

spas·tic (spas′tik), *Pathol.* **—***adj.* **1.** pertaining to, of the nature of, or characterized by spasm, esp. tonic spasm. **—***n.* **2.** a person given to such spasms, esp. one who has cerebral palsy. [< L *syastic(us)* afflicted with spasms < Gk *spastikós* of a spasm. See SPASM, -TIC] **—spas′ti·cal·ly,** *adv.*

spat[1] (spat), *n.*, *v.*, **spat·ted, spat·ting.** **—***n.* **1.** a petty quarrel. **2.** a light blow; slap; smack. **—***v.i.* **3.** to splash or spatter. **—***v.t.* **4.** to strike lightly; slap. [? imit.]

spat[2] (spat), *v.* a pt. and pp. of **spit.**

spat[3] (spat), *n.* a short gaiter worn over the instep and usually fastened under the foot with a strap. [short for SPATTERDASH]

spat[4] (spat), *n.* **1.** the spawn of an oyster or similar shellfish. **2.** a young oyster. **3.** young oysters collectively. [? c. SPIT[1]]

spate (spāt), *n.* **1.** a sudden outpouring of words, emotion, etc. **2.** *Brit.* **a.** a flood. **b.** a river flooding its banks. **c.** a sudden or heavy rainstorm. [?]

spa·tha·ceous (spə thā′shəs), *adj.* *Bot.* **1.** of the nature of or resembling a spathe. **2.** having a spathe. [< NL *spathāce-(us)* = L *spath(a)* (see SPATHE) + *-āceus;* see -ACEOUS]

spathe (spāth), *n.* *Bot.* a bract or pair of bracts, often large and colored, subtending or enclosing a spadix or flower cluster. [< L *spath(a)* < Gk *spáthē* blade, sword, stem] **—spathed,** *adj.*

spath·ic (spath′ik), *adj.* *Mineral.* like spar. [< G *Spat* (earlier sp., *Spath*) spar + -IC]

spa·tial (spā′shəl), *adj.* **1.** of or pertaining to space. **2.** existing or occurring in space. Also, **spacial.** [< L *spati(um)* space + -AL[1]] **—spa·ti·al·i·ty** (spā′shē al′i tē), *n.* **—spa′tial·ly,** *adv.*

spa·ti·o·tem·po·ral (spā′shē ō tem′pər əl), *adj.* **1.** pertaining to space-time. **2.** of or pertaining to both space and time. [< L *spati(um)* space + -o- + TEMPORAL[1]] **—spa′ti·o·tem′po·ral·ly,** *adv.*

spat·ter (spat′ər), *v.t.* **1.** to scatter in small particles or drops. **2.** to splash with small particles of something, esp. so as to soil or stain. **3.** to defame. **—***v.i.* **4.** to send out small particles or drops, as falling water. **5.** to strike a surface in or as in a shower, as bullets. **—***n.* **6.** the act or the sound of spattering. **7.** a splash or spot of something spattered. [perh. < D *spatt(en)* (to) burst, spout + -ER[6]] **—spat′ter·ing·ly,** *adv.*

spat·ter·dash (spat′ər dash′), *n.* a long gaiter to protect the trousers or stockings, as from mud while riding. **—spat′ter·dashed′,** *adj.*

spat·ter·dock (spat′ər dok′), *n.* **1.** a yellow-flowered pond lily, *Nuphar advena,* common in stagnant waters. **2.** any other water lily of the genera *Nuphar* and *Nymphaea,* esp. one having yellow flowers.

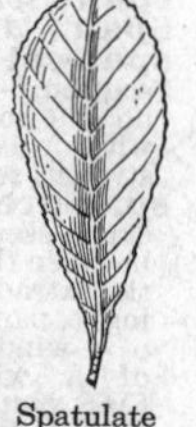

Spatulate leaf

spat·u·la (spach′ə lə), *n.* an implement with a broad, flat, usually flexible blade, used for blending foods or removing them from cooking utensils, mixing drugs, spreading plasters and paints, etc. [< L: a broad piece. See SPATHE, -ULE] **—spat′u·lar,** *adj.*

spat·u·late (spach′ə lit, -lāt′), *adj.* **1.** shaped like a spatula; rounded more or less like a spoon. **2.** *Bot.* having a broad, rounded end and a narrow, attenuate base, as a leaf. [< NL *spatulāt(us)*]

spa·vin (spav′in), *n.* *Vet. Pathol.* **1.** a disease of the hock joint of horses in which enlargement occurs due to collection of fluids **(bog spavin),** bony growth **(bone spavin),** or distention of the veins **(blood spavin). 2.** an excrescence or enlargement so formed. [ME *spaveyne* < OF (*e*)*spavain, esparvain* swelling < ?]

spav·ined (spav′ind), *adj.* **1.** suffering from or affected with spavin. **2.** being in a decrepit condition: *a spavined old car.* [late ME *spaveyned*]

spawn (spôn), *n.* **1.** *Zool.* the mass of eggs deposited by fishes, amphibians, mollusks, crustaceans, etc. **2.** *Bot.* the mycelium of mushrooms, esp. of the species grown for the market. **3.** *Usually Disparaging.* progeny, offspring, or brood. —*v.i.* **4.** to deposit eggs or sperm directly into the water, as fishes. —*v.t.* **5.** to produce (spawn). **6.** to give birth to; give rise to. **7.** to produce in large number. **8.** to plant with mycelium. [ME *spawn*(*en*), prob. < AF (*e*)*spaundre* (OF *espandre*) (to) EXPAND] —**spawn′er,** *n.*

spay (spā), *v.t.* *Vet. Med.* to remove the ovaries of (an animal). [ME *spay*(*en*) < AF (*e*)*speï*(*er*) (to) cut with a sword (OF *espeer*) < *espee* sword; see ÉPÉE]

S.P.C.A., Society for the Prevention of Cruelty to Animals.

S.P.C.C., Society for the Prevention of Cruelty to Children.

speak (spēk), *v.,* **spoke** or (*Archaic*) **spake; spo·ken** or (*Archaic*) **spoke; speak·ing.** —*v.i.* **1.** to utter words or articulate sounds with the ordinary voice; talk. **2.** to communicate vocally. **3.** to converse. **4.** to deliver an address, discourse, etc. **5.** to make a statement in written or printed words. **6.** to communicate by any means; convey significance: *Actions speak louder than words.* **7.** to emit a sound, as a musical instrument; make a noise or report. **8.** (of dogs) to bark when ordered. —*v.t.* **9.** to utter vocally and articulately. **10.** to express or make known, esp. with the voice. **11.** to declare by any means of communication. **12.** to use, or be able to use, in oral utterance, as a language. **13.** *Naut.* to communicate with (a passing vessel) at sea, as by voice or signal. **14.** *Archaic.* to speak to or with. **15. so to speak,** figuratively speaking. **16. speak for, a.** to speak in behalf of. **b.** to choose or have reserved: *This item is already spoken for.* **17. to speak of,** worth mentioning: *The country has no mineral resources to speak of.* [ME *spek*(*en*), OE *specan,* var. of *sprecan;* c. G *sprechen;* cf. OHG *spehhan*] —**speak′a·ble,** *adj.*
—**Syn. 1.** SPEAK, CONVERSE, TALK mean to make vocal sounds, usually for purposes of communication. To SPEAK is to utter one or more words, not necessarily connected; it usually implies conveying information and may apply to anything from an informal remark to a formal address before an audience: *to speak sharply; to speak at a convention.* To CONVERSE is to exchange ideas with someone by speaking: *to converse with a friend.* To TALK is to utter intelligible sounds, sometimes without regard to content: *The child is learning to talk.* **9.** pronounce, articulate.

speak·eas·y (spēk′ē′zē), *n., pl.* **-eas·ies.** a place where alcoholic beverages are illegally sold. Also, **speak′eas′y.**

speak·er (spē′kər), *n.* **1.** a person who speaks. **2.** a person who speaks formally; orator. **3.** (*usually cap.*) the presiding officer of the U.S. House of Representatives, the British House of Commons, or other such legislative assembly. **4.** a loudspeaker. **5.** a book of selections for practice in declamation. [ME] —**speak′er·ship′,** *n.*

Spea·ker (spē′kər), *n.* **Tris(tram E.),** 1888–1958, U.S. baseball player.

speak·ing (spē′king), *n.* **1.** the act, utterance, or discourse of a person who speaks. **2. speakings,** literary works composed for recitation; oral literature. —*adj.* **3.** that speaks; giving information as if by speech: *a speaking proof of a thing.* **4.** highly expressive: *speaking eyes.* **5.** lifelike: *a speaking likeness.* **6.** used in, suited to, or involving speaking or talking: *the speaking voice.* **7.** of or pertaining to declamation. **8. be on speaking terms (with), a.** to know (a person) only casually. **b.** (in negative sense) to refuse to speak with, as on account of a quarrel or misunderstanding: *They haven't been on speaking terms for ten years.* [ME]

speak′ing in tongues′, a prayer characterized chiefly by incomprehensible speech, originating in primitive Christianity and now practiced by Pentecostal groups in ecstatic forms of worship. Also called **gift of tongues.**

speak′ing tube′, a tube for conveying the voice to a distance, as from one part of a building to another.

spear[1] (spēr), *n.* **1.** a weapon for thrusting or throwing, consisting of a long wooden staff to which a sharp head, as of iron or steel, is attached. **2.** a soldier or other person armed with such a weapon; spearman: *an army of 40,000 spears.* **3.** some similar weapon or instrument, as one for use in fishing. **4.** the act of spearing. —*v.t.* **5.** to pierce with or as with a spear. —*v.i.* **6.** to go or penetrate like a spear. [ME, OE *spere;* c. D, G *speer*] —**spear′er,** *n.*

spear[2] (spēr), *n.* **1.** a sprout or shoot of a plant, as a blade of grass, an acrospire of grain, etc. —*v.i.* **2.** to sprout; shoot; send up or rise in a spear or spears. [var. of SPIRE[1], ? influenced by SPEAR[1]]

spear·fish (spēr′fish′), *v., n., pl.* (*esp. collectively*) **-fish,** (*esp. referring to two or more kinds or species*) **-fish·es.** —*v.i.* **1.** to fish underwater, as a scuba diver, using a spearlike implement propelled manually or mechanically. —*n.* **2.** any of several billfishes of the genus *Tetrapturas,* resembling the sailfish but having the first dorsal fin less developed.

spear′ gun′, a spearfishing device for shooting a barbed missile under water, usually by means of gas under pressure, a strong rubber band, or a powerful spring.

spear·head (spēr′hed′), *n.* **1.** the sharp-pointed head that forms the piercing end of a spear. **2.** any person or thing that leads an attack, undertaking, etc. —*v.t.* **3.** to act as a spearhead for. [ME]

spear·man (spēr′mən), *n., pl.* **-men.** a person who is armed with or uses a spear. [ME]

spear·mint (spēr′mint′), *n.* an aromatic herb, *Menta spicata,* used for flavoring.

spear′ side′, the male side, or line of descent, of a family (distinguished from *distaff side*).

spear·wort (spēr′wûrt′), *n.* any of several buttercups, esp. *Ranunculus Flammula,* having lanceolate leaves. [ME *sperewort,* OE *sperewyrt.* See SPEAR[1], WORT[2]]

spec., **1.** special. **2.** specially. **3.** specification.

spe·cial (spesh′əl), *adj.* **1.** of a distinct or particular kind or character: *a special kind of key.* **2.** having a particular function, purpose, application, etc.: *a special messenger.* **3.** dealing with particulars; specific: *a special statement.* **4.** distinguished or different from what is ordinary or usual. **5.** extraordinary; exceptional: *special importance.* **6.** great; dear: *a special friend.* —*n.* **7.** a special person or thing. **8.** a train used for a particular purpose. **9.** a special edition of a newspaper. **10.** a temporary, arbitrary reduction in the price of regularly stocked goods, esp. food; a special offer or price. **11.** *Television.* a single program not forming part of a regular series. [ME (*e*)*special* < L *speciāl*(*is*) of a given species = *speci*(*ēs*) SPECIES + *-ālis* -AL[1]] —**spe′cial·ly,** *adv.*
—**Syn. 4.** singular. SPECIAL, PARTICULAR, SPECIFIC refer to something pointed out for attention and consideration. SPECIAL means given unusual treatment because of being uncommon: *a special sense of a word.* PARTICULAR implies something selected from the others of its kind and set off from them for attention: *a particular variety of orchid.* SPECIFIC implies plain and unambiguous indication of one definite instance, example, etc.: *a specific instance of cowardice.* —**Ant. 1.** general.

spe′cial court′-martial, *U.S. Mil.* a court-martial established to try violations of military law less serious than those tried by a general court-martial but more serious than those tried by a summary court-martial.

spe′cial deliv′ery, delivery of mail outside the regularly scheduled hours upon the payment of an extra fee. —**spe′cial-de·liv′er·y,** *adj.*

spec′ial draw′ing rights′, the reserve asset created through the International Monetary Fund as a supplement to gold and U.S. dollars, for use among the member governments in settling international payments. *Abbr.:* SDR, S.D.R.

spe′cial effect′, Usually, **special effects.** *Motion Pictures, Television.* any artificial device that aids in producing a variety of illusions on the screen, as of thunder, lightning, etc.

Spe′cial Forc′es, U.S. military personnel trained to organize, instruct, and supervise foreign forces engaged in antiguerrilla and counterinsurgence operations.

spe·cial·ise (spesh′ə līz′), *v.i., v.t.,* **-ised, -is·ing.** *Chiefly Brit.* specialize. —**spe′cial·i·sa′tion,** *n.*

spe·cial·ism (spesh′ə liz′əm), *n.* devotion or restriction to a particular pursuit, branch of study, etc.

spe·cial·ist (spesh′ə list), *n.* **1.** a person who devotes himself to one subject or to one particular branch of a subject or pursuit. **2.** a medical practitioner who devotes his attention to a particular class of diseases, patients, etc. **3.** *U.S. Army.* an enlisted person of one of six grades having technical or administrative duties, corresponding to the grades of corporal through sergeant major but not requiring the exercise of command. **4.** *Stock Exchange.* a member of an exchange charged with executing orders for other members and maintaining a fair and orderly market in a particular group of stocks to which he confines his activities.

spe·ci·al·i·ty (spesh′ē al′i tē), *n., pl.* **-ties.** *Chiefly Brit.* specialty. [ME *specialite* < LL *specialitāt-;* see SPECIALTY]

spe·cial·ize (spesh′ə līz′), *v.,* **-ized, -iz·ing.** —*v.i.* **1.** to pursue some special line of study, work, etc.; have a specialty. **2.** *Biol.* (of an organism or one of its organs) to modify or differentiate in order to adapt to a special function or environment. —*v.t.* **3.** to invest with a special character, function, etc. **4.** to adapt to special conditions. **5.** to specify. Also, *esp. Brit.,* **specialise.** [< F *spécialis*(*er*)] —**spe′cial·i·za′tion,** *n.*

spe′cial ju′ry, *Law.* **1.** See **struck jury. 2.** See **blue-ribbon jury.**

spe′cial or′ders, *Mil.* a set of instructions from a headquarters affecting the activity or status of an individual or group of individuals. Cf. **general orders.**

spe′cial plead′ing, *Law.* a pleading that alleges special or new matter in avoidance of the allegations made by the opposite side.

spe′cial ses′sion, a session, as of a legislature or council, called to meet in addition to those held regularly.

spe′cial staff′, *Mil.* all staff officers assigned to headquarters of a division or higher unit who are not members of the general staff or personal staff.

spe′cial the′ory of relativ′ity, *Physics.* See under **relativity** (def. 2).

spe·cial·ty (spesh′əl tē), *n., pl.* **-ties,** *adj.* —*n.* **1.** the state or condition of being special. **2.** a special subject of study, line of work, or the like. **3.** an article particularly dealt in, manufactured, etc. **4.** an article of unusual or superior design or quality. **5.** a new article; novelty. **6.** an article with such strong consumer demand that it is at least partially removed from price competition. **7.** a special or particular point, item, matter, characteristic, or peculiarity. **8.** *Law.* a special agreement, contract, etc., under seal. —*adj.* **9.** *Theat.* (in vaudeville) **a.** performing or performed in an unusual manner, esp. one that involves dexterity or ingenuity: *specialty actor; specialty act.* **b.** (of a song or dance) isolated from the rest of the show: *specialty number.* Also, *esp. Brit.,* **speciality.** [ME *specialte* < MF (*e*)*specialte* < LL *specialitāt-* (s. of *specialitās*). See SPECIAL, -ITY]

spe·ci·a·tion (spē′shē ā′shən), *n.* *Biol.* the process by which new species are formed. [SPECI(ES) + -ATION]

spe·cie (spē′shē, -sē), *n.* **1.** coin; coined money. **2. in specie, a.** in the same kind or manner. **b.** (of money) in coin. **c.** *Law,* in the identical shape, form, etc., as specified. [< L (*in*) *speciē* (in) kind; see SPECIES]

spe·cies (spē′shēz, -sēz), *n., pl.* **-cies. 1.** a class of individuals having some common characteristics or qualities; distinct sort or kind. **2.** *Biol.* the major subdivision of a genus or subgenus, regarded as the basic category of biological classification, composed of related individuals that resemble one another and are able to breed among themselves but not able to breed with members of another species. **3.** *Logic.* **a.** one of the classes of things included with other classes in a genus. **b.** the set of things within one of these classes. **4.** *Eccles.* **a.** the external form or appearance of the bread or the wine in the Eucharist. **b.** either of the Eucharistic elements.

5. **the species,** the human race; mankind. 6. *Obs.* specie; coin. [< L: appearance, sort, form = *spec-* look, behold + *-i-* thematic vowel + *-ēs* n. suffix]

specif., 1. specific. 2. specifically.

spec·i·fi·a·ble (spes′ə fī′ə bəl), *adj.* capable of being specified.

spe·cif·ic (spi sif′ik), *adj.* 1. having a special application, bearing, or reference; specifying, explicit, or definite. 2. specified, precise, or particular: *a specific sum of money.* 3. peculiar or proper to something, as qualities, characteristics, or effects. 4. of a special or particular kind. 5. *Biol.* of or pertaining to a species: *specific characters.* 6. *Med.* a. (of a disease) produced by a special cause or infection. b. (of a remedy) having special effect in the prevention or cure of a certain disease. 7. *Immunol.* (of an antigen or antibody) having a particular effect on only one antigen or antibody or affecting it in only one way. 8. *Com.* noting customs or duties levied in fixed amounts per unit, as quantity, weight, or volume. 9. *Physics.* a. designating a physical constant that, for a particular substance, is expressed as the ratio of the quantity in the substance to the quantity in an equal volume of a standard substance, as water or air. b. designating a physical constant that expresses a property or effect as a quantity per unit length, area, volume, or mass. —*n.* 10. something specific, as a statement, quality, etc. 11. *Med.* a specific remedy. [< ML *specific(us)* = L *speci(ēs)* SPECIES + *-ficus* -FIC] —**spe·cif′i·cal·ly,** *adv.* —**spec·i·fic·i·ty** (spes′ə fis′i tē), *n.* —**Syn.** 1. See **special.** —**Ant.** 2. vague.

spec·i·fi·ca·tion (spes′ə fə kā′shən), *n.* 1. the act of specifying. 2. a detailed description of requirements, dimensions, materials, etc., as of a proposed building. 3. something specified, as an item in a bill of particulars. 4. the act of making specific. 5. the state of having a specific character. [< ML *specificātiōn-* (s. of *specificātiō*) = *specificāt(us)* mentioned, described (ptp. of *specificāre;* see SPECIFIC, -ATE[1]) + *-iōn-* -ION]

specif′ic grav′ity, *Physics.* the ratio of the density of any substance to the density of some other substance taken as standard, water being the standard for liquids and solids, and hydrogen or air being the standard for gases. Also called **relative density.** —**spe·cif′ic-grav′i·ty,** *adj.*

specif′ic heat′, *Physics.* 1. the number of calories required to raise the temperature of 1 gram of a substance 1°C, or the number of BTU's per pound per degree F. 2. (originally) the ratio of the thermal capacity of a substance to that of standard material.

specif′ic im′pulse, *Rocketry.* a measure of the efficiency with which a rocket engine utilizes its propellants, equal to the number of pounds of thrust produced per pound of propellant burned per second.

specif′ic vol′ume, *Physics.* volume per unit mass; the reciprocal of density.

spec·i·fy (spes′ə fī′), *v.,* **-fied, -fy·ing.** —*v.t.* 1. to mention or name specifically; state in detail. 2. to give a specific character to. 3. to name or state as a condition. —*v.i.* 4. to make a specific mention or statement. [ME *specyfy* < OF *specifi(er)* < ML *specificāre.* See SPECIFICATION, -FY] —**spec·i·fi·ca·tive** (spes′ə fə kā′tiv), *adj.* —**spec′i·fi·ca′tive·ly,** *adv.* —**spec′i·fi′er,** *n.*

spec·i·men (spes′ə mən), *n.* 1. a part or an individual taken as exemplifying or typifying a whole mass or number. 2. (in medicine, microbiology, etc.) a sample, as of urine, tissue, etc., for examination or study. 3. *Informal.* a particular or peculiar kind of person. [< L: mark, example, indication, sign = *spec-* look + *-i-* -I- + *-men* n. suffix denoting result or means] —**Syn.** 1. type, model, pattern. See **example.**

spe·ci·os·i·ty (spē′shē os′i tē), *n., pl.* **-ties.** 1. the state of being specious or plausible. 2. something pleasing to the eye but deceptive. 3. *Obs.* the state or quality of being beautiful. [< LL *speciōsitās* good looks, beauty]

spe·cious (spē′shəs), *adj.* 1. apparently good or right but lacking real merit; not genuine. 2. pleasing to the eye but deceptive. 3. *Obs.* pleasing to the eye. [< L *speciōs(us)* fair, beautiful = *speci(ēs)* SPECIES + *-ōsus* -OUS] —**spe′cious·ly,** *adv.* —**spe′cious·ness,** *n.* —**Syn.** 2. false, misleading.

speck (spek), *n.* 1. a small spot differing in color or substance from that of the surface or material upon which it appears or lies. 2. a very little bit or particle. 3. something appearing small by comparison or by reason of distance. —*v.t.* 4. to mark with or as with a speck or specks. [ME *specke,* OE *specca;* c. D *spikkel*] —**speck·ed·ness** (spek′id nis), *n.* —**speck′less,** *adj.*

speck·le (spek′əl), *n., v.,* **-led, -ling.** —*n.* 1. a small speck, spot, or mark, as on skin. 2. speckled coloring or marking. —*v.t.* 3. to mark with or as with speckles. [late ME] —**speck′led·ness,** *n.*

speck′led trout′. See **brook trout.**

specs (speks), *n.pl. Informal.* 1. spectacles; eyeglasses. 2. specifications. [by shortening]

spec·ta·cle (spek′tə kəl), *n.* 1. anything presented to the sight or view, esp. something of a large-scale, impressive kind. 2. a public show or display. 3. **spectacles.** eyeglasses (often used with *pair of*). 4. Often, **spectacles.** a. something resembling spectacles in shape or function. b. any of various devices suggesting or resembling spectacles. 5. *Obs.* a spyglass. 6. **make a spectacle of oneself,** to behave badly in public. [ME < L *spectācul(um)* < *spectāre,* freq. of *specere.* See SPECIES, -CLE]

spec·ta·cled (spek′tə kəld), *adj.* 1. provided with or wearing spectacles. 2. (of an animal) having a marking resembling a pair of spectacles.

spec·tac·u·lar (spek tak′yə lər), *adj.* 1. of or like a spectacle; marked by or given to an impressive, large-scale display. 2. dramatically daring or thrilling. —*n.* 3. an elaborate television production. Cf. **special** (def. 15). 4. an impressive, large-scale display. [< L *spectācul(um)* (see SPECTACLE) + -AR[1]] —**spec·tac·u·lar·i·ty** (spek tak′yə lar′i tē), *n.* —**spec·tac′u·lar·ly,** *adv.*

spec·tate (spek′tāt), *v.i.,* **-tat·ed, -tat·ing.** to be present as a spectator. [back formation from SPECTATOR]

spec·ta·tor (spek′tā tər, spek tā′-), *n.* 1. a person who looks on; onlooker; observer. 2. a person who is present at and views a spectacle, display, or the like. [< L < *spectātus,* ptp. of *spectāre.* See SPECTACLE, -OR[2]] —**spec·ta·to·ri·al** (spek′tə tōr′ē əl, -tôr′-), *adj.*

spec·ter (spek′tər), *n.* 1. a ghost, esp. one of a terrifying nature. 2. some source of terror or dread: *the specter of disease.* Also, *esp. Brit.,* **spec′tre.** [< L *spectr(um);* see SPECTRUM] —**Syn.** 1. phantom, apparition. See **ghost.**

spec·tra (spek′trə), *n.* a pl. of **spectrum.**

spec·tral (spek′trəl), *adj.* 1. of or pertaining to a specter; ghostly. 2. resembling a specter. 3. of, pertaining to, or produced by a spectrum or spectra. 4. resembling or suggesting a spectrum or spectra. [< L *spectr(um)* (see SPECTRUM) + -AL[1]] —**spec·tral′i·ty, spec′tral·ness,** *n.* —**spec′tral·ly,** *adv.*

spectro-, a combining form of **spectrum:** *spectrometer.*

spec·tro·bo·lom·e·ter (spek′trō bō lom′i tər), *n. Physics.* an instrument consisting of a spectroscope and a bolometer, for determining the distribution of energy in a spectrum. —**spec·tro·bo·lo·met·ric** (spek′trō bō′lə me′trik), *adj.*

spec·tro·gram (spek′trə gram′), *n.* a representation or photograph of a spectrum.

spec·tro·graph (spek′trə graf′, -gräf′), *n.* a spectroscope for photographing or producing a representation of a spectrum. —**spec·trog·ra·pher** (spek trog′rə fər), *n.* —**spec·tro·graph·ic** (spek′trə graf′ik), *adj.* —**spec′tro·graph′i·cal·ly,** *adv.* —**spec·trog′ra·phy,** *n.*

spec·tro·he·li·o·gram (spek′trō hē′lē ə gram′), *n.* a photograph of the sun made with a spectroheliograph.

spec·tro·he·li·o·graph (spek′trō hē′lē ə graf′, -gräf′), *n.* an apparatus for making photographs of the sun with a monochromatic light. —**spec·tro·he·li·o·graph·ic** (spek′trō hē′lē ə graf′ik), *adj.*

spec·trol·o·gy (spek trol′ə jē), *n.* the study of ghosts, phantoms, or apparitions. [< L *spectr(um)* SPECTER + -O- + -LOGY] —**spec·tro·log·i·cal** (spek′trə loj′i kəl), *adj.* —**spec′tro·log′i·cal·ly,** *adv.*

spec·trom·e·ter (spek trom′i tər), *n. Optics.* an optical device for measuring wavelengths, deviation of refracted rays, and angles between faces of a prism, esp. an instrument consisting of a slit through which light passes, a collimator, a prism that deviates the light, and a telescope through which the deviated light is examined. —**spec·tro·met·ric** (spek′trə me′trik), *adj.* —**spec·trom′e·try,** *n.*

spec·tro·pho·tom·e·ter (spek′trō fō tom′i tər), *n.* an instrument for making photometric comparisons between parts of spectra. —**spec·tro·pho·to·met·ric** (spek′trō fō′tə me′trik), *adj.* —**spec′tro·pho′to·met′ri·cal·ly,** *adv.* —**spec′tro·pho·tom′e·try,** *n.*

spec·tro·scope (spek′trə skōp′), *n. Optics.* an optical device for observing the spectrum of light or radiation from any source, consisting essentially of a slit through which the radiation passes, a collimating lens, a prism, and a telescope through which the spectrum is viewed. —**spec·tro·scop·ic** (spek′trə skop′ik), **spec′tro·scop′i·cal,** *adj.* —**spec′tro·scop′i·cal·ly,** *adv.* —**spec·tros·co·py** (spek tros′kə pē, spek′trə skō′pē), *n.* —**spec·tros·co·pist** (spek tros′kə pist), *n.*

spec·trum (spek′trəm), *n., pl.* **-tra** (-trə), **-trums.** 1. *Physics.* a. an array of entities, as light waves or particles, ordered in accordance with the magnitudes of a common physical property, as wavelength or mass: often the band of colors produced when sunlight is passed through a prism, comprising red, orange, yellow, green, blue, indigo, and violet. b. this band or series of colors together with extensions at the ends, which are not visible to the eye, but which can be studied by means of photography, heat effects, etc., and which are produced by the dispersion of radiant energy other than ordinary light rays. 2. a broad range of varied but related ideas or objects that form a continuous series or sequence: *the spectrum of political beliefs.* [< L: appearance, form < *spectāre;* see SPECTACLE]

spec′trum anal′ysis, the determination of the constitution or condition of bodies and substances by means of the spectra they produce.

spec·u·lar (spek′yə lər), *adj.* 1. pertaining to or having the properties of a mirror. 2. (of a reflection) regular, like that of a mirror (opposed to *diffuse*). 3. pertaining to a speculum. [< L *speculār(is)* (*specul(um)* a mirror = *spec-* look (see SPECIES) + *-ul-* -ULE) + *-āris* -AR[1]] —**spec′u·lar·ly,** *adv.*

spec·u·late (spek′yə lāt′), *v.i.,* **-lat·ed, -lat·ing.** 1. to engage in thought or reflection; meditate (often fol. by *on, upon,* or a clause). 2. to indulge in conjectural thought. 3. to engage in any business transaction involving considerable risk for the chance of large gains. [< L *speculāt(us)* observed, watched, examined; see SPECULATOR] —**Syn.** 1. think, reflect, cogitate. 2. conjecture, guess, surmise, theorize.

spec·u·la·tion (spek′yə lā′shən), *n.* 1. the contemplation or consideration of some subject. 2. a single instance or process of consideration. 3. a conclusion or opinion reached by such contemplation. 4. conjectural consideration of a matter; conjecture or surmise. 5. engagement in business transactions involving considerable risk for the chance of large gains. 6. a speculative commercial venture or undertaking. [ME *speculacioun* < LL *speculātiōn-* (s. of *speculātiō*) exploration, observation] —**Syn.** 3. supposition, theory.

spec·u·la·tive (spek′yə lā′tiv, -lə tiv), *adj.* 1. pertaining to or of the nature of speculation, contemplation, conjecture, or abstract reasoning. 2. theoretical, rather than practical. 3. given to speculation, as persons, the mind, etc. 4. of the nature of or involving commercial or financial speculation. 5. engaging in or given to such speculation. [ME *speculatif* < LL *speculātīv(us)*] —**spec′u·la′tive·ly,** *adv.* —**spec′u·la′tive·ness,** *n.*

spec·u·la·tor (spek′yə lā′tər), *n.* 1. a person who is engaged in commercial or financial speculation. 2. a person who makes advance purchases of tickets, as to games, theatrical performances, etc., that are likely to be in demand, for resale later at a higher price. 3. a person who is devoted to mental speculation. [< L: explorer = *speculāt(us),* ptp. of *speculārī* (*specul(a)* lookout = *spec(ere)* (to) look at + *-ula* fem. suffix + *-ātus* -ATE[1]) + *-or* -OR[2]]

spec·u·la·to·ry (spek′yə lə tōr′ē, -tôr′ē), *adj. Archaic.* speculative. [< L *speculāt(us)* (see SPECULATOR) + -ORY[1]]

spec·u·lum (spek′yə ləm), *n., pl.* **-la** (-lə), **-lums.** 1. a mirror or reflector, esp. one of polished metal, as on a reflecting telescope. 2. *Surg.* an instrument for rendering a part accessible to observation, as by enlarging an orifice. 3. *Ornith.* a lustrous or specially colored area on the wing of certain birds. [< L: mirror = *spec(ere)* (to) behold + *-ulum* -ULE]

sped (sped), *v.* a pt. and pp. of **speed.**

speech (spēch), *n.* **1.** the faculty or power of speaking; oral communication. **2.** the act of speaking. **3.** something spoken; an utterance, remark, or declaration. **4.** oral communication to an audience for a given purpose. **5.** any single utterance of an actor in the course of a play, motion picture, etc. **6.** the form of utterance characteristic of a particular people or region; a language or dialect. **7.** manner of speaking, as of a person. **8.** a field of study devoted to the theory and practice of oral communication. **9.** *Archaic.* rumor. [ME *speche,* OE *spǣc,* var. of *sprǣc;* c. G *Sprache*] —**Syn. 1.** parlance, parley, conversation. SPEECH, LANGUAGE refer to the means of communication used by people. SPEECH is the expression of ideas and thoughts by means of articulate vocal sounds, or the faculty of thus expressing ideas and thoughts. LANGUAGE is a set of conventional signs, used conventionally and not necessarily articulate or even vocal (any set of signs, signals, or symbols that convey meaning, including written words, may be called language): *a spoken language.* Thus, LANGUAGE is the set of conventions, and SPEECH is the action of putting these to use: *He couldn't understand the speech of the natives because it was in a foreign language.* **3.** observation, assertion, asseveration, comment, mention, talk. **4.** talk, discourse. SPEECH, ADDRESS, ORATION, HARANGUE are terms for a communication to an audience. SPEECH is the general word, with no implication of kind or length, or whether planned or not. An ADDRESS is a rather formal, planned speech, appropriate to a particular subject or occasion. An ORATION is a polished, rhetorical address, given usually on a notable occasion, that employs eloquence and studied methods of delivery. A HARANGUE is a violent, informal speech, often addressed to a casual audience, and intended to arouse strong feeling (sometimes to lead to mob action). **6.** tongue, patois.

speech′ clin′ic, a place at which specialists in speech therapy reeducate those with a speech handicap.

speech′ commu′nity, *Linguistics.* the aggregate of all the people who use a given language or dialect.

speech′ correc′tion, the reeducation of speech habits that deviate from accepted speech standards.

speech′ form′. See **linguistic form.**

speech·i·fy (spē′chə fī′), *v.i.,* **-fied, -fy·ing.** to make a speech or speeches; harangue. —**speech′i·fi′er,** *n.*

speech·less (spēch′lis), *adj.* **1.** temporarily deprived of speech by strong emotion, exhaustion, etc. **2.** characterized by absence or loss of speech: *speechless joy.* **3.** lacking the faculty of speech; dumb. **4.** not expressed in speech or words. **5.** refraining from speech. [ME *specheles,* OE *spǣclēas*] —**speech′less·ly,** *adv.* —**speech′less·ness,** *n.* —**Syn. 1.** dumfounded, shocked, mute. See **dumb. 3.** silent, mute. —**Ant. 1–3.** loquacious, voluble, talkative.

speech·mak·er (spēch′mā′kər), *n.* a person who delivers a speech or speeches. —**speech′mak′ing,** *n.*

speech′ sound′, *Phonet.* **1.** any of the set of distinctive sounds of a given language. Cf. **phoneme. 2.** any audible, elemental, acoustic event occurring in speech: *"Go" contains the speech sound "o."* Cf. **phone**[2]. **3.** any of the sounds of the entire phonetic system of a language. Cf. **allophone.**

speed (spēd), *n., v.,* **sped** or **speed·ed, speed·ing.** —*n.* **1.** rapidity in moving, going, etc.; swiftness; celerity: *moderate speed.* **2.** relative rapidity in moving, going, etc.; rate of motion or progress: *the speed of light.* **3.** *Auto.* a transmission gear ratio. **4.** *Photog.* **a.** the sensitivity of a film or paper to light. **b.** the length of time a shutter is opened to expose film. **c.** the largest opening at which a lens can be used. **5.** *Slang.* a stimulating drug, as amphetamine or Methedrine. **6.** *Optics, Photog.* See **f number. 7.** *Archaic.* success or prosperity. **8. at full** or **top speed, a.** at the greatest speed possible. **b.** to the maximum of one's capabilities: with great rapidity. —*v.t.* **9.** to promote the success of (an affair, undertaking, etc.); further or expedite. **10.** to direct (the steps, way, etc.) with speed. **11.** to increase the rate of speed of (usually fol. by *up*): *to speed up industrial production.* **12.** to bring to a particular speed, as a machine. **13.** to cause to move, go, or proceed with speed. **14.** *Archaic.* to cause to succeed or prosper. —*v.i.,* **15.** to move, go, etc., with speed or rapidity. **16.** to drive a vehicle at a rate that exceeds the legally established maximum. **17.** to increase the rate of speed or progress (usually fol. by *up*). **18.** to get on or fare in a specified or particular manner. **19.** *Archaic.* to succeed or prosper. [ME *spede* good luck, OE *spēd;* c. D *spoed,* OHG *spōt;* akin to OE *spōwan* to prosper, succeed] —**speed′er,** *n.* —**Syn. 1, 2.** fleetness, alacrity, dispatch, expedition; hurry. SPEED, VELOCITY, QUICKNESS, RAPIDITY, CELERITY, HASTE refer to swift or energetic movement or operation. SPEED (originally prosperity or success) may apply to human or nonhuman activity and emphasizes the rate in time at which something travels or operates: *the speed of light, of a lens, of an automobile, of thought.* VELOCITY, a more learned or technical term, is sometimes interchangeable with SPEED: *the velocity of light;* it is commonly used to refer to high rates of speed, linear or circular: *velocity of a projectile.* QUICKNESS, a native word, and RAPIDITY, a synonym of Latin origin, suggest speed of movement or operation on a small or subordinate scale; QUICKNESS applies more to people (*quickness of mind, of bodily movement*), RAPIDITY more to things, often in a technical or mechanical context: *the rapidity of moving parts; a lens of great rapidity.* CELERITY, a somewhat literary synonym of Latin origin, refers usually to human movement or operation and emphasizes expedition, dispatch, or economy in an activity: *the celerity of his response.* HASTE refers to the energetic activity of human beings under stress; it often suggests lack of opportunity for care or thought: *to marry in haste.* **11.** accelerate. **15.** See **rush**[1].

speed·boat (spēd′bōt′), *n.* a motorboat designed for high speeds.

speed′ light′, *Photog.* an electronic flash lamp. Also called **speed′ lamp′.**

speed′ lim′it, the maximum speed at which a vehicle is legally permitted to travel, as within a specific area, on a certain road, under given conditions, etc.

speed·om·e·ter (spē dom′i tər, spi-), *n.* a device on an automobile or other vehicle for recording the rate of travel in miles per hour and, often, the distance covered.

speed-read (spēd′rēd′), *v.t., v.i.,* **-read, -read·ing.** to read faster than normal, esp. by acquired techniques of skimming, controlled eye-movements, etc. —**speed′-read′er,** *n.* —**speed′-read′ing,** *n.*

speed·ster (spēd′stər), *n. Informal.* **1.** a person who drives at high speeds, esp. exceeding the legal speed limit. **2.** an athlete known for his speed in running, as in track, basketball, or the like. **3.** an animal known for its speed, as a race horse.

speed′ trap′, a section of a road where hidden policemen, radar, etc., check the speed of motorists and strictly enforce traffic regulations.

speed-up (spēd′up′), *n.* **1.** an increasing of speed. **2.** an imposed increase in the rate of production without a corresponding increase in the rate of pay. Also, **speed′up′.**

speed·way (spēd′wā′), *n.* **1.** a road or course for fast driving, motoring, or the like, or on which more than ordinary speed is allowed. **2.** a track on which automobile or motorcycle races are held.

speed·well (spēd′wel′), *n.* any of several herbs, shrubs, or small trees of the genus *Veronica.* [so called because its petals fade and fall early]

speed·y (spē′dē), *adj.,* **speed·i·er, speed·i·est. 1.** characterized by speed; rapid; swift; fast. **2.** prompt; not delayed: *a speedy recovery.* [ME *spedy*] —**speed′i·ly,** *adv.* —**speed′i·ness,** *n.* —**Syn. 1.** quick. **2.** expeditious.

speel (spēl), *v.t., v.i. Scot. and North Eng.* to climb; ascend; mount. Also, **speil** (spēl). [?]

speer (spēr), *v.i., v.t. Scot. and North Eng.* to ask. Also, **speir** (spēr). [ME *spere, spire,* OE *spyr(ian)* (to) make tracks, trace, ask about; c. Icel *spyrja;* akin to SPOOR]

speiss (spīs), *n. Metall.* a product obtained in smelting certain ores, consisting of one or more metallic arsenides, as of iron, nickel, etc. [< G *Speise,* lit., food]

spe·lae·an (spi lē′ən), *adj.* of, pertaining to, or inhabiting a cave or caves. Also, **spe·le′an.** [< NL *spēlae(us)* (adj., for L *spēlaeum* < Gk *spēlaion* cave) + -AN]

spe·le·ol·o·gy (spē′lē ol′ə jē), *n.* the exploration and study of caves. Also, **spe′lae·ol′o·gy.** [< L *spēlae(um)* (see SPELAEAN) + -O- + -LOGY] —**spe·le·o·log·i·cal, spe·lae·o·log·i·cal** (spē′lē ə loj′i kəl), *adj.* —**spe′le·ol′o·gist, spe′lae·ol′o·gist,** *n.*

spell[1] (spel), *v.,* **spelled** or **spelt, spell·ing.** —*v.t.* **1.** to name or write the letters of (a word, syllable, etc.). **2.** (of letters) to form (a word, syllable, etc.). **3.** to signify; amount to: *This delay spells disaster for us.* —*v.i.* **4.** to express words by letters, often as specified: *to spell poorly.* **5. spell out, a.** to read with difficulty, as letter by letter. **b.** *Informal.* to explain something explicitly and painstakingly; make the meaning unmistakable. **c.** to write out in full, unabbreviated form. [ME *spell(en)* < OF *(e)spell(er)* < some Gmc tongue; cf. OE *spellian* to talk < *spell* SPELL[2]] —**spell′a·ble,** *adj.*

spell[2] (spel), *n.* **1.** a magic word, phrase, or form of words; charm; incantation. **2.** a state of enchantment. **3.** any irresistible influence; fascination. [ME, OE *spell* discourse; c. OHG *spel,* Goth *spill,* Icel *spjall* tale; akin to OE *spellian,* Icel *spjalla,* Goth *spillon,* etc. (see SPELL[1])] —**spell′-like′,** *adj.*

spell[3] (spel), *n.* **1.** a course or period of work or other activity. **2.** a turn of work so taken. **3.** a turn, bout, fit, or period of anything experienced, as an illness. **4.** an indefinite interval or space of time. **5.** a period of weather of a specified kind: *a hot spell.* **6.** *Australian.* a rest period. —*v.t.* **7.** to take the place of for a time; relieve. **8.** *Australian.* to declare or give a rest period to. —*v.i.* **9.** *Australian.* to have or take a rest period. [ME *spel(en),* OE *spelian* to be substitute for, OE *gespellia* substitute; akin to OE *spala* substitute]

spell·bind (spel′bīnd′), *v.t.,* **-bound, -bind·ing.** to hold or bind by, or as by, a spell; enchant; entrance; fascinate. [deduced from SPELLBOUND]

spell·bind·er (spel′bīn′dər), *n.* a speaker, esp. a politician, who holds his audience spellbound.

spell·bound (spel′bound′), *adj.* bound by or as by a spell; enchanted or fascinated.

spell·er (spel′ər), *n.* **1.** a person who spells words. **2.** Also called **spell′ing book′.** an elementary textbook or manual to teach spelling. [late ME]

spell·ing (spel′ing), *n.* **1.** the manner in which words are spelled; orthography. **2.** a group of letters representing a word. **3.** the act of a speller. [late ME]

spell′ing bee′, a spelling competition won by the individual or team spelling the greatest number of words correctly.

spell′ing pronuncia′tion, a pronunciation based on spelling, usually a variant of the traditional pronunciation. The spelling pronunciation of *waistcoat* is (wāst′kōt′) rather than (wes′kət).

Spell·man (spel′mən), *n.* **Francis Joseph, Cardinal,** 1889–1967, U.S. Roman Catholic clergyman: archbishop of New York 1939–67.

spelt[1] (spelt), *v.* a pt. and pp. of **spell**[1].

spelt[2] (spelt), *n.* a wheat, *Triticum spelta,* native to southern Europe and western Asia, used chiefly for livestock feed. [ME, OE < LL *spelta;* cf. OHG *spelza,* G *Spelt*]

spel·ter (spel′tər), *n.* zinc, esp. in the form of ingots. [akin to MD *speauter*]

spe·lunk (spi lungk′), *v.i.* to explore caves. [< L *spēlunc(a)* a cave < Gk *spēlynx;* see SPELAEAN]

spe·lun·ker (spi lung′kər), *n.* a person who explores caves.

spence (spens), *n. Brit. Dial.* a pantry. [late ME *spense, spence,* by aphesis < MF *despense* pantry < L *dispensa,* n. use of fem. of *dispensus,* ptp. of *dispendere* to weigh out; see DISPENSE]

spen·cer[1] (spen′sər), *n.* **1.** a short, close-fitting jacket, frequently trimmed with fur, worn in the 19th century by women and children. **2.** a man's close-fitting jacket, having a collar and lapels and reaching just below the waist. [named after G. J. *Spencer* (1758–1834), English earl]

spen·cer[2] (spen′sər), *n. Naut.* a large gaff sail, usually loose-footed, hooped to a trysail mast abaft a square-rigged foremast or abaft the mainmast of a ship or bark. [? after the surname]

Spen·cer (spen′sər), *n.* **Herbert,** 1820–1903, English philosopher, whose system of thought was based on evolutionary theory. —**Spen·ce·ri·an·ism** (spen sēr′ē ə niz′əm), *n.*
Spen·ce·ri·an (spen sēr′ē ən), *adj.* **1.** of Herbert Spencer or his philosophy. —*n.* **2.** a follower of Herbert Spencer.
Spen·ce·ri·an (spen sēr′ē ən), *adj.* pertaining to a system of penmanship, characterized by clear, rounded letters slanting to the right. [named after P. R. *Spencer* (d. 1864), American handwriting expert]
spend (spend), *v.*, **spent, spend·ing.** —*v.t.* **1.** to pay out, disburse, or expend (money, resources, etc.). **2.** to employ (labor, time, etc.) on some object, in some proceeding, etc. **3.** to pass (time) in a particular manner, place, etc. **4.** to use up, consume, or exhaust. **5.** to give (one's blood, life, etc.) for some cause. —*v.i.* **6.** to spend money, time, etc. [ME *spend(en)*, OE (*a*)*spendan* < WGmc < L *expendere* to pay out, EXPEND; cf. G *spenden*]
—**Syn. 1.** SPEND, DISBURSE, EXPEND refer to paying out money. SPEND is the general word: *We spend more for living expenses now.* DISBURSE implies spending from a specific source or sum to meet specific obligations, or paying in definite allotments: *The treasurer has authority to disburse funds.* EXPEND is more formal, and implies spending for some definite and (usually) sensible or worthy object: *to expend most of one's salary on necessities.* **2.** use, apply, devote. —**Ant. 1.** earn, keep.
spend·a·ble (spen′də bəl), *adj.* available for spending.
spend·er (spen′dər), *n.* a person who spends, esp. excessively or lavishly; spendthrift. [ME]
Spen·der (spen′dər), *n.* **Stephen,** born 1909, English poet and critic.
spend′ing mon′ey, money for small personal expenses.
spend·thrift (spend′thrift′), *n.* **1.** a person who spends his money extravagantly or wastefully; prodigal. —*adj.* **2.** extravagant or wasteful; prodigal.
Spe·ner (shpā′nər), *n.* **Phi·lipp Ja·kob** (fē′lēp yä′kôp), 1635–1705, German theologian: founder of Pietism. —**Spe·ner·ism** (shpā′nə riz′əm, spā′-), *n.*
Speng·ler (speng′glər; *Ger.* shpeng′glər), *n.* **Os·wald** (oz′wôld; *Ger.* ôs′vält), 1880–1936, German philosopher. —**Speng·le·ri·an** (speng glēr′ē ən, shpeng-), *adj.*
Spen·ser (spen′sər), *n.* **Edmund,** c1552–99, English poet.
Spen·se·ri·an (spen sēr′ē ən), *adj.* **1.** of or characteristic of Spenser or his work. —*n.* **2.** an imitator of Spenser. **3.** See **Spenserian stanza. 4.** verse in Spenserian stanzas.
Spense′rian son′net, a sonnet employing the rhyme scheme *abab, bcbc, cdcd, ee.*
Spense′rian stan′za, the stanza used by Spenser in his verse allegory *The Faerie Queene* (1590–96) and employed since by other poets, consisting of eight iambic pentameter lines and a final Alexandrine, with a rhyme scheme of *ababbcbcc.*
spent (spent), *v.* **1.** pt. and pp. of **spend.** —*adj.* **2.** used up, consumed, or exhausted.
Spen·ta Main·yu (spen′tə mīn′yōō), *Zoroastrianism.* the good and creative spirit that is the offspring of Ahura Mazda.
sperm[1] (spûrm), *n.* **1.** See **spermatic fluid. 2.** a male reproductive cell; spermatozoon. [late ME *sperme* < LL *sperma* < Gk *spérma* seed = *sper-* (root of *speírein* to sow) + *-ma* n. suffix] —**sper·ma·toid** (spûr′mə toid′), *adj.* —**sper′mous,** *adj.*
sperm[2] (spûrm), *n.* **1.** spermaceti. **2.** See **sperm whale. 3.** See **sperm oil.** [by shortening]
sperm-, var. of **spermo-** before a vowel: *spermine.*
-sperm, var. of **spermo-,** as final element of a compound word: *gymnosperm.*
sper·ma·cet·i (spûr′mə set′ē, -sē′tē), *n.* *Chem., Pharm.* a waxy solid, obtained from the oil in the head of the sperm whale: used chiefly in the manufacture of cosmetics and as an emollient in ointments. [< ML *sperma cētī* sperm of whale (see SPERM[1], CET-); r. ME *sperma cete* < ML *sperma cētē* sperm of whales (L *cētē* < Gk *kḗtē* whales)]
-spermal, a word element used to form adjectives corresponding to nouns with stems ending in **-sperm.**
sper·mar·y (spûr′mə rē), *n., pl.* **-ries.** an organ in which spermatozoa are generated; testis. [< NL *spermāri(um)*]
spermat-, var. of **spermato-** before a vowel: *spermatid.*
sper·mat·ic (spûr mat′ik), *adj.* **1.** of, pertaining to, or resembling sperm; seminal; generative. **2.** pertaining to a spermary. [< LL *spermatic(us)* < Gk *spermatikós* relating to seed = *spermat-* (s. of *spérma*) SPERM[1] + *-ikos* -IC] —**sper·mat′i·cal·ly,** *adv.*
spermat′ic cord′, *Anat.* the cord by which a testis is suspended in the scrotum, containing the vas deferens, the blood vessels and nerves of the testis, etc.
spermat′ic flu′id, the male generative fluid; semen.
sper·ma·tid (spûr′mə tid), *n.* one of the cells that result from the meiotic divisions of a spermatocyte and mature into spermatozoa.
sper·ma·ti·um (spûr mā′shē əm), *n., pl.* **-ti·a** (-shē ə). *Bot.* **1.** the nonmotile male gamete of a red alga. **2.** a minute, colorless cell, believed to be a male reproductive body, developed within spermogonia. [< NL < Gk *spermátion* = *spermat-* (s. of *spérma*) SPERM[1] + *-ion* dim. suffix]
spermato-, a learned borrowing from Greek, meaning "seed," used with this meaning and as a combining form of **sperm**[1] in the formation of compound words: *spermatogonium.* Cf. **sperm-, -sperm, -spermal, spermat-, -spermic, spermo-, -spermous.** [< Gk *spermat-* (s. of *spérma;* see SPERM[1]) + -o-]
sper·mat·o·cyte (spûr mat′ə sīt′, spûr′mə tə-), *n.* *Biol.* a male germ cell in the maturation stage. —**sper′ma·to·cyt′·al,** *adj.*
sper·mat·o·gen·e·sis (spûr mat′ə jen′i sis, spûr′mə tə-), *n.* *Biol.* the origin and development of spermatozoa. [< NL] —**sper·ma·to·ge·net·ic** (spûr′mə tō jə net′ik, spər mat′ō-), *adj.*
sper·mat·o·go·ni·um (spûr mat′ə gō′nē əm, spûr′mə-tə-), *n., pl.* **-ni·a** (-nē ə). *Biol.* one of the undifferentiated germ cells giving rise to spermatocytes. [< NL] —**sper·mat′o·go′ni·al,** *adj.*
sper·mat·o·phore (spûr mat′ə fōr′, -fôr′, spûr′mə tə-), *n.* *Zool.* a special case or capsule containing a number of spermatozoa, produced by the male of certain insects, mollusks, annelids, etc., and some vertebrates.
sper·mat·o·phyte (spûr mat′ə fīt′, spûr′mə tə-), *n.* any of the *Spermatophyta,* a primary division or group of plants comprising those that bear seeds. [modeled on NL *spermatophyta*] —**sper·ma·to·phyt·ic** (spûr′mə tə fit′ik, spər mat′ə-), *adj.*
sper·ma·to·zo·id (spûr′mə tə zō′id, spûr-mat′ə-), *n.* *Bot.* a motile male gamete produced in an antheridium. [SPERMATOZO(ON) + -ID[3]]
sper·ma·to·zo·on (spûr′mə tə zō′ən, -on, spûr mat′ə-), *n., pl.* **-zo·a** (-zō′ə). *Biol.* one of the minute, usually actively motile gametes in semen, which serve to fertilize the ovum; a mature male reproductive cell. Also, **sper′ma·to·zo′ön.** [< NL] —**sper′·ma·to·zo′al, sper′ma·to·zo′an, sper′ma·to·zo′ic,** *adj.*

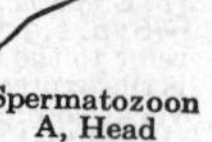

Spermatozoon
A, Head
B, Neck
C, Tail

-spermic, a word element used to form adjectives corresponding to nouns with stems ending in **-sperm.** [< NL *-spermicus*]
sperm·ine (spûr′mēn, -min), *n.* *Biochem., Pharm.* a base, $H_2N(CH_2)_3NH(CH_2)_4NH(CH_2)_3NH_2$, found esp. in semen, sputum, pancreatic tissue, and certain yeasts: used chiefly as a nerve stimulant. [SPERM- + -INE[2]]
sper·mi·o·gen·e·sis (spûr′mē ō jen′i sis), *n.* *Biol.* the development of a spermatozoon from a spermatid. [< NL *spermio-* (comb. form of *spermium;* see SPERM[1]) + GENESIS] —**sper·mi·o·ge·net·ic** (spûr′mē ō jə net′ik), *adj.*
spermo-, a combining form of **sperm**[1], used also with the meaning "seed," "germ," "semen," in the formation of compound words: *spermophyte.* Also, *esp. before a vowel,* **sperm-.**
sper·mo·go·ni·um (spûr′mə gō′nē əm), *n., pl.* **-ni·a** (-nē ə). *Bot.* one of the cup- or flask-shaped receptacles in which the spermatia of certain thallophytic plants are produced.
sperm′ oil′, *Chem.* a yellow liquid obtained from the sperm whale, used chiefly as a lubricant in light machinery.
sper·mo·phile (spûr′mə fīl′, -fil), *n.* any of various burrowing rodents of the squirrel family, esp. of the genus *Citellus* (or *Spermophilus*), as the ground squirrels or susliks, sometimes sufficiently numerous to do much damage to crops. [SPERMO- + -PHILE, modeled on NL *spermophilus*]
sper·mo·phyte (spûr′mə fīt′), *n.* *Bot.* spermatophyte. [modeled on NL *spermophyta*]
sper·mous (spûr′məs), *adj.* of or pertaining to sperm.
-spermous, a word element used to form adjectives corresponding to nouns with stems ending in **-sperm:** *gymnospermous.*
sperm′ whale′, a large, square-snouted whale, *Physeter catodon,* valued for its oil and spermaceti.
sper·ry·lite (sper′ə līt′), *n.* a mineral, platinum arsenide, $PtAs_2$, a minor ore of platinum. [named after F. L. *Sperry,* 19th-century Canadian chemist, who found it; see -LITE]
spew (spyōō), *v.t.* **1.** to eject from the stomach through the mouth; vomit. **2.** to cast forth, gush, or eject. —*v.i.* **3.** to discharge the contents of the stomach through the mouth; vomit. —*n.* **4.** that which is spewed; vomit. Also, **spue.** [ME; OE *spīw(an);* c. G *speien,* Goth *speiwan,* Icel *spýja,* L *spuere*]
Spey·er (shpī′ər), *n.* a city in SW West Germany, on the Rhine. 39,800 (est. 1963). Also called **Spires.**
Spe·zia (*It.* spe′tsyä), *n.* See **La Spezia.**
sp. gr., specific gravity.
sphaero-, var. of **sphero-.**
sphag·num (sfag′nəm), *n.* any soft moss of the genus *Sphagnum,* found chiefly on the surface of bogs, used in potting and packing plants, dressing wounds, etc. [< NL, alter. of Gk *sphágnos* a moss] —**sphag′nous,** *n.*
sphal·er·ite (sfal′ə rīt′, sfā′lə-), *n.* a very common mineral, zinc sulfide, ZnS, usually containing a little cadmium, the principal ore of zinc and cadmium; blackjack. [< Gk *sphaler(ós)* slippery, deceptive + -ITE[1]]
sphen-, a learned borrowing from Greek meaning "wedge," used in the formation of compound words: *sphenic.* [< NL < Gk *sphḗn* wedge]
sphene (sfēn), *n.* a mineral, calcium titanium silicate, $CaTiSiO_5$. Also called **titanite.** [< Gk *sphḗn* wedge]
sphe·nic (sfē′nik), *adj.* wedge-shaped.
sphe·noid (sfē′noid), *adj.* Also, **sphe·noi′dal. 1.** wedge-shaped. **2.** *Anat.* of or pertaining to the compound bone of the base of the skull, at the roof of the pharynx. —*n.* **3.** *Anat.* the sphenoid bone. [< NL *sphēnoīd(ēs)* < Gk *sphēnoeidḗs*]
spher·al (sfēr′əl), *adj.* **1.** of or pertaining to a sphere. **2.** spherical. **3.** symmetrical; perfect in form. [< LL *sphaerāl(is)*]
sphere (sfēr), *n., v.,* **sphered, spher·ing.** —*n.* **1.** a solid geometric figure generated by the revolution of a semicircle about its diameter; a round body whose surface is at all points equidistant from the center. **2.** any rounded body approximately of this form. **3.** a planet or star; heavenly body. **4.** See **celestial sphere. 5.** *Astron.* any of the transparent, concentric, spherical shells, or layers, in which, according to ancient belief, the planets, stars, and other heavenly bodies were set. **6.** the place or environment within which a person or thing exists. **7.** a field of something specified: *a sphere of knowledge.* —*v.t.* **8.** to enclose in or as in a sphere. **9.** to form into a sphere. [< LL *sphēr(a),* var. of L *sphaera* globe < Gk *sphaîra* ball; r. ME *spere* < OF (*e*)*spere* < LL *spēra,* as above] —**Syn. 2.** See **ball**[1]. **6.** area, province, realm, domain.
-sphere, a combining form of **sphere** (*planisphere*), having a special use in the names of the layers of gases and the like, surrounding the earth and other celestial bodies (*ionosphere*).
sphere′ of in′fluence, 1. any area in which one nation wields dominant power over another or others. **2.** a region where underdeveloped countries are exploited and dominated by a powerful and often imperialistic state.
spher·i·cal (sfer′i kəl), *adj.* **1.** having the form of a sphere; globular. **2.** formed in or on a sphere, as a geometrical figure. **3.** of or pertaining to a sphere or spheres. **4.** pertaining to the heavenly bodies, or to their supposed revolving spheres or shells. **5.** pertaining to the heavenly bodies regarded astrologically as exerting influence on mankind and events. Also, **spher′ic.** [< LL *sphēric(us)* (see SPHERICS[1])

+ -AL[1]] —**spher′i·cal′i·ty,** *n.* —**spher′i·cal·ly,** *adv.* —**Syn. 1.** rounded.

spher′ical aberra′tion, variation in focal length of a lens or mirror from center to edge, due to its spherical shape.

spher′ical an′gle, *Geom.* an angle formed by arcs of great circles of a sphere.

spher′ical geom′etry, the branch of geometry that deals with figures on spherical surfaces.

spher′ical pol′ygon, *Geom.* a closed figure formed by arcs of great circles of a sphere.

spher′ical tri′angle, *Geom.* a triangle formed by arcs of great circles of a sphere.

spher′ical trigonom′etry, the branch of trigonometry that deals with spherical triangles.

sphe·ric·i·ty (sfi ris′i tē), *n.* the state of being spherical. [< NL *sphēricitāt-* (s. of *sphēricitās*) = LL *sphēric(us)* (see SPHERICS[1]) + *-itāt-* -ITY]

spher·ics[1] (sfer′iks), *n.* (*construed as sing.*) the geometry and trigonometry of figures formed on the surface of a sphere. [< LL *sphēric(us)* < Gk *sphairikós.* See SPHERE, -IC, -ICS]

spher·ics[2] (sfer′iks), *n.* *Radio.* (*construed as pl.*) atmospherics. [by shortening]

sphero-, a combining form of **sphere:** *spherometer.* Also, **sphaero-, -sphere.**

sphe·roid (sfēr′oid), *Geom.* —*n.* **1.** a solid geometrical figure generated by rotating an ellipse about one of its axes. —*adj.* **2.** spheroidal. [< L *sphaeroīd(ēs)* < Gk *sphairoeidḗs*]

sphe·roi·dal (sfi roid′əl), *adj.* **1.** pertaining to a spheroid or spheroids. **2.** shaped like a spheroid; approximately spherical. Also, **sphe·roi′dic.** —**sphe·roi′dal·ly, sphe·roi′di·cal·ly,** *adv.*

sphe·roi·dic·i·ty (sfēr′oi dis′i tē), *n.* the state of being spheroidal.

sphe·rom·e·ter (sfi rom′i tər), *n.* an instrument for measuring the curvature of surfaces. [SPHERO- + -METER, modeled on F *sphéromètre*]

spher·ule (sfer′o͞ol, -yo͞ol, sfēr′-), *n.* a small sphere or spherical body. [< LL *sphaerul(a)*] —**spher·u·lar** (sfer′yo͞o lər, sfēr′-), *adj.*

spher·u·lite (sfer′o͝o līt′, -yo͝o-, sfēr′-), *n.* a rounded aggregate of radiating crystals found in obsidian and other glassy igneous rocks.

spher·y (sfēr′ē), *adj.* **1.** having the form of a sphere; spherelike. **2.** pertaining to or resembling a heavenly body; starlike.

sphinc·ter (sfingk′tər), *n.* *Anat.* a circular band of voluntary or involuntary muscle that encircles an orifice of the body or one of its hollow organs. [< LL < Gk *sphinktḗr* = *sphink-* (var. of *sphing-*, root of *sphíngein* to hold tight) + *-tēr* suffix denoting agent] —**sphinc′ter·al, sphinc·te·ri·al** (sfingk tēr′ē əl), *adj.*

sphin·go·sine (sfing′gə sēn′, -sin), *n.* *Biochem.* a basic unsaturated amino alcohol, $C_{18}H_{33}(OH)_2NH_2$. [*sphingo-* (< Gk *sphíngein* to draw tight) + *-s-* connective + -INE[2]]

sphinx (sfingks), *n., pl.* **sphinx·es, sphin·ges** (sfin′jēz). **1.** (in ancient Egypt) **a.** a figure of an imaginary creature having a human or animal head on the body of a lion. **b.** (*usually cap.*) the colossal recumbent stone figure of this kind near the pyramids of Giza. **2.** (*cap.*) *Class. Myth.* a monster, usually represented as having the head and breast of a woman, the body of a lion, and the wings of an eagle. She proposed a riddle to Oedipus and killed herself when he answered it correctly. **3.** a mysterious, inscrutable person or thing. [late ME < L < Gk = *sphink-* (see SPHINCTER) + *-s* nom. sing. ending; lit., she who holds (her victims) fast]

Sphinx (Egyptian)

sphinx′ moth′. See **hawk moth.**

sphra·gis·tic (sfrə jis′tik), *adj.* of or pertaining to seals or signet rings. [< LGk *sphrāgistik(ós)* = Gk *sphrāgist(ós)* (ptp. of *sphrāgízein* to seal < *sphrāgís* a seal) + *-ikos* -IC]

sp. ht., specific heat.

sphyg·mic (sfig′mik), *adj.* *Physiol., Med.* of or pertaining to the pulse. [< Gk *sphygmik(ós)* = *sphygm(ós)* SPHYGMUS + *-ikos* -IC]

sphygmo-, a combining form of **sphygmus:** *sphygmometer.*

sphyg·mo·graph (sfig′mə graf′, -gräf′), *n.* an instrument for recording the rapidity, strength, and uniformity of the arterial pulse. —**sphyg·mo·graph·ic** (sfig′mə graf′ik), *adj.* —**sphyg·mog·ra·phy** (sfig mog′rə fē), *n.*

sphyg·mo·ma·nom·e·ter (sfig′mō mə nom′i tər), *n.* *Physiol.* an instrument for measuring the pressure of the blood in an artery.

sphyg·mom·e·ter (sfig mom′i tər), *n.* *Physiol.* an instrument for measuring the strength of the pulse. —**sphyg·mo·met·ric** (sfig′mə me′trik), *adj.*

sphyg·mus (sfig′məs), *n.* *Physiol.* the pulse. [< NL < Gk *sphygmós* a throbbing, pulsation; cf. ASPHYXIA]

Sphygmomanometer

spic (spik), *n.* *Offensive.* a Spanish-American person. Also, **spick, spik.** [? from a mispronunciation of SPEAK]

spi·ca (spī′kə), *n., pl.* **-cae** (-sē), **-cas** for 1, 2. **1.** spike[2]. **2.** a type of bandage extending from an extremity to the trunk by means of successive turns and crosses. **3.** (*cap.*) *Astron.* a first-magnitude star in the constellation Virgo. [< L: ear of grain]

spi·cate (spī′kāt), *adj.* *Bot.* **1.** having spikes, as a plant. **2.** arranged in spikes, as flowers. **3.** in the form of a spike, as in inflorescence. [< L *spīcāt(us)* = *spīc(a)* SPICA + *-ātus* -ATE[1]]

spic·ca·to (spi kä′tō; *It.* spēk kä′tō), *adj.* (esp. of violin music) performed with short, abrupt, rebounding motions of the bow. [< It = *spicc-* (s. of *spiccare* to detach) + *-ato* < L *-ātus* -ATE[1]]

spice (spīs), *n., v.,* **spiced, spic·ing.** —*n.* **1.** any of a class of pungent or aromatic substances of vegetable origin, as pepper, cinnamon, or cloves, used as seasoning, preservatives, etc. **2.** such substances taken as a whole. **3.** *Literary.* a spicy or aromatic odor or fragrance. **4.** a piquant, interesting element or quality; zest; piquancy. **5.** anything that gives zest. **6.** *Archaic.* a small quantity of something; trace; bit. —*v.t.* **7.** to prepare or season with a spice or spices. **8.** to give zest, piquancy, or interest to by adding something. [ME, OE < LL *spīcea aromatic herb, n. use of fem. of L *spīceus* pertaining to plants with spiky tufts or heads = *spīc(a)* SPIKE[2] + *-eus* -EOUS; confused with L *speciēs* shape, form, kind, sort, whence LL *speciēs* (pl.) spices]

spice·ber·ry (spīs′ber′ē, -bə rē), *n., pl.* **-ries. 1.** the checkerberry, or American wintergreen, *Gaultheria procumbens.* **2.** a Caribbean myrtaceous tree, *Eugenia rhombea*, cultivated in Florida for its black or orange fruit.

spice·bush (spīs′bo͝osh′), *n.* **1.** a yellow-flowered, lauraceous shrub, *Lindera Benzoin*, of North America, whose bark and leaves have a spicy odor. **2.** a North American shrub, *Calycanthus occidentalis*, having fragrant, light-brown flowers. Also called **benjamin-bush.**

Spice′ Is′lands, Moluccas.

spic·er·y (spī′sə rē), *n., pl.* **-er·ies** for 3. **1.** spices. **2.** spicy flavor or fragrance. **3.** *Archaic.* a storeroom or place for spices. [ME *spicerie* < OF *(e)spicerie*]

spic·ey (spī′sē), *adj.,* **spic·i·er, spic·i·est.** spicy.

spick (spik), *n.* spic.

spick-and-span (spik′ən span′), *adj.* **1.** spotlessly clean and neat: *a spick-and-span kitchen.* **2.** perfectly new; fresh. [short for *spick-and-span-new*, alliterative extension of SPAN-NEW]

spic·u·la (spik′yə lə), *n., pl.* **-lae** (-lē′). a spicule. [< NL, ML = L *spīc(a)* SPIKE[2] + *-ula* -ULE]

spic·u·late (spik′yə lāt′, -lit), *adj.* **1.** having the form of a spicule. **2.** having, covered with, or consisting of spicules. Also, **spic·u·lar** (spik′yə lər). [< L *spīculāt(us)* = *spīcul(um)* (see SPICULE) + *-ātus* -ATE[1]]

spic·ule (spik′yo͞ol), *n.* **1.** a small or minute, slender, sharp-pointed body or part; a small, needlelike crystal, process, or the like. **2.** *Zool.* one of the small, hard, calcareous or siliceous bodies that serve as the skeletal elements of various animals. [< L *spīcul(um)* = *spīc(a)* SPIKE[2] + *-ulum* -ULE]

spic·u·lum (spik′yə ləm), *n., pl.* **-la** (-lə). *Zool.* a small, needlelike body, part, process, or the like. [< L; see SPICULE]

spic·y (spī′sē), *adj.,* **spic·i·er, spic·i·est. 1.** seasoned with or containing spice: *a spicy salad dressing.* **2.** of the nature of or suggestive of spice. **3.** abounding in or yielding spices. **4.** aromatic or fragrant. **5.** piquant or pungent: *spicy criticism.* **6.** slightly improper or risqué. Also, **spicey.** —**spic′i·ly,** *adv.* —**spic′i·ness,** *n.* —**Syn. 5.** hot, sharp, peppery.

Spider, (def. 1), *Argiope aurantia* (Length ¾ in.)

spi·der (spī′dər), *n.* **1.** any of numerous predaceous arachnids of the order *Araneae* (*Araneida*), most of which spin webs that serve as nests and as traps for prey. **2.** (loosely) any of various other arachnids resembling or suggesting these. **3.** a frying pan, originally one with legs or feet. **4.** a trivet or tripod, as for supporting a pot or pan on a hearth. **5.** *Mach.* a part having a number of radiating spokes or arms. [ME *spithre*, OE *spīthra;* c. Dan *spinder*, lit., spinner; see SPIN]

spi′der crab′, any of various crabs having long, slender legs and a small, triangular body.

spi′der mon′key, any of several tropical American monkeys of the genus *Ateles*, having a slender body, long, slender limbs, and a long, prehensile tail.

Spider monkey, genus *Ateles* (Total length 4½ ft.; tail 2½ ft.)

spi′der pha′eton, a lightly built carriage with a very high body and large, slender wheels, having a covered seat for the driver and an open seat on the back for a footman.

spi′der web′, the web, made of interlaced threads of viscous fluid that harden on exposure to air, that is spun by a spider to catch its prey. Also, **spi′der's web′.**

spi·der·wort (spī′dər wûrt′), *n.* **1.** any herb of the genus *Tradescantia*, having blue, purple, or rose-colored flowers. **2.** any of several related plants.

spi·der·y (spī′də rē), *adj.* **1.** like a spider or a spider web. **2.** full of spiders.

spie·gel·ei·sen (spē′gəl ī′zən), *n.* a lustrous, crystalline pig iron containing a large amount of manganese, used in making steel. Also called **spie′gel, spie′gel i′ron.** [< G = *Spiegel* mirror + *Eisen* iron]

spiel (spēl, shpēl), *n.* *Informal.* a usually colorful, practiced talk or speech, as for the purpose of enticing customers. [< G (dial.): gossip, talk; cf. SPELL[2]]

spiel·er (spē′lər), *n.* a barker, as at a circus side show. [< G; see SPIEL, -ER[1]]

spi·er (spī′ər), *n.* *Archaic.* a person who spies, watches, or discovers. [ME]

spiff·y (spif′ē), *adj.,* **spiff·i·er, spiff·i·est.** *Slang.* spruce; smart; fine. Also, **spif·fing** (spif′ing). [dial. *spiff* well-dressed (< ?) + -Y[1]] —**spiff′i·ly,** *adv.*

spig·ot (spig′ət), *n.* **1.** a faucet or cock for controlling the flow of liquid from a pipe or the like. **2.** a small peg or plug for stopping the vent of a cask. **3.** a peg or plug for stopping the passage of liquid in a faucet or cock. [ME *spigot*, perh.

< OF *(e)spigot < OPr *espig(a)* (< L *spīca* SPIKE[2]) + OF *-ot* dim. suffix]

spik (spik), *n.* spic.

spike[1] (spīk), *n., v.,* **spiked, spik·ing.** —*n.* **1.** a naillike fastener, 3 to 12 inches long and proportionately thicker than a common nail, for fastening together heavy timbers or railroad track. **2.** a sharply pointed object or part, used in a weapon, barrier, etc. **3.** one of a number of naillike metal projections on the heel and sole of a shoe, as of a baseball player or a runner, for improving traction. **4. spikes,** a pair of shoes having such projections. **5.** the straight, unbranched antler of a young deer. **6.** a young mackerel about six inches long. —*v.t.* **7.** to fasten or secure with a spike or spikes. **8.** to provide or set with a spike or spikes. **9.** to pierce with or impale on a spike or spikes, as in baseball. **10.** to render (a muzzleloading gun) useless by driving a spike into the touchhole. **11.** to make ineffective; frustrate the action or purpose of: *to spike a rumor; to spike someone's chances for promotion.* **12.** *Informal.* to add alcoholic liquor to (a drink). [ME *spik(e)* < Scand or D; cf. Icel *spīk* splinter, Sw *spik,* MD *spike* nail; c. OE *spīc-* (in *spīcing* nail); all << L *spīca* (see SPIKE[2])]

spike[2] (spīk), *n.* **1.** an ear, as of wheat or other grain. **2.** *Bot.* an inflorescence in which the flowers are sessile or apparently so, along an elongated, unbranched axis. [< L *spīc(a)* spike, sharp point, ear of grain; akin to SPILE[1], SPINE, SPIRE[1]]

spike′ heel′, (on a woman's shoe) a very high heel tapering to a narrow base.

spike′ lav′ender, a lavender, *Lavandula latifolia,* having spikes of pale-purple flowers, and yielding an oil used in painting.

spike·let (spīk′lit), *n. Bot.* a small or secondary spike in grasses; one of the flower clusters, the unit of inflorescence, consisting of two or more flowers and subtended by one or more glumes variously disposed around a common axis.

spike·nard (spīk′nərd, -närd), *n.* **1.** an aromatic, East Indian valerianaceous plant, *Nardostachys Jatamansi,* believed to be the nard of the ancients. **2.** an aromatic substance used by the ancients, supposed to be obtained from this plant. **3.** any of various other plants, esp. an American araliaceous herb, *Aralia racemosa,* having an aromatic root. [ME < ML *spīca nardī.* See SPIKE[2], NARD]

spik·y (spī′kē), *adj.,* **spik·i·er, spik·i·est. 1.** having a spike or spikes. **2.** having the form of a spike; spikelike. —**spik′i·ly,** *adv.* —**spik′i·ness,** *n.*

spile[1] (spīl), *n., v.,* **spiled, spil·ing.** —*n.* **1.** a peg or plug of wood, esp. one used as a spigot. **2.** a spout for conducting sap from the sugar maple. **3.** a heavy wooden stake or pile. —*v.t.* **4.** to stop up (a hole) with a spile or peg. **5.** to furnish with a spigot or spout, as for drawing off a liquid. **6.** to tap by means of a spile. **7.** to furnish, strengthen, or support with spiles or piles. [< MD or MLG *spile* splinter, peg; c. G *Speil;* akin to SPIKE[1], SPINE, SPIRE[1]]

spile[2] (spīl), *v.t., v.i.,* **spiled, spil·ing,** *n. Eye Dial.* spoil.

spil·i·kin (spil′ə kin), *n.* spillikin.

spil·ing (spī′ling), *n.* piles; spiles collectively.

spill[1] (spil), *v.,* **spilled** or **spilt, spill·ing,** *n.* —*v.t.* **1.** to cause or allow to run or fall from a container, esp. accidentally or unintentionally. **2.** to shed (blood), as in killing or wounding. **3.** to scatter haphazardly. **4.** *Naut.* to lose (wind) from a sail. **5.** *Slang.* to divulge, disclose, or tell: *Don't spill the secret.* —*v.i.* **6** (of a liquid, loose particles, etc.) to run or fall from a container, esp. accidentally or unintentionally. **7. spill the beans.** See **bean** (def. 7). —*n.* **8.** a spilling, as of liquid. **9.** a spillway. **10.** *Informal.* a fall from a horse, vehicle, or the like. [ME *spill(en),* OE *spillan* to destroy, c. MHG, MD *spillen;* akin to SPOIL]

spill[2] (spil), *n.* **1.** a splinter. **2.** a slender piece of wood or a twisted paper, for lighting candles, lamps, etc. **3.** a peg made of metal. **4.** a small pin for stopping a cask; spile. [ME *spille;* akin to SPILE[1]]

spill·age (spil′ij), *n.* **1.** the act, process, or an instance of spilling. **2.** an amount that spills or is spilled.

spil·li·kin (spil′ə kin), *n.* **1.** a jackstraw. **2. spillikins,** (*construed as sing.*) the game of jackstraws. Also, **spilikin.** [var. of *spellican* < obs. D *spelleken* = *spelle* peg, pin + *-ken* -KIN]

spill·o·ver (spil′ō′vər), *n.* **1.** the act of spilling over. **2.** something that is spilled over; overflow.

spill·way (spil′wā′), *n.* a passageway through which surplus water escapes as from a reservoir.

spilt (spilt), *v.* a pt. and pp. of **spill**[1].

spilth (spilth), *n.* **1.** spillage (def. 1). **2.** something that is spilled. **3.** refuse or trash. [SPILL[1] + -TH[1]]

spin (spin), *v.,* **spun** or (*Archaic*) **span; spun; spin·ning;** *n.* —*v.t* **1.** to make (yarn or thread), esp. by drawing out, twisting, and winding fibers. **2.** to produce (a thread, cobweb, or the like) by extruding from the body a natural viscous matter that hardens in the air, as spiders, silkworms, etc. **3.** to cause to turn around rapidly, as on an axis; twirl; whirl. **4.** to produce, fabricate, or evolve in a manner suggestive of spinning thread: *to spin a tale.* **5.** to draw out, protract, or prolong (often fol. by *out*): *He spun the project out for over three years.* —*v.i.* **6.** to revolve or rotate rapidly. **7.** to produce a thread from the body, as a spider. **8.** to produce yarn or thread by spinning. **9.** to move or travel rapidly. **10.** to have a sensation of whirling; reel: *My head began to spin, and I fainted.* —*n.* **11.** the act of causing something to spin. **12.** a spinning motion. **13.** a downward movement or trend, esp. one that is sudden, alarming, etc.: *Steel prices went into a spin.* **14.** a short ride or drive for pleasure. **15.** Also called **tail-spin, tail spin.** *Aeron.* a maneuver in which an airplane dives in such a way as to describe a helix. **16.** *Physics.* the component of angular momentum of a particle or atom that the particle has when at rest. [ME *spinne(n),* OE *spinnan;* c. D, G *spinnen,* Icel *spinna,* Goth *spinnan*] —**Syn. 4.** narrate, relate. **5.** extend, lengthen. **6.** gyrate. See **turn.**

spi·na·ceous (spi nā′shəs), *adj.* pertaining to or of the nature of spinach; belonging to the *Chenopodiaceae,* the spinach or goosefoot family of plants. [< NL *Spin(acia)* spinach + -ACEOUS]

spin·ach (spin′ich), *n.* **1.** an herbaceous annual, *Spinacia oleracea,* cultivated for its succulent leaves. **2.** the leaves. [< MF *(e)spinache, (e)spinage* < OSp *espinaca,* alter. of Ar *isfānākh* < Pers]

spi·nal (spīn′ᵊl), *adj.* **1.** of, pertaining to, or belonging to a spine or thornlike structure, esp. to the backbone. —*n.* **2.** *Med.* a spinal anesthetic. [< LL *spīnāl(is)* = L *spīn(a)* SPINA + *-ālis* -AL[1]] —**spi′nal·ly,** *adv.*

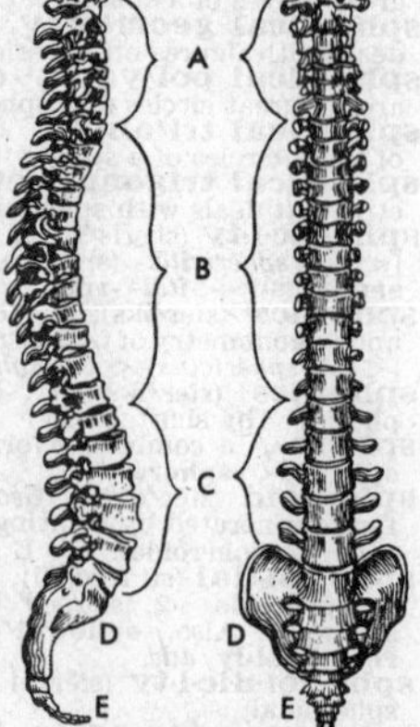

Spinal column (Human) Vertebrae: A, Seven cervical; B, Twelve dorsal; C, Five lumbar; D, Five sacral; E, Four caudal or coccygeal, forming a coccyx

spi′nal anesthe′sia, *Med.* anesthesia produced by the injection of an anesthetic into the spinal canal, reducing sensitivity to pain without causing loss of consciousness.

spi′nal canal′, the tube formed by the vertebrae in which the spinal cord and its membranes are located.

spi′nal col′umn, the series of vertebrae in a vertebrate animal forming the axis of the skeleton and protecting the spinal cord; spine; backbone. Also called **vertebral column.**

spi′nal cord′, the cord of nerve tissue extending through the spinal canal of the spinal column.

spi′nal tap′, the withdrawal of spinal fluid, for analysis or replacement by an anesthetic.

spin′ cast′ing, spinning (def. 2). —**spin′ cast′er.**

spin·dle (spin′dᵊl), *n., v.,* **-dled, -dling.** —*n.* **1.** a rod, used in hand spinning to twist into thread the fibers drawn from the mass on the distaff, and on which the thread is wound as it is spun. **2.** one of the rods of a spinning machine that bear the bobbins on which the spun thread is wound. **3.** any of various rodlike machine parts, esp. one that rotates; an axis, arbor, or mandrel. **4.** a slender, turned piece of wood, used esp. in furniture and carpentry. **5.** a measure of yarn, containing, for cotton, 15,120 yards, and for linen, 14,400 yards. **6.** *Biol.* the fine threads of achromatic material arranged within the cell in a spindle-shaped manner during mitosis. **7.** a narrow, upright spike on which business papers are impaled to keep them conveniently accessible. —*v.t.* **8.** to give the form of a spindle to. **9.** to provide or equip with a spindle or spindles. **10.** to impale (a card or paper) on a spindle. —*v.i.* **11.** to shoot up or grow into a long, slender stalk or stem, as a plant. [ME *spindel* (with intrusive *d*), OE *spin(e)l;* see SPIN, -LE; c. G *Spindel*]

spin·dle·legs (spin′dᵊl legz′), *n., pl.* **-legs** for 2. **1.** (*construed as pl.*) long, thin legs. **2.** (*construed as sing.*) *Informal.* a tall, thin person with such legs. —**spin·dle-leg·ged** (spin′dᵊl leg′id, -legd′), *adj.*

spin·dle·shanks (spin′dᵊl shangks′), *n., pl.* **-shanks.** (*construed as sing. or pl.*) spindlelegs. —**spin·dle-shanked** (spin′dᵊl shangkt′), *adj.*

spin′dle tree′, **1.** a European shrub, *Euonymus europaeus,* whose wood was formerly used for making spindles. **2.** any of various allied plants.

spin·dling (spind′ling), *adj.* **1.** long or tall and slender, often disproportionately so. **2.** growing into a long, slender stalk or stem. —*n.* **3.** a spindling person or thing.

spin·dly (spind′lē), *adj.,* **-dli·er, -dli·est.** long or tall, thin, and usually frail.

spin·drift (spin′drift′), *n.* spray swept by a violent wind along the surface of the sea. Also, **spoondrift.** [var. of Scot *speendrift* SPOONDRIFT]

spine (spīn), *n.* **1.** the spinal or vertebral column; backbone. **2.** any backbonelike part. **3.** a stiff, pointed process or appendage on an animal, as a quill of a porcupine. **4.** strength of character or will. **5.** a ridge, as of ground or rock. **6.** a sharp-pointed, hard or woody outgrowth on a plant; thorn. **7.** *Bookbinding.* the portion of a book that covers the binding; backbone. [late ME < L *spīn(a)* backbone; akin to SPIKE[1], SPILE[1], SPIRE[1]] —**spined,** *adj.*

spi·nel (spi nel′, spin′ᵊl), *n.* **1.** any of a group of minerals composed principally of oxides of magnesium, aluminum, iron, manganese, chromium, etc., characterized by their hardness and octahedral crystals. **2.** a mineral of this group, essentially magnesium aluminate, $MgAl_2O_4$, some varieties being used as gems. Also called **spi·nelle′.** [< F *spinelle* < It *spinell(a)* = *spin(a)* thorn (< L) + *-ella* dim. suffix (< L *-illa*)]

spine·less (spīn′lis), *adj.* **1.** having no spines or quills. **2.** having no spine or backbone. **3.** without strength of character. —**Syn. 3.** weak, irresolute, indecisive. —**Ant. 3.** strong, resolute.

spinel′ ru′by. See **ruby spinel.**

spi·nes·cent (spī nes′ənt), *adj.* **1.** *Bot.* **a.** becoming spinelike. **b.** ending in a spine. **c.** bearing spines. **2.** *Zool.* somewhat spinelike; coarse, as hair. [< LL *spīnēscent-* (s. of *spīnēscēns* growing thorny, prp. of *spīnēscere*). See SPINE, -ESCENT] —**spi·nes′cence,** *n.*

spin·et (spin′it), *n.* **1.** a small upright piano. **2.** a small transversely strung harpsichord. **3.** a small square piano. **4.** Also called **spin′et or′gan.** a small electric or electronic organ. [aph. var. of obs. *espinette* < F < It *spinetta,* possibly named after G. *Spinetti,* Venetian craftsman said to have invented it c1500]

spin′ fish′ing, spinning (def. 2). —**spin′ fish′erman.**

spi·nif·er·ous (spī nif′ər əs), *adj.* abounding in or covered with spines; spiny. Also, **spi·nig·er·ous** (spī nij′ər əs). [< LL *spīnifer* spine-bearing (see SPINE, -I-, -FER) + -OUS]

spin·i·fex (spin′ə feks′), *n.* any of the spiny grasses of the genus *Spinifex,* chiefly of Australia, used to bind sand on seashores. [< NL = L *spīn(a)* SPINE + *-i-* -I- + *-fex* maker (*fec-,* var. of *fac-,* of *facere* make + *-s* nom. sing. ending)]

spin·na·ker (spin′ə kər), *n. Naut.* a large, triangular sail carried by yachts as a headsail when running before the wind or when the wind is abaft the beam. [appar. SPIN + *(mo)naker*, var. of MONIKER; but said to be alter. of *Sphinx*, name of first yacht making regular use of this sail]

spin·ner (spin′ər), *n.* **1.** a person or thing that spins. **2.** *Angling.* a lure, as a spoon, that revolves in the water in trolling and casting. [ME *spinnere*]

spin·ner·et (spin′ə ret′), *n.* an organ or part by means of which a spider, insect larva, or the like, spins a silky thread for its web or cocoon.

spin·ner·y (spin′ə rē), *n., pl.* **-ner·ies.** a spinning mill.

spin·ney (spin′ē), *n., pl.* **-neys.** *Brit.* a small wood, thicket, or grove. [ME < MF *(e)spinei* (masc.), *(e)spinaie* (fem.); cf. L *spinēt(um)* thicket of thorns = *spīn(a)* thorn (see SPINE) + *-ētum* collective suffix]

spin·ning (spin′ing), *n.* **1.** the act or process of converting fibrous substances into yarn or thread. **2.** Also called **spin casting, spin fishing.** *Angling.* act or technique of casting a relatively light lure attached to a threadlike line wound on a stationary spool. [ME] —**spin′ning·ly,** *adv.*

spin′ning frame′, a machine for drawing, twisting, and winding yarn.

spin′ning jen′ny, an early spinning machine having more than one spindle and enabling a person to make a number of yarns simultaneously.

spin′ning mule′, mule[1] (def. 4).

spin′ning ring′, ring[1] (def. 19).

spin′ning wheel′, a device formerly used for spinning yarn or thread, consisting essentially of a single spindle driven by a large wheel operated by hand or foot. [late ME]

Spinning wheel

spin-off (spin′ôf′, -of′), *n.* **1.** *Com.* a process of reorganizing a corporation whereby the capital stock of a division or subsidiary or of a newly affiliated company is transferred to the stockholders of the parent corporation without an exchange of any part of the stock of the latter. **2.** anything derived from something already in existence without detriment to it.

spi·nose (spī′nōs, spī nōs′), *adj.* *Chiefly Biol.* full of spines; spiniferous; spinous. [< L *spīnōs(us)*] —**spi′nose·ly,** *adv.* —**spi·nos·i·ty** (spī nos′i tē), *n.*

spi·nous (spī′nəs), *adj.* **1.** covered with or having spines. **2.** armed with or bearing sharp-pointed processes, as an animal; spiniferous. **3.** spinelike. [< L *spīnōsus* (see SPINOSE), with -OUS r. -OSE[1]]

spi′nous proc′ess, *Anat., Zool.* a spinelike process of a bone, esp. the dorsal projection from the center of the arch of a vertebra.

Spi·no·za (spi nō′zə), *n.* **Ba·ruch** (bə ro͝ok′) or **Be·ne·dict de** (ben′ə dikt də), 1632–77, Dutch rationalist philosopher. —**Spi·no′zism,** *n.* —**Spi·no′zist,** *n.*

spin·ster (spin′stər), *n.* **1.** a woman beyond the usual age for marrying and still unmarried. **2.** *Chiefly Law.* any woman who has never married. **3.** a woman whose occupation is spinning yarn or thread. [ME *spinnestere*] —**spin′ster·hood′,** *n.* —**spin′ster·ish,** *adj.*

spin·thar·i·scope (spin thar′i skōp′), *n.* *Physics.* an instrument for observing scintillations produced by alpha particles on a phosphorescent screen. [< Gk *spintharí(s)* dim. of *spinthḗr* spark + -SCOPE]

spin′ the bot′tle, a game in which a boy or girl spins a bottle and receives a kiss from the member of the opposite sex at whom the bottle points on coming to rest.

spi·nule (spī′nyo͞ol, spin′yo͞ol), *n.* *Zool., Bot.* a small spine. [< L *spīnul(a)*. See SPINE, -ULE] —**spin·u·lose** (spin′yə lōs′, spīn′-), *adj.*

spin·y (spī′nē), *adj.,* **spin·i·er, spin·i·est. 1.** abounding in or having spines; thorny. **2.** covered with or having sharp-pointed processes, as an animal. **3.** resembling a spine; spinelike. **4.** troublesome or difficult to handle; thorny: *a spiny problem.* —**spin′i·ness,** *n.*

spin′y ant′eater, echidna.

spin·y-finned (spī′nē find′), *adj.* *Ichthyol.* having fins with sharp bony rays, as an acanthopterygian.

spin′y lob′ster, any of several edible crustaceans of the family *Palinuridae*, differing from the true lobsters in having a spiny shell and lacking the large pincers.

spi·ra·cle (spī′rə kəl, spir′ə-), *n.* **1.** a hole for breathing or ventilation. **2.** *Zool.* **a.** an aperture or orifice through which air or water passes in the act of respiration, as the blowhole of a cetacean. **b.** an opening in the head of sharks and rays through which water is drawn and passed over gills. **c.** one of the external orifices of a tracheal respiratory system, usually on the sides of the body. [< L *spīrācul(um)* air hole = *spīrā(re)* (to) breathe + *-culum* -CLE] —**spi·rac·u·lar** (spī rak′yə lər, spi-), *adj.*

spi·rae·a (spī rē′ə), *n.* spirea.

spi·ral (spī′rəl), *n., adj., v.,* **-raled, -ral·ing** or (*esp. Brit.*) **-ralled, -ral·ling.** —*n.* **1.** *Geom.* a plane curve generated by a point moving round a fixed point while constantly receding from or approaching it. **2.** a helix. **3.** a single circle or ring of a spiral or helical curve or object. **4.** a spiral or helical object, formation, or form. **5.** *Football.* a type of kick or pass in which the ball turns on its longer axis as it flies through the air. **6.** *Econ.* a continuous, accelerating increase or decrease in costs, wages, prices, etc. —*adj.* **7.** formed like or running in a spiral. **8.** formed like or running in a helix. **9.** of or of the nature of a spire or coil. —*v.i.* **10.** to take a spiral form or course. —*v.t.* **11.** to cause to take a spiral form or course. [< ML *spīrāl(is)* = L *spīr(a)* coil (see SPIRE[2]) + *-ālis* -AL[1]] —**spi′ral·ly,** *adv.*

Spirals (def. 4)

spi′ral gear′, (not in technical use) See **helical gear.**

spi′ral neb′ula, *Astron.* a galaxy having a spiral structure.

spi′ral spring′, a form of spring consisting of a wire coiled in a helix. See illus. at **spring.**

spi·rant (spī′rənt), *Phonet.* —*n.* **1.** fricative (def. 2). —*adj.* **2.** spirantal. [< L *spīrant-* (s. of *spīrāns*, prp. of *spīrāre* to breathe) = *spīr-* breathe + *-ant-* -ANT]

spi·ran·tal (spī ran′təl), *adj.* *Phonet.* fricative (def. 1). Also, **spirant, spi·ran·tic** (spī ran′tik).

spire[1] (spīər), *n., v.,* **spired, spir·ing.** —*n.* **1.** a tall, acutely pointed pyramidal roof or rooflike construction upon a tower, roof, etc.; steeple. **2.** a similar construction forming the upper part of a steeple. See illus. at **steeple. 3.** a sprout or shoot of a plant. —*v.i.* **4.** to shoot or rise into spirelike form; rise or extend to a height in the manner of a spire. [ME; OE *spīr* spike, blade; c. Icel *spīra* stalk, MD *spier*, MLG *spīr* shoot, sprout, sprig; akin to SPIKE[1], SPILE[1], SPINE]

spire[2] (spīər), *n.* **1.** a coil or spiral. **2.** one of the series of convolutions of a coil or spiral. **3.** *Zool.* the upper, convoluted part of a spiral shell, above the aperture. [< L *spīr(a)* < Gk *speîra* a coil, twist]

spi·re·a (spī rē′ə), *n.* any rosaceous herb or shrub of the genus *Spiraea*, having racemes, cymes, panicles, or corymbs of small, white or pink flowers, certain species of which are cultivated as ornamentals. Also, **spiraea.** [< L *spīraea* < Gk *speiraía* privet]

spired (spīərd), *adj.* having a spire: *a spired tower.*

spi·reme (spī′rēm), *n.* *Biol.* the chromatin of a cell nucleus when in a continuous or segmented threadlike form during mitosis. [< Gk *speírēm(a)* coil. See SPIRE[2], -EME]

Spires (spīərz), *n.* Speyer.

spi·rif·er·ous (spī rif′ər əs), *adj.* **1.** having a spire or spiral upper part, as a univalve shell. **2.** having spiral appendages, as a brachiopod. [< NL *spirifer* (see SPIRE[2], -I-, -FER) + -OUS]

spi·ril·lum (spī ril′əm), *n., pl.* **-ril·la** (-ril′ə). *Bacteriol.* **1.** any of several spirally twisted, aerobic bacteria of the genus *Spirillum*, certain species of which are pathogenic for man. See diag. at **bacteria. 2.** any of various similar microorganisms. [< NL = L *spīr(a)* (see SPIRE[2]) + *-illum* dim. suffix] —**spi·ril′lar,** *adj.*

spir·it (spir′it), *n.* **1.** the incorporeal part of man in general or of an individual, or an aspect of this, such as the mind or soul. **2.** this part, or such an aspect, with relation to the religious, intellectual, cultural, or other concerns proper to it: *things of the spirit.* **3.** a supernatural, incorporeal being, as a ghost. **4.** a fairy, sprite, or elf. **5.** an angel or demon. **6.** (*cap.*) the divine influence as an agency working in the heart of man. **7.** (*cap.*) the third person of the Trinity; Holy Spirit. **8.** the soul or heart as the seat of feelings or sympathies. **9. spirits,** feelings or mood with regard to exaltation or depression: *low spirits; good spirits.* **10.** excellent disposition or attitude in terms of vigor, courage, etc.; mettle: *a man of spirit.* **11.** temper or disposition: *meek in spirit.* **12.** an individual as characterized by his temper or disposition: *a few brave spirits.* **13.** the dominant tendency or character of anything: *the spirit of the age.* **14.** vigorous sense of membership in a group: *college spirit.* **15.** the true or basic meaning or intent of a statement, document, etc. (opposed to *letter*): *the spirit of the law.* **16.** *Chem.* the essence or active principle of a substance as extracted in liquid form, esp. by distillation. **17.** Often, **spirits.** a strong distilled alcoholic liquor. **18.** *Chiefly Brit.* alcohol. **19.** *Pharm.* a solution in alcohol of an essential or volatile principle; essence. **20.** any of certain subtle fluids formerly supposed to permeate the body. **21. the Spirit,** God. —*adj.* **22.** pertaining to something that works by burning alcoholic spirits: *a spirit stove.* —*v.t.* **23.** to animate with fresh ardor or courage; inspirit. **24.** to encourage; urge on or stir up, as to action. **25.** to carry off mysteriously or secretly (often fol. by *away* or *off*): *His captors spirited him away.* [ME < L *spīrit(us)* breathing = *spīri-* (akin to *spīrā-*, s. of *spīrāre* to breathe) + *-tus* n. suffix] —**Syn. 1.** life, mind, consciousness. **3.** apparition, phantom. See **ghost. 4.** goblin, hobgoblin. **10.** energy, zeal, ardor. **11.** attitude, mood, humor. **15.** essence, sense, intention, significance.

spir·it·ed (spir′i tid), *adj.* having or showing mettle, courage, vigor, liveliness, etc.: *a spirited defense of poetry.* —**spir′it·ed·ly,** *adv.* —**Syn.** animated, energetic, lively, vigorous.

spir′it gum′, a special glue used in fastening false hair or whiskers to an actor's face.

spir·it·ism (spir′i tiz′əm), *n.* the doctrine or practices of spiritualism. —**spir′it·ist,** *n.*

spir·it·less (spir′it lis), *adj.* **1.** without spirit. **2.** without ardor, vigor, zeal, animation, etc. —**spir′it·less·ly,** *adv.*

spir′it lev′el, a device for determining true horizontal or vertical direction by the centering of a bubble in a slightly curved glass tube or tubes filled with alcohol or ether.

A B

Spirit level
A, Glass tube for determining horizontals; B, Glass tube for determining verticals

spir′it of harts′horn, *Chem.* a suffocating, aqueous solution of about 28.5 percent ammonia gas: used chiefly as a detergent, for removing stains, and in the manufacture of ammonium salts. Also, **spir′its of harts′horn.**

spi·ri·to·so (spir′i tō′sō; *It.* spē′rē tô′sô), *adj.* *Music.* spirited; lively. [< It; see SPIRIT, -OSE[1]]

spir·i·tous (spir′i təs), *adj.* *Archaic.* of the nature of spirit; immaterial, ethereal, or refined.

spir′its of tur′pentine, *Chem.* See **oil of turpentine.** Also, **spir′it of tur′pentine.**

spir·it·u·al (spir′i cho͞o əl), *adj.* **1.** of, pertaining to, or consisting of spirit; incorporeal. **2.** of or pertaining to the spirit or its concerns as distinguished from bodily or worldly existence or its concerns. **3.** of or pertaining to spirits or to spiritualists; supernatural or spiritualistic. **4.** characterized by or suggesting predominance of the spirit or things of the spirit. **5.** of or pertaining to the spirit as the seat of the moral or religious nature. **6.** of or pertaining to sacred things or matters; religious. **7.** of or belonging to the church; ecclesiastical: *lords spiritual and temporal.* **8.** of or pertaining to the conscious thoughts and emotions. —*n.* **9.** a spiritual or religious song, esp. of a type that originated among Negroes of the southern U.S. **10.** the realm of things of the spirit. [ME < ML *spīrituāl(is)* = *spīritu-* (s.

of L *spīritus* SPIRIT) + *-ālis* -AL[1]; r. ME *spirituel* < MF] —**spir′it·u·al·ly,** *adv.* —**spir′it·u·al·ness,** *n.*

spir′itual death′, death (def. 8).

spir·it·u·al·ise (spir′i cho͞o ə līz′), *v.t.*, **-ised, -is·ing.** *Chiefly Brit.* spiritualize. —**spir′it·u·al·i·sa′tion,** *n.*

spir·it·u·al·ism (spir′i cho͞o ə liz′əm), *n.* **1.** the belief or doctrine that the spirits of the dead communicate with the living, esp. through mediums. **2.** the practices or the phenomena associated with this belief. **3.** the belief that all reality is spiritual. **4.** *Metaphys.* any of various doctrines maintaining that the ultimate reality is spirit or mind. Cf. **absolute idealism, personalism. 5.** a spiritual quality or tendency. **6.** insistence on spirituality, as in philosophy or religion.

spir·it·u·al·ist (spir′i cho͞o ə list), *n.* **1.** an adherent of spiritualism. **2.** a person who is preoccupied with spiritual matters.

spir·it·u·al·i·ty (spir′i cho͞o al′i tē), *n.*, *pl.* **-ties. 1.** the quality or fact of being spiritual. **2.** incorporeal or immaterial nature. **3.** a predominantly spiritual character as shown in thoughts or actions. **4.** Often, **spiritualities.** property or revenue of the church or of an ecclesiastic in his official capacity. [late ME < ML *spīrituālitās*]

spir·it·u·al·ize (spir′i cho͞o ə līz′), *v.t.*, **-ized, -iz·ing. 1.** to make spiritual. **2.** to invest with a spiritual meaning. Also, *esp. Brit.*, **spiritualise.** —**spir′it·u·al·i·za′tion,** *n.*

spir·it·u·al·ty (spir′i cho͞o əl tē), *n.*, *pl.* **-ties. 1.** Often, **spiritualties.** spirituality (def. 4). **2.** the body of ecclesiastics; the clergy. [late ME *spiritualte* < MF; see SPIRITUALITY]

spi·ri·tu·el (spir′i cho͞o el′; *Fr.* spē rē tʏel′), *adj.* showing or having a refined and graceful mind or wit. Also, *referring to a woman,* **spi′ri·tu·elle′.** [< F: lit., SPIRITUAL]

spir·it·u·ous (spir′i cho͞o əs), *adj.* **1.** containing, of the nature of, or pertaining to alcohol; alcoholic. **2.** (of alcoholic beverages) distilled, rather than fermented. [SPIRIT + -OUS (with *-u-* of L *spīritus*)]

spir·i·tus as·per (spir′i təs as′pər; *Lat.* spē′rē to͝os′ äs′per). See **rough breathing.** [< LL]

spir·i·tus fru·men·ti (spir′i təs fro͞o men′tī), whiskey. [< NL: lit., the spirit (or life) of grain]

spir·i·tus le·nis (spir′i təs lē′nis; *Lat.* spē′rē to͝os′ le′nis). See **smooth breathing.** [< LL]

spiro-[1], a learned borrowing from Latin meaning "respiration," used in the formation of compound words: *spirograph.* [comb. form of L *spīrāre* to breathe]

spiro-[2], a learned borrowing from Latin and Greek meaning "coil," "spiral," used in the formation of compound words: *spirochete.* [comb. form of L *spīra* < Gk *speîra* coil]

spi·ro·chete (spī′rə kēt′), *n.* *Bacteriol.* any of several spiral-shaped bacteria of the order *Spirochaetales*, certain species of which are pathogenic for man and animals. Also, **spi′ro·chaete′.** [< NL *spirochaet(a)*. See SPIRO-[2], CHAETO-] —**spi′ro·chet′al, spi′ro·che′tic,** *adj.*

spi·ro·che·to·sis (spī′rə kē tō′sis), *n.* *Pathol.* a disease caused by infection with a spirochete. Also, **spi′ro·chae·to′sis.** —**spi·ro·che·tot·ic, spi·ro·chae·tot·ic** (spī′rə kē tot′ik), *adj.*

spi·ro·graph (spī′rə graf′, -gräf′), *n.* an instrument for recording respiratory movements. —**spi·ro·graph·ic** (spī′rə graf′ik), *adj.*

spi·ro·gy·ra (spī′rə jī′rə), *n.* *Bot.* a widely distributed fresh-water green alga of the genus *Spirogyra.* [< NL = *spiro-* SPIRO-[2] + *-gyra*, alter. of Gk *gŷros* circle or *gyrōs* round]

spi·roid (spī′roid), *adj.* more or less spiral; resembling a spiral. [< NL *spīroīd(ēs)* < Gk *speiroeidēs*. See SPIRO-[2], -OID]

spi·rom·e·ter (spī rom′i tər), *n.* an instrument for determining the capacity of the lungs.

spirt (spûrt), *v.i.*, *v.t.*, *n.* spurt.

spir·u·la (spir′yə lə, -o͝o lə), *n.*, *pl.* **-lae** (-lē′) any cephalopod of the genus *Spirula*, having a flat, spiral shell that is partly inside and partly outside the posterior part of the body. [< NL < LL: twisted cake. See SPIRE[2], -ULE]

spir·y[1] (spīər′ē), *adj.* **1.** having the form of a spire, slender shoot, or tapering pointed body; tapering up to a point like a spire. **2.** abounding in spires or steeples. [SPIRE[1] + -Y[1]]

spir·y[2] (spī′rē), *adj.* spiral or coiled; coiling; helical. [SPIRE[2] + -Y[1]]

spit[1] (spit), *v.*, **spit** or **spat, spit·ting,** *n.* —*v.i.* **1.** to eject saliva from the mouth; expectorate. **2.** to sputter: *grease spitting on the fire.* —*v.t.* **3.** to eject from the mouth (often fol. by *out*): *Spit out the seeds.* **4.** to throw out or emit like saliva: *The kettle spat boiling water over the stove.* —*n.* **5.** saliva, esp. when ejected. **6.** the act of spitting. **7.** *Entomol.* spittle. **8. spit and image,** *Informal.* exact likeness; counterpart. Also, **spitting image.** [ME *spitt(en)*, OE *spittan*; c. G (dial.) *spitzen* to spit; akin to OE *spǣtan* to spit, *spātl* spittle] —**spit′ter,** *n.*

spit[2] (spit), *n.*, *v.*, **spit·ted, spit·ting.** —*n.* **1.** a pointed rod or bar for thrusting through and holding meat that is to be cooked before or over a fire. **2.** any of various rods, pins, etc. **3.** a narrow point of land or shoal extending from the shore. —*v.t.* **4.** to pierce, stab, or transfix, as with a spit. [ME *spite*, OE *spit(u)*; c. MD, MLG *spit, spet*, OHG *spiz* spit; akin to Icel *spíta* peg, and to SPIKE[1], SPILE[1], SPINE, SPIRE[1]] —**spit′ter,** *n.*

spit·al (spit′əl), *n.* *Obs.* **1.** a hospital, esp. one for lazars. **2.** a shelter on a highway. [alter. of *spittle*, ME *spitel* < ML *hospitale*; see HOSPITAL]

spit′ and pol′ish, *Informal.* great care in maintaining smart appearance and crisp efficiency. —**spit-and-pol·ish** (spit′ən pol′ish), *adj.*

spit·ball (spit′bôl′), *n.* **1.** a small ball or lump of chewed paper used as a missile. **2.** *Baseball.* a pitch, now illegal, made to curve by moistening one side of the ball with saliva or perspiration.

spitch·cock (spich′kok′), *v.t.* **1.** to split, cut up, and broil or fry (an eel). **2.** to treat severely. [? OE *spic* fat bacon + *cuc*, var. of *cwic* QUICK; from the way the eel moves about in cooking as if alive]

spit′ curl′, a tight curl of hair, usually pressed against the forehead or cheek.

spite (spīt), *n.*, *v.*, **spit·ed, spit·ing.** —*n.* **1.** a malicious desire to harm, annoy, or humiliate another person. **2.** a particular instance of such an attitude or action; grudge. **3.** *Obs.* something that causes vexation; annoyance. **4. in spite of,** in disregard or defiance of; notwithstanding; despite. —*v.t.* **5.** to treat with spite or malice. **6.** to annoy or thwart, out of spite. **7.** to fill with spite; vex; offend. **8. cut off one's nose to spite one's face.** See **nose** (def. 13). [ME; aph. var. of DESPITE] —**Syn. 1.** malevolence, maliciousness, rancor. See **grudge. 4.** See **notwithstanding. 6.** injure, hurt, harm.

spite·ful (spīt′fəl), *adj.* full of or revealing spite or malice; malicious. [late ME] —**spite′ful·ly,** *adv.*

—**Syn.** vengeful, rancorous. SPITEFUL, REVENGEFUL, VINDICTIVE refer to a desire to inflict a wrong or injury on someone, usually in return for one received. SPITEFUL implies a mean or malicious desire for (often petty) revenge: *a spiteful attitude toward a former friend.* REVENGEFUL is a strong word, implying a deep, powerful, and continued intent to repay a wrong: *a fierce and revengeful spirit.* VINDICTIVE does not imply action necessarily, but stresses the unforgiving nature of the avenger: *a vindictive look.* —**Ant.** benevolent.

spit·fire (spit′fīər′), *n.* **1.** a person, esp. a girl or woman, of fiery temper. **2.** (*cap.*) a British fighter plane with a single engine used by the RAF throughout World War II.

Spit·head (spit′hed′), *n.* a roadstead off the S coast of England between Portsmouth and the Isle of Wight.

Spits·ber·gen (spits′bûr′gən), *n.* a group of islands in the Arctic Ocean, N of and belonging to Norway. 1200 (est. 1959); 24,293 sq. mi. Also, **Spitz′ber′gen.** Norwegian, **Svalbard.**

spit′ting im′age, *Informal.* See **spit**[1] (def. 8). [from the phrase *spit and image* (see SPIT[1]) by confusion of *spit and* with *spittin'*]

spit·tle (spit′əl), *n.* **1.** saliva; spit. **2.** *Entomol.* a frothy or spitlike secretion exuded by spittle insects. [b. ME *spit* (n.) (see SPIT[1]) and *spetil*, OE *spǣtl*, var. of *spātl* saliva]

spit′tle in′sect, froghopper. Also called **spit′tle bug′.**

spit·toon (spi to͞on′), *n.* a cuspidor.

spitz (spits), *n.* any of several dogs having a stocky body, a thick coat, erect, pointed ears, and a tail curved over the back, as a chow chow or Pomeranian. [< G *spitz* pointed]

spiv (spiv), *n.* *Brit. Informal.* a petty criminal. [back formation from dial. *spiving* smart; akin to SPIFFY]

splanch·nic (splangk′nik), *adj.* of or pertaining to the viscera; visceral. [< NL *splanchnic(us)* < Gk *splanchnikós* = *splánchn(a)* entrails (pl.) + *-ikos* -IC]

splanchno-, a learned borrowing from Greek meaning "viscera." [comb. form of Gk *splánchna* entrails (pl.)]

splash (splash), *v.t.* **1.** to wet or soil by dashing water, mud, etc., upon. **2.** to fall upon (something) in scattered masses or particles, as a liquid does. **3.** to dash (water, mud, etc.) about in scattered masses or particles. —*v.i.* **4.** to dash a liquid or semiliquid substance about. **5.** to fall, move, or go with a splash or splashes. **6.** to dash with force in scattered masses or particles, as a liquid or semiliquid substance. **7.** (of a space vehicle) to land on a body of water (usually fol. by *down*). —*n.* **8.** the act of splashing. **9.** the sound of splashing. **10.** a quantity of some liquid or semiliquid substance splashed upon or in a thing. **11.** a spot caused by something splashed. **12.** a patch, as of color or light. **13.** a striking show or an ostentatious display. [alter. of PLASH[1]] —**splash′er,** *n.*

splash·board (splash′bōrd′, -bôrd′), *n.* **1.** a board, guard, or screen to protect something from being splashed. **2.** *Naut.* washboard (def. 3).

splash·down (splash′doun′), *n.* the landing of a space vehicle on a body of water.

splash′ guard′, a large flap behind a rear tire, as on a truck, to prevent mud, water, etc., from being splashed onto a vehicle following.

splash·y (splash′ē), *adj.*, **splash·i·er, splash·i·est. 1.** making a splash or splashes. **2.** full of or marked by splashes or irregular spots; spotty. **3.** making an ostentatious display; showy. —**splash′i·ness,** *n.*

splat[1] (splat), *n.* a broad, flat piece of wood, either pierced or solid, forming the center upright part of a chair back or the like. [? akin to OE *splātan* to split]

splat[2] (splat), *n.* a sound made by splattering or slapping. [back formation from SPLATTER]

splat·ter (splat′ər), *v.t.*, *v.i.* to spatter, as by splashing. [b. SPLASH and SPATTER]

splay (splā), *v.t.* **1.** to spread out, expand, or extend. **2.** to form with an oblique angle; make slanting; bevel. **3.** to make with a splay or splays. **4.** to disjoin; dislocate. —*v.i.* **5.** to have an oblique or slanting direction. **6.** to spread or flare. —*n.* **7.** a surface that makes an oblique angle with another, as where an opening for a window or door widens from inside to outside. —*adj.* **8.** spread out; wide and flat; turned outward. **9.** oblique or awry. [aph. var. of DISPLAY]

S, Splay (def. 7)

splay·foot (splā′fo͝ot′), *n.*, *pl.* **-feet,** *adj.* —*n.* **1.** a broad, flat foot, esp. one turned outward. **2.** *Pathol.* this condition as a deformity; flatfoot. —*adj.* **3.** Also, **splay′foot′ed.** of, pertaining to, or afflicted with splayfoot.

spleen (splēn), *n.* **1.** a highly vascular, glandular, ductless organ, situated in man at the cardiac end of the stomach, serving chiefly in the formation of lymphocytes, in the destruction of worn-out erythrocytes, and as a reservoir for blood. **2.** this organ conceived of as the seat of spirit and courage or of such emotions as mirth, ill humor, or melancholy. **3.** ill humor, peevish temper, or spite. **4.** *Archaic.* melancholy. **5.** *Obs.* caprice. [ME < L *splēn* < Gk *splḗn*; akin to Skt *plīhán*, L *liēn* spleen] —**spleen′ish,** *adj.* —**Syn. 3.** petulance, rancor; wrath, ire, anger.

spleen·ful (splēn′fəl), *adj.* **1.** full of or displaying spleen. **2.** ill-humored; irritable or peevish; spiteful. —**spleen′ful·ly,** *adv.*

spleen·wort (splēn′wûrt′), *n.* any of various temperate and tropical ferns of the genus *Asplenium*, certain species of which are grown as ornamentals. [SPLEEN + WORT[2]]

spleen·y (splē′nē), *adj.*, **spleen·i·er, spleen·i·est.** abundant in spleen.

splen-, var. of **spleno-** before a vowel: *splenectomy.*

splen·dent (splen′dənt), *adj.* **1.** shining or lustrous. **2.** eminent or illustrious. [late ME < L *splendent-* (s. of *splendēns*, prp. of *splendēre* to shine) = *splend-* shine + *-ent-* -ENT]

splen·did (splen′did), *adj.* **1.** magnificent or sumptuous. **2.** grand or superb, as beauty. **3.** distinguished or glorious. **4.** strikingly admirable or fine: *splendid talents.* **5.** *Rare.* brilliant in appearance, color, etc. [< L *splendid(us)* brilliant = *splend-* shine + *-idus* -ID[4]] **—splen′did·ly,** *adv.* **—splen′did·ness,** *n.* **—Syn. 1.** luxurious, dazzling. See **magnificent. 3.** renowned, famed; celebrated, eminent, brilliant; noble. **4.** excellent.

splen·dif·er·ous (splen dif′ər əs), *adj. Informal.* splendid or magnificent; fine (often used facetiously or ironically). [late ME < LL *splend(ōr)ifer* bringing brightness. See SPLENDOR, -I-, -FEROUS] **—splen·dif′er·ous·ly,** *adv.* **—splen·dif′er·ous·ness,** *n.*

splen·dor (splen′dər), *n.* **1.** the quality of being magnificent, glorious, or sumptuous. **2.** an instance or display of imposing pomp or grandeur: *the splendor of the coronation.* **3.** brilliance; radiance: *the splendor of the morning.* Also, *esp. Brit.,* **splen′dour.** [< L *splendor* = *splend-* (root of *splendēre* to shine) + *-or* -OR[1]; r. ME *splendure* < AF] **—splen′dor·ous, splen·drous** (splen′drəs), *adj.*

sple·nec·to·my (spli nek′tə mē), *n., pl.* **-mies.** *Surg.* excision or removal of the spleen.

sple·net·ic (spli net′ik), *adj.* Also, **sple·net′i·cal, splen·i·tive** (splen′i tiv). **1.** of the spleen; splenic. **2.** irritable; peevish; spiteful. **3.** *Obs.* affected with, characterized by, or tending to produce melancholy. **—***n.* **4.** a splenetic person. [< L *splēnētic(us)*] **—sple·net′i·cal·ly,** *adv.* **—Syn. 2.** irascible, testy, petulant.

splen·ic (splē′nik, splen′ik), *adj.* of, pertaining to, connected with, or affecting the spleen: *splenic nerves.* [< L *splēnic(us)* < Gk *splēnikós*]

sple·ni·us (splē′nē əs), *n., pl.* **-ni·i** (-nē ī′). *Anat.* a broad muscle on each side of the back of the neck and the upper part of the thoracic region, the action of which draws the head backward and assists in turning it. [< NL, alter. of L *splēnium* < Gk *splēníon* plaster, patch] **—sple′ni·al,** *adj.*

spleno-, a learned borrowing from Greek, used as the combining form of **spleen** in compound words: *splenomegaly.* Also, *esp. before a vowel,* **splen-.** [comb. form repr. Gk *splḗn*]

sple·no·meg·a·ly (splē′nə meg′ə lē, splen′ə-), *n. Pathol.* enlargement of the spleen. Also, **sple·no·me·ga·li·a** (splē′nō mə gā′lē ə, -gāl′yə, splen′ō-).

spleu·chan (splo͞o′ḵʜən), *n. Scot., Irish Eng.* a small pouch, esp. for carrying tobacco or money. Also, **spleu·ghan** (splo͞o′ḵʜən). [< Gael *spliuchan*]

A B C

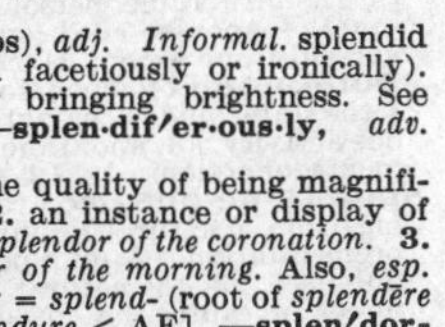

Splices
A, Short splice; B, Eye splice; C, Long splice

splice (splīs), *v.,* **spliced, splic·ing,** *n.* **—***v.t.* **1.** to join together or unite (two sections of rope) by the interweaving of strands. **2.** to unite (timbers) by overlapping and binding their ends. **3.** to unite (film, magnetic tape, or the like) by butting and cementing. **4.** to join or unite. **—***n.* **5.** a union or junction made by splicing. [< MD *spliss(en)*; akin to SPLIT] **—splic′er,** *n.*

spline (splīn), *n., v.,* **splined, splin·ing.** **—***n.* **1.** a long, narrow, thin strip of wood, metal, etc.; slat. **2.** a long, flexible strip of wood or the like, used in drawing curves. **3.** *Mach.* any of a series of uniformly spaced ridges on a shaft, parallel to its axis and fitting inside corresponding grooves in the hub of a gear, etc., to transmit torque. **4.** *Building Trades.* a thin strip of material inserted into the edges of two boards, acoustic tiles, etc., to make a butt joint between them; feather. **—***v.t. Mach.* **5.** to provide with a spline or key. **6.** to provide with a keyway. [EAnglian dial. word, perh. akin to SPLINT; cf. OE *splin* spindle]

splint (splint), *n.* **1.** a thin piece of wood or other rigid material used to immobilize a fractured or dislocated bone or to maintain any part of the body in a fixed position. **2.** one of a number of thin strips of wood woven together to make a chair seat, basket, etc. **3.** *Vet. Med.* an exostosis or bony enlargement of a splint bone of a horse or a related animal. **4.** *Armor.* **a.** any of a number of narrow plates forming a piece of armor. **b.** a partial vambrace protecting only the outer part of the arm. **—***v.t.* **5.** to secure, hold in position, or support by means of a splint or splints, as a fractured bone. [ME < MD or MLG *splinte;* akin to Norw *splint* peg; see SPLINTER]

splint′ bone′, one of the rudimentary, splintlike metacarpal or metatarsal bones of the horse or some allied animal, one on each side of the back of each cannon bone.

splin·ter (splin′tər), *n.* **1.** a small, thin, sharp piece of wood, bone, or the like, split or broken off from the main body. **2.** See **splinter group. 3.** a splint. **—***v.t.* **4.** to split or break into splinters. **5.** to break off (something) in splinters. **6.** to split or break (a larger group) into separate factions or independent groups. **—***v.i.* **7.** to be split or broken into splinters. **8.** to break off in splinters. [ME < MD or MLG; see SPLINT] **—splin′ter·y,** *adj.* **—Syn. 1.** sliver. **8.** separate, part, split.

splin′ter group′, a small organization that becomes separated from or acts apart from a larger group or other small groups, as because of disagreement.

split (split), *v.* **split, split·ting,** *n., adj.* **—***v.t.* **1.** to divide or separate from end to end or into layers: *to split a log in two.* **2.** to separate by cutting, chopping, etc.: *to split a piece from a block.* **3.** to divide into distinct parts or portions (often fol. by *up*): *We split up our rations.* **4.** to divide (persons) into different groups, factions, etc., as by discord: *to split a political party.* **5.** to divide between two or more persons, groups, etc.; share: *We split a bottle of wine.* **6.** to separate into parts by interposing something: *to split an infinitive.* **7.** *Chem.* to divide (molecules or atoms) by cleavage. **8.** to issue additional shares of (stock) to stockholders, thereby dividing their interest into a larger number of shares. **—***v.i.* **9.** to divide, break, or separate. **10.** to become separated, as a part from a whole. **11.** to part or separate, as through disagreement. **12.** to divide or share something with another or others. **13.** *Slang.* to leave; depart: *Man, let's split.* **14. split hairs.** See **hair** (def. 12). **15. split the difference.** See **difference** (def. 11). **—***n.* **16.** the act of splitting. **17.** a crack, tear, or fissure caused by splitting. **18.** a piece or part separated by or as by splitting. **19.** a breach or rupture, as between persons. **20.** a faction, party, etc., formed by a rupture or schism. **21.** *Colloq.* an ice-cream dish made from sliced fruit, usually a banana, and ice cream, and covered with syrup and nuts. **22.** a bottle, as for wine, containing about 6 ounces. **23.** Often, **splits.** the feat of separating the legs while sinking to the floor, until they extend at right angles to the body. **24.** *Bowling.* an arrangement of the pins remaining after the first bowl in two separated groups. **25.** the act of splitting a stock. **—***adj.* **26.** that has undergone splitting; parted lengthwise; cleft. **27.** disunited; divided: *a split opinion.* **28.** (of a stock) having undergone a split. [< MD *splitt(en)*; akin to MLG *splīten*, G *spleissen* to split] **—split′ter,** *n.*

Split (splēt), *n.* a seaport in W Yugoslavia: Roman ruins. 109,000 (1961). Italian, **Spalato.**

split′ deci′sion, *Boxing.* a decision of a bout on whose outcome the referee and judges did not unanimously agree.

split′ infin′itive, *Gram.* an expression in which a word or group of words, esp. an adverb or adverbial phrase, comes between *to* and its accompanying verb form in an infinitive, as in *to readily understand.*

—Usage. In Latin, the infinitive is one word, hence cannot be split. In the 17th century, modeling English style on Latin style and grammar was considered the epitome of good writing; and writers and Latin scholars, such as John Dryden, inveighed against the practice of using sentences like *To really get to know someone you have to have lived with him.* But in a sentence like the preceding, placing *really* anywhere else makes for awkward phrasing. Although there is nothing inherent in English grammar or style to forbid the use of a split infinitive, most teachers and careful stylists follow the "rule" against using it.

split-lev·el (split′lev′əl), *adj.* noting a house having a room or rooms that are somewhat above or below adjacent rooms.

split′ personal′ity, *Psychol.* a functionally dissociated personality having distinct, sometimes autonomous personality structures each of a complexity comparable to that of a normal individual. Also called **multiple personality.**

split′ sec′ond, **1.** a fraction of a second. **2.** an infinitesimal amount of time; instant. **—split′-sec′ond,** *adj.*

split′ tick′et, *U.S. Pol.* **1.** a ballot on which not all votes have been cast for candidates of the same party. **2.** a ticket on which not all the candidates nominated by a party are members of the party. Cf. **straight ticket.**

split-up (split′up′), *n.* a splitting or separating into two or more parts, groups, etc.

splore (splōr, splôr), *n. Scot.* a frolic; revel; carousal. [? aph. var. of EXPLORE]

splosh (splosh), *v.t., v.i., n.* splash.

splotch (sploch), *n.* **1.** a large, irregular spot; blot; stain. **—***v.t.* **2.** to mark with splotches. **—***v.i.* **3.** to be susceptible to stains or blots. **4.** to cause stains, blots, or spots. [? b. OE *splott* spot, blot, patch (of land) and PATCH]

splotch·y (sploch′ē), *adj.,* **splotch·i·er, splotch·i·est.** marked or covered with splotches.

splurge (splûrj), *v.,* **splurged, splurg·ing,** *n.* **—***v.i.* **1.** to indulge oneself in the purchase of some luxury or pleasure, esp. a costly one. **2.** to show off. **—***v.t.* **3.** to spend (money) lavishly or ostentatiously. **—***n.* **4.** an ostentatious display, esp. an extravagantly expensive one. [? b. SPLASH and SURGE]

splut·ter (splut′ər), *v.i.* **1.** to talk rapidly and somewhat incoherently, as when confused or excited. **2.** to make a sputtering sound or emit particles of something explosively, as meat being roasted. **3.** to fly or fall in particles or drops; spatter, as a liquid. **—***v.t.* **4.** to utter hastily and confusedly or incoherently; sputter. **5.** to spatter or bespatter. **—***n.* **6.** spluttering utterance or talk; noise or fuss. **7.** a sputtering or spattering, as of liquid. [b. SPLASH and SPUTTER]

Spock (spok), *n.* **Benjamin (Mc·Lane)** (mə klān′), born 1903, U.S. pediatrician, educator, and spokesman against U.S. involvement in the Vietnam War.

Spode (spōd), *n.* **1. Josiah,** 1733–97, and his son, **Josiah,** 1754–1827, English potters. **2.** Also called **Spode′ chi′na.** *Trademark.* china or porcelain manufactured by the Spodes or the firm which they established.

spod·u·mene (spoj′o͝o mēn′), *n.* a mineral, lithium aluminum silicate, $LiAlSi_2O_6$. [< F *spodumène* < G *Spodumen* < Gk *spodoúmen(os)* being burnt to ashes = *spodou-* (< *spodós* wood ash) + *-menos* passive suffix]

spoil (spoil), *v.,* **spoiled** or **spoilt, spoil·ing,** *n.* **—***v.t.* **1.** to damage or harm (something), esp. with reference to its excellence, value, usefulness, etc. **2.** to impair the character of (someone) by excessively indulgent treatment. **3.** *Archaic.* **a.** to plunder, pillage, or despoil. **b.** to carry off as booty. **—***v.i.* **4.** to become bad, or unfit for use, as food or other perishable substances. **5.** to plunder, pillage, or rob. **6. be spoiling for,** *Informal.* to be very eager for. **—***n.* **7.** Often, **spoils.** booty, loot, or plunder. **8.** waste material, as that which is cast up in excavating. [ME *spoil(en)* < MF *(e)spoillie(r)* < L *spoliāre* to despoil = *spoli(um)* booty + *-āre* inf. suffix] **—Syn. 1.** disfigure, destroy, demolish, mar.

spoil·age (spoi′lij), *n.* **1.** the act of spoiling. **2.** the state of being spoiled. **3.** material or the amount of material that is spoiled.

spoil·er (spoi′lər), *n.* **1.** a person or thing that spoils. **2.** *Aeron.* a device used to break up the airflow around an aerodynamic surface, as an aircraft wing, in order to provide bank or descent control. **3.** *Sports Slang.* a person or team that defeats, and spoils the reputation or winning record of, a favored opponent.

spoil·five (spoil′fīv′), *n. Cards.* a game played by two to ten persons having five cards each.

spoils·man (spoilz′mən), *n., pl.* **-men.** **1.** a person who seeks or receives a share in political spoils. **2.** an advocate of the spoils system in politics.

spoil·sport (spoil′spôrt′, -spōrt′), *n.* a person whose conduct spoils the pleasure of others.

spoils′ sys′tem, *Chiefly U.S.* the practice by which public offices with their emoluments are at the disposal of the victorious party.

spoilt (spoilt), *v.* a pt. and pp. of **spoil.**

Spo·kane (spō kan′), *n.* a city in E Washington. 170,516 (1970).

spoke[1] (spōk), *v.* **1.** a pt. of **speak.** **2.** *Archaic.* pp. of **speak.**

spoke[2] (spōk), *n., v.,* **spoked, spok·ing.** —*n.* **1.** one of the bars, rods, or rungs radiating from the hub or nave of a wheel and supporting the rim or felloe. **2.** a handlelike projection from the rim of a wheel, as a ship's steering wheel. **3.** a rung of a ladder. —*v.t.* **4.** to fit or furnish with or as with spokes. [ME; OE *spāca;* c. D *speek,* G *Speiche*] —**spoke′less,** *adj.*

spo·ken (spō′kən), *v.* **1.** a pp. of **speak.** —*adj.* **2.** uttered or expressed by speaking; oral (opposed to *written*): *the spoken word.* **3.** speaking, or using speech, as specified (usually used in combination): *My father was an extremely pleasant-spoken man.*

spoke·shave (spōk′shāv′), *n.* a cutting tool, having a blade set between two handles, for dressing curved edges of wood and forming round bars and shapes.

Spokeshave

spokes·man (spōks′mən), *n., pl.* **-men.** a person who speaks for another or for a group. [SPOKE[1] (used as n.) + 's[1] + MAN[1]]

spokes·wom·an (spōks′wŏŏm′ən), *n., pl.* **-wom·en.** a woman who speaks for another person or for a group.

spo·li·ate (spō′lē āt′), *v.t., v.i.,* **-at·ed, -at·ing.** to plunder, rob, or ruin. [< L *spoliāt(us),* ptp. of *spoliāre* to spoil. See SPOIL, -ATE[1]]

spo·li·a·tion (spō′lē ā′shən), *n.* **1.** the act or an instance of plundering or despoiling. **2.** the authorized plundering of neutrals at sea in time of war. **3.** *Law.* the destruction or material alteration of a bill of exchange, will, or the like. **4.** the act of spoiling or damaging something. [late ME < L *spoliātiōn-* (s. of *spoliātiō*)]

spon·da·ic (spon dā′ik), *adj. Pros.* **1.** of or pertaining to a spondee. **2.** constituting a spondee. **3.** consisting of or characterized by spondees. Also, **spon·da′i·cal.** [< LL *spondaic(us),* metathetic var. of *spondīacus* < Gk *spondeiakós* = *spondeî(os)* SPONDEE + *-akos,* var. of *-ikos* -IC]

spon·dee (spon′dē), *n. Pros.* a foot of two syllables, both of which are long in quantitative meter or stressed in accentual meter. [< L *spondē(us)* < Gk *spondeîos* < *spondḗ* ceremonial]

spondyl-, a learned borrowing from Greek meaning "vertebra," used in the formation of compound words: *spondylitis.* Also, *esp. before a vowel,* **spondylo-.** [comb. form of L *spondylus* < Gk *spóndylos* vertebra, whorl, mussel]

spon·dy·li·tis (spon′dəlī′tis), *n. Pathol.* inflammation of the vertebrae. [< NL]

sponge (spunj), *n., v.,* **sponged, spong·ing.** —*n.* **1.** any aquatic, chiefly marine animal of the phylum *Porifera,* having a porous structure and usually a horny, siliceous or calcareous skeleton or framework, occurring in large, complex, sessile, often plantlike colonies. **2.** the light, yielding, porous, fibrous skeleton or framework of certain animals or colonies of this group from which the living matter has been removed, characterized by readily absorbing water: used in cleaning surfaces, etc. **3.** any of various similar substances. **4.** *Informal.* a person who lives at the expense of others. **5.** *Metall.* a porous mass of fine, loosely cohering, metallic particles, as of platinum, obtained in a reduction process. **6.** *Surg.* a sterile surgical dressing of absorbent material for wiping or absorbing blood or other fluids during an operation. **7.** *Cookery.* **a.** dough raised with yeast, as for bread. **b.** a sweet spongy pudding. **8. throw in the sponge,** *Slang.* to concede defeat. —*v.t.* **9.** to wipe or rub with or as with a wet sponge. **10.** to wipe out or efface with or as with a sponge (often fol. by *out*). **11.** to take up or absorb with or as with a sponge (often fol. by *up*). **12.** *Informal.* to obtain by imposing on another's good nature. —*v.i.* **13.** to take in or soak up liquid by absorption. **14.** to gather sponges. **15.** *Informal.* to live at the expense of others (often fol. by *on* or *off*). [ME, OE < L *spong(ia), spong(ea)* < Gk *spongiā́*] —**sponge′like′,** *adj.* —**Syn. 4.** leech. **9.** wash.

sponge′ bath′, a bath in which the bather is cleaned by a wet sponge or damp cloth without getting into a tub or shower.

sponge′ cake′, a light, sweet cake made with eggs but no shortening.

sponge′ cloth′, **1.** a cotton fabric loosely woven of coarse yarn in any of various weaves. **2.** ratiné.

spong·er (spun′jər), *n.* **1.** *Informal.* a person who habitually borrows or lives at the expense of others; parasite. **2.** a person or thing that sponges.

sponge′ rub′ber, a light, spongy rubber, usually prepared by bubbling carbon dioxide through or whipping air into latex, used for padding, insulation, gaskets, etc.; foam rubber.

spon·gin (spun′jin), *n.* a scleroprotein occurring in the form of fibers that form the skeleton of certain sponges.

spong·i·o·blast (spun′jē ō blast′), *n. Embryol.* one of the primordial cells in the embryonic brain and spinal cord capable of developing into neuroglia. [*spongio-* (comb. form of Gk *spongiā́* SPONGE) + -BLAST] —**spon′gi·o·blas′tic,** *adj.*

spon·gy (spun′jē), *adj.,* **-gi·er, -gi·est.** **1.** of the nature of or resembling a sponge; light, porous, or readily compressible, as pith or bread. **2.** having the absorbent characteristics of a sponge. **3.** of or pertaining to a sponge. **4.** porous but hard, as bone. —**spon′gi·ly,** *adv.* —**spon′gi·ness,** *n.*

spon·sion (spon′shən), *n.* **1.** a pledge or promise, esp. one made on behalf of another. **2.** the act of becoming surety for another. [< L *sponsiōn-* (s. of *sponsiō*) guarantee = *spons(us)* (ptp. of *spondēre*) + *-iōn-* -ION]

spon·son (spon′sən), *n.* **1.** a structure projecting from the side or main deck of a vessel to support a gun or the outer edge of a paddle box. **2.** a buoyant appendage at the gunwale of a canoe to resist capsizing. [var. of EXPANSION]

spon·sor (spon′sər), *n.* **1.** a person who vouches or is responsible for a person or thing. **2.** a person, firm, etc., that finances and buys the time to broadcast a radio or television program so as to advertise a product, political party, etc. **3.** a person who makes a pledge or promise on behalf of another. **4.** a person who answers for an infant at baptism, making the required professions and assuming responsibility for the child's religious upbringing; godfather or godmother. —*v.t.* **5.** to act as sponsor for; promise, vouch, or answer for. [< L: answerable person = *spons(us)* (see SPONSION) + *-or* -OR[2]] —**spon·so·ri·al** (spon sōr′ē əl, -sôr′-), *adj.* —**spon′sor·ship′,** *n.* —**Syn. 1.** patron, backer. **2.** advertiser.

spon·ta·ne·i·ty (spon′tə nē′i tē, -nā′-), *n., pl.* **-ties** for 2, 3. **1.** the state, quality, or fact of being spontaneous. **2.** spontaneous activity. **3. spontaneities,** spontaneous impulses, movements, or actions. [< LL *spontāne(us)* SPONTANEOUS + -ITY]

spon·ta·ne·ous (spon tā′nē əs), *adj.* **1.** coming or resulting from a natural impulse or tendency; without effort or premeditation. **2.** (of a person) given to acting upon sudden impulses. **3.** (of natural phenomena) arising from internal forces or causes. **4.** produced by natural process. [< LL *spontāneus* = L *spont(e)* willingly + *-āneus* (*-ān-* -AN + *-eus* -EOUS)] —**spon·ta′ne·ous·ly,** *adv.* —**spon·ta′ne·ous·ness,** *n.* —**Syn. 1.** unpremeditated.

sponta′neous combus′tion, the ignition of a substance or body from the rapid oxidation of its own constituents, without heat from any external source.

sponta′neous genera′tion, *Biol.* abiogenesis.

spon·toon (spon tōōn′), *n.* a shafted weapon having a pointed blade with a crossbar at its base, used by infantry officers in the 17th and 18th centuries. Also called **half-pike.** [< F *(e)sponton* < It *spunton(e)* = *s-* EX-[1] + *puntone* kind of weapon (*punt(o)* POINT + *-one* aug. suffix)]

spoof (spōōf), *n.* **1.** a mocking imitation of someone or something; lampoon or parody. **2.** a hoax; prank. —*v.t.* **3.** to mock (something or someone) lightly and good-humoredly; kid. **4.** to fool by a hoax. —*v.i.* **5.** to scoff at something lightly and good-humoredly; kid. [after a game invented and named by A. Roberts (1852–1933), British comedian]

spook (spōōk), *n.* **1.** *Informal.* a ghost; specter. **2.** *Slang.* an espionage agent; spy. —*v.t.* **3.** to haunt; inhabit or appear in or to as a ghost or specter. **4.** *Informal.* to frighten; scare. —*v.i.* **5.** *Informal.* to become frightened or scared. [< D; c. G *Spuk*]

spook·y (spōō′kē), *adj.,* **spook·i·er, spook·i·est.** *Informal.* **1.** like or befitting a spook; suggestive of spooks. **2.** eerie; scary. —**spook′i·ly,** *adv.*

spool (spōōl), *n.* **1.** any cylindrical object or device on which something is wound. **2.** the material or quantity of material that this holds wound on such a device. —*v.t.* **3.** to wind on a spool. **4.** to unwind from a spool (usually fol. by *off* or *out*). [ME *spole* < MD or MLG; c. G *Spule*]

spoon (spōōn), *n.* **1.** a utensil for use in eating, stirring, measuring, ladling, etc., consisting of a small, shallow bowl with a handle. **2.** a spoonful. **3.** *Angling.* a lure consisting of a piece of metal shaped like the bowl of a spoon. **3.** *Golf.* a club with a wooden head whose face has a greater slope than the brassie or driver. **4. born with a silver spoon in one's mouth,** born into a wealthy family. —*v.t.* **5.** to eat with, take up, or transfer in or as in a spoon. **6.** to hollow out or shape like a spoon. **7.** *Games.* **a.** to push or shove (a ball) with a lifting motion instead of striking it soundly, as in croquet or golf. **b.** to hit (a ball) up in the air, as in cricket. —*v.i.* **8.** *Informal.* to show affection or love, esp. in an openly sentimental manner. **9.** *Games.* to spoon a ball. **10.** *Angling.* to fish with a spoon. [ME; OE *spōn;* c. LG *spon,* Icel *spōnn,* G *Span* chip, Gk *sphḗn* wedge; see SPHENE]

Spoonbill,
Ajaia ajaja
(Length about 3 ft.)

spoon·bill (spōōn′bil′), *n.* **1.** any of several wading birds of the genera *Platalea* and *Ajaia,* related to the ibises, having a long, flat bill with a spoonlike tip. **2.** any of various birds having a similar bill, as the shoveler duck. **3.** the paddlefish.

spoon′ bread′, **1.** a baked dish made with corn meal, milk, eggs, and shortening, served as an accompaniment to meat. **2.** *Dial.* any of various types of biscuits shaped by dropping batter into a baking pan from a spoon.

spoon·drift (spōōn′drift′), *n.* spindrift. [*spoon,* var. of *spoom* to scud (? akin to FOAM) + DRIFT]

spoon·er·ism (spōō′nə riz′əm), *n.* the transposition of initial or other sounds of words, usually by accident, as in *a blushing crow* for *a crushing blow.* [after W. A. *Spooner* (1844–1930), Englishman noted for such slips; see -ISM]

spoon·ey (spōō′nē), *adj.,* **spoon·i·er, spoon·i·est,** *n., pl.* **spoon·ies.** spoony[1].

spoon-fed (spōōn′fed′), *adj.* **1.** fed with a spoon. **2.** treated with excessive solicitude; pampered. **3.** given no opportunity to act or think for oneself.

spoon-feed (spōōn′fēd′, -fēd′), *v.t.,* **-fed, -feed·ing.** to cause to be spoon-fed.

spoon·ful (spōōn′fŏŏl), *n., pl.* **-fuls.** **1.** the amount that a spoon can hold. **2.** a small quantity. [ME *sponeful*]

spoon′ hook′, *Angling.* a fishhook equipped with a spoon lure.

spoon·y[1] (spōō′nē), *adj.,* **spoon·i·er, spoon·i·est.** *Informal.* **1.** foolishly or sentimentally amorous. **2.** *Chiefly Brit.* foolish; silly. [SPOON + -Y[1]] —**spoon′i·ly,** *adv.*

spoon·y[2] (spōō′nē), *n., pl.* **spoon·ies.** **1.** a person who is foolishly or sentimentally amorous. **2.** *Chiefly Brit.* a simple or foolish person. [SPOON + -Y[2]]

spoor (spŏŏr, spōr, spôr), *n.* **1.** a track or trail, esp. of a wild animal. —*v.t., v.i.* **2.** to track by or follow a spoor. [< SAfrD; c. OE, Icel *spor,* G *Spur;* cf. SPEER]

spor-, var. of **sporo-** before a vowel: *sporangium.*

Spor·a·des (spôr′ə dēz′; *Gk.* spô rä′thes), *n.pl.* two groups of Greek islands in the Aegean: the one off the E coast of Greece; the other including the Dodecanese, off the SW coast of Asia Minor.

spo·rad·ic (spō rad′ik, spô-, spə-), *adj.* **1.** (of similar things or occurrences) appearing or happening at irregular intervals in time; occasional. **2.** appearing in scattered or isolated instances, as a disease. **3.** isolated, as a single instance of something. **4.** occurring in widely separated places. Also, **spo·rad′i·cal.** [< ML *sporadic(us)* < Gk *sporadikós* = *sporad-* (s. of *sporás* strewn, akin to *sporá* SPORE) + *-ikos* -IC] —**spo·rad′i·cal·ly,** *adv.* —**spo·ra·dic·i·ty** (spōr′ə dis′i tē, spôr′-), *n.* —**Syn. 3.** separate, unconnected. —**Ant. 1.** continuous.

spo·ran·gi·um (spō ran′jē əm, spô-), *n., pl.* **-gi·a** (-jē ə). *Bot.* the case or sac in which the asexual spores are produced in cryptogams and phanerogams. Also called **spore′ case′.** [< NL = *spor-* SPOR- + Gk *angeîon* vessel] —**spo·ran′gi·al,** *adj.*

spore (spōr, spôr), *n., v.,* **spored, spor·ing.** —*n.* **1.** *Biol.* a walled, single-to-many-celled reproductive body of an organism, capable of giving rise to a new individual either directly or indirectly. **2.** a germ, germ cell, seed, or the like. —*v.i.* **3.** to bear or produce spores. [< NL *spor(a)* < Gk *sporá* sowing, seed, akin to *speírein* to sow; see SPERM[1]] —**spo′ral,** *adj.* —**spo′roid,** *adj.*

-spore, var. of **sporo-,** as final element of compound words: *endospore.*

spori-, var. of **sporo-** before elements of Latin origin: *sporiferous.*

spo·rif·er·ous (spō rif′ər əs, spô-), *adj.* bearing spores.

sporo-, a combining form of **spore:** *sporophyte.* Also, **spor-, -spore, spori-.** Cf. **-sporous.**

spo·ro·carp (spōr′ə kärp′, spôr′-), *n. Bot.* (in higher fungi, lichens, and red algae) a many-celled body developed for the formation of spores.

spo·ro·cyst (spōr′ə sist′, spôr′-), *n. Zool.* **1.** a walled body resulting from the multiple division of a sporozoan, which produces one or more sporozoites. **2.** a stage in development of trematodes that gives rise, asexually, to cercaria. —**spo·ro·cys·tic** (spōr′ə sis′tik, spôr′-), *adj.*

spo·ro·gen·e·sis (spōr′ə jen′i sis, spôr′-), *n. Biol.* **1.** the production of spores; sporogony. **2.** reproduction by means of spores. —**spo·rog·e·nous** (spō roj′ə nəs, spô-), *adj.*

spo·ro·go·ni·um (spōr′ə gō′nē əm, spôr′-), *n., pl.* **-ni·a** (-nē ə). *Bot.* the sporangium of mosses and liverworts. —**spo′ro·go′ni·al,** *adj.*

spo·rog·o·ny (spō roj′ə nē, spô-), *n. Biol.* (in certain sporozoans) the multiple fission of an encysted zygote or oocyte, resulting in the formation of sporozoites.

spo·ro·phore (spōr′ə fōr′, spôr′ə fôr′), *n. Bot.* a simple or branched fungus hypha specialized to bear spores. —**spo·ro·phor·ic** (spōr′ə fôr′ik, -for′-, spôr′-), **spo·roph·o·rous** (spō rof′ər əs, spô-), *adj.*

spo·ro·phyll (spōr′ə fil, spôr′-), *n. Bot.* a modified leaf that bears sporangia. Also, **spo′ro·phyl.** —**spo·ro·phyl·la·ry** (spōr′ə fil′ə rē, spôr′-), *adj.*

spo·ro·phyte (spōr′ə fīt′, spôr′-), *n. Bot.* the asexual form of a plant in the alternation of generations (opposed to *gametophyte*). —**spo·ro·phyt·ic** (spōr′ə fit′ik, spôr′-), *adj.*

-sporous, a word element used to form adjectives corresponding to nouns with stems ending in **-spore:** *homosporous.*

spo·ro·zo·an (spōr′ə zō′ən, spôr′-), *n.* **1.** any parasitic protozoan of the class *Sporozoa,* certain species of which cause malaria. —*adj.* **2.** belonging or pertaining to the *Sporozoa.*

spo·ro·zo·ite (spōr′ə zō′īt, spôr′-), *n. Zool.* one of the minute, active bodies into which the spore of certain *Sporozoa* divides, each developing into an adult individual. [< NL *Sporozo(a)* name of class + -ITE[1]]

spor·ran (spor′ən), *n.* (in Scottish Highland costume) a large purse for men, commonly of fur, worn, suspended from a belt, in front of the kilt. [< ScotGael *sporan;* c. Ir *sparān* purse]

S

S, Sporran

sport (spōrt, spôrt), *n.* **1.** an athletic activity requiring skill or physical prowess and often of a competitive nature. **2.** diversion; recreation. **3.** jest or fun: *to say something in sport.* **4.** mockery or ridicule: *to make sport of someone.* **5.** something or someone subject to the whims or vicissitudes of fate, circumstances, etc. **6.** *Informal.* a sportsmanlike or accommodating person. **7.** *Informal.* a person interested in sports as an occasion for gambling. **8.** *Biol.* an animal, plant, or part of a plant that shows an unusual or singular deviation from the normal or parent type; mutation. **9.** *Obs.* amorous dalliance. —*adj.* **10.** suitable for outdoor or informal wear: *sport clothes.* **11.** having to do with sports. —*v.i.* **12.** to amuse oneself with some pleasant pastime or recreation. **13.** to engage in some open-air or athletic pastime or sport. **14.** to trifle with someone or something. **15.** to mock, scoff, or tease. **16.** *Bot.* to mutate. —*v.t.* **17.** *Informal.* to wear, display, carry, etc., esp. with ostentation; show off. [late ME; aph. var. of DISPORT] —**sport′ful,** *adj.* —**Syn. 1.** game. **2.** fun, entertainment. See **play. 12.** romp, caper. **14.** toy.

sport·ing (spōr′ting, spôr′-), *adj.* **1.** engaging in, disposed to, or interested in open-air or athletic sports. **2.** concerned with or suitable for such sports: *sporting equipment.* **3.** sportsmanlike. **4.** interested in or connected with sports or pursuits involving betting or gambling.

sport′ing chance′, an even or fair opportunity for a favorable outcome in an enterprise, as winning in a game of chance or in any kind of contest: *They gave the less experienced players a sporting chance by handicapping the experts.*

sport′ing house′, **1.** *Informal.* a brothel. **2.** *Archaic.* an establishment, as a tavern or inn, catering to gamblers or sportsmen.

sport′ing la′dy, *Informal.* a prostitute.

spor·tive (spōr′tiv, spôr′-), *adj.* **1.** playful or frolicsome. **2.** pertaining to or of the nature of a sport or sports. **3.** *Biol.* mutative. **4.** *Archaic.* ardent; wanton. —**spor′tive·ly,** *adv.* —**spor′tive·ness,** *n.* —**Syn. 1.** jocular, gay, sprightly.

sports (spōrts, spôrts), *adj.* **1.** of or pertaining to a sport or sports, esp. of the open-air or athletic kind: *a sports festival.* **2.** (of garments, equipment, etc.) suitable for use in open-air sports, or for outdoor or informal use. [see SPORT]

sports′ car′, a small, high-powered automobile, usually seating two persons. Also, **sport′ car′.**

sports·cast (spōrts′kast′, -käst′, spôrts′-), *n.* a newscast concerning sports. [modeled on *broadcast*] —**sports′cast′er,** *n.*

sport′ shirt′, a shirt for informal wear by men, having a squared-off shirttail that may be left outside the trousers. Also, **sports′ shirt′.** Cf. **dress shirt.**

sports′ jack′et, a man's jacket, often of textured wool or colorful pattern, cut somewhat fuller than the jacket of a business suit, for informal wear with unmatching slacks.

sports·man (spōrts′mən, spôrts′-), *n., pl.* **-men. 1.** a man who engages in sports, esp. in some open-air sport, as hunting, fishing, etc. **2.** a person who exhibits qualities especially esteemed in those who engage in sports, as fairness, courtesy, etc. —**sports′man·like′, sports′man·ly,** *adj.*

sports·man·ship (spōrts′mən ship′, spôrts′-), *n.* **1.** the character, practice, or skill of a sportsman. **2.** sportsmanlike conduct, as fairness, courtesy, being a cheerful loser, etc.

sports·wear (spōrts′wâr′, spôrts′-), *n.* informal clothing; originally, clothing for wear while playing golf or tennis, bicycling, etc.

sports·wom·an (spōrts′wŏŏm′ən, spôrts′-), *n., pl.* **-wom·en.** a woman who engages in sports.

sports·writ·er (spōrts′rī′tər, spôrts′-), *n.* a journalist who reports on or writes about sports and sporting events.

sport·y (spōr′tē, spôr′-), *adj.,* **sport·i·er, sport·i·est.** *Informal.* **1.** flashy; showy. **2.** smart in dress, behavior, etc. **3.** like or befitting a sportsman. —**sport′i·ly,** *adv.* —**sport′i·ness,** *n.*

spor·u·late (spôr′yə lāt′, spor′-), *v.i.,* **-lat·ed, -lat·ing.** *Biol.* to undergo multiple division resulting in the production of spores. —**spor′u·la′tion,** *n.*

spor·ule (spôr′yōōl, spor′-), *n. Biol.* a spore, esp. a small one. [< NL *sporul(a).* See SPORE, -ULE] —**spor·u·lar** (spôr′yə lər), *adj.*

spot (spot), *n., v.,* **spot·ted, spot·ting,** *adj.* —*n.* **1.** a rounded mark or stain made by foreign matter. **2.** something that mars one's character or reputation; blemish; flaw. **3.** a pimple. **4.** a comparatively small, usually roundish, part of a surface differing from the rest in color, texture, character, etc. **5.** a place or locality. **6.** Usually, **spots.** places of entertainment or sightseeing interest. **7.** See **spot announcement. 8.** a specific position, as in a sequence: *You have the second spot on the program.* **9.** *Cards.* **a.** one of various traditional, geometric drawings of a club, diamond, heart, or spade on a playing card for indicating suit and value. **b.** any playing card from a two through a ten. **10.** *Informal.* a pip, as on dice or dominoes. **11.** *Slang.* a piece of paper money of a specified number of dollars in value: *a five-spot.* **12.** Also called **spot′ illustra′tion.** a small drawing, usually black and white, appearing within or accompanying a text. **13.** *Chiefly Brit. Informal.* **a.** a small quantity of anything. **b.** a drink: *a spot of tea.* **14.** a small, sciaenoid food fish, *Leiostomus xanthurus,* of the eastern coast of the U.S. **15.** *Informal.* spotlight (def. 1). **16. hit the spot,** *Slang.* to satisfy a want or need. **17. in a (bad) spot,** *U.S. Slang.* in an uncomfortable or dangerous predicament. **18. on the spot, a.** at once; instantly. **b.** at the very place in question. **c.** *U.S. Slang.* in a difficult or embarrassing position. —*v.t.* **19.** to stain or mark with spots. **20.** to sully; blemish. **21.** *Informal.* to recognize; identify by seeing. **22.** to place or position on a particular place: *to spot a billiard ball.* **23.** to scatter in various places. **24.** *Mil.* to observe (the results of gunfire at or near a target) for the purpose of correcting aim. **25.** (in gymnastics) to watch or assist (a performer) in order to prevent injury. —*v.i.* **26.** to make a spot or stain. **27.** to become spotted, as some fabrics when spattered with water. —*adj.* **28.** made, paid, delivered, etc., at once: *a spot sale.* [ME *spotte;* c. MD, LG *spot* speck, Icel *spotti* bit] —**Syn. 2.** taint, stigma. **5.** locale, site. **20.** stain, taint, stigmatize.

spot′ announce′ment, a brief radio or television announcement, usually a commercial.

spot′ check′, a random sampling or quick sample investigation.

spot·less (spot′lis), *adj.* **1.** free from spots or dirt. **2.** irreproachable; pure; undefiled: *a spotless reputation.* [late ME] —**spot′less·ly,** *adv.* —**spot′less·ness,** *n.*

spot·light (spot′līt′), *n.* **1.** a strong, focused light thrown upon a particular spot to make some object, person, or group especially conspicuous. **2.** a lamp for producing such a light. **3.** the area of immediate or conspicuous public attention. —*v.t.* **4.** to direct the beam of a spotlight upon; light with a spotlight. **5.** to make conspicuous; call attention to; emphasize.

Spot·syl·va·ni·a (spot′sil vā′nē ə, -vān′yə), *n.* a village in NE Virginia: battles between the armies of Grant and Lee, May 8–21, 1864.

spot·ted (spot′id), *adj.* **1.** marked with or characterized by a spot or spots. **2.** sullied; blemished. [ME]

spot′ted ad′der. See **milk snake.**

spot′ted ca′vy, paca.

spot′ted fe′ver, *Pathol.* **1.** any of several fevers characterized by spots on the skin, esp. as in cerebrospinal meningitis or typhus fever. **2.** See **tick fever** (def. 1).

spot′ted hye′na, an African hyena, *Crocuta crocuta,* having a yellowish-gray coat with brown or black spots. Also called **laughing hyena.** See illus. at **hyena.**

spot′ted sand′piper, a North American sandpiper, *Actitis macularia,* having brownish-gray upper parts and white underparts, that is spotted with black in the summer, See illus. at **sandpiper.**

spot·ter (spot′ər), *n.* **1.** a person who looks for and removes spots from clothing in a dry-cleaning establishment. **2.** (in civil defense) a civilian who watches for enemy airplanes. **3.** *Informal.* a person employed to watch the activity and behavior of others, esp. employees, as for evidence of dishonesty. **4.** *Mil.* the person who determines for the gunner the fall of shots in relation to the target. **5.** a person or thing that spots.

spot·ty (spot′ē), *adj.* **-ti·er, -ti·est.** **1.** full of, having, or occurring in spots: *spotty coloring.* **2.** irregular or uneven in quality or character: *a spotty performance.* [ME] —**spot′ti·ly,** *adv.* —**spot′ti·ness,** *n.*

spot-weld (spot′weld′), *v.t.* **1.** to weld (two pieces of metal) together in a small area or spot by the application of heat and pressure. —*n.* **2.** a welded joint made by this process.

spous·al (spou′zəl), *n.* **1.** Often, **spousals.** the ceremony of marriage; nuptials. —*adj.* **2.** nuptial; matrimonial. [ME *spousaille,* aph. var. of *espousaille* ESPOUSAL] —**spous′al·ly,** *adv.*

spouse (*n.* spous, spouz; *v.* spouz, spous), *n., v.,* **spoused, spous·ing.** —*n.* **1.** either member of a married pair in relation to the other; one's husband or wife. —*v.t.* **2.** *Obs.* to join, give, or take in marriage. [ME < OF *spus* (masc.), *spuse* (fem.) < L *spons(us), spons(a)* pledged (man, woman), n. uses of ptp. of *spondēre* to pledge] —**spouse′hood,** *n.* —**spouse′less,** *adj.*

spout (spout), *v.t.* **1.** to emit or discharge forcibly (a liquid, granulated substance, etc.) in a jet or continuous stream. **2.** *Informal.* to state or declaim volubly or in an oratorical manner. —*v.i.* **3.** to discharge, as a liquid, in a jet or continuous stream. **4.** to issue forth with force, as liquid or other material through a narrow orifice. —*n.* **5.** a pipe, tube or liplike projection through or by which a liquid is discharged, poured, or conveyed. **6.** a trough or shoot for discharging or conveying grain, flour, etc. **7.** a waterspout. **8.** a continuous discharge from or as from a spout. [ME *spoute(n);* c. D *spuiten;* akin to Icel *spȳta* to SPIT[1]]

spp., species (pl. of **specie**).

S.P.Q.R., the Senate and People of Rome. Also, **SPQR** [< L *Senātus Populusque Rōmānus*]

sprad·dle (sprad′əl), *v.,* **-dled, -dling.** —*v.t.* **1.** to straddle. —*v.i.* **2.** to sprawl. [< Scand; cf. Norw *spradla* to thrash about, c. OHG *spratalōn* in same sense]

sprad·dle-leg·ged (sprad′əl leg′id, -legd′), *adj.* **1.** moving with or having the legs wide apart: *a spraddle-legged walk.* —*adv.* **2.** with the legs sprawled, spread apart, etc.

sprag (sprag), *n.* **1.** a pole or bar hinged to the rear axle of a cart or the like to prevent it from rolling downhill. **2.** *Mining.* a short timber for propping up loose walls or spacing two sets. [special use of dial. *sprag* twig, OE *sprǣc(g)* shoot, slip; c. Sw (dial.) *spragg(e)* branch; akin to SPRIG]

sprain (sprān), *v.t.* **1.** to overstrain or wrench (the ankle, wrist, or other part of the body at a joint) so as to injure without fracture or dislocation. —*n.* **2.** a violent straining or wrenching of the parts around a joint, without dislocation. **3.** the condition of being sprained. [?] —**Syn. 1.** twist. See **strain**[1].

sprang (sprang), *v.* a pt. of **spring.**

sprat (sprat), *n.* a small, herringlike, marine fish, *Clupea sprattus,* of Europe. [var. of earlier *sprot,* ME, OE *sprott* sprat (c. G *Sprott*); appar. same word as OE *sprott* sprout, twig, whence OE *sprytan* to sprout; akin to SPROUT]

sprat·tle (sprat′əl), *n.* *Scot.* a struggle; fight. [metathetic var. of *spartle* to scatter, itself alter. of *sparple* (ME < OF *(e)sparpeill(er)* < ?)]

sprawl (sprôl), *v.i.* **1.** to be stretched or spread out in an unnatural or ungraceful manner. **2.** to sit or lie in a relaxed position with the limbs spread out carelessly or ungracefully. **3.** to extend or be distributed in a straggling or irregular manner. **4.** to crawl awkwardly with the aid of all the limbs; scramble. —*v.t.* **5.** to stretch out (the limbs) as in sprawling. —*n.* **6.** the act or an instance of sprawling; a sprawling posture. [ME *spraule(n),* OE *spreawlian;* c. North Fris *spraweli*]

sprawl·y (sprô′lē), *adj.,* **sprawl·i·er, sprawl·i·est.** tending to sprawl; straggly.

spray[1] (sprā), *n.* **1.** water or other liquid broken up into small or fine particles and blown or falling through the air. **2.** a jet of fine particles of liquid discharged from an atomizer or other device for direct application to a surface. **3.** a liquid to be discharged or applied in such a jet. **4.** an apparatus or device for discharging such a liquid. **5.** a quantity of small objects, flying or discharged through the air. —*v.t.* **6.** to scatter in the form of fine particles. **7.** to apply as a spray. **8.** to sprinkle or treat with a spray. —*v.i.* **9.** to scatter spray; discharge a spray. **10.** to issue as spray. [< MD *spraeien;* c. MHG *spreien* to sprinkle] —**spray′er,** *n.* —**spray′like′,** *adj.*

spray[2] (sprā), *n.* **1.** a single, slender shoot, twig, or branch with its leaves, flowers, or berries. **2.** a group or bunch of cut flowers, leafy twigs, etc., arranged decoratively and for display, as in a vase. **3.** an ornament having a similar form. [ME; akin to SPRAG] —**spray′like′,** *adj.*

spray′ gun′, a device consisting of a container from which liquid is sprayed through a nozzle by air pressure from a pump.

spread (spred), *v.,* **spread, spread·ing,** *n.* —*v.t.* **1.** to draw, stretch, or open out, as something rolled or folded. **2.** to distribute over a relatively great area of space or time (often fol. by *out*). **3.** to set out in full: *We spread our lunch on the grass.* **4.** to apply in a thin layer or coating: *to spread butter on bread.* **5.** to set or prepare (a table), as for a meal. **6.** to diffuse, disseminate, or scatter. **7.** to force apart. **8.** *Phonet.* to extend the aperture between the lips laterally, so as to reduce it vertically, during an utterance. Cf. **round**[1] (def. 44), **unround.** —*v.i.* **9.** to become stretched out or extended. **10.** to extend or be distributed over a considerable area or time. **11.** to admit of being spread or applied in a thin layer, as a soft substance. **12.** to become shed abroad, diffused, or disseminated. **13.** to be forced apart. —*n.* **14.** expansion, extension, or diffusion. **15.** *Finance.* **a.** the difference between the prices bid and asked of stock or a commodity for a given time. **b.** a type of straddle in which the call price is placed above and the put price is placed below the current market quotation. **16.** capacity for spreading: *the spread of an elastic material.* **17.** a stretch, expanse, or extent of something: *a spread of timber.* **18.** a cloth covering for a bed, table, or the like, esp. a bedspread. **19.** *Informal.* an abundance of food set out on a table; feast. **20.** any food preparation for spreading on bread, crackers, etc., as jam or peanut butter. **21.** *Aeron.* wingspan. **22.** *Journalism.* **a.** an extensive, varied treatment of a subject. **b.** an advertisement, photograph, or the like, covering several columns, a full page, or two facing pages. **23.** *Informal.* a farm or ranch. [ME *sprede(n)* OE *sprǣdan;* c. MD *spreden,* G *spreiten*] —**spread′a·ble,** *adj.* —**Syn. 1.** unfold, unroll, expand.

spread′ ea′gle, **1.** a representation of an eagle with outspread wings: used as an emblem of the U.S. **2.** an acrobatic figure in skating.

spread-ea·gle (spred′ē′gəl), *adj., v.,* **-gled, -gling.** —*adj.* **1.** having or suggesting the form of a spread eagle. **2.** lying prone with arms and legs outstretched. —*v.t.* **3.** to stretch out (something) in the manner of a spread eagle. —*v.i.* **4.** to assume the position or perform the acrobatic figure of a spread eagle.

spread·er (spred′ər), *n.* **1.** a person or thing that spreads. **2.** a small knife used for spreading butter, jelly, etc. **3.** a machine for dispersing bulk material: *manure spreader.* **4.** a device for spacing or keeping apart two objects, as electric wires. **5.** *Naut.* a strut for spreading shrouds on a mast.

spread·sheet (spred′shēt′), *n.* **1.** *Accounting.* a work sheet that is arranged in the manner of a mathematical matrix and contains a multicolumn analysis of related entries for easy reference on a single sheet. **2.** *Computer Technol.* See **electronic spreadsheet.**

spree (sprē), *n.* **1.** a lively frolic or outing. **2.** a bout or spell of drinking to intoxication; binge; carousal. **3.** a period, spell, or bout of indulgence, as of a particular wish, craving, or whim. **4.** a period or outburst of activity. [?]

S
S, Spreader

Spree (shprā), *n.* a river in East Germany, flowing N through Berlin to the Havel River. 220 mi. long.

spri·er (sprī′ər), *adj.* a comparative of **spry.**

spri·est (sprī′ist), *adj.* a superlative of **spry.**

sprig (sprig), *n., v.,* **sprigged, sprig·ging.** —*n.* **1.** a small spray of some plant with its leaves, flowers, etc. **2.** an ornament having the form of such a spray. **3.** a shoot, twig, or small branch. **4.** a youth or young fellow. **5.** Also called **dowel pin.** a headless brad. —*v.t.* **6.** to mark or decorate (fabrics, pottery, etc.) with a design of sprigs. **7.** to fasten with brads. **8.** to remove a sprig or sprigs from (a plant). [akin to SPRAG, SPRAY[2]]

sprig·gy (sprig′ē), *adj.,* **-gi·er, -gi·est.** possessing sprigs or small branches.

spright·ful (sprīt′fəl), *adj.* sprightly. [*spright* (sp. var. of SPRITE) + -FUL]

spright·ly (sprīt′lē), *adj.,* **-li·er, -li·est,** *adv.* —*adj.* **1.** animated, vivacious, or gay; lively. —*adv.* **2.** in a sprightly manner. [*spright* (sp. var. of SPRITE) + -LY] —**spright′li·ness,** *n.* —**Syn. 1.** spirited, buoyant, spry.

spring (spring), *v.,* **sprang** or, often, **sprung; sprung; spring·ing;** *n., adj.* —*v.i.* **1.** to rise or leap suddenly and swiftly. **2.** to act swiftly upon release, as a mechanism operated by the elasticity of a part. **3.** to issue or arise suddenly (often fol. by *forth, out,* or *up*): *Flames sprang up everywhere.* **4.** to come into being within a short time (usually fol. by *up*): *Industries sprang up in the suburbs.* **5.** to come into being by growth, as a plant. **6.** to proceed or originate from a specified source. **7.** to be descended (usually fol. by *from*): *to spring from the aristocracy.* **8.** to rise or extend upward. **9.** to come or appear suddenly, as if at a bound: *An objection sprang to mind.* **10.** to start or rise from cover, as a game bird. **11.** to become bent or warped, as boards. **12.** to shift or work loose, as parts of a mechanism. **13.** to explode, as a mine. **14.** *Archaic.* to begin to appear, as day, light, etc.; dawn. —*v.t.* **15.** to cause to act swiftly, as a mechanism. **16.** to cause to shift, bend, warp, etc., under pressure. **17.** to cause to split or crack, as a timber. **18.** to develop by or as by the shifting, warping, or cracking of a structural member: *The boat sprang a leak.* **19.** to stretch or bend (a spring or other resilient device) beyond its elastic tolerance. **20.** to bring out, disclose, produce, make, etc., suddenly: *to spring a joke.* **21.** to leap over. **22.** *Slang.* to secure the release of (someone) from confinement, as of jail, military service, or the like. **23.** to explode (a mine). —*n.* **24.** a leap or bound. **25.** a sudden movement caused by the release of something elastic. **26.** a bouncy, elastic quality, as in a person's walk. **27.** elasticity or resilience. **28.** a structural defect or injury caused by a warp, crack, etc. **29.** an issue of water from the earth, taking the form, on the surface, of a stream or body of water. **30.** an elastic contrivance or body, as a strip or wire of steel coiled spirally, that recovers its shape after being compressed, bent, or stretched. **31.** the season between winter and summer: in the Northern Hemisphere from the vernal equinox to the summer solstice; in the Southern Hemisphere from the autumnal equinox to the winter solstice. **32.** the first stage and freshest period: *the spring of life.* **33.** Also called **springing.** *Archit.* **a.** the point at which an arch rises from its support. **b.** the rise or the angle of the rise of an arch. **34.** *Archaic.* the dawn, as of day, light, etc. —*adj.* **35.** of, pertaining to, characteristic of, or suitable for the season of spring: *spring flowers.* **36.** resting on or con-

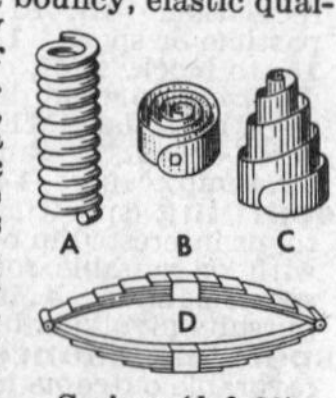

Springs (def. 30)
A, Spiral; B, Coil; C, Volute; D, Leaf

taining mechanical springs. [ME *springe(n)*, OE *springan;* c. D, G *springen*, Icel *springa*] —**spring′like′,** *adj.*
—**Syn. 1.** jump, bound, hop, vault. **2.** recoil, rebound. **3.** shoot, dart, fly. **6.** emerge, flow. **11.** bend, warp.

spring′ beau′ty, any American portulacaceous spring herb of the genus *Claytonia*, esp. *C. virginica*, having a raceme of white or pink flowers.

spring·board (spring′bōrd′, -bôrd′), *n.* **1.** a resilient board used as an aid in diving or gymnastics. **2.** *Informal.* a starting point, esp. in a discussion, argument, etc.

spring·bok (spring′bok′), *n., pl.* **-boks,** (*esp. collectively*) **-bok.** a gazelle, *Antidorcas marsupialis*, of southern Africa, noted for its habit of springing into the air when alarmed. [< SAfrD. See SPRING, BUCK[1]]

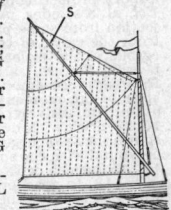

Springbok
(2½ ft. high at shoulder; length 5 ft.; horns 15 in.)

spring·buck (spring′buk′), *n., pl.* **-bucks,** (*esp. collectively*) **-buck.** springbok.

spring′ chick′en, 1. a young chicken, esp. a broiler or fryer. **2.** *Slang.* a young person.

spring-clean·ing (spring′klē′ning), *n.* a complete cleaning of a place, as a home, done traditionally in the spring of the year.

springe (sprinj), *n., v.,* **springed, spring·ing.** —*n.* **1.** a snare for catching small game. —*v.t.* **2.** to catch in a springe. —*v.i.* **3.** to set a springe or springes. [ME, var. of *sprenge*, lit., something that is made to spring < *sprenge(n)* (to) make spring, OE *sprengan*, causative of *springan* to SPRING]

spring·er (spring′ər), *n.* **1.** a person or thing that springs. **2.** *Archit.* the first voussoir above the impost of an arch. [ME]

English springer spaniel
(18½ in. high at shoulder)

spring′er span′iel, a dog of either of two breeds of medium-sized spaniels, used for flushing and retrieving game. Cf. **English springer spaniel, Welsh springer spaniel.**

spring′ fe′ver, a listless, lazy, or restless feeling commonly associated with the beginning of spring.

Spring·field (spring′fēld′), *n.* **1.** a city in SW Massachusetts, on the Connecticut River. 163,905 (1970). **2.** a city in SW Missouri. 120,096 (1970). **3.** a city in and the capital of Illinois, in the central part. 91,753 (1970). **4.** a city in W Ohio. 81,941 (1970). **5.** a town in SE Pennsylvania, near Philadelphia. 29,006 (1970). **6.** a city in W Oregon. 27,220 (1970).

Spring′field ri′fle, a bolt-operated, magazine-fed, .30-caliber rifle adopted by the U.S. Army in 1903 and used during World War I. Also called **Springfield 1903.** [named after SPRINGFIELD, Mass., from U.S. arsenal there]

spring·halt (spring′hôlt′), *n.* *Vet. Pathol.* stringhalt. [alter. by assoc. with SPRING]

spring·head (spring′hed′), *n.* **1.** a spring or fountainhead from which a stream flows. **2.** the source of something.

spring·house (spring′hous′), *n., pl.* **-hous·es** (-hou′ziz). a small storehouse built over a spring or part of a brook, for keeping such foods as meat and dairy products cool and fresh.

spring·ing (spring′ing), *n.* **1.** the act of a person or thing that springs. **2.** the type or arrangement of springs with which a machine is equipped. **3.** spring (def. 33). [ME]

spring′ lamb′, a lamb born in the late winter or early spring and sold for slaughter prior to July 1.

spring·let (spring′lit), *n.* a small spring of water.

Springs (springz), *n.* a city in the E Republic of South Africa, SE of Johannesburg. 137,253 (1960).

spring·tail (spring′tāl′), *n.* any of numerous small, wingless insects of the order *Collembola*, having a ventral, forked appendage on the abdomen that is suddenly extended to spring the insect into the air.

spring′ tide′, 1. the large rise and fall of the tide at or soon after the new or the full moon. See diag. at **tide**[1]. **2.** anything that is swift and abundant: *a spring tide of compliments.*

spring·time (spring′tīm′), *n.* **1.** the season of spring. **2.** the first or earliest period: *the springtime of love.* Also called **spring·tide** (spring′tīd′).

spring′ train′ing, a program of physical exercise, practice, and exhibition games followed by a baseball team in the early spring, before the start of the regular baseball season.

Spring′ Val′ley, a town in SW California, near San Diego. 29,742 (1970).

spring·wood (spring′wo͝od′), *n.* the part of an annual ring of wood, characterized by large, thin-walled cells, that is formed during the first part of the growing season. Cf. **summerwood.**

spring·y (spring′ē), *adj.,* **spring·i·er, spring·i·est. 1.** characterized by spring or elasticity; flexible; resilient. **2.** (of land) abounding in or having springs of water. —**spring′i·ly,** *adv.* —**spring′i·ness,** *n.* —**Syn. 1.** buoyant, bouncy.

sprin·kle (spring′kəl), *v.,* **-kled, -kling,** *n.* —*v.t.* **1.** to scatter (a liquid, powder, etc.) in drops or particles. **2.** to disperse or distribute here and there. **3.** to cover (a surface or object) partially in all areas with drops or particles of some material. **4.** to diversify with a pattern or random distribution of objects, marks, etc. —*v.i.* **5.** to scatter or disperse liquid, a powder, etc., in drops or particles. **6.** to be sprinkled. **7.** to rain slightly (often used impersonally with *it* as subject): *It may sprinkle this evening.* —*n.* **8.** the act or an instance of sprinkling. **9.** something used for sprinkling. **10.** a light rain. **11.** a small quantity or number. [ME *sprenkle;* c. D *sprenkelen*, G *sprenkeln;* akin to OE *sprengan* to sprinkle, make (things) spring, scatter, causative of *springan* to SPRING] —**Syn. 1.** distribute, rain.

sprin·kler (spring′klər), *n.* **1.** any of various devices for sprinkling, as a perforated ring or small stand with a revolving nozzle to which a hose is attached for watering a lawn. **2.** a person who sprinkles.

sprin′kler sys′tem, a system of sprinklers for extinguishing fires in a building.

sprin·kling (spring′kling), *n.* **1.** a small quantity or number of things scattered here and there. **2.** a small quantity sprinkled or to be sprinkled. [late ME *sprenclyng*]

sprin′kling can′. See **watering pot.**

sprint (sprint), *v.i.* **1.** to race or move at full speed, esp. for a short distance, as in running or rowing. —*v.t.* **2.** to traverse in sprinting: *to sprint a half mile.* —*n.* **3.** a short race at full speed. **4.** a short burst of speed during a race. [OE **sprintan* (cf. *gesprintan* to emit); c. Sw (obs.) *sprenta*, Icel *spretta*, OHG *sprinzan* to jump up] —**sprint′er,** *n.*

S, Sprit

sprit (sprit), *n.* *Naut.* a small pole or spar crossing a fore-and-aft sail diagonally from the mast to the upper aftermost corner, serving to extend the sail. [ME *spret*, OE *sprēot;* c. D, G *Spriet;* akin to SPROUT]

sprite (sprīt), *n.* an elf, fairy, or goblin. [ME *sprit* < OF *(e)sprit* < L *spīrit(us)* SPIRIT] —**Syn.** See **fairy.**

sprit·sail (sprit′sāl′; *Naut.* sprit′səl), *n.* *Naut.* **1.** a sail extended by a sprit. **2.** a square sail set on a yard crossed under a bowsprit. [late ME *sprete seyle* (see SPIRIT, SAIL); cf. D *sprietzeil*]

sprock·et (sprok′it), *n.* *Mach.* a toothed wheel engaging with a conveyor or power chain. Also called **sprock′et wheel′.** [*sprock-* (metathetic var. of *spork-*, OE *spor(a)* SPUR[1] + *-k* suffix) + -ET]

Sprockets

sprout (sprout), *v.i.* **1.** to begin to grow, as a plant from a seed. **2.** (of a seed or plant) to put forth buds or shoots. **3.** to develop or grow quickly. —*v.t.* **4.** to cause to sprout. **5.** to remove sprouts from: *Sprout and boil the potatoes.* —*n.* **6.** a shoot of a plant. **7.** a new growth from a germinating seed or from a rootstock, tuber, bud, or the like. **8. sprouts.** See **Brussels sprout.** [ME *spr(o)uten*, OE *sprūtan;* c. MD *sprūten*, G *spriessen* to sprout; akin to Gk *speírein* to scatter]

spruce[1] (spro͞os), *n.* **1.** any evergreen, coniferous tree of the genus *Picea*, having short, angular, needle-shaped leaves attached singly around twigs. **2.** any of various allied trees, as the Douglas fir and the hemlock spruce. **3.** the wood of any such tree. —*adj.* **4.** made from the wood of a spruce tree or trees. **5.** containing or abounding in spruce trees. [late ME, special use of *Spruce* sandhi var. of *Pruce* < OF *Pruce* < ML *Prussia*, var. of *Borussia* Prussia, whence the timber came]

spruce[2] (spro͞os), *adj.,* **spruc·er, spruc·est,** *v.,* **spruced, spruc·ing.** —*adj.* **1.** trim in dress or appearance; neat; smart; dapper. —*v.t.* **2.** to make spruce or smart (usually fol. by *up*). —*v.i.* **3.** to make oneself spruce (usually fol. by *up*). [obs. *spruce jerkin*, orig. jerkin made of *spruce leather*, i.e., leather imported from Prussia (see SPRUCE[1]), hence fine, smart, etc.]

spruce′ beer′, a fermented beverage made with spruce leaves and twigs, or an extract from them.

sprue[1] (spro͞o), *n.* **1.** *Foundry.* **a.** an opening through which molten metal is poured into a mold. **b.** the waste metal left in this opening after casting. **2.** *Metalworking.* a channel in a forging die permitting the die to clear that part of the rough piece not being forged. [?]

sprue[2] (spro͞o), *n.* *Pathol.* a chronic disease, occurring chiefly in the tropics, characterized by diarrhea, ulceration of the mucous membrane of the digestive tract, and a smooth, shining tongue. [< D *spruw;* c. MLG *sprüwe* tumor < ?]

sprung (sprung), *v.* a pt. and pp. of **spring.**

sprung′ rhythm′, a poetic rhythm characterized by the use of strongly accented syllables, often in juxtaposition, accompanied by an indefinite number of unaccented syllables in each foot, of which the accented syllable is the essential component.

spry (sprī), *adj.,* **spry·er, spry·est** or **spri·er, spri·est.** active and brisk; nimble; energetic. [?] —**spry′ly,** *adv.* —**Syn.** agile, lively, animated.

spt., seaport.

spud (spud), *n., v.,* **spud·ded, spud·ding.** —*n.* **1.** *Informal.* a potato. **2.** a spadelike instrument, esp. one with a narrow blade, as for digging up roots. —*v.t.* **3.** to remove with a spud. [late ME *spudde* a kind of knife < ?]

spue (spyo͞o), *v.t., v.i.,* **spued, spu·ing,** *n.* spew.

spume (spyo͞om), *v.,* **spumed, spum·ing,** *n.* —*v.t.* **1.** to eject or discharge as or like foam or froth; spew (often fol. by *forth*). —*v.i.* **2.** to foam; froth. —*n.* **3.** foam, froth, or scum. [ME < L *spūm(a)* foam, froth = *spū-* (var. of *spu-* in *spuere* to spit out; see SPEW) + *-ma* n. suffix] —**spu′mous, spum′y,** *adj.*

spu·mes·cent (spyo͞o mes′ənt), *adj.* foamy or foamlike; frothy. —**spu·mes′cence,** *n.*

spu·mo·ne (spə mō′nē, -nā; *It.* spo͞o mô′ne), *n.* an Italian ice cream, usually containing layers of various colors and flavors and chopped fruit or nuts. Also, **spu·mo·ni** (spə-mō′nē). [< It = *spum(a)* SPUME + *-one* aug. suffix]

spun (spun), *v.* **1.** a pt. and pp. of **spin.** —*adj.* **2.** formed by or as by spinning.

spunk (spungk), *n.* **1.** *Informal.* pluck; spirit or mettle. **2.** touchwood, tinder, or punk. [b. SPARK[1] + and obs. *funk* spark, touchwood (c. D *vonk*, G *Funke*)]

spunk·y (spung′kē), *adj.,* **spunk·i·er, spunk·i·est.** *Informal.* plucky; spirited. —**spunk′i·ly,** *adv.* —**spunk′i·ness,** *n.*

spun′ silk′, 1. yarn produced by spinning silk waste and short, broken filaments from which the sericin has been removed. **2.** a fabric woven from this yarn.

spun′ yarn′, 1. yarn produced by spinning fibers into a continuous strand. **2.** *Naut.* cord formed of rope yarns loosely twisted together.

spur (spûr), *n., v.,* **spurred, spur·ring.** —*n.* **1.** a device attached to the heel of a boot, used by a rider to urge a horse forward. **2.** anything that goads, impels, or urges to action, speed, or achievement. **3.** *Ornith.* a stiff, usually sharp, horny process on the leg of various birds, esp. the domestic rooster. **4.** a sharp, piercing or cutting instrument fastened to the leg of a gamecock in cockfighting; gaff. **5.** *Phys. Geog.* a ridge or line of elevation projecting from or subordinate to the main body of a mountain or mountain range. **6.** a short, projecting part of any kind. **7.** *Bot.* **a.** a slender, usually hollow, projection from some part of a flower, as from the calyx of the larkspur or the corolla of the violet. **b.** a short shoot bearing flowers, as in fruit trees. **8.** *Railroads.* See **spur track. 9. on the spur of the moment,** without deliberation; impulsively; suddenly. —*v.t.* **10.** to prick with or as with a spur or spurs; incite or urge on. **11.** to strike or wound with the spur, as a gamecock. **12.** to furnish with spurs or a spur. —*v.i.* **13.** to goad or urge one's horse with spurs; ride quickly. [ME *spure,* OE *spur(a)*; c. OHG *sporo,* Icel *spori* spur; akin to SPURN] —**Syn. 1, 2.** goad. **2.** incitement, provocation. **10.** goad, provoke.

A

B

Spurs (def. 1)
A, Hunt spur
B, Rowel spur

spurge (spûrj), *n.* any of numerous plants of the genus *Euphorbia,* having a milky juice and flowers with no petals or sepals. [late ME < MF *(e)spurge,* appar. back formation from *espurgier* < L *expurgāre* to cleanse. See EX-[1], PURGE]

spur′ gear′, *Mach.* a gear having straight teeth cut on the rim parallel to the axis of rotation.

Spur gear

spurge′ lau′rel, a laurellike shrub, *Daphne Laureola,* of southern and western Europe and western Asia, having evergreen leaves and green axillary flowers.

spu·ri·ous (spyo͝or′ē əs), *adj.* **1.** not genuine, authentic, or true. **2.** of illegitimate birth; bastard. **3.** *Biol.* (of two or more parts, plants, etc.) having a similar appearance but a different structure. [< L *spurius;* see -OUS] —**spu′ri·ous·ly,** *adv.* —**Syn. 1.** false, sham. —**Ant. 1.** genuine.

spurn (spûrn), *v.t.* **1.** to reject with disdain; scorn. **2.** to treat with contempt; despise. **3.** *Obs.* to kick. —*v.i.* **4.** to show disdain or contempt (usually fol. by *at*). —*n.* **5.** disdainful rejection. **6.** contemptuous treatment. **7.** a kick. [ME *spurn(en),* OE *spurnan;* c. Icel *sporna,* OS, OHG *spurnan* to kick; akin to L *spernere* to put away] —**Syn. 1.** See **refuse**[1]. **6.** contumely. —**Ant. 1.** accept.

spur·rey (spûr′ē, spur′ē), *n., pl.* **-reys.** spurry.

spur·ri·er (spûr′ē ər, spur′-), *n.* a maker of spurs. [ME *sporier*]

spur·ry (spûr′ē, spur′ē), *n., pl.* **-ries.** any of several caryophyllaceous herbs of the genus *Spergula,* esp. *S. arvensis,* having white flowers and numerous whorled, linear leaves.

spurt (spûrt), *v.i.* **1.** to gush or issue suddenly in a stream or jet, as a liquid; spout. **2.** to show marked, usually increased, activity or energy for a short period. —*v.t.* **3.** to expel or force out suddenly in a stream or jet, as a liquid; spout. —*n.* **4.** a sudden, forceful gush or jet of or as of liquid. **5.** a brief or sudden outburst of energy, increased activity, etc. Also, **spirt.** [var. of *spirt,* by metathesis from ME *sprutten,* OE *sprytian* to spring, come forth; akin to OE *sprytting* a shoot, sprout, increase; and to SPROUT] —**Syn. 1.** well, spring. **4.** spout. —**Ant. 1.** drip, ooze.

spur′ track′, *Railroads.* a short branch track leading from the main track, and connected with it at one end only. Also called **stub track.**

spur′ wheel′. See **spur gear.**

sput·nik (spo͝ot′nik, sput′-; *Russ.* spo͞ot′nik), *n.* a man-made satellite launched by the Soviet Union. Sputnik I was the first artificial satellite to be orbited, 1957. [< Russ; lit. fellow wayfarer = *s-* with + *put′* path + *-nik* agent suffix]

sput·ter (sput′ər), *v.i.* **1.** to emit particles, sparks, etc., forcibly or explosively. **2.** to eject particles of saliva from the mouth, as when speaking angrily or excitedly. **3.** to utter or spit out words or sounds explosively or incoherently, as when angry or flustered. —*v.t.* **4.** to emit (anything) forcibly and in small particles, as if by spitting. **5.** to eject (saliva, food, etc.) in small particles explosively and involuntarily, as in excitement. **6.** to utter explosively and incoherently. —*n.* **7.** the act or sound of sputtering. **8.** explosive, incoherent utterance. **9.** matter ejected in sputtering. [*sput-* (var. of SPOUT) + -ER[6]; c. D *sputteren*] —**sput′ter·ing·ly,** *adv.*

spu·tum (spyo͞o′təm), *n., pl.* **-ta** (-tə). matter, as saliva mixed with mucus, expectorated from the mouth, as in diseases of the respiratory tract. [< L *spūtum,* n. use of neut. of *spūtus,* ptp. of *spuere* to spit]

Spuy′ten Duy′vil Creek′ (spīt′ən dī′vəl), a channel in New York City at the north end of Manhattan Island, connecting the Hudson and Harlem rivers.

spy (spī), *n., pl.* **spies,** *v.,* **spied, spy·ing.** —*n.* **1.** a person employed by a government to obtain secret information or intelligence about another country. **2.** any person who clandestinely seeks information concerning persons, projects, or the like, esp. for profit: *an industrial spy.* **3.** the act of spying. —*v.i.* **4.** to observe secretively or furtively with hostile intent (often fol. by *on* or *upon*). **5.** to search for or examine something closely or carefully. —*v.t.* **6.** to examine or look for closely or carefully. **7.** to discover or find out by observation or scrutiny. **8.** to catch sight of suddenly; espy; descry: *to spy a rare bird overhead.* [ME *spi(en),* aph. var. of *espien* to ESPY]

spy·glass (spī′glas′, -gläs′), *n.* a small telescope.

Sq., **1.** Squadron. **2.** Square (used in street names).

sq., **1.** sequence. **2.** the following; the following one. [< L *sequēns*] **3.** squadron. **4.** square.

sq. ft., square foot; square feet.

sq. in., square inch; square inches.

sq. m., square meter; square meters.

sq. mi., square mile; square miles.

sqq., the following; the following ones. [< L *sequentia*]

squab (skwob), *n., pl.* **squabs,** (*esp. collectively for 1*) **squab,** *adj.* —*n.* **1.** a nestling pigeon, marketed when fully grown but still unfledged. **2.** a short, stout person. **3.** a thickly stuffed, soft cushion. —*adj.* **4.** short and thick or broad. **5.** (of a bird) unfledged or newly hatched. [< Scand; cf. dial Sw *skvabb* loose fat flesh, dial. Norw *skvabb* soft wet mass]

squab·ble (skwob′əl), *v.,* **-bled, -bling,** *n.* —*v.i.* **1.** to engage in a petty quarrel. —*n.* **2.** a petty quarrel. [< Scand; cf. dial. Sw *skvabbel* to quarrel, Norw *skvabbe* to gabble; perh. akin to SCUFFLE] —**Syn. 1.** quarrel, wrangle, bicker, fight.

squab·by (skwob′ē), *adj.,* **-bi·er, -bi·est.** short and stout; squat.

squad (skwod), *n., v.,* **squad·ded, squad·ding.** —*n.* **1.** a small number of soldiers, commonly 10 men led usually by a sergeant; the smallest military unit. **2.** any small group or party of persons organized for a particular purpose. —*v.t.* **3.** to form into squads. **4.** to assign to a squad. [< F *(e)squade,* alter. of *esquadre* < Sp *escuadra* SQUARE; so called from square shape of formation]

squad′ car′, an automobile used by policemen, equipped with a radiotelephone for communicating with police headquarters.

squad·ron (skwod′rən), *n.* **1.** an armored cavalry or cavalry unit consisting of two or more troops, a headquarters, and various supporting units. **2.** *U.S. Air Force.* **a.** the basic administrative and tactical unit, smaller than a group and composed of two or more flights. **b.** a flight formation. **3.** *U.S. Navy.* two or more divisions of ships or aircraft, usually of the same type. **4.** a number of persons grouped or united together for some purpose; group. —*v.t.* **5.** to form into a squadron or squadrons. [< It *squadron(e)* = *squadr(a)* SQUARE + *-one* aug. suffix]

squal·id (skwol′id, skwôl′-), *adj.* **1.** foul and repulsive, as from lack of care or cleanliness. **2.** wretched; sordid. [< L *squālid(us)* dirty = *squāl-* (root of *squālēre* to be dirty from neglect) + *-idus* -ID[4]] —**squal′id·ly,** *adv.* —**squa·lid·i·ty** (skwo lid′i tē), *n.* —**Syn. 1.** unclean. See **dirty.** —**Ant.** splendid.

squall[1] (skwôl), *n.* **1.** a sudden, violent gust of wind, often accompanied by rain, snow, or sleet. **2.** a sudden disturbance or commotion. —*v.i.* **3.** to blow as a squall. [? special use of SQUALL[2]] —**squall′ish,** *adj.*

squall[2] (skwôl), *v.i.* **1.** to cry or scream loudly and violently. —*n.* **2.** the act or sound of squalling. [< Scand; cf. Icel *skvala* to shout] —**squall′er,** *n.*

squall′ line′, *Meteorol.* a line or extended narrow region along a cold front within which squalls or thunderstorms occur, often several hundred miles long.

squal·ly (skwô′lē), *adj.,* **-li·er, -li·est.** **1.** characterized by squalls. **2.** *Informal.* threatening.

squal·or (skwol′ər, skwō′lər), *n.* **1.** the condition of being squalid. **2.** wretchedness; sordidness. [< L *squālor* dirtiness. See SQUALID, -OR[1]] —**Ant.** splendor.

squam-, a combining form of **squama:** *squamation.*

squa·ma (skwā′mə), *n., pl.* **-mae** (-mē). a scale or scalelike part, as of epidermis or bone. [< L: scale]

squa·mate (skwā′māt), *adj.* provided or covered with squamae or scales; scaly. [< LL *squāmāt(us)*]

squa·ma·tion (skwā mā′shən), *n.* **1.** the state of being squamate. **2.** the arrangement of the squamae or scales of an animal.

squa·mo·sal (skwə mō′səl), *adj.* **1.** *Anat.* of or pertaining to the thin, scalelike portion of the temporal bone that is situated on the side of the skull behind the ear. **2.** *Zool.* of or pertaining to a corresponding bone in other vertebrates. **3.** squamous. —*n.* **4.** a squamosal bone.

squa·mous (skwā′məs), *adj.* **1.** covered with or formed of squamae or scales. **2.** scalelike: *squamous cells.* Also, **squamosal, squa·mose** (skwā′mōs, skwə mōs′). [< L *squāmōsus.* See SQUAM-, -OUS, -OSE[1]] —**squa′mous·ly,** *adv.* **squa′mose·ly,** *adv.*

squam·u·lose (skwam′yə lōs′, skwā′myə-), *adj.* furnished or covered with small scales. [< L *squāmul(a)* (see SQUAM-, -ULE) + -OSE[1]]

squan·der (skwon′dər), *v.t.* **1.** to spend or use (money, time, etc.) extravagantly or wastefully. **2.** to scatter. —*n.* **3.** extravagant or wasteful expenditure. [?] —**Syn. 1.** waste, dissipate. —**Ant. 1.** save.

square (skwâr), *n., v.,* **squared, squar·ing,** *adj.,* **squar·er, squar·est,** *adv.* —*n.* **1.** a rectangle having all four sides of equal length. **2.** anything having this form or a form approximating it. **3.** an open area or plaza in a city or town. **4.** a rectangularly shaped area on a game board, as in chess or checkers. **5.** a try square, T square, or the like. **6.** *Math.* **a.** the second power of a quantity, expressed as $a^2 = a \times a$, where a is the quantity. **b.** a quantity that is the second power of another: *Four is the square of two.* **7.** *Slang.* a person who is ignorant of or uninterested in current fads, ideas, manners, tastes, etc. **8. on the square,** *Informal.* straightforward; honest; just.
—*v.t.* **9.** to reduce to square or rectangular form or cross section. **10.** to mark out in one or more squares or rectangles. **11.** to test with measuring devices for deviation from a right angle, straight line, or plane surface. **12.** *Math.* **a.** to multiply (a number or quantity) by itself; raise to the second power. **b.** to describe or find a square that is equivalent in area to: *to square a circle.* **13.** to bring to the form of a right angle or right angles. **14.** to even the score of (a contest). **15.** to set (the shoulders and back) in an erect posture so they form an angle similar to a right angle. **16.** to make straight, level, or even: *Square the cloth on the table.* **17.** to regulate, as by a standard; adapt; adjust. **18.** to adjust harmoniously or satisfactorily (often fol. by *with*). **19.** to pay off; settle: *to square a debt.* **20.** *Slang.* **a.** to bribe (someone). **b.** to settle (a matter) by means of a bribe.
—*v.i.* **21.** to accord or agree (often fol. by *with*). **22. square away,** *Informal.* to prepare; get ready. **23. square off,** to assume a posture of defense or offense, as in boxing.
—*adj.* **24.** formed with or as a right angle: *a square corner.* **25.** formed as a square or cube. **26.** noting any unit of area measurement having the form of a square and designated by a unit of linear measurement forming a side of the square: *one square foot.* **27.** noting a system of area measurement in terms of such units. **28.** (of an area) equal to a square of a

specified length on a side: *five miles square.* **29.** at right angles, or perpendicular. **30.** *Naut.* at right angles to the mast and the keel, as a yard. **31.** having a square or rectangular section: *a square bar.* **32.** having a solid, sturdy form, esp. when characterized by a rectilinear or angular outline. **33.** straight, level, or even, as a surface or surfaces. **34.** leaving no balance of debt on either side; having all accounts settled. **35.** *Informal.* candid or honest. **36.** *Informal.* substantial or satisfying: *a square meal.* **37.** *Slang.* conventional or conservative in style or taste.
—*adv.* **38.** so as to be square; in square or rectangular form. **39.** at right angles. **40.** *Informal.* fairly, honestly, or straightforwardly. [ME < OF *(e)squarre* < VL **exquadra* < **exquadrāre* (L *ex-* EX-[1] + *quadrāre* to square)]

square′ brack′et, *Print.* bracket (def. 5).

square′ dance′, **1.** a dance, as a quadrille, by a set of couples arranged in a square or in some set form. **2.** hoedown (def. 1). —**square′ danc′er.**

square-dance (skwâr′dans′, -däns′), *v.i.*, **-danced, -danc·ing.** to participate in a square dance.

square′ deal′, *Informal.* a fair and honest arrangement or transaction.

squared′ pa′per, paper, as graph paper, ruled in a pattern of squares.

square′ foot′, a unit of area measurement equal to a square measuring one foot on each side. *Abbr.:* ft^2, sq. ft.

square·head (skwâr′hed′), *n.* *Offensive.* **1.** a German. **2.** a Scandinavian.

square′ inch′, a unit of area measurement equal to a square measuring one inch on each side. *Abbr.:* in^2, sq. in.

square′ joint′. See **straight joint** (def. 2). —**square′-joint′ed,** *adj.*

square′ knot′, a common knot in which the ends come out alongside of the standing parts. See illus. at **knot.**

square·ly (skwâr′lē), *adv.* **1.** in a square shape, form, or manner. **2.** directly; without evasion; in a straightforward manner. **3.** in an honest or open manner; fairly.

square′ meas′ure, a system of units for the measurement of surfaces or areas in squares.

square′ me′ter, a unit of area measurement equal to a square measuring one meter on each side. *Abbr.:* m^2, sq. m.

square′ mile′, a unit of area measurement equal to a square measuring one mile on each side. *Abbr.:* mi^2, sq. mi.

square′ num′ber, a number that is the square of another integer, as 1 of 1, 4 of 2, 9 of 3, etc.

square′ one′, *Informal.* the original condition, idea, etc., from which one starts or makes a new beginning: *If this plan fails, we'll have to go back to square one.*

square′ pian′o, a piano having a rectangular horizontal body.

square-rigged (skwâr′rigd′), *adj.* *Naut.* having square sails as the principal sails. —**square′-rig′ger,** *n.*

square′ root′, a quantity of which a given quantity is the square: *The square root of 36 is 6.*

square′ sail′, *Naut.* a sail set beneath a horizontal yard, the normal position of which, when not trimmed to the wind, is directly athwartships. See diag. at **sail.**

square′ shoot′er, *Informal.* an honest, fair person. —**square′ shoot′ing.**

square-shoul·dered (skwâr′shōl′dərd), *adj.* having the shoulders held back, giving a straight form to the upper part of the back.

square·toed (skwâr′tōd′), *adj.* having a broad, square toe, as a shoe.

square′ yard′, a unit of area measurement equal to a square measuring one yard on each side. *Abbr.:* yd^2, sq. yd.

squar′ing the cir′cle, *Math.* the insoluble problem of constructing, by the methods of Euclidean geometry, a square equal in area to a given circle.

squar·ish (skwâr′ish), *adj.* approximately square. —**squar′ish·ly,** *adv.*

squar·rose (skwar′ōs, skwo rōs′), *adj.* *Biol.* denoting any rough or ragged surface. [< L *squarrōs(us)* scurfy, scabby] —**squar′rose·ly,** *adv.*

squash[1] (skwosh), *v.t.* **1.** to press into a flat mass or pulp; crush. **2.** to suppress or put down; quash. —*v.i.* **3.** to be pressed into a flat mass or pulp, as after falling heavily. **4.** to admit of being squashed. **5.** to make a splashing sound as a result of being squashed. —*n.* **6.** the act of squashing. **7.** the fact of squashing or of being squashed. **8.** something squashed or crushed. **9.** Also called **squash′ rac′quets.** a game for two or four persons, similar to racquets but played on a smaller court and with a racket having a round head and a long handle. **10.** Also called **squash′ ten′nis.** a game for two persons, resembling squash racquets except that the ball is larger and livelier, and the racket is shaped like a tennis racket. **11.** *Brit.* a beverage made from fruit juice and soda water: *lemon squash.* [< MF *(e)squasser* < VL **exquassāre.* See EX-[1], QUASH]

squash[2] (skwosh), *n., pl.* **squash·es,** (*esp. collectively*) **squash. 1.** the fruit of any of various vinelike, tendril-bearing plants of the genus *Curcurbita,* used as a vegetable, esp. *C. moschata* and *C. maxima.* **2.** any of these plants. [< Narragansett *askūtasquash,* lit., vegetables eaten green]

squash′ bug′, a dark brown hemipterous insect, *Anasa tristis,* that sucks the sap from the leaves of squash, pumpkin, and other cucurbitaceous plants.

squash·y (skwosh′ē), *adj.,* **squash·i·er, squash·i·est. 1.** easily squashed; pulpy. **2.** soft and wet, as the ground after rain. **3.** having a squashed appearance. —**squash′i·ly,** *adv.*

squat (skwot), *v.,* **squat·ted** or **squat, squat·ting,** *adj., n.* —*v.i.* **1.** to sit in a low or crouching position with the legs drawn up closely beneath or in front of the body; sit on one's haunches or heels. **2.** to crouch down or cower, as an animal. **3.** to settle on land, esp. public or new land, without title, right, or payment of rent. **4.** to settle on public land under government regulation, in order to acquire title. —*v.t.* **5.** to cause to squat. —*adj.* **6.** (of a person, animal, the body, etc.) short and thickset. **7.** low and thick or broad: *The building had a squat shape.* **8.** seated or being in a squatting position; crouching. —*n.* **9.** the act or fact of squatting. **10.** a squatting position or posture. [ME *squatt(en)* < OF *(e)squate(r), (e)squati(r)* = *es-* EX-[1] + *quatir* < VL **coactīre* to compress = L *coact(us)* ptp. of *cōgere* to compress (*co-* co- + *-ac-* drive (var. of *ag-*) + *-tus* ptp. suffix) + *-īre* inf. suffix]

squat·ter (skwot′ər), *n.* **1.** a person or thing that squats. **2.** a person who settles on land, esp. public or new land, without title, right, or payment of rent. **3.** a person who settles on land under government regulation, in order to acquire title.

squat′ter sov′ereignty, *U.S. Hist.* (used contemptuously by its opponents) See **popular sovereignty** (def. 2).

squat′ter's right′, a claim to real property, esp. public land, that may be granted to a person who has openly and continuously occupied it without legal authority for a number of years.

squat·ty (skwot′ē), *adj.,* **-ti·er, -ti·est.** short and thick; low and broad. —**squat′ti·ly,** *adv.*

squaw (skwô), *n.* a North American Indian woman, esp. a wife. [< some Algonquian tongue; cf. Natick *squa* a female]

squaw·fish (skwô′fish′), *n., pl.* (*esp. collectively*) **-fish,** (*esp. referring to two or more kinds or species*) **-fish·es. 1.** any of several large, voracious cyprinid fishes of the genus *Ptychocheilus,* found in the rivers of the western U.S. and Canada. **2.** a viviparous perch, *Taenioloca lateralis,* found off the Pacific Coast of the U.S.

squawk (skwôk), *v.i.* **1.** to utter a loud, harsh cry, as a duck or other fowl when frightened. **2.** *Slang.* to complain loudly and vehemently. —*v.t.* **3.** to utter or give forth with a squawk. —*n.* **4.** a loud, harsh cry or sound. **5.** *Slang.* a loud, vehement complaint. [b. SQUALL[2] and HAWK[3]]

squawk′ box′, *Slang.* the speaker of a public-address system or of an intercommunication system.

squaw′ man′, a white or other non-Indian man married to a North American Indian woman.

squaw·root (skwô′ro͞ot′, -ro͝ot′), *n.* a fleshy, leafless, orobanchaceous plant, *Conopholis americana,* of eastern North America, found in clusters, esp. under oaks. [from its former use by Indians in treating female ailments]

squeak (skwēk), *n.* **1.** a short, sharp, shrill cry; a sharp, high-pitched sound. **2.** *Informal.* an escape from danger, death, etc. (usually qualified by *narrow* or *close*). —*v.i.* **3.** to utter or emit a squeak or squeaky sound. —*v.t.* **4.** to utter or sound with a squeak, or squeaks. **5. squeak by** or **through,** to succeed, win, etc., by a very narrow margin. [ME *squeke,* perh. < Scand; cf. Sw *skväka* to croak]

squeak·y (skwē′kē), *adj.,* **squeak·i·er, squeak·i·est.** squeaking; tending to squeak. —**squeak′i·ly,** *adv.*

squeal (skwēl), *n.* **1.** a somewhat prolonged, sharp, shrill cry, as of pain, fear, surprise, etc. —*v.i.* **2.** to utter or emit a squeal or squealing sound. **3.** *Slang.* to turn informer; inform. —*v.t.* **4.** to utter or produce with a squeal. [ME *squel(en);* imit.] —**squeal′er,** *n.*

squeam·ish (skwē′mish), *adj.* **1.** easily shocked by anything immodest; prudish. **2.** fastidious or dainty. **3.** easily nauseated or disgusted. [late ME *squemish,* var. of *squemes, squaymes* < *squaymour* < AF *(e)scoymo(u)s* < ?] —**squeam′ish·ly,** *adv.* —**Syn. 1.** modest. **2.** finical, finicky, delicate.

squee·gee (skwē′jē, skwē jē′), *n., v.,* **-geed, -gee·ing.** —*n.* **1.** an implement edged with rubber or the like, for removing water from windows after washing, sweeping water from wet decks, etc. **2.** a similar and smaller device, esp. for removing surplus water from photographic prints. —*v.t.* **3.** to sweep or scrape with or as with a squeegee. Also, **squilgee, squillagee, squillgee.** [? rhyming compound based on SQUEEZE]

squeez·a·ble (skwē′zə bəl), *adj.* **1.** easily squeezed, compressed, or the like. **2.** evoking a desire to squeeze or embrace; huggable; cuddly. —**squeez′a·bil′i·ty, squeez′a·ble·ness,** *n.* —**squeez′a·bly,** *adv.*

squeeze (skwēz), *v.,* **squeezed, squeez·ing,** *n.* —*v.t.* **1.** to press forcibly together; compress. **2.** to extract from a thing by crushing it: *to squeeze juice from an orange.* **3.** to thrust forcibly, as into a confined space. **4.** to press or hug firmly. **5.** *Informal.* to extort, as money, by financial or emotional pressure or the like. **6.** *Informal.* to extort or exact money, advantages, etc., from. **7.** *Baseball.* **a.** to enable (a runner on third base) to score on a squeeze play (often fol. by *in*). **b.** to score (a run) in this way (often fol. by *in*). —*v.i.* **8.** to exert a compressing force. **9.** to force a way through or into some narrow or crowded place (usually fol. by *through, in,* etc.). —*n.* **10.** the act or fact of squeezing. **11.** the fact of being squeezed. **12.** a hug or close embrace. **13.** a small quantity or amount of anything obtained by squeezing. **14.** *Informal.* coercion intended to obtain money, advantages, etc. **15.** *Baseball.* See **squeeze play.** [? var. of obs. *squize,* OE *cwӯsan* to squeeze (initial *s* by false division of words in sandhi)]

squeeze′ bot′tle, a flexible bottle, usually of plastic, the contents of which can be forced out by squeezing.

squeeze′ play′, *Baseball.* a play in which the runner starts for home as soon as the pitcher makes a motion to pitch, and the batter bunts.

squelch (skwelch), *v.t.* **1.** to strike or press with crushing force; crush down; squash. **2.** *Informal.* to suppress or silence (a person), as with a crushing retort. —*v.i.* **3.** to make a splashing sound. **4.** to tread heavily in water, mud, etc., with such a sound. —*n.* **5.** a squelched or crushed mass of anything. **6.** a splashing sound. **7.** *Informal.* the act or instance of squelching a person. [var. of *quelch* in same sense (? QUELL + (QUA)SH); initial *s* perh. from SQUASH[1]] —**squelch′er,** *n.* —**squelch′ing·ly,** *adv.*

sque·teague (skwē tēg′), *n., pl.* (*esp. collectively*) **-teague,** (*esp. referring to two or more kinds or species*) **-teagues. 1.** an Atlantic food fish, *Cynoscion regalis,* of the croaker family. **2.** any of several other Atlantic fishes of the same genus; sea trout. [< Narragansett *pesukwiteag,* lit., they give glue (i.e., serve as material for glue-making)]

squib (skwib), *n., v.,* **squibbed, squib·bing.** —*n.* **1.** a short and witty or sarcastic saying or writing. **2.** a firework, consisting of a tube or ball filled with powder, that burns with a hissing noise, terminating usually in a slight explosion. —*v.i.* **3.** to write or use squibs. **4.** to shoot a squib. **5.** to explode with a small, sharp sound. **6.** to move swiftly and irregularly. —*v.t.* **7.** to assail in squibs or lampoons. **8.** to toss, shoot, or utilize as a squib. [?]

squid (skwid), *n., pl.* (*esp. collectively*) **squid,** (*esp. referring to two or more kinds or species*) **squids.** any of several ten-armed cephalopods, as of the genera *Loligo* and *Ommastrephes,* having a slender body and a pair of rounded or triangular caudal fins and varying in length from 4–6 inches to 60–80 feet. [?]

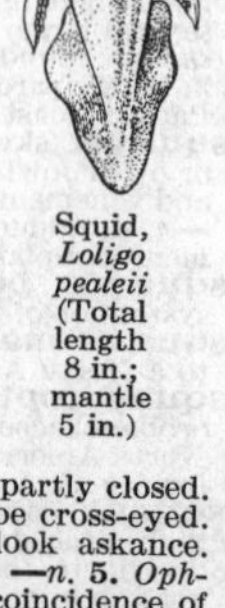

Squid, *Loligo pealeii* (Total length 8 in.; mantle 5 in.)

squig·gle (skwig′əl), *n., v.,* **-gled, -gling.** —*n.* **1.** a short, irregular curve or twist, as in writing or drawing. —*v.i.* **2.** to move in, or appear as squiggles. —*v.t.* **3.** to form in or cause to appear as squiggles; scribble. [b. SQUIRM and WRIGGLE] —**squig′gly,** *adj.*

squil·gee (skwil′jē, skwil jē′), *n., v.t.,* **-geed, -gee·ing.** squeegee. [unexplained var.]

squill (skwil), *n.* **1.** the bulb of the sea onion, *Urginea maritima,* cut into thin slices and dried, and used as an expectorant. **2.** the plant itself. [< L *squill(a),* var. of *scilla* < Gk *skílla*]

squil·la (skwil′ə), *n., pl.* **squil·las, squil·lae** (skwil′ē). See **mantis shrimp.** [< L; see SQUILL]

squil·la·gee (skwil′ə jē′), *n., v.t.,* **-geed, -gee·ing.** squeegee.

squill·gee (skwil′jē, skwil jē′), *n., v.t.,* **-geed, -gee·ing.** squeegee.

squinch (skwinch), *n. Archit.* a small arch, system of corbeling, or the like, built across the interior angle between two walls, as in a square tower for supporting an oblique side of a superimposed octagonal spire. [var. of *scunch,* short for *scuncheon,* ME *sconch(e)on* < MF *(e)scoinson, (e)sconchon = es-* EX-[1] + *conch-* (< L *cune(us)* wedge) + *-on* n. suffix]

squint (skwint), *v.i.* **1.** to look with the eyes partly closed. **2.** *Ophthalm.* to be affected with strabismus; be cross-eyed. **3.** to look or glance obliquely or sidewise; look askance. —*v.t.* **4.** to close (the eyes) partly in looking. —*n.* **5.** *Ophthalm.* a condition of the eye consisting in noncoincidence of the optic axes; strabismus. **6.** *Informal.* a quick glance. —*adj.* **7.** looking obliquely; looking with a side glance; looking askance. **8.** *Ophthalm.* (of the eyes) affected with strabismus. [aph. var. of ASQUINT] —**squint′ing·ly,** *adv.*

squint-eyed (skwint′īd′), *adj.* **1.** affected with or characterized by strabismus. **2.** looking obliquely or askance.

squint·y (skwin′tē), *adj.,* **squint·i·er, squint·i·est.** characterized by or having a squint.

squir·ar·chy (skwīər′är kē), *n., pl.* **-chies.** *Chiefly Brit.* squirearchy. —**squir·ar′chal, squir·ar′chi·cal,** *adj.*

squire (skwīər), *n., v.,* **squired, squir·ing.** —*n.* **1.** (in England) a country gentleman, esp. the chief landed proprietor in a district. **2.** (formerly) an aspirant to knighthood acting as the personal servant of a knight; esquire. **3.** a personal attendant, as of a person of rank. **4.** a man who accompanies or escorts a woman. **5.** *U.S.* a title applied to a justice of the peace, local judge, or other local dignitary of a rural district or small town. —*v.t.* **6.** to attend as, or in the manner of, a squire. **7.** to escort (a woman), as to a dance or social gathering. [ME *squier;* aph. var. of ESQUIRE]

squire·ar·chy (skwīər′är kē), *n., pl.* **-chies.** *Chiefly Brit.* the class of squires or landed gentry. Also, **squirarchy.** —**squire·ar′chal, squire·ar′chi·cal,** *adj.*

squi·reen (skwī rēn′), *n. Chiefly Irish Eng.* the landowner of a small estate; a squire of a small domain. [SQUIRE + *-een,* dim. suffix of Ir orig.]

squirm (skwûrm), *v.i.* **1.** to wriggle or writhe. **2.** to feel or display discomfort or distress, as from embarrassment or pain. —*n.* **3.** the act of squirming; a squirming or wriggling movement. [? b. SQUID and WORM] —**squirm′ing·ly,** *adv.*

squirm·y (skwûr′mē), *adj.,* **squirm·i·er, squirm·i·est.** characterized by squirming.

squir·rel (skwûr′əl, skwur′- *or, esp. Brit.,* skwer′əl), *n., pl.* **-rels,** (*esp. collectively*) **-rel. 1.** any of numerous arboreal, bushy-tailed rodents of the genus *Sciurus,* of the family *Sciuridae.* **2.** any of various other members of the family *Sciuridae,* as the chipmunks and flying squirrels. **3.** the pelt or fur of such an animal. [ME *squirel* < AF *(e)scuirel* (cf. OF *escuireul*) << LL *sciūr(us)* (< Gk *skíouros* = *ski(á)* shade + *ourá* tail) + *-ellus* dim. suffix]

Gray squirrel, *Sciurus carolinensis* (Total length 21 in.; tail 10 in.)

squir′rel cage′, 1. a cage containing a cylindrical framework that is rotated by a squirrel or other small animal running inside of it. **2.** *Informal.* any situation that seems to be endlessly without goal or achievement.

squir′rel corn′, an American, papaveraceous herb, *Dicentra canadensis,* having finely dissected leaves and cream-colored flowers.

squirt (skwûrt), *v.i.* **1.** to eject liquid in a jet, as from a narrow orifice. —*v.t.* **2.** to cause (liquid or a viscous substance) to spurt or issue in a jet, as from a narrow orifice. **3.** to wet or bespatter with a liquid or viscous substance so ejected. —*n.* **4.** the act of squirting. **5.** a spurt or jetlike stream, as of water. **6.** an instrument for squirting, as a syringe. **7.** a small quantity of liquid or viscous substance squirted. **8.** *Informal.* an insignificant, annoying fellow, esp. one who is small or young. [late ME *squirt(en),* appar. var. of *swirten*]

squirt′ gun′, 1. See **spray gun. 2.** See **water pistol.**

squirt′ing cu′cumber, a cucurbitaceous plant, *Ecballium Elaterium,* of the Mediterranean region, whose ripened fruit forcibly ejects the seeds and juice.

squish (skwish), *v.t.* **1.** *Dial.* to squeeze or squash. —*v.i.* **2.** (of water, soft mud, etc.) to make a gushing or splashing sound when walked in or on. —*n.* **3.** a squishing sound. [alter. of SQUASH]

squish·y (skwish′ē), *adj.,* **squish·i·er, squish·i·est. 1.** soft and wet. **2.** softly gurgling or splashing.

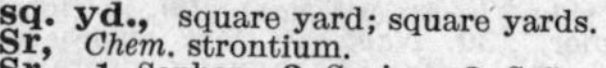

sq. yd., square yard; square yards.

Sr, *Chem.* strontium.

Sr., **1.** Senhor. **2.** Senior. **3.** Señor. **4.** Sir.

Sra., **1.** Senhora. **2.** Señora.

SRBM, short-range ballistic missile.

S. Res., Senate resolution. Also, **S.R.**

sri (shrē), *n. Hindustani.* Mr.; Sir. [lit., majesty, holiness]

Sri Lan·ka (srē läng′kə), an island republic in the Indian Ocean, S of India: a member of the British Commonwealth. 14,500,000; 25,332 sq. mi. *Cap.:* Colombo. Formerly, **Ceylon.**

Sri·na·gar (srē nug′ər), *n.* a city in and the capital of Kashmir, on the Jhelum River. 403,000.

S.R.O., standing room only.

Srta., **1.** Senhorita. **2.** Señorita.

SS, 1. See **SS Troops. 2.** steamship. **3.** supersonic.

ss, (in prescriptions) a half. [< L *sēmis*]

S/S, steamship.

SS., **1.** Saints. [< L *sancti*] **2.** See **SS Troops.**

ss., **1.** to wit; namely (used esp. on legal documents, as an affidavit, pleading, etc., to verify the place of action). [< L *scilicet*] **2.** sections. **3.** *Baseball.* shortstop.

S.S., **1.** See **SS Troops. 2.** steamship. **3.** Sunday School.

SS.D., Most Holy Lord: a title of the pope. [< L *Sanctissimus Dominus*]

SSE, south-southeast. Also, **S.S.E., s.s.e.**

SSI, a type of electronic microminiaturization in which approximately 100 transistors may be concentrated on a single integrated-circuit chip. Cf. **LSI, MSI.** [S(MALL-)S(CALE) I(NTEGRATION)]

SSM, surface-to-surface missile.

SSR, Soviet Socialist Republic. Also, **S.S.R.**

SS Troops, an elite military unit of the Nazi party, serving as Hitler's bodyguard and as a special police force. [< G *S(chutz)s(taffel)* protective echelon]

SSW, south-southwest. Also, **S.S.W., s.s.w.**

-st[1], var. of **-est**[1]: *first; least.*

-st[2], var. of **-est**[2]: *hadst; wouldst; dost.*

St., **1.** Saint. **2.** statute; statutes. **3.** Strait. **4.** Street.

st., **1.** stanza. **2.** statute; statutes. **3.** stet. **4.** stone (weight). **5.** strait. **6.** street.

s.t., short ton.

Sta., **1.** Santa. **2.** Station.

stab (stab), *v.,* **stabbed, stab·bing,** *n.* —*v.t.* **1.** to pierce or wound with or as with a pointed weapon. **2.** to thrust, plunge, or jab at or into a person or thing. —*v.i.* **3.** to thrust with or as with a knife. **4. stab (someone) in the back,** *Slang.* to do harm to, esp. to a friend or an unsuspecting person. —*n.* **5.** the act of stabbing. **6.** a thrust or blow with or as with a pointed weapon. **7.** *Informal.* a brief attempt; try. **8.** a wound made by stabbing. **9.** a sudden, brief, and usually painful, sensation; pang. **10. stab in the back,** *Slang.* an act of treachery. [ME, var. of *stob* in same sense; ? v. use of ME *stob* stick] —**Syn. 1.** spear, penetrate.

Sta·bat Ma·ter (stä′bät mä′ter, stā′bat mā′tər), **1.** (*italics*) a Latin hymn, composed in the 13th century, that is sung or chanted to commemorate the sorrows of the Virgin Mary at the Cross. **2.** a musical setting for this. [lit., the mother was standing]

stab·bing (stab′ing), *adj.* **1.** penetrating; piercing: *a stabbing pain.* **2.** emotionally wounding. **3.** incisive or trenchant. —**stab′bing·ly,** *adv.*

sta·bile (*adj.* stā′bil, -bəl *or, esp. Brit.,* -bīl; *n.* stā′bēl *or, esp. Brit.,* -bīl), *adj.* **1.** fixed in position; stable. —*n.* **2.** a stationary, abstract sculpture that presents different forms as the viewer walks around it. Cf. **mobile** (def. 6). [< L *stabilis* = *sta-* (s. of *stāre* to stand) + *-bilis* -BLE]

sta·bi·lise (stā′bə līz′), *v.t., v.i.,* **-lised, -lis·ing.** *Chiefly Brit.* stabilize. —**sta′bi·li·sa′tion,** *n.*

sta·bi·lis·er (stā′bə lī′zər), *n. Brit.* stabilizer.

sta·bil·i·ty (stə bil′i tē), *n., pl.* **-ties. 1.** the state or quality of being stable. **2.** firmness in position. **3.** continuance without change; permanence. **4.** *Chem.* resistance or the degree of resistance to chemical change or disintegration. **5.** resistance to change, esp. sudden change or deterioration. **6.** reliable steadiness, as of character. **7.** the ability of an object to maintain or restore its equilibrium when acted upon by forces tending to displace it. **8.** a vow that binds a monk to reside for life in one monastery. [< L *stabilitāt-* (s. of *stabilitās*); see STABILE, -TY[2]; r. ME *stablete* < OF < L]

sta·bi·lize (stā′bə līz′), *v.,* **-lized, -liz·ing.** —*v.t.* **1.** to make or hold stable, firm, or steadfast. **2.** to maintain at a given or unfluctuating level or quantity. —*v.i.* **3.** to become stabilized. Also, *esp. Brit.,* **stabilise.** —**sta′bi·li·za′tion,** *n.*

sta·bi·liz·er (stā′bə lī′zər), *n.* **1.** a person or thing that stabilizes. **2.** *Aeron.* a device for maintaining the stability of an aircraft, as the fixed, horizontal tail surface on an airplane. **3.** *Naut.* **a.** a mechanical device for counteracting the roll of a vessel, consisting of a pair of retractable fins so pivoted as to oppose a downward force with an upward one, and vice versa. **b.** a gyrostabilizer. **4.** any of various substances added to foods, chemical compounds, or the like, to prevent deterioration or the loss of desirable properties. Also, *esp. Brit.,* **stabiliser.**

sta·ble[1] (stā′bəl), *n., v.,* **-bled, -bling.** —*n.* **1.** a building for the lodging and feeding of horses, cattle, etc. **2.** a collection of animals housed in such a building. **3.** *Horse Racing.* **a.** an establishment where race horses are kept and trained. **b.** the horses belonging to, or the persons connected with, such an establishment. —*v.t.* **4.** to put or lodge in or as in a stable. [ME *stable* < OF *(e)stable* < L *stabul(um)* standing room]

sta·ble[2] (stā′bəl), *adj.* **1.** not likely to overturn or collapse. **2.** able or likely to continue or last; enduring or permanent. **3.** resistant to sudden change or deterioration. **4.** reliable and steady, as in character, emotions, or attitudes. **5.** *Physics.* having the ability to react to a disturbing force by maintaining or reestablishing position, form, etc. **6.** *Chem.* not readily decomposing, as a compound; resisting molecular or chemical change. [ME < OF *(e)stable* < L *stabil(is)* STABILE] —**sta′bly,** *adv.* —**Syn. 1.** fixed, strong, sturdy.

sta·ble·boy (stā′bəl boi′), *n.* a man or boy who works in or performs various tasks around a stable.

sta·ble·man (stā′bəl mən, -man′), *n., pl.* **-men** (-mən, -men′). a man who works in a stable.

sta·ble·mate (stā′bəl māt′), *n.* a horse sharing a stable with another.

sta·bling (stā′bling), *n.* **1.** accommodation for horses or other draft or farm animals in a stable or stables. **2.** stables collectively. [ME]

stab·lish (stab′lish), *v.t. Archaic.* establish. [ME *stablisse(n),* aph. var. of ESTABLISH]

stacc., *Music.* staccato.

stac·ca·to (stə kä′tō), *adj., adv., n., pl.* **-tos, -ti** (-tē). —*adj.* **1.** *Music.* composed of notes played as a series of completely separate sounds: *a staccato passage.* Cf. **legato. 2.** composed of or characterized by a series of detached sounds or elements. —*adv.* **3.** in a staccato manner. —*n.* **4.** *Music.* **a.** a staccato passage. **b.** performance of such passages. **5.** something that is abruptly discontinuous or disjointed in quality or character. [< It: disconnected (ptp. of *staccare,* aph. var. of *distaccare* to DETACH)]

Staccato notes

stack (stak), *n.* **1.** a large, usually conical, circular, or rectangular pile of hay, straw, or the like. **2.** a tall, more or less orderly pile or heap. **3.** Often, **stacks.** a set of bookshelves ranged compactly one above the other, as in a library. **4. stacks,** the area or part of a library in which the books are stored or kept. **5.** a number of chimneys or flues grouped together. **6.** smokestack. **7.** *Mil.* a conical, free-standing group of three rifles placed on their butts and hooked together. **8.** an English measure for coal and wood, equal to 108 cubic feet. **9.** *Games.* **a.** a given quantity of chips that can be bought at one time, as in poker. **b.** the quantity of chips held by a player at a given point. **10. blow one's stack,** *Slang.* to lose one's temper, esp. to display one's fury, as by shouting. —*v.t.* **11.** to pile or arrange in a stack. **12.** to cover or load with something in stacks or piles. **13.** to arrange (a pack or cards in a pack) so as to cheat. —*v.i.* **14.** to be arranged in or form a stack. [ME *stak* < Scand; cf. Icel *stakkr* haystack; akin to Russ *stog* haystack]

stacked (stakt), *adj. Slang.* (of a woman) having an attractively proportioned, voluptuous figure.

stac·te (stak′tē), *n.* one of the sweet spices used in the holy incense of the ancient Hebrews. Ex. 30:34. [ME < L *stactē* < Gk *staktḗ,* fem. of *staktós* (ptp. of *stázein* to fall in drops) = *stak-* (var. of *stag-* s. of *stágma* drop) + *-tos* adj. suffix]

stad·dle (stad′ᵊl), *n.* **1.** the lower part of a stack of hay or the like. **2.** a supporting frame for such a stack. **3.** any supporting framework or base. [ME *stathel,* OE *stathol* base, support; c. OHG *stadal* barn, Icel *stöthull* milking place]

stad·hold·er (stad′hōl′dər), *n.* **1.** the chief magistrate of the former republic of the United Provinces of the Netherlands. **2.** (formerly in the Netherlands) the viceroy or governor of a province. Also, **stadtholder.** [< D *stadhouder* = *stad* city (see STEAD) + *houder* HOLDER]

sta·di·a[1] (stā′dē ə), *n.* **1.** a method of surveying in which distances are read by noting the interval on a graduated rod intercepted by two parallel cross hairs (**sta′dia hairs′** or **sta′dia wires′**) mounted in the telescope of a surveying instrument, the rod being placed at one end of the distance to be measured and the surveying instrument at the other. —*adj.* **2.** of or pertaining to such a method of surveying. [prob. special use of STADIA[2]]

sta·di·a[2] (stā′dē ə), *n.* a pl. of **stadium.**

sta′dia rod′, *Survey.* rod (def. 17).

sta·di·om·e·ter (stā′dē om′i tər), *n.* **1.** an instrument for measuring the lengths of curves, dashed lines, etc., by running a toothed wheel over them. **2.** *Survey.* an obsolete form of the tachymeter. [STADI(UM) + -O- + -METER]

sta·di·um (stā′dē əm), *n., pl.* **-di·ums, -di·a** (-dē ə). **1.** a sports arena, usually oval or horseshoe-shaped, with tiers of seats for spectators. **2.** an ancient Greek course for foot races, typically semicircular, with tiers of seats for spectators. **3.** an ancient Greek and Roman unit of length, the Athenian unit being equal to about 607 feet. **4.** a stage in a process or in the life of a plant or animal. **5.** *Entomol.* the period between molts. [< L < Gk *stádion* racecourse]

stadt·hold·er (stat′hōl′dər), *n.* stadholder.

Staël-Hols·tein (stäl′ôl sten′), *n.* **Anne Louise Germaine Neck·er** (AN lwēz zhER men′ ne kER′), **Baronne de** (*Madame de Staël*), 1766–1817, French writer.

staff[1] (staf, stäf), *n., pl.* **staves** (stāvz) or **staffs** for 1–3, 8, 9; **staffs** for 4–7; *adj., v.* —*n.* **1.** a stick, pole, or rod for aid in walking or climbing, for use as a weapon, etc. **2.** a rod or wand serving as an ensign of office or authority. **3.** a pole on which a flag is hung or displayed. **4.** a group of assistants to an executive. **5.** a group of persons charged with carrying out the work of an establishment or executing some undertaking. **6.** *Mil.* **a.** a body of officers without command authority, appointed to assist a commanding officer. **b.** the parts of any military force concerned with administrative matters, planning, etc., rather than with participation in combat. **7.** the members of an organization that serve only in auxiliary or advisory capacity on a given project. **8.** Also called **stave.** *Music.* a set of five horizontal lines, together with the corresponding four spaces between them, on which music is written. **9.** *Archaic.* the shaft of a spear or lance. —*adj.* **10.** of or pertaining to a military or organizational staff: *a staff member.* **11.** (of certain professional persons) working full-time on the staff of a corporation, newspaper or magazine company, etc., rather than self-employed or practicing privately: *a staff writer.* —*v.t.* **12.** to provide with a staff of workers. [ME *staf,* OE *stæf;* c. D *staf,* Icel *stafr,* G *Stab* staff, Skt *stabh-* support]

staff[2] (staf, stäf), *n.* a composition of plaster and fibrous material used for a temporary finish and in ornamental work. [? < G *Stoff* STUFF]

Staf·fa (staf′ə), *n.* an island in W Scotland, in the Hebrides: site of Fingal's Cave.

staff·er (staf′ər, stä′fər), *n.* **1.** a member of a staff of employees. **2.** *Journalism.* an editorial employee, esp. a writer.

staff′ of′ficer, *Mil.* a commissioned officer who is a member of a staff.

staff′ of life′, bread, considered as the mainstay of the human diet.

Staf·ford (staf′ərd), *n.* **1.** a city in and the county seat of Staffordshire, in central England. 47,814 (1961). **2.** Staffordshire.

Staf·ford·shire (staf′ərd shēr′, -shər), *n.* a county in central England. 1,733,887 (1961); 1154 sq. mi. *Co. seat:* Stafford. Also called **Stafford, Staffs** (stafs).

Staf′fordshire ter′rier, one of an English breed of stocky dogs having a short coat of any of various colors.

staff′ sec′tion, *Mil.* section (def. 10b).

staff′ ser′geant, *U.S.* **1.** *Air Force.* a noncommissioned officer ranking below a technical sergeant and above an airman first class. **2.** *Army.* a noncommissioned officer ranking above a sergeant and below a sergeant first class. **3.** *Marine Corps.* a noncommissioned officer ranking below a gunnery sergeant and above a sergeant.

stag (stag), *n., adj., adv., v.,* **stagged, stag·ging.** —*n.* **1.** an adult male deer. **2.** the male of various other animals. **3.** *Informal.* a man unaccompanied by a woman at a social gathering. **4.** a swine or bull castrated after maturation of the sex organs. —*adj.* **5.** for or of men only: *a stag dinner.* —*adv.* **6.** not accompanied by a female companion: *He went stag to the dance.* —*v.i.* **7.** *Informal.* (of a man) to attend a social function, as a dance, without a female partner or date. **8.** *Brit.* to be an informer or spy. —*v.t.* **9.** *Brit.* to inform or spy on. [ME *stagge,* OE **stagga;* akin to Icel *steggr* male fox]

stag′ bee′tle, any of numerous lamellicorn beetles of the family *Lucanidae,* some of the males of which have mandibles resembling the antlers of a stag.

stag′ bush′. See **black haw** (def. 1).

stage (stāj), *n., v.,* **staged, stag·ing.** —*n.* **1.** any of the individual phases or periods of a process or series. **2.** a platform for the performance in public of actors, musicians, lecturers, etc. **3.** (in a theater) this platform with the area of the building that serves it. **4. the stage,** the theatrical profession. **5.** a stagecoach. **6.** a place of stopping or rest on a journey. **7.** the distance between one such place and the next. **8.** *Entomol.* any one of the major time periods in the development of an insect, as the embryonic, larval, pupal, and imaginal stages. **9.** *Econ., Sociol.* a major phase of the economic or sociological life of man or society: *the patriarchal stage.* **10.** *Geol.* any of the several divisions of stratified rocks forming a period, corresponding to a single age. **11.** the small platform of a microscope on which the object to be examined is placed. **12.** *Radio.* an element in a complex mechanism, as a tube and its accessory structures in a multiple amplifier. **13.** *Rocketry.* a section of a rocket containing a rocket engine or cluster of rocket engines, usually separable from other such sections when its propellant is exhausted. —*v.t.* **14.** to represent, produce, or exhibit on or as on a stage. **15.** to perform or cause to be performed publicly or conspicuously. [ME < OF *(e)stage* (F *étage*) < VL **static(um)* standing-place = *stat(us)* STATUS + *-icum,* neut. of *-icus* -IC]

stage′ busi′ness, business (def. 10).

stage·coach (stāj′kōch′), *n.* (formerly) a horse-drawn passenger coach traveling regularly over a fixed route.

Stagecoach

stage·craft (stāj′kraft′, -kräft′), *n.* skill in or the art of writing, adapting, or staging plays.

stage′ direc′tion, 1. instruction, as to actors' movements, written into the script of a play. **2.** the art and technique of a stage director.

stage′ direc′tor, the person who directs a theatrical production.

stage′ door′, a door at the back or side of a theater, used by performers and theater personnel.

stage′ fright′, nervousness felt by a performer or speaker when appearing before an audience.

stage·hand (stāj′hand′), *n.* a person who moves properties, scenery, etc., in a theatrical production.

stage′ left′, *Theat.* the part of the stage that is left of center as one faces the audience.

stage-man·age (stāj′man′ij), *v.,* **-aged, -ag·ing.** —*v.t.* **1.** to work as a stage manager for (a theatrical presentation). **2.** to arrange or stage in order to produce a spectacular effect: *to stage-manage a costume ball.* **3.** to arrange or direct unobtrusively or in secret. —*v.i.* **4.** to work as a stage manager. [back formation from STAGE MANAGER]

stage′ man′ager, a person responsible for the technical details of a theatrical production.

stag·er (stā′jər), *n.* **1.** a person of experience in some profession, way of life, etc. **2.** *Archaic.* an actor.

stage′ right′, *Theat.* the part of the stage that is right of center as one faces the audience.

stage-struck (stāj′struk′), *adj.* **1.** obsessed with the desire to become an actor or actress. **2.** overly impressed by theatrical people, customs, etc.

stage′ whis′per, a loud whisper on a stage, meant to be heard by the audience.

stage·y (stā′jē), *adj.,* **stag·i·er, stag·i·est.** stagy.

stag·fla·tion (stag′flā′shən), *n.* a condition of simultaneously declining business activity, increasing unemployment, and rapid inflation. [STAG(NATION) + (IN)FLATION]

Stagg (stag), *n.* **Amos Alonzo,** 1862–1965, U.S. football coach.

stag·ger (stag′ər), *v.i.* **1.** to walk or stand unsteadily. **2.** to falter or vacillate. —*v.t.* **3.** to cause to walk or stand unsteadily. **4.** to astound, shock, or bewilder. **5.** to cause to falter. **6.** to arrange in a manner that avoids symmetry or coincidence. **7.** *Aeron.* to arrange (the wings of a bi-

plane or the like) so that the entering edge of an upper wing is either in advance of or behind that of a corresponding lower wing. —*n.* **8.** the act of staggering; a reeling or tottering movement or motion. **9.** a staggered order or arrangement. **10. staggers.** Also called **blind staggers, mad staggers.** (*construed as sing.*) *Vet. Pathol.* any of various forms of cerebral and spinal disease in horses, cattle, and other animals, characterized by blindness, a staggering gait, sudden falling, etc. [earlier *stacker* to reel, ME *stakere* < Scand; cf. Icel *stakra* = *stak(a)* to stagger + *-ra* freq. suffix; akin to STAKE[1]] —**stag′ger·ing·ly,** *adv.*
—**Syn. 1.** STAGGER, REEL, TOTTER suggest an unsteady manner of walking. To STAGGER is successively to lose and regain one's equilibrium and the ability to maintain one's direction: *to stagger with exhaustion, a heavy load, intoxication.* To REEL is to sway dizzily and be in imminent danger of falling: *to reel when faint with hunger.* TOTTER suggests moving slowly and unsteadily, as if afraid of the immediate likelihood of falling from weakness or feebleness, and is used particularly of infants or the very aged: *An old man tottered along with a cane.* **4.** confound, dumfound. **6.** alternate.

stag·ger·bush (stag′ər bo͝osh′), *n.* an American ericaceous shrub, *Lyonia mariana*, poisonous to animals.

stag·hound (stag′hound′), *n.* a hound trained to hunt stags and other large animals.

stag·ing (stā′jiṅg), *n.* **1.** the act, process, or manner of presenting a play on the stage. **2.** a temporary platform or structure of posts and boards for support, as in building; scaffolding. [ME]

stag′ing ar′ea, an area, as a port of embarkation, where troops are assembled and readied for transportation to a new field of operations.

Sta·gi·ra (stə jī′rə), *n.* an ancient town in NE Greece, in Macedonia on the E Chalcidice peninsula: birthplace of Aristotle. Also, **Sta·gi·ros** (stə jī′ros), **Sta·gi·rus** (stə jī′rəs). —**Stag·i·rite** (staj′ə rīt′), *n.*

stag′ line′, the men at a dance who are not accompanied by a female partner or date.

stag·nant (stag′nənt), *adj.* **1.** (of water, air, etc.) not flowing or running. **2.** stale or foul from standing, as a pool of water. **3.** characterized by lack of development, advancement, or useful activity: *a stagnant economy.* [< L *stagnant-* (s. of *stagnāns*, prp. of *stagnāre* to STAGNATE) = *stagn(um)* pool of standing water + *-ant-* -ANT] —**stag′nan·cy, stag′nance,** *n.*

stag·nate (stag′nāt), *v.i.*, **-nat·ed, -nat·ing. 1.** to cease to run or flow, as water or air. **2.** to be or become stale or foul from standing, as a pool of water. **3.** to stop developing, advancing, or being usefully active. [< L *stagnāt(us)* (ptp. of *stagnāre*). See STAGNANT, -ATE[1]] —**stag·na′tion,** *n.*

stag′ par′ty, a social gathering for men only.

stag·y (stā′jē), *adj.*, **stag·i·er, stag·i·est. 1.** of, pertaining to, or suggestive of the stage. **2.** theatrical; unnatural. Also, **stagey.** —**stag′i·ly,** *adv.* —**stag′i·ness,** *n.*

staid (stād), *adj.* **1.** of settled or sedate character; not flighty or capricious. **2.** *Rare.* fixed, settled, or permanent. —*v.* **3.** a pt. and pp. of **stay**[1]. —**staid′ly,** *adv.*
—**Syn. 1.** proper, serious, decorous, solemn. STAID, SEDATE, SETTLED indicate a sober and composed type of conduct. STAID indicates an ingrained seriousness and propriety that shows itself in complete decorum; a colorless kind of correctness is indicated: *a staid old maid.* SEDATE applies to a person who is noticeably quiet, composed, and sober in conduct: *a sedate and dignified young man.* A person who is SETTLED has become fixed, esp. in a sober or determined way, in his manner, judgments, or mode of life: *He is young to be so settled in his ways.* —**Ant. 1.** wild, frivolous.

stain (stān), *n.* **1.** a discoloration produced by foreign matter that has penetrated into or chemically reacted with a material. **2.** a natural spot or patch of color different from that of the basic color, as on the body of an animal. **3.** a permanent impairment to one's reputation; stigma. **4.** coloration produced by a dye that penetrates a substance. **5.** a dye made into a solution for coloring any of various materials. **6.** a reagent or dye used in treating a specimen for microscopic examination. —*v.t.* **7.** to discolor with spots or streaks of foreign matter. **8.** to color or dye with a stain. **9.** to bring reproach or dishonor upon; blemish. **10.** to sully with guilt; corrupt. —*v.i.* **11.** to produce a stain. **12.** to become stained, or admit of being stained. [late ME *steyne(n)* < Scand; cf. Icel *steina* to paint; in some senses, aph. var. of DISTAIN] —**stain′a·bil′i·ty,** *n.* —**stain′a·ble,** *adj.* —**stain′er,** *n.* —**Syn. 3.** blot, taint. **7.** spot, streak, soil, dirty. **9.** sully, taint, dishonor.

stained′ glass′, glass that has been colored, esp. by having pigments baked onto its surface or by having various metallic oxides fused into it. —**stained′-glass′,** *adj.*

stain·less (stān′lis), *adj.* **1.** having no stain; spotless. **2.** made of stainless steel. **3.** resistant to staining or rusting. —*n.* **4.** flatware made of stainless steel.

stain′less steel′, alloy steel having a chromium content of at least 4 percent so as to resist rust and the like.

stair (stâr), *n.* **1.** one of a flight or series of steps for going from one level to another, as in a building. **2. stairs,** a flight of steps, or a series of such flights. **3.** a series or flight of steps; stairway: *a winding stair.* [ME *stey(e)r*, OE *stǣger;* c. D, LG *steiger* landing; akin to STY[2]]

stair·case (stâr′kās′), *n.* a flight of stairs with its framework, banisters, etc., or a series of such flights.

stair·head (stâr′hed′), *n.* the top of a staircase.

stair·way (stâr′wā′), *n.* a passageway from one level (of a building) to another, consisting o a series of stairs; staircase.

stair·well (stâr′wel′), *n.* the vertical shaft or opening containing a stairway. Also, **stair′ well′.**

stake[1] (stāk), *n.*, *v.*, **staked, stak·ing.** —*n.* **1.** a stick or post pointed at one end for driving into the ground as a boundary mark, part of a fence, support for a plant, etc. **2.** (formerly) a tall post customarily used to hold a person for execution by burning. **3.** one of a number of vertical posts fitting into sockets or staples on the edge of the platform of a truck or other vehicle, as to retain the load. **4.** *Mormon Ch.* a division of ecclesiastical territory, consisting of a number of wards. **5. pull up stakes,** *Informal.* to leave one's job, place of residence, etc. —*v.t.* **6.** to mark with or as with stakes, as boundaries (often fol. by *off* or *out*). **7.** to possess, claim, or reserve a share of (land). **8.** to separate or close off by a barrier of stakes. **9.** to support with a stake or stakes, as a plant: *to stake tomato vines.* **10.** to tether or secure to a stake, as an animal. **11.** to fasten with a stake or stakes. **12. stake out,** *Slang.* to keep (a location or suspect) under police surveillance. [ME; OE *staca* pin; c. D *staak*, G *Stake*, Icel *-staki* (in *lȳsistaki* candlestick); akin to STICK[1]] —**Syn. 1.** pale, picket, pike.

stake[2] (stāk), *n.*, *v.*, **staked, stak·ing.** —*n.* **1.** something that is wagered in a game, race, or contest. **2.** a monetary or commercial involvement in something, as in hope of gain. **3.** a personal or emotional interest, involvement, or share. **4.** the funds with which a gambler operates. **5.** Often, **stakes.** something to be gained or lost. **6. stakes,** *Poker.* the cash values assigned to the various chips, bets, and raises: *Our stakes are 5, 10, and 25 cents.* **7. at stake,** in danger of being lost, as something that has been wagered; critically involved. —*v.t.* **8.** to risk (something) upon a game or an event of uncertain outcome. **9.** *Informal.* to furnish (someone) with necessaries or resources, esp. money: *He staked me to a good meal.* [? < D *stake(n)* (to) fix, place, or special use of STAKE[1]] —**Syn. 1.** wager. **1, 8.** bet. **8.** jeopardize.

Staked′ Plain′. See **Llano Estacado.**

stake·hold·er (stāk′hōl′dər), *n.* the holder of the stakes of a wager.

stake·out (stāk′out′), *n.* *Slang.* the surveillance of a location or suspect by the police. [n. use of v. phrase *stake out*]

stake′ race′, *Horse Racing.* a race in which part of the prize or purse is put up by the owners of the horses nominated to run in the race. Also, **stakes′ race′.**

Sta·kha·nov·ism (stə kä′nə viz′əm, stə ka′no-), *n.* (in the Soviet Union) a method for increasing production by rewarding individual initiative, developed in 1935. [named after A. G. *Stakhanov* (b. 1905) Russian efficiency expert; see -ISM]

Sta·kha·nov·ite (stə kä′nə vīt′, -kan′ə-), *n.* a worker rewarded under Stakhanovism. [STAKHANOV(ISM) + -ITE[1]]

sta·lac·ti·form (stə lak′tə fôrm′), *adj.* resembling or shaped like a stalactite. [STALACT(ITE) + -I- + -FORM]

sta·lac·tite (stə lak′tīt, stal′ək tīt′), *n.* an icicle-shaped deposit, usually of calcium carbonate, hanging from the roof of a cave or the like, and formed by the dripping of percolating calcareous water. [< NL *stalactit(es)* < Gk *stalakt(ós)* dripping (*stalak-*, var. of *stalag-*, s. of *stalássein* to drip + *-tos* verbid suffix) + *-ites* -ITE[1]] —**stal·ac·tit·ic** (stal′ək tit′ik), **stal′ac·tit′i·cal,** *adj.*

stalac′tite work′, (in Islamic architecture) intricate decorative corbeling in the form of squinches and portions of pointed vaults.

A, Stalactite
B, Stalagmite

sta·lag (stal′əg; *Ger.* shtä′läk), *n.* a German camp for prisoners of war, esp in World War II. [< G, short for *Sta(mm)lag(er)*, group camp; akin to STEM[1], LAIR]

sta·lag·mite (stə lag′mīt, stal′əg mīt′), *n.* a deposit, usually of calcium carbonate, resembling an inverted stalactite, formed on the floor of a cave or the like by the dripping of percolating calcareous water. See illus. at **stalactite.** [< NL *stalagmite(s)* < Gk *stálagm(a)* (akin to *stalássein;* see STALACTITE) + *-ites* -ITE[1]] —**stal·ag·mit·ic** (stal′əg mit′ik), **stal′ag·mit′i·cal,** *adj.*

St. Al·bans (ôl′bənz), a city in W Hertfordshire, in SE England: cathedral. 50,276 (1961).

stale[1] (stāl), *adj.*, **stal·er, stal·est,** *v.* —*adj.* **1.** not fresh; vapid or flat, as beverages; dry or hardened, as bread. **2.** having ceased to be novel or interesting. **3.** (of a person) affected with weariness, boredom, etc., from overwork or monotony. **4.** *Law.* having lost force or effectiveness through absence of action, as a claim. —*v.t.*, *v.i.* **5.** to make or become stale. [ME; akin to MD *stel* in same sense; ? akin to STAND or to STALE[2]] —**Ant. 1.** fresh.

stale[2] (stāl), *v.i.*, **staled, stal·ing.** (of livestock) to urinate. [late ME *stale(n)* (to) urinate; c. G *stallen*, Dan *stalle*, Norw, Sw *stalla*, F *estaller* (< OFrankish); akin to Gk *stalássein* to drip (see STALAGMITE), Breton *staot* urine]

stale·mate (stāl′māt′), *n.*, *v.*, **-mat·ed, -mat·ing.** —*n.* **1.** *Chess.* a position in which a player cannot move any piece except his king and cannot move his king without putting it in check, the result being a draw. **2.** any position or situation in which no action can be taken; deadlock. —*v.t.* **3.** to subject to a stalemate. **4.** to bring to a standstill. [late ME *stale* stalemate (whence AF *estale*) (appar. special use of STALE[1]) + MATE[2]] —**Syn. 2.** impasse.

Sta·lin (stä′lin, -lēn), *n.* **1. Joseph V.** (*Iosif Vissarionovich Dzhugashvili* or *Dzugashvili*), 1879–1953, Russian political leader: secretary general of the Communist party 1922–53; premier of the U.S.S.R. 1941–53. **2.** Also, **Sta·li·no** (*Russ.* stä′li no). a former name of **Donetsk. 3.** former name of **Varna. 4.** former name of **Brașov.**

Sta·lin·a·bad (*Russ.* stä′li nä bät′), *n.* former name of **Dyushambe.**

Sta·lin·grad (stä′lin grad′; *Russ.* stä′lin grät′), *n.* a former name of **Volgograd.**

Sta·lin·ism (stä′li niz′əm), *n.* the principles of communism associated with Joseph Stalin, characterized esp. by the rigid suppression of dissident political or ideological views, the concentration of power in one person, and by an aggressive international policy. —**Sta′lin·ist,** *adj.*, *n.*

Sta·linsk (*Russ.* stä′linsk), *n.* former name of **Novokuznetsk.**

stalk[1] (stôk), *n.* **1.** the stem or main axis of a plant. **2.** any slender supporting or connecting part of a plant, as the petiole of a leaf or the peduncle of a flower. **3.** a stem, shaft, or slender supporting part of anything. [ME *stalke*, OE *stæl(a)* + *-k* suffix]

stalk[2] (stôk), *v.i.* **1.** to pursue or approach prey, quarry, etc., stealthily. **2.** to walk with measured, stiff strides. **3.** to range about or be abroad in a menacing manner. **4.** *Obs.* to walk or go stealthily along. —*v.t.* **5.** to pursue (game, a person, etc.) stealthily. —*n.* **6.** the act or an instance of stalking game or victims. **7.** a slow, stiff stride or gait. [ME *stalke,* OE (*be*)*stealc*(*ian*) (to) move stealthily, STEAL = *stal*(*u*) stealing + *-k* suffix]

stalk·ing-horse (stô′king hôrs′), *n.* **1.** a horse or a figure of a horse behind which a stalking hunter hides. **2.** anything put forward to mask plans or efforts; pretext. **3.** *Politics.* a candidate used to conceal the candidacy of a more important candidate or to draw votes from a rival.

stalk·less (stôk′lis), *adj.* **1.** having no stalk. **2.** *Bot.* sessile.

stalk·y (stô′kē), *adj.,* **stalk·i·er, stalk·i·est.** **1.** abounding in stalks. **2.** stalklike; long and slender. —**stalk′i·ly,** *adv.* —**stalk′i·ness,** *n.*

stall[1] (stôl), *n.* **1.** a compartment in a stable or shed for the accommodation of one animal. **2.** a stable or shed for horses or cattle. **3.** a booth or stand for the display or sale of merchandise: *a butcher's stall.* **4.** one of a number of fixed enclosed seats in the choir or chancel of a church for the use of the clergy. **5.** a pew. **6.** any small compartment for a specific activity or housing a specific thing: *a shower stall.* **7.** a rectangular space marked off or reserved for parking a car or other vehicle, as in a parking lot. **8.** an instance or the condition of causing an engine, or a vehicle powered by an engine, to stop by supplying it with a poor fuel mixture or by overloading it. **9.** *Aeron.* an instance or the condition of causing an airplane to fly at an angle of attack greater than the angle of maximum lift, causing loss of control and a downward spin. **10.** a protective covering for a finger or toe, as various guards and sheaths or one finger of a glove. **11.** *Brit.* a chairlike seat in a theater, separated from others by arms or rails, esp. one in the front section of the parquet. —*v.t.* **12.** to assign to, put, or keep in a stall or stalls, as an animal or a car. **13.** to confine in a stall for fattening, as cattle. **14.** to cause (a motor or the vehicle it powers) to stop by supplying it with a poor fuel mixture or overloading it. **15.** to put (an airplane) into a stall. **16.** to bring to a standstill; check the progress or motion of, esp. unintentionally. —*v.i.* **17.** (of an engine, car, airplane, etc.) to be stalled. **18.** to come to a standstill; be brought to a stop. **19.** to occupy a stall, as an animal. [ME; OE *steall;* c. G *Stall,* Icel *stallr;* akin to OE *stellan,* G *stellen* to put, place]

stall[2] (stôl), *Informal.* —*n.* **1.** a pretext used to delay or deceive. —*v.i.* **2.** to delay, esp. by evasion or deception. —*v.t.* **3.** to delay or put off, esp. by evasion or deception. [ME *stal*(*e*) decoy bird (whence AF *estale* decoy pigeon), OE *stæl-* decoy (in *stælhrān* decoy reindeer); akin to STALL[1]]

stal·lion (stal′yən), *n.* an uncastrated adult male horse, esp. one used for breeding. [ME *stalon* < OF (*e*)*stalon* = *stal-* (< Gmc; see STALL[1]) + *-on* n. suffix]

stal·wart (stôl′wərt), *adj.* **1.** strongly and stoutly built; sturdy and robust. **2.** strong and brave; valiant. **3.** firm, steadfast, or uncompromising. —*n.* **4.** a physically stalwart person. **5.** a steadfast or uncompromising partisan. [ME (Scot), var. of *stalward,* earlier *stalwurthe,* OE *stǣlwirthe* serviceable = *stǣl* (contr. of *stathol* STADDLE) + *wierthe* WORTH] —**Syn. 2.** intrepid, fearless. —**Ant. 2.** fearful.

stal·worth (stôl′wərth), *adj. Archaic.* stalwart.

Stam·bul (stäm bo͞ol′), *n.* Istanbul. Also, **Stam·boul** (stäm bo͞ol′; *Fr.* stäN bo͞ol′).

sta·men (stā′mən), *n., pl.* **sta·mens, stam·i·na** (stam′ə nə). *Bot.* the pollen-bearing organ of a flower, consisting of the filament and the anther. [< L: warp in upright loom, thread, filament = *stā*(*re*) (to) stand + *-men* n. suffix; akin to Gk *stēmōn* warp, Skt *sthāman* place < *sthā-* STAND]

Stam·ford (stam′fərd), *n.* a city in SW Connecticut. 108,798 (1970).

stamin-, var. of **stamini-** before a vowel: *staminate.*

stam·i·na[1] (stam′ə nə), *n.* strength of physical constitution; power to endure disease, fatigue, privation, etc. [< L, pl. of *stāmen* thread (see STAMEN); namely, the life threads spun by the Fates] —**Syn.** endurance, resistance, health.

stam·i·na[2] (stam′ə nə), *n.* a pl. of **stamen.**

stam·i·nal[1] (stam′ə n^{ə}l), *adj. Bot.* of or pertaining to stamens. Also, **sta·min·e·al** (stə min′ē əl). [STAMIN(A)[2] + -AL[1]]

stam·i·nal[2] (stam′ə n^{ə}l), *adj.* of or pertaining to stamina or endurance. [STAMIN(A)[1] + -AL[1]]

stam·i·nate (stam′ə nit, -nāt′), *adj. Bot.* **1.** having a stamen or stamens. **2.** having stamens but no pistils.

stamini-, a combining form of **stamen:** *staminiferous.* Also, *esp. before a vowel,* **stamin-.** [comb. form repr. L *stāmin-* (s. of *stāmen*); see -I-]

stam·i·nif·er·ous (stam′ə nif′ər əs), *adj. Bot.* bearing or having a stamen or stamens. Also, **stam·i·nig·er·ous** (stam′ə-nij′ər əs).

stam·i·no·di·um (stam′ə nō′dē əm), *n., pl.* **-di·a** (-dē ə). *Bot.* **1.** a sterile or abortive stamen. **2.** a part resembling such a stamen. Also, **stam·i·node** (stam′ə nōd′). [STAMIN- + -ODE[1] + -IUM]

stam·i·no·dy (stam′ə nō′dē), *n. Bot.* the metamorphosis of any of various flower organs, as a sepal or a petal, into a stamen. [STAMINODIUM, with -Y[3] r. -IUM]

stam·mel (stam′əl), *n. Obs.* **1.** a coarse wool, often dyed red, formerly used for undergarments. **2.** a bright red color, as of such a cloth. [< MF (*e*)*stamel* = *estame* (< L *stāmen* warp; see STAMEN) + *-el* n. suffix]

stam·mer (stam′ər), *v.i.* **1.** to speak with involuntary breaks and pauses, or with spasmodic repetitions of syllables or sounds. —*v.t.* **2.** to say with a stammer (often fol. by *out*). —*n.* **3.** a stammering mode of utterance. **4.** a stammered utterance. [ME; OE *stamer*(*ian*) (c. G *stammern*) = *stam* stammering + *-erian* -ER[2]; akin to Icel *stamma* to stammer, Goth *stams* stammering] —**stam′mer·er,** *n.* —**stam′mer·ing·ly,** *adv.*
—**Syn. 1.** pause, hesitate, falter. STAMMER, STUTTER mean to speak with some form of difficulty. STAMMER, the general term, suggests a speech difficulty that results in broken or inarticulate sounds and sometimes in complete stoppage of speech; it may be temporary, caused by sudden excitement, confusion, embarrassment, or other emotion, or it may be so deep-seated as to require special treatment for its correction. STUTTER, the parallel term preferred in technical usage, designates a broad range of defects that produce spasmodic interruptions of the speech rhythm, repetitions, or prolongations of sounds or syllables: *The child's stutter was no mere stammer of embarrassment.*

stamp (stamp), *v.t.* **1.** to strike or beat with a forcible, downward thrust of the foot. **2.** to bring (the foot) down forcibly or smartly on the ground, floor, etc. **3.** to extinguish, crush, etc., with a forcible downward thrust of the foot (usually fol. by *out*): *to stamp out a fire.* **4.** to suppress or quell (a rebellion, uprising, etc.) quickly through the use of overwhelming force (usually fol. by *out*). **5.** to crush or pound with or as with a pestle. **6.** to impress with a particular mark or device, as to indicate genuineness, approval or ownership. **7.** to impress (a design, word, mark, etc.) on a paper or the like. **8.** to affix a postage stamp to (a letter, envelope, etc.). **9.** to characterize, distinguish, or reveal. —*v.i.* **10.** to bring the foot down forcibly or smartly. **11.** to walk with forcible or heavy, resounding steps. —*n.* **12.** See **postage stamp.** **13.** the act or an instance of stamping. **14.** a die or block for impressing or imprinting. **15.** a design or legend made with such a die or block. **16.** an official mark indicating genuineness, validity, payment of a duty or charge, etc. **17.** an official seal or device appearing on a business or legal document to show that a tax has been paid. **18.** something serving as visible evidence of character or quality. **19.** character, kind, or type: *a man of serious stamp.* **20.** See **trading stamp.** **21.** an instrument for stamping, crushing, or pounding. [early ME *stamp*(*en*) (to) pound (c. G *stampfen*); r. OE *stempan;* akin to Icel *stappa* to stamp, Gk *stémbein* to shake up] —**Syn. 4.** eliminate, squash, quash. See **abolish. 6.** label, imprint. **6, 15.** brand. **15.** pattern, mark, print, seal. **19.** sort, description, mold, cast, style.

Stamp′ Act′, *Amer. Hist.* an act of the British Parliament for raising revenue in the American colonies by requiring that documents and articles of commerce bear an official stamp.

stam·pede (stam pēd′), *n., v.,* **-ped·ed, -ped·ing.** —*n.* **1.** a sudden, frenzied rush or headlong flight of a herd of frightened animals, esp. cattle or horses. **2.** any headlong general flight or rush. **3.** *Western U.S., Canadian.* a celebration, including a rodeo, contests, exhibitions, dancing, etc. **4.** (in the Northwest U.S. and W Canada) a rodeo. —*v.i.* **5.** to scatter or flee in a stampede. **6.** to make a general rush. —*v.t.* **7.** to cause to stampede. **8.** to rush or overrun (a place, exits, etc.). [< AmerSp (*e*)*stampid*(*a*), Sp = *estamp*(*ar*) (to) stamp + *-ida* n. suffix]

stamp·er (stam′pər), *n.* **1.** a person or thing that stamps. **2.** an employee in a post office who applies postmarks and cancels postage stamps. **3.** a pestle, esp. one in a stamp mill. [ME *stampere*]

stamp′ing ground′, *Informal.* a place that a person frequents; a favorite haunt.

stamp′ mill′, *Metall.* a mill or machine in which ore is crushed to powder by means of heavy stamps.

stance (stans), *n.* **1.** the position or bearing of the body while standing. **2.** a mental or emotional position adopted with respect to something. **3.** *Sports.* the relative position of the feet, as in addressing a golf ball or in making a stroke. [< F < It *stanz*(*a*) station; see STANZA] —**Syn. 1, 2.** posture. **2.** attitude. **3.** placement.

stanch[1] (stônch, stanch, stänch), *v.t.* **1.** to stop the flow of (a liquid, esp. blood). **2.** to stop the flow of blood or other liquid from (a wound, leak, etc.). **3.** *Archaic.* to check, allay, or extinguish. —*v.i.* **4.** to stop flowing, as blood. Also, **staunch.** [ME *sta*(*u*)*nche*(*n*) < OF (*e*)*stanch*(*i*)*e*(*r*) (to) close, stop, slake (thirst) < VL **stanticāre* = L *stanti-* (s. of *stāns,* prp. of *stāre* to STAND) + *-cāre* causative suffix] —**stanch′a·ble,** *adj.* —**stanch′er,** *n.*

stanch[2] (stônch, stänch, stanch), *adj.* staunch[2]. —**stanch′ly,** *adv.* —**stanch′ness,** *n.*

stan·chion (stan′shən), *n.* **1.** an isolated upright structural support. —*v.t.* **2.** to furnish with stanchions. **3.** to support by or secure to a stanchion or stanchions. [ME *stanchon* < OF (*e*)*stanchon* = *estanche* (var. of *estance,* prob. < VL **stantia* = L *stant-* (s. of *stāns* prp. of *stāre* to STAND) + *-ia* -Y) + *-on* n. suffix]

stand (stand), *v.,* **stood, stand·ing,** *n., pl.* **stands** for 34–49, **stands, stand** for 50. —*v.i.* **1.** (of a person) to be upright with the whole weight of the body on the feet. **2.** to rise to one's feet (often fol. by *up*). **3.** to be located: *The asylum stands upon the hill.* **4.** to be as erected or built: *an old house still standing.* **5.** to halt or to be temporarily motionless or inactive. **6.** to move as specified by shifting a standing position: *Stand aside, everyone!* **7.** to continue in effect: *My offer still stands.* **8.** to be or remain in a specified state or condition: *I stand corrected. They stand in danger of a lawsuit. The thermometer stood at 80 degrees.* **9.** (of a substance or mixture) to be left alone or without interference. **10.** (of water outdoors) to be or become stagnant. **11.** to make a public profession of oneself or one's attitudes as specified: *to stand for free trade; to stand as sponsor for a baby.* **12.** to remain firm or steadfast: *I still stand your friend.* **13.** (of a person) to have a specified measure in height. **14.** *Chiefly Brit.* to be or become a candidate, as for public office. **15.** *Naut.* to take or hold a particular course at sea. **16.** (of a male domestic animal, esp. a stud) to be available as a sire, usually for a fee.
—*v.t.* **17.** to cause to stand; set upright; set. **18.** to face or experience, as an attack or ordeal. **19.** to endure or undergo without harm or damage or without giving way. **20.** to endure or tolerate: *He cannot stand criticism.* **21.** *Informal.* to treat: *I'll stand you to a drink.* **22.** to perform the duty of or participate in as part of one's job or duty: *to stand watch aboard ship.* **23. stand a chance,** to have a chance or possibility, as of winning or surviving. **24. stand by, a.** to be faithful to, as in trouble. **b.** to adhere to (a promise or the like). **c.** to stand ready; wait. **25. stand for, a.** to represent; symbolize: *"P.S." stands for "postscript."* **b.** to advocate; favor. **c.** *Informal.* to tolerate; allow. **26. stand on, a.** to depend on; rest on: *The case stands on his testimony.* **b.** to be particular about; demand: *to stand on ceremony.* **27. stand out, a.** to be conspicuous or prominent. **b.** to persist in oppo-

sition or resistance; be inflexible. **28. stand pat,** to refuse to change or to accept changes. **29. stand to reason.** See **reason** (def. 10). **30. stand up, a.** to rise to one's feet. **b.** to remain convincing, as an argument. **c.** to remain durable. **d.** *Slang.* to fail to keep an appointment with someone. **31. stand up to,** to meet or deal with fearlessly; confront: *to stand up to a bully.* —*n.* **32.** the act of standing. **33.** a cessation of motion; halt; standstill. **34.** a determined effort for or against something, esp. a final defensive effort. **35.** a determined policy, position, attitude, etc., taken or maintained. **36.** the place in which a person or thing stands; station. **37.** See **witness stand. 38.** a raised platform, as for a speaker or a band. **39. stands,** a raised section of seats for spectators; grandstand. **40.** a framework on or in which articles are placed for support, exhibition, etc. **41.** a piece of furniture in any of various forms, on or in which to put articles (often used in combination): *a hatstand.* **42.** a small, light table. **43.** a stall, booth, or the like, where articles are displayed for sale or where some business is carried on: *a fruit stand.* **44.** a site or location for business. **45.** a place or station occupied by vehicles available for hire: *a taxicab stand.* **46.** the growing trees, or those of a particular species or grade, in a given area. **47.** a standing growth, as of grass or wheat. **48.** a halt of a theatrical company on tour, to give a performance or performances: *a series of one-night stands.* **49.** hive (def. 2). **50.** *Archaic.* a complete set of arms or accoutrements for one soldier. [ME; OE *stand(an)*; c. Icel *standa, standan;* akin to L *stā(re),* Skt *sthā-* stand]
—**Syn. 12.** continue, persist. **17.** place, put, fix. **18.** meet, resist, oppose. **20.** abide, stomach. See **bear**[1]. **46.** crop.

stand·ard (stan′dərd), *n.* **1.** something considered by an authority or by general consent as a basis of comparison; an approved model. **2.** anything, as a rule or principle, that is used as a basis for judgment. **3.** an average or normal requirement, quality, level, etc.: *His work this week hasn't been up to his usual standard.* **4. standards,** morals, ethics, habits, etc., established by authority, custom, or an individual as acceptable. **5.** the authorized exemplar of a unit of weight or measure. **6.** a certain commodity, esp. gold or silver, in or by which a basic monetary unit is stated. **7.** the legally established content of full-weight coins. **8.** the prescribed degree of fineness for gold or silver. **9.** a musical piece of sufficiently enduring popularity to be made part of a permanent repertoire. **10.** a flag indicating the presence of a sovereign or public official. **11.** a flag, emblematic figure, or other object used as the emblem of an army, fleet, etc. **12.** something that stands or is placed upright. **13.** an upright support or supporting part. **14.** *Hort.* a plant trained or grafted to have a single, erect, treelike stem. **15.** *Bot.* vexillum (def. 3). —*adj.* **16.** serving as a model or as a basis for judgment or comparison. **17.** of recognized excellence: *a standard book on a subject.* **18.** usual, common, or customary. **19.** conforming in pronunciation, grammar, vocabulary, etc., to the usage that is generally considered to be correct or preferred. **20.** fulfilling specific requirements as established by an authority, law, rule, custom, etc. [ME < OF, prob. alter. of Frankish **standord* (cf. G *Standort* standing point), conformed to *-ard* -ARD]
—**Syn. 1, 2.** gauge, basis, pattern, guide. STANDARD, CRITERION refer to the basis for making a judgment. A STANDARD is an authoritative principle or rule that usually implies a model or pattern for guidance, by comparison with which the quantity, excellence, correctness, etc., of other things may be determined: *She could serve as the standard of good breeding.* A CRITERION is a rule or principle used to judge the value, suitability, probability, etc., of something, without necessarily implying any comparison: *Wealth is no criterion of a man's worth.* **11.** ensign, banner, pennant. **16.** guiding.

stand·ard-bear·er (stan′dərd bâr′ər), *n.* **1.** an officer or soldier of a military unit who bears a standard. **2.** a conspicuous leader of a movement, political party, or the like. [late ME]

stan·dard·bred (stan′dərd bred′), *n.* (*often cap.*) one of an American breed of trotting and pacing horses used chiefly for harness racing.

stand′ard devia′tion, *Statistics.* a measure of dispersion in a frequency distribution, equal to the square root of the mean of the squares of the deviations from the arithmetic mean of the distribution.

stand′ard dol′lar, the basic monetary unit of the U.S., containing $15^{5}/_{21}$ grains of gold, 0.900 fine.

Stand′ard Eng′lish, the English language as written and spoken by literate people in both formal and informal usage and that is universally current while incorporating regional differences.

stand′ard gauge′. See under **gauge** (def. 11). Also, *esp. in technical use,* **stand′ard gage′.** —**stand′ard-gauge′, stand′ard-gage′,** *adj.* —**stand′ard-gauged′, stand′ard-gaged′,** *adj.*

stand·ard·ise (stan′dər dīz′), *v.t., v.i.,* **-ised, -is·ing.** *Chiefly Brit.* standardize. —**stand′ard·i·sa′tion,** *n.*

stand·ard·ize (stan′dər dīz′), *v.,* **-ized, -iz·ing.** —*v.t.* **1.** to bring to or make of an established standard size, weight, quality, strength, or the like. —*v.i.* **2.** to become standardized. —**stand′ard·i·za′tion,** *n.*

stand′ard of liv′ing, the grade or level of subsistence and comfort in everyday life maintained by a group or individual. Also called **living standard.**

stand′ard time′, the civil time officially adopted for a country or region, usually the civil time of some specific meridian lying within the region. The standard time zones in the U.S. (**Eastern time, Central time, Mountain time, Pacific time, Yukon time, Alaska time,** and **Bering time**) use the civil times of the 75th, 90th, 105th, 120th, 135th, 150th, and 165th meridians respectively, the difference of time between one zone and the next being exactly one hour. See diag. at **time zone.**

stand-by (stand′bī′), *n., pl.* **-bys,** *adj.* —*n.* **1.** a person or thing that can be relied upon in an emergency. **2.** the situation of being in readiness, as of a passenger to occupy canceled accommodations (sometimes prec. by *on*). —*adj.* **3.** kept available for use in an emergency, shortage, etc. Also, **stand′by′.**

stand·ee (stan dē′), *n. Informal.* a spectator who stands, as in a theater, at a concert, etc., either because no seats are available or because standing room is cheaper than a seat.

stand·fast (stand′fast′, -fäst′), *n.* an unyielding position.

stand-in (stand′in′), *n.* **1.** a substitute for a motion-picture star during the preparation of lighting, cameras, etc., or in dangerous scenes. **2.** any substitute.

stand·ing (stan′ding), *n.* **1.** rank or status, esp. with respect to social, economic, or personal position, reputation, etc. **2.** good position, reputation, or credit. **3.** length of existence or continuance: *a friend of long standing.* **4.** the act of a person or thing that stands. **5.** a place where a person or thing stands. —*adj.* **6.** having an erect or upright position: *a standing lamp.* **7.** performed in or from an erect position: *a standing jump.* **8.** still or stagnant, as water; stationary. **9.** continuing without cessation or change; lasting or permanent. **10.** out of use; idle: *a standing engine.* **11.** *Naut.* noting any of various objects or assemblages of objects fixed in place or position, unless moved for adjustment or repairs: *standing bowsprit.* [ME]

stand′ing ar′my, a permanently organized military force maintained by a nation.

stand′ing broad′ jump′. See under **broad jump.**

stand′ing commit′tee, a permanent committee, as of a legislature, dealing with a designated subject.

stand′ing mar′tingale, martingale (def. 1).

stand′ing or′der, 1. an order or instruction always in effect. **2. standing orders,** *Parl. Proc.* the rules ensuring continuity of procedure during the meetings of an assembly.

stand′ing rig′ging, *Naut.* rigging remaining permanently in position, as shrouds, stays, etc.

stand′ing room′, room or space in which to stand, as in a theater, stadium, etc.

stand′ing wave′, *Physics.* a wave in a medium in which each point on the axis of the wave has an associated constant amplitude ranging from zero at the nodes to a maximum at the antinodes. Also called **stationary wave.**

stand·ish (stan′dish), *n. Archaic.* a stand for ink, pens, and other writing materials. [perh. STAND + DISH]

Stan·dish (stan′dish), *n.* **Myles** or **Miles** (mīlz), c1584–1656, military leader in Plymouth Colony, born in England.

stand-off (stand′ôf′, -of′), *n.* **1.** a standing off or apart; aloofness. **2.** a tie or draw, as in a game. **3.** something that counterbalances. —*adj.* **4.** standing off or apart; aloof; reserved. Also, **stand′off′.**

stand-off·ish (stand′ô′fish, -of′ish), *adj.* somewhat aloof or reserved; cold and unfriendly. Also, **stand′off′ish.**

stand′ oil′, a thick oil made by heating linseed oil to temperatures of 600°F and higher, used chiefly as a medium in paints.

stand·out (stand′out′), *n.* **1.** something or someone showing remarkable superiority. —*adj.* **2.** outstanding; superior. Also, **stand′-out′.**

stand·pipe (stand′pīp′), *n.* a vertical pipe or tower into which water is pumped to obtain a required head.

stand·point (stand′point′), *n.* **1.** the point or place at which a person stands to view something. **2.** the mental position, attitude, etc., from which a person views and judges things. [modeled on G *Standpunkt*]

St. An·drews (an′dro͞oz), a seaport in E Fife, in E Scotland: resort; golf courses. 10,350 (est. 1964).

St. Andrew's cross, a cross composed of four diagonal arms of equal length; saltire. See illus. at **cross.**

stand·still (stand′stil′), *n.* a state of cessation of movement or action; halt; stop.

stand-up (stand′up′), *adj.* **1.** standing erect or upright, as a collar. **2.** involving or requiring a standing position. **3.** characterized by an erect or bold stance: *a stand-up batter who hits many doubles.* **4.** *Theat.* (of a comedian) delivering a comic monologue while alone on the stage.

Stan′ford-Bi·net′ test′ (stan′fərd bi nā′), *Psychol.* a revised version of the Binet-Simon scale, prepared for use in the U.S. [named after *Stanford* University, Palo Alto, California and A. BINET]

stang (stang), *v. Obs.* pt. of **sting.**

stan·hope (stan′hōp′, stan′əp), *n.* a light, open, one-seated, horse-drawn carriage with two or four wheels, the body of which is hung on four springs. [named after Fitzroy *Stanhope* (1787–1864), British clergyman]

Stan·hope (stan′hōp′, stan′əp), *n.* **Philip Dor·mer** (dôr′mər). See **Chesterfield, 4th Earl of.**

Stan·i·slav·ski (stan′i släv′skē, -släf′-; *Russ.* stä ni släf′-skē), *n.* **Kon·stan·tin** (kon stän tēn′), 1863–1938, Russian actor, producer, and director. Also, **Stan′i·slav′sky.**

Stanislav′ski Meth′od, method (def. 5). Also called **Stanislav′ski Sys′tem.** [named after K. STANISLAVSKI]

Sta·ni·sła·wów (*Pol.* stä′nē slä′vo͝of), *n.* a city in the SW Ukraine, in the SW Soviet Union in Europe: formerly in Poland. 66,000 (1959). German, **Stan·is·lau** (shtä′nis-lou′). Russian, **Sta·ni·sla·vov** (stä′ni slä′vof).

stank (stangk), *v.* a pt. of **stink.**

Stan·ley (stan′lē), *n.* **1. Sir Henry Morgan** (originally *John Rowlands*), 1841–1904, English explorer in Africa. **2. Mount,** a mountain with two summits, in central Africa, between Uganda and the Democratic Republic of the Congo: highest peak in the Ruwenzori group. 16,790 ft. **3.** the chief town of the Falkland Islands. 1074 (1964).

Stan′ley Falls′, a group of seven cataracts of the Congo River, in the NE Democratic Republic of the Congo, on the equator.

Stan′ley Pool′, a lake on the boundary between the W Democratic Republic of the Congo and the S Republic of Congo, formed by the widening of the Congo River. ab. 20 mi. long; ab. 15 mi. wide.

Stan·ley·ville (stan′lē vil′), *n.* former name of **Kisangani.**

stann-, a combining form of **stannum:** *stannite.*

stan·na·ry (stan′ə rē), *n., pl.* **-ries. 1.** a tin-mining region or district. **2.** *Brit.* a place where tin is mined or smelted. [late ME < ML *stannāri(a)* tin mine = LL *stann(um)* STANNUM + *-āria* -ARY]

stan·nic (stan′ik), *adj. Chem.* of or containing tin, esp. in the tetravalent state.

stan′nic sul′fide, *Chem.* a powder, SnS_2, usually used suspended in lacquer or varnish for gilding and bronzing.

stan·nite (stan′īt), *n.* a mineral, copper iron tin sulfide, Cu_2FeSnS_4: an ore of tin.

stan·nous (stan′əs), *adj.* *Chem.* containing tin, esp. in the bivalent state.

stan·num (stan′əm), *n.* tin. [< LL: tin, L: alloy of silver and lead; perh. < Celt]

Sta·no·voi (stä′no voi′), *n.* a mountain range in the E Soviet Union in Asia: a watershed between the Pacific and Arctic oceans; highest peak, 8143 ft.

St. Anthony's cross. See **tau cross.**

Stan·ton (stan′tᵊn), *n.* **1. Edwin Mc·Mas·ters** (mək-mas′tərz, -mä′stərz), 1814–69, U.S. statesman: Secretary of War 1862–67. **2. Mrs. Elizabeth Ca·dy** (kā′dē), 1815–1902, U.S. social reformer.

stan·za (stan′zə), *n.* *Pros.* an arrangement of a certain number of lines, usually four or more, sometimes having a fixed length, meter, or rhyme scheme, forming a division of a poem. [< It: room, station, stopping place (pl. *stanze*) < VL **stantia* = L *stant-* (s. of *stāns*, prp. of *stāre* to STAND) + *-ia* -Y³] —**stan′zaed,** *adj.* —**stan·za·ic** (stan zā′ik), **stan·za′i·cal,** *adj.* —**Syn.** See **verse.**

sta·pe·li·a (stə pē′lē ə), *n.* any asclepiadaceous plant of the genus *Stapelia*, of southern Africa, having short, fleshy, leafless stems and flowers that are oddly colored or mottled and in most species emit a fetid odor, as of carrion. [named after J. B. van *Stapel* (d. 1636), Dutch botanist; see -IA]

sta·pes (stā′pēz), *n., pl.* **sta·pes, sta·pe·dez** (stə pē′dēz). *Anat.* the outer, stirrup-shaped bone of a chain of three small bones in the middle ear of man and other mammals. Also called **stirrup.** Cf. **incus** (def. 1), **malleus.** [< NL, ML: stirrup] —**sta·pe·di·al** (stə pē′dē əl), *adj.*

staph (staf), *n.* *Informal.* staphylococcus. [by shortening]

staphylo-, a learned borrowing from Greek, where it meant "bunch of grapes," "uvula," used with these meanings and also with reference to the palate and to staphylococcus in the formation of compound words: *staphyloplasty.* [comb. form repr. Gk *staphylḗ*]

staph·y·lo·coc·cus (staf′ə lə kok′əs), *n., pl.* **-coc·ci** (-kok′sī). *Bacteriol.* any of several spherical bacteria of the genus *Staphylococcus*, occurring in pairs, tetrads, and irregular clusters, certain species of which, as *S. aureus*, can be pathogenic for man. —**staph·y·lo·coc·cal** (staf′ə lə kok′əl), **staph·y·lo·coc·cic** (staf′ə lə kok′sik), *adj.*

staph·y·lo·plas·ty (staf′ə lə plas′tē), *n.* the remedying of defects of the soft palate by plastic surgery. —**staph′y·lo·plas′tic,** *adj.*

staph·y·lor·rha·phy (staf′ə lôr′ə fē, -lor′-), *n., pl.* **-phies.** the uniting of a cleft palate by plastic surgery.

sta·ple¹ (stā′pəl), *n., v.,* **-pled, -pling.** —*n.* **1.** a short piece of wire bent so as to bind together papers, sections of a book, or the like, by having the ends driven through and clinched. **2.** a similar, often U-shaped piece of wire or metal with pointed ends for driving into a surface to hold a hasp, pin, bolt, etc. —*v.t.* **3.** to secure or fasten by a staple or staples. [ME *stapel*, OE *stapol* support, post; c. MD *stapel* foundation, Icel *stöpull* pillar, G *Stapel* stake]

sta·ple² (stā′pəl), *n., adj., v.,* **-pled, -pling.** —*n.* **1.** a principal raw material or commodity grown or manufactured in a locality. **2.** a principal commodity in a mercantile field; goods in steady demand or of known or recognized quality. **3.** a basic or necessary item of food, as bread or salt. **4.** any basic or principal item, thing, feature, element, etc. **5.** the fiber of wool, cotton, flax, etc., considered with reference to length and fineness. **6.** *Textiles.* a standard length of textile fibers, representing the average of such fibers taken collectively: *long-staple cotton.* —*adj.* **7.** chief or prominent among the products exported or produced by a country or district. **8.** basic, chief, or principal: *staple industries.* **9.** principally used: *staple subjects of conversation.* —*v.t.* **10.** to sort or classify according to the staple or fiber, as wool. [ME *stapel* < MD: warehouse, mart; see STAPLE¹]

sta·pler¹ (stā′plər), *n.* **1.** a machine for fastening together sheets of paper with wire staples. **2.** a wire-stitching machine, esp. one used in bookbinding. [STAPLE¹ + -ER¹]

sta·pler² (stā′plər), *n.* **1.** a person who staples, as wool. **2.** a merchant who deals in a staple or staples. [STAPLE² + -ER¹]

star (stär), *n., adj., v.,* **starred, star·ring.** —*n.* **1.** any of the heavenly bodies, except the moon, appearing as luminous points in the sky at night. **2.** *Astron.* any of the large, self-luminous, heavenly bodies, as the sun. **3.** any heavenly body. **4.** *Astrol.* a heavenly body, esp. a planet, considered as influencing mankind and events. **5.** a person's destiny, fortune, temperament, etc., regarded as influenced and determined by the stars. **6.** a conventionalized figure usually having five or six points radiating from or disposed about a center. **7.** a medal, sticker, printed symbol, etc., formed like or containing this figure. **8.** such a figure used as a designation of rank, distinction, etc. **9.** *Jewelry.* a brilliant with six facets of equilateral triangles immediately beneath the table, instead of the normal eight. **10.** *Print.* an asterisk. **11.** a person who has a leading part in a theatrical performance or other entertainment. **12.** a person who is prominent in some other field, as of entertainment or sports. **13.** a white spot on the forehead of a horse. —*adj.* **14.** celebrated, prominent, or distinguished; preeminent: *a star basketball player; a star reporter.* **15.** of or pertaining to a star or stars. —*v.t.* **16.** to set with or as with stars; spangle. **17.** to present (a performer) as a star. **18.** to feature as a star: *This movie stars Marlon Brando.* **19.** to mark with a star or asterisk. —*v.i.* **20.** to shine as a star; to be brilliant or prominent. **21.** (of a performer) to appear as a star. [ME *sterre*, OE *steorra*; c. OHG *sterra*; akin to OHG *sterno*, Icel *stjarna*, Goth *stairno*, L *stella*, Gk *astḗr*, Skt *str*] —**star′less,** *adj.*

star′ ap′ple, **1.** the edible fruit of a West Indian, sapotaceous tree, *Chrysophyllum Cainito*, which when cut across exhibits a star-shaped figure within. **2.** the tree itself.

Sta·ra Za·go·ra (stä′rä zä gô′rä), a city in central Bulgaria. 88,951 (1964).

star·board (stär′bərd), *n.* **1.** the right-hand side of or direction from a boat or aircraft, facing forward. Cf. **port²** (def. 1). —*adj.* **2.** of, pertaining to, or located to the starboard. **3.** *Naut.* (of a tack) with the wind striking the starboard side of the vessel. —*adv.* **4.** toward the right side. —*v.t., v.i.* **5.** to turn (the helm) to starboard. [ME *sterbord*, OE *stēorbord* = *stēor* steering (see STEER¹) + *bord* side (see BOARD)]

starch (stärch), *n.* **1.** a white, tasteless, solid carbohydrate, $(C_6H_{10}O_5)_n$, occurring in the form of minute granules in the seeds, tubers, and other parts of plants, and forming an important constituent of rice, corn, wheat, beans, potatoes, and many other vegetable foods. **2.** a commercial preparation of this substance used to stiffen textile fabrics in laundering. **3. starches,** foods rich in natural starch. **4.** *Informal.* vigor; energy; stamina; boldness. —*v.t.* **5.** to stiffen or treat with starch, as a shirt collar. [ME *sterche(n)*, OE *stercean* to make stiff, strengthen < *stearc* STARK¹; c. G *stärken* to strengthen] —**starch′less,** *adj.* —**starch′like′,** *adj.*

Star′ Cham′ber, **1.** a former court of inquisitorial and criminal jurisdiction in England, primarily composed of royal councillors, that sat without a jury and that became noted for its arbitrary methods and severe punishments: abolished in 1641. **2.** any tribunal, committee, or the like, that proceeds by arbitrary or unfair methods.

starch′ syr′up, glucose (def. 2).

starch·y (stär′chē), *adj.,* **starch·i·er, starch·i·est.** **1.** of, pertaining to, or of the nature of starch. **2.** containing starch. **3.** stiffened with starch. **4.** stiff and formal, as in manner. —**starch′i·ly,** *adv.* —**starch′i·ness,** *n.*

star-crossed (stär′krôst′, -krost′), *adj.* thwarted or opposed by the stars; ill-fated: *star-crossed lovers.*

star′ cut′, a gem cut having a hexagonal table surrounded by six facets in the form of equilateral triangles.

star·dom (stär′dəm), *n.* **1.** the world or class of professional stars, as of the stage. **2.** the status of a star or preeminent performer.

star′ dust′, **1.** a mass of distant stars appearing as tiny particles of dust. **2.** *Informal.* an extremely and naïvely romantic quality: *There was star dust in her eyes.*

stare (stâr), *v.,* **stared, star·ing,** *n.* —*v.i.* **1.** to gaze fixedly and intently, esp. with the eyes wide open. **2.** to be boldly or obtrusively conspicuous. **3.** (of hair, feathers, etc.) to stand on end; bristle. —*v.t.* **4.** to stare at. **5.** to effect or have a certain effect on by staring: *to stare one out of countenance.* **6. stare down,** to intimidate with a stare. **7. stare one in the face,** to be urgent or impending, as a deadline. —*n.* **8.** a staring gaze; a fixed look with the eyes wide open. [ME; OE *star(ian)*; c. D *staren*, Icel *stara*, G *starren*] —**Syn. 1.** See **gaze.**

sta·re de·ci·sis (stâr′ē di sī′sis), *Law.* the doctrine that principles of law established by judicial decision be accepted as authoritative in cases similar to those from which such principles were derived. [< L: to stand by things (that have been) settled]

star′ fac′et, *Jewelry.* (in a brilliant) any of the eight small facets of the crown immediately below the table.

star·fish (stär′fish′), *n., pl.* (*esp. collectively*) **-fish,** (*esp. referring to two or more kinds or species*) **-fish·es.** any echinoderm of the class *Asteroidea*, having the body radially arranged, usually in the form of a star, with five or more rays or arms radiating from a central disk; asteroid.

Starfish,
Asterias rubens
(Diameter 3½ in.)

star·flow·er (stär′flou′ər), *n.* any of several plants having starlike flowers, as the star-of-Bethlehem or a primulaceous plant of the genus *Trientalis.*

star·gaze (stär′gāz′), *v.i.,* **-gazed, -gaz·ing.** **1.** to gaze at or observe the stars. **2.** to daydream. [back formation from STARGAZER]

star·gaz·er (stär′gā′zər), *n.* **1.** a person who stargazes, as an astronomer or astrologer. **2.** a daydreamer. **3.** an impractical idealist. **4.** any of several marine fishes of the family *Uranoscopidae*, having the eyes at the top of the head.

star′ grass′, any of various grasslike plants having star-shaped flowers or a stellate arrangement of leaves, as an American, amaryllidaceous plant, *Hypoxis hirsuta.*

stark (stärk), *adj.* **1.** sheer, utter, downright, or complete: *stark madness.* **2.** harsh, grim, or desolate: *a stark landscape.* **3.** extremely simple or severe: *a stark interior.* **4.** stiff or rigid in substance, muscles, etc. **5.** rigid in death. —*adv.* **6.** utterly, absolutely, or quite: *stark mad.* [ME; OE *stearc* stiff, firm; c. G *Stark* strong; akin to Icel *sterkr* strong; see STARCH, STARE] —**stark′ly,** *adv.* —**stark′ness,** *n.* —**Syn. 1.** mere, pure, absolute, entire.

Stark (stärk), *n.* **John,** 1728–1822, American Revolutionary War general.

stark-nak·ed (stärk′nā′kid), *adj.* absolutely naked. [r. *start-naked*; ME *start*, OE *steort* tail; c. D *staart*, Icel *stertr*, OHG *sterz*]

star·let (stär′lit), *n.* a young actress promoted and publicized as a future star.

star·light (stär′līt′), *n.* **1.** the light emanating from the stars. —*adj.* **2.** of or pertaining to starlight. **3.** Also, **star′light′ed.** starlit. [late ME]

star·like (stär′līk′), *adj.* **1.** of the shape of or like a star. **2.** shining like a star.

Starling,
Sturnus vulgaris
(Length 8½ in.)

star·ling (stär′ling), *n.* **1.** any of numerous Old World, passerine birds of the family *Sturnidae*, esp. *Sturnus vulgaris*, introduced into North America from Europe. **2.** *Brit.* any of various American birds of the family *Icteridae.* [ME; OE *stærling* = *stær* starling (c. OHG *stara*, Icel *stari*) + *-ling* -LING¹; akin to OE *stearn* TERN, L *sturnus* starling]

star·lit (stär′lit), *adj.* lighted by the stars: *a starlit night.*

star′-nosed mole′ (stär′nōzd′), a North American mole, *Condylura cristata,* having a starlike ring of fleshy processes around the end of the snout. Also, **star′nose mole′.** Also called **star′nose′.**

Star′ of Beth′lehem, the star that guided the Magi to the manger of the infant Jesus in Bethlehem. Matt. 2:1–10.

star-of-Beth·le·hem (stär′əv beth′lē-əm, -li hem′), *n., pl.* **stars-of-Beth·le·hem.** an Old World, liliaceous plant, *Ornithogalum umbellatum,* having star-shaped flowers.

Star′ of Da′vid, a figure symbolic of Judaism, consisting of a six-pointed star formed of two identical equilateral triangles placed one upon the other so that each side of one is trisected by two sides of the other triangle. Also called **Magen David, Mogen David, Shield of David.**

Star of David

starred (stärd), *adj.* **1.** set or studded with or as with stars. **2.** (of a performer) presented as a star. **3.** decorated or marked with a star. [ME]

star′ route′, a mail-delivery route between postal stations, given on contract to a private carrier.

star·ry (stär′ē), *adj.,* **-ri·er, -ri·est. 1.** abounding with or lighted by stars. **2.** of, pertaining to, or proceeding from the stars. **3.** of the nature of or consisting of stars. **4.** resembling a star; star-shaped or stellate. [late ME]

star·ry-eyed (stär′ē īd′), *adj.* excessively romantic or idealistic.

Stars′ and Bars′, the flag adopted by the Confederate States of America.

Stars′ and Stripes′, the national flag of the U.S., consisting of 13 horizontal stripes, alternately red and white, and of a blue canton containing 50 white stars. Also called **Old Glory, The Star-Spangled Banner.**

star′ sap′phire, a sapphire, cut cabochon, exhibiting asterism in the form of a colorless six-rayed star.

star′ shell′, an artillery shell that bursts in the air and produces a bright light to illuminate enemy positions.

star-span·gled (stär′spang′gəld), *adj.* spangled with stars.

Star′-Spangled Ban′ner, The, 1. See **Stars and Stripes. 2.** (*italics*) the national anthem of the United States of America, based on a poem written by Francis Scott Key on September 14, 1814, and set by him to the melody of the English song *To Anacreon in Heaven:* officially adopted by the U.S. Congress in 1931.

star-stud·ded (stär′stud′id), *adj.* **1.** lighted by or full of stars. **2.** exhibiting or characterized by the presence of many preeminent performers, as a motion picture or play.

start (stärt), *v.i.* **1.** to begin, as on a journey or activity. **2.** to appear or come suddenly into action, life, view, etc. **3.** to spring, move, or dart suddenly from a position or place. **4.** to give a sudden, involuntary jerk, jump, or twitch, as from a shock of surprise, or pain. **5.** to protrude or emerge: *eyes seeming to start from their sockets.* **6.** (of an object) to spring, slip, or work loose from a place where it has been fastened. **7.** to be among the entrants in a race or the initial participants in a game or contest. —*v.t.* **8.** to set moving, going, or acting. **9.** to bring into existence, operation, or effect: *to start a new business.* **10.** to begin work upon: *to start a book.* **11.** to enable or help (someone) in beginning a journey, career, etc. **12.** to cause or choose to be an entrant in a game or contest. **13.** to cause (an object) to work loose from a place where it has been fastened. **14.** to rouse (game) from its lair or covert; flush. **15.** *Archaic.* to startle. —*n.* **16.** the beginning of an action, journey, etc. **17.** a signal to move, proceed, or begin, as on a course or in a race. **18.** a place or time at which something begins. **19.** the first or beginning part of anything. **20.** a sudden, springing movement from a position. **21.** a sudden, involuntary jerking movement of the body, as from surprise or pain. **22.** a lead or advance of specified amount, as over competitors or pursuers. **23.** the position or advantage of one who starts first. **24.** a chance, opportunity, aid, or encouragement given to a person starting on a course or career. **25.** the action of parts that work loose from their fastenings. **26.** the resulting break or opening. **27.** *Archaic.* an outburst or sally, as of emotion, wit, or fancy. [ME *sterten* (c. MHG *sterzen*); r. OE *styrtan,* c. G *stürzen*] —**Syn. 10.** See **begin. 16.** commencement, onset.

start·er (stär′tər), *n.* **1.** a person or thing that starts. **2.** a person who gives the signal to begin a race, the running of a bus or elevator, etc. **3.** a self-starter. **4.** one who or that which starts in a race or contest. **5.** a culture of bacteria used to start a particular fermentation. **6.** sourdough (def. 1).

star·tle (stär′tᵊl), *v.,* **-tled, -tling.** —*v.t.* **1.** to disturb or agitate, as with something surprising. **2.** to cause to start involuntarily, by or as by a sudden shock. —*v.i.* **3.** to start involuntarily, as from surprise or alarm. —*n.* **4.** something that startles. [ME *stertle* to rush, caper; akin to OE *steartlian* to kick, struggle] —**star′tling·ly,** *adv.* —**Syn. 1.** scare, frighten, astonish. See **shock**[1]. —**Ant. 1.** calm.

start-up (stärt′up′), *n.* **1.** the act or fact of starting something; a setting in motion. —*adj.* **2.** of or pertaining to an investment made to start a new project, operation, etc., esp. in an industrial enterprise: *high start-up costs.* Also, **start′up′.** [n. use of v. phrase *start up*]

star·va·tion (stär vā′shən), *n.* **1.** the act or an instance of starving. **2.** the condition of being starved. —*adj.* **3.** liable or seeming to cause starving: *a starvation diet.*

starva′tion wag′es, wages below the level necessary for subsistence.

starve (stärv), *v.,* **starved, starv·ing.** —*v.i.* **1.** to die or perish from lack of food or nourishment. **2.** to be in the process of perishing or suffering severely from hunger. **3.** to feel a strong need or craving (usually fol. by *for*): *The child was starving for affection.* **4.** *Chiefly Brit. Dial.* to perish or suffer extremely from cold. **5.** *Obs.* to die. —*v.t.* **6.** to cause to starve; kill, weaken, or reduce by lack of food. **7.** to subdue, or force to some condition or action, by hunger. **8.** to cause to suffer for lack of something needed or craved. **9.** *Chiefly Brit. Dial.* to cause to perish or to suffer extremely from cold. [ME *sterve(n),* OE *steorfan* to die; c. G *sterben*] —**starved·ly** (stärvd′lē, stär′vid-), *adv.* —**starv′er,** *n.*

starve·ling (stärv′ling), *n.* **1.** a person, animal, or plant that is starving. —*adj.* **2.** starving; suffering from lack of nourishment. **3.** poor in condition or quality.

Star′ Wars′, a U.S. weapons research program begun in 1984 to explore technologies, including ground- and space-based lasers, for destroying attacking missiles and warheads. Also called **Strategic Defense Initiative.**

stash (stash), *Informal.* —*v.t.* **1.** to put by or away, as for safekeeping or future use, esp. in a secret place (usually fol. by *away*). —*n.* **2.** a secret hiding place. **3.** something kept or hidden away. [b. STOW and CACHE]

stas·i·mon (stas′ə mon′), *n., pl.* **-ma** (-mə). *Greek.* (in ancient Greek drama) a choral ode, esp. in tragedy, divided into strophe and antistrophe. [lit: standing (neut.)]

sta·sis (stā′sis, stas′is), *n.* **1.** the state of equilibrium or inactivity caused by opposing equal forces. **2.** *Pathol.* stagnation in the flow of any of the fluids of the body, as of the blood in an inflamed area. [< Gk: state of standing = *sta-* (s. of *histánai* to stand; akin to L *stāre* to STAND) + *-sis* -SIS]

-stat, a learned borrowing from Greek meaning "standing," "stationary," "set," used in the formation of compound words, esp. in names of instruments that maintain something in a stable, stationary, or constant state: *thermostat; rheostat.* [< Gk *-statēs* = *sta-* (s. of *histánai* to make stand) + *-itēs* n. agent suffix]

stat., 1. (in prescriptions) immediately. [< L *statim*] **2.** statuary. **3.** statue. **4.** statute.

sta·tant (stāt′ᵊnt), *adj. Heraldry.* (of an animal) represented as standing with all feet on the ground: *a bear statant.* [< L *stat(us)* (ptp. of *stāre;* see STATUS) + -ANT]

state (stāt), *n., adj., v.,* **stat·ed, stat·ing.** —*n.* **1.** the condition of a person or thing with respect to circumstances, qualities, etc.: *a state of disrepair; in a terrible state.* **2.** condition with respect to structure, form, phase, etc.: *water in a gaseous state; the larval state.* **3.** the status or dignity of a person. **4.** a quality or condition that enhances or reflects one's dignity, rank, etc.: *to travel in state.* **5.** a particular emotional condition: *to be in a nervous state.* **6.** an agitated emotional condition: *You are in a state, aren't you?* **7.** a politically unified population occupying a specific area of land; nation. **8.** (*sometimes cap.*) any of the territories, each with its own government, that are combined under a federal government. **9.** governmental activity or concern: *affairs of state.* **10. lie in state,** (of a corpse) to be exhibited publicly with honors before burial. **11. the state,** civil government as distinguished from individuals, ecclesiastical authority, etc. **12. the States,** *Informal.* the United States. —*adj.* **13.** of or pertaining to the central civil government or authority. **14.** of, pertaining to, maintained by, or under the authority of one of the commonwealths that make up a federal union: *a Texas state highway.* **15.** of a ceremonial nature or for ceremonial purposes. —*v.t.* **16.** to declare or set forth, esp. in a precise, formal, or authoritative manner. **17.** to say (something), esp. in an emphatic way; assert. [ME *stat,* partly var. of *estat* (see ESTATE), partly < L *stat(us)* condition (see STATUS); in defs. 8–12 < L *status* (*rērum*) state of things or *status* (*reī publicae*) state of the republic]
—**Syn. 1.** STATE, CONDITION, SITUATION, STATUS are terms for existing circumstances or surroundings. STATE is the general word, often with no concrete implications or material relationships: *the present state of affairs.* CONDITION carries an implication of a relationship to causes and circumstances: *The conditions made flying impossible.* SITUATION suggests an arrangement of circumstances, related to one another and to the character of a person: *He was master of the situation.* STATUS carries official or legal implications; it suggests a complete picture of interrelated circumstances as having to do with rank, position, standing, a stage reached in progress, etc.: *the status of negotiations.*

state′ bank′, *U.S.* a bank chartered by a state.

state′ cap′italism, a form of capitalism in which the central government controls most of the capital, industry, natural resources, etc.

State′ Col′lege, a city in central Pennsylvania. 33,778.

state·craft (stāt′kraft′, -kräft′), *n.* the art of government.

stat·ed (stā′tid), *adj.* **1.** fixed or settled: *a stated price.* **2.** explicitly set forth; declared as fact. **3.** recognized or official.

state′ flow′er, the floral symbol of a state of the U.S.

state·hood (stāt′ho͝od), *n.* the status or condition of being a state, esp. of the U.S.

state·house (stāt′hous′), *n., pl.* **-hous·es** (-hou′ziz). *U.S.* (*sometimes cap.*) the building in which the legislature of a state sits; a state capitol.

state·less (stāt′lis), *adj.* lacking nationality.

state·ly (stāt′lē), *adj.,* **-li·er, -li·est,** *adv.* —*adj.* **1.** majestic; imposing in magnificence, elegance, etc.: *a stately home.* **2.** dignified. —*adv.* **3.** in a stately manner. [late ME *statly*] —**state′li·ness,** *n.* —**Syn. 1.** grand, magnificent.

state′ med′icine. See **socialized medicine.**

state·ment (stāt′mənt), *n.* **1.** something stated. **2.** a detailed or explicit communication. **3.** any one of a number of assertions: *We think some of his statements are highly questionable.* **4.** *Com.* an abstract of an account, as one rendered to show the balance due. **5.** an appearance of a theme, subject, or motif within a musical composition. **6.** the act or manner of stating something. [STATE (v.) + -MENT]

Stat′en Is′land (stat′ᵊn), an island facing New York Bay, comprising Richmond borough of New York City. 295,443 (1970); 64½ sq. mi.

state′ of the art′, the scientific and technical level attained at a given time, as in the computer industry. —**state′-of-the-art′,** *adj.*

state′ of war′, a condition marked by armed conflict between or among states, with or without a formal declaration of war.

state′ police′, a police force under state authority.

sta·ter (stā′tər), *n.* any of various gold or silver or electrum coin units or coins of the ancient Greek states or cities. [< LL < Gk *statḗr,* akin to *histánai* to place in the balance]

state·room (stāt′ro͞om′, -ro͝om′), *n.* a private room or compartment on a ship, train, etc. [STATE (adj.) + ROOM]

state's′ attor′ney, *U.S.* (in judicial proceedings) the legal representative of the State.

state's' ev'idence, *U.S.* **1.** evidence given by an accomplice in a crime who becomes a voluntary witness against the other defendants. **2.** any evidence for the State, esp. in criminal trials.

States-Gen·er·al (stāts′jen′ər əl), *n.* **1.** the parliament of the Netherlands. **2.** *Fr. Hist.* the legislative body in France before the French Revolution.

state·side (stāt′sīd′), *adj.* **1.** being in or toward the U.S. —*adv.* **2.** in or toward the U.S. Also, **State′side′.** [(the) STATES + SIDE[1]]

states·man (stāts′mən), *n., pl.* **-men. 1.** a man who is experienced in the art of government or versed in the administration of government affairs. **2.** a man who exhibits great wisdom and ability in dealing with important public issues. [STATE + 's[1] + MAN[1], modeled on *steersman;* cf. the phrase *ship of state*] —**states′man·like′, states′man·ly,** *adj.* —**states′man·ship′,** *n.* —**Syn. 1.** See **politician.**

state′ so′cialism, the theory, doctrine, and movement advocating a planned economy controlled by the state.

States′ of the Church′. See **Papal States.**

states′′ right′er, a person who opposes U.S. federal intervention in the affairs of the separate states, supporting his position by a strict interpretation of the Constitution of the United States.

states′′ rights′, *U.S.* the rights belonging to the various states, esp. with reference to the strict interpretation of the Constitution.

States′ Rights′ Democrat′ic par′ty, a political party formed by dissident Southern Democrats who opposed the candidacy of Harry Truman in 1948.

state′ troop′er, a member of a police force in the U.S. operated by a state government and having statewide jurisdiction.

state′ univer′sity, *U.S.* a public university maintained by the government of a state.

state·wide (stāt′wīd′), *adj.* **1.** (*sometimes cap.*) extending throughout all parts of a state. —*adv.* **2.** (*sometimes cap.*) throughout a state.

stat·ic (stat′ik), *adj.* Also, **stat′i·cal. 1.** pertaining to or characterized by a fixed or stationary condition. **2.** showing or admitting of little or no change. **3.** lacking movement, development, or vitality. **4.** *Sociol.* referring to a condition of social life bound by tradition. **5.** *Elect.* pertaining to or noting static electricity. **6.** *Physics.* acting by mere weight without producing motion: *static pressure.* —*n.* **7.** *Elect.* **a.** static or atmospheric electricity. **b.** interference with radio or radar signals as a result of electrical disturbances. [< NL *static(us)* < G *statikós* = *sta-* (s. of *histánai* to make stand) + *-tikos* -TIC] —**stat′i·cal·ly,** *adv.*

stat′ic electric′ity, *Elect.* the electricity contained or produced by charged bodies.

stat·ics (stat′iks), *n.* (*construed as sing.*) the branch of mechanics that deals with bodies at rest or forces in equilibrium. [see STATIC, -ICS]

stat′ic tube′, a tube for measuring the static pressure of a fluid in motion, so placed in the fluid as not to be affected by the pressure changes caused by the motion of the fluid.

sta·tion (stā′shən), *n.* **1.** a place or position in which a person or thing is normally located. **2.** a stopping place for trains or other land conveyances, for the transfer of freight or passengers. **3.** a place for the local conduct of a service or business: *a police station; a gasoline station.* **4.** a building or group of buildings belonging to any such place. **5.** the rank, social standing, etc., of an individual. **6.** *Mil.* a military place of duty. **7.** *Navy.* a place or region to which a ship or fleet is assigned for duty. **8.** (formerly in India) the area in which the British officials of a district or the officers of a garrison resided. **9.** *Radio and Television.* **a.** a studio room or building from which broadcasts originate. **b.** a person or an organization originating and broadcasting messages or programs. **c.** a specific frequency or band of frequencies assigned to a regular or special broadcaster: *tune to the Civil Defense station.* **d.** the complete equipment used in transmitting and receiving broadcasts. **10.** *Biol.* a particular area or type of region where a given animal or plant is found. **11.** *Australian.* a ranch with its buildings, land, etc., esp. for raising sheep. **12.** *Survey.* **a.** a point where an observation is taken. **b.** a precisely located reference point. **c.** a length of 100 feet along a survey line. **13.** Also called **cross section.** *Naval Archit.* any of a series of lines on the lines plan of a hull, corresponding to the location of a frame. —*v.t.* **14.** to assign a station to; place or post in a station or position. [< L *statiōn-* (s. of *statiō*) a standing still, standing place = *stat(us)* (ptp. of *stāre* to stand) + *-iōn-* -ION; r. ME *stacioun* < AF] —**sta′tion·al,** *adj.*
—**Syn. 1.** situation, location. **2.** STATION, DEPOT, and TERMINAL are not properly synonyms. A STATION is a stopping place along a route where passengers may get on and off trains or other vehicles: *Union Station.* A DEPOT is a storehouse or warehouse: *a depot in the wing of the station building.* In the early days in the U.S., the station waiting room and the freight depot were usually in the same building and, as a result, the names were confused. A TERMINAL is, literally, at the end of a rail, bus, or other transportation line, but STATION has become the more common word and is applied generally to both a stopping place along a route and the end of a route. **14.** position, locate, establish, set, fix.

sta′tion a′gent, a person who manages a small railroad station.

sta·tion·ar·y (stā′shə ner′ē), *adj., n., pl.* **-ar·ies.** —*adj.* **1.** standing still; not moving. **2.** having a fixed position; not movable. **3.** established in one place; not itinerant or migratory. **4.** remaining in the same condition or state; not changing. —*n.* **5.** a person or thing that is stationary. [< L *statiōnāri(us)*] —**sta·tion·ar·i·ly** (stā′shə ner′ə lē, stā′shə nâr′-), *adv.*

sta′tionary en′gine, an engine mounted in a fixed position, as one used to drive a generator. —**sta′tionary engineer′.**

sta′tionary wave′. See **standing wave.**

sta′tion break′, *Radio and Television.* an interval between or during programs for identifying the station, making announcements, etc.

sta·tion·er (stā′shə nər), *n.* **1.** a person who sells stationery. **2.** *Archaic.* **a.** a bookseller. **b.** a publisher. [ME *stacio(u)ner* < ML *statiōnār(ius)* (see STATIONARY) of dealers with permanent shops as distinguished from itinerant vendors]

Sta′tioners' Com′pany, a company or guild of the City of London comprised of booksellers, printers, and the like, incorporated in 1557.

sta·tion·er·y (stā′shə ner′ē), *n.* **1.** writing paper. **2.** writing materials, as pens, pencils, paper, etc.

sta′tion house′, 1. See **police station. 2.** See **fire station.**

sta·tion·mas·ter (stā′shən mas′tər, -mä′stər), *n.* a person in charge of a railroad station; station agent.

sta′tions of the cross′, *Eccles.* a series of 14 representations of successive incidents from the Passion of Christ, each with a wooden cross, visited in sequence, for prayer and meditation. Also, **Sta′tions of the Cross′.**

sta·tion-to-sta·tion (stā′shən tə stā′shən), *adj.* **1.** (of a long-distance telephone call) chargeable upon speaking with anyone at the number called. —*adv.* **2.** from one station to another. **3.** by telephone at station-to-station rates. Cf. **person-to-person** (defs. 1, 3).

sta′tion wag′on, *U.S.* an automobile with one or more rows of folding or removable seats behind the driver and an area behind the seats into which suitcases, parcels, etc., can be loaded through a tailgate.

stat·ism (stā′tiz əm), *n.* **1.** the principle of concentrating extensive economic and political controls in the state. **2.** support of the sovereignty of a state. —**stat′ist,** *n., adj.*

sta·tis·tic (stə tis′tik), *n.* a numerical fact or datum. [< NL *statistic(us).* See STATUS, -ISTIC]

sta·tis·ti·cal (stə tis′ti kəl), *adj.* of, pertaining to, consisting of, or based on statistics. [STATISTIC(S) + -AL[1]] —**sta·tis′ti·cal·ly,** *adv.*

stat·is·ti·cian (stat′i stish′ən), *n.* an expert in or compiler of statistics.

sta·tis·tics (stə tis′tiks), *n.* **1.** (*construed as sing.*) the science that deals with the collection, classification, analysis, and interpretation of numerical facts or data, and that, by use of mathematical theories of probability, imposes order and regularity on aggregates of more or less disparate elements. **2.** (*construed as pl.*) the numerical facts or data themselves. [see STATISTIC, -ICS]

Sta·ti·us (stā′shē əs), *n.* **Pub·li·us Pa·pin·i·us** (pub′lē əs pə pin′ē əs), A.D. c45–c96, Roman poet.

sta·tive (stā′tiv), *adj.* (of a verb) expressing a state. [< NL *statīv(us),* L = *stat(us)* (ptp. of *stāre* to stand) + *-īvus* -IVE]

stat·o·blast (stat′ə blast′), *n.* *Zool.* (in certain bryozoans) an asexually produced group of cells encased in a chitinous covering that can survive unfavorable conditions and germinate to produce a new colony. [*stato-* (comb. form of Gk *statós* standing; akin to STATUS, STATIC) + -BLAST]

stat·o·cyst (stat′ə sist′), *n.* *Zool.* (in certain invertebrates) a sense organ consisting of a sac enclosing sensory hairs and particles of sand, lime, etc., that has an equilibrating function serving to indicate position in space. [*stato-* (see STATOBLAST) + -CYST]

stat·o·lith (stat′əlith), *n.* *Zool.* any of the granules of lime, sand, etc., contained within a statocyst. [*stato-* (see STATOBLAST) + -LITH] —**stat′o·lith′ic,** *adj.*

sta·tor (stā′tər), *n.* *Elect.* a portion of a machine that remains fixed with respect to rotating parts, esp. the collection of stationary parts in the magnetic circuits of a machine (opposed to *rotor*). [< NL, L: one that stands. See STATUS, -OR[2]]

stat·o·scope (stat′ə skōp′), *n.* **1.** an aneroid barometer for registering minute variations of atmospheric pressure. **2.** *Aeron.* an instrument for detecting a small rate of rise or fall of an aircraft. [*stato-* (see STATOBLAST) + -SCOPE]

stat·u·ar·y (stach′ōō er′ē), *n., pl.* **-ar·ies,** *adj.* —*n.* **1.** statues collectively. **2.** a group or collection of statues. —*adj.* **3.** of, pertaining to, or suitable for statues. [< L *statuāri(us)*]

stat·ue (stach′ōō), *n.* a three-dimensional work of art, as a representation of a person or animal or an abstract form. [ME < MF < L *statu(a)* = *statu(s)* (see STATUS) + *-a* fem. ending]

stat·ued (stach′ōōd), *adj.* having or ornamented with statues.

Stat′ue of Lib′erty, a large copper statue, on Liberty Island, in New York harbor: presented to the U.S. by France, and designed by F.A. Bartholdi; unveiled 1886.

stat·u·esque (stach′ōō esk′), *adj.* like or suggesting a statue, as in massive or majestic dignity, grace, or beauty. —**stat′u·esque′ly,** *adv.* —**stat′u·esque′ness,** *n.*

stat·u·ette (stach′ōō et′), *n.* a small statue. [< F]

stat·ure (stach′ər), *n.* **1.** the height of an animal body, esp. of a person. **2.** the height of any object. **3.** degree of development attained; level of achievement. [ME < OF *(e)stature* < L *statūr(a).* See STATUS, -URE] —**Syn. 3.** status; importance.

sta·tus (stā′təs, stat′əs), *n.* **1.** the position of an individual in relation to another or others. **2.** a state or condition of affairs. **3.** *Law.* the standing of a person before the law. [< L = *sta-* (var. s. of *stāre* to STAND) + *-tus* n. use of *-tus* ptp. suffix] —**Syn. 2.** See **state.**

sta′tus quo′ (kwō), the existing state or condition. Also called **sta′tus in quo′.** [< L: lit., state in which]

sta′tus sym′bol, an object, habit, style of living, etc., by which the social or economic status of the possessor may be or is intended to be judged.

stat·u·ta·ble (stach′ōō tə bəl), *adj.* prescribed, authorized, or permitted by statute. —**stat′u·ta·ble·ness,** *n.* —**stat′u·ta·bly,** *adv.*

stat·ute (stach′ōōt, -ŏŏt), *n.* **1.** *Law.* an enactment made by a legislature and expressed in a formal document. **2.** *Internat. Law.* an instrument annexed or subsidiary to an international agreement, as a treaty. **3.** a permanent rule established by an organization, corporation, etc., to govern its internal affairs. [ME *statut* < OF *(e)statut* < LL *statūt(um)*, neut. of L *statūtus* (ptp. of *statuere* to make stand, set up) = *statū-* (see STATUS) + *-tus* ptp. suffix] —**Syn. 1.** act, law, ordinance.

stat′ute mile′, mile (def. 1).

stat′ute of limita′tions, *Law.* a statute defining the period within which action may be taken on some legal issue. Cf. **laches.**

stat·u·to·ry (stach′o͝o tôr′ē, -tōr′ē), *adj.* **1.** of, pertaining to, or of the nature of a statute. **2.** prescribed or authorized by statute. **3.** (of an offense) recognized by statute; legally punishable. —**stat′u·to′ri·ly,** *adv.*

stat′utory law′, the written law as distinguished from the unwritten law or common law. Also called **stat′ute law′.**

stat′utory offense′, *Law.* a wrong punishable under a statute, rather than at common law. Also called **stat′utory crime′.**

stat′utory rape′, *U.S. Law.* sexual intercourse with a girl under the age of consent.

St. Au·gus·tine (ô′gə stēn′), a seacoast city in NE Florida: founded by the Spanish 1565; oldest city in the U.S.; resort. 12,352 (1970).

staunch[1] (stônch), *v.t., v.i.* stanch[1].

staunch[2] (stônch, stänch), *adj.* **1.** characterized by firmness, steadfastness, or loyalty. **2.** strong; substantial. Also, **stanch.** [late ME *sta(u)nch* watertight < MF *(e)stanche* (fem.), *estanc* (masc.) < *estancher* to STANCH[1]] —**staunch′ly,** *adv.* —**staunch′ness,** *n.* —**Syn. 1.** constant, true, faithful. See **steadfast. 2.** stout, sound.

stau·ro·lite (stôr′ə līt′), *n.* a mineral, basic iron aluminum silicate, $HFeAl_5Si_2O_{13}$, often occurring in crystals twinned in the form of a cross. [< Gk *staurό(s)* cross + -LITE] —**stau·ro·lit·ic** (stôr′ə lit′ik), *adj.*

stau·ro·scope (stôr′ə skōp′), *n. Obs.* an optical instrument for determining the position of the planes of light vibration in sections of crystals. [< Gk *staurό(s)* cross + -SCOPE] —**stau·ro·scop·ic** (stôr′ə skop′ik), *adj.* —**stau′ro·scop′i·cal·ly,** *adv.*

Sta·vang·er (stä väng′ər), *n.* a seaport in SW Norway. 78,435 (est. 1965).

stave (stāv), *n., v.,* **staved or stove, stav·ing.** —*n.* **1.** one of the thin, narrow, shaped pieces of wood which form the sides of a cask, tub, or similar vessel. **2.** a stick, rod, pole, or the like. **3.** a rung of a ladder, chair, etc. **4.** *Pros.* **a.** a verse or stanza of a poem or song. **b.** the alliterating sound in a line of verse, as the *w*-sound in *wind in the willows.* **5.** *Music.* staff[1] (def. 8). —*v.t.* **6.** to break in a stave or staves of (a cask or barrel) so as to release the wine, liquor, or other contents. **7.** to release (wine, liquor, etc.) by breaking the cask or barrel. **8.** to break or crush (something) inward (often fol. by *in*). **9.** to break (a hole) in, esp. in the hull of a boat. **10.** to break to pieces; splinter; smash. **11.** to furnish with a stave or staves. **12.** to beat with a stave or staff. —*v.i.* **13.** to become staved in, as a boat; break in or up. **14. stave off, a.** to put, ward, or keep off, as by force or evasion. **b.** to prevent in time; forestall. [ME; back formation from STAVES] —**Syn. 4.** See **verse.**

staves (stāvz), *n.* **1.** a pl. of **staff**[1]. **2.** pl. of **stave.**

staves·a·cre (stāvz′ā′kər), *n.* **1.** a larkspur, *Delphinium staphisagria,* having violently emetic and cathartic poisonous seeds. **2.** the seeds themselves. [late ME *staphisagre* < L *staphis agria* < Gk *staphís* raisin + *agría* wild (fem.)]

Stav·ro·pol (stäv′ʀo pol′), *n.* a city in the SW RSFSR, in the S Soviet Union in Europe. 162,000 (est. 1964). Formerly, **Voroshilovsk.**

stay[1] (stā), *v.,* **stayed or staid, stay·ing,** *n.* —*v.i.* **1.** to spend some time at a place, in a situation, with a person or group, etc. **2.** to continue to be at a place, in someone's company, etc.: *Can't you stay a while?* **3.** to continue to be as specified: *Stay well!* **4.** to reside temporarily. **5.** to come to a halt or pause. **6.** *Informal.* to continue or endure, as in a task or competition (usually fol. by *with*). **7.** *Poker.* to continue in a hand by matching an ante, bet, or raise. **8.** *Archaic.* to cease or desist. **9.** *Archaic.* to stand firm. —*v.t.* **10.** to stop or halt. **11.** to hold back, detain, or restrain. **12.** to suppress or quell (an emotion, violence, etc.). **13.** to appease or satisfy temporarily the cravings of (the stomach, appetite, etc.). **14.** to remain through or during (a period of time): *They stayed several days in each of the major European cities.* **15.** to remain to the end of; remain beyond (usually fol. by *out*). **16.** to endure (the demands of a contest, task, etc.). **17.** *Archaic.* to await. —*n.* **18.** the act of stopping or being stopped. **19.** a stop, halt, or pause. **20.** a sojourn or temporary residence: *a week's stay in Miami.* **21.** *Law.* suspension of a judicial proceeding. **22.** *Obs.* a cause of stoppage or restraint; obstacle. [late ME *staie(n)* < AF *(e)stai(er),* OF *estai-,* s. of *ester* < L *stāre* to STAND] —**Syn. 1.** abide, sojourn. **2.** remain. **5.** delay. **11.** obstruct, arrest, check, curb, prevent. **13.** curb, allay. **18.** interruption, break. —**Ant. 1.** leave.

stay[2] (stā), *n., v.,* **stayed, stay·ing.** —*n.* **1.** something used to support or steady a thing; prop; brace. **2.** a flat strip of steel, plastic, etc., used esp. for stiffening corsets, collars, etc. **3. stays,** *Chiefly Brit.* a corset. —*v.t.* **4.** to support, prop, or hold up (sometimes fol. by *up*). **5.** to sustain or strengthen mentally or spiritually. [appar. same as STAY[3]; cf. OF *estayer* to hold in place, support, perh. < ME *steye* STAY[3]]

stay[3] (stā), *n., v.,* **stayed, stay·ing.** *Chiefly Naut.* —*n.* **1.** any of various strong ropes or wires for steadying masts, funnels, etc. **2. in stays, a.** (of a fore-and-aft-rigged vessel) heading into the wind with sails shaking, as in coming about. **b.** (of a square-rigged vessel) with the fore yards aback, as in tacking. Cf. **iron** (def. 11a). —*v.t.* **3.** to support or secure with a stay or stays: *to stay a mast.* **4.** to put (a ship) on the other tack. —*v.i.* **5.** (of a ship) to change to the other tack. [ME *stey(e),* OE *stæg;* c. G *Stag*]

stay-at-home (stā′ət hōm′), *n.* a person who stays at home a good deal; homebody.

stay′ing pow′er, ability or strength to last or endure.

stay·sail (stā′sāl′; *Naut.* stā′səl), *n. Naut.* any sail set on a stay, as a triangular sail between two masts. See diag. at **ship.**

S.T.B., **1.** Bachelor of Sacred Theology. [< L *Sacrae Theologiae Baccalaureus*] **2.** Bachelor of Theology. [< L *Scientiae Theologicae Baccalaureus*]

St. Ber·nard (sānt′ bər närd′; *for 1, 2 also Fr.* sᴀɴ bᴇʀ ɴᴀʀ′), **1. Great,** a mountain pass between SW Switzerland and NW Italy, in the Pennine Alps: Napoleon led his army through it in 1800; location of a hospice. 8108 ft. high. **2. Little,** a mountain pass between SE France and NW Italy, in the Alps, S of Mont Blanc. 7177 ft. high. **3.** See **Saint Bernard.**

St. Bri·euc (sᴀɴ brē œ′), a city in NW France. 47,307 (1962).

St. Catharines, a city in SE Ontario, in SE Canada. 84,472 (1961).

St. Charles, a city in E Missouri, on the Missouri River. 31,834 (1970).

St. Christopher. See **St. Kitts.**

St. Clair (sānt′ klâr′; *for 1 also* sing′klâr, sin′-), **1. Arthur,** 1736–1818, American Revolutionary War general, born in Scotland: 1st governor of the Northwest Territory, 1787–1802. **2.** a river in the N central U.S. and S Canada, flowing S from Lake Huron to Lake St. Clair, forming part of the boundary between Michigan and Ontario. 41 mi. long. **3. Lake,** a lake between SE Michigan and Ontario, Canada. 26 mi. long; 460 sq. mi.

St. Clair Shores, a city in SE Michigan, near Detroit. 88,093 (1970).

St. Cloud (sānt′ kloud′ *for 1;* sᴀɴ klo͞o′ *for 2*), **1.** a city in central Minnesota, on the Mississippi. 39,691 (1970). **2.** a suburb of Paris in N France, on the Seine: former royal palace. 26,746 (1962).

St. Croix (kroi), **1.** Also called **Santa Cruz.** a U.S. island in the N Lesser Antilles: the largest of the Virgin Islands. 31,779 (1970); 80 sq. mi. **2.** a river flowing from NW Wisconsin along the boundary between Wisconsin and Minnesota into the Mississippi. 164 mi. long. **3.** a river in the NE United States and SE Canada, forming a part of the boundary between Maine and New Brunswick, flowing into Passamaquoddy Bay. 75 mi. long.

St. Cyr-l'É·cole (sᴀɴ sēʀ lā kôl′), a town in N France, W of Versailles: military academy. 9610 (1962).

std., standard.

S.T.D., Doctor of Sacred Theology. [< L *Sacrae Theologiae Doctor*]

St. Den·is (sānt′ den′is; *Fr.* sᴀɴ də nē′), **1. Ruth,** 1880?–1968, U.S. dancer. **2.** a suburb of Paris in N France: famous abbey, the burial place of many French kings. 95,072 (1962). **3.** a seaport in and the capital of Réunion island, in the Indian Ocean. 41,863 (est. 1960).

Ste., (referring to a woman) Saint. [< F *Sainte*]

stead (sted), *n.* **1.** the place of a person or thing as occupied by a successor or substitute: *The nephew of the queen came in her stead.* **2.** *Obs.* a place or locality. **3. stand in good stead,** to be useful to, esp. in a critical situation. —*v.t.* **4.** *Archaic.* to be of service, advantage, or avail to. [ME, OE *stede;* c. G *Stätte* place; akin to G *Stadt,* Icel *stathr,* Goth *staths;* see STATION, STASIS]

stead·fast (sted′fast′, -fäst′, -fəst), *adj.* **1.** fixed in direction; steadily directed: *a steadfast gaze.* **2.** firm, as in purpose, resolution, etc. **3.** firmly established, as an institution or a state of affairs. **4.** firmly fixed in place or position. Also, **stedfast.** [ME *stedefast,* OE *stedefæst*] —**stead′fast′ly,** *adv.* —**stead′fast′ness,** *n.*

—**Syn. 2.** sure, dependable, reliable, constant, unwavering. STEADFAST, STAUNCH, STEADY imply a sureness and continuousness that may be depended upon. STEADFAST literally means fixed in place, but is chiefly used figuratively to indicate undeviating constancy or resolution: *steadfast in one's faith.* STAUNCH literally means watertight, as of a vessel, and therefore strong and firm; figuratively, it is used of loyal support that will endure strain: *a staunch advocate of free trade.* Literally, STEADY is applied to that which is relatively firm in position or continuous in movement or duration; figuratively, it implies sober regularity or persistence: *to work at a steady pace.* **3, 4.** stable. —**Ant. 2.** capricious, variable.

stead·ing (sted′ing), *n. Scot. and North Eng.* **1.** the farmhouse, barns, and all outbuildings on a farm. **2.** a building lot or site.

stead·y (sted′ē), *adj.,* **stead·i·er, stead·i·est,** *interj., n., pl.* **stead·ies,** *v.,* **stead·ied, stead·y·ing,** *adv.* —*adj.* **1.** firmly placed or fixed; stable in position or equilibrium: *a steady ladder.* **2.** even or regular in movement or rhythm. **3.** free from change, variation, or interruption; uniform; continuous. **4.** regular or habitual: *a steady customer.* **5.** firm; unfaltering: *a steady gaze; a steady hand.* **6.** steadfast or unwavering; resolute: *a steady purpose.* **7.** *Naut.* (of a vessel) keeping nearly upright, as in a heavy sea. **8. go steady,** *Informal.* to date exclusively one person of the opposite sex. —*interj.* **9.** be calm; control yourself. —*n.* **10.** *Informal.* a person of the opposite sex whom one dates exclusively. —*v.t.* **11.** to make or keep steady, as in position, movement, action, character, etc. —*v.i.* **12.** to become steady. —*adv.* **13.** in a firm or steady manner: *Hold the ladder steady.* —**stead′i·er,** *n.* —**stead′i·ly,** *adv.* —**stead′i·ness,** *n.* —**stead′y·ing·ly,** *adv.* —**Syn. 1.** balanced. **3.** undeviating, invariable. **6.** See **steadfast.**

stead′y-state′ the′ory (sted′ē stāt′), *Astron.* the theory that the universe does not go through a cycle of explosion and contraction but is unlimited and will constantly expand. Cf. **big-bang theory.**

steak (stāk), *n.* **1.** a slice of meat, esp. beef or fish, cooked by broiling, frying, etc. **2.** chopped meat prepared in the same manner as a steak. [ME *steike* < Scand; cf. Icel *steik,* akin to *steikja* to roast on a spit, *stikna* to be roasted; see STICK[1]]

steak·house (stāk′hous′), *n., pl.* **-hous·es** (-hou′ziz). a restaurant specializing in beefsteak.

steak′ knife′, a sharp dinner knife having a steel blade that is usually serrated.

steak′ tar′tare. See **tartar steak.**

steal (stēl), *v.,* **stole, sto·len, steal·ing,** *n.* —*v.t.* **1.** to take (the property of another or others) without permission or right, esp. secretly or by force. **2.** to appropriate (ideas, credit, words, etc.) without right or acknowledgment. **3.** to take, get, or win artfully or surreptitiously. **4.** to move, bring, convey, or put secretly or quietly; smuggle (usually fol. by *away, from, in, into,* etc.). **5.** *Baseball.* (of a base runner) to gain (a base) without the help of a walk or batted ball, as by running to it during the delivery of a pitch. —*v.i.* **6.** to commit or practice theft. **7.** to move, go, or come secretly, quietly, or unobserved. **8.** to pass, happen, etc., imperceptibly, gently, or gradually: *The years steal by.* **9.** *Baseball.* (of a base runner) to advance a base without the help of a walk or batted ball. **10. steal someone's thunder,** to appropriate or use another's idea, plan, words, etc. —*n.* **11.** something stolen or plagiarized. **12.** *Informal.* something acquired at a cost far below its real value; bargain. **13.** *Baseball.* the act of advancing a base by stealing. [ME *stele(n),* OE *stelan;* c. G *stehlen,* Icel *stela,* Goth *stilan*] —**steal′er,** *n.* —**Syn. 1.** pilfer, purloin, filch.

steal·age (stē′lij), *n.* **1.** the act of stealing. **2.** losses due to theft.

stealth (stelth), *n.* **1.** secret, clandestine, or surreptitious procedure. **2.** *Obs.* a furtive departure or entrance. **3.** *Obs.* **a.** an act of stealing; theft. **b.** the thing stolen; booty. [ME *stelthe;* cf. OE *stælthing* theft. See STEAL, -TH[1]] —**stealth′ful,** *adj.* —**stealth′ful·ly,** *adv.* —**stealth′less,** *adj.*

stealth·y (stel′thē), *adj.,* **stealth·i·er, stealth·i·est.** done, characterized, or acting by stealth; furtive: *stealthy footsteps.* —**stealth′i·ly,** *adv.* —**stealth′i·ness,** *n.* —**Syn.** surreptitious, secret, clandestine, sly.

steam (stēm), *n.* **1.** water in the form of an invisible gas or vapor. **2.** the mist formed when the gas or vapor from boiling water condenses in the air. **3.** an exhalation of a vapor or mist. **4.** *Informal.* power or energy. **5. blow off** or **let off steam,** *Slang.* to give vent to one's repressed emotions, esp. by talking or behaving in an unrestrained manner. —*v.i.* **6.** to emit or give off steam or vapor. **7.** to rise or pass off in the form of steam or vapor. **8.** to become covered with condensed steam, as a window or other surface (often fol. by *up*). **9.** to generate or produce steam, as in a boiler. **10.** to move or travel by the agency of steam. **11.** *Informal.* to be angry or show anger. —*v.t.* **12.** to expose to or treat with steam, as in order to heat, cook, soften, etc. —*adj.* **13.** operated by or employing steam. **14.** conducting steam: *a steam line.* **15.** of or pertaining to steam. [ME *steme,* OE *stēam;* c. D *stoom*] —**steam′less,** *adj.*

steam′ bath′, **1.** a bath of steam, usually in a specially equipped room or enclosure, for cleansing or refreshing oneself. **2.** a special room or establishment for such a bath.

steam·boat (stēm′bōt′), *n.* a steam-driven vessel, esp. a small one or one used on inland waters.

steam′ boil′er, a receptacle in which water is boiled to generate steam.

steam′ en′gine, an engine worked by steam, typically one in which a sliding piston in a cylinder is moved by the expansive action of the steam generated in a boiler. —**steam′-en′gine,** *adj.*

steam·er (stē′mər), *n.* **1.** something propelled or operated by steam, as a steamship. **2.** a person or thing that steams. **3.** a device or container in which something is steamed. **4.** See **soft-shell clam.** —*v.i.* **5.** to travel by steamship.

steam′er bas′ket, a basket, usually decorated, containing elaborately arranged fruits, sweets, and the like, sent to a person departing on a trip, esp. by ship.

steam′er chair′. See **deck chair.**

steam′er rug′, **1.** a coarse, heavy lap robe used by ship passengers sitting in deck chairs. **2.** rug (def. 3).

steam′er trunk′, a rectangular traveling trunk low enough to slide under a bunk on a ship.

steam′ fit′ter, a person who installs and repairs steam-pipes and their accessories. —**steam′ fit′ting.**

steam′ heat′, heat obtained by the circulation of steam in pipes, radiators, etc.

steam′ i′ron, an electric iron with a water chamber from which steam is emitted onto the fabric being ironed.

steam′ point′, the temperature at which water vapor condenses at a pressure of one atmosphere, represented by 100°C and 212°F. Cf. **ice point.**

steam·roll·er (stēm′rō′lər), *n.* Also, **steam′ roll′er. 1.** a heavy, steam-powered vehicle having a roller for crushing, compacting, or leveling materials used for a road or the like. **2.** (not in technical use) any powered vehicle having a roller for this purpose. —*v.t.* **3.** to move, go over, crush, or defeat as with a steamroller or an overpowering force. —*adj.* **4.** suggestive of a steamroller; ruthlessly overpowering: *steamroller tactics.* Also, **steam′-roll′er** (for defs. 3, 4).

steam′ room′, a steam-filled and -heated room to induce sweating, as in a Turkish bath.

steam·ship (stēm′ship′), *n.* a large commercial power vessel, esp. one driven by steam.

steam′ shov′el, a machine for digging or excavating operated by its own engine and boiler.

Steam shovel

steam′ ta′ble, a boxlike table or counter, usually of stainless steel, with receptacles in the top into which containers of food may be fitted to be kept warm by steam or hot water.

steam·tight (stēm′tīt′), *adj.* impervious to steam under pressure. —**steam′tight′ness,** *n.*

steam·y (stē′mē), *adj.,* **steam·i·er, steam·i·est. 1.** consisting of or resembling steam. **2.** full of or abounding in steam; emitting steam. **3.** covered with or as with condensed steam. **4.** hot and humid.

Ste. Anne de Beau·pré (sānt an′ də bō prā′; *Fr.* sɑɴ tɑɴ də bō prā′), a village in S Quebec, in SE Canada, on the St. Lawrence, NE of Quebec: Roman Catholic shrine. 1878 (1961).

ste·ap·sin (stē ap′sin), *n.* *Biochem.* the lipase of the pancreatic juice. [STEA(R)- + (PE)PSIN]

stear-, var. of **stearo-** before a vowel: *stearate.*

ste·a·rate (stē′ə rāt′, stēr′āt), *n.* *Chem.* a salt or ester of stearic acid.

ste·ar·ic (stē ar′ik, stēr′ik), *adj.* **1.** of or pertaining to suet or fat. **2.** of or derived from stearic acid.

stear′ic ac′id, *Chem.* a waxlike solid, $CH_3(CH_2)_{16}COOH$, the most common fatty acid, occurring as the glyceride in animal fats: used chiefly in the manufacture of soaps, stearates, candles, and cosmetics.

ste·a·rin (stē′ər in, stēr′in), *n.* **1.** *Chem.* any of the three glyceryl esters of stearic acid, esp. $C_3H_5(C_{18}H_{35}O_2)_3$. **2.** the crude commercial form of stearic acid, used chiefly in the manufacture of candles. Also, **ste·a·rine** (stē′ər in, -ə rēn′, stēr′in). [< F *stéarine* < Gk *stéar* fat, grease + F *-ine* -INE[2], -IN[2]]

stearo-, a learned borrowing from Greek, where it meant "fat", used with this meaning, and with reference to stearic acid and its related compounds, in the formation of compound words: *stearoptene.* Also, *esp. before a vowel,* **stear-.** [comb. form repr. Gk *stéar* fat, grease. Cf. STEATO-]

ste·a·rop·tene (stē′ə rop′tēn), *n.* *Chem.* the oxygenated solid part of an essential oil (opposed to *eleoptine*). [STEARO- + Gk *ptēn(ós)* winged, volatile; cf. ELAEOPTENE]

ste·a·tite (stē′ə tīt′), *n.* soapstone. [< L *steatīt(s).* See STEATO-, -ITE[1]] —**ste·a·tit·ic** (stē′ə tit′ik), *adj.*

steato-, a learned borrowing from Greek meaning "fat," "tallow"; used in the formation of compound words: *steatopygia.* Also, *esp. before a vowel,* **steat-.** [< Gk *steat-* (s. of *stéar;* see STEARO-) + -o-]

ste·a·to·py·gi·a (stē′ə tō pī′jē ə, -pij′ē ə), *n.* extreme accumulation of fat on and about the buttocks, esp. of women, as among the Hottentots, Bushmen, and certain other South African peoples. Also, **ste·a·to·py·gy** (stē′ə tə-pī′jē, stē′ə top′i jē). [STEATO- + Gk *pyg(ḗ)* buttocks + *-ia* -IA] —**ste·a·to·pyg·ic** (stē′ə tō pij′ik), **ste·a·to·py·gous** (stē′ə tō pī′gəs, -top′ə gəs), *adj.*

ste·a·tor·rhe·a (stē′ə tə rē′ə), *n.* *Pathol.* the presence of excess fat in the stools, usually caused by disease of the pancreas or intestine, and characterized by chronic diarrhea and weight loss. Also, **ste′a·tor·rhoe′a.**

sted·fast (sted′fast′, -fäst′, -fəst), *adj.* steadfast. —**sted′fast′ly,** *adv.* —**sted′fast′ness,** *n.*

steed (stēd), *n.* a horse, esp. a high-spirited horse for riding. [ME *stēde,* OE *stēda* stallion < *stōd* STUD[2]; cf. G *Stute*]

steek (stēk, stāk), *v.t.* *Scot.* to shut, close, fasten or lock (a window, door, or the like). [ME (north) *steke,* OE *stic(ian)* (to) prick, stab, whence STITCH[1]]

steel (stēl), *n.* **1.** any of various modified forms of iron, artificially produced, having a carbon content less than that of pig iron and more than that of wrought iron, and having varying qualities of hardness, elasticity, and strength. **2.** a thing or things made of this metal. **3. steels,** stocks or bonds of companies producing this metal. **4.** a sword. —*adj.* **5.** pertaining to or made of steel. **6.** like steel in color, hardness, or strength. —*v.t.* **7.** to fit with steel, as by pointing, edging, or overlaying. **8.** to cause to resemble steel in some way. **9.** to render firmly determined upon or prepared for an action or occurrence. [ME, OE (north) *stēle;* c. D *staal,* G *Stahl,* Icel *stāl*]

steel′ band′, *Music.* a band, native to Trinidad and common in other Caribbean islands, using steel oil drums cut to various heights and tuned to specific pitches.

steel′ blue′, dark bluish gray.

Steele (stēl), *n.* **Sir Richard,** 1672–1729, English essayist, journalist, dramatist, and political leader; born in Ireland.

steel′ engrav′ing, *Print.* **1.** a method of incising letters, designs, etc., on steel. **2.** the imprint, as on paper, from a plate of engraved steel.

steel′ gray′, dark metallic gray with a bluish tinge.

steel·head (stēl′hed′), *n., pl.* **-heads,** (*esp. collectively*) **-head.** a silvery rainbow trout that migrates to the sea before returning to fresh water to spawn.

steel·mak·ing (stēl′mā′king), *n.* the manufacture of steel.

steel′ mill′, an establishment where steel is made and often manufactured into girders, rails, etc. Also called **steelworks.**

steel′ wool′, a mass of fine, threadlike steel shavings, used for scouring, polishing, etc.

steel·work (stēl′wûrk′), *n.* **1.** steel parts or articles. **2.** the steel frame or girders of a skyscraper.

steel·work·er (stēl′wûr′kər), *n.* a person employed in steel manufacturing.

steel·works (stēl′wûrks′), *n., pl.* **-works.** (*construed as sing. or pl.*) See **steel mill.**

steel·y (stē′lē), *adj.,* **steel·i·er, steel·i·est. 1.** consisting or made of steel. **2.** resembling or suggesting steel, as in color, strength, or hardness. —**steel′i·ness,** *n.*

steel·yard (stēl′yärd′, stil′yərd), *n.* a portable balance with two unequal arms, the longer one having a movable counterpoise, and the shorter one bearing a hook or the like for holding the object to be weighed.

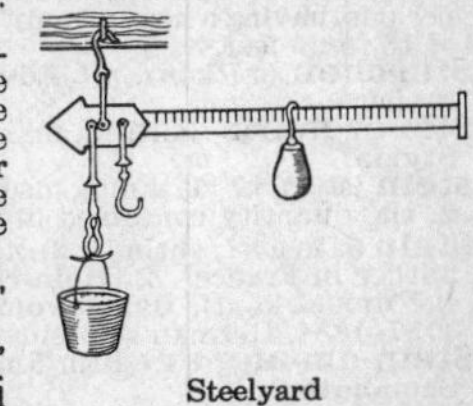

Steelyard

Steen (stān), *n.* **Jan** (yän), 1626–79, Dutch painter.

steen·bok (stēn′bok′, stān′-), *n., pl.* **-boks,** (*esp. collectively*) **-bok.** a small antelope, *Raphicerus campestris,* of grassy areas of eastern and southern Africa. Also, **steinbok.** [< SAfrD: stone buck]

steep[1] (stēp), *adj.* **1.** having a slope or pitch approaching the vertical, or a relatively high gradient, as a hill, an ascent, stairs, etc. **2.** (of a price or amount) unduly high; exorbitant. —*n.* **3.** a steep place; declivity, as of a hill.

[ME *stepe,* OE *stēap;* akin to STOOP[1]] —**steep′ly,** *adv.* —**Syn. 1.** precipitous, abrupt. —**Ant. 1.** flat.

steep[2] (stēp), *v.t.* **1.** to soak in water or other liquid, as to soften, cleanse, or extract some constituent. **2.** to wet thoroughly in or with a liquid; drench; saturate; imbue. **3.** to saturate or imbue with some pervading influence or agency: *an incident steeped in mystery.* —*v.i.* **4.** to lie soaking in a liquid. —*n.* **5.** the act, process, or state of steeping. **6.** the state of being steeped. **7.** a liquid in which something is steeped. [ME *stepe;* c. Sw *stöpa*]

steep·en (stē′pən), *v.t., v.i.* to make or become steeper.

stee·ple (stē′pəl), *n.* **1.** an ornamental construction, usually ending in a spire, erected on a roof or tower of a church, public building, etc. **2.** a tower terminating in such a construction. **3.** a spire. [ME *stepel,* OE *stēpel* tower. See STEEP[1], -LE] —**stee′pled,** *adj.* —**stee′ple·like′,** *adj.*

A, Steeple
B, Spire

stee·ple·bush (stē′pəl bo͝osh′), *n.* the hardhack. [so called because of its steeple-like blossom shoots]

stee·ple·chase (stē′pəl chās′), *n., v.,* **-chased, -chas·ing.** —*n.* **1.** a horse race over a turf course furnished with artificial ditches, hedges, and other obstacles over which the horses must jump. **2.** a point-to-point race. **3.** a foot race run on a cross-country course or over a course having obstacles. —*v.i.* **4.** to ride or run in a steeplechase. [so called because the course was kept by sighting a church steeple] —**stee′ple·chas′er,** *n.*

stee·ple·jack (stē′pəl jak′), *n.* a person who builds or repairs steeples, towers, or the like.

steer[1] (stēr), *v.t.* **1.** to guide the course of (something in motion): *to steer a bicycle.* **2.** to follow or pursue (a particular course). **3.** *Informal.* to direct the course of, as with advice; guide. —*v.i.* **4.** to direct the course of a vessel, vehicle, airplane, etc. **5.** (of a vessel, vehicle, airplane, etc.) to admit of being steered or steered in a certain manner. **6. steer clear of,** to stay away from; shun; avoid. —*n.* **7.** *Informal.* a suggestion about a course of action; tip. [ME *stere,* OE *steor(an)* < *steor* steering; c. G *steuern,* Icel *stȳra,* Goth *stiurjan*] —**Syn. 1.** direct, pilot.

steer[2] (stēr), *n.* a castrated male bovine, esp. one raised for beef; ox. [ME; OE *stēor;* c. D, G *Stier,* Icel *stjōrr,* Goth *stiur*]

steer[3] (stēr), *v.t., v.i., n. Brit. Dial.* stir[1].

steer·age (stēr′ij), *n.* **1.** a part or division of a ship, formerly the part containing the steering apparatus. **2.** (in a passenger ship) the part or accommodations alloted to the passengers who have booked passage at the cheapest rate. [late ME *sterage*]

steer·age·way (stēr′ij wā′), *n. Naut.* sufficient speed to permit a vessel to be maneuvered.

steer′ing commit′tee, a committee, esp. of a deliberative or legislative body, charged with preparing the agenda of a session.

steer′ing gear′, the apparatus or mechanism for steering a ship, automobile, bicycle, airplane, etc.

steer′ing wheel′, a wheel held and turned by the driver, pilot, or the like, in steering an automobile, ship, etc.

steers·man (stērz′mən), *n., pl.* **-men. 1.** a person who steers a ship; helmsman. **2.** a person who drives a machine. [ME *steresman,* OE *stēoresmann*]

steeve[1] (stēv), *v.,* **steeved, steev·ing,** *n.* —*v.t.* **1.** to pack tightly, as cotton or other cargo in a ship's hold. —*n.* **2.** a long derrick or spar, with a block at one end, used in stowing cargo in a ship's hold. [late ME *steve(n),* prob. < Sp *(e)stiba(r)* (to) cram < L *stīpāre* to stuff, pack tightly; akin to OE *stīf* STIFF]

steeve[2] (stēv), *v.,* **steeved, steev·ing,** *n. Naut.* —*v.i.* **1.** (of a bowsprit or the like) to incline upward at an angle instead of extending horizontally. —*v.t.* **2.** to set (a spar) at an upward inclination. —*n.* **3.** the angle that a bowsprit or the like makes with the horizontal. [?; cf. OE *stīfig* steep]

Stef·ans·son (stef′ən sən), *n.* **Vil·hjal·mur** (vil′hyoul′mer), 1879–1962, U.S. arctic explorer, born in Canada.

Stef·fens (stef′ənz), *n.* **(Joseph) Lincoln,** 1866–1936, U.S. author and journalist.

stego-, a learned borrowing from Greek meaning "cover," used in the formation of compound words: *stegosaur.* [comb. form of Gk *stégos* roof]

steg·o·saur (steg′ə sôr′), *n.* any herbivorous dinosaur of the genus *Stegosaurus,* from the Jurassic and Cretaceous periods, having a heavy, bony armor, and growing to a length of 18 to 25 feet.

Stegosaur,
Stegosaurus stenops
(Length 20 ft.)

Stei·chen (stī′kən), *n.* **Edward,** 1879–1973, U.S. photographer.

Stei·er·mark (shtī′ər märk′), *n.* German name of **Styria.**

stein (stīn), *n.* **1.** a mug, usually earthenware, esp. for beer. **2.** the quantity contained in a stein. [< G: lit., stone]

Stein (stīn *for 1;* shtīn *for 2*), *n.* **1. Gertrude,** 1874–1946, U.S. author in France. **2. Hein·rich Frie·drich Karl** (hīn′rikh frē′drikh kärl), **Baron vom und zum** (fôm o͝ont tso͞om), 1757–1831, German statesman.

Stein·am·ang·er (shtīn′äm äng′ər), *n.* German name of **Szombathely.**

Stein·beck (stīn′bek), *n.* **John (Ernst)** (ûrnst), 1902–68, U.S. novelist: Nobel prize 1962.

Stein·berg (stīn′burg), *n.* **Saul,** born 1914, U.S. cartoonist and illustrator, born in Rumania.

stein·bok (stīn′bok), *n., pl.* **-boks,** *(esp. collectively)* **-bok. 1.** steenbok. **2.** an ibex.

Stein·er (stī′nər; *Ger.* shtī′nər), *n.* **Ru·dolf** (ro͞o′dolf; *Ger.* ro͞o′dôlf), 1861–1925, German social philosopher and founder of anthroposophy, born in Hungary.

Stein′heim man′ (shtīn′hīm, stīn′-), a prehistoric man, probably of the second interglacial period, known from a skull found in West Germany. [named after *Steinheim am Murr,* Germany]

Stein·metz (stīn′mets), *n.* **Charles Pro·te·us** (prō′tē əs), 1865–1923, U.S. electrical engineer, born in Germany.

ste·la (stē′lə), *n., pl.* **ste·lae** (stē′lē). stele (defs. 1, 2).

ste·le (stē′lē, stēl *for 1, 2;* stēl, stē′lē *for 3*), *n., pl.* **ste·lai** (stē′lī), **ste·les** (stē′lēz, stēlz). **1.** an upright stone slab or pillar bearing an inscription or design and serving as a monument, marker, or the like. **2.** *Archit.* a prepared surface on the face of a building, rock, etc., bearing an inscription or the like. **3.** *Bot.* the central cylinder or cylinders of vascular and related tissue in the stem, root, petiole, leaf, etc., of the higher plants. Also, **stela** (for defs. 1, 2). [< Gk *stḗlē,* akin to *histánai,* L *stāre* to STAND] —**ste·lar** (stē′lər), *adj.*

St. Elias, Mount, a mountain on the boundary between Alaska and Canada, a peak of the St. Elias Mountains. 18,008 ft.

St. Elias Mountains, a mountain range between SE Alaska and the SW Yukon territory. Highest peak, Mount Logan, 19,850 ft.

Stel′la Polar′is (stel′ə), Polaris.

stel·lar (stel′ər), *adj.* **1.** of or pertaining to the stars; consisting of stars. **2.** like a star, as in brilliance, shape, etc. **3.** pertaining to a preeminent performer, athlete, etc. [< LL *stellār(is)* = *stell(a)* star + *-āris* -AR[1]]

stel·late (stel′it, -āt), *adj.* being or arranged in the form of a conventionalized figure of a star; star-shaped. Also, **stel′lat·ed.** [< L *stellāt(us)* starry = *stell(a)* STAR + *-ātus* -ATE[1]] —**stel′late·ly,** *adv.*

stel·lif·er·ous (ste lif′ər əs), *adj.* having or abounding with stars or star-shaped markings. [< L *stellifer* star-bearing (*stell(a)* star + *-i-* -I- + *-fer* -FER) + -OUS; see -FEROUS]

stel·lu·lar (stel′yə lər), *adj.* **1.** having the form of a small star or small stars. **2.** spotted with star-shaped specks of color. [< LL *stellul(a)* (*stell(a)* star + *-ula* -ULE) + -AR[1]] —**stel′lu·lar·ly,** *adv.*

St. El·mo's fire (el′mōz). See **corona discharge.** Also called **St. Elmo's light, St. Ulmo's fire, St. Ulmo's light.** [named after *St. Elmo* (d. A.D. 303), patron saint of sailors]

stem[1] (stem), *n., v.,* **stemmed, stem·ming.** —*n.* **1.** the ascending axis of a plant, whether above or below ground, which ordinarily grows in an opposite direction to the root or descending axis. **2.** the stalk that supports a leaf, flower, or fruit. **3.** the main body of that portion of a tree, shrub, or other plant, that is above ground; trunk; stalk. **4.** a petiole; peduncle; pedicel. **5.** a stalk of bananas. **6.** something resembling or suggesting a leaf or flower stalk. **7.** a long, slender part: *the stem of a tobacco pipe.* **8.** a projection from the rim of a watch, having on its end a knob for winding the watch. **9.** the circular rod in some locks around which the key fits and rotates. **10.** the rod or spindle by which a valve is operated from outside. **11.** the stock or line of descent of a family; ancestry or pedigree. **12.** *Gram.* the underlying form, often consisting of a root plus an affix, to which the inflectional endings of a word are added. Cf. **base**[1] (def. 18), **theme** (def. 4). **13.** *Music.* the vertical line forming part of a note. **14.** the main or relatively thick stroke of a letter in printing. —*v.t.* **15.** to remove the stem from (a leaf, fruit, etc.). —*v.i.* **16.** to arise or originate: *This project stems from last week's lecture.* [ME; OE *stemn, stefn* = *ste-* (mutated var. of *sta-;* see STAND) + *-mn-* suffix; akin to G *Stamm* stem, tribe, Icel *stamn, stafn* stem of a ship; see STAFF[1]] —**stem′less,** *adj.* —**stem′like′,** *adj.* —**Syn. 11.** lineage, race.

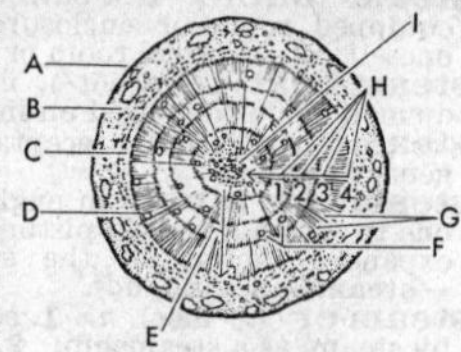

Stem of a dicotyledonous plant (Transverse section)
A, Epidermis; B, Cork; C, Cortex; D, Phloem; E, Xylem; F, Resin canals; G, Xylem rays; H, Annual rings; I, Pith

stem[2] (stem), *v.,* **stemmed, stem·ming,** *n.* —*v.t.* **1.** to stop, check, or restrain. **2.** to dam up; stop the flow of (a stream, river, or the like). **3.** to tamp, plug, or make tight, as a hole or joint. **4.** *Scot.* to stanch (bleeding). **5.** *Skiing.* to maneuver (a ski or skis) in executing a stem. —*v.i.* **6.** *Skiing.* to execute a stem. —*n.* **7.** *Skiing.* the act or instance of a skier pushing the heel of one or both skis outward so that the heels are far apart, as in making certain turns or slowing down. [ME *stemme* < Scand; cf. Icel *stemma;* c. G *stemmen* to prop]

stem[3] (stem), *v.t.,* **stemmed, stem·ming. 1.** to make headway against (a tide, current, gale, etc.). **2.** to make progress against (any opposition). [v. use of STEM[4]] —**Syn. 1.** breast.

stem[4] (stem), *n. Naut.* **1.** (at the bow of a vessel) an upright into which the side timbers or plates are jointed. **2.** the forward part of a vessel (often opposed to *stern*). [OE *stefn, stemn* prow, stern; special use of STEM[1]]

stemmed (stemd), *adj.* **1.** having a stem or a specified kind of stem (often used in combination): *a long-stemmed rose.* **2.** having the stem or stems removed: *stemmed cherries.*

stem·mer[1] (stem′ər), *n.* **1.** a person who removes stems. **2.** a device for removing stems, as from tobacco, grapes, etc. [STEM[1] + -ER[1]]

stem·mer[2] (stem′ər), *n.* an implement for stemming or tamping. [STEM[2] + -ER[1]]

stem·mer·y (stem′ə rē), *n., pl.* **-mer·ies.** a factory or other place where tobacco leaves are stripped. [STEM[1] + -ERY]

stem′ turn′, *Skiing.* a turn in which a skier stems one ski in the direction to be turned and brings the other ski parallel.

stem·ware (stem′wâr′), *n.* glass or crystal vessels, esp. for beverages and desserts, having rounded bowls mounted on footed stems.

stem-wind·er (stem′wīn′dər), *n.* a stem-winding watch.

stem-wind·ing (stem′wīn′ding), *adj.* wound by turning a knob at the stem.

stench (stench), *n.* an offensive smell or odor; stink. [ME; OE *stenc* odor (good or bad); akin to G *Stank* and to STINK]

sten·cil (sten′səl), *n., v.,* **-ciled, -cil·ing** or (*esp. Brit.*) **-cilled, -cil·ling.** —*n.* **1.** a thin sheet of cardboard or other impervious material having perforations through which paint, ink, etc., applied on one side will pass through to form a design or legend on a surface against which the sheet rests. **2.** a design or legend produced on a surface by this method. —*v.t.* **3.** to mark or paint (a surface) by means of a stencil. **4.** to produce (a design or legend) by means of a stencil. [earlier *stanesile,* ME *stansele* to ornament with diverse colors or spangles < MF (*e*)*stancele*(*r*) < *estencele* a spark, ornamental spangle < VL **stincilla,* metathetic var. of L *scintilla* SCINTILLA] —**sten′cil·er;** *esp. Brit.,* **sten′cil·ler,** *n.*

Stencil

Sten·dhal (sten däl′, stan-; *Fr.* stăn dal′), *n.* (pen name of *Marie Henri Beyle*) 1783–1842, French novelist and critic.

sten·o (sten′ō), *n., pl.* **sten·os** for 1. **1.** a stenographer. **2.** the art or practice of a stenographer; stenography. [by shortening; see STENO-]

steno-, a learned borrowing from Greek meaning "narrow," "close," used in the formation of compound words: *stenography.* [< Gk *stenó*(*s*)]

sten·o·graph (sten′ə graf′, -gräf′), *n.* **1.** any of various keyboard instruments for writing in shorthand, as by means of phonetic or arbitrary symbols. **2.** a character written in shorthand. —*v.t.* **3.** to write in shorthand.

ste·nog·ra·pher (stə nog′rə fər), *n.* a person who specializes in taking dictation in shorthand. Also, **ste·nog′ra·phist.**

ste·nog·ra·phy (stə nog′rə fē), *n.* the art of writing in shorthand. —**sten·o·graph·ic** (sten′ə graf′ik), **sten′o·graph′i·cal,** *adj.* —**sten′o·graph′i·cal·ly,** *adv.*

sten·o·ha·line (sten′ə hā′līn, -lin, -hal′īn, -in), *adj. Ecol.* (of a plant or animal) restricted to an environment of only slightly varying salinity. [STENO- + Gk *hálin*(*os*) of salt = *hál*(*s*) salt + *-inos* -INE[1]]

ste·no·sis (sti nō′sis), *n. Pathol.* narrowing of a passage or vessel. [< NL < Gk *sténōsis.* See STENO-, -OSIS] —**ste·not·ic** (sti not′ik), *adj.*

sten·o·ther·mal (sten′ə thûr′məl), *adj. Ecol.* (of a plant or animal) able to withstand only slight variations in temperature. Also, **sten′o·ther′mic.** Cf. **eurythermal.**

sten·o·top·ic (sten′ə top′ik), *adj. Ecol.* (of a plant or animal) able to tolerate only limited variations in conditions of the environment, as in temperature, humidity, etc. [STENO- + Gk *tóp*(*os*) place + -IC; see TOPIC]

sten·o·type (sten′ə tīp′), *n.* **1.** a keyboard machine resembling a typewriter, used in a system of phonetic shorthand. **2.** the symbols typed in one stroke on this machine.

sten·o·typ·y (sten′ə tī′pē), *n.* shorthand in which alphabetic letters or types are used to produce shortened forms of words or groups of words. —**sten·o·typ·ic** (sten′ə tip′ik), *adj.* —**sten′o·typ′ist,** *n.*

Sten·tor (sten′tôr), *n.* **1.** (in the *Iliad*) a Greek herald with a loud voice. **2.** (*l.c.*) a person having a very loud voice.

sten·to·ri·an (sten tōr′ē ən, -tôr′-), *adj.* very loud or powerful in sound: *a stentorian voice.* Also, **sten·to·ri·ous** (sten tōr′ē əs, -tôr′-).

step (step), *n., v.,* **stepped, step·ping.** —*n.* **1.** a movement made by lifting the foot and setting it down again in a new position, accompanied by a shifting of the body in the direction of the new position. **2.** such a movement followed by a movement of equal distance of the other foot. **3.** the space passed over or the distance measured by one movement of the foot in such a movement. **4.** the sound made by the foot in making such a movement. **5.** a mark or impression made by the foot on the ground; footprint. **6.** the manner of walking; gait; stride. **7.** a rhythm, pace, or pattern conformed to in walking, marching, or dancing. **8.** conformity to such a rhythm, pace, or pattern. **9. steps,** a person's movements or course in walking or running. **10.** any of a series of distinct successive stages in a process or the attainment of an end. **11.** rank, degree, or grade, as on a vertical scale. **12.** a support for the foot in ascending or descending. **13.** a very short distance. **14.** *Music.* **a.** a degree of the staff or of the scale. **b.** the interval between two adjacent scale degrees; second. Cf. **semitone, whole step. 15. steps,** *Brit.* a stepladder. **16.** an offset part of anything. **17.** *Naut.* a socket, frame, or platform for supporting the lower end of a mast. **18. in step, a.** moving in time to a rhythm or with the corresponding step of others. **b.** in harmony or conformity. **19. out of step, a.** not moving or proceeding in time to a rhythm; not corresponding to the step of others. **b.** not in harmony or conformity. **20. take steps,** to set about putting something into operation; begin to act. **21. watch one's step,** *Informal.* to proceed with caution; behave prudently. —*v.i.* **22.** to move in steps. **23.** to walk, esp. for a few strides or a short distance: *Step over to the bar.* **24.** to move with measured steps, as in a dance. **25.** to go briskly or fast, as a horse. **26.** to put the foot down; tread by intention or accident: *to step on a cat's tail.* —*v.t.* **27.** to walk (a number of paces or a certain distance). **28.** to move or set (the foot) in taking a step. **29.** to measure (a distance, ground, etc.) by steps (sometimes fol. by *off* or *out*). **30.** to make or arrange in the manner of a series of steps. **31.** *Naut.* to fix (a mast) in its step. **32. step down, a.** to lower or decrease by degrees. **b.** to relinquish one's authority or control; resign. **33. step on it,** *Slang.* to hasten; hurry up. **34. step up,** to raise or increase by degrees: *to step up production.* [ME *stepp*(*en*), OE *steppan;* c. OHG *stepfan;* akin to STAMP]

step-, a prefix indicating connection between members of a family by the remarriage of a parent and not by blood: *stepbrother.* [ME; OE *stēop-;* c. G *stief-,* Icel *stjūp-* step-; akin to OE *āstēpan* to bereave, *bestēpan* to deprive (of children)]

step·broth·er (step′bruth′ər), *n.* the son of one's stepfather or stepmother by a former marriage. [late ME]

step·child (step′chīld′), *n., pl.* **-chil·dren.** a child of one's husband or wife by a former marriage. [ME; OE *stēopcild*]

step·dame (step′dām′), *n. Archaic.* a stepmother. [late ME]

step·daugh·ter (step′dô′tər), *n.* a daughter of one's husband or wife by a former marriage. [ME *stepdohter,* OE *stēopdohtor*]

step-down (step′doun′), *adj. Elect.* serving to reduce or decrease voltage: *a step-down transformer.*

step·fa·ther (step′fä′thər), *n.* a man who succeeds one's father as the husband of one's mother. [ME *stepfader,* OE *stēopfæder*]

Ste·phen (stē′vən), *n.* **1. Saint,** died A.D. c35, first Christian martyr. **2. Saint,** c975–1038, first king of Hungary 997–1038. **3.** (*Stephen of Blois*) 1097?–1154, king of England 1135–54. **4. Sir Leslie,** 1832–1904, English critic, biographer, and philosopher; father of Virginia Woolf.

Stephen I, Saint, died A.D. 257?, pope 254–257.

Stephen II, died A.D. 757, pope 752–757.

Stephen III, died A.D. 772, pope 768–772.

Stephen IV, died A.D. 817, pope 816–817.

Stephen V, died A.D. 891, pope 885–891.

Stephen VI, died A.D. 897, pope 896–897.

Stephen VII, died A.D. 931, pope 928–931.

Stephen VIII, died A.D. 942, pope 939–942.

Stephen IX, died 1058, pope 1057–58.

Ste·phens (stē′vənz), *n.* **1. Alexander Hamilton,** 1812–1883, U.S. statesman: vice president of the Confederacy 1861–65. **2. James,** 1882–1950, Irish poet and novelist.

Ste·phen·son (stē′vən sən), *n.* **1. George,** 1781–1848, English inventor and engineer. **2.** his son **Robert,** 1803–59, English engineer.

step-in (step′in′), *Clothing.* —*adj.* **1.** put on by being stepped into. —*n.* **2. step-ins,** panties. **3.** any step-in garment.

step·lad·der (step′lad′ər), *n.* **1.** a ladder having flat steps or treads in place of rungs. **2.** any ladder, esp. a tall one with a hinged frame opening up to form four supporting legs.

step·moth·er (step′muth′ər), *n.* a woman who succeeds one's mother as the wife of one's father. [ME *stepmoder,* OE *stēopmōdor*]

Step·ney (step′nē), *n.* a borough of E London, England. 91,940 (1961).

step·par·ent (step′pâr′ənt, -par′-), *n.* a stepfather or stepmother.

steppe (step), *n.* **1.** an extensive plain, esp. one without trees. **2. the Steppes, a.** the vast Russian grasslands, esp. those in the S and E European and W and SW Asian parts of the Soviet Union. **b.** See **Kirghiz Steppe.** [< Russ *step'*]

step·per (step′ər), *n.* a person or animal that steps, esp. a horse that lifts its front legs high at the knee.

step′ping stone′, 1. a stone, or one of a line of stones, in shallow water, etc., that is stepped on in crossing. **2.** a stone for use in mounting. **3.** any means or stage of advancement or improvement. Also, **step′ping·stone′.** [ME]

step·sis·ter (step′sis′tər), *n.* the daughter of one's stepfather or stepmother by a former marriage. [late ME]

step·son (step′sun′), *n.* a son of one's husband or wife by a former marriage. [ME *stepsone,* OE *stēopsunu*]

step′ turn′, *Skiing.* a turn in which a skier steps slightly outward with one ski in the direction to be turned, and then brings the other ski around so that both skis are parallel.

step-up (step′up′), *n.* **1.** an increase or rise in rate or quantity. —*adj.* **2.** effecting or allowing for an increase. **3.** *Elect.* serving to increase voltage: *a step-up transformer.*

step·wise (step′wīz′), *adv.* **1.** in a steplike arrangement. **2.** *Music.* by proceeding to an adjacent tone: *The melody ascends stepwise.* —*adj.* **3.** *Music.* moving from one adjacent tone to another.

-ster, a suffix used in forming nouns, often derogatory, referring esp. to occupation, habit, or association: *songster; gamester; trickster.* [ME, OE *-estre;* c. D *-ster,* MLG *-*(*e*)*ster*]

ster., sterling.

ste·ra·di·an (stə rā′dē ən), *n. Geom.* a solid angle at the center of a sphere subtending a section on the surface equal in area to the square of the radius of the sphere. *Abbr.:* s [STERE(O)- + RADIAN]

ster·co·ra·ceous (stûr′kə rā′shəs), *adj. Physiol.* consisting of, resembling, or pertaining to dung or feces. Also, **ster·co·rous** (stûr′kər əs). [< L *stercor-* (s. of *stercus*) dung + -ACEOUS]

ster·co·ric·o·lous (stûr′kə rik′ə ləs), *adj.* living in dung. [*stercor-* (see STERCORACEOUS) + -I- + -COLOUS]

ster·cu·li·a·ceous (stûr kyōō′lē ā′shəs), *adj.* belonging to the *Sterculiaceae,* a family of trees and shrubs comprising the cacao and kola nut trees. [< NL *sterculi*(*a*) (special use of *Sterculius* Roman god of manuring) + -ACEOUS]

stere (stēr), *n. Metric System.* a cubic meter equivalent to 35.315 cubic feet or 1.3080 cubic yards, used to measure cordwood. *Abbr.:* s [< F *stère* < Gk *stere*(*ós*) solid]

ster·e·o (ster′ē ō′, stēr′-), *n., pl.* **ster·e·os,** *adj., v.* —*n.* **1.** a system or the equipment for reproducing stereophonic sound. **2.** stereophonic sound reproduction. **3.** stereoscopic photography. **4.** a stereoscopic photograph. **5.** *Print.* stereotype (defs. 1, 2). —*adj.* **6.** pertaining to stereophonic sound, stereoscopic photography, etc. —*v.t.* **7.** *Print.* stereotype (def. 5). [by shortening]

stereo-, a learned borrowing from Greek, where it meant "solid," used with reference to hardness, solidity, three-dimensionality in the formation of compound words: *stereochemistry; stereogram; stereoscope.* Also, *esp. before a vowel,* **stere-.** [< Gk *stereó*(*s*)]

stereo., stereotype.

ster·e·o·chem·is·try (ster′ē ō kem′i strē, stēr′-), *n.* the branch of chemistry that deals with the determination of the relative positions in space of the atoms or groups of atoms in a compound and with the effects of these positions on the properties of the compound. —**ster·e·o·chem·ic** (ster′ē ō-kem′ik, stēr′-), **ster′e·o·chem′i·cal,** *adj.*

ster·e·o·chrome (ster′ē ə krōm′, stēr′-), *n.* a picture produced by a process in which water glass is used as a vehicle or as a preservative coating. [back formation from STEREOCHROMY]

ster·e·o·chro·my (ster′ē ə krō′mē, stēr′-), *n.* the stereochrome process. Also called **waterglass painting.** [STEREO- + -*chromy* (see -CHROME, -Y[3])] —**ster′e·o·chro′mic, ster·e·o·chro·mat·ic** (ster′ē ō krə mat′ik, -krō-, stēr′-), *adj.*

ster·e·o·gram (ster′ē ə gram′, stēr′-), *n.* **1.** a diagram or picture representing objects in a way to give the impression of solidity. **2.** a stereograph.

ster·e·o·graph (ster′ē ə graf′, -gräf′, stēr′-), *n.* **1.** a single or double picture for a stereoscope. —*v.t.* **2.** to make a stereograph of.

ster·e·og·ra·phy (ster′ē og′rə fē, stēr′-), *n.* **1.** the art of delineating the forms of solid bodies on a plane. **2.** a branch of solid geometry dealing with the construction of regularly defined solids. —**ster·e·o·graph·ic** (ster′ē ə graf′ik, stēr′-), **ster′e·o·graph′i·cal,** *adj.* —**ster′e·o·graph′i·cal·ly,** *adv.*

ster·e·o·i·som·er·ism (ster′ē ō ī som′ə riz′əm, stēr′-), *n.* *Chem.* the isomerism ascribed to different relative positions of the atoms or groups of atoms in the molecules displaying optical activity organic compounds.

ster·e·om·e·try (ster′ē om′i trē, stēr′-), *n.* the measurement of volumes. [< NL *stereometria*] —**ster·e·o·met·ric** (ster′ē ə me′trik, stēr′-), **ster′e·o·met′ri·cal,** *adj.* —**ster′e·o·met′ri·cal·ly,** *adv.*

ster·e·o·phon·ic (ster′ē ə fon′ik, stēr′-), *adj.* of or noting, or having a system of separately placed microphones or loudspeakers for enhancing the realism of reproduced sound. Cf. **monophonic** (def. 2). —**ster′e·o·phon′i·cal·ly,** *adv.* —**ster·e·oph·o·ny** (ster′ē of′ə nē, stēr′-, ster′ē ə fō′nē, stēr′-), *n.*

ster·e·op·sis (ster′ē op′sis, stēr′-), *n.* stereoscopic vision.

ster·e·op·ti·con (ster′ē op′tə kən, -kon′, stēr′-), *n.* *Optics.* a projector usually consisting of two complete lanterns arranged so that one picture appears to dissolve while the next is forming. [STERE(O)- + Gk *optikṓn* (neut.) OPTIC] —**ster′e·op′ti·can,** *adj.* —**ster·e·op·ti·cian** (ster′ē op tish′ən, stēr′-), *n.*

ster·e·o·scope (ster′ē ə skōp′, stēr′-), *n.* an optical instrument through which two pictures of the same object, taken from slightly different points of view, are viewed, one by each eye, producing the effect of a single picture of the object, with the appearance of depth or relief.

ster·e·o·scop·ic (ster′ē ə skop′ik, stēr′-), *adj.* **1.** noting or pertaining to three-dimensional vision or any of the means of giving an illusion of such vision in the viewing of pictures. **2.** of or characterized by a stereoscope or stereoscopy. Also, **ster′e·o·scop′i·cal.** —**ster′e·o·scop′i·cal·ly,** *adv.*

ster·e·os·co·py (ster′ē os′kə pē, stēr′-), *n.* **1.** the study of the stereoscope and its techniques. **2.** three-dimensional vision.

ste·re·o·tape (ster′ē ə tāp′, stēr′-), *n.* a magnetic tape for recording and reproducing stereophonic sound.

ster·e·o·tax·is (ster′ē ə tak′sis, stēr′-), *n.* *Biol.* movement of an organism in response to contact with a solid. —**ster·e·o·tac·tic** (ster′ē ə tak′tik, stēr′-), *adj.* —**ster′e·o·tac′ti·cal·ly,** *adv.*

ster·e·ot·o·my (ster′ē ot′ə mē, stēr′-), *n.* the technique of cutting solids, as stones, to specified forms and dimensions. —**ster·e·o·tom·ic** (ster′ē ə tom′ik, stēr′-), **ster′e·o·tom′i·cal,** *adj.* —**ster′e·ot′o·mist,** *n.*

ster·e·ot·ro·pism (ster′ē o′trə piz′əm, stēr′-), *n.* *Biol.* a tropism determined by contact with a solid.

ster·e·o·type (ster′ē ə tīp′, stēr′-), *n.*, *v.*, **-typed, -typ·ing.** —*n.* **1.** a process of making metal printing plates by taking a mold of composed type or the like in papier-mâché or other material and then taking from this mold a cast in type metal. **2.** a plate made by this process. **3.** an idea, expression, etc., lacking in originality and inventiveness; a set form. **4.** *Sociol.* a standardized conception or image invested with special meaning and held in common by members of a group. —*v.t.* **5.** to make a stereotype of. **6.** to give a fixed form to. —**ster′e·o·typ′er, ster′e·o·typ′ist,** *n.* —**ster·e·o·typ·ic** (ster′ē ə tip′ik, stēr′-), **ster′e·o·typ′i·cal,** *adj.*

ster·e·o·typed (ster′ē ə tīpt′, stēr′-), *adj.* **1.** reproduced in or by stereotype plates. **2.** fixed or settled in form; hackneyed; conventional. —**Syn. 2.** See **commonplace.**

ster·e·o·typ·y (ster′ē ə tī′pē, stēr′-), *n.* the stereotype process.

ster·ic (ster′ik, stēr′-), *adj.* *Chem.* of or pertaining to the spatial relationships of atoms in a molecule. Also, **ster′i·cal.** [STERE- + -IC] —**ster′i·cal·ly,** *adv.*

ster·i·lant (ster′ə lənt), *n.* *Chem.* a sterilizing agent.

ster·ile (ster′il *or, esp. Brit.,* -īl), *adj.* **1.** free from living germs or microorganisms: *sterile surgical instruments.* **2.** incapable of producing offspring; not producing offspring. **3.** barren; not producing vegetation: *sterile soil.* **4.** *Bot.* **a.** noting a plant in which reproductive structures fail to develop. **b.** bearing no stamens or pistils. **5.** not productive of results, ideas, etc.; fruitless. [< L *steril(is)* unfruitful] —**ste·ril·i·ty** (stə ril′i tē), *n.* —**Syn. 1.** uncontaminated, unpolluted, antiseptic. **2.** infecund, unfruitful. **3.** fruitless.

ster·i·lise (ster′ə līz′), *v.t.*, **-lised, -lis·ing.** *Chiefly Brit.* sterilize. —**ster′i·lis′a·ble,** *adj.* —**ster′i·lis′er,** *n.*

ster·i·li·za·tion (ster′ə li zā′shən *or, esp. Brit.,* -lī-), *n.* **1.** the act of sterilizing. **2.** the condition of being sterilized. **3.** the destruction of all living microorganisms, as pathogenic or saprophytic bacteria, vegetative forms, and spores. Also, *esp. Brit.,* **ster′i·li·sa′tion.**

ster·i·lize (ster′ə līz′), *v.t.*, **-lized, -liz·ing. 1.** to free of microorganisms, usually by bringing to a high temperature. **2.** to destroy the ability to reproduce by removing the sex organs or inhibiting their functions. **3.** to make (land) barren or unproductive. Also, *esp. Brit.,* **sterilise.** —**ster′i·liz′a·ble,** *adj.* —**ster′i·liz′er,** *n.*

ster·i·lized (ster′ə līzd′), *adj.* (at an air terminal) closed to all except boarding passengers who have been screened by electronic metal-detection devices against skyjacking weapons: *a sterilized concourse.* Also, **sterile.**

ster·let (stûr′lit), *n.* a small sturgeon, *Acipenser ruthenus,* found in the areas of the Black and Caspian seas, valued as a source of caviar. [< Russ *sterlyad′*]

ster·ling (stûr′ling), *adj.* **1.** of, pertaining to, or noting British money. **2.** (of silver) having the standard fineness of .925. **3.** made of silver of this fineness. **4.** thoroughly excellent: *a man of sterling worth.* —*n.* **5.** the standard of fineness for gold coin in the United Kingdom, presently 0.91666. **6.** silver having a fineness of .925, now used esp. in the manufacture of table utensils, jewelry, etc. **7.** manufactured articles of sterling silver. **8.** sterling flatware. [ME: name of a silver coin; OE *steorling (see STAR, -LING[1]) with reference to the little star on some of the mintages]

ster′ling bloc′, those countries whose currency values are contingent upon or based on the pound sterling. Also called **ster′ling ar′ea.**

Ster′ling Heights′, a city in SE Michigan, N of Detroit. 61,365 (1970).

Ster·li·ta·mak (sterʟ′li tä mäk′), *n.* a city in the RSFSR in the E Soviet Union in Europe, W of the Southern Urals. 131,000 (est. 1962).

stern[1] (stûrn), *adj.* **1.** firm, strict, or uncompromising: *stern discipline.* **2.** hard, harsh, or severe. **3.** rigorous or austere; of an unpleasantly serious character: *stern times.* **4.** grim or forbidding: *a stern face.* [ME; OE *styrne.* See STARE, STARVE] —**stern′ly,** *adv.* —**stern′ness,** *n.*
—**Syn. 1, 2.** adamant, unrelenting. STERN, SEVERE, HARSH agree in referring to methods, aspects, manners, or facial expressions. STERN implies uncompromising, inflexible firmness: *a stern but loving parent.* SEVERE implies strictness, lack of sympathy, and a tendency to impose a hard discipline on others: *a severe judge.* HARSH suggests a great severity and roughness, and cruel treatment of others: *a harsh critic.*

stern[2] (stûrn), *n.* **1.** the after part of a vessel (often opposed to *stem*). **2.** the back or rear of anything. [ME *sterne* < Scand; cf. Icel *stjōrn* steering (done aft; see STERNPOST)]

Stern (stûrn), *n.* **Isaac,** born 1920, U.S. violinist, born in Russia.

ster·nal (stûr′nəl), *adj.* of or pertaining to the sternum. [< NL *sternāl(is).* See STERNUM, -AL[1]]

stern′ chas′er, a cannon mounted at or near the stern of a sailing ship, facing aft.

Sterne (stûrn), *n.* **Laurence,** 1713–68, English novelist.

stern·fore·most (stûrn′fōr′mōst, -fôr′- *or, esp. Brit.,* -məst), *adv.* **1.** *Naut.* with the stern foremost. **2.** awkwardly; with difficulty.

stern·most (stûrn′mōst *or, esp. Brit.,* -məst), *adj.* *Naut.* **1.** farthest aft. **2.** nearest the stern.

Sterno (stûr′nō), *n.* *Trademark.* flammable hydrocarbon jelly packaged in a small can for use as a portable heat source for cooking.

sterno-, a combining form of **sternum.** Also, *esp. before a vowel,* **stern-.**

stern·post (stûrn′pōst′), *n.* *Naut.* an upright member rising from the after end of a keel; a rudderpost or propeller post.

stern′ sheets′, *Naut.* the after part of an open boat.

ster·num (stûr′nəm), *n., pl.* **-na** (-nə), **-nums.** *Anat., Zool.* a bone or series of bones extending along the middle line of the ventral portion of the body of most vertebrates, consisting in man of a flat, narrow bone connected with the clavicles and the true ribs; breastbone. [< NL < Gk *stérnon* chest, breastbone]

ster·nu·ta·tion (stûr′nyə tā′shən), *n.* the act of sneezing. [< L *sternūtātiōn-* (s. of *sternūtātiō*) = *sternūtāt(us)* (ptp. of *sternūtāre,* freq. of *sternuere* to sneeze) + *-iōn-* -ION]

ster·nu·ta·tor (stûr′nyə tā′tər), *n.* *Chemical Warfare.* a chemical agent causing nose irritation, coughing, etc. [back formation from STERNUTATORY]

ster·nu·ta·to·ry (stər nōō′tə tōr′ē, -tôr′ē, -nyōō′-), *adj., n., pl.* **-ries.** —*adj.* **1.** Also, **ster·nu′ta·tive.** causing or tending to cause sneezing. —*n.* **2.** a sternutatory substance. [< LL *sternūtātōri(us)* = *sternūtāt(us)* + *-ōrius* -ORY[1]]

stern·ward (stûrn′wərd), *adv.* toward the stern; astern.

stern·way (stûrn′wā′), *n.* **1.** *Naut.* the movement of a vessel backward, or stern foremost. **2. have sternway on,** (of a vessel) to move or be moving backward.

stern·wheel (stûrn′hwēl′, -wēl′), *n.* *Naut.* a paddle wheel at the stern of a vessel. —**stern′-wheel′,** *adj.*

stern·wheel·er (stûrn′hwē′lər, -wē′-), *n.* a boat propelled by a paddle wheel at the stern.

Sternwheeler

ster·oid (ster′oid, stēr′-), *Biochem.* —*n.* **1.** any of a large group of fat-soluble organic compounds, as the sterols, bile acids, and sex hormones, most of which have specific physiological action. —*adj.* **2.** Also, **ste·roi·dal** (ste roid′əl, sti-). pertaining to or characteristic of a steroid. [STER(OL) + -OID]

ster·ol (ster′ōl, -ol, stēr′-), *n.* *Biochem.* any of a group of solid, mostly unsaturated, polycyclic alcohols, as cholesterol and ergosterol, derived from plants or animals. [abstracted from such words as *cholesterol, ergosterol,* etc.]

ster·tor (stûr′tər), *n.* a heavy snore or a heavy snoring sound accompanying respiration in certain diseases. [< L *stert-* (s. of *stertere* to snore) + -OR[1]]

ster·to·rous (stûr′tər əs), *adj.* **1.** characterized by stertor or heavy snoring. **2.** breathing in this manner. —**ster′to·rous·ly,** *adv.* —**ster′to·rous·ness,** *n.*

stet (stet), *v.,* **stet·ted, stet·ting.** —*v.i.* **1.** let it stand (used as a direction, as on a printer's proof, to retain material previously cancelled). —*v.t.* **2.** to mark (a manuscript, printer's proof, etc.) with the word "stet." [< L, pres. subj. 3rd pers. sing. of *stāre* to stand]

stetho-, a learned borrowing from Greek meaning "chest," used in the formation of compound words: *stethoscope.* [comb. form of Gk *stēthos*]

steth·o·scope (steth′ə skōp′), *n.* *Med.* an instrument used in auscultation to convey sounds in the chest or other parts of the body to the ear of the examiner. —**ste·thos·co·py** (ste thos′kə pē, steth′ə skō′-), *n.*

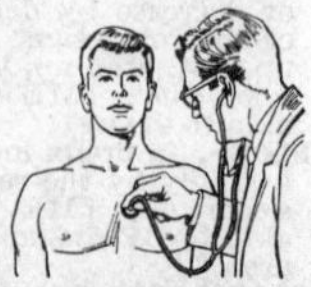

Stethoscope

steth·o·scop·ic (steth′ə skop′ik), *adj.* **1.** pertaining to the stethoscope or to stethoscopy. **2.** made or obtained by the stethoscope. Also, **steth′o·scop′i·cal.** —**steth′o·scop′i·cal·ly,** *adv.*

St.-É·tienne (saN tā tyen′), *n.* a city in SE France. 221,775.

Stet·son (stet′sən), *n.* (*often l.c.*) *Slang.* a felt hat with a broad brim and high crown, esp. one worn as part of a cowboy's outfit. [after the trademark]

Stet·tin (shte tēn′), *n.* a seaport in NW Poland: formerly in Germany. 370,000. Polish, **Szczecin.**

Stet·tin·i·us (stə tin′ē əs), *n.* **Edward Reil·ley** (rī′lē), 1900–49, U.S. industrialist: Secretary of State 1944–45.

Steu·ben (sto͞o′bən, styo͞o′-, sto͞o ben′, styo͞o-; *Ger.* shtoi′-bən), *n.* **Frie·drich Wil·helm Lu·dolf Ger·hard Au·gus·tin von** (frē′drikh vil′helm lo͞o′dôlf gār′härt ou′go͞os tēn′ fən) (*Baron Steuben*), 1730–94, Prussian major general in the American Revolutionary army.

Steu·ben·ville (sto͞o′bən vil′, styo͞o′-), *n.* a city in E Ohio, on the Ohio River. 30,771 (1970).

St. Eu·sta·ti·us (yo͞o stā′shē əs, -shəs), an island in the Netherlands Antilles, in the E West Indies. 1421; 7 sq. mi.

ste·ve·dore (stē′vi dōr′, -dôr′), *n., v.,* **-dored, -dor·ing.** —*n.* **1.** a firm or individual engaged in loading or unloading a vessel. —*v.t.* **2.** to load or unload the cargo of (a ship). —*v.i.* **3.** to load or unload a vessel. [< Sp (*e*)*stibador* = *estib*(*ar*) (to) pack, stow (see STEEVE[1]) + *-ad-* -ATE[1] + *-or* -OR[2]]

ste′vedore's knot′, a knot that forms a lump in a line to prevent it from passing through a hole or grommet.

Ste·ven·age (stē′və nij), *n.* a town in N Hertfordshire, in SE England. 73,300.

Ste·vens (stē′vənz), *n.* **1. John Cox** (koks), 1749–1838, U.S. engineer and inventor. **2. John Paul,** born 1920, U.S. jurist: associate justice of the U.S. Supreme Court since 1975. **3. Thaddeus,** 1792–1868, U.S. abolitionist and political leader. **4. Wallace,** 1879–1955, U.S. poet.

Ste·ven·son (stē′vən sən), *n.* **1. Ad·lai Ew·ing** (ad′lā yo͞o′ing), 1835–1914, vice president of the U.S. 1893–97. **2.** his grandson, **Adlai E(wing),** 1900–65, U.S. statesman and diplomat: ambassador to the U.N. 1960–65. **3. Robert Louis,** (*Robert Lewis Balfour Stevenson*), 1850–94, Scottish novelist, essayist, and poet.

stew[1] (sto͞o, styo͞o), *v.t.* **1.** to cook (food) by simmering or slow boiling. —*v.i.* **2.** to undergo cooking by simmering or slow boiling. **3.** *Informal.* to fret, worry, or fuss. **4. stew in one's own juice,** to suffer the consequences of one's own actions. —*n.* **5.** a preparation of meat, fish, or other food cooked by stewing, esp. a mixture of meat and vegetables. **6.** *Informal.* a state of agitation, uneasiness, or worry. **7. stews,** a disreputable neighborhood of slums, brothels, etc. [late ME *stue*(*n*) (to) take a vapor bath < MF (*e*)*stuve*(*r*) < VL **extūfāre* = *ex-* EX-[1] + **tūf*(*us*) steam < Gk *týphos*]

stew[2] (sto͞o, styo͞o), *n. Slang.* stewardess. [by shortening]

stew·ard (sto͞o′ərd, styo͞o′-), *n.* **1.** a person who manages another's property or financial affairs, or who administers anything as the agent of another or others. **2.** a person who has charge of the household affairs of another. **3.** an employee who has charge of the table, wine, servants, etc., in a club, restaurant, or the like. **4.** a person who attends to the domestic concerns of persons on board a vessel, as in overseeing maids and waiters. **5.** an employee on a ship, train, or airplane who waits on and is responsible for the comfort of passengers. **6.** a person appointed by an organization or group to supervise the affairs of that group at certain functions. **7.** *U.S. Navy.* a petty officer in charge of officer's quarters and mess. —*v.t.* **8.** to act as steward of; manage. —*v.i.* **9.** to act or serve as steward. [ME; OE *stīweard, stigweard* = *stig* hall (see STY[1]) + *weard* WARD[2]]

stew·ard·ess (sto͞o′ər dis, styo͞o′-), *n.* a female flight attendant.

Stew·art (sto͞o′ərt, styo͞o′-), *n.* **1.** Also, **Stuart.** See **Darnley, Lord Henry. 2. Du·gald** (do͞o′gəld, dyo͞o′-), 1753–1828, Scottish philosopher. **3. Potter,** 1915–85, U.S. jurist: associate justice of the U.S. Supreme Court 1958–81.

Stew′art Is′land, one of the islands of New Zealand, S of South Island. 329; 670 sq. mi.

stew·bum (sto͞o′bum′, styo͞o′-), *n. Slang.* a drunken bum.

stewed (sto͞od, styo͞od), *adj.* **1.** cooked by simmering or slow boiling, as food. **2.** *Slang.* intoxicated; drunk. [late ME]

stew·pan (sto͞o′pan′, styo͞o′-), *n.* a pan for stewing; saucepan.

St. Ex., Stock Exchange.

stg., sterling.

St. Gal·len (sänt′ gä′lən; *Ger.* zängkt′ gä′lən), **1.** a canton in NE Switzerland. 384,800; 777 sq. mi. **2.** a city in and the capital of this canton. 77,800. French, **St. Gall** (saN gal′).

stge., storage.

St. George's (jôr′jiz), a seaport in and the capital of the island of Grenada, in the SW part. 6657.

St. George's Channel, a channel between Wales and Ireland, connecting the Irish Sea and the Atlantic. 100 mi. long; 50–90 mi. wide.

St.-Ger·main-en-Laye (saN zher ma′näN lā′), *n.* a city in N France, near Paris: royal chateau and forest; treaties 1570, 1632, 1679, 1919. 40,471. Also called **St.-Germain** (saN zher maN′).

St. Got·thard (sänt′ got′ərd; *Ger.* zängkt′ gôt′härt), **1.** a mountain range in S Switzerland: a part of the Alps; highest peak, 10,490 ft. **2.** a mountain pass over this range. 6935 ft. high. French, **St. Go·thard** (saN gô tar′). Italian, **San Gottardo.**

St. He·le·na (hə lē′nə), **1.** a British island in the S Atlantic: Napoleon's exile 1815–21. 5147; 47 sq. mi. **2.** a British colony comprising this island, Ascension Island, and the Tristan da Cunha group. 5147; 126 sq. mi. *Cap.:* Jamestown.

St. Hel·ens (hel′inz), **1.** a city in SW Lancashire, in NW England, near Liverpool. 194,700. **2. Mount,** an active volcano in NW United States, S of Seattle, Washington: major eruptions 1980. ab. 9677 ft.

St. Hel·ier (sänt′ hel′yər; *Fr.* saN te lyā′), a seaport on the island of Jersey in the English Channel: resort. 28,135.

sthe·ni·a (sthə nī′ə, sthē′nē ə), *n. Pathol.* strength; excessive vital force. Cf. **asthenia.** [< NL, abstracted from ASTHENIA]

sthen·ic (sthen′ik), *adj.* sturdy; heavily and strongly built. [abstracted from ASTHENIC]

Sthe·no (sthē′nō, sthen′ō), *n. Class. Myth.* one of the three Gorgons.

stibi-, a combining form of **stibium:** *stibial.* Also, *esp. before a vowel,* **stib-.**

stib·i·al (stib′ē əl), *adj.* of or resembling antimony.

stib·ine (stib′ēn, -in), *n.* **1.** *Chem.* a poisonous gas, SbH_3. **2.** any derivative of this compound in which the hydrogen atoms are replaced by one or more organic groups.

stib·i·um (stib′ē əm), *n. Chem.* antimony. [late ME < L < Gk *stíbi* (var. of *stímmi* < Egypt *stm*)]

stib·nite (stib′nīt), *n.* a soft mineral, antimony sulfide, Sb_2S_3, lead-gray in color with a metallic luster: the most important ore of antimony. [STIB(I)NE (in obs. sense of stibnite) + -ITE[1]]

stich (stik), *n.* a verse or line of poetry. [< Gk *stích*(*os*) row, line, verse]

stich·ic (stik′ik), *adj.* **1.** pertaining to or consisting of stichs or verses. **2.** composed of lines of the same metrical form throughout. [< Gk *stichikós*] —**stich′i·cal·ly,** *adv.*

sti·chom·e·try (sti kom′i trē), *n.* the practice of writing a prose text in lines the length of which corresponds to divisions in the sense and indicate phrasal rhythms. —**stich·o·met·ric** (stik′ə me′trik), **stich′o·met′ri·cal,** *adj.* —**stich′o·met′ri·cal·ly,** *adv.*

sti·cho·myth·i·a (stik′ə mith′ē ə), *n.* dramatic dialogue, as in a Greek play, characterized by brief exchanges between two characters, each of whom usually speaks in one line of verse. Also, **sti·chom·y·thy** (sti kom′ə thē). [< Gk = *sticho*(*s*) (see STICH) + *-mythia* (*mŷth*(*os*) speech, story + *-ia* -IA)] —**stich′o·myth′ic,** *adj.*

-stich·ous, *Bot., Zool.* a word element referring to rows: *distichous.* [< LL *-stichus* < Gk *-stichos,* as comb. form; see STICH]

stick[1] (stik), *n., v.,* **sticked, stick·ing.** —*n.* **1.** a branch or shoot from a tree or shrub. **2.** a relatively long and slender piece of wood. **3.** a long piece of wood for use in carpentry. **4.** a rod or wand. **5.** a baton. **6.** *Chiefly Brit.* a walking stick or cane. **7.** a club or cudgel. **8.** a long, slender piece of anything. **9.** *Sports.* an implement used to drive or propel a ball or puck, as a crosse or a hockey stick. **10.** *Aeron.* a lever by which the longitudinal and lateral motions of an airplane are controlled. **11.** *Naut.* a mast or spar. **12.** *Print.* See **composing stick. 13.** *Mil.* a group of bombs so arranged as to be released in a row across a target. **14.** *Slang.* a marijuana cigarette; reefer. **15. the sticks,** *U.S. Informal.* any region distant from cities or towns, as rural districts; the country. —*v.t.* **16.** to furnish (a plant, vine, etc.) with a stick or sticks in order to prop or support. **17.** *Print.* to set (type) in a composing stick. [ME *stikke,* OE *sticca*]

stick[2] (stik), *v.,* **stuck, stick·ing,** *n.* —*v.t.* **1.** to pierce or puncture with something pointed. **2.** to kill by stabbing: *to stick a pig.* **3.** to insert (something pointed) so as to pierce or puncture. **4.** to fasten in position by thrusting a point or end into something: *to stick a peg in a pegboard.* **5.** to fasten in position by or as by something thrust through: *to stick a painting on the wall.* **6.** to put or hold something pointed; impale: *to stick a marshmallow on a fork.* **7.** to decorate or furnish with things piercing the surface: *to stick a cushion full of pins.* **8.** to furnish or adorn with things attached or set here and there. **9.** to place upon a stick or pin for exhibit: *to stick butterflies.* **10.** to place or set in a specified position; put: *Stick the chair in the corner.* **11.** to fasten or attach by causing to adhere: *to stick a stamp on a letter.* **12.** to bring to a standstill; render unable to proceed or go back (usually used in the passive): *The car was stuck in the mud.* **13.** to tolerate; endure: *He couldn't stick the job more than three days.* **14.** to confuse or puzzle; bewilder; perplex; nonplus: *The problem stuck him.* **15.** *Informal.* to impose something disagreeable upon (a person or persons).
—*v.i.* **16.** to have the point piercing or embedded in something: *The arrow stuck in the tree.* **17.** to remain attached by adhesion. **18.** to hold, cleave, or cling. **19.** to remain persistently or permanently: *a fact that sticks in the mind.* **20.** to remain firm, as in resolution, opinion, etc. **21.** to keep or remain steadily or unremittingly, as to a task. **22.** to become fastened, hindered, checked, or stationary by some obstruction. **23.** to be at a standstill, as from difficulties. **24.** to be embarrassed or puzzled; hesitate or scruple (usually fol. by *at*). **25.** to be thrust or placed so as to extend or protrude (usually fol. by *through, out,* etc.). **26. stick around,** *Slang.* to wait in the vicinity; linger. **27. stick by** or **to,** to maintain one's attachment or loyalty to; remain faithful. **28. stick one's neck out.** See **neck** (def. 15). **29. stick something out,** *Informal.* to stay with to the end; endure. **30. stick to one's guns.** See **gun**[1] (def. 9). **31. stick to the** or **one's ribs,** *Informal.* to be substantial and nourishing, as a hearty meal. **32. stick up,** *Slang.* to rob, esp. at gunpoint. **33. stick up for,** *Informal.* to speak in favor of; come to the defense of; support.
—*n.* **34.** a thrust with a pointed instrument; stab. **35.** a stoppage or standstill. **36.** something causing delay or difficulty. **37.** the quality of adhering or of causing things to adhere. **38.** something causing adhesion. [ME *stike*(*n*), OE *stician;* akin to G *stechen* to sting, L *-stig-* in *instīgāre* (see INSTIGATE)] —**stick′a·bil′i·ty,** *n.* —**stick′a·ble,** *adj.*
—**Syn. 1.** penetrate, spear, transfix, pin. **11.** glue, cement, paste. **17.** STICK, ADHERE, COHERE mean to cling to or be tightly attached to something. ADHERE implies that one kind of material clings tenaciously to another; COHERE adds the idea that a thing is attracted to and held by something like itself: *Particles of sealing wax cohere and form a mass which will adhere to tin.* STICK, a more colloquial and general term, is used particularly when a third kind of material is involved: *A gummed label will stick to a package.*

stick·ball (stik′bôl′), *n.* a form of baseball played with a rubber ball and a broomstick or the like.

stick·er (stik′ər), *n.* **1.** an adhesive label. **2.** a persistent, diligent person, esp. one who adheres closely to rules, plans, etc. **3.** *Informal.* something, as a problem or riddle, that puzzles one.

stick′er price′, the manufacturer's suggested retail price, esp. on a new automobile, from which a discount is usually given.

stick·ful (stik′fo͝ol′), *n., pl.* **-fuls.** *Print.* the amount of set type that a composing stick will hold, usually about two column inches.

stick′ing plas′ter, an adhesive cloth or other material for holding bandages or the like in place.

stick-in-the-mud (stik′in *th*ə mud′), *n. Informal.* someone who avoids or rejects new activities, ideas, or attitudes.

stick·le (stik′əl), *v.i.,* **-led, -ling.** **1.** to argue or haggle insistently, esp. on trivial matters. **2.** to raise objections; scruple; demur. [ME *stightle* to set in order, freq. of obs. *stighte,* OE *stiht(an)* (to) arrange; c. G *stiften,* Icel *stétta* to set up]

stick·le·back (stik′əl bak′), *n., pl.* (*esp. collectively*) **-back,** (*esp. referring to two or more kinds or species*) **-backs.** any of the small pugnacious, spiny-backed fishes of the family *Gasterosteidae,* found in northern fresh waters and sea inlets. [late ME *stykylbak,* OE *sticol* scaly + *bæc* BACK[1]]

Stickleback, *Eucalia inconstans* (Length 2½ in.)

stick·ler (stik′lər), *n.* **1.** a person who insists on something rigidly (usually fol. by *for*): *a stickler for ceremony.* **2.** any puzzling or difficult problem.

stick·out (stik′out′), *n. Informal.* a person or thing that is outstanding or conspicuous.

stick·pin (stik′pin′), *n.* a decorative straight pin holding an ascot or necktie in place.

stick·seed (stik′sēd′), *n.* any of the boraginaceous herbs of the genus *Lappula,* having prickly seeds that adhere to clothing.

stick′ shift′, a manually operated transmission for a motor vehicle with a shift lever set either in the floor or on the steering column.

stick·tight (stik′tīt′), *n.* **1.** a composite herb, *Bidens frondosa,* having flat, barbed achenes that adhere to clothing or fur. **2.** any of several other plants of this genus. **3.** the barbed achene of any of these plants.

stick-to-it-ive (stik′to͞o′it iv, -i tiv), *adj. Informal.* tenaciously resolute; persevering: *Stick-to-it-ive people get ahead.* [adj. use of v. phrase *stick to it;* see -IVE] **—stick′-to′-it-ive·ness,** *n.*

stick·up (stik′up′), *n. Slang.* a holdup; robbery.

stick·weed (stik′wēd′), *n.* ragweed.

stick·y (stik′ē), *adj.,* **stick·i·er, stick·i·est.** **1.** having the property of adhering, as glue; adhesive. **2.** covered with adhesive or viscid matter: *sticky hands.* **3.** (of the weather or climate) hot and humid. **4.** requiring careful treatment; awkwardly difficult. **—stick′i·ly,** *adv.* **—stick′i·ness,** *n.*

stick·y-fin·gered (stik′ē fing′gərd), *adj.* prone to steal.

Stieg·litz (stēg′lits), *n.* **Alfred,** 1864–1946, U.S. photographer.

stiff (stif), *adj.* **1.** rigid or firm; difficult or impossible to bend or flex: *a stiff collar.* **2.** not moving or working easily: *a stiff motor.* **3.** (of a person or animal) not supple; moving with difficulty, as from cold, age, etc. **4.** strong; forceful; powerful: *stiff winds.* **5.** strong or potent to the taste or system, as a beverage. **6.** resolute; firm in purpose; stubborn. **7.** stubbornly maintained: *a stiff battle.* **8.** firm against any tendency to decrease, as stock-market prices. **9.** rigidly formal, as people or manners. **10.** lacking ease and grace; awkward: *a stiff style of writing.* **11.** excessively regular or formal, as a design. **12.** laborious or difficult, as a task. **13.** severe or harsh, as a penalty or demand. **14.** excessive; unusually high or great. **15.** firm from tension; taut. **16.** relatively firm in consistency, as semisolid matter; thick. **17.** dense or compact; not friable: *stiff soil.* **18.** *Naut.* (of a vessel) having a high resistance to rolling; stable (opposed to *crank*). **—***n.* **19.** *Slang.* **a.** a dead body; corpse. **b.** a drunk. **20.** *Slang.* **a.** a fellow: *lucky stiff; poor stiff.* **b.** a tramp; hobo. **c.** a laborer. **—***adv.* **21.** in or to a firm or rigid state. **22.** completely, intensely, or extremely: *to be bored stiff; to be scared stiff.* [ME; OE *stīf;* c. G *steif;* akin to STIFLE[1], STEEVE[1]] **—stiff′ish,** *adj.* **—stiff′ly,** *adv.* **—stiff′ness,** *n.* **—Syn. 1.** unbending, unyielding. See **firm**[1]. **6.** obstinate, pertinacious. **9.** reserved, constrained.

stiff-arm (stif′ärm′), *v.t., n.* straight-arm.

stiff·en (stif′ən), *v.t.* **1.** to make stiff. **—***v.i.* **2.** to become stiff. **3.** to become tense, as in bracing oneself for or drawing back from shock. **—stiff′en·er,** *n.*

stiff-necked (stif′nekt′), *adj.* **1.** having a stiff neck. **2.** stubborn; refractory. **—stiff-neck·ed·ly,** (stif′nek′id lē, -nekt′lē), *adv.* **—stiff′-neck′ed·ness,** *n.*

sti·fle[1] (stī′fəl), *v.,* **-fled, -fling.** **—***v.t.* **1.** to kill by impeding respiration; smother. **2.** to suppress, curb, or withhold. **3.** to quell, crush, or end by force. **—***v.i.* **4.** to become stifled. **5.** to suffer from difficulty in breathing, as in a close atmosphere. [< Scand; cf. Icel *stīfla* to stop up; akin to STIFF] **—sti′fler,** *n.* **—Syn. 1.** suffocate, strangle, choke. **2.** check. **3.** prevent, preclude. **—Ant. 2, 3.** encourage.

sti·fle[2] (stī′fəl), *n.* (in a horse or other quadruped) the joint that is between the femur and the tibia and joins the hind leg and the body, corresponding anatomically to the human knee. Also called **sti′fle joint′.** [ME < ?]

sti·fling (stī′fling), *adj.* suffocating; oppressively close. **—sti′fling·ly,** *adv.*

stig·ma (stig′mə), *n., pl.* **stig·ma·ta** (stig′mə tə, stig-mä′tə, -mat′ə), **stig·mas.** **1.** a stain or reproach, as on one's reputation. **2.** *Med.* **a.** a mark on the skin, esp. one characteristic of a defect, disease, etc.: *the stigmata of leprosy.* **b.** a mark on the skin that bleeds during certain mental states, as in hysteria. **3.** *Zool.* **a.** a small mark, spot, or pore on an animal or organ. **b.** the eyespot of a protozoan. **c.** an entrance into the respiratory system of insects. **4.** *Bot.* the part of a pistil which receives the pollen. **5. stigmata,** marks resembling the wounds of the crucified body of Christ, said to be supernaturally impressed on the bodies of certain holy persons. **6.** *Archaic.* a mark made by a branding iron on the skin of a criminal or slave. [< L < Gk: tattoo mark = *stig-* (s. of *stízein* to tattoo) + *-ma* n. suffix denoting result of action]

stig·mas·ter·ol (stig mas′tə rōl′, -rôl′), *n. Biochem.* a steroid, $C_{29}H_{48}O$, used chiefly as a raw material in the manufacture of progesterone. [< NL *(Physo)stigm(a)* (see PHYSOSTIGMINE) + STEROL]

stig·mat·ic (stig mat′ik), *adj.* Also, **stig·mat′i·cal.** **1.** pertaining to a stigma, mark, spot, or the like. **2.** *Bot.* pertaining to or having the character of a stigma. **3.** *Optics.* converging to a point; anastigmatic. **—***n.* **4.** one marked with supernatural stigmata. [< ML *stigmatic(us)* = *stigmat-* (s. of Gk *stígma*) STIGMA + *-icus* -IC] **—stig·mat′i·cal·ly,** *adv.* **—stig·mat′i·cal·ness,** *n.*

stig·ma·tise (stig′mə tīz′), *v.t.,* **-tised, -tis·ing.** *Chiefly Brit.* stigmatize. **—stig′ma·ti·sa′tion,** *n.* **—stig′ma·tis′er,** *n.*

stig·ma·tism (stig′mə tiz′əm), *n. Optics.* the property of a lens that is stigmatic. [*stigmat-* (see STIGMATIC) + -ISM]

stig·ma·tize (stig′mə tīz′), *v.t.,* **-tized, -tiz·ing.** **1.** to mark with a stigma or brand. **2.** to set some mark of disgrace or infamy upon. **3.** to produce stigmata, marks, spots, or the like, on. Also, *esp. Brit.,* **stigmatise.** [< ML *stigmatiz(āre)* = *stigmat-* (see STIGMATIC) + *-izāre* -IZE] **—stig′-ma·ti·za′tion,** *n.* **—stig′ma·tiz′er,** *n.*

stil·bes·trol (stil bes′trōl, -trôl, -trol), *n. Pharm.* diethylstilbestrol. Also, **stil·boes′trol.** [STILB(ENE) + ESTR(US) + -OL[1]]

stil·bite (stil′bīt), *n.* a white-to-brown or red zeolite mineral, a hydrous silicate of calcium and aluminum, occurring in sheaflike aggregates of crystals and in radiated masses. [< Gk *stílb-* (s. of *stílbein* to shine) + -ITE[1]]

stile[1] (stīl), *n.* **1.** a series of steps or rungs used for passing over a wall or fence. **2.** a turnstile. [ME; OE *stigel* < *stīgan* to climb, c. G *steigen*]

stile[2] (stīl), *n. Carpentry, Furniture.* any of various upright members framing panels or the like, as in a paneled door, chest of drawers, etc. Cf. **rail**[1] (def. 7). [perh. < D *stijl* pillar, prop]

sti·let·to (sti let′ō), *n., pl.* **-tos, -toes,** *v.,* **-toed, -to·ing.** **—***n.* **1.** a short dagger with a slender blade. **2.** a small pointed instrument for making eyelet holes in needlework. **—***v.t.* **3.** to stab or kill with a stiletto. [< It = *stil(o)* dagger (< L *stilus* STYLUS) + *-etto* -ETTE]

Stil·i·cho (stil′ə kō′), *n.* **Fla·vi·us** (flā′vē əs), A.D. 359?–408, Roman general and statesman.

still[1] (stil), *adj.* **1.** remaining in place or at rest; motionless; stationary: *to stand still.* **2.** free or refraining from sound or noise. **3.** subdued or low in sound; hushed: *a still murmur.* **4.** free from turbulence or commotion; peaceful; calm: *the still air.* **5.** not flowing, as water. **6.** not effervescent, as wine. **7.** *Photog.* noting, pertaining to, or used for making single photographs, as opposed to a motion picture. **—***n.* **8.** stillness or silence: *the still of the night.* **9.** *Photog.* a single photographic print, as of one of the frames of a motion-picture film. **—***adv.* **10.** at this or that time; as previously: *Are you still here?* **11.** up to this or that time; as yet. **12.** in the future as in the past: *Objections will still be made.* **13.** even; in addition; yet (used to emphasize a comparative). **14.** even then; yet; nevertheless. **15.** without sound or movement: *Sit still!* **16.** at or to a greater distance or degree. **17.** *Archaic.* steadily; constantly; always. **—***conj.* **18.** and yet; but yet; nevertheless: *It was futile, still they fought.* **19. still and all,** *U.S.* nevertheless. **—***v.t.* **20.** to silence or hush (sounds, voices, etc.). **21.** to calm, appease, or allay. **22.** to subdue or cause to subside. **—***v.i.* **23.** to become still or quiet. [ME, OE *stille;* c. G *still;* akin to STALL[1]]

—Syn. 1. unmoving, inert, quiescent. **2.** soundless, mute. STILL, QUIET, HUSHED, NOISELESS, SILENT indicate the absence of noise and of excitement or activity accompanied by sound. STILL indicates the absence of sound or movement: *The house was still.* QUIET implies relative freedom from noise, activity, or excitement: *a quiet engine; a quiet vacation.* HUSHED implies the suppression of sound or noise: *a hushed whisper.* NOISELESS and SILENT characterize that which does not reveal its presence or movement by any sound: *a noiseless footstep; silent dissent.* **4.** serene. **8.** quiet, hush, calm. **18.** See **but**[1]. **20.** quiet, muffle. **21.** soothe.

still[2] (stil), *n.* **1.** a distilling apparatus, consisting of a vessel in which a liquid is heated and vaporized and a cooling device or coil for condensing the vapor. **2.** a distillery. **—***v.t., v.i.* **3.** to distill. [aph. var. of DISTILL]

Still (stil), *n.* **Andrew Taylor,** 1828–1917, U.S. founder of osteopathy.

still·birth (stil′bûrth′), *n.* **1.** the birth of a dead child or organism. **2.** a fetus dead at birth.

still·born (stil′bôrn′), *adj.* **1.** dead when born. **2.** ineffectual; abortive; fruitless.

stil·li·form (stil′ə fôrm′), *adj.* drop-shaped; globular. [*stilli-* (comb. form of L *stilla* drop) + -FORM]

still′ life′, *pl.* **still lifes.** *Fine Arts, Photography.* **1.** the category of subject matter in which inanimate objects are represented. **2.** a representation of inanimate objects as of a bowl of fruit. **—still′-life′,** *adj.*

still·ness (stil′nis), *n.* **1.** absence of motion. **2.** silence; quiet; hush. [ME *stilnesse,* OE *stilnes*]

Still′son wrench′ (stil′sən), *Trademark.* a monkey wrench with a pivoted, adjustable jaw that grips pipes, bars, etc., more tightly when pressure is exerted on the handle.

Still·wa·ter (stil′wô′tər, -wot′ər), *n.* a city in N Oklahoma. 31,126 (1970).

stil·ly (*adv.* stil′lē; *adj.* stil′ē), *adv.* **1.** quietly; silently. **—***adj.* **2.** *Chiefly Literary.* still; quiet. [ME; OE *stillice*]

stilt (stilt), *n.* **1.** one of two poles, each with a support for the foot at some distance above the bottom end, enabling the wearer to walk with his feet above the ground. **2.** one of several posts supporting a structure built above the surface of land or water. **3.** any of several limicoline birds, esp. of the genus *Himantopus,* found chiefly in marshes, having long legs, a long neck, and a slender bill. **—***v.t.* **4.** to raise on or as on stilts. [ME *stilte;* c. LG *stilte* pole, G *Stelze*] —**stilt′like′,** *adj.*

stilt·ed (stil′tid), *adj.* **1.** stiffly dignified or formal, as speech, literary style, etc.; pompous. **2.** *Archit.* (of an arch) resting on imposts treated in part as downward continuations of the arch.

Stil·ton (stil′tᵊn), *n.* a waxy, white cheese, veined with mold: made principally in England. [after *Stilton,* place in England where it was first sold]

Stil·well (stil′wel, -wəl), *n.* **Joseph W.** ("*Vinegar Joe*"), 1883–1946, U.S. general.

stime (stīm), *n. Scot., Irish Eng.* the smallest bit; a drop, taste, or glimpse. [ME, perh. var. (by mishearing) of *skime < Scand; cf. Icel *skīma,* c. OE *scīma* ray, light]

Stim·son (stim′sən), *n.* **Henry L(ewis),** 1867–1950, U.S. statesman: Secretary of War 1911–13, 1940–45; Secretary of State 1929–33.

stim·u·lant (stim′yə lənt), *n.* **1.** *Physiol., Med.* something that temporarily quickens some vital process or functional activity. **2.** any food or beverage that stimulates, as coffee or tea. **3.** a stimulus or incentive. —*adj.* **4.** *Physiol., Med.* temporarily quickening some vital process or functional activity. **5.** stimulating. Cf. **depressant.** [< L *stimulant-* (s. of *stimulāns,* prp. of *stimulāre* to goad). See STIMULUS, -ANT]

stim·u·late (stim′yə lāt′), *v.,* **-lat·ed, -lat·ing.** —*v.t.* **1.** to rouse to action or effort, as by encouragement or pressure; incite. **2.** *Physiol., Med.* to excite (a nerve, gland, etc.) to its functional activity. **3.** to invigorate by a food or beverage containing a stimulant. —*v.i.* **4.** to act as a stimulus or stimulant. [< L *stimulāt(us)* (ptp. of *stimulāre* to goad). See STIMULUS, -ATE¹] —**stim·u·la·bil·i·ty** (stim′yə lə bil′i tē), *n.* —**stim′u·la·ble,** *adj.* —**stim′u·lat′ing·ly,** *adv.* —**stim′u·la′tor, stim′u·lat′er,** *n.* —**stim′u·la′tion,** *n.*

stim·u·la·tive (stim′yə lā′tiv), *adj.* **1.** serving to stimulate. —*n.* **2.** a stimulating agency.

stim·u·lus (stim′yə ləs), *n., pl.* **-li** (-lī′). **1.** something that incites or quickens action, feeling, thought, etc. **2.** *Physiol., Med.* something that excites an organism or part to functional activity. [< L: a goad] —**Syn. 1.** incitement, provocation.

sti·my (stī′mē), *n., pl.* **-mies,** *v.t.,* **-mied, -my·ing.** stymie.

sting (sting), *v.,* **stung** or (*Archaic or Obs.*) **stang; stung; sting·ing;** *n.* —*v.t.* **1.** to prick or wound with a sharp-pointed, often venom-bearing organ. **2.** to affect painfully or irritatingly as a result of contact, as certain plants do. **3.** to cause to smart or to feel a sharp pain. **4.** to cause mental or moral anguish. **5.** to goad or drive, as by sharp irritation. **6.** *Slang.* to cheat or take advantage of, esp. to overcharge; soak. —*v.i.* **7.** to use, have, or wound with a sting, as bees. **8.** to cause a sharp, smarting pain. **9.** to cause acute mental pain or irritation: *The memory of that insult still stings.* **10.** to feel acute mental pain or irritation. **11.** to feel a smarting pain, as from the sting of an insect or from a blow. —*n.* **12.** the act or an instance of stinging. **13.** a wound, pain, or smart caused by stinging. **14.** any sharp physical or mental pain. **15.** anything or an element in anything that wounds, pains, or irritates. **16.** the capacity to wound or pain: *Satire has a sting.* **17.** a sharp stimulus or incitement. **18.** *Bot.* a glandular hair on certain plants, as nettles, that emits an irritating fluid. **19.** *Zool.* any of various sharp-pointed, often venom-bearing organs of insects and other animals capable of inflicting painful or dangerous wounds. **20.** *Slang.* **a.** See **confidence game. b.** an ostensibly illegal operation, as the buying of stolen goods or the bribing of public officials, used by undercover investigators to collect evidence of wrongdoing. [ME; OE *sting(an);* c. Icel *stinga* to pierce, Goth *-stangan* (in *usstangan* to pull out)] —**sting′ing·ly,** *adv.* —**sting′ing·ness,** *n.* —**sting′less,** *adj.*

sting·a·ree (sting′ə rē′, sting′ə rē′), *n.* stingray.

sting·er (sting′ər), *n.* **1.** a person or thing that stings. **2.** an animal or plant having a stinging organ. **3.** the sting or stinging organ of an insect or other animal. **4.** a cocktail made of brandy and crème de menthe.

sting′ing hair′, *Bot.* sting (def. 18).

stin·go (sting′gō), *n. Chiefly Brit. Slang.* **1.** strong beer or ale. **2.** vitality or vigor. [STING + -O; cf. BLOTTO, STINKO]

sting·ray (sting′rā′), *n.* any of the rays, esp. of the family *Dasyatidae,* having a long, flexible tail armed near the base with a strong, serrated bony spine with which they can inflict severe and very painful wounds. Also, **stingaree.**

Stingray, *Dasyatis centroura* (Width 5 ft.; total length 10 ft.; tail 7¼ ft.)

stin·gy¹ (stin′jē), *adj.,* **-gi·er, -gi·est. 1.** reluctant to give or spend; niggardly; penurious. **2.** scanty or meager. [dial. *stingy* spiky, hence bad-tempered = *stinge* (OE *steng* stake) + -Y¹; akin to STING] —**stin′gi·ly,** *adv.* —**stin′gi·ness,** *n.* —**Syn. 1.** parsimonious, miserly. —**Ant. 1.** generous.

sting·y² (sting′ē), *adj.* capable of stinging or having a sting. [STING + -Y¹]

stink (stingk), *v.,* **stank** or, often, **stunk; stunk; stink·ing;** *n.* —*v.i.* **1.** to emit a strong offensive smell. **2.** to be offensive to propriety. **3.** *Slang.* to be disgustingly inferior. **4.** *Slang.* to have a large quantity of something, esp. money (usually fol. by *of* or *with*). —*v.t.* **5.** to cause to stink (often fol. by *up*). —*n.* **6.** a strong offensive smell; stench. **7.** *Slang.* an unpleasant fuss; scandal. **8. stinks,** (*construed as sing.*) *Brit. Slang.* chemistry or natural science as a course of study. [ME *stink(en),* OE *stincan;* c. G *stinken.* Cf. STENCH]

stink·ard (sting′kərd), *n. Obs.* a despicable person; stinker. —**stink′ard·ly,** *adv.*

stink′ bomb′, a small bomb made to emit a foul smell on exploding.

stink′ bug′, any of numerous flat, hemipterous insects of the family *Pentatomidae* that emit a disagreeable odor.

stink·er (sting′kər), *n.* **1.** a person or thing that stinks. **2.** *Slang.* a mean or despicable person; louse. **3.** *Slang.* something of inferior quality, as a play, novel, etc. **4.** *Slang.* something difficult. **5.** any device emitting an offensive odor, as a stink bomb, stinkpot, etc.

stink·horn (stingk′hôrn′), *n.* any of various rank-smelling, basidiomycetous fungi of the genus *Phallus,* esp. *P. impudicus.*

stink·ing (sting′king), *adj.* **1.** foul-smelling. **2.** contemptible; disgusting: *a stinking shame.* [ME *stinkinge,* OE *stincende*] —**stink′ing·ly,** *adv.* —**stink′ing·ness,** *n.* —**Syn. 1.** smelly, putrid, rotten, putrescent, rank.

stink′ing smut′, bunt³.

stink·o (sting′kō), *adj. Slang.* drunk. [STINK + (BLOTT)O]

stink·pot (stingk′pot′), *n.* a jar containing foul-smelling combustibles or other materials that generate offensive and suffocating vapors, formerly used in warfare.

stink·weed (stingk′wēd′), *n.* any of various rank-smelling plants, as the jimson weed.

stink·y (sting′kē), *adj.,* **stink·i·er, stink·i·est.** foul-smelling; stinking.

stint¹ (stint), *v.t.* **1.** to limit to a certain amount, number, etc., often unduly. **2.** *Archaic.* to bring to an end; check. —*v.i.* **3.** to be frugal. **4.** *Archaic.* to cease action; desist. —*n.* **5.** limitation or restriction, esp. as to amount. **6.** a limited, prescribed, or expected quantity, share, rate, etc.: *to exceed one's stint.* **7.** *Obs.* a pause; halt. [ME; OE *stynt(an)* (to) make blunt, dull; c. Icel *stytta* to shorten; cf. STUNT¹] —**stint′ed·ly,** *adv.* —**stint′ed·ness,** *n.* —**stint′er,** *n.* —**stint′ing·ly,** *adv.* —**stint′less,** *adj.* —**Syn. 1.** confine, restrain. **5.** restraint, constraint. **6.** allotment, portion.

stint² (stint), *n.* any of various small sandpipers. [late ME *stynte,* appar. OE *stynte or *stynta, lit., the foolish one < *stunt* foolish; see STUNT¹, STINT¹]

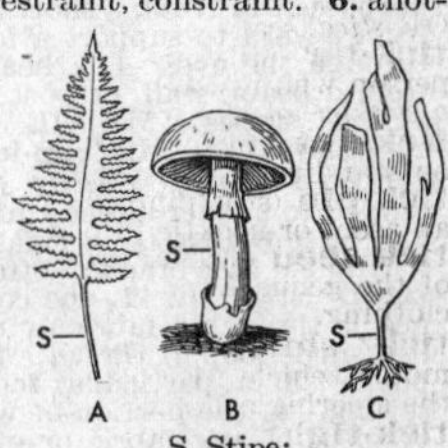

S, Stipe; A, Fern; B, Mushroom; C, Kelp

stipe (stīp), *n.* **1.** *Bot.* a stalk or slender support, as the petiole of a fern frond, the stem supporting the pileus of a mushroom, or a stalklike elongation of the receptacle of a flower. **2.** *Zool.* a stemlike part, as a footstalk; stalk. [< F: < L *stīp(es)* post, tree trunk or branch, log; see STIFF]

sti·pel (stī′pəl), *n. Bot.* a secondary stipule situated at the base of a leaflet of a compound leaf. [< NL *stipell(a),* alter. of L *stipula* (see STIPULE), with *-ella* r. *-ula* -ULE] —**sti·pel·late** (stī pel′it, -āt, stī′pə lit, -lāt′), *adj.*

sti·pend (stī′pend), *n.* **1.** fixed or regular pay; salary. **2.** any periodic payment, esp. a scholarship allowance. [late ME *stipend(i)e* < L *stīpendi(um)* soldier's pay = *stī-* (for *stipi-,* s. of *stips* a coin) + *pend-* weigh out, pay (see PEND) + *-ium* n. suffix] —**sti′pend·less,** *adj.* —**Syn.** See **pay**¹.

sti·pen·di·ar·y (stī pen′dē er′ē), *adj., n., pl.* **-ar·ies.** —*adj.* **1.** receiving a stipend. **2.** paid for by a stipend. **3.** pertaining to or of the nature of a stipend. —*n.* **4.** a person who receives a stipend. [< L *stīpendiāri(us)* = *stīpendi(um)* STIPEND + *-ārius* -ARY]

sti·pes (stī′pēz), *n., pl.* **stip·i·tes** (stip′i tēz′). **1.** *Zool.* the second joint in a maxilla of crustaceans and insects. **2.** *Bot.* a stipe. [< L; see STIPE]

stip·ple (stip′əl), *v.,* **-pled, -pling,** *n.* —*v.t.* **1.** to paint, engrave, or draw by means of dots or small touches. —*n.* Also, **stip′pling. 2.** the method of painting, engraving, etc. by stippling. **3.** stippled work. [< D *stippel(en),* freq. of *stippen* to dot, speckle < *stip* point, dot] —**stip′pler,** *n.*

stip·u·late¹ (stip′yə lāt′), *v.,* **-lat·ed, -lat·ing.** —*v.i.* **1.** to make an express demand or arrangement as a condition of agreement (often fol. by *for*). —*v.t.* **2.** to arrange expressly or specify in terms of agreement: *to stipulate a price.* **3.** to require as an essential condition in making an agreement. **4.** to promise, in making an agreement. [< L *stipulāt(us)* (ptp. of *stipulārī* to demand a formal agreement) = *stipul-* firm (see STIPULE) + *-ātus* -ATE¹] —**stip·u·la·ble** (stip′yə lə bəl), *adj.* —**stip′u·la′tor,** *n.* —**stip·u·la·to·ry** (stip′yə lə tôr′ē, -tōr′ē), *adj.*

stip·u·late² (stip′yə lit, -lāt′), *adj. Bot.* having stipules. [< NL *stipulāt(us)*]

stip·u·la·tion (stip′yə lā′shən), *n.* **1.** the act of stipulating. **2.** a condition, demand, or promise in an agreement or contract. [< L *stipulātiōn-* (s. of *stipulātiō*)]

S, Stipule; A, Dog rose, *Rosa canina;* B, Pea, *Pisum satium;* C, Pansy, *Viola tricolor hortensis*

stip·ule (stip′yo͞ol), *n. Bot.* one of a pair of lateral appendages at the base of a leaf petiole in many plants. [< L *stipul(a)* stalk, n. use of fem. of *stipulus firm (recorded in LL); akin to STIPES; see STIFF] —**stip′u·lar,** *adj.*

stir¹ (stûr), *v.,* **stirred, stir·ring,** *n.* —*v.t.* **1.** to agitate (a liquid or other substance) with a continuous or repeated movement of an implement or one's hand. **2.** to move, esp. in a slight way: *He would not stir a finger to help them.* **3.** to set in tremulous, fluttering, or irregular motion. **4.** to move briskly; bestir: *to stir oneself.* **5.** to rouse from inactivity, indifference, etc. (usually fol. by *up*). **6.** to incite, instigate, or prompt (usually fol. by *up*). **7.** to affect strongly; excite. **8.** *Archaic.* to bring up for notice or discussion. **9.** *Archaic.* to disturb; trouble. —*v.i.* **10.** to move, esp. slightly or lightly. **11.** to move around, esp. briskly; be active. **12.** to be in circulation, current, or afoot. **13.** to become active, as from some rousing impulse. **14.** to be emotionally moved. —*n.* **15.** the act of stirring or moving. **16.** movement, esp. brisk and busy movement. **17.** the sound made by stirring or moving slightly. **18.** a state or occasion of general excitement; commotion. **19.** a mental impulse, sensation, or feeling. **20.** a jog, poke, or thrust. [ME *stir(en)*, OE *styrian*; c. G *stören*; akin to Icel *styrr* disturbance; see STORM] —**stir′ra·ble,** *adj.* —**stir′rer,** *n.* —**Syn. 6.** rouse. **16.** bustle. **18.** fuss, uproar. See **ado.**

stir[2] (stûr), *n. Slang.* prison. [? var. of obs. *steer*, OE *stēor* discipline, restraint, punishment]

stir-cra·zy (stûr′krā′zē), *adj. Slang.* mentally ill because of long imprisonment.

stir-fry (stûr′frī′), *v.t.,* **-fried, -fry·ing.** to cook (food) quickly by cutting it into small pieces and stirring it constantly in a lightly oiled frying pan over high heat: the most common method of Chinese cookery.

Stir·ling (stûr′ling), *n.* **1.** Also called **Stir·ling·shire** (stûr′ling shēr′, -shər). a county in central Scotland. 144,858 (1961); 451 sq. mi. **2.** its county seat, on the Forth River. 27,503 (est. 1964).

stirps (stûrps), *n., pl.* **stir·pes** (stûr′pēz). **1.** a stock; family or branch of a family; line of descent. **2.** *Law.* one from whom a family is descended. **3.** *Biol. Obs.* a family, superfamily, or permanent variety. [< L: rootstock, trunk]

stir·ring (stûr′ing), *adj.* **1.** rousing, exciting, or thrilling. **2.** moving, active, or lively. [ME *stiringe*, OE *styriende*] —**stir′ring·ly,** *adv.*

stir·rup (stûr′əp, stir′-, stur′-), *n.* **1.** a loop, ring, or other contrivance of metal, wood, leather, etc., suspended from the saddle of a horse to support the rider's foot. **2.** any of various similar supports or clamps used for special purposes. **3.** *Naut.* a short rope with an eye at the end hung from a yard to support a footrope, the footrope being rove through the eye. **4.** a heavy metal strap or casting hung from a beam, wall, or post to support one end of a timber. **5.** *Anat.* stapes. [ME; OE *stigrāp* (*stige* ascent + *rāp* ROPE); c. G *Stegreif*] —**stir′rup·less,** *adj.* —**stir′rup·like′,** *adj.*

stir′rup cup′, *Chiefly Brit.* a farewell drink, esp. one offered to a rider already mounted for departure.

stir′rup pump′, a small hand pump held steady by a stirruplike foot bracket, often used in fire fighting.

stitch[1] (stich), *n.* **1.** one complete movement of a threaded needle through a fabric or material such as to leave behind it a single loop of thread. **2.** the loop of thread disposed in place. **3.** a particular mode of disposing the thread in sewing. **4.** the portion of work produced. **5.** a thread, bit, or piece of any fabric or of clothing: *every stitch of clothes.* **6.** the least bit of anything: *He wouldn't do a stitch of work.* **7.** a sudden, sharp pain, esp. in the intercostal muscles. —*v.t.* **8.** to work upon, join, mend, or fasten with stitches; sew. **9.** to put staples through for fastening: *to stitch cartons.* —*v.i.* **10.** to make stitches, join together, or sew. [ME *stiche*, OE *stice*; c. G *Stich* prick; akin to STICK[2]] —**stitch′er,** *n.* —**stitch′like′,** *adj.*

stitch[2] (stich), *n. Brit. Dial.* a distance, as in walking. [ME *sticche*, OE *stycce* piece; c. G *Stück*]

stitch·er·y (stich′ə rē), *n.* needlework. [STITCH[1] + -ERY]

stitch·ing (stich′ing), *n.* **1.** the act of a person or thing that stitches. **2.** a series or line of stitches. **3.** mending by means of sewing.

stitch·wort (stich′wûrt′), *n.* any of certain herbs of the genus *Stellaria* (or *Alsine*), as *S. Holostea*, of the Old World, having white flowers. [ME *stichewort*, OE *sticwyrt* agrimony]

stith·y (stith′ē, stith′ē), *n., pl.* **stith·ies,** *v.,* **stith·ied, stith·y·ing.** —*n.* **1.** an anvil. **2.** a forge or smithy. —*v.t.* **3.** *Obs.* to forge. [ME *stithie*, var. of *stethie* < Scand; cf. Icel *stethja* (acc. of *stethi*); akin to STAND]

sti·ver (stī′vər), *n.* **1.** Also, **stuiver.** a former nickel coin of the Netherlands, equal to five Dutch cents. **2.** the smallest possible amount: *not a stiver of work.* [< D *stuiver*]

St. John (sānt′jon′; *for 1 also* sin′jən), **1. Henry, 1st Viscount Bolingbroke.** See **Bolingbroke, 1st Viscount. 2.** an island of the Virgin Islands of the United States, in the E West Indies. 1729 (1970); ab. 20 sq. mi. **3. Lake,** a lake in SE Canada, in Quebec province, draining into the Saguenay River. 365 sq. mi. **4.** a river in the NE United States and SE Canada, flowing NE and E from Maine to New Brunswick province and then S to the Bay of Fundy. 450 mi. long. **5.** See **St. John's.**

St. Johns, a river flowing N and E through NE Florida into the Atlantic. 276 mi. long.

St. John's, 1. a seaport in and the capital of Newfoundland, on the SE part of the island. 63,633 with suburbs (1961). **2.** a seaport on and the capital of Antigua, in the E West Indies. 21,637 (1960). Also, **St. John.**

St. John's-bread (jonz′bred′), carob.

St. John's Day. See **Midsummer Day.**

St. John's Eve. See **Midsummer Eve.** Also called **St. John's Night.**

St.-John's-wort (sānt′jonz′wûrt′), *n.* any of various herbs or shrubs of the genus *Hypericum*, having yellow flowers. [so named because gathered on eve of St. John the Baptist's day to ward off evil]

St. Joseph, a city in NW Missouri, on the Missouri River. 72,691 (1970).

stk., stock.

St. Kitts (kits), one of the Leeward Islands, in the E West Indies: a member of the West Indies Associated States; formerly a British colony. 38,291 (1960); 68 sq. mi. Also called **St. Christopher.**

St. Kitts-Ne·vis-An·guil·la (kits′nē′vis ang gwil′ə), a former British colony in the Leeward Islands, in the E West Indies: comprising St. Kitts, Nevis, Anguilla, and adjacent small islands; a member of the West Indies Associated States. 56,591 (est. 1964); 155 sq. mi.

St. Lawrence, 1. a river in SE Canada, flowing NE from Lake Ontario, forming part of the boundary between New York and Ontario, and emptying into the Gulf of St. Lawrence. 760 mi. long. **2. Gulf of,** an arm of the Atlantic between SE Canada and Newfoundland.

St. Lawrence Seaway, a waterway system developed jointly by the U.S. and Canada permitting deep-draft vessels to travel from the Atlantic Ocean up the St. Lawrence River, through a series of channels, canals, and locks, to all Great Lakes ports. 182 miles long.

stlg., sterling.

St. Lô (saN lō′), a city in NW France: World War II battle 1944. 16,072 (1962).

St. Lou·is (sānt′ lo͞o′is, lo͞o′ē), a port in E Missouri, on the Mississippi. 622,236 (1970).

St. Louis Park, a city in E Minnesota, near Minneapolis. 48,922 (1970).

St. Lu·ci·a (lo͞o′shē ə, -sē ə), one of the Windward Islands, in the E West Indies: formerly a British colony; independent since 1979. 120,000; 238 sq. mi. *Cap.:* Castries.

St. Ma·lo (saN MA lō′), **1.** a fortified seaport in NW France, on the Gulf of St. Malo: resort; surrendered by German forces August 1944. 17,800 (1962). **2. Gulf of,** an arm of the English Channel in NW France. 60 mi. wide.

St. Mar·tin (sānt′ mär′tən, -tin; *Fr.* saN MAR taN′), an island in the N Leeward Islands, in the E West Indies, divided in two parts: the N section is a dependency of Guadeloupe. 4502 (1963); 20 sq. mi.; the S section is an administrative part of the Netherlands Antilles. 3643 (1963); 17 sq. mi.

St. Mar·ys (mâr′ēz), a river in the north-central U.S. and S Canada, forming the boundary between NE Michigan and Ontario, flowing SE from Lake Superior into Lake Huron. 63 mi. long. Cf. **Sault Ste. Marie.**

St.-Mi·hiel (saN mē yel′), *n.* a town in NE France, on the Meuse River, NW of Nancy: captured by American forces 1918. 5366 (1962).

St. Mo·ritz (mō rits′, mō-, mə-; mōr′its, môr′-), a resort town in SE Switzerland: center for winter sports. 3751 (1960); 6037 ft. high.

St. Na·zaire (saN NA ZAR′), a seaport in W France, on the Loire estuary. 59,181 (1962).

sto·a (stō′ə), *n., pl.* **sto·as, sto·ai** (stō′ī), **sto·ae** (stō′ē). **1.** *Gk. Archit.* a portico, usually a detached portico of considerable length, that is used as a promenade or meeting place. **2.** (*usually cap.*) *Philos.* any of the three phases of Stoicism, early, middle, and late. [< Gk *stoá*]

stoat (stōt), *n.* the ermine, *Mustela erminea*, esp. when in brown summer pelage. [ME *stote* < ?]

stob (stob), *n. Chiefly Dial.* a post. [ME; var. of STUB[1]]

stoc·ca·do (stə kä′dō), *n., pl.* **-dos.** *Archaic.* a thrust with a rapier or other pointed weapon. Also, **stoc·ca·ta** (stə kä′tə). [alter. of It *stoccata* = *stocc(o)* swordpoint, dagger (< Gmc; cf. OE *stocc* stake) + *-ata* -ADE[1]; *-ado* < Sp, as in *renegado*]

sto·chas·tic (stə kas′tik), *adj. Statistics.* of or pertaining to a process involving a randomly determined sequence of observations, each of which is considered as a sample of one element from a probability distribution. Stochastic variation implies randomness as opposed to a fixed rule or relation in passing from one observation to the next in order. [< Gk *stochastik(ós)* = *stochas-* (var. s. of *stocházesthai* to aim at) + *-tikos* -TIC] —**sto·chas′ti·cal·ly,** *adv.*

stock (stok), *n.* **1.** a supply of goods kept on hand for sale to customers by a merchant, distributor, etc.; inventory. **2.** a quantity of something accumulated, as for future use. **3.** livestock. **4.** *Theat.* a stock company: *to appear in summer stock.* **5.** *Finance.* **a.** the outstanding capital of a company or corporation. **b.** the shares of a particular company or corporation. **c.** a stock certificate. **d.** (formerly) a tally or stick used in transactions between a debtor and a creditor. **6.** *Hort.* **a.** a stem in grafting in which the bud or scion is inserted. **b.** a stem, tree, or plant that furnishes slips or cuttings. **7.** the trunk or main stem of a tree or other plant. **8.** the type from which a group of animals or plants has been derived. **9.** a race or other related group of animals or plants. **10.** the original progenitor of a family. **11.** a line of descent; a tribe, race, or ethnic group. **12.** *Anthropol.* a major division of mankind according to race. **13.** *Linguistics.* a category consisting of language families that are considered likely to be related by common origin. Cf. **family** (def. 11), **phylum** (def. 2). **14.** any grouping of related languages. **15.** the center of a wheel; hub. **16.** the handle of a whip, fishing rod, etc. **17.** *Firearms.* the wooden or metal piece to which the barrel and mechanism of a rifle are attached. **18.** the trunk or stump of a tree, left standing. **19.** (formerly) a log or block of wood. **20.** a dull or stupid person. **21.** something lifeless or senseless. **22.** the main upright part of anything, esp. a supporting structure. **23. stocks, a.** a former instrument of punishment consisting of a framework with holes for securing the ankles and, sometimes, the wrists, used to expose an offender to public derision. Cf. **pillory** (def. 1). **b.** a frame in which a horse or other animal is secured in a standing position for shoeing or for a veterinary operation. **c.** the frame on which a boat rests while under construction. **24.** *Metall.* **a.** material being smelted in a blast furnace. **b.** a metal piece to be forged. **25.** the raw material from which something is made. **26.** *Naut.* a transverse piece of wood or metal near the ring occurring on some anchors. **27.** *Cookery.* the liquor or broth prepared by boiling meat, fish, etc., and used esp. for soups and sauces. **28.** any of several plants of the genus *Mathiola*, esp. *M. incana*, having fragrant white, blue, purple, reddish, or yellowish flowers. **29.** a rhizome or rootstock. **30.** *Zool.* a compound organism. **31.** a bandlike collar or a neckcloth. **32.** *Cards.* the portion of a pack of cards that, in certain games, is left on the table, to be drawn from as occasion requires. **33.** *Railroads.* See **rolling stock. 34.** *Obs.* the frame of a plow to which the share, handles, etc., are attached. **35. lock, stock, and barrel.** See **lock**[1] (def. 7). **36. take** or **put stock in,** *Informal.* to put confidence in or attach importance to; believe; trust. —*adj.* **37.** kept regularly on hand, as for use or sale. **38.** having as one's job the care of a firm's inventory. **39.** of the common or ordinary type; banal; commonplace. **40.** of, pertaining to, or devoted to the breeding and raising of

Stocks (def. 23a)

livestock. **41.** of or pertaining to the stock of a company or corporation. **42.** *Theat.* **a.** pertaining to stock plays or pieces, or to a stock company. **b.** appearing together in a repertoire, as a company. **c.** forming part of a repertoire, as a play. **d.** being a character type fixed by convention, as in the commedia dell'arte.
—*v.t.* **43.** to furnish with a stock or supply. **44.** to furnish with livestock. **45.** to lay up in store, as for future use. **46.** to fasten to or provide with a stock, as a rifle, plow, etc. **47.** *Obs.* to put in the stocks as a punishment.
—*v.i.* **48.** to lay in a stock of something (often fol. by *up*). [ME; OE *stoc(c)* stump, stake, post, log; c. G *Stock*, Icel *stokkr* tree trunk] —**stock′er,** *n.* —**stock′like′,** *adj.*
—**Syn. 1.** store, supply. **11.** lineage, family. **16.** haft. **39.** ordinary, usual.

stock·ade (sto kād′), *n., v.,* **-ad·ed, -ad·ing.** —*n.* **1.** *Fort.* a defensive barrier consisting of strong posts or timbers fixed upright in the ground. **2.** an enclosure made with posts and stakes. **3.** *U.S. Mil.* a prison for military personnel. —*v.t.* **4.** to protect, fortify, or encompass with a stockade. [< MF *(e)stocade,* var. of *estacade* < Sp *estacad(a).* See STAKE[1], -ADE[1]]

stock·breed·er (stok′brē′dər), *n.* a person who breeds and raises livestock. —**stock′breed′ing,** *adj.*

stock·brok·er (stok′brō′kər), *n.* a broker, esp. one employed by a member firm of a stock exchange, who buys and sells stocks and other securities for his customers. —**stock·brok·er·age** (stok′brō′kər ij), *n.*

stock′ car′, **1.** a standard model of automobile converted for racing purposes. **2.** *Railroads.* a boxcar for carrying livestock. —**stock′-car′,** *adj.*

stock′ certif′icate, a certificate evidencing ownership of one or more shares of stock in a corporation.

stock′ com′pany, 1. *Finance.* a company or corporation whose capital is divided into shares represented by stock. **2.** *Theat.* a company acting a repertoire of plays, usually at its own theater.

stock′ exchange′, 1. a building or marketplace where stocks and other securities are bought and sold. **2.** an association of brokers and dealers in stocks and bonds.

stock′ farm′, a farm devoted to breeding livestock. —**stock′ farm′er.** —**stock′ farm′ing.**

stock·fish (stok′fish′), *n., pl.* (*esp. collectively*) **-fish,** (*esp. referring to two or more kinds or species*) **-fish·es.** fish, as the cod or haddock, cured by splitting and drying in the air without salt. [ME *stokfish* < MD *stokvisch.* See STOCK, FISH]

stock·hold·er (stok′hōl′dər), *n.* **1.** a holder or owner of stock in a corporation. **2.** *Australian.* an owner of livestock, as a rancher.

Stock·holm (stok′hōm, -hōlm; *Swed.* stôk′hôlm′), *n.* the chief seaport in and the capital of Sweden, in the SE part. 665,202; with suburbs, 1,493,546.

stock·i·net (stok′ə net′), *n.* **1.** *Chiefly Brit.* an elastic machine-knitted fabric for undergarments, stockings, etc. **2.** a stitch in knitting, all knit on the right side and all purl on the wrong side. [earlier *stocking-net*]

stock·ing (stok′ing), *n.* **1.** a close-fitting covering for the foot and part of the leg, usually knitted. **2.** something resembling such a covering. **3.** *Brit.* stockinet (def. 2). **4. in one's stocking feet,** wearing stockings, but without shoes. —**stock′inged,** *adj.* —**stock′ing·less,** *adj.*

stock′ing cap′, a long, conical, knitted cap, usually with a tassel or pompon at the tip.

stock′ing mask′, a stocking or panty hose used as a face mask to conceal one's identity, as in a holdup.

stock′ in trade′, 1. the requisites for carrying on a business, esp. goods kept on hand for sale. **2.** resources or abilities peculiar to an individual or group or employed for a specific purpose: *A sense of style is part of the stock in trade of any writer.* Also, **stock′-in-trade′.**

stock·ish (stok′ish), *adj.* like a block of wood; stupid. —**stock′ish·ly,** *adv.* —**stock′ish·ness,** *n.*

stock·job·ber (stok′job′ər), *n.* **1.** a stock salesman, esp. one who sells or promotes worthless securities. **2.** *Brit.* a stock-exchange operator who acts as an intermediary between brokers but does not do business with the public. —**stock′job′ber·y, stock′job′bing,** *n.*

stock·less (stok′lis), *adj.* having no stock, as an anchor.

stock·man (stok′mən *or, for 3,* -man′), *n., pl.* **-men** (-mən *or, for 3,* -men′). **1.** *U.S. and Australia.* a man who raises livestock. **2.** a man employed on a stock farm. **3.** a man in charge of a stock of goods, as in a warehouse.

stock′ mar′ket, 1. a particular market where stocks and bonds are traded; stock exchange. **2.** the market for securities, esp. stocks, throughout a nation.

stock·pile (stok′pīl′), *n., v.,* **-piled, -pil·ing.** —*n.* **1.** a supply of material, as for construction or maintenance. **2.** a large supply of some metal, food, etc., held in reserve, esp. for use during a shortage. **3.** a quantity, as of munitions or weapons, accumulated for possible future use. —*v.t.* **4.** to accumulate for future use. —*v.i.* **5.** to accumulate in a stockpile. —**stock′pil′er,** *n.*

Stock·port (stok′pōrt′, -pôrt′), *n.* a city in NE Cheshire, in NW England, near Manchester. 142,469 (1961).

stock′ rais′ing, the breeding and raising of livestock. —**stock′ rais′er.**

stock·room (stok′rōōm′, -rŏŏm′), *n.* a room in which a stock of materials or goods is kept for use or sale.

stock-still (stok′stil′), *adj.* motionless. [ME *stok still*]

stock·tak·ing (stok′tā′king), *n.* **1.** the examination or counting over of materials or goods on hand. **2.** the act of appraising a present situation, condition, etc., in terms of accomplishments, degree of progress, and ultimate goals.

stock′ tick′er, ticker (def. 1).

Stock·ton (stok′tən), *n.* **1. Frank R.** (*Francis Richard Stockton*), 1834–1902, U.S. novelist and short-story writer. **2.** a city in central California, on the San Joaquin River. 109,963 (1970).

Stock·ton-on-Tees (stok′tən on tēz′, -ôn-), *n.* a seaport in SE Durham, in NE England, near the mouth of the Tees River. 109,963 (1971).

stock·y (stok′ē), *adj.,* **stock·i·er, stock·i·est. 1.** of sturdy form or build, and, usually, short. **2.** having a strong, stout stem, as a plant. [late ME *stokky*] —**stock′i·ly,** *adv.* —**stock′i·ness,** *n.*

stock·yard (stok′yärd′), *n.* an enclosure with pens, sheds, etc., for the temporary keeping of livestock.

stodge (stoj), *v.,* **stodged, stodg·ing,** *n.* —*v.t.* **1.** to stuff full, esp. with food or drink; gorge. —*v.i.* **2.** *Informal.* to trudge. —*n.* **3.** food that is particularly filling. [?; in some senses b. *stoff* (earlier form of STUFF) and GORGE]

stodg·y (stoj′ē), *adj.,* **stodg·i·er, stodg·i·est. 1.** heavy, dull, or uninteresting; boring. **2.** heavy, as food. **3.** unduly formal and traditional. **4.** dull; graceless or inelegant: *a stodgy business suit.* —**stodg′i·ly,** *adv.* —**stodg′i·ness,** *n.*

stoe·chi·om·e·try (stē′kē om′i trē), *n.* stoichiometry. —**stoe·chi·o·met·ri·cal·ly** (stē′kē ə me′trik lē), *adv.*

sto·gey (stō′gē), *n., pl.* **-geys.** stogy.

sto·gy (stō′gē), *n., pl.* **-gies. 1.** a long, slender, roughly made, inexpensive cigar. **2.** a coarse, heavy boot or shoe. [*stog(a)* (short for *Conestoga,* town in Pennsylvania) + -Y[2]]

Sto·ic (stō′ik), *adj.* **1.** of or pertaining to the school of philosophy founded by Zeno, who taught that men should be free from passion, unmoved by joy or grief, and submit without complaint to unavoidable necessity. **2.** (*l.c.*) stoical. —*n.* **3.** a member or adherent of the Stoic school of philosophy. **4.** (*l.c.*) a person who maintains or affects the mental attitude advocated by the Stoics. [< L *Stōic(us)* < Gk *Stōïkós* = *stōi-* (var. s. of *stoá* STOA) + *-ikos* -IC]

sto·i·cal (stō′i kəl), *adj.* **1.** impassive; characterized by a calm, austere fortitude befitting the Stoics. **2.** (*cap.*) of or pertaining to the Stoics. —**sto′i·cal·ly,** *adv.* —**sto′i·cal·ness,** *n.* —**Syn. 1.** imperturbable, cool.

stoi·chei·om·e·try (stoi′kē om′i trē), *n.* stoichiometry. —**stoi·chei·o·met·ri·cal·ly** (stoi′kē ə me′trik lē), *adv.*

stoi·chi·o·met·ric (stoi′kē ə me′trik), *adj.* *Chem.* **1.** of or pertaining to stoichiometry. **2.** pertaining to or involving substances that are in the exact proportions required for a given reaction. Also, **stoi′chi·o·met′ri·cal.** [< Gk *stoicheî-o(n)* component (akin to *stíchos* STICH) + -METRIC] —**stoi′chi·o·met′ri·cal·ly,** *adv.*

stoi·chi·om·e·try (stoi′kē om′i trē), *n.* **1.** the calculation of the quantities of chemical elements or compounds involved in chemical reactions. **2.** the branch of chemistry dealing with relationships of combining elements, esp. quantitatively. Also, **stoechiometry, stoicheiometry.** [< Gk *stoicheîo(n)* (see STOICHIOMETRIC) + -METRY]

Sto·i·cism (stō′i siz′əm), *n.* **1.** the philosophy of the Stoics. **2.** (*l.c.*) conduct conforming to the precepts of the Stoics, as repression of emotion, indifference to pleasure or pain, etc. —**Syn. 2.** See **patience.**

stoke (stōk), *v.,* **stoked, stok·ing.** —*v.t.* **1.** to poke, stir up, and feed (a fire). **2.** to tend the fire of (a furnace); supply with fuel. —*v.i.* **3.** to shake up the coals of a fire. **4.** to tend a fire or furnace; act or serve as a stoker. [< D *stoke(n)* (to) feed or stock a fire; see STOCK]

stoke·hold (stōk′hōld′), *n.* See **fire room.**

stoke·hole (stōk′hōl′), *n.* **1.** a hole in a furnace through which the fire is stoked. **2.** See **fire room.**

Stoke-on-Trent (stōk′on trent′, -ôn-), *n.* a city in N Staffordshire, in central England, on the Trent River: pottery and china. 265,506 (1961). Also, **Stoke′-up·on-Trent′.** Cf. **Potteries.**

stok·er (stō′kər), *n.* **1.** a laborer employed to tend and fuel a furnace. **2.** *Chiefly Brit.* the fireman on a locomotive. **3.** a mechanical device for supplying coal or other solid fuel to a furnace. [< D; see STOKE, -ER[1]] —**stok′er·less,** *adj.*

Stokes′-Ad′ams syn′drome (stōks′ad′əmz), *Med.* a combination of symptoms characterizing a condition resembling epilepsy, caused by blockage and consequent independence of beat between the auricle and ventricle. Also called **Stokes′-Ad′ams disease′, Adams-Stokes syndrome, Adams-Stokes disease.** [named after W. *Stokes* (1804–78), and R. *Adams* (1791–1875), Irish physicians]

Sto·kow·ski (stə kou′skē, -kôf′-, -kôv′-), *n.* **Le·o·pold (An·to·ni Sta·ni·slaw)** (lē′ə pōld′ än tō′nē stä nē′släf), 1882–1977, U.S. orchestra conductor, born in England.

STOL (es′tôl′), *n.* a convertiplane capable of becoming airborne after a short takeoff run, having forward speeds comparable to those of conventional aircraft. [*s(hort) t(ake) o(ff and) l(anding)*]

stole[1] (stōl), *v.* pt. of **steal.**

stole[2] (stōl), *n.* **1.** an ecclesiastical vestment consisting of a narrow strip of silk or other material worn over the shoulders or, by deacons, over the left shoulder only. Cf. **tippet** (def. 2). **2.** a woman's shoulder scarf of fur or other material. Cf. **tippet** (def. 1). **3.** *Archaic.* a long robe, esp. one worn by Roman matrons. [ME, OE < L *stol(a)* < Gk *stolḗ* clothing, robe; akin to Gk *stéllein* to array, OE *stellan* to place, put] —**stole′like′,** *adj.*

sto·len (stō′lən), *v.* pp. of **steal.**

stol·id (stol′id), *adj.* not easily stirred or moved mentally; unemotional; impassive. [< L *stolid(us)* immovable, dull, stupid; akin to STILL[1], STOLE[2]] —**sto·lid·i·ty** (stə lid′i tē), **stol′id·ness,** *n.* —**stol′id·ly,** *adv.*

stol·len (stō′lən; *Ger.* shtô′lən), *n.* a sweetened bread made from raised dough, usually containing nuts, raisins, and citron. [< G (dial.) *Stolle, Stollen,* lit., post, prop (with reference to its shape); c. STALL[1]]

sto·lon (stō′lən), *n.* **1.** *Bot.* a prostrate stem at or just below the surface of the ground, that produces new plants from buds at its tips or nodes. **2.** *Zool.* a rootlike extension in a compound organism, usually giving rise to new zooids by budding. [< L *stolōn-* (s. of *stolō*) branch, shoot, twig] —**sto·lon·ic** (stō lon′ik), *adj.*

sto·ma (stō′mə), *n., pl.* **sto·ma·ta** (stō′mə tə, stom′ə-, stō mä′tə), **sto·mas. 1.** *Bot.* any of various small apertures, esp. one of the minute orifices or slits in the epidermis of leaves, stems, etc. **2.** *Zool.* a mouth or ingestive opening, esp. when in the form of a small or simple aperture. Also, **stomate.** [< NL < Gk: mouth]

stom·ach (stum′ək), *n.* **1.** *Anat., Zool.* **a.** a saclike enlargement of the alimentary canal, as in man and certain animals, forming an organ for storing, diluting, and digesting food.

b. such an organ or an analogous portion of the alimentary canal when divided into two or more sections or parts. **c.** any one of these sections. **2.** any analogous digestive cavity or tract in invertebrates. **3.** the part of the body containing the stomach; belly or abdomen. **4.** appetite for food. **5.** desire, inclination, or liking: *I have no stomach for this trip.* **6.** *Obs.* **a.** spirit; courage. **b.** pride; haughtiness. **c.** resentment; anger. —*v.t.* **7.** to take into or retain in the stomach. **8.** to endure or tolerate. **9.** *Obs.* to be offended at or resent. [late ME *stomak* < L *stomach(us)* gullet, stomach < Gk *stómachos,* orig. opening; akin to STOMA]

stom′ach ache′, pain in the stomach or abdomen; gastralgia; colic. —**stom′ach-ach′y,** *adj.*

stom·ach·er (stum′ə kər), *n.* a richly ornamented garment covering the stomach and chest, worn by both sexes in the 15th and 16th centuries, and later worn under a bodice by women. [late ME]

Stomacher

sto·mach·ic (stō mak′ik), *adj.* Also, **sto·mach′i·cal. 1.** of or pertaining to the stomach; gastric. **2.** beneficial to the stomach. —*n.* **3.** a stomachic agent or drug. [< L *stomachic(us)* < Gk *stomachikós*] —**sto·mach′i·cal·ly,** *adv.*

stom′ach pump′, *Med.* a suction pump for removing the contents of the stomach, used esp. in cases of poisoning.

stom′ach sweet′bread, sweetbread (def. 1).

stom′ach tooth′, a lower canine milk tooth of infants.

stom′ach worm′, a nematode, *Haemonchus contortus,* parasitic in the stomach of sheep, cattle, and related animals. Also called **wireworm.**

stom·ach·y (stum′ə kē), *adj.* **1.** *Brit. Dial.* irritable; quick to take offense. **2.** paunchy.

stomat-, var. of **stomato-** before a vowel: *stomatitis.*

sto·ma·ta (stō′mə tə, stom′ə-), *n.* pl. of **stoma.**

stom·a·tal (stom′ə tᵊl, stō′mə-), *adj.* **1.** of, pertaining to, or of the nature of a stoma. **2.** having stomata.

sto·mate (stō′māt), *n.* stoma.

sto·mat·ic (stō mat′ik), *adj.* **1.** of or pertaining to the mouth. **2.** stomatal. [< Gk *stomatikós*]

sto·ma·ti·tis (stō′mə tī′tis, stom′ə-), *n. Pathol.* inflammation of the mouth. —**sto·ma·tit·ic** (stō′mə tit′ik, stom′ə-), *adj.*

stomato-, a learned borrowing from Greek meaning "mouth," used in the formation of compound words: *stomatoplasty.* Also, *esp. before a vowel,* **stomat-.** Cf. **-stome, -stomous, -stomy.** [< Gk *stomat-,* s. of *stóma;* see STOMA]

sto·ma·tol·o·gy (stō′mə tol′ə jē, stom′ə-), *n.* the science dealing with the mouth and its diseases. —**sto·ma·to·log·ic** (stō′mə tᵊloj′ik), **sto′ma·to·log′i·cal,** *adj.* —**sto′ma·tol′o·gist,** *n.*

sto·ma·to·plas·ty (stō′mə tə plas′tē, stom′ə-), *n.* plastic surgery of the mouth. —**stom′a·to·plas′tic,** *adj.*

sto·ma·to·pod (stō′mə tə pod′, stom′ə-), *n.* any crustacean of the order *Stomatopoda,* having a carapace that does not cover the posterior thorax and a broad abdomen bearing gills on the appendages.

stom·a·tous (stom′ə təs, stō′mə-), *adj.* stomatal.

-stome, a learned borrowing from Greek meaning "mouth," used to indicate a mouthlike opening in the formation of compound words: *cyclostome.* Cf. **stomato-, -stomous, -stomy.** [comb. form repr. Gk *stóma* mouth, and *stómion* little mouth]

sto·mo·dae·um (stō′mə dē′əm, stom′ə-), *n., pl.* **-dae·a** (-dē′ə). stomodeum. —**sto′mo·dae′al,** *adj.*

sto·mo·de·um (stō′mə dē′əm, stom′ə-), *n., pl.* **-de·a** (-dē′ə). *Embryol.* a depression in the ectoderm of the oral region of a young embryo that develops into the mouth and oral cavity. [< NL < Gk *stóm(a)* STOMA + *hodaíon* (neut. sing.) on the way; akin to -ODE[2]] —**sto′mo·de′al,** *adj.*

-stomous, a word element used to form adjectives corresponding to nouns with stems ending in **-stome:** *monostomous.*

stomp (stomp), *v.t., v.i.* **1.** *Informal.* stamp (defs. 1–5, 10, 11). —*n.* **2.** *Informal.* stamp (def. 21). **3.** a jazz composition, marked by a driving rhythm and a fast tempo. **4.** a dance to this music. [var. of STAMP] —**stomp′er,** *n.*

-stomy, a combining form used in names of surgical operations for making an artificial opening: *cystostomy.* [< Gk *-stomia* < *stóma* mouth. See -STOME, -Y[3]]

stone (stōn), *n., pl.* **stones** for 1–5, 7–17; **stone** for 6; *adj.; v.,* **stoned, ston·ing.** —*n.* **1.** the hard substance, formed from mineral and earth material, of which rocks consist. **2.** a rock or particular piece or kind of rock. **3.** a piece of rock quarried and worked. **4.** a piece of rock of small or moderate size, as a pebble. **5.** See **precious stone. 6.** one of various units of weight, esp. the British unit equivalent to 14 pounds. **7.** something resembling a small piece of rock. **8.** any small, hard seed, as of a date; pit. **9.** *Bot.* the hard endocarp of a drupe, as of a peach. **10.** *Med.* **a.** a calculous concretion in the body, as in the gall bladder. **b.** a disease arising from such a concretion. **11.** a gravestone or tombstone. **12.** a grindstone. **13.** a millstone. **14.** a hailstone. **15.** *Building Trades.* any of various artificial materials imitating cut stone or rubble. **16.** *Print.* a table with a smooth surface, formerly made of stone, on which page forms are composed. **17.** (in lithography) any surface on which an artist draws or etches a picture or design from which a lithograph is made. **18.** Usually, **stones.** *Obs.* the testes. **19. cast the first stone,** to be the first to condemn or blame a wrongdoer. **20. leave no stone unturned,** to exhaust every possibility in attempting to achieve one's goal. —*adj.* **21.** made of or pertaining to stone. **22.** made of stoneware. —*v.t.* **23.** to throw stones at. **24.** to put to death by pelting with stones. **25.** to provide, fit, pave, line, face or fortify with stones. **26.** to rub (something) with or on a stone. **27.** to remove stones from, as fruit. **28.** *Obs.* to make insensitive or unfeeling. [ME; OE *stān;* c. D *steen,* G *Stein,* Icel *steinn,* Goth *stains;* akin to Gk *stía* pebble, L *stīria* icicle; basic sense, something hard] —**ston′a·ble, stone′a·ble,** *adj.* —**stone′less,** *adj.* —**stone′less·ness,** *n.* —**stone′like′,** *adj.* —**ston′er,** *n.*

Stone (stōn), *n.* **1. Edward Du·rell** (dŏŏ rel′, dyŏŏ-), 1902–78, U.S. architect. **2. Har·lan Fiske** (här′lən), 1872–1946, U.S. jurist: Chief Justice of the U.S. 1941–46. **3. Lucy,** 1818–93, U.S. suffragist.

Stone′ Age′, the period in the history of mankind, preceding the Bronze Age and the Iron Age, and marked by the use of stone implements and weapons: subdivided into the Paleolithic, Mesolithic, and Neolithic periods.

stone-blind (stōn′blīnd′), *adj.* completely blind. [late ME (north) *staneblynde* blind as a stone] —**stone′-blind′ness,** *n.*

stone-broke (stōn′brōk′), *adj. Informal.* having no money whatsoever.

stone·chat (stōn′chat′), *n.* any of several small Old World thrushes, esp. of the genus *Saxicola,* as *S. torquata.* [STONE + CHAT, so called from its warning cry which sounds like a clash of stones]

stone-cold (stōn′kōld′), *adj.* completely cold, as a radiator, a corpse, etc.

stone·crop (stōn′krop′), *n.* **1.** any plant of the genus *Sedum,* esp. a mosslike herb, *Sedum acre,* having small yellow flowers, frequently growing on rocks and walls. **2.** any of various related plants. [ME *stooncrop,* OE *stāncrop*]

stone·cut·ter (stōn′kut′ər), *n.* **1.** a person who cuts or carves stone. **2.** a machine for cutting or dressing stone. —**stone′cut′ting,** *n.*

stoned (stōnd), *adj. Slang.* **1.** drunk; intoxicated. **2.** under the influence of marijuana or a drug.

stone-dead (stōn′ded′), *adj.* dead beyond any doubt; completely lifeless. [ME (north) *standed*]

stone-deaf (stōn′def′), *adj.* completely deaf.

stone·fly (stōn′flī′), *n., pl.* **-flies.** any of numerous drab-colored, membranous-winged insects of the order *Plecoptera,* having aquatic larvae often found under stones in streams.

stone′ fruit′, a fruit with a stone or hard endocarp, as a peach or plum; drupe.

Stone·henge (stōn′henj), *n.* a prehistoric monument on Salisbury Plain, Wiltshire, England, consisting mainly of a large circle of megalithic posts and lintels.

stone′ lil′y, a fossil crinoid.

stone′ mar′ten, a marten, *Mustela foina,* of Europe and Asia, having a white mark on the throat and breast.

stone·ma·son (stōn′mā′sən), *n.* a person who builds with or dresses stone. —**stone′ma′son·ry,** *n.*

Stone′ Moun′tain, a mountain in NW Georgia, near Atlanta: sculptures of Confederate heroes.

stone′ pars′ley, an umbelliferous herb, *Sison amomum,* of Eurasia, bearing aromatic seeds.

Stone′ Riv′er, a river in central Tennessee, flowing NW to the Cumberland River. Cf. **Murfreesboro** (def. 1).

stone·roll·er (stōn′rō′lər), *n.* **1.** an American minnow, *Campostoma anomalum,* named from its habit of moving stones in constructing its nest. **2.** any of several other minnows or suckers with similar habits.

stone's′ throw′, a short distance.

stone·wall (stōn′wôl′), *v.t., v.i.* **1.** *U.S. Informal.* to block, stall, or resist, esp. intentionally. **2.** *Brit.* to filibuster.

Stone′wall Jack′son (stōn′wôl′). See **Jackson, Thomas Jonathan.**

stone·ware (stōn′wâr′), *n.* a hard, opaque, vitrified ceramic ware.

stone·work (stōn′wûrk′), *n.* **1.** any construction, as walls or the like, of stone; stone masonry. **2.** the techniques, processes, work, or art of dressing, setting, or designing in stone. [ME *stoonwerk,* OE *stānweorc*] —**stone′work′er,** *n.*

stone·wort (stōn′wûrt′), *n.* a green alga of the class *Charophyceae,* having a jointed plant body frequently encrusted with lime and usually growing in fresh water.

ston·ey (stō′nē), *adj.,* **ston·i·er, ston·i·est.** stony.

ston·y (stō′nē), *adj.,* **ston·i·er, ston·i·est. 1.** full of or abounding in stones or rock. **2.** pertaining to or characteristic of stone. **3.** resembling or suggesting stone, esp. in its hardness. **4.** unfeeling; merciless; obdurate: *a stony heart.* **5.** without expression, as the eyes or face: *a hard, stony stare.* **6.** petrifying; stupefying: *stony fear.* **7.** having a stone or stones, as fruit. [ME; OE *stānig*] —**ston′i·ly,** *adv.* —**ston′i·ness,** *n.* —**Syn. 1.** rocky, pebbly. **4.** hard.

ston′y cor′al, a true coral or madrepore consisting of numerous anthozoan polyps imbedded in the calcareous material that they secrete.

Ston′y Point′, a village in SE New York, on the Hudson: site of a fort in the Revolutionary War. 8270 (1970).

stood (stŏŏd), *v.* pt. and pp. of **stand.**

stooge (stōōj), *n., v.,* **stooged, stoog·ing.** —*n.* **1.** *Informal.* an entertainer who feeds lines to the main comedian and usually serves as the butt of his jokes. **2.** *Slang.* any underling, assistant, or accomplice. —*v.i.* **3.** *Slang.* to act as a stooge. [?]

stook (stŏŏk, stōōk), *Brit.* —*n.* **1.** shock[2] (def. 1). —*v.t.* **2.** shock[2] (def. 2). [ME *stouk,* OE *stūc* heap; c. MLG *stūke,* G *Stauche;* akin to STOCK] —**stook′er,** *n.*

stool (stōōl), *n.* **1.** a single seat on legs or a pedestal and without arms or a back. **2.** a short, low support on which to stand, step, kneel, etc. **3.** *Hort.* the stump, base, or root of a plant from which propagative organs are produced, as shoots for layering. **4.** the base of plants which annually produce new stems or shoots. **5.** a cluster of shoots or stems springing up from such a base or from any root, or a single shoot or layer. **6.** a bird fastened to a pole or perch and used as a decoy. **7.** an artificial duck or other bird used as a decoy by hunters. **8.** a toilet bowl, water closet, or the like. **9.** the mass of matter evacuated from the bowels at one movement. **10.** a ledge forming the inside sill of a window. **11.** a seat considered as symbolic of authority. —*v.i.* **12.** to put forth shoots from the base or root, as a plant; form a stool. [ME; OE *stōl;* c. G *Stuhl,* Icel *stóll,* Goth *stols* chair; all < *stō-* (< IE root of STAND) + *-l* suffix as in OSlav *stolu* seat]

stool′ pi′geon, 1. a pigeon used as a decoy. **2.** Also called **stool·ie** (stōō′lē). *Slang.* a person employed or acting as a decoy or informer, esp. for the police.

stoop[1] (stōōp), *v.i.* **1.** to bend the head and shoulders, or the body generally, forward and downward from an erect position. **2.** to carry the head and shoulders habitually bowed forward: *to stoop from age.* **3.** (of trees, precipices, etc.) to bend, bow, or lean. **4.** to descend from one's level of dignity; condescend; deign. **5.** to swoop down, as a hawk at prey. **6.**

Rare. to submit; yield. —*v.t.* **7.** to bend (oneself, one's head, etc.) forward and downward. **8.** *Archaic.* to abase, humble, or subdue. —*n.* **9.** the act or an instance of stooping. **10.** a stooping position or carriage of body. **11.** a descent from dignity. **12.** a downward swoop, as of a hawk. [ME *stoup(en)*, OE *stūpian;* c. MD *stūpen* to bend, bow; akin to STEEP[1]] —**stoop′er,** *n.* —**stoop′ing·ly,** *adv.* —**Syn. 1.** lean, crouch. See **bend**[1].

stoop[2] (stōōp), *n.* *U.S.* a small raised platform, approached by steps and sometimes having a roof and seats, at the entrance of a house; a small porch. [< D *stoep;* c. MLG *stope,* OHG *stuofa* step in a stair; akin to OE *stōpel* footprint, *stōp,* preterit of *steppan* to STEP]

stoop[3] (stōōp), *n.* *Brit. Dial.* a post or prop. [ME *stoupe* < *stulpe* post; c. MLG *stolpe,* Icel *stolpi* post; akin to STELE]

stoop[4] (stōōp), *n.* stoup.

stoop′ ball′, a game resembling baseball, in which a ball is thrown forcibly against a stairway or wall so that it rebounds into the air, bases and runs being awarded depending on the number of bounces the ball takes before being caught by the opposing player or team.

stop (stop), *v.,* **stopped** or (*Archaic*) **stopt; stop·ping;** *n.* —*v.t.* **1.** to cease from, leave off, or discontinue. **2.** to cause to cease; put an end to. **3.** to interrupt, arrest, or check (a course, proceeding, process, etc.). **4.** to cut off, intercept, or withhold. **5.** to restrain, hinder, or prevent (usually fol. by *from*). **6.** to prevent from proceeding, operating, etc. **7.** to block, obstruct, or close (a passageway, channel, etc.) (usually fol. by *up*): *She stopped up the sink with a paper towel. He stopped the hole in the tire with a patch.* **8.** to fill the hole or holes in (a wall, a decayed tooth, etc.). **9.** to close (a container, tube, etc.) with a cork, plug, or the like. **10.** to close the external orifice of (the ears, nose, etc.). **11.** *Sports.* **a.** to check (a stroke, blow, etc.); parry; ward off. **b.** to defeat (an opposing player or team): **c.** *Boxing.* to defeat by a knockout or technical knockout: *Louis stopped Conn in the 13th round.* **12.** *Banking.* to notify a bank to refuse payment of (a check). **13.** *Bridge.* to have an honor card and a sufficient number of protecting cards to keep an opponent from continuing to win in (a suit). **14.** *Music.* **a.** to close (a finger hole) in order to produce a particular note from a wind instrument. **b.** to press down (a string of a violin, viola, etc.) to alter the pitch of the tone produced from it. —*v.i.* **15.** to come to a stand, as in a course or journey; halt. **16.** to cease moving, proceeding, speaking, etc.; pause; desist. **17.** to cease; come to an end. **18.** to halt for a brief visit (often fol. by *at, in,* or *by*). **19. stop down,** *Photog.* to reduce the diaphragm opening of (a camera). **20. stop off,** to halt for a brief stay at some point on the way elsewhere. **21. stop out,** to mask (certain areas of an etching plate, photographic negative, etc.) with varnish, paper, or the like, to prevent their being etched, printed, etc. **22. stop over,** to stop in the course of a journey, as for the night. —*n.* **23.** the act of stopping. **24.** a cessation or arrest of movement, action, operation, etc.; end. **25.** a stay or sojourn made at a place, as in the course of a journey. **26.** a place where buses or other vehicles halt to load or unload passengers. **27.** a closing or filling up. **28.** a blocking or obstructing. **29.** a plug or other stopper for an opening. **30.** an obstacle or hindrance. **31.** any part or device that serves to check or control movement or action in a mechanism. **32.** *Archit.* a feature terminating a molding or chamfer. **33.** *Com.* **a.** an order to refuse payment of a check. **b.** See **stop order. 34.** *Music.* **a.** the act of closing a finger hole or pressing a string of an instrument in order to produce a particular note. **b.** a device or contrivance, as on an instrument, for accomplishing this. **c.** (in an organ) a graduated set of pipes of the same kind and giving tones of the same quality. **d.** a knob or handle which is drawn out or pushed back to permit or prevent the sounding of such a set of pipes or to control some other part of the organ. **35.** *Naut.* a piece of small line used to lash or fasten something, as a furled sail. **36.** *Phonet.* **a.** an articulation that interrupts the flow of air from the lungs. Cf. **continuant. b.** a consonant sound characterized by stop articulation, as *p, b, t, d, k,* and *g.* **37.** *Photog.* the diaphragm opening of a lens, esp. as indicated by an F number. **38.** any of various marks used as punctuation at the end of a sentence, esp. a period. **39.** (used in the body of a telegram or cablegram to indicate a punctuation period.) **40.** *Zool.* a depression in the face of certain animals, esp. dogs, marking the division between the forehead and the projecting part of the muzzle. [ME *stopp(en),* OE *-stoppian;* c. D, LG *stoppen,* G *stopfen;* all < WGmc < VL **stuppāre* to plug with oakum < L *stuppa* < Gk *stýppē* oakum] —**stop′pa·ble,** *adj.* —**Syn. 3.** STOP, ARREST, CHECK, HALT imply causing a cessation of movement or progress (literal or figurative). STOP is the general term for the idea: *to stop a clock.* ARREST usually refers to stopping by imposing a sudden and complete restraint: *to arrest development.* CHECK implies bringing about an abrupt, partial, or temporary stop: *to check a trotting horse.* To HALT means to make a temporary stop, esp. one resulting from a command: *to halt a company of soldiers.* **5.** thwart, obstruct, impede. **16.** quit. —**Ant. 1–3, 15–17, 23, 24.** start.

stop′ bath′, *Photog.* an acid bath or rinse for stopping the action of a developer before fixing a negative or print.

stop·cock (stop′kok′), *n.* cock[1] (def. 5).

stope (stōp), *n., v.,* **stoped, stop·ing.** —*n.* **1.** any excavation made in a mine to remove the ore that has been rendered accessible by the shafts and drifts. —*v.i., v.t.* **2.** to mine or work by stopes. [appar. < LG *stope;* see STOOP[2]]

stop·gap (stop′gap′), *n.* **1.** something that fills the place of something lacking; temporary substitute; makeshift. —*adj.* **2.** makeshift. [n., adj. use of v. phrase *stop a gap*]

stop·light (stop′līt′), *n.* **1.** a taillight that lights up as the driver of a vehicle steps on the brake pedal to slow down or stop. **2.** See **traffic light.**

stop-off (stop′ôf′, -of′), *n.* stopover. [n. use of v. phrase *stop off*]

stop′ or′der, an order from a customer to a broker to sell a security if the market price drops below a designated level.

stop·o·ver (stop′ō′vər), *n.* **1.** a brief stop in the course of a journey, as to eat or sleep. **2.** such a stop made with the privilege of proceeding later on the same ticket.

stop·page (stop′ij), *n.* **1.** the act or an instance of stopping; cessation of activity. **2.** the state of being stopped. [late ME; see STOP, -AGE]

stop′ pay′ment, an order by the drawer of a check to his bank not to pay a specified check.

stopped′ diapa′son. See under **diapason** (def. 4).

stop·per (stop′ər), *n.* **1.** a person or thing that stops. **2.** a plug, cork, bung, or other piece for closing a bottle, tube, drain, or the like. —*v.t.* **3.** to close, secure, or fit with a stopper. [late ME] —**stop′per·less,** *adj.*

stop·ple (stop′əl), *n., v.,* **-pled, -pling.** —*n.* **1.** a stopper for a bottle or the like. —*v.t.* **2.** to close or fit with a stopple. [late ME *stoppel.* See STOP, -LE]

stopt (stopt), *v.* *Archaic.* a pt. and pp. of **stop.**

stop·watch (stop′woch′), *n.* a watch with a hand or hands that can be stopped or started at any instant, used for precise timing, as in races.

stor·a·ble (stôr′ə bəl, stōr′-), *adj.* **1.** capable of being stored for considerable time without loss of freshness or usability. —*n.* **2.** Usually, **storables.** articles that are storable. —**stor′a·bil′i·ty,** *n.*

stor·age (stôr′ij, stōr′-), *n.* **1.** the act of storing. **2.** the state or fact of being stored. **3.** capacity or space for storing. **4.** a place, as a room or building, for storing. **5.** the price charged for storing goods. **6.** *Computer Technol.* memory (def. 10).

stor′age bat′tery, *Elect.* **1.** a voltaic battery consisting of two or more storage cells. **2.** See **storage cell.**

stor′age cell′, *Elect.* a cell whose energy can be renewed by passing a current through it in the direction opposite to that of the flow of current generated by the cell. Also called **secondary cell, storage battery.**

sto·rax (stôr′aks, stōr′-), *n.* **1.** a solid resin with a vanilla-like odor, obtained from a small styracaceous tree, *Styrax officinalis:* formerly used in medicine and perfumery. **2.** a liquid balsam (**liquid storax**) obtained from species of liquidambar, esp. from the wood and inner bark of *Liquidambar orientalis* (**Levant storax**), a tree of Asia Minor: used chiefly in medicine and perfumery. **3.** any shrub or tree of the genus *Styrax,* having racemes of showy, white flowers. [late ME < LL, var. of L *styrax* < Gk]

store (stôr, stōr), *n., v.,* **stored, stor·ing.** —*n.* **1.** an establishment where merchandise is sold. **2.** a stall, room, floor, or building for housing a retail business. **3.** a supply or stock of something. **4. stores,** supplies of food, clothing, or other requisites. **5.** *Chiefly Brit.* a storehouse or warehouse. **6.** quantity, esp. great quantity; abundance. **7. in store, a.** in readiness or reserve. **b.** about to happen; imminent. **8. set** or **lay store by,** to have high regard for. —*v.t.* **9.** to supply or stock with something. **10.** to accumulate or put away for future use (usually fol. by *up* or *away*). **11.** to deposit in a storehouse, warehouse, etc. **12.** (in data processing) **a.** to put (data) into a memory unit. **b.** to retain (data) in a memory unit. —*v.i.* **13.** to take in or hold supplies, goods, etc., for future use. **14.** to remain fresh and usable for considerable time on being stored. [ME *store(n),* aph. var. of *astoren* < OF *estore(r)* < L *instaurāre* to set up, renew = *in-* IN-[2] + *staur-* (akin to Gk *staurós* cross and to STEER[1]) + *-āre* inf. suffix]

store-bought (stôr′bôt′, stōr′-), *adj.* commercially made and purchased at a store rather than homemade, as clothes or baked goods.

store·front (stôr′frunt′, stōr′-), *n.* **1.** the side of a store facing a street, usually containing display windows. —*adj.* **2.** located or operating in a room or rooms behind a storefront: *a storefront community center.*

store·house (stôr′hous′, stōr′-), *n., pl.* **-hous·es** (-hou′ziz). **1.** a building in which things are stored. **2.** any repository or source of abundant supplies, as of facts: *He was a storehouse of information.* [ME *storhous*]

store·keep·er (stôr′kē′pər, stōr′-), *n.* **1.** *Chiefly U.S.* a tradesman who owns a store. **2.** a person who has charge of or operates a store or stores. **3.** *U.S. Navy.* a petty officer in charge of a supply office afloat or ashore. —**store′keep′ing,** *n.*

store·room (stôr′rōōm′, -rŏŏm′, stōr′-), *n.* a room in which supplies or goods are stored.

sto·rey (stôr′ē, stōr′ē), *n., pl.* **-reys.** *Chiefly Brit.* story[2].

sto·ried[1] (stôr′ēd, stōr′-), *adj.* **1.** recorded or celebrated in history or legend: *the storied cities of ancient Greece.* **2.** ornamented with designs representing historical, legendary, or similar subjects. [STORY[1] + -ED[3]]

sto·ried[2] (stôr′ēd, stōr′-), *adj.* having stories or floors (often used in combination): *a two-storied house.* Also, *esp. Brit.,* **sto′reyed.** [STORY[2] + -ED[3]]

White stork, *Ciconia ciconia* (Length 3½ ft.)

stork (stôrk), *n., pl.* **storks,** (*esp. collectively*) **stork. 1.** any of several wading birds of the family *Ciconiidae,* related to the ibises and herons, having long legs and a long neck and bill. Cf. **white stork. 2.** the symbol of the birth of a child: *a visit from the stork.* [ME; OE *storc;* c. Icel *storkr,* G *Storch;* akin to STARK; the bird presumably owes its name to the rigidity of its stiltlike legs] —**stork′like′,** *adj.*

stork's-bill (stôrks′bil′), *n.* **1.** geranium (def. 2). **2.** heron's-bill.

storm (stôrm), *n.* **1.** a disturbance of the normal condition of the atmosphere, manifesting itself by winds of unusual force or direction, often accompanied by rain, snow, hail, etc. **2.** a heavy fall of rain, snow, or hail, or a violent outbreak of thunder and lightning, unaccompanied by strong winds. **3.** (on the Beaufort scale) a wind of 64–72 miles per hour. **4.** a violent military assault. **5.** a heavy or sudden volley or discharge. **6.** a violent disturbance of affairs, as a civil, political, social, or domestic commotion. **7.** a violent outbreak of expression. **8.** *Informal.* See **storm window. 9. storm in a teacup,** a great to-do about trivia. —*v.i.* **10.** (of the wind or weather) to blow, rain, snow, hail, etc., esp. with violence (usually used impersonally with *it* as subject): *It stormed all day.* **11.** to rage or complain violently. **12.** to deliver a violent attack or fire, as with artillery. **13.** to rush to an assault or attack. **14.** to rush angrily. **—***v.t.* **15.** to subject to or as to a storm. **16.** to utter or say with angry vehemence. **17.** to attack or assault (persons, places, or things): *to storm a fortress.* [ME, OE; c. D *storm,* Icel *stormr,* G *Sturm;* akin to STIR[1]] **—storm′less,** *adj.* **—storm′like′,** *adj.* **—Syn. 1.** gale, hurricane, tornado, cyclone, squall.

storm·bound (stôrm′bound′), *adj.* confined, detained, or isolated by storms: *a stormbound ship.*

storm′ cel′lar, a cellar or underground chamber for refuge during violent storms; cyclone cellar.

storm′ cen′ter, 1. the center of a cyclonic storm, the area of lowest pressure and of comparative calm. **2.** a center of disturbance, tumult, trouble, or the like.

storm′ door′, a supplementary outside door, usually glazed, for protecting the main door.

storm′ pet′rel. See **stormy petrel.**

storm·proof (stôrm′pro͞of′), *adj.* protected from or not affected by storms.

Storms (stôrmz), *n.* **Ocean of.** See **Oceanus Procellarum.**

storm′ sig′nal, 1. a visual signal, as a flag, giving advance notice of a heavy storm, used esp. along coastal areas. **2.** See **storm warning** (def. 3).

storm′ troop′er, a member of the Nazi paramilitary organization or Sturmabteilung, noted esp. for their brutality; Brown Shirt.

storm′ warn′ing, 1. a showing of storm signals. **2.** an announcement, esp. by radio, of a heavy storm. **3.** any sign of approaching trouble.

storm′ win′dow, a supplementary, protective window sash. Also called **storm′ sash′.**

storm·y (stôr′mē), *adj.,* **storm·i·er, storm·i·est. 1.** affected, characterized by, or subject to storms; tempestuous. **2.** characterized by violent commotion, actions, etc. [ME; OE *stormig*] **—storm′i·ly,** *adv.* **—storm′i·ness,** *n.*

storm′y pet′rel, any of several small sea birds of the family *Hydrobatidae,* usually having black or sooty-brown plumage with a white rump, esp. *Hydrobates pelagicus,* of the eastern North Atlantic and Mediterranean. Also called **storm petrel.**

sto·ry[1] (stôr′ē, stôr′ē), *n., pl.* **-ries,** *v.,* **-ried, -ry·ing.** **—***n.* **1.** a narrative, either true or fictitious, in prose or verse; tale. **2.** a fictitious tale, shorter and less elaborate than a novel. **3.** such narratives or tales as a branch of literature: *song and story.* **4.** the plot or succession of incidents of a novel, poem, drama, etc. **5.** a narration of an incident or a series of events or an example of these that is or may be narrated, as an anecdote or joke. **6.** a narration of the events in the life of a person or the existence of a thing, or such events as a subject for narration. **7.** a report or account of a matter; statement or allegation. **8.** *Informal.* a lie. **9.** *Obs.* history. **—***v.t.* **10.** to ornament with pictured scenes. **11.** *Obs.* to tell the history or story of. [ME *storie* < AF (*e*)*storie* < L *historia* HISTORY] **—sto′ry·less,** *adj.* **—Syn. 1.** legend, fable, romance; anecdote, chronicle. **5.** recital.

sto·ry[2] (stôr′ē, stôr′ē), *n., pl.* **-ries. 1.** a complete horizontal section of a building, having one continuous or practically continuous floor. **2.** the set of rooms on the same floor or level of a building. **3.** any major horizontal architectural division, as of a façade, the wall of a nave, etc. **4.** a horizontal layer or division of any structure or formation. Also, *esp. Brit.,* **storey.** [late ME *storie* < AL *historia* picture decorating a building, a part of the building so decorated, hence floor, story, L *historia* HISTORY]

sto·ry·board (stôr′ē bôrd′, stôr′ē bôrd′), *n.* a panel or panels on which a sequence of sketches depict the significant changes of action and scene in a planned film, as for a movie, television show, or advertisement.

sto·ry·book (stôr′ē bo͝ok′, stôr′-), *n.* a book that contains a story or stories, esp. for children.

sto′ry line′, plot[1] (def. 2).

sto·ry·tell·er (stôr′ē tel′ər, stôr′-), *n.* **1.** a person who tells or writes stories or anecdotes. **2.** *Informal.* a person who tells trivial falsehoods; fibber.

sto·ry·tell·ing (stôr′ē tel′ing, stôr′-), *n.* the telling or writing of stories or anecdotes.

stoss (stōs; *Ger.* shtōs), *adj. Geol.* noting or pertaining to the side, as of a hill, dale, etc., that receives or has received the thrust of a glacier or other impulse. [< G: thrust, push]

sto·tin·ka (stô ting′kä), *n., pl.* **-ki** (-kē). a minor coin of Bulgaria, the 100th part of a lev. [< Bulg]

St.-Ouen (SAN twäN′), *n.* a suburb of Paris in N France. 52,103 (1962).

stoup (sto͞op), *n.* **1.** a basin for holy water, as at the entrance of a church. **2.** *Scot. and North Eng.* a drinking vessel, as a cup or tankard. [late ME *stowp* < Scand; cf. Icel *staup* cup; c. OE *stēap* flagon; see STEEP[1]]

Stoup (def. 1)

stour (sto͝or), *n.* **1.** *Brit. Dial.* **a.** tumult or confusion. **b.** a storm. **2.** *Archaic.* armed combat; battle. **3.** *Obs.* a time of tumult. [ME < OF (*e*)*stour* battle < Gmc; akin to STORM]

stout (stout), *adj.* **1.** bulky in figure; corpulent; or thickset. **2.** brave or dauntless: *a stout heart; stout fellows.* **3.** firm or resolute: *stout resistance.* **4.** strong of body, hearty, or sturdy: *stout seamen.* **5.** strong in substance or body, as a beverage. **6.** strong and thick or heavy: *a stout cudgel.* **—***n.* **7.** *Brewing.* a dark, sweet brew made of roasted malt and having a higher percentage of hops than porter. **8.** porter of extra strength. **9.** a garment size designed for a stout man. [ME < OF (*e*)*stout* bold, proud < Gmc; cf. MD *stout* bold, MLG *stolt,* MHG *stolz* proud] **—stout′ish,** *adj.* **—stout′ly,** *adv.* **—stout′ness,** *n.*

—Syn. 1. portly, fleshy. STOUT, FAT, PLUMP imply corpulence of body. STOUT describes a heavily built but usually strong and healthy body: *a handsome stout lady.* FAT suggests an unbecoming fleshy stoutness; it may, however, apply also to a hearty fun-loving type of stout person: *a fat old man; fat and jolly.* PLUMP connotes a pleasing roundness and is often used as a euphemistic equivalent for stout, fleshy, etc.: *a plump figure attractively dressed.*

stout-heart·ed (stout′här′tid), *adj.* brave and resolute; dauntless. **—stout′-heart′ed·ly,** *adv.* **—stout′-heart′ed·ness,** *n.*

stove[1] (stōv), *n.* **1.** an apparatus that furnishes heat for warmth, cooking, etc., commonly using coal, oil, gas, or electricity as a source of power. **2.** a heated chamber or box for some special purpose, as a drying room or a kiln for firing pottery. [late ME; OE *stofa* hot-air bathroom; c. D *stoof,* G *Stube* room (orig. heated room)]

stove[2] (stōv), *v.* a pt. and pp. of **stave.**

stove′ bolt′, a small bolt, similar to a machine screw but with a coarser thread. See illus. at **bolt.**

stove·pipe (stōv′pīp′), *n.* **1.** a pipe, as of sheet metal, serving as a stove chimney or to connect a stove with a chimney flue. **2.** *U.S. Informal.* See **stovepipe hat.**

stove′pipe hat′, *U.S. Informal.* a tall silk hat.

sto·ver (stō′vər), *n.* **1.** coarse roughage used as livestock feed. **2.** *Chiefly U.S.* stalks and leaves, not including grain, of such forages as corn and sorghum. **3.** *Brit. Dial.* fodder minus the grain portion. [ME; aph. var. of ESTOVER]

stow[1] (stō), *v.t.* **1.** to put in a place or receptacle, as for storage or reserve; pack: *He stowed the cargo in the hold.* **2.** to fill (a place or receptacle) by packing. **3.** (of a place or receptacle) to afford room for; hold. **4.** *Slang.* to stop; break off: *Stow the talk!* **5.** *Obs.* to lodge or quarter. **6. stow away,** to conceal oneself aboard a ship or airplane in order to obtain free transportation or elude pursuers. [ME *stow(en),* OE *stōwigan* to keep, hold back (lit., to place) < *stōw* place; akin to *-sto-* place, in Icel *eldstō* fireplace, Goth *stojan* to judge (lit., to place)] **—stow′a·ble,** *adj.*

stow[2] (sto͞o, stou), *v.t. Brit. Dial.* to cut close or trim, esp. to crop (a sheep's ears) or prune (a tree or shrub). [< Scand; cf. Icel *stūfr* stump, *stȳfa* to cut off]

stow·age (stō′ij), *n.* **1.** the act or operation of stowing. **2.** the state or manner of being stowed. **3.** room or accommodation for stowing something. **4.** that which is stowed or to be stowed. **5.** a charge for stowing goods.

stow·a·way (stō′ə wā′), *n.* a person who conceals himself aboard a ship or airplane in order to obtain free transportation or elude pursuers.

Stowe (stō), *n.* **1. Harriet (Elizabeth) Beecher,** 1811–96, U.S. abolitionist and novelist (daughter of Lyman Beecher). **2.** a town in N Vermont: ski resort. 435 (1970).

STP, a hallucinogenic drug similar to but more potent than LSD. [after the trademark of an automobile-oil additive]

St. Paul, a port in and the capital of Minnesota, in the SE part, on the Mississippi. 309,828 (1970).

St. Petersburg, 1. a seaport in W Florida, on Tampa Bay: seaside winter resort. 216,232 (1970). **2.** a former name (1703–1914) of **Leningrad.**

St. Pierre (sānt′ pyâr′; *Fr.* SAN pyeR′), **1.** a city on Réunion Island, in the Indian Ocean. 33,874 (est. 1965). **2.** a former city on Martinique, in the French West Indies: destroyed 1902, with the entire population of 26,000, by an eruption of the volcano Mt. Pelée.

St. Pierre and Miq·ue·lon (mik′ə lon′; *Fr.* mēk lôN′), two small groups of islands off the S coast of Newfoundland: an overseas territory of France. 5134 (1960); 93 sq. mi. *Cap.:* St. Pierre.

St. Quen·tin (sānt′ kwen′tᵊn; *Fr.* SAN kän taN′), a city in N France, on the Somme. 62,579 (1962).

str., 1. steamer. **2.** strait. **3.** *Music.* string; strings.

stra·bis·mus (strə biz′məs), *n.* *Ophthalm.* a disorder of vision due to the turning of one eye or both eyes from the normal position; squint; cross-eye. [< NL < Gk *strabismós* = *strab(ós)* squinting + *-ismos* -ISM] **—stra·bis′mal, stra·bis′mic, stra·bis′mi·cal,** *adj.* **—stra·bis′mal·ly,** *adv.*

Stra·bo (strā′bō), *n.* 63? B.C.–A.D. 21?, Greek geographer and historian.

Stra·chey (strā′chē), *n.* **(Giles) Lyt·ton** (jīlz lit′ᵊn), 1880–1932, English biographer and literary critic.

strad·dle (strad′ᵊl), *v.,* **-dled, -dling,** *n.* **—***v.i.* **1.** to walk, stand, or sit with the legs wide apart. **2.** to stand wide apart, as the legs. **3.** *Informal.* to favor or appear to favor both sides of an issue; maintain an equivocal position. **—***v.t.* **4.** to walk, stand, or sit with one leg on each side of; stand or sit astride of: *to straddle a horse.* **5.** to spread (the legs) wide apart. **6.** to favor or appear to favor both sides of (an issue, political division, etc.). **—***n.* **7.** the act or an instance of straddling. **8.** the distance straddled over. **9.** *Finance.* an option consisting of a put and a call combined, both at the same current market price and for the same specified period. [OE *strād* (preterit of *strīdan* to STRIDE) + -LE] **—strad′dler,** *n.* **—strad′dling·ly,** *adv.*

Stra·di·va·ri (strad′ə vâr′ē; *It.* strä′dē vä′rē), *n.* **An·to·nio** (än tô′nyô), 1644?–1737, Italian violinmaker.

Strad·i·var·i·us (strad′ə vâr′ē əs), *n.* **1.** a violin or other instrument made by Stradivari or his family. **2.** See **Stradivari, Antonio.**

strafe (strāf, sträf), *v.,* **strafed, straf·ing,** *n.* **—***v.t.* **1.** to attack with machine-gun fire from an airplane or airplanes. **—***n.* **2.** a strafing attack. [< G *strafe(n)* (to) punish] **—straf′er,** *n.*

Straf·ford (straf′ərd), *n.* **1st Earl of** (*Thomas Wentworth*), 1593–1641, English statesman: chief adviser of Charles I of England.

strag·gle (strag′əl), *v.i.,* **-gled, -gling. 1.** to stray from the road, course, or line of march. **2.** to wander about in a scattered fashion; ramble. [b. STRAY and DRAGGLE] **—strag′gler,** *n.* **—strag′gling·ly,** *adv.*

strag·gly (strag′lē), *adj.*, **-gli·er, -gli·est.** straggling.

straight (strāt), *adj.* **1.** without a bend, angle, or curve; direct: *a straight path.* **2.** exactly vertical or horizontal. **3.** evenly formed or set: *straight shoulders.* **4.** without circumlocution; frank: *straight speaking.* **5.** honest, honorable, or upright, as dealings or persons. **6.** right or correct, as thinking or a thinker. **7.** in the proper order or condition: *Things are straight now.* **8.** continuous or unbroken: *in straight succession.* **9.** *U.S.* thoroughgoing or unreserved: *a straight Republican.* **10.** unmodified or unaltered: *a straight comedy.* **11.** *U.S.* undiluted, as whiskey. **12.** *Theat.* (of acting) straightforward; not striving for effect. **13.** *Journalism.* written or to be written in a direct and objective manner: *Treat it as straight news.* **14.** *Cards.* containing cards in consecutive denomination, as a two, three, four, five, and six, in various suits. **15.** *Slang.* normal, legal, or conforming; not perverted, illicit, or deviant. —*adv.* **16.** in a straight line: *to walk straight.* **17.** in an even form or position: *pictures hung straight.* **18.** in an erect posture: *to stand straight.* **19.** directly: *to go straight home.* **20.** honestly, honorably, or virtuously: *to live straight.* **21.** without intricate involvement; directly to the point: *He can think straight.* **22.** in a steady course (often fol. by *on*): *to keep straight on after the second traffic light.* **23.** into the proper form or condition: *to put a room straight.* **24.** *Journalism.* directly and objectively. **25.** without personal embellishments, additions, etc.: *Tell the story straight.* **26. straight off,** immediately; straightaway. Also, **straight away.** —*n.* **27.** the condition of being straight. **28.** a straight form or position. **29.** a straight line. **30.** a straight part, as of a racecourse. **31.** *Poker.* a sequence of five consecutive cards of various suits. Cf. **sequence** (def. 8). [ME; orig. ptp. of STRETCH] —**straight′ly,** *adv.* —**straight′ness,** *n.* —**Syn. 4.** open, direct. **5.** virtuous, just, fair, equitable. —**Ant. 1.** crooked. **4.** devious.

straight′ and nar′row, the way of virtuous or proper conduct: *After his release from prison he followed the straight and narrow.*

straight′ an′gle, the angle formed by two radii of a circle that are drawn to the extremities of an arc equal to one half of the circle; an angle of 180°.

straight-arm (strāt′ärm′), *Football.* —*v.t.* **1.** to push (a potential tackler) away by holding the arm out straight. —*n.* **2.** the act or an instance of straight-arming.

straight·a·way (strāt′ə wā′), *adj.* **1.** straight onward, without turn or curve, as a racecourse. —*n.* **2.** a straightaway course or part. —*adv.* **3.** Also, **straightway.** immediately; right away.

straight′ chain′, *Chem.* an open chain of atoms, usually carbon, with no side chains attached to it. Cf. **branched chain.**

straight′ chair′, a chair with a straight back, esp. one which is unupholstered and has straight legs and straight arms or no arms.

straight·edge (strāt′ej′), *n.* a bar or strip of wood or metal having at least one long edge of sufficiently reliable straightness for use in drawing.

straight·en (strāt′ᵊn), *v.t., v.i.* to make or become straight in position, character, conduct, etc. —**straight′en·er,** *n.*

straight′ face′, a serious facial expression that conceals one's true feelings, esp. a suppression of the desire to laugh. —**straight′-faced′,** *adj.*

straight′ flush′, *Poker.* a sequence of five consecutive cards of the same suit.

straight·for·ward (strāt′fôr′wərd), *adj.* **1.** going or directed straight ahead. **2.** direct; not roundabout. **3.** free from crookedness or deceit; honest. —*adv.* **4.** Also, **straight′for′wards.** straight ahead; directly or continuously forward. —**straight′for′ward·ly,** *adv.* —**straight′for′ward·ness,** *n.* —**Syn. 1.** undeviating, unswerving. —**Ant. 1, 2.** devious.

straight′ jack′et. See **strait jacket.**

straight′ joint′, **1.** *Building Trades.* a continuous joint made by the termination of parallel members, as floorboards or bricks, at the same line. **2.** Also called **square joint.** *Carpentry.* a joint between two timbers having no overlap and no dowels to bind them together.

straight-laced (strāt′lāst′), *adj.* strait-laced. —**straight-lac·ed·ly** (strāt′lā′sid lē, -lāst′lē), *adv.* —**straight′-lac′ed·ness,** *n.*

straight-line (strāt′līn′), *adj.* *Mach.* noting a machine or mechanism the working parts of which act or are arranged in a straight line.

straight′ man′, an entertainer who plays a foil for a comedian.

straight-out (strāt′out′), *adj.* *U.S. Informal.* **1.** thoroughgoing: *a straight-out Democrat.* **2.** frank; aboveboard.

Straight′ Range′, a mountain range in the second quadrant of the face of the moon in the Mare Imbrium. ab. 40 mi. long with highest peaks about 6,000 ft.

straight′ ra′zor, a razor having a stiff blade made of steel that is hinged to a handle into which it folds.

straight′ shoot′er, a forthright, honest person.

straight′ tick′et, *U.S. Politics.* a ballot on which all votes have been cast for candidates of the same party. Cf. **split ticket.**

straight′ time′, **1.** the time or number of hours established as standard for a specific work period in a particular industry. **2.** the rate of pay established for the period (distinguished from *overtime*). —**straight′-time′,** *adj.*

straight·way (strāt′wā′), *adv.* straightaway. [late ME]

straight′ whis′key, *U.S.* pure, unblended whiskey of 80 to 110 proof.

strain[1] (strān), *v.t.* **1.** to draw tight or taut; stretch, esp. to the utmost tension: *to strain a rope.* **2.** to exert to the utmost. **3.** to impair, injure, or weaken (a muscle, tendon, etc.) by stretching or overexertion. **4.** to cause mechanical deformation in (a body or structure) as the result of stress. **5.** to stretch beyond the proper point or limit: *to strain the meaning of a word.* **6.** to make excessive demands upon: *to strain one's luck.* **7.** to pour (liquid containing solid matter) through a filter, sieve, or the like, in order to hold back the denser solid constituents: *to strain gravy.* **8.** to draw off (clear or pure liquid) by means of a filter or sieve: *to strain the water from spinach.* **9.** to hold back (solid particles) from liquid matter by means of a filter or sieve: *to strain seeds from orange juice.* **10.** to clasp tightly in the arms, the hand, etc.: *The mother strained her child close to her breast.* **11.** *Obs.* to constrain, as to a course of action. —*v.i.* **12.** to pull forcibly: *a dog straining at a leash.* **13.** to stretch one's muscles, nerves, etc., to the utmost. **14.** to make violent physical efforts; strive hard. **15.** to be subjected to tension or stress; suffer strain. **16.** to filter, percolate, or ooze. **17.** to trickle or flow. —*n.* **18.** any force or pressure tending to alter shape, cause a fracture, etc. **19.** an injury resulting from this. **20.** strong muscular or physical effort. **21.** great effort or striving after some goal, object, or effect. **22.** an injury to a muscle, tendon, etc., due to excessive tension; sprain. **23.** deformation of a body or structure as a result of an applied force. **24.** condition of being strained or stretched. **25.** severe, trying, or fatiguing pressure or effect: *the strain of hard work.* **26.** a flow or burst of language, eloquence, etc.: *the lofty strain of Cicero.* **27.** Often, **strains.** a passage of music or songs, as rendered or heard: *the strains of the nightingale.* **28.** *Music.* a section of a piece of music, more or less complete in itself. **29.** a passage or piece of poetry. **30.** the tone, style, or spirit of an utterance, writing, etc.: *a humorous strain.* [ME *strein(en)* < OF *(e)strein-*, s. of *estreindre* to press tightly, grip < L *stringere* to bind, tie, draw tight. See STRINGENT, STRANGURY] —**strain′ing·ly,** *adv.* —**strain′less,** *adj.* —**strain′less·ly,** *adv.*
—**Syn. 1.** tighten. **3.** STRAIN, SPRAIN imply a wrenching, twisting, and stretching of muscles and tendons. To STRAIN is to stretch tightly, make taut, wrench, tear, cause injury to, by long-continued or sudden and too violent effort or movement: *to strain one's heart by over-exertion, one's eyes by reading small print.* To SPRAIN is to strain excessively (but without dislocation) by a sudden twist or wrench, the tendons and muscles connected with a joint, esp. those of the ankle or wrist: *to sprain an ankle.* **7.** filter, sieve. **20.** exertion. **22.** wrench.

strain[2] (strān), *n.* **1.** the body of descendants of a common ancestor, as a family or stock. **2.** any of the different lines of ancestry united in a family or an individual. **3.** a group of plants distinguished from other plants of the variety to which it belongs by some intrinsic quality; race. **4.** an artificial variety of a species of domestic animal or cultivated plant. **5.** a variety, esp. of microorganisms. **6.** ancestry or descent. **7.** a streak or trace. **8.** a kind or sort. [ME *strene*, OE *strēon* lineage, race, stock, tribe, akin to *strīenan* to beget]

strained (strānd), *adj.* affected or produced by effort; forced; not natural or spontaneous: *strained hospitality; a strained smile.* —**strained·ly** (strānd′lē, strā′nid-), *adv.* —**strained′ness,** *n.*

strain·er (strā′nər), *n.* **1.** a person or thing that strains. **2.** a filter, sieve, or the like, for straining liquids. [ME]

strain′ing piece′, (in a queen-post roof) a horizontal beam uniting the tops of the two queen posts, and resisting the thrust of the roof. Also called **strain′ing beam′.**

strait (strāt), *n.* Often, **straits. 1.** (*construed as sing.*) a narrow passage of water connecting two large bodies of water. **2.** a position of difficulty, distress, or need. —*adj.* *Archaic.* **3.** narrow: *Strait is the gate.* **4.** affording little space; confined in area. **5.** strict, as in requirements or principles. [ME *streit* < OF *(e)streit* < L *strict(us)* prp. of *stringere* to bind; see STRAIN[1]] —**strait′ly,** *adv.* —**strait′ness,** *n.* —**Syn. 2.** dilemma, predicament, plight. —**Ant. 2.** ease.

strait·en (strāt′ᵊn), *v.t.* **1.** to put into difficulties, esp. financial ones. **2.** to restrict in range, extent, amount, pecuniary means, etc. **3.** *Archaic.* **a.** to make narrow. **b.** to confine within narrow limits.

strait′ jack′et, a garment made of strong material and designed to bind the arms, as of a violently insane or delirious person. Also, **straight jacket.**

strait-jack·et (strāt′jak′it), *v.t.* to put in or as in a strait jacket.

strait-laced (strāt′lāst′), *adj.* **1.** excessively strict in conduct or morality; puritanical; prudish. **2.** *Archaic.* tightly laced, as a bodice. Also, **straight-laced.** —**strait-lac′ed·ly** (strāt′lā′sid lē, -lāst′lē), *adv.* —**strait′-lac′ed·ness,** *n.*

Straits′ dol′lar (strāts), a former silver coin and monetary unit of the Straits Settlements.

Straits′ Set′tlements, a former British crown colony in SE Asia: included the settlements of Singapore, Penang, Malacca, and Labuan. *Cap.:* Singapore.

strake (strāk), *n.* *Naut.* a continuous course of planks or plates forming a hull shell, deck, the side of a deckhouse, etc. [ME; appar. akin to STRETCH] —**straked,** *adj.*

Stral·sund (shträl′zo͝ont), *n.* a seaport in N East Germany: a member of the medieval Hanseatic League; besieged by Wallenstein 1628. 65,275 (est. 1955).

stra·mo·ni·um (strə mō′nē əm), *n.* **1.** See **jimson weed. 2.** the dried leaves of the jimson weed, used as an analgesic, antispasmodic, etc. [< NL < ?]

strand[1] (strand), *v.t.* **1.** to drive or leave (a ship, fish, etc.) aground or ashore. **2.** to bring into or leave in a helpless position (usually used in the passive): *He was stranded in the middle of nowhere.* —*v.i.* **3.** to be driven or left ashore; run aground. **4.** to be halted or struck by a difficult situation. —*n.* **5.** the land bordering the sea, a lake, or a river; shore. [ME, OE; c. G *Strand*, D *strand*, Icel *strǫnd;* akin to STREW]

strand[2] (strand), *n.* **1.** a number of fibers, threads, or yarns plaited or twisted together to form a unit of a rope, cord, or the like. **2.** a similar part of a wire rope. **3.** a rope made of such twisted or plaited fibers. **4.** a fiber or filament, as in animal or plant tissue. **5.** a tress of hair. **6.** a string of pearls, beads, etc. —*v.t.* **7.** to form (a rope, cable, etc.) by twisting strands together. [?] —**strand′less,** *adj.*

Strand, the (strand), a street parallel to the Thames, in W central London, England: famous for hotels and theaters.

strand′ line′, a shoreline, esp. one from which the sea or a lake has receded.

strange (strānj), *adj.*, **strang·er, strang·est,** *adv.* —*adj.* **1.** unusual, extraordinary, or curious: *a strange remark to make.* **2.** estranged, alienated, etc., as a result of being out of one's natural environment. **3.** situated, belonging, or coming from outside of one's own locality; foreign, alien: *a strange place.* **4.** outside of one's previous experience; hitherto unknown; unfamiliar: *strange faces.* **5.** unaccustomed to or inexperienced in; unacquainted (usually fol. by *to*): *I'm strange to this part of the job.* **6.** distant or reserved; shy. —*adv.* **7.** Also, **strange′ly.** in a strange manner. [ME < OF *(e)strange* < L *extrāne(us)* EXTRANEOUS] —**strange′ness,** *n.*
—**Syn. 1.** bizarre, singular. STRANGE, PECULIAR, ODD, QUEER refer to that which is out of the ordinary. STRANGE implies that the thing or its cause is unknown or unexplained; it is unfamiliar and unusual: *a strange expression.* That which is PECULIAR mystifies or exhibits qualities not shared by others: *peculiar behavior.* That which is ODD is irregular or unconventional, and sometimes approaches the bizarre: *an odd custom.* QUEER sometimes adds to ODD the suggestion of something abnormal and eccentric: *queer in the head.* **6.** aloof. —**Ant. 4–6.** familiar.

stran·ger (strān′jər), *n.* **1.** an individual with whom one has had no personal acquaintance: *He is a perfect stranger to me.* **2.** a newcomer in a place or locality: *a stranger in town.* **3.** a person who is unacquainted with or unaccustomed to something (usually fol. by *to*): *He is no stranger to poverty.* **4.** a person who is not a member of a family, group, community, or the like, as a guest or outsider: *Our town shows hospitality to strangers.* **5.** *Law.* a person who is not privy or party to an act, proceeding, etc. [late ME < MF *(e)strangier.* See STRANGE, -ER[2]] —**stran′ger·like′,** *adj.*
—**Syn. 2, 4.** STRANGER, ALIEN, FOREIGNER all refer to someone regarded as outside of or distinct from a particular group. STRANGER may apply to one who does not belong to some social, professional, national, or other group, or may apply to a person with whom one is not acquainted. ALIEN emphasizes a difference in political allegiance and citizenship from that of the country in which one is living. FOREIGNER emphasizes a difference in language, customs, and background. —**Ant. 1.** acquaintance.

stran·gle (straŋ′gəl), *v.*, **-gled, -gling.** —*v.t.* **1.** to kill by squeezing the throat in order to compress the windpipe and prevent the intake of air, as with the hands or a tightly drawn cord. **2.** to kill by stopping the breath in any manner; choke; stifle; suffocate. **3.** to prevent the continuance, growth, rise, or action of; suppress: *Suburbs strangled the city.* —*v.i.* **4.** to be choked, stifled, or suffocated. [ME *strangel(en)* < OF *(e)strangle(r)* < L *strangulāre* < Gk *strangalân* < *strangál(ē)* halter, akin to *strangós* twisted] —**stran′gler,** *n.* —**Syn. 1.** garrote, throttle, choke. **2.** smother.

stran′gle hold′, 1. *Wrestling.* an illegal hold by which an opponent's breath is choked off. **2.** any force or influence which restricts the free actions or development of a person or group.

stran·gles (straŋ′gəlz), *n.* (*construed as sing.*) *Vet. Pathol.* distemper[1] (def. 1b). [pl. of obs. *strangle* act of strangling]

stran·gu·late (straŋ′gyə lāt′), *v.t.*, **-lat·ed, -lat·ing. 1.** *Pathol., Surg.* to compress or constrict (a duct, intestine, vessel, etc.) so as to prevent circulation or suppress function. **2.** to strangle. [< L *strangulāt(us)* strangled = *strangul-* (s. of *strangulāre* to strangle) + *-ātus* -ATE[1]] —**stran·gu·la·ble** (straŋ′gyə lə bəl), *adj.* —**stran′gu·la′tion,** *n.* —**stran′gu·la′tive,** *adj.* —**stran·gu·la·to·ry** (straŋ′gyə lə tôr′ē, -tōr′ē), *adj.*

stran′gulated her′nia, a hernia in which the protruding organ is so constricted as to stop blood circulation.

stran·gu·ry (straŋ′gyə rē), *n.* *Pathol.* a condition of the urinary organs in which the urine is emitted painfully and drop by drop. [< L *strangūria* < Gk *strangouriā* = *strang(ós)* flowing drop by drop + *oûr(on)* urine + *-ia* -Y[3]]

strap (strap), *n.*, *v.*, **strapped, strap·ping.** —*n.* **1.** a narrow strip of flexible material, esp. leather, as for fastening or holding things together. **2.** a looped band by which an item may be held, pulled, lifted, etc., as a bootstrap. **3.** a suspended loop of leather or a metal ring that standing passengers may hold on to in a public conveyance. **4.** a strop for a razor. **5.** a long, narrow object or piece of something; strip; band. **6.** See **shoulder strap. 7.** *Mach.* a shallow metal fitting surrounding and retaining other parts, as on the end of a rod. **8.** *Naut., Mach.* strop (def. 2). **9.** watchband. —*v.t.* **10.** to fasten or secure with a strap or straps. **11.** to fasten (a thing) around something in the manner of a strap. **12.** to sharpen on a strap or strop: *to strap a razor.* **13.** to beat or flog with a strap. [var. of STROP]

strap·hang·er (strap′haŋ′ər), *n.* *Informal.* a passenger who stands in a crowded bus or subway train and holds onto a strap or other support suspended from above. —**strap′hang′ing,** *n.*

strap-hinge (strap′hinj′), *n.* a hinge having a flap, esp. a long one, attached to one face of a door or the like. See illus. at **hinge.**

strap·less (strap′lis), *adj.* **1.** without a strap or straps. **2.** designed and made without shoulder straps: *a strapless evening gown.*

strap·pa·do (strə pā′dō, -pä′-), *n.*, *pl.* **-does. 1.** an old form of torture in which the victim was hoisted by a rope fastened to his wrists and then abruptly dropped to a point just short of the ground. **2.** the instrument used for this purpose. [alter. of MF *strapade* or its source, It *strappata* a sharp pull or tug = *strapp-* (s. of *strappare* to snatch < Gmc; cf. dial. G *strapfen* to stretch tight) + *-ata* -ADE[1]]

strapped (strapt), *adj.* *Informal.* needy; wanting: *The company is rather strapped for funds.*

strap·per (strap′ər), *n.* **1.** a person or thing that straps. **2.** *Informal.* a large, robust person.

strap·ping[1] (strap′iŋ), *adj.* **1.** powerfully built; robust. **2.** *Informal.* large; whopping. [STRAP + -ING[2]]

strap·ping[2] (strap′iŋ), *n.* **1.** a beating given with or as with a strap. **2.** straps collectively. [STRAP + -ING[1]]

Stras·bourg (stras′bûrg, sträz′bo͝org; *Fr.* STRAZ BO͞OR′), *n.* a fortress city in NE France, near the Rhine: cathedral; taken by Allied forces November 1944. 233,549 (1962). German, **Strass·burg** (s͟htRäs′bo͝oRk).

strass (stras), *n.* a flint glass with a high lead content, used to imitate gemstones. [< G, named after J. *Strasser,* 18th-century German jeweler who invented it]

stra·ta (strā′tə, strat′ə, strä′tə), *n.* **1.** a pl. of **stratum. 2.** (*usually considered nonstandard.*) stratum.

strat·a·gem (strat′ə jəm), *n.* **1.** a plan, scheme, or trick for surprising or deceiving an enemy. **2.** any artifice, ruse, or trick to attain a goal or to gain an advantage over an adversary. [< MF *stratagème* or its source, It *stratagemma* war ruse < L *stratēgēma* < Gk *stratḗgēma* instance of generalship < *stratēgein* to be in command] —**Syn. 1, 2.** See **trick.**

stra·tal (strāt′əl), *adj.* of a stratum or strata. [STRAT(UM) + -AL[1]]

stra·te·gic (strə tē′jik), *adj.* **1.** pertaining to, characterized by, or of the nature of strategy. **2.** important in or essential to strategy. **3.** (of an action, as a military operation or a move in a game) forming an integral part of a stratagem: *a strategic move in a game of chess.* **4.** *Mil.* **a.** intended to render the enemy incapable of making war, as by the destruction of materials, factories, etc.: *a strategic bombing mission.* **b.** essential to the conduct of a war: *Copper is a strategic material.* Also, **stra·te′gi·cal.** [< Gk *stratēgik(ós)* = *stratēg(ós)* army leader (*strat(ós)* army + *-ēgos* leader: *ēg-* var. s. of *ágein* to lead + *-os* n. suffix) + *-ikos* -IC] —**stra·te′gi·cal·ly,** *adv.*

Strate′gic Defense′ Ini′tiative. See **Star Wars.**

stra·te·gics (strə tē′jiks), *n.* (*construed as sing.*) strategy (def. 2). [see STRATEGIC, -ICS]

strat·e·gist (strat′i jist), *n.* an expert in strategy, as in warfare.

strat·e·gy (strat′i jē), *n.*, *pl.* **-gies. 1.** a plan, method, or series of maneuvers or stratagems for obtaining a specific goal or result. **2.** Also, **strategics.** the science or art of planning and directing large military movements and operations. **3.** the use or an instance of using this science or art. **4.** skillful use of a stratagem. [< Gk *stratēgía* generalship = *stratēg-* (see STRATEGIC) + *-ia* -Y[3]]
—**Syn. 2.** In military usage, a distinction is made between STRATEGY and TACTICS. STRATEGY is the utilization of all of a nation's forces, through large-scale, long-range planning and development, to ensure security or victory. TACTICS deals with the use and deployment of troops in combat.

Strat·ford (strat′fərd), *n.* **1.** a town in SW Connecticut, near Bridgeport: Shakespeare theater. 49,775 (1970). **2.** a city in SE Ontario, in S Canada: Shakespeare theater. 20,467 (1961).

Strat′ford de Red′cliffe (də red′klif), **1st Viscount** (*Stratford Canning*), 1786–1880, English diplomat.

Strat·ford-on-A·von (strat′fərd on ā′vən, -ôn-), *n.* a town in SW Warwickshire, in central England, on the Avon River: birthplace and burial place of Shakespeare. 16,847 (1961). Also, **Strat′ford-up·on-A′von.**

strath·spey (strath′spā′, strath′spā′), *n.* a slow Scottish dance in quadruple meter. [after *Strath Spey* a Scottish locality]

strati-, a combining form of **stratum:** *stratiform.*

stra·tic·u·late (strə tik′yə lit, -lāt′), *adj.* (of a geological formation) composed of thin, continuous strata. [STRATI- + -CULE + -ATE[1]] —**stra·tic′u·la′tion,** *n.*

strat·i·fi·ca·tion (strat′ə fə kā′shən), *n.* **1.** the act or an instance of stratifying. **2.** a stratified state or appearance. **3.** *Sociol.* the division of society according to rank, caste, or class: *stratification of feudal society.* **4.** *Geol.* **a.** formation of strata; deposition or occurrence in strata. **b.** a stratum. [< NL *strātificātiōn-* (s. of *strātificātiō*)]

strat·i·form (strat′ə fôrm′), *adj.* **1.** *Geol.* occurring as a bed or beds; arranged in strata. **2.** *Meteorol.* (of a cloud) having predominantly horizontal development.

strat·i·fy (strat′ə fī′), *v.*, **-fied, -fy·ing.** —*v.t.* **1.** to form or place strata or layers. **2.** to preserve or germinate (seeds) by placing them between layers of earth. **3.** *Sociol.* to arrange in a hierarchical order, esp. according to graded status levels. —*v.i.* **4.** to form strata. **5.** *Geol.* to lie in beds or layers. **6.** *Sociol.* to develop hierarchically, esp. as graded status levels. [modeled on NL *strātificāre.* See STRATI-, -FY]

stratig., stratigraphy.

stra·tig·ra·phy (strə tig′rə fē), *n.* a branch of geology dealing with the classification, correlation, and interpretation of stratified rocks. —**stra·tig·ra·pher** (strə tig′rə fər), **stra·tig′ra·phist,** *n.* —**strat·i·graph·ic** (strat′ə graf′ik), **strat′i·graph′i·cal,** *adj.* —**strat′i·graph′i·cal·ly,** *adv.*

strato-, a combining form representing **stratus** (*stratocumulus*) and sometimes specialized as a combining form of **stratosphere.** [< NL, comb. form repr. L *strātus* a spreading out. See STRATUS]

stra·toc·ra·cy (strə tok′rə sē), *n.*, *pl.* **-cies.** a form of government in which political power is vested in the army or a military class. [< Gk *strató(s)* army + -CRACY] —**strat·o·crat** (strat′ə krat′), *n.* —**strat·o·crat·ic** (strat′ə krat′ik), *adj.*

stra·to·cu·mu·lus (strā′tō kyo͞o′myə ləs, strat′ō-), *n.*, *pl.* **-lus.** a cloud of a class characterized by large dark, rounded masses, usually in groups, lines, or waves.

strat·o·sphere (strat′ə sfēr′), *n.* the region of the upper atmosphere extending upward from the tropopause to about 15 miles above the earth. [STRAT(UM + ATM)OSPHERE] —**strat·o·spher·ic** (strat′ə sfer′ik), *adj.*

stra·tum (strā′təm, strat′əm, strä′təm), *n.*, *pl.* **stra·ta** (strā′tə, strat′ə, strä′tə), **stra·tums. 1.** a layer of material, often one of a number of parallel layers one upon another. **2.** one of a number of portions or divisions likened to layers or levels: *an allegory with many strata of meaning.* **3.** *Geol.* a single bed of sedimentary rock, generally consisting of one kind of matter representing continuous deposition. **4.** *Biol.* a layer of tissue; lamella. **5.** *Ecol.* (in a plant community) a layer of vegetation, usually of the same or similar height. **6.** a layer of the ocean or the atmosphere distinguished by natural or arbitrary limits. **7.** *Sociol.* a level or grade of a people or population with reference to social position, education, etc. [< L: lit., a cover, n. use of neut. of *strātus.* See STRATUS] —**stra′tous,** *adj.*

stra·tus (strā′təs, strat′əs), *n.*, *pl.* **-tus.** a cloud of a class characterized by a gray horizontal layer with a uniform base. [< NL, L, ptp. of *sternere* to spread]

Straus (strous; *Ger.* s͟htrous), *n.* **Os·car** (os′kər; *Ger.* ôs′kär), 1870–1954, Austrian composer.

Strauss (strous; *Ger.* s͟htrous), *n.* **1. Da·vid Frie·drich** (dä′vēt frē′driкн), 1808–74, German theologian, philosopher, and author. **2. Jo·hann** (yō′hän), 1804–49, Austrian orchestra conductor and composer. **3.** his son, **Johann,** 1825–1899, Austrian orchestra conductor and composer. **4. Rich·ard** (ric͟h′ərd; *Ger.* riкн′ärt), 1864–1949, German orchestra conductor and composer.

Stra·vin·sky (strə vin′skē; *Russ.* strä vēn′ski), *n.* **I·gor Fë·do·ro·vich** (ē′gôr fyô′də rō′vic͟h; *Russ.* e′gôr fyô′do-rô′vic͟h), 1882–1971, U.S. composer, born in Russia.

straw (strô), *n.* **1.** a single stalk or stem, esp. of wheat, rye, oats, and barley. **2.** a mass of such stalks, esp. after drying and threshing, used as fodder. **3.** material, fibers, etc., made from such stalks, as used for making hats, baskets, etc. **4.** the value of one such stalk; trifle; least bit: *not to care a straw.* **5.** a tube, usually of paper or glass, for sucking up a beverage from a container. **6.** a straw hat. **7. catch, clutch, or grasp at a straw or straws,** to seize at any chance, no matter how slight, of saving onself from calamity. **—*adj.* 8.** of, pertaining to, containing, or made of straw: *a straw hat.* **9.** of little value or consequence; worthless. [ME; OE *strēaw;* akin to STREW] **—straw′y,** *adj.*

straw·ber·ry (strô′ber′ē, -bə rē), *n., pl.* **-ries. 1.** the fruit of any stemless, rosaceous herb of the genus *Fragaria,* consisting of an enlarged fleshy receptacle bearing achenes on its exterior. **2.** the plant bearing it. [ME; OE *strēawberige.* See STRAW, BERRY]

straw′berry blonde′, 1. reddish blonde. **2.** a woman with reddish-blonde hair.

straw′berry bush′, wahoo[2].

straw′berry mark′, a small, reddish, slightly raised birthmark.

straw′berry shrub′, any of several shrubs of the genus *Calycanthus,* having purplish-red flowers.

straw′berry toma′to, the small, edible, tomatolike fruit of a solanaceous plant, *Physalis pruinosa.*

straw′berry tree′, an evergreen, ericaceous shrub or tree, *Arbutus Unedo,* bearing a strawberrylike fruit.

straw·board (strô′bōrd′, -bôrd′), *n.* coarse paperboard made of straw pulp, used in packing, for making boxes, etc.

straw′ boss′, *U.S. Informal.* a member of a work crew who acts as a boss; assistant foreman.

straw·hat (strô′hat′), *adj.* noting or pertaining to a summer theater situated outside an urban or metropolitan area. [so called from the wearing of straw hats in summer]

straw′ man′, 1. a mass of straw formed to resemble a man, as for a scarecrow. **2.** a person used by another to disguise his own activities, as a perjured witness. **3.** a weak or unimportant person, argument, theory, etc.

straw′ vote′, *U.S.* an unofficial vote taken to obtain an indication of the trend of opinion on a particular issue.

straw·worm (strô′wûrm′), *n.* **1.** caddisworm. **2.** jointworm.

stray (strā), *v.i.* **1.** to deviate from the direct course, leave the proper place, or go beyond the proper limits, esp. without a fixed course or purpose: *to stray from the main road.* **2.** to wander; roam. **3.** to go astray; deviate, as from a moral or philosophical course. **4.** to digress or become distracted. **—*n.* 5.** a domestic animal found wandering at large or without an owner. **6.** any homeless or friendless person or animal. **—*adj.* 7.** straying or having strayed, as a domestic animal. **8.** found or occurring apart from others or as an isolated or casual instance; incidental or occasional. [ME *stray(en),* aph. var. of *astraien, estraien* < MF *estraie(r)* < VL **extrāgāre* for **extrāvagāre* (cf. ML *extrāvagārī*) to wander out of bounds. See EXTRAVAGANT] **—stray′er,** *n.*

streak (strēk), *n.* **1.** a long, narrow mark, smear, band of color, or the like: *streaks of mud.* **2.** a flash of lightning; bolt. **3.** a portion or layer of something, distinguished by color or nature from the rest; a vein or stratum: *streaks of fat in meat.* **4.** a vein, strain, or admixture of anything: *a streak of humor.* **5.** *U.S. Informal.* a spell or run: *a winning streak.* **6.** *Mineral.* the line of powder obtained by scratching a mineral or rubbing it upon a hard, rough white surface, often differing in color from the mineral in the mass, and forming an important distinguishing character. **7.** *Bacteriol.* the inoculation of a medium with a loop that contains the material to be inoculated, by passing the loop in a direct or zigzag line over the medium, without scratching the surface. **—*v.t.* 8.** to mark with a streak or streaks; form streaks on. **9.** to dispose, arrange, smear, spread, etc., in the form of a streak or streaks. **—*v.i.* 10.** to become streaked. **11.** to run, go, work, etc., rapidly. **12.** to flash, as lightning. **13.** to engage in the prank or fad of streaking. [ME *strek(e),* akin to *strik(e),* OE *strica* STROKE[1], line, mark; c. G *Strich*] **—streaked·ly** (strēkt′lē, strē′kid lē), *adv.* **—streaked′ness,** *n.* **—streak′er,** *n.* **—streak′like′,** *adj.*

streak·ing (strē′king), *n.* (esp. among college students) a prank or fad of dashing briefly in the nude across a campus, street, etc., in public view.

streak·y (strē′kē), *adj.,* **streak·i·er, streak·i·est. 1.** occurring as a streak or in streaks. **2.** marked with or characterized by streaks. **3.** *Informal.* varying or uneven in quality. **—streak′i·ly,** *adv.* **—streak′i·ness,** *n.*

stream (strēm), *n.* **1.** a body of water flowing in a channel or watercourse, as a river, rivulet, or brook. **2.** a steady current in water, as in a river or the ocean. **3.** any flow of water or other liquid or fluid: *streams of blood.* **4.** a current or flow of air, gas, or the like. **5.** a beam or trail of light. **6.** a continuous flow or succession of anything: *a stream of words.* **7. on stream,** in or into manufacturing operation. **—*v.i.* 8.** to flow, pass, or issue in a stream, as water, tears, blood, etc. **9.** to send forth or throw off a stream; run or flow (often fol. by *with*): *eyes streaming with tears.* **10.** to extend in a beam or trail, as light: *Sunlight streamed in through the windows.* **11.** to move or proceed continuously like a flowing stream, as a procession. **12.** to wave or float outward, as a flag in the wind. **13.** to hang in a loose, flowing manner, as long hair. **—*v.t.* 14.** to send forth or discharge in a stream. **15.** to cause to stream or float outward, as a flag. [ME *streem,* OE *strēam;* c. G *Strom,* Icel *straumr;* akin to SERUM]
—Syn. 1–4. STREAM, CURRENT refer to a steady flow. In this use they are interchangeable. In the sense of running water, however, a STREAM is a flow which may be as small as a brook or as large as a river: *A number of streams have their sources in mountains.* CURRENT refers to the most rapidly moving part of the stream: *This river has a swift current.*

stream·er (strē′mər), *n.* **1.** something that streams: *streamers of flame.* **2.** a long, narrow flag or pennant. **3.** a long, flowing ribbon, feather, or the like, used for ornament, as in dress. **4.** a stream of light, esp. one appearing in some forms of the aurora borealis. **5.** banner (def. 6).

stream·let (strēm′lit), *n.* a small stream; rivulet.

stream·line (strēm′līn′), *n., v.,* **-lined, -lin·ing. —*n.* 1.** a teardrop contour offering the least possible resistance to a current of air, water, etc. **2.** the path of a particle that is flowing steadily and without turbulence in a fluid past an object. **—*v.t.* 3.** to make streamlined. **4.** to alter (a routine, process, plan, etc.) in order to make it more efficient, esp. by simplifying.

stream·lined (strēm′līnd′), *adj.* **1.** having a surface designed to offer the least possible resistance to a current of air, water, etc. **2.** designed or organized to give maximum efficiency; compact. **3.** modernized; up-to-date.

stream′line flow′, *Hydraulics.* the flow of a fluid past an object such that the velocity at any fixed point in the fluid is constant or varies in a regular manner. Cf. **turbulent flow.**

stream·lin·er (strēm′lī′nər), *n.* something that is streamlined, esp. a locomotive or passenger train.

stream′ of con′sciousness, *Psychol.* thought regarded as a succession of states constantly moving forward in time.

stream-of-con·scious·ness (strēm′əv kon′shəs nis), *adj.* of, pertaining to, or characterized by writing in which a character's thoughts or perceptions are presented in a manner that simulates the process of consciousness as it normally occurs when there is no constraint to follow logic or distinguish between various levels of reality.

stream·y (strē′mē), *adj.,* **stream·i·er, stream·i·est. 1.** abounding in streams or watercourses. **2.** flowing in a stream; streaming. [late ME *stremy*] **—stream′i·ness,** *n.*

streek (strēk), *v.t. Brit. Dial.* **1.** to stretch (one's limbs), as on awakening or by exercise. **2.** to extend (one's hand or arm), as in reaching for or offering an object. **3.** to stretch out or prepare (a corpse) for burial. [ME (north) *streke,* var. of *strecchen* to STRETCH] **—streek′er,** *n.*

street (strēt), *n.* **1.** a public thoroughfare, usually paved, in a village, town, or city, including the sidewalk or sidewalks. **2.** such a thoroughfare together with adjacent buildings, lots, etc. **3.** the roadway of such a thoroughfare, as distinguished from the sidewalk: *to cross a street.* **4.** a main way or thoroughfare, as distinguished from a lane, alley, or the like. **5.** the inhabitants or frequentors of a street. **—*adj.* 6.** of, in, on, or adjoining a street: *a street floor.* **7.** appropriate for general wear in public: *a street dress.* [ME; OE *strēt, strǣt;* c. D *straat,* G *Strasse;* all << L (*via*) *strāta* paved (road); see STRATUS]
—Syn. 1. STREET, ALLEY, AVENUE, BOULEVARD all refer to public ways or roads in municipal areas. A STREET is a road in a village, town, or city, esp. a road lined with buildings. An ALLEY is a narrow street or footway, esp. at the rear of or between rows of buildings or lots. An AVENUE is properly a prominent street, often one bordered by fine residences and impressive buildings, or with a row of trees on each side. A BOULEVARD is a beautiful, broad street, lined with trees, esp. used as a promenade. In some cities STREET and AVENUE are used interchangeably, the only difference being that those running in one direction are given one designation and those crossing them are given the other.

street′ Ar′ab, a homeless child who lives by begging or stealing.

street·car (strēt′kär′), *n. U.S.* a public vehicle running regularly along certain streets, usually on rails, as a trolley car or trolley bus.

street′ clean′er, a sanitation worker who cleans streets or sidewalks.

street·light (strēt′līt′), *n.* a light, usually supported by a lamppost, for illuminating a street, road, etc.

street′ peo′ple, 1. the people of a neighborhood, esp. a crowded big-city neighborhood or ghetto, who frequent the streets of their area. **2.** wandering hippies, students, and others who have no permanent address.

street′ the′ater, the presentation of plays by travelling companies on the streets, in parks, etc., often with the use of temporary or mobile stages.

street·walk·er (strēt′wô′kər), *n.* a prostitute who solicits on the streets. **—street′walk′ing,** *n.*

street-wise (strēt′wīz′), *adj.* having a tough-minded, practical familiarity with the sordid aspects of modern urban life, esp. as a result of growing up on the streets of a large city. Also, **streetwise.** Also called **street-smart** (strēt′smärt′).

strength (strengkth, strength), *n.* **1.** the quality or state of being strong; bodily or muscular power; vigor. **2.** mental power, force, or vigor. **3.** moral power, firmness, or courage. **4.** power by reason of influence, authority, resources, numbers, etc. **5.** number, as of men or ships in a force or body: *a regiment with a strength of 3000.* **6.** effective force, potency or cogency, as of inducements or arguments: *the strength of his plea.* **7.** power of resisting force, strain, wear, etc. **8.** vigor of action, language, feeling, etc. **9.** amount; quantity; proportion: *The alcoholic strength of brandy far exceeds that of wine.* **10.** intensity, as of light, color, sound, flavor, or odor: *coffee of normal strength.* **11.** something or someone that is a source of power or encouragement: *The Bible was her strength and joy.* **12.** power to rise or remain firm in prices: *The pound declined in strength.* **13. on the strength of,** on the basis of; relying on. [ME *strengthe,* OE *strength(u)* = *streng-* (mutated var. of STRONG) + *-thu* -TH[1]]
—Syn. 4. STRENGTH, POWER, FORCE, MIGHT suggest capacity

to do something. STRENGTH is inherent capacity to manifest energy, to endure, and to resist. POWER is capacity to do work and to act. FORCE is the exercise of power: *One has the power to do something. He exerts force when he does it. He has sufficient strength to complete it.* MIGHT is power or strength in a great degree: *the might of an army.*

strength·en (strengk′thən, streng′-), *v.t.* **1.** to make stronger; give strength to. —*v.i.* **2.** to gain strength; grow stronger. [ME *strengthne(n)*] —**strength′en·er,** *n.*

stren·u·ous (stren′yo͞o əs), *adj.* **1.** vigorous, energetic, or zealously active: *a strenuous person; a strenuous intellect.* **2.** characterized by or requiring vigorous exertion: *a strenuous exercise.* [< L *strēnuus;* see -OUS] —**stren′u·ous·ly,** *adv.* —**stren′u·ous·ness,** *n.* —**Syn. 1.** See **active.**

strep (strep), *Informal.* —*n.* **1.** streptococcus. —*adj.* **2.** streptococcal: *strep throat.* [by shortening]

stre·pi·tous (strep′i təs), *adj.* boisterous; noisy. Also, **strep′i·tant.** [< L *strepit(us)* noise + -OUS]

strepto-, a learned borrowing from Greek meaning "twined," used in the formation of compound words: *streptococcus.* [comb. form of Gk *streptós* pliant, twisted, twined = *strep-* (var. s. of *stréphein* to twist) + *-tos* ptp. suffix]

strep·to·coc·cus (strep′tə kok′əs), *n., pl.* **-coc·ci** (-kok′sī). *Bacteriol.* any of several spherical or oval bacteria of the genus *Streptococcus,* occurring in pairs or chains, certain species of which are pathogenic for man, causing scarlet fever, tonsillitis, etc. —**strep·to·coc·cal** (strep′tə kok′əl), **strep·to·coc·cic** (strep′tə kok′sik), *adj.*

strep·to·ki·nase (strep′tō kī′nās, -kin′ās), *n. Pharm.* fibrinolysin (def. 2).

strep·to·my·cin (strep′tō mī′sin), *n. Pharm.* an antibiotic, $C_{21}H_{39}N_7O_{12}$, produced by a soil actinomycete, *Streptomyces griseus,* and used chiefly in the treatment of tuberculosis. [STREPTO- + MYC- + -IN[2]]

strep·to·thri·cin (strep′tō thrī′sin), *n. Pharm.* an antibacterial substance produced by the soil fungus, *Actinomyces lavendulae.* [STREPTO- + *thric-* (var. of TRICH-) + -IN[2]]

stress (stres), *n.* **1.** importance or significance attached to a thing; emphasis: *to lay stress upon good manners.* **2.** *Phonet.* emphasis in the form of prominent relative loudness of a syllable or a word as a result of special effort in utterance. **3.** *Pros.* accent or emphasis on syllables in a metrical pattern. **4.** emphasis in melody, rhythm, etc.; beat. **5.** the physical pressure, pull, or other force exerted on one thing by another; strain. **6.** *Mech., Physics.* **a.** the action on a body of any system of balanced forces whereby strain or deformation results. **b.** the amount of such action, usually measured in number of pounds per square inch. **c.** the internal resistance or reaction of an elastic body to the external forces applied to it. **7.** *Physiol.* any stimulus, as fear or pain, that disturbs or interferes with the normal physiological equilibrium of an organism. **8.** physical, mental, or emotional strain or tension. —*v.t.* **9.** to lay stress on; emphasize. **10.** *Phonet.* to pronounce (a syllable or a word) with prominent loudness. Cf. **accent** (def. 13). **11.** to subject to stress or strain. [ME *stresse,* aph. var. of *distresse* DISTRESS] —**stress′less,** *adj.* —**stress′less·ness,** *n.*

-stress, a feminine equivalent of **-ster:** *seamstress; songstress.* [-ST(E)R + -ESS]

stress·ful (stres′fəl), *adj.* full of stress or tension: *the stressful days before a war.* —**stress′ful·ly,** *adv.*

stretch (strech), *v.t.* **1.** to draw out or extend (oneself, a body, limbs, wings, etc.) to the full length or extent (often fol. by *out*): *to stretch oneself out on the ground.* **2.** to hold out, reach forth, or extend (the hand or something held, the head, etc.). **3.** to cause (something) to reach, extend, or spread from one point or place to another: *to stretch a rope across a road.* **4.** to draw tight or taut: *to stretch the strings of a violin.* **5.** to strain to the utmost, as by exertion: *She stretched herself to provide for the family.* **6.** to lengthen, widen, distend, or enlarge by tension: *to stretch a rubber band.* **7.** to draw out, extend, or enlarge unduly: *The jacket was stretched at the elbows.* **8.** to extend, force, or make serve beyond the normal or proper limits; strain: *to stretch the imagination; to stretch money to keep within a budget.* —*v.i.* **9.** to recline at full length (usually fol. by *out*): *to stretch out on a couch.* **10.** to extend the hand or to reach, as for something. **11.** to extend over a distance or area or in a particular direction: *The forest stretches for miles.* **12.** to stretch oneself by extending the limbs and straining the muscles to the utmost: *to stretch and yawn.* **13.** to become stretched, or admit of being stretched, to greater length, width, etc., as any elastic or ductile material. —*n.* **14.** the act or an instance of stretching. **15.** state of being stretched. **16.** a continuous length, distance, tract, or expanse: *a stretch of meadow.* **17.** *Horse Racing.* the homestretch of a race track. **18.** elasticity or capacity for extension. **19.** *Slang.* a term of imprisonment: *He's doing a stretch in the pen.* —*adj.* **20.** made of synthetic or composite yarn having a sufficiently low denier to permit increased elasticity: *stretch socks.* [ME *strecche(n),* OE *streccan;* c. D *strekken,* G *strecken;* akin to OE *stræc* firm, hard, MD *strac* stiff. See STARE, STARK] —**stretch′a·bil′i·ty,** *n.* —**stretch′a·ble,** *adj.* —**Syn. 6.** See **lengthen.** —**Ant. 6, 13.** shorten, shrink.

stretch·er (strech′ər), *n.* **1.** a litter, usually of canvas stretched on a frame, for carrying the sick, wounded, or dead. **2.** a person or thing that stretches. **3.** any of various instruments for extending, widening, distending, etc. **4.** a bar, beam, or fabricated material, serving as a tie or brace. **5.** *Masonry.* a brick or stone laid in a wall so that its longer edge is exposed or parallel to the surface. Cf. **header** (def. 4a). **6.** *Furniture.* **a.** a framework connecting and bracing the legs of a piece of furniture. **b.** one member of this framework. **7.** one of the thin, sliding rods connecting the canopy and handle of an umbrella. [late ME]

stretch·er-bear·er (strech′ər bâr′ər), *n.* a man who helps carry a stretcher, as in removing wounded from a battlefield.

stretch·y (strech′ē), *adj.,* **stretch·i·er, stretch·i·est.** **1.** having a tendency to stretch, esp. excessively. **2.** capable of being stretched; elastic. —**stretch′i·ness,** *n.*

stret·ta (stret′ə), *n., pl.* **stret·te** (stret′ā), **stret·tas.** stretto. [< It; fem. of STRETTO]

stret·to (stret′ō), *n., pl.* **stret·ti** (stret′ē), **stret·tos.** *Music.* **1.** the close overlapping of statements of the subject in a fugue, each voice entering immediately after the preceding one. **2.** (in a nonfugal composition) a concluding passage played at a faster tempo. Also, **stretta.** [< It: lit., narrow < L *strict(us).* See STRICT, STRAIT]

strew (stro͞o), *v.t.,* **strewed, strewn** or **strewed, strewing.** **1.** to let fall separately or in separate pieces or particles over a surface; scatter or sprinkle: *to strew sawdust.* **2.** to cover or overspread (a surface, place, etc.) with something scattered or sprinkled: *to strew a floor with sawdust.* **3.** to be scattered or sprinkled over (a surface): *Sawdust strewed the floor.* **4.** to spread widely: *to strew rumors among the troops.* [ME *strew(en),* OE *strewian;* c. G *streuen,* Icel *strā,* Goth *straujan;* akin to L *sternere* to spread (see STRATUS)] —**strew′er,** *n.* —**Syn. 1, 4.** broadcast. —**Ant. 1.** gather.

stri·a (strī′ə), *n., pl.* **stri·ae** (strī′ē). **1.** a slight or narrow furrow, ridge, stripe, or streak, esp. one of a number in parallel arrangement: *striae of muscle fiber.* **2.** *Geol.* any of a number of scratches or parallel grooves on the surface of a rock, resulting from the action of moving ice, as of a glacier. **3.** *Mineral.* any of a series of parallel lines or tiny grooves on the surface of a crystal, or on a cleavage face of a crystal, due to its molecular organization. [< L: furrow, channel]

stri·ate (*v.* strī′āt; *adj.* strī′it, -āt), *v.,* **-at·ed, -at·ing,** *adj.* —*v.t.* **1.** to mark with striae; furrow; stripe; streak. —*adj.* **2.** striated. [< L *striāt(us)* (ptp. of *striāre*) = *stri-* (see STRIA) + *-ātus* -ATE[1]]

stri·at·ed (strī′ā tid), *adj.* marked with striae; furrowed; striped; streaked.

stri·a·tion (strī ā′shən), *n.* **1.** striated condition or appearance. **2.** a stria; one of many parallel striae.

strick (strik), *n.* **1.** a group of any of the major bast fibers prepared for conversion into sliver form. **2.** any of the pieces cut from a layer of carded and combed silk. [ME *strik,* perh. < OE *stric* a word of uncertain meaning; akin to STRIKE]

strick·en (strik′ən), *adj.* **1.** a pp. of **strike. 2.** beset or afflicted, as with disease, trouble, or sorrow: *stricken areas; a stricken family.* **3.** deeply affected, as with grief, fear, or other emotions. **4.** characterized by or showing the effects of affliction, misfortune, a mental blow, etc. **5.** hit or wounded by a weapon, missile, or the like. —**strick′en·ly,** *adv.*

strick·le (strik′əl), *n., v.,* **-led, -ling.** —*n.* **1.** a straightedge used for sweeping off heaped-up grain to the level of the rim of a measure. **2.** *Foundry.* a template rotated to generate a mold surface symmetrical about one axis. **3.** an implement for sharpening scythes, composed typically of a piece of wood smeared with grease and sand. —*v.t.* **4.** to sweep off or remove with a strickle. [ME *strikyll,* OE *stricel;* akin to STRIKE]

strict (strikt), *adj.* **1.** characterized by or acting in close conformity with requirements or principles: *a strict observance of rituals.* **2.** stringent or exacting in or in enforcing rules, requirements, obligations, etc.; stern; severe: *strict laws; a strict judge.* **3.** closely or rigorously enforced or maintained: *strict silence.* **4.** exact or precise: *a strict statement of facts.* **5.** conservative; narrowly or carefully limited: *a strict interpretation of the Constitution.* **6.** absolute, perfect, or complete: *told in strict confidence.* [< L *strict(us)* = *stric-* (*strig-,* var. s. of *stringere* to draw tight) + *-tus* ptp. suffix] —**strict′ness,** *n.* —**Syn. 1.** narrow, illiberal, austere. STRICT, RIGID, RIGOROUS, STRINGENT imply inflexibility, severity, and an exacting quality. STRICT implies great exactness, esp. in the observance or enforcement of rules: *strict discipline.* RIGID, literally stiff or unbending, applies to that which is inflexible: *rigid economy.* RIGOROUS, with the same literal meaning, applies to that which is severe, exacting, and uncompromising, esp. in action or application: *rigorous self-denial.* STRINGENT applies to that which is vigorously exacting and severe: *stringent measures to suppress disorder.* **4.** accurate, scrupulous. —**Ant. 1.** flexible, lax.

stric·tion (strik′shən), *n.* the act of drawing tight, constricting, or straining. [< LL *strictiōn-* (s. of *strictiō*). See STRICT, -ION]

strict·ly (strikt′lē), *adv.* in a strict manner; precisely; stringently: *strictly speaking.*

stric·ture (strik′chər), *n.* **1.** an adverse criticism or remark; censure. **2.** an abnormal contraction of any passage or duct of the body. **3.** a restriction or limitation. **4.** *Obs.* strictness. [< LL *strictūr(a)* tightening = L *strict(us)* (see STRICT) + *-ūra* -URE] —**stric′tured,** *adj.*

stride (strīd), *v.,* **strode, strid·den** (strid′ən), **strid·ing,** *n.* —*v.i.* **1.** to walk with long steps, as with vigor, haste, or arrogance. **2.** to take a long step: *to stride across a puddle.* **3.** to straddle. —*v.t.* **4.** to walk with long steps along, on, through, over, etc.: *to stride the deck.* **5.** to pass over or across in one long step: *to stride a ditch.* **6.** to straddle. —*n.* **7.** a striding manner or gait. **8.** a long step in walking. **9.** (in animal locomotion) the act of progressive movement completed when all the feet are returned to the same relative position as at the beginning. **10.** the distance covered by such a movement. **11.** a regular or steady course, pace, etc.: *to hit one's stride.* **12.** a step forward in development or progress. **13. take something in one's stride,** to deal with calmly or successfully. [ME *stride(n),* OE *strīdan;* c. D *strijden,* LG *strīden* to stride; akin to STRADDLE] —**strid′er,** *n.* —**strid′ing·ly,** *adv.*

stri·dent (strīd′ənt), *adj.* making or having a harsh sound; grating; creaking. [< L *strīdent-* (s. of *strīdēns*), prp. of *strīd(ēre)* (to) make a harsh noise; see -ENT] —**stri′dence, stri′den·cy,** *n.* —**stri′dent·ly,** *adv.*

stri·dor (strī′dər), *n.* **1.** a harsh, grating, or creaking sound. **2.** *Pathol.* a harsh respiratory sound due to any of various forms of obstruction of the breathing passages. [< L = *strīd-* (see STRIDENT) + *-or* -OR[1]]

strid·u·late (strij′ə lāt′), *v.i.,* **-lat·ed, -lat·ing.** to produce a harsh or grating sound, as a cricket does, by rubbing together certain parts of the body; shrill. [back formation from *stridulation.* See STRIDUL(OUS), -ATION] —**strid′u·la′tion,** *n.* —**strid·u·la·to·ry** (strij′ə lə tôr′ē, -tōr′ē), *adj.*

strid·u·lous (strij′ə ləs), *adj.* producing or having a harsh or grating sound. Also, **strid′u·lant.** [< L *strīdulus* = *strīd-* (see STRIDENT) + *-ulus* -ULOUS] —**strid′u·lous·ly,** *adv.* —**strid′u·lous·ness,** *n.*

strife (strīf), *n.* **1.** vigorous or bitter conflict, discord, or antagonism. **2.** a quarrel, struggle, or clash: *armed strife.* **3.**

competition or rivalry. **4.** *Archaic.* strenuous effort. [ME *strif,* OF *(e)strif;* see STRIVE] —**strife′ful,** *adj.* —**strife′less,** *adj.* —**Syn. 1.** difference, disagreement. **2.** conflict.

strig·i·form (strij′ə fôrm′), *adj.* of, pertaining, or belonging to the order *Strigiformes,* comprising the owls. [< NL *Strigiform(ēs)* name of the order = *strig-* (s. of *strix*) screech owl + *-i-* -I- + *-form-* -FORM]

strig·il (strij′əl), *n.* an instrument for scraping the skin, used by ancient Greeks and Romans at the bath and gymnasium. [< L *strigil(is)* = *strig-* (var. s. of *stringere* to touch lightly; see STREAK, STRIKE) + *-ilis* -ILE] —**strig·il·ate** (strij′ə lit, -lāt′), *adj.*

stri·gose (strī′gōs, stri gōs′), *adj.* **1.** *Bot.* set with stiff bristles of hairs; hispid. **2.** *Zool.* marked with fine, closely set ridges, grooves, or points. [< L *strig(a)* furrow, row of bristles (see STRIGIL) + -OSE¹]

strike (strīk), *v.,* **struck** or (*Obs.*) **strook; struck** or (*esp. for 27–30*) **strick·en** or (*Obs.*) **strook; strik·ing;** *n.* —*v.t.* **1.** to deal a blow or stroke to, as with the fist, a weapon, or a hammer; hit. **2.** to inflict, deliver, or deal (a blow, stroke, attack, etc.). **3.** to drive so as to cause impact: *to strike the hands together.* **4.** to thrust forcibly: *Brutus struck a dagger into the dying Caesar.* **5.** to produce (fire, sparks, light, etc.) by percussion, friction, etc. **6.** to cause (a match) to ignite by friction. **7.** (of some natural or supernatural agency) to smite or blast: *May God strike you dead!* **8.** to come into forcible contact or collision with; hit into or against: *The ship struck a rock.* **9.** to reach or fall upon (the eyes, ears, etc.), as light or sound: *A shrill peal of bells struck their ears.* **10.** to enter the mind of; occur to: *A happy thought struck him.* **11.** to catch or arrest (the sight, hearing, etc.): *the first object that strikes one's eye.* **12.** to impress strongly: *a picture that strikes one's fancy.* **13.** to impress in a particular manner: *How does it strike you?* **14.** to come upon or find (oil, ore, etc.) in drilling, prospecting, or the like. **15.** to send down or put forth (a root), as a plant, cutting, etc. **16.** to arrive at or achieve by or as by balancing: *to strike a compromise.* **17.** to take apart or pull down (a structure or object, as a tent). **18.** to remove from the stage (the scenery and properties of an act or scene): *to strike a set.* **19.** *Naut.* **a.** to lower or take down (a sail, mast, etc.). **b.** to lower (a sail, flag, etc.) as a salute or as a sign of surrender. **20.** *Angling.* **a.** (of a fish) to snatch at (the bait). **b.** to hook (a fish that has taken the bait) by making a sharp jerk on the line. **21.** to harpoon (a whale). **22.** to make level, smooth, or even, as a measure of grain or salt, by drawing a strickle across the top. **23.** to efface, cancel, or cross out, with or as with the stroke of a pen (usually fol. by *out*). **24.** to impress or stamp (a coin, medal, etc.) by printing or punching. **25.** to remove or separate with or as with a cut (usually fol. by *off*). **26.** to indicate (the hour of day) by a stroke or strokes, as a clock: *to strike 12.* **27.** to afflict suddenly, as with disease, suffering, or death (often fol. by *down*): *The plague struck Europe.* **28.** to overwhelm emotionally, as with terror, fear, etc.; affect deeply. **29.** to make blind, dumb, etc., suddenly, as if by a blow. **30.** to implant or induce (a feeling): *to strike fear into a person.* **31.** to start or move suddenly into (vigorous movement): *The horse struck a gallop.* **32.** to assume (an attitude or posture): *He likes to strike a noble pose.* **33.** to cause (chill, warmth, etc.) to pass or penetrate quickly. **34.** to come upon or reach in traveling or in a course of procedure: *We struck Rome before dark.* **35.** to make, conclude, or ratify (an agreement, treaty, etc.). **36.** to estimate or determine (a mean or average). **37.** to leave off (work) or stop (working) as a coercive measure. **38.** (of a union or union member) to declare or engage in a suspension of work against (a factory, employer, industry, etc.) until certain demands are met. **39.** *Law.* to choose from a given panel the persons to serve on (a jury).
—*v.i.* **40.** to deal or aim a blow or stroke, as with the fist, a weapon, or a hammer; make an attack. **41.** to knock, rap, or tap. **42.** to hit or dash on or against something, as a moving body does; collide. **43.** to run upon a bank, rock, or other obstacle, as a ship does. **44.** to fall, as light or sound does (fol. by *on* or *upon*). **45.** to make an impression on the mind, senses, etc., as something seen or heard. **46.** to come suddenly or unexpectedly (usually fol. by *on* or *upon*): *to strike on a new way of doing a thing.* **47.** to sound by percussion: *The clock strikes.* **48.** to be indicated by or as by such percussion: *The hour has struck.* **49.** to ignite or be ignited by friction, as a match. **50.** to make a stroke, as in swimming or as with an oar in rowing. **51.** to produce a sound, music, etc., by touching a string or playing upon an instrument. **52.** to take root, as a slip of a plant. **53.** to go, proceed, or advance: *They struck out at dawn.* **54.** (of a union or union member) to engage in a suspension of work until an employer or industry meets certain demands. **55. a.** *U.S. Army.* to act as a voluntary paid servant to a commissioned officer. **b.** *U.S. Navy.* to work hard; strive (fol. by *for*): *He is striking for yeoman.* **56.** *Naut.* **a.** to lower the flag or colors, esp. as a salute or as a sign of surrender. **b.** to run up the white flag of surrender. **57.** *Angling.* (of fish) to swallow or take the bait. **58. strike home, a.** to deal an effective blow. **b.** to have the intended effect; hit the mark. **59. strike it rich, a.** to come upon a valuable mineral or oil deposit. **b.** to have sudden or unexpected financial success. **60. strike off, a.** *Print.* to print. **b.** to remove or cancel, as from a record, list, etc. **61. strike out, a.** *Baseball.* to put out or be put out by a strike-out. **b.** (of a person or effort) to fail. **c.** to lose favor. **62. strike up, a.** to begin to play or to sing: *The orchestra struck up a waltz.* **b.** to bring into being; commence; begin: *to strike up an acquaintance.*
—*n.* **63.** the act or an instance of striking. **64.** work stoppage or a withdrawal of workers' services, as to compel an employer to accede to workers' demands or in protest against terms or conditions imposed by an employer. **65.** *Baseball.* **a.** a pitch that is swung at and missed by the batter. **b.** a pitch that passes through the strike zone and is not swung at by the batter. **c.** a foul tip caught by the catcher or a foul bunt when there are already two strikes against the batter. **d.** a ball hit foul and not caught on the fly when there are less than two strikes against the batter. Cf. **ball¹** (def. 4). **66.** *Bowling.* **a.** the knocking down of all of the pins with the first bowl. **b.** the score so made. Cf. **spare** (def. 21). **67.** *Horol.* the striking mechanism of a timepiece. **68.** *Brewing.* the degree of excellence or strength of beer, ale, etc. **69.** *Angling.* **a.** a pull on the line, made by the fish in the process of taking the bait. **b.** a sharp jerk on the line, made in order to set the hook in the mouth of the fish. **70.** *Coining.* a quantity of coins struck at one time. **71.** *Geol.* **a.** the direction of the line formed by the intersection of the bedding plane of a bed or stratum of sedimentary rock with a horizontal plane. **b.** the direction or trend of a structural feature, as an anticlinal axis or the lineation resulting from metamorphism. **72.** the discovery of a rich vein of ore in mining, of petroleum in boring, etc. **73. have two strikes against one,** to be in an unfavorable or a critical position. [ME, OE *strīc(an);* c. G *streichen.* See STREAK, STRIGIL] —**strike′less,** *adj.*
—**Syn. 1.** STRIKE, HIT, KNOCK imply suddenly bringing one body in contact with another. STRIKE suggests such an action in a general way: *to strike a child.* HIT is less formal than STRIKE, and often implies giving a single blow, but usually a strong one and definitely aimed: *to hit a baseball.* To KNOCK is to strike, often with a tendency to displace the object struck; it also means to strike repeatedly: *to knock someone down; to knock at a door.* See **beat.** —**Ant. 1.** miss.

strike·bound (strīk′bound′), *adj.* closed by a strike of workers: *a strikebound factory.*

strike·break·er (strīk′brā′kər), *n.* a person who takes part in breaking a strike either by working or by furnishing workers for the employer.

strike·break·ing (strīk′brā′king), *n.* action directed at breaking up a strike of workers.

strike′ fault′, *Geol.* a fault, the trend of which is parallel to the strike of the affected rocks.

strike-out (strīk′out′), *n.* *Baseball.* an out made by a batter to whom three strikes have been charged.

strike·o·ver (strīk′ō′vər), *n.* the act or an instance of typing over an error without erasing it.

strik·er (strī′kər), *n.* **1.** a person or thing that strikes. **2.** a worker who is on strike. **3.** the clapper in a clock that strikes the hours or rings an alarm. **4.** *U.S. Army.* an enlisted man who acts as a voluntary paid servant to a commissioned officer. **5.** *U.S. Navy.* an enlisted man in training for a specific technical rating.

strike′ zone′, *Baseball.* the area above home plate extending from the batter's knees to his shoulders.

strik·ing (strī′king), *adj.* **1.** that strikes. **2.** exceptional; outstanding; impressive: *a woman of striking beauty.* **3.** noticeable; conspicuous: *a striking lack of enthusiasm.* **4.** being on strike. —**strik′ing·ly,** *adv.* —**strik′ing·ness,** *n.*

strik′ing train′, *Horol.* the gear train of the striking mechanism of a timepiece. Cf. **going train.**

Strind·berg (strind′bûrg, strin′-; *Swed.* strin′bar′yə), *n.* **(Jo·han) Au·gust** (yōō′hän ou′gŏŏst), 1849–1912, Swedish novelist, dramatist, and essayist.

string (string), *n., v.,* **strung; strung** or (*Rare*) **stringed; string·ing.** —*n.* **1.** a slender cord or thick thread for binding or tying; line. **2.** something resembling a cord or thread. **3.** a narrow strip of flexible material, as cloth or leather, for tying parts together: *the strings of a bonnet.* **4.** a necklace consisting of a number of beads, pearls, or the like, threaded or strung on a cord; strand: *a string of pearls.* **5.** any series of things arranged or connected in a line or following closely one after another. **6.** a group of animals belonging to one owner or managed by one man: *a string of race horses.* **7.** (in a musical instrument) a tightly stretched cord or wire that produces a tone when caused to vibrate, as by plucking, striking, or the friction of a bow. **8. strings, a.** stringed instruments, esp. those played with a bow. **b.** players on such instruments in an orchestra or band. **9.** a bowstring. **10.** a cord or fiber in a plant. **11.** the tough piece uniting the two parts of a pod: *the strings of beans.* **12.** *Archit.* **a.** a stringcourse. **b.** Also called **stringer.** one of the sloping sides of a stair, supporting the treads and risers. **13.** *Billiards, Pool.* **a.** a stroke made by each player from the head of the table to the opposite cushion and back, to determine, by means of the resultant positions of the cue balls, who shall open the game. **b.** Also called **string line.** a line from behind which the cue ball is placed after being out of play. **14.** a group of contestants or players listed in accordance with their skill: *He made the second string on the football team.* **15.** Usually, **strings.** *Informal.* conditions or limitations on a proposal: *a generous offer with no strings attached.* **16. pull strings or wires,** to gain or attempt to gain one's objectives by means of influential friends, associates, etc.
—*v.t.* **17.** to furnish with or as with a string or strings. **18.** to extend or stretch (a cord, thread, etc.) from one point to another. **19.** to thread on or as on a string: *to string beads.* **20.** to connect in or as in a line; arrange in a series or succession: *He knows how to string words together.* **21.** *Music.* to equip (a bow or instrument) with new strings. **22.** to provide or adorn with something suspended or slung: *a room strung with festoons.* **23.** to deprive of a string or strings; strip the strings from: *to string beans.* **24.** to make tense, as the sinews, nerves, mind, etc. **25.** *Informal.* to kill by hanging (usually fol. by *up*).
—*v.i.* **26.** to form into or move in a string or series: *The ideas string together coherently.* **27.** to form into a string or strings, as a glutinous substance does when pulled: *Good taffy doesn't break—it strings.* **28. string along,** *Slang.* **a.** to go along in agreement: *She found she couldn't string along with their modern notions.* **b.** to keep (a person) waiting or in a state of uncertainty. **c.** to deceive; cheat. [ME, OE *streng;* c. D *streng,* G *Strang;* akin to L *stringere* to bind] —**string′less,** *adj.* —**string′like′,** *adj.*

string′ bass′ (bās). See **double bass.**

string′ bean′, any of various kinds of bean the unripe pods of which are used as food, usually after stripping off the fibrous thread along the side.

string·course (string′kōrs′, -kôrs′), *n.* *Archit.* a horizontal band or course, as of stone, often molded and sometimes richly carved.

S, Stringcourse

stringed (stringd), *adj.* fitted with strings (often used in combination): *a five-stringed banjo.*

stringed′ in′strument, a musical instrument having strings played with the fingers or with a plectrum or a bow.

strin·gen·cy (strin′jən sē), *n., pl.* **-cies. 1.** stringent character or condition. **2.** strictness; closeness; rigor: *the stringency of school discipline.* **3.** tightness; straitness. [STRING(ENT) + -ENCY]

strin·gen·do (strin jen′dō; *It.* strēn jen′dô), *adj., adv. Music.* progressively quickening the tempo. [< It = *string(ere)* to compress + *-endo* ger. suffix (< L *-endum*); see STRINGENT]

strin·gent (strin′jənt), *adj.* **1.** rigorously binding or exacting; severe. **2.** compelling or urgent: *stringent necessity.* **3.** convincing or forcible: *stringent arguments.* [< L *stringent-* (s. of *stringēns*), prp. of *string(ere)* (to) draw tight; see -ENT] —**strin′gent·ly,** *adv.* —**Syn. 1.** See **strict. 3.** forceful, powerful.

string·er (string′ər), *n.* **1.** a person or thing that strings. **2.** a long horizontal timber connecting upright posts. **3.** *Archit.* string (def. 12b). **4.** *Journalism.* a part-time newspaper correspondent covering his local area for a paper published elsewhere. **5.** a stout string, rope, etc., on which a fisherman strings the fish he has caught, by passing it through the gills and mouth, so that he may carry them or put them back in the water to keep them alive or fresh. [late ME]

string·halt (string′hôlt′), *n. Vet. Pathol.* a nerve disorder in horses, causing exaggerated flexing movements of the hind legs in walking. Also, **springhalt.** —**string′halt′ed, string′halt′y,** *adj.* —**string′halt′ed·ness,** *n.*

string′ line′, *Billiards, Pool.* string (def. 13b).

string·piece (string′pēs′), *n.* a long, usually horizontal piece of timber, beam, etc., for strengthening, connecting, or supporting a framework.

string′ quartet′, 1. a musical composition, usually in three or four movements, for four stringed instruments, typically two violins, viola, and cello. **2.** the players forming a group for the performance of such quartets.

string′ tie′, a short, very narrow, unflared necktie, usually tied in a bow.

string·y (string′ē), *adj.,* **string·i·er, string·i·est. 1.** resembling a string or strings. **2.** consisting of strings or stringlike pieces. **3.** coarsely or toughly fibrous, as meat. **4.** sinewy or wiry, as a person. **5.** ropy, as a glutinous liquid. —**string′i·ness,** *n.*

strip[1] (strip), *v.,* **stripped** or **stript, strip·ping.** —*v.t.* **1.** to deprive of covering, clothing, or the like: *to strip a fruit of its rind.* **2.** to take away or remove: *to strip a rind from a fruit.* **3.** to deprive or divest: *to strip a tree of its fruit.* **4.** to clear out or empty: *to strip a house of its contents.* **5.** to dismantle; remove the components of or deprive of equipment: *to strip a ship of rigging.* **6.** to take from; rob or plunder. **7.** to separate the leaves from the stalks of (tobacco). **8.** *Mach.* to break off or grind the thread of (a screw, bolt, etc.) or the teeth of (a gear), as by applying too much force. **9.** to draw the last milk from (a cow), esp. by a stroking and compressing movement. **10.** to draw out (milk) in this manner. —*v.i.* **11.** to strip something. **12.** to remove one's clothes. **13.** to perform a striptease. **14.** to become stripped: *Bananas strip easily.* [ME *strippe,* OE **strypp(an)* (cf. MHG *strupfen* to strip off); r. ME *stripe, strepe, strupe,* OE *(be)strȳp(an)* (to) rob, plunder; c. D *stroopen*]
—**Syn. 1.** uncover, peel. **6.** despoil. STRIP, DEPRIVE, DISPOSSESS, DIVEST imply more or less forcibly taking something away from someone. To STRIP is to take something completely (often violently) from a person or thing so as to leave in a destitute or powerless state: *to strip a man of all his property.* To DEPRIVE is to take away forcibly or coercively what one has, or to withhold what one might have: *to deprive one of his income.* To DISPOSSESS is to deprive of the holding or use of something: *to dispossess the renters of a house.* DIVEST usually means depriving of rights, privileges, powers, or the like: *to divest a king of authority.*

strip[2] (strip), *n., v.,* **stripped, strip·ping.** —*n.* **1.** a narrow piece, comparatively long and usually of uniform width. **2.** a continuous series of drawings or pictures illustrating incidents, conversation, etc., as a comic strip. **3.** *Aeron.* See **landing strip. 4.** *Philately.* three or more stamps joined either in a horizontal or vertical row. **5.** (*sometimes cap.*) a street or avenue densely lined on both sides by a large variety of retail stores, gas stations, restaurants, bars, etc. —*v.t.* **6.** to cut, tear, or form into strips. **7.** *Print.* to combine (a piece of film) with another, esp. for making a combination plate of lines and halftones. [late ME < MLG *strippe* strap; see STRIPE[1]]

strip′ crop′ping, the growing of different crops on alternate strips of ground that usually follow the contour of the land, in order to minimize erosion. Also called **strip farming.**

stripe[1] (strīp), *n., v.,* **striped, strip·ing.** —*n.* **1.** a relatively long, narrow band of a different color, appearance, weave, material, or nature from the rest of a surface or thing: *the stripes of a zebra.* **2.** a fabric or material containing such a band or bands. **3.** a strip of braid, tape, or the like, esp. one that is worn on a military or other uniform as a badge of rank, service, good conduct, wounds, etc. **4.** a strip, or long, narrow piece of anything: *a stripe of beach.* **5.** style, variety, sort, or kind: *a man of quite a different stripe.* —*v.t.* **6.** to mark or furnish with a stripe or stripes. [ME < MD or MLG *stripe*] —**stripe′less,** *adj.*

stripe[2] (strīp), *n.* a stroke with a whip, rod, etc., as in punishment. [late ME, perh. special use of STRIPE[1] in sense of WALE[1]]

striped (strīpt, strī′pid), *adj.* having stripes or bands.

striped′ bass′ (bas), an American game fish, *Roccus saxatilis,* having blackish stripes along each side.

strip·er (strī′pər), *n. Slang.* **1.** a naval officer who wears stripes on the sleeve of his uniform: *a four-striper.* **2.** an enlisted man of any of the armed services who wears stripes on his sleeve denoting years of service: *a six-striper.*

strip′ farm′ing. See **strip cropping.**

strip·ing (strī′ping), *n.* **1.** the act of decorating or otherwise providing with stripes: *The striping of the boat proceeded slowly.* **2.** a striped pattern: *the striping of the zebra.*

strip·ling (strip′ling), *n.* a youth. [ME; see STRIP[2], -LING[1]]

strip′ map′, a narrow map charting only the immediate territory to be traversed, which appears as a long, narrow strip.

strip′ min′ing, mining in an open pit after removal of the earth and rock covering a mineral deposit.

strip·per (strip′ər), *n.* **1.** a person or thing that strips. **2.** Also called **ecdysiast, stripteaser.** a woman who performs a striptease.

strip′ pok′er, a game of poker in which the losers in a hand remove articles of clothing.

stript (stript), *v.* a pt. and pp. of **strip.**

strip·tease (strip′tēz′), *n., v.,* **-teased, -teas·ing.** —*n.* **1.** a burlesque act in which a woman dancer removes her garments one at a time to the accompaniment of music. —*v.i.* **2.** to do a striptease.

strip·teas·er (strip′tē′zər), *n.* stripper (def. 2).

strip·y (strī′pē), *adj.,* **strip·i·er, strip·i·est.** marked with stripes.

strive (strīv), *v.i.,* **strove, striv·en** (striv′ən), **striv·ing. 1.** to exert oneself vigorously; try hard. **2.** to make strenuous efforts toward any goal: *to strive for success.* **3.** to contend in opposition, battle, or any conflict; compete. **4.** to struggle vigorously, as in opposition or resistance: *to strive against fate.* **5.** *Obs.* to rival; vie. [ME *strive(n)* < OF *(e)strive(r)* (to) quarrel, compete, strive < Gmc; cf. obs. D *strijven,* G *streben* to strive] —**striv′er,** *n.* —**striv′ing·ly,** *adv.* —**Syn. 1.** See **try. 3, 4.** struggle, fight.

strobe (strōb), *n.* **1.** *Informal.* stroboscope. —*adj.* **2.** stroboscopic. [shortening of STROBOSCOPE]

stro·bi·la (strō bī′lə), *n. Zool.* the entire body of a tapeworm. [< NL < Gk *strobīlē,* plug of lint shaped like a fir cone; see STROBILE]

strob·ile (strob′il), *n. Bot.* **1.** the somewhat conical multiple fruit of the pine, fir, etc. **2.** a conelike mass of sporophylls found in certain club mosses and ferns. [< NL *strobilus* < Gk *strōbīlos* fir cone < *strōbos* a whirling] —**strob·i·loid** (strob′ə loid′), *adj.*

stro·bo·scope (strō′bə skōp′, strob′ə-), *n.* **1.** a device for studying the motion of a body, esp. one in rapid revolution or vibration, by making the motion appear to slow down or stop, as by periodically illuminating the body or viewing it through widely spaced openings in a revolving disk. **2.** *Photog.* **a.** Also called **stro′boscop′ic lamp′.** a lamp capable of producing an extremely short, brilliant burst of light, for synchronization with a camera having a high shutter speed, in order to photograph a rapidly moving object, for such a short duration that it will appear to be standing still. **b.** the device for holding and firing such a lamp. [< Gk *strōbo(s)* action of whirling + -SCOPE] —**stro·bo·scop·ic** (strō′bə skop′ik, strob′ə-), **stro′bo·scop′i·cal,** *adj.* —**stro·bos·co·py** (strə bos′kə pē), *n.*

strode (strōd), *v.* pt. of **stride.**

stro·ga·noff (strô′gə nôf′, strō′-), *adj.* (of meat) sautéed with onion, and cooked in a sauce of sour cream, seasonings, and, usually, mushrooms. [named after P. *Stroganoff,* 19th-century Russian count and diplomat]

stroke[1] (strōk), *n., v.,* **stroked, strok·ing.** —*n.* **1.** the act or an instance of striking, as with the fist, a weapon, a hammer, etc.; a blow. **2.** a hitting of or upon anything. **3.** a striking of a clapper or hammer, as on a bell. **4.** the sound produced by this. **5.** a throb or pulsation, as of the heart. **6.** something likened to a blow in its effect, as in causing pain, injury, or death; an attack of apoplexy or paralysis. **7.** a vigorous movement, as if in dealing a blow. **8.** *Sports.* a hitting of a ball, as the swinging hit of tennis or the controlled jabbing or thrusting with the cue of pool and billiards. **9.** a single complete movement, esp. one continuously repeated in some process. **10.** *Mech.* **a.** one of a series of alternating continuous movements of something back and forth over or through the same line. **b.** the complete movement of a moving part, esp. a reciprocating part, in one direction. **11.** *Swimming.* **a.** a method of swimming: *The crawl is a rapid stroke.* **b.** each successive movement of the arms and legs. **12.** *Rowing.* **a.** a single pull of the oar. **b.** the manner or style of moving the oars. **c.** Also called **stroke oar.** the oarsman nearest to the stern of the boat, to whose strokes those of the other oarsmen must conform. **13.** a movement of a pen, pencil, brush, graver, or the like. **14.** a mark traced by or as if by one movement of a pen, pencil, brush, or the like. **15.** *Brit.* virgule. **16.** a distinctive or effective touch in a literary composition. **17.** an act, piece, or amount of work, activity, etc.: *to refuse to do a stroke of work.* **18.** an attempt to attain some object: *a bold stroke for liberty.* **19.** a measure adopted for a particular purpose. **20.** a feat or achievement: *a stroke of genius.* **21.** a sudden or chance happening, as of luck or fortune. —*v.t.* **22.** to mark with a stroke or strokes, as of a pen; cancel, as by a stroke of a pen. **23.** *Rowing.* **a.** to row as a stroke oar of (a boat or crew). **b.** to set the stroke for the crew of (a boat). **24.** *Sports.* to hit (a ball), as with a deliberate, smooth swing of a bat or club. [ME, OE **strāc* (whence *strācian* to STROKE[2]); c. G *Streich;* akin to STRIKE] —**Syn. 1.** rap, tap, knock, pat. **1, 6.** See **blow**[1]. **5.** beat, thump; rhythm.

stroke[2] (strōk), *v.,* **stroked, strok·ing,** *n.* —*v.t.* **1.** to pass the hand or an instrument over (something) lightly or with little pressure; rub gently, as in soothing or caressing. —*n.* **2.** the act or an instance of stroking; a stroking movement. [ME, OE *strāc(ian);* c. G *streichen;* akin to STRIKE]

stroke′ oar′, *Rowing.* **1.** the oar nearest to the stern of the boat. **2.** stroke[1] (def. 12c).

stroke′ play′, *Golf.* See **medal play.**

stroll (strōl), *v.i.* **1.** to walk leisurely as inclination directs; ramble: *to stroll along the beach.* **2.** to wander or rove from place to place; roam: *strolling Gypsies.* —*v.t.* **3.** to saunter along or through: *to stroll the countryside.* —*n.* **4.** a leisurely walk; ramble; saunter: *a short stroll before supper.* [? akin to *streel* < Ir *straoill-* wander, loiter, trail] —**Syn. 1.** meander.

stroll·er (strō′lər), *n.* **1.** a person who takes a leisurely walk. **2.** a wanderer; vagrant. **3.** an itinerant performer. **4.** a four-wheeled, often collapsible, chairlike carriage in which small children are pushed.

stro·ma (strō′mə), *n., pl.* **-ma·ta** (-mə tə). **1.** *Anat.* **a.** the colorless, spongelike framework of an erythrocyte or other cell. **b.** the supporting framework, usually of connective tissue, of an organ, as distinguished from the parenchyma. **2.** (in certain fungi) a compact, somatic mass of fungous tissue, in or on which the fructifications may be developed. [< LL < Gk *strôma* bed covering; akin to L *sternere, strātum;* see STRAW, STREW] —**stro·mat·ic** (strō mat′ik), **stro′mal, stro′ma·tous,** *adj.*

Strom·bo·li (strom′bē lə; *It.* strôm′bô lē), *n.* **1.** an island off the NE coast of Sicily, in the Lipari group. **2.** an active volcano on this island. 3040 ft.

strong (strông, strong), *adj.*, **strong·er** (strông′gər, strong′-), **strong·est** (strông′gist, strong′-), *adv.* —*adj.* **1.** having, showing, or able to exert great bodily or muscular power; physically vigorous or robust. **2.** accompanied or delivered by great physical, mechanical, etc., power or force: *a strong handshake; With one strong blow the machine stamped out a fender.* **3.** mentally powerful or vigorous: *His mind is still strong.* **4.** especially able, competent, or powerful in a specific field or respect: *She's very strong in mathematics.* **5.** of great moral power, firmness, or courage. **6.** powerful in influence, authority, resources, or means of prevailing: *a strong nation.* **7.** compelling; of great force, effectiveness, potency, or cogency: *strong arguments.* **8.** able to resist strain, force, wear, attack, etc.: *strong walls; strong defense.* **9.** having a great store of wealth or capable of managing money well: *a strong economy.* **10.** firm or uncompromising; unfaltering. **11.** fervent; zealous; thoroughgoing: *He's a strong Democrat.* **12.** strenuous or energetic; vigorous: *strong efforts.* **13.** moving or acting with force or vigor: *strong winds.* **14.** distinct or marked; vivid, as impressions, resemblance or contrast, etc.: *He bears a strong resemblance to his grandfather.* **15.** intense, as light or color. **16.** having a large proportion of the effective or essential properties or ingredients; concentrated: *strong tea.* **17.** (of a beverage or food) containing alcohol or much alcohol: *strong drink.* **18.** having a high degree of flavor or odor: *strong cheese.* **19.** having an unpleasant or offensive flavor or odor, esp. in the process of decay: *strong butter.* **20.** *Com.* characterized by steady or advancing prices. **21.** *Gram.* **a.** (of Germanic verbs) having vowel change in the root in inflected forms, as the English verbs *sing, sang, sung; ride, rode, ridden.* **b.** (of Germanic nouns and adjectives) inflected with endings that are generally distinctive of case, number, and gender, as German *alter Mann* "old man." **22.** (of a syllable in a verse) stressed. **23.** *Optics.* having great magnifying or refractive power: *a strong microscope.* —*adv.* **24.** strongly. [ME, OE *strang;* c. Icel *strangr,* MD *stranc;* akin to G *streng* severe, strict, L *stringere* to tie; see STRINGENT] —**strong′ish,** *adj.* —**strong′ness,** *n.* —**Syn. 1.** mighty, sturdy, hardy, stalwart. **4.** capable, efficient. **5.** valiant, brave. **7.** persuasive, cogent. **10.** unwavering, resolute. **11.** fervid, vehement. **14.** stark, sharp. **15.** brilliant, vivid. **18.** pungent, aromatic, sharp, piquant, hot, spicy, biting. **19.** smelly, rank. —**Ant. 1.** weak.

strong-arm (strông′ärm′, strong′-), *Informal.* —*adj.* **1.** using, involving, or threatening the use of physical force or violence to gain an objective: *strong-arm methods.* —*v.t.* **2.** to use violent methods upon; assault. **3.** to rob by force.

strong·box (strông′boks′, strong′-), *n.* a strongly made, lockable box or chest for storing valuables or money.

strong′ breeze′, *Meteorol.* (on the Beaufort scale) a wind of 25–30 miles per hour.

strong′ gale′, *Meteorol.* (on the Beaufort scale) a wind of 47–54 miles per hour.

strong·hold (strông′hōld′, strong′-), *n.* **1.** a well-fortified place; fortress. **2.** a place that serves as the center of a group or of a person holding a controversial viewpoint. [late ME]

strong·ly (strông′lē, strong′-), *adv.* **1.** in a strong, forceful, or vehement manner. **2.** so as to be strong: *a strongly fortified gate.* [ME *strongliche,* OE *stranglīce.* See STRONG, -LY]

strong′ man′, **1.** a man who performs remarkable feats of strength, as in a circus. **2.** a person who controls by force; dictator. Also, **strong′man′.**

strong-mind·ed (strông′mīn′did, strong′-), *adj.* having or showing an obstinate mind or vigorous mental powers. —**strong′-mind′ed·ly,** *adv.* —**strong′-mind′ed·ness,** *n.*

strong·room (strông′rōōm′, -rŏŏm′, strong′-), *n.* *Chiefly Brit.* a fireproof, burglarproof room in which valuables are kept.

strong-willed (strông′wild′, strong′-), *adj.* **1.** having a powerful will; resolute. **2.** stubborn; obstinate.

stron·gyle (stron′jil), *n.* any nematode of the family *Strongylidae,* parasitic as an adult in the intestine of mammals, esp. horses. Also, **stron′gyl.** [< NL *Strongyl(us)* name of type genus < Gk *strongýlos* round, spherical]

stron·gy·lo·sis (stron′jə lō′sis), *n.* *Vet. Pathol.* a disease, esp. of horses, caused by an infestation by strongyles and characterized in serious cases by weakness and anemia. [< NL = *Strongyl(us)* STRONGYLE + *-ōsis* -OSIS]

stron·ti·a (stron′shē ə, -shə), *n.* *Chem.* **1.** Also called **strontium oxide.** an amorphous powder, SrO, resembling lime in its general character: used chiefly in the manufacture of strontium salts. **2.** See **strontium hydroxide.** [alter. of STRONTIAN; see -IA]

stron·ti·an (stron′shē ən, -shən), *n.* strontianite. [short for *Strontian earth,* mineral first found in *Strontian* parish, Argyllshire, Scotland]

stron·ti·an·ite (stron′shē ə nīt′, -shə nīt′), *n.* a mineral, strontium carbonate, $SrCO_3$, a minor ore of strontium.

stron·ti·um (stron′shē əm, -shəm, -tē əm), *n.* *Chem.* a bivalent, metallic element whose compounds resemble those of calcium, found in nature only in the combined state, as in strontianite: used in fireworks, flares, and tracer bullets. *Symbol:* Sr; *at. wt.:* 87.62; *at. no.:* 38; *sp. gr.:* 2.6. [STRONT(IAN) + -IUM]

strontium 90, *Chem.* a harmful radioactive isotope of strontium, produced in certain nuclear reactions and present in their fallout. Also called **radiostrontium.**

stron′tium hydrox′ide, *Chem.* a white powder, $Sr(OH)_2$, or its crystalline octahydrate (**stron′tium hy′drate**): used chiefly in the refining of beet sugar. Also called **strontia.**

stron′tium ox′ide, *Chem.* strontia (def. 1).

strook (strŏŏk), *v.* *Obs.* a pt. and pp. of **strike.**

strop (strop), *n.*, *v.* **stropped, strop·ping.** —*n.* **1.** a strip, usually of leather, used for sharpening razors. **2.** Also, **strap.** *Naut., Mach.* **a.** a rope or a band of metal surrounding and supporting a block, deadeye, etc. **b.** a metal band surrounding the pulley of a block to transmit the load on the pulley to its hook or shackle. —*v.t.* **3.** to sharpen on or as on a strop. [ME, OE; c. D, LG *strop;* prob. < L *stropp(us),* var. of *struppus* strap]

stro·phan·thin (strō fan′thin), *n.* *Pharm.* a very poisonous glycoside or mixture of glycosides obtained from the dried, ripe seeds of a strophanthus, esp. *Strophanthus Kombe,* used as a cardiac stimulant. [STROPHANTH(US) + -IN²]

stro·phan·thus (strō fan′thəs), *n.*, *pl.* **-thus·es. 1.** any apocynaceous shrub or small tree of the genus *Strophanthus,* chiefly of tropical Africa. **2.** the dried, ripe seed of any of these plants, which yields the drug strophanthin. [< NL = Gk *stróph(os)* twine + *ánthos* flower]

stro·phe (strō′fē), *n.* **1.** the part of an ancient Greek choral ode sung by the chorus when moving from right to left. **2.** the movement performed by the chorus during the singing of this part. **3.** the first of the three series of lines forming the divisions of each section of a Pindaric ode. **4.** (in modern poetry) any separate section or extended movement in a poem, distinguished from a stanza in that it does not follow a regularly repeated pattern. [< Gk *strophḗ* a twist, turning about, akin to *stréphein* to turn; see STREPTO-] —**Syn. 3.** See **verse.**

stroph·ic (strof′ik, strō′fik), *adj.* **1.** Also, **stroph′i·cal.** consisting of, pertaining to, or characterized by a strophe or strophes. **2.** *Music.* (of a song) having the same music for each successive stanza. —**stroph′i·cal·ly,** *adv.*

stroud (stroud), *n.* a coarse woolen cloth, blanket, or garment formerly used by the British in bartering with the North American Indians. [named after *Stroud* in Gloucestershire, England, where woolens are made]

strove (strōv), *v.* pt. of **strive.**

strow (strō), *v.*, **strowed, strown** or **strowed, strowing.** *Archaic.* strew. [ME *strow(en),* var. of *strewen* to STREW]

stroy (stroi), *v.t.* *Archaic.* to destroy. —**stroy′er,** *n.*

struck (struk), *v.* **1.** pt. and a pp. of **strike.** —*adj.* **2.** (of a factory, industry, etc.) closed or otherwise affected by a strike of workers.

struck·en (struk′ən), *v.* a pp. of **strike.**

struck′ ju′ry, *Law.* a jury obtained by special agreement between the opposing attorneys, who take turns in eliminating members of the impaneled group until 12 remain.

struck′ meas′ure, a measure, esp. of grain, even with the top of a receptacle.

struc·tur·al (struk′chər əl), *adj.* **1.** of or pertaining to structures or construction. **2.** pertaining or essential to a structure. **3.** *Biol.* pertaining to organic structure; morphological. **4.** *Geol.* of or pertaining to geological structure, as of rock. **5.** *Chem.* pertaining to or showing the arrangement or mode of attachment of the atoms that constitute a molecule of a substance. Cf. **structural formula. 6.** noting or pertaining to the interrelationship of elements, as in a field of study. —**struc′tur·al·ly,** *adv.*

struc′tural for′mula, *Chem.* a chemical formula showing the diagrammatic linkage of the atoms in a molecule, as H–O–H. Cf. **empirical formula, molecular formula.**

struc′tural geol′ogy, the branch of geology dealing with the structure and distribution of rocks.

struc·tur·al·ism (struk′chər ə liz′əm), *n.* **1.** any theory that embodies structural principles. **2.** See **structural psychology.** —**struc′tur·al·ist,** *n., adj.* —**struc′tur·al·is′tic,** *adj.*

struc′tural isom′erism, *Chem.* See under **isomerism** (def. 1).

struc′tural linguis′tics, the branch of linguistics concerned with the structural aspect of language.

struc′tural psychol′ogy, psychology centering on the analysis of the structure or content of conscious mental states by introspective methods. Also called **structuralism.**

struc·ture (struk′chər), *n., v.,* **-tured, -tur·ing.** —*n.* **1.** the manner in which something is constructed. **2.** something that is constructed, as a building or work of civil engineering. **3.** the manner in which the elements of anything are organized or interrelated. **4.** anything composed of organized or interrelated elements. **5.** *Biol.* the construction and arrangement of tissues, parts, or organs. **6.** *Geol.* **a.** the attitude of beds or strata of sedimentary rocks, as indicated by the dip and strike. **b.** the coarser composition of a rock, as contrasted with its texture. **7.** the manner in which atoms in a molecule are joined to each other, esp. in organic chemistry where it is represented by a diagram or model of the molecular arrangement. **8.** *Sociol.* the pattern or organization of elements in a society or culture. —*v.t.* **9.** to give a structure, organization, or arrangement to; construct a systematic framework for. [< L *structūr(a)* = *struc-* (var. s. of *struere* to put together) + *-t-* ptp. suffix + *-ūra* -URE] —**Syn. 1.** system, form, configuration.

stru·del (strōōd′əl; *Ger.* shtrōō′dəl), *n.* a pastry consisting of fruit, cheese, or some other filling rolled in paper-thin dough and baked. [< G: lit., eddy, whirlpool]

strug·gle (strug′əl), *v.,* **-gled, -gling,** *n.* —*v.i.* **1.** to contend resolutely with an adversary or adverse conditions. **2.** to contend resolutely with a task or problem. **3.** to advance with violent effort: *to struggle through mud.* —*v.t.* **4.** to move or place with an effort. **5.** to make (one's way) with violent effort. —*n.* **6.** the act or process or an instance of struggling. **7.** a war, fight, conflict, or contest of any kind. [late ME *strugle* = *strug-* (? b. STR(UT + T)UG) + *-le* -LE] —**Syn. 1.** oppose, contest, fight, conflict. **6.** endeavor, exertion. **7.** encounter, skirmish.

strug′gle for exist′ence, the competition in nature among organisms of a population to maintain themselves in a given environment and to survive to reproduce others of their kind.

strum (strum), *v.,* **strummed, strum·ming,** *n.* —*v.t.* **1.** to play on (a stringed musical instrument) by running the fingers lightly across the strings. **2.** to produce (notes, a melody, etc.) by such playing: *to strum a tune.* —*v.i.* **3.** to play on a stringed musical instrument by running the fingers lightly across the strings. —*n.* **4.** the act of strumming. **5.** the sound produced by strumming. [? b. STR(ING + TH)UMB, or imit.]

stru·ma (stro͞o′mə), *n., pl.* **-mae** (-mē). **1.** *Pathol.* **a.** scrofula. **b.** goiter. **2.** *Bot.* a cushionlike swelling on an organ, as that at one side of the base of the capsule in many mosses. [< L: scrofulous tumor]

Stru·ma (stro͞o′mä), *n.* a river in S Europe, flowing SE through SW Bulgaria and NE Greece into the Aegean. 225 mi. long.

stru·mose (stro͞o′mōs, stro͞o mōs′), *adj.* *Bot.* having a struma or strumae. [< L *strūmōs(us).* See STRUMA, -OSE[1]]

strum·pet (strum′pit), *n.* a prostitute; harlot. [ME < ?]

strung (strung), *v.* **1.** pt. and pp. of **string. 2. strung out,** *Slang.* so heavily addicted to a drug as to be sick, dazed, or agitated.

strut[1] (strut), *v.,* **strut·ted, strut·ting,** *n.* —*v.i.* **1.** to walk with a vain, pompous bearing, as if expecting to impress observers. —*n.* **2.** the act of strutting. **3.** a strutting walk or gait. [ME *stroute,* OE *strūt(ian)* (to) stand out stiffly, struggle < **strūt* (whence ME *strut* strife); akin to STRUT[2]] —**Syn. 1.** parade, flourish. STRUT and SWAGGER refer esp. to carriage in walking. STRUT implies swelling pride or pompousness; to walk with a stiff, pompous, affected, self-conscious gait: *A turkey struts about the barnyard.* SWAGGER implies a domineering, sometimes jaunty, superiority or challenge and a self-important manner: *to swagger down the street.*

strut[2] (strut), *n., v.,* **strut·ted, strut·ting.** —*n.* **1.** any of various structural members, as in trusses, primarily intended to resist longitudinal compression. —*v.t.* **2.** to brace or support by means of a strut or struts. [cf. LG *strutt* stiff]

stru·thi·ous (stro͞o′thē əs), *adj.* resembling or related to the ostriches or other ratite birds. [< LL *strūthi-*(shortened s. of *strūthiō* < Gk *strouthíō(n)* ostrich) + -OUS]

Stru·ve (stro͞o′və), *n.* **O.,** an elliptical walled plain in the second quadrant of the face of the moon. ab. 113 mi. long and 96 mi. wide. Also called **Otto Struve.**

strych·nic (strik′nik), *adj.* of, pertaining to, or obtained from strychnine. [< NL *Strychn(os)* (see STRYCHNINE) + -IC]

strych·nine (strik′nin, -nēn, -nīn), *n.* *Pharm.* a poison, $C_{21}H_{22}N_2O_2$, used as an antidote for poisoning by depressant drugs because of its stimulating effect on the central nervous system. Also, **strych·ni·a** (strik′nē ə), **strych·ni·na** (strik′-ni nə). [< F = NL *Strychn(os)* < Gk: a kind of nightshade + F *-ine* -INE[2]]

strych·nin·ism (strik′ni niz′əm), *n.* *Pathol.* a condition induced by an overdose or by excessive use of strychnine.

St. Swith′in's Day′ (swith′ənz), July 15: rain on this day is superstitiously believed to portend 40 consecutive days of rain.

St. Thomas, 1. an island in the Virgin Islands of the United States, in the E West Indies. 28,960 (1970); 32 sq. mi. **2.** former name of **Charlotte Amalie. 3.** Portuguese, **São Tomé, São Thomé.** an island in the republic of St. Thomas and Principe. **4.** a city in and the capital of St. Thomas and Principe. 4500.

St. Thomas and Principe, a republic in the Gulf of Guinea, off the W coast of Africa, comprising the islands of St. Thomas and Principe: a former overseas province of Portugal; independent since 1975. 80,000; 372 sq. mi. *Cap.:* St. Thomas. Official name, **São Tomé e Principe.**

Stu·art (sto͞o′ərt, styo͞o′-), *n.* **1.** a member of the royal family that ruled in Scotland from 1371 to 1714 and in England from 1603 to 1714. **2. Charles Edward** (*"the Young Pretender"* or *"Bonnie Prince Charlie"*), 1720–80, grandson of James II. **3.** Also, **Stewart.** See **Darnley, Lord Henry. 4. Gilbert,** 1755–1828, U.S. painter. **5. James Ewell Brown** (*"Jeb"*), 1833–64, Confederate general in the Civil War. **6. James Francis Edward.** Also called **James III.** (*"the Old Pretender"*), 1688–1766, English prince. **7. Jesse Hilton,** 1907–84, U.S. writer. **8. Mary.** See **Mary, Queen of Scots.**

stub[1] (stub), *n., v.,* **stubbed, stub·bing.** —*n.* **1.** a short projecting part. **2.** the end of a fallen tree, shrub, or plant left fixed in the ground; stump. **3.** a short remaining piece, as of a pencil, candle, or cigar. **4.** something unusually short, as a short, thick, or worn nail. **5.** (in a checkbook, receipt book, etc.) the inner end of each leaf, for keeping a record of the content of the part filled out and torn away. **6.** the returned portion of a ticket. **7.** a short-pointed, blunt pen. —*v.t.* **8.** to strike accidentally against a projecting object: *I stubbed my toe on the step.* **9.** to clear of stubs, as land. **10.** to dig up by the roots; grub up (roots). [ME, OE *stubb*]

stub[2] (stub), *adj.* stocky; squat. [special use of STUB[1]]

stub·bed (stub′id, stubd), *adj.* **1.** reduced to or resembling a stub; short and thick; stumpy. **2.** abounding in or rough with stubs.

stub·ble (stub′əl), *n.* **1.** Usually, **stubbles.** the stumps of grain and other stalks left in the ground when the crop is cut. **2.** such stumps collectively. **3.** any short, rough growth, as of beard. [ME *stuble* < OF *(e)stuble* < VL **stupul(a)* for L *stipula* STIPULE] —**stub′bled, stub′bly,** *adj.*

stub·born (stub′ərn), *adj.* **1.** unreasonably obstinate; obstinately perverse. **2.** fixed or set in purpose or opinion; resolute. **3.** obstinately maintained, as a course of action: *a stubborn resistance.* **4.** difficult to work, control, subdue, etc. [ME *stiborn(e)*; appar. < OE *stybb,* var. of *stubb* STUB[1] + *-orn* adj. suffix (< ?)] —**stub′born·ly,** *adv.* —**stub′born·ness,** *n.* —**Syn. 1.** contrary, refractory, headstrong, obdurate. **2.** persevering. STUBBORN, OBSTINATE, DOGGED, PERSISTENT imply fixity of purpose or condition, and resistance to change. STUBBORN and OBSTINATE both imply resistance to advice, entreaty, remonstrance, or force; but STUBBORN implies more of innate quality and is the more frequently used when referring to inanimate things: *stubborn disposition; stubborn difficulties.* DOGGED implies pertinacity and grimness in doing something, esp. in the face of discouragements: *dogged determination.* PERSISTENT implies having staying or lasting qualities, resoluteness, and perseverance: *persistent questioning.* —**Ant. 1.** tractable. **2.** irresolute.

Stubbs (stubz), *n.* **William,** 1825–1901, English historian and bishop.

stub·by (stub′ē), *adj.,* **-bi·er, -bi·est. 1.** of the nature of or resembling a stub. **2.** short and thick or broad; thickset or squat: *stubby fingers.* **3.** consisting of or abounding in stubs. **4.** bristly, as the hair or beard. —**stub′bi·ness,** *n.*

stub′ track′. See **spur track.**

stuc·co (stuk′ō), *n., pl.* **-coes, -cos,** *v.,* **-coed, -co·ing.** —*n.* **1.** an exterior finish for masonry or frame walls, usually composed of cement, sand, and hydrated lime mixed with water and laid on wet. **2.** any of various fine plasters for decorative work, moldings, etc. —*v.t.* **3.** to cover or ornament with stucco. [< It < Gmc; cf. OHG *stucki* piece, crust, G *Stück,* OE *stycce*]

stuc·co·work (stuk′ō wûrk′), *n.* moldings, decorative work, or a finish made of stucco.

stuck (stuk), *v.* **1.** a pt. and pp. of **stick**[2]. **2. stuck on,** *Slang.* infatuated with.

stuck-up (stuk′up′), *adj.* *Informal.* snobbishly conceited. —**stuck′-up′ness,** *n.*

stud[1] (stud), *n., v.,* **stud·ded, stud·ding.** —*n.* **1.** a boss, knob, nailhead, or other protuberance projecting from a surface or part, esp. as an ornament. **2.** a buttonlike object mounted on a shank that is passed through an article of clothing to fasten it. **3.** any of a number of slender, upright members of wood, steel, etc., forming the frame of a wall or partition and covered with plasterwork, siding, etc. **4.** any of various projecting pins, lugs, or the like, on machines or other implements. —*v.t.* **5.** to set with or as with studs, bosses, or the like. **6.** to scatter over with things set at intervals. **7.** to set or scatter (objects) at intervals over a surface: *to stud raisins over a cake.* **8.** (of objects) to lie scattered over: *Raisins studded the cake.* **9.** to furnish with or support by studs. [ME *stude,* OE *stud(u)* post; c. MHG *stud;* Icel *stoth* post]

stud[2] (stud), *n.* **1.** a studhorse or stallion. **2.** an establishment, as a farm, in which horses are kept for breeding. **3.** a number of horses, usually for racing or hunting, bred or kept by one owner. **4.** a male animal, as a bull or ram, kept for breeding. **5.** a herd of animals kept for breeding. **6.** *Poker.* See **stud poker. 7. at** or **in stud,** (of a male animal) offered for the purpose of breeding. —*adj.* **8.** of, associated with, or pertaining to a studhorse or studhorses. **9.** retained for breeding purposes. [ME, OE *stōd;* c. Icel *stōth;* akin to STAND]

stud·book (stud′bo͝ok′), *n.* a genealogical register of a stud; a book giving the pedigree of horses.

stud·ding (stud′ing), *n.* **1.** a number of studs, as in a wall or partition. **2.** timbers or manufactured objects for use as studs.

stud·ding·sail (stud′ing sāl′; *Naut.* stun′səl), *n.* *Naut.* a light sail, sometimes set outboard of either of the leeches of a square sail and extended by booms. Also, **stunsail, stuns'l.** [*studding* (< ?) + SAIL]

stu·dent (sto͞od′ənt, styo͞od′-), *n.* **1.** a person formally engaged in learning, esp. one enrolled in an institution of secondary or higher education. **2.** any person who studies, investigates, or carefully examines a subject. —*adj.* **3.** of, by, or pertaining to students, esp. of colleges or universities: *a student song; a student demonstration.* [late ME < L *student-* (s. of *studēns,* prp.) = *stud-* (s. of *studēre* to take pains) + *-ent-* -ENT; r. *studiant* < MF] —**Syn. 1, 2.** See **pupil**[1].

stu′dent coun′cil, a representative body composed chiefly of students chosen by their classmates to organize social and extracurricular activities and to participate in the government of a school or college.

stu′dent lamp′, a table lamp whose light source can be adjusted in height.

Stu′dent Nonvi′olent (now Na′tional) Coor′dinating Commit′tee. See **SNCC.**

stu′dent nurse′, a person, esp. a woman, who is training to be a nurse in a nursing school or a hospital.

stu′dent teach′er, a person studying to be a teacher, who does closely supervised teaching in an elementary or secondary school. Also called **intern, practice teacher, pupil teacher.** —**stu′dent teach′ing.**

stud·horse (stud′hôrs′), *n.* a stallion kept for breeding. [OE *stōdhors*]

stud·ied (stud′ēd), *adj.* **1.** marked by or suggestive of conscious effort: *studied simplicity.* **2.** carefully deliberated: *a studied approval.* **3.** *Archaic.* learned. —**stud′ied·ly,** *adv.* —**stud′ied·ness,** *n.* —**Syn. 1.** deliberate. **1, 2.** considered. See **elaborate.** —**Ant. 1.** unpremeditated.

stu·di·o (sto͞o′dē ō′, styo͞o′-), *n., pl.* **-di·os. 1.** the workroom or atelier of an artist, as a painter or sculptor. **2.** a place for instruction or experimentation in one of the performing arts. **3.** a room or set of rooms specially equipped for broadcasting radio or television programs, making phonograph records, etc. **4.** a place where motion pictures are made. **5.** See **studio apartment.** [It: lit., STUDY]

stu′dio apart′ment, an apartment consisting of one main room, a kitchen or kitchenette, and a bathroom.

stu′dio couch′, an upholstered couch, usually without a back, convertible into a bed, as by sliding a bedframe out from beneath it and covering the frame with the mattress that forms the upper thickness of the upholstery.

stu·di·ous (sto͞o′dē əs, styo͞o′-), *adj.* **1.** disposed or given to study: *a studious boy.* **2.** characterized by study or a disposition to study: *studious tastes.* **3.** zealous, assiduous, or painstaking: *studious care.* [< L *studiōs(us)* = *studi(um)* (see STUDY) + *-ōsus* -OUS] —**stu′di·ous·ly,** *adv.* —**stu′di·ous·ness,** *n.*

stud′ pok′er, *Cards.* **1.** a variety of poker in which each player is dealt one card face down in the first round and one card face up in each of the next four rounds, each of the last four rounds being followed by a betting interval. **2.** any similar variety of poker, as seven-card stud. [STUD[2] + POKER[2]]

stud·y (stud′ē), *n., pl.* **stud·ies,** *v.,* **stud·ied, stud·y·ing.** —*n.* **1.** application of the mind to the acquisition of knowledge, as by reading, investigation, or reflection: *long hours of study.* **2.** the acquirement of knowledge or skill in a particular branch of learning, science, or art: *the study of law.* **3.** Often, **studies.** a personal effort to gain knowledge: *to pursue one's studies.* **4.** something studied or to be studied. **5.** a detailed examination and analysis of a subject, phenomenon, etc. **6.** a written account of this, or its findings. **7.** a well-defined, organized branch of learning or knowledge. **8.** zealous endeavor or assiduous effort. **9.** the object of such endeavor or effort. **10.** deep thought, reverie, or a state of abstraction. **11.** a room, in a house or other building, set apart for private study, reading, writing, or the like. **12.** *Music.* étude. **13.** *Literature.* **a.** a literary composition executed for exercise or as an experiment in a particular method of treatment. **b.** such a composition dealing in detail with a particular subject, as a single main character. **14.** *Art.* something produced as an educational exercise, as a memorandum of things observed, or as a guide for a finished work. **—*v.i.*** **15.** to apply oneself to the acquisition of knowledge, as by reading or investigation. **16.** to apply oneself; endeavor. **17.** to think deeply, reflect, or consider. **—*v.t.*** **18.** to apply oneself to acquiring a knowledge of or skill in (a subject). **19.** to examine or investigate carefully and in detail. **20.** to observe attentively; scrutinize: *to study a person's face.* **21.** to read carefully or intently. **22.** to endeavor to learn or memorize, as a part in a play. **23.** to consider, as something to be achieved or devised. **24.** to think out, as the result of careful consideration or devising. [ME *studie* < OF (*e*)*studie* < L *studi*(*um*) = *stud-* (s. of *studēre* to be busy with) + *-ium* -Y³] **—Syn. 1.** research, reading, thought. **7.** subject, field, area. **11.** library, den. **19, 20.** STUDY, CONSIDER, REFLECT, WEIGH imply fixing the mind upon something, generally doing so with a view to some decision or action. STUDY implies an attempt to obtain a grasp of something by methodical or exhaustive thought: *to study a problem.* To CONSIDER is to fix the thought upon something and give it close attention before making a decision or beginning an action: *consider ways and means.* REFLECT implies looking back quietly over past experience and giving it consideration: *reflect on similar cases in the past.* WEIGH implies a deliberate and judicial estimate, as by a balance: *weigh a decision.*

stud′y hall′, **1.** (in some schools) a room used solely or chiefly for studying. **2.** a period of time in a school day set aside for study and doing homework.

stuff (stuf), *n.* **1.** the material of which anything is made. **2.** material, objects, or items of some unspecified kind. **3.** inward character, qualities, or capabilities: *to have good stuff in one.* **4.** *Informal.* **a.** a specialty or special skill: *to do one's stuff.* **b.** action or talk of a particular kind: *rough stuff.* **5.** worthless things or matter. **6.** worthless or foolish ideas, talk, or writing: *stuff and nonsense.* **—*v.t.*** **7.** to fill (a receptacle or aperture) with solidly packed contents. **8.** to fill or line with some kind of material as a padding or packing. **9.** to fill or cram with food. **10.** (of poultry or other food) to fill with a stuffing. **11.** to fill the preserved skin of (a dead animal) with material, retaining its natural form and appearance for display. **12.** *U.S.* to put fraudulent votes into (a ballot box). **13.** to thrust or cram (something) into a receptacle or aperture. **14.** to pack tightly in a confined place; crowd together. **15.** to stop up or plug; block or choke (usually fol. by *up*). **—*v.i.*** **16.** to cram oneself with food; eat gluttonously; gorge. [ME < OF (*e*)*stoffe* = *estoffe*(*r*) (to) stock, equip < Gmc, cf. MHG *stopfen* to stop up, fill, stuff; see STOP] **—Syn. 5.** waste, rubbish, trash. **6.** nonsense, twaddle, balderdash. **7.** crowd, press, stow. **15.** obstruct.

stuffed′ der′ma, kishke.

stuffed′ shirt′, *Informal.* a pompous, self-satisfied, and inflexible person.

stuff·ing (stuf′ing), *n.* **1.** the act of a person or thing that stuffs. **2.** that with which anything is or may be stuffed. **3.** seasoned bread crumbs or other filling used to stuff poultry or other food.

stuff′ing box′, *Mach.* a device for preventing leakage of gases or liquids along a moving rod or shaft at the point at which it leaves an enclosed space.

stuff′ing nut′, *Mach.* a nut on a stuffing box that serves to condense packing and tighten the seal.

stuff·y (stuf′ē), *adj.*, **stuff·i·er, stuff·i·est.** **1.** close; poorly ventilated. **2.** oppressive, as stale air. **3.** troubled with a sensation of obstruction in the respiratory passages: *a stuffy nose.* **4.** dull or tedious. **5.** self-important; pompous. **6.** rigid or old-fashioned in attitudes, esp. in matters of personal behavior. **—stuff′i·ly,** *adv.* **—stuff′i·ness,** *n.*

stui·ver (stī′vər), *n.* stiver (def. 1).

Stu·ka (stōō′kə; *Ger.* shtōō′kä), *n.* a German two-seated dive bomber with a single engine, used by the Luftwaffe in World War II. [< G *Stu*(*rz*)*ka*(*mpfflugzeug*) dive bomber = *Sturz* dive + *Kampfflugzeug* battle plane]

stull (stul), *n.* *Mining.* **1.** a timber prop. **2.** a timber wedged in place between two walls of a stope as part of a protective covering or platform. [cf. G *Stollen* prop]

St. Ul·mo's fire (ul′mōz). See **St. Elmo's fire.** Also called **St. Ulmo's light.**

stul·ti·fy (stul′tə fī′), *v.t.*, **-fied, -fy·ing.** **1.** to make, or cause to appear, foolish or ridiculous. **2.** to render absurdly or wholly futile or ineffectual. **3.** *Law.* to allege or prove (oneself or another) to be of unsound mind. [< LL *stultificāre*) = L *stult*(*us*) stupid + -I- + *-ficāre* -FY] **—stul′ti·fi·ca′tion,** *n.*

stum (stum), *n.*, *v.*, **stummed, stum·ming.** **—*n.*** **1.** unfermented or partly fermented grape juice. **2.** wine in which increased fermentation has taken place because of the addition of stum. **—*v.t.*** **3.** to increase the fermentation of (wine) by adding stum. [< D *stom* dumb, dull; cf. F *vin muet*, G *stummer Wein*, in the same sense]

stum·ble (stum′bəl), *v.*, **-bled, -bling,** *n.* **—*v.i.*** **1.** to strike the foot against something, as in walking or running, so as to stagger or fall; trip. **2.** to walk or go unsteadily. **3.** to make a slip, mistake, or blunder. **4.** to proceed in a hesitating or blundering manner, as in action or speech (often fol. by *along*). **5.** to discover, arrive at, or meet with accidentally or unexpectedly (usually fol. by *on, upon, across*, etc.): *They stumbled on a little village.* **—*v.t.*** **6.** to cause to stumble; trip. **7.** to give pause to; puzzle or perplex. **—*n.*** **8.** the act of stumbling. **9.** a slip or blunder. [ME; c. Norw *stumla* to grope and stumble in the dark; akin to STAMMER] **—stum′bling·ly,** *adv.*

stum·ble·bum (stum′bəl bum′), *n.* *Slang.* **1.** a clumsy, second-rate prizefighter. **2.** a clumsy, incompetent person.

stum′bling block′, an obstacle or hindrance to progress, belief, or understanding.

stump (stump), *n.* **1.** the lower end of a tree or plant left after the main part falls or is cut off. **2.** the part of a limb of the body remaining after the rest has been cut off. **3.** a short remnant, as of a candle; stub. **4.** any basal part remaining after the main or more important part has been removed. **5.** an artificial leg. **6. stumps,** *Informal.* legs: *Stir your stumps!* **7.** a heavy step or gait, as of a wooden-legged or lame person. **8.** the figurative place of political speechmaking: *to go on the stump.* **9.** *Furniture.* a support for the front end of the arm of a chair, sofa, etc. **10.** a short, thick roll of paper, soft leather, etc., for rubbing pencil, charcoal, or crayon drawings in order to achieve subtle gradations of tone in representing light and shade. **11.** *Cricket.* each of the three upright sticks that, with the two bails laid on top of them, form a wicket. **—*v.t.*** **12.** to reduce to a stump; truncate; lop. **13.** to clear of stumps, as land. **14.** *Chiefly Southern U.S.* to stub, as one's toe. **15.** to nonplus, embarrass, or render completely at a loss: *This riddle stumps me.* **16.** *Informal.* to make political campaign speeches to or in: *to stump a state.* **17.** *Cricket.* (of the wicketkeeper) to put (a batsman) out by knocking down a stump or by dislodging a bail with the ball held in the hand at a moment when the batsman is off his ground. **18.** to tone or modify (a crayon drawing, pencil rendering, etc.) by means of a stump. **—*v.i.*** **19.** to walk heavily or clumsily, as if with a wooden leg. **20.** *Informal.* to make political campaign speeches; electioneer. [ME *stumpe*; c. MD *stomp*(*e*), G *Stumpf*; akin to STAMP] **—stump′er,** *n.*

stump·age (stum′pij), *n.* **1.** standing timber with reference to its value. **2.** the right to cut such timber on the land of another. **3.** the value of such timber.

stump·y (stum′pē), *adj.*, **stump·i·er, stump·i·est.** **1.** of the nature of or resembling a stump. **2.** short and thick; stubby; stocky. **3.** abounding in stumps: *a stumpy field.*

stun (stun), *v.*, **stunned, stun·ning,** *n.* **—*v.t.*** **1.** to deprive of consciousness or coordination by or as by a blow, fall, etc. **2.** to astonish; astound; amaze. **3.** to daze or bewilder by distracting noise. **—*n.*** **4.** the act of stunning. **5.** the condition of being stunned. [ME *ston*(*i*)*e*(*n*), *stune*(*n*), OE *stunian* to crash, resound (OF *estoner* to shake, make resound < ME); see ASTONISH] **—Syn. 1.** dizzy. See **shock**¹. **2.** overwhelm, confound. **3.** stupefy.

stung (stung), *v.* a pt. and pp. of **sting.**

stunk (stungk), *v.* a pt. and pp. of **stink.**

stun·ner (stun′ər), *n.* **1.** a person or thing that stuns. **2.** *Chiefly Brit. Informal.* a person or thing of striking excellence, beauty, etc.

stun·ning (stun′ing), *adj.* **1.** causing, capable of causing, or liable to stun. **2.** of striking beauty or excellence.

stun·sail (stun′səl), *n.* studdingsail. Also, **stun′s′l.** [syncopated var. of STUDDINGSAIL]

stunt¹ (stunt), *v.t.* **1.** to stop or slow down the growth or development of. **—*n.*** **2.** a stop or hindrance in growth or development. **3.** arrested development. **4.** a creature hindered from attaining its proper growth. [dial. adj. *stunt* dwarfed, stubborn (in ME, OE: stupid); c. MHG *stunz*, Icel *stuttr* short; akin to STINT¹]

stunt² (stunt), *n.* **1.** a performance of skill or dexterity, as in athletics; feat. **2.** any remarkable feat performed chiefly to attract attention. **—*v.i.*** **3.** to do a stunt or stunts. **—*v.t.*** **4.** to use in doing stunts: *to stunt an airplane.* [?]

stunt′ man′, *Motion Pictures.* a person who substitutes for an actor in scenes requiring hazardous or acrobatic feats. Also, *referring to a woman,* **stunt′ girl′.**

stu·pa (stōō′pə), *n.* *Buddhism.* a dome-shaped or pyramidal monument to Buddha or a Buddhist saint. [< Skt *stūpa* topknot, top of the head, dome]

stupe¹ (stōōp, styōōp), *n.* flannel or other cloth soaked in hot water and applied to the skin as a counterirritant. [< L *stūp*(*a*), var. of *stuppa* < Gk *stýppē* flax, hemp, tow]

stupe² (stōōp), *n.* *Slang.* a stupid person. [by shortening]

stu·pe·fa·cient (stōō′pə fā′shənt, styōō′-), *adj.* **1.** stupefying; producing stupor. **—*n.*** **2.** a drug or agent that produces stupor. [< L *stupefacient-* (s. of *stupefaciēns*) benumbing = *stupe-* senseless + *-facient-* -FACIENT]

stu·pe·fac·tion (stōō′pə fak′shən, styōō′-), *n.* **1.** the act of stupefying. **2.** the state of being stupefied; stupor; numbness of the faculties. **3.** overwhelming amazement. [< NL *stupefactiōn-* (s. of *stupefactiō*) senseless state = *stupe-* senseless + *fac-* make + *-tiōn-* -TION]

stu·pe·fac·tive (stōō′pə fak′tiv, styōō′-), *adj.* serving to stupefy. [< ML *stupefactīv*(*us*) < L *stupe* senseless + *fac-* make + *-t-* ptp. suffix + *-īvus* -IVE]

stu·pe·fy (stōō′pə fī′, styōō′-), *v.t.*, **-fied, -fy·ing.** **1.** to put into a state of little or no sensibility, as with heat, cold, a narcotic, etc.; benumb the faculties of; put into a stupor. **2.** to stun, as with a strong emotion. **3.** to overwhelm with amazement; astound; astonish. [< MF *stupefi*(*er*) = *stupe-* (< L *stupe-* senseless) + *-fier* -FY] **—stu′pe·fy′ing·ly,** *adv.*

stu·pen·dous (stōō pen′dəs, styōō-), *adj.* **1.** causing amazement; astounding; marvelous: *stupendous news.* **2.** amazingly large or great; immense. [< L *stupendus*, ger. of *stupēre* to be astonished] **—stu·pen′dous·ly,** *adv.* **—Syn. 1.** extraordinary. **2.** colossal, vast, gigantic, prodigious.

stu·pid (stōō′pid, styōō′-), *adj.* **1.** lacking ordinary activity and keenness of mind; mentally slow; dull. **2.** characterized by, indicative of, or proceeding from mental dullness; foolish; senseless: *a stupid act.* **3.** tediously dull or uninteresting, esp. because of lack of meaning or sense. **4.** in a state of stupor; stupefied. [< L *stupid*(*us*) = *stup-* senseless + *-idus* -ID⁴] **—stu′pid·ly,** *adv.* **—stu′pid·ness,** *n.* **—Syn. 1.** witless, dumb. See **foolish.** **3.** vapid, pointless, inane, asinine. See **dull.** **—Ant. 1.** bright, clever.

stu·pid·i·ty (stōō pid′i tē, styōō-), *n.*, *pl.* **-ties** for 2. **1.** the state, quality, or fact of being stupid. **2.** a stupid act, notion, speech, etc. [< L *stupiditāt-* (s. of *stupiditās*)]

stu·por (stōō′pər, styōō′-), *n.* **1.** a state of suspended or deadened sensibility. **2.** a state of mental torpor or apathy; stupefaction. [< L: astonishment, insensibility = *stup-* senseless + *-or* -OR¹] **—stu′por·ous,** *adj.*

stur·dy¹ (stûr′dē), *adj.*, **-di·er, -di·est.** **1.** strongly built;

stalwart; robust: *sturdy young athletes.* **2.** strong, as in substance or structure. **3.** firm; courageous or indomitable. **4.** of strong or hardy growth, as a plant. [ME *stourdi* < OF *(e)stourdi* dazed, stunned, violent, reckless (ptp. of *estourdir* < ?)] —**stur′di·ly,** *adv.* —**stur′di·ness,** *n.* —**Syn. 1.** hardy, muscular, brawny. **3.** resolute, unconquerable. —**Ant. 1.** weak.

stur·dy² (stûr′dē), *n. Vet. Pathol.* gid. [< OF *estourdi* gid; see STURDY¹]

Sturgeon, *Acipenser oxyrhynchus* (Length to 12 ft.)

stur·geon (stûr′jən), *n., pl.* (*esp. collectively*) **-geon,** (*esp. referring to two or more kinds or species*) **-geons.** any of various large ganoid fishes of the family *Acipenseridae,* found in fresh and salt waters of the North Temperate Zone: valued for their flesh and as a source of caviar and isinglass. [ME < AF < OF *(e)sturgeon* < Gmc; cf. OE *styria,* Icel *styrja,* OHG *sturio* (G *Stör*)]

Sturm·ab·tei·lung (shtŏŏʀm′äp′tī′lŏŏng), *n.* See **storm troopers.** [< G = *Sturm* storm, troop of storm troopers + *Abteilung* division, department]

Sturm und Drang (shtŏŏʀm′ ŏŏnt dʀäng′), a movement in German literature of the late 18th century, characterized chiefly by impetuosity of manner, exaltation of the individual, opposition to established forms, and extreme nationalism. [< G: lit., storm and stress]

stut·ter (stut′ər), *v.i.* **1.** to speak in such a way that the speech rhythm is interrupted by repetitions, blocks or spasms, or prolongations of sounds or syllables. —*v.t.* **2.** to speak (words, sentences, etc.) with a stutter. —*n.* **3.** a form of speech characterized by stuttering. [< ME *stutt(en)* (to) stutter; akin to dial. *stoit* to move, lurch] —**stut′ter·er,** *n.*—**stut′ter·ing·ly,** *adv.* —**Syn. 1.** See **stammer.**

Stutt·gart (stut′gärt, stŏŏt′-; *Ger.* shtŏŏt′gäʀt), *n.* a city in W West Germany. 594,100.

Stuy·ve·sant (stī′vi sənt), *n.* **Peter,** 1592–1672, Dutch colonial administrator in the Americas: last governor of New Netherlands 1646–64.

St. Vincent, 1. a former British colony, comprising St. Vincent Island and the N Grenadines, in the S Windward Islands, in the SE West Indies: independent since 1979. 109,743; 150 sq. mi. *Cap.:* Kingstown. Official name, **St. Vincent and the Grenadines. 2. Cape,** the SW tip of Portugal: naval battle 1797.

St. Vi·tus's dance (vī′tə siz), *Pathol.* chorea (def. 2). Also, **St. Vitus dance.** [named after *St. Vitus* (3rd century), patron saint of those afflicted with chorea]

sty¹ (stī), *n., pl.* **sties,** *v.,* **stied, sty·ing.** —*n.* **1.** a pen or enclosure for swine; pigpen. **2.** any filthy place or abode. —*v.t.* **3.** to keep or lodge in or as in a sty. —*v.i.* **4.** to live in or as in a sty. [ME, OE *stig;* c. Icel *stī,* D *stijg,* G *Steige*]

sty² (stī), *n., pl.* **sties.** *Ophthalm.* a circumscribed inflammatory swelling, like a small boil, on the edge of the eyelid. Also, **stye.** [by false division of ME *styanye* sty (*styan,* OE *stīgend* sty, lit., rising + *ye* EYE) taken to be *sty on eye*]

Styg·i·an (stij′ē ən), *adj.* **1.** of or pertaining to the river Styx or to Hades. **2.** dark or gloomy. **3.** infernal; hellish. **4.** (of an oath or vow) binding; irrevocable or inviolable. [< L *Stygi(us)* < Gk *Stýgios* (*Styg-,* s. of *Stýx* STYX + *-ios* adj. suffix) + -AN]

styl-¹, var. of **stylo-¹** before a vowel: *stylar.*

styl-², var. of **stylo-²** before a vowel: *stylite.*

sty·lar (stī′lər), *adj.* having the shape of a style or stylus; resembling a pen, pin, or peg. [STYL-¹ + -AR¹]

style (stīl), *n., v.* **styled, styl·ing.** —*n.* **1.** a particular kind, sort, or type, as with reference to form, appearance, or character: *the baroque style.* **2.** a particular, distinctive, or characteristic mode of action or manner of acting: *to do things in a grand style.* **3.** a mode of living, esp. one that is fashionable or luxurious. **4.** a mode of fashion, as in dress; elegance; smartness. **5.** the mode of expressing thought in writing or speaking that is characteristic of a group, person, etc.: *to write in the style of Faulkner; a familiar style; a pompous style.* **6.** (in a literary composition) the mode and form of expression, as distinguished from the content. **7.** a descriptive or distinguishing appellation, esp. a legal, official, or recognized title. **8.** Also, **stylus. a.** an instrument used by the ancients for writing on waxed tablets. **b.** something resembling or suggesting such an instrument. **c.** a pointed instrument for drawing, etching, or writing. **9.** the gnomon of a sundial. **10.** a method of reckoning time. Cf. **New Style, old style** (def. 2). **11.** *Bot.* a narrow, usually cylindrical and more or less filiform extension of the ovary that, when present, bears the stigma at its apex. **12.** *Zool.* a small, slender, pointed process or part. **13.** the rules or customs of typography, punctuation, spelling, etc., used by a newspaper, publishing house, etc. —*v.t.* **14.** to call by a given title or appellation; denominate; name. **15.** to design in accordance with a given or new style. **16.** to bring into conformity with a specific style or give a specific style to. —*v.i.* **17.** to do decorative work with a style or stylus. [ME < L *styl(us),* sp. var. of *stilus* tool for writing, hence, written composition, style; see STYLUS] —**Syn. 4.** chic. See **fashion.**

style·book (stīl′bŏŏk′), *n.* **1.** a book containing rules of usage in typography, punctuation, etc., employed by printers, editors, and writers. **2.** a book featuring styles or fashions, as for dressmaking.

sty·let (stī′lit), *n.* **1.** a stiletto or dagger. **2.** any similar sharp-pointed instrument. **3.** *Med.* **a.** a probe. **b.** a wire run through the length of a catheter, cannula, or needle to make it rigid or to clear it. **4.** *Zool.* style (def. 12). [< F < MF *stilet* < It *stilett(o)* STILETTO; *-y-* < L *stylus.* See STYLE, STYLUS]

sty·li·form (stī′lə fôrm′), *adj.* having the shape of an ancient style or stylus; stylar. [earlier *stiliform* < NL *stiliform(is)* < L *stil(us)* STYLUS + -I- + *-formis* -FORM]

styl·ise (stī′līz), *v.t.,* **-ised, -is·ing.** *Chiefly Brit.* stylize. —**styl′i·sa′tion,** *n.* —**styl′is·er,** *n.*

styl·ish (stī′lish), *adj.* characterized by or conforming to the present style; smart or chic. —**styl′ish·ly,** *adv.* —**styl′ish·ness,** *n.*

styl·ist (stī′list), *n.* **1.** a master of style, esp. in writing or speaking. **2.** a designer or consultant in a field subject to changes of style, esp. clothing or interior decoration.

sty·lis·tic (stī lis′tik), *adj.* of or pertaining to style. Also, **sty·lis′ti·cal.** —**sty·lis′ti·cal·ly,** *adv.*

sty·lite (stī′līt), *n. Eccles. Hist.* one of a class of solitary ascetics who lived on the top of high pillars or columns. [< LGk *stylī́tē(s)* = *stŷl(os)* STYL-² + *-ītēs* -ITE¹] —**sty·lit·ic** (stī lit′ik), *adj.*

styl·ize (stī′līz), *v.t.,* **-ized, -iz·ing.** to design in or cause to conform to a particular style, as of representation or treatment in art; conventionalize. Also, *esp. Brit.,* **stylise.** —**styl′i·za′tion,** *n.* —**styl′iz·er,** *n.*

stylo-¹, a learned borrowing from Latin used to represent **style** or **styloid** in the formation of compound words: *stylography.* Also, *esp. before a vowel,* **styl-.** [comb. form of L *stilus.* See STYLUS, -O-]

stylo-², a learned borrowing from Greek meaning "column," "pillar," "tube," used in the formation of compound words: *stylolite.* Also, *esp. before a vowel,* **styl-.** [< Gk, comb. form of *stŷlos* pillar]

sty·lo·bate (stī′lə bāt′), *n. Archit.* (in a classical temple) a course of masonry forming the foundation for a colonnade, esp. the outermost colonnade. [< L *stylobatē(s), stylobata* < Gk = *stŷlo(s)* STYLO-² + *-batēs* (*ba-* (s. of *baínein* to step) + *-tēs* suffix denoting agent)]

sty·lo·graph (stī′lə graf′, -gräf′), *n.* a fountain pen in which the writing point is a fine, hollow tube instead of a nib. Also called **sty′lograph′ic pen′.**

sty·lo·graph·ic (stī′lə graf′ik), *adj.* **1.** of or pertaining to a stylograph. **2.** of, pertaining to, or used in stylography. Also, **sty′lo·graph′i·cal.** —**sty′lo·graph′i·cal·ly,** *adv.*

sty·log·ra·phy (stī log′rə fē), *n.* the art of writing, tracing, drawing, etc., with a style or stylus.

sty·loid (stī′loid), *adj.* **1.** resembling a style; slender and pointed. **2.** *Anat.* pertaining to several bony processes on the temporal bone, radius, ulna, etc. [< NL *styloid(es)*]

sty·lo·lite (stī′lə līt′), *n. Geol.* an irregular columnar structure in certain limestones, the columns being approximately at right angles to the bedding planes. —**sty·lo·lit·ic** (stī′lə-lit′ik), *adj.*

sty·lo·po·di·um (stī′lə pō′dē əm), *n., pl.* **-di·a** (-dē ə). *Bot.* a glandular disk or expansion surmounting the ovary in umbelliferous plants and supporting the styles.

sty·lus (stī′ləs), *n., pl.* **-li** (-lī), **-lus·es. 1.** style (def. 8). **2.** a needle used for cutting a phonograph record. **3.** a needle for reproducing the sounds of a phonograph record. **4.** any of various pointed wedges used to punch holes in paper or other material, as in writing Braille. **5.** any of various pens for tracing a line automatically, as on a recording seismograph. [< L *stilus* stake, pointed writing instrument; sp. with *-y-* from fancied derivation < Gk *stŷlos* column]

sty·mie (stī′mē), *n., v.,* **-mied, -mie·ing.** —*n.* **1.** *Golf.* (on a putting green) an instance of a ball's lying on a direct line between the cup and the ball of an opponent about to putt. **2.** a situation or problem presenting such difficulties as to discourage or defeat any attempt to deal with or resolve it. —*v.t.* **3.** to hinder, block, or thwart. Also, **stymy.** [?]

Stym·pha′li·an birds′ (stim fā′lē ən, -fāl′yən), *Class. Myth.* a flock of annoying or dangerous birds of Arcadia that were driven away or killed by Hercules as one of his labors. [after lake *Stymphalus* in Arcadia; see -IAN]

sty·my (stī′mē), *n., pl.* **-mies,** *v.t.,* **-mied, -my·ing.** stymie

styp·tic (stip′tik), *adj.* Also, **styp′ti·cal. 1.** causing the contraction of organic tissue; astringent; binding. **2.** capable of checking hemorrhage or bleeding, as a drug; hemostatic. —*n.* **3.** a styptic agent or substance. [late ME < LL *stýptic(us)* < Gk *styptikós* contractile = *stýp-* (s. of *stýphein* to contract) + *-tikos* -TIC] —**styp·tic·i·ty** (stip tis′i tē), *n.*

styp′tic pen′cil, a pencil-shaped stick of a paste containing alum or a similar styptic agent, used to stanch the bleeding of minor cuts and abrasions, as those occurring in shaving.

Styr (stēr), *n.* a river in the W Soviet Union in Europe, in NW Ukraine flowing N to the Pripet River. 300 mi. long.

sty·ra·ca·ceous (stī′rə kā′shəs), *adj.* belonging to the *Styracaceae* or storax family of shrubs and trees. [*styrac-* (s. of STYRAX) + -ACEOUS]

sty·rax (stī′raks), *n.* any plant of the genus *Styrax,* comprising the storaxes. [var. of STORAX]

sty·rene (stī′rēn, stēr′ēn), *n. Chem.* a liquid, $C_6H_5CH{=}CH_2$, that polymerizes to a clear, transparent material and copolymerizes with other materials to form synthetic rubbers. Also called **vinylbenzene.** Cf. **polystyrene.** [*styr-* (shortened s. of STYRAX) + -ENE]

sty′rene res′in, *Chem.* a transparent thermoplastic resin formed by polymerizing styrene.

Styr·i·a (stēr′ē ə), *n.* a province in SE Austria: formerly a duchy. 1,192,100; 6327 sq. mi. *Cap.:* Graz. German, **Steiermark.**

Sty·ro·foam (stī′rə fōm′), *n. Trademark.* a light, durable polystyrene foam used as a packing and insulating material.

Sty·ron (stī′rən), *n.* **William,** born 1925, U.S. author.

Styx (stiks), *n. Class. Myth.* a river in the lower world over which the souls of the dead were ferried by Charon.

su-, var. of **sub-** before *sp: suspect.*

su·a·ble (sōō′ə bəl), *adj.* liable to or capable of being sued. —**su′a·bil′i·ty,** *n.* —**su′a·bly,** *adv.*

Sua·kin (swä′kēn), *n.* a seaport in NE Sudan, on the Red Sea. 5511.

sua·sion (swā′zhən), *n.* the act or an instance of advising, urging, or attempting to persuade; persuasion. [< L *suāsiōn-* (s. of *suāsiō*) = *suās(us),* ptp. of *suādēre* to advise + *-iōn-* -ION] —**sua·sive** (swā′siv), *adj.* —**sua′sive·ly,** *adv.* —**sua′sive·ness,** *n.*

suave (swäv), *adj.* **1.** (of persons or their manner, speech, etc.) smoothly agreeable or polite; agreeably or blandly urbane. **2.** blandly agreeable; mild: *suave, perfumed breezes.* **3.** polished or smooth in texture. [< F < L *suāv(is)* sweet] —**suave′ly,** *adv.* —**Syn. 1.** sophisticated, worldly. —**Ant. 1.** blunt.

suav·i·ty (swä′vi tē, swav′i-), *n., pl.* **-ties. 1.** a suave or smoothly agreeable quality. **2. suavities,** suave or courteous actions or manners; amenities. Also, **suave′ness.** [late ME < L *suāvitāt-* (s. of *suāvitās*)]

sub (sub), *n.*, *v.*, **subbed, sub·bing.** —*n.* **1.** submarine. **2.** substitute. **3.** *Photog. Informal.* a substratum. —*v.i.* **4.** to act as a substitute for another. —*v.t.* **5.** *Photog. Informal.* to coat (a film or plate) with a substratum. [shortened form]

sub-, **1.** a prefix occurring originally in loan words from Latin the stems of which are sometimes not used as words (*subject; subtract; subvert*); on this model, attached freely to elements of any origin and used with the meaning "under," "below," "beneath" (*subalpine*), "slightly," "imperfectly," "nearly" (*subcolumnar*), "secondary," "subordinate" (*subcommittee; subplot*). **2.** *Chem.* **a.** a prefix indicating a basic compound: *subacetate.* **b.** a prefix indicating that the element is present in a relatively small proportion, i.e., in a low oxidation state: *subchloride; suboxide.* Also, **su-, suc-, suf-, sug-, sum-, sup-, sus-.** [< L, comb. form repr. *sub* (prep.); akin to HYPO-]

sub., **1.** subscription. **2.** substitute. **3.** subway.

sub·ac·e·tate (sub as′i tāt′), *n.* *Chem.* a basic salt of acetic acid.

sub·ac·id (sub as′id), *adj.* **1.** slightly or moderately acid or sour: *a subacid fruit.* **2.** (of a person or his speech, temper, etc.) somewhat biting or sharp. —**sub·a·cid·i·ty** (sub′ə sid′i tē), **sub·ac′id·ness,** *n.* —**sub·ac′id·ly,** *adv.*

sub·a·cute (sub′ə kyōōt′), *adj.* somewhat or moderately acute. —**sub′a·cute′ly,** *adv.*

su·ba·dar (sōō′bə där′), *n.* (formerly, in India) **1.** a provincial governor of the Mogul empire. **2.** the chief native officer of a company of native troops in the British Indian Service. Also, **su′bah·dar′.** [< Urdu < Pers = *sūbah* province + *dār* holding, holder]

sub·al·pine (sub al′pīn, -pin), *adj.* **1.** pertaining to the regions at the foot of the Alps. **2.** *Bot.* growing on mountains below the limit of tree growth, and above the foothill, or montane, zone.

sub·al·tern (sub ôl′tərn *or, esp. for 2, 5,* sub′əl tûrn′), *adj.* **1.** lower in rank; subordinate: *a subaltern employee.* **2.** *Logic.* noting the relation of a particular proposition to a universal proposition having the same subject, predicate, and quality. —*n.* **3.** a person who has a subordinate position. **4.** *Brit. Mil.* a commissioned officer below the rank of captain. **5.** *Logic.* a subaltern proposition. [< LL *subaltern(us)* = *sub-* SUB- + *alternus* ALTERNATE]

sub·al·ter·nate (sub ôl′tər nit, -al′-), *adj.* **1.** subordinate; inferior. **2.** *Bot.* placed singly along an axis, but tending to become grouped oppositely. [< ML *subalternāt(us)* (ptp. of *subalternāre* to subordinate) = *subaltern(us)* SUBALTERN + *-ātus* -ATE[1]]

sub·a·quat·ic (sub′ə kwat′ik, -ə kwot′-), *adj.* living or growing partly on land, partly in water.

sub·a·que·ous (sub ā′kwē əs, -ak′wē-), *adj.* **1.** existing or situated under water. **2.** occurring or performed under water. **3.** used under water.

sub·ar·id (sub ar′id), *adj.* moderately arid.

sub·as·sem·bly (sub′ə sem′blē), *n., pl.* **-blies.** a structural assembly, as of electronic or machine parts, forming part of a larger assembly.

sub·at·om (sub at′əm), *n.* any component of an atom.

sub·a·tom·ic (sub′ə tom′ik), *adj.* *Physics.* **1.** of or pertaining to a process that occurs within an atom. **2.** noting or pertaining to a particle or particles contained in an atom, as electrons, protons, or neutrons.

sub·au·di·tion (sub′ô dish′ən), *n.* **1.** the act or an instance of understanding or mentally supplying something not expressed. **2.** something mentally supplied; understood or implied meaning. [< LL *subauditiōn-* (s. of *subauditiō*) understanding, i.e., supplying an omitted word]

sub·ax·il·la·ry (sub ak′sə ler′ē), *adj.* *Bot.* situated or placed beneath an axil.

sub·base·ment (sub′bās′mənt), *n.* a basement or one of a series of basements below a main basement.

sub·bass (sub′bās′), *n.* *Music.* a pedal stop producing the lowest tones of an organ.

sub·bing (sub′ing), *n.* *Photog.* **1.** the act or process of applying a substratum. **2.** the material used for a substratum.

sub·cal·i·ber (sub kal′ə bər), *adj.* *Mil.* **1.** (of a projectile) having a diameter less than the caliber of the gun from which it is fired. **2.** used in firing such a projectile: *a subcaliber gun.*

sub·ce·les·tial (sub′si les′chəl), *adj.* **1.** being beneath the heavens; terrestrial. **2.** mundane; worldly. —*n.* **3.** a subcelestial being.

sub·cel·lar (sub′sel′ər), *n.* a cellar below a main cellar.

sub·cen·tral (sub sen′trəl), *adj.* near or almost at the center. —**sub·cen′tral·ly,** *adv.*

subch., subchapter.

sub·chas·er (sub′chā′sər), *n.* See **submarine chaser.**

sub·chlo·ride (sub klōr′īd, -id, -klôr′-), *n.* *Chem.* a chloride containing a relatively small proportion of chlorine, as mercurous chloride.

sub·class (sub′klas′, -kläs′), *n.* **1.** a primary division of a class. **2.** *Biol.* a category of related orders within a class. —*v.t.* **3.** to place in a subclass.

sub·cla·vi·an (sub klā′vē ən), *Anat.* —*adj.* **1.** situated or extending beneath the clavicle, as certain arteries or veins. **2.** pertaining to such an artery, vein, etc. —*n.* **3.** a subclavian artery, vein, or the like. [< NL *subclāvi(us)* (*sub-* SUB- + *clāv(is)* key + *-ius* adj. suffix) + -AN]

subcla′vian groove′, *Anat.* either of two shallow depressions on the first rib, one for the subclavian artery and the other for the subclavian vein.

sub·cli·max (sub klī′maks), *n.* *Ecol.* the imperfect development of a climax community because of some factor, as repeated fires in a forest, that arrests the normal succession.

sub·clin·i·cal (sub klin′i kəl), *adj.* *Pathol.* (of a disease, deficiency, etc.) having symptoms too mild to be detected by the usual clinical examination and tests.

sub·co·lum·nar (sub′kə lum′nər), *adj.* almost or imperfectly columnar.

sub·com·mit·tee (sub′kə mit′ē), *n.* a secondary committee appointed out of a main committee.

sub·com·pact (*adj.* sub′kəm pakt′; *n.* sub′kom′pakt), *adj.* **1.** of a size smaller than a compact automobile: *a subcompact car.* —*n.* **2.** Also called **mini.** a subcompact automobile.

sub·con·scious (sub kon′shəs), *adj.* **1.** existing or operating in the mind beneath or beyond consciousness. **2.** imperfectly or not wholly conscious. —*n.* **3.** the totality of mental processes of which the individual is not aware. —**sub·con′scious·ly,** *adv.* —**sub·con′scious·ness,** *n.*

sub·con·ti·nent (sub kon′tᵊnənt, sub′kon′-), *n.* **1.** a large, relatively self-contained land mass forming a subdivision of a continent: *the subcontinent of India.* **2.** a large land mass, as Greenland, that is smaller than any of the usually recognized continents. —**sub·con·ti·nen·tal** (sub′kon tᵊnen′tᵊl), *adj.*

sub·con·tract (*n.* sub kon′trakt, sub′kon′-; *v.* sub′kən trakt′), *n.* **1.** a contract by which one agrees to render services or to provide materials necessary for the performance of another contract. —*v.t.* **2.** to make a subcontract for. —*v.i.* **3.** to make a subcontract.

sub·con·trac·tor (sub kon′trak tər, sub′kon′-, sub′kən trak′tər), *n.* a person who or business that contracts to provide some service or material necessary for the performance of another's contract.

sub·cor·tex (sub kôr′teks, sub′kôr′-), *n., pl.* **-ti·ces** (-ti sēz′). *Anat.* the portions of the brain situated beneath the cerebral cortex, considered as a whole.

sub·crit·i·cal (sub krit′i kəl), *adj.* *Physics.* pertaining to a state, value, or quantity of material, esp. radioactive material, that is less than critical.

sub·cul·ture (*v.* sub kul′chər; *n.* sub′kul′chər), *v.,* **-tured, -tur·ing,** *n.* —*v.t.* **1.** *Bacteriol.* to cultivate (a bacterial strain) again on a new medium. —*n.* **2.** *Bacteriol.* a culture derived in this manner. **3.** *Sociol.* a group having social, economic, ethnic, or other traits distinctive enough to distinguish it from others within the same culture or society. —**sub·cul′tur·al,** *adj.*

sub·cu·ta·ne·ous (sub′kyōō tā′nē əs), *adj.* **1.** situated or lying under the skin, as tissue. **2.** performed or introduced under the skin, as an injection by a syringe. **3.** living below the several layers of the skin, as certain parasites. [< LL *subcutāneus*] —**sub′cu·ta′ne·ous·ly,** *adv.*

sub·dea·con (sub dē′kən, sub′dē′-), *n.* a member of the clerical order next below that of deacon. [ME *subdecon, -dekene* < LL *subdiacon(us)*]

sub·deb (sub′deb′), *n.* *Informal.* subdebutante. [shortened form]

sub·deb·u·tante (sub deb′yōō tänt′, -tant′), *n.* a young girl who has not yet made her debut into society.

sub·di·ac·o·nate (sub′dī ak′ə nit, -nāt′), *n.* the office or dignity of a subdeacon.

sub·di·vide (sub′di vīd′, sub′di vīd′), *v.,* **-vid·ed, -vid·ing.** —*v.t.* **1.** to divide (something already divided) into smaller parts. **2.** to divide into parts. **3.** to divide (a plot, tract of land, etc.) into building lots. —*v.i.* **4.** to become separated into divisions or subdivisions. [< LL *subdīvid(ere)*] —**sub′di·vid′er,** *n.*

sub·di·vi·sion (sub′di vizh′ən), *n.* **1.** the act or fact of subdividing. **2.** a division of a large division. **3.** a portion of land divided into lots for real-estate development. [< LL *subdīvīsiōn-* (s. of *subdīvīsiō*) = *subdīvīs(us)* (ptp. of *subdīvidere* to SUBDIVIDE) + *-iōn-* -ION]

sub·dom·i·nant (sub dom′ə nənt), *n.* **1.** *Music.* the fourth tone of a scale, next below the dominant. —*adj.* **2.** less than or not quite dominant.

sub·du·al (səb dōō′əl, -dyōō′-), *n.* **1.** the act or an instance of subduing. **2.** the state of being subdued.

sub·duct (səb dukt′), *v.t.* *Archaic.* to take away; subtract. [< L *subduct(us)* taken away, ptp. of *subdūcere* = *sub-* SUB- + *dūcere* to lead] —**sub·duc′tion,** *n.*

sub·due (səb dōō′, -dyōō′), *v.t.,* **-dued, -du·ing.** **1.** to conquer and bring into subjection. **2.** to overpower by superior force; overcome. **3.** to bring under mental or emotional control, as by persuasion or intimidation. **4.** to repress (feelings, impulses, etc.). **5.** to bring (land) under cultivation. **6.** to reduce the intensity, force, or vividness of (sound, light, color, etc.); tone down; soften. **7.** to allay (inflammation, infection, etc.). [ME *so(b)due, -dewe* < AF **sodue(r)* (to) overcome, MF *soduire* to deceive, seduce < L *subdūcere* to take away (see SUBDUCT); meaning in E (and AF) < L *subdere*] —**sub·du′a·ble,** *adj.* —**sub·du′a·ble·ness,** *n.* —**sub·du′a·bly,** *adv.* —**sub·du′er,** *n.* —**Syn. 1.** subjugate, vanquish. See **defeat. 3.** tame, discipline.

sub·dued (səb dōōd′, -dyōōd′), *adj.* **1.** quiet; repressed; controlled. **2.** lowered in intensity or strength; reduced in fullness of tone, as a color or voice; muted.

su·be·re·ous (sōō bēr′ē əs), *adj.* of the nature of or

sub′ab′bot, *n.*
sub′ad·min′is·tra′tive, *adj.*
sub′ad·min′is·tra′tor, *n.*
sub·a′gen·cy, *n., pl.* **-cies.**
sub·a′gent, *n.*
sub′al·li′ance, *n.*
sub′ar′e·a, *n.*
sub′ar′ti·cle, *n.*
sub′as·so′ci·a′tion, *n.*
sub′at·tor′ney, *n., pl.* **-neys.**
sub·av′er·age, *adj.*
sub′branch′, *n.*
sub′breed′, *n.*
sub′bu′reau, *n., pl.* **-reaus, -reaux.**
sub·cat′e·go′ry, *n., pl.* **-ries.**
sub′cell′, *n.*
sub′chap′ter, *n.*
sub′chief′, *n.*
sub′civ·i·li·za′tion, *n.*
sub′clan′, *n.*
sub′clas·si·fi·ca′tion, *n.*
sub·clas′si·fy′, *v.t.,* **-fied, -fy·ing.**
sub′clause′, *n.*
sub′clerk′, *n.*
sub·cli′mate, *n.*
sub′com·mand′er, *n.*
sub′com·mis′sion, *n.*
sub′com·mis′sion·er, *n.*
sub′con·stel·la′tion, *n.*
sub·coun′cil, *n.*
sub·cra′ni·al, *adj.*
sub′cu·ra′tor, *n.*
sub′def·i·ni′tion, *n.*
sub′de·part′ment, *n.*
sub′de·part·men′tal, *adj.*
sub·de′pot, *n.*
sub·di′a·lect′, *n.*
sub′di·rec′tor, *n.*
sub′dis·tinc′tion, *n.*
sub′dis′trict, *n.*
sub·ech′o, *n., pl.* **-ech·oes.**
sub·ed′i·tor, *n.*
sub·el′e·ment, *n.*
sub′el·e·men′tal, *adj.*
sub·en′try, *n., pl.* **-tries.**
sub·ep′och, *n.*

resembling cork; suberose. [< L *sūbereus* = *sūber* cork + *-eus* -EOUS]

su·ber·ic (sōō ber′ik), *adj.* of or pertaining to cork. [< L *sūber* cork + -IC]

suber′ic ac′id, *Chem.* a dibasic acid, $HOOC(CH_2)_6COOH$, used chiefly in plastics and plasticizers.

su·ber·in (sōō ber′in), *n.* *Bot.* a waxlike substance, occurring in cork cell walls, that on alkaline hydrolysis yields suberic acid. [< L *sūber* cork + -IN[2]; cf. F *subérine*]

su·ber·ise (sōō′bə rīz′), *v.t.*, **-ised, -is·ing.** *Chiefly Brit.* suberize.

su·ber·i·za·tion (sōō′bər i zā′shən or, *esp. Brit.*, -bə rī-), *n.* *Bot.* the impregnation of cell walls with suberin, causing the formation of cork. Also, *esp. Brit.*, **su′ber·i·sa′tion.**

su·ber·ize (sōō′bə rīz′), *v.t.*, **-ized, -iz·ing.** *Bot.* to convert into cork tissue. Also, *esp. Brit.*, **suberise.** [< L *sūber* cork + -IZE]

su·ber·ose (sōō′bə rōs′), *adj.* of the nature of cork; corklike; corky. Also, **su·ber·ous** (sōō′bər əs). [< NL *suberōs(us)* = L *sūber* cork + *-ōsus* -OSE[1]]

sub·fam·i·ly (sub fam′ə lē, -fam′lē, sub′fam′ə lē, -fam′-lē), *n., pl.* **-lies.** **1.** *Biol.* a category of related genera within a family. **2.** *Linguistics.* (in the classification of related languages within a family) a category of a higher order than a branch. Cf. **branch** (def. 7), **family** (def. 11).

sub·floor (sub′flōr′, -flôr′), *n.* a rough floor beneath a finished floor.

sub·freez·ing (sub′frē′zing), *adj.* below the freezing point.

sub·fusc (sub fusk′), *adj.* **1.** subfuscous; dusky. **2.** dark and dull; dingy; drab. [< L *subfusc(us)* SUBFUSCOUS]

sub·fus·cous (sub fus′kəs), *adj.* slightly dark, dusky, or somber. [< L *subfuscus.* See SUB-, FUSCOUS]

sub·ge·nus (sub jē′nəs), *n., pl.* **-gen·er·a** (-jen′ər ə), **-ge·nus·es.** *Biol.* a category of related species within a genus. [< NL] —**sub·ge·ner·ic** (sub′jə ner′ik), *adj.*

sub·gla·cial (sub glā′shəl), *adj.* **1.** beneath a glacier. **2.** formerly beneath a glacier: *a subglacial deposit.*

sub·grade (sub′grād′), *Civ. Eng., Building Trades.* —*n.* **1.** the prepared earth surface on which a pavement or the ballast of a railroad track is placed. —*adj.* **2.** beneath the finished ground level of a project.

sub·group (sub′grōōp′), *n.* **1.** a subordinate group, or a division of a group. **2.** *Chem.* a vertical division of a group in the periodic table; family.

sub·gum (sub′gum′), *adj.* *Chinese-American Cookery.* prepared with mixed vegetables, as with water chestnuts, mushrooms, and bean sprouts. [Cantonese Pidgin for mixed vegetable dishes]

sub·head (sub′hed′), *n.* (in written or printed matter) **1.** a title or heading of a subdivision. **2.** a subordinate division of a title or heading, as of a headline. Also, **sub′head′ing.**

sub·he·dral (sub hē′drəl), *adj.* (of mineral crystals in igneous rocks) having a partial or incomplete crystal face or form.

sub·hu·man (sub hyōō′mən *or, often,* -yōō′-), *adj.* **1.** less than or not quite human. **2.** almost human.

sub·in·dex (sub in′deks), *n., pl.* **-di·ces** (-di sēz′). **1.** an index to a part or subdivision of a larger category. **2.** inferior (def. 9).

sub·in·feu·date (sub′in fyōō′dāt), *v.t., v.i.*, **-dat·ed, -dat·ing.** to grant subinfeudation (to). Also, **sub′in·feud′.** [back formation from SUBINFEUDATION]

sub·in·feu·da·tion (sub′in fyōō dā′shən), *n.* *Feudal Law.* **1.** the granting of a portion of an estate by a feudal tenant to a subtenant. **2.** the tenure established. **3.** the estate or fief so created.

sub·in·feu·da·to·ry (sub′in fyōō′də tōr′ē, -tôr′ē), *n., pl.* **-ries,** *adj.* —*n.* **1.** a person who holds by subinfeudation. —*adj.* **2.** of or pertaining to subinfeudation. [SUBINFEUDA-T(ION) + -ORY[1]]

sub·in·ter·val (sub in′tər vəl), *n.* *Math.* an interval that is a subset of a given interval.

sub·ir·ri·gate (sub ir′ə gāt′), *v.t.*, **-gat·ed, -gat·ing.** to irrigate beneath the surface of the ground. —**sub′ir·ri·ga′tion,** *n.*

su·bi·to (sōō′bi tō′; *It.* sōō′bē tô), *adv.* (as a musical direction) suddenly; abruptly: *subito pianissimo.* [< It < L, abl. sing. neut. of *subitus* sudden = *sub-* SUB- + *-i-* (root of *ire* to go) + *-tus* ptp. suffix]

subj., **1.** subject. **2.** subjective. **3.** subjectively. **4.** subjunctive.

sub·ja·cent (sub jā′sənt), *adj.* **1.** situated or occurring underneath or below; underlying. **2.** forming a basis. **3.** lower than but not directly under something. [< L *subjacent-* (s. of *subjacēns*) underlying (prp. of *subjacēre*) = *sub-* SUB- + *jac-* lie + *-ent-* -ENT] —**sub·ja′cen·cy,** *n.* —**sub·ja′cent·ly,** *adv.*

sub·ject (*n., adj.* sub′jikt; *v.* səb jekt′), *n.* **1.** a matter or topic that forms the basis of a conversation, train of thought, investigation, etc. **2.** a branch of knowledge as a course of study. **3.** a motive, cause, or ground: *a subject for complaint.* **4.** something or someone represented or treated of in a work of art, literary composition, etc. **5.** the principal melodic motive or phrase in a musical composition, esp. a fugue. **6.** a person who owes allegiance to, or is under the domination of, a sovereign or state. **7.** a person who undergoes some form of treatment at the hands of others. **8.** a person, animal, or corpse that undergoes medical or scientific treatment or investigation. **9.** *Gram.* syntactic unit that functions as one of the two main constituents of a simple sentence, the other being the predicate, and that consists of a noun, noun phrase, or noun substitute that often refers to the person or thing performing the action or being in the state expressed by the predicate, as *He* in *He gave notice.* **10.** *Logic.* the term of a proposition concerning which the predicate is affirmed or denied. **11.** *Philos.* **a.** that which thinks, feels, perceives, intends, etc., as contrasted with the objects of thought, feeling, etc. **b.** the self or ego. **c.** *Metaphysics.* that in which qualities or attributes inhere; substance. —*adj.* **12.** being under the domination, control, or influence of something (often fol. by *to*). **13.** being under the dominion, rule, or authority of a sovereign, state, etc. (often fol. by *to*). **14.** open or exposed (usually fol. by *to*): *subject to ridicule.* **15.** dependent upon something (usually fol. by *to*): *His consent is subject to your approval.* **16.** being under the necessity of undergoing something (usually fol. by *to*): *All men are subject to death.* **17.** liable; prone (usually fol. by *to*): *subject to headaches.* —*v.t.* **18.** to bring under domination, control, or influence (usually fol. by *to*). **19.** to cause to undergo the action of something specified; expose (usually fol. by *to*): *to subject metal to intense heat.* **20.** to make liable or vulnerable (usually fol. by *to*): *to subject oneself to ridicule.* **21.** *Obs.* to place beneath something; make subjacent. [< L *subject(us)* thrown under (ptp. of *subicere*), hence as n. *subjectus* (masc.), person of inferior status, *subjectum* (neut.), basis = *sub-* SUB- + *jec-* throw + *-tus* ptp. suffix; r. ME *suget* < OF] —**sub·ject′a·bil′i·ty,** *n.* —**sub·ject′a·ble,** *adj.* —**sub′ject·less,** *adj.* —**sub′ject-like′,** *adj.*

—**Syn. 1, 4.** SUBJECT, THEME, TOPIC are often interchangeable to express the material being considered in a speech or written composition. SUBJECT is a broad word for whatever is treated of in writing, speech, art, etc.: *the subject for discussion.* THEME and TOPIC are usually narrower and apply to some limited or specific part of a general subject. A THEME is often the underlying conception of a discourse or composition, perhaps not put into words but easily recognizable: *The theme of a need for reform runs throughout his work.* A TOPIC is the statement of what is to be treated in a section of a composition: *The topic is treated fully in this section.* **13.** subordinate, subservient. **15.** contingent.

sub·jec·ti·fy (səb jek′tə fī′), *v.t.*, **-fied, -fy·ing.** **1.** to make subjective. **2.** to identify with (a subject) or interpret subjectively. Cf. **objectify.**

sub·jec·tion (səb jek′shən), *n.* **1.** the act of subjecting. **2.** the state or fact of being subjected. [ME < L *subjectiōn-* (s. of *subjectiō*) a throwing under = *subject-* (see SUBJECT) + *-iōn-* -ION]

sub·jec·tive (səb jek′tiv), *adj.* **1.** existing in the mind; belonging to the thinking subject rather than to the object of thought (opposed to *objective*). **2.** pertaining to or on the part of an individual; personal; individual: *a subjective evaluation.* **3.** placing emphasis or reliance on one's own moods, attitudes, opinions, etc. **4.** *Philos.* relating to or of the nature of an object as it is known in the mind as distinct from a thing in itself. **5.** relating to properties or specific conditions of the mind as distinguished from general or universal experience. **6.** pertaining to the subject or substance in which attributes inhere; essential. **7.** *Gram.* **a.** pertaining to or constituting the subject of a sentence. **b.** (in English and certain other languages) noting a case specialized for that use, as *He* in *He hit the ball.* **c.** similar to such a case in meaning. Cf. **nominative** (def. 1). **8.** *Obs.* characteristic of a political subject; submissive. [< L *subjectīv(us)* = *subject(um)* (neut. of *subjectus;* see SUBJECT) + *-īvus* -IVE] —**sub·jec′tive·ly,** *adv.* —**sub·jec·tiv·i·ty** (sub′jek tiv′i tē), **sub·jec′tive·ness,** *n.* —**Syn. 1.** mental. **6.** substantial, inherent.

subjec′tive ide′alism, *Philos.* a doctrine that the world has no existence independent of sensations or ideas.

sub·jec·tiv·ism (səb jek′tə viz′əm), *n.* **1.** *Epistemology.* the doctrine that all knowledge is limited to experiences by the self, and that transcendent knowledge is impossible. **2.** *Ethics.* **a.** any of various theories maintaining that moral judgments are statements concerning the emotional or mental reactions of the individual or the community. **b.** any of several theories holding that certain states of thought or feeling are the highest good. —**sub·jec′tiv·ist,** *n.* —**sub·jec′ti·vis′tic,** *adj.* —**sub·jec′ti·vis′ti·cal·ly,** *adv.*

sub′ject mat′ter, the subject or substance of a discussion, book, writing, etc., as distinguished from its form or style.

sub·join (səb join′), *v.t.* to add at the end, as of something said or written; append. [< MF *subjoin(dre)*]

sub·join·der (səb join′dər), *n.* something subjoined, as an additional comment. [SUB- + *-joinder,* as in *rejoinder*]

sub ju·di·ce (sub jōō′di sē′; *Lat.* sōōb yōō′di ke′), before a judge or court; awaiting judicial determination. [< L]

sub·ju·gate (sub′jə gāt′), *v.t.*, **-gat·ed, -gat·ing.** **1.** to bring under complete control or subjection; conquer; master. **2.** to make submissive or subservient; enslave. [< LL *subjugāt(us)* (ptp. of *subjugāre*) = *sub-* SUB- + *jug(um)* yoke + *-ātus* -ATE[1]] —**sub·ju·ga·ble** (sub′jə gə bəl), *adj.* —**sub′ju·ga′tion,** *n.* —**sub′ju·ga′tor,** *n.* —**Syn. 1, 2.** overcome, vanquish, reduce, overpower.

sub·junc·tion (səb jungk′shən), *n.* **1.** the act of subjoining. **2.** the state of being subjoined. **3.** something subjoined; subjoinder. [< LL *subjunctiōn-* (s. of *subjunctiō*) a subjoining]

sub·junc·tive (səb jungk′tiv), *Gram.* —*adj.* **1.** (in English and certain other languages) noting or pertaining to the mood or mode of a verb that may be used for subjective, doubtful, hypothetical, or grammatically subordinate statements or questions, as the mood of *be* in *if this be treason.* Cf. **imperative** (def. 3), **indicative** (def. 2). —*n.* **2.** the subjunctive mood or mode. **3.** a verb in the subjunctive mood or form. [< LL *subjunctīv(us)* = *subjunct(us)* (ptp. of *subjungere* to subjoin: *sub-* SUB- + *junc-* (< *jung-* join) + *-tus* ptp. suffix) + *-īvus* -IVE] —**sub·junc′tive·ly,** *adv.*

—**Usage.** Speakers of standard English usually use the subjunctive in contrary-to-fact and other subordinate clauses where it applies, as *were* in *If I were king . . .,* and *I wish he were here.* Although the subjunctive seems to be disappearing from the speech of many, its proper use is still a mark of the educated speaker.

sub·king·dom (sub king′dəm, sub′king′-), *n.* *Biol.* a category of related phyla within a kingdom.

sub·lap·sar·i·an·ism (sub′lap sâr′ē ə niz′əm), *n.* *Theol.* infralapsarianism. [< NL *sublapsāri(us)* (L *sub-* SUB- + *laps(us)* a fall + *-ārius* -ARY) + -AN + -ISM] —**sub′lap·sar′i·an,** *adj., n.*

sub·lease (*n.* sub′lēs′; *v.* sub lēs′), *n., v.*, **-leased, -leas·ing.** —*n.* **1.** a lease granted by a person who is himself a lessee of a property, as an apartment. —*v.t.* **2.** to grant a sublease of. **3.** to take or hold a sublease of. —**sub·les·see** (sub′le sē′), *n.* —**sub·les·sor** (sub les′ôr, sub′le sôr′), *n.*

sub·let (*v.* sub let′; *n.* sub′let′, sub let′), *v.*, **-let, -let·ting,**

sub·frac′tion, *n.* **sub·frac′tion·al,** *adj.* **sub·func′tion,** *n.* **sub·i′tem,** *n.*

n. —*v.t.* **1.** to sublease. **2.** to let under a subcontract: *to sublet work.* —*n.* **3.** a sublease. **4.** a property obtained by subleasing, as an apartment.

sub·lieu·ten·ant (sub′lo͞o ten′ənt), *n.* a subordinate lieutenant: not used in U.S. Armed Forces. —**sub′lieu·ten′an·cy,** *n.*

sub·li·mate (*v.* sub′lə māt′; *n., adj.* sub′lə mit, -māt′), *v.,* **-mat·ed, -mat·ing,** *n., adj.* —*v.t.* **1.** *Psychol.* to divert the energy of (a sexual or other biological impulse) from its immediate goal to one of a higher social, moral, or aesthetic nature or use. **2.** *Chem.* **a.** to sublime (a solid substance); extract by this process. **b.** to refine or purify (a substance). **3.** to make nobler or purer. —*v.i.* **4.** to become sublimated; undergo sublimation. —*n.* **5.** *Chem.* **a.** the crystals, deposit, or material obtained when a substance is sublimated. **b.** See **mercuric chloride.** —*adj.* **6.** purified or exalted; sublimated. [< L *sublīmāt(us)* (ptp. of *sublīmāre* to elevate) = *sublīm(is)* SUBLIME + *-ātus* -ATE[1]] —**sub·li·ma·ble** (sub′lə mə bəl), *adj.* —**sub′li·ma′tion,** *n.*

sub·lime (sə blīm′), *adj., n., v.,* **-limed, -lim·ing.** —*adj.* **1.** elevated or lofty in thought, language, etc. **2.** impressing the mind with a sense of grandeur or power; inspiring awe, veneration, etc. **3.** supreme or outstanding: *a sublime dinner.* **4.** *Archaic.* **a.** of lofty bearing. **b.** haughty. **5.** *Archaic.* raised high; high up. —*n.* **6. the sublime, a.** the realm of things that are sublime. **b.** the quality of sublimity. —*v.t.* **7.** to make higher, nobler, or purer. **8.** *Chem.* **a.** to convert (a solid substance) by heat into a vapor, which on cooling condenses again to solid form, without apparent liquefaction. **b.** to cause to be given off by this or some analogous process. —*v.i.* **9.** *Chem.* to volatilize from the solid state to a gas and then condense again as a solid without passing through the liquid state. [< L *sublīm(is)* high = *sub-* SUB- + *-līm-* lintel + *-is* adj. suffix] —**sub·lime′ly,** *adv.* —**Syn. 1.** exalted, noble. **2.** magnificent, superb.

Sublime′ Porte′ (pōrt, pôrt), official name of **Porte.**

sub·lim·i·nal (sub lim′ə nᵊl, -lī′mə-), *adj.* *Psychol.* noting, pertaining to, or employing stimuli that exist or operate below the threshold of consciousness. [SUB- + L *līmin-* (s. of *līmen*) threshold + -AL[1]] —**sub·lim′i·nal·ly,** *adv.*

sub·lim·i·ty (sə blim′i tē), *n., pl.* **-ties** for 2. **1.** the state or quality of being sublime. **2.** a sublime person or thing. [< L *sublīmitāt-* (s. of *sublīmitās*) height]

sub·lin·gual (sub liŋ′gwəl), *Anat.* —*adj.* **1.** situated under the tongue, or on the underside of the tongue. —*n.* **2.** a sublingual gland, artery, or the like. [< NL *sublinguāl(is)*]

sub·lu·nar·y (sub′lo͞o ner′ē, sub lo͞o′nə rē), *adj.* **1.** situated beneath the moon or between the earth and the moon. **2.** characteristic of or pertaining to the earth; terrestrial. **3.** mundane or worldly. Also, **sub·lu·nar** (sub lo͞o′nər). [< LL *sublūnār(is).* See SUB-, LUNAR]

sub·ma·chine′ gun′ (sub′mə shēn′), a lightweight automatic or semiautomatic gun, fired from the shoulder or hip.

sub·mar·gin·al (sub mär′jə nᵊl), *adj.* **1.** *Biol.* near the margin. **2.** below the margin. **3.** (of land) not worth cultivating; unproductive. —**sub·mar′gin·al·ly,** *adv.*

sub·ma·rine (*n.* sub′mə rēn′, sub′mə rēn′; *adj.* sub′mə rēn′), *n., adj.* —*n.* **1.** a ship that can be submerged and navigated under water. **2.** something situated or living under the surface of the sea, as a plant or animal. —*adj.* **3.** situated, occurring, operating, or living under the surface of the sea. **4.** of, pertaining to, or carried on by a submarine or submarines: *submarine warfare.*

sub′marine chas′er, a small patrol vessel designed for military operations against submarines. Also called **subchaser.**

sub·ma·rin·er (sub′mə rē′nər, səb mar′ə nər), *n.* a member of a submarine crew.

sub·max·il·la (sub′mak sil′ə), *n., pl.* **-max·il·lae** (-mak sil′ē). *Anat., Zool.* the lower jaw or lower jawbone.

sub·max·il·lar·y (sub mak′sə ler′ē, sub′mak sil′ə rē), *adj.* of or pertaining to the lower jaw or lower jawbone.

submax′illary gland′, *Anat.* either of a pair of salivary glands located beneath the lower jaw on the sides.

sub·me·di·ant (sub mē′dē ənt), *n.* *Music.* the sixth tone of a scale, being midway between the subdominant and the upper tonic. Also called **superdominant.**

sub·merge (səb mûrj′), *v.,* **-merged, -merg·ing.** —*v.t.* **1.** to put or sink below the surface of water or any other enveloping medium. **2.** to cover or overflow with water; immerse. —*v.i.* **3.** to sink or plunge under water or beneath the surface of any enveloping medium. [< L *submerge(re).* See SUB-, MERGE] —**sub·mer′gence,** *n.* —**Syn. 1.** submerse.

sub·merged (səb mûrjd′), *adj.* **1.** under the surface of water or any other enveloping medium. **2.** destitute; impoverished. **3.** hidden or unknown: *submerged facts.*

sub·mer·gi·ble (səb mûr′jə bəl), *adj.* submersible. —**sub·mer′gi·bil′i·ty,** *n.*

sub·merse (səb mûrs′), *v.t.,* **-mersed, -mers·ing.** to submerge. [< L *submers(us)* (ptp. of *submergere* to SUBMERGE) = *sub-* SUB- + *merg-* dip + *-tus* ptp. suffix] —**sub·mer·sion** (səb mûr′zhən, -shən), *n.*

sub·mersed (səb mûrst′), *adj.* **1.** submerged. **2.** *Bot.* growing under water.

sub·mers·i·ble (səb mûr′sə bəl), *adj.* **1.** capable of being submerged. **2.** capable of functioning while submerged: *a submersible pump.* —*n.* **3.** a ship capable of submerging and operating under water; submarine. —**sub·mers′i·bil′i·ty,** *n.*

sub·me·tal·lic (sub′mə tal′ik), *adj.* somewhat or imperfectly metallic.

sub·mi·cro·scop·ic (sub′mī krə skop′ik), *adj.* too small to be seen through a microscope. Also, **sub′mi·cro·scop′i·cal.** —**sub′mi·cro·scop′i·cal·ly,** *adv.*

sub·min·i·a·ture (sub min′ē ə chər), *n.* **1.** See **subminiature camera.** —*adj.* **2.** noting or pertaining to subminiature cameras, their accessories, and to systems of photography employing them. **3.** smaller than miniature, as certain electronic components.

submin′iature cam′era, a very small, palm-sized, still camera for taking photographs on 16-millimeter or similar film. Also called **subminiature.**

sub·min·i·a·tur·ize (sub min′ē ə chə rīz′), *v.t.,* **-ized, -iz·ing.** to design or manufacture (equipment, esp. electronic equipment) of a greatly reduced scale. —**sub·min′i·a·tur·i·za′tion,** *n.*

sub·miss (səb mis′), *adj.* *Archaic.* submissive. [< L *submiss(us)* (ptp. of *submittere*) = *sub-* SUB- + *mitt-* send + *-tus* ptp. suffix]

sub·mis·sion (səb mish′ən), *n.* **1.** the act or an instance of submitting. **2.** the condition of having submitted. **3.** submissive conduct or attitude. **4.** something that is submitted, as for consideration. **5.** *Law.* an agreement to abide by the decision of an arbitrator or arbitrators. [late ME < L *submissiōn-* (s. of *submissiō*) a letting down]

sub·mis·sive (səb mis′iv), *adj.* **1.** inclined or ready to submit; unresistingly or humbly obedient: *submissive servants.* **2.** marked by or indicating submission: *a submissive reply.* —**sub·mis′sive·ly,** *adv.* —**sub·mis′sive·ness,** *n.* —**Syn. 1.** tractable, compliant, amenable. **2.** resigned, subdued.

sub·mit (səb mit′), *v.,* **-mit·ted, -mit·ting.** —*v.t.* **1.** to give over or yield to the power or authority of another (often used reflexively). **2.** to subject to some kind of treatment or influence. **3.** to present for consideration. **4.** to state or urge with deference; suggest or propose (usually fol. by a clause): *I submit that full proof should be required.* —*v.i.* **5.** to yield oneself to the power or authority of another. **6.** to allow oneself to be subjected to some kind of treatment. **7.** to defer to another's judgment, opinion, decision, etc. [< L *submitt(ere)* (to) lower, reduce, yield = *sub-* SUB- + *mittere* to send] —**sub·mit′ta·ble, sub·mis·si·ble** (səb mis′ə bel), *adj.* —**sub·mit′tal,** *n.* —**sub·mit′ting·ly,** *adv.* —**Syn. 1.** comply, obey, resign. See **yield.** —**Ant. 1.** fight.

sub·mon·tane (sub mon′tān), *adj.* **1.** under or beneath a mountain or mountains. **2.** at or near the foot of mountains. [< LL *submontān(us)* = *sub-* SUB- + *mont-* (s. of *mōns*) mountain + *-ānus* -ANE]

sub·mul·ti·ple (sub mul′tə pəl), *n.* **1.** a number that is contained by another number an integral number of times without a remainder: *The number 3 is a submultiple of 12.* —*adj.* **2.** pertaining to or noting a quantity that is a submultiple.

sub·nor·mal (sub nôr′məl), *adj.* **1.** below the normal; less than or inferior to the normal. **2.** being less than average in any psychological trait, esp. intelligence. —*n.* **3.** a subnormal person. —**sub′nor·mal′i·ty,** *n.*

sub·o·ce·an·ic (sub′ō shē an′ik), *adj.* **1.** occurring or existing below the floor of the ocean: *suboceanic oil.* **2.** of, pertaining to, or existing on the floor of the ocean: *suboceanic plants.*

sub·or·bit·al (sub ôr′bi tᵊl), *adj.* **1.** (of a spacecraft) not in orbit; not achieving an altitude and velocity resulting in a ballistic trajectory circling the earth at least once. **2.** *Anat.* situated below the orbit of the eye.

sub·or·der (sub′ôr′dər), *n.* *Biol.* a category of related families within an order.

sub·or·di·nal (sub ôr′dᵊnᵊl), *adj.* of, pertaining to, or ranked as a suborder.

sub·or·di·nar·y (sub ôr′dᵊner′ē), *n., pl.* **-nar·ies.** *Heraldry.* an ordinary, as a quarter, canton, inescutcheon, or bordure.

sub·or·di·nate (*adj., n.* sə bôr′dᵊnit; *v.* sə bôr′dᵊnāt′), *adj., n., v.,* **-nat·ed, -nat·ing.** —*adj.* **1.** placed in or belonging to a lower order or rank. **2.** of less importance; secondary. **3.** subject to or under the authority of a superior. **4.** subservient or inferior. **5.** subject; dependent. **6.** *Gram.* **a.** acting as a modifier, as *when I finished,* which is subordinate to *They were glad* in *They were glad when I finished.* **b.** noting or pertaining to a subordinating conjunction. **7.** *Obs.* submissive. —*n.* **8.** a subordinate person or thing. —*v.t.* **9.** to place in a lower order or rank. **10.** to make secondary (usually fol. by *to*): *to subordinate work to pleasure.* **11.** to make subject, subservient, or dependent (usually fol. by *to*). [< ML *subordināt(us)* (ptp. of *subordināre*) = L *sub-* SUB- + *ordin-* (s. of *ordō*) rank, order + *-ātus* -ATE[1]] —**sub·or′di·nate·ly,** *adv.* —**sub·or′di·na′tion,** *n.* —**sub·or·di·na·tive** (sə bôr′dᵊnā′tiv, -bôr′dᵊnə-), *adj.* —**Syn. 2.** ancillary. **8.** inferior. —**Ant. 2.** superior; primary.

subor′dinate clause′, *Gram.* a clause that modifies the principal clause, as *when he arrived* in the sentence *I was there when he arrived.*

subor′dinating conjunc′tion, *Gram.* a conjunction introducing a subordinate clause, as *when* in *They were glad when I finished.* Also, **subor′dinate conjunc′tion.** Cf. **coordinating conjunction.**

sub·or·di·na·tion·ism (sə bôr′dᵊnā′shə niz′əm), *n.* *Theol.* the doctrine that the first person of the Holy Trinity is superior to the second and the second to the third. —**sub·or′di·na′tion·ist,** *n.*

sub·orn (sə bôrn′), *v.t.* **1.** to bribe or induce (someone) unlawfully or secretly to perform some misdeed or to commit a crime. **2.** *Law.* to induce (a person, esp. a witness) to give false testimony. [< L *suborn(āre)* (to) instigate secretly = *sub-* SUB- + *ornāre* to equip; see ADORN] —**sub·or·na·tion** (sub′ôr nā′shən), *n.* —**sub·or·na·tive** (sə bôr′nə tiv), *adj.* —**sub·orn′er,** *n.*

Su·bo·ti·ca (*Serbo-Croatian.* so͞o′bô′ti tsä), *n.* a city in NE Yugoslavia. 77,000 (est. 1964). Hungarian, **Szabadka.**

sub·ox·ide (sub ok′sīd, -sid), *n.* *Chem.* the oxide of an element that contains the smallest proportion of oxygen.

sub·phy·lum (sub fī′ləm), *n., pl.* **-la** (-lə). *Biol.* a category of related classes within a phylum. —**sub·phy′lar,** *adj.*

sub·plot (sub′plot′), *n.* a secondary plot, as in a play or novel; underplot. Cf. **counterplot** (def. 2).

sub·poe·na (sə pē′nə, səb-), *n., v.,* **-naed, -na·ing.** *Law.*

sub·mem′ber, *n.*
sub·men′tal, *adj.*
sub′mo·lec′u·lar, *adj.*
sub·nu′cle·us, *n., pl.* **-cle·i, -cle·us·es.**
sub·of′fice, *n.*
sub·of′fi·cer, *n.*
sub′of·fi′cial, *n.*
sub·par′a·graph′, *n.*
sub′part′, *n.*
sub′par·ti′tion, *n.*
sub·pat′tern, *n.*

—*n.* **1.** the usual writ for the summoning of witnesses or the submission of evidence, as records, documents, etc., before a court or other official body. —*v.t.* **2.** to serve with a subpoena. Also, **sub·pe′na.** [ME < L *sub poenā* under penalty]

sub·prin·ci·pal (sub prin′sə pəl, sub′prin′-), *n.* **1.** an assistant or deputy principal. **2.** *Music.* (in an organ) a subbass of the open diapason class.

sub·rep·tion (səb rep′shən), *n.* **1.** *Canon Law.* a concealment of the pertinent facts in a petition, as for dispensation or favor, that in certain cases nullifies the grant. **2.** a fallacious representation or an inference from it. [< L *subreptiōn-* (s. of *subreptiō*) a stealing < *subrept(us)* (ptp. of *subripere*) = *sub-* SUB- + *rep-* (var. of *rap-* seize) + *-tus* ptp. suffix + *-iōn-* -ION] —**sub·rep·ti·tious** (sub′rep tish′əs), *adj.*

sub·ro·gate (sub′rō gāt′), *v.t.*, **-gat·ed, -gat·ing.** **1.** to put into the place of another; substitute for another. **2.** *Civil Law.* to substitute a claim against one person for a claim against another person. [< L *subrogāt(us)* (ptp. of *subrogāre* to nominate (someone) as a substitute) = *sub-* SUB- + *rog-* request + *-ātus* -ATE[1]] —**sub′ro·ga′tion,** *n.*

sub ro·sa (sub rō′zə), confidentially; secretly; privately. [< L: lit., under the rose, from the ancient use of the rose at meetings as a symbol of the sworn confidence of the participants]

sub·rou·tine (sub′rōō tēn′), *n.* *Computer Technol.* a sequence of coded instructions directing a computer to perform a specific operation in the solution of a problem.

sub·scap·u·lar (sub skap′yə lər), *Anat.* —*adj.* **1.** situated beneath or on the deep surface of the scapula, as a muscle. —*n.* **2.** a subscapular muscle, artery, etc. Also, **sub·scap′u·lar′y.**

sub·scribe (səb skrīb′), *v.*, **-scribed, -scrib·ing.** —*v.t.* **1.** to give, pay, or pledge (a sum of money) as a contribution, investment, etc. **2.** to append one's signature or mark to (a document), as in approval or attestation of its contents. **3.** to append, as one's signature, at the bottom of a document or the like. —*v.i.* **4.** to give, pledge, or pay money as a contribution, investment, etc. **5.** to obtain a subscription to a magazine, newspaper, etc. **6.** to append one's signature or mark to a document or the like, as to show approval or attestation of its contents. **7.** to give one's consent; sanction: *I will not subscribe to popular fallacies.* [< L *subscrībe(re)* = *sub-* SUB- + *scrībere* to write] —**sub·scrib′er,** *n.*

sub·script (sub′skript), *adj.* **1.** written below (distinguished from *adscript, superscript*). **2.** inferior (def. 7). —*n.* **3.** inferior (def. 9). [< L *subscrīpt(us)* (ptp. of *subscrībere* to SUBSCRIBE) = *sub-* SUB- + *scrīp-* (var. of *scrīb-* write) + *-tus* ptp. suffix]

sub·scrip·tion (səb skrip′shən), *n.* **1.** a sum of money given or pledged as a contribution, investment, etc. **2.** the right to receive a periodical for a sum paid, usually for an agreed number of issues. **3.** *Chiefly Brit.* the dues paid by a member of a club, society, etc. **4.** a fund raised through sums of money subscribed. **5.** the act of appending one's signature or mark, as to a document. **6.** a signature or mark thus appended. **7.** something written beneath or at the end of a thing. **8.** assent, agreement, or approval. **9.** *Eccles.* assent to or acceptance of a body of principles or doctrines. [< L *subscrīptiōn-* (s. of *subscrīptiō*) a writing beneath. See SUBSCRIPT, -ION] —**sub·scrip·tive** (səb-skrip′tiv), *adj.*

sub·se·quence (sub′sə kwəns), *n.* **1.** the state or fact of being subsequent. **2.** a subsequent occurrence, event, etc.; sequel. [SUBSEQU(ENT) + -ENCE]

sub·se·quent (sub′sə kwənt), *adj.* **1.** occurring or coming later or after: *subsequent events.* **2.** following in order or succession; succeeding: *a subsequent section in a treaty.* [< L *subsequent-* (s. of *subsequēns*) following (prp. of *subsequī*) = *sub-* SUB- + *sequ-* follow + *-ent-* -ENT] —**sub′se·quent·ly,** *adv.*

sub·serve (səb sûrv′), *v.t.*, **-served, -serv·ing.** **1.** to be useful or instrumental in promoting (a purpose, action, etc.). **2.** *Obs.* to serve as a subordinate. [< L *subserv(īre)* = *sub-* SUB- + *servīre* (*serv(us)* servant, slave + *-īre* inf. suffix)]

sub·ser·vi·ent (səb sûr′vē ənt), *adj.* **1.** serving or acting in a subordinate capacity; subordinate. **2.** servile; excessively submissive; obsequious: *subservient persons; subservient conduct.* [< L *subservient-* (s. of *subserviēns*, prp. of *subservīre*. See SUBSERVE, -ENT] —**sub·ser′vi·ence, sub·ser′vi·en·cy,** *n.* —**sub·ser′vi·ent·ly,** *adv.*

sub·set (sub′set′), *n.* **1.** a set that is a part of a larger set. **2.** *Math.* a particular set selected from the elements of a given set.

sub·shrub (sub′shrub′), *n.* a plant consisting of a woody, perennial base with annual, herbaceous shoots. —**sub′shrub′by,** *adj.*

sub·side (səb sīd′), *v.i.*, **-sid·ed, -sid·ing.** **1.** to sink to a low or lower level. **2.** to become quiet, less active, or less violent; abate: *The laughter subsided.* **3.** to sink or fall to the bottom; settle; precipitate. [< L *subsīde(re)* = *sub-* SUB- + *sīdere* to sit, settle; akin to *sedēre* to be seated; see SIT] —**sub·sid·ence** (səb sīd′əns, sub′si dəns), *n.* —**sub·sid′er,** *n.* —**Syn. 1.** decline, descend. **2.** diminish, wane, ebb. —**Ant. 1.** rise. **2.** increase.

sub·sid·i·ar·y (səb sid′ē er′ē), *adj.*, *n.*, *pl.* **-ar·ies.** —*adj.* **1.** serving to assist or supplement; auxiliary; supplementary. **2.** subordinate or secondary: *subsidiary issues.* —*n.* **3.** a subsidiary thing or person. **4.** See **subsidiary company.** [< L *subsidiāri(us)*. See SUBSIDY, -ARY] —**sub·sid·i·ar·i·ly** (səb sid′ē âr′ə lē, -sid′ē er′-), *adv.* —**sub·sid′i·ar′i·ness,** *n.*

subsid′iary coin′, a coin having a value less than that of the monetary unit.

subsid′iary com′pany, a company whose controlling interest is owned by another company.

sub·si·dize (sub′si dīz′), *v.t.*, **-dized, -diz·ing.** **1.** to furnish or aid with a subsidy. **2.** to purchase the assistance of by the payment of a subsidy. **3.** to secure the cooperation of by bribery; buy over. —**sub′si·diz′a·ble,** *adj.* —**sub′si·di·za′tion,** *n.* —**sub′si·diz′er,** *n.*

sub·si·dy (sub′si dē), *n.*, *pl.* **-dies.** **1.** a direct pecuniary aid furnished by a government to a private commercial enterprise, a charity organization, or the like. **2.** a grant or contribution of money. **3.** money formerly granted by the English Parliament to the crown for special needs. [late ME *subsidie* < AF < L *subsidi(um)* auxiliary force, reserve, help = *subsid-* stay behind (see SUBSIDE) + *-ium* n. suffix; see -Y[3]]

sub·sist (səb sist′), *v.i.* **1.** to exist; continue in existence. **2.** to remain alive; live, as on food, resources, etc. **3.** to have existence in, or by reason of, something. **4.** *Philos.* **a.** to have timeless or abstract existence, as a number, relation, etc. **b.** to have existence, esp. independent existence. —*v.t.* **5.** to provide sustenance or support for; maintain. [< L *subsist(ere)* (to) remain = *sub-* SUB- + *sistere* to stand, make stand] —**sub·sist′ing·ly,** *adv.*

sub·sist·ence (səb sis′təns), *n.* **1.** the state or fact of subsisting or existing. **2.** the providing of sustenance or support. **3.** means of supporting life; a living or livelihood. **4.** the source from which food and other items necessary to exist are obtained. **5.** *Philos.* **a.** existence, esp. of an independent entity. **b.** the quality of having timeless or abstract existence. **c.** mode of existence or that by which a substance is individualized. [late ME < LL *subsistentia* = *subsist-* (see SUBSIST) + *-entia* -ENCE]

sub·sist·ent (səb sis′tənt), *adj.* **1.** subsisting, existing, or continuing in existence. **2.** inherent: *subsistent qualities of character.* —*n.* **3.** *Philos.* an existent, as a concept or an object. [< L *subsistent-* (s. of *subsistēns*, prp.). See SUBSIST, -ENT]

sub·so·cial (sub sō′shəl), *adj.* without a definite social structure. —**sub·so′cial·ly,** *adv.*

sub·soil (sub′soil′), *n.* the bed or stratum of earth or earthy material immediately under the surface soil. Also called **undersoil.**

sub·so·lar (sub sō′lər), *adj.* **1.** situated beneath the sun or between the earth and the sun. **2.** between the tropics.

sub·son·ic (sub son′ik), *adj.* **1.** noting or pertaining to a speed less than that of sound in air at the same height above sea level. **2.** infrasonic.

sub·spe·cies (sub spē′shēz, sub′spē′shēz), *n.*, *pl.* **-cies.** a subdivision of a species, esp. a geographical or ecological subdivision. —**sub·spe·cif·ic** (sub′spi sif′ik), *adj.* —**sub′spe·cif′i·cal·ly,** *adv.*

subst., **1.** substantive. **2.** substantively. **3.** substitute.

sub·stance (sub′stəns), *n.* **1.** that of which a thing consists; physical matter or material: *form and substance.* **2.** a species of matter of definite chemical composition: *a metallic substance.* **3.** the subject matter of thought, discourse, study, etc. **4.** substantial or solid character or quality. **5.** consistency; body: *soup without much substance.* **6.** the meaning or gist, as of speech or writing. **7.** something that has separate or independent existence. **8.** *Philos.* **a.** that which exists by itself and in which accidents or attributes inhere. **b.** the essential part of a thing; essence. **9.** possessions, means, or wealth. [ME < L *substantia* essence (lit., that which stands under, i.e., underlies) = *sub-* SUB- + *-stant-* (s. of *stāns*, prp. of *stāre* to stand) + *-ia* -Y[3]; see -ANCE] —**sub′stance·less,** *adj.* —**Syn. 3.** theme, subject. **6.** essence, significance, import.

sub·stand·ard (sub stan′dərd), *adj.* **1.** below standard or less than adequate. **2.** *Linguistics.* noting or pertaining to a dialect or variety of a language or a feature of usage that is often considered by others to mark its user as uneducated or socially inferior.

sub·stan·tial (səb stan′shəl), *adj.* **1.** of ample or considerable amount, quantity, size, etc. **2.** of a corporeal or material nature; tangible. **3.** of solid character or quality; firm, stout, or strong: *a substantial fabric.* **4.** basic or essential; fundamental. **5.** wealthy or influential. **6.** of real worth, value, or effect: *substantial reasons.* **7.** pertaining to the substance, matter, or material of a thing. **8.** of or pertaining to the essence of a thing. —*n.* **9.** something substantial. [ME *substancial* < LL *substantiāl(is)* = L *substanti(a)* SUBSTANCE + *-ālis* -AL[1]] —**sub·stan′ti·al′i·ty, sub·stan′tial·ness,** *n.* —**sub·stan′tial·ly,** *adv.* —**Syn. 3.** stable, sound. **6.** valid, important. —**Ant. 1.** immaterial.

sub·stan·tial·ism (səb stan′shə liz′əm), *n.* *Philos.* the doctrine that substantial noumena exist as a basis for phenomena. —**sub·stan′tial·ist,** *n.*

sub·stan·ti·ate (səb stan′shē āt′), *v.t.*, **-at·ed, -at·ing.** **1.** to establish by proof or competent evidence: *to substantiate a charge.* **2.** to give substantial existence to. **3.** to affirm as having substance; strengthen: *to substantiate a friendship.* [< NL *substantiāt(us)* (ptp. of *substantiāre*). See SUBSTANCE, -ATE[1]] —**sub·stan′ti·a′tion,** *n.* —**sub·stan′ti·a′tive,** *adj.* —**sub·stan′ti·a′tor,** *n.* —**Syn. 1.** prove.

sub·stan·tive (sub′stən tiv), *n.* *Gram.* **1.** a noun. **2.** a pronoun or other word or phrase functioning or inflected like a noun. —*adj.* **3.** *Gram.* **a.** pertaining to substantives. **b.** used in a sentence like a noun: *a substantive adjective.* **c.** expressing existence: *"to be" is a substantive verb.* **4.** having independent existence; independent. **5.** belonging to the real nature or essential part of a thing; essential. **6.** real or actual. **7.** of considerable amount or quantity. **8.** *Law.* pertaining to the rules of right (opposed to *adjective*). **9.** (of dye colors) attaching directly to the material without the aid of a mordant (opposed to *adjective*). [ME < LL *substantīvus* = L *substant-* (s. of *substāns*) standing under (see SUBSTANCE) + *-īvus* -IVE] —**sub·stan·ti·val** (sub′stən tī′vəl), *adj.* —**sub′stan·ti′val·ly,** *adv.* —**sub′stan·tive·ly,** *adv.* —**sub′stan·tive·ness,** *n.*

sub·stan·tiv·ize (sub′stən tə vīz′), *v.t.*, **-ized, -iz·ing.** to use (an adjective, verb, etc.) as a substantive; to convert into a substantive.

sub·sta·tion (sub′stā′shən), *n.* a subsidiary station, esp. a branch of a post office.

sub·stit·u·ent (sub stich′ōō ənt), *n.* **1.** *Chem.* an atom or atomic group that takes the place of another atom or group present in the molecule of the original compound. —*adj.* **2.** having been or capable of being substituted. [< L *substituent-* (s. of *substituēns* (prp.) putting in place of) = *substitu-* (see SUBSTITUTE) + *-ent-* -ENT]

sub′pop·u·la′tion, *n.*	**sub′re′gion,** *n.*	**sub′sat·u·ra′tion,** *n.*	**sub·sec′tion,** *n.*
sub·prov′ince, *n.*	**sub′rule′,** *n.*	**sub·sched′ule,** *n.*	**sub·seg′ment,** *n.*
sub′race′, *n.*	**sub′sale′,** *n.*	**sub′sect′,** *n.*	**sub·se′ries,** *n.*, *pl.* **-ries.**

sub·sti·tute (sub′sti to͞ot′, -tyo͞ot′), *n.*, *v.*, **-tut·ed, -tut·ing,** *adj.* —*n.* **1.** a person or thing acting or serving in place of another. **2.** *Gram.* a word that functions as a replacement for any member of a class of words or constructions, as *do* in *He doesn't know but I do.* **3.** *Naut.* repeater (def. 9). —*v.t.* **4.** to put (a person or thing) in the place of another. **5.** to take the place of; replace. —*v.i.* **6.** to act as a substitute. **7.** *Chem.* to replace one or more elements or groups in a compound by other elements or groups. —*adj.* **8.** of or pertaining to a substitute or to substitutes. **9.** composed of substitutes. [< L *substitūt(us)* (ptp. of *substituere* to put in place of) = *sub-* SUB- + *stitū-*, var. of *statū-* cause to stand (see STATUS) + *-tus* ptp. suffix] —**sub′sti·tut′a·ble,** *adj.* —**sub′sti·tut′er,** *n.* —**sub′sti·tut′ing·ly,** *adv.* —**sub′sti·tu′tion,** *n.* —**sub′sti·tu′tion·al, sub·sti·tu·tion·ar·y** (sub′sti to͞o′shə ner′ē, -tyo͞o′-), *adj.* —**sub′sti·tu′tion·al·ly,** *adv.*

sub·sti·tu·tive (sub′sti to͞o′tiv, -tyo͞o′-), *adj.* **1.** serving as or capable of serving as a substitute. **2.** pertaining to or involving substitution. —**sub′sti·tu′tive·ly,** *adv.*

sub·strate (sub′strāt), *n.* **1.** a substratum. **2.** *Biochem.* the substance acted upon by an enzyme or ferment. **3.** *Electronics.* a supporting material on which a circuit is formed or fabricated. [var. of SUBSTRATUM]

sub·stra·tum (sub strā′təm, -strat′əm, sub′strā′təm, -strat′əm), *n.*, *pl.* **-stra·ta** (-strā′tə, -strat′ə, -strā′tə, -strat′ə). **1.** that which is spread or laid under something else; a stratum or layer lying under another. **2.** something that underlies or serves as a basis or foundation. **3.** *Agric.* the subsoil. **4.** *Biol.* the base or material on which an organism lives. [< NL] —**sub·stra′tive, sub·stra′tal,** *adj.*

sub·struc·tion (sub struk′shən), *n.* a foundation or substructure. [< L *substructiōn-* (s. of *substructiō*) foundation = *substruct(us)*, ptp. of *substruere* to lay a foundation + *-iōn-* -ION] —**sub·struc′tion·al,** *adj.*

sub·struc·ture (sub struk′chər, sub′struk′-), *n.* a structure forming the foundation of a building or other construction. —**sub·struc′tur·al,** *adj.*

sub·sume (səb so͞om′), *v.t.*, **-sumed, -sum·ing.** **1.** to consider (an idea, term, proposition, etc.) as part of a more comprehensive one. **2.** to bring (a case, instance, etc.) under a rule. **3.** to take up into a more inclusive classification. [< NL *subsume(re)* = L *sub-* SUB- + *sumere* to take; see RESUME] —**sub·sum′a·ble,** *adj.*

sub·sump·tion (səb sump′shən), *n.* **1.** the act of subsuming. **2.** the state of being subsumed. **3.** something that is subsumed. **4.** a proposition subsumed under another. [< NL *subsumptiōn-* (s. of *subsumptiō*) a subjoining = *sub-sumpt(us)*, ptp. of *subsumere* to SUBSUME + *-iōn-* -ION] —**sub·sump′tive,** *adj.*

sub·tan·gent (sub tan′jənt), *n.* *Geom.* the part of the *x*-axis cut off between the ordinate of a given point of a curve and the tangent at that point.

sub·teen (sub′tēn′), *n.* a young person approaching the teens or adolescence.

sub·tem·per·ate (sub tem′pər it), *adj.* of, pertaining to, or occurring in the colder parts of the Temperate Zone.

sub·ten·ant (sub ten′ənt), *n.* a person who rents from a tenant. —**sub·ten′an·cy,** *n.*

sub·tend (səb tend′, sub-), *v.t.* **1.** *Geom.* to extend under or be opposite to: *a chord subtending an arc.* **2.** *Bot.* (of a leaf, bract, etc.) to enclose or embrace (a flower or the like) in its axil. **3.** to form or mark the outline or boundary of. [< L *subtend(ere)* (to) stretch beneath = *sub-* SUB- + *tendere* to stretch; see TEND[1]]

B A C
Chord AC subtends arc ABC

sub·ten·ure (sub ten′yər), *n.* the tenancy of a subtenant.

subter-, a formal element occurring in loan words from Latin (*subterfuge*): used, with the meaning "under," "below," in the formation of compound words (*subternatural*). [< L *subter-* below, underhand, in secret < *subter* (adv., prep.) underneath = *sub-* SUB- + *-ter* comp. suffix (see FURTHER)]

sub·ter·fuge (sub′tər fyo͞oj′), *n.* an artifice or expedient used to evade a rule, escape a consequence, hide something, etc. [< LL *subterfug(ium)* = L *subterfug(ere)* (to) evade (*subter-* SUBTER- + *fugere* to flee) + *-ium* n. suffix]

sub·ter·nat·u·ral (sub′tər nach′ər əl, -nach′rəl), *adj.* below what is natural; less than natural.

sub·ter·rane (sub′tə rān′, sub′tə rān′), *n.* a cave or subterranean room. Also, **sub′ter·rain′, sub·ter·rene** (sub′tə-rēn′, sub′tə rēn′). [< L *subterrān(eus)* = *sub-* SUB- + *terr(a)* earth + *-āneus* composite adj. suffix (*-ān(us)* -ANE + *-eus* -EOUS)]

sub·ter·ra·ne·an (sub′tə rā′nē ən), *adj.* Also, **sub′ter-ra′ne·ous.** **1.** existing, situated, or operating below the surface of the earth; underground. **2.** existing or operating out of sight or secretly; hidden or secret. —*n.* **3.** a person or thing that is subterranean. **4.** a subterrane. [< L *subterrāne(us)* (see SUBTERRANE) + -AN] —**sub′ter·ra′ne-an·ly, sub′ter·ra′ne·ous·ly,** *adv.*

sub·ter·res·tri·al (sub′tə res′trē əl), *adj.* subterranean.

sub·tile (sut′əl, sub′til), *adj.* *Archaic.* subtle. [ME < L *subtīlis* fine (lit., finely woven) = *sub-* SUB- + *tēl(a)* web (< *texla; see TEXT) + *-is* adj. suffix] —**sub′tile·ly,** *adv.* —**sub′tile·ness,** *n.*

sub·til·ise (sut′əlīz′, sub′tə līz′), *v.t.*, *v.i.*, **-ised, -is·ing.** *Chiefly Brit.* subtilize. —**sub′til·i·sa′tion,** *n.* —**sub′til-is′er,** *n.*

sub·til·ize (sut′əlīz′, sub′tə līz′), *v.*, **-ized, -iz·ing.** —*v.t.* **1.** to elevate in character; sublimate. **2.** to make (the mind, senses, etc.) keen or discerning; sharpen. **3.** to introduce subtleties into or argue subtly about. **4.** to make thin, rare, or more fluid or volatile; refine. —*v.i.* **5.** to make subtle distinctions or to argue subtly. [< ML *subtīliz(āre)* = *subtīl(is)* SUBTLE + *-izāre* -IZE] —**sub′til·i·za′tion,** *n.* —**sub′til·iz′er,** *n.*

sub·til·ty (sut′əl tē, sub′til-), *n.*, *pl.* **-ties.** *Archaic.* subtlety. Also, **sub·til·i·ty** (sub til′i tē).

sub·ti·tle (sub′tīt′əl), *n.*, *v.*, **-tled, -tling.** —*n.* **1.** a secondary or subordinate title of a literary work, usually of explanatory character. **2.** a repetition of the leading words in the full title of a book at the head of the first page of text. **3.** *Motion Pictures.* **a.** the text of dialogue, speeches, etc., translated into another language and projected on the lower part of the screen. **b.** (in silent motion pictures) a title or caption. —*v.t.* **4.** to give a subtitle to. —**sub·tit·u·lar** (sub-tich′ə lər, -tit′yə-), *adj.*

sub·tle (sut′əl), *adj.* **1.** thin, tenuous, or rarefied, as a fluid or an odor. **2.** fine or delicate in meaning or intent; difficult to perceive or understand: *subtle irony.* **3.** delicate or faint and mysterious: *a subtle smile.* **4.** characterized by or requiring mental acuteness, penetration or discernment: *a subtle understanding; a subtle philosophy.* **5.** cunning, wily, or crafty: *a subtle liar.* **6.** insidious in operation: *subtle poison.* **7.** skillful, clever, or ingenious: *a subtle painter.* [ME *sotil* < OF < L *subtīl(is)* SUBTILE (mute *b* of mod. sp. < L)] —**sub′tle·ness,** *n.* —**sub′tly,** *adv.*

sub·tle·ty (sut′əl tē), *n.*, *pl.* **-ties.** **1.** the state or quality of being subtle. **2.** delicacy or nicety of character or meaning; acuteness or penetration of mind; delicacy of discrimination. **3.** a fine-drawn distinction; refinement of reasoning. **4.** something subtle. [ME *sutilte* < OF < L *subtīlitāt-* (s. of *subtīlitās*) fineness = *subtīl(is)* SUBTILE + *-tāt-* -TY[2]]

sub·ton·ic (sub ton′ik), *n.* the seventh tone of a scale, being the next below the upper tonic.

sub·top·ic (sub′top′ik, sub top′-), *n.* a topic that is included within another topic.

sub·tor·rid (sub tôr′id, -tor′-), *adj.* subtropical.

sub·to·tal (sub tōt′əl, sub′tōt′-), *n.*, *adj.*, *v.*, **-taled, -tal·ing** or (*esp. Brit.*) **-talled, -tal·ling.** —*n.* **1.** the total of a part of a group or column of figures, as in an accounting statement. —*adj.* **2.** somewhat less than complete; not total. —*v.t.* **3.** to determine a subtotal for (a column). —*v.i.* **4.** to determine a subtotal.

sub·tract (səb trakt′), *v.t.* **1.** to withdraw or take away, as a part from a whole. **2.** *Math.* to take (one number or quantity) from another; deduct. —*v.i.* **3.** to take away something or a part, as from a whole. [< L *subtract(us)* (ptp. of *subtrahere* to draw away from underneath) = *sub-* SUB- + *trac-* (pt., ptp. s. of *trahere* to draw) + *-tus* ptp. suffix] —**sub·tract′er,** *n.* —**Syn. 1, 3.** deduct. —**Ant. 1–3.** add.

sub·trac·tion (səb trak′shən), *n.* **1.** the act or an instance of subtracting. **2.** *Math.* the operation or process of finding the difference between two numbers or quantities, denoted by a minus sign (−). [late ME < LL *subtractiōn-* (s. of *subtractiō*) a withdrawing]

sub·trac·tive (səb trak′tiv), *adj.* **1.** tending to subtract; having power to subtract. **2.** *Math.* (of a quantity) that is to be subtracted; having the minus sign (−).

sub·tra·hend (sub′trə hend′), *n.* *Math.* a number that is subtracted from another. Cf. **minuend.** [< L *subtrahen-d(um)*, neut. ger. of *subtrahere;* see SUBTRACT]

sub·treas·ur·y (sub trezh′ə rē, sub′trezh′-), *n.*, *pl.* **-ur·ies.** a subordinate or branch treasury. —**sub·treas′-ur·er,** *n.* —**sub·treas′ur·er·ship′,** *n.*

sub·trop·i·cal (sub trop′i kəl), *adj.* **1.** bordering on the tropics; nearly tropical. **2.** pertaining to or occurring in a region between tropical and temperate; subtorrid; semitropical.

sub·trop·ics (sub trop′iks), *n.pl.* subtropical regions.

sub·type (sub′tīp′), *n.* **1.** a subordinate type. **2.** a special type included within a more general type. —**sub·typ·i·cal** (sub-tip′i kəl), *adj.*

su·bu·late (so͞o′byə lit, -lāt′), *adj.* **1.** awl-shaped. **2.** *Bot., Zool.* slender, more or less cylindrical, and tapering to a point. [< NL *subulat(us)* = L *sūbul(a)* awl + *-ātus* -ATE[1]]

Subulate leaves

sub·urb (sub′ûrb), *n.* **1.** a district lying immediately outside a city or town, esp. a smaller residential community. **2.** an outlying part. [ME < L *suburb(ium)* = *sub-* SUB- + *urb(s)* city + *-ium* n. suffix] —**sub′urbed,** *adj.*

sub·ur·ban (sə bûr′bən), *adj.* **1.** pertaining to, inhabiting, or being in a suburb or the suburbs of a city or town. **2.** characteristic of a suburb or suburbs. —*n.* **3.** a suburbanite. **4.** See **station wagon.** [< L *suburbān(us)*]

sub·ur·ban·ite (sə bûr′bə nīt′), *n.* a person who lives in a suburb of a city or large town.

sub·ur·bi·a (sə bûr′bē ə), *n.* **1.** suburbs or suburbanites collectively. **2.** the social or cultural aspects of life in suburbs.

sub·ur·bi·car·i·an (sə bûr′bə kâr′ē ən), *adj.* **1.** being near the city of Rome. **2.** designating any of the dioceses surrounding the city of Rome. [< LL *suburbicāri(us)* (L *suburb(ium)* SUBURB + *-ic(us)* -IC + *-āri(us)* -ARY) + -AN]

sub·vene (səb vēn′), *v.i.*, **-vened, -ven·ing.** to arrive or occur as a support or relief. [< L *subven(īre)* = *sub-* SUB- + *venīre* to come]

sub·ven·tion (səb ven′shən), *n.* **1.** a grant of money, as by a government or some other authority, in aid or support of some institution or undertaking, esp. in connection with science or the arts. **2.** the furnishing of aid or relief. [< LL *subventiōn-* (s. of *subventiō*) official grant in aid = *subvent(us)* (ptp. of *subvenīre: subven-* (see SUBVENE) + *-tus* ptp. suffix) + *-iōn-* -ION] —**sub·ven′tion·ar′y,** *adj.*

sub ver·bo (so͝ob wer′bō; *Eng.* sub vûr′bō), *Latin.* (used as a direction to a reference) under the word or heading.

sub·ver·sion (səb vûr′zhən, -shən), *n.* **1.** the act or an instance of subverting. **2.** the state of being subverted; destruction. **3.** something that subverts or overthrows. [late ME < LL *subversiōn-* (s. of *subversiō*) an overthrowing]

sub·ver·sive (səb vûr′siv), *adj.* **1.** tending to subvert or advocating subversion, esp. in an attempt to overthrow or cause the destruction of an established or legally constituted government. —*n.* **2.** a person who adopts subversive principles or policies. *All subversives had to leave the country.* [<

sub·sur′face, *adj.* **sub·ter′ri·to′ry,** *n.*, *pl.* **-ries.** **sub′tribe′,** *n.* **sub·u′nit,** *n.*
sub′sys′tem, *n.* **sub·tu′nic,** *n.* **sub′va·ri′e·ty,** *n.*, *pl.* **-ties.**

L *subvers(us)* (ptp. of *subvertere* to SUBVERT) + -IVE] —**sub·ver′sive·ly,** *adv.* —**sub·ver′sive·ness,** *n.*

sub·vert (səb vûrt′), *v.t.* **1.** to overthrow (something established or existing). **2.** to cause the downfall, ruin, or destruction of. **3.** to undermine the principles of; corrupt. [ME *subvert(en)* < L *subvertere* to overthrow = *sub-* SUB- + *vertere* to turn] —**sub·vert′er,** *n.*

sub·vo·cal (sub vō′kəl), *adj.* mentally formulated as words, esp. without vocalization.

sub vo·ce (so͝ob wō′ke; *Eng.* sub vō′sē), *Latin.* (used as a direction to a reference) under the specified word. [lit., under the voice, i.e., utterance]

sub·way (sub′wā′), *n.* **1.** Also called, *Brit.,* **tube, underground.** *U.S.* an underground electric railroad, usually in a large city. **2.** *Chiefly Brit.* a short tunnel or underground passageway for pedestrians, automobiles, etc.; underpass.

sub-ze·ro (sub zēr′ō), *adj.* **1.** indicating or recording lower than zero on some scale, esp. on the Fahrenheit scale. **2.** characterized by or appropriate for sub-zero temperatures.

suc-, var. of **sub-** before *c: succeed.*

suc·cah (so͞o kä′; *Eng.* so͝ok′ə), *n., pl.* **suc·coth** (so͞o kôt′), *Eng.* **suc·cahs.** *Hebrew.* sukkah.

suc·ce·da·ne·um (suk′si dā′nē əm), *n., pl.* **-ne·a** (-nē ə). a substitute. [< L, neut. sing. of *succēdāneus* = *suc-* SUC- + *cēd(ere)* (to) come, go + *-āneus* composite adj. suffix (*-ān(us)* -AN + *-eus* -EOUS)] —**suc′ce·da′ne·ous,** *adj.*

suc·ceed (sək sēd′), *v.i.* **1.** to happen or terminate according to desire; turn out successfully; have the desired result: *Our efforts succeeded.* **2.** to thrive, prosper, grow, or the like: *Grass will not succeed in this dry soil.* **3.** to accomplish what is attempted or intended: *We succeeded in our efforts to start the car.* **4.** to attain success in some popularly recognized form, as wealth or standing. **5.** to follow or replace another by descent, election, appointment, etc. (often fol. by *to*). **6.** to come next after something else in an order or series. —*v.t.* **7.** to come after and take the place of, as in an office or estate. **8.** to come next after in an order or series, or in the course of events; follow. [late ME < L *succēde(re)* (to) go (from) under, follow, prosper = *suc-* SUC- + *cēdere* to go (see CEDE)] —**suc·ceed′a·ble,** *adj.* —**suc·ceed′er,** *n.* —**suc·ceed′ing·ly,** *adv.* —**Syn. 5.** See **follow.** —**Ant. 1, 3, 4.** fail. **8.** precede.

suc·cès d'es·time (syk se des tēm′), *French.* success won by reason of critical respect rather than by popularity.

suc·cess (sək ses′), *n.* **1.** the favorable or prosperous termination of attempts or endeavors. **2.** the attainment of wealth, position, honors, or the like. **3.** a successful performance or achievement. **4.** a thing or a person that is successful. **5.** *Obs.* outcome. [< L *success(us)* (n.) < ptp. of *succēdere* (see SUCCEED) = *suc-* SUC- + *cessus* (*ced-* come, go + *-tus* ptp. suffix)] —**suc·cess′less,** *adj.*

suc·cess·ful (sək ses′fəl), *adj.* **1.** achieving or having achieved success. **2.** having attained wealth, position, honors, or the like. **3.** resulting in or attended with success. —**suc·cess′ful·ly,** *adv.* —**suc·cess′ful·ness,** *n.*

suc·ces·sion (sək sesh′ən), *n.* **1.** the coming of one person or thing after another in order, sequence, or in the course of events. **2.** a number of persons or things following one another in order or sequence. **3.** the right, act, or process by which one person succeeds to the office, rank, estate, or the like, of another. **4.** the order or line of those entitled to succeed one another. **5.** the descent or transmission of a throne, dignity, estate, or the like. [ME < L *successiōn-* (s. of *successiō*) a following (someone) in office. See SUCCESS, -ION] —**suc·ces′sion·al,** *adj.* —**suc·ces′sion·al·ly,** *adv.* —**Syn. 2.** See **series.**

suc·ces·sive (sək ses′iv), *adj.* **1.** following in order or in uninterrupted sequence; consecutive: *three successive days.* **2.** following another in a regular sequence. **3.** characterized by or involving succession. [< ML *successīv(us)*] —**suc·ces′sive·ly,** *adv.* —**suc·ces′sive·ness,** *n.*

suc·ces·sor (sək ses′ər), *n.* **1.** a person or thing that succeeds or follows. **2.** a person who succeeds another in an office, position, or the like. [< L = *success-* (see SUCCESS) + *-or* -OR[2]; r. ME *successour* < AF] —**suc·ces′sor·al,** *adj.*

suc·cinct (sək singkt′), *adj.* **1.** expressed in few words; concise; terse. **2.** characterized by conciseness or verbal brevity. **3.** compressed into a small area, scope, or compass. **4.** *Archaic.* **a.** drawn up, as by a girdle. **b.** close-fitting. **c.** encircled, as by a girdle. [< L *succinct(us)* girt from below, tucked up, ready, concise = *suc-* SUC- + *cinctus* (ptp.) (*cing-* gird + *-tus* ptp. suffix)] —**suc·cinct′ly,** *adv.* —**suc·cinct′ness,** *n.*

suc·cin·ic (sək sin′ik), *adj.* **1.** pertaining to or obtained from amber. **2.** *Chem.* of or derived from succinic acid. [< L *succin(um)* amber + -IC; cf. F *succinique*]

succin′ic ac′id, *Chem.* a solid, $HOOC(CH_2)_2COOH$, used chiefly in the manufacture of lacquers, dyes, and perfume.

suc·cor (suk′ər), *n.* **1.** help; relief; aid; assistance. **2.** a person or thing that gives help, relief, aid, etc. —*v.t.* **3.** to help or relieve in difficulty, need, or distress; aid; assist. Also, *esp. Brit.,* **suc′cour.** [ME *sucur(en)* (v.) < OF *sucurir(r)* < L *succurrere* to go beneath, run to help = *suc-* SUC- + *currere* to run (see CURRENT)] —**suc′cor·a·ble;** *esp. Brit.,* **suc′cour·a·ble,** *adj.* —**suc′cor·er;** *esp. Brit.,* **suc′cour·er,** *n.* —**Syn.** support. See **help.**

suc·co·ry (suk′ə rē), *n., pl.* **-ries.** chicory. [< MLG *suckerie,* perh. < ML, b. L *succ(us)* juice + *(cich)orium* (< Gk *kichōreia* (pl.) CHICORY)]

suc·co·tash (suk′ə tash′), *n.* a cooked dish of kernels of corn mixed with shell beans, esp. lima beans. [< Narragansett *msiquatash,* lit., fragments]

suc·coth (so͞o kôt′), *n. Hebrew.* a pl. of **succah.**

Suc·coth (so͝ok′əs; *Heb.* so͞o kôt′), *n. Judaism.* Sukkoth.

suc·cu·ba (suk′yə bə), *n.* a succubus. [< LL: strumpet = *suc-* SUC- + *cub-* (s. of *cubāre* to lie down) + *-a* fem. suffix]

suc·cu·bus (suk′yə bəs), *n., pl.* **-bi** (-bī′). **1.** a demon in female form, said to have sexual intercourse with men in their sleep. Cf. **incubus** (def. 1). **2.** any demon or evil spirit. **3.** a strumpet or prostitute. [late ME < ML, var. of SUCCUBA with masc. inflexion (< *incubus* INCUBUS) but unchanged meaning]

suc·cu·lent (suk′yə lənt), *adj.* **1.** full of juice; juicy. **2.** rich in desirable qualities. **3.** affording mental nourishment. **4.** (of a plant) having fleshy and juicy tissues. [< LL *succulent(us)* = *succu(s)* (var. of *sūcus*) juice + *-lentus* adj. suffix] —**suc′cu·lence, suc′cu·len·cy,** *n.* —**suc′cu·lent·ly,** *adv.*

suc·cumb (sə kum′), *v.i.* **1.** to give way to superior force; yield. **2.** to yield to disease, wounds, old age, etc.; die. [late ME < L *succumb(ere)* = *suc-* SUC- + *-cumbere,* var. of *cubāre* to lie down] —**suc·cumb′er,** *n.*

suc·cuss (sə kus′), *v.t.* **1.** to shake up; shake. **2.** *Med.* to shake (a patient) in order to determine if a fluid is present in the thorax or elsewhere. [< L *succuss(us)* tossed up (ptp. of *succutere*) = *suc-* SUC- + *cut-* (s. of *-cutere,* var. of *quatere* to shake) + *-tus* ptp. suffix]

suc·cus·sion (sə kush′ən), *n.* the act of succussing. [< L *succussiōn-* (s. of *succussiō*) a tossing up = *successūs(us)* (see SUCCUSS) + *-iōn* -ION] —**suc·cus·sive** (sə kus′iv), *adj.*

such (such), *adj.* **1.** of the kind, character, degree, extent, etc., of that or those indicated or implied: *Such a man is dangerous.* **2.** like or similar: *tea, coffee, and such commodities.* **3.** (used preceding an attributive adjective) so or in such a manner or degree: *such terrible deeds.* **4.** (used with omission of an indication or comparison) of so extreme a kind: *He is such a liar.* **5.** being the person or thing or the persons or things indicated. **6.** definite but not specified: *Allow such an amount for food and rent, and the rest for other things.* —*pron.* **7.** such a person or thing or such persons or things: *kings, princes, and such.* **8.** someone or something indicated or exemplified. **9. as such.** See **as**[1] (def. 22). **10. such as, a.** of the kind specified: *A plan such as you propose will never succeed.* **b.** for example. [ME, OE *swilc;* c. G *solch,* Icel *slīkr,* Goth *swaleiks* = *swa* so + *leiks* LIKE[1]]

such·like (such′līk′), *adj.* **1.** of any such kind; similar. —*pron.* **2.** persons or things of such a kind. [late ME]

such·ness (such′nis). *n.* a fundamental, intrinsic, or characteristic quality or condition: *seraphic indifference to the suchness of his surroundings.*

suck (suk), *v.t.* **1.** to draw into the mouth by action of the lips and tongue, thereby producing a partial vacuum. **2.** to draw (water, moisture, air, etc.) by or as if by suction. **3.** to apply the lips or mouth to and draw upon by producing a partial vacuum, esp. for extracting fluid contents: *to suck an orange.* **4.** to put into the mouth and draw upon: *Stop sucking your thumb!* **5.** to take into the mouth and dissolve by the action of the tongue, saliva, etc.: *to suck a piece o candy.* —*v.i.* **6.** to draw something in by producing a partial vacuum in the mouth, esp. to draw milk from the breast. **7.** to draw or be drawn by or as if by suction. **8.** (of a pump) to draw air instead of water, as when the water is low or a valve is defective. **9. suck in,** *Slang.* to deceive; cheat; defraud. **10. suck off,** *Slang* (*usually vulgar*). to perform fellatio on. —*n.* **11.** the act or an instance of sucking. **12.** a sucking force. **13.** the sound produced by sucking. **14.** that which is sucked, as nourishment drawn from the breast. **15.** a whirlpool. [ME *souk(en),* OE *sūcan;* c. L. *sūgere;* akin to SOAK] —**suck′less,** *adj.*

suck·er (suk′ər), *n.* **1.** a person or thing that sucks. **2.** *Informal.* a person easily cheated, deceived, or imposed upon. **3.** an infant or a young animal that is suckled, esp. a suckling pig. **4.** a part or organ of an animal adapted for sucking nourishment, or for adhering to an object as by suction. **5.** any of several fresh-water, mostly North American cyprinoid fishes of the family *Catostomidae,* often used for food. **6.** *Informal.* a lollipop. **7.** the piston of a pump that works by suction, or the valve of such a piston. **8.** a pipe or tube through which something is drawn or sucked. **9.** *Bot.* a shoot rising from a subterranean stem or root. —*v.t.* **10.** to strip off suckers or shoots from (a plant). —*v.i.* **11.** to send out suckers or shoots, as a plant. [late ME]

Sucker, *Catostomus commersoni* (Length to 2¼ ft.)

suck·er·fish (suk′ər fish′), *n., pl.* **-fish·es,** (*esp. collectively*) **-fish.** remora (def. 1).

suck·fish (suk′fish′), *n., pl.* (*esp. collectively*) **-fish,** (*esp. referring to two or more kinds or species*) **-fish·es.** remora (def. 1).

suck′ing louse′. See under **louse** (def. 1).

suck·le (suk′əl), *v.,* **-led, -ling.** —*v.t.* **1.** to nurse at the breast. **2.** to nourish or bring up. **3.** to put to suck. —*v.i.* **4.** to suck at the breast. [late ME; see SUCK, -LE]

suck·ling (suk′ling), *n.* an infant or a young animal that is not yet weaned.

Suck·ling (suk′ling), *n.* **Sir John,** 1609–42, English poet.

sucr-, a combining form meaning "sugar": *sucrose.* [< F *sucr(e)* SUGAR]

su·crase (so͞o′krās), *n. Biochem.* invertase.

Su·cre (so͞o′kre), *n.* **1. An·to·nio Jo·sé de** (än tô′nyô hô se′ the), 1793–1830, Venezuelan general and South American liberator: 1st president of Bolivia 1826–28. **2.** a city in and the nominal capital of Bolivia, in the S part. 57,090. **3.** (*l.c.*) a cupronickel coin and monetary unit of Ecuador, equal to 100 centavos. *Abbr.:* S.

su·crose (so͞o′krōs), *n. Chem.* a crystalline disaccharide, $C_{12}H_{22}O_{11}$, the sugar obtained from the sugar cane, the sugar beet, and sorghum, and forming the greater part of maple sugar; sugar.

suc·tion (suk′shən), *n.* **1.** the act, process, or condition of sucking. **2.** the force that, by a pressure differential, attracts a substance to the region of lower pressure. **3.** the act or process of producing such a force. [< LL *suctiōn-* (s. of *suctiō*) a sucking = L *suct(us)* (ptp. of *sūgere: sug-* + *-tus* ptp. suffix) + *-iōn-* -ION] —**suc′tion·al,** *adj.*

suc′tion pump′, a pump for raising water or other fluids by suction, consisting essentially of a vertical cylinder in which a piston works up and down.

suc′tion stop′, *Phonet.* click (def. 3).

suc·to·ri·al (suk tōr′ē əl, -tôr′-), *adj.* **1.** adapted for sucking or suction, as an organ; functioning as a sucker for imbibing or adhering. **2.** having sucking organs; imbibing or adhering by suckers. [< NL *suctōri(us)* (L *suct(us)* (see SUCTION) + *-ōrius* -ORY[1]) + -AL[1]]

Su·dan (so͞o dan′), *n.* **1.** French, **Soudan.** a region in N Africa, S of the Sahara and Libyan deserts, extending from the Atlantic to the Red Sea. **2. Democratic Republic of the.** Formerly, **Anglo-Egyptian Sudan.** a republic in NE Africa, S of Egypt and bordering on the Red Sea: a former condominium of Egypt and Great Britain. 16,400,000; 967,500 sq. mi. *Cap.:* Khartoum.

Su·da·nese (so͞od/ᵊnēs/, -ᵊnēz/), *n., pl.* **-nese,** *adj.* —*n.* **1.** a native or inhabitant of Sudan. —*adj.* **2.** of or pertaining to Sudan or its inhabitants. Also, **Soudanese.**

Sudan/ grass/, a sorghum, *Sorghum vulgare sudanensis,* introduced into the U.S. from Africa, grown for hay and pasture.

Su·dan·ic (so͞o dan/ik), *adj.* **1.** belonging to a residual category in former classifications of languages that consists of the non-Bantu, non-Hamitic languages of the Sudan. These have since been classified into families. **2.** of or pertaining to the Sudan or the Sudanese.

su·dar·i·um (so͞o dâr/ē əm), *n., pl.* **-dar·i·a** (-dâr/ē ə). (in ancient Rome) a cloth, usually of linen, for wiping the face; handkerchief. [< L = *sūd-* (s. of *sūdāre* to sweat) + *-ārium* -ARY]

su·da·to·ri·um (so͞o/də tōr/ē əm, -tôr/-), *n., pl.* **-to·ri·a** (-tōr/ē ə, -tôr/-). a hot-air bath for inducing sweating. [< L = *sūdāt(us)* (ptp. of *sūdāre* to sweat) + *-ōrium* -ORY[2]]

su·da·to·ry (so͞o/də tōr/ē, -tôr/ē), *adj., n., pl.* **-ries.** —*adj.* **1.** pertaining to or causing sweating. **2.** pertaining to a sudatorium. —*n.* **3.** a sudatorium. [< L *sūdātōri(us)* = *sūdāt(us)* (see SUDATORIUM) + *-ōrius* -ORY[1]]

Sud·bur·y (sud/ber/ē, -bə rē, -brē), *n.* a city in S Ontario, in S Canada. 80,120 (1961).

sudd (sud), *n.* (in the White Nile) floating vegetable matter that often obstructs navigation. [< Ar: lit., an obstructing]

sud·den (sud/ᵊn), *adj.* **1.** happening, coming, made, or done quickly, without warning, or unexpectedly: *a sudden attack; a sudden smile.* **2.** occurring without transition from the previous form, state, etc.; abrupt: *a sudden turn; a sudden slope.* **3.** *Archaic.* **a.** quickly made or provided. **b.** impetuous; rash. —*adv.* **4.** *Poetic.* suddenly. —*n.* **5.** *Obs.* an unexpected occasion or occurrence. **6. all of a sudden,** without warning; unexpectedly; suddenly. [< ME *sodain* < MF < L *subitān(eus)* going or coming stealthily = *subit(us)* sudden, taking by surprise (see SUBITO) + *-āneus* adj. suffix (*-ān(us)* -AN + *-eus* -EOUS)] —**sud/den·ly,** *adv.* —**sud/den·ness,** *n.* —**Syn. 1, 2.** unforeseen, unanticipated. SUDDEN, UNEXPECTED, ABRUPT describe acts, events, or conditions for which there has been no preparation or gradual approach. SUDDEN refers to the quickness of an occurrence, although the event may have been expected; it can be interchangeable with ABRUPT: *a sudden change in the weather.* UNEXPECTED emphasizes the lack of preparedness for what occurs or appears: *an unexpected crisis.* ABRUPT characterizes something involving a swift adjustment; the effect is often unpleasant, unfavorable, or the cause of dismay: *The road came to an abrupt end.* —**Ant. 1, 2.** gradual, foreseen.

sud/den death/, *Sports.* an overtime period in which a tied contest is won and play is stopped immediately after one of the contestants scores, as in football, or goes ahead, in a specified period or unit of play, as in basketball.

Su·der·mann (zo͞o/dər män/), *n.* **Her·mann** (her/män), 1857–1928, German dramatist and novelist.

Su·de·ten (so͞o dāt/ᵊn; *Ger.* zo͞o dāt/ᵊn), *n.* **1.** Also, **Su·de·tes** (so͞o dē/tēz). a mountain range in E central Europe, extending along the N boundary of Czechoslovakia between the Oder and Neisse rivers. **2.** a native or inhabitant of the Sudetenland. **3.** Sudetenland.

Su·de·ten·land (so͞o dāt/ᵊn land/; *Ger.* zo͞o dāt/ᵊn länt/), *n.* a mountainous region in N and NW Czechoslovakia, including the Sudeten and the Erz Gebirge: annexed by Germany 1938; returned to Czechoslovakia 1945. Also called **Sudeten.**

su·dor·if·er·ous (so͞o/də rif/ər əs), *adj.* bearing or secreting sweat. [< LL *sūdōrifer* (L *sūdor* sweat; see -I-, -FER) + -OUS] —**su/dor·if/er·ous·ness,** *n.*

su·dor·if·ic (so͞o/də rif/ik), *adj.* **1.** causing sweat; diaphoretic. —*n.* **2.** a sudorific agent. [< NL *sūdōrific(us)* (L *sūdor* sweat; see -I-, -FIC)]

Su·dra (so͞o/drə), *n.* a Hindu of the lowest caste, that of the workers. Cf. **Brahman** (def. 1), **Kshatriya, Vaisya.** [< Skt *śūdra*]

suds (sudz), *n.* (*construed as pl.*) **1.** soapy water. **2.** foam made by soap; lather. **3.** *Slang.* beer. [? < MD *sudse* marsh; akin to SODDEN]

suds·y (sud/zē), *adj.,* **suds·i·er, suds·i·est. 1.** consisting of, containing, or producing foamy lather. **2.** resembling or suggesting suds.

sue (so͞o), *v.,* **sued, su·ing.** —*v.t.* **1.** to institute process in law against, or bring a civil action against. **2.** *Rare.* to make petition or appeal to. **3.** *Archaic.* to woo or court. —*v.i.* **4.** to institute legal proceedings, or bring suit. **5.** to make petition or appeal: *to sue for peace.* **6.** *Archaic.* to court a woman. [ME *suen, siwen* < OF *sivre* < VL **sequere,* for L *sequī* to follow] —**su/er,** *n.*

Sue (so͞o; *Fr.* sʏ), *n.* **Eu·gène** (œ zhen/) (pen name of *Marie Joseph Sue*) 1804–57, French novelist.

suede (swād), *n.* **1.** kid or other leather finished with a soft, napped surface, on the flesh side or on the outer side after removal of a thin outer layer. **2.** Also called **suede/ cloth/.** a fabric with a napped surface resembling this. [< F (*gants de*) *Suède* (gloves from) Sweden]

su·et (so͞o/it), *n.* the hard fatty tissue about the loins and kidneys of beef, sheep, etc., used in cookery or processed to yield tallow. [late ME *sewet* < AF **suet* = *su-, sew* (< L *sēbum* tallow) + *-et* -ET] —**su/et·y,** *adj.*

Sue·to·ni·us (swi tō/nē əs), *n.* (*Gaius Suetonius Tranquillus*) A.D. 75–150, Roman historian.

su/et pud/ding, a pudding made of chopped beef suet and flour, boiled or steamed, often with raisins, spices, etc.

Su·ez (so͞o ez/, so͞o/ez), *n.* **1.** a seaport in NE Egypt, near the S end of the Suez Canal. 275,000. **2. Gulf of,** a NW arm of the Red Sea, W of the Sinai Peninsula. **3. Isthmus of,** an isthmus in NE Egypt, joining Africa and Asia. 72 mi. wide.

Su/ez Canal/, a canal in NE Egypt, cutting across the Isthmus of Suez and connecting the Mediterranean and the Red Sea. 107 mi. long.

suf-, var. of **sub-** before *f: suffer.*

suf., suffix. Also, **suff.**

Suff., 1. Suffolk. **2.** suffragan.

suf·fer (suf/ər), *v.i.* **1.** to undergo or feel pain or distress: *The patient is still suffering.* **2.** to sustain injury or loss: *One's health suffers from overwork.* **3.** to undergo a penalty, esp. of death. **4.** to be the object of some action. **5.** *Obs.* to endure or hold out patiently. —*v.t.* **6.** to undergo, be subjected to, or endure (pain, distress, injury, loss, or anything unpleasant). **7.** to undergo or experience (any action, process, or condition): *to suffer change.* **8.** to tolerate or allow: *I do not suffer fools gladly.* **9.** to allow or permit (to do or be as stated): *Will you suffer us to leave?* [ME *suff(e)re(n)* < L *suffer(re)* = *suf-* SUF- + *fer-* bear; cf. OF *sofrir* < VL **sufferīre*] —**suf/fer·a·ble,** *adj.* —**suf/fer·a·ble·ness,** *n.* —**suf/fer·a·bly,** *adv.* —**suf/fer·er,** *n.* —**Syn. 6.** sustain. **8.** stomach, stand, abide.

suf·fer·ance (suf/ər əns, suf/rəns), *n.* **1.** passive permission resulting from lack of interference; tolerance, esp. of something wrong or illegal (usually prec. by *on* or *by*). **2.** capacity to endure pain, hardship, etc.; endurance. **3.** *Archaic.* suffering; misery. **4.** *Archaic.* patient endurance. [ME *suffrance,* OF *soufrance,* < LL *sufferentia*]

suf·fer·ing (suf/ər ing, suf/ring), *n.* **1.** the state of a person or thing that suffers. **2.** something suffered; pain. —**Syn. 1.** distress. **2.** agony, torment.

suf·fice (sə fīs/, -fīz/), *v.,* **-ficed, -fic·ing.** —*v.i.* **1.** to be enough or adequate, as for needs, purposes, etc. —*v.t.* **2.** to be enough or adequate for; satisfy. [late ME *suffice(n)* < L *suffice(re)* = *suf-* SUF- + *-ficere,* var. of *facere* to make, do; r. ME *suffise(n)* < OF]

suf·fi·cien·cy (sə fish/ən sē), *n., pl.* **-cies. 1.** the state or fact of being sufficient; adequacy. **2.** a sufficient number or amount; enough. **3.** adequate provision or supply, esp. of wealth. [< LL *sufficientia* = L *suffici-* (see SUFFICE) + *-entia* -ENCY]

suf·fi·cient (sə fish/ənt), *adj.* **1.** adequate for the purpose; enough. **2.** *Logic.* (of a condition) such that its existence is inevitably accompanied by the occurrence of a given event or the existence of a given thing. Cf. **necessary** (def. 4c). **3.** *Archaic.* competent. [late ME < L *sufficient-* (s. of *sufficiēns*) sufficing = *suffici-* (see SUFFICE) + *-ent-* -ENT] —**suf·fi/cient·ly,** *adv.*

suf·fix (*n.* suf/iks; *v.* suf/iks, sə fiks/), *n.* **1.** *Gram.* an affix that follows the element to which it is added, as *-ly* in *kindly.* **2.** something added to the end of something else. —*v.t.* **3.** *Gram.* to add as a suffix. **4.** to affix at the end of something. **5.** to fix or put under. —*v.i. Gram.* **6.** to admit a suffix. **7.** to add a suffix. [< NL *suffix(um),* n. use of neut. of L *suffixus* (ptp. of *suffīgere* to fasten) = *suf-* SUF- + *fixus;* see FIX] —**suf·fix·al** (suf/ik səl), *adj.* —**suf·fix·ion** (sə fik/shən), *n.*

suf·fo·cate (suf/ə kāt/), *v.,* **-cat·ed, -cat·ing.** —*v.t.* **1.** to kill by preventing the access of air to the blood through the lungs or analogous organs, as gills; strangle. **2.** to impede the respiration of. **3.** to discomfort by a lack of fresh or cool air. **4.** to overcome or extinguish; suppress. —*v.i.* **5.** to become suffocated; stifle; smother. **6.** to be uncomfortable due to a lack of fresh or cool air. [< L *suffōcātus* (ptp. of *suffōcāre* to choke, stifle) = *suf-* SUF- + *fōc-* (var. of *fauc-,* s. of *faucēs* throat) + *-ātus* -ATE[1]] —**suf/fo·cat/ing·ly,** *adv.* —**suf/fo·ca/tion,** *n.* —**suf/fo·ca/tive,** *adj.*

Suf·folk (suf/ək), *n.* **1.** a county in E England, divided for administrative purposes into East Suffolk and West Suffolk. **2.** one of an English breed of sheep having a black face and legs, noted for mutton of high quality. **3.** one of an English breed of chestnut draft horses having a deep body and short legs. [OE *sūthfolk* south folk]

Suffr., suffragan.

suf·fra·gan (suf/rə gən), *adj.* **1.** assisting or auxiliary to, as applied to any bishop in relation to the archbishop or metropolitan who is his superior or as applied to an assistant or subsidiary bishop without ordinary jurisdiction, as in the Church of England. **2.** (of a see or diocese) subordinate to an archiepiscopal or metropolitan see. —*n.* **3.** a suffragan bishop. [ME *suffragane* < ML *suffragān(eus)* voting = *suffrāg(ium)* SUFFRAGE + *-āneus* (*-ān(us)* -AN + *-eus* -EOUS)]

suf·frage (suf/rij), *n.* **1.** the right to vote, esp. in a political election. **2.** a vote given in favor of a proposed measure, candidate, or the like. **3.** *Eccles.* a prayer, esp. a short intercessory prayer or petition. [ME < L *suffrāg(ium)* voting tablet, vote = L *suffrāg(ārī)* (to) vote for, support + *-ium* n. suffix]

suf·fra·gette (suf/rə jet/), *n.* a woman advocate of female suffrage. —**suf/fra·get/tism,** *n.*

suf·fra·gist (suf/rə jist), *n.* an advocate of the grant or extension of political suffrage, esp. to women. —**suf/fra·gism,** *n.*

suf·fru·ti·cose (sə fro͞o/tə kōs/), *adj.* woody at the base and herbaceous above. [< NL *suffruticōs(us)* = L *suf-* SUF- + *frutic-* (s. of *frutex* shrub, bush) + *-ōsus* -OSE[1]]

suf·fu·mi·gate (sə fyo͞o/mə gāt/), *v.t.,* **-gat·ed, -gat·ing.** to fumigate from below; apply fumes or smoke to. [< L *suffūmigāt(us).* See SUF-, FUMIGATE] —**suf·fu/mi·ga/tion,** *n.*

suf·fuse (sə fyo͞oz/), *v.t.,* **-fused, -fus·ing.** to overspread with or as with a liquid, color, etc. [< L *suffūs(us)* (ptp. of *suffundere*). See SUF-, FUSE[2]] —**suf·fused·ly** (sə fyo͞ozd/lē, -fyo͞o/zid-), *adv.* —**suf·fu·sion** (sə fyo͞o/zhən), *n.* —**suf·fu·sive** (sə fyo͞o/siv), *adj.*

Su·fi (so͞o/fē), *n., pl.* **-fis.** a member of an ascetic, retiring, and mystical Muslim sect. [< Ar, lit., (man) of wool = *sūf* wool + *-ī* suffix of appurtenance] —**Su·fism** (so͞o/fiz-əm), **Su·fi·ism** (so͞o/fē iz/əm), *n.* —**Su·fis/tic,** *adj.*

sug-, var. of **sub-** before *g: suggest.*

sug·ar (sho͝og/ər), *n.* **1.** a sweet, crystalline substance, $C_{12}H_{22}O_{11}$, obtained chiefly from the juice of the sugar cane and the sugar beet, and present in sorghum, maple sap, etc.: used extensively as an ingredient and flavoring and as a fermenting agent in the manufacture of certain alcoholic beverages; sucrose. Cf. **beet sugar, cane sugar. 2.** *Chem.* a member of the same class of carbohydrates, as glucose and fructose. **3.** *Informal.* a term of endearment for a loved one; sweetheart; honey. **—v.t. 4.** to cover, sprinkle, mix, or sweeten with sugar. **5.** to make agreeable. **—v.i. 6.** to form sugar or sugar crystals. **7.** to make maple sugar. [ME *sugre, sucre* < MF *sucre* < ML *succār(um)* < It *zucchero* < Ar *sukkar* << Skt *śárkarā*] **—sug′ar·less,** *adj.*

sug′ar ap′ple, sweetsop.

sug′ar beet′, a beet, *Beta vulgaris,* having a white root, cultivated for the sugar it yields.

sug·ar·ber·ry (shŏŏg′ər ber′ē), *n., pl.* **-ries.** a hackberry, *Celtis laevigata,* of the southern U.S.

sug·ar·bush (shŏŏg′ər bŏŏsh′), *n. U.S., Canada.* an orchard or grove of sugar maples.

sug′ar can′dy, a confection made by boiling pure sugar until it hardens.

sug′ar cane′, a tall grass, *Saccharum officinarum,* of tropical and warm regions, having a stout, jointed stalk, and constituting the chief source of sugar.

sug·ar-coat (shŏŏg′ər kōt′), *v.t.* **1.** to cover with sugar: *to sugar-coat a pill.* **2.** to make (something difficult or distasteful) appear more pleasant or acceptable.

sug′ar corn′, See **sweet corn.**

sug′ar dad′dy, *Informal.* a wealthy, usually older, man who spends freely on a young woman in return for her companionship or intimacy.

sug·ar·house (shŏŏg′ər hous′), *n., pl.* **-hous·es** (-hou′ziz). a shed or other building where maple syrup or maple sugar is made.

sug′ar loaf′, a large, approximately conical loaf or mass of hard refined sugar.

Sug′arloaf Moun′tain, a mountain in SE Brazil in Rio de Janeiro, at the entrance to Guanabara Bay. 1280 ft. Portuguese, **Pão de Açúcar.**

sug′ar ma′ple, any of several maples having a sweet sap, esp. *Acer saccharum* (the state tree of New York, Vermont, West Virginia, and Wisconsin), yielding a hard wood used for making furniture and being the chief source of maple sugar. **—sug′ar-ma′ple,** *adj.*

sug′ar of lead′ (led), *Chem.* See **lead acetate.**

sug′ar of milk′, lactose.

sug′ar or′chard, *Chiefly New England.* sugarbush.

sug′ar pine′, a tall pine, *Pinus Lambertiana,* of California, Oregon, etc., having cones 20 inches long.

sug·ar·plum (shŏŏg′ər plum′), *n.* a small sweetmeat made of sugar with various flavoring and coloring ingredients; a bonbon.

sug·ar-tit (shŏŏg′ər tit′), *n.* a piece of cloth containing moist sugar, wrapped to resemble a nipple and used to pacify an infant. Also, **sug·ar-teat** (shŏŏg′ər tēt′).

sug·ar·y (shŏŏg′ə rē), *adj.* **1.** of, containing, or resembling sugar. **2.** sweet; excessively sweet. **3.** dulcet; honeyed; cloying; deceitfully agreeable. **—sug′ar·i·ness,** *n.*

sug·gest (səg jest′, sə-), *v.t.* **1.** to mention or introduce (an idea, proposition, plan, etc.) for consideration or possible action: *The architect suggested that the building be restored.* **2.** to propose (a person or thing) as suitable or possible for some purpose. **3.** (of things) to prompt the consideration, making, doing, etc., of: *The glove suggests that she was at the scene of the crime.* **4.** to bring before a person's mind indirectly or without plain expression. **5.** to call (something) up in the mind through association or natural connection of ideas. [< L *suggest(us)* brought up (ptp. of *suggerere*) = *sug-* SUG- + *ges-* (pt., ptp. s. of *gerere* to carry, display) + *-tus* ptp. suffix] **—sug·gest′er,** *n.* **—sug·gest′ing·ly,** *adv.* **—Syn. 2.** recommend, advise. **4.** indicate, imply.

sug·gest·i·ble (səg jes′tə bəl, sə-), *adj.* **1.** subject to or easily influenced by suggestion. **2.** that may be suggested. **—sug·gest′i·bil′i·ty, sug·gest′i·ble·ness,** *n.* **—sug·gest′i·bly,** *adv.*

sug·ges·tion (səg jes′chən, -jesh′-, sə-), *n.* **1.** the act of suggesting. **2.** the state of being suggested. **3.** something suggested, as a piece of advice. **4.** a slight trace: *He speaks English with just a suggestion of a foreign accent.* **5.** the calling up in the mind of one idea by another through the association of ideas. **6.** the idea thus called up. **7.** *Psychol.* **a.** the process of inducing thought or action without resorting to techniques of persuasion or giving rise to reflection; the offering of a stimulus in such a way as to produce an uncritical response. **b.** the thought or action induced in this way. [ME *suggestio(u)n* incitement to evil < ML, L *suggestiōn-* (s. of *suggestiō*)] **—Syn. 1, 3.** See **advice.**

sug·ges·tive (səg jes′tiv, sə-), *adj.* **1.** that suggests; referring to other thoughts, persons, etc. **2.** rich in suggestions or controversial ideas; leading to further thought; provocative: *a suggestive critical essay.* **3.** evocative; presented partially or sketchily rather than in detail: *a suggestive form.* **4.** that suggests or implies something improper or indecent; risqué. **—sug·ges′tive·ly,** *adv.* **—sug·ges′tive·ness,** *n.*

Su·har·to (sŏŏ här′tō), *n.* born 1925, Indonesian army officer and statesman; president since 1968.

su·i·cid·al (sōō′i sīd′əl), *adj.* **1.** pertaining to, involving, or suggesting suicide. **2.** tending or leading to suicide. **3.** foolishly or rashly dangerous. **—su′i·cid′al·ly,** *adv.*

su·i·cide (sōō′i sīd′), *n., v.,* **-cid·ed, -cid·ing.** **—n. 1.** the intentional taking of one's own life. **2.** destruction of one's own interests or prospects: *Speculation in stocks can be financial suicide.* **3.** a person who intentionally takes his own life. **—v.i. 4.** to commit suicide. **—v.t. 5.** to kill (oneself). [< NL *suicīd(ium), -cīda* = L *suī,* gen. sing. of refl. pron. + *-cīdium, -cīda* -CIDE]

su·i ge·ne·ris (sōō′ē ge′ne ris; *Eng.* sōō′ī jen′ər is), *Latin.* of his, her, its, or their own kind; unique.

su·i ju·ris (sōō′ī jŏŏr′is, sōō′ē), *Law.* capable of managing one's affairs or assuming legal responsibility. [< L: of one's own right]

su·int (sōō′int, swint), *n.* the natural grease of the wool of sheep, consisting of a mixture of fatty matter and potassium salts, used as a source of potash and in the preparation of ointments. [< F = *su-* (*su(er)* < L *sūdāre* to sweat) + *-int* < ?]

Suisse (swēs), *n.* French name of **Switzerland.**

suit (sōōt), *n.* **1.** a set of clothing, armor, or the like, intended for wear together, esp. as outer garments. **2.** a set of men's garments of the same color and fabric, consisting of trousers, a fitted jacket, and often a vest. Cf. **slack suit** (def. 1). **3.** a similarly matched set of women's garments, consisting of a skirt and jacket, and sometimes a topcoat. Cf. **slack suit** (def. 2). **4.** *Law.* the act, the process, or an instance of suing in a court of law; legal prosecution; lawsuit. **5.** *Cards.* one of the four sets or classes (spades, hearts, diamonds, and clubs) into which a common deck of playing cards is divided. **6.** the wooing or courting of a woman. **7.** the act of making a petition or an appeal. **8.** a petition, as to a person of rank or station. **9. follow suit, a.** *Cards.* to play a card of the same suit as that led. **b.** to follow the example of another. **—v.t. 10.** to make appropriate, adapt, or accommodate, as one thing to another: *to suit the punishment to the crime.* **11.** to be appropriate or becoming to: *Blue suits you very well.* **12.** to be or prove satisfactory, agreeable, or acceptable to; satisfy or please: *The arrangements suit me.* **13.** to provide with a suit, as of clothing or armor; clothe; array. **—v.i. 14.** to be appropriate or suitable; accord. **15.** to be satisfactory, agreeable, or acceptable. [ME *siute, sute, suite* < AF, OF, akin to *sivre* to follow. See SUE, SUITE] **—suit′like′,** *adj.*

suit·a·ble (sōō′tə bəl), *adj.* such as to suit; appropriate; fitting; becoming. **—suit′a·bil′i·ty, suit′a·ble·ness,** *n.* **—suit′a·bly,** *adv.*

suit·case (sōōt′kās′), *n.* an oblong valise.

suite (swēt *or, for 3 often,* sōōt), *n.* **1.** a number of things forming a series or set. **2.** a connected series of rooms to be used together: *a large suite at the Waldorf.* **3.** a set of furniture, esp. for one room: *bedroom suite.* **4.** a company of followers or attendants; a train or retinue. **5.** *Music.* **a.** an ordered series of instrumental dances, in the same or related keys, commonly preceded by a prelude. **b.** an ordered series of instrumental movements of any character. [< F, appar. metathetic var. of OF *siute* (see SUIT); akin to SUE, SUITOR]

suit·ed (sōō′tid), *adj.* **1.** being appropriate: *He is well suited to his job.* **2.** being compatible or consistent with.

suit·ing (sōō′ting), *n.* any fabric for making suits.

Suit′land-Sil′ver Hill′ (sōōt′lənd), a town in S Maryland, near Washington, D.C. 30,355 (1970).

suit·or (sōō′tər), *n.* **1.** a man who courts or woos a woman. **2.** *Law.* a petitioner or plaintiff. **3.** a person who sues or petitions for anything. [late ME *s(e)utor, suitour* < AF < L *secūtor* = (*secū-,* ptp. s. of *sequī* to follow + *-tus* ptp. suffix) + *-or* -OR[2]]

Sui·yüan (swē′yʏän′), *n.* a former province in N China, now a part of Inner Mongolian Autonomous Area. *Cap.:* Kweihsui. 127,413 sq. mi.

Su·kar·no (sōō kär′nō), *n.* **Ach·med** (äk′med), 1901–1970, Indonesian statesman: president 1945–67. Also, **Soekarno.**

su·ki·ya·ki (sōō′kē yä′kē, sŏŏk′ē-; *Jap.* skē yä′kē), *n.* a Japanese dish made with meat, soy sauce, bean curd, and greens, often cooked over direct heat at the table. [< Jap]

suk·kah (sōō kä′; *Eng.* sŏŏk′ə), *n., pl.* **suk·koth** (sōō kōt′), *Eng.* **suk·kahs.** *Hebrew.* a temporary structure in which meals are eaten during Sukkoth. Also, **succah.** [lit., booth]

suk·koth (sōō kōt′), *n. Hebrew.* a pl. of **sukkah.**

Suk·koth (sŏŏk′əs; *Heb.* sōō kōt′), *n.* a Jewish festival, beginning on the 15th day of Tishri and celebrated for either eight or nine days, that commemorates the post-Exodus period, during which the Jews wandered in the wilderness and lived in huts. Also, **Succoth.** Cf. **Simhath Torah, sukkah.** [< Heb: booths]

Su·la·we·si (sōō′lä wā′sē), *n.* Indonesian name of **Celebes.**

sul·cate (sul′kāt), *adj.* having long, narrow grooves or channels, as plant stems, or furrowed or cleft, as hoofs. Also, **sul′cat·ed.** [< L *sulcāt(us)* (ptp. of *sulcāre* to plow). See SULCUS, -ATE[1]] **—sul·ca′tion,** *n.*

sul·cus (sul′kəs), *n., pl.* **-ci** (-sī). **1.** a furrow or groove. **2.** *Anat.* a groove or fissure, esp. a fissure between two convolutions of the brain. [< L: furrow]

Su·lei·man I (sōō′lə män′, -lā-; sōō′lā män′), ("*the Magnificent*") 1495?–1566, sultan of the Ottoman Empire 1520–66. Also, **Soliman I, Solyman I.**

sulf-, a combining form of **sulfur:** *sulfarsphenamine.* Also, **sulph-.**

sul·fa (sul′fə), *Pharm.* **—adj. 1.** related chemically to sulfanilamide. **2.** pertaining to, consisting of, or involving a sulfa drug or drugs. **—n. 3.** See **sulfa drug.** Also, **sulpha.** [short for SULFANILAMIDE]

sulfa-, a combining form representing sulfa drugs: *sulfathiazole.* Also, **sulpha-,** *esp. before a vowel,* **sulf-, sulph-.** [see SULFA]

sul·fa·di·a·zine (sul′fə dī′ə zēn′, -zin), *n. Pharm.* a sulfanilamide derivative, $NH_2C_6H_4SO_2NHC_4H_3N_2$, used in the treatment of pneumococcal, staphylococcal, streptococcal, and gonococcal infections. Also, **sulphadiazine.**

sul′fa drug′, *Pharm.* any of a group of drugs closely related in chemical structure to sulfanilamide, having a bacteriostatic rather than a bacteriocidal effect: used in the treatment of various diseases, wounds, burns, and the like. Also called **sulfa, sulfonamide.**

sul·fa·nil·a·mide (sul′fə nil′ə mīd′, -mid), *n. Pharm.* a crystalline amide of sulfanilic acid, $NH_2C_6H_4SO_2NH_2$, used chiefly in the treatment of infections caused by hemolytic streptococci, gonococci, and the like. Also, **sulphanilamide.** [SULF- + *anil-* (from *anilic acid;* see ANIL) + AMIDE]

sul′fa·nil′ic ac′id (sul′fə nil′ik, sul′-), *Chem.* a solid, the para form of $H_2NC_6H_4SO_3H \cdot H_2O$, used chiefly as an intermediate in the manufacture of dyes. Also, **sulphanilic acid.** [SULF- + *anilic* (see ANIL, -IC)]

sulfan′ilyl group′, *Chem.* the para form of the group $H_2NC_6H_4SO_2$–, derived from sulfanilic acid. Also called **sulfan′ilyl rad′ical.** **—sul·fan·i·lyl** (sul fan′ə lil), *adj.*

sul·fa·pyr·a·zine (sul′fə pēr′ə zēn′, -zin), *n. Pharm.* a sulfa drug, $C_{10}H_{10}N_4O_2S$, used chiefly in the treatment of infections caused by staphylococci or gonococci.

sul·fa·pyr·i·dine (sul′fə pēr′i dēn′, -din), *n. Pharm.* a sulfanilamide derivative, $NH_2C_6H_4SO_2NHC_5H_4N$, formerly used for infections caused by pneumococci, now used primarily for a particular dermatitis.

sulf·ar·se·nide (sul fär′sə nīd′, -nid), *n. Chem.* any compound containing an arsenide and a sulfide.

sulf·ars·phen·a·mine (sulf′ärs fen′ə mēn′, -min), *n. Pharm.* a powder, $C_{14}H_{14}As_2N_2Na_2O_8S_2$, formerly used in the treatment of syphilis.

sul·fate (sul′fāt), *n., v.,* **-fat·ed, -fat·ing.** **—n. 1.** *Chem.* a salt or ester of sulfuric acid. —*v.t.* **2.** to combine, treat, or impregnate with sulfuric acid, a sulfate, or sulfates. **3.** to convert into a sulfate. **4.** *Elect.* to form a deposit of lead-sulfate compound on the lead electrodes of a storage battery. —*v.i.* **5.** to become sulfated. Also, **sulphate.** [earlier *sulphate* < NL *sulphātum*] —**sul·fa′tion,** *n.*

sul′fate pa′per, paper made from sulfate pulp.

sul′fate proc′ess, *Chem.* a process for making wood pulp by digesting wood chips in an alkaline liquor containing caustic soda and sodium sulfate. Also called **kraft process.**

sul′fate pulp′, wood pulp made by the sulfate process.

sul·fa·thi·a·zole (sul′fə thī′ə zōl′, -zôl′, -zol′), *n. Pharm.* a sulfanilamide derivative, $NH_2C_6H_4SO_2NHC_3H_2NS$, formerly used in the treatment of pneumonia and staphylococcal infections, but now largely replaced because of its toxicity.

sulf·hy·dryl (sulf hī′dril), *adj. Chem.* mercapto. Also, **sulphydryl.** [SULF- + HYDR-[2] + -YL]

sul·fide (sul′fīd), *n. Chem.* a compound of sulfur with a more electropositive element or, less often, a group. Also, **sulphide.**

sul·fi·nyl (sul′fə nil), *adj. Chem.* containing the sulfinyl group; thionyl. Also, **sulphinyl.** [SULF- + -IN[2] + -YL]

sul′finyl group′, *Chem.* the bivalent group, >SO. Also called **sul′finyl rad′ical.**

sul·fite (sul′fīt), *n. Chem.* a salt or ester of sulfurous acid. Also, **sulphite.** —**sul·fit·ic** (sul fit′ik), *adj.*

sul′fite pa′per, paper made from sulfite pulp.

sul′fite proc′ess, *Chem.* a process for making wood pulp by digesting wood chips in an acid liquor consisting of sulfurous acid and a salt, usually calcium bisulfite.

sul′fite pulp′, wood pulp made by the sulfite process.

sul·fo (sul′fō), *adj. Chem.* containing the sulfo group; sulfonic. [abstracted from SULFONIC]

sul′fo group′, *Chem.* the univalent group, SO_3H–, derived from sulfuric acid. Also called **sulfo radical.**

sul·fon·a·mide (sul fon′ə mīd′, sul′fə nam′id), *n. Pharm.* See **sulfa drug.** Also, **sulphonamide.** [*sulfon-* abstracted from SULFONIC + AMIDE]

sul·fo·nate (sul′fə nāt′), *n., v.,* **-nat·ed, -nat·ing.** *Chem.* —*n.* **1.** an ester or salt derived from a sulfonic acid. —*v.t.* **2.** to make into a sulfonic acid, as by treating an aromatic hydrocarbon with concentrated sulfuric acid. **3.** to introduce the sulfonic group into (an organic compound). Also, **sulphonate.** [SULFON(IC) + -ATE[2], r. -IC]

sul·fo·na·tion (sul′fə nā′shən), *n. Chem.* the process of attaching the sulfonic acid group, $-SO_3H$, directly to carbon in an organic compound. Also, **sulphonation.**

sul·fone (sul′fōn), *n. Chem.* any of a class of organic compounds containing the bivalent group, $-SO_2-$, united with two hydrocarbon groups. Also, **sulphone.**

sul·fon·ic (sul fon′ik), *adj. Chem.* sulfo. Also, **sulphonic.**

sulfon′ic ac′id, *Chem.* any of the strong acids of the structure RSO_2OH that give neutral sodium salts: used in the synthesis of phenols, dyes, and other substances.

sul·fo·ni·um (sul fō′nē əm), *n. Chem.* the positively charged group, H_3S^+, its salts, or their substitute products, as trimethylsulfonium iodide, $(CH_3)_3SI$. Also, **sulphonium.** [<NL = *sulf-* SULF- + *-onium,* abstracted from AMMONIUM]

sul′fo·nyl chlo′ride (sul′fə nil), *Chem.* noting the group, $-SO_2Cl$, as in benzenesulfonyl chloride, $C_6H_5SO_2Cl$. [SULFON(IC) + -YL]

sul′fo rad′ical. See **sulfo group.**

sul·fur (sul′fər), *n.* **1.** Also, **sulphur.** *Chem.* a nonmetallic element that exists in several forms, the ordinary one being a yellow rhombic crystalline solid: used esp. in making gunpowder and matches, in medicine, and in vulcanizing rubber. *Symbol:* S; *at. wt.:* 32.064; *at. no.:* 16; *sp. gr.:* 2.07 at 20° C. **2.** sulphur (def. 2). [ME *sulphur* < L, sp. var. of *sulfur*]

sul·fur-bot·tom (sul′fər bot′əm), *n.* sulphur-bottom. Also called **sul′fur-bottom whale′.**

sul′fur but′terfly, any of various yellow or orange butterflies of the family *Pieridae.*

sul′fur diox′ide, *Chem.* a suffocating gas, SO_2, formed when sulfur burns: used chiefly in the manufacture of chemicals such as sulfuric acid, in preserving fruits and vegetables, and in bleaching, disinfecting, and fumigating.

sul′fur dye′, *Chem.* any of the class of dyes produced by heating an organic compound with sulfur or sodium polysulfide, used chiefly to dye cotton.

sul·fu·re·ous (sul fyŏŏr′ē əs), *adj.* **1.** consisting of, containing, or pertaining to sulfur. **2.** resembling sulfur, esp. in color. Also, **sulphureous.** [< L *sulfureus*] —**sul·fu′re·ous·ly,** *adv.* —**sul·fu′re·ous·ness,** *n.*

sul·fu·ric (sul fyŏŏr′ik), *adj. Chem.* of or containing sulfur, esp. in the hexavalent state. Also, **sulphuric.** [modeled on F *sulfurique*]

sulfu′ric ac′id, *Chem.* an oily, corrosive liquid, H_2SO_4, usually produced from sulfur dioxide: used chiefly in the manufacture of fertilizers, chemicals, explosives, dyes, and in petroleum refining. Also called **oil of vitriol.**

sul·fu·rize (sul′fyə rīz′, -fə-), *v.t.,* **-rized, -riz·ing.** **1.** to combine, treat, or impregnate with sulfur. **2.** to fumigate with sulfur dioxide. Also, **sulphurize.** [< F *sulfuris(er)*] —**sul′fu·ri·za′tion,** *n.*

sul·fur·ous (sul′fər əs, sul fyŏŏr′əs), *adj.* **1.** relating to sulfur. **2.** of the yellow color of sulfur. **3.** containing tetravalent sulfur. Also, **sulphurous.** [< L *sulfurōs(us)*] —**sul′fur·ous·ly,** *adv.* —**sul′fur·ous·ness,** *n.*

sul′furous ac′id, *Chem.* a liquid, H_2SO_3, having a suffocating odor, known mainly by its salts, which are sulfites: used chiefly in organic synthesis and as a bleach.

sul′fur spring′, a spring the water of which contains naturally occurring sulfur compounds.

sul′fur triox′ide, *Chem.* a corrosive solid, SO_3, used as an intermediate in the manufacture of sulfuric acid.

sul·fur·yl (sul′fə ril, -fyə ril), *adj. Chem.* containing the sulfuryl group $>SO_2$, as sulfuryl chloride; sulfonyl.

sul′furyl group′, *Chem.* the bivalent group $>SO_2$, derived from sulfuric acid. Also called **sul′furyl rad′ical.**

sulk (sulk), *v.i.* **1.** to remain silent or hold oneself aloof in a sullen, ill-humored, or offended manner. —*n.* **2.** a state or fit of sulking. **3. sulks,** ill-humor shown by sulking: *to be in the sulks.* **4.** Also, **sulk′er.** a person who sulks. [back formation from SULKY]

sulk·y (sul′kē), *adj.,* **sulk·i·er, sulk·i·est,** *n., pl.* **sulk·ies.** —*adj.* **1.** marked by or given to sulking; sullenly ill-humored, resentful, or aloof. **2.** gloomy or dull: *sulky weather.* —*n.* **3.** a light, two-wheeled, one-horse carriage for one person. [akin to OE *solcen-* lazy (in *solcennes* laziness), NFris *sulkig* sulky] —**sulk′i·ly,** *adv.* —**sulk′i·ness,** *n.* —**Syn. 1.** moody, surly, morose. —**Ant. 1.** cheerful, good-natured.

Sul·la (sul′ə), *n.* (*Lucius Cornelius Sulla Felix*) 138–78 B.C., Roman general and statesman: dictator 82–79.

sul·lage (sul′ij), *n.* **1.** refuse or waste; sewage. **2.** silt; sediment. **3.** *Metall.* scoria floating on molten metal in a ladle. [? < OE *sol* mud + -AGE; see SULLY]

sul·len (sul′ən), *adj.* **1.** showing irritation or ill humor by a gloomy silence or reserve. **2.** persistently and silently ill-humored; morose. **3.** indicative of gloomy ill humor. **4.** gloomy or dismal, as weather, sounds, etc. **5.** sluggish, as a stream. **6.** *Obs.* malignant, as planets or influences. [ME *solein* < ?] —**sul′len·ly,** *adv.* —**sul′len·ness,** *n.* —**Syn. 1.** See **cross. 2.** sulky, moody. **4.** cheerless, somber, mournful. **5.** slow, stagnant. —**Ant. 1, 2.** cheerful.

Sul·li·van (sul′ə vən), *n.* **1. Annie** (*Anne Mansfield Sullivan Macy*), 1866–1936, U.S. teacher of Helen Keller. **2. Sir Arthur (Seymour),** 1842–1900, English composer: collaborator with Sir William Gilbert. **3. Harry Stack** (stak), 1892–1949, U.S. psychiatrist and psychoanalyst. **4. John L(awrence),** 1858–1918, U.S. boxer: world heavyweight champion 1882–92. **5. Louis Hen·ri** (hen′rē), 1856–1924, U.S. architect.

sul·ly (sul′ē), *v.,* **-lied, -ly·ing,** *n., pl.* **-lies.** —*v.t.* **1.** to soil, stain, or tarnish. **2.** to mar the purity or luster of; defile: *to sully a reputation.* —*v.i.* **3.** to become sullied, soiled, or tarnished. —*n.* **4.** *Obs.* a stain; soil. [OE *soli(an)* (to) become defiled, akin to *sol* mud, slough] —**sul′li·a·ble,** *adj.* —**Syn. 1.** taint, blemish, contaminate. **2.** dirty, disgrace, dishonor.

Sul·ly (sul′ē; *for 1 also Fr.* SY lē′), *n.* **1. Ma·xi·mi·lien de Bé·thune** (MAK sē mē lyaN′ də bā TYN′), **Duc de,** 1560–1641, French statesman. **2. Thomas,** 1783–1872, U.S. painter, born in England.

Sul·ly-Pru·dhomme (SY lē′PRY dôm′), *n.* **Re·né Fran·çois Ar·mand** (RƏ nā′ FRÄN SWA′ AR mäN′), 1839–1907, French poet and critic: Nobel prize 1901.

sul·pha (sul′fə), *adj., n. Pharm.* sulfa.

sulpha-, var. of **sulfa-.** Also, *esp. before a vowel,* **sulph-.**

sul·pha·di·a·zine (sul′fə dī′ə zēn′, -zin), *n. Pharm.* sulfadiazine.

sul·pha·nil·a·mide (sul′fə nil′ə mīd′, -mid), *n. Pharm.* sulfanilamide.

sul′pha·nil′ic ac′id (sul′fə nil′ik, sul′-), *Chem.* See **sulfanilic acid.**

sul·phate (sul′fāt), *n., v.t., v.i.,* **-phat·ed, -phat·ing.** sulfate. —**sul·pha′tion,** *n.*

sul·phide (sul′fīd), *n. Chem.* sulfide.

sul·phi·nyl (sul′fə nil), *adj. Chem.* sulfinyl.

sul·phite (sul′fīt), *n. Chem.* sulfite. —**sul·phit·ic** (sul-fit′ik), *adj.*

sul·phon·a·mide (sul fon′ə mīd′, sul′fə nam′id), *n. Pharm.* sulfonamide.

sul·pho·nate (sul′fə nāt′), *n., v.t.,* **-nat·ed, -nat·ing.** *Chem.* sulfonate.

sul·pho·na·tion (sul′fə nā′shən), *n. Chem.* sulfonation.

sul·phone (sul′fōn), *n. Chem.* sulfone.

sul·phon·ic (sul fon′ik), *adj. Chem.* sulfonic.

sul·pho·ni·um (sul fō′nē əm), *n. Chem.* sulfonium.

sul·phur (sul′fər), *n.* **1.** sulfur (def. 1). **2.** yellow with a greenish tinge; lemon color. [var. of SULFUR]

sul·phur-bot·tom (sul′fər bot′əm), *n.* a grayish to bluish-gray whalebone whale, *Sibbaldus musculus,* of arctic seas, having yellowish underparts: the largest mammal that has ever lived. Also called **sul′phur-bottom whale′, sulfur-bottom, sulfur-bottom whale, blue whale.**

sul·phu·re·ous (sul fyŏŏr′ē əs), *adj.* sulfureous. —**sul·phu′re·ous·ly,** *adv.* —**sul·phu′re·ous·ness,** *n.*

sul·phu·ric (sul fyŏŏr′ik), *adj. Chem.* sulfuric.

sul·phu·rize (sul′fyə rīz′, -fə-), *v.t.,* **-rized, -riz·ing.** *Chem.* sulfurize. —**sul′phu·ri·za′tion,** *n.*

sul·phur·ous (sul′fər əs, sul fyŏŏr′əs), *adj.* **1.** sulfurous. **2.** pertaining to the fires of hell; hellish or satanic. **3.** fiery or heated. —**sul′phur·ous·ly,** *adv.* —**sul′phur·ous·ness,** *n.*

sul·phy·dryl (sul fī′dril), *adj. Chem.* sulfhydryl.

sul·tan (sul′tᵊn), *n.* **1.** the sovereign of an Islamic country. **2.** (*cap.*) any of the former sovereigns of Turkey. [< ML *sultān(us)* < Ar *sulṭān* dominion, sovereign] —**sul·tan·ic** (sul tan′ik), *adj.* —**sul′tan·like′,** *adj.* —**sul′tan·ship′,** *n.*

sul·tan·a (sul tan′ə, -tä′nə), *n.* **1.** a wife, sister, daughter, or mother of a sultan. **2.** a mistress, esp. of a king. **3.** *Chiefly Brit.* a small, seedless raisin. [< It, fem. of *sultano* SULTAN]

sul·tan·ate (sul′tᵊnāt′), *n.* **1.** the office or rule of a sultan. **2.** the territory ruled over by a sultan.

sul·try (sul′trē), *adj.,* **-tri·er, -tri·est.** **1.** oppressively hot and humid or moist; sweltering: *a sultry day.* **2.** oppressively hot; emitting great heat: *the sultry sun.* **3.** characterized by or associated with sweltering heat: *sultry work in the fields.* **4.** characterized by or arousing heated temper or passion: *a sultry brunette.* [*sult(e)r* (var. of SWELTER) + -Y[1]] —**sul′tri·ly,** *adv.* —**sul′tri·ness,** *n.*

Su′lu Archipel′ago, an island group in the SW Philippines, separating the Celebes Sea from the Sulu Sea. 390,000 (est. 1965); 1086 sq. mi. *Cap.:* Jolo.

Su′lu Sea′, a sea in the W Pacific, between the SW Philippines and Borneo.

Sulz·ber·ger (sulz′bûr′gər), *n.* **Arthur Hays,** 1891–1968, U.S. newspaper publisher.

sum (sum), *n., v.,* **summed, sum·ming.** —*n.* **1.** the aggregate of two or more numbers, magnitudes, quantities, or particulars as determined by the mathematical process of addition; total: *The sum of 6 and 8 is 14.* **2.** a particular aggregate or total, esp. with reference to money: *The expenses came to an* *enormous sum.* **3.** an indefinite amount or quantity, esp. of money: *to lend small sums.* **4.** a series of numbers or quantities to be added up. **5.** an arithmetical problem to be solved, or such a problem worked out and having the various steps shown. **6.** the substance or gist of a matter, comprehensively or broadly viewed or expressed. **7.** concise or brief form: *in sum.* **8.** a summary. —*v.t.* **9.** to combine into an aggregate or total (often fol. by *up*). **10.** to ascertain the sum of, as by addition. **11.** to bring into or contain in a small compass (often fol. by *up*). **12. sum up,** to bring into or contain in a brief and comprehensive statement; summarize; recapitulate. —*v.i.* **13.** to amount (usually fol. by *to* or *into*). [ME *summe* < L *summa* (n.) < *summa* (adj.), fem. of *summus* highest, superl. of *super(us)*; see SUPER] —**Syn. 1.** See **number.**

SUM, surface-to-underwater missile.

sum-, var. of **sub-** before *m: summon.*

su·mac (shōō′mak, sōō′-), *n.* **1.** any of several anacardiaceous shrubs or small trees of the genus *Rhus.* **2.** a preparation of the dried and powdered leaves, bark, etc., of certain species of *Rhus,* esp. *R. coriaria* of southern Europe, used esp. in tanning. **3.** the wood of these trees. Also, **su′mach.** [ME < ML < Ar *summāq*]

Su·ma·tra (sŏŏ mä′trə), *n.* a large island in the W part of Indonesia. 15,439,000 (est. 1961); 164,147 sq. mi. —**Su·ma′tran,** *adj., n.*

Sum·ba (sōōm′bä), *n.* one of the Lesser Sunda Islands, in Indonesia, S of Celebes. 250,852 (est. 1961); 4306 sq. mi. Also called **Sandalwood Island.** Dutch, **Soemba.**

Sum·ba·wa (sōōm bä′wä), *n.* one of the Lesser Sunda Islands, in Indonesia: destructive eruption in 1815 of Mt. Tambora. 194,819 (est. 1961); 5965 sq. mi. Dutch, **Soembawa.**

Su·mer (sōō′mər), *n.* an ancient region in southern Mesopotamia containing a number of independent cities and city-states, some possibly established as early as 5000 B.C. See map at **Chaldea.**

Su·me·ri·an (sōō mēr′ē ən, -mer′-), *adj.* **1.** of or pertaining to Sumer, its people, or their language. —*n.* **2.** a native or inhabitant of Sumer. **3.** a language of unknown affinities that was the language of the Sumerians and had, in the late 4th and 3rd millenniums B.C., a well-developed literature that is preserved in pictographic and cuneiform writing and represents the world's oldest extant written documents.

sum·ma (sŏŏm′ə, sum′ə), *n., pl.* **sum·mae** (sŏŏm′ī, sum′ē), **sum·mas.** a comprehensive work covering or summarizing a particular field or subject. [< L; see SUM]

sum·ma cum lau·de (sŏŏm′ə kŏŏm lou′dā, -də, -dē; sum′ə kum lô′dē), with highest praise: used in diplomas to grant the highest of three special honors for grades above the average. Cf. **cum laude, magna cum laude.** [< L]

sum·mand (sum′and, sum and′, sə mand′), *n.* a part of a sum. [< ML *summand(us),* ger. of *summāre* to total or sum < *summ(a)* SUM]

sum·ma·rise (sum′ə rīz′), *v.t.,* **-rised, -ris·ing.** *Chiefly Brit.* summarize. —**sum′ma·ris′a·ble,** *adj.* —**sum′ma·ri·sa′tion,** *n.* —**sum′ma·ris′er,** *n.*

sum·ma·rize (sum′ə rīz′), *v.t.,* **-rized, -riz·ing. 1.** to make a summary of; state or express in a concise form. **2.** to constitute a summary of. —**sum′ma·riz′a·ble,** *adj.* —**sum′ma·ri·za′tion,** *n.* —**sum′ma·riz′er, sum′mar·ist,** *n.*

sum·ma·ry (sum′ə rē), *n., pl.* **-ries,** *adj.* —*n.* **1.** a comprehensive and usually brief abstract, recapitulation, or compendium of previously stated facts or statements. —*adj.* **2.** brief and comprehensive; concise. **3.** direct and prompt; unceremoniously fast: *to treat someone with summary dispatch.* **4.** (of legal proceedings) conducted without the various steps of a formal trial. [< L *summāri(um).* See SUM, -ARY] —**sum·mar·i·ly** (sə mer′ə lē, sum′ər ə-), *adv.* —**sum·mar′i·ness,** *n.*

—**Syn. 1.** outline, précis. SUMMARY, BRIEF, DIGEST, SYNOPSIS are terms for a short version of a longer work. A SUMMARY is a brief statement or restatement of main points, esp. as a conclusion to a work: *the summary of a chapter.* A BRIEF is a detailed outline, by heads and subheads, of a discourse (usually legal) to be completed: *a brief for an argument.* A DIGEST is an abridgement of an article, book, etc., or an organized arrangement of material under heads and titles: *a digest of a popular novel.* A SYNOPSIS is a compressed statement of the plot of a novel, play, etc.: *a synopsis of* Hamlet.

sum·ma·tion (sə mā′shən), *n.* **1.** the act or process of summing. **2.** the result of this; an aggregate or total. **3.** a review or recapitulation of previously stated facts or statements, often with a final conclusion or conclusions drawn from them. **4.** *Law.* the final arguments in a case. [< ML *summātiōn-* (s. of *summātiō*) = *summāt(us)* (ptp. of *summāre* to SUM: *summ-* + *-ātus* -ATE[1]) + *-iōn-* -ION] —**sum·ma′tion·al,** *adj.*

sum·mer[1] (sum′ər), *n.* **1.** the season between spring and autumn: in the Northern Hemisphere, from the summer solstice to the autumnal equinox, and in the Southern Hemisphere from the winter solstice to the vernal equinox. **2.** a period of hot, usually sunny weather: *We had no real summer last year.* **3.** the period of finest development, perfection, or beauty previous to any decline: *the summer of life.* —*adj.* **4.** of, pertaining to, or characteristic of summer. **5.** suitable for or used during the summer. —*v.i.* **6.** to spend or pass the summer. —*v.t.* **7.** to keep, feed, or manage during the summer. [ME *sumer,* OE *sumor;* c. D *zomer,* G *Sommer,* Icel *sumar* summer, Skt *samā* half-year, year, OIr *sam,* Welsh *haf* summer] —**sum′mer·less,** *adj.* —**sum′mer·like′,** *adj.*

sum·mer[2] (sum′ər), *n.* **1.** a principal beam or girder, as one running between girts to support joists. **2.** a stone laid upon a pier, column, or wall, from which one or more arches spring: usually molded or otherwise treated like the arch or arches springing from it. **3.** a beam or lintel. [ME *somer* < AF < OF *somier* packhorse, beam < VL **saumār(ius)* = L *sagm(a)* packsaddle (< Gk) + *-ārius* -ARY]

sum′mer camp′, a camp, esp. one attended by children during the summer, providing facilities for sleeping and eating, and usually for sports, handicrafts, etc.

sum·mer·house (sum′ər hous′), *n., pl.* **-hous·es** (-hou′ziz). a simple, often rustic structure in a park or garden, intended to provide a shady, cool place in the summer. [ME *sumer hous*]

sum·mer·ize (sum′ə rīz′), *v.t.,* **-ized, -iz·ing. 1.** to protect in hot weather for future use: *to summerize a snowmobile.* **2.** to prepare for hot weather, as by adding an air conditioner.

sum·mer·sault (sum′ər sôlt′), *n., v.i.* somersault. Also, **sum·mer·set** (sum′ər set′).

sum′mer sau′sage, dried or smoked sausage that keeps without refrigeration.

sum′mer school′, 1. study programs offered by a high school, college, or university during the summer to those who wish to obtain their degrees more quickly, who must make up credits, or who wish to supplement their education. **2.** a school offering such programs.

sum′mer sol′stice, *Astron.* the solstice on or about June 21st that marks the beginning of summer in the Northern Hemisphere.

sum′mer squash′, any of several squashes of the variety *Cucurbita Pepo Melopepo,* that mature in the late summer or early autumn and are used as a vegetable in an unripe state.

sum′mer stock′, 1. the production of plays, musical comedy, etc., during the summer, often by a repertory group. **2.** summer theaters collectively or their productions.

sum′mer the′ater, a theater that operates during the summer, esp. in a suburban or resort area.

sum·mer·time (sum′ər tīm′), *n.* **1.** the summer season. **2.** *Brit.* See **daylight-saving time.** [late ME *somertyme*]

sum·mer·wood (sum′ər wŏŏd′), *n.* the part of an annual ring of wood, characterized by compact, thick-walled cells, formed during the later part of the growing season.

sum·mer·y (sum′ə rē), *adj.* of, like, or appropriate for summer. —**sum′mer·i·ness,** *n.*

sum·ming-up (sum′ing up′), *n., pl.* **sum·mings-up.** a summation or statement made for the purpose of reviewing the basic concepts or principles of an argument, story, explanation, or the like.

sum·mit (sum′it), *n.* **1.** the highest point or part, as of a hill, a line of travel, or any object; top; apex. **2.** the highest point of attainment or aspiration: *the summit of one's ambition.* **3.** the highest state or degree. **4.** the highest level of diplomatic or other governmental officials: *a meeting at the summit.* —*adj.* **5.** between heads of state: *a summit conference.* [late ME *somete* < OF = *som* top (< L *summ(um),* n. use of neut. of *summus* highest; see SUM) + *-ete* -ET] —**sum′mit·al,** *adj.* —**sum′mit·less,** *adj.* —**Syn. 1.** peak, pinnacle. **2, 3.** acme, zenith, culmination. —**Ant. 1.** base.

sum·mit·ry (sum′i trē), *n., pl.* **-ries. 1.** the art or conduct of a summit conference. **2.** the idea or belief that international negotiations can best be handled at summit conferences.

sum·mon (sum′ən), *v.t.* **1.** to call or order to some duty, task, or performance; call upon to do something. **2.** to call for the presence of, as by command, message, or signal; call (usually fol. by *to, away, from,* etc.). **3.** to call or notify to appear at a specified place, esp. before a court: *to summon a defendant.* **4.** to call into action; rouse; call forth (often. fol. by *up*): *to summon up all one's courage.* **5.** to call upon (a person, army, etc.) to surrender. [< ML *summon(ēre)* (to) summon (L: to remind unofficially, suggest) = *sum-* SUM- + *monēre* to remind, warn; r. ME *somon(en)* < OF *semond(re), somond(re)*] —**sum′mon·a·ble,** *adj.* —**sum′mon·er,** *n.* —**Syn. 1–3.** See **call.**

sum·mons (sum′ənz), *n., pl.* **-mons·es. 1.** an authoritative command, message, or signal by which one is summoned. **2.** a request, demand, or call to do something: *a summons to surrender.* **3.** *Law.* **a.** a call or citation by authority to appear before a court or a judicial officer. **b.** the writ by which the call is made. **4.** an authoritative call or notice to appear at a specified place, as for a particular purpose or duty. **5.** a call issued for the meeting of an assembly or parliament. [ME *somons* < AF, OF *somonse* (n. use of fem. of *somons,* ptp. of *somondre* to summon) < VL **summonsa* (irreg. formation), r. L *summonita,* fem. ptp. of *summonēre;* see SUMMON]

sum·mum bo·num (sŏŏm′ŏŏm bō′nŏŏm; *Eng.* sum′əm bō′nəm), *Latin.* the highest or chief good.

Sum·ner (sum′nər), *n.* **Charles,** 1811–74, U.S. statesman.

su·mo (sōō′mō), *n.* a form of wrestling in Japan in which a contestant wins by forcing his opponent out of the ring or by causing him to touch the ground with any part of his body other than the soles of his feet, contestants usually being men of great height and weight. [< Jap *sumō*]

sump (sump), *n.* **1.** a pit, well, or the like, in which water or other liquid is collected. **2.** *Mach.* a chamber at the bottom of a machine, pump, circulation system, etc., into which a fluid drains before recirculation or in which wastes gather before disposal. **3.** *Mining.* **a.** a space where water is allowed to collect at the bottom of a shaft or below a passageway. **b.** a pilot shaft or tunnel pushed out in front of a main bore. [late ME *sompe* < MLG or MD *sump;* c. G *Sumpf;* akin to SWAMP]

sump·ter (sump′tər), *n.* *Archaic.* a packhorse or mule. [ME *sompter* < OF *sometier* packhorse driver < VL **saumatār(ius)* = L *sagmat-* (s. of *sagma;* see SUMMER[2]) + *-ārius* -ARY]

sump·tu·ar·y (sump′chōō er′ē), *adj.* pertaining to, dealing with, or regulating expense or expenditure. [< L *sumptuāri(us)* = *sumptu(s)* expense + *-ārius* -ARY; *sumptus* < *sumptus* taken, spent (ptp. of *sūmere*) = *sum-* + *-p-* (transition sound) + *-tus* ptp. suffix]

sump′tuary law′, 1. a law regulating personal expenditures, esp. on food and dress, often perpetuating distinctions in social class. **2.** a law based on the police power of the state but regulating personal habits that offend the moral or religious beliefs of the community.

sump·tu·ous (sump′chōō əs), *adj.* **1.** entailing great expense, as from fine workmanship, choice materials, etc.; costly. **2.** luxuriously fine; splendid or superb. [late ME < L *sumptuōs(us)* = *sumptu(s)* expense (see SUMPTUARY) + *-ōsus* -OUS] —**sump′tu·ous·ly,** *adv.* —**sump′tu·ous·ness,** *n.*

Sum·ter (sum′tər, sump′-), *n.* See **Fort Sumter.**

Su·my (sōō′mi), *n.* a city in the NE Ukraine, in the S Soviet Union in Europe. 123,000 (est. 1964).

sun (sun), *n., v.,* **sunned, sun·ning.** —*n.* **1.** the star that is the central body of the solar system, around which the planets revolve and from which they receive light and heat: its mean distance from the earth is about 93,000,000 miles, its diameter about 864,000 miles, and its mass about 330,000 times that of the earth. **2.** the sun as it appears at a given time, in a given location, etc.: *the noonday sun; the Florida sun.* **3.** a self-luminous heavenly body; star. **4.** sunshine; the heat and light from the sun: *to be exposed to the sun.* **5.** *Chiefly Literary.* **a.** clime; climate. **b.** glory; splendor. **6.** *Archaic.* **a.** a day. **b.** a year. **c.** sunrise or sunset: *They traveled hard from sun to sun.* **7. place in the sun,** a favorable or advantageous position; prominence; recognition. —*v.t.* **8.** to expose to the sun's rays. **9.** to warm, dry, etc., in the sunshine. **10.** to put, bring, make, etc., by exposure to the rays of the sun. —*v.i.* **11.** to expose oneself to the rays of the sun. [ME, OE *sunne;* c. G *Sonne,* Icel *sunna,* Goth *sunno*] —**sun′like′,** *adj.*

Sun-and-planet gear

Sun., Sunday. Also, **Sund.**

sun′-and-plan′et gear′ (sun′ən-plan′it), *Mach.* a planetary epicyclic gear train.

sun·back (sun′bak′), *adj.* (of a garment) cut low to expose the back for sunbathing or coolness.

sun′ bath′, exposure of the body to the direct rays of the sun or a sun lamp, esp. to acquire a sun tan.

sun·bathe (sun′bāth′), *v.i.,* **-bathed, -bath·ing.** to take a sun bath. —**sun′bath′er,** *n.*

sun·beam (sun′bēm′), *n.* a beam or ray of sunlight. [ME *sunnebem,* OE *sun(ne)bēam*] —**sun′beamed′, sun′beam′y,** *adj.*

Sun·belt (sun′belt′), *n. Informal.* the southern and southwestern region of the U.S.

sun·bird (sun′bûrd′), *n.* any of various small, brightly colored, Old World birds of the family *Nectariniidae.*

sun·bon·net (sun′bon′it), *n.* a large bonnet of cotton or other light material shading the face and projecting down over the neck. —**sun′bon′net·ed,** *adj.*

sun·bow (sun′bō′), *n.* a bow or arc of prismatic colors like a rainbow, appearing in the spray of cataracts, waterfalls, fountains, etc.

sun·burn (sun′bûrn′), *n., v.,* **-burned** or **-burnt, -burn·ing.** —*n.* **1.** superficial inflammation of the skin caused by exposure to the rays of the sun or a sun lamp. —*v.t., v.i.* **2.** to affect or be affected with sunburn.

sun·burst (sun′bûrst′), *n.* **1.** a burst of sunlight. **2.** a firework, piece of jewelry, ornament, or the like, resembling the sun with rays issuing in all directions.

sun-cured (sun′kyo͝ord′), *adj.* cured or preserved by exposure to the rays of the sun, as meat, fruit, etc.

sun·dae (sun′dē, -dā), *n.* ice cream topped with fruit, syrup, whipped cream, nuts, etc. [? special use of *Sunday*]

Sun′da Is′lands (sun′də; *Du.* so͞on′dä), a chain of islands in the Malay Archipelago, including Borneo, Sumatra, Java, and Celebes **(Greater Sunda Islands)**; and a group of smaller islands extending E from Java to Timor **(Lesser Sunda Islands).** Also, **Soenda Islands.**

sun′ dance′, a religious ceremony associated with the sun, performed by the Plains Indians at the summer solstice.

Sun′da Strait′, a strait between Sumatra and Java, connecting Java Sea and Indian Ocean. 20–65 mi. wide.

Sun·day (sun′dē, -dā), *n.* **1.** the first day of the week, observed as the Sabbath by most Christian sects. **2. a month of Sundays,** an indeterminately great length of time. —*adj.* **3.** of, pertaining to, or characteristic of Sunday. **4.** used, done, taking place, or being as indicated only on or as on Sundays. [ME *sun(nen)day,* OE *sunnandæg,* trans. of L *diēs sōlis,* itself trans. of Gk *hēmĕra hēlίou* day of the sun; c. G *Sonntag,* etc.] —**Sun′day·like′,** *adj.*

—**Syn. 1.** SUNDAY, SABBATH are not properly synonyms. SUNDAY is the first day of the week in most Western countries, and among most Christians it is observed as the Sab bath. The SABBATH is the day on which the fourth Com mandment enjoins abstention from work of all kinds. It is a day of special religious devotion by most Christians on Sunday, by Jews on Saturday, and by Muslims on Friday.

Sun·day (sun′dē, -dā), *n.* **William Ash·ley** (ash′lē), ("*Billy Sunday*"), 1862–1935, U.S. evangelist.

Sun′day clothes′, *Informal.* one's best or newest clothing, as saved for Sundays and special occasions. Also called **Sun′day best′.**

Sun′day driv′er, a person who drives a car infrequently and tends to drive slowly, overcautiously, or with pauses to look at his surroundings, as one who drives only on Sundays.

Sun·day-go-to-meet·ing (sun′dē gō′tə mēt′ᵊn, -mē′tiŋ, -dā-), *adj. Informal.* most presentable; best: *Sunday-go-to-meeting dress.*

Sun′day paint′er, a nonprofessional painter, usually unschooled, who paints as a hobby.

Sun′day punch′, *Informal.* the most powerful punch of a boxer, esp. the punch used in trying to gain a knockout.

Sun′day school′, **1.** a school for religious instruction on Sunday. **2.** the members of such a school.

sun′ deck′, a raised, open area, as a roof, terrace, or ship's deck, that is exposed to the sun.

sun·der (sun′dər), *v.t.* **1.** to separate; part; divide; sever. —*v.i.* **2.** to become separated; part. [ME *sundr(en),* OE *-sundrian;* c. G *sondern,* Icel *sundra;* see ASUNDER] —**sun′der·a·ble,** *adj.* —**sun′der·er,** *n.*

Sun·der·land (sun′dər lənd), *n.* a seaport in E Durham, in NE England. 298,000.

sun·dew (sun′do͞o′, -dyo͞o′), *n.* any of several small bog plants of the genus *Drosera,* having sticky hairs that trap insects. [< D *sondauw* (cf. G *Sonnentau*), trans. of L *rōs sōlis* dew of the sun]

sun·di·al (sun′dī′əl, -dīl′), *n.* an instrument that indicates the time of day by means of the position, on a graduated plate or surface, of the shadow of the gnomon as it is cast by the sun.

Sundial

sun′ disk′, **1.** the disk of the sun. **2.** a figure or representation of this, esp. in religious symbolism.

Sun disk, Ancient Egyptian (def. 2)

sun·dog (sun′dôg′, -dog′), *n.* **1.** parhelion. **2.** a small or incomplete rainbow. [?]

sun·down (sun′doun′), *n.* sunset, esp. the time of sunset.

sun·down·er (sun′dou′nər), *n. Australian.* a hobo, originally one who arrived at a station near sundown in order to avoid having to work in exchange for food and shelter.

sun·dries (sun′drēz), *n.pl.* sundry things or items, esp. small, miscellaneous items of little value. Cf. **notion** (def. 5). [n. pl. use of SUNDRY]

sun·dry (sun′drē), *adj.* **1.** various or diverse. —*pron.* **2. all and sundry,** everybody, collectively and individually. [ME; OE *syndrig* private, separate]

Sunds·vall (sunts′väl), *n.* a seaport in E Sweden, on the Gulf of Bothnia. 93,992.

sun·fish (sun′fish′), *n., pl.* (*esp. collectively*) **-fish,** (*esp. referring to two or more kinds or species*) **-fish·es. 1.** the ocean sunfish, *Mola mola.* **2.** any of various other fishes of the family *Molidae.* **3.** any of several small, fresh-water, spiny-rayed fishes of the genus *Lepomis,* of North America, having a deep, compressed body.

sun·flow·er (sun′flou′ər), *n.* any of several herbs of the genus *Helianthus,* as *H. annus* (the state flower of Kansas), having showy, yellow-rayed flowers and edible, oil-producing seeds. [trans. of L *flōs sōlis* flower of the sun]

Sun′flower State′, Kansas (used as a nickname).

sung (suŋ), *v.* a pt. and pp. of **sing.**

Sung (so͝oŋ), *n.* a dynasty in China, A.D. 960–1279, characterized by a high level of achievement in painting, ceramics, and philosophy.

Sun·ga·ri (so͞on gär′ē, so͝oŋ är′-), *n.* a river in NE China, flowing NW and NE through E and central Manchuria into the Amur River. 800 mi. long.

sun′ gear′, *Mach.* (in an epicyclic train) the central gear around which the planet gears revolve.

Sung·kiang (so͝oŋ′gyäŋ′), *n.* a former province in NE China, now a part of the Inner Mongolian Autonomous Region. 79,151 sq. mi.

sun·glass (sun′glas′, -gläs′), *n.* See **burning glass.**

sun·glass·es (sun′glas′iz, -glä′siz), *n.pl.* spectacles with colored or tinted lenses for protecting the eyes from the glare of sunlight.

sun·glow (sun′glō′), *n.* a diffused, hazy light seen around the sun, caused by particles of foreign matter in the atmosphere.

sun-god (sun′god′), *n.* **1.** the sun considered or personified as a deity. **2.** a god identified or associated with the sun.

sunk (suŋk), *v.* **1.** a pt. and pp. of **sink. 2.** *Slang.* beyond help; done for; washed up.

sunk·en (suŋ′kən), *v.* **1.** a pp. of **sink.** —*adj.* **2.** having sunk or been sunk beneath the surface; submerged. **3.** having settled to a lower level, as walls. **4.** situated or lying on a lower level: *a sunken living room.* **5.** hollow; depressed: *sunken cheeks.*

sun′ lamp′, **1.** a lamp for generating ultraviolet rays, used as a therapeutic device, for obtaining an artificial sun tan, etc. **2.** a lamp used in motion-picture photography, having an arrangement of parabolic mirrors for directing and concentrating the light.

sun·less (sun′lis), *adj.* **1.** lacking sun or sunlight; dark. **2.** dismal; gloomy; cheerless. —**sun′less·ness,** *n.*

sun·light (sun′līt′), *n.* sunshine. [ME *sonnelihť*]

sunn (sun), *n.* **1.** a tall, East Indian, fabaceous shrub, *Crotalaria juncea,* having slender branches and yellow flowers, and an inner bark that yields a fiber used for making ropes, sacking, etc. **2.** the fiber. Also called **sunn′ hemp′.** [< Hindi *san* < Skt *śāṇā*]

Sun·na (so͝on′ə), *n.* the traditional portion of Muslim Law, claimed to be based on the words and acts of Muhammad, but not attributed directly to him. Also, **Sun′nah.** [< Ar *sunnah* way, path, rule]

Sun·nite (so͝on′īt), *n. Islam.* a member of one of the two great religious divisions of Islam, regarding the first four caliphs as legitimate successors of Muhammad and stressing the importance of Sunna. Also called **Sun·ni** (so͝on′ē). Cf. **Shiite.**

sun·ny (sun′ē), *adj.,* **-ni·er, -ni·est. 1.** abounding in sunshine. **2.** exposed to, lighted, or warmed by the direct rays of the sun. **3.** pertaining to or proceeding from the sun; solar. **4.** resembling the sun. **5.** cheery, cheerful, or joyous: *a sunny disposition.* [ME] —**sun′ni·ly,** *adv.* —**sun′ni·ness,** *n.*

sun′ny side′, **1.** the part upon which sunlight falls. **2.** a pleasant or hopeful aspect or part. **3.** some age less than one specified: *You're still on the sunny side of thirty.*

sun′ny-side up′ (sun′ē sīd′), (of an egg) fried without being turned over, so that the yolk is visible and liquid inside.

Sun·ny·vale (sun′ē vāl′), *n.* a city in central California, south of San Francisco. 95,408 (1970).

sun′ porch′, a windowed porch or porchlike room having more window than wall area, intended to receive large amounts of sunlight. Also called **sun′ par′lor, sun′ room′.**

sun·rise (sun′rīz′), *n.* **1.** the rise or ascent of the sun above the horizon in the morning. **2.** the atmospheric and scenic phenomena accompanying this. **3.** the time when half the sun has risen above the horizon. [short for ME *sunrising*]

sun·roof (sun′ro͞of′), *n.* an automobile roof with a section that may be slid open manually or electrically.

sun·set (sun′set′), *n.* **1.** the setting or descent of the sun below the horizon in the evening. **2.** the atmospheric and scenic phenomena accompanying this. **3.** the time when the sun sets. [ME; in OE: west]

sun′set law′, a legislative bill or provision requiring an automatic review by a certain date of the effectiveness of a government program, agency, etc., before new funds can be authorized for its continuance.

sun·shade (sun′shād′), *n.* something used as a protection from the rays of the sun, as an awning or a parasol.

sun·shine (sun′shīn′), *n.* **1.** the shining of the sun; direct light of the sun. **2.** cheerfulness or happiness. **3.** a source of cheer or happiness. **4.** the effect of the sun in lighting and heating a place. **5.** a place where the rays of the sun fall. [ME *sunnesin*, alter. of OE *sunnscīn* = *sunn(an)* sun's + *scīn* brightness] —**sun′shine′less,** *adj.* —**sun′shin′y,** *adj.*

Sun′shine State′, Florida (used as a nickname).

sun·spot (sun′spot′), *n.* one of the dark patches that appear periodically on the surface of the sun, affecting terrestrial magnetism and other terrestrial phenomena.

sun·stroke (sun′strōk′), *n.* *Pathol.* a frequently fatal affection due to prolonged exposure to the sun's rays or to excessive heat, marked by sudden prostration and symptoms resembling those of apoplexy. Also called **insolation.**

sun·struck (sun′struk′), *adj.* affected with sunstroke.

sun·suit (sun′so͞ot′), *n.* a playsuit consisting of a halter and shorts.

sun′ tan′, a browning of the skin resulting from exposure to the rays of the sun or a sun lamp. Also, **sun′tan′.**

sun·tans (sun′tanz′), *n.* (*construed as pl.*) a tan military uniform for summer wear.

sun·up (sun′up′), *n.* sunrise.

Sun′ Val′ley, a village in S central Idaho: winter resort.

sun·ward (sun′wərd), *adv.* **1.** Also, **sun′wards.** toward the sun. —*adj.* **2.** directed toward the sun.

sun·wise (sun′wīz′), *adv.* in a clockwise direction.

Sun Yat-sen (so͝on′ yät′sen′), 1867–1925, Chinese political and revolutionary leader.

su·o ju·re (so͞o′ō yo͞o′re; *Eng.* so͞o′ō jo͝or′ē), *Latin.* in one's own right.

su·o lo·co (so͞o′ō lō′kō), *Latin.* in one's rightful place.

Suo·mi (swô′mē), *n.* Finnish name of **Finland.**

sup[1] (sup), *v.*, **supped, sup·ping.** —*v.i.* **1.** to eat supper. —*v.t.* **2.** to provide with supper. [ME *s(o)up(en)* < OF *soupe(r)* (to) take supper < Gmc; cf. OE *sūpan* to swallow, taste, sip. See SUP[2], SOP]

sup[2] (sup), *v.*, **supped, sup·ping,** *n.* —*v.t.* **1.** to take (liquid food, or any liquid) into the mouth in small quantities; sip. —*v.i.* **2.** to take liquid into the mouth in small quantities. —*n.* **3.** a mouthful or sip of liquid food or of drink. [ME *supp(en)*, var. of *soupen*, OE *sūpan;* c. G *saufen* to drink. Cf. SIP, SOP, SUP[1], SOUP]

sup-, var. of **sub-** before *p: suppose.*

sup., **1.** superior. **2.** superlative. **3.** supine. **4.** supplement. **5.** supplementary. **6.** supra.

Sup. Ct., **1.** Superior Court. **2.** Supreme Court.

su·per (so͞o′pər), *n.* **1.** *Informal.* **a.** superintendent. **b.** supervisor. **c.** supernumerary. **2.** *Com.* an article of a superior quality, grade, size, etc. **3.** *Entomol.* the portion of a hive in which honey is stored. **4.** *U.S. Informal.* supercalendered paper. —*adj. Informal.* **5.** superfine. **6.** first-rate. **7.** of the highest degree, power, etc. **8.** of an extreme or excessive degree. [by shortening, or special use of SUPER-]

super-, a formal element occurring in loan words from Latin (*supersede*); used, with the meaning "above," "beyond," in the formation of compound words with second elements of any origin (*superman; superhighway*). [comb. form of L prep. and v. prefix *super* above, beyond, in addition, to an especially high degree]

su·per·a·ble (so͞o′pər ə bəl), *adj.* capable of being overcome; surmountable. [< L *superābil(is)* = *superā-* overcome (*super-* SUPER- + *-ā v.* suffix) + *-bilis* -BLE] —**su′per·a·bil′i·ty, su′per·a·ble·ness,** *n.* —**su′per·a·bly,** *adv.*

su·per·a·bound (so͞o′pər ə bound′), *v.i.* **1.** to abound beyond something else. **2.** to be very abundant (usually fol. by *in* or *with*). [late ME < LL *superabund(āre)* = *super-* SUPER- + *abundāre* to ABOUND]

su·per·a·bun·dant (so͞o′pər ə bun′dənt), *adj.* exceedingly abundant; more than sufficient; excessive. [late ME < LL *superabundant-* (s. of *superabundāns*) superabounding] —**su′per·a·bun′dance,** *n.* —**su′per·a·bun′dant·ly,** *adv.*

su·per·add (so͞o′pər ad′), *v.t.* to add over and above; add besides. [< L *superadd(ere)*] —**su·per·ad·di·tion** (so͞o′pər-ə dish′ən), *n.* —**su′per·ad·di′tion·al,** *adj.*

su·per·an·nu·ate (so͞o′pər an′yo͞o āt′), *v.*, **-at·ed, -at·ing.** —*v.t.* **1.** to allow to retire from service or office on a pension because of age or infirmity. **2.** to set aside as out of date. —*v.i.* **3.** to be or become old or out of date. [back formation from SUPERANNUATED]

su·per·an·nu·at·ed (so͞o′pər an′yo͞o ā′tid), *adj.* **1.** retired because of age or infirmity. **2.** too old for use, work, or service. **3.** antiquated or obsolete: *superannuated ideas.* [alter. (with *-u-* of ANNUAL) of ML *superannāt(us)* over a year old (said of cattle) + -ED[2]; *superannātus* = *super ann(um)* beyond a year + *-ātus* -ATE[1]] —**su′per·an′nu·a′tion,** *n.*

su·perb (so͝o pûrb′, sə-), *adj.* **1.** admirably fine or excellent. **2.** sumptuous; rich; grand. **3.** of a proudly imposing appearance or kind; majestic. [< L *superb(us)* proud, superior, excellent = *super-* SUPER- + *-bus* suffix akin to *fuī* I have been; see BE] —**su·perb′ly,** *adv.* —**su·perb′ness,** *n.* —**Syn. 2.** elegant. See **magnificent.** —**Ant. 2.** inferior.

su·per·bomb (so͞o′pər bom′), *n.* a highly destructive bomb, esp. the hydrogen bomb.

su·per·cal·en·der (so͞o′pər kal′ən dər), *n.* **1.** a roll or set of rolls for giving a high finish to paper. —*v.t.* **2.** to finish paper in a supercalender.

su·per·car·go (so͞o′pər kär′gō, so͞o′pər kär′-), *n.*, *pl.* **-goes, -gos.** a merchant-ship officer who is in charge of the cargo and the commercial concerns of the voyage. [< Sp *sobrecargo* with *sobre-* over (< L *super*) Latinized; r. *supracargo* (with *supra-* for Sp *sobre-*); see CARGO]

su·per·car·ri·er (so͞o′pər kar′ē ər), *n.* a large aircraft carrier, as a nuclear-powered one.

su·per·charge (so͞o′pər chärj′), *v.t.*, **-charged, -charg·ing.** **1.** to charge with an abundant or excessive amount, as of energy, emotion, tension, etc. **2.** to supply air to (an internal-combustion engine) at greater than atmospheric pressure.

su·per·charg·er (so͞o′pər chär′jər), *n.* a mechanism for forcing air into an internal-combustion engine in order to increase engine power.

su·per·cil·i·ar·y (so͞o′pər sil′ē er′ē), *adj.* *Anat., Zool.* **1.** of or pertaining to the eyebrow. **2.** having a conspicuous line or marking over the eye, as certain birds. **3.** situated on the frontal bone at the level of the eyebrow. [< NL *superciliar(is).* See SUPERCILIUM, -ARY]

su′percil′iary ridge′. See **supraorbital ridge.**

su·per·cil·i·ous (so͞o′pər sil′ē əs), *adj.* haughtily disdainful, as a person, his expression, bearing, etc. [< L *superciliōs(us).* See SUPERCILIUM, -OUS] —**su′per·cil′i·ous·ly,** *adv.* —**su′per·cil′i·ous·ness,** *n.* —**Syn.** arrogant, scornful.

su·per·cil·i·um (so͞o′pər sil′ē əm), *n.*, *pl.* **-cil·i·a** (-sil′ē ə). *Archit.* **1.** the fillet above the cyma of a cornice. **2.** (on an Attic base) either of the fillets above and below the scotia. [< L: eyebrow, haughtiness = *super-* SUPER- + *cilium* eyelid]

su·per·class (so͞o′pər klas′, -kläs′), *n.* *Biol.* **1.** a category of related classes within a subphylum. **2.** a subphylum.

su·per·con·duc·tiv·i·ty (so͞o′pər kon′duk tiv′i tē), *n.* *Physics.* the disappearance of electrical resistance shown by certain metals at temperatures near absolute zero and by new classes of ceramic oxides at temperatures well above this. —**su·per·con·duc·tion** (soo′pər kən duk′ shən), *n.* —**su′per·con·duc′tive, su′per·con·duct′ing,** *adj.*

su·per·con·duc·tor (so͞o′pər kən duk′tər), *n.* a material or device that loses all electrical resistance when cooled below a certain temperature.

su·per·cool (so͞o′pər ko͞ol′), *v.t.* **1.** to cool (a liquid) below its freezing point without producing solidification or crystallization. —*v.i.* **2.** to become supercooled.

su·per·crat (so͞o′pər krat′), *n.* *Informal.* a high-ranking bureaucrat, esp. one of cabinet rank. [SUPER + (BUREAU)-CRAT]

su·per·dom·i·nant (so͞o′pər dom′ə nənt), *n.* *Music.* submediant.

su·per-du·per (so͞o′pər do͞o′pər, -dyo͞o′-), *adj.* *Informal.* very super; marvelous or colossal.

su·per·e·go (so͞o′pər ē′gō, -eg′ō), *n.*, *pl.* **-gos.** *Psychoanal.* the part of the psyche that functions like the conscience in mediating between the drives of the id and learned values or ideals.

su·per·el·e·va·tion (so͞o′pər el′ə vā′shən), *n.* bank[1] (def. 6).

su·per·em·i·nent (so͞o′pər em′ə nənt), *adj.* of superior eminence, rank, or dignity; distinguished or conspicuous. [< L *superēminent-* (s. of *superēminēns*) overtopping] —**su′per·em′i·nence,** *n.* —**su′per·em′i·nent·ly,** *adv.*

su·per·er·o·gate (so͞o′pər er′ə gāt′), *v.i.*, **-gat·ed, -gat·ing.** to do more than duty requires. [< LL *supererogāt(us)* (ptp. of *supererogāre* to pay out in addition) = *super-* SUPER- + *ērogātus* paid out = *ērog-* (*ē-* E- + *rog-* ask) + *-ātus* -ATE[1]] —**su′per·er′o·ga′tion,** *n.* —**su′per·er′o·ga′tor,** *n.*

su·per·e·rog·a·to·ry (so͞o′pər ə rog′ə tôr′ē, -tôr′ē), *adj.* **1.** going beyond the requirements of duty. **2.** greater than that required; superfluous. [< ML *supererogātōri(us).* See SUPEREROGATE, -ORY[1]] —**su′per·e·rog′a·to′ri·ly,** *adv.*

su·per·fam·i·ly (so͞o′pər fam′ə lē, -fam′lē), *n.*, *pl.* **-lies.** *Biol.* a category of related families within an order or suborder.

su·per·fec·ta (so͞o′pər fek′tə), *n.* a type of betting, esp. on horse races, in which the bettor must select the first-, second-, third-, and fourth-place finishers in exact order of finish. Cf. **exacta, trifecta.**

su·per·fe·cun·da·tion (so͞o′pər fē′kən dā′shən, -fek′ən-), *n.* the fertilization of two or more ova discharged at the same ovulation by successive acts of sexual intercourse.

su·per·fe·ta·tion (so͞o′pər fē tā′shən), *n.* the fertilization of an ovum in a female mammal already pregnant. [< L *superfetāt(us)* (ptp. of *superfētāre* to conceive again while still pregnant) = *super-* SUPER- + *fētātus* = *fēt-* pregnant + *-ātus* -ATE[1]] —**su′per·fe′tate,** *adj.*

su·per·fi·cial (so͞o′pər fish′əl), *adj.* **1.** of or pertaining to the surface. **2.** being at, on, or near the surface: *a superficial cut.* **3.** external or outward only: *a superficial resemblance.* **4.** concerned merely with what is on the surface or obvious. **5.** shallow; not profound. **6.** apparent rather than real. **7.** insubstantial or insignificant. [< LL *superficāl(is)* = L *superfici(ēs)* SUPERFICIES + *-ālis* -AL[1]] —**su·per·fi·ci·al·i·ty** (so͞o′pər fish′ē al′i tē), **su′per·fi′cial·ness,** *n.* —**su′per·fi′cial·ly,** *adv.*

su·per·fi·ci·es (so͞o′pər fish′ē ēz′, -fish′ēz), *n.*, *pl.* **-ci·es.** **1.** the surface, outer face, or outside of a thing. **2.** the outward appearance, esp. as distinguished from the inner nature. [< L = *super-* SUPER- + *-ficiēs,* var. of *faciēs* face]

su·per·fine (so͞o′pər fīn′), *adj.* **1.** extra fine; unusually fine: *superfine sugar.* **2.** excessively refined; overnice.

su·per·flu·id (so͞o′pər flo͞o′id), *Physics.* —*n.* **1.** a fluid that exhibits frictionless flow, very high heat conductivity, and other unusual physical properties, helium below 2.186° K being the only known example. —*adj.* **2.** of superfluid.

su·per·flu·i·ty (so͞o′pər flo͞o′i tē), *n.*, *pl.* **-ties** for 2, 3. **1.** the state of being superfluous. **2.** an excessive amount. **3.** something superfluous, as a luxury. [late ME *superfluite* < OF < L *superfluitāt-* (s. of *superfluitās*). See SUPERFLUOUS]

su·per·flu·ous (so͝o pûr′flo͞o əs), *adj.* **1.** being more than sufficient; excessive. **2.** unnecessary or needless. **3.** *Obs.* possessing or spending more than enough; extravagant. [late ME < L *superfluus* = *super-* SUPER- + *flu-* (s. of *fluere* to flow) + *-us* -OUS] —**su·per′flu·ous·ly,** *adv.* —**su·per′flu·ous·ness,** *n.* —**Syn. 1.** extra; redundant.

Su·per·for·tress (so͞o′pər fôr′tris), *n.* *U.S. Mil.* a heavy, long-range, four-engined bomber used during World War II, specifically the B-29 and the B-50. Also called **Su·per·fort** (so͞o′pər fôrt′, -fōrt′). [SUPER- + (FLYING) FORTRESS]

su·per·fuse (so͞o′pər fyo͞oz′), *v.t.*, **-fused, -fus·ing.** *Obs.* to pour. [< L *superfūs(us)* (ptp.) poured on or over = *super-* SUPER- + *-fūsus* = *fūd-* (root of *fundere* to pour) + *-tus* ptp. suffix] —**su·per·fu·sion** (so͞o′pər fyo͞o′zhən), *n.*

su·per·gal·ax·y (so͞o′pər gal′ək sē), *n.*, *pl.* **-ax·ies.** *Astron.* a system of galaxies. —**su·per·ga·lac·tic** (so͞o′pər-gə lak′tik), *adj.*

su′per·gi′ant star′ (so͞o′pər jī′ənt), *Astron.* an exceptionally luminous star whose diameter is more than 100 times that of the sun, as Betelgeuse or Antares.

su·per·gla·cial (so͞o′pər glā′shəl), *adj.* **1.** on the surface of a glacier. **2.** believed to have come from the surface of a glacier: *superglacial debris.*

su·per·heat (*n.* so͞o′pər hēt′; *v.* so͞o′pər hēt′), *n.* **1.** the state of being superheated. **2.** the amount of superheating. —*v.t.* **3.** to heat to an extreme degree or to a very high temperature. **4.** to heat (a liquid) above its boiling point without the formation of bubbles of vapor. **5.** to heat (a gas, as steam not in contact with water) to such a high degree that its temperature may be lowered or its pressure increased without the conversion of any of the gas into liquid. —**su′per·heat′er,** *n.*

su·per·het·er·o·dyne (so͞o′pər het′ər ə dīn′), *Radio.* —*adj.* **1.** noting, pertaining to, or using a method of receiving radio signals by which the incoming modulated wave is changed by the heterodyne process to a lower frequency and then submitted to stages of radio-frequency amplification with subsequent detection and audio-frequency amplification. —*n.* **2.** a superheterodyne receiver. [SUPER(SONIC) + HETERODYNE]

su′per·high fre′quency (so͞o′pər hī′), *Radio.* any frequency between 3,000 and 30,000 megacycles per second. *Abbr.:* SHF

su·per·high·way (so͞o′pər hī′wā′), *n.* a main highway designed for travel at high speeds, having more than one lane for each direction of traffic.

su·per·hu·man (so͞o′pər hyo͞o′mən *or, often,* -yo͞o′-), *adj.* **1.** above or beyond what is human; having a higher nature or greater powers than man has: *a superhuman being.* **2.** exceeding ordinary human power, achievement, experience, etc.: *a superhuman effort.* [< NL *superhūmān(us)*] —**su·per·hu·man·i·ty** (so͞o′pər hyo͞o man′i tē *or, often,* -yo͞o-), **su′per·hu′man·ness,** *n.* —**su′per·hu′man·ly,** *adv.*

su·per·im·pose (so͞o′pər im pōz′), *v.t.,* **-posed, -pos·ing.** **1.** to impose, place, or set over, above, or on something else. **2.** to put or join as an addition (usually fol. by *on* or *upon*). —**su·per·im·po·si·tion** (so͞o′pər im′pə zish′ən), *n.*

su·per·in·cum·bent (so͞o′pər in kum′bənt), *adj.* **1.** lying on something else. **2.** situated above; overhanging. **3.** exerted from above, as pressure. [< L *superincumbent-* (s. of *superincumbēns*) lying on] —**su′per·in·cum′bence, su′per·in·cum′ben·cy,** *n.* —**su′per·in·cum′bent·ly,** *adv.*

su·per·in·duce (so͞o′pər in do͞os′, -dyo͞os′), *v.t.,* **-duced, -duc·ing.** to bring in or induce as an added feature, circumstance, etc.; superimpose. [< L *superindūce(re)*] —**su·per·in·duc·tion** (so͞o′pər in duk′shən), *n.*

su·per·in·tend (so͞o′pər in tend′, so͞o′prin-), *v.t.* **1.** to oversee and direct (work, processes, etc.). **2.** to exercise supervision over (an institution, district, etc.). [< LL *superintend(ere)*] —**Syn.** supervise, manage, conduct.

su·per·in·tend·en·cy (so͞o′pər in ten′dən sē, so͞o′prin-), *n., pl.* **-cies.** **1.** a district or place under a superintendent. **2.** the position or work of a superintendent. **3.** Also, **su′per·in·tend′ence.** the act or process of superintending; supervision. [< ML *superintendentia.* See SUPERINTEND, -ENCY]

su·per·in·tend·ent (so͞o′pər in ten′dənt, so͞o′prin-), *n.* Also called, *Informal,* **super. 1.** a person who oversees or directs some work, enterprise, organization, etc.; supervisor. **2.** a person who is responsible for the maintenance and general supervision of a building. —*adj.* **3.** superintending. [< ML *superintendent-* (s. of *superintendēns*) superintending]

su·pe·ri·or (sə pēr′ē ər, so͝o-), *adj.* **1.** higher in station, rank, degree, etc. **2.** above the average in excellence, merit, intelligence, etc. **3.** of higher grade or quality. **4.** greater in quantity or amount. **5.** showing a consciousness of superiority to others. **6.** not yielding or susceptible (usually fol. by *to*): *to be superior to temptation.* **7.** higher in place or position: *superior ground.* **8.** *Bot.* **a.** situated above some other organ. **b.** (of a calyx) seeming to originate from the top of the ovary. **c.** (of an ovary) free from the calyx. **9.** *Anat., Zool.* (of an organ or part) higher in place or position; situated above another. Cf. **inferior** (def. 5). **10.** *Print.* written or printed high on a line of text, as the "2" in a^2b; superscript. Cf. **inferior** (def. 7). **11.** *Astron.* **a.** (of a planet) having an orbit outside that of the earth. **b.** (of an inferior planet) noting a conjunction in which the sun is between the earth and the planet. —*n.* **12.** one superior to another or others. **13.** Also called **superscript.** *Print.* a letter, number, or symbol written or printed high on a line of text. Cf. **inferior** (def. 9). **14.** *Eccles.* the head of a monastery, convent, or the like. [ME < L = *super(us)* situated above + *-ior* comp. suffix; see -ER[4]] —**su·pe′ri·or·ly,** *adv.*

Su·pe·ri·or (sə pēr′ē ər, so͝o-), *n.* **1. Lake,** a lake in the N central United States and S Canada: the northernmost of the Great Lakes; the largest body of fresh water in the world. 350 mi. long; 31 820 sq. mi.; greatest depth, 1290 ft. **2.** a port in NW Wisconsin, on Lake Superior. 32,237 (1970).

supe′rior court′, **1.** the court of general jurisdiction in many states of the United States. **2.** a court that has general jurisdiction above that of inferior courts.

su·pe·ri·or·i·ty (sə pēr′ē ôr′i tē, -or′-, so͝o-), *n.* the quality or condition of being superior. [< ML *superioritāt-* (s. of *superioritās*)]

superior′ity com′plex, an exaggerated feeling of one's own superiority.

su·per·ja·cent (so͞o′pər jā′sənt), *adj.* lying above or upon something else. [< L *superjacent-* (s. of *superjacēns*) lying over or upon]

su·per·jet (so͞o pər jet′), *n. Informal.* a giant jet plane.

superl., superlative.

su·per·la·tive (sə pûr′lə tiv, so͝o-), *adj.* **1.** of the highest kind or order. **2.** excessive or exaggerated, as in language. **3.** *Gram.* of, pertaining to, or noting the highest degree of the comparison of adjectives and adverbs, as *best,* the superlative form of *good.* Cf. **comparative** (def. 4), **positive** (def. 18). —*n.* **4.** a superlative person or thing. **5.** the utmost degree; acme. **6.** *Gram.* **a.** the superlative degree. **b.** a form in the superlative. [< LL *superlātīv(us)* = L *superlāt(us)* hyperbolical (*super-* SUPER- + *-lātus* carried, ptp. of *ferre* to bear) + *-īvus* -IVE; r. ME *superlatif* < OF] —**su·per′la·tive·ly,** *adv.* —**su·per′la·tive·ness,** *n.*

su·per·lu·na·ry (so͞o′pər lo͞o′nə rē), *adj.* **1.** situated above or beyond the moon. **2.** celestial, rather than earthly. Also, **su′per·lu′nar.** [SUPER- + (SUB)LUNARY]

su·per·man (so͞o′pər man′), *n., pl.* **-men. 1.** a man of superhuman powers. **2.** an ideal superior being conceived by Nietzsche as the product of human evolution. [trans. of G *Übermensch*]

su·per·mar·ket (so͞o′pər mär′kit), *n.* a large, self-service retail market that sells food.

su·per·nal (so͝o pûr′nəl), *adj.* **1.** heavenly, celestial, or divine. **2.** lofty; of more than human excellence, powers, etc. **3.** being on high or in the sky or visible heavens. [late ME < MF = *supern-* (< L *supern(us)* upper) + *-al* -AL[1]] —**su·per′nal·ly,** *adv.*

su·per·na·tant (so͞o′pər nāt′ənt), *adj.* floating above or on the surface. [< L *supernatant-* (s. of *supernatāns*) floating] —**su·per·na·ta·tion** (so͞o′pər nə tā′shən), *n.*

su·per·na·tion·al (so͞o′pər nash′ə nəl), *adj.* **1.** extremely or fanatically devoted to a nation. **2.** tending to involve, or extending authority over, more than one nation; international. —**su′per·na′tion·al·ism,** *n.* —**su′per·na′tion·al·ist,** *n.* —**su′per·na′tion·al·ly,** *adv.*

su·per·nat·u·ral (so͞o′pər nach′ər əl), *adj.* **1.** of, pertaining to, or being above or beyond what is explainable by natural laws or phenomena. **2.** of, pertaining to, or characteristic of God or a deity. **3.** exceeding normal or expected capability; preternatural: *a missile of supernatural speed.* **4.** of or relating to ghosts, goblins, etc.; eerie; occult. —*n.* **5.** a being, occurrence, etc., considered as supernatural or of supernatural origin. **6.** direct influence or action of a god on earthly affairs. **7. the supernatural, a.** supernatural beings, behavior, and occurrences collectively. **b.** supernatural forces and the supernatural plane of existence. [< ML *supernātūrāl(is)*] —**su′per·nat′u·ral·ly,** *adv.* —**su′per·nat′u·ral·ness,** *n.* —**Syn. 1.** See **miraculous.**

su·per·nat·u·ral·ism (so͞o′pər nach′ər ə liz′əm), *n.* **1.** supernatural character or agency. **2.** belief in the doctrine of supernatural or divine agency as manifested in the world, in human events, etc. —**su′per·nat′u·ral·ist,** *n., adj.* —**su′per·nat′u·ral·is′tic,** *adj.*

su·per·nor·mal (so͞o′pər nôr′məl), *adj.* **1.** in excess of the normal or average. **2.** lying beyond normal or natural powers of comprehension: *supernormal intimations.* —**super·nor·mal·i·ty** (so͞o′pər nôr mal′i tē), **su′per·nor′malness,** *n.* —**su′per·nor′mal·ly,** *adv.*

su·per·no·va (so͞o′pər nō′və), *n., pl.* **-vae** (-vē), **-vas.** *Astron.* an extremely bright nova that emits from ten million to a hundred million times as much light as the sun.

su·per·nu·mer·ar·y (so͞o′pər no͞o′mə rer′ē, -nyo͞o′-), *adj., n., pl.* **-ar·ies.** —*adj.* **1.** being in excess of the usual, proper, or prescribed number; extra. **2.** associated with a regular body or staff as an assistant or substitute in case of necessity. —*n.* **3.** a supernumerary or extra person or thing. **4.** a supernumerary official or employee. **5.** *Theat.* a person who appears onstage without speaking lines or as part of a crowd; walk-on. [< LL *supernumerāri(us)*]

su·per·or·der (so͞o′pər ôr′dər), *n. Biol.* a category of related orders within a class or subclass.

su·per·or·di·nate (*adj., n.* so͞o′pər ôr′dənit; *v.* so͞o′pər-ôr′dənāt′), *adj., n., v.,* **-nat·ed, -nat·ing.** —*adj.* **1.** of higher degree in condition or rank. —*n.* **2.** a superordinate person or thing. —*v.t.* **3.** to elevate to superordinate position. [SUPER- + (SUB)ORDINATE]

su·per·or·gan·ic (so͞o′pər ôr gan′ik), *adj. Sociol., Anthropol.* of or pertaining to the structure of cultural elements within society conceived as independent of and superior to the individual members of society. —**su′per·or·gan′i·cism,** *n.* —**su′per·or·gan′i·cist,** *n.*

su·per·ox·ide (so͞o′pər ok′sīd, -sid), *n. Chem.* peroxide (defs. 1a, b). Also called **hyperoxide.**

su·per·pa·tri·ot (so͞o′pər pā′trē ət, so͞o′pər pā′-; *esp. Brit.,* so͞o′pər pa′trē ət, so͞o′pər pa′-), *n.* a person who is patriotic to an extreme. —**su·per·pa·tri·ot·ic** (so͞o′pər-pā′trē ot′ik; *esp. Brit.,* so͞o′pər pa′trē ot′ik), *adj.* —**su′per·pa′tri·ot′i·cal·ly,** *adv.* —**su′per·pa′tri·ot·ism,** *n.*

su·per·phos·phate (so͞o′pər fos′fāt), *n.* **1.** a mixture, prepared with sulfuric acid, of calcium acid phosphate and calcium sulfate, used chiefly as a fertilizer. **2.** a mixture prepared with phosphoric acid, used as a fertilizer.

su·per·phys·i·cal (so͞o′pər fiz′i kəl), *adj.* above or beyond what is physical; hyperphysical.

su·per·pose (so͞o′pər pōz′), *v.t.,* **-posed, -pos·ing. 1.** to place above or upon something else, or one upon another; superimpose. **2.** *Geom.* to place one figure in the space occupied by another, so that the two coincide throughout their whole extent. [< F *superpos(er)*] —**su′per·pos′a·ble,** *adj.* —**su·per·po·si·tion** (so͞o′pər pə zish′ən), *n.*

su·per·pow·er (so͞o′pər pou′ər), *n.* **1.** power that is extremely great in scope or magnitude. **2.** a nation capable of influencing the acts and policies of other nations. —**su′per·pow′ered,** *adj.*

su·per·race (so͞o′pər rās′), *n.* a race, class, or people allegedly superior to another or others.

su·per·ra·tion·al (so͞o′pər rash′ə nəl), *adj.* beyond the scope or range of reason; intuitional. —**su′per·ra′tion·al′i·ty,** *n.* —**su′per·ra′tion·al·ly,** *adv.*

su·per·sat·u·rate (so͞o′pər sach′ə rāt′), *v.t.,* **-rat·ed, -rat·ing.** to increase the concentration of (a solution) beyond saturation. —**su′per·sat′u·ra′tion,** *n.*

su·per·scribe (so͞o′pər skrīb′, so͞o′pər skrīb′), *v.t.,* **-scribed, -scrib·ing. 1.** to write (words, letters, one's name, etc.) above or on something. **2.** to inscribe or mark with writing at the top or on the outside or surface of. [< L *superscrībe(re)* = *super-* SUPER- + *scrībere* to write; see SCRIBE[1]]

su·per·script (so͞o′pər skript′), *adj.* **1.** superior (def. 10). —*n.* **2.** superior (def. 13). **3.** *Obs.* an address on a letter. [< L *superscrīpt(us)* (ptp. of *superscrībere* to SUPERSCRIBE) = *super-* SUPER- + *scrīptus* written; see SCRIPT]

su·per·scrip·tion (so͞o′pər skrip′shən), *n.* **1.** the act of superscribing. **2.** that which is superscribed. **3.** an address on a letter, parcel, or the like. **4.** *Pharm.* the sign ℞, meaning "take," at the beginning of a prescription. [< LL *superscrīptiōn-* (s. of *superscrīptiō*) a writing above. See SUPERSCRIPT, -ION]

su·per·sede (so͞o′pər sēd′), *v.t.,* **-sed·ed, -sed·ing. 1.** to replace in power, authority, effectiveness, etc. **2.** to set aside or cause to be set aside as void, useless, or obsolete, usually in favor of something mentioned. **3.** to succeed to the position, function, office, etc., of; supplant. [< L *supersed(ēre)* (to) sit above or upon, forbear = *super-* SUPER- + *sedēre* to SIT] —**su′per·sed′a·ble,** *adj.* —**su′per·sed′er,** *n.* —**su·per·se·dure** (so͞o′pər sē′jər), **su·per·ses·sion** (so͞o′pər sesh′ən), *n.* —**Syn. 1.** See **replace.**

su·per·se·de·as (so͞o′pər sē′dē əs, -as′), *n., pl.* **-de·as.** *Law.* a writ ordering a stoppage or suspension of a judicial proceeding. [< L, 2nd sing. pres. subj. of *supersedēre* to SUPERSEDE, the writ being so named because *supersedeas,* i.e., you shall desist, occurs in it]

su·per·sen·si·ble (so͞o′pər sen′sə bəl), *adj.* being above or beyond perception by the senses; beyond the reach of the senses. —**su′per·sen′si·bly,** *adv.*

su·per·sen·si·tive (so͞o′pər sen′si tiv), *adj.* **1.** extremely or excessively sensitive. **2.** hypersensitive (def. 2). —**su′per·sen′si·tive·ness,** *n.*

su·per·sen·so·ry (so͞o′pər sen′sə rē), *adj.* **1.** supersensible. **2.** independent of the organs of sense.

su·per·son·ic (so͞o′pər son′ik), *adj.* **1.** greater than the speed of sound waves through air. **2.** capable of achieving such speed: *a supersonic plane.* **3.** ultrasonic. —**su′per·son′i·cal·ly,** *adv.*

su·per·son·ics (so͞o′pər son′iks), *n.* (*construed as sing.*) the branch of science that deals with supersonic phenomena. [see SUPERSONIC, -ICS]

su·per·state (so͞o′pər stāt′), *n.* **1.** a state or a governing power presiding over states subordinated to it. **2.** an extremely powerful centralized government.

su·per·sti·tion (so͞o′pər stish′ən), *n.* **1.** an irrational belief in or notion of the ominous significance of a particular thing, circumstance, or the like. **2.** a system or collection of such beliefs. **3.** a custom or act based on such a belief. **4.** irrational fear of what is unknown, esp. in connection with religion. **5.** any blindly accepted belief or notion. [< L *superstitiōn-* (s. of *superstitiō*) = *superstit-* (s. of *superstes*) standing beyond, outliving + *-iōn-* -ION]

su·per·sti·tious (so͞o′pər stish′əs), *adj.* **1.** of the nature of, characterized by, or proceeding from superstition: *superstitious fears.* **2.** pertaining to or connected with superstition: *superstitious legends.* **3.** believing in or full of superstition. [< L *superstitiōs(us)* = *superstiti-* (shortened s. of *superstitiō* SUPERSTITION) + *-ōsus* -OUS] —**su′per·sti′tious·ly,** *adv.* —**su′per·sti′tious·ness,** *n.*

su·per·stra·tum (so͞o′pər strā′təm, -strat′əm), *n., pl.* **-stra·ta** (-strā′tə, -strat′ə), **-stra·tums.** an overlying stratum or layer.

su·per·struc·ture (so͞o′pər struk′chər), *n.* **1.** the part of a building or construction entirely above its foundation or basement. **2.** any structure built on something else. **3.** *Naut.* any construction built above the main deck of a vessel as an upward continuation of the sides. Cf. **deckhouse. 4.** the part of a bridge that rests on the piers and abutments. —**su′per·struc′tur·al,** *adj.*

su·per·sub·tle (so͞o′pər sut′əl), *adj.* extremely or excessively subtle. —**su′per·sub′tle·ty,** *n.*

su·per·tank·er (so͞o′pər tang′kər), *n.* a tanker with a capacity of over 75,000 tons.

su·per·tax (so͞o′pər taks′), *n.* **1.** *Chiefly Brit.* a tax in addition to a normal tax, as one upon income above a certain amount. **2.** *U.S.* a surtax.

su·per·ti·tle (so͞o′pər tīt′əl), *n., v.,* **-tled, -tling.** —*n.* **1.** (esp. in opera) a translation of a text, as a libretto, projected onto a screen above the stage during performance. —*v.t.* **2.** to provide supertitles for.

su·per·ton·ic (so͞o′pər ton′ik), *n.* *Music.* the second tone of a scale, being the next above the tonic.

su·per·vene (so͞o′pər vēn′), *v.i.,* **-vened, -ven·ing. 1.** to take place or occur as something additional or extraneous. **2.** to ensue. [< L *superven(īre)* = *super-* SUPER- + *venīre* to come] —**su·per·ven·ience** (so͞o′pər vēn′yəns), **su·per·ven·tion** (so͞o′pər ven′shən), *n.* —**su′per·ven′ient,** *adj.*

su·per·vise (so͞o′pər vīz′), *v.t.,* **-vised, -vis·ing.** to oversee (a process, work, workers, etc.) during execution or performance; superintend. [< ML *supervīs(us)*]

su·per·vi·sion (so͞o′pər vizh′ən), *n.* the act or function of supervising; superintendence. [< ML *supervīsiōn-* (s. of *supervīsiō*) oversight = *super-* SUPER- + *vīsiōn-* VISION]

su·per·vi·sor (so͞o′pər vī′zər), *n.* **1.** a person who supervises; superintendent. **2.** *Educ.* an official responsible for assisting teachers in the preparation of syllabuses, in devising teaching methods, etc., esp. in public schools. **3.** *U.S.* an elected administrative officer in some states. [< ML] —**su′per·vi′sor·ship′,** *n.*

su·per·vi·so·ry (so͞o′pər vī′zə rē), *adj.* of, pertaining to, or having supervision.

su·pi·nate (so͞o′pə nāt′), *v.,* **-nat·ed, -nat·ing.** —*v.t.* **1.** to turn to a supine position; rotate (the hand or forearm) so that the palmar surface is upward. —*v.i.* **2.** to become supinated. [< L *supīnāt(us)* (ptp. of *supīnāre* to lay face up)]

su·pi·na·tion (so͞o′pə nā′shən), *n.* **1.** rotation of the hand or forearm so that the palmar surface is facing upward. **2.** a comparable motion of the foot. **3.** the position assumed as the result of this rotation.

su·pi·na·tor (so͞o′pə nā′tər), *n.* *Anat.* a muscle used in supination. [< NL]

su·pine (*adj.* so͞o pīn′; *n.* so͞o′pīn), *adj.* **1.** lying on the back. **2.** inactive, passive, or inert. **3.** (of the hand) having the palm upward. —*n.* **4.** (in Latin) a noun form derived from verbs, appearing only in the accusative and the dative-ablative, as *dictū* in *mīrābile dictū,* "wonderful to say." **5.** (in English) the simple infinitive of a verb preceded by *to.* **6.** an analogous form in some other language. [< L *supīn(us)* lying face up, inactive] —**su·pine′ly,** *adv.* —**su·pine′ness,** *n.*

supp., supplement. Also, **suppl.**

sup·per (sup′ər), *n.* **1.** the evening meal, esp. when dinner is served at midday. **2.** any light evening meal, esp. one taken late in the evening. [ME *sup(p)er* < OF *souper,* n. use of *souper* to SUP[1]]

sup′per club′, a night club, esp. a small, luxurious one.

sup·plant (sə plant′, -plänt′), *v.t.* **1.** to take the place of (another), as through force, scheming, or the like. **2.** to replace (one thing) by something else. [ME *supplante(n)* < L *supplantāre* to trip up, overthrow. See SUP-, PLANT] —**sup·plan·ta·tion** (sup′lan tā′shən), *n.* —**sup·plant′er,** *n.*

sup·ple (sup′əl), *adj.,* **-pler, -plest,** *v.,* **-pled, -pling.** —*adj.* **1.** able to bend readily without damage; pliant; flexible. **2.** characterized by ease in bending; limber; lithe: *a supple dancer.* **3.** characterized by mental adaptability. **4.** compliant or yielding. **5.** obsequious; servile. —*v.t., v.i.* **6.** to make or become supple. [ME *souple* < OF: soft, yielding < L *supplic-* kneeling, submissive] —**sup′ple·ness,** *n.*

sup·ple·jack (sup′əl jak′), *n.* **1.** a strong, pliant cane or walking stick. **2.** any of various climbing shrubs with strong stems suitable for making walking sticks.

sup·ple·ly (sup′lē), *adv.* supply[2].

sup·ple·ment (*n.* sup′lə mənt; *v.* sup′lə ment′), *n.* **1.** something added to complete a thing, supply a deficiency, or reinforce or extend a whole. **2.** a part added to a book, document, etc., to supply additional or later information, correct errors, or the like. **3.** an additional part of a newspaper or other periodical. **4.** *Math.* the quantity by which an angle or an arc falls short of 180° or a semicircle. —*v.t.* **5.** to complete, add to, or extend by a supplement; form a supplement or addition to. **6.** to supply (a deficiency). [ME < L *supplēment(um)* that by which anything is made full = *sup-* SUP- + *plē-* (s. of *plēre* to fill) + *-mentum* -MENT] —**sup′ple·men·ta′tion,** *n.* —**sup′ple·ment′er,** *n.* —**Syn. 1.** reinforcement, extension, addition. **2.** addendum. **5.** See **complement.**

sup·ple·men·tal (sup′lə men′təl), *adj.* supplementary (def. 1). —**sup′ple·men′tal·ly,** *adv.*

sup·ple·men·ta·ry (sup′lə men′tə rē), *adj., n., pl.* **-ries.** —*adj.* **1.** of the nature of or forming a supplement; additional. —*n.* **2.** a person or thing that is supplementary.

sup′plemen′tary an′gle, *Math.* either of two angles that added together produce an angle of 180°.

sup·ple·tion (sə plē′shən), *n.* *Gram.* the use in inflection or derivation of an allomorph that is not related in form to the primary allomorph of a morpheme, as the use of *better* as the comparative of *good.* [< ML *supplētiōn-* (s. of *supplētiō*) a filling up = *supplēt(us),* ptp. of *supplēre* to make complete, (*sup-* SUP- + *plē-* s. of *plēre* to fill + *-tus* ptp. suffix) + *-iōn-* -ION]

sup·ple·tive (sə plē′tiv, sup′li tiv), *adj.* *Gram.* characterized by or serving to indicate suppletion. [< ML *supplētīv(us)* = L *supplēt(us)* (ptp. of *supplēre* to fill up; see SUPPLETION) + *-īvus* -IVE]

sup·ple·to·ry (sup′li tōr′ē, -tôr′ē), *adj.* supplying a deficiency. [< LL *supplētōri(us)*] —**sup′ple·to′ri·ly,** *adv.*

sup·pli·ance (sup′lē əns), *n.* appeal; entreaty; plea. Also, **sup′pli·an·cy.** [SUPPLI(ANT) + -ANCE]

sup·pli·ant (sup′lē ənt), *n.* **1.** a person who supplicates; petitioner. —*adj.* **2.** supplicating. **3.** expressive of supplication, as words or actions. [late ME < MF, prp. of *supplier* < L *supplicāre* to kneel, beseech, SUPPLICATE] —**sup′pli·ant·ly,** *adv.* —**sup′pli·ant·ness,** *n.*

sup·pli·cant (sup′lə kənt), *adj.* **1.** supplicating. —*n.* **2.** a suppliant. [< L *supplicant-* (s. of *supplicāns,* prp. of *supplicāre* to SUPPLICATE) = *supplic-* (see SUPPLE) + *-ant-* -ANT]

sup·pli·cate (sup′lə kāt′), *v.,* **-cat·ed, -cat·ing.** —*v.i.* **1.** to make humble and earnest entreaty. —*v.t.* **2.** to pray humbly to; entreat or petition humbly. **3.** to ask for by humble entreaty. [< L *supplicāt(us)* (ptp. of *supplicāre* to kneel)] —**sup′pli·cat′ing·ly,** *adv.* —**Syn. 2.** implore, beseech.

sup·pli·ca·tion (sup′lə kā′shən), *n.* the act of supplicating; humble prayer, entreaty, or petition. [late ME < L *supplicātiōn-* (s. of *supplicātiō*), lit., a kneeling]

sup·pli·ca·to·ry (sup′lə kə tōr′ē, -tôr′ē), *adj.* making or expressing supplication. [< ML *supplicātōri(us)*]

sup·ply[1] (sə plī′), *v.,* **-plied, -ply·ing,** *n., pl.* **-plies.** —*v.t.* **1.** to provide (a person, establishment, etc.) with what is lacking or needed (often fol. by *with*): *to supply someone clothing; to supply a community with electricity.* **2.** to provide (something wanting or needed): *to supply electricity to a community.* **3.** to make up, compensate for, or satisfy (a deficiency, need, etc.). **4.** to fill or occupy as a substitute. —*v.i.* **5.** to substitute for another, esp. in the pulpit of a church. —*n.* **6.** the act of furnishing, providing, etc. **7.** that which is provided: *a city's water supply.* **8.** a quantity of something on hand or available, as for use; a stock or store. **9.** Usually, **supplies.** a provision, stock, or store of food or other things necessary for maintenance. **10.** *Econ.* the quantity of a commodity that is in the market and available for purchase, esp. at a particular price. **11. supplies,** *Mil.* **a.** all items necessary for the equipment, maintenance, and operation of a military command. **b.** procurement, distribution, maintenance, and salvage of supplies. **12.** a person who fills a vacancy or takes the place of another, esp. temporarily. **13.** *Obs.* reinforcements. **14.** *Obs.* aid. [late ME *sup(p)lie(n)* < MF *souplie(r),* var. of *soupleer* < L *supplēre* to fill up = *sup-* SUP- + *plēre* to fill] —**sup·pli′a·ble,** *adj.* —**sup·pli′er,** *n.*

sup·ply[2] (sup′lē), *adv.* in a supple manner or way; supplely.

sup·ply-side (sə plī′sīd′), *adj.* *Econ.* of or pertaining to a theory that a nation can regain its economic stability and curb inflation by increasing its supply of goods and services, and that this can be achieved by reducing taxes and passing other legislation designed to encourage business investment and growth.

sup·ply-sid·er (sə plī′sī′dər), *n.* one who supports or advocates supply-side economics.

sup·port (sə pōrt′, -pôrt′), *v.t.* **1.** to bear or hold up (a load, structure, part, etc.). **2.** to sustain or withstand (weight, pressure, strain, etc.). **3.** to provide (a person, family, etc.) with the means of sustaining life. **4.** to sustain (a person, his spirits, etc.) under affliction. **5.** to uphold and aid (a person, cause, principle, etc.); back. **6.** to corroborate (a statement, opinion, etc.). **7.** to endure or tolerate, esp. with patience. **8.** to act with or second (a leading actor), as on a stage. —*n.* **9.** the act or an instance of supporting. **10.** the state of being supported. **11.** that which serves as a foundation, prop. **12.** maintenance, as of a person or family. **13.** a person or thing that supports, as financially: *The pension was his only support.* **14.** a thing or a person that gives aid or assistance. **15.** the material, as canvas or wood, on which a picture is painted. [ME *supporte(n)* < MF *supporte(r)* < ML *supportāre* to endure (L: to convey) = *sup-* SUP- + *portāre* to carry; see PORT[5]] —**sup·port′ing·ly,** *adv.* —**sup·port′less,** *adj.* —**sup·port′less·ly,** *adv.*

—**Syn. 1, 5.** SUPPORT, MAINTAIN, SUSTAIN, UPHOLD all

mean to hold up and to preserve. To SUPPORT is to hold up or add strength to, literally or figuratively: *The columns support the roof.* To MAINTAIN is to support so as to preserve intact: *to maintain an attitude of defiance.* To SUSTAIN, a rather elevated word, suggests completeness and adequacy in supporting: *The court sustained his claim.* UPHOLD applies esp. to supporting or backing another, as in a statement, opinion, or belief: *to uphold the rights of a minority.* **5.** abet, encourage; help. **12.** sustenance, keep. See **living.**

sup·port·a·ble (sə pōr′tə bəl, -pôr′-), *adj.* capable of being supported; endurable. **—sup·port′a·bil′i·ty, sup·port′a·ble·ness,** *n.* **—sup·port′a·bly,** *adv.*

sup·port·er (sə pōr′tər, -pôr′-), *n.* **1.** a person or thing that supports. **2.** a jockstrap. **3.** a device, usually of elastic cotton webbing, for supporting some part of the body. **4.** a garter, esp. one attached to a garter belt or girdle. **5.** an adherent or follower, backer. **6.** *Heraldry.* either of two human or animal figures flanking and supporting an escutcheon in an achievement of arms. [late ME]

sup·port·ive (sə pōr′tiv, -pôr′-), *adj.* providing support.

sup·pose (sə pōz′), *v.*, **-posed, -pos·ing.** **—***v.t.* **1.** to assume (something), as for the sake of argument. **2.** (used in the imperative) to consider as a possibility suggested or an idea or plan proposed: *Suppose we wait until tomorrow.* **3.** to believe or assume as true; take for granted: *I suppose you'll leave now.* **4.** to think, or hold as an opinion: *What do you suppose he will do?* **5.** to make or involve the assumption of, as a proposition, theory, etc. **6.** to require logically; imply; presuppose. **7.** to expect, as facts, circumstances, etc. **—***v.i.* **8.** to assume something; presume; think. [ME *suppose(n)* < OF *suppose(r)* = *sup-* SUP- (< ML *suppōnere* to suppose) + *poser* to POSE[1]] **—sup·pos′a·ble,** *adj.* **—sup·pos′a·bly,** *adv.* **—sup·pos′er,** *n.*

sup·posed (sə pōzd′, -pō′zid), *adj.* **1.** assumed as true, regardless of fact; hypothetical: *a supposed case.* **2.** accepted or believed as true, without positive knowledge. **3.** merely thought to be such; imagined: *to sacrifice real for supposed gains.* **—sup·pos·ed·ly** (sə pō′zid lē), *adv.*

sup·po·si·tion (sup′ə zish′ən), *n.* **1.** the act of supposing. **2.** an assumption or hypothesis. [late ME < L *suppositiōn-* (s. of *suppositiō* substitution); E meaning by assoc. with SUPPOSE) = *supposit(us)* (ptp. of *suppōnere* to substitute) + *-iōn-* -ION] **—sup′po·si′tion·al,** *adj.* **—sup′po·si′tion·al·ly,** *adv.* **—sup′po·si′tion·less,** *adj.*

sup·po·si·tious (sup′ə zish′əs), *adj.* **1.** formed from or growing out of supposition: *suppositious evidence.* **2.** supposititious. [shortened form of SUPPOSITITIOUS]

sup·pos·i·ti·tious (sə poz′i tish′əs), *adj.* **1.** fraudulently substituted; spurious. **2.** hypothetical. [< L *supposit*ī*cius* = *supposit(us)* (ptp. of *suppōnere;* see SUPPOSITION) + *-icius* -ITIOUS] **—sup·pos′i·ti′tious·ness,** *n.*

sup·pos·i·tive (sə poz′i tiv), *adj.* **1.** of the nature of or involving supposition. **2.** supposititious or false. **3.** *Gram.* expressing supposition, as the words *if, granting,* or *provided.* **—***n.* **4.** *Gram.* a suppositive word. [< LL *suppositīv(us)* = *supposit(us)* (see SUPPOSITION) + *-īvus* -IVE] **—sup·pos′i·tive·ly,** *adv.*

sup·pos·i·to·ry (se poz′i tōr′ē, -tôr′ē), *n., pl.* **-ries.** a solid, conical mass of medicinal substance for inserting into the rectum or vagina. [late ME < ML *suppositōri(um)* = *supposit(us)* (see SUPPOSITITIOUS) + *-ōrium* -ORY[2]]

sup·press (sə pres′), *v.t.* **1.** to put an end to the activities of (a person, body of persons, etc.). **2.** to do away with by or as by authority; abolish; stop (a practice, custom, etc.). **3.** to keep in or repress (a feeling, smile, groan, etc.). **4.** to withhold from disclosure or publication. **5.** to stop or arrest (a flow, hemorrhage, cough, etc.). **6.** to vanquish or subdue (a revolt, rebellion, etc.); quell; crush. [late ME < L *suppress(us)* pressed under (ptp. of *supprimere*) = *sup-* SUP- + *pressus;* see PRESS[1]] **—sup·pressed·ly** (sə prest′lē, -pres′-id lē), *adv.* **—sup·press′i·ble,** *adj.* **—sup·pres′sive,** *adj.* **—sup·pres′sive·ly,** *adv.* **—sup·pres′sor, sup·press′er,** *n.*

sup·pres·sant (sə pres′ənt), *n.* a drug, chemical, etc., that suppresses an undesirable action or condition: *a cough suppressant.* [SUPPRESS + -ANT]

sup·pres·sion (sə presh′ən), *n.* **1.** the act of suppressing. **2.** the state of being suppressed. **3.** *Psychoanal.* conscious inhibiting or suppressing, as of an impulse or memory. [< L *suppressiōn-* (s. of *suppressiō*) a pressing under]

sup·pu·rate (sup′yə rāt′), *v.i.*, **-rat·ed, -rat·ing.** to produce or discharge pus, as a wound; maturate. [< L *suppūrāt(us)* (ptp. of *suppūrāre*) = *sup-* SUP- + *pūr-* (s. of *pūs*) PUS + *-ātus* -ATE[1]]

sup·pu·ra·tion (sup′yə rā′shən), *n.* **1.** the process of suppurating. **2.** the matter produced by suppuration; pus. [< L *suppūrātiōn-* (s. of *suppūrātiō*) a forming of pus]

sup·pu·ra·tive (sup′yə rā′tiv), *adj.* **1.** suppurating. **2.** promoting suppuration. **—***n.* **3.** a medicine that promotes suppuration. [< ML *suppūrātīv(us)*]

supr., **1.** superior. **2.** supreme.

su·pra (so͞o′prə), *adv.* above, esp. when used in referring to parts of a text. Cf. **infra.** [< L (adv., prep.): on the upper side, above, over; akin to SUPER-]

supra-, a learned borrowing from Latin meaning "above," equivalent to **super-** but emphasizing location or position and used in the formation of compound words: *supraorbital.*

su·pra·lap·sar·i·an (so͞o′prə lap sâr′ē ən), *n.* **1.** a person who believes in supralapsarianism. **—***adj.* **2.** of supralapsarians or supralapsarianism. [< NL *suprālapsāri(us)* (L *suprā-* SUPRA- + *laps(us)* a fall + *-ārius* -ARY) + -AN]

su·pra·lap·sar·i·an·ism (so͞o′prə lap sâr′ē ə niz′əm), *n.* *Theol.* the doctrine that the decree of election preceded the creation and Fall of man (opposed to *infralapsarianism*).

su·pra·lim·i·nal (so͞o′prə lim′ə nᵊl), *adj.* *Psychol.* existing or operating above the threshold of consciousness. **—su′pra·lim′i·nal·ly,** *adv.*

su·pra·mo·lec·u·lar (so͞o′prə mə lek′yə lər), *adj.* **1.** having an organization more complex than that of a molecule. **2.** composed of an aggregate of molecules.

su·pra·na·tion·al (so͞o′prə nash′ə nᵊl), *adj.* outside or beyond the authority of one national government, as a project or policy. **—su′pra·na′tion·al·ism,** *n.*

su·pra·or·bit·al (so͞o′prə ôr′bi tᵊl), *adj.* situated above the eye socket. [< NL *suprāorbitāl(is)* = L *suprā-* SUPRA- + *orbit(a)* ORBIT + *-ālis* -AL[1]]

su′praor′bital ridge′, *Anat.* a bony protrusion over the eyes. Also called **superciliary ridge.**

su·pra·pro·test (so͞o′prə prō′test), *n.* *Law.* an acceptance or a payment of a bill by a third person after protest for nonacceptance or nonpayment by the drawee. [alter. of It *sopra protesto* upon protest]

su·pra·re·nal (so͞o′prə rēn′ᵊl), *Anat.* **—***adj.* **1.** situated above or on the kidney. **—***n.* **2.** a suprarenal part, esp. the suprarenal gland. [< NL *suprārēnāl(is)*]

su′prare′nal gland′. See **adrenal gland.**

su·pra·seg·men·tal (so͞o′prə seg men′tᵊl), *adj.* **1.** above, beyond, or in addition to a segment or segments. **2.** *Linguistics.* pertaining to or noting junctural or prosodic phonemic features.

su·prem·a·cist (sə prem′ə sist, so͝o-), *n.* a person who believes in or advocates the supremacy of a particular group, esp. a racial group: *a white supremacist.*

su·prem·a·cy (sə prem′ə sē, so͝o-), *n.* **1.** the state of being supreme. **2.** supreme authority or power.

su·preme (sə prēm′, so͝o-), *adj.* **1.** highest in rank or authority; paramount; sovereign; chief. **2.** of the highest quality, degree, character, etc. **3.** greatest, utmost, or extreme. **4.** last or final; ultimate. [< L *suprēm(us)*, superl. of *super(us)* upper] **—su·preme′ly,** *adv.* **—su·preme′ness,** *n.*

Supreme′ Be′ing, God.

supreme′ command′er, the military, naval, or air officer commanding all allied forces in a theater of war.

Supreme′ Court′, *U.S.* **1.** the highest court of the nation. **2.** (in most states) the highest court of the state.

Supreme′ Court′ of Ju′dicature, an English court formed in 1873 from several superior courts and consisting of a court of original jurisdiction **(High Court of Justice)** and an appellate court **(Court of Appeal).**

supreme′ sac′rifice, the sacrifice of one's own life.

Supreme′ So′viet, the legislature of the Soviet Union, consisting of an upper house **(Soviet of the Union),** and a lower house **(Soviet of Nationalities).** Also called **Supreme′ Coun′cil.**

Supt., superintendent. Also, **supt.**

Sur (so͝or), *n.* a town in S Lebanon, on the Mediterranean Sea: site of ancient port of Tyre. 12,000 (est. 1963).

sur-[1], a prefix corresponding to **super-** but mainly attached to stems not used as words and having figurative applications (*survive; surname*), used esp. in legal terms (*surrebuttal*). [ME < OF < L *super-* SUPER-]

sur-[2], var. of **sub-** before *r: surrogate.*

su·ra (so͝or′ə), *n.* *Islam.* any of the 114 chapters of the Koran. Also, **surah.** [< Ar *sūrah*, lit., row, step, rung]

Su·ra·ba·ya (so͝or′ə bä′yə), *n.* a seaport on NE Java: naval base. 989,734 (est. 1961). Also, **Su′ra·ba′ja.** Dutch, **Soerabaja.**

su·rah[1] (so͝or′ə), *n.* a soft, twilled silk or rayon fabric. [appar. var. of SURAT]

su·rah[2] (so͝or′ə), *n.* *Islam.* sura.

Su·ra·jah Dow·lah (sə rä′jə dou′lə), Siraj-ud-daula.

Su·ra·kar·ta (so͝or′ə kär′tə), *n.* a city on central Java, in central Indonesia. 363,167 (1961). Formerly, **Solo.**

Su·rat (so͝o rat′, so͝or′et), *n.* a seaport in W Gujarat, in W India: first British settlement in India 1612. 288,000 (1961).

sur·cease (sûr sēs′), *n., v.*, **-ceased, -ceas·ing.** **—***n.* **1.** cessation; end. **—***v.i. Archaic.* **2.** to cease from some action; desist. **3.** to come to an end. **—***v.t.* **4.** *Archaic.* to cease from; leave off. [SUR[1]- + CEASE; r. late ME *sursese(n)* < MF *sursis* (ptp. of *surseoir* < L *supersedēre* to forbear; see SUPERSEDE) < L *supersess(us)* (ptp.)]

sur·charge (*n.* sûr′chärj′; *v.* sûr chärj′, sûr′chärj′), *n., v.*, **-charged, -charg·ing.** **—***n.* **1.** an additional charge, tax, or cost. **2.** an excessive sum or price charged. **3.** an additional or excessive load or burden. **4.** *Philately.* **a.** an overprint that alters the face value of a stamp to which it has been applied. **b.** a stamp bearing such an overprint. **5.** *Law.* act of surcharging. **—***v.t.* **6.** to subject to an additional charge, tax, fee, etc. **7.** to overcharge for goods. **8.** to show an omission in (an account); omit a credit toward (an account). **9.** *Philately.* to print a surcharge on (a stamp). **10.** to put an additional or excessive burden upon. [late ME < MF *surcharg(i)er*] **—sur·charg′er,** *n.*

sur·cin·gle (sûr′sing′gəl), *n.* **1.** a belt or girth that passes around the belly of a horse and over the blanket, pack, saddle, etc., and is buckled on the horse's back. **2.** a beltlike fastening for a garment, esp. a cassock. [late ME *surcengle* < MF *sur-* SUR-[1] + *cengle* belt < L; see CINGULUM]

Surcoat (13th century)

sur·coat (sûr′kōt′), *n.* **1.** a garment worn over medieval armor, often embroidered with heraldic arms. **2.** an outer coat or other outer garment. [ME *surcote* < MF]

sur·cu·lose (sûr′kyə lōs′), *adj.* *Bot.* producing suckers. [< L *surculōs(us)* = *surcul(us)* (*sūr(us)* branch, twig + *-culus* -CLE, -CULE) + *-ōsus* -OSE[1]]

surd (sûrd), *adj.* **1.** *Phonet.* voiceless (opposed to *sonant*). **2.** *Math. Obs.* (of a quantity) not capable of being expressed in rational numbers; irrational. **—***n.* **3.** *Phonet.* a voiceless consonant (opposed to *sonant*). **4.** *Math. Obs.* a surd quantity. [< L *surd(us)* dull-sounding, deaf]

sure (sho͝or), *adj.*, **sur·er, sur·est,** *adv.* **—***adj.* **1.** free from doubt as to the reliability, character, action, etc., of something (often fol. by *of*): *to be sure of one's facts.* **2.** confident, as of something expected. **3.** convinced, fully persuaded, or positive. **4.** assured or certain beyond question: *His death is sure.* **5.** worthy of confidence; reliable; stable. **6.** unfailing: *a sure cure.* **7.** unerring: *a sure aim.* **8.** admitting of no doubt or question: *sure proof.* **9.** inevitable: *Death is sure.* **10.** destined; bound inevitably; certain: *He is sure to come.* **11.** *Obs.* secure; safe. **12. be sure,** to take care (to be or do as specified); be certain: *Be sure to close the windows.* **13. for sure,** as a certainty; surely. **14. make sure,** to be or arrange to be absolutely certain. **15. sure enough,** *Informal.* as might have been supposed; actually; certainly. **16. to be sure, a.** without doubt; surely; certainly. **b.** admittedly. —*adv. Informal.* **17.** surely; undoubtedly. **18.** inevitably. **19.** of course; yes. [ME *sur(e)* < MF *sur,* OF *seur* < L *sēcūr(us)* SECURE] —**sure′ness,** *n.*

—**Syn. 1.** SURE, CERTAIN, POSITIVE, CONFIDENT indicate full belief and trust that something is true. SURE, CERTAIN, and POSITIVE are often used interchangeably. SURE, the simplest and most general, expresses mere absence of doubt. CERTAIN suggests that there are definite reasons that have freed one from doubt. CONFIDENT emphasizes the strength of the belief or the certainty of expectation felt. POSITIVE implies emphatic certainty, which may even become overconfidence or dogmatism. **5.** certain, trustworthy, solid, steady. **7.** accurate, precise. **9.** unavoidable.

—**Usage. 17.** Although many educated speakers use SURE when they mean SURELY—chiefly because it has become an idiomatic cliché—it is considered to be somewhat less than standard usage and should not be used instead of SURELY except in informal situations.

sure-e·nough (shŏŏr′i nuf′), *adj. Dial.* real; genuine.

sure-fire (shŏŏr′fīər′), *adj. Informal.* sure to work.

sure-foot·ed (shŏŏr′fŏŏt′id), *adj.* **1.** not likely to stumble, slip, or fall. **2.** proceeding surely. —**sure′-foot′ed·ly,** *adv.* —**sure-foot′ed·ness,** *n.*

sure·ly (shŏŏr′lē), *adv.* **1.** firmly; unerringly; without missing, slipping, etc. **2.** undoubtedly, assuredly, or certainly. **3.** (in emphatic utterances that are not necessarily sustained by fact) assuredly: *Surely you are mistaken.* **4.** inevitably or without fail. **6.** yes, indeed. [ME *surliche*] —**Usage. 2.** See **sure.**

sure′ thing′, *Informal.* **1.** something that is or is supposed to be a certain success, as a bet, business venture, etc. **2.** surely; for sure; O.K.; roger (often used as an interjection).

sure·ty (shŏŏr′i tē, shŏŏr′tē), *n., pl.* **-ties. 1.** security against loss or damage or for the fulfillment of an obligation, the payment of a debt, etc.; a pledge, guaranty, or bond. **2.** a person who has made himself responsible for another, as a sponsor, godparent, or bondsman. **3.** the state or quality of being sure. **4.** certainty. **5.** that which makes sure; ground of confidence or safety. **6.** a person who is legally responsible for the debt, default, or delinquency of another. **7.** assurance, esp. self-assurance. [ME *surte* < MF; OF *seurte* < L *sēcūritāt-* SECURITY]

surf (sûrf), *n.* **1.** the swell of the sea that breaks upon a shore or upon shoals. **2.** the mass or line of foamy water caused by the breaking of the sea upon a shore. —*v.i.* **3.** to engage in surfboarding. [earlier *suff,* var. of SOUGH¹] —**surf′a·ble,** *adj.* —**surf′like′,** *adj.*

—**Syn. 1.** See **wave.**

sur·face (sûr′fis), *n., adj., v.,* **-faced, -fac·ing.** —*n.* **1.** the outer face, outside, or exterior boundary of a thing. **2.** any face of a body or thing: *the six surfaces of a cube.* **3.** extent or area of outer face. **4.** the outward appearance, esp. as distinguished from the inner nature. **5.** *Geom.* any figure having only two dimensions; part or all of the boundary of a solid. **6.** land or sea transportation, rather than air, underground, or undersea transportation. **7.** *Aeron.* an airfoil. —*adj.* **8.** of, on, or pertaining to the surface; external. **9.** apparent rather than real; superficial. **10.** of, pertaining to, or via land or sea: *surface travel; surface mail.* —*v.t.* **11.** to finish the surface of. —*v.i.* **12.** (of something submerged) to rise to the surface. **13.** *Mining.* **a.** to wash surface deposits of ore-bearing mineral. **b.** to mine at or near the surface. **14.** to work on or at the surface. [< F = *sur-* SUR-¹ + *face* FACE, appar. modeled on L *superficies* SUPERFICIES] —**sur′face·less,** *adj.* —**sur′fac·er,** *n.*

sur′face-ac·tive a′gent (sûr′fis ak′tiv), *Chem.* any substance that when dissolved in water or an aqueous solution reduces its surface tension or the interfacial tension between it and another liquid. Also called **surfactant.**

sur′face bound′ary lay′er, *Meteorol.* the thin layer of air adjacent to the earth's surface, usually considered to be less than 300 feet high. Also called **sur′face lay′er, friction layer, ground layer.**

sur′face plate′, *Mach.* a flat plate used by machinists for testing surfaces that are to be made perfectly flat.

sur′face ten′sion, *Physics.* the elasticlike force existing in the surface of a body, esp. a liquid, tending to minimize the area of the surface, and manifested in capillarity, the constriction of the surface of a liquid, etc.

sur·face-to-air (sûr′fis tōō âr′), *adj.* (of a missile, message, etc.) capable of traveling from the surface of the earth to a target in the atmosphere.

sur·face-to-sur·face (sûr′fis tə sûr′fis), *adj.* (of a missile, message, etc.) capable of traveling from a base on the surface of the earth to a target also on the surface.

sur·face-to-un·der·wa·ter (sûr′fis tōō un′dər wô′tər, -wot′ər), *adj.* (of a missile, message, etc.) traveling from the surface of the earth to a target underwater: *a surface-to-underwater antisubmarine missile.*

sur·fac·tant (sər fak′tənt), *n. Chem.* See **surface-active agent.** [shortening of *surf(ace)-act(ive) a(ge)nt*]

surf·bird (sûrf′bûrd′), *n.* a shore bird, *Aphriza virgata,* of the Pacific coast of North and South America, related to the turnstones.

surf·board (sûrf′bōrd′, -bôrd′), *n.* a long, narrow board on which a person stands, kneels, or lies in surfboarding.

surf·board·ing (sûrf′bōr′ding, -bôr′-), *n.* a sport in which a person stands, kneels, or lies prone on a surfboard and rides the crest of a breaking wave toward the shore. Also called **surfing, surfriding.** —**surf′board′er,** *n.*

surf·boat (sûrf′bōt′), *n.* a strong, buoyant rowboat with high ends, adapted for passing through surf.

surf′ cast′ing, *Angling.* the act, technique, or sport of fishing by casting from the shoreline into the sea, usually using heavy-duty tackle.

sur·feit (sûr′fit), *n.* **1.** excess; an excessive amount. **2.** excess or overindulgence in eating or drinking. **3.** an uncomfortable feeling due to excessive eating or drinking. **4.** general disgust caused by excess or satiety. —*v.t.* **5.** to bring to a state of surfeit. **6.** to satiate. —*v.i.* **7.** to indulge in anything to excess. [late ME *surfait* < MF *s(e)urfait* (n. use of ptp. of *surfaire* to overdo) = *sur-* SUR-¹ + *fait* < L *fact(us)* (see FACT), ptp. of *facere* to do] —**Syn. 1.** superabundance.

surf·fish (sûrf′fish′), *n., pl.* (*esp. collectively*) **-fish,** (*esp. referring to two or more kinds or species*) **-fish·es. 1.** surfperch. **2.** any of several sciaenid fishes, as *Umbrina roncador,* found along the Pacific coast of North America.

surf·ing (sûr′fing), *n.* surfboarding. Also called **surf·riding** (sûrf′rī′ding). —**surf′er, surf′rid′er,** *n.*

surf·perch (sûrf′pûrch′), *n., pl.* (*esp. collectively*) **-perch,** (*esp. referring to two or more kinds or species*) **-perch·es.** any of several viviparous fishes of the family *Embiotocidae,* found in the shallow waters along the Pacific coast of North America. Also called **surffish.**

surf·y (sûr′fē), *adj.,* **surf·i·er, surf·i·est.** abounding with surf; forming or resembling surf.

surg., **1.** surgeon. **2.** surgery. **3.** surgical.

surge (sûrj), *n., v.,* **surged, surg·ing.** —*n.* **1.** a strong, wavelike forward movement, rush, or sweep. **2.** a strong, swelling, wavelike volume or body of something. **3.** the rolling swell of the sea. **4.** the swelling and rolling sea. **5.** a swelling wave; billow. **6.** *Elect.* **a.** a sudden rush or burst of current or voltage. **b.** a violent oscillatory disturbance. **7.** *Naut.* a slackening or slipping back, as of a rope or cable. —*v.i.* **8.** (of a ship) to rise and fall, toss about, or move along on the waves: *to surge at anchor.* **9.** to rise, roll, move, or swell forward in or like waves. **10.** to rise as if by a heaving or swelling force. **11.** *Elect.* **a.** to increase suddenly, as current or voltage. **b.** to oscillate violently. **12.** *Naut.* **a.** to slack off or loosen a rope or cable around a capstan or windlass. **b.** to slip back, as a rope. —*v.t.* **13.** to cause to surge or roll in or as if in waves. **14.** *Naut.* to slacken (a rope). [? < L *surge(re)* (to) spring up, arise, stand up] —**surge′less,** *adj.*

sur·geon (sûr′jən), *n.* a physician who specializes in surgery. [ME *surgien* < AF, alter. of OF *cirurgien* CHIRURGEON]

sur·geon·fish (sûr′jən fish′), *n., pl.* (*esp. collectively*) **-fish,** (*esp. referring to two or more kinds or species*) **-fish·es.** any tropical, coral-reef fish of the family *Acanthuridae,* with one or more spines near the base of the tail fin. [so called from the resemblance of its spines to a surgeon's instruments]

sur′geon gen′eral, *pl.* **surgeons general. 1.** the chief of medical services in one of the armed forces. **2.** (*cap.*) the head of the U.S. Bureau of Public Health or, in some states, of a state health agency.

sur′geon's knot′, a knot resembling a reef knot, used by surgeons for tying ligatures and the like.

sur·ger·y (sûr′jə rē), *n., pl.* **-ger·ies** for 4, 5. **1.** the art, practice, or work of treating diseases, injuries, or deformities by operation, esp. with instruments. **2.** the branch of medicine concerned with such treatment. **3.** treatment, as an operation, performed by a surgeon. **4.** a room or place for surgical operations. **5.** *Brit.* the consulting office, examining room, and dispensary of a general medical practitioner; doctor's office. [ME *surgerie* < OF *cirurg(er)ie* CHIRURGERY]

Surg. Gen., Surgeon General.

sur·gi·cal (sûr′ji kəl), *adj.* **1.** pertaining to or involving surgery. **2.** used in surgery. [SURG(EON) + -ICAL] —**sur′gi·cal·ly,** *adv.*

Su·ri·ba·chi (sŏŏr′ə bä′chē), *n.* an extinct volcano on Iwo Jima: World War II battle 1945.

su·ri·cate (sŏŏr′ə kāt′), *n.* a small, burrowing, South African carnivore, *Suricata suricatta,* related to the mongooses. [earlier *surikate* < F < D *suri-kat* macaque]

Suricate
(Total length 21 in.; tail 8½ in.)

Su′rinam cher′ry, a myrtaceous tree, *Eugenia uniflora,* of Brazil.

Su·ri·name (sŏŏr′ə näm′, -nam′; *Du.* sʏ′rē nä′mə), *n.* a republic on the NE coast of South America: formerly a territory of the Netherlands; independent since 1975. 414,000; 60,230 sq. mi. *Cap.:* Paramaribo. Formerly, **Su·ri·nam** (sŏŏr′ə näm′, -nam′), **Dutch Guiana, Netherlands Guiana.**

sur·ly (sûr′lē), *adj.,* **-li·er, -li·est. 1.** churlishly rude or bad-tempered. **2.** unfriendly or hostile; menacingly irritable. **3.** dark or dismal; menacing; threatening. **4.** *Obs.* lordly; arrogant. [sp. var. of obs. *sirly* (SIR + -LY) lordly, arrogant] —**sur′li·ly,** *adv.* —**sur′li·ness,** *n.*

sur·mise (*v.* sər mīz′; *n.* sər mīz′, sûr′mīz), *v.,* **-mised, -mis·ing,** *n.* —*v.t.* **1.** to think or infer without certain or strong evidence; conjecture. —*v.i.* **2.** to conjecture or guess. —*n.* **3.** a matter of conjecture. **4.** an idea or thought of something as being possible or likely. **5.** a conjecture or opinion. [late ME *surmise(n)* < AF, MF *surmis(e)* (ptp. of *surmet(t)re* to accuse < L *supermittere* to throw upon) = *sur-* SUR-¹ + *mis(e)* < L *miss(us), -a* = *mit-* send + *-tus, -ta* ptp. suffix] —**sur·mis′a·ble,** *adj.* —**sur·mised·ly** (sər mīzd′lē, -mī′zid-), *adv.* —**sur·mis′er,** *n.* —**Syn. 1.** imagine, suppose, suspect. See **guess. 3.** possibility, likelihood.

sur·mount (sər mount′), *v.t.* **1.** to get over or across (barriers, obstacles, etc.). **2.** to prevail over: *to surmount tremendous odds.* **3.** to get to the top of; mount upon. **4.** to be on top of or above. **5.** to furnish with something placed on top or above. **6.** *Obs.* **a.** to surpass in excellence. **b.** to exceed in amount. [late ME *surmounte(n)* < AF, MF *surmonte(r).* See SUR-¹, MOUNT¹] —**sur·mount′a·ble,** *adj.* —**sur·mount′a·ble·ness,** *n.* —**sur·mount′er,** *n.*

sur·mul·let (sər mul′it), *n.* a goatfish, esp. one of the European species used for food. [< F *surmulet,* MF *sormulet* = *sor* reddish brown (see SORREL¹) + *mulet* MULLET]

sur·name (*n.* sûr′nām′; *v.* sûr′nām′, sûr nām′), *n., v.,* **-named, -nam·ing.** —*n.* **1.** Also called **last name.** the name that a person has in common with the other members of his family, as distinguished from his given name; family name. **2.** a descriptive name added to a person's name or names; epithet. —*v.t.* **3.** to give a surname to; call by a surname. [ME; see SUR-¹, NAME; modeled on OF *surnom*]

sur·pass (sər pas′, -päs′), *v.t.* **1.** to go beyond in amount, extent, or degree; be greater than; exceed. **2.** to go beyond in excellence or achievement; be superior to; excel. **3.** to be beyond the range or capacity of; transcend. [< MF *surpass(er)*] —**sur·pass′a·ble,** *adj.* —**Syn. 2.** beat, outstrip. See **excel.**

sur·pass·ing (sər pas′ing, -pä′sing), *adj.* **1.** of a large amount or high degree; exceeding, excelling, or extraordinary. —*adv.* **2.** *Archaic.* in a surpassing manner; extraordinarily. —**sur·pass′ing·ly,** *adv.* —**sur·pass′ing·ness,** *n.*

sur·plice (sûr′plis), *n.* **1.** a loose-fitting, broad-sleeved white vestment, worn over the cassock. **2.** a garment in which the two halves of the front cross each other diagonally. [ME *surplis* < AF *surpliz,* syncopated var. of OF *surpeliz* < ML *superpellīc(ium) (vestimentum)* over-pelt (garment), neut. of *superpellīcius* (adj.) = L *super-* SUPER- + *pellīt(us)* pelt-clad + *-ius* adj. suffix] —**sur′pliced,** *adj.*

Surplice

sur·plus (sûr′plus, -pləs), *n.* **1.** that which remains above what is used or needed. **2.** an amount, quantity, etc., greater than needed. **3.** *U.S.* agricultural produce or a quantity of food grown by a nation or area in excess of its needs. **4.** *Accounting.* **a.** the excess of assets over liabilities accumulated throughout the existence of a business, excepting assets against which stock certificates have been issued; excess of net worth over capital-stock value. **b.** an amount of assets in excess of what is requisite to meet liabilities. —*adj.* **5.** being a surplus. [late ME < OF < ML *superplus.* See SUPER-, PLUS] —**Syn. 1.** superabundance. —**Ant. 1.** deficiency.

sur·plus·age (sûr′plus ij), *n.* **1.** a surplus amount. **2.** an excess of words.

sur·print (sûr′print′), *v.t.* **1.** to print over with additional marks or matter; overprint. **2.** to print (additional marks, a new address, etc.) over something already printed. —*n.* **3.** something surprinted.

sur·pris·al (sər prī′zəl), *n.* **1.** the act of surprising. **2.** the state of being surprised. **3.** a surprise.

sur·prise (sər prīz′), *v.,* **-prised, -pris·ing,** *n.* —*v.t.* **1.** to strike or occur to with a sudden feeling of unexpected wonder. **2.** to come upon or discover suddenly and unexpectedly. **3.** to make an unexpected assault on (an unprepared army, fort, person, etc.). **4.** to elicit suddenly and without warning. **5.** to lead or bring unawares, as into doing something not intended. —*n.* **6.** the act or an instance of surprising. **7.** a completely unexpected occurrence, appearance, or statement. **8.** a sudden, unexpected attack or assault. **9.** a coming upon unexpectedly. **10.** a state or feeling of sudden wonder. **11.** something that excites this feeling. **12. take by surprise, a.** to come upon unawares. **b.** to astonish; amaze. [late ME < AF, MF *surpris(e)* (ptp. of *surprendre* = *sur-* SUR-[1] + *pris(e)* < L *prens(us), -sa* = *prend-* take + *-tus, -ta* ptp. suffix] —**sur·pris·ed·ly** (sər prī′zid lē, -prīzd′-), *adv.* —**sur·pris′er,** *n.*
—**Syn. 1.** SURPRISE, ASTONISH, AMAZE, ASTOUND mean to strike with wonder because of unexpectedness, strangeness, unusualness, etc. To SURPRISE is to take unawares or to affect with wonder: *surprised at receiving a telegram.* To ASTONISH is to strike with wonder by something unlooked for, startling, or seemingly inexplicable: *astonished at someone's behavior.* To AMAZE is to astonish so greatly as to disconcert or bewilder: *amazed at his stupidity.* To ASTOUND is to so overwhelm with surprise that one is unable to think or act: *astounded by a sudden calamity.* **10.** amazement, astonishment.

sur·pris·ing (sər prī′zing), *adj.* **1.** causing surprise, wonder, or astonishment. **2.** unexpected. —**sur·pris′ing·ly,** *adv.* —**sur·pris′ing·ness,** *n.*

sur·ra (so͝or′ə), *n.* *Vet. Pathol.* an often fatal infectious disease of horses, camels, elephants, and dogs caused by a blood-infecting protozoan parasite, *Trypanosoma evansi,* transmitted by the bite of horseflies and characterized by fever, anemia, and emaciation. [< Marathi *sūra* heavy breathing sound]

Sur·re·al·ism (sə rē′ə liz′əm), *n.* (*often l.c.*) a style of art and literature developed principally in the 20th century, stressing the subconscious or nonrational significance of imagery arrived at by automatism or the exploitation of chance effects, unexpected juxtapositions, symbolic objects, etc. [< F *surréalisme.* See SUR-[1], REALISM] —**Sur·re′al·ist,** *n., adj.* —**Sur·re′al·is′tic,** *adj.* —**Sur·re′al·is′ti·cal·ly,** *adv.*

sur·re·but·tal (sûr′ri but′ᵊl), *n.* *Law.* the giving of evidence to meet a defendant's rebuttal.

sur·re·but·ter (sûr′ri but′ər), *n.* *Law.* a plaintiff's reply to a defendant's rebutter.

sur·re·join·der (sûr′ri join′dər), *n.* *Law.* a plaintiff's reply to a defendant's rejoinder.

sur·ren·der (sə ren′dər), *v.t.* **1.** to yield (something) to the possession or power of another; deliver up possession of on demand or under duress. **2.** to give (oneself) up, as to the police. **3.** to give (oneself) up to some influence, course, emotion, etc. **4.** to give up, abandon, or relinquish (comfort, hope, etc.). **5.** to yield or resign (an office, privilege, etc.) in favor of another. **6.** *Obs.* to return: *to surrender thanks.* —*v.i.* **7.** to give oneself up, as into the power of another; submit or yield. —*n.* **8.** the act or an instance of surrendering. **9.** *Insurance.* the voluntary abandonment of a life-insurance policy by the owner for any of its nonforfeiture values. **10.** the deed by which a legal surrendering is made. [late ME < AF = OF *surrendre* to give up = *sur-* SUR-[1] + *rendre* to RENDER] —**sur·ren′der·er,** *n.* —**Syn. 1.** See **yield. 4.** renounce; relinquish, abandon, forgo. **7.** capitulate. **8.** capitulation, relinquishment.

sur·rep·ti·tious (sûr′əp tish′əs), *adj.* **1.** obtained, done, made, etc., by stealth. **2.** acting in a stealthy way. **3.** obtained by subreption; subreptitious. [< L *surreptīcius* stolen, clandestine = *surrept(us),* ptp. of *surripere* to steal (*sur-* SUR-[2] + *rep-,* var. of *rap-* snatch, RAPE[1] + *-tus* ptp. suffix) + *-icius* -ITIOUS] —**sur′rep·ti′tious·ly,** *adv.* —**sur′rep·ti′tious·ness,** *n.*

sur·rey (sûr′ē, sur′ē), *n., pl.* **-reys.** a light, four-wheeled, two-seated carriage, with or without a top, for four persons. [after SURREY, the county]

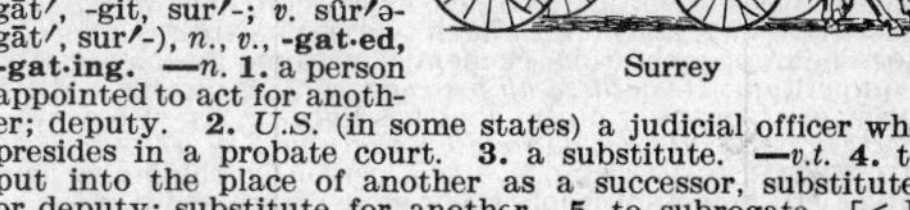
Surrey

Sur·rey (sûr′ē, sur′ē), *n.* **1. Earl of** (*Henry Howard*), 1517?–47, English poet. **2.** a county in SE England, bordering S London. 1,733,036 (1961); 722 sq. mi. *Co. seat:* Guildford.

sur·ro·gate (*n.* sûr′ə gāt′, -git, sur′-; *v.* sûr′ə gāt′, sur′-), *n., v.,* **-gat·ed, -gat·ing.** —*n.* **1.** a person appointed to act for another; deputy. **2.** *U.S.* (in some states) a judicial officer who presides in a probate court. **3.** a substitute. —*v.t.* **4.** to put into the place of another as a successor, substitute, or deputy; substitute for another. **5.** to subrogate. [< L *surrogāt(us),* assimilated var. of *subrogātus;* see SUBROGATE] —**sur′ro·gate·ship′,** *n.* —**sur′ro·ga′tion,** *n.*

sur′rogate moth′er, 1. a person who acts in the place of another person's biological mother. **2.** an animal that is given another's offspring to raise or another's embryo to carry to term. **3.** a woman who carries to term an artificially inseminated embryo for the sperm donor and another woman. **4.** a woman whose egg is extracted for transfer to another woman's uterus; an egg donor.

sur·round (sə round′), *v.t.* **1.** to enclose on all sides; encompass. **2.** to form an enclosure round; encircle. **3.** to enclose (a body of troops, a fort or town, etc.) so as to cut off communication or retreat. —*n.* **4.** *Archit.* a feature forming a border to an opening or panel. **5.** something that surrounds, as the area, border, etc., around an object or central space. [SUR-[1] + ROUND; r. late ME *surounde(n)* < AF *surounde(r),* MF *suronder* < LL *superundāre* to overflow = L *super-* SUPER- + *undāre* to flood < *und(a)* wave; see UNDULATE] —**sur·round′ed·ly,** *adv.*

sur·round·ing (sə roun′ding), *n.* **1.** something that surrounds. **2. surroundings,** things, circumstances, conditions, etc., that surround one; environment. **3.** the act of encircling. —*adj.* **4.** enclosing or encircling. **5.** being the environment. [late ME (n.)]

sur·roy·al (sûr roi′əl), *n.* See **crown antler.** [ME *surryal*]

sur·sum cor·da (so͝or′so͞om kōr′dä, kôr′-), *Eccles.* the words, "Lift up your hearts," said by the celebrant of the Mass to the congregation just before the preface. [< L]

sur·tax (*n.* sûr′taks′; *v.* sûr′taks′, sûr taks′), *n.* **1.** an additional or extra tax on something already taxed. **2.** one of a graded series of additional taxes levied on incomes exceeding a certain amount. —*v.t.* **3.** to charge with a surtax. [cf. SUPERTAX, F *surtaxe*]

Sur·tees (sûr′tēz), *n.* **Robert Smith,** 1805–64, English editor and writer.

surv., 1. surveying. **2.** surveyor.

sur·veil·lance (sər vā′ləns, -vāl′yəns), *n.* **1.** a watch kept over a person, group, etc., esp. over a suspect, prisoner, or the like. **2.** supervision or superintendence. [< F = *surveill(er)* (to) watch over (*sur-* SUR-[1] + *veiller* < L *vigilāre* to watch; see VIGIL) + *-ance* -ANCE] —**Syn. 2.** care, control, management.

sur·veil·lant (sər vā′lənt, -vāl′yənt), *adj.* **1.** exercising surveillance. —*n.* **2.** a person who exercises surveillance. [< F = *surveill-* watch (see SURVEILLANCE) + *-ant* -ANT]

sur·vey (*v.* sər vā′; *n.* sûr′vā, sər vā′), *v., n. pl.* **-veys.** —*v.t.* **1.** to take a general or comprehensive view of or appraise, as a situation. **2.** to view in detail, as in order to ascertain condition, value, etc. **3.** to determine the exact form, extent, etc., of (a tract of land, section of a country, etc.) by linear and angular measurements and the application of the principles of geometry and trigonometry. —*v.i.* **4.** to survey land; practice surveying. —*n.* **5.** the act or an instance of surveying. **6.** a formal or official examination of the particulars of something. **7.** a statement or description embodying the result of this. **8.** a sampling, or partial collection, of facts, figures, or opinions taken and used to approximate or indicate what a complete collection and analysis might reveal. **9.** the act of determining the exact form, boundaries, position, etc., as of a tract of land or section of a country, by linear measurements, angular measurements, etc. **10.** the plan or description resulting from such an operation. **11.** an agency for making determinations. [late ME *survei(en)* < AF *surveie(r),* MF *survee(i)r, -veoir* to oversee = *sur-* SUR-[1] + *vee(i)r* < L *vidēre* to see] —**sur·vey′a·ble,** *adj.*

survey., surveying.

sur·vey·ing (sər vā′ing), *n.* **1.** the science or scientific method of making surveys of land. **2.** the occupation of a person who makes land surveys. **3.** the act of a person who surveys.

sur·vey·or (sər vā′ər), *n.* **1.** a person whose occupation is surveying. **2.** an overseer or supervisor. **3.** *Chiefly Brit.* a person who inspects something officially for the purpose of ascertaining condition, value, etc. **4.** (formerly) a U.S. customs official responsible for ascertaining the value of imported merchandise. [late ME *surveio(u)r* < AF, MF = *survei-* (see SURVEY) + *-o(u)r* -OR[2]] —**sur·vey′or·ship′,** *n.*

survey′or's chain′. See under **chain** (def. 8a).

survey′or's meas′ure, a system of units of length used in surveying land, based on the surveyor's chain of 66 feet and its 100 links of 7.92 inches.

sur·viv·al (sər vī′vəl), *n.* **1.** the act or fact of surviving. **2.** a person or thing that survives or endures. —*adj.* **3.** of or pertaining to the food, clothing, equipment, etc., necessary to or aiding a person's survival in adverse circumstances.

surviv′al of the fit′test, *Biol.* the fact or the principle of the survival of the forms of animal and vegetable life best fitted for existing conditions, while related but less fit forms become extinct. Cf. **natural selection.**

sur·vive (sər vīv′), *v.,* **-vived, -viv·ing.** —*v.i.* **1.** to remain alive after the death of another, or in spite of a mortally dangerous occurrence or situation. **2.** to remain or continue

in existence or use. —*v.t.* **3.** to continue to live or exist after the death, cessation, or occurrence of. **4.** to endure or live in spite of (an affliction, adversity, misery, etc.). [late ME < MF *surviv(re)* < L *supervīvere* = *super-* SUPER- + *vīvere* to live; see VIVID] —**sur·viv′a·bil′i·ty,** *n.* —**sur·viv′a·ble,** *adj.*
—**Syn. 1.** persist, succeed. SURVIVE, OUTLIVE refer to remaining alive longer than someone else or after some event. SURVIVE usually means to succeed in keeping alive against odds, to live after some event which has threatened a person: *to survive an automobile accident.* It is also used of living longer than another person (usually a relative), but, today, mainly in the passive, as in the fixed expression: *The deceased is survived by his wife and children.* OUTLIVE stresses capacity for endurance, the time element, and sometimes a sense of competition: *He outlived all his enemies.* It is also used, however, of a person or object that has lived or lasted beyond a certain point: *He has outlived his usefulness.*

sur·vi·vor (sər vī′vər), *n.* **1.** a person or thing that survives. **2.** *Law.* the one of two or more designated persons, as joint tenants or others having a joint interest, who outlives the other or others.

sur·vi·vor·ship (sər vī′vər ship′), *n.* **1.** the state of being a survivor. **2.** *Law.* a right of a person to property on the death of another person having a joint interest.

sus-, var. of **sub-** before *c, p, t: susceptible.*

Su·sa (so͞o′sä), *n.* a ruined city in W Iran: the capital of ancient Elam; palaces of Darius and Artaxerxes I. Biblical name, **Shushan.**

Su·san·na (so͞o zan′ə), *n.* a book of the Apocrypha, comprising the 13th chapter of Daniel in the Douay Bible.

sus·cep·tance (sə sep′təns), *n.* *Elect.* the imaginary component of admittance, equal to the quotient of the negative of the reactance divided by the sum of the squares of the reactance and resistance. *Symbol:* B [SUSCEPT(IBILITY) + -ANCE]

sus·cep·ti·bil·i·ty (sə sep′tə bil′i tē), *n., pl.* **-ties. 1.** the state or character of being susceptible. **2.** capacity for receiving mental or moral impressions; tendency to be emotionally affected. **3. susceptibilities,** capacities for emotion; sensitive feelings; emotional vulnerability. **4.** *Elect.* the ratio of the magnetization produced in a substance to the magnetizing force. [< ML *susceptibilitāt-* (s. of *susceptibilitās*)] —**Syn. 2.** See **sensibility.**

sus·cep·ti·ble (sə sep′tə bəl), *adj.* **1.** admitting or capable of treatment of a specified kind (usually fol. by *of* or *to*): *susceptible of a high polish; susceptible to various interpretations.* **2.** accessible or especially liable or subject to some influence, mood, agency, etc. (usually fol. by *to*). **3.** capable of being affected emotionally; impressionable. [< LL *susceptibil(is)* = *suscept(us),* ptp. of *suscipere* to take up, support (*sus-* SUS- + *cep-* var. of *cap-* take + *-tus* ptp. suffix) + *-ibilis* -IBLE] —**sus·cep′ti·ble·ness,** *n.* —**sus·cep′ti·bly,** *adv.*

sus·cep·tive (sə sep′tiv), *adj.* **1.** receptive. **2.** susceptible. [< LL *susceptīv(us)* = *suscept(us)* (see SUSCEPTIBLE) + *-īvus* -IVE] —**sus·cep·tiv·i·ty** (sus′ep tiv′i tē), **sus·cep′tive·ness,** *n.*

su·shi (so͞o′shē), *n.* *Japanese Cookery.* a preparation of cooled cooked rice, dressed with seasoned vinegar and often shaped into fingers, then garnished with a variety of raw seafood, vegetables, and seaweed. [< Jap]

sus·lik (sus′lik), *n.* **1.** a common ground squirrel or spermophile, *Citellus* (or *Spermophilus*) *citellus,* of Europe and Asia. **2.** the fur of this animal. [< Russ]

Sus·lov (so͞os′lof), *n.* **Mi·kha·il An·dre·e·vich** (mi кнä ēl′ än dʀe′yə vich), 1902–82, Russian government official: former member of the Presidium.

sus·pect (*v.* sə spekt′; *n.* sus′pekt; *adj.* sus′pekt, sə spekt′), *v.t.* **1.** to believe to be guilty, false, etc., with insufficient or no proof. **2.** to believe to be rightly chargeable with something stated, usually something wrong, on little or no evidence. **3.** to believe to be the case or to be likely; surmise. —*v.i.* **4.** to believe something, esp. something evil or wrong, to be the case. —*n.* **5.** a person who is suspected, as of a crime. —*adj.* **6.** suspected; open to or under suspicion. [late ME *suspecte(n)* < L *suspect(āre)* = *su-* SU- + *spec-* (var. of *spic-* look) + *-t-* intensive suffix + *-āre* v. suffix] —**sus·pect′er,** *n.* —**sus·pect′i·ble,** *adj.* —**sus′pect·less,** *adj.*
—**Syn. 1.** distrust, mistrust, doubt. **3.** guess, suppose.

sus·pend (sə spend′), *v.t.* **1.** to support from above; hang. **2.** to keep (particles) in suspension. **3.** to defer to a later occasion, as the deliverance of an opinion or a judicial sentence. **4.** to halt or interrupt (something in process): *to suspend operations.* **5.** to render temporarily void (a law, rule, policy, etc.). **6.** to punish by temporary exclusion from work, school attendance, etc. **7.** to keep in anxiety or suspense. **8.** *Music.* to prolong (a note or tone) into the next chord. —*v.i.* **9.** to come to a stop, usually temporarily. **10.** to stop payment, as from being unable to meet financial obligations. **11.** to be suspended. [ME *suspend(en)* < L *suspende(re)* (to) hang up = *sus-* SUS- + *pendere* to PEND; see SUSPENSE] —**sus·pend′i·bil′i·ty,** *n.* —**sus·pend′i·ble,** *adj.* —**Syn. 3.** withhold, delay. **4.** hold up, intermit. See **interrupt.**

suspend′ed anima′tion, a state of temporary cessation of the vital functions.

sus·pend·er (sə spen′dər), *n.* **1.** Usually, **suspenders.** Also called, *esp. Brit.,* **braces.** *Chiefly U.S.* adjustable straps or bands worn over the shoulders with the ends buttoned or clipped to the waistband of the trousers to support them. **2.** *Brit.* garter (def. 1). **3.** a person or thing that suspends.

sus·pense (sə spens′), *n.* **1.** a state or condition of mental uncertainty or excitement, as from awaiting a decision or outcome. **2.** a state of mental indecision. **3.** an undecided or doubtful condition, as of affairs. **4.** the state or condition of being suspended. [ME < ML *suspens(um)* deferment, suspension, uncertainty, n. use of neut. of L *suspens(us)* hung up, doubtful, in suspense (ptp. of *suspendere* to hang up, leave undecided) = *sus-* SUS- + *pensus* = *pend-* hang + *-tus* ptp. suffix] —**sus·pense′ful,** *adj.* —**Syn. 1.** doubt, incertitude. **2.** hesitation, vacillation, irresolution. —**Ant. 1.** certainty. **2.** decision.

suspense′ account′, *Bookkeeping.* an account in which items are temporarily entered until their final disposition is determined.

sus·pen·sion (sə spen′shən), *n.* **1.** the act of suspending. **2.** the state of being suspended. **3.** the temporary interruption of an activity or state, voiding of a law or policy, etc. **4.** stoppage of payment of debts or claims because of financial inability or insolvency. **5.** *Chem.* **a.** the state in which the particles of a substance are mixed with a fluid but are undissolved. **b.** a substance in such a state. **6.** *Physical Chem.* a system consisting of small particles kept dispersed by agitation or by the molecular motion in the surrounding medium. **7.** something on or by which something else is suspended or hung. **8.** something that is suspended or hung. **9.** the arrangement of springs, shock absorbers, hangers, etc., connecting the wheel-suspension units or axles to the chassis frame of an automobile or other vehicle. **10.** *Music.* **a.** the prolongation of a tone in one chord into the following chord, usually producing a temporary dissonance. **b.** the tone so prolonged. [< L *suspensiōn-* (s. of *suspensiō*). See SUSPENSE, -ION] —**Syn. 3.** cessation, abeyance, hiatus.

suspen′sion bridge′, a bridge having a deck suspended from cables anchored at their extremities and usually raised on towers.

suspen′sion points′, *Print.* a series of periods used as an ellipsis. Also called **breaks.**

sus·pen·sive (sə spen′siv), *adj.* **1.** pertaining to or characterized by suspension. **2.** undecided in mind. **3.** pertaining to or characterized by suspense. **4.** (of words, phrases, etc.) characterized by or expressing suspense. **5.** having the effect of suspending the operation of something. [< ML *suspensīv(us).* See SUSPENSE, -IVE] —**sus·pen′sive·ly,** *adv.* —**sus·pen′sive·ness,** *n.*

sus·pen·soid (sə spen′soid), *n.* *Physical Chem.* a sol having a solid disperse phase. Cf. **emulsoid.** [SUSPENS(ION) + (COLL)OID]

sus·pen·sor (sə spen′sər), *n.* a suspensory ligament, muscle, bandage, etc. [< NL; see SUSPENSE, -OR²]

sus·pen·so·ry¹ (sə spen′sə rē), *adj.* **1.** serving or fitted to suspend or hold up, as a ligament, muscle, bandage, etc. **2.** suspending the operation of something. [< L *suspens(us)* (see SUSPENSE) + -ORY¹]

sus·pen·so·ry² (sə spen′sə rē), *n., pl.* **-ries.** suspensor. [< L *suspens(us)* (see SUSPENSE) + -ORY²]

suspen′sory lig′ament, *Anat.* any of several tissues that suspend certain organs or parts of the body, esp. the transparent, delicate web of fibrous tissue that supports the crystalline lens.

sus·pi·cion (sə spish′ən), *n.* **1.** the act of suspecting. **2.** the state of mind of a person who suspects. **3.** an instance of suspecting. **4.** the state of being suspected. **5.** a notion that something is the case. **6.** a slight trace, hint, or suggestion: *a suspicion of a smile.* —*v.t.* **7.** *Nonstandard.* to suspect. [late ME < L *suspīciōn-* (s. of *suspīciō*) = *suspīc-* (var. of *suspic-,* base of *suspicere* to look from below, SUSPECT) + *-iōn-* -ION; r. ME *suspecioun* < AF << L *suspectiōn-* mistrust] —**sus·pi′cion·less,** *adj.*
—**Syn. 2.** doubt, mistrust. SUSPICION, DISTRUST are terms for a feeling that appearances are not reliable. SUSPICION is the positive tendency to doubt the trustworthiness of appearances and therefore to believe that one has detected possibilities of something unreliable, unfavorable, menacing, or the like: *to feel suspicion about the honesty of a prominent man.* DISTRUST may be a passive want of trust, faith, or reliance in a person or thing: *to feel distrust of one's own ability.* **5.** supposition, conjecture, guess. —**Ant. 2.** trust.

sus·pi·cious (sə spish′əs), *adj.* **1.** tending to cause or excite suspicion; questionable. **2.** inclined to suspect, esp. inclined to suspect evil. **3.** full of or feeling suspicion. **4.** expressing or indicating suspicion: *a suspicious glance.* [ME < L *suspīciōs(us)* = *suspīci-* (see SUSPICION) + *-ōsus* -OUS; r. ME *suspecious* < AF] —**sus·pi′cious·ly,** *adv.* —**sus·pi′cious·ness,** *n.*

sus·pire (sə spīᵊr′), *v.i.,* **-pired, -pir·ing.** *Chiefly Literary.* **1.** to sigh. **2.** to breathe. [< L *suspīr(āre)* = *su-* SU- + *spīrāre* to breathe] —**sus·pi·ra·tion** (sus′pə rā′shən), *n.*

Sus·que·han·na (sus′kwə han′ə), *n.* a river flowing S from central New York through E Pennsylvania and NE Maryland into Chesapeake Bay. 444 mi. long.

Sus·sex (sus′iks), *n.* **1.** a county in SE England: divided for administrative purposes into East Sussex and West Sussex. **2.** a kingdom of the Anglo-Saxon heptarchy in SE England. See map at **Mercia**

Sus′sex span′iel, one of an English breed of short-legged spaniels having a golden liver-colored coat.

sus·tain (sə stān′), *v.t.* **1.** to support, hold, or bear up from below. **2.** to bear (a burden, charge, etc.). **3.** to undergo (injury, loss, etc.) without yielding. **4.** to keep (a person, the mind, the spirits, etc.) from giving way. **5.** to keep up or keep going, as an action or process. **6.** to supply with food, drink, and other necessities of life. **7.** to provide for (an institution or the like). **8.** to support (a cause or the like) by aid or approval. **9.** to uphold as valid, just, or correct, as a claim or the person making it. **10.** to confirm or corroborate. [ME *suste(i)n(en)* < AF, OF *susteni(r)* < L *sustinēre* to uphold = *sus-* SUS- + *-tinēre,* var. of *tenēre* to hold] —**sus·tain′a·ble,** *adj.* —**sus·tain·ed·ly** (sə stā′nid lē, -stānd′-), *adv.* —**sus·tain′ing·ly,** *adv.* —**sus·tain′ment,** *n.* —**Syn. 1.** carry. See **support. 3.** bear. **5.** maintain. **6.** nurture; back, abet, help. **10.** establish, ratify.

sus·tain·er (sə stā′nər), *n.* **1.** a person or thing that sustains. **2.** *Rocketry.* (of a multistage rocket or guided missile) **a.** any stage that sustains flight after the burnout of the booster. **b.** the rocket engine or cluster of engines contained in such a stage. [late ME *sosteynere*]

sus·te·nance (sus′tə nəns), *n.* **1.** means of sustaining life; nourishment. **2.** means of livelihood. **3.** the process of sustaining. **4.** the state of being sustained. [ME *sustena(u)nce* < AF, var. of OF *sostenance*]

sus·ten·tac·u·lar (sus′tən tak′yə lər), *adj.* *Anat.* supporting. [< L *sustentācul(um)* a prop, support (*sustentā-* (see SUSTENTATION) + *-culum* suffix denoting means or instrument) + -AR¹]

sus·ten·ta·tion (sus′tən tā′shən), *n.* **1.** maintenance in being or activity. **2.** provision with means or funds. **3.** means of sustaining life; sustenance. [ME < L *sustentātiōn-* (s. of *sustentātiō*) an upholding = *sustentāt(us)* (ptp. of *sustentāre*) freq. of *sustinēre* to SUSTAIN + *-iōn-* -ION]

—**sus·ten·ta·tive** (sus′tən tā′tiv, sə sten′tə tiv), *adj.* —**sus′ten·ta′tion·al,** *adj.*

sus·ten·tion (sə sten′shən), *n.* **1.** the act of sustaining. **2.** the state or quality of being sustained. [*susten-* (see SUSTAIN) + -TION, modeled on *detention, retention* (cf. *detain, retain*)] —**sus·ten·tive** (sə sten′tiv), *adj.*

sus·ti·ne·o a·las (so͝os tin′e ō′ ä′läs; *Eng.* su stin′ē ō′ ā′las), *Latin.* I sustain the wings: motto of the U.S. Air Force.

su·sur·rant (so͝o sûr′ənt), *adj.* softly murmuring; whispering. [< L *susurrant-* (s. of *susurrāns*) whispering (prp. of *susurrāre*). See SUSURRUS, -ANT]

su·sur·ra·tion (so͞o′sə rā′shən), *n.* a soft murmur; whisper. [< LL *susurrātiōn-* (s. of *susurrātiō*) = *susurrāt(us)* (ptp. of *susurrāre;* see SUSURRANT) + *-iōn-* -ION]

su·sur·rous (so͝o sûr′əs), *adj.* full of whispering or rustling sounds. [SUSURR(US) + -OUS]

su·sur·rus (so͝o sûr′əs), *n., pl.* **-rus·es.** a soft murmuring or rustling sound; whisper. [< L: a whisper]

Suth·er·land (suth′ər lənd), *n.* **1. Joan,** born 1926, Australian soprano: in the U.S. **2.** Also called **Suth·er·land·shire** (suth′ər lənd shēr′, -shər). a county in N Scotland. 13,240 (est. 1965); 2028 sq. mi. *Co. seat:* Dornoch.

Suth′erland Falls′, a waterfall in New Zealand, on SW South Island. 1904 ft. high.

Sut·lej (sut′lej), *n.* a river in S Asia, flowing W and SW from SW Tibet through NW India into the Indus River in W Pakistan. 900 mi. long.

sut·ler (sut′lər), *n.* (formerly) a merchant who followed an army and sold provisions to the soldiers. [< obs. D *soeteler* (now *zoetelaar*) = *soetel(en)* (to) do befouling work (akin to SOOT) + *-er* -ER[1]] —**sut′ler·ship′,** *n.*

su·tra (so͞o′trə), *n.* **1.** *Hinduism.* a collection of aphorisms relating to some aspect of the conduct of life. **2.** *Pali,* **sut·ta** (so͝ot′ə). *Buddhism.* any of the sermons of Buddha. [< Skt *sūtra* thread, connective cord, rule, technical manual]

sut·tee (su tē′, sut′ē), *n.* **1.** a former Hindu practice whereby a widow immolated herself on the funeral pyre of her husband. **2.** a Hindu widow who so immolated herself. [< Skt *satī* good woman, n. use of fem. of *sat* good (lit., being), prp. of *as* to be] —**sut·tee′ism,** *n.*

Sut·ter (sut′ər), *n.* **John Augustus,** 1803–80, U.S. frontiersman born in Germany.

Sut′ter's Mill′, the location of John Sutter's mill in central California, NE of Sacramento, near which gold was found in 1848, precipitating the gold rush of 1849.

Sut·ton Hoo (sut′ᵊn ho͞o′), an archaeological site in Suffolk, England.

su·ture (so͞o′chər), *n., v.,* **-tured, -tur·ing.** —*n.* **1.** *Surg.* **a.** a joining of the lips or edges of a wound or the like by stitching or some similar process. **b.** a method of doing this. **c.** one of the stitches or fastenings employed. **2.** *Anat.* **a.** the line of junction of two bones, esp. of the skull, in an immovable articulation. **b.** the articulation itself. **3.** *Zool., Bot.* the junction or line of junction of contiguous parts, as the line of closure between the valves of a bivalve shell. **4.** a seam as formed in sewing. **5.** a sewing together or a joining as by sewing. —*v.t.* **6.** to unite by or as by a suture. [< L *sūtūr(a)* seam, suture = *sūt(us)* (ptp. of *suere* to SEW) + *-ūra* -URE] —**su′tur·al,** *adj.* —**su′tur·al·ly,** *adv.*

Su·va (so͞o′vä), *n.* a seaport in and the capital of Fiji, on Viti Levu island. 96,000.

Su·vo·rov (so͝o vô′rof), *n.* **A·le·ksan·dr Va·si·le·vich** (ä′le ksän′dər vä sē′lə vich), (*Count Suvorov Rymnikski, Prince Itliski*), 1729–1800, Russian field marshal.

Su·wan·nee (sə won′ē, -wô′nē; swon′ē, swô′nē), *n.* a river in SE Georgia and N Florida, flowing SW to the Gulf of Mexico. 240 mi. long. Also, **Swanee.**

su·ze·rain (so͞o′zə rin, -rān′), *n.* **1.** a sovereign or a state exercising political control over a dependent state. **2.** *Hist.* a feudal overlord. —*adj.* **3.** characteristic of or being a suzerain. [< F = *sus* above (< L *susum,* var. of *sursum,* contr. of *subversum,* neut. of *subversus* upturned]

su·ze·rain·ty (so͞o′zə rin tē, -rān′-), *n., pl.* **-ties. 1.** the position or authority of a suzerain. **2.** the domain or area subject to a suzerain. [< F *suzeraineté,* MF *susereneté*]

Su·zu·ki (so͝o zo͞o′kē), *n.* **Zen·ko** (zen′kō), born 1911, Japanese statesman: prime minister since 1980.

S.V., Holy Virgin. [< L *Sancta Virgō*]

s.v., **1.** See **sub verbo. 2.** See **sub voce.**

Sval·bard (sväl′bär), *n.* Norwegian name of **Spitsbergen.**

svelte (svelt, sfelt), *adj.,* **svelt·er, svelt·est. 1.** slender, esp. gracefully slender in figure; lithe. **2.** suave; blandly urbane. [< F < It *svelt(o)* < VL *(e)xvellit(um)* pulled out (r. L *ēvulsum,* ptp. of *ēvellere*)]

Sverd·lovsk (sverd lôfsk′), *n.* a city in the W RSFSR, in the W Soviet Union in Asia, on the E slope of the central Ural Mountains: execution of Czar Nicholas and his family 1918. 1,204,000. Formerly, **Ekaterinburg.**

Sve·ri·ge (sve′rē ye), *n.* Swedish name of **Sweden.**

Sviz·ze·ra (zvēt′tse rä), *n.* Italian name of **Switzerland.**

SW, 1. shortwave. **2.** southwest. **3.** southwestern.

Sw, Swedish (def. 3).

Sw., 1. Sweden. **2.** Swedish.

S.W., 1. South Wales. **2.** southwest. **3.** southwestern.

S.W.A., South-West Africa.

swab (swob), *n., v.,* **swabbed, swab·bing.** —*n.* **1.** a large mop used on shipboard for cleaning decks, living quarters, etc. **2.** a bit of sponge, cloth, cotton, or the like, sometimes fixed to a stick, for cleansing the mouth of a sick person or for applying medicaments, drying areas, etc. **3.** the material collected with a swab as a specimen. **4.** a brush or wad of absorbent material for cleaning the bore of a firearm. —*v.t.* **5.** to clean with or as with a swab. **6.** to take up or apply, as moisture, with or as with a swab. **7.** to pass (a mop, sponge, or the like) over a surface. Also, **swob.** [back formation from SWABBER]

Swab., 1. Swabia. **2.** Swabian.

swab·ber (swob′ər), *n.* **1.** a person who uses a swab. **2.** a swab; mop. [< D *zwabber* = *zwabb(en)* (to) move back and forth + *-er* -ER[1]; cf. ME *swabben* to sway (< D or LG); akin to OE *swīfan* to revolve, sweep, G *schweifen*]

Swa·bi·a (swā′bē ə), *n.* **1.** a medieval duchy in SW Germany: it comprised the area now included in Baden-Württemberg and Bavaria. **2.** a district in SW Bavaria, in S West Germany. ab. 3900 sq. mi. *Cap.:* Augsburg. German, **Schwaben.** —**Swa′bi·an,** *adj., n.*

swad·dle (swod′ᵊl), *v.,* **-dled, -dling,** *n.* —*v.t.* **1.** to bind (an infant, esp. a newborn infant) with long, narrow strips of cloth to prevent free movement. **2.** to wrap (anything) round with bandages. —*n.* **3.** a long, narrow strip of cloth used for swaddling or bandaging. [ME *swathel,* OE *swæthel* swaddling band; akin to SWATHE]

swad′dling clothes′, 1. clothes consisting of long, narrow strips of cloth for swaddling an infant. **2.** long garments for an infant. **3.** the period of infancy or immaturity, as of a person, or incipience, as of a thing. **4.** rigid supervision or restriction of actions or movements, as of the immature. Also called **swad′dling bands′** (for defs. 1, 2).

Swa·de·shi (swə dā′shē), *adj.* (formerly, in British India) made in India: a designation used to encourage the boycott of foreign goods. [< Bengali *svadesī* = *sva-* self, own + *desī* native]

swag[1] (swag), *n., v.,* **swagged, swag·ging.** —*n.* **1.** a suspended wreath, drapery, or the like; festoon. **2.** a wreath, spray, or cluster of foliage, flowers, or fruit. **3.** a swale. **4.** a swaying or lurching movement. —*v.i.* **5.** to move heavily or unsteadily with a swaying movement. **6.** to hang loosely and heavily; sink down. —*v.t.* **7.** to cause to sway, sink, or sag. **8.** to hang or adorn with swags. [prob. < Scand; cf. Norw *svagga* to sway]

swag[2] (swag), *n., v.,* **swagged, swag·ging.** —*n.* **1.** *Slang.* **a.** plunder; booty. **b.** money; valuables. **2.** *Australian.* a traveler's bundle containing personal belongings, cooking utensils, food, etc. —*v.i.* **3.** *Australian.* to travel about carrying one's bundle of personal belongings. [special uses of SWAG[1]]

swage (swāj), *n., v.,* **swaged, swag·ing.** —*n.* **1.** a tool for bending cold metal to a required shape. **2.** a tool, die, or stamp for giving a particular shape to metal on an anvil, in a stamping press, etc. **3.** See **swage block.** —*v.t.* **4.** to bend or shape by means of a swage. **5.** to reduce or taper (an object), as by forging or squeezing. [ME *souage* < MF] —**swag′er,** *n.*

swage′ block′, an iron block containing holes and grooves of various sizes, used for heading bolts and shaping objects not easily worked on an anvil.

swag·ger (swag′ər), *v.i.* **1.** to walk or strut with a defiant or insolent air. **2.** to boast or brag noisily. —*v.t.* **3.** to bring, drive, force, etc., by blustering. —*n.* **4.** swaggering manner, conduct, or walk. —**swag′ger·er,** *n.* —**Syn. 2, 4.** bluster. **4.** affectation, braggadocio.

swag′ger stick′, a short, batonlike stick sometimes carried by army officers, soldiers, etc. Also called, *esp. Brit.,* **swag′ger cane′.**

swag·man (swag′mən), *n., pl.* **-men.** *Australian.* a tramp, hobo, or vagabond.

Swa·hi·li (swä hē′lē), *n., pl.* **-lis,** (*esp. collectively*) **-li. 1.** a member of a Bantu people of Zanzibar and the neighboring coast of Africa. **2.** the Bantu language of the Swahili people: a lingua franca of E Africa and parts of Zaïre. —**Swa·hi′li·an,** *adj.*

swain (swān), *n.* **1.** a lover. **2.** a country lad. **3.** a country gallant. [early ME *swein* servant < Scand; cf. Icel *sveinn* boy, lad, c. OE *swān,* OHG *swein*] —**swain′ish,** *adj.* —**swain′ish·ness,** *n.*

S.W.A.K., sealed with a kiss (written at the end of a love letter or on the envelope). Also, **SWAK** (swak).

swale (swāl), *n.* a low place in a tract of land, usually moister and often having ranker vegetation than the adjacent higher land. [late ME; orig. a cool, shady, wet spot < Scand; cf. Icel *svalr* cool; akin to SWILL]

swal·low[1] (swol′ō), *v.t.* **1.** to take into the stomach by drawing through the throat or esophagus with a voluntary muscular action, as food or drink. **2.** to take in so as to envelop (often fol. by *up*): *The crowd swallowed him up.* **3.** *Informal.* to accept without question. **4.** to accept without opposition. **5.** to suppress (emotion, a laugh, a sob, etc.) as if by drawing it down one's throat. **6.** to take back; retract. **7.** to enunciate poorly; mutter. —*v.i.* **8.** to perform the act of swallowing. —*n.* **9.** the act or an instance of swallowing. **10.** a quantity swallowed. **11.** capacity for swallowing. **12.** Also called **crown, throat.** *Naut., Mach.* the space in a block, between the groove of the sheave and the shell, through which the rope runs. [ME *swalwen,* var. of *swelwen,* OE *swelgan;* c. G *schwelgen;* akin to Icel *svelgja*] —**swal′low·a·ble,** *adj.* —**swal′low·er,** *n.* —**Syn. 1.** eat, gulp, drink. **2.** engulf. **10.** gulp, draught, drink.

swal·low[2] (swol′ō), *n.* **1.** any of numerous small, long-winged, passerine birds of the family *Hirundinidae,* noted for their swift, graceful flight and for the extent and regularity of their migrations. **2.** any of several unrelated, swallowlike birds. [ME *swalwe,* OE *swealwe;* c. G *Schwalbe,* Icel *svala*] —**swal′low·like′,** *adj.*

swal′low dive′, *Chiefly Brit.* See **swan dive.**

swal·low·tail (swol′ō tāl′), *n.* **1.** the tail of a swallow or a deeply forked tail like that of a swallow. **2.** any of several butterflies of the genus *Papilio,* characterized by elongated hind wings that resemble the tail of a swallow.

Tiger swallowtail, *Papilio glaucus* (Wingspread to 4 in.)

swal·low-tailed (swol′ō tāld′), *adj.* **1.** having a deeply forked tail like that of a swallow, as various birds. **2.** having an end or part suggesting a swallow's tail.

swal′low-tailed coat′. See **tail coat.**

swal·low·wort (swol′ō wûrt′), *n.* **1.** celandine (def. 1). **2.** any of several asclepiadaceous plants, esp. an herb, *Vincetoxicum officinale* (or *Cynanchum Vincetoxicum*), of Europe, having an emetic root formerly used as an antidote.

swam (swam), *v.* pt. of **swim.**

swa·mi (swä′mē), *n., pl.* **-mies. 1.** an honorific title given to a Hindu religious teacher. **2.** a wise man; pundit or sage. Also, **swamy.** [< Skt *svāmī* lord, master]

swamp (swomp), *n.* **1.** a tract of wet, spongy land, often having a growth of certain types of trees and other vegetation, but unfit for cultivation. —*v.t.* **2.** to flood or drench with water or the like. **3.** to sink or fill (a boat) with water. **4.** to plunge or cause to sink in or as if in a swamp. **5.** to overwhelm, esp. with an excess of something. **6.** to render helpless. **7.** to remove trees and underbrush from (a specific area) (often fol. by *out*). **8.** to trim (felled trees) into logs, as at a logging camp or sawmill. —*v.i.* **9.** to fill with water and sink, as a boat. **10.** to sink or be stuck in a swamp or something likened to a swamp. **11.** to overwhelm, as with work, demands, etc. [? < D *zwamp* fen; akin to SUMP and to MLG *swamp*, Icel *svöppr* sponge] —**swamp′ish,** *adj.*

swamp′ cy′press. See **bald cypress.**

swamp·er (swom′pər), *n.* **1.** *Informal.* a person who inhabits, works in, or is familiar with swamps. **2.** a handyman. **3.** a worker who trims felled trees into logs. **4.** *Archaic.* the assistant driver of a mule train, camel caravan, or the like.

swamp′ fe′ver, *Pathol., Vet. Pathol.* malaria (def. 1).

Swamp′ Fox′. See **Marion, Francis.**

swamp·land (swomp′land′), *n.* land or an area covered with swamps.

swamp·y (swom′pē), *adj.,* **swamp·i·er, swamp·i·est. 1.** of the nature of, resembling, or abounding in swamps. **2.** found in swamps. —**swam′pi·ness,** *n.*

swa·my (swä′mē), *n., pl.* **-mies.** swami.

Mute Swan, *Cygnus olor* (Length 5 ft.)

swan[1] (swon), *n.* **1.** any of several large, stately, aquatic birds of the subfamily *Anserinae*, of the family *Anatidae*, having a long, slender neck and usually pure-white plumage in the adult. **2.** a person or thing of unusual grace or purity. **3.** *Literary.* a person who sings sweetly; a poet. **4.** (*cap.*) *Astron.* the constellation Cygnus. [ME, OE; c. G *Schwan*, Icel *svanr*] —**swan′like′,** *adj.*

swan[2] (swon), *v.i. U.S. Dial.* to swear: *I swan, that's a big one!* [dial. (north) *I s'wan* I shall warrant; see WARRANT]

swan′ dive′, *Fancy Diving.* a forward dive in which the arms are outstretched first crosswise and then, before the water is entered, above the head. Also called, *esp. Brit.*, **swallow dive.**

Swa·nee (swon′ē, swô′nē), *n.* Suwannee.

swang (swang), *v. Archaic and Dial.* pt. of **swing**[1].

swan·herd (swon′hûrd′), *n.* a person who tends swans. [ME]

swank (swangk), *n.* **1.** *Informal.* dashing smartness, as in dress or appearance; style. **2.** a swagger. —*adj.* **3.** *Informal.* pretentiously stylish. —*v.i.* **4.** to swagger in behavior; show off. [cf. Scot *swank* lively, prob. back formation from OE *swancor* lithe; akin to MD *swanc* supple, MHG *swanken* to sway]

swank·y (swang′kē), *adj.,* **swank·i·er, swank·i·est.** *Informal.* **1.** swank. **2.** luxurious. —**swank′i·ly,** *adv.* —**swank′i·ness,** *n.*

swan′ maid′en, a legendary maiden in many Indo-European and Asian tales, capable of transforming herself into a swan.

swan·ner·y (swon′ə rē), *n., pl.* **-ner·ies.** a place where swans are kept and raised.

swan's-down (swonz′doun′), *n.* **1.** the down or under plumage of a swan, used for trimming, powder puffs, etc. **2.** a fine, soft, thick woolen cloth. Also, **swans′down′.**

Swan·sea (swon′sē, -zē), *n.* a seaport in S Wales. 190,500.

swan·skin (swon′skin′), *n.* **1.** the skin of a swan, with the feathers on. **2.** a twill-weave flannel, closely woven and napped, for work clothes.

swan′ song′, the last work, act, utterance, or achievement of a person, group, period, etc., before death, retirement, dissolution, etc. [so called from the belief that the dying swan sings]

swan-up·ping (swon′up′ing), *n. Brit.* the taking up of young swans to mark them with nicks on the beak for identification by the owners.

swap (swop), *v.,* **swapped, swap·ping,** *n.* —*v.t.* **1.** to exchange, barter, or trade, as one thing for another. —*v.i.* **2.** to make an exchange. —*n.* **3.** an exchange: *He got the radio in a swap.* Also, **swop.** [ME *swappe(n)* (to) strike, strike hands (in bargaining); c. dial. G *schwappen* to box (the ear)] —**swap′per,** *n.*

swa·raj (swə räj′), *n.* **1.** (in India) self-government. **2.** (*cap.*) (formerly, in British India) the political party supporting this principle and opposed to British rule. [< Skt *svārājya* = *sva-* self, one's own + *rāj-* king, ruler + *-ya* suffix making abstract n.] —**swa·raj′ism,** *n.* —**swa·raj′ist,** *n., adj.*

sward (swôrd), *n.* **1.** the grassy surface of land; turf. **2.** a stretch of turf; a growth of grass. —*v.t.* **3.** to cover with sward or turf. —*v.i.* **4.** to become covered with sward. [ME; OE *sweard* skin, rind; c. G *Schwarte* rind, OFris *swarde* scalp]

sware (swâr), *n. Archaic.* pt. of **swear.**

swarm[1] (swôrm), *n.* **1.** a body of honeybees that emigrate from a hive. **2.** a body of bees settled together, as in a hive. **3.** a great number of things or persons, esp. in motion; horde. **4.** *Biol.* a group or aggregation of free-floating or free-swimming cells or organisms. —*v.i.* **5.** (of bees) to emigrate from a hive. **6.** to move about, along, forth, etc., in great numbers, as things or persons. **7.** to congregate, hover, or occur in groups or multitudes; be exceedingly numerous, as in a place or area. **8.** (of a place) to abound or teem (usually fol. by *with*): *The beach swarms with children.* **9.** *Biol.* to move or swim about in a swarm. —*v.t.* **10.** to swarm about, over, or in; throng; overrun. **11.** to produce a swarm of. [ME; OE *swearm;* c. G *Schwarm* swarm, Icel *svarmr* tumult] —**swarm′er,** *n.* —**Syn. 3.** host. See **crowd**[1]. **7.** crowd, throng.

swarm[2] (swôrm), *v.t., v.i.* to climb by clasping with the legs and hands or arms. [?]

swarm′ spore′, *Biol.* any minute, motile, naked reproductive body; zoospore; planogamete.

swart (swôrt), *adj.* swarthy. Also, *Archaic,* **swarth.** [ME; OE *sweart;* c. G *schwarz*, Icel *svatr*, Goth *swarts;* akin to L *sordēs* filth] —**swart′ness,** *n.*

swarth[1] (swôrth), *n.* sward; greensward. [ME; OE *swearth*, var. of *sweard* skin, rind; see SWARD]

swarth[2] (swôrth), *adj. Archaic.* swarthy. [unexplained var. of SWART]

swarth·y (swôr′thē, -thē), *adj.,* **swarth·i·er, swarth·i·est.** (of the skin, complexion, etc.) dark-colored. [unexplained var. of *swarty*] —**swarth′i·ly,** *adv.* —**swarth′i·ness,** *n.*

swash (swosh, swôsh), *v.i.* **1.** to splash, as things in water, or as water does. **2.** to dash around, as things in violent motion. **3.** to swagger. —*v.t.* **4.** to dash (water or other liquid) around, down, etc. —*n.* **5.** a swashing movement or the sound of it. **6.** the surging or dashing of water, waves, etc. **7.** the sound made by such dashing. **8.** the ground over which water washes. **9.** a channel of water through or behind a sandbank. [imit.] —**swash′ing·ly,** *adv.*

swash·buck·ler (swosh′buk′lər, swôsh′-), *n.* a swaggering swordsman, soldier, or adventurer; daredevil. Also called **swash′er.**

swash·buck·ling (swosh′buk′ling, swôsh′-), *adj.* **1.** characteristic of a swashbuckler. —*n.* **2.** the activities, deeds, or adventures of a swashbuckler. Also, **swash′buck′ler·ing.**

swash′ let′ter, an ornamental italic capital letter having a flourish extending beyond the body of the type.

swas·ti·ka (swos′ti kə *or, esp. Brit.,* swas′-), *n.* **1.** a geometrical figure used as a symbol or an ornament in the Old World and in America since prehistoric times, consisting of a cross with arms of equal length, each arm having a continuation at right angles, and all four continuations extending either clockwise or counterclockwise. **2.** this figure with clockwise arms as the official emblem of the Nazi party and the Third Reich. [< Skt *svastika* good luck sign = *su-* good, well + *as-* be + *-ti-* abstract n. suffix + *-ka* adj. suffix] —**swas′ti·kaed,** *adj.*

A B
Swastikas
A, Oriental and American Indian;
B, Nazi

swat[1] (swot), *v.,* **swat·ted, swat·ting,** *n.* —*v.t.* **1.** to hit; slap; smack. **2.** *Baseball.* to hit (a ball) powerfully, usually for a long distance. —*n.* **3.** a smart blow; slap; smack. **4.** *Baseball.* a powerfully hit ball. Also, **swot.** [orig. var. of SQUAT] —**swat′ter,** *n.*

swat[2] (swot), *v. Dial.* pt. and pp. of **sweat.**

Swat (swät), *n.* **1.** a former princely state in NW India: now a part of Pakistan, in the province of West Pakistan. **2.** Also, **Swati.** a Muslim inhabitant of Swat.

SWAT (swot), *n.* a special section of some law enforcement agencies trained and equipped to deal with especially dangerous or violent situations, as when hostages are being held (often used attributively). Also, **S.W.A.T.** [*S*(*pecial*) *W*(*eapons*) *a*(*nd*) *T*(*actics*)]

swatch (swoch), *n.* **1.** a sample of cloth or other material. **2.** a sample, patch, or characteristic specimen of anything. [? akin to SWITCH]

swath (swoth, swôth), *n.* **1.** the space covered by the stroke of a scythe or the cut of a mowing machine. **2.** the piece or strip so cut. **3.** grass, grain, or the like, cut and thrown together in a line. **4.** a strip, belt, or long and narrow extent of anything. **5. cut a swath,** to attract considerable notice. Also, **swathe.** [ME; OE *swæth* footprint; c. G *Shwade*]

swathe[1] (swoth, swāth), *v.,* **swathed, swath·ing,** *n.* —*v.t.* **1.** to wrap, bind, or swaddle with bands. **2.** to bandage. **3.** to enfold or envelop, as wrappings do. **4.** to wrap (cloth, rope, etc.) around something. —*n.* **5.** a wrapping or bandage. [ME; late OE *swathian* < OE *swæth bandage (in *swathium*, dat. pl.); c. Icel *svatha*] —**swath′a·ble, swathe′a·ble,** *adj.* —**swath′er,** *n.*

swathe[2] (swoth, swāth), *n.* swath.

Swa·ti (swä′tē), *n., pl.* **-tis,** (*esp. collectively*) **-ti.** Swat (def. 2).

Swa·tow (swä′tou′), *n.* a seaport in E Kwantung, in SE China. 400,000.

swats (swats), *n.* (*construed as pl.*) *Scot.* sweet, new beer or ale. [cf. OE *swatan* beer (pl.)]

sway (swā), *v.i.* **1.** to move or swing to and fro, as something fixed at one end or resting on a support. **2.** to move or incline to one side or in a particular direction. **3.** to incline in opinion, sympathy, etc. **4.** to fluctuate or vacillate, as in opinion. **5.** to wield power; exercise rule. —*v.t.* **6.** to cause to move to and fro or to incline from side to side. **7.** to cause to move to one side or in a particular direction. **8.** *Naut.* to hoist or raise (a yard, topmast, or the like) (usually fol. by *up*). **9.** to cause to fluctuate or vacillate. **10.** to influence (the mind, emotions, etc., or a person). **11.** to cause to swerve, as from a purpose. **12.** to dominate; direct. **13.** *Archaic.* **a.** to wield, as a weapon or scepter. **b.** to rule; govern. —*n.* **14.** the act of swaying; swaying movement. **15.** rule or dominion. **16.** dominating power or influence. [ME *sweye(n)* < Scand; cf. Icel *sveigja* to sway; akin to MLG *swājen* to sway] —**sway′a·ble,** *adj.* —**sway′er,** *n.* —**sway′ful,** *adj.* —**sway′ing·ly,** *adv.* —**Syn. 1.** wave. See **swing**[1]. **3.** lean, bend, tend. **5.** reign, govern. **15.** sovereignty, authority, mastery. **16.** control.

sway-back (swā′bak′), *Vet. Pathol.* —*n.* **1.** an excessive or abnormal downward curvature of the spinal column in the dorsal region, esp. of horses. —*adj.* **2.** sway-backed. Also, **sway′back′.**

sway-backed (swā′bakt′), *adj. Vet. Pathol.* having a sway-back. Also, **sway′backed′, sway-back.**

Swa·zi (swä′zē), *n., pl.* **-zis,** (*esp. collectively*) **-zi.** a member of a Bantu tribe of Zulu descent found in SE Africa.

Swa·zi·land (swä′zē land′), *n.* a kingdom in SE Africa between S Mozambique and SE Transvaal in the Republic of South Africa, formerly a British protectorate. 480,000; 6704 sq. mi. *Cap.:* Mbabane.

SWbS, See **southwest by south.**

SWbW, See **southwest by west.**

swear (swâr), *v.,* **swore** or (*Archaic*) **sware; sworn; swear·ing.** —*v.i.* **1.** to make a solemn declaration or affirmation by some sacred being or object, as the Deity or the Bible. **2.** to bind oneself by oath (usually fol. by *to*); vow. **3.** to give evidence or make any statement on oath (usually fol. by *to*). **4.** to use profane oaths or language. —*v.t.* **5.** to declare, affirm, attest, etc., by swearing by a deity, some sacred object, etc. **6.** to affirm, assert, or say with solemn earnestness. **7.** to promise or undertake on oath or in a solemn manner; vow. **8.** to testify or state on oath. **9.** to take (an oath), as in order to give solemnity or force to a declaration, promise, etc. **10.** to bind by an oath. **11. swear by, a.** to name (a sacred being or thing) as one's witness or guarantee in swearing. **b.** *Informal.* to have confidence in; rely on. **c.** to have certain knowledge of. **12. swear in,** to admit to office or service by administering an oath. **13. swear off,** *Informal.* to resolve to give up something, esp. intoxicating beverages. **14. swear out,** to secure (a warrant for arrest) by making an accusation under oath. [ME *swere(n),* OE *swerian;* G *schwören,* Icel *sverja;* akin to Goth *swaran* to swear; see ANSWER] —**swear′er,** *n.* —**swear′ing·ly,** *adv.* —**Syn. 1.** declare, affirm, avow. **3.** depose, testify. **4.** imprecate. See **curse.**

sweat (swet), *v.,* **sweat** or **sweat·ed, sweat·ing,** *n.* —*v.i.* **1.** to excrete watery fluid through the pores of the skin; perspire, esp. freely or profusely. **2.** to exude moisture, as green plants piled in a heap. **3.** to gather moisture from the surrounding air by condensation. **4.** (of moisture or liquid) to ooze or be exuded. **5.** *Informal.* to experience distress, as from anxiety. **6.** (of tobacco) to ferment. **7.** *Obs.* to suffer punishment.
—*v.t.* **8.** to excrete (perspiration, moisture, etc.) through the pores of the skin. **9.** to exude in drops or small particles. **10.** to send forth or get rid of with or like perspiration (often fol. by *out* or *off*). **11.** to wet or stain with perspiration. **12.** to cause (a person, a horse, etc.) to perspire. **13.** to cause to exude moisture, esp. as a step in some industrial process: *to sweat tobacco leaves.* **14.** to earn, produce, or obtain by hard work. **15.** to cause to lose (weight) as by perspiring or hard work (often fol. by *off* or *out*). **16.** to cause, force, or bring pressure on (a person, an animal, etc.) to work hard. **17.** to employ (workers) at low wages, for long hours, or under other unfavorable conditions. **18.** *Metall.* to heat (an alloy) in order to remove a constituent melting at a lower temperature than the alloy as a whole. **19.** to remove bits of metal from (gold coins) by shaking together. Cf. **clip**[1] (def. 4). **20.** to cause (tobacco) to ferment. **21. sweat blood,** *Slang.* **a.** to be under a strain; work strenuously. **b.** to wait anxiously; worry. **22. sweat (something) out,** *Slang.* **a.** to wait until the end of; endure. **b.** to work arduously at or toward (a goal, solution, etc.).
—*n.* **23.** the process of sweating or perspiring. **24.** that which is secreted from sweat glands. **25.** a state or a period of sweating. **26.** *Informal.* a state of anxiety or impatience. **27.** a process of inducing sweating or of being sweated, as in medical treatment. **28.** moisture exuded from something or gathered on a surface. **29.** an exuding of moisture, as by a substance. **30.** an inducing of such exudation, as in some industrial process. **31.** a run given to a horse for exercise. [ME *swete(n),* OE *swǣtan* to sweat < *swāt* sweat; c. D *zweet,* G *Schweiss,* Icel *sveiti,* Skt *svedas;* akin to L *sūdor,* Gk *hidrōs*] —**sweat′less,** *adj.*
—**Syn. 24.** See **perspiration.**

sweat·band (swet′band′), *n.* a band lining the bottom of the inside of the crown of a hat or cap to protect it against sweat from the head.

sweat′ bee′, any of several bees of the family *Halictidae* that are attracted by perspiration.

sweat·box (swet′boks′), *n.* **1.** a device for sweating tobacco leaves, figs, raisins, etc. **2.** *Slang.* a narrow box or cell for confining a prisoner.

sweat·er (swet′ər), *n.* **1.** a knitted jacket or jersey, in pullover or cardigan style, with or without sleeves. **2.** a person or thing that sweats.

sweat′er girl′, *Slang.* a girl or young woman with a shapely bosom, esp. one who wears tight sweaters to emphasize her bosom.

sweat′ gland′, *Anat.* one of the minute, coiled, tubular glands of the skin that secrete sweat.

sweat′ing sick′ness, a febrile epidemic disease, esp. of the 15th and 16th centuries: characterized by profuse sweating and frequently fatal in a few hours.

sweat′ pants′, loose-fitting, cotton-jersey trousers with close-fitting or elastic cuffs and a drawstring at the waist, worn esp. by athletes to prevent chill or, while exercising, to induce sweating.

sweat′ shirt′, a loose, collarless, cotton-jersey pullover, usually long-sleeved, worn esp. by athletes to prevent chill or, while exercising, to induce sweating.

sweat·shop (swet′shop′), *n.* a shop employing workers at low wages, for long hours, and under poor conditions.

sweat·y (swet′ē), *adj.,* **sweat·i·er, sweat·i·est. 1.** covered, moist, or stained with sweat. **2.** causing sweat. **3.** laborious. [late ME *swety*] —**sweat′i·ly,** *adv.* —**sweat′i·ness,** *n.*

Swed., **1.** Sweden. **2.** Swedish.

Swede (swēd), *n.* a native or inhabitant of Sweden. [< MD or MLG; c. G *Schwede;* cf. OE *Swēon* (pl.), Icel *Svēar, Svíar,* L *Suiōnes*]

Swe·den (swēd′ᵊn), *n.* a kingdom in N Europe, in the E part of the Scandinavian Peninsula. 8,200,000; 173,394 sq. mi. *Cap.:* Stockholm. Swedish, **Sverige.**

Swe·den·borg (swēd′ᵊn bôrg′; *Sw.* svād′ᵊn bôʀ′yᵊ), *n.* **E·ma·nu·el** (i man′yo͞o əl; *Sw.* e mä′no͞o əl), (*Emanuel Swedberg*), 1688–1772, Swedish scientist and philosopher.

Swe·den·bor·gi·an (swēd′ᵊn bôr′jē ən, -gē-), *adj.* **1.** pertaining to Emanuel Swedenborg, to his religious doctrines, or to the body of followers adhering to these doctrines and constituting the New Jerusalem Church. —*n.* **2.** a believer in the religious doctrines of Swedenborg. —**Swe′den·bor′gi·an·ism, Swe′den·borg′ism,** *n.*

Swed·ish (swē′dish), *adj.* **1.** of or pertaining to Sweden, its inhabitants, or their language. —*n.* **2.** the people of Sweden collectively. **3.** a Germanic language, the language of Sweden and parts of Finland, closely related to Danish and Norwegian. *Abbr.:* Sw, Sw., Swed.

Swed′ish massage′, a massage employing techniques of manipulation and muscular exercise systematized in Sweden in the 19th century.

Swed′ish tur′nip, rutabaga. [so called because introduced (into Great Britain) from Sweden]

swee·ny (swē′nē), *n.* *Vet. Pathol.* atrophy of the shoulder muscles in horses. Also, **swinney.** [cf. dial. G *Schweine,* PaG *Schwinne* atrophy, OE *swindan* to pine away, disappear]

sweep[1] (swēp), *v.,* **swept, sweep·ing,** *n.* —*v.t.* **1.** to move or remove (dust, dirt, etc.) by passing a broom, brush, or the like, through, over, or back and forth over the surface occupied (often fol. by *away, out,* etc.). **2.** to clear or clean (a floor, room, chimney, etc.) of dirt, litter, or the like, by means of a broom or brush. **3.** to move, bring, take, etc., by or as by a steady, driving stroke or a series of short strokes. **4.** to pass or draw (something) over a surface, or about, along, etc., with a steady, continuous stroke or movement. **5.** to make (a path, opening, etc.) by clearing a space with or as with a broom. **6.** to clear (a surface, place, etc.) of something on or in it. **7.** to pass over (a surface, region, etc.) with a steady, driving movement or unimpeded course. **8.** to direct the eyes, a gaze, etc., over (a region, area, etc.). **9.** to direct (the eyes, gaze, etc.) over a region, surface, or the like. **10.** to win a complete or overwhelming victory in (a contest). **11.** to win (every game, round, etc., of a series of contests). —*v.i.* **12.** to sweep a floor, room, etc., with or as with a broom. **13.** to move steadily and strongly or swiftly (usually fol. by *along, down, by, into,* etc.). **14.** to pass in a swift but stately manner. **15.** to move, pass, or extend in a continuous course, esp. a wide curve or circuit. **16.** to conduct an underwater search by towing a drag under the surface of the water. —*n.* **17.** the act of sweeping, esp. a moving, removing, clearing, etc., by or as by the use of a broom. **18.** the steady, driving motion or swift onward course of something moving with force or without interruption. **19.** a swinging or curving movement or stroke. **20.** reach, range, or compass, as of something that extends around or encircles. **21.** a continuous extent or stretch: *a broad sweep of sand.* **22.** a curving, esp. widely or gently curving, line, form, part, or mass. **23.** matter removed or gathered by sweeping. **24.** a leverlike device for raising or lowering a bucket in a well. **25.** a large oar used in small vessels to assist the rudder or to propel the craft. **26.** an overwhelming victory in a contest or series of contests. **27.** one of the sails of a windmill. **28.** *Chiefly Brit.* a chimney sweeper. **29.** *Cards.* **a.** *Whist.* the winning of all the tricks in a hand. Cf. **slam**[2] (def. 1). **b.** *Casino.* a pairing or combining, and hence taking, of all the cards on the board. [ME *swep(en);* cf. OE *geswēpa* sweepings < *swāp(an)* (to) sweep; c. G *schweifen*] —**sweep′a·ble,** *adj.*

sweep[2] (swēp), *n.* *Slang.* a sweepstakes. [by shortening]

sweep·back (swēp′bak′), *n.* *Aeron.* the shape of, or the angle formed by, an airplane wing or other airfoil the leading or trailing edge of which slopes backward from the fuselage. [n. use of v. phrase *sweep back*]

sweep·er (swē′pər), *n.* **1.** a person or thing that sweeps. **2.** See **carpet sweeper.** **3.** a janitor. [ME]

sweep′ hand′, *Horol.* a hand, usually a second hand, centrally mounted with the minute and hour hands of a timepiece and reaching to the edge of the dial.

sweep·ing (swē′ping), *adj.* **1.** of wide range or scope. **2.** passing over a wide area. **3.** moving or passing steadily and forcibly on. **4.** (of the outcome of a contest) decisive; overwhelming. —*n.* **5.** the act of a person or thing that sweeps. **6. sweepings,** matter swept out or up: *Put the sweepings in the trash can.* [late ME (n.)] —**sweep′ing·ly,** *adv.* —**sweep′ing·ness,** *n.*

sweeps (swēps), *n.* *Slang.* a sweepstakes.

sweep·stake (swēp′stāk′), *n.* a sweepstakes.

sweep·stakes (swēp′stāks′), *n.* (*construed as sing. or pl.*) **1.** a race or other contest for which the prize consists of the stakes contributed by the various competitors. **2.** the prize itself. **3.** a lottery in which winning tickets are selected at random, each winning-ticket number then being matched to one of the horses nominated for or entered in a specific race, and the amounts paid the winners being determined by the finishing order of the horses that run. **4.** lottery (def. 2). **5.** any gambling transaction in which each of a number of persons contributes a stake, and the stakes are awarded to one or several winners.

sweet (swēt), *adj.* **1.** having the taste or flavor characteristic of sugar, honey, etc. **2.** producing one of the four basic taste sensations; not bitter, sour, or salt. **3.** not rancid or stale; fresh: *This milk is still sweet.* **4.** not salt or salted: *sweet butter.* **5.** pleasing to the ear; musical. **6.** pleasing or fresh to the smell; fragrant. **7.** pleasing or agreeable. **8.** pleasant in disposition or manners, as a person, action, etc. **9.** dear; beloved; precious. **10.** easily managed or done. **11.** (of wine) not dry; containing unfermented, natural sugar. **12.** sentimental, cloying, or unrealistic. **13.** (of air) fresh; free from odor, staleness, etc. **14.** free from acidity or sourness, as soil. **15.** *Chem.* **a.** devoid of corrosive or acidic substances. **b.** (of gasoline or the like) containing no sulfur compounds. **16.** (of jazz or ballroom dance music) performed with a regular beat, moderate tempo, lack of improvisation, and an emphasis on warm tone and clearly outlined melody. **17. sweet on,** *Informal.* infatuated with; in love with. —*adv.* **18.** in a sweet manner; sweetly. —*n.* **19.** a sweet flavor, smell, or sound; sweetness. **20.** something that is sweet or causes or gives a sweet flavor, smell, or sound. **21. sweets, a.** *Informal.* candied sweet potatoes. **b.**

pie, cake, candy, and other foods high in sugar content. **22.** *Chiefly Brit.* **a.** a piece of candy; sweetmeat or bonbon. **b.** a sweet dish or dessert. **23.** something pleasant to the mind or feelings. **24.** a beloved person. **25.** *Informal.* (in direct address) darling; sweetheart. [ME, OE *swēte;* c. OS *swōti,* OHG *swuozi,* G *süss;* akin to Goth *suts,* D *zoet,* Icel *sætr,* Gk *hēdýs* sweet, L *suād(us)* persuasive, *suāvis* sweet] —**sweet′less,** *adj.* —**sweet′ly,** *adv.* —**sweet′ness,** *n.* —**Syn. 1.** sugary, honeyed, syrupy, saccharine. **3.** clean, new. **5.** melodious, mellifluous. **6.** redolent, aromatic, scented. —**Ant. 1.** sour.

Sweet (swēt), *n.* **Henry,** 1845–1912, English philologist and linguist.

sweet′ alys′sum, a cruciferous garden plant, *Lobularia maritima,* having small, white or violet flowers.

sweet-and-sour (swēt′ən sour′, -sou′ər), *adj.* cooked with sugar and vinegar or lemon juice, and often with additional seasoning.

sweet′ bas′il. See under **basil.**

sweet′ bay′, **1.** bay[4] (def. 1). **2.** an American magnolia, *Magnolia virginiana,* having fragrant, white, globular flowers.

sweet·bread (swēt′bred′), *n.* **1.** Also called **stomach sweetbread.** the pancreas of an animal, esp. a calf or a lamb, used for food. **2.** Also called **throat sweetbread.** the thymus gland of such an animal, used for food.

sweet·bri·er (swēt′brī′ər), *n.* a rose, *Rosa Eglanteria,* of Europe and central Asia, having a tall stem, stout prickles often mixed with bristles, and single pink flowers. Also, **sweet′bri′ar.**

sweet′ cher′ry, **1.** a cherry, *Prunus avium,* characterized by its reddish-brown bark and pyramidal manner of growth. **2.** the edible, sweet fruit of this tree.

sweet′ cic′ely, any of several umbelliferous plants, as a European herb, *Myrrhis odorata,* used as a potherb, or certain North American herbs of the genus *Osmorhiza.*

sweet′ ci′der. See under **cider.**

sweet′ clo′ver, melilot.

sweet′ corn′, **1.** any of several varieties of corn, esp. *Zea Mays saccharata,* having sweet edible kernels. **2.** the young and tender ears of corn, esp. when used as a table vegetable; green corn.

sweet·en (swēt′ən), *v.t.* **1.** to make sweet, as by adding sugar. **2.** to make mild or kind; soften. **3.** to make (the breath, room air, etc.) sweet or fresh, as with a mouthwash, spray, etc. **4.** to make (the stomach, soil, etc.) less acidic, as by taking certain preparations, spreading chemicals, etc. **5.** *Informal.* **a.** to enhance the value of (loan collateral) by including additional or especially valuable securities. **b.** to enhance the value or attractiveness of (any proposition, holding, etc.). **6.** *Informal.* to replenish (an alcoholic drink) before the original portion is finished. **7.** *Poker Slang.* to increase (a pot) by adding stakes before opening. —*v.i.* **8.** to become sweet or sweeter. —**sweet′en·er,** *n.*

sweet·en·ing (swēt′ən ning, swēt′ning), *n.* **1.** something that sweetens food, beverages, etc., as sugar, saccharin, etc. **2.** the process of causing something to be or become sweet.

sweet′ fern′, a small, North American shrub, *Comptonia peregrina* (*Myrica asplenifolia*), having aromatic, fern-like leaves.

sweet′ flag′, an araceous plant, *Acorus Calamus,* having long, sword-shaped leaves and a pungent, aromatic rootstock.

sweet′ gale′, a shrub, *Myrica Gale,* growing in marshy places and having an aromatic odor.

sweet′ gum′, **1.** the American liquidambar, *Liquidambar Styraciflua.* **2.** the hard reddish-brown wood of this tree, used for making furniture. **3.** the amber balsam exuded by this tree, used in perfumes and medicines. Also called **copalm** (for defs. 1, 2).

sweet·heart (swēt′härt′), *n.* **1.** either of a pair of lovers in relation to the other. **2.** (often used as a term of endearment) a beloved person. **3.** *Informal.* a generous, friendly person. [ME *swete herte*]

sweet·ie (swē′tē), *n.* **1.** *Informal.* sweetheart (defs. 1, 2). **2.** Usually, **sweeties.** *Brit.* candy; sweets.

sweet·ing (swē′ting), *n.* **1.** a sweet variety of apple. **2.** *Archaic.* sweetheart. [ME *sweting*]

sweet·ish (swē′tish), *adj.* somewhat sweet. —**sweet′ish·ly,** *adv.* —**sweet′ish·ness,** *n.*

sweet′ mar′joram, a fragrant herb, *Majorana hortensis,* grown for its leaves for use in cookery.

sweet·meat (swēt′mēt′), *n.* **1.** a highly sweetened food, as preserves, candy, or, formerly, cakes or pastry. **2.** Usually, **sweetmeats.** any sweet delicacy of the confectionery or candy kind, as candied fruit, bonbons, etc. [ME *swete mete,* OE *swētmete*]

sweet′ or′ange. See under **orange** (def. 2).

sweet′ pea′, an annual climbing plant, *Lathyrus odoratus,* having sweet-scented flowers.

sweet′ pep′per, **1.** a variety of pepper, *Capsicum frutescens grossum,* having a mild-flavored, bell-shaped or somewhat oblong fruit. **2.** the fruit itself, used as a vegetable. Also called **bell pepper.**

sweet′ pota′to, **1.** a convolvulaceous plant, *Ipomoea Batatas,* grown for its sweet, edible, tuberous roots. **2.** the edible root itself. **3.** *Informal.* ocarina.

sweet-scent·ed (swēt′sen′tid), *adj.* having a pleasant and sweet smell; fragrant.

sweet′ shop′, *Brit.* a store that sells candy.

sweet·sop (swēt′sop′), *n.* **1.** a sweet, pulpy fruit having a thin, tuberculate rind, borne by a tree or shrub, *Annona squamosa,* of tropical America. **2.** the tree or shrub. Also called **sugar apple.**

sweet′ talk′, *Informal.* cajolery; soft soap.

sweet-talk (swēt′tôk′), *v.t., Informal.* to use cajoling words on in order to persuade; soft-soap.

sweet′ tooth′, a liking or craving for candy and other sweets.

sweet′ vibur′num, the sheepberry, *Viburnum Lentago.*

sweet′ wil′liam, a perennial pink, *Dianthus barbatus,* having showy clusters of small, variously colored flowers. Also, **sweet′ Wil′liam.**

swell (swel), *v.,* **swelled, swelled** or **swol·len, swell·ing,** *n., adj.* —*v.i.* **1.** to grow in bulk, as by absorption of moisture, inflation, distention, the process of growth, or the like. **2.** to rise in waves, as the sea. **3.** to well up, as a spring or as tears. **4.** to bulge out, as a sail, the middle of a cask, etc. **5.** to grow in amount, degree, force, etc. **6.** to increase gradually in volume or intensity, as sound. **7.** to arise and grow within a person, as a feeling or emotion. **8.** to become puffed up with pride. —*v.t.* **9.** to cause to grow in bulk. **10.** to cause to increase gradually in loudness: *to swell a musical tone.* **11.** to cause (a thing) to bulge out or be protuberant. **12.** to increase in amount, degree, force, etc. **13.** to affect with a strong, expansive emotion. **14.** to puff up with pride. —*n.* **15.** the act of swelling or the condition of being swollen. **16.** inflation or distention. **17.** a protuberant part. **18.** a wave, esp. when long and unbroken, or a series of such waves. **19.** a gradually rising elevation of the land. **20.** an increase in amount, degree, force, etc. **21.** a gradual increase in loudness of sound. **22.** *Music.* **a.** a gradual increase (crescendo) followed by a gradual decrease (diminuendo) in loudness or force of musical sound. **b.** the sign (<>) for indicating this. **c.** a device, as in an organ, by which the loudness of tones may be varied. **23.** a swelling of emotion within a person. **24.** *Slang.* **a.** a fashionably dressed person; dandy. **b.** a socially prominent person. —*adj. Slang.* **25.** (of things) stylish; elegant: *a swell hotel.* **26.** (of persons) fashionably dressed or socially prominent. **27.** first-rate; fine. [ME; OE *swell(an);* c. D *zwellen,* G *schwellen,* Icel *svella;* akin to Goth *(uf)swalleins* pride] —**Syn. 1.** dilate, distend, expand. **4.** protrude. **9.** inflate, expand. **12.** augment. **16.** swelling. **17.** bulge, protuberance. **18.** billow. **26, 27.** grand. —**Ant. 1.** contract. **12.** decrease, diminish.

swell′ box′, a chamber containing a set of pipes in a pipe organ or of reeds in a reed organ, and having movable slats or shutters that can be opened or closed to increase or diminish tonal volume.

swelled′ head′, *Informal.* an inordinately grand opinion of oneself. —**swelled′-head′ed,** *adj.* —**swelled′-head′ed·ness,** *n.*

swell·fish (swel′fish′), *n., pl.* (*esp. collectively*) **-fish,** (*esp. referring to two or more kinds or species*) **-fish·es.** puffer (def. 2).

swell′ front′, *Furniture.* a horizontally convex front, as of a chest of drawers. Also called **bow front.** Cf. **bombé.**

swell·head (swel′hed′), *n.* *Informal.* a vain, arrogant person. —**swell′head′ed,** *adj.* —**swell′head′ed·ness,** *n.*

swell·ing (swel′ing), *n.* **1.** the act of a person or thing that swells. **2.** the condition of being or becoming swollen. **3.** a swollen part. **4.** *Pathol.* an abnormal enlargement or protuberance. [late ME]

swel·ter (swel′tər), *v.i.* **1.** to suffer from oppressive heat. —*v.t.* **2.** to oppress with heat. **3.** *Archaic.* to exude, as venom. —*n.* **4.** a sweltering condition. [ME *swelt(e)r(en)* = *swelt(en)* (OE *sweltan* to die; c. Icel *svelta,* Goth *swiltan*) + *-eren* -ER[6]]

swel·ter·ing (swel′tər ing), *adj.* **1.** suffering from oppressive heat. **2.** characterized by oppressive heat. —**swel′ter·ing·ly,** *adv.*

swept (swept), *v.* pt. and pp. of **sweep.**

swept·back (swept′bak′), *adj.* *Aeron.* **1.** (of the leading edge of an airfoil) forming an obtuse angle with the fuselage. **2.** (of an aircraft or missile) having wings of this type.

swept·wing (swept′wing′), *adj.* *Aeron.* (of an aircraft, winged missile, etc.) having sweptback wings. [SWEPT(BACK) + WING]

swerve (swûrv), *v.,* **swerved, swerv·ing,** *n.* —*v.i.* **1.** to turn aside abruptly in movement or direction. —*v.t.* **2.** to cause to turn aside. —*n.* **3.** an act of swerving. [ME; OE *sweorf(an)* (to) rub, file; c. D *zwerven* to rove, Icel *sverfa* to file, OHG *swerban,* Goth *afswairban* to wipe off] —**swerv′a·ble,** *adj.* —**swerv′er,** *n.*

swev·en (swev′ən), *n.* *Archaic.* a vision; dream. [ME; OE *swefn;* akin to Icel *sofa* to sleep, L *somnus,* Gk *hýpnos* sleep]

swift (swift), *adj.* **1.** moving or capable of moving with great speed. **2.** coming, happening, or performed quickly. **3.** quick to act or respond. —*adv.* **4.** swiftly. —*n.* **5.** any of numerous long-winged, swallowlike birds of the family *Apodidae,* related to the hummingbirds and noted for their rapid flight. **6.** an adjustable device upon which a hank of yarn is placed in order to wind off skeins or balls. [ME, OE; akin to OE *swīfan* to revolve, Icel *svīfa* to rove; see SWIVEL] —**swift′ly,** *adv.* —**swift′ness,** *n.* —**Syn. 1.** speedy. See **quick. 2.** expeditious. **3.** ready, eager, alert. —**Ant. 1.** slow.

Swift (swift), *n.* **Jonathan,** 1667–1745, English satirist and clergyman, born in Ireland.

swift-foot·ed (swift′fo͝ot′id), *adj.* swift in running.

swig[1] (swig), *n., v.,* **swigged, swig·ging.** *Informal.* —*n.* **1.** an amount of liquid, esp. liquor, taken in one swallow; draught. —*v.t., v.i.* **2.** to drink heartily or greedily. [? akin to SWAG[1]] —**swig′ger,** *n.*

swig[2] (swig), *v.i.,* **swigged, swig·ging.** *Naut.* to haul on a rope while taking up its slack (sometimes fol. by *off* or *to*). [? var. of SWAG[1]]

swill (swil), *n.* **1.** liquid or partly liquid food, esp. kitchen refuse, for animals. **2.** kitchen refuse in general; garbage. **3.** any liquid mess; slop. **4.** a deep draught of liquor. —*v.i.* **5.** to drink greedily or excessively. —*v.t.* **6.** to guzzle. **7.** to feed (animals) with swill. **8.** *Chiefly Brit. Informal.* to wash by rinsing or flooding with water. [ME *swile(n),* OE *swilian,* var. of *swillan*] —**swill′er,** *n.*

swim (swim), *v.,* **swam, swum, swim·ming,** *n.* —*v.i.* **1.** to move in water by using the limbs, fins, tail, etc. **2.** to float on the surface of water or some other liquid. **3.** to move, rest, or be suspended in air as if swimming in water. **4.** to move, glide, or go smoothly over a surface. **5.** to be immersed in or flooded with a liquid. **6.** to be dizzy or giddy. —*v.t.* **7.** to move along in or cross (a body of water) by swimming. **8.** to perform (a particular stroke) in swimming. **9.** to cause to swim or float. —*n.* **10.** the act, an instance, or a period of swimming. **11.** a smooth, gliding movement. **12. in the swim,** alert to or actively engaged in current affairs, social activities, etc. [ME *swimm(en),* OE *swimman;*

c. G *schwimmen*, D *zwemmen*, Icel *svimma*] —**swim′ma·ble,** *adj.* —**swim′mer,** *n.*

swim′ blad′der. See **air bladder** (def. 2).

swim′ fin′, one of a pair of flippers.

swim·mer·et (swim′ə ret′), *n.* (in many crustaceans) one of a number of abdominal limbs or appendages, usually adapted for swimming and for carrying eggs.

swim·ming (swim′ing), *n.* **1.** the act of a person or thing that swims. **2.** the skill or technique of a person who swims. **3.** the sport or a contest based on the ability to swim. —*adj.* **4.** capable of, knowing how to, or in the act of propelling oneself in water by moving the limbs, fins, tail, etc. **5.** used in or for swimming. **6.** immersed in or overflowing with water or some other liquid. **7.** having a sensation of dizziness. [ME; OE *swimmende*] —**swim′ming·ness,** *n.*

swim·ming·ly (swim′ing lē), *adv.* without difficulty; with great success.

swim′ming pool′, a tank or large artificial basin, usually of concrete, for filling with water for swimming.

swim·suit (swim′so͞ot′), *n.* See **bathing suit.**

swim·wear (swim′wâr′), *n.* clothing, such as bathing suits, trunks, etc., worn for swimming or at a beach.

Swin·burne (swin′bərn), *n.* **Algernon Charles,** 1837–1909, English poet and critic.

swin·dle (swin′dəl), *v.*, **-dled, -dling,** *n.* —*v.t.* **1.** to cheat out of money or other assets. **2.** to obtain by fraud or deceit. —*v.i.* **3.** to defraud or cheat. —*n.* **4.** the act of swindling or a fraudulent transaction or scheme. **5.** any fraud. [back formation from *swindler* < G *Schwindler* giddy-minded, irresponsible person, promoter of wildcat schemes, cheat < *schwindeln* to be dizzy (hence dizzy-minded, irresponsible), defraud = *schwind-* (akin to OE *swindan* to languish) + *-eln* freq. suffix] —**swin′dle·a·ble,** *adj.* —**swin′dler,** *n.* —**swin′dling·ly,** *adv.* —**Syn. 1.** cozen, dupe, trick, gull.

swin′dle sheet′, *Slang.* an expense account.

swine (swīn), *n., pl.* **swine. 1.** the domestic hog. **2.** any artiodactyl animal of the family *Suidae*, of the Old World, or of the closely related New World family, *Tayassuidae*, comprising the peccaries. **3.** a coarse, gross, or brutishly sensual person. **4.** any contemptible man. [ME; OE *swīn*; c. G *Schwein* hog, L *suīnus* (adj.) porcine; akin to sow[2]] —**swine′like′,** *adj.*

swine·herd (swīn′hûrd′), *n.* a man who tends swine. [ME; late OE *swȳnhyrde*]

swing[1] (swing), *v.*, **swung** or (*Archaic and Dial.*) **swang; swung; swing·ing;** *n., adj.* —*v.t.* **1.** to cause to move to and fro, sway, or oscillate, as something suspended from above. **2.** to cause to move in alternate directions or in either direction around a fixed point, on an axis, or on a line of support, as a door on hinges. **3.** to move (the hand or something held) with an oscillating or rotary movement: *to swing a club around one's head.* **4.** *Aeron.* to pull or turn (a propeller) by hand, esp. in order to start the engine. **5.** to cause to move in a new direction, in a curve, or as if around a central point. **6.** to suspend so as to hang freely, as a hammock or a door. **7.** *U.S. Informal.* to influence or manage as desired: *to swing votes; swing a business deal.* **8.** to direct, change, or shift (one's attention, interest, opinion, support, etc.). —*v.i.* **9.** to move back and forth, esp. with regular motion, as of a body supported from the end or ends. **10.** to move to and fro in a swing. **11.** to move in alternate directions or in either direction around a point, an axis, or a line of support. **12.** to move in a curve as if around a central point. **13.** to move with a free, swaying motion. **14.** to be suspended so as to hang freely, as a bell. **15.** to move by grasping a support with the hands and drawing up the arms or using the momentum of the swaying body. **16.** to direct, change, or shift one's attention, interest, opinion, support, etc. **17.** to hit at someone or something with the hand or something grasped in the hand. **18.** *Slang.* **a.** to have or be characterized by a modern, lively, active, and knowledgeable attitude, life, or atmosphere; be hip: *She may be 45, but she swings. Las Vegas swings all year.* **b.** (of two persons) to be in rapport. **c.** to engage uninhibitedly in sexual activities. **d.** (of married couples) to exchange partners for sexual activities. **19.** *Informal.* to suffer death by hanging. —*n.* **20.** the act, manner, or progression of swinging. **21.** the amount or extent of such movement. **22.** a curving movement or course. **23.** a moving of the body with a free, swaying motion. **24.** a blow or stroke with the hand or an object grasped in the hands. **25.** a steady, marked rhythm or movement, as of verse or music. **26.** a regular upward or downward movement in any business activity. **27.** *Informal.* a work period coming between the regular day and night shifts. **28.** freedom of action. **29.** active operation; progression: *to get into the swing of things.* **30.** something that is swung or that swings. **31.** a seat suspended from above by means of a loop of rope or between ropes or rods, on which a person, esp. a child, may sit and swing to and fro for recreation. **32. in full swing,** *Informal.* **a.** working at the highest or most efficient speed. **b.** fully under way. —*adj.* **33.** of or pertaining to a swing. **34.** determining or capable of determining the outcome of an election, decision, etc. **35.** designed or constructed to permit swinging or hanging. **36.** *Informal.* relieving other workers when needed, as at night. [ME *swing(en)*, OE *swingan*; c. G *schwingen*] —**swing′a·ble,** *adj.*
—**Syn. 1.** wave. **9.** SWING, SWAY, OSCILLATE, ROCK suggest a movement back and forth. SWING expresses the comparatively regular motion to and fro of a body supported from the end or ends, esp. from above: *A lamp swings from the ceiling.* To SWAY is to swing gently and is used esp. of fixed objects or of persons: *Young oaks sway in the breeze.* OSCILLATE refers to the smooth, regular, alternating movement of a body within certain limits between two fixed points. ROCK indicates the slow and regular movement back and forth of a body, as on curved supports: *A cradle rocks.* **20.** sway, vibration, oscillation. **21.** range, scope, sweep, play.

swing[2] (swing), *n., v.*, **swung, swing·ing.** —*n.* **1.** Also called **swing music.** a smooth, flowing style of jazz, popular esp. in the 1930's and often arranged for a large dance band. —*v.t.* **2.** to play (a piece of music) in the style of swing. [special use of SWING[1]]

swinge[1] (swinj), *v.t.*, **swinged, swinge·ing.** *Archaic.* to thrash; punish. [ME *swenge(n)* (to) shake, smite, OE *swengan*, caus. of *swingan* to swing or denominative of OE *sweng* a blow]

swinge[2] (swinj), *v.t.*, **swinged, swinge·ing.** *Dial.* to singe. [special use of SWINGE[1] by assoc. with SINGE]

swinge·ing (swin′jing), *adj.* *Chiefly Brit.* enormous; thumping. [SWINGE[1] + -ING[2]]

swing·er[1] (swing′ər), *n.* **1.** a person or thing that swings. **2.** *Slang.* an active and modern person. **3.** *Slang.* **a.** a person who is very uninhibited sexually. **b.** one of a married couple who exchange partners with other couples for sexual activities. [SWING[1] + -ER[1]]

swing·er[2] (swin′jər), *n.* *Archaic.* a person or thing that swinges. [SWINGE[1] + -ER[1]]

swing·ing (swing′ing), *adj., superl.* **-ing·est. 1.** characterized by or capable of swinging, being swung, or causing to swing. **2.** used for swinging upon, by, from, or in: *the swinging tire in a playground.* **3.** *Slang.* first-rate. **4.** *Slang.* lively and modern; hip. —**swing′ing·ly,** *adv.*

swing′ing door′, a door that swings open on being pushed or pulled from either side and then swings closed by itself.

swin·gle (swing′gəl), *n., v.*, **-gled, -gling.** —*n.* **1.** the swipple of a flail. **2.** a wooden instrument shaped like a large knife, for beating flax or hemp. —*v.t.* **3.** to clean (flax or hemp) by beating and scraping with a swingle. [ME *swingel*, OE *swingell* rod (c. MD *swinghel*) = *swing-* (see SWING[1]) + *-el* instrumental suffix]

swin·gle·tree (swing′gəl trē′), *n.* whiffletree. [late ME]

swing′ mu′sic, swing[2] (def. 1).

swing′ shift′, 1. a work shift in industry from midafternoon until midnight. **2.** the group of workers on such a shift. —**swing′ shift′er.**

swing·y (swing′ē), *adj.*, **swing·i·er, swing·i·est.** characterized by swing; lively; swinging.

swin·ish (swī′nish), *adj.* **1.** like or befitting swine; hoggish. **2.** brutishly gross or sensual. [ME] —**swin′ish·ly,** *adv.* —**swin′ish·ness,** *n.*

Swin·ner·ton (swin′ər tən), *n.* **Frank (Arthur),** 1884–1982, English novelist and critic.

swin·ney (swin′ē), *n.* *Vet. Pathol.* sweeny.

swipe (swīp), *n., v.*, **swiped, swip·ing.** —*n.* *Informal.* **1. a.** a strong, sweeping blow, as with a cricket bat or golf club. **b.** a sideswipe. **2.** a person who rubs down horses in a stable; groom. —*v.t.* **3.** *Informal.* to strike with a sweeping blow. **4.** *Slang.* to steal. [akin to SWEEP[1]; c. G *schweifen*]

swipes (swīps), *n.* (*construed as pl.*) *Brit. Informal.* **1.** poor, watery, or spoiled beer. **2.** malt liquor in general, esp. beer and small beer. [? n. pl. use of *swipe* to drink down at one gulp, var. of SWEEP[1]]

swip·ple (swip′əl), *n.* the freely swinging part of a flail, which falls upon the grain in threshing; swingle. Also, **swi′ple.** [ME *swipyl*, var. of *swepyl* = *swep(en)* (to) SWEEP[1] + *-yl* instrumental suffix]

swirl (swûrl), *v.i.* **1.** to move around or along with a whirling motion; whirl; eddy. **2.** to be dizzy or giddy. —*v.t.* **3.** to cause to whirl; twist. —*n.* **4.** a swirling movement. **5.** a twist, as of hair. **6.** any curving, twisting line, shape, or form. **7.** confusion; disorder. [late ME (north) < Scand; cf. Norw *svirla*, c. D *zwirrelen* to whirl, G (dial.) *schwirrlen* to totter; all < a root **swir-* (whence Dan *svirre* to whirl, G *schwirren* to whir) + freq. *l-* suffix] —**swirl′ing·ly,** *adv.*

swirl·y (swûr′lē), *adj.*, **swirl·i·er, swirl·i·est.** swirling, whirling, or twisted.

swish (swish), *v.i.* **1.** to move with or make a sibilant sound, as a slender rod cutting sharply through the air. **2.** to rustle, as silk. —*v.t.* **3.** to flourish, whisk, etc., with a swishing movement or sound. **4.** to bring, take, cut, etc., with or as with such a movement or sound. **5.** to flog or whip. —*n.* **6.** a swishing movement or sound. **7.** a stick or rod for flogging. **8.** a stroke with such a stick or rod. **9.** *Slang.* a male homosexual with effeminate traits. —*adj.* *Informal.* **10.** fancy; elegant. **11.** effeminate. [imit.] —**swish′er,** *n.* —**swish′ing·ly,** *adv.*

swish·y (swish′ē), *adj.*, **swish·i·er, swish·i·est. 1.** causing, giving rise to, or characterized by a swishing sound or motion. **2.** swish (def. 11).

Swiss (swis), *adj.* **1.** of, pertaining to, associated with, or characteristic of Switzerland or its inhabitants. —*n.* **2.** a native or inhabitant of Switzerland. **3.** any thin, crisp fabric made in Switzerland, esp. Swiss muslin. **4.** Also called **Swiss′ cheese′.** a firm, pale-yellow or whitish cheese containing many holes, made usually from half-skimmed cow's milk. [< F *Suisse* < MHG *Swīz*]

Swiss′ chard′. See under **chard.**

Swiss·er (swis′ər), *n.* Swiss (def. 2).

SwissF, Swiss French.

Swiss′ French′, a group of French dialects spoken in Switzerland.

Swiss′ Guard′, a member of a corps of Swiss bodyguards protecting the pope.

Swiss′ mus′lin, a crisp, sheer muslin often ornamented with raised dots or figures **(dotted swiss),** used chiefly for making curtains and women's summer clothes.

Swiss′ steak′, a thick slice of steak dredged in flour and pounded, browned, and braised with tomatoes, onions, and other vegetables.

Swit., Switzerland.

switch (swich), *n.* **1.** a slender, flexible shoot, rod, etc., used esp. in whipping. **2.** the act of whipping or beating with or as with such an object; a stroke, lash, or whisking movement. **3.** a slender growing shoot, as of a plant. **4.** a bunch or tress of long hair or some substitute, worn by women to supplement their own hair. **5.** *Elect.* a device for turning on or off or directing an electric current, or making or breaking a circuit. **6.** *Railroads.* a track structure for diverting moving trains or rolling stock from one track to another. **7.** a turning, shifting, or changing. **8.** a tuft of hair at the end of the tail of some animals, as of the cow or lion. —*v.t.* **9.** to whip with a switch or the like. **10.** to move, swing, or whisk (a cane, a fishing line, etc.). **11.** to shift or exchange. **12.** to turn, shift, or divert. **13.** *Elect.* to connect, disconnect, or redirect (an electric circuit or the device it serves) by operating a switch (often fol. by *off* or *on*). **14.** *Railroads.* **a.** to move or transfer (a train, car, etc.) from one set of tracks to another. **b.** to drop or add (cars) or to make up (a train). —*v.i.* **15.** to strike with or as with a switch. **16.** to change direction or course. **17.** to exchange or replace something with another. **18.** to be shifted, turned, etc., by means of a switch. **19.** to move back and forth briskly, as a cat's tail. [earlier *swits, switz;* cf. LG (Hanoverian) *schwutsche* switch] —**switch′er,** *n.* —**switch′like′,** *adj.*

switch·back (swich′bak′), *n.* **1.** a highway, as in a mountainous area, having many hairpin curves. **2.** *Railroads.* a zigzag track arrangement for climbing a steep grade.

switch·blade (swich′blād′), *n.* a pocketknife, the blade of which is held by a spring and released by pressure on a button. Also called **switch′blade knife′.**

switch·board (swich′bōrd′, -bôrd′), *n. Elect.* a structural unit containing switches and instruments necessary to complete telephone circuits manually.

switched-on (swicht′on′, -ôn′), *adj. Slang.* turned-on (def. 1).

switch′ en′gine, *Railroads.* a locomotive for switching rolling stock in a yard.

switch′ hit′ter, *Baseball.* a player who can bat either right-handed or left-handed. Also, **switch′-hit′ter.**

switch·man (swich′mən), *n., pl.* **-men.** **1.** a person who has charge of a switch or switches on a railroad. **2.** a person who assists in moving cars in a railroad yard or terminal.

switch·o·ver (swich′ō′vər), *n.* a changeover. [n. use of v. phrase *switch over*]

switch·yard (swich′yärd′), *n.* a railroad yard in which rolling stock is distributed or made up into trains.

swith (swith), *adv. Chiefly Brit. Dial.* immediately; quickly. Also, **swithe.** [ME, OE *swīthe* (adv.) strongly = *swīth* strong (c. Goth *swinths* strong, Icel *svinnr,* G (*ge*)*schwind* fast) + *-e* adv. suffix] —**swith′ly,** *adv.*

swith·er (swith′ər), *n. Brit. Dial.* a state of confusion, excitement, or perplexity. [cf. OE *swithrian* to dwindle, fail]

Swith·in (swith′in, swith′-), *n.* **Saint,** died A.D. 862, English ecclesiastic: bishop of Winchester 852?–862. Also, **Swith′un.**

Switz., Switzerland.

Switz·er (swit′sər), *n.* Swiss (def. 2). [< MHG = *Swītz* Switzerland + *-er* -ER[1]]

Swit·zer·land (swit′sər lənd), *n.* a republic in central Europe. 6,333,200; 15,944 sq. mi. *Cap.:* Bern. French, **Suisse.** German, **Schweiz.** Italian, **Svizzera.**

swive (swīv), *v.,* **swived, swiv·ing.** *Archaic.* —*v.t.* **1.** to copulate with. —*v.i.* **2.** to copulate. [ME *swiven,* OE *swīfan* to move, wend, sweep. See SWIVEL]

swiv·el (swiv′əl), *n., v.,* **-eled, -el·ing** or (*esp. Brit.*) **-elled, -el·ling.** —*n.* **1.** a fastening device that allows the thing fastened to turn round freely upon it. **2.** such a device consisting of two parts, each of which turns round independently, as a compound link of a chain. **3.** a pivoted support for a gun. **4.** a swivel gun. —*v.t.* **5.** to turn or pivot on or as on a swivel. **6.** to fasten by a swivel. —*v.i.* **7.** to turn on or as on a swivel, pivot, or the like. [ME *swiv-* (akin to OE *swīfan* to revolve, Icel *svīfa* to turn) + *-el* instrumental suffix]

swiv′el chair′, a chair whose seat turns round horizontally on a swivel.

swiv′el gun′, a gun mounted on a pedestal so that it can be turned from side to side or up and down.

swiz·zle (swiz′əl), *n.* a tall drink of rum, lime juice, sugar, and crushed ice. [?]

swiz′zle stick′, a small rod for stirring drinks.

swob (swob), *n., v.t.,* **swobbed, swob·bing.** swab.

swol·len (swō′lən), *v.* **1.** a pp. of **swell.** —*adj.* **2.** enlarged by or as by swelling; tumid. **3.** turgid or bombastic. —**swol′len·ly,** *adv.* —**swol′len·ness,** *n.*

swoon (swōōn), *v.i.* **1.** to faint; lose consciousness. **2.** to enter a state of hysterical rapture or ecstasy. —*n.* **3.** a faint or syncope. Also, *Archaic,* **swound.** [ME *swo*(*w*)*ne*(*n*) (to) faint, OE (*ge*)*swōgen* in a swoon] —**swoon′ing·ly,** *adv.*

swoop (swōōp), *v.i.* **1.** to sweep down through the air, as a bird upon prey. **2.** to come down upon something in a sudden, swift attack (often fol. by *down* and *on* or *upon*). —*v.t.* **3.** to take, lift, scoop up, or remove with or as with one sweeping motion (often fol. by *up, away,* or *off*). —*n.* **4.** the act or an instance of swooping; a sudden, swift descent. [var. (with close *ō*) of ME *swopen,* OE *swāpan* to sweep]

swoosh (swōōsh), *v.i.* **1.** to move with or make a rustling, swirling, or brushing sound. **2.** to pour out swiftly. —*v.t.* **3.** to cause to make or move with a rustling, swirling, or brushing sound. —*n.* **4.** a swirling or rustling sound or movement. [imit.]

swop (swop), *v.t., v.i.,* **swopped, swop·ping,** *n.* swap.

sword (sōrd, sôrd), *n.* **1.** a weapon consisting typically of a long, pointed, straight or slightly curved blade with a sharp edge or edges, fixed in a hilt or handle. **2.** this weapon as the symbol of military power, punitive justice, etc. **3.** a cause of death or destruction. **4.** war, combat, slaughter, or violence; military force or power. **5. at swords' points,** mutually ready to begin hostilities; opposed. **6. cross swords, a.** to engage in combat; fight. **b.** to disagree violently; argue. **7. put to the sword,** to slay; execute. [ME; OE *sweord;* c. G *Schwert,* D *zwaard,* Icel *sverth*] —**sword′less,** *adj.* —**sword′like′,** *adj.*

sword′ bay′onet, a short sword that may be attached to the muzzle of a gun and used as a bayonet.

sword-bear·er (sôrd′bâr′ər), *n. Brit.* an official who carries the sword of state on ceremonial occasions, as before the sovereign. [ME *swerd berer*]

sword′ belt′, a military belt from which a sword may be hung.

sword·craft (sōrd′kraft′, -kräft′, sôrd′-), *n.* **1.** skill in or the art of swordplay. **2.** military skill or power.

sword′ dance′, any of various dances, usually performed by men, employing the ceremonial use of swords. —**sword′ danc′er.**

sword′ fern′, any fern of the genus *Nephrolepis,* esp. *N. exaltata,* characterized by sword-shaped, pinnate fronds.

sword·fish (sōrd′fish′, sôrd′-), *n., pl.* **-fish·es,** (*esp. collectively*) **-fish.** a large, marine food fish, *Xiphias gladius,* having the upper jaw elongated into a swordlike structure.

sword′ grass′, any of various grasses or plants having swordlike or sharp leaves, as the sword lily.

sword′ knot′, a looped strap, ribbon, or the like, attached to the hilt of a sword as a support or ornament.

sword′ lil′y, a gladiolus.

sword·man (sōrd′mən, sôrd′-), *n., pl.* **-men.** swordsman. [ME *swerdman*] —**sword′man·ship′,** *n.*

Swordfish
(Length to 15 ft.)

sword·play (sōrd′plā′, sôrd′-), *n.* the action or technique of wielding a sword. —**sword′play′er,** *n.*

swords·man (sōrdz′mən, sôrdz′-), *n., pl.* **-men.** **1.** a person who uses or is skilled in the use of a sword. **2.** a fencer. **3.** a soldier. —**swords′man·ship′,** *n.*

sword·tail (sōrd′tāl′, sôrd′-), *n.* any of several small, brightly colored, viviparous, fresh-water fishes of the genus *Xiphophorus,* found in Central America, having the lower part of the caudal fin elongated into a swordlike structure.

swore (swōr, swôr), *v.* a pt. of **swear.**

sworn (swōrn, swôrn), *v.* **1.** pp. of **swear.** —*adj.* **2.** having taken an oath. **3.** bound by or as by an oath or pledge. **4.** avowed; affirmed.

swot[1] (swot), *v.t.,* **swot·ted, swot·ting,** *n.* swat[1]. —**swot′ter,** *n.*

swot[2] (swot), *v.,* **swot·ted, swot·ting,** *n. Brit. Slang.* —*v.i.* **1.** to study or work hard. —*n.* **2.** a student who studies hard; grind. [ME *swot,* OE *swāt* perspiration; see SWEAT]

swound (swound, swōōnd), *v.i., n. Archaic.* swoon. [late ME < *swoun* SWOON + meaningless *-d*]

'swounds (zwoundz, zoundz, zwōōndz), *interj. Obs.* zounds. [short for *God's wounds*]

Swtz., Switzerland.

swum (swum), *v.* pp. of **swim.**

swung (swung), *v.* a pt. and pp. of **swing.**

swung′ dash′, a mark of punctuation (~) used in place of a word or part of a word previously spelled out.

sy-, var. of **syn-** before *s* followed by a consonant and before *z: systaltic; syzygy.*

Syb·a·ris (sib′ə ris), *n.* an ancient Greek city in S Italy: noted for its wealth and luxury; destroyed 510 B.C.

Syb·a·rite (sib′ə rīt′), *n.* **1.** an inhabitant of Sybaris. **2.** (*l.c.*) a person devoted to luxury and pleasure. [< L *Sybarīt*(*a*) < Gk *Sybarī́tēs*] —**syb·a·rit·ism** (sib′ə rī tiz′əm), *n.* —**Syn. 2.** sensualist.

Syb·a·rit·ic (sib′ə rit′ik), *adj.* **1.** of, pertaining to, or characteristic of the Sybarites. **2.** (*l.c.*) pertaining to or characteristic of a sybarite. Also, **Syb′a·rit′i·cal.** [< L *Sybarīticus* < Gk *Sybarītikós*] —**Syb′a·rit′i·cal·ly,** *adv.*

syc·a·mine (sik′ə min, -mīn′), *n.* a tree mentioned in the New Testament, probably the black mulberry. [< L *sȳcamīn*(*us*) < Gk *sȳkáminos* < Sem; cf. Heb *shiqmāh* mulberry tree, sycamore (*y* < Gk *sŷkon* fig)]

syc·a·more (sik′ə mōr′, -môr′), *n.* **1.** *U.S.* the plane tree or buttonwood, *Platanus occidentalis.* **2.** *Brit.* the sycamore maple. **3.** a tree, *Ficus Sycomorus,* of the Near East, related to the common fig, bearing an edible fruit. [ME *sicomore* < OF < L *sȳcomor*(*us*) < Gk *sȳkómoros* = *sŷko*(*n*) fig + *móron* mulberry, appar. by folk etym. < Sem; cf. Heb *shiqmāh* sycamore]

syc′amore ma′ple, a maple, *Acer Pseudo-Platanus* of Europe and western Asia, grown as a shade tree.

syce (sīs), *n.* (in India) a groom; stableman. Also, **saice, sice.** [< Urdu *sā'is* < Ar]

sy·cee (sī sē′), *n.* fine, uncoined silver in lumps of various sizes usually bearing a banker's or assayer's stamp or mark, formerly used in China as a medium of exchange. Also called **sycee′ sil′ver.** [< dial. Chin *sai szi,* Cantonese for Mandarin *hsi ssŭ* fine silk: so called because it can be made into wire as fine as silk thread]

Sy·chem (shē′kəm, -kem, shek′əm, -em), *n.* Shechem.

sy·co·ni·um (sī kō′nē əm), *n., pl.* **-ni·a** (-nē ə). *Bot.* a multiple fruit developed from a hollow fleshy receptacle containing numerous flowers, as in the fig. [< NL < Gk *sŷkon* fig + NL *-ium* -IUM]

syc·o·phan·cy (sik′ə fən sē), *n.* **1.** self-seeking or servile flattery. **2.** the character or conduct of a sycophant. [< L *sycophantia* < Gk *sykophantía* = *sykophant-* (see SYCOPHANT) + *-ia* -CY]

syc·o·phant (sik′ə fənt), *n.* a self-seeking, servile flatterer; fawning parasite. [< L *sycophant*(*a*) < Gk *sykophánt*(*ēs*) informer, lit., fig-shower (i.e., one who makes the fig sign; see FIG) = *sŷko*(*n*) fig + *phan-* (s. of *phaínein* to show) + *-tēs* agentive suffix] —**syc·o·phan·tic** (sik′ə fan′tik), **syc′o·phan′ti·cal, syc′o·phant′ish,** *adj.* —**syc′o·phan′ti·cal·ly, syc′o·phant′ish·ly,** *adv.* —**Syn.** toady.

sy·co·sis (sī kō′sis), *n. Pathol.* an inflammatory disease of the hair follicles, characterized by a pustular eruption. [< NL < Gk *sýkōsis* = *sŷk*(*on*) fig + *-ōsis* -OSIS]

Syd·ney (sid′nē), *n.* **1. Sir Philip.** See **Sidney, Sir Philip.** **2.** a seaport in and the capital of New South Wales, in SE Australia. 2,183,388 with suburbs (1961). **3.** a seaport on NE Cape Breton Island, Nova Scotia, in SE Canada. 33,617 (1961).

Sy·e·ne (sī ē′nē), *n.* ancient name of **Aswan.**

sy·e·nite (sī′ə nīt′), *n.* a granular igneous rock consisting chiefly of orthoclase and oligoclase with hornblende, biotite, or augite. [< L *syēnīte*(*s*) (*lapis*) (stone) of SYENE < Gk *syēnī́tes* (*líthos*); see -ITE[1]] —**sy·e·nit·ic** (sī′ə nit′ik), *adj.*

syl-, var. of **syn-** before *l: syllepsis.*

syll., **1.** syllable. **2.** syllabus.

syl·la·bar·y (sil′ə ber′ē), *n., pl.* **-bar·ies.** **1.** a list or catalog of syllables. **2.** a set of written symbols, each of which represents a syllable, used to write a given language: *the Japanese syllabary.* [< NL *syllabāri*(*um*)]

syl·la·bi (sil′ə bī′), *n.* a pl. of **syllabus.**

syl·lab·ic (si lab′ik), *adj.* **1.** of, pertaining to, or consisting of a syllable or syllables. **2.** pronounced with careful distinction of syllables. 3. of, pertaining to, or noting poetry based on a specific number of syllables, as distinguished from poetry depending on stresses or quantities. 4. *Phonet.* syllable-forming or syllable-dominating; sonantal. —*n.* 5. *Phonet.* a syllabic sound. [< LL *syllabic(us)* < Gk *syllabikós*] —**syl·lab′i·cal·ly,** *adv.*

syl·lab·i·cate (si lab′ə kāt′), *v.t.*, **-cat·ed, -cat·ing.** to syllabify. [back formation from *syllabication* < ML *syllabicātiōn-* (s. of *syllabicātiō*)] —**syl·lab′i·ca′tion,** *n.*

syl·lab·i·fy (si lab′ə fī′), *v.t.*, **-fied, -fy·ing.** to form or divide into syllables. [< NL *syllabificāre.* See SYLLABLE, -IFY] —**syl·lab′i·fi·ca′tion,** *n.*

syl·la·bise (sil′ə bīz′), *v.t.*, **-bised, -bis·ing.** *Chiefly Brit.* syllabize.

syl·la·bism (sil′ə biz′əm), *n.* 1. the use of syllabic characters, as in writing. 2. division into syllables. [< L *syllab(a)* SYLLABLE + -ISM]

syl·la·bize (sil′ə bīz′), *v.t.*, **-bized, -biz·ing.** to syllabify. Also, *esp. Brit.*, **syllabise.** [< ML *syllabiz(āre)* < Gk *syllabízein.* See SYLLABLE, -IZE]

syl·la·ble (sil′ə bəl), *n.*, *v.*, **-bled, -bling.** —*n.* 1. a segment of speech typically produced with a single pulse of air pressure from the lungs, and consisting of a center of relatively great sonority with or without one or more accompanying sounds of relatively less sonority: "*Man,*" "*eye,*" "*strength,*" *and* "*sixths*" *are English words of one syllable.* 2. (in writing systems) a character or a set of characters representing more or less exactly such an element of speech. 3. the least portion or amount of speech or writing; the least mention: *Do not breathe a syllable of all this.* —*v.t.* 4. to utter in syllables; articulate. 5. to represent by syllables. —*v.i.* 6. to utter syllables; speak. [late ME *sillable* < AF; MF *sillabe* < L *syllab(a)* < Gk *syllabḗ* = *syl-* SYL- + *lab-* (s. of *lambánein* to take) + *-ē* n. suffix]

syl·la·bub (sil′ə bub′), *n.* sillabub.

syl·la·bus (sil′ə bəs), *n.*, *pl.* **-bus·es, -bi** (-bī′). 1. an outline or other brief statement of the main points of a discourse, the subjects of a course of lectures, the contents of a curriculum, etc. 2. *Law.* a short summary of the legal basis of a court's decision appearing at the beginning of a reported case. [< LL < L *sittybus* or *sillybus* title slip on a book < Gk *sittýba* or *síllybos* < ?]

syl·lep·sis (si lep′sis), *n.*, *pl.* **-ses** (-sēz). *Gram.* the use of a word or expression to perform two syntactic functions, esp. to modify two or more words of which at least one does not agree in number, case, or gender, as the use of *are* in *Neither he nor we are willing.* [< L < Gk = *syl-* SYL- + *lēp-* (var. of *lab-*, *lamb-*, s. of *lambánein* to take and of *syllabḗ* syllable) + *-sis* -SIS] —**syl·lep·tic** (si lep′tik), *adj.* —**syl·lep′ti·cal·ly,** *adv.*

syl·lo·gise (sil′ə jīz′), *v.i.*, *v.t.*, **-gised, -gis·ing.** *Chiefly Brit.* syllogize. —**syl′lo·gi·sa′tion,** *n.* —**syl′lo·gis′er,** *n.*

syl·lo·gism (sil′ə jiz′əm), *n.* 1. *Logic.* an argument whose conclusion is supported by two premises, of which one **(major premise)** contains the term **(major term)** that is the predicate of the conclusion, and the other **(minor premise)** contains the term **(minor term)** that is the subject of the conclusion; common to both premises is a term **(middle term)** that is excluded from the conclusion. A typical form is "All A is B; all B is C; therefore all A is C." 2. deductive reasoning. 3. an extremely subtle, sophisticated, or deceptive argument. [< L *syllogism(us)* < Gk *syllogismós* = *syllog-* (see SYLLOGIZE) + *-ismos* -ISM; r. ME *silogime* < OF]

syl·lo·gis·tic (sil′ə jis′tik), *adj.* Also, **syl′lo·gis′ti·cal.** 1. of or pertaining to a syllogism. 2. like or consisting of syllogisms. —*n.* 3. the part of logic that deals with syllogisms. 4. syllogistic reasoning. [< L *syllogistic(us)* < Gk *syllogistikós* = *syllogist(ós)* verbid of *syllogízesthai* (see SYLLOGIZE) + *-ikos* -IC] —**syl′lo·gis′ti·cal·ly,** *adv.*

syl·lo·gize (sil′ə jīz′), *v.i.*, *v.t.*, **-gized, -giz·ing.** to argue or reason by syllogism. Also, *esp. Brit.*, **syllogise.** [ME *silogyse(n)* < LL *syllogizā(re)* < Gk *syllogíz(esthai)* (to) reason = *syl-* SYL- + *logízesthai* to reckon, infer = *lóg(os)* discourse + *-izesthai* -IZE] —**syl′lo·gi·za′tion,** *n.* —**syl′lo·giz′er,** *n.*

sylph (silf), *n.* 1. a slender, graceful girl or woman. 2. one of a race of dainty, imaginary beings supposed to inhabit the air. [< NL *sylph(ēs)* (pl.), coined by Paracelsus; appar. b. *sylva* (var. sp. of L *silva* forest) + Gk *nýmphē* NYMPH] —**sylph′ic,** *adj.* —**sylph′like′, sylph′ish, sylph′y,** *adj.*
—**Syn.** 2. SYLPH, SALAMANDER, UNDINE (NYMPH), GNOME were imaginary beings inhabiting the four elements once believed to make up the physical world. All except the GNOMES were female. SYLPHS dwelt in the air and were light, dainty, and airy beings. SALAMANDERS dwelt in fire: "*a salamander that . . . lives in the midst of flames*" (Addison). UNDINES were water spirits: *By marrying a man, an undine could acquire a mortal soul.* (They were also called NYMPHS, though nymphs were ordinarily minor divinities of nature who dwelt in woods, hills, and meadows as well as in waters.) GNOMES were little old men or dwarfs, dwelling in the earth: *ugly enough to be king of the gnomes.*

sylph·id (sil′fid), *n.* 1. a little or young sylph. —*adj.* 2. Also, **sylph·id·ine** (sil′fi din, -dīn′). of, pertaining to, or characteristic of a sylph. [< F *sylphide*]

syl·va (sil′və), *n.*, *pl.* **-vas, -vae** (-vē). silva. [< L]

syl·van (sil′vən), *adj.* 1. of, pertaining to, or inhabiting the woods. 2. consisting of or abounding in woods or trees; wooded; woody. 3. made of trees, branches, boughs, etc. —*n.* 4. a person dwelling in a woodland region. 5. a mythical deity or spirit of the woods. Also, **silvan.** [< L *sylvān(us)*, var. of *silvānus* = *silv(a)* forest + *-ānus* -AN]

syl·van·ite (sil′və nīt′), *n.* a mineral, gold-silver telluride, $(AuAg)Te_2$, silver-white with metallic luster, often occurring in crystals so arranged as to resemble written characters: an ore of gold. [named after (TRAN)SYLVAN(IA); see -ITE[1]]

Syl·va·nus (sil vā′nəs), *n.*, *pl.* **-ni** (-nī). Silvanus.

Syl·ves·ter I (sil ves′tər), **Saint,** died A.D. 335, pope 314–335. Also, **Silvester I.**

Sylvester II, (*Gerbert*) died 1003, French ecclesiastic: pope 999–1003. Also, **Silvester II.**

syl·vi·cul·ture (sil′və kul′chər), *n.* silviculture. [*sylv-* (s. of L *sylva, silva,* forest) + -I- + CULTURE]

syl·vite (sil′vīt), *n.* a common mineral, potassium chloride, KCl, colorless to milky-white or red: the most important source of potassium. Also, **syl·vin, syl·vine** (sil′vin). [< L (*sal digestivus*) *Sylv(ii)* digestive salt of Sylvius (Latinized name of Jacques *Dubois* (d. 1555), French anatomist) + -ITE[1]; cf. F *sylvine*]

sym-, var. of **syn-** before *b, p, m: symbol; symphony; symmetry.*

sym., 1. symbol. 2. *Chem.* symmetrical. 3. symphony. 4. symptom.

sym·bi·ont (sim′bī ont′, -bē-), *n.* *Biol.* an organism living in a state of symbiosis. [< Gk *symbiount-* (s. of *symbioûs*) aorist participle of *symbioûn* to live together; see SYMBIOSIS] —**sym·bi·on·tic** (sim′bī on′tik, -bē-), *adj.*

sym·bi·o·sis (sim′bī ō′sis, -bē-), *n.*, *pl.* **-ses** (-sēz). *Biol.* the living together of two dissimilar organisms, esp. when this association is mutually beneficial. [< Gk *symbíōsis* = *sym-* SYM- + *bio-* (s. of *bioûn* to live) + *-ōsis* -OSIS] —**sym·bi·ot·ic** (sim′bī ot′ik, -bē-) **sym′bi·ot′i·cal,** *adj.* —**sym′bi·ot′i·cal·ly,** *adv.*

sym·bol (sim′bəl), *n.*, *v.*, **-boled, -bol·ing** or (*esp. Brit.*) **-bolled, -bol·ling.** —*n.* 1. something used for or regarded as representing something else; a material object representing something, often something immaterial; emblem, token, or sign. 2. a letter, figure, or other character or mark or a combination of letters or the like used to represent something: *the algebraic symbol* x; *the chemical symbol Au.* —*v.t.* 3. to symbolize. [< L *symbol(um)* < Gk *sýmbolon* sign = *sym-* SYM- + *-bolon,* neut. var. of *bolḗ, bólos* a throw]

sym·bol·ic (sim bol′ik), *adj.* 1. serving as a symbol of something (often fol. by *of*). 2. of, pertaining to, or expressed by a symbol. 3. characterized by or involving the use of symbols: *a highly symbolic poem.* 4. (in semantics, esp. formerly) pertaining to a class of words which expressed only relations. Cf. **notional** (def. 6). Also, **sym·bol′i·cal.** [< LL *symbolic(us)* < Gk *symbolikós*] —**sym·bol′i·cal·ly,** *adv.* —**sym·bol′i·cal·ness,** *n.*

symbol′ic log′ic, a modern development of formal logic employing a special notation or symbolism capable of manipulation in accordance with precise rules. Also called **mathematical logic.**

sym·bol·ise (sim′bə līz′), *v.t.*, *v.i.*, **-ised, -is·ing.** *Chiefly Brit.* symbolize. —**sym′bol·i·sa′tion,** *n.*

sym·bol·ism (sim′bə liz′əm), *n.* 1. the practice of representing things by symbols, or of investing things with a symbolic meaning or character. 2. a set or system of symbols. 3. symbolic meaning or character. 4. the principles and practice of symbolists in art or literature. 5. (*cap.*) *Literature.* the style of writing, themes, viewpoint, etc., of the French and Belgian Symbolists of the late 19th century and of their followers.

sym·bol·ist (sim′bə list), *n.* 1. a person who uses symbols or symbolism. 2. a person versed in the study or interpretation of symbols. 3. *Literature, Fine Arts.* **a.** a writer or artist who seeks to express or evoke emotions, ideas, etc., by the use of symbolic language, imagery, color, etc. **b.** (*usually cap.*) a member of a group of chiefly French and Belgian poets and writers of the late 19th century characterized by a rejection of naturalism and the use of evocative images and associations to convey states of experience. —*adj.* 4. of or pertaining to symbolists or symbolism. —**sym′bol·is′tic, sym′bol·is′ti·cal,** *adj.* —**sym′bol·is′ti·cal·ly,** *adv.*

sym·bol·ize (sim′bə līz′), *v.*, **-ized, -iz·ing.** —*v.t.* 1. to be a symbol of; stand for or represent in the manner of a symbol. 2. to represent by a symbol or symbols. 3. to regard or treat as symbolic. —*v.i.* 4. to use symbols. Also, *esp. Brit.*, **symbolise.** [< NL *symboliz(āre)*] —**sym′bol·i·za′tion,** *n.*

sym·bol·o·gy (sim bol′ə jē), *n.* 1. the study of symbols. 2. the use of symbols; symbolism. [by haplology, *symbolo-* (comb. form of SYMBOL) + -LOGY] —**sym·bo·log·i·cal** (sim′bə loj′i kəl), *adj.* —**sym·bol′o·gist,** *n.*

Sy·ming·ton (sī′ming tən), *n.* **(William) Stuart,** born 1901, U.S. politician: Democratic senator from Missouri since 1952.

Sym·ma·chus (sim′ə kəs), *n.* **Saint,** died A.D. 514, pope 498–514.

sym·met·al·lism (sim met′əliz′əm), *n.* the use of two (or more) metals, such as gold and silver, combined in assigned proportions as a monetary standard. [SYM- + *-metallism,* as in *bimetallism*]

sym·met·ri·cal (si me′tri kəl), *adj.* 1. characterized by or exhibiting symmetry; well-proportioned, as a body or whole; regular in form or arrangement of corresponding parts. 2. *Geom.* **a.** noting two points in a plane such that the line segment joining the points is bisected by an axis: *points (1, 1) and (1, −1) are symmetrical with respect to the x-axis.* **b.** noting a set consisting of pairs of points having this relation with respect to the same axis. 3. *Bot.* **a.** divisible into two similar parts by more than one plane passing through the center; actinomorphic. **b.** (of a flower) having the same number of parts in each whorl. 4. *Chem.* **a.** having a structure that exhibits a regular repeated pattern of the component parts. **b.** noting a benzene derivative in which three substitutions have occurred at alternate carbon atoms. 5. *Pathol.* affecting corresponding parts simultaneously, as certain diseases. Also, **sym·met′ric.** [SYMMETR(Y) + -ICAL] —**sym·met′ri·cal·ly,** *adv.* —**sym·met′ri·cal·ness,** *n.*

sym·me·trise (sim′i trīz′), *v.t.*, **-trised, -tris·ing.** *Chiefly Brit.* symmetrize. —**sym′me·tri·sa′tion,** *n.*

sym·me·trize (sim′i trīz′), *v.t.*, **-trized, -triz·ing.** to make symmetrical. —**sym′me·tri·za′tion,** *n.*

sym·me·try (sim′i trē), *n.*, *pl.* **-tries.** 1. the correspondence in size, form, and arrangement of parts on opposite sides of a plane, line, or point; regularity of form or arrangement with reference to corresponding parts. 2. the proper or due proportion of the parts of a body or whole to one another with regard to size and form; excellence of proportion. 3. beauty based on or characterized by such excellence of proportion. 4. *Math.* a rotation or translation of a plane

figure that leaves the figure unchanged although its position may be altered. [< L *symmetria* < Gk *symmetría* commensurateness]
—**Syn. 1.** concord, correspondence. SYMMETRY, BALANCE, PROPORTION, HARMONY are terms used, particularly in the arts, to denote qualities based upon a correspondence or agreement, usually pleasing, among the parts of a whole. SYMMETRY implies either a quantitative equality of parts or a unified system of subordinate parts: *the perfect symmetry of pairs of matched columns; the symmetry of a well-ordered musical composition.* BALANCE implies equality of parts, often as a means of emphasis: *Balance in sentences may emphasize the contrast in ideas.* PROPORTION depends less upon equality of parts than upon that agreement among them that is determined by their relation to a whole: *The dimensions of the room gave a feeling of right proportion.* HARMONY, a technical term in music, may also suggest the pleasing quality that arises from a just ordering of parts in other forms of artistic composition: *harmony of line, color, phrase, ideas.*

Sym·onds (sim′əndz), *n.* **John Add·ing·ton** (ad′ing tən), 1840–93, English poet, essayist, and critic.

Sy·mons (sī′mənz), *n.* **Arthur,** 1865–1945, English poet and critic, born in Wales.

sym·pa·thec·to·my (sim′pə thek′tə mē), *n., pl.* **-mies.** *Med.* **1.** surgery that interrupts a part of the nerve pathways of the sympathetic or involuntary nervous system, as that of the glands, heart, or smooth muscle. **2.** a like interruption by chemical means. [SYMPATH(ETIC) + -ECTOMY]

sym·pa·thet·ic (sim′pə thet′ik), *adj.* **1.** characterized by, proceeding from, exhibiting, or feeling sympathy; sympathizing; compassionate: *a sympathetic listener.* **2.** acting or affected by, of the nature of, or pertaining to a special affinity or mutual relationship. **3.** looking upon with favor (often fol. by *to* or *toward*): *He is sympathetic to the project.* **4.** *Anat., Physiol.* pertaining to that portion of the autonomic nervous system consisting of nerves and ganglia that arise from the thoracic and lumbar regions of the spinal cord, and functioning in opposition to the parasympathetic system, as in stimulating heartbeat, dilating the pupil of the eye, etc. **5.** *Physics.* noting or pertaining to vibrations, sounds, etc., produced by a body as the direct result of similar vibrations in a different body. [< NL *sympathēticus*). See SYM-, PATHETIC] —**sym′pa·thet′i·cal·ly,** *adv.* —**Syn. 1.** commiserating, kind, tender, affectionate.

sym′pathet′ic ink′. See **invisible ink.**

sym′pathet′ic mag′ic, magic based on the belief that one thing or event can influence another at a distance as a result of a continuing, nonphysical connection between them.

sym′pathet′ic strike′. See **sympathy strike.**

sym·pa·thin (sim′pə thin), *n.* *Biochem.* a hormonelike substance, secreted by sympathetic nerve endings, that serves to increase the heart rate, constrict the arterioles of the skin and mucous membranes, and dilate the arterioles of the skeletal and cardiac muscles. [SYMPATH(ETIC) + -IN[2]]

sym·pa·thise (sim′pə thīz′), *v.i.,* **-thised, -this·ing.** *Chiefly Brit.* sympathize. —**sym′pa·this′er,** *n.* —**sym′pa·this′ing·ly,** *adv.*

sym·pa·thize (sim′pə thīz′), *v.i.,* **-thized, -thiz·ing. 1.** to be in sympathy or agreement of feeling; share in a feeling or feelings (often fol. by *with*). **2.** to feel a compassionate sympathy, as for suffering or trouble (often fol. by *with*). **3.** to express sympathy or condole (often fol. by *with*). **4.** to be in approving accord, as with a person, cause, etc. **5.** to agree, correspond, or accord. [< MF *sympathise(r)* = *sympath(ie)* SYMPATHY + *-iser* -ISE] —**sym′pa·thiz′er,** *n.* —**sym′pa·thiz′ing·ly,** *adv.*

sym·pa·thy (sim′pə thē), *n., pl.* **-thies,** *adj.* —*n.* **1.** harmony of or agreement in feeling, as between persons or on the part of one person with respect to another. **2.** a quality of mutual relations between people or things whereby whatever affects one also affects the other. **3.** the ability to share the feelings of another, esp. in sorrow or trouble; compassion or commiseration. **4. sympathies,** feelings or impulses of compassion. **5.** favorable or approving accord; favor or approval: *He viewed the plan with sympathy and publicly backed it.* **6.** agreement, consonance, or accord. —*adj.* **7.** acted or done out of sympathy: *a sympathy vote.* [< L *sympathīa* < Gk *sympátheia* = *sympathḗ(s)* sympathetic (*sym-* SYM- + *páth(os)* suffering, sensation + *-ēs* adj. suffix) + *-ia* -Y[3]]

sym′pathy strike′, a strike by a body of workers, not because of grievances against their own employer, but by way of endorsing and aiding another body of workers on strike. Also called **sympathetic strike.**

sym·pet·al·ous (sim pet′əl əs), *adj.* *Bot.* gamopetalous.

sym·phon·ic (sim fon′ik), *adj.* **1.** *Music.* of, for, pertaining to, or having the character of a symphony or symphony orchestra. **2.** of or pertaining to symphony or harmony of sounds. **3.** characterized by similarity of sound, as words. —**sym·phon′i·cal·ly,** *adv.*

symphon′ic po′em, *Music.* a free-form composition, scored for a symphony orchestra, in which a literary or pictorial "plot" is treated with considerable program detail. Also called **tone poem.**

sym·pho·ni·ous (sim fō′nē əs), *adj.* harmonious; in harmonious agreement or accord. —**sym·pho′ni·ous·ly,** *adv.*

sym·pho·nise (sim′fə nīz′), *v.i.,* **-nised, -nis·ing.** *Chiefly Brit.* symphonize.

sym·pho·nist (sim′fə nist), *n.* a composer who writes symphonies.

sym·pho·nize (sim′fə nīz′), *v.i.,* **-nized, -niz·ing.** to play or sound together harmoniously. Also, *esp. Brit.,* **symphonise.** [SYMPHON(Y) + -IZE]

sym·pho·ny (sim′fə nē), *n., pl.* **-nies. 1.** *Music.* **a.** an elaborate composition for orchestra, usually in four movements, the first of which is in sonata form, the others being in any of various other forms, as rondo, scherzo, etc. **b.** an instrumental piece forming an overture to or an interlude in an opera, oratorio, etc. **2.** See **symphony orchestra. 3.** harmony of sounds. **4.** *Archaic.* agreement; concord. [ME *symfonye* < OF *symphonie* < L *symphōnia* concert < Gk *symphōnía* harmony. See SYM-, -PHONY]

sym′phony or′chestra, a large orchestra composed of wind, string, and percussion instruments and organized to perform symphonic compositions.

sym·phy·sis (sim′fi sis), *n., pl.* **-ses** (-sēz′). **1.** *Anat., Zool.* **a.** the growing together, or the fixed or nearly fixed union, of bones, as that of the two halves of the lower jaw in man, or of the pubic bones in the anterior part of the pelvic girdle. **b.** a line of junction or articulation so formed. **2.** *Bot.* a coalescence or growing together of parts. [< NL < Gk *sýmphysis* a growing together = *sym-* SYM- + *phýsis* = *phý(ein)* (to) grow + *-sis* -SIS] —**sym·phys·i·al, sym·phys·e·al** (sim fiz′ē əl), *adj.* —**sym·phys·tic** (sim fis′tik), *adj.*

sym·po·si·ac (sim pō′zē ak′), *adj.* **1.** of, pertaining to, or suitable for a symposium. —*n.* **2.** *Archaic.* a symposium. [< L *symposiac(us)* < Gk *symposiakós.* See SYMPOSIUM, -AC]

sym·po·si·arch (sim pō′zē ärk′), *n.* **1.** the president, director, or master of a symposium. **2.** a toastmaster. [< Gk *symposíarch(os).* See SYMPOSIUM, -ARCH]

sym·po·si·um (sim pō′zē əm), *n., pl.* **-si·ums, -si·a** (-zē ə). **1.** a meeting or conference for the discussion of some subject, esp. a meeting at which several speakers discuss a topic before an audience. **2.** a collection of opinions expressed or articles contributed by several persons on a given subject or topic. **3.** (in ancient Greece and Rome) a party, usually following a dinner, for drinking and conversation. [< L < Gk *sympósion* a drinking together = *sym-* SYM- + *po-* (var. s. of *pínein* to drink) + *-sion* composite n. suffix]

symp·tom (simp′təm), *n.* **1.** a sign or indication of something. **2.** *Pathol.* a phenomenon that arises from and accompanies a particular disease or disorder and serves as an indication of it. [< LL *symptōm(a)* < Gk *sýmptōma* occurrence, that which falls together with something = *sym-* SYM- + *ptō-* (var. s. of *píptein* to fall) + *-ma* n. suffix] —**symp′tom·less,** *adj.*

symp·to·mat·ic (simp′tə mat′ik), *adj.* **1.** pertaining to a symptom or symptoms. **2.** of the nature of or constituting a symptom; indicative (often fol. by *of*). **3.** according to symptoms: *a symptomatic classification of disease.* Also, **symp′to·mat′i·cal.** [< ML *symptōmaticus*) = LL *symptōmat-* (s. of *symptōma*) SYMPTOM + *-icus* -IC] —**symp′to·mat′i·cal·ly,** *adv.*

symp·tom·a·tol·o·gy (simp′tə mə tol′ə jē), *n.* **1.** the branch of medical science dealing with symptoms. **2.** the collective symptoms of a patient or disease. Cf. **syndrome.** [< NL *symptōmatologia* = LL *symptōmat-* (s. of *symptōma*) SYMPTOM + *-o-* -O- + *-logia* -LOGY]

syn-, a prefix occurring in loan words from Greek, having the same function as **co-** (*synthesis; synoptic*); meaning "with," "together," used in the formation of compound words (*synsepalous*). Also, **sy-, syl-, sym-, sys-.** [< Gk, comb. form repr. *sýn*]

syn., 1. synonym. **2.** synonymous. **3.** synonymy.

syn·aer·e·sis (si ner′i sis), *n.* *Phonet.* **1.** the contraction of two syllables or two vowels into one, esp. the contraction of two vowels so as to form a diphthong. **2.** synizesis. Also, **syneresis.** [< LL < Gk *synaíresis* act of taking together = *syn-* SYN- + *haire-* (s. of *haireîn* to take) + *-sis* -SIS]

syn·aes·the·sia (sin′is thē′zhə, -zhē ə, -zē ə), *n.* synesthesia. —**syn·aes·thet·ic** (sin′is thet′ik), *adj.*

syn·a·gogue (sin′ə gog′, -gôg′), *n.* **1.** a Jewish house of worship. **2.** an assembly or congregation of Jews for the purpose of religious worship. Also, **syn′a·gog.** [ME *synagoge* < eccl. L *synagōg(a)* < Gk *synagōgḗ* assembly, meeting = *syn-* SYN- + *agōgḗ,* n. use of fem. of *agōgós* (adj.) gathering < *ágein* to bring, lead; akin to L *agere* to drive] —**syn·a·gog·i·cal** (sin′ə goj′i kəl), **syn·a·gog·al** (sin′ə-gog′əl, -gô′gəl), *adj.*

syn·a·loe·pha (sin′əlē′fə), *n.* the blending of two successive vowels into one. Also, **syn′a·le′pha, syn·a·le·phe** (sin′əlē′fē). [< NL < Gk *synaloiphḗ, synaliphḗ* = *syn-* SYN- + *aloiph-, aliph-* (var. stems of *aleíphein* to smear) + *-ē* n. suffix]

syn·apse (sin′aps, si naps′), *n.* *Physiol.* the region of contact between the axon of one neuron and the dendrite or cell body of another neuron, across which nerve impulses are transmitted in one direction only. [back formation from *synapses,* pl. of SYNAPSIS]

syn·ap·sis (si nap′sis), *n., pl.* **-ses** (-sēz). **1.** *Biol.* the conjugation of homologous chromosomes, one from each parent, during early meiosis. **2.** *Physiol.* synapse. [< NL < Gk *sýnapsis* junction = *synap-* (s. of *synáptein* to make contact = *syn-* SYN- + *háptein* to touch) + *-sis* -SIS] —**syn·ap·tic** (si nap′tik), **syn·ap′ti·cal,** *adj.* —**syn·ap′ti·cal·ly,** *adv.*

syn·ar·thro·sis (sin′är thrō′sis), *n., pl.* **-ses** (-sēz). *Anat.* immovable articulation; a fixed or immovable joint; suture. [< NL < Gk *synárthrōsis* = *synarthrō-* (s. of *synarthroûsthai* to be joined by articulation = *syn-* SYN- + *árthro(n)* joint + *-esthai* inf. suffix) + *-sis* -SIS]

sync (singk), *Motion Pictures, Television Informal.* —*n.* **1.** Also, **synch** (singk). synchronization: *The picture and the sound track were out of sync.* —*v.i., v.t.* **2.** to synchronize. [shortened form]

syn·carp (sin′kärp), *n.* *Bot.* **1.** an aggregate fruit. **2.** a collective fruit. [< NL *syncarp(ium)* = *syncarp(us)* SYNCARPOUS + *-ium* n. suffix]

syn·car·pous (sin kär′pəs), *adj.* *Bot.* **1.** of the nature of or pertaining to a syncarp. **2.** composed of or having united carpels. [< NL *syncarpus*] —**syn·car·py** (sin′kär pē), *n.*

syn·cat·e·gor·e·mat·ic (sin kat′ə gôr′ə mat′ik, -gor′-), *adj.* *Logic.* of or pertaining to a word or term, as *all,* that has no independent significance and must be used in combination in a proposition.

synchro-, a combining form of **synchronized** and **synchronous:** *synchroscope; synchrotron.*

syn·chro·flash (sing′krə flash′), *adj.* of or pertaining to photography employing a device that synchronizes the firing of the flash bulb with the exact time that the camera shutter opens.

syn·chro·mesh (sing′krə mesh′), *n.* *Auto.* a shifting mechanism for synchronizing the speeds of two gears to be meshed.

syn·chro·nal (sing′krə nᵊl), *adj.* synchronous. [< NL *synchron(us)* SYNCHRONOUS + -AL[1]]

syn·chron·ic (sin kron′ik), *adj. Linguistics.* having reference to the facts of a linguistic system as it exists at one point in time without reference to its history. Also, **syn·chron′i·cal.** Cf. **diachronic.** [< LL *synchron(us)* SYNCHRONOUS + -IC] —**syn·chron′i·cal·ly,** *adv.*

synchron′ic linguis′tics, the study of the existing features of a language or languages at a given point in time.

syn·chro·nise (sing′krə nīz′), *v.i., v.t.,* **-nised, -nis·ing.** *Chiefly Brit.* synchronize. —**syn′chro·ni·sa′tion,** *n.* —**syn′chro·nis′er,** *n.*

syn·chro·nism (sing′krə niz′əm), *n.* **1.** coincidence in time; contemporaneousness; simultaneousness. **2.** the arrangement or treatment of synchronous things or events in conjunction, as in a history. **3.** a tabular arrangement of historical events and personages, synchronized according to their dates. **4.** *Physics, Elect.* the state of being synchronous. [< ML *synchronism(us)* < Gk *synchronismós* = *sýnchron(os)* SYNCHRONOUS + *-ismos* -ISM] —**syn′chro·nis′tic, syn′chro·nis′ti·cal,** *adj.* —**syn′chro·nis′ti·cal·ly,** *adv.*

syn·chro·nize (sing′krə nīz′), *v.,* **-nized, -niz·ing.** —*v.i.* **1.** to occur at the same time or coincide or agree in time. **2.** to go on, move, operate, work, etc., at the same rate and exactly together; recur together. **3.** *Motion Pictures, Television.* (of action and sound) to coincide in a scene. —*v.t.* **4.** to cause to indicate the same time, as one timepiece with another: *Synchronize your watches.* **5.** to cause to go on, move, operate, work, etc., at the same rate and exactly together. **6.** to assign to the same time or period, as in a history. **7.** *Motion Pictures, Television.* **a.** to arrange (sound) so as to coincide with the action of a scene. **b.** to make action and sound coincide in (a scene). Also, *esp. Brit.,* **synchronise.** [< Gk *synchronízein* (to) be contemporary with = *sýnchron(os)* SYNCHRONOUS + *-izein* -IZE] —**syn′chro·ni·za′tion,** *n.* —**syn′chro·niz′er,** *n.*

syn·chro·nous (sing′krə nəs), *adj.* **1.** occurring at the same time; coinciding in time; contemporaneous; simultaneous. **2.** going on at the same rate and exactly together; recurring together. **3.** *Physics, Elect.* having the same frequency and zero phase difference. [< LL *synchronus* < Gk *sýnchronos* = *syn-* SYN- + *chrón(os)* time + *-os* -OUS] —**syn′chro·nous·ly,** *adv.* —**syn′chro·nous·ness,** *n.*

syn·chro·scope (sing′krə skōp′), *n.* an instrument for determining the difference in phase between two related motions, as those of two aircraft engines or two electric generators. Also, **syn·chron·o·scope** (sin kron′ə skōp′).

syn·chro·tron (sing′krə tron′), *n. Physics.* a type of cyclotron consisting of magnetic sections alternately spaced with sections in which the particles are electrostatically accelerated.

syn·clas·tic (sin klas′tik), *adj. Math.* (of a surface) having principal curvatures of similar sign at a given point. Cf. **anticlastic.** [SYN- + Gk *klast(ós)* broken + -IC]

syn·cli·nal (sin klīn′ᵊl, sing′kli nᵊl), *adj.* **1.** sloping downward in opposite directions so as to meet in a common point or line. **2.** *Geol.* **a.** inclining upward on both sides from a median line or axis, as a downward fold of rock strata. **b.** pertaining to such a fold. [SYN- + Gk *klín(ein)* (to) lean + -AL[1]] —**syn·cli′nal·ly,** *adv.*

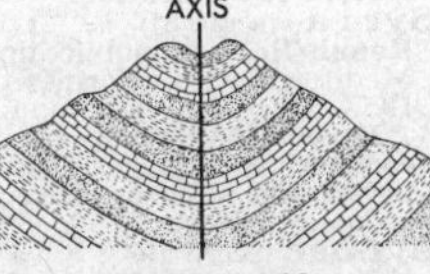

Synclinal folds

syn·cline (sing′klīn, sin′-), *n. Geol.* a synclinal fold. [back formation from SYNCLINAL]

syn·co·pate (sing′kə pāt′, sin′-), *v.t.,* **-pat·ed, -pat·ing.** **1.** *Music.* **a.** to place (the accents) on beats that are normally unaccented. **b.** to treat (a passage, piece, etc.) in this way. **2.** *Gram.* to contract (a word) by omitting one or more sounds from the middle, as in reducing *Gloucester* to *Gloster.* [< ML *syncopāt(us)* (ptp. of *syncopāre* to shorten by syncope). See SYNCOPE, -ATE[1]] —**syn′co·pa′tor,** *n.*

syn·co·pat·ed (sing′kə pā′tid, sin′-), *adj.* **1.** marked by syncopation: *syncopated rhythm.* **2.** cut short; abbreviated.

syn·co·pa·tion (sing′kə pā′shən, sin′-), *n.* **1.** *Music.* a shifting of the normal accent, usually by stressing the normally unaccented beats. **2.** Also called **counterpoint, counterpoint rhythm.** *Pros.* the use of rhetorical stress at variance with the metrical stress of a line of verse, as the stress on *and* and *of* in *Come praise Colonus' horses and come praise/The wine-dark of the wood's intricacies.* **3.** *Gram.* a syncope. [< ML *syncopātiōn-* (s. of *syncopātiō*)]

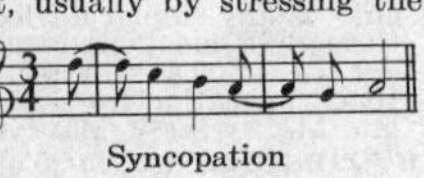
Syncopation

syn·co·pe (sing′kə pē, -pē′, sin′-), *n.* **1.** *Gram.* the contraction of a word by omitting one or more sounds from the middle, as in the reduction of *never* to *ne'er.* **2.** *Pathol.* brief loss of consciousness associated with transient cerebral anemia, as in heart block, sudden lowering of the blood pressure, etc.; fainting. [late ME < LL < Gk *synkopḗ* a cutting short = *syn-* SYN- + *kop-* (s. of *kóptein* to cut) + *-ē* n. suffix] —**syn·cop·ic** (sin kop′ik), **syn′co·pal,** *adj.*

syn·cre·tism (sing′kri tiz′əm, sin′-), *n.* **1.** the attempted reconciliation or union of different or opposing principles, practices, or parties, as in philosophy or religion. **2.** *Gram.* the merging, as by historical change in a language, of two or more inflectional categories in a specified environment. [< NL *syncretism(us)* < Gk *synkrētismós* union of Cretans, hence a united front of two opposing parties against a common foe < *synkrētíz(ein)* (to) SYNCRETIZE, with *-ismos* -ISM r. *-izein* -IZE] —**syn·cret·ic** (sin kret′ik), **syn·cret′i·cal, syn·cre·tis·tic** (sing′kri tis′tik, sin′-), **syn′cre·tis′ti·cal,** *adj.*

syn·cre·tize (sing′kri tīz′, sin′-), *v.t., v.i.,* **-tized, -tiz·ing.** to attempt to combine or unite, as different or opposing principles, parties, etc. [< NL *syncrētiz(āre)* < Gk *synkrētíz(ein)* (to) form a confederation = *syn-* SYN- + *Krēt-* (s. of *Krḗs*) a Cretan + *-izein* -IZE; see SYNCRETISM]

syn·cri·sis (sing′kri sis, sin′-), *n. Rhet. Obs.* the comparison of opposites. [< LL < Gk *sýnkrisis* combination, comparison = *syn-* SYN- + *kri-* (s. of *krínein* to separate) + *-sis* -SIS]

synd., **1.** syndicate. **2.** syndicated.

syn·dac·tyl (sin dak′til), *adj.* **1.** having certain digits joined together. —*n.* **2.** a syndactyl animal. Also, **syn·dac′tyle.** —**syn·dac·tyl·ism** (sin dak′tᵊliz′əm), *n.*

syn·det·ic (sin det′ik), *adj.* **1.** serving to unite or connect; connective; copulative. **2.** *Gram.* conjunctive (def. 3c). Also, **syn·det′i·cal.** [< Gk *syndetik(ós)* = *sýndet(os)* bound together (*syn-* SYN- + *de-* (s. of *deîn* to bind) + *-tos* verbal adj. suffix) + *-ikos* -IC] —**syn·det′i·cal·ly,** *adv.*

syn·dic (sin′dik), *n.* **1.** *Brit.* a person chosen to represent and transact business for a corporation, as a university. **2.** a civil magistrate having different powers in different countries. [< F < LL *syndic(us)* city official < Gk *sýndikos* counsel for defendant = *syn-* SYN- + *dik-* (s. of *díkē*) justice + *-os* n. suffix] —**syn′dic·ship′,** *n.*

syn·di·cal (sin′di kəl), *adj.* **1.** noting or pertaining to a union of persons engaged in a particular trade. **2.** of or pertaining to syndicalism. [< F]

syn·di·cal·ism (sin′di kə liz′əm), *n.* **1.** a doctrine of revolutionary trade unionism, developed chiefly in the late 19th century, advocating principally the abolition of the state, which was to be replaced by a loose federation of industrial workers. **2.** an economic system in which workers own and manage industry. [< F *syndicalisme*] —**syn′di·cal·ist,** *adj., n.* —**syn′di·cal·is′tic,** *adj.*

syn·di·cate (*n.* sin′də kit; *v.* sin′də kāt′), *n., v.,* **-cat·ed, -cat·ing.** —*n.* **1.** a group of individuals or organizations combined or making a joint effort to undertake some specific duty or carry out specific transactions or negotiations. **2.** *Journalism.* an agency that buys articles, photographs, comic strips, etc., and sells and distributes them for simultaneous publication in a number of newspapers or periodicals. **3.** a council or body of syndics. —*v.t.* **4.** to combine into a syndicate. **5.** to supply for simultaneous publication in a number of newspapers or periodicals. [< MF *syndicat* board of syndics] —**syn′di·ca′tion,** *n.*

syn·drome (sin′drōm, sin′drə mē′), *n.* **1.** *Pathol., Psychiatry.* a group of symptoms that together are characteristic of a specific condition, disease, or the like. **2.** the pattern of symptoms that characterize or indicate a particular social condition. [< NL < Gk *syndromḗ* concurrence, combination = *syn-* SYN- + *drom-* (var. s. of *drameîn* to run) + *-ē* n. suffix] —**syn·drom·ic** (sin drom′ik), *adj.*

syn·ec·do·che (si nek′də kē), *n. Rhet.* a figure of speech in which a part is used for the whole or the whole for a part, the special for the general or the general for the special, as in "ten sail" for ten ships or "a Croesus" for a rich man. [< L < Gk *synekdochḗ* = *syn-* SYN- + *ekdochḗ* act of receiving from another = *ek-* EC- + *doch-* (var. s. of *déchesthai* to receive) + *-ē* n. suffix] —**syn·ec·doch·ic** (sin′ik dok′ik), **syn′ec·doch′i·cal,** *adj.* —**syn′ec·doch′i·cal·ly,** *adv.*

syn·e·cious (si nē′shəs), *adj.* synoicous. [SYN- + *eci-* (< Gk *oikía* house) + -OUS]

syn·e·col·o·gy (sin′ə kol′ə jē), *n.* the branch of ecology dealing with the relations between plant and animal communities and their environments. —**syn·ec·o·log·ic** (sin′ek-ə loj′ik), **syn′ec·o·log′i·cal,** *adj.*

syn·er·e·sis (si ner′i sis), *n.* **1.** synaeresis. **2.** *Physical Chem.* the contraction of a gel accompanied by the exudation of liquid. [var. of SYNAERESIS]

syn·er·get·ic (sin′ər jet′ik), *adj.* working together; cooperative. [< Gk *synergētik(ós)* = *syn-* SYN- + *-ergētikos;* see ENERGETIC]

syn·er·gism (sin′ər jiz′əm, si nûr′jiz-), *n.* the joint action of agents, as drugs, that when taken together increase each other's effectiveness. [< NL *synergism(us)* = Gk *synerg(ós)* (*syn-* SYN- + *érg(on)* work + *-os* adj. suffix) + NL *-ismus* -ISM]

syn·er·gist (sin′ər jist, si nûr′-), *n.* **1.** *Physiol., Med.* a body organ, medicine, etc., that cooperates with another or others to produce or enhance an effect. **2.** *Chem., Pharm.* any admixture to a substance for increasing the effectiveness of one or more of its properties. [< NL *synergist(a)* = Gk *synerg(ós)* (see SYNERGISM) + NL *-ista* -IST]

syn·er·gis·tic (sin′ər jis′tik), *adj.* working together; synergetic. [SYNERG(ISM) or SYNERG(IST) + -ISTIC] —**syn′er·gis′ti·cal·ly,** *adv.*

syn·er·gy (sin′ər jē), *n., pl.* **-gies.** **1.** combined action. **2.** the cooperative action of two or more muscles, nerves, stimuli, drugs, etc. [< NL *synergia* < Gk *synergía* = *synerg(ós)* (see SYNERGISM) + *-ia* -Y[3]] —**syn·er·gic** (si nûr′jik), *adj.*

syn·e·sis (sin′i sis), *n. Gram.* a construction in which an expected grammatical agreement in form is replaced by an agreement in meaning, as in *the committee are,* where a plural verb is used with a singular noun. [< NL < Gk: understanding, intelligence = *syn-* SYN- + *(h)e-* (s. of *hiénai* to throw, send) + *-sis* -SIS]

syn·es·the·sia (sin′is thē′zhə, -zhē ə, -zē ə), *n.* a sensation produced in one modality when a stimulus is applied to another modality, as when the hearing of a certain sound induces the visualization of a certain color. Also, **synaesthesia.** [< NL] —**syn·es·thet·ic** (sin′is thet′ik), *adj.*

syn·fu·el (sin′fyōō′əl), *n.* See **synthetic fuel.** [SYN(THETIC) + FUEL]

syn·ga·my (sing′gə mē), *n. Biol.* union of gametes, as in fertilization or conjugation; sexual reproduction. —**syn·gam·ic** (sin gam′ik), **syn·ga·mous** (sing′gə məs), *adj.*

Synge (sing), *n.* **John Mil·ling·ton** (mil′ing tən), 1871–1909, Irish dramatist.

syn·gen·e·sis (sin jen′i sis), *n. Biol.* sexual reproduction. [< NL] —**syn·ge·net·ic** (sin′jə net′ik), *adj.*

syn·i·ze·sis (sin′i zē′sis), *n. Phonet.* the combination into one syllable of two vowels (or of a vowel and a diphthong) that do not form a diphthong. Also called **synaeresis.** [< LL < Gk *synízēsis* = *syn-* SYN- + *(h)izē-* (s. of *hízein* to sit) + *-sis* -SIS]

syn·od (sin′əd), *n.* **1.** an assembly of ecclesiastics or other church delegates, convoked pursuant to the law of the church, for the discussion and decision of ecclesiastical affairs; ecclesiastical council. **2.** any council. [late ME < L *synod(us)* < Gk *sýnodos* meeting = *syn-* SYN- + *hodós* way] —**syn′od·al,** *adj.*

syn·od·ic (si nod′ik), *adj. Astron.* pertaining to a conjunction, or to two successive conjunctions of the same bodies. Also, **syn·od′i·cal.** [< LL *synodic(us)* < Gk *synodikós*] —**syn·od′i·cal·ly,** *adv.*

syn·oi·cous (si noi′kəs), *adj. Bot.* having male and female flowers on one head, as in many composite plants. Also, **synecious, syn·oe·cious** (si nē′shəs). [< Gk *sýnoikos* dwelling in the same house = *syn-* SYN- + *oik-* (s. of *oîkos, oikía* house, *oikeîn* to dwell) + *-os* -OUS] —**syn·oi′cous·ly, syn·oe′cious·ly,** *adv.* —**syn·oi′cous·ness, syn·oe′cious·ness,** *n.*

syn·o·nym (sin′ə nim), *n.* **1.** a word having the same or nearly the same meaning as another in the language, as *joyful, elated, glad.* **2.** a word or expression accepted as another name for something, as *Arcadia* for *pastoral simplicity.* **3.** *Bot., Zool.* a rejected scientific name, other than a homonym. [< LL *synonym(um)* < Gk *synṓnymon,* n. use of neut. of *synṓnymos* SYNONYMOUS; r. ME *sinonyme* < MF] —**syn′o·nym′ic, syn′o·nym′i·cal,** *adj.* —**syn·o·nym·i·ty** (sin′ə nim′i tē), *n.*

syn·on·y·mise (si non′ə mīz′), *v.t.,* **-mised, -mis·ing.** *Chiefly Brit.* synonymize.

syn·on·y·mize (si non′ə mīz′), *v.t.,* **-mized, -miz·ing.** to give synonyms for (a word, name, etc.); furnish with synonyms.

syn·on·y·mous (si non′ə məs), *adj.* having the character of synonyms or a synonym; equivalent in meaning; expressing or implying the same idea. [< LL *synonymus* < Gk *synṓnymos* = *syn-* SYN- + *-ōnym-* -ONYM + *-os* -OUS] —**syn·on′y·mous·ly,** *adv.* —**syn·on′y·mous·ness,** *n.*

syn·on·y·my (si non′ə mē), *n., pl.* **-mies** for 3, 4. **1.** the quality of being synonymous; equivalence in meaning. **2.** the study of synonyms. **3.** a set, list, or system of synonyms. **4.** *Bot., Zool.* **a.** a list of the scientific names for a particular species or other group, or for various species, etc., with discriminations or explanatory matter. **b.** these names collectively, whether listed or not. [< LL *synōnymia* < Gk. See SYNONYMOUS, -Y[3]]

synop., synopsis.

syn·op·sis (si nop′sis), *n., pl.* **-ses** (-sēz). **1.** a brief or condensed statement giving a general view of some subject. **2.** a compendium of heads or short paragraphs giving a view of the whole. **3.** a brief summary of the plot of a novel, motion picture, play, etc. [< LL < Gk *sýnopsis* = *syn-* SYN- + *op-* (suppletive s. of *horân* to see; cf. AUTOPSY) + *-sis* -SIS] —**Syn.** condensation, abstract, précis. See **summary.**

syn·op·sise (si nop′sīz), *v.t.,* **-sised, -sis·ing.** *Chiefly Brit.* synopsize.

syn·op·size (si nop′sīz), *v.t.,* **-sized, -siz·ing.** to make a synopsis of; summarize. [SYNOPS(IS) + -IZE]

syn·op·tic (si nop′tik), *adj.* **1.** pertaining to or constituting a synopsis; affording or taking a general view of the principal parts of a subject. **2.** (*often cap.*) taking a common view: used chiefly in reference to the first three Gospels **(synop′tic Gos′pels),** Matthew, Mark, and Luke, from their similarity in content, order, and statement. Also, **syn·op′ti·cal.** [< Gk *synoptik(ós)* = *synop-* (see SYNOPSIS) + *-tikos* -TIC] —**syn·op′ti·cal·ly,** *adv.*

synop′tic chart′, a chart showing the distribution of meteorological conditions over a wide region at a given moment.

syn·o·vi·a (si nō′vē ə), *n. Physiol.* a lubricating fluid resembling the white of an egg, secreted by certain membranes, as those of the joints. [< NL = *syn-* SYN- + L *ov-* (s. of *ōvum* egg) + *-ia* -IA] —**syn·o′vi·al,** *adj.* —**syn·o′vi·al·ly,** *adv.*

syn·o·vi·tis (sin′ə vī′tis), *n. Pathol.* inflammation of a synovial membrane. [SYNOV(IA) + -ITIS] —**syn·o·vit·ic** (sin′ə vit′ik), *adj.*

syn·sep·al·ous (sin sep′ə ləs), *adj. Bot.* gamosepalous.

syn·tac·tic (sin tak′tik), *adj.* of or pertaining to syntax. Also, **syn·tac′ti·cal.** [< NL *syntactic(us)* < Gk *syntaktikós* = *syntakt(ós)* ordered, arranged together, verbid of *syntássein* to arrange together (*syn-* SYN- + *tak-* < *tag-* root of *tássein* + *-tos* adj. suffix) + *-ikos* -IC] —**syn·tac′ti·cal·ly,** *adv.*

syntac′tic construc′tion, *Gram.* a construction that has no bound forms among its immediate constituents.

syn·tax (sin′taks), *n. Linguistics.* **1.** the study of the structure of grammatical sentences in a language. **2.** the pattern or structure of the word order in a sentence and phrase. [short for earlier *syntaxis* < LL < Gk = *syntak-* (var. of *syntag-*; see SYNTACTIC) + *-sis* -SIS]

syn·the·sis (sin′thi sis), *n., pl.* **-ses** (-sēz′). **1.** the combining of the constituent elements of separate material or abstract entities into a single or unified entity (opposed to *analysis*). **2.** a complex whole formed by combining. **3** *Chem.* the forming of a more complex substance or compound from elements or simpler compounds. **4.** a process of reasoning in which the conclusion is reached directly from given propositions and established or assumed principles. **5.** *Philos.* See under **Hegelian dialectic.** [< L < Gk *sýnthesis* = *syn-* SYN- + *the-* (s. of *tithénai* to put, place) + *-sis* -SIS] —**syn′the·sist,** *n.*

syn·the·sise (sin′thi sīz′), *v.t.,* **-sised, -sis·ing.** *Chiefly Brit.* synthesize. —**syn′the·si·sa′tion,** *n.* —**syn′the·sis′er,** *n.*

syn·the·size (sin′thi sīz′), *v.,* **-sized, -siz·ing.** —*v.t.* **1.** to form (a material or abstract entity) by combining parts or elements (opposed to *analyze*). **2.** *Chem.* to combine (constituent elements) into a single or unified entity. **3.** to treat synthetically. —*v.i.* **4.** to make or form a synthesis. Also, **synthetize.** [SYNTHES(IS) + -IZE] —**syn′the·si·za′tion,** *n.* —**syn′the·siz′er,** *n.*

syn·the·siz·er (sin′thi sīz′ər), *n.* **1.** a person or thing that synthesizes. **2.** an electronic apparatus capable of generating, modifying, and combining a wide range of sounds, used esp. in music.

syn·thet·ic (sin thet′ik), *adj.* Also, **syn·thet′i·cal. 1.** of, pertaining to, proceeding by, or involving synthesis (opposed to *analytic*). **2.** *Chem.* noting or pertaining to compounds formed by chemical reaction in a laboratory, as opposed to those of natural origin. **3.** (of a language) characterized by a relatively widespread use of affixes, rather than separate words, to express syntactic relationships: Latin is a synthetic language, while English is analytic. Cf. **analytic** (def. 3), **polysynthetic. 4.** *Logic.* of or pertaining to a noncontradictory proposition in which the predicate is not included in, or entailed by, the subject. **5.** not real or genuine; artificial; feigned: *a synthetic chuckle at a poor joke.* —*n.* **6.** something made by a synthetic, or chemical, process. [< NL *synthetic(us)* < Gk *synthetikós* = *synthet(ós)* placed together, verbid of *syntithénai* to put together (*syn-* SYN- + *the-,* s. of *tithénai* + *-tos* adj. suffix) + *-ikos* -IC] —**syn·thet′i·cal·ly,** *adv.*

synthet′ic fu′el, fuel in the form of liquid or gas manufactured from coal or in the form of oil extracted from shale or tar sands.

synthet′ic rub′ber, any of several substances similar to natural rubber in properties and uses, produced by the polymerization of an unsaturated hydrocarbon, as butylene or isoprene, or by the copolymerization of such hydrocarbons with styrene, butadiene, or the like.

syn·the·tise (sin′thi tīz′), *v.t.,* **-tised, -tis·ing.** *Chiefly Brit.* synthetize. —**syn′the·ti·sa′tion,** *n.* —**syn′the·tis′er,** *n.*

syn·the·tize (sin′thi tīz′), *v.t.,* **-tized, -tiz·ing.** to synthesize. [< Gk *synthetíze(sthai)*; see SYNTHETIC, -IZE] —**syn′the·ti·za′tion,** *n.* —**syn′the·tiz′er,** *n.*

syph·i·lis (sif′ə lis), *n. Pathol.* a chronic infectious disease, caused by a spirochete, *Treponema pallidum,* usually venereal in origin but often congenital, and affecting almost any organ or tissue in the body. [< NL, coined by G. Fracastoro (1478–1553), Italian physician and poet, author of Latin poem *Syphilis,* with a shepherd, *Syphilus,* as chief character and first sufferer of the disease]

syph·i·lit·ic (sif′ə lit′ik), *adj.* **1.** pertaining to, noting, or affected with syphilis. —*n.* **2.** a person affected with syphilis. [< NL *syphiliticus(us).* See SYPHILIS, -TIC] —**syph′i·lit′i·cal·ly,** *adv.*

syph·i·loid (sif′ə loid′), *adj.* resembling syphilis.

syph·i·lol·o·gy (sif′ə lol′ə jē), *n.* the science dealing with the study of syphilis. —**syph′i·lol′o·gist,** *n.*

sy·phon (sī′fən), *n., v.t., v.i.* siphon.

Syr., **1.** Syria. **2.** Syriac. **3.** Syrian.

syr., *Pharm.* syrup.

Syr·a·cuse (sir′ə kyōōs′, sēr′-), *n.* **1.** a city in central New York. 197,297 (1970). **2.** Italian, **Siracusa.** a seaport in SE Sicily: ancient city founded by the Carthaginians 734 B.C.; battles 413 B.C., 212 B.C. 90,333 (1961). —**Syr′a·cu′san,** *adj., n.*

Syr Dar·ya (sēr där′yä), a river in the SW Soviet Union in Asia, flowing NW from the Tien Shan Mountains to the Aral Sea. 1300 mi. long. Ancient name, **Jaxartes.**

Syr·ette (si ret′), *n. Trademark.* a collapsible tube with an attached hypodermic needle for the subcutaneous administration of medication.

Syr·i·a (sēr′ē ə), *n.* **1.** Official name, **Syr′ian Ar′ab Repub′lic.** a republic in SW Asia at the E end of the Mediterranean: a former part of the United Arab Republic 1958–61; with Lebanon, a French mandate 1920–43. 7,200,000; 71,227 sq. mi. *Cap.:* Damascus. **2.** an ancient country in W Asia, including the present Syria, Lebanon, Israel, and adjacent areas: a part of the Roman Empire 64 B.C.–A.D. 636.

Syr·i·ac (sēr′ē ak′), *n.* a form of Aramaic used by various Eastern Churches. [< L *Syriac(us)* < Gk *Syriakós*]

Syr·i·an (sēr′ē ən), *adj.* **1.** of or pertaining to Syria or its inhabitants. —*n.* **2.** a native or inhabitant of Syria. [late ME *Sirien* < MF]

sy·rin·ga (sə ring′gə), *n.* **1.** any shrub of the genus *Philadelphus,* certain species of which are cultivated as ornamentals, esp. *P. coronarius,* having fragrant, white flowers. **2.** a lilac of the genus *Syringa.* [< NL < Gk *syring-* (s. of *sŷrinx* SYRINX) + *-a* n. suffix]

sy·ringe (sə rinj′, sir′inj), *n., v.,* **-ringed, -ring·ing.** —*n.* **1.** *Med.* a small device consisting of a tube, narrowed at its outlet, and fitted with either a piston or a rubber bulb for drawing in a quantity of fluid and ejecting it in a stream, for cleaning wounds, injecting fluids into the body, etc. **2.** any similar device for pumping and spraying liquids through a small aperture. **3.** See **hypodermic syringe.** —*v.i.* **4.** to cleanse, wash, inject, etc., by means of a syringe. [back formation from LL *syringēs,* pl. of *syrinx* SYRINX; r. late ME *syring* < ML *syringa*] —**sy·ringe′ful,** *adj.*

sy·rin·ge·al (sə rin′jē əl), *adj. Ornith.* of, pertaining to, or connected with the syrinx. [*syringe-* (var. s. of SYRINX) + -AL[1]]

sy·rin·go·my·e·li·a (sə ring′gō mī ē′lē ə), *n. Pathol.* a disease of the spinal cord in which the nerve tissue is replaced by a cavity filled with fluid. [*syringo-* (comb. form of Gk *sŷrinx* SYRINX) + *myelia* (MYEL- + -IA)] —**sy·rin·go·my·el·ic** (sə ring′gō mī el′ik), *adj.*

syr·inx (sir′ingks), *n., pl.* **sy·rin·ges** (sə rin′jēz), **syr·inx·es. 1.** *Ornith.* the vocal organ of birds, situated at or near the bifurcation of the trachea into the bronchi. **2.** (*cap.*) *Class. Myth.* a mountain nymph of Arcadia: in order to protect her chastity from Pan, she was transformed into the reed from which Pan then made the panpipe. **3.** a panpipe. **4.** a narrow corridor in an ancient Egyptian tomb. [(partly through L) < Gk: pipe, tube]

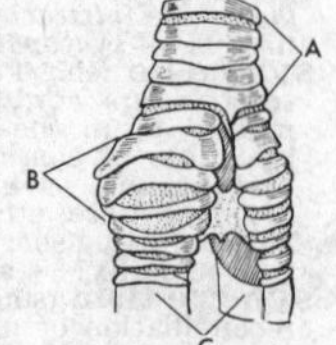

Syrinx (of passerine bird) A, Tracheal rings; B, Bronchial rings; C, Right and left bronchi

syr·phid (sûr′fid), *n.* See **syrphid fly.** Also, **syr·phi·an** (sûr′fē ən). [< Gk *sýrph(os)* gnat + -ID[2]]

syr′phid fly′, any of numerous beelike or wasplike flies of the family *Syrphidae* that feed on the nectar and pollen of flowers, and have larvae that feed on decaying vegetation or are predaceous on aphids. Also, **syr′phus fly′** (sûr′fəs).

Syr′tis Ma′jor (sûr′tis), an area in the northern hemisphere and near the equator of Mars, appearing as a dark region when viewed telescopically from the earth.

syr·up (sir′əp, sûr′-), *n.* **1.** any of various thick, sweet liquids prepared for cooking or table use from molasses, glucose, etc., mixed with water and often a flavoring agent. **2.** any of various preparations consisting of fruit juices, water, etc., boiled with sugar. **3.** *Pharm.* **a.** a concentrated sugar solution containing medication or flavoring. **b.** Also called **simple syrup.** an official U.S.P. solution of 850 grams of sucrose and sufficient water to make a total volume of 1000 cubic centimeters, used as a vehicle for medication. Also, **sirup.** [< ML *syrup(us)* < Ar *sharāb* a drink; r. ME *sirop* < MF] —**syr′up·like′,** *adj.*

syr·up·y (sir′ə pē), *adj.* **1.** having the appearance or quality of syrup; thick or sweet. **2.** sentimental or mawkish. Also, **sirupy.**

sys-, var. of **syn-** before *s: syssarcosis.*

sys·sar·co·sis (sis′är kō′sis), *n., pl.* **-ses** (-sēz). *Anat.* the union of bones by muscle. [< NL < Gk *syssárkōsis* = *syssark-*, s. of *syssarkoûsthai* to be likewise overgrown with flesh (*sys-* SIS- + *sark-* SARC-) + *-ōsis* -OSIS]

syst., system.

sys·tal·tic (si stôl′tik, -stal′-), *adj.* *Physiol.* **1.** rhythmically contracting. **2.** of the nature of contraction. **3.** characterized by alternate contraction and dilatation, as the action of the heart. [< LL *systaltic(us)* < Gk *systaltikós* = *systalt(ós)* contracted, verbid of *systéllein* to put together, (*sy-* SY- + *stal-* var. s. of *stéllein* to place + *-tos* adj. suffix) + *-ikos* -IC]

sys·tem (sis′təm), *n.* **1.** an assemblage or combination of things or parts forming a complex or unitary whole: *a mountain system; a railroad system.* **2.** any assemblage or set of correlated members. **3.** an ordered and comprehensive assemblage of facts, principles, methods, etc., in a particular field: *a system of philosophy.* **4.** any formulated, regular, or special method or plan of procedure. **5.** a method or manner of arrangement or procedure. **6.** a number of heavenly bodies associated and acting together according to certain natural laws: *the solar system.* **7.** *Astron.* a hypothesis or theory of the disposition and arrangements of the heavenly bodies by which their phenomena, motions, changes, etc., are explained: *the Copernican system.* **8.** *Biol.* **a.** an assemblage of organs or related tissues concerned with the same function. **b.** the body considered as a functioning unit. **9.** a method or scheme of classification. **10.** *Geol.* a major division of rocks comprising sedimentary deposits and igneous masses formed during a geological period. **11.** *Crystall.* one of the six primary divisions in the classification of crystals by form, as hexagonal, isometric, monoclinic, orthorhombic, tetragonal, or triclinic. **12.** *Physical Chem.* a combination of two or more phases, as a binary system, each of which consists of one or more substances, that is attaining or is in equilibrium. **13.** the structure of society, business, politics, etc. **14.** any unit of equipment for audio reproduction, esp. in high fidelity or stereo: *a speaker system.* **15.** Often, **systems. a.** *Computer Technol.* an organized set of computer programs designed to control the operation of computers and associated equipment and to provide various facilities to users of the equipment. **b.** procedures usually involving people and machines in which units are clearly defined and organized to achieve specific objectives. [< LL *systēm(a)* < Gk *sýstēma* whole compounded of several parts = *sy-* SY- + *stē-* (var. s. of *histánai* to cause to stand; akin to L *stāre* to STAND) + *-ma* n. suffix denoting result of action] —**sys′tem·less,** *adj.* —**Syn. 1.** organization. **8b.** organism.

sys·tem·at·ic (sis′tə mat′ik), *adj.* **1.** having, showing, or involving a system, method, or plan: *a systematic course of reading; systematic efforts.* **2.** characterized by system or method; methodical: *a systematic person; systematic habits.* **3.** arranged in or comprising an ordered system: *systematic theology.* Also, **sys′tem·at′i·cal.** [< LL *systēmatic(us)* < Gk *systēmatikós* = *systēmat-* (s. of *sýstēma*) SYSTEM + *-ikos* -IC] —**sys′tem·at′ic·ness,** *n.* —**sys′tem·at′i·cal·ly,** *adv.* —**Syn. 2.** See **orderly.**

sys·tem·at·ics (sis′tə mat′iks), *n.* (*construed as sing.*) the study of systems or of classification. [see SYSTEMATIC, -ICS]

sys·tem·a·tise (sis′tə mə tīz′), *v.t.,* **-tised, -tis·ing.** *Chiefly Brit.* systematize. —**sys′tem·a·ti·sa′tion,** *n.* —**sys′tem·a·tis′er,** *n.*

sys·tem·a·tism (sis′tə mə tiz′əm), *n.* **1.** the practice of systematizing. **2.** adherence to system or method. [SYSTEMAT(IZE) + -ISM]

sys·tem·a·tist (sis′tə mə tist), *n.* **1.** a person who constructs or adheres to a system, order, or method. **2.** a naturalist engaged in classification. [< Gk *systēmat-* (s. of *sýstēma*) SYSTEM + -IST]

sys·tem·a·tize (sis′tə mə tīz′), *v.t.,* **-tized, -tiz·ing.** to arrange in or according to a system; reduce to a system; make systematic. Also, *esp. Brit.,* **systematise; systemize.** [< Gk *systēmat-* (s. of *sýstēma*) SYSTEM + -IZE] —**sys′tem·a·ti·za′tion,** *n.* —**sys′tem·a·tiz′er,** *n.* —**Syn.** organize, order, articulate.

sys·tem·a·tol·o·gy (sis′tə mə tol′ə jē), *n.* the science of systems or their formation. [< Gk *systēmat-* (s. of *sýstēma*) SYSTEM + -O- + -LOGY]

sys·tem·ic (si stem′ik), *adj.* **1.** of or pertaining to a system. **2.** *Physiol., Pathol.* **a.** pertaining to or affecting the entire bodily system or the body as a whole. **b.** pertaining to a particular system of parts or organs of the body. **3.** absorbed by a plant so as to be lethal to insects that feed on it. —*n.* **4.** a systemic insecticide. —**sys·tem′i·cal·ly,** *adv.*

sys·tem·ise (sis′tə mīz′), *v.t.,* **-ised, -is·ing.** *Chiefly Brit.* systemize. —**sys′tem·is′a·ble,** *adj.* —**sys′tem·i·sa′tion,** *n.* —**sys′tem·is′er,** *n.*

sys·tem·ize (sis′tə mīz′), *v.t.,* **-ized, -iz·ing.** systematize. —**sys′tem·iz′a·ble,** *adj.* —**sys′tem·i·za′tion,** *n.* —**sys′tem·iz′er,** *n.*

sys′tems anal′ysis, the methodical study and evaluation of an activity, such as a business, to identify its desired objectives in order to determine procedures by which these objectives can be gained. —**sys′tems an′alyst.**

sys′tems design′, **1.** the analyzing and organizing of a problem to make it suitable for solution or processing by electronic equipment. **2.** the organizing of a system of interrelated information-processing equipment to perform a given function or pattern of functions.

sys·to·le (sis′tə lē′, -lē), *n.* **1.** *Physiol.* the normal rhythmical contraction of the heart during which the blood in the chambers is forced onward. Cf. **diastole** (def. 1). **2.** *Class. Pros.* the shortening of a syllable regularly long. [< Gk *systolḗ* = *sy-* SY- + *stolḗ* = *stol-* (var. s. of *stéllein* to send, place) + *-ē* n. suffix; cf. DIASTOLE, SYSTALTIC] —**sys·tol·ic** (si stol′ik), *adj.*

systol′ic pres′sure, *Med.* the highest arterial pressure of the blood, occurring just after systole of the left ventricle.

Syz·ran (siz′RÄn), *n.* a city in the RSFSR, in the E Soviet Union in Europe, on the Volga. 159,000 (est. 1962).

syz·y·gy (siz′i jē), *n., pl.* **-gies.** **1.** *Astron.* the conjunction or opposition of two heavenly bodies; a point in the orbit of a body, as the moon, at which it is in conjunction with or in opposition to the sun. **2.** *Class. Pros.* a group or combination of two feet, sometimes restricted to a combination of two feet of different kinds. **3.** any two related things, either alike or opposite. [< LL *sýzygia* < Gk *syzygía* union, pair = *sýzyg(os)* yoked together (*sy-* SY- + *zyg-*, root of *zeugnýnai* to yoke + *-os* adj. suffix) + *-ia* -Y³] —**sy·zyg·i·al** (si zij′ē əl), **syz·y·get·ic** (siz′i jet′ik), **syz·y·gal** (siz′ə gəl), *adj.*

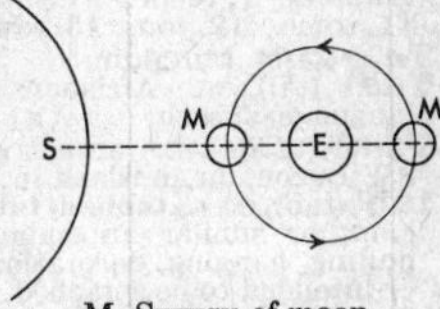

M, Syzygy of moon
S, Sun; E, Earth

Sza·bad·ka (so′bot ko), *n.* Hungarian name of **Subotica.**

Szcze·cin (shche tsēn′), *n.* Polish name of **Stettin.**

Sze·chwan (se′chwän′; *Chin.* su′chwän′), *n.* a province in SW China. 72,160,000 (est. 1957); 219,691 sq. mi. *Cap.:* Chengtu. Also, **Sze′chuan′.**

Sze·ged (se′ged), *n.* a city in S Hungary, on the Tisza River. 107,326 (est. 1963). German, **Sze·ge·din** (se′gə din).

Szell (sel), *n.* **George,** 1897–1970, U.S. pianist and conductor, born in Hungary.

Szent-Györ·gyi (sent jûr′jē; *Hung.* sent dyœr′dyi), *n.* **Al·bert** (al′bərt; *Hung.* ôl′beRt), born 1893, U.S. biochemist, born in Hungary: Nobel prize for medicine 1937.

Szi·ge·ti (sig′i tē, si get′ē; *Hung.* si′ge tē), *n.* **Joseph,** 1892–1973, U.S. violinist, born in Hungary.

Szi·lard (sil′ärd), *n.* **Leo,** 1898–1964, U.S. physicist, born in Hungary.

Szold (zōld), *n.* **Henrietta,** 1860–1945, U.S. Zionist: founded Hadassah in 1912.

Szom·bat·hely (sôm′bät hā′, -he′yᵊ), *n.* a city in W Hungary: founded A.D. 48. 57,000 (est. 1962). German, **Steinamanger.**

T

DEVELOPMENT OF MAJUSCULE								
NORTH SEMITIC	GREEK	ETR.	LATIN		MODERN		
					GOTHIC	ITALIC	ROMAN
+	X	T	T	T	T	𝕿	*T*	T

DEVELOPMENT OF MINUSCULE					
ROMAN CURSIVE	ROMAN UNCIAL	CAROL. MIN.	MODERN		
			GOTHIC	ITALIC	ROMAN
τ	T	τ	t	*t*	t

The twentieth letter of the English alphabet developed from North Semitic *taw*. The symbol has changed but little in its long history, and its minuscule (t) is only a slight variant of the capital.

T, t (tē), *n., pl.* **T's** or **Ts, t's** or **ts. 1.** the 20th letter of the English alphabet, a consonant. **2.** any spoken sound represented by the letter *T* or *t*, as in *table, altar,* or *cat.* **3.** something having the shape of a T. **4.** a written or printed representation of the letter *T* or *t.* **5.** a device, as a printer's type, for reproducing the letter *T* or *t.* **6. to a T,** exactly; perfectly: *That job would suit you to a T.* Also, **to a tee.**

T, tesla; teslas.

T, 1. the 20th in order or in a series, or, when *I* is omitted, the 19th. **2.** absolute temperature. **3.** surface tension. **4.** *Math.* a symbol followed by a subscript indicating the relation between points and closed sets in topological spaces.

t, *Statistics.* distribution.

't, a shortened form of *it,* before or after a verb, as in *'twas, 'tis, do't, see't.*

T-, *U.S. Mil.* (in designations of aircraft) trainer: *T-11.*

t-, *Chem.* tertiary.

-t, var. of **-ed** used in forming the past tense or past participle of certain verbs, usually occurring when the final consonant of the stem is voiceless and there is internal vowel change in the root: *slept.* [ptp.: ME, OE *-t, -(e)d,* OE *-od;* past tense: ME, OE *-te, -(e)de,* OE *-ode*]

T., 1. tablespoon; tablespoonful. **2.** Territory. **3.** township. **4.** Tuesday.

t., 1. *Football.* tackle. **2.** taken from. **3.** tare. **4.** teaspoon; teaspoonful. **5.** temperature. **6.** in the time of. [< L *tempore*] **7.** tenor. **8.** *Gram.* tense. **9.** territory. **10.** time. **11.** tome. **12.** ton. **13.** town. **14.** township. **15.** transitive.

Ta, *Chem.* tantalum.

Taal (täl), *n.* Afrikaans (usually prec. by *the*). [< D: language, speech; c. TALE]

Ta·al (tä äl′), *n.* an active volcano in the Philippines, on SW Luzon, on an island in Taal Lake. 1050 ft.

tab¹ (tab), *n., v.,* **tabbed, tab·bing.** —*n.* **1.** a small flap, strap, loop, or similar appendage, as on a garment, used for pulling, hanging, decoration, etc. **2.** a small piece attached or intended to be attached, as to an automobile license plate. **3.** a small projection from a paper, card, or folder, used as an aid in filing. **4.** *Aeron.* a small airfoil hinged to the rear portion of a control surface, as to an elevator, aileron, or rudder. Cf. **trim tab. 5. keep tab** or **tabs on,** *Informal.* to keep an account of; check on; observe. —*v.t.* **6.** to furnish or ornament with a tab or tabs. **7.** to name or designate. [?]

tab² (tab), *n.* **1.** tabulator (def. 2). [by shortening] **2.** *Informal.* an unpaid bill, as in a restaurant; check. [short for TABULATION]

tab., 1. (in prescriptions) tablet. [< L *tabella*] **2.** table; tables.

tab·a·nid (tab′ə nid), *n.* **1.** any of numerous bloodsucking, dipterous insects of the family *Tabanidae,* comprising the deer flies and horseflies. —*adj.* **2.** belonging or pertaining to the family *Tabanidae.* [back formation from NL *tabānidae,* based on L *tabān(us)* horse fly; see -IDAE]

tab·ard (tab′ərd), *n.* **1.** a loose, usually sleeveless, outer garment, worn by a knight over his armor. **2.** an official garment of a herald, emblazoned with the arms of his master. **3.** a short coat, with or without sleeves, formerly worn outdoors. [ME < OF *tabart*] —**tab′ard·ed,** *adj.*

Tabard (def. 2)

tab·a·ret (tab′ə rit), *n.* a durable silk or acetate fabric having alternating stripes of satin and moire, for drapery and upholstery. [? akin to TABBY]

Ta·bas·co (tə bas′kō; *Sp.* tä väs′kō), *n.* a state in SE Mexico, on the Gulf of Campeche. 496,340 (1960); 9783 sq. mi. *Cap.:* Villahermosa.

Ta·bas·co (tə bas′kō), *n. Trademark.* a pungent condiment sauce prepared from the fruit of a variety of capsicum.

tab·by (tab′ē), *n., pl.* **-bies,** *adj., v.,* **-bied, -by·ing.** —*n.* **1.** a cat with a striped or brindled coat. **2.** a domestic cat, esp. a female one. **3.** a gossipy old maid; spinster. **4.** See **plain weave. 5.** a watered silk fabric, or any other watered material, as moreen. —*adj.* **6.** striped or brindled. **7.** made of or resembling tabby. —*v.t.* **8.** to give a wavy or watered appearance to, as silk. [back formation from F *tabis* (taken as pl.), MF *(a)tabis* silk cloth < ML *attābi* < Ar *'attābī,* short for *Al 'attābīya* quarter of Baghdad where first made, lit., the quarter of (Prince) 'Attab]

tab·er·nac·le (tab′ər nak′əl), *n., v.,* **-led, -ling.** —*n.* **1.** a temporary dwelling, as a tent or hut. **2.** a dwelling place. **3.** *Judaism.* the portable sanctuary used by the Jews from the time of their post-Exodus wandering in the wilderness to the building of Solomon's Temple. Ex. 25–27. **4.** any place or house of worship, esp. one designed for a large congregation. **5.** a canopied niche or recess, as for an image or icon. **6.** *Eccles.* an ornamental receptacle for the reserved Eucharist. **7.** the human body as the temporary abode of the soul. **8.** *Naut.* a raised support holding a mast in such a way that it can be readily lowered to the deck. —*v.t., v.i.* **9.** to place or dwell in, or as in, a tabernacle. [ME < eccl. L *tabernācul(um)* tent, booth, double dim. of *taberna* hut, shed, TAVERN] —**tab·er·nac·u·lar** (tab′ər nak′yə lər), *adj.*

ta·bes (tā′bēz), *n. Pathol.* **1.** a gradually progressive emaciation. **2.** See **tabes dorsalis.** [< L: wasting, decay, akin to *tābēre* to waste away]

ta·bes·cent (tə bes′ənt), *adj.* wasting away; becoming emaciated or consumed. [< L *tābēscent-,* s. of *tābēscēns,* prp. of *tābēscere.* See TABES, -ESCENT] —**ta·bes′cence,** *n.*

ta′bes dor·sa′lis (dôr sā′lis), *Pathol.* syphilis of the spinal cord and its appendages, characterized by various sensory disturbances and, in the later stages, by loss of muscular control and paralysis. Also called **locomotor ataxia.** [< NL: lit., tabes of the back]

tab′ key′, tabulator (def. 2).

tab·la·ture (tab′lə chər), *n.* **1.** a tabular space, surface, or structure. **2.** *Music.* any of various systems of musical notation using letters, numbers, or other signs to indicate the strings, frets, or keys to be played. [< F < It *tavolatur(a)* = *tavolat(o)* wooden floor, wainscoting (< L *tabulātum;* see TABULATE) + *-ura* -URE]

ta·ble (tā′bəl) *n., v.,* **-bled, -bling,** *adj.* —*n.* **1.** an article of furniture consisting of a flat, slablike top supported by one or more legs. **2.** such a piece of furniture specifically used for serving food to those seated at it. **3.** the food served at a table. **4.** the service used at a table. **5.** a group of persons at a table, as for a meal, game, or business transaction. **6.** a gaming table. **7.** a flat or plane surface; a level area. **8.** a tableland or plateau. **9.** *Archit.* **a.** a course or band, esp. of masonry, having a distinctive form or position. **b.** a distinctively treated surface on a wall. **10. tables, a.** tablets on which laws were inscribed by the ancients: *the Twelve Tables of Rome.* **b.** the laws themselves. **11.** an arrangement of words, numbers, or signs, or combinations of them, as in parallel columns, to exhibit a set of facts or relations in a definite, compact, and comprehensive form; a synopsis or scheme. **12.** *Jewelry.* **a.** the upper horizontal surface of a faceted gem. **b.** a gem with such a surface. **13. on the table,** *U.S. Parl. Proc.* postponed. **14. turn the tables,** to reverse an existing situation so that it may be used against persons or groups in opposition: *Fortune turned the tables and we won.* Also, **turn the tables on. 15. under the table,** *Informal.* **a.** drunk. **b.** as a bribe: *She gave money under the table to get the apartment.* **16. wait (on) table,** to work as a waiter; serve food. —*v.t.* **17.** to place (a card, money, etc.) on a table. **18.** to enter in or form into a table or list. **19.** *U.S. Parl. Proc.* to lay aside a proposal, resolution, etc.) for future discussion, or for an indefinite period of time. —*adj.* **20.** of, for, pertaining to, or for use on a table: *a table radio.* **21.** suitable for serving at a table or for eating or drinking: *table grapes.* [ME; OE *tablu, tabule,* var. of *tabula* < L: plank, tablet] —**ta′ble·less,** *adj.*

tab·leau (tab′lō, ta blō′), *n., pl.* **tab·leaux** (tab′lōz, tablōz′), **tab·leaus. 1.** a picture, as of a scene. **2.** a picturesque grouping of persons or objects; a striking scene. **3.** a representation of a picture, statue, scene, etc., by one or more persons suitably costumed and posed. [< F: board, picture, MF *tablel,* dim. of *table* TABLE]

ta·bleau vi·vant (tᴀ blō′ vē väɴ′), *pl.* **ta·bleaux vi·vants** (tᴀ blō′ vē väɴ′). *French.* tableau (def. 3). [lit., living picture]

ta·ble·cloth (tā′bəl klôth′, -kloth′), *n., pl.* **-cloths** (-klôthz′, -klothz′, -klôths′, -kloths′). a cloth for covering the top of a table, esp. during a meal.

ta·ble d'hôte (tab′əl dōt′, tä′bəl; *Fr.* tᴀ blᵊ dōt′), *pl.* **ta·bles d'hôte** (tab′əlz dōt′, tä′bəlz; *Fr.* tᴀ blᵊ dōt′). a meal of prearranged courses served at a fixed time and price to the guests at a restaurant. Cf. **à la carte, prix fixe.** [< F: lit., the host's table] —**ta′ble-d'hôte′,** *adj.*

ta·ble-hop (tā′bəl hop′), *v.i.,* **-hopped, -hop·ping.** *Informal.* to move about in a restaurant, night club, or the like, chatting with people at various tables. —**ta′ble-hop′per,** *n.*

ta·ble·land (tā′bəl land′), *n.* an elevated and generally level region of considerable extent; plateau.

ta′ble lin′en, tablecloths, napkins, etc.

Ta′ble Moun′tain, a mountain in the Republic of South Africa, near Cape Town. 3550 ft.

ta′ble salt′, salt (def. 1).

ta·ble·spoon (tā′bəl spo͞on′, -spo͝on′), *n.* **1.** a spoon larger than a teaspoon or a dessert spoon, used in serving food at the table and as a standard measuring unit in recipes. **2.** a tablespoonful.

ta·ble·spoon·ful (tā′bəl spo͞on′fo͝ol, -spo͝on′-), *n., pl.* **-fuls. 1.** the amount a tablespoon can hold. **2.** *Cookery.* a volumetric measure equal to ½ fluid ounce; three teaspoonfuls. *Abbr.:* T., tbs.

tab·let (tab′lit), *n., v.,* **-let·ed, -let·ing** or **-let·ted, -let·ting.** —*n.* **1.** a number of sheets of writing paper, office forms, etc., fastened together at the edge; pad. **2.** a flat slab or surface, esp. one bearing or intended to bear an inscription, carving, or the like. **3.** a thin, flat leaf or sheet of rigid material, used for writing or marking on, esp. one of a pair or set fastened together. **4. tablets,** the set as a whole. **5.** a small, flat, or flattish cake or piece of some solid or solidified substance, as a drug, chemical, soap, or the like. —*v.t.* **6.** to furnish or mark with a tablet or plaque. **7.** to mark or inscribe (memoranda, notes, etc.) on a tablet. **8.** to form into tablets, cakes, etc. [ME *tablette* < MF *tablete.* See TABLE, -ET]

ta′ble talk′, informal conversation at meals.

ta′ble ten′nis, a variety of tennis played on a table, using small paddles and a hollow celluloid or plastic ball.

ta·ble·ware (tā′bəl wâr′), *n.* the dishes, utensils, etc., used at the table.

ta′ble wine′, a wine that contains not more than 14 percent alcohol and is usually served with meals.

tab·loid (tab′loid), *n.* **1.** a newspaper whose pages are approximately 11 x 15 inches, about half the size of a standard-size newspaper page. **2.** such a newspaper that concentrates on sensational news, usually heavily illustrated. —*adj.* **3.** compressed or condensed in or as in a tabloid. **4.** luridly sensational: *tabloid reporting.* [TABL(ET) + -OID] —**tab′loid·ism,** *n.*

ta·boo (tə bo͞o′, ta-), *adj., n., pl.* **-boos,** *v.,* **-booed, -boo·ing.** —*adj.* **1.** proscribed by society as improper and unacceptable: *taboo words.* **2.** (among the Polynesians and other peoples of the South Pacific) separated or set apart as sacred or profane; forbidden for general use. —*n.* **3.** a prohibition or interdiction of anything; exclusion from use or practice. **4.** exclusion from social relations; ostracism. **5.** (among the Polynesians and other peoples of the South Pacific) the system or practice of setting things apart as sacred or forbidden for general use. —*v.t.* **6.** to put under a taboo; prohibit or forbid. **7.** to ostracize (a person, group, etc.). Also, **tabu.** [< Tongan *tabu* set apart, inviolable] —**Syn. 1, 2.** prohibited, banned. **6.** See **forbid.**

ta·bor (tā′bər), *n.* **1.** a small drum formerly used to accompany oneself on a pipe or fife. —*v.i.* **2.** to play upon or as upon a tabor; drum. —*v.t.* **3.** to strike or beat, as on a tabor. Also, **ta′bour.** [ME < OF *tab(o)ur* << Pers *tabūrāk* drum] —**ta′bor·er, ta′bour·er,** *n.*

T, Tabor

Ta·bor (tā′bər), *n.* **Mount,** a mountain in N Israel, E of Nazareth. 1929 ft.

tab·o·ret (tab′ə rit, tab′ə ret′), *n.* **1.** a low seat without back or arms, for one person; stool. **2.** a frame for embroidery. **3.** a small tabor. Also, **tab′ou·ret.** [var. of *tabouret* < F: lit., small drum. See TABOR, -ET]

tab·o·rin (tab′ər in), *n.* a small tabor. [< MF *tabourin*]

Ta·briz (tä brēz′), *n.* a city in and the capital of Azerbaijan province, in NW Iran. 403,413 (est. 1967).

ta·bu (tə bo͞o′, ta-), *adj., n., v.t.* taboo.

tab·u·lar (tab′yə lər), *adj.* **1.** of, pertaining to, or arranged in a table or systematic arrangement by columns, rows, etc., as statistics. **2.** ascertained from or computed by the use of tables. **3.** having the form of a table, tablet, or tablature. [< L *tabulār(is)* pertaining to a board or tablet. See TABLE, -AR[1]] —**tab′u·lar·ly,** *adv.*

ta·bu·la ra·sa (tab′yə lə rā′sə, rä′-; *Lat.* tä′bo͞o lä′ rä′sä), *pl.* **ta·bu·lae ra·sae** (tab′yə lē′ rā′sē, rä′-; *Lat.* tä′bo͝o lī′ rä′sī). a mind not yet affected by experiences, impressions, etc. [< L: scraped tablet; clean slate]

tab·u·lar·ise (tab′yə lə rīz′), *v.t.,* **-ised, -is·ing.** *Chiefly Brit.* tabularize. —**tab′u·lar·i·sa′tion,** *n.*

tab·u·lar·ize (tab′yə lə rīz′), *v.t.,* **-ized, -iz·ing.** to tabulate. —**tab′u·lar·i·za′tion,** *n.*

tab·u·late (*v.* tab′yə lāt′; *adj.* tab′yə lit, -lāt′), *v.,* **-lat·ed, -lat·ing,** *adj.* —*v.t.* **1.** to put or arrange in a tabular, systematic, or condensed form; formulate tabularly. —*v.i.* **2.** to set or operate the tabulator on a typewriter. —*adj.* **3.** shaped like a table or tablet; tabular. **4.** having transverse dissepiments, as certain corals. [< L *tabulāt(us)* boarded, planked. See TABLE, -ATE[1]] —**tab′u·la·ble,** *adj.* —**tab′u·la′tion,** *n.*

tab·u·la·tor (tab′yə lā′tər), *n.* **1.** a person or thing that tabulates. **2.** Also called **tab, tab key.** a typewriter key for moving the carriage a set number of spaces to the left each time it is depressed, used for typing material in columns, for fixed indentions, and the like.

tac·a·ma·hac (tak′ə mə hak′), *n.* **1.** any of certain resinous substances, used in incenses, ointments, etc. **2.** any tree, as of the genera *Bursera* and *Protium,* yielding such a product. **3.** See **balsam poplar.** Also, **tac·a·ma·hac·a** (tak′ə mə hak′ə), **tacmahack.** [< Sp *tacama(ha)c(a)* < Nahuatl *tecomahca* smelling copal]

tace (tas, tās), *n. Armor.* tasset.

ta·cet (tach′it, tā′sit, tä′ket), *v. imperative. Music.* be silent (directing an instrument or voice not to play or sing). [< L: lit., (it) is silent]

tach (tak), *n. Informal.* tachometer. [by shortening]

tache (tach), *n. Archaic.* a buckle; clasp. Also, **tach.** [late ME < MF < Gmc. See TACK[1]]

tach′i·na fly′ (tak′ə nə), any of numerous dipterous insects of the family *Tachinidae,* the larvae of which are parasitic on caterpillars, beetles, and other insects. [< NL *Tachina* genus of flies < Gk *tachinē,* c. *tach(ýs)* swift + *-inē,* fem. of *-inos* -INE[1]]

Ta Ch'ing (dä′ ching′), Ch'ing.

tachisto-, a learned borrowing from Greek meaning "swiftest," used in the formation of compound words: *tachistoscope.* Cf. **tacho-, tachy-.** [< Gk *táchisto(s),* superl. of *tachýs* swift]

ta·chis·to·scope (tə kis′tə skōp′), *n. Psychol.* an apparatus for exposing visual stimuli, as pictures, letters, or words, for an extremely brief period: used esp. for testing perception. —**ta·chis·to·scop·ic** (tə kis′tə skop′ik), *adj.* —**ta·chis′to·scop′i·cal·ly,** *adv.*

tacho-, a learned borrowing from Greek meaning "speed," used in the formation of compound words: *tachometer.* Cf. **tachisto-, tachy-.** [comb. form repr. Gk *táchos;* akin to *tachýs* swift]

ta·chom·e·ter (ta kom′i tər, tə-), *n.* **1.** any of various instruments for measuring or indicating velocity or speed, as of a machine, a river, the blood, etc. **2.** an instrument measuring revolutions per minute, as of an engine. —**tach·o·met·ri·cal·ly** (tak′ə me′trik lē), *adv.* —**ta·chom′e·try,** *n.*

tachy-, a learned borrowing from Greek meaning "swift," used in the formation of compound words: *tachygraphy.* Cf. **tachisto-, tacho-.** [< Gk, comb. form of *tachýs*]

tach·y·car·di·a (tak′ə kär′dē ə), *n. Med.* excessively rapid heartbeat.

tach·y·graph (tak′ə graf′, -gräf′), *n.* **1.** tachygraphic writing. **2.** a person who writes or is skilled in writing tachygraphy.

ta·chyg·ra·phy (ta kig′rə fē, tə-), *n.* the Greek and Roman handwriting used for rapid stenography and writing. —**ta·chyg′ra·pher, ta·chyg′ra·phist,** *n.* —**tach·y·graph·ic** (tak′ə graf′ik), **tach′y·graph′i·cal,** *adj.* —**tach′y·graph′i·cal·ly,** *adv.*

tach·y·lyte (tak′ə līt′), *n.* a black, glassy form of basalt, readily fusible and of a high luster. Also, **tach′y·lite′.** —**tach·y·lit·ic** (tak′ə lit′ik), *adj.*

ta·chym·e·ter (ta kim′i tər, tə-), *n. Survey.* any of several instruments for determining, in a single operation, distances, directions, and differences of elevation.

ta·chym·e·try (ta kim′i trē, tə-), *n. Survey.* the science of measuring distances with a tachymeter. [< F *tachymétrie*]

tac·it (tas′it), *adj.* **1.** silent; saying nothing: *a tacit partner.* **2.** understood without being openly expressed; implied: *tacit approval.* **3.** unvoiced or unspoken: *a tacit prayer.* [< L *tacit(us)* silent, ptp. of *tacēre;* c. Goth *thahan;* akin to Icel *thegja*] —**tac′it·ly,** *adv.* —**tac′it·ness,** *n.* —**Syn. 2.** implicit. **3.** unexpressed, unsaid. —**Ant. 3.** expressed.

tac·i·turn (tas′i tûrn′), *adj.* **1.** inclined to silence; reserved in speech. **2.** dour, stern, and silent in expression and manner. [< L *taciturn(us),* quiet = *tacit(us)* silent + *-urnus* adj. suffix of time] —**tac′i·tur′ni·ty,** *n.* —**tac′i·turn′ly,** *adv.* —**Syn. 1.** uncommunicative, reticent.

Tac·i·tus (tas′i təs), *n.* **Pub·li·us Cornelius** (pub′lē əs), A.D. c55–c120, Roman historian. —**Tac·i·te·an** (tas′i tē′ən), *adj.*

tack[1] (tak), *n.* **1.** a short, sharp-pointed nail, usually with a flat, broad head. **2.** a stitch, esp. a long stitch used in fastening seams, preparatory to a more thorough sewing. **3.** a fastening, esp. of a temporary kind. **4.** stickiness, as of nearly dry paint or glue; adhesiveness. **5.** *Naut.* **a.** a rope for extending the weather clew of a course. **b.** the weather clew of a course. **c.** the lower forward corner of a fore-and-aft sail. **d.** a line secured to the lower outboard corner of a studdingsail to haul it to the end of the boom. **e.** the heading of a sailing vessel, when sailing close-hauled, with reference to the wind direction. **f.** a course run obliquely against the wind. **g.** one of the series of straight runs that make up the zigzag course of a ship proceeding to windward. **6.** a course of action, esp. one differing from some preceding course. **7.** the gear used in equipping a horse, including saddle, bridle, etc. **8. on the wrong tack,** under a misapprehension; in error; astray. —*v.t.* **9.** to fasten by a tack or tacks. **10.** to secure by some slight or temporary fastening. **11.** to join together; unite; combine. **12.** to attach as something supplementary; append; annex (often fol. by *on* or *onto*). **13.** *Naut.* **a.** to change the course of (a sailing vessel) to the opposite tack. **b.** to navigate (a sailing vessel) by a series of tacks. **14.** to equip (a horse) with tack. —*v.i.* **15.** *Naut.* **a.** to change the course of a sailing vessel. **b.** (of a sailing vessel) to change course. **c.** to proceed to windward by a series of tacks, the wind being alternately on one bow and then on the other. **16.** to take or follow a zigzag course or route. **17.** to change one's course of action, conduct, ideas, etc. **18.** to equip a horse with tack (usually fol. by *up*): *Please tack up quickly.* [ME *tak* buckle, clasp, nail (later, tack); c. G *Zacke* prong, D *tak* twig. See TACHE] —**tack′er,** *n.* —**tack′less,** *adj.*

tack[2] (tak), *n.* food; fare. [?]

tack′ ham′mer, a light hammer for driving tacks, often magnetized to hold the tack to the head.

tack·le (tak′əl *or, for 2,* tā′kəl), *n., v.,* **-led, -ling.** —*n.* **1.** equipment, apparatus, or gear, esp. for fishing. **2.** any system of leverage using pulleys, as a combination of ropes and blocks for hoisting, lowering, and shifting objects or materials; purchase. **3.** *Naut.* the gear and running rigging for handling a vessel or performing some task on a vessel. **4.** an act of tackling, as in football; a seizing or grasping. **5.** *Football.* either of the linemen stationed between a guard and an end. **6.** (formerly) tack[1] (def. 7). —*v.t.* **7.** to undertake to handle, master, solve, etc.: *to tackle a difficult problem.* **8.** to deal with (a person) on some problem, issue, etc. **9.** to harness (a horse). **10.** *Football.* to seize, stop, or throw down (a ball-carrier). —*v.i.* **11.** *Football.* to tackle an opponent having the ball. [ME *takel* gear < MLG; akin to TAKE] —**tack′ler,** *n.*

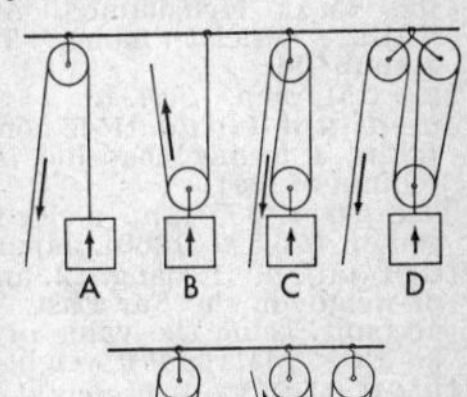

Tackles (def. 2)
A, Single whip; B, Runner; C, Gun tackle; D, Luff tackle; E, Single Spanish burton; F, Bell purchase

tack·ling (tak′ling), *n. Archaic.* equipment; tackle. [late ME]

tack′ room′, a room in or near a stable for storing saddles, harnesses, and other tack.

tack·y[1] (tak′ē), *adj.,* **tack·i·er, tack·i·est.** sticky; adhesive. [TACK[1] + -Y[1]] —**tack′i·ness,** *n.*

tack·y[2] (tak′ē), *adj.,* **tack·i·er, tack·i·est.** *Informal.* shabby or dowdy in appearance. [?]

Ta·clo·ban (tä klō′bän), *n.* a seaport on NE Leyte, in the central Philippines. 56,703 (est. 1960).

tac·ma·hack (tak′mə hak′), *n.* tacamahac.

Tac·na-A·ri·ca (täk′nä ä rē′kä), *n.* a maritime region in W South America: long in dispute between Chile and Peru; annexed by Chile 1883; divided into a Peruvian department **(Tac′na)** and a Chilean department **(Arica)** as a result of arbitration in 1929.

ta·co (tä′kō; *Sp.* tä′kô), *n., pl.* **-cos** (-kōz; *Sp.* -kôs). a tortilla folded into a turnover or roll with a filling, usually fried. [< MexSp < Sp: bung, snack]

Ta·co·ma (tə kō′mə), *n.* **1.** a seaport in W Washington, on Puget Sound. 154,581 (1970). **2. Mount.** See **Rainier, Mount.** —**Ta·co′man,** *n.*

tac·o·nite (tak′ə nīt′), *n.* a low-grade iron ore, containing about 27 percent iron and 51 percent silica. [*Tacon(ic)* mountain range (east of Hudson river) + -ITE[1]]

tact (takt), *n.* **1.** a keen sense of what to say or do to avoid giving offense; skill in dealing with difficult or delicate situations. **2.** a keen feeling or sense for what is appropriate, tasteful, or aesthetically pleasing; taste; discrimination. [< L *tact(us)* sense of touch = *tact-* (ptp. s. of *tangere* to touch) + *-us* n. suffix (4th decl.)] —**Syn. 1.** perception, sensitivity; diplomacy, poise, aplomb.

tact·ful (takt′fəl), *adj.* having or manifesting tact. —**tact′ful·ly,** *adv.* —**tact′ful·ness,** *n.* —**Syn.** adroit, skillful, clever. —**Ant.** tactless.

tac·tic (tak′tik), *n.* **1.** tactics. **2.** a system or a detail of tactics. —*adj.* **3.** of or pertaining to arrangement or order; tactical. [NL *tactic(us)* < Gk *taktikós* fit for arranging or ordering = *tak-* (verbid s. of *tássein, táttein* to arrange, place in order) + *-tikos* -TIC]

tac·ti·cal (tak′ti kəl), *adj.* **1.** of or pertaining to tactics, esp. military tactics. **2.** characterized by skillful tactics or by adroit maneuvering, technique, or procedure. —**tac′ti·cal·ly,** *adv.*

tac·ti·cian (tak tish′ən), *n.* a person who is adept in planning tactics.

tac·tics (tak′tiks), *n.* **1.** (*usually construed as sing.*) the art or science of disposing military forces for battle and maneuvering them in battle. **2.** (*construed as pl.*) the maneuvers themselves. **3.** (*construed as pl.*) any maneuvers for gaining advantage or success. [see TACTIC, -ICS] —**Syn. 1.** See **strategy.**

tac·tile (tak′til, -tīl), *adj.* **1.** of, pertaining to, endowed with, or affecting the sense of touch. **2.** perceptible to the touch; capable of being touched; tangible. [< L *tactil(is)* tangible = *tact-* (ptp. s. of *tangere* to touch) + *-ilis* -ILE] —**tac·til·i·ty** (tak til′i tē), *n.*

tac·tion (tak′shən), *n.* touch; contact. [< L *tactiōn-* (s. of *tactiō*) a touching = *tact-* (ptp. s. of *tangere* to touch) + *-iōn-* -ION]

tact·less (takt′lis), *adj.* lacking tact; undiplomatic; offendingly blunt: *a tactless remark.* —**tact′less·ly,** *adv.* —**tact′less·ness,** *n.*

tac·tu·al (tak′cho͞o əl), *adj.* **1.** of or pertaining to the sense of touch. **2.** communicating or imparting the sensation of contact; arising from or due to touch. [< L *tactu(s)* touch (see TACT) + -AL[1]] —**tac′tu·al·ly,** *adv.*

Ta·cu·ba·ya (tä′ko͞o bä′yä), *n.* a former city in the Federal District of Mexico: now a district of Mexico City; national observatory.

tad (tad), *n.* *U.S. Informal.* a small child, esp. a boy. [short for TADPOLE]

Ta·djik (tä′jik), *n., pl.* **-djik** for 1. **1.** Tajik. **2.** Tadzhikistan.

tad·pole (tad′pōl′), *n.* the aquatic larva or immature form of frogs, toads, etc., esp. after the enclosure of the gills and before the appearance of the forelimbs and the resorption of the tail. [late ME *taddepol* = *tadde* TOAD + *pol* POLL (head)]

Tadpoles in early stages of growth

Ta·dzhik (tä′jik), *n., pl.* **-dzhik** for 1. **1.** Tajik. **2.** Tadzhikistan.

Ta·dzhik·i·stan (tə jik′i stan′, -stän′; *Russ.* tä ji ki stän′), *n.* a constituent republic of the Soviet Union in Asia, N of Afghanistan. 2,500,000 (est. 1965). 55,019 sq. mi. *Cap.:* Dyushambe. Also called **Tadjik, Tadzhik, Tajik.** Official name, **Ta′dzhik So′viet So′cialist Repub′lic.**

tae (tā), *prep. Scot.* to.

tae·di·um vi·tae (tī′dē o͝om′ wē′tī; *Eng.* tē′dē əm vī′tē), *Latin.* a feeling that life is unbearably wearisome. [lit., tedium of life]

Tae·gu (tī′go͞o′), *n.* a city in SE South Korea: commercial center. 676,692 (1960). Japanese, **Taikyu.**

tael (tāl), *n.* **1.** liang. **2.** any of various other similar units of weight in the Far East. **3.** a former Chinese money of account, being the value of this weight of standard silver. [< Pg < Malay *tahil* weight]

ta′en (tān), *v. Archaic.* taken. [ME *(y)tan, tane, tain,* var. of TAKEN]

tae·ni·a (tē′nē ə), *n., pl.* **-ni·ae** (-nē ē′). **1.** *Class. Antiq.* a headband or fillet. **2.** *Anat.* a ribbonlike structure, as certain bands of white nerve fibers in the brain. **3.** any tapeworm of the genus *Taenia,* parasitic in man and other mammals. Also, **tenia.** [< L < Gk *tainía* band, ribbon]

tae·ni·a·cide (tē′nē ə sīd′), *Med.* —*adj.* **1.** Also, **tae′ni·a·cid′al, teniacidal.** destroying tapeworms. —*n.* **2.** an agent that destroys tapeworms. Also, **teniacide.**

tae·ni·a·fuge (tē′nē ə fyo͞oj′), *Med.* —*adj.* **1.** expelling tapeworms, as a medicine. —*n.* **2.** an agent or medicine for expelling tapeworms from the body. Also, **teniafuge.**

tae·ni·a·sis (tē nī′ə sis), *n. Pathol.* the condition of being infested with tapeworms. Also, **teniasis.**

taf·fa·rel (taf′ər əl, -ə rel′), *n. Archaic.* taffrail. Also, **taf′fe·rel.** [< MD *tafereel,* var. (by dissimilation) of *tafeleel* < F (dial.) *tavlel* TABLEAU]

taf·fe·ta (taf′i tə), *n.* **1.** a smooth, crisp, lustrous fabric of acetate, nylon, rayon, or silk in plain weave. **2.** any of various other fabrics of silk, linen, wool, etc., in use at different periods in history. —*adj.* **3.** of or resembling taffeta. [ME *taffata* < ML << Pers *tāftah* silken or linen cloth, n. use of ptp. of *tāftan* to twist, spin]

taf′feta weave′. See **plain weave.**

taff·rail (taf′rāl′), *n. Naut.* **1.** the upper part of the stern of a vessel. **2.** a rail above or around the stern of a vessel. [syncopated var. of TAFFAREL; *-ai-* repr. D *-ee-*]

T, Taffrail (def. 2)

taf·fy (taf′ē), *n.* **1.** a candy made of sugar or molasses boiled down, often with butter, nuts, etc. **2.** *Informal.* flattery. Also, *esp. Brit.,* **toffee, toffy.** [var. of TOFFEE]

taf·i·a (taf′ē ə), *n.* a type of rum made in Haiti from lower grades of molasses, refuse sugar, or the like. Also, **taf′fi·a.** [< F (WInd Creole dial.); aph. var. of *ratafia* RATAFIA]

Ta·fi·lelt (tä fē′lelt), *n.* a large, populated, agricultural oasis in SE Morocco: date-growing center. ab. 200 sq. mi. Also, **Ta·fi·la·let** (tä′fē lä′let).

Taft (taft), *n.* **1. Robert A(l·phon·so)** (al fon′sō), 1889–1953, U.S. lawyer, senator, and political leader (son of William Howard). **2. William Howard,** 1857–1930, 27th president of the U.S. 1909–13; Chief Justice of the U.S. Supreme Court 1921–30.

tag[1] (tag), *n., v.,* **tagged, tag·ging.** —*n.* **1.** a piece or strip of strong paper, etc., for attaching by one end to something as a mark or label: *The price is on the tag.* **2.** any small, loosely attached, or hanging part or piece; tatter. **3.** a hard tip at the end of a shoelace, cord, or the like. **4.** *Angling.* a small piece of tinsel, or the like, tied to the shank of a hook at the body of an artificial fly. **5.** the very end or concluding part, as the final speech in a play. **6.** an addition to a speech or writing, as the moral of a fable. **7.** a quotation added for special effect. **8.** a descriptive word or phrase applied to a person, group, etc., as a label or means of identification; epithet. **9.** *Informal.* a person who follows another closely, as to spy upon him. **10.** a curlicue in writing. **11.** a lock of hair. **12.** a matted lock of wool on a sheep. **13.** *Fox Hunting.* the white tip of the tail of a fox. **14.** *Obs.* the rabble. —*v.t.* **15.** to furnish with a tag or tags; attach a tag to. **16.** to append as a tag, addition, or afterthought, to something else. **17.** to attach or give an epithet to; label. **18.** to give a traffic ticket to. **19.** to hold accountable for something; attach blame to. **20.** to set a price on; fix the cost of. **21.** *Informal.* to follow closely: *I tagged him to an old house at the outskirts of town.* **22.** to remove the tags of wool from (a sheep). —*v.i.* **23.** *Informal.* to follow closely: *to tag after someone; to tag along behind someone.* [late ME *tagge;* c. MLG, Norw *tagge,* Sw *tagg* pointed protruding part; akin to TACK[1]] —**tag′like′,** *adj.*

tag[2] (tag), *n., v.,* **tagged, tag·ging.** —*n.* **1.** a children's game in which one player chases the others till he touches one of them, the one caught then becoming pursuer. **2.** *Baseball.* the act or an instance of tagging a base runner. —*v.t.* **3.** to touch in or as in the game of tag. **4.** *Baseball.* **a.** to touch (a base runner) with the ball held in the hand or glove. **b.** *Slang.* to hit (a pitched ball) solidly. **5.** *Boxing.* to strike (an opponent) with a powerful blow. [? special use of TAG[1]]

Ta·ga·log (tä gä′log, tag′ə log′), *n., pl.* **-logs,** (*esp. collectively*) **-log** for 1. **1.** a member of a Malayan people native to Luzon, in the Philippines. **2.** the principal Indonesian language of the Philippines.

Ta·gan·rog (tä′gän rôk′), *n.* **1.** a seaport in the S Soviet Union in Europe, on the Gulf of Taganrog. 220,000 (est. 1962). **2. Gulf of,** a NE arm of the Sea of Azov.

tag′ day′, *U.S.* a day on which contributions to a fund are solicited, each contributor receiving a tag.

tag′ end′, **1.** the last or final part of something. **2.** a random scrap, fragment, or remnant.

tag·ger (tag′ər), *n.* **1.** a person or thing that tags. **2.** **taggers,** *Metall.* iron or tin plate in very thin sheets.

tag·meme (tag′mēm), *n. Linguistics.* the smallest unit of grammatical form. Cf. **glosseme, morpheme.** [< Gk *tágm(a)* arrangement < *táss(ein)* (to) arrange + -EME]

Ta·gore (tə gōr′, -gôr′, tä′gôr), *n.* **Sir Ra·bin·dra·nath** (rə bēn′drə nät′), 1861–1941, Hindu poet.

tag·rag (tag′rag′), *n.* **1.** riffraff; rabble. **2.** a tatter. [TAG[1] + RAG[1]]

tag′ sale′. See **garage sale.**

Ta·gus (tā′gəs), *n.* a river in SW Europe, flowing W through central Spain and Portugal to the Atlantic at Lisbon. 566 mi. long. Spanish, **Tajo.** Portuguese, **Tejo.**

Ta·hi·ti (tə hē′tē, tä-, tī′tē), *n.* the principal island of the Society Islands, in the S Pacific. 44,710 (1956); 402 sq. mi. *Cap.:* Papeete.

Ta·hi·tian (tə hē′shən, -tē ən, tä-), *adj.* **1.** of or pertaining to Tahiti, its inhabitants, or their language. —*n.* **2.** a native or inhabitant of Tahiti. **3.** the Polynesian language of Tahiti.

Ta·hoe (tä′hō, tā′-), *n.* **Lake,** a lake in E California and W Nevada, in the Sierra Nevada Mountains: resort. ab. 200 sq. mi.; 6225 ft. above sea level.

tah·sil·dar (tə sēl där′), *n.* an official of the revenue department in India. Also, **tah·seel·dar′.** [< Urdu < Pers *taḥṣīl* collection (< Ar) + *-dār* agent suffix]

Tai (tī, tä′ē), *n., adj.* Thai.

Tai·chung (tī′jo͝ong′), *n.* a city on W Taiwan. 336,280 (est. 1963). Japanese, **Tai·chu** (tī′cho͞o′).

Ta·if (tä′if), *n.* a city in W Saudi Arabia. 53,954 (1963).

tai·ga (tī′gə), *n.* the coniferous, evergreen forests of subarctic lands, covering vast areas of northern North America and Eurasia. [< Russ < Turkic; akin to Turk *dağ* mountain]

Tai·ho·ku (tī′hô ko͞o′), *n.* Japanese name of **Taipei.**

Tai·kyu (tī kyo͞o′), *n.* Japanese name of **Taegu.**

tail[1] (tāl), *n.* **1.** the hindmost part of an animal, esp. that forming a distinct, flexible appendage to the trunk. **2.** something resembling or suggesting this in shape or position: *the tail of a kite.* **3.** the hinder, bottom, or end part of anything. **4.** the inferior or unwanted part of anything. **5.** a long braid or tress of hair. **6.** *Astron.* the luminous stream extending from the head of a comet. **7.** the reverse of a coin (opposed to *head*). **8.** a retinue; train. **9.** *Aeron.* the rear portion of an airplane or the like. **10.** the lower part of a pool or stream. **11. tails, a.** See **tail coat. b.** full-dress attire. **12.** *Slang (vulgar).* coitus or a woman considered as an object of coitus. —*adj.* **13.** coming from behind: *a tail breeze.* **14.** being in the back or rear; *a tail gun on an airplane.* —*v.t.* **15.** to form or furnish with a tail. **16.** to form or constitute the tail or end of (a procession, retinue, etc.). **17.** to join or attach (one thing) at the tail or end of another. **18.** *Building Trades.* to fasten (a beam, stone, etc.) by one end. **19.** to dock the tail of (a horse, dog, etc.). **20.** *Informal.* to follow in order to observe: *to tail a suspect.* —*v.i.* **21.** to form, or move or pass in, a line or column suggestive of a tail. **22.** (of a boat) to have or take a position with the stern in a particular direction. **23.** to recede or disappear gradually. **24.** *Building Trades.* (of a beam, stone, etc.) to be fastened by one end. **25.** *Informal.* to follow close behind. [ME; OE *tæl;* c. Icel *tagl* horse's tail, Goth *tagl* hair, MHG *zagel* tail, MLG *tagel* rope end] —**tail′less,** *adj.* —**tail′less·ly,** *adv.* —**tail′less·ness,** *n.* —**tail′like′,** *adj.*

tail[2] (tāl), *Law.* —*n.* **1.** the limitation of an estate to a person and the heirs of his body, or some particular class of such heirs. —*adj.* **2.** limited to a specified line of heirs; being in tail. [ME *taille* (n.) (< MF; see TAILLE); late ME *taille* (adj.) < AF: cut, shaped, limited, ptp. of *tailler* = OF *tailler* < LL *tāliāre.* See TAILOR] —**tail′less,** *adj.*

tail·back (tāl′bak′), *n.* *Football.* the offensive back who lines up farthest behind the line of scrimmage.

tail·board (tāl′bōrd′, -bôrd′), *n.* the tailgate, esp. of a wagon or truck.

tail′ coat′. a man's fitted coat, cutaway over the hips and descending in a pair of tapering skirts behind, usually black and worn as part of full evening dress. Also, **tail′coat′.** Also called **tails, dress coat, swallow-tailed coat.**

tail′ end′, **1.** See **rear end.** **2.** the concluding or final part or section; tag end.

tail·er (tā′lər), *n.* a person or thing that tails.

tail·first (tāl′fûrst′), *adv.* with the rear part foremost.

tail·gate[1] (tāl′gāt′), *n.*, *v.*, **-gat·ed, -gat·ing.** —*n.* **1.** the board or gate at the back of a wagon, truck, station wagon, etc., which can be removed or let down for convenience in loading or unloading. —*v.i.* **2.** to follow or drive hazardously close to the rear of another vehicle. —*v.t.* **3.** to follow or drive hazardously close to the rear of (another vehicle). [TAIL[1] + GATE]

tail·gate[2] (tāl′gāt′), *n.* *Jazz.* a style of playing the trombone, esp. in Dixieland jazz, distinguished esp. by the use of melodic counterpoint and long glissandi. [so called from the usual seat of trombonists in trucks in parades]

tail·ings (tā′liṅgz), *n., pl.* **1.** *Building Trades.* gravel, aggregate, etc., too large to pass through a given screen. **2.** the residue of any product, as in mining; leavings.

taille (tāl; *Fr.* tä′yᵊ), *n., pl.* **tailles** (tālz; *Fr.* tä′yᵊ). **1.** *French Hist.* a tax levied by a king or seigneur on his subjects or on lands held under him. **2.** (in dressmaking) the waist or bodice of a garment. [< F: lit., a cutting < *tailler,* OF *taillier* to cut, limit, tax; see TAILOR]

tail·light (tāl′līt′), *n.* a warning light, usually red, at the rear of an automobile, train, etc. Also called, *Brit.,* **tail′ lamp′.**

tai·lor (tā′lər), *n.* **1.** a person whose occupation is the making, mending, or altering of suits, coats, and other outer garments. —*v.i.* **2.** to do the work of a tailor. —*v.t.* **3.** to make by tailor's work. **4.** to fit or furnish with clothing. **5.** to fashion or adapt to a particular taste, purpose, etc. [ME < AF *tailour,* OF *tailleor* = *taill(ier)* (to) cut (< LL *tāliāre* < L *tālea* a cutting, lit., heel piece; see TALLY) + *-or* -OR[2]]

tai·lor·bird (tā′lər bûrd′), *n.* any of several small Asian passerine birds, esp. of the genus *Orthotomus,* that stitch leaves together to form and conceal their nests.

tai·lored (tā′lərd), *adj.* **1.** (of a woman's garment) in a simple or plain style with fitted lines. Cf. **dressmaker** (def. 2). **2.** having simple, straight lines and a neat appearance: *tailored slipcovers.* [TAILOR + -ED[2]]

tai·lor·ing (tā′lər iṅg), *n.* **1.** the business or work of a tailor. **2.** the skill or craftsmanship of a tailor.

tai·lor-made (*adj.* tā′lər mād′; *n.* tā′lər mād′, -mād′), *adj.* **1.** tailored. **2.** custom-made; made-to-order; made-to-measure. **3.** fashioned to a particular taste, purpose, etc. —*n.* **4.** Usually, **tailor-mades.** a tailor-made garment.

tail·piece (tāl′pēs′) *n.* **1.** a piece added at the end; an end piece or appendage. **2.** *Print.* a small decorative design at the end of a chapter or at the bottom of a page. **3.** (in a musical instrument of the violin family) a triangular piece of wood to which the lower ends of the strings are fastened.

tail·pipe (tāl′pīp′), *n.* an exhaust pipe located at the rear of a vehicle, as a car or jet-engine airplane.

tail·race (tāl′rās′), *n.* **1.** the race, flume, or channel leading away from a water wheel or the like. **2.** *Mining.* the channel for conducting tailings or refuse away in water.

tails (tālz), *adj., adv.* (of a coin) with the reverse facing up: *On the next toss, the coin came up tails.* Cf. **heads.**

tail′ skid′, *Aeron.* a runner under the tail of an airplane.

tail·spin (tāl′spin′), *n.* **1.** spin (def. 15). **2.** *Informal.* a sudden and helpless collapse into failure, confusion, or the like. Also, **tail′ spin′.**

tail·stock (tāl′stok′), *n.* a movable or sliding support for the dead center of a lathe or grinder. [TAIL[1] + STOCK]

tail·wind (tāl′wind′), *n.* a wind coming from directly behind a moving aircraft or vessel.

Tai·myr′ Penin′sula (tī mēr′), a peninsula in the N Soviet Union in Asia, between the Kara and Nordenskjöld seas. Also, **Tai·mir′ Penin′sula.**

tain (tān), *n.* **1.** a thin tin plate. **2.** tin foil for the backs of mirrors. [< F: silvering, foil, aph. var. of *étain* tin]

Tai·nan (tī′nän′), *n.* a city on SW Taiwan. 375,101 (est. 1963).

Taine (tān; *Fr.* ten), *n.* **Hip·po·lyte A·dolphe** (ē pô lēt′ A dôlf′), 1828–93, French literary critic and historian.

Tai·no (tī′nō), *n., pl.* **-nos,** (*esp. collectively*) **-no** for 1. **1.** a member of an extinct Arawakan Indian tribe of the West Indies. **2.** the language of the Taino.

taint (tānt), *n.* **1.** a trace of something bad, offensive, or harmful. **2.** a trace of infection, contamination, or the like. **3.** a trace of dishonor or discredit. **4.** *Obs.* color or tint. —*v.t.* **5.** to modify by or as by a trace of something offensive or deleterious. **6.** to infect, contaminate, or corrupt. **7.** to sully or tarnish (a person's name, reputation, etc.). **8.** *Obs.* to color or tint. —*v.i.* **9.** to become tainted. [ME *taynt* (aph. var. of *attaint* struck, attainted, ptp. of ATTAIN) + late ME *taynt* < AF *teint(er)* (to) color, dye, tinge, v. use of ptp. of *teindre* < L *tingere* to TINGE] —**taint′less,** *adj.* —**Syn. 1.** defect, spot, flaw, fault. **1, 7.** blemish, stain. **6.** defile, pollute, poison.

Tai·pei (tī′pā′; *Chin.* tī′bā′), *n.* a city in N Taiwan: provisional capital of the Republic of China. 1,076,649 (1965). Also, **Tai′peh′.** Japanese, **Taihoku.**

Tai·ping (tī′piṅg′), *n.* a person who participated in the unsuccessful rebellion (**Tai′ping′ Rebel′lion**), 1850–64, against the Manchu dynasty. [< Chin = *t'ai* great + *p'ing* peace]

Tai·wan (tī′wän′), *n.* a Chinese island separated from the SE coast of China by Formosa Strait: seat of the Republic of China since 1949. 12,257,000 (est. 1964); 13,890 sq. mi. *Cap.:* Taipei. Also called **Formosa.**

Tai·wan·ese (tī′wä nēz′, -nēs′), *adj., n., pl.* **-ese.** —*adj.* **1.** of or pertaining to Taiwan or its people. —*n.* **2.** a native or inhabitant of Taiwan.

Tai′wan′ Strait′. See **Formosa Strait.**

Tai·yüan (tī′yʏän′), *n.* a city in and the capital of Shansi, in N China. 1,020,000 (est. 1957). Formerly, **Yangkü.**

Ta·iz (ta iz′), *n.* a city in S Yemen. 80,000 (est. 1966). Also, **Ta'izz′.**

Ta·jik (tä′jik), *n., pl.* **-jik. 1.** a person of Iranian descent in Tadzhikistan and vicinity. **2.** Tadzhikistan. Also, **Tadjik, Tadzhik.**

Taj Ma·hal (täzh′ mə häl′, täj′), a white marble mausoleum built at Agra, India, by the Mogul emperor Shah Jahan (fl. 1628–58) for his favorite wife. [< Urdu: crown (i.e., finest) of buildings; reminiscent of queen's title: *mumtāz-i-mahall* Exalted One of the abode < Pers]

Ta·jo (tä′hô), *n.* Spanish name of **Tagus.**

Ta·ka·ma·tsu (tä′kä mä′tso͝o), *n.* a seaport on NE Shikoku, in SW Japan. 241,843 (1964).

Ta·kao (tä kou′), *n.* Kaohsiung.

take (tāk), *v.,* **took, tak·en, tak·ing,** *n.* —*v.t.* **1.** to get into one's hands or possession by voluntary action: *to take a book from the table.* **2.** to get into one's possession by force or artifice: *to take a bone from a snarling dog.* **3.** to seize or capture. **4.** to catch (fish, game, etc.). **5.** to hold, grasp, or grip. **6.** to pick from a number; select. **7.** to receive and accept willingly (something given or offered): *to take a bribe; to take advice.* **8.** to receive or adopt (a person) into some relation: *to take a wife.* **9.** to receive, react, or respond to in a specified manner: *She took the news hard.* **10.** to receive as a payment or charge. **11.** to gain for use by payment, lease, etc.: *to take a box at the opera.* **12.** to secure regularly or periodically by payment; subscribe to. **13.** to obtain from a source; derive. **14.** to obtain or exact as compensation: *to take revenge; to take no payment.* **15.** to receive into the body or system, as by swallowing or inhaling. **16.** to have for one's benefit or use: *to take a nap; to take a bath.* **17.** to be subjected to or undergo with equanimity: *to take a heat treatment; to take punishment.* **18.** to enter into the enjoyment of (recreation, a holiday, etc.): *to take a vacation.* **19.** to carry off or remove. **20.** to end (a life): *He took his own life.* **21.** to subtract or deduct: *If you take 2 from 5, that leaves 3.* **22.** to carry with one. **23.** to convey or transport: *We took them for a ride in the country. Will this bus take me across town?* **24.** to use as a means of transportation: *She takes the bus to work.* **25.** to get on or board (a means of transportation) at a given time or place: *He'll take the train at three.* **26.** (of a road, path, etc.) to serve as a means of conducting to or through some place or region: *These stairs will take you up to the attic.* **27.** to conduct or escort: *to take someone out for dinner.* **28.** to convey to a new state or condition: *His ambition and perseverance took him quickly to the top of his field.* **29.** to succeed in getting over, through, or around (some obstacle); clear; negotiate: *He took the corner at top speed.* **30.** to come upon suddenly; catch: *to take someone by surprise.* **31.** to get or contract; catch: *He took cold over the weekend.* **32.** to attack or affect, as with a disease. **33.** to be capable of attaining as a result of some action or treatment: *Most leathers take a high polish.* **34.** to absorb or become impregnated with; be susceptible to: *Waxed paper will not take ink.* **35.** to attract, captivate, or charm: *She took his fancy. The ribbon took her eye.* **36.** to require: *It takes courage to do that.* **37.** to employ for some specified or implied purpose: *to take measures to check an evil.* **38.** to proceed to occupy: *to take a seat.* **39.** to occupy; fill (time, space, etc.): *His hobby takes most of his spare time.* **40.** to use up; consume: *This car takes a great deal of oil.* **41.** to avail oneself of: *He took the opportunity to leave.* **42.** to do, perform, execute, etc.: *to take a walk; to take a swing at someone.* **43.** to go into or enter: *Take the next road to the left.* **44.** to adopt and enter upon (a way, course, etc.): *to take the path of least resistance.* **45.** to act or perform: *to take the part of the hero.* **46.** to make (a reproduction, picture, or photograph): *to take home movies.* **47.** to make a picture, esp. a photograph, of: *The photographer took us sitting down.* **48.** to write down: *to take a letter in shorthand.* **49.** to study: *to take ballet.* **50.** to deal with; treat: *to take things in their proper order.* **51.** to proceed to handle in some manner: *to take a matter under consideration.* **52.** to assume or adopt (a symbol, badge, or the like) as a token of office: *to take the veil; to take the throne.* **53.** to assume the obligation of: *to take responsibility; to take an oath.* **54.** to assume or adopt as one's own: *He took the side of the speaker.* **55.** to assume or appropriate as if by right. **56.** to determine by examination, observation, etc.: *to take someone's pulse; to take the census.* **57.** to experience (a certain feeling or state of mind): *to take pride in one's appearance.* **58.** to form and hold in the mind: *to take a gloomy view.* **59.** to apprehend mentally; understand: *Do you take my meaning, sir?* **60.** to understand in a specified way: *You must not take his remark as an insult.* **61.** *Chess.* to capture (a piece). **62.** *Slang.* to cheat or victimize. **63.** *Informal.* to win from, as in betting or at cards: *He took me for $5 at the poker game.* **64.** *Gram.* to be used with (a certain form, accent, case, mood, etc.). **65.** *Law.* to acquire property. **66.** *Baseball.* to allow (a pitch) to go by without swinging at it. **67.** to have sexual intercourse with. —*v.i.* **68.** to catch or engage, as a lock. **69.** to strike root, as a plant. **70.** to adhere, as ink or dye. **71.** to win favor or acceptance, as a person or thing. **72.** to have the intended result or effect, as a medicine: *The vaccination took.* **73.** to enter into possession, as of an estate. **74.** to detract (usually fol. by *from*): *So much make-up takes from her appearance.* **75.** to apply or devote oneself: *He took to his studies.* **76.** to make one's way; proceed; go. **77.** to fall or become: *He took sick and had to go home.* **78.** to admit of being photographed in a particular manner: *a model who takes exceptionally well.* **79.** to admit of being moved or separated: *This crib takes apart for easy storage.* **80. take after, a.** to resemble (another person, as a parent) physically, temperamentally, etc. **b.** Also, **take off after, take out after.** to follow; chase. **81. take back, a.** to regain possession of. **b.** to return, as for exchange. **c.** to retract. **82. take down, a.** to move from a higher to a lower level or place. **b.** to pull apart or take apart; dismantle. **c.** to write down; record. **d.** to humble. **83. take in, a.** to permit to enter; admit. **b.** to alter (an article of clothing) so as to make smaller. **c.** to provide lodging for. **d.** to include; encompass. **e.** to grasp the meaning of; comprehend. **f.** to furl (a sail). **g.** to deceive; trick; cheat. **h.** to observe; notice. **84. take it, a.** to acquiesce to; accept: *I'll take it on your say-so.* **b.** *Slang.* to be able to resist or endure hardship, abuse, etc.: *He can't take it the way he used to.* **c.** to understand: *I take it that you're not interested.* **85. take it out of,** *Informal.* **a.** to exhaust; enervate: *Every year the winter takes it out of him.* **b.** to exact payment from: *They took it out of his pay.* **86. take it out on,** *Informal.* to cause (someone else) to suffer for one's own misfortune or dissatisfaction. **87. take off, a.** to remove: *to take off one's coat.* **b.** to abduct. **c.** *Informal.* to depart; leave. **d.** to leave the ground, as an airplane. **e.** to withdraw, as from service: *He was taken off the night shift.* **f.** to remove by death; kill. **g.** to make a copy of; reproduce. **h.** to subtract, as a discount; deduct. **i.** *Informal.* to burlesque; satirize. **88. take on, a.** to hire; employ. **b.** to undertake; assume. **c.** to acquire: *The situation begins to take on a new light.* **d.** to contend against: *to take on a bully.* **e.** *Informal.* to show great emotion; become excited. **89. take out, a.** to remove; withdraw: *to take out a handkerchief.* **b.** to procure by application: *to take out an insurance policy.* **c.** to escort; invite: *He takes out my sister now and then.* **d.** to set out; start: *They took out for the nearest beach.* **90. take over,** to assume management of or responsibility for. **91. take to, a.** to devote or apply oneself to; become habituated to: *to take to drink.* **b.** to respond favorably to; begin to like: *They took to each other at once.* **c.** to go to for an extended period of time: *to take to one's bed.* **d.** to have recourse to; resort to: *She took to nagging to get her own way.* **92. take up, a.** to occupy oneself with the study or practice of. **b.** to lift or pick up. **c.** to occupy (space). **d.** to consume; use up; absorb. **e.** to begin to advocate or support. **f.** to continue; resume: *We took up where we had left off.* **g.** to assume (duties). **93. take up with,** *Informal.* to become friendly with; keep company with. —*n.* **94.** the act of taking. **95.** something that is taken. **96.** the quantity of fish, game, etc., taken at one time. **97.** *Slang.* money taken in, esp. profits. **98.** *Journalism.* a portion of copy assigned to a linotype operator or compositor. **99.** *Motion Pictures.* **a.** a scene, or a portion of a scene, photographed without any interruption or break. **b.** an instance of such continuous operation of the camera. **100.** a recording of a musical performance. **101.** *Med.* a successful inoculation. **102. on the take,** *Slang.* in search of personal profit at the expense of others. [ME *take(n)*, late OE *tacan* < Scand (cf. Icel *taka* to take); c. MD *taken* to grasp; akin to Goth *tekan* to touch] —**tak′a·ble, take′a·ble,** *adj.* —**tak′er,** *n.* —**Syn. 1.** acquire, secure, procure. See **bring. 6.** choose. **35.** delight, interest, engage. **36.** need, demand. **37.** use. **56.** ascertain. —**Ant. 1.** give.

take·down (tāk′doun′), *adj.* **1.** made or constructed so as to be easily dismantled or disassembled. —*n.* **2.** the act of taking down. **3.** a firearm designed to be swiftly disassembled or assembled. **4.** the point of separation of two or more of the parts of such a firearm. Also, **take′-down′.**

take′-home pay′ (tāk′hōm′), the amount of salary remaining after all deductions, as of withholding tax, pension contribution, etc., have been made. Also called **take′-home′.**

take-in (tāk′in′), *n.* *Informal.* a deception or fraud.

tak·en (tā′kən), *v.* pp. of **take.**

take·off (tāk′ôf′, -of′), *n.* **1.** a taking or setting off; the leaving of the ground, as in leaping or in beginning a flight in an airplane. **2.** *Informal.* a humorous or satirical imitation; burlesque. Also, **take′-off′.**

take·out (tāk′out′), *n.* **1.** the act or fact of taking out. **2.** something taken out or made to be taken out, as food in a restaurant for consumption elsewhere. **3.** *Bridge.* a bid in a suit or denomination different from the one bid by one's partner. —*adj.* **4.** Also, **take-′out′.** made to be taken out of a restaurant or serving food for consumption elsewhere: *take-out coffee; a take-out barbecue shop.*

take·o·ver (tāk′ō′vər), *n.* the act of seizing, appropriating, or arrogating authority, control, management, etc. Also, **take′-o′ver.**

take-up (tāk′up′), *n.* **1.** the act of taking up. **2.** *Mach.* **a.** uptake (def. 3). **b.** any of various devices for taking up slack, winding in, or compensating for the looseness of parts due to wear.

tak·ing (tā′king), *n.* **1.** the act of a person or thing that takes. **2.** the state of being taken. **3.** something that is taken. **4. takings,** receipts. **5.** *Archaic.* a state of agitation or distress. —*adj.* **6.** captivating, winning, or pleasing. **7.** *Obs.* infectious or contagious. [ME *takyng* (n.)]

Ta·ku (tä′ko͞o′), *n.* a fortified city in E Hopeh, in NE China, E of Tientsin: battles 1860, 1900.

tal·a·poin (tal′ə poin′), *n.* a small, yellowish guenon monkey, *Cercopithecus talapoin,* of western Africa. [< F; special use (orig. jocular) of *talapoin* Buddhist monk << Mon *tala pôi* my lord (title, proper to such monks)]

ta·lar·i·a (tə lâr′ē ə), *n.pl.* *Class. Myth.* the wings or winged sandals on the feet of Hermes, or Mercury. [< L, neut. pl. of *tālāris* = *tāl(us)* ankle + *āris* -AR¹]

Ta·la·ve·ra de la Rei·na (tä′lä ve′rä ᵺe lä rā′nä), a city in central Spain, on the Tagus River: British and Spanish defeat of the French 1809. 21,728 (est. 1960).

Tal·bot (tôl′bət), *n.* **Charles, Duke of Shrewsbury,** 1660–1718, British statesman: prime minister 1714.

talc (talk), *n.*, *v.*, **talcked** or **talced** (talkt), **talck·ing** or **talc·ing** (tal′king). —*n.* Also, **tal·cum** (tal′kəm). **1.** a green-to-gray, soft mineral, hydrous magnesium silicate, $H_2Mg_3(SiO_3)_4$, used in making lubricants, talcum powder, electrical insulation, etc. **2.** See **talcum powder.** —*v.t.* **3.** to treat or rub with talc. [< ML *talc(um)* < Ar *ṭalq* mica < Pers *talk*]

Tal·ca (täl′kä), *n.* a city in central Chile. 69,864 (est. 1959).

Tal·ca·hua·no (täl′kä wä′nô), *n.* a seaport in central Chile. 102,323 (est. 1963).

talc·ose (tal′kōs, tal kōs′), *adj.* containing or composed largely of talc. Also, **talc·ous** (tal′kəs).

tal′cum pow′der, a powder made of purified, usually perfumed talc, for toilet purposes. [< ML *talcum* TALC]

tale (tāl), *n.* **1.** a narrative that relates the details of some real or imaginary event, incident, or case; story. **2.** a literary composition having the form of such a narrative, as Chaucer's *Canterbury Tales.* **3.** a falsehood; fib. **4.** a rumor or piece of gossip, often malicious or untrue. **5.** *Archaic.* enumeration; count. **6.** *Obs.* talk; discourse. [ME; OE *talu*; c. D *taal* speech, language, G *Zahl* number, Icel *tala* number, speech. See TELL¹]

tale·bear·er (tāl′bâr′ər), *n.* a person who spreads gossip that may cause trouble or harm. —**tale′bear′ing,** *adj.*, *n.*

tal·ent (tal′ənt), *n.* **1.** a special natural ability or aptitude: *a talent for drawing.* **2.** a capacity for achievement or success; ability: *young men of talent.* **3.** *Informal.* a talented person. **4.** a group of persons with special ability: *the local talent.* **5.** any of various ancient units of weight, as a unit of Palestine and Syria equal to 3000 shekels, or a unit of Greece equal to 6000 drachmas. **6.** any of various ancient Hebrew or Attic monetary units equal in value to that of a talent weight of gold, silver, or other metal. **7.** *Obs.* inclination or disposition. [ME, OE *talente* < L *talenta,* pl. of *talentum* < Gk *tálanton* balance, weight, monetary unit; in obs. sense desire < ML *talentum*] —**Syn. 1.** capability, gift. See **ability.**

tal·ent·ed (tal′ən tid), *adj.* having special ability; gifted.

tal′ent scout′, a person who recruits persons of marked ability in a certain profession, as for the theater or baseball.

ta·ler (tä′lər), *n.*, *pl.* **-ler, -lers.** thaler.

ta·les (tā′lēz), *n.* *Law.* **1.** (*construed as pl.*) jurors selected from among those present in court to fill vacancies in the original panel. **2.** (*construed as sing.*) the order or writ summoning them. [< ML *tālēs* (*dē circumstantibus*) such (of the bystanders)]

tales·man (tālz′mən, tā′lēz mən), *n.*, *pl.* **-men.** *Law.* a person summoned as one of the tales.

tale·tell·er (tāl′tel′ər), *n.* **1.** a person who tells tales or stories; narrator. **2.** a person who tells falsehoods. **3.** a telltale. —**tale′tell′ing,** *adj.*, *n.*

tali-, a learned borrowing from Latin meaning "ankle," used in the formation of compound words: *taligrade.* [comb. form repr. L *tālus*]

Ta·lien (dä′lyen′), *n.* Chinese name of **Dairen.**

tal·i·grade (tal′ə grād′), *adj.* *Zool.* walking on the outer side of the foot.

tal·i·on (tal′ē ən), *n.* See **lex talionis.** [< L *tāliōn-* (s. of *tāliō*), akin to OIr *im-thānad* exchange; r. late ME *talioun* < AF]

tal·i·ped (tal′ə ped′), *adj.* **1.** (of a foot) twisted or distorted out of shape or position. **2.** (of a person) clubfooted. —*n.* **3.** a taliped person or animal.

tal·i·pes (tal′ə pēz′), *n.* **1.** a clubfoot. **2.** the condition of being clubfooted. [TALI- + L *pēs* foot]

tal·i·pot (tal′ə pot′), *n.* a tall palm, *Corypha umbraculifera,* of southern India and Ceylon, having large leaves used for making fans and umbrellas, for covering houses, and in place of writing paper. Also called **tal′ipot palm′.** [< Malayan *tālipat* < Skt *tālapattra* = *tāla* fan palm + *pattra* leaf]

tal·is·man (tal′is mən, -iz-), *n.*, *pl.* **-mans.** **1.** an object supposed to possess occult powers and worn as an amulet or charm. **2.** any amulet or charm. [< F or Sp << Ar *tilsam* < Gk *télesma* payment = *teles-* (var. s. of *teleîn* to complete, perform) + *-ma* n. suffix] —**tal·is·man·ic** (tal′is man′ik, -iz-), **tal′is·man′i·cal,** *adj.* —**tal′is·man′i·cal·ly,** *adv.*

talk (tôk), *v.i.* **1.** to communicate or exchange ideas, information, etc., by speaking: *to talk about poetry.* **2.** to consult or confer: *Talk with your adviser.* **3.** to spread a rumor or tell a confidence; gossip. **4.** to chatter or prate. **5.** to employ speech; perform the act of speaking. **6.** to deliver a speech, lecture, etc. **7.** to give or reveal confidential or incriminating information. **8.** to communicate ideas by means other than speech, as by writing, signs, or signals. **9.** to make sounds imitative or suggestive of speech. —*v.t.* **10.** to express in words; utter: *to talk sense.* **11.** to use (a specified language or idiom) in speaking or conversing: *They talk French together for practice.* **12.** to discuss: *to talk politics.* **13.** to bring, put, influence, etc., by talk: *to talk a person to sleep.* **14. talk back,** to reply rudely or disrespectfully. **15. talk big,** *Informal.* to speak boastingly; brag. **16. talk down, a.** to outtalk; subdue by talking. **b.** to speak disparagingly of; belittle. **c.** Also, **talk in.** to give landing instructions by radio to a pilot who is hampered by snow, fog, etc. **17. talk down to,** to speak condescendingly to; patronize. **18. talk over,** to weigh in conversation; consider; discuss. **19. talk shop.** See **shop** (def. 6). **20. talk up, a.** to promote interest in; discuss enthusiastically. **b.** to speak without hesitation; speak distinctly and openly. —*n.* **21.** the act of talking; speech; conversation, esp. of a familiar or informal kind. **22.** an informal speech or lecture. **23.** a conference. **24.** report or rumor; gossip. **25.** a subject or occasion of talking, esp. of gossip. **26.** mere empty speech: *That's just a lot of talk.* **27.** a way of talking: *a halting, lisping talk.* **28.** language, dialect, or lingo. **29.** signs or sounds imitative or suggestive of speech, as the noise made by loose parts in a mechanism. [ME *talk(i)en* < TALE; (with *-k* suffix) c. EFris *talken*] —**talk′a·bil′i·ty,** *n.* —**talk′a·ble,** *adj.* —**talk′er,** *n.* —**Syn. 1.** See **speak. 2.** discuss.

talk·a·thon (tô′kə thon′), *n.* an unusually long speech or discussion, esp. on a matter of public interest, as a Congressional filibuster, a televised question-and-answer session with a political candidate, etc. [TALK + -ATHON, modeled on *marathon*]

talk·a·tive (tô′kə tiv), *adj.* inclined to talk a great deal. —**talk′a·tive·ly,** *adv.* —**talk′a·tive·ness,** *n.*
—**Syn.** wordy, verbose, prolix. TALKATIVE, GARRULOUS, LOQUACIOUS agree in referring to a person who talks a great deal. TALKATIVE is a mildly unfavorable word applied to a person who is in the habit of talking a great deal and often without significance: *a talkative child.* The GARRULOUS person talks with wearisome persistence about trivial things: *a garrulous old woman.* A LOQUACIOUS person, intending to be sociable, talks continuously: *a loquacious hostess.*

talk·ie (tô′kē), *n. Informal.* See **talking picture.** [TALK + (MOV)IE]

talk·ing (tô′kiŋ), *n.* **1.** the act of a person who talks; conversation. —*adj.* **2.** that talks; having the power of speech or of mimicking speech: *a talking parrot.* **3.** talkative or talky. **4.** (of reading matter) having its contents converted into a recording, so that they may be heard instead of being read, esp. for use by the blind: *a talking book.*

talk′ing machine′, an early-model phonograph.

talk′ing pic′ture, a motion picture with accompanying synchronized sound.

talk′ing point′, a fact or feature that aids or supports one side, as in an argument or competition.

talk·ing-to (tô′kiŋ to͞o′), *n., pl.* **-tos.** *Informal.* a scolding.

talk′ show′, *Radio and Television.* a show in which the host interviews or chats with guests.

talk·y (tô′kē), *adj.,* **talk·i·er, talk·i·est. 1.** having or containing excessive talk, dialogue, etc. **2.** talkative.

tall (tôl), *adj.* **1.** having a relatively great height: *a tall boy; tall grass.* **2.** having stature or height as specified: *a man six feet tall.* **3.** *Informal.* extravagant; difficult to believe: *a tall tale.* **4.** *Obs.* **a.** seemly; proper. **b.** fine; handsome. [ME: big, bold, comely, proper, ready, OE *getale* (pl.) quick, ready, competent; c. OHG *gizal* quick] —**tall′ness,** *n.* —**Syn. 2.** See **high.** —**Ant. 1.** short.

tal·lage (tal′ij), *n.* **1.** a tax paid by a feudal tenant to his lord. **2.** a compulsory tax levied by a feudal lord. [ME *taillage* < OF < *taill(ier)* (to) cut, tax (see TAILOR) < LL *tāliāre* to cut; see -AGE]

Tal·la·has·see (tal′ə has′ē), *n.* a city in and the capital of Florida, in the N part. 72,586 (1970).

tall·boy (tôl′boi′), *n.* **1.** *Eng. Furniture.* **a.** a chest of drawers supported by a low stand. Cf. **highboy. b.** a chest-on-chest. **2.** a tall chimney pot.

Tal·ley·rand-Pé·ri·gord (tal′i rand′per′ə gôr′; *Fr.* TA-le RÄN′pā RĒ GÔR′), *n.* **Charles Mau·rice de** (sharl mô-RĒS′ də), **Prince de Bé·né·vent** (də bā nā vȧN′), 1754–1838, French statesman.

Tal·linn (täl′lin), *n.* a seaport in and the capital of Estonia, in the NW Soviet Union in Europe, on the Gulf of Finland. 328,000 (est. 1965). Also, **Tal′lin.** Russian, **Revel.** German, **Reval.**

tall·ish (tô′lish), *adj.* rather tall.

tal·lith (tä′lis; *Heb.* tä lēt′), *n., pl.* **tal·li·toth** (*Heb.* tä lē tôt′), *Eng.* **tal·lai·sim** (tä lā′sim), **tal·lith·es.** *Judaism.* a shawllike garment, usually of wool or silk, having zizith: worn at prayer by Jewish males. [< Heb: a cover, garment]

Tallith

tall′ oil′ (täl), a resinous secondary product resulting from the manufacture of chemical wood pulp: used in the manufacture of soaps, paints, etc. [< Sw *tallolja* = *tall* pine (c. Icel. *thöll* young pine tree) + *olja* oil]

tal·low (tal′ō), *n.* **1.** the fatty tissue or suet of animals. **2.** the harder fat of sheep, cattle, etc., separated by melting from the fibrous and membranous matter naturally mixed with it, and used to make candles, soap, etc. **3.** any of various similar fatty substances: *vegetable tallow.* —*v.t.* **4.** to smear with tallow. [ME *talow. talgh;* c. G *Talg* (< LG)]

tal·low·y (tal′ō ē), *adj.* resembling tallow in consistency, color, etc.; fatty. Also, **tal′low·like′.** [late ME *talwy*] —**tal′low·i·ness,** *n.*

tal·ly (tal′ē), *n., pl.* **-lies,** *v.,* **-lied, -ly·ing.** —*n.* **1.** Also called **tal′ly stick′.** a stick of wood with notches cut to indicate the amount of a debt or payment, often split lengthwise across the notches, the debtor retaining one piece and the creditor the other. **2.** a notch or mark made on or in a tally. **3.** anything on which a score or account is kept. **4.** an account or reckoning, as of the score of a game. **5.** a number or group of items recorded. **6.** a mark made to register a certain number of items. **7.** a number of objects serving as a unit of computation. **8.** a ticket, label, or mark used as a means of identification, classification, etc. **9.** anything corresponding to another thing as a counterpart or duplicate. —*v.t.* **10.** to mark or enter on a tally; register; record. **11.** to count or reckon up. **12.** to furnish with a tally or identifying label. **13.** to cause to correspond or agree. —*v.i.* **14.** to correspond, as one part of a tally with the other; accord or agree. [late ME *taly* < ML *talia,* var. of L *tālea* rod, cutting, lit., heel-piece < *tālus* heel] —**tal′li·er,** *n.* —**Syn. 4.** inventory, score, register. **10.** enroll, list, enter. **11.** enumerate, calculate.

tal·ly·ho (*n., v.* tal′ē hō′; *interj.* tal′ē hō′), *interj., n., pl.* **-hos,** *v.* **-hoed** or **-ho'd, -ho·ing.** —*interj.* **1.** the cry of a huntsman on first sighting the fox. —*n.* **2.** a cry of "tallyho." —*v.t.* **3.** to arouse by crying "tallyho," as to the hounds. —*v.i.* **4.** to utter a cry of "tallyho." [cf. F *tayau* hunter's cry]

tal·ly·man (tal′ē mən), *n., pl.* **-men.** a person who tallies or keeps account of something.

Tal·mud (täl′mo͝od, -məd, tal′-), *n.* the collection of Jewish law and tradition consisting of the Mishnah and the Gemara. [< Heb: orig., instruction] —**Tal·mud·ic** (täl-mo͞o′dik, -myo͞o′-, -mo͝od′ik, -mud′-, tal-), **Tal·mud′i·cal,** *adj.* —**Tal′mud·ism,** *n.*

Tal·mud·ist (täl′mo͝o dist, tal′mə-), *n.* **1.** one of the writers or compilers of the Talmud. **2.** a person who accepts or supports the doctrines of the Talmud. **3.** a person versed in the Talmud.

tal·on (tal′ən), *n.* **1.** a claw, esp. of a bird of prey. **2.** the shoulder on the bolt of a lock against which the key presses in sliding the bolt. **3.** *Cards.* the cards left over after the deal; stock. [late ME *taloun* < AF = OF *talon* < VL **tālōn-*, s. of **tālō* for L *tālus* heel] —**tal′oned,** *adj.*

Ta·los (tā′los), *n. Class. Myth.* **1.** the inventive nephew of Daedalus, by whom he was jealously slain. **2.** a man of brass made for Minos as a guardian of Crete.

ta·luk (tä′lo͝ok, tä lo͝ok′), *n.* (in India) **1.** a hereditary estate. **2.** a subdivision of a revenue district. Also, **ta·lu·ka, ta·loo·ka** (tä lo͞o′kə). [< Urdu *ta'alluq* estate < Ar]

ta·lus[1] (tā′ləs), *n., pl.* **-li** (-lī). *Anat.* the uppermost of the proximal row of bones of the tarsus; anklebone. [< L: ankle, anklebone, die (OL **taxlus*). See TASSEL]

ta·lus[2] (tā′ləs), *n., pl.* **-lus·es. 1.** a slope. **2.** *Geol.* a sloping mass of rocky fragments at the base of a cliff. **3.** *Fort.* the slope of the face of a work. [< F: pseudo-learned alter. of OF *talu* slope < L *talūtium* a slope indicating the presence of gold, prob. of Iberian origin]

tam (tam), *n.* tam-o'-shanter.

tam·a·ble (tā′mə bəl), *adj.* able to be tamed. Also, **tameable.** —**tam′a·bil′i·ty, tam′a·ble·ness,** *n.*

ta·ma·le (tə mä′lē), *n.* a Mexican dish made of minced and seasoned meat that has been packed in cornmeal dough, wrapped in corn husks, and steamed. [back formation from MexSp *tamales,* pl. of *tamal* < Nahuatl *tamalli*]

ta·man·dua (tä′män dwä′), *n.* an arboreal, tropical American anteater, *Tamandua tetradactyla.* Also, **tam·an·du** (tam′ən do͞o′). [< Pg < Tupi: lit., ant-trapper]

tam·a·rack (tam′ə rak′), *n.* **1.** an American larch, *Larix laricina,* yielding a useful timber. **2.** any of several related, very similar trees. **3.** the wood of these trees. [< Algonquian]

ta·ma·rao (tä′mə rou′), *n., pl.* **-raos.** tamarau.

ta·ma·rau (tä′mə rou′), *n.* a small wild buffalo, *Bubalus (Anoa) mindorensis,* of Mindoro in the Philippines, having thick, brown hair and short, massive horns. Also, **tamarao, timarau.** [< Tagalog]

tam·a·rin (tam′ə rin), *n.* any South American marmoset of the genera *Saguinus* or *Leontideus.* [< F < Carib (Galibi dial.)]

Tamarin, *Saguinus oedipus* (Total length 22 in.; tail 1 ft.)

tam·a·rind (tam′ə rind), *n.* **1.** the pod of a large, tropical, caesalpiniaceous tree, *Tamarindus indica,* containing seeds enclosed in a juicy acid pulp that is used in beverages and food. **2.** the tree itself. [< ML *tamarind(us)* << Ar *tamr-hindī* date of India]

tam·a·risk (tam′ə risk), *n.* any Old World tropical plant of the genus *Tamarix,* esp. *T. gallica,* an ornamental Mediterranean shrub or small tree having slender, feathery branches. [ME *tamarisc(us)* < LL, var. of L *tamarix*]

ta·ma·sha (tə mä′shə), *n.* (in the East Indies) a spectacle; entertainment. [< Urdu < Ar *tamāshā* a stroll]

Ta·ma·tave (tä′mä täv′), *n.* a seaport on E Madagascar. 39,627 (1960).

Ta·mau·li·pas (tä′mou lē′päs), *n.* a state in NE Mexico, bordering on the Gulf of Mexico. 1,024,182 (1960); 30,731 sq. mi. *Cap.:* Ciudad Victoria.

Ta·ma·yo (tä mä′yō), *n.* **Ru·fi·no** (ro͞o fē′nô), born 1899, Mexican painter.

tam·bac (tam′bak), *n.* tombac.

Tam·bo·ra (täm′bō rä′, -bô-), *n.* an active volcano in Indonesia, on N Sumbawa: eruption 1815. 9042 ft.

tam·bour (tam′bo͝or), *n.* **1.** *Music.* a drum. **2.** a circular frame consisting of two hoops, one fitting within the other, in which cloth is stretched for embroidering. **3.** embroidery done on such a frame. **4.** *Furniture.* a flexible shutter used as a desk top or in place of a door, composed of a number of closely set wood strips attached to a piece of cloth, the whole sliding in grooves along the sides or at the top and bottom. —*v.t., v.i.* **5.** to embroider on a tambour. [late ME: drum < MF << Ar *ṭanbūr* lute, confused with Pers *tabūrāk* drum. See TABOR]

T, Tambour (in bedside stand)

tam·bou·rin (tam′bo͝o rin; *Fr.* täN bo͞o RAN′), *n., pl.* **-rins** (-rinz; *Fr.* -RAN′). a long narrow drum of Provence. [< F < Pr *tamborin,* dim. of *tambor* TAMBOUR]

tam·bou·rine (tam′bə rēn′), *n.* a small drum consisting of a circular frame with a skin stretched over it and several pairs of metal jingles attached to the frame, played by striking with the knuckles, shaking, and the like. [late ME *tamboryne* < MFlem *tamborijn* small drum < MF *tambourin* or ML *tamborīnum.* See TAMBOUR, -INE[1]] —**tam′bou·rin′ist,** *n.*

Tambourine

Tam·bov (täm bôf′), *n.* a city in the RSFSR, in the central Soviet Union in Europe, SE of Moscow. 199,000 (est. 1964).

tam·bu·ra (tam bo͝or′ə), *n.* an Asian musical instrument of the lute family having a small, round body and a long neck. Also, **tam·bou′ra, tam·bur** (täm bŏŏr′). [< Pers *ṭanbūr* < Ar *ṭunbūr*]

Tam·bur·laine (tam′bər lān′), *n.* Tamerlane.

tame (tām), *adj.*, **tam·er, tam·est,** *v.*, **tamed, tam·ing.** **—***adj.* **1.** changed from the wild or savage state; domesticated: *a tame bear.* **2.** tractable, docile, or submissive, as a person, the disposition, etc. **3.** lacking in excitement; dull; insipid: *a very tame party.* **4.** spiritless or cowardly. **5.** cultivated or improved by cultivation, as a plant, its fruit, etc. **—***v.t.* **6.** to make tame; domesticate; make tractable; subdue. **7.** to deprive of courage, ardor, or interest. **8.** to soften; tone down. **9.** to harness or control; render useful, as a source of power. **10.** to cultivate, as land, plants, etc. [ME; OE *tam;* c. D *tam,* Icel *tamr,* G *zahm;* akin to OE *temman,* Icel *temja,* Goth *gatamjan,* L *domāre* to tame] **—tame′ly,** *adv.* **—tame′ness,** *n.* **—tam′er,** *n.*

tame·a·ble (tā′mə bəl), *adj.* tamable. **—tame′a·bil′i·ty, tame′a·ble·ness,** *n.*

tame·less (tām′lis), *adj.* untamed or untamable. **—tame′less·ly,** *adv.* **—tame′less·ness,** *n.*

Tam·er·lane (tam′ər lān′), *n.* (*Timur Lenk*) 1336?–1405, Tartar conqueror in southern and western Asia: ruler of Samarkand 1369–1405. Also, **Tamburlaine.** Also called **Timour, Timur.**

Tam·il (tam′əl, tum′-, tä′məl), *n., pl.* **-ils,** (*esp. collectively*) **-il,** *adj.* **—***n.* **1.** a member of a people of Dravidian stock of southern India and Ceylon. **2.** the Dravidian language of the Tamils, spoken in India from Madras southward and in Ceylon on the N and E coasts. **—***adj.* **3.** of or pertaining to the Tamils or their language.

Tamil Nadu (nä′dōō), a large state in S India: formerly a presidency. 41,199,168; 50,110 sq. mi. Also, **Tam·il·nad** (tam′əl näd, tum-). Formerly, **Madras.**

tam·is (tam′ē, -is), *n., pl.* **tam·ises** (tam′ēz, -i siz). a worsted cloth mesh, used as a strainer. Also, **tammy.** [< F: sieve < ?; cf. OE *temes* sieve, c. MLG *temes,* MD *temse*]

Tam·ma·ny (tam′ə nē), *n.* **1.** See **Tammany Hall.** **—***adj.* **2.** pertaining to, involving, or characteristic of the membership or methods of Tammany Hall. **—Tam′ma·ny·ism,** *n.* **—Tam′ma·ny·ite′,** *n.*

Tam′many Hall′, a powerful Democratic political organization in New York City, founded in 1789 as a fraternal benevolent society (**Tam′many Soci′ety**). [named after *Tammany* (var. of *Tamanen, Tammenund*), 17th-century Delaware Indian chief, later facetiously referred to as patron saint of U.S.]

Tam·mer·fors (täm′mər fôrs′), *n.* Swedish name of **Tampere.**

Tam·muz (tä′mŏŏz; *Heb.* tä mōōz′), *n.* the tenth month of the Jewish calendar. Cf. **Jewish calendar.** [< Heb]

tam·my[1] (tam′ē), *n.* a fabric of mixed fibers, often heavily glazed, used for linings and undergarments. Also, **tam′mie.** [? back formation from obs. F *tamise* kind of glossy cloth (taken as pl.)]

tam·my[2] (tam′ē), *n., pl.* **-mies.** tamis.

tam-o'-shan·ter (tam′ə shan′tər), *n.* a cap of Scottish origin, usually made of wool, having a round, flat top that projects all around the head and often a pompon at its center. Also called **tam.** [named after the hero of *Tam O'Shanter,* a poem (1791) by Robert Burns]

Tam-o'-shanter

tamp (tamp), *v.t.* **1.** to force in or down by repeated, rather light, strokes; pack in tightly by tapping: *He tamped the tobacco in his pipe.* **2.** (in blasting) to fill (the hole made by the drill) with earth or the like after the powder or explosive has been placed in it, to contain the explosion. [? back formation from *tampin* (obs. var. of TAMPION), taken as prp. (*-in* -ING[2])]

Tam·pa (tam′pə), *n.* a seaport in W Florida, on Tampa Bay: fishing resort. 277,767 (1970).

Tam′pa Bay′, an inlet of the Gulf of Mexico, in W Florida. ab. 27 mi. long.

tam·per[1] (tam′pər), *v.i.* **1.** to meddle, esp. for the purpose of altering, damaging, or misusing (usually fol. by *with*) **2.** to engage secretly or improperly in something. **3.** to engage in underhand or corrupt dealings, as in order to influence improperly (usually fol. by *with*). [prob. var. of TEMPER (v.)] **—tam′per·er,** *n.*

tam·per[2] (tam′pər), *n.* a person or thing that tamps. [TAMP + -ER[1]]

Tam·pe·re (täm′pe re), *n.* a city in SW Finland. 165,928. Swedish, **Tammerfors.**

Tam·pi·co (tam pē′kō; *Sp.* täm pē′kô), *n.* a seaport in E Mexico. 240,500.

tam·pi·on (tam′pē ən), *n.* a plug or stopper placed in the muzzle of a piece of ordnance when not in use, to keep out dampness and dust. Also, **tompion.** [late ME *tampyon,* var. of *tampon* < MF, nasalized var. of OF *tapon* < *tape* plug < Gmc. See TAP[2]]

tam·pon (tam′pon), *n.* **1.** *Med.* a plug of cotton or the like for insertion into a body orifice, wound, etc. **2.** a two-headed drumstick for playing drum rolls. **—***v.t.* **3.** *Med.* to fill or plug with a tampon. [< F; see TAMPION]

tam-tam (tum′tum′, tam′tam′), *n.* **1.** a gong with indefinite pitch. **2.** tom-tom. [var. of TOM-TOM]

tan[1] (tan), *v.*, **tanned, tan·ning,** *n., adj.*, **tan·ner, tan·nest.** **—***v.t.* **1.** to convert (a hide) into leather, esp. by soaking or steeping in a bath prepared from tanbark or other materials. **2.** to make brown by exposure to ultraviolet rays, as of the sun. **3.** *Informal.* to thrash; spank. **—***v.i.* **4.** to become tanned. **5. tan one's hide,** *Informal.* to beat someone soundly. **—***n.* **6.** the brown color imparted to the skin by exposure to the sun or open air. **7.** yellowish brown; light brown. **8.** tanbark. **—***adj.* **9.** used in or pertaining to tanning processes, materials, etc. [ME *tanne(n),* late OE *tannian* < ML *tannāre* < *tannum* oak bark, tanbark < Gmc; cf. OHG *tanna* oak, fir, akin to D *den* fir] **—tan′na·ble,** *adj.* **—tan′nish,** *adj.*

tan[2] (tan), *n.* tangent.

Ta·na (tä′nä), *n.* **1.** a river in E Africa, in Kenya, flowing SE to the Indian Ocean. 500 mi. long. **2.** Also, **Tsana. Lake,** a lake in NW Ethiopia: the source of the Blue Nile. 1100 sq. mi.

Ta·nach (tä näkh′), *n.* *Hebrew.* the Old Testament, being the three Jewish divisions of the Pentateuch or Torah, the Prophets or *Nebiim,* and the Hagiographa or *Ketubim,* taken as a whole. [vocalization of Heb *TNK* for *Tōrah* law + *Nebhī'im* prophets + *Kethūbhim* (other) writings]

Scarlet tanager, *Piranga olivacea* (Length 7 in.)

tan·a·ger (tan′ə jər), *n.* any of numerous small, usually brightly colored passerine birds of the family *Thraupidae,* of the New World. [< NL *tanagra,* metathetic var. of Tupi *tangara*]

Tan·a·gra (tan′ə grə), *n.* a town in ancient Greece, in Boeotia: ancient tombs containing terra-cotta figurines; Spartan victory over the Athenians 457 B.C.

tan·a·grine (tan′ə grin), *adj.* of or pertaining to the tanagers; belonging to the tanager family. [< NL *tanagr(a)* TANAGER + -INE[1]]

Tan·a·na (tan′ə nä′), *n.* a river flowing NW from E Alaska to the Yukon River. ab. 650 mi. long.

Ta·na·na·rive (*Fr.* ta na na rēv′; *Eng.* tə nan′ə rēv′), *n.* a city in and the capital of Madagascar, in the central part. 400,000. Also called **Antananarivo.**

tan·bark (tan′bärk′), the bark of the oak, hemlock, etc., bruised and broken by a mill: used in tanning hides and for spreading on the floors of indoor arenas.

Tan·cred (taŋ′krid), *n.* 1078?–1112, Norman leader in the 1st Crusade.

T&E, travel and entertainment.

tan·dem (tan′dəm), *adv.* **1.** one following or behind the other: *to drive horses tandem.* **2. in tandem, a.** in single file. **b.** in association or partnership. **—***adj.* **3.** having animals, seats, parts, etc., arranged tandem or one behind another. **—***n.* **4.** a team of horses so harnessed. **5.** a two-wheeled carriage with a high driver's seat, drawn by two or more horses in tandem. **6.** any of various mechanisms having a tandem arrangement, esp. a truck or trailer having the axles close together. [special use (orig. facetious) of L *tandem* at length, finally = *tam* so far + *-dem* demonstrative suffix]

Tandem (def. 5)

tan′dem bi′cycle, a bicycle for two or more persons, having seats and corresponding sets of pedals arranged in tandem.

Ta·ney (tô′nē), *n.* **Roger Brooke,** 1777–1864, U.S. jurist: Chief Justice of the U.S. 1836?–64.

tang[1] (taŋ), *n.* **1.** a strong taste or flavor. **2.** a pungent or distinctive odor. **3.** a touch or suggestion of something; slight trace. **4.** a long and slender projecting strip, tongue, or prong forming part of an object, as a chisel or knife, and serving as a means of attachment for another part, as a handle or stock. **—***v.t.* **5.** to furnish with a tang. [ME *tange* < Scand; cf. Icel *tangi* pointed object; akin to TONGS]

tang[2] (taŋ), *n.* **1.** a sharp ringing or twanging sound; clang. **—***v.t., v.i.* **2.** to ring or twang; clang. [imit]

Tang (täŋ), *n.* a dynasty in China, A.D. 618–907, marked by the invention of printing and the high development of poetry. Also, **T'ang.** [< Chin (Peking) *T'ang*]

Tan·ga (taŋ′gə), *n.* a seaport in NE Tanzania. 143,878 (1979).

Tan·gan·yi·ka (tan′gən yē′kə, taŋ′-), *n.* **1.** a former country in E Africa: formed the larger part of German East Africa; British trusteeship (**Tan′ganyi′ka Ter′ritory**) 1946–61; became independent 1961; now the mainland part of Tanzania. 14,734,000; 361,800 sq. mi. *Cap.:* Dar es Salaam. **2. Lake,** a lake in central Africa, between Zaïre and Tanzania: the longest fresh-water lake in the world. ab. 450 mi. long; 30–40 mi. wide; 12,700 sq. mi. **—Tan′gan·yi′kan,** *adj., n.*

Tanganyi′ka and Zan′zibar, United Republic of, former name of **Tanzania.**

tan·ge·lo (tan′jə lō′), *n., pl.* **-los.** **1.** a hybrid citrus tree produced by crossing the tangerine and the grapefruit. **2.** the tart fruit of this tree. [TANG(ERINE) + (POM)ELO]

tan·gen·cy (tan′jən sē), *n.* the state of being tangent. [TANG(ENT) + -ENCY]

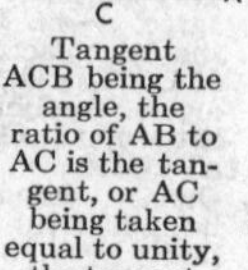

Tangent ACB being the angle, the ratio of AB to AC is the tangent, or AC being taken equal to unity, the tangent is AB

tan·gent (tan′jənt), *adj.* **1.** in immediate physical contact; touching. **2.** *Geom.* touching at a single point or along one line. **—***n.* **3.** *Geom.* a line or a plane that touches a curve or a surface at a point so that it is closer to the curve in the vicinity of the point than any other line or plane drawn through the point. **4.** *Trig.* **a.** (in a right triangle) the ratio of the side opposite a given angle to the side adjacent to the angle. **b.** (of an angle) a trigonometric function equal to the ratio of the ordinate of the end point of the arc to the abscissa of this end point, the origin being at the center of the circle on which the arc lies and the initial point of the arc being on the x-axis. *Abbr.:* tan **c.** (originally) a straight line perpendicular to the radius of a circle at one end of an arc and extending from this point to the produced radius which cuts off the arc at its other end. **5.** *Survey.* the straight portion of a survey line between curves, as in railroad or highway alignment. **6. off on** or **at a tangent,** digressing suddenly from one course of action or thought and turning to another. [< L *tangent-* (s. of *tangēns,* prp. of *tangere* to touch) in phrase *linea tangēns* touching line; see -ENT] **—Syn. 1.** meeting, abutting.

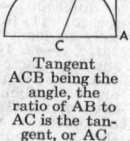

tan·gen·tial (tan jen′shəl), *adj.* **1.** pertaining to or of the nature of a tangent; being or moving in the direction of a tangent. **2.** merely touching; slightly connected. **3.** divergent or digressive, as from a subject under consideration. Also, **tan·gen·tal** (tan jen′tᵊl). —**tan·gen′tial·ly, tan·gen′tal·ly,** *adv.*

tan·ge·rine (tan′jə rēn′), *n.* **1.** a small, loose-skinned variety of mandarin orange. **2.** a deep or reddish orange color. —*adj.* **3.** of the color tangerine; reddish-orange. [TANG(I)ER + -INE[1]]

tan·gi·ble (tan′jə bəl), *adj.* **1.** capable of being touched; material or substantial. **2.** real or actual, rather than imaginary or visionary: *the tangible benefits of sunshine.* **3.** definite; not vague or elusive: *no tangible grounds for suspicion.* **4.** (of an asset) having actual physical existence, as real estate, chattels, etc., and therefore capable of being assigned a value in monetary terms. —*n.* **5.** something tangible, esp. a tangible asset. [< L *tangibil(is)* = *tang(ere)* (to) touch + *-ibil(is)* -IBLE] —**tan′gi·bil′i·ty, tan′gi·ble·ness,** *n.* —**tan′gi·bly,** *adv.*

Tan·gier (tan jēr′), *n.* a seaport in N Morocco, on the W Strait of Gibraltar: capital of the former Tangier Zone. 243,600.

Tangier′ Zone′, a former internationalized zone on the Strait of Gibraltar: became a part of Morocco 1956. Cf. **Morocco** (def. 1).

tan·gle (taŋ′gəl), *v.*, **-gled, -gling,** *n.* —*v.t.* **1.** to bring together into a mass of confusedly interlaced or intertwisted parts; snarl. **2.** to involve in something that complicates, involves, obstructs, or overgrows. **3.** to catch and hold in or as in a net or snare. —*v.i.* **4.** to be or become tangled. **5.** *Informal.* to come into conflict; fight or argue. —*n.* **6.** a complicated, intricate, or involved condition. **7.** a confused jumble: *a tangle of ropes; a tangle of contradictory statements.* [ME *tangil*, nasalized var. of *tagil* entangle < Scand; cf. Sw (dial) *taggla* to disarrange] —**tan′gle·ment,** *n.* —**tan′gler,** *n.* —**tan′gly,** *adj.*

tan·gle·ber·ry (taŋ′gəl ber′ē), *n., pl.* **-ries.** a huckleberry, *Gaylussacia frondosa,* of the eastern U.S.

Tan·gle·wood (taŋ′gəl wo͝od′), *n.* See under **Lenox.**

tan·go (taŋ′gō), *n., pl.* **-gos,** *v.*, **-goed, -go·ing.** —*n.* **1.** a ballroom dance of Spanish-American origin. **2.** (*cap.*) a word used in communications to represent the letter *T.* —*v.i.* **3.** to dance the tango. [< AmerSp < ?]

Tan·guy (täN gē′), *n.* **Yves** (ēv), 1900–55, French painter, in the U.S. after 1939.

tang·y (taŋ′ē), *adj.*, **tang·i·er, tang·i·est.** having a tang. [TANG[1] + -Y[1]]

tanh, hyperbolic tangent. [TAN(GENT) + H(YPERBOLIC)]

Ta·nis (tā′nis), *n.* an ancient city in Lower Egypt, in the Nile delta. Biblical, **Zoan.**

tan·ist (tan′ist, thô′nist), *n.* *Hist.* the heir apparent to a Celtic chief, chosen by election among the tribe during the chief's lifetime. [< Ir, Gaelic *tānaiste* second, substitute, heir by election]

tan·ist·ry (tan′i strē, thô′ni-), *n.* the system of succession by tanists.

Tan·jore (tan jōr′, -jôr′), *n.* a city in E Madras, in SE India. 140,470.

tank (taŋk), *n.* **1.** a large receptacle, container, or structure for holding a liquid or gas. **2.** *Mil.* an armored, self-propelled combat vehicle, armed with cannon and machine guns and moving on a caterpillar tread. **3.** *Dial.* a natural or artificial pool, pond, or lake. **4.** *Slang.* a large prison cell for more than one occupant, as for prisoners awaiting a hearing. —*v.t.* **5.** to put or store in a tank. [< Gujarati *tānkh* reservoir, lake + Pg *tanque,* contr. of *estanque* pond, lit., something dammed up < *estancar* (< VL **stanticāre*) to dam up, weaken]

tan·ka (täŋ′kə), *n., pl.* **-kas, -ka.** *Pros.* a Japanese poem consisting of 31 syllables in 5 lines, with 5 syllables in the first and third lines and 7 in the others. [< Jap = *tan* short + *ka* verse]

tank·age (taŋ′kij), *n.* **1.** the capacity of a tank or tanks. **2.** the act or process of storing liquid in a tank. **3.** the fee charged for such storage.

tank·ard (taŋ′kərd), *n.* a large drinking mug, usually with a hinged cover. [ME: bucket; cf. MD *tanckaert,* MF *tanquart*]

Tankard (18th century)

tank·er (taŋ′kər), *n.* a ship, airplane, or truck designed to carry oil or other liquid in bulk.

tank′ farm′, an area or expanse of land for oil storage tanks.

tank′ farm′ing, hydroponics.

tank·ful (taŋk′fo͝ol), *n., pl.* **-fuls.** the quantity a tank holds.

tank·ship (taŋk′ship′), *n.* a ship for carrying bulk cargoes of liquids; tanker.

tank′ suit′, a simple one-piece bathing suit, usually of cotton or wool knit.

tank′ town′, **1.** a town where trains stop to take on a supply of water. **2.** any small, unimportant town.

tan·nage (tan′ij), *n.* **1.** the act or process of tanning. **2.** the product of tanning; that which is tanned.

tan·nate (tan′āt), *n.* *Chem.* a salt of tannic acid. [TANN(IN) + -ATE[2]]

tan·nen·baum (tan′ən boum′), *n.* a Christmas tree. [< G: lit., fir tree]

Tan·nen·berg (tän′ən berkh′), *n.* a village formerly in East Prussia, now in N Poland: German victory over the Russians 1914.

tan·ner[1] (tan′ər), *n.* a person whose occupation is to tan hides. [ME, OE *tannere.* See TAN, -ER[1]]

tan·ner[2] (tan′ər), *adj.* comparative of **tan[1]**. [TAN[1] + -ER[4]]

tan·ner[3] (tan′ər), *n.* *Brit. Slang.* a sixpenny piece. [?]

tan·ner·y (tan′ə rē), *n., pl.* **-ner·ies.** a place where tanning is done.

Tann·häu·ser (tan′hoi′zər, -hou′-; *Ger.* tän′hoi′zər), *n.* a Middle High German lyric poet of the 13th century: a well-known legend tells of his stay with Venus in the Venusberg and his later repentance.

tan·nic (tan′ik), *adj.* *Chem.* of, pertaining to, or derived from tan or tanning. [TAN or TANN(IN) + -IC]

tan·nin (tan′in), *n.* *Chem.* any of a group of astringent vegetable principles or compounds, as the reddish compound which gives the tanning properties to oak bark or the whitish compound which occurs in large quantities in nutgalls (**tan′nic ac′id**). [earlier *tanin* < F. See TAN, -IN[2]]

tan·ning (tan′iŋ), *n.* **1.** the process or art of converting hides or skins into leather. **2.** a browning or darkening of the skin, as by exposure to the sun. **3.** *Informal.* a thrashing; whipping. [late ME]

Tan′nu Tu′va Peo′ple's Repub′lic (tan′o͞o to͞o′və), former name of **Tuva Autonomous Soviet Socialist Republic.** Also called **Tan′nu Tu′va.** —**Tan′nu Tu′van.**

Ta·no·an (tä′nō ən), *n.* a language family of which the three surviving languages are spoken in several pueblos, including Taos, in northern New Mexico. [*Tano* Pueblo Indian group + -AN]

tan·sy (tan′zē), *n., pl.* **-sies.** any composite plant of the genus *Tanacetum,* esp. a strong-scented, weedy, Old World herb, *T. vulgare,* having corymbs of yellow flowers. [late ME < OF *tanesie,* aph. var. of *atanesie* < ML *athanasia* < Gk: immortality = *a-* A-[6] + *-thanasia* mortality. See THANATOS, -Y[3]]

Tan·ta (tän′tä), *n.* a city in the N United Republic of Egypt, in the Nile delta. 240,500.

tan·ta·late (tan′tᵊlāt′), *n.* *Chem.* a salt of any tantalic acid. [TANTAL(UM) + -ATE[2]]

tan·tal·ic (tan tal′ik), *adj.* *Chem.* of or pertaining to tantalum, esp. in the pentavalent state. [TANTAL(UM) + -IC]

tantal′ic ac′id, *Chem.* an acid, $HTaO_3$, that forms complex salts or tantalates.

tan·ta·lise (tan′tᵊlīz′), *v.t.*, **-lised, -lis·ing.** *Chiefly Brit.* tantalize. —**tan′ta·li·sa′tion,** *n.*

tan·ta·lite (tan′tᵊlīt′), *n.* a mineral, iron tantalate, $FeTa_2O_6$, usually containing manganese and columbium: the principal ore of tantalum. [TANTAL(UM) + -ITE[1]]

tan·ta·lize (tan′tᵊlīz′), *v.t.*, **-lized, -liz·ing.** to torment with or as with the sight or prospect of something desired that cannot be reached or attained; tease by arousing expectations. Also, *esp. Brit.,* **tantalise.** [TANTAL(US) + -IZE] —**tan′ta·li·za′tion,** *n.* —**Ant.** satisfy.

tan·ta·liz·ing (tan′tᵊlī′ziŋ), *adj.* provoking or arousing expectation, interest, or desire, esp. that which remains unobtainable. Also, *esp. Brit.,* **tan′ta·lis′ing.** —**tan′ta·liz′ing·ly;** *esp. Brit.,* **tan′ta·lis′ing·ly,** *adv.*

tan·ta·lous (tan′tᵊləs), *adj.* *Chem.* containing trivalent tantalum. [TANTAL(UM) + -OUS]

tan·ta·lum (tan′tᵊləm), *n.* *Chem.* a gray, hard, rare, metallic element with a very high melting point, occurring in columbite and usually associated with niobium: used, because of its resistance to corrosion by most acids, for chemical, dental, and surgical instruments and apparatus and in electrolytic rectifiers and capacitors. *Symbol:* Ta; *at. wt.:* 180.948; *at. no.:* 73; *sp. gr.:* 16.6. [< NL; named after TANTALUS]

Tan·ta·lus (tan′tᵊləs), *n.* *Class. Myth.* a Phrygian king, who for his crimes was condemned to remain in Tartarus, standing, unable to drink or eat, chin deep in water with fruit-laden branches hanging above his head.

tan·ta·mount (tan′tə mount′), *adj.* equivalent, as in value, force, effect, or signification. [adj. use of obs. n., itself n. use of obs. verb < AF *tant amunter* or It *tanto montare* to amount to as much. See TANTO, AMOUNT]

tan·ta·ra (tan′tər ə, tan tar′ə, -tär′ə), *n.* a blast of a trumpet or horn. [< L *(tara)tantara;* imit.]

tan·tiv·y (tan tiv′ē), *adv., adj., n., pl.* **-tiv·ies,** *interj.* —*adv.* **1.** at full gallop: *to ride tantivy.* —*adj.* **2.** swift; rapid. —*n.* **3.** a gallop; rush. —*interj.* **4.** (used as a hunting cry when the chase is at full speed.) [?]

tant mieux (täN myœ′), *French.* so much the better.

tan·to (tän′tō; *It.* tän′tô), *adv.* too much; so much (used as a musical direction). [It < L *tantum* so much]

tant pis (täN pē′), *French.* so much the worse.

Tan·tra (tun′trə), *n.* **1.** *Hinduism.* any of several books of esoteric doctrine regarding rituals, disciplines, meditation, etc., composed in the form of dialogues between Shiva and his Shakti. **2.** Also called **Tan·trism** (tun′triz əm). the philosophy or doctrine of these books.

Tan·tri·ka (tun′trə kə), *n.* **1.** Also called **Tan·trist** (tun′trist). an adherent of Tantra. —*adj.* **2.** of or pertaining to Tantra. Also, **Tan·tric, Tan·trik** (tun′trik). [var. of *Tantric.* See TANTRA, -IC]

tan·trum (tan′trəm), *n.* a violent demonstration of rage or frustration. [?]

Tan·za·ni·a (tan′zə nē′ə, tan zan′ē ə; *Swahili* tän zä-nē′ä), *n.* a republic in E Africa, comprising the former country of Tanganyika, the islands of Zanzibar and Pemba, and adjacent small islands: formed 1964. 16,500,000; 362,820 sq. mi. *Cap.:* Dar es Salaam. Formerly, **United Republic of Tanganyika and Zanzibar.**

Tao (dou, tou), *n.* **1.** (in philosophical Taoism) that by virtue of which all things happen or exist. **2.** the rational basis of human activity or conduct. **3.** a universal, regarded as an ideal attained to a greater or lesser degree by those embodying it. [< Chin: the way]

Tao·ism (dou′iz əm, tou′-), *n.* **1.** a Chinese religion and philosophical system traditionally founded by Lao-tzu, advocating a life of complete simplicity and naturalness and of noninterference with the course of natural events, in order to attain a happy existence in harmony with the Tao. **2.** a later form of this religion, having a pantheon of many gods and advocating alchemy, divination, and magic to attain longevity and immortality. —**Tao′ist,** *n., adj.* —**Tao·is′tic,** *adj.*

Taos (tous), *n., pl.* **Taos** for 2. **1.** a Tanoan language spoken in two villages in New Mexico. **2.** a member of an American Indian people occupying a pueblo in New Mexico. **3.** a town in N New Mexico: resort; art colony. 2163 (1960).

tap[1] (tap), *v.*, **tapped, tap·ping,** *n.* —*v.t.* **1.** to strike or touch gently. **2.** to make, put, etc., with light blows: *to tap a nail into a wall.* **3.** to strike (the fingers, the foot, a pencil, etc.) upon or against something, esp. with repeated light blows. **4.** to add a thickness of leather to the sole or heel of (a boot or shoe), as in repairing. —*v.i.* **5.** to strike a surface lightly but audibly; rap. —*n.* **6.** a light blow or rap. **7.** a sound made by this. **8.** a thickness of leather added to the sole or heel of a shoe, as in repairing. **9.** a piece of metal attached to the toe or heel of a shoe, as for reinforcement or for making the tapping of a dancer audible. [late ME *tappe(n)*, var. of early ME *teppen*; prob. imit.] —**tap′per,** *n.*

tap[2] (tap), *n., v.,* **tapped, tap·ping.** —*n.* **1.** a faucet or cock. **2.** the liquor drawn through a particular faucet or cock. **3.** a cylindrical stick, long plug, or stopper for closing an opening through which liquid is drawn, as in a cask. **4.** a tool for cutting screw threads into the cylindrical surface of a round opening. **5.** *Surg.* the withdrawal of fluid: *spinal tap.* **6.** *Elect.* a connection brought out of a winding at some point between its extremities, for controlling the voltage ratio. **7.** the act or an instance of wiretapping. **8.** *Archaic.* a particular kind or quality of drink. **9. on tap, a.** ready to be drawn and served, as beer from a barrel. **b.** furnished with a tap or cock, as a barrel containing liquor. **c.** *Informal.* ready for immediate use; available. —*v.t.* **10.** to draw liquid from (a vessel or container). **11.** to draw off (liquid) by removing or opening a tap or by piercing a container. **12.** to draw the tap or plug from or pierce (a cask or other container). **13.** to draw upon resources or stores of any kind. **14.** to connect into secretly so as to receive the message being transmitted: *to tap a telephone.* **15.** to furnish (a cask, container, pipe, etc.) with a tap. **16.** to cut a screw thread into the surface of (an opening). **17.** to open outlets from (power lines, highways, pipes, etc.). [ME *tappe*, OE *tæppa*; c. D *tap*, OHG *zapfo*; Icel *tappi*] —**tap′per,** *n.*

ta·pa (tä′pə), *n.* **1.** the bark of the paper mulberry. **2.** Also, **ta′pa cloth′.** a cloth of the Pacific islands made by pounding this or similar barks flat and thin, used for clothing and floor covering. [< Polynesian]

Ta·pa·jós (tä′pə zhôs′), *n.* a river flowing NE through central Brazil to the Amazon. 500 mi. long.

tap′ dance′, a dance in which the rhythm or rhythmical variation is audibly tapped out with the toe or heel by a dancer wearing shoes with special hard soles or with taps.

tap-dance (tap′dans′, -däns′), *v.i.,* **-danced, -danc·ing.** to perform a tap dance. —**tap′-danc′er,** *n.*

tape (tāp), *n., v.,* **taped, tap·ing.** —*n.* **1.** a long, narrow strip of cloth, mainly used as a means of attaching or binding, and in many forms having one surface adhesive. **2.** a long, narrow strip of paper, metal, etc. **3.** See **tape measure. 4.** a string stretched across the finishing line in a race and broken by the winning contestant as he crosses. **5.** the ribbon of paper on which stock-market quotations are printed by a ticker. **6.** See **magnetic tape. 7.** a magnetic tape carrying prerecorded sound. —*v.t.* **8.** to furnish with a tape or tapes. **9.** to tie up, bind, or attach with tape. **10.** to measure with or as with a tape measure. **11.** to record or prerecord on magnetic tape. [ME, unexplained var. of *tappe*, OE *tæppe* strip (of cloth), lit., part torn off; akin to MLG *teppen* to tear, pluck] —**tap′er,** *n.* —**tape′less,** *adj.* —**tape′like′,** *adj.*

tape′ deck′, a simplified tape recorder, lacking a power amplifier and speaker of its own.

tape′ grass′, a fresh-water plant, *Vallisneria spiralis*, that has long, ribbonlike leaves and grows under water. Also called **eelgrass, wild celery.**

tape′ machine′, a tape recorder.

tape′ meas′ure, a long, flexible strip or ribbon of cloth, metal, etc., marked with subdivisions of the foot or meter and used for measuring. Also called **tape·line** (tāp′līn′).

tape′ play′er, a small machine for playing magnetic tape recordings.

ta·per (tā′pər), *v.i.* **1.** to become smaller or thinner toward one end. **2.** to grow gradually lean. —*v.t.* **3.** to cause gradually to become smaller toward one end. **4.** to reduce gradually. **5. taper off, a.** to become gradually more slender toward one end. **b.** to cease by degrees; diminish. —*n.* **6.** gradual diminution of width or thickness in an elongated object. **7.** a candle, esp. a very slender one. **8.** a long wick coated with wax, tallow, or the like, as for use in lighting candles or gas. [ME, OE, var. of *tapur*, dissimilated var. of **papur* PAPER] —**ta′per·ing·ly,** *adv.*

tape-re·cord (tāp′ri kôrd′), *v.t.* to record on magnetic tape.

tape′ record′er, an electric machine for recording and playing back signals, as sound, television pictures, or telemetry data, on magnetic tape.

tape′ record′ing, 1. a magnetic tape on which speech, music, etc., have been recorded. **2.** the act of recording on magnetic tape.

tap·es·try (tap′i strē), *n., pl.* **-tries,** *v.,* **-tried, -try·ing.** —*n.* **1.** a fabric consisting of a warp upon which colored threads are woven by hand to produce a design, often pictorial, used for wall hangings, furniture coverings, etc. **2.** a similar reproduction woven by machinery. —*v.t.* **3.** to furnish, cover, or adorn with tapestry. [late ME *tapst(e)ry*, *tapistry* < MF *tapisserie* carpeting. See TAPIS, -ERY] —**tap′es·try·like′,** *adj.*

tap′estry Brus′sels. See under **Brussels carpet.**

ta·pe·tum (tə pē′təm), *n., pl.* **-ta** (-tə). **1.** *Bot.* a layer of cells often investing the archespore in a developing sporangium and absorbed as the spores mature. **2.** *Anat., Zool.* any of certain membranous layers or the like, as in the choroid or retina. [< NL, special use of ML *tapētum* coverlet (L, only pl.) < Gk *tapēt-* (s. of *tápēs*) carpet, rug] —**ta·pe′tal,** *adj.*

tape·worm (tāp′wûrm′), *n.* any of various flat or tapelike worms of the class *Cestoda* that lack an alimentary canal and are parasitic when adult in the alimentary canal of man and other vertebrates.

tap·hole (tap′hōl′), *n.* *Metall.* a hole in a blast furnace, steelmaking furnace, etc., through which molten metal or slag is tapped off.

tap·house (tap′hous′), *n., pl.* **-hous·es** (-hou′ziz). *Brit.* an inn or tavern where liquor is kept on tap for sale.

tap·i·o·ca (tap′ē ō′kə), *n.* a food substance prepared from cassava in granular, flake, pellet, or flour form, used in puddings, as a thickener, etc. [< Pg < Tupi *tipioca*, lit., juice (of cassava) squeezed out, i.e., pulp after squeezing]

tapio′ca snow′. See **snow pellets.**

ta·pir (tā′pər), *n., pl.* **-pirs,** (*esp. collectively*) **-pir.** any of several large, stout, hoofed quadrupeds of the family *Tapiridae*, somewhat resembling swine and having a long, flexible snout. [< Tupi *tapira*]

Tapir, *Tapirus terrestris* (3 ft. high at shoulder; length 6½ ft.)

tap·is (tap′ē, tap′is, ta pē′), *n., pl.* **tap·is. 1.** a carpet, tapestry, or other covering. **2. on the tapis,** under consideration or discussion. [< MF; OF *tapiz* << Gk *tapētion* = *tapēt-* (s. of *tápēs*) carpet + *-ion* dim. suffix]

tap·pet (tap′it), *n.* *Mach.* a sliding rod, intermittently struck by a cam, for moving another part, as a valve.

tap·ping[1] (tap′ing), *n.* **1.** the act of a person or thing that taps or strikes lightly. **2.** the sound produced by this. [late ME; see TAP[1], -ING[1]]

tap·ping[2] (tap′ing), *n.* **1.** the act of a person or thing that taps casks, telephone conversations, etc. **2.** something that is drawn by tapping. [TAP[2] + -ING[1]]

tap·pit-hen (tap′it hen′), *n.* *Scot.* **1.** a hen with a crest or topknot. **2.** a tankard, esp. a large one, with a knob or ornament projecting from the top of its lid. [*tappit* (Scot var. of *topped;* see TOP[1]) + HEN]

tap·room (tap′ro͞om′, -ro͝om′), *n.* *Chiefly Brit.* a barroom.

tap·root (tap′ro͞ot′, -ro͝ot′), *n.* *Bot.* a main root descending downward from the radicle and giving off small lateral roots. See illus. at **root**[1].

taps (taps), *n., pl.* **taps.** (*construed as sing.*) *U.S. Mil.* a bugle call or, less commonly, a drum signal sounded at night as an order to extinguish unauthorized lights or performed as a postlude to a military funeral or a memorial service. [prob. *tap(too)*, var. of TATTOO[1] + -S[3]]

tar[1] (tär), *n., v.,* **tarred, tar·ring,** *adj.* —*n.* **1.** any of various dark-colored viscid products obtained by the destructive distillation of certain organic substances, as coal or wood. **2.** coal-tar pitch. **3.** (not in technical use) smoke solids or components: *cigarette tar.* **4. beat, knock, or whale the tar out of,** to beat mercilessly. —*v.t.* **5.** to smear or cover with or as with tar. **6. tar and feather,** to coat (a person) with tar and feathers as a punishment or humiliation. —*adj.* **7.** of or characteristic of tar. **8.** covered or smeared with tar; tarred. [ME *tarr(e)*, *ter(re)*, OE *teru* (nom.), *terwes* (gen.); c. D, G *teer*, Icel *tjara;* akin to TREE]

tar[2] (tär), *n.* *Informal.* a sailor. [? short for TARPAULIN]

Tar·a (tar′ə), *n.* a village in the NE Republic of Ireland, NW of Dublin: home of the ancient Irish kings.

ta·ran·tass (tä′rän täs′), *n.* a large, four-wheeled Russian carriage mounted on two parallel longitudinal wooden bars. Also, **ta′ran·tas′.** [< Russ *tarantas*]

tar·an·tel·la (tar′ən tel′ə), *n.* a rapid, whirling southern Italian dance in very quick sextuple meter, and formerly supposed to be a remedy for tarantism. [< It, after *Taranto* TARANTO + *-ella* n. suffix. See TARANTISM]

tar·ant·ism (tar′ən tiz′əm), *n.* a nervous condition characterized by an uncontrollable impulse to dance, prevalent esp. in S Italy from the 15th to the 17th century: popularly attributed to the bite of the tarantula. Also, **tarentism.** Cf. **tarantula** (def. 3). [< NL *tarantism(us)*. See TARANTO, -ISM]

Ta·ran·to (tä′rän tô), *n.* **1.** Ancient name, **Tarentum.** a fortified seaport in SE Italy, on the Gulf of Taranto: founded by the Greeks in the 8th century B.C.; naval base. 191,515 (1961). **2. Gulf of,** an arm of the Ionian Sea, in S Italy. 85 mi. long.

Tarantula, *Dugesiella hentzi* (Body length 2 in.)

ta·ran·tu·la (tə ran′chə lə), *n., pl.* **-las, -lae** (-lē′). **1.** any of several large, hairy spiders of the family *Theraphosidae*, as *Dugesiella hentzi*, of the southwestern U.S., having a painful but not highly venomous bite. **2.** any of various related spiders. **3.** a large wolf spider, *Lycosa tarantula*, of southern Europe, having a bite once thought to be the cause of tarantism. [< ML < It *tarantola*. See TARANTO, -ULE]

Ta·ra·wa (tä rä′wä, tä′rä wä′), *n.* one of the Gilbert Islands, in the central Pacific; capital of Kiribati: U.S. victory over Japanese forces, Nov. 1943. 19,000; 14 sq. mi.

ta·rax·a·cum (tə rak′sə kəm), *n.* *Pharm.* the dried roots of any of several composite plants of the genus *Taraxacum*, as the dandelion, *T. officinale*, or *T. laevigatum*, used as a tonic and aperient. [< NL < Ar *ṭarakhshaqūn* wild chicory, ? < Pers]

Tar·bell (tär′bel′), *n.* **Ida Minerva,** 1857–1944, U.S. author.

Tarbes (tarb), *n.* a city in SW France. 50,715 (1962).

tar·boosh (tär bo͞osh′), *n.* a tasseled cloth or felt cap worn by Muslim men. Also, **tar·bush′.** [< Ar *ṭarbūsh*]

tar·di·grade (tär′də grād′), *adj.* **1.** slow in pace or movement. **2.** belonging or pertaining to the phylum *Tardigrada*. —*n.* **3.** any microscopic, chiefly herbivorous invertebrate of the phylum *Tardigrada*, related to the arthropods, living in water, on mosses, lichens, etc. [< L *tardigrad(us)* slow-paced. See TARDY, -GRADE]

tar·dy (tär′dē), *adj.,* **-di·er, -di·est. 1.** late; behind time; not on time. **2.** moving or acting slowly. **3.** delaying through reluctance. [abstracted from late ME *tarditee* < L *tarditās* = *tardi-* (comb. form of *tardus* slow) + *-tās* -TY[2]; r. late ME *tardive* < MF] —**tar′di·ly,** *adv.* —**tar′di·ness,** *n.*

tare[1] (târ), *n.* **1.** any of various vetches, esp. *Vicia sativa*. **2.** the seed of a vetch. **3.** *Bible.* a noxious weed, probably the darnel. [ME: vetch; akin to D *tarwe* wheat]

tare[2] (târ), *n., v.,* **tared, tar·ing.** —*n.* **1.** the weight of the container or wrapping holding goods. **2.** a deduction from the gross weight to allow for this. **3.** the weight of a vehicle without cargo, passengers, etc. **4.** a counterweight used in chemical analysis to balance the weight of a container. —*v.t.* **5.** to ascertain, note, or allow for the tare of. [late ME < MF (= ML, It, Pr, Sp, Pg *tara*, Sp *atara*) << Ar *ṭarḥah* what one throws away < *ṭaraḥa* to throw away]

tare[3] (târ), *v.* *Archaic.* pt. and pp. of **tear.**

tar·ent·ism (tar′ən tiz′əm), *n.* tarantism.

Ta·ren·tum (tə ren′təm), *n.* ancient name of **Taranto.**

targe (tärj), *n.* *Archaic.* a small, round shield; target or buckler. [ME < OF < Scand (cf. Icel *targa* round shield; c. OHG *zarga* rim, ring); r. OE *targe, targa* < Scand]

tar·get (tär′git), *n.* **1.** an object, as one marked with concentric circles, to be aimed at in shooting practice or in competitions. **2.** any thing to be struck with missiles. **3.** a goal or end to be attained. **4.** an object of abuse, scorn, derision, etc.; butt. **5.** any of various disklike markers intended to be visible at considerable distances. **6.** a small shield, usually round, carried by a foot soldier; buckler. —*v.t.* **7.** to make a target of. [late ME < MF *targuete*, var. of *targete* small shield. See TARGE, -ET]

tar′get date′, the date set or aimed at for the commencement or completion of some effort.

Tar·gum (tär′go͝om; *Heb.* täʀ go͞om′), *n., pl.* **Targums,** *Heb.* **Tar·gu·mim** (täʀ go͞o mēm′). a translation or paraphrase in Aramaic of a book or division of the Old Testament. [< Aram: paraphrase, interpretation] —**Tar·gum′ic,** *adj.* —**Tar′gum·ist,** *n.*

Târ·gu-Mu·res (tiʀ′go͞o mo͞o′ʀesh), *n.* a city in central Rumania. 75,450 (est. 1964).

Tar·heel (tär′hēl′), *n.* a native or inhabitant of North Carolina (the **Tarheel State**) (used as a nickname). [TAR[1] + HEEL[1]; point of nickname uncertain]

Tar′heel State′, North Carolina (used as a nickname).

tar·iff (tar′if), *n.* **1.** an official schedule of duties or customs imposed by a government on imports or exports. **2.** any duty or rate of duty in such a schedule. **3.** any charge or fare, as of a railroad or bus line. —*v.t.* **4.** to subject to a tariff. **5.** to put a valuation on according to a tariff. [earlier *tariffa* < It < Ar *ta'rīf* information, akin to *'arafa* to make known]

Ta·rim (tä′rēm′), *n.* a river in NW China, in Sinkiang province. ab. 1300 mi. long.

Ta′rim′ Ba′sin, a region in W China between the Tien Shan and Kunlun mountain ranges. ab. 350,000 sq. mi.

Tar·king·ton (tär′king tən), *n.* **(Newton) Booth,** 1869–1946, U.S. novelist and playwright.

Tar·lac (tär′läk), *n.* a city on central Luzon, in the N Philippines. 64,597 (1960).

tar·la·tan (tär′lə tən), *n.* a thin, open, stiff cotton fabric, not washable. Also, **tar′le·tan.** [< F *tarlatane*, dissimilated var. of *tarnatane* kind of cloth orig. imported from India < ?]

Tar·mac (tär′mak), *n.* **1.** *Trademark.* a bituminous binder, similar to tarmacadam, for surfacing roads, airport runways, parking areas, etc. **2.** (*l.c.*) *Chiefly Brit.* a road, airport runway, parking area, etc., paved with Tarmac, tarmacadam, or a layer of tar.

tar·mac·ad·am (tär′mə kad′əm), *n.* a paving material consisting of coarse crushed stone covered with a mixture of tar and bitumen.

tarn (tärn), *n.* a small mountain lake or pool. [ME *terne* < Scand; cf. Icel *tjörn* pond, pool]

tar·na·tion (tär nā′shən), *Dial.* —*interj.* **1.** damnation. —*n.* **2.** damnation; hell (used as a euphemism): *Where in tarnation is that boy?* —*adv.* **3.** damned. [dial. *'tar(nal)* damned (var. of ETERNAL) + (DAM)NATION]

tar·nish (tär′nish), *v.t.* **1.** to dull the luster of (a metallic surface), esp. by oxidation; discolor. **2.** to diminish or destroy the purity of; stain; sully: *The scandal tarnished his reputation.* —*v.i.* **3.** to grow dull or discolored; lose luster. **4.** to become sullied. —*n.* **5.** a dull coating on metal, caused by tarnishing. **6.** the condition of being tarnished. **7.** a stain or blemish. [< MF *terniss-*, long s. of *ternir* to dull, deaden < *terne* dull, wan < Gmc; cf. OHG *tarni*, c. OS *derni*, OE *dierne* hidden, obscure; see -ISH[2]] —**tar′nish·a·ble,** *adj.* —**Syn. 2.** blemish, soil. —**Ant. 1.** brighten.

Tar·no·pol (tär nô′pôl), *n.* Polish name of **Ternopol.**

Tar·nów (täʀ′no͝of), *n.* a city in SE Poland, E of Cracow. 74,000 (est. 1963).

ta·ro (tär′ō, târ′ō), *n., pl.* **-ros.** either of two stemless, araceous plants, *Colocasia esculenta* or *C. antiquorum*, cultivated in tropical regions, esp. the Pacific islands, for the tuberous, starchy, edible root. [< Polynesian]

ta·rot (ta rō′), *n.* *Cards.* any of a set of 22 playing cards bearing allegorical representations, used for fortunetelling. [back formation from *tarots* (pl.) < MF < It *tarocchi*, pl. of *tarocco* < ?]

tarp (tärp), *n.* *Informal.* tarpaulin. [by shortening]

tar·pan (tär pan′), *n.* a wild horse, *Equus przewalskii*, of central Asia, believed to be a subspecies of the domestic horse. [< Kirghiz]

tar·pau·lin (tär pô′lin, tär′pə lin), *n.* a protective covering of canvas or other material waterproofed with tar, paint, or wax. [earlier *tarpauling*. See TAR[1], PALL[1], -ING[1]]

Tar·pe·ia (tär pē′ə), *n.* *Class. Myth.* a vestal virgin who betrayed Rome to the Sabines and was crushed under their shields when she claimed a reward.

Tar·pe′ian Rock′ (tär pē′ən), a rock on the Capitoline Hill in ancient Rome, from which criminals were hurled. [< L (*mons*) *Tarpēi(us)* Tarpeian (hill) + -AN]

tar·pon (tär′pən), *n., pl.* **-pons,** (*esp. collectively*) **-pon.** a large game fish, *Tarpon atlanticus*, found in the warmer waters of the Atlantic Ocean. [?; c. D *tarpoen*]

Tarpon
(Length to 8 ft.)

Tar·quin (tär′kwin), *n.* **1.** (*Lucius Tarquinius Priscus*) died 578 B.C., king of Rome 616–578. **2.** (*Lucius Tarquinius Superbus*) ("*the Proud*") died 498 B.C., king of Rome 534–510. Also, **Tar·quin·i·us** (tär kwin′ē əs).

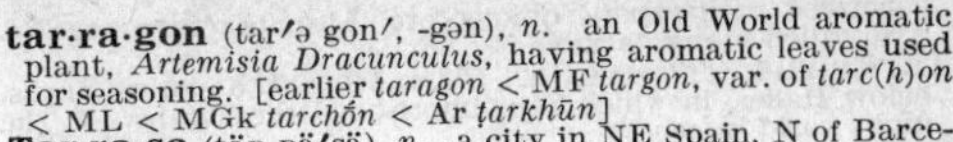

tar·ra·gon (tar′ə gon′, -gən), *n.* an Old World aromatic plant, *Artemisia Dracunculus*, having aromatic leaves used for seasoning. [earlier *taragon* < MF *targon*, var. of *tarc(h)on* < ML < MGk *tarchṓn* < Ar *ṭarkhūn*]

Tar·ra·sa (täʀ ʀä′sä), *n.* a city in NE Spain, N of Barcelona. 78,702 (1955).

tar·ri·ance (tar′ē əns), *n.* *Archaic.* **1.** delay. **2.** sojourn. [TARRY[1] + -ANCE]

tar·ry[1] (tar′ē), *v.*, **-ried, -ry·ing,** *n., pl.* **-ries.** —*v.i.* **1.** to remain or stay, as in a place; sojourn. **2.** to delay or be tardy in acting, starting, etc.; linger or loiter. **3.** to wait. —*v.t.* **4.** *Archaic.* to wait for. —*n.* **5.** *Archaic.* a stay; sojourn. [ME *tarye*] —**tar′ri·er,** *n.* —**Syn. 3.** See **wait.**

tar·ry[2] (tär′ē), *adj.*, **-ri·er, -ri·est.** of or like tar; smeared with tar. [TAR[1] + -Y[1]] —**tar′ri·ness,** *n.*

Tar·ry·town (tar′ē toun′), *n.* a village in SE New York, on the Hudson River. 11,115 (1970).

tars-, var. of **tarso-** before a vowel: *tarsal.*

tar·sal (tär′səl), *adj.* **1.** of or pertaining to the tarsus of the foot. **2.** pertaining to the tarsi of the eyelids. —*n.* **3.** a tarsal bone, joint, or the like.

Tarsier
(Total length 13 in.; tail 8 in.)

tar′ sand′, *Geol.* bituminous sand or sandstone from which petroleum can be obtained.

Tar·shish (tär′shish), *n.* an ancient country, of uncertain location, mentioned in the Bible. I Kings 10:22.

tar·si·a (tär′sē ə, tär sē′ə), *n.* intarsia. [< It; see INTARSIA]

tar·si·er (tär′sē ər), *n.* a small, arboreal, nocturnal primate of the genus *Tarsius*, of Indonesia and the Philippines, having a long thin tail and very large eyes. [< F = *tarse* TARSUS + *-ier* -ER[2]]

tarso-, a combining form of **tarsus:** *tarsometatarsus.* Also, *esp. before a vowel,* **tars-.**

tar·so·met·a·tar·sus (tär′sō met′ə tär′səs), *n., pl.* **-si** (-sī). *Ornith.* the large bone in the lower leg of a bird with which the toe bones articulate, formed by the fusion of tarsal and metatarsal bones. —**tar′so·met′a·tar′sal,** *adj.*

tar·sus (tär′səs), *n., pl.* **-si** (-sī). **1.** *Anat., Zool.* the proximal segment of the foot; the collection of bones between the tibia and the metatarsus, entering into the construction of the ankle joint. **2.** the small plate of connective tissue along the border of an eyelid. **3.** tarsometatarsus. **4.** the distal part of the leg of an insect, usually subdivided in the adult into 2 to 5 segments. [< NL < Gk *tarsós* the flat (of the foot)]

Tar·sus (tär′səs), *n.* a city in S Turkey, near the Mediterranean, on the Cydnus River: important seaport of ancient Cilicia; birthplace of Saint Paul. 57,035 (1965).

tart[1] (tärt), *adj.* **1.** sharp to the taste; sour or acid. **2.** sharp in character, spirit, or expression; cutting; caustic: *a tart remark.* [ME; OE *teart* sharp, rough; akin to D *tarten* to defy, MHG *traz* defiance] —**tart′ly,** *adv.* —**tart′ness,** *n.*

tart[2] (tärt), *n.* **1.** a small pie filled with cooked fruit or other sweetened preparation, usually having no top crust. **2.** *U.S. Slang.* a prostitute. **3.** *Chiefly Brit. Slang.* a girl or woman, esp. one of questionable morals. [late ME *tarte* < MF; cf. ML *tarta*]

tar·tan[1] (tär′tᵊn), *n.* **1.** a woolen or worsted cloth woven with stripes of different colors and widths crossing at right angles, worn chiefly by the Scottish Highlanders, each clan having one or more such distinctive plaids. **2.** a design of such a plaid known by the name of the clan wearing it. **3.** any plaid. —*adj.* **4.** of, pertaining to, or resembling tartan. **5.** made of tartan. [var. of *tertane* < MF *tertaine* (OF *tiretaine*) linsey-woolsey]

tar·tan[2] (tär′tᵊn), *n.* a single-masted vessel with a lateen sail and a jib, used in the Mediterranean. Also, **tar·tan·a** (tär tan′ə, -tä′nə). [earlier *tartane* < F, prob. < Pr *tartana* falcon, from the custom of using bird names for ships]

tar·tar (tär′tər), *n.* **1.** a hard, brownish or brownish-yellow deposit on the teeth, consisting of salivary secretion, food particles, and various salts, as calcium carbonate and phosphate. **2.** the deposit from wines, potassium bitartrate. [ME < ML *tartar(um)* < LGk *tártaron*; r. ME *tartre* < MF] —**tar′tar·ous,** *adj.*

Tar·tar (tär′tər), *n.* **1.** a member of any of the various tribes, chiefly Mongolian and Turkish, that overran Asia and much of eastern Europe in the Middle Ages. **2.** any of the descendants of this people. **3.** Tatar (def. 1). **4.** (*often l.c.*) a savage, intractable person. —*adj.* **5.** of or pertaining to a Tartar or Tartars. **6.** Tatar (def. 3). Also, **Tatar** (for defs. 1, 2, 4, 5). [late ME < ML *Tartar(us)* (? var. of **Tātārus* < Pers *Tātār*, by assoc. with TARTARUS); r. ME *Tartre* < MF]

Tar·tar (tär′tər), *n.* *Obs.* Tartarus.

Tar′tar Auton′omous So′viet So′cialist Repub′lic. See **Tatar Autonomous Soviet Socialist Republic.**

Tar·tar·e·an (tär târ′ē ən), *adj.* of or pertaining to Tartarus; infernal. [< L *Tartare(us)* of TARTARUS (see -EOUS) + -AN]

tar′tar emet′ic, *Chem., Pharm.* a poisonous powder, $K(SbO)C_4H_4O_6 \cdot \frac{1}{2}H_2O$, used as a mordant for dyeing, and as an expectorant, diaphoretic, and emetic. Also called **antimony potassium tartrate, potassium antimonyl tartrate.**

Tar·tar·i·an (tär târ′ē ən), *adj.* of, pertaining to, or characteristic of a Tartar or the Tartars; Tartar.

tar·tar·ic (tär târ′ik, -tär′-), *adj.* pertaining to or derived from tartar.

tartar′ic ac′id, *Chem.* an organic compound, $HOOC(CHOH)_2COOH$, existing in four isomeric forms, the commonest being a white powder: used in effervescent beverages, baking powders, confections, photography, and tanning.

tar′tar sauce′, a mayonnaise dressing, usually with chopped pickles, onions, olives, and green herbs added. Also, **tar′tare sauce′.** [< F *sauce tartare*]

tar′tar steak′, chopped beefsteak seasoned with salt and pepper and served uncooked, often with a raw egg and

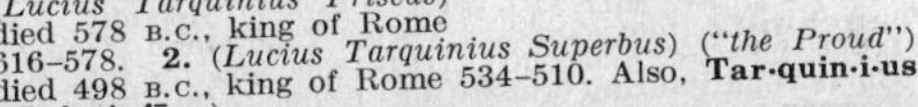

act, āble, dâre, ärt; ebb, ēqual; if, īce; hot, ōver, ôrder; oil; bo͝ok; o͞oze; out; up, ûrge; ə = *a* as in *alone*; chief; sing; shoe; thin; that; zh as in *measure*; ᵊ as in *button* (butᵊn). fire (fīᵊr). See the full key inside the front cover.

garnished with capers, onions, etc. Also, **tar′tare steak′.** Also called **steak tartare.**

Tar·ta·rus (tär′tər əs), *n. Class. Myth.* **1.** a sunless abyss, below Hades, in which Zeus imprisoned the Titans. **2.** the underworld in general.

Tar·ta·ry (tär′tə rē), *n.* the historical name of the region, of indefinite extent, in E Europe and Asia that was overrun by the Tartars in the Middle Ages. Also, **Tatary.** [ME *Tartarye* < MF *Tartarie* < ML *Tartaria*]

tart·let (tärt′lit), *n. Brit.* a small pie.

tar·trate (tär′trāt), *n. Chem.* a salt or ester of tartaric acid. [*tartr-* (comb. form repr. TARTAR) + -ATE[2]] —**tar′-trat·ed,** *adj.*

Tar·tu (tär′to͞o), *n.* a city in SE Estonia, in the W Soviet Union. 74,000 (1959). German, **Dorpat.** Russian, **Yurev.**

Tar·zan (tär′zən, -zan), *n. Often facetious.* a man of superior physical strength and virility. [from the hero of a series of jungle stories created by E. R. BURROUGHS]

Ta·shi La·ma (tä′shē lä′mə), any of a succession of Tibetan monks and spiritual leaders, second in importance only to the Dalai Lama. Also called **Panchen Lama, Panchen Rimpoche.** [after *Tashi* (*Lumpo*) name of monastery of which this Lama is abbot]

Tash·kent (täsh kent′), *n.* a city in and the capital of Uzbekistan, in the SW Soviet Union in Asia. 1,090,000 (1965). Also, **Tash·kend′.**

task (task, täsk), *n.* **1.** a definite piece of work assigned to or expected of a person; duty. **2.** any piece of work. **3.** a matter of considerable labor or difficulty. **4.** *Obs.* a tax or impost. **5. take to task,** to call to account; blame; censure. —*v.t.* **6.** to subject to severe or excessive labor or exertion; put a strain upon (powers, resources, etc.). **7.** to impose a task on. **8.** *Obs.* to tax. [ME < ML *tasca,* metathetic var. of *taxa* TAX] —**Syn. 1, 2.** job, assignment.

task′ force′, 1. *Mil.* a temporary grouping of units under one commander, formed for the purpose of carrying out a specific operation or mission. **2.** a group or committee formed for analyzing, investigating, or solving a specific problem.

task·mas·ter (task′mas′tər, täsk′mä′stər), *n.* **1.** a person whose function is to assign tasks to others, esp. burdensome tasks. **2.** a person who supervises rigorously the work of others.

task·work (task′wûrk′, täsk′-), *n.* work paid for by the job; piecework. [late ME *taske werke*]

Tasm., Tasmania.

Tas·man (taz′mən; *Du.* täs′män′), *n.* **A·bel Jans·zoon** (ä′bəl yän′sōn), 1602?–59, Dutch navigator and explorer.

Tas·ma·ni·a (taz mā′nē ə), *n.* an island S of Australia: a state of the Commonwealth of Australia. 350,340 (1961); 26,215 sq. mi. *Cap.:* Hobart. Formerly, **Van Diemen's Land.** —**Tas·ma′ni·an,** *adj., n.*

Tasma′nian dev′il, a small, ferocious, carnivorous marsupial, *Sarcophilus harrisii,* of Tasmania, having a black coat with white patches.

Tasmanian devil (Total length 3 ft.; tail 10½ in.)

Tasma′nian wolf′, the thylacine. Also called **Tasma′nian ti′ger.**

Tas′man Sea′ (taz′mən), a part of the Pacific Ocean between SE Australia and New Zealand.

tass (tas), *n. Chiefly Scot.* **1.** a cup or small goblet, esp. an ornamental one. **2.** the contents of a cup or goblet; a small draught, as of liquor. Also, **tassie.** [late ME *tasse* < MF < Ar *ṭass, ṭassah* basin < Pers *tast* cup]

Tass (tas, täs), *n.* an official press agency of the Soviet Union. Also, **TASS** [< Russ *T*(*elegrafnoye*) *A*(*genstvo*) *S*(*ovyetskovo*) *S*(*oyuza*) Telegraph Agency of the Soviet Union]

tasse (tas), *n. Armor.* tasset. [back formation from MF *tassete* TASSET]

tas·sel (tas′əl), *n., v.,* **-seled, -sel·ing** or (*esp. Brit.*) **-selled, -sel·ling.** —*n.* **1.** a pendent ornament, consisting of small cords or strands hanging from a roundish knob or head. **2.** something resembling this, as the inflorescence of certain plants, esp. that at the summit of a stalk of corn. —*v.t.* **3.** to furnish or adorn with tassels. **4.** to form into a tassel or tassels. **5.** to remove the tassel from (growing corn) in order to improve the crop. —*v.i.* **6.** (of corn) to put forth tassels. [ME < OF: fastening for cloak < LL **tassell*(*us*), b. L *tessella* (dim. of *tessera* die for gaming) and *taxillus* (dim. of *tālus* die for gaming). See TESSELLATE, TALUS[1]]

tas·set (tas′it), *n. Armor.* either of two pieces of plate armor hanging from the fauld to protect the upper parts of the thighs. Also, **tace, tasse.** [< F *tassette,* MF *tassete* = *tasse* pouch (< MHG *tasche,* lit., pendent object) + *-ete* -ET]

tass·ie (tas′ē), *n. Chiefly Scot.* tass.

Tas·so (tas′ō; *It.* täs′sô), *n.* **Tor·qua·to** (tôr kwä′tô), 1544–95, Italian poet.

taste (tāst), *v.,* **tast·ed, tast·ing,** *n.* —*v.t.* **1.** to experience, try, or detect the flavor of (something in the mouth). **2.** to eat or drink a little of. **3.** to experience (pleasures, sorrows, etc.), esp. in limited amounts. **4.** *Archaic.* to enjoy or appreciate the flavor of something. —*v.i.* **5.** to experience, try, or detect a flavor or flavors. **6.** to eat or drink a little (usually fol. by *of*): *She tasted of the cake.* **7.** to have a particular flavor (often fol. by *of*): *The milk tastes sour. This bread tastes of mold.* **8.** to experience pleasures, sorrows, etc., slightly (usually fol. by *of*). —*n.* **9.** the act of tasting food or drink. **10.** the sense by which the flavors of things are perceived when they are brought into contact with the tongue. **11.** the quality perceived by this sense; flavor. **12.** a small quantity tasted; a morsel, bit, or sip. **13.** a personal inclination to enjoy or appreciate certain things (often fol. by *for*). **14.** the sense of what is fitting, harmonious, or beautiful. **15.** the attitude of a place or period as to what is beautiful or harmonious. **16.** an artistic or decorative manner or style reflecting this attitude. **17.** the sense of what may be done or said without giving offense or committing an impropriety. **18.** a slight experience of pleasure, sorrow, etc., or a source of these: *a taste of the whip.* **19.** *Obs.* a test or trial. [ME *taste*(*n*) (to) touch, taste < OF *taster* to touch, explore by touching (MF also to taste); c. It *tastare,* Pr, OSp *tastar;* < ?] —**Syn. 1.** savor. **11.** TASTE, FLAVOR, SAVOR refer to a quality that is perceived when a substance is placed upon the tongue. TASTE is the general word: *the taste of roast beef.* FLAVOR is a characteristic taste, usually of a pleasing kind, as of some ingredient put into the food: *lemon flavor.* SAVOR implies pleasing scent as well as taste or flavor, and connotes enjoyment in tasting: *The sauce has an excellent savor.* **13.** fondness, disposition, appreciation, predisposition. **14.** discernment, perception, judgment. —**Ant. 13.** antipathy.

taste′ bud′, one of numerous small, flask-shaped bodies chiefly in the epithelium of the tongue, which are the end organs for the sense of taste.

taste·ful (tāst′fəl), *adj.* having, displaying, or in accordance with good taste. —**taste′ful·ly,** *adv.* —**taste′ful-ness,** *n.*

taste·less (tāst′lis), *adj.* **1.** having no taste or flavor; insipid. **2.** dull or uninteresting. **3.** lacking in good taste; showing lack of good taste. —**taste′less·ly,** *adv.* —**taste′-less·ness,** *n.*

tast·er (tā′stər), *n.* **1.** a person who tastes, esp. one skilled in distinguishing the qualities of liquors, tea, etc., by the taste. **2.** a container for taking samples or tasting. **3.** a person employed or ordered to taste the food and drink prepared for a king, dictator, etc., to ascertain the presence of poison. [ME *tastour* < AF]

tast·y (tā′stē), *adj.,* **tast·i·er, tast·i·est. 1.** good-tasting; savory. **2.** *Informal.* having or showing good taste; tasteful. —**tast′i·ly,** *adv.* —**tast′i·ness,** *n.*

tat (tat), *v.i., v.t.,* **tat·ted, tat·ting.** to do, or make by, tatting. [back formation from TATTING]

ta-ta (tä tä′), *n. Chiefly Brit.* good-by. [?]

Ta·tar (tä′tər), *n.* **1.** any of several Turkic languages of W central Asia and E Europe. **2.** Tartar (defs. 1, 2, 4). —*adj.* **3.** of or pertaining to Tatar. **4.** Tartar (def. 5). Also, **Tartar** (for defs. 1, 3). [see TARTAR] —**Ta·tar·i·an** (tä târ′ē ən), **Ta·tar·ic** (tä tar′ik) *adj.*

Ta′tar Auton′omous So′viet So′cialist Repub′lic, an administrative division of the RSFSR, in the E Soviet Union in Europe. 2,847,000 (1959); ab. 25,900 sq. mi. *Cap.:* Kazan. Also, **Tartar Autonomous Soviet Socialist Republic.**

Ta·ta·ry (tä′tə rē), *n.* Tartary.

Tate (tāt), *n.* **1. Sir Henry,** 1819–99, English merchant and philanthropist: founder of the English National Gallery of Art **(Tate′ Gal′lery). 2. (John Or·ley) Allen** (ôr′lē), 1899–1979, U.S. poet and critic.

ta·ter (tā′tər), *n. Dial.* potato. Also, **'ta′ter.** [by aphesis, and addition of hiatus-filling *r*]

tat·ou·ay (tat′o͞o ā′, tä′to͞o ī′), *n.* an armadillo, *Tatoua unicintus,* of tropical South America. [< Sp *tatuay* < Pg < Guarani *tatu-ai* = *tatu* armadillo + *ai* worthless (i.e., not edible)]

Ta′tra Moun′tains (tä′trä), a mountain range in N Czechoslovakia and S Poland: a part of the central Carpathian Mountains. Highest peak, Gerlachovka, 8737 ft. Also called **High Tatra.**

tat·ter (tat′ər), *n.* **1.** a torn piece hanging loose from or torn off the main part, as of a garment, flag, etc. **2. tatters,** torn or ragged clothing. —*v.t.* **3.** to tear or wear to tatters. —*v.i.* **4.** to become ragged. [(n.) late ME < Scand; cf. Icel *tötturr* rag, akin to OE *tætteca* rag, shred; (v.) back formation from TATTERED]

tat·ter·de·mal·ion (tat′ər di māl′yən, -mal′-), *n.* a person in tattered clothing; a ragged fellow. [first written *tatter-de-mallian* and rhymed with *Italian;* see TATTER; *-demallian* < ?]

tat·tered (tat′ərd), *adj.* **1.** torn to tatters; ragged: *a tattered flag.* **2.** wearing ragged clothing.

tat·ter·sall (tat′ər sôl′), *n.* **1.** a fabric with brightly colored crossbars in a tartan pattern. —*adj.* **2.** made of this fabric. [after *Tattersall's,* London horse market, where brightly-colored blankets were used]

tat·ting (tat′ing), *n.* **1.** the act or process of making a kind of knotted lace of cotton or linen thread with a shuttle. **2.** such lace. [?]

tat·tle (tat′əl), *v.,* **-tled, -tling,** *n.* —*v.i.* **1.** (esp. among children) to disclose information, as a secret, about another person, esp. out of spite or malice. **2.** to chatter or gossip. —*v.t.* **3.** to utter idly; disclose by gossiping. **4. tattle on,** to betray by tattling: *She tattled on her brother.* —*n.* **5.** act of tattling. **6.** idle talk; chatter; gossip. [late ME < MFlem *tatelen;* c. MLG *tatelen* to prattle, tattle] —**tat′tling·ly,** *adv.*

tat·tler (tat′lər), *n.* **1.** a person who tattles; telltale. **2.** any of several shore birds of the genus *Heteroscelus,* having a loud, whistling cry. **3.** any of various related shore birds having shrill cries, as the yellowlegs.

tat·tle·tale (tat′əl tāl′), *n.* **1.** a talebearer or informer, esp. among children. —*adj.* **2.** telltale; revealing.

tat·too[1] (ta to͞o′; *esp. Brit.* tə to͞o′), *n., pl.* **-toos. 1.** a signal on a drum, bugle, or trumpet at night, for soldiers or sailors to go to their quarters. **2.** a knocking or strong pulsation: *My heart beat a tattoo on my ribs.* **3.** *Brit.* an outdoor military pageant or display. [earlier *taptoo* < D *taptoe,* lit., the tap(room) is to (i.e., shut)]

tat·too[2] (ta to͞o′), *n., pl.* **-toos,** *v.,* **-tooed, -too·ing.** —*n.* **1.** the act or practice of marking the skin with indelible patterns, pictures, legends, etc., by making punctures in it and inserting pigments. **2.** a picture, legend, etc., so made. —*v.t.* **3.** to mark with tattoos. **4.** to put (designs or legends) on the skin. [< Marquesan *tatu;* r. *tattow* < Tahitian *tatau*] —**tat·too′er, tat·too′ist,** *n.*

tat·ty (tat′ē), *adj.* vulgar; crude; cheap. [perh. akin to OE *tætec* tatter, rag]

Ta·tum (tā′təm), *n.* **Edward Law·rie** (lôr′ē), 1909–75 U.S. biochemist: Nobel prize for medicine 1958.

tau (tô, tou), *n.* **1.** the 19th letter of the Greek alphabet (T, τ). **2.** tav. [ME < L < Gk < Sem; cf. Heb *tāw*]

Tauch·nitz (toukн′nits), *n.* **Karl Chri·stoph Trau·gott** (kärl kris′tôf trou′gôt), 1761–1836, and his son, **Karl Chris·ti·an Phi·lipp** (kris′tē än′ fē′lip, fil′ip), 1798–1844, German printers and publishers.

tau′ cross′, a T-shaped cross. Also called **Saint Anthony's cross.** See illus. at **cross.**

taught (tôt), *v.* pt. and pp. of **teach.**

taunt[1] (tônt, tänt), *v.t.* **1.** to challenge or reproach in a sarcastic, insulting, or jeering manner; mock. **2.** to provoke by taunts. —*n.* **3.** an insulting gibe or sarcasm, used to challenge or reproach. **4.** *Obs.* an object of insulting gibes or scornful reproaches. [?] —**taunt′er,** *n.* —**taunt′ing·ly,** *adv.* —**Syn. 1.** flout, insult. **2, 3.** jeer. See **ridicule.**

taunt[2] (tônt, tänt), *adj.* *Naut.* tall and well-stayed, as a mast. [akin to *ataunt* in phrase *all ataunt* fully rigged (said of a ship); cf. F *boire d'autant* to drink a great deal]

Taun·ton (tän′tᵊn *for 1;* tôn′tᵊn *for 2*), *n.* **1.** a city in SE Massachusetts. 43,756 (1970). **2.** a city in and the county seat of Somersetshire, in SW England. 35,178 (1961).

taupe (tōp), *n.* a dark brownish gray, sometimes tinged with purple, yellow, or green. [< F < L *talpa* mole]

taur-, var. of **tauro-** before a vowel: *taurine.*

tauri-, var. of **tauro-.**

tau·ri·form (tôr′ə fôrm′), *adj.* shaped like a bull or the head or horns of a bull. [< L *tauriform(is)*]

tau·rine[1] (tôr′īn, -in), *adj.* **1.** of, pertaining to, or resembling a bull. **2.** pertaining to the zodiacal sign Taurus. [< L *taurīn(us)*]

tau·rine[2] (tôr′ēn, -in), *n.* *Chem.* a crystalline substance, $H_2NCH_2CH_2SO_3H$, obtained from the bile of animals, used in biochemical research. [TAUR(OCHOLIC) + -INE[2]]

tauro-, a learned borrowing from Latin and Greek meaning "bull," used in the formation of compound words: *tauromachy.* Also, **taur-, tauri-.** [comb. form repr. L *taurus,* Gk *taûros*]

tau′rocho′lic ac′id, *Chem.* an acid, $C_{26}H_{45}NO_7S$, occurring as a sodium salt in the bile of carnivorous animals. —**tau·ro·cho·lic** (tôr′ə kō′lik, -kol′ik), *adj.*

tau·rom·a·chy (tô rom′ə kē), *n.* the art or technique of bullfighting. [< Sp *tauromaquia* < Gk *tauromachía*] —**tau·ro·ma·chi·an** (tôr′ə mā′kē ən), *adj.*

Tau·rus (tôr′əs), *n., gen.* **Tau·ri** (tôr′ī) for 1. **1.** *Astron.* the Bull, a zodiacal constellation between Gemini and Aries, containing the bright star Aldebaran. **2.** *Astrol.* the second sign of the zodiac. See illus. at **zodiac.** [< L]

Tau·rus (tôr′əs), *n.* a mountain range in S Turkey: highest peak, 12,251 ft.

taut (tôt), *adj.* **1.** tightly drawn; tense; not slack. **2.** emotionally or mentally strained or tense: *taut nerves.* **3.** in good order or condition; tidy; neat. [earlier *taught,* ME *tought;* akin to TOW[1]] —**taut′ly,** *adv.* —**taut′ness,** *n.*

taut·en (tôt′ᵊn), *v.t., v.i.* to make or become taut.

tauto-, a learned borrowing from Greek meaning "same," used in the formation of compound words: *tautomerism.* [< Gk, comb. form of *tautó,* contr. of *tò autó* the same]

tau·tog (tô tog′, -tôg′), *n.* a black food fish, *Tautoga onitis,* found along the North Atlantic coast of the U.S. [< Narragansett *tautauog,* pl. of *tautau* sheepshead]

tau·tol·o·gise (tô tol′ə jīz′), *v.i.,* **-gised, -gis·ing.** *Chiefly Brit.* tautologize.

tau·tol·o·gism (tô tol′ə jiz′əm), *n.* *Rare.* **1.** the use of tautology. **2.** a tautology.

tau·tol·o·gize (tô tol′ə jīz′), *v.i.,* **-gized, -giz·ing.** to use tautology. Also, *esp. Brit.,* **tautologise.**

tau·tol·o·gy (tô tol′ə jē), *n., pl.* **-gies. 1.** needless repetition of an idea in different words, as in "widow woman." **2.** an instance of such repetition. **3.** *Logic.* **a.** a law that can be shown on the basis of certain rules to exclude no logical possibilities. **b.** an instance of such a law. [< LL *tautologia* < Gk] —**tau·to·log·i·cal** (tôt′ᵊloj′i kəl), **tau′to·log′ic, tau·tol·o·gous** (tô tol′ə gəs), *adj.* —**tau′to·log′i·cal·ly, tau·tol′o·gous·ly,** *adv.*

tau·to·mer (tô′tə mər), *n.* *Chem.* a compound that exhibits tautomerism. [back formation from TAUTOMERISM]

tau·tom·er·ism (tô tom′ə riz′əm), *n.* *Chem.* the ability of certain organic compounds to react in isomeric structures which differ from each other in the position of a hydrogen atom and a double bond. [TAUTO- + (ISO)MERISM] —**tau·to·mer·ic** (tô′tə mer′ik), *adj.*

tau·tom·er·ize (tô tom′ə rīz′), *v.,* **-ized, -iz·ing.** —*v.i.* **1.** to undergo tautomerism. —*v.t.* **2.** to cause to undergo tautomerism. —**tau·tom′er·iz′a·ble,** *adj.* —**tau·tom′er·i·za′tion,** *n.*

tau·to·nym (tô′tə nim), *n.* *Bot., Zool.* a scientific name in which the generic and the specific names are the same, as *Chloris chloris* (the greenfinch). [< Gk *tautónym(os)* of the same name] —**tau′to·nym′ic, tau·ton·y·mous** (tô ton′ə məs), *adj.* —**tau·ton′y·my,** *n.*

tav (täv, täf; *Heb.* täv, täf), *n.* the 23rd letter of the Hebrew alphabet. Also, **taw.** [< Heb]

tav·ern (tav′ərn), *n.* **1.** a place where liquors are sold to be consumed on the premises. **2.** a public house for travelers and others; inn. [ME *taverne* < OF < L *taberna* hut, inn, wine shop] —**Syn. 1.** bar; pub. **2.** hostelry. See **hotel.**

tav·ern·er (tav′ər nər), *n.* **1.** *Archaic.* the owner of a tavern. **2.** *Obs.* a frequenter of taverns. [ME < AF = OF *tavernier*]

taw[1] (tô), *n.* **1.** a playing marble used as a shooter. **2.** a game in which marbles are arranged in the center of a circle drawn or scratched on the ground, the object being to knock out as many as possible from the circle; ringer. **3.** Also called **taw′ line′.** the line from which the players shoot. —*v.i.* **4.** to shoot a marble. [? special use of OE *getawu* tools]

taw[2] (tô), *v.t.* **1.** to prepare or dress (some raw material) for use or further manipulation. **2.** to transform an animal skin into white leather by the application of minerals, emulsions, etc. **3.** *Archaic.* to flog. [ME *tawe(n),* OE *tawian;* c. D *touwen,* Goth *taujan*] —**taw′er,** *n.*

taw[3] (täv, täf; *Heb.* täv, täf), *n.* tav.

taw·dry (tô′drē), *adj.,* **-dri·er, -dri·est.** (of finery, trappings, etc.) gaudy; showy and cheap. [short for *(Sain)t Audrey* lace, after the neck lace sold at St. Audrey's fair in Ely, England; *St. Audrey* (OE *Aethelthrȳth,* d. A.D. 679), Northumbrian queen and patron saint of Ely, according to tradition died of a throat tumor in punishment of her youthful liking for neck lace] —**taw′dri·ly,** *adv.* —**taw′dri·ness,** *n.* —**Syn.** flashy.

taw·ney (tô′nē), *adj.,* **-ni·er, -ni·est,** *n.* tawny.

taw·ny (tô′nē), *adj.,* **-ni·er, -ni·est,** *n.* —*adj.* **1.** of a dark yellowish or dull yellowish-brown color. —*n.* **2.** a shade of brown tinged with yellow; dull yellowish brown. [ME *tauny* < AF *taune* < MF *tané,* ptp. of *taner* to TAN] —**taw′ni·ly,** *adv.* —**taw′ni·ness,** *n.*

taws (tôz, täz), *n., pl.* **taws.** *Chiefly Scot.* a leather whip having its tip divided into smaller strips, used to punish students. [pl. of *taw* < Scand; cf. Icel *tang* string, rope, c. OE *tēag* TIE]

tax (taks), *n.* **1.** a sum of money levied upon incomes, property, sales, etc., by a government for its support or for specific facilities or services. **2.** a burdensome charge, obligation, duty, or demand. —*v.t.* **3.** (of a government) **a.** to impose a tax on (a person, business, etc.). **b.** to levy a tax in consideration of the possession or occurrence of (income, goods, sales, etc.), usually in proportion to the value of money involved. **4.** to lay a burden on; make serious demands on: *to tax one's resources.* **5.** to censure, reprove, or accuse: *to tax a person with laziness.* **6.** *Archaic.* to estimate or determine the amount or value of. [ME *taxe(n)* < ML *taxāre* to tax, appraise, L: to appraise, handle, freq. of *tangere* to touch] —**tax′er,** *n.* —**tax′ing·ly,** *adv.* —**tax′less,** *adj.* —**Syn. 1.** duty, impost, levy.

tax-, var. of **taxo-** before a vowel: *taxeme.* Also, **taxi-.**

tax·a·ble (tak′sə bəl), *adj.* **1.** subject to tax: *a taxable gain.* —*n.* **2.** Usually, **taxables.** persons, items of property, etc., that are subject to tax. [ME] —**tax′a·bil′i·ty, tax′a·ble·ness,** *n.* —**tax′a·bly,** *adv.*

tax·a·ceous (tak sā′shəs), *adj.* belonging to the *Taxaceae,* or yew family of trees and shrubs. [< NL *taxāceus* = L *tax(us)* yew + *-āceus* -ACEOUS]

tax·a·tion (tak sā′shən), *n.* **1.** the act of taxing. **2.** the fact of being taxed. **3.** a tax imposed. **4.** the revenue raised by taxes. [< ML *taxātiōn-* (s. of *taxātiō*) an appraising (see TAX, -ATION); r. ME *taxacioun* < AF] —**tax·a′tion·al,** *adj.*

tax-de·duct·i·ble (taks′di duk′tə bəl), *adj.* noting an item the value or cost of which is deductible from the gross amount on which a tax is calculated.

tax·eme (tak′sēm), *n.* *Linguistics.* a feature of the arrangement of elements in a construction, as selection, order, phonetic modification, or modulation. —**tax·e′mic,** *adj.*

tax′ eva′sion, a deliberate failure to pay taxes, usually by not filing or by falsifying a tax return.

tax-ex·empt (taks′ig zempt′), *adj.* **1.** not subject or liable to taxation. **2.** *U.S.* bearing interest that is exempt from federal income tax and from state income tax in the state of origin: *tax-exempt municipal bonds.* —*n.* **3.** a tax-exempt bond.

tax·i (tak′sē), *n., pl.* **tax·is** or **tax·ies,** *v.,* **tax·ied, tax·i·ing** or **tax·y·ing.** —*n.* **1.** a taxicab. —*v.i.* **2.** to ride or travel in a taxicab. **3.** (of an airplane) to move on the ground or on water under its own power. —*v.t.* **4.** to cause (an airplane) to taxi. [short for TAXICAB]

taxi-, var. of **taxo-:** *taxidermy.* Also, **tax-.**

tax·i·cab (tak′sē kab′), *n.* a public passenger vehicle, esp. an automobile, usually fitted with a taximeter. [TAXI(METER) + CAB]

tax′i danc′er, a girl or woman employed, as by a dance hall, to dance with patrons who pay a fee for each dance or for a set period of time. [so called because such a dancer, like a taxi, is hired for the occasion]

tax·i·der·my (tak′si dûr′mē), *n.* the art of preparing and preserving the skins of animals and of stuffing and mounting them in lifelike form. [TAX- + Gk *-dermia;* see -DERM, -Y[3]] —**tax′i·der′mal, tax′i·der′mic,** *adj.* —**tax′i·der′mist,** *n.*

tax·i·me·ter (tak′sē mē′tər, tak sim′i tər), *n.* a device fitted to a taxicab or other vehicle, for automatically computing and indicating the fare due. [alter. of *taxameter* < G < *Taxa* (< ML: tax, charge) + *-meter* -METER]

tax·is[1] (tak′sis), *n.* **1.** arrangement or order, as in one of the physical sciences. **2.** *Biol.* movement of an organism in a particular direction in response to an external stimulus. **3.** *Surg.* the replacing of a displaced part, or the reducing of a hernial tumor or the like, by manipulation without cutting. [< NL < Gk *táxis* = *tak-* (var. s. of *tássein* to arrange, put in order) + *-sis* -SIS]

tax·is[2] (tak′sēz), *n.* a pl. of **taxi.**

-taxis, a combining form of **taxis**[1]: *heterotaxis.* Cf. **tax-, taxo-, -taxy.**

tax·ite (tak′sīt), *n.* *Petrog.* a lava appearing to be formed from fragments, because of its parts having different colors, textures, etc. [TAX- + -ITE[1]] —**tax·it·ic** (tak sit′ik), *adj.*

taxo-, a combining form of **taxis**[1]: *taxonomy.* Also, **tax-, taxi-.**

tax·on·o·my (tak son′ə mē), *n.* **1.** the science or technique of classification. **2.** the science dealing with the identification, naming, and classification of organisms. [F *taxonomie*] —**tax·o·nom·ic** (tak′sə nom′ik), **tax′o·nom′i·cal,** *adj.* —**tax′o·nom′i·cal·ly,** *adv.* —**tax·on′o·mist, tax·on′o·mer,** *n.*

tax·pay·er (taks′pā′ər), *n.* **1.** a person who pays a tax or is subject to taxation. **2.** a building that yields only enough rent to defray the taxes on the property on which it stands. —**tax′pay′ing,** *adj.*

tax′ rate′, the percentage of income, property value, or the like, to be paid as a tax.

tax′ return′, return (def. 24).

tax′ shel′ter, any financial arrangement (as a certain kind of investment, deduction, or allowance) which results in a reduction or elimination of taxes due. —**tax-shel·tered** (taks′shel′tərd), *adj.*

tax′ stamp′, a stamp required to be affixed to certain products, documents, etc., to indicate that a tax has been paid.

tax′ ti′tle, *Law.* a title, acquired by the purchaser at a forced sale of property for nonpayment of taxes.

-taxy, var. of **-taxis:** *heterotaxy.* [< Gk *-taxia.* See TAXIS[1], -Y[3]]

Tay (tā), *n.* **1.** a river flowing through central Scotland into the Firth of Tay. 118 mi. long. **2. Firth of,** an estuary of the North Sea, off the coast of central Scotland. 25 mi. long.

Ta·ÿg·e·te (tā ij′i tē), *n.* *Class. Myth.* one of the Pleiades and the mother, by Zeus, of Lacedaemon.

Tay·lor (tā′lər), *n.* **1. Bay·ard** (bī′ərd, bā′-), (*James Bayard*), 1825–78, U.S. poet, novelist, and travel writer. **2. Jeremy,** 1613–67, English prelate and theological writer. **3. Zachary** ("*Old Rough and Ready*"), 1784–1850, 12th president of the U.S. 1849–50: major general during the Mexican War and commander of the army of the Rio Grande in 1846. **4.** a city in SE Michigan, near Detroit. 70,020 (1970).

Tay′-Sachs′ disease′ (tā′saks′), *Pathol.* a rare, fatal disease, occurring chiefly in infants and children, esp. of Jewish extraction and of eastern European origin, characterized by a red spot on the retina, gradual blindness, and loss of weight, and believed to be of genetic origin.

taz·za (tät′sə; *It.* tät′tsä), *n., pl.* **-zas,** *It.* **-ze** (-tse). a shallow, saucerlike, ornamental bowl, often having handles and usually on a high base or pedestal. [< It < Ar *ṭassah* basin. See TASS]

TB, 1. tubercle bacillus. **2.** tuberculosis. Also, **T.B., Tb**

Tb, *Chem.* terbium.

t.b., 1. trial balance. **2.** tubercle bacillus. **3.** tuberculosis.

T-bar (tē′bär′), *n.* **1.** Also called **tee.** (in construction work) a rolled metal bar or beam with a cross section resembling a T. See illus. at **shape. 2.** See **T-bar lift.**

T′-bar lift′, a ski lift having a T-shaped bar against which two skiers may lean. Also called **T-bar.**

Tbi·li·si (tbi lē′sē), *n.* a city in and the capital of Georgia, in the SW Soviet Union on the Kura River. 805,000 (1965). Formerly, **Tiflis.**

T-bill (tē′bil′), *n. Informal.* See **treasury bill.** [by shortening]

T′-bone steak′ (tē′bōn′), a loin steak having some tenderloin, characterized by its T-shaped bone.

tbs., tablespoon; tablespoonful. Also, **tbsp.**

TC, Trusteeship Council (of the United Nations).

Tc, *Chem.* technetium.

tc., tierce; tierces.

TCBM, transcontinental ballistic missile.

Tchad (chᴀd), *n.* French name of **Chad.**

Tchai·kov·sky (chī kôf′skē), *n.* **Peter Il·yich** (il′yich) or **Pë·tr Il·ich** (pyô′tər il yēch′), 1840–93, Russian composer. Also, **Tschaikovsky, Tschaikowsky.** Russian, **Chaikovski.**

tcher·vo·netz (cher vô′nits), *n., pl.* **-von·tzi** (-vôn′tsē). chervonets.

tchr., teacher.

TD, touchdown; touchdowns.

T.D., 1. Traffic Director. **2.** Treasury Department.

Te, *Chem.* tellurium.

tea (tē), *n.* **1.** the dried and prepared leaves of a shrub, *Thea sinensis.* **2.** the shrub itself, extensively cultivated in China, Japan, India, etc., and having fragrant white flowers. **3.** a somewhat bitter, aromatic beverage prepared by infusing tea leaves in boiling water, served hot or iced. **4.** any of various infusions prepared from the leaves, flowers, etc., of other plants, and used as beverages or medicines. **5.** See **beef tea. 6.** *Brit.* a light afternoon or evening meal. **7.** a social gathering at which tea is served. **8.** *Slang.* marijuana. **9. one's cup of tea,** suitable, appropriate, or attractive to one. [< Chin (Amoy dial.) *t'e;* c. Mandarin *ch'a*]

tea′ bag′, a container of thin paper or cloth holding a measured amount of tea leaves, usually for making an individual serving of tea.

tea′ ball′, a perforated metal ball in which tea leaves are placed to be immersed in boiling water to make tea.

tea·ber·ry (tē′ber′ē, -bə rē), *n., pl.* **-ries.** the spicy red fruit of the American wintergreen, *Gaultheria procumbens.*

tea′ bis′cuit, a small, round biscuit, usually shortened and sweetened.

tea′ cad′dy, *Chiefly Brit.* a small box, can, or chest for holding tea leaves.

tea·cake (tē′kāk′), *n.* **1.** (in the U.S.) a small cake, cooky, tart, or the like, for serving with tea or punch. **2.** (in England) a light, flat, sweet cake with raisins, usually buttered and served hot with tea.

tea·cart (tē′kärt′), *n.* a small, wheeled table used in serving tea; tea wagon.

teach (tēch), *v.,* **taught, teach·ing.** —*v.t.* **1.** to impart knowledge of or skill in; give instruction in: *He teaches mathematics.* **2.** to impart knowledge or skill to; give instruction to: *He teaches a large class.* —*v.i.* **3.** to impart knowledge or skill; give instruction. [ME *teche(n),* OE *tǣcan;* akin to TOKEN] —**Syn. 2, 3.** instruct, tutor, educate.

Teach (tēch), *n.* **Edward** ("*Blackbeard*"), died 1718, English pirate and privateer in the Americas.

teach·a·ble (tē′chə bəl), *adj.* **1.** capable of being instructed, as a person; docile. **2.** capable of being taught, as a subject. —**teach′a·bil′i·ty, teach′a·ble·ness,** *n.* —**teach′a·bly,** *adv.*

teach·er (tē′chər), *n.* a person who teaches or instructs, esp. as a profession; instructor. [ME *techer*] —**teach′er·less,** *adj.* —**teach′er·ship′,** *n.*

teach′er bird′, *U.S. Dial.* the ovenbird, *Seiurus aurocapillus.*

teach′ers col′lege a college offering courses for the training of teachers.

teach-in (tēch′in′), *n., pl.* **teach-ins.** a prolonged period of uninterrupted lectures, speeches, etc., esp. conducted at a college or university by members of the faculty and invited guests, as an expression of social protest.

teach·ing (tē′ching), *n.* **1.** the act or profession of a person who teaches. **2.** something that is taught. **3.** Often, **teachings.** doctrines or precepts. [ME *teching*]

teach′ing aid′, material used by a teacher to supplement classroom instruction or to stimulate the interest of students.

teach′ing fel′low, a holder of a teaching fellowship.

teach′ing fel′lowship, a fellowship providing a student in a graduate school with free tuition and expenses but stipulating that he assume some teaching duties.

teach′ing machine′, an automatic device that presents the user with items of information in planned sequence, registers his response, and informs him of its acceptability.

tea′ co′zy, cozy (def. 3).

tea·cup (tē′kup′), *n.* **1.** a cup in which tea is served, usually of small or moderate ize. **2.** a teacupful.

tea·cup·ful (tē′kup fŏŏl′), *n., pl.* **-fuls.** the amount a teacup will hold, equal to four fluid ounces.

tea′ dance′, a dance held at teatime.

tea·house (tē′hous′), *n., pl.* **-hous·es** (-hou′ziz). a restaurant or other establishment, esp. in the Orient, where tea and refreshments are served.

teak (tēk), *n.* **1.** a large East Indian verbenaceous tree, *Tectona grandis,* yielding a hard, durable, resinous, yellowish-brown wood used for shipbuilding, making furniture, etc. **2.** any of various similar trees or woods. [earlier *teke* < Pg *teca* < Malayalam *tēkka*]

tea·ket·tle (tē′ket′əl), *n.* a portable kettle with a cover, spout, and handle, used for boiling water.

teak·wood (tēk′wŏŏd′), *n.* the wood of the teak.

teal (tēl), *n., pl.* **-teals,** (*esp. collectively*) **-teal** for 1. **1.** any of several small, fresh-water ducks. **2.** Also called **teal′ blue′.** a medium to dark greenish blue. [ME *tele;* akin to D *taling,* MLG *telink*]

team (tēm), *n.* **1.** a number of persons associated in some joint action, as one of the sides in a game or contest. **2.** two or more draft animals harnessed together. **3.** one or more draft animals together with the harness and the vehicle drawn. **4.** *Archaic.* a family of young animals, esp. ducks or pigs. **5.** *Obs.* offspring or progeny; race or lineage. —*v.t.* **6.** to join together in a team. **7.** to convey or transport by means of a team. —*v.i.* **8.** to drive a team. **9.** to gather or join in a team, a band, or a cooperative effort (usually fol. by *up, together,* etc.). —*adj.* **10.** of, pertaining to, or performed by a team: *a team sport; team effort.* [ME *teme,* OE *tēam* childbearing, brood, offspring, set of draft beasts; c. D *toom* bridle, reins, G *Zaum,* Icel *taumr*]

team·mate (tēm′māt′), *n.* a member of the same team.

team·ster (tēm′stər), *n.* a person who drives teams or a truck for hauling, esp. as an occupation.

team′ teach′ing, a program by which two or more teachers integrate their subjects, such as literature and history, into one course to create a broader perspective for the students.

team·work (tēm′wûrk′), *n.* **1.** cooperative or coordinated effort by a group of persons acting together as a team or for a common cause. **2.** work done with a team.

Tea·neck (tē′nek′), *n.* a township in NE New Jersey. 42,355 (1970).

tea′ par′ty, a social gathering, usually in the afternoon, at which tea and other light refreshments are served.

tea·pot (tē′pot′), *n.* a container with a lid, spout, and handle, in which tea is made and from which it is poured.

tea·poy (tē′poi), *n.* **1.** a small three-legged table or stand. **2.** a small table for use in serving tea. [< Hindi *tīpāi,* alter. (with *t-* from *tir-* < Skt *tri* three) of Pers *sīpǣ* three-legged stand]

tear[1] (tēr), *n.* **1.** a drop of the saline, watery fluid continually secreted by the lacrimal glands between the surface of the eye and the eyelid, serving to moisten and lubricate these parts and keep them clear of foreign particles. **2.** this fluid appearing in or flowing from the eye as the result of emotion, esp. grief. **3.** something resembling or suggesting a tear, as a drop of a liquid or a tearlike mass of a solid substance having a teardrop shape. **4. tears,** grief; sorrow. **5. in tears,** in the act of weeping. —*v.i.* **6.** to fill up and overflow with tears, as the eyes. [ME *teer,* OE (WS) *tēar* (var. of *teagor*) = *tæher* (north); c. OHG *zahar,* Icel *tār,* Goth *tagr,* Gk *dákry,* etc.]

tear[2] (târ), *v.,* **tore** or (*Archaic*) **tare; torn** or (*Archaic*) **tare; tear·ing;** *n.* —*v.t.* **1.** to pull apart or in pieces by force, esp. so as to leave ragged or irregular edges. **2.** to pull or snatch violently; wrench away with force: *to tear a book from someone's hands.* **3.** to harrow or disrupt: *a country torn by civil war.* **4.** to lacerate. **5.** to produce or effect by rending: *to tear a hole in one's coat.* —*v.i.* **6.** to become shredded or separated into parts. **7.** to make a rip or rent. **8.** to move with great haste. **9.** to attempt to rip off or away (usually fol. by *at*). **10. tear into,** *Informal.* **a.** to attack impulsively and heedlessly. **b.** to attack verbally. **11. tear up,** to rip into small shreds. —*n.* **12.** the act of tearing. **13.** a rent or fissure. **14.** *Slang.* a spree. [ME *tere(n),* OE *teran;* c. D *teren,* G *zehren* to consume, Goth *(dis)tairan* to destroy, Gk *dérein* to flay, etc.] —**tear′a·ble,** *adj.* —**tear′er,** *n.*

—**Syn. 1.** TEAR, REND, RIP mean to pull apart. To TEAR is to split the fibers of something by pulling apart: *to tear open a letter.* REND emphasizes the force or violence in tearing apart or in pieces: *to rend one's clothes in grief.* RIP implies vigorous tearing asunder, esp. along a seam or line: *to rip the sleeves out of a coat.* **3.** shatter, afflict. **5.** cut, mangle. **13.** rip.

tear·drop (tēr′drop′), *n.* **1.** a tear or something suggesting a tear. **2.** something shaped like a drop of a thin liquid, having a globular form at the bottom, tapering to a point at the top.

tear·ful (tēr′fəl), *adj.* **1.** full of tears; weeping. **2.** causing tears, as of sympathy. —**tear′ful·ly,** *adv.* —**tear′ful·ness,** *n.*

tear′ gas′ (tēr), a gas that makes the eyes smart and water, thus producing a temporary blindness, used in warfare, to quell riots, etc.

tear-gas (tēr′gas′), *v.t.,* **-gassed, -gas·sing.** to subject to tear gas.

tear·ing (târ′ing), *adj.* violently hasty: *in a tearing hurry.* [TEAR[2] + -ING[2]] —**tear′ing·ly,** *adv.*

tear-jerk·er (tēr′jûr′kər), *n. Informal.* a pathetic story, play, movie, or the like. Also, **tear′jerk′er.**

tear·less (tēr′lis), *adj.* **1.** not weeping or shedding tears. **2.** unable to shed tears. —**tear′less·ly,** *adv.* —**tear′less·ness,** *n.*

tea·room (tē′rōōm′, -rŏŏm′), *n.* a room or shop where tea and other refreshments are served to customers.

tea′ rose′, *Hort.* any of several cultivated varieties of roses having a scent resembling that of tea.

tear′ sheet′ (târ), a sheet or page torn from a publication, esp. one containing an advertisement and sent to the advertiser as proof of publication.

tear·y (tēr′ē), *adj.,* **tear·i·er, tear·i·est. 1.** of or like tears. **2.** tearful. [ME *tery*] —**tear′i·ly,** *adv.*

Teas·dale (tēz′dāl′), *n.* **Sara,** 1884–1933, U.S. poet.

tease (tēz), *v.*, **teased, teas·ing,** *n.* —*v.t.* **1.** to irritate or provoke with persistent petty distractions, trifling raillery, or other annoyance, often in sport. **2.** to pull apart or separate the adhering fibers of (wool or the like), as in combing or carding. **3.** to ruffle (the hair) by holding it at the ends and combing toward the scalp so as to give body to a hairdo. **4.** to raise a nap on (cloth) with teasels; teasel. —*v.i.* **5.** to provoke or disturb a person or animal by importunity or persistent petty annoyances. —*n.* **6.** a person who teases or annoys. **7.** the act of teasing. **8.** the state of being teased. [ME *tese(n)*, OE *tǣsan* to pull, tear, comb; c. MLG *tesen*, OHG *zeisan* to pluck] —**teas′ing·ly,** *adv.* —**Syn. 1.** See **bother.** —**Ant. 1.** mollify.

tea·sel (tē′zəl), *n.*, *v.*, **-seled, -sel·ing** or (*esp. Brit.*) **-selled, -sel·ling.** —*n.* **1.** any dipsacaceous herb of the genus *Dipsacus*, having prickly leaves and flower heads. **2.** the dried flower head or bur of the herb *D. fullonum*, used for teasing or teaseling cloth. **3.** any mechanical contrivance used for teaseling. —*v.t.* **4.** to raise a nap on (cloth) with teasels; dress by means of teasels. Also, **teazel, teazle.** [ME *tesel*, OE *tǣsel;* akin to TEASE] —**tea′sel·er;** *esp. Brit.*, **tea′sel·ler,** *n.*

teas·er (tē′zər), *n.* **1.** a person or thing that teases. **2.** *Theat.* a drapery or flat piece across the top of the proscenium arch which masks the flies and together with the tormentors helps form a frame for the stage opening. **3.** *Print., Journalism.* kicker (def. 5).

tea′ serv′ice, 1. a set of chinaware for preparing and drinking hot beverages, esp. tea. **2.** a set of silver or other metalware for preparing and serving hot beverages, esp. tea. Also called **tea′ set′.**

tea′ shop′, 1. a tearoom. **2.** *Brit.* a restaurant that specializes in serving light meals and snacks; lunchroom.

tea·spoon (tē′spo͞on′, -spo͝on′), *n.* **1.** a small spoon for stirring tea, coffee, etc. **2.** a teaspoonful.

tea·spoon·ful (tē′spo͞on fo͝ol′, -spo͝on-), *n.*, *pl.* **-fuls. 1.** the amount a teaspoon can hold. **2.** *Cookery.* a volumetric measure equal to 1/6 fluid ounce; 1/3 tablespoonful. *Abbr.:* t., tsp.

teat (tēt, tit), *n.* the protuberance on the breast or udder in female mammals, except the monotremes, through which the milk ducts discharge; nipple or mammilla. [ME *tete* < OF < Gmc; see TIT[2]]

tea′ ta′ble, a small table for holding a tea service and cups, plates, etc., for several people.

tea·time (tē′tīm′), *n.* the time at which tea is served or taken, usually in the late afternoon.

tea′ tow′el, a dishtowel.

tea′ wag′on, teacart.

tea·zel (tē′zəl), *n.*, *v.t.*, **-zeled, -zel·ing** or (*esp. Brit.*) **-zelled, -zel·ling.** teasel.

tea·zle (tē′zəl), *n.*, *v.t.*, **-zled, -zling.** teasel.

Te·bet (tā′vəs; *Heb.* tā vāt′), *n.* the fourth month of the Jewish calendar. Also, **Tevet.** Cf. **Jewish calendar.** [ME *tebeth* < LL < Heb *tēbhēth*]

tech., 1. technical. **2.** technically. **3.** technician. **4.** technological. **5.** technology. Also, **techn.**

tech·ne·ti·um (tek nē′shē əm, -shəm), *n.* *Chem.* an element of the manganese family, not found in nature, but obtained in the fission of uranium or by the bombardment of molybdenum. *Symbol:* Tc; *at. wt.:* 99; *at. no.:* 43; *sp. gr.:* 11.5. [Gk *technēt(ós)* artificial (< *technásthai* to make, contrive; see TECHNIC) + -IUM]

tech·nic (tek′nik *or, for 1,* tek nēk′), *n.* **1.** technique. **2.** a technicality. **3. technics,** (*construed as sing. or pl.*) the study or science of an art or of arts in general, esp. the mechanical or industrial arts. —*adj.* **4.** technical. [(n.): earlier *technica* < Gk *techniká*, neut. pl. of *technikós* of art and craft = *téchn(ē)* art, craft + *-ikos* -IC; (adj.): < Gk *technik(ós)*]

tech·ni·cal (tek′ni kəl), *adj.* **1.** pertaining to or suitable for an art, science, or the like: *technical skill.* **2.** peculiar to or characteristic of a particular art, science, profession, trade, etc. **3.** meaningful or of interest to persons of specialized knowledge rather than to laymen: *a technical article in a science journal.* **4.** concerned with or dwelling on technicalities, as a person in an explanation or argument. **5.** skilled in or familiar in a practical way with a particular art, trade, etc. **6.** pertaining to or connected with the mechanical or industrial arts and the applied sciences. **7.** considered from a point of view in accordance with a stringent interpretation of the rules. —**tech′ni·cal·ly,** *adv.*

tech·ni·cal·i·ty (tek′nə kal′i tē), *n.*, *pl.* **-ties** for 2, 3. **1.** the characteristic of being technical. **2.** the use of technical methods or terms. **3.** something that is technical; a technical point, detail, or expression.

tech′nical knock′out, *Boxing.* the termination of a bout to prevent severe or disabling injury to the boxer who is losing. *Abbr.:* TKO, T.K.O.

tech′nical ser′geant, 1. *U.S. Air Force.* a noncommissioned officer ranking below a master sergeant and above a staff sergeant. **2** *U.S. Army.* (formerly) a noncommissioned officer below a master sergeant and above a staff sergeant: now corresponds to sergeant first class.

tech·ni·cian (tek nish′ən), *n.* **1.** a person who is trained or skilled in the technicalities of a subject. **2.** a person who is skilled in the technique of an art, as music or painting. **3.** *U.S. Army.* (formerly) one of several grades above private, given to specialists who are enlisted men: now called specialist. [TECHNIC + -IAN; see -ICIAN]

Tech·ni·col·or (tek′nə kul′ər), *n.* *Trademark.* a system of making color motion pictures by superimposing the three primary colors to produce a final colored print. —**Tech·ni·col·ored** (tek′nə kul′ərd), *adj.*

tech·nique (tek nēk′), *n.* **1.** the manner, methods, or ability with which a person fulfills the technical requirements of his particular art or field of endeavor. **2.** the body of specialized procedures and methods used in any specific field, esp. in an area of applied science. **3.** technical skill; ability to apply procedures or methods so as to effect a desired result. **4.** *Informal.* method of projecting personal charm, appeal, etc.: *He has the greatest technique with women.* [< F: technical (adj.), technic (n.) < Gk; see TECHNIC]

techno-, a learned borrowing from Greek where it meant "art," "skill," used in the formation of compound words to refer to "technique," "technology," etc.: *technography.* [comb. form repr. Gk *téchnē* art, skill. See TECHNIC]

tech·noc·ra·cy (tek nok′rə sē), *n.*, *pl.* **-cies. 1.** a theory and movement advocating control of industrial resources, reform of financial institutions, and reorganization of the social system according to the findings of technologists and engineers. **2.** a system of government in which this theory is applied. **3.** any application of this theory. —**tech·no·crat** (tek′nə krat′), *n.* —**tech′no·crat′ic,** *adj.*

tech·nog·ra·phy (tek nog′rə fē), *n.* the description and study of the arts and sciences in their geographical and ethnic distribution and historical development.

technol., 1. technological. **2.** technology.

tech·no·log·i·cal (tek′nə loj′i kəl), *adj.* **1.** of or pertaining to technology; relating to science and industry. **2.** *Econ.* caused by technical advances in production methods: *technological unemployment.* Also, **tech′no·log′ic.** —**tech′no·log′i·cal·ly,** *adv.*

tech·nol·o·gy (tek nol′ə jē), *n.* **1.** the branch of knowledge that deals with industrial arts, applied science, engineering, etc. **2.** the application of knowledge for practical ends, as in a particular field: *educational technology.* **3.** the terminology of an art, science, etc.; technical nomenclature. **4.** a technological process, invention, method, or the like. **5.** the sum of the ways in which a social group provide themselves with the material objects of their civilization. [< Gk *technología* systematic treatment. See TECHNO-, -LOGY] —**tech·nol′o·gist,** *n.*

Tech. Sgt., Technical Sergeant.

tech·y (tech′ē), *adj.*, **tech·i·er, tech·i·est.** tetchy. —**tech′i·ly,** *adv.* —**tech′i·ness,** *n.*

tec·ton·ic (tek ton′ik), *adj.* **1.** of or pertaining to building or construction; constructive; architectural. **2.** *Geol.* **a.** pertaining to the structure of the earth's crust. **b.** referring to the forces or conditions within the earth that cause movements of the crust, as earthquakes, folds, faults, or the like. **c.** designating the results of such movements: *tectonic valleys.* [< LL *tectonic(us)* < Gk *tektonikós* pertaining to construction = *tekton-* (s. of *téktōn*) carpenter + *-ikos* -IC]

tec·ton·ics (tek ton′iks), *n.* (*construed as sing.*) **1.** the science or art of assembling, shaping, or ornamenting materials in construction; the constructive arts in general. **2.** structural geology. [see TECTONIC, -ICS]

tec·trix (tek′triks), *n.*, *pl.* **tec·tri·ces** (tek′tri sēz′, tek trī′sēz). *Ornith.* covert (def. 8). [< NL, fem. of L *tector* = *tect(us)* covered (ptp. of *tegere*) + *-or* -OR[2]; see -TRIX] —**tec·tri·cial** (tek trish′əl), *adj.*

Te·cum·seh (ti kum′sə), *n.* 1768?–1813, American Indian chief of the Shawnee tribe. Also, **Te·cum·tha** (ti kum′thə).

ted (ted), *v.t.*, **ted·ded, ted·ding.** to spread out for drying, as newly mown hay. [late ME *tedde*, OE **teddan;* c. Icel *tethja* to manure, OHG *zettan* to spread, Gk *dateisthai* to divide] —**ted′der,** *n.*

ted·dy (ted′ē), *n.*, *pl.* **-dies.** Often, **teddies.** a one-piece undergarment, consisting of a chemise and loose-fitting underpants, worn by women. [?]

ted′dy bear′, a toy bear, esp. a stuffed one. [named after Theodore Roosevelt, who was called *Teddy;* he is said to have spared or saved the life of a bear cub while hunting]

Ted′dy boy′, (*often l.c.*) a rebellious British youth of the early 1960's affecting Edwardian dress.

Te De·um (tā dā′o͝om, tē dē′əm), **1.** an ancient Latin hymn of praise to God, sung regularly at matins in the Roman Catholic Church and, usually, in an English translation, at Morning Prayer in the Anglican Church, as well as at services of thanksgiving. **2.** a musical setting of this hymn. **3.** a service of thanksgiving in which this hymn forms a prominent part. [first two words of the hymn, which begins: *Tē Deum laudāmus* thee, God, we praise]

te·di·ous (tē′dē əs, tē′jəs), *adj.* **1.** marked by dullness; long and tiresome. **2.** causing weariness or boredom, as through verbosity. [late ME < ML, LL *taediōs(us).* See TEDIUM, -OUS] —**te′di·ous·ly,** *adv.* —**te′di·ous·ness,** *n.* —**Syn. 1.** wearing, boring, tiring, monotonous, dull.

te·di·um (tē′dē əm), *n.* the quality or state of being tedious; monotony. [< L *taedium*]

tee[1] (tē), *n.* **1.** the letter *T* or *t.* **2.** something shaped like a T, as a three-way joint used in fitting pipes together. **3.** T-bar (def. 1). **4.** the mark aimed at in various games, as curling. **5. to a tee.** See **T, t** (def. 6). —*adj.* **6.** having a crosspiece at the top; shaped like a T.

tee[2] (tē), *n.*, *v.*, **teed, tee·ing.** *Golf.* —*n.* **1.** Also called **tee′ing ground′.** the starting place, usually a hard mound of earth, at the beginning of play for each hole. **2.** a small wooden, plastic, metal, or rubber peg from which the ball is driven, as in teeing off. —*v.t.* **3.** to place (the ball) on a tee. **4. tee off,** to strike the ball from a tee. [?]

teem[1] (tēm), *v.i.* **1.** to abound or swarm; be prolific or fertile (usually fol. by *with*). **2.** *Obs.* to be or become pregnant; bring forth young. —*v.t.* **3.** *Obs.* to produce (offspring). [ME *teme(n)*, OE *tēman, tīeman* to produce (offspring). See TEAM] —**teem′er,** *n.* —**teem′ing·ly,** *adv.*

teem[2] (tēm), *v.t.*, *v.i.* to empty or pour out; discharge. [ME *teme(n)* < Scand; cf. Icel *tæma* to empty, *tōmr* empty, c. OE *tōm* free from]

teen[1] (tēn), *n.* **1.** *Archaic.* suffering; grief. **2.** *Obs.* injury; harm. [ME *tene*, OE *tēona;* c. OFris *tiona*, OS *tiono*, Icel *tjōn*]

teen[2] (tēn), *adj.* **1.** teen-age. —*n.* **2.** Also, **teen·er** (tē′nər). a teen-ager. [by shortening]

-teen, a suffix used to form cardinal numerals from thirteen to nineteen. [ME, OE *-tēne*, comb. form of TEN; c. D *-tien*, G *-zehn*]

teen-age (tēn′āj′), *adj.* of, pertaining to, or characteristic of a teen-ager. Also, **teen′age′, teen′-aged′, teen′aged′.**

teen-ag·er (tēn′ā′jər), *n.* a person in his or her teens. Also, **teen′ag′er.**

teens (tēnz), *n. pl.* the numbers 13 through 19, esp. in a

progression, as the 13th through the 19th years of a lifetime or of a given or implied century. [independent pl. use of -TEEN]
teen·sy-ween·sy (tēn′sē wēn′sē), *adj. Baby Talk.* tiny; small. Also, **teent′sy-weent′sy, teen′sie-ween′sie.** [alter. of TEENY-WEENY]
tee·ny (tē′nē), *adj.*, **-ni·er, -ni·est.** *Informal.* tiny. [b. TINY + WEE]
tee·ny·bop·per (tē′nē bop′ər), *n.* a young teenage girl of the late 1960's who closely followed teenage fads.
tee·ny-wee·ny (tē′nē wē′nē), *adj. Baby Talk.* tiny; small. Also, **tee′nie-wee′nie.** [TEENY + WEENY]
tee·pee (tē′pē), *n.* tepee.
Tees (tēz), *n.* a river in N England, flowing E along the boundary between Durham and Yorkshire to the North Sea. 70 mi. long.
tee′ shirt′, T-shirt.
tee·ter (tē′tər), *Chiefly U.S.* —*v.i.* **1.** to seesaw. **2.** to move unsteadily. —*v.t.* **3.** to tip (something) up and down; move unsteadily. —*n.* **4.** a seesaw. **5.** a seesaw motion; wobble. [northern var. of ME *titeren* < Scand; cf. Icel *titra;* c. G *zittern* to tremble, quiver]
tee·ter·board (tē′tər bōrd′, -bôrd′), *n.* a seesaw. Also called **tee·ter-tot·ter** (tē′tər tot′ər).
teeth (tēth), *n.* pl. of **tooth.** —**teeth′less,** *adj.*
teethe (tēth), *v.i.*, **teethed, teeth·ing.** to grow teeth; cut one's teeth. [late ME *teth,* OE **tēthan* (only ptp. is recorded)]
teeth′ing ring′, a circular ring, usually of plastic, ivory, bone, etc., on which a teething baby may bite.
tee·to·tal (tē tōt′əl), *adj.*, *v.*, **-taled, -tal·ing** or (*esp. Brit.*) **-talled, -tal·ling.** —*adj.* **1.** of, pertaining to, advocating, or pledged to total abstinence from intoxicating drink. **2.** *Informal.* absolute; complete. —*v.i.* **3.** to practice teetotalism. [reduplicated var. of TOTAL, coined by R. Turner, of Preston, England, in 1833, in a speech advocating total abstinence from alcoholic drinks] —**tee·to′tal·ly,** *adv.*
tee·to·tal·er (tē tōt′əl ər), *n.* a person who abstains totally from intoxicating drink. Also, **tee·to′tal·ist.**
tee·to·tum (tē tō′təm), *n.* a kind of die having four sides, each marked with a different initial letter, spun with the fingers in an old game of chance. [earlier *T totum,* alter. of *totum* (name of toy < L *tōtum,* neut. of *tōtus* all) by prefixing its initial letter, which stood on one side of the toy]
Tef·lon (tef′lon), *n. Trademark.* polytetrafluoroethylene.
teg·men (teg′mən), *n., pl.* **-mi·na** (-mə nə). **1.** a cover, covering, or integument. **2.** *Bot.* the delicate inner integument or coat of a seed. [< L: covering, syncopated var. of *tegumen* = *tegu-* (var. s. of *tegere* to cover) + *-men* n. suffix] —**teg·mi·nal** (teg′mə nəl), *adj.*
Te·gu·ci·gal·pa (te gōō′sē gäl′pä), *n.* a city in and the capital of Honduras, in the S part. 270,645.
teg·u·lar (teg′yə lər), *adj.* **1.** pertaining to or resembling a tile. **2.** consisting of or arranged like tiles. [< L *tēgu(la)* tile + -AR¹] —**teg′u·lar·ly,** *adv.*
teg·u·ment (teg′yə mənt), *n.* a covering or investment; integument. [< L *tegument(um)* = *tegu-* (see TEGMEN) + *-mentum* -MENT] —**teg·u·men·tal** (teg′yə men′təl), **teg·u·men·ta·ry** (teg′yə men′tə rē), *adj.*
te-hee (tē hē′), *interj., n., v.*, **-heed, -hee·ing.** —*interj.* **1.** the sound of a tittering laugh. —*n.* **2.** a titter; snicker. —*v.i.* **3.** to titter; snicker. [ME; OE *tæg tæg;* imit.]
Te·he·ran (te′hə ran′, -rän′, tē′ə-, tā′ə-; *Pers.* te hrän′), *n.* a city in and the capital of Iran, in the N part: World War II conference of Roosevelt, Churchill, and Stalin 1943. 3,150,000. Also, **Te·hran′.**
Te·huan·te·pec (tə wän′tə pek′; *Sp.* te wän′te pek′), *n.* **1. Isthmus of,** an isthmus in S Mexico, between the Gulf of Tehuantepec and the Gulf of Campeche. 125 mi. wide at its narrowest point. **2. Gulf of,** an inlet of the Pacific, off the S coast of Mexico. ab. 300 mi. wide.
Tei·de (*Sp.* tā′the), *n.* **Pi·co de** (pē′kō the), a volcanic peak in the Canary Islands, on Tenerife. 12,190 ft. Also called **Pico de Tenerife, Pico de Teneriffe, Pico de Teyde.**
te ig·i·tur (tā ij′i tōōr′), *Church Latin.* thee therefore: the first words in the canon of the Mass in the Roman rite.
Tei·re·si·as (tī rē′sē əs), *n.* Tiresias.
Te·jo (te′zhōō), *n.* Portuguese name of **Tagus.**
tek·tite (tek′tīt), *n. Geol.* any of several kinds of small glassy bodies, in various forms, the exact origin of which is unknown. [< Gk *tēkt(ós)* molten + -ITE¹]
tel-¹, var. of **tele-¹:** *telesthesia.*
tel-², var. of **tele-²:** *telencephalon.* Properly, this form should occur wherever the following element begins with a vowel; however, **teleo-** is more frequently found.
tel., **1.** telegram. **2.** telegraph. **3.** telephone.
tel·aes·the·sia (tel′is thē′zhə, -zhē ə, -zē ə), *n.* telesthesia.
Tel A·mar·na (tel′ ə mär′nə). See **Tell el Amarna.**
tel·a·mon (tel′ə mon′), *n., pl.* **tel·a·mo·nes** (tel′ə mō′nēz). *Archit.* atlas (def. 8). [< L < Gk: bearer, support; identified with TELAMON]
Tel·a·mon (tel′ə mən), *n. Class. Myth.* an Argonaut and friend of Hercules, and the father of Ajax and Teucer.
Tel·a·mo′ni·an A′jax (tel′ə mō′nē ən), Ajax (def. 1).
tel·an·gi·ec·ta·sis (tel an′jē ek′tə sis), *n., pl.* **-ses** (-sēz′). *Pathol.* chronic dilatation of the capillaries and other small blood vessels, as seen in the faces of alcoholics and those exposed to raw, cold climates. [< NL < Gk *tél(os)* end + *angeî(on)* receptacle + *éktasis* extension] —**tel·an·gi·ec·tat·ic** (tel an′jē ek tat′ik), *adj.*
Tel A·viv (tel′ ə vēv′), *n.* a city in W Israel. 392,900 with Jaffa (est. 1963).
tele-¹, a learned borrowing from Greek meaning "distant," esp. "transmission over a distance," used in the formation of technical terms: *telegraph.* Also, **tel-, telo-.** [comb. form repr. Gk *têle* far]
tele-², a learned borrowing from Greek meaning "end," "complete," used in the formation of compound words: *telestich.* Also, **tel-, teleo-, telo-.** [comb. form repr. Gk *télos* end, and *téleios* perfected]
tel·e·cast (tel′ə kast′, -käst′), *v.*, **-cast** or **-cast·ed, -cast·ing,** *n.* —*v.t., v.i.* **1.** to broadcast by television. —*n.* **2.** a television broadcast. [TELE(VISION + BROAD)CAST] —**tel′e·cast′er,** *n.*
tel·e·com·mu·ni·cate (tel′ə kə myōō′nə kāt′), *v.t.*, **-cat·ed, -cat·ing.** to transmit (data, sound, images, etc.) by telecommunications. [back formation from TELECOMMUNICATIONS] —**tel′e·com·mu′ni·ca′tor,** *n.*
tel·e·com·mu·ni·ca·tions (tel′ə kə myōō′nə kā′shənz), *n.* Sometimes, **telecommunication.** (*construed as sing.*) the transmission of information, as words, sounds, or images, usually over great distances, in the form of electromagnetic signals, as by telegraph, telephone, radio, or television.
tel·e·du (tel′i dōō′), *n.* a small, dark-brown, skunklike mammal, *Mydaus javensis,* of the mountains of Java, Sumatra, and Borneo. [< Malay]
teleg., **1.** telegram. **2.** telegraph. **3.** telegraphy.
tel·e·gen·ic (tel′ə jen′ik), *adj.* having physical qualities or characteristics that televise well. [TELE-¹ + (PHOTO)-GENIC] —**tel′e·gen′i·cal·ly,** *adv.*
tel·eg·no·sis (tel′ə nō′sis, tel′əg-), *n.* supernatural or occult knowledge; clairvoyance. [TELE-¹ + -GNOSIS]
Te·leg·o·nus (tə leg′ə nəs), *n. Class. Myth.* a son of Odysseus and Circe who unknowingly killed his father and eventually married Penelope.
te·leg·o·ny (tə leg′ə nē), *n. Genetics.* the supposed influence of a previous sire upon the progeny subsequently borne by the same mother to other sires. [TELE-¹ + -GONY] —**tel·e·gon·ic** (tel′ə gon′ik), *adj.*
tel·e·gram (tel′ə gram′), *n.* a message or communication sent by telegraph. —**tel′e·gram′mic, tel·e·gram·mat·ic** (tel′ə grə mat′ik), *adj.*
tel·e·graph (tel′ə graf′, -gräf′), *n.* **1.** an apparatus or system for transmitting messages or signals to a distant place by means of an electric device. —*v.t.* **2.** to transmit or send (a message) by telegraph. **3.** to send a message to (a person) by telegraph. **4.** *Informal.* to divulge or indicate unwittingly to one's opponent (one's next offensive move); broadcast. —*v.i.* **5.** to send a message by telegraph. —**te·leg·ra·pher** (tə leg′rə fər); *esp. Brit.*, **te·leg′ra·phist,** *n.* —**tel′e·graph′ic, tel′e·graph′i·cal,** *adj.*
tel·e·graph·o·scope (tel′ə graf′ə skōp′), *n.* an early type of facsimile telegraph.
te·leg·ra·phy (tə leg′rə fē), *n.* the technique or practice of constructing or operating telegraphs.
tel·e·ki·ne·sis (tel′ə ki nē′sis, -kī-), *n.* the production of motion in a body, apparently without the application of material force: a power long claimed by spiritualistic mediums. [TELE-¹ + Gk *kínēsis* movement] —**tel·e·ki·net·ic** (tel′ə-ki net′ik, -kī-), *adj.*
Tel el A·mar·na (tel′ el ə mär′nə). See **Tell el Amarna.**
Te·lem·a·chus (tə lem′ə kəs), *n. Class. Myth.* the son of Odysseus and Penelope who helped Odysseus to kill the suitors of Penelope.
Te·le·mann (tā′lə män′), *n.* **Ge·org Phi·lipp** (gā′ōrk fē′lip, fil′ip), 1681–1767, German composer.
tel·e·mark (tel′ə märk′), *n.* (*sometimes cap.*) *Skiing.* a turn in which the tip of one ski placed far forward is gradually angled inward in the direction of turn. [named after *Telemark,* a Norwegian county]
te·lem·e·ter (tə lem′i tər, tel′ə mē′tər), *n.* **1.** any of certain devices or attachments for determining distances by measuring the angle subtending a known distance. **2.** *Elect.* the complete measuring, transmitting, and receiving apparatus for indicating, recording, or integrating at a distance, by electrical translating means, the value of a quantity. —**tel·e·met·ric** (tel′ə me′trik), *adj.* —**te·lem·e·try** (tə lem′i trē), *n.*
tel·en·ceph·a·lon (tel′en sef′ə lon′), *n., pl.* **-lons, -la** (-lə). *Anat.* the anterior section of the forebrain comprising the cerebrum and related structures. —**tel·en·ce·phal·ic** (tel′en sə fal′ik), *adj.*
teleo-, var. of **tele-²:** *teleology.*
tel·e·ol·o·gy (tel′ē ol′ə jē, tē′lē-), *n. Philos.* **1.** the doctrine that final causes exist. **2.** the study of the evidences of design or purpose in nature. **3.** such design or purpose. **4.** the belief that purpose and design are a part of or are apparent in nature. **5.** (in vitalist philosophy) the doctrine that phenomena are guided not only by mechanical forces but that they also move toward certain goals of self-realization. [< NL *teleologia.* See TELEO-, -LOGY] —**tel·e·o·log·i·cal** (tel′ē ə loj′i kəl, tē′lē-), **tel′e·o·log′ic,** *adj.* —**tel′e·o·log′i·cal·ly,** *adv.* —**tel′e·ol′o·gism,** *n.*
tel·e·ost (tel′ē ost′, tē′lē-), *adj.* **1.** belonging or pertaining to the *Teleostei,* a group of bony fishes including most living species. —*n.* **2.** a teleost fish. [back formation from NL *teleosteī* (pl.). See TELE-², OSTEO-] —**tel′e·os′te·an,** *adj., n.*
te·lep·a·thist (tə lep′ə thist), *n.* **1.** a student of or believer in telepathy. **2.** a person having telepathic power.
te·lep·a·thy (tə lep′ə thē), *n.* communication between minds by some means other than sensory perception. —**tel·e·path·ic** (tel′ə path′ik), *adj.* —**tel′e·path′i·cal·ly,** *adv.*
tel·e·phone (tel′ə fōn′), *n., v.*, **-phoned, -phon·ing.** —*n.* **1.** an apparatus or system for transmission of sound or speech to a distant point by an electric device. —*v.t.* **2.** to speak to by telephone. **3.** to send (a message) by telephone. —*v.i.* **4.** to send a message by telephone. —**tel′e·phon′er,** *n.*
tel′ephone book′, a directory containing an alphabetical list of telephone subscribers in a city or other area, together with their addresses and telephone numbers. Also called **tel′ephone direc′tory, phone book, phone directory.**
tel′ephone booth′, a booth containing a public telephone. Also called, *esp. Brit.*, **tel′ephone box′.**
tel′ephone pole′. See **utility pole.**
tel·e·phon·ic (tel′ə fon′ik), *adj.* **1.** of or pertaining to a telephone system. **2.** carrying sound to a distance. —**tel′e·phon′i·cal·ly,** *adv.*
te·leph·o·ny (tə lef′ə nē), *n.* the construction or operation of telephones or telephonic systems.
Tel·e·pho·to (tel′ə fō′tō), *adj.* **1.** *Trademark.* noting or pertaining to a lens construction for producing a relatively large image with a focal length shorter than that required by an ordinary lens producing an image of the same size. **2.** (*l.c.*) noting or pertaining to telephotography. [(def. 2) short for TELEPHOTOGRAPH]
tel·e·pho·to·graph (tel′ə fō′tə graf′, -gräf′), *n.* **1.** a picture transmitted by wire or radio. **2.** *Rare.* a photograph taken with a Telephoto lens.
tel·e·pho·tog·ra·phy (tel′ə fə tog′rə fē), *n.* **1.** photogra-

phy of distant objects, using a Telephoto lens. **2.** facsimile (def. 2). —**tel·e·pho·to·graph·ic** (tel′ə fō′tə graf′ik), *adj.*

tel·e·port (tel′ə pōrt′, -pôrt′), *v.t.* to transport (a body) by telekinesis. [TELE-[1] + PORT[5]] —**tel′e·por·ta′tion, tel′e·por′tage,** *n.*

tel·e·print·er (tel′ə prin′tər), *n.* a teletypewriter. [TELE(TYPE) + PRINTER]

Tel·e·prompt·er (tel′ə promp′tər), *n. Trademark.* an off-screen device for unrolling a magnified script so that it is visible to the performers or speakers on a television program.

tel·e·ran (tel′ə ran′), *n. Electronics.* a system of aircraft navigation using radar to provide a map of the sky above an airfield, which, together with the map of the airfield itself and other pertinent data, is transmitted by television to the airplane approaching the field. [short for *Tele(vision) R(adar) A(ir) N(avigation)*]

tel·e·scope (tel′i skōp′), *n., v.,* **-scoped, -scop·ing.** —*n.* **1.** an optical instrument for making distant objects appear larger and therefore nearer. One of the two principal forms **(refracting telescope)** consists essentially of an objective lens set into one end of a tube and an adjustable eyepiece or combination of lenses set into the other end of a tube that slides into the first and through which the enlarged object is viewed directly, the other **(reflecting telescope)** having a concave mirror that gathers light from the object and focuses it into an adjustable eyepiece or combination of lenses through which the reflection of the object is enlarged and viewed. —*v.t.* **2.** to force together, one into another, or force into something else, in the manner of the sliding tubes of a jointed telescope. **3.** to shorten or condense. —*v.i.* **4.** to slide together, or into something else. **5.** to be driven one into another, as railroad cars in a collision. **6.** to be or become shortened or condensed. [TELE-[1] + -SCOPE; r. *telescopium* (< NL) and *telescopio* (< It)]

tel·e·scop·ic (tel′i skop′ik), *adj.* **1.** of, pertaining to, or of the nature of a telescope. **2.** obtained by means of a telescope: *a telescopic view of the moon.* **3.** seen by a telescope; visible only through a telescope. **4.** far-seeing: *a telescopic eye.* **5.** consisting of parts that slide one within another. Also, **tel′e·scop′i·cal.** —**tel′e·scop′i·cal·ly,** *adv.*

te·les·co·py (tə les′kə pē), *n.* the use of the telescope. —**te·les′co·pist,** *n.*

tel·e·sis (tel′i sis), *n. Sociol.* deliberate, purposeful utilization of the processes of nature and society to obtain particular goals. [< Gk: completion]

Te·les·pho·rus (tə les′fər əs), *n.* pope A.D. 125?–136?.

tel·es·the·sia (tel′is thē′zhə, -zhē ə, -zē ə), *n.* sensation or perception received at a distance without the normal operation of the recognized sense organs. Also, **telaesthesia.** —**tel·es·thet·ic** (tel′is thet′ik), **tel′aes·thet′ic,** *adj.*

te·les·tich (tə les′tik, tel′i stik′), *n. Pros.* a poem in which the last letters of successive lines form a word, a phrase, or the like. Cf. **acrostic.**

tel·e·thon (tel′ə thon′), *n.* a television broadcast lasting several hours, esp. one soliciting support for a charity, political candidate, etc. [TELE-[1] + *-thon,* modeled after *marathon*]

Tel·e·type (tel′i tīp′), *n., v.,* **-typed, -typ·ing.** —*n.* **1.** *Trademark.* a teletypewriter. —*v.t.* **2.** (*l.c.*) to send by Teletype. —*v.i.* **3.** (*l.c.*) to operate a Teletype.

Tel·e·type·set·ter (tel′i tīp′set′ər, tel′i tīp′-), *n. Trademark.* an apparatus, actuated by punched paper tape, for operating automatically a Linotype or other similar machine. *Abbr.:* TTS —**tel′e·type′set′ting,** *n.*

tel·e·type·writ·er (tel′i tīp′rī′tər, tel′i tīp′-), *n.* a telegraphic apparatus by which signals are sent by striking the letters and symbols of the keyboard of an instrument resembling a typewriter and are received by and reproduced on a similar instrument.

tel·e·typ·ist (tel′i tī′pist), *n.* a teletypewriter operator.

tel·e·vise (tel′ə vīz′), *v.t., v.i.,* **-vised, -vis·ing.** to send or receive by television. [back formation from TELEVISION]

tel·e·vi·sion (tel′ə vizh′ən), *n.* **1.** the broadcasting of a still or moving image via radiowaves to receivers that project it on a picture tube for viewing at a distance from the point of origin. **2.** the process involved. **3.** the field of television broadcasting. **4.** a set for receiving television broadcasts. [TELE-[1] + VISION] —**tel·e·vi·sion·al** (tel′ə vizh′ə nᵊl), *adj.* —**tel′e·vi′sion·al·ly,** *adv.* —**tel·e·vi·sion·ar·y** (tel′ə vizh′ə ner′ē), *adj.*

tel′evision sta′tion, station (def. 9).

tel·e·vi·sor (tel′ə vī′zər), *n.* an apparatus for transmitting or receiving television. [TELEVISE + -OR[2]]

Tel·ex (tel′eks), *n.* **1.** *Trademark.* a two-way teletypewriter service channeled through a public telecommunications system for instantaneous, direct communication between private subscribers at remote locations. —*v.t.* **2.** (*l.c.*) to send by Telex. [*tel(eprinter) ex(change)*]

tel·fer (tel′fər), *n., adj., v.t.* telpher. —**tel′fer·age,** *n.*

te·li·um (tē′lē əm, tel′ē-), *n., pl.* **te·li·a** (tē′lē ə, tel′ē ə). *Bot.* the sorus of the rust fungi. [< NL < Gk *téleion,* neut. of *téleios* perfected] —**te′li·al,** *adj.*

tell[1] (tel), *v.,* **told, tell·ing.** —*v.t.* **1.** to give an account or narrative of; narrate; relate (a story, tale, etc.). **2.** to make known by speech or writing (a fact, news, information, etc.); communicate. **3.** to announce or proclaim. **4.** to utter (the truth, a lie, etc.). **5.** to express in words (thoughts, feelings, etc.). **6.** to reveal or divulge (something secret or private). **7.** to discern or distinguish: *to tell twins apart; Can you tell who that is from here?* **8.** to bid or command: *Tell him to stop.* —*v.i.* **9.** to give an account or report: *Tell me about your trip.* **10.** to give evidence or be an indication: *Time will tell.* **11.** to disclose something secret or private; tattle: *She knows who did it, but she won't tell.* **12.** to determine or predict: *Who can tell what tomorrow may bring?* **13.** to produce a marked or severe effect: *The strain was telling on his health.* **14. tell off,** *Informal.* to rebuke severely; scold. **15. tell on,** to tattle on (someone). [ME *telle(n),* OE *tellan* to relate, count; c. D *tellen* to reckon, count, Icel *telja* to count, say, OHG *zellēn.* See TALE] —**tell′a·ble,** *adj.* —**Syn. 1.** recount, describe, report. **2.** impart. **4.** speak. **6.** disclose, acknowledge, confess. **7.** recognize.

tell[2] (tel), *n.* an artificial mound consisting of the accumulated remains of one or more ancient settlements (often used as part of a place name). [< Ar *tall* hillock]

Tell (tel), *n.* **William.** See **William Tell.**

Tell el A·mar·na (tel′ el ə mär′nə), a village in central Arab Republic of Egypt, on the Nile: site of the ancient Egyptian capital of Ikhnaton. Also, **Tell′-el-A·mar′na, Tel el Amarna, Tel Amarna.**

tell·er (tel′ər), *n.* **1.** a person or thing that tells, relates, or communicates; narrator. **2.** a person employed in a bank to receive or pay out money over the counter. **3.** a person who tells, counts, or enumerates, as one appointed to count votes in a legislative body. [ME] —**tell′er·ship′,** *n.*

Tel·ler (tel′ər), *n.* **Edward,** born 1908, U.S. physicist, born in Hungary.

tell·ing (tel′ing), *adj.* **1.** having force or effect; effective; striking: *a telling blow.* **2.** revealing; indicative of much otherwise unnoticed: *a telling analysis.* —**tell′ing·ly,** *adv.*

Tel·loh (te lō′), *n.* a village in SE Iraq, between the lower Tigris and Euphrates: site of Lagash. Also, **Tel·lo′.**

tell·tale (tel′tāl′), *n.* **1.** a person who heedlessly or maliciously reveals private or confidential matters; tattler; talebearer. **2.** a thing serving to reveal or disclose something. **3.** any of various registering devices, as a time clock. **4.** a row of strips hung over a track to warn trainmen atop freight trains when they are approaching a low bridge, tunnel, or the like. **5.** *Yachting.* (on a sailboat) a feather, string or similar device used to indicate the relative direction of the wind. —*adj.* **6.** that reveals or betrays what is not intended to be known: *a telltale blush.* **7.** giving notice or warning of something, as a mechanical device.

tellur-, *Chem.* a prefix indicating the presence of tellurium: *tellurite.*

tel·lu·ri·an[1] (te lo͝or′ē ən), *adj.* **1.** of or characteristic of the earth or its inhabitants; terrestrial. —*n.* **2.** an inhabitant of the earth. [< L *tellūri-* (s. of *tellūs*) earth + -AN]

tel·lu·ri·an[2] (te lo͝or′ē ən), *n.* tellurion.

tel·lu·ric[1] (te lo͝or′ik), *adj.* **1.** of or pertaining to the earth; terrestrial. **2.** of or proceeding from the earth or soil. [< L *tellūri-* (s. of *tellūs*) earth + -IC]

tel·lu·ric[2] (te lo͝or′ik), *adj. Chem.* **1.** of or containing tellurium, esp. in the hexavalent state. **2.** containing tellurium in a higher valence state than the corresponding tellurous compound.

tel·lu·ride (tel′yə rīd′, -rid), *n. Chem.* a binary compound of tellurium with an electropositive element or group.

tel·lu·ri·on (te lo͝or′ē on′), *n.* an apparatus for showing the manner in which the diurnal rotation and annual revolution of the earth and the obliquity of its axis produce the alternation of day and night and the changes of the seasons. Also, **tellurian.** [< L *tellūri-* (s. of *tellūs*) earth + Gk *-on,* neut. of *-os* adj. suffix]

tel·lu·rite (tel′yə rīt′), *n.* **1.** *Chem.* a salt of tellurous acid as sodium tellurite, Na_2TeO_3. **2.** a rare mineral, tellurium dioxide, TeO_2.

tel·lu·ri·um (te lo͝or′ē əm), *n. Chem.* a rare, lustrous, brittle, crystalline, silver-white element resembling sulfur in its properties, and usually occurring in nature combined with gold, silver, or other metals of high atomic weight: used in the manufacture of alloys and as a coloring agent in glass and ceramics. *Symbol:* Te; *at. wt.:* 127.60; *at. no.:* 52; *sp. gr.:* 6.24. [< L *tellūr-* (s. of *tellūs*) earth + (URAN)IUM]

tel·lu·rous (tel′yər əs, te lo͝or′əs), *adj. Chem.* containing tetravalent tellurium.

Tel·lus (tel′əs), *n.* an ancient Roman goddess of the earth, marriages, and fertility, identified with the Greek Gaea.

tel·ly (tel′ē), *n., pl.* **-lies.** *Brit. Informal.* **1.** television. **2.** a television set. [by shortening and alter.]

telo-[1], var. of **tele-**[1].

telo-[2], var. of **tele-**[2]: *telophase.*

tel·o·phase (tel′ə fāz′), *n. Biol.* the final stage of mitosis in which new nuclei are formed. —**tel′o·pha′sic,** *adj.*

tel·pher (tel′fər), *n.* **1.** a traveling unit, car, or carrier in a telpherage. —*adj.* **2.** of or pertaining to a system of telpherage. —*v.t.* **3.** to transport by means of a telpherage. Also, **telfer.** [alter. of *telephore.* See TELE-[1], -PHORE]

tel·pher·age (tel′fər ij), *n.* a transportation system in which telphers are suspended from or run on wire cables or the like, esp. one operated by electricity. Also, **telferage.**

tel·son (tel′sən), *n.* the last segment, or an appendage of the last segment, of certain arthropods, as the middle flipper of a lobster's tail. [< Gk: boundary, limit] —**tel·son·ic** (tel son′ik), *adj.*

Tel·star (tel′stär′), *n. Trademark.* one of a series of low-altitude, active communications satellites for broadband microwave communications and satellite tracking in space.

Tel·u·gu (tel′o͝o go͞o′), *n., pl.* **-gus,** (*esp. collectively*) **-gu,** *adj.* —*n.* **1.** a Dravidian language spoken in SE India in the region N of Madras. **2.** a member of the people speaking this language. —*adj.* **3.** of Telugu or the Telugu.

tem·blor (tem′blər, -blôr; *Sp.* tem blôr′), *n., pl.* **-blors,** *Sp.* **-blo·res** (-blô′res). *Chiefly U.S.* a tremor; earthquake. [< Sp: lit., a quaking < *tembl(ar)* (to) quake (? b. L *timēre* to fear and LL *tremulāre* to quake; see TREMBLE) + *-or* -OR[1]]

tem·er·ar·i·ous (tem′ə râr′ē əs), *adj.* reckless; rash. [< L *temerārius* = *temer(e)* blindly, heedlessly + *-ārius* -ARY] —**tem′er·ar′i·ous·ly,** *adv.* —**tem′er·ar′i·ous·ness,** *n.*

te·mer·i·ty (tə mer′i tē), *n.* reckless boldness; rashness. [late ME *temeryte* < L *temeritās* hap, chance, rashness = *temer(e)* by chance, rashly + *-itās* -ITY] —**Syn.** audacity, effrontery, foolhardiness.

Tem·es·vár (te′mesh vär′), *n.* Hungarian name of **Timișoara.**

temp., **1.** temperature. **2.** temporary. **3.** in the time of. [< L *tempore*]

Tem·pe (tem′pē), *n.* **1. Vale of,** a valley in E Greece, in Thessaly, between Mounts Olympus and Ossa. **2.** a city in central Arizona, near Phoenix. 63,550 (1970).

tem·per (tem′pər), *n.* **1.** a particular state of mind or feelings. **2.** habit of mind, esp. with respect to irritability or patience; disposition: *an even temper.* **3.** heat of mind or passion, shown in outbursts of anger, resentment, etc. **4.** calm disposition or state of mind: *to be out of temper.* **5.** a substance added to something to modify its properties or qualities. **6.** *Metall.* **a.** the degree of hardness and strength imparted to a metal, as by quenching, heat treatment, or cold working. **b.** the percentage of carbon in tool steel. **c.** the operation of tempering. **7.** *Archaic.* a middle course; compromise. **8.** *Obs.* the constitution or character of a substance. **—***v.t.* **9.** to moderate or mitigate: *to temper justice with mercy.* **10.** to soften or tone down. **11.** to bring to a proper, suitable, or desirable state by or as by blending or admixture. **12.** to moisten, mix, and work up into proper consistency, as clay or mortar. **13.** *Metall.* to impart strength or toughness to (steel or cast iron) by heating it to some temperature below the transformation point, maintaining it there for some time, then cooling it under controlled conditions. **14.** to tune (a keyboard instrument) so as to make the tones available in different keys or tonalities. **—***v.i.* **15.** to be or become tempered. [ME *tempre(n),* OE *temprian* < L *temperāre* to divide or proportion duly, temper] **—tem′per·a·bil′i·ty,** *n.* **—tem′per·a·ble,** *adj.* **—tem′per·er,** *n.* **—Syn. 1.** nature, condition. **2.** humor. See **disposition. 3.** irritation. **4.** equanimity, composure. **10.** See **modify.**

tem·per·a (tem′pər ə), *n.* **1.** a technique of painting in which an emulsion consisting of water and pure egg yolk or a mixture of egg and oil is used as a binder or medium, characterized by its film-forming properties and rapid drying rate. **2.** a painting executed in this technique. **3.** a water paint used in this technique in which the egg-water or egg-oil emulsion is used as a binder. Cf. **distemper**[2] (defs. 1, 2). [< It, short for *pingere a tempera* painting in distemper.

tem·per·a·ment (tem′pər ə mənt, -prə mənt), *n.* **1.** the unique physical constitution of an individual that permanently affects his manner of thinking, feeling, and acting; natural disposition. **2.** unusual personal attitude or nature as manifested by peculiarities of feeling, temper, action, etc. **3.** *Music.* **a.** the tuning of a keyboard instrument so that the instrument may be played in all keys without further tuning. **b.** a particular system of doing this. **4.** *Obs.* temperature. [late ME < L *temperāment(um)* due mixture = *temperā(re)* (to) mix properly + *-mentum* -MENT] **—Syn. 1.** nature, make-up. See **disposition.**

tem·per·a·men·tal (tem′pər ə men′tᵊl, -prə men′-), *adj.* **1.** having or exhibiting a strongly marked, individual temperament. **2.** moody, irritable, or sensitive. **3.** given to erratic behavior. **4.** of or pertaining to temperament; constitutional. **—tem′per·a·men′tal·ly** *adv.*

tem·per·ance (tem′pər əns, tem′prəns), *n.* **1.** moderation or self-restraint in action, statement, etc.; self-control. **2.** habitual moderation or total abstinence in the indulgence of alcoholic liquors. [ME *temperaunce* < AF < L *temperantia* self-control]

tem·per·ate (tem′pər it, tem′prit), *adj.* **1.** moderate or self-restrained; not extreme in opinion, statement, etc. **2.** moderate as regards indulgence, esp. in alcoholic liquors. **3.** not excessive in degree, as things, qualities, etc. **4.** moderate in respect to temperature; not subject to prolonged extremes of hot or cold weather. [ME *temperat* = L *temperāt(us),* ptp. of *temperāre* to control] **—tem′per·ate·ly,** *adv.* **—tem′per·ate·ness,** *n.* **—Syn. 1.** continent, sober, dispassionate. **—Ant. 1.** unrestrained.

Tem′perate Zone′, *Geog.* the part of the earth's surface lying between the tropic of Cancer and the Arctic Circle in the Northern Hemisphere or between the tropic of Capricorn and the Antarctic Circle in the Southern Hemisphere, and characterized by having a climate that is warm in the summer, cold in the winter, and moderate in the spring and fall.

tem·per·a·ture (tem′pər ə chər, -prə chər), *n.* **1.** a measure of the warmth or coldness of an object or substance with reference to some standard value. The temperature of two systems is the same when the systems are in thermal equilibrium. **2.** *Physiol., Pathol.* **a.** the degree of heat in a living body, esp. the human body. **b.** the excess of this above the normal: in man this is about 98.6°F or about 37°C. **3.** *Obs.* temperament. [< L *temperātūra* a tempering]

tem′perature gra′dient, *Meteorol.* rate of change of temperature with distance.

Tem′per·a·ture-Hu·mid′i·ty In′dex (tem′pər ə chər hyo͞o mid′i tē *or, often,* -yo͞o-, -prə chər-), a number representing an estimate of the effect of temperature and moisture on humans, computed by multiplying the sum of dry-bulb and wet-bulb temperature readings by 0.4 and adding 15, with 65 regarded as the highest comfortable Index. *Abbr.:* T.H.I.

tem·pered (tem′pərd), *adj.* **1.** having a temper or disposition of a specified character (usually used in combination): *a good-tempered child.* **2.** *Music.* tuned in equal temperament. **3.** lessened or mitigated. **4.** properly moistened or mixed, as clay. **5.** *Metall.* of or pertaining to steel or cast iron that has been tempered.

tem·pest (tem′pist), *n.* **1.** an extensive current of wind rushing with great velocity and violence, esp. one attended with rain, hail, or snow; a violent storm. **2.** a violent commotion, disturbance, or tumult. **3. tempest in a teapot,** considerable commotion over an insignificant matter. [ME *tempeste* < OF < VL **tempesta* for L *tempestās* season, weather, storm = *tempes-* (var. of *tempus* time) + *-tās* -TY[2]]

tem·pes·tu·ous (tem pes′cho͞o əs), *adj.* **1.** characterized by or subject to tempests: *the tempestuous ocean.* **2.** of the nature of or resembling a tempest: *a tempestuous wind.* **3.** tumultuous; turbulent. [< L *tempestuōs(us)* < *tempestus,* var. of *tempestās* TEMPEST; see -OUS] **—tem·pes′tu·ous·ly,** *adv.* **—tem·pes′tu·ous·ness,** *n.* **—Syn. 2.** violent, stormy.

tem·pi (tem′pē), *n.* a pl. of **tempo.**

Tem·plar (tem′plər), *n.* **1.** a member of a religious military order founded by Crusaders in Jerusalem about 1118, and suppressed in 1312. **2.** (*often l.c.*) a barrister or other person occupying chambers in the Temple, London. **3.** a member of the Masonic order, Knights Templars. Also called **Knight Templar.** [< ML *templār(ius)* (see TEMPLE[1], -AR[2]); r. ME *templer* < AF (see -ER[2])]

tem·plate (tem′plit), *n.* templet. [TEM(PLET) + PLATE[1]]

tem·ple[1] (tem′pəl), *n.* **1.** an edifice or place dedicated to the service or worship of a deity or deities. **2.** (*usually cap.*) any of the three successive houses of worship in Jerusalem in use by the Jews in Biblical times. **3.** a Reform or Conservative synagogue. **4.** any place or object in which God dwells, as the body of a Christian. I Cor. 6:19. **5.** a Mormon church. **6.** (*cap.*) either of two establishments of the medieval Templars, one in London and the other in Paris. **7.** (*cap.*) either of two groups of buildings (**Inner Temple** and **Middle Temple**) on the site of the Templars' former establishment in London, occupied by two of the Inns of Court. **8.** a building used by the Templars in the U.S. [ME, var. of ME, OE *tempel* < L *templum* place thought of as holy, orig. something cut off; akin to TEMPLE[2]] **—tem′pled,** *adj.* **—tem′ple-like′,** *adj.*

tem·ple[2] (tem′pəl), *n.* **1.** the flattened region on each side of the forehead in man. **2.** a corresponding region in certain animals. **3.** either of the sidepieces of a pair of spectacles, extending back above the ears. [ME < MF < VL **tempula* < L *tempora* the temples, pl. (taken as fem. sing.) of *tempus* period of time, orig. a part (of space or time) marked out or cut off]

tem·ple[3] (tem′pəl), *n.* a device in a loom for keeping the cloth stretched. [late ME *tempylle* < MF *temple* < L *templum* purlin, small piece of timber. See TEMPLE[1]]

Tem·ple (tem′pəl), *n.* **1. Sir William,** 1628–99, English essayist and diplomat. **2.** a city in central Texas. 33,431 (1970).

Tem′ple Cit′y, a city in SW California, near Los Angeles. 31,040 (1970).

Tem′ple of Ar′temis, the large temple at Ephesus, dedicated to Artemis. Cf. **Seven Wonders of the World.**

tem·plet (tem′plit), *n.* **1.** a pattern, mold, or the like, usually consisting of a thin plate of wood or metal, serving as a gauge or guide in mechanical work. **2.** *Building.* a horizontal piece of timber or stone, set into a wall to receive and distribute the pressure of a girder, beam, or the like. Also, **template.** [< F, dim. of *temple* TEMPLE[3]; see -ET]

tem·po (tem′pō), *n., pl.* **-pos, -pi** (-pē). **1.** *Music.* relative rapidity or rate of movement, usually indicated by such terms as *adagio, allegro,* etc., or by reference to the metronome. **2.** characteristic rate, rhythm, or pattern of work or activity: *the tempo of city life.* [< It < L *tempus* time]

tem·po·ral[1] (tem′pər əl, tem′prəl), *adj.* **1.** of or pertaining to time. **2.** pertaining to or concerned with the present life or this world; worldly: *temporal joys.* **3.** enduring for a time only; temporary; transitory (opposed to *eternal*). **4.** *Gram.* of or pertaining to the verbal tenses or to time. **5.** secular, lay, or civil, as opposed to ecclesiastical. [ME < L *temporāl(is)* = *tempor-* (s. of *tempus*) time + *-ālis* -AL[1]] **—tem′po·ral·ly,** *adv.* **—tem′po·ral·ness,** *n.*

tem·po·ral[2] (tem′pər əl, tem′prəl), *Anat.* **—***adj.* **1.** of, pertaining to, or situated near the temple or a temporal bone. **—***n.* **2.** any of several parts in the temporal region, esp. the temporal bone. [< L *temporāl(is)* = *tempor-* (s. of *tempus*) TEMPLE[2] + *-ālis* -AL[1]]

tem′poral bone′, *Anat.* either of a pair of compound bones, forming part of the sides and base of the skull.

tem·po·ral·i·ty (tem′pə ral′i tē), *n., pl.* **-ties. 1.** temporal character or nature; temporariness. **2.** Usually, **temporalities.** temporal possession, revenue, or the like, as of the church or clergy. [ME *temporalite* < LL *temporālitās*]

tem·po·rar·y (tem′pə rer′ē), *adj., n., pl.* **-rar·ies. —***adj.* **1.** lasting, existing, serving, or effective for a time only; not permanent. **—***n.* **2.** an office worker hired through an agency on a per diem basis. [< L *temporāri(us)* = *tempor-* (s. of *tempus*) time + *-ārius* -ARY] **—tem·po·rar·i·ly** (tem′pə râr′ə lē, tem′pə rer′-), *adv.* **—tem′po·rar′i·ness,** *n.*

—Syn. 1. impermanent, passing. TEMPORARY, TRANSIENT, TRANSITORY agree in referring to that which is not lasting or permanent. TEMPORARY implies an arrangement established with no thought of continuance but with the idea of being changed soon: *a temporary structure.* TRANSIENT describes something that is in the process of passing by and will therefore last or stay only a short time: *a transient condition.* TRANSITORY describes an innate characteristic by which a thing, by its very nature, lasts only a short time: *Life is transitory.* **—Ant. 1.** permanent.

tem·po·rise (tem′pə rīz′), *v.i.,* **-rised, -ris·ing.** *Chiefly Brit.* temporize. **—tem′po·ri·sa′tion,** *n.* **—tem′po·ris′er,** *n.* **—tem′po·ris′ing·ly,** *adv.*

tem·po·rize (tem′pə rīz′), *v.i.,* **-rized, -riz·ing. 1.** to be indecisive or evasive to gain time or delay acting. **2.** to comply with the time or occasion. **3.** to treat or parley so as to gain time (usually fol. by *with*). **4.** to come to terms (usually fol. by *with*). **5.** to effect a compromise (usually fol. by *between*). [< ML *temporiz(āre)* (to) hang back, delay = *tempor-* (s. of *tempus*) time + *-izāre* -IZE] **—tem′po·ri·za′tion,** *n.* **—tem′po·riz′er,** *n.* **—tem′po·riz′ing·ly,** *adv.*

tempt (tempt), *v.t.* **1.** to entice or allure to do something often regarded as unwise or wrong. **2.** to allure, appeal strongly to, or invite: *The offer tempts me.* **3.** to put to the test in a venturesome way; risk provoking; provoke: *to tempt one's fate.* **4.** *Obs.* to try or test. [ME *tempt(en)* < L *temptāre* to test, tempt] **—tempt′a·ble,** *adj.* **—Syn. 2.** inveigle, decoy, lure. **—Ant. 1.** dissuade.

temp·ta·tion (temp tā′shən), *n.* **1.** the act of tempting; enticement or allurement. **2.** something that tempts, entices, or allures. **3.** the fact or state of being tempted, esp. to evil. **4.** an instance of this. [ME *temptacion* < L *temptātiōn-* (s. of *temptātiō*) a testing] **—temp·ta′tion·al,** *adj.*

tempt·er (temp′tər), *n.* **1.** a person or thing that tempts, esp. to evil. **2. the Tempter,** Satan; the devil. [ME *temptour* < L *temptātōr-* (s. of *temptātor*). See TEMPT, -ATOR]

tempt·ing (temp′ting), *adj.* that tempts; enticing or inviting. **—tempt′ing·ly,** *adv.* **—tempt′ing·ness,** *n.* **—Syn.** attractive, alluring, seductive. **—Ant.** repellent.

tempt·ress (temp′tris), *n.* a female tempter.

tem·pu·ra (tem′po͞o rä′, tem po͝or′ə), *n.* *Japanese Cookery.* seafood or vegetables dipped in batter and deep-fried. [< Jap: fried food]

tem·pus fu·git (tem′po͝os fo͞o′git; *Eng.* tem′pəs fyo͞o′jit), *Latin.* time flies.

Te·mu·co (te mo͞o′kô), *n.* a city in S Chile. 111,980 (1960).

ten (ten), *n.* **1.** a cardinal number, nine plus one. **2.** a symbol for this number, as 10 or X. **3.** a set of this many persons or things. **4.** a playing card with ten pips. **5.** Also called **ten's place.** *Math.* **a.** (in a mixed number) the position of the second digit to the left of the decimal point. **b.** (in a whole number) the position of the second digit from the right. **6.** *Informal.* a ten-dollar bill. **7. take ten,** *Informal.* to rest from what one is doing, esp. for ten minutes. —*adj.* **8.** amounting to ten in number. [ME, OE *tēn(e), tīen(e)*; c. D *tien*, G *zehn*, Icel *tīu*, Goth *taihun*, L *decem*, Gk *déka*, Skt *daśa*]

ten-, an element occurring in loan words from Latin (*tenant*), used with the meaning "hold," in the formation of technical terms: *tenaculum.* [< L *ten(ēre)* (to) hold]

ten., **1.** tenor. **2.** *Music.* tenuto.

ten·a·ble (ten′ə bəl), *adj.* capable of being held, maintained, or defended. [< F: that can be held. See TEN-, -ABLE] —**ten′a·bil′i·ty, ten′a·ble·ness,** *n.* —**ten′a·bly,** *adv.*

ten·ace (ten′ās′), *n.* *Whist, Bridge.* a sequence of two high cards that lack an intervening card to be in consecutive order, as the ace and queen. [< Sp *tenaza* tongs, tenace (in card games) < *tenaz* < L *tenāc-* (s. of *tenāx*) TENACIOUS; cf. ML *tenācēs* forceps]

te·na·cious (tə nā′shəs), *adj.* **1.** holding fast; characterized by keeping a firm hold (often fol. by *of*): *a tenacious grip on my arm; tenacious of old habits.* **2.** highly retentive: *a tenacious memory.* **3.** pertinacious, persistent, stubborn, or obstinate. **4.** adhesive or sticky; viscous or glutinous. **5.** holding together; cohesive; not easily pulled asunder. [TENACI(TY) + -OUS] —**te·na′cious·ly,** *adv.* —**te·na′cious·ness,** *n.*

te·nac·i·ty (tə nas′i tē), *n.* the quality or property of being tenacious. [< L *tenācitās* < *tenāci-* (s. of *tenāx*) holding fast + *-tās* -TY[2]] —**Syn.** See **perseverance.**

te·nac·u·lum (tə nak′yə ləm), *n., pl.* **-la** (-lə). *Surg.* a small, sharp-pointed hook set in a handle, used for seizing and picking up parts in operations and dissections. [< LL: holding tool = *tenā-* (s. of *tenāx*) holding fast (see TEN-) + *-ulum* suffix denoting instrument]

te·naille (te nāl′), *n.* *Fort.* an outwork containing one or two reentering angles, raised in the main ditch between two bastions and immediately in front of a curtain. Also, **te·nail′.** [< MF: lit., forceps, pincers < LL *tenācula* (pl.); see TENACULUM]

ten·an·cy (ten′ən sē), *n., pl.* **-cies.** **1.** a holding, as of lands, by any kind of title; tenure. **2.** the period of a tenant's occupancy. **3.** occupancy or enjoyment of a position, post, situation, etc. **4.** *Archaic.* a piece of land held by a tenant. [TENANT + -CY; cf. ML *tenantia*, var. of *tenentia*; see -ANCY]

ten·ant (ten′ənt), *n.* **1.** a person or group that rents and occupies land, a house, an office, or the like, from another for a period of time; lessee. **2.** an occupant or inhabitant of any place. —*v.t.* **3.** to hold or occupy as a tenant, dwell in; inhabit. —*v.i.* **4.** to dwell or live (usually fol. by *in*). [ME *tena(u)nt* < AF; MF *tenant*, n. use of prp. of *tenir* to hold < L *tenēre.* See TEN-, -ANT] —**ten′ant·less,** *adj.* —**ten′ant·like′,** *adj.*

ten′ant farm′er, a person who rents farmland from another and pays with cash or with a portion of the produce.

ten·ant·ry (ten′ən trē), *n.* **1.** tenants collectively; the body of tenants on an estate. **2.** the state or condition of being a tenant. [ME]

ten′-cent store′ (ten′sent′, -sent′), five-and-ten.

tench (tench), *n., pl.* **tench·es,** (*esp. collectively*) **tench.** a fresh-water cyprinoid fish, *Tinca tinca*, found in Europe. [ME *tenche* < MF, OF < LL *tinca*]

Ten′ Command′ments, the precepts spoken by God to Israel, delivered to Moses on Mount Sinai; the Decalogue. Ex. 20; 24:12, 34; Deut. 5.

tend[1] (tend), *v.i.* **1.** to be disposed or inclined in action, operation, or effect to do something: *The particles tend to unite.* **2.** to be disposed toward an idea, emotion, way of thinking, etc. **3.** (of a journey, course, road, etc.) to lead or be directed in a particular direction (usually fol. by *to, toward,* etc.). [ME *tende(n)* < MF *tendre* < L *tendere* to stretch, extend, proceed]

tend[2] (tend), *v.t.* **1.** to attend to by work or services, care, etc.: *to tend a fire.* **2.** to look after; watch over and care for; minister to or wait on with service: *to tend the sick.* **3.** *Naut.* to handle or attend to (a rope). —*v.i.* **4.** to attend by action, care, etc. (usually fol. by *to*). **5. tend on** or **upon,** *Archaic.* to attend or wait upon; minister to; serve. [ME *tende(n)*, aph. var. of ATTEND]

tend·ance (ten′dəns), *n.* **1.** attention; care; ministration, as to the sick. **2.** *Archaic.* servants or attendants. [aph. var. of ATTENDANCE]

ten·den·cious (ten den′shəs), *adj.* tendentious. —**ten·den′cious·ly,** *adv.* —**ten·den′cious·ness,** *n.*

ten·den·cy (ten′dən sē), *n., pl.* **-cies.** **1.** a natural or prevailing disposition to move, proceed, or act in some direction or toward some point, end, or result: *the tendency of falling bodies toward the earth.* **2.** an inclination, bent, or predisposition to something. **3.** a special and definite purpose in a novel or other literary work. [< ML *tendentia*]

ten·den·tious (ten den′shəs), *adj.* having or showing a definite tendency, bias, or purpose: *a tendentious novel.* Also, **tendencious, ten·den·tial** (ten den′shəl). [< ML *tendenti(a)* TENDENCY + -OUS] —**ten·den′tious·ly, ten·den′tial·ly,** *adv.* —**ten·den′tious·ness,** *n.*

ten·der[1] (ten′dər), *adj.* **1.** soft or delicate in substance; not hard or tough: *a tender steak.* **2.** weak or delicate in constitution; not strong or hardy. **3.** young or immature: *children of tender age.* **4.** delicate, soft, or gentle: *the tender touch of her hand.* **5.** easily moved to sympathy or compassion; kind: *a tender heart.* **6.** affectionate or loving; sentimental or amatory: *a tender glance.* **7.** acutely or painfully sensitive: *a tender bruise.* **8.** easily distressed: *a tender conscience.* **9.** of a delicate or ticklish nature; requiring tactful handling: *a tender subject.* **10.** *Naut.* crank[2] (def. 1). —*v.t.* **11.** to make tender. [ME, var. of *tendre* < OF < L *tenerum, teneram*, acc. of *tener* tender] —**ten′der·ly,** *adv.* —**ten′der·ness,** *n.*

ten·der[2] (ten′dər), *v.t.* **1.** to present formally for acceptance. **2.** to offer or proffer. **3.** *Law.* to offer, as money or goods, in payment of a debt or other obligation. —*n.* **4.** the act of tendering; an offer of something for acceptance. **5.** something tendered or offered, esp. money, as in payment. **6.** *Com.* an offer to execute certain work, supply certain commodities, etc., at a given cost; bid. **7.** *Law.* an offer, as of money or goods, in payment of a debt or other obligation. [earlier *tendre*, n. use of AF *tendre* to extend, offer. See TEND[1]] —**ten′der·a·ble,** *adj.* —**ten′der·er,** *n.* —**Syn. 1.** See **offer. 4.** proposal, proffer.

ten·der[3] (ten′dər), *n.* **1.** a person who tends; a person who attends to or takes charge of someone or something. **2.** an auxiliary vessel employed to attend to one or more other vessels, as for supplying provisions. **3.** a dinghy carried or towed by a yacht. **4.** *Railroads.* a car attached to a steam locomotive for carrying fuel and water. [late ME; aph. var. of ATTENDER]

ten·der·foot (ten′dər fo͝ot′), *n., pl.* **-foots, -feet** (-fēt′). **1.** a raw, inexperienced person; novice. **2.** a newcomer to the ranching and mining regions of the western U.S., unused to hardships. **3.** one in the lowest rank of the Boy Scouts of America or Girl Scouts of America.

ten·der-heart·ed (ten′dər här′tid), *adj.* soft-hearted; sympathetic. —**ten′der-heart′ed·ly,** *adv.* —**ten′der-heart′ed·ness,** *n.*

ten·der·ise (ten′də rīz′), *v.t.,* **-ised, -is·ing.** *Chiefly Brit.* tenderize. —**ten′der·i·sa′tion,** *n.* —**ten′der·is′er,** *n.*

ten·der·ize (ten′də rīz′), *v.t.,* **-ized, -iz·ing.** to make (meat) tender, as by pounding or by means of a chemical process or treatment. —**ten′der·i·za′tion,** *n.* —**ten′der·iz′er,** *n.*

ten·der·loin (ten′dər loin′), *n.* **1.** (in beef or pork) the tender meat of the muscle running through the sirloin and terminating before the ribs. **2.** a cut of beef lying between the sirloin and ribs. **3.** (*cap.*) **a.** (formerly) a district in New York City noted for corruption and vice: so called because police there could eat well from their bribes. **b.** a similar district in any U.S. city.

ten′der of′fer, a public solicitation by a corporation to shareholders of another corporation to purchase stock of the latter above the current market price.

ten·di·nous (ten′də nəs), *adj.* **1.** of the nature of or resembling a tendon. **2.** consisting of tendons. [< early NL *tendin-* (r. ML *tendōn-*, s. of *tendō*) TENDON + -OUS]

ten·don (ten′dən), *n.* *Anat.* a cord or band of dense, tough, inelastic, white, fibrous tissue, serving to connect a muscle with a bone or part; sinew. [< ML *tendōn-* (s. of *tendō*) < Gk *ténōn* sinew (with *-d-* from L *tendere* to stretch)]

T, Tendrils of fox grape, *Vitis Labrusca*

ten·dril (ten′dril), *n.* *Bot.* a filiform, leafless organ of climbing plants, often growing in spiral form, which attaches itself to or twines around some other body, so as to support the plant. [earlier *tendrel*, var. (? by dissimilation) of ME *tendren, tendron* < MF *tendron* shoot, sprout, cartilage] —**ten′dril·lar, ten′dril·ous,** *adj.* —**ten′dril·ly,** *adj.*

Ten·e·brae (ten′ə brā′), *n.* (*construed as sing. or pl.*) *Rom. Cath. Ch.* the office of matins and lauds sung during Holy Week to commemorate the Crucifixion. [< L: lit., darkness]

ten·e·brif·ic (ten′ə brif′ik), *adj.* producing darkness. [< L *tenebr(ae)* darkness + -I- + -FIC]

ten·e·brous (ten′ə brəs), *adj.* dark; gloomy; obscure. Also, **te·neb·ri·ous** (tə neb′rē əs). [late ME < L *tenebrōs(us).* See TENEBRAE, -OUS] —**ten′e·brous·ness, te·neb′ri·ous·ness,** *n.*

Ten·e·dos (ten′i dos′, -dōs′; *Gk.* ten′e thôs), *n.* an island in the Aegean, near the entrance to the Dardanelles, belonging to Turkey. Also called **Bozcaada.**

ten·e·ment (ten′ə mənt), *n.* **1.** any house or building to live in; dwelling house. **2.** See **tenement house. 3.** a portion of a house or building occupied by a tenant as a separate dwelling. **4.** *Law.* any species of property, as lands, houses, rents, an office, a franchise, etc., that may be held or treated as real property. **5. tenements,** freehold interests in things immovable considered as subjects of property. [ME < ML *tenēment(um)* = L *tenē(re)* (to) hold + *-mentum* -MENT] —**ten·e·men·tal** (ten′ə men′tᵊl), **ten·e·men·ta·ry** (ten′ə men′tə rē), *adj.* —**ten′e·ment·ed,** *adj.*

ten′ement house′, an apartment house, esp. one in the poorer, crowded parts of a large city.

Ten·er·ife (ten′ə rif′, -rēf′; *Sp.* te′ne rē′fe), *n.* **1.** the largest of the Canary Islands, off the NW Coast of Africa. 321,949 (1950); 794 sq. mi. *Cap.:* Santa Cruz de Tenerife. **2. Pi·co de** (pē′kô the). See **Teide, Pico de.** Also, **Ten′er·iffe′.**

te·nes·mus (tə nez′məs, -nes′-), *n.* *Pathol.* the urgent feeling of need to urinate or defecate, without the ability to do so. [< ML, var. of L *tēnesmos* < Gk *teinesmós* = *teín(ein)* (to) stretch + *-esmos* n. suffix]

ten·et (ten′it, tē′nit), *n.* any opinion, doctrine, dogma, etc., held as true. [< L: he holds] —**Syn.** belief.

ten·fold (*adj.* ten′fōld′; *adv.* ten′fōld′), *adj.* **1.** comprising ten parts or members. **2.** ten times as great or as much. —*adv.* **3.** in tenfold measure. [ME; OE *tienfeald*]

ten′-gal·lon hat′ (ten′gal′ən), a man's broad-brimmed hat with a high crown, worn esp. in the western and southwestern U.S. [so called from its size]

10-gauge (ten′gāj′), *n.* **1.** Also called **10-gauge shotgun.** a shotgun using a shell of approx. .775 in. in diameter. **2.** the shell itself.

Ten·gri Khan (teng′grē kän′, ᴋʜän′), a mountain in central Asia, on the boundary between the Soviet Union and China: highest peak of the Tien Shan Mountains. ab. 23,950 ft.

Ten·gri Nor (teng′grē nôr′, nōr′), a salt lake in E Tibet, NW of Lhasa. ab. 700 sq. mi.; 15,186 ft. above sea level.

te·ni·a (tē′nē ə), *n., pl.* **-ni·ae** (-nē ē′). taenia.

te·ni·a·cide (tē′nē ə sīd′), *Med.* —*adj.* **1.** Also, **te′ni·a·ci′dal.** taeniacide. —*n.* **2.** taeniacide.

te·ni·a·fuge (tē′nē ə fyōōj′), *adj., n. Med.* taeniafuge.

te·ni·a·sis (ti nī′ə sis), *n. Pathol.* taeniasis.

Ten·iers (ten′yərz; *Flem.* tə nērs′; *Fr.* te nyā′), *n.* **1.** **David** ("*the Elder*"), 1582–1649, Flemish painter and engraver. **2.** his son, **David** ("*the Younger*"), 1610–90, Flemish painter.

Tenn., Tennessee.

ten·ner (ten′ər), *n. Informal.* **1.** *U.S.* a ten-dollar bill. **2.** *Brit.* a ten-pound note.

Ten·nes·see (ten′i sē′), *n.* **1.** a state in the SE United States. 3,924,164 (1970); 42,246 sq. mi. *Cap.:* Nashville. *Abbr.:* Tenn., TN **2.** a river flowing from E Tennessee through N Alabama, W Tennessee, and SW Kentucky into the Ohio near Paducah. 652 mi. long. —**Ten′nes·se′an,** *adj., n.*

Ten′nessee Val′ley Author′ity. See **TVA.**

Ten′nessee Walk′ing Horse′, one of a breed of saddle horses developed largely from Standardbred and Morgan stock.

Ten·niel (ten′yəl), *n.* **Sir John,** 1820–1914, English caricaturist and illustrator.

ten·nis (ten′is), *n.* a game played on a rectangular court by two players or two pairs of players equipped with rackets, in which a ball is driven back and forth over a low net that divides the court in half. Cf. **lawn tennis.** [late ME *tenetz* < AF, impv. pl. of *tenir* to hold < L *tenēre*]

Tennis court

ten′nis ball′, a hollow ball used in tennis, made of rubber with a fuzzy covering of woven Dacron, nylon, or wool.

ten′nis shoe′, a sports shoe with a rubber sole and a stitched canvas upper that laces over the instep.

Ten·ny·son (ten′i sən), *n.* **Alfred, Lord** (*1st Baron*), 1809–1892, English poet: poet laureate 1850–92.

teno-, a learned borrowing from Greek meaning "tendon," used in the formation of compound words: *tenotomy.* [comb. form repr. Gk *ténōn*]

Te·noch·ti·tlán (te nôch′tē tlän′), *n.* the capital of the Aztec empire: now the site of Mexico City.

ten·on (ten′ən), *n.* **1.** a projection formed on the end of a timber or the like for insertion into a mortise of the same dimensions. See illus. at **mortise.** —*v.t.* **2.** to provide with a tenon. **3.** to join by or as by a tenon. **4.** to join securely. [late ME < MF = *ten(ir)* (to) hold (< L *tenēre*) + *-on* n. suffix] —**ten′on·er,** *n.*

ten·or (ten′ər), *n.* **1.** the course of thought or meaning that runs through something written or spoken; purport; drift. **2.** continuous course, progress, or movement. **3.** *Music.* **a.** the adult male voice intermediate between the baritone and the alto or countertenor. **b.** a part sung by or written for such a voice. **c.** a singer with such a voice. **d.** an instrument corresponding in compass to this voice, esp. the viola. **4.** *Obs.* quality, character, or condition. —*adj.* **5.** *Music.* of, pertaining to, or having the compass of, a tenor. [< ML, L: course, etc. = *ten(ēre)* to hold + *-or* -OR[1]; r. ME *ten(o)ur* < AF] —**ten′or·less,** *adj.*

ten′or clef′, *Music.* a sign locating middle C on the next to the top line of the staff. See illus. at **C clef.**

ten·o·rite (ten′ə rīt′), *n.* a mineral, cupric oxide, CuO. [named after G. *Tenore* (d. 1861), President of Naples Academy; see -ITE[1]]

te·nor·rha·phy (tə nôr′ə fē, -nor′-), *n., pl.* **-phies.** *Surg.* suture of a tendon.

te·not·o·my (tə not′ə mē), *n., pl.* **-mies.** *Surg.* the cutting or division of a tendon. —**te·not′o·mist,** *n.*

ten·pen·ny (ten′pen′ē, -pə nē), *adj.* **1.** noting a nail three inches in length. *Abbr.:* 10d. **2.** worth or costing 10 cents.

ten·pin (ten′pin′), *n.* **1.** one of the pins used in tenpins. **2.** **tenpins,** (*construed as sing.*) a form of bowling, played with ten wooden pins at which a ball is bowled to knock them down.

ten·rec (ten′rek), *n.* any of several insectivorous mammals of the family *Tenrecidae,* of Madagascar, having a long, pointed snout, certain species of which are spiny and tailless. [< F < Malagasy *tàndraka*]

Tenrec, *Tenrec ecaudatus* (Length 14 in.)

tense[1] (tens), *adj.,* **tens·er, tens·est,** *v.,* **tensed, tens·ing.** —*adj.* **1.** stretched tight, as a cord, fiber, etc.; drawn taut; rigid. **2.** in a state of mental or nervous strain; high-strung; taut: *a tense person.* **3.** characterized by a strain upon the nerves or feelings: *a tense moment.* **4.** *Phonet.* pronounced with relatively tense tongue muscles; narrow. Cf. **lax**[2] (def. 7). —*v.t., v.i.* **5.** to make or become tense. [< L *tens(us)* stretched, taut, ptp. of *tendere;* see TEND[1]] —**tense′ly,** *adv.* —**tense′ness,** *n.* —**Ant. 1–3.** relaxed.

tense[2] (tens), *n.* **1.** a category of verb inflection specifying time and duration. **2.** a set of such categories or constructions in a particular language. [ME *tens* < MF < L *tempus* time] —**tense′less,** *adj.* —**tense′less·ly,** *adv.* —**tense′less·ness,** *n.*

ten·si·ble (ten′sə bəl), *adj.* capable of being stretched; tensile. [< NL *tensibil(is)*] —**ten′si·bil′i·ty, ten′si·ble·ness,** *n.* —**ten′si·bly,** *adv.*

ten·sile (ten′səl, -sil *or, esp. Brit.,* -sīl), *adj.* **1.** of or pertaining to tension: *tensile strain.* **2.** capable of being stretched or drawn out; ductile. [< NL *tensil(is)*] —**ten·sil′i·ty, ten′sile·ness,** *n.* —**ten′sile·ly,** *adv.*

ten′sile strength′, the resistance of a material to longitudinal stress, measured by the minimum amount of longitudinal stress required to rupture the material.

ten·sim·e·ter (ten sim′i tər), *n.* an instrument for measuring vapor pressure. [TENSI(ON) + -METER]

ten·si·om·e·ter (ten′sē om′i tər), *n.* an instrument for measuring longitudinal stress in wires, structural beams, etc. [TENSIO(N) + -METER]

ten·sion (ten′shən), *n.* **1.** the act of stretching or straining. **2.** the state of being stretched or strained. **3.** mental or emotional strain; suspense, anxiety, or excitement. **4.** a strained relationship between individuals, nations, etc. **5.** (not in current use) pressure, esp. of a vapor. **6.** *Mech.* **a.** the longitudinal deformation of an elastic body that results in its elongation. **b.** the force producing such deformation. **7.** *Elect.* electromotive force; potential. **8.** *Mach.* a device for stretching or pulling something. [< L *tensiōn-* (s. of *tensiō*) a stretching] —**ten′sion·al,** *adj.* —**ten′sion·less,** *adj.*

ten·si·ty (ten′si tē), *n.* the state of being tense. [< ML *tensitās*]

ten·sive (ten′siv), *adj.* stretching or straining. [TENS(ION) + -IVE; cf. F *tensif*]

ten·sor (ten′sər, -sôr), *n.* **1.** *Anat.* a muscle that stretches or tightens some part of the body. **2.** *Math.* a set of functions that are transformed in a particular way when changing from one coordinate system to another. [< NL: stretcher] —**ten·so·ri·al** (ten sōr′ē əl, -sôr′-), *adj.*

ten's′ place′, ten (def. 5).

ten-spot (ten′spot′), *n. Slang.* **1.** a playing card having ten pips on its face. **2.** a ten-dollar bill.

ten-strike (ten′strīk′), *n.* **1.** *Tenpins.* a strike. **2.** *Informal.* any act which is completely successful.

tent[1] (tent), *n.* **1.** a portable shelter of skins, coarse cloth, or esp. canvas supported by one or more poles and usually extended by ropes fastened to pegs in the ground. —*v.t.* **2.** to provide with or lodge in tents; cover as with a tent. —*v.i.* **3.** to live in a tent; encamp. [ME *tente* < OF < L *tenta,* fem. of *tentus* extended, stretched, ptp. of *tendere;* cf. *tentōrium* tent] —**tent′less,** *adj.* —**tent′like′,** *adj.*

tent[2] (tent), *n. Brit.* a dark, sweet wine from Spain. [alter. of Sp *tinto* dark red. See TINT[1]]

ten·ta·cle (ten′tə kəl), *n.* **1.** *Zool.* any of various slender, flexible processes or appendages in animals, esp. invertebrates, that serve as organs of touch, prehension, etc.; feeler. **2.** *Bot.* a sensitive filament or process, as one of the glandular hairs of the sundew. [< NL *tentācul(um)* = L *tentā(re)* (var. of *temptāre* to feel, probe) + *-culum* instrumental suffix] —**ten·tac·u·lar** (ten tak′yə lər), *adj.* —**ten′ta·cle·like′, ten·tac′u·loid′,** *adj.*

ten·ta·cled (ten′tə kəld), *adj.* having tentacles. Also, **ten·tac·u·lat·ed** (ten tak′yə lā′tid).

tent·age (ten′tij), *n.* tents collectively; equipment or supply of tents.

ten·ta·tion (ten tā′shən), *n.* a method of making mechanical adjustments or the like by a succession of trials. [< L *tentātiōn-* (s. of *tentātiō*) trial, var. of *temptātiō.* See TEMPTATION]

ten·ta·tive (ten′tə tiv), *adj.* **1.** of the nature of or made or done as a trial, experiment, or attempt; experimental. **2.** unsure; not definite or positive; hesitant. [< ML *tentātīv(us)* = L *tentāt(us)* tried (ptp. of *tentāre,* var. of *temptāre*) + *-īvus* -IVE] —**ten′ta·tive·ly,** *adv.* —**ten′ta·tive·ness,** *n.*

tent′ cat′erpillar, the larva of any of several moths of the genus *Malacosoma,* that live gregariously in tentlike webs and feed on the leaves of shade trees.

tent·ed (ten′tid), *adj.* **1.** covered with or living in a tent or tents. **2.** shaped like a tent.

ten·ter (ten′tər), *n.* **1.** a framework on which cloth in the process of manufacture is stretched so it may set or dry evenly. **2.** *Obs.* a tenterhook. —*v.t.* **3.** to stretch (cloth) on a tenter or tenters. —*v.i.* **4.** to be capable of being tentered. [ME *tente* to stretch (< L *tentus,* var. of *tensus* TENSE[1]) + -ER[1]; r. ME *teyntur* < ?]

ten·ter·hook (ten′tər hŏŏk′), *n.* **1.** one of the hooks or bent nails that hold cloth stretched on a tenter. **2.** **on tenterhooks,** in a state of uneasy suspense or painful anxiety.

tent′ fly′, fly[1] (def. 23).

tenth (tenth), *adj.* **1.** next after ninth; being the ordinal number for ten. **2.** being one of ten equal parts. —*n.* **3.** one of ten equal parts, esp. of one (1/10). **4.** the member of a series preceding the eleventh and following the ninth. **5.** *Music.* **a.** a tone distant from another tone by an interval of an octave and a third. **b.** the interval between such tones. **c.** the harmonic combination of such tones. **6.** Also called **tenth's′ place′.** (in decimal notation) the position of the first digit to the right of the decimal point. [ME *tenthe.* See TEN, -TH[2], TITHE] —**tenth′ly,** *adv.*

tent·mak·er (tent′mā′kər), *n.* a person who makes tents.

tent′ show′, an exhibition or performance, esp. of a circus, presented in a tent.

tent′ stitch′, a short, slanting stitch used in embroidery. Cf. **petit point** (def. 1).

ten·u·is (ten′yōō is), *n., pl.* **ten·u·es** (ten′yōō ēz′). *Gk. Grammar.* an unaspirated, voiceless plosive. [< L: thin, fine, slender]

te·nu·i·ty (tə nōō′i tē, -nyōō′-, te-), *n.* **1.** the state of being tenuous. **2.** slenderness. **3.** thinness of consistency; rarefied condition. [< L *tenuitās* thinness. See TENUI(S), -TY[2]]

ten·u·ous (ten′yōō əs), *adj.* **1.** thin or slender in form. **2.** thin in consistency; rare or rarefied. **3.** of slight importance or significance; unsubstantial. **4.** lacking a sound basis; poorly supported; weak. [TENU(ITY) + -OUS] —**ten′u·ous·ly,** *adv.* —**ten′u·ous·ness,** *n.* —**Syn. 1.** attenuated. **3.** insignificant, unimportant. —**Ant. 1.** thick. **3.** important, substantial.

ten·ure (ten′yər), *n.* **1.** the holding or possessing of anything: *the tenure of an office.* **2.** the holding of property, esp. real property, of a superior in return for services to be rendered. **3.** the period or term of holding something. **4.** status assuring an employee of permanence in his position or employment. [ME < AF; OF *teneure* < VL **tenitura* = **tenit(us)* held (for L *tentus,* ptp. of *tenēre*) + *-ura* -URE] —**ten·u·ri·al** (ten yŏŏr′ē əl), *adj.* —**ten·u′ri·al·ly,** *adv.*

te·nu·to (tə nōō′tō; *It.* te nōō′tô), *adj., n., pl.* **-tos,** *It.* **-ti** (-tē). *Music.* —*adj.* **1.** (a musical direction, of a note, chord, or rest) held to the full time value. —*n.* **2.** a note, chord, or rest held longer than its normal duration; a hold. **3.** the sign indicating this. [< It: held (ptp. of *tenere*) < VL **tenutus* for L *tentus*]

Ten·zing (ten′zing), *n.* (*Norgay*) 1913?–86, Nepalese mountain climber who scaled Mt. Everest 1953.

te·o·cal·li (tē′ə kal′ē; *Sp.* te′ô kä′yē), *n., pl.* **-cal·lis**

(-kal′ēz; *Sp.* -kä′yēs). a ceremonial structure of the Aztecs, consisting of a truncated, terraced pyramid supporting a temple. [< Nahuatl = *teo(tl)* god + *calli* house]

te·o·sin·te (tē′ə sin′tē), *n.* a tall annual grass, *Euchlaena mexicana,* of Mexico and Central America, closely related to corn, and sometimes cultivated as a fodder plant. [< MexSp = Nahuatl *teo(tl)* god + *centli, cintli* dry ear of maize]

te·pee (tē′pē), *n.* a tent or wigwam of the American Indians. Also, **teepee, tipi.** [< Siouan *tipi* tent = *ti* to dwell + *pi* used for]

Tepee

tep·e·fy (tep′ə fī′), *v.t., v.i.,* **-fied, -fy·ing.** to make or become tepid or lukewarm. [< L *tepe-* (s. of *tepēre* to be tepid) + -FY] —**tep·e·fac·tion** (tep′ə fak′shən), *n.*

teph·rite (tef′rīt), *n. Petrog.* a basaltic rock consisting essentially of pyroxene and plagioclase with nepheline or leucite. [< Gk *tephr(ós)* ash-colored + -ITE¹] —**teph·rit·ic** (tef rit′ik), *adj.*

Te·pic (te pēk′), *n.* a city in and the capital of Nayarit, in W central Mexico. 114,512.

tep·id (tep′id), *adj.* moderately warm; lukewarm: *tepid water.* [late ME < L *tepid(us)* lukewarm] —**te·pid′i·ty, tep′id·ness,** *n.* —**tep′id·ly,** *adv.*

tep·i·dar·i·um (tep′i dâr′ē əm), *n., pl.* **-dar·i·a** (-dâr′ē ə). (in an ancient Roman bath) a room having a lukewarm bath. [< L; see TEPID, -ARY]

TEPP, *Chem.* See **tetraethyl pyrophosphate.**

te·qui·la (tə kē′lə), *n.* a strong liquor from Mexico, distilled from fermented mash of an agave, *Agave tequilana.* [after *Tequila,* a district in Mexico]

ter-, a learned borrowing from Latin meaning "thrice," used in the formation of compound words: *tercentennial.* [< L, comb. form of *ter;* akin to *tres* THREE]

ter., 1. terrace. 2. territory.

ter·a·phim (ter′ə fim), *n. pl., sing.* **ter·aph** (ter′əf). idols or images revered by the ancient Hebrews and kindred peoples, apparently as household gods. [< Heb (pl.); r. ME *theraphym* < L *theraphim* (Vulgate) < Gk *theraphin* (Septuagint)]

terat-, var. of **terato-** before a vowel: *teratoid.*

ter·a·tism (ter′ə tiz′əm), *n.* **1.** love or worship of the monstrous. **2.** *Biol.* a monstrosity, esp. a malformed fetus.

terato-, a learned borrowing from Greek meaning "monster," used in the formation of compound words: *teratology.* Also, *esp. before a vowel,* **terat-.** [< Gk *térat-* (s. of *téras*) monster, marvel + -o-]

ter·a·toid (ter′ə toid′), *adj. Biol.* resembling a monster.

ter·a·tol·o·gy (ter′ə tol′ə jē), *n. Biol.* the science or study of monstrosities or abnormal formations in animals or plants. —**ter·a·to·log·i·cal** (ter′ə tᵊloj′i kəl), *adj.* —**ter′a·tol′o·gist,** *n.*

ter·bi·a (tûr′bē ə), *n. Chem.* an amorphous white powder, TbO_3. Also called **ter′bium ox′ide.** [< NL: TERB(IUM) + -IA]

ter·bi·um (tûr′bē əm), *n. Chem.* a rare-earth, metallic element. *Symbol:* Tb; *at. no.:* 65; *at. wt.:* 158.924; *sp. gr.:* 8.25. [after *(Yt)terb(y),* Swedish town where found] —**ter′bic,** *adj.*

ter′bium met′al, *Chem.* any of a subgroup of rare-earth metals, of which the cerium and yttrium metals comprise the other two subgroups. Cf. **rare-earth element.**

Ter Borch (tər bôrkh′), *n.* **Ge·rard** (gä′rärt), 1617–81, Dutch painter. Also, **Ter·borch′, Ter·burg** (tər bo͝orkh′).

terce (tûrs), *n. Eccles.* tierce (def. 3). [late ME var. of TIERCE]

Ter·cei·ra (tər sā′rə), *n.* an island in the Azores, in the N Atlantic. 90,409; 153 sq. mi. *Cap.:* Angra do Heroismo.

ter·cel (tûr′səl), *n. Falconry.* the male of a hawk, esp. of a gerfalcon or peregrine. Also, **terce·let** (tûrs′lit), **tiercel.** [ME < MF < LL **tertiol(us)* = L *terti(us)* third + *-olus* dim. suffix; so named from the belief that only a third of birds of species are male]

ter·cen·te·nar·y (tûr sen′tᵊner′ē, tûr′sen ten′ə rē), *adj., n., pl.* **-nar·ies.** —*adj.* **1.** pertaining to 300 years or a period of 300 years. **2.** marking the completion of such a period: *a tercentenary celebration.* —*n.* **3.** a 300th anniversary or its celebration. Also, **ter′cen·ten′ni·al.**

ter·cet (tûr′sit, tûr set′), *n.* **1.** *Pros.* a group of three lines rhyming together or connected by rhyme with the adjacent group or groups of three lines. **2.** *Music.* triplet (def. 5). [< F < It *terzetto,* dim. of *terzo* third < L *tertius.* See -ET]

tereb′ic ac′id, *Chem.* an acid, $C_7H_{10}O_4$, formed by the oxidation of certain terpenes. [TEREB(INTH) + -IC] —**te·reb·ic** (tə reb′ik, -rē′bik), *adj.*

ter·e·binth (ter′ə binth), *n.* an anacardiaceous tree, *Pistacia Terebinthus,* of the Mediterranean regions, yielding Chian turpentine. [< L *terebinth(us)* < Gk *terébinthos* turpentine tree; r. ME *therebinte* < MF]

ter·e·bin·thi·nate (ter′ə bin′thə nāt′), *adj.* of, pertaining to, or resembling turpentine.

ter·e·bin·thine (ter′ə bin′thin), *adj.* **1.** terebinthinate. **2.** of or pertaining to the terebinth.

te·re·do (te rē′dō), *n., pl.* **-re·dos, -re·di·nes** (-rēd′ᵊnēz′). a shipworm of the genus *Teredo.* [< L < Gk *terēdṓn* wood-boring worm]

te·re·fah (tə rä fä′; *Eng.* trā′fə, tə rā′-), *adj. Hebrew.* unfit for use according to Jewish law; not kosher. Also, **trefah, tref.**

Ter·ence (ter′əns), *n.* (*Publius Terentius Afer*) c190–159? B.C., Roman playwright.

Te·re·sa (tə rē′sə, -zə; *for 2 also Sp.* te re′sä), *n.* **1. Mother** (*Agnes Gonxha Bojaxhiu*), born 1910, Albanian nun: Nobel peace prize 1979 for work in the slums of Calcutta, India. **2. Saint.** See **Theresa, Saint.**

Te·re·si·na (ti ri zē′nə), *n.* a port in NE Brazil, on the Parnahiba River. 230,168. Formerly, **Therezina.**

te·rete (tə rēt′, ter′ēt), *adj.* **1.** slender and smooth, with a circular transverse section. **2.** cylindrical or slightly tapering. [earlier *teret* < L *teret-* (s. of *teres*) smooth and round, akin to *terere* to rub]

Te·re·us (tēr′ē əs, tēr′yo͞os), *n. Class. Myth.* a Thracian prince, the husband of Procne, who raped his sister-in-law Philomela and was changed into a hoopoe as a punishment.

ter·gi·ver·sate (tûr′ji vər sāt′), *v.i.,* **-sat·ed, -sat·ing.** **1.** to change repeatedly one's attitude or opinions with respect to a cause, subject, etc. **2.** to turn renegade. [< L *tergiversāt(us)* (ptp. of *tergiversārī* to turn one's back) = *tergi-* (comb. form of *tergum* back) + *versātus,* ptp. of *versāre,* freq. of *vertere* to turn; see -ATE¹] —**ter′gi·ver·sa′tion,** *n.* —**ter′gi·ver·sa′tor, ter·gi·ver·sant** (tûr′ji vûr′sənt), *n.* —**ter·gi·ver·sa·to·ry** (tûr′ji vûr′sə tōr′ē, -tôr′ē), *adj.*

ter·gum (tûr′gəm), *n., pl.* **-ga** (-gə). *Zool.* the dorsal surface of a body segment of an arthropod. [< L: the back] —**ter′gal,** *adj.*

Ter·hune (tər hyo͞on′), *n.* **Albert Pay·son** (pā′sən), 1872–1942, U.S. novelist and short-story writer.

ter·i·ya·ki (ter′i yä′kē), *n. Japanese Cookery.* meat or fish marinated in seasoned soy sauce and grilled. [< Jap]

term (tûrm), *n.* **1.** a word or group of words designating something, esp. in a particular field, as *atom* in physics, *quietism* in theology. **2.** any word or group of words considered as a member of a construction or utterance. **3.** the time or period through which something lasts. **4.** a period of time to which limits have been set: *elected for a term of four years.* **5.** one of two or more divisions of a school year, during which instruction is regularly provided. **6.** an appointed or set time or date, as for the payment of rent, interest, wages, etc. **7. terms, a.** conditions with regard to payment, price, charge, rates, wages, etc. **b.** conditions or stipulations limiting what is proposed to be granted or done: *the terms of a treaty.* **c.** footing or standing; relations: *on good terms with someone.* **8.** *Algebra, Arith.* each of the members of which an expression, a series of quantities, or the like, is composed, as one of two or more parts of an algebraic expression. **9.** *Logic.* **a.** the subject or predicate of a categorical proposition. **b.** the word or expression denoting the subject or predicate of a categorical proposition. **10.** *Law.* **a.** the period of time for which an estate is enjoyed. **b.** the period during which a court holds its session. **11.** termination of pregnancy; parturition. **12.** *Archaic.* **a.** end, conclusion, or termination. **b.** boundary or limit. **13. bring to terms,** to force to agree to stated demands or conditions; bring into submission. **14. come to terms,** to reach an agreement. —*v.t.* **15.** to apply a particular term or name to; name; call; designate. [ME *terme* < OF < L *term(inus)* boundary, limit, end; akin to Gk *térmōn* limit] —**term′ly,** *adv.*

term., 1. terminal. 2. termination.

ter·ma·gant (tûr′mə gənt), *n.* **1.** a violent, turbulent, or brawling woman. **2.** (*cap.*) a mythical deity popularly believed in the Middle Ages to be worshiped by the Muslims and introduced into morality plays as a violent, overbearing personage in long robes. —*adj.* **3.** violent; turbulent; brawling; shrewish. [ME *Termagaunt,* earlier *Tervagaunt,* alter. of OF *Tervagan* (see def. 2)] —**ter′ma·gant·ly,** *adv.*

term′ day′, a fixed or appointed day, as for the payment of money due; a quarter day. [ME *term dai*]

term·er (tûr′mər), *n.* a person who is serving a term, esp. in prison (usually used in combination): *a first-termer.*

ter·mi·na·ble (tûr′mə nə bəl), *adj.* **1.** that may be terminated. **2.** (of an annuity) coming to an end after a certain term. [< L *termināre* to end + -ABLE] —**ter′mi·na·bil′i·ty, ter′mi·na·ble·ness,** *n.* —**ter′mi·na·bly,** *adv.*

ter·mi·nal (tûr′mə nᵊl), *adj.* **1.** situated at or forming the end or extremity of something: *a terminal feature of a vista.* **2.** occurring at or forming the end of a series, succession, or the like; closing; concluding. **3.** pertaining to or lasting for a term or definite period; occurring at fixed terms or in every term: *terminal payments.* **4.** pertaining to, situated at, or forming the terminus of a railroad. **5.** *Bot.* growing at the end of a branch or stem, as a bud, inflorescence, etc. **6.** pertaining to or placed at a boundary, as a landmark. **7.** occurring at or causing the end of life. —*n.* **8.** a terminal part of a structure; end or extremity. **9.** *Railroads.* a major assemblage of station, yard, maintenance, and repair facilities, as at a terminus, at which trains originate or terminate, or at which they are distributed or combined. **10.** *Computer Technol.* any device for entering information into a computer or receiving information from it, as a keyboard with video display unit or a printer, either adjoining the computer or at some distance from it. **11.** *Elect.* **a.** the mechanical device by means of which an electric connection to an apparatus is established. **b.** the point of current entry to, or point of current departure from, any conducting component in an electric circuit. **12.** *Archit.* **a.** a herm or term. **b.** a carving or the like at the end of something, as a finial. [late ME < L *terminal(is)* = *termin(us)* end, limit + *-ālis* -AL¹] —**ter′mi·nal·ly,** *adv.*

ter′minal leave′, the final leave granted to a member of the armed forces just before discharge, equal to the total unused leave accumulated during active service.

ter·mi·nate (tûr′mə nāt′), *v.,* **-nat·ed, -nat·ing.** —*v.t.* **1.** to bring to an end; put an end to. **2.** to occur at or form the conclusion of. **3.** to bound or limit spatially; form or be situated at the extremity of. —*v.i.* **4.** to end, conclude, or cease. **5.** to come to an end (often fol. by *at, in,* or *with*). **6.** to issue or result (usually fol. by *in*). [v. use of late ME *terminate* (adj.) limited < L *termināt(us),* ptp. of *termināre*] —**ter′mi·na′tive,** *adj.* —**ter′mi·na′tive·ly,** *adv.*

ter·mi·na·tion (tûr′mə nā′shən), *n.* **1.** the act of terminating. **2.** the fact of being terminated. **3.** the place or part where anything terminates; bound. **4.** an end or extremity; close or conclusion. **5.** an issue or result. **6.** *Gram.* a suffix or ending. [late ME *terminacion* < L *terminātiōn-* (s. of *terminātiō*) decision] —**ter′mi·na′tion·al,** *adj.*

ter·mi·na·tor (tûr′mə nā′tər), *n.* **1.** a person or thing that terminates. **2.** *Astron.* the dividing line between the illuminated and the unilluminated part of a satellite or planet, esp. the moon. [< LL]

ter·mi·na·to·ry (tûr′mə nə tōr′ē, -tôr′ē), *adj.* pertaining to or forming the extremity or boundary; terminal; terminating.

ter·mi·nol·o·gy (tûr′mə nol′ə jē), *n., pl.* **-gies. 1.** the system of terms belonging or peculiar to a science, art, or specialized subject; nomenclature: *the terminology of botany.* **2.** the science of terms, as in particular sciences or arts. [< ML *termin(us)* TERM + -O- + -LOGY] —**ter·mi·no·log·i·cal** (tûr′mə nəloj′i kəl), *adj.* —**ter′mi·no·log′i·cal·ly,** *adv.* —**ter′mi·nol′o·gist,** *n.*

term′ insur′ance, 1. life insurance for a stipulated term of years only, the beneficiary being paid the face value of the policy upon death during the term, but nothing being paid upon survival at the completion of the term. **2.** any type of insurance policy issued for a specific term.

ter·mi·nus (tûr′mə nəs), *n., pl.* **-ni** (-nī′), **-nus·es. 1.** the end or extremity of anything. **2.** either end of a railroad line. **3.** *Brit.* the station or the town at the end of a railway or bus route. **4.** the point toward which anything tends; goal or end. **5.** a boundary or limit. **6.** a boundary post or stone. **7.** (*cap.*) the ancient Roman god of boundaries and landmarks. [< L: boundary, limit, end]

ter·mi·nus ad quem (teʀ′mi no͝os′ äd kwem′; *Eng.* tûr′mə nəs ad kwem′), *Latin.* the end to which; final or latest limiting point.

ter·mi·nus a quo (teʀ′mi no͝os′ ä kwō′; *Eng.* tûr′mə nəs ā kwō′), *Latin.* the end from which; beginning; starting point; earliest limiting point.

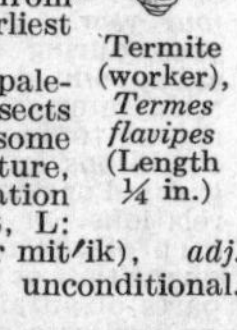
Termite (worker), *Termes flavipes* (Length ¼ in.)

ter·mite (tûr′mīt), *n.* any of numerous pale-colored, soft-bodied, chiefly tropical, social insects of the order *Isoptera* that feed on wood, some being highly destructive to buildings, furniture, etc. Also called **white ant.** [back formation from *termitēs,* pl. of NL *termes* white ant, L: wood-eating worms] —**ter·mit·ic** (tər mit′ik), *adj.*

term·less (tûrm′lis), *adj.* **1.** not limited; unconditional. **2.** boundless; endless.

term·or (tûr′mər), *n.* *Law.* a person who has an estate for a term of years or for life. [TERM + -OR²; r. ME *termur* < AF *termer* (see -ER²)]

term′ pa′per, a long essay, report, or the like, written by a student as an assignment over the course of a term or semester.

tern¹ (tûrn), *n.* any of numerous aquatic birds of the subfamily *Sterninae* of the family *Laridae,* related to the gulls but usually having a more slender body and bill, smaller feet, a long, deeply forked tail, and a more graceful flight. [< Dan *terne* or Norw *terna;* c. Icel *therna*]

Tern, *Sterna hirundo* (Length 15 in.; wingspread 2½ ft.)

tern² (tûrn), *n.* **1.** a set of three. **2.** three winning numbers drawn together in a lottery. [ME *terne* < MF < It *terno* < L *ternī* three each, triad, akin to *ter* thrice]

ter·na·ry (tûr′nə rē), *adj., n., pl.* **-ries.** —*adj.* **1.** consisting of or involving three; threefold; triple. **2.** third in order or rank. **3.** based on the number three. **4.** *Chem.* **a.** consisting of three different elements or groups. **b.** (formerly) consisting of three atoms. **5.** *Math.* having three variables. —*n.* **6.** a group of three. [late ME < L *ternāri(us)* made up of three]

ter′nary form′, a musical form in three sections with the third usually an exact repetition of the first.

ter·nate (tur′nit, -nāt), *adj.* **1.** consisting of three; arranged in threes. **2.** *Bot.* **a.** consisting of three leaflets, as a compound leaf. **b.** having leaves arranged in whorls of three, as a plant. [< NL *ternāt(us)*] —**ter′nate·ly,** *adv.*

Ternate leaves A, Laburnum, *Laburnum laburnum;* B, Rosinweed, *Silphium trifoliatum*

Ter·na·te (teʀ nä′te), *n.* an island in E Indonesia, W of Halmahera: important source of spices. 53 sq. mi.

terne′ met′al (tûrn), an alloy of lead and tin used for plating. [TERNE-(PLATE) + METAL]

terne·plate (tûrn′plāt′), *n.* steel plate coated with terne metal. [obs. *terne* (< F: dull; see TARNISH) + PLATE¹]

Ter·ni (teʀ′nē), *n.* a city in central Italy. 95,207 (1961).

ter·ni·on (tûr′nē ən), *n.* a set or group of three; triad. [< L *terniōn-* (s. of *terniō*) triad. See TERN², -ION]

Ter·no·pol (tyeʀ nô′pôl′yᵊ), *n.* a city in the W Ukraine, in the SW Soviet Union in Europe: formerly in Poland. 52,000 (1959). Polish, **Tarnopol.**

ter·pene (tûr′pēn), *n.* *Chem.* **1.** (originally) any of a class of monocyclic hydrocarbons of the formula $C_{10}H_{16}$, obtained from plants. **2.** any of a number of derivatives of this class. [alter. of TEREBENE, with *p* from TURPENTINE] —**ter′pene·less,** *adj.* —**ter·pe·nic** (tûr pē′nik), *adj.*

ter·pin·e·ol (tûr pin′ē ōl′, -ôl′, -ol′), *n.* *Chem.* any of several tertiary alcohols having the formula $C_{10}H_{17}OH$, used chiefly in the manufacture of perfumes. [*terpine* (TERP(ENE) + -INE²) + -OL²]

Terp·sich·o·re (tûrp sik′ə rē), *n.* **1.** *Class. Myth.* the Muse of dancing and choral song **2.** (*l.c.*) choreography; the art of dancing. [< L < Gk *Terpsichórē;* n. use of fem. of *terpsíchoros* enjoying the dance; see CHORUS]

terp·si·cho·re·an (tûrp′sə kə rē′ən, tûrp′sə kōr′ē ən, -kôr′-), *adj.* **1.** pertaining to dancing. **2.** (*cap.*) of or pertaining to Terpsichore. —*n.* **3.** *Informal.* a dancer.

terr., 1. terrace. **2.** territory.

ter·ra (ter′ə), *n.* earth; land. [< L]

ter′ra al′ba (al′bə), any of various white, earthy or powdery substances, as pipe clay, gypsum, kaolin, or magnesia. [< L: white earth]

ter·race (ter′əs), *n., v.,* **-raced, -rac·ing.** —*n.* **1.** a raised level with a vertical or sloping front or sides faced with masonry, turf, or the like, esp. one of a series of levels rising one above another. **2.** the top of such a construction, used as a platform, garden, road, etc. **3.** a nearly level strip of land with a more or less abrupt descent along the margin of the sea, a lake, or a river. **4.** the flat roof of a house. **5.** an open, often paved area connected to a house and serving as an outdoor living area. —*v.t.* **6.** to form into or furnish with a terrace or terraces. [earlier *terrasse* < MF < ML *terrācea* heap of earth, n. use of fem. of L **terrāceus.* See TERRA, -ACEOUS]

ter′ra cot′ta (kot′ə), **1.** a hard, fired clay, brownish-red in color when unglazed, that is used for architectural ornaments, structural units, pottery, and as a material for sculpture. **2.** something made of terra cotta. **3.** a brownish-orange color like that of unglazed terra cotta. [< It: lit., baked earth < L *terra cocta*] —**ter′ra-cot′ta,** *adj.*

ter′ra fir′ma (fûr′mə), firm or solid earth; dry land (as opposed to water or air). [< L]

ter·rain (tə rān′, ter′ān), *n.* **1.** a tract of land, esp. as considered with reference to its natural features, military advantages, etc. **2.** *Geol.* terrane. [< F << VL **terrān(um),* n. use of neut. of **terrānus* of land. See TERRA, -AN]

ter·ra in·cog·ni·ta (teʀ′ʀä in kōg′ni tä′; *Eng.* ter′ə in kog′ni tə, in′kog nē′-), *Latin.* an unknown or unexplored land, region, or subject.

Ter·ra·my·cin (ter′ə mī′sin), *n.* *Pharm., Trademark.* oxytetracycline.

ter·rane (tə rān′, ter′ān), *n.* *Geol.* any rock formation or series of formations. Also, **terrain.** [sp. var. of TERRAIN]

ter·ra·pin (ter′ə pin), *n.* **1.** any of several edible North American turtles of the family *Emydidae,* found in fresh or brackish waters, esp. the diamondback terrapin. **2.** any of various similar turtles. [earlier *torope* < Algonquian (Va.); see -IN¹]

ter·ra·que·ous (ter ā′kwē əs, -ak′wē-), *adj.* consisting of land and water, as the earth.

ter·rar·i·um (te râr′ē əm), *n., pl.* **-rar·i·ums, -rar·i·a** (-râr′ē ə). a vivarium for land animals (distinguished from *aquarium*).

ter·ras (tə ras′), *n.* trass.

ter·raz·zo (tə raz′ō, -räz′ō; *It.* teʀ ʀät′tsô), *n.* a mosaic flooring or paving composed of chips of broken stone, usually marble, and cement. [< It: balcony, terraced or flat roof. See TERRACE]

Ter·re Haute (ter′ə hōt′, ter′ē hut′), a city in W Indiana, on the Wabash River. 70,335 (1970).

ter·rene (te rēn′, tə-), *adj.* **1.** earthly; worldly. **2.** earthy. —*n.* **3.** the earth. **4.** a land or region. [ME < L *terrēn(us)* pertaining to earth. See TERRA, -ENE] —**ter·rene′ly,** *adv.*

terre·plein (ter′plān′), *n.* *Fort.* the top platform or horizontal surface of a rampart where guns are mounted. [< F < ML *terrā plēnus,* lit., full with earth, i.e., a fill. See TERRA, PLENUM]

ter·res·tri·al (tə res′trē əl), *adj.* **1.** pertaining to, consisting of, or representing the earth as distinct from other planets. **2.** of or pertaining to land as distinct from water. **3.** *Bot.* **a.** growing on land; not aquatic. **b.** growing in the ground; not epiphytic or aerial. **4.** *Zool.* living on the ground; not aquatic, arboreal, or aerial. **5.** of or pertaining to the earth or this world; worldly; mundane. —*n.* **6.** an inhabitant of the earth. [late ME < L *terrestri(s)* pertaining to earth + -AL¹] —**ter·res′tri·al·ly,** *adv.* —**Syn. 1.** terrene. See **earthly.** —**Ant. 1.** celestial.

terres′trial globe′. See under **globe** (def. 3).

ter·ret (ter′it), *n.* one of the round loops or rings on the saddle of a harness, through which the driving reins pass. [late ME *teret,* unexplained var. of ME *toret* < MF, OF *tor* ring (see TOUR) + *-et* -ET]

ter·ri·ble (ter′ə bəl), *adj.* **1.** distressing; severe: *a terrible winter.* **2.** extremely bad; horrible. **3.** exciting terror or great fear; dreadful; awful. [late ME < L *terribil(is)* = *terr(ēre)* (to) frighten + *-ibilis* -IBLE] —**ter′ri·ble·ness,** *n.* —**Syn. 3.** frightful, appalling, horrible. —**Ant. 3.** delightful.

ter·ri·bly (ter′ə blē), *adv.* **1.** in a terrible manner. **2.** *Informal.* extremely: *It's terribly late. You're terribly nice.*

ter·ric·o·lous (te rik′ə ləs), *adj.* *Bot., Zool.* living on or in the ground. [< L *terri-* (comb. form of *terra* earth) + -COLOUS]

ter·ri·er (ter′ē ər), *n.* one of any of several breeds of usually small dogs, used originally to pursue game and drive it out of its hole or burrow. [< MF, short for *chien terrier,* lit., dog of the earth (< ML *terrārius;* see TERRA, -IER); so called because used to start badgers from their burrows; r. late ME *terrere* < AF]

ter·rif·ic (tə rif′ik), *adj.* **1.** *Informal.* extraordinarily great, intense, or good: *terrific speed.* **2.** causing terror; terrifying. [< L *terrific(us)* frightening = *terr(ēre)* (to) frighten + *-i-* -I- + *-ficus* -FIC] —**ter·rif′i·cal·ly,** *adv.* —**Syn. 1.** fine, excellent, extraordinary, remarkable.

ter·ri·fy (ter′ə fī′), *v.t.,* **-fied, -fy·ing.** to fill with terror; make greatly afraid. [< L *terrifi(cāre)* = *terr(ēre)* (to) frighten + *-ificāre* -IFY] —**ter′ri·fi′er,** *n.* —**ter′ri·fy′ing·ly,** *adv.* —**Syn.** See **frighten.**

ter·rig·e·nous (te rij′ə nəs), *adj.* **1.** produced by the earth. **2.** *Geol.* noting or pertaining to sediments on the sea bottom derived directly from the neighboring land, or to the rocks formed primarily by the consolidation of such sediments. [< L *terrigenus* = *terr(a)* earth + *-i-* -I- + *-genus* -GENOUS]

ter·ri·to·ri·al (ter′i tōr′ē əl, -tôr′-), *adj.* **1.** of or pertaining to territory or land. **2.** of, pertaining to, associated with, or restricted to a particular territory or district; local. **3.** (of an animal) characterized by territoriality. **4.** (*cap.*) of or pertaining to a Territory of the U.S. **5.** (*cap.*) *Mil.* organized on a local basis for home defense: *the British Territorial Army.* —*n.* **6.** (*cap.*) a member of the British Territorial Army. **7.** a soldier in a territorial army. [< LL *territōriāl(is)*] —**ter′ri·to′ri·al·ly,** *adv.*

ter·ri·to·ri·al·ise (ter′i tōr′ē ə līz′, -tôr′-), *v.t.,* **-ised, -is·ing.** *Chiefly Brit.* territorialize. —**ter′ri·to′ri·al·i·sa′tion,** *n.*

ter·ri·to·ri·al·ism (ter′i tōr′ē ə liz′əm, -tôr′-), *n.* **1.** landlordism. **2.** Also called **territo′rial sys′tem.** the theory of church policy according to which the supreme ecclesiastical authority is vested in the civil power. —**ter′ri·to′ri·al·ist,** *n.*

ter·ri·to·ri·al·i·ty (ter′i tōr′ē al′i tē, -tôr′-), *n.* **1.** territorial quality, condition, or status. **2.** the behavior of an animal in defending its territory.

ter·ri·to·ri·al·ize (ter′i tōr′ē ə līz′, -tôr′-), *v.t.,* **-ized, -iz·ing. 1.** to extend by adding new territory. **2.** to reduce to the status of a territory. Also, *esp. Brit.*, **territorialise.** —**ter′ri·to′ri·al·i·za′tion,** *n.*

territo′rial wa′ters, the waters of a littoral state that are regarded as under the jurisdiction of the state: commonly, those waters within three miles of the shore. Also, **territo′rial wa′ter.**

ter·ri·to·ry (ter′i tōr′ē, -tôr′ē), *n., pl.* **-ries. 1.** any tract of land; region or district. **2.** the land and waters belonging to or under the jurisdiction of a state, sovereign, etc. **3.** any separate tract of land belonging to a state. **4.** (*cap.*) *Govt. U.S.* (formerly) a region not admitted to the Union as a state but having its own legislature, with a governor and other officers appointed by the President and confirmed by the Senate. **5.** a field or sphere of action, thought, etc. **6.** the region or district assigned to a representative, agent, or the like, as for making sales. **7.** the area which an animal defends against intruders of the same species. [late ME < L *territōri(um)* land around a town, district = *terr(a)* land + *-i-* -I- + *-tōrium* abstracted from other words in *-tōrium* with local sense; see -ORY[2]]

ter·ror (ter′ər), *n.* **1.** intense, sharp, overmastering fear: *to be frantic with terror.* **2.** a feeling, instance, or cause of intense fear: *to be a terror to evildoers.* [< L = *terr(ēre)* (to) frighten + *-or* -OR[1]; r. ME *terrour* < AF] —**ter′ror·ful,** *adj.* —**ter′ror·less,** *adj.*
—**Syn. 1.** alarm, dismay, consternation. TERROR, HORROR, PANIC, FRIGHT all imply extreme fear in the presence of danger or evil. TERROR implies an intense fear that is somewhat prolonged and may refer to imagined or future dangers: *frozen with terror.* HORROR implies a sense of shock at a danger that is also evil: *to recoil in horror.* PANIC and FRIGHT both imply a sudden shock of fear. PANIC is uncontrolled and unreasoning fear, often groundless, that may be prolonged: *The mob was in a panic.* FRIGHT is usually of short duration: *a spasm of fright.* —**Ant. 1.** calm.

ter·ror·ism (ter′ə riz′əm), *n.* **1.** the use of terrorizing methods. **2.** the state of fear and submission so produced. **3.** a terroristic method of governing or of resisting a government.

ter·ror·ist (ter′ər ist), *n.* **1.** a person who uses or favors terrorizing methods. **2.** (formerly) a member of a political group in Russia aiming at the demoralization of the government by terror. **3.** an agent or partisan of the revolutionary tribunal during the Reign of Terror in France. [TERROR + -IST; cf. F *terroriste*] —**ter′ror·is′tic,** *adj.*

ter·ror·ize (ter′ə rīz′), *v.t.,* **-ized, -iz·ing. 1.** to fill or overcome with terror. **2.** to dominate or coerce by intimidation. Also, *esp. Brit.*, **ter′ror·ise′.** —**ter′ror·i·za′tion,** *n.* —**ter′ror·iz′er,** *n.* —**Syn.** See **frighten.**

ter·ror-strick·en (ter′ər strik′ən), *adj.* overwhelmed by terror; terrified.

ter·ry (ter′ē), *n., pl.* **-ries,** *adj.* —*n.* **1.** the loop formed by the pile of a fabric when left uncut. **2.** Also, **ter′ry cloth′.** a pile fabric with loops on both sides, as in a Turkish towel. —*adj.* **3.** having the pile loops uncut: *terry velvet.* [? var. of TERRET]

Ter·ry (ter′ē), *n.* **Ellen (Alicia** or **Alice),** 1848?–1928, English actress.

terse (tûrs), *adj.,* **ters·er, ters·est.** neatly or effectively concise; brief and pithy, as language: *a terse review of the novel.* [< L *ters(us)*, ptp. of *tergēre* to rub off, wipe off, clean, polish] —**terse′ly,** *adv.* —**terse′ness,** *n.* —**Syn.** succinct, compact, neat, concentrated; curt.

ter·tial (tûr′shəl), *Ornith.* —*adj.* **1.** pertaining to any of a set of flight feathers situated on the basal segment of a bird's wing. —*n.* **2.** a tertial feather. [< L *terti(us)* third + -AL[1]]

ter·tian (tûr′shən), *adj.* **1.** *Pathol.* (of a fever, ague, etc.) characterized by paroxysms that recur every other day. —*n.* **2.** *Pathol.* a tertian fever or ague. [ME *terciane* < L (*febris*) *tertiāna* tertian (fever) = *terti(us)* third + *-āna*, fem. of *-ānus* -AN]

ter·ti·ar·y (tûr′shē er′ē, tûr′shə rē), *adj., n., pl.* **-ar·ies.** —*adj.* **1.** of the third order, rank, formation, etc.; third. **2.** being or constituting the third stage, degree, etc. **3.** *Chem.* **a.** noting or containing a carbon atom united to three other carbon atoms. **b.** formed by replacement of three atoms or groups. **4.** (*cap.*) *Geol.* noting or pertaining to the period forming the earlier part of the Cenozoic era, occurring from 1,000,000 to 70,000,000 years ago. See table at **era. 5.** *Ornith.* tertial. **6.** *Eccles.* noting or pertaining to a branch, or third order, of certain religious orders. —*n.* **7.** (*cap.*) *Geol.* the Tertiary period or system. **8.** *Ornith.* a tertial feather. **9.** (*often cap.*) *Eccles.* a member of a tertiary branch of a religious order. [< L *tertiāri(us)* of third part or rank = *terti(us)* third + *-ārius* -ARY]

ter′tiary col′or, a color, as gray or brown, produced by mixing two secondary colors.

ter·ti·um quid (tûr′shē əm kwid′; *Lat.* teʀ′tē ŏŏm′ kwid′), something related in some way to two things, but distinct from both; something intermediate between two things. [< L, trans. of Gk *tríton ti* some third thing]

Ter·tul·li·an (tər tul′ē ən, -tul′yən), *n.* (*Quintus Septimius Florens Tertullianus*) A.D. c160–c230, Carthaginian theologian.

ter·va·lent (tûr vā′lənt), *adj. Chem.* **1.** trivalent. **2.** possessing three different valences, as cobalt with valences 2, 3, and 4. —**ter·va′lence, ter·va′len·cy,** *n.*

ter·za ri·ma (tert′sə rē′mə; *It.* teʀ′tsä ʀē′mä), *Pros.* an Italian form of iambic verse consisting of eleven-syllable lines arranged in tercets, the middle line of each tercet rhyming with the first and last lines of the following tercet. [< It: third rhyme]

tes·la (tes′lə), *n.* a unit of magnetic induction equal to one weber per square meter. *Abbr.:* T [named after N. TESLA]

Tes·la (tes′lə), *n.* **Ni·ko·la** (nik′ō lə), 1856–1943, U.S. electrical engineer and inventor, born in Croatia.

TESOL (tē′sôl, tes′əl), *n.* teaching English to speakers of other languages.

tes·se·late (tes′ə lāt′), *v.t.,* **-lat·ed, -lat·ing,** *adj.* tessellate.

tes·sel·late (*v.* tes′ə lāt′; *adj.* tes′ə lit, -lāt′), *v.,* **-lat·ed, -lat·ing,** *adj.* —*v.t.* **1.** to form of small squares or blocks, as floors, pavements, etc.; form or arrange in a checkered or mosaic pattern. —*adj.* **2.** tessellated. [< L *tessellāt(us)* mosaic = *tessell(a)* small square stone (dim. of *tessera* TESSERA) + *-ātus* -ATE[1]]

tes·sel·lat·ed (tes′ə lā′tid), *adj.* **1.** of, pertaining to, or like a mosaic. **2.** arranged in or having the appearance of a mosaic; checkered. Also, **tes′se·lat′ed.**

tes·sel·la·tion (tes′ə lā′shən), *n.* **1.** the art or practice of tessellating. **2.** tessellated form or arrangement. **3.** tessellated work. Also, **tes′se·la′tion.**

tes·ser·a (tes′ər ə), *n., pl.* **tes·ser·ae** (tes′ə rē′). **1.** each of the small pieces used in mosaic work. **2.** a small square of bone, wood, or the like, used in ancient times as a token, tally, ticket, due, etc. [< L < Gk (Ionic) *tésseres* four]

tes·ser·act (tes′ə rakt′), *n.* the generalization of a cube to four dimensions. [< Gk *tésser(es)* four + *akt(ís)* ray]

tes·si·tu·ra (tes′i tŏŏr′ə; *It.* tes′sē tōō′ʀä), *n., pl.* **-tu·ras,** *It.* **-tu·re** (-tōō′ʀe). the general pitch level of a vocal or instrumental part in musical composition: *an uncomfortably high tessitura.* [< It: lit., texture < L *textura* TEXTURE]

test[1] (test), *n.* **1.** the means by which the presence, quality, or genuineness of anything is determined; a means of trial. **2.** the trial of the quality of something: *to put to the test.* **3.** a particular process or method for trying or assessing. **4.** a form of examination for evaluating the performance, capabilities, traits, or achievements of an individual. **5.** *Chem.* **a.** the process of detecting the presence of an ingredient in a substance, or of determining the nature of a substance, commonly by the addition of a reagent. **b.** the result obtained by such means. **6.** *Brit.* a cupel for refining or assaying metals. —*v.t.* **7.** to subject to a test of any kind; try. **8.** *Chem.* to subject to a chemical test. —*v.i.* **9.** to undergo a test or trial; try out. **10.** to conduct a test. [ME: cupel < MF < L *testū* earthen pot with lid; akin to TEST[2]] —**test′a·bil′i·ty,** *n.* —**test′a·ble,** *adj.* —**test′ing·ly,** *adv.* —**Syn. 1.** proof, assay. See **trial. 7.** assay, prove, examine.

test[2] (test), *n.* **1.** *Zool.* the hard, protective shell or covering of certain invertebrates, as echinoderms or tunicates. **2.** *Bot.* testa. [< L *testa* tile, shell, covering. See TEST[1]]

Test., Testament.

tes·ta (tes′tə), *n., pl.* **-tae** (-tē). *Bot.* the outer, usually hard, integument or coat of a seed. Also, **test.** [< L; see TEST[2]]

tes·ta·ceous (te stā′shəs), *adj.* **1.** of, pertaining to, or derived from shells. **2.** having a test or shell-like covering. **3.** *Bot., Zool.* of a brick-red, brownish-red, or brownish-yellow color. [< L *testāceus* shell-covered = *test(a)* (see TEST[2]) + *-āceus* -ACEOUS]

tes·ta·cy (tes′tə sē), *n.* the state of being testate. [TESTA(TE) + -CY]

tes·ta·ment (tes′tə mənt), *n.* **1.** *Law.* **a.** a will, esp. one that relates to the disposition of one's personal property. **b.** will[2] (def. 8). **2.** a covenant, esp. between God and man. **3.** (*cap.*) either the New Testament or the Old Testament. [ME < L *testāment(um)* will = *testā(rī)* (to) bear witness (see TESTATE) + *-mentum* -MENT; in sense, covenant < eccl. L, mistranslation of Gk *diathḗkē*]

tes·ta·men·ta·ry (tes′tə men′tə rē), *adj.* **1.** of, pertaining to, or of the nature of a testament or will. **2.** given, bequeathed, done, or appointed by will. **3.** set forth or contained in a will. Also, **tes′ta·men′tal.** [late ME < L *testamentāri(us)*]

tes·tate (tes′tāt), *adj.* having made and left a valid will. [late ME < L *testāt(us)*, ptp. of *testārī* to bear witness, make a will < *testis* witness]

tes·ta·tor (tes′tā tər, te stā′tər), *n.* **1.** a person who makes a will. **2.** a person who has died leaving a valid will. [< L; see TESTATE, -OR[2]; r. late ME *testatour* < AF]

tes·ta·trix (te stā′triks), *n., pl.* **tes·ta·tri·ces** (te stā′tri sēz′, tes′tə trī′sēz). a female testator. [< LL; fem. of TESTATOR]

test′ ban′, an agreement by nations producing atomic bombs to refrain from nuclear tests in the atmosphere. —**test′-ban′,** *adj.*

test′ case′, a legal action taken, sometimes deliberately by agreement of both parties, with a special view to determining the position of the law on some matter, as the constitutionality of a statute.

test·ee (te stē′), *n.* one who is tested, as by a scholastic examination.

test·er[1] (tes′tər), *n.* a person or thing that tests. [TEST[1] + -ER[1]]

tes·ter[2] (tes′tər), *n.* a canopy, as over a bed, altar, etc. [ME < ML *testrum* canopy of a bed; akin to L *testa* covering. See TEST[2]]

tes·ter[3] (tes′tər), *n.* the teston of Henry VIII. [earlier *testorn*, var. of TESTON, with *-r-* from MF *testart* teston]

tes·tes (tes′tēz), *n.* pl. of **testis.**

tes·ti·cle (tes′ti kəl), *n.* testis. [< L *testicul(us)*. See TESTIS, -CLE]

tes·tic·u·lar (te stik′yə lər), *adj. Bot.* testiculate. [< L *testicul(us)* TESTICLE + -AR[1]]

tes·tic·u·late (te stik′yŏŏ lit), *adj. Bot.* **1.** shaped like a testis. **2.** having tubers shaped like testes, as certain orchids. [< LL *testiculāt(us)*. See TESTICLE, -ATE[1]]

tes·ti·fy (tes′tə fī′), *v.,* **-fied, -fy·ing.** —*v.i.* **1.** to bear witness; give or afford evidence. **2.** to make solemn declaration. **3.** *Law.* to give testimony under oath or solemn affirmation, usually in court. —*v.t.* **4.** to bear witness to; affirm as fact or truth; attest. **5.** to give or afford evidence of in any manner. **6.** to declare, profess, or acknowledge openly. **7.** *Law.* to state or declare under oath or affirmation, usually in court. [ME *testifye* < L *testificārī* to bear witness = *testi(s)* witness + *-ficārī* -FY] —**tes·ti·fi·ca·tion** (tes′tə fə kā′shən), *n.* —**tes′ti·fi′er,** *n.*

tes·ti·mo·ni·al (tes′tə mō′nē əl), *n.* **1.** a written declaration certifying to a person's character, conduct, or qualifications, or to the value, excellence, etc., of a thing; a letter or written statement of recommendation. **2.** something given or done as an expression of esteem, admiration, or gratitude. —*adj.* **3.** pertaining to or serving as a testimonial: *a testimonial dinner for the retiring dean.* [late ME < LL *testimōniāl(is)*]

tes·ti·mo·ny (tes′tə mō′nē), *n., pl.* **-nies. 1.** *Law.* the statement or declaration of a witness under oath or affirmation

tion, usually in court. **2.** evidence in support of a fact or statement; proof. **3.** open declaration or profession, as of faith. **4.** the Decalogue as inscribed on the two tables of the law. Ex. 16:34; 25:16. [late ME < L *testimōni(um)* = *testi(s)* witness + *-mōnium* -MONY] —**Syn. 1.** deposition, attestation. See **evidence. 2.** corroboration. **3.** affirmation.

tes·tis (tes′tis), *n., pl.* **-tes** (-tēz). *Anat., Zool.* the male gonad or reproductive gland; either of two oval glands located in the scrotum. [< L]

tes·ton (tes′tən, te sto͞on′), *n.* **1.** a former silver coin of France, equal at various times to between 10 and 14½ sols. **2.** a former silver coin of England, issued by Henry VII, Henry VIII, and Edward VI, equal originally to 12 pence, later to sixpence. Also, **tes·toon** (te sto͞on′). [< F < It *testone,* aug. of *testa* head < L; see TESTA]

tes·tos·ter·one (te stos′tə rōn′), *n.* **1.** *Biochem.* the sex hormone, $C_{19}H_{28}O_2$, secreted by the testes, that stimulates the development of masculine characteristics. **2.** *Pharm.* a commercially prepared synthetic form of this compound. [*testo-* (comb. form of TESTIS) + STER(OL) + -ONE]

test′ pa′per, 1. *U.S.* the paper bearing the student's answers to an examination. **2.** *Chem.* paper impregnated with a reagent, as litmus, which changes color when acted upon by certain substances.

test′ pat′tern, *Television.* a geometric design broadcast to receivers for testing the quality of transmission.

test′ pi′lot, a pilot employed to fly newly developed and experimental aircraft.

test′ tube′, a hollow cylinder of thin glass with one end closed, used in chemical and biological laboratories.

test-tube (test′to͞ob′, -tyo͞ob′), *adj.* **1.** produced in or as in a test tube; synthetic or experimental. **2.** generated by artificial insemination: *a test-tube baby.*

tes·tu·di·nal (te sto͞od′ənəl, -styo͞od′-), *adj.* pertaining to or resembling a tortoise or tortoise shell. Also, **tes·tu·di·nar·i·an** (te sto͞od′ənâr′ē ən, -styo͞od′-). [< L *testūdin-* (s. of *testūdō*) tortoise + -AL[1]]

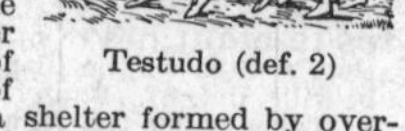
Testudo (def. 2)

tes·tu·di·nate (te sto͞od′ənit, -ənāt′, -styo͞od′-), *adj.* **1.** formed like the carapace of a tortoise; arched; vaulted. **2.** chelonian. —*n.* **3.** a turtle. [< L *testūdināt-(us).* See TESTUDINAL, -ATE[1]]

tes·tu·do (te sto͞o′dō, -styo͞o′-), *n., pl.* **tes·tu·di·nes** (te sto͞od′ənēz′, -styo͞od′-). *Fort.* **1.** (among the ancient Romans) a movable shelter with a strong and usually fireproof arched roof, used for protection of soldiers in siege operations. **2.** a shelter formed by overlapping shields, held by soldiers above their heads. [< L: lit., tortoise; akin to TEST[2]]

tes·ty (tes′tē), *adj.,* **-ti·er, -ti·est.** irritably impatient; touchy. [late ME *testi,* alter. of MF *testu* headstrong; r. ME *testif* < MF. See TEST[2], -IVE] —**tes′ti·ly,** *adv.* —**tes′ti·ness,** *n.* —**Syn.** tetchy, edgy, snappish, cross, irascible.

te·tan·ic (tə tan′ik), *adj.* **1.** *Pathol.* pertaining to, of the nature of, or characterized by tetanus. **2.** *Med.* noting a remedy that acts on the nerves and through them on the muscles, and that if taken in overdoses, causes tetanic spasms of the muscles and death. Cf. **tetany.** Also, **te·tan′i·cal.** [< L *tetanic(us)* < Gk *tetanikós*] —**te·tan′i·cal·ly,** *adv.*

tet·a·nise (tet′ənīz′), *v.t.,* **-nised, -nis·ing.** *Chiefly Brit.* tetanize. —**tet′a·ni·sa′tion,** *n.*

tet·a·nize (tet′ənīz′), *v.t.,* **-nized, -niz·ing.** *Physiol.* to induce tetanus in (a muscle). —**tet′a·ni·za′tion,** *n.*

tet·a·nus (tet′ənəs), *n.* **1.** *Pathol.* an infectious, often fatal disease, caused by a bacterium that enters the body through wounds, and characterized by tonic spasms and rigidity of voluntary muscles, esp. those of the neck and lower jaw. Cf. **lockjaw. 2.** Also called **tet′anus bacil′lus.** *Bacteriol.* the bacterium, *Clostridium tetani,* causing this disease. **3.** *Physiol.* a state of sustained contraction of a muscle, during which the muscle does not relax to its initial length or tension, induced by a rapid succession of stimuli. [< L < Gk *tétanos* spasm (of muscles), tetanus] —**tet′a·noid′,** *adj.*

tet·a·ny (tet′ənē), *n.* *Pathol.* a state marked by severe, intermittent tonic contractions and muscular pain, frequently due to a deficiency of calcium salts. [< NL *tetania.* See TETANUS, -Y[3]]

tetarto-, a learned borrowing from Greek meaning "one fourth," used in the formation of compound words: *tetartohedral.* [comb. form repr. Gk *tétartos;* akin to L *quartus*]

te·tar·to·he·dral (ti tär′tō hē′drəl), *adj.* (of a crystal) having one fourth the planes or faces required by the maximum symmetry of the system to which it belongs. —**te·tar′to·he′dral·ly,** *adv.* —**te·tar′to·he′drism,** *n.*

tetched (techt), *adj.* touched; slightly mad. [late ME *techyd* marked (confused in sense with *touched* a little crazy) = *teche* mark, spot, blemish, taint (< MF, OF < Gmc; akin to TOKEN) + *-ed* -ED[3]]

tetch·y (tech′ē), *adj.,* **tetch·i·er, tetch·i·est.** irritable; touchy. Also, **techy.** [? *tetch* (see TETCHED) + -Y[1]] —**tetch′i·ly,** *adv.* —**tetch′i·ness,** *n.*

tête-à-tête (tāt′ə tāt′; *Fr.* te tA tet′), *adj., n., pl.* **tête-à-têtes,** *Fr.* **tête-à-tête,** *adv.* —*adj.* **1.** of, between, or for two persons only. —*n.* **2.** a private conversation, usually between two persons. —*adv.* **3.** (of two persons) together in private: *to sit tête-à-tête.* [< F: lit., head to head]

tête-bêche (tet besh′), *adj.* *Philately.* of or pertaining to a pair of stamps that have been printed with one stamp inverted. [< F = *tête* head + *bêche,* reduced from *béchevet* head (of bed) the wrong way]

tête-de-pont (*Fr.* tet də pôN′), *n., pl.* **têtes-de-pont** (*Fr.* tet də pôN′). *Fort.* bridgehead. [< F]

teth (tes; *Heb.* tet), *n.* the ninth letter of the Hebrew alphabet. [< Heb]

teth·er (teth′ər), *n.* **1.** a cord, chain, or the like, by which a movable or moving object is fastened to a fixed object. **2.** the utmost length to which one can go in action; the utmost extent or limit of ability or resources. **3. at the end of one's tether,** at the end of one's resources, patience, or strength. —*v.t.* **4.** to fasten or confine with or as with a tether. [ME *tethir* < Scand; cf. Icel *tjōthr,* c. D *tuier*]

Te·thys (tē′this), *n.* *Class. Myth.* a Titaness, a daughter of Uranus and Gaea, the wife of Oceanus and mother of the Oceanids and river gods.

Te·ton (tēt′ən), *n., pl.* **-tons,** (*esp. collectively*) **-ton** for **1. 1.** a member of a Dakota people of the western U.S. **2.** a dialect of the Dakota language.

Te′ton Range′ (tēt′ən), a mountain range in NW Wyoming and SE Idaho: a part of the Rocky Mountains. Highest peak, Grand Teton, ab. 13,700 ft.

tet·ra (te′trə), *n., pl.* (*esp. collectively*) **-ra,** (*esp. referring to two or more kinds or species*) **-ras.** any of several tropical, fresh-water fishes of the family *Characidae,* often kept in aquariums. [shortening of NL *tetragonopterus.* See TETRAGON, -O-, -PTEROUS]

tetra-, a learned borrowing from Greek meaning "four," used in the formation of compound words: *tetrabranchiate.* Also, *esp. before a vowel,* **tetr-.** [< Gk, comb. form of *téttara*]

tet·ra·ba·sic (te′trə bā′sik), *adj.* *Chem.* **1.** (of an acid) having four atoms of hydrogen replaceable by basic atoms or groups. **2.** containing four basic atoms or groups having a valence of one. —**tet·ra·ba·sic·i·ty** (te′trə bā sis′i tē), *n.*

tet·ra·brach (te′trə brak′), *n.* *Class. Pros.* a metrical foot or word of four short syllables. [< Gk *tetrábrachys* having four short syllables. See TETRA-, BRACHY-]

tet·ra·bran·chi·ate (te′trə braŋ′kē it, -āt′), *adj.* belonging or pertaining to the *Tetrabranchiata,* a subclass or order of cephalopods with four gills, including the pearly nautilus and numerous fossil forms.

tet·ra·chlo·ride (te′trə klōr′īd, -id, -klôr′-), *n.* *Chem.* a chloride containing four atoms of chlorine.

tet·ra·chord (te′trə kôrd′), *n.* *Music.* a diatonic series of four tones, the first and last separated by a perfect fourth. [< Gk *tetráchord(os)* having four strings] —**tet′ra·chor′dal,** *adj.*

te·trac·id (te tras′id), *n.* *Chem.* a base or alcohol containing four hydroxyl groups.

tet·ra·cy·cline (te′trə sī′klīn, -klin), *n.* *Pharm.* an antibiotic, $C_{22}H_{24}H_2O_8$, used to treat a broad variety of infections.

tet·rad (te′trad), *n.* **1.** a group of four. **2.** the number four. **3.** *Chem.* a tetravalent or quadrivalent element, atom, or group. [< Gk *tetrad-* (s. of *tetrás*) group of four]

te·trad·y·mite (te trad′ə mīt′), *n.* a mineral, bismuth telluride and sulfide, Bi_2Te_2S, occurring in soft-gray to black foliated masses. [< Gk *tetrádym(os)* fourfold (see TETRA-, DIDYMOUS) + -ITE[1]; modeled on G *Tetradymit*]

tet′ra·eth·yl lead′ (te′trə eth′əl led′), *Chem.* a poisonous liquid, $(C_2H_5)_4Pb$, used as an antiknock agent in gasoline. Also called **lead tetraethyl.**

tetraeth′yl pyrophos′phate, *Chem.* a poisonous liquid, $(C_2H_5)_4P_2O_7$, used as an insecticide and as a rodenticide. Also called **TEPP**

tet·ra·gon (te′trə gon′), *n.* *Rare.* a plane figure having four angles or sides; a quadrangle or quadrilateral. [< Gk *tetrágōn(on)* quadrangle]

te·trag·o·nal (te trag′ə nəl), *adj.* **1.** pertaining to or having the form of a tetragon. **2.** *Crystall.* noting or pertaining to that system of crystallization in which all three axes are at right angles to one another, two being equal in length and the third being of a different length. Cf. **system** (def. 11). —**te·trag′o·nal·ly,** *adv.* —**te·trag′o·nal·ness,** *n.*

tet·ra·gram (te′trə gram′), *n.* a word of four letters. [< LGk *tetrágramm(on),* n. use of neut. of *tetrágrammos* having four letters. See TETRA-, -GRAM[1]]

Tet·ra·gram·ma·ton (te′trə gram′ə ton′), *n.* the four letters *yod, he, vav, he* (used to represent the Hebrew word for God, transliterated consonantally usually as *YHVH,* now pronounced as *Adonai* or *Elohim* in substitution for the original and now forbidden pronunciation uttered inaudibly by the high priest on Yom Kippur until the destruction of the Second Temple). [late ME < Gk, n. use of neut. of *tetragrámmatos* having four letters = *tetra-* TETRA- + *grammat-* (s. of *grámma*) letter + *-os* adj. suffix]

tet·ra·he·dral (te′trə hē′drəl), *adj.* **1.** pertaining to or having the form of a tetrahedron. **2.** having four lateral planes in addition to the top and bottom. [TETRAHEDR(ON) + -AL[1]] —**tet′ra·he′dral·ly,** *adv.*

tet·ra·he·drite (te′trə hē′drīt), *n.* a mineral, essentially copper and antimony sulfide, approximately Cu_3SbS_3, but often containing silver or other elements, sometimes occurring in tetrahedral crystals: an important ore of silver. [TETRAHEDR(ON) + -ITE[1], modeled on G *Tetraedrit*]

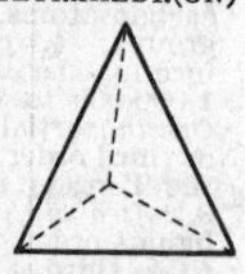
Tetrahedron

tet·ra·he·dron (te′trə hē′drən), *n., pl.* **-drons, -dra** (-drə). **1.** *Geom.* a solid contained by four plane faces; a triangular pyramid. **2.** any of various objects resembling a tetrahedron in the distribution of its faces or apexes. [TETRA- + -HEDRON, modeled on LGk *tetráedron,* n. use of neut. of *tetráedros* four-sided]

te·tral·o·gy (te tral′ə jē), *n., pl.* **-gies. 1.** a series of four related dramas, operas, novels, etc. **2.** a group of four dramas, three tragic and one satiric, performed consecutively at the festival of Dionysus in ancient Athens. [< Gk *tetralogía*]

te·tram·er·ous (te tram′ər əs), *adj.* **1.** consisting of or divided into four parts. **2.** *Bot.* (of flowers) having four members in each whorl. [< NL *tetramerus* < Gk *tetramerḗs* having four parts] —**te·tram′er·ism,** *n.*

te·tram·e·ter (te tram′i tər), *n.* **1.** *Pros.* a verse of four feet. **2.** *Class. Pros.* a line consisting of four dipodies in trochaic, iambic, or anapestic meter. —*adj.* **3.** consisting of four metrical feet. [< L *tetrametr(us)* < Gk *tetrámetros* having four measures]

tet·ra·pet·al·ous (te′trə pet′ələs), *adj.* *Bot.* having four petals.

tet·ra·pod (te′trə pod′), *n.* an object, as a caltrop, having four projections radiating from one central node: no matter how the object is placed, three of the projections will form a supporting tripod and the fourth will point directly upward. [< NL *tetrapod(us)* < Gk *tetrapod-* (s. of *tetrápous*) four-footed. See TETRA-, -POD]

te·trap·o·dy (te trap′ə dē), *n., pl.* **-dies.** *Pros.* a measure consisting of four feet. [< Gk *tetrapodía.* See TETRA-, -POD, -Y[3]] —**tet·ra·pod·ic** (te′trə pod′ik), *adj.*

te·trap·ter·ous (te trap′tər əs), *adj.* **1.** *Zool.* having four wings or winglike appendages. **2.** *Bot.* having four winglike appendages. [< Gk *tetrápteros*]

te·trarch (tē′trärk, te′-), *n.* **1.** any ruler of a fourth part, division, etc. **2.** a subordinate ruler. **3.** one of four joint rulers or chiefs. **4.** the ruler of the fourth part of a country or province in the ancient Roman Empire. [< LL *tetrarcha,* var. of L *tetrarchēs* < Gk *tetrárchēs.* See TETR-, -ARCH] —**te·trarch·ate** (tē′trär kāt′, -kit, te′trär-), **te·trar·chy** (tē′trär kē, te′trär-), *n.* —**te·trar·chic** (ti trär′kik), **te·trar′chi·cal,** *adj.*

tet·ra·spo·ran·gi·um (te′trə spō ran′jē əm, -spô-), *n., pl.* **-gi·a** (-jē ə). *Bot.* a sporangium containing four asexual spores.

tet·ra·spore (te′trə spōr′, -spôr′), *n. Bot.* one of the four asexual spores produced within a tetrasporangium. —**tet·ra·spor·ic** (te′trə spôr′ik, -spor′-), **tet·ra·spor·ous** (te′trə spôr′əs, -spor′-, ti tras′pər-), *adj.*

A

B

Tetrapterous fruit of silverbell tree, *Halesia Carolina;* A, Full view B, Transverse section

tet·ra·stich (te′trə stik, te tras′tik), *n. Pros.* a strophe, stanza, or poem consisting of four lines. [< L *tetrastichon* < Gk, n. use of neut. of *tetrástichos.* See TETRASTICHOUS] —**tet·ra·stich·ic** (te′trə stik′ik), **te·tras·ti·chal** (te tras′ti kəl), *adj.*

te·tras·ti·chous (te tras′ti kəs), *adj. Bot.* **1.** arranged in a spike of four vertical rows, as flowers. **2.** having four such rows of flowers, as a spike. [< NL *tetrastichus* < Gk *tetrástichos* having four lines or rows. See TETRA-, STICH]

tet·ra·syl·la·ble (te′trə sil′ə bəl), *n. Pros.* a word or line of verse of four syllables. —**tet·ra·syl·lab·ic** (te′trə si lab′ik), **tet′ra·syl·lab′i·cal,** *adj.*

tet·ra·tom·ic (te′trə tom′ik), *adj. Chem.* **1.** having four atoms in the molecule. **2.** having a valence of four. **3.** containing four replaceable atoms or groups.

tet·ra·va·lent (te′trə vā′lənt, te trav′ə-), *adj. Chem.* **1.** having a valence of four, as Pt^{+4}. **2.** quadrivalent. —**tet′ra·va′lence, tet′ra·va′len·cy,** *n.*

Te·traz·zi·ni (te′trə zē′nē; *It.* te′tʀät tsē′nē), *n.* **Lu·i·sa** (lo͞o ē′zä), 1874–1940, Italian operatic soprano.

tet·rode (te′trōd), *n. Electronics.* a vacuum tube containing four electrodes, usually a plate, two grids, and a cathode.

te·trox·ide (te trok′sīd, -sid), *n. Chem.* an oxide whose molecule contains four atoms of oxygen.

tet·ryl (te′tril), *n. Chem.* a yellow solid, $(O_2N)_3C_6H_2N(CH_3)NO_2$, used as a chemical indicator and as a detonator and bursting charge in small-caliber projectiles.

tet·ter (tet′ər), *n. Pathol.* any of various cutaneous diseases, as herpes, eczema, impetigo, etc. [ME; OE *teter*]

Te·tuán (te twän′), *n.* a seaport in N Morocco, on the Mediterranean: former capital of the Spanish zone of Morocco. 101,352 (1960).

Tet·zel (tet′səl), *n.* **Jo·hann** (yō′hän), 1465?–1519, German monk: antagonist of Martin Luther. Also, **Tezel.**

Teut., **1.** Teuton. **2.** Teutonic.

Teu·to·bur·ger Wald (*Ger.* toi′tō bo͝oʀ′gəʀ vält′), a chain of wooded hills in N West Germany, in Westphalia: Romans defeated by German tribes A.D. 9.

Teu·ton (to͞ot′ən, tyo͞ot′-), *n.* **1.** a member of a Germanic people or tribe first mentioned in the 4th century B.C. and supposed to have dwelt in Jutland. **2.** a native of Germany or a person of German origin. —*adj.* **3.** Teutonic. [< L *Teuton(ēs), Teutonī* (pl.) tribal name < Gmc]

Teu·ton·ic (to͞o ton′ik, tyo͞o-), *adj.* **1.** of or pertaining to the ancient Teutons. **2.** of, pertaining to, or characteristic of the Teutons or Germans; German. **3.** noting or pertaining to the northern European stock that includes the German, Dutch, Scandinavian, British, and related peoples. **4.** (of languages) Germanic. **5.** Nordic. —*n.* **6.** Germanic. —**Teu·ton′i·cal·ly,** *adv.*

Teu·ton·i·cism (to͞o ton′i siz′əm, tyo͞o-), *n.* **1.** the character or spirit of the Teutons, esp. the Germans. **2.** a Teutonic characteristic. **3.** a Germanism.

Teuton′ic Or′der, a religious military order founded c1190 in the Holy Land by German crusaders. Also called **Teuton′ic Knights′.**

Teu·ton·ise (to͞ot′ənīz′, tyo͞ot′-), *v.t., v.i.,* **-ised, -is·ing.** *Chiefly Brit.* Teutonize. —**Teu′ton·i·sa′tion,** *n.*

Teu·ton·ism (to͞ot′əniz′əm, tyo͞ot′-), *n.* the spirit, culture, or civilization of the Teutons. —**Teu′ton·ist,** *n.*

Teu·ton·ize (to͞ot′əniz′, tyo͞ot′-), *v.t., v.i.,* **-ized, -iz·ing.** to make or become Teutonic. Also, *esp. Brit.,* **Teutonise.** —**Teu′ton·i·za′tion,** *n.*

Te·ve·re (te′ve ʀe), *n.* Italian name of the **Tiber.**

Te·vet (tā′vəs; *Heb.* tā vāt′), *n.* Tebet.

Tewkes·bur·y (to͞oks′ber′ē, -bə rē, tyo͞oks′-), *n.* a town in N Gloucestershire, in W England: final defeat of the Lancastrians in the Wars of the Roses 1471. 5814 (1961).

Tex., **1.** Texan. **2.** Texas.

Tex·ar·kan·a (tek′sär kan′ə), *n.* **1.** a city in NE Texas. 30,497 (1970). **2.** a city in SW Arkansas: contiguous with but politically independent of Texarkana, Texas. 21,682 (1970).

tex·as (tek′səs), *n. U.S. Naut.* **1.** a deckhouse on a texas deck for the accommodation of officers. **2.** See **texas deck.** [after TEXAS, from the fact that the officers' accommodation was the most spacious on the Mississippi steamboats where cabins were named after states]

Tex·as (tek′səs), *n.* a state in the S United States. 11,196,730 (1970); 267,339 sq. mi. *Cap.:* Austin. *Abbr.:* Tex., TX —**Tex′an,** *adj., n.*

Tex′as Cit′y, a city in SE Texas, on Galveston Bay. 38,908 (1970).

tex′as deck′, *U.S. Naut.* the uppermost deck of an inland or western river steamer. [see TEXAS]

Tex′as fe′ver, an infectious blood disease of cattle, transmitted by ticks.

Tex′as lea′guer, *Baseball.* a fly that falls safely between converging infielders and outfielders.

Tex′as long′horn, (in southwestern U.S.) one of a nearly extinct breed of long-horned beef cattle developed from stock introduced into North America from Spain.

Tex′as Rang′ers, the mounted police force of the state of Texas, originally a semiofficial group of settlers organized to fight the Indians.

text (tekst), *n.* **1.** the main body of matter in a manuscript, book, newspaper, etc., as distinguished from notes, appendixes, headings, illustrations, etc. **2.** the actual, original words of an author or speaker. **3.** any of the various forms in which a writing exists: *The text is a medieval transcription.* **4.** any theme or topic; subject. **5.** the words of a song or the like. **6.** a textbook. **7.** a short passage of the Scriptures, esp. one chosen in proof of a doctrine or as the subject of a sermon. **8.** the letter of the Holy Scripture or the Scriptures themselves. **9.** *Print.* **a.** See **black letter. b.** type, as distinguished from illustrations, margins, etc. [ME < ML *text(us)* wording, L: structure (of an utterance), texture (of cloth); see TEXTURE] —**text′less,** *adj.*

text·book (tekst′bo͝ok′), *n.* a book used by students as a standard work for a particular branch of study. —**text′book′ish,** *adj.*

tex·tile (teks′til, -tīl), *n.* **1.** any material that is woven. **2.** a material, as a fiber or yarn, used in or suitable for weaving. —*adj.* **3.** woven or capable of being woven: *textile fabrics.* **4.** of or pertaining to weaving. [< L *textil(is)* woven, *textile* woven fabric = *text(us)* woven (ptp. of *texere* to weave) + *-ilis, -ile* -ILE]

tex·tu·al (teks′cho͞o əl), *adj.* **1.** of or pertaining to the text: *textual errors.* **2.** based on or conforming to the text, as of the Scriptures: *a textual interpretation of the Bible.* [late ME < ML *textu(s)* wording (see TEXT) + -AL[1]; r. ME *textuel* < MF] —**tex′tu·al·ly,** *adv.*

tex′tual crit′icism. See **lower criticism.** —**tex′tual crit′ic.**

tex·tu·al·ism (teks′cho͞o ə liz′əm), *n.* strict adherence to the text, esp. of the Scriptures.

tex·tu·al·ist (teks′cho͞o ə list), *n.* **1.** a person who adheres closely to the text, esp. of the Scriptures. **2.** a person who is well versed in the text of the Scriptures.

tex·tu·ar·y (teks′cho͞o er′ē), *adj., n., pl.* **-ar·ies.** —*adj.* **1.** of or pertaining to the text; textual. —*n.* **2.** a textualist. [< ML *textu(s)* wording (see TEXT) + -ARY]

tex·ture (teks′chər), *n., v.,* **-tured, -tur·ing.** —*n.* **1.** the characteristic structure of the interwoven or intertwined threads, strands, or the like, that make up a textile fabric: *rough texture.* **2.** the characteristic physical structure given to a material by the size, shape, density, arrangement, and proportions of its elementary parts: *soil of a sandy texture.* **3.** an essential part or quality; essence. **4.** *Fine Arts.* **a.** the characteristic visual and tactile quality of the surface of a work of art resulting from the way in which the materials are used. **b.** the imitation of the tactile quality of represented objects. **5.** anything produced by weaving; woven fabric. —*v.t.* **6.** to make by or as by weaving. **7.** to give texture or a particular texture to. [late ME < L *textūra* web = *text(us)* woven (ptp. of *texere*) + *-ūra* -URE] —**tex′tur·al,** *adj.* —**tex′tur·al·ly,** *adv.* —**tex′ture·less,** *adj.*

tex′tured vege′table pro′tein (teks′chərd), a nutritious meat substitute made from soybeans.

tex·tur·ize (teks′chə rīz′), *v.t.,* **-ized, -iz·ing.** to form into texture or patterns.

Tey·de (tā′t͟he), *n.* **Pi·co de** (pē′kô t͟he). See **Teide.**

Te·zel (tet′səl), *n.* **Johann.** See **Tetzel, Johann.**

T formation, *Football.* an offensive formation in which the quarterback lines up behind the center, with the fullback about three yards behind the quarterback and the halfbacks on opposite sides of and about one yard from the fullback.

tfr., transfer.

t.g., *Biol.* type genus.

TGIF, Thank God it's Friday.

T-group (tē′gro͞op′), *n.* a group of persons engaged in sensitivity training. [*T(raining) group*]

Th, *Chem.* thorium.

-th[1], a suffix referring to condition, quality, or action, formerly used to form abstract nouns from adjectives or verbs (*warmth; bath*) or from stems not used as words (*depth*). [ME *-th(e),* OE *-thu, -tho, -th;* c. Icel *-th,* Goth *-itha*]

-th[2], a suffix used in the formation of ordinal numbers (*fourth; tenth*), in some cases, added to altered stems of the cardinal (*fifth; twelfth*). [ME *-(e)the, -te,* OE *-(o)tha, -(o)the;* c. Icel *-thi, -di,* L *-tus,* Gk *-tos*]

-th[3], var. of **-eth[1]:** *doth.*

Th., Thursday.

T.H., (formerly) Territory of Hawaii.

Thack·er·ay (thak′ə rē), *n.* **William Make·peace** (māk′pēs′), 1811–63, English novelist, born in India.

Thai (tī, tä′ē), *n.* **1.** Also called **Thai·land·er** (tī′lan′dər, -lən-), a native or descendant of a native of Thailand. **2.** Also called **Siamese.** a member of the Kadai family of languages and the official language of Thailand. **3.** a group of languages, including Shan, Lao, and Thai, that are spoken over a wide area of SE Asia and that constitute a branch of the Kadai family of languages. —*adj.* **4.** of, designating, or pertaining to the Thai languages or to the peoples that speak them. **5.** of Thailand; Siamese. Also, **Tai.**

Thai·land (tī′land′, -lənd), *n.* a kingdom in SE Asia: official name of Siam 1939–45 and since 1949. 40,000,000; 198,242 sq. mi. *Cap.:* Bangkok.

Tha·ïs (thā′is), *n.* fl. late 4th century A.D., Athenian hetaera: mistress of Alexander the Great and Ptolemy I.

thal·a·men·ceph·a·lon (thal′ə men sef′ə lon′), *n., pl.* **-lons, -la** (-lə). *Anat.* the diencephalon. [THALAM(US) + ENCEPHALON] —**thal·a·men·ce·phal·ic** (thal′ə men′sə fal′ik), *adj.*

thal·a·mus (thal′ə məs), *n., pl.* **-mi** (-mī′). **1.** *Anat.* the middle part of the diencephalon through which sensory impulses pass to reach the cerebral cortex. **2.** *Bot.* **a.** a receptacle or torus. **b.** thallus. [< NL; L *thalamus* bedroom < Gk *thálamos*] —**tha·lam·ic** (thə lam′ik), *adj.* —**tha·lam′i·cal·ly,** *adv.*

tha·las·sic (thə las′ik), *adj.* **1.** of or pertaining to the seas and oceans. **2.** of or pertaining to the seas and gulfs. **3.** growing, living, or found in the sea; marine. [< Gk *thálass(a)* sea + -IC]

tha·ler (tä′lər), *n., pl.* **-ler, -lers.** any of various former large coins of various German states; dollar. Also, **taler.** [< G; see DOLLAR]

Tha·les (thā′lēz), *n.* c640–546? B.C., Greek philosopher, born in Miletus.

Tha·li·a (thə lī′ə, thā′lē ə, thāl′yə), *n. Class. Myth.* the Muse of comedy and idyllic poetry. [< L < Gk, special use of *tháleia* blooming; akin to THALLUS]

tha·lid·o·mide (thə lid′ə mīd′, tha-), *n. Chem.* a crystalline solid, $C_{13}H_{10}N_2O_4$, formerly used as a tranquilizer: when taken during pregnancy it sometimes causes abnormalities in the fetus. [THAL(LIC) + (IM)IDO- + (*glutar*)*imide* (GLUT(EN) + (TART)AR(IC) + -IMIDE)]

thal·lic (thal′ik), *adj. Chem.* of or containing thallium, esp. in the trivalent state.

thal·li·um (thal′ē əm), *n. Chem.* a rare metallic element. *Symbol:* Tl; *at. wt.:* 204.37; *at. no.:* 81; *sp. gr.:* 11.85 at 20°C. [< NL = *thall-* (< Gk *thallós* green stalk) + *-ium* -IUM; named after green line in its spectrum]

thal·loid (thal′oid), *adj. Bot.* resembling or consisting of a thallus.

thal·lo·phyte (thal′ə fīt′), *n.* any plant of the phylum or division *Thallophyta*, comprising the algae, fungi, and lichens, in which the plant body of the larger species is typically a thallus. [< NL *thallophyt(a)* (pl.). See THALLUS, -O-, -PHYTE] —**thal·lo·phyt·ic** (thal′ə fit′ik), *adj.*

thal·lous (thal′əs), *adj. Chem.* containing univalent thallium. Also, **thal·li·ous** (thal′ē əs).

thal·lus (thal′əs), *n., pl.* **thal·li** (thal′ī), **thal·lus·es.** *Bot.* a simple vegetative plant body undifferentiated into true leaves, stem, and root: the plant body of typical thallophytes. [< NL < Gk *thallós* young shoot, twig] —**thal′loid,** *adj.*

Thames (temz *for 1, 2;* thāmz, tāmz, temz *for 3*), *n.* **1.** a river in S England, flowing E through London to the North Sea. 209 mi. long. **2.** a river in SE Canada, in Ontario province, flowing SW to Lake St. Clair. 160 mi. long. **3.** an estuary in SE Connecticut, flowing S past New London to Long Island Sound. 15 mi. long.

than (than; *unstressed* thən), *conj.* **1.** (used after comparative adjectives and adverbs and certain other words, such as *other, otherwise, else,* etc., to introduce the second member of a comparison, both members being usually of the same case): *He is taller than I am.* **2.** (used after some adverbs and adjectives expressing choice or diversity, such as *anywhere, different, other, otherwise,* etc., to introduce an alternative or denote a difference in kind, place, style, identity, etc.): *I had no choice other than that. You won't find such freedom anywhere than in the U.S.* **3.** when: *We barely arrived than it was time to leave.* —*prep.* **4.** in relation to; by comparison with (usually fol. by a pronoun in the objective case): *He is a person than whom I can imagine no one more courteous.* [ME, OE *than(ne)* than, then, when; c. G *dann, denn,* Goth *than.* See THEN] —**Usage. 2.** See **different.**

than·age (thā′nij), *n.* **1.** the tenure by which lands were held by a thane. **2.** the land so held. **3.** the office, rank, or jurisdiction of a thane. [late ME < AL *thanag(ium)*]

thanato-, a learned borrowing from Greek meaning "death," used in the formation of compound words: *thanatopsis.* [comb. form repr. Gk *thánatos*]

than·a·tol·o·gy (than′ə tol′ə jē), *n.* the interdisciplinary study of death and dying, esp. of ways to lessen the physical and psychological suffering of the terminally ill, and the apprehensions, guilt feelings, and sense of loss of their families. [THANATO- + -LOGY] —**than′a·tol′o·gist,** *n.*

than·a·top·sis (than′ə top′sis), *n.* a view or contemplation of death.

Than·a·tos (than′ə tos′), *n.* an ancient Greek personification of death. —**Than·a·tot·ic** (than′ə tot′ik), *adj.*

thane (thān), *n.* **1.** *Early Eng. Hist.* a member of any of several classes of men ranking between earls and ordinary freemen, and holding lands of the king or lord by military service. **2.** *Scot. Hist.* the chief of a clan, who became one of the king's barons. Also, **thegn.** [late ME, sp. var. (Scot) of ME *thain, thein,* OE *thegn;* c. G *Degen* warrior, hero]

thank (thangk), *v.t.* **1.** to express gratitude, appreciation, or acknowledgment to. **2. have oneself to thank,** to be personally to blame; have the responsibility. —*n.* **3.** Usually, **thanks.** a grateful feeling or acknowledgment of a benefit, favor, or the like, expressed by words or otherwise. **4. thanks,** I thank you (a common elliptical expression used in acknowledging a favor, service, courtesy, or the like). **5. thanks to,** because of; owing to. [ME *thanke(n),* OE *thancian* (c. D, G *danken*) < *thanc* gratitude, orig. thoughtfulness, thought. See THINK[1]] —**thank′er,** *n.*

thank·ful (thangk′fəl), *adj.* feeling or expressing gratitude or appreciation. [ME; OE *thancful.* See THANK, -FUL] —**thank′ful·ly,** *adv.* —**thank′ful·ness,** *n.* —**Syn.** beholden, obliged. See **grateful.**

thank·less (thangk′lis), *adj.* **1.** not likely to be appreciated or rewarded; unappreciated: *a thankless job.* **2.** not feeling or expressing gratitude or appreciation; ungrateful: *a thankless child.* —**thank′less·ly,** *adv.* —**thank′less·ness,** *n.*

thanks·giv·er (thangks′giv′ər), *n.* a person who gives thanks.

thanks·giv·ing (thangks′giv′ing), *n.* **1.** the act of giving thanks; grateful acknowledgment of benefits or favors, esp. to God. **2.** an expression of thanks, esp. to God. **3.** a public celebration in acknowledgment of divine favor or kindness. **4.** a day set apart for giving thanks to God. **5.** (*cap.*) *U.S.* See **Thanksgiving Day.** [THANK + -S[3] + GIVING]

Thanksgiv′ing Day′, **1.** (in the United States) a national holiday for giving thanks to God, now observed on the fourth Thursday of November. **2.** (in Canada) a national holiday for giving thanks to God, observed on the second Monday in October.

thank·wor·thy (thangk′wûr′thē), *adj.* deserving gratitude.

thank-you (thangk′yōō′), *adj.* expressing one's gratitude or thanks: *a thank-you note.*

Thant (thänt, tänt, thant), *n.* **U.** See **U Thant.**

Thap·sus (thap′səs), *n.* an ancient town on the coast of Tunisia.

Thar′ Des′ert (tûr, tär), a desert in NW India and S Pakistan. ab. 100,000 sq. mi. Also called **Indian Desert.**

Tha·sos (thä′sôs), *n.* a Greek island in the N Aegean. 13,316; ab. 170 sq. mi.

that (that; *unstressed* thət), *pron. and adj., pl.* **those;** *adv.; conj.* —*pron.* **1.** (used to indicate a person, thing, etc., as pointed out or present, before mentioned, supposed to be understood, or by way of emphasis): *That is her mother.* **2.** (used to indicate one of two or more persons, things, etc., already mentioned, referring to the one more remote in place, time, or thought; opposed to *this*): *This is Alexandra and that is Nicky.* **3.** (used to indicate one of two or more persons, things, etc., already mentioned, implying a contrast or contradistinction; opposed to *this*): *This suit fits better than that.* **4.** (used as the subject or object of a relative clause, esp. one defining or restricting the antecedent, sometimes replaceable by *who, whom,* or *which*): *the horse that he bought.* **5.** (used as the object of a preposition, the preposition standing at the end of a relative clause): *the farm that I spoke of.* **6.** (used in various special or elliptical constructions): *fool that he is.* —*adj.* **7.** (used to indicate a person, place, thing, or degree as indicated, mentioned before, present, or as well-known or characteristic): *That woman is her mother. Those little mannerisms of hers make me sick.* **8.** (used to indicate the more remote in time, place, or thought of two persons, things, etc., already mentioned; opposed to *this*): *This room is his and that one is mine.* **9.** (used to imply mere contradistinction; opposed to *this*): *not this house, but that one.* —*adv.* **10.** (used with adjectives and adverbs of quantity or extent) to the extent or degree indicated: *Don't take that much. The fish was that big.* **11.** *Dial.* (used to modify an adjective or another adverb) to such an extent: *He was that weak he could hardly stand.* —*conj.* **12.** (used to introduce a subordinate clause as the subject or object of the principal verb or as the necessary complement to a statement made, or a clause expressing cause or reason, purpose or aim, result or consequence, etc.): *That he will come is certain.* **13.** (used elliptically to introduce a sentence or exclamatory clause expressing desire, surprise, indignation, or other strong feeling): *That boy!* [ME, OE *thæt;* c. D *dat,* G *das(s),* Icel *that,* Gk *tó,* Skt *tád*] —**Usage.** See **which.**

that-a·way (that′ə wā′), *adv. Dial.* **1.** in or toward the direction pointed out: *They went that-away.* **2.** in the manner indicated: *You better do it that-away.* Also, **that′a·way′, that′-a-way′.** [alter. of *that way*]

thatch (thach), *n.* **1.** Also, **thatching.** a material, as straw, rushes, leaves, or the like, used to cover roofs, grain stacks, etc. **2.** a covering of such a material. **3.** any of various palms, the leaves of which are used for thatching. **4.** the hair covering the head: *a thatch of unruly red hair.* —*v.t.* **5.** to cover with or as with thatch. [ME *thacch(en),* var. of *thecchen,* OE *theccan* to cover, hide; c. D *dekken,* G *decken,* Icel *thekja;* see DECK] —**thatch′er,** *n.* —**thatch′less,** *adj.*

Thatch·er (thach′ər), *n.* **Margaret (Hilda),** born 1925, British statesman: leader of the Conservative party since 1975; prime minister since 1979.

thatch·ing (thach′ing), *n.* thatch (def. 1). [ME *thecchyng*]

that's (thats), **1.** contraction of *that is: That's mine.* **2.** contraction of *that has: That's got more leaves.*

thaumato-, a learned borrowing from Greek meaning "miracle," "wonder," used in the formation of compound words: *thaumatology.* [< Gk, comb. form of *thaumat-* (s. of *thaûma*)]

thau·ma·tol·o·gy (thô′mə tol′ə jē), *n.* the study or description of miracles.

thau·ma·trope (thô′mə trōp′), *n.* a card with different pictures on opposite sides (as a horse on one side and a rider on the other), which appear to combine when twirled rapidly. [THAUMA(TO)- + -TROPE] —**thau·ma·trop·i·cal** (thô′mə trop′i kəl), *adj.*

thau·ma·turge (thô′mə tûrj′), *n.* a worker of wonders or miracles. Also, **thau′ma·tur′gist.**

thau·ma·tur·gic (thô′mə tûr′jik), *adj.* **1.** pertaining to a thaumaturge or to thaumaturgy. **2.** having the powers of a thaumaturge. Also, **thau′ma·tur′gi·cal.** [< NL *thaumaturgic(us)* = *thaumaturg(us)* wonderworker (< Gk *thaumatourgós: thaumat-* THAUMATO- + *-ourgos;* see -URGY) + *-icus* -IC]

thau·ma·tur·gy (thô′mə tûr′jē), *n.* the working of wonders or miracles; magic. [< Gk *thaumatourgía*]

thaw (thô), *v.i.* **1.** to pass or change from a frozen to a liquid or semiliquid state; melt. **2.** to be freed from the physical effect of frost or extreme cold (sometimes fol. by *out*): *Sit by the fire and thaw out.* **3.** (of the weather) to become warm enough to melt ice and snow: *It will probably thaw today.* **4.** to become less hostile, tense, or aloof. —*v.t.* **5.** to cause to change from a frozen to a liquid or semiliquid state; melt. **6.** to free from the physical effect of frost or extreme cold; bring to a more normal temperature, esp. to room temperature. **7.** to make less hostile, tense, or aloof. —*n.* **8.** the act or process of thawing. **9.** (in winter or in areas where freezing weather is the norm) weather warm enough to melt ice and snow. **10.** a period of such weather. **11.** a reduction or easing in tension or hostility. [ME *thawe(n),* OE *thawian;* c. D *dooien,* Icel *theyja*] —**thaw′less,** *adj.* —**Syn. 1.** See **melt. 2.** warm. —**Ant. 1.** freeze.

Thay·er (thā′ər, thâr), *n.* **Sylvanus,** 1785–1872, U.S. army officer and educator.

Th.B., Bachelor of Theology. [< L *Theologicae Baccalaureus*]

Th.D., Doctor of Theology. [< L *Theologicae Doctor*]

the[1] (*stressed* thē; *unstressed before a consonant* thə; *unstressed before a vowel* thē), *definite article.* **1.** (used, esp. before a noun, with a specifying or particularizing effect, as opposed to the indefinite or generalizing force of the indefinite article *a* or *an*): *the book you gave me.* **2.** (used to mark a proper noun, natural phenomenon, ship, building, time, point of the compass, branch of endeavor, or field of study as something well-known or unique): *the Alps; the* Queen Elizabeth; *the past; the West.* **3.** (used with or as part of a title): *the Duke of Wellington.* **4.** (used to mark a noun as indicating the best-known, most approved, most important, most satisfying, etc.): *the* *skiing center of the U.S.* **5.** (used to mark a noun as being used generically): *The dog is a quadruped.* **6.** (used in place of a possessive pronoun, to note a part of the body or a personal belonging): *Has the leg mended?* **7.** (used before adjectives that are used substantively, to note an individual, a class or number of individuals, or an abstract idea): *to visit the sick; from the sublime to the ridiculous.* **8.** (used before a modifying adjective to specify or limit its modifying effect): *He took the wrong road.* **9.** (used to indicate one particular decade of a lifetime or of a century): *the gay nineties.* **10.** (one of many of a class or type, as of a manufactured item, as opposed to an individual one): *Did you listen to the radio last night?* **11.** enough: *She didn't have the courage to leave.* **12.** (used distributively, to note any one separately); for, to, or in each; a or an: *at one dollar the pound.* [ME, OE, uninflected var. of demonstrative pronoun. See THAT]

the[2] (thə, thē), *adv.* **1.** (used to modify an adjective or adverb in the comparative degree and to signify "in or by that," "on that account," "in or by so much," or "in some or any degree"): *He looks the better for his rest.* **2.** (used in correlative constructions to modify an adjective or adverb in the comparative degree, in one instance with relative force and in the other with demonstrative force, and signifying "by how much . . . by so much" or "in what degree . . . in that degree"): *the more the merrier; The bigger they are, the harder they fall.* [ME; OE *thē, thȳ,* instrumental case of demonstrative pronoun. See THAT]

the-, var. of **theo-** before a vowel: *thearchy.*

the·a·ceous (thē ā′shəs), *adj.* belonging to the *Theaceae,* or tea family of plants. [< NL *the(a)* tea + -ACEOUS]

the·an·throp·ic (thē′an throp′ik), *adj.* of or pertaining to both God and man; both divine and human.

the·an·thro·pism (thē an′thrə piz′əm), *n.* **1.** the doctrine of the union of the divine and human natures, or the manifestation of God as man in Christ. **2.** the attribution of human nature to the gods. —**the·an′thro·pist,** *n.*

the·ar·chy (thē′är kē), *n., pl.* **-chies. 1.** the rule or government of God or of a god. **2.** an order or system of deities. [< eccl. Gk *thearchía*] —**the·ar′chic,** *adj.*

theat., theater.

the·a·ter (thē′ə tər, thēᵊ′-), *n.* **1.** a building, part of a building, or outdoor area for housing dramatic presentations, stage entertainments, or motion-picture shows. **2.** the audience at a theatrical or motion-picture performance: *The theater wept.* **3.** a room or hall, fitted with tiers of seats rising like steps, used for lectures, anatomical demonstrations, etc. **4. the theater,** dramatic performances as a branch of art; the drama. **5.** dramatic works collectively, as of literature, a nation, or an author (often prec. by *the*): *the theater of Ibsen.* **6.** the quality or effectiveness of dramatic performance. **7.** a place of action; field of operations. **8.** a natural formation of land rising by steps or gradations. Also, *esp. Brit.,* **theatre.** [ME *theatre* < L *theātr(um)* < Gk *théātron* seeing place, theater = *theâ(sthai)* (to) view + *-tron* -TRON]

the·a·ter·go·er (thē′ə tər gō′ər, thēᵊ′-), *n.* a playgoer. Also, *esp. Brit.,* **the′a·tre·go′er.**

the·a·ter-in-the-round (thē′ə tər in thə round′, thēᵊ′-), *n.* See **arena theater.** Also, *esp. Brit.,* **the′atre-in-the-round′.**

The′ater of the Absurd′, (*sometimes l.c.*) an avant-garde style of playwriting and theatrical presentation in which standard or realistic conventions of plot, characterization, and thematic structure are ignored or distorted for ideational or aesthetic reasons, and in which the irrational nature of reality and man's isolation in the world are often stressed. Also, *esp. Brit.,* **The′atre of the Absurd′.**

the·a·tre (thē′ə tər, thēᵊ′-), *n. Chiefly Brit.* theater.

the·at·ri·cal (thē a′tri kəl), *adj.* Also, **the·at′ric. 1.** of or pertaining to the theater, or dramatic or scenic representations: *theatrical performances.* **2.** artificial, pompous, or extravagantly histrionic. —*n.* **3. theatricals, a.** dramatic performances, now esp. as given by amateurs. **b.** professional actors. [< LL *theātric(us)* (see THEATRICS) + -AL[1]] —**the·at·ri·cal·i·ty** (thē a′tri kal′i tē), **the·at′ri·cal·ness,** *n.* —**the·at′ri·cal·ly,** *adv.*

the·at·ri·cal·ism (thē a′tri kə liz′əm), *n.* conduct suggesting theatrical actions or mannerisms, esp. of an extravagant or exhibitionistic sort.

the·at·rics (thē a′triks), *n.* **1.** (*construed as sing.*) the art of staging plays and other stage performances. **2.** (*construed as pl.*) exaggerated, artificial, or histrionic mannerisms, actions, or words. [*theatric* < LL *theātric(us)* < Gk *theātrikós.* See THEATER, -ICS]

The·ba·id (thē′bā id, -bē-), *n.* the ancient region surrounding Thebes, in Egypt.

the·ba·ine (thē′bə ēn′, thi bā′ēn, -in), *n. Chem.* a poisonous alkaloid, $C_{19}H_{21}NO_3$, present in opium but having a strychninelike effect. [< NL *thēba(ia)* opium of Thebes, Egypt (alter. of L *Thēbaea,* fem. of *Thēbaeus* Theban) + -INE[2]]

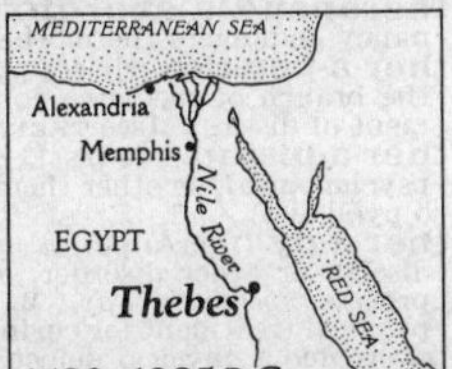

Thebes (thēbz), *n.* **1.** an ancient city in Upper Egypt, on the Nile; its ruins are in the modern towns of Karnak and Luxor: a former capital of Egypt. **2.** a city of ancient Greece, in Boeotia: a rival of ancient Athens. —**The·ba·ic** (thi bā′ik), *adj.* **The·ban** (thē′bən), *adj., n.*

the·ca (thē′kə), *n., pl.* **-cae** (-sē). **1.** a case or receptacle. **2.** *Bot.* **a.** a sac, cell, or capsule. **b.** a sporangium. **3.** *Anat., Zool.* a case or sheath enclosing an organ, structure, etc., as the horny covering of an insect pupa. [< L < Gk *thḗkē* case, cover, akin to *tithénai* to place, put] —**the′cal,** *adj.*

the·cate (thē′kit, -kāt), *adj.* having or being contained in a theca. [THEC(A) + -ATE[1]]

thé dan·sant (tā dän säɴ′), *pl.* **thés dan·sants** (tā dän säɴ′). *French.* See **tea dance.**

thee (thē), *pron.* **1.** the objective case of **thou:** *With this ring, I thee wed.* **2.** thou (now used chiefly by the Friends). [ME; OE *thē* (orig. dat.; later dat. and acc.); c. LG *di,* G *dir,* Icel *thēr.* See THOU]

thee·lin (thē′lin), *n. Biochem.* estrone. [irreg. < Gk *thêl(ys)* female + -IN[2]]

thee·lol (thē′lōl, -lôl, -lol), *n. Biochem.* estriol. [THEEL(IN) + -OL[1]]

theft (theft), *n.* **1.** the act of stealing; the wrongful taking and carrying away of the personal goods or property of another; larceny. **2.** an instance of this. **3.** *Archaic.* something stolen. [ME; OE *thēfth, thēofth;* see THIEF, -TH[1]]

thegn (thān), *n.* thane. —**thegn′ly,** *adj.*

The·ia (thē′ə, thī′ə), *n. Class. Myth.* a Titaness, the daughter of Gaea and Uranus, and mother by her brother Hyperion of Eos, Helios, and Selene.

the·ine (thē′ēn, -in), *n.* caffeine, esp. in tea. [< NL *the(a)* TEA + -INE[2]]

their (thâr; *unstressed* thər), *pron.* **1.** a form of the possessive of **they** used as an attributive adjective, before a noun: *their home; their rights as citizens.* **2.** *Nonstandard.* (used after an indefinite singular antecedent in place of the definite masculine form "his" or the definite feminine form "her"): *Somebody left their book on the table.* Cf. **theirs.** [ME < Scand; cf. Icel *theirra* of those. See THEY] —**Usage.** See **me.**

theirs (thârz), *pron.* **1.** a form of the possessive case of **they** used as a predicate adjective, after a noun or without a noun: *Are you a friend of theirs? It is theirs.* **2.** *Nonstandard.* (used after an indefinite singular antecedent in place of the definite masculine form "his" or the definite feminine form "hers"): *I have my book; does everybody else have theirs?* **3.** something that belongs to them: *Theirs is the white house.*

the·ism (thē′iz əm), *n.* **1.** the belief in one God as the creator and ruler of the universe, without rejection of revelation (distinguished from *deism*). **2.** belief in the existence of God or gods (opposed to *atheism*). —**the·ist** (thē′ist), *n., adj.* —**the·is′tic, the·is′ti·cal,** *adj.* —**the·is′ti·cal·ly,** *adv.*

Theiss (tīs), *n.* German name of **Tisza.**

the·li·tis (thi lī′tis), *n. Pathol.* inflammation of the nipple. [< Gk *thēl(ḗ)* nipple + -ITIS]

them (them; *unstressed* thəm), *pron.* **1.** the objective case of **they,** both as direct and indirect object: *We saw them yesterday. I gave them the books.* —*adj.* **2.** *Nonstandard.* those: *He don't want them books.* [ME *theym* < Scand; cf. Icel *theim* to those. See THEY]

the·mat·ic (thē mat′ik), *adj.* **1.** of or pertaining to a theme. **2.** *Gram.* **a.** (of a word or words) of, pertaining to, or producing a theme or themes. **b.** (of a letter) pertaining to the theme or stem. The thematic vowel is the vowel that ends the stem and precedes the inflectional ending of a word form, as *i* in Latin *audiō* "I hear." [< Gk *thematik(ós)* of the subject, stem (in grammar) = *themat-* (s. of *théma*) THEME + *-ikos* -IC] —**the·mat′i·cal·ly,** *adv.*

theme (thēm), *n.* **1.** a subject of discourse, discussion, meditation, or composition; topic. **2.** a short, informal essay, esp. a school composition. **3.** *Music.* a principal melodic subject in a musical composition. **4.** *Gram.* the element common to all or most of the forms of an inflectional paradigm, often consisting of a root with certain formative elements or modifications. Cf. **stem**[1] (def. 12). [ME *t(h)eme* < ML, L *thema* (pronounced *tema*) < Gk: proposition, deposit, akin to *tithénai* to put, set down] —**theme′less,** *adj.* —**Syn. 1.** thesis.

theme′ park′, an amusement park whose attractions are based on one or several themes, as fairy tales, cartoon characters, American history, or jungle wildlife.

theme′ song′, a melody identifying or identified with a radio or television program, dance band, etc.

The·mis (thē′mis), *n. Class. Myth.* a Titaness, the daughter of Uranus and Gaea and the mother of the Moerae and the Horae.

The·mis·to·cles (thə mis′tə klēz′), *n.* 527?–460? B.C., Athenian statesman.

them·selves (thəm selvz′), *pron. pl.* **1.** an emphatic form of **them** or **they:** *The authors themselves left the theater.* **2.** a reflexive form of **them:** *They washed themselves quickly.* **3.** *Nonstandard.* (used after an indefinite singular antecedent in place of the definite masculine "himself" or the definite feminine "herself"): *No one who ignores the law can call themselves a good citizen.* **4.** their usual, normal, characteristic selves: *After a hot meal and a few hours rest, they were themselves again.* [THEM + SELVES; r. *themself* (ME *thamself*); see SELF] —**Usage.** See **myself.**

then (then), *adv.* **1.** at that time: *Prices were lower then.* **2.** immediately or soon afterward: *The rain stopped and then began again.* **3.** next in order of time: *We ate, then we started home.* **4.** at the same time: *At first the water seemed blue, then gray.* **5.** next in order of place: *Standing beside Charlie is Hazel, then Uncle Harry, then Aunt Agatha.* **6.** in addition; besides; also: *I love my job, and then it pays so well.* **7.** in that case; as a consequence; in those circumstances. **8.** since that is so; as it appears; therefore. **9. then and there,** at that moment; at once. —*adj.* **10.** being; being such; existing or being at the time indicated: *the then prime minister.* —*n.* **11.** that time: *We have not been back since then.* [ME, var. of *thenne,* OE *thænne.* See THAN] —**Syn. 8.** See **therefore.**

the·nar (thē′när), *n.* **1.** *Anat.* the fleshy mass of the outer side of the palm of the hand. **2.** the fleshy prominence or ball of muscle at the base of the thumb. —*adj.* **3.** of or pertaining to the thenar. [< Gk: palm of hand or sole of foot]

thence (thens), *adv.* **1.** from that place: *I went first to Paris and thence to Rome.* **2.** from that time; thenceforth. **3.** from that source. **4.** from that fact; therefore. [ME *thennes* = *thenne* (earlier *thenene,* OE *thanon(e)* thence) + *-es* -S[1]]

thence·forth (thens′fôrth′, -fōrth′, thens′fôrth′, -fōrth′), *adv.* from that time onward. Also, **thence·for·ward** (thens′fôr′wərd), **thence′for′wards.** [ME *thennes forth,* OE *thanonforth.* See THENCE, FORTH]

theo-, a learned borrowing from Greek meaning "god," used in the formation of compound words: *tehocrat.* Also, *esp. before a vowel,* **the-.** [< Gk, comb. form of *theós*]

the·o·bro·mine (thē′ə brō′mēn, -min), *n. Pharm.* a poisonous powder, $C_7H_8N_4O_2$, used chiefly as a diuretic, myocardial stimulant, and vasodilator. [< NL *theobrom(a)* genus of trees typified by cacao (< Gk *theo-* THEO- + *brôma* food) + -INE[2]]

the·o·cen·tric (thē′ə sen′trik), *adj.* having God as the focus of interest. —**the·o·cen·tric·i·ty** (thē′ō sen tris′i tē), *n.* —**the′o·cen′trism, the·o·cen·tri·cism** (thē′ō sen′tri-siz′əm), *n.*

the·oc·ra·cy (thē ok′rə sē), *n., pl.* **-cies.** **1.** a form of government in which God or a deity is recognized as the supreme civil ruler. **2.** a system of government by priests claiming a divine commission. **3.** a state under such a form of government. [< Gk *theokratía*. See THEO-, -CRACY] —**the·o·crat·ic** (thē′ə krat′ik), **the′o·crat′i·cal,** *adj.* —**the′o·crat′i·cal·ly,** *adv.*

the·oc·ra·sy (thē ok′rə sē), *n.* **1.** a mingling of the attributes of several deities into one, esp. in the minds of worshipers. **2.** union of the personal soul with God, as in Neoplatonism. [< Gk *theokrāsía* = *theo-* THEO- + *krās(is)* a mingling + *-ia* -Y[3]]

the·o·crat (thē′ə krat′), *n.* **1.** a person who rules, governs as a representative of God or a deity, or is a member of the ruling group in a theocracy, as a divine king or a high priest. **2.** a person who favors theocracy. [back formation from *theocratic* < Gk *theokrat(ía)* THEOCRACY + -IC]

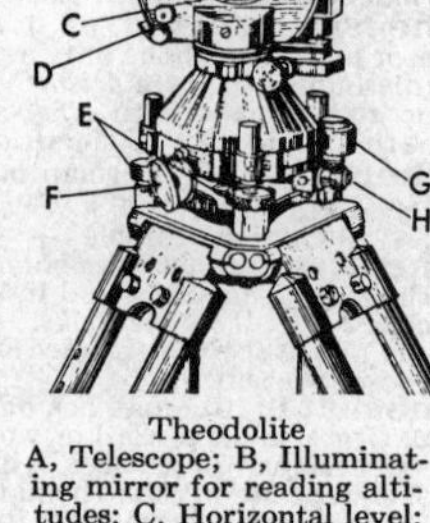

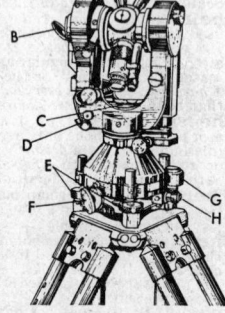

Theodolite
A, Telescope; B, Illuminating mirror for reading altitudes; C, Horizontal level; D, Reflector for collimation level; E, Leveling screw; F, Illuminating mirror for reading azimuths; G, Circular level; H, Eyepiece for optical centering

The·oc·ri·tus (thē ok′ri təs), *n.* fl. c270 B.C., Greek poet. —**The·oc·ri·te·an** (thē ok′ri-tē′ən), **The·oc′ri·tan,** *adj.*

the·od·i·cy (thē od′i sē), *n., pl.* **-cies.** a vindication of the goodness of God in respect to the existence of evil. [THEO- + Gk *dík(ē)* justice + -Y[3], modeled on F *théodicée*, a coinage of Leibniz] —**the·od′i·ce′an,** *adj.*

the·od·o·lite (thē od′ᵊlīt′), *n. Survey.* a precision instrument having a telescopic sight for establishing horizontal and sometimes vertical angles. Cf. **transit** (def. 5). [< NL *theodolit(us)* < ?] —**the·od·o·lit·ic** (thē od′ᵊlit′ik), *adj.*

The·o·do·ra (thē′ə dōr′ə, -dôr′ə), *n.* A.D. 508–548, Byzantine empress: consort of Justinian I.

The·o·dore I (thē′ə dōr′, -dôr′), died A.D. 649, pope 642–649.

Theodore II, pope A.D. 897.

The·od·o·ric (thē od′ə rik), *n.* A.D. 454?–526, king of the Ostrogoths and founder of the Ostrogothic monarchy in Italy: ruler of Italy 493–526.

The·o·do·si·us I (thē′ə dō′shē əs, -shəs), ("*the Great*") A.D. 346?–395, Roman emperor of the Eastern Roman Empire 379–395: made Christianity the official state religion of the Roman Empire. —**The·o·do·sian** (thē′ə dō′shən, -shē ən), *adj.*

the·og·o·ny (thē og′ə nē), *n., pl.* **-nies.** **1.** the origin of the gods. **2.** an account of this; a genealogical account of the gods. [< Gk *theogonía*] —**the·o·gon·ic** (thē′ə gon′ik), *adj.* —**the·og′o·nist,** *n.*

theol., 1. theologian. **2.** theological. **3.** theology.

the·o·lo·gian (thē′ə lō′jən, -jē ən), *n.* a person who is versed in theology, esp. Christian theology; divine. [THEOLOGY + -AN; r. late ME *theologien* < MF]

the·o·log·i·cal (thē′ə loj′i kəl), *adj.* **1.** of, pertaining to, or involved with theology: *a theological student.* **2.** based upon the nature and will of God as revealed to man. Also, **the′o·log′ic.** [< ML *theologicāl(is)* = *theologic(us)* (< Gk *theologikós*; see THEOLOGY, -IC) + *-ālis* -AL[1]] —**the′o·log′i·cal·ly,** *adv.*

theolog′ical vir′tue, one of the three graces, faith, hope, and charity, perfecting the natural virtues.

the·ol·o·gise (thē ol′ə jīz′), *v.i., v.t.,* **-gised, -gis·ing.** *Chiefly Brit.* theologize. —**the·ol′o·gi·sa′tion,** *n.* —**the·ol′o·gis′er,** *n.*

the·ol·o·gize (thē ol′ə jīz′), *v.,* **-gized, -giz·ing.** —*v.i.* **1.** to theorize or speculate upon theological subjects. —*v.t.* **2.** to make theological; treat theologically. [< ML *theologiz(āre)*] —**the·ol′o·gi·za′tion,** *n.* —**the·ol′o·giz′er,** *n.*

the·ol·o·gy (thē ol′ə jē), *n., pl.* **-gies.** **1.** the field of study, thought, and analysis that treats of God, His attributes, and His relations to the universe; the science or study of divine things or religious truth; divinity. **2.** a particular form, system, branch, or course of this science or study. [< LL *theologia* < Gk]

the·om·a·chy (thē om′ə kē), *n., pl.* **-chies.** a battle with or among the gods. [< LL *theomachia* < Gk]

the·o·mor·phic (thē′ə môr′fik), *adj.* having the form or likeness of God. [< Gk *theómorph(os)*. See THEO-, -MORPHOUS, -MORPHIC] —**the′o·mor′phism,** *n.*

the·op·a·thy (thē op′ə thē), *n.* religious emotion excited by the contemplation of God. [THEO- + (SYM)PATHY] —**the·o·pa·thet·ic** (thē′ə pə thet′ik), **the·o·path·ic** (thē′ə-path′ik), *adj.*

the·oph·a·ny (thē of′ə nē), *n., pl.* **-nies.** a manifestation or appearance of God or of a god to man. [< LL *theophania* < LGk *theopháneia*] —**the·o·phan·ic** (thē′ə fan′ik), **the·oph′a·nous,** *adj.*

The·o·phras·tus (thē′ə fras′təs), *n.* 372?–287 B.C., Greek philosopher and natural scientist.

the·o·phyl·line (thē′ə fil′ēn, -in), *n. Pharm.* a poisonous alkaloid, $C_7H_8N_4O_2$, an isomer of theobromine, used, chiefly in the form of aminophylline, to relieve bronchial spasms in asthma and in treating certain heart conditions. [*theo-*, irreg. comb. form repr. NL *thea* TEA + -PHYLL + -INE[2]]

theor., theorem.

the·or·bo (thē ôr′bō), *n., pl.* **-bos.** an obsolete bass lute with two sets of strings attached to separate peg boxes, one above the other, on the neck. [< It *teorba*, var. of *tiorba*, special use of Venetian *tiorba*, var. of *tuorba* traveling bag << Turk *torba* bag; so called from the bag it was carried in] —**the·or′bist,** *n.*

Theorbo

the·o·rem (thē′ə rəm, thēr′əm), *n.* **1.** *Math.* a theoretical proposition, statement, or formula embodying something to be proved from other propositions or formulas. **2.** a rule or law, esp. one expressed by an equation or formula. **3.** *Logic.* a proposition that can be deduced from the premises or assumptions of a system. **4.** an idea, belief, method, or statement generally accepted as true or worthwhile without proof. [< LL *theōrēm(a)* < Gk *theṓrēma* spectacle, hence, subject for contemplation, thesis (to be proved) = *theōr(eîn)* (to) view + *-ēma* -EME] —**the·o·re·mat·ic** (thē′ər ə mat′ik, thēr′ə-), *adj.* —**the′o·re·mat′i·cal·ly,** *adv.*

the·o·ret·i·cal (thē′ə ret′i kəl), *adj.* **1.** of, pertaining to, or consisting in theory; not practical (distinguished from *applied*). **2.** existing only in theory; hypothetical. **3.** given to, forming, or dealing with theories; speculative. Also, **the′o·ret′ic.** [< LL *theōrētic(us)* < Gk *theōrētikós* = *theōrēt(ós)* to be seen (verbid of *theōreîn* to view) + *-ikos* -IC + -AL[1]] —**the′o·ret′i·cal·ly,** *adv.*

theoret′ical arith′metic, arithmetic (def. 2).

the·o·re·ti·cian (thē′ər i tish′ən, thēr′i-), *n.* a person who deals with or is expert in the theoretical side of a subject: *a military theoretician.* [THEORETIC(S) + -IAN]

the·o·ret·ics (thē′ə ret′iks), *n.* (*construed as sing.*) the theoretical or speculative part of a science or subject. [see THEORETIC(AL), -ICS]

the·o·rise (thē′ə rīz′), *v.i.,* **-rised, -ris·ing.** *Chiefly Brit.* theorize. —**the′o·ri·sa′tion,** *n.* —**the′o·ris′er,** *n.*

the·o·rist (thē′ə rist), *n.* **1.** a person who theorizes. **2.** a person who deals mainly with the theory of a subject: *a theorist in medical research.*

the·o·rize (thē′ə rīz′), *v.i.,* **-rized, -riz·ing.** to form a theory or theories. Also, *esp. Brit.,* **theorise.** [< ML *theōriz(āre)*] —**the′o·ri·za′tion,** *n.* —**the′o·riz′er,** *n.*

the·o·ry (thē′ə rē, thēr′ē), *n., pl.* **-ries.** **1.** a coherent group of general propositions used as principles of explanation for a class of phenomena: *Newton's theory of gravitation.* **2.** a proposed explanation whose status is still conjectural, in contrast to well-established propositions that are regarded as reporting matters of actual fact. **3.** *Math.* a body of principles, theorems, or the like, belonging to one subject: *number theory.* **4.** the branch of a science or art that deals with its principles or methods, as distinguished from its practice: *music theory.* **5.** guess or conjecture. [< LL *theōria* < Gk *theōría* a viewing, contemplating = *theōr(eîn)* (to) view + *-ia* -Y[3]] —**Syn. 1.** THEORY, HYPOTHESIS are both often used colloquially to mean an untested idea or opinion. A THEORY properly is a more or less verified or established explanation accounting for known facts or phenomena: *the theory of relativity.* A HYPOTHESIS is a conjecture put forth as a possible explanation of certain phenomena or relations, and serves as a basis of argument or experimentation by which to reach the truth: *This idea is offered only as a hypothesis.* **2.** rationale, guess.

the′ory of games′. See **game theory.**

the′ory of relativ′ity, *Physics.* relativity (def. 2).

theos., 1. theosophical. **2.** theosophy.

Theosoph′ical Soci′ety, a society founded by Madame Blavatsky and others, in New York in 1875, advocating a world-wide eclectic religion based largely on Brahmanic and Buddhistic teachings.

the·os·o·phy (thē os′ə fē), *n.* **1.** any of various forms of philosophical or religious thought claiming a mystical insight into the divine nature. **2.** the system of belief and practice of the Theosophical Society. [< ML *theosophia* < LGk. See THEO, -SOPHY] —**the·o·soph·i·cal** (thē′ə sof′i kəl), **the′o·soph′ic,** *adj.* —**the′o·soph′i·cal·ly,** *adv.* —**the·os′o·phism,** *n.* —**the·os′o·phist,** *n.*

The·o·to·co·pou·los (the′ô tô kô′po͞o lôs), *n.* **Do·men·i·kos** (thô men′ē kôs). See **El Greco.**

therapeut., 1. therapeutic. **2.** therapeutics. Also, **therap.**

ther·a·peu·tic (ther′ə pyo͞o′tik), *adj.* of or pertaining to the treating or curing of disease; curative. Also, **ther′a·peu′ti·cal.** [< NL *therapeutic(us)* < Gk *therapeutikós* = *therapeu-* (s. of *therapeúein* to attend, treat medically) + *-tikos* -TIC] —**ther′a·peu′ti·cal·ly,** *adv.*

therapeu′tic abor′tion, abortion induced when pregnancy endangers the mother's health.

ther·a·peu·tics (ther′ə pyo͞o′tiks), *n.* (*construed as sing.*) the branch of medicine concerned with the remedial treatment of disease. [see THERAPEUTIC, -ICS]

ther·a·pist (ther′ə pist), *n.* a person trained in physical, psychological, or other therapy. Also, **ther·a·peu·tist** (ther′ə pyo͞o′tist).

ther·a·py (ther′ə pē), *n., pl.* **-pies.** **1.** the treatment of a disease or other disorder, as by some remedial or curative process: *speech therapy.* **2.** a curative power or quality. **3.** physical treatment for curing or rehabilitating a patient or to overcome a physical defect, as by exercise, heat treatments, etc. **4.** treatment of the psychologically or socially maladjusted, as by psychoanalysis. [< NL *therapīa* < Gk *therapeía* healing]

Ther·a·va·da (ther′ə vä′də), *n. Buddhism.* Hinayanist name for **Hinayana.**

there (thâr), *adv.* **1.** in or at that place (opposed to *here*): *He is there now.* **2.** at that point in an action, speech, etc.: *He stopped there for applause.* **3.** in that matter, particular, or respect: *His anger was justified there.* **4.** to or into that place; thither: *We went there last year.* **5.** (used by way of calling attention to something or someone): *There they go.* **6.** (used in interjectional phrases to express approval, encouragement, etc.): *There's a good boy!* **7.** in or at that place where you are: *Well, hi there!* —*pron.* **8.** (used to introduce a sentence or clause in which the verb comes before its subject or has no complement): *There is no hope.* **9.** that place: *He comes from there too.* **10.** that point. —*n.* **11.** that state or condition: *from there on.* —*adj.* **12.** (used after a demonstrative pronoun or after a noun modified by a demonstrative adjective, for emphasis): *Ask that man there.* **13.** *Nonstandard.* (used between a demonstrative adjective and the noun it modifies, for emphasis): *Ask that there man.* —*interj.* **14.** an exclamation used to express satisfaction, relief, encouragement, consolation, etc.: *There! It's done.* [ME; OE *thǣr;* c. D *daar,* OHG *dār;* akin to Goth, Icel *thar;* all with adv. suffix *-r.* See THAT]

there-, a prefix meaning "that (place)," "that (time)," etc., used in combination with certain adverbs and prepositions: *thereafter.*

there·a·bouts (thâr′ə bouts′), *adv.* **1.** about or near that place or time: *last June or thereabouts.* **2.** about that number, amount, etc.: *a dozen or thereabouts.* Also, **there′a·bout′.** [ME *ther aboute,* OE *thǣr abūtan.* See THERE-, ABOUT, -S[1]]

there·af·ter (thâr′af′tər, -äf′-), *adv.* **1.** after that in time or sequence; afterwards. **2.** *Obs.* accordingly. [ME *ther after,* OE *thǣr æfter*]

there·a·gainst (thâr′ə genst′ *or, esp. Brit.,* -gānst′), *adv. Archaic.* against that. [late ME *ther agenst;* r. ME *thereageyns*]

there·at (thâr′at′), *adv.* **1.** at that place or time; there. **2.** because of that; thereupon. [ME *ther at,* OE *thǣr æt*]

there·by (thâr′bī′, thâr′bī′), *adv.* **1.** by that; by means of that. **2.** in that connection or relation: *Thereby hangs a tale.* **3.** by or near that place. **4.** *Scot.* about that number, quantity, or degree. [ME *therby,* OE *thǣrbī*]

there·for (thâr′fôr′), *adv.* for or in exchange for that or this; for it: *a refund therefor.* [ME *therfor*]

there·fore (thâr′fōr′, -fôr′), *adv.* in consequence of that; as a result; consequently: *I think; therefore I am.* [ME *ther(e)fore,* var. of *therfor* THEREFOR]
—**Syn.** hence, whence. THEREFORE, WHEREFORE, ACCORDINGLY, CONSEQUENTLY, SO, THEN agree in introducing a statement resulting from, or caused by, what immediately precedes. THEREFORE (for this or that reason) and WHEREFORE (for which reason) imply exactness of reasoning; they are esp. used in logic, law, mathematics, etc., and in a formal style of speaking or writing. ACCORDINGLY (in conformity with the preceding) and CONSEQUENTLY (as a result, or sequence, or effect of the preceding) are less formal. So (because the preceding is true or this being the case) and THEN (since the preceding is true) are conversational in tone.

there·from (thâr′frum′, -from′), *adv.* from that place, thing, etc. [ME]

there·in (thâr′in′), *adv.* **1.** in or into that place or thing. **2.** in that matter, circumstance, etc. [ME *therin,* OE *thǣrin*]

there·in·af·ter (thâr′in af′tər, -äf′-), *adv.* afterward in that document, statement, etc.

there·in·to (thâr′in′to͞o, thâr′in to͞o′), *adv.* **1.** into that place or thing. **2.** into that matter, circumstance, etc. [ME *thar into*]

ther·e·min (ther′ə min), *n.* a musical instrument with electronic tone generation, the pitch and tone volume being controlled by the distance between the player's hands and two metal rods serving as antennas. [named after Leo *Theremin* (b. 1896), Russian inventor] —**ther′e·min′ist,** *n.*

there·of (thâr′uv′, -ov′), *adv.* **1.** of that or it. **2.** from or out of that origin or cause. [ME *therof,* OE *thǣrof*]

there·on (thâr′on′, -ôn′), *adv.* **1.** on or upon that or it. **2.** immediately after that; thereupon. [ME *ther on,* OE *thǣron*]

there's (thârz), **1.** contraction of *there is.* **2.** contraction of *there has.*

The·re·sa (tə rē′sə, -zə; *Sp.* te re′sä), *n.* **Saint,** 1515–82, Spanish Carmelite nun, mystic, and writer. Also, **Teresa.** Also called **There′sa of A′vi·la** (ä′vē lä′).

there·to (thâr′to͞o′), *adv.* **1.** to that place, thing, etc. **2.** to that matter, circumstance, etc. **3.** *Archaic.* in addition to that. Also, **there·un·to** (thâr′un to͞o′, thâr′un′to͞o). [ME *therto,* OE *thǣrtō*]

there·to·fore (thâr′tə fōr′, -fôr′), *adv.* before or until that time. [ME *ther tofore.* See THERE, HERETOFORE]

there·un·der (thâr′un′dər), *adv.* **1.** under or beneath that. **2.** under the authority of or in accordance with that. [ME *therunder,* OE *thǣrunder*]

there·up·on (thâr′ə pon′, -pôn′, thâr′ə pon′, -pôn′), *adv.* **1.** immediately following that. **2.** in consequence of that. **3.** upon that or it. **4.** with reference to that. [ME *ther uppon*]

there·with (thâr′with′, -with′), *adv.* **1.** with that. **2.** in addition to that. **3.** following upon that; thereupon. [ME *ther(e)with,* OE *thǣrwith*]

there·with·al (thâr′with ôl′, -with-), *adv.* **1.** together with that; in addition to that. **2.** following upon that. [ME *ther withal*]

The·re·zi·na (*Port.* te′re zē′nə), *n.* former name of **Teresina.**

the·ri·ac (thēr′ē ak′), *n.* molasses; treacle. Also, **the·ri·a·ca** (thə rī′ə kə). [< L *thēriac(a)* antidote to poison < Gk *thēriakē,* fem. of *thēriakós* = *thēri(on)* wild beast + *-akos* -AC; r. ME *tiriake,* OE *tȳriaca* < ML] —**the·ri′a·cal,** *adj.*

the·ri·an·throp·ic (thēr′ē an throp′ik), *adj.* **1.** being partly bestial and partly human in form. **2.** of or pertaining to deities conceived or represented in such form. [< Gk *thēri(on)* beast + ANTHROP- + -IC] —**the·ri·an·thro·pism** (thēr′ē an′thrə piz′əm), *n.*

the·ri·o·mor·phic (thēr′ē ə môr′fik), *adj.* (of deities) thought of or represented as having the form of beasts. Also, **the′ri·o·mor′phous.** [< Gk *thēriómorph(os)* beast-shaped (*thērío(n)* wild beast + *-morphos* -MORPHOUS) + -IC] —**the′ri·o·morph′,** *n.*

therm (thûrm), *n. Physics.* any of several units of heat, as one equivalent to 1000 large calories or 100,000 British thermal units. Also, **therme.** [< Gk *thérm(ē)* heat]

therm-, var. of **thermo-** before a vowel: *thermal.*

-therm, var. of **thermo-** as final element in compound words: *isotherm.*

therm., thermometer.

Ther·ma (thûr′mə), *n.* ancient name of **Salonika.**

ther·mae (thûr′mē), *n.* (*construed as pl.*) **1.** hot springs; hot baths. **2.** a public bathing establishment of the ancient Greeks or Romans. [< L < Gk *thérmai,* pl. of *thérmē* heat]

ther·mal (thûr′məl), *adj.* **1.** Also, **thermic.** of, pertaining to, or caused by heat or temperature: *thermal capacity.* **2.** of, pertaining to, or of the nature of thermae: *thermal waters.* —*n.* **3.** a rising current of warm air. [THERM- + -AL[1]] —**ther′mal·ly,** *adv.*

ther′mal bar′rier, *Aeronaut., Rocketry.* the limiting speed imposed on a supersonic object by aerodynamic heating effects.

ther′mal spring′, a spring having waters of a temperature higher than the mean temperature of the surrounding locale.

ther′mal u′nit, a unit of heat energy or of the equivalent of heat energy in work.

therme (thûrm), *n. Physics.* therm.

therm·el (thûr′mel), *n.* thermocouple. [THERM- + EL(ECTRIC)]

ther·mic (thûr′mik), *adj.* thermal (def. 1).

Ther·mi·dor (thûr′mi dôr′; *Fr.* ter mē dôr′), *n.* (in the French Revolutionary calendar) the 11th month of the year, extending from July 19th to August 17th. Also called **Fervidor.** [< F < Gk *thérmē* heat + *dôr(on)* gift]

Ther·mi·do·ri·an (thûr′mi dōr′ē ən, -dôr′-), *n.* a member of the French moderate group who participated in the downfall of Robespierre and his followers on the 9th Thermidor (July 27th), 1794. Also, **Ther′mi·do′re·an.** [< F *thermidorien.* See THERMIDOR, -IAN]

therm·i·on (thûrm′ī′ən, thûr′mē ən), *n. Physics.* an ion emitted by an incandescent material. —**therm·i·on·ic** (thûrm′ī on′ik, thûr′mē-), *adj.*

therm′ion′ic cur′rent, an electric current produced by the flow of thermions.

therm·i·on·ics (thûrm′ī on′iks, thûr′mē-), *n.* (*construed as sing.*) the branch of physics that deals with thermionic phenomena. [see THERMIONIC, -ICS]

therm′ion′ic tube′, *Electronics.* a vacuum tube in which the cathode is heated electrically to cause the emission of electrons by thermal agitation. Also called, *Brit.,* **thermionic valve.**

therm′ion′ic valve′, *Brit.* **1.** See **vacuum tube. 2.** See **thermionic tube.**

ther·mis·tor (thər mis′tər), *n. Electronics.* a resistor whose action depends upon changes of its resistance material with changes in temperature. [THERM- + (RES)ISTOR]

ther·mite (thûr′mīt), *n.* a mixture of finely divided metallic aluminum and ferric oxide that when ignited produces extremely high temperatures: used in welding, incendiary bombs, etc. [THERM- + -ITE[1]]

thermo-, a learned borrowing from Greek meaning "heat," "hot," used in the formation of compound words: *thermoplastic.* Also, **therm-, -therm.** [< Gk, comb. form of *thermós* hot, *thérmē* heat]

ther·mo·bar·o·graph (thûr′mō bär′ə graf′, -gräf′), *n. Physics.* a device consisting of a thermograph and a barograph, for recording simultaneously the temperature and pressure of a gas.

ther·mo·ba·rom·e·ter (thûr′mō bə rom′i tər), *n.* **1.** an instrument for measuring atmospheric pressure, and sometimes altitude, from its effect upon the boiling point of a liquid. **2.** a barometer so constructed that it may also be used as a thermometer.

ther·mo·chem·is·try (thûr′mō kem′i strē), *n.* the branch of chemistry dealing with the relationship between chemical action and heat. —**ther′mo·chem′i·cal,** *adj.* —**ther′mo·chem′i·cal·ly,** *adv.* —**ther′mo·chem′ist,** *n.*

ther·mo·cou·ple (thûr′mə kup′əl), *n. Physics.* a device for measuring temperature, consisting essentially of two dissimilar metallic conductors joined at their ends: when the two junctions are maintained at different temperatures an electromotive force proportional to the temperature difference is induced. Also called **thermel, thermoelectric couple, thermoelectric thermometer.**

ther·mo·cur·rent (thûr′mō kûr′ənt, -kur′-), *n.* a thermoelectric current.

thermodynam., thermodynamics.

ther·mo·dy·nam·ic (thûr′mō dī nam′ik), *adj.* **1.** of or pertaining to thermodynamics. **2.** using or producing heat. Also, **ther′mo·dy·nam′i·cal.** —**ther′mo·dy·nam′i·cal·ly,** *adv.*

ther·mo·dy·nam·ics (thûr′mō dī nam′iks, -di-), *n.* (*construed as sing.*) the science concerned with the relations between heat and mechanical energy or work, and the conversion of one into the other: modern thermodynamics deals with the properties of systems for the description of which temperature is a necessary coordinate. —**ther′mo·dy·nam′i·cist,** *n.*

ther·mo·e·lec·tric (thûr′mō i lek′trik), *adj.* of, pertaining to, or involving the direct relationship between heat and electricity. Also, **ther′mo·e·lec′tri·cal.** —**ther′mo·e·lec′tri·cal·ly,** *adv.*

ther′moelec′tric cou′ple, *Physics.* thermocouple.

ther′moelec′tric effect′, *Physics.* the production of electromotive force, as in a thermocouple.

ther·mo·e·lec·tric·i·ty (thûr′mō i lek tris′i tē, -ē′lek-), *n.* electricity generated by heat or temperature difference, as in a thermocouple.

ther′moelec′tric thermom′eter, *Physics.* thermocouple.

ther′mo·e·lec·tro·mo′tive force′ (thûr′mō i lek′trə mō′tiv, thûr′-), the electromotive force developed by the thermoelectric effect.

ther·mo·e·lec·tron (thûr′mō i lek′tron), *n. Physics.* an electron emitted by an incandescent material.

ther·mo·gen·e·sis (thûr′mō jen′i sis), *n.* the production of heat, esp. in an animal body by physiological processes. —**ther·mo·ge·net·ic** (thûr′mō jə net′ik), *adj.*

ther·mog·e·nous (thər moj′ə nəs), *adj.* producing heat; thermogenetic.

ther·mo·graph (thûr′mə graf′, -gräf′), *n.* a recording thermometer.
ther·mo·la·bile (thûr′mō lā′bil), *adj.* *Biochem.* subject to destruction or loss of characteristic properties by the action of moderate heat, as certain toxins and ferments (opposed to *thermostable*).
ther·mol·y·sis (thər mol′i sis), *n.* **1.** *Physiol.* the dispersion of heat from the body. **2.** *Chem.* dissociation by heat. —**ther·mo·lyt·ic** (thûr′mə lit′ik), *adj.*
ther·mo·mag·net·ic (thûr′mō mag net′ik), *adj.* **1.** *Physics.* of or pertaining to the effect of heat on the magnetic properties of a substance. **2.** of or pertaining to the effect of a magnetic field on a conductor of heat.
ther·mom·e·ter (thər mom′i tər), *n.* an instrument for measuring temperature, typically consisting of a sealed glass tube containing a column of liquid, as mercury, that rises and falls with temperature changes, the temperature being read from a calibrated scale marked on the tube or its frame. —**ther·mo·met·ric** (thûr′mə me′trik), **ther′mo·met′ri·cal,** *adj.* —**ther′mo·met′ri·cal·ly,** *adv.*
ther·mom·e·try (thər mom′i trē), *n.* **1.** the branch of physics dealing with the measurement of temperature. **2.** the science of the construction and use of thermometers.

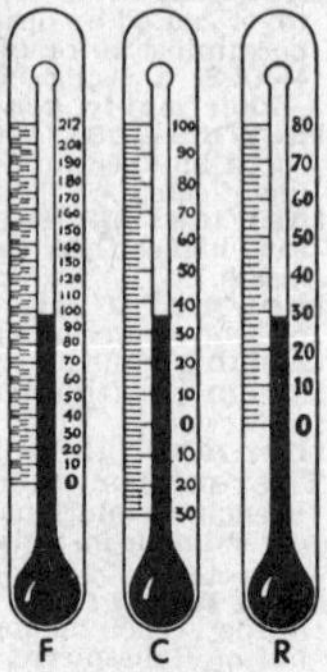

Thermometers
F, Fahrenheit
C, Centigrade (Celsius)
R, Réaumur

ther·mo·mo·tor (thûr′mə mō′tər), *n.* an engine operated by heat, esp. one driven by the expansive force of hot air.
ther·mo·nu·cle·ar (thûr′mō no͞o′klē ər, -nyo͞o′-), *adj.* of, pertaining to, or involving a thermonuclear reaction: *thermonuclear power.*
ther′monu′clear bomb′. See **hydrogen bomb.**
ther′monu′clear reac′tion, *Chem., Physics.* a nuclear-fusion reaction that takes place between the nuclei of a gas, esp. hydrogen, heated to a temperature of several million degrees.
ther·mo·pile (thûr′mə pīl′), *n.* *Physics.* a device consisting of a number of thermocouples joined in series, used for generating thermoelectric current or for detecting and measuring radiant energy, as from a star.
ther·mo·plas·tic (thûr′mə plas′tik), *adj.* **1.** soft and pliable whenever heated, as some plastics, without any change of the inherent properties. —*n.* **2.** a plastic of this type. —**ther·mo·plas·tic·i·ty** (thûr′mō pla stis′i tē), *n.* 
Ther·mop·y·lae (thər mop′ə lē′), *n.* a pass in E Greece: important entry into the south from the north; Persian defeat of the Spartans 480 B.C.
Ther·mos (thûr′məs), *n.* *Trademark.* See **vacuum bottle.**
ther·mo·scope (thûr′mə skōp′), *n.* a device for giving an approximation of the temperature change of a substance by noting the corresponding change in its volume. —**ther·mo·scop·ic** (thûr′mə skop′ik), **ther′mo·scop′i·cal,** *adj.*
ther·mo·set·ting (thûr′mō set′ing), *adj.* noting any plastic, as one of the urea resins, that sets when heated and cannot be remolded.
ther·mo·si·phon (thûr′mō sī′fən, -fon), *n.* an arrangement of siphon tubes that induces the circulation of water in a heating apparatus.
ther·mo·sphere (thûr′mə sfēr′), *n.* the region of the upper atmosphere in which temperature increases continuously with altitude.
ther·mo·sta·ble (thûr′mə stā′bəl), *adj.* *Biochem.* capable of being subjected to a moderate degree of heat without loss of characteristic properties, as certain toxins and ferments (opposed to *thermolabile*). —**ther′mo·sta·bil′i·ty,** *n.*
ther·mo·stat (thûr′mə stat′), *n.* a device that functions to establish and maintain a desired temperature automatically or signals a change in temperature for manual adjustment. —**ther′mo·stat′ic,** *adj.* —**ther′mo·stat′i·cal·ly,** *adv.*
ther·mo·stat·ics (thûr′mə stat′iks), *n.* (*construed as sing.*) *Rare.* the branch of physics dealing with thermal equilibrium.
ther·mo·tax·is (thûr′mə tak′sis), *n.* **1.** *Biol.* movement of an organism toward or away from a source of heat. **2.** *Physiol.* the regulation of the bodily temperature. —**ther·mo·tac·tic** (thûr′mə tak′tik), **ther′mo·tax′ic,** *adj.*
ther·mo·ten·sile (thûr′mə ten′səl, -sil *or, esp. Brit.,* -sīl), *adj.* *Rare.* pertaining to tensile strength as affected by changes of temperature.
ther·mo·ther·a·py (thûr′mō ther′ə pē), *n.* treatment of disease by means of heat, either moist or dry.
ther·mot·ro·pism (thər mo′trə piz′əm), *n.* *Biol.* oriented growth of an organism in response to heat. —**ther·mo·trop·ic** (thûr′mə trop′ik), *adj.*
-thermy, a combining form referring to heat, used in the formation of nouns: *diathermy.* [< NL *-thermia;* see -THERM, -Y[3]]
the·roid (thēr′oid), *adj.* having animal propensities or characteristics; brutish. [< Gk *thēroeid(ḗs)* = *thḗr* wild beast + *-oeidēs* -OID]
Ther·si·tes (thər sī′tēz), *n.* (in the *Iliad*) a Greek known for his ugliness, deformity, and foulmouthed, quarrelsome nature. [< L < Gk = *thérs(os)* (dial. var. of *thársos* audacity) + *-ītēs* -ITE[1]]
ther·sit·i·cal (thər sit′i kəl), *adj.* scurrilous; foulmouthed; grossly abusive. [THERSIT(ES) + -ICAL]
Thes., Thessalonians.
the·sau·rus (thi sôr′əs), *n., pl.* **-sau·ri** (-sôr′ī). **1.** a dictionary of synonyms and antonyms. **2.** any dictionary, encyclopedia, or other comprehensive reference book. **3.** a storehouse, repository, or treasury. **4.** *Computer Technol.* an index to information stored in a computer. [< L < Gk *thēsaurós* treasure, treasury]
these (thēz), *pron., adj.* pl. of **this.**
The·seus (thē′sē əs, -so͞os), *n.* *Class. Myth.* an Attic hero, the son of Aegeus, the husband of Phaedra, and the father of Hippolytus. His adventures included the killing of the robber Procrustes, the slaying of the Minotaur, battles against the Amazons and the Centaurs, and an attempt to abduct Persephone. —**The·se·an** (thi sē′ən), *adj.*
the·sis (thē′sis), *n., pl.* **-ses** (-sēz). **1.** a proposition stated or put forward for consideration, esp. one to be proved or maintained against objections. **2.** a subject for a composition or essay. **3.** a monograph embodying original research, esp. one presented by a candidate for a master's degree. **4.** *Music.* the downward stroke in conducting; downbeat. Cf. **arsis** (def. 1). **5.** *Pros.* **a.** the unstressed part of a metrical foot. **b.** (less commonly) the stressed part of a metrical foot. Cf. **arsis** (def. 2). **6.** *Philos.* See under **Hegelian dialectic.** [ME < L < Gk: a setting down, something set down = *the-* (s. of *tithénai* to put, set down) + *-sis* -SIS]
Thes·pi·an (thes′pē ən), *adj.* **1.** of or characteristic of Thespis. **2.** (*often l.c.*) pertaining to tragedy or to the dramatic art in general. —*n.* **3.** (*usually l.c.*) an actor or actress.
Thes·pis (thes′pis), *n.* fl. 6th century B.C., Greek poet.
Thess., Thessalonians.
Thes·sa·lo·ni·an (thes′ə lō′nē ən), *adj.* **1.** of or pertaining to Thessalonike or its inhabitants. —*n.* **2.** a native or inhabitant of Thessalonike.
Thes·sa·lo·ni·ans (thes′ə lō′nē ənz), *n.* (*construed as sing.*) either of two books of the New Testament, I Thessalonians or II Thessalonians, written by Paul.
Thes·sa·lo·ni·ke (thes′ä lô nē′kē), *n.* official name of **Salonika.** Ancient, **Thes·sa·lon·i·ca** (thes′ə lon′ə kə, -ə lō nī′kə).
Thes·sa·ly (thes′ə lē), *n.* a region in E Greece: a former division of ancient Greece. 695,385 (1961); 5208 sq. mi. —**Thes·sa·li·an** (the sā′lē ən), *adj., n.*
the·ta (thā′tə, thē′-), *n.* the eighth letter of the Greek alphabet (Θ, θ). [< Gk < Sem. See TETH]
thet·ic (thet′ik), *adj.* positive; dogmatic. Also, **thet′i·cal.** [< Gk *thetik(ós)* = *thet(ós)* placed, set (verbid of *tithénai* to lay down) + *-ikos* -IC] —**thet′i·cal·ly,** *adv.*
The·tis (thē′tis), *n.* *Class. Myth.* a Nereid, the wife of Peleus and the mother of Achilles.
the·ur·gy (thē′ûr jē), *n., pl.* **-gies. 1.** a system of beneficent magic practiced by the Egyptian Platonists and others. **2.** the working of a divine or supernatural agency in human affairs. [< LL *theūrgia* < Gk *theourgía* magic. See THE-, -URGY] —**the·ur′gic, the·ur′gi·cal,** *adj.* —**the·ur′gi·cal·ly,** *adv.* —**the′ur·gist,** *n.*
thew (thyo͞o), *n.* **1.** Usually, **thews.** a muscle or sinew. **2. thews,** physical strength. [ME; OE *thēaw* custom, usage; c. OHG *thau* (later *dau*) discipline; akin to L *tuērī* to watch] —**thew′y,** *adj.*
thew·less (thyo͞o′lis), *adj.* **1.** cowardly; timid. **2.** without muscles; weak. [ME *theweles*]
they (thā), *pron.pl., poss.* **their** or **theirs,** *obj.* **them. 1.** nominative plural of **he, she,** and **it. 2.** people in general: *They say he's rich.* **3.** *Nonstandard.* (used with an indefinite singular antecedent in place of the definite masculine "he" or the definite feminine "she"): *Whoever is of voting age, whether they are interested in politics or not, should vote.* [ME < Scand; cf. Icel *their* those, c. OE *thā*, pl. of *thæt* THAT]
they'd (thād), **1.** contraction of *they had.* **2.** contraction of *they would.*
they'll (thāl), **1.** contraction of *they will.* **2.** contraction of *they shall.*
they're (thâr), contraction of *they are.*
they've (thāv), contraction of *they have.*
thi-, var. of **thio-** (*thiazine*), properly occurring before a vowel but not systematically employed (cf. *thioaldehyde*).
T.H.I., See **Temperature-Humidity Index.**
thi′a·ce′tic ac′id (thī′ə sē′tik, -ə set′ik, thī′-), *Chem.* See **thioacetic acid.**
thi·a·mine (thī′ə mēn′, -min), *n.* *Biochem.* a crystalline compound of the vitamin B complex, $C_{12}H_{17}ClN_4OS$, essential for normal functioning of the nervous system, a deficiency of which results chiefly in beriberi and other nerve disorders: occurring in many natural sources, as green peas, liver, and esp. the seed coats of cereal grains. Also, **thi·a·min** (thī′ə min). Also called **vitamin B_1, aneurin, aneurine.**
thi·a·zine (thī′ə zēn′, -zin), *n.* *Chem.* any of a class of compounds containing a ring composed of one atom each of sulfur and nitrogen and four atoms of carbon.
thi·a·zole (thī′ə zōl′), *n.* *Chem.* **1.** a colorless, slightly water-miscible liquid, C_3H_3NS, having a disagreeable odor. **2.** any of various derivatives of this substance, used as dyes or reagents.
Thi·bet (ti bet′), *n.* Tibet. —**Thi·bet′an,** *adj., n.*
Thich (tik, tich), *n.* a Vietnamese religious title applied to a Buddhist: used before the proper name. [< Vietnamese: lit., Buddhist]
thick (thik), *adj.* **1.** having relatively great extent in the smallest dimension or between surfaces. **2.** measured between opposite surfaces or across the smallest dimension: *a board one inch thick.* **3.** composed of or containing objects, particles, etc., close together; dense: *a thick forest, a thick fog.* **4.** (of a liquid) heavy or viscous: *a thick soup.* **5.** deep or profound: *thick darkness.* **6.** extreme; decided; pronounced: *a thick German accent.* **7.** not properly articulated; indistinct: *thick speech.* **8.** abounding in things, persons, or matter close together: *a room thick with guests; a table thick with dust.* **9.** *Informal.* close in friendship; intimate. **10.** mentally slow; stupid; dull. **11.** disagreeably excessive or exaggerated: *They thought it a bit thick when he called himself a genius.* **12.** *Archaic.* dull of sense perception. —*adv.* **13.** in a thick manner. **14.** close together; densely. **15.** in a manner to produce something thick: *Slice the cheese thick.* **16. lay it on thick,** *Informal.* to praise excessively; flatter. —*n.* **17.** the thickest, densest, or most crowded part: *in the thick of the fight.* **18. through thick and thin,** under favorable and unfavorable conditions; steadfastly.

[ME *thikke*, OE *thicce;* c. D *dik*, G *dick;* akin to Icel *thykkr*, Ir *tiugh*] —**thick′ish,** *adj.* —**thick′ly,** *adv.*

thick·en (thik′ən), *v.t., v.i.* **1.** to make or become thick or thicker. **2.** to make or grow more intense, profound, intricate, or complex: *The plot thickens.* [late ME *thikne* < Scand; cf. Icel *thykkna*]

thick·en·er (thik′ə nər), *n.* **1.** something that thickens. **2.** an apparatus for the sedimentation and removal of solids suspended in various liquids.

thick·en·ing (thik′ə ning), *n.* **1.** a making or becoming thick. **2.** a thickened part or area; swelling. **3.** something used to thicken; thickener.

thick·et (thik′it), *n.* a thick or dense growth of shrubs, bushes, or small trees; a thick coppice. [OE *thiccet* = *thicce* THICK + *-et* n. suffix]

thick·head·ed (thik′hed′id), *adj.* **1.** (of an animal) having a thick head. **2.** (of a person) dull-witted; stupid. —**thick′head′ed·ly,** *adv.* —**thick′head′ed·ness,** *n.*

thick·leaf (thik′lēf′), *n., pl.* **-leaves** (-lēvz′). any succulent herb or shrub of the genus *Crassula.*

thick·ness (thik′nis), *n.* **1.** the state or quality of being thick. **2.** the measure of the smallest dimension of a solid figure: *a board of two-inch thickness.* **3.** the thick part or body of something. **4.** a layer, stratum, or ply: *three thicknesses of cloth.* [ME *thiknesse*, OE *thicnes*]

thick·set (*adj.* thik′set′; *n.* thik′set′), *adj.* **1.** set thickly or in close arrangement; dense: *a thickset hedge.* **2.** studded or furnished thickly; closely packed: *a sky thickset with stars.* **3.** heavily or solidly built; stocky: *a thickset young man.* —*n.* **4.** a thicket. [ME *thikke sette* thickly set]

thick-skinned (thik′skind′), *adj.* **1.** having a thick skin. **2.** insensitive or hardened to criticism, reproach, rebuff, etc. —**Syn. 2.** insensitive, obtuse, callous.

thick-witted (thik′wit′id), *adj.* lacking intelligence; thickheaded; dull; stupid. —**thick′-wit′ted·ly,** *adv.* —**thick′-wit′ted·ness,** *n.*

thief (thēf), *n., pl.* **thieves.** a person who steals, esp. secretly or without open force; a person guilty of theft. [ME; OE *thēof;* c. D *dief*, G *Dieb*, Icel *thjōfr*, Goth *thiufs*] —**Syn.** burglar, pickpocket, highwayman. THIEF, ROBBER refer to a person who steals. A THIEF takes the goods or property of another by stealth without the latter's knowledge: *a horse thief; like a thief in the night.* A ROBBER trespasses upon the house, property, or person of another and makes away with things of value, even at the cost of violence: *A robber held up two women on the street.*

Thiers (tyer), *n.* **Louis A·dolphe** (lwē A dôlf′), 1797–1877, French statesman: president 1871–73.

Thieu (tyōō′), *n.* **Ngu·yen van** (əngōō′yen′ vän′, nōō′-). See **Nguyen van Thieu.**

thieve (thēv), *v.,* **thieved, thiev·ing.** —*v.t.* **1.** to take by theft; steal. —*v.i.* **2.** to act as a thief; commit theft; steal. [OE *thēofian* < *thēof* THIEF] —**thiev′ing·ly,** *adv.*

thieve·less (thēv′lis), *adj. Scot.* **1.** not cordial, affectionate, or emotional; cold. **2.** thowless. [? misreading of *theueless*, sp. var. of THEWLESS]

thiev·er·y (thē′və rē), *n., pl.* **-er·ies.** the practice or an instance of thieving; theft.

thiev·ish (thē′vish), *adj.* **1.** given to thieving. **2.** of, pertaining to, or characteristic of a thief. [late ME *thevisch, thefyische*] —**thiev′ish·ly,** *adv.* —**thiev′ish·ness,** *n.*

thigh (thī), *n.* **1.** the part of the lower limb in man between the hip and the knee. **2.** the corresponding part of the hind limb of other animals; the femoral region. **3.** (in birds) **a.** the true femoral region that is hidden by the skin or feathers of the body. **b.** the segment below, containing the fibula and tibia. **4.** *Entomol.* the femur. [ME; OE *thēoh;* c. D *dij*, OHG *dioh*, Icel *thjō*]

thigh·bone (thī′bōn′), *n.* femur (def. 1). [late ME *the bane*]

thig·mo·tax·is (thig′mə tak′sis), *n. Biol.* movement of an organism toward or away from any object that provides a mechanical stimulus; stereotaxis. [< Gk *thigm(a)* touch + -o- + -TAXIS] —**thig·mo·tac·tic** (thig′mə tak′tik), *adj.*

thig·mo·tro·pism (thig mo′trə piz′əm), *n. Biol.* oriented growth of an organism in response to mechanical contact. [< Gk *thigm(a)* touch + -o- + -TROPISM] —**thig·mo·trop·ic** (thig′mə trop′ik), *adj.*

thill (thil), *n.* either of the pair of shafts of a vehicle between which a single animal is harnessed to pull it. [ME *thille* shaft, OE: plank. See DEAL[2]]

thim·ble (thim′bəl), *n.* **1.** a small cap, usually of metal, worn on the fingertip to protect it when pushing a needle through cloth in sewing. **2.** *Mech.* any of various devices or attachments likened to this. **3.** *Naut.* a metal ring with a concave groove on the outside, used to line the outside of a ring of rope forming an eye. [ME *thym(b)yl*, OE *thȳmel;* akin to Icel *thumall* thumb of a glove. See THUMB]

thim·ble·ber·ry (thim′bəl ber′ē), *n., pl.* **-ries.** any of several American raspberries bearing a thimble-shaped fruit, esp. the black raspberry, *Rubus occidentalis.*

thim·ble·ful (thim′bəl fo͝ol′), *n., pl.* **-fuls. 1.** the amount that a thimble will hold. **2.** a small quantity, esp. of liquid.

thim·ble·rig (thim′bəl rig′), *n., v.,* **-rigged, -rig·ging.** —*n.* **1.** a sleight-of-hand swindling game in which the operator palms a pellet or pea while appearing to cover it with one of three thimblelike cups, and then, moving the cups about, offers to bet that no one can tell under which cup the pellet or pea lies. —*v.t.* **2.** to cheat by or as by thimblerig. —**thim′ble·rig′ger,** *n.*

thim·ble·weed (thim′bəl wēd′), *n.* any of various plants having a thimble-shaped fruiting head, as the anemone, *Anemone virginiana*, and the rudbeckia, *Rudbeckia laciniata.*

Thim·bu (tim′bōō), *n.* a city in and the capital of Bhutan, in the W part.

thi·mer·o·sal (thī mûr′ə sal′, -mer′-), *n. Pharm.* a powder, $C_9H_9HgNaO_2S$, used chiefly as an antiseptic; sodium ethylmercurithiosalicylate. [? THI- + MER(CURY) + -o- + SAL(ICYLATE)]

thin (thin), *adj.,* **thin·ner, thin·nest,** *adv., v.,* **thinned, thin·ning.** —*adj.* **1.** having relatively little extent in the smallest dimension or between surfaces. **2.** having little flesh; spare; lean: *a thin man.* **3.** composed of or containing objects, particles, etc., widely separated; sparse: *thin vegetation.* **4.** of relatively low consistency or viscosity: *thin soup.* **5.** rarefied: *thin air.* **6.** scant; not abundant or plentiful. **7.** without solidity or substance; flimsy: *a thin excuse.* **8.** lacking fullness or volume; weak and shrill: *a thin voice.* **9.** lacking body, richness, or strength: *a thin wine.* **10.** lacking in chroma; of light tint. **11.** *Photog.* (of a developed negative) lacking in density or contrast through underdevelopment or underexposure. —*adv.* **12.** in a thin manner. **13.** sparsely; not densely. **14.** so as to produce something thin: *Slice the ham thin.* —*v.t.* **15.** to make thin or thinner (often fol. by *down, out,* etc.). —*v.i.* **16.** to become thin or thinner (often fol. by *down, out, off,* etc.): *The crowd is thinning out.* [ME, OE *thynne;* c. D *dun*, G *dünn*, Icel *thunnr;* akin to OIr *tana*, L *tenuis* thin, Gk *tany-* long] —**thin′ly,** *adv.* —**thin′ness,** *n.* —**Syn. 2.** slim, slender, skinny, lank, scrawny. THIN, GAUNT, LEAN agree in referring to a person having little flesh. THIN applies often to a person in an unnaturally reduced state, as from sickness, overwork, lack of food, or the like: *a thin, dirty little waif.* GAUNT suggests the angularity of bones prominently displayed in a thin face and body: *to look ill and gaunt.* LEAN usually applies to a person or animal that is naturally thin: *looking lean but healthy after an outdoor vacation.* **6.** meager. **7.** weak. **15.** dilute.

thine (thīn), *pron.* **1.** the possessive case of **thou** used as a predicate adjective, after a noun or without a noun. **2.** the possessive case of **thou** used as an attributive adjective before a noun beginning with a vowel or vowel sound: *thine eyes; thine honor.* Cf. **thy. 3.** that which belongs to thee: *Thine is the power and the glory.* [ME, OE *thīn;* c. Icel *thinn*, Goth *theins*, G *dein.* See THOU]

thing (thing), *n.* **1.** a material object without life or consciousness; an inanimate object. **2.** some entity, object, or creature that is not or cannot be specifically designated or precisely described: *The stick had a brass thing on it.* **3.** anything that is or may become an object of thought. **4.** Often, **things.** matters; affairs: *Things are going well now.* **5.** a fact, circumstance, or state of affairs. **6.** an action, deed or event: *to do great things.* **7.** a particular, respect, or detail. *perfect in all things.* **8.** aim or objective: *The thing is to reach this line with the ball.* **9.** a useful or appropriate object, method, etc.: *This is just the thing for your insomnia.* **10. things, a.** outer clothing or apparel: *Come on in and let me take your things.* **b.** personal possessions or belongings: *Pack your things and go!* **c.** implements, utensils, or other articles for service: *I'll wash the breakfast things.* **11.** a task; chore: *I've got a lot of things to do today.* **12.** a living being or creature: *His daughter's a pretty little thing.* **13.** a thought or statement: *I have just one thing to say to you.* **14.** *Informal.* a peculiar attitude or feeling toward something; mental quirk; phobia: *She has a thing about cats.* **15.** *Slang.* something special or unique that one feels disposed to do: *to do her thing; to find your own thing.* **16.** something that is signified or represented, as distinguished from a word, symbol, or idea representing it. **17.** *Law.* anything that may be the subject of a property right. [ME, OE; c. D *ding*, G *Ding* thing; earlier, meeting; cf. Icel *thing* assembly]

thing·a·ma·bob (thing′ə mə bob′), *n. Informal.* thingumbob.

thing-in-it·self (thing′in it self′), *n., pl.* **things-in-them·selves** (thingz′in them selvz′). *Kantianism.* reality as it is apart from experience, or apart from the categories of understanding and the a priori forms of consciousness, space, and time. Cf. **noumenon** (def. 3). [trans. of G *Ding an sich*]

thing·u·ma·jig (thing′ə mə jig′), *n. Informal.* thingumbob.

thing·um·bob (thing′əm bob′), *n. Informal.* a gadget or other thing for which the speaker does not know or has forgotten the name. Also, **thingamabob, thing·a·ma·jig** (thing′ə mə jig′), **thing·u·ma·bob** (thing′ə mə bob′), **thing-umajig.** [*thingum* (facetious Latinized var. of THING) + BOB[2]]

think[1] (thingk), *v.,* **thought, think·ing,** *adj.* —*v.i.* **1.** to have a conscious mind, to some extent capable of reasoning, remembering experiences, making rational decisions, etc. **2.** to employ one's mind rationally and objectively in evaluating or dealing with a given situation. **3.** to have a certain thing as the subject of one's thoughts (usually fol. by *of* or *about*). **4.** to call something to one's conscious mind (usually fol. by *of*). **5.** to consider something as a possible action, choice, etc. (usually fol. by *about* or *of*). **6.** to invent or conceive of something (usually fol. by *of*). **7.** to have consideration or regard for someone (usually fol. by *of*). **8.** to esteem a person or thing as indicated (usually fol. by *of*): *to think badly of someone.* —*v.t.* **9.** to have or form in the mind as an idea, conception, etc. **10.** to have as an opinion or belief. **11.** to consider for evaluation or for possible action upon (usually fol. by *over*). **12.** to regard as specified: *He thought me unkind.* **13.** to believe to be true of someone or something: *to think evil of the neighbors.* **14.** to analyze or evolve rationally (usually fol. by *out*). **15.** to have as a plan or intention. **16.** to anticipate or expect (usually fol. by an infinitive clause). **17. think better of,** to reconsider (a course of action); change one's mind about. **18. think fit,** to consider advisable or appropriate: *By all means, go if you think fit.* **19. think up,** to devise or contrive by thinking; conceive. —*adj.* **20.** of or pertaining to thinking or thought. [ME *thinke*, var. of *thenke(n)*, OE *thencan;* c. D, G *denken*, Icel *thekkja*, Goth *thagkjan*. See THANK]

think[2] (thingk), *v.i.,* **thought, think·ing.** *Obs.* to seem or appear (used impersonally with an indirect object). Cf. **methinks.** [ME *thinke*, OE *thyncan;* c. D *dunken*, G *dünken*, Icel *thykkja*, Goth *thugkjan*]

think·a·ble (thing′kə bəl), *adj.* **1.** capable of being thought or conceived by the mind. **2.** capable of being considered as possible; conceivable.

think·er (thing′kər), *n.* **1.** a person who thinks, esp. in a specified way or manner: *Your child is a slow thinker.* **2.** a person who has cultivated or exercised to an unusually great extent the faculty of thought, as a philosopher, theorist, or scholar. [ME *thenkare*]

think′ fac′tory, *Informal.* See **think tank.**

think·ing (thing′king), *adj.* **1.** rational; reasoning: *Man is a thinking animal.* **2.** thoughtful; reflective; studious.

—*n.* **3.** thought; judgment; reflection. [ME *thenking* (n.)] —**think′ing·ly,** *adv.*

think′ing cap′, a state of mind marked by concentration.

think′ tank′, *Informal.* a research institute or other organization of scholars, social or physical scientists, etc., esp. one employed by government to solve complex problems or predict future developments in military and social areas. Also called **think factory.**

thin·ner¹ (thin′ər), *n.* **1.** a liquid, as turpentine, used to dilute paint, varnish, rubber cement, etc., to the desired or proper consistency. **2.** a person or thing that thins.

thin·ner² (thin′ər), *adj.* comparative of **thin.**

thin·nish (thin′ish), *adj.* somewhat thin.

thin-skinned (thin′skind′), *adj.* **1.** having a thin skin. **2.** sensitive to criticism or rebuff; easily offended; touchy.

thi·o (thī′ō), *adj. Chem.* containing sulfur, esp. in place of oxygen. [< Gk *theîon* sulfur]

thio-, a learned borrowing from Greek meaning "sulfur": used in chemical nomenclature to indicate the replacement of part or all of the oxygen atoms in a compound by sulfur; often used to designate sulfur analogues of oxygen compounds. Also, *esp. before a vowel,* **thi-.** [comb. form repr. Gk *theîon*]

thi′oace′tic ac′id, *Chem.* a fuming liquid, CH_3COSH, used as a reagent and tear gas. Also, **thiacetic acid.** —**thi·o·a·ce·tic** (thī′ō ə sē′tik, -set′ik), *adj.*

thi′o ac′id, *Chem.* an acid in which part or all of the oxygen has been replaced by sulfur.

thi·o·al·de·hyde (thī′ō al′də hīd′), *n. Chem.* any of a class of compounds formed by the action of hydrogen sulfide on aldehydes and regarded as aldehydes with the oxygen replaced by sulfur.

thi′o·al′lyl e′ther (thī′ō al′il). See **allyl sulfide.**

thi·o·car·bam·ide (thī′ō kär bam′īd, -id), *n. Chem.* thiourea.

thi·o·cy·a·nate (thī′ō sī′ə nāt′), *n. Chem.* a salt or ester of thiocyanic acid, as sodium thiocyanate, NaSCN.

thi′ocyan′ic ac′id, *Chem.* an unstable acid, HSCN, known chiefly in the form of its salts. —**thi·o·cy·an·ic** (thī′ō sī an′ik), *adj.*

thi·o·cy·a·no (thī′ō sī′ə nō′), *adj. Chem.* containing the thiocyano group. [THIO- + CYANO-³]

thiocy′ano group′, *Chem.* the univalent group, –SCN, derived from thiocyanic acid. Also called **thiocy′ano rad′ical.**

thi·ol (thī′ōl, -ôl, -ol), *Chem.* —*n.* **1.** mercaptan. —*adj.* **2.** mercapto. [THI- + -OL¹]

thi·on·ic (thī on′ik), *adj. Chem.* of or pertaining to sulfur. [< Gk *theîon* sulfur + -IC]

thion′ic ac′id, *Chem.* any of the five acids of sulfur of the type $H_2S_nO_6$, where *n* is a number from two to six.

thi·o·nin (thī′ə nin), *n. Chem.* a thiazine derivative, used as a violet dye, as in staining microscopic objects. [< Gk *theîon* sulfur + -IN²]

thi·o·nyl (thī′ə nil), *adj. Chem.* sulfinyl. [< Gk *theîon* sulfur + -YL]

thi·o·pen·tal (thī′ə pen′tᵊl), *n. Pharm.* a barbiturate, $C_{11}H_{18}N_2O_2S$, usually administered intravenously: used chiefly as an anesthetic in surgery and as a truth serum. Also called **thi′open′tal so′dium.** [THIO- + PENT- + -AL³]

thi·o·pen·tone (thī′ə pen′tōn), *n. Pharm., Brit.* thiopental. Also called **thi′open′tone so′dium.**

thi·o·phene (thī′ə fēn′), *n. Chem.* a liquid, C_4H_4S, used chiefly as a solvent and in organic synthesis. Also, **thi·o·phen** (thī′ə fen′). [THIO- + *-phene,* final var. of PHEN-]

thi·o·sul·fate (thī′ō sul′fāt), *n. Chem.* a salt or ester of thiosulfuric acid.

thi′osulfu′ric ac′id, *Chem.* an acid, $H_2S_2O_3$, that may be regarded as sulfuric acid with one oxygen atom replaced by one sulfur atom. —**thi·o·sul·fu·ric** (thī′ō sul fyo͝or′ik), *adj.*

thi·o·u·ra·cil (thī′ō yo͝or′ə sil), *n. Pharm.* a bitter powder, $C_4H_4N_2OS$, used chiefly in treating hyperthyroidism by reducing the activity of the thyroid gland. [THIO- + *uracil* (UR-¹ + AC(ETIC) + -IL)]

thi·o·u·re·a (thī′ō yo͞o rē′ə, -yo͝or′ē ə), *n. Chem.* a solid, $CS(NH_2)_2$, used chiefly in photography, in organic synthesis, and the vulcanization of rubber. Also called **thiocarbamide.** [< NL]

third (thûrd), *adj.* **1.** next after the second; being the ordinal number for three. **2.** being one of three equal parts. **3.** *Auto.* pertaining to the third highest gear transmission ratio: *third gear.* **4.** rated, graded, or ranked one level below the second: *He's third engineer on the ship.* —*n.* **5.** a third part, esp. of one (⅓). **6.** the third member of a series. **7.** *Auto.* third gear. **8.** a person or thing next after second in rank, precedence, order. **9.** Usually, **thirds.** *Law.* **a.** the third part of the personal property of a deceased husband, which under certain circumstances goes absolutely to the widow. **b.** a widow's dower. **10.** *Music.* **a.** a tone on the third degree from a given tone (counted as the first). **b.** the interval between such tones. **c.** the harmonic combination of such tones. **11.** *Baseball.* See **third base.** —*adv.* **12.** in the third place; thirdly. [ME *thirde,* OE (north) *thirda,* var. of *thridda;* c. D *derde,* G *dritte,* Goth *thridja,* Icel *thrithi,* Gk *trítos,* L *tertius,* Skt *tṛtīya.* See THREE]

third′ base′, *Baseball.* **1.** the third in counterclockwise order of the bases from home plate. **2.** the playing position of the fielder covering the area of the infield near this base. —**third′ base′man.**

third′ class′, **1.** the class, grade, or rank immediately below the second. **2.** the least costly class of accommodations on trains, in hotels, etc. Cf. **tourist class. 3.** (in the U.S. postal system) the class of mail consisting of merchandise not exceeding 16 ounces and of written or printed material, as books, manuscripts, circulars, or the like, not sealed against postal inspection.

third-class (thûrd′klas′, -kläs′), *adj.* **1.** of the third class. **2.** of poor or less desirable quality; inferior. —*adv.* **3.** by third-class accommodations: *to travel third-class.*

third′ degree′, **1.** *Chiefly U.S.* intensive questioning or rough treatment, esp. by the police, in order to get information or a confession. **2.** the degree of master mason in Freemasonry.

third-de·gree (thûrd′də grē′), *v.,* **-greed, -gree·ing,** *adj.* —*v.t.* **1.** to subject to the third degree. —*adj.* **2.** of or pertaining to the third degree.

third′-degree burn′, *Pathol.* See under **burn¹** (def. 31).

third′ dimen′sion, **1.** the additional dimension by which a solid object is distinguished from a planar projection of itself or from any planar object. **2.** something that heightens the reality, vividness, or significance of a factual account, sequence of happenings, etc.

third′ estate′, the third of the three estates or political orders: the commons in France or England.

third′ eye′lid. See **nictitating membrane.**

third′ fin′ger, the finger next to the little finger; ring finger.

third′ force′, a political faction or party, etc., occupying an intermediate position between two other forces.

third·hand (*adj.* thûrd′hand′; *adv.* thûrd′hand′), *adj.* **1.** previously used or owned by two successive people. **2.** (loosely) secondhand, esp. in poor condition. **3.** obtained through two intermediates successively; twice removed from the original source. —*adv.* **4.** after two other users or owners: *He bought the guitar thirdhand.* **5.** indirectly.

Third′ Interna′tional, an international organization (1919–43), founded in Moscow, uniting Communist groups of various countries and advocating the spread of Communism by violent revolution. Also called **Communist International.** Cf. **international** (def. 5).

third′ law′ of mo′tion. See under **law of motion.**

third′ law′ of thermodynam′ics. See under **law of thermodynamics.**

third·ly (thûrd′lē), *adv.* in the third place; third.

third′ man′, **1.** *Cricket.* **a.** the position of a fielder on the off side between slip and point. **b.** the fielder occupying this position. **2.** *Lacrosse.* **a.** the position of a player who is first in the line of defense between center and goal. **b.** the player occupying this position.

third′ mar′ket, the trading of listed securities off the stock-exchange floor, typically in the over-the-counter market, as through nonmember firms of the exchanges for cut-rate commissions.

third′ mate′, the officer of a merchant vessel next in command beneath the second mate. Also called **third′ of′ficer.**

third′ par′ty, **1.** any party to an incident, case, quarrel, etc., who is incidentally involved. **2.** (in a two-party system) a political party formed as a dissenting or independent group from members of one or both of the two major parties.

third′ par′ty proce′dure, *Law.* impleader.

third′ per′son, *Gram.* **1.** the person that is used by the speaker of an utterance in referring to anything or to anyone other than himself or the one or ones to whom he is speaking. **2.** a linguistic form or the group of linguistic forms referring to this grammatical person, as any of certain verb forms or pronouns: *"He goes" contains a pronoun and a verb form in the third person.* **3.** in or referring to such a grammatical person or linguistic form: *"He," "she," "it," and "they" are third person pronouns, singular and plural, nominative case.*

third′ rail′, a supplementary rail, laid beside the two regular rails of the track of an electric railroad to carry the electric current. Cf. **shoe** (def. 7).

third-rate (thûrd′rāt′), *adj.* **1.** of the third rate or class. **2.** inferior: *a third-rate performance.* —**third′-rat′er,** *n*

Third′ Reich′, Germany during the Nazi regime 1933-45.

Third′ Repub′lic, the republic in France 1870–1940.

Third′ World′, (*sometimes l.c.*) the group of developing nations, esp. of Asia and Africa, that do not align themselves with, or are not committed to, the policies of either the United States or the Soviet Union.

thirl (thûrl), *v.t., v.i. Brit. Dial.* **1.** to pierce. **2.** to thrill. [ME *thirle,* OE *thyr(e)lian* < *thyrel* hole. See NOSTRIL]

thirst (thûrst), *n.* **1.** a sensation of dryness in the mouth and throat caused by need of liquid. **2.** the physical condition resulting from this need. **3.** a strong or eager desire; craving: *a thirst for knowledge.* —*v.i.* **4.** to feel thirst; be thirsty. **5.** to have a strong desire. [ME *thirst(en)* (v.), OE *thyrstan* < *thurst* (n.); c. D *dorst,* G *Durst,* Icel *thorsti,* Goth *thaurstei;* modern *thirst* (n.) has its *-i-* from v. or adj.; see THIRSTY, TOAST] —**thirst′er,** *n.* —**Syn. 3.** eagerness, yearning, hunger, appetite.

thirst·y (thûr′stē), *adj.,* **thirst·i·er, thirst·i·est. 1.** feeling or having thirst; craving liquid. **2.** needing moisture, as soil. **3.** eagerly desirous; eager. **4.** *Informal.* causing thirst: *Digging is thirsty work.* [ME *thirsti,* OE *thyrstig;* akin to G *durstig,* Skt *tṛṣita*] —**thirst′i·ly,** *adv.* —**thirst′i·ness,** *n.*

thir·teen (thûr′tēn′), *n.* **1.** a cardinal number, 10 plus 3. **2.** a symbol for this number, as 13 or XIII. **3.** a set of this many persons or things. —*adj.* **4.** amounting to 13 in number. [ME *thrittene,* OE *thrēotēne;* c. D *dertien,* G *dreizehn,* Icel *threttān.* See THREE, -TEEN]

thir·teenth (thûr′tēnth′), *adj.* **1.** next after the twelfth; being the ordinal number for 13. **2.** being one of 13 equal parts. —*n.* **3.** a thirteenth part, esp. of one (¹/₁₃). **4.** the thirteenth member of a series. [THIRTEEN + -TH²; r. ME *thrittenthe* (see THREE, TENTH), OE *thrytēotha* (see TITHE)]

thir·ti·eth (thûr′tē ith), *adj.* **1.** next after the twenty-ninth; being the ordinal number for 30. **2.** being one of 30 equal parts. —*n.* **3.** a thirtieth part, esp. of one (¹/₃₀). **4.** the thirtieth member of a series. [THIRTY + -TH²; r. ME *thrittythe,* OE *thrītegtha*]

thir·ty (thûr′tē), *n., pl.* **-ties,** *adj.* —*n.* **1.** a cardinal number, 10 times 3. **2.** a symbol for this number, as 30 or XXX. **3.** a set of this many persons or things. **4. thirties,** the numbers, years, degrees, or the like, between 30 and 39, as in referring to numbered streets, indicating the years of a lifetime or of a century, or degrees of temperature. —*adj.* **5.** amounting to 30 in number. [ME *thritty,* OE *thrītig* = *thrī* THREE + *-tig* -TY¹; c. D *dertig,* G *dreissig,* Icel *thrjātīu*]

.38 (thûr′tē āt), *n., pl.* **.38s, .38′s. 1.** a pistol or revolver using a cartridge approx. .38 in. in diameter. **2.** the cartridge itself.

.30-′06 (thûr′tē ō′siks′), *n.* **1.** a .30 caliber bolt-action rifle, developed in 1903 and improved in 1906, originally for military use, now used for hunting. **2.** a rifle cartridge having a diam. of .30 inch, used with this rifle. Also, **.30/′06.**

thir·ty·pen·ny (thûr′tē pen′ē), *adj.* noting a nail 4½ inches long. *Symbol:* 30d

thir′ty-sec′ond note′ (thûr′tē sek′ənd), *Music.* a note having 1/32 of the time value of a whole note; demisemiquaver. See illus. at **note.**

thir′ty-sec′ond rest′, *Music.* a rest equal in value to a thirty-second note. See illus. at **rest**[1].

.30–30 (thûr′tē thûr′tē), *n.* **1.** a rifle using a cartridge approx. .30 in. in diameter, originally having a powder charge of 30 grains but now of various charges. **2.** the cartridge itself.

thir·ty-two·mo (thûr′tē to͞o′mō), *n., pl.* **-mos,** for 2, *adj.* —*n.* **1.** a book size of about 3¼ × 5½ inches, determined by printing on sheets folded to form 32 leaves or 64 pages. *Abbr.:* 32mo, 32° **2.** a book of this size. —*adj.* **3.** printed, folded, or bound as a thirty-twomo. Also, **thir′ty-two′mo.**

Thir′ty Years′′ War′, the war (1618–48), fought chiefly in central Europe, from which France emerged as the most powerful nation on the Continent.

this (t͟his), *pron. and adj., pl.* **these** (t͟hēz), *adv.* —*pron.* **1.** (used to indicate a person, thing, idea, state, event, time, remark, etc., as present, near, just mentioned or pointed out, supposed to be understood, or by way of emphasis): *This is my hat.* **2.** (used to indicate one of two or more persons, things, etc., already mentioned, referring to the one nearer in place, time, or thought; opposed to *that*): *This is Liza and that is Amy.* **3.** (used to indicate one of two or more persons, things, etc., already mentioned, implying a contrast or contradistinction; opposed to *that*): *I'd take that instead of this.* **4.** what is about to follow: *Now hear this! Watch this!* —*adj.* **5.** (used to indicate a person, place, thing, or degree as present, near, just indicated or mentioned, or as well-known or characteristic): *These people are my friends. This problem has worried me for a long time.* **6.** (used to indicate the nearer in time, place, or thought of two persons, things, etc., already mentioned; opposed to *that.*) **7.** (used in place of an indefinite article for emphasis): *I was walking down the street when I heard this explosion.* **8.** (used to imply mere contradistinction; opposed to *that.*) —*adv.* **9.** (used with adjectives and adverbs of quantity or extent) to the extent or degree indicated: *this far; this softly.* [ME, OE; c. G *dies,* Icel *thissi*]

Thistle, *Onopordum Acanthium* (Height to 9 ft.)

This·be (thiz′bē), *n. Class. Myth.* See **Pyramus and Thisbe.**

this·tle (this′əl), *n.* **1.** any of various prickly, composite plants having showy, purple flower heads, esp. of the genus *Cirsium,* as an herb, *C. lanceolatum,* and the Scottish thistle, *Onopordum Acanthium,* the national emblem of Scotland. **2.** any of various other prickly plants. [ME, OE *thistel;* c. D *distel,* G *Distel,* Icel *thistill*] —**this·tly** (this′lē, -ə lē), *adj.*

this·tle·down (this′əl doun′), *n.* the mature, silky pappus of a thistle.

thith·er (thit͟h′ər, t͟hit͟h′-), *adv.* **1.** Also, **thith·er·ward** (thit͟h′ər wərd, t͟hit͟h′-), **thith′er·wards.** to or toward that place or point; there. —*adj.* **2.** on the farther or other side, or in the direction away from the person speaking; farther; more remote. [late ME, var. of ME, OE *thider,* alter. of OE *thæder* (*-i-* from *hider* HITHER); akin to Icel *thathra* there, Goth *thathro* thence, Skt *tātra* there, thither]

thith·er·to (thit͟h′ər to͞o′, t͟hit͟h′-, thit͟h′ər to͞o′, t͟hit͟h′-), *adv. Rare.* up to that time; until then. [late ME *thidir to*]

tho (t͟hō), *conj., adv. Informal.* though. Also, **tho′.**

Thole[1]

thole[1] (thōl), *n.* a pin, sometimes one of a pair, inserted into a gunwale to provide a fulcrum for an oar. Also called **thole-pin** (thōl′pin′). [ME *tholle,* OE *tholl;* c. LG *dolle,* Icel *thollr;* akin to Icel *thöll* young fir tree]

thole[2] (thōl), *v.t.,* **tholed, thol·ing.** *Chiefly Scot.* to suffer; bear; endure. [ME; OE *thol(ian);* c. Icel *thola,* Goth *thulan;* akin to L *tolerāre,* Gk *tlênai* to bear, endure]

tho·los (thō′los), *n., pl.* **-loi** (-loi). (in classical architecture) **1.** a circular building. **2.** a circular subterranean tomb, lined with masonry. [< Gk: lit., rotunda]

Thom·as (tom′əs), *n.* **1.** an apostle who demanded proof of Christ's Resurrection. John 20:24–29. **2. Dyl·an (Mar·lais)** (dil′ən mär′lā), 1914–53, Welsh poet and short-story writer. **3. George Henry,** 1816–70, Union general in the U.S. Civil War. **4. Norman (Mat·toon)** (mə to͞on′), 1884–1968, U.S. socialist leader and political writer. **5. Seth,** 1785–1859, U.S. clock designer and manufacturer.

Thom·as à Beck·et (tom′əs ə bek′it), **Saint.** See **Becket, Saint Thomas à.**

Thom·as à Kem·pis (tom′əs ə kem′pis). See **Kempis, Thomas à.**

Thom′as Aqui′nas (tom′əs), **Saint.** See **Aquinas, Saint Thomas.**

Thom·as of Er·cel·doune (tom′əs əv ûr′səl do͞on′), ("*Thomas the Rhymer*") c1220–97?, Scottish poet.

Thom·as of Wood·stock (tom′əs əv wo͝od′stok′), **Duke of Gloucester,** 1355–97, English prince (son of Edward III).

Tho·mism (tō′miz əm, thō′-), *n.* the theological and philosophical system of Thomas Aquinas, the basis of 13th-century scholasticism. —**Tho′mist,** *n.; adj.* —**Tho·mis′tic,** *adj.*

Thomp·son (tomp′sən, tom′-), *n.* **1. Benjamin, Count Rumford,** 1753–1814, English physicist and diplomat, born in the U.S. **2. Francis,** 1859–1907, English poet.

Thomp′son seed′less, **1.** a yellow, seedless variety of grape used in producing raisins. **2.** the vine bearing this fruit, grown in California. Also called **Thomp′son seed′less grape′.** [named after W. B. *Thompson* (1869–1930), American horticulturist]

Thomp′son submachine′ gun′, a portable, .45-caliber, automatic weapon, designed to be fired from the shoulder or hip. Also called **Tommy gun.** [named after J. T. *Thompson* (1860–1940), American army officer who aided in its invention]

Thom·son (tom′sən), *n.* **1. James,** 1700–48, English poet, born in Scotland. **2. James** (pen name: *B.V.*) ("*Poet of Despair*"), 1834–82, Scottish poet. **3. Sir Joseph John,** 1856–1940, English physicist: Nobel prize 1906. **4. Virgil,** born 1896, U.S. composer and music critic. **5. Sir William.** See **Kelvin, 1st Baron.**

thong (thông, thong), *n.* **1.** a narrow strip of hide or leather used as a fastening or as the lash of a whip. **2.** a similar strip of some other material, as for fastening sandals. [ME; OE *thwong;* akin to Icel *thvengr* strap, *thvinga* to compel]

thong′ leath′er, whang (def. 3b).

Thor (thôr), *n.* **1.** *Scand. Myth.* the god of thunder, rain, and farming, represented as riding a chariot drawn by goats and wielding the hammer Miölnir. **2.** *U.S.* a surface-to-surface intermediate range ballistic missile. [OE *Thōr* < WScand; cf. Icel *Thōrr,* c. ODan *Thūr,* lit., THUNDER]

thorac-, var. of **thoraco-** before a vowel: *thoracic.*

tho·rac·ic (thō ras′ik, thô-), *adj.* of or pertaining to the thorax. Also, **tho·ra·cal** (thōr′ə kəl, thôr′-). [< ML *thōrācic(us)* < Gk *thōrākikós*]

thorac′ic duct′, *Anat.* the main trunk of the lymphatic system, passing along the spinal column in the thoracic cavity and conveying a large amount of lymph and chyle into the venous circulation.

thoraco-, a combining form of **thorax:** *thoracoplasty.* Also, *esp. before a vowel,* **thorac-.** [comb. form repr. Gk *thōrāk-* (s. of *thōrāx*) chest + -o-]

tho·ra·cop·a·gus (thōr′ə kop′ə gəs, thôr′-), *n. Pathol.* a fetal monster consisting of twins joined at the thorax. [< NL < THORACO- + Gk *pág(os)* fixation + L *-us* n. suffix]

tho·ra·co·plas·ty (thōr′ə kō plas′tē, thôr′-), *n., pl.* **-ties.** *Surg.* the operation removing selected portions of the bony chest wall or ribs to compress part of the underlying lung or an abnormal pleural space, usually in the treatment of tuberculosis.

tho·ra·cot·o·my (thōr′ə kot′ə mē, thôr′-), *n., pl.* **-mies.** *Surg.* incision into the chest wall.

tho·rax (thōr′aks, thôr′-), *n., pl.* **tho·rax·es, tho·ra·ces** (thōr′ə sēz′, thôr′-). **1.** the part of the trunk in man and higher vertebrates between the neck and the abdomen, containing the cavity, enclosed by the ribs, sternum, and certain vertebrae, in which the heart, lungs, etc., are situated; chest. **2.** a corresponding part in other animals. **3.** (in insects) the portion of the body between the head and the abdomen. [late ME < L < Gk *thōrāx* breastplate, trunk, thorax]

Tho·ra·zine (thōr′ə zēn′, thôr′-), *n. Pharm., Trademark.* chlorpromazine.

Tho·reau (thōr′ō, thôr′ō, thə rō′, thə rō′), *n.* **Henry David,** 1817–62, U.S. naturalist and author.

tho·ri·a (thōr′ē ə, thôr′-), *n. Chem.* a white powder, ThO_2, used chiefly in incandescent mantles, as the Welsbach gas mantle. [THORI(UM) + *-a,* modeled on *magnesia*]

tho·ri·a·nite (thōr′ē ə nīt′, thôr′-), *n.* a rare mineral, mainly thoria, ThO_2, but also containing uranium, cerium, and other rare-earth metals, notable for its radioactivity: a minor source of thorium. [*thorian* (THORIA + -AN) + -ITE[1]]

tho·rite (thōr′īt, thôr′-), *n.* a rare mineral, thorium silicate, $ThSiO_4$. [*thor-* (as in THORIA, THORIUM) + -ITE[1], modeled on Sw *thorit*]

tho·ri·um (thōr′ē əm, thôr′-), *n. Chem.* a grayish-white, lustrous, somewhat ductile and malleable, radioactive, metallic element, used as a source of nuclear energy, in sun-lamp and vacuum-tube filament coatings, and in alloys. *Symbol:* Th; *at. wt.:* 232.038; *sp. gr.:* 11.2. Cf. **thoria.** [THOR + -IUM]

tho′rium se′ries, *Chem.* the radioactive series that starts with thorium and ends with a stable isotope of lead of mass number 208.

thorn (thôrn), *n.* **1.** a sharp excrescence on a plant, esp. a sharp-pointed, aborted branch; spine; prickle. **2.** any of various thorny shrubs or trees, esp. the hawthorns of the genus *Crataegus.* **3.** the wood of any of these trees. **4.** the runic character þ for *th* as in *thin,* borrowed into the Latin alphabet as used for Old English and Icelandic. **5. thorn in one's flesh or side,** a source of continual irritation or suffering. —*v.t.* **6.** to prick with a thorn. [ME, OE; c. D *doorn,* G *Dorn,* Icel *thorn,* Goth *thaurnus*] —**thorn′less,** *adj.* —**thorn′less·ness,** *n.* —**thorn′like′,** *adj.*

Thorn (tôʀn), *n.* German name of **Torun.**

thorn′ ap′ple (thôrn), **1.** any poisonous, solanaceous plant of the genus *Datura,* the species of which bear capsules covered with prickly spines, esp. the jimson weed, *D. Stramonium.* **2.** the fruit of certain hawthorns of the genus *Crataegus.*

thorn·back (thôrn′bak′), *n.* **1.** a European skate, *Raja clavata,* with short spines on the back and tail. **2.** a California ray, *Platyrhinoidis triseriatus,* belonging to the guitarfish group.

Thorn·dike (thôrn′dīk′), *n.* **Edward Lee,** 1874–1949, U.S. psychologist and lexicographer.

Thorn·ton (thôrn′tən, -tᵊn), *n.* **William,** 1759–1828, U.S. architect, born in the British Virgin Islands.

thorn·y (thôr′nē), *adj.,* **thorn·i·er, thorn·i·est. 1.** abounding in or characterized by thorns; spiny; prickly. **2.** thornlike. **3.** overgrown with thorns or brambles. **4.** painful; vexatious: *a thorny predicament.* **5.** full of difficulties, complexities, or controversial points: *a thorny question.* [ME; OE *thornig*] —**thorn′i·ly,** *adv.* —**thorn′i·ness,** *n.*

thor·o (thûr′ō, thur′ō), *adj. Informal.* thorough.

thor·ough (thûr′ō, thur′ō), *adj.* **1.** executed without negligence or omissions: *a thorough search.* **2.** accustomed to neglecting or omitting nothing: *a thorough worker.* **3.** complete or perfect in all respects: *thorough enjoyment.* **4.** *Archaic.* extending or passing through. —*adv., prep.* **5.** *Archaic.* through. [ME; OE *thuruh,* var. of *thurh* THROUGH] —**thor′ough·ly,** *adv.* —**thor′ough·ness,** *n.* —**Syn. 1.** unqualified, total. —**Ant. 1.** partial.

thor′ough bass′ (bās), *Music.* **1.** a bass part written out in full throughout an entire piece and accompanied by figures that indicate the successive chords of the harmony. **2.** the method of indicating harmonies by such figures.

thor′ough brace′, either of two strong braces or bands of leather supporting the body of a coach or other vehicle and connecting the front and back springs.
thor·ough·bred (thûr′ō bred′, -ə bred′, thur′-), *adj.* **1.** of pure or unmixed breed, stock, or race, as a horse or other animal; bred from the purest and best blood. **2.** (*sometimes cap.*) of or pertaining to the Thoroughbred breed of horses. **3.** (of a person) having good breeding or education. **—*n.* 4.** (*cap.*) any of a breed of horses, to which all race horses belong, originally developed in England by crossing Arabian stallions with European mares. **5.** a thoroughbred animal. **6.** a well-bred or well-educated person.
thor·ough·fare (thûr′ō fâr′, -ə fâr′, thur′-), *n.* **1.** a road, street, or the like, that leads at each end into another street. **2.** a major road or highway. **3.** a passage or way through: *no thoroughfare.* **4.** a strait, river, or the like, affording passage. [ME *thurghfare*]
thor·ough·go·ing (thûr′ō gō′ing, -ə gō′-, thur′-), *adj.* **1.** doing things thoroughly. **2.** carried out to the full extent; thorough. **3.** complete; unqualified: *a thoroughgoing knave.* **—thor′ough·go′ing·ness,** *n.*
thor·ough·paced (thûr′ō pāst′, -ə pāst′, thur′-), *adj.* **1.** trained to go through all the possible paces, as a horse. **2.** thoroughgoing; complete or perfect.
thor·ough·pin (thûr′ō pin′, -ə pin′, thur′-), *n.* *Vet. Pathol.* an abnormal swelling just above the hock of a horse, usually appearing on both sides of the leg and sometimes causing lameness.
thor·ough·wort (thûr′ō wûrt′, -ə wûrt′, thur′-), *n.* boneset.
thorp (thôrp), *n.* *Archaic.* a hamlet; village. Also, **thorpe.** [ME, OE; c. G *Dorf,* Icel *thorp* village, Goth *thaurp* field]
Thorpe (thôrp), *n.* **James Francis** (“*Jim*”), 1888–1953, U.S. athlete.
Thor·vald·sen (tōōr′väl′sən), *n.* **Al·bert Ber·tal** (äl′bert bar′təl), 1770–1844, Danish sculptor. Also, **Thor·wald·sen** (tōōr′väl′sən).
those (thōz), *pron., adj.* pl. of **that.** [late ME *those, thoos,* pl. of THAT, earlier ME *thos,* OE *thās,* pl. of THIS]
Thoth (thōth, tōt), *n.* *Egyptian Religion.* the god of wisdom, learning, and magic, inventor of numbers and letters, and scribe of all the gods, represented as a man with the head either of an ibis or of a baboon: identified by the Greeks with Hermes.

Thoth

thou[1] (thou), *pron., sing., nom.* **thou;** *poss.* **thy** or **thine;** *obj.* **thee;** *pl., nom.* **you** or **ye;** *poss.* **your** or **yours;** *obj.* **you** or **ye;** *v.* **—*pron.* 1.** *Archaic* (*except in some elevated or ecclesiastical prose*), *Poetic,* or *Brit. Dial.* the personal pronoun of the second person singular in the nominative case (used to denote the person or thing addressed): *Thou shalt not kill.* **—*v.t.* 2.** to address as “thou.” **—*v.i.* 3.** to use “thou” in discourse. [ME; OE *thū;* c. G, MD *du,* Icel *thū,* Goth *thu,* Ir *tu,* Welsh, Cornish *ti,* L *tū,* Doric Gk *tý,* Lith *tu,* OSlav *ty;* akin to Skt *tvam*]
thou[2] (thou), *n., pl.* **thous,** (*as after a numeral*) **thou.** *Slang.* one thousand dollars, pounds sterling, etc. [by shortening]
though (thō), *conj.* **1.** (used in introducing a subordinate clause, which is often marked by ellipsis) notwithstanding that; in spite of the fact that: *Though he tried very hard, he failed the course.* **2.** even if; granting that (often prec. by *even*). **3. as though,** as if: *It seems as though the place is deserted.* **—*adv.* 4.** for all that; however. [ME, var. of *thoh* < Scand; cf. Icel *thō* < proto-Norse **thauh,* c. Goth *thauh* OE *thēah,* G *doch*]
—Usage. Among some purists there is a traditional objection to the use of THOUGH in place of ALTHOUGH as a conjunction. However, the latter (earlier *all though*) was originally an emphatic form of the former and there is nothing in modern English usage to justify such a distinction.
thought[1] (thôt), *n.* **1.** the product of mental activity; that which one thinks: *a body of thought.* **2.** a single act or product of thinking; idea or notion: *to collect one's thoughts.* **3.** the act or process of thinking; mental activity: *Thought as well as action wearies us.* **4.** the capacity or faculty of thinking, reasoning, imagining, etc. **5.** a consideration or reflection: *Thought of death terrified him.* **6.** meditation, contemplation, or recollection: *deep in thought.* **7.** intention, design, or purpose, esp. a half-formed or imperfect intention: *We had some thought of going to Alaska.* **8.** anticipation or expectation: *I had no thought of seeing you here.* **9.** consideration, attention, care, or regard: *She took no thought of her appearance.* **10.** a judgment, opinion, or belief: *According to his thought, all violence is evil.* **11.** the intellectual activity or the ideas, opinions, etc., characteristic of a particular place, class, or time: *Greek thought.* **12.** *Rare.* a very small amount; a touch; bit; trifle: *The steak is a thought underdone.* [ME *thoght* OE (*ge*)*thōht;* c. D *gedachte;* akin to THANK, THINK[1]] **—Syn. 2.** concept. See **idea. 3.** reflection, cogitation.
thought[2] (thôt), *v.* pt. and pp. of **think.**
thought·ful (thôt′fəl), *adj.* **1.** occupied with or given to thought; contemplative; meditative; reflective: *in a thoughtful mood.* **2.** characterized by or manifesting careful thought: *a thoughtful essay.* **3.** careful, heedful, or mindful: *to be thoughtful of one's safety.* **4.** showing consideration for others; considerate. [ME] **—thought′ful·ly,** *adv.* **—thought′ful·ness,** *n.*
—Syn. 1. pensive. **3.** regardful, discreet, prudent, wary, circumspect. **4.** attentive, solicitous. THOUGHTFUL, CONSIDERATE mean taking thought for the comfort and the good of others. THOUGHTFUL implies providing little attentions, offering services, or in some way looking out for the comfort or welfare of others: *It was thoughtful of you to send the flowers.* CONSIDERATE implies sparing others annoyance or discomfort and being careful not to hurt their feelings: *not considerate, only polite.*
thought·less (thôt′lis), *adj.* **1.** not thinking enough; careless or heedless. **2.** characterized by or showing lack of thought. **3.** lacking in consideration for others; inconsiderate; tactless. **4.** devoid of or lacking capacity for thought. **—thought′less·ly,** *adv.* **—thought′less·ness,** *n.* **—Syn. 1.** negligent, neglectful, reckless. **3.** inattentive, remiss.
thought-out (thôt′out′), *adj.* produced by or showing the results of much thought: *a carefully thought-out argument.*
thou·sand (thou′zənd), *n., pl.* **-sands,** (*as after a numeral*) **-sand,** *adj.* **—*n.* 1.** a cardinal number, 10 times 100. **2.** a symbol for this number, as 1000 or M. **3. thousands,** the numbers between 1000 and 999,999, as in referring to an amount of money. **4.** Also called **thou′sand's place′. a.** (in a mixed number) the position of the fourth digit to the left of the decimal point. **b.** (in a whole number) the position of the fourth digit from the right. **—*adj.* 5.** amounting to 1000 in number. [ME; OE *thūsend;* c. D *duizend,* OHG *dūsunt,* Icel *thūsund,* Goth *thūsindi*]
thou·sand·fold (*adj.* thou′zənd fōld′; *adv.* thou′zənd-fōld′), *adj.* **1.** having a thousand elements or parts. **2.** a thousand times as great or as much. **—*adv.* 3.** Also, **thou′-sand·fold′ly.** in a thousandfold manner or measure. [ME *thowsand folde,* OE *thūsendfealde*]
Thou′sand Is′land dress′ing, a mayonnaise seasoned with pickles, pimientos, sweet peppers, etc.
Thou′sand Is′lands, a group of about 1500 islands in S Canada and the N United States, in the St. Lawrence River at the outlet of Lake Ontario: summer resorts.
Thou′sand Oaks′, a city in S California. 35,873 (1970).
thou·sandth (thou′zəndth, -zəntth), *adj.* **1.** last in order of a series of a thousand. **2.** being one of a thousand equal parts. **—*n.* 3.** a thousandth part, esp. of one (1/1000). **4.** the thousandth member of a series. **5.** Also, **thou′sandth's place′.** (in decimal notation) the position of the third digit to the right of the decimal point.
thow·less (thou′lis), *adj.* *Scot.* listless; without energy or spirit. Also, **thieveless.** [ME *thowles* (Scot), var. of THEWLESS]
Thrace (thrās), *n.* **1.** an ancient region of varying extent in the E part of the Balkan Peninsula: later a Roman province; now in Bulgaria, Turkey, and Greece. **2.** a modern region corresponding to the S part of the Roman province: now divided between Greece (**Western Thrace**) and Turkey (**Eastern Thrace**).
Thra·cian (thrā′shən), *adj.* **1.** of or pertaining to Thrace or its inhabitants. **—*n.* 2.** a native or inhabitant of Thrace. **3.** an Indo-European language that was the language of ancient Thrace. [< L *Thrāci*(*us*) of Thrace (< Gk *Thrāikios* = *Thrāik*(*ē*) THRACE + *-ios* adj. suffix) + -AN]
Thra·co-Phryg·i·an (thrā′kō frij′ē ən), *n.* **1.** a hypothetical branch of Indo-European implying a special genetic affinity between the meagerly attested Thracian and Phrygian languages. **—*adj.* 2.** of, belonging to, or pertaining to Thraco-Phrygian. [*Thraco-* < Gk *Thrāiko-,* comb. form of *Thrāikē* Thrace; see PHRYGIAN]
thrall (thrôl), *n.* **1.** a person who is in bondage; bondman; slave. **2.** a person who is completely dominated by some power over his mind. **3.** slavery; thralldom. **—*v.t.* 4.** *Archaic.* to put or hold in thralldom; enslave. [ME; OE *thræl* < Scand; cf. Icel *thræll* slave]
thrall·dom (thrôl′dəm), *n.* the state of being a thrall; bondage; slavery; servitude. Also, **thral′dom.** [ME *thraldom*]
thrash (thrash), *v.t.* **1.** to beat soundly in punishment; flog. **2.** to defeat thoroughly. **3.** thresh. **—*v.i.* 4.** to toss or plunge about wildly or violently. **5.** thresh. **6. thrash out** or **over.** See **thresh** (def. 5). **—*n.* 7.** the act or an instance of thrashing; beating; blow. **8.** thresh. **9.** *Swimming.* the upward and downward movement of the legs, as in the crawl. [var. of THRESH] **—Syn. 1.** maul, drub. See **beat.**
thrash·er (thrash′ər), *n.* **1.** a person or thing that thrashes. **2.** any of several long-tailed, thrushlike birds, esp. of the genus *Toxostoma,* related to the mockingbirds. **3.** thresher (def. 3).
thrash·ing (thrash′ing), *n.* **1.** a flogging; whipping. **2.** the act of a person or thing that thrashes. **3.** a pile or quantity of threshed grain or the grain threshed at one time.
Thras·y·bu·lus (thras′ə byōō′ləs), *n.* died c389 B.C., Athenian patriot and general.
thrave (thrāv), *n.* *Chiefly Scot.* **1.** a measure for grain or straw, usually 24 sheaves. **2.** a large number. [late ME < EScand; cf. Sw *thrave,* akin to OE, ME, *threfe* < WScand]
thraw (thrô, thrä), *v.t.* *Scot.* **1.** to twist; distort. **2.** to oppose; thwart; vex. [ME *thrawe,* OE *thrawu* THROE]
thrawn (thrôn, thrän), *adj.* *Scot.* **1.** twisted; crooked; distorted. **2.** contrary; peevish; perverse. [Scot. and dial. var. of THROWN]
thread (thred), *n.* **1.** a fine cord of flax, cotton, or other fibrous material spun out to considerable length, esp. when composed of two or more filaments twisted together. **2.** twisted filaments or fibers of any kind used for sewing. **3.** one of the lengths of yarn forming the warp or weft of a woven fabric. **4.** a filament or fiber of glass or other ductile substance. **5.** *Ropemaking.* **a.** any of a number of fibers twisted into a yarn. **b.** a yarn, esp. as enumerated in describing small stuff. **6.** something having the fineness or slenderness of a filament: *a thread of smoke.* **7.** the helical ridge of a screw. **8.** that which runs through the whole course of something, connecting successive parts: *He lost the thread of the story.* **9. threads,** *Slang.* clothes. **—*v.t.* 10.** to pass the end of a thread through the eye of (a needle). **11.** to fix (beads, pearls, etc.) upon a thread that is passed through; string. **12.** to make (one's way), as among obstacles. **13.** to cut a thread on or in (a bolt, hole, etc.). **14.** to place and arrange thread, yarn, etc., in position on (a sewing machine, loom, textile machine, etc.). **—*v.i.* 15.** to thread one's way, as among obstacles. **16.** to move in a threadlike course; wind or twine. **17.** *Cookery.* (of boiling syrup) to form a fine thread when poured from a spoon. [ME *threed,* OE *thrǣd;* c. D *draad,* Icel *thrathr* thread, G *Draht* wire. See THROW] **—thread′er,** *n.* **—thread′less,** *adj.* **—thread′like′,** *adj.*
thread·bare (thred′bâr′), *adj.* **1.** (of a piece of textile) having the nap worn off so as to lay bare the threads of the warp and woof. **2.** meager, scanty, or poor. **3.** hackneyed; trite. **4.** wearing threadbare clothes. [ME *thredbare*] **—thread′bare′ness,** *n.* **—Syn. 3.** shopworn, stereotyped.
thread·worm (thred′wûrm′), *n.* any of various nematode worms, esp. the pinworm.
thread·y (thred′ē), *adj.,* **thread·i·er, thread·i·est. 1.** consisting of or resembling a thread or threads; fibrous; filamentous. **2.** stringy or viscid, as a liquid. **3.** (of the

pulse) thin and feeble. **4.** (of sound, the voice, etc.) lacking fullness; weak; feeble. —**thread′i·ness,** *n.*

threap (thrēp), *n. Scot. and North Eng.* **1.** an argument; quarrel. **2.** a hostile charge; accusation. [ME *threpe,* OE *thrēapian* to blame] —**threap′er,** *n.*

threat (thret), *n.* **1.** a declaration of an intention or determination to inflict punishment, injury, etc., in retaliation for, or conditionally upon, some action or course; menace: *He confessed under the threat of imprisonment.* **2.** an indication or warning of probable trouble: *the threat of a storm.* —*v.t., v.i.* **3.** *Archaic.* to threaten. [ME *threte,* OE *thrēat* pressure, oppression; c. Icel *thraut* hardship, bitter end; akin to OE *thrēatian* to press, threaten, *thrēotan* to vex, *thrietan* to compel] —**threat′ful,** *adj.* —**threat′ful·ly,** *adv.*

threat·en (thret′ᵊn), *v.t.* **1.** to utter a threat against; menace: *He threatened the boy with a beating.* **2.** to be a menace or source of danger to. **3.** to offer by way of a threat. **4.** to give an ominous indication of: *The clouds threaten rain.* —*v.i.* **5.** to utter or use threats. **6.** to indicate impending evil or mischief. [ME *thretne(n),* OE *thrēatnian,* var. of *thrēatian* to press, threaten] —**threat′en·er,** *n.* —**threat′en·ing·ly,** *adv.* —**Syn. 2.** endanger. **4.** presage, portend, augur, forebode.

three (thrē), *n.* **1.** a cardinal number, 2 plus 1. **2.** a symbol for this number, as 3 or III. **3.** a set of this many persons or things. **4.** a playing card, die face, or half of a domino face with three pips. —*adj.* **5.** amounting to three in number. [ME; OE *thrēo,* var. of *thrīo,* fem., neut. of *thrī(e);* c. D *drie,* G *drei,* Icel *thrīr,* Goth *threis,* Gk *treîs,* L *trēs,* Ir *trī,* Skt *trī, trāyas*]

three-and-a-half·pen·ny (thrē′ənd ə haf′pen′ē, -häf′-), *adj. Carpentry.* noting a shingle nail 1⅜ inches long. *Abbr.:* 3½d

three-bag·ger (thrē′bag′ər), *n. Baseball Slang.* triple (def. 6).

three′-base hit′ (thrē′bās′), *Baseball.* triple (def. 6).

three-col·or (thrē′kul′ər), *adj.* **1.** having or using three colors. **2.** noting or pertaining to a photomechanical process for making reproductions, as of paintings, usually by making three plates, each corresponding to a primary color, and printing superimposed impressions from them in three correspondingly colored inks.

three-cor·nered (thrē′kôr′nərd), *adj.* **1.** having three corners. **2.** pertaining to or involving three persons, parties, or things. [ME *thre cornerid*]

3-D (thrē′dē′), *adj. Informal.* **1.** of, pertaining to, or representing something in three dimensions; three-dimensional: *3-D movies.* —*n.* **2.** a medium for representing things as in three dimensions.

three-deck·er (thrē′dek′ər), *n.* **1.** (formerly) one of a class of sailing warships that carried guns on three decks. **2.** a sandwich made of three slices of bread interlaid with two layers of filling. **3.** something having three layers, levels, or tiers. Also called **triple-decker** (for defs. 2, 3).

three-di·men·sion·al (thrē′di men′shə nᵊl), *adj.* having, or seeming to have, the dimension of depth as well as width and height.

three·fold (thrē′fōld′), *adj.* **1.** comprising three parts, members, or aspects; triple. **2.** three times as great or as much; treble. —*adv.* **3.** in threefold manner or measure; trebly. [ME *threfold,* OE *thrifeald*]

three′-four′ time′ (thrē′fōr′, -fôr′). See **three-quarter time.**

three-gait·ed (thrē′gā′tid), *adj. Manège.* noting a horse trained to walk, trot, and canter, as for pleasure riding and showing. Cf. **five-gaited.**

Three′ Mile′ Is′land, an island in the Susquehanna River, near Middletown, Pennsylvania, SE of Harrisburg: scene of a near-disastrous accident at a nuclear plant in 1979.

three′-mile lim′it (thrē′mīl′), *Internat. Law.* the limit of the marine belt of three miles, which is included within the jurisdiction of the state possessing the coast.

three·pence (thrip′əns, threp′-, thrup′-; thrē′pens′), *n.* **1.** (*construed as sing. or pl.*) *Brit.* a sum of three pennies. **2.** a cupronickel coin of the United Kingdom, a quarter of a shilling. Also, **thrippence, thruppence.**

three·pen·ny (thrip′ə nē, threp′-, thrup′-; thrē′pen′ē), *adj.* **1.** of the amount or value of threepence. **2.** *Carpentry.* **a.** noting a nail 1¼ inches long. **b.** noting a fine nail 1⅛ inches long. *Abbr.:* 3d

three-phase (thrē′fāz′), *adj. Elect.* **1.** noting or pertaining to a circuit, system, or device that is energized by three electromotive forces differing in phase by one third of a cycle, or 120°. **2.** having three phases.

three-piece (thrē′pēs′), *adj.* **1.** *Clothing.* consisting of three matching or harmonious pieces, as an ensemble of coat, skirt, and blouse for a woman or a suit of a jacket, vest, and trousers for a man. **2.** having three parts.

three′-point land′ing (thrē′point′), *Aeron.* an aircraft landing in which the two wheels of the main landing gear and the tail or nose wheel touch the ground simultaneously.

three-quar·ter (thrē′kwôr′tər), *adj.* **1.** consisting of or involving three quarters of a whole or of the usual length. **2.** (of the face) midway between the full-faced view and profile: *a three-quarter view.* Also, **three-quar·ters** (thrē′kwôr′tərz).

three′-quar′ter bind′ing, *Bookbinding.* a binding in which the material used for the back extends farther over the covers than in half binding.

three′-quar′ter nel′son. See under **nelson.**

three′-quar′ter time′, *Music.* the meter of a musical composition having a time signature of ¾ and three quarter notes or their equivalents in each measure. Also called **three-four time, waltz time.**

three′-ring cir′cus (thrē′ring′), **1.** a circus having three adjacent rings in which performances take place simultaneously. **2.** something spectacular, tumultuous, or full of confused action. Also, **three′-ringed′ cir′cus.**

Three′ Riv′ers, a city in S Quebec, in SE Canada, on the St. Lawrence. 53,477 (1961). French, **Trois-Rivières.**

three R's, reading, 'riting, and 'rithmetic, regarded as the fundamentals of education.

three·score (thrē′skōr′, -skôr′), *adj.* being or containing three times twenty; sixty. [ME *thre scoor*]

three·some (thrē′səm), *adj.* **1.** consisting of three; threefold. **2.** performed or played by three persons. —*n.* **3.** a group of three. **4.** *Golf.* a match in which one contestant, playing his own ball, competes against two opponents who play, alternately, with one ball. [ME *thresum*]

three-spot (thrē′spot′), *n.* a playing card, an upward face of a die, or a domino half bearing three pips.

three′ u′nities, the. See under **unity** (def. 8).

three′-way bulb′ (thrē′wā′), a light bulb that can be switched to three successive degrees of illumination.

three-wheel·er (thrē′hwē′lər, -wē′-), *n.* a vehicle equipped with three wheels, as a tricycle or some small, experimental, or early-model cars.

threm·ma·tol·o·gy (threm′ə tol′ə jē), *n. Biol.* the science of breeding or propagating animals and plants under domestication. [< Gk *thremmato-* (comb. form of *thrémma* nursling) + -LOGY]

thre·node (thrē′nōd, thren′ōd), *n.* threnody. [by alter.; see ODE]

thren·o·dy (thren′ə dē), *n., pl.* **-dies.** a poem, speech, or song of lamentation, esp. for the dead; dirge; funeral song. [< Gk *thrēnōidía* = *thrên(os)* dirge + *-ōid(ḗ)* song (see ODE) + *-ia* -Y[3]] —**thre·no·di·al** (thri nō′dē əl), **thre·nod·ic** (thri nod′ik), *adj.* —**thren·o·dist** (thren′ə dist), *n.*

thre·o·nine (thrē′ə nēn′, -nin), *n. Biochem.* an essential amino acid, $CH_3CHOHCH(NH_2)COOH$. [*threon-* (alter. of Gk *erythrón,* neut. of *erythrós* red; see ERYTHRO-) + -INE[2]]

thresh (thresh), *v.t.* **1.** to separate the grain or seeds from (a cereal plant or the like) by some mechanical means. **2.** to beat as if with a flail. —*v.i.* **3.** to thresh wheat, grain, etc. **4.** to deliver blows as if with a flail. **5. thresh out** or **over,** to talk over thoroughly and vigorously in order to reach a decision, conclusion, or understanding. —*n.* **6.** the act of threshing. Also, **thrash.** [ME *thresche(n),* OE *threscan;* c. G *dreschen,* Goth *thriskan;* akin to Icel *thriskja,* D *dorsen*]

thresh·er (thresh′ər), *n.* **1.** a person or thing that threshes. **2.** a person who separates grain or seeds from wheat, rye, etc. **3.** Also, **thrasher.** Also called **thresh′er shark′.** a large shark of the genus *Alopias,* esp. *A. vulpinus,* that threshes the water with its long tail to drive together the small fish on which it feeds. [ME *thressher*]

thresh′ing machine′, *Agric.* a machine for removing the grains and seeds from straw and chaff.

thresh·old (thresh′ōld, thresh′hōld), *n.* **1.** the sill of a doorway. **2.** the entrance to a house or building. **3.** any place or point of entering or beginning. **4.** Also called **limen.** *Psychol., Physiol.* the point at which a stimulus is of sufficient intensity to begin to produce an effect. [ME *threschold,* OE *threscold, threscwald;* c. Icel *threskōldr,* dial. Sw *träskvald;* akin to THRESH in old sense trample, tread; *-old, -wald* unexplained]

threw (thrōō), *v.* a pt. of **throw.**

thrice (thrīs), *adv.* **1.** three times, as in succession; on three occasions. **2.** in threefold quantity or degree. **3.** very; greatly; extremely. [ME *thries* = obs. *thrie* thrice (OE *thrīga*) + *-s* -s[1]]

thrift (thrift), *n.* **1.** economical management; economy; frugality. **2.** any alpine and maritime, plumbaginaceous plant of the genus *Armeria,* having pink or white flowers, esp. *A. maritima,* noted for its vigorous growth. **3.** any of various allied plants. **4.** vigorous growth, as of a plant. **5.** *Obs.* prosperity. [ME < Scand; cf. Icel *thrift* prosperity. See THRIVE]

thrift·less (thrift′lis), *adj.* **1.** without thrift; improvident; wasteful. **2.** *Archaic.* useless or pointless. [ME: unsuccessful] —**thrift′less·ly,** *adv.* —**thrift′less·ness,** *n.*

thrift·shop (thrift′shop′), *n.* a retail store, sometimes run for a charity, that sells second-hand goods at reduced prices.

thrift·y (thrif′tē), *adj.,* **thrift·i·er, thrift·i·est. 1.** practicing thrift or economical management; frugal: *a thrifty housewife.* **2.** thriving. [ME] —**thrift′i·ly,** *adv.* —**thrift′i·ness,** *n.* —**Syn. 1.** sparing, saving. See **economical.** —**Ant. 1.** wasteful.

thrill (thril), *v.t.* **1.** to affect with a sudden wave of keen emotion or excitement, as to produce a tremor or tingling sensation through the body. **2.** to utter or send forth tremulously, as a melody. —*v.i.* **3.** to affect one with a wave of emotion or excitement. **4.** to be stirred by a tremor or tingling sensation of emotion or excitement: *He thrilled at the thought of home.* **5.** a sudden wave of keen emotion or excitement, sometimes manifested as a tremor or tingling sensation passing through the body. —*n.* **6.** something that produces or is capable of producing such a sensation: *a story full of thrills.* [ME; metathetic var. of THIRL]

thrill·er (thril′ər), *n.* **1.** *Informal.* an exciting, suspenseful play or story, esp. a mystery story. **2.** a person or thing that thrills.

thrill·ing (thril′ing), *adj.* **1.** producing sudden, strong, and deep emotion or excitement. **2.** producing a tremor, as by chilling. —**thrill′ing·ly,** *adv.*

thrip·pence (thrip′əns), *n.* threepence.

thrips (thrips), *n., pl.* **thrips.** any of several minute insects of the order *Thysanoptera,* that have long, narrow wings fringed with hairs and that feed on plants. [< NL < Gk: woodworm = *thrīp-* (? c. DRIVE) + *-s* nom. sing. ending]

thrive (thrīv), *v.i.,* **throve** or **thrived, thrived** or **thriv·en** (thriv′ən), **thriv·ing. 1.** to prosper; be fortunate or successful. **2.** to grow or develop vigorously; flourish. [ME *thrive(n)* < Scand; cf. Icel *thrīfask* to thrive, reflexive of *thrīfa* to grasp] —**thriv′ing·ly,** *adv.* —**Ant.** languish.

thro (thrōō), *prep. Archaic.* through. Also, **thro′.**

throat (thrōt), *n.* **1.** the passage from the mouth to the stomach or to the lungs, including the fauces, pharynx, esophagus, larynx, and trachea. **2.** some analogous or similar narrowed part or passage. **3.** the front of the neck below the chin and above the collarbone. **4.** the narrow opening between a fireplace and its flue or smoke chamber, often closed by a damper. **5.** *Naut., Mach.* swallow[1] (def. 12). **6.** *Naut.* Also called **nock.** the forward upper corner of a quadrilateral fore-and-aft sail. **7.** the forward edge of the opening in the vamp of a shoe. **8. cut one's own throat,**

to cause one's own ruin or failure. **9. jump down someone's throat,** *Slang.* to give someone a scolding; berate. **10. lump in one's throat,** a tight or uncomfortable feeling in the throat, esp. from emotion. **11. ram something down someone's throat,** *Informal.* to force someone to agree to or accept something. **12. stick in one's throat,** to be difficult of expression: *The words of sympathy stuck in her throat.* —*v.t.* **13.** to make a throat in; provide with a throat. **14.** to utter or express from or as from the throat; utter throatily. [ME, OE *throte, throta, throtu;* akin to OHG *drozza* throat, Icel *throti* swelling. See THROTTLE]

throat·latch (thrōt′lach′), *n.* a strap that passes under a horse's throat and helps to hold a bridle or halter in place.

throat′ sweet′bread, sweetbread (def. 2).

throat·y (thrō′tē), *adj.,* **throat·i·er, throat·i·est.** produced or modified in the throat, as sounds; guttural; husky; hoarse. —**throat′i·ly,** *adv.* —**throat′i·ness,** *n.*

throb (throb), *v.,* **throbbed, throb·bing,** *n.* —*v.i.* **1.** to beat with increased force or rapidity, as the heart under the influence of emotion or excitement; palpitate. **2.** to feel or exhibit emotion: *He throbbed at the happy thought.* **3.** to pulsate; vibrate. —*n.* **4.** the act of throbbing. **5.** a violent beat or pulsation, as of the heart. [ME *throbbant* (adj.) throbbing < ?] —**throb′bing·ly,** *adv.* —**Syn. 3.** See **pulsate.**

throe (thrō), *n.* **1.** a violent spasm or pang; paroxysm. **2.** a sharp attack of emotion. **3. throes, a.** any violent convulsion or struggle: *the throes of battle.* **b.** the agony of death. **c.** the pains of childbirth. [ME *throwe,* alter. of *thrawe* (-*o*- from OE *thrōwian* to suffer, be in pain), OE *thrawu;* c. Icel *thrā* (in *līkthrā* leprosy); akin to Ir *trū* wretch]

throm·bin (throm′bin), *n.* *Biochem.* the substance or ferment that causes the coagulation of blood.

thrombo-, a learned borrowing from Greek meaning "clot (of blood)," used in the formation of compound words: *thrombocyte.* Also, *esp. before a vowel,* **thromb-.** [< Gk, comb. form of *thrómbos* clot, lump]

throm·bo·cyte (throm′bə sīt′), *n.* *Anat.* one of the minute, nucleate cells that aid coagulation in the blood of vertebrates that do not have blood platelets.

throm·bo·gen (throm′bə jen′), *n.* *Biochem.* prothrombin.

throm·bo·ki·nase (throm′bō kī′nās, -kin′ās), *n.* *Biochem.* thromboplastin.

throm·bo·phle·bi·tis (throm′bō fli bī′tis), *n.* *Pathol.* the presence of a thrombus in a vein accompanied by irritation of the vessel wall. [< NL]

throm·bo·plas·tic (throm′bə plas′tik), *adj.* *Biochem.* causing or accelerating blood-clot formation.

throm·bo·plas·tin (throm′bə plas′tin), *n.* **1.** *Biochem.* any of the class of lipoproteins, containing cephalin or other phosphatides, that are found in most animal tissue, esp. in the blood platelets, and that serve to convert prothrombin to thrombin in the presence of calcium ions. **2.** *Pharm.* a commercial form of this substance, obtained from the brains of cattle, used chiefly as a local hemostatic and as a laboratory reagent in blood prothrombin tests. Also called **thrombokinase.** [THROMBO- + -PLAST + -IN[2]]

throm·bo·sis (throm bō′sis), *n.* *Pathol.* intravascular coagulation of the blood in any part of the circulatory system, as in the heart, arteries, veins, or capillaries. [< NL < Gk: a curdling. See THROMB-, -OSIS] —**throm·bot·ic** (throm bot′ik), *adj.*

throm·bus (throm′bəs), *n., pl.* **-bi** (-bī). *Pathol.* a fibrinous clot that forms in and obstructs a blood vessel or that forms in one of the chambers of the heart. [< NL < Gk *thrómbos* clot, lump]

throne (thrōn), *n., v.,* **throned, thron·ing.** —*n.* **1.** the chair or seat occupied by a sovereign, bishop, or other exalted personage on ceremonial occasions, usually raised on a dais and covered with a canopy. **2.** the office or dignity of a sovereign: *He came to the throne by succession.* **3.** sovereign power or authority: *to address one's pleas to the throne.* **4.** the occupant of a throne; sovereign. **5.** an episcopal office or authority: *the diocesan throne.* **6.** See **mercy seat** (def. 2). **7. thrones,** an order of angels. Cf. **angel** (def. 1). —*v.t., v.i.* **8.** to sit on or as on a throne. [ME < L *thron(us)* < Gk *thrónos* high seat; r. ME *trone* < OF]

throng (thrông, throng), *n.* **1.** a multitude of people crowded or assembled together. **2.** a great number of things crowded or considered together. —*v.i.* **3.** to assemble, collect, or go in large numbers; crowd. —*v.t.* **4.** to crowd or press upon; jostle. **5.** to fill or occupy with or as with a crowd: *He thronged the picture with stars.* **6.** to bring or drive together into or as into a crowd, heap, or collection. **7.** to fill by crowding or pressing into: *They thronged the small room.* [ME; OE *gethrang;* c. D *drang,* G *Drang* pressure, Icel *thröng;* akin to obs. *thring* to press] —**Syn. 1.** horde, host; assemblage. See **crowd**[1].

thros·tle (thros′əl), *n.* **1.** *Brit., Chiefly Literary.* the song thrush. **2.** a machine for spinning wool, cotton, etc., in which the twisting and winding are simultaneous and continuous. [ME, OE; c. D *drossel,* G *Drossel;* akin to Icel *thröstr,* L *turdus* thrush]

throt·tle (throt′əl), *n., v.,* **-tled, -tling.** —*n.* **1.** a lever, pedal, handle, etc., for controlling or manipulating a throttle valve. **2.** See **throttle valve. 3.** *Rare.* the throat, gullet, or windpipe. —*v.t.* **4.** to stop the breath of by compressing the throat; strangle. **5.** to choke or suffocate in any way. **6.** to compress by fastening something tightly around. **7.** to silence or check as if by choking: *His message was throttled by censorship.* **8.** *Mach.* **a.** to obstruct or check the flow of (a fluid), as to control the speed of an engine. **b.** to reduce the pressure of (a fluid) by passing it from a smaller area to a larger one. [(n.) prob. dim. of ME *throte* THROAT (cf. G *Drossel*); (v.) late ME *throtel,* freq. of *throte(n)* (to) cut the throat of (someone), strangle < THROAT] —**throt′tler,** *n.*

throt′tle valve′, a valve for throttling the working fluid of an engine, refrigerator, etc.

through (thrōō), *prep.* **1.** in at one end, side, or surface and out at the other: *to pass through a tunnel.* **2.** past: *to go through a stop sign without stopping.* **3.** from one to the other of; between or among the individual members or parts of: *to swing through the trees.* **4.** over the surface of, by way of, or within the limits or medium of: *He flies through the air with the greatest of ease.* **5.** during the whole period of; throughout: *He worked through the night.* **6.** having reached the end of: *to be through one's work.* **7.** to and including: *from 1900 through 1950.* **8.** having finished successfully: *to get through an examination.* **9.** by the means or agency of: *It was through him they found out.* **10.** by reason of or in consequence of: *to run away through fear.* **11.** in at the first step of a process, treatment, or method of handling, completing subsequent steps or stages in order, and finished, accepted, or out of the last step or stage: *The body of a car passes through 147 stages on the production line. The new tax bill finally got through Congress.* —*adv.* **12.** in at one end, side, or surface and out at the other: *to push a needle through.* **13.** all the way; along the whole distance: *This train goes through to Boston.* **14.** from the beginning to the end: *to read a letter through.* **15.** to the end: *to carry a matter through.* **16.** to a favorable or successful conclusion: *He barely managed to pull through.* **17.** having completed an action, process, relationship, etc.: *Please be still until I'm through.* **18. through and through, a.** through the whole extent of; thoroughly: *wet through and through.* **b.** from beginning to end; in all respects: *an aristocrat through and through.* **19. through with, a.** finished with. **b.** at the end of all relations or dealings with: *My sister again insists that she's through with men.* —*adj.* **20.** having completed an action, process, etc.; finished. **21.** passing or extending from one end, side, or surface to the other. **22.** traveling, conveying, or extending the full distance with little or no interruption: *a through train.* **23.** (of a road, route, way, course, etc., or of a ticket, routing order, etc.) admitting continuous or direct passage; having no interruption, obstruction, or hindrance: *a through highway; a through ticket to Boston.* [ME, metathetic var. of *thourgh,* OE *thurh;* c. G *durch;* akin to OE *therh,* Goth *thairh* through, OHG *derh* perforated, OE *thyrel* full of holes (adj.), hole (n.). See THIRL, NOSTRIL] —**Syn. 9.** See **by.**

through·ly (thrōō′lē), *adv.* *Archaic.* thoroughly. [late ME]

through·out (thrōō out′), *prep.* **1.** in or to every part of; everywhere in: *They searched throughout the house.* **2.** from the beginning to the end of: *He was bored throughout the play.* —*adv.* **3.** in every part: *rotten throughout.* **4.** at every moment or point: *Follow my plan throughout.* **5.** from the beginning to the end. [ME *throw out,* OE *thurh ūt*]

through·put (thrōō′pŏŏt′), *n.* the amount of raw material processed within a given time, esp. by an electronic computer. Also, **thruput.** [n. use of v. phrase *put through,* modeled on *output*]

through′ street′, a street on which the traffic has the right of way over vehicles entering or crossing at intersections.

through·way (thrōō′wā′), *n.* thruway.

throve (thrōv), *v.* a pt. of **thrive.**

throw (thrō), *v.,* **threw, thrown, throw·ing,** *n.* —*v.t.* **1.** to propel or cast in any way, esp. to project or propel from the hand by a sudden forward motion or straightening of the arm and wrist: *to throw a ball.* **2.** to hurl or project (a missile), as a gun does. **3.** to project or cast (light, a shadow, etc.). **4.** to project (the voice) so as to cause to appear to be coming from a place different from the source, as in ventriloquism. **5.** to direct or send forth (words, a glance, etc.). **6.** to put or cause to go or come into some place, position, condition, etc., as if by hurling: *to throw a man into prison; to throw a bridge across a river.* **7.** to put on, off, or away hastily: *to throw a shawl over one's shoulders.* **8.** *Mach.* **a.** to move (a lever or the like) in order to connect or disconnect parts of an apparatus or mechanism: *to throw the switch.* **b.** to connect, engage, disconnect, or disengage by such a procedure: *to throw the current.* **9.** to shape on a potter's wheel: *He threw the clay into a vase.* **10.** to exert or bring to bear (influence, resources, or power or authority of any kind): *The FBI threw every available agent into the case.* **11.** to deliver (a blow or punch): *He threw a hard left to the chin.* **12.** *Cards.* to play (a card). **13.** to cause to fall to the ground, as an opponent in wrestling. **14.** *Informal.* to lose (a game, race, or other contest) intentionally, as for a bribe. **15.** to cast (dice). **16.** (of an animal, as a horse) to cause (a rider) to fall off; unseat. **17.** (of domestic animals) to bring forth (young). **18.** *Textiles.* to twist (filaments) without attenuation in the production of yarn or thread. **19.** *Informal.* to overcome with astonishment or confusion; astonish; confuse: *Her nastiness really threw me.*

—*v.i.* **20.** to cast, fling, or hurl a missile or the like. **21. throw a party,** to give a party. **22. throw away, a.** to dispose of; discard. **b.** to employ wastefully; squander. **c.** to fail to use (a chance opportunity, etc.); miss: *He threw away a college education.* **23. throw down the gauntlet** or **glove.** See **gauntlet**[1] (def. 3). **24. throw in,** *Informal.* **a.** to add as a bonus or extra. **b.** to bring into (a discussion, plan, etc.) as an addition; interpolate. **c.** *Cards.* to abandon (a hand). **25. throw in the sponge.** See **sponge** (def. 8). **26. throw in the towel.** See **towel** (def. 2). **27. throw off, a.** to free oneself of; cast aside. **b.** to escape from; elude. **c.** to give off; discharge. **d.** to confuse; fluster: *The jeers threw the performers off.* **28. throw oneself at someone** or **someone's head,** (of a woman) to strive to attract the romantic interest of. **29. throw oneself into,** to engage in with energy or enthusiasm. **30. throw oneself on** or **upon someone,** to commit oneself to another's mercy, generosity, support, etc. **31. throw out, a.** to cast away; remove; discard. **b.** to bring up for consideration; propose. **c.** to put out of mind, as a plan; reject. **d.** *Baseball.* to cause to be out by throwing the ball to a fielder, esp. an infielder, in time to prevent a batter or runner from reaching base safely: *The shortstop threw the batter out at first.* **e.** to eject (a person) from a place, esp. forcibly; remove. **32. throw over,** to foresake (a person, esp. a lover or spouse); abandon. **33. throw together, a.** to make in a hurried and haphazard manner. **b.** to cause (persons) to associate. **34. throw up, a.** to vomit. **b.** to build hastily. **c.** to point out, as an error; criticize (usually fol. by *to*): *He threw up her mistakes to her until she couldn't stand it any longer.*

—*n.* **35.** the act or an instance of throwing or casting; cast; fling. **36.** the distance to which anything is or may be thrown: *a stone's throw.* **37.** *Mach.* **a.** the distance between the center of a crankshaft and the center of the crankpins, equal to one half of the piston stroke. **b.** the distance between the center of a crankshaft and the center of an eccentric. **c.** the movement of a reciprocating part in one direction. **38.** a scarf, boa, or the like. **39.** a light blanket, as for use when reclining on a sofa; afghan. **40.** a cast of dice. **41.** the number thrown with a pair of dice. **42.** *Wrestling.*

the act, method, or an instance of throwing an opponent. [ME *throw(en)*, *thrawen*, OE *thrāwan* to twist, turn; c. D *draaien*, G *drehen* to turn, spin, twirl, whirl; akin to L *terere*, Gk *teírein* to rub away] —**throw′er,** *n.*
—**Syn. 1.** fling, launch, send. THROW, CAST, PITCH, TOSS imply projecting something through the air. THROW is the general word, often used with an adverb that indicates direction, destination, etc.: *to throw a rope to someone, the paper away.* CAST is a formal word for THROW, now usually used in certain idiomatic expressions (*to cast a net, black looks; cast down;* the compound *broadcast,* etc.): *to cast off a boat.* PITCH implies throwing with some force and definite aim: *to pitch a baseball.* To TOSS is to throw lightly, as with an underhand or sidewise motion, or to move irregularly up and down or back and forth: *to toss a bone to a dog.*

throw·a·way (thrō′ə wā′), *n.* any advertisement designed to be distributed in quantity to individuals, as a broadside.

throw·back (thrō′bak′), *n.* **1.** an act of throwing back. **2.** a setback or check. **3.** the reversion to an ancestral or earlier type or character; atavism. **4.** an example of this.

throw′ing stick′, 1. a slinglike device used in various primitive societies for propelling a weapon, as a spear, javelin, or the like. **2.** *Australian.* a boomerang.

thrown (thrōn), *v.* a pp. of **throw.**

throw′ rug′. See **scatter rug.**

throw·ster (thrō′stər), *n.* *Textiles.* a person who throws silk or man-made filaments. [late ME *throwestre*]

thru (thro͞o), *prep., adv., adj.* *Informal.* through.

thrum[1] (thrum), *v.,* **thrummed, thrum·ming,** *n.* —*v.i.* **1.** to play on a stringed instrument, as a guitar, by plucking the strings, esp. in an idle manner. **2.** to sound when thrummed on, as a guitar or similar stringed instrument. **3.** to drum or tap idly with the fingers. —*v.t.* **4.** to play (a stringed instrument or a melody on it) by plucking the strings, esp. idly. **5.** to drum or tap idly on. **6.** to recite or tell in a monotonous way. —*n.* **7.** the act or sound of thrumming; dull, monotonous sound. [imit.] —**thrum′mer,** *n.*

thrum[2] (thrum), *n., v.,* **thrummed, thrum·ming.** —*n.* **1.** one of the unwoven ends of the warp threads in a loom, left attached to the loom when the web is cut off. **2. thrums,** the row of such threads. **3.** any short piece of waste thread or yarn, esp. as a tuft or fringe of threads at the edge of a piece of cloth. **4.** Often, **thrums.** *Naut.* short bits of rope yarn used for making mats. —*v.t.* **5.** *Naut.* to insert short pieces of rope yarn through (canvas) and thus give it a rough surface, as for wrapping about a part to prevent chafing. **6.** *Archaic.* to furnish or cover with thrums, ends of thread, or tufts. [ME *throm* endpiece, OE *-thrum* ligament; c. OHG *drum* endpiece; akin to Icel *thröm(r)* brim, edge, L *terminus*, Gk *térma* end]

thrum·my (thrum′ē), *adj.,* **-mi·er, -mi·est.** of or abounding in thrums; shaggy or tufted.

thrup·pence (thrup′əns), *n.* threepence.

thru·put (thro͞o′po͝ot′), *n.* throughput.

thrush[1] (thrush), *n.* **1.** any of numerous, cosmopolitan, passerine birds of the family *Turdidae*, many species of which are noted as songbirds. **2.** any of various unrelated, superficially similar birds, as the water thrushes. **3.** *Slang.* a female professional singer, esp. of popular songs. [ME *thrusche*, OE *thrȳsce;* c. OHG *drōsca*]

Wood thrush, *Hylocichla mustelina* (Length 8 in.)

thrush[2] (thrush), *n.* **1.** *Pathol.* a disease, esp. in children, characterized by whitish spots and ulcers on the membranes of the mouth, fauces, etc., caused by a parasitic fungus, *Candida albicans.* **2.** (in horses) a diseased condition of the frog of the foot. [akin to Dan *troske*, Sw *torsk*]

thrust (thrust), *v.,* **thrust, thrust·ing,** *n.* —*v.t.* **1.** to push forcibly; shove; put or drive with force. **2.** to impose acceptance of; put boldly into some position, condition, etc.: *to thrust oneself into a conversation between others.* **3.** to stab or pierce, as with a sword. **4.** to extend; present: *He thrust his fist in front of my face.* —*v.i.* **5.** to push against something. **6.** to push or force one's way, as against obstacles or through a crowd. **7.** to make a thrust, lunge, or stab at something. —*n.* **8.** the act or an instance of thrusting. **9.** an organized military attack; assault; offensive. **10.** a driving force producing impact, as of a remark, policy, etc. **11.** *Mech.* a pushing force or pressure exerted by a thing or a part against a contiguous one. **12.** *Mech.* a linear reactive force exerted by a propeller, propulsive gases, etc., to propel a vessel, aircraft, etc. **13.** *Geol.* a compressive strain in the crust of the earth, which, in its most characteristic development, produces reversed or thrust faults. **14.** *Archit.* the downward and outward force exerted by an arch on each side. [ME *thrust(en)*, *thrysten* < Scand; cf. Icel *thrȳsta* to thrust] —**thrust′er,** *n.* —**Syn. 6.** shove.

thrust′ fault′, *Geol.* a fault along an inclined plane in which the side or hanging wall appears to have moved upward with respect to the lower side or footwall (contrasted with *gravity fault*).

thru·way (thro͞o′wā′), *n.* a limited-access toll highway providing a means of direct transportation between distant areas for high-speed automobile traffic. Also, **throughway.**

Thu·cyd·i·des (tho͞o sid′i dēz′), *n.* c460–c400 B.C., Greek historian.

thud (thud), *n., v.,* **thud·ded, thud·ding.** —*n.* **1.** a dull sound, as of a heavy blow or fall. **2.** a blow causing such a sound. —*v.t., v.i.* **3.** to beat or strike with a dull sound of heavy impact. [ME *thudd(en)*, OE *thyddan* to strike, press] —**thud′ding·ly,** *adv.*

thug (thug), *n.* **1.** a cruel or vicious ruffian, robber, or murderer. **2.** (*sometimes cap.*) one of a former group of professional robbers and murderers in India, who strangled their victims. [< Hindi *ṭhag*, lit., rogue, cheat] —**thug·ger·y** (thug′ə rē), *n.* —**thug′gish,** *adj.*

thug·gee (thug′ē), *n.* (*sometimes cap.*) (in India) robbery and strangulation committed by thugs. [< Hindi *ṭhagī*]

thu·ja (tho͞o′jə), *n.* any tree of the genus *Thuja*, comprising the arborvitaes. Also, **thuya.** [< NL, ML *thuia* < MGk *thyía*, for Gk *thýa* kind of African tree]

Thu·le (tho͞o′lē, thyo͞o′-, to͞o′-), *n.* **1.** (among the ancient Greeks and Romans) the most northerly region of the world. **2.** See **ultima Thule. 3.** a settlement in NW Greenland: site of U.S. air base. 603 (1962). [< L < Gk *Thoúlē;* r. ME, OE *Tyle* < L *Thȳlē* < Gk]

thu·li·a (tho͞o′lē ə), *n.* *Chem.* a greenish-white powder, TmO_3, that on gentle heating exhibits a reddish incandescence. Also called **thu′lium ox′ide.** [< NL; see THULE, -IA]

thu·li·um (tho͞o′lē əm), *n.* *Chem.* a rare-earth metallic element. *Symbol:* Tm; *at. wt.:* 168.934; *at. no.:* 69; *sp. gr.:* 9.32. [< NL; see THULE, -IUM]

thumb (thum), *n.* **1.** the short, thick, inner digit of the hand in man, next to the forefinger. **2.** the corresponding digit in other animals; pollex. **3.** the part of a glove or mitten for containing the thumb. **4. all thumbs,** awkward, esp. in using one's hands; clumsy; bungling. **5. thumbs down,** a gesture or expression of dissent or disapproval. **6. under one's thumb,** under the power or influence of. —*v.t.* **7.** to soil or wear with the fingers in handling, as the pages of a book. **8.** to glance through (the pages of a book, leaflet, etc.) quickly; leaf. **9.** to play (a guitar or other instrument) with or as with the thumbs. **10.** (of a hitchhiker) to solicit or get (a ride) by pointing the thumb in the desired direction of travel. **11. thumb one's nose (at), a.** to put one's thumb to one's nose and extend the fingers, as a crude gesture of defiance or contempt. **b.** to reject or turn down contemptuously. [ME; OE *thūma;* c. D *duim*, OS, OHG *dūmo* (G *Daumen*), ON *thumall;* akin to L *tumēre* to swell. See TUMOR]

thumb′ in′dex, a series of labeled notches cut along the fore edge of a book, to indicate the divisions or sections.

thumb-in·dex (thum′in′deks), *v.t.* to provide (a book) with a thumb index.

thumb·nail (thum′nāl′), *n.* **1.** the nail of the thumb. —*adj.* **2.** very small or brief; concise: *a thumbnail description of Corsica.*

thumb·screw (thum′skro͞o′), *n.* **1.** a screw, the head of which is so constructed that it may be turned easily with the thumb and a finger. **2.** Often, **thumbscrews.** an old instrument of torture by which one or both thumbs were compressed.

thumb·stall (thum′stôl′), *n.* a protective sheath of rubber, leather, or the like, for the thumb.

thumb·tack (thum′tak′), *n.* **1.** a tack with a large, flat head, designed to be thrust into a board or other fairly soft object by the pressure of the thumb. —*v.t.* **2.** to attach or tack by means of a thumbtack or thumbtacks.

thump (thump), *n.* **1.** a blow with something thick and heavy, producing a dull sound; a heavy knock. **2.** the sound made by such a blow. —*v.t.* **3.** to strike or beat with something thick and heavy, so as to produce a dull sound; pound. **4.** (of an object) to strike against (something) heavily and noisily. —*v.i.* **5.** to strike, beat, or fall heavily, with a dull sound. **6.** to walk with heavy steps; pound. **7.** to palpitate or beat violently, as the heart. [imit.] —**thump′er,** *n.*

thump·ing (thum′ping), *adj.* **1.** of, like, or pertaining to a thump. **2.** *Informal.* strikingly great; exceptional: *a thumping victory at the polls.* —**thump′ing·ly,** *adv.*

Thun (to͞on), *n.* **1.** a city in central Switzerland, on the Aar River, near the Lake of Thun. 29,034 (1960). **2. Lake of.** German, **Thuner See.** a lake in central Switzerland, formed by a widening in the course of the Aar River. 10 mi. long.

thun·der (thun′dər), *n.* **1.** a loud, explosive, resounding noise produced by the sudden expansion of air heated by a lightning discharge. **2.** any loud, resounding noise: *the thunder of applause.* **3.** a threatening or startling utterance, as a denunciation. **4. steal someone's thunder,** to destroy the effect of a performance, remark, etc., by anticipating it. —*v.i.* **5.** to give forth thunder (usually used impersonally with *it* as subject): *It thundered last night.* **6.** to make a loud, resounding noise like thunder: *The artillery thundered in the hills.* **7.** to utter loud or vehement denunciations, threats, or the like. **8.** to move or go with a loud noise or violent action: *The train thundered through the village.* —*v.t.* **9.** to strike, drive, inflict, give forth, etc., with loud noise or violent action. [ME; OE *thunor;* c. D *donder*, G *Donner;* Icel *thōrr* Thor, lit., thunder; akin to OE *thunian*, L *tonāre* to thunder]

thun·der·a·tion (thun′də rā′shən), *interj.* (used as an exclamation of surprise or petulance.)

thun·der·bird (thun′dər bûrd′), *n.* (in the myths of some North American Indians) a huge, supernatural bird capable of producing thunder, lightning, and rain.

thun·der·bolt (thun′dər bōlt′), *n.* **1.** a flash of lightning accompanied by thunder. **2.** an imaginary bolt or dart conceived as the material destructive agent cast to earth in a flash of lightning: *the thunderbolts of Jove.* **3.** any of various fossils, stones, or mineral concretions formerly supposed to have been cast to earth with lightning. [late ME]

thun·der·clap (thun′dər klap′), *n.* a crash of thunder. [ME *thonder clappe*]

thun·der·cloud (thun′dər kloud′), *n.* cumulonimbus. Also, **thun′der·clouds′.**

thun·der·head (thun′dər hed′), *n.* *Meteorol.* **1.** incus (def. 2). **2.** cumulonimbus.

thun·der·ing (thun′dər ing), *adj.* **1.** of, pertaining to, or accompanied by thunder. **2.** producing a noise or effect like thunder. **3.** *Informal.* very great; extraordinary. —*n.* **4.** thunder. [ME *thundring*, OE *thunring* thunder] —**thun′der·ing·ly,** *adv.*

thun·der·ous (thun′dər əs), *adj.* producing thunder or a loud noise like thunder: *thunderous applause.* —**thun′der·ous·ly,** *adv.*

thun·der·peal (thun′dər pēl′), *n.* a thunderclap.

thun·der·show·er (thun′dər shou′ər), *n.* a shower accompanied by thunder and lightning.

thun·der·squall (thun′dər skwôl′), *n.* a combined squall and thunderstorm.

thun·der·stick (thun′dər stik′), *n.* bull-roarer.

thun·der·stone (thun′dər stōn′), *n.* any of various stones, fossils, etc., formerly believed to have fallen as thunderbolts.

thun·der·storm (thun′dər stôrm′), *n.* a transient storm of lightning and thunder, usually with rain and gusty winds. Also called **electrical storm.**

thun·der·struck (thun′dər struk′), *adj.* overcome with consternation; confounded; astounded. Also, **thun·der·strick·en** (thun′dər strik′ən).

Thu·ner See (to͞o′nᴇʀ zā′), German name of Lake of Thun.

Thur., Thursday.

Thur·ber (thûr′bər), *n.* **James (Gro·ver)** (grō′vər), 1894–1961, U.S. writer and caricaturist.

thu·ri·ble (tho͝or′ə bəl), *n.* a censer. [late ME *turrible, thoryble* < L *t(h)ūribul(um)* censer = *thūri-* (s. of *thūs*) incense + *-bulum* instrumental suffix]

thu·ri·fer (tho͝or′ə fər), *n.* the person who carries the thurible in a religious ceremony. [< NL, n. use of L *t(h)ūrifer* (adj.) = *t(h)ūri-* (s. of *t(h)ūs*) incense + *-fer* -FER]

Thu·rin·gi·a (tho͝o rin′jē ə, -jə), *n.* a former state in central Germany: formed from duchies and principalities. German, **Thü·ring·en** (ᴛʏ′ʀɪŋ ən). —**Thu·rin′gi·an,** *adj., n.*

Thurin′gian For′est, a forested mountain region in central East Germany: a resort area. German, **Thü·ring·er Wald** (ᴛʏ′ʀɪŋ əʀ vält′).

Thur·mond (thûr′mənd), *n.* **Strom** (strom), born 1902, U.S. senator from South Carolina since 1955.

Thurs., Thursday.

Thurs·day (thûrz′dē, -dā), *n.* the fifth day of the week, following Wednesday. *Abbr.:* Th., Thur., Thurs. [ME; OE *Thursdæg* < ODan *Thūrsdagr,* lit., Thor's day; r. OE *Thunres dæg,* c. D *donderdag,* G *Donnerstag* (all repr. Gmc trans. of LL *diēs Jovis*). See THOR, THUNDER, DAY]

Thurs′day Is′land, an island in Torres Strait between NE Australia and New Guinea; part of Queensland: pearl fishing. 2140 (1955); 1½ sq. mi.

Thurs·days (thûrz′dēz, -dāz), *adv.* on Thursdays; every Thursday: *Thursdays I go to French class.*

thus (thus), *adv.* **1.** in the way indicated; in this way: *Stated thus, the problem seems trivial.* **2.** in accordance with this; so; consequently: *It is late, and thus you must go.* **3.** to this extent or degree: *thus far.* **4.** as an example; for instance. [ME, OE; c. D *dus*] —**Usage.** See **thusly.**

thus·ly (thus′lē), *adv. Informal.* thus. —**Usage.** Since THUS is an adverb, THUSLY is avoided by careful speakers as a grammatical tautology.

thu·ya (tho͞o′yə), *n.* thuja.

thwack (thwak), *v.t.* **1.** to strike or beat vigorously with something flat; whack. —*n.* **2.** a sharp blow with something flat; whack. [imit.] —**thwack′er,** *n.*

thwart (thwôrt), *v.t.* **1.** to oppose successfully; prevent from accomplishing a purpose. **2.** to frustrate or baffle (a plan, purpose, etc.). **3.** *Archaic.* **a.** to cross. **b.** to extend across. —*n.* **4.** a seat across a boat, esp. one used by an oarsman. **5.** a transverse member spreading the gunwales of a canoe or the like. —*adj.* **6.** passing or lying crosswise or across; cross; transverse. **7.** adverse; unfavorable. **8.** *Archaic.* perverse; obstinate. —*prep., adv.* **9.** across; athwart. [ME *thwert* (adv.) < Scand; cf. Icel *thvert* across, neut. of *thverr* transverse, c. OE *thweorh* crooked, cross, Goth *thwairhs* cross, angry] —**thwart′ed·ly,** *adv.* —**Syn. 1.** hinder, obstruct.

thy (thī), *pron.* the possessive case of **thou** (used as an attributive adjective before a noun beginning with a consonant sound): *thy kingdom.* Cf. **thine.** [ME; var. of THINE]

Thyes′tean ban′quet, *Literary.* a dinner at which human flesh is eaten.

Thy·es·tes (thī es′tēz), *n. Class. Myth.* a son of Pelops and brother and rival of Atreus. He unknowingly ate the flesh of his own sons, which Atreus served to him at a dinner in punishment for his having committed adultery with Atreus' wife. Thyestes then pronounced a curse on the house of Atreus. —**Thy·es·te·an** (thī es′tē ən, thī′e stē′ən), **Thy·es′ti·an,** *adj.*

thy·la·cine (thī′lə sīn′, -sin), *n.* a carnivorous, wolflike marsupial, *Thylacinus cynocephalus,* of Tasmania, tan with black stripes across the back. [< NL *Thȳlacīn(us)* = *thȳlac-* (< Gk *thȳlakos* pouch) + *-īnus* -INE[1]]

Thylacine (Total length 6 ft.; tail 2 ft.)

thyme (tīm; *spelling pron.* thīm), *n.* any menthaceous plant of the genus *Thymus,* as a low subshrub, *T. vulgaris,* a common garden herb having aromatic leaves used for seasoning. [ME < L *thym(um)* < Gk *thȳmon*]

thym·e·lae·a·ceous (thim′ə lē ā′shəs), *adj.* belonging to the *Thymelaeaceae,* a family of chiefly Old World trees, shrubs, and herbs comprising the mezereon, leatherwood, etc. [< NL *Thymelae(a)* genus name (< Gk *thymelaía* = *thȳm(on)* THYME + *elaía* olive tree) + -ACEOUS]

thym·ic[1] (tī′mik), *adj.* pertaining to or derived from thyme. [THYM(E) + -IC]

thym·ic[2] (thī′mik), *adj.* of or pertaining to the thymus. [THYM(US) + -IC]

thy·mol (thī′mōl, -mol), *n. Chem., Pharm.* a crystalline solid, $(CH_3)_2CHC_6H_3(CH_3)OH$, having a pungent taste and odor, used chiefly in perfumery, embalming, and as a fungicide and antiseptic. Also called **thyme′ cam′phor, thym′ic ac′id** (tī′mik).

thy·mus (thī′məs), *n., pl.* **-mus·es, -mi** (-mī). *Anat.* a glandular body or ductless gland of uncertain function found in vertebrate animals, lying in the thorax near the base of the neck in man and becoming vestigial in the adult. Also called **thy′mus gland′.** [< NL < Gk *thȳmos* sweetbread, lit., thymelike excrescence]

thyr-, a combining form of **thyroid:** *thyroxine.* Also, **thyreo-, thyro-.**

thy·roid (thī′roid), *adj.* **1.** of or pertaining to the thyroid gland. **2.** of or pertaining to the largest cartilage of the larynx, forming the projection known in men as the Adam's apple. —*n.* **3.** See **thyroid gland. 4.** the thyroid cartilage. **5.** an artery, vein, etc., in the thyroid region. **6.** *Med.* a preparation made from the thyroid glands of certain animals, used in treating hypothyroid conditions. [var. of *thyreoid* < Gk *thyreoeid(ēs)* shield-shaped = *thyre(ós)* oblong shield (lit., doorlike object: *thȳr(a)* DOOR + *-eos* -EOUS) + *-oeidēs* -OID]

thy·roid·ec·to·my (thī′roi dek′tə mē), *n., pl.* **-mies.** *Surg.* excision of all or a part of the thyroid gland.

thy′roid gland′, *Anat.* a bilobate endocrine gland on both sides of the trachea, connected below the larynx by a thin isthmus of tissue: its secretion regulates the rates of metabolism and body growth.

thy·roi·dot·o·my (thī′roi dot′ə mē), *n., pl.* **-mies.** *Surg.* incision of the thyroid gland.

thy·rox·ine (thī rok′sēn, -sin), *n.* **1.** *Biochem.* the hormone of the thyroid gland, $C_{15}H_{11}O_4NI_4$, that regulates the metabolic rate. **2.** *Pharm.* a commercial form of this compound, obtained from the thyroid glands of animals or synthesized, used in the treatment of hypothyroidism. Also, **thy·rox·in** (thī rok′sin). [THYR- + *-oxine,* abstracted from *toxine* TOXIN]

thyr·soid (thûr′soid), *adj. Bot.* having somewhat the form of a thyrsus. Also, **thyr·soi′dal.** [< Gk *thyrsoeid(ēs)* thyrsuslike. See THYRSUS, -OID]

thyr·sus (thûr′səs), *n., pl.* **-si** (-sī). **1.** Also, **thyrse** (thûrs). *Bot.* a form of mixed inflorescence, as in the lilac, in which the primary ramification is centripetal or indeterminate and the secondary and successive ramifications are centrifugal or determinate. **2.** *Gk. Antiq.* a staff tipped with a pine cone and sometimes twined with ivy and vine branches, borne by Dionysus and his votaries. [< L < Gk *thýrsos* Bacchic staff, stem of plant]

thy·sa·nu·ran (thī′sə no͝or′ən, -nyo͝or′-, this′ə-), *adj.* **1.** belonging or pertaining to the order *Thysanura,* comprising the bristletails. —*n.* **2.** a thysanuran insect. [< NL *Thysanur(a)* (< Gk *thýsan(os)* tassel + *ourá* tail) + -AN]

thy·self (thī self′), *pron.* **1.** an emphatic appositive to *thou* or *thee.* **2.** a substitute for reflexive *thee.* [ME *thi self;* r. OE *thē self.* See THEE, THY, SELF]

Thys·sen (tis′ən), *n.* **Fritz** (fʀits), 1873–1951, German industrialist.

ti[1] (tē), *n., pl.* **tis.** *Music.* **1.** the syllable for the seventh tone of a diatonic scale. **2.** (in the fixed system of solmization) the tone B. Cf. **sol-fa** (def. 1). [substituted for *si* to avoid confusion with the sharp of *sol.* See GAMUT]

ti[2] (tē), *n., pl.* **tis.** a tropical, palmlike plant, *Cordyline australis.* [< Polynesian]

Ti, *Chem.* titanium.

Ti·a Jua·na (tē′ə wä′nə; *Sp.* tē′ä hwä′nä), Tijuana.

Tian Shan (tyän′ shän′). See **Tien Shan.**

ti·ar·a (tē ar′ə, -är′ə, -âr′ə), *n.* **1.** a jeweled, ornamental coronet worn by women. **2.** *Rom. Cath. Ch.* the pope's crown, consisting of three coronets on top of which are an orb and a cross. **3.** a high headdress, or turban, worn by the ancient Persians and others. [< L < Gk: kind of turban] —**ti·ar′aed,** *adj.*

Ti·ber (tī′bər), *n.* a river in central Italy, flowing through Rome into the Mediterranean. 244 mi. long. Italian, **Tevere.**

Ti·be·ri·as (tī bēr′ē əs), *n.* **Lake.** See **Galilee, Sea of.**

Ti·be·ri·us (tī bēr′ē əs), *n.* (*Tiberius Claudius Nero Caesar*) 42 B.C.–A.D. 37, Roman emperor A.D. 14–37.

Ti·bet (ti bet′), *n.* a country in S Asia, N of the Himalayas: under the suzerainty of China: the highest country in the world, average elevation ab. 16,000 ft. 1,270,000 (est. 1957); 471,660 sq. mi. *Cap.:* Lhasa. Also, **Thibet.** Chinese, **Sitsang.**

Ti·bet·an (ti bet′ᵊn, tib′i tᵊn), *adj.* **1.** of or pertaining to Tibet, its inhabitants, or their language. —*n.* **2.** a member of the native Mongolian race of Tibet. **3.** the Sino-Tibetan language of Tibet, esp. in its standard literary form. Also, **Thibetan.**

Ti·bet·o-Bur·man (ti bet′ō bûr′mən), *n.* a subfamily of Sino-Tibetan languages, including esp. Tibetan and Burmese.

tib·i·a (tib′ē ə), *n., pl.* **tib·i·ae** (tib′ē ē′), **tib·i·as. 1.** *Anat.* the inner of the two bones of the leg, extending from the knee to the ankle and articulating with the femur and the talus; shinbone. **2.** *Zool.* **a.** a corresponding bone in a horse or other hoofed quadruped, extending from the stifle to the hock. **b.** (in insects) the fourth segment of the leg, between the femur and tarsus. [< L: shinbone] —**tib′i·al,** *adj.*

Ti·bul·lus (ti bul′əs), *n.* **Al·bi·us** (al′bē əs), c54–c19 B.C., Roman poet.

Ti·bur (tī′bər), *n.* ancient name of **Tivoli.**

tic (tik), *n. Pathol.* **1.** a sudden spasmodic, painless, involuntary muscular contraction, as of the face. **2.** See **tic douloureux.** [< F; c. It *ticche*]

-tic, a suffix occurring in adjectives of Greek origin (*analytic*), used esp. in the formation of adjectives from nouns with stems in **-sis:** *neurotic.* [< Gk *-tikos;* cf. -IC]

ti·cal (ti käl′, -kôl′, tē′kəl), *n., pl.* **-cals, -cal. 1.** a former Thai unit of weight, equal to 231.5 grains, or about half an ounce. **2.** a former silver coin and monetary unit of Siam, equal to 100 satang: replaced in 1928 by the baht. **3.** baht. [< Siamese < Pg < Malay *tikal*]

tic dou·lou·reux (tik′ do͞o′lo͞o ro͞o′; *Fr.* tēk do͞o lo͞o-ʀœ′), *Pathol.* paroxysmal darting pain and muscular twitching in the face. [< F: lit., painful tic]

tick[1] (tik), *n.* **1.** a slight, sharp, recurring click, tap, or beat, as of the mechanism of a clock. **2.** *Chiefly Brit. Informal.* a moment or instant. **3.** a small dot, mark, or check, as used to mark off an item on a list, serve as a reminder, etc. —*v.i.* **4.** to emit or produce a tick, like that of a clock. **5.** to pass as with ticks of a clock: *The hours ticked by.* —*v.t.* **6.** to sound or announce by a tick or ticks: *The clock ticked the minutes.* **7.** to mark with a tick or ticks; check (usually fol. by *off*): *to tick off the items on the memo.* **8. tick (someone) off,** *Chiefly Brit. Informal.* to reprimand; tell off: *She ticked me off for being late.* **9. what makes one tick,** the motive or guiding principle of one's behavior. [late ME *tek* little touch; akin to D *tik* a touch, pat, Norw *tikka* to touch or shove slightly. See TICKLE]

Tick, *Dermacentor variabilis* (Length ¼ in.)

tick[2] (tik), *n.* any of numerous bloodsucking arachnids of the order *Acarina,* including the families *Ixodidae* and *Argasidae,* somewhat larger than the related mites and having a barbed proboscis for attachment to the skin of warm-blooded vertebrates. [ME *teke, tyke,* OE *ticia* (? for *tiica* or *ticca*); akin to LG *tieke,* G *Zecke*]

tick[3] (tik), *n.* **1.** the cloth case of a mattress, pillow, etc., containing hair, feathers, or the like. **2.** *Informal.* ticking. Also called **bedtick.** [ME *tikke, teke, tyke* (c. D *tijk*, G *Zieche*) << L *tēca, thēca* < Gk *thḗkē* case]

tick[4] (tik), *n.* *Chiefly Brit. Informal.* **1.** a score or account. **2. on tick,** on credit or trust: *We bought our telly on tick.* [short for TICKET]

tick·er (tik′ər), *n.* **1.** a telegraphic receiving instrument that automatically prints stock prices, market reports, etc., on a tape. **2.** *Slang.* the heart.

tick′er-tape parade′ (tik′ər tāp′), a parade honoring a dignitary, hero, or the like, in which ticker tapes, confetti, etc., are showered into the streets from buildings along the way.

tick·et (tik′it), *n.* **1.** a slip, usually of paper or cardboard, serving as evidence that the holder has paid his fare or admission or is entitled to some service, right, or the like: *a railroad ticket; a theater ticket.* **2.** a written or printed slip of paper, cardboard, etc., affixed to something to indicate its nature, price, or the like; label or tag. **3.** *U.S.* a list of candidates nominated by a political party or faction. **4.** a summons issued for a traffic or parking violation. **5.** the license of a ship's officer or of an aviation pilot. **6.** *Informal.* the proper thing: *That's the ticket. Warm milk and toast is just the ticket for you.* —*v.t.* **7.** to attach a ticket to; distinguish by means of a ticket; label. **8.** *U.S.* to furnish with a ticket, as on a railroad. [earlier *tiket* < MF *etiquet* memorandum. See ETIQUETTE]

tick′et of leave′, *pl.* **tickets of leave.** *Brit.* (formerly) a permit allowing a convict to leave prison, under certain restrictions, and go to work before his full term had been served, somewhat similar to a certificate of parole. Also, **tick′et-of-leave′.**

tick′et-of-leave′ man′ (tik′it əv lēv′), *Brit.* (formerly) a convict granted a ticket of leave.

tick′ fe′ver, 1. any fever transmitted by ticks, as Rocky Mountain spotted fever which attacks man. **2.** See **Texas fever.**

tick·ing (tik′ing), *n.* **1.** a strong cotton fabric, usually twilled, used esp. in making ticks. **2.** a similar cloth in satin weave or Jacquard, used esp. for mattress covers.

tick·le (tik′əl), *v.*, **-led, -ling,** *n.* —*v.t.* **1.** to touch or stroke lightly with the fingers, a feather, etc., so as to excite a tingling sensation in; titillate. **2.** to poke in some sensitive part of the body so as to excite spasmodic laughter. **3.** to excite agreeably; gratify: *to tickle someone's vanity.* **4.** to excite amusement in: *The clown tickled the kids.* —*v.i.* **5.** to be affected with a tingling sensation, as from light touches or strokes: *I tickle all over.* **6.** to produce such a sensation. **7. tickled pink,** *Informal.* greatly pleased. —*n.* **8.** the act or an instance of tickling. **9.** a tickling sensation. [ME *tikele(n)*; freq. of TICK[1] (in obs. sense) to touch lightly]

tick·ler (tik′lər), *n.* **1.** a person or thing that tickles. **2.** a memorandum book, card file, or the like, organized by date and kept to refresh the memory as to appointments, payments due, etc.

tick′ler coil′, *Radio.* the coil by which the plate circuit of a vacuum tube is inductively coupled with the grid circuit in the process of regeneration.

tick·lish (tik′lish), *adj.* **1.** sensitive to tickling. **2.** requiring careful or delicate handling or action; difficult; risky: *a ticklish situation.* **3.** (of a person) extremely sensitive; touchy: *Father is ticklish about being interrupted.* **4.** unstable or easily upset, as a boat; unsteady. —**tick′lish·ly,** *adv.* —**tick′lish·ness,** *n.*

tick·seed (tik′sēd′), *n.* **1.** any of various plants having seeds resembling ticks, as a coreopsis or the bugseed. **2.** See **tick trefoil.**

tick·tack (tik′tak′), *n.* **1.** a repetitive sound of ticking, tapping, knocking, clicking, etc.: *the ticktack of high heels in the corridor.* **2.** a device for making a tapping sound, as against a window or door in playing a practical joke. —*v.i.* **3.** to make a repeated ticking or tapping sound. Also, **tictac.** [imit. See TICK[1]]

tick-tack-toe (tik′tak tō′), *n.* a simple game, played on a grid having nine compartments, in which two players, one marking X's and the other 0's, take turns marking the compartments until one has succeeded in placing three marks lined up in a horizontal, vertical, or diagonal row. Also, **tick-tack-too** (tik′tak to͞o′), **tic-tac-toe, tit-tat-toe.** [imit. of sound of bringing a pencil down on slate, the essential action in a children's game from which this name is derived; see TICKTACK]

tick·tock (tik′tok′), *n.* **1.** an alternating ticking sound, as that made by a clock. —*v.i.* **2.** to emit or produce a ticking sound, like that of a clock. Also, **tictoc.** [imit.]

tick′ tre′foil, any leguminous plant of the genus *Desmodium*, having trifoliolate leaves and jointed pods with hooked hairs by which they adhere to objects.

Ti·con·der·o·ga (tī′ kon də rō′gə), *n.* a village in NE New York, on Lake Champlain: site of French fort captured by the English 1759 and by Americans under Ethan Allen 1775. 3268 (1970).

tic·tac (tik′tak′), *n.*, *v.i.*, **-tacked, -tack·ing.** ticktack.

tic-tac-toe (tik′tak tō′), *n.* tick-tack-toe.

tic·toc (tik′tok′), *n.*, *v.i.*, **-tocked, -tock·ing.** ticktock.

t.i.d., (in prescriptions) three times a day. [< L *ter in diē*]

tid·al (tīd′ᵊl), *adj.* **1.** of, pertaining to, characterized by, or subject to tides: *a tidal current.* **2.** dependent on the state of the tide as to time of departure: *a tidal steamer.* —**tid′al·ly,** *adv.*

tid′al ba′sin, an artificial body of water open to a river, etc., subject to tidal action.

ti′dal da′tum, (in a hydrographic survey) a curved surface representing one phase of a tide, usually mean low water, taken as a datum level. Also called **datum plane.**

tid′al flat′, tideland that is flat or nearly flat and often muddy or marshy.

tid′al wave′, 1. (not in technical use) a large, destructive ocean wave, produced by a seaquake, hurricane, or strong wind. Cf. **tsunami. 2.** either of the two great wavelike swellings of the ocean surface that move around the earth on opposite sides and give rise to tide, caused by the attraction of the moon and sun. **3.** any widespread or powerful movement, opinion, or tendency: *a tidal wave of public indignation.*

tid·bit (tid′bit′), *n.* **1.** a delicate bit or morsel of food. **2.** a choice or pleasing bit of anything, as news or gossip. Also, *esp. Brit.*, **titbit.** [TIDE[1] (in sense of feast day) + BIT[2]]

tid·dly (tid′lē), *adj.* *Chiefly Brit. Slang.* slightly drunk; tipsy. [dial.: little (OE *tīdlic* timely). See TIDE[1], -LY]

tid·dly·winks (tid′lē wingks′), *n.* (*construed as sing.*) a game played on a flat surface, in which players attempt to snap small plastic disks into a cup by pressing the edges of the disks with larger disks. Also, **tid·dle·dy·winks** (tid′ᵊl dē wingks′). [pl. of *tiddlywink* (TIDDLY + dial. *wink*, var. of WINCH), referring to the counter used to snap the pieces into place]

tide[1] (tīd), *n.*, *v.*, **tid·ed, tid·ing.** —*n.* **1.** the periodic rise and fall of the waters of the ocean and its inlets, produced by the attraction of the moon and sun and occurring about every 12 hours. **2.** the inflow, outflow, or current of water at any given place resulting from the waves of tides. **3.** See **flood tide. 4.** a stream or current. **5.** anything that alternately rises and falls, increases and decreases, etc.: *the tide of the seasons.* **6.** current, tendency, or drift, as of events, ideas, action, etc.: *the tide of international events.* **7.** any extreme or critical period or condition: *The tide of her illness is at its height.* **8.** a season or period in the course of the year, day, etc. (now used chiefly in combination): *wintertide; eventide.* **9.** *Eccles.* a period of time that includes and follows an anniversary, festival, etc. **10.** *Archaic.* a suitable time or occasion. **11.** *Obs.* an extent of time. **12. turn the tide,** to reverse the course of events, esp. from one extreme to another. —*v.i.* **13.** to flow as the tide; flow to and fro. **14.** to float or drift with the tide. —*v.t.* **15.** to carry, as the tide does. **16. tide over,** to assist in getting over a period of difficulty or distress. [ME; OE *tīd* time, hour; c. D *tijd*, Icel *tīth*, G *Zeit*; akin to TIME] —**tide′less,** *adj.* —**tide′less·ness,** *n.* —**tide′like′,** *adj.*

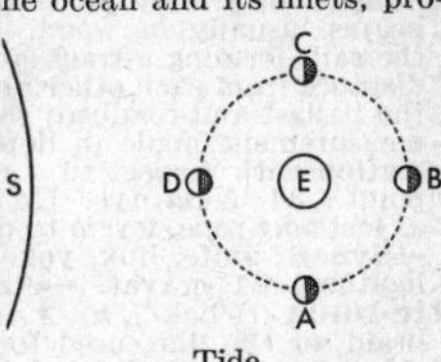

Tide
S, Sun; E, Earth;
A, C, Moon at neap tide;
B, D, Moon at spring tide

tide[2] (tīd), *v.i.*, **tid·ed, tid·ing.** *Archaic.* to happen or befall. [ME; OE *tīda(n)* (to) happen. See BETIDE]

tide′ gate′, 1. a gate through which water flows when the tide is in one direction and which closes automatically when the tide is in the opposite direction. **2.** a restricted passage, as a strait, through which the tide flows swiftly.

tide·land (tīd′land′), *n.* land alternately exposed and covered by the ordinary ebb and flow of the tide.

tide·mark (tīd′märk′), *n.* **1.** a mark left by the highest or lowest point of a tide. **2.** the point that something or someone has reached, receded below, or risen above: *He has reached the tidemark of his prosperity.*

tide′ race′, 1. a swift tidal current. **2.** a tideway.

tide·rip (tīd′rip′), *n.* a rip caused by conflicting tidal currents or by a tidal current crossing a rough bottom.

tide·wa·ter (tīd′wô′tər, -wot′ər), *n.* **1.** water affected by the flow and ebb of the tide. **2.** the water covering tideland at flood tide. **3.** seacoast.

tide·way (tīd′wā′), *n.* **1.** a channel in which a tidal current runs. **2.** the rush of a tidal current through a channel or stream. **3.** tideland. Also, **tide′ way′.**

ti·dings (tī′dingz), *n.* (*sometimes construed as sing.*) news, information, or report: *sad tidings.* [ME; OE *tīdung*; c. D *tijding*, G *Zeitung* news; akin to Icel *tīthindi*]

ti·dy (tī′dē), *adj.*, **-di·er, -di·est,** *v.*, **-died, -dy·ing,** *n.*, *pl.* **-dies.** —*adj.* **1.** neat, orderly, or trim, as in appearance or dress. **2.** clearly organized and systematic: *a tidy mind.* **3.** tolerably good; acceptable: *They worked out a tidy arrangement agreeable to all.* **4.** *Informal.* considerable: *a tidy sum.* —*v.t., v.i.* **5.** to make (something) tidy or neat (often fol. by *up*). —*n.* **6.** any of various articles for keeping things tidy, as a boxlike device with small drawers and compartments. **7.** an antimacassar. [ME *tidi, tidy* seasonable, hence good; c. D *tijdig*] —**ti′di·ly,** *adv.* —**ti′di·ness,** *n.* —**Ant. 1.** messy, sloppy.

ti·dy·tips (tī′dē tips′), *n.*, *pl.* **-tips.** a showy, composite plant, *Layia elegans*, of California, having flowers with bright yellow rays.

tie (tī), *v.*, **tied, ty·ing,** *n.* —*v.t.* **1.** to bind, fasten, or attach with a cord, string, or the like, drawn together and knotted. **2.** to draw together the parts of with a knotted string or the like: *to tie a bundle tight.* **3.** to fasten by tightening and knotting the string or strings of: *to tie one's shoes.* **4.** to draw or fasten together into a knot, as a cord: *to tie one's shoelace.* **5.** to form by looping and interlacing, as a knot or bow. **6.** to fasten, join, or connect in any way. **7.** *Angling.* to design and make (an artificial fly). **8.** to bind or join closely or firmly: *Great affection tied them.* **9.** to confine, restrict, or limit: *The weather tied him to the house.* **10.** to bind or oblige, as to do something. **11.** to make the same score as; equal in a contest. **12.** *Music.* to connect (notes) by a tie.
—*v.i.* **13.** to make a tie, bond, or connection. **14.** to make or be the same score; be equal in a contest: *The teams tied for first place in the league.* **15. tie down,** to limit one's activities; confine; curtail: *He finds that a desk job ties him down.* **16. tie in,** to connect or be connected; be consistent:

His story ties in with the facts. **17. tie one on,** *Slang.* to get drunk. **18. tie up, a.** to fasten securely by tying. **b.** to wrap; bind. **c.** to hinder; impede. **d.** to bring to a stop; make inactive. **e.** to invest or place (money) in such a way as to render unavailable for other uses. **f.** to place (property) under such conditions or restrictions as to prevent sale or alienation. **g.** to moor a ship. **h.** to engage or occupy completely: *I can't see you now, I'm all tied up.*
—*n.* 19. something with which anything is tied. **20.** a cord, string, or the like, used for tying, fastening, binding, or wrapping something. **21.** a necktie. **22.** a bow tie. **23.** a low shoe fastened with a lace. **24.** a knot, esp. an ornamental one; bow. **25.** anything that fastens, secures, or unites. **26.** a bond or connection of affection, kinship, business, mutual interest, etc., between two or more people, groups, nations, or the like. **27.** a state of equality in the result of a contest, as in points scored or votes obtained, among competitors: *The game ended in a tie.* **28.** a match or contest in which this occurs. **29.** any of various structural members, as beams or rods, for keeping two objects, as rafters or the haunches of an arch, from spreading or separating. **30.** *Music.* a curved line connecting two notes on the same line or space to indicate that the sound is to be sustained for their joint value, not repeated. **31.** *Railroads.* any of a number of closely spaced transverse beams, usually of wood, for holding the rails forming a track at the proper distance from each other and for transmitting train loads to the ballast and roadbed; sleeper. **32.** bride[2]. **33.** *Survey.* a measurement made to determine the position of a survey station with respect to a reference mark or other isolated point. **34.** *Naut.* tye. [ME *tie(n)*, OE *tīgan* (v.), *tēag* (n.); c. Icel *taug* rope, *teygja* to draw. See TUG, TOW[1]]
—Syn. 6. unite, link, yoke. **10.** obligate. **20.** rope, band, ligature. **21.** cravat. **—Ant. 1.** loose, loosen.

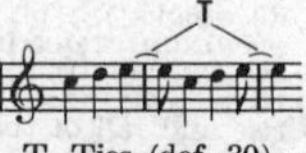

T, Ties (def. 30)

tie·back (tī′bak′), *n.* **1.** a strip or loop of material, heavy braid, or the like, used for holding a curtain back to one side. **2.** a curtain having such a device.

tie′ beam′, a horizontal timber or the like for connecting two structural members to keep them from spreading apart, as a beam connecting the feet of two principal rafters in a roof truss.

Tieck (tēk), *n.* **Lud·wig** (lo͞ot′viKH, lo͞od′-), 1773–1853, German writer.

tie·clasp (tī′klasp′, -kläsp′), *n.* an ornamental metal clasp for securing the two ends of a necktie to a shirt front.

tie-dye (tī′dī′), *n., v.,* **-dyed, -dye·ing. —*n.* 1.** an American Indian method of dyeing fabric, now simplified by students and others to tying off areas of clothing, draperies, etc. and dyeing each in a vivid color or abstract pattern. **—*v.t.* 2.** to dye in this method.

tie-in (tī′in′), *adj.* **1.** pertaining to or designating a sale in which the buyer in order to get the item desired must also purchase another item or items. **2.** of or pertaining to two or more products advertised, sold, obtained, or allotted together. **—*n.* 3.** a tie-in sale or advertisement. **4.** an item in a tie-in sale or advertisement. **5.** any direct or indirect link, relationship, or connection: *There is a tie-in between smoking and cancer.*

tie·mann·ite (tē′mə nīt′), *n.* a mineral, mercuric selenide, HgSe. [named in 1855 after W. *Tiemann*, German scientist who found it; see -ITE[1]]

Tien Shan (tyen′ shän′), a mountain range in central Asia, in China and the Soviet Union. Highest peak, Tengri Khan, ab. 23,950 ft. Also, **Tian Shan.**

Tien·tsin (tin′tsin′; *Chin.* tyen′jin′), *n.* a port in E Hopeh, in NE China. 3,220,000 (est. 1957).

tie·pin (tī′pin′), *n.* a straight pin, usually with an ornamented head and a sheath or clasp for its point, for holding together the ends of a necktie or to pin them to a shirt front. Also called **scarfpin.**

Tie·po·lo (tē ep′ə lō′; *It.* tye′pô lô), *n.* **Gio·van·ni Bat·ti·sta** (jō vä′nē bə tē′stə; *It.* jô vän′nē bät tē′stä), 1696–1770, Italian painter.

tier[1] (tēr), *n.* **1.** one of a series of rows or ranks rising one behind or above another, as of seats in an amphitheater. **2.** one of a number of galleries, as in a theater. **3.** a layer; level; stratum. **—*v.t.* 4.** to arrange in tiers. **—*v.i.* 5.** to rise in tiers. [earlier also *tire, tyre, teare* < MF, OF *tire, tiere* order, row < Gmc; cf. OE, OS *tīr*, OHG *zēri* glory, adornment]

ti·er[2] (tī′ər), *n.* **1.** a person or thing that ties. **2.** *U.S. Dial.* a child's apron or pinafore. [TIE + -ER[1]]

tierce (tērs), *n.* **1.** an old measure of capacity equivalent to one third of a pipe, or 42 wine gallons. **2.** a cask or vessel holding this quantity. **3.** Also, **terce.** *Eccles.* the third of the seven canonical hours, or the service for it, originally fixed for the third hour of the day (or 9 a.m.). **4.** *Fencing.* the third of eight defensive positions. **5.** *Piquet.* a sequence of three cards of the same suit, as an ace, king, and queen **(tierce′ ma′jor)** or a king, queen, and jack **(tierce′ mi′nor). 6.** *Obs.* a third or third part. [ME < MF, fem. of *tiers* < L *tertius* third]

tierced (tērst), *adj.* *Heraldry.* (of an escutcheon) divided vertically or horizontally into three equal parts: *an escutcheon tierced in pale.*

tier·cel (tēr′səl), *n.* *Falconry.* tercel.

tier·ce·ron (tēr′sər ən), *n.* (in a ribbed vault) a diagonal rib, other than an ogive, springing from a point of support. See **vault[1].** [< F = *tierce* TIERCE + *-r-* (< ?) + *-on* -OON]

tie′ rod′, 1. an iron or steel rod serving as a structural tie, esp. one keeping the lower ends of a roof truss, arch, etc., from spreading. **2.** *Auto.* a rod connecting the wheels that turn to steer a vehicle.

Tier·ra del Fue·go (tyeR′Rä del fwe′gô), a group of islands at the S tip of South America, separated from the mainland by the Strait of Magellan: the eastern part (9765, est. 1953; 8074 sq. mi.) belongs to Argentina and the western part (4768, 1952; 19,402 sq. mi.) belongs to Chile.

tiers é·tat (tyeR zā tA′), *French.* See **third estate.**

tie′ tack′, a pin with an ornamental head, for pinning through the ends of a necktie to hold it to a shirt.

tie-up (tī′up′), *n.* **1.** a temporary stoppage or slowing of business, traffic, telephone service, etc., as due to a strike, storm, or accident. **2.** the act or state of tying up. **3.** the state of being tied up. **4.** an involvement, connection, or entanglement: *his tie-up with the crime syndicate.* **5.** a mooring place.

tiff[1] (tif), *n.* **1.** a slight or petty quarrel. **2.** a slight fit of annoyance, bad mood, or the like. **—*v.i.* 3.** to have a petty quarrel. **4.** to be in a tiff. [?]

tiff[2] (tif), *n.* *Archaic.* liquor. [?]

tif·fa·ny (tif′ə nē), *n., pl.* **-nies.** a sheer, mesh fabric of silk, cotton, or man-made fibers. [prob. < obs. F *tiphanie* Epiphany < LL *theophania*. See THEOPHANY]

Tif·fa·ny (tif′ə nē), *n.* **1. Charles Lewis,** 1812–1902, U.S. jeweler. **2.** his son, **Louis Com·fort** (kum′fərt), 1848–1933, U.S. artist and designer of glassware.

Tif′fany glass′, an iridescent art glass, introduced by L. C. Tiffany c1890 and used by him for blown vases, flower holders, etc.

Tif′fany set′ting, a setting, as in a ring, in which the stone is held with prongs. [named after C. L. TIFFANY]

tif·fin (tif′in), *Brit.* **—*n.* 1.** lunch. **—*v.i.* 2.** to eat lunch. [var. of **tiffing* lunching. See TIFF[2]]

Tif·lis (tif′lis; *Russ.* tif lēs′), *n.* former name of **Tbilisi.**

ti·ger (tī′gər), *n., pl.* **-gers,** (*esp. collectively for 1, 2*) **-ger. 1.** a large, carnivorous, tawny-colored, black-striped feline, *Panthera tigris*, of Asia, ranging in several races from India and the Malay Peninsula to Siberia. **2.** the cougar, jaguar, thylacine, or other animal resembling the tiger. **3.** *Informal.* an especially energetic, dynamic, or hard-working person. **4.** *U.S.* an additional cheer (often the word *tiger*) at the end of a round of cheering. [ME *tigre*, OE *tīgras* (pl.) < L *tīgris, tigris* < Gk *tígris*] **—ti′ger·like′,** *adj.*

Tiger, *Panthera tigris*
(Total length 10 ft.; tail 3 ft.)

ti′ger bee′tle, any of numerous active, usually brightly colored beetles of the family *Cicindelidae* that prey on other insects.

ti′ger cat′, 1. any of several felines, as the ocelot, margay, etc., that resemble the tiger in coloration or ferocity but are smaller. **2.** a spotted marsupial cat, *Dasyurops maculatus*. **3.** a domestic cat having a striped coat resembling that of a tiger.

ti·ger·eye (tī′gər ī′), *n.* tiger's-eye.

ti·ger·ish (tī′gər ish), *adj.* **1.** tigerlike, as in power, fierceness, courage, coloration, etc. **2.** fiercely cruel; bloodthirsty; relentless. Also, **tigrish. —ti′ger·ish·ly,** *adv.* **—ti′ger·ish·ness,** *n.*

ti′ger lil′y, 1. a lily, *Lilium tigrinum*, having dull-orange flowers spotted with black and small bulbs or bulbils in the axils of the leaves. **2.** any lily, esp. *L. pardalinum*, of similar coloration.

ti′ger moth′, any of numerous moths of the family *Arctiidae*, many of which have conspicuously striped or spotted wings.

ti′ger sal′amander, a salamander, *Ambystoma tigrinum*, common in North America, having a dark body marked with yellowish spots or bars. See **salamander.**

ti·ger's-eye (tī′gərz ī′), *n.* **1.** a golden-brown chatoyant stone used for ornament, formed by the alteration of crocidolite and consisting essentially of quartz colored by iron oxide. **2.** a glass coating or glaze giving the covered object the appearance of this stone. Also, **tigereye.**

ti′ger shark′, a large shark, *Galeocerdo cuvier*, found in warm seas, noted for its voracious habits.

ti′ger swal′lowtail, a yellow swallowtail butterfly, *Papilio glaucus*, of eastern North America, having the forewings striped with black. See illus. at **swallowtail.**

tight (tīt), *adj.* **1.** firmly or closely fixed in place; not easily moved; secure: *a tight knot.* **2.** drawn or stretched so as to be tense; taut. **3.** affording little or no extra room; fitting closely, esp. too closely: *a tight collar.* **4.** difficult to deal with or manage: *to be in a tight situation.* **5.** of such close or compacted texture, or fitted together so closely, as to be impervious to water, air, steam, etc.: *a good, tight roof.* **6.** concise or terse: *a tight style of writing.* **7.** firm or rigid: *his tight control of the company.* **8.** packed closely or full; affording little leeway: *a tight schedule.* **9.** *Informal.* nearly even; close: *a tight race.* **10.** *Informal.* parsimonious; stingy. **11.** *Slang.* drunk; tipsy. **12.** *Com.* **a.** (of a commodity) difficult to obtain. **b.** (of money) difficult to borrow, as because of high interest rate. **c.** (of a market) characterized by scarcity or eager demand. **13.** *Chiefly Dial.* competent or skillful. **14.** *Chiefly Dial.* **a.** tidy. **b.** neatly or well built or made. **—*adv.* 15.** Also, **tight′ly.** in a tight manner; securely; closely: *Shut the door tight. The shirt fit tight across the shoulders.* [late ME, sandhi var. of *thight* dense, solid, OE *-thīht* (as in *magathīht* belly-strong); c. Icel *thēttr* tight, D, G *dicht* tight, close, dense] **—tight′ness,** *n.*
—Syn. 10. close, niggardly, frugal, sparing.

tight·en (tīt′ən), *v.t., v.i.* to make or become tight or tighter. **—tight′en·er,** *n.*

tight·fist·ed (tīt′fis′tid), *adj.* parsimonious; stingy; tight.

tight·knit (tīt′nit′), *adj.* well-organized and integrated.

tight-lipped (tīt′lipt′), *adj.* not speaking or saying much; taciturn.

tight·rope (tīt′rōp′), *n.* a rope or wire cable stretched tight, on which acrobats perform feats of balancing.

tights (tīts), *n.* (*construed as pl.*) a skintight garment for the lower part of the body and the legs, worn by acrobats, dancers, etc.

tight·wad (tīt′wod′), *n.* *Informal.* a stingy person.

Tig·lath-pi·le·ser I (tig′lath pi lē′zər, -pī-), died 1102? B.C., king of Assyria c1115–1102?.

Tiglath-pileser III, died 727 B.C., king of Assyria 745–727.

Ti·gré (tē grā′), *n.* a former kingdom in E Africa: now a province in N Ethiopia. *Cap.:* Aduwa.

ti·gress (tī′gris), *n.* **1.** a female tiger. **2.** a fierce, aggressive or cruel woman. [earlier *tigresse* < F; see TIGER, -ESS]

Ti·gris (tī′gris), *n.* a river in SW Asia, flowing SE from SE Turkey through Iraq, joining the Euphrates to form the Shatt-al-Arab. 1150 mi. long.

ti·grish (tī′grish), *adj.* tigerish.

Ti·hwa (*Chin.* dē′hwä′), *n.* Urumchi.

Ti·jua·na (tē′ə wä′nə; *Sp.* tē hwä′nä), *n.* a city in NW Mexico, on the Mexico-U.S. border. 244,290 (est. 1965). Also called **Tia Juana.**

tike (tīk), *n.* tyke.

til (til, tēl), *n.* the sesame plant. [< Hindi: sesame]

'til (til), *prep., conj. Nonstandard.* until; till. Also, **til.** [aph. var. of UNTIL]

Til·burg (til′bûrg; *Du.* til′bœrkh), *n.* a city in the S Netherlands. 141,580 (1962).

til·bur·y (til′ber′ē, -bə rē), *n., pl.* **-ries.** a light two-wheeled carriage without a top. [named after its inventor, a 19th-century English coachbuilder]

til·de (til′də), *n.* **1.** a diacritic (~) placed over a letter, as in Spanish over the first *n* in *mañana*, to indicate a palatal nasal sound. **2.** a similar mark used in some texts to indicate the omission of a word, syllable, or phrase: *The inflected forms of "walk" are "walk, ~ed, ~ing."* [< Sp < L *titul(us)* superscription. See TITLE]

Til·den (til′dən), *n.* **1. Samuel Jones,** 1814–86, U.S. statesman. **2. William Ta·tem, Jr.** (tā′təm), 1893–1953, U.S. tennis player.

tile (tīl), *n., v.,* **tiled, til·ing.** —*n.* **1.** a thin slab or bent piece of baked clay, sometimes painted or glazed, used for various purposes, as to form one of the units of a roof covering, pavement, or revetment. **2.** any of various similar slabs or pieces, as of stone or metal. **3.** tiles collectively; tiling. **4.** a pottery tube or pipe used for draining land. **5.** any of various hollow or cellular units of burnt clay or other materials, as gypsum or cinder concrete, for building walls, partitions, floors, and roofs, or for fireproofing steelwork or the like. —*v.t.* **6.** to cover with or as with tiles. [ME; OE *tīgele* (c. G *Ziegel*) < L *tēgul(a)*] —**tile′like′,** *adj.* —**til′er,** *n.*

tile·fish (tīl′fish′), *n., pl.* (*esp. collectively*) **-fish,** (*esp. referring to two or more kinds or species*) **-fish·es.** a large, brilliantly colored food fish, *Lopholatilus chamaeleonticeps*, found in the Atlantic Ocean.

til·i·a·ceous (til′ē ā′shəs), *adj.* belonging to the *Tiliaceae*, or linden family of plants. [< LL *tiliāceus* = L *tili(a)* lime tree + *-āceus* -ACEOUS]

til·ing (tī′ling), *n.* **1.** the operation of covering with tiles. **2.** tiles collectively; tile. **3.** a tiled surface. [late ME *tylynge*]

till[1] (til), *prep.* **1.** up to the time of; until: *to fight till death.* **2.** before (used in negative constructions): *He did not come till today.* **3.** near or at a specified time: *till evening.* **4.** *Scot. and North Eng.* **a.** to. **b.** unto. —*conj.* **5.** to the time that or when; until. **6.** before (used in negative constructions). [ME; OE (north) *til* < Scand; cf. Icel *til* to, akin to OE *till* station, G *Ziel* goal. See TILL[2]]

till[2] (til), *v.t.* **1.** to labor, as by plowing, harrowing, etc., upon (land) for the raising of crops; cultivate. **2.** to plow. —*v.i.* **3.** to cultivate the soil. [ME *tile(n)*, OE *tilian* to strive after, get, till; c. D *telen* to breed, cultivate, G *zielen* to aim (at)]

till[3] (til), *n.* **1.** a drawer, box, or the like, as in a shop or bank in which money is kept. **2.** a drawer, tray, or the like, as in a cabinet or chest, for keeping valuables. [late ME *tylle*, n. use of *tylle* to draw, OE *-tyllan* (in *fortyllan* to seduce); akin to L *dolus* trick, Gk *dólos* bait (for fish), any cunning contrivance, treachery]

till[4] (til), *n.* **1.** *Geol.* glacial drift consisting of an unassorted mixture of clay, sand, gravel, and boulders. **2.** a stiff clay. [?]

till·a·ble (til′ə bəl), *adj.* able to be tilled; arable.

till·age (til′ij), *n.* **1.** the operation, practice, or art of tilling land. **2.** tilled land.

til·lands·i·a (ti lan′dzē ə), *n.* any tropical and subtropical American bromeliaceous plants of the genus *Tillandsia*, most of which are epiphytic on trees, as Spanish moss. [named after E. *Tillands*, 17th-century Finno-Swedish botanist; see -IA]

till·er[1] (til′ər), *n.* a person who tills; farmer. [ME *tiliere.* See TILL[2], -ER[1]]

till·er[2] (til′ər), *n. Naut.* a bar or lever fitted to the head of a rudder, for turning the rudder in steering. [late ME < AF *teiler* weaver's beam, AL *tēlār(ium)* < L *tēl(a)* warp + *-ārium* -ARY] —**till′er·less,** *adj.*

till·er[3] (til′ər), *n.* **1.** a plant shoot that springs from the root or bottom of the original stalk. **2.** a sapling. —*v.i.* **3.** (of a plant) to put forth new shoots from the root or around the bottom of the original stalk. [OE *telgor* twig, shoot; akin to *telge* rod, Icel *tjalga* branch, *telgja* to cut]

Til·lich (til′ik; *Ger.* til′ikh), *n.* **Paul Jo·han·nes** (pôl yō han′is; *Ger.* poul yō hän′is), 1886–1965, U.S. philosopher and theologian, born in Germany.

Til·lot·son (til′ət sən), *n.* **John,** 1630–94, English clergyman: archbishop of Canterbury 1691–94.

Til·ly (til′ē) *n.* **Count Jo·han Tser·claes von** (yō′hän tser kläs′ fən), 1559–1632, German general in the Thirty Years' War.

til·ly-val·ly (til′ē val′ē), *interj. Archaic.* (esp. in exclamations of annoyance or impatience) fiddlesticks! Also, **til·ly-fal·ly** (til′ē fal′ē). [?]

Til·sit (til′zit), *n.* former name of **Sovetsk.**

tilt[1] (tilt), *v.t.* **1.** to cause to lean, incline, slope, or slant. **2.** to rush at or charge, as in a joust. **3.** to hold poised for attack, as a lance. —*v.i.* **4.** to move into or assume a sloping position or direction. **5.** to strike, thrust, or charge with a lance or the like (usually fol. by *at*). **6.** to engage in a joust, tournament, or similar contest. **7. tilt at windmills,** to contend against imaginary opponents or injustices. —*n.* **8.** the act or an instance of tilting. **9.** the state of being tilted; a sloping position. **10.** a slope. **11.** a joust or any other contest. **12.** a dispute; controversy. **13.** a thrust of a weapon, as at a tilt or joust. **14. full tilt,** with full force or speed; directly. [ME *tylte(n)* (to) upset, tumble < Scand; cf. dial. Norw *tylta* to tiptoe, *tylten* unsteady; akin to OE *tealt* unsteady, *tealtian* to totter, amble, MD *touteren* to sway]

tilt[2] (tilt), *n.* **1.** a cover of coarse cloth, canvas, etc., as for a wagon. **2.** an awning. —*v.t.* **3.** to furnish with a tilt. [ME, var. of *tild*, OE *teld*; c. G *Zelt* tent, Icel *tjald* tent, curtain]

tilth (tilth), *n.* **1.** the act or operation of tilling land; tillage. **2.** the state of being tilled or under cultivation. **3.** the physical condition of soil in relation to plant growth. **4.** land that is tilled or cultivated. [ME, OE. See TILL[2], -TH[1]]

tilt′ ham′mer, a drop hammer used in forging, consisting of a pivoted lever with a heavy head at one end.

tilt′-top ta′ble (tilt′top′), a pedestal table having a top that can be tilted vertically.

tilt·yard (tilt′yärd′), *n.* a courtyard or other area for tilting.

Tim., *Bible.* Timothy.

ti·ma·rau (tē′mə rou′), *n.* tamarau.

Tim·a·ru (tim′ə rōō′), *n.* a seaport on the E coast of South Island, in S New Zealand. 23,308 (1957).

tim·bal (tim′bəl), *n.* a kettledrum. Also, **tymbal.** [< F, MF *timbale* = OF *timb(re)* drum (see TIMBRE) + MF *(attab)al* < Sp *atabal* < Ar *aṭ-ṭabl* the drum]

tim·bale (tim′bəl; *Fr.* tan bal′), *n., pl.* **-bales** (-bəlz; *Fr.* -bal′). a small pastry shell filled with a meat, fish, or vegetable mixture and richly sauced. [< F: lit., kettledrum. See TIMBAL]

tim·ber (tim′bər), *n.* **1.** the wood of growing trees suitable for structural uses. **2.** growing trees themselves. **3.** wooded land. **4.** wood, esp. when suitable or adapted for various building purposes. **5.** a single piece of wood forming part of a structure or the like: *A timber fell from the roof.* **6.** *Naut.* (in a ship's frame) one of the curved pieces of wood that spring upward and outward from the keel; rib. **7.** personal character or quality: *He's being talked up as presidential timber.* —*v.t.* **8.** to furnish with timber. **9.** to support with timber. —*interj.* **10.** a lumberjack's call to warn those in the vicinity that a cut tree is about to fall to the ground. [ME, OE; orig. house, building material; c. Icel *timbr* timber, G *Zimmer* room; akin to Goth *timrjan*, Gk *démein* to build. See DOME] —**tim′ber·less,** *adj.*

tim·bered (tim′bərd), *adj.* **1.** made of or furnished with timber. **2.** covered with growing trees; wooded: *timbered acres.* [late ME *timbred*]

tim·ber·head (tim′bər hed′), *n. Naut.* **1.** the top end of a timber, rising above the deck and serving for belaying ropes. **2.** a bollard resembling this in position and use.

tim′ber hitch′, a knot or hitch on a spar or the like, made by taking a turn on the object, wrapping the end around the standing part of the rope, and then wrapping it several times around itself.

tim·ber·ing (tim′bər ing), *n.* **1.** building material of wood. **2.** timberwork. [ME *timbrung*]

tim·ber·jack (tim′bər jak′), *n.* a person whose occupation is logging; logger.

tim·ber·land (tim′bər land′), *n.* land covered with timber-producing forests.

tim′ber line′, **1.** the altitude above sea level at which timber ceases to grow. **2.** the arctic or antarctic limit of tree growth. —**tim′ber-line′,** *adj.*

tim′ber wolf′, the American gray wolf, *Canis lupus*, esp. the subspecies *C. lupus occidentalis*, of heavily forested parts of Canada and the northern U.S.

tim·ber·work (tim′bər wûrk′), *n.* structural work formed of timbers. [ME *timberwerk*]

tim·bre (tim′bər; *Fr.* tan′brə), *n.* **1.** *Acoustics, Phonet.* the characteristic quality of a sound, independent of pitch and loudness but dependent on the relative strengths of the components of different frequencies, determined by resonance. **2.** *Music.* the characteristic quality of sound produced by a particular instrument or voice; tone color. [< F: sound (orig. of bell), MF: bell, timbrel, drum, OF: drum < MGk *tímban(on)*, var. of Gk *týmpanon* drum]

tim·brel (tim′brəl), *n.* a tambourine or similar instrument. [ME *timbre* drum (see TIMBRE) + *-el* dim. suffix]

Tim·buk·tu (tim′buk tōō′, tim buk′tōō), *n.* **1.** French, **Tombouctou.** a town in central Mali, in W Africa, near the Niger River. 6000 (est. 1961). **2.** any faraway place.

time (tīm), *n., adj., v.,* **timed, tim·ing.** —*n.* **1.** the system of sequential relations that any event has to any other, as past, present, or future; indefinite continuous duration regarded as that in which events succeed one another. **2.** finite duration (contrasted with *eternity*). **3.** a system or method of measuring or reckoning the passage of time: *mean time; Greenwich Time.* **4.** a period or interval, as between two events: *a long time.* **5.** a particular period considered as distinct from other periods: *Youth is the best time of life.* **6.** Often, **times. a.** a period in the history of the world or contemporary with the life or activities of a notable person: *prehistoric times; in Lincoln's time.* **b.** the period or era now or previously present: *a sign of the times.* **c.** a period considered with reference to its events or prevailing conditions, tendencies, ideas, etc.: *hard times; a time of war.* **7.** a prescribed or allotted period, as of one's life or for payment of a debt. **8.** the end of a prescribed or allotted period, as of one's life or a period of gestation: *When her time came she was delivered of a boy.* **9.** a period with reference to personal experience: *to have a good time.* **10.** a period of work of an employee, or the pay for it; working hours or days or an hourly or daily pay rate. **11.** *Informal.* a term of enforced duty or imprisonment: *to serve time in the army; to do time in prison.* **12.** the period necessary for or occupied by something: *The time of the baseball game was two hours and two minutes.* **13.** leisure time; sufficient or spare time: *We had no time for a vacation. I have no time to stop now.* **14.** a particular or definite point in time, as indicated by a clock: *What time is it?* **15.** a particular part of a year, day, etc.; season or period: *lunch time; Christmas time.* **16.** an appointed, fit, due, or proper instant or period: *There is a time for everything.* **17.** the particular point in time when an event is scheduled to take place: *train time; curtain time.* **18.** an indefinite, frequently prolonged period or duration in the future: *Time will tell if what we have done here today was right.* **19.** the right occasion or opportunity: *to watch one's time.* **20.** each occasion of a recurring action or event: *It's Joe's time at bat.* **21. times,** used as a multiplicative word in phrasal combinations expressing how many instances of a quantity or factor are taken together: *Two goes into six three times.* **22.** *Drama.* one of the three unities. Cf. **unity** (def. 8). **23.** *Pros.* a unit or a group of units in the measurement of meter. **24.** *Music.* **a.** tempo; relative rapidity of movement. **b.** the metrical duration of a note or rest. **c.** proper or characteristic tempo. **d.** the general movement of a particular kind of musical composition with reference to its rhythm, metrical structure, and tempo. **e.** the movement of a dance or the like to music so arranged: *waltz time.* **25.** *Mil.* rate of marching, calculated on the number of paces taken per minute: *double time; quick time.* **26.** *Embryol.* the period of gestation. **27. against time,** in an effort to finish something within a limited period. **28. ahead of time,** before the time due; early. **29. at one time, a.** once; in a former time: *At one time I lived in Japan.* **b.** at the same time; at once: *They all tried to talk at one time.* **30. at times,** at intervals; occasionally. **31. behind the times,** old-fashioned; dated. **32. for the time being,** temporarily; for the present: *Let's forget about it for the time being.* **33. from time to time,** on occasion; occasionally; at intervals. **34. in good time, a.** at the right time. **b.** in advance of the right time; early: *We arrived in good time.* **35. in no time,** in a very brief time; almost at once: *They cleaned the entire house in no time.* **36. in time, a.** early enough: *to come in time for dinner.* **b.** in the future; eventually: *In time he'll see what is right.* **c.** in the correct rhythm or tempo. **37. keep time, a.** to record time, as a watch or clock does. **b.** to mark or observe the tempo. **c.** to perform rhythmic movements in unison. **38. kill time,** to occupy oneself with some activity to make time pass quickly. **39. make good, bad,** etc., **time,** to maintain or achieve a good, bad, etc., rate of speed in traveling: *I made bad time because of the detour.* **40. make time,** to move quickly, esp. in an attempt to recover lost time. **41. many a time,** again and again; frequently. **42. mark time, a.** to suspend progress temporarily, as to await developments; fail to advance. **b.** *Mil.* to move the feet alternately as in marching, but without advancing. **43. on time, a.** at the specified time; punctually. **b.** on, or in accordance with, the installment plan. **44. out of time,** not in the proper rhythm. **45. pass the time of day,** to converse briefly with or greet someone: *The women would stop in the market to pass the time of day.* **46. take one's time,** to be slow or leisurely; dawdle. **47. time after time,** again and again; repeatedly; often. Also, **time and time again, time and again. 48. time of life,** (one's) age: *At your time of life you must be careful not to overdo things.* **49. time of one's life,** *Informal.* a time or period with respect to keen pleasure enjoyed: *They had the time of their lives on their trip to Europe.* —*adj.* **50.** of, pertaining to, or showing the passage of time. **51.** (of an explosive device) containing a clock so that it will detonate at the desired moment: *a time bomb.* **52.** *Com.* payable a stated period of time after presentment. **53.** of or pertaining to purchases on the installment plan. —*v.t.* **54.** to ascertain or record the time, duration, or rate of: *to time a race.* **55.** to fix the duration of. **56.** to fix the interval between (actions, events, etc.): *They timed their strokes at six per minute.* **57.** to regulate as to time, as a train, clock, etc. **58.** to appoint or choose the moment or occasion for; schedule: *He timed the attack perfectly.* **59.** to mark the rhythm or measure of, as in music. **60.** *Music.* to classify (notes or syllables) according to meter, accent, rhythm, etc. —*v.i.* **61.** to keep time; sound or move in unison. [ME; OE *tīma* (n.); c. Icel *tīmi;* akin to TIDE[1]] —**Syn. 4.** period, term, spell, span. **6.** epoch, era, age, date.

time′ and a half′, a rate of pay for overtime work equal to one and one half times the regular hourly wage.

time′ and mo′tion stud′y, the systematic analysis of the motions and time required to perform a specific operation with a view to seeking more efficient methods of production. Also called **time study, motion study.**

time′ belt′. See **time zone.**

time-bind·ing (tīm′bīn′ding), *n.* the distinctively human attribute of preserving memories and records of experiences for the use of subsequent generations.

time′ bomb′, a bomb that may be set to explode at a specific time.

time′ cap′sule, a receptacle containing documents or objects typical of the current period, placed in the earth or in a cornerstone for discovery in the future.

time·card (tīm′kärd′), *n.* a card for recording an employee's times of arrival and departure from a job.

time′ clock′, **1.** a clock with an attachment that records the exact times of arrival and departure on a timecard. **2. punch a time clock,** to have a job requiring use of a time clock or fastidious observance of regulations governing arrival and departure times.

time-con·sum·ing (tīm′kən so͞o′ming), *adj.* (of an action) requiring or wasting much time.

time′ depos′it, *Banking.* a deposit that can be withdrawn by the depositor only after he has given advance notice or after an agreed period of time has elapsed.

time′ expo′sure, *Photog.* a long exposure in which the shutter is opened and closed by hand or by a mechanism other than the automatic mechanism of the shutter.

time-hon·ored (tīm′on′ərd), *adj.* revered or respected because of antiquity and long continuance: *a time-honored custom.* Also, *esp. Brit.,* **time′-hon′oured.**

time′ immemo′rial, **1.** time in the distant past beyond memory or record. **2.** *Law.* time beyond legal memory, fixed by statute in England as prior to the beginning of the reign of Richard I (1189).

time·keep·er (tīm′kē′pər), *n.* **1.** an official appointed to time, regulate, and record the duration of a sports contest or its component parts. **2.** a timepiece. **3.** a person employed to keep account of the hours of work done by others. —**time′keep′ing,** *n.*

time-lag (tīm′lag′), *n.* the period of time between two closely related events, phenomena, etc., as between stimulus and response.

time′-lapse photog′raphy (tīm′laps′), the photographing on motion-picture film of a slow and continuous process at regular intervals, esp. by exposing a single frame at a time, for projection at a higher speed.

time·less (tīm′lis), *adj.* **1.** without beginning or end; eternal; everlasting. **2.** referring or restricted to no particular time: *the timeless beauty of great music.* —**time′-less·ly,** *adv.* —**time′less·ness,** *n.*

time′ lim′it, a period of time within which an action or procedure must be done or completed.

time′ loan′, a loan repayable at a specified date. Cf. **call loan.**

time′ lock′, a lock, as for the door of a bank vault, equipped with a mechanism that makes it impossible to operate the lock within certain hours.

time·ly (tīm′lē), *adj.* **1.** occurring at a suitable time; seasonable: *a timely warning.* **2.** *Archaic.* early. —*adv.* **3.** opportunely. **4.** *Archaic.* early or soon. [ME *tim(e)liche,* OE *tīmlīc*] —**time′li·ness,** *n.* —**Syn. 1.** See **opportune.**

time′ machine′, an imaginary machine that enables a person to travel back and forth in time at command.

time′ note′, *Com.* a note payable within a specified number of days after it is presented.

time′ of day′, **1.** a definite time as shown by a timepiece; the hour: *Can you tell me the time of day?* **2.** *Informal.* a minimum of attention: *He wouldn't give her the time of day.*

time·ous (tī′məs), *adj.* *Scot.* **1.** early. **2.** timely. [TIME + -OUS; r. late ME (Scot) *tymys;* see -ISH[1]] —**time′ous·ly,** *adv.*

time-out (tīm′out′), *n.* **1.** Also, **time′out′.** a brief suspension of activity; intermission; break. **2.** *Sports.* a short interruption in a regular period of play during which a referee or other official stops the clock so that the players may rest, deliberate, make substitutions, etc.

time·piece (tīm′pēs′), *n.* **1.** an apparatus for measuring and recording the progress of time; chronometer. **2.** a clock or a watch.

tim·er (tī′mər), *n.* **1.** a person who measures or records time; timekeeper. **2.** a device for indicating or measuring elapsed time, as a stopwatch. **3.** a device for controlling machinery, appliances, or the like, in a specified way at a predetermined time: *an oven timer.* **4.** (in an internal-combustion engine) a set of points actuated by a cam which automatically times current for the spark.

times (tīmz), *prep.* multiplied by: *Two times four is eight.*

time·sav·ing (tīm′sā′ving), *adj.* (of methods, devices, etc.) reducing the time spent or required to do something. —**time′sav′er,** *n.*

time·serv·er (tīm′sûr′vər), *n.* a person who shapes his conduct to conform with the opinions of the time or of persons in power, esp. for selfish ends; toady. —**time′serv′ing,** *adj., n.*

time′ shar′ing, a system or service in which a number of subscribers at remote locations simultaneously use a single multiple-access computer. —**time′-shar′ing,** *adj.*

time′ sig′nal, a signal sent electrically or by radio to indicate a precise moment of time as a means of checking or regulating timepieces.

time′ sig′nature, *Music.* a numerical or other indication showing the meter, usually placed after the key signature.

times′ sign′. See **multiplication sign.**

Times′ Square′, a wide intersection extending from 42nd to 47th Streets where Broadway and Seventh Avenue intersect in central Manhattan, New York City: theaters, restaurants, etc.

time′ stud′y. See **time and motion study.**

time·ta·ble (tīm′tā′bəl), *n.* **1.** a schedule showing the times at which railroad trains, airplanes, etc., arrive and depart. **2.** any schedule or plan designating the times at or within which certain things occur or are scheduled to occur: *a timetable of space research.*

time·work (tīm′wûrk′), *n.* work done and paid for by the hour or day. Cf. **piecework.** —**time′work′er,** *n.*

time·worn (tīm′wōrn′, -wôrn′), *adj.* **1.** showing the effects of age or antiquity; antiquated. **2.** commonplace; trite; hackneyed.

time′ zone′, one of the 24 regions or divisions of the globe approximately coinciding with meridians at successive hours from the observatory at Greenwich, England. Also called **time belt.**

Time zones of the continental United States

tim·id (tim′id), *adj.* **1.** lacking in self-assurance or courage; timorous; shy. **2.** characterized by or indicating fear. [< L *timid(us)* fearful = *tim(ēre)* (to) fear + *-idus* -ID[4]] —**ti·mid′i·ty, tim′id·ness,** *n.* —**tim′id·ly,** *adv.* —**Syn. 1.** fearful, fainthearted. See **cowardly.**

tim·ing (tī′ming), *n.* **1.** *Theat.* the act of adjusting the tempo of the various parts of a production or performance to achieve maximum effect. **2.** *Sports.* the control of the speed of a stroke, blow, etc., in order that it may reach its maximum at the proper moment. **3.** the selecting of the best time or speed for doing something in order to achieve the desired or maximum result. 4. the act or an instance of observing and recording the elapsed time of an act, contest, etc.

Ti·mi·șoa·ra (tē′mē shwä′rä), *n.* a city in W Rumania. 152,230 (est. 1964). Hungarian, **Temesvár.**

ti·moc·ra·cy (tī mok′rə sē), *n., pl.* **-cies.** 1. a form of government in which a certain amount of property is a requisite as a qualification for office. 2. a form of government in which love of honor is the dominant motive of the rulers. [earlier *timocratie* < Gk *tīmokratía* = *tīmo-* (comb. form of *tīmḗ* honor, worth) + *-kratia* -CRACY] —**ti·mo·crat·ic** (tī′mə krat′ik), **ti′mo·crat′i·cal,** *adj.*

Ti·mon (tī′mən), *n.* c320–c230 B.C., Greek philosopher.

Ti·mor (tē′môr), *n.* 1. an island in the Malay Archipelago: largest and easternmost of the Lesser Sunda Islands; W half belongs to Indonesia, E half belongs to Portugal. 2. Also called **Indonesian Timor.** Formerly, **Netherlands Timor.** the W part of this island. 569,927 (est. 1961); 5765 sq. mi. 3. Also called **Portuguese Timor.** a Portuguese overseas territory comprising the E part of this island. 496,000 (est. 1959); 7330 sq. mi. *Cap.:* Dili.

tim·or·ous (tim′ər əs), *adj.* 1. full of fear; fearful. 2. subject to fear; timid. 3. characterized by or indicating fear. [late ME < ML *timōrōs(us)* (L *timōr-* (s. of *timor*) fear + *-ōsus* -OUS); r. late ME *tymerous, tumerous,* etc. < MF *temerous*] —**tim′or·ous·ly,** *adv.* —**tim′or·ous·ness,** *n.* —**Syn. 1.** See **cowardly.**

Ti′mor Sea′, an arm of the Indian Ocean, between Timor and NW Australia.

Ti·mo·shen·ko (tim′ə sheng′kō; *Russ.* tē′mo shen′ko), *n.* **Si·mion Kon·stan·ti·no·vich** (si myôn′ kôn′stän tē′no-vich), born 1895, Russian general.

tim·o·thy (tim′ə thē), *n.* a coarse grass, *Phleum pratense,* having cylindrical spikes, used as fodder. Also called **tim′othy grass′.** [named after *Timothy* Hanson, American farmer who grew this grass and spread its cultivation in the early 18th century]

Tim·o·thy (tim′ə thē), *n.* 1. a disciple and companion of the apostle Paul, to whom Paul is supposed to have addressed two Epistles. 2. either of these Epistles, I Timothy or II Timothy.

Ti·mour (ti mo͝or′), *n.* Tamerlane. Also, **Ti·mur′.**

tim·pa·ni (tim′pə nē), *n.pl.* (*often construed as sing.*) a set of kettledrums, esp. as used in an orchestra or band. Also, **tympani.** [< It, pl. of *timpano* kettledrum < L *tympan(um)* < Gk *týmpanon*] —**tim′pa·nist,** *n.*

tin (tin), *n., adj., v.,* **tinned, tin·ning.** —*n.* 1. *Chem.* a low-melting, malleable, ductile metallic element nearly approaching silver in color and luster: used in plating and in making alloys, tinfoil, and soft solders. *Symbol:* Sn; *at. wt.:* 118.69; *at. no.:* 50; *sp. gr.:* 7.31 at 20°C. 2. See **tin plate.** 3. *Chiefly Brit.* **a.** any shallow pan, esp. one used in baking. **b.** See **tin can** (def. 1). —*adj.* 4. made of tin or tin plate. 5. mean; worthless; counterfeit. 6. indicating the tenth event of a series, as a wedding anniversary. —*v.t.* 7. *Metall.* **a.** to cover or coat with tin. **b.** to coat with soft solder. 8. *Chiefly Brit.* to preserve or pack (esp. food) in cans; can. [ME, OE; c. D, Icel *tin,* G *Zinn*] —**tin′like′,** *adj.*

tin·a·mou (tin′ə mo͞o′), *n.* any of several birds of the family *Tinamidae,* of South and Central America, related to the ratite birds but superficially resembling the gallinaceous birds. [< F < Carib *tinamu* (Galibi dial.)]

tin·cal (ting′käl, -kôl), *n.* the former Oriental name of crude native borax. [< Malay *tingkal*]

tin′ can′, 1. a sealed metal can for food or other perishables, esp. one made of tin-plated sheet steel. 2. *U.S. Navy Slang.* a destroyer.

tinct (tingkt), *n.* 1. *Literary.* tint; tinge; coloring. —*adj.* 2. *Archaic Literary.* tinged; colored; flavored. —*v.t. Obs.* 3. to tinge or tint, as with color. 4. to imbue. [< L *tinct(us),* ptp. of *tingere* to dye, color, tinge]

tinct., tincture.

tinc·to·ri·al (tingk tōr′ē əl, -tôr′-), *adj.* pertaining to coloring or dyeing. [< L *tinctōri(us)* of or related to dipping, dyeing (see TINCT, -ORY[1]) + -AL[1]] —**tinc·to′ri·al·ly,** *adv.*

tinc·ture (tingk′chər), *n., v.,* **-tured, -tur·ing.** —*n.* 1. *Pharm.* a solution of alcohol or of alcohol and water, containing animal, vegetable, or chemical drugs. 2. a slight infusion, as of some element or quality. 3. a trace; smack or smattering; tinge. 4. *Heraldry.* any of the colors, metals, or furs used for the fields, charges, etc., of an escutcheon or achievement of arms. 5. *Obs.* a dye or pigment. —*v.t.* 6. to impart a tint or color to; tinge. 7. to imbue or infuse with something. [< L *tinctūr(a)* dyeing]

Tin·dal (tin′dᵊl), *n.* 1. **Matthew,** c1655–1733, English deist. 2. Also, **Tin′dale. William.** See **Tyndale, William.**

tin·der (tin′dər), *n.* 1. a highly flammable material or preparation formerly used for catching the spark from a flint and steel struck together for fire or light. 2. any dry substance that readily takes fire from a spark. [ME; OE *tynder;* akin to Icel *tundr,* G *Zunder,* OE *-tendan* (as in *ātendan* to set on fire), Goth *tundnan* to catch fire, G *-zünden* in *entzünden* to kindle] —**tin′der·like′,** *adj.* —**tin′der·y,** *adj.*

tin·der·box (tin′dər boks′), *n.* 1. a box for holding tinder, usually fitted with a flint and steel. 2. a potential source or place of violence, war, or the like.

tine (tīn), *n.* a sharp, projecting point or prong, as of a fork. Also, *esp. Brit.,* **tyne.** [late ME *tyne,* ME, OE *tind;* c. Icel *tindr,* OHG *zint*] —**tined,** *adj.*

tin·e·a (tin′ē ə), *n. Pathol.* any of several skin diseases caused by fungi; ringworm. [< NL; in L: gnawing worm] —**tin′e·al,** *adj.*

tin′ ear′, *Slang.* 1. See **cauliflower ear.** 2. an inability to distinguish all or certain sounds or tones.

tin·e·id (tin′ē id), *n.* 1. a moth of the family *Tineidae,* comprising the clothes moths. —*adj.* 2. belonging or pertaining to the family *Tineidae.* [< NL *Tineid(ae).* See TINEA, -ID[2]]

tin′ fish′, *Slang.* a torpedo.

tin′ foil′, tin, or an alloy of tin and lead, in a thin sheet, for use as a wrapping. —**tin′-foil′,** *adj.*

ting (ting), *v.t., v.i.* 1. to cause to make or to make a high, clear, ringing sound. —*n.* 2. a tinging sound. [imit.; see TANG[2]]

ting-a-ling (ting′ə ling′), *n.* a repeated tinkling sound, as of a small bell. [imit. rhyming compound]

tinge (tinj), *v.,* **tinged, tinge·ing** or **ting·ing,** *n.* —*v.t.* 1. to impart a trace or slight degree of some color to; tint. 2. to impart a slight taste or smell to. —*n.* 3. a slight degree of coloration. 4. a slight admixture; trace: *a tinge of garlic; a tinge of anger.* [late ME < L *ting(ere)* (to) dye, color]

tin·gle (ting′gəl), *v.,* **-gled, -gling,** *n.* —*v.i.* 1. to have a sensation of slight prickles, stings, or tremors, as from cold, a sharp blow, excitement, etc. 2. to cause such a sensation. —*n.* 3. a tingling sensation. 4. the tingling action of cold, a blow, excitement, etc. [ME; var. of TINKLE] —**tin′gler,** *n.* —**ting′ling·ly,** *adv.*

tin′ god′, a self-important, dictatorial person in a position of authority.

tin′ hat′, a steel or aluminum safety helmet, as worn by soldiers, construction workers, loggers, etc.

tin·horn (tin′hôrn′), *Slang.* —*n.* 1. someone, esp. a gambler, who pretends to be important but actually has little ability, influence, or money. —*adj.* 2. cheap and insignificant; small-time: *a tinhorn racket.*

tink·er (ting′kər), *n.* 1. a mender of pots, kettles, pans, etc., usually an itinerant. 2. an unskillful or clumsy worker; bungler. 3. a jack-of-all-trades. 4. the act or an instance of tinkering. 5. *Scot., Irish, Eng.* **a.** a gypsy. **b.** any itinerant worker. **c.** a wanderer. **d.** a beggar. 6. a small mackerel, *Pneumatophorus grex,* found off the Atlantic coast of the U.S. —*v.i.* 7. to do the work of a tinker. 8. to work unskillfully or clumsily at anything. 9. to busy oneself futilely with a thing: *Stop tinkering with that clock and take it to the repair shop.* —*v.t.* 10. to mend as a tinker. 11. to repair in an unskillful way. [ME *tinkere,* syncopated var. of *tinekere* worker in tin] —**tink′er·er,** *n.*

tink′er's dam′, something worthless or trivial; nothing at all: *It's not worth a tinker's dam.* Also, **tink′er's damn′.**

tin·kle (ting′kəl), *v.,* **-kled, -kling,** *n.* —*v.i.* 1. to give forth or make a succession of short, light, ringing sounds, as a small bell. 2. to run one's fingers lightly over a keyboard instrument or to play such an instrument simply or badly. —*v.t.* 3. to cause to tinkle or jingle. —*n.* 4. a tinkling sound or tune. 5. the act or an instance of tinkling. [ME, freq. of obs. *tink* (v.) to clink; imit.]

tin·kly (ting′klē), *adj.,* **-kli·er, -kli·est.** tinkling or producing a tinkling sound.

tin′ liz′zie (liz′ē), *Slang.* a small, cheap automobile.

tin·man (tin′mən), *n., pl.* **-men.** a tinsmith.

tinned (tind), *adj.* 1. coated or plated with tin. 2. *Chiefly Brit.* preserved or packed in a can, as food; canned.

tin·ner (tin′ər), *n.* a tinsmith.

tin·ni·tus (ti nī′təs), *n. Pathol.* a ringing sensation of sound in the ears. [< L: a tinkling = *tinnīt-* (ptp. s. of *tinnīre* to tinkle) + *-us* n. suffix]

tin·ny (tin′ē), *adj.,* **-ni·er, -ni·est.** 1. of or like tin. 2. containing tin. 3. lacking in timbre or resonance: *a tinny piano.* 4. not strong or durable. 5. having the taste of tin. —**tin′ni·ly,** *adv.* —**tin′ni·ness,** *n.*

tin-pan (tin′pan′), *adj.* harsh, tinny, or clanging; noisy. Also, **tin′-pan′ny.**

Tin′ Pan Al′ley, 1. the district of a city, esp. New York City, where most of the popular music is published. 2. the composers or publishers of popular music as a group.

tin′ plate′, thin iron or steel sheet coated with tin. Also, **tin′plate′.**

tin-plate (tin′plāt′), *v.t.,* **-plat·ed, -plat·ing.** to coat (iron or steel sheet) with tin. —**tin′ plat′er.**

tin·sel (tin′səl), *n., adj., v.,* **-seled, -sel·ing** or (*esp. Brit.*) **-selled, -sel·ling.** —*n.* 1. a glittering, metallic, inexpensive substance, used in strips, threads, etc., to produce a sparkling effect. 2. a metallic yarn, usually wrapped around a core yarn of silk, rayon, or cotton, for weaving brocade or lamé. 3. any showy pretense. 4. a fabric, formerly in use, of silk or wool interwoven with threads of gold, silver, or, later, copper. —*adj.* 5. consisting of or containing tinsel. 6. showy; gaudy; tawdry. —*v.t.* 7. to adorn with or as with tinsel. 8. to make showy or gaudy. [by aphesis < MF *estincelle* (OF *estincele*) a spark, flash < VL **stincilla,* metathetic var. of L *scintilla* SCINTILLA; first used attributively in phrases *tinsel satin, tinsel cloth*] —**tin′sel·like′,** *adj.*

tin·smith (tin′smith′), *n.* a person who makes or repairs tinware or items of other light metals.

tin′ sol′dier, a miniature toy soldier of cast metal.

tin′ spir′it, Often, **tin spirits.** any of a group of solutions containing tin salts, used in dyeing.

tin·stone (tin′stōn′), *n.* cassiterite.

tint (tint), *n.* 1. a gradation or variety of a color; hue. 2. a color diluted with white, or one of less than maximum purity, chromo, or saturation. 3. any delicate or pale color. 4. *Engraving.* a uniform shading. 5. Also called **tint′ block′.** *Print.* a faintly or lightly colored background to an illustration. 6. any of various commercial dyes for the hair. —*v.t.* 7. to apply a tint or tints to; color slightly or delicately; tinge. [var. of TINCT] —**tint′er,** *n.* —**tint′less,** *adj.*

Tin·tag′el Head′ (tin taj′əl), a cape in SW England, on the W coast of Cornwall.

tin·tin·nab·u·lar (tin′ti nab′yə lər), *adj.* of or pertaining to bells or bell ringing. Also, **tin·tin·nab·u·lar·y** (tin′ti nab′yə ler′ē), **tin′tin·nab′u·lous.** [< L *tintinnābul(um)* bell (*tintinnā(re)* (to) ring + *-bulum* instrumental suffix) + -AR[1]]

tin·tin·nab·u·la·tion (tin′ti nab′yə lā′shən), *n.* the ringing or sound of bells. [< L *tintinnābul(um)* bell (see TINTINNABULAR) + -ATION]

Tin·to·ret·to (tin′tə ret′ō; *It.* tēn′tô ret′tô), *n.* **Il** (ēl), (*Jacopo Robusti*), 1518–94, Venetian painter.

tin·type (tin′tīp′), *n.* a positive photograph made on a sensitized sheet of enameled tin or iron; ferrotype.

tin·ware (tin′wâr′), *n.* articles made of tin plate.

tin·work (tin′wûrk′), *n.* 1. something made of tin. 2. such things collectively.

tin·works (tin′wûrks′), *n., pl.* **-works.** (*construed as sing. or pl.*) an establishment for the mining or processing of tin or for the making of tinware.

ti·ny (tī′nē), *adj.*, **-ni·er, -ni·est.** very small; minute; wee. [late ME *tine* very small (< ?) + -Y[1]] —**ti′ni·ly,** *adv.* —**ti′ni·ness,** *n.* —**Syn.** little, diminutive, teeny.

-tion, a suffix occurring in words of Latin origin, used to form abstract nouns from verbs or stems not identical with verbs, whether as expressing action (*revolution; commendation*), or a state (*contrition; starvation*), or associated meanings (*relation; temptation*). Also, **-ation, -cion, -ion, -sion, -xion.** [< L *-tiōn-* (s. of *-tiō*) = *-t(us)* ptp. suffix + *-iōn-* -ION]

-tious, a suffix originally occurring in adjectives borrowed from Latin (*fictitious*); on this model, used with stems of other origin (*bumptious*). Also, **-ious, -ous.** [< L *-tiōs(us)* = *-t(us)* ptp. suffix + *-iōsus* -IOUS]

tip[1] (tip), *n.*, *v.*, **tipped, tip·ping.** —*n.* **1.** a slender or pointed end or extremity, esp. of anything long or tapered. **2.** the top, summit, or apex. **3.** a small piece or part, as of metal, leather, etc., forming or covering the extremity of something: *a cane with a rubber tip.* **4.** Also called **tip-in.** an insert, as an illustration or map, pasted to a page of a book, magazine, etc. —*v.t.* **5.** to furnish with a tip. **6.** to serve as or form the tip of. **7.** to mark or adorn the tip of. **8.** to remove the tip or stem of (berries or certain fruits or vegetables). **9.** **tip in,** *Bookbinding.* to paste the inner margin of (a map, illustration, or other plate) into a signature before gathering. [ME; cf. D, LG, Dan *tip*, Sw *tipp*, G *zipf-* in *Zipfel* tip] —**tip′less,** *adj.*

tip[2] (tip), *v.*, **tipped, tip·ping,** *n.* —*v.t.* **1.** to incline or tilt. **2.** to overturn, upset, or overthrow (often fol. by *over*). **3.** to remove or lift (one's hat or cap) in salutation. **4.** *Brit.* to dump or dispose of by dumping: *The maid tipped the rubbish.* —*v.i.* **5.** to assume a slanting or sloping position; incline. **6.** to tilt up at one end and down at the other; slant. **7.** to be overturned or upset. **8.** to tumble or topple (usually fol. by *over*). —*n.* **9.** the act of tipping. **10.** the state of being tipped. **11.** *Brit.* a dump for refuse, as that from a mine. [earlier *tipe*, ME *type* to upset, overturn] —**tip′pa·ble,** *adj.*

tip[3] (tip), *n.*, *v.*, **tipped, tip·ping.** —*n.* **1.** a small present of money given in return for a service; gratuity. **2.** a piece of private information, as for use in betting, a news story, etc. **3.** a useful hint or idea. —*v.t.* **4.** to give a small gratuity to. —*v.i.* **5.** to give a gratuity. **6.** **tip off,** *Informal.* **a.** to give private information about or to inform. **b.** to warn of impending danger or trouble. [? special use of TIP[4]] —**tip′less,** *adj.* —**tip′pa·ble,** *adj.* —**tip′per,** *n.*

tip[4] (tip), *n.*, *v.*, **tipped, tip·ping.** —*n.* **1.** a light, smart blow; tap. **2.** *Baseball.* a batted ball that glances off the bat. Cf. **foul tip.** —*v.t.* **3.** to strike or hit lightly. **4.** *Baseball.* to strike (the ball) with a glancing blow. [? < LG; cf. G *tippen* to tap < LG]

ti′ palm′, ti[2].

tip·cart (tip′kärt′), *n.* a cart with a body that can be tipped or tilted to empty it of its contents.

ti·pi (tē′pē), *n.*, *pl.* **-pis.** tepee.

tip-in[1] (tip′in′), *n.* *Basketball.* tap-in.

tip-in[2] (tip′in′), *n.* tip[1] (def. 4).

tip-off (tip′ôf′, -of′), *n.* *Informal.* **1.** the act of tipping off. **2.** a hint or warning: *They got a tip-off on the raid.*

Tip·pe·ca·noe (tip′ə kə no͞o′), *n.* a river in N Indiana, flowing SW to the Wabash: battle 1811. 200 mi. long.

Tip·per·ar·y (tip′ə râr′ē), *n.* **1.** a county in Munster province, in the S Republic of Ireland. 123,822 (1961); 1643 sq. mi. **2.** a town in this county. 4507 (est. 1966).

tip·pet (tip′it), *n.* **1.** a scarf, usually of fur or wool, for covering the neck or the neck and shoulders. Cf. **stole**[2] (def. 2). **2.** *Eccles.* a band of silk or the like worn around the neck with the ends pendent in front. Cf. **stole**[2] (def. 1). **3.** a long, narrow, pendent part of a hood, sleeve, etc. [ME]

tip·ple[1] (tip′əl), *v.*, **-pled, -pling,** *n.* —*v.t.* **1.** to drink (intoxicating liquor), esp. repeatedly, in small quantities. —*v.i.* **2.** to drink intoxicating liquor, esp. habitually or to some excess. —*n.* **3.** intoxicating liquor. [back formation from ME *tipeler* tapster = *tipel-* TAP[2] (c. D *tepel* teat) + *-er* -ER[1]. See TIPSY] —**tip′pler,** *n.*

tip·ple[2] (tip′əl), *n.* **1.** a device that tilts or overturns a freight car to dump its contents. **2.** a place where loaded cars are emptied by tipping. [n. use of *tipple* to tumble, freq. of TIP[2]]

tip′ sheet′, a publication containing the latest information, tips, and predictions, esp. of business, stock-market conditions, horse racing results, etc.

tip·staff (tip′staf′, -stäf′), *n.*, *pl.* **-staves** (-stāvz′, -stavz′, -stävz′), **-staffs.** **1.** an attendant or crier in a court of law. **2.** a staff tipped with metal, formerly carried as a badge of office, as by such an attendant or a constable. **3.** any official who formerly carried such a staff. [TIPP(ED) (see TIP[1], -ED[3]) + STAFF]

tip·ster (tip′stər), *n.* *Informal.* a person who furnishes tips, as for betting.

tip·sy (tip′sē), *adj.*, **-si·er, -si·est.** **1.** slightly intoxicated or drunk. **2.** characterized by or due to intoxication; unsteady. **3.** askew or crooked; uneven. [obs. *tip* strong drink (? back formation from TIPPLE[1]) + *-sy* adj. suffix. Cf. obs. *bumpsy* in same sense] —**tip′si·ly,** *adv.* —**tip′si·ness,** *n.*

tip·toe (tip′tō′), *n.*, *v.*, **-toed, -to·ing,** *adj.*, *adv.* —*n.* **1.** the tip or end of a toe. **2.** **on tiptoe, a.** on the tips of one's toes. **b.** expectant; eager: *With Christmas coming, the children were on tiptoe.* **c.** stealthily; cautiously. —*v.i.* **3.** to move or go on tiptoe, as with caution or stealth. —*adj.* **4.** characterized by standing or walking on tiptoe. **5.** straining upward. **6.** eagerly expectant. **7.** cautious; stealthy. —*adv.* **8.** eagerly or cautiously; on tiptoe. [ME *tiptoon* (pl.)]

tip·top (tip′top′), *n.* **1.** the extreme top or summit. **2.** *Informal.* the highest point or degree of quality. —*adj.* **3.** at the very top. **4.** *Informal.* of the highest quality. —*adv.* **5.** in a tiptop manner; very well: *It's shaping up tiptop.*

ti·rade (tī′rād, tī rād′), *n.* **1.** a prolonged outburst of bitter, outspoken denunciation. **2.** a long, vehement speech. **3.** a passage with a single theme or idea, as in dramatic poetry. [< F: lit., a stretch, (continuous) pulling < It *tirata*, n. use of fem. of *tirato*, ptp. of *tirare* to draw, pull, fire (a shot)] —**Syn. 2.** harangue.

ti·rail·leur (tē RA yœR′), *n.*, *pl.* **-leurs** (-yœR′). *French.* **1.** skirmisher; sharpshooter. **2.** one of the native infantry units formerly organized by the French in North Africa, Senegal, and Indochina.

Ti·ran (tē rän′), *n.* **1.** **Strait of,** a strait between the Gulf of Aqaba and the Red Sea. 10 mi. long; 5 mi. wide. **2.** an island in the mouth of this strait.

Ti·ra·na (tē rä′nä), *n.* a city in and the capital of Albania, in the central part. 175,000. Albanian, **Ti·ra·në** (tē rä′ne).

tire[1] (tīər), *v.*, **tired, tir·ing,** *n.* —*v.t.* **1.** to reduce or exhaust the strength of, as by exertion; make weary; fatigue. **2.** to exhaust the interest, patience, etc., of, as by long continuance or by dullness; bore. —*v.i.* **3.** to have the strength reduced or exhausted, as by labor or exertion; become fatigued; be sleepy. **4.** to have one's interest, patience, etc., exhausted; become bored (usually fol. by *of*): *He has tired of waiting.* —*n.* **5.** *Brit. Dial.* fatigue. [late ME (Scot) *tyre*, OE *tȳr(ian)*, var. of *tēorian* to weary, be wearied] —**Syn. 2.** exasperate, irk.

tire[2] (tīər), *n.*, *v.*, **tired, tir·ing.** —*n.* **1.** a ring or band of rubber, either solid or hollow and inflated, for placing over the rim of a wheel to provide traction, resistance to wear, etc. **2.** a metal band attached to the outside of the felloes and forming the tread of a wagon wheel. —*v.t.* **3.** to furnish with tires. Also, *Brit.*, **tyre.** [late ME *tyre;* special use of TIRE[3]]

Tire[2] (Cross section) A, Rim of wheel; B, Bead; C, Inner tube; D, Tread; E, Sidewall

tire[3] (tīər), *v.*, **tired, tir·ing,** *n.* *Archaic.* —*v.t.* **1.** to attire or array. **2.** to dress (the head or hair), esp. with a headdress. —*n.* **3.** attire or dress. **4.** a headdress. [ME; aph. var. of ATTIRE]

tire′ chain′, a network of chains fitting over the tire of a car, truck, or other vehicle, to increase traction and prevent skidding on roads covered with ice or snow.

tired[1] (tīərd), *adj.* **1.** exhausted, as by exertion; fatigued or sleepy. **2.** weary or bored (usually fol. by *of*): *He's tired of eating the same food every day.* **3.** hackneyed; stale, as a joke, phrase, theatrical performance, or the like. **4.** *Informal.* impatient or disgusted: *You make me tired.* [ME *tyred.* See TIRE[1], -ED[2]]
—**Syn. 1.** enervated. TIRED, EXHAUSTED, FATIGUED, WEARIED, WEARY suggest a condition in which a large part of one's energy and vitality has been consumed. A person who is TIRED has used up a considerable part of his bodily or mental resources: *to feel tired at the end of the day.* A person who is EXHAUSTED is completely drained of energy and vitality, usually because of arduous or long-sustained effort: *exhausted after a hard run.* A person who is FATIGUED has consumed energy to a point where rest and sleep are demanded: *feeling rather pleasantly fatigued.* A person who is WEARIED has been under protracted exertion or strain: *wearied by a long vigil.* WEARY suggests a more permanent condition than wearied: *weary of struggling against misfortunes.* —**Ant. 1.** rested; energetic, tireless.

tired[2] (tīərd), *adj.* having a tire or tires. [TIRE[2] + -ED[3]]

tire·less (tīər′lis), *adj.* untiring; indefatigable: *a tireless worker.* —**tire′less·ly,** *adv.* —**tire′less·ness,** *n.*

Ti·re·si·as (tī rē′sē əs, -shē əs), *n.* *Class. Myth.* a prophet who, blinded by Athena because he saw her bathing, was awarded the gift of prophecy by her as a consolation: said to have lived both as a man and as a woman.

tire·some (tīər′səm), *adj.* **1.** causing or liable to cause a person to tire; wearisome. **2.** annoying or vexatious. —**Syn. 1.** dull, fatiguing, humdrum. —**Ant. 1.** interesting; exciting, stimulating.

tire·wom·an (tīər′wo͝om′ən), *n.*, *pl.* **-wom·en.** *Archaic.* a lady's maid.

Ti·rich Mir (tē′rich mēr′), a mountain in N Pakistan, on the border of Afghanistan: highest peak of the Hindu Kush Mountains. 25,230 ft.

tir′ing room′, *Archaic.* a dressing room, esp. in a theater. [aph. var. of *attiring room*]

ti·ro (tī′rō), *n.*, *pl.* **-ros.** tyro.

Tir·ol (tir′ol, tī′rōl, ti rōl′; *Ger.* tē RŌL′), *n.* Tyrol.

Ti·ro·le·an (ti rō′lē ən), *adj.*, *n.* Tyrolean.

Tir·o·lese (tir′ə lēz′, -lēs′), *adj.*, *n.*, *pl.* **-lese.** Tyrolese.

Ti·ros (tī′rōs), *n.* *U.S.* a satellite for transmitting television pictures of the earth's cloud cover.

Tir·pitz (tiR′pits), *n.* **Al·fred von** (äl′fRāt fən), 1849–1930, German admiral and statesman.

Tir·so de Mo·li·na (tēR′sô the mô lē′nä), (*Gabriel Téllez*) 1571?–1648, Spanish dramatist.

Tir·u·chi·ra·pal·li (tir′o͝o chir ə pul′ē, ti ro͞o′chi rä′pə lē), *n.* a city in central Madras, in S India, on the Cauvery River. 249,900 (1961). Formerly, **Trichinopoly.**

Tir·yns (tir′inz), *n.* an ancient city in Greece, in Peloponnesus: excavated ruins.

'tis (tiz), a contraction of *it is.*

ti·sane (ti zan′; *Fr.* tē ZAN′), *n.*, *pl.* **-sanes** (-zanz′; *Fr.* -ZAN′). *Obs.* a ptisan. [< F]

Tish·ah b'Ab (tish′ə bôv′; *Heb.* tē shä′ bə äv′), a Jewish fast day observed on the ninth day of Ab in memory of the destruction of the First and Second Temples. Also, **Tish·ah b'Av** (tish′ə bôv′). Also called **Ninth of Ab.** [< Heb: ninth (day) of Ab]

Tish·ri (tish′rā, -rē; *Heb.* tēsh RĒ′), *n.* the first month of the Jewish calendar. Cf. **Jewish calendar.** [< Heb]

Ti·siph·o·ne (ti sif′ə nē′), *n.* *Class. Myth.* one of the Furies.

tis·sue (tish′o͞o), *n.*, *v.*, **-sued, -su·ing.** —*n.* **1.** *Biol.* an aggregate of similar cells and cell products forming a definite kind of structural material in an animal or plant. **2.** any of several kinds of soft gauzy papers: *cleansing tissue.* **3.** See **tissue paper.** **4.** a woven fabric, esp. one of light or gauzy texture, originally woven with gold or silver. **5.** an interwoven or interconnected series or mass: *a tissue of falsehoods.* **6.** a piece of thin writing paper on which carbon copies are made. —*v.t.* *Archaic.* **7.** to weave, esp. with threads of gold and silver. **8.** to clothe or adorn with tissue. [ME *tissew*, var. of *tissu* < MF, OF, n. use of ptp. of *tistre* to weave < L *texere*] —**tis′su·al,** *adj.* —**tis′su·ey,** *adj.*

tis′sue cul′ture, **1.** the science of cultivating animal tissue in a prepared medium. **2.** the process itself.

tis′sue pa′per, a very thin, almost transparent paper used for wrapping, in packing, etc.

Ti·sza (*Hung.* tē′so), *n.* a river in S central Europe, flowing from the Carpathian Mountains through E Hungary and NE Yugoslavia into the Danube N of Belgrade. 800 mi. long. German, **Theiss.**

tit[1] (tit), *n. Archaic.* **1.** a girl or young woman; hussy. **2.** a small or poor horse; nag. [ME *tite-* (in *titemose* TITMOUSE); c. Norw *tite* titmouse; akin to Icel *tittr* tack, pin. See TIT[2]]

tit[2] (tit), *n.* **1.** a teat. **2.** *Slang.* a female breast. [ME *titte*, OE *titt;* c. MLG, MD *titte*, G *Zitze*, Norw *titta;* akin to TIT[1]]

Tit., Titus.

tit., title.

Ti·tan (tīt′ən), *n.* **1.** *Class. Myth.* **a.** any of the sons of Uranus and Gaea, including Coeus, Crius, Cronus, Hyperion, Iapetus, and Oceanus. **b.** Also, **Ti′tan·ess.** any of the sisters of these, including Mnemosyne, Phoebe, Rhea, Tethys, Themis, and Theia. **c.** any of the offspring of the children of Uranus and Gaea. **2. the Titan,** Helios. **3.** (*usually l.c.*) a person or thing of enormous size, strength, power, influence, etc.: *a titan of industry.* **4.** *U.S.* a surface-to-surface intercontinental ballistic missile. —*adj.* **5.** (*l.c.*) titanic; gigantic. [late ME: the sun < L < Gk]

ti·tan·ate (tīt′ənāt′), *n. Chem.* a salt of titanic acid. [TITAN(IUM) + -ATE[2]]

ti·tan·ic[1] (tī tan′ik, ti-), *adj. Chem.* of or containing titanium, esp. in the tetravalent state. [TITAN(IUM) + -IC]

ti·tan·ic[2] (tī tan′ik), *adj.* **1.** Also, **titan.** of enormous size, strength, power, etc.; gigantic. **2.** (*cap.*) of, pertaining to, or characteristic of the Titans. [< Gk *Titanik(ós).* See TITAN, -IC] —**ti·tan′i·cal·ly,** *adv.*

titan′ic ac′id, *Chem.* **1.** See **titanium dioxide. 2.** any of various acids derived from titanium dioxide.

titan′ic ox′ide, *Chem.* See **titanium dioxide.**

Ti·tan·ism (tīt′əniz′əm), *n.* (*sometimes l.c.*) the characteristic Titan spirit or quality, esp. of revolt against tradition, convention, and established order.

ti·tan·ite (tīt′ənīt′), *n. Mineral.* sphene. [< G *Titanit.* See TITANIUM, -ITE[1]]

ti·ta·ni·um (tī tā′nē əm), *n. Chem.* a dark-gray or silvery, lustrous, very hard, light, corrosion-resistant, metallic element: used in metallurgy to remove oxygen and nitrogen from steel and to toughen it. *Symbol:* Ti; *at. wt.:* 47.90; *at. no.:* 22; *sp. gr.:* 4.5 at 20°C.

tita′nium diox′ide, *Chem.* a white powder, TiO_2, used chiefly in white pigments. Also called **tita′nium ox′ide, titanic acid, titanic oxide.**

Ti·tan·om·a·chy (tīt′ənom′ə kē), *n. Class. Myth.* the unsuccessful revolt of the family of Iapetus against Zeus. [< Gk *tītānomachía*]

ti·tan·o·saur (tī tan′ə sôr′, tīt′ənə sôr′), *n.* any amphibious, herbivorous dinosaur of the genus *Titanosaurus*, from the Cretaceous period. [< NL *Tītānosaur(us)*]

ti·tan·ous (tī tan′əs, ti-), *adj. Chem.* containing trivalent titanium. [TITAN(IUM) + -OUS]

tit·bit (tit′bit′), *n. Chiefly Brit.* tidbit. [rhyming compound, by alter.]

ti·ter (tī′tər, tē′-), *n. Chem.* the strength of a solution as determined by titration with a standard substance. Also, *esp. Brit.,* **titre.** [< F *titre* title, qualification, fineness of alloyed gold or silver < L *titulus* TITLE]

tit′ for tat′, with an equivalent retaliation, as a blow for a blow.

tith·a·ble (tī′thə bəl), *adj.* liable to be tithed; subject to the payment of tithes. [late ME *tythable*]

tithe (tīth), *n., v.,* **tithed, tith·ing.** —*n.* **1.** Sometimes, **tithes.** the tenth part of agricultural produce, goods, or personal income set apart as an offering to God or for works of mercy, or the same amount regarded as an obligation or tax for the support of the church, priesthood, or the like. **2.** any tax, levy, or the like, of one-tenth. **3.** a tenth part or any indefinitely small part of anything. —*v.t.* **4.** to give or pay a tithe or tenth of. **5.** to give or pay tithes on. **6.** to exact a tithe from (a person, community, parish, etc.). **7.** to levy a tithe on (crops, income, etc.). —*v.i.* **8.** to give or pay a tithe. Also, *Brit.,* **tythe.** [(n.) ME *ti(ghe)the*, OE *teogotha* tenth; (v.) ME *tithe(n)*, OE *te(o)g(o)thian* to take the tenth of] —**tithe′less,** *adj.* —**tith′er,** *n.*

tith·ing (tī′thing), *n.* **1.** a tithe. **2.** a giving or an exacting of tithes. **3.** a company of householders, originally 10 in number, in the old English system of frankpledge. **4.** a rural division in England, originally regarded as one tenth of a hundred. [ME; OE *tigething*]

Ti·tho·nus (ti thō′nəs), *n. Class. Myth.* a son of Laomedon, beloved by Eos (Aurora): he was granted immortality by Zeus through the offices of Eos, but without eternal youth, which he neglected to request: in old age he asked Eos to take back the gift and was metamorphosed into a grasshopper.

ti·ti[1] (tē tē′), *n., pl.* **-tis.** any of various small reddish or grayish monkeys of the genus *Callicebus*, of South America. [< Sp < Aymaran]

ti·ti[2] (tē′tē), *n., pl.* **-tis.** any of the cyrillaceous shrubs or small trees of the southern U.S., esp. *Cliftonia monophylla* and *Cyrilla racemiflora*, having glossy leaves and racemes of fragrant white flowers. [< AmerInd]

Ti·tian (tish′ən), *n.* **1.** (*Tiziano Vecellio*) c1477–1576, Italian painter. **2.** (*l.c.*) a reddish or golden brown: *titian hair.* —**Ti′tian·esque′,** *adj.*

Ti·ti·ca·ca (tē′tē kä′kä), *n.* **Lake,** a lake on the boundary between S Peru and W Bolivia, in the Andes: the largest lake in South America; the highest large lake in the world. 3200 sq. mi.; 12,508 ft. above sea level.

tit·il·late (tit′əlāt′), *v.t.,* **-lat·ed, -lat·ing.** **1.** to excite a tingling sensation in, as by touching or stroking lightly. **2.** to excite agreeably, esp. superficially. [< L *tītillāt(us)*, ptp. of *tītillāre* to tickle; see -ATE[1]] —**tit′il·lat′ing·ly,** *adv.* —**tit′il·la′tion,** *n.* —**tit′il·la′tive,** *adj.*

tit·i·vate[1] (tit′ə vāt′), *v.,* **-vat·ed, -vat·ing.** *Informal.* —*v.t.* **1.** to make smart or spruce. —*v.i.* **2.** to make oneself smart or spruce. [earlier *tidivate* (TIDY + (ELE)VATE; i.e., tidy up)] —**tit′i·va′tion,** *n.* —**tit′i·va′tor,** *n.*

tit·i·vate[2] (tit′ə vāt′), *v.t.,* **-vat·ed, -vat·ing.** titillate. [by alter.]

tit·lark (tit′lärk′), *n.* any of several small, larklike birds, esp. a pipit.

ti·tle (tīt′əl), *n., v.,* **-tled, -tling.** —*n.* **1.** the distinguishing name of a book, poem, picture, piece of music, or the like. **2.** a descriptive heading or caption, as of a chapter or other part of a book. **3.** See **title page. 4.** a descriptive or distinctive appellation, esp. one belonging to a person by right of rank, office, attainment, etc.: *the title of Lord Mayor.* **5.** *Sports.* the championship. **6.** an established right to something. **7.** a ground or basis for a claim. **8.** anything that provides such a ground. **9.** *Law.* **a.** legal right to the possession of property, esp. real property. **b.** the ground or evidence of such right. **c.** the instrument constituting evidence of such right. **d.** a unity combining all of the requisites to complete legal ownership. **e.** a division of a statute, lawbook, etc., esp. one larger than an article or section. **f.** (in pleading) the designation of one's basis for judicial relief; the cause of action sued upon, as contract, tort, etc. **10.** *Eccles.* **a.** a fixed sphere of work and source of income. **b.** any of certain Roman Catholic churches in Rome, the nominal incumbents of which are cardinals. **11.** Usually, **titles.** *Motion Pictures, Television.* **a.** any written matter inserted into the film or program, esp. the list of actors, technicians, writers, etc., contributing to it; credits. **b.** subtitle (def. 3). —*v.t.* **12.** to furnish with a title; entitle. [ME, var. of *titel*, OE *titul* < L *titul(us)* superscription, title] —**Syn. 4.** See **name. 12.** term, call, style.

ti′tled (tīt′əld), *adj.* having a title of nobility: *a titled family.*

ti′tle deed′, a deed containing evidence of ownership.

ti·tle·hold·er (tīt′əl hōl′dər), *n.* **1.** a person who holds a title. **2.** *Sports.* Also called **ti·tlist** (tīt′list). a present champion.

ti′tle page′, the page at the beginning of a volume that indicates the title, author's or editor's name, and usually the publisher and the place and date of publication.

ti′tle role′, (in a play, opera, etc.) the role or character from which the title is derived.

ti·tlist (tīt′list), *n. Sports.* a titleholder; champion.

tit·mouse (tit′mous′), *n., pl.* **-mice** (-mīs′). any of numerous small, passerine birds of the family *Paridae*, esp. of the genus *Parus*, having soft, thick plumage and a short, stout, conical bill. Cf. **tufted titmouse.** [ME *tit(e)mose* (see TIT[1]); *mose*, OE *māse* titmouse; c. G *Meise* titmouse, Icel *meis-* in *meisingr* kind of bird; modern *mouse* by folk etym.]

Tufted titmouse, *Parus bicolor* (Length 6 in.)

Ti·to (tē′tō), *n.* **Marshal** (*Josip Broz*), 1891–1980, president of Yugoslavia 1953–80.

Ti·to·grad (tē′tō grad′), *n.* a city in and the capital of Montenegro, in S Yugoslavia. 39,000 (est. 1964). Formerly, **Podgorica, Podgoritsa.**

Ti·to·ism (tē′tō iz′əm), *n.* a form of communism associated with Tito, characterized by the assertion by a satellite state of its national interests in opposition to Soviet rule.

ti·trant (tī′trənt), *n. Chem.* the reagent added in a titration. [TIT(E)R + -ANT]

ti·trate (tī′trāt, ti′-), *v.t., v.i.,* **-trat·ed, -trat·ing.** *Chem.* to ascertain the quantity of a given constituent present in (a solution) by adding a liquid reagent of known strength and measuring the volume necessary to convert the constituent to another form. [TIT(E)R + -ATE[1]] —**ti·trat′a·ble, ti·tra·ble** (tī′trə bəl), *adj.* —**ti·tra′tion,** *n.*

ti·tre (tī′tər, tē′-), *n. Chiefly Brit.* titer.

tit-tat-toe (tit′tat tō′), *n.* tick-tack-toe.

tit·ter (tit′ər), *v.i.* **1.** to laugh in a half-restrained, self-conscious, or affected way, as from nervousness or in ill-suppressed amusement. —*n.* **2.** a tittering laugh. [? < Scand; cf. Icel *titra* to quiver, Sw (dial.) *tittra* to giggle] —**tit′ter·er,** *n.* —**tit′ter·ing·ly,** *adv.* —**Syn. 1.** snicker, snigger, giggle, laugh.

tit·tle (tit′əl), *n.* **1.** a dot or other small mark in writing or printing, used as a diacritic, punctuation, etc. **2.** a particle, jot, or whit. [ME *titel*, OE *titul* < ML *titul(us)* mark over letter or word. See TITLE]

tit·tle-tat·tle (tit′əl tat′əl), *n., v.,* **-tled, -tling.** —*n.* **1.** gossip or chatter. —*v.i.* **2.** to gossip or chatter. [gradational compound based on *tittle* to whisper, gossip] —**tit′tle-tat′tler,** *n.*

tit·tup (tit′əp), *n., v.,* **-tuped, -tup·ing** or (*esp. Brit.*) **-tupped, -tup·ping.** *Chiefly Brit.* —*n.* **1.** an exaggerated prancing, bouncing movement or manner of moving. —*v.i.* **2.** to move in an exaggerated prancing or bouncing way, as a spirited horse. [dial. *tit* a jerk, twitch (ME *titte*) + (GALL)OP] —**tit′tup·py,** *adj.*

tit·ty (tit′ē), *n., pl.* **-ties.** a teat. [TIT[2] + -Y[2]]

tit·u·lar (tich′ə lər, tit′yə-), *adj.* **1.** of, pertaining to, or of the nature of a title. **2.** having a title, esp. of rank. **3.** in title only; nominal; having the title but none of the associated duties, powers, etc.: *He is only the titular head of the company.* **4.** from whom or which a title or name is taken: *His titular saint is Michael.* **5.** designating any of the Roman Catholic churches in Rome whose nominal incumbents are cardinals. —*n.* **6.** a person who bears a title. **7.** a person from whom or something from which a title or name is taken. **8.** *Eccles.* a person entitled to a benefice but not required to perform its duties. [< L *titul(us)* TITLE + -AR[1]] —**tit·u·lar·i·ty** (tich′ə lar′i tē, tit′yə-), *n.* —**tit′u·lar·ly,** *adv.*

tit·u·lar·y (tich′ə ler′ē, tit′yə-), *adj., n., pl.* **-lar·ies.** titular. [< L *titul(us)* TITLE + -ARY]

Ti·tus (tī′təs), *n.* **1.** a disciple and companion of the apostle Paul, to whom Paul is supposed to have addressed an Epistle. **2.** this New Testament Epistle. **3.** (*Flavius Sabinus Vespasianus*) A.D. 40?–81, Roman emperor 79–81.
Ti·tus·ville (tī′təs vil′), *n.* **1.** a town in NW Pennsylvania: first oil well in U.S. drilled 1859. 7,331 (1970). **2.** a city in central Florida. 30,515 (1970).
Ti·u (tē′o͞o), *n.* *Eng. Myth.* a god of the sky and of war, the equivalent of Tyr in Scandinavian mythology. [var. of OE *Tiw* god of war. See TUESDAY]
Tiv·o·li (tiv′ə lē; *It.* tē′vô lē), *n.* a town in central Italy, E of Rome: Roman ruins. 34,235 (1961). Ancient, **Tibur.**
tiz·zy (tiz′ē), *n., pl.* **-zies.** *Informal.* a dither. [?]
Tji·re·bon (chir′ē bôn′), *n.* a seaport on N Java, in S central Indonesia. 158,299 (1961).
TKO, *Boxing.* See **technical knockout.** Also, **T.K.O.**
TL, trade-last. Also, **T.L.**
Tl, *Chem.* thallium.
Tlal·pan (tläl pän′), *n.* a city in S Mexico: near site of a large mound erected by a prehistoric people. 18,141 (1956).
Tlax·ca·la (tläs kä′lä), *n.* a state in SE central Mexico. 347,334 (1960); 1554 sq. mi.
TLC, tender, loving care.
Tlem·cen (tlem sen′), *n.* a city in NW Algeria. 83,000 (1960). Also, **Tlem·sen′.**
Tlin·git (tliŋ′git), *n., pl.* **-gits,** (*esp. collectively*) **-git. 1.** a member of any of a number of American Indian peoples of the coastal regions of southern Alaska and northern British Colombia. **2.** the language of the Tlingit, a Na-Dene language related to Athapaskan.
Tlin·kit (tliŋ′kit), *n., pl.* **-kits,** (*esp. collectively*) **-kit.** Tlingit.
TM, trademark.
Tm, *Chem.* thulium.
T-man (tē′man′), *n., pl.* **T-men.** *U.S. Informal.* a special investigator of the Department of the Treasury.
tme·sis (tə mē′sis, mē′sis), *n.* the interpolation of one or more words between the parts of a compound word, as *be thou ware* for *beware.* [< L < Gk: a cutting = *tmē-* (var. s. of *témnein* to cut) + *-sis* -SIS]
TN, Tennessee (approved esp. for use with zip code).
tn., ton.
Tng., training.
TNT, *Chem.* a yellow, flammable solid, $CH_3C_6H_2(NO_2)_3$, derived from toluene by nitration, a high explosive unaffected by ordinary friction or shock: used in explosive devices and as an intermediate in the preparation of dyestuffs and photographic chemicals. Also, **T.N.T.** Also called **trinitrotoluene, trinitrotoluol.**
T number, *Photog.* one of a series of calibrations of lens openings according to the intensity of the light actually transmitted by the lens.
to (to͞o; *unstressed* to͝o, tə), *prep.* **1.** (used for expressing motion or direction toward a point, person, place, or thing approached and reached, as opposed to *from*): *He came to the house.* **2.** (used for expressing motion or direction toward something) in the direction of; toward: *from north to south.* **3.** (used for expressing limit of movement or extension): *He grew to six feet.* **4.** (used for expressing contact or contiguity) on; against; beside; upon: *Apply varnish to the surface.* **5.** (used for expressing a point of limit in time) before; until: *to this day; It is ten minutes to six. We work from nine to five.* **6.** (used for expressing purpose, intention, destination, or appointed end): *going to the rescue; sentenced to jail.* **7.** (used for expressing a result or a resulting state or condition): *to his dismay; He tore it to pieces.* **8.** (used for expressing the object of inclination or desire): *They drink to his health.* **9.** (used for expressing the object of a right or claim): *claimants to an estate.* **10.** (used for expressing limit in degree, condition, or amount): *amounting to $1000; Tomorrow's high will be 75 to 80°.* **11.** (used for expressing addition or accompaniment) with: *He added insult to injury. They danced to the music. Where is the top to this box?* **12.** (used for expressing attachment or adherence): *He held to his opinion.* **13.** (used for expressing comparison or opposition): *inferior to last year's crop; The score is eight to seven.* **14.** (used for expressing agreement or accordance) according to; by: *a position to one's liking; to the best of my knowledge.* **15.** (used for expressing reference, reaction, or relation): *What will he say to this?* **16.** (used for expressing a relative position): *parallel to the roof.* **17.** (used for expressing a proportion or ratio of number or quantity): *12 to the dozen; 20 miles to the gallon.* **18.** (used for indicating or supplying the dative case, for connecting a verb with its complement, or for indicating or limiting the application of an adjective, noun, or pronoun): *Give it to me. I refer to your work.* **19.** (used to indicate that a following verb is an infinitive (Does he want *to invest?*) or to represent an infinitive that is not expressed (Yes, he wants *to*).) **20.** *Math.* raised to the power indicated: *Three to the fourth is 81* ($3^4 = 81$). —*adv.* **21.** toward a point, person, place, or thing implied or understood. **22.** toward a contact point or closed position: *Pull the door to.* **23.** toward a matter, action, or work: *We turned to with a will.* **24.** into a state of consciousness: *after he came to.* **25. to and fro,** alternately in opposite directions: *The wind was whipping the playground swings to and fro.* [ME, OE *tō;* c. D *te, toe,* G *zu*]
toad (tōd), *n.* **1.** any of numerous tailless amphibians, esp. of the family *Bufonidae,* that have dry, warty skin and that are chiefly terrestrial, entering water only during the breeding season. **2.** any of various toadlike animals, as certain lizards. **3.** a person or thing as an object of disgust or aversion. [ME *tode,* OE *tāde, tādi(g)e*] —**toad′-ish, toad′like′,** *adj.* —**toad′ish·ness,** *n.* —**toad′less,** *adj.*

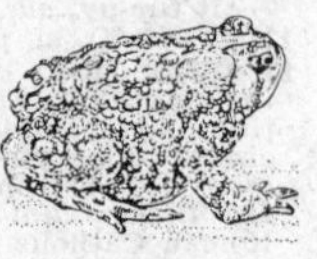

Toad, *Bufo americanus* (Length 3 to 4 in.)

toad·eat·er (tōd′ē′tər), *n.* a toady.
toad·fish (tōd′fish′), *n., pl.* (*esp. collectively*) **-fish,** (*esp. referring to two or more kinds or species*) **fish·es. 1.** any of several thick-headed, wide-mouthed fishes of the family *Batrachoididae,* as *Opsanus tau,* found along the Atlantic coast of the U.S. **2.** puffer (def. 2).
toad·flax (tōd′flaks′), *n.* **1.** a common, European, scrophulariaceous plant, *Linaria vulgaris,* having showy yellow-and-orange flowers, naturalized as a weed in the U.S. **2.** any plant of the same genus.

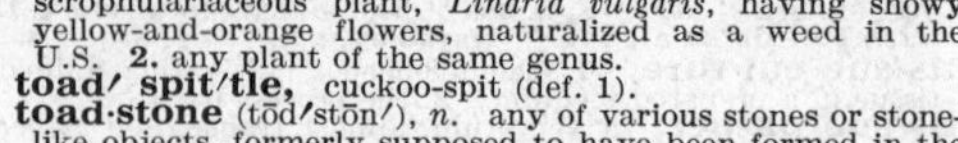

toad′ spit′tle, cuckoo-spit (def. 1).
toad·stone (tōd′stōn′), *n.* any of various stones or stonelike objects, formerly supposed to have been formed in the head or body of a toad, worn as jewels.
toad·stool (tōd′sto͞ol′), *n.* **1.** any of various fleshy fungi having a stalk with an umbrellalike cap. **2.** a poisonous mushroom, as distinguished from an edible one. [ME *tadstol*]
toad·y (tō′dē), *n., pl.* **toad·ies,** *v.,* **toad·ied, toad·y·ing.** —*n.* **1.** an obsequious sycophant; a fawning flatterer. —*v.i.* **2.** to be a toady. —*v.t.* **3.** to be the toady to. [TOAD + -Y[2]] —**toad′y·ish,** *adj.* —**toad′y·ism,** *n.* —**Syn. 1.** fawner, yes man.
to-and-fro (to͞o′ən frō′), *adj., n., pl.* **-fros,** *adv.* —*adj.* **1.** back-and-forth: *to-and-fro motion.* —*n.* **2.** a continuous or regular movement backward and forward; an alternating movement, flux, flow, etc.: *the to-and-fro of the surf.* —*adv.* **3.** to (def. 25).
toast[1] (tōst), *n.* **1.** sliced bread that has been browned and given a crisp surface by dry heat. —*v.t.* **2.** to brown, as bread, by exposure to heat. **3.** to heat or warm thoroughly at a fire. —*v.i.* **4.** to become toasted. [ME *toste(n)* < MF *toste(r)* < L *tōst(us)* for **torsitus,* ptp. of *torrēre* to roast, parch; akin to Icel *thurr* dry. See TORRID, THIRST]
toast[2] (tōst), *n.* **1.** a salutation uttered immediately before drinking in honor of a person, event, etc. **2.** the act or an instance of thus drinking. **3.** a person who is celebrated with or as with the spirited homage of a toast: *She was the toast of the town.* —*v.t.* **4.** to drink to the health of or in honor of. —*v.i.* **5.** to propose or drink a toast. [fig. use of TOAST[1] (n.)]
toast·er[1] (tō′stər), *n.* an instrument or appliance for toasting bread, muffins, etc. [TOAST[1] + -ER[1]]
toast·er[2] (tō′stər), *n.* a person who proposes or joins in a toast to someone or something. [TOAST[2] + -ER[1]]
toast·mas·ter (tōst′mas′tər, -mä′stər), *n.* a person who presides at a dinner, introducing the speakers and proposing toasts. Also, *referring to a woman,* **toast·mis·tress** (tōst′-mis′tris).
toast·y (tō′stē), *adj.,* **toast·i·er, toast·i·est. 1.** characteristic of or resembling toast: *toasty aromas.* **2.** cozily warm.
Tob., Tobit.
to·bac·co (tə bak′ō), *n., pl.* **-cos, -coes. 1.** any solanaceous plant of the genus *Nicotiana,* esp. one of those species, as *N. Tabacum,* whose leaves are prepared for smoking or chewing or as snuff. **2.** the prepared leaves, as used in cigarettes, cigars, and pipes. **3.** any of various similar plants of other genera. [< Sp *tabaco* < Arawak (? < Guarani): a pipe for smoking the plant, or roll of leaves smoked, or the plant]
to·bac·co·nist (tə bak′ə nist), *n.* a dealer in tobacco, cigarettes, and cigars. [TOBACCO + *-n-* connective + -IST]
To·ba·go (tō bā′gō), *n.* an island in the SE West Indies, off the NE coast of Venezuela: formerly a British colony in the Federation of the West Indies; now part of Trinidad and Tobago. 33,333 (1960); 116 sq. mi. —**To·ba·go·ni·an** (tō′bə-gō′nē ən, -gōn′yən), *n.*
to-be (tə bē′), *adj.* future; soon to be (usually used in combination): *bride-to-be.*
To·bey (tō′bē), *n.* **Mark,** 1890–1976, U.S. painter.
To·bit (tō′bit), *n.* **1.** a book of the Apocrypha. **2.** a devout Jew whose story is recorded in this book.
to·bog·gan (tə bog′ən), *n.* **1.** a long, narrow, flat-bottomed sled made of a thin board curved upward and backward at the front, used esp. in the sport of coasting over snow or ice. —*v.i.* **2.** to use, or coast on, a toboggan. **3.** to fall rapidly, as prices, one's fortune, etc. [< CanF *tabagane,* etc. < Micmac *tobâgun* something used for dragging] —**to·bog′gan·er, to·bog′gan·ist,** *n.*
To·bol (to bôl′yᵊ), *n.* a river in the W Soviet Union in Asia, flowing NE to the Irtish River. 800 mi. long.
To·bolsk (to bôlsk′), *n.* a town in the W RSFSR, in the W Soviet Union in Asia, on the Irtish River near its confluence with the Tobol. 46,700 (1959).
to·by (tō′bē), *n., pl.* **-bies.** a mug in the form of a stout old man wearing a three-cornered hat. Also, **To′by, To′by jug′.** [abbr. of *Tobias*]
To·can·tins (tô′kän tēns′), *n.* a river in E Brazil, flowing N to the Pará River. 1700 mi. long.
toc·ca·ta (tə kä′tə; *It.* tôk kä′tä), *n. pl.* **-te** (-tē; *It.* -te). *Music.* a virtuoso composition in the style of an improvisation, for a keyboard instrument. [< It: lit., touched, ptp. fem. of *toccare* to TOUCH]

Toby (18th century)

Toch (tōkh), *n.* **Ernst** (ernst), 1887–1964, Austrian composer.
To·char·i·an (tō kâr′ē ən, -kär′-), *n.* **1.** a member of a central Asian people of high culture, who were assimilated with other peoples about the 11th century A.D. **2.** the language of the Tocharians, an extinct Indo-European language, records of which date from A.D. c600 to c1000. —*adj.* **3.** of or pertaining to the Tocharians or their language. Also, **Tokharian.** [< Gk *Tochár(oi)* Tocharians + -IAN]
toch·er (tokh′ər), *n.* *Scot. and North Eng.* a dowry. [< Ir *tochar,* var. of *tachar* a providing, provision]
to·col·o·gy (tō kol′ə jē), *n.* obstetrics. Also, **tokology.** [< Gk *tóko(s)* child(birth) + -LOGY]
to·coph·er·ol (tō kof′ə rōl′, -rôl′, -rol′), *n.* *Biochem.* one of several alcohols that comprise the dietary factor known as vitamin E, occurring in wheat-germ oil, lettuce or spinach leaves, egg yolk, etc. Cf. **vitamin E.** [< Gk *tóko(s)* child(birth) + *phér(ein)* (to) carry, bear + -OL[1]]
Tocque·ville (tōk′vil, tok′-; *Fr.* tôk vēl′), *n.* **A·le·xis Charles Hen·ri Mau·rice Clé·rel de** (A lek sē′ SHARL äN RĒ′ mô RĒS′ klā REL′ də), 1805–59, French statesman and author.
toc·sin (tok′sin), *n.* **1.** a signal, esp. of alarm, sounded on a

bell or bells. **2.** a bell used to sound an alarm. [< F < Pr *tocasenh* = *toca(r)* (to) TOUCH, strike + *senh* sign, bell < L *sign(um)* sign, in ML, also bell]

tod (tod), *n.* **1.** an English unit of weight, chiefly for wool, commonly equal to 28 pounds but varying locally. **2.** a load. **3.** a bushy mass, esp. of ivy. [late ME *todde;* akin to EFris *todde* small load, Icel *toddi* piece, slice]

to·day (tə dā′), *n.* **1.** this present day. **2.** this present time or age: *the world of today.* —*adv.* **3.** on this present day. **4.** at the present time; in these days: *Today you seldom see horses.* Also, **to-day′.** [ME; OE *tō dæg.* See TO, DAY]

tod·dle (tod′əl), *v.*, **-dled, -dling,** *n.* —*v.i.* **1.** to walk with short, unsteady steps, as a child or an old person. —*n.* **2.** the act of toddling. **3.** an unsteady gait. [b. TO(TTER + WA)DDLE]

tod·dler (tod′lər), *n.* **1.** a person who toddles, esp. a small child roughly between the ages of one and three. **2.** a range of garment sizes for very young children.

tod·dy (tod′ē), *n., pl.* **-dies. 1.** a drink made of alcoholic liquor and hot water, sweetened and sometimes spiced with cloves. **2.** the sap of the toddy palm, often fermented and drunk. [var. of *tarrie* < Hindi *tārī* palmyra palm juice = *tār* palmyra palm (< Skt *tāla*) + *-ī* suffix of appurtenance]

tod′dy palm′, an East Indian palm, *Caryota urens,* yielding toddy.

to-do (tə do͞o′), *n., pl.* **-dos.** *Informal.* bustle; fuss: *They made a great to-do over the dinner.* [n. use of infinitive phrase; see TO, DO¹, ADO] —**Syn.** See **ado.**

to·dy (tō′dē), *n., pl.* **-dies.** any of several small, insectivorous, West Indian birds of the family *Todidae,* related to the kingfishers, having brightly colored green and red plumage. [< NL *Todī,* pl. of *Todus* genus name; L: small bird]

toe (tō), *n., v.,* **toed, toe·ing.** —*n.* **1.** one of the terminal digits of the foot in man. **2.** an analogous part in certain animals, as the hoof of a horse. **3.** the forepart of anything worn on the foot, as of a shoe or stocking. **4.** a part resembling a toe in shape or position. **5.** *Mach.* **a.** a journal or part placed vertically in a bearing, as the lower end of a vertical shaft. **b.** a curved partial cam lifting the flat surface of a follower and letting it drop; wiper. **6.** *Golf.* the outer end of the head of a club. **7. on one's toes,** *Informal.* energetic; alert; ready. **8. step** or **tread on (someone's) toes,** to offend (a person); encroach on the territory or domain of (another). —*v.t.* **9.** to furnish with a toe or toes. **10.** to touch or reach with the toes: *The pitcher toed the mound, wound up, and threw a fast ball.* **11.** to kick with the toe. —*v.i.* **12.** to stand, walk, etc., with the toes in a specified position: *to toe in.* **13.** to tap with the toe, as in dancing. **14. toe the line.** See **line**¹ (def. 42). [ME; OE *tā;* c. G *Zeh(e),* Icel *tā,* D *teen;* akin to L *digitus* DIGIT] —**toe′less,** *adj.* —**toe′like′,** *adj.*

toe′ crack′, a sand crack on the front of a horse's hoof.

toed (tōd), *adj.* having a toe or toes.

toe′ dance′, a dance performed on the tips of the toes, usually ballet.

toe-dance (tō′dans′, -däns′), *v.i.,* **-danced, -danc·ing.** to perform a toe dance. —**toe′ danc′er.**

toe·hold (tō′hōld′), *n.* **1.** a small ledge or niche just large enough to support the toes, as in climbing. **2.** any slight or initial support, influence, advantage, progress, or the like. **3.** *Wrestling.* a hold in which an opponent's foot is twisted.

toe·nail (tō′nāl′), *n.* **1.** a nail of a toe. **2.** *Carpentry.* a nail driven obliquely. —*v.t.* **3.** *Carpentry.* to secure with oblique nailing.

toe·shoe (tō′sho͞o′), *n.* *Ballet.* a heelless dance slipper fitted with a thick, leather-covered wooden toe to enable the ballet dancer to toe-dance.

toff (tof), *n.* *Brit. Informal.* a dandy. [? var. of TUFT]

tof·fee (tô′fē, tof′ē), *n.* *Chiefly Brit.* taffy. Also, **tof′fy.**

toft (tôft, toft), *n.* *Brit. Dial.* **1.** the site of a house and outbuildings. **2.** a house site and its adjoining arable land. [ME, late OE < Scand; cf. Icel *topt* homestead]

to·fu (tō′fo͞o), *n.* a soft, bland, white cheeselike food made from curdled soybean milk, high in protein content, used originally in Oriental cookery but now in a wide variety of soups and main dishes. [< Jap]

tog (tog), *n., v.,* **togged, tog·ging.** —*n.* **1.** a coat. **2.** Usually, **togs,** clothes. —*v.t.* **3.** to dress (often fol. by *out* or *up*). [appar. short for obs. *tog(e)man(s)* cloak, coat = *toge* (late ME < L *toga* TOGA) + *-mans* obs. cant suffix < ?]

to·ga (tō′gə), *n., pl.* **-gas, -gae** (-jē). **1.** (in ancient Rome) the loose outer garment worn by citizens when appearing in public. **2.** a robe of office, a professorial gown, or some other distinctive garment. [< L: lit., a covering. See TEGMEN] —**to·gaed** (tō′gəd), *adj.*

Toga (def. 1)

to·gate (tō′gāt), *adj.* of or pertaining to ancient Rome: *the togate provinces.* [< L *togāt(us).* See TOGA, -ATE¹]

to·gat·ed (tō′gā tid), *adj.* **1.** peaceful. **2.** clad in a toga. [< L *togāt(us)* clad in a toga (see TOGATE) + -ED²]

to·geth·er (to͝o geth′ər, tə-), *adv.* **1.** into or in one gathering, company, mass, place, etc. **2.** into or in union, proximity, contact, or collision: *to sew things together.* **3.** into or in relationship, association, etc.: *to bring strangers together.* **4.** taken or considered collectively or conjointly: *This one cost more than all the others together.* **5.** (of a single thing) into or in a condition of unity, compactness, or coherence: *The argument does not hang together well.* **6.** at the same time; simultaneously: *You cannot have both together.* **7.** without interruption: *for days together.* **8.** in cooperation; with united action; conjointly: *to undertake a task together.* **9.** with mutual action; reciprocally: *to confer together.* [late ME; earlier *togedere, togadere,* OE *tōgædere;* c. OFris *togadera*]

to·geth·er·ness (to͝o geth′ər nis, tə-), *n.* **1.** the quality, state, or condition of being together. **2.** warm fellowship, as among members of a family.

tog·ger·y (tog′ə rē), *n.* *Informal.* clothes; togs.

tog·gle (tog′əl), *n., v.,* **-gled, -gling.** —*n.* **1.** a pin, bolt, or rod placed transversely through a chain, an eye or loop in a rope, etc., as to bind it temporarily to another chain or rope similarly treated. **2.** a toggle joint, or a device having one. **3.** an ornamental, rod-shaped button for inserting into a large buttonhole, loop, or frog, used esp. on sports clothes. —*v.t.* **4.** to furnish with a toggle or toggles. **5.** to bind or fasten with a toggle or toggles. [? var. of TACKLE] —**tog′gler,** *n.*

tog′gle bolt′, an anchor bolt having two hinged wings, ordinarily held open by a spring, for engaging the rough sides of a hole drilled in masonry or the inner surface of a hollow wall.

tog′gle joint′, *Mach.* any of various devices consisting basically of a rod that can be inserted into an object and then manipulated so that the inserted part spreads, becomes offset, or turns at a right angle to the exterior part, allowing it to be used as a support, handle, linkage, lever, etc.

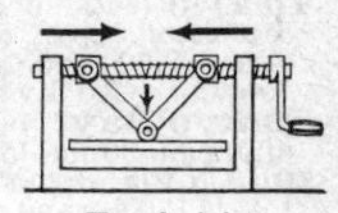
Toggle joint

tog′gle switch′, *Elect.* a switch in which a projecting knob or arm, moving through a small arc, causes the contacts to open or close an electric circuit, as the household light switch.

To·go (tô′gô *for 1;* tō′gō *for 2*), *n.* **1. Shi·ge·no·ri** (shē′gē nô′rē), 1882–1950, Japanese political leader and diplomat. **2. Republic of,** an independent country in W Africa: formerly a French mandate 1922–46 and trusteeship 1946–60 in E Togoland. 2,197,900; 21,830 sq. mi. *Cap.:* Lomé.

To·go·land (tō′gō land′), *n.* a former German protectorate in W Africa, on the Gulf of Guinea: E part is now the Republic of Togo; W part, a British mandate 1922–46 and trusteeship 1946–57, is now part of Ghana. —**To′go·land′er,** *n.*

toil¹ (toil), *n.* **1.** hard and continuous work or exhausting labor. **2.** a laborious task. **3.** *Archaic.* battle; strife; struggle. —*v.i.* **4.** to engage in hard and continuous work; labor arduously. **5.** to move or travel with difficulty, weariness, or pain. —*v.t.* **6.** *Archaic.* to accomplish or produce by toil. [ME *toile* (n.), *toil(en)* (v.) < AF *toil* contention, *toile(r)* (to) contend < L *tudiculāre* to stir up, beat < *tudicula* machine for crushing olives = *tudi-* (s. of *tundere* to beat) + *-cula* -CULE] —**toil′er,** *n.* —**Syn. 1.** exertion. See **work. 4.** strive, moil. —**Ant. 1.** indolence, sloth.

toil² (toil), *n.* **1.** a net or series of nets to trap game. **2.** Usually, **toils.** any snare, trap, difficulty, etc. [< F *toile* < L *tēl(a)* web]

toile (twäl), *n.* any of various transparent linens and cottons. [< F: linen cloth, canvas. See TOIL²]

toi·let (toi′lit), *n.* **1.** a bathroom fixture consisting of a bowl, a detachable, hinged seat and usually a lid, and a device for flushing with water, used for defecation and urination. **2.** a bathroom. **3.** a dressing room, esp. one containing a bath. **4.** the act or process of dressing, including bathing, arranging the hair, etc.: *to make one's toilet.* **5.** See **toilet set. 6.** the dress or costume of a person; any particular costume. **7.** *Surg.* the cleansing of the part or wound after an operation, esp. in the peritoneal cavity. **8.** *Archaic.* See **dressing table.** Also, **toilette** (for defs. 4, 6). [< F *toilette* small cloth, doily, dressing table. See TOIL², -ET]

toi′let pa′per, a soft, absorbent paper used in bathrooms for personal cleanliness. Also called **toi′let tis′sue.**

toi·let·ry (toi′li trē), *n., pl.* **-ries.** an article or substance used in grooming, making up, etc.

toi′let set′, the articles used in grooming, as a mirror, brush, comb, etc., esp. when of a matching design.

toi·lette (toi let′; *Fr.* TWA let′), *n., pl.* **-lettes** (-lets′; *Fr.* -let′). toilet (defs. 4, 6).

toi′let train′ing, the training of a very young child to control and regulate bowel and bladder movements and use the toilet.

toi′let wa′ter, a scented liquid used as a light perfume; cologne.

toil·ful (toil′fəl), *adj.* characterized by or involving toil; toilsome. —**toil′ful·ly,** *adv.*

toil·some (toil′səm), *adj.* characterized by or involving toil; laborious. —**toil′some·ly,** *adv.* —**toil′some·ness,** *n.*

toil·worn (toil′wōrn′, -wôrn′), *adj.* **1.** worn by toil: *toilworn hands.* **2.** worn out or aged by toil: *a toilworn farmer.*

To·jo (tō′jō), *n.* **Hi·de·ki** (hē′de kē′), 1885–1948, Japanese general.

to·kay (tō kā′), *n.* a gecko, *Gecko gecko,* of the Malay Archipelago and southeastern Asia. [< Malay *toke*]

To·kay (tō kā′), *n.* **1.** an aromatic wine made from Furmint grapes grown in the district surrounding Tokay, a town in NE Hungary. **2.** a sweet, strong white wine made in California. [< Hung]

to·ken (tō′kən), *n.* **1.** something meant or serving to represent or indicate some fact, event, feeling, etc.; sign: *to wear black as a token of mourning.* **2.** a characteristic indication or mark of something; symbol: *His shabby suit is a token of his poverty.* **3.** a memento; souvenir; keepsake: *The seashell was a token of their trip to Atlantic City.* **4.** something used to indicate authenticity, authority, etc.; emblem; badge: *He wore his robes as a token of office.* **5.** Also called **to′ken coin′.** a stamped piece of metal, issued as a limited medium of exchange, as for bus fares. **6.** anything of only nominal value. **7.** a part conceived of as representing the whole; sample; indication. **8.** *Philos.* a specific instance of the use of a word, expression, symbol, etc. *Cat* and *cat* are two tokens of the same type. Cf. **type** (def. 9b). **9. by the same token, a.** in proof of which. **b.** moreover; furthermore. **10. in token of,** as a sign of; in evidence of. —*v.t.* **11.** to be a token of; signify; betoken. —*adj.* **12.** serving as a token: *a token gift.* **13.** slight; perfunctory; minimal: *token resistance.* [ME; OE *tāc(e)n;* c. Icel *teikn,* Goth *taikn,* G *Zeichen* sign, mark. See TEACH]

to·ken·ism (tō′kə niz′əm), *n.* the practice of admitting a very limited number of Negroes into business organizations, schools, etc., in token conformity with legislation and public opinion regarding civil rights. [TOKEN + -ISM]

to′ken pay′ment, a small payment binding an agreement or acknowledging a debt.

To·khar·i·an (tō kâr′ē ən, -kär′-), *n.* Tocharian.

To·klas (tō′kləs), *n.* **Alice B.,** 1877–1967, U.S. author in France: friend and companion of Gertrude Stein.

to·kol·o·gy (tō kol′ə jē), *n.* tocology.

to·ko·no·ma (tō′kə nō′mə), *n.* (in Japanese architecture) a shallow alcove for the display of *kakemono* or flower arrangements. [< Jap]

To·ku·ga·wa (tō′ko͞o gä′wä), *n.* a member of a powerful family in Japan that ruled as shoguns 1603–1867.

To·ku·shi·ma (tō′ko͞o shē′mä), *n.* a seaport on NE Shikoku, in SW Japan. 239,000.

To·ky·o (tō′kē ō′; *Jap.* tô′kyô), *n.* a seaport in and the capital of Japan, on Tokyo Bay: one of the world's largest cities. 8,500,000. Also, **To′ki·o′.** Formerly, **Edo, Yedo, Yeddo.** —**To′ky·o·ite′,** *n.*

To′kyo Bay′, an inlet of the Pacific, in SE Honshu Island of Japan. 30 mi. long; 20 mi. wide.

to·la (tō′lä), *n.* a unit of weight in India: the government tola is 180 ser and equals 180 English grains, the weight of a silver rupee. [< Hindi < Skt *tulā* balance, scale, weight]

to·lan (tō′lan), *n.* *Chem.* a solid, unsaturated compound, $C_6H_5C{\equiv}CC_6H_5$, used in organic synthesis. [TOL(UENE) + *-an*, var. of -ANE]

tol·booth (tōl′bo͞oth′), *n., pl.* **-booths** (-bo͞othz′, -bo͞oths′). **1.** *Chiefly Scot.* **a.** a town jail. **b.** a town hall or guild hall, esp. a place where tolls are paid. **2.** tollbooth (def. 1).

told (tōld), *v.* **1.** pt. and pp. of **tell. 2. all told,** counting everyone or everything; in all.

tole (tōl), *v.t.,* **toled, tol·ing.** toll[1] (def. 6).

To·le·do (tə lē′dō; *for 1, 3, 4, also Sp.* tô le′t͟hô), *n.* **1. Fran·cis·co de** (fʀän sēs′kô t͟he), c1515–84?, Spanish administrator: viceroy of Peru 1569–81. **2.** a port in NW Ohio, on Lake Erie. 383,818 (1970). **3.** a city in central Spain, on the Tagus River: the capital of Spain under the Romans. 38,136 (est. 1960). **4.** a sword or sword blade of finely tempered steel, as formerly made in Toledo, Spain.

tol·er·a·ble (tol′ər ə bəl), *adj.* **1.** capable of being tolerated; endurable. **2.** fairly good; not bad. **3.** *Informal.* in fair health. [late ME < L *tolerābil(is)* = *tolerā(re)* (to) endure + *-bilis* -BLE] —**tol′er·a·ble·ness, tol′er·a·bil′i·ty,** *n.* —**tol′er·a·bly,** *adv.* —**Syn. 1.** bearable. **2.** passable.

tol·er·ance (tol′ər əns), *n.* **1.** a fair and objective attitude toward those whose opinions, practices, race, religion, nationality, or the like, differ from one's own; freedom from bigotry. **2.** a fair and objective attitude toward opinions and practices that differ from one's own. **3.** any liberal, undogmatic viewpoint. **4.** the act or capacity of enduring; endurance: *My tolerance of noise is limited.* **5.** *Med.* the power to endure or resist the action of a drug, poison, etc. **6.** *Mach.* **a.** the permissible range of variation in a dimension of an object. **b.** the permissible variation of an object or objects in some characteristic such as hardness, weight, or quantity. **7.** *Coining.* a permissible deviation in the fineness and weight of coin. [late ME < L *tolerantia.* See TOLERANT, -ANCE] —**Syn. 1, 2.** liberality, impartiality, open-mindedness. TOLERANCE, TOLERATION agree in allowing the right of something that one may not approve. TOLERANCE suggests a liberal spirit toward the views and actions of others: *tolerance toward religious minorities.* TOLERATION may imply the allowance or sufferance of conduct that one might or should rightly oppose: *toleration of graft.*

tol·er·ant (tol′ər ənt), *adj.* **1.** showing or favoring tolerance; forbearing. **2.** *Med.* able to endure or resist the action of a drug, poison, etc. [< L *tolerant-* (s. of *tolerāns*), prp. of *tolerāre* to bear. See TOLERATE, -ANT] —**tol′er·ant·ly,** *adv.*

tol·er·ate (tol′ə rāt′), *v.t.,* **-at·ed, -at·ing. 1.** to allow without prohibition or hindrance; permit. **2.** to endure without repugnance; put up with: *I can tolerate laziness, but not sloth.* **3.** *Med.* to endure or resist the action of (a drug, poison, etc.). **4.** *Obs.* to experience, undergo, or sustain, as pain or hardship. [< L *tolerāt(us),* ptp. of *tolerāre* to bear (akin to THOLE[2]); see -ATE[1]] —**tol′er·a′tive,** *adj.* —**tol′er·a′tor,** *n.* —**Syn. 2.** support, endure, accept.

tol·er·a·tion (tol′ə rā′shən), *n.* **1.** the act or an instance of tolerating, esp. something that is not actually approved; forbearance. **2.** allowance by a government of the exercise of religions other than the established one. [< L *tolerātiōn-* (s. of *tolerātiō*)] —**tol′er·a′tion·ism,** *n.* —**tol′er·a′tion·ist,** *n.* —**Syn. 1.** See **tolerance.**

tol·i·dine (tol′i dēn′, -din), *n.* *Chem.* any of several isomeric derivatives of biphenyl containing two methyl and two amino groups, esp. the ortho isomer which is used as a reagent and in the preparation of dyes. [TOL(UENE) + -ID[3] + -INE[2]]

To·li·ma (tô lē′mä), *n.* a volcano in W Colombia, in the Andes. 18,438 ft.

toll[1] (tōl), *v.t.* **1.** to cause (a large bell) to sound with single strokes slowly and regularly repeated. **2.** to sound or strike (a knell, the hour, etc.) by such strokes. **3.** to announce (a death) by this means. **4.** to ring a knell for (a dying or dead person). **5.** to summon or dismiss by tolling. **6.** Also, **tole.** to allure; entice. —*v.i.* **7.** to sound with slow, single, repeated strokes, as a bell. —*n.* **8.** act of tolling a bell. **9.** one of the strokes made in tolling a bell. **10.** the sound made. [ME *toll(en)*; akin to OE *-tyllan,* in *fortyllan* to attract, allure]

toll[2] (tōl), *n.* **1.** a payment or fee exacted, as by the state, for some right or privilege, as for passage along a road or over a bridge. **2.** (formerly in England) the right to take such payment. **3.** a payment for a long-distance telephone call. **4.** a tax, duty, or tribute, as for services, use of facilities, etc. **5.** the extent of loss, damage, suffering, etc., resulting from some action or calamity: *The toll was 300 persons dead or missing.* **6.** a compensation for services, as for grinding corn or for transportation or transmission. —*v.t.* **7.** to collect (something) as toll. **8.** to impose a tax or toll on (a person). —*v.i.* **9.** to collect toll; levy toll. [ME, OE (c. D *tol,* Icel *tollr,* G *Zoll*), assimilated var. of OE *toln* < LL *tolōn(ēum),* for *telōnēum* < Gk *telṓnion* tollhouse, akin to *telṓnēs* tax collector, *télos* tax] —**toll′er,** *n.* —**Syn. 3.** tariff, levy, impost.

toll′ bar′, a barrier, esp. a gate, across a road or bridge, where toll is collected.

toll·booth (tōl′bo͞oth′), *n., pl.* **-booths** (-bo͞othz′, -bo͞oths′). **1.** a booth, as at a bridge or the entrance to a toll road, where a toll is collected. **2.** *Chiefly Scot.* tolbooth (def. 1.). [ME *tolbothe*]

toll′ bridge′, a bridge at which a toll is charged.

toll′ call′, any telephone call involving a higher base rate than that fixed for a local message.

Tol·ler (tô′lər, tol′ər; *Ger.* tô′ləʀ), *n.* **Ernst** (ûrnst; *Ger.* eʀnst), 1893–1939, German dramatist.

toll·gate (tōl′gāt′), *n.* a gate where toll is collected.

toll·house (tōl′hous′), *n., pl.* **-hous·es** (-hou′ziz). a booth at a tollgate, occupied by a tollkeeper. [late ME *tolhowse*]

toll′house cook′y, a crisp cooky containing bits of chocolate and sometimes chopped nuts.

toll·keep·er (tōl′kē′pər), *n.* the collector at a tollgate.

toll′ road′, a road or highway on which a toll is exacted from each traveler, vehicle, or the like, that passes along it.

Tol·stoy (tol′stoi, tōl′-; *Russ.* tol stoi′), *n.* **Lev** (*Russ.* lef) or **Leo Ni·ko·la·e·vich** (*Russ.* ni ko lä′yə vich), **Count,** 1828–1910, Russian novelist and social critic. Also, **Tol′stoi.** —**Tol′stoy·an, Tol′stoi·an,** *adj., n.* —**Tol′stoy·ism,** *n.*

Tol·tec (tol′tek), *n., pl.* **-tecs,** (*esp. collectively*) **-tec,** *adj.* —*n.* **1.** a member of an Indian people living in central Mexico before the Aztec conquest. —*adj.* **2.** Also, **Tol′tec·an.** of or pertaining to the Toltecs.

to·lu (tô lo͞o′, tə-), *n.* a fragrant yellowish-brown balsam or resin obtained from a South American tree, *Myroxylon balsamum,* used as a stomachic and expectorant, and in perfumery. Also called **to·lu′ bal′sam, to·lu′ res′in, balsam of tolu.** [after *Tolú* (now Santiago de Tolú) in Colombia, where balsam is obtained]

tol·u·ate (tol′yo͞o āt′), *n.* *Chem.* a salt or ester of any of the three isomeric toluic acids. [TOLU(ENE) + -ATE[2]]

To·lu·ca (tô lo͞o′kä), *n.* **1.** a city in and the capital of Mexico state, in S central Mexico. 141,726. **2.** an extinct volcano in central Mexico, in Mexico state. 15,026 ft.

tol·u·ene (tol′yo͞o ēn′), *n.* *Chem.* a flammable liquid, $C_6H_5CH_3$, having a benzenelike odor, obtained chiefly from coal tar and petroleum, used in the manufacture of TNT and other organic compounds. Also called **methylbenzene.**

tolu′ic ac′id, *Chem.* any of three isomeric acids having the formula $CH_3C_6H_4COOH$: derivatives of toluene. —**to·lu·ic** (tə lo͞o′ik, tol′yo͞o ik), *adj.*

to·lu·i·dine (tə lo͞o′i dēn′, -din), *n.* *Chem.* any of three isomeric amines having the formula $CH_3C_6H_4NH_2$, used in the dye and drug industries. Cf. **meta-toluidine, ortho-toluidine, para-toluidine.** [TOLU(ENE) + -ID[3] + -INE[2]]

tol·u·ol (tol′yo͞o ōl′), *n.* *Chem.* **1.** toluene. **2.** the commercial form of toluene.

tolu′ tree′, a South American leguminous tree, *Myroxylon balsamum,* yielding tolu.

tol′uyl group′, *Chem.* any of three univalent isomeric groups having the formula $CH_3C_6H_4CO–$, derived from toluic acids. Also called **tol′uyl rad′ical.** —**tol·u·yl** (tol′yo͞o il), *adj.*

tol′yl group′, *Chem.* any of three univalent, isomeric groups having the formula $CH_3C_6H_4–$, derived from toluene. Also called **tol′yl rad′ical.** Cf. **meta, ortho, para**[2]. —**tol·yl** (tol′il), *adj.*

tom (tom), *n.* **1.** the male of various animals: *tom turkey.* **2.** a tomcat. [special use of *Tom* given name]

Tomahawk (def. 1)

tom·a·hawk (tom′ə hôk′), *n.* **1.** a light ax used by the North American Indians as a weapon and tool. **2.** any of various similar weapons or implements. **3.** (in Australia) a stone hatchet used by the aborigines. —*v.t.* **4.** to attack, wound, or kill with or as with a tomahawk. [earlier *tomahack* < Algonquian (Virginia dial.)]

to·man (tə män′), *n.* a paper money of Iran, equal to 10 rials. [< Pers *tōmān, tūmān,* of Mongolian orig.]

Tom′ and Jer′ry, a hot drink made of rum and water or milk, beaten eggs, spices, and sugar. [named after the principal characters in *Life in London* (1821) by Pierce Egan (d. 1849), English writer]

to·ma·to (tə mā′tō, -mä′-), *n., pl.* **-toes. 1.** a solanaceous plant, *Lycopersicon esculentum,* bearing a mildly acid, pulpy fruit, commonly red, used as a vegetable. **2.** *Slang.* a girl or woman. [earlier *tomate* < Sp < Nahuatl *tomatl*]

tomb (to͞om), *n.* **1.** an excavation in earth or rock for the burial of a corpse; a grave or other burial place. **2.** a mausoleum, burial chamber, or the like. **3.** a monument for housing a corpse. **4.** a structure erected in memory of a dead person; cenotaph. **5.** any structure having an air of sepulchral sadness. —*v.t.* **6.** to entomb; bury. [early ME *tumbe* < AF = OF *tombe* < LL *tumba* < Gk *týmbos* burial mound; akin to L *tumēre* to swell. See TUMOR, TUMULUS, THUMB] —**tomb′al,** *adj.* —**tomb′less,** *adj.* —**tomb′like′,** *adj.*

tom·bac (tom′bak), *n.* an alloy, used to imitate gold, containing from 70 to 92 percent copper with zinc and sometimes tin and other materials. Also, **tambac.** [< D *tombak* < Pg *tambaca* < Malay *tambâga* copper < Skt *tāmraka;* r. earlier *tombaga* < Malay, as above]

Tom·big·bee (tom big′bē), *n.* a river flowing S through NE Mississippi and SW Alabama to the Mobile River. 525 mi. long.

tom·bo·lo (tom′bə lō′), *n., pl.* **-los.** a sand bar connecting an island to the mainland or to another island. [< It < L *tumul(us)* mound. See TUMULUS]

Tom·bouc·tou (tôɴ bo͝ok to͞o′), *n.* French name of **Timbuktu.**

tom·boy (tom′boi′), *n.* a romping, boisterous, boyish young girl. —**tom′boy′ish,** *adj.* —**tom′boy′ish·ly,** *adv.* —**tom′boy′ish·ness,** *n.*

tomb·stone (to͞om′stōn′), *n.* a stone marker, usually inscribed, on a tomb or grave.

tom·cat (tom′kat′), *n.* a male cat.

tom·cod (tom′kod′), *n., pl.* (*esp. collectively*) **-cod,** (*esp. referring to two or more kinds or species*) **-cods. 1.** either of two small cods, *Microgadus tomcod,* of the Atlantic Ocean, or *M. proximus,* of the Pacific Ocean. **2.** any of various similar fishes. [TOM (THUMB) + COD[1]]

Tom′ Col′lins, a tall drink containing gin, lemon or lime juice, and carbonated water, sweetened and served with ice. [said to have been named after its inventor]

tome (tōm), *n.* **1.** any book, esp. a very heavy, large, or learned one. **2.** one volume of two or more in the same format comprising a work of considerable length. [< F < L *tom(us)* < Gk *tómos* slice, piece, roll of paper, book, akin to *témnein* to cut]

-tome, a learned borrowing from Greek meaning "cutting," used esp. in the formation of scientific terms: *microtome; osteotome.* Cf. **-tomic**[1], **tomo-, -tomous, -tomy.** [comb. form repr. Gk *tomḗ* a cutting; *tómos* a cut, slice; *-tomon*, neut. of *-tomos* -cutting]

to·men·tose (tə men′tōs, tō′men tōs′), *adj. Bot., Entomol.* closely covered with down or matted hair. [< NL *tōmentōs(us)*. See TOMENTUM, -OSE[1]]

to·men·tum (tə men′təm), *n., pl.* **-ta** (-tə). *Bot.* pubescence consisting of longish, soft, entangled hairs pressed close to the surface. [< NL, special use of L *tōmentum* stuffing (of wool, hair, etc.) for cushions]

tom·fool (tom′fo͞ol′), *n.* **1.** a grossly foolish or stupid person; a silly fool. **—*adj.* 2.** being or characteristic of a tomfool. [ME *Thome fole* Tom the fool] **—tom′fool′ish,** *adj.* **—tom′fool′ish·ness,** *n.*

tom·fool·er·y (tom′fo͞o′lə rē), *n., pl.* **-er·ies. 1.** foolish or silly behavior. **2.** a silly act, matter, or thing.

-tomic[1], a combination of **-tome** and **-ic** used to form adjectives from nouns with stems in **-tome:** *microtomic.*

-tomic[2], a combination of **-tomy** and **-ic** used to form adjectives from nouns with stems in **-tomy:** *dichotomic.*

tom·my (tom′ē), *n., pl.* **-mies.** (*sometimes cap.*) See **Tommy Atkins.** [by shortening]

Tom′my At′kins, *pl.* **Tommy Atkins.** any private of the British army.

Tom′my gun′, 1. See **Thompson submachine gun. 2.** *Informal.* any submachine gun. [by shortening]

tom·my·rot (tom′ē rot′), *n.* nonsense; utter foolishness. [*tommy* simpleton (see TOMFOOL) + ROT]

tomo-, a combining form meaning "a cut," "section," used in the formation of compound words: *tomography.* [comb. form repr. Gk *tómos* a cut, section; cf. -TOME]

to·mog·ra·phy (tə mog′rə fē), *n. Med.* x-ray photography of a selected plane in the body.

to·mor·row (tə môr′ō, -mor′ō), *n.* **1.** the day following today. **2.** a future period or time: *Today's youth are the leaders of tomorrow.* **—*adv.* 3.** on the morrow; on the day following today. **4.** at some future time. Also, **to-mor′row.** [ME *to morwe(n)*, OE *to morgen(ne)*]

-tomous, a suffix of adjectives indicating a cut or division of a certain kind: *dichotomous.* [-TOME or -TOMY + -OUS]

tom·pi·on (tom′pē ən), *n.* tampion.

Tomp·kins (tomp′kinz), *n.* **Daniel D.,** 1774–1825, U.S. politician and jurist: vice president of the U.S. 1817–25.

Tomsk (tômsk), *n.* a city in the central RSFSR, in the SW Soviet Union in Asia, E of the Ob River. 293,000 (est. 1964).

Tom′ Thumb′, 1. See **Stratton, Charles Sherwood. 2.** a diminutive hero of folk tales. **3.** an extremely small person; dwarf.

tom·tit (tom′tit′), *n. Brit. Dial.* **1.** a titmouse. **2.** any of various other small birds, as the wren. [TOM (THUMB) + TIT[1]]

tom-tom (tom′tom′), *n.* **1.** an American Indian or Oriental drum of indefinite pitch, commonly played with the hands. **2.** a dully repetitious drumbeat or similar sound. Also, **tam-tam.** [< Hindi *tamtam*, repetitive compound; imit.]

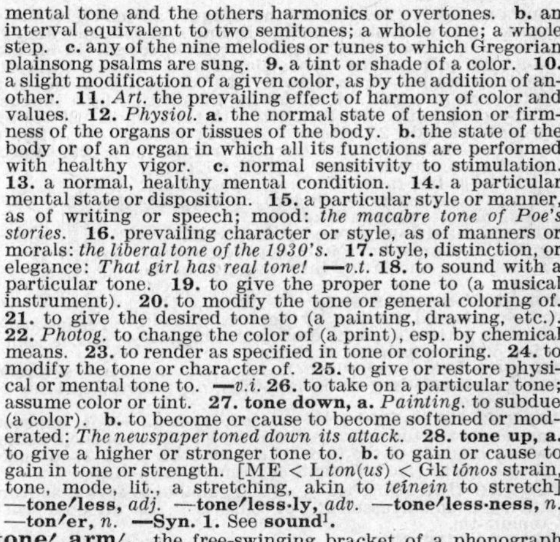
Tom-tom

-tomy, a suffix meaning "a cutting," used esp. in relation to a surgical operation (*appendectomy; phlebotomy*) or sometimes a division (*dichotomy*). Cf. **-tome, -tomic**[2], **tomo-, -tomous.** [repr. Gk *-tomia*; see -TOME, -Y[3]]

ton[1] (tun), *n.* **1.** a unit of weight, equivalent to 2000 pounds avoirdupois **(short ton)** in the U.S. and 2240 pounds avoirdupois **(long ton)** in Great Britain. **2.** Also called **freight ton.** a unit of volume for freight that weighs one ton, varying with the type of freight measured, as 40 cubic feet of oak timber, 20 bushels of wheat, etc. **3.** See **metric ton. 4.** See **displacement ton. 5.** a unit of volume used in transportation by sea, commonly equal to 40 cubic feet **(shipping ton** or **measurement ton). 6.** a unit of internal capacity of ships, equal to 100 cubic feet **(register ton). 7.** Often, **tons.** *Informal.* a great quantity; a lot: *tons of wedding presents.* [ME; var. of TUN]

ton[2] (*Fr.* tôN), *n., pl.* **tons** (*Fr.* tôN). **1.** high fashion; stylishness. **2.** the current fashion, style, or vogue. [< F < L *ton(us)*. See TONE] **—ton·ish, ton·nish** (ton′ish), *adj.* **—ton′ish·ly, ton′nish·ly,** *adv.* **—ton′ish·ness, ton′nish·ness,** *n.*

-ton, a suffix formerly used to form nouns from adjectives: *simpleton; singleton.* [var. of dial. *tone* ONE. See TOTHER]

ton·al (tōn′əl), *adj. Music.* pertaining to tonality. [< ML *tonāl(is)*] **—ton′al·ly,** *adv.*

to·nal·i·ty (tō nal′i tē), *n., pl.* **-ties. 1.** *Music.* **a.** the sum of relations, melodic and harmonic, existing between the tones of a scale or musical system. **b.** a particular scale or system of tones; a key. **2.** (in painting, graphics, etc.) the system of tones or tints, or the color scheme, of a picture. **—to·nal′i·tive,** *adj.*

tone (tōn), *n., v.,* **toned, ton·ing. —*n.* 1.** any sound considered with reference to its quality, pitch, strength, source, etc.: *shrill tones.* **2.** quality or character of sound. **3.** vocal sound; the sound made by vibrating muscular bands in the larynx. **4.** a particular expressive quality, way of sounding, modulation, or intonation of the voice. **5.** an accent peculiar to a person, people, locality, etc., or a characteristic mode of sounding words in speech. **6.** stress of voice on a syllable of a word. **7.** *Linguistics.* any of the musical pitches or movements in pitch that are characteristic of a given language and that in certain languages serve to distinguish meaning. Cf. **tone language. 8.** *Music.* **a.** a musical sound of definite pitch, consisting of several relatively simple constituents called partial tones, the lowest of which is called the fundamental tone and the others harmonics or overtones. **b.** an interval equivalent to two semitones; a whole tone; a whole step. **c.** any of the nine melodies or tunes to which Gregorian plainsong psalms are sung. **9.** a tint or shade of a color. **10.** a slight modification of a given color, as by the addition of another. **11.** *Art.* the prevailing effect of harmony of color and values. **12.** *Physiol.* **a.** the normal state of tension or firmness of the organs or tissues of the body. **b.** the state of the body or of an organ in which all its functions are performed with healthy vigor. **c.** normal sensitivity to stimulation. **13.** a normal, healthy mental condition. **14.** a particular mental state or disposition. **15.** a particular style or manner, as of writing or speech; mood: *the macabre tone of Poe's stories.* **16.** prevailing character or style, as of manners or morals: *the liberal tone of the 1930's.* **17.** style, distinction, or elegance: *That girl has real tone!* **—*v.t.* 18.** to sound with a particular tone. **19.** to give the proper tone to (a musical instrument). **20.** to modify the tone or general coloring of. **21.** to give the desired tone to (a painting, drawing, etc.). **22.** *Photog.* to change the color of (a print), esp. by chemical means. **23.** to render as specified in tone or coloring. **24.** to modify the tone or character of. **25.** to give or restore physical or mental tone to. **—*v.i.* 26.** to take on a particular tone; assume color or tint. **27. tone down, a.** *Painting.* to subdue (a color). **b.** to become or cause to become softened or moderated: *The newspaper toned down its attack.* **28. tone up, a.** to give a higher or stronger tone to. **b.** to gain or cause to gain in tone or strength. [ME < L *ton(us)* < Gk *tónos* strain, tone, mode, lit., a stretching, akin to *teínein* to stretch] **—tone′less,** *adj.* **—tone′less·ly,** *adv.* **—tone′less·ness,** *n.* **—ton′er,** *n.* **—Syn. 1.** See **sound**[1].

tone′ arm′, the free-swinging bracket of a phonograph containing the pickup. Also called **pickup arm.**

tone′ clus′ter, *Music.* a group of adjacent notes played on a keyboard instrument or similar groupings occurring in orchestral music.

tone′ col′or, *Music.* quality of tone; timbre.

tone-deaf (tōn′def′), *adj. Pathol.* unable to distinguish differences in pitch in musical sounds when producing or hearing them. **—tone′ deaf′ness.**

tone′ lan′guage, a language, as Swedish, Chinese, Yoruba, or Serbo-Croatian, in which words that are otherwise phonologically identical are distinguished by having different pitches or pitch contour.

ton·eme (tō′nēm), *n.* a phoneme consisting of a contrastive feature of tone in a tone language. [TONE + -EME]

tone′ po′em, *Music.* See **symphonic poem.** Cf. **program music.**

tone′ row′, *Music.* a series of tones in which no tone is duplicated: used in serial technique. Also called **twelve-tone row.**

to·net·ic (tō net′ik), *adj.* noting or pertaining to the phonetic study of tone in language. [TONE + (PHON)ETIC] **—to·net′i·cal·ly,** *adv.*

to·net·ics (tō net′iks), *n.* (*construed as sing.*) the phonetic study of tone in language. [TONE + (PHON)ETICS] **—to·ne·ti·cian** (tō′ni tish′ən), *n.*

to·nette (tō net′), *n.* a small, end-blown flute of simple construction and narrow range.

ton-force (tun′fōrs′, -fôrs′), *n.* two thousand pound-force. *Abbr.:* tonf

tong[1] (tông, tong), *n.* **1.** tongs. **—*v.t.* 2.** to lift, seize, gather, hold, or handle with tongs, as logs or oysters. **—*v.i.* 3.** to use or work with tongs. [ME, OE; c. D *tang*, G *Zange* pair of tongs or pincers; akin to Gk *dáknein* to bite]

tong[2] (tông, tong), *n.* **1.** (in China) an association, society, or political party. **2.** (among Chinese living in the U.S.) a fraternal organization or secret society, formerly believed to engage extensively in criminal activities. [< Chin *t'ang* meeting place]

ton·ga (tong′gə), *n.* a light, two-wheeled, horse-drawn vehicle used in India. [< Hindi *tāṅgā*]

Ton·ga (tong′gə), *n.* a Polynesian kingdom consisting of three groups of islands in the S Pacific, NE of New Zealand: a former British protectorate. 100,105; ab. 270 sq. mi. *Cap.:* Nukualofa. Also called **Ton′ga Is′lands, Friendly Islands.**

Ton·gan (tong′gən), *n.* **1.** a native or inhabitant of Tonga. **2.** a Polynesian language, the language of the Tongans. **—*adj.* 3.** of or pertaining to Tonga, its people, or their language. [TONG(A) + -AN]

Tong·king (tong′king′), *n.* Tonkin.

tong·man (tong′mən), *n., pl.* **-men.** a member of a Chinese tong.

tongs (tôngz, tongz), *n.* (*usually construed as pl.*) any of various implements consisting of two arms hinged, pivoted, or otherwise fastened together, for seizing, holding, or lifting something (usually used with *pair of*).

tongue (tung), *n., v.* **tongued, tongu·ing. —*n.* 1.** the usually movable organ in the floor of the mouth in man and most vertebrates, functioning in eating, in tasting, and, in man, in speaking. **2.** an analogous organ in invertebrate animals. **3.** the tongue of an animal, as an ox, beef, or sheep, used for food. **4.** the human tongue as the organ of speech. **5.** the faculty or power of speech: *Have you lost your tongue?* **6.** a manner or character of speech: *a flattering tongue.* **7.** the language or dialect of a particular people, region, or nation. **8.** a people or nation distinguished by its language. Is. 66:18; Rev. 5:9. **9. tongues,** a form of incomprehensible speech delivered in moments of religious ecstasy. **10.** an object that resembles an animal's tongue in shape, position, or function. **11.** a strip of leather under the lacing or fastening of a shoe. **12.** a suspended object of metal for striking the interior of a bell; clapper. **13.** a vibrating reed or similar structure in a musical instrument. **14.** the pole extending from a carriage or other vehicle between the animals drawing it. **15.** a projecting strip along the center of the edge or end of a board, for fitting into a groove in another board. **16.** a narrow strip of land extending into a body of water; cape. **17.** *Mach.* a long, narrow projection on a machine. **18.** the pin of a buckle, brooch, etc. **19. hold one's tongue,** to refrain from or cease speaking; keep silent. **20. on the tip of one's tongue, a.** on the verge of being uttered. **b.** barely escaping one's memory. **21. slip of the tongue,** an inadvertent remark. **22. with one's tongue in one's cheek,** mockingly; insincerely. Also, **with tongue in cheek, tongue in cheek.** —*v.t.* **23.** to articulate (tones played on a clarinet, trumpet, etc.) by strokes of the tongue. **24.** *Carpentry.* **a.** to cut a tongue on (a board). **b.** to join or fit together by a tongue-and-groove joint. **25.** to touch with the tongue. **26.** to reproach or scold. **27.** *Archaic.* to speak or utter. —*v.i.* **28.** to tongue tones played on a clarinet, trumpet, etc. **29.** to project like a tongue or tongues. [ME, OE *tunge;* c. D *tong,* Icel *tunga,* G *Zunge,* Goth *tuggo;* akin to L *lingua* (earlier *dingua*)] —**tongue′less,** *adj.* —**tongue′like′,** *adj.*

tongue′-and-groove′ joint′ (tung′ən grōōv′), *Carpentry.* a joint between boards, a tongue on one fitting into a groove in the other.

Tongue-and-groove joint

tongue′ depres′sor, a broad, thin piece of wood for use by doctors to hold down a patient's tongue during an examination of the mouth and throat.

tongue-lash (tung′lash′), *v.t., v.i.* to scold severely.

tongue-lash·ing (tung′lash′ing), *n.* a severe scolding or reprimand.

tongue-tie (tung′tī′), *n., v.,* **-tied, -ty·ing.** —*n.* **1.** impeded motion of the tongue caused esp. by shortness of the frenum, which binds it to the floor of the mouth. —*v.t.* **2.** to make tongue-tied. [back formation from TONGUE-TIED]

tongue-tied (tung′tīd′), *adj.* **1.** unable to speak, as from shyness, embarrassment, or surprise. **2.** affected with tongue-tie.

tongue′ twist′er, a word or sequence of words difficult to pronounce, esp. rapidly, because of alliteration of consonant sounds with slight variations, as "Rubber baby buggy bumpers" or "The Leith police dismisseth us."

ton·ic (ton′ik), *n.* **1.** a medicine that invigorates or strengthens. **2.** anything invigorating physically, mentally, or morally. **3.** *Music.* the first degree of the scale; the keynote. **4.** carbonated quinine water for mixing with alcoholic drinks to make highballs. —*adj.* **5.** pertaining to, maintaining, increasing, or restoring the tone or health of the body or an organ, as a medicine. **6.** invigorating physically, mentally, or morally. **7.** *Physiol., Pathol.* **a.** pertaining to tension, as of the muscles. **b.** marked by continued muscular tension: *a tonic spasm.* **8.** using differences in tone or pitch to distinguish between words that are otherwise phonemically identical: *a tonic language.* **9.** pertaining to tone or accent in speech. **10.** *Phonet.* accented, esp. with primary accent. **11.** *Music.* **a.** of or pertaining to a tone or tones. **b.** pertaining to or founded on the keynote, or first tone, of a musical scale: *a tonic chord.* [< Gk *tonik(ós)* pertaining to stretching or tones] —**ton′i·cal·ly,** *adv.*

ton′ic ac′cent, vocal accent, or syllabic stress, in pronunciation or speaking.

to·nic·i·ty (tō nis′i tē), *n.* **1.** a tonic quality or condition. **2.** the state of bodily tone. **3.** *Physiol.* the normal elastic tension of living muscles, arteries, etc., by which the tone of the system is maintained.

ton′ic sol-fa′, a system of singing characterized by emphasis upon tonality or key relationship, in which tones are indicated by the initial letters of the syllables of the *sol-fa* system rather than by conventional staff notation.

ton′ic spasm′, *Med.* See under **spasm** (def. 1).

to·night (tə nīt′), *n.* **1.** this present or coming night. —*adv.* **2.** on this present night. **3.** *Obs.* during last night. Also, **to-night′.** [ME, OE *tō niht*]

ton′ka bean′ (tong′kə), **1.** the fragrant, black, almond-shaped seed of a tall, leguminous tree of the genus *Dipteryx* (or *Coumarouna*), esp. *D. odorata,* of tropical South America, used in perfumes and snuff, and as a substitute for vanilla. **2.** the tree itself. [*tonka* ? < Tupi]

Ton·kin (ton′kin′, tong′kin′), *n.* **1.** a former state in N French Indochina, now part of North Vietnam. **2. Gulf of,** an arm of the South China Sea, W of Hainan, bordering China and North Vietnam. 300 mi. long. Also, **Tongking, Tonking** (ton′king′, tong′-).

Ton·le Sap (ton′lā säp′), a lake in W Cambodia, draining into the Mekong River.

ton·let (tun′lit), *n.* *Armor.* a skirt of plates. [< F *tonnelet* keg, MF, prob. dim. of *tonel* cask, from the resemblance to the arrangement of staves]

ton·nage (tun′ij), *n.* **1.** the capacity of a merchant vessel, expressed either in units of weight, as deadweight tons, or of volume, as gross tons. **2.** ships collectively considered with reference to their carrying capacity or together with their cargoes. **3.** a duty on ships or boats at so much per ton of cargo or freight, or according to the capacity in tons. Also, **tunnage.** [ME: duty < OF]

tonne (tun), *n.* See **metric ton.**

ton·neau (tu nō′), *n., pl.* **-neaus, -neaux** (-nōz′). **1.** a rear part or compartment of an automobile body, containing seats for passengers. **2.** a complete automobile body having such a rear part. **3.** a tight-fitting cover for the cockpit of a small sports car, to protect it from the weather when parking when the top is down. **4.** millier. [< F: kind of vehicle; also, cask; OF *tonel* cask. See TUNNEL]

to·nom·e·ter (tō nom′i tər), *n.* **1.** an instrument for measuring the frequencies of tones. **2.** any of various physiological instruments, as for measuring the tension within the eyeball, or for determining blood pressure. **3.** *Physical Chem.* an instrument for measuring vapor pressure. [< Gk *tóno(s)* tension, tone + -METER] —**ton·o·met·ric** (ton′ə me′trik, tō′nə-), *adj.* —**to·nom′e·try,** *n.*

A, Tonsil
B, Adenoids

tons′ bur′den, *Naut.* the weight of cargo that a vessel can carry, expressed in long tons.

ton·sil (ton′səl), *n.* *Anat.* a prominent oval mass of lymphoid tissue on each side of the fauces. [< L *tōnsill(ae)* (pl.) the tonsils] —**ton′sil·lar, ton′sil·ar,** **ton·sil·lar·y** (ton′sə ler′ē), *adj.*

ton·sil·lec·to·my (ton′sə lek′tə mē), *n., pl.* **-mies.** *Surg.* the operation of excising or removing one or both tonsils. [< L *tōnsill(ae)* tonsils + -ECTOMY]

ton·sil·li·tis (ton′sə lī′tis), *n.* *Pathol.* inflammation of a tonsil or the tonsils. [< L *tōnsill(ae)* tonsils + -ITIS] —**ton·sil·lit·ic** (ton′sə lit′ik), *adj.*

ton·sil·lot·o·my (ton′sə lot′ə mē), *n., pl.* **-mies.** *Surg.* incision or excision of a portion of a tonsil. [< L *tōnsill(ae)* tonsils + -o- + -TOMY]

ton·so·ri·al (ton sōr′ē əl, -sôr′-), *adj.* of or pertaining to barbers or barbering. [< L *tōnsōri(us)* of shaving (*tōns(us),* ptp. of *tondēre* to shave + *-ōrius* -ORY[1]) + -AL[1]]

ton·sure (ton′shər), *n., v.,* **-sured, -sur·ing.** —*n.* **1.** the act of cutting the hair. **2.** the act of shaving the head or of some part of it, esp. as a religious practice or rite. **3.** the part of a cleric's head, usually the crown, left bare by shaving the hair. **4.** the state of being shorn. —*v.t.* **5.** to subject to tonsure. [ME < L *tōnsūr(a)* a shearing = *tōns(us)* (ptp. of *tondēre* to shear, clip, shave) + *-ūra* -URE]

ton·tine (ton′tēn, ton tēn′), *n.* **1.** an annuity scheme in which subscribers share a common fund with the benefit of survivorship, the survivors' shares being increased as the subscribers die, until the whole goes to the last survivor. **2.** the annuity shared. **3.** the share of each subscriber. **4.** the group of subscribers. **5.** any of various forms of life insurance based on the tontine scheme. [< F; named after Lorenzo *Tonti,* Neapolitan banker who started the scheme in France about 1653. See -INE[1]]

to·nus (tō′nəs), *n.* *Physiol.* a normal state of continuous slight tension in muscle tissue that facilitates its response to stimulation. [< NL, special use of L *tonus* < Gk *tónos* TONE]

ton·y (tō′nē), *adj.,* **ton·i·er, ton·i·est.** *Slang.* high-toned; stylish: *a tony nightclub.*

To·ny (tō′nē), *n., pl.* **-nies.** *U.S.* one of a group of awards made annually for achievements in theatrical production and performance. [after the nickname of *Antoinette Perry* (1888–1946), U.S. actress and theatrical producer]

too (tōō), *adv.* **1.** in addition; also; moreover: *young, clever, and rich too.* **2.** to an excessive extent or degree: *too sick to travel.* **3.** more, as specified, than should be. **4.** extremely; very: *It was too nice of you to come.* **5.** used as an affirmative to contradict a negative statement: *I am too!* **6. only too.** See **only** (def. 6). [sp. var. of TO (adv.)]

took (tŏŏk), *v.* pt. of **take.**

Tooke (tŏŏk), *n.* **(John) Horne** (hôrn), 1736–1812, English politician and philologist.

tool (tōōl), *n.* **1.** an implement, esp. one held in the hand, as a hammer, saw, file, etc., for performing or facilitating mechanical operations. **2.** the cutting or machining part of a lathe, drill, or similar machine. **3.** the machine itself; a machine tool. **4.** a person manipulated by another for his own ends. **5.** *Slang* (*usually vulgar*). the penis. —*v.t.* **6.** to provide with tools. **7.** to work or shape with a tool. **8.** to work decoratively with a hand tool. **9.** to drive (a car or other vehicle). —*v.i.* **10.** to work with a tool or tools. **11.** to drive or ride in a vehicle. [ME; OE *tōl;* c. Icel *tōl* tools; akin to TAW[2]] —**tool′er,** *n.* —**tool′less,** *adj.* —**Syn. 1.** TOOL, IMPLEMENT, INSTRUMENT, UTENSIL refer to contrivances for doing work. A TOOL is a contrivance held in and worked by the hand, for assisting the work of (esp.) mechanics or laborers: *a carpenter's tools.* An IMPLEMENT is any tool or contrivance designed or used for a particular purpose: *agricultural implements.* An INSTRUMENT is anything used in doing a certain work or producing a certain result, esp. that which requires delicacy, accuracy, or precision: *surgical or musical instruments.* A UTENSIL is esp. an article for domestic use: *kitchen utensils.* When used figuratively of human agency, TOOL is generally used in a contemptuous sense; INSTRUMENT, in a neutral or good sense: *a tool of unscrupulous men; an instrument of Providence.*

tool·box (tōōl′boks′), *n.* a box or case, often with compartments, in which tools are kept.

tool·house (tōōl′hous′), *n., pl.* **-hous·es** (-hou′ziz). toolshed.

tool·ing (tōō′ling), *n.* **1.** ornamental work or markings made with a tool or tools. **2.** *Mach.* the planning and arrangement of tools for a particular manufacturing process.

tool·mak·er (tōōl′mā′kər), *n.* a machinist skilled in the building and reconditioning of tools, jigs, etc. —**tool′mak′ing,** *n.*

tool·room (tōōl′rōōm′, -rŏŏm′), *n.* a room, as in a machine shop, in which tools are stored, repaired, produced, etc., for the workmen of the shop.

tool·shed (tōōl′shed′), *n.* a small building where tools are stored, often behind a house. Also called **toolhouse.**

Toombs (tōōmz), *n.* **Robert,** 1810–85, U.S. lawyer, orator, and Confederate statesman and army officer.

toon (tōōn), *n.* **1.** a meliaceous tree, *Toona ciliata* (or *Cedrela Toona*), of the East Indies and Australia, yielding an aromatic red wood resembling mahogany, used for furniture, carving, etc. **2.** the wood. [< Hindi *tūn* < Skt *tunna*]

toot[1] (tōōt), *v.i.* **1.** (of a horn or whistle) to give forth its characteristic sound. **2.** to make a similar sound. **3.** to sound or blow a horn or other wind instrument. —*v.t.* **4.** to cause (a horn or other wind instrument) to sound. **5.** to sound (notes, music, etc.) on a horn or the like. —*n.* **6.** an act or sound of tooting. [akin to LG, G *tuten,* D *toeten,* Sw *tuta* in same sense; orig. imit.] —**toot′er,** *n.*

toot[2] (tōōt), *n.* *Informal.* a period or instance of drunken revelry; binge; spree. [?]

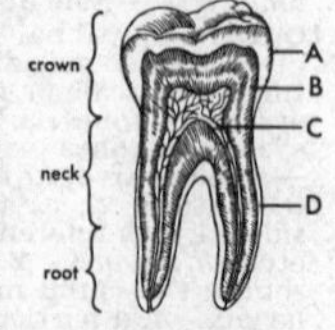

Tooth (Human)
A, Enamel;
B, Dentin; C, Pulp;
D, Cementum

tooth (tōōth), *n., pl.* **teeth,** *v.,* **toothed** (tōōtht, tōōthd), **tooth·ing** (tōō′thing, -thing). —*n.* **1.** (in most vertebrates) one of the hard bodies or processes usually attached in a row to each jaw, serving for the prehension and mastication of food, as weapons, etc., and in mammals typically composed chiefly of dentin surrounding a sensitive pulp and covered on the crown with enamel. **2.** (in invertebrates) any of various similar or analogous processes occurring in the mouth or alimentary canal, or on a shell. **3.** any projection resembling or suggesting a tooth, as on a comb, rake, or saw. **4.** *Mach.* any of the uniform projections on a gear, rack, or sprocket, by which it drives, or is driven. **5.** taste, relish, or liking. **6.** a rough surface created on drawing paper, canvas for oil painting, or the like. **7. by the skin of one's teeth,** by an extremely narrow margin; barely. **8. in the teeth of, a.** so as to face or confront: *in the teeth of the wind.* **b.** in defiance of; in opposition to: *in the teeth of public opinion.* **9. to the teeth,** entirely; fully: *armed to the teeth.* —*v.t.* **10.** to furnish with teeth. [ME; OE *tōth;* c. D *tand,* Icel *tönn,* G *Zahn;* akin to Goth *tunthus,* L *dēns,* Gk *odoús,* Skt *dánta*] —**tooth′less,** *adj.* —**tooth′less·ly,** *adv.* —**tooth′less·ness,** *n.* —**tooth′like′,** *adj.*

tooth·ache (to͞oth′āk′), *n.* a pain in or about a tooth. [ME *tothache,* OE *tōthæce*]

tooth′ and nail′, with all one's resources or energy; fiercely: *We fought tooth and nail but lost.*

tooth·brush (to͞oth′brush′), *n.* a small brush with a long handle, for cleaning the teeth.

toothed′ whale′, any whale of the suborder *Odontoceti,* having conical teeth in one or both jaws and feeding on fish, squid, etc. Cf. **whalebone whale.**

tooth·paste (to͞oth′pāst′), *n.* a dentifrice in paste form.

tooth·pick (to͞oth′pik′), *n.* a small pointed piece of wood, plastic, etc., for removing substances, esp. food particles, from between the teeth.

tooth′ pow′der, a dentifrice in the form of a powder.

tooth′ shell′, **1.** any marine mollusk of the class *Scaphopoda,* having a curved, tapering shell that is open at both ends. **2.** the shell itself.

tooth·some (to͞oth′səm), *adj.* **1.** pleasing to the taste; palatable. **2.** attractive or desirable. —**tooth′some·ly,** *adv.* —**tooth′some·ness,** *n.*

tooth·wort (to͞oth′wûrt′), *n.* **1.** a European, orobanchaceous plant, *Lathraea Squamaria,* having a rootstock covered with toothlike scales. **2.** any cruciferous plant of the genus *Dentaria,* having toothlike projections upon the creeping rootstock.

tooth·y (to͞o′thē, -thē), *adj.,* **tooth·i·er, tooth·i·est.** having or displaying conspicuous teeth: *a toothy smile.* —**tooth′i·ly,** *adv.* —**tooth′i·ness,** *n.*

too·tle (to͞ot′əl), *v.,* **-tled, -tling,** *n.* —*v.i.* **1.** to toot gently or repeatedly on a flute or the like. —*n.* **2.** the sound so made. —**too′tler,** *n.*

toots (to͝ots), *n.* *Informal.* an affectionate or flippant form of address for a girl or woman; honey; baby.

toot·sy (to͝ot′sē), *n., pl.* **-sies.** *Informal.* **1.** a foot. **2.** toots. [dial. *toot* foot (lit., something that peeps or sticks out, n. use of *toot* to protrude, OE *tōtian*) + *-sy* hypocoristic suffix]

Too·woom·ba (tə wo͝om′bə), *n.* a city in SE Queensland, in E Australia. 50,134 (1961).

top[1] (top), *n., adj., v.,* **topped, top·ping.** —*n.* **1.** the uppermost point, area, surface, or section of anything; apex; summit. **2.** a part or feature that forms this. **3.** a lid or cover for a box or the like. **4.** a rooflike cover for a vehicle. **5.** the maximum intensity, amount, etc.: *at the top of one's voice; a price of five dollars, at the top.* **6.** the position of greatest honor, authority, etc. **7.** one's head: *from top to toe.* **8.** the part of a plant that grows above ground, esp. of an edible root. **9.** the first or foremost part; beginning: *Take it from the top.* **10.** *Naut.* a platform surrounding the head of a lower mast on a ship, and serving as a foothold, a means of extending the upper rigging, etc. **11.** *Bridge.* **a.** the best card of a suit in a player's hand. **b.** (in duplicate bridge) the best score on a hand. **12.** *Sports.* **a.** a stroke that hits the ball above its center. **b.** the forward spin given to the ball by such a stroke. **13.** *Baseball.* the first half of an inning. **14.** *Jewelry.* crown (def. 20). **15. blow one's top,** *Slang.* **a.** to become enraged; lose one's temper. **b.** to become insane. **16. on top,** successful; victorious; dominant. **17. on top of, a.** over or upon. **b.** in addition to; over and above. **c.** close upon; following upon. **d.** in complete control, as of a problem. **18. over the top,** *Mil.* over the top of the parapet before a trench, as in issuing to charge against the enemy. —*adj.* **19.** pertaining to, situated at, or forming the top; highest; uppermost; upper: *the top shelf.* **20.** highest in degree; greatest: *to pay top prices.* **21.** foremost, chief, or principal. —*v.t.* **22.** to furnish with a top or topping. **23.** to be at or constitute the top of. **24.** to reach the top of. **25.** to rise above. **26.** to exceed in height, amount, etc. **27.** to surpass, excel, or outdo: *That tops everything!* **28.** to remove the top of; crop; prune: *to top a tall tree.* **29.** *Chem.* to distill off only the most volatile part of a mixture. **30.** *Sports.* **a.** to strike (the ball) above its center, giving it a forward spin. **b.** to make (a stroke) by hitting the ball in this manner. —*v.i.* **31.** to rise aloft. **32. top off,** to climax or complete, esp. in an exceptional manner; finish: [ME, OE; c. D *top,* G *Zopf,* Icel *toppr* top, tuft] —**Syn. 1.** zenith, acme, peak, pinnacle.

top[2] (top), *n.* **1.** a child's toy, often inversely conical, with a point on which it is made to spin. **2. sleep like a top,** to sleep soundly. [ME, OE; c. Fris, Flem *top*]

top-, var. of **topo-** before a vowel: *toponym.*

to·paz (tō′paz), *n.* **1.** a mineral, a fluosilicate of aluminum, usually occurring in prismatic orthorhombic crystals of various colors, and used as a gem. **2.** a yellow variety of quartz; false topaz. **3.** either of two South American hummingbirds, *Topaza pella* or *T. pyra,* having chiefly red and crimson plumage and a yellowish-green throat with a topaz sheen. [< L *topaz(us)* < Gk *tópazos;* r. ME *topace* < OF < L] —**to·paz·ine** (tō′pə zēn′, -zin), *adj.*

to·paz·o·lite (tō paz′ə līt′), *n.* a yellow or olive-green variety of andradite garnet found in Piedmont. [*topazo-* (comb. form repr. Gk *tópazos* TOPAZ) + -LITE]

to′paz quartz′, citrine (def. 2).

top′ banan′a, *Slang.* a leading comedian in musical comedy, burlesque, vaudeville, etc.

top′ boot′, a high boot, esp. one having a cuff of a different material, color, etc., from the rest of the boot.

top′ brass′, *U.S. Slang.* brass (def. 7)

top·coat (top′kōt′), *n.* a lightweight overcoat.

top′ cross′, *Genetics.* the progeny of the cross of a variety with one inbred line.

top′ dog′, *Informal.* a predominant person, group, or nation, esp. in a competition.

top-draw·er (top′drôr′), *adj.* of or pertaining to the highest level in rank, excellence, or importance: *a top-drawer secret.*

top-dress (top′dres′), *v.t.* to manure (land) on the surface.

top′ dress′ing, a dressing of manure on the surface of land.

tope[1] (tōp), *v.,* **toped, top·ing.** —*v.i.* **1.** to drink alcoholic liquor habitually and to excess. —*v.t.* **2.** to drink (liquor) habitually and to excess. [var. of obs. *top* to drink, in phrase *top off = tip off* to drink (a full helping) at a draught; special use of *top* to tilt. See TOPPLE]

tope[2] (tōp), *n.* a small shark, *Galeorhinus galeus,* found along the European coast. [akin to *toper* dogfish (Norfolk dial.)]

Tope[3] (East Indian)

tope[3] (tōp), *n.* (in Buddhist countries) a dome-shaped monument, usually for religious relics. [< Hindi *tōp*]

to·pec·to·my (tə pek′tə mē), *n., pl.* **-mies.** *Surg.* excision of part of the cerebral cortex for the relief of unmanageable pain or esp. as a treatment for certain kinds of mental disease. [TOP + ECTOMY]

to·pee (tō pē′, tō′pē), *n.* (in India) a lightweight helmet or sun hat made of pith. Also, **topi.** [< Hindi: hat]

To·pe·ka (tə pē′kə), *n.* a city in and the capital of Kansas, in the NE part, on the Kansas River. 125,011 (1970).

top·er (tō′pər), *n.* a hard drinker or chronic drunkard.

top·flight (top′flīt′), *adj.* outstandingly excellent, superior, or expert; first-rate.

top·full (top′fo͝ol′), *adj.* full to the utmost; brimful.

top·gal·lant (top′gal′ənt; *Naut.* tə gal′ənt), *Naut.* —*n.* **1.** See **topgallant sail.** **2.** *Archaic.* a top at the head of a topmast. —*adj.* **3.** of or pertaining to a topgallant mast.

topgal′lant mast′, *Naut.* **1.** a mast fixed to the head of a topmast on a square-rigged vessel. **2.** a section of an extended topmast on which the topgallant yards are carried.

topgal′lant sail′, *Naut.* a sail or either of two sails set on the yard or yards of a topgallant mast. Also called **topgallant.** See diag. at **ship.**

top·ham·per (top′ham′pər), *n.* *Naut.* **1.** the light upper sails and their gear and spars, sometimes used to refer to all spars and gear above the deck. **2.** any unnecessary weight, either aloft or about the upper decks.

top′ hat′, a tall, cylindrical hat with a stiff brim usually slightly curved on the sides, worn by men esp. on formal occasions. Cf. **opera hat, silk hat.**

top-heav·y (top′hev′ē), *adj.* **1.** having the top disproportionately heavy; liable to fall from too great weight above. **2.** *Finance.* overcapitalized. —**top′-heav′i·ly,** *adv.* —**top′-heav′i·ness,** *n.*

To·phet (tō′fet), *n.* *Bible.* **1.** a shrine near Jerusalem, where children were offered as sacrifices to Moloch. **2.** the place of punishment for the wicked after death; hell. Also, **To·pheth** (tō′fet). [ME << Heb *Tōpheth* a place-name]

top-hole (top′hōl′), *adj.* *Brit. Slang.* first-rate.

to·phus (tō′fəs), *n., pl.* **-phi** (-fī). *Pathol.* a calcareous concretion formed in the soft tissue about a joint, in the pinna of the ear, etc., esp. in gout; a gouty deposit. [< L, var. sp. of *tōfus* TUFA] —**to·pha·ceous** (tə fā′shəs), *adj.*

to·pi (tō pē′, tō′pē), *n., pl.* **-pis.** topee.

to·pi·ar·y (tō′pē er′ē), *adj., n., pl.* **-ar·ies.** *Hort.* —*adj.* **1.** (of a plant) clipped or trimmed into fantastic shapes. **2.** of, pertaining to, or characterized by such trimming. —*n.* **3.** topiary work; the topiary art. **4.** a garden containing such work. [< L *topiāri(us)* pertaining to landscape gardening or to ornamental gardens = *topi-* (< Gk *tópi(on),* dim. of *tópos* place) + *-ārius* -ARY]

top·ic (top′ik), *n.* **1.** a subject of conversation or discussion. **2.** the subject or theme of a discourse or of one of its parts. **3.** *Rhet., Logic.* a general field of considerations from which arguments can be drawn. **4.** a general rule or maxim. [< L *topic(a)* (pl.) < Gk *(tà) topiká* name of work by Aristotle (lit., things pertaining to commonplaces) = *tóp(oi)* commonplaces + *-ika,* neut. pl. of *-ikos* -IC; see TOPO-] —**Syn. 2.** thesis, subject matter. See **subject.**

top·i·cal (top′i kəl), *adj.* **1.** pertaining to or dealing with matters of current or local interest: *a topical reference.* **2.** pertaining to the subject of a discourse, composition, or the like. **3.** of a place; local. **4.** *Med.* of, pertaining to, or applied to a particular part of the body; local. [< Gk *topik(ós)* local, pertaining to commonplaces (see TOPO-, -IC) + -AL[1]] —**top′i·cal·ly,** *adv.*

top·i·cal·i·ty (top′ə kal′i tē), *n., pl.* **-ties** for 2. **1.** the state or quality of being topical. **2.** a detail or matter of current or local interest.

top′ic sen′tence, an introductory sentence that expresses the essential idea of a paragraph or larger section. Also, **top′ical sen′tence.**

top′ kick′, *Mil. Slang.* a first sergeant.

top·knot (top′not′), *n.* **1.** a knot or tuft of hair on the top of the head. **2.** a knot or bow of ribbon worn on the top of the head. **3.** a tuft or crest of feathers on the head of a bird.

top·less (top′lis), *adj.* **1.** lacking an upper part: *a topless bathing suit.* **2.** wearing no clothing above the waist: *a topless waitress.* **3.** featuring dancers, singers, etc., who wear no clothing above the waist: *a topless bar.* **4.** extremely high: *a topless mountain.* **5.** *Obs.* without a peer. —**top′less·ness,** *n.*

top-lev·el (top′lev′əl), *adj.* *Informal.* high-level: *a top-level meeting.*

top·loft·y (top′lôf′tē, -lof′-), *adj.* *Informal.* condescending; haughty. —**top′loft′i·ly,** *adv.* —**top′loft′i·ness,** *n.*

top·mast (top′mast′, -mäst′; *Naut.* top′məst), *n.* *Naut.* the mast next above a lower mast, usually formed as a separate spar from the lower mast and used to support the yards or rigging of a topsail or topsails.

top·min·now (top′min′ō), *n., pl.* (*esp. collectively*) **-now,** (*esp. referring to two or more kinds or species*) **-nows.** any of several small, surface-swimming cyprinodont fishes of the egg-laying family *Cyprinodontidae* and the live-bearing family *Poeciliidae*.

top·most (top′mōst′ *or, esp. Brit.,* -məst), *adj.* highest; uppermost: *the topmost bough of the tree.*

top·notch (top′noch′), *adj. Informal.* first-rate: *a topnotch job.*

topo-, a learned borrowing from Greek meaning "place," "local," used in the formation of compound words: *topography; topology.* Also, *esp. before a vowel,* **top-.** [comb. form of Gk *tópos* place, commonplace]

topog., 1. topographical. 2. topography.

to·pog·ra·pher (tə pog′rə fər), *n.* a specialist in topography. [< Gk *topográph(os)* topographer + -ER¹]

top′ograph′ic map′, a map showing topographic features, usually by means of contour lines.

to·pog·ra·phy (tə pog′rə fē), *n., pl.* **-phies. 1.** the detailed mapping or description of the features of a relatively small area, district, or locality. **2.** the relief features or surface configuration of an area. [late ME *topographye* < LL *topographia* < Gk] —**top·o·graph·ic** (top′ə graf′ik), **top′o·graph′i·cal,** *adj.* —**top′o·graph′i·cal·ly,** *adv.*

to·pol·o·gy (tə pol′ə jē), *n. Math.* the study of the properties of geometric forms that remain invariant under certain transformations, as bending, stretching, etc. Also called **analysis situs.** —**top·o·log·ic** (top′ə loj′ik), **top′o·log′i·cal,** *adj.* —**top′o·log′i·cal·ly,** *adv.* —**to·pol′o·gist,** *n.*

top·o·nym (top′ə nim), *n.* **1.** a place name. **2.** a name derived from the name of a place.

to·pon·y·my (tə pon′ə mē), *n.* **1.** the study of toponyms. **2.** *Anat.* the nomenclature of the regions of the body. —**top·o·nym·ic** (top′ə nim′ik), **top′o·nym′i·cal,** *adj.*

top·per (top′ər), *n.* **1.** a person or thing that tops. **2.** a woman's loose topcoat, usually lightweight and shorter than a standard-length coat. **3.** *Informal.* See **top hat.**

top·ping (top′ing), *n.* **1.** the act of a person or thing that tops. **2.** something that forms a top, esp. a garnish or sauce spread over food. —*adj.* **3.** rising above something else; overtopping. **4.** *Chiefly Brit. Informal.* excellent; wonderful.

top·ple (top′əl), *v.,* **-pled, -pling.** —*v.i.* **1.** to fall forward, as from weakness; pitch; tumble down. **2.** to lean over or jut, as if threatening to fall. —*v.t.* **3.** to cause to topple. **4.** to overthrow, as from a position of authority. [earlier *top* to tilt, topple (see TOPE¹) + -LE]

top′ round′, a cut of beef taken from inside the round, which is below the rump and above the upper leg. Cf. **bottom round.**

tops (tops), *adj.* **1.** ranked among the highest, as in ability, performance, comprehensiveness, quality, etc. —*n.* **2. the tops,** a person or thing that is outstanding.

top·sail (top′sāl′; *Naut.* top′səl), *n. Naut.* a sail, or either of a pair of sails, set immediately above the lowermost sail of a mast and supported by a topmast. [ME *topseil*]

top-se·cret (top′sē′krit), *adj. U.S. Govt., Mil.* (of information, a document, etc.) **1.** bearing the classification *top-secret,* the highest level of classified information. **2.** limited to persons authorized to use information, documents, etc., so classified.

top′ ser′geant, *Mil. Slang.* a first sergeant.

top·side (top′sīd′), *n.* **1.** the upper side. **2.** Usually, **topsides.** *Naut.* the outer surface of a hull above the water. —*adj.* **3.** of, pertaining to, or located on the topside. —*adv.* **4.** Also, **top′sides′.** up on the deck.

top·soil (top′soil′), *n.* **1.** the surface or upper part of the soil. —*v.t.* **2.** to cover (land) with topsoil.

top·sy-tur·vy (top′sē tûr′vē), *adv., adj., n., pl.* **-vies.** —*adv.* **1.** with the top where the bottom should be; upside down. **2.** in or into a state of confusion or disorder. —*adj.* **3.** turned upside down; inverted; reversed. **4.** confused or disorderly. —*n.* **5.** a state of confusion or disorder. [? var. of *top syd turvye* topside down (with loss of *d* before *t*); *turvy,* var. of *tervy* = obs. *terve* to turn over (c. OHG *zerben*) + -Y¹]

Toque

toque (tōk), *n.* **1.** a velvet hat with a narrow, sometimes turned-up brim, a full crown, and usually a plume, worn esp. in the 16th century. **2.** a brimless and close-fitting hat for women, in any of several shapes. **3.** tuque. [< F; r. earlier *toock, towk* (< Pg *touca* coif), *tock, tocque* (< It *tocca* cap), *toke* (< Sp *toca* headdress); all perh. < Basque *tauka* hat]

tor (tôr), *n.* a rocky pinnacle; a peak of a bare or rocky mountain or hill. [ME; OE *torr* < Celt; cf. Gael *torr* hill, mound, Ir *torr,* Welsh *twr* heap, pile]

To·rah (tōr′ə, tôr′ə; *Heb.* tô rä′), *n.* **1.** the Pentateuch, being the first of the three Jewish divisions of the Old Testament. Cf. **Tanach. 2.** the Old Testament itself. **3.** the entire body of Jewish law as contained chiefly in the Old Testament and the Talmud. Also, **To′ra.** [< Heb *tōrāh* instruction, law]

tor·bern·ite (tôr′bər nīt′), *n.* a mineral, hydrated copper uranium phosphate, $CuU_2P_2O_{12}\cdot12H_2O$, a minor ore of uranium; copper uranite. Also called **chalcolite.** [named after *Torbern* Bergman (1735–84), Swedish chemist; see -ITE¹]

torch (tôrch), *n.* **1.** a light consisting of a stick or rod having a flammable substance at the upper end. **2.** such a light as a symbol of enlightenment or learning. **3.** any of various devices that produce a hot flame for soldering, burning off paint, etc. **4.** *Brit.* a flashlight. **5. carry the** or **a torch for,** *Slang.* to be in love with, esp. to suffer from unrequited love for. [ME *torche* < OF < VL **torca* something twisted. See TORQUE] —**torch′less,** *adj.* —**torch′like′,** *adj.*

torch·bear·er (tôrch′bâr′ər), *n.* **1.** a person who carries a torch. **2.** a leader in a movement, campaign, etc.

tor·chère (tôr shâr′), *n.* a tall stand for a candelabrum. [< F < *torche* TORCH¹ + *-ère,* fem. of *-er* -ER²]

tor·chier (tôr chēr′), *n.* a floor lamp for indirect lighting, having its source of light within a reflecting bowl. Also, **tor·chiere′.** [var. of TORCHÈRE]

torch·light (tôrch′līt′), *n.* the light of a torch or torches.

tor′chon lace′ (tôr′shon; *Fr.* tôr shôN′), a linen or cotton lace with loosely twisted threads in simple, open patterns. [*torchon* < F: duster, dishcloth, lit., something to wipe with = *torch(er)* (to) wipe (< *torche* a twist) + *-on* n. suffix]

torch′ sing′er, a singer, esp. a woman, who specializes in singing torch songs.

torch′ song′, a popular song concerned with unhappiness or failure in love.

torch·wood (tôrch′wo͝od′), *n.* **1.** any of various resinous woods suitable for making torches, as the wood of the rutaceous tree, *Amyris balsamifera,* of Florida, the West Indies, etc. **2.** any of the trees yielding these woods.

Tor·de·si·llas (tôr′the sē′lyäs), *n.* a town in NW Spain, SW of Valladolid: treaty 1494. 4515 (1950).

tore¹ (tōr, tôr), *v.* pt. of **tear².**

tore² (tōr, tôr), *n.* a torus. [< F < L *tor(us)*]

tor·e·a·dor (tôr′ē ə dôr′; *Sp.* tô′re ä thôr′), *n.* a bullfighter; torero. [< Sp = *toread(o)* (ptp. of *torear* to bait a bull < *toro* bull < L *taur(us),* akin to STEER²; *-ado* < L *-ātus* -ATE¹) + *-or* -OR²]

tor′eador pants′, close-fitting slacks that extend below the knee, worn by women esp. for sports.

to·re·ro (tə râr′ō; *Sp.* tô re′rô), *n., pl.* **-re·ros** (-râr′ōz; *Sp.* -re′rôs). a bullfighter, esp. a matador. [< Sp < LL *taurār(ius)* = L *taur(us)* bull (see STEER²) + *-ārius* -ER²]

to·ri (tōr′ē, tôr′ē), *n.* pl. of **torus.**

tor·ic (tôr′ik, tor′-), *adj.* noting or pertaining to a lens with a surface forming a portion of a torus, used for eyeglasses. [TOR(US) + -IC]

Torii

to·ri·i (tôr′ē ē′, tōr′-), *n., pl.* **to·ri·i.** a gateway or portal consisting of two upright wooden posts connected at the top by two horizontal crosspieces, commonly found at the entrance to Japanese Shinto temples. [< Jap]

To·ri·no (tô rē′nô), *n.* Italian name of **Turin.**

tor·ment (*v.* tôr ment′; *n.* tôr′ment), *v.t.* **1.** to afflict with great bodily or mental suffering; pain. **2.** to worry or annoy excessively. **3.** to throw into commotion; stir up; disturb. —*n.* **4.** a state of great bodily or mental suffering; agony; misery. **5.** something that causes great bodily or mental pain or suffering. **6.** *Archaic.* **a.** an instrument of torture, as the rack or the thumbscrew. **b.** the torture inflicted. [ME *torment(en)* (v.), *torment* (n.) < LL *torment(āre)* (v.), L *torment(um)* (n.), lit., an instrument (of torture) worked by twisting, earlier **torquementum.* See TORQUE, -MENT] —**tor·ment′ed·ly,** *adv.* —**tor·ment′ing·ly,** *adv.* —**Syn. 1.** harry, hector, vex, distress, agonize. **2.** plague, needle, trouble. **4.** torture, distress, anguish.

tor·men·til (tôr′men til), *n.* a low, rosaceous herb, *Potentilla Tormentilla,* of Europe, having small, bright-yellow flowers, and a strongly astringent root used in medicine and in tanning and dyeing. [ME *tormentille* < ML *tormentill(a)* = L *torment(um)* TORMENT + *-illa* dim. suffix]

tor·men·tor (tôr men′tər), *n.* **1.** a person or thing that torments. **2.** *Theat.* a curtain or framed structure behind the proscenium at both sides of the stage, for screening the wings from the audience. Cf. **teaser** (def. 2). **3.** *Motion Pictures.* a sound-deadening screen used during the taking of scenes to prevent echo and reverberation. Also, **tor·ment′er.** [ME *tormento(u)r* < AF; OF *tormenteor* < LL **tormentātōr-*]

torn (tōrn, tôrn), *v.* pp. of **tear².**

tor·na·do (tôr nā′dō), *n., pl.* **-does, -dos. 1.** a localized, violently destructive windstorm occurring over land, esp. in the midwestern U.S., and characterized by a long, funnel-shaped cloud, composed of condensation and containing debris, that extends to the ground and marks the path of greatest destruction. Cf. **waterspout** (def. 2). **2.** a violent squall or whirlwind of small extent, as one of those occurring during the summer on the west coast of Africa. [appar. by metathesis < Sp *tronada* thunderstorm, n. use of fem. of *tronado,* ptp. of *tronar* < L *tonāre* to thunder; r. 16th-century *ternado,* with unexplained *e*] —**tor·nad·ic** (tôr nad′ik), *adj.* —**tor·na′do·like′,** *adj.*

torna′do cloud′, tuba (def. 2).

to·ro (tô′rô), *n., pl.* **-ros** (-rôs). *Spanish.* a bull, *Bos taurus africanus* (*ibericus*), bred esp. for combat in the bullring.

to·roid (tōr′oid, tôr′-), *n. Geom.* **1.** a surface generated by the revolution of any closed plane curve or contour about an axis lying in its plane. **2.** the solid enclosed by such a surface. [TOR(US) + -OID]

To·ron·to (tə ron′tō), *n.* a city in and the capital of Ontario, in SE Canada, on Lake Ontario. 672,407 (1961). —**To·ron·to′ni·an,** *adj., n.*

to·rose (tōr′ōs, tôr′-, tō rōs′, tô-), *adj.* **1.** *Bot.* cylindrical, with swellings or constrictions at intervals; knobbed. **2.** *Zool.* bulging. Also, **to·rous** (tōr′əs, tôr′-). [< L *torōs(us)* bulging, full of muscle = *tor(us)* muscle + *-ōsus* -OSE¹]

tor·pe·do (tôr pē′dō), *n., pl.* **-does,** *v.,* **-doed, -do·ing.** —*n.* **1.** a self-propelled, elongated missile containing explosives, launched from a submarine or other warship, for destroying enemy ships. **2.** a submarine mine. **3.** a cartridge of gunpowder, dynamite, or the like, exploded in an oil well to facilitate the extraction of oil from the well. **4.** a detonating device fastened to a rail and exploded as a signal when run over by a locomotive. **5.** *U.S. Slang.* a gangster who hires himself out as a murderer. —*v.t.* **6.** to attack, hit, damage, or destroy with or as with a torpedo or torpedoes. [< L *torpēdō* numbness, torpidity, crampfish = *torpē(re)* (to) be stiff (see TORPID) + *-dō* suffix denoting state or condition] —**tor·pe′do·like′,** *adj.*

torpe′do boat′, a small, fast, highly maneuverable boat used for torpedoing enemy shipping.

tor·pe′do-boat destroy′er (tôr pē′dō bōt′), a vessel somewhat larger than the ordinary torpedo boat, designed for destroying torpedo boats or as a more powerful form of torpedo boat.

tor·pe·do·man (tôr pē′dō man′, -mən), *n., pl.* **-men** (-men′, -mən). a petty officer or warrant officer responsible for the maintenance, use, and repair of underwater weapons and equipment.

torpe′do tube′, a tube through which a self-propelled torpedo is launched.

tor·pid (tôr′pid), *adj.* **1.** inactive or sluggish, as a bodily organ. 2. slow; dull; apathetic; lethargic. 3. dormant, as a hibernating or estivating animal. [< L *torpid(us)* numb = *torp(ēre)* (to) be stiff or numb + *-idus* -ID[4]] —**tor·pid′i·ty, tor′pid·ness,** *n.* —**tor′pid·ly,** *adv.* —**Syn. 2.** indolent. —**Ant. 1.** energetic.

tor·por (tôr′pər), *n.* **1.** a state of suspended physical powers and activities. **2.** sluggish inactivity or inertia. **3.** dormancy, as of a hibernating animal. **4.** lethargic dullness or indifference; apathy. [< L: numbness = *torp(ēre)* (to) be stiff or numb + *-or* -OR[1]] —**Syn. 3.** sleepiness, slumber, drowsiness. **4.** stolidity, listlessness.

tor·por·if·ic (tôr′pə rif′ik), *adj.* causing torpor.

tor·quate (tôr′kwit, -kwāt), *adj. Zool.* ringed about the neck, as with feathers or a color; collared. [< L *torquāt(us)* adorned with a necklace = *torqu(ēs)* twisted neck chain + *-ātus* -ATE[1]]

Tor·quay (tôr kē′), *n.* a municipal borough in S Devonshire, in SW England: seaside resort. 53,915 (1961).

torque (tôrk), *n.* **1.** *Mech.* something that produces or tends to produce torsion or rotation. **2.** *Mach.* the measured ability of a rotating element, as of a gear or shaft, to overcome turning resistance. **3.** *Optics.* the rotational effect on plane-polarized light passing through certain liquids or crystals. **4.** a twisted narrow band, usually of precious metal, worn as an ornament esp. by the ancient Gauls and Britons. [back formation from TORQUES, the *s* being taken as pl. sign]

Tor·que·ma·da (tôʀ′ke mä′t͟hä), *n.* **To·más de** (tô-mäs′ de), 1420–98, Spanish inquisitor general.

tor·ques (tôr′kwēz), *n. Zool.* a ringlike band or formation about the neck, as of feathers, hair, or integument of distinctive color or appearance; collar. [< L: twisted necklace or collar = *torquē(re)* (to) twist (akin to Gk *trépein*) + *-s* nom. sing. ending]

torr (tôr), *n.* a unit of pressure, being the pressure necessary to support a column of mercury one millimeter high at 0°C and standard gravity, equal to 1333.2 microbars. [named after Evangelista TORR(ICELLI)]

Tor·rance (tôr′əns, tor′-), *n.* a city in SW California, SW of Los Angeles. 134,584 (1970).

Tor·re del Gre·co (tôʀ′ʀe del gʀe′kô), a city in SW Italy, near Naples. 77,851 (1961).

tor·re·fy (tôr′ə fī′, tor′-), *v.t.*, **-fied, -fy·ing.** to subject to fire or intense heat, as drugs, ores, etc. [< L *torrefacere* to make dry or hot = *torrē(re)* (to) dry up, parch, scorch + *facere* -FY; see TORRID] —**tor·re·fac·tion** (tôr′ə fak′shən, tor′-), *n.*

Tor·rens (tôr′ənz, tor′-), *n.* **Lake,** a salt lake in Australia, in E South Australia. 130 mi. long; 25 ft. below sea level.

tor·rent (tôr′ənt, tor′-), *n.* **1.** a stream of water flowing with great rapidity and violence. **2.** a rushing, violent, or abundant stream of anything. **3.** a violent downpour of rain. [< L *torrent-* (s. of *torrēns*) seething, lit., burning, prp. of *torrēre* to burn, parch; see -ENT]

tor·ren·tial (tô ren′shəl, to-, tə-), *adj.* **1.** pertaining to or having the nature of a torrent. **2.** resembling a torrent in rapidity or violence. **3.** falling in torrents: *torrential rains.* **4.** produced by the action of a torrent. **5.** violent, vehement, or impassioned. —**tor·ren′tial·ly,** *adv.*

Tor·re·ón (tôʀ′ʀe ôn′), *n.* a city in N Mexico. 212,900 (est. 1965).

Tor·res Bo·det (tôʀ′ʀes bô t͟het′), **Jai·me** (hī′me), 1902–74, Mexican poet, statesman, and diplomat.

Tor′res Strait′ (tôr′iz, tor′-), a strait between NE Australia and S New Guinea. 80 mi. wide.

Tor·ri·cel·li (tôr′i chel′ē; *It.* tôʀ′ʀē chel′lē), *n.* **E·van·ge·lis·ta** (e vän′je lē′stä), 1608–47, Italian physicist. —**Tor′ri·cel′li·an,** *adj.*

tor·rid (tôr′id, tor′-), *adj.* **1.** subject to parching or burning heat from the sun, as a geographical area. **2.** oppressively hot, parching, or burning, as climate, weather, air, etc. **3.** ardent; passionate: *a torrid love story.* [< L *torrid(us)* dried up, parched = *torr(ēre)* (to) parch, burn (see TORRENT, THIRST) + *-idus* -ID[4]] —**tor·rid′i·ty, tor′rid·ness,** *n.* —**tor′rid·ly,** *adv.* —**Syn. 1.** tropical. **2.** scorching, fiery. —**Ant. 1.** arctic. **2.** frigid. **3.** cool.

Tor′rid Zone′, the part of the earth's surface between the tropics of Cancer and Capricorn.

Tor·ring·ton (tôr′ing tən, tor′-), *n.* a city in NW Connecticut. 31,952 (1970).

tor·sade (tôr sād′), *n.* **1.** a twisted cord. **2.** any ornamental twist, as of velvet. [< F: twisted fringe = *tors* twisted (see TORSE) + *-ade* -ADE[1]]

torse (tôrs), *n. Heraldry.* a wreath of twisted silks of two alternating tinctures, usually a metal and a color, depicted supporting a crest or coronet, often upon a helmet. [< MF: wreath, n. use of fem. of *tors* twisted < LL *tors(us),* ptp., r. L *tortus,* ptp. of *torquēre* to twist]

tor·si (tôr′sē), *n.* a pl. of **torso.**

tor·si·bil·i·ty (tôr′sə bil′i tē), *n.* ability to be twisted. [TORSI(ON) + (A)BILITY]

tor·sion (tôr′shən), *n.* **1.** the act of twisting. **2.** the state of being twisted. **3.** *Mech.* **a.** the twisting of an object by two equal and opposite torques. **b.** the internal torque so produced. [late ME *torcion* < medical L *torsiōn-* (s. of *torsiō*) a griping or wringing of the bowels = LL *tors(us)* twisted (see TORSE) + *-iōn-* -ION] —**tor′sion·al,** *adj.* —**tor′sion·al·ly,** *adv.*

tor′sion bal′ance, an instrument for measuring small forces, as electric attraction or repulsion, by determining the amount of twisting they cause in a slender wire or filament.

tor′sion bar′, a metal bar having elasticity when subjected to torsion: used as a spring.

torsk (tôrsk), *n., pl.* **torsks,** (*esp. collectively*) **torsk. 1.** a cod. **2.** cusk (def. 1). [< Norw; ON *thorskr,* akin to *thurr* dry. See THIRST]

tor·so (tôr′sō), *n., pl.* **-sos, -si** (-sē). **1.** the trunk of the human body. **2.** a sculptured form representing the trunk of a nude female or male figure. [< It: stalk, trunk of statue < L *thyrs(us)* < Gk *thýrsos* wand, stem]

tort (tôrt), *n. Law.* a civil wrong, not including a breach of contract, for which the injured party is entitled to compensation. [ME < legal L *tort(um)* wrong, injustice, n. use of neut. of L *tortus* twisted, ptp. of *torquēre* to twist, wring]

torte (tôrt; *Ger.* tôʀ′tə), *n., pl.* **tortes** (tôrts), *Ger.* **tor·ten** (tôʀ′tᵊn). a rich cake, esp. one containing little or no flour, usually made with eggs, crumbs, and ground nuts. [< G << LL *tōrt(a)* round cake (of bread) < ?]

tort-fea·sor (tôrt′fē′zər, -zôr, -fē′-), *n. Law.* a person who commits a tort. [< AF *tortfesor* wrongdoer = F *tortfaiseur.* See TORT, FEASANCE, -OR[2]]

tor·ti·col·lis (tôr′tə kol′is), *n. Pathol.* a condition in which the neck is twisted and the head inclined to one side, caused by spasmodic contraction of the muscles of the neck. Also called **wryneck.** [< NL = L *tort(us)* twisted (see TORT) + *-i-* -I- + *coll(um)* neck + *-is* nom. suffix]

tor·tile (tôr′til), *adj.* twisted; coiled. [< L *tortil(is)* = *tort(us)* twisted (see TORT) + *-ilis* -ILE]

tor·til·la (tôr tē′ə; *Sp.* tôʀ tē′yä), *n., pl.* **-til·las** (-tē′əz; *Sp.* -tē′yäs). *Mexican Cookery.* a round, flat, unleavened bread made from corn meal. [< Sp = *tort(a)* cake (see TORTE) + *-illa* < L, dim. suffix]

tor·tious (tôr′shəs), *adj. Law.* of the nature of or pertaining to a tort. [ME *torcious* < AF = *torci(on)* TORSION + *-ous* -OUS; meaning influenced by TORT] —**tor′tious·ly,** *adv.*

tor·toise (tôr′təs), *n.* **1.** a turtle, esp. a terrestrial turtle. **2.** a very slow person or thing. [var. of earlier (15th-century) *tortuse, tortose, tortuce,* ME *tortuca* < ML << LL *tartarūcha* (fem.) of Tartarus < Gk *tartaroûchos* (the tortoise being regarded as an infernal animal); ML form influenced by L *tortus* crooked, twisted; see TORT]

tor′toise shell′, 1. a horny substance of a mottled brown and yellow coloration, composing the plates that form the carapace of a hawksbill turtle, used for making combs and ornamental articles, inlaying, etc. **2.** any of various imitations of this. **3.** any of several nymphalid butterflies of the genus *Nymphalis,* as *N. californica.*

tor·toise-shell (tôr′təs shel′), *adj.* **1.** mottled or variegated like tortoise shell, esp. with yellow and brown and sometimes other colors. **2.** made of tortoise shell.

tor′toise-shell cat′. See **calico cat.**

tor′toise-shell tur′tle. See **hawksbill turtle.**

Tor·to·la (tôr tō′lə), *n.* the principal island of the British Virgin Islands, in the NE West Indies.

tor·to·ni (tôr tō′nē), *n.* **1.** a rich ice cream, often containing chopped cherries or topped with crushed almonds or macaroons. **2.** See **biscuit tortoni.** [? named after an Italian caterer in Paris in the 19th century]

tor·tri·cid (tôr′tri sid), *n.* **1.** any of numerous moths of the family *Tortricidae,* characterized by broad wings and forewings each with a truncated tip, the larvae of which are usually leaf rollers. —*adj.* **2.** belonging or pertaining to the family *Tortricidae.* [back formation from NL *Tortrīcidae* = *tortrīc-* (s. of *tortrix,* fem. of L *tortor* torturer, lit., twister; see TORT, -OR[2]) + *-idae* -ID[2]]

Tor·tu·ga (tôr to͞o′gə), *n.* an island off the N coast of and belonging to Haiti: formerly a pirate stronghold. 23 mi. long; 70 sq. mi. French, **La Tortue.**

tor·tu·os·i·ty (tôr′cho͞o os′i tē), *n., pl.* **-ties. 1.** the state of being tortuous. **2.** a twist, bend, or crook. [< LL *tortuōsitās*]

tor·tu·ous (tôr′cho͞o əs), *adj.* **1.** full of twists, turns, or bends; twisting, winding, or crooked: *a tortuous path through the woods.* **2.** not direct or straightforward. **3.** deceitfully indirect or morally crooked. [late ME < L *tortuōs(us)* = *tortu(s)* a twisting + *-ōsus* -OUS] —**tor′tu·ous·ly,** *adv.* —**tor′tu·ous·ness,** *n.* —**Syn. 1.** bent, sinuous, serpentine.

tor·ture (tôr′chər), *n., v.,* **-tured, -tur·ing.** —*n.* **1.** the act of inflicting excruciating pain, esp. as a means of punishment or coercion. **2.** a method of inflicting such pain. **3.** Often, **tortures.** the pain or suffering caused or undergone. **4.** extreme anguish of body or mind; agony. **5.** a cause of severe pain or anguish. —*v.t.* **6.** to subject to torture. **7.** to afflict with severe pain of body or mind. **8.** to twist, force, or bring into some unnatural shape. [< LL *tortūr(a)* a twisting, torment, torture. See TORT, -URE] —**tor′tured·ly,** *adv.* —**tor′tur·er,** *n.* —**tor′ture·some, tor′tur·ous,** *adj.* —**tor′tur·ing·ly,** *adv.* —**tor′tur·ous·ly,** *adv.*

To·ruń (tô′ʀo͞on′yᵊ), *n.* a city in N Poland, on the Vistula. 110,000 (est. 1963). German, **Thorn.**

to·rus (tōr′əs, tôr′-), *n., pl.* **to·ri** (tōr′ī, tôr′ī). **1.** *Archit.* a large convex molding, more or less semicircular in profile, commonly forming the lowest member of the base of a column. See illus. at **molding. 2.** *Geom.* **a.** Also called **anchor ring.** a doughnut-shaped surface generated by the revolution of a conic, esp. a circle, about an exterior line lying in its plane. **b.** the solid enclosed by such a surface. **3.** *Bot.* **a.** the receptacle of a flower. **b.** a thickening of the wall membrane in the bordered pits occurring in the tracheid cells of the wood of many conifers. **4.** *Anat.* a rounded ridge; a protuberant part. [< L: bulge, rounded molding]

To·ry (tōr′ē, tôr′ē), *n., pl.* **-ries,** for 1–5, *adj.* —*n.* **1.** a member of the Conservative party in Great Britain or Canada. **2.** a member of a political party in Great Britain from the late 17th century to about 1832 that favored the authority of the king over Parliament and the preservation of the existing social and political order: succeeded by the Conservative party. **3.** (*often l.c.*) an advocate of conservative principles. **4.** a person who supported the British cause in the American Revolution; a loyalist. **5.** (in the 17th century) an outlawed Irish royalist. —*adj.* **6.** of, belonging to, or characteristic of the Tories. **7.** being a Tory. [< Ir *tōraidhe, tōiridhe* highwayman, persecuted person = *tōir* chase, pursuit + *-idhe* n. suffix] —**To′ry·ish,** *adj.*

To·ry·ism (tōr′ē iz′əm, tôr′-), *n.* **1.** the act or fact of being a Tory. **2.** the principles and beliefs of Tories.

Tos·ca·na (tôs kä′nä), *n.* Italian name of **Tuscany.**

Tos·ca·ni·ni (tos′kə nē′nē; *It.* tôs′kä nē′nē), *n.* **Ar·tu·ro** (är to͝or′ō; *It.* äʀ to͞o′ʀô), 1867–1957, Italian orchestra conductor, in the U.S. after 1928.

tosh (tosh), *n. Brit. Slang.* nonsense. [? b. TRASH and BOSH]

toss (tôs, tos), *v.,* **tossed** or (*Poetic*) **tost; toss·ing;** *n.* —*v.t.* **1.** to throw, pitch, or fling, esp. to throw lightly or carelessly. **2.** to throw or send from one to another, as in play: *to toss a ball.* **3.** to jerk or move from place to place with rapid, irregular motions. **4.** to throw, raise, or jerk upward suddenly, as the head. **5.** to interject (remarks, suggestions, etc.) in a sudden, offhand manner. **6.** to throw (a coin) into the air, as in order to decide something by the side turned up when it falls. **7.** to stir or mix (a salad) lightly and gently until the ingredients are coated with the dressing. —*v.i.* **8.** to pitch, rock, sway, or move irregularly. **9.** to fling or jerk oneself or move restlessly about, esp. on a bed or couch: *to toss in one's sleep.* **10.** to move with a fling of the body. **11. toss off, a.** to accomplish quickly or easily. **b.** to consume rapidly, esp. to drink something up in one swallow. —*n.* **12.** act of tossing. **13.** a pitching about or up and down. **14.** a throw or pitch. **15.** a tossing of a coin to decide something; toss-up. **16.** a sudden fling or jerk of the body, esp. a quick upward or backward movement of the head. [appar. < Scand; cf. dial. Sw *tossa* to spread, strew] —**toss′er,** *n.* —**Syn. 1.** See **throw.**

tossed′ sal′ad, a salad consisting of one or more greens, tomatoes, onion slices, etc., with a dressing, and mixed with a large fork and spoon.

toss·pot (tôs′pot′, tos′-), *n.* a tippler; drunkard.

toss·up (tôs′up′, tos′-), *n.* **1.** toss (def. 15). **2.** *Informal.* an even choice or chance.

tost (tôst, tost), *v.* a pt. and pp. of **toss.**

tot[1] (tot), *n.* **1.** a small child. **2.** *Chiefly Brit.* a small portion of a beverage, esp. a dram of liquor. **3.** a small quantity of anything. [? short for TOTTERER]

tot[2] (tot), *v.t., v.i.,* **tot·ted, tot·ting.** to add; total (often fol. by *up*). [< L: so much, so many]

to·tal (tōt′əl), *adj., n., v.,* **-taled, -tal·ing** or (*esp. Brit.*) **-talled, -tal·ling.** —*adj.* **1.** constituting or comprising the whole of something; entire: *the total expenditure.* **2.** of or pertaining to the whole of something: *the total effect of a play.* **3.** complete in extent or degree; absolute; utter: *a total failure.* —*n.* **4.** the total amount; sum; aggregate. **5.** the whole or entirety of anything. —*v.t.* **6.** to bring to a total; add up. **7.** to reach a total of; amount to. **8.** *Slang.* to wreck or demolish completely: *He totaled his new car in the accident.* —*v.i.* **9.** to amount (often fol. by *to*). [ME < ML *tōtāl(is)* = L *tōt(us)* entire + *-ālis* -AL[1]] —**Syn. 1.** complete. **4, 5.** entirety, totality. **5.** See **whole.**

to′tal deprav′ity, *Calvinism.* the doctrine that man's entire nature is corrupt as a result of the Fall.

to′tal eclipse′, an eclipse in which the surface of the eclipsed body is completely obscured. Cf. **annular eclipse.**

to·tal·ise (tōt′əlīz′), *v.t.,* **-ised, -is·ing.** *Chiefly Brit.* totalize. —**to′tal·i·sa′tion,** *n.*

to·tal·i·tar·i·an (tō tal′i târ′ē ən), *adj.* **1.** of or pertaining to a centralized government in which those in control grant neither recognition nor tolerance to parties of differing opinion. —*n.* **2.** an adherent of totalitarian principles. —**Syn. 1.** arbitrary, oppressive, tyrannical.

to·tal·i·tar·i·an·ism (tō tal′i târ′ē ə niz′əm), *n.* **1.** the practices and principles of a totalitarian regime: *the totalitarianism of Nazi Germany.* **2.** absolute control by the state or a governing branch of a highly centralized institution: *Totalitarianism aims at suppressing initiative as well as individualism.* **3.** the character or quality of an autocratic or authoritarian individual, group, government, or state: *the totalitarianism of the father in their patriarchal household.*

to·tal·i·ty (tō tal′i tē), *n., pl.* **-ties. 1.** the state of being total; entirety. **2.** something that is total or constitutes a total. **3.** *Astron.* total obscuration in an eclipse.

To·tal·i·za·tor (tōt′əli zā′tər), *n.* *Trademark.* **1.** an apparatus for indicating the total of operations, measurements, etc. **2.** pari-mutuel (def. 2).

to·tal·ize (tōt′əlīz′), *v.t.,* **-ized, -iz·ing.** to make total; combine into a total. Also, *esp. Brit.,* **totalise.** —**to′tal·i·za′tion,** *n.*

to·tal·iz·er (tōt′əlī′zər), *n.* **1.** a person or thing that totals. **2.** a totalizator. **3.** a machine for adding and subtracting.

to·tal·ly (tōt′əlē), *adv.* wholly; entirely; completely.

to′tal recall′, the ability to remember with complete, detailed accuracy.

to·ta·quine (tō′tə kwēn′, -kwin), *n.* *Pharm.* a water-insoluble powder obtained from cinchona bark, used in medicine chiefly as an antimalarial. [var. of *totaquina* < NL = L *tōta* (fem. of *tōtus* all) + Sp *quina* cinchona bark < Kechua *kina* bark]

tote (tōt), *v.,* **tot·ed, tot·ing,** *n.* *Informal.* —*v.t.* **1.** to carry, as on one's back or in one's arms. **2.** to carry on one's person: *to tote a gun.* **3.** to transport or convey, as on a vehicle or boat. —*n.* **4.** something that is toted. [? < Angolese *tota* to pick up, carry] —**tot′a·ble,** *adj.* —**tot′er,** *n.*

tote′ bag′, a capacious handbag, used by women esp. for carrying packages or small items.

tote′ board′, *Informal.* pari-mutuel (def. 2).

to·tem (tō′təm), *n.* **1.** a natural object or an animate being, as an animal or bird, assumed as the emblem of a clan, family, or group. **2.** an object or natural phenomenon with which a primitive family or sib considers itself closely related. [< Ojibwa *ototeman* his brother-sister kin] —**to·tem·ic** (tō tem′ik), *adj.* —**to·tem′i·cal·ly,** *adv.*

to·tem·ism (tō′tə miz′əm), *n.* **1.** the practice of having totems. **2.** the system of tribal division according to totems.

to′tem pole′, a pole or post carved and painted with totemic figures, erected by Indians of the northwest coast of North America.

Totem pole

toth·er (tuth′ər), *adj., pron.* *Dial.* that other; the other. Also, **t'oth′er.** [ME var. of *that other*]

toti-, a learned borrowing from Latin meaning "entire," "entirely," used in the formation of compound words: *totipalmation.* [comb. form repr. L *tōtus*]

to·ti·pal·mate (tō′tə pal′mit, -māt), *adj.* *Ornith.* having all four toes fully webbed.

Totipalmate foot

to·ti·pal·ma·tion (tō′tə pal mā′shən), *n.* totipalmate condition or formation.

Tot·le·ben (tôt′le ben, tot le′-), *n.* **Franz E·du·ard I·va·no·vich** (fränts e′do͞o ärt′ i vä′no vich), **Count,** 1818–84, Russian military engineer and general.

Tot·ten·ham (tot′ənəm), *n.* a city in E Middlesex, in SE England, a part of Greater London. 113,126 (1961).

tot·ter (tot′ər), *v.i.* **1.** to walk or go with faltering steps, as if from extreme weakness. **2.** to show signs of unsteadiness or of imminent collapse. —*n.* **3.** act of tottering; an unsteady movement or gait. [ME *toter(en)* (to) swing, perh. back formation from OE *totrida* a swing, lit., a rider (*rida*) on a projecting part (*tot*); cf. Icel *tota* toe (of a shoe), *toti* snout] —**Syn. 1. stagger. 2.** waver.

tot·ter·ing (tot′ər ing), *adj.* **1.** walking unsteadily or shakily, as a person. **2.** lacking security or stability; threatening to collapse; precarious. —**tot′ter·ing·ly,** *adv.*

tot·ter·y (tot′ə rē), *adj.* tottering; shaky.

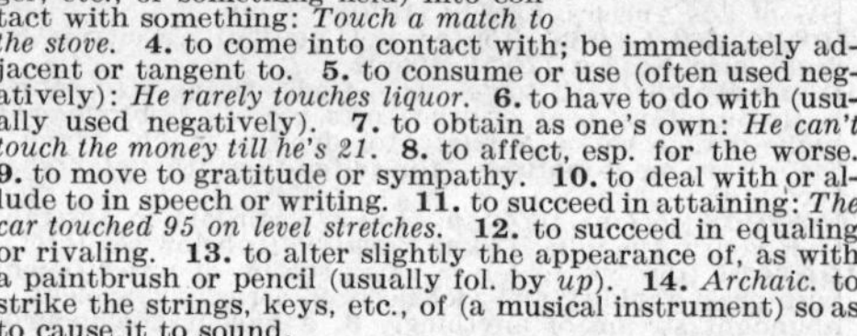

Toucan, *Ramphastos monilis* (Length 22 in.)

tou·can (to͞o′kan, to͞o kän′), *n.* any of several usually brightly colored, fruit-eating birds of the family *Ramphastidae,* of tropical America, having a very large bill. [< F < Pg *tucano* < Tupi *tucana*]

touch (tuch), *v.t.* **1.** to put the hand, finger, etc., on or into contact with (something) so as to feel it. **2.** to feel, pat, or tap, as with the hand or an instrument. **3.** to bring (the hand, finger, etc., or something held) into contact with something: *Touch a match to the stove.* **4.** to come into contact with; be immediately adjacent or tangent to. **5.** to consume or use (often used negatively): *He rarely touches liquor.* **6.** to have to do with (usually used negatively). **7.** to obtain as one's own: *He can't touch the money till he's 21.* **8.** to affect, esp. for the worse. **9.** to move to gratitude or sympathy. **10.** to deal with or allude to in speech or writing. **11.** to succeed in attaining: *The car touched 95 on level stretches.* **12.** to succeed in equaling or rivaling. **13.** to alter slightly the appearance of, as with a paintbrush or pencil (usually fol. by *up*). **14.** *Archaic.* to strike the strings, keys, etc., of (a musical instrument) so as to cause it to sound.
—*v.i.* **15.** to place the hand, finger, etc., on or in contact with something. **16.** to come into or be in contact. **17.** to make a stop or a short call at a place, as a ship or those on board (usually fol. by *at*). **18. touch down,** (of an airplane) to land. **19. touch off, a.** to cause to ignite or explode. **b.** to give rise to. **20. touch on** or **upon,** to mention a subject briefly or casually; treat of in passing. **21. touch up, a.** to make minor improvements in the appearance of. **b.** to modify or improve (a painting, photograph, etc.) by adding small strokes or making slight changes. **c.** to rouse by or as by striking.
—*n.* **22.** the sense by which an object or material is perceived or known by contact with the body, esp. the fingers. **23.** a quality of an object or material, experienced when it is felt; feeling; feel. **24.** the act of touching. **25.** an instance of touching or of being touched. **26.** a relationship of communication: *Let's keep in touch.* **27.** a relationship of objective or sensitive understanding: *out of touch with reality.* **28.** skill based on an acute tactile sense. **29.** skill based on acute sensitivity or perception of any kind. **30.** a minor stroke, as with a paintbrush or pencil. **31.** a detail that enhances the quality of a work of art or the like. **32.** the characteristic manner of a musician in playing an instrument, esp. a keyboard instrument. **33.** the responsiveness of the action of a keyboard instrument. **34.** the characteristic manner of any person practicing an art or skill. **35.** a mild onset of an illness: *a touch of fever.* **36.** a minute amount or trace of something. **37.** *Slang.* **a.** the act of approaching someone for money as a gift or a loan. **b.** the obtaining of money in this manner. **c.** the money obtained. **d.** a person considered from the standpoint of the relative ease with which he will lend money. [ME *to(u)che* < OF *tochie(r)* < VL **toccāre* to knock, strike, touch, based on an imitation of a knocking sound] —**touch′a·ble,** *adj.* —**touch′er,** *n.* —**touch′less,** *adj.*

touch′ and go′, 1. quick action or movement: *the touch and go of city traffic.* **2.** a precarious or delicate state of affairs. —**touch-and-go** (tuch′ən gō′), *adj.*

touch·back (tuch′bak′), *n.* *Football.* a play in which the ball is downed after having been kicked into the end zone by the opposing team or having been recovered or intercepted there, or in which it has been kicked beyond the end zone. Cf. **safety** (def. 4a).

touch·down (tuch′doun′), *n.* **1.** *Football.* the act or an instance of scoring six points by being in possession of the ball on or behind the opponent's goal line. **2.** *Rugby.* the act of a player who touches the ball on or to the ground inside his own in-goal.

tou·ché (to͞o shā′), *interj.* **1.** *Fencing.* (an expression used to indicate a hit or touch.) **2.** (an expression used for acknowledging a telling remark or rejoinder.) [< F: lit., touched]

touched (tucht), *adj.* **1.** moved; stirred. **2.** slightly crazy; unbalanced: *touched in the head.*

touch′ foot′ball, an informal variety of football in which touching, usually with both hands, replaces tackling.

touch·hole (tuch′hōl′), *n.* (formerly) the vent at the breech of a gun through which the charge was ignited.

touch·ing (tuch′ing), *adj.* **1.** affecting; moving: *a touching scene of farewell.* **2.** that touches. —*prep.* **3.** in reference or relation to; concerning; about: *He addressed them touching future plans.* —**touch′ing·ly,** *adv.* —**Syn. 1.** piteous; impressive. **2.** tangent.

touch·line (tuch′līn′), *n.* *Rugby, Soccer.* any of the outer lines bordering the playing field.
touch·stone (tuch′stōn′), *n.* **1.** a black siliceous stone used to test the purity of gold and silver by the color of the streak produced on it by rubbing it with either metal. **2.** a test or criterion for the qualities of a thing.
touch′ sys′tem, a system of typing in which each finger is trained to operate one or more specified keys, thereby enabling a person to type without looking at the keyboard.
touch-tack·le (tuch′tak′əl), *n.* See **touch football.**
Touch-Tone (tuch′tōn′), *n.* *Trademark.* a system of calling a telephone number by push buttons that electronically activate audio frequencies to transmit a digit (instead of the conventional mechanical dial).
touch-up (tuch′up′), *n.* the act or process of making minor improvements in appearance.
touch·wood (tuch′wo͝od′), *n.* **1.** wood converted into an easily ignitible substance by the action of certain fungi, and used as tinder; punk. **2.** amadou.
touch·y (tuch′ē), *adj.*, **touch·i·er, touch·i·est. 1.** apt to take offense on slight provocation; irritable. **2.** requiring caution, tactfulness, or expert handling; precarious; risky. **3.** sensitive to touch. **4.** easily ignited, as tinder. [var. of TECHY, by assoc. with TOUCH] —**touch′i·ly,** *adv.* —**touch′i·ness,** *n.* —**Syn. 1.** testy, irascible, edgy, snappish, cranky.
tough (tuf), *adj.* **1.** strong and durable; not easily broken or cut. **2.** not brittle or tender. **3.** difficult to masticate, as food: *a tough steak.* **4.** capable of great endurance; sturdy; hardy: *tough troops.* **5.** not easily influenced, as a person; unyielding; stubborn. **6.** hardened; incorrigible: *a tough criminal.* **7.** difficult to perform, accomplish, or deal with. **8.** hard to bear or endure: *tough luck.* **9.** vigorous; severe; violent: *a tough struggle.* **10.** *U.S.* vicious; rough; rowdyish. —*n.* **11.** *U.S.* a ruffian; rowdy. —*v.t.* **12. tough it out,** to endure or bear hardship, adversity, or the like. [ME; OE *tōh;* cf. D *taai,* G *zäh(e)*] —**tough′ish,** *adj.* —**tough′ly,** *adv.* —**tough′ness,** *n.* —**Syn. 1.** firm, strong, hard.
tough·en (tuf′ən), *v.t., v.i.* to make or become tough or tougher. —**tough′en·er,** *n.*
tough·ie (tuf′ē), *n.* *Informal.* **1.** a tough person, esp. one who is belligerent. **2.** a difficult problem or situation.
tough-mind·ed (tuf′mīn′did), *adj.* **1.** characterized by a practical, unsentimental attitude or point of view. **2.** strong-willed; vigorous; not easily swayed. —**tough′-mind′ed·ly,** *adv.* —**tough′-mind′ed·ness,** *n.*
tough·y (tuf′ē), *n., pl.* **tough·ies.** toughie.
Toul (to͞ol), *n.* a fortress town in NE France, on the Moselle: siege 1870. 15,031 (1962).
Tou·lon (to͞o lôɴ′), *n.* a seaport in SE France: naval base. 172,586 (1962).
Tou·louse (to͞o lo͞oz′), *n.* a city in S France, on the Garonne River. 330,570 (1962).
Tou·louse-Lau·trec (to͞o lo͞os′lō trek′, -lə-, -lo͞oz′-; *Fr.* to͞o lo͞oz′lō tʀek′), *n.* **Hen·ri Ma·rie Ray·mond de** (äɴ ʀē′ mᴀ ʀē′ ʀā môɴ′ də), 1864–1901, French painter and lithographer.
tou·pee (to͞o pā′), *n.* **1.** a man's wig. **2.** a patch of false hair for covering a bald spot. **3.** (formerly) a curl or an artificial lock of hair on the top of the head, esp. as a crowning feature of a periwig. [var. of *toupet* < F = OF *to(u)p* tuft (< Gmc; see TOP[1]) + *-et* -ET]
tour (to͝or), *v.i.* **1.** to travel from place to place. **2.** to travel from city to city with a theatrical company. —*v.t.* **3.** to travel through (a place). **4.** (of a manager) to send or take (a theatrical company, its production, etc.) from city to city. —*n.* **5.** the act of moving in a predetermined manner from place to place. **6.** a long journey including the visiting of a number of places in sequence. **7.** a journey of a theatrical company from town to town to fulfill engagements: *to go on tour.* **8.** *Chiefly Mil.* a period of duty at one place. [ME < MF < L *tor(nus)* < Gk *tórnos* tool for making a circle. See TURN] —**Syn. 1, 3.** visit. **6.** trip, expedition.
tou·ra·co (to͝or′ə kō′), *n., pl.* **-cos.** any of several large, brightly colored birds of the family *Musophagidae,* of Africa, having a helmetlike crest. Also, **turaco.** [< WAfr]
Tou·raine (to͞o ren′; *Fr.* to͞o ʀen′), *n.* a former province in W France. *Cap.:* Tours.
Tou·rane (to͞o rän′), *n.* former name of **Danang.**
tour·bil·lion (to͝or bil′yən), *n.* **1.** a whirlwind or something resembling a whirlwind. **2.** a firework that rises spirally. [late ME *turbilloun* < MF *to(u)rbillon* < VL **turbiliōnem,* dissimilated var. of **turbiniōnem,* acc. of **turbiniō* whirlwind. See TURBINE]
Tour·coing (to͞oʀ kwaɴ′), *n.* a city in N France, near the Belgian border. 90,105 (1962).
tour de force (to͝or′ də fôrs′, -fôrs′; *Fr.* to͞oʀ də fôʀs′), *pl.* **tours de force** (to͝or′ də fôrs′, -fôrs′; *Fr.* to͞oʀ də fôʀs′). **1.** an exceptional achievement using the full skill, ingenuity, resources, etc., of a person, country, or group. **2.** such an achievement by a performer, writer, artist, etc., that is unlikely to be equaled by him or anyone else; stroke of genius. **3.** a feat requiring unusual strength, skill, or ingenuity. [< F: feat of strength or skill]
Tou·ré (*Fr.* to͞o ʀā′), *n.* **Sé·kou** (sā′ko͞o), 1922–84, Guinean political leader: president 1958–84.
tour′ing car′, an open automobile designed for five or more passengers.
tour·ism (to͝or′iz əm), *n.* **1.** the activity or practice of touring, esp. for pleasure. **2.** the occupation of providing local transportation, lodging, food, etc., for tourists.
tour·ist (to͝or′ist), *n.* **1.** a person who makes a tour, esp. for pleasure. **2.** See **tourist class.** —*adv.* **3.** in tourist-class accommodations, or by tourist-class conveyance.
tour′ist class′, the least costly class of accommodations on regularly scheduled ships and airplanes. Cf. **third class** (def. 2). —**tour′ist-class′,** *adj., adv.*
tour′ist court′, *Obsolesc.* motel.
tour′ist home′, a private home with rooms for rent, usually for one night, to tourists, travelers, etc.
tour·is·tic (to͝o ris′tik), *adj.* of, pertaining to, or typical of tourists or tourism. Also, **tour·is′ti·cal.** —**tour·is′ti·cal·ly,** *adv.*
tour·ist·y (to͝or′i stē), *adj.* *Often Disparaging.* **1.** of or pertaining to tourists: *a touristy attitude.* **2.** popular with or catering to tourists.
tour·ma·line (to͝or′mə lin, -lēn′), *n.* a mineral, essentially a complex silicate containing boron, aluminum, etc., usually black but having various colored, transparent varieties used as gems. Also, **tour·ma·lin** (to͝or′mə lin), **turmaline.** [earlier *tourmalin* < G *Turmalin* < Sinhalese *toramalli* carnelian; see -IN[2]] —**tour·ma·lin·ic** (to͝or′mə lin′ik), *adj.*
Tour·nai (to͝or nā′; *Fr.* to͞oʀ ne′), *n.* a city in W Belgium, on the Scheldt River. 33,197 (est. 1964). Also, **Tour·nay′.**
tour·na·ment (to͝or′nə mənt, tûr′-), *n.* **1.** a trial of skill in some game, in which competitors play a series of contests: *a chess tournament.* **2.** a meeting for contests in a variety of sports, as between teams of different nations. **3.** *Hist.* **a.** a ceremonial contest or martial sport in which mounted and armored combatants fought with blunted weapons. **b.** a series of knightly contests held at one time and place. [ME *tornement* < OF *torneiement* = *tornei(er)* (to) TOURNEY + *-ment* -MENT]
Tour·neur (tûr′nər), *n.* **Cyril,** 1575?–1626, English dramatist.
tour·ney (to͝or′nē, tûr′-), *n., pl.* **-neys,** *v.,* **-neyed, -ney·ing.** —*n.* **1.** a tournament. —*v.i.* **2.** to contend or engage in a tournament. [ME *tourney(en)* < OF *torneie(r)* < VL **tornidiare* to wheel, keep turning. See TURN]
tour·ni·quet (tûr′nə kit, to͝or′-), *n.* *Surg.* any device for arresting bleeding by forcibly compressing a blood vessel, as a pad pressed down by a screw, a bandage tightened by twisting, etc. [< F < *tourn(er)* (to) TURN]
Tours (to͝or; *Fr.* to͞oʀ), *n.* a city in W France, on the Loire River: Charles Martel defeated the Saracens near here A.D. 732. 96,472 (1962).
tou·sle (tou′zəl), *v.,* **-sled, -sling,** *n.* —*v.t.* **1.** to handle roughly. **2.** to disorder or dishevel: *The wind tousled our hair.* —*n.* **3.** a disheveled or rumpled mass, esp. of hair. **4.** a disordered, disheveled, or tangled condition. Also, **touzle.** [late ME *tousel* = *-t(o)use(n)* + -LE; c. LG *tüseln*]
tous-les-mois (to͞o′lə mwä′), *n.* a large-grained farinaceous food resembling arrowroot, obtained from a South American canna, *Canna edulis,* and used in baby food. [< F: all the months, prob. alter. of French Antilles *toloman,* native name]
Tous·saint L'Ou·ver·ture (*Fr.* to͞o saɴ′ lo͞o vᴇʀ tʏʀ′), (*Francis Dominique Toussaint*) 1743–1803, Haitian military and political leader.
tout (tout), *Informal.* —*v.t.* **1.** to solicit support for importunately. **2.** to describe flatteringly or boastfully. **3.** to give a tip on (a race horse, etc.), esp. in order to indicate a probable winner. **4.** *Horse Racing.* **a.** to provide information on (a horse) running in a particular race, esp. for a fee. **b.** to spy on (a horse in training) in order to gain information for the purpose of betting. **5.** to watch; spy on. —*v i.* **6.** to solicit business, employment, votes, or the like, importunately. **7.** *Horse Racing.* to act as a tout. —*n.* **8.** a person who solicits business, employment, support, or the like, importunately. **9.** *Horse Racing.* a person who gives information on a horse, esp. for a fee. [late ME *tute* to look out, peer; akin to OE *tōtian* to peep out, dial *toot* protrude]
tout à fait (to͞o tᴀ fe′), *French.* entirely. [lit., wholly to fact]
tout à l'heure (to͞o tᴀ lœʀ′), *French.* **1.** presently; very soon. **2.** just a moment ago; just now. [lit., wholly to the hour]
tout de suite (to͞ot swēt′), *French.* at once; immediately. [lit., wholly consecutively]
tout en·sem·ble (to͞o täɴ säɴ′blᵊ), *French.* **1.** all together. **2.** the assemblage of parts or details, as in a work of art, considered as forming a whole.
tout le monde (to͞olᵊ môɴd′), *French.* everyone; everybody. [lit., the whole world]
tou·zle (tou′zəl), *v.t.,* **-zled, -zling,** *n.* tousle.
to·va·rich (to vä′ʀishch; *Eng.* tō vär′ish), *n.* *Russian.* comrade. Also, **to·va′rish, to·va′risch.**
tow[1] (tō), *v.t.* **1.** to drag or pull (a car, boat, etc.) by means of a rope, chain, or other device; haul. —*n.* **2.** the act or an instance of towing. **3.** the state of being towed. **4.** something being towed. **5.** a truck, boat, etc., that tows. **6.** a rope, chain, or other device for towing. **7.** See **ski tow. 8. in tow, a.** in the state of being towed. **b.** under one's guidance; in one's charge. **c.** as a follower, admirer, or companion. **9. under tow,** in the condition of being towed; in tow. [ME *towe(n),* OE *togian* to pull by force, drag; c. MHG *zogen* to draw, tug, drag. See TUG] —**Syn. 1.** trail, draw, tug.
tow[2] (tō), *n.* **1.** the fiber of flax, hemp, or jute prepared for spinning by scutching. **2.** the shorter, less desirable flax fibers separated from line fibers in hackling. **3.** man-made filaments prior to spinning. —*adj.* **4.** made of tow: *tow cloth.* [ME; OE *tōw-* (in *tōwlīc* pertaining to thread, *tōwhūs* spinning house); akin to Icel *tō* wool]
tow·age (tō′ij), *n.* **1.** the act of towing. **2.** the state of being towed. **3.** the price or charge for towing.
to·ward (*prep.* tōrd, tôrd, tə wôrd′; *adj.* tōrd, tôrd), *prep.* Also, **to·wards′. 1.** in the direction of. **2.** with a view to obtaining or having; for: *They're saving money toward a new house.* **3.** in the area or vicinity of; near. **4.** turned to; facing. **5.** shortly before; close to: *toward midnight.* **6.** as a help or contribution to: *to give money toward a person's expenses.* **7.** with respect to; as regards. —*adj.* **8.** *Rare.* that is to come soon; imminent. **9.** *Rare.* going on; in progress; afoot: *There is work toward.* **10.** propitious; favorable. **11.** *Obs.* promising or apt, as a student. **12.** *Obs.* compliant; docile. [ME; OE *tōweard.* See TO, -WARD]
to·ward·ly (tōrd′lē, tôrd′-), *adj.* *Archaic.* **1.** apt to learn; promising. **2.** docile; tractable. **3.** propitious; seasonable.
tow·a·way (tō′ə wā), *n.* **1.** an illegally parked automotive vehicle hauled away by the police department, usually subject to both a towing charge and parking fine. —*adj.* **2.** of or designating a towaway: *a towaway zone.*

tow·boat (tō′bōt′), *n.* **1.** a powered boat used esp. on inland waterways to push groups of barges. **2.** tugboat.
tow′ car′, wrecker (def. 3).
tow·el (tou′əl), *n.*, *v.*, **-eled, -el·ing** or (*esp. Brit.*) **-elled, -el·ling.** —*n.* **1.** an absorbent cloth or paper for wiping and drying something wet, esp. one for the hands, face, or body after washing or bathing. **2. throw in the towel,** *Slang.* to concede defeat; give up; yield. —*v.t.* **3.** to wipe or dry with a towel. [ME < OF *toaille* cloth for washing or wiping < WGmc **thwahliō* > OHG *dwahilla*]
tow·el·ette (tou′ə let′), *n.* a small paper towel, usually premoistened, sold in a sealed moisture-retaining wrapper.
tow·el·ing (tou′ə ling), *n.* a narrow fabric of cotton or linen in plain, twill, or huck weave, used for hand or dish towels. Also, *esp. Brit.*, **tow′el·ling.**
tow·er[1] (tou′ər), *n.* **1.** a building or structure high in proportion to its lateral dimensions. **2.** any of various fully enclosed fireproof housings for vertical communications, as staircases, between the stories of a building. **3.** any structure, contrivance, or object that resembles or suggests a tower. **4.** a tall, movable structure used in ancient and medieval siege operations. —*v.i.* **5.** to rise or extend far upward, as a tower does. **6.** to rise above or surpass others. **7.** *Falconry.* (of a hawk) to rise straight into the air; ring up. [ME *tour*, earlier *tur*, *tor* < OF < L *turr(is)* (but note OE *tor(r)*, *tur* < L *turris*) < Gk *týrris*] —**tow′er·less,** *adj.* —**tow′er·like′,** *adj.* —**tow′er·y,** *adj.*
tow·er[2] (tō′ər), *n.* a person or thing that tows.
tow·er·ing (tou′ər ing), *adj.* **1.** very high or tall; lofty: *a towering oak.* **2.** surpassing others; preeminent. **3.** rising to an extreme degree of violence or intensity: *a towering rage.* **4.** beyond the proper or usual limits; inordinate; excessive. —**tow′er·ing·ly,** *adv.* —**Syn. 1.** elevated.
Tow′er of Ba′bel. See under **Babel.** (def. 1).
Tow′er of Lon′don, a fortress in London, England: originally a royal palace, later a prison, now a group of buildings containing an arsenal and museum.
tow·er·y (tou′ə rē), *adj.* **1.** having towers. **2.** very tall; lofty: *towery oaks.*
tow·head (tō′hed′), *n.* **1.** a head of very light blond, almost white, hair. **2.** a person with such hair. [TOW[2] + HEAD] —**tow′head′ed,** *adj.*
tow·hee (tou′hē, tō′hē), *n.* any of several longtailed, North American finches of the genus *Pipilo.* Also called **tow′hee bun′ting.** [imit.]
tow·line (tō′līn′), *n.* a line, hawser, or the like, by which anything is or may be towed. [OE *tohlīne* towline]
tow·mond (tou′mənd), *n.* *Scot.* twelvemonth. Also, **tow·mont** (tou′mənt). [late ME (Scot) *towlmonyth* < Scand; cf. Icel. *tōlfmānathr* twelvemonth]
town (toun), *n.* **1.** a thickly populated area, usually smaller than a city and larger than a village, having fixed boundaries and certain local powers of government. **2.** *U.S.* a township. **3.** any urban area, as contrasted with its surrounding countryside. **4.** the inhabitants of a town; townspeople; citizenry. **5.** the particular town or city in mind or referred to: *out of town.* **6.** the main business or shopping area in a town or city; downtown. **7.** *Brit.* a village or hamlet in which a periodic market or fair is held. **8. go to town,** *Slang.* to do or plan well, efficiently, or speedily. **9. on the town,** *Slang.* in quest of entertainment in a city's night clubs, bars, etc. **10. paint the town.** See **paint** (def. 14). —*adj.* **11.** of, pertaining to, characteristic of, or belonging to a town. [ME *toun*, *tun*, OE *tūn* walled or fenced place (whence courtyard, farm, village); c. Icel *tūn* homefield, G *Zaun* fence] —**town′ish,** *adj.* —**town′less,** *adj.*
town′ clerk′, a town official who keeps the records, issues licenses, calls the town meeting, etc.
town′ cri′er, (formerly) a person employed by a town to make public announcements or proclamations, usually by shouting in the streets.
town′ hall′, a building that houses the offices of a town government, often used for public assemblies.
town′ house′, **1.** a house in the city, esp. as distinguished from a house in the country. **2.** a rather luxurious private house in a large city. **3.** one of a group of houses that are joined by common side walls. Also, **town′house′.**
town′ meet′ing, **1.** a general meeting of the inhabitants of a town. **2.** a meeting of the qualified voters of a town.
town·scape (toun′skāp′), *n.* **1.** a scene, either pictorial or natural, of a town or city. **2.** the planning and building of urban structures with special concern for aesthetically pleasing results. [TOWN + *-scape*, modeled on LANDSCAPE]
Town′send plan′ (toun′zənd), a pension plan, proposed in the U.S. in 1934 but never passed, that would have awarded $200 monthly to persons over 60 who were no longer gainfully employed, provided that such allowance was spent in the U.S. within 30 days. [named after Francis E. *Townsend* (1867–1960), American reformer, its proposer]
towns·folk (tounz′fōk′), *n.pl.* townspeople.
town·ship (toun′ship), *n.* **1.** (in the U.S. and Canada) an administrative division of a county, with varying corporate powers. **2.** (in U.S. surveys of public land) a region or district approximately six miles square, containing 36 sections. **3.** *Eng. Hist.* one of the local divisions or districts of a large parish. **4.** (in Australia) a small town or settlement serving as the business center of a rural area. [late ME *tounship*, OE *tūnscipe*]
towns·man (tounz′mən), *n.*, *pl.* **-men. 1.** a native or inhabitant of a town. **2.** a native or inhabitant of one's own town. [ME, OE *tūnesman*]
towns·peo·ple (tounz′pē′pəl), *n.pl.* **1.** the inhabitants of a town. **2.** people who were raised in a town or city, as contrasted with country-bred people. Also called **townsfolk.**
Towns·ville (tounz′vil), *n.* a seaport on the E coast of Queensland, in E Australia. 82,500.
towns·wom·an (tounz′wo͝om′ən), *n.*, *pl.* **-wom·en.** a woman inhabitant of a town.
tow·path (tō′path′, -päth′), *n.*, *pl.* **-paths** (-pathz′, -päthz′, -paths′, -päths′). a path along the bank of a canal or river, for use in towing boats.
tow·rope (tō′rōp′), *n.* a rope, hawser, or the like, used in towing boats.
Tow·son (tou′sən), *n.* a town in central Maryland, near Baltimore. 77,799 (1970).
tow′ truck′, wrecker (def. 3).
tox-, var. of **toxo-** before a vowel: *toxemia.*
tox·al·bu·min (tok′sal byo͞o′mən), *n.* *Biochem.* any poisonous protein occurring in certain bacterial cultures or plants and in snake venoms.
tox·a·phene (tok′sə fēn′), *n.* *Chem.* a solid whose principal constituent is chlorinated camphene, used as an insecticide and as a rodenticide. [TOX- + (C)A(M)PHENE]
tox·e·mi·a (tok sē′mē ə), *n.* *Pathol.* a condition of illness due to the presence in the bloodstream of toxins, caused by the ingestion of foods contaminated with poisons, by self-produced toxins, as in toxemia of pregnancy, or especially by toxic metabolic by-products from pathogenic microorganisms of a local infection. Also, **tox·ae′mi·a.** —**tox·e·mic** (tok sē′mik, -sem′ik), *adj.*
tox·ic (tok′sik), *adj.* **1.** of, pertaining to, affected with, or caused by a toxin or poison: *a toxic condition.* **2.** acting as or having the effect of a poison; poisonous. [< LL *toxic(us)* poisonous, adj. use of L *toxicum* poison < Gk *toxikón* (orig. short for *toxikôn phármakon*, lit., bow poison, i.e., poison used on arrows)] —**tox′i·cal·ly,** *adv.*
toxic-, var. of **toxico-** before a vowel: *toxicity.*
tox·i·cant (tok′sə kənt), *adj.* **1.** toxic. —*n.* **2.** a poison. [< ML *toxicant-* (s. of *toxicāns*), prp. of *toxicāre* to poison]
tox·i·ca·tion (tok′sə kā′shən), *n.* poisoning. [< ML *toxicātiōn-* (s. of *toxicātiō*) = *toxicāt(us)* poisoned (ptp. of *toxicāre*; see TOXIC, -ATE[1]) + *-iōn-* -ION]
tox·ic·i·ty (tok sis′i tē), *n.* the quality, relative degree, or specific degree of being toxic or poisonous.
toxico-, a combining form of **toxic:** *toxicology.* Also, *esp. before a vowel,* **toxic-.** Cf. **toxo-.**
tox·i·co·gen·ic (tok′sə kō jen′ik), *adj.* *Pathol.* generating or producing toxic products or poisons.
toxicol., toxicology.
tox·i·col·o·gy (tok′sə kol′ə jē), *n.* the science dealing with the effects, antidotes, detection, etc., of poisons. —**tox·i·co·log·i·cal** (tok′sə kə loj′i kəl), **tox′i·co·log′ic,** *adj.* —**tox′i·co·log′i·cal·ly,** *adv.* —**tox′i·col′o·gist,** *n.*
tox·i·co·sis (tok′sə kō′sis), *n.* *Pathol.* an abnormal condition produced by the action of a poison.
tox′ic-shock′ syn′drome (tok′sik shok′), a rare, sometimes fatal, disease contracted by and developing rapidly in women, esp. those under 30, who use tampons during menstruation: characterized by high fever, vomiting, and diarrhea, and thought to be caused by the release and rapid spread of bacterial infection in the vagina. Also called **TSS**
tox·in (tok′sin), *n.* any of a group of poisonous, usually unstable compounds generated by microorganisms, plants, or animals. Certain toxins are produced by specific pathogenic microorganisms and are the causative agents in various diseases, as tetanus, diphtheria, etc.; some are capable of inducing the production of antibodies. [TOX(IC) + -IN[2]] —**Syn.** See **poison.**
tox·in-an·ti·tox·in (tok′sin an′ti tok′sin, -an′tē-; -an′ti-tok′sin, -an′tē-), *n.* *Immunol.* a mixture of toxin and antitoxin, formerly used to induce active immunity against certain diseases, esp. diphtheria.
toxo-, var. of **toxico-:** *toxoplasmosis.* Also, *esp. before a vowel,* **tox-.**
tox·oid (tok′soid), a toxin rendered nontoxic by treatment with chemical agents or by physical means and used for administration into the body in order to produce specific immunity by stimulating the production of antibodies.
tox·o·plas·mo·sis (tok′sō plaz mō′sis), *n.* *Vet. Pathol.* an infection caused by the protozoan parasite *Toxoplasma gondii*, affecting dogs, cats, and other animals, and sometimes man. —**tox′o·plas′mic,** *adj.*
toy (toi), *n.* **1.** an object, often a small representation of something familiar, as an animal, object, person, etc., for children to play with; plaything. **2.** something of little or no value or importance; trifle. **3.** something diminutive, esp. in comparison with like objects. **4.** an animal of a breed or variety noted for smallness of size: *The winning poodle at the dog show was a toy.* **5.** a close-fitting cap of linen or wool, with flaps coming down to the shoulders, formerly worn by women in Scotland. —*adj.* **6.** made or designed for use as a toy: *a toy gun.* **7.** of or resembling a toy, esp. in smallness of size. —*v.i.* **8.** to play; sport. **9.** to act idly or without seriousness; trifle: *Stop toying with your food!* **10.** to dally amorously; flirt without serious intention. [ME *toye* dalliance] —**toy′er,** *n.* —**toy′less,** *adj.* —**toy′like′,** *adj.*
To·ya·ma (tô′yä mä′), *n.* a city on W Honshu, in central Japan. 290,000.
Toyn·bee (toin′bē), *n.* **Arnold J(oseph),** 1889–1975, English historian.
To·yo·ha·shi (tô′yô hä′shē), *n.* a seaport on S Honshu, in central Japan. 285,000.
to·yon (tō′yən), an evergreen, rosaceous shrub or small tree, *Photinia* (*Heteromeles*) *arbutifolia*, of California, having white flowers and bright-red berries. [var. of *tollon* < MexSp]
tp., **1.** township. **2.** troop.
tr, *Music.* trill.
tr., **1.** trace. **2.** train. **3.** transitive. **4.** translated. **5.** translation. **6.** translator. **7.** transpose. **8.** treasurer. **9.** trust. **10.** trustee.
tra·be·at·ed (trā′bē ā′tid), *adj.* *Archit.* **1.** constructed with a beam or on the principle of a beam, as an entablature or flat ceiling. **2.** denoting a form of architecture or system of construction employing beams or lintels exclusively. Also, **tra·be·ate** (trā′bē it, -āt′). [*trabeate* (v.), back formation from TRABEATION (< L *trabē(s)* beam + -ATION) + -ED[3]] —**tra′be·a′tion,** *n.*
tra·bec·u·la (trə bek′yə lə), *n.*, *pl.* **-lae** (-lē′). **1.** *Anat.*, *Bot.* a structural part resembling a small beam or crossbar. **2.** *Bot.* one of the projections from the cell wall that extends across the cell cavity of the ducts of certain plants, or the plate of cells across the cavity of the sporangium of a moss. [< NL; in L: little beam = *trabē(s)* beam + *-cula* -CULE] —**tra·bec′u·lar, tra·bec·u·late** (trə bek′yə lit, -lāt′), *adj.*
Trab·zon (*Turkish.* träb zôn′), *n.* official name of **Trebizond.**

trace[1] (trās), *n.*, *v.*, **traced, trac·ing.** —*n.* **1.** a surviving mark, sign, or evidence of the former existence, influence, or action of some agent or event; vestige. **2.** a barely discernible indication or evidence of some quantity, quality, characteristic, expression, etc.: *the trace of a smile.* **3.** an extremely small amount of some chemical component. **4.** the track left by the passage of a man, animal, or object. **5.** a trail or path, esp. through wild or open territory, made by the passage of people, animals, or vehicles. **6.** Also called **engram.** *Neurol., Psychol.* a structural change in the nervous system effected by an experience, considered to be the physical basis of memory. **7.** a tracing, drawing, or sketch of something. **8.** a lightly drawn line, as the record drawn by a self-registering instrument —*v.t.* **9.** to follow the footprints, track, or traces of. **10.** to follow, make out, or determine the course or line of: *to trace a river to its source.* **11.** to follow (footprints, evidence, the history or course of something, etc.). **12.** to follow the course, development, or history of: *to trace a political movement.* **13.** to ascertain by investigation; find out; discover: *The police were unable to trace the whereabouts of the missing girl.* **14.** to draw (a line, outline, figure, etc.). **15.** to make a plan, diagram, or map of. **16.** to copy (a drawing, plan, etc.) by following the lines of the original on a superimposed transparent sheet. **17.** to make an impression or imprinting of (a design, pattern, etc.). —*v.i.* **18.** to go back in history, ancestry, or origin; date back in time: *Her family traces back to Paul Revere.* **19.** to follow a course, trail, etc.; make one's way. [late ME < MF *trac(i)e(r)* < VL **tractiāre* < L *tractus*, ptp. of *trahere* to draw, drag. See TRACT[1]] —**trace′less,** *adj.* —**trace′less·ly,** *adv* —**Syn. 2.** hint, suggestion. **4.** spoor, trail, record. **9.** trail. —**Ant. 3.** abundance, plethora.

trace[2] (trās), *n.* **1.** either of the two straps, ropes, or chains by which a carriage, wagon, or the like, is drawn by a harnessed horse or other draft animal. **2. kick over the traces,** to throw off restraint; become independent or defiant. [ME *trais* < MF, pl. of *trait* strap for harness, action of drawing < L *tract(us)* a drawing, dragging; see TRACT[1]]

trace·a·ble (trā′sə bəl), *adj.* **1.** capable of being traced. **2.** logically attributable or ascribable (usually fol. by *to*). —**trace′a·bil′i·ty, trace′a·ble·ness,** *n.* —**trace′a·bly,** *n.*

trace′ el′ement, *Biochem.* an element found in plants and animals in minute quantities and believed to be a critical factor in physiological processes. Also called **microelement.**

trac·er (trā′sər), *n.* **1.** a person or thing that traces. **2.** a person whose business or work is the tracing of missing property, parcels, persons, etc. **3.** an inquiry form sent from point to point to trace a missing shipment, parcel, or the like. **4.** Also called **trac′er ammuni′tion.** ammunition containing a chemical substance that causes a projectile to trail smoke or fire so as to make its path visible. **5.** the chemical substance contained in such ammunition. **6.** a substance, usually radioactive, traced through a biological, chemical, or physical system, as the human body, in order to study the system.

Window tracery

trac′er bul′let, a bullet containing a tracer.

trac·er·y (trā′sə rē), *n.*, *pl.* **-er·ies.** **1.** ornamental work consisting of ramified ribs, bars, or the like, as in the upper part of a Gothic window, in panels, screens, etc. **2.** any delicate, interlacing work of lines, threads, etc., as in carving, embroidery, etc.; network.

trache-, var. of **tracheo-** before a vowel: *tracheitis.*

tra·che·a (trā′kē ə *or, esp. Brit.*, trə kē′ə), *n.*, *pl.* **tra·che·ae** (trā′kē ē′ *or, esp. Brit.*, trə kē′ē). **1.** *Anat., Zool.* the tube in man and other air-breathing vertebrates extending from the larynx to the bronchi, serving as the principal passage for conveying air to and from the lungs; the windpipe. **2.** (in insects and other arthropods) one of the air-conveying tubes of the respiratory system. **3.** *Bot.* vessel (def. 4). [< ML < Gk *trācheîa*, short for *artēría trācheîa* rough artery, i.e., windpipe] —**tra′che·al,** *adj.*

tra·che·ate (trā′kē āt′, -it *or, esp. Brit.*, trə kē′it), *adj.* (of an arthropod) having tracheae. [< NL *Tracheāt(a)* name of the class, n. use of neut. pl. of *tracheāt(us).* See TRACHE-, -ATE[1]]

tra·che·id (trā′kē id), *n.* *Bot.* an elongated, tapering xylem cell having lignified, pitted, intact walls, adapted for conduction and support. Cf. **vessel** (def. 4). —**tra·che·i·dal** (trə kē′i dᵊl, trā′kē īd′ᵊl), *adj.*

tra·che·i·tis (trā′kē ī′tis), *n.* *Pathol.* inflammation of the trachea.

tracheo-, a combining form of **trachea:** *tracheotomy.* Also, *esp. before a vowel,* **trache-.**

tra·che·o·phyte (trā′kē ə fīt′), *n.* any plant of the division *Tracheophyta*, characterized by a vascular system and comprising the pteridophytes and spermatophytes. [< NL *Tracheophyta*]

tra·che·ot·o·my (trā′kē ot′ə mē), *n.*, *pl.* **-mies.** *Surg.* the operation of cutting into the trachea. —**tra′che·ot′o·mist,** *n.*

tra·cho·ma (trə kō′mə), *n.* *Ophthalm.* a contagious inflammation of the conjunctiva and cornea, characterized by the formation of granulations and scarring. [< Gk *trāchōma* roughness = *trāch(ýs)* rough + *-ōma* -OMA] —**tra·chom·a·tous** (trə kom′ə təs, -kō′mə-), *adj.*

tra·chyte (trā′kīt, trak′īt), *n.* a fine-grained igneous rock consisting essentially of alkali feldspar and one or more subordinate minerals, as hornblende or mica: the volcanic equivalent of syenite. [< F < Gk *trāchýtē(s)* roughness] —**trach·y·toid** (trak′i toid′, trā′ki-), *adj.*

trac·ing (trā′sing), *n.* **1.** the act of a person or thing that traces. **2.** something that is produced by tracing. **3.** a copy of a drawing, map, plan, etc., made by tracing on a transparent sheet placed over the original.

track (trak), *n.* **1.** a structure consisting of a pair of parallel lines of rails with their crossties that provides a road for railroad trains. **2.** a wheel rut. **3.** evidence, as a mark or a series of marks, that something has passed. **4.** Usually, **tracks.** footprints or other marks left by an animal, person, or vehicle. **5.** a path made or beaten by or as by the feet of men or animals; trail. **6.** a line of travel or motion: *the track of a bird.* **7.** a course or route followed. **8.** a course of action, conduct, or procedure: *He couldn't solve the problem because he started out on the wrong track.* **9.** a path or course made or laid out for some particular purpose. **10.** *Sports.* **a.** a course laid out for running or racing. **b.** the group of sports performed on a track, as running or hurdling, as distinguished from field events. **c.** both track and field events as a whole. **11.** *Auto.* the distance between the centers of the treads of either the front or rear wheels of a vehicle, measured along the ground in inches. **12.** *Computer Technol.* a series of binary cells on the magnetic drum or tape of a computer, so arranged as to allow data to be read from one cell at a time. **13. keep track of,** to follow the course or progress of; keep informed about. **14. lose track of,** to fail to keep informed about; neglect to keep a record of. **15. make tracks,** *Informal.* to go or depart in a hurry: *to make tracks for the store before closing time.* **16. off the track,** departing from the objective or the subject at hand; astray. **17. on the track of,** in search or pursuit of; close upon. **18. on the wrong side of the tracks,** from a lower-class background or from a poor part of a community. —*v.t.* **19.** to follow or pursue the track, traces, or footprints of. **20.** to follow (a track, course, etc.). **21.** to make one's way through; traverse. **22.** *Aerospace.* to follow the flight path of and collect data from (a rocket, satellite, etc.). **23.** *U.S.* **a.** to leave footprints on (often fol. by *up* or *on*): *Don't track up my clean floor with your muddy shoes!* **b.** to make a trail of footprints with (dirt, snow, or the like): *The dog tracked mud all over the living room rug.* **24.** to furnish with a track or tracks, as for railroad trains. —*v.i.* **25.** to follow or pursue a track or trail. **26.** to run in the same track, as the wheels of a vehicle. **27.** to be in alignment, as one gearwheel with another. **28.** to have a specified span between wheels or runners. **29. track down,** to pursue until caught or captured; follow: *tracking down a killer.* [late ME *trak* < MF *trac*, perh. < Scand; cf. Icel *trathk* trodden spot, Norw *trakke* to trample; akin to TREAD] —**track′a·ble,** *adj.* —**track′er,** *n.* —**Syn. 3.** trace, record, spoor. **19.** stalk, hunt.

track·age (trak′ij), *n.* **1.** the whole quantity of track owned by a railroad. **2.** the right of one railroad company to use the tracks of another. **3.** the money paid for this right.

track′ and field′, a group of sports performed indoors or outdoors, including running, pole-vaulting, broad-jumping, etc. —**track′-and-field′,** *adj.*

track′ing sta′tion, *Aerospace.* an outpost, ship, building, or room equipped with the instrumentation necessary for following the flight path of, communicating with, and collecting data from, a rocket, man-made satellite, etc.

track·lay·er (trak′lā′ər), *n.* See **section hand.**

track·less (trak′lis), *adj.* **1.** showing no tracks, as a snow-covered meadow. **2.** not making or leaving a track. **3.** not on tracks: *a trackless streetcar.* —**track′less·ly,** *adv.*

track·man (trak′mən), *n.*, *pl.* **-men.** *U.S.* **1.** a man who assists in inspecting, installing, or maintaining railroad tracks. **2.** trackwalker.

track′ meet′, a series of athletic contests such as running, jumping, etc.

track′ rec′ord, a record of achievements or performance, esp. in competition: *The track record of economists recently has been disappointing.*

track′ shoe′, **1.** the part of a track-brake mechanism that slows or stops a vehicle. **2.** a light, heelless, leather shoe having either steel spikes for use outdoors on a cinder or dirt track, or a rubber sole for use indoors on a board floor.

track·walk·er (trak′wô′kər), *n.* *U.S.* a man employed to walk over and inspect a certain section of railroad track at intervals. Also called **trackman.**

tract[1] (trakt), *n.* **1.** an expanse or area of land, water, etc.; region; stretch. **2.** *Anat.* **a.** a definite region or area of the body, esp. a group, series, or system of related parts or organs: *the digestive tract.* **b.** a bundle of nerve fibers having a common origin and destination. **3.** a stretch or period of time; interval; lapse. [late ME *tracte* < L *tract(us)* stretch (of space or time), a drawing out, n. use of *tractus*, ptp. of *trahere* to draw] —**Syn. 1.** district, territory.

tract[2] (trakt), *n.* a brief treatise, pamphlet, or leaflet for general distribution, usually on a religious or political topic. [late ME *tracte* < L *tract(ātus)* TRACTATE] —**Syn.** essay, homily, disquisition.

trac·ta·ble (trak′tə bəl), *adj.* **1.** easily managed; docile; yielding. **2.** easily worked, shaped, or otherwise handled; malleable. [< L *tractābil(is)* = *tractā(re)* (to) handle, deal with (freq. of *trahere* to draw) + *-bilis* -BLE] —**trac′ta·bil′i·ty, trac′ta·ble·ness,** *n.* —**trac′ta·bly,** *adv.* —**Syn. 1.** manageable, willing, governable. —**Ant. 1.** stubborn.

Trac·tar·i·an·ism (trak târ′ē ə niz′əm), *n.* the religious opinions and principles of the Oxford movement, esp. in its early phase, given in a series of 90 papers called *Tracts for the Times*, published at Oxford, England, 1833–41. —**Trac·tar′i·an,** *n.*, *adj.*

trac·tate (trak′tāt), *n.* a treatise; tract. [late ME < L *tractāt(us)* handling, treatment, treatise, n. use of *tractātus*, ptp. of *tractāre* to handle, treat, freq. of *trahere* to draw]

trac·tile (trak′til), *adj.* **1.** that can be drawn out in length; ductile. **2.** capable of being drawn. [< L *tract(us)* (see TRACT[1]) + -ILE] —**trac·til′i·ty,** *n.*

trac·tion (trak′shən), *n.* **1.** the adhesive friction of a body on some surface, as a wheel on a rail or a tire on a road. **2.** action of drawing a body, vehicle, train, or the like, along a surface, as a road, track, railroad, waterway, etc. **3.** *Med.* the deliberate and prolonged pulling of a muscle, organ, or the like, as by weights, to correct dislocation, relieve pressure, etc. **4.** act of drawing or pulling. **5.** state of being drawn. [< ML *tractiōn-* (s. of *tractiō*) act of drawing] —**trac′tion·al,** *adj.*

trac′tion en′gine, a locomotive operating on surfaces other than tracks and pulling heavy loads, as fallen logs.

trac·tive (trak′tiv), *adj.* having or exerting traction; drawing. [< L *tract(us)* (see TRACT[1]) + -IVE]

trac·tor (trak′tər), *n.* **1.** a powerful motor-driven vehicle with large, heavy treads, used for pulling farm machinery, other vehicles, etc. **2.** a short truck with a body containing only a cab for the driver, used for pulling a trailer or semitrailer to form a tractor-trailer. **3.** a propeller mounted at the front of an airplane, thus exerting a pull. **4.** Also called **trac′tor air′plane.** an airplane with its propeller or propellers so mounted. [< L *tract(us)* (see TRACT[1]) + -OR[2]]

trac·tor-trail·er (trak′tər trā′lər), *n.* a combination trucking unit consisting of a tractor and a trailer or semitrailer.

trade (trād), *n., v.,* **trad·ed, trad·ing,** *adj.* —*n.* **1.** act or process of buying, selling, or exchanging commodities, at either wholesale or retail prices, within a country or between countries: *domestic trade; foreign trade.* **2.** a purchase, sale, or exchange. **3.** any occupation pursued as a business or livelihood. **4.** some line of skilled manual or mechanical work; craft: *the trade of a carpenter; printer's trade.* **5.** people engaged in a particular line of business: *a lecture of interest only to the trade.* **6.** market: *an increase in the tourist trade.* **7.** a field of business activity: *a magazine for the furniture trade.* **8.** the body of customers of a business establishment. **9. trades.** See **trade winds.** —*v.t.* **10.** to buy and sell; barter; traffic in. **11.** to exchange: *to trade seats with a person.* **12.** to buy and sell (securities or commodities) frequently, esp. for short-term profits. —*v.i.* **13.** to carry on trade. **14.** to traffic (usually fol. by *in*): *a tyrant who trades in human lives.* **15.** to make an exchange. **16.** to make one's purchases; shop; buy: *I trade at Mr. Martin's store exclusively.* **17. trade in,** to give (a used article) as payment to be credited toward a purchase: *We trade in our car every three years.* **18. trade off,** to exchange something for or with another. —*adj.* **19.** of or pertaining to trade or commerce. **20.** used by, serving, or intended for a particular trade: *trade journal.* **21.** Also, **trades.** composed of members of a trade: *trade council.* [ME: course, path, track < MLG, MD < OS *trada;* c. OHG *trata;* akin to TREAD] —**trad′a·ble, trade′a·ble,** *adj.* —**trade′less,** *adj.*

—**Syn. 1.** business, barter, dealing. TRADE, COMMERCE, TRAFFIC refer to the exchanging of commodities for other commodities or money. TRADE is the general word: *a brisk trade between the nations.* COMMERCE applies to trade on a large scale and over an extensive area: *international commerce.* TRAFFIC may refer to a particular kind of trade; but it usually suggests the travel, transportation, and activity associated with or incident to trade: *the white-slave traffic; heavy traffic on the railroads.* **3.** vocation, employment. See **occupation. 10.** TRADE, BARGAIN, BARTER, SELL refer to exchange or transfer of ownership for some kind of material consideration. TRADE conveys the general idea, but often means to exchange articles of more or less even value: *to trade with Argentina.* BARGAIN suggests a somewhat extended period of coming to terms: *to bargain about the price of a horse.* BARTER applies esp. to exchanging goods, wares, labor, etc., with no transfer of money for the transaction: *to barter wheat for machinery.* SELL implies transferring ownership, usually for a sum of money: *to sell a car.*

trade-in (trād′in′), *n.* **1.** goods given in whole or, usually, part payment of a purchase: *We used our old car as a trade-in for the new one.* **2.** a business transaction involving a trade-in. —*adj.* **3.** of or pertaining to the valuation of goods used in a trade-in: *trade-in value; trade-in price.* **4.** of or pertaining to such a business transaction: *trade-in terms.*

trade-last (trād′last′, -läst′), *n. Informal.* a flattering remark relayed to the person so complimented by someone who heard it, in exchange for the report of a similar compliment made about himself. *Abbr.:* TL, T.L. [?]

trade·mark (trād′märk′), *n.* **1.** the name, symbol, figure, letter, word, or mark adopted and used by a manufacturer or merchant in order to designate his goods and to distinguish them from any others. A trademark is usually registered with a governmental agency to assure its exclusive use by its owner. —*v.t.* **2.** to stamp or otherwise place a trademark designation upon. **3.** to register the trademark of.

trade′ name′, 1. a word or phrase used in a trade to designate a business, firm, or a particular class of goods. **2.** the name or style under which a firm does business.

trade-off (trād′ôf′), *n.* the exchange of one thing for another, esp. to effect a compromise. Also, **trade′off′.**

trad·er (trā′dər), *n.* **1.** a person who trades; a merchant or businessman. **2.** a ship used in trade, esp. foreign trade. **3.** a member of a stock exchange trading for himself and not for his customers. —**trad′er·ship′,** *n.*

trade′ route′, any route usually taken by merchant ships, caravans, etc.

trad·es·can·ti·a (trad′is kan′shē ə, -shə), *n.* any plant of the genus *Tradescantia,* comprising the spiderworts. [< NL; named after (John) *Tradescant* (1608–62), English gardener to Charles I; see -IA]

trade′ school′, a high school giving instruction chiefly in the skilled trades.

trade′ se′cret, a secret process, technique, method, etc., used to advantage in a trade, business, profession, etc.

trades·man (trādz′mən), *n., pl.* **-men. 1.** a man engaged in trade. **2.** *Chiefly Brit.* a shopkeeper.

trades·peo·ple (trādz′pē′pəl), *n.pl.* **1.** those persons who are engaged in trade; tradesmen. **2.** *Chiefly Brit.* shopkeepers collectively. Also, **trades·folk** (trādz′fōk′).

trades·wom·an (trādz′wo͝om′ən), *n., pl.* **-wom·en.** a woman engaged in trade.

trade′ un′ion, 1. a labor union of craftsmen or workers in related crafts, as distinguished from general workers or a union including all workers in an industry. **2.** See **labor union.** —**trade′-un′ion,** *adj.* —**trade′ un′ionism.** —**trade′ un′ionist.**

trade′ winds′, the nearly constant easterly winds that dominate most of the tropics and subtropics throughout the world, blowing mainly from the northeast in the Northern Hemisphere, and from the southeast in the Southern Hemisphere. Also, **trade′ wind′.** Also called **trades.**

trad′ing post′, 1. a store, established in an unsettled or thinly settled region by a trader or trading company, in which inhabitants of the region may exchange local products for the goods they wish to purchase. **2.** *Stock Exchange.* post[2] (def. 6).

trad′ing stamp′, a stamp given as a premium by a retailer to a customer, specified quantities of these stamps being exchangeable for various articles.

tra·di·tion (trə dish′ən), *n.* **1.** the handing down of statements, beliefs, legends, customs, etc., from generation to generation, esp. by word of mouth or by practice. **2.** that which is so handed down. **3.** *Theol.* **a.** (among Jews) an unwritten body of laws and doctrines, or any one of them, held to have been received from Moses and handed down orally from generation to generation. **b.** (among Christians) a body of teachings, or any one of them, held to have been delivered by Christ and His apostles but not committed to writing. **4.** *Law.* delivery; transfer. [ME *tradicion* < L *trāditiōn-* (s. of *trāditiō*) a handing over or down, transfer, surrender, betrayal = *trādit(us)* given over, ptp. of *trādere* (*trā-,* var. of *trāns-* TRANS- + *-ditus,* var. of *datus* given; see DATE[1]) + *-iōn-* -ION] —**tra·di′tion·less,** *adj.*

tra·di·tion·al (trə dish′ə nəl), *adj.* **1.** of or pertaining to tradition. **2.** handed down by tradition. **3.** in accordance with tradition. Also, **tra·di·tion·ar·y** (trə dish′ə ner′ē). [< ML *trāditiōnāl(is)*] —**tra·di′tion·al′i·ty,** *n.* —**tra·di′tion·al·ly,** *adv.*

tra·di·tion·al·ism (trə dish′ə nəlizm), *n.* **1.** adherence to tradition as authority, esp. in matters of religion. **2.** a system of philosophy according to which all knowledge of religious truth is derived from divine revelation and received by traditional instruction. —**tra·di′tion·al·ist,** *n., adj.* —**tra·di′tion·al·is′tic,** *adj.*

tradi′tional log′ic, formal logic based on syllogistic formulas, esp. as developed by Aristotle.

tra·di·tion·ist (trə dish′ə nist), *n.* **1.** a traditionalist. **2.** a person who records, transmits, or is versed in traditions.

trad·i·tive (trad′i tiv), *adj.* traditional. [TRADIT(ION) + -IVE]

tra·duce (trə do͞os′, -dyo͞os′), *v.t.,* **-duced, -duc·ing.** to speak maliciously and falsely of; slander; defame; malign: *to traduce someone's character.* [< L *trādūc(re),* var. of *trānsdūcere* to transfer, display, expose = *trāns-* TRANS- + *dūcere* to lead] —**tra·duce′ment,** *n.* —**tra·duc′er,** *n.* —**tra·duc′ing·ly,** *adv.* —**Syn.** vilify, asperse, depreciate.

tra·du·cian·ism (trə do͞o′shə niz′əm, -dyo͞o′-), *n. Theol.* the doctrine that the human soul is propagated along with the body. Cf. **creationism.** [< eccl. L *trādūciān(us)* believer in inheritance of original sin or of soul (*trāduci-,* s. of *trādux* lineage (L: vine led across for propagation; see TRADUCE) + *-ānus* -AN) + -ISM] —**tra·du′cian·ist, tra·du′cian** *n., adj.* —**tra·du′cian·is′tic,** *adj.*

Tra·fal·gar (trə fal′gər; *Sp.* trä′fäl gär′), *n.* **Cape,** a cape on the SW coast of Spain, W of Gibraltar: British naval victory over the French and Spanish fleets 1805.

traf·fic (traf′ik), *n., v.,* **-ficked, -fick·ing.** —*n.* **1.** the movement of vehicles, ships, persons, etc., in an area, along a street, through an air lane, over a water route, etc. **2.** the vehicles, persons, etc., moving in an area, along a street, etc. **3.** the transportation of goods for the purpose of trade, by sea, land, or air: *ships of traffic.* **4.** trade; buying and selling; commercial dealings. **5.** trade between different countries or places; commerce. **6.** the business done by a railroad or other carrier in the transportation of freight or passengers. **7.** the aggregate of freight, passengers, telephone or telegraph messages, etc., handled, esp. in a given period. **8.** trade or dealing in some specific commodity or service, often of an illegal nature: *the vast traffic in narcotics.* —*v.i.* **9.** to carry on traffic, trade, or commercial dealings. **10.** to trade or deal in a specific commodity or service, often of an illegal nature (usually fol. by *in*): *to traffic in guns for revolutionary forces.* [earlier *traffyk* < MF *trafique* (n.), *trafique(r)* (v.) < It *traffic(o)* (n.), *trafficare* (v.)] —**traf′fick·er,** *n.* —**traf′fic·less,** *adj.* —**Syn. 4.** See **trade.**

traf′fic cir′cle, a circular arrangement placed at the intersection of two or more roads in order to facilitate the passage of vehicles from one road to another. Also called **rotary;** *Brit.,* **roundabout.**

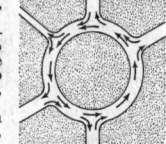

Traffic circle

traf′fic cop′, *Informal.* a policeman who directs the flow of motor vehicles, usually at an intersection.

traf′fic court′, a court that passes on alleged violations of traffic laws.

traf′fic is′land, a raised or marked-off area between lanes of a roadway, used by pedestrians to get out of the flow of traffic, as a place for traffic signals, for separating lanes, etc.

traf′fic jam′, a slowing down or stopping of vehicles on a highway or road, caused by overcrowding, an accident, etc. —**traf′fic-jammed′,** *adj.*

traf′fic light′, a set of electrically operated signal lights used to direct or control traffic at intersections. Also called **traf′fic sig′nal, traf′fic control′ sig′nal.**

traf′fic man′ager, 1. a person who supervises the transportation of goods for his employer. **2.** a person in a transportation company who sets rates or fares, schedules space, etc., for freight or passengers. **3.** an office employee, responsible for routing items of business within a company for appropriate action by various departments.

traf′fic pat′tern, *Aeron.* a system of courses about an airfield that aircraft are assigned to fly when taking off, landing, or preparing to land.

trag·a·canth (trag′ə kanth′), *n.* **1.** a mucilaginous substance derived from various low, spiny, Asian shrubs of the genus *Astragalus,* esp. *A. gummifer:* used to impart firmness to pills and lozenges, stiffen calicoes, etc. **2.** the plants themselves. [< L *tragacantha* goat's thorn < Gk *tragákantha* = *trág(os)* goat + *ákantha* thorn. See TRAGEDY, ACANTHO-]

tra·ge·di·an (trə jē′dē ən), *n.* **1.** an actor noted for his performances in tragedy. **2.** a writer of tragedy. [TRAGEDY + -AN: r. ME *tragedien* < MF]

tra·ge·di·enne (trə jē′dē en′), *n.* an actress noted for her performances in tragedy. [< F, fem. of *tragédien* TRAGEDIAN]

trag·e·dy (traj′i dē), *n., pl.* **-dies. 1.** a dramatic composition, often in verse, dealing with a serious or somber theme, typically that of a noble person whose character is flawed by a single weakness, as pride, envy, etc., which causes him to break a divine law or moral precept and which leads inevitably to his downfall or destruction. **2.** the branch of drama that is concerned with this form of composition. **3.** the art and theory of writing and producing tragedies. **4.** any literary composition, as a novel, dealing with a somber theme carried to a tragic conclusion. **5.** the tragic element of drama, of literature generally, or of life. **6.** a lamentable, dreadful, or fatal event or affair; calamity; disaster. [ME *tragedie* < ML *tragēdia*, var. of L *tragoedia* < Gk *tragōidía* = *trág(os)* goat + *ōidē* song (see ODE) + *-ia* -Y[3]; reason for name variously explained]

trag·ic (traj′ik), *adj.* **1.** of, pertaining to, or characteristic of tragedy: *the tragic drama.* **2.** extremely mournful, melancholy, or pathetic: *a tragic plight.* **3.** dreadful, calamitous, disastrous, or fatal: *a tragic event.* Also, **trag′i·cal.** [< L *tragic(us)* < Gk *tragikós* of tragedy = *trág(os)* goat + *-ikos* -IC] —**trag′i·cal·ly,** *adv.* —**trag′i·cal·ness,** *n.*

trag′ic flaw′, *Literature.* the defect in the character of a tragic hero causing his downfall.

trag·i·com·e·dy (traj′i kom′i dē), *n., pl.* **-dies. 1.** a dramatic or other literary composition combining elements of both tragedy and comedy. **2.** an incident, or series of incidents, of mixed tragic and comic character. [< LL *tragicōmoedia*, syncopated var. of L *tragico-cōmoedia*. See TRAGIC, -O-, COMEDY] —**trag·i·com·ic** (traj′i kom′ik), **trag′i·com′i·cal,** *adj.* —**trag′i·com′i·cal·ly,** *adv.*

trag·o·pan (trag′ə pan′), *n.* any of several Asian pheasants of the genus *Tragopan*, having two fleshy, erectile horns on the head and wattles on the throat. [< NL, special use of L *tragopān* fabulous Ethiopian bird < Gk = *trágo(s)* goat + *Pān* PAN]

tra·gus (trā′gəs), *n., pl.* **-gi** (-jī). *Anat.* a fleshy prominence at the front of the external opening of the ear. [< LL < Gk *trágos* hairy part of ear, lit., he-goat]

trail (trāl), *v.t.* **1.** to drag or let drag along the ground or other surface; draw or drag along behind. **2.** to bring or have floating after itself or oneself: *a racing car trailing clouds of dust.* **3.** to follow the track, trail, or scent of; track. **4.** *U.S. Informal.* to follow along behind (another or others), as in a race. **5.** *Mil.* to carry (a firearm, etc.) in the right hand in an oblique position, with the muzzle forward and the butt near the ground. —*v.i.* **6.** to be drawn or dragged along the ground or some other surface. **7.** to stream from or float after something moving. **8.** to follow as if drawn along. **9.** to go slowly, lazily, or wearily along. **10.** to change gradually or wander from a course, so as to become weak, ineffectual, etc. (usually fol. by *off* or *away*): *Her voice trailed off into silence. The conversation trailed off into absurdities.* **11.** to be losing in a contest: *The home team was trailing 20 to 15.* **12.** to follow a track or scent, as of game. **13.** (of a plant) to extend itself in growth along the ground rather than taking root or clinging by tendrils, etc. —*n.* **14.** a path or track made across a wild region, over rough country, or the like, by the passage of men or animals: *to follow the trail.* **15.** the track, scent, or the like, left by an animal, person, or thing. **16.** something that is trailed or that trails behind, as the train of a skirt or robe. **17.** a stream of dust, smoke, light, people, vehicles, etc., behind something moving. **18.** *Artillery.* the part of a gun carriage that rests on the ground when the piece is unlimbered. [ME *trail(en)*, OE *træglian* to tear off, drag; c. MD *traghelen* to drag; akin to Latvian *dragât* to tear off, drag] —**trail′less,** *adj.* —**Syn. 14.** See **path.**

trail′ bike′, a motorcycle adapted for traveling on rough terrain, trails, etc.

trail·blaz·er (trāl′blā′zər), *n.* **1.** a person who blazes a trail for others to follow through unsettled country or wilderness; pathfinder. **2.** a pioneer in any field of endeavor. —**trail′blaz′ing,** *adj.*

trail′ boss′, (in Western U.S.) a person responsible for driving a herd of cattle.

trail·er (trā′lər), *n.* **1.** a person or thing that trails. **2.** a large van or wagon drawn by an automobile, truck, or tractor, used esp. in hauling freight by road. **3.** a vehicle attached to an automobile and used as a mobile home or place of business, usually equipped with furniture, kitchen facilities, etc. **4.** a trailing plant. **5.** an advertisement for a forthcoming motion picture, shown as part of the program of a motion-picture theater.

trail′er camp′, an area where house trailers may be parked, usually having running water, electrical outlets, etc. Also called **trail′er court′, trail′er park′.**

trail′ing arbu′tus, arbutus (def. 2).

trail′ing edge′, *Aeron.* the rear edge of a propeller blade or airfoil.

trail′ rope′, a guide rope on an aerostat.

train (trān), *n.* **1.** *Railroads.* a self-propelled, connected group of rolling stock. **2.** a line or procession of persons, vehicles, animals, etc., traveling together. **3.** *Mil.* an aggregation of vehicles, animals, and men accompanying an army to carry supplies, baggage, ammunition, etc. **4.** a series or row of objects or parts. **5.** *Mach.* a connected set of three or more rotating elements, usually gears, through which force is transmitted, or motion or torque changed. **6.** order, esp. proper order: *Matters were in good train.* **7.** something that is drawn along; a trailing part. **8.** an elongated part of a skirt or robe trailing behind on the ground. **9.** a line or succession of persons or things following after. **10.** a body of followers or attendants; retinue. **11.** a succession or series of proceedings, events, ideas, etc. **12.** the series of results or circumstances following or proceeding from an event, action, etc.; aftermath: *Disease came in the train of war.* **13.** a succession of connected ideas; course of reasoning: *to lose one's train of thought.* **14.** a line of combustible material, as gunpowder, for leading fire to an explosive charge. —*v.t.* **15.** to develop or form the habits, thoughts, or behavior of (a child or other person) by discipline and instruction: *to train an unruly boy.* **16.** to make proficient by instruction and practice, as in some art, profession, or work: *to train soldiers.* **17.** to make (a person) fit by proper exercise, diet, practice, etc., as for some athletic feat or contest. **18.** to discipline and instruct (an animal), as in the performance of tasks or tricks. **19.** to treat or manipulate so as to bring into some desired form, position, direction, etc.: *You can train your hair to lie down by combing it daily.* **20.** to bring to bear on some object; point, aim, or direct, as a firearm, telescope, eye, etc. —*v.i.* **21.** to give the discipline and instruction, drill, practice, etc., designed to impart proficiency or efficiency. **22.** to undergo discipline and instruction, drill, etc. **23.** to get oneself into condition for an athletic feat or contest through exercise, diet, practice, etc. **24.** to travel or go by train. [late ME *traine* < MF *train(er)*, OF *trahiner* < VL **tragīnāre* < **tragīna* something dragged or drawn (cf. ML *tragīna* carriage), akin to L *trahere* to draw] —**train′a·ble,** *adj.* —**Syn. 3.** convoy. **9.** file, column.

train·band (trān′band′), *n.* *Eng. Hist.* a company of trained militia organized in London and elsewhere in the 16th, 17th, and 18th centuries. [TRAIN(ED) + BAND[1]]

trained′ nurse′. See **graduate nurse.**

train·ee (trā nē′), *n.* **1.** a person receiving training, esp. vocational training; apprentice. **2.** an enlisted person undergoing military training.

train·er (trā′nər), *n.* **1.** a person who trains athletes for contests or feats. **2.** a person who trains race horses or other animals for contests, feats, or show. **3.** *U.S. Mil.* an aircraft used in training aircrew members, esp. pilots.

train·ing (trā′ning), *n.* **1.** the education, instruction, or discipline of a person or thing that is being trained. **2.** the status or condition of a person who has been trained. [late ME] —**Syn. 1.** See **education.**

train′ing school′, **1.** a school that provides training in some art, profession, or vocation. **2.** an institution for the detention and education of juvenile delinquents.

train′ing ship′, a ship equipped for training men in seamanship, as for naval service.

train·man (trān′mən), *n., pl.* **-men.** a member of the crew that operates a railroad train, usually an assistant to the conductor, such as a brakeman or flagman.

train·mas·ter (trān′mas′tər, -mä′stər), *n.* a person who has charge of operations over one portion of a railroad.

train′ oil′, oil obtained from the blubber of whales or from seals, walruses, or other marine animals. [earlier *trane* train oil (< MD: whale oil, drop, tear; c. G *Träne* tear)]

traipse (trāps), *v.,* **traipsed, traips·ing,** *n. Informal.* —*v.i.* **1.** to walk or go aimlessly or idly or without finding or reaching one's goal: *We traipsed all over town looking for a copy of the book.* —*v.t.* **2.** *Dial.* to walk over; tramp: *to traipse the fields.* —*n.* **3.** *Dial.* a tiring walk. [earlier *trapse*, unexplained var. of *trape*, non-nasalized var. of TRAMP]

trait (trāt), *n.* **1.** a distinguishing characteristic or quality, esp. of one's personal nature: *several bad traits of character.* **2.** a pen or pencil stroke. **3.** a stroke, touch, or strain, as of some quality. [< MF: lit., something drawn < L *tract(us)*. See TRACT[1]] —**Syn. 1.** peculiarity, attribute, property.

trai·tor (trā′tər), *n.* **1.** a person who betrays another, a cause, or any trust. **2.** a person who betrays his country by violating his allegiance; one guilty of treason. Also, *referring to a woman,* **trai·tress** (trā′tris). [ME *traitur* < OF < L *trāditōr-*, obl. s. of *trāditor* betrayer. See TRADITOR] —**trai′tor·ship′,** *n.*

trai·tor·ous (trā′tər əs), *adj.* **1.** having the character of a traitor; treacherous; perfidious. **2.** characteristic of a traitor. **3.** of the nature of treason; treasonable. —**trai′tor·ous·ly,** *adv.* —**trai′tor·ous·ness,** *n.* —**Syn.** disloyal, treasonous.

Tra·jan (trā′jən), *n.* (*Marcus Ulpius Nerva Trajanus*) A.D. 53?–117, Roman emperor 98–117.

tra·ject (trə jekt′), *v.t.* *Archaic.* to transport, transmit, or transpose. [< L *trāject(us)* (ptp. of *trāicere* to cast, throw over or across) = *trā-* (var. of *trāns-* TRANS-) + *-jec-* (var. of *jac-*, s. of *iacere* to throw) + *-tus* ptp. suffix] —**tra·jec′tion,** *n.*

tra·jec·to·ry (trə jek′tə rē), *n., pl.* **-ries. 1.** the curve described by a projectile, rocket, or the like, in its flight. **2.** the path described by a body moving under the action of given forces. **3.** *Geom.* a curve or surface that cuts all the curves or surfaces of a given system at a constant angle. [< NL *trājectōria*, n. use of fem. of ML *trājectōrius* casting over] —**tra·jec·tile** (trə jek′tᵊl, -tīl), *adj.* —**tra·jec·tion** (trə jek′shən), *n.*

Tra·lee (trə lē′), *n.* a city in and the county seat of Kerry, in the SW Republic of Ireland. 10,723 (1961).

tram[1] (tram), *n., v.,* **trammed, tram·ming.** —*n.* **1.** *Brit.* a streetcar. **2.** a tramway; tramroad. **3.** a truck or car on rails for carrying loads in a mine. **4.** the vehicle or cage of an overhead carrier. —*v.t., v.i.* **5.** to convey or travel by tram. [< MFlem: shaft of a cart or wheelbarrow; akin to L *trabs* beam, tree] —**tram′less,** *adj.*

tram[2] (tram), *n., v.,* **trammed, tram·ming.** —*n.* **1.** trammel (def. 3). —*v.t.* **2.** *Mach.* to adjust (something) correctly. [short for TRAMMEL]

tram[3] (tram), *n.* silk that has been slightly or loosely twisted, used weftwise in weaving silk fabrics. Cf. **organzine.** [var. of *trame* < F < L *trāma* weft, See TRANS-]

tram·mel (tram′əl), *n., v.,* **-meled, -mel·ing** or (*esp. Brit.*) **-melled, -mel·ling.** —*n.* **1.** Usually, **trammels.** hindrances or impediments to free action; restraints. **2.** an instrument for drawing ellipses. **3.** Also called **tram.** a device used to align or adjust parts of a machine. **4.** a fowling net. **5.** a contrivance hung in a fireplace to support pots, kettles, etc., over the fire. **6.** a fetter or shackle, esp. one used in training a horse to amble. —*v.t.* **7.** to involve or hold in trammels; hamper; restrain. **8.** to catch or entangle in or as in a net. [late ME *tramayle* < MF *tramail*, var. of *tremail* three-mesh net < LL *trēmacul(um)* = L *trē(s)* three + *macula* mesh] —**tram′mel·er;** *esp. Brit.,* **tram′mel·ler,** *n.* —**Syn. 1.** hobble, curb, inhibition. **8.** hinder, impede, obstruct, encumber.

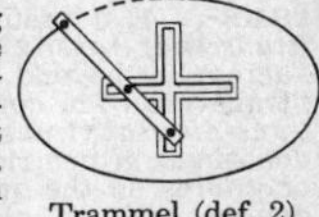

Trammel (def. 2)

tra·mon·tane (trə mon′tān, tram′ən tān′), *adj.* Also, **transmontane. 1.** being or situated beyond the mountains, esp. the Alps as viewed from Italy. **2.** of, pertaining to, or coming from the other side of the mountains. **3.** foreign;

barbarous. —*n.* **4.** a person who lives beyond the mountains: formerly applied by the Italians to the peoples beyond the Alps, and by the latter to the Italians. **5.** a foreigner; outlander; barbarian. [< It *tramontano* < L *trānsmontān(us)* beyond the mountains. See TRANS-, MOUNT², -AN]

tramp (tramp), *v.i.* **1.** to tread or walk with a firm, heavy, resounding step. **2.** to tread heavily or trample (usually fol. by *on* or *upon*): *to tramp on a person's toes.* **3.** to walk steadily; march; trudge. **4.** to go on a walking excursion or expedition; hike. **5.** to go about as a vagabond or tramp. **6.** to make a voyage on a tramp steamer. —*v.t.* **7.** to tramp or walk heavily or steadily through or over. **8.** to traverse on foot: *to tramp the streets.* **9.** to tread or trample underfoot: *to tramp grapes in order to make wine.* **10.** to travel over as a tramp. —*n.* **11.** act of tramping. **12.** a firm, heavy, resounding tread. **13.** the sound made by such a tread. **14.** a long, steady walk; trudge. **15.** a person who travels about on foot from place to place, esp. a vagabond living on occasional jobs or gifts of money or food. **16.** a sexually promiscuous girl or woman. **17.** a freight vessel that does not run regularly between fixed ports, but takes a cargo wherever shippers desire. **18.** a piece of iron affixed to the sole of a shoe. [ME *tramp(en)* (to) stamp; c. LG *trampen;* akin to Goth *ana-trimpan* to press hard upon. See TRAIPSE, TRAMPLE] —**tramp′er,** *n.* —**tramp′ish,** *adj.* —**tramp′ish·ly,** *adv.* —**tramp′ish·ness,** *n.* —**Syn. 15.** vagrant, bum, hobo.

tram·ple (tram′pəl), *v.,* **-pled, -pling,** *n.* —*v.i.* **1.** to tread or step heavily and noisily; stamp. **2.** to tread heavily, roughly, or crushingly (usually fol. by *on, upon,* or *over*): *to trample on a flower bed.* —*v.t.* **3.** to tread heavily, roughly, or carelessly on or over; tread underfoot. **4.** to put out or extinguish by trampling (usually fol. by *out*): *to trample out a fire.* —*n.* **5.** act of trampling. **6.** sound of trampling. [ME *trample(n)* (to) stamp (c. G *trampeln*), freq. of TRAMP] —**tram′pler,** *n.*

tram·po·line (tram′pə lēn′, tram′-pə lēn′, tram′pə lin), *n.* a sheet, usually of canvas, attached by resilient cords or springs to a horizontal frame, used as a springboard in tumbling. [var. of *trampolin* < Sp < It *trampolino* springboard = *trampol(i)* stilts (< Gmc; see TRAMPLE) + *-ino* -INE¹] —**tram′po·lin′er, tram′po·lin′ist,** *n.*

Trampoline

tramp′ steam′er, tramp (def. 17).

tram·road (tram′rōd′), *n.* (in a mine) a small railroad for trams.

tram·way (tram′wā′), *n.* **1.** a crude railroad of wooden rails, or wooden rails capped with metal treads. **2.** Also called **ropeway.** a system for hauling passengers and freight in vehicles suspended from a cable or cables supported by a series of towers, hangers, etc.

trance (trans, träns), *n., v.,* **tranced, tranc·ing.** —*n.* **1.** a half-conscious state, seemingly between sleeping and waking, in which ability to function voluntarily may be suspended. **2.** a dazed or bewildered condition. **3.** a state of complete mental absorption or deep musing. **4.** an unconscious, cataleptic, or hypnotic condition. **5.** *Spiritualism.* a temporary state in which a medium, with suspension of personal consciousness, is controlled by an intelligence from without and used as a means of communication, as from the dead. —*v.t.* *Archaic.* **6.** to put in a trance; stupefy. **7.** to entrance; enrapture. [ME *traunce* state of extreme dread, swoon, dazed state < MF *transe,* lit., passage (from life to death) < *transir* to go across, pass over < L *trānsīre* = *trāns-* TRANS- + *-īre* to go] —**tranced·ly** (transt′lē, tran′sid lē), *adv.* —**trance′like′,** *adj.*

tranfd., transferred.

tran·quil (trang′kwil), *adj.* **1.** free from commotion or tumult; peaceful; quiet; calm: *a tranquil country place.* **2.** free from or unaffected by disturbing emotions; unagitated; serene; placid: *a tranquil life.* [earlier *tranquill* < L *tranquill(us)* quiet, calm, still] —**tran′quil·ly,** *adv.* —**tran′quil·ness,** *n.* —**Syn. 1.** See **peaceful.** —**Ant. 2.** agitated.

tran·quil·ize (trang′kwə līz′), *v.t., v.i.,* **-ized, -iz·ing.** to make or become tranquil. Also, **tranquillize;** *esp. Brit.,* **tranquillise.** —**tran′quil·i·za′tion,** *n.*

tran·quil·iz·er (trang′kwə lī′zər), *n.* **1.** a person or thing that tranquilizes. **2.** a drug that has a sedative or calming effect without inducing sleep. Also, **tran′quil·liz′er;** *esp. Brit.,* **tran′quil·lis′er.**

tran·quil·lise (trang′kwə līz′), *v.t., v.i.,* **-lised, -lis·ing.** *Chiefly Brit.* tranquilize. —**tran′quil·li·sa′tion,** *n.*

Tran·quil·li·ta·tis (trang kwil′ē tä′tis), *n.* **Mare.** See **Mare Tranquillitatis.**

tran·quil·li·ty (trang kwil′i tē), *n.* quality or state of being tranquil; calmness; peacefulness; quiet; serenity. Also, **tran·quil′i·ty.** [ME *tranquillite* < L *tranquillitās*]

Tran·quil·li·ty (trang kwil′i tē), *n.* **Sea of.** See **Mare Tranquillitatis.**

tran·quil·lize (trang′kwə līz′), *v.t., v.i.,* **-lized, -liz·ing.** tranquilize.

trans-, **1.** a prefix occurring in loan words from Latin (*transcend; transfix*); on this model, used with the meaning "across," "beyond," "through," "changing thoroughly," "transverse," in combination with elements of any origin: *trans-Siberian; transempirical; transvalue.* **2.** *Chem.* a prefix denoting a geometric isomer having a pair of identical atoms or groups on the opposite sides of two atoms linked by a double bond. Cf. **cis-** (def. 2). **3.** *Astron.* a prefix denoting something farther from the sun (than a given planet): *trans-Martian; trans-Neptunian.* [< L, comb. form of *trāns* (adv. and prep.)]

trans., **1.** transaction; transactions. **2.** transfer. **3.** transferred. **4.** transitive. **5.** translated. **6.** translation. **7.** translator. **8.** transportation. **9.** transpose. **10.** transverse.

trans·act (tran sakt′, -zakt′), *v.t.* **1.** to carry on or conduct (business, negotiations, activities, etc.) to a conclusion or settlement. —*v.i.* **2.** to carry on or conduct business, negotiations, etc. [< L *trānsact(us)* carried out, accomplished (ptp. of *trānsigere*) = *trāns-* TRANS- + *ag(ere)* (to) drive, lead + *-tus* ptp. suffix] —**trans·ac′tor,** *n.* —**Syn. 1.** enact, settle, manage, negotiate, conduct. See **perform.**

trans·ac·tion (tran sak′shən, -zak′-), *n.* **1.** act of transacting; fact of being transacted. **2.** an instance or process of transacting something. **3.** something that is transacted, esp. a business agreement. **4. transactions,** the published reports of the proceedings, as papers read, addresses delivered, discussions, etc., at the meetings of a learned society or the like. [late ME < L *trānsactiōn-* (s. of *trānsactiō*) completion, transaction] —**trans·ac′tion·al,** *adj.* —**trans·ac′tion·al·ly,** *adv.*

trans·al·pine (trans al′pin, -pīn, tranz-), *adj.* **1.** situated beyond the Alps, esp. toward the north as viewed from Italy. **2.** passing or extending across or through the Alps. **3.** of, pertaining to, or characteristic of peoples or lands beyond the Alps. —*n.* **4.** a native or inhabitant of a country beyond the Alps. [< L *trānsalpīn(us)*]

Transal′pine Gaul′. See under **Gaul** (def. 1).

trans·at·lan·tic (trans′ət lan′tik, tranz′-), *adj.* **1.** crossing or reaching across the Atlantic. **2.** situated beyond the Atlantic.

trans·ca·lent (trans kā′lənt), *adj.* permitting the passage of heat. [TRANS- + L *calent-* (s. of *calēns*), prp. of *calēre* to be hot; see -ENT] —**trans·ca·len·cy** (trans kā′lən sē), *n.*

Trans·cau·ca·sia (trans′kô kā′zhə, -shə), *n.* a region in the S Soviet Union in Europe, S of the Caucasus Mountains, between the Black and Caspian seas: constituted a republic 1922–36 (**Transcauca′sian So′cialist Fed′erated So′viet Repub′lic**); area now includes the Soviet republics of Armenia, Azerbaijan, and Georgia. —**Trans·cau·ca·sian** (trans′kô kā′zhən, -shən, -kazh′ən, -kash′-), *adj., n.*

trans·ceiv·er (tran sē′vər), *n.* *Radio.* a transmitter and receiver combined in one unit. [TRANS(MITTER) + (RE)CEIVER]

tran·scend (tran send′), *v.t.* **1.** to rise above or go beyond the limits of; overpass; exceed: *kindness that transcends mere courtesy.* **2.** to outdo or exceed in excellence, degree, etc.; surpass; excel. **3.** *Theol.* (of the Deity) to be above and independent of (the universe, time, etc.). —*v.i.* **4.** to be transcendent or superior; excel. [ME < L *trānscend(ere)* (to) surmount = *trāns-* TRANS- + *scandere* to climb] —**tran·scend′ing·ly,** *adv.*

tran·scend·ence (tran sen′dəns), *n.* quality or state of being transcendent. Also, **tran·scend′en·cy.** [< ML *trānscendentia.* See TRANSCENDENT, -ENCE]

tran·scend·ent (tran sen′dənt), *adj.* **1.** going beyond ordinary limits; surpassing; exceeding. **2.** superior or supreme. **3.** *Theol.* (of the Deity) transcending the universe, time, etc. Cf. **immanent** (def. 3). **4.** *Kantianism.* transcending experience; not realizable in human experience. Cf. **transcendental** (def. 4). [< L *trānscendent-* (s. of *trānscendēns*), prp. of *trānscendere.* See TRANSCEND, -ENT] —**tran·scend′ent·ly,** *adv.* —**tran·scend′ent·ness,** *n.*

tran·scen·den·tal (tran′sen den′tᵊl), *adj.* **1.** transcendent, surpassing, or superior. **2.** being beyond ordinary or common experience, thought, or belief; supernatural. **3.** abstract or metaphysical. **4.** *Philos.* **a.** beyond the contingent and accidental in human experience, but not beyond all human knowledge. **b.** *Kantianism.* of, pertaining to, based upon, or concerned with the a priori elements in experience that condition human knowledge. Cf. **transcendent** (def. 4). **5.** *Math.* **a.** (of a quantity or number) not a root of any algebraic equation having integral coefficients. **b.** (of a function) not expressible by the operations of addition, subtraction, multiplication, or division, as $y = \sin x$. **c.** (of an equation) involving transcendental functions. —*n.* **6.** *Math.* a transcendental number, as π or e. [< ML *trānscendentāl(is)*] —**tran′scen·den·tal′i·ty,** *n.* —**tran′scen·den′tal·ly,** *adv.*

tran·scen·den·tal·ism (tran′sen den′tᵊliz′əm), *n.* **1.** transcendental character, thought, or language. **2.** Also called **transcenden′tal philos′ophy.** any philosophy based upon the doctrine that the principles of reality are to be discovered by the study of the processes of thought, or a philosophy emphasizing the intuitive and spiritual above the empirical: in America, associated with Emerson. [< G *Transcendentalism(us)*] —**tran′scen·den′tal·ist,** *n., adj.*

trans·con·ti·nen·tal (trans′kon tᵊnen′tᵊl), *adj.* **1.** passing or extending across a continent. **2.** on the other, or far, side of a continent. —**trans′con·ti·nen′tal·ly,** *adv.*

tran·scribe (tran skrīb′), *v.t.,* **-scribed, -scrib·ing.** **1.** to make a written or typewritten copy of (dictated material, notes taken during a lecture, or other spoken material). **2.** to make an exact copy of (a document, text, etc.). **3.** to write out in another language or alphabet; translate or transliterate. **4.** *Phonet.* to represent (speech sounds) in written phonetic or phonemic symbols. **5.** *Radio.* to make a recording of (a program, announcement, etc.) for broadcasting. **6.** *Music.* to arrange (a composition) for a medium other than that for which it was originally written. [< L *trānscrībere*) (to) copy off = *trāns-* TRANS- + *scrībere* to write. See SHRIVE, SCRIBE] —**tran·scrib′er,** *n.*

tran·script (tran′skript), *n.* **1.** a written, typewritten, or printed copy; something transcribed or made by transcribing. **2.** an exact copy or reproduction, esp. one having an official status. **3.** a form of something as rendered from one alphabet or language into another. **4.** an official report supplied by a scholar or college on the record of an individual student, listing subjects studied, credits and grades received, etc. [late ME < L *trānscript(um)* thing copied (neut. of ptp. of *trānscrībere* to TRANSCRIBE); r. ME *transcrit* < OF; see SCRIPT]

tran·scrip·tion (tran skrip′shən), *n.* **1.** act of transcribing. **2.** a transcript; copy. **3.** *Music.* **a.** the arrangement of a composition for a medium other than that for which it was originally written. **b.** a composition so arranged. **4.** *Radio.* a phonograph record. [< L *trānscriptiōn-* (s. of *trānscriptiō*)] —**tran·scrip′tion·al,** *adj.* —**tran·scrip′tion·al·ly,** *adv.*

trans′-A·dri·at′ic, *adj.*
trans-Af′ri·can, *adj.*
trans′-Al·le·ghe′ni·an, *adj.*
trans′-Al·ta′ic, *adj.*
trans′-A·mer′i·can, *adj.*
trans′-An·de′an, *adj.*
trans′-Ant·arc′tic, *adj.*
trans-Ap′en·nine′, *adj.*
trans′-A·ra′bi·an, *adj.*
trans-Arc′tic, *adj.*
trans′-A·si·at′ic, *adj.*
trans′-Aus·tral′ian, *adj.*
trans-Bal′tic, *adj.*
trans·bor′der, *adj.*
trans′-Ca·na′di·an, *adj.*
trans-Cas′pi·an, *adj.*

—**tran·scrip·tive** (tran skrip′tive), *adj.* —**tran·scrip′tive·ly,** *adv.*

trans·cur·rent (trans kûr′ənt, -kur′-, tranz-), *adj.* running or extending across or transversely. [< L *trānscurrent-* (s. of *trānscurrēns*) running across, prp. of *trānscurrere*]

trans·duc·er (trans do͞o′sər, -dyo͞o′-, tranz-), *n.* a device that receives energy from one system and retransmits it, often in a different form, to another. [*transduce* to transfer (see TRADUCE) + -ER[1]]

tran·sect (tran sekt′), *v.t.* to cut across; dissect transversely. —**tran·sec′tion,** *n.*

tran·sept (tran′sept), *n. Archit.* **1.** any major transverse part of the body of a church, usually crossing the nave at the entrance to the choir and often similar to the nave in cross section and appearance. **2.** an arm of this, on either side of the central aisle of a church. [< AL *transept(um).* See TRANS-, SEPTUM] —**tran·sep′tal,** *adj.* —**tran·sep′tal·ly,** *adv.*

trans·e·unt (tran′sē ənt), *adj. Philos.* (of a mental act) producing an effect outside of the mind. Also, **transient.** Cf. **immanent** (def. 2). [< L *trānseunt-*, oblique s. of *trānsiēns* passing beyond; see TRANSIENT]

transf., 1. transfer. **2.** transferred.

trans·fer (*v.* trans fûr′, trans′fər; *n.* trans′fər), *v.*, **-ferred, -fer·ring,** *n.* —*v.t.* **1.** to convey or remove from one place, person, etc., to another. **2.** to cause to pass from one person to another, as thought, qualities, power, etc.; transmit. **3.** *Law.* to make over the possession or control of: *to transfer a title to land.* **4.** to imprint, impress, or otherwise convey (a drawing, design, pattern, etc.) from one surface to another. —*v.i.* **5.** to remove oneself or be moved from one place to another. **6.** to withdraw from one school, college, or the like, and enter another: *He transferred from Rutgers to Tulane.* **7.** to be moved from one place to another: *The entire military unit will transfer to overseas duty.* **8.** to change by means of a transfer from one bus, train, or the like, to another. —*n.* **9.** the act of transferring. **10.** the fact of being transferred. **11.** means or system of transferring. **12.** a point or place for transferring. **13.** a ticket, issued with or without extra charge, entitling a passenger to continue his journey on another bus, train, or the like. **14.** a drawing, design, pattern, or the like, that is or may be transferred to another surface, usually by direct contact. **15.** a person who changes or is changed from one college, military unit, business department, etc., to another. **16.** *Law.* a conveyance, by sale, gift, or otherwise, of real or personal property, to another. **17.** *Finance.* act of having the ownership of a stock or registered bond transferred on the books of the issuing corporation or its agent. [ME *transferre* < L = *trāns-* TRANS- + *ferre* to bear, carry] —**trans·fer′a·bil′i·ty,** *n.* —**trans·fer′a·ble, trans·fer′ra·ble,** *adj.* —**trans·fer′rer,** *n.*

trans·fer·al (trans fûr′əl), *n.* transference; transfer. Also, **transferral.**

trans·fer·ee (trans′fə rē′), *n.* **1.** a person who is transferred or removed, as from one place to another. **2.** *Law.* a person to whom a transfer is made, as of property.

trans·fer·ence (trans fûr′əns, trans′fər əns), *n.* **1.** the act or process of transferring. **2.** the fact of being transferred. **3.** *Psychoanal.* **a.** the shift of emotions, esp. those experienced in childhood, from one person or object to another, esp. the transfer of feelings about a parent to an analyst. **b.** displacement (def. 6). [< NL *trānsferentia*]

trans·fer·en·tial (trans′fə ren′shəl), *adj.* of, pertaining to, or involving transference. [< NL *trānsferenti(a)* TRANSFERENCE + -AL[1]]

trans·fer·or (trans fûr′ər), *n. Law.* a person who makes a transfer, as of property.

trans·fer·ral (trans fûr′əl), *n.* transferal.

trans·fig·u·ra·tion (trans′fig yə rā′shən, trans fig′-), *n.* **1.** the act of transfiguring. **2.** the state of being transfigured. **3.** (*cap.*) the supernatural and glorified change in the appearance of Jesus on the mountain. Matt. 17:1–9. **4.** (*cap.*) the church festival commemorating this, observed on August 6. [ME *transfiguracion* < L *trānsfigūrātiōn-* (s. of *trānsfigūrātiō*) change of shape]

trans·fig·ure (trans fig′yər), *v.t.*, **-ured, -ur·ing. 1.** to change in outward form or appearance; transform, change, or alter. **2.** to change so as to glorify, exalt, or idealize. [ME < L *trānsfigūr(āre)* (to) change in shape] —**trans·fig′ure·ment,** *n.* —**Syn. 2.** transmute, renew.

trans·fi·nite (trans fī′nīt), *adj.* **1.** going beyond or surpassing the finite. —*n.* **2.** See **transfinite number.**

transfi′nite num′ber, *Math.* an infinite cardinal or ordinal number.

trans·fix (trans fiks′), *v.t.*, **-fixed** or **-fixt, -fix·ing. 1.** to pierce through with or as with a pointed weapon; impale. **2.** to hold or fasten with or on something that pierces. **3.** to make or hold motionless with amazement, awe, terror, etc. [< L *trānsfīx(us)* pierced through (ptp. of *trānsfīgere*) = *trāns-* TRANS- + *fīxus* (*fīg-* pierce + *-sus* ptp. suffix)] —**trans·fix·ion** (trans fik′shən), *n.*

trans·form (*v.* trans fôrm′; *n.* trans′fôrm), *v.t.* **1.** to change in form, appearance, or structure; metamorphose. **2.** to change in condition, nature, or character; convert. **3.** *Elect.* to increase or decrease (voltage and current characteristics) as by means of a transformer. **4.** *Math.* to change the form of (a figure, expression, etc.) without in general changing the value. **5.** *Physics.* to change into another form of energy. —*v.i.* **6.** to undergo a change in form, appearance, or character; become transformed. —*n.* **7.** *Gram., Logic.* transformation (def. 5). [ME *transforme* < L *trānsformā(re)* (to) change in shape] —**trans·form′a·ble,** *adj.* —**trans·form′a·tive,** *adj.* —**Syn. 1.** transfigure.

trans·for·ma·tion (trans′fər mā′shən), *n.* **1.** the act or process of transforming. **2.** the state of being transformed. **3.** change in form, appearance, nature, or character. **4.** a wig or hairpiece for a woman. **5.** *Gram., Logic.* Also called **transform.** one of a set of algebraic formulas used to express the relations between elements, sets, etc., that form parts of a given system, as of the grammar of a language. **6.** *Math.* **a.** the act, process, or result of transforming or mapping. **b.** function (def. 4). [late ME < LL *trānsformātiōn-* (s. of *trānsformātiō*) change of shape] —**trans′for·ma′tion·al,** *adj.*

transforma′tional gram′mar, a system of grammatical analysis that uses transformations to express the relations between different elements in a sentence, clause, or phrase, or between different forms of a word, phrase, etc., as between the passive and active forms of a verb.

trans·form·er (trans fôr′mər), *n.* **1.** a person or thing that transforms. **2.** *Elect.* an electric device consisting essentially of two or more windings, which by electromagnetic induction transfers electric energy from one set of one or more circuits to another set of one or more circuits such that the frequency of the energy remains unchanged while the voltage and current usually change.

trans·form·ism (trans fôr′miz əm), *n. Biol.* the doctrine of gradual transformation of one species into another by descent with modification through many generations. [TRANSFORM + -ISM, modeled on F *transformisme*]

trans·form·ist (trans fôr′mist), *n.* a person who adheres to transformism. [TRANSFORM + -IST, modeled on F *transformiste*] —**trans′form·is′tic,** *adj.*

trans·fuse (trans fyo͞oz′), *v.t.*, **-fused, -fus·ing. 1.** to transfer or pass from one source to another; transmit; impart; instill: *to transfuse a love of literature to one's students.* **2.** to diffuse into or through; permeate; infuse. **3.** *Med.* **a.** to transfer (blood) from the veins or arteries of one person or animal into those of another. **b.** to inject, as a saline solution, into a blood vessel. **4.** *Archaic.* to pour from one container into another. [late ME < L *trānsfūs(us)* decanted, ptp. of *trānsfundere*] —**trans·fus′er,** *n.* —**trans·fus′i·ble, trans·fus′a·ble,** *adj.* —**trans·fu·sive** (trans fyo͞o′siv), *adj.*

trans·fu·sion (trans fyo͞o′zhən), *n.* **1.** the act or process of transfusing. **2.** *Med.* **a.** the direct transferring of blood, plasma, or the like, from one person or animal into another. **b.** the injecting of bottled blood or a solution of a salt, sugar, etc., into a blood vessel. [< L *trānsfūsiōn-* (s. of *trānsfūsiō*) decanting, intermingling]

trans·gress (trans gres′, tranz-), *v.i.* **1.** to break or violate a law, command, moral code, etc.; offend; sin (usually fol. by *against*). —*v.t.* **2.** to pass over or go beyond (a limit, boundary, etc.). **3.** to go beyond the limits imposed by (a law, command, etc.); violate; infringe; break. [< L *trānsgress(us)* having stepped across (ptp. of *trānsgredī*) = *trāns-* TRANS- + *gressus* = *gred-* (var. of *grad-* step; see GRADE) + *-tus* ptp. suffix] —**trans·gres′sive,** *adj.* —**trans·gres′sive·ly,** *adv.* —**trans·gres′sor,** *n.* —**Syn. 1.** err, trespass. **3.** disobey. —**Ant. 3.** obey.

trans·gres·sion (trans gresh′ən, tranz-), *n.* the act of transgressing; violation of a law, command, etc.; sin. [late ME < L *trānsgressiōn-* (s. of *trānsgressiō*) a stepping across]

tran·ship (tran ship′), *v.t.*, *v.i.*, **-shipped, -ship·ping.** transship. —**tran·ship′ment,** *n.*

trans·hu·mance (trans hyo͞o′məns *or, often,* -yo͞o′-), *n.* the seasonal migration of livestock, and the people who tend them, between lowlands and adjacent mountains. [< F = *transhum(er)* (to) shift ground (modeled on Sp *trashumar;* see TRANS-, HUMUS) + *-ance* -ANCE] —**trans·hu′mant,** *adj.*

tran·sience (tran′shəns, -zhəns), *n.* transient state or quality. Also, **tran′sien·cy.** [TRANSI(ENT) + -ENCE]

tran·sient (tran′shənt, -zhənt), *adj.* **1.** not lasting, enduring, or permanent; transitory. **2.** lasting only a short time; existing briefly; temporary: *transient authority.* **3.** staying only a short time: *the transient guests at a hotel.* **4.** *Philos.* transeunt. —*n.* **5.** a person or thing that is transient, esp. a temporary guest, boarder, or the like. **6.** *Physics.* the nonperiodic portion of a wave or signal. [alter. of earlier *transeunt* (see TRANSEUNT), with *-ie-* from L *transiēns* (nom. sing.) passing, prp. of *transīre* to pass by, lit., go across; see -ENT] —**tran′sient·ly,** *adv.* —**tran′sient·ness,** *n.* —**Syn. 2.** fleeting, flitting. See **temporary.** —**Ant. 2.** permanent.

tran′sient modula′tion, *Music.* a modulation of a temporary nature. Also called **passing modulation.**

tran·sil·i·ent (tran sil′ē ənt, -sil′yənt), *adj.* leaping or passing from one thing or state to another. [< L *trānsilient-* (s. of *trānsiliēns*) leaping across, prp. of *trānsilīre* = *trāns-* TRANS- + *-sili-* (var. s. of *salīre* to leap) + *-ent-* -ENT] —**tran·sil′i·ence,** *n.*

trans·il·lu·mi·nate (trans′i lo͞o′mə nāt′, tranz′-), *v.t.*, **-nat·ed, -nat·ing. 1.** to cause light to pass through. **2.** *Med.* to throw a strong light through (an organ or part) as a means of diagnosis. —**trans′il·lu′mi·na′tion,** *n.* —**trans′il·lu′mi·na′tor,** *n.*

tran·sis·tor (tran zis′tər), *n.* **1.** *Electronics.* an electronic device made of semiconducting material and equipped with three or more electrodes: it performs functions similar to those of a vacuum tube, but can be very much smaller in size and consumes much less power. **2.** *Informal.* a transistorized radio. —*adj.* **3.** *Informal.* transistorized: *a transistor radio.* [TRANS(FER) + (RES)ISTOR]

tran·sis·tor·ize (tran zis′tə rīz′), *v.t.*, **-ized, -iz·ing.** *Electronics.* to equip with or convert to a circuit employing transistors.

trans·it (tran′sit, -zit), *n.*, *v.*, **-it·ed, -it·ing.** —*n.* **1.** the act or fact of passing across or through; passage from one place to another. **2.** conveyance or transportation from one to another, as of persons or goods. **3.** a means or system of public transportation chiefly for passengers, esp. in an urban area. **4.** a transition or change. **5.** *Astron.* **a.** the passage of a heavenly body across the meridian of a given location or through the field of a telescope. **b.** the passage of Mercury or Venus across the disk of the sun, or of a satellite or its shadow across the face of its primary. **6.** *Survey.* Also called **trans′it in′strument.** an instrument, as a theodolite, having a telescope that can be transited, used for measuring horizontal and sometimes vertical angles. —*v.t.* **7.** to pass across or through. **8.** *Survey.* to turn (the telescope of a transit) in a vertical plane to reverse its direction; plunge. **9.** *Astron.* to cross (a meridian, celestial body, etc.). —*v.i.* **10.** to pass over or through something; make a transit. **11.** *Astron.* to make a transit across a meridian, celestial

trans′-Dan·u′bi·an, *adj.*
trans·des′ert, *adj.*
trans′-E·gyp′tian, *adj.*
trans′e·qua·to′ri·al, *adj.*
trans′fron·tier′, *adj.*
trans′-Him·a·lay′an, *adj.*
trans′-His·pan′ic, *adj.*
trans·isth′mi·an, *adj.*

body, etc. [late ME < L *trānsit(us)* a going across, passage, n. use of *trānsitus* crossed (ptp. of *trānsīre*) = *trāns-* TRANS- + *-i-* go + *-tus* ptp. suffix] —**tran′sit·a·ble,** *adj.*

tran·si·tion (tran zish′ən, -sish′-; *Brit.* tran sizh′ən), *n.* **1.** movement, passage, or change from one position, state, stage, subject, concept, etc., to another; change: *the transition from a monarchy to a democracy; the transition from adolescence to adulthood.* **2.** *Music.* **a.** a passing from one key to another; modulation. **b.** a brief modulation; a modulation used in passing. **c.** a sudden, unprepared modulation. **3.** a passage from one scene to another in a novel, play, or the like. [< L *trānsitiōn-* (s. of *trānsitiō*) a going across = *trānsit(us)* (see TRANSIT) + *-iōn-* -ION] —**tran·si′tion·al, tran·si′tion·a′ry,** *adj.* —**tran·si′tion·al·ly,** *adv.*

transi′tion el′ement, *Chem.* any element in either of the three series of elements with atomic numbers 21–30, 39–48, 57–80, and 89–103, that in a given inner orbital has less than a full quota of electrons.

tran·si·tive (tran′si tiv, -zi-), *adj.* **1.** *Gram.* having the nature of a transitive verb. **2.** characterized by or involving transition; transitional; intermediate. **3.** passing over to or affecting something else; transeunt. —*n.* **4.** *Gram.* See **transitive verb.** [< LL *trānsitīv(us)* = L *trānsit(us)* (see TRANSIT) + *-īvus* -IVE] —**tran′si·tive·ly,** *adv.* —**tran′si·tive·ness, tran′si·tiv′i·ty,** *n.*

tran′sitive verb′, *Gram.* a verb that is accompanied by a direct object and from which a passive can be formed, as *deny, rectify, elect.*

tran·si·to·ry (tran′si tôr′ē, -tōr′ē, -zi-), *adj.* **1.** not lasting, enduring, permanent, or eternal. **2.** lasting only a short time; brief; short-lived; temporary. [ME *transitorie* < eccl. L *trānsitōri(us)* fleeting (see TRANSIT, -ORY[1]); r. ME *transitoire* < MF] —**tran·si·to·ri·ly** (tran′si tôr′ə lē, -tōr′-, tran′si tôr′-, -tōr′-, -zi-), *adv.* —**tran′si·to′ri·ness,** *n.* —**Syn. 2.** See **temporary.** —**Ant. 2.** permanent.

trans′it theod′olite, a theodolite having a telescope that can be transited.

Trans·jor·dan (trans jôr′dᵊn, tranz-), *n.* an area east of the Jordan River, in SW Asia: a British mandate (1921–23); an amirate (1923–49); now the major part of the kingdom of Jordan. Also, **Trans-Jor′dan.**

transl., 1. translated. **2.** translation. **3.** translator.

trans·late (trans lāt′, tranz-; trans′lāt, tranz′-), *v.,* **-lat·ed, -lat·ing.** —*v.t.* **1.** to turn (something written or spoken) from one language into another: *to translate English books into Spanish.* **2.** to change the form, condition, nature, etc., of; transform: *to translate wishes into deeds.* **3.** to explain in terms that can be more easily understood; interpret. **4.** *Mech.* to cause (a body) to move without rotation or angular displacement; subject to translation. **5.** *Telegraphy.* to retransmit or forward (a message), as by a relay. **6.** *Eccles.* to move (a bishop) from one see to another. **7.** to convey or remove to heaven without natural death. —*v.i.* **8.** to provide or make a translation; act as translator. **9.** to admit of translation; to be capable of translation. [ME < L *trānslāt(us)* transferred (ptp. of *transferre*) = *trāns-* TRANS- + *-lātus* carried, borne (ptp. of *ferre* to BEAR[1]), earlier **tlātus* = **tlā-* (akin to THOLE[2]) + *-tus* ptp. suffix] —**trans·lat′a·bil′i·ty, trans·lat′a·ble·ness,** *n.* —**trans·lat′a·ble,** *adj.* —**trans·la·tor** (trans lā′tər, tranz-; trans′lā tər, tranz′-), **trans·lat′er,** *n.*

trans·la·tion (trans lā′shən, tranz-), *n.* **1.** the rendering of something into another language. **2.** a version in a different language: *a new translation of Plato.* **3.** change or conversion to another form, appearance, etc.; transformation: *a swift translation of thought into action.* **4.** the act or process of translating. **5.** the state of being translated. **6.** *Mech.* motion in which all particles of a body move with the same velocity along parallel paths. **7.** *Telegraphy.* the retransmitting or forwarding of a message, as by relay. [< L *trānslātiōn-* (s. of *trānslātiō*) a transferring; r. ME *translacioun* < AF] —**trans·la′tion·al,** *adj.*

trans·la·tive (trans lā′tiv, tranz-; trans′lā-, tranz′-), *adj.* **1.** of or pertaining to the transfer of something from one person, position, or place to another. **2.** of translation; serving to translate. [< L *trānslātīv(us)*]

trans·lit·er·ate (trans lit′ə rāt′, tranz-), *v.t.,* **-at·ed, -at·ing.** to change (letters, words, etc.) into corresponding characters of another alphabet or language. [TRANS- + L *lītera* LETTER[1] + -ATE[1]] —**trans·lit′er·a′tion,** *n.* —**trans·lit′er·a′tor,** *n.*

trans·lo·cate (trans lō′kāt, tranz-), *v.t.,* **-cat·ed, -cat·ing.** to move or transfer from one place to another; cause to change location; displace; dislocate. —**trans′lo·ca′tion,** *n.*

trans·lu·cent (trans lo͞o′sənt, tranz-), *adj.* **1.** permitting light to pass through but diffusing it so that persons, objects, etc., on the opposite side are not clearly visible: *Frosted window glass is translucent but not transparent.* **2.** easily understandable; lucid. [< L *trānslūcent-* (s. of *trānslūcēns*) shining through, prp. of *trānslūcēre*] —**trans·lu′cence, trans·lu′cen·cy,** *n.* —**trans·lu′cent·ly,** *adv.* —**Syn.** See **transparent.** —**Ant.** opaque.

trans·lu·nar·y (trans′lo͞o ner′ē, tranz′-; trans lo͞o′nə rē, tranz-), *adj.* **1.** situated beyond or above the moon; superlunary. **2.** celestial, rather than earthly. **3.** ideal; visionary. Also, **trans·lu·nar** (trans′lo͞o′nər, tranz′-; trans lo͞o′nər, tranz-). [TRANS- + *lunary* < L *lūnāri(s)* LUNAR; see -ARY]

trans·ma·rine (trans′mə rēn′, tranz′-), *adj.* **1.** being on or coming from the opposite side of the sea or ocean. **2.** being or crossing over the sea or ocean. [< L *trānsmarīn(us)*]

trans·mi·grant (trans mī′grənt, tranz-; trans′mə grənt, tranz′-), *n.* **1.** a person or thing that transmigrates. —*adj.* **2.** passing from one place or state to another. [< L *trānsmigrant-* (s. of *trānsmigrāns*), prp. of *trānsmigrāre*]

trans·mi·grate (trans mī′grāt, tranz-), *v.i.,* **-grat·ed, -grat·ing. 1.** to move or pass from one place to another. **2.** to migrate from one country to another in order to settle there. **3.** (of the soul) to be reborn at death in another body. [late ME < L *trānsmigrāt(us)* moved off (ptp. of *trānsmigrāre*)] —**trans·mi′gra·tor,** *n.* —**trans·mi·gra·to·ry** (trans mī′grə tôr′ē, -tōr′ē, tranz-), **trans·mi′gra·tive,** *adj.*

trans·mi·gra·tion (trans′mī grā′shən, tranz′-), *n.* **1.** the act of transmigrating. **2.** the passage of a soul at death into another body; metempsychosis. Cf. **reincarnation.** [ME *transmigracion* < LL *trānsmigrātiōn-* (s. of *trānsmigrātiō*) removal]

trans·mis·si·ble (trans mis′ə bəl, tranz-), *adj.* capable of being transmitted. [< L *trānsmiss(us)* transmitted (see TRANSMISSION) + -IBLE] —**trans·mis′si·bil′i·ty,** *n.*

trans·mis·sion (trans mish′ən, tranz-), *n.* **1.** the act or process of transmitting. **2.** the fact of being transmitted. **3.** something that is transmitted. **4.** *Mach.* **a.** transference of force between machines or mechanisms, often with changes of torque and speed. **b.** a compact, enclosed unit of gears or the like for this purpose, as in an automobile. **5.** *Radio.* the broadcasting of electromagnetic waves from the transmitting station to the receiving station. [< L *trānsmissiōn-* (s. of *trānsmissiō*) a sending across = *trānsmiss(us)* sent across (ptp. of *trānsmittere*) + *-iōn-* -ION] —**trans·mis·sive** (trans mis′iv, tranz-), *adj.* —**trans·mis′sive·ly,** *adv.* —**trans·mis′sive·ness,** *n.*

trans·mit (trans mit′, tranz-), *v.,* **-mit·ted, -mit·ting.** —*v.t.* **1.** to send or forward, as to a recipient or destination; dispatch; convey. **2.** to communicate, as information, news, etc. **3.** to pass or spread (disease, infection, etc.) to another. **4.** to pass on (a genetic character) from parent to offspring. **5.** *Physics.* **a.** to cause (light, heat, sound, etc.) to pass through a medium. **b.** to convey or pass along (an impulse, force, motion, etc.). **c.** to permit (light, heat, etc.) to pass through: *Glass transmits light.* **6.** *Radio.* to emit (electromagnetic waves). —*v.i.* **7.** to send a signal by wire or radio waves. **8.** to pass on a right or obligation to heirs or descendants. [ME *transmitte* < L *trānsmitte(re)* (to) send across = *trāns-* TRANS- + *mittere* to send] —**trans·mit′ta·ble, trans·mit′ti·ble,** *adj.* —**Syn. 2.** bear. See **carry.**

trans·mit·tal (trans mit′ᵊl, tranz-), *n.* transmission (defs. 1–3).

trans·mit·tance (trans mit′ᵊns, tranz-), *n.* **1.** transmission (defs. 1–3). **2.** *Physics.* the ratio of the radiant flux transmitted through and emerging from a body to the total flux incident on it.

trans·mit·ter (trans mit′ər, tranz-), *n.* **1.** a person or thing that transmits. **2.** Also called **transmit′ting set′.** *Radio.* a device for sending electromagnetic waves; the part of a broadcasting apparatus that generates and modulates the radiofrequency current and conveys it to the antenna. **3.** the part of a telephonic or telegraphic apparatus that converts sound waves or mechanical movements into electrical signals.

trans·mog·ri·fy (trans mog′rə fī′, tranz-), *v.t.,* **-fied, -fy·ing.** to change in appearance or form, esp. strangely or grotesquely; transform. [vulgar or humorous coinage] —**trans·mog′ri·fi·ca′tion,** *n.*

trans·mon·tane (trans mon′tān, tranz-), *adj.* tramontane. [< L *trānsmontān(us)*]

trans·mu·ta·tion (trans′myo͞o tā′shən, tranz′-), *n.* **1.** the act or process of transmuting. **2.** the fact or state of being transmuted. **3.** change into another nature, substance, form, or condition. **4.** *Biol.* the transformation of one species into another. Cf. **transformism. 5.** *Physics.* any process in which a nuclide is transformed into a different nuclide, usually one of a different element. **6.** *Alchemy.* the supposed conversion of base metals into metals of greater value, esp. into gold or silver. [ME *transmutacion* < L *trānsmūtātiōn-* (s. of *trānsmūtātiō*) a changing, shifting = *trānsmūtāt(us)* (ptp. of *trānsmutāre*) + *-iōn-* -ION] —**trans′mu·ta′tion·al, trans·mut·a·tive** (trans myo͞o′tə tiv, tranz-), *adj.* —**trans′mu·ta′tion·ist,** *n.*

trans·mute (trans myo͞ot′, tranz-), *v.t., v.i.,* **-mut·ed, -mut·ing.** to change from one nature, substance, form, or condition into another; transform. [ME < L *trānsmūt(āre)* (to) shift = *trāns-* TRANS- + *mūtāre* to change; see MUTABLE] —**trans·mut′a·bil′i·ty, trans·mut′a·ble·ness,** *n.* —**trans·mut′a·ble,** *adj.* —**trans·mut′a·bly,** *adv.* —**trans·mut′er,** *n.* —**Syn.** convert, alter, metamorphose.

trans·na·tion·al (trans nash′ə nᵊl, tranz-), *adj.* going beyond national boundaries or solely national interests.

trans·o·ce·an·ic (trans′ō shē an′ik, tranz′-), *adj.* **1.** extending across or traversing the ocean: *a transoceanic cable.* **2.** situated or living beyond the ocean.

tran·som (tran′səm), *n.* **1.** a crosspiece separating a door or the like from a window or fanlight above it. **2.** a window above such a crosspiece. **3.** a crossbar of wood or stone, dividing a window horizontally. **4.** *Naut.* **a.** a flat termination to a stern, above the water line. **b.** framework running athwartships in way of the sternpost of a steel or iron vessel, used as a support for the frames of the counter. [late ME < L *trāns(tr)um* crossbeam (with loss of second *-tr-* by dissimilation) = *trāns-* TRANS- + *-trum* instrumental suffix] —**tran′somed,** *adj.*

T, Transom (def. 4a)

tran·son·ic (tran son′ik), *adj.* *Chiefly Aeron.* close to the speed of propagation of sound; moving at 700–780 miles per hour at sea level.

transon′ic bar′rier. See **sound barrier.**

transp., 1. transparent. **2.** transportation.

trans·pa·cif·ic (trans′pə sif′ik), *adj.* **1.** passing or extending across the Pacific. **2.** beyond or on the other side of the Pacific.

trans·pa·dane (trans′pə dān′, trans pā′dān), *adj.* on the farther side, esp. the northern side of the Po River. [< L *trānspadān(us)* = *trāns-* TRANS- + *Pad(us)* Po + *-ānus* -ANE]

trans·par·en·cy (trans pâr′ən sē, -par′-), *n., pl.* **-cies. 1.** Also, **trans·par′ence.** the quality or state of being transparent. **2.** something transparent, esp. a picture, design, or the like, on glass or some translucent substance, made visible by light shining through from behind. **3.** *Photog.*

trans-Mar′tian, *adj.*
trans′-Med·i·ter·ra′ne·an, *adj.*
trans′-Mon·go′li·an, *adj.*
trans·mu′tu·al, *adj.*
trans·nat′ur·al, *adj.*
trans′-Nep·tu′ni·an, *adj.*
trans-Ni′ger, *adj.*
trans·nor′mal, *adj.;* **-ly,** *adv.*
trans·or′bi·tal, *adj.*
trans′o·var′i·an, *adj.*
trans′-Pan·a·ma′ni·an, *adj.*

the proportion of the light that is passed through the emulsion on an area of a photographic image. [< ML *trānspārentia.* See TRANSPARENT, -ENCY]

trans·par·ent (trans pâr′ənt, -par′-), *adj.* **1.** having the property of transmitting rays of light through its substance so that bodies situated beyond or behind can be distinctly seen, as opposed to opaque, and usually distinguished from translucent. **2.** admitting the passage of light through interstices. **3.** so sheer as to permit light to pass through; diaphanous. **4** open; frank or candid. **5.** easily seen through, recognized, or detected: *his transparent excuses.* **6.** manifest; obvious: *a story with a transparent plot.* **7.** *Obs.* shining through, as light. [late ME < ML *trānspārent-* (s. of *trānspārēns*) showing through (prp. of *trānspārēre*) = L *trāns-* TRANS- + *pārent-* (s. of *pārēns*) appearing (prp. of *pārēre*); see -ENT] —**trans·par′ent·ly,** *adv.* —**trans·par′ent·ness,** *n.* —**Syn. 1.** clear, pellucid, limpid. TRANSPARENT, TRANSLUCENT agree in describing material that light rays can pass through. That which is TRANSPARENT allows objects to be seen clearly through it: *Clear water is transparent.* That which is TRANSLUCENT allows light to pass through, diffusing it, however, so that objects beyond are not distinctly seen: *Ground glass is translucent.* —**Ant. 1.** opaque. **4.** secretive.

tran·spic·u·ous (tran spik′yo͞o əs), *adj.* transparent. [< NL *trānspicuus* = *trāns-* TRANS- + (*per*)*spicuus* transparent; see PERSPICUOUS] —**tran·spic′u·ous·ly,** *adv.*

trans·pierce (trans pērs′), *v.t.*, **-pierced, -pierc·ing.** to pierce through; penetrate; pass through.

tran·spire (tran spīər′), *v.*, **-spired, -spir·ing.** —*v.i.* **1.** to occur; happen; take place. **2.** to emit or give off waste matter, etc., through the surface, as of the body, of leaves, etc. **3.** to escape, as moisture, odor, etc., through or as through pores. **4.** to be revealed or become known. —*v.t.* **5.** to emit or give off (waste matter, watery vapor, an odor, etc.) through the surface, as of the body, of leaves, etc. [TRANS- + obs. *spire* to breathe < L *spīr(āre)*] —**tran·spir′a·ble,** *adj.* —**tran·spi·ra·tion** (tran′spə rā′shən), *n.* —**tran·spir·a·to·ry** (tran spīər′ə tôr′ē, -tôr′ē), *adj.*

trans·plant (*v.* trans plant′, -plänt′; *n.* trans′plant′, -plänt′), *v.t.* **1.** to remove (a plant) from one place and plant it in another. **2.** *Surg.* to transfer (an organ, a portion of tissue, etc.) from one part of the body to another or from one person or animal to another. **3.** to move from one place to another. **4.** to bring (a family, colony, etc.) from one country, region, etc., to another for settlement; relocate. —*n.* **5.** the act or process of transplanting. **6.** something transplanted. [late ME < LL *trānsplant(āre)*] —**trans·plant′a·ble,** *adj.* —**trans′plan·ta′tion,** *n.* —**trans·plant′er,** *n.*

tran·spon·der (tran spon′dər), *n.* a radio or radar transceiver, used in radar beacons, that automatically transmits a reply promptly on reception of a certain signal. Also, **tran·spon′dor.** [TRANS(MITTER) + (RES)PONDER]

trans·pon·tine (trans pon′tin, -tīn), *adj.* **1.** across or beyond a bridge. **2.** on the southern side of the Thames in London. [TRANS- + L *pont-* (s. of *pōns*) bridge + -INE[1]]

trans·port (*v.* trans pōrt′, -pôrt′; *n.* trans′pōrt′, -pôrt′), *v.t.* **1.** to carry, move, or convey from one place to another. **2.** to carry away by strong emotion; enrapture. **3.** to send into banishment, esp. to a penal colony. **4.** *Obs.* to kill. —*n.* **5.** the act of transporting or conveying; conveyance. **6.** a means of transporting or conveying, as a truck, bus, etc. **7.** a ship or airplane employed for transporting troops, military supplies, etc. **8.** an airplane carrying freight or passengers as part of a transportation system. **9.** a system of public travel. **10.** transportation (def. 4). **11.** strong emotion; ecstatic joy, bliss, etc. **12.** a convict sent into banishment, esp. to a penal colony. [late ME < L *trānsport(āre)* (to) carry across] —**trans·port′a·ble,** *adj.* —**trans·port′a·bil′i·ty,** *n.* —**trans·port′ed·ly,** *adv.* —**trans·port′er,** *n.* —**trans·port′ive,** *adj.* —**Syn. 1.** See **carry. 3.** banish, exile. **7.** troopship. **11.** rapture, ecstasy.

trans·por·ta·tion (trans′pər tā′shən), *n.* **1.** the act of transporting. **2.** the state of being transported. **3.** the means of transport or conveyance. **4.** the business of conveying people, goods, etc. **5.** price of travel or transport by public conveyance; fare. **6.** banishment, as of a criminal to a penal colony; deportation.

trans·pose (trans pōz′), *v.*, **-posed, -pos·ing.** —*v.t.* **1.** to change the relative position, order, or sequence of; cause to change places; interchange: *to transpose the third and fourth letters of a word.* **2.** *Algebra.* to bring (a term) from one side of an equation to the other, with corresponding change of sign. **3.** *Music.* to reproduce in a different key by raising or lowering in pitch. **4.** *Archaic.* to transfer or transport. **5.** *Obs.* to transform; transmute. —*v.i.* **6.** to perform a piece of music in a key other than the one in which it is written: *Accompanists must learn to transpose at sight.* [ME < MF *transpos(er)*] —**trans·pos′a·bil′i·ty,** *n.* —**trans·pos′a·ble,** *adj.* —**trans·pos′er,** *n.* —**Syn. 1.** rearrange. **2.** invert.

trans·po·si·tion (trans′pə zish′ən), *n.* **1.** the act of transposing. **2.** the state of being transposed. **3.** a transposed form of something. Also, **trans·pos·al** (trans pō′zəl). [< ML *trānspositiōn-* (s. of *trānspositiō*). See TRANS-, POSITION] —**trans′po·si′tion·al, trans·pos·i·tive** (trans poz′i tiv), *adj.*

trans·sex·u·al (trans sek′sho͞o əl), *n.* **1.** a person who, though not a homosexual, psychologically identifies with the opposite sex. **2.** such a person whose sex has been changed by surgery and hormone treatment.

trans·ship (trans ship′), *v.*, **-shipped, -ship·ping.** —*v.t.* **1.** to transfer from one ship, truck, freight car, or other conveyance to another. —*v.i.* **2.** to change from one ship or other conveyance to another. Also, **tranship.** —**trans·ship′ment,** *n.*

Trans′-Si·be′ri·an Rail′road (trans′sī bēr′ē ən, trans′-), a railroad traversing Siberia and Manchuria, from Chelyabinsk in the Ural Mountains to Vladivostok: over 4000 mi. long.

tran·sub·stan·ti·ate (tran′səb stan′shē āt′), *v.t.*, **-at·ed, -at·ing. 1.** to change from one substance into another; transmute. **2.** *Theol.* to cause (the substance of bread and wine) to undergo transubstantiation. [v. use of late ME *transsubstanciate* (adj.) < ML *trānssubstantiāt(us)*, ptp. of *trānssubstantiāre.* See TRANS-, SUBSTANCE, -ATE[1]] —**tran′sub·stan′tial,** *adj.* —**tran′sub·stan′tial·ly,** *adv.*

tran·sub·stan·ti·a·tion (tran′səb stan′shē ā′shən), *n.* **1.** the changing of one substance into another. **2.** *Rom. Cath. Ch.* (in the Eucharist) the conversion of the whole substance of the bread and wine into the body and blood of Christ, only the external appearance of bread and wine remaining. [ME *transubstanciacioun* < ML *trānssubstantiātiōn-* (s. of *trānssubstantiātiō*)] —**tran′sub·stan′ti·a′tion·al·ist,** *n.*

tran·su·date (tran′so͝o dāt′), *n.* transudation (def. 2). [< NL *trānsūdāt(us)*, ptp. of *trānsūdāre* to TRANSUDE; see -ATE[1]]

tran·su·da·tion (tran′so͝o dā′shən), *n.* **1.** the act or process of transuding. **2.** a substance that has transuded. [< NL *trānsūdātiōn-* (s. of *trānsūdātiō*)]

tran·sude (tran so͞od′), *v.i.*, **-sud·ed, -sud·ing.** to pass or ooze through pores or interstices, as a fluid. [< NL *trānsūd(āre)* = L *trāns-* TRANS- + *sūdāre* to SWEAT]

trans·u·ran·ic (trans′yo͝o ran′ik, tranz′-), *adj.* *Chem., Physics.* noting or pertaining to an element having a higher atomic number than that of uranium. Also, **trans·u·ra·ni·an** (trans′yo͝o rā′nē ən, tranz′-), **trans′u·ra′ni·um.**

Trans·vaal (trans väl′, tranz-), *n.* a province in the NE Republic of South Africa. 6,225,052 (1960); 110,450 sq. mi. *Cap.:* Pretoria. Formerly, **South African Republic.**

trans·val·ue (trans val′yo͞o, tranz-), *v.t.*, **-ued, -u·ing.** to reestimate the value of, esp. on a basis differing from accepted standards; reappraise; reevaluate. —**trans′val·u·a′tion,** *n.*

trans·ver·sal (trans vûr′səl, tranz-), *adj.* **1.** transverse. —*n.* **2.** *Geom.* a line intersecting two or more lines. [late ME < ML *trānsversāl(is)*] —**trans·ver′sal·ly,** *adv.*

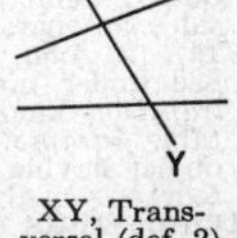

XY, Transversal (def. 2)

trans·verse (trans vûrs′, tranz-; trans′vûrs, tranz′-), *adj.* **1.** lying or being across or in a cross direction; cross; athwart. **2.** (of a flute) having a mouth hole in the side of the tube, near its end, across which the player's breath is directed. —*n.* **3.** something that is transverse. **4.** a direct city route or road that cuts through a park or other area of light traffic; shortcut. [< L *trānsvers(us)* going or lying across, athwart. See TRAVERSE] —**trans·verse′ly,** *adv.* —**trans·verse′ness,** *n.*

trans′verse sec′tion. See **cross section.**

trans′verse wave′, *Physics.* a wave in which the direction of displacement is perpendicular to the direction of propagation, as a surface wave of water. Cf. **longitudinal wave.**

trans·ves·tism (trans ves′tiz əm, tranz-), *n.* the practice of wearing clothing appropriate to the opposite sex, often as a manifestation of homosexuality. Also, **trans·ves·ti·tism** (trans ves′ti tiz′əm, tranz-). [*transvest* to clothe across, i.e., in violation of custom (now obs.; see TRANS-, VEST) + -ISM; modeled on G *Transvestismus*] —**trans·ves′tic,** *adj.* —**trans·ves·tite** (trans ves′tīt, tranz-), *n.*, *adj.*

Tran·syl·va·ni·a (tran′sil vā′nē ə, -vān′yə), *n.* a region and former province in central Rumania: formerly part of Hungary. 24,027 sq. mi. —**Tran′syl·va′ni·an,** *adj.*, *n.*

Tran′sylva′nian Alps′, a mountain range in S Rumania, forming a SW extension of the Carpathian Mountains. Highest peak, Mt. Negoiul, 8345 ft.

trap[1] (trap), *n.*, *v.*, **trapped** or (*Archaic*) **trapt; trap·ping.** —*n.* **1.** a contrivance used for catching game or other animals, as a mechanical device that springs shut suddenly, a pitfall, or a snare. **2.** any device, stratagem, trick, or the like, for catching a person unawares. **3.** any of various devices for removing undesirable substances from a moving fluid, vapor, etc., as water from steam or cinders from coal gas. **4.** an arrangement in a pipe, as a double curve or a U-shaped section, in which liquid remains and forms a seal for preventing the passage or escape of air or of gases through the pipe from behind or below. **5. traps,** the percussion instruments of a jazz or dance band. **6.** *Trapshooting, Skeet.* a device for hurling clay pigeons into the air. **7.** *Chiefly Brit.* a carriage, esp. a light, two-wheeled one. **8.** See **trap door. 9.** *Sports.* the act or an instance of trapping a ball. **10.** *Slang.* mouth: *Keep your trap shut.* —*v.t.* **11.** to catch in a trap; ensnare: *to trap foxes.* **12.** to catch by stratagem, artifice, or trickery. **13.** to furnish or set with traps. **14.** to provide (a drain or the like) with a trap. **15.** to stop and hold by a trap, as air in a pipe. **16.** *Sports.* **a.** to catch (a ball) as it rises after having just hit the ground. **b.** *Baseball.* to catch (a base runner) away from a base, usually by a throw: *He was trapped off first by a quick throw from the catcher.* —*v.i.* **17.** to set traps for game. **18.** to engage in the business of trapping animals for their furs. **19.** *Trapshooting, Skeet.* to work the trap. [ME *trappe*, OE *træppe*; c. MD, MFlem *trappe* trap; akin to OE *treppan* to tread, G *Treppe* staircase, ladder, D *trap* step, kick, stair, ladder] —**trap′like′,** *adj.*

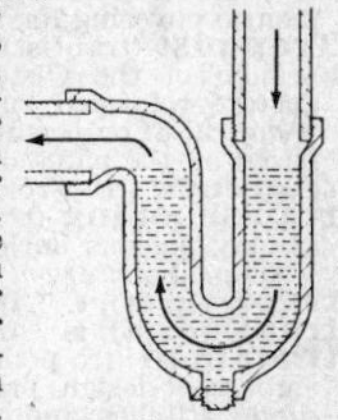
Trap[1] (def. 4)

—**Syn. 1, 2.** TRAP, PITFALL, SNARE apply to literal or figurative contrivances for deceiving and catching animals or people. Literally, a TRAP is a mechanical contrivance for catching animals, the main feature usually being a spring: *a trap baited with cheese for mice.* Figuratively, TRAP suggests the scheme of one person to take another by surprise and gain an advantage from him: *a trap for the unwary.* A PITFALL is (usually) a concealed pit arranged for the capture of large animals or of men who may fall into it; figuratively, it

trans·per′son·al, *adj.*; **-ly,** *adv.*
trans·po′lar, *adj.*
trans′-Pyr·e·ne′an, *adj.*
trans′-Sa·har′an, *adj.*
trans·shape′, *v.t.*, **-shaped, -shap·ing.**
trans′-Si·be′ri·an, *adj.*
trans′-U·ra′li·an, *adj.*

is any concealed danger, error, or source of disaster. A SNARE is a device for entangling birds, rabbits, etc., with intent to capture; figuratively, it implies enticement and inveiglement: *a snare for small animals.* **2.** ambush, maneuver.

trap[2] (trap), *v.*, **trapped** or (*Archaic*) **trapt; trap·ping;** *n.* —*v.t.* **1.** to furnish with or as with trappings; caparison. —*n.* **2. traps,** *Informal.* personal belongings; baggage. **3.** *Obs.* a cloth or covering for a horse; caparison. [ME *trappe* < ?]

trap[3] (trap), *n.* *Geol.* any of various fine-grained, dark-colored igneous rocks having a more or less columnar structure, esp. some form of basalt. Also called **traprock.** [< Sw *trapp*, var. of *trappa* stair (so named from their looks) < MLG *trappe.* See TRAP[1]]

tra·pan (trə pan′), *n., v.t.,* **-panned, -pan·ning.** *Archaic.* trepan[2]. —**tra·pan′ner,** *n.*

Tra·pa·ni (trä′pä nē), *n.* a seaport in NW Sicily. 75,537 (1961).

trap′ door′, 1. a door or the like, flush or nearly so with the surface of a floor, ceiling, roof, etc. **2.** the opening that it covers. —**trap′-door′,** *adj.*

trap′-door spi′der, any of several burrowing spiders of the family *Ctenizidae*, that construct a tubular nest with a hinged lid.

tra·peze (tra pēz′), *n.* a gymnastic apparatus consisting of a short bar attached horizontally to the ends of two suspended ropes. [< F, special use of *trapèze* TRAPEZIUM]

trapeze′ art′ist, a person who performs, esp. professionally, on a trapeze. Also called **tra·pez′ist.**

tra·pe·zi·form (trə pē′zə fôrm′), *adj.* formed like a trapezium.

tra·pe·zi·um (trə pē′zē əm), *n., pl.* **-zi·ums, -zi·a** (-zē ə). **1.** *Geom.* **a.** (in Euclidean geometry) any rectilinear quadrilateral plane figure not a parallelogram. **b.** a quadrilateral plane figure of which no two sides are parallel. **c.** *Brit.* trapezoid (def. 1a). **2.** *Anat.* the greater multangular bone. See under **multangulum.** [< NL < Gk *trapézion* kind of quadrilateral, lit., small table = *trápez(a)* table (aph. var. of **tetrápeza* object having four feet: *tetra-* four + *péza* foot) + *-ion* dim. suffix] —**tra·pe′zi·al,** *adj.*

Trapezium (def. 1b)

tra·pe·zi·us (trə pē′zē əs), *n., pl.* **-us·es.** *Anat.* a broad, flat muscle on each side of the upper and back part of the neck, shoulders, and thorax, the action of which raises, rotates, or draws back the shoulders and pulls the head backward or to one side. [< NL, short for *trapezius musculus* trapeziform muscle]

trapezo-, a learned borrowing from Greek meaning "table," "trapezium," used in the formation of compound words: *trapezohedron.* [comb. form of Gk *trápeza* table, *trapézion* trapezium]

tra·pe·zo·he·dron (trə pē′zə hē′drən, trap′i-), *n., pl.* **-drons, -dra** (-drə). *Crystall.* a crystal form having all faces trapeziums. —**tra·pe′zo·he′dral,** *adj.*

trap·e·zoid (trap′i zoid′), *n.* **1.** *Geom.* **a.** a quadrilateral plane figure having two parallel and two nonparallel sides. **b.** *Brit.* trapezium (def. 1b). **2.** *Anat.* the lesser multangular bone. See under **multangulum.** —*adj.* **3.** Also, **trap′e·zoi′dal.** *Geom.* of, pertaining to, or having the form of a trapezoid. [< NL *trapezoid(ēs)* < LGk *trapezoeidḗs* trapezium]

Trapezoid (def. 1a)

trap·per (trap′ər), *n.* a person whose business is the trapping of animals for their furs.

trap·pings (trap′ingz), *n.* (*construed as pl.*) **1.** articles of equipment or dress, esp. of an ornamental character. **2.** conventional or characteristic articles of dress or adornment. **3.** Sometimes, **trapping.** an ornamental covering for a horse; caparison. [ME]

Trap·pist (trap′ist), *n.* **1.** *Rom. Cath. Ch.* a member of a branch of the Cistercian order, observing the extremely austere reformed rule established at La Trappe in 1664. —*adj.* **2.** of or pertaining to the Trappists. [< F *trappiste*, based on the name of the monastery]

trap·rock (trap′rok′), *n.* trap[3].

trap·shoot·ing (trap′sho͞o′ting), *n.* the sport of shooting at clay pigeons hurled into the air from a trap. Cf. **skeet.** —**trap′shoot′er,** *n.*

trapt[1] (trapt), *v.* *Archaic.* pt. and pp. of **trap**[1].

trapt[2] (trapt), *v.* *Archaic.* pp. of **trap**[2].

tra·pun·to (trə po͝on′tō), *n., pl.* **-tos.** quilting having an embossed design produced by outlining the pattern with single stitches and then padding it with yarn or cotton. [< It: embroidery; as adj., embroidered, lit., pricked through (ptp. of *trapungere*) = *tra-* (< L *trā-*, var. of *trāns-* TRANS-) + *-punto* < L *punct(us)* = *pung-* (s. of *pungere* to prick) + *-tus* ptp. suffix; see PUNCTURE]

trash[1] (trash), *n.* **1.** anything worthless or useless; rubbish. **2.** foolish or pointless ideas, talk, or writing; nonsense. **3.** a worthless or disreputable person. **4.** such persons collectively. **5.** literary or artistic material of poor or inferior quality. **6.** broken or torn bits, as twigs, splinters, or rags. **7.** something that is broken or lopped off from anything in preparing it for use. **8.** the refuse of sugar cane after the juice has been expressed. —*v.t.* **9.** to remove the outer leaves of (a growing sugar-cane plant). **10.** to free from superfluous twigs or branches. **11.** *Slang.* to put in disarray or cause minor damage to in anger or protest: *He trashed his room in a fit of rage.* [ME *trasches* (pl.), appar. c. Norw *trask* rubbish; akin to OE *trus* brushwood, Icel *tros* rubbish]

trash[2] (trash), *v.t.* *Obs.* **1.** to hinder; retard; restrain. **2.** to hold (a dog or other animal) in check by a cord or leash. —*n.* **3.** *Brit. Dial.* a cord or leash for holding an animal, esp. a hunting dog, in check. [? var. of TRACE[2]]

trash′ can′, a container for the disposal of dry waste matter.

trash·y (trash′ē), *adj.*, **trash·i·er, trash·i·est.** of the nature of trash; useless or worthless. —**trash′i·ness,** *n.*

Tra·si·me·no (trä′sē me′nô), *n.* a lake in central Italy, in Umbria near Perugia: Romans defeated by Hannibal 217 B.C. ab. 50 sq. mi. Also called **Lake of Perugia.** Latin, **Tras·i·me·nus** (tras′ə mē′nəs).

trass (tras), *n.* a rock, common along the Rhine, composed chiefly of comminuted pumice or other volcanic material, used for making hydraulic cement. Also, **terras.** [< D *tras*, earlier *tarasse* < early It *terrazza* worthless earth. See TERRACE]

trau·ma (trou′mə, trô′-), *n., pl.* **-ma·ta** (-mə tə), **-mas. 1.** *Pathol.* **a.** a body injury produced by violence or any thermal, chemical, or other extrinsic agent. **b.** the condition resulting from the injury; traumatism. **2.** *Psychiatry.* a startling experience that has a lasting effect on mental life; shock. [< Gk *traûma* wound]

trau·mat·ic (trə mat′ik, trou-, trô-), *adj.* **1.** of, pertaining to, or produced by a trauma or wound. **2.** adapted to the cure of wounds. [< LL *traumatic(us)* < Gk *traumatikós* pertaining to wounds = *traumat-* (s. of *traûma* TRAUMA) + *-ikos* -IC] —**trau·mat′i·cal·ly,** *adv.*

trau·ma·tism (trou′mə tiz′əm, trô′-), *n.* *Pathol.* **1.** any abnormal condition produced by a trauma. **2.** the trauma or wound itself. [< LGk *traumatism(ós)* a wounding]

trau·ma·tize (trou′mə tīz′, trô′-), *v.t.*, **-tized, -tiz·ing. 1.** *Pathol.* to injure (tissues) by force or by thermal, chemical, electrical, etc., agents. **2.** *Psychiatry.* to cause a trauma in (a person's mind): *to be traumatized by a childhood experience.* [< Gk *traumatíz(ein)* (to) wound. See TRAUMATIC, -IZE] —**trau′ma·ti·za′tion,** *n.*

trav., 1. traveler. **2.** travels.

tra·vail (trə vāl′, trav′āl, trav′əl), *n.* **1.** painfully difficult or burdensome work; toil. **2.** pain, anguish, suffering, etc., resulting from mental or physical hardship. **3.** the labor and pain of childbirth. —*v.i.* **4.** to suffer the pangs of childbirth; be in labor. **5.** *Archaic.* to toil or exert oneself. [ME *travaill(en)* < OF *travaill(i)e(r)* (to) torment < VL **trepaliāre* to torture < LL *trepāli(um)* torture chamber, lit., instrument of torture made with three stakes. See TRI-, PALE[3]] —**Syn. 1.** labor, work, moil. **2.** torment, agony.

Trav·an·core (trav′ən kōr′, -kôr′), *n.* a former state in SW India: merged 1949 with Cochin to form a new state (**Trav′ancore and Co′chin**), reorganized 1956 to form the larger part of Kerala state.

trave[1] (trāv), *n.* *Archit.* a section or bay formed by crossbeams. [< MF *trave* < L *trab-* (s. of *trabs*) beam, timber]

trave[2] (trāv), *n.* a device to inhibit a wild or untrained horse or one being shod. [ME; OE *træf* framework, building, heathen temple < L *trab-* (s. of *trabs*). See TRAVE[1]]

trav·el (trav′əl), *v.*, **-eled, -el·ing** or (*esp. Brit.*) **-elled, -el·ling,** *n.* —*v.i.* **1.** to go from one place to another or from place to place, as by car, train, plane, or ship; take a trip; journey: *to travel for pleasure.* **2.** to move from one place or point to another. **3.** to proceed or advance in any way. **4.** to go from place to place as a representative of a business firm. **5.** to associate or consort (usually fol. by *with*): *He travels with a wealthy crowd.* **6.** *Informal.* to move with speed. **7.** to move in a fixed course, as a piece of mechanism. **8.** to pass, or be transmitted, as light, sound, etc. —*v.t.* **9.** to travel, journey, or pass through or over, as a country or road. **10.** to journey or traverse (a specified distance): *We traveled a hundred miles today.* **11.** to cause to journey; drive. —*n.* **12.** the act of traveling, esp. in distant or foreign places; journeying: *the difficulties of travel in midwinter.* **13. travels, a.** journeys; wanderings: *to set out on one's travels.* **b.** journeys as the subject of a written account or literary work: *a book of travels.* **14.** the coming and going of persons or conveyances along a way of passage; traffic. **15.** *Mach.* **a.** the complete movement of a moving part, esp. a reciprocating part, in one direction, or the distance traversed. **b.** length of stroke. **16.** movement or passage in general. [ME *travaill(en)* (to) journey; special use of TRAVAIL]

tra′vel a′gency, a business that accommodates travelers, as by securing tickets, arranging for reservations, giving information, etc. Also called **trav′el bu′reau.**

trav′el a′gent, 1. a person who arranges trips. **2.** a person or firm that owns or operates a travel agency.

trav·eled (trav′əld), *adj.* **1.** having traveled, esp. to distant places; experienced in travel. **2.** used by travelers: *a heavily-traveled road.* Also, *esp. Brit.*, **travelled.** [late ME]

trav·el·er (trav′ə lər, trav′lər), *n.* **1.** a person or thing that travels. **2.** a person who travels or has traveled in distant places or foreign lands. **3.** See **traveling salesman. 4.** *Naut.* **a.** a metal ring or thimble fitted to move freely on a rope, spar, or rod. **b.** the rope, spar, or rod itself. **c.** a ring, block, or other fitting, either attached to the sheet of a fore-and-aft sail or through which the sheet is rove, that slides from side to side on a metal rod fastened to the deck. Also, *esp. Brit.*, **traveller.** [ME *travaillour*]

trav′eler's check′, a check, usually one of a set, sold by a bank or the like, that may be cashed by countersigning in the presence of a payee and is widely accepted by financial and commercial firms. Also, **trav′elers check′.**

trav′eling sales′man, a representative of a business firm who travels in an assigned territory soliciting orders for his company's products or services. Also called **commercial traveler, traveler.**

trav·elled (trav′əld), *adj.* *Chiefly Brit.* traveled.

trav·el·ler (trav′ə lər, trav′lər), *n.* *Chiefly Brit.* traveler.

trav·e·logue (trav′ə lôg′, -log′), *n.* a motion picture or an illustrated lecture describing travels. Also, **trav′e·log′.**

trav·erse (trav′ərs, trə vûrs′), *v.*, **-ersed, -ers·ing,** *n., adj., adv.* —*v.t.* **1.** to pass or move over, along, or through. **2.** to go to and fro over or along. **3.** to extend across or over: *A covered bridge traverses the stream.* **4.** to go up, down, or across (a rope, mountain, hill, etc.) at an angle: *The climbers traversed the east face of the mountain with ease.* **5.** to cause to move laterally. **6.** to look over, examine, or consider carefully; survey; inspect. **7.** to go counter to; obstruct; oppose; thwart. **8.** to contradict or deny. **9.** *Law.* **a.** (in the law of pleading) to deny formally (an allegation of fact set forth in a previous pleading). **b.** to join issue upon. **10.** to turn and point (a gun) in any direction. **11.** *Naut.* to brace (a yard) fore and aft. —*v.i.* **12.** to pass along or go across something; cross; cross over. **13.** to turn laterally, as a gun. **14.** *Fencing.* to glide the blade toward the hilt of the contestant's foil while applying pressure to the blade. —*n.* **15.** the act of passing across, over, or through. **16.** something that crosses, obstructs, or thwarts; obstacle. **17.** a transversal or similar line. **18.** a place where one may traverse or cross; crossing. **19.** a bar, strip, rod, or other structural part placed or extending across; crosspiece; crossbar. **20.** a railing, lattice, or screen serving as a barrier. **21.** *Naut.* **a.** the zigzag track of a vessel compelled by contrary winds or currents to sail on different courses. **b.** each of the runs in a single direction made in such sailing. **22.** *Fort.* **a.** a defensive barrier, parapet, or the like, placed transversely. **b.** a defensive barrier thrown across the terreplein or the covered way of a fortification to protect it from enfilade fire. **23.** *Gunnery.* the horizontal turning of a gun so as to make it point in any required direction. **24.** *Mach.* **a.** the motion of a lathe tool or grinding wheel along a piece of work. **b.** a part moving along a piece of work in this way, as the carriage of a lathe. **25.** *Survey.* a series of distances and angles or bearings connecting successive instrument stations of a survey. **26.** *Law.* a formal denial of some matter of fact alleged by the other side. —*adj.* **27.** lying, extending, or passing across; transverse. —*adv.* **28.** *Obs.* across; crosswise; transversely. [(v.) ME *travers(en)* < MF *traverse(r)* (to) cross < LL *trānsversāre* < *trānsvers(us)* TRANSVERSE; (n.) ME *travers(e)* < MF *traverse* (<< L *trānsversa* something lying across, fem. of *trānsversus*) and *travers* (<< L *trānsversum* passage across, neut. of *trānsversus*)] —**tra·vers′a·ble,** *adj.* —**tra·vers′al,** *n.* —**tra·vers′er,** *n.* —**Syn. 1.** cross. **7.** hinder, impede. **8.** counter, dispute, challenge.

trav′erse rod′, a horizontal rod upon which drapes slide to open or close when pulled by cords.

trav·er·tine (trav′ər tin, -tēn′), *n.* a form of limestone deposited by springs, esp. hot springs, used in Italy for building. Also, **trav·er·tin** (trav′ər tin). [< It *travertin(o)* = *tra-* across (< L *trāns-* TRANS-) + *(ti)vertino* < L *Tīburtīn(us)* = *Tīburt-* (s. of *Tībur*s) the territory of Tibur + *-īnus* -INE[1]]

trav·es·ty (trav′i stē), *n., pl.* **-ties,** *v.,* **-tied, -ty·ing.** —*n.* **1.** a literary or artistic burlesque of a serious work or subject, characterized by grotesque or ludicrous incongruity of style, treatment, subject matter, etc. **2.** a literary or artistic composition so inferior in quality as to seem merely a grotesque imitation of its model. **3.** any grotesque or debased likeness or imitation: *a travesty of justice.* —*v.t.* **4.** to make a travesty on; burlesque; counterfeit; mock. [< F *travesti* disguised, ptp. of *travestir* < It *travestire* to disguise = *tra-* (< L *trāns-* TRANS-) + *vestire* to clothe < L *vestīre;* see VEST]

tra·vois (trə voi′), *n., pl.* **-vois** (-voiz′). a sledlike vehicle, formerly used by the Plains Indians, consisting of two poles joined by a frame, for drawing by an animal. [pseudo-F for *travoy* (rhyming with *boy*), repr. var. pronunciation of F *travail* TRAVE[2] < ?]

trawl (trôl), *n.* **1.** Also called **trawl′ net′.** a strong fishing net for dragging along the sea bottom to catch deep-dwelling fish. **2.** Also called **trawl′ line′.** a buoyed line used in sea fishing, having numerous short lines with baited hooks attached at intervals. —*v.i.* **3.** to fish with a trawl net. **4.** to fish with a trawl line. **5.** to troll. —*v.t.* **6.** to catch with a trawl net or a trawl line. **7.** to drag (a trawl net). **8.** to troll. [late ME *trawelle* < MD *traghel* dragnet, *traghelen* to drag; c. TRAIL[1]]

trawl·er (trô′lər), *n.* any of various vessels used in fishing with a trawl net.

tray (trā), *n.* **1.** a flat, shallow container or receptacle, usually with slightly raised edges, used typically for carrying, holding, or displaying articles of food, glass, china, etc. **2.** a removable receptacle of this shape in a cabinet, box, trunk, or the like, sometimes forming a drawer. **3.** a tray and its contents: *to have a breakfast tray in one's room; to examine a tray of diamonds.* [ME; OE *trēg, trīg;* c. Sw (obs.) *trö* corn measure; akin to TREE]

treach·er·ous (trech′ər əs), *adj.* **1.** characterized by faithlessness or readiness to betray trust; disloyal; perfidious; traitorous. **2.** deceptive, untrustworthy, or unreliable. **3.** unstable or insecure, as footing. **4.** dangerous; hazardous. [ME *trecherous* < AF = *trecher* deceiver (*trech-* deceive + *-er* -ER[2]) + *-ous* -OUS. Cf. F *tricheur* trickster] —**treach′er·ous·ly,** *adv.* —**treach′er·ous·ness,** *n.* —**Syn. 1.** unfaithful, faithless, treasonous. **2.** deceitful. —**Ant. 1.** loyal. **2.** reliable.

treach·er·y (trech′ə rē), *n., pl.* **-er·ies. 1.** violation of faith; betrayal of trust; treason. **2.** an act of perfidy, faithlessness, or treason. [ME *trecherie* < MF, OF *trech(ier)* (to) deceive + *-erie* -ERY] —**Syn. 1.** See **disloyalty.** —**Ant. 1.** loyalty.

trea·cle (trē′kəl), *n.* **1.** *Brit.* **a.** molasses, esp. that which is drained from the vats used in sugar refining. **b.** a mild mixture of molasses, corn syrup, etc., used in cooking or as a table syrup. **2.** contrived or unrestrained sentimentality. **3.** *Pharm. Obs.* any of various medicinal compounds, formerly used as antidotes for poisonous bites or for poisons. **4.** *Obs.* a sovereign remedy. [ME, var. of *triacle* antidote < MF, OF < L *thēriaca* < Gk *thēriakḗ,* n. use of fem. of *thēriakós* = *thērí(on)* reptile (*thḗr* wild beast + *-ion* dim. suffix) + *-akos* -AC] —**trea·cly** (trē′klē), *adj.*

tread (tred), *v.,* **trod** or (*Archaic*) **trode; trod·den** or **trod; tread·ing;** *n.* —*v.t.* **1.** to step or walk on, about, in, or along. **2.** to trample or crush underfoot. **3.** to form by the action of walking or trampling: *to tread a path.* **4.** to treat with disdainful harshness or cruelty; crush; oppress. **5.** to perform by walking or dancing: *to tread a measure.* **6.** (of a male bird) to copulate with (a female bird). —*v.i.* **7.** to set down the foot or feet in walking; step; walk. **8.** to step, walk, or trample so as to press, crush, or injure (usually fol. by *on* or *upon*): *to tread on grapes; to tread upon a person's foot.* **9.** (of a male bird) to copulate. **10. tread on someone's toes** or **corns,** to offend or irritate someone. **11. tread the boards** or **stage,** to play a role on the stage; act, esp. professionally. **12. tread water,** *Swimming.* to maintain the body erect in the water with the head above the surface, usually by a pumping up-and-down movement of the legs and sometimes the arms. —*n.* **13.** the action of treading, stepping, or walking. **14.** the sound of footsteps. **15.** manner of treading or walking: *a stealthy tread.* **16.** a single step, as in walking. **17.** any of various things or parts on which a person or thing treads, stands, or moves. **18.** the part of the undersurface of the foot or of a shoe that touches the ground. **19.** the horizontal upper surface of a step in a stair, on which the foot is placed. **20.** the part of a wheel, tire, or runner that bears on the road, rail, etc. **21.** the pattern raised on or cut into the face of a rubber tire. [ME *tred(en),* OE *tredan;* c. D *treden,* G *treten;* akin to Goth *trudan,* Icel *trotha*] —**tread′er,** *n.*

trea·dle (tred′əl), *n., v.,* **-dled, -dling.** —*n.* **1.** a lever or the like worked by continual action of the foot to impart motion to a machine. **2.** a platform, as on a bus, trolley car, etc., for actuating an exit door. —*v.i.* **3.** to work a treadle. [ME, OE *tredel* stairstep, lit., something that one treads or steps on. See TREAD]

tread·mill (tred′mil′), *n.* **1.** an apparatus for producing rotary motion by the weight of men or animals, treading on a succession of moving steps or a belt that forms a continuous path. **2.** a monotonous, wearisome routine of work or other activity in which there is little or no satisfactory progress.

treas., 1. treasurer. **2.** treasury. Also, **Treas.**

trea·son (trē′zən), *n.* **1.** violation by a subject of his allegiance to his sovereign or to the state; high treason. **2.** *U.S.* such a violation directed against the United States, and consisting only in levying war against the U.S. or in adhering to its enemies or giving them aid and comfort. **3.** *Rare.* the betrayal of a trust or confidence; breach of faith; treachery. [ME *tre(i)so(u)n* < AF; OF *traïson* < L *trāditiōn-* (s. of *trāditiō*) a handing over, betrayal. See TRADITION]
—**Syn. 1.** TREASON, SEDITION mean disloyalty or treachery to one's country or its government. TREASON is any attempt to overthrow the government or impair the well-being of a state to which one owes allegiance: the crime of giving aid or comfort to the enemies of one's government. SEDITION is any act, writing, speech, etc., directed unlawfully against state authority, the government, or the constitution or calculated to bring it into contempt or to incite others to hostility, ill will, or disaffection; it does not amount to treason and therefore is not a capital offense. **2.** See **disloyalty.**

trea·son·a·ble (trē′zə nə bəl), *adj.* **1.** of the nature of treason. **2.** involving treason; traitorous. [ME *tresonabill*] —**trea′son·a·ble·ness,** *n.* —**trea′son·a·bly,** *adv.*

trea·son·ous (trē′zə nəs), *adj.* treasonable. —**trea′son·ous·ly,** *adv.*

treasr., treasurer.

treas·ure (trezh′ər), *n., v.,* **-ured, -ur·ing.** —*n.* **1.** wealth or riches stored or accumulated, esp. in the form of precious metals, money, jewels, or plate. **2.** wealth, rich materials, or valuable things. **3.** any thing or person greatly valued or highly prized: *This book was his chief treasure.* —*v.t.* **4.** to retain carefully or keep in store, as in the mind. **5.** to regard or treat as precious; prize; cherish. **6.** to put away for security or future use, as money; lay up in store. [early ME *tresor* < OF < L *thēsaur(us)* storehouse, hoard. See THESAURUS] —**treas′ur·a·ble,** *adj.* —**treas′ure·less,** *adj.* —**Syn. 1, 6.** hoard. **5.** value, esteem.

treas′ure house′, 1. a building, room, or chamber used as a storage place for valuables; treasury. **2.** a place, source, or the like, where many things of value or worth may be found: *Reading is the key to the treasure house of ideas.*

treas·ure-house (trezh′ər hous′), *n., pl.* **-hous·es** (-hou′ziz). See **treasure house.**

treas′ure hunt′, a game in which hidden objects are sought competitively with the use of written directions or clues.

Treas′ure Is′land, a man-made island in San Francisco Bay, in W California: naval base. 380 acres.

treas·ur·er (trezh′ər ər), *n.* **1.** a person who is in charge of treasure or a treasury. **2.** an officer of a government, corporation, association, club, etc., who is charged with the receipt, care, and disbursement of money. [ME *tresorer* < AF < LL *thēsaurār(ius).* See THESAURUS, -ER[2]]

treas·ure-trove (trezh′ər trōv′), *n.* **1.** *Law.* any money, bullion, or the like, of unknown ownership, found hidden in the earth or any other place. **2.** anything of the nature of treasure that one finds; a valuable discovery: *Mother's attic was a treasure-trove when we were furnishing our apartment.* [< AF *tresor trové* treasure found]

treas·ur·y (trezh′ə rē), *n., pl.* **-ur·ies. 1.** a place where the funds of the government, a corporation, etc., are deposited, kept, and disbursed. **2.** the funds or revenue of a government, public or private corporation, etc. **3.** (*cap.*) the department of government that has control over the collection, management, and disbursement of the public revenue. **4.** a building, room, chest, or other place for the preservation of treasure or valuable objects. **5.** a collection or supply of excellent or highly prized writings, works of art, etc.: *a treasury of American poetry.* [ME *tresorie* < OF]

treas′ury bill′, an obligation of the U.S. government represented by promissory notes in denominations ranging from $1000 to $1,000,000, with a maturity of about 90 days but bearing no interest, and sold periodically at a discount on the market.

treas′ury bond′, any of various interest-bearing bonds issued by the U.S. Department of the Treasury and usually maturing over a long period of time.

treas′ury certif′icate, an obligation of the U.S. government represented by certificates in denominations ranging from $1000 to $1,000,000, maturing in one year or less with interest periodically payable by the redemption of coupons.

treas′ury note′, a note or bill issued by the U.S. Department of the Treasury, receivable as legal tender for all debts.

treas′ury stock′, outstanding shares of stock reacquired and held by the issuing corporation.

treat (trēt), *v.t.* **1.** to act or behave toward (a person) in some specified way: *to treat someone with respect.* **2.** to consider or regard in a specified way, and deal with accordingly: *to treat a matter as unimportant.* **3.** to deal with (a disease, patient, etc.) in order to relieve or cure, as a physician does. **4.** to deal with in speech or writing; discuss. **5.** to deal with, develop, or represent artistically, esp. in some specified manner or style: *to treat a theme realistically.* **6.** to subject to some agent or action in order to bring about a particular result: *to treat a substance with an acid.* **7.** to entertain; give hospitality to: *He treats visiting dignitaries in the lavish surroundings of his country estate.* **8.** to provide food, entertainment, gifts, etc., at one's own expense: *He treated them to dinner.* —*v.i.* **9.** to deal with a subject in speech or writing; discourse (often fol. by *of*): *a work that treats of the caste system in India.*

10. to give, or bear the expense of, a treat: *Is it my turn to treat?* 11. to carry on negotiations with a view to a settlement; discuss terms of settlement; negotiate. —*n.* 12. an entertainment of food, drink, amusement, etc., given by way of compliment or as an expression of friendly regard. 13. anything that affords particular pleasure or enjoyment: *This cool breeze is a real treat.* 14. the act of treating. 15. one's turn or time to treat. [ME *trete(n)* < OF *tretie(r), traitie(r)* < L *tractāre* to drag, handle < treat *tract(us)* drawn, ptp. of *trahere* to DRAG. See TRACT[1]] —**treat′a·ble,** *adj.* —**treat′er,** *n.* —**Syn.** 5. handle. 11. bargain, settle. 12. party.

trea·tise (trē′tis), *n.* a formal and systematic exposition in writing of the principles of a subject, generally longer and more detailed than an essay. [ME *tretis* < AF *tretiz.* See TREAT]

treat·ment (trēt′mənt), *n.* 1. the act or manner of treating. 2. action or behavior toward a person, animal, etc. 3. the systematic effort to cure illness and relieve symptoms, as with medicines, surgery, etc.; therapy. 4. literary or artistic handling, esp. with reference to style. 5. subjection to some agent or action.

trea·ty (trē′tē), *n., pl.* **-ties.** 1. a formal agreement between two or more nations in reference to peace, alliance, commerce, etc. 2. the formal document embodying such an international agreement. 3. any agreement or compact. 4. *Archaic.* negotiation with a view to settlement. 5. *Obs.* entreaty. [ME *trete* < AF < L *tractāt(us)* TRACTATE] —**trea′ty·less,** *adj.*

trea′ty port′, *Hist.* any of the ports in China, Japan, or Korea through which trade with foreign countries was permitted by special treaty.

Treb·bia (tʀeb′byä), *n.* a river in N Italy, flowing N into the Po at Piacenza: Romans defeated by Hannibal near here 218 B.C. 70 mi. long.

Treb·i·zond (treb′i zond′), *n.* 1. a medieval empire in NE Asia Minor 1204–1461. 2. Official name, **Trabzon.** a seaport in NE Turkey, on the Black Sea: an ancient Greek colony; capital of the medieval empire of Trebizond. 65,598 (1965).

tre·ble (treb′əl), *adj., n., v.,* **-bled, -bling.** —*adj.* 1. threefold; triple. 2. *Music.* a. of or pertaining to the highest part in harmonized music; soprano. b. of the highest pitch or range, as a voice part, voice, singer, or instrument. c. high in pitch; shrill. —*n.* 3. *Music.* a. the treble or soprano part. b. a treble voice, singer, or instrument. 4. a high or shrill voice or sound. 5. the highest-pitched peal of a bell. —*v.t., v.i.* 6. to make or become three times as much or as many; triple. [ME < MF < L *tripl(us)* TRIPLE] —**tre·bly** (treb′lē), *adv.*

tre′ble clef′, *Music.* a sign that locates the G above middle C, placed on the second line of the staff, counting up; G clef. Also called **violin clef.** See illus. at **clef.**

tre′ble staff′, *Music.* a staff, bearing a treble clef.

Tre·blin·ka (tʀe bleng′kä; *Eng.* trə bling′kə), *n.* a Nazi concentration camp in Poland, near Warsaw.

treb·u·chet (treb′yŏŏ shet′), *n.* a medieval engine of war having a pivoted beam with a heavy weight at one end and a sling for a missile at the other, the sling being pulled down for loading and released suddenly for hurling heavy missiles forcefully, so as to make a break in a wall, defense, etc. Also, **tre·buck·et** (trē′buk′it). [ME < MF = *trebuch(er)* (to) overturn, fall *(tre(s)* across, over, TRANS- + *buc* trunk of body < Gmc; cf. OE *buc* belly) + *-et* -ET]

tre·cen·to (trā chen′tō; *It.* tʀe chen′tô), *n.* *(often cap.)* the 14th century, with reference to Italy, and esp. to its art or literature. [< It, short for *mille trecento* a thousand three hundred] —**tre·cen′tist,** *n.*

tre cor·de (trā kôr′dā; *It.* tʀe kôʀ′de), with the soft pedal released (used as a musical direction in piano playing). [< It: lit., three strings]

tree (trē), *n., v.,* **treed, tree·ing.** —*n.* 1. a perennial plant having a permanent, woody, self-supporting main stem or trunk, ordinarily growing to a considerable height, and usually developing branches at some distance from the ground. 2. any of various shrubs, bushes, and herbaceous plants, as the banana, resembling a tree in form and size. 3. something resembling a tree in shape, as a clothes tree. 4. See **family tree.** 5. a pole, post, beam, bar, handle, or the like, as one forming part of some structure. 6. a saddletree. 7. a treelike group of crystals, as one forming in an electrolytic cell. 8. a gallows or gibbet. 9. *Archaic.* the cross on which Christ was crucified. 10. See **Christmas tree.** 11. **up a tree,** *Informal.* in a difficult or embarrassing situation; at a loss; stumped. —*v.t.* 12. to drive into or up a tree, as a hunted animal. 13. to stretch or shape on a tree, as a boot. 14. to furnish (a structure) with a tree, as a post or beam. [ME; OE *trēo(w)*; c. OFris, Icel *trē*, OS *treo*, Goth *triu;* akin to Gk *drŷs* oak, Skt, Avestan *dru* wood] —**tree′less,** *adj.* —**tree′less·ness,** *n.* —**tree′like′,** *adj.*

Tree (trē), *n.* **Sir Herbert Beer·bohm** (bēr′bōm), *(Herbert Beerbohm),* 1853–1917, English actor and theater manager (brother of Sir Max Beerbohm).

tree′ farm′, a tree-covered area managed as a business enterprise under a plan of reforestation that makes continuous production of timber possible.

tree′ fern′, any of various ferns, mostly tropical and chiefly of the family *Cyatheaceae*, that attain the size of trees, sending up a straight trunklike stem with foliage at the summit.

tree′ frog′, any of various arboreal frogs, esp. of the family *Hylidae*, usually having adhesive disks at the tip of each toe.

tree′ heath′, the brier, *Erica arborea.*

tree′ house′, a small house, esp. one for children to play in, built or placed in the branches of a tree.

tree·lined (trē′līnd), *adj.* having a line or lines of trees: *a treelined road.*

tree·nail (trē′nāl′, tren′əl, trun′əl), *n.* a wooden pin for fastening together timbers, as those of ships. Also, **trenail.** [ME *trenayl*]

tree′ of heav′en, an Asian simarubaceous tree, *Ailanthus altissima*, having rank-smelling flowers, often planted as a shade tree.

tree′ of knowl′edge of good′ and e′vil, the tree in the Garden of Eden bearing the forbidden fruit that was tasted by Adam and Eve. Gen. 2:17; 3:6–24. Also called **tree′ of knowl′edge.**

tree′ of life′, 1. a tree in the Garden of Eden that yielded food giving everlasting life. Gen 2:9; 3:22. 2. a tree in the heavenly Jerusalem with leaves for the healing of the nations. Rev. 22:2.

Tree′ Plant′ers State′, Nebraska (used as a nickname).

tree′ sur′gery, the repair of damaged trees, as by the removal of diseased parts, filling of cavities, etc. —**tree′ sur′geon.**

tree′ toad′. See **tree frog.**

tree·top (trē′top′), *n.* the top of a tree; the uppermost branches of a tree.

tre·fah (tʀā fä′; *Eng.* trā′fə), *adj.* *Hebrew.* terefah. Also, **tref** (*Eng.* trāf).

tre·foil (trē′foil), *n.* 1. any leguminous plant of the genus *Trifolium*, having usually digitate leaves of three leaflets and reddish, purple, yellow, or white flower heads, comprising the common clovers. 2. any of various similar plants. 3. an ornamental figure or structure resembling a trifoliolate leaf. 4. such an ornamental figure used by the Girl Scouts as its official emblem. —*adj.* 5. of, pertaining to, or shaped like a trefoil. [late ME < AF *trifoil* < L *trifol(ium)* triple leaf, the three-leaved plant, clover = *tri-* TRI- + *folium* leaf]

tre′foil arch′, *Archit.* an arch having the intrados on either side of the center formed like a cusp.

tre·ha·lose (trē′hə lōs′), *n.* *Chem.* a disaccharide, $C_{12}H_{22}O_{11}$, found in yeast, certain fungi, etc., and used to identify certain bacteria. [< NL *trehala* sugary substance forming the pupal covering of certain Asiatic beetles (< Turk *tīgālah* (< Pers) + -OSE[2]]

treil·lage (trā′lij), *n.* latticework; a lattice or trellis. [< F = *treille* vine-arbor, TRELLIS + *-age* -AGE]

Treitsch·ke (tʀīch′kə), *n.* **Hein·rich von** (hīn′ʀiᴋʜ fən), 1834–96, German historian.

trek (trek), *v.,* **trekked, trek·king,** *n.* —*v.i.* 1. to travel or migrate, esp. slowly or with difficulty. 2. (in South Africa) to travel by ox wagon. —*v.t.* 3. (in South Africa) (of a draft animal) to draw (a vehicle or load). —*n.* 4. a journey or trip, esp. one involving difficulty or hardship. 5. (in South Africa) a migration or expedition, as by ox wagon. 6. (in South Africa) a stage of a journey, esp. by ox wagon, between one stopping place and the next. [< D *trekk(en)* (to) draw, travel] —**trek′ker,** *n.*

Trellis (def. 3)

Tre·law·ney (tri lô′nē), *n.* **Edward John,** 1792–1881, English adventurer and author.

trel·lis (trel′is), *n.* 1. a frame or structure of latticework; lattice. 2. a framework of this kind used as a support for growing vines, climbing plants, etc. 3. a summerhouse, gazebo, arch, etc., made chiefly or completely of latticework. —*v.t.* 4. to furnish with a trellis. 5. to enclose in a trellis. 6. to train or support on a trellis: *trellised vines.* 7. to form into or like a trellis; interlace. [late ME *trelis* < MF *trelis* < LL *trilīcius* (r. L *trilīx*) woven with three threads = L *tri-* TRI- + *līci(um)* thread + *-us* adj. suffix] —**trel′lis·like′,** *adj.*

trel·lis·work (trel′is wûrk′), *n.* latticework.

trem·a·tode (trem′ə tōd′, trē′mə-), *n.* any parasitic platyhelminth or flatworm of the class *Trematoda*, having one or more external suckers; fluke. [< NL *Trematod(a)* class name < Gk *trēmatṓd(ēs)* having holes = *trēmat-* (s. of *trēma*) hole + *-ōdēs* -ODE[1]]

trem·ble (trem′bəl), *v.,* **-bled, -bling,** *n.* —*v.i.* 1. to shake involuntarily with quick, short movements, as from fear, excitement, weakness, or cold; quake; quiver; shake. 2. to be troubled or concerned with fear, apprehension, or the like. 3. (of things) to be affected with vibratory motion. 4. to be tremulous, as light, sound, etc.: *His voice trembled as he spoke.* —*n.* 5. the act of trembling. 6. a state or fit of trembling. 7. **trembles,** *(construed as sing.)* a. *Pathol.* any condition or disease characterized by continued trembling or shaking, as ague. b. See **milk sickness.** c. *Vet. Pathol.* a toxic condition of cattle and sheep caused by the eating of white snakeroot and characterized by muscular tremors. [ME < MF *trembl(er)* < ML *tremulāre* < L *tremul(us)* TREMULOUS; r. ME *trem(e)le(n)* < ML *tremulāre*] —**trem′bler,** *n.* —**trem′bling·ly,** *adv.* —**Syn.** 1. shudder. See **shake.** 3. oscillate.

trem·bly (trem′blē), *adj.,* **-bli·er, -bli·est.** quivering; tremulous; shaking.

tre·men·dous (tri men′dəs), *adj.* 1. *Informal.* extraordinarily great in size, amount, or intensity. 2. dreadful or awful, as in character or effect; exciting fear; frightening; terrifying. 3. *Informal.* extraordinary in excellence: *a tremendous piano player.* [< L *tremendus* dreadful, to be shaken by = *trem(ere)* (to) shake, quake + *-endus* fut. pass. part. suffix] —**tre·men′dous·ly,** *adv.* —**tre·men′dous·ness,** *n.* —**Syn.** 1. See **huge.**

tre·mis·sis (tri mis′is), *n., pl.* **-mis·ses** (-mis′ēz). 1. Also called **triens.** a gold coin of the Eastern Roman Empire, the third part of a solidus, first issued in the 3rd century B.C. 2. a Merovingian gold coin imitating this. [< LL = L *tre(s)* three + *-missis* as in *semissis* = *semis* SEMI- + *as* AS[2]]

trem·o·lant (trem′ə lənt), *adj.* having a tremulous or vibrating tone, as certain pipes of an organ. [< G < It *tremolant(e)* TREMULANT]

trem·o·lite (trem′ə līt′), *n.* a variety of amphibole, $Ca_2Mg_5Si_8O_{22}(OH)_2$, usually occurring in bladed crystals. [named after *Tremol(a)*, valley in Switzerland; see -ITE[1]]

trem·o·lo (trem′ə lō′), *n., pl.* **-los.** *Music.* 1. a tremulous or vibrating effect produced on certain instruments and in the human voice, as to express emotion. 2. a mechanical device in an organ by which such an effect is produced. [< It: trembling < L *tremul(us)* TREMULOUS]

trem·or (trem′ər, trē′mər), *n.* 1. involuntary shaking of the body or limbs, as from disease, fear, weakness, or excitement; a fit of trembling. 2. any tremulous or vibratory movement; vibration: *The earth tremors lasted all night.* **3.** a trembling or quivering effect, as of light. **4.** a quavering sound, as of the voice. [ME < L: a trembling = *trem(ere)* (to) tremble + *-or* -OR¹] —**trem′or·less·ly,** *adv.* —**trem′or·ous,** *adj.* —**Syn. 1.** shudder, shiver, quaver, quiver.

trem·u·lant (trem′yə lənt), *adj.* trembling; tremulous. [< ML *tremulant-* (s. of *tremulāns*) prp. of *tremulāre* to TREMBLE; see -ANT]

trem·u·lous (trem′yə ləs), *adj.* **1.** (of persons, the body, etc.) characterized by trembling, as from fear, nervousness, or weakness. **2.** timid; timorous; fearful. **3.** (of things) vibratory, shaking, or quivering. **4.** (of writing) done with a trembling hand. [< L *tremulus* = *trem(ere)* (to) tremble + *-ulus* adj. suffix denoting qualities] —**trem′u·lous·ly,** *adv.* —**trem′u·lous·ness,** *n.* —**Syn. 2.** frightened; afraid.

tre·nail (trē′nāl′, tren′ᵊl, trun′ᵊl), *n.* treenail.

trench (trench), *n.* **1.** *Fort.* a long, narrow excavation in the ground, the earth from which is thrown up in front to serve as a shelter from the enemy's fire. **2. trenches,** a system of such excavations and their embankments. **3.** a deep furrow, ditch, or cut. **4.** *Phys. Geog.* a long, steep-sided, narrow depression of great depth in the ocean floor. —*v.t.* **5.** to surround or fortify with a trench or trenches; entrench. **6.** to cut a trench or trenches in. **7.** to set or place in a trench. **8.** to form (a furrow, ditch, etc.) by cutting into or through something. **9.** to make a cut in; cut into; carve. **10.** *Obs.* to sever or slash. —*v.i.* **11.** to dig a trench or trenches. **12.** *Obs.* to enter so as to affect intimately (usually fol. by *into* or *unto*). **13. trench on** or **upon, a.** to encroach or infringe on. **b.** to come close to; verge on: *His remarks were trenching on poor taste.* [ME *trenche* path made by cutting < OF: act of cutting, a cut < *trenchier* to cut < VL **trincāre* for L *truncāre* to lop; see TRUNCATE]

Trench (trench), *n.* **Richard Chen·e·vix** (shen′ə vē), 1807–86, English clergyman and scholar, born in Ireland.

trench·ant (tren′chənt), *adj.* **1.** incisive or keen, as language or a person: *trenchant wit.* **2.** vigorous; effective; energetic: *a trenchant policy of political reform.* **3.** clearly or sharply defined; clear-cut; distinct. **4.** *Archaic.* sharp-edged: *a trenchant blade.* [ME *tranchaunt* < AF = OF *trenchant,* prp. of *trenchier* to cut. See TRENCH, -ANT] —**trench′an·cy,** *n.* —**trench′ant·ly,** *adv.* —**Syn. 1.** sharp, biting, acute.

trench′ coat′, a waterproof, usually double-breasted, belted overcoat, with large pockets and straps on the shoulders and lower sleeves.

trench·er (tren′chər), *n.* **1.** a person who digs trenches. **2.** *Archaic.* **a.** a rectangular or circular flat piece of wood on which meat or other food is served or carved. **b.** such a piece of wood and the food on it. **c.** food; the pleasures of good eating. [ME *trenchour* something to cut with or on < AF, MF *trencheoir.* See TRENCH, -ORY²]

trench·er·man (tren′chər mən), *n., pl.* **-men. 1.** a person who has a hearty appetite; heavy eater. **2.** *Archaic.* a hanger-on; parasite.

trench′ fe′ver, *Pathol.* a recurrent fever, often suffered by soldiers in trenches in World War I, caused by a rickettsia transmitted by the body louse.

trench′ foot′, *Pathol.* a disease of the feet due to exposure to cold and wet, formerly common among soldiers serving in trenches.

trench′ knife′, a short knife for stabbing, sometimes equipped with brass knuckles as a guard, used in modern warfare in hand-to-hand combat.

trench′ mor′tar, a portable, muzzle-loaded mortar, usually having a smooth bore, fired at high angles of elevation to reach concealed enemy targets.

trench′ mouth′. See **Vincent's angina.** [so called from the high incidence among soldiers in the trenches]

trench′ war′fare, combat in which each side occupies a system of protective trenches.

trend (trend), *n.* **1.** the general course or prevailing tendency; drift: *trends in the teaching of foreign languages; the trend of events.* **2.** style; vogue: *the new trend in women's apparel.* **3.** the general direction followed by a road, river, coastline, or the like. —*v.i.* **4.** to have a general tendency, as events, conditions, etc. **5.** to tend to take a particular direction; extend in some direction indicated. **6.** to veer or turn off in a specified direction, as a river or mountain range. [ME *trend(en),* OE *trendan;* akin to OE *trinde* ball, D *trent* circumference, Sw *trind* round. See TRINDLE, TRUNDLE] —**Syn. 5.** stretch, run, incline.

trend·y (trend′ē), *adj.,* **-i·er, i·est. 1.** of, in, or pertaining to the most recent trend or style. **2.** up-to-date, stylish, or chic: *the trendy young generation.*

Treng·ga·nu (treng gä′nōō), *n.* a state in Malaysia, on the SE Malay Peninsula. 317,049 (est. 1961); 5050 sq. mi. *Cap.:* Kuala Trengganu.

Trent (trent), *n.* **1.** Italian, **Trento.** Ancient, **Tridentum.** a city in N Italy, on the Adige River. 74,766 (1961). **2. Council of,** the ecumenical council of the Roman Catholic Church that met at Trent intermittently from 1545 to 1563: defined church doctrine and condemned the Reformation. **3.** a river in central England, flowing NE from Staffordshire to the Humber. 170 mi. long.

trente et qua·rante (tränt′ ā kə ränt′; *Fr.* tʀäɴ tā ka ʀäɴt′). See **rouge et noir.** [< F: thirty and forty]

Tren·ti·no-Al·to A·di·ge (tʀen tē′nô äl′tô ä′dē je), a region in NE Italy. 785,491 (1961); 5256 sq. mi.

Tren·to (tʀen′tô), *n.* Italian name of **Trent.**

Tren·ton (tren′tᵊn), *n.* a city in and the capital of New Jersey, in the W part, on the Delaware River: Washington defeated Hessian troops here 1776. 104,638 (1970).

tre·pan¹ (tri pan′), *n., v.,* **-panned, -pan·ning.** —*n.* **1.** a tool for cutting shallow holes by removing a core. **2.** *Surg.* an obsolete form of the trephine resembling a carpenter's bit and brace. —*v.t.* **3.** *Mach.* **a.** to cut circular disks out of plate stock using a rotating cutter. **b.** to cut a concentric groove around a bored or drilled hole. **4.** to operate upon with a trepan; perforate by a trepan; trephine. [late ME *trepane* < ML *trepan(um)* crown saw < Gk *trýpanon* borer, akin to *trýpa* hole, *trypân* to bore] —**trep·a·na·tion** (trep′ə nā′shən), *n.* —**tre·pan′ner,** *n.*

tre·pan² (tri pan′), *n., v.,* **-panned, -pan·ning.** *Archaic.* —*n.* **1.** a person who ensnares or entraps others. **2.** a stratagem; a trap. —*v.t.* **3.** to ensnare or entrap. **4.** to entice. **5.** to cheat or swindle. Also, **trapan.** [earlier *trapan* = TRAP¹ + *-an* < ?]

tre·pang (tri pang′), *n.* any of various wormlike holothurians or sea cucumbers, as *Holothuria edulis,* used as food in China. [< Malay *trīpang*]

tre·phine (tri fīn′, -fēn′), *n., v.,* **-phined, -phin·ing.** *Surg.* —*n.* **1.** a small circular saw with a center pin mounted on a strong hollow metal shaft to which is attached a transverse handle: used in surgery to remove circular disks of bone from the skull. —*v.t.* **2.** to operate upon with a trephine. [sp. var. of *trefine,* orig. *trafine,* b. *trapan* (var. of TREPAN¹) and L phrase *trēs fīnēs* the three ends (the inventor's explanation)] —**treph·i·na·tion** (tref′ə nā′shən), *n.*

trep·i·da·tion (trep′i dā′shən), *n.* **1.** tremulous fear, alarm, or agitation; perturbation. **2.** trembling or quivering movement; vibration; tremor. **3.** *Pathol.* rapid, repeated, muscular flexion and extension of muscles of the extremities or lower jaw; clonus. [< L *trepidātiōn-* (s. of *trepidātiō*) = *trepidāt(us)* hurried, alarmed (ptp. of *trepidāre;* see INTREPID, -ATE¹) + *-iōn-* -ION] —**Syn. 1.** trembling, fright.

trep·o·ne·ma (trep′ə nē′mə), *n., pl.* **-mas, -ma·ta** (-mə tə). any of several anaerobic spirochetes of the genus *Treponema,* certain species of which are parasitic in and pathogenic for man and warm-blooded animals. [< NL: genus name < Gk *trép(ein)* (to) turn + *-o-* -O- + *nêma* thread]

trep·o·ne·ma·to·sis (trep′ə nē′mə tō′sis), *n.* *Pathol.* an infection caused by an organism of the genus *Treponema,* as syphilis or yaws. [< NL *Treponemat-* (s. of *Treponema;* see TREPONEMA) + -OSIS]

tres·pass (tres′pəs, -pas′), *n.* **1.** *Law.* **a.** an unlawful act on the person, property, or rights of another, committed with force, actual or implied. **b.** a wrongful entry upon the lands of another. **c.** the action to recover damages for a trespass. **2.** an encroachment or intrusion. **3.** an offense, sin, or wrong. —*v.i.* **4.** *Law.* to commit a trespass. **5.** to encroach on a person's privacy, time, etc.; infringe (usually fol. by *on* or *upon*). **6.** to commit a transgression or offense; transgress; offend; sin. [ME *trespas* < OF < *trespasser* = *tres-* (< L *trāns-* TRANS-) + *passer* to PASS] —**tres′pass·er,** *n.* —**Syn. 2.** invasion, infringement. **3.** transgression, fault, misdeed; crime, misdemeanor. **4, 5.** TRESPASS, ENCROACH, INFRINGE, INTRUDE imply overstepping boundaries and assuming possession of others' property or crowding onto the rights of others. To TRESPASS is to pass unlawfully within the boundaries of another's property: *Hunters trespassed on the farmer's fields.* To ENCROACH is to creep, as it were, gradually and often stealthily, upon territory, rights, or privileges, so that a footing is imperceptibly established: *The sea encroached upon the land.* To INFRINGE is to break in upon or invade rights, customs, or the like, by violating or disregarding them: *to infringe upon a patent.* To INTRUDE is to thrust oneself into the presence of a person or into places or circumstances where one is not welcome: *to intrude into a private conversation.*

tress (tres), *n.* **1.** Usually, **tresses.** long locks or curls of unbraided or unbound hair, esp. those of a woman. **2.** *Archaic.* a plait or braid of hair, esp. of a woman. [ME *tresse* < MF: plait or braid of hair < ?]

tressed (trest), *adj.* **1.** (of the hair) arranged or formed into tresses; braided; plaited. **2.** having tresses (usually used in combination): *auburn-tressed; golden-tressed.* [ME]

tres·sure (tresh′ər), *n.* *Heraldry.* a narrower diminutive of the orle, usually ornamented with fleurs-de-lis at the edges and often doubled. [late ME < MF = *tress(er)* (to) braid, plait (< *tresse* TRESS) + *-ure* -URE; r. ME *tressour* < MF *tresseor, tressoir*] —**tres′sured,** *adj.*

tres·tine (tres′tīn), *n.* See **royal antler.** [? < L *trēs* three + TINE]

tres·tle (tres′əl), *n.* **1.** a frame typically composed of a horizontal bar or beam rigidly joined or fitted at each end to the top of a transverse A-frame, used as a barrier, a transverse support for planking, etc.; horse. **2.** *Civ. Eng.* **a.** one of a number of bents, having sloping sides of framework or piling, for supporting the deck or stringers of a bridge. **b.** a bridge made of these. [ME *trestel* < MF; OF *trestre* (by dissimilation) < L *trānstr(um)* crossbeam. See TRANSOM]

Trestle (def. 2b)

tres·tle·tree (tres′əl trē′), *n.* *Naut.* either of a pair of timbers or metal shapes lying along the tops of the hounds or cheeks of a mast to support crosstrees or a top.

tres·tle·work (tres′əl wûrk′), *n.* a structural system composed of trestles.

tret (tret), *n.* (formerly) an allowance for waste, after deduction for tare. [< AF, var. of *trait* TRAIT]

Tre·vel·yan (tri vel′yən, -vil′-), *n.* **1. George Macaulay,** 1876–1962, English historian. **2.** his father, **Sir George Otto,** 1838–1928, English writer and statesman.

Treves (trēvz), *n.* Trier. French, **Trèves** (tʀev).

Tre·vi·so (tʀe vē′zô), *n.* a city in NE Italy: medieval palaces and cathedral. 75,185 (1961).

trews (trōōz), *n.* (*construed as pl.*) close-fitting tartan trousers, worn esp. by certain Scottish regiments. [< Ir and ScotGael *triubhas* < OF *trebus* breeches]

trey (trā), *n.* a playing card or a die having three pips. [ME < MF *trei(s)* < L *trēs* three]

trez·tine (trez′tīn), *n.* See **royal antler.**

trf, **1.** transfer. **2.** tuned-radio-frequency.

tri-, a learned borrowing from Latin or Greek meaning "three," used in the formation of compound words: *triacid; triatomic.* [ME < L, comb. form repr. L *trēs, tria,* Gk *treîs, tria* three]

tri·a·ble (trī′ə bəl), **1.** subject or liable to judicial trial. **2.** *Obs.* that may be tried, attempted, or tested. [late ME < AF; see TRY, -ABLE] —**tri′a·ble·ness,** *n.*

tri·ac·id (trī as′id), *adj. Chem.* **1.** capable of combining with three molecules of a monobasic acid: *a triacid base.* **2.** noting acid salts containing three replaceable hydrogen atoms.

tri·ad (trī′ad), *n.* **1.** a group of three, esp. of three closely related or associated persons or things. **2.** *Chem.* **a.** an element, atom, or group having a valence of three. Cf. **monad** (def. 2), **dyad** (def. 3). **b.** a group of three closely related compounds or elements, as isomers or halides. **3.** *Music.* a chord of three tones, esp. one consisting of a given tone with its major or minor third and its perfect, augmented, or diminished fifth. [< L *triad-* (s. of *trias*) < Gk; see TRI-, -AD] —**tri·ad′ic,** *adj.* —**tri′ad·ism,** *n.*

tri·age (trē äzh′), *n., adj., v.,* **-aged, ag·ing.** —*n.* **1.** the process of sorting victims, as of a battle or disaster, to determine priority or appropriate place of medical treatment. **2.** the determination of priorities for action in an emergency. —*adj.* **3.** of, pertaining to, or performing the task of triage: *a triage officer.* —*v.t.* **4.** to act on or in by triage: *to triage a crisis.* [< F: lit., sorting, selecting]

tri·al (trī′əl, trīl), *n.* **1.** *Law.* **a.** the examination before a judicial tribunal of the facts put in issue in a cause, often including issues of law as well as of fact. **b.** the determination of a person's guilt or innocence by due process of law. **2.** the act of trying, testing, or putting to the proof. **3.** test; proof. **4.** an attempt or effort to do something. **5.** a tentative or experimental action in order to ascertain results; experiment. **6.** the state or position of a person or thing being tried or tested; probation. **7.** subjection to suffering or grievous experiences; a distressed or painful state: *comfort in the hour of trial.* **8.** an affliction or trouble. **9.** a trying, distressing, or annoying thing or person. —*adj.* **10.** of, pertaining to, or employed in a trial. **11.** done or made by way of trial, test, proof, or experiment. **12.** used in testing, experimenting, etc. **13.** acting or serving as a sample, experimental specimen, etc.: *a trial offer.* [TRY + -AL[2]]
—**Syn. 2, 3, 5.** examination, proof. TRIAL, EXPERIMENT, TEST imply an attempt to find out something or to find out about something. TRIAL is the general word for a trying of anything: *articles sent for ten days' free trial.* EXPERIMENT looks to the future, and is a trial conducted to prove or illustrate the truth or validity of something, or an attempt to discover something new: *an experiment in chemistry.* TEST is a stronger and more specific word, referring to a trial under approved and fixed conditions, or a final and decisive trial as a conclusion of past experiments: *a test of a new airplane.*

tri′al and er′ror, experimentation or investigation in which various methods or means are tried and faulty ones eliminated. —**tri′al-and-er′ror,** *adj.*

tri′al bal′ance, *Bookkeeping.* a statement of all the open debit and credit items, made preliminary to balancing a double-entry ledger.

tri′al balloon′, a tentative or initial statement, policy, program, or the like, issued publicly as a means of determining reactions in advance of a final or full scale one.

tri′al law′yer, a lawyer who specializes in appearing before a court of law on behalf of his clients.

tri′al mar′riage, a nonconjugal relationship in which a man and woman agree to live together for a specified period of time, esp. in the expectation of having the period terminate in legal marriage. Cf **companionate marriage.**

tri′al run′, a preliminary performance of action in order to ascertain results, as of the operation of a ship, the effectiveness of a play, etc.; an initial trial or test of something.

tri·an·gle (trī′ang′gəl), *n.* **1.** a closed plane figure having three sides and three angles. **2.** a flat triangular piece, usually of plastic, with straight edges, used in connection with a T square for drawing perpendicular lines, geometric figures, etc. **3.** any three-cornered or three-sided figure, object, or piece: *a triangle of land.* **4.** a musical percussion instrument that consists of a steel rod bent into triangular shape, open at one corner, and is struck with a small, straight steel rod. **5.** a group of three; triad. **6.** a situation involving three persons, esp. one in which two people are in love with a third. [ME < L *triangul(um),* n. use of neut. of *triangulus* three-cornered] —**tri′an·gled,** *adj.*

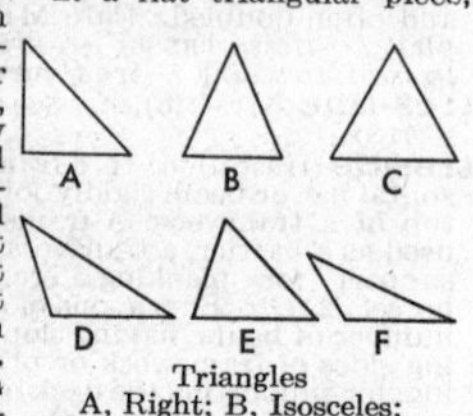

Triangles
A, Right; B, Isosceles; C, Equilateral; D, Obtuse; E, Acute; F, Scalene

tri·an·gu·lar (trī ang′gyə lər), *adj.* **1.** pertaining to or having the form of a triangle; three-cornered. **2.** having a triangle as base or cross section: *a triangular prism.* **3.** comprising three parts or elements; triple. **4.** pertaining to or involving a group of three, as three persons, parties, or things. [< L *triangulār(is).* See TRIANGLE, -AR[1]] —**tri·an·gu·lar·i·ty** (trī ang′gyə lar′i tē), *n.* —**tri·an′gu·lar·ly,** *adv.*

tri·an·gu·late (*adj.* trī ang′gyə lit, -lāt′; *v.* trī ang′gyə-lāt′), *adj., v.,* **-lat·ed, -lat·ing.** —*adj.* **1.** composed of or marked with triangles. —*v.t.* **2.** to make triangular. **3.** to divide into triangles. **4.** to survey (an area) by triangulation. [< ML *triangulāt(us),* ptp. of *triangulāre* to make triangles]

tri·an·gu·la·tion (trī ang′gyə lā′shən), *n. Survey., Navig.* **1.** a technique for establishing the distance between two points or the relative position of two or more points by using such points as vertices of a triangle or series of triangles, such that each has a side of known or measurable length (**base** or **base line**) that permits the size of the angles of the triangle and the length of its other two sides to be established by observations taken from the two ends of the base line. **2.** the triangles thus formed and measured. [< ML *triangulātiōn-* (s. of *triangulātiō*) the making of triangles]

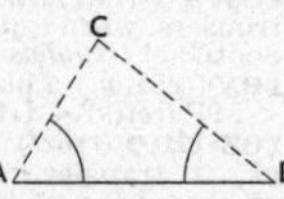

Triangulation
A, B, Points known; C, Point visible from both A and B, the position of which is plotted by measuring angles A and B

tri·ar·chy (trī′är kē), *n., pl.* **-chies.** **1.** government by three persons. **2.** a set of three joint rulers; triumvirate. **3.** a country divided into three governments. [< Gk *triarchía* triumvirate]

Tri·as·sic (trī as′ik), *Geol.* —*adj.* **1.** noting or pertaining to a period of the Mesozoic era occurring from 180,000,000 to 220,000,000 years ago; characterized by volcanic activity and the advent of dinosaurs and marine reptiles. See table at **era.** —*n.* **2.** the Triassic period or system. Also, **Tri·as** (trī′əs). [< L *trias* group of three (see TRIAD) + -IC; so called because it has three subdivisions]

tri·ath·lon (trī ath′lon), *n.* an athletic contest comprising three consecutive events, usually swimming, bicycling, and distance running. —**tri·ath′lete,** *n.*

tri·at′ic stay′ (trī at′ik), *Naut.* **1.** a backstay for the head of a fore-and-aft-rigged topmast, running down to the head of the lower mast next aft. **2.** a horizontal wire running aft from a fore topmast head to some other point for hoisting signals. [? TRI- + -ATE[1] + -IC]

tri·a·tom·ic (trī′ə tom′ik), *adj. Chem.* **1.** having three atoms in a molecule. **2.** having three replaceable hydrogen atoms. **3.** having three replaceable hydroxyl groups. —**tri′a·tom′i·cal·ly,** *adv.*

tri·ax·i·al (trī ak′sē əl), *adj.* having three axes.

tri·a·zine (trī′ə zēn′, -zin, trī az′ēn, -in), *n. Chem.* **1.** any of a group of three compounds having the formula $C_3H_3N_3$. **2.** any of a number of their derivatives.

tri·a·zole (trī′ə zōl′, trī az′ōl), *n. Chem.* **1.** any of a group of four compounds containing three nitrogen and two carbon atoms arranged in a five-membered ring and having the formula $C_2H_3N_3$. **2.** any of a number of their derivatives. —**tri·a·zol·ic** (trī′ə zol′ik), *adj.*

trib·ade (trib′əd), *n.* a woman who practices tribadism, esp. a female homosexual who assumes the male role. [< F < L *tribad-* (s. of *tribas*) < Gk: lit., rubbing = *tríb(ein)* (to) rub + *-ad-* -ADE[2]] —**tri·bad·ic** (tri bad′ik), *adj.*

trib·a·dism (trib′ə diz′əm), *n.* lesbianism.

trib·al (trī′bəl), *adj.* of, pertaining to, or characteristic of a tribe or tribes: *tribal customs; a tribal dance.* —**trib′al·ly,** *adv.*

trib·al·ism (trī′bə liz′əm), *n.* **1.** the customs and beliefs of tribal life and society. **2.** strong loyalty to one's own tribe, party, or group. —**trib′al·ist,** *n.*

tri·ba·sic (trī bā′sik), *adj. Chem.* **1.** (of an acid) having three atoms of hydrogen replaceable by basic atoms or groups. **2.** containing three atoms or groups, each having a valence of one, as tribasic sodium phosphate, Na_3PO_4.

tribe (trīb), *n.* **1.** any aggregate of people united by ties of descent from a common ancestor, community of customs and traditions, adherence to the same leaders, etc. **2.** a local division of an aboriginal people. **3.** a class or type of animals, plants, articles, or the like. **4.** *Stockbreeding.* a group of animals, esp. cattle, descended through the female line from a common female ancestor. **5.** *Biol.* **a.** a category in the classification of plants and animals between a family and a genus or, sometimes, between an order and a family. **b.** any group of plants or animals. **6.** a company, group, or number of persons. **7.** *Facetious.* **a.** *Often Disparaging.* a class or set of persons. **b.** a family. **8.** *Rom. Hist.* **a.** any one of three divisions of the people representing the Latin, Sabine, and Etruscan settlements. **b.** any of the later political divisions of the people. **9.** *Gk. Hist.* a phyle. [ME < L *trib(us)* tribe, orig. each of the three divisions of the Roman people]

tribes·man (trībz′mən), *n., pl.* **-men.** a member of a tribe.

tribo-, a learned borrowing from Greek meaning "friction," used in the formation of compound words: *triboelectricity.* [comb. form repr. Gk *tríbein* to rub]

tri·bo·e·lec·tric·i·ty (trī′bō i lek tris′i tē, -ē′lek-, trib′ō-), *n. Elect.* electricity generated by friction. —**tri·bo·e·lec·tric** (trī′bō i lek′trik, trib′ō-), *adj.*

tri·bo·lu·mi·nes·cence (trī′bō lo͞o′mə nes′əns, trib′ō-), *n. Physics.* luminescence produced by friction. —**tri′bo·lu′mi·nes′cent,** *adj.*

tri·brach (trī′brak, trib′rak), *n. Pros.* a foot of three short syllables. [< L *tribrach(ys)* < Gk *tríbrachys* = *tri-* TRI- + *brachýs* short; see BRACHY-] —**tri·brach′ic,** *adj.*

trib·u·la·tion (trib′yə lā′shən), *n.* **1.** grievous trouble; severe trial or suffering. **2.** an instance of this; an affliction, trouble, etc. [ME < L *trībulātiōn-* (s. of *trībulātiō*) distress, trouble = *trībulāt(us)* oppressed (ptp. of *trībulāre*), lit., threshed (= *trībul(um)* threshing platform (*trī-* perf. s. of *terere* to rub, crush + *-bulum* n. suffix of instrument) + *-ātus* -ATE[1]) + *-iōn-* -ION] —**Syn. 1.** hardship, distress, adversity.

tri·bu·nal (trī byo͞on′ᵊl, tri-), *n.* **1.** a court of justice. **2.** a place or seat of judgment. [< L: judgment seat = *tribūn(us)* TRIBUNE[1] + *-āl(e)* neut. of *-ālis* -AL[1]]

trib·u·nate (trib′yə nit, -nāt′), *n. Hist.* **1.** the office of tribune. **2.** a body of tribunes. [< L *tribūnāt(us)*]

trib·une[1] (trib′yo͞on *or, esp. Brit.,* tri′byo͞on), *n.* **1.** a person who upholds or defends the rights of the people. **2.** *Rom. Hist.* **a.** any of various administrative officers, esp. one of 10 officers elected to protect the interests and rights of the plebeians from the patricians. **b.** any of the six officers of a legion who rotated in commanding the legion during the year. [ME < L *tribūn(us),* orig., the head of a TRIBE]

trib·une[2] (trib′yo͞on), *n.* **1.** a raised platform for a speaker; a dais, rostrum, or pulpit. **2.** a raised part or gallery with seats, as in a church. **3.** (in a Christian basilica) the bishop's throne, occupying a recess or apse at one end. **4.** the apse itself. [< ML *tribūn(a)*; r. L *tribūnāle* TRIBUNAL]

trib·u·tar·y (trib′yə ter′ē), *n., pl.* **-tar·ies,** *adj.* —*n.* **1.** a stream contributing its flow to a larger stream or other body of water (opposed to *distributary*). **2.** a person or nation that pays tribute, as in acknowledgment of subjugation. —*adj.* **3.** (of a stream) flowing into a larger stream or other body of water. **4.** furnishing subsidiary aid; contributory; auxiliary. **5.** paying or required to pay tribute. **6.** paid as tribute. **7.** subject; subjugated; subordinate: *a tributary nation.* [ME < L *tribūtāri(us)* of tribute] —**trib′u·tar′i·ly,** *adv.*

trib·ute (trib′yo͞ot), *n.* **1.** a gift, testimonial, compliment, or the like, given as due or in acknowledgment of gratitude, esteem, or regard. **2.** a stated sum or other valuable consideration paid by one sovereign or state to another in acknowledgment of subjugation or as the price of peace, security, protection, or the like. **3.** a rent, tax, or the like, as that paid by a subject to a sovereign. **4.** any exacted or enforced payment or contribution. **5.** obligation or liability to make such payment. [ME *tribut* < L *tribūt(um)* a levied payment (n. use of neut. of ptp. of *tribuere* to assign, allot) =

tribū- (ptp. s. of *tribuere*) + *-tum* neut. of *-tus* ptp. suffix]
—Syn. 1. recognition, commendation, eulogy. **4.** levy, toll, impost, duty.

trice[1] (trīs), *n.* a very short time; moment or instant: *She added the figures in a trice.* [late ME *tryse;* special use of TRICE[2]]

trice[2] (trīs), *v.t.*, **triced, tric·ing.** *Naut.* **1.** to pull or haul with a rope. **2.** to haul up and fasten with a rope (usually fol. by *up*). [ME < MD *trisen* to hoist = *trīse* pulley + *-en* inf. suffix]

tri·cen·ten·ni·al (trī/sen ten/ē əl), *adj.*, *n.* tercentenary.

tri·ceps (trī/seps), *n.*, *pl.* **-ceps·es** (-sep siz), **-ceps.** *Anat.* a muscle having three heads or points of origin, esp. the muscle on the back of the upper arm whose action straightens the elbow. [< L: three-headed = *tri-* TRI- + *-ceps* headed, akin to *caput* head]

trich-, var. of **tricho-** before a vowel: *trichite.*

tri·chi·a·sis (tri kī/ə sis), *n.* *Pathol.* a condition in which the eyelashes grow inward. [< LL < Gk *trichíasis.* See TRICH-, -IASIS]

tri·chi·na (tri kī/nə), *n.*, *pl.* **-nae** (-nē). a nematode, *Trichinella spiralis,* the adults of which live in the intestine and produce larvae that encyst in the muscle tissue. [< NL < Gk *trīchina,* n. use of fem. of *trīchinos* of hair. See TRICH-, -INE[1]]

trich·i·nise (trik/ə nīz/), *v.t.*, **-nised, -nis·ing.** *Chiefly Brit.* trichinize. **—trich/i·ni·sa/tion,** *n.*

trich·i·nize (trik/ə nīz/), *v.t.*, **-nized, -niz·ing.** *Pathol.* to infect with trichinae. **—trich/i·ni·za/tion,** *n.*

Trich·i·nop·o·ly (trik/ə nop/ə lē), *n.* former name of **Tiruchirapalli.**

trich·i·no·sis (trik/ə nō/sis), *n.* *Pathol.* a disease resulting from infestation with *Trichinella spiralis,* caused by ingestion of undercooked infested meat, esp. pork, and characterized by fever, muscle weakness, diarrhea, etc. Also, **trich·i·ni·a·sis** (trik/ə nī/ə sis). [TRICHIN(A) + -OSIS]

trich·i·nous (trik/ə nəs), *adj.* *Pathol.* **1.** pertaining to or of the nature of trichinosis. **2.** infected with trichinae. [TRICHIN(A) + -OUS]

trich·ite (trik/īt), *n.* *Petrog.* any of various minute, hairlike mineral bodies occurring in certain vitreous igneous rocks, esp. obsidian. **—tri·chit·ic** (tri kit/ik), *adj.*

tri·chlo·ride (trī klôr/īd, -id, -klôr/-), *n.* *Chem.* a chloride having three atoms of chlorine, as ferric chloride, $FeCl_3$.

tri·chlo/ro·phe·nox·y·a·ce/tic ac/id (trī klôr/ə fə-nok/sē ə sē/tik, -set/ik, -klôr/-, -klôr/-, -klôr/-), *Chem.* a water-insoluble solid, $Cl_3C_6H_2OCH_2CO_2H$, used chiefly for killing weeds. Also called **2, 4, 5–T.** [TRI- + CHLORO-[2] + PHEN- + OXY-[2] + ACETIC]

tricho-, a learned borrowing from Greek meaning "hair," used in the formation of compound words: *trichocyst.* Also, *esp. before a vowel,* **trich-.** [< Gk *tricho-,* comb. form of *thríx,* (*thrichós* gen.)]

trich·o·cyst (trik/ə sist/), *n.* *Zool.* an organ of offense and defense embedded in the outer protoplasm of many infusorians, consisting of a small elongated sac containing a fine, hairlike filament capable of being ejected. **—trich/o·cyst/ic,** *adj.*

trich·o·gyne (trik/ə jīn/, -jin), *n.* *Bot.* a hairlike prolongation of a carpogonium, serving as a receptive organ for the spermatium. **—trich·o·gyn·i·al** (trik/ə jin/ē əl), **trich/o·gyn/ic,** *adj.*

trich·oid (trik/oid), *adj.* resembling hair; hairlike.

tri·chol·o·gy (tri kol/ə jē), *n.* the science dealing with the study of the hair and its diseases. **—tri·chol/o·gist,** *n.*

tri·chome (trī/kōm, trik/ōm), *n.* *Bot.* an outgrowth from the epidermis of plants, as a hair. [< Gk *trichō̄m(a)* growth of hair. See TRICH-, -OMA] **—tri·chom·ic** (tri kom/ik), *adj.*

trich·o·mon·ad (trik/ə mon/ad), *n.* any flagellate protozoan of the genus *Trichomonas,* parasitic in man or animals. [< NL *Trichomonad-* (s. of *Trichomonas*) genus name] **—trich·o·mon·a·dal** (trik/ə mon/ə dᵊl), **trich·o·mon·al** (trik/ə mon/ᵊl, -mōn/-, tri kom/ə nᵊl), *adj.*

trich·o·mo·ni·a·sis (trik/ə mə nī/ə sis), *n.* **1.** *Pathol.* infestation with a trichomonad, as vaginitis characterized by a persistent discharge and itching, caused by the trichomonad *Trichomonas vaginalis.* **2.** *Vet. Pathol.* **a.** a venereal disease of domestic cattle, characterized by pus in the uterine cavity, sterility, and abortion, caused by the trichomonad *T. fetus.* **b.** a disease of birds, characterized by diarrhea, and caused by one of several trichomonads. [TRICHOMON(AD) + -IASIS]

tri·chot·o·my (tri kot/ə mē), *n.*, *pl.* **-mies.** **1.** division into three parts, classes, categories, etc. **2.** an instance of such a division, as in thought, structure, or object. **3.** the three-part division of man into body, spirit, and soul. [? < NL **trichotomia* = Gk *trichotom(eín)* (to) trisect + NL *-ia* -Y[3]] **—trich·o·tom·ic** (trik/ə tom/ik), **tri·chot/o·mous,** *adj.* **—tri·chot/o·mous·ly,** *adv.*

tri·chro·ism (trī/krō iz/əm), *n.* *Crystall.* pleochroism of a biaxial crystal such that it exhibits three different colors when viewed from three different directions under transmitted light. **—tri·chro/ic,** *adj.*

tri·chro·mat (trī/krō mat/, -krə-), *n.* *Ophthalm.* a person who possesses full trichromatism. [back formation from TRICHROMATIC]

tri·chro·mat·ic (trī/krō mat/ik, -krə-), *adj.* **1.** pertaining to the use or combination of three colors, as in printing or in color photography. **2.** pertaining to, characterized by, or involving three colors. **3.** *Ophthalm.* of, pertaining to, or exhibiting trichromatism. Also, **tri·chro·mic** (trī krō/mik).

tri·chro·ma·tism (trī krō/mə tiz/əm), *n.* **1.** the quality or condition of being trichromatic. **2.** the use or combination of three colors, as in printing or photography. **3.** *Ophthalm.* Also, **tri·chro·ma·top·si·a** (trī krō/mə top/sē ə). normal vision, in which the retina responds to all colors. Cf. **dichromatism** (def. 2), **monochromatism** (def. 2).

tri·cit·y (trī/sit/ē, -sit/ē), *adj.* **1.** of or pertaining to a metropolitan area consisting of three separate but interdependent cities. **—***n.* **2.** any one of three such cities.

trick (trik), *n.* **1.** a crafty or underhanded device, maneuver, stratagem, or the like, intended to deceive or cheat; artifice; ruse; wile. **2.** an optical illusion. **3.** a roguish or mischievous act; practical joke; prank: *He likes to play tricks on his friends.* **4.** a foolish, childish, or disgraceful action. **5.** a clever or ingenious device or expedient; adroit technique: *a rhetorical trick; the tricks of the trade.* **6.** the art or knack of doing something skillfully: *You seem to have mastered the trick of making others laugh.* **7.** a clever or dexterous feat intended to entertain, amuse, etc.: *He taught his dog some amazing tricks.* **8.** a feat of magic or legerdemain: *card tricks.* **9.** a behavioral peculiarity; trait; habit; mannerism. **10.** a turn; stint; tour of duty. **11.** *Cards.* **a.** the group or set of cards played and won in one round. **b.** a point or scoring unit. **c.** a card that is a potential winner. **12.** *Informal.* a child or young girl: *a cute little trick.* **13.** a specific period when a person is to perform a particular action; turn of duty; shift. **14.** *Heraldry.* a preliminary sketch of a coat of arms. **15. do** or **turn the trick,** to achieve the desired effect or result: *Another turn of the pliers should do the trick.* **—***adj.* **16.** of, pertaining to, characterized by, or involving tricks: *trick shooting; trick riding.* **17.** designed or used for tricks: *a trick chair; a trick horse.* **—***v.t.* **18.** to deceive by trickery. **19.** to cheat or swindle (usually fol. by *out of*): *tricked out of his paycheck.* **20.** to beguile by trickery (usually fol. by *into*). **21.** to dress, array, or deck, esp. ostentatiously or decoratively (often fol. by *out* or *up*). **—***v.i.* **22.** to practice trickery or deception; cheat. **23.** to play tricks; trifle (usually fol. by *with*). [late ME *trik* < ONF *trique* deceit < *trikier* to deceive < VL **triccare,* var. of L *trīcārī* to play tricks] **—trick/er,** *n.* **—trick/ing·ly,** *adv.* **—trick/less,** *adj.*
—Syn. 1. deception. TRICK, ARTIFICE, RUSE, STRATAGEM are terms for crafty or cunning devices that are intended to deceive. TRICK, the general term, refers usually to an underhanded act designed to cheat someone, but it sometimes refers merely to a pleasurable deceiving of the senses: *to win by a trick.* Like TRICK, but to a greater degree, ARTIFICE emphasizes the cleverness, ingenuity, or cunning with which the proceeding is devised: *an artifice of diabolical ingenuity.* RUSE and STRATAGEM emphasize the purpose for which the trick is designed; RUSE is the more general term of the two, and STRATAGEM sometimes implies a more elaborate procedure or a military application: *He gained entrance by a ruse. His stratagem gave the army command of the hill.* **18.** See **cheat.**

trick·er·y (trik/ə rē), *n.*, *pl.* **-er·ies.** **1.** the use or practice of tricks or stratagems to deceive; artifice; deception. **2.** a trick used to deceive. **—Syn. 1.** See **deceit.**

trick·ish (trik/ish), *adj.* tricky. **—trick/ish·ly,** *adv.* **—trick/ish·ness,** *n.*

trick/ knee/, a knee subject to a condition in which the joint suddenly stiffens or abandons its support.

trick·le (trik/əl), *v.*, **-led, -ling,** *n.* **—***v.i.* **1.** to flow or fall by drops, or in a small, gentle stream: *Tears trickled down her cheeks.* **2.** to come, go, or pass bit by bit, slowly, or irregularly: *Subscriptions trickled into the office. The guests trickled out of the room.* **—***v.t.* **3.** to cause to trickle. **—***n.* **4.** a trickling flow or stream. **5.** a small, slow, or irregular quantity of anything coming, going, or proceeding: *a trickle of visitors throughout the day.* [ME; sandhi var. of obs. *strickle* = STRIKE (in obs. sense, flow) + -LE] **—trick/ling·ly,** *adv.*

trick/ or treat/, the traditional Halloween custom, practiced by children, of calling on neighbors, usually uttering the phrase "trick or treat" as a threat to play a trick if candies, pennies, etc., are not given them.

trick·ster (trik/stər), *n.* **1.** a deceiver; cheat; fraud. **2.** a person who plays tricks. **3.** a mischievous supernatural figure appearing in various guises in the folklore and mythology of many primitive peoples. **—trick/ster·ing,** *n.*

trick·sy (trik/sē), *adj.*, **-si·er, -si·est.** **1.** given to tricks; mischievous; playful; prankish. **2.** *Archaic.* tricky; crafty; wily. **3.** *Archaic.* difficult to handle or deal with. **4.** *Archaic.* fashionably trim; spruce; smart. [? *tricks* (pl. of TRICK) + -Y[1]]

trick·y (trik/ē), *adj.*, **trick·i·er, trick·i·est.** **1.** given to or characterized by deceitful tricks; crafty; wily. **2.** skilled in clever tricks or dodges. **3.** deceptive, uncertain, or difficult to deal with or handle. **—trick/i·ly,** *adv.* **—trick/i·ness,** *n.*
—Syn. 1. artful, sly, shrewd. **2.** skillful, cunning, adroit. **3.** unpredictable, unreliable, perilous.

tri·clin·ic (trī klin/ik), *adj.* *Crystall.* noting or pertaining to a system of crystallization in which the three axes are unequal and intersect at oblique angles. Cf. **system** (def. 11). [TRI- + Gk *klī́n(ein)* (to) lean, slope + -IC]

tri·clin·i·um (trī klin/ē əm), *n.*, *pl.* **-clin·i·a** (-klin/ē ə). *Rom. Hist.* **1.** a couch extending along three sides of a table, for reclining on at meals. **2.** a dining room, esp. one containing such a couch. [< L < Gk *triklī́nion,* dim. of *trí̄klīnos* having three couches (adj.), dining room so furnished (n.) = *tri-* TRI- + *klī́n(ē)* couch + *-os* adj. suffix; see CLINIC]

tric·o·lette (trik/ə let/), *n.* a knitted fabric of silk or man-made yarn, used for apparel. [TRICO(T + FLANNE)LETTE]

tri·col·or (trī/kul/ər), *adj.* **1.** Also, **tri/col/ored;** *esp. Brit.,* **tri/col/oured.** having three colors. **—***n.* **2.** a flag having three colors. **3.** (*often cap.*) the national flag of France, adopted during the French Revolution, consisting of vertical bands of blue, white, and red. Also, *esp. Brit.,* **tri/col/our.** [< LL *tricolor*]

tri·corn (trī/kôrn), *adj.* **1.** having three horns or hornlike projections; three-cornered. **—***n.* **2.** Also, **tri/corne.** a hat with the brim turned up on three sides; cocked hat. [< L *tricorn(is)* having three horns = *tri-* TRI- + *corn(u)* HORN + *-is* adj. suffix]

tri·cor·nered (trī/kôr/nərd), *adj.* having three corners; tricorn: *a tricornered hat.*

tri·cos·tate (trī kos/tāt), *adj.* *Bot., Zool.* having three ribs, costae, or raised lines.

tri·cot (trē/kō; *Fr.* trē kō/), *n.* **1.** a warp-knit fabric, usually of nylon, with each side different. **2.** a kind of worsted cloth. [< F: knitting, knitted fabric, sweater < *tricoter* to knit << Gmc; akin to G *stricken* to knit]

tri·crot·ic (trī krot/ik), *adj.* *Physiol.* **1.** having three arterial beats for one heartbeat, as certain pulses. **2.** pertaining to such a pulse. [< Gk *trikrot(os)* with triple beat (*tri-* TRI- + *krótos* beat) + -IC] **—tri·cro·tism** (trī/krə tiz/əm, trik/rə-), *n.*

tri·cus·pid (trī kus/pid), *adj.* **1.** Also, **tri·cus/pi·dal.** having three cusps or points, as a tooth. Cf. **bicuspid.** 2. *Anat.* of, pertaining to, or affecting the tricuspid valve. —*n.* 3. *Anat.* a tricuspid part, as a tooth. [< L *tricuspid-* (s. of *tricuspis*) having three points]

tricus′pid valve′, *Anat.* the valve, consisting of three triangular flaps of tissue between the right auricle and ventricle of the heart, that prevents the blood from flowing back into the auricle. Cf. **mitral valve.**

tri·cy·cle (trī′si kəl), *n.* 1. a child's vehicle having one large front wheel, two small rear wheels, and propelled by foot pedals. 2. a velocipede with three wheels propelled by pedaling or the use of hand levers. [< F]

tri·cy·clic (trī sī′klik, -sik′lik), *adj.* pertaining to or embodying three cycles.

tri·dent (trīd′ənt), *n.* 1. a three-pronged instrument or weapon. 2. *Rom. Hist.* a three-pronged spear used in gladiatorial combats. 3. *Class. Myth.* the three-pronged spear forming a characteristic attribute of the sea god Poseidon, or Neptune. —*adj.* 4. Also, **tri·den·tal** (trī den′təl). having three prongs or tines. [< L *trident-* (s. of *tridēns*) having three teeth]

tri·den·tate (trī den′tāt), *adj.* having three teeth or toothlike parts or processes.

Tri·den·tine (trī den′tin, -tīn, tri-), *adj.* 1. of or pertaining to the city of Trent. 2. of or pertaining to the Council of Trent. 3. conforming to the decrees and doctrines of the Council of Trent. [< ML *Tridentīnus,* adj. use of L *Tridentīnus* tribesman of Tridentum; see -INE[1]]

Tri·den·tum (trī den′təm), *n.* ancient name of **Trent.**

tri·di·men·sion·al (trī′di men′shə nəl), *adj.* having three dimensions. —**tri′di·men′sion·al′i·ty,** *n.*

tri·e·cious (trī ē′shəs), *adj. Bot.* trioecious.

tried (trīd), *v.* 1. pt. and pp. of **try.** —*adj.* 2. tested and proved good, dependable, or trustworthy. 3. subjected to hardship, worry, trouble, or the like.

tri·en·ni·al (trī en′ē əl), *adj.* 1. occurring every three years. 2. lasting three years. —*n.* 3. a third anniversary. 4. something that appears or occurs every three years. 5. triennium. [TRIENNI(UM) + -AL[1]] —**tri·en′ni·al·ly,** *adv.*

tri·en·ni·um (trī en′ē əm), *n., pl.* **-en·ni·ums, -en·ni·a** (-en′ē ə). a period of three years. [< L: period of three years = *trienni(s)* pertaining to three years (*tri-* TRI- + *-ennis,* akin to *annus* year) + *-um* neut. n. suffix]

tri·ens (trī′enz), *n., pl.* **tri·en·tes** (trī en′tēz). 1. a copper coin of ancient Rome, issued during the Republic, a third part of an as. 2. tremissis (def. 1). [< L: third part]

tri·er (trī′ər), *n.* a person or thing that tries or tests.

Trier (trēr), *n.* a city in W West Germany, on the Moselle River. 87,400 (1963). Also called **Treves.** French, **Trèves.**

tri·er·arch (trī′ə rärk′), *n. Gk. Hist.* 1. the commander of a trireme. 2. (in Athens) a citizen required to fit out a trireme for the public service. [< Gk *triḗrarch(os)* = *triḗr(ēs)* having three banks of oars (adj.), trireme (n.) + *archós* commander. See TRI-, -ARCH]

tri·er·ar·chy (trī′ə rär′kē), *n., pl.* **-chies.** *Gk. Hist.* 1. the office of a trierarch. 2. trierarchs collectively. 3. (in Athens) the duty of fitting out or furnishing triremes for the public service. [< Gk *triērarchía*]

Tri·este (trē est′; *It.* trē es′te), *n.* 1. a seaport in NE Italy, on the Gulf of Trieste. 273,390 (1961). 2. **Free Territory of,** an area bordering the N Adriatic: N zone, including the city of Trieste (86 sq. mi.), a part of Italy; S zone (199 sq. mi.) incorporated into Yugoslavia. 3. **Gulf of,** an inlet at the N end of the Adriatic, in NE Italy. 20 mi. wide.

tri·fa·cial (trī fā′shəl), *adj.* trigeminal.

tri·fec·ta (trī′fek′tə), *n.* a type of betting, esp. on a horse race, in which the bettor must select the first-, second-, and third-place finishers in exact order. Also called **triple.** Cf. **exacta, quinella, superfecta.** [TRI(PLE) (PER)FECTA]

tri·fid (trī′fid), *adj.* cleft into three parts or lobes. [< L *trifid(us)* split in three]

tri·fle (trī′fəl), *n., v.,* **-fled, -fling.** —*n.* 1. something of very little value, importance, or significance. 2. a small quantity or amount of anything, as money; a little. 3. pewter of medium hardness. 4. *English Cookery.* a dessert consisting of custard or some substitute and usually containing cake soaked in wine or liqueur, and jam, fruit, or the like. —*v.i.* 5. to deal lightly or without due seriousness or respect (usually fol. by *with*): *Don't trifle with me today.* 6. to amuse oneself; dally. 7. to play or toy by handling or fingering (usually fol. by *with*): *He sat trifling with a pen.* 8. to act or talk in an idle or frivolous way. 9. to waste time; idle. —*v.t.* 10. to pass or spend (time) idly or frivolously. [ME *trufle* idle talk < OF; ME *treoflen* to mock < OF *trufler* to make sport of] —**tri′fler,** *n.* —**Syn. 5, 6.** play, toy.

tri·fling (trī′fling), *adj.* 1. of very little importance; trivial; insignificant: *a trifling matter.* 2. of small value, cost, or amount: *a trifling sum.* 3. frivolous; shallow; light: *trifling conversation.* 4. *U.S. Dial.* mean; worthless. —*n.* 5. idle or frivolous conduct, talk, etc. 6. foolish delay or waste of time. [late ME] —**tri′fling·ly,** *adv.* —**tri′fling·ness,** *n.* —**Syn.** 1. unimportant, inconsequential. See **petty.** 2. negligible, piddling.

tri·fo·cal (*adj.* trī fō′kəl; *n.* trī fō′kəl, trī′fō′kəl), *adj.* 1. *Optics.* having three foci. 2. (of an eyeglass lens) having three portions, one for near, one for intermediate, and one for far vision. —*n.* 3. **trifocals,** eyeglasses with trifocal lenses.

tri·fo·li·ate (trī fō′lē it, -āt′), *adj.* 1. having three leaflets, leaflike parts, lobes, or foils; trefoil. 2. *Bot.* trifoliolate. Also, **tri·fo′li·at′ed.**

tri·fo·li·o·late (trī fō′lē ə lāt′), *adj. Bot.* 1. (of a compound leaf) having three leaflets. 2. (of a plant) having leaves with three leaflets.

tri·fo·li·um (trī fō′lē əm), *n.* any plant of the genus *Trifolium,* comprising the trefoils. [< L: triple leaf]

Triforium

tri·fo·ri·um (trī fôr′ē əm, -fōr′-), *n., pl.* **-fo·ri·a** (-fôr′ē ə, -fōr′-). *Archit.* (in a church) the wall at the side of the nave, choir, or transept, corresponding to the space between the vaulting or ceiling and the roof of an aisle, often having a blind arcade or an opening in a gallery. [< AL, special use of ML *triforium* kind of gallery, lit., something with three openings = L *tri-* TRI- + *for-* opening + *-ium* n. suffix (neut. of *-ius* adj. suffix)] —**tri·fo′ri·al,** *adj.*

tri·form (trī′fôrm′), *adj.* 1. formed of three parts; in three divisions. 2. existing or appearing in three different forms. 3. combining three different forms. Also, **tri′formed′.** [< L *triform(is)*]

tri·fur·cate (*v.* trī fûr′kāt; *adj.* trī fûr′kit, -kāt), *v.,* **-cat·ed, -cat·ing,** *adj.* —*v.i.* 1. to divide into three forks or branches. —*adj.* 2. Also, **tri·fur′cat·ed.** divided into three forks or branches. —**tri′fur·ca′tion,** *n.*

trig[1] (trig), *n. Informal.* trigonometry. [by shortening]

trig[2] (trig), *adj., v.,* **trigged, trig·ging.** —*adj. Chiefly Brit.* 1. neat, trim, or spruce. 2. in good physical condition; sound; well —*v.t.* 3. *Brit. Dial.* to make trim, smart, etc. (often fol. by *up* or *out*). [ME < Scand; cf. Icel *tryggr* loyal, safe; c. Goth *triggws* true, faithful. See TRUE] —**trig′ness,** *n.*

trig[3] (trig), *v.,* **trigged, trig·ging,** *n.* —*v.t. Dial.* 1. to support or prop, as with a wedge. 2. to act as a check on (the moving of wheels, vehicles, etc.). —*n.* 3. a wedge or block used to prevent a wheel, cask, or the like, from rolling. [? < Scand; cf. Icel *tryggja* to make fast, secure]

trig., 1. trigonometric. 2. trigonometrical. 3. trigonometry.

tri·gem·i·nal (trī jem′ə nəl), *adj. Anat.* —*adj.* 1. of or pertaining to the trigeminal nerve. —*n.* 2. See **trigeminal nerve.** [< NL *trigemin(us),* L: triple (*tri-* TRI- + *geminus* twin, double) + -AL[1]]

trigem′inal nerve′, *Anat.* either one of the fifth pair of cranial nerves, consisting of motor fibers that innervate the muscles of mastication, and of sensory fibers that conduct impulses from the head and face to the brain.

trig·ger (trig′ər), *n.* 1. a small projecting tongue in a firearm that, when pressed by the finger, actuates the mechanism for discharging the weapon. 2. a device, as a lever, the pulling or pressing of which releases a detent or spring. 3. anything, as an act, event, etc., that initiates or precipitates a reaction or series of reactions. 4. **quick on the trigger,** *Informal.* quick to act or respond; impetuous; alert. —*v.t.* 5. to initiate or precipitate a reaction or series of reactions. 6. to fire or explode (a gun, missile, etc.) by pulling a trigger or releasing a triggering device. [earlier *tricker* < D *trekker* = *trekk(en)* (to) pull + *-er* -ER[1]]

trig′ger fin′ger, any finger, usually the forefinger, that presses the trigger of a gun.

trig·ger·fish (trig′ər fish′), *n., pl.* (*esp. collectively*) **-fish,** (*esp. referring to two or more kinds or species*) **-fish·es.** any of various compressed, deep-bodied fishes of the genus *Balistes* and allied genera, chiefly found in tropical seas, having an anterior dorsal fin with three stout spines.

trig·ger-hap·py (trig′ər hap′ē), *adj. Informal.* 1. ready to fire a gun, missile, etc., at the least provocation, regardless of the situation or probable consequences. 2. foolhardy and irresponsible in matters of great importance, esp. in advocating an action that could result in war.

tri·glyc·er·ide (trī glis′ə rīd′, -ər id), *n. Chem.* an ester obtained from glycerol by the esterification of three hydroxyl groups with fatty acids. Cf. **glyceride.**

tri·glyph (trī′glif′), *n. Archit.* a member of a Doric frieze, separating two consecutive metopes. [< L *trīglyph(us)* < Gk *tríglyphos* thrice-grooved = *tri-* TRI- + *glyph(ḗ)* GLYPH + *-os* adj. suffix]

tri·go (trē′gō; *Sp.* trē′gô), *n., pl.* **-gos** (-gōz; *Sp.* -gôs). wheat; field of wheat. [< Sp < L *trīticum* wheat = *trīt(us)* ground, rubbed to pieces (ptp. of *terere*) + *-icum* -IC]

tri·gon (trī′gon), *n.* 1. an ancient Greek stringed instrument with a triangular shape. 2. *Archaic.* a triangle. [< L *trigōn(um)* triangle < Gk *trígōnon,* n. use of neut. of *trígōnos* three-angled]

trigon., 1. trigonometric. 2. trigonometrical. 3. trigonometry.

trig·o·nal (trig′ə nəl), *adj.* 1. of, pertaining to, or shaped like a triangle; having three angles; triangular. 2. *Crystall.* having threefold symmetry. —**trig′o·nal·ly,** *adv.*

trig′onomet′ric func′tion, *Math.* a function, as sine, cosine, etc., expressed as the ratio of the sides of a right triangle. Also called **circular function.**

trig·o·nom·e·try (trig′ə nom′i trē), *n.* the branch of mathematics that deals with the relations between the sides and angles of plane or spherical triangles, and the calculations based on them. [< NL *trigōnometria,* lit., triangle measuring. See TRIGON, -METRY] —**trig·o·no·met·ric** (trig′ə nə me′trik), **trig′o·no·met′ri·cal,** *adj.* —**trig′o·no·met′ri·cal·ly,** *adv.*

tri·graph (trī′graf, -gräf), *n.* a group of three letters representing a single speech sound, as *eau* in *beau.* —**tri·graph′ic,** *adj.*

tri·he·dral (trī hē′drəl), *adj.* 1. *Geom.* having, or formed by, three planes meeting in a point: *a trihedral angle.* —*n.* 2. the figure formed by three lines of different planes, meeting at a point.

tri·he·dron (trī hē′drən), *n., pl.* **-drons, -dra** (-drə). *Geom.* the figure determined by three planes meeting in a point.

tri·hy·drate (trī hī′drāt), *n. Chem.* a hydrate that contains three molecules of water, as potassium pyrophosphate, $K_4P_2O_7 \cdot 3H_2O$. —**tri·hy′drat·ed,** *adj.*

tri·ju·gate (trī′jo͞o gāt′, trī jo͞o′git, -gāt), *adj. Bot.* having three pairs of leaflets. Also, **tri·ju·gous** (trī′jo͞o gəs, trī jo͞o′-).

tri·lat·er·al (trī lat′ər əl), *adj.* having three sides. [< L *trilater(us)* three-sided + -AL[1]] —**tri·lat′er·al′i·ty,** *n.* —**tri·lat′er·al·ly,** *adv.*

tril·by (tril′bē), *n., pl.* **-bies.** *Chiefly Brit.* a hat of soft felt with an indented crown. Also, **tril′by hat′.** [named after heroine of *Trilby,* novel (1894) by George Du MAURIER]

tri·lin·e·ar (trī lin′ē ər), *adj.* of, pertaining to, or bounded by three lines.

tri·lin·gual (trī ling′gwəl), *adj.* employing, speaking, or involving three languages: *a trilingual edition of the plays of Shakespeare in English, French, and Italian.* [< L *trilingu(is)* triple-tongued + -AL[1]] —**tri·lin′gual·ism,** *n.* —**tri·lin′gual·ly,** *adv.*

tri·lit·er·al (trī lit′ər əl), *adj.* using or consisting of three letters.

trill[1] (tril), *v.t.* **1.** to sing or play with a vibratory or quavering effect. **2.** *Phonet.* to produce (a trill). **3.** (of birds, insects, etc.) to sing or utter in a succession of rapidly alternating sounds. —*v.i.* **4.** to resound vibrantly, or with a rapid succession of sounds, as the voice, song, laughter, etc. **5.** to utter or make a sound or succession of sounds resembling such singing. **6.** to execute a shake or trill with the voice or on a musical instrument. —*n.* **7.** act or sound of trilling. **8.** *Music.* rapid alternation of two adjacent tones; shake. **9.** a similar sound, or succession of sounds, uttered or made by a bird, an insect, a person laughing, etc. **10.** *Phonet.* **a.** a sequence of rapid, vibratory movements produced in any free articulator or membrane, often causing a corresponding sequence of contacts between the vibrating articulator and another surface. **b.** a speech sound produced by such a trill. [< It *trill(o)* quaver or warble in singing << Gmc; cf. D *trillen* to vibrate, late ME *trille* to shake or rock (something)]

Trill[1] (def. 8)

trill[2] (tril), *Archaic.* —*v.i.* **1.** to flow in a thin stream; trickle. —*v.t.* **2.** to cause to flow in a thin stream. [ME *trille* to make (something) turn; to roll, flow (said of tears, water) < Scand; cf. Dan *trille* to roll (said, e.g., of tears and of a wheelbarrow). See TRILL[1]]

Tril·ling (tril′ing), *n.* **Lionel,** 1905–75, U.S. critic and author.

tril·lion (tril′yən), *n., pl.* **-lions,** (*as after a numeral*) **-lion,** *adj.* —*n.* **1.** a cardinal number represented, in the U.S. and France, by one followed by 12 zeros, and, in Great Britain and Germany, by one followed by 18 zeros. —*adj.* **2.** amounting to one trillion in number. [< F, c. It *trillione* = *tr(i)*- TRI- + *(m)illione* MILLION] —**tril′lionth,** *n., adj.*

tril·li·um (tril′ē əm), *n.* any liliaceous herb of the genus *Trillium,* having a whorl of three leaves from the center of which rises a solitary flower. [< NL: genus name, appar. alter. (by Linnaeus) of Sw *trilling* triplet, alluding to the foliation]

tri·lo·bate (trī lō′bāt, trī′lə bāt′), *adj.* having three lobes. Also, **tri·lo′bat·ed, tri·lobed** (trī′lōbd′).

Trilobate leaf

tri·lo·bite (trī′lə bīt′), *n.* any marine arthropod of the extinct group *Trilobita,* from the Paleozoic era, having a flattened, oval body varying in length from an inch or less to two feet: one of the earliest known fossils. [< NL *Trilobītes* = Gk *trílob(os)* three-lobed (see TRI-, LOBE) + *-ītes* -ITE[1]] —**tri·lo·bit·ic** (trī′lə bit′ik), *adj.*

Trilobite, *Griffithides bufo* (Length 1¼ in.)

tri·loc·u·lar (trī lok′yə lər), *adj. Bot., Zool.* having three loculi, chambers, or cells.

tril·o·gy (tril′ə jē), *n., pl.* **-gies.** a series or group of three plays, novels, operas, etc., that, although individually complete, are closely related in theme, sequence, or the like. [< Gk *trilogía*]

trim (trim), *v.,* **trimmed, trim·ming,** *n., adj.,* **trim·mer, trim·mest,** *adv.* —*v.t.* **1.** to put into a neat or orderly condition by clipping, paring, pruning, etc. **2.** to remove (something superfluous or dispensable) by or as by cutting (often fol. by *off*). **3.** to cut down, as to a required size or shape. **4.** *Aeron.* to level off (an airship or airplane) in flight. **5.** *Naut.* **a.** to distribute the load of (a ship) so that the ship sits well in the water. **b.** to stow or arrange, as cargo. **c.** to adjust (the sails or yards) with reference to the direction of the wind and the course of the ship. **6.** to decorate or adorn with ornaments or embellishments: *to trim a Christmas tree.* **7.** to arrange goods in (a store window) as a display. **8.** to prepare or adjust (a lamp, fire, etc.) for proper burning. **9.** *Informal.* **a.** to rebuke or reprove. **b.** to beat or thrash. **c.** to defeat. **10.** *Obs.* to equip. —*v.i.* **11.** *Naut.* **a.** to assume a particular position or trim in the water, as a vessel. **b.** to adjust sails or yards with reference to the direction of the wind and the course of a vessel. **12.** to pursue a neutral or cautious policy between parties. **13.** to change one's views for reasons of expediency. —*n.* **14.** the condition, order, or fitness of a person or thing for action, work, use, etc. **15.** *Naut.* **a.** the set of a ship in the water. **b.** the condition of a ship with reference to her fitness for sailing. **c.** the adjustment of the sails, rigging, etc., with reference to the direction of the wind and the course of the ship. **16.** a person's dress, adornment, or appearance. **17.** material used for decoration or embellishment; trimming. **18.** decoration of a store window for the display of merchandise; window dressing. **19.** a trimming by cutting, clipping, or the like. **20.** a haircut that restores the neatness of a previous cut. **21.** that which is cut off or eliminated. **22.** *Aeron.* the attitude of an airplane with respect to all three axes, at which balance occurs in forward flight under no controls. **23.** *Building Trades.* woodwork or moldings used to decorate or border openings or wall surfaces. **24.** *Auto.* **a.** the upholstery, knobs, handles, and other equipment inside a motor car. **b.** ornamentation on the exterior of an automobile. —*adj.* **25.** pleasingly neat or smart in appearance: *trim lawns.* **26.** in good condition or order. **27.** *Archaic.* properly prepared or equipped. **28.** *Obs.* good, excellent, or fine. —*adv.* **29.** trimly. [OE *trymman, trymian* to strengthen, prepare < *trum* strong, active; akin to Ir *dron* strong, Gk *drymós* coppice, L *dūrus* hard. See TREE] —**trim′ly,** *adv.* —**trim′mer,** *n.* —**trim′ness,** *n.* —**Syn. 1.** shear, shave, cut, lop. **6.** deck, ornament, embellish. **17.** adornment, embellishment, garnish. **26.** trig, spruce.

tri·ma·ran (trī′mə ran′), *n.* a vessel similar to a catamaran but having three separate hulls. [TRI- + *-maran* (as in CATAMARAN)]

trim·er·ous (trim′ər əs), *adj.* **1.** *Bot.* (of flowers) having three members in each whorl. **2.** *Entomol.* having three segments or parts. [< NL *trimerus* = *trimer-* (< Gk *trimer(ḗs)* having three parts; see TRI-, -MER) + *-us* -OUS]

tri·mes·ter (trī mes′tər), *n.* **1.** a term or period of three months. **2.** one of the three approximately equal terms into which the year is divided by some colleges, schools, etc. [< F *trimestre* < L *trimēstris* of three months = *tri-* TRI- + *-mēstris,* var. of *mēnstruus* monthly; see MENSTRUAL] —**tri·mes′tral, tri·mes′tri·al,** *adj.*

trim·e·ter (trim′i tər), *Pros.* —*n.* **1.** a verse of three measures or feet. —*adj.* **2.** consisting of three measures or feet. **3.** *Class. Pros.* composed of six feet or three dipodies. [< L *trimetr(us)* having three measures < Gk *trímetros*]

tri·met·ric (trī me′trik), *adj.* **1.** pertaining to or consisting of a trimeter or trimeters. **2.** *Crystall.* orthorhombic. Also, **tri·met′ri·cal.**

trimet′ric projec′tion, *Geom.* a three-dimensional projection with three different linear scales at arbitrary angles.

tri·met·ro·gon (trī me′trə gon′), *adj.* of or pertaining to a system of aerial photography using three cameras, one pointed directly downward and the others at 60° to it. [TRI- + Gk *métro(n)* measure + -GON]

trim·ming (trim′ing), *n.* **1.** anything used or serving to decorate or complete: *the trimmings of a Christmas tree.* **2.** Usually, **trimmings.** an accompaniment or garnish to a main dish: *roast turkey with all the trimmings.* **3. trimmings,** pieces cut off in trimming, clipping, or pruning. **4.** the act of a person or thing that trims. **5.** *Informal.* a reproving. **6.** *Informal.* a beating or thrashing. **7.** *Informal.* a defeat.

tri·mo·lec·u·lar (trī′mə lek′yə lər), *adj. Chem.* pertaining to or having a total of three molecules.

tri·month·ly (trī munth′lē), *adj.* occurring, taking place, done, or acted upon every three months.

tri·morph (trī′môrf), *n. Crystall.* **1.** a substance existing in three structurally distinct forms; a trimorphous substance. **2.** any of the three forms. [< Gk *trímorph(os)* having three forms. See TRI-, -MORPH]

tri·mor·phism (trī môr′fiz əm), *n.* **1.** *Zool.* the occurrence of three forms distinct in structure, coloration, etc., among animals of the same species. **2.** *Bot.* the occurrence of three different forms of flowers, leaves, etc., on the same plant or on distinct plants of the same species. **3.** *Crystall.* the property of some substances of crystallizing in three structurally distinct forms. **4.** the property or condition of occurring in three distinct forms. [< Gk *trímorph(os)* TRIMORPH + -ISM] —**tri·mor′phic, tri·mor′phous,** *adj.*

A B C
Trimorphism (def. 2) A, Long style; B, Intermediate style; C, Short style

tri·mo·tored (trī mō′tərd), *adj.* having three engines, as an airplane.

trim′ tab′, *Aeron.* an independently controlled tab set in the trailing edge of a control surface, as an elevator, aileron, or rudder, to hold it in a position suitable for stabilizing the aircraft in a flight attitude.

Tri·mur·ti (tri mŏŏr′tē), *n.* (in later Hinduism) a trinity consisting of Brahma the Creator, Vishnu the Preserver, and Shiva the Destroyer. [< Skt = *tri* THREE + *mūrti* shape]

Tri·na·cri·a (tri nā′krē ə, trī-), *n.* ancient name of **Sicily.**

Tri·na·cri·an (tri nā′krē ən, trī-), *adj. Archaic.* Sicilian.

tri·nal (trīn′əl), *adj.* threefold; triple; trine. [< LL *trīnāl(is).* See TRINE, -AL[1]]

tri·na·ry (trī′nə rē), *adj.* consisting of three parts, or proceeding by three; ternary. [< LL *trīnāri(us)* of three kinds = *trīn(ī)* three apiece (*tri-* three + *-nī* each) + *-ārius* -ARY]

Trin·co·ma·lee (tring′kō mə lē′), *n.* a seaport in E Sri Lanka. 39,000. Also, **Trin′co·ma·li′.**

trine (trīn), *adj.* **1.** threefold; triple. **2.** *Astrol.* of or pertaining to the trigon aspect of two planets distant from each other 120°, or the third part of the zodiac. —*n.* **3.** a set or group of three; triad. **4.** (*cap.*) the Trinity. **5.** *Astrol.* the trine aspect of two planets. [ME < L *trīn(us)* = *trī-* three + *-nus* -fold]

Trin·i·dad (trin′i dad′; *Sp.* trē′nē thäth′), *n.* an island in the SE Lesser Antilles, in the E West Indies, off the NE coast of Venezuela: formerly a British colony in the Federation of the West Indies; now part of Trinidad and Tobago. 945,210; 1864 sq. mi. —**Trin′i·dad′i·an,** *adj., n.*

Trin′idad and Toba′go, an independent republic in the West Indies, comprising the islands of Trinidad and Tobago: member of the British Commonwealth. 1,073,800; 1980 sq. mi. *Cap.:* Port-of-Spain.

Trin·i·tar·i·an (trin′i târ′ē ən), *adj.* **1.** believing in the doctrine of the Trinity. **2.** of or pertaining to the Trinity. —*n.* **3.** a person who believes in the doctrine of the Trinity. [< NL *trīnitāri(us)* of the Trinity (see TRINITY, -ARY) + -AN] —**Trin′i·tar′i·an·ism,** *n.*

trinitro-, *Chem.* a combination of **tri-** and **nitro-:** *trinitrotoluene.*

tri·ni·tro·ben·zene (trī nī′trō ben′zēn, -ben zēn′), *n. Chem.* any of three compounds having the formula $C_6H_3(NO_2)_3$, capable of more explosive power than TNT.

tri·ni·tro·cre·sol (trī nī′trō krē′sōl, -sôl, -sol), *n. Chem.* a compound, $CH_3C_6H(OH)(NO_2)_3$, used in high explosives.

tri·ni·tro·glyc·er·in (trī nī′trō glis′ər in), *n. Chem.* nitroglycerin.

tri·ni·tro·tol·u·ene (trī nī′trō tol′yo͞o ēn′), *n. Chem.* See **TNT.** Also, **tri·ni·tro·tol·u·ol** (trī nī′trō tol′yo͞o ōl′, -ôl′, -ol′).

Trin·i·ty (trin′i tē), *n., pl.* **-ties** for 3. **1.** the union of three persons, Father, Son, and Holy Ghost, in one Godhead, or the threefold personality of the one Divine Being. **2.** See **Trinity Sunday. 3.** (*l.c.*) a group of three; triad.

4. (*l.c.*) the state of being threefold or triple. [ME *trinite* < OF < LL *trīnitāt-* (s. of *trīnitās*) triad, trio, trinity = *trīn(us)* threefold (see TRINE) + *-itāt-* -ITY]

Trin′ity Sun′day, the Sunday after Pentecost, observed as a festival in honor of the Trinity.

trin·ket (tring′kit), *n.* **1.** a small ornament, piece of jewelry, etc., usually of little value. **2.** anything of trivial value. [?]

tri·no·mi·al (trī nō′mē əl), *adj.* **1.** *Algebra.* consisting of or pertaining to three terms. **2.** *Biol.* **a.** pertaining to a scientific name comprising three terms, as of genus, species, and subspecies or variety. **b.** characterized by the use of such names. —*n.* **3.** *Algebra.* an expression that is a sum or difference of three terms, as $3x + 2y + z$ or $3x^3 + 2x^2 + x$. **4.** *Biol.* a trinomial name. [TRI- + (BI)NOMIAL] —**tri·no′mi·al·ly,** *adv.*

tri·o (trē′ō), *n., pl.* **tri·os.** **1.** a musical composition for three voices or instruments. **2.** a company of three singers or players. **3.** a subordinate division of a minuet, scherzo, etc., usually in a contrasted key and style. **4.** any group of three persons or things. [< It = *tri-* TRI- + *(du)o* two]

tri·ode (trī′ōd), *n.* *Electronics.* a vacuum tube containing three elements, usually plate, grid, and cathode. [TRI- + (ELECTR)ODE]

tri·oe·cious (trī ē′shəs), *adj.* *Bot.* of or pertaining to a species having male, female, and hermaphrodite flowers on different plants. Also, **triecious.** [< NL *trioeci(a)* pl. name of the order (Gk *tri-* TRI- + *oikía* pl. of *oikíon* = *oîk(os)* house + *-ion* dim. suffix) + -OUS]

tri·o·let (trī′ə lit), *n.* a short poem of fixed form, having a rhyme scheme of *ab, aa, abab,* and having the first line repeated as the fourth and seventh lines, and the second line repeated as the eighth. [< F: lit., little trio]

tri·ox·ide (trī ok′sīd, -sid), *n.* *Chem.* an oxide containing three oxygen atoms, as As_2O_3.

trip (trip), *n., v.,* **tripped, trip·ping.** —*n.* **1.** a journey or voyage: *to win a trip to Paris.* **2.** a run made by a boat, train, bus, or the like, between two points. **3.** See **round trip.** **4.** a single course of travel taken as part of one's duty, work, etc.: *his daily trip to the bank.* **5.** a stumble; misstep. **6.** a sudden impeding or catching of a person's foot so as to throw him down. **7.** a slip, mistake, error, or blunder. **8.** a light, nimble step or movement of the feet. **9.** *Mach.* a projecting object mounted on a moving part for striking a control lever to control the actions of some machine. **10.** *Slang.* **a.** an instance or period of being under the influence of a hallucinogenic drug, esp. LSD. **b.** the euphoria, illusions, etc., experienced during such period. —*v.i.* **11.** to stumble. **12.** to make a mistake, as in conversation, conduct, etc. **13.** to step lightly or nimbly; skip. **14.** to tip or tilt. **15.** *Slang.* to be under the influence of a hallucinogenic drug, esp. LSD (sometimes fol. by *out*). —*v.t.* **16.** to cause to stumble (often fol. by *up*): *The rug tripped him up.* **17.** to cause to fail; hinder, obstruct, or overthrow. **18.** to cause to make a slip or error. **19.** to catch in a slip or error. **20.** to tip or tilt. **21.** *Naut.* **a.** to break out (an anchor) by turning it over or lifting it from the bottom by a line attached to its crown. **b.** to tip or turn (a yard) from a horizontal to a vertical position. **22.** to operate, start, or set free (a mechanism, weight, etc.) by suddenly releasing a catch, clutch, or the like. **23.** *Mach.* to release or operate suddenly (a catch, clutch, etc.). **24.** *Archaic.* to perform with a light or tripping step, as a dance. **25.** **trip the light fantastic,** to go dancing. [ME *trippen* to step lightly < MD (whence also MF *triper;* note single *p*); akin to OE *treppan* to tread]
—**Syn.** **1.** excursion, tour, jaunt, junket. TRIP, EXPEDITION, JOURNEY, PILGRIMAGE, VOYAGE are terms for a course of travel made to a particular place, usually for some specific purpose. TRIP is the general word, indicating going any distance and returning, by walking or any means of locomotion, for either business or pleasure, and in either a hurried or a leisurely manner: *a trip to Europe; a vacation trip; a bus trip.* An EXPEDITION, made often by an organized company, is designed to accomplish a specific purpose: *an archaeological expedition.* JOURNEY indicates a trip of considerable length, wholly or mainly by land, for business or pleasure or other reasons, and is now applied to travel that is more leisurely or more fatiguing than a trip; a return is not necessarily indicated: *the long journey to Siam.* A PILGRIMAGE is made as to a shrine, from motives of piety or veneration: *a pilgrimage to Lourdes.* A VOYAGE is travel by water or air, usually for a long distance and for business or pleasure; if by water, leisure is indicated: *a voyage around the world.*

tri·part·ed (trī pär′tid), *adj.,* divided into three parts. Also, **tri′part′.** [late ME: alter. of TRIPARTITE; see -ED[2]]

tri·par·tite (trī pär′tīt), *adj.* **1.** divided into or consisting of three parts. **2.** *Bot.* divided into three parts by incisions that extend nearly to the base, as a leaf. **3.** involving, participated in, or made by three parties. [late ME < L *tripartīt(us)* divided into three parts = *tri-* TRI- + *partītus,* ptp. of *partīre* to divide; see PART, -ITE[2]]

Tripartite leaf

tri·par·ti·tion (trī′pär tish′ən, trip′ər-), *n.* division into three parts.

tripe (trīp), *n.* **1.** the first and second divisions of the stomach of a ruminant, esp. oxen, sheep, or goats, used as food. **2.** *Slang.* **a.** something spoken or written that is false or worthless. **b.** something that is inferior or worthless or that does not meet expected standards. [ME < OF < ?]

tri·pe·dal (trī′pi dəl, trī pēd′əl, trip′i dəl), *adj.* having three feet. [< L *tripedāl(is)*]

tri·per·son·al (trī pûr′sə nəl), *adj.* (*sometimes cap.*) consisting of or existing in three persons, as the Godhead.

tri·per·son·al·i·ty (trī′pûr sə nal′i tē), *n.* (*sometimes cap.*) the state or condition of being tripersonal; existence in three persons, as the Godhead.

tri·pet·al·ous (trī pet′əl əs), *adj.* *Bot.* having three petals.

trip·ham·mer (trip′ham′ər), *n.* *Mach.* a heavy hammer raised and then let fall by means of some tripping device, as a cam. Also, **trip′ ham′mer.**

tri·phen·yl·meth·ane (trī fen′əl meth′ān, -fēn′-), *n.* *Chem.* a colorless solid, $(C_6H_5)_3CH$, from which many dyes are derived.

tri′phos·phor′ic ac′id (trī′fos fôr′ik, -for′-, trī′-), the hypothetical acid, $H_5P_3O_{10}$, known chiefly by its salts.

triph·thong (trif′thông, -thong, trip′-), *n.* **1.** *Phonet.* a monosyllabic speech-sound sequence made up of three differing vowel qualities, as in some dialectal pronunciations of *our.* **2.** (not in technical use) a trigraph. [< NL *triphthong(us)* < MGk *tríphthongos* with three vowels = *tri-* TRI- + *phthóngos* voice, sound] —**triph·thong·al** (trif thông′gəl, -thong′-, trip-), *adj.*

triph·y·lite (trif′ə līt′), *n.* a mineral, a rare phosphate of lithium, iron, and manganese, usually occurring in masses of a bluish or greenish color. Also called **triph·y·line** (trif′ə lēn′, -lin). [TRI- + PHYLE + -ITE[1]; r. *triphyline* < G *Triphylin*]

tri·pin·nate (trī pin′āt), *adj.* *Bot.* bipinnate, as a leaf, with the divisions also pinnate. Also, **tri·pin′nat·ed.** —**tri·pin′nate·ly,** *adv.*

tri·ple (trip′əl), *adj., n., v.,* **-pled, -pling.** —*adj.* **1.** threefold; consisting of three parts: *a triple knot.* **2.** of three kinds; threefold in character or relationship. **3.** three times as great. —*n.* **4.** an amount, number, etc., that is three times as great as another. **5.** a group, set, or series of three; something threefold; triad. **6.** Also called **three-base hit.** *Baseball.* a base hit that enables a batter to reach third base safely. **7.** trifecta. —*v.t.* **8.** to make triple. —*v.i.* **9.** to become triple. **10.** *Baseball.* to make a three-base hit. [late ME < L *triplus* = *tri-* TRI- + *(du)plus* DUPLE] —**tri·ply** (trip′lē), *adv.*

Tri′ple Alli′ance, **1.** the alliance (1882–1915) between Germany, Austria-Hungary, and Italy. **2.** a league (1717) of France, Great Britain, and the Netherlands against Spain. **3.** a league (1668) of England, Sweden, and the Netherlands against France.

tri′ple bond′, *Chem.* a chemical linkage consisting of three covalent bonds between two atoms of a molecule, represented in chemical formulas by three lines or six dots, as CH≡CH or CH⋮⋮CH.

tri·ple-deck·er (trip′əl dek′ər), *n.* three-decker (defs. 2, 3).

Tri′ple Entente′, **1.** an informal alliance (1894–1917) between Great Britain, France, and Russia counterbalancing the Triple Alliance. **2.** the member nations of this entente.

tri′ple play′, *Baseball.* a play in which three put-outs are made.

tri′ple rhyme′. See under **feminine rhyme.**

tri·plet (trip′lit), *n.* **1.** any of three children or offspring born at the same birth. **2.** **triplets,** three offspring born at one birth. **3.** any group or combination of three. **4.** *Pros.* three successive verses or lines, esp. when rhyming and of the same length; a stanza of three lines. **5.** Also called **tercet.** *Music.* a group of three notes to be performed in the time of two ordinary notes of the same kind.

tri·ple·tail (trip′əl tāl′), *n., pl.* (*esp. collectively*) **-tail,** (*esp. referring to two or more kinds or species*) **-tails.** a large food fish, *Lobotes surinamensis,* found in the warmer waters of the Atlantic Ocean and the Mediterranean Sea, having the lobes of its dorsal and anal fins extending backward and with the caudal fin suggesting a three-lobed tail.

tri′ple threat′, **1.** an expert in three different fields or in three different skills in the same field. **2.** *Football.* a back who is proficient at running, passing, and punting.

tri·plex (trip′leks, trī′pleks), *adj.* **1.** threefold; triple. —*n.* **2.** an apartment having three floors. [< L: threefold = *tri-* TRI- + *-plex,* nom. sing. of *-plic-* -fold; see PLY[2]]

trip·li·cate (*n., adj.* trip′lə kit, -kāt′; *v.* trip′lə kāt′), *n., adj., v.,* **-cat·ed, -cat·ing.** —*n.* **1.** a group, series, or set of three identical copies (usually prec. by *in*). —*adj.* **2.** having or consisting of three identical parts; threefold. **3.** noting the third copy or item. —*v.t.* **4.** to make three copies of something. **5.** to make three times as great. [< L *triplicātus* (ptp. of *triplicāre* to triple) = *triplic-* (s. of *triplex*) TRIPLEX + *-ātus* -ATE[1]] —**trip′li·ca′tion,** *n.*

tri·plic·i·ty (tri plis′i tē), *n., pl.* **-ties.** **1.** the quality or state of being triple. **2.** a group or combination of three; triad. **3.** *Astrol.* a set of three signs of the zodiac. [ME *triplicite* < LL *triplicitās* threefold state. See TRIPLEX, -ITY]

trip·loid (trip′loid), *Biol.* —*adj.* **1.** having a chromosome number that is three times the basic or haploid number. —*n.* **2.** a triploid cell or organism. —**trip′loi·dy,** *n.*

tri·pod (trī′pod), *n.* **1.** a stool, table, pedestal, etc., with three legs. **2.** a three-legged stand or support, as for a camera, telescope, etc. [< L *tripod-* (s. of *tripūs*) < Gk *tripod-* (s. of *trípous*) three-footed. See TRI-, -POD]

trip·o·dal (trip′ə dəl), *adj.* **1.** pertaining to or having the form of a tripod. **2.** Also, **tri·pod·ic** (trī pod′ik). having three feet or legs.

trip·o·dy (trip′ə dē), *n., pl.* **-dies.** *Pros.* a measure of three feet. [< Gk *tripodía.* See TRI-, -POD, -Y[3]]

Trip·o·li (trip′ə lē; *It.* trē′pô lē), *n.* **1.** Also, **Trip·o·li·ta·ni·a** (trip′ə li tā′nē ə; *It.* trē′pô lē tä′nyä). one of the former Barbary States of N Africa; now a part of Libya. **2.** a seaport in and a capital of Libya, in the NW part. 551,477. **3.** a seaport in N Lebanon, on the Mediterranean. 175,000. **4.** (*l.c.*) any of several siliceous substances, as rottenstone and infusorial earth, used chiefly in polishing.

tri·pos (trī′pos), *n., pl.* **-pos·es.** any of various final honors examinations at Cambridge University, England.

trip·per (trip′ər), *n.* **1.** a person or thing that trips. **2.** *Mach.* **a.** a tripping mechanism; a trip. **b.** an apparatus causing a signal or other operating device to be tripped or activated. **3.** *Brit. Informal.* an excursionist. **4.** *Slang.* a person who is under the influence of a hallucinogenic drug, esp. LSD.

trip·pet (trip′it), *n.* *Mach.* a projection, cam, or the like, for striking some part at regular intervals. [late ME *trypet*]

trip·ping (trip′ing), *adj.* **1.** light and quick, as a step or pace. **2.** proceeding with a light, easy movement or rhythm. —**trip′ping·ly,** *adv.*

trip·tane (trip′tān), *n.* *Chem.* a colorless liquid, $(CH_3)_2CHC(CH_3)_3$, having high antiknock properties as a fuel:

used chiefly as an admixture to aviation gasolines. [short for *trimethyl butane* (with *p* r. *b* before *t*). See TRI-, METHYL]

trip·ter·ous (trip′tər əs), *adj. Bot.* three-winged; having three wings or winglike expansions.

Trip·tol·e·mus (trip tol′ə məs), *n. Class. Myth.* a favorite of Demeter; inventor of the plow and patron of agriculture, connected with the Eleusinian mysteries. Also, **Trip·tol′e·mos.**

trip·tych (trip′tik), *n.* **1.** *Fine Arts.* a set of three panels or compartments side by side, bearing pictures, carvings, or the like. **2.** an ancient hinged, three-leaved writing tablet for use with a stylus. [< Gk *tríptych(os)* of three plates = *tri-* TRI- + *ptych-* (s. of *ptýx*) plate + *-os* adj. suffix]

Trip·u·ra (trip′ər ə), *n.* a union territory in NE India. 1,142,005 (1961); 4033 sq. mi. *Cap.:* Agartala.

tri·que·trous (trī kwē′trəs, -kwe′-), *adj.* **1.** three-sided; triangular. **2.** having a triangular cross section. [< L *triquetrus* triangular = *tri-* TRI- + *-quetros* cornered]

tri·ra·di·ate (trī rā′dē āt′), *adj.* having or consisting of three rays or raylike processes. Also, **tri·ra′di·at′ed.** —**tri·ra′di·ate′ly,** *adv.*

tri·reme (trī′rēm), *n. Class. Hist.* a galley with three tiers of oars on each side, used chiefly as a warship. [< L *trirēm(is)* having three banks of oars = *tri-* TRI- + *rēm(us)* oar + *-is* adj. suffix]

tri·sac·cha·ride (trī sak′ə rīd′, -ər id), *n. Chem.* a carbohydrate composed of three monosaccharide units, and hydrolyzable to a monosaccharide or a mixture of monosaccharides.

tri·sect (trī sekt′), *v.t.* to divide into three parts, esp. into three equal parts. —**tri·sec·tion** (trī sek′shən), *n.* —**tri·sec′tor,** *n.*

tri·sep·al·ous (trī sep′ə ləs), *adj. Bot.* having three sepals.

tri·sep·tate (trī sep′tāt), *adj. Bot., Zool.* having three septa.

tri·se·ri·al (trī sēr′ē əl), *adj.* arranged in three series or rows.

tris·kel·i·on (tri skel′ē on′, -ən), *n., pl.* **tris·kel·i·a** (tri-skel′ē ə). a symbolic figure consisting of three legs, arms, or branches, usually curved, radiating from a common center, as the device of Sicily and the Isle of Man. Also, **tris·kele** (tris′kēl). [< Gk *triskel(ēs)* three-legged (*tri-* TRI- + *skél(os)* leg + *-ēs* adj. suffix) + *-ion* dim. suffix]

Tris·me·gis·tus (tris′mi jis′təs), *n.* See **Hermes Trismegistus.**

tris·mus (triz′məs, tris′-), *n., pl.* **-mus·es.** *Pathol.* **1.** a spasm of the jaw muscles that makes it difficult to open the mouth. **2.** lockjaw. [< NL < Gk *trismós* a grinding] —**tris′mic,** *adj.*

tris·oc·ta·he·dron (tris ok′tə hē′drən), *n., pl.* **-drons, -dra** (-drə). a solid bounded by 24 identical faces in groups of three, each group corresponding to one face of an octahedron. [< Gk *trís* thrice + OCTAHEDRON] —**tris·oc′ta·he′dral,** *adj.*

Tris·tan (tris′tən, -tan; *Ger.* tris′tän), *n.* Tristram. Also, **Tris·tam** (tris′təm, -tam).

Tris·tan da Cu·nha (tris′tən də ko͞on′yə), a group of four volcanic islands in the S Atlantic; dependency of St. Helena: volcanic eruption 1961. 40 sq. mi.

tri-state (trī′stāt′), *adj.* **1.** pertaining to a territory made up of three adjoining states, esp. of the U.S. **2.** pertaining to the three adjoining parts of such states. Also, **tri′state′.**

triste (trēst), *adj. French.* sad; melancholy.

tris·tesse (trēs tes′), *n. French.* sadness or sorrow; melancholy.

trist·ful (trist′fəl), *adj. Archaic.* full of sadness; sorrowful. [late ME] —**trist′ful·ly,** *adv.* —**trist′ful·ness,** *n.*

tris·tich (tris′tik), *n. Pros.* a strophe, stanza, or poem consisting of three lines. —**tris·tich′ic,** *adj.*

tris·tich·ous (tris′tə kəs), *adj.* arranged in three rows. [< Gk *trístichos* of three rows or verses. See TRI-, -STICHOUS]

Tris·tram (tris′trəm, -tram), *n.* one of the knights of the Round Table, whose love for Iseult, wife of King Mark, is the subject of many romances. Also, **Tristan, Tris·trem** (tris′trəm), **Tristam.**

tri·sul·fide (trī sul′fīd, -fid), *n. Chem.* a sulfide containing three sulfur atoms.

tri·syl·la·ble (trī sil′ə bəl, tri-), *n.* a word of three syllables, as *pendulum.* [modeled on Gk *trisýllabos* having three syllables] —**tri·syl·lab·ic** (trī′si lab′ik, tris′i-), **tri′syl·lab′i·cal,** *adj.* —**tri′syl·lab′i·cal·ly,** *adv.* —**tri·syl′lab·ism,** *n.*

trit·an·o·pi·a (trit′^{ə}nō′pē ə), *n. Ophthalm.* a defect of vision in which the retina fails to respond to blue and yellow. [< NL = *trit-* (< Gk *trít(os)* third) + *an-* AN-[1] + *-opia* -OPIA] —**trit·an·op·ic** (trit′^{ə}nop′ik), *adj.*

trite (trīt), *adj.,* **trit·er, trit·est. 1.** lacking in freshness or effectiveness because of excessive repetition; hackneyed; stale. **2.** characterized by hackneyed expressions, ideas, etc. **3.** *Archaic.* rubbed or worn by use. [< L *trītus* worn, common = *trī-* (ptp. s. of *terere* to rub, wear down) + *-tus* ptp. suffix] —**trite′ly,** *adv.* —**trite′ness,** *n.* —**Syn. 1.** ordinary. See **commonplace.** —**Ant. 1.** original.

tri·the·ism (trī′thē iz′əm), *n. Theol.* belief in three Gods, esp. in the doctrine that the three persons of the Trinity are three distinct Gods. —**tri′the·ist,** *n., adj.* —**tri′the·is′tic, tri′the·is′ti·cal,** *adj.*

trit·i·um (trit′ē əm, trish′əm), *n. Chem.* an isotope of hydrogen having an atomic weight of three. [< NL = *trit-* (< Gk *trítos* third: *tri-* TRI- + *-tos* adj. suffix) + *-ium* -IUM]

tri·ton (trī′ton), *n. Physics.* a positively charged particle consisting of a proton and two neutrons, equivalent to the nucleus of an atom of tritium. Cf. **deuteron.** [< Gk *tríton,* neut. of *trítos* third]

Tri·ton (trīt′^{ə}n), *n.* **1.** *Class. Myth.* a son of Poseidon and Amphitrite, represented as having the head and trunk of a man and the tail of a fish, and as using a conch-shell trumpet. **2.** (*l.c.*) any of various marine gastropods of the family *Tritonidae,* esp. of the genus *Triton,* having a large, spiral, often beautifully colored shell. **3.** (*l.c.*) the shell of a triton. —**Tri·ton·ic** (trī ton′ik), *adj.*

tri·tone (trī′tōn′), *n. Music.* an interval consisting of three whole tones; an augmented fourth. [< ML *tritonus* < Gk *trítonos* having three tones. See TRI-, TONE]

trit·u·rate (trich′ə rāt′), *v.,* **-rat·ed, -rat·ing,** *n.* —*v.t.* **1.** to reduce to fine particles or powder by rubbing, grinding, bruising, or the like; pulverize. —*n.* **2.** a triturated substance. **3.** trituration (def. 3). [< LL *trītūrātus* (ptp. of *trītūrāre* to thresh) = L *trītūr(a)* a threshing (*trītus* rubbed, crushed (see TRITE) + *-ūra* -URE) + *-ātus* -ATE[1]] —**trit′u·ra′tor,** *n.* —**trit′u·ra·ble,** *adj.*

trit·u·ra·tion (trich′ə rā′shən), *n.* **1.** the act of triturating. **2.** the state of being triturated. **3.** *Pharm.* **a.** a mixture of a medicinal substance with sugar of milk, triturated to an impalpable powder. **b.** any triturated substance. [< LL *trītūrātiōn-* (s. of *trītūrātiō*)]

tri·umph (trī′əmf), *n.* **1.** the act, fact, or condition of being victorious or highly successful. **2.** exultation resulting from this. **3.** *Rom. Hist.* the ceremonial entrance into Rome of a victorious commander, authorized by the senate as the highest military honor. Cf. **ovation** (def. 2). —*v.i.* **4.** to gain a victory or be highly successful. **5.** to gain mastery; prevail: *to triumph over fear.* **6.** to exult over victory; rejoice over success. **7.** to be elated or glad; rejoice proudly; glory. **8.** to celebrate a triumph, as a victorious Roman commander. —*v.t.* **9.** *Obs.* to conquer; triumph over. [ME *triumphe,* OE *triumpha* < L *triumphus,* OL *triumpus;* cf. Gk *thríambos* Dionysiac procession] —**tri′umph·er,** *n.* —**Syn. 1.** success. See **victory. 2.** jubilation. **4.** succeed.

tri·um·phal (trī um′fəl), *adj.* **1.** of, pertaining to, celebrating, or commemorating a triumph or victory: *a triumphal banquet; a triumphal ode.* **2.** triumphant (def. 2). [late ME < L *triumphālis*]

trium′phal arch′, a monumental archway built to commemorate a victory, as in war.

tri·um·phant (trī um′fənt), *adj.* **1.** having achieved victory or success; victorious; successful. **2.** exulting over victory; rejoicing over success; exultant. **3.** *Archaic.* triumphal (def. 1). **4.** *Obs.* splendid; magnificent. [< L *triumphant-,* s. of *triumphāns,* prp. of *triumphāre* to triumph] —**tri·um′phant·ly,** *adv.*

tri·um·vir (trī um′vər), *n., pl.* **-virs, -vi·ri** (-və rī′). **1.** *Rom. Hist.* one of three officers or magistrates having the same function. **2.** any of three persons associated in any office or position of authority. [< L: lit., one man of three, back formation from *trium virōrum* of three men] —**tri·um′vi·ral,** *adj.*

tri·um·vi·rate (trī um′vər it, -və rāt′), *n.* **1.** *Rom. Hist.* **a.** the office or magistracy of a triumvir. **b.** a government of three officers or magistrates functioning jointly. **2.** any association of three persons. **3.** any group or set of three. [< L *triumvirātus*]

tri·une (trī′yo͞on), *adj.* three in one; constituting a trinity in unity, as the Godhead. [TRI- + L *ūn(us)* one]

tri·u·ni·tar·i·an (trī yo͞o′ni târ′ē ən), *n.* Trinitarian. [TRIUNE + *-itarian* as in UNITARIAN]

tri·u·ni·ty (trī yo͞o′ni tē), *n., pl.* **-ties.** Trinity (defs. 3, 4).

tri·va·lent (trī vā′lənt, triv′ə lənt), *adj. Chem.* having a valence of three. —**tri·va′lence, tri·va′len·cy,** *n.*

tri·valve (trī′valv′), *adj.* **1.** having three valves, as a shell. —*n.* **2.** a trivalve shell.

Tri·van·drum (tri van′drəm), *n.* a city in and the capital of Kerala, in S India: Vishnu pilgrimage center. 239,800 (1961).

triv·et (triv′it), *n.* **1.** a small metal plate with short legs, esp. one put under a hot platter or dish to protect a table. **2.** a three-legged metal stand placed over a fire to support cooking vessels or the like. [ME *trevet,* OE *trefet,* appar. b. of OE *thrifēte* three-footed and L *triped-,* s. of *tripēs* three-footed (with VL *-e-* for L *-i-*)]

triv·i·a (triv′ē ə), *n.pl.* matters or things that are very unimportant, inconsequential, or inessential; trifles; trivialities. [appar. back formation from TRIVIAL]

triv·i·al (triv′ē əl), *adj.* **1.** of very little importance or value; trifling; insignificant: *Don't bother me with trivial matters.* **2.** commonplace; ordinary. [ME < L *triviālis* belonging to the crossroads, (hence) common = *tri-* TRI- + *vi(a)* road + *-ālis* -AL[1]] —**triv′i·al·ly,** *adv.* —**triv′i·al·ness,** *n.* —**Syn. 1.** unimportant, inconsequential, frivolous. See **petty.** —**Ant. 1.** important.

triv·i·al·ism (triv′ē ə liz′əm), *n.* **1.** trivial character. **2.** something trivial.

triv·i·al·i·ty (triv′ē al′i tē), *n., pl.* **-ties** for 2. **1.** something trivial. **2.** a trivial quality or character.

triv·i·um (triv′ē əm), *n., pl.* **triv·i·a** (triv′ē ə). (during the Middle Ages) the lower division of the seven liberal arts, comprising grammar, rhetoric, and logic. Cf. **quadrivium.** [< ML, special use of L *trivium* public place, lit., place where three roads meet. See TRIVIAL]

tri·week·ly (trī wēk′lē), *adv., adj., n., pl.* **-lies.** —*adv.* **1.** every three weeks. **2.** three times a week. —*adj.* **3.** occurring or appearing every three weeks. **4.** occurring or appearing three times a week. —*n.* **5.** a triweekly publication.

-trix, a feminine suffix of agent nouns corresponding to masculine *-tor: aviatrix.* Cf. **-tress, -ess, -or**[2]. [< L, fem. of *-tor*]

TRM, trademark.

Tro·as (trō′as), *n.* a region in NW Asia Minor surrounding ancient Troy. Also called **the Tro·ad** (trō′ad).

Tro′bri·and Is′lands (trō′brē änd′, -ənd), a group of islands north of the eastern end of New Guinea: part of the Australian Territory of New Guinea. 100,000 (est. 1961); 170 sq. mi.

tro·car (trō′kär), *n. Surg.* a sharp-pointed instrument enclosed in a cannula, used for withdrawing fluid from a cavity, as the abdominal cavity, etc. Also, **trochar.** [earlier *trocart* < F, lit., three-sided = *tro-* (var. of *trois* three) + *cart,* var. of *carre* side < L *quadra* something square]

tro·cha·ic (trō kā′ik), *Pros.* —*adj.* **1.** pertaining to the trochee. 2. consisting of or employing a trochee or trochees. —*n.* 3. a trochee. 4. Usually, **trochaics.** a verse or poem written in trochees. [< L *trochaic(us)* < Gk *trochaïkós.* See TROCHEE, -IC] —**tro·cha′i·cal·ly,** *adv.*

tro·chal (trō′kəl), *adj. Zool.* resembling a wheel. [< Gk *troch(ós)* wheel + -AL¹]

tro·chan·ter (trō kan′tər), *n.* 1. *Anat., Zool.* a prominence or process on the upper part of the femur of many vertebrates serving for the attachment of muscles. 2. *Entomol.* (in an insect) the usually small second segment of the leg, between the coxa and femur. [< NL < Gk *trochantḗr* ball on which the hipbone turns in its socket. See TROCHE] —**tro·chan·ter·ic** (trō′kən ter′ik), **tro·chan′ter·al,** *adj.*

tro·char (trō′kär), *n. Surg.* trocar.

tro·che (trō′kē), *n. Pharm.* a small tablet or lozenge, usually a circular one, made of medicinal substance worked into a paste with sugar and mucilage or the like, and dried. [back formation from *troches,* earlier *tro(s)chies,* late ME *trocis* (taken as pl.) < MF *trocisse* < L *trochiscus* < Gk *trochískos* = *troch(ós)* wheel (akin to *tréchein* to run) + *-iskos* dim. suffix]

tro·chee (trō′kē), *n. Pros.* a foot of two syllables, a long followed by a short in quantitative meter, or a stressed followed by an unstressed in accentual meter. [< L *trochae(us)* < Gk *trochaîos* running = *troch-* (var. s. of *tréchein* to run) + *-aios* adj. suffix]

troch·el·minth (trok′əl minth), *n.* any invertebrate of the phylum *Trochelminthes* (now usually broken up into several phyla), comprising the rotifers, gastrotrichs, and several other forms. [back formation from NL *trochelminthes* phylum name = Gk *troch(ós)* wheel + *helminth-* HELMINTH]

troch·i·lus (trok′ə ləs), *n., pl.* **-li** (-lī′). 1. a hummingbird. 2. *Rare.* **a.** any of several small, Old World warblers, as the willow warbler, *Phylloscopus trochilus.* **b.** See **crocodile bird.** [< L < Gk *tróchilos* Egyptian courser (crocodile bird) = *troch-* (var. s. of *tréchein* to run) + *-ilos* dim. suffix]

troch·le·a (trok′lē ə), *n., pl.* **-le·ae** (-lē ē′). *Anat.* a pulleylike structure or arrangement of parts affording a smooth surface upon which another part glides, as a tendon or bone. [< L: pulley block or sheave < Gk *trochilía.* See TROCHILUS]

troch·le·ar (trok′lē ər), *adj.* 1. *Anat.* of, pertaining to, or connected with a trochlea. 2. *Physiol., Anat.* pulleylike. 3. *Bot.* circular and contracted in the middle so as to resemble a pulley. Also, **troch·le·ar·i·form** (trok′lē ar′ə fôrm′).

tro·choid (trō′koid), *n.* 1. *Geom.* a curve traced by a point on a radius or an extension of the radius of a circle that rolls, without slipping, on a curve, another circle, or a straight line. —*adj.* 2. rotating on an axis, as a wheel. [< Gk *trochoeidḗs* round like a wheel. See TROCHE, -OID] —**tro·choi′dal,** *adj.* —**tro·choi′dal·ly,** *adv.*

Trochoid
A, b > a
B, b < a

troch·o·phore (trok′ə fōr′, -fôr′), *n. Zool.* a ciliate, free-swimming larva common to several groups of invertebrates. [< Gk *trochó(s)* wheel + -PHORE]

trod (trod), *v.* a pt. and pp. of **tread.**

trod·den (trod′ən), *v.* a pp. of **tread.**

trode (trōd), *v. Archaic.* pt. and pp. of **tread.**

trog·lo·dyte (trog′lə dīt′), *n.* 1. a cave man or cave dweller. 2. a person, as a hermit, living in seclusion or in a primitive state. [< L *trōglodyta* < Gk *trōglodýtēs* one who creeps into holes, cave dweller = *trōglo-* (comb. form of *trṓglē* a gnawed hole; see TROGON) + *dý(ein)* (to) creep into + *-tēs* agent suffix] —**trog·lo·dyt·ic** (trog′lə dit′ik), **trog′lo·dyt′i·cal,** *adj.*

tro·gon (trō′gon), *n.* any of several brilliantly colored birds of the family *Trogonidae,* esp. of the genus *Trogon,* of tropical and subtropical regions. [< NL < Gk *trṓgōn,* prp. of *trṓgein* to gnaw] —**tro·gon·oid** (trō′gə noid′), *adj.*

troi·ka (troi′kə), *n.* 1. a Russian carriage or wagon drawn by a team of three horses abreast. 2. a team of three horses driven abreast. 3. triumvirate (defs. 2, 3). [< Russ = *troye* THREE + *-ka* n. suffix]

Troi·lus (troi′ləs, trō′ə-), *n. Class. Myth. and Medieval Legend.* a warrior son of Priam, mentioned by Homer and Vergil and later represented as the lover of Cressida.

trois (trwä), *n. French.* the number 3.

Trois-Ri·vières (trwä rē vyer′), *n.* French name of **Three Rivers.**

Tro·jan (trō′jən), *adj.* 1. of or pertaining to ancient Troy or its inhabitants. —*n.* 2. a native or inhabitant of Troy. 3. a person who shows pluck, determination, or energy: *to work like a Trojan.* [ME, OE *Trōiān* < L *Trōiānus* = *Trōi(a)* TROY + *-ānus* -AN]

Tro′jan Horse′, 1. *Class. Myth.* a gigantic hollow wooden horse, left by the Greeks upon their pretended abandonment of the siege of Troy. The Trojans, regarding the horse as a sacrifice to Athena, opened the city gates and took it into Troy. Greek soldiers concealed in the horse opened the gates to the Greek army at night and conquered the city. 2. a person or thing that is designed to undermine or destroy from within.

Tro′jan War′, *Class. Myth.* a ten-year war waged by the confederated Greeks under Agamemnon against the Trojans to avenge the abduction of Helen, wife of Menelaus, by Paris, son of the Trojan king Priam, and ending in the plundering and burning of Troy.

tro·land (trō′lənd), *n. Ophthalm.* photon (def. 2). [named after L. T. *Troland,* (1889–1932), American psychologist and physicist]

troll¹ (trōl), *v.t.* 1. to sing or utter in a full, rolling voice. 2. to sing in the manner of a round or catch. 3. to fish by trolling. 4. to move (the line or bait) in fishing. 5. to cause to turn round and round; roll. —*v.i.* 6. to sing with a full, rolling voice; give forth full, rolling tones. 7. to be uttered or sounded in such tones. 8. to fish with a moving line, as one trailed behind a boat. 9. to roll; turn round and round. 10. *Archaic.* to move nimbly, as the tongue in speaking. —*n.* 11. a song whose parts are sung in succession; a round. 12. the act of trolling. 13. a lure used in trolling for fish. 14. the fishing line containing the lure and hook for use in trolling. [ME *trolle(n)* to roll, stroll < MF *troller* to run here and there < MHG *trollen* to walk or run with short steps] —**troll′er,** *n.*

troll² (trōl), *n.* (in Scandinavian folklore) any of a race of supernatural beings, sometimes conceived as giants and sometimes as dwarfs, inhabiting caves or subterranean dwellings. [< Scand; cf. Icel *troll* giant, demon]

trol·ley (trol′ē), *n., pl.* **-leys,** *v.,* **-leyed, -ley·ing.** —*n.* 1. a trolley car. 2. a pulley or truck traveling on an overhead track and serving to support and move a suspended object. 3. a grooved metallic wheel or pulley carried on the end of a pole by an electric car or locomotive, and held in contact with an overhead conductor, usually a suspended wire (**trol′ley wire′**), from which it collects the current. 4. any of various other devices for collecting current for such a purpose. 5. a small truck or car operated on a track, as in a mine or factory. 6. *Brit.* any of various low carts or vehicles, as a railway handcar, costermonger's cart, etc. —*v.t., v.i.* 7. to convey or go by trolley. [TROLL¹ (n.) + -EY²]

trol′ley bus′, a passenger bus operating on tires and having an electric motor that draws power from overhead wires. Also called **trol′ley coach′.**

trol′ley car′, a streetcar propelled electrically by current taken by means of a trolley from a conducting wire strung overhead or running beneath a slot between the tracks.

trol′ley line′, 1. the route of a trolley car or trolley bus. 2. a transportation system using trolley cars or trolley buses.

trol·lop (trol′əp), *n.* 1. an untidy or slovenly woman; slattern. 2. an immoral or promiscuous woman, esp. a prostitute. [earlier *trollops;* akin to TROLL¹] —**trol′lop·y,** *adj.*

Trol·lope (trol′əp), *n.* **Anthony,** 1815–82, English novelist.

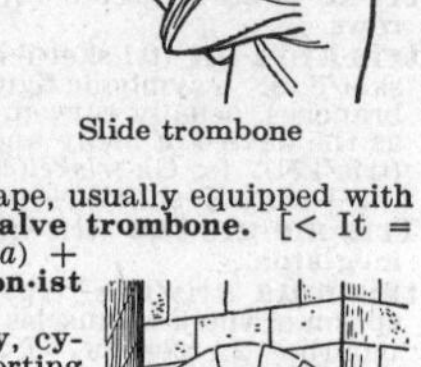
Slide trombone

trom·bi·di·a·sis (trom′bə dī′ə sis), *n. Vet. Pathol.* the condition of being infested with chiggers. Also, **trom·bi·di·o·sis** (trom′bi dī ō′sis). [< NL *trombid(ium)* genus name + -IASIS]

trom·bone (trom bōn′, trom′bōn), *n.* a musical wind instrument consisting of a cylindrical metal tube expanding into a bell and bent twice in U shape, usually equipped with a slide (**slide trombone**). Cf. **valve trombone.** [< It = *tromb(a)* trumpet (< OHG *trumba*) + *-one* aug. suffix] —**trom·bon·ist** (trom′bō nist, trom bō′-), *n.*

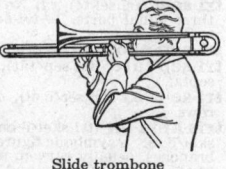

trom·mel (trom′əl), *n.* a rotary, cylindrical or conical screen for sorting ores, coal, gravel, etc., according to size. [< G *Trommel* drum]

trompe (tromp), *n.* 1. *Metall.* a device formerly used for inducing a blast of air upon the hearth of a forge by means of a current of falling water. 2. *Masonry.* a squinchlike structure for supporting an eccentric load having the form of a part of a cone, a sphere, or a vault. [< F: lit., TRUMP³]

trompe l'oeil (trômp′ lā′; *Fr.* trônp lœ′yᵊ), 1. visual deception, esp. in paintings in which objects are rendered in extremely fine detail emphasizing the illusion of tactile and spatial qualities. 2. a painting, mural, or panel of wallpaper designed to create such an effect. [< F: lit., trick of the eye]

-tron, a learned borrowing from Greek denoting an instrument, used in the formation of compound words: *cyclotron.* [< Gk *-tron*]

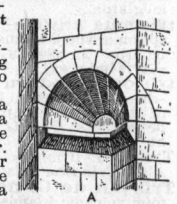

Trompes (def. 2)
A, At exterior angle
B, At interior angle

tro·na (trō′nə), *n.* a mineral, hydrous sodium carbonate and bicarbonate, $Na_2CO_3 \cdot NaHCO_3 \cdot 2H_2O$, occurring in dried or partly evaporated lake basins. [< Sw < Ar *trōn,* aph. var. of *natrūn* NATRON]

Trond·heim (trôn′hām), *n.* a seaport in central Norway, on Trondheim Fiord. 113,582 (est. 1965). Formerly, **Nidaros, Trond·hjem** (trôn′yem).

Trond′heim Fiord′, an inlet of the North Sea, extending into N Norway. 80 mi. long.

troop (tro͞op), *n.* 1. an assemblage of persons or things; company; band. 2. *Mil.* an armored cavalry or cavalry unit consisting of two or more platoons and a headquarters group. 3. **troops, a.** a group of soldiers, police, etc. **b.** soldiers, esp. enlisted persons: *How many American troops served overseas in World War II?* 4. a unit of Boy Scouts or Girl Scouts usually having a maximum of 32 members under the guidance of an adult leader. 5. a herd, flock, or swarm. 6. *Archaic.* a band or troupe of actors. —*v.i.* 7. to gather in a company; flock together. 8. to come, go, or pass in great numbers; throng. 9. to walk, as if in a march; go: *troop down to breakfast.* 10. to associate or consort (usually fol. by *with*). —*v.t.* 11. *Brit. Mil.* to carry (the flag or colors) in a ceremonial way before troops. [< F *troupe* back formation from *troupeau* herd < Gmc; see THORP]
—**Syn.** 1. body, group, crowd. See **company.** 6. TROOP, TROUPE both mean a band, company, or group. TROOP has various meanings as indicated in the definitions above. With the spelling TROUPE the word has the specialized meaning of a company of actors, singers, acrobats, or other performers.

troop′ car′rier, 1. a transport airplane used for carrying troops and their equipment. 2. an armored vehicle for transporting infantry troops and equipment.

troop·er (tro͞o′pər), *n.* 1. a horse-cavalry soldier. 2. a mounted policeman. 3. See **state trooper.** 4. a cavalry horse. 5. *Chiefly Brit.* a troopship.

troop·ship (tro͞op′ship′), *n.* a ship for the transportation of military troops; transport.

trop (trō), *adv. French.* too; too many; too much.

trop-, var. of **tropo-** before a vowel: *tropism.*

tro·pae·o·lum (trō pē′ə ləm), *n., pl.* **-lums, -la** (-lə). any plant of the genus *Tropaeolum*, comprising the nasturtiums. [< NL = L *tropae(um)* TROPHY + *-olum*, neut. of *-olus* dim. suffix]

-tropal, a suffix identical in meaning with **-tropic,** used to form adjectives from stems in **-trope.** [-TROPE + -AL[1]]

trope (trōp), *n.* **1.** *Rhet.* **a.** any literary or rhetorical device, as metaphor, metonymy, synecdoche, and irony, that consists in the use of words in other than their literal sense. **b.** an instance of this. Cf. **figure of speech. 2.** a phrase, sentence, or verse formerly interpolated in a liturgical text to amplify or embellish. [< L *tropus* figure in rhetoric < Gk *trópos* turn, turning, turn or figure of speech, akin to *trépein* to turn]

-trope, var. of **tropo-,** occurring as the final element in compound words: *heliotrope.* Cf. **-tropal, -tropic, -tropism, -tropous, -tropy.**

troph-, var. of **tropho-** before a vowel: *trophic.*

troph·ic (trof′ik), *adj.* *Physiol.* of or pertaining to nutrition; concerned in nutritive processes. [< Gk *trophikós* pertaining to food] —**troph′i·cal·ly,** *adv.*

tro·phied (trō′fēd), *adj.* adorned with trophies.

tropho-, a learned borrowing from Greek meaning "nourishment," used in the formation of compound words: *trophoplasm.* Also, *esp. before a vowel,* **troph-.** [comb. form of Gk *trophḗ* nourishment, food; akin to *tréphein* to feed, nourish]

troph·o·blast (trof′ə blast′), *n.* *Embryol.* the layer of extraembryonic ectoderm that chiefly nourishes the embryo or develops into fetal membranes with nutritive functions. —**troph′o·blas′tic,** *adj.*

troph·o·plasm (trof′ə plaz′əm), *n.* *Biol.* the kind of protoplasm that is regarded as forming the nutritive part of a cell. —**troph′o·plas′mic, troph·o·plas·mat·ic** (trof′ə-plaz mat′ik), *adj.*

tro·phy (trō′fē), *n., pl.* **-phies. 1.** anything taken in war, hunting, competition, etc., esp. when preserved as a memento; spoil, prize, or award. **2.** anything serving as a token or evidence of victory, valor, skill, etc. **3.** a carving, painting, or other representation of objects, as weapons or armor, associated with or symbolic of victory or achievement. [earlier *trophe* < F *trophée* < L *trop(h)aeum* < Gk *trópaion,* n. use of neut. of *trópaios,* Attic var. of *tropaîos* of turning or putting to flight = *trop(ḗ)* a turning (akin to *trépein* to turn) + *-aios* adj. suffix. See TROPE]

-trophy, a combining form referring to nourishment or growth, used in the formation of compound words: *hypertrophy.* [< Gk *-trophía* nutrition = *troph(ḗ)* food + *-ia* -Y]

trop·ic (trop′ik), *n.* **1.** *Geog.* **a.** either of two corresponding parallels of latitude on the terrestrial globe, one **(tropic of Cancer)** about 23½° N, and the other **(tropic of Capricorn)** about 23½° S of the equator, being the boundaries of the Torrid Zone. **b. the tropics,** the regions lying between and near these parallels of latitude; the Torrid Zone and neighboring regions. **2.** *Astron.* **a.** either of two circles on the celestial sphere, one lying in the same plane as the tropic of Cancer, the other in the same plane as the tropic of Capricorn. **b.** *Obs.* either of the two solstitial points, at which the sun reaches its greatest distance north and south of the celestial equator. —*adj.* **3.** of, pertaining to, characteristic of, or occurring in the tropics; tropical. [ME < L *tropicus* < Gk *tropikós* pertaining to a turn = *tróp(os)* turn + *-ikos* -IC]

-tropic, a combination of **-trope** and **-ic,** used in the formation of adjectives from stems in **-trope:** *geotropic.* Also, **-tropal.** [see TROPIC]

trop·i·cal (trop′i kəl *for 1, 2;* trō′pi kəl *for 3*), *adj.* **1.** pertaining to, characteristic of, occurring in, or inhabiting the tropics. **2.** used in or suitable for the tropics. **3.** pertaining to, characterized by, or of the nature of a trope or tropes; metaphorical. —**trop′i·cal′i·ty,** *n.* —**trop′i·cal·ly,** *adv.*

trop′ical fish′, any of numerous small, usually brightly-colored fishes indigenous to the tropics that are kept and bred in aquariums.

trop·i·cal·ise (trop′i kə līz′), *v.t.,* **-ised, -is·ing.** *Chiefly Brit.* tropicalize. —**trop′i·cal·i·sa′tion,** *n.*

trop·i·cal·ize (trop′i kə līz′), *v.t.,* **-ized, -iz·ing.** to adapt or make suitable for use in tropical regions. —**trop′i·cal·i·za′tion,** *n.*

trop′ical year′, year (def. 3b).

trop′ic bird′, any of several totipalmate sea birds of the family *Phaethontidae,* found chiefly in tropical regions, having white plumage with black markings and a pair of greatly elongated central tail feathers.

trop′ic of Can′cer. See under **tropic** (def. 1a).

trop′ic of Cap′ricorn. See under **tropic** (def. 1a).

tro·pism (trō′piz əm), *n.* *Biol.* an orientation of an organism to an external stimulus, as light, esp. by growth rather than by movement. [separate use of -TROPISM] —**tro·pis·mat·ic** (trō′piz mat′ik), *adj.* —**tro·pis·tic** (trō pis′tik), *adj.*

-tropism, a combination of **-trope** and **-ism,** used in the formation of nouns from stems in **-trope:** *heliotropism.*

tropo-, a learned borrowing from Greek meaning "turn," "turning," often indicating a change, or an attraction to a given thing, used in the formation of compound words: *tropophilous.* Also, *esp. before a vowel,* **trop-.** Cf. **-trope, -tropism, -tropy, -tropal, -tropic, -tropous.** [comb. form repr. Gk *trópos* turn, *tropḗ* turning]

tro·pol·o·gy (trō pol′ə jē), *n., pl.* **-gies** for 2. **1.** the use of figurative language in speech or writing. **2.** a treatise on figures of speech or tropes. **3.** the use of a Scriptural text so as to give it a moral interpretation or significance apart from its direct meaning. [< LL *tropologi(a)* < Gk. See TROPE, -LOGY] —**trop·o·log·ic** (trop′ə loj′ik), **trop′o·log′i·cal,** *adj.*

trop·o·pause (trop′ə pôz′), *n.* *Meteorol.* the boundary, or transitional layer, between the troposphere and the stratosphere.

tro·poph·i·lous (trō pof′ə ləs), *adj.* *Ecol.* adapted to a climate characterized by marked environmental changes.

trop·o·sphere (trop′ə sfēr′), *n.* *Meteorol.* the inner layer of the atmosphere, varying in height between about 6 miles and 12 miles, within which nearly all cloud formations occur and weather conditions manifest themselves. —**trop·o·spher·ic** (trop′ə sfer′ik), *adj.*

-tropous, a combination of **-trope** and **-ous,** used in the formation of adjectives from nouns ending in **-trope:** *heterotropous.* Cf. **-tropic, -tropal.** [< Gk *-tropos* pertaining to a turn]

-tropy, a combination of **-trope** and **-y,** used in the formation of nouns: *allotropy.* Cf. **-tropism.** [< Gk *-tropía.* See -TROPE, -Y[3]]

Tros·sachs (tros′əks), *n.* a valley in central Scotland, in Perth county, near Loch Katrine.

trot (trot), *v.,* **trot·ted, trot·ting,** *n.* —*v.i.* **1.** (of a horse) to go at a gait between a walk and a run, in which the legs move in diagonal pairs, but not quite simultaneously. **2.** to go at a quick, steady pace; move briskly; bustle; hurry. —*v.t.* **3.** to cause to trot. **4.** to ride at a trot. **5.** to lead at a trot. **6.** to execute by trotting. **7. trot out,** *Informal.* **a.** to bring forward for inspection. **b.** to bring to the attention of; introduce; submit: *He trots out his old jokes at every party.* —*n.* **8.** the gait of a horse, dog, or other quadruped, when trotting. **9.** the sound made by an animal when trotting. **10.** the jogging gait of a human being, between a walk and a run. **11.** *Harness Racing.* a race for trotters. **12.** brisk, continuous movement or activity: *I've been on the trot all afternoon.* **13.** *U.S. Slang.* a literal translation used illicitly in doing schoolwork; crib; pony. **14. the trots,** *Slang.* diarrhea. [ME *trotte(n)* < MF *troter* < Gmc; akin to OHG *trottōn* to tread, (> MHG *trotten* to run)]

troth (trôth, trōth), *n.* *Archaic.* **1.** faithfulness, fidelity, or loyalty: *by my troth.* **2.** truth or verity: *in troth.* **3.** one's word or promise, esp. in engaging oneself to marry. [ME *trowthe, trouthe,* OE *trēowth.* See TRUTH]

troth·plight (trôth′plīt′, trōth′-), *Archaic.* —*n.* **1.** engagement to be married; betrothal. —*v.t.* **2.** to betroth. —*adj.* **3.** betrothed. [ME *trouth plight* having plighted troth, betrothed]

trot·line (trot′līn′), *n.* a strong fishing line strung across a stream, or deep into a river, having individual hooks attached by smaller lines at intervals.

Trot·sky (trot′skē; *Russ.* trôt′skē), *n.* **Leon** (*Lev* or *Leib Davidovich Bronstein*), 1879–1940, Russian revolutionary and writer; minister of war 1918–25. Also, **Trot′ski.**

Trot·sky·ism (trot′skē iz′əm), *n.* the form of communism advocated by Leon Trotsky, based on an immediate, world-wide revolution by the proletariat. —**Trot′sky·ite′, Trot′sky·ist,** *n., adj.*

Trot′skyist Interna′tional. See **Fourth International.**

trot·ter (trot′ər), *n.* **1.** an animal that trots, esp. a horse bred and trained for harness racing. **2.** a person who moves about briskly and constantly. **3.** the foot of an animal, esp. of a sheep or pig, used as food. [ME]

tro·tyl (trō′til, -tēl), *n.* *Chem.* See **TNT.** [(TRINI)TROT(OLUENE) + -YL]

trou·ba·dour (tro͞o′bə dōr′, -dôr′, -do͝or′), *n.* **1.** one of a class of medieval lyric poets who flourished principally in southern France from the 11th to 13th centuries, and wrote songs and poems of a complex metrical form in langue d'oc, chiefly on themes of courtly love. Cf. **trouvère. 2.** any wandering singer or minstrel. [< F < Pr *trobador* = *trob(ar)* to find, compose (see TROVER) + *-ador* < L *-ātor* -ATOR]

trou·ble (trub′əl), *v.,* **-bled, -bling,** *n.* —*v.t.* **1.** to disturb the mental calm and contentment of; worry; distress; agitate. **2.** to put to inconvenience, exertion, pains, or the like: *May I trouble you to shut the door?* **3.** to cause bodily pain, discomfort, or disorder to; afflict: *Her arthritis troubles her greatly.* **4.** to annoy, vex, or bother. **5.** to disturb, agitate, or stir up (liquid) so as to make it turbid. —*v.i.* **6.** to put oneself to inconvenience, extra effort, or the like. **7.** to be distressed; worry. —*n.* **8.** difficulty, annoyance, or harassment: *It would be no trouble at all to advise you.* **9.** an unfortunate or distressing position, circumstance, or occurrence; misfortune: *financial trouble.* **10.** civil disorder, disturbance, or conflict. **11.** a physical disorder, disease, ailment, etc.; ill health. **12.** effort, exertion, or inconvenience in accomplishing some action, deed, etc. **13.** something or someone that is a cause or source of disturbance, annoyance, etc. **14. in trouble,** *Informal.* being pregnant out of wedlock (used as a euphemism). [ME *trouble(n)* < OF *troubler* < VL **turbulare* < **turbulus* turbid, back formation from L *turbulentus* TURBULENT] —**trou′bled·ly,** *adv.* —**trou′bling·ly,** *adv.* —**Syn. 1.** concern, upset. **4.** hector, harass. **13.** trial, affliction. —**Ant. 1.** mollify; delight.

trou·ble·mak·er (trub′əl mā′kər), *n.* a person who causes trouble for others. —**trou′ble·mak′ing,** *n.*

trou·ble·shoot (trub′əl sho͞ot′), *v.i.,* **-shoot·ed** or **-shot, -shoot·ing.** to act or be employed as a troubleshooter. Also, **trou′ble-shoot′.** [back formation from TROUBLESHOOTER]

trou·ble·shoot·er (trub′əl sho͞o′tər), *n.* **1.** a person with special skill in resolving disputes, impasses, etc., as in business, national, or international affairs. **2.** an expert in discovering and eliminating the cause of trouble in mechanical equipment, power lines, etc. Also, **trou′ble-shoot′er.**

trou·ble·some (trub′əl səm), *adj.* **1.** causing trouble, annoyance, or difficulty; vexatious. **2.** laborious; difficult. **3.** *Archaic.* full of distress or affliction. —**Syn. 1.** perplexing, galling, harassing. **2.** arduous, hard, burdensome.

trou′ble spot′, an area in which trouble exists or is expected to develop.

trou·blous (trub′ləs), *adj.* *Archaic.* **1.** characterized by trouble; unsettled: *troublous times.* **2.** causing disturbance: *a troublous preacher.* [late ME *troub(e)lous* = *trouble* turbid (< MF < VL **turbulus;* see TROUBLE) + -OUS] —**trou′blous·ly,** *adv.* —**trou′blous·ness,** *n.*

trou-de-loup (tro͞od′əlo͞o′), *n., pl.* **trous-de-loup** (tro͞od′ə-lo͞o′). *Mil.* a conical or pyramidal pit with a pointed stake fixed vertically in the center, rows of which are dug in front of a fortification to hinder an enemy's approach, formerly used chiefly against cavalry. [< F: lit., wolfhole]

trough (trôf, trof; *dial.* trôth, troth), *n.* **1.** a long, narrow, open receptacle, usually boxlike in shape, used chiefly to hold water or food for animals. **2.** a channel or gutter. **3.** any long depression or hollow, as between two ridges or waves. **4.** *Meteorol.* an elongated area of relatively low pressure. [ME; OE *trōh;* c. D, G, Icel *trog*] —**trough′like′,** *adj.*

trounce (trouns), *v.t.,* **trounced, trounc·ing. 1.** to beat severely; thrash. **2.** to punish. **3.** to defeat. [?]

troupe (tro͞op), *n., v.,* **trouped, troup·ing.** *Theat.* **—*n.* 1.** a company, band, or group of singers, actors, or other performers, esp. one that travels about. **—*v.i.* 2.** to travel as a member of a theatrical company; barnstorm. [< F: TROOP] **—Syn. 1.** See **troop.**

troup·er (tro͞o′pər), *n.* **1.** an actor, esp. in a touring company. **2.** an experienced, devoted, and dependable performer, esp. a veteran actor.

troup·i·al (tro͞o′pē əl), *n.* any of several American birds of the family *Icteridae,* esp. one with brilliantly colored plumage, as *Icterus icterus,* of South America. [< F *troupiale* (so called from its gregariousness). See TROOP, -IAL]

trou·ser (trou′zər), *adj.* of or pertaining to trousers: *trouser cuffs.* [back formation from TROUSERS]

trou·sers (trou′zərz), *n.* (*construed as pl.*) **1.** Sometimes, **trou′ser.** Also called **pants.** a rather loose-fitting outer garment for the lower part of the body, having legs, usually of full length. Cf. **Bermuda shorts, breeches, knickers** (def. 1), **short** (def. 24a), **slacks. 2.** pantalets. [*trouse* (var. of TREWS) + (DRAW)ERS]

trous·seau (tro͞o′sō, tro͞o sō′), *n., pl.* **-seaux** (-sōz, -sōz′), **-seaus.** an outfit of clothing, household linen, etc., for a bride. [< F < MF *troussel* small bundle = *trusse* bundle (see TRUSS) + *-el* < L *-ellus* dim. suffix]

trout (trout), *n., pl.* (*esp. collectively*) **trout,** (*esp. referring to two or more kinds or species*) **trouts. 1.** any of several game fishes of the genus *Salmo,* related to the salmon. Cf. **brown trout, rainbow trout. 2.** any of various game fishes of the salmon family of the genera *Salvelinus* and *Cristovomer.* Cf. **brook trout** (def. 1), **char**[2], **Dolly Varden** (def. 2). **3.** any of several unrelated fishes, as a bass, *Micropterus salmoides,* a drum of the genus *Cynoscion,* or a greenling of the genus *Hexagrammos.* [ME *trou(h)te,* OE *truht* < L *tructa* < Gk *trṓktēs* gnawer, a sea fish = *trṓg(ein)* (to) gnaw + *-tēs* n. suffix] **—trout′like′,** *adj.*

Brook trout, *Salvelinus fontinalis* (Length 1½ ft.)

trout·perch (trout′pûrch′), *n., pl.* **-perch·es,** (*esp. collectively*) **-perch.** a North American, fresh-water fish, *Percopsis omiscomaycas,* resembling both trouts and perches.

trou·vère (tro͞o vâr′; *Fr.* tʀo͞o vɛʀ′), *n., pl.* **-vères** (-vârz′; *Fr.* -vɛʀ′). one of a class of medieval poets who flourished in northern France during the 12th and 13th centuries, wrote in langue d'oïl, and composed chiefly the chansons de geste and works on the themes of courtly love. Also, **trouveur.** Cf. **troubadour** (def. 1). [< F; OF *troveor* = *trov(er)* (to) find, compose (see TROVER) + *-eor* < L *-ātor* -ATOR]

trou·veur (tro͞o vûr′; *Fr.* tʀo͞o vœʀ′), *n., pl.* **-veurs** (-vûrz′; *Fr.* -vœʀ′). trouvère.

Trou·ville (tʀo͞o vēl′), *n.* a seaport in NW France, on the English Channel: resort. 6822 (1962). Also called **Trouville-sur-Mer** (tʀo͞o vēl′syʀ mɛʀ′).

trove (trōv), *n.* something valuable or pleasing, esp. something that has been kept hidden or is discovered. [short for TREASURE TROVE]

tro·ver (trō′vər), *n.* *Law.* an action for the recovery of the value of personal property wrongfully converted by another to his own use. [< MF, OF: to find, orig., stir up < L *turbāre* to disturb. See TURBID]

trow (trō), *v.i.* *Archaic.* to believe, think, or suppose. [ME *trowe(n),* OE *trēow(i)an* to believe < *trēow* belief; akin to Icel *trūa,* G *trauen,* Goth *trauan* to trust, believe. See TRUST, TRUE]

trow·el (trou′əl), *n., v.,* **-eled, -el·ing** or (*esp. Brit.*) **-elled, -el·ling. —*n.* 1.** any of various tools having a flat blade with a handle, used for depositing and working mortar, plaster, etc. **2.** a similar tool with a curved, scooplike blade, used in gardening. **—*v.t.* 3.** to apply, shape, smooth, or dig with or as with a trowel. [ME < OF *truelle* < LL *truella* = L *tru(a)* ladle + *-ella* dim. suffix]

troy (troi), *adj.* expressed or computed in troy weight. [ME *troye,* named after TROYES, France, where it was standard]

Troy (troi), *n.* **1.** Latin, **Ilium.** Greek, **Ilion.** an ancient ruined city in NW Asia Minor: site of Trojan War. **2.** a city in E New York, on the Hudson River. 62,918 (1970). **3.** a city in SE Michigan, near Detroit. 39,419 (1970).

Troyes (tʀwä), *n.* a city in NE France, SE of Paris, on the Seine: cathedrals. 68,898 (1962).

troy′ weight′, a system of weights in use for precious metals and gems.

trp, *Mil.* troop.

tru·an·cy (tro͞o′ən sē), *n., pl.* **-cies. 1.** the act or state of being truant. **2.** an instance of being truant. Also, **truantry.**

tru·ant (tro͞o′ənt), *n.* **1.** a student who stays away from school without permission. **2.** a person who shirks or neglects his duty. **—*adj.* 3.** absent from school without permission. **4.** neglectful of duty or responsibility; idle. **5.** of, pertaining to, or characteristic of a truant. **—*v.i.* 6.** to be truant. [ME < OF: vagrant, beggar < Celt; cf. Welsh *truan* wretched, wretch]

tru′ant of′ficer, a public-school official who investigates unauthorized absences from school.

tru·ant·ry (tro͞o′ən trē), *n., pl.* **-ries.** truancy.

truce (tro͞os), *n.* **1.** a suspension of hostilities for a specified period of time by mutual agreement of the warring parties; armistice. **2.** an agreement or treaty establishing this. [ME *trewes,* pl. of *trewe,* OE *trēow* belief, pledge, treaty. See TROW[1]]

Tru·cial O·man (tro͞o′shəl ō män′), a former name of **United Arab Emirates.** Also called **Tru′cial Coast′, Tru′cial Sheik′doms, Tru′cial States′.**

truck[1] (truk), *n.* **1.** any of various forms of vehicle for carrying loads, freight, etc., usually consisting of either a single self-propelled unit or of a trailer vehicle hauled by a tractor unit. **2.** Also called **hand truck.** a barrowlike frame with low wheels, used to move heavy objects. **3.** any of various wheeled devices for moving loads. **4.** a group of two or more pairs of wheels in one frame, for supporting one end of a railroad car, locomotive, etc. **5.** *Naut.* a circular or square piece of wood fixed on the head of a mast or the top of a flagstaff, usually containing small holes for signal halyards. **—*v.t.* 6.** to transport by a truck or trucks. **7.** to put on a truck. **—*v.i.* 8.** to convey articles or goods on a truck. **9.** to drive a truck. [back formation from *truckle* wheel. See TRUCKLE[2]]

truck[2] (truk), *n.* **1.** *U.S.* vegetables raised for the market. **2.** *Informal.* trash or rubbish: *That's a lot of truck.* **3.** *Informal.* dealings: *I'll have no truck with him.* **4.** barter. **5.** See **truck system. —*v.t.* 6.** to exchange; trade; barter. **—*v.i.* 7.** to exchange commodities; barter. [ME *trukien* < OF *troquer* to exchange]

truck[3] (truk), *n.* **1.** a shuffling jitterbug step. **—*v.i.* 2.** to dance with such steps. [special use of TRUCK[1]]

truck·age (truk′ij), *n.* **1.** conveyance by a truck or trucks. **2.** the charge for this.

truck·driv·er (truk′drī′vər), *n.* a person who drives a truck.

truck·er[1] (truk′ər), *n.* **1.** a person who drives a truck; truckdriver. **2.** a person whose business is trucking goods.

truck·er[2] (truk′ər), *n.* *U.S.* a truck farmer.

truck′ farm′, *U.S.* a farm for the growing of vegetables for the market. Also called **truck′ gar′den.** Cf. **market garden. —truck′ farmer. —truck′ farming.**

truck·ing[1] (truk′ing), *n.* the art or business of conveying articles or goods on trucks. [TRUCK[1] + -ING[1]]

truck·ing[2] (truk′ing), *n.* **1.** *U.S.* the growing of vegetables for the market. **2.** commercial bartering. [TRUCK[2] + -ING[1]]

truck·le[1] (truk′əl), *v.i.,* **-led, -ling.** to submit or yield obsequiously or tamely (usually fol. by *to*). [special use of obs. *truckle* to sleep on truckle bed. See TRUCKLE[2]] **—truck′ler,** *n.*

truck·le[2] (truk′əl), *n.* See **trundle bed.** [late ME *trocle* sheave, roller < AF < L *trochlea* pulley. See TROCHLEA]

truck′le bed′. See **trundle bed.**

truck·load (truk′lōd′), *n.* **1.** an amount comprising a full or almost full load on a truck. **2.** the minimum weight legally required for making shipments at a rate (**truck′load rate′**) below that charged for shipments under this minimum.

truck·man (truk′mən), *n., pl.* **-men. 1.** a person who drives a truck. **2.** a man who is in the business of trucking goods, produce, etc.

truck′ sys′tem, the system of paying wages in goods instead of money. Also called **truck.**

truck′ trac′tor, *Auto.* a motor truck with a short body and no cargo space, for hauling semitrailers.

truck′ trail′er, *Auto.* a trailer designed to be drawn by a truck tractor or other motor truck.

truc·u·lent (truk′yə lənt, tro͞o′kyə-), *adj.* **1.** fierce; cruel; savagely brutal. **2.** brutally harsh; vitriolic; scathing. **3.** aggressively hostile; belligerent. [< L *truculentus* = *trucu-* (comb. form of *trux* savage, grim) + *-lentus* -LENT] **—truc′u·lence, truc′u·len·cy,** *n.* **—truc′u·lent·ly,** *adv.* **—Ant. 1.** amiable, gentle.

Tru·deau (tro͞o dō′), *n.* **Pi·erre Elliot** (pē âr′), **born 1919, Canadian statesman: prime minister 1968–79 and 1980–84.**

trudge (truj), *v.,* **trudged, trudg·ing,** *n.* **—*v.i.* 1.** to walk, esp. laboriously or wearily. **—*v.t.* 2.** to walk laboriously or wearily along or over. **—*n.* 3.** a laborious or tiring walk; tramp. [? TR(EAD + DR)UDGE] **—Syn. 1.** tramp. See **pace**[1].

trudg·en (truj′ən), *n.* *Swimming.* a stroke in which a double overarm motion and a scissors kick are used. Also called **trudg′en stroke′.** [named after John *Trudgen* (1852–1902), British swimmer]

true (tro͞o), *adj.,* **tru·er, tru·est,** *n., adv., v.,* **trued, tru·ing** or **true·ing. —*adj.* 1.** in accordance with or not contrary to fact. **2.** having a basis in fact: *not fiction, but a true story.* **3.** being really such; authentic: *true vanilla flavoring.* **4.** being such in the best or most desirable sense: *true statesmanship.* **5.** loyal; faithful. **6.** reflecting sincerely one's feelings or intentions: *true amusement.* **7.** exact; accurate; of the proper form: *a true copy; a true surface.* **8.** characterized by truth or accuracy; sure: *a true intuition; a true aim.* **9.** *Biol.* conforming to the type, norm, or standard of structure of a particular group; typical: *The lion is a true cat.* **10.** *Stockbreeding.* purebred. **11.** *Navig.* (of a bearing, course, etc.) determined in relation to true north. **12.** *Archaic.* truthful. **13. come true,** to come to realization: *a dream that comes true.* **—*n.* 14.** exact or accurate formation, position, or adjustment: *to be out of true.* **15. the true,** that which is true; truth. **—*adv.* 16.** in a true manner; truly; truthfully. **17.** exactly or accurately. **18.** in conformity with the ancestral type: *to breed true.* **—*v.t.* 19.** to make true; shape, adjust, place, etc., exactly or accurately. [ME *trewe,* OE *trēowe* loyal, trusty, honest (see TROW, TRUCE); akin to G *treu,* D *trouw,* Goth *triggws,* Icel *tryggr*] **—Syn. 1.** factual, veracious. **5.** trustworthy; staunch, constant, steady, unwavering.

true′ bill′, *Law.* a bill of indictment endorsed by a grand jury as being sufficiently supported by evidence to justify a hearing of the case.

true-blue (tro͞o′blo͞o′), *adj.* unwaveringly loyal or faithful; staunch.

true·born (tro͞o′bôrn′), *adj.* genuinely or authentically so because of birth.

true′ bug′, bug[1] (def. 1).

true′ course′, *Navig.* a course whose bearing is given relative to the geographical meridian. Cf. **compass course, magnetic course.**

true′ fly′, fly[2] (def. 1).

true′ fres′co, fresco (def. 1).

true·heart·ed (tro͞o′här′tid), *adj.* **1.** faithful; loyal. **2.** honest; sincere. Also, **true′-heart′ed.** [late ME] **—true′heart′ed·ness,** *n.*

true′ jade′, jadeite or nephrite.

true′ lev′el, an imaginary surface everywhere perpendicular to the plumb line, or line of gravity.

true-life (trōō′līf′), *adj.* (of a story) depicting everyday life accurately; not fictional; realistic. Also, **true-to-life** (trōō′tə līf′).

true·love (trōō′luv′), *n.* **1.** a sweetheart; a truly loving or loved person. **2.** the herb Paris, *Paris quadrifolia,* having a whorl of four leaves suggesting a truelove knot. [ME *trewe love,* OE *trēow lufu*]

true′love knot′, a complicated ornamental knot, esp. a double knot having two interlacing bows, regarded as an emblem of true love or interwoven affections. Also called **true′ lov′er's knot′, true′-lov′er's knot′.**

true′ north′, *Navig.* the direction of the north pole from a given point.

true·pen·ny (trōō′pen′ē), *n., pl.* **-nies.** *Archaic.* a trusty, honest fellow.

true′ rib′, *Anat.* one member of the first seven pairs of ribs that are attached in man to the sternum by costal cartilages.

truffe (tʀyf), *n. French.* **1.** truffle. **2.** *Slang.* peasant; boor.

truf·fle (truf′əl, trōō′fəl), *n.* **1.** any of several subterranean, edible, ascomycetous fungi of the genus *Tuber.* **2.** any of various similar fungi of other genera. [appar. < Vaudois (Swiss) *trufla* << VL **tūfera* < Oscan-Umbrian *tūfer,* c. L *tūber* truffle. See TUBER[1]]

tru·ism (trōō′iz əm), *n.* a self-evident, obvious truth. —**tru·is′tic, tru·is′ti·cal,** *adj.* —**Syn.** cliché, platitude.

Tru·jil·lo (trōō hē′ō; *Sp.* tʀōō hē′yô), *n.* **1. Ra·fa·el Le·on·i·das** (raf′ā el′ lē on′i dəs; *Sp.* rä′fä el′ le′ô-nē′thäs), *(Rafael Leonidas Trujillo Molina),* 1891–1961, Dominican general and politician: president 1930–38, 1942–52. **2.** a seaport in NW Peru. 129,470 (est. 1966).

Truk′ Is′lands (truk), a group of the Caroline Islands, in the N Pacific: an important Japanese naval base in World War II. 21,041 (1970); ab. 50 sq. mi.

trull (trul), *n.* a prostitute; strumpet. [< G *Trulle,* var. of *Trudel* loose woman]

tru·ly (trōō′lē), *adv.* **1.** in accordance with fact or truth; truthfully. **2.** exactly; accurately; correctly. **3.** rightly; properly; duly. **4.** really; genuinely; authentically. **5.** indeed; verily. **6.** sincerely: *yours truly.* **7.** *Archaic.* faithfully; loyally. [ME *treuli,* OE *trēowlīce*]

Tru·man (trōō′mən), *n.* **Harry S,** 1884–1972, 33rd president of the U.S. 1945–53.

Trum·bull (trum′bəl), *n.* **1. John,** 1756–1843, U.S. painter. **2.** his father, **Jonathan,** 1710–85, U.S. statesman. **3.** a city in SW Connecticut. 31,394 (1970).

tru·meau (trōō mō′; *Fr.* tʀy mō′), *n., pl.* **-meaux** (-mōz′; *Fr.* -mō′). *Archit.* a column supporting a tympanum of a doorway at its center. See illus. at **tympanum.** [< F]

trump[1] (trump), *n.* **1.** *Cards.* **a.** any playing card of a suit that for the time outranks the other suits, such a card being able to take any card of another suit. **b.** Often, **trumps.** (*construed as sing.*) the suit itself. **2.** *Informal.* a fine person; brick. —*v.t.* **3.** *Cards.* to take with a trump. **4.** to excel; surpass; outdo. —*v.i.* **5.** *Cards.* **a.** to play a trump. **b.** to take a trick with a trump. **6. trump up,** to devise deceitfully or dishonestly, as an accusation; fabricate. [unexplained var. of TRIUMPH]

trump[2] (trump), *Archaic or Poetic.* —*n.* **1.** trumpet. **2.** its sound. —*v.i.* **3.** to blow a trumpet. [ME *trompe* < OF < OHG *trumpa,* var. of *trumba* trumpet]

trump card (trump′ kärd′ *for 1;* trump′ kärd′ *for 2*), **1.** *Cards.* trump[1] (def. 1a). **2.** *Informal.* something that gives one person or group the advantage over another: *The surprise witness was his trump card.*

trumped-up (trumpt′up′), *adj.* spuriously devised; fabricated: *He was arrested on some trumped-up charge.*

Trum·pel·dor (trum′pəl dôr′), *n.* **Joseph,** 1880–1920, Palestinian hero and Zionist leader, born in Russia.

trump·er·y (trum′pə rē), *n., pl.* **-ries,** *adj.* —*n.* **1.** something without use or value. **2.** nonsense; twaddle. **3.** *Archaic.* worthless finery. —*adj.* **4.** of little or no value; worthless. [late ME *trompery* deceit < MF *tromperie* = *tromp(er)* to deceive + *-erie* -ERY]

trum·pet (trum′pit), *n.* **1.** *Music.* **a.** any of a family of brass wind instruments with a powerful, penetrating tone, consisting of a tube commonly curved once or twice around on itself and having a cup-shaped mouthpiece at one end and a flaring bell at the other. **b.** an organ stop having a tone resembling that of a trumpet. **c.** a trumpeter. **2.** something used as or resembling a trumpet, esp. in sound. **3.** a sound like that of a trumpet. **4.** the loud shrill cry of an animal, esp. an elephant. **5.** See **ear trumpet. 6. trumpets,** any of several pitcher plants of the southeastern U.S. —*v.i.* **7.** to blow a trumpet. **8.** to emit a loud, trumpet-like cry, as an elephant. —*v.t.* **9.** to sound on a trumpet. **10.** to utter with a sound like that of a trumpet. **11.** to proclaim loudly or widely. [ME *trumpette, trompette* < F; see TRUMP[2], -ET] —**trum′pet·like′,** *adj.*

Trumpet (def. 1a)

trum′pet creep′er, any climbing, bignoniaceous plant of the genus *Campsis,* esp. *C. radicans,* of the southern U.S., having large, red, trumpet-shaped flowers.

trum·pet·er (trum′pi tər), *n.* **1.** a person who plays a trumpet; trumpet player. **2.** a person who proclaims, extols, or eulogizes. **3.** any of several large, South American birds of the family *Psophiidae,* esp. *Psophia crepitans,* related to the cranes and rails, having a loud, harsh, prolonged cry. **4.** See **trumpeter swan. 5.** one of a breed of domestic pigeons.

trum′peter swan′, a large North American wild swan, *Olor buccinator,* having a sonorous cry.

trum′pet hon′eysuckle, an American honeysuckle, *Lonicera sempervirens,* having large, tubular flowers, deep-red outside and yellow within.

trum·pet·weed (trum′pit wēd′), *n.* any of several eupatoriums, as a boneset, *Eupatorium perfoliatum,* and the joe-pye weeds, *E. maculatum* and *E. purpureum.*

Truncate leaf

truncate (trung′kāt), *v.,* **-cat·ed, -cat·ing,** *adj.* —*v.t.* **1.** to shorten by cutting off a part; cut short: *Truncate detailed explanations.* —*adj.* **2.** truncated. **3.** *Biol.* **a.** square or broad at the end, as if cut off transversely. **b.** lacking the apex, as certain spiral shells. [< L *truncātus* lopped (ptp. of *truncāre*). See TRUNK, -ATE[1]] —**trun′cate·ly,** *adv.*

trun·cat·ed (trung′kā tid), *adj.* **1.** shortened by or as by having a part cut off. **2.** (of a geometric figure or solid) having the apex, vertex, or end cut off by a plane. **3.** *Crystall.* (of a crystal) having angles or edges cut off or replaced by a single plane. **4.** *Biol.* truncate (def. 3). **5.** *Pros.* (of a line of verse) lacking at the beginning or end one or more unstressed syllables needed to fill out the metrical pattern.

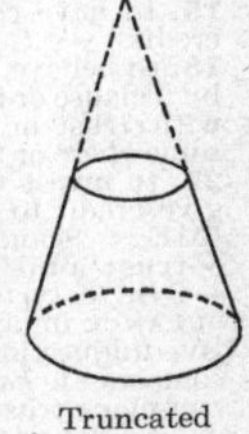
Truncated cone

trun·ca·tion (trung kā′shən), *n.* **1.** the act or process of truncating. **2.** the quality or state of being truncated. **3.** *Pros.* the omission of one or more unaccented syllables at the beginning or the end of a line of verse. [< LL *truncātiōn-* (s. of *truncātiō*)]

trun·cheon (trun′chən), *n.* **1.** *Chiefly Brit.* the club carried by a policeman; billy. **2.** a staff representing an office or authority; baton. **3.** *Obs.* a club or cudgel. **4.** *Obs.* the shaft of a spear. —*v.t.* **5.** *Archaic.* to beat with a club. [ME *tronchon* fragment < MF < VL **trunciōn-,* s. of **trunciō* lit., a lopping. See TRUNK, -ION]

trun·dle (trun′dəl), *v.,* **-dled, -dling,** *n.* —*v.t.* **1.** to cause (a circular object) to roll along; roll. **2.** to convey or move in a wagon, cart, or other wheeled vehicle; wheel. **3.** *Archaic.* to cause to rotate; twirl; spin. —*v.i.* **4.** to roll along, as a circular object. **5.** to move on or as on a wheel or wheels. —*n.* **6.** a small wheel, roller, or the like. **7.** a lantern wheel. **8.** each of the bars of a lantern wheel. **9.** *Obs.* a truck or carriage on low wheels. [var. of obs. *trindle* roll, trundle, ME *trindel,* OE *tryndel* circle, ring. See TREND] —**trun′dler,** *n.*

trun′dle bed′, a low bed moving on casters, usually pushed under another bed when not in use. Also called **truckle bed.**

trunk (trungk), *n.* **1.** the main stem of a tree, as distinct from the branches and roots. **2.** a large, sturdy box or chest for holding or transporting clothes, personal effects, etc. **3.** *U.S.* a large compartment in an automobile in which luggage and other articles may be kept. **4.** the body of man or an animal excluding the head and limbs; torso. **5.** the main channel, artery, or line in a river, railroad, highway, canal, or other tributary system. **6.** *Telephony, Telegraphy.* a telephone line or channel between two central offices or switching devices. **7.** *Anat.* the main body of an artery, nerve, or the like, as distinct from its branches. **8.** the long, cylindrical nasal appendage of the elephant. **9. trunks, a.** brief shorts, loose-fitting or tight, worn by men chiefly for boxing, swimming, and track. **b.** *Obs.* See **trunk hose. 10.** *Naut.* **a.** a large enclosed passage through the decks or bulkheads of a vessel, for cooling, ventilation, or the like. **b.** any of various watertight casings in a vessel, as the vertical one above the slot for a centerboard in the bottom of a boat. —*adj.* **11.** of, pertaining to, or noting a main channel or line, as of a railroad, river, etc. [late ME *trunke* < L *truncus* stem, trunk, stump, n. use of *truncus* (adj.) lopped] —**trunk′less,** *adj.*

trunk′ cab′in, a cabin of a yacht that presents a long, low profile with a relatively unbroken line fore and aft.

trunk′ call′, *Chiefly Brit.* a long-distance phone call.

trunk·fish (trungk′fish′), *n., pl.* (*esp. collectively*) **-fish,** (*esp. referring to two or more kinds or species*) **-fish·es.** any plectognath fish of the family *Ostraciontidae,* found in warm seas, having a boxlike body encased in bony, polygonal plates. Also called **boxfish.**

trunk′ hose′, full, baglike breeches reaching to the middle of the thigh, worn in the 16th and 17th centuries.

trunk′ line′, **1.** a major long-distance transportation line. **2.** trunk (def. 6).

trun·nion (trun′yən), *n.* **1.** either of the two cylindrical projections on a cannon, one on each side, for supporting the cannon on its carriage. **2.** any of various similar supports for machinery. [< F *trognon* trunk, stump, core (of fruit)] —**trun′nioned,** *adj.*

truss (trus), *v.t.* **1.** to tie, bind, or fasten. **2.** to make fast with skewers, thread, or the like, as the wings or legs of a fowl in preparation for cooking. **3.** to furnish or support with a truss or trusses. **4.** to tie or secure (the body) closely or tightly; bind (often fol. by *up*). **5.** *Falconry.* (of a hawk, falcon, etc.) to grasp (prey) firmly. —*n.* **6.** *Engineering, Building Trades.* any of various structural frames usually based on the geometric rigidity of the triangle and composed of straight members subject to longitudinal compression, tension, or both, so disposed as to function as a beam or cantilever to support bridges, roofs, etc. **7.** *Med.* an apparatus consisting of a pad usually supported by a belt for maintaining a hernia in a reduced state. **8.** *Hort.* a compact terminal cluster or head of flowers. **9.** *Naut.* a device for supporting a standing yard, having a pivot permitting the yard to swing horizontally when braced. [ME *trusse(n)* < OF *tr(o)usser,* var. of *torser* < VL **torciare* < **torca* bundle, TORCH] —**truss′er,** *n.*

truss′ bridge′, a bridge in which the loads are supported by trusses.

trust (trust), *n.* **1.** belief in and reliance on the integrity, strength, ability, surety, etc., of a person or thing. **2.** confident expectation of something; hope. **3.** confidence in the certainty of future payment for property or goods received; credit: *to sell merchandise on trust.* **4.** a person or thing that is reliable or trustworthy. **5.** the condition of one to whom

something has been entrusted. **6.** the obligation or responsibility imposed on one in whom confidence or authority is placed: *a position of trust.* **7.** charge; custody; care. **8.** something committed or entrusted to one's care for use or safekeeping, as an office, duty, or the like; responsibility; charge. **9.** *Law.* a fiduciary relationship in which one person (the trustee) holds the title to property (the trust estate or trust property) for the benefit of another (the beneficiary). **10.** *Com.* an illegal combination of industrial or commercial companies in which the stock is controlled by a central board of trustees, thus making it possible to control prices, destroy competition, etc. **11.** *Archaic.* reliability. **12. in trust,** left in the care or guard of another: *The money will be kept in trust for her children.* —*adj.* **13.** *Law.* of or pertaining to trusts or a trust. —*v.i.* **14.** to rely upon or place confidence in someone or something (usually fol. by *in* or *to*). **15.** to have confidence; hope. **16.** to sell merchandise on credit. —*v.t.* **17.** to have trust or confidence in; rely on. **18.** to believe. **19.** to expect confidently; hope (usually fol. by a clause or infinitive as object). **20.** to commit or consign with trust or confidence. **21.** to permit to remain or go somewhere or to do something without fear of consequences. **22.** to invest with a trust; entrust with something. **23.** to give credit to (a person) for goods, services, etc., supplied. [ME < Scand; cf. Icel *traust* trust, c. G *Trost* comfort] —**trust′a·bil′i·ty,** *n.* —**trust′a·ble,** *adj.* —**trust′er,** *n.*
—**Syn. 1.** certainty, belief, faith. TRUST, CONFIDENCE, ASSURANCE imply a feeling of security. TRUST implies instinctive unquestioning belief in and reliance upon something or someone: *to have trust in one's parents.* CONFIDENCE implies conscious trust because of good reasons, definite evidence, or past experience: *to have confidence in the outcome of events.* ASSURANCE implies absolute confidence and certainty: *to feel an assurance of victory.* **8.** commitment, commission.

trust′ account′, *Banking U.S.* a savings account over which the depositor, as trustee, has sole control during his lifetime, after which any balance in the account becomes payable to the beneficiary. Also called **trustee′ account′.**

trust′bust′er, *n.* a federal official who seeks to dissolve business trusts, esp. through vigorous application of anti-trust regulations.

trust′ com′pany, a company or corporation organized to exercise the functions of a trustee, but usually engaging also in other banking and financial activities.

trus·tee (tru stē′), *n., v.* **-teed, -tee·ing.** *Law.* —*n.* **1.** a person, usually one of a body of persons, appointed to administer the affairs of a company, institution, etc. **2.** a person who holds the title to property for the benefit of another. **3.** (in New England) a garnishee. **4.** a trusty. —*v.t.* **5.** to place in the hands of a trustee or trustees.

trustee′ proc′ess, *Law.* (in New England) garnishment (def. 2).

trus·tee·ship (tru stē′ship), *n.* **1.** *Law.* the office or function of a trustee. **2.** the administrative control of a territory granted to a country by a body (**Trustee′ship Coun′cil**) of the United Nations. **3.** See **trust territory.**

trust·ful (trust′fəl), *adj.* full of trust; confiding. —**trust′ful·ly,** *adv.* —**trust′ful·ness,** *n.*

trust′ fund′, money, securities, property, etc., held in trust.

trust·ing (trus′ting), *adj.* that trusts; confiding; trustful: *a trusting child.* —**trust′ing·ly,** *adv.* —**trust′ing·ness,** *n.*

trust·less (trust′lis), *adj.* **1.** not worthy of trust; faithless; unreliable; false. **2.** distrustful; suspicious. —**trust′less·ly,** *adv.* —**trust′less·ness,** *n.*

trust′ ter′ritory, a territory under the administrative control of a country designated by the United Nations.

trust·wor·thy (trust′wûr′thē), *adj.* deserving of trust or confidence; dependable; reliable. —**trust′wor′thi·ly,** *adv.* —**trust′wor′thi·ness,** *n.* —**Syn.** honest, faithful. See **reliable.**

trust·y (trus′tē), *adj.,* **trust·i·er, trust·i·est,** *n., pl.* **trust·ies.** —*adj.* **1.** that may be trusted or relied on; trustworthy; reliable. **2.** *Archaic.* trustful. —*n.* **3.** a person or thing that is trusted, esp. a convict to whom special privileges are granted. —**trust′i·ly,** *adv.* —**trust′i·ness,** *n.*

truth (trōōth), *n., pl.* **truths** (trōōthz). **1.** true or actual state of a matter: *the truth about one's health.* **2.** conformity with fact or reality; verity: *the truth of a statement.* **3.** a verified or indisputable fact, proposition, principle, or the like: *mathematical truths.* **4.** state or character of being true. **5.** actuality or actual existence. **6.** (*often cap.*) ideal or fundamental reality apart from and transcending perceived experience: *the truth of the universe.* **7.** agreement with a standard or original. **8.** honesty; integrity; truthfulness. **9.** an obvious or accepted fact; truism; platitude. **10.** accuracy, as of position or adjustment. **11. in truth,** in reality; in fact; actually. [ME *treuthe,* OE *trēowth* (c. Icel *tryggth* faith). See TRUE, -TH[1]] —**truth′less,** *adj.* —**truth′less·ness,** *n.* —**Syn. 1.** fact. **2.** veracity. **8.** sincerity, candor, frankness. **10.** precision, exactness. —**Ant. 1.** falsehood. **2, 4, 8.** falsity.

truth·ful (trōōth′fəl), *adj.* **1.** telling the truth, esp. habitually: *a truthful person.* **2.** conforming to truth: *a truthful statement.* **3.** corresponding with reality. —**truth′ful·ly,** *adv.* —**truth′ful·ness,** *n.*

truth-func·tion (trōōth′fungk′shən), *n.* *Logic.* a statement so constructed from other statements that its truth-value depends only on the truth-value of the other statements rather than their meanings.

truth′ se′rum, a drug that induces in the subject a desire to talk or a state of heightened suggestibility, used in psychotherapy and in interrogation to discover repressed or consciously withheld information. Also called **truth′ drug′.**

truth′ ta′ble, *Logic.* a table drawn up to show the truth-value of a compound logical statement for every possible combination of the truth-values of its component propositions.

truth-val·ue (trōōth′val′yōō), *n.* *Logic.* the property of a proposition according to which it is either true or false.

try (trī), *v.,* **tried, try·ing,** *n., pl.* **tries.** —*v.t.* **1.** to attempt to do or accomplish by deliberate effort. **2.** to test the effect or result of (often fol. by *out*). **3.** to endeavor to evaluate by experiment or experience. **4.** to attempt to open (a door, window, etc.) in order to find out whether it is locked. **5.** *Law.* to examine and determine judicially, as a cause of action; determine judicially the guilt or innocence of (a person). **6.** to put to a severe test; subject to strain, as of endurance, patience, etc.; tax: *to try one's patience.* **7.** to melt down (fat, blubber, etc.) to obtain the oil; render (usually fol. by *out*). —*v.i.* **8.** to make an attempt or effort; strive. **9. try on,** to put on an article of clothing in order to judge its appearance and fit. **10. try out,** to use experimentally; test. —*n.* **11.** an attempt; effort. **12.** *Rugby.* a goal that earns a score of three points. [ME *trie(n)* to try (a legal case) < AF *trier* = OF: to sift, cull]
—**Syn. 1, 8.** TRY, ATTEMPT, ENDEAVOR, STRIVE imply putting forth effort toward a specific end. TRY is the verb in most general use, transitively and intransitively: *Try your best. Try with all you have.* ATTEMPT, a transitive verb, is more formal and often carries the idea of more effort: *He attempted the impossible.* ENDEAVOR, usually intransitive, suggests resolve and continuous effort, esp. in the face of difficulties: *to endeavor to overcome obstacles.* STRIVE, intransitive, implies hard and earnest exertion to accomplish something difficult or laborious: *to strive mightily at a difficult task.*

try·ing (trī′ing), *adj.* extremely annoying, difficult, or the like: *a trying experience.* —**try′ing·ly,** *adv.* —**try′ing·ness,** *n.*

try·ma (trī′mə), *n., pl.* **-ma·ta** (-mə tə). *Bot.* a drupaceous nut having a fibrous or fleshy epicarp which is ultimately dehiscent, as in the walnut and hickory. [< NL < Gk; hole = *trȳ(ein)* (to) rub down, wear away + *-ma* n. suffix marking result]

try·out (trī′out′), *n.* a trial or test to ascertain fitness for some purpose.

tryp′a·fla′vine neu′tral (trip′ə flā′vin, -vēn, trī′pə-, trip′ə-, trī′pə-), *Chem.* acriflavine. [< Gk *trȳpa* hole + FLAVINE]

tryp·a·no·some (trip′ə nə sōm′, tri pan′ə-), *n.* any minute, flagellate protozoan of the genus *Trypanosoma,* parasitic in the blood or tissues of man and other vertebrates, usually transmitted by insects, often causing serious diseases, as African sleeping sickness. [< Gk *trȳpano-* (comb. form of *trȳpanon* borer) + -SOME[3]] —**tryp′a·no·so′mal, tryp·a·no·som·ic** (trip′ə nə som′ik), *adj.*

tryp·a·no·so·mi·a·sis (trip′ə nō sō mī′ə sis, tri pan′ō-), *n.* *Pathol.* any infection caused by a trypanosome.

tryp·sin (trip′sin), *n.* *Biochem.* a proteolytic enzyme of the pancreatic juice, capable of converting proteins into peptone. [for **tripsin* < Gk *trîps(is)* friction (*trīb(ein)* (to) rub + *-sis* -SIS) + -IN[2]; so called because first obtained by rubbing the pancreas with glycerin] —**tryp·tic** (trip′tik), *adj.*

tryp·to·phan (trip′tə fan′), *n.* *Biochem.* an essential amino acid, $(C_8H_6N)CH_2CH(NH_2)COOH$, occurring in the seeds of some leguminous plants, released from proteins by tryptic digestion, and important in the nutrition of animals. Also, **tryp·to·phane** (trip′tə fān′). [< *trypto-* (comb. form of Gk *triptós* rubbed) + -PHAN(E)]

try·sail (trī′sāl′; *Naut.* trī′səl), *n.* *Naut.* a triangular or quadrilateral sail having its luff hooped or otherwise bent to a mast, used for lying to or keeping a vessel headed into the wind; spencer.

try′sail mast′, *Naut.* a small auxiliary mast for a fore-and-aft sail, fastened just abaft the mainmast or foremast of a sailing vessel; used esp. on the mainmast of the snow or with spencers.

try′ square′, a device for testing the squareness of carpentry work or the like, or for laying out right angles, consisting of a pair of straight-edges fixed at right angles to one another.

Try square

tryst (trist, trīst), *n.* **1.** an appointment to meet at a certain time and place, esp. one arranged clandestinely by lovers. **2.** an appointed meeting. **3.** an appointed place of meeting. [ME *triste* < OF: appointed station in a hunt, ambush < Gmc; cf. Goth *trausti* agreement, arrangement, akin to ME *trist* confidence (OE **tryst*). See TROW[1], TRUST] —**tryst′er,** *n.* —**Syn. 1, 2.** assignation. **1–3.** rendezvous.

tryst′ing place′ (tris′ting, trī′sting), a place for a meeting, esp. a secret meeting of lovers; rendezvous.

TS, 1. toolshed. **2.** top secret.

tsa·di (tsä′dē, sä′dē; *Heb.* tsä′dē), *n.* sadhe.

Tsa·na (tsä′nä), *n.* **Lake.** See **Tana, Lake.**

tsar (zär, tsär), *n.* czar.

tsar·e·vitch (zär′ə vich, tsär′-), *n.* czarevitch.

tsa·rev·na (zä rev′nə, tsä-), *n.* czarevna.

tsa·ri·na (zä rē′nə, tsä-), *n.* czarina.

tsar·ism (zär′iz əm, tsär′-), *n.* czarism.

tsar·ist (zär′ist, tsär′-), *adj., n.* czarist.

tsa·ris·tic (zä ris′tik, tsä-), *adj.* czarist.

Tsa·rit·syn (tsä rit′sin; *Russ.* tsä rē′tsin), *n.* a former name of **Volgograd.**

tsa·rit·za (zä rit′sə, tsä-), *n.* czaritza.

Tschai·kov·sky (chī kôf′skē), *n.* **Peter Il·yich** (il′yich). See **Tchaikovsky, Peter Ilyich.** Also, **Tschai·kow′sky.**

tscher·no·sem (*Russ.* cher′noz yôm′), *n.* a soil common in cool or temperate semiarid climates, very black and rich in humus and carbonates. Also, **chernozem.** [< Russ: lit., black earth, equiv. to *cherno-,* for *cherny* black + *zem* earth]

Tse·li·no·grad (tse′li no grät′), a city in W Kazakstan, in the SW Soviet Union in Asia. 150,000 (est. 1964). Formerly, **Akmolinsk.**

tset′se fly′ (tset′sē, tsē′tsē), any of several bloodsucking, African flies of the genus *Glossina* that act as a vector of sleeping sickness and other trypanosome infections of man and domestic animals. Also, **tzetze fly.** Also called **tset′se, tzetze.** [< Bantu (Bechuana)]

T.S.F., wireless telegraph. [< F *t(élégraphie) s(ans) f(il)*]

T.Sgt., Technical Sergeant.

T-shirt (tē′shûrt′), *n.* a lightweight shirt, close-fitting and with a round neckline and short sleeves, worn esp. as an undershirt by men and boys. Also, **tee-shirt.** [named from its shape]

Tsi·nan (jē′nän′), *n.* a city in and the capital of Shantung, in NE China. 862,000 (est. 1957).

Tsing·hai (ching′hī′), *n.* Chinghai.

Tsing·tao (tsing′tou′; *Chin.* ching′dou′), *n.* a seaport in E Shantung, in E China. Municipal district, 1,300,000.
Tsing·yuan (ching′yyän′), *n.* a city in N Hopeh, in NE China. 350,000. Formerly, **Paoting.**
Tsin·kiang (jin′gyäng′), *n.* a seaport in SE Fukien, in SE China, on Formosa Strait. 130,000. Formerly, **Chuanchow.**
Tsin·ling Shan (chin′ling′ shän′), a mountain range in central China: highest peak over 12,000 ft.
Tsiol·kov·sky (tsyôl kôf′skē), *n.* **Kon·stan·tin E·duar·do·vich** (kon stän tēn′ e doo̅är′do vich), 1857–1935, Russian inventor and rocket expert.
Tsi·tsi·har (tsē′tsē′här′; *Chin.* chē′chē′här′), *n.* a city in NW Heilungkiang, in NE China. 760,000. Also, **Chichihar, Chichihaerh, Tsi′tsi′haerh′.**
tsk (*pronounced as an alveolar click; spelling pron.* tisk), *interj.* **1.** (used as an exclamation of commiseration, annoyance, impatience, etc.) —*n.* **2.** an exclamation of "tsk." —*v.i.* **3.** to utter the exclamation "tsk." Also, **tsk′tsk′.**
tsp., 1. teaspoon. **2.** teaspoonful.
T square, a T-shaped ruler, used primarily in mechanical drawing, having a short crosspiece that slides along the edge of the drawing board as a guide to the perpendicular longer section in making parallel lines, right angles, etc., and as a support for triangles.

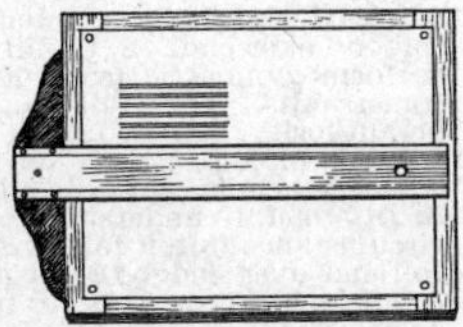
T square on drawing board

TSS, See **toxic-shock syndrome.**
tsu·ba (tso͞o′bə; *Jap.* tsŏŏ bä′), *n., pl.* **-ba.** the metal plate, usually elliptical, serving as the guard of a Japanese sword or knife, having an opening for the tang. [< Jap]
tsu·na·mi (tsŏŏ nä′mē), *n.* an unusually large sea wave produced by a seaquake or undersea volcanic eruption. [< Jap = *tsu* harbor + *nami* wave] —**tsu·na·mic** (tsŏŏ-nä′mik, -nam′ik), *adj.*
Tsu·shi·ma (tso͞o′shē mä′), *n.* two adjacent Japanese islands between Korea and Kyushu: Russian fleet defeated by Japanese fleet 1905. 58,672; 271 sq. mi.
TTS, Teletypesetter.
Tu., Tuesday.
Tu·a·mo′tu Archipel′ago (to͞o′ä mô′to͞o), a group of French islands in the S Pacific. 6664; 332 sq. mi. Also called **Low Archipelago, Paumotu Archipelago.**
Tua·reg (twä′reg), *n.* **1.** a Berber or Hamitic-speaking member of the Muslim nomads of the Sahara. **2.** the language of the Tuaregs, an Afro-Asian language of the Berber subfamily.
tu·a·ta·ra (to͞o′ə tä′rə), *n.* a nocturnal, lizardlike reptile, *Sphaenodon punctatum,* of islands near the coast of New Zealand: the only surviving rhynchocephalian. Also, **tu·a·te·ra** (to͞o′ə tā′rə). [< Maori = *tua* dorsal + *tara* spine]

Tuatara
(Length to 2½ ft.)

Tu·a·tha De Da·nann (tho͞o′ə hə dā dä′nən), *Irish Legend.* a race of gods or demigods who defeated the Fomorians and ruled Ireland during a golden age. Also, **Tu′atha de Da′naan, Tu′atha De′.**
tub (tub), *n., v.,* **tubbed, tub·bing.** —*n.* **1.** a bathtub. **2.** a broad, round, open container, usually having handles. **3.** the amount a tub will hold. **4.** *Naut. Disparaging.* an old, slow, or clumsy vessel. **5.** *Brit. Informal.* a bath in a bathtub. **6.** *Mining.* an ore car; tram. —*v.t.* **7.** to place or keep in a tub. **8.** *Brit. Informal.* to bathe in a bathtub. —*v.i.* **9.** *Brit. Informal.* to bathe oneself in a bathtub. [ME *tubbe* < MFlem *tobbe,* c. LG *tubbe*] —**tub′ba·ble,** *adj.* —**tub′ber,** *n.* —**tub′like′,** *adj.*
tu·ba (to͞o′bə, tyo͞o′-), *n., pl.* **-bas, -bae** (-bē). **1.** *Music.* a valved, brass wind instrument having a low range. **2.** Also called **funnel cloud, pendant cloud, tornado cloud.** *Meteorol.* a rapidly whirling, funnel-shaped cloud form hanging from a cloud base, esp. that of a cumulonimbus or cumulus. Cf. **tornado** (def. 1), **waterspout** (def. 2). [< L: trumpet; akin to TUBE]

Tuba (def. 1)

tub·al (to͞o′bəl, tyo͞o′-), *adj. Anat.* pertaining to a tube.
Tu·bal-cain (to͞o′bəl kān′, tyo͞o′-), *n.* the son of Lamech and Zillah. Gen. 4:22. Also, **Tu′bal-cain′.**
tu·bate (to͞o′bāt, tyo͞o′-), *adj.* having or forming a tube or tubes; tubular.
tub·by (tub′ē), *adj.,* **-bi·er, -bi·est. 1.** short and fat. **2.** having a dull, thumping sound. —**tub′bi·ness,** *n.*
tube (to͞ob, tyo͞ob), *n., v.,* **tubed, tub·ing.** —*n.* **1.** a hollow, usually cylindrical body of metal, glass, rubber, or other material, used esp. for conveying or containing liquids or gases. **2.** a small, collapsible cylinder of metal or plastic sealed at one end and having a capped opening at the other from which paint, toothpaste, etc., may be squeezed. **3.** *Anat., Zool.* any hollow, cylindrical vessel or organ: *the bronchial tubes.* **4.** *Bot.* **a.** any hollow, elongated body or part. **b.** the united lower portion of a gamopetalous corolla or a gamosepalous calyx. **5.** a tubular tunnel, esp. under water, in which an underground railroad runs. **6.** *Informal.* the railroad itself. **7.** See **inner tube. 8.** *Electronics.* See **electron tube. 9.** *Brit.* subway (def. 1). —*v.t.* **10.** to furnish with a tube or tubes. **11.** to convey or enclose in a tube. **12.** to make tubular. [< L *tub(us)* pipe] —**tube′like′,** *adj.*
tube′ foot′, one of numerous small, tubular processes on the body surface of most echinoderms.
tu·ber¹ (to͞o′bər, tyo͞o′-), *n.* **1.** *Bot.* a fleshy, usually oblong or rounded thickening or outgrowth of a subterranean stem or shoot, as the potato. **2.** *Anat.* a rounded swelling or protuberance; a tuberosity; a tubercle. [< L: bump, swelling. See TRUFFLE] —**tu′ber·less,** *adj.* —**tu′ber·oid′,** *adj.*
tu·ber² (to͞o′bər, tyo͞o′-), *n.* a person or thing that forms, installs, or operates with tubes. [TUBE + -ER¹]
tu·ber·cle (to͞o′bər kəl, tyo͞o′-), *n.* **1.** a small rounded projection or excrescence, as on a bone, on the surface of the body, or on a plant. **2.** *Pathol.* **a.** a small, firm, rounded nodule or swelling. **b.** such a swelling as the characteristic lesion of tuberculosis. [< L *tūberculum*]

A
B
Tubercle bacillus
A, Bacillus
B, Blood cell

tu′bercle bacil′lus, the bacterium, *Mycobacterium tuberculosis,* causing tuberculosis.
tubercul-, var. of **tuberculo-** before a vowel: *tuberculin.*
tu·ber·cu·lar (tŏŏ bûr′kyə lər, tyŏŏ-), *adj.* **1.** pertaining to tuberculosis; tuberculous. **2.** of, pertaining to, or of the nature of a tubercle or tubercles. **3.** characterized by or having tubercles. —*n.* **4.** a person affected with tuberculosis. —**tu·ber′cu·lar·ly,** *adv.*
tu·ber·cu·late (tŏŏ bûr′kyə lit, -lāt′, tyŏŏ-), *adj.* **1.** Also, **tu·ber′cu·lat′ed.** having tubercles. **2.** tubercular. [< NL *tuberculātus*] —**tu·ber′cu·la′tion,** *n.*
tu·ber·cule (to͞o′bər kyo͞ol′, tyo͞o′-), *n. Bot.* a nodule, esp. on the roots of certain legumes. [< L *tūberculum*]
tu·ber·cu·lin (tŏŏ bûr′kyə lin, tyŏŏ-), *n. Med.* a sterile liquid prepared from cultures of the tubercle bacillus, used in the diagnosis and treatment of tuberculosis.
tuber′culin test′, a test for tuberculosis in which a hypersensitive reaction to a given quantity of tuberculin indicates a past or present tubercular condition.
tuberculo-, a combining form representing **tubercle:** *tuberculosis.* Also, *esp. before a vowel,* **tubercul-.** [< L *tūbercul(um)* tubercle + -o-]
tu·ber·cu·loid (tŏŏ bûr′kyə loid′, tyŏŏ-), *adj.* **1.** resembling a tubercle. **2.** resembling tuberculosis.
tu·ber·cu·lo·sis (tŏŏ bûr′kyə lō′sis, tyŏŏ-), *n. Pathol.* **1.** an infectious disease that may affect almost any tissue of the body, esp. the lungs, caused by the organism *Mycobacterium tuberculosis,* and characterized by tubercles. **2.** this disease when affecting the lungs; pulmonary phthisis; consumption. Also called **TB.** [< NL]
tu·ber·cu·lous (tŏŏ bûr′kyə ləs, tyŏŏ-), *adj.* **1.** tubercular. **2.** affected with tuberculosis. —**tu·ber′cu·lous·ly,** *adv.*
tu·ber·cu·lum (tŏŏ bûr′kyə ləm, tyŏŏ-), *n., pl.* **-la** (-lə). a tubercle. [< NL]
tube·rose¹ (to͞ob′rōz′, tyo͞ob′-, to͞o′bə rōz′, tyo͞o′-), *n.* a bulbous, amaryllidaceous plant, *Polianthes tuberosa,* cultivated for its spike of fragrant, creamy-white, lilylike flowers. [< L *tūberōsa,* fem. of *tūberōsus* TUBEROSE²]
tu·ber·ose² (to͞o′bə rōs′, tyo͞o′-), *adj.* tuberous. [< L *tūberōsus* knobby. See TUBER¹, -OSE¹]
tu·ber·os·i·ty (to͞o′bə ros′i tē, tyo͞o′-), *n., pl.* **-ties.** a rough projection or protuberance of a bone, as for the attachment of a muscle. [< ML *tūberōsitās.* See TUBEROSE², -ITY]
tu·ber·ous (to͞o′bər əs, tyo͞o′-), *adj.* **1.** characterized by the presence of rounded or wartlike prominences or tubers. **2.** *Bot.* bearing tubers. **3.** having the nature of or resembling a tuber. Also, **tuberose.** [< L *tūberōsus* knobby]
tu′berous root′, a true root so thickened as to resemble a tuber, but bearing no buds or eyes. See illus. at **root.**
tubi-, a combining form representing **tube:** *tubiform.* [< L *tub(us)* + -I-]
tu·bi·form (to͞o′bə fôrm′, tyo͞o′-), *adj.* shaped like a tube.
tub·ing (to͞o′bing, tyo͞o′-), *n.* **1.** material in the form of a tube: *glass tubing.* **2.** tubes collectively. **3.** a piece of tube.
Tub·man (tub′mən), *n.* **William Va·can·a·rat Shadrach** (və kan′ə rat′), 1895–1971, president of Liberia 1944–71.
tu·bu·lar (to͞o′byə lər, tyo͞o′-), *adj.* **1.** of or pertaining to a tube or tubes. **2.** having the form or shape of a tube; tubiform. **3.** *Physiol., Pathol.* noting a respiratory sound resembling that produced by a current of air passing through a tube. [< NL *tubulāris;* see TUBULE, -AR¹] —**tu′bu·lar′i·ty,** *n.* —**tu′bu·lar·ly,** *adv.*
tu·bu·late (*adj.* to͞o′byə lit, -lāt′, tyo͞o′-; *v.* to͞o′byə lāt′, tyo͞o′-), *adj., v.,* **-lat·ed, -lat·ing.** —*adj.* **1.** Also, **tu′bu·lat′ed.** shaped like or having a tube. —*v.t.* **2.** to form into or furnish with a tube. [< L *tubulātus*] —**tu′bu·la′tion,** *n.* —**tu′bu·la′tor,** *n.*
tu·bule (to͞o′byo͞ol, tyo͞o′-), *n.* a small tube. [< L *tubulus* = *tub(us)* pipe + *-ulus* -ULE]
tubuli-, a combining form of **tubule** or **tubular:** *tubuliflorous.*
tu·bu·li·flo·rous (to͞o′byə lə flôr′əs, -flôr′-, tyo͞o′-) *adj. Bot.* having the corolla tubular in all the perfect flowers of a head, as certain composite plants.
tu·bu·lous (to͞o′byə ləs, tyo͞o′-), *adj.* **1.** containing or consisting of tubes. **2.** having the form of a tube; tubular. **3.** *Bot.* having tubular flowers. [< NL *tubulōsus*] —**tu′bu·lous·ly,** *adv.*
tu·bu·lure (to͞o′byə lər, tyo͞o′-), *n.* a short tubular opening, as in a glass jar or at the top of a retort. [< F]
tu·chun (do͞o′jyn′), *n. Chinese Hist.* **1.** the title of a military governor of a province during the period 1916–25. **2.** a war lord. [< Chin: lit., overseer of troops]
tuck (tuk), *v.t.* **1.** to thrust in the loose end or edge of (a garment, covering, etc.) so as to hold closely in place (often fol. by *in, up,* etc.). **2.** to cram or hide in a close place. **3.** to cover snugly in or as in this manner: *She tucked the children into bed.* **4.** to pull up into or as into a fold or folds (usually fol. by *in, up,* etc.). **5.** *Needlework.* to sew tucks in. **6.** *Slang.* to eat or drink (often fol. by *away*). —*v.i.* **7.** to draw together; contract; pucker. **8.** *Needlework.* to make tucks. —*n.* **9.** something tucked or folded in. **10.** *Sewing.* a fold made by doubling cloth upon itself and stitching parallel with the edge of the fold, used for decoration or for shortening or fitting a garment. **11.** *Naut.* the part of a vessel where the after ends of the outside planking or plating unite at the sternpost. [ME *t(o)uke(n)* to stretch (cloth), torment, OE

tūcian to torment; akin to MLG *tucken* to tug, G *zucken* to jerk. See TOW¹]

tuck·a·hoe (tuk′ə hō′), *n.* the edible, underground sclerotium of the fungus *Poria cocos,* found on the roots of trees in the southern United States. Also called **Indian bread.** [< Algonquian (Va. dial.) *tockawhoughe* it is globular]

tuck·er¹ (tuk′ər), *n.* **1.** a person or thing that tucks. **2.** a piece of linen, muslin, or the like, worn by women around the neck and shoulders. **3.** chemisette. **4.** *Australian.* food. [ME *tokere.* See TUCK¹, -ER¹]

tuck·er² (tuk′ər), *v.t.* *U.S. Informal.* to weary; tire; exhaust (often fol. by *out*). [TUCK¹ + -ER⁶]

tuck·et (tuk′it), *n.* a trumpet fanfare. [ME *tukke* to beat, sound (said of a drum) < MF (north.) *toker* to strike, TOUCH + -ET]

Tuc·son (to͞o′son, to͞o son′), *n.* a city in S Arizona: health resort. 262,933 (1970).

Tu·cu·mán (to͞o′ko͞o män′), *n.* a city in NW Argentina. 287,004 (1960).

-tude, a suffix appearing in abstract nouns (generally formed from Latin adjectives or participles) of Latin origin (*latitude; altitude*); on this model, used in the formation of new nouns: *platitude.* [< L *-tūdo* > also F *-tude*]

Tu·dor (to͞o′dər, tyo͞o′-), *n.* **1.** **Mary.** See **Mary I.** **2.** a member of the royal family that ruled in England from 1485 to 1603. —*adj.* **3.** pertaining or belonging to the English royal house of Tudor. **4.** of, pertaining to, or characteristic of the periods of the reigns of the Tudor sovereigns: *Tudor architecture.*

Tu′dor arch′, a four-centered arch, the inner pair of curves having a radius much greater than that of the outer pair. See illus. at **arch.**

tu·e·bor (to͞o e′bōr; *Eng.* to͞o ē′bôr, tyo͞o-), *v.* *Latin.* I will defend: motto on the coat of arms of Michigan.

Tues., Tuesday.

Tues·day (to͞oz′dē, -dā, tyo͞oz′-), *n.* the third day of the week, following Monday. [ME *tewesday,* OE *tīwesdæg* (c. OHG *zīestac,* Icel *tȳsdagr,* etc.), orig. phrase *Tīwes daeg* Tiu's day, translating L *diēs Martis* day of Mars. See TIU, DAY]

Tues·days (to͞oz′dēz, -dāz, tyo͞oz′-), *adv.* on Tuesdays.

tu·fa (to͞o′fə, tyo͞o′-), *n.* *Geol.* **1.** Also called **calc-tufa, calc-tuff.** a porous limestone formed from calcium carbonate deposited by springs or the like. Cf. **travertine.** **2.** (not in technical use) tuff. [< It *tufo* < L *tōfus*] —**tu·fa·ceous** (to͞o fā′shəs, tyo͞o-), *adj.*

tuff (tuf), *n.* *Geol.* a fragmental rock consisting of the smaller kinds of volcanic detritus, usually more or less stratified. Also called **volcanic tuff.** [< F *tuf* < It *tufo.* See TUFA] —**tuff·a·ceous** (tuf ā′shəs), *adj.*

tuft (tuft), *n.* **1.** a bunch or cluster of small, usually soft and flexible parts, as feathers, leaves, etc., attached or fixed closely together at the base and loose at the upper ends. **2.** a cluster of cut threads, used as a decorative finish attached to the tying or holding threads of mattresses, quilts, etc. —*v.t.* **3.** to furnish or decorate with a tuft or tufts. **4.** to arrange in a tuft or tufts. —*v.i.* **5.** to form into or grow in a tuft or tufts. [ME, var. of *toft(e)* < MF *tofe* (< Gmc; akin to TOP¹) + inorganic *-t*] —**tuft′er,** *n.*

tuft·ed (tuf′tid), *adj.* **1.** furnished or decorated with tufts. **2.** formed into or growing in a tuft or tufts.

tuft′ed tit′mouse, a gray titmouse, *Parus bicolor,* of the eastern and midwestern U.S., having a crested head. See illus. at **titmouse.**

tuft·y (tuf′tē), *adj.,* **tuft·i·er, tuft·i·est.** **1.** abounding in tufts. **2.** covered or adorned with tufts. **3.** growing in or forming tufts. —**tuft′i·ly,** *adv.*

tug (tug), *v.,* **tugged, tug·ging,** *n.* —*v.t.* **1.** to pull at with force, vigor, or effort. **2.** to move by pulling forcibly; drag; haul. **3.** to tow (a vessel) by means of a tugboat. —*v.i.* **4.** to pull with force or effort: *to tug at a stuck drawer.* **5.** to strive hard; labor; toil. —*n.* **6.** the act or an instance of tugging; pull; haul. **7.** a strenuous contest between opposing forces, groups, or persons; struggle. **8.** tugboat. **9.** that by which something is tugged, as a rope or chain. **10.** (on a harness) **a.** trace² (def. 1). **b.** any of various supporting or pulling parts. [ME *toggen,* akin to OE *togian* to, TOW¹] —**tug′ger,** *n.* —**tug′less,** *adj.*

tug·boat (tug′bōt′), *n.* a small, powerful boat for towing or pushing ships, barges, etc.

tug′ of war′, **1.** an athletic contest between two teams pulling on opposite ends of a rope. **2.** a hard-fought, critical struggle for supremacy.

tu·i (to͞o′ē), *n.* a black, New Zealand honey eater, *Prosthemadera novae-zealandiae,* having a patch of white feathers on each side of the throat. Also called **parson bird.** [< Maori]

Tui·ler·ies (twē′lə rēz; *Fr.* twēlᵊ rē′), *n.* a former royal palace in Paris: begun by Catherine de Médicis in 1564; burned by supporters of the Commune in 1871. A public park **(Tui′leries Gar′dens)** now occupies the site.

tuille (twēl), *n.* (loosely) a tasset. [late ME *toile* < MF *tuille,* var. of *teuille* < L *tēgula* TILE]

tu·i·tion (to͞o ish′ən, tyo͞o-), *n.* **1.** the charge or fee for instruction. **2.** teaching or instruction, as of pupils. **3.** *Archaic.* guardianship or custody. [late ME *tuicion* a looking after, guarding < L *tuitiōn-* (s. of *tuitiō*) = *tuit(us)* watched over (ptp. of *tuērī*) + *-iōn-* -ION] —**tu·i′tion·al, tu·i·tion·ar·y** (to͞o ish′ə ner′ē, tyo͞o-), *adj.*

Tu·la (to͞o′lä, -lə), *n.* a city in the W RSFSR, in the central Soviet Union in Europe, S of Moscow. 360,000 (est. 1964).

tu·la·re·mi·a (to͞o′lə rē′mē ə), *n.* *Pathol., Vet. Pathol.* a disease of rabbits, squirrels, etc., caused by a bacterium, *Pasturella tularensis* (or *Bacterium tularense*), transmitted to man by insects or by the handling of infected animals, resembling the plague and taking the form in man of an irregular fever lasting several weeks. Also, **tu′la·rae′mi·a.** Also called **rabbit fever.** [*Tulare,* California county where first found + -EMIA] —**tu′la·re′mic, tu′la·rae′mic,** *adj.*

tu·le (to͞o′lē; *Sp.* to͞o′le), *n., pl.* **-les** (-lēz; *Sp.* -les). either of two large bulrushes, *Scirpus lacustris* or *S. californicus,* found in California and adjacent regions in inundated lands and marshes. [< Sp < Nahuatl *tullin*]

tu·lip (to͞o′lip, tyo͞o′-), *n.* **1.** any liliaceous plant of the genus *Tulipa,* cultivated in many varieties, and having large, showy, usually erect, cup-shaped or bell-shaped flowers of various colors. **2.** a flower or bulb of such a plant. [earlier *tulipa* < NL, appar. back formation from It *tulipano* (taken as adj.) < Turk *tülbend* turban (from a fancied likeness); see TURBAN] —**tu′lip·like′,** *adj.*

tu′lip tree′, a North American, magnoliaceous tree, *Liriodendron Tulipifera,* having tuliplike flowers and yielding a wood used in making furniture: the state tree of Indiana, Kentucky, and Tennessee. Also called **tu′lip pop′lar.**

tu·lip·wood (to͞o′lip wo͝od′, tyo͞o′-), *n.* **1.** the wood of the tulip tree. **2.** any of various striped or variegated woods of other trees. **3.** any of these trees.

tulle (to͞ol; *Fr.* tʏl), *n.* a thin, fine net of acetate, nylon, rayon, or silk, for millinery, dresses, etc. [< F, named after *Tulle,* France, where first made]

Tul·ly (tul′ē), *n.* See **Cicero, Marcus Tullius.**

Tul·sa (tul′sə), *n.* a city in NE Oklahoma: center of a rich oil-producing region. 330,350 (1970).

Tu·luá (to͞o lwä′), *n.* a city in W Colombia. 151,370 (est. 1964).

tum·ble (tum′bəl), *v.,* **-bled, -bling,** *n.* —*v.i.* **1.** to fall or roll end over end. **2.** to fall or decline rapidly; drop. **3.** to perform gymnastic feats of skill and agility, as leaps or somersaults. **4.** to fall suddenly from a position of power or authority. **5.** to fall in ruins; collapse; topple. **6.** to stumble or fall (usually fol. by *over*): *to tumble over a sled.* **7.** to go, come, get, etc., in a hasty and confused way. **8.** *Informal.* to understand or become aware of some fact or circumstance (often fol. by *to*). —*v.t.* **9.** to cause to fall or roll end over end. **10.** to put in a disordered or rumpled condition. **11.** to cause to fall from a position of authority or power; overthrow; topple. **12.** to cause to fall or collapse in ruins. **13.** to subject to the action of a tumbling barrel. —*n.* **14.** an act of tumbling or falling. **15.** a gymnastic or acrobatic feat. **16.** an accidental fall; spill. **17.** a drop in value, as of stocks. **18.** a fall from a position of power or authority. **19.** a response indicating interest, affection, etc.: *She wouldn't give me a tumble.* **20.** tumbled condition; disorder or confusion. **21.** a confused heap. [ME *tum(b)le(n)* to dance in acrobatic style (c. D *tuimelen,* LG *tummeln,* etc.), freq. of ME *tomben,* OE *tumbian,* c. Icel *tumba,* akin to OHG *tūmōn* to reel (? < OLG). Cf. F *tomber* to fall < Gmc]

tum·ble·bug (tum′bəl bug′), *n.* any of several dung beetles that roll balls of dung in which they deposit their eggs and in which the young develop.

tum·ble-down (tum′bəl doun′), *adj.* dilapidated; ruined; rundown: *He lived in a tumble-down shack.*

tum·bler (tum′blər), *n.* **1.** a person who performs leaps, somersaults, and other bodily feats. **2.** (in a lock) any locking or checking part that when lifted or released by the action of a key or the like, allows the bolt to move. **3.** a stemless drinking glass having a flat bottom and no handle. **4.** (in a gunlock) a leverlike piece that by the action of a spring forces the hammer forward when released by the trigger. **5.** *Mach.* **a.** a part moving a gear into place in a selective transmission. **b.** a single cog or cam on a rotating shaft, transmitting motion to a part with which it engages. **6.** a tumbling barrel. **7.** one of a breed of domestic pigeons, noted for the habit of tumbling backward in flight. **8.** a toy that is weighted and rounded at the bottom so as to rock when touched. [TUMBLE + -ER¹. Cf. LG *tümeler* drinking cup, kind of pigeon]

tum′bler gear′, *Mach.* a transmission having gears actuated by a tumbler.

tum·ble·weed (tum′bəl wēd′), *n.* *U.S.* any of various plants, as an amaranth, *Amaranthus graecizans,* whose branching upper part becomes detached from the roots in autumn and is driven about by the wind.

tum·bling (tum′bling), *n.* the act, practice, or art of performing acrobatic tumbles.

tum′bling bar′rel, a rotating drum for subjecting materials or objects, loosely placed inside, to a tumbling action, as for mixing or polishing.

tum·brel (tum′brəl), *n.* **1.** one of the carts used during the French Revolution to convey victims to the guillotine. **2.** a dumpcart, esp. one for carrying dung. **3.** *Obs.* a two-wheeled covered cart accompanying artillery, for carrying tools, ammunition, etc. Also, **tum′bril.** [late ME *tumberell* ducking stool < ML *tumberellus* < OF *tumberel* dumpcart = *tomber* to fall (see TUMBLE) + *-rel* -REL]

tu·me·fa·ci·ent (to͞o′mə fā′shənt, tyo͞o′-), *adj.* tumefying; causing to swell. [< L *tumefacient-,* s. of *tumefaciēns* causing to swell (prp. of *tumefacere*). See TUMEFY, -ENT]

tu·me·fac·tion (to͞o′mə fak′shən, tyo͞o′-), *n.* the act of making or becoming swollen or tumid. [< medical L *tumefactiōn-* (s. of *tumefactiō* a causing to swell) = *tumefact(us)* made to swell, swollen (ptp. of *tumefacere* TUMEFY) + *-iōn-* -ION]

tu·me·fy (to͞o′mə fī′, tyo͞o′-), *v.t., v.i.,* **-fied, -fy·ing.** to make or become swollen or tumid. [back formation from *tumefied,* Anglicization of L *tumefactus* caused to swell (ptp. of *tumefacere*) = *tumē(re)* (to) swell + *-factus* made, done; see FACT, -FY, -ED²]

tu·mes·cent (to͞o mes′ənt, tyo͞o-), *adj.* swelling; slightly tumid. [< L *tumescent-* (s. of *tumescēns* beginning to swell, prp. of *tumescere*) = *tum(ēre)* (to) swell + *-escent-* -ESCENT] —**tu·mes′cence,** *n.*

tu·mid (to͞o′mid, tyo͞o′-), *adj.* **1.** swollen, or affected with swelling, as a part of the body. **2.** pompous or inflated, as language; turgid; bombastic. **3.** seeming to swell; bulging. [< L *tumidus* swollen = *tum(ēre)* (to) swell + *-idus* -ID⁴] —**tu·mid′i·ty, tu′mid·ness,** *n.* —**tu′mid·ly,** *adv.* —**Syn.** **1.** distended, turgid. —**Ant. 1.** deflated.

tum·my (tum′ē), *n., pl.* **-mies.** *Informal.* stomach or abdomen. [nursery form: *(s)tummi(ck),* dial. var. of STOMACH]

tu·mor (to͞o′mər, tyo͞o′-), *n.* *Pathol.* an abnormal or diseased swelling in any part of the body, esp. a more or less circumscribed overgrowth of new tissue that is autonomous, differs in structure from the part in which it grows, and serves no useful purpose; neoplasm. Also, *esp. Brit.,* **tu′mour.** [< L: a swelling, swollen state = *tum(ēre)* (to) swell + *-or* -OR¹] —**tu′mor·like′,** *adj.* —**tu′mor·ous, tu′mor·al,** *adj.*

tump·line (tump′līn′), *n.* a strap or sling passed around the chest or forehead to help support a pack carried on a person's back. [< *tump,* of Algonquian orig. + LINE¹]

tu·mu·lar (to͞o′myə lər, tyo͞o′-), *adj.* of, pertaining to, resembling, or characterized by a tumulus or tumuli. [< L *tumul(us)* mound + -AR[1]]

tu·mu·lous (to͞o′myə ləs, tyo͞o′-), *adj.* having mounds; full of mounds; tumular. Also, **tu·mu·lose** (to͞o′myə lōs′, tyo͞o′-). [< L *tumulōsus.* See TUMULUS, -OUS]

tu·mult (to͞o′məlt, tyo͞o′-), *n.* **1.** violent and noisy commotion or disturbance of a crowd or mob; uproar. **2.** turbulent mental or emotional disturbance. [late ME *tumult(e)* < L *tumultus* an uproar, lit., a rising = *tum(ēre)* (to) swell (with anger) + *-ul-* formative suffix (see TUMULUS) + *-tus* suffix of action and its result] —**Syn. 1.** disorder, turbulence. See **ado. 2.** excitement, perturbation.

tu·mul·tu·ous (to͞o mul′cho͞o əs, tyo͞o-), *adj.* **1.** full of tumult or riotousness; marked by disturbance and uproar. **2.** highly disturbed or agitated, as the mind or emotions. [< L *tumultuōsus*] —**tu·mul′tu·ous·ly,** *adv.* —**tu·mul′tu·ous·ness,** *n.* —**Syn. 1.** uproarious, turbulent, violent. **2.** distraught. —**Ant.** calm, quiet.

tu·mu·lus (to͞o′myə ləs, tyo͞o′-), *n., pl.* **-lus·es, -li** (-lī′). **1.** *Archeol.* an artificial mound, esp. over a grave; barrow. **2.** *Geol.* a domelike swelling or mound formed in congealed lava. [< L: mound, swelling = *tum(ēre)* (to) swell + *-ulus* suffix of place]

tun (tun), *n., v.,* **tunned, tun·ning.** —*n.* **1.** a large cask. **2.** a measure of capacity for wine, etc., usually equivalent to 252 wine gallons. —*v.t.* **3.** to put into or store in a tun or tuns. [ME, OE *tunne,* c. D *ton,* G *Tonne* (< LG), Icel *tunna*]

tu·na[1] (to͞o′nə), *n., pl.* (*esp. collectively*) **-na,** (*esp. referring to two or more kinds or species*) **-nas. 1.** any of several large food and game fishes of the family *Scombridae,* found in temperate and tropical seas. Cf. **albacore. 2.** any of various related fishes. **3.** Also called **tu′na fish′.** the flesh of the tuna, used as food. [< AmerSp, var. of Sp *atún* < Ar *tūn* < Gk *thýnnos* TUNNY]

Bluefin tuna, *Thunnus thynnus* (Length to 14 ft.)

tu·na[2] (to͞o′nə, tyo͞o′-), *n.* **1.** any of various prickly pears, esp. either of two erect, treelike species, *Opuntia Tuna* or *O. megacantha,* of Mexico, bearing a sweet, edible fruit. **2.** the fruit of these plants. [< Sp < Taino]

tun·a·ble (to͞o′nə bəl, tyo͞o′-), *adj.* capable of being tuned. Also, **tuneable.** —**tun′a·ble·ness,** *n.* —**tun′a·bly,** *adv.*

Tun′bridge Wells′ (tun′brij′), a city in SW Kent, in SE England: mineral springs; resort. 39,855 (1961).

tun·dra (tun′drə, to͝on′-), *n.* one of the vast, nearly level, treeless plains of the arctic regions of Europe, Asia, and North America. [< Russ: marshy plain]

tune (to͞on, tyo͞on), *n., v.,* **tuned, tun·ing.** —*n.* **1.** a succession of musical sounds forming an air or melody. **2.** state of being in the proper pitch: *to be in tune.* **3.** agreement in pitch; unison; harmony. **4. change (one's) tune,** to reverse one's views; change one's mind. **5. sing a different tune,** to change one's opinion, attitude, behavior, etc. **6. to the tune of,** *Informal.* at a price or cost of. —*v.t.* **7.** to adjust (a musical instrument) to a correct or given standard of pitch (often fol. by *up*). **8.** to bring into harmony. **9.** to adjust (a motor, mechanism, or the like) for proper functioning. **10.** *Radio.* to adjust a receiving apparatus so as to receive (the signals of a particular transmitting station). **11.** to put into or cause to be in a receptive condition, mood, etc. —*v.i.* **12.** to put a musical instrument in tune (often fol. by *up*). **13.** to be in harmony or accord; become responsive. **14. tune in, a.** to adjust a radio so as to receive (signals). **b.** *Slang.* to pay attention to or understand a person, situation, etc. **15. tune out, a.** to adjust a radio so as to avoid (interference, static, etc.). **b.** *Slang.* to refuse or cease to attend to a person, situation, etc. **16. tune up, a.** to cause a group of musical instruments to be brought to the same pitch. **b.** to bring into proper operating order, as a motor. [ME; unexplained var. of TONE]

tune·a·ble (to͞o′nə bəl, tyo͞o′-), *adj.* tunable. —**tune′a·ble·ness,** *n.* —**tune′a·bly,** *adv.*

tune·ful (to͞on′fəl, tyo͞on′-), *adj.* **1.** full of melody; melodious. **2.** producing musical sounds or melody. —**tune′ful·ly,** *adv.* —**tune′ful·ness,** *n.* —**Syn. 1.** musical, harmonious, dulcet, sweet. —**Ant. 1.** discordant.

tune·less (to͞on′lis, tyo͞on′-), *adj.* **1.** unmelodious; unmusical. **2.** making or giving no music; silent. —**tune′less·ly,** *adv.*

tun·er (to͞o′nər, tyo͞o′-), *n.* **1.** a person or thing that tunes. **2.** the portion of a radio receiver producing an output suitable for feeding into a detector and adjustable for selecting a desired signal. **3.** a radio without an amplifier, speakers, etc., usually coupled with a high-fidelity or stereophonic amplifier and speakers.

tune·smith (to͞on′smith′, tyo͞on′-), *n.* *Informal.* a person who composes popular music or songs.

tune-up (to͞on′up′, tyo͞on′-), *n.* an adjustment, as of a motor, to improve working order or condition.

tung′ oil′ (tung), a yellow drying oil derived from the seeds of a Chinese tree, *Aleurites Fordii,* used in varnishes, linoleum, etc. [half translation, half adoption of Chinese *yu t'ung* oil of tung tree]

tung·state (tung′stāt), *n.* *Chem.* a salt of any tungstic acid. [TUNGST(EN) + -ATE[2]]

tung·sten (tung′stən), *n.* *Chem.* a rare, metallic element having a high melting point: used in alloys, electric-lamp filaments, etc. *Symbol:* W; *at. wt.:* 183.85; *at. no.:* 74; *sp. gr.:* 19.3. [< Sw = *tung* heavy + *sten* stone] —**tung·sten·ic** (tung sten′ik), *adj.*

tung′sten lamp′, an incandescent electric lamp in which the filament is made of tungsten.

tung′sten steel′, an alloy steel containing tungsten.

tung·stic (tung′stik), *adj.* *Chem.* of or containing tungsten, esp. in the pentavalent or hexavalent state. [TUNGST(EN) + -IC]

tung′stic ac′id, *Chem.* **1.** a hydrate of tungsten trioxide, $H_2WO_4 \cdot H_2O$, used in the manufacture of tungsten-lamp filaments. **2.** any of a group of acids derived from tungsten.

tung·stite (tung′stīt), *n.* a mineral tungsten trioxide, WO_3. [TUNGST(EN) + -ITE[1]]

Tung·ting (do͝ong′ting′), *n.* a lake in S China, in Hunan province. 1450 sq. mi.

Tun·gus (to͝on go͝oz′), *n., pl.* **-gus·es,** (*esp. collectively*) **-gus. 1.** a member of a Mongoloid people living in eastern Siberia. **2.** the northern group of Tungusic languages. Also, **Tunguz.**

Tun·gus·ic (to͝on go͝oz′ik), *n.* **1.** a branch of the Altaic family of languages, including Manchu. —*adj.* **2.** of or pertaining to the Tunguses or Tungusic.

Tun·gus·ka (to͝on go͝os′kä), *n.* any of three tributaries of the Yenesei River in the central Soviet Union in Asia: includes the Lower Tunguska 2000 mi. long; the Upper Tunguska or the lower course of the Angara; and the Stony Tunguska ab. 975 mi. long.

Tun·guz (to͝on go͝oz′), *n., pl.* **-guz·es,** (*esp. collectively*) **-guz.** Tungus.

tu·nic (to͞o′nik, tyo͞o′-), *n.* **1.** a gownlike outer garment, with or without sleeves and sometimes belted, worn by the ancient Greeks and Romans. **2.** a garment with a short skirt, worn by women for sports. **3.** *Eccles.* a tunicle. **4.** *Anat., Zool.* any covering or investing membrane or part, as of an organ. **5.** *Bot.* a natural integument. [OE **tunice* (occurs in acc. case *tunican*) < L *tunica*]

tu·ni·ca (to͞o′nə kə, tyo͞o′-), *n., pl.* **-cae** (-sē′). *Anat., Zool., Bot.* a tunic. [< NL, special use of L *tunica* tunic]

tu·ni·cate (to͞o′nə kit, -kāt′, tyo͞o′-), *n.* **1.** *Zool.* any marine chordate of the subphylum *Tunicata,* having a saclike body enclosed in a thick membrane or tunic, from which protrude two openings or siphons for the ingress and egress of water. —*adj.* Also, **tu′ni·cat′ed. 2.** (esp. of the *Tunicata*) having a tunic or covering. **3.** of or pertaining to the tunicates. **4.** *Bot.* having or consisting of a series of concentric layers, as a bulb. [< L *tunicātus* wearing a tunic]

tu·ni·cle (to͞o′ni kəl, tyo͞o′-), *n.* *Eccles.* a vestment worn over the alb by subdeacons, as at the celebration of the Mass, and by bishops. [ME < L *tunicula* = *tunic(a)* tunic + *-ula;* see -ULE, -CLE]

tun′ing fork′, a steel instrument consisting of a stem with two prongs, producing a musical tone of definite, constant pitch when struck, and serving as a standard for tuning musical instruments, making acoustical experiments, and the like.

Tuning fork

Tu·nis (to͞o′nis, tyo͞o′-), *n.* **1.** a city in and the capital of Tunisia, in the NE part. 944,000. **2.** one of the former Barbary States in N Africa, once notorious for its pirates: constitutes modern Tunisia.

Tu·ni·sia (to͞o nē′zhə, -shə, -nizh′ə, -nish′ə), *n.* a republic in N Africa, on the Mediterranean: a French protectorate until 1956. 6,000,000; 48,330 sq. mi. *Cap.:* Tunis. —**Tu·ni′sian,** *adj., n.*

Tun·ker (tung′kər), *n.* Dunker.

tun·nage (tun′ij), *n.* tonnage.

tun·nel (tun′əl), *n., v.,* **-neled, -nel·ing** or (*esp. Brit.*) **-nelled, -nel·ling.** —*n.* **1.** an underground passageway, as for trains, automobiles, etc., through or under an obstruction, as a city, mountain, river, harbor, or the like. **2.** an approximately horizontal gallery or corridor in a mine. **3.** the burrow of an animal. **4.** *Dial.* a funnel. **5.** *Obs.* the flue of a chimney. —*v.t.* **6.** to construct a passageway through or under. **7.** to make or excavate (a tunnel or underground passage). —*v.i.* **8.** to make a tunnel or tunnels. [late ME *tonel* < MF *tonele, tonnelle* funnel-shaped net, fem. of *tonne* cask, dim. of *tonne* TUN] —**tun′nel·er;** *esp. Brit.,* **tun′nel·ler,** *n.* —**tun′nel·like′,** *adj.*

tun′nel disease′, *Pathol.* **1.** See **caisson disease. 2.** hookworm (def. 2).

Tun·ney (tun′ē), *n.* **James Joseph** ("*Gene*"), 1897–1978, U.S. boxer: world heavyweight champion 1926–28.

tun·ny (tun′ē), *n., pl.* (*esp. collectively*) **-ny,** (*esp. referring to two or more kinds or species*) **-nies.** *Chiefly Brit.* tuna[1]. [< ML *tunnīna* false tunny (by apocope), n. use of fem. of *tunnīnus* tunnylike = *tunn(us)* tunny (var. of L *thynnus* < Gk *thýnnos*) + *-īnus* -INE[1]]

Tuo·ne·la (twô′ne lə), *n.* *Finnish Myth.* the afterworld, an island on which the sun and moon never shine. Also called **Manala.**

tup (tup), *n., v.,* **tupped, tup·ping.** —*n.* **1.** *Chiefly Brit.* a male sheep; ram. **2.** the head of a falling, hammerlike mechanism, as of a steam hammer or pile driver. —*v.t.* **3.** *Chiefly Brit.* (of a ram) to copulate with (a ewe). —*v.i.* (of a ewe) to copulate. [ME *tope, tupe* ram]

tu·pe·lo (to͞o′pə lō′), *n., pl.* **-los. 1.** any of several cornaceous trees of the genus *Nyssa,* esp. the black gum, *N. sylvatica,* or *N. aquatica,* of deep swamps and river bottoms of the southern U.S. **2.** the strong, tough wood of any of these trees. [< Creek (*i*)*to opelwa* swamp tree]

Tu·pi (to͞o pē′, to͞o′pē), *n., pl.* **-pis,** (*esp. collectively*) **-pi. 1.** a member of any of several related Indian peoples living in the valleys of various Brazilian rivers, esp. the Amazon. **2.** a language belonging to the Tupi-Guarani family of languages and spoken in northern Brazil by the Tupi Indians. Also, **Tu·pí′.** —**Tu·pi′an,** *adj.*

Tu·pi-Gua·ra·ni (to͞o pē′gwär′ə nē′, to͞o′pē-), *n.* a family of Indian languages including Tupi, Guarani, lingua geral, and many others of central South America. —**Tu·pi-Gua·ra·ni·an** (to͞o′pē gwə rä′nē ən), *adj., n.*

tup·pence (tup′əns), *n.* *Brit.* twopence.

tup·pen·ny (tup′ə nē), *adj.* twopenny (def. 1).

Tu·pun·ga·to (to͞o′po͞on gä′tô), *n.* a mountain between Argentina and Chile, in the Andes. ab. 21,490 ft.

tuque (to͞ok, tyo͞ok), *n.* a heavy stocking cap worn in Canada. Also, **toque.** [< CanF, var. of TOQUE]

tu quo·que (to͞o kwō′kwe; *Eng.* to͞o kwō′kwē, tyo͞o), *Latin.* thou too: a retort charging an accuser with a similar crime or failing.

tu·ra·co (to͝or′ə kō′), *n., pl.* **-cos.** touraco.

Tu·ra·ni·an (to͝o rā′nē ən, tyo͝o-), *adj.* **1.** belonging or pertaining to a group of Asian peoples or languages comprising nearly all of those that are neither Indo-European nor Semitic; allophylian. **2.** *Obs.* Ural-Altaic. —*n.* **3.** a member of any of the peoples speaking a Turanian, esp. a Ural-Altaic, language. **4.** a member of any of the Ural-Altaic peoples. [< Pers *Tūrān* Turkestan + -IAN]

tur·ban (tûr′bən), *n.* **1.** a man's headdress worn chiefly by Muslims in southern Asia, consisting of a long cloth of silk, linen, cotton, etc., wound either about a cap or directly around the head. **2.** any headdress resembling this. **3.** any of various off-the-face hats for women that are close-fitting, of a soft fabric, and brimless or having a narrow, sometimes draped, brim. [earlier *torbant,* var. of *tulbant* < Turk (var. of *tülbend*) < Pers *dulband*] —**tur′baned,** *adj.* —**tur′ban·less,** *adj.* —**tur′ban·like′,** *adj.*

Turban

tur·bel·lar·i·an (tûr′bə lâr′ē ən), *adj.* **1.** belonging to the *Turbellaria,* a class of platyhelminths or flatworms, mostly aquatic, and having cilia on the body surface. —*n.* **2.** a turbellarian platyhelminth. [< NL *Turbellāria* (L *turbell(ae)* a stir, row (pl. dim. of *turba* turmoil) + *-āria,* neut. pl. of *-ārius* -ARY) + -AN]

tur·bid (tûr′bid), *adj.* **1.** unclear or murky because of stirred-up sediment; clouded; opaque: *turbid water.* **2.** thick or dense, as smoke, clouds, etc. **3.** confused; muddled; disturbed: *turbid thinking; turbid passions.* [< L *turbidus* disturbed = *turb(āre)* (to) disturb (< *turba* turmoil) + *-idus* -ID[4]] —**tur·bid′i·ty, tur′bid·ness,** *n.* —**tur′bid·ly,** *adv.*

tur·bi·dim·e·ter (tûr′bi dim′i tər), *n.* a device for measuring the turbidity of water or other liquids. —**tur′bi·dim′e·try,** *n.* —**tur·bi·di·met·ric** (tûr′bi di me′trik), *adj.* —**tur′bi·di·met′ri·cal·ly,** *adv.*

tur·bi·nal (tûr′bə nəl), *adj.* **1.** turbinate. —*n.* **2.** *Anat.* a turbinate bone. [< L *turbin-* (s. of *turbō* a whirlwind, a top) + -AL[1]]

tur·bi·nate (tûr′bə nit, -nāt′), *adj.* Also, **tur′bi·nat′ed.** **1.** scroll-like; whorled; spiraled. **2.** *Anat.* of or pertaining to certain scroll-like, spongy bones of the nasal passages in man and other vertebrates. **3.** inversely conical. —*n.* **4.** a turbinate shell. **5.** *Anat.* a turbinate bone. [< L *turbinātus* shaped like a top = *turbin-* (s. of *turbō* a top) + *-ātus* -ATE[1]] —**tur′bi·na′tion,** *n.*

tur·bine (tûr′bin, -bīn), *n.* any of various machines having a rotor, usually with vanes or blades, driven by the pressure, momentum, or reactive thrust of a moving fluid, as steam, water, hot gases, or air, either occurring in the form of free jets or as a fluid passing through and entirely filling a housing around the rotor. [< F < L *turbin-,* s. of *turbō* something that spins, e.g., a top, a spindle; akin to TURBID]

tur·bit (tûr′bit), *n.* one of a breed of domestic pigeons having a stout, roundish body, a short head and beak, and a ruffled breast and neck. [var. of TURBOT; appar. applied to bird because, like the fish, it is toplike in outline]

turbo-, a combining form of **turbine:** *turbojet.* [TURB(INE) + -O-]

tur·bo-e·lec·tric (tûr′bō i lek′trik), *adj.* noting, pertaining to, or utilizing machinery that includes a generator driven by a turbine: *turbo-electric engine; turbo-electric propulsion.*

tur·bo·fan (tûr′bō fan′), *n.* fanjet (def. 1).

tur·bo·jet (tûr′bō jet′), *n.* **1.** See **turbojet engine. 2.** an airplane equipped with one or more turbojet engines.

tur′bo·jet en′gine, a jet-propulsion engine in which air from the atmosphere is compressed for combustion by a turbine-driven compressor.

tur·bo·prop (tûr′bō prop′), *n.* **1.** See **turbo-propeller engine. 2.** an airplane equipped with one or more turbo-propeller engines.

tur′bo-pro·pel·ler en′gine (tûr′bō prə pel′ər), *Aeron.* a jet engine with a turbine-driven propeller that produces thrust augmenting the thrust of the jet exhaust. Also called **propjet engine, turboprop, tur′boprop en′gine.**

tur·bo·su·per·charg·er (tûr′bō so͞o′pər chär′jər), *n.* a supercharger driven by a turbine turned by a stream of exhaust gases from the engine.

tur·bot (tûr′bət), *n., pl.* (*esp. collectively*) **-bot,** (*esp. referring to two or more kinds or species*) **-bots. 1.** a European flatfish, *Psetta maxima,* having a diamond-shaped body. **2.** any of several other flatfishes. [ME *turbut* < AF (OF *tourbot*) < ML *turb(o)* turbot (in L, top; appar. applied to the fish because of its outline; see TURBINE) + *-ut-* F *-ot* n. suffix]

tur·bu·lence (tûr′byə ləns), *n.* **1.** the quality or state of being turbulent; violent disorder or commotion. **2.** *Hydraulics.* the haphazard secondary motion caused by eddies within a moving fluid. **3.** *Meteorol.* irregular motion of the atmosphere, as that indicated by gusts and lulls in the wind. Also, **tur′bu·len·cy.** [< LL *turbulentia.* See TURBULENT, -ENCE]

tur·bu·lent (tûr′byə lənt), *adj.* **1.** being in a state of agitation or tumult; disturbed: *turbulent feelings or emotions.* **2.** characterized by, or showing disturbance, disorder, etc.: *the turbulent years.* **3.** given to acts of violence and aggression. [< L *turbulentus* restless = *turbu-* (comb. form of *turba* turmoil) + *-lentus* full of] —**tur′bu·lent·ly,** *adv.*

tur′bulent flow′, *Hydraulics.* the flow of a fluid past an object such that the velocity at any fixed point in the fluid varies irregularly. Cf. **streamline flow.**

Tur·co (tûr′kō), *n., pl.* **-cos.** *Often Disparaging.* (formerly) an Algerian serving in the light infantry of the French army; a Zouave. [< F < It: lit., Turk]

Turco-, a combining form of **Turkish.** Also, **Turko-.** [< F < It]

Tur·co·man (tûr′kə mən), *n., pl.* **-mans. 1.** Turkoman. **2.** Turkmen.

turd (tûrd), *n. Slang* (*vulgar*). a piece of excrement. [ME; OE *tord*]

tu·reen (to͝o rēn′, tyo͝o-), *n.* a large, deep, covered dish for serving soup, stew, or other foods. [earlier *terrene* < F *terrine* earthenware dish, n. use of fem. of LL **terrīnus* earthen = L *terr(a)* earth + *-īnus* -INE[1]]

Tu·renne (ty REN′), *n.* **Hen·ri de la Tour d'Au·vergne de** (äN RĒ′ də LA to͞oR′ dō VERN′y[ə] də), 1611–75, French general and marshal.

turf (tûrf), *n., pl.* **turfs,** (*esp. Brit.*) **turves;** *v.* —*n.* **1.** a layer of matted earth formed by grass and plant roots. **2.** a block or piece of peat dug for fuel. **3.** *Slang.* the neighborhood over which a street gang asserts its authority. **4. the turf, a.** the track over which horse races are run. **b.** the practice or sport of racing horses. —*v.t.* **5.** to cover with turf or sod. [ME, OE, c. D *turf,* G *Torf* (< LG), Icel *torf,* akin to Skt *darbha* tuft of grass] —**turf′less** *adj.* —**turf′like′,** *adj.*

turf·man (tûrf′mən), *n., pl.* **-men.** a person who is devoted to horse racing, esp. one who keeps a racing stable.

turf·y (tûr′fē), *adj.,* **turf·i·er, turf·i·est. 1.** covered with or consisting of grassy turf. **2.** resembling turf. **3.** of, pertaining to, or characteristic of horse racing. —**turf′i·ness,** *n.*

Tur·ge·nev (to͞oR ge′nyəf), *n.* **I·van Ser·ge·e·vich** (i vän′ SER ge′yə vich), 1818–83, Russian novelist. Also, **Tur·ge′·niev.**

tur·gent (tûr′jənt), *adj. Obs.* swelling; swollen; turgid. [< L *turgent-* (s. of *turgēns* swelling, prp. of *turgēre*)] —**tur′·gen·cy,** *n.* —**tur′gent·ly,** *adv.*

tur·ges·cent (tûr jes′ənt), *adj.* becoming swollen; swelling. [< L *turgescent-* (s. of *turgescēns* beginning to swell, prp. of *turgescere*) = *turg(ēre)* (to) swell + *-escent-* -ESCENT] —**tur·ges′cence, tur·ges′cen·cy,** *n.*

tur·gid (tûr′jid), *adj.* **1.** swollen; distended; tumid. **2.** inflated, overblown, or pompous; bombastic. [< L *turgidus* = *turg(ēre)* (to) swell + *-idus* -ID[4]] —**tur·gid′i·ty, tur′gid·ness,** *n.* —**tur′gid·ly,** *adv.*

tur·gite (tûr′jīt), *n.* an iron ore, a hydrated ferric oxide, related to limonite but containing less water.

tur·gor (tûr′gər), *n.* **1.** *Plant Physiol.* the normal distention or rigidity of plant cells, resulting from the pressure exerted from within against the cell walls by the cell contents. **2.** the state of being swollen or distended. [< LL = L *turg(ēre)* (to) swell (out) + *-or* -OR[1]]

Tur·got (TYR gō′), *n.* **Anne Ro·bert Jacques** (AN RÔ BER′ zhäk) (*Baron de l'Aulne*), 1727–81, French statesman, financier, and economist.

Tu·rin (to͝or′in, tyo͝or′-, to͝o rin′, tyo͝o-), *n.* a city in NW Italy, on the Po: capital of the Kingdom of Italy 1860–65. 1,188,689. Italian, **Torino.**

Turk (tûrk), *n.* **1.** a native or inhabitant of Turkey. **2.** (formerly) a native or inhabitant of the Ottoman Empire. **3.** a member of any of the peoples speaking Turkic languages. **4.** one of a breed of Turkish horses closely related to the Arabian horse. **5.** any Turkish horse. **6.** See **Young Turk. 7.** *Obs.* a Muslim. [ME < Turkish *Türk;* cf. ML *Turcus,* MGk *Toûrkos,* MF *Turc,* It *Turco,* Pers *turk*]

Turk, Turkish (def. 4).

Turk., **1.** Turkey. **2.** Turkish.

Tur·ke·stan (tûr′ki stan′, -stän′), *n.* a vast region in W and central Asia, E of the Caspian Sea: includes territory in the S central part of Sinkiang province in China **(Eastern Turkestan** or **Chinese Turkestan),** a strip of N Afghanistan, and the area **(Russian Turkestan)** comprising the republics of Kazakstan, Kirghizia, Tadzhikistan, Turkmenistan, and Uzbekistan. Also, **Turkistan.**

tur·key (tûr′kē), *n., pl.* **-keys,** (*esp. collectively*) **-key. 1.** a large, gallinaceous bird of the family *Meleagrididae,* esp. *Meleagris gallopava,* of America, that typically has green, reddish-brown, and yellowish-brown plumage of a metallic luster, and that is domesticated in most parts of the world. **2.** the flesh of this bird, used as food. **3.** *Slang.* a poor and unsuccessful theatrical production; flop. **4. talk turkey,** *Informal.* to talk frankly or seriously. [short for *Turkey cock* and *Turkey hen* cock and hen of Turkey, first applied to guinea fowl, later (by confusion) to the American bird]

Turkey (Domestic)

Tur·key (tûr′kē), *n.* a republic in W Asia and SE Europe. 40,000,000; 296,184 sq. mi. (286,928 sq. mi. in Asia; 9257 sq. mi. in Europe). *Cap.:* Ankara. Cf. **Ottoman Empire.**

tur′key buz′zard. See **turkey vulture.**

tur′key cock′, **1.** the male of the turkey. **2.** a strutting, pompous, conceited person.

Tur′key red′, **1.** a bright red produced in fabrics by madder, alizarin, or synthetic dyes. **2.** cotton cloth of this color.

tur′key trot′, a dance, to ragtime music, popular in the early 20th century.

tur·key-trot (tûr′kē trot′), *v.i.,* **-trot·ted, -trot·ting.** to dance the turkey trot.

tur′key vul′ture, a blackish-brown vulture, *Cathartes aura,* of Central and South America and the southern U.S., having a bare, red head and neck. Also called **turkey buzzard.** See illus. at **vulture.**

Tur·ki (tûr′kē, to͝or′-), *n.* **1.** the Turkic languages of central Asia, taken collectively. —*adj.* **2.** of or pertaining to Turki or to the peoples speaking these languages. [< Pers = *turk* TURK + *-ī* suffix of appurtenance]

Tur·kic (tûr′kik), *n.* **1.** a branch of the Altaic language family comprising languages of central and southwest Asia and eastern Europe, as Turkish, Azerbaijani, Turkmen, Uzbek, Kirghiz, and Yakut. —*adj.* **2.** of or pertaining to Turkic or Turkic-speaking peoples.

Turk·ish (tûr′kish), *adj.* **1.** of, pertaining to, characteristic of, or derived from Turkey or the Turks. **2.** of or pertaining to the language of Turkey. **3.** (loosely) Turkic. —*n.* **4.** the language of Turkey; Ottoman Turkish. *Abbr.:* Turk **5.** (loosely) Turkic. —**Turk′ish·ly,** *adv.* —**Turk′ish·ness,** *n.*

Turk′ish bath′, a bath in which the bather first perspires copiously in a steam room, is then given a rubdown and a massage, and then takes an ice-cold shower.

Turk′ish delight′, a candy made of fruit juice and gelatin, cubed and dusted with sugar. Also called **Turk′ish paste′.**

Turk′ish Empire′. See **Ottoman Empire.**

Turk′ish rug′, any of a large variety of handwoven rugs

produced in Turkey, characterized by coarse, heavy yarn and a long, uneven pile. Also called **Turk′ish car′pet.**

Turk′ish tobac′co, an aromatic tobacco, grown chiefly in Turkey and Greece, used in cigarettes.

Turk′ish tow′el, a thick, cotton towel with a long nap usually composed of uncut loops. Also, **turk′ish tow′el.**

Turk·ism (tûr′kiz əm), *n.* the culture, beliefs, principles, practices, etc., of the Turks.

Tur·ki·stan (tûr′ki stan′, -stän′), *n.* Turkestan.

Turk·man (tûrk′mən), *n., pl.* **-men.** a native or inhabitant of Turkmenistan. [alter. of TURKOMAN] **—Turk·me·ni·an** (tûrk mē′nē ən), *adj.*

Turk·men (tûrk′men), *n.* the language of the Turkman people, a Turkic language spoken mostly east of the Caspian Sea in the Turkmen S.S.R. but also in parts of European Russia, Iran, and the Caucasus. Also, **Turkoman, Turcoman.** [< Pers *Turkmēn* Turkoman]

Turk·me·ni·stan (tûrk′me ni stan′, -stän′), *n.* a constituent republic of the Soviet Union in Asia, bordering the Caspian Sea, Iran, and Afghanistan. 1,900,000 (est. 1965); 188,417 sq. mi. *Cap.:* Ashkhabad. Also called **Turkomen.** Official name, **Turk′men So′viet So′cialist Repub′lic.**

Turko-, var. of **Turco-.** [appar. back formation from TURKOMAN]

Tur·ko·man (tûr′kə mən), *n., pl.* **-mans. 1.** a member of a Turkish people consisting of a group of tribes that inhabit the region near the Aral Sea and parts of Iran and Afghanistan. **2.** Turkmen. Also, **Turcoman.** [< ML *Turcomannus* < Pers *turkumān* Turklike person = *turk* Turk + *-u-* + *mān-(dan)* (to) resemble]

Tur·ko·men (tûr′kə men′, -mən), *n.* Turkmenistan.

Turks′ and Cai′cos Is′lands (tûrks; kī′kōs), two groups of islands in the SE Bahamas: a dependency of Jamaica. 5716 (est. 1960); ab. 166 sq. mi. *Cap.:* Grand Turk.

Turk's-head (tûrks′hed′), *n.* a turbanlike knot of small cords, made around a rope, spar, etc.

Tur·ku (to͝or′ko͞o), *n.* a seaport in SW Finland. 138,299 (est. 1965). Swedish, **Åbo.**

tur·ma·line (tûr′mə lēn′), *n.* tourmaline.

tur·mer·ic (tûr′mər ik), *n.* **1.** the aromatic rhizome of an East Indian, zingiberaceous plant, *Curcuma longa.* **2.** a powder prepared from it, used as a condiment, as in curry powder, or as a yellow dye, a medicine, etc. **3.** the plant itself. **4.** any of various similar substances or plants. [earlier *tarmaret* < ML *terra merita* merited earth, unexplained name for curcuma]

tur′meric pa′per, paper treated with turmeric: used to indicate the presence of alkalis, which turn it brown, or of boric acid, which turns it reddish-brown.

tur·moil (tûr′moil), *n.* **1.** a state of great commotion, confusion, or disturbance; tumult; agitation; disquiet. **2.** *Obs.* harassing labor. [TUR(N) + MOIL] **—Syn. 1.** turbulence, disorder, uproar. See **agitation. —Ant. 1.** order, quiet.

turn (tûrn), *v.t.* **1.** to cause to move around on an axis or about a center; rotate: *to turn a wheel.* **2.** to cause to move around or partly around, as for the purpose of opening, closing, tightening, etc. **3.** to reverse the position or placement of. **4.** to bring the lower layers of (sod, soil, etc.) to the surface, as in plowing. **5.** to change the position of, by or as by rotating; move into a different position: *to turn the handle one notch.* **6.** to change or alter the course of; divert; deflect. **7.** to change the tendency or trend of. **8.** to change or alter the nature, character, or appearance of. **9.** to render or make by some change. **10.** to change the color of (leaves). **11.** to cause to become sour, ferment, or the like: *Warm weather turns milk.* **12.** to cause (the stomach) to reject food, liquid, etc.; affect with nausea. **13.** to change from one language or form of expression to another; translate. **14.** to put or apply to some use or purpose. **15.** to go or pass around or to the other side of: *to turn a street corner.* **16.** to get beyond or pass (a certain age, time, etc.): *His son just turned four.* **17.** to direct toward, away from, or in a specified direction. **18.** to shape (a piece of metal, wood, etc.) into rounded form with a cutting tool while rotating on a lathe. **19.** to bring into a rounded or curved form in any way. **20.** to form or express gracefully: *to turn a phrase well.* **21.** to cause to go; send; drive. **22.** to revolve in the mind; ponder (often fol. by *over*). **23.** to persuade (a person) to change or reorder the course of his life. **24.** to cause to be antagonistic toward: *to turn a son against his father.* **25.** to keep circulating (money, goods, etc.). **26.** to reverse or remake (a garment, shirt collar, etc.). **27.** to curve, bend, or twist. **28.** to twist out of position; wrench: *He turned his ankle.* **29.** to bend back or blunt (the edge of a blade). **30.** to perform (a gymnastic feat) by rotating or revolving: *to turn a somersault.* **31.** to disorder or upset the placement or condition of. **32.** *Obs.* **a.** to convert. **b.** to pervert.
—*v.i.* **33.** to move around on an axis or about a center; rotate. **34.** to move partly around through the arc of a circle, as a door on a hinge. **35.** to hinge or depend (usually fol. by *on* or *upon*): *The question turns on this point.* **36.** to direct or set one's course toward, away from, or in a particular direction. **37.** to direct one's thought, desire, etc., toward or away from someone or something. **38.** to give or apply one's interest, effort, etc., to something; pursue: *He turned to the study and practice of medicine.* **39.** to change or reverse a course so as to face or go in a different or the opposite direction: *to turn to the right.* **40.** to shift the body about as if on an axis. **41.** to assume a curved form; bend. **42.** to become blunted or dulled by bending, as the cutting edge of a knife, saw, etc. **43.** (of the stomach) to be affected with nausea. **44.** to be affected with giddiness or dizziness. **45.** to change or transfer one's loyalties; defect. **46.** to make a sudden, usually unexpected change or reversal of position in order to resist or attack: *The big cats suddenly turned on their trainer.* **47.** to change an attitude or policy. **48.** to change or alter, as in nature or appearance. **49.** to become sour, rancid, or the like, as milk or butter. **50.** to change color: *The leaves began to turn in October.* **51.** to change so as to be; become: *a lawyer turned poet; to turn pale.* **52.** to put about or tack, as a ship. **53. turn down, a.** to turn over; fold down. **b.** to refuse or reject (a person, request, etc.). **54. turn in, a.** to hand in; submit: *to turn in a resignation.* **b.** to inform on or deliver up. **c.** *Informal.* to go to bed; retire. **55. turn off, a.** to stop the flow of (water, gas, etc.), as by closing a faucet or valve. **b.** to extinguish (a light). **c.** to drive a vehicle or walk onto (a side road) from a main road. **d.** *Slang.* to cause (someone) to lose interest; to bore or discourage. **56. turn on, a.** to cause (water, gas, etc.) to flow, as by opening a valve. **b.** to switch on (a light). **c.** to put into operation; activate. **d.** to start suddenly to affect or show: *She turned on the charm and won him over.* **e.** *Slang.* to induce (a person) to take a narcotic drug. **f.** *Slang.* to take or attain euphoria by taking a narcotic drug. **g.** *Slang.* to excite or stimulate (someone). **h.** Also, **turn upon.** to become hostile to. **57. turn out, a.** to extinguish (a light). **b.** to produce as the result of labor. **c.** to be revealed: *It turns out that she's the admiral's daughter.* **d.** to be or become ultimately: *All the children turned out to be successes.* **58. turn over, a.** to move from one side to another. **b.** to put in reverse position; invert. **c.** to transfer; give. **d.** (of an engine) to start. **e.** *Com.* to purchase and then sell (goods or commodities). **f.** *Com.* to do business or sell goods to the amount of (a specified sum). **g.** *Com.* to invest or recover (capital) in some transaction or in the course of business. **59. turn the tables.** See **table** (def. 14). **60. turn the tide.** See **tide**[1] (def. 12). **61. turn to, a.** to apply to for aid; appeal to. **b.** to begin to attend to or work at something: *We'd better turn to and clean up this place.* **c.** to change to: *The ice turned to water.* **62. turn up, a.** to fold (material, a hem, cuffs, etc.) up or over in order to alter a garment. **b.** to bring to the surface by digging. **c.** to uncover, find. **d.** to intensify or increase. **e.** to happen; occur. **f.** to appear; arrive. **g.** to be recovered.
—*n.* **63.** a movement of partial or total rotation: *a slight turn of the handle.* **64.** act of changing or reversing position or posture as by a rotary movement: *a turn of the head.* **65.** a time or opportunity for action that comes in due rotation or order: *It's my turn to pay the bill.* **66.** act of changing or reversing the course or direction: *to make a turn to the right.* **67.** a place or point at which such a change occurs. **68.** a single revolution, as of a wheel. **69.** act of turning so as to face or go in a different direction. **70.** direction, drift, or trend. **71.** any change, as in nature, circumstances, etc.; alteration; modification: *a turn for the better.* **72.** the point or time of change. **73.** rounded or curved form. **74.** the shape or mold in which something is formed or cast. **75.** a passing or twisting of one thing around another, as of a rope around a mast. **76.** state or manner of being twisted. **77.** a single circular or convoluted shape, as of a coiled or wound rope. **78.** a small latch operated by a turning knob or lever. **79.** a distinctive form or style of expression or language. **80.** a short walk, ride, or the like, out and back, esp. by different routes: *Let's go for a turn in the car.* **81.** natural inclination, bent, tendency, or aptitude: *the turn of his mind.* **82.** a spell or period of work; shift. **83.** an attack of illness or the like. **84.** an act of service or disservice. **85.** requirement, exigency, or need: *This will serve your turn.* **86.** treatment or rendering, esp. with reference to the form or content of a work of literature, art, etc.; twist. **87.** *Stock Exchange.* a complete securities transaction that includes both a purchase and sale. **88.** *Music.* a melodic embellishment or grace, commonly consisting of a principal tone with two auxiliary tones, one above and the other below it. **89.** *Chiefly Brit.* an individual stage performance, esp. in a vaudeville theater or music hall. **90.** *Mil.* a drill movement by which a formation changes fronts. **91. at every turn,** in every instance; constantly. **92. by turns,** one after another; alternately. **93. in turn,** in due order of succession. **94. out of turn, a.** not in the correct succession. **b.** imprudently or indiscreetly: *to speak out of turn.* **95. take turns,** to succeed one another in order; rotate; alternate. **96. to a turn,** to just the proper degree; to perfection: *a steak done to a turn.* [ME *turnen,* OE *turnian* < L *tornāre* to turn in a lathe, round off < *tornus* lathe < Gk *tórnos* tool for making circles] **—turn′a·ble,** *adj.*
—Syn. 8. metamorphose, transmute, transform. **20.** fashion, mold. **33, 34.** TURN, REVOLVE, ROTATE, SPIN indicate moving in a more or less rotary, circular fashion. TURN is the general and popular word for motion on an axis or around a center, but it is used also of motion that is less than a complete circle: *A gate turns on its hinges.* REVOLVE refers esp. to movement in an orbit around a center, but is sometimes exchangeable with ROTATE, which refers only to the motion of a body around its own center or axis: *The moon revolves about the earth. The earth rotates on its axis.* To SPIN is to rotate very rapidly: *A top spins.* **63.** gyration, revolution. **71.** deviation, bend, twist, variation. **81.** talent, proclivity.

turn·a·bout (tûrn′ə bout′), *n.* **1.** the act of turning in a different or opposite direction. **2.** a change of opinion, loyalty, etc. **3.** a reciprocal action; act of doing to someone exactly as he has done to someone else.

turn·a·round (tûrn′ə round′), *n.* **1.** turnabout. **2.** change of allegiance, opinion, mood, policy, etc. **3.** a place or area having sufficient room for a vehicle to turn around.

turn·buck·le (tûrn′buk′əl), *n.* a rotating link or sleeve having one or two internal screw threads, used to connect or unite two threaded parts.

Turnbuckle (Open)

turn′ but′ton, button (def. 6).

turn·coat (tûrn′kōt′), *n.* **1.** a person who changes to the opposite party or faction, reverses his principles, etc. **2.** a renegade or traitor.

turn·down (tûrn′doun′), *adj.* that is or that may be turned down; folded or doubled down: *a turndown collar.*

turned′ com′ma, *Brit.* See **quotation mark.** Also called **inverted comma.**

turned-on (tûrnd′on′, -ôn′), *adj. Slang.* **1.** lively and chic; switched-on. **2.** full of or characterized by excitement. **3.** under the influence of a narcotic or hallucinogen, as marijuana.

turn·er[1] (tûr′nər), *n.* **1.** a person or thing that turns or is employed in turning. **2.** a large spatula used for turning over pancakes, eggs, etc., in cooking. **3.** a person who fashions or shapes objects on a lathe. [ME; see TURN, -ER[1]]

turn·er[2] (tûr′nər, tŏŏr′-), *n.* a member of a turnverein; a tumbler or gymnast. [< G *Turner* gymnast < *turnen* to exercise < F *tourner* to TURN]

Tur·ner (tûr′nər), *n.* **1. Frederick Jackson,** 1861–1932, U.S. historian. **2. Joseph Mal·lord William** (mal′ərd), 1775–1851, English painter. **3. Nat,** 1800–31, American black slave leader: led uprising of slaves in Virginia, 1831.

turn·er·y (tûr′nə rē), *n., pl.* **-er·ies. 1.** the process or art of forming or shaping objects on a lathe. **2.** objects or articles fashioned on a lathe collectively. **3.** a workshop where such work is done.

turn·hall (tûrn′hôl′), *n.* a hall or building in which turners or gymnasts practice or perform. [< G *Turnhalle* = *turn(en)* (to) practice gymnastics + *Halle* hall]

turn·ing (tûr′ning), *n.* **1.** the act of a person or thing that turns. **2.** the act of reversing position. **3.** a place or point at which something changes direction. **4.** the forming of objects on a lathe. **5.** an object turned on a lathe. **6.** the act of shaping something: *the turning of verses.* [ME, OE]

turn′ing point′, 1. a point at which a decisive change takes place. **2.** a point at which something changes direction, esp. a high or low point on a graph.

tur·nip (tûr′nip), *n.* **1.** the thick, fleshy, edible root of either of two cruciferous plants, the white-fleshed *Brassica Rapa,* or the yellow-fleshed rutabaga. **2.** the plant itself. **3.** the root of this plant used as a vegetable. [earlier *turnepa* = TURN (with reference to its rounded shape) + *nepe* NEEP]

turn·key (tûrn′kē′), *n., pl.* **-keys,** *adj.* **—***n.* **1.** a person who has charge of the keys of a prison; jailer. **—***adj.* **2.** of, involving, or resulting from an arrangement under which a private contractor develops a project, building, etc., for sale when completely ready for occupancy or operation: *turnkey housing.*

turn·off (tûrn′ôf′, -of′), *n.* **1.** a small road that branches off from a larger one. **2.** a place at which one changes from one's course. **3.** an act or instance of turning off.

turn·out (tûrn′out′), *n.* **1.** the gathering of persons who come to an exhibition, party, spectacle, or the like. **2.** a quantity of production; output. **3.** the act of turning out. **4.** the manner or style in which a person or thing is equipped, dressed, etc. **5.** equipment; outfit. **6.** a short side track or area that enables trains, automobiles, etc., to pass one another. **7.** *Railroads.* a track structure permitting a train to leave a given track for a branching or parallel track. Cf. **crossover** (def. 4). **8.** *Brit.* **a.** a labor strike. **b.** a worker who is on strike; striker.

turn·o·ver (tûrn′ō′vər), *n.* **1.** the act or result of turning over; upset. **2.** the number of workers replaced in a business or industry in a specified period. **3.** the rate of such replacement, esp. as compared with the average number of employees. **4.** the total amount of business done in a given time. **5.** the rate at which items are sold and restocked. **6.** a change from one position, opinion, etc., to another. **7.** a reorganization of a political organization, business, etc. **8.** a baked pastry with a sweet savory filling in which half the dough is turned over the filling and the edges sealed. **—***adj.* **9.** that is or may be turned over. **10.** having a part that turns over, as a collar.

turn·pike (tûrn′pīk′), *n.* **1.** a high-speed highway, esp. one maintained by tolls. **2.** (formerly) a barrier preventing passage on a highway until a toll was paid; tollgate. [late ME *turnepike* road barrier. See TURN, PIKE[2]]

turn·sole (tûrn′sōl′), *n.* **1.** any of several plants that turn with the sun. **2.** heliotrope. (def. 2). **3.** a European, euphorbiaceous plant, *Chrozophora tinctoria,* yielding a purple dye. **4.** the dye itself. [ME *turnesole* < MF *tournesol* the dye obtained from the plant < It *tornasole* the plant = *tornar(e)* to turn + *sole* sun]

turn·spit (tûrn′spit′), *n.* **1.** a roasting spit that can be rotated. **2.** a person or thing that operates such a spit.

turn·stile (tûrn′stil′), *n.* **1.** a structure of four horizontally revolving arms pivoted atop a post and set in an opening in a fence to allow the passage of people while barring that of cattle. **2.** a similar device set up in an entrance to bar passage until a charge is paid, to control passage, to record the number of persons passing through, etc.

turn·stone (tûrn′stōn′), *n.* any of several small, limicoline birds of the genus *Arenaria,* esp. a New World turnstone, characterized by the habit of turning over stones in search of food.

turn·ta·ble (tûrn′tā′bəl), *n.* **1.** the rotating disk on which the record in a phonograph rests. **2.** *Railroads.* a rotating, track-bearing platform, used for turning locomotives and cars around. **3.** a rotating stand used in sculpture, metalwork, and ceramics.

turn·up (tûrn′up′), *n.* **1.** something that turns up or is turned up. **2.** *Brit.* a cuff on a pair of trousers. **—***adj.* **3.** that is or may be turned up.

Tur·nus (tûr′nəs), *n.* *Rom. Legend.* an Italian king and rival of Aeneas for Lavinia. He was finally killed by Aeneas.

turn·ver·ein (tûrn′və rīn′; *Ger.* tŏŏʀn′feʀ īn′), *n.* an athletic club, esp. of gymnasts. [< G: gymnastic club = *turn(en)* (to) practice gymnastics + *Verein* union]

tur·pen·tine (tûr′pən tīn′), *n., v.,* **-tined, -tin·ing. —***n.* **1.** any of various oleoresins derived from coniferous trees, esp. the longleaf pine, *Pinus palustris,* and yielding a volatile oil and a resin when distilled. **2.** an oleoresin exuding from the terbinth, *Pistacia Terebinthus.* **3.** See **oil of turpentine.** **—***v.t.* **4.** to treat with turpentine. **5.** to gather or take crude turpentine from (trees). [late ME, r. ME *ter(e)bentyn(e)* < ML *ter(e)bentīna* < L *terebinthīna,* n. use of fem. of *terebinthinus* of the turpentine tree = *terebinth(us)* turpentine tree (< Gk *terébinthos*) + *-īnus* -INE[1]] **—tur·pen·tin·ic** (tûr′pən tin′ik), **tur·pen·tin·ous** (tûr′pən tin′əs, -tī′nəs), **tur·pen·tin·y** (tûr′pən tī′nē), *adj.*

tur·peth (tûr′pith), *n.* **1.** the purgative root of a convolvulaceous plant, *Operculina turpethum,* of the East Indies. **2.** the plant itself. [< ML *turpethum* < Ar *turbid;* r. late ME *tubit* < MF < Ar *turbid*]

tur·pi·tude (tûr′pi tōōd′, -tyōōd′), *n.* **1.** baseness or depravity. **2.** a base or depraved act. [late ME < L *turpitūdō* = *turpi(s)* base, vile + *-tūdō* -TUDE]

tur·quoise (tûr′koiz, -kwoiz), *n.* **1.** Also, **tur′quois.** an opaque mineral, a basic hydrous copper aluminum phosphate often containing a small amount of iron, sky-blue or greenish-blue in color, cut cabochon as a gem. **2.** Also called **tur′quoise blue′.** a greenish blue or bluish green. [< F: Turkish (stone) = *Turc* TURK + *-oise,* fem. of *-ois* -ESE; r. ME *turkeis* < MF]

tur·ret (tûr′it, tur′-), *n.* **1.** a small tower, usually one forming part of a larger structure, as of a castle or fortress. **2.** Also called **turrethead.** a pivoted attachment on a lathe or the like for holding a number of tools. **3.** *Navy, Army.* a low, towerlike, heavily armored structure, usually revolving horizontally, within which guns are mounted. **4.** *Fort.* (formerly) a tall structure, usually moved on wheels, employed in breaching or scaling a fortified place, a wall, or the like. [ME *turet* < MF *turete* = OF *tur* tower (< L *turris*) + *-ete* -ET]

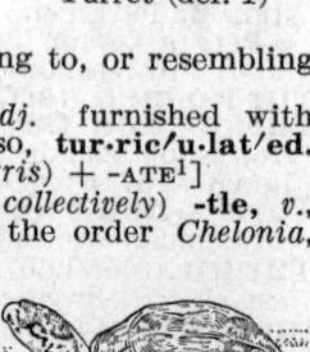
Turret (def. 1)

tur·ret·ed (tûr′i tid, tur′-), *adj.* **1.** furnished with a turret or turrets. **2.** having a turretlike part or parts. **3.** *Zool.* having whorls in the form of a long or towering spiral, as certain shells.

tur·ret·head (tûr′it hed′, tur′-), *n.* *Mach.* turret (def. 2).

tur′ret lathe′, a lathe fitted with a turret.

turri-, a learned borrowing from Latin meaning "tower," used in the formation of compound words: *turrical.* [comb. form of L *turris* tower]

tur·ri·cal (tûr′i kəl), *adj.* of, pertaining to, or resembling a turret. [TURR(I)- + -ICAL]

tur·ric·u·late (tə rik′yə lit, -lāt′), *adj.* furnished with or resembling a turret or turrets. Also, **tur·ric′u·lat′ed.** [< L *turricul(a)* little tower (dim. of *turris*) + -ATE[1]]

tur·tle[1] (tûr′tᵊl), *n., pl.* **-tles,** (*esp. collectively*) **-tle,** *v.,* **-tled, -tling. —***n.* **1.** any reptile of the order *Chelonia,* comprising aquatic and terrestrial species having the trunk enclosed in a shell consisting of a dorsal carapace and a ventral plastron. **2.** (not in technical use) an aquatic turtle as distinguished from a terrestrial one. Cf. **tortoise** (def. 1). **3. turn turtle,** to overturn. **—***v.i.* **4.** to catch turtles, esp. as a business. [adaptation (influenced by TURTLE[2]) of F *tortue* < ML *tortuca* TORTOISE] **—tur′tler,** *n.*

Box turtle[1], *Terrapene carolina* (Length 6 in.)

tur·tle[2] (tûr′tᵊl), *n.* *Archaic.* a turtledove. [ME, OE, var. of *turtur* turtledove < L, sound imit.]

tur·tle·dove (tûr′tᵊl duv′), *n.* any of several small to medium-sized, Old World doves of the genus *Streptopelia,* esp. *S. turtur,* of Europe, having a long, graduated tail. [ME *turtildove* = *turtil* TURTLE[2] + *dove* DOVE[1]]

tur·tle·head (tûr′tᵊl hed′), *n.* any scrophulariaceous herb of the genus *Chelone,* of North America. [TURTLE[1] + HEAD, so called from the appearance of its flower]

tur·tle·neck (tûr′tᵊl nek′), *n.* **1.** a high, close-fitting collar, appearing esp. on pullover sweaters. **2.** a sweater with such a collar.

turves (tûrvz), *n.* *Chiefly Brit.* pl. of **turf.**

Tus·ca·loo·sa (tus′kə lōō′sə), *n.* a city in W Alabama. 65,773 (1970).

Tus·can (tus′kən), *adj.* **1.** of, pertaining to, or characteristic of Tuscany, its people, or their dialect. **2.** *Archit.* noting or pertaining to one of the five classical orders, basically a simplified Roman Doric, with unfluted columns and with no decoration other than moldings. Cf. **composite** (def. 3), **Corinthian** (def. 4), **Doric** (def. 2), **Ionic** (def. 1). See illus. at **order.** **—***n.* **3.** the standard literary form of the Italian language. **4.** any Italian dialect of Tuscany. **5.** a native of Tuscany. [ME < L *tuscānus* Etruscan = *Tusc(i)* the Etruscans + *-ānus* -AN]

Tus·ca·ny (tus′kə nē), *n.* a region in W central Italy: formerly a grand duchy. 3,267,374 (1961); 8879 sq. mi. Italian, **Toscana.**

Tus·ca·ro·ra (tus′kə rōr′ə, -rôr′ə), *n., pl.* **-ras,** (*esp. collectively*) **-ra. 1.** a member of an Indian people living originally in North Carolina and later, after their admission into the Iroquois confederacy, in New York. **2.** an Iroquoian language, the language of the Tuscarora people.

tusch·e (tŏŏsh; *Ger.* tŏŏsh′ə), *n.* a greaselike liquid used in lithography as a medium receptive to lithographic ink, and in etching and silkscreen as a resist. [< G *Tusche,* from *tuschen* to lay on color or ink < F *toucher* to touch]

Tus·cu·lum (tus′kyə ləm), *n.* an ancient city of Latium, SE of Rome. **—Tus′cu·lan,** *adj.*

tush[1] (tush), *interj.* **1.** (used as an exclamation of impatience, disdain, contempt, etc.) **—***n.* **2.** an exclamation of "tush." [sound imit.]

tush[2] (tush), *n.* **1.** one of the four canine teeth of the horse. **2.** a tusk. [ME, OE *tusc.* See TUSK] **—tushed,** *adj.*

tusk (tusk), *n.* **1.** (in certain animals) a tooth developed to great length, usually one of a pair, as in the elephant, walrus, etc., but single in the narwhal. **2.** a long, pointed, or protruding tooth. **3.** a projection resembling the tusk of an animal. **4.** Also called **gain.** *Carpentry.* a diagonally cut shoulder at the end of a timber for strengthening a tenon. **—***v.t.* **5.** to dig up or tear off with the tusks. **6.** to gore with a tusk. **—***v.i.* **7.** to dig up or thrust at the ground with the tusks. [ME; OE *tusc* (also, *tux*), c. OFris *tusk;* akin to TOOTH] **—tusk′less,** *adj.* **—tusk′like′,** *adj.*

Tus·ke·gee (tus kē′gē), *n.* a city in E Alabama: location of Tuskegee Institute. 11,028 (1970).

tusk·er (tus′kər), *n.* an animal with tusks, as an elephant or a wild boar.

tus·sah (tus′ə), *n.* **1.** a tan silk from India. Cf. **Shantung** (def. 3a). **2.** the silkworm of an oriental moth of the genus *Antheraea,* as *A. mylitta,* that produces this silk. Also, **tus′seh, tus·ser, tus·sor** (tus′ər), **tus·sore** (tus′ōr, -ôr), **tus·sur** (tus′ər). Also called **wild silk.** [earlier *tusser* < Hind *tasar* shuttle < Skt *tasara, trasara* kind of silkworm]

tus·sis (tus′is), *n.* *Pathol.* a cough, esp. a persistent one. [< L: cough]

tus·sive (tus′iv), *adj. Pathol.* of or pertaining to a cough. [< L *tuss(is)* cough + -IVE]

tus·sle (tus′əl), *v.*, **-sled, -sling,** *n.* —*v.i.* **1.** to struggle or fight roughly or vigorously; wrestle; scuffle. —*n.* **2.** a struggle or scuffle. **3.** any vigorous struggle, conflict, etc. [var. of earlier *touse* to tease, pull (ME *-tuse(n)*) + -LE]

tus·sock (tus′ək), *n.* a tuft or clump of growing grass or the like. [appar. akin to MHG *zūsach* thicket < *zūse* lock (of hair), brushwood. See TOUSLE, -OCK] —**tus′socked,** *adj.*

tus′sock moth′, any of several moths of the family *Lymantriidae*, the larvae of which have characteristic tufts of hair on the body and feed on the leaves of various deciduous trees.

Tus·tin-Foothills (tus′tən fo͝ot′hilz), *n.* a town in SW California. 26,598 (1970).

tut (*pronounced as an alveolar click; spelling pron.* tut), *interj.*, *n.*, *v.*, **tut·ted, tut·ting.** —*interj.* **1.** (used as an exclamation of contempt, impatience, reproach, etc.) —*n.* **2.** an exclamation of "tut." —*v.i.* **3.** to utter the exclamation "tut." Also called **tut-tut.**

Tut·ankh·a·men (to͞ot′äng̃k ä′mən), *n.* 14th century B.C., a king of Egypt of the 18th dynasty. Also, **Tut′-ankh·a′mon, Tut′ankh·a′mun, Tut·enkh·a·mon** (to͞ot′-eng̃k ä′mən).

tu·te·lage (to͞ot′əlij, tyo͞ot′-), *n.* **1.** the act or fact of guarding, protecting, or guiding; guardianship. **2.** instruction; teaching; guidance. **3.** the state of being under a guardian or a tutor. [< L *tūtēl(a)* watching + -AGE]

tu·te·lar·y (to͞ot′əler′ē, tyo͞ot′-), *adj.*, *n.*, *pl.* **-lar·ies.** —*adj.* **1.** having the position of guardian or protector: *a tutelary saint.* **2.** of or pertaining to a guardian or guardianship. —*n.* **3.** a person, deity, or saint with tutelary powers. Also, **tu·te·lar** (to͞ot′əler, tyo͞ot′-). [< L *tūtēlārius* guardian]

tu·tor (to͞o′tər, tyo͞o′-), *n.* **1.** a person employed to instruct another, esp. privately. **2.** a teacher of academic rank lower than instructor in some American universities and colleges. **3.** a teacher without institutional connection who assists students in preparing for examinations. **4.** (esp. at Oxford and Cambridge) a university officer responsible for teaching and supervising a number of undergraduates. —*v.t.* **5.** to act as a tutor to. **6.** to have the guardianship, instruction, or care of. **7.** to instruct underhandedly; coach. **8.** *Archaic.* to train, school, or discipline. —*v.i.* **9.** to act as a tutor. **10.** to study privately with a tutor. [ME < L: protector] —**tu′tor·ship′,** *n.*

tu·tor·age (to͞o′tər ij, tyo͞o′-), *n.* **1.** the office, authority, or care of a tutor. **2.** the charge for instruction by a tutor.

tu·to·ri·al (to͞o tôr′ē əl, -tōr′-, tyo͞o-), *adj.* **1.** pertaining to or exercised by a tutor. —*n.* **2.** a session of intensive instruction by a tutor. [< L *tūtōri(us)* of a guardian + -AL[1]]

tuto′rial sys′tem, a system of education, esp. in some colleges, in which instruction is given personally by tutors, who also act as general advisers.

tu·toy·er (to͞o′twä yā′, tyo͞o′-; *Fr.* ty twa yā′), *v.t.*, **-toy·ered** or **-toy·ed** (-twä yād′), **-toy·er·ing** (-twä yā′-ing̃). to address (someone) familiarly, esp. in French, using the singular forms of "you." [< F = *tu* you + *toi* you (acc.) + *-er* inf. suffix]

tut·ti (to͞o′tē; *It.* to͞ot′tē), *adj.*, *n.*, *pl.* **-tis.** *Music.* —*adj.* **1.** all; all the voices or instruments together. **2.** intended for all of these together. —*n.* **3.** a tutti passage or movement. **4.** the tonal product or effect of a tutti performance. [< It, pl. of *tutto* all]

tut·ti-frut·ti (to͞o′tē fro͞o′tē), *n.* a variety of fruits, usually candied and minced, used in ice cream, confections, etc. [< It: lit., all the fruits]

tut-tut (*pronounced as two alveolar clicks; spelling pron.* tut′tut′), *interj.*, *n.*, *v.i.*, **-tut·ted, -tut·ting.** tut.

tut·ty (tut′ē), *n.* an impure oxide of zinc obtained esp. from the flues of smelting furnaces, used chiefly as a polishing powder. [ME *tutie* < late OF < ML *tūtia* ? < Pers]

tu·tu (to͞o′to͞o; *Fr.* ty ty′), *n.*, *pl.* **-tus** (-to͞oz; *Fr.* -ty′). a short, full skirt, worn by ballerinas. [< F]

Tu·tu (to͞o′to͞o), *n.* **Des·mond (Mpi·lo)** (dez′mənd əm pē′-lō), born 1931, South African Anglican clergyman and civil-rights activist: Nobel peace prize 1984.

Tu·tu·i·la (to͞o′to͞o ē′lä), *n.* the largest of the islands of American Samoa: excellent harbor at Pago Pago. 24,973 (1970); 53 sq. mi. —**Tu′tu·i′lan,** *adj.*, *n.*

Tu′va Auton′omous So′viet So′cialist Repub′lic (to͞o′və), an administrative division of the RSFSR, in the S Soviet Union in Asia: formerly an independent republic in Mongolia. 259,000; ab. 64,000 sq. mi. *Cap.*: Kyzyl. Also, **Tu·vin′i·an Auton′omous So′viet So′cialist Repub′lic** (to͞o vin′ē ən). Formerly, **Tannu Tuva.**

Tu·va·lu (to͞o′və lo͞o′), *n.* an independent group of islands in the central Pacific, S of the equator: a former British colony, independent since 1978. 5817; 10 sq. mi. *Cap.*: Funafuti. Formerly, **Ellice Islands, Lagoon Islands.**

tux (tuks), *n. Informal.* a tuxedo. [by shortening]

tux·e·do (tuk sē′dō), *n.*, *pl.* **-dos.** See **dinner jacket** (def. 1). Also, **Tux·e′do.** [short for *Tuxedo coat*, named after country club at Tuxedo Park, N.Y.]

Tux·tla Gu·tiér·rez (to͞os′tlä go͞o tyeʀ′ʀes), *n.* a city in and the capital of Chiapas, in SE Mexico. 69,326.

tu·yère (twē yâr′, to͞o-, twēr; *Fr.* ty yeʀ′), *n.*, *pl.* **tu·yères** (twē yârz′, to͞o-, twērz′; *Fr.* ty yeʀ′). *Metall.* an opening through which the blast of air enters a blast furnace, cupola forge, or the like, to facilitate combustion. Also, **tu·yer** (twē yâr′, to͞o-, twēr). [< F < *tuyau* pipe < Gmc]

TV, television.

TVA, *U.S. Govt.* Tennessee Valley Authority: a board, created in 1933, charged with developing the Tennessee River and its tributaries to promote their use for cheap electric power, irrigation, flood control, etc.

TV dinner, a meal, usually consisting of meat, potato, and a vegetable, packaged in a partitioned tray of aluminum foil, quick frozen, and requiring only heating before serving.

Tver (*Russ.* tveʀ), *n.* former name of **Kalinin.**

TVP, *Trademark.* See **textured vegetable protein.**

twad·dle (twod′əl), *n.*, *v.*, **-dled, -dling.** —*n.* **1.** trivial, feeble, silly, or tedious talk or writing. —*v.i.* **2.** to talk in a trivial, feeble, silly, or tedious manner; prate. —*v.t.* **3.** to utter as twaddle. [var. of *twattle*] —**twad′dler,** *n.*

twain (twān), *adj.*, *n. Archaic.* two. [ME *twayn*, OE *twēgen*]

Twain (twān), *n.* **Mark** (pen name of *Samuel Langhorn Clemens*), 1835–1910, U.S. author and humorist.

twang (twang̃), *v.i.* **1.** to give out a sharp, vibrating sound, as the string of a musical instrument or a bowstring. **2.** to have a sharp, nasal tone, as the human voice. —*v.t.* **3.** to cause to make a sharp, vibrating sound, as a string of a musical instrument or of a bow. **4.** to produce (music) with a twanging sound. **5.** to speak with a sharp, nasal tone. **6.** to pull the string of (an archer's bow). —*n.* **7.** the sharp, ringing sound produced by plucking or suddenly releasing a tense string. **8.** a sound or quality of speech resembling this. **9.** the act or an instance of plucking or picking. [sound imit.] —**twang′y,** *adj.*

twas (twuz, twoz; *unstressed* twəz), contraction of *it was.*

twat (twät), *n. Slang (vulgar).* the vulva. [orig. unknown]

twat·tle (twot′əl), *n.*, *v.i.*, *v.t.*, **-tled, -tling.** *Brit. Dial.* twaddle.

tway·blade (twā′blād′), *n.* any of various orchidaceous plants, esp. of the genera *Listera*, *Ophrys*, or *Liparis*, characterized by two nearly opposite broad leaves. [dial. *tway* (apocopated form of OE *twēgen* twain) + BLADE]

tweak (twēk), *v.t.* **1.** to seize and pull with a jerk and twist. **2.** to pull or pinch the nose of, esp. gently. —*n.* **3.** act of tweaking; a sharp, twisting pull or jerk. [akin to TWITCH]

tweed (twēd), *n.* **1.** a coarse wool cloth in a variety of weaves and colors, produced esp. in Scotland. **2. tweeds,** garments made of this cloth. [appar. back formation from Scot *tweedling* twilling (now obs.) < ?]

Tweed (twēd), *n.* **1. William Mar·cy** (mär′sē) ("*Boss Tweed*"), 1823–78, U.S. politician. **2.** a river flowing E from S Scotland along part of the NE boundary of England into the North Sea. 97 mi. long.

twee·dle (twēd′əl), *v.*, **-dled, -dling.** —*v.i.* **1.** to produce high-pitched, modulated sounds, as a singer, bird, etc. **2.** to perform lightly upon a musical instrument.

Twee·dle·dum and Twee·dle·dee (twēd′əl dum′ ən twēd′əl dē′), two persons or things only nominally different; a nearly identical pair. [humorous imit. coinage, appar. first applied as nicknames to Handel and Giovanni Bononcini, 1670–1750, Italian composer, with reference to their musical rivalry < *tweedle* imit. word for a shrill note]

Tweeds·muir (twēdz′myo͝or), *n.* **Baron.** See **Buchan.**

tweed·y (twē′dē), *adj.*, **tweed·i·er, tweed·i·est.** **1.** made of or resembling tweed, as in texture or appearance. **2.** wearing tweeds, esp. as a mark of a casual or outdoor life.

'tween (twēn), *prep.* contraction of *between.* [ME *twene*, aph. var. of *atwene* or *betwene*]

'tween′ deck′, *Naut.* any space between two continuous decks in the hull of a vessel.

tweet (twēt), *n.* **1.** the weak chirp of a young or small bird. —*v.i.* **2.** to chirp. [imit.]

tweet·er (twē′tər), *n.* a small loudspeaker designed for the reproduction of high-frequency sounds.

tweeze (twēz), *v.t.*, **tweezed, tweez·ing.** to pluck, as with tweezers. [back formation from TWEEZERS]

tweez·er (twē′zər), *n.* tweezers.

tweez·ers (twē′zərz), *n.pl.* small pincers or nippers for plucking out hairs, taking up small objects, etc. [pl. of *tweezer* (after *scissors*, *pincers*, etc.) = *tweeze* (earlier *(e)twees(e)* < F *étuis*, pl. of *étui*, OF *etuier* to keep < L *studiāre* to care for) + -ER[1]]

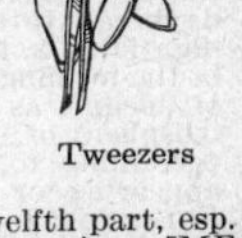

Tweezers

twelfth (twelfth), *adj.* **1.** next after the eleventh; being the ordinal number for 12. **2.** being one of 12 equal parts. —*n.* **3.** a twelfth part, esp. of one ($^1/_{12}$). **4.** the twelfth member of a series. [ME *twelfthe*, *twelfte*, OE *twelfta* = *twelf* TWELVE + *-ta* -TH[2]]

Twelfth′ Day′, Epiphany: formerly observed as the last day of the Christmas festivities.

Twelfth′ Night′, **1.** the evening before Twelfth Day, formerly observed with various festivities. **2.** the evening of Twelfth Day itself. [ME; OE *twelftan niht*]

Twelfth·tide (twelfth′tīd′), *n.* the season of Twelfth Night and Twelfth Day.

twelve (twelv), *n.* **1.** a cardinal number, 10 plus 2. **2.** a symbol for this number, as 12 or XII. **3.** a set of this many persons or things. **4. the Twelve,** the 12 apostles chosen by Christ. —*adj.* **5.** amounting to 12 in number. [ME *twelve*, inflected form of *twelf*, OE *twelfe*, lit., (ten and) two leave, i.e. two left over; c. OFris *twel(e)f*, Goth *twalif*, OHG *zwelif*, Icel *tōlf*; cf. Lith *dvýlika*]

12-gauge (twelv′gāj′), *n.* **1.** Also called **12-gauge shotgun.** a shotgun using a shell approx. .729 in. in diameter and of varying length. **2.** the shell itself.

twelve′-mile lim′it (twelv′mīl′), offshore boundary of a state, extending 12 miles at sea. Cf. **three-mile limit.**

twelve·mo (twelv′mō), *n.*, *pl.* **-mos,** *adj.* duodecimo.

twelve·month (twelv′munth′), *n. Chiefly Brit.* a year.

twelve′ pa′triarchs. See under **patriarch** (def. 3).

twelve·pen·ny (twelv′pen′ē), *adj.* noting a nail 3¼ inches long. *Abbr.*: 12d

twelve-tone (twelv′tōn′), *adj. Music.* **1.** based on or incorporating the twelve-tone technique. **2.** using or advocating the twelve-tone technique.

twelve′-tone′ row′ (rō). See **tone row.**

twelve′-tone′ technique′, *Music.* a modern system of tone relationships in which the 12 tones of an octave are not centered around any one tone, but are unified by a selected order of tones for a given composition.

twen·ti·eth (twen′tē ith), *adj.* **1.** next after the nineteenth; being the ordinal number for 20. **2.** being one of 20 equal parts. —*n.* **3.** a twentieth part, esp. of one ($^1/_{20}$). **4.** the twentieth member of a series. [ME *twentithe*, OE *twentigotha*]

twen·ty (twen′tē), *n.*, *pl.* **-ties,** *adj.* —*n.* **1.** a cardinal number, 10 times 2. **2.** a symbol for this number, as 20 or XX. **3.** a set of this many persons or things. **4. twenties,**

the numbers, years, degrees, or the like, between 20 and 29, as in referring to numbered sheets, indicating the years of a lifetime or of a century, or degrees of temperature. **5.** *Informal.* a twenty-dollar bill. —*adj.* **6.** amounting to 20 in number. [ME; OE *twēntig;* c. OFris *tw(e)intich,* OHG *zweinzug* (G *zwanzig*), Goth *twai tigjus* two tens]

28-gauge (twen′tē āt′gāj′), *n.* **1.** Also called **28-gauge shotgun.** a shotgun using a shell approx. .550 in. in diameter and of varying length. **2.** the shell itself.

twen·ty-five·pen·ny (twen′tē fīv′pen′ē), *adj.* noting a nail 4¼ inches long. *Abbr.:* 25d

20-gauge (twent′tē gāj′), *n.* **1.** Also called **20-gauge shotgun,** a shotgun using a shell approx. .615 in. in diameter and of varying length. **2.** the shell itself.

twen·ty-one (twen′tē wun′), *n.* **1.** a cardinal number, 20 plus 1. **2.** Also called **blackjack.** a gambling game at cards, in which the object is to obtain from the dealer cards whose values add up to, or close to, 21. —*adj.* **3.** amounting to 21 in number.

twen·ty·pen·ny (twen′tē pen′ē), *adj.* noting a nail four inches long. *Abbr.:* 20d

twen·ty-twen·ty (twen′tē twen′tē), *adj.* *Ophthalm.* having normal visual acuity.

.22 (twen′tē to͞o′), *n., pl.* **.22s, .22's.** **1.** a rifle or pistol using a cartridge .22 in. in diameter and of varying length. **2.** the cartridge itself. Also, **twen′ty-two′.**

'twere (twûr; *unstressed* twər), contraction of *it were.*

twerp (twûrp), *n.* *Slang.* an insignificant or despicable fellow. Also, **twirp.** [?]

Twi (chwē, chē), *n.* a dialect that is spoken and written in Ghana, belongs to the Kwa group of languages, and is mutually intelligible with Fanti.

twi-, a word element meaning "two," "twice": *twibill.* [ME, OE; c. G *zwie-* (OHG *zwi-*), L *bi-.* See TWO]

twi·bill (twī′bil′), *n.* a double-bladed battle-ax. [ME, OE]

twice (twīs), *adv.* **1.** two times. **2.** on two occasions. **3.** in twofold quantity or degree. [ME *twies* = *twie* twice (OE *twiga*) + *-s* -s¹]

twice-laid (twīs′lād′), *adj.* **1.** made from strands of used rope. **2.** made from makeshift or used material.

twice-told (twīs′tōld′), *adj.* having been told before; related two times. [late ME]

Twick·en·ham (twik′ə nəm), *n.* a city in S Middlesex, in SE England, on the Thames, near London. 100,822 (1961).

twid·dle (twid′ᵊl), *v.,* **-dled, -dling,** *n.* —*v.t.* **1.** to turn about or play with lightly or idly, esp. with the fingers; twirl. —*v.i.* **2.** to play or trifle idly with something; fiddle. **3.** to turn about lightly; twirl. **4. twiddle one's thumbs,** to do nothing; be idle. —*n.* **5.** the act of twiddling. [TW(ITCH + F)IDDLE]

twig¹ (twig), *n.* a slender shoot or branch of a tree or other plant. [ME; OE *twig, twigge,* orig. (something) divided in two; akin to OHG *zwīg* (G *Zweig*), D *twijg;* cf. Skt *dvikās* double] —**twig′less,** *adj.* —**twig′like′,** *adj.*

twig² (twig), *v.,* **twigged, twig·ging.** *Brit.* —*v.t.* **1.** to look at; observe. **2.** to see; perceive. **3.** to understand. —*v.i.* **4.** to understand. [? < Celt]

twig′ gir′dler. See under **girdler** (def. 2).

twig·gy (twig′ē), *adj.,* **-gi·er, -gi·est.** of, pertaining to, or resembling a twig or twigs.

twi·light (twī′līt′), *n.* **1.** the soft, diffused light from the sky when the sun is below the horizon, either from daybreak to sunrise or, more commonly, from sunset to nightfall. **2.** the period in the morning or, more commonly, in the evening during which this light prevails. **3.** a period of decline, as after one of maturity and vigor. **4.** an atmosphere or state of uncertainty or gloom. —*adj.* **5.** of, pertaining to, or resembling twilight; dim; obscure. **6.** appearing or flying at twilight; crepuscular. [ME; see TWI-, LIGHT]

Twi′light of the Gods′, *Teutonic Myth.* Ragnarok; Götterdämmerung.

twi′light sleep′, *Med.* a state of semiconsciousness, usually produced by scopolamine and morphine, used chiefly to effect relatively painless childbirth.

twi′light zone′, **1.** the lowest level of the ocean to which light can reach. **2.** an ill-defined area between two distinct conditions.

twill (twil), *n.* **1.** a fabric with a twill weave. **2.** See **twill weave.** —*v.t.* **3.** to weave in the manner of a twill. **4.** to weave in twill construction. [Scot and north var. of *twilly,* ME *twyle,* OE *twili(c),* half trans., half adoption of L *bilic-* (s. of *bilix*) having double thread. See TWI-]

'twill (twil), a contraction of *it will.*

twill′ weave′, one of the basic weave structures in which the filling threads are woven over and under two or more warp yarns producing a characteristic diagonal pattern. Also called **twill.** Cf. **plain weave, satin weave.**

Twill weave

twin (twin), *n., adj., v.,* **twinned, twin·ning.** —*n.* **1.** either of two children or animals brought forth at a birth. **2.** either of two persons or things closely related to or closely resembling each other. **3.** Also called **twin room.** a type of hotel accommodation with twin beds for occupancy by two persons. Cf. **double** (def. 12). **4.** Also called **hemitrope.** *Crystall.* a compound crystal consisting of two or more parts or crystals definitely oriented each to the other; macle. **5. Twins,** *Astron., Astrol.* the constellation or sign of Gemini. —*adj.* **6.** being two, or one of two, children or animals born at the same birth. **7.** being two persons or things closely related to or closely resembling each other. **8.** being one of a pair; identical: *a twin peak.* **9.** consisting of two similar parts or elements joined or connected: *a twin vase.* **10.** *Bot., Zool.* occurring in pairs; didymous. **11.** *Crystall.* of the nature of a twin; hemitrope. **12.** *Obs.* twofold or double. —*v.t.* **13.** to pair or couple. **14.** to furnish a counterpart to; match. **15.** *Crystall.* to form into a twin. **16.** *Obs.* to conceive or bring forth twins. —*v.i.* **17.** to bring forth twins. **18.** *Obs.* to be paired or coupled. [ME; OE *(ge)twinn;* akin to OFris *twīne,* Goth *twaihnai,* Icel *tvinn(r)* double]

twin′ bed′, a single bed, esp. one of a matching pair in a bedroom.

twin·ber·ry (twin′ber′ē, -bə rē), *n., pl.* **-ries.** **1.** the partridgeberry, *Mitchella repens.* **2.** a North American honeysuckle shrub, *Lonicera involucrata,* having involucrate flowers of various colors.

twin′ bill′, *Sports Slang.* a doubleheader, as in baseball.

twin-born (twin′bôrn′), *adj.* born at the same birth.

Twin′ Cit′ies, the cities of St. Paul and Minneapolis.

twine (twīn), *n., v.,* **twined, twin·ing.** —*n.* **1.** a strong thread or string composed of two or more strands twisted together. **2.** the act of twining, twisting, or interweaving. **3.** a coiled or twisted object or part; convolution. **4.** a twist or turn in anything. **5.** a knot or tangle. —*v.t.* **6.** to twist together; interweave. **7.** to form by or as by twisting together: *to twine a wreath.* **8.** to twist (one strand, thread, or the like) with another; interlace. **9.** to insert with a twisting or winding motion (usually fol. by *in* or *into*): *She twined her fingers in her hair.* **10.** to clasp or enfold (something) around something else (usually fol. by *about, around,* etc.). **11.** to wreathe or wrap: *She twined the bridal arch with flowers.* —*v.i.* **12.** to wind around something; twist itself in spirals (usually fol. by *about, around,* etc.). **13.** to wind in a sinuous or meandering course. [ME; OE *twīn,* lit., a double or twisted thread; c. D *twijn;* akin to Icel *tvinni,* G *Zwirn* thread, twine]

twin-en·gine (twin′en′jən), *adj.* having two engines of equal power as prime movers: *a twin-engine airplane.*

twin·flow·er (twin′flou′ər), *n.* either of two slender, creeping, evergreen, caprifoliaceous plants, *Linnaea borealis,* of Europe, or *L. americana,* of North America, having pink or purplish nodding flowers borne in pairs.

twinge (twinj), *n., v.,* **twinged, twing·ing.** —*n.* **1.** a sudden, sharp pain. **2.** a sharp mental or emotional pain or prick; pang. —*v.t.* **3.** to affect (the body or mind) with a sudden, sharp pain or pang. **4.** *Obs.* to pinch; tweak; twitch. —*v.i.* **5.** to have or feel a sudden, sharp pain. [ME *twenge(n),* OE *twengan* to pinch]

twi·night (twī′nīt′), *adj.* *Baseball.* noting or pertaining to a doubleheader in which the first game begins late in the afternoon and the second game begins in the evening under lights. [TWI(LIGHT) + NIGHT]

twin·jet (twin′jet′), *n.* a jet aircraft with two engines.

twin·kle (twiŋ′kəl), *v.,* **-kled, -kling,** *n.* —*v.i.* **1.** to shine with a flickering gleam of light, as a star, distant light, etc. **2.** to sparkle in the light. **3.** (of the eyes) to be bright with amusement, pleasure, etc. **4.** to flicker, as light. **5.** *Archaic.* to wink; blink. —*v.t.* **6.** to emit (light) flickeringly. **7.** *Archaic.* to wink (the eyes or eyelids). —*n.* **8.** a flickering or intermittent brightness or light. **9.** a scintillating brightness in the eyes; sparkle. **10.** the time required for a wink; twinkling. **11.** *Archaic.* a wink. [ME *twinkle(n),* OE *twinclian*]

twin·kling (twiŋ′kliŋ), *n.* **1.** the act of something that twinkles. **2.** the time required for a wink; an instant. **3.** *Archaic.* winking; a wink. [ME]

twin′-lens re′flex (twin′lenz′), a type of reflex camera in which the image passes through one lens to the ground glass and through a second lens to the film, the lenses being coupled for focusing.

twinned (twind), *adj.* **1.** born two at one birth. **2.** closely or intimately associated, joined, or united; coupled; paired.

twin·ning (twin′iŋ), *n.* **1.** the bearing of two children at one birth. **2.** the coupling of two persons or things; union. **3.** *Crystall.* the union of crystals to form a twin. [ME *twynnynge.* See TWIN, -ING¹]

twin′ room′, twin (def. 3).

twin-screw (twin′skro͞o′), *adj.* *Naut.* (of a vessel) having two screw propellers, which usually revolve in opposite directions.

twirl (twûrl), *v.t.* **1.** to cause to rotate rapidly; spin; revolve; whirl. **2.** to twiddle. **3.** to wind idly, as about something. **4.** *Baseball Slang.* to pitch. —*v.i.* **5.** to rotate rapidly; whirl. **6.** to turn quickly. **7.** *Baseball Slang.* to pitch. —*n.* **8.** act of rotating rapidly; whirl. **9.** a spiral or convolution. [TW(IST + WH)IRL] —**twirl′er,** *n.*

twirp (twûrp), *n.* twerp.

twist (twist), *v.t.* **1.** to combine, as two or more strands or threads, by winding together; intertwine. **2.** to form by or as by winding strands together. **3.** to entwine (one thing) with another. **4.** to wind or coil (something) about something else. **5.** to alter in shape, as by turning the ends in opposite directions. **6.** to turn sharply or wrench out of place; sprain. **7.** to pull, tear, or break off by turning forcibly. **8.** to contort (the features). **9.** to distort the meaning or form of; pervert. **10.** to cause to become mentally or emotionally distorted; warp. **11.** to cause to move with a rotary motion, as a ball pitched in a curve. **12.** to turn (something) from one direction to another, as by rotating or revolving. —*v.i.* **13.** to be or become intertwined. **14.** to wind or twine about something. **15.** to writhe or squirm. **16.** to take a zigzag or spiral form or course. **17.** to turn so as to face in another direction. **18.** to change shape under forcible turning or twisting. **19.** to move with a progressive rotary motion, as a ball pitched in a curve. **20.** to dance the twist. —*n.* **21.** a deviation in direction; curve; bend; turn. **22.** a rotary motion or spin. **23.** anything formed by or as by twisting. **24.** act or process of twining things together. **25.** a distortion or perversion, as of meaning or form. **26.** an eccentric attitude or bias. **27.** a spiral arrangement or form. **28.** a spiral movement or course. **29.** an irregular bend; crook; kink. **30.** a sudden, unanticipated change of course, as of events. **31.** a novel treatment, method, etc. **32.** the changing of the shape of anything by or as by turning the ends in opposite directions. **33.** the stress causing this alteration; torque. **34.** a twisting action, force, or stress; torsion. **35.** a strong, twisted silk thread, used esp. for working buttonholes. **36.** the direction of twisting in weaving yarn. **37.** a loaf or roll of dough twisted and baked. **38.** a strip of citrus peel that has been twisted and placed in a drink to add flavor. **39.** a kind of tobacco manufactured in the form of a rope or thick cord. **40.** a vigorous dance characterized by strongly rhythmic twisting motions of the body. **41.** *Slang.* a girl or woman. [ME *twiste(n)* (to) divide < *twist* divided object, rope, OE *-twist;* c. D *twisten* to quarrel, G *Zwist* a quarrel. See TWI-] —**twist′a·bil′i·ty,** *n.* —**twist′a·ble,** *adj.* —**twist′ed·ly,** *adv.* —**twist′ing·ly,** *adv.*

twist′ drill′, *Mach.* a cylindrical drill bit with one or more deep helical grooves.

twist·er (twis′tər), *n.* **1.** a person or thing that twists. **2.** a ball pitched or moving with a spin. **3.** *U.S. Informal.* a whirlwind or tornado.

twit (twit), *v.*, **twit·ted, twit·ting,** *n.* —*v.t.* **1.** to taunt, tease, ridicule, etc. **2.** to reproach or upbraid. —*n.* **3.** the act or an instance of twitting. **4.** a derisive reproach; taunt; gibe. [aph. var. of obs. *atwite*, ME *atwiten*, OE *ætwītan* to taunt = *æt-* AT + *wītan* to blame] —**Syn. 1.** deride, mock, rally, chaff.

twitch (twich), *v.t.* **1.** to tug or pull at with a quick, short movement; pluck. **2.** to jerk rapidly. **3.** to move (a part of the body) with a sudden, jerking motion. **4.** to pinch or pull at sharply and painfully. —*v.i.* **5.** to move spasmodically or convulsively; jerk; jump. **6.** to give a sharp, sudden pull; tug; pluck (usually fol. by *at*). **7.** to ache or hurt with a sharp, shooting pain; twinge. —*n.* **8.** a quick, jerky movement of the body, or of some part of it. **9.** a short, sudden pull or tug; jerk. **10.** a twinge or pang. [ME *twicche(n)*; akin to OE *twiccian* to pluck; c. G *zwicken* to pinch] —**twitch′er,** *n.* —**twitch′ing·ly,** *adv.*

twitch′ grass′. See **couch grass.** [m. *quitch grass*]

twit·ter (twit′ər), *v.i.* **1.** to utter a succession of small, tremulous sounds, as a bird. **2.** to talk lightly and rapidly; chatter. **3.** to titter; giggle. **4.** to tremble with excitement. —*v.t.* **5.** to express by twittering. —*n.* **6.** act of twittering. **7.** a twittering sound. **8.** a state of tremulous excitement. [ME *twiter;* akin to G *zwitschern*]

twit·ter·y (twit′ə rē), *adj.* **1.** given to or characterized by twittering. **2.** tremulous; shaky.

'twixt (twikst), *prep.* contraction of *betwixt*.

two (to͞o), *n.* **1.** a cardinal number, 1 plus 1. **2.** a symbol for this number, as 2 or II. **3.** a set of this many persons or things. **4.** a playing card, die face, or half of a domino face with two pips. **5. in two,** into two separate parts, as halves. **6. put two and two together,** to draw a correct conclusion from the given circumstances; infer. —*adj.* **7.** amounting to two in number. [ME; OE *twā*; c. G *zwei;* cf. L *duo*, Gk *dýo*]

2-A (to͞o′ā′), *n.* **1.** a U.S. Selective Service classification designating a person other than an agricultural worker or student having an occupational deferment. **2.** a person so classified. Also, **II-A.**

two-bag·ger (to͞o′bag′ər), *n.* *Baseball Slang.* double (def. 19).

two′-base hit′ (to͞o′bās′), *Baseball.* double (def. 19).

two-bit (to͞o′bit′), *adj.* *Slang.* **1.** costing twenty-five cents. **2.** inferior; small-time: *a two-bit actor.*

two′ bits′, *Slang.* twenty-five cents.

two-by-four (to͞o′bī fôr′, -fôr′, -bə-), *adj.* **1.** two units thick and four units wide, esp. in inches. **2.** *Slang.* unimportant; insignificant; two-bit. **3.** *Informal.* lacking adequate space; cramped. —*n.* **4.** a timber measuring two inches by four inches in cross section. **5.** something, as a room or apartment, that is small or cramped.

2-C (to͞o′sē′), *n.* **1.** a U.S. Selective Service classification designating an agricultural worker having a deferment. **2.** a person so classified. Also, **II-C.**

two-cy·cle (to͞o′sī′kəl), *adj.* noting or pertaining to an internal-combustion engine in which a complete cycle in each cylinder requires two strokes, one to admit and compress air or an air-fuel mixture and one to ignite fuel, do work, and scavenge the cylinder. Cf. **four-cycle.**

two-di·men·sion·al (to͞o′di men′shə nəl), *adj.* **1.** having the dimensions of height and width only. **2.** (of a work of art) having its elements organized in terms of a flat surface, esp. emphasizing the vertical and horizontal character of the picture plane. **3.** (in a literary work) superficial, as in character development. —**two′-di·men′sion·al′i·ty,** *n.* —**two′-di·men′sion·al·ly,** *adv.*

two-edged (to͞o′ejd′), *adj.* **1.** having two edges, as a sword. **2.** cutting or effective both ways.

two-faced (to͞o′fāst′), *adj.* **1.** having two faces. **2.** deceitful, hypocritical. —**two-fac·ed·ly** (to͞o′fā′sid lē, -fāst′lē), *adv.* —**two′-fac′ed·ness,** *n.*

two·fer (to͞o′fər), *n.* *Theat.* a card or ticket entitling the holder to purchase theater tickets at a reduced price. [from the phrase *two for* (the price of one, a nickel, etc.)]

two-fist·ed (to͞o′fis′tid), *adj.* **1.** having two fists and being able to use them. **2.** *U.S. Informal.* strong and vigorous.

two·fold (to͞o′fōld′), *adj.* **1.** having two elements or parts. **2.** twice as great or as much; double. —*adv.* **3.** in twofold measure; doubly. [ME]

two-four (to͞o′fôr′, -fôr′), *adj.* *Music.* (of a meter) having two quarter notes or their equivalent to a measure.

2, 4-D, a slightly water-soluble powder $C_6H_3(OCH_2COOH)Cl_2$, used as a weed killer. Also called **dichlorophenoxyacetic acid.** [*2, 4-d(ichlorophenoxyacetic acid)*]

2, 4, 5-T, See **trichlorphenoxyacetic acid.**

two-hand·ed (to͞o′han′did), *adj.* **1.** having two hands. **2.** ambidextrous. **3.** involving or requiring the use of both hands. **4.** requiring or engaged in by two persons. [late ME *too-honded*] —**two′-hand′ed·ly,** *adv.*

two-mast·er (to͞o′mas′tər, -mä′stər), *n.* *Naut.* a vessel rigged with two masts.

two′-name pa′per (to͞o′nām′), *Banking.* commercial paper having more than one obligor.

two′-par·ty sys′tem (to͞o′pär′tē), *Govt.* a political system consisting chiefly of two major parties, more or less equal in strength.

two·pence (tup′əns), *n.* **1.** (*construed as sing. or pl.*) *Brit.* a sum of two pennies. **2.** a trifle. Also, **tuppence.** [ME *two pens*]

two·pen·ny (tup′ə nē), *adj.* **1.** Also, **tuppenny.** of the amount or value of twopence. **2.** noting a nail one inch long. *Abbr.:* 2d

two-phase (to͞o′fāz′), *adj.* *Elect.* diphase.

two-piece (to͞o′pēs′), *adj.* **1.** having or consisting of two parts or pieces, esp. two matching pieces of a clothing ensemble: *a two-piece bathing suit.* —*n.* **2.** Also, **two′-piec′er.** a two-piece garment.

two-ply (to͞o′plī′), *adj.* consisting of two thicknesses, layers, strands, or the like: *two-ply knitting yarn.*

2-S (to͞o′es′), *n.* **1.** a U.S. Selective Service classification designating a student having a deferment. **2.** a person so classified. Also, **II-S.**

two-seat·er (to͞o′sē′tər), *n.* a vehicle accommodating two persons.

Two′ Sic′ilies, a former kingdom in Sicily and S Italy that existed intermittently from 1130 to 1861.

two-sid·ed (to͞o′sī′did), *adj.* **1.** having two sides; bilateral. **2.** having two aspects or characters.

two·some (to͞o′səm), *adj.* **1.** consisting of two; twofold. **2.** performed or played by two persons. —*n.* **3.** two together; couple; duo. **4.** *Golf.* a match between two persons. [ME (north); see TWO, -SOME[2]]

two-spot (to͞o′spot′), *n.* a playing card or the upward face of a die having two pips, or a domino one half of which bears two pips.

two-step (to͞o′step′), *n.* a ballroom dance in duple meter, marked by sliding steps.

two-suit·er (to͞o′so͞ot′ər), *n.* a man's lightweight valise or suitcase that can accommodate two suits.

two-time (to͞o′tīm′), *v.t.*, **-timed, -tim·ing.** *Slang.* to be unfaithful to a lover or spouse. —**two′-tim′er,** *n.*

two-tone (to͞o′tōn′), *adj.* having two colors or two shades of the same color. Also, **two′-toned′.**

'twould (two͝od), contraction of *it would.*

two-way (to͞o′wā′), *adj.* **1.** providing for or allowing movement or communication in opposite directions, or both to and from a place. **2.** involving two parties or participants, as a relationship or agreement. **3.** entailing responsibilities, obligations, etc., on both such parties.

twp., township.

TX, Texas (approved esp. for use with zip code).

-ty[1], a suffix of numerals denoting multiples of ten: *twenty; thirty.* [OE *-tig;* c. OFris *-tich*, Goth *-tigjus*, Icel *-tigr*, G *-zig*]

-ty[2] a suffix occurring in nouns of Latin origin, denoting quality, state, etc.: *unity; enmity.* [ME *-te(e)* < OF *-te* (m.), *-tet* (fem.) < L *-tāt-* (obl. of *-tās*)]

Ty., Territory.

Ty·burn (tī′bərn), *n.* a former place of public execution in London, England.

Ty·che (tī′kē), *n.* the ancient Greek goddess of fortune, identified by the Romans with Fortuna. [< Gk *týchē* luck, fortune]

Ty·cho (tī′kō), *n.* a crater in the third quadrant of the face of the moon, having an extensive ray system. ab. 56 mi. in diam.

ty·coon (tī ko͞on′), *n.* **1.** a businessman having great wealth and power. **2.** (*often cap.*) a title used to refer to the shogun of Japan. [< Jap *taikun* = Chin *tai* great (dial. var. of *ta*) + *kiun* prince (dial. var. of *chün*)]

Ty·de·us (tī′dē əs, -dyo͞os, tid′ē əs), *n.* *Class. Myth.* the father of Diomedes: one of the Seven against Thebes.

tye (tī), *n.* *Naut.* a chain for hoisting an upper yard at its middle, hauled upon by the halyard tackle. Also, **tie.** [ME; see TIE]

ty·ing (tī′ing), *v.* ppr. of **tie.**

tyke (tīk), *n.* **1.** a cur; mongrel. **2.** *Chiefly Scot.* a boor. **3.** a small child. Also, **tike.** [ME < Icel *tīk* bitch]

Ty·ler (tī′lər), *n.* **1. John,** 1790–1862, 10th president of the United States 1841–45. **2. Moses Coit** (koit), 1835–1900, U.S. historian and educator. **3. Wat** (wot) or **Walter,** died 1381, English rebel: leader of the peasants' revolt of 1381. **4.** a city in E Texas. 57,770 (1970).

tym·bal (tim′bəl), *n.* timbal.

tym·pan (tim′pən), *n.* **1.** drum. **2.** *Print.* a padlike device interposed between the platen or its equivalent and the sheet to be printed, in order to soften and equalize the pressure. **3.** See **tympanic membrane.** [< L *tympan(um)* TYMPANUM]

tym·pa·ni (tim′pə nē), *n. pl.* timpani.

tym·pan·ic (tim pan′ik), *adj.* pertaining or belonging to a tympanum, esp. the tympanic membrane of the ear.

tympan′ic bone′, *Anat., Zool.* (in mammals) a bone of the skull, supporting the tympanic membrane and enclosing part of the tympanum or middle ear.

tympan′ic mem′brane, *Anat., Zool.* a membrane separating the tympanum or middle ear from the passage of the external ear; eardrum.

tym·pa·nist (tim′pə nist), *n.* a person who plays the kettledrum or other percussion instruments in an orchestra. [< L *tympanista* < Gk *tympanistḗs* = *tympan(ízein)* (to) beat a drum + *-istēs* -IST]

tym·pa·ni·tes (tim′pə nī′tēz), *n.* *Pathol.* distention of the abdominal wall, as in peritonitis, caused by the accumulation of gas or air in the intestine or peritoneal cavity. [< NL < Gk *tympanī́tēs* pertaining to a drum] —**tym·pa·nit·ic** (tim′pə nit′ik), *adj.*

tym·pa·ni·tis (tim′pə nī′tis), *n.* *Pathol.* inflammation of the middle ear. [TYMPAN(UM) + -ITIS]

tym·pa·num (tim′pə nəm), *n., pl.* **-nums, -na** (-nə). **1.** *Anat., Zool.* **a.** See **middle ear. b.** See **tympanic membrane. 2.** *Archit.* **a.** the recessed, usually triangular space enclosed between the cornices of a pediment, often decorated with sculpture. **b.** a similar space between an arch and the horizontal head of a door or window below. **3.** *Elect.* the diaphragm of a telephone. [< L < Gk *týmpanon* drum]

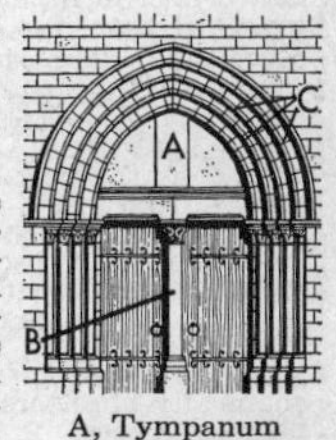

A, Tympanum (def. 2b); B, Trumeau; C, Orders of arches

tym·pa·ny (tim′pə nē), *n.* **1.** *Pathol.* tympanites. **2.** *Archaic.* inflated or pretentious style; bombast; turgidity. [< ML *tympanias* < Gk *tympanías*]

Tyn·dale (tin′dəl), *n.* **William,** c1492–1536, English religious reformer, translator of the Bible into English: martyred 1536. Also, **Tindal, Tindale.**

Tyn·dall (tin′dəl), *n.* **John,** 1820–93, English physicist.

Tyn′dall effect′, *Physics.* the scattering and polarization of light passing through a system of particles, as a solution of colloidal particles. [named after John TYNDALL]

Tyn·dar·e·us (tin dâr′ē əs), *n. Class. Myth.* the husband of Leda and father of Clytemnestra, Castor, and, according to some authors, Pollux. Also, **Tyn·dar′e·os.**

tyne (tīn), *n. Chiefly Brit.* tine[1].

Tyne (tīn), *n.* a river in NE England, in Northumberland, flowing E into the North Sea. ab. 30 mi. long.

Tyne·mouth (tīn′məth, tin′-), *n.* a seaport in SE Northumberland, in NE England, at the mouth of the Tyne River. 70,112 (1961).

typ., 1. typographer. 2. typographic. 3. typographical. 4. typography.

typ·al (tī′pəl), *adj.* 1. of, pertaining to, or constituting a type. 2. serving as a type; typical.

type (tīp), *n., v.,* **typed, typ·ing.** —*n.* **1.** a number of things or persons sharing a particular characteristic, or set of characteristics, that causes them to be regarded as a group, more or less precisely defined or designated; class; category. **2.** a thing or person regarded as a member of a class or category: *This is some type of mushroom.* **3.** *Informal.* a person, regarded as reflecting or typifying a certain line of work, environment, etc.: *a couple of civil service types.* **4.** a thing or person that represents perfectly or in the best way a class or category; model. **5.** *Print.* **a.** a rectangular piece or block, now usually of metal, having on its upper surface a letter or character in relief. **b.** such pieces or blocks collectively. **c.** a printed character or printed characters. **d.** face (defs. 17b, c). **6.** *Biol.* **a.** a genus or species that most nearly exemplifies the essential characteristics of a higher group. **b.** the one or more specimens on which the description and naming of a species is based. **7.** *Agric.* the inherited features of an animal or breed: *dairy type.* **8.** the pattern or model from which something is made. **9.** *Philos.* **a.** a classification of logical propositions according to a particular hierarchy, in which individuals, classes of individuals, and classes of classes, etc., are treated as progressively higher entities. **b.** the form of a word, expression, symbol, etc., as opposed to a specific instance of its use. In the expression "Mary, Mary" there is one type and two tokens. Cf. **token** (def. 8). **10.** an image or figure produced by impressing or stamping. **11.** a symbol of something in the future, as an Old Testament event serving as a prefiguration of a New Testament event. **12.** See **blood group.** —*v.t.* **13.** to typewrite. **14.** to reproduce in type or in print. **15.** *Med.* to ascertain the blood group of (a blood sample). **16.** to typecast. **17.** to typify, symbolize, or represent. **18.** to represent prophetically; foreshadow; prefigure. —*v.i.* **19.** to typewrite. [late ME < L *typus* < Gk *týpos* blow, impression] —**Syn. 1.** sort, classification, form, stamp. **4.** sample, example, prototype.

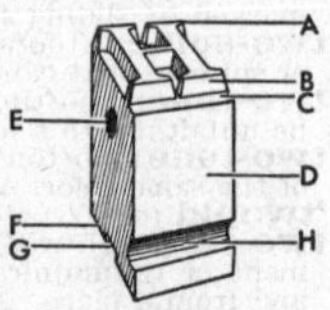

A B C D E F G H

Type (def. 5a) A, Serif; B, Beard or neck; C, Shoulder; D, Body; E, Pin mark; F, Foot; G, Groove; H, Nick

-type, a suffix representing **type** (*prototype*), esp. used of photographic processes: *ferrotype.* Cf. **typo-.**

type·bar (tīp′bär), *n.* one of a series of thin metal bars on a typewriter that holds the type and is actuated by the keys.

type-cast (tīp′kast′, -käst′), *v.,* **-cast, -cast·ing,** *adj. Print.* —*v.t., v.i.* **1.** to cast (type). —*adj.* **2.** (of text to be printed) having the type already cast. —**type′-cast′er,** *n.*

type·cast (tīp′kast′, -käst′), *v.t.,* **-cast, -cast·ing.** *Theat.* to cast (a performer) according to his physical type, manner, or personality, etc., according to the mental image the audience has of him.

type·face (tīp′fās′), *n.* face (defs. 17b, c).

type′ found′er, a person engaged in the making of metallic types. —**type′ found′ing.** —**type′ found′ry.**

type′ ge′nus, *Biol.* the genus that is formally held to be typical of the family or other higher group to which it belongs.

type-high (tīp′hī′), *adj. Print.* of a height equal to the distance from the foot to the face of a type: 0.918 inch.

type′ local′ity, *Biol.* the locality in which a type specimen was collected.

type′ met′al, an alloy for making printing types, consisting chiefly of lead and antimony.

type·script (tīp′skript′), *n.* **1.** a typewritten copy, as of a literary composition. **2.** typewritten matter. [TYPE + SCRIPT (formed on model of *manuscript*)]

type·set (tīp′set′), *v.,* **-set, -set·ting,** *adj.* —*v.t.* **1.** to set (textual matter) in type. —*adj.* **2.** (of written, textual matter) set in type. [back formation from TYPESETTER]

type·set·ter (tīp′set′ər), *n.* **1.** a person who sets or composes type; compositor. **2.** a typesetting machine.

type·set·ting (tīp′set′ing), *n.* **1.** the process or action of setting type. —*adj.* **2.** used for setting type.

type′ spe′cies, *Biol.* the species of a genus that is regarded as the best example of the generic characters; the species from which a genus is named.

type′ spec′imen, *Biol.* an individual animal or plant from which the description of a species has been prepared.

type·write (tīp′rīt′), *v.t., v.i.,* **-wrote, -writ·ten, -writ·ing.** to write by means of a typewriter; type. [back formation from TYPEWRITER]

type·writ·er (tīp′rī′tər), *n.* **1.** a machine for writing mechanically in letters and characters like those produced by printers' types. **2.** *Print.* a type style which gives the appearance of typewritten copy. **3.** a typist.

type·writ·ing (tīp′rī′ting), *n.* **1.** the act or art of using a typewriter. **2.** printed work done on a typewriter.

type·writ·ten (tīp′rit′ən), *v.* pp. of **typewrite.**

typh-, var. of **typho-** before a vowel: *typhoid.*

typh·li·tis (tif lī′tis), *n. Pathol.* inflammation of the cecum. [< Gk *typhl(ós)* blind + -ITIS] —**typh·lit·ic** (tif lit′ik), *adj.*

typh·lol·o·gy (tif lol′ə jē), *n.* the sum of scientific knowledge concerning blindness. [< Gk *typhlo-* (comb. form of *typhlós* blind) + -LOGY]

typho-, a combining form representing **typhus** and **typhoid.** Also, *esp. before a vowel,* **typh-.**

Ty·phoe·us (tī fē′əs), *n. Class. Myth.* a monster with a hundred serpent heads, fiery eyes, and a terrifying voice. Zeus set him on fire with thunderbolts and flung him down into Tartarus under Mount Etna. —**Ty·phoe′an,** *adj.*

ty·phoid (tī′foid), *Pathol.* —*n.* **1.** Also called **ty′phoid fe′ver.** an infectious, often fatal, febrile disease, characterized by intestinal inflammation and ulceration, caused by the typhoid bacillus. —*adj.* **2.** resembling typhus; typhous. **3.** typhoidal.

ty·phoi·dal (tī foid′əl), *adj. Pathol.* of, pertaining to, or resembling typhoid.

ty′phoid bacil′lus, the bacterium, *Salmonella typhosa,* causing typhoid fever.

ty·phoi·din (tī foi′din), *n. Med.* a culture of dead typhoid bacillus used by cutaneous inoculation to detect the presence of typhoid infection.

ty·phon (tī′fon), *n.* a signal horn operated by compressed air or steam. [appar. after TYPHON]

Ty·phon (tī′fon), *n. Class. Myth.* a monster and a son of Typhoeus, often identified with Typhoeus.

ty·phoon (tī fōōn′), *n.* **1.** a tropical cyclone or hurricane of the western Pacific area and the China seas. **2.** a violent storm or tempest of India. [< Chin *tai fung* great wind; influenced by Gk *typhôn* violent wind] —**ty·phon·ic** (tī fon′ik), *adj.*

ty·phus (tī′fəs), *n. Pathol.* an acute, infectious disease characterized by great prostration, severe nervous symptoms, and a peculiar eruption of reddish spots on the body: now regarded as due to a specific microorganism transmitted by lice and fleas. Also called **ty′phus fe′ver.** [< NL < Gk *týphos* vapor] —**ty′phous,** *adj.*

typ·i·cal (tip′i kəl), *adj.* **1.** of the nature of or serving as a type or representative specimen. **2.** conforming to a particular type. **3.** *Biol.* exemplifying most nearly the essential characteristics of a higher group in natural history, and forming the type. **4.** characteristic or distinctive: *a person's typical walk.* **5.** pertaining to, of the nature of, or serving as a type or emblem; symbolic. Also, **typ′ic.** [< ML *typicāl(is)* = LL *typic(us)* (< Gk *typikós* = *týp(os)* TYPE + *-ikos* -IC) + *-ālis* -AL[1]] —**typ′i·cal·ly,** *adv.* —**typ′i·cal·ness, typ′i·cal′i·ty,** *n.*

typ·i·fy (tip′ə fī′), *v.t.,* **-fied, -fy·ing.** **1.** to serve as the typical specimen of. **2.** to symbolize or prefigure. **3.** to represent by a type or symbol. [< L *typ(us)* TYPE + -IFY] —**typ′i·fi·ca′tion,** *n.*

typ·ist (tī′pist), *n.* a person who operates a typewriter.

ty·po (tī′pō), *n., pl.* **-pos.** *Informal.* See **typographical error.** [shortened form]

typo-, a combining form representing **type:** *typography; typology.* Cf. **-type.**

typo., 1. typographer. 2. typographic. 3. typographical. 4. typography.

typog., 1. typographer. 2. typographic. 3. typographical. 4. typography.

ty·pog·ra·pher (tī pog′rə fər), *n.* a person skilled or engaged in typography. [TYPOGRAPH(Y) + -ER[1]]

ty·po·graph·ic (tī′pə graf′ik), *adj.* of or pertaining to typography. Also, **ty′po·graph′i·cal.** [< NL *typographic(us)* = ML *typograph(ia)* TYPOGRAPHY + *-icus* -IC] —**ty′po·graph′i·cal·ly,** *adv.*

typograph′ical er′ror, an error in printed or typewritten matter resulting from striking the improper key of a keyboard, from mechanical failure, or the like.

ty·pog·ra·phy (tī pog′rə fē), *n.* **1.** the art or process of printing with type. **2.** the work of setting and arranging types and of printing from them. **3.** the general character or appearance of printed matter. [< NL *typographia* = Gk *týpo(s)* type + *-graphia* -GRAPHY]

ty·pol·o·gy (tī pol′ə jē), *n.* **1.** a systematic classification or study of types. **2.** symbolism. —**ty·po·log·i·cal** (tī′pə loj′i kəl), **ty′po·log′ic,** *adj.* —**ty′po·log′i·cal·ly,** *adv.* —**ty·pol′o·gist,** *n.*

ty·poth·e·tae (tī poth′i tē′, tī′pə thē′tē), *n. pl.* printers, esp. master printers: used in the names of associations of printers. [< NL = Gk *týpo(s)* type + *-thetai,* Latinized pl. of Gk *thétēs* one who places; see THETIC]

typp (tip), *n. Textiles.* a number representing the aggregate of thousands of yards of yarn weighing one pound. [*t(housand)y(ards) p(er) p(ound)*]

typw., 1. typewriter. 2. typewritten.

Tyr (tēr, tʏr), *n. Scand. Myth.* the god of victory, usually regarded as the son of Odin and Frigg.

ty·ran·ni·cal (ti ran′i kəl, tī-), *adj.* unjustly cruel, harsh, or severe; arbitrary or oppressive; despotic. Also, **ty·ran′nic.** [< L *tyrannic(us)* (< Gk *tyrannikós* = *týrann(os)* TYRANT + *-ikos* -IC) + -AL[1]] —**ty·ran′ni·cal·ly,** *adv.* —**Syn.** dictatorial; imperious, domineering.

ty·ran·ni·cide (ti ran′i sīd′, tī-), *n.* **1.** the act of killing a tyrant. **2.** a person who kills a tyrant. [< L *tyrannicīda, -ium.* See TYRANT, -CIDE] —**ty·ran′ni·cid′al,** *adj.*

tyr·an·nise (tir′ə nīz′), *v.i., v.t.,* **-nised, -nis·ing.** *Chiefly Brit.* tyrannize.

tyr·an·nize (tir′ə nīz′), *v.,* **-nized, -niz·ing.** —*v.i.* **1.** to exercise absolute power, esp. cruelly or oppressively (often fol. by *over*). **2.** to govern despotically, cruelly, or oppressively. **3.** to govern as a tyrant. —*v.t.* **4.** to govern tyrannically. [< F *tyranniser*(r) < LL *tyrannizāre* = *tyrann(us)* TYRANT + *-izāre* -IZE]

ty·ran·no·saur (ti ran′ə sôr′, tī-), *n.* a carnivorous dinosaur of the genus *Tyrannosaurus,* from the late Cretaceous period of North America, that walked upright on its hind feet. [< NL *tyrrano-* (comb. form of L *tyrannus* tyrant) + -SAUR]

tyr·an·nous (tir′ə nəs), *adj.* tyrannical. [ME < L *tyrann(us)* TYRANT + -OUS] —**tyr′an·nous·ly,** *adv.*

tyr·an·ny (tir′ə nē), *n., pl.* **-nies.** **1.** arbitrary or unrestrained exercise of power; despotic abuse of authority. **2.** the government or rule of a tyrant. **3.** a state ruled by a tyrant. **4.** oppressive government on the part of any ruler. **5.** undue severity or harshness. **6.** a tyrannical act or proceeding. [ME *tyrannie* < OF < ML *tyrannia* = L *tyrann(us)* TYRANT + *-ia* -Y[3]]

ty·rant (tī′rənt), *n.* **1.** a king or ruler who uses his power oppressively or unjustly. **2.** any despotic person. **3.** a tyrannical or compulsory influence. **4.** an absolute ruler, esp. one in ancient Greece or Sicily. [ME *tirant* < OF < L *tyrann(us)* < Gk *týrannos*] —**Syn. 1.** despot, autocrat, dictator.

ty′rant fly′catcher, flycatcher (def. 2).

tyre (tīᵊr), *n., v.t.,* **tyred, tyr·ing.** *Brit.* tire[2].

Tyre (tīᵊr), *n.* an ancient seaport of Phoenicia.

Tyr·i·an (tir′ē ən), *adj.* **1.** of or pertaining to ancient Tyre or its people. **2.** of the color of Tyrian purple. [< L *tyri(us)* (< Gk *týri(os)* < *Týros* TYRE) + -AN]

Tyr′ian pur′ple, 1. Also called **Tyr′ian dye′.** a highly prized purple dye of classical antiquity, an indigo derivative originally obtained from a certain shellfish and later synthetically produced. **2.** a vivid, purplish red.

ty·ro (tī′rō), *n., pl.* **-ros.** a beginner in learning anything; novice. Also, **tiro.** [< L *tīro* recruit] —**ty·ron·ic** (tī ron′ik), adj. —**Syn.** neophyte, learner.

ty·ro·ci·dine (tī′rə sīd′ᵊn, -sī′dēn), *n.* *Pharm.* an antibacterial substance, obtained from tyrothricin: used chiefly in treating infections caused by Gram-positive bacteria. Also, **ty·ro·ci·din** (tī′rə sīd′ᵊn). [TYRO(SINE) + -CIDE + -INE[1]]

Tyr·ol (tir′ol, tī′rōl, ti rōl′; *Ger.* tē ʀōl′), *n.* **1.** an alpine region in W Austria and N Italy: a former Austrian crown land. **2.** a province in W Austria. 462,612 (1961); 4883 sq. mi. *Cap.:* Innsbruck. Also, **Tirol.**

Ty·ro·le·an (ti rō′lē ən), *adj.* **1.** of, pertaining to, or characteristic of the Tyrol or its inhabitants. —*n.* **2.** a native or inhabitant of the Tyrol. Also, **Tirolean, Tyrolese.** [TYROL + *-ean* (var. of -IAN)]

Tyr·o·lese (tir′ə lēz′, -lēs′), *adj., n., pl.* **-lese.** Tyrolean. Also, **Tirolese.**

Ty·rone (ti rōn′), *n.* a county in W Northern Ireland. 133,919 (1961); 1218 sq. mi. *Co. seat:* Omagh.

ty·ro·si·nase (tī′rō si nās′, tir′ō-), *n.* *Biochem.* an oxidizing enzyme, found in plant and animal tissues, that catalyzes the aerobic oxidation of tyrosine into melanin and other pigments.

ty·ro·sine (tī′rə sēn′, -sin, tir′ə-), *n.* *Biochem.* an amino acid, $HOC_6H_4CH_2CH(NH_2)COOH$, resulting from the hydrolysis of proteins. [< Gk *tȳrós* cheese + -INE[2]]

ty·ro·thri·cin (tī′rō thrī′sin, -thris′in), *n.* *Pharm.* an antibiotic powder consisting chiefly of a mixture of gramicidin and tyrocidine: used chiefly for treating local infections caused by Gram-positive bacteria. [< NL *Tyrothric-* (s. of *Tyrothrix*) name of genus of bacteria (= Gk *tȳró(s)* cheese + *thríx* hair) + -IN[2]]

Tyrr (tēr, tʏr), *n.* Tyr.

Tyr·rhe′ni·an Sea′ (ti rē′nē ən), a part of the Mediterranean, bounded by W Italy, Corsica, Sardinia, and Sicily.

Tyr·tae·us (tûr tē′əs), *n.* fl. 7th century B.C., Greek poet.

tythe (tīth), *n., v.t., v.i.,* **tythed, tyth·ing.** *Brit.* tithe.

Tyu·men (tyo͞o men′), *n.* a city in the SW RSFSR, in the W Soviet Union in Asia. 200,000 (est. 1964).

tzad·dik (tsä dēk′; *Eng.* tsä′dik), *n., pl.* **tzad·di·kim** (tsä dē kēm′; *Eng.* tsä dē′kim, -dik′im). *Hebrew.* zaddik.

tzar (zär, tsär), *n.* czar.

tzar·e·vich (zär′ə vich, tsär′-), *n.* czarevitch.

tza·rev·na (zä rev′nə, tsä-), *n.* czarevna.

tza·ri·na (zä rē′nə, tsä-), *n.* czarina.

tzar·ism (zär′iz əm, tsär′-), *n.* czarism.

tzar·ist (zär′ist, tsär′-), *adj., n.* czarist.

tza·ris·tic (zä ris′tic, tsä-), *adj.* czarist.

tza·rit·za (zä rit′sə, tsä-), *n.* czaritza.

tzet′ze fly′ (tset′sē, tsēt′-). See **tsetse fly.** Also called **tzet′ze.**

Tzi·gane (tsi gän′), *adj.* **1.** (*often l.c.*) of, consisting of, or pertaining to Gypsies: *Tzigane music.* —*n.* **2.** a Gypsy, esp. a Hungarian one. [< F < Russ *tzygan* (c. Ukr *tzigán*) < Hung *cigány* gypsy, Romany < ?]

Tzi·ga·ny (tsi gä′nē), *adj., n., pl.* **-nies.** Tzigane.

tzim·mes (tsim′is), *n.* *Yiddish.* fuss; uproar; hullabaloo. [lit., a mixed dish, stew]

tzi·tzith (tsit′sis; *Heb.* tsē tsēt′), *n.* (*construed as sing. or pl.*) *Judaism.* zizith.

DEVELOPMENT OF MAJUSCULE								
NORTH SEMITIC	GREEK		ETR.	LATIN		MODERN		
						GOTHIC	ITALIC	ROMAN
Y	Ч	Y	Y	V	V	𝔘	*U*	U

DEVELOPMENT OF MINUSCULE					
ROMAN CURSIVE	ROMAN UNCIAL	CAROL. MIN.	MODERN		
			GOTHIC	ITALIC	ROMAN
u	u	u	𝔲	*u*	u

The twenty-first letter of the English alphabet developed as a transformation of North Semitic *waw* into Greek *upsilon* (*υ*). (See also **F** and **W.**) In Etruscan, the *u*-sound was signified by V, and Classical Latin monumental writing later used the V for both U and V. U and V were used interchangeably for both sounds in the early Middle Ages, with V appearing in the monumental writing and U in the manuscripts. Their separation did not crystallize until after the Middle Ages.

U, u (yo͞o), *n., pl.* **U's** or **Us, u's** or **us. 1.** the 21st letter of the English alphabet, a vowel. **2.** any spoken sound represented by the letter *U* or *u*, as in *uncle, pure,* or *Uccello.* **3.** something having the shape of a **U. 4.** a written or printed representation of the letter *U* or *u.* **5.** a device, as a printer's type, for reproducing the letter *U* or *u.*

U (yo͞o), *adj. Informal.* characteristic of or appropriate to the upper class, esp. of Great Britain. [*u*(*pper class*)]

U (o͞o), *n.* a Burmese title of respect applicable to a man: used before the proper name.

U, 1. the 21st in order or in a series, or, when *I* is omitted, the 20th. **2.** *Chem.* uranium.

U., 1. uncle. **2.** and [< G *und*] **3.** uniform. **4.** union. **5.** unit. **6.** united. **7.** university. **8.** upper.

u., 1. and. [< G *und*] **2.** uniform. **3.** unit. **4.** upper.

U-235, *Chem.* See **uranium 235.** Also, **U 235.**

U-238, *Chem.* See **uranium 238.** Also, **U 238.**

UAM, underwater-to-air missile.

u·a ma·u ke e·a o ka a·i·na i ka po·no (o͞o′ä mä′o͝o kä ā′ä ō kä ä′ē nä′ ē kä pō′nō), *Hawaiian.* the life of the land is maintained by righteousness: motto of Hawaii.

u. & l.c., *Print.* upper and lower case.

U.A.R., See **United Arab Republic.**

UAW, United Automobile Workers (full name: International Union of United Automobile, Aerospace, and Agricultural Implement Workers of America). Also, **U.A.W.**

U·ban·gi (yo͞o baŋ′gē, o͞o bäŋ′-), *n.* **1.** French, **Oubangi.** a river in W central Africa, forming part of the boundary between Zaïre and the Central African Republic, flowing W and S into the Congo River. 700 mi. long. **2.** a woman of the Sara tribe in the Central African Republic whose lips are pierced and stretched around flat wooden disks.

U·ban·gi-Sha·ri (yo͞o baŋ′gē shär′ē, o͞o bäŋ′-), *n.* former name of the **Central African Republic.** French, **Oubangi-Chari.**

U·be (o͞o′be; *Jap.* o͝o be′), *n.* a seaport on W Honshu, in W Japan. 161,905 (1964).

Ü·ber·mensch (ʏ′bər mensh′), *n., pl.* **-mensch·en** (-men′-shən). *German.* superman (def. 2).

u·bi·e·ty (yo͞o bī′i tē), *n.* the property of having a definite location at any given time. [< ML **ubietāt-* = L *ubi* where + *-etāt-* var. of *-itāt-* -ITY]

u·biq·ui·tous (yo͞o bik′wi təs), *adj.* being everywhere, esp. at the same time; omnipresent: *ubiquitous fog.* Also, **u·biq·ui·tar·y** (yo͞o bik′wi ter′ē). [UBIQUIT(Y) + -OUS] —**u·biq′ui·tous·ly,** *adv.* —**u·biq′ui·tous·ness,** *n.*

u·biq·ui·ty (yo͞o bik′wi tē), *n.* the state or capacity of being everywhere, esp. at the same time; omnipresence. [< F *ubiquité,* OF *ubiquite* < VL **ubiquitāt-* = L *ubiqu*(*e*) everywhere + *-tāt-* -TY[2]]

u·bi su·pra (o͞o′bē so͞o′prä; *Eng.* yo͞o′bī so͞o′prə), *Latin.* See **u.s.** (def. 1).

U-boat (yo͞o′bōt′), *n.* a German submarine. [< G *U-Boot,* short for *Unterseeboot,* lit., undersea boat]

U bolt, a bar of iron bent into the form of the letter *U,* fitted with a screw thread and nut at each end.

u.c., *Print.* upper case.

U·ca·ya·li (o͞o′kä yä′lē), *n.* a river in W South America, flowing N from E Peru and joining the Marañón to form the Amazon. 1200 mi. long.

Uc·cel·lo (o͞o chel′ō; *It.* o͞ot chel′lô), *n.* **Pa·o·lo** (pä′ô lô), (*Paolo di Dono*), 1397–1475, Italian painter.

U·dai·pur (o͞o dī′po͝or, o͞o′dī po͝or′), *n.* **1.** a city in S Rajasthan, in NW India. 111,100 (1961). **2.** Also called **Mewar,** a former state in NW India: merged into Rajasthan state 1948.

U·dall (yo͞o′dôl *or, for 1,* yo͞od′əl), *n.* **1.** Also called **Uvedale. Nicholas,** 1505–56, English translator and playwright, esp. of comedy. **2. Stewart Lee,** born 1920, U.S. politician: Secretary of the Interior 1961–69.

ud·der (ud′ər), *n.* a mamma or mammary gland, as in cows. [ME *uddre,* OE *ūder;* c. G *Euter,* L *ūber,* Gk *oûthar,* Skt *ū́dhar*]

U·di·ne (o͞o′dē ne), *n.* a city in NE Italy. 85,205 (1961).

u·do (o͞o′dō), *n., pl.* **u·dos.** a plant, *Aralia cordata,* cultivated esp. in Japan and China for its edible shoots. [< Jap]

u·dom·e·ter (yo͞o dom′i tər), *n.* a rain gauge. [< F *udomètre* < L *ūd*(*us*) wet + F *-o-* -o- + *-mètre* -METER] —**u·do·met·ric** (yo͞o′də me′trik), *adj.* —**u·dom′e·try,** *n.*

Ue·le (wā′lə), *n.* a river in central Africa flowing W from the NE Democratic Republic of the Congo to the Ubangi River. 700 mi. long.

U·fa (o͞o fä′), *n.* a city in the W RSFSR, in the E Soviet Union in Europe. 666,000 (1965).

UFO (*sometimes* yo͞o′fō), unidentified flying object.

U·gan·da (yo͞o gan′də, o͞o gän′dä), *n.* an independent state in E Africa, between NE Zaïre and Kenya: member of the British Commonwealth of Nations; formerly a British protectorate. 12,700,000; 93,981 sq. mi. *Cap.:* Kampala. —**U·gan′dan,** *adj., n.*

U·ga·rit (o͞o′gə rēt′), *n.* an ancient city in Syria, N of Latakia, on the site of modern Ras Shamra.

ugh (o͝oᴋʜ, uᴋʜ, u, o͝o; *spelling pron.* ug), *interj.* **1.** (used as an exclamation of disgust, aversion, or the like.) —*n.* **2.** the sound of a cough, grunt, or the like.

ug·li·fy (ug′lə fī′), *v.t.,* **-fied, -fy·ing.** to make ugly. —**ug′li·fi·ca′tion,** *n.* —**ug′li·fi′er,** *n.*

ug·ly (ug′lē), *adj.,* **-li·er, -li·est. 1.** very unattractive or unpleasant to look at. **2.** disagreeable or unpleasant; objectionable: *ugly remarks; ugly weather.* **3.** morally revolting: *ugly crime.* **4.** threatening trouble or danger: *ugly symptoms.* **5.** mean; hostile or quarrelsome: *an ugly mood.* [ME *ugly, uglike* < ON *ugglig*(*r*) fearful, dreadful = *ugg*(*r*) fear + *-ligr* -LY] —**ug′li·ly,** *adv.* —**ug′li·ness,** *n.* —**Syn. 1.** unsightly, homely. **4.** ominous. —**Ant. 1.** beautiful.

ug′ly cus′tomer, a hostile or dangerous person.

ug′ly duck′ling, an unattractive or unpromising child who becomes a beautiful or much-admired adult. [after the story of the same name by Hans Christian Andersen]

U·gri·an (o͞o′grē ən, yo͞o′-), *adj.* **1.** noting or pertaining to a race or ethnological group including the Magyars and related peoples of western Siberia and the northeastern Soviet Union in Europe. —*n.* **2.** a member of any of the Ugrian peoples. **3.** Ugric. [< Russ *Ugri* (pl.) (ORuss *ugreninu* Hungarians) + -AN]

U·gric (o͞o′grik, yo͞o′-), *n.* **1.** a branch of the Uralic family of languages, consisting of Hungarian and two languages, Ostyak and Vogul, spoken in western Siberia. —*adj.* **2.** Ugrian. [UGR(IAN) + -IC]

Ugro-, a combining form of **Ugric-:** *Ugro-Finnic.*

U·gro-Fin·nic (o͞o′grō fin′ik, yo͞o′-), *n., adj.* Finno-Ugric.

UHF, See **ultrahigh frequency.** Also, **uhf**

uh-huh (uɴ hu′), *interj.* (used to indicate an affirmative answer.)

uh·lan (o͞o′län, yo͞o′lən), *n.* **1.** one of a group of lancers in a light-cavalry unit, first appearing in Europe in the Polish army. **2.** one of such a group as later developed into heavy cavalry in western European armies, esp. in Germany. Also, **ulan.** [< G < Pol *ulan* << Turk *oğlan* boy, lad]

Uh·land (o͞o′länt), *n.* **Jo·hann Lud·wig** (yō′hän lo͞ot′viᴋʜ, lo͞od′), 1787–1862, German poet and writer.

uh-uh (uɴ′uɴ′, uɴ′uɴ′, uɴ′uɴ′), *interj.* (used to indicate a negative answer.)

u.i., ut infra.

Ui·gur (wē′go͝or), *n.* **1.** a member of a Turkish people dominant in Mongolia and eastern Turkestan from the 8th to 12th centuries A.D. **2.** the Turkic language of the Uigurs. —*adj.* **3.** of, pertaining to, or characteristic of the Uigurs. Also, **Ui′ghur.** —**Ui·gu′ri·an, Ui·ghu′ri·an, Ui·gu′ric, Ui·ghu′ric,** *adj.*

u·in·ta·ite (yo͞o in′tə īt′), *n.* gilsonite. Also, **u·in′tah·ite′.** [named after the UINTA (MOUNTAINS); see -ITE[1]]

U·in′ta Moun′tains (yo͞o in′tə), a mountain range in NE Utah, part of the Rocky Mountains. Highest peak, Kings Peak, 13,498 ft.

uit·land·er (īt′lan′dər, oit′-; *Du.* œit′län′dər), *n.* (*often cap.*) a foreigner, esp. a British settler in the former Boer republics. [< SAfrD: outsider]

U·ji·ji (o͞o jē′jē), *n.* a town in W Tanzania, on Lake Tanganyika: Stanley found Livingstone here 1871. 20,000 (1970).

Uj·pest (o͞oi′pesht′), *n.* a suburb of Budapest, in N Hungary.

U.K., See **United Kingdom.**

u·kase (yo͞o′kās, yo͞o kāz′), *n.* **1.** (in czarist Russia) an edict or order of the czar having the force of law. **2.** any order or proclamation by an absolute or arbitrary authority. [< F < Russ *ukáz,* ORuss *ukazŭ* = *u-* away + *-kaz-* show]

Ukr., Ukraine.

U·kra·i·na (o͞o′kʀä ē′nä), *n.* Russian name of **Ukraine.**

U·kraine (yo͞o krān′, -krīn′, yo͞o′krān), *n.* a constituent republic of the Soviet Union, in S Europe: rich agricultural region. 49,478,000; ab. 223,000 sq. mi. *Cap.:* Kiev. Russian, **Ukraina.** Official name, **Ukrain′ian So′viet So′cialist Repub′lic.**

U·krain·i·an (yo͞o krā′nē ən, -krī′-), *adj.* **1.** of or pertaining to the Ukraine, its people, or their language. —*n.* **2.** a native or inhabitant of the Ukraine. **3.** Also called **Little Russian.** a Slavic language closely related to Russian.

u·ku·le·le (yo͞o′kə lā′lē; *Hawaiian.* o͞o′ko͝o lā′lā), *n.* a small musical instrument resembling a guitar. Also, **u′ke·le′le.** [< Hawaiian: lit., flea]

Ukulele

UL, Underwriters' Laboratories (used esp. on labels for electrical appliances approved by this nonprofit safety-testing organization).

'u·la·ma (o͞o′lä mä′), *n.* (*construed as pl.*) ulema.

u·lan (o͞o′län, yo͞o′lən), *n.* uhlan.

U·lan Ba·tor (o͞o′län bä′tôr), a city in and the capital of the Mongolian People's Republic, in E central Asia: former holy city. 282,000. Chinese, **Kulun.** Formerly, **Urga.**

U·lan U·de (o͞o′län o͞o′də), a city in the SE RSFSR, in

the S Soviet Union in Asia, near Lake Baikal. 209,000.

ul·cer (ul′sər), *n.* **1.** *Pathol.* a sore open either to the surface of the body or to a natural cavity, and accompanied by the disintegration of tissue, the formation of pus, etc. **2.** any chronically corrupting or disrupting condition, element, etc. [ME < L *ulcer-* (s. of *ulcus*); c. Gk *hélkos*]

ul·cer·ate (ul′sə rāt′), *v.*, **-at·ed, -at·ing.** —*v.i.* **1.** to form an ulcer; become ulcerous. —*v.t.* **2.** to cause an ulcer on or in. [< L *ulcerāt(us)* (ptp. of *ulcerāre*) made sore = *ulcer-* (see ULCER) + *-ātus* -ATE[1]] —**ul′cer·a′tion,** *n.*

ul·cer·a·tive (ul′sə rā′tiv, -sər ə tiv), *adj.* **1.** causing ulceration. **2.** of the nature of or characterized by ulceration. [< ML *ulcerātīv(us)*]

ul·cer·ous (ul′sər əs), *adj.* **1.** of the nature of an ulcer or ulcers; characterized by the formation of ulcers. **2.** affected with an ulcer or ulcers. [< L *ulcerōs(us)* full of sores, ulcerous] —**ul′cer·ous·ly,** *adv.* —**ul′cer·ous·ness,** *n.*

-ule, a suffix, usually having diminutive force, occurring originally in nouns borrowed from Latin: *globule; granule.* [< L *-ulus*]

u·le·ma (o͞o′lə mä′), *n.* (*construed as pl.*) the doctors of Muslim religion and law, esp. in Turkey. Also, **'ulama.** [< Ar *ulemā* learned men]

-ulent, an adjective suffix meaning "abounding in," occurring in words of Latin origin: *fraudulent.* [< L *-ulentus*]

Ul·fi·las (ul′fi ləs), *n.* A.D. c311–c382, Christian bishop to the Goths: translated Bible into the Gothic language. Also, **Ul·fi·la** (ul′fi lə), **Wulfila.**

ul·lage (ul′ij), *n.* **1.** the amount by which the contents fall short of filling a container. **2.** the quantity of wine, liquor, or the like, remaining in a container after evaporation or leakage. [< AF *ulliage,* OF *ouillage,* etc., wine needed to fill a cask = *(a)ouill(er)* (to) fill (a cask) (< *ouil* eye, hole < L *oculus*) + *-age* -AGE] —**ul′laged,** *adj.*

Ulm (o͝olm), *n.* a port in E Baden-Württemberg, in S West Germany, on the Danube. 94,400 (1963).

ul·ma·ceous (ul mā′shəs), *adj.* belonging to the *Ulmaceae,* or elm family of trees and shrubs. [< NL *Ulmāce(ae)* name of genus (L *ulm(us)* elm tree + *-āceae* -ACEAE) + -OUS]

ul·na (ul′nə), *n., pl.* **-nae** (-nē), **-nas.** **1.** *Anat.* the bone of the forearm on the side opposite to the thumb. Cf. **radius** (def. 7). **2.** a corresponding bone in the forelimb of other vertebrates. [< L: elbow; c. Gk *ōlénē,* OE *eln* ELL[2]] —**ul′nar,** *adj.*

-ulose, var. of **-ulous,** used in scientific terminology with the meaning "characterized by" or "abounding in": *granulose; ramulose.* [< L *-ulōsus.* See -ULE, -OSE[1]]

u·lot·ri·chous (yo͞o lo′trə kəs), *adj.* belonging to a group of people whose hair is woolly or crisply curly. [< NL *Ulotrich(ī)* name of the genus (< Gk *oulótrich-* (s. of *oulóthrix*) with curly hair + L *-ī* nom. pl. ending) + -OUS]

-ulous, an adjective suffix meaning "tending to": *granulous; credulous.* [< L *-ulōsus* or *-ulus.* See -ULE, -OUS]

Ul·pi·an (ul′pē ən), *n.* (*Domitius Ulpianus*) died A.D. 288?, Roman jurist.

Ul·ster (ul′stər), *n.* **1.** a former province in Ireland, now comprising Northern Ireland and a part of the Republic of Ireland. **2.** a province in N Republic of Ireland. 217,524 (1961); 3123 sq. mi. **3.** *Informal.* See **Northern Ireland.** **4.** (*l.c.*) a long, loose, heavy overcoat, originally of Irish frieze, now also of any of various other woolen cloths.

Ul·ster·man (ul′stər mən), *n., pl.* **-men.** a native or inhabitant of Ulster.

ult., **1.** ultimate. **2.** ultimately. **3.** ultimo.

ul·te·ri·or (ul tēr′ē ər), *adj.* **1.** being beyond what is seen or avowed; intentionally kept concealed: *ulterior motives.* **2.** coming at a subsequent time or stage: *ulterior action.* **3.** lying beyond or outside of some specified or understood boundary; more remote: *a suggestion ulterior to the purposes of the present discussion.* [< L: farther, comp. of *ulter* beyond, far] —**ul·te′ri·or·ly,** *adv.*

ul·ti·ma (ul′tə mə), *n.* the last syllable of a word. [< L, fem. of *ultimus,* superl. of *ulter* far]

ul·ti·mate (ul′tə mit), *adj.* **1.** last; furthest or farthest; ending a process or series. **2.** maximum; decisive or conclusive: *the ultimate authority.* **3.** highest; not subsidiary: *ultimate goal in life.* **4.** basic; fundamental; representing a limit beyond which further progress, as in investigation or analysis, is impossible: *ultimate principles.* **5.** final; total: *the ultimate cost of a project.* —*n.* **6.** the final point; final result. **7.** a fundamental fact or principle. [< LL *ultimāt(us)* having come to an end (ptp. of *ultimāre*) = L *ultim(us)* last, most distant (see ULTIMA) + *-ātus* -ATE[1]] —**ul′ti·mate·ly,** *adv.* —**ul′ti·mate·ness,** *n.* —**Syn. 1.** extreme, remotest, uttermost. **2.** supreme. **5.** See **last**[1]. —**Ant. 5.** first.

ul′timate constit′uent, *Gram.* a basic, irreducible element, as a morpheme, in a construction. Cf. **immediate constituent.**

ul·ti·ma Thu·le (ul′tə mə tho͞o′lē; *Lat.* o͝ol′ti mä′ to͞o′le), **1.** (*italics*) *Latin.* the highest degree attainable. **2.** the farthest point; the limit of any journey. **3.** the point believed by the ancients to be farthest north. Also called **Thule.** [lit., farthest Thule]

ul·ti·ma·tum (ul′tə mā′təm, -mä′-), *n., pl.* **-tums, -ta** (-tə). **1.** a final, uncompromising demand or set of terms issued by a party to a dispute. **2.** a final proposal or statement of conditions. [< NL, LL, neut. of *ultimātus.* See ULTIMATE]

ul·ti·mo (ul′tə mō′), *adj.* *Obsolesc.* of the month preceding the current one: *our letter of the 12th ultimo. Abbr.:* ult., ulto. Cf. **instant** (def. 6), **proximo.** [< L *ultimō* (*mēnse* or *diē*) in the last (month) or on the last (day)]

ulto., ultimo.

ul·tra (ul′trə), *adj.* **1.** going beyond what is usual or ordinary; excessive; extreme. —*n.* **2.** an extremist, as in politics, religion, etc. [< L *ultrā,* adv. and prep., beyond, on the other side, farther, special use of abl. sing. fem. of *ulter* beyond]

ultra-, a combining form of **ultra:** *ultramarine.*

ul·tra·cen·tri·fuge (ul′trə sen′trə fyo͞oj′), *n., v.,* **-fuged, -fug·ing.** *Physical Chem.* —*n.* **1.** a high-speed centrifuge for subjecting sols or solutions to forces many times that of gravity and producing concentration differences depending on the weight of the micelle or molecule. —*v.t.* **2.** to subject to the action of an ultracentrifuge. —**ul·tra·cen·trif·u·gal** (ul′trə sen trif′yə gəl), *adj.* —**ul′tra·cen·trif′u·gal·ly,** *adv.*

ul·tra·con·ser·va·tive (ul′trə kən sûr′və tiv), *adj.* **1.** extremely conservative, esp. in politics. —*n.* **2.** an ultraconservative person or group.

ul·tra·crit·i·cal (ul′trə krit′i kəl), *adj.* overly critical.

ul·tra·fil·ter (ul′trə fil′tər), *n.* *Physical Chem.* **1.** a filter for purifying sols, having a membrane with pores sufficiently small to prevent the passage of the suspended particles. —*v.t.* **2.** to purify by means of an ultrafilter. —**ul·tra·fil·tra·tion** (ul′trə fil trā′shən), *n.*

ul′tra·high fre′quency (ul′trə hī′, -hī′), *Radio.* any frequency between 300 and 3,000 megacycles per second. *Abbr.:* UHF, uhf —**ul′tra·high′-fre′quen·cy,** *adj.*

ul·tra·ism (ul′trə iz′əm), *n.* **1.** extremism. **2.** an extremist point of view or act. —**ul′tra·ist,** *n., adj.* —**ul′tra·is′tic,** *adj.*

ul·tra·light (ul′trə līt′), *n.* a small, simple, single-seat airplane, technically designated as weighing less than 254 lbs., having a top speed of no more than 63 mph, and holding no more than 5 gallons of fuel.

ul·tra·ma·rine (ul′trə mə rēn′), *n.* **1.** a blue pigment consisting of powdered lapis lazuli. **2.** a similar artificial blue pigment. **3.** any of various other pigments. **4.** a deep-blue color. —*adj.* **5.** beyond the sea. **6.** of the color ultramarine. [< ML *ultrāmarīn(us)*]

ul·tra·mi·crom·e·ter (ul′trə mī krom′i tər), *n.* a micrometer capable of measuring extremely small magnitudes.

ul·tra·mi·cro·scope (ul′trə mī′krə skōp′), *n.* an instrument that uses scattering phenomena to detect the position of objects too small to be seen by an ordinary microscope. —**ul·tra·mi·cro·scop·ic** (ul′trə mī′krə skop′ik), **ul′tra·mi′cro·scop′i·cal,** *adj.* —**ul·tra·mi·cros·co·py** (ul′trə mī kros′kə pē), *n.*

ul·tra·mod·ern (ul′trə mod′ərn), *adj.* very advanced in ideas or techniques: *an ultramodern automobile.* —**ul′tra·mod′ern·ism,** *n.* —**ul′tra·mod′ern·ist,** *n.*

ul·tra·mon·tane (ul′trə mon tān′), *adj.* **1.** beyond the mountains. **2.** of or pertaining to the area south of the Alps, esp. Italy. **3.** *Rom. Cath. Ch.* of, pertaining to, or advocating ultramontanism. **4.** (formerly) north of the Alps; tramontane. —*n.* **5.** a person who lives beyond the mountains. **6.** a person living south of the Alps. **7.** *Rom. Cath. Ch.* a person who supports ultramontanism. **8.** (formerly) a person living to the north of the Alps. [< ML *ultrāmontān(us)* = L *ultrā* ULTRA- + *montānus* of, belonging to a MOUNTAIN]

ul·tra·mon·ta·nism (ul′trə mon′tᵊniz′əm), *n.* (*sometimes cap.*) the policy of the party in the Roman Catholic Church that favors increasing and enhancing the power and authority of the pope. Cf. **Gallicanism.** [< F *ultramontanisme.* See ULTRAMONTANE, -ISM] —**ul′tra·mon′ta·nist,** *n.*

ul·tra·mun·dane (ul′trə mun′dān, -mun dān′), *adj.* **1.** outside or beyond the earth or the orbits of the planets. **2.** outside the sphere of physical existence. [< LL *ultrāmundān(us)*]

ul·tra·na·tion·al·ism (ul′trə nash′ə nᵊliz′əm), *n.* excessive devotion to the interests of a nation. —**ul′tra·na′tion·al,** *adj.*

ul·tra·na·tion·al·ist (ul′trə nash′ə nᵊlist), *n.* **1.** an advocate of ultranationalism. —*adj.* **2.** Also, **ul′tra·na′tion·al·is′tic.** of or pertaining to ultranationalism or ultranationalists. —**ul′tra·na′tion·al·is′ti·cal·ly,** *adv.*

ul·tra·red (ul′trə red′), *n.* (not in technical use) infrared.

ul·tra·short (ul′trə shôrt′), *adj.* **1.** extremely short. **2.** *Radio.* having a wavelength below 10 meters or a frequency above 30 megahertz.

ul·tra·son·ic (ul′trə son′ik), *adj.* noting or pertaining to a frequency above the audio-frequency range. —**ul′tra·son′i·cal·ly,** *adv.*

ul·tra·son·ics (ul′trə son′iks), *n.pl.* (*construed as sing.*) the branch of science that deals with ultrasonic phenomena. [see ULTRASONIC, -ICS]

ul·tra·struc·ture (ul′trə struk′chər), *n.* *Biol.* the submicroscopic, elemental structure of protoplasm. —**ul′tra·struc′tur·al,** *adj.*

Ul·tra·suede (ul′trə swād′), *n.* *Trademark.* a washable, synthetic, suedelike fabric.

ul·tra·trop·i·cal (ul′trə trop′i kəl), *adj.* **1.** outside the tropics. **2.** hotter than the average or usual tropical climate.

ul·tra·vi·o·let (ul′trə vī′ə lit), *adj.* **1.** beyond the violet in the spectrum; radiation with wavelengths shorter than 4000 angstrom units. **2.** pertaining to or producing such radiation. —*n.* **3.** ultraviolet radiation. Cf. **infrared.**

ul·tra vi·res (ul′trə vī′rēz), *Law.* beyond the legal power or authority of an individual or corporation (opposed to *intra vires*). [< L: lit., beyond strength]

ul·u·lant (yo͞ol′yə lənt, ul′-), *adj.* howling; ululating. [< L *ululant-* (s. of *ululāns*), prp. of *ululāre.* See ULULATE, -ANT]

ul·u·late (yo͞ol′yə lāt′, ul′-), *v.i.,* **-lat·ed, -lat·ing.** **1.** to howl, as a dog or a wolf; hoot, as an owl. **2.** to utter howling sounds, as in shrill, wordless lamentation; wail. **3.** to lament loudly and shrilly. [< L *ululāt(us)* howled (ptp. of *ululāre*) = *ulul(a)* owl (imit.) + *-ātus* -ATE[1]] —**ul′u·la′tion,** *n.*

-ulus, a diminutive suffix occurring in loan words from Latin: *calculus.* [< L *-ulus;* cf. -ULE]

Ul·ya·novsk (o͞o lyä′nofsk), *n.* a city in the W RSFSR, in the E Soviet Union in Europe. 256,000 (est. 1964).

U·lys·ses (yo͞o lis′ēz), *n.* Latin name for **Odysseus.**

-um, a formal element occurring in loan words from Latin: *rostrum; addendum.* [< L *-um,* neut. sing. nom. or acc. ending]

U·may·yad (o͞o mī′yad), *n.* Omayyad.

um·bel (um′bəl), *n.* *Bot.* an inflorescence in which a number of flower stalks or pedicels, nearly equal in length, spread from a common center. [< L *umbel(la)* a sunshade, parasol = *umb(ra)* a shadow, shade + *-ella* dim. suffix]

um·bel·late (um′bə lit, -lāt′), *adj.* having or forming an umbel or umbels. [< NL *umbellāt(us)* = L *umbell(a)* (see UMBEL) + *-ātus* -ATE[1]] —**um′bel·lar, um′bel·lat′ed,** *adj.* —**um′bel·late·ly,** *adv.*

um·bel·let (um′bə lit), *n.* an umbellule. [< L *umbell(a)* (see UMBEL) + -ET]

um·bel·lif·er·ous (um′bə lif′ər əs), *adj.* **1.** bearing an umbel or umbels. **2.** belonging or pertaining to the *Umbelliferae* (or *Ammiaceae*), a family of plants comprising the carrot, celery, parsnip, parsley, and other similar plants; apiaceous. [< NL *umbellifer* (*umbelli-* comb. form of L *umbella* (see UMBEL) + *-fer* -FER) + -OUS]

um·bel·lule (um′bəl yōōl′, um bel′yōōl), *n.* one of the secondary umbels in a compound umbel. [< NL *umbellul(a)* = L *umbell(a)* (see UMBEL) + *-ula* -ULE] —**um·bel·lu·late** (um bel′yə lit, -lāt′), *adj.*

um·ber (um′bər), *n.* **1.** an earth consisting chiefly of a hydrated oxide of iron and some oxide of manganese, used in its natural state as a brown pigment or, after heating, as a reddish-brown pigment. **2.** the color of such a pigment; dark dusky brown or dark reddish brown. **3.** the European grayling, *Thymallus thymallus.* **4.** *Brit. Dial.* shade; shadow. —*adj.* **5.** of the color umber. —*v.t.* **6.** to color with or as with umber. [ME *umbre, umber* shade, shadow < OF *umbre* < L *umbr(a)*]

Um·ber·to (*It.* ōōm bɛʀ′tô), *n.* See **Humbert I.**

um·bil·i·cal (um bil′i kəl), *adj.* **1.** of, pertaining to, or characteristic of an umbilicus or umbilical cord. **2.** joined together by or as by an umbilical cord; heavily dependent in a close relationship. **3.** adjacent to or located near the navel; central to the abdomen: *the umbilical region.* [< ML *umbilīcāl(is)* = L *umbilīc(us)* (see UMBILICUS) + *-ālis* -AL[1]] —**um·bil′i·cal·ly,** *adv.*

umbil′ical cord′, **1.** *Anat.* a cord or funicle connecting the embryo or fetus with the placenta of the mother and transmitting nourishment from the mother. **2.** *Rocketry Slang.* **a.** a service cable connected to a rocket at its launching site and detached at takeoff. **b.** a strong life line connecting an astronaut working in space outside his vehicle to the vehicle, and supplying him with air, a communication system, etc.

um·bil·i·cate (um bil′ə kit, -kāt′), *adj.* **1.** having the form of an umbilicus or navel. **2.** having an umbilicus. Also, **um·bil′i·cat′ed.** [< L *umbilīcāt(us)* = *umbilīc(us)* (see UMBILICUS) + *-ātus* -ATE[1]]

um·bil·i·ca·tion (um bil′ə kā′shən), *n.* **1.** a central navellike depression. **2.** an umbilicate condition or formation. [UMBILIC(US) + -ATION]

um·bil·i·cus (um bil′ə kəs, um′bə lī′kəs), *n., pl.* **-bil·i·ci** (-bil′i sī′, -bə lī′sī). **1.** *Anat.* the depression in the center of the surface of the abdomen indicating the point of attachment of the umbilical cord to the embryo; navel. **2.** *Bot., Zool.* a navellike formation, as the hilum of a seed. [< L *umbilīcus* navel, middle, center; c. Gk *omphalós*]

um·bil·i·form (um bil′ə fôrm′), *adj.* having the form of an umbilicus. [UMBILI(CUS) + -FORM]

um′ble pie′ (um′bəl). See **humble pie** (def. 1).

um·bo (um′bō), *n., pl.* **um·bo·nes** (um bō′nēz), **um·bos.** **1.** a boss on a shield, as one at the center of a circular shield. **2.** any similar boss or protuberance. **3.** *Zool.* the beak of a bivalve shell; the protuberance of each valve above the hinge. **4.** *Anat.* the depressed area on the outer surface of the tympanic membrane. [< L *umbō* boss (of a shield), knob, projecting part] —**um·bon·ic** (um bon′ik), *adj.*

um·bo·nal (um′bə nəl), *adj.* **1.** having the shape or appearance of an umbo; bosslike: *an umbonal structure.* **2.** of, pertaining to, or near the umbo: *the umbonal region.* Also, **um·bon·ic** (um bon′ik). [< L *umbōn-* (s. of *umbō*) UMBO + -AL[1]]

um·bo·nate (um′bə nit, -nāt′), *adj.* **1.** having an umbo or projecting boss. **2.** shaped like an umbo; having a rounded convex form: *an umbonate fungus.* [< L *umbōn-* (s. of *umbō*) (see UMBO) + -ATE[1]]

um·bra (um′brə), *n., pl.* **-brae** (-brē). **1.** shade; shadow. **2.** the invariable or characteristic accompaniment or companion of a person or thing. **3.** the complete or perfect shadow of an opaque body, as a planet, where the light from the source of illumination is completely cut off. Cf. **penumbra** (def. 1). **4.** the dark central portion of a sunspot. Cf. **penumbra** (def. 2). **5.** a phantom or shadowy apparition, as of someone or something not physically present; ghost; spectral image. [< L: shade, shadow] —**um′bral,** *adj.*

um·brage (um′brij), *n.* **1.** offense; annoyance or displeasure. **2.** the slightest indication or vaguest feeling of suspicion, doubt, hostility, or the like. **3.** leaves that afford shade, as the foliage of trees. **4.** *Archaic.* shade or shadows, as cast by trees. **5.** *Archaic.* a shadowy appearance or semblance of something. [late ME < OF < L *umbrātic(um)* < *umbrātus* (ptp. of *umbrāre* to shade) = *umbr(a)* shade + *-āticum* -AGE] —**Syn. 1.** pique, grudge, resentment.

um·bra·geous (um brā′jəs), *adj.* **1.** creating or providing shade; shady: *an umbrageous tree.* **2.** apt to take offense. —**um·bra′geous·ly,** *adv.* —**um·bra′geous·ness,** *n.*

um·brel·la (um brel′ə), *n.* **1.** a light, small, portable, usually circular cover for protection from rain or sun, consisting of a fabric held on a collapsible frame of thin ribs radiating from the top of a carrying stick or handle. **2.** the saucer- or bowl-shaped, gelatinous body of a jellyfish; the bell. **3.** something that covers or protects from above, as military aircraft safeguarding surface forces. **4.** any general kind of protection: *a price umbrella.* **5.** the power of a major nation, corporation, etc., to defend or protect another: *Japan is under the American nuclear umbrella.* —*adj.* **6.** shaped like or intended to perform the function of an umbrella. **7.** having the quality or function of covering or applying simultaneously to a group of similar items or elements: *an umbrella patent; umbrella legislation.* [< It *ombrella,* earlier var. of *ombrello* < LL *umbrella* (with influence of L *umbra* shade) < L *umbella.* See UMBEL] —**um·brel′la·less,** *adj.* —**um·brel′la·like′,** *adj.*

umbrel′la bird′, any of several South American birds of the genus *Cephalopterus,* as *C. ornatus,* having an umbrellalike crest above the head.

umbrel′la leaf′, a North American berberidaceous herb, *Diphylleia cymosa,* having either a large peltate, umbrellalike, lobed, basal leaf or two smaller similar leaves on a flowering stem.

umbrel′la tree′, **1.** an American magnolia, *Magnolia tripetala,* having large leaves in umbrellalike clusters. **2.** any of various other trees resembling an umbrella, as a tropical American moraceous tree, *Musanga Smithii.*

Um·bri·a (um′brē ə; *It.* ōōm′bʀē ä′), *n.* **1.** an ancient district in central and N Italy. **2.** a region in central Italy. 788,546 (1961); 3270 sq. mi.

Um·bri·an (um′brē ən), *adj.* **1.** of or pertaining to Umbria, its inhabitants, or their language. —*n.* **2.** a native or inhabitant of Umbria. **3.** the extinct Italic language of the ancient Umbrians.

um·brif·er·ous (um brif′ər əs), *adj.* casting or making shade. [< L *umbrifer* shade-bringing, shady (*umbri-* comb-form of *umbra* shade + *-fer* -FER) + -OUS] —**um·brif′er·ous·ly,** *adv.*

u·mi·ak (ōō′mē ak′), *n.* an open Eskimo boat that consists of a wooden frame covered with skins and provided with several thwarts: used for transport of goods and passengers. Also, **oomiak, oomiac, u′mi·ac′.** [< Greenland Eskimo: boat used exclusively for women]

Umiak

um·laut (ŏŏm′lout), *Gram.* —*n.* **1.** (of vowels in Germanic languages) assimilation in which a vowel is influenced by a following vowel or semivowel. **2.** a diacritic (¨) placed over a vowel, as *ä, ö, ü,* to indicate a sound different from that of the vowel without the diacritic, esp. as so used in German. Cf. **dieresis.** —*v.t.* **3.** to modify by umlaut. **4.** to write an umlaut over. [< G = *um-* about (changed) + *Laut* sound]

ump (ump), *n., v.t., v.i., Slang.* umpire. [shortened form]

um·pir·age (um′pīər ij, -pər ij), *n.* **1.** the office or authority of an umpire. **2.** the decision of an umpire; arbitrament.

um·pire (um′pīər), *n., v.,* **-pired, -pir·ing.** —*n.* **1.** a person selected to rule on the plays in a game. **2.** a person selected to settle disputes about the application of settled rules or usages; a person agreed on by disputing parties to arbitrate their differences. —*v.t.* **3.** to act as umpire in (a game). **4.** to decide or settle (a controversy, dispute, or the like) as umpire; arbitrate. —*v.i.* **5.** to act as umpire. [ME *umpere,* var. of *noumpere* (cf. APRON) < OF *nomper, nonper* not equal (arbiter). See NON-, PEER[1]] —**Syn. 2.** See **judge.**

ump·teen (ump′tēn′), *adj. Informal.* innumerable; many. [*umpt(y),* var. of *-enty,* as in twenty + -TEEN]

ump·teenth (ump′tēnth′), *adj. Informal.* of an indefinitely large number in succession: *He was the umpteenth person to arrive.* Also, **um·teenth** (um′tēnth′).

UMT, See **universal military training.**

UMW, United Mine Workers. Also, **U.M.W.**

un (ən), *pron. Dial.* one: *He's a bad un. Young uns.* Also, **'un.**

UN, See **United Nations** (def. 1). Also, **U.N.**

un-[1], a prefix meaning "not," freely used as an English formative, giving negative or opposite force in adjectives and their derivative adverbs and nouns (*unfair; unfairly; unfairness; unfelt; unseen; unfitting; unformed; unheard-of*), and less freely used in certain other nouns (*unfaith; unrest; unemployment*). [ME, OE *un-, on-;* c. D *on-,* Goth, G *un-,* Icel *ū-, ō-;* akin to L *in-,* Gk *an-, a-.* See A-[6], AN-[1]] —**Syn.** See **in-**[3].

un-[2], a prefix freely used in English to form verbs expressing a reversal of some action or state, or removal, deprivation, release, etc. (*unbend; uncork; unfasten,* etc.), or to intensify the force of a verb already having such a meaning (*unloose*). [ME, OE *un-, on-;* c. Goth *and-,* D *ont-,* G *-ent;* akin to L *ante,* Gk *antí;* cf. ANTE-, ANTI-]

un·a·bat·ed (un′ə bā′tid), *adj.* with undiminished force, power, or vigor. —**un′a·bat′ed·ly,** *adv.*

un·a·ble (un ā′bəl), *adj.* lacking the necessary power, competence, etc., to accomplish some specified act: *He was unable to swim.* [ME]

un·a·bridged (un′ə brijd′), *adj.* **1.** not abridged or shortened, as a book. —*n.* **2.** a dictionary that has not been reduced in size by omission of terms or definitions; the most comprehensive edition of a given dictionary.

un·ac·cent·ed (un ak′sen tid, un′ak sen′-), *adj.* without an accent mark; unstressed.

un·ac·com·mo·dat·ed (un′ə kom′ə dā′tid), *adj.* **1.** not accommodated; not adapted. **2.** not having accommodations. **3.** not furnished with something wanted or needed; not given satisfaction.

un·ac·com·pa·nied (un′ə kum′pə nēd), *adj.* **1.** not accompanied; alone. **2.** *Music.* without an accompaniment.

un·ac·com·plished (un′ə kom′plisht), *adj.* **1.** not accomplished; incomplete or not carried out. **2.** without accomplishments; inexpert.

un·ac·count·a·ble (un′ə koun′tə bəl), *adj.* **1.** unexplained; inexplicable; not in accordance with understood relations of cause and effect; strange. **2.** exempt from being called to account; not answerable. —**un′ac·count′a·ble·ness, un′ac·count′a·bil′i·ty,** *n.* —**un′ac·count′a·bly,** *adv.*

un·ac·count·ed-for (un′ə koun′tid fôr′), *adj.* not accounted for; unexplained: *Four planes came back, but two are unaccounted-for.*

un·ac·cus·tomed (un′ə kus′təmd), *adj.* **1.** unusual; unfamiliar. **2.** not habituated. —**un′ac·cus′tomed·ness,** *n.*

u·na cor·da (ōō′nə kôr′də; *It.* ōō′nä kôʀ′dä), with the soft pedal depressed (a musical direction in piano playing). [< It: lit., one string]

un′a·bashed′, *adj.*
un′a·bash′ed·ly, *adv.*
un′ab·bre′vi·at′ed, *adj.*
un′ab·solved′, *adj.*
un′ab·sorb′a·ble, *adj.*
un′ab·sorbed′, *adj.*
un′ab·sorb′ent, *adj.*
un′a·bused′, *adj.*
un′ac·a·dem′ic, *adj.*
un′ac·cen′tu·at′ed, *adj.*
un′ac·cep′ta·ble, *adj.*
un′ac·cept′ed, *adj.*
un′ac·ci·den′tal, *adj.*
un′ac·claimed′, *adj.*
un′ac′cli·mat′ed, *adj.*
un′ac·cli′ma·tized′, *adj.*
un′ac·com′mo·dat′ing, *adj.*
un′ac·cord′ed, *adj.*
un′ac·count′ed, *adj.*
un′ac·cred′it·ed, *adj.*
un′ac·knowl′edged, *adj.*
un′a·cous′ti·cal, *adj.;* **-ly,** *adv.*
un′ac·quaint′ed, *adj.*
un′ac·quit′ted, *adj.*
un·act′ed, *adj.*
un·ac′tion·a·ble, *adj.*
un·ac′tu·at′ed, *adj.*

un·ad·vised (un′ad vīzd′), *adj.* **1.** without advice; uninformed. **2.** imprudent; rash; ill-advised. [ME *onavised*] —**un·ad·vis·ed·ly** (un′ad vī′zid lē), *adv.* —**un′ad·vis′ed·ness,** *n.*

un·af·fect·ed[1] (un′ə fek′tid), *adj.* free from affectation; sincere; genuine; unpretentious. [UN-[1] + AFFECTED[2]] —**un′af·fect′ed·ly,** *adv.* —**un′af·fect′ed·ness,** *n.* —**Syn.** plain, natural, simple, artless; naïve, guileless.

un·af·fect·ed[2] (un′ə fek′tid), *adj.* not affected, acted upon, or influenced; unchanged; unaltered. [UN-[1] + AFFECTED[1]] —**Syn.** unmoved, untouched, unimpressed.

U·na·las·ka (o͞o′nə las′kə, un′ə las′-), *n.* an island off the coast of SW Alaska, one of the Aleutian Islands: site of the Dutch Harbor naval base. ab. 75 mi. long.

un·al·loyed (un′ə loid′), *adj.* pure; not mixed: *unalloyed metals.*

un·al·ter·a·ble (un ôl′tər ə bəl), *adj.* not capable of being altered. Also, **inalterable.** —**un·al′ter·a·bly,** *adv.*

un-A·mer·i·can (un′ə mer′i kən), *adj.* **1.** not American. **2.** not characteristic of or proper to the U.S.; foreign to or opposed to its character, standards, ideals, etc. —**un′-A·mer′i·can·ism,** *n.*

U·na·mu·no (o͞o′nə mo͞o′nō; *Sp.* o͞o′nä mo͞o′nô), *n.* **Miguel de** (mē gel′ de), 1864–1936, Spanish philosopher, poet, novelist, and essayist.

un·a·neled (un′ə nēld′), *adj. Archaic.* not having received extreme unction.

u·na·nim·i·ty (yo͞o′nə nim′i tē), *n.* the state or quality of being unanimous; a consensus or undivided opinion. [ME *unanimite* < MF < L *ūnanimitāt-* (s. of *ūnanimitās*) = *ūnanim(us)* UNANIMOUS + *-itāt-* -ITY] —**Syn.** harmony, unity, unison, concert. —**Ant.** disagreement.

u·nan·i·mous (yo͞o nan′ə məs), *adj.* **1.** being in complete accord; agreed. **2.** characterized by or showing complete accord. [< L *ūnanim(us)* (*ūn(us)* one + *animus* mind, heart, feeling) + -OUS] —**u·nan′i·mous·ly,** *adv.* —**u·nan′i·mous·ness,** *n.*

un·an·swer·a·ble (un an′sər ə bəl), *adj.* **1.** not having a known or discoverable answer: *an unanswerable question.* **2.** not open to dispute or rebuttal; irrefutable. —**un·an′swer·a·ble·ness,** *n.* —**un·an′swer·a·bly,** *adv.*

un·ap·peal·a·ble (un′ə pē′lə bəl), *adj.* **1.** not appealable to a higher court, as a cause. **2.** incapable of being appealed from, as a judgment. —**un′ap·peal′a·ble·ness,** *n.* —**un′ap·peal′a·bly,** *adv.*

un·ap·proach·a·ble (un′ə prō′chə bəl), *adj.* **1.** not capable of being approached; remote; unreachable. **2.** impossible to equal or rival. —**un′ap·proach′a·ble·ness,** *n.* —**un′ap·proach′a·bly,** *adv.*

un·ap·pro·pri·at·ed (un′ə prō′prē ā′tid), *adj.* **1.** not set apart or voted for some purpose or use, as money, revenues, etc. **2.** not taken into possession by any person.

un·apt (un apt′), *adj.* **1.** not appropriate; unfit; unsuitable. **2.** not disposed or likely. **3.** deficient in aptitude or capacity; slow; dull. [ME] —**un·apt′ly,** *adv.* —**un·apt′ness,** *n.*

un·ar·gued (un är′gyo͞od), *adj.* **1.** not subject to argument or discussion. **2.** undebated; unopposed by argument; admitted.

un·arm (un ärm′), *v.t.* to deprive or relieve of weapons; disarm. [ME *unarme*]

un·armed (un ärmd′), *adj.* **1.** without weapons or armor. **2.** not having claws, thorns, scales, etc., as animals or plants. [ME]

un·a·shamed (un′ə shāmd′), *adj.* **1.** not ashamed; not restrained by embarrassment or consciousness of moral guilt. **2.** open; unconcealed; unabashed. —**un·a·sham·ed·ly** (un′ə shā′mid lē), *adv.* —**un′a·sham′ed·ness,** *n.*

un·as·sail·a·ble (un′ə sā′lə bəl), *adj.* **1.** not open to attack or assault, as by military force, argument, etc. **2.** not subject to denial or loss. —**un′as·sail′a·ble·ness,** *n.* —**un′as·sail′a·bly,** *adv.*

un·as·sum·ing (un′ə so͞o′ming), *adj.* modest; unpretentious. —**un′as·sum′ing·ly,** *adv.* —**un′as·sum′ing·ness,** *n.*

un·at·tached (un′ə tacht′), *adj.* **1.** not attached. **2.** not connected or associated with any particular body, group, organization, or the like; independent. **3.** not engaged or married.

un·at·tend·ed (un′ə ten′did), *adj.* **1.** without attendance; lacking an audience, spectators, etc. **2.** not accompanied; not associated with, as a concomitant effect or result. **3.** not cared for or ministered to; not waited on, as an invalid. **4.** not accompanied, as by an attendant or companion; alone. **5.** not taken in charge or watched over. **6.** unheeded; not listened to; disregarded. **7.** not tended to; not done or carried out, as a task (usually fol. by *to*).

un·a·vail·ing (un′ə vā′ling), *adj.* ineffectual; futile. —**un′a·vail′ing·ly,** *adv.*

un·a·void·a·ble (un′ə voi′də bəl), *adj.* **1.** incapable of being avoided; inevitable. **2.** incapable of being made null or void. —**un′a·void′a·ble·ness,** *n.* —**un′a·void′a·bly,** *adv.*

un·a·ware (un′ə wâr′), *adj.* **1.** not aware; unconscious. —*adv.* **2.** unawares. [ME *uniwar, ungewar;* c. OE *gewær* and *unwær*] —**un′a·ware′ly,** *adv.* —**un′a·ware′ness,** *n.*

un·a·wares (un′ə wârz′), *adv.* **1.** while not aware or conscious of a thing oneself; unknowingly or inadvertently. **2.** without warning; suddenly; unexpectedly: *to come upon someone unawares.*

un·backed (un bakt′), *adj.* **1.** without backing or support. **2.** not supported by bets. **3.** not endorsed. **4.** never having been mounted by a rider, as a horse.

un·baked (un bākt′), *adj.* **1.** not baked. **2.** crude; immature.

un·bal·ance (un bal′əns), *v.,* **-anced, -anc·ing,** *n.* —*v.t.* **1.** to throw or put out of balance. **2.** to disorder or derange, as the mind. —*n.* **3.** unbalanced condition.

un·bal·anced (un bal′ənst), *adj.* **1.** not balanced or not properly balanced. **2.** lacking steadiness and soundness of judgment. **3.** mentally disordered; deranged. **4.** (of an account) not adjusted; not brought to an equality of debits and credits.

un·bal·last·ed (un bal′ə stid), *adj.* **1.** not ballasted. **2.** not properly steadied or regulated.

un·bar (un bär′), *v.t.,* **-barred, -bar·ring.** **1.** to remove a bar or bars from. **2.** to open; unlock; unbolt: *to unbar a door.* [ME *unbarre(n)*]

un·bat·ed (un bā′tid), *adj.* **1.** unabated. **2.** *Archaic.* not blunted, as a lance or fencer's foil.

un·bear·a·ble (un bâr′ə bəl), *adj.* not bearable; unendurable; intolerable. [late ME] —**un·bear′a·ble·ness,** *n.* —**un·bear′a·bly,** *adv.*

un·beat·en (un bēt′ən), *adj.* **1.** not struck or pounded. **2.** not defeated or never defeated. **3.** untrodden: *unbeaten paths.*

un·be·com·ing (un′bi kum′ing), *adj.* unattractive; unsuitable, as apparel, a fashion, habit, etc.; detracting from one's appearance, character, or reputation; creating an unfavorable impression: *an unbecoming hat; unbecoming language.* —**un′be·com′ing·ly,** *adv.* —**un′be·com′ing·ness,** *n.* —**Syn.** unapt, unfit. See **improper.**

un·be·got·ten (un′bi got′ən), *adj.* **1.** not yet begotten; as yet unborn. **2.** without a beginning; eternal.

un·be·known (un′bi nōn′), *adj.* unknown; unperceived; without one's knowledge (usually fol. by *to*). Also, **un·be·knownst** (un′bi nōnst′). [UN-[1] + *beknown* (late ME *beknowe,* ptp. of *bynowe*); see BE-, KNOW]

un·be·lief (un′bi lēf′), *n.* state or quality of not believing; incredulity or skepticism, esp. in matters of doctrine or religious faith. [ME *unbelefe*]

un·be·liev·er (un′bi lē′vər), *n.* **1.** a person who does not believe; skeptic. **2.** a person who does not accept any, or some particular, religious belief.

un·be·liev·ing (un′bi lē′ving), *adj.* **1.** not believing; skeptical. **2.** not accepting any, or some particular, religious belief. [late ME] —**un′be·liev′ing·ly,** *adv.* —**un′be·liev′ing·ness,** *n.*

un·belt (un belt′), *v.t.* **1.** to remove the belt from. **2.** to remove by undoing a supporting belt: *to unbelt a sword.*

un·bend (un bend′), *v.,* **-bent** or (*Archaic*) **-bend·ed; -bend·ing.** —*v.t.* **1.** to release from the strain of effort or close application; relax by laying aside formality or ceremony. **2.** to release from tension, as a bow. **3.** to straighten from a bent form or position. **4.** *Naut.* **a.** to loose or untie, as a sail, rope, etc. **b.** to unfasten from spars or stays, as sails. —*v.i.* **5.** to relax the strictness of formality or ceremony; act in an easy, genial manner. **6.** to become unbent. [late ME] —**un·bend′a·ble,** *adj.*

un·bend·ing (un ben′ding), *adj.* **1.** not bending; rigid;

un′a·dapt′a·ble, *adj.*
un′a·dapt′ed, *adj.*
un′ad·dressed′, *adj.*
un′ad·journed′, *adj.*
un′ad·ju′di·cat′ed, *adj.*
un′ad·just′a·ble, *adj.;* **-bly,** *adv.*
un′ad·just′ed, *adj.*
un′a·dorned′, *adj.*
un′a·dul′ter·at′ed, *adj.*
un′ad·van·ta′geous, *adj.;* **-ly,** *adv.*
un′ad·ven′tur·ous, *adj.*
un·ad′ver·tised′, *adj.*
un′ad·vis′a·ble, *adj.*
un′aes·thet′ic, *adj.*
un′af·fil′i·at′ed, *adj.*
un′a·fraid′, *adj.*
un·aged′, *adj.*
un′ag·gres′sive, *adj.;* **-ly,** *adv.;* **-ness,** *n.*
un·ag′ing, *adj.*
un·ag′i·tat′ed, *adj.*
un·aid′ed, *adj.*
un·aimed′, *adj.*
un·aired′, *adj.*
un′a·larmed′, *adj.*
un′a·larm′ing, *adj.*
un·al′ien·a·ble, *adj.*
un·al′ien·at′ed, *adj.*
un·al′ien·at′ing, *adj.*
un′a·ligned′, *adj.*
un′al·layed′, *adj.*
un′al·le′vi·at′ed, *adj.*
un′al·lied′, *adj.*
un′al·low′a·ble, *adj.*
un·al′pha·bet·ized′, *adj.*
un·al′ter·ing, *adj.*
un′am·big′u·ous, *adj.;* **-ly,** *adv.*
un′am·bi′tious, *adj.*
un·a′mi·a·ble, *adj.*
un·am′i·ca·ble, *adj.*
un·am′or·tized′, *adj.*
un·am′pli·fied′, *adj.*
un′a·mused′, *adj.*
un′a·mus′ing, *adj.*
un′an·a·lyt′ic, *adj.*
un′an·a·lyt′i·cal, *adj.*
un·an′a·lyz′a·ble, *adj.*
un·an′a·lyzed′, *adj.*
un·an′i·mat′ed, *adj.*
un′an·nexed′, *adj.*
un′an·nounced′, *adj.*
un′an·tic′i·pat′ed, *adj.*
un′a·pol′o·get′ic, *adj.*
un′a·pol′o·get′i·cal·ly, *adv.*
un′ap·par′ent, *adj.*
un′ap·peal′ing, *adj.*
un′ap·peas′a·ble, *adj.*
un′ap·peased′, *adj.*
un·ap′pe·tis′ing, *adj.*
un·ap′pe·tiz′ing, *adj.;* **-ly,** *adv.*
un·ap′pli·ca·ble, *adj.;* **-ble·ness,** *n.;* **-bly,** *adv.*
un′ap·plied′, *adj.*
un′ap·point′ed, *adj.*
un′ap·por′tioned, *adj.*
un′ap·pre′ci·at′ed, *adj.*
un′ap·pre′ci·a′tive, *adj.*
un′ap·pre·hen′sive, *adj.*
un′ap·proved′, *adj.*
un′ap·prov′ing, *adj.;* **-ly,** *adv.*
un·ar′gu·a·ble, *adj.*
un·ar′mored, *adj.*
un·ar′moured, *adj.*
un′ar·rest′ed, *adj.*
un·art′ful, *adj.;* **-ly,** *adv.;* **-ness,** *n.*
un′ar·tic′u·late, *adj.;* **-ly,** *adv.*
un′ar·tic′u·lat′ed, *adj.*
un′ar·tic′u·la′tive, *adj.*
un′ar·tis′tic, *adj.*
un′as·cer·tain′a·ble, *adj.*
un·as′pi·rat′ed, *adj.*
un′a·spir′ing, *adj.*
un′as·sailed′, *adj.*
un′as·ser′tive, *adj.*
un′as·sessed′, *adj.*
un′as·sign′a·ble, *adj.*
un′as·signed′, *adj.*
un′as·sim′i·lat′ed, *adj.*
un′as·sist′ed, *adj.*
un′as·sort′ed, *adj.*
un′as·sumed′, *adj.*
un′a·toned′, *adj.*
un′a·ton′ing, *adj.*
un′at·tain′a·ble, *adj.*
un′at·tained′, *adj.*
un′at·tempt′ed, *adj.*
un′at·test′ed, *adj.*
un′at·tract′ed, *adj.*
un′at·trac′tive, *adj.*
un′aus·pi′cious, *adj.*
un′au·then′tic, *adj.*
un′au·then′ti·cat′ed, *adj.*
un·au′thor·ized′, *adj.*
un′a·vail′a·bil′i·ty, *n.*
un′a·vail′a·ble, *adj.*
un′a·venged′, *adj.*
un′a·waked′, *adj.*
un·awed′, *adj.*
un·bap′tized, *adj.*
un·barbed′, *adj.*
un·based′, *adj.*
un·beat′a·ble, *adj.*
un′be·fit′ting, *adj.*
un′be·grudged′, *adj.*
un′be·hold′en, *adj.*
un′be·loved′, *adj.*

inflexible. **2.** firm; unyielding. —**un·bend′ing·ly,** *adv.* —**un·bend′ing·ness,** *n.*

un·bent (un bent′), *v.* **1.** pt. and pp. of **unbend.** —*adj.* **2.** not bent; unbowed. **3.** not forced to yield or submit.

un·be·seem·ing (un′bi sē′ming), *adj.* unbecoming.

un·bi·ased (un bī′əst), *adj.* not biased; unprejudiced; impartial. Also, *esp. Brit.,* **un·bi′assed.** —**un·bi′ased·ly;** *esp. Brit.,* **un·bi′assed·ly,** *adv.* —**Syn.** fair, equitable, neutral.

un·bid·den (un bid′ᵊn), *adj.* **1.** not commanded; spontaneous. **2.** not bidden, asked, or summoned. Also, **un·bid′.** [ME *unbiden,* OE *unbēden*]

un·bind (un bīnd′), *v.t.,* **-bound, -bind·ing. 1.** to release from bonds or restraint, as a prisoner; free. **2.** to unfasten or loose, as a bond or tie. [ME; OE *unbind(an)*; c. G *entbinden*]

un·bit·ted (un bit′id), *adj.* **1.** not bitted or bridled. **2.** not controlled.

un·blenched (un blencht′), *adj. Archaic.* undaunted.

un·blessed (un blest′), *adj.* **1.** excluded from or lacking a blessing. **2.** unhallowed. **3.** unhappy; wretched. Also, **un·blest′.** [ME] —**un·bless·ed·ness** (un bles′id nis), *n.*

un·blink·ing (un bling′king), *adj.* **1.** not blinking. **2.** without displaying response, as surprise, confusion, chagrin, etc. **3.** not varying or wavering. —**un·blink′ing·ly,** *adv.*

un·blush·ing (un blush′ing), *adj.* **1.** shameless. **2.** not blushing. —**un·blush′ing·ly,** *adv.* —**un·blush′ing·ness,** *n.*

un·bod·ied (un bod′ēd), *adj.* **1.** incorporeal; disembodied. **2.** lacking a form; formless; shapeless.

un·bolt (un bōlt′), *v.t.* **1.** to open (a door, window, etc.) by or as by removing a bolt; unlock; unfasten. **2.** to release, as by the removal of threaded bolts.

un·bolt·ed[1] (un bōl′tid), *adj.* not fastened or secured, as with a bolt or bolts. [UN-[1] + BOLT[1] + -ED[2]]

un·bolt·ed[2] (un bōl′tid), *adj.* not sifted, as grain. [UN-[1] + BOLT[2] + -ED[2]]

un·bon·net (un bon′it), *v.i.* **1.** to uncover the head, as in respect. —*v.t.* **2.** to take off the bonnet from.

un·bon·net·ed (un bon′i tid), *adj.* bareheaded.

un·born (un bôrn′), *adj.* **1.** not yet born; yet to come; future: *unborn generations.* **2.** not yet delivered; still existing in the mother's womb: *an unborn baby.* **3.** existing without birth or beginning. [ME; OE *unboren*]

un·bos·om (un bo͝oz′əm, -bo͞o′zəm), *v.t.* **1.** to disclose (a confidence, secret, etc.). —*v.i.* **2.** to disclose one's thoughts, feelings, or the like, esp. in confidence. **3. unbosom oneself,** to disclose one's personal thoughts, feelings, etc., to another person; confide in someone. —**un·bos′om·er,** *n.*

un·bound (un bound′), *v.* **1.** pt. and pp. of **unbind.** —*adj.* **2.** not bound, as a book. **3.** free; not attached, as by a chemical bond: *unbound electrons.*

un·bound·ed (un boun′did), *adj.* **1.** unlimited; boundless. **2.** unrestrained; uncontrolled. —**un·bound′ed·ly,** *adv.* —**un·bound′ed·ness,** *n.* —**Syn. 1.** limitless, vast, infinite.

un·bowed (un boud′), *adj.* **1.** not bowed or bent. **2.** not yielding or submitting, as to defeat; not subjugated. [ME]

un·brace (un brās′), *v.t.,* **-braced, -brac·ing. 1.** to remove the braces of. **2.** to free from tension; relax. **3.** to weaken. [ME *unbrace(n)* (to) free of clothing or armor]

un·breathed (un brēthd′), *adj.* **1.** not breathed: *unbreathed air.* **2.** not disclosed; uncommunicated, as a secret.

un·bred (un bred′), *adj.* **1.** not taught or trained. **2.** not bred or mated, as a stock animal; not yet bred.

un·bri·dle (un brīd′ᵊl), *v.t.,* **-dled, -dling. 1.** to remove the bridle from (a horse, mule, etc.). **2.** to free from restraint. [ME *unbridle(n)*]

un·bro·ken (un brō′kən), *adj.* **1.** whole; intact. **2.** uninterrupted; continuous. **3.** not tamed, as a horse. **4.** undisturbed; unimpaired. [ME] —**un·bro′ken·ly,** *adv.* —**un·bro′ken·ness,** *n.* —**Syn. 1.** complete, entire.

un·build (un bild′), *v.t.,* **-built, -build·ing.** to demolish (something built); raze.

un·bun·dle (un bun′dᵊl), *v.,* **-dled, -dling.** —*v.t.* **1.** to separate (the charges for related products and services usually offered in a single transaction at one all-inclusive price). —*v.i.* **2.** to separate such charges.

un·bur·den (un bûr′dᵊn), *v.t.* **1.** to free from a burden. **2.** to relieve (one's mind, conscience, etc.) by disclosure or confession of something. **3.** to cast off or get rid of, as a burden or something burdensome; disclose; reveal.

un·but·ton (un but′ᵊn), *v.t.* **1.** to free (buttons) from buttonholes; unfasten or undo. **2.** to unfasten by or as by unbuttoning. —*v.i.* **3.** to unfasten a button or one's buttons. [ME *unboten(en)*]

un·but·toned (un but′ᵊnd), *adj.* **1.** not buttoned. **2.** not furnished with buttons. **3.** not restrained; free or open.

UNC, United Nations Command. Also, **U.N.C.**

un·called-for (un kôld′fôr′), *adj.* **1.** not called for; not required or wanted. **2.** unwarranted or unjustified; improper: *an uncalled-for criticism.*

un·can·ny (un kan′ē), *adj.* **1.** having or seeming to have a supernatural or inexplicable basis; beyond the ordinary or normal; extraordinary. **2.** mysterious; frightening, as by superstitious dread; uncomfortably strange. —**un·can′ni·ly,** *adv.* —**un·can′ni·ness,** *n.* —**Syn. 2.** See **weird.**

un·cap (un kap′), *v.,* **-capped, -cap·ping.** —*v.t.* **1.** to remove a cap or hat from (the head of a person). **2.** to remove a cap or cover from (a bottle, container, etc.). —*v.i.* **3.** to remove the cap from the head, as in respect.

un·cared-for (un kârd′fôr′), *adj.* **1.** not cared for; for which no liking, fondness, or affection is felt or shown. **2.** untended or neglected; unkempt.

un·case (un kās′), *v.t.,* **-cased, -cas·ing. 1.** to remove from a case; remove the case from. **2.** to remove the cover from; put on view. **3.** to make known; reveal.

un·caused (un kôzd′), *adj.* not resulting from some antecedent cause; self-existent.

un·cer·e·mo·ni·ous (un′ser ə mō′nē əs), *adj.* **1.** without ceremony or ritual; informal. **2.** abrupt, as with less than the normal courtesy; hasty; rude. —**un′cer·e·mo′ni·ous·ly,** *adv.* —**un′cer·e·mo′ni·ous·ness,** *n.*

un·cer·tain (un sûr′tᵊn), *adj.* **1.** not definitely ascertainable or fixed, as in time of occurrence, number, quality, etc. **2.** not confident, assured, or free from hesitancy. **3.** not clearly or precisely determined; indefinite; unknown: *a manuscript of uncertain origin.* **4.** vague; indistinct; not perfectly apprehended. **5.** subject to change; capricious; unstable. **6.** dependent on chance or unpredictable factors; doubtful; of unforeseeable outcome or effect. **7.** unsteady or flickering, as light. [ME] —**un·cer′tain·ly,** *adv.* —**un·cer′tain·ness,** *n.* —**Syn. 1.** unsure, unpredictable. **3.** unsettled, undetermined. **5.** unreliable. **7.** irregular.

un·cer·tain·ty (un sûr′tᵊn tē), *n., pl.* **-ties. 1.** the state of being uncertain; doubt; hesitancy. **2.** an instance of uncertainty, doubt, etc. **3.** unpredictability; indeterminacy or indefiniteness. [ME]

uncer′tainty prin′ciple, *Physics.* the principle of quantum mechanics, formulated by Heisenberg, that the accurate measurement of either of two related quantities, as position and momentum or energy and time, produces uncertainties in the measurement of the other. Also called **indeterminacy principle.**

un·chan·cy (un chan′sē, -chän′-), *adj. Chiefly Scot.* **1.** unlucky. **2.** dangerous.

un·charge (un chärj′), *v.t.,* **-charged, -charg·ing.** *Obs.* **1.** to free from a load; unload. **2.** to acquit. [ME]

un·charged (un chärjd′), *adj.* not charged, esp. with electricity; electrically neutral: *an uncharged battery; an uncharged particle.*

un·char·i·ta·ble (un char′i tə bəl), *adj.* deficient in charity; unkind; harsh; unforgiving; censorious; merciless. [ME] —**un·char′i·ta·ble·ness,** *n.* —**un·char′i·ta·bly,** *adv.*

un·char·tered (un chär′tərd), *adj.* **1.** not chartered: *an unchartered company.* **2.** without regulation; lawless.

un·chaste (un chāst′), *adj.* **1.** not chaste, virtuous, or pure. **2.** characterized by sexual transgression or excess; bawdy. [ME] —**un·chaste′ly,** *adv.* —**un·chaste′ness, un·chas·ti·ty** (un chas′ti tē), *n.*

un·chris·tian (un kris′chən), *adj.* **1.** not Christian. **2.** unworthy of Christians. **3.** not conforming to Christian teaching or principles. —**un·chris′tian·ly,** *adv.*

un·church (un chûrch′), *v.t.* **1.** to expel (individuals) from a church; excommunicate. **2.** to deprive of the character and rights of a church.

un·churched (un chûrcht′), *adj.* not being a member of a church; not attending any church.

un·ci·a (un′chē ə), *n., pl.* **-ci·ae** (-chē ē′). a bronze coin of ancient Rome, the 12th part of an as. [< L; c. Gk *ounkía*]

un·ci·al (un′shē əl, -shəl), *adj.* **1.** designating, written in, or pertaining to a form of majuscule writing having more curves than capitals have and used chiefly in Greek and Latin manuscripts from about the 3rd to the 9th century A.D. —*n.* **2.** an uncial letter. **3.** uncial writing. **4.** a manuscript written in uncials. [< L *unciāl(is).* See UNCIA, -AL[1]] —**un′ci·al·ly,** *adv.*

Uncials (Latin) 8th century

un·ci·form (un′sə fôrm′), *adj.* **1.** hook-shaped. —*n.* **2.** *Anat.* hamate (def. 3). [< NL *unciform(is)* = L *unc(us)* a hook, barb (c. Gk *ónkos*) + *-formis* -FORM]

un·ci·na·ri·a·sis (un′sə nə rī′ə sis), *n. Pathol.* hookworm (def. 2). [< NL *Uncinār(ia)* name of the genus (L *uncīn(us)* hooked + *-āria* -ARIA) + *-iasis* -IASIS]

un·ci·nate (un′sə nit, -nāt′), *adj. Biol.* hooked; bent at the end like a hook. [< L *uncīnāt(us)* furnished with hooks = *uncīn(us)* hooked (*uncus* hook + *-īnus* -INE[1]) + *-ātus* -ATE[1]]

Uncinate prickles

UNCIO, United Nations Conference on International Organization.

un·cir·cum·cised (un sûr′kəm sīzd′), *adj.* **1.** not circumcised. **2.** not Jewish or not of Jewish birth; gentile. **3.** heathen; unregenerate. [ME]

un·cir·cum·ci·sion (un′sûr kəm sizh′ən), *n.* **1.** the state or condition of being uncircumcised. **2.** people who are not circumcised; gentiles. Rom. 2:26.

un·civ·il (un siv′əl), *adj.* **1.** without good manners; rude; impolite; discourteous. **2.** uncivilized. —**un·ci·vil·i·ty** (un′si vil′i tē), **un·civ′il·ness,** *n.* —**un·civ′il·ly,** *adv.* —**Syn. 1.** disrespectful, uncouth, boorish, unmannerly.

un·civ·i·lized (un siv′ə līzd′), *adj.* barbarous; unenlightened. Also, *esp. Brit.,* **un·civ′i·lised′.** —**un·civ·i·liz·ed·ly;** *esp. Brit.,* **un·civ·i·lis·ed·ly** (un siv′ə lī′zid lē, -līzd′-), *adv.* —**un·civ′i·liz′ed·ness;** *esp. Brit.,* **un·civ′i·lis′ed·ness,** *n.*

un·clad (un klad′), *v.* **1.** a pt. and pp. of **unclothe.** —*adj.* **2.** naked or nude; undressed.

---

un·blam′a·ble, *adj.*
un·bleached′, *adj.*
un·blem′ished, *adj.*
un·block′, *v.t.*
un·boned′, *adj.*
un·braid′, *v.t.*
un·brand′ed, *adj.*
un·break′a·ble, *adj.*
un·brib′a·ble, *adj.;* **-bly,** *adv.*
un·bridge′a·ble, *adj.*
un·bridged′, *adj.*
un·broth′er·ly, *adj.*
un·bruised′, *adj.*
un·brushed′, *adj.*
un·buck′le, *v.t.,* **-led, -ling.**
un·budg′et·ed, *adj.*
un·budg′ing, *adj.*
un·bur′ied, *adj.*
un·burned′, *adj.*
un·burnt′, *adj.*
un·cake′, *v.t.,* **-caked, -cak·ing.**
un·can′celed, *adj.*
un·can′celled, *adj.*
un·car′ing, *adj.*
un·car′pet·ed, *adj.*
un·cashed′, *adj.*
un·cas′trat·ed, *adj.*
un′cat·e·gor′i·cal, *adj.;* **-ly,** *adv.*
un·caught′, *adj.*
un·ceas′ing, *adj.;* **-ly,** *adv.*
un·cel′e·brat′ed, *adj.*
un·cen′sored, *adj.*
un·cen′sured, *adj.*
un·cer′ti·fied′, *adj.*
un·chain′, *v.t.*
un·chal′lenge·a·ble, *adj.*
un·chal′lenged, *adj.*
un·chal′leng·ing, *adj.*
un·change′a·ble, *adj.*
un·changed′, *adj.*
un·chang′ing, *adj.*
un·chap′er·oned′, *adj.*
un′char·ac·ter·is′tic, *adj.*
un′char·ac·ter·is′ti·cal·ly, *adv.*
un·charred′, *adj.*
un·chart′ed, *adj.*
un·char′y, *adj.*
un·chas′tened, *adj.*
un·chas′tised, *adj.*
un·checked′, *adj.*
un·cheer′ful, *adj.;* **-ly,** *adv.;* **-ness,** *n.*
un·cher′ished, *adj.*
un·chilled′, *adj.*
un·chiv′al·rous, *adj.*
un·cho′sen, *adj.*
un·chris′tened, *adj.*

un·clasp (un klasp′, -kläsp′), *v.t.* **1.** to undo the clasp or clasps of; unfasten. **2.** to release from the grasp: *to unclasp a sword handle.* **—*v.i.*** **3.** to become unclasped, as the hands, arms, etc. **4.** to release or relax the grasp.

un·clas·si·fied (un klas′ə fīd′), *adj.* **1.** not assigned to a class or category; not arranged according to characteristics. **2.** (of data, documents, etc.) not belonging to a category that is restricted for reasons of security; not secret.

un·cle (ung′kəl), *n.* **1.** a brother of one's father or mother. **2.** an aunt's husband. **3.** a familiar title applied to any elderly man. **4.** *Slang.* a pawnbroker. **5.** (*cap.*) a word formerly used in communications to represent the letter *U.* [ME < AF *uncle,* OF *oncle* < L *avuncul(us)* mother's brother = *av(us)* grandfather + *-unculus* double dim. suffix]

un·clean (un klēn′), *adj.* **1.** not clean; dirty. **2.** morally impure; evil; vile: *an unclean attitude.* **3.** *Chiefly Biblical.* having a physical or moral blemish so as to be impure according to the laws, esp. the dietary or ceremonial laws. [ME *unclene,* OE *unclǣne*] **—un·clean′ness,** *n.* **—Syn. 1.** soiled, filthy. **2.** base, unchaste, sinful, corrupt.

un·clean·ly[1] (un klēn′lē), *adv.* in an unclean manner. [ME *onclenlich,* OE *unclǣnlīc.* See UNCLEAN, -LY]

un·clean·ly[2] (un klen′lē), *adj.* not cleanly; unclean. [OE *unclǣnlīche.* See UN-[1], CLEANLY] **—un·clean′li·ness,** *n.*

un·clench (un klench′), *v.t., v.i.* to open or become opened from a clenched state or position.

Un′cle Sam′, a personification of the government or people of the U.S.: represented as a tall, lean man with white chin whiskers, wearing a blue tailcoat, red-and-white-striped trousers, and a top hat with a band of stars. [extension of the initials U.S.]

Un′cle Tom′, (*sometimes l.c.*) *Contemptuous.* a Negro who is abjectly servile or deferential to whites. [so called after the leading character in *Uncle Tom's Cabin* (1852), a novel by Harriet Beecher Stowe] **—Un′cle Tom′ism.**

un·clinch (un klinch′), *v.t., v.i.* unclench.

un·cloak (un klōk′), *v.t.* **1.** to remove the cloak from. **2.** to reveal; expose. **—*v.i.*** **3.** to take off the cloak or the outer garments generally.

un·clog (un klog′), *v.t.,* **-clogged, -clog·ging.** to free of an obstruction or impediment: *to unclog a drain; to unclog a traffic artery.*

un·close (un klōz′), *v.t., v.i.,* **-closed, -clos·ing.** to bring or come out of a closed state; open. [ME *unclose(n)*]

un·clothe (un klōth′), *v.t.,* **-clothed** or **-clad, -cloth·ing.** **1.** to strip of clothes. **2.** to remove a covering from; lay bare, as by removing garments. [ME *unclothe(n)*]

un·co (ung′kō), *adj., adv., n., pl.* **-cos.** *Scot. and North Eng.* **—*adj.*** **1.** remarkable; extraordinary. **—*adv.*** **2.** remarkably; extremely. **—*n.*** **3.** something extraordinary or unusual; novelty. [var. of UNCOUTH]

un·com·fort·a·ble (un kumf′tə bəl, -kum′fər tə bəl), *adj.* **1.** causing discomfort or distress; painful; irritating. **2.** in a state of discomfort; uneasy; conscious of stress or strain. **—un·com′fort·a·ble·ness,** *n.* **—un·com′fort·a·bly,** *adv.*

un·com·mer·cial (un′kə mûr′shəl), *adj.* **1.** not engaged in or involved with commerce or trade. **2.** not in accordance with commercial principles or practices.

un·com·mit·ted (un′kə mit′id), *adj.* not committed, esp. not pledged or bound to follow a prescribed course of action.

un·com·mon (un kom′ən), *adj.* **1.** not common; unusual; rare. **2.** unusual in amount or degree; above the ordinary. **3.** exceptional or remarkable; outstanding. **—un·com′mon·ness,** *n.* **—Syn. 1.** scarce, infrequent; odd, singular, strange, peculiar, queer. **2.** extraordinary.

un·com·mon·ly (un kom′ən lē), *adv.* **1.** in an uncommon or unusual manner or degree. **2.** exceptionally; outstandingly. **3.** rarely; infrequently.

un·com·mu·ni·ca·tive (un′kə myōō′nə kā′tiv, -nə kə-tiv), *adj.* not disposed to impart information, opinions, etc.; reserved; taciturn. **—un′com·mu′ni·ca′tive·ly,** *adv.* **—un′com·mu′ni·ca′tive·ness,** *n.*

un·com·pro·mis·ing (un kom′prə mī′zing), *adj.* **1.** not admitting of compromise or adjustment of differences; making no concessions; inaccessible to flexible bargaining; unyielding. **2.** without reservation or exception; undeviating; absolute. **—un·com′pro·mis′ing·ly,** *adv.* **—un·com′pro·mis′ing·ness,** *n.* **—Syn. 1.** rigid, firm, steadfast, obstinate.

un·con·cern (un′kən sûrn′), *n.* **1.** freedom from anxiety. **2.** absence of feeling or concern; indifference. **—Syn.** nonchalance, insouciance. See **indifference.**

un·con·cerned (un′kən sûrnd′), *adj.* **1.** not involved or interested; disinterested. **2.** not caring; unworried; free from solicitude or anxiety. **—un·con·cern·ed·ly** (un′kən sûr′nid-lē), *adv.* **—un′con·cern′ed·ness,** *n.*

un·con·di·tion·al (un′kən dish′ə nəl), *adj.* not limited by conditions; absolute. **—un′con·di′tion·al·ly,** *adv.* **—un′con·di′tion·al·ness, un′con·di′tion·al′i·ty,** *n.* **—Syn.** complete, unqualified, categorical.

un·con·di·tioned (un′kən dish′ənd), *adj.* **1.** not subject to conditions; absolute. **2.** *Psychol.* not proceeding from or dependent on a conditioning of the individual; natural; innate. Cf. **conditioned** (def. 3). **—un′con·di′tioned·ness,** *n.*

un·con·form·a·ble (un′kən fôr′mə bəl), *adj.* **1.** not conformable; not conforming. **2.** *Geol.* indicating discontinuity of any type in stratigraphic sequence. **—un′con·form′a·bil′i·ty,** *n.* **—un′con·form′a·bly,** *adv.*

un·con·form·i·ty (un′kən fôr′mi tē), *n., pl.* **-ties.** **1.** lack of conformity; incongruity; inconsistency. **2.** *Geol.* **a.** a discontinuity in rock sequence indicating interruption of sedimentation, commonly accompanied by erosion of rocks below the break. **b.** the interface between such strata.

un·con·nec·ted (un′kə nek′tid), *adj.* **1.** not connected; not joined together or attached. **2.** without connection; not related causally, logically, etc.; incoherent. **—un′con·nect′ed·ly,** *adv.* **—un′con·nect′ed·ness,** *n.*

un·con·scion·a·ble (un kon′shə nə bəl), *adj.* **1.** not guided by conscience; unscrupulous. **2.** not in accordance with what is just or reasonable. **3.** excessive; extortionate. **—un·con′scion·a·ble·ness,** *n.* **—un·con′scion·a·bly,** *adv.*

un·con·scious (un kon′shəs), *adj.* **1.** not conscious; without awareness, sensation, or cognition. **2.** temporarily devoid of consciousness. **3.** not endowed with mental faculties: *the unconscious stones.* **4.** not perceived at the level of awareness; occurring below the level of conscious thought: *an unconscious impulse.* **5.** not consciously realized, planned, or done. **—*n.*** **6. the unconscious,** *Psychoanal.* the part of the mind containing the psychic material of which the ego is unaware. **—un·con′scious·ly,** *adv.* **—un·con′scious·ness,** *n.*

un·con·sti·tu·tion·al (un′kon sti tōō′shə nəl, -tyōō′-), *adj.* **1.** not constitutional; unauthorized by or inconsistent with the constitution, as of a country. **2.** contrary to the Constitution of the United States. **—un′con·sti·tu′tion·al·ism,** *n.* **—un′con·sti·tu′tion·al′i·ty,** *n.* **—un′con·sti·tu′tion·al·ly,** *adv.*

un·con·ven·tion·al (un′kən ven′shə nəl), *adj.* not conventional; not bound by or conforming to convention, rule, or precedent; free from conventionality: *an unconventional artist; an unconventional use of color.* **—un′con·ven′tion·al′i·ty,** *n.* **—un′con·ven′tion·al·ly,** *adv.*

un·cork (un kôrk′), *v.t.* to draw the cork from.

un·count·a·ble (un koun′tə bəl), *adj.* **1.** not countable; incapable of having the total precisely ascertained. **2.** indefinitely large in number; infinite.

un·count·ed (un koun′tid), *adj.* **1.** not counted. **2.** innumerable. [ME *uncountit*]

un·cou·ple (un kup′əl), *v.,* **-pled, -pling.** **—*v.t.*** **1.** to release the coupling or link between; disconnect. **—*v.i.*** **2.** to become unfastened; let go. [ME]

un·court·ly (un kôrt′lē), *adj.* **1.** not courtly; rude. **2.** not conforming to the customs or usage of a royal court. **—un·court′li·ness,** *n.*

un·couth (un kōōth′), *adj.* **1.** awkward, clumsy, or unmannerly. **2.** strange and ungraceful in appearance or form. **3.** unusual or strange. [ME; OE *uncūth* (*un-* UN-[1] + *cūth* known, ptp.); c. D *onkond*] **—un·couth′ly,** *adv.* **—un·couth′ness,** *n.* **—Syn. 1.** discourteous, rude, boorish.

un·cov·e·nant·ed (un kuv′ə nən tid), *adj.* **1.** not agreed to or promised by covenant. **2.** not having joined in a covenant.

un·cov·er (un kuv′ər), *v.t.* **1.** to lay bare; disclose; reveal. **2.** to remove the cover or covering from. **3.** to remove a hat from (the head). **—*v.i.*** **4.** to remove a cover or covering. **5.** to take off one's hat as a gesture of respect. [ME *uncover(en)*]

un·cov·ered (un kuv′ərd), *adj.* **1.** having no cover or covering. **2.** having the head bare. **3.** not protected by collateral or other security, as a note. [ME *uncovert*]

un·crit·i·cal (un krit′i kəl), *adj.* **1.** not inclined or able to judge, esp. by the application of comparative standards. **2.** undiscriminating; not applying or not guided by the standards of analysis. **—un·crit′i·cal·ly,** *adv.*

un·crown (un kroun′), *v.t.* **1.** to deprive or divest of a crown. **2.** to reduce from dignity or preeminence. [ME *uncroun(en)*]

un·crowned (un kround′), *adj.* **1.** not crowned; not having yet assumed the crown. **2.** having royal rank or power without occupying the royal office. [ME *uncrouned*]

unc·tion (ungk′shən), *n.* **1.** an act of anointing, esp. as a medical treatment or ritual symbol. **2.** *Relig.* **a.** the oil used in religious rites, as in anointing the sick or dying. **b.** See **extreme unction.** **3.** something soothing or comforting. **4.** a soothing, sympathetic, and persuasive quality in discourse, esp. on religious subjects. **5.** a professional, conventional, or affected earnestness or fervor in utterance. [ME *unctioun* <

un·claimed′, *adj.*
un·clar′i·fied′, *adj.*
un·clas′si·cal, *adj.*
un·clas′si·fi′a·ble, *adj.*
un·cleaned′, *adj.*
un·clear′, *adj.*
un·cleared′, *adj.*
un·cloud′ed, *adj.*
un·clut′tered, *adj.*
un′co·ag′u·lat′ed, *adj.*
un·cocked′, *adj.*
un·coil′, *v.*
un′col·lect′ed, *adj.*
un′col·lect′i·ble, *adj.*
un·col′ored, *adj.*
un·col′oured, *adj.*
un·combed′, *adj.*
un′com·bined′, *adj.*
un·com′fort·ed, *adj.*
un·com′fort·ing, *adj.*
un′com·mend′a·ble, *adj.*
un′com·pan′ion·a·ble, *adj.*
un·com′pen·sat′ed, *adj.*
un′com·pet′i·tive, *adj.*
un′com·plain′ing, *adj.;* **-ly,** *adv.*
un′com·pli′ant, *adj.*
un·com′pli·cat′ed, *adj.*
un·com′pli·men′ta·ry, *adj.*
un′com·pound′ed, *adj.*
un′com·pre·hend′ed, *adj.*
un′com·pre·hend′ing, *adj.;* **-ly,** *adv.*
un′com·pre·hen′si·ble, *adj.;* **-ble·ness,** *n.;* **-bly,** *adv.*
un′con·ced′ed, *adj.*
un′con·cert′ed, *adj.*
un′con·clud′ed, *adj.*
un′con·demned′, *adj.*
un′con·densed′, *adj.*
un′con·du′cive, *adj.*
un′con·fessed′, *adj.*
un′con·fined′, *adj.*
un′con·fused′, *adj.*
un′con·fut′ed, *adj.*
un′con·gen′ial, *adj.*
un·con′quer·a·ble, *adj.*
un·con′quered, *adj.*
un′con·sci·en′tious, *adj.;* **-ly,** *adv.;* **-ness,** *n.*
un·con′se·crat′ed, *adj.*
un′con·sec′u·tive, *adj.*
un′con·sent′ing, *adj.*
un′con·sid′ered, *adj.*
un′con·soled′, *adj.*
un′con·sol′i·dat′ed, *adj.*
un′con·strained′, *adj.*
un′con·straint′, *n.*
un′con·strict′ed, *adj.*
un′con·sumed′, *adj.*
un·con′sum·mat′ed, *adj.*
un′con·tam′i·nat′ed, *adj.*
un·con′tem·plat′ed, *adj.*
un′con·test′ed, *adj.*
un′con·tra·dict′a·ble, *adj.;* **-ly,** *adv.*
un′con·tra·dict′ed, *adj.*
un′con·trite′, *adj.*
un′con·trived′, *adj.*
un′con·trol′la·ble, *adj.;* **-bly,** *adv.*
un′con·trolled′, *adj.*
un′con·ver′sant, *adj.*
un′con·vert′ed, *adj.*
un′con·vert′i·ble, *adj.*
un′con·vinced′, *adj.*
un′con·vinc′ing, *adj.;* **-ly,** *adv.*
un·cooked′, *adj.*
un′co·op′er·a′tive, *adj.*
un′co·or′di·nat′ed, *adj.*
un·cop′y·right′ed, *adj.*
un·cor′dial, *adj.*
un′cor·rect′ed, *adj.*
un′cor·rob′o·rat′ed, *adj.*
un′cor·rupt′ed, *adj.*
un·cour′te·ous, *adj.*
un·crate′, *v.t.,* **-crat·ed, -crat·ing.**
un′cre·at′ed, *adj.*
un′cre·a′tive, *adj.;* **-ly,** *adv.*
un·cred′it·a·ble, *adj.*
un·crip′pled, *adj.*
un·cross′, *v.t.*
un·crowd′ed, *adj.*
un·crys′tal·lized′, *adj.*

L *unctiōn-* (s. of *unctiō*) anointing, besmearing = *unct(us)* smeared, anointed (ptp. of *ungere, unquere*) + *-iōn-* -ION]

unc·tu·ous (ungk′cho͞o əs), *adj.* **1.** of the nature of or characteristic of an unguent or ointment; oily; greasy. **2.** characterized by excessive piousness or moralistic fervor; excessively smooth, suave, or smug. **3.** having an oily or soapy feel, as certain minerals. [< ML *unctuōs(us)* = L *unct(um)* ointment, n. use of neut. of *unctus* (see UNCTION) + *-ōsus* -OUS] —**unc·tu·os·i·ty** (ungk′cho͞o os′i tē), **unc′tu·ous·ness,** *n.* —**unc′tu·ous·ly,** *adv.*

un·cut (un kut′), *adj.* **1.** not cut. **2.** not shortened or condensed; unabridged. **3.** in the original form; neither reduced in size nor given shape, as a diamond. [ME *unkitt*]

un·damped (un dampt′), *adj.* **1.** not damped or dampened; undiminished, as in energy, vigor, etc.: *undamped spirits.* **2.** *Physics.* (of an oscillation) having constant or increasing amplitude.

un·daunt·ed (un dôn′tid), *adj.* **1.** undismayed; not discouraged; not forced to abandon purpose or effort. **2.** undiminished in courage or valor; not giving way to fear; intrepid. [late ME] —**un·daunt′ed·ly,** *adv.* —**un·daunt′ed·ness,** *n.*

un·dé (un dā′), *adj.* *Heraldry.* wavy, esp. when the curves are relatively abrupt and close. Also, **un·dée′.** [< AF (c. OF *onde*) < L *undāt(us)* (ptp. of *undāre* to make waves) = *und(a)* wave + *-ātus* -ATE[1]]

un·dec·a·gon (un dek′ə gon′), *n.* a polygon having 11 angles and 11 sides. [< L *undec(im)* eleven = *ūn(us)* one + *decem* ten + *-a-* connective vowel + -GON]

un·de·ceive (un′di sēv′), *v.t.,* **-ceived, -ceiv·ing.** to free from deception, fallacy, or mistake. —**un′de·ceiv′a·ble,** *adj.* —**un′de·ceiv′er,** *n.*

un·de·cid·ed (un′di sī′did), *adj.* **1.** not decided or determined. **2.** not having one's mind firmly made up; irresolute. —**un′de·cid′ed·ly,** *adv.* —**un′de·cid′ed·ness,** *n.*

un·de·fined (un′di fīnd′), *adj.* **1.** without fixed limits; indefinite in form, extent, or application. **2.** not given meaning or significance, as by a definition; unexplained. —**un·de·fin·ed·ly** (un′di fī′nid lē, -fīnd′-), *adv.* —**un′de·fin′ed·ness,** *n.*

un·de·ni·able (un′di nī′ə bəl), *adj.* **1.** not capable of being disputed or controverted; inescapable. **2.** not open to refusal. **3.** unquestioned as to quality, merit, etc.; indisputably good. —**un′de·ni′a·ble·ness,** *n.* —**un′de·ni′a·bly,** *adv.* —**Syn. 1.** incontrovertible; obvious, evident.

un·der (un′dər), *prep.* **1.** beneath and covered by: *under a table; under a tree.* **2.** below the surface of: *under water.* **3.** at a point or position lower or further down than. **4.** in the position or state of supporting, enduring, etc.: *to sink under a heavy load.* **5.** beneath the heading or within the category of: *Classify the books under "Fiction" and "General."* **6.** as designated, indicated, or represented by: *to register under a new name.* **7.** below in degree, amount, etc.; less than: *purchased under cost.* **8.** below in rank; of less dignity, importance, or the like. **9.** subject to the authority, direction, or supervision of. **10.** subject to the instruction or advice of: *to study violin under Heifetz.* **11.** subject to the influence, condition, force, etc.: *under these circumstances; born under the sign of Taurus.* **12.** protected, controlled, or watched by: *under guard.* **13.** authorized, warranted, or attested by: *under one's hand or seal.* **14.** in accordance with: *under the provisions of the law.* **15.** during the rule or administration of: *new laws passed under the new Congress.* **16.** in the state or process of: *under repair.* —*adv.* **17.** below or beneath something: *Go over the fence, not under.* **18.** beneath the surface. **19.** in a lower place. **20.** in a lower degree, amount, etc.: *selling blouses for $6 and under.* **21.** in a subordinate position or condition. **22.** in or into subjection or submission. **23. go under, a.** to give in; succumb; yield. **b.** *Informal.* to fail in business. —*adj.* **24.** beneath. **25.** lower in position. **26.** lower in degree, amount, etc. **27.** lower in rank or condition. **28.** subject to the control, effect, etc., as of a person, drug, or force (used predicatively) under hypnosis; under anesthetic. [ME, OE; c. D *onder,* G *unter,* OIcel *undir,* L *infra* below] —**Syn. 2.** See **below.**

under-, a prefixal attributive use of *under,* as to indicate place or situation below or beneath (*underbrush; undertow*); lower in grade or dignity (*undersheriff; understudy*); of lesser degree, extent, or amount (*undersized*); or insufficiency (*underfeed*).

un·der·a·chieve (un′dər ə chēv′), *v.i.,* **-a·chieved, -a·chiev·ing.** *Educ.* (of a student) to perform below the potential indicated by his scores on tests of mental ability. —**un′der·a·chieve′ment,** *n.* —**un′der·a·chiev′er,** *n.*

un·der·act (un′dər akt′), *v.t., v.i.* to underplay.

un·der·age[1] (un′dər āj′), *adj.* lacking the required age, esp. that of legal maturity. [UNDER- + AGE]

un·der·age[2] (un′dər ij), *n.* shortage; deficiency in amount. [UNDER- + -AGE]

un·der·arm (un′dər ärm′), *adj.* **1.** of, applicable to, or associated with the region under the arm. **2.** underhand: *an underarm pitch in softball.* —*adv.* **3.** underhand.

un·der·armed (un′dər ärmd′), *adj.* not having sufficient weapons.

un·der·bel·ly (un′dər bel′ē), *n., pl.* **-lies. 1.** the lower abdomen; posterior ventral area, as of an animal's body. **2.** the vital area most vulnerable to attack; the weakest point: *the soft underbelly of Europe.*

un·der·bid (un′dər bid′), *v.,* **-bid, -bid·ding.** —*v.t.* **1.** to make a bid lower than that of (another bidder); make an offer at a lower price than (a competing offer). **2.** *Bridge.* to bid less than the value of (one's hand). —*v.i.* **3.** *Bridge.* to bid less than one's hand is worth. —**un′der·bid′der,** *n.*

un·der·bred (un′dər bred′), *adj.* **1.** having inferior breeding or manners; vulgar. **2.** not of pure breed, as a horse. —**un·der·breed·ing** (un′dər brē′ding), *n.*

un·der·brush (un′dər brush′), *n.* shrubs, small trees, etc., growing under large trees in a wood or forest. Also, **un·der·bush** (un′dər bo͝osh′).

un·der·buy (un′dər bī′), *v.,* **-bought, -buy·ing.** —*v.t.* **1.** to buy more cheaply than (another). **2.** to buy at less than the actual value. —*v.i.* **3.** to buy an insufficient quantity, as of supplies or stock in trade.

un·der·cap·i·tal·ize (un′dər kap′i tᵊlīz′; *Brit. also* un′dər kə pit′ᵊlīz′), *v.t.,* **-ized, -iz·ing.** to provide an insufficient amount of capital for (a business enterprise).

un·der·car·riage (un′dər kar′ij), *n.* **1.** the supporting framework underneath a vehicle, as an automobile; the structure to which the wheels, tracks, or the like, are attached. **2.** the portions of an aircraft that are below the body.

un·der·charge (*v.* un′dər chärj′; *n.* un′dər chärj′), *v.,* **-charged, -charg·ing,** *n.* —*v.t.* **1.** to charge (a purchaser) less than the proper or fair price. **2.** to charge (a stated amount) less than the proper price. **3.** to put an insufficient charge or load into. —*n.* **4.** a charge or price less than is proper or customary. **5.** an insufficient charge or load.

un·der·class·man (un′dər klas′mən, -kläs′-), *n., pl.* **-men.** a freshman, sophomore, or junior in a school or college.

un·der·clothes (un′dər klōz′, -klōthz′), *n.pl.* clothes worn under outer clothes, esp. those worn next to the skin. Also called **underclothing.**

un·der·cloth·ing (un′dər klō′thing), *n.* **1.** underwear. **2.** underclothes.

un·der·coat (un′dər kōt′), *n.* **1.** a coat or jacket worn under another. **2.** *Zool.* a growth of short fur or hair lying beneath a longer growth. **3.** a coat of paint or the like applied under the finishing coat. **4.** a paint, sealer, or the like, specially prepared for use underneath a finishing coat.

un·der·coat·ing (un′dər kō′ting), *n.* a protective seal applied to the underside of an automobile to reduce corrosion and vibration.

un·der·cool (un′dər ko͞ol′), *v.t.* *Chem.* **1.** to cool less than necessary for a given process or purpose. **2.** to supercool.

un·der·cov·er (un′dər kuv′ər, un′dər kuv′-), *adj.* **1.** working or done in secret. **2.** engaged in spying or securing confidential information: *an undercover agent.*

un·der·croft (un′dər krôft′, -kroft′), *n.* a vault or chamber under the ground, esp. in a church. [ME]

un·der·cur·rent (un′dər kûr′ənt, -kur′-), *n.* **1.** a current, as of air or water, that flows below the upper currents or surface. **2.** an underlying, hidden tendency, often at variance with the obvious significance of words, actions, etc.

un·der·cut (un′dər kut′), *v.,* **-cut, -cut·ting,** *n., adj.* —*v.t.* **1.** to cut under or beneath. **2.** to cut away material from so as to leave a portion overhanging, as in carving or sculpture. **3.** to sell at a lower price or work for a lower wage than another, as a competitor. **4.** *Golf.* to hit (the ball) so as to cause a backspin. **5.** *Tennis.* to slice (the ball) using an underhand motion. —*v.i.* **6.** to undercut material, a competitor, a ball, etc. —*n.* **7.** a cut or a cutting away underneath. **8.** a notch cut in a tree to determine the direction in which the tree is to fall and to prevent splitting. **9.** *Golf.* a backspin. **10.** *Tennis.* a slice or cut made with an underhand motion. **11.** *Chiefly Brit.* a tenderloin of beef including the fillet. —*adj.* **12.** having or resulting from an undercut.

un·der·de·vel·op (un′dər di vel′əp), *v.t.* to develop (something) short of the required amount: *to underdevelop film.* —**un′der·de·vel′op·ment,** *n.*

un·der·de·vel·ope (un′dər di vel′əp), *v.t.,* **-oped, -op·ing.** underdevelop. —**un′der·de·vel′ope·ment,** *n.*

un·der·de·vel·oped (un′dər di vel′əpt), *adj.* **1.** improperly or insufficiently developed. **2.** *Photog.* (of a negative) less developed than is normal, so as to produce a relatively dark positive lacking in contrast. **3.** (of a nation or geographical area) having a standard of living or level of industrial production well below that possible with financial or technical aid. Cf. **developing.**

un·der·do (un′dər do͞o′), *v.i., v.t.,* **-did, -done, -do·ing.** to do less than is usual or requisite.

un·der·dog (un′dər dôg′, -dog′), *n.* **1.** a person who is expected to lose in a contest or conflict. **2.** a victim of social or political injustice.

un·der·done (un′dər dun′), *adj.* **1.** (of food) not thoroughly cooked; not cooked enough. **2.** *Chiefly Brit.* (of meat) rare.

un·der·drain (*n.* un′dər drān′; *v.* un′dər drān′), *n.* **1.** a drain placed beneath the surface of cultivated fields, streets, etc. —*v.t.* **2.** to equip or supply with an underdrain or underdrains.

un·der·drain·age (un′dər drā′nij), *n.* drainage of agricultural lands and removal of excess water and of alkali by drains buried beneath the surface.

un·der·draw·ers (un′dər drôrz′), *n.* (*construed as pl.*) an undergarment for the lower part of the body, typically covering at least part of the legs. Cf. **drawer** (def. 2).

un·der·dress (un′dər dres′), *v.i.,* **-dressed, -dress·ing.** to clothe oneself less completely or formally than is usual or fitting for the circumstances.

un·der·em·ployed (un′dər em ploid′), *adj.* **1.** employed at a job that does not use one's maximum skill, ability, etc. **2.** not utilized fully. —*n.* **3.** workers collectively who are underemployed, as Negroes who cannot find jobs that make full use of their skills, abilities, etc. —**un′der·em·ploy′ment,** *n.*

un·der·es·ti·mate (*v.* un′dər es′tə māt′; *n.* un′dər es′-

un·cul′ti·va·ble, *adj.*
un·cul′ti·vat′ed, *adj.*
un·cul′tured, *adj.*
un·curbed′, *adj.*
un·cured′, *adj.*
un·cu′ri·ous, *adj.*
un·curl′, *v.*
un·cus′tom·ar′y, *adj.*
un·dam′aged, *adj.*
un·dat′ed, *adj.*
un·daugh′ter·ly, *adj.*
un′de·bat′a·ble, *adj.*
un′de·cayed′, *adj.*
un′de·cay′ing, *adj.*
un′de·ci′pher·a·ble, *adj.*
un′de·clared′, *adj.*
un′de·clin′a·ble, *adj.*
un·dec′o·rat′ed, *adj.*
un′de·feat′ed, *adj.*
un′de·fend′ed, *adj.*
un′de·fen′si·ble, *adj.*
un′de·fin′a·ble, *adj.*
un′de·lin′e·at′ed, *adj.*
un′de·liv′er·a·ble, *adj.*
un′de·mand′ing, *adj.*
un′dem·o·crat′ic, *adj.*
un′de·mon′stra·ble, *adj.;* **-bly,** *adv.*
un′de·mon′stra·tive, *adj.*
un′de·nied′, *adj.*
un′de·nom′i·na′tion·al, *adj.*
un′de·pend′a·ble, *adj.*

un′der·cap′tain, *n.*
un′der·clad′, *adj.*
un′der·clerk′, *n.*
un′der·clothed′, *adj.*
un′der·cook′, *v.t.*
un′der·cor·rect′, *v.*
un′der·dose′, *n.*
un′der·dose′, *v.t.,* **-dosed, -dos·ing.**
un′der·eat′, *v.i.,* **-ate, -eat·en, -eat·ing.**
un′der·ed′u·cat′ed, *adj.*

tə mit, -māt′), v., -mat·ed, -mat·ing, n. —v.t. 1. to estimate at too low a value, rate, or the like. —v.i. 2. to make an estimate that is too low. —n. 3. an estimate that is too low. —un′der·es′ti·ma′tion, n.

un·der·ex·pose (un′dər ik spōz′), v.t., -posed, -pos·ing. to expose (a film) to insufficient light or to sufficient light for too short a period.

un·der·ex·po·sure (un′dər ik spō′zhər), n. 1. inadequate exposure, as of photographic film. 2. a photographic negative or print that is imperfect because of insufficient exposure.

un·der·feed (un′dər fēd′ for 1; un′dər fēd′ for 2), v.t., -fed, -feed·ing. 1. to feed insufficiently. 2. to feed with fuel from beneath.

un·der·foot (un′dər fo͝ot′), adv. 1. under the foot or feet; on the ground; underneath or below. —adj. 2. lying under the foot or in a position to be trodden upon. 3. forming an obstruction, as to walking; in the way. [ME *underfot*]

un·der·fur (un′dər fûr′), n. the fine, soft, thick, hairy coat under the longer and coarser outer hair in certain animals, as seals, otters, and beavers.

un·der·gar·ment (un′dər gär′mənt), n. an article of underwear.

un·der·gird (un′dər gûrd′), v.t., -gird·ed or -girt, -gird·ing. 1. to strengthen; secure, as by passing a rope or chain under and around. 2. to give fundamental support to; provide with a sound or secure basis.

un·der·glaze (un′dər glāz′), *Ceram.* —adj. 1. (of a color) applied to a piece before the piece is glazed. —n. 2. color or decoration applied to a piece before it is glazed.

un·der·go (un′dər gō′), v.t., -went, -gone, -go·ing. 1. to be subjected to; experience: *to undergo surgery.* 2. to endure; sustain; suffer: *to undergo sustained deprivation.* [ME *undergon*] —un′der·go′er, n. —Syn. 2. bear, tolerate.

un·der·grad (un′dər grad′), n., adj. *Informal.* an undergraduate. [by shortening]

un·der·grad·u·ate (un′dər graj′o͞o it), n. 1. a student in a university or college who has not taken his first degree. —adj. 2. having the standing of an undergraduate. 3. of, for, or characteristic of undergraduates.

un·der·ground (adv., adj. un′dər ground′; n. un′dər-ground′), adv. 1. beneath the surface of the ground. 2. in concealment or secrecy; not openly. —adj. 3. existing, situated, operating, or taking place beneath the surface of the ground. 4. used, or for use, underground. 5. hidden or secret; not open. 6. *Informal.* a. published or produced to reflect nonconformist or radical views on social, racial, and political problems: *an underground newspaper.* b. avant-garde; experimental: *an underground movie.* c. critical of or attacking the established society or system. d. offbeat or inexpensive: *an underground gourmet.* —n. 7. the place or region beneath the surface of the ground. 8. an underground space or passage. 9. a secret organization fighting the established government or occupation forces. 10. *Chiefly Brit.* subway (def. 1). 11. (*often cap.*) *Informal.* a group identified with or leading avant-garde or radical movements in the arts or in politics.

un′derground rail′road, 1. Also called **un′derground rail′way.** a railroad running through a continuous tunnel, as under city streets; subway. 2. *U.S. Hist.* (before the abolition of slavery) a system of helping fugitive slaves escape to Canada or other places of safety.

un·der·grown (un′dər grōn′, un′dər grōn′), adj. 1. not grown to normal size. 2. having an undergrowth. [ME]

un·der·growth (un′dər grōth′), n. 1. low-lying vegetation or small trees growing beneath or among larger trees; underbrush. 2. the condition of being undergrown or undersized. 3. short, fine hair underlying longer, outer wool or fur.

un·der·hand (un′dər hand′), adj. 1. not open and aboveboard; secret and crafty or dishonorable. 2. executed with the hand below the level of the shoulder and the palm turned upward and forward. —adv. 3. with the hand below the level of the shoulder and the palm turned upward and forward: *to bowl underhand.* 4. secretly; stealthily; slyly. [ME *under hande,* OE *underhand*] —Syn. 1. stealthy, sly.

un·der·hand·ed (un′dər han′did), adj. 1. underhand. 2. short-handed. —un′der·hand′ed·ly, adv. —un′der·hand′ed·ness, n.

un·der·housed (un′dər houzd′), adj. 1. (of a community) not having enough dwellings. 2. (of a family, group, or the like) having inadequate or poor housing.

un·der·hung (un′dər hung′), adj. *Anat.* 1. (of the lower jaw) projecting beyond the upper jaw. 2. having the lower jaw so projecting.

un·der·laid (un′dər lād′), adj. 1. placed or laid underneath, as a foundation or substratum. 2. having an underneath layer (often fol. by *with*): *courtesy underlaid with reserve.* —v. 3. pt. and pp. of **underlay.**

un·der·lap (un′dər lap′), v.t., -lapped, -lap·ping. to extend partly under (something).

un·der·lay (v. un′dər lā′; n. un′dər lā′), v., -laid, -lay·ing, n. —v.t. 1. to place under or beneath. 2. to raise or support with something laid underneath. 3. to extend across the bottom of. —n. 4. something underlaid. 5. *Print.* a piece or pieces of paper put under types or cuts to bring them to the proper height for printing. [ME]

un·der·let (un′dər let′), v.t., -let, -let·ting. 1. to let below the true value. 2. to sublet.

un·der·lie (un′dər lī′), v.t. -lay, -lain, -ly·ing. 1. to lie under or beneath; be situated under. 2. to be at the basis of; form the foundation of. 3. *Gram.* to function as the root morpheme or original or basic form of (a derived form): *The form "boy" underlies "boyish."* 4. *Finance.* to be prior to (another right or security) in order of claim. [ME *underly,* OE *underlicgan*] —un′der·li′er, n.

un·der·line (v. un′dər līn′, un′dər līn′; n. un′dər līn′), v., -lined, -lin·ing, n. —v.t. 1. to mark with a line or lines underneath; underscore. 2. to indicate the importance of; emphasize, as by stressing or italicizing. —n. 3. *Print.* a caption under an illustration. —un·der·lin·e·a·tion (un′dər-lin′ē ā′shən), n.

un·der·ling (un′dər ling), n. a subordinate, esp. one of slight importance. [ME, OE]

un·der·lit (un′dər lit′), adj. lacking adequate light.

un·der·ly·ing (un′dər lī′ing), adj. 1. lying or situated beneath, as a substratum. 2. fundamental; basic. 3. implicit; discoverable only by close scrutiny or analysis. 4. *Finance.* prior to another right or security in order of claim: *underlying mortgage.* —v. 5. ppr. of **underlie.**

un·der·manned (un′dər mand′), adj. lacking a normal or sufficient work force; understaffed; short-handed.

un·der·mine (un′dər mīn′ or, esp. for 2, 3, un′dər mīn′), v.t., -mined, -min·ing. 1. to make an excavation under; dig or tunnel beneath. 2. to weaken or cause to collapse by removing underlying support, as by digging away the foundation. 3. to injure or destroy by secret means or in imperceptible stages. [ME *undermine(n)*] —un′der·min′er, n.

un·der·most (un′dər mōst′), adj., adv. lowest, as in position, status, or the like.

un·der·neath (un′dər nēth′), prep. 1. below the surface or level of, esp. directly or vertically beneath. 2. under the control of; in a lower position than, as in a hierarchy of authority. 3. hidden, disguised, or misrepresented, as by a false appearance. —adv. 4. below; at a lower level or position; on the underside. —adj. 5. lower; situated below or under. —n. 6. the bottom; underside; lowest part. [ME *undernethe,* OE *underneoth(an).* See UNDER, BENEATH]

un·der·nour·ish (un′dər nûr′ish, -nur′-), v.t. to furnish with less than the food requirements for good health or normal development. —un′der·nour′ish·ment, n.

un·der·pants (un′dər pants′), n.pl. drawers or shorts worn under outer clothing, usually next to the skin.

un·der·part (un′dər pärt′), n. 1. the lower part or side, as of an animal, object, etc. 2. an auxiliary or secondary part or role.

un·der·pass (un′dər pas′, -päs′), n. a passage running underneath, esp. a passage for pedestrians or vehicles, crossing under a railroad, road, etc.

un·der·pay (un′dər pā′), v.t., -paid, -pay·ing. to pay less than is usual or deserved. —un′der·pay′ment, n.

un·der·pin (un′dər pin′), v.t., -pinned, -pin·ning. 1. to prop up or support from below; strengthen, as by reinforcing a foundation. 2. to replace or strengthen the foundation of (a building or the like). 3. to furnish a foundation for; corroborate.

un·der·pin·ning (un′dər pin′ing), n. 1. a system of supports beneath a wall or the like. 2. **underpinnings,** *Informal.* a. the legs. b. underwear, esp. women's underwear.

un′der·pitch vault′ (un′dər pich′), a construction having a central vault intersected by vaults of lower pitch. See illus. at **vault**[1].

un·der·play (un′der plā′, un′dər plā′), v.t. 1. to act (a part) subtly and with restraint. —v.i. 2. to achieve an effect in acting with a minimum of emphasis.

un·der·plot (un′dər plot′), n. subplot.

un·der·price (un′dər prīs′), v.t., -priced, -pric·ing. 1. to price (goods or services) lower than the standard price or fair value. 2. to undercut (a competitor) by underselling him or setting prices below actual cost.

un·der·priv·i·leged (un′dər priv′ə lijd, -priv′lijd), adj. denied the enjoyment of the normal privileges or rights of a society because of low economic and social status.

un·der·proof (un′dər pro͞of′), adj. containing a smaller proportion of alcohol than proof spirit.

un·der·prop (un′dər prop′), v.t., -propped, -prop·ping. to prop underneath; support; uphold. —un′der·prop′per, n.

un·der·quote (un′dər kwōt′), v.t., -quot·ed, -quot·ing. 1. to offer (goods or services) at a price lower than the market price or some other quoted price; offer at a price reduced by (a specified amount). 2. to quote a price lower than that of (a specified competitor).

un·der·rate (un′dər rāt′), v.t., -rat·ed, -rat·ing. to rate too low; underestimate.

un·der·ripe (un′dər rīp′), adj. not completely ripe.

un·der·run (un′dər run′), v., -ran, -run, -run·ning, n. —v.t. 1. to run, pass, or go under. 2. *Naut.* a. to pass beneath (a stretched rope, net, etc.) in a boat or the like for the purpose of inspection or repairs. b. to lay out (tackle) in proper order and readiness. —n. 3. something that runs or passes underneath, as a current.

un·der·score (v. un′dər skôr′, -skōr′; n. un′dər skôr′, -skōr′), v., -scored, -scor·ing, n. —v.t. 1. to mark with a line or lines underneath; underline, as for emphasis. 2. to stress; emphasize. —n. 3. a line drawn beneath something written or printed. 4. background music for a film or stage production.

un·der·sea (un′dər sē′), adj. 1. located, carried on, or designed for use under the surface of the sea. —adv. 2. underseas.

un·der·seas (un′dər sēz′), adv. beneath the surface of the sea.

un·der·sec·re·tar·i·at (un′dər sek′ri târ′ē ət, un′dər-sek′rə ter′-), n. a department or section of a ministry of which an undersecretary is in charge.

un·der·sec·re·tar·y (un′dər sek′ri ter′ē), n., pl. -tar·ies. a secretary subordinate to a principal secretary. Also, **un′der sec′re·tar′y.**

un·der·sell (un′dər sel′), v.t., -sold, -sell·ing. 1. to sell merchandise more cheaply than. 2. to advertise (something) with restraint; understate the merits of, as of merchandise offered to a prospective purchaser. —un′der·sell′er, n.

un·der·set (un′dər set′), n. a current of water below the surface and flowing in a direction contrary to the water on the surface. [ME *undersett(en)*]

un′der·fi·nance′, v.t., -nanced, -nanc·ing.
un′der·fur′nished, adj.
un′der·glow′, n.
un′der·lay′er, n.
un′der·lip′, n.
un′der·men′tioned, adj.
un′der·named′, adj.
un′der·of′fi·cer, n.
un′der·of·fi′cial, n.
un′der·peo′pled, adj.
un′der·pop′u·lat′ed, adj.
un′der·pop′u·la′tion, n.
un′der·pow′ered, adj.
un′der·praise′, v.t.
un′der·pro·duce′, v.i., -duced, -duc·ing.
un′der·pro·duc′tion, n.
un′der·ri′pened, adj.
un′der·serv′ant, n.

un·der·sher·iff (un′dər sher′if), *n.* a sheriff's deputy, esp. a deputy on whom the sheriff's duties devolve when the office is vacant. [late ME] —**un′der·sher′iff·ship′,** *n.*

un·der·shirt (un′dər shûrt′), *n.* a collarless undergarment, usually of cotton and either sleeveless and low-cut or with sleeves, worn chiefly by men and children.

un·der·shoot (un′dər shōōt′, un′dər shōōt′), *v.*, **-shot, -shoot·ing.** —*v.t.* **1.** to shoot or launch a projectile that strikes under or short of (a target). **2.** *Aeron.* (of an aircraft or pilot) to land short of (a landing strip) because of a too rapid loss of altitude. —*v.i.* **3.** to shoot or launch a projectile so as to strike under or short of a target.

un·der·shorts (un′dər shôrts′), *n.pl.* short underpants for men and boys.

un·der·shot (un′dər shot′), *adj.* **1.** having the front teeth of the lower jaw projecting in front of the upper teeth, as a bulldog. **2.** driven by water passing beneath: *an undershot vertical water wheel.* —*v.* **3.** pt. and pp. of **undershoot.**

un′dershot wheel′, a water wheel on a horizontal axis turned by the force of water passing beneath it.

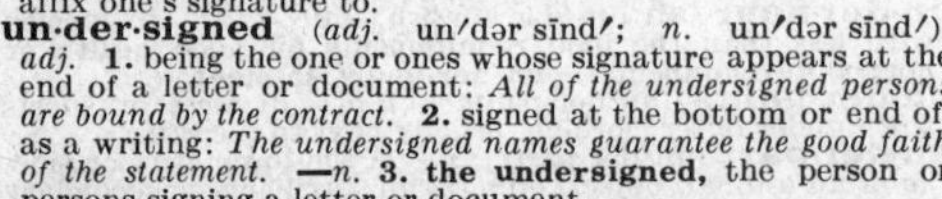
Undershot wheel

un·der·shrub (un′dər shrub′), *n.* a low shrub.

un·der·side (un′dər sīd′), *n.* an under or lower side.

un·der·sign (un′dər sīn′, un′dər-sīn′), *v.t.* to sign one's name under or at the end of (a letter or document); affix one's signature to.

un·der·signed (*adj.* un′dər sīnd′; *n.* un′dər sīnd′), *adj.* **1.** being the one or ones whose signature appears at the end of a letter or document: *All of the undersigned persons are bound by the contract.* **2.** signed at the bottom or end of, as a writing: *The undersigned names guarantee the good faith of the statement.* —*n.* **3. the undersigned,** the person or persons signing a letter or document.

un·der·sized (un′dər sīzd′), *adj.* smaller than the usual or normal size.

un·der·skirt (un′dər skûrt′), *n.* a skirt, as a petticoat, worn under another skirt or a dress.

un·der·slung (un′dər slung′), *adj.* **1.** suspended from an upper support, as the chassis of a vehicle from the axles. **2.** supported from above; placed or suspended below the source of support. **3.** more massive at the bottom than the top; squat.

un·der·soil (un′dər soil′), *n.* subsoil.

un·der·spin (un′dər spin′), *n.* backspin.

un·der·staffed (un′dər staft′, -stäft′), *adj.* having an insufficient number of personnel: *The hospital is understaffed.*

un·der·stand (un′dər stand′), *v.*, **-stood, -stand·ing.** —*v.t.* **1.** to perceive the meaning of; grasp the idea of; comprehend: *to understand Spanish.* **2.** to be thoroughly familiar with; apprehend clearly the character, nature, or subtleties of: *to understand a trade; to understand a poem.* **3.** to assign a meaning to; interpret: *He understood her suggestion as a complaint.* **4.** to grasp the significance or importance of. **5.** to regard as firmly communicated; take as agreed or settled: *I understand that you will repay this loan in 30 days.* **6.** to learn or hear: *I understand that you are going out of town.* **7.** to accept as true; believe. **8.** to construe in a particular way: *You are to understand the phrase literally.* **9.** to supply mentally (something that is not expressed). —*v.i.* **10.** to perceive what is meant; grasp the information conveyed. **11.** to accept tolerantly or sympathetically: *If you cannot do it, I will understand.* **12.** to have knowledge or background, as on a particular subject: *He understands about boats.* **13.** to have a systematic interpretation or rationale, as in a field or area of knowledge. [ME; OE *understond(an)*; c. D *onderstaan*] —**Syn. 1.** See **know.**

un·der·stand·a·ble (un′dər stan′də bəl), *adj.* capable of being understood; comprehensible. —**un′der·stand′a·ble·ness, un′der·stand′a·bil′i·ty,** *n.* —**un′der·stand′a·bly,** *adv.*

un·der·stand·ing (un′dər stan′ding), *n.* **1.** the mental process of a person who comprehends; comprehension; personal interpretation: *His understanding is unequal to the task. My understanding of the word does not agree with yours.* **2.** intellectual faculties; intelligence; mind: *a quick understanding.* **3.** superior power of discernment; enlightened intelligence. **4.** knowledge of or familiarity with a particular thing; skill in dealing with or handling something. **5.** a state of cooperative or mutually tolerant relations between people. **6.** a mutual agreement, esp. of a private, unannounced, or tacit kind. **7.** an agreement regulating joint activity or settling differences, often informal or preliminary in character. **8.** *Philos.* the power of abstract thought; logical power. —*adj.* **9.** characterized by understanding; prompted by, based on, or demonstrating comprehension, intelligence, discernment, empathy, or the like. [ME *understandynge*, OE *understandincge* (n.). See UNDERSTAND, -ING[1], -ING[2]] —**un′der·stand′ing·ly,** *adv.* —**un′der·stand′ing·ness,** *n.*

un·der·state (un′dər stāt′), *v.t.*, **-stat·ed, -stat·ing.** to state or represent less strongly or strikingly than the facts would bear out; set forth in restrained, moderate, or weak terms. —**un′der·state′ment,** *n.*

un·der·stood (un′dər stŏŏd′), *v.* **1.** pt. and pp. of **understand.** —*adj.* **2.** agreed upon; assented to. **3.** implied but not stated; left unexpressed.

un·der·stra·tum (un′dər strā′təm, -strat′əm), *n.*, *pl.* **-stra·ta** (-strā′tə, -strat′ə), **-strat·ums.** a substratum.

un·der·stud·y (un′dər stud′ē), *v.*, **-stud·ied, -stud·y·ing,** *n.*, *pl.* **-stud·ies.** —*v.t.* **1.** to study (a part) in order to replace the regular actor or actress when necessary. **2.** to act as understudy to (an actor or actress). —*n.* **3.** a person trained and retained to act as substitute for an actor or actress.

un·der·take (un′dər tāk′), *v.*, **-took, -tak·en, -tak·ing.** —*v.t.* **1.** to take on oneself, as a task or performance. **2.** to promise, agree, or obligate oneself to perform a task, duty, or the like. **3.** to warrant or guarantee (fol. by a clause): *The sponsors undertake that the proposal meets all the legal requirements.* **4.** to take in charge; assume the duty of attending to. **5.** *Obs.* to engage with, as in a duel. —*v.i.* **6.** *Archaic.* to take on oneself any task or responsibility. **7.** *Archaic.* to engage oneself by promise; give a guarantee, or become surety. [ME]

un·der·tak·er (un′dər tā′kər *for 1;* un′dər tā′kər *for 2*), *n.* **1.** a person who undertakes something. **2.** Also called **mortician.** a person whose business it is to prepare the dead for burial and to arrange funerals. [ME]

un·der·tak·ing (un′dər tā′king *for 1–3;* un′dər tā′king *for 4*), *n.* **1.** the act of a person who undertakes any task or responsibility. **2.** a task, enterprise, etc., undertaken. **3.** a promise; pledge; guarantee. **4.** the business of an undertaker or funeral director. [ME]

un·der-the-coun·ter (un′dər thə koun′tər), *adj.* **1.** (of merchandise) sold clandestinely. **2.** illegal; unauthorized: *under-the-counter payments.*

un·der-the-ta·ble (un′dər thə tā′bəl), *adj.* transacted in secret or in an underhanded manner.

un·der·things (un′dər thingz′), *n.pl.* women's underclothes.

un·der·thrust (un′dər thrust′), *n.* *Geol.* a thrust fault in which the footwall was the one that moved (opposed to *overthrust*).

un·der·tint (un′dər tint′), *n.* a subdued tint.

un·der·tone (un′dər tōn′), *n.* **1.** a low or subdued tone, as of a voice. **2.** an underlying quality or element; undercurrent. **3.** a subdued color; a color modified by an underlying color.

un·der·took (un′dər tŏŏk′), *v.* pt. of **undertake.**

un·der·tow (un′dər tō′), *n.* **1.** the seaward, subsurface flow or draft of water from waves breaking on a beach. **2.** any strong current below the surface of a body of water, moving in a direction different from that of the surface current.

un·der·trick (un′dər trik′), *n.* *Bridge.* a trick that a declarer failed to win as part of his contract. Cf. **overtrick.**

un·der·trump (un′dər trump′), *v.t., v.i.* *Cards.* to trump with a lower trump than has already been played.

un·der·vest (un′dər vest′), *n.* *Brit.* an undershirt.

un·der·waist (un′dər wāst′), *n.* a blouse worn under another.

un·der·wa·ter (un′dər wô′tər, -wot′ər), *adj.* **1.** existing or occurring under water. **2.** designed to be used under water. **3.** located below a ship's waterline. —*adv.* **4.** beneath the water.

un·der·wear (un′dər wâr′), *n.* clothing worn next to the skin under outer clothes. Also called **underclothing.**

un·der·weight (*n.* un′dər wāt′; *adj.* un′dər wāt′), *n.* **1.** deficiency in weight below a standard or requirement. —*adj.* **2.** lacking the usual, required, or proper weight.

un·der·went (un′dər went′), *v.* pt. of **undergo.**

un·der·wing (un′dər wing′), *n.* one of the hind wings of an insect.

un·der·wood (un′dər wŏŏd′), *n.* **1.** woody shrubs or small trees growing among taller trees. **2.** a clump or stretch of such growth. [ME *underwode*]

un·der·world (un′dər wûrld′), *n.* **1.** the criminal element of human society. **2.** the imagined abode of departed souls or spirits; Hades. **3.** a region below the surface, as of the earth or a body of water. **4.** the opposite side of the earth; the antipodes. **5.** *Archaic.* the earth.

un·der·write (un′dər rīt′), *v.*, **-wrote, -writ·ten, -writ·ing.** —*v.t.* **1.** to write under or at the foot of, esp. under other written matter. **2.** to sign one's name, as to a document. **3.** to concur with (a statement, decision, testimony, etc.) by or as by signing one's name to it. **4.** to bind oneself to support (an undertaking) with money. **5.** to guarantee the sale of (a security issue to be offered to the public for subscription). **6.** *Insurance.* **a.** to write one's name at the end of (a policy), thereby becoming liable in case of certain losses specified in the policy. **b.** to insure. **c.** to assume liability to the extent of (a specified sum) by way of insurance. —*v.i.* **7.** to underwrite something. **8.** to carry on the business of an underwriter. [late ME, trans. of L *subscrībere* to write underneath, sign, subscribe. See SUBSCRIBE]

un·der·writ·er (un′dər rī′tər), *n.* **1.** a person who underwrites insurance policies or carries on insurance as a business. **2.** a person who underwrites an issue or issues of securities.

un·de·served (un′di zûrvd′), *adj.* unjustified; not merited: *undeserved praise.* —**un·de·serv·ed·ly** (un′di zûr′vid lē), *adv.*

un·de·serv·ing (un′di zûr′ving), *adj.* unqualified for a reward, assistance, or the like, because of one's actions or qualities: *undeserving of praise.* —**un′de·serv′ing·ly,** *adv.*

un·de·sign·ing (un′di zī′ning), *adj.* not characterized by underhand schemes; without an ulterior design. —**un′de·sign′ing·ly,** *adv.*

un·de·sir·a·ble (un′di zīər′ə bəl), *adj.* **1.** not desirable or attractive; objectionable. —*n.* **2.** a person or thing that is undesirable. **3.** a person of doubtful or negative value to a group or to society in general. —**un′de·sir′a·bly,** *adv.*

undesir′able dis′charge, *U.S.* a discharge under other than honorable conditions of a person from military service by administrative action.

un·did (un did′), *v.* pt. of **undo.**

un·dies (un′dēz), *n.pl.* women's or children's underwear. [shortening and alter. of UNDERWEAR]

un′de·scrib′a·ble, *adj.;* **-bly,** *adv.*
un′de·sired′, *adj.*
un′de·sir′ous, *adj.*
un′de·spair′ing, *adj.;* **-ly,** *adv.*
un′de·stroyed′, *adj.*
un′de·tach′a·ble, *adj.*
un′de·tached′, *adj.*
un′de·tec′ted, *adj.*
un′de·ter′mi·na·ble, *adj.*
un′de·ter′mined, *adj.*
un′de·terred′, *adj.*
un′de·vel′oped, *adj.*
un·de′vi·at′ing, *adj.*
un′di·ag·nosed′, *adj.*

un′der·spend′, *v.*, **-spent, -spend·ing.**
un′der·stock′, *v.t.*
un′der·sup·ply′, *v.t.*, **-plied, -ply·ing;** *n.*
un′der·sur′face, *n.*
un′der·trained′, *adj.*
un′der·val′ue, *v.t.*, **-ued, -u·ing.**
un′der·wave′, *n.*
un′der·wind′, *v.t.*, **-wound, -wind·ing.**

un·dine (un dēn′, un′dēn, -dīn), *n.* one of a group of female water spirits. According to Paracelsus, when an undine married a mortal and bore a child, she received a soul. [< NL *undina* (coined by Paracelsus) = L *und(a)* wave, water + *-īna* -INE[1]] **—Syn.** See **sylph.**

un·di·rect·ed (un′di rek′tid, -dī-), *adj.* **1.** not directed; not guided. **2.** bearing no address, as a letter.

un·dis·posed (un′di spōzd′), *adj.* **1.** not disposed of. **2.** not favorably inclined; not prepared; unwilling. [ME]

un·dis·so·ci·at·ed (un′di sō′shē ā′tid, -sē ā′-), *adj. Chem.* not dissociated, esp. into ions or into simpler molecules.

un·dis·tin·guished (un′di sting′gwisht), *adj.* **1.** without any claim to distinction. **2.** unnoticed; inconspicuous.

un·do (un dōō′), *v.t.*, **-did, -done, -do·ing. 1.** to reverse the effect of; cause to be as if never done. **2.** to do away with; erase; efface. **3.** to bring to ruin or disaster; destroy. **4.** to unfasten, loosen, or open. **5.** *Archaic.* to explain; interpret. [ME; OE *undōn;* c. D *ontdoen*]

un·do·ing (un dōō′ing), *n.* **1.** the reversing of what has been done; annulling. **2.** a bringing to destruction, ruin, or disaster. **3.** a cause of destruction or ruin. **4.** act of unfastening, loosing, or opening. [ME]

un·done[1] (un dun′), *adj.* not done; not accomplished or completed. [ME *un-dun.* See UN-[1], DONE]

un·done[2] (un dun′), *v.* **1.** pp. of **undo.** **—***adj.* **2.** brought to destruction or ruin. **3.** unfastened.

un·doubt·ed (un dou′tid), *adj.* not doubted or disputed; accepted as beyond doubt. [ME] **—un·doubt′ed·ly,** *adv.*

un·draw (un drô′), *v.*, **-drew, -drawn, -draw·ing.** **—***v.t.* **1.** to draw open or aside. **—***v.i.* **2.** to be drawn open or aside. [ME: to withdraw]

un·dress (un dres′), *v.*, **-dressed** or **-drest, -dress·ing,** *n., adj.* **—***v.t.* **1.** to take the clothes off (a person); disrobe. **2.** to strip or divest of or as of a covering; expose. **3.** to remove the dressing from (a wound, sore, etc.). **—***v.i.* **4.** to take off one's clothes. **—***n.* **5.** dress of a style designed to be worn on other than highly formal or ceremonial occasions; informal dress, as opposed to full dress. **6.** dress of a style not designed to be worn in public; dishabille; negligée. **—***adj.* **7.** of or pertaining to clothing of a style less formal than full dress: *undress uniform.*

un·dressed (un drest′), *adj.* **1.** not dressed; not specially prepared. **2.** (of leather) having a napped finish on the flesh side. [ME]

Und·set (ōōn′set), *n.* **Sig·rid** (sig′rid; *Nor.* si′grI), 1882–1949, Norwegian novelist: Nobel prize 1928.

un·due (un dōō′, -dyōō′), *adj.* **1.** unwarranted; excessive. **2.** inappropriate; unjustifiable; improper. **3.** not owed or currently payable. [ME *undewe*]

un·du·lant (un′jə lənt, un′dyə-, -də-), *adj.* undulating; characterized by a wavelike motion or pattern. [UNDUL(ATE) + -ANT] **—un′du·lance,** *n.*

un′dulant fe′ver, *Pathol.* brucellosis.

un·du·late (*v.* un′jə lāt′, un′dyə-, -də-; *adj.* un′jə lit, -lāt′, un′dyə-, -də-), *v.*, **-lat·ed, -lat·ing,** *adj.* **—***v.i.* **1.** to move with a sinuous or wavelike motion. **2.** to have a wavy form or surface. **—***v.t.* **3.** to cause to move in waves. **4.** to give a wavy form to. **—***adj.* **5.** Also, **un′du·lat′ed.** having a wavelike or rippled form, surface, edge, etc.; wavy. [< L *undulāt(us)* waved = *undul(a)* (dim. of *unda* wave) + *-ātus* -ATE[1]] **—un′du·la′tor,** *n.*

un·du·la·tion (un′jə lā′shən, un′dyə-, -də-), *n.* **1.** the act of undulating; a wavelike motion. **2.** a wavy form or outline. **3.** one of a series of wavelike bends, curves, or elevations. **4.** *Physics.* **a.** a wave. **b.** the motion of waves.

un·du·la·to·ry (un′jə lə tōr′ē, -tôr′ē, un′dyə-, -də-), *adj.* **1.** Also, **un′du·lar.** moving in undulations. **2.** having the form or appearance of waves. Also, **un·du·la·tive** (un′jə lā′tiv, un′dyə-, -də-).

un′dulatory the′ory, *Physics.* See **wave theory.**

un·du·ly (un dōō′lē, -dyōō′-), *adv.* **1.** excessively. **2.** in an inappropriate, unjustifiable, or improper manner. [ME *undewely.* See UNDUE, -LY]

un·dy·ing (un dī′ing), *adj.* deathless; immortal; unending. [ME] **—un·dy′ing·ly,** *adv.*

un·earned (un ûrnd′), *adj.* **1.** not received in exchange for labor or services; not gained by lawful work or employment. **2.** not earned; unmerited; undeserved.

un′earned in′come, income received from property, as interest, dividends, or the like.

un′earned in′crement, the increase in the value of property, esp. land, due to causes other than labor or expenditure by the owner.

un·earth (un ûrth′), *v.t.* **1.** to dig or get out of the earth; dig up. **2.** to uncover or bring to light by search, inquiry, etc. [ME *unerth(en)*]

un·earth·ly (un ûrth′lē), *adj.* **1.** seeming not to belong to this world. **2.** supernatural; ghostly. **3.** absurdly peculiar. **—un·earth′li·ness,** *n.* **—Syn. 2.** preternatural, spectral. See **weird.**

un·eas·y (un ē′zē), *adj.*, **-eas·i·er, -eas·i·est. 1.** not easy in body or mind; restless. **2.** not easy in manner; constrained. **3.** not conducive to ease. [ME *unesy*] **—un·ease′,** *n.* **—un·eas′i·ly,** *adv.* **—un·eas′i·ness,** *n.*

UNEF, United Nations Emergency Force.

un·em·ploy·a·ble (un′em ploi′ə bəl), *adj.* **1.** unacceptable or unsuitable for employment. **—***n.* **2.** an unemployable individual.

un·em·ployed (un′em ploid′), *adj.* **1.** not employed; without a job; out of work. **2.** not currently in use. **3.** not productively used. **—***n.* **4. the unemployed,** persons who do not have jobs. **—Syn. 1.** unoccupied, idle, jobless.

un·em·ploy·ment (un′em ploi′mənt), *n.* the state of being unemployed, esp. involuntarily.

unemploy′ment compensa′tion, *U.S.* an allowance of money, fixed in amount and duration by statute, paid to an unemployed working person by a government agency.

un·e·qual (un ē′kwəl), *adj.* **1.** (of two or more persons or things) not equal in some respect. **2.** not adequate, as in amount, power, ability, etc. (usually fol. by *to*): *strength unequal to a task.* **3.** not evenly proportioned or balanced; not having the parts alike or symmetrical. **4.** uneven or variable. **5.** inequitable; unfair; unjust. **—un·e′qual·ly,** *adv.*

un·e·qualed (un ē′kwəld), *adj.* not equaled; supreme; matchless. Also, *esp. Brit.*, **un·e′qualled.** **—Syn.** peerless, unrivaled, inimitable, incomparable.

un·e·quiv·o·cal (un′i kwiv′ə kəl), *adj.* not equivocal; unambiguous; clear; having only one possible meaning or interpretation. **—un′e·quiv′o·cal·ly,** *adv.* **—un′e·quiv′o·cal·ness,** *n.* **—Syn.** obvious, explicit, unmistakable.

un·err·ing (un ûr′ing, -er′-), *adj.* **1.** not erring; not going astray or missing the mark. **2.** undeviatingly accurate. **3.** unfailingly right or appropriate. **—un·err′ing·ly,** *adv.* **—un·err′ing·ness,** *n.* **—Syn. 2, 3.** infallible.

UNESCO (yōō nes′kō), *n.* an agency of the United Nations charged with administering programs for coordinated action in education, science, and the arts. [*U(nited) N(ations) E(ducational), S(cientific, and) C(ultural) O(rganization)*]

un·es·sen·tial (un′ə sen′shəl), *adj.* **1.** not of prime importance; not indispensable. **—***n.* **2.** an unessential thing; nonessential. **—un′es·sen′tial·ly,** *adv.* **—Syn. 1.** unnecessary, dispensable, unimportant.

un·e·ven (un ē′vən), *adj.* **1.** not level or flat; rough; rugged. **2.** irregular; varying; not uniform. **3.** not equitable or fair; one-sided: *an uneven contest.* **4.** not equally balanced or symmetrical. **5.** (of a number) odd; not divisible into two equal integers: *The number 3 is uneven.* [ME; OE *unefen;* c. G *uneben*] **—un·e′ven·ly,** *adv.* **—un·e′ven·ness,** *n.*

un·e·vent·ful (un′i vent′fəl), *adj.* not eventful; placid, routine, or ordinary. **—un′e·vent′ful·ly,** *adv.* **—un′e·vent′ful·ness,** *n.*

un·ex·am·pled (un′ig zam′pəld, -zäm′-), *adj.* unprecedented; unparalleled; unlike anything previously known.

un·ex·cep·tion·a·ble (un′ik sep′shə nə bəl), *adj.* not offering any basis for exception or objection; beyond criticism. **—un′ex·cep′tion·a·ble·ness, un′ex·cep′tion·a·bil′i·ty,** *n.* **—un′ex·cep′tion·a·bly,** *adv.*

un·ex·cep·tion·al (un′ik sep′shə nəl), *adj.* **1.** not exceptional; commonplace or ordinary. **2.** admitting of no exception to the general rule. **3.** unexceptionable. **—un′ex·cep′tion·al·ly,** *adv.*

un·ex·pect·ed (un′ik spek′tid), *adj.* not expected; unforeseen; surprising. **—un′ex·pect′ed·ly,** *adv.* **—un′ex·pect′ed·ness,** *n.* **—Syn.** unanticipated. See **sudden.**

un·ex·pend·a·ble (un′ik spen′də bəl), *adj.* **1.** essential; absolutely required. **2.** not capable of being expended; in-

un′dif·fer·en′ti·at′ed, *adj.*
un′dif·fused′, *adj.*
un′di·gest′ed, *adj.*
un·dig′ni·fied′, *adj.*
un′di·lut′ed, *adj.*
un′di·min′ished, *adj.*
un·dimmed′, *adj.*
un′dip·lo·mat′ic, *adj.*
un′dis·bursed′, *adj.*
un′dis·cerned′, *adj.*
un′dis·cern′i·ble, *adj.;* **-bly,** *adv.*
un′dis·cern′ing, *adj.*
un′dis·charged′, *adj.*
un·dis′ci·plined, *adj.*
un′dis·closed′, *adj.*
un′dis·cour′aged, *adj.*
un′dis·cov′er·a·ble, *adj.*
un′dis·cov′ered, *adj.*
un′dis·crim′i·nat′ing, *adj.;* **-ly,** *adv.*
un′dis·guised′, *adj.*
un′dis·mayed′, *adj.*
un′dis·pelled′, *adj.*
un′dis·played′, *adj.*
un′dis·proved′, *adj.*
un′dis·put′a·ble, *adj.*
un′dis·put′ed, *adj.*
un′dis·solved′, *adj.*
un′dis·tilled′, *adj.*
un′dis·tin′guish·a·ble, *adj.*
un′dis·tin′guish·ing, *adj.;* **-ly,** *adv.*
un′dis·tressed′, *adj.*
un′dis·trib′ut·ed, *adj.*
un′dis·turbed′, *adj.*
un′di·ver′si·fied′, *adj.*
un′di·vid′ed, *adj.*
un′di·vulged′, *adj.*
un·doc′u·ment·ed, *adj.*
un′dog·mat′ic, *adj.*
un′do·mes′ti·cat′ed, *adj.*
un·doubt′a·ble, *adj.*
un·doubt′ing, *adj.*
un·drained′, *adj.*
un′dra·mat′ic, *adj.*
un·drape′, *v.t.*, **-draped, -drap·ing.**
un·dreamed′, *adj.*
un·dreamt′, *adj.*
un·drink′a·ble, *adj.*
un·du′ti·ful, *adj.*
un·dyed′, *adj.*
un·eat′a·ble, *adj.*
un·eat′en, *adj.*
un′e·co·nom′ic, *adj.*
un′e·co·nom′i·cal, *adj.;* **-ly,** *adv.*
un·ed′i·ble, *adj.*
un·ed′i·fy′ing, *adj.*
un·ed′u·ca·ble, *adj.*
un·ed′u·cat′ed, *adj.*
un′e·man′ci·pat′ed, *adj.*
un′em·bar′rassed, *adj.*
un′em·bel′lished, *adj.*
un′e·mo′tion·al, *adj.*
un′em·phat′ic, *adj.*
un·emp′tied, *adj.*
un′en·closed′, *adj.*
un′en·cum′bered, *adj.*
un′en·dan′gered, *adj.*
un·end′ed, *adj.*
un·end′ing, *adj.;* **-ly,** *adv.*
un′en·dorsed′, *adj.*
un′en·dowed′, *adj.*
un′en·dur′a·ble, *adj.;* **-bly,** *adv.*
un′en·dur′ing, *adj.*
un′en·forced′, *adj.*
un′en·gaged′, *adj.*
un′en·joy′a·ble, *adj.*
un′en·joyed′, *adj.*
un′en·light′ened, *adj.*
un′en·light′en·ing, *adj.*
un′en·riched′, *adj.*
un′en·rolled′, *adj.*
un′en·slaved′, *adj.*
un′en·sured′, *adj.*
un′en·tan′gled, *adj.*
un·en′tered, *adj.*
un·en′ter·pris′ing, *adj.*
un′en·ter·tain′ing, *adj.*
un′en·thu′si·as′tic, *adj.*
un′en·thu′si·as′ti·cal·ly, *adv.*
un·en′vi·a·ble, *adj.*
un·en′vied, *adj.*
un·en′vi·ous, *adj.;* **-ly,** *adv.*
un·en′vy·ing, *adj.;* **-ly,** *adv.*
un′e·quipped′, *adj.*
un′e·rased′, *adj.*
un′es·cap′a·ble, *adj.;* **-bly,** *adv.*
un′es·cort′ed, *adj.*
un′es·sayed′, *adj.*
un′es·tab′lished, *adj.*
un·es·thet′ic, *adj.*
un·es′ti·mat′ed, *adj.*
un·eth′i·cal, *adj.;* **-ly,** *adv.*
un′e·vad′ed, *adj.*
un′ex·act′ing, *adj.;* **-ly,** *adv.*
un′ex·ag′ger·at′ed, *adj.*
un′ex·alt′ed, *adj.*
un·ex′ca·vat′ed, *adj.*
un′ex·ceed′ed, *adj.*
un′ex·celled′, *adj.*
un′ex·change′a·ble, *adj.*
un′ex·cit′ed, *adj.*
un′ex·cit′ing, *adj.*
un′ex·cus′a·ble, *adj.;* **-bly,** *adv.*
un′ex·cused′, *adj.*
un·ex′e·cut′ed, *adj.*
un·ex′er·cised′, *adj.*
un′ex·haust′ed, *adj.;* **-ly,** *adv.*

exhaustible. **3.** not available for expenditure. —**un′ex·pend′a·ble·ness,** *n.* —**un′ex·pend′a·bly,** *adv.*

un·ex·pressed (un′ik sprest′), *adj.* **1.** not expressed; not indicated or communicated, as in words, intimations, or the like: *an unexpressed desire.* **2.** tacit; understood without explicit statement: *an unexpressed agreement.*

un·fail·ing (un fā′ling), *adj.* **1.** not failing; completely dependable. **2.** inexhaustible; endless, as resources or a supply. [ME] —**un·fail′ing·ly,** *adv.* —**un·fail′ing·ness,** *n.*

un·fair (un fâr′), *adj.* **1.** not fair; not conforming to approved standards of ethics or the like. **2.** disproportionate; undue: *an unfair advantage.* [ME; OE *unfæger;* c. OIcel *ūfagr*] —**un·fair′ly,** *adv.* —**un·fair′ness,** *n.*

un·faith·ful (un fāth′fəl), *adj.* **1.** not faithful; false to duty, obligation, or promises; faithless; disloyal. **2.** guilty of adultery. **3.** not accurate or complete; inexact. **4.** *Obs.* unbelieving; infidel. [ME *unfeithful*] —**un·faith′ful·ly,** *adv.* —**un·faith′ful·ness,** *n.* —**Syn. 1.** deceitful, treacherous.

un·fa·mil·iar (un′fə mil′yər), *adj.* **1.** not familiar; not acquainted or conversant. **2.** unaccustomed; unusual. —**un·fa·mil·i·ar·i·ty** (un′fə mil′ē ar′i tē), *n.* —**un′fa·mil′iar·ly,** *adv.*

un·fas·ten (un fas′ən, -fä′sən), *v.t.* **1.** to release from or as from fastenings; detach. **2.** to undo or open (something fastened). —*v.i.* **3.** to become unfastened. [ME *unfastne(n)*]

un·fa·thered (un fä′thərd), *adj.* **1.** having no father; fatherless. **2.** of illegitimate or unknown paternity; bastard. **3.** not ascribable to a particular author or source: *unfathered tales.*

un·fa·vor·a·ble (un fā′vər ə bəl), *adj.* **1.** not favorable; disadvantageous. **2.** inauspicious. Also, *esp. Brit.,* **un·fa′vour·a·ble.** [ME] —**un·fa′vor·a·bly;** *esp. Brit.,* **un·fa′vour·a·bly,** *adv.*

Unfed′erated Ma′lay States′, a former group of five native states in the Malay Peninsula, under indirect British control and forming a part of the former Federation of Malaya: now part of the federation of Malaysia. 24,347 sq. mi.

un·feel·ing (un fē′ling), *adj.* **1.** not feeling; insensible or insensate. **2.** unsympathetic; callous. [ME; OE *unfelende*] —**un·feel′ing·ly,** *adv.* —**un·feel′ing·ness,** *n.* —**Syn. 1.** numb. **2.** hard-hearted. See **hard.** —**Ant. 2.** sympathetic.

un·feigned (un fānd′), *adj.* not feigned; sincere; genuine. [ME *unfeynid*] —**un·feign·ed·ly** (un fā′nid lē), *adv.*

un·fet·ter (un fet′ər), *v.t.* **1.** to release from fetters. **2.** to free from restraint; liberate. [ME *unfeteren*]

un·fil·i·al (un fil′ē əl), *adj.* not befitting a son or daughter; violating the customary duty or obligation of a child to a parent. —**un·fil′i·al·ly,** *adv.*

un·fin·ished (un fin′isht), *adj.* **1.** not finished; incomplete or unaccomplished. **2.** lacking some special finish or surface treatment, as polish, paint, etc. **3.** (of cloth) not sheared following the looming process.

unfin′ished wor′sted, men's suiting of worsted yarns, given a slight nap.

un·fit (un fit′), *adj., v.,* **-fit** or **-fit·ted; -fit·ting.** —*adj.* **1.** not adapted or suited; unsuitable. **2.** unqualified or incompetent. **3.** not in a physically fit condition. —*v.t.* **4.** to render unfit or unsuitable; disqualify. —**un·fit′ly,** *adv.* —**un·fit′ness,** *n.* —**Syn. 1.** inappropriate, unapt. **2.** incapable.

un·fix (un fiks′), *v.t.,* **-fixed** or **-fixt, -fix·ing. 1.** to render no longer fixed; unfasten. **2.** to unsettle, as the mind, habits, etc.

un·flap·pa·ble (un flap′ə bəl), *adj. Slang.* not easily upset or confused, esp. in a crisis; imperturbable. [UN-[1] + FLAP (def. 18a) + -ABLE] —**un·flap·pa·bil·i·ty** (un flap′ə bil′i tē), *n.* —**un·flap′pa·bly,** *adv.*

un·fledged (un flejd′), *adj.* **1.** not fledged; without feathers sufficiently developed for flight, as a young bird. **2.** immature; callow.

un·flinch·ing (un flin′ching), *adj.* not flinching; undiminished or unwavering: *unflinching courage.* —**un·flinch′ing·ly,** *adv.*

un·fold (un fōld′), *v.t.* **1.** to bring out of a folded state; spread or open out. **2.** to spread out or lay open to view. **3.** to reveal or disclose in words, esp. by careful or systematic exposition; set forth; explain. —*v.i.* **4.** to become unfolded; open. **5.** to develop. **6.** to become clear, apparent, or known. [ME; OE *unfeald(an);* c. G *entfalten*]

un·for·get·ta·ble (un′fər get′ə bəl), *adj.* impossible to forget: *scenes of unforgettable beauty.* —**un′for·get′ta·bly,** *adv.*

un·formed (un fôrmd′), *adj.* **1.** not definitely shaped; shapeless or formless. **2.** undeveloped; crude. **3.** not formed; not created. [ME *unfourmed*]

un·for·tu·nate (un fôr′chə nit), *adj.* **1.** suffering from bad luck. **2.** unfavorable or inauspicious: *an unfortunate turn of events.* **3.** to be regretted or deplored: *an unfortunate remark.* —*n.* **4.** Usually, **unfortunates.** people who are generally unfortunate. —**un·for′tu·nate·ly,** *adv.* —**Syn. 1.** unsuccessful.

un·found·ed (un foun′did), *adj.* **1.** without factual or rational foundation. **2.** not established; not founded. —**un·found′ed·ly,** *adv.* —**un·found′ed·ness,** *n.*

un·friend·ed (un fren′did), *adj.* without friends.

un·friend·ly (un frend′lē), *adj.,* **-li·er, -li·est,** *adv.* —*adj.* **1.** not of friendly or kindly disposition; unsympathetic; aloof. **2.** hostile; antagonistic. **3.** unfavorable, as an environment. —*adv.* **4.** in an unfriendly manner. [ME *unfrendly*] —**un·friend′li·ness,** *n.*

un·frock (un frok′), *v.t.* **1.** to deprive of ecclesiastical rank, authority, and function. **2.** to divest or strip of a frock.

un·fruit·ful (un fro͞ot′fəl), *adj.* **1.** not providing satisfaction or a desired result; unprofitable. **2.** not producing offspring; sterile. **3.** not yielding fruit, crops, etc. [ME] —**un·fruit′ful·ly,** *adv.* —**un·fruit′ful·ness,** *n.*

ung., (in prescriptions) ointment. [< L *unguentum*]

un·gain·ly (un gān′lē), *adj.* **1.** not graceful; awkward; clumsy. **2.** coarse or uncouth. —*adv.* **3.** in an awkward manner. [ME *ungaynly* (adv.)] —**un·gain′li·ness,** *n.*

Un·ga·va (ung gä′və, -gā′-), *n.* a region in NE Canada, comprising the larger part of the peninsula of Labrador: incorporated into Quebec province 1912.

un·gen·er·ous (un jen′ər əs), *adj.* **1.** stingy; miserly. **2.** uncharitable; petty. —**un·gen′er·ous·ly,** *adv.*

un·gird (un gûrd′), *v.t.,* **-gird·ed** or **-girt, -gird·ing. 1.** to loosen or remove a girdle or belt from. **2.** to loosen or remove by unfastening a belt.

un·girt (un gûrt′), *adj.* **1.** having a girdle loosened or removed. **2.** slack; relaxed; not taut or pulled together. [ME *ungyrt*]

un·god·ly (un god′lē), *adj.,* **-li·er, -li·est. 1.** not accepting God or a particular religious doctrine; irreligious; atheistic. **2.** sinful; wicked; impious; not conforming to religious tenets or canons. **3.** *Informal.* dreadful; insufferable: *an ungodly hour to drop in.* —**un·god′li·ness,** *n.* —**Syn. 2.** profane, evil.

un·got·ten (un got′ən), *adj.* **1.** not obtained or gained. **2.** *Obs.* not begotten. Also, **un·got′.** [ME]

un·gov·ern·a·ble (un guv′ər nə bəl), *adj.* impossible to govern, rule, or restrain; uncontrollable. —**un·gov′ern·a·bly,** *adv.*

un·gra·cious (un grā′shəs), *adj.* **1.** discourteous; unpleasant; ill-mannered; rude. **2.** unpleasant; disagreeable; unrewarding. **3.** *Obs.* ungraceful; unpleasing. [ME] —**un·gra′cious·ly,** *adv.* —**un·gra′cious·ness,** *n.*

un·gram·mat·i·cal (un′grə mat′i kəl), *adj.* grammatically incorrect or awkward. —**un′gram·mat′i·cal·ly,** *adv.*

un·grate·ful (un grāt′fəl), *adj.* **1.** not displaying gratitude; not giving due return or recompense. **2.** unpleasant; distasteful; repellent: *an ungrateful task.* —**un·grate′ful·ly,** *adv.* —**un·grate′ful·ness,** *n.*

un·grudg·ing (un gruj′ing), *adj.* not begrudging; not stinting; wholehearted. —**un·grudg′ing·ly,** *adv.*

un·gual (ung′gwəl), *adj.* of, pertaining to, bearing, or shaped like a nail, claw, or hoof. [< L *ungu(is)* a nail, claw, hoof (c. Gk *ónyx*) + -AL[1]]

un·guard·ed (un gär′did), *adj.* **1.** not guarded; unprotected or unshielded. **2.** open; frank; guileless. **3.** not cautious or discreet; careless. —**un·guard′ed·ly,** *adv.* —**un·guard′ed·ness,** *n.* —**Syn. 1.** defenseless. **3.** indiscreet.

un·guent (ung′gwənt), *n.* an ointment or salve, usually liquid or semiliquid, for application to wounds, sores, etc. [< L *unguent(um)* = *unguent-* (s. of *unguēns,* prp. of *ungu(ere)* (to) anoint; see -ENT) + *-um* n. suffix] —**un·guen·tar·y** (ung′gwən ter′ē), *adj.*

un·guen·tum (ung gwen′təm), *n., pl.* **-ta** (-tə). (in prescriptions) ointment. [< L]

un·guic·u·late (ung gwik′yə lit, -lāt′), *adj.* Also, **un·guic′u·lat′ed. 1.** bearing or resembling a nail or claw. **2.** *Zool.* having nails or claws, as distinguished from hoofs. **3.** *Bot.* having a clawlike base, as certain petals. —*n.* **4.** an unguiculate animal. [< NL *unguiculāt(us)* = L *unguicul(us)* fingernail (*ungu(is)* (see UNGUIS) + *-i-* -I- + *-culus* -CULE) + *-ātus* -ATE[1]]

un·gui·nous (ung′gwə nəs), *adj.* resembling, containing, or consisting of fat or oil; greasy; oily. [< L *unguinōs(us)* = *unguin-* (s. of *unguen*) ointment + *-ōsus* -OUS]

un·guis (ung′gwis), *n., pl.* **-gues** (-gwēz). **1.** a nail, claw, or hoof. **2.** *Bot.* the clawlike base of certain petals. [< L *unguis* a nail, claw, hoof; c. Gk *ónyx*]

un·gu·la (ung′gyə lə), *n., pl.* **-lae** (-lē′). **1.** *Geom.* a part of a cylinder, cone, or the like, between the base and a plane oblique to the base. **2.** *Bot.* an unguis. [< L *ungula* a claw, hoof, talon, dim. of *unguis* UNGUIS]

Ungula

un·gu·lar (ung′gyə lər), *adj.* pertaining to or of the nature of an ungula; ungual.

---

un′ex·pend′ed, *adj.*
un′ex·pe′ri·enced, *adj.*
un·ex′pi·at′ed, *adj.*
un′ex·pired′, *adj.*
un′ex·plain′a·ble, *adj.;* **-bly,** *adv.*
un′ex·plained′, *adj.*
un′ex·plic′it, *adj.*
un′ex·plod′ed, *adj.*
un′ex·ploit′ed, *adj.*
un′ex·plored′, *adj.*
un′ex·posed′, *adj.*
un′ex·pres′sive, *adj.*
un′ex·punged′, *adj.*
un·ex′pur·gat′ed, *adj.*
un′ex·tend′ed, *adj.*
un′ex·tin′guished, *adj.*
un·fad′ed, *adj.*
un·fad′ing, *adj.*
un·fal′ter·ing, *adj.;* **-ly,** *adv.*
un·fash′ion·a·ble, *adj.;* **-bly,** *adv.*
un·fa′ther·ly, *adj.*
un·fath′omed, *adj.*
un′fa·tigued′, *adj.*
un·fa′vored, *adj.*
un·feared′, *adj.*
un·fear′ful, *adj.;* **-ly,** *adv.*
un·fear′ing, *adj.*
un·fea′si·ble, *adj.*
un·fea′tured, *adj.*
un·fed′, *adj.*
un·fed′er·at′ed, *adj.*
un·felt′, *adj.*
un·fem′i·nine, *adj.*
un·fence′, *v.t.,* **-fenced, -fenc·ing.**
un′fer·ment′ed, *adj.*
un·fer′ti·lized′, *adj.*
un·fes′tive, *adj.*
un·filled′, *adj.*
un·filmed′, *adj.*
un·fil′tered, *adj.*
un·fired′, *adj.*
un·fished′, *adj.*
un·fit′ting, *adj.;* **-ly,** *adv.*
un·flag′ging, *adj.;* **-ly,** *adv.*
un·flat′ter·ing, *adj.*
un·fla′vored, *adj.*
un′for·bear′ing, *adj.*
un′for·bid′den, *adj.*
un′for·bid′ding, *adj.*
un·force′a·ble, *adj.*
un·forced′, *adj.*
un′fore·bod′ing, *adj.*
un′fore·known′, *adj.*
un′fore·see′a·ble, *adj.*
un′fore·see′ing, *adj.*
un′fore·seen′, *adj.*
un·for′est·ed, *adj.*
un′fore·told′, *adj.*
un·for′feit·ed, *adj.*
un′for·get′ful, *adj.*
un′for·giv′a·ble, *adj.;* **-bly,** *adv.*
un′for·giv′en, *adj.*
un′for·giv′ing, *adj.*
un′for·got′ten, *adj.*
un·for′mu·lat′ed, *adj.*
un′for·sak′en, *adj.*
un·for′ti·fied′, *adj.*
un·fought′, *adj.*
un·found′, *adj.*
un·framed′, *adj.*
un·free′, *v.t.,* **-freed, -free·ing,** *adj.*
un·freeze′, *v.* **-froze, -fro·zen, -freez·ing.**
un·fre′quent·ed, *adj.*
un·fri′a·ble, *adj.;* **-ble·ness,** *n.*
un′ful·filled′, *adj.*
un·fun′ny, *adj.*
un·furl′, *v.*
un·fur′nished, *adj.*
un·fur′rowed, *adj.*
un·gal′lant, *adj.;* **-ly,** *adv.*
un·gar′nished, *adj.*
un·gath′ered, *adj.*
un·gen′ial, *adj.;* **-ly,** *adv.*
un′gen·teel′, *adj.*
un·gen′tle, *adj.;* **-tly,** *adv.*
un·gen′tle·man·ly, *adj.*
un·gift′ed, *adj.*
un·glazed′, *adj.*
un·gov′erned, *adj.*
un·graced′, *adj.*
un·grace′ful, *adj.;* **-ly,** *adv.*
un·grad′ed, *adj.*
un·grained′, *adj.*
un·grat′i·fied′, *adj.*
un·grat′i·fy′ing, *adj.*
un·ground′ed, *adj.*
un·guid′ed, *adj.*

un·gu·late (ung′gyə lit, -lāt′), *adj.* **1.** having hoofs. **2.** belonging or pertaining to the *Ungulata,* a former group comprising all hoofed mammals. **3.** hooflike. —*n.* **4.** a hoofed mammal. [< LL *ungulāt(us)* having claws or hoofs]

un·hair (un hâr′), *v.t.* **1.** to remove the hair from. **2.** to remove the guard hairs from (a pelt or animal skin). —*v.i.* **3.** to become hairless. [ME *unheere(n)*]

un·hal·low (un hal′ō), *v.t.* to desecrate; profane.

un·hal·lowed (un hal′ōd), *adj.* **1.** not hallowed or consecrated. **2.** impious, wicked, or sinful. [ME *unhalewed*]

un·hand (un hand′), *v.t.* to take the hand or hands from; release from a grasp; let go.

un·hand·some (un han′səm), *adj.* **1.** lacking good looks; plain or ugly. **2.** ungracious; discourteous; unseemly. **3.** ungenerous; illiberal. —**un·hand′some·ly,** *adv.*

un·hap·py (un hap′ē), *adj.,* **-pi·er, -pi·est. 1.** sad; miserable; wretched. **2.** unfortunate; regrettable or deplorable. **3.** unfavorable or inauspicious. **4.** *Obs.* causing trouble; reprehensible; troublesome. [ME: causing misfortune, objectionable] —**un·hap′pi·ly,** *adv.* —**un·hap′pi·ness,** *n.* —**Syn. 1.** sorrowful, downcast, disconsolate.

un·har·ness (un här′nis), *v.t.* **1.** to strip of harness; detach the harness from (a horse, mule, etc.). **2.** *Archaic.* to divest of armor, as a knight or warhorse. [ME *onharnes(en)*]

un·health·y (un hel′thē), *adj.,* **-health·i·er, -health·i·est. 1.** not in a state of good or normal health. **2.** symptomatic of or resulting from bad health. **3.** not conducive to good health. **4.** morally bad, harmful, or contaminating. —**un·health′i·ly,** *adv.* —**Syn. 1.** sickly, delicate, frail. **3.** unhealthful, unhygienic.

un·heard (un hûrd′), *adj.* **1.** not heard; not perceived by the ear. **2.** not given a hearing or audience. **3.** *Archaic.* unheard-of. [ME *unherd*]

un·heard-of (un hûrd′uv′, -ov′), *adj.* **1.** never heard of; unknown: *an unheard-of artist.* **2.** never known before; unprecedented. **3.** outrageous.

un·helm (un helm′), *v.t. Archaic.* to deprive of the helm or helmet. [ME *unhelm(en)*]

un·hes·i·tat·ing (un hez′i tā′ting), *adj.* **1.** without hesitation. **2.** unwavering; unfaltering; steadfast. —**un·hes′i·tat′ing·ly,** *adv.*

un·hinge (un hinj′), *v.t.,* **-hinged, -hing·ing. 1.** to remove from hinges. **2.** to throw into confusion or turmoil; upset; unbalance.

un·ho·ly (un hō′lē), *adj.,* **-li·er, -li·est. 1.** not holy; not sacred or hallowed. **2.** characterized by wickedness or depravity. **3.** dreadful or disagreeable: *to rise at an unholy hour.* [ME; OE *unhālig* (c. D *onheilig,* OIcel *ūheilagr*)] —**un·ho′li·ness,** *n.*

un·hook (un ho͝ok′), *v.t.* **1.** to detach by or as by releasing a hook. **2.** to unfasten or open by undoing a hook or hooks. —*v.i.* **3.** to become unhooked.

un·hoped-for (un hōpt′fôr′), *adj.* unexpected; unanticipated.

un·horse (un hôrs′), *v.t.,* **-horsed, -hors·ing. 1.** to cause to fall from a horse. **2.** to dislodge, as from office. [ME *unhorse(n)*]

un·hou·seled (un hou′zəld), *adj. Archaic.* not having received the Eucharist.

un·hur·ried (un hûr′ēd, -hur′-), *adj.* not hurried; leisurely; deliberate. —**un·hur·ried·ly** (un hûr′id lē, -ēd-, -hur′-), *adv.*

uni-, a formal element occurring in loan words from Latin (*universe*): used, with the meaning "one," in the formation of compound words (*unicycle*). [< L, comb. form of *ūnus*]

U·ni·at (yo͞o′nē at′), *n.* a member of an Eastern church that is in union with the Roman Catholic Church, acknowledges the Roman pope as supreme in matters of faith, but maintains its own liturgy, discipline, and rite. Also, **U·ni·ate** (yo͞o′nē it, -āt′). [< Russ] —**U′ni·at·ism,** *n.*

u·ni·ax·i·al (yo͞o′nē ak′sē əl), *adj.* **1.** having one axis. **2.** *Crystall.* (of a crystal) having one direction in which no double refraction occurs. **3.** *Bot.* (of a plant) having a primary stem that does not branch and that terminates in a flower. —**u′ni·ax′i·al·ly,** *adv.*

u·ni·cam·er·al (yo͞o′nə kam′ər əl), *adj.* consisting of a single chamber, as a legislative assembly. [UNI- + L *camer(a)* CHAMBER + -AL[1]] —**u′ni·cam′er·al·ism,** *n.* —**u′ni·cam′er·al·ly,** *adv.*

UNICEF (yo͞o′ni sef′), *n.* an agency, created by the United Nations General Assembly in 1946, concerned with improving the health and nutrition of children and mothers throughout the world. [*U(nited) N(ations) I(nternational) C(hildren's) E(mergency) F(und)*]

u·ni·cel·lu·lar (yo͞o′ni sel′yə lər), *adj.* having or consisting of a single cell or individual structural unit. —**u′ni·cel′lu·lar′i·ty,** *n.*

u·ni·corn (yo͞o′nə kôrn′), *n.* **1.** a mythical creature resembling a horse and having a single horn in the center of its forehead: often symbolic of chastity or purity. **2.** an animal mentioned in the Bible: now believed to be a wild ox or rhinoceros. Deut. 33:17. [ME *unicorne* < L *unicorn(is)* one-horned = L *uni-* UNI- + *corn(u)* HORN + *-is* adj. suffix]

Unicorn

u·ni·cos·tate (yo͞o′nə kos′tāt, -kô′stāt), *adj.* **1.** having only one costa, rib, or ridge. **2.** *Bot.* (of a leaf) having only one primary or prominent rib, the midrib.

u·ni·cy·cle (yo͞o′nə sī′kəl), *n.* a one-wheeled vehicle, usually pedal-driven. —**u′ni·cy′clist,** *n.*

un′iden′tified fly′ing ob′ject. See **flying saucer.**

u·ni·di·rec·tion·al (yo͞o′ni di rek′shə nəl, -dī-), *adj.* operating or moving in one direction only.

u·ni·face (yo͞o′nə fās′), *n. Numis.* a coin or medal having a blank reverse.

u·ni·fi·a·ble (yo͞o′nə fī′ə bəl), *adj.* capable of being unified.

u·nif·ic (yo͞o nif′ik), *adj.* unifying; uniting.

u·ni·fi·ca·tion (yo͞o′nə fə kā′shən), *n.* **1.** the process of unifying or uniting; union. **2.** the state or condition of being unified. [UNI- + -FICATION, modeled on *purify, purification*]

u·ni·fi·lar (yo͞o′nə fī′lər), *adj.* having or involving only one thread, wire, or the like.

u·ni·fo·li·ate (yo͞o′nə fō′lē it, -āt′), *adj.* **1.** having only one leaf. **2.** unifoliolate.

u·ni·fo·li·o·late (yo͞o′nə fō′lē ə lāt′), *adj. Bot.* **1.** compound in structure yet having only one leaflet, as the orange. **2.** bearing such leaves.

Unifoliolate leaf

u·ni·form (yo͞o′nə fôrm′), *adj.* **1.** identical, as from example to example, place to place, or moment to moment: *a uniform nationwide building code.* **2.** without variations in detail: *a uniform surface.* **3.** consistent; unvarying: *uniform kindness.* —*n.* **4.** a suit or the items of dress worn by all the members of a given rank, profession, or organization on specified occasions. **5.** a word used in communications to represent the letter *U.* —*v.t.* **6.** to make uniform. **7.** to clothe in or furnish with a uniform. [< L *uniform(is).* See UNI-, -FORM] —**u′ni·form′ly,** *adv.* —**Syn. 1.** invariable, constant, regular. **2.** undiversified, unvariegated. —**Ant. 1.** irregular.

U′niform Code′ of Mil′itary Jus′tice, the body of laws and legal procedures of the armed forces: replaced the Articles of War in 1951.

u·ni·form·i·tar·i·an (yo͞o′nə fôr′mi târ′ē ən), *adj.* **1.** supporting, adhering to, conforming to, or derived from a theory or doctrine about uniformity. **2.** *Geol.* noting or pertaining to the thesis that early geological processes are not different from those observed now. —*n.* **3.** a person who accepts or supports a uniformitarian theory. —**u′ni·form′i·tar′i·an·ism,** *n.*

u·ni·form·i·ty (yo͞o′nə fôr′mi tē), *n., pl.* **-ties. 1.** the state or quality of being uniform; overall sameness or homogeneity; absence of diversity or variation. **2.** something that is uniform. [ME *uniformite* < MF *uniformite* < LL *ūniformitāt-* (s. of *ūniformitās*)]

u·ni·fy (yo͞o′nə fī′), *v.t.,* **-fied, -fy·ing.** to form into a single unit or a harmonious whole. [< LL *ūnificāre*] —**u′ni·fi′er,** *n.*

u·nij·u·gate (yo͞o nij′ə gāt′, yo͞o′ni jo͞o′git, -gāt), *adj. Bot.* (of a pinnate leaf) having only a single pair of leaflets. [< L *ūnijug(us)* having one yoke = *ūni-* UNI- + *jug(um)* YOKE + -ATE[1]]

Unijugate leaf

u·ni·lat·er·al (yo͞o′nə lat′ər əl), *adj.* **1.** relating to, occurring on, or involving one side only. **2.** pertaining to, affecting, or proceeding from only one of a number of sides or parties in a controversy, transaction, etc. **3.** having only one side or surface; without a reverse side or inside, as a Möbius strip. **4.** *Law.* noting or pertaining to a contract under which one party makes a promise in exchange for a certain action on the part of another. **5.** *Bot.* having all the parts disposed on one side of an axis, as an inflorescence. **6.** through forebears of one sex only, as the mother's or father's line. Cf. **bilateral** (def. 5). [< NL *ūnilaterāl(is)*] —**u′ni·lat′er·al·ly,** *adv.*

u·ni·lobed (yo͞o′nə lōbd′), *adj.* having or consisting of a single lobe, esp. of the maxilla of an insect.

u·ni·loc·u·lar (yo͞o′nə lok′yə lər), *adj. Bot., Zool.* having or consisting of only one loculus, chamber, or cell.

un·im·peach·a·ble (un′im pē′chə bəl), *adj.* above suspicion; impeccable; blameless. **un′im·peach′a·ble·ness,** *n.* —**un′im·peach′a·bly,** *adv.*

un·im·pos·ing (un′im pō′zing), *adj.* not imposing; unimpressive.

un·im·proved (un′im pro͞ovd′), *adj.* **1.** not developed to full potential, as resources or the mind. **2.** not showing improvement, as one's health, appearance, etc. **3.** (of land) not cleared, cultivated, or built on. **4.** not used to advantage, as an opportunity; neglected.

un·in·cor·po·rat·ed (un′in kôr′pə rā′tid), *adj.* **1.** not chartered as a corporation; lacking the powers and immunities of a corporate enterprise. **2.** not chartered as a self-governing village or city; lacking the tax, police, and other powers conferred by the state on incorporated towns: *an unincorporated hamlet.* **3.** not combined into a single body or unit; not made part of; not included: *Many unincorporated research notes are appended to the text of the book.*

un·hack′neyed, *adj.*
un·hailed′, *adj.*
un·ham′pered, *adj.*
un·hand′i·capped′, *adj.*
un·hard′ened, *adj.*
un·harmed′, *adj.*
un·harm′ful, *adj.*
un′har·mo′ni·ous, *adj.;* **-ly,** *adv.*
un·har′rowed, *adj.*
un·har′vest·ed, *adj.*
un·hatched′, *adj.*
un·healed′, *adj.*
un·heat′ed, *adj.*
un·heed′ed, *adj.;* **-ly,** *adv.*
un·heed′ful, *adj.;* **-ly,** *adv.*
un·heed′ing, *adj.*
un·helped′, *adj.*
un·help′ful, *adj.*
un·her′ald·ed, *adj.*
un′he·ro′ic, *adj.*
un·hewn′, *adj.*
un·hin′dered, *adj.*
un·hitch′, *v.t.*
un·hon′ored, *adj.*
un·hon′oured, *adj.*
un·hood′, *v.t.*
un·housed′, *adj.*
un·hung′, *adj.*
un·hurt′, *adj.*
un′hy·gi·en′ic, *adj.*
un·hy′phen·at′ed, *adj.*
un′i·de′al, *adj.*
un′i·den′ti·fi′a·ble, *adj.*
un′i·den′ti·fied′, *adj.*
un′id·i·o·mat′ic, *adj.*
un′id·i·o·mat′i·cal·ly, *adv.*
un′il·lu′mi·nat′ed, *adj.*
un′il·lu′mi·nat′ing, *adj.*
un·il′lus·trat′ed, *adj.*
un′il·lus′tra·tive, *adj.*
un′im·ag′i·na·ble, *adj.;* **-bly,** *adv.*
un′im·ag′i·na′tive, *adj.;* **-ly,** *adv.*
un′im·ag′ined, *adj.*
un′im·bued′, *adj.*
un′im·paired′, *adj.*
un′im·pas′sioned, *adj.*
un′im·ped′ed, *adj.*
un′im·por′tant, *adj.*
un′im·pressed′, *adj.*
un′im·pres′sion·a·ble, *adj.*
un′im·pres′sive, *adj.;* **-ly,** *adv.*
un′in·closed′, *adj.*
un·in′cu·bat′ed, *adj.*
un′in·cum′bered, *adj.*
un′in·dem′ni·fied′, *adj.*
un′in·dorsed′, *adj.*

un·in·hib·it·ed (un′in hib′i tid), *adj.* **1.** not inhibited or restricted. **2.** not restrained, as by social convention or usage. —**un′in·hib′it·ed·ly,** *adv.* —**un′in·hib′it·ed·ness,** *n.*

un·in·spired (un′in spīᵊrd′), *adj.* not inspired; not creative or spirited; unimaginative; lifeless: *an uninspired performance; an uninspired teacher.*

un·in·struct·ed (un′in struk′tid), *adj.* **1.** uninformed; uneducated. **2.** not furnished with orders or instructions. —**un′in·struct′ed·ly,** *adv.*

un·in·tel·li·gent (un′in tel′i jənt), *adj.* **1.** deficient in intelligence; dull; stupid. **2.** not endowed with a mind. —**un′-in·tel′li·gence,** *n.* —**un′in·tel′li·gent·ly,** *adv.*

un·in·tel·li·gi·ble (un′in tel′i jə bəl), *adj.* not intelligible; not capable of being understood. —**un′in·tel′li·gi·bil′i·ty, un′in·tel′li·gi·ble·ness,** *n.* —**un′in·tel′li·gi·bly,** *adv.*

un·in·ter·est·ed (un in′tər i stid, -tris tid, -tə res′tid), *adj.* **1.** having or showing no interest; indifferent. **2.** not having an interest, esp. a financial interest. —**un·in′ter·est·ed·ly,** *adv.* —**Syn. 1.** See **disinterested.**

u·ni·oc·u·lar (yo͞o′nē ok′yə lər), *adj.* monocular.

un·ion (yo͞on′yən), *n.* **1.** the act of uniting. **2.** the state of being united. **3.** something formed by uniting two or more things; combination. **4.** a number of persons, states, etc., joined or associated together for some common purpose. **5.** a group of states or nations united into one political body, as that of the American colonies at the time of the Revolution. **6. the Union.** See **United States. 7.** a device emblematic of union used in a flag or ensign, as the blue area of the U.S. flag. **8.** act of uniting or of being united in marriage or sexual intercourse. **9.** an organization of workers; a labor union or trade union. **10.** any of various devices for connecting parts of machinery, pipes, or the like. **11.** *Textiles.* **a.** a fabric of two kinds of yarn. **b.** a yarn of two or more fibers. [ME < MF < LL *ūniōn-* (s. of *ūniō*) = L *ūn(us)* one + *-iōn-* -ION] —**Syn. 2.** UNION, UNITY agree in referring to a oneness, either created by putting together, or by being undivided. A UNION is a state of being united, a combination, as the result of joining two or more things into one: *to promote the union between two families; the Union of England and Scotland.* UNITY is the state or inherent quality of being one, single, individual, and indivisible (often as a consequence of union): *to find unity in diversity; to give unity to a work of art.* **4.** association. See **alliance. 8.** wedlock.

Un·ion (yo͞on′yən), *n.* a township in NE New Jersey. 53,077 (1970).

un′ion card′, a card identifying a worker as a member of a particular union.

un′ion cat′alog, a library catalog listing in alphabetical sequence the contents of several catalogs, often those of separate libraries.

Un′ion Cit′y, a city in NE New Jersey. 58,537 (1970).

un·ion·ise (yo͞on′yə nīz′), *v.t., v.i.,* **-ised, -is·ing.** *Chiefly Brit.* unionize[1]. —**un′ion·i·sa′tion,** *n.*

un·ion·ism (yo͞on′yə niz′əm), *n.* **1.** the principle of union, esp. trade unionism. **2.** attachment to a union. **3.** (*cap.*) loyalty to the United States at the time of the Civil War.

un·ion·ist (yo͞on′yə nist), *n.* **1.** a person whose activities or beliefs are characterized by unionism. **2.** a member of a trade union. **3.** (*cap.*) an adherent of Unionism. **4.** *Brit. Politics.* (formerly) an upholder of the legislative union of Great Britain and Ireland. —**un′ion·is′tic,** *adj.*

un·ion·ize[1] (yo͞on′yə nīz′), *v.,* **-ized, -iz·ing.** —*v.t.* **1.** to form into a union. **2.** to organize (workers) into a union. **3.** to subject to the rules of a union. —*v.i.* **4.** to form a union. **5.** (of workers) to join a union. Also, *esp. Brit.,* **unionise.** [UNION + -IZE] —**un′ion·i·za′tion,** *n.*

un·i·on·ize[2] (un ī′ə nīz′), *v.t.,* **-ized, -iz·ing.** to remove the ionization of (a gas, a particle, or the like). [UN-[2] + IONIZE]

un′ion jack′, **1.** a jack consisting of the union of a national flag or ensign, as the U.S. jack, formed from the blue area of the U.S. national flag. **2.** any flag whose overall design is a union. **3.** (*caps.*) the British national flag.

Un′ion of South′ Af′rica, former name of the Republic of South Africa.

Un′ion of So′viet So′cialist Repub′lics, official name of the **Soviet Union.** *Abbr.:* U.S.S.R., USSR

un′ion shop′, a shop, business, etc., in which membership in a union is made a condition of employment.

un′ion suit′, a close-fitting undergarment, esp. worn by men and children, combining drawers and shirt in one piece.

u·nip·a·rous (yo͞o nip′ər əs), *adj.* **1.** *Zool.* producing only one egg or offspring at a time. **2.** *Bot.* (of a cyme) producing only one axis at each branching. [< NL *ūniparus*]

u·ni·per·son·al (yo͞o′nə pûr′sə nᵊl), *adj.* **1.** consisting of or existing as one person only. **2.** *Gram.* used in only one person, esp. the third person singular, as certain verbs. —**u′ni·per′son·al′i·ty,** *n.*

u·ni·pla·nar (yo͞o′nə plā′nər), *adj.* confined to a single plane or two-dimensional continuum.

u·ni·pod (yo͞o′nə pod′), *n.* something that is formed with a single leg or foot, as a one-legged support for a camera.

u·ni·po·lar (yo͞o′nə pō′lər), *adj.* *Physics.* having or pertaining to a single magnetic or electric pole. —**u·ni·po·lar·i·ty** (yo͞o′nə pō lar′i tē), *n.*

u·nip·o·tent (yo͞o nip′ə tᵊnt), *adj.* *Biol.* (of cells) capable of developing into only one type of cell or tissue.

u·nique (yo͞o nēk′), *adj.* **1.** existing as the only one or as the sole example; single; solitary in type or characteristics. **2.** having no like or equal; standing alone in quality; incomparable. —*n.* **3.** the embodiment of unique characteristics. [< F < L *ūnic(us)* = *ūn(us)* one + *-icus* -IC] —**u·nique′ly,** *adv.* —**u·nique′ness,** *n.* —**Syn. 2.** peerless.

u·ni·sep·tate (yo͞o′ni sep′tāt), *adj.* having only one septum or partition, as a silicle.

u·ni·sex (yo͞o′nə seks′), *adj.* of, noting, or engaged in a design, type, or style that is for use or wear by both sexes alike: *unisex clothes; a unisex shop; the unisex fashion.*

u·ni·sex·u·al (yo͞o′ni sek′sho͞o əl), *adj.* **1.** of or pertaining to one sex only. **2.** having only male or female organs in one individual, as an animal or a flower. —**u′ni·sex′u·al′i·ty,** *n.* —**u′ni·sex′u·al·ly,** *adv.*

u·ni·son (yo͞o′ni sən, -zən), *n.* **1.** coincidence in pitch of two or more musical tones, voices, etc. **2.** the musical interval of a perfect prime. **3.** the performance of musical parts at the same pitch or at the octave. **4.** a sounding together in octaves, esp. of male and female voices or of higher and lower instruments of the same class. **5.** a condition in which all members behave in the same way at the same time. **6.** perfect accord; harmony. [< ML *ūnison(us)* of a single sound = L *ūni-* UNI- + *sonus* sound]

u·nis·o·nous (yo͞o nis′ə nəs), *adj.* being in unison. Also, **u·nis′o·nal, u·nis′o·nant.** [< ML *ūnison(us)*]

u·nit (yo͞o′nit), *n.* **1.** any of a number of things, parts, items, etc., that are equivalent or identical. **2.** any of a number of more or less similar things, organizations, etc., having a specified or implied purpose: *a housing unit; a unit of rolling stock.* **3.** something that forms a united whole. **4.** a specific abstract quantity, used for purposes of measurement. **5.** the least positive integer; one. **6.** Also called **unit's place. a.** (in a mixed number) the position of the first digit to the left of the decimal point. **b.** (in a whole number) the position of the first digit from the right. **7.** *Educ.* a standard of measurement of academic accomplishment in terms of a specified number of hours of class or laboratory. **8.** *Mil.* an organized body of soldiers, varying in size and constituting a subdivision of a larger body. **9.** *Immunol., Pharm.* **a.** the measured amount of a substance necessary to cause a certain effect: used when a substance cannot readily be isolated in pure form and its activity determined directly. **b.** the amount necessary to cause a specific effect upon a specific animal or upon animal tissues. [appar. back formation from UNITY]

Unit., Unitarian.

U·ni·tar·i·an (yo͞o′ni târ′ē ən), *n.* **1.** a member of a Christian denomination founded upon the doctrine that God is one being, rejecting the doctrine of the Trinity, emphasizing tolerance of difference in religious opinion, and giving each congregation complete control over its affairs. **2.** a person who espouses any form of Protestantism maintaining that God is one being and rejecting the doctrine of the Trinity. **3.** (*l.c.*) an advocate of unity or centralization, as in government. —*adj.* **4.** of or pertaining to the Unitarians or their doctrines. **5.** (*l.c.*) unitary. [< NL *unitari(us)* (L *ūnit(ās)* UNITY + *-ārius* -ARY) + -AN]

U·ni·tar·i·an·ism (yo͞o′ni târ′ē ə niz′əm), *n.* **1.** the beliefs, principles, and practices of Unitarians. **2.** (*l.c.*) any system advocating unity or centralization, as in government.

u·ni·tar·y (yo͞o′ni ter′ē), *adj.* **1.** of or pertaining to a unit or units. **2.** of, pertaining to, characterized by, or aiming toward unity. **3.** of the nature of a unit; indivisible; whole. **4.** *Govt.* noting or pertaining to a system of government in which the executive, legislative, and judicial powers of each state in a body of states are vested in a central authority. [UNIT or UNIT(Y) + -ARY]

u′nit cell′, *Crystall.* the simplest unit of a regular lattice.

u′nit char′acter, *Genetics.* a character, usually controlled by a single gene, that is transmitted as a unit in heredity.

u·nite (yo͞o nīt′), *v.,* **u·nit·ed, u·nit·ing.** —*v.t.* **1.** to join, combine, or incorporate so as to form a single unit or whole. **2.** to cause to adhere. **3.** to cause (persons) to be in a state of mutual sympathy, or to have a common opinion or attitude. **4.** to exhibit or embody in combination, as qualities. —*v.i.* **5.** to become or to act as a single entity. **6.** (of persons) to act together, as in a common cause. **7.** (of persons) to share a common opinion, attitude, or bond of sympathy. **8.** to be joined together. [ME *unite(n)* < L *ūnīt(us)* joined together, united (ptp. of *ūnīre*) = *ūn(us)* one + *-ītus* -ITE[1]] —**Syn. 1, 5.** amalgamate, consolidate, merge. See **join.**

u·nit·ed (yo͞o nī′tid), *adj.* **1.** made into, or caused to act as, a single entity. **2.** formed or produced by the uniting of things or persons: *a united effort.* —**u·nit′ed·ly,** *adv.*

Unit′ed Ar′ab Emir′ates, an independent federation of seven Arab emirates, on the S Coast **(Pirate Coast)** of the Persian Gulf: formerly under British protection. 200,000 (est. 1972). 32,000 sq. mi. *Cap.:* Abu Dhabi. Formerly, **Trucial Coast, Trucial Oman, Trucial Sheikdoms, Trucial States.**

Unit′ed Ar′ab Repub′lic, former name (1958–71) of **Arab Republic of Egypt.**

Unit′ed Breth′ren, a Protestant denomination founded in 1800, characterized by Wesleyan beliefs and practices.

unit′ed front′, a coalition formed to oppose a force that menaces the interests, otherwise usually diverging, of all the members.

Unit′ed King′dom, a kingdom in NW Europe, consisting of Great Britain and Northern Ireland: formerly comprising Great Britain and Ireland 1801–1922. 55,900,000; 93,377 sq. mi. *Cap.:* London. *Abbr.:* U.K. Official name, **Unit′ed King′dom of Great′ Brit′ain and North′-ern Ire′land.**

Unit′ed Na′tions, **1.** an international organization, with headquarters in New York City, formed to promote international peace, security, and cooperation under the terms of the charter signed by 51 founding countries in San Francisco in 1945. *Abbr.:* UN **2.** the nations that signed the joint declaration in Washington, D.C., January 2, 1942, pledging to employ full resources against the Axis powers.

Unit′ed Na′tions Day′, October 24, observed in commemoration of the founding of the United Nations.

Unit′ed Na′tions Organiza′tion, the United Nations.

Unit′ed Prov′inces, **1.** former name of **Uttar Pradesh. 2.** *Hist.* the seven northern provinces in the Low Countries

---

un′in·fect′ed, *adj.*
un′in·flam′ma·ble, *adj.*
un·in′flu·enced, *adj.*
un′in·flu·en′tial, *adj.*
un′in·form′a·tive, *adj.*
un′in·formed′, *adj.*
un′in·hab′it·a·ble, *adj.*
un′in·hab′it·ed, *adj.*
un′in·i′ti·at′ed, *adj.*
un·in′jured, *adj.*
un′in·quis′i·tive, *adj.*
un′in·spir′ing, *adj.;* **-ly,** *adv.*
un′in·struc′tive, *adj.*
un′in·sur′a·ble, *adj.*
un′in·sured′, *adj.*
un′in·tel·lec′tu·al, *adj.*
un′in·tend′ed, *adj.;* **-ly,** *adv.*
un·in′ter·est·ing, *adj.;* **-ly,** *adv.*
un′in·ter·rupt′ed, *adj.;* **-ly,** *adv.*
un′in·ven′tive, *adj.*
un′in·vest′ed, *adj.*
un′in·vit′ed, *adj.*
un′in·vit′ing, *adj.;* **-ly,** *adv.*
un′in·voked′, *adj.*
un′in·volved′, *adj.*
un·i′roned, *adj.*

that declared their independence from Spain in 1581: now part of the Netherlands.

Unit′ed Prov′inces of A′gra and Oudh′, former official name of **Uttar Pradesh.**

Unit′ed States′, a republic comprising 48 conterminous states, the District of Columbia, and Alaska in North America, and Hawaii in the N Pacific. 215,118,000; conterminous United States, 3,022,387 sq. mi.; continental United States and Hawaii, 3,615,122 sq. mi. *Cap.:* Washington, D.C. *Abbr.:* U.S. Also called **United States of America, America.**

Unit′ed States′ Air′ Force′, the permanent or regular military air force of the United States, established in 1947 as a separate service under the authority of the Department of Defense: a branch of the U.S. Army before 1947. *Abbr.:* USAF

Unit′ed States′ Ar′my, the permanent or regular military land force of the United States under the authority of the Department of Defense since 1947. *Abbr.:* USA

Unit′ed States′ Informa′tion A′gency, a U.S. federal agency that distributes information concerning the people of the United States and the U.S. government and its policies in foreign countries. *Abbr.:* USIA

Unit′ed States′ Marine′ Corps′, a branch of the U.S. Navy, usually employed in amphibious landing operations and organized and equipped as soldiers. *Abbr.:* USMC

Unit′ed States′ Na′vy, the permanent or regular naval force of the United States, serving under the authority of the Department of Defense since 1947. *Abbr.:* USN

Unit′ed States′ of Amer′ica. See **United States.** *Abbr.:* U.S.A., USA

Unit′ed States′ of Indone′sia, former official name of the Republic of Indonesia.

Unit′ed States′ Post′al Ser′vice, an independent federal agency created in 1971 to replace the Post Office Department.

u′nit fac′tor, *Biol.* a gene; a substance that functions as the hereditary unit for a single character.

u·ni·tive (yo͞o′ni tiv), *adj.* **1.** capable of causing unity or serving to unite. **2.** marked by or involving union. [< LL *ūnītīvus* uniting = L *ūnīt(us)* (see UNITE) + *-īvus* -IVE] —**u′ni·tive·ly,** *adv.*

u·ni·tize (yo͞o′ni tīz′), *v.t.,* **u·ni·tized, u·ni·tiz·ing. 1.** to make into one unit by welding parts together: *unitized construction.* **2.** to make or separate into units. **3.** to separate into autonomous parts, as the branch office of a large company. —**u′ni·ti·za′tion,** *n.* —**u′ni·tiz′er,** *n.*

u′nit price′, 1. rate[1] (def. 3). **2.** a price for a service or commodity that includes all incidental extra costs.

u′nit pric′ing, the system of indicating the cost of a consumer product in terms of a standard unit of measure, as so much per pound, quart, or yard, in addition to the price per can, bottle, or piece.

u′nit rule′, *U.S.* (in national conventions of the Democratic party) a rule whereby states may sometimes vote as units, not recognizing minority votes within the delegation.

u′nit's place′, unit (def. 6).

u′nit train′, *Railroads.* a train with freight cars that remain coupled from a shipping point to a destination, chiefly for hauling huge loads of one commodity, such as coal or wheat.

u·ni·ty (yo͞o′ni tē), *n., pl.* **-ties. 1.** the state of being one single entity; oneness. **2.** the state of being combined with others to form a greater whole. **3.** the state of being a complete or harmonious combination of elements. **4.** something that is the result of such a combination. **5.** complete accord among persons regarding attitudes, opinions, intentions, etc. **6.** *Math.* the number one; a quantity regarded as one. **7.** (in literature and art) harmony among the parts or elements of a work producing a single major effect. **8.** one of the three principles of dramatic structure **(the three unities)** derived from Aristotelian aesthetics by which a play is limited in action to one day **(u′nity of time′)** and one place **(u′nity of place′),** and to a single plot **(u′nity of ac′tion).** [ME *unite* < OF *unite* < L *ūnitāt-* (s. of *ūnitās*) = *ūn(us)* one + *-itāt-* -ITY] —**Syn. 1.** singleness, singularity, individuality. See **union. 7.** concert, harmony.

Univ., 1. Universalist. **2.** University.

univ., 1. universal. **2.** universally. **3.** university.

u·ni·va·lent (yo͞o′nə vā′lənt, yo͞o niv′ə-), *adj.* **1.** *Chem.* having a valence of one; monovalent. **2.** *Genetics.* (of a chromosome) single; unpaired; not possessing or joining its homologous chromosome in synapsis. —**u′ni·va′lence,** *n.*

u·ni·valve (yo͞o′nə valv′), *adj.* Also, **u′ni·valved′, u·ni·val·vu·lar** (yo͞o′nə val′vyə lər). **1.** having one valve. **2.** (of a shell) composed of a single valve or piece. —*n.* **3.** a univalve mollusk or its shell.

u·ni·ver·sal (yo͞o′nə vûr′səl), *adj.* **1.** of, pertaining to, or characteristic of all or the whole. **2.** applicable or effective everywhere or in all cases: *a universal language.* **3.** affecting, concerning, or involving all: *universal military training.* **4.** existing or prevailing everywhere. **5.** versed in or embracing many or all skills, branches of learning, etc. **6.** of or pertaining to the universe. **7.** *Logic.* (of a proposition) asserted of every member of a class. **8.** *Mach.* noting any of various machines, tools, or devices widely adaptable in position, range of use, etc. —*n.* **9.** *Logic.* a universal proposition. **10.** *Philos.* **a.** a general term or concept or the generic nature that such a term signifies; a Platonic idea or Aristotelian form. **b.** a metaphysical entity that remains unchanged in character in a series of changes or changing relations. **11.** See **universal joint.** [ME *universal* < MF < L *ūniversāl(is)*] —**u′ni·ver′sal·ness,** *n.*

u′niver′sal cou′pling. See **universal joint.**

u·ni·ver·sal·ise (yo͞o′nə vûr′sə līz′), *v.t.,* **-ised, -is·ing.** *Chiefly Brit.* universalize. —**u′ni·ver′sal·i·sa′tion,** *n.*

u·ni·ver·sal·ism (yo͞o′nə vûr′sə liz′əm), *n.* **1.** universal character; universality. **2.** a universal range of knowledge, interests, or activities. **3.** (*cap.*) the doctrine that emphasizes the universal fatherhood of God and the final salvation of all men.

u·ni·ver·sal·ist (yo͞o′nə vûr′sə list), *n.* **1.** a person characterized by universalism, as in knowledge, interests, or activities. **2.** (*cap.*) a member of a Christian denomination advocating Universalism. —*adj.* **3.** (*cap.*) Also, **U′ni·ver′sal·is′tic.** of or pertaining to Universalism or Universalists.

u·ni·ver·sal·i·ty (yo͞o′nə vər sal′i tē), *n.* **1.** the character or state of being universal; existence or prevalence everywhere. **2.** relation, extension, or applicability to all. **3.** possession of a universal range of knowledge, interests, etc. [ME *universalite* < LL *ūniversālit(ās)*]

u·ni·ver·sal·ize (yo͞o′nə vûr′sə līz′), *v.t.,* **-ized, -iz·ing.** to make universal. Also, *esp. Brit.,* **universalise.** —**u′ni·ver′sal·i·za′tion,** *n.*

u′niver′sal joint′, *Mach.* a coupling between rotating shafts set at an angle to one another, allowing for rotation in three planes. Also called **universal, universal coupling.**

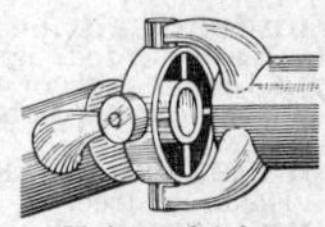

Universal joint

u·ni·ver·sal·ly (yo͞o′nə vûr′sə lē), *adv.* in a universal manner; in every instance or place; without exception. [ME]

u′niver′sal mil′itary train′ing, a program for maintaining army manpower, requiring all young male citizens, excepting those exempt for specific reasons, as physical or mental defects, to serve for a period of active and reserve duty. *Abbr.:* UMT

u·ni·verse (yo͞o′nə vûrs′), *n.* **1.** the totality of known or supposed objects and phenomena throughout space; the cosmos; macrocosm. **2.** the whole world, esp. that of mankind. **3.** a world or sphere in which something exists or prevails. **4.** *Logic.* See **universe of discourse.** [< L *ūnivers(um),* neut. of *ūniversus* = *ūni-* UNI- + *versus* (ptp. of *vertere* to turn)]

u′niverse of dis′course, *Logic.* the aggregate of all the objects, attributes, and relations assumed or implied in a given discussion.

u·ni·ver·si·ty (yo͞o′nə vûr′si tē), *n., pl.* **-ties.** an institution of learning of the highest level, comprising a college of liberal arts, a program of graduate studies, and several professional schools, and authorized to confer both undergraduate and graduate degrees. [ME *universite* < OF < ML *ūniversitāt-* (s. of *ūniversitās*), LL: guild, corporation, L: totality. See UNIVERSE, -ITY]

Univer′sity Cit′y, a city in E Missouri, near St. Louis. 46,309 (1970).

u·niv·o·cal (yo͞o niv′ə kəl), *adj.* having only one meaning. [< LL *univocus.* See UNI-, VOCAL] —**u·niv′o·cal·ly,** *adv.*

un·just (un just′), *adj.* **1.** not just; lacking in justice or fairness: *unjust criticism.* **2.** *Archaic.* unfaithful or dishonest. [ME] —**un·just′ly,** *adv.* —**Syn. 1.** inequitable, unfair, prejudiced, biased; undeserved.

un·kempt (un kempt′), *adj.* **1.** not combed, as hair. **2.** being in a neglected or untidy condition; disheveled; messy. **3.** unpolished; rough; crude. [var. of *unkembed* = UN-[1] + *kembed,* ptp. of obs. *kemb* to comb (ME *kembe,* OE *cemban*] —**un·kempt′ly,** *adv.* —**un·kempt′ness,** *n.*

un·ken·nel (un ken′əl), *v.t.,* **-neled, -nel·ing** or (*esp. Brit.*) **-nelled, -nel·ling. 1.** to drive or release from or as from a kennel. **2.** to reveal; disclose.

un·kind (un kīnd′), *adj.* **1.** lacking in kindness or consideration. **2.** lacking in sympathy or mercy; severe. [ME] —**un·kind′ness,** *n.*

un·kind·ly (un kīnd′lē), *adj.* **1.** not kindly; unkind. **2.** inclement or bleak, as weather. —*adv.* **3.** in an unkind manner. **4.** as being unkind: *to take a comment unkindly.* [ME] —**un·kind′li·ness,** *n.*

un·knight·ly (un nīt′lē), *adj.* **1.** unworthy of a knight. **2.** not like a knight. —*adv.* **3.** in a manner unworthy of a knight. —**un·knight′li·ness,** *n.*

un·knit (un nit′), *v.,* **-knit·ted** or **-knit, -knit·ting.** —*v.t.* **1.** to untie or unfasten (a knot, tangle, etc.); unravel (something knitted); undo. **2.** to weaken, undo, or destroy. **3.** to smooth out (something wrinkled). —*v.i.* **4.** to become undone. [ME *unknytte(n),* OE *uncnyttan*]

un·know·a·ble (un nō′ə bəl), *adj.* **1.** not knowable; incapable of being known or understood. —*n.* **2.** something that is unknowable. **3. the Unknowable,** the postulated reality lying behind all phenomena but not cognizable by any of the processes of the mind. [ME] —**un·know′a·ble·ness,** *n.* —**un·know′a·bly,** *adv.*

un·know·ing (un nō′ing), *adj.* not knowing; ignorant or unaware. [ME] —**un·know′ing·ly,** *adv.*

un·known (un nōn′), *adj.* **1.** not known; not within the range of knowledge, experience, or understanding. **2.** not discovered, explored, identified, or ascertained. —*n.* **3.** a person, thing, factor, etc., that is unknown. **4.** *Math.* a symbol representing an unknown quantity: in algebra, analysis, etc., frequently represented by a letter from the last part of the alphabet, as *x, y,* or *z.* [ME *unknow(e)n*] —**un·known′ness,** *n.*

Un′known Sol′dier, an unidentified soldier killed in battle and buried with honors, his tomb serving as a memorial to all the unidentified dead of a nation's armed forces. The tomb of the American Unknown Soldier, killed in World War I, is located in the Arlington National Cemetery in Virginia. Also called, *Brit.,* **Un′known War′rior.**

un·lace (un lās′), *v.t.,* **-laced, -lac·ing. 1.** to loosen or undo the lacing or laces of (a pair of boots, a corset, etc.). **2.** to loosen or remove (the garment of) by or as by undoing laces. [ME *unlace(n)*]

un·lade (un lād′), *v.,* **-lad·ed, -lad·ing.** —*v.t.* **1.** to take the lading, load, or cargo from; unload. **2.** to discharge (a load or cargo). —*v.i.* **3.** to unload a cargo. [ME *unlade(n)*]

un·laid (un lād′), *adj.* **1.** not laid or placed. **2.** (of dead bodies) not laid out. **3.** not laid or twisted, as a rope. [ME *unleyd*]

un·joint′ed, *adj.*
un·jus′ti·fi′a·ble, *adj.;* **-bly,** *adv.*
un·jus′ti·fied′, *adj.*
un·kept′, *adj.*
un·kin′dled, *adj.*
un·king′ly, *adj., adv.*
un·kink′, *v.*
un·kissed′, *adj.*
un·knot′, *v.t.*
un·la′beled, *adj.*
un·la′belled, *adj.*
un·la′bored, *adj.*
un·la′boured, *adj.*
un·la′den, *adj.*
un′la·ment′ed, *adj.*

un·lash (un lash′), *v.t.* to loosen, unfasten, or detach, as something lashed or tied fast.

un·law·ful (un lô′fəl), *adj.* **1.** not lawful; contrary to law; illegal; not sanctioned by law. **2.** born out of wedlock; illegitimate. [ME *unlaweful*] —**un·law′ful·ly,** *adv.* —**un·law′ful·ness,** *n.* —**Syn. 1.** illicit. **2.** bastard, natural.

un·lay (un lā′), *v.t.,* **-laid, -lay·ing. 1.** to separate (a strand) from a rope. **2.** to untwist (a rope) in order to separate its strands.

un·lead·ed (un led′id), *adj.* nonleaded.

un·learn (un lûrn′), *v.t.* **1.** to forget or lose knowledge of. **2.** to discard or put aside certain knowledge as being false or harmful. —*v.i.* **3.** to lose or discard knowledge. [ME *unlerne(n)*]

un·learn·ed (un lûr′nid *for 1;* un lûrnd′ *for 2, 3*), *adj.* **1.** uneducated; ignorant. **2.** not having been learned, as a lesson, skill, or the like. **3.** known or acquired without being learned, as behavior. [ME *unlerned*] —**un·learn′ed·ly,** *adv.*

un·leash (un lēsh′), *v.t.* to release from or as from a leash; set free.

un·leav·ened (un lev′ənd), *adj.* (of bread, cake, cookies, etc.) containing no leaven or leavening agent.

un·less (un les′), *conj.* **1.** except under the circumstances that: *Don't shoot unless you're attacked.* —*prep.* **2.** except; but; save: *Nothing will come of it, unless disaster.* [ME *onlesse* = *on* ON (prep.) + *lesse* LESS; orig. meaning, for less (than)]

un·let·tered (un let′ərd), *adj.* **1.** uneducated; ignorant. **2.** illiterate. **3.** not marked with letters, as a tombstone. [ME]

un·li·censed (un lī′sənst), *adj.* **1.** having no license. **2.** done or undertaken without license or permission; unauthorized. **3.** unrestrained; unbridled.

un·like (un līk′), *adj.* **1.** not similar or identical; different, dissimilar, or unequal. —*prep.* **2.** dissimilar to; different from. **3.** not typical or characteristic of: *It is unlike her to be cross.* [ME *unlik*] —**un·like′ness,** *n.* —**Syn. 1.** diverse.

un·like·ly (un līk′lē), *adj.* **1.** not likely to be or occur; improbable. **2.** holding little prospect of success; unpromising. —*adv.* **3.** in an unlikely way. [ME *unlikli*] —**un·like′li·hood′, un·like′li·ness,** *n.*

un·lim·ber (un lim′bər), *v.t.* **1.** to detach (a gun) from its limber or prime mover. **2.** to make ready for use or action. —*n.* **3.** the act of changing a gun from traveling to firing position.

un·lim·it·ed (un lim′i tid), *adj.* **1.** without limitations or restrictions. **2.** boundless; limitless; infinite; vast. **3.** without any qualification or exception: *unlimited surrender.* [ME] —**un·lim′it·ed·ly,** *adv.* —**Syn. 1.** unconstrained, unrestrained, unfettered. **2.** unbounded.

un·link (un lingk′), *v.t.* **1.** to separate the links of; unfasten. **2.** to detach or separate by or as by undoing one or more connecting links. —*v.i.* **3.** to become detached.

un·list·ed (un lis′tid), *adj.* **1.** not listed; not entered in a list. **2.** (of a security) not admitted to trading privileges on an exchange.

un·live (un liv′), *v.t.,* **-lived, -liv·ing. 1.** to undo or annul (past life, experiences, etc.). **2.** to live so as to make amends for.

un·load (un lōd′), *v.t.* **1.** to take the load from. **2.** to remove or discharge (freight, passengers, etc.). **3.** to remove the charge from (a firearm). **4.** to relieve of anything burdensome, oppressive, etc. —*v.i.* **5.** to unload freight, passengers, etc.

un·lock (un lok′), *v.t.* **1.** to undo the lock of (a door, chest, etc.), esp. with a key. **2.** to open or release by or as by undoing a lock. **3.** to lay open; disclose. —*v.i.* **4.** to become unlocked. —**un·lock′a·ble,** *adj.*

un·looked-for (un lŏŏkt′fôr′), *adj.* not expected or anticipated.

un·loose (un lōōs′), *v.t.,* **-loosed, -loos·ing. 1.** to loosen or relax, as one's grasp. **2.** to let loose or set free; release from bonds, shackles, etc.; free from restraint. **3.** to undo or untie (a fastening, knot, etc.); unfasten. [ME *unloosen*]

un·loos·en (un lōō′sən), *v.t.* to unloose. [ME *unlosnen*]

un·love·ly (un luv′lē), *adj.* **1.** not lovely; without beauty or charm. **2.** unattractive or repellent in character; unpleasant; disagreeable; objectionable. [ME] —**un·love′li·ness,** *n.*

un·luck·y (un luk′ē), *adj.,* **-luck·i·er, -luck·i·est. 1.** (of a person) not lucky; lacking good fortune; ill-fated. **2.** (of an event or circumstance) inauspicious; ominous. —**un·luck′i·ly,** *adv.* —**Syn.** hapless, unsuccessful, ill-omened.

un·made (un mād′), *adj.* **1.** not made. **2.** *Falconry.* unmanned (def. 2). [ME]

un·make (un māk′), *v.t.,* **-made, -mak·ing. 1.** to cause to be as if never made; undo; destroy; ruin. **2.** to depose from office or authority; demote in rank. **3.** to alter radically the nature of. [ME *unmake(n)*] —**un·mak′er,** *n.*

un·man (un man′), *v.t.,* **-manned, -man·ning. 1.** to deprive of courage or fortitude; break down the manly spirit of. **2.** to deprive of virility; emasculate; castrate. **3.** *Archaic.* to deprive of the character of man.

un·man·ly (un man′lē), *adj.* **1.** not manly; weak, timid, or cowardly. **2.** womanish; effeminate. —*adv.* **3.** *Archaic.* in an unmanly manner. [ME] —**un·man′li·ness,** *n.*

un·manned (un mand′), *adj.* **1.** without the physical presence of men in control: *an unmanned spacecraft.* **2.** *Falconry.* (of a captured hawk) untrained for hunting with a master; unmade.

un·man·nered (un man′ərd), *adj.* **1.** lacking good manners; rude or ill-bred. **2.** without affectation or insincerity; ingenuous.

un·man·ner·ly (un man′ər lē), *adj.* **1.** not mannerly; impolite; discourteous; coarse. —*adv.* **2.** *Archaic.* with ill manners. [ME] —**un·man′ner·li·ness,** *n.*

un·marked (un märkt′), *adj.* **1.** having no scars, scratches, or other blemishes: *His face was unmarked by the accident.* **2.** having no added notations, corrections, or the like: *an unmarked copy of the report.* **3.** (of an examination paper, student's report, or the like) not yet graded or corrected by a teacher. **4.** (of a grave) not having a tombstone or other identifying marker.

un·mask (un mask′, -mäsk′), *v.t.* **1.** to strip a mask or disguise from. **2.** to reveal the true character of; disclose; expose. **3.** *Mil.* to reveal the presence of (guns) by firing. —*v.i.* **4.** to put off one's mask; appear in true nature. —**un·mask′er,** *n.*

un·mean·ing (un mē′ning), *adj.* **1.** devoid of sense or significance, as words or actions; empty. **2.** expressionless or unintelligent, as the face. —**un·mean′ing·ly,** *adv.* —**un·mean′ing·ness,** *n.*

un·meas·ured (un mezh′ərd), *adj.* **1.** not capable of being measured. **2.** without bounds or limits. **3.** *Pros., Music.* not metrical. [ME *unmesured*] —**un·meas′ur·a·ble,** *adj.* —**un·meas′ur·a·ble·ness,** *n.* —**un·meas′ured·ly,** *adv.* —**Syn. 1.** immense, vast. **2.** unstinting, lavish.

un·meet (un mēt′), *adj.* not meet; unbecoming; unseemly. [ME *unmete,* OE *unmǣte*] —**un·meet′ly,** *adv.*

un·men·tion·a·ble (un men′shə nə bəl), *adj.* **1.** unfit to be mentioned. —*n.* **2.** something that is not to be mentioned. **3. unmentionables, a.** trousers or breeches. **b.** *Facetious.* undergarments.

un·mer·ci·ful (un mûr′si fəl), *adj.* **1.** merciless; relentless; pitiless. **2.** inconsiderately or pitilessly excessive: *an unmerciful length of time.* —**un·mer′ci·ful·ly,** *adv.*

un·mind·ful (un mīnd′fəl), *adj.* not mindful; unaware; heedless; forgetful; neglectful. [ME *unmyndeful*] —**un·mind′ful·ly,** *adv.* —**un·mind′ful·ness,** *n.* —**Syn.** inattentive, negligent, unobservant.

un·mis·tak·a·ble (un′mi stā′kə bəl), *adj.* not mistakable; clear; evident; obvious. —**un′mis·tak′a·bly,** *adv.* —**Syn.** obvious, patent.

un·mit·i·gat·ed (un mit′ə gā′tid), *adj.* **1.** not mitigated. **2.** unqualified or absolute: *an unmitigated cad.* —**un·mit′i·gat′ed·ly,** *adv.*

un·mixed (un mikst′), *adj.* not mixed; pure. —**un·mix·ed·ly** (un mik′sid lē, -mikst′lē), *adv.*

un·mor·al (un môr′əl, -mor′-), *adj.* amoral; nonmoral. —**un·mo·ral·i·ty** (un′mə ral′i tē, -mô-), *n.* —**un·mor′al·ly,** *adv.* —**Syn.** See **immoral.**

unmoved′ mov′er, *Aristotelianism.* See **prime mover** (def. 2).

un·mov·ing (un mōō′ving), *adj.* **1.** not moving; still; motionless. **2.** not stirring the emotions.

un·mu·si·cal (un myōō′zi kəl), *adj.* **1.** not musical; deficient in melody, harmony, or the like. **2.** not fond of or skilled in music. —**un·mu′si·cal·ly,** *adv.*

un·muz·zle (un muz′əl), *v.t.,* **-zled, -zling. 1.** to remove a muzzle from (a dog, cat, etc.). **2.** to free from restraint, as speech or expression.

un·named (un nāmd′), *adj.* **1.** without a name; nameless. **2.** not indicated or mentioned by name.

un·nat·u·ral (un nach′ər əl, -nach′rəl), *adj.* **1.** contrary to the laws or course of nature. **2.** at variance with the character or nature of a person, animal, or plant. **3.** at variance with what is normal or to be expected. **4.** not genuine or spontaneous; artificial or affected. **5.** lacking human qualities or sympathies; monstrous; inhuman. **6.** *Obs.* lacking a valid or natural claim; illegitimate. [ME] —**un·nat′u·ral·ly,** *adv.* —**un·nat′u·ral·ness,** *n.* —**Syn. 3.** irregular, anomalous, aberrant. **5.** heartless.

un·nec·es·sar·y (un nes′i ser′ē), *adj.* not necessary; needless; unessential. —**un·nec·es·sar·i·ly** (un nes′i sâr′ə lē, -nes′i ser′-), *adv.*

un·nerve (un nûrv′), *v.t.,* **-nerved, -nerv·ing.** to deprive of courage, determination; render ineffectual. —**Syn.** discourage, shake, fluster, disconcert. —**Ant.** steel.

un·num·bered (un num′bərd), *adj.* **1.** countless; innumerable. **2.** not identified with numerals. **3.** uncounted. [ME *unnoumbred*]

UNO, United Nations Organization. Also, **U.N.O.**

un·oc·cu·pied (un ok′yə pīd′), *adj.* **1.** without occupants; empty; vacant. **2.** not busy or active; idle. [ME]

un·latch′, *v.*
un·leased′, *adj.*
un·life′like′, *adj.*
un·light′ed, *adj.*
un·lik′a·ble, *adj.*
un·lined′, *adj.*
un·liq′ui·dat′ed, *adj.*
un·lit′, *adj.*
un·liv′a·ble, *adj.*
un·lo′cat·ed, *adj.*
un·lov′a·ble, *adj.*
un·loved′, *adj.*
un·lov′ing, *adj.*
un·lu′bri·cat′ed, *adj.*
un·mag′ni·fied′, *adj.*
un·maid′en·ly, *adj.*
un·man′age·a·ble, *adj.*
un′ma·nip′u·lat′ed, *adj.*
un′man·u·fac′tured, *adj.*
un·mar′ket·a·ble, *adj.*
un·marred′, *adj.*
un·mar′riage·a·ble, *adj.*
un·mar′ried, *adj.*
un·mas′tered, *adj.*
un·matched′, *adj.*
un·mat′ted, *adj.*
un′ma·tured′, *adj.*
un·meant′, *adj.*
un′me·chan′ic·al, *adj.*
un·med′i·cat′ed, *adj.*
un′me·lo′di·ous, *adj.*
un·melt′ed, *adj.*
un·mem′o·rized′, *adj.*
un·men′aced, *adj.*
un·mend′ed, *adj.*
un·men′tioned, *adj.*
un·mer′chant·a·ble, *adj.*
un·mer′it·ed, *adj.*
un′me·thod′i·cal, *adj.*
un·met′ri·cal, *adj.*
un·mil′i·tar′y, *adj.*
un·min′gled, *adj.*
un·mirth′ful, *adj.;* **-ly,** *adv.*
un′mis·tak′en, *adj.*
un·mod′u·lat′ed, *adj.*
un·mold′ed, *adj.*
un′mo·lest′ed, *adj.*
un·mol′li·fied′, *adj.*
un·mo′ti·vat′ed, *adj.*
un·mount′ed, *adj.*
un·mourned′, *adj.*
un·mov′a·ble, *adj.*
un·moved′, *adj.*
un·mown′, *adj.*
un·muf′fle, *v.t.,* **-fled, -fling.**
un·mys′ti·fied′, *adj.*
un·nam′a·ble, *adj.*
un·name′a·ble, *adj.*
un·nav′i·ga·ble, *adj.*
un·nav′i·gat′ed, *adj.*
un·need′ed, *adj.*
un·need′ful, *adj.;* **-ly,** *adv.*
un·ne·go′ti·a·ble, *adj.*
un′ne·go′ti·at′ed, *adj.*
un·neigh′bor·ly, *adj.*
un·note′wor′thy, *adj.*
un·no′tice·a·ble, *adj.;* **-bly,** *adv.*
un·no′ticed, *adj.*
un·nur′tured, *adj.*
un′ob·jec′tion·a·ble, *adj.*
un′ob·liged′, *adj.*
un′ob·lig′ing, *adj.*
un′ob·nox′ious, *adj.*
un′ob·scured′, *adj.*
un′ob·serv′ant, *adj.*
un′ob·served′, *adj.*
un′ob·serv′ing, *adj.*
un′ob·struct′ed, *adj.*
un′ob·tain′a·ble, *adj.*
un′ob·tained′, *adj.*
un′ob·trud′ing, *adj.*
un′ob·tru′sive, *adj.;* **-ly,** *adv.;* **-ness,** *n.*

un·or·gan·ized (un ôr′gə nīzd′), *adj.* **1.** not organized; without organic structure. **2.** not formed into a systematized whole. **3.** not thinking or acting methodically. **4.** not having membership in a labor union: *organized and unorganized labor.* Also, *esp. Brit.*, **un·or′gan·ised′.**

un·pack (un pak′), *v.t.* **1.** to empty (a container) of its contents. **2.** to remove (something) from a container. **3.** to remove a pack or load from (a horse, vehicle, etc.). —*v.i.* **4.** to remove the contents of a container. [ME *unpakke(n)*]

un·paged (un pājd′), *adj.* (of a publication) having unnumbered pages.

un·par·al·leled (un par′ə leld′), *adj.* not paralleled; unequaled or unmatched. Also, *esp. Brit.*, **un·par′al·lelled′.** —**Syn.** matchless, unrivaled.

un·par·lia·men·ta·ry (un′pär lə men′tə rē), *adj.* not parliamentary; at variance with or contrary to the methods employed by parliamentary bodies. —**un′par·lia·men′ta·ri·ly,** *adv.*

un·peg (un peg′), *v.t.*, **-pegged, -peg·ging. 1.** to remove the peg or pegs from. **2.** to open, unfasten, or unfix by or as if by removing a peg or pegs.

un·peo·ple (un pē′pəl), *v.t.*, **-pled, -pling.** to deprive of people; depopulate.

un·pile (un pīl′), *v.*, **-piled, -pil·ing.** —*v.t.* **1.** to remove from a pile or a piled condition: *to unpile boxes; to unpile a heap of stones.* —*v.i.* **2.** to become removed from a pile or a piled condition.

un·pin (un pin′), *v.t.*, **-pinned, -pin·ning. 1.** to remove a pin or pins from. **2.** to unfasten by or as by removing a pin.

un·pleas·ant (un plez′ənt), *adj.* not pleasant; displeasing; disagreeable. —**un·pleas′ant·ly,** *adv.* —**Syn.** unappetizing, obnoxious, noisome.

un·pleas·ant·ness (un plez′ənt nis), *n.* **1.** the quality or state of being unpleasant. **2.** something that is displeasing or offensive.

un·plug (un plug′), *v.t.*, **-plugged, -plug·ging.** to remove a plug or plugs from.

un·plumbed (un plumd′), *adj.* **1.** not plumbed; not measured with a plumb line. **2.** not deeply or thoroughly understood or explored.

un′polished rice′, a partly refined rice, hulled and deprived of its germ but retaining some bran.

un·po·lite (un′pə līt′), *adj.* impolite. —**un′po·lite′ly,** *adv.* —**un′po·lite′ness,** *n.*

un·pop·u·lar (un pop′yə lər), *adj.* **1.** not popular; disliked, disapproved, or ignored by the public. **2.** in disfavor with a particular person or group of persons. —**un·pop·u·lar·i·ty** (un′pop yə lar′i tē), *n.* —**un·pop′u·lar·ly,** *adv.*

un·prac·ti·cal (un prak′ti kəl), *adj.* impractical. —**un·prac′ti·cal·ly,** *adv.*

un·prac·ticed (un prak′tist), *adj.* **1.** not trained or skilled; inexpert: *an unpracticed actor.* **2.** not practiced; not usually or generally done or put into effect. Also, *esp. Brit.*, **un·prac′tised.**

un·prec·e·dent·ed (un pres′i den′tid), *adj.* without previous instance; never before known or experienced; unexampled or unparalleled.

un·pre·dict·a·ble (un′pri dik′tə bəl), *adj.* **1.** not predictable; not to be foreseen or foretold. —*n.* **2.** something that is unpredictable. —**un′pre·dict′a·bil′i·ty, un′pre·dict′a·ble·ness,** *n.* —**un′pre·dict′a·bly,** *adv.*

un·prej·u·diced (un prej′ə dist), *adj.* **1.** not prejudiced; without preconception; unbiased; impartial. **2.** *Obs.* not damaged; unimpaired. —**un·prej′u·diced·ly,** *adv.* —**Syn. 1.** See **fair**[1].

un·pre·ten·tious (un′pri ten′shəs), *adj.* not pretentious; simple; modest; unaffected. —**un′pre·ten′tious·ly,** *adv.* —**un′pre·ten′tious·ness,** *n.* —**Syn.** humble, unpretending, plain, open, easy.

un·prin·ci·pled (un prin′sə pəld), *adj.* **1.** lacking or not based on moral scruples or principles. **2.** not instructed in the principles of something (usually fol. by *in*). —**un·prin′ci·pled·ness,** *n.* —**Syn. 1.** tricky, dishonest.

un·print·a·ble (un prin′tə bəl), *adj.* improper or unfit for print, esp. because of obscenity or offensive nature. —**un·print′a·ble·ness,** *n.* —**un·print′a·bly,** *adv.*

un·pro·fes·sion·al (un′prə fesh′ə nəl), *adj.* **1.** not professional; not pertaining to or characteristic of a profession. **2.** at variance with or contrary to professional standards or ethics: *unprofessional conduct.* **3.** not belonging to a profession; nonprofessional. **4.** not done with professional competence; amateurish. **5.** *Sports.* nonprofessional. —*n.* **6.** a person who is not a professional; amateur. —**un′pro·fes′sion·al·ly,** *adv.*

un·prom·is·ing (un prom′i sing), *adj.* unlikely to be favorable or successful. —**un·prom′is·ing·ly,** *adv.*

un·qual·i·fied (un kwol′ə fīd′), *adj.* **1.** not qualified; not fit; lacking the requisite qualifications. **2.** not modified or restricted in any way; without reservations; absolute; complete. —**un·qual′i·fi′a·ble,** *adj.* —**un·qual′i·fied′ly,** *adv.* —**un·qual′i·fied′ness,** *n.* —**Syn. 1.** unfit, incompetent. **2.** unmitigated.

un·ques·tion·a·ble (un kwes′chə nə bəl), *adj.* **1.** not open to question; beyond doubt or dispute; certain. **2.** above criticism; unexceptionable: *a man of unquestionable principles.* —**un·ques′tion·a·ble·ness,** *n.* —**un·ques′tion·a·bly,** *adv.* —**Syn. 1.** incontrovertible, incontestable.

un·ques·tioned (un kwes′chənd), *adj.* **1.** not called into question; undisputed. **2.** not inquired into or investigated. **3.** not interrogated: *an unquestioned witness.*

un·qui·et (un kwī′it), *adj.* **1.** agitated; restless; disordered; turbulent or tumultuous. **2.** mentally or emotionally disturbed; vexed or perturbed; uneasy. **3.** *Archaic.* not silent; noisy. —*n.* **4.** a state of agitation, turbulence, disturbance, etc. —**un·qui′et·ly,** *adv.* —**un·qui′et·ness,** *n.* —**Syn. 1.** restive, fidgety. **2.** nervous; upset, disturbed.

un·quote (un kwōt′), *v.i.*, **-quot·ed, -quot·ing.** to close a quotation (often used with the word *quote,* which notes the opening of the quotation): *The candidate said, quote, I am unalterably opposed to this policy, unquote.*

un·rav·el (un rav′əl), *v.*, **-eled, -el·ing** or (*esp. Brit.*) **-elled, -el·ling.** —*v.t.* **1.** to separate or disentangle the threads of (a fabric, rope, etc.). **2.** to free from complications; make plain or clear; solve: *to unravel a mystery.* —*v.i.* **3.** to become unraveled. —**un·rav′el·er;** *esp. Brit.*, **un·rav′el·ler,** *n.* —**un·rav′el·ment,** *n.*

un·read (un red′), *adj.* **1.** not read. **2.** lacking in knowledge gained by reading. **3.** having little knowledge of a specific field. [ME *unred*]

un·read·a·ble (un rē′də bəl), *adj.* **1.** not readable; undecipherable; illegible. **2.** not interesting to read; dull; tedious. **3.** extraordinarily difficult to read or comprehend; obscure; incomprehensible. —**un·read′a·bil′i·ty, un·read′a·ble·ness,** *n.* —**un·read′a·bly,** *adv.*

un·read·y (un red′ē), *adj.* **1.** not ready; not made ready: *The new stadium is as yet unready for use.* **2.** not in a state of readiness; unprepared: *He was emotionally unready for success.* **3.** lacking in presence of mind: *Awkward situations often found him unready.* **4.** *Brit. Dial.* not dressed. [ME *unredy*] —**un·read′i·ness,** *n.*

un·re·al (un rē′əl, -rēl′), *adj.* **1.** not real or actual. **2.** imaginary; fanciful; illusory; delusory; fantastic. **3.** lacking in truth; not genuine; false; artificial. —**un·re′al·ly,** *adv.* —**Syn.** sham, spurious; fictitious, theoretical; vague.

un·re·al·i·ty (un′rē al′i tē), *n., pl.* **-ties. 1.** lack of reality; quality of being unreal. **2.** something that is unreal, invalid, imaginary, or illusory. **3.** incompetence or impracticality.

un·re·al·iz·a·ble (un rē′ə lī′zə bəl), *adj.* **1.** with no possibility of realization, as an ideal. **2.** incapable of being sensed or understood; unthinkable. Also, *esp. Brit.*, **un′re·al·is′a·ble.**

un·re·al·ized (un rē′ə līzd′), *adj.* **1.** not made real or actual; not resulting in accomplishment, as a task, aim, etc. **2.** not known or suspected: *unrealized talent.* Also, *esp. Brit.*, **un·re′al·ised′.**

un′of·fend′ed, *adj.*
un′of·fend′ing, *adj.*
un′of·fen′sive, *adj.;* **-ly,** *adv.*
un·of′fered, *adj.*
un′of·fi′cial, *adj.;* **-ly,** *adv.*
un′of·fi′cious, *adj.;* **-ly,** *adv.*
un·o′pen, *adj.*
un·o′pened, *adj.*
un′op·posed′, *adj.*
un′op·pressed′, *adj.*
un′op·pres′sive, *adj.;* **-ly,** *adv.*
un′or·dained′, *adj.*
un′o·rig′i·nal, *adj.*
un′or·na·men′tal, *adj.*
un·or′na·ment′ed, *adj.*
un·or′tho·dox, *adj.;* **-ly,** *adv.*
un′os·ten·ta′tious, *adj.;* **-ly,** *adv.*
un·owned′, *adj.*
un·pac′i·fied′, *adj.*
un·paid′, *adj.*
un·paired′, *adj.*
un·pal′at·a·ble, *adj.;* **-bly,** *adv.*
un·par′don·a·ble, *adj.;* **-bly,** *adv.*
un·par′doned, *adj.*
un′pa·ren′tal, *adj.;* **-ly,** *adv.*
un·part′ed, *adj.*
un·pas′teur·ized′, *adj.*
un·pat′ent·ed, *adj.*
un′pa·tri·ot′ic, *adj.*
un·paved′, *adj.*
un·pay′ing, *adj.*
un·peace′ful, *adj.;* **-ly,** *adv.*
un·ped′i·greed′, *adj.*
un·pen′e·trat′ed, *adj.*
un·pen′sioned, *adj.*
un·pep′pered, *adj.*
un′per·ceiv′a·ble, *adj.;* **-bly,** *adv.*
un′per·ceived′, *adj.*
un′per·cep′tive, *adj.;* **-ly,** *adv.*
un′per·fect′ed, *adj.*
un′per·formed′, *adj.*
un′per·plexed′, *adj.*
un′per·suad′a·ble, *adj.;* **-bly,** *adv.*
un′per·suad′ed, *adj.*
un′per·sua′sive, *adj.;* **-ly,** *adv.*
un′per·turb′a·ble, *adj.*
un′per·turbed′, *adj.*
un′phil·o·soph′i·cal, *adj.;* **-ly,** *adv.*
un·picked′, *adj.*
un·pit′ied, *adj.*
un·pit′y·ing, *adj.*
un·placed′, *adj.*
un·plait′, *v.t.*
un·plant′ed, *adj.*
un·play′a·ble, *adj.*
un·played′, *adj.*
un·pleased′, *adj.*
un·pleas′ing, *adj.*
un·pledged′, *adj.*
un·plowed′, *adj.*
un′po·et′ic, *adj.*
un′po·et′i·cal, *adj.;* **-ly,** *adv.*
un·point′ed, *adj.*
un·poised′, *adj.*
un·po′lar·ized′, *adj.*
un·pol′ished, *adj.*
un·pol′i·tic, *adj.*
un′po·lit′i·cal, *adj.*
un·polled′, *adj.*
un′pol·lut′ed, *adj.*
un·pol′ym·er·ised′, *adj.*
un·pol′ym·er·ized′, *adj.*
un·pon′dered, *adj.*
un·pop′u·lat′ed, *adj.*
un·posed′, *adj.*
un′pos·sess′ing, *adj.*
un′pos·ses′sive, *adj.;* **-ly,** *adv.*
un·prac′ti·ca·ble, *adj.*
un′pre·dict′ed, *adj.*
un′pre·med′i·tat′ed, *adj.*
un′pre·pared′, *adj.*
un′pre·par′ed·ness, *n.*
un′pre·pos·sess′ing, *adj.*
un′pre·scribed′, *adj.*
un′pre·sent′a·ble, *adj.;* **-bly,** *adv.*
un′pre·served′, *adj.*
un·pressed′, *adj.*
un′pre·sump′tu·ous, *adj.*
un′pre·vail′ing, *adj.*
un′pre·vent′a·ble, *adj.*
un′pre·vent′ed, *adj.*
un·probed′, *adj.*
un·proc′essed, *adj.*
un′pro·claimed′, *adj.*
un′pro·cur′a·ble, *adj.*
un′pro·duc′tive, *adj.;* **-ly,** *adv.;* **-ness,** *n.*
un′pro·fessed′, *adj.*
un·prof′it·a·ble, *adj.;* **-bly,** *adv.*
un′pro·gres′sive, *adj.;* **-ly,** *adv.*
un′pro·hib′it·ed, *adj.*
un·prompt′ed, *adj.*
un′pro·nounce′a·ble, *adj.*
un′pro·nounced′, *adj.*
un′pro·pi′tious, *adj.;* **-ly,** *adv.*
un′pro·por′tion·ate, *adj.;* **-ly,** *adv.*
un′pro·posed′, *adj.*
un′pro·pound′ed, *adj.*
un·pros′per·ous, *adj.*
un′pro·tect′ed, *adj.*
un′pro·test′ing, *adj.;* **-ly,** *adv.*
un·proved′, *adj.*
un·prov′en, *adj.*
un′pro·vid′ed, *adj.*
un′pro·voked′, *adj.*
un·pub′lished, *adj.*
un·punc′tu·al, *adj.*
un·pun′ished, *adj.*
un·pu′ri·fied′, *adj.*
un·quelled′, *adj.*
un·quench′a·ble, *adj.*
un·quenched′, *adj.*
un·ques′tion·ing, *adj.;* **-ly,** *adv.*
un·quot′a·ble, *adj.*
un·raised′, *adj.*
un·raked′, *adj.*
un·rat′ed, *adj.*
un′re·al·is′tic, *adj.*
un′re·al·is′ti·cal·ly, *adv.*

un·rea·son (un rē′zən), *n.* **1.** inability or unwillingness to think or act rationally; irrationality. **2.** lack of reason or sanity; madness; confusion; disorder; chaos. —*v.t.* **3.** to upset or disrupt the reason or sanity of. [ME *un-reson*]

un·rea·son·a·ble (un rē′zə nə bəl, -rēz′nə-), *adj.* **1.** acting at variance with or contrary to reason; not guided by reason, sound judgment, or good sense; irrational. **2.** not in accordance with practical realities, as attitude, behavior, etc.; inappropriate. **3.** excessive, immoderate, or exorbitant: *unreasonable demands.* **4.** not having the faculty of reason. [ME *unresonabel*] —**un·rea′son·a·ble·ness,** *n.* —**un·rea′son·a·bly,** *adv.* —**Syn. 1, 2.** senseless, foolish, silly. **2.** preposterous, absurd. **3.** extravagant.

un·rea·son·ing (un rē′zə ning), *adj.* not reasoning or exercising reason; irrational. —**un·rea′son·ing·ly,** *adv.*

un·re·con·struct·ed (un′rē kən struk′tid), *adj.* **1.** stubbornly maintaining earlier positions, beliefs, etc. **2.** *U.S. Hist.* (of Southern states) not accepting the conditions for reinstatement in the Union after the Civil War.

un·reel (un rēl′), *v.t.* **1.** to unwind from or as from a reel. —*v.i.* **2.** to become unreeled. —**un·reel′a·ble,** *adj.* —**un·reel′er,** *n.*

un·re·fined (un′ri fīnd′), *adj.* **1.** not refined; not purified: *unrefined metal.* **2.** coarse or crude; lacking in refinement of taste, manners, language, etc. —**Syn. 1.** unpurified, crude. **2.** uncultured, rude, boorish, vulgar.

un·re·flect·ed (un′ri flek′tid), *adj.* **1.** not reflected on; not given consideration. **2.** not cast back, as light, heat, an image, etc.

un·re·flect·ing (un′ri flek′ting), *adj.* not reflecting; unthinking: *an unreflecting, self-satisfied man.* —**un′re·flect′ing·ly,** *adv.*

un·re·flec·tive (un′ri flek′tiv), *adj.* not reflective; thoughtless; lacking in due deliberation; heedless; rash. —**un′re·flec′tive·ly,** *adv.*

un·re·gen·er·ate (un′ri jen′ər it), *adj.* Also, **un·re·gen·er·at·ed** (un′ri jen′ə rā′tid). **1.** not regenerate; not renewed in heart and mind or reborn in spirit; unrepentant: *an unregenerate sinner.* **2.** unconvinced by or unconverted to a particular religion, sect, cause, etc.; unreconstructed. **3.** obstinate: *an unregenerate reactionary.* —*n.* **4.** an unregenerate person. —**un·re·gen·er·a·cy** (un′ri jen′ər ə sē), *n.* —**un′re·gen′er·ate·ly,** *adv.*

un·re·lent·ing (un′ri len′ting), *adj.* **1.** not relenting; not yielding in determination; inflexible. **2.** not easing or slackening; maintaining speed, effort, vigor, etc.: *unrelenting progress.* —**un′re·lent′ing·ly,** *adv.* —**un′re·lent′ing·ness,** *n.* —**Syn. 1.** relentless, implacable, inexorable. **2.** unremitting; constant; unfailing.

un·re·li·gious (un′ri lij′əs), *adj.* **1.** irreligious. **2.** neither religious nor irreligious; nonreligious; secular. [ME] —**un′re·li′gious·ly,** *adv.*

un·re·mit·ting (un′ri mit′ing), *adj.* not slackening or abating; incessant: *unremitting noise; unremitting attention.* —**un′re·mit′ting·ly,** *adv.* —**un′re·mit′ting·ness,** *n.* —**Syn.** continuous, constant, perpetual.

un·re·pair (un′ri pâr′), *n.* lack of repair; disrepair; dilapidation. —**un′re·paired′,** *adj.*

un·re·serve (un′ri zûrv′), *n.* absence of reserve; frankness; candor.

un·re·served (un′ri zûrvd′), *adj.* **1.** not reserved; without reservation; unqualified: *unreserved approval.* **2.** free from reserve; frank; open: *unreserved behavior.* —**un·re·serv·ed·ly** (un′ri zûr′vid lē), *adv.* —**un′re·serv′ed·ness,** *n.* —**Syn. 1.** complete, unlimited. **2.** ingenuous, candid.

un·rest (un rest′), *n.* **1.** lack of rest; uneasiness; disquiet. **2.** strong, almost rebellious, dissatisfaction and agitation: *political unrest.* [ME]

un·rid·dle (un rid′əl), *v.t.*, **-dled, -dling.** to solve (a riddle, mystery, etc.). —**un·rid′dler,** *n.*

un·rig (un rig′), *v.t.*, **-rigged, -rig·ging. 1.** to strip of rigging, as a ship. **2.** to strip of equipment. **3.** *Chiefly Brit. Dial.* to undress.

un·right·eous (un rī′chəs), *adj.* **1.** not righteous; not upright or virtuous; wicked; sinful; evil. **2.** unfair or unjust. [ME *unrightwyse,* OE *unrihtwīs*] —**un·right′eous·ly,** *adv.* —**un·right′eous·ness,** *n.*

un·rip (un rip′), *v.t.*, **-ripped, -rip·ping. 1.** to undo by ripping; cut or tear open; rip. **2.** to make known; disclose; reveal.

un·ripe (un rīp′), *adj.* **1.** not ripe; immature. **2.** too early; premature. [ME *unrype,* OE *unripe*] —**un·ripe′ly,** *adv.* —**un·ripe′ness,** *n.*

un·ri·valed (un rī′vəld), *adj.* having no rival or competitor; having no equal; peerless; incomparable. Also, *esp. Brit.,* **un·ri′valled.**

un·robe (un rōb′), *v.t., v.i.*, **-robed, -rob·ing.** to disrobe; undress.

un·roll (un rōl′), *v.t.* **1.** to open or spread out (something rolled or coiled). **2.** to lay open; display; reveal. **3.** *Obs.* to strike from a roll or register. —*v.i.* **4.** to become unrolled or spread out. **5.** to become continuously visible or apparent: *The landscape unrolled before his eyes.* [ME *unroll(en)*]

un·root (un ro͞ot′, -ro͝ot′), *v.t.* **1.** to uproot; eradicate. —*v.i.* **2.** to become unrooted. [ME *unroot(en)*]

un·round (un round′), *v.t. Phonet.* to articulate (an ordinarily rounded vowel) without rounding the lips. Cf. **round**[1] (def. 44), **spread** (def. 8).

UNRRA (un′rə), United Nations Relief and Rehabilitation Administration. Also, **U.N.R.R.A.**

un·ruf·fled (un ruf′əld), *adj.* **1.** calm; steady; unflustered. **2.** not ruffled, as a garment; smooth. —**un·ruf′fled·ness,** *n.* —**Syn. 1.** unperturbed, tranquil, serene, composed.

un·ru·ly (un ro͞o′lē), *adj.*, **-li·er, -li·est.** not submissive or conforming to rule; ungovernable; intractable. [ME *unruely* = *un-* UN-[1] + *ruly, ruely* governable, controllable; see RULE, -Y[1]] —**un·ru′li·ness,** *n.* —**Syn.** disobedient, unmanageable, uncontrollable.

un·sad·dle (un sad′əl), *v.*, **-dled, -dling.** —*v.t.* **1.** to take the saddle from. **2.** to cause to fall or dismount from a saddle; unhorse. —*v.i.* **3.** to take the saddle from a horse. [ME; cf. D, Flem *ontsadelen,* OHG *intsatalōn*]

un·said[1] (un sed′), *v.* pt. and pp. of **unsay.**

un·said[2] (un sed′), *adj.* not said; thought but not mentioned or discussed; unstated.

un·sat·is·fac·to·ry (un′sat is fak′tə rē), *adj.* not satisfactory; not satisfying or meeting one's demands; inadequate. —**un′sat·is·fac′to·ri·ly,** *adv.* —**Syn.** disappointing, insufficient.

un·sat·u·rat·ed (un sach′ə rā′tid), *adj.* **1.** not saturated; having the power to dissolve still more of a substance. **2.** *Chem.* (of an organic compound) having a double or triple bond and capable of taking on elements or groups by direct chemical combination without the liberation of other elements or compounds, as ethylene, $CH_2{=}CH_2$. —**un·sat·u·rate** (un sach′ər it, -ə rāt′), *n.* —**un′sat·u·ra′tion,** *n.*

un·sa·vor·y (un sā′və rē), *adj.* **1.** not savory; tasteless or insipid: *an unsavory meal.* **2.** unpleasant in taste or smell; distasteful. **3.** unappealing or disagreeable, as a pursuit: *Poor teachers can make education unsavory.* **4.** socially or morally objectionable. Also, *esp. Brit.,* **un·sa′vour·y.** [ME] —**un·sa′vor·i·ly;** *esp. Brit.,* **un·sa′vour·i·ly,** *adv.* —**un·sa′vor·i·ness;** *esp. Brit.,* **un·sa′vour·i·ness,** *n.*

un·say (un sā′), *v.t.*, **-said, -say·ing.** to retract (something said). [ME *unsayen*]

un·scathed (un skāthd′), *adj.* not scathed; unharmed; uninjured. [ME]

un·schooled (un sko͞old′), *adj.* **1.** not schooled, taught, or trained. **2.** not acquired or artificial; natural.

un·sci·en·tif·ic (un′sī ən tif′ik), *adj.* **1.** not scientific; not in accordance with the requirements of science. **2.** not conforming to the principles or methods of science. **3.** lacking scientific knowledge. —**un′sci·en·tif′i·cal·ly,** *adv.*

un·scram·ble (un skram′bəl), *v.t.*, **-bled, -bling. 1.** to bring out of a scrambled condition; restore to order or intelligibility. **2.** to make (a scrambled radio or telephonic message) comprehensible.

un·screw (un skro͞o′), *v.t.* **1.** to draw or loosen a screw or screws from (a hinge, bracket, etc.). **2.** to unfasten (something) by withdrawing screws. **3.** to open (a jar, bottle, can, etc.) by turning the lid or cover. —*v.i.* **4.** to permit of being unscrewed.

un·scru·pu·lous (un skro͞o′pyə ləs), *adj.* not scrupulous; conscienceless; unprincipled. —**un·scru′pu·lous·ly,** *adv.* —**un·scru′pu·lous·ness, un·scru·pu·los·i·ty** (un skro͞o′pyə los′i tē), *n.*

un·seal (un sēl′), *v.t.* **1.** to break or remove the seal of; open. **2.** to free from constraint, as a person's speech or behavior. [ME] —**un·seal′a·ble,** *adj.*

un·sealed (un sēld′), *adj.* **1.** not sealed; not stamped or marked with a seal: *unsealed cargo.* **2.** not shut or closed with or as if with a seal: *an unsealed letter.* **3.** not verified, certain, or confirmed. [ME *unseled*]

un·seam (un sēm′), *v.t.* to open the seam or seams of; undo; rip apart.

un·search·a·ble (un sûr′chə bəl), *adj.* not searchable;

---

un·rea′soned, *adj.*
un′re·buked′, *adj.*
un′re·cep′tive, *adj.;* **-ly,** *adv.*
un·reck′oned, *adj.*
un′re·claimed′, *adj.*
un·rec′og·niz′a·ble, *adj.;* **-bly,** *adv.*
un·rec′og·nized′, *adj.*
un′rec·om·mend′ed, *adj.*
un·rec′om·pensed′, *adj.*
un′rec·on·cil′a·ble, *adj.;* **-bly,** *adv.*
un·rec′on·ciled′, *adj.*
un′re·cord′ed, *adj.*
un·rec′ti·fied′, *adj.*
un′re·formed′, *adj.*
un′re·freshed′, *adj.*
un·reg′i·ment′ed, *adj.*
un·reg′is·tered, *adj.*
un′re·gret′ted, *adj.*
un·reg′u·lat′ed, *adj.*
un′re·hearsed′, *adj.*
un′re·lat′ed, *adj.*
un′re·li′a·ble, *adj.;* **-bly,** *adv.*
un′re·lieved′, *adj.*
un·rem′e·died, *adj.*
un′re·mem′bered, *adj.*
un′re·mit′ted, *adj.*
un′re·morse′ful, *adj.;* **-ly,** *adv.*
un′re·mov′a·ble, *adj.*
un′re·moved′, *adj.*
un′re·mu′ner·at′ed, *adj.*
un′re·mu′ner·a′tive, *adj.*
un·ren′dered, *adj.*
un′re·newed′, *adj.*
un′re·nowned′, *adj.*
un·rent′ed, *adj.*
un′re·paid′, *adj.*
un′re·pealed′, *adj.*
un′re·pent′ant, *adj.*
un′re·pent′ed, *adj.*
un′re·pent′ing, *adj.;* **-ly,** *adv.*
un′re·place′a·ble, *adj.*
un′re·placed′, *adj.*
un′re·port′ed, *adj.*
un′rep·re·sent′a·tive, *adj.*
un′rep·re·sent′ed, *adj.*
un′re·pressed′, *adj.*
un′re·prieved′, *adj.*
un′rep·ri·mand′ed, *adj.*
un′re·proved′, *adj.*
un′re·quest′ed, *adj.*
un′re·quit′ed, *adj.*
un′re·sent′ed, *adj.*
un′re·sent′ful, *adj.;* **-ly,** *adv.*
un′re·signed′, *adj.*
un′re·sist′ant, *adj.*
un′re·sist′ed, *adj.*
un′re·sist′ing, *adj.*
un′re·solved′, *adj.*
un′re·spect′ful, *adj.;* **-ly,** *adv.*
un′re·spon′sive, *adj.;* **-ly,** *adv.;* **-ness,** *n.*
un·rest′ed, *adj.*
un·rest′ing, *adj*
un′re·strained′, *adj.*
un′re·strain′ed·ly, *adv.*
un′re·straint′, *n.*
un′re·strict′ed, *adj.;* **-ly,** *adv.*
un′re·ten′tive, *adj.*
un′re·tract′ed, *adj.*
un′re·turned′, *adj.*
un′re·vealed′, *adj.*
un′re·veal′ing, *adj.*
un′re·venged′, *adj.*
un′re·vised′, *adj.*
un′re·voked′, *adj.*
un′re·ward′ed, *adj.*
un′re·ward′ing, *adj.*
un·rhymed′, *adj.*
un·rhyth′mic, *adj.*
un·rhyth′mi·cal, *adj.;* **-ly,** *adv.*
un·right′ful, *adj.;* **-ly,** *adv.*
un·ri′pened, *adj.*
un′ro·man′tic, *adj.*
un′ro·man′ti·cal·ly, *adv.*
un′ro·man′ti·cised′, *adj.*
un·roof′, *v.t.*
un·ruled′, *adj.*
un·safe′, *adj.;* **-ly,** *adv.*
un·safe′ty, *n.*
un·saint′ly, *adj.*
un′sal·a·bil′i·ty, *n.*
un·sal′a·ble, *adj.*
un·sale′a·ble, *adj.*
un·salt′ed, *adj.*
un·sanc′ti·fied′, *adj.*
un·sanc′tioned, *adj.*
un·san′i·tar′y, *adj.*
un·sat′ed, *adj.*
un·sa′ti·a·ble, *adj.;* **-bly,** *adv.*
un·sa′ti·at′ed, *adj.*
un·sat′is·fied′, *adj.*
un·saved′, *adj.*
un·say′a·ble, *adj.*
un·scaled′, *adj.*
un·scanned′, *adj.*
un·scarred′, *adj.*
un·scent′ed, *adj.*
un·scep′ti·cal, *adj.*
un·sched′uled, *adj.*
un·schol′ar·ly, *adv.*
un·scratched′, *adj.*
un·screened′, *adj.*
un·scrip′tur·al, *adj.*

not lending itself to research or exploration; inscrutable; mysterious: *the unsearchable ways of the universe.* [ME *unserchable*] —**un·search′a·ble·ness,** *n.* —**un·search′a·bly,** *adv.*

un·sea·son·a·ble (un sē′zə nə bəl), *adj.* **1.** not seasonable; out of season; unseasonal: *unseasonable weather.* **2.** not befitting the occasion; untimely; ill-timed; inopportune. [ME] —**un·sea′son·a·ble·ness,** *n.* —**un·sea′son·a·bly,** *adv.*

un·sea·soned (un sē′zənd), *adj.* **1.** (of things) not seasoned; not matured, dried, etc., by due seasoning. **2.** (of persons) not inured to a climate, work, etc.; inexperienced. **3.** (of food) not flavored with seasoning.

un·seat (un sēt′), *v.t.* **1.** to dislodge from a seat, esp. to throw from a saddle, as a rider; unhorse. **2.** to remove from political office.

un·se·cured (un′si kyŏŏrd′), *adj.* **1.** not secured, esp. not backed by any form of collateral: *an unsecured loan.* **2.** not made secure, as a door, lock of hair, etc.

un·seem·ly (un sēm′lē), *adj.* **1.** not seemly; not in keeping with established standards of taste or form; unbecoming or indecorous; improper in speech, conduct, etc. —*adv.* **2.** in an unseemly manner. [ME] —**un·seem′li·ness,** *n.* —**Syn. 1.** unbefitting, inappropriate. See **improper.**

un·seen (un sēn′), *adj.* **1.** not seen; unperceived; unobserved; invisible. **2.** recognized or comprehended without prior study, as a text or musical score.

un·seg·re·gat·ed (un seg′rə gā′tid), *adj.* not segregated, esp. not subject to racial division; integrated.

un·self·ish (un sel′fish), *adj.* not selfish; disinterested; altruistic; magnanimous. —**un·self′ish·ly** *adv.* —**un·self′ish·ness,** *n.*

un·set·tle (un set′əl), *v.*, **-tled, -tling.** —*v.t.* **1.** to alter from a settled state; make unstable. **2.** to shake or weaken (beliefs, feelings, etc.); cause doubt or uncertainty about. **3.** to vex or agitate the mind or emotions of; upset. —*v.i.* **4.** to become unfixed or disordered. —**un·set′tle·ment,** *n.*

un·set·tled (un set′əld), *adj.* **1.** not settled; not fixed or stable; unorganized; disorganized. **2.** continuously moving or changing; not situated in one place. **3.** wavering or uncertain, as in opinions, behavior, etc.; unstable. **4.** not populated or settled, as a region. **5.** undetermined, as a point at issue; undecided; doubtful. **6.** not adjusted, closed, or disposed of, as an account, estate, or law case. **7.** liable to change; inconstant; variable. —**un·set′tled·ness,** *n.* —**Syn. 1, 3, 5.** UNSETTLED, UNSTABLE, UNSTEADY imply a lack of fixity, firmness, and dependability. That which is UNSETTLED is not fixed or determined: *unsettled weather; unsettled claims.* That which is UNSTABLE is wavering, changeable; easily moved, shaken, or overthrown: *unstable equilibrium; an unstable government.* That which is UNSTEADY is infirm or shaky in position or movement: *unsteady on one's feet; unsteady of purpose.* **5.** indeterminate, unsure. **7.** vacillating, fickle, faltering, irresolute. —**Ant. 1, 3.** stable.

un·sex (un seks′), *v.t.* **1.** to deprive of sexual power; render impotent. **2.** to deprive (a person) of the character and qualities appropriate to one's sex.

un·shack·le (un shak′əl), *v.t.*, **-led, -ling. 1.** to free from shackles; unfetter. **2.** to free from restraint, as conversation.

un·sheathe (un shēth′), *v.t.*, **-sheathed, -sheath·ing. 1.** to draw from a sheath, as a sword, knife, or the like. **2.** to bring or put forth from a covering, threateningly or otherwise.

un·ship (un ship′), *v.*, **-shipped, -ship·ping.** —*v.t.* **1.** to put or take off from a ship, as passengers or cargo. **2.** to remove from the place proper for its use, as an oar, tiller, etc. —*v.i.* **3.** to become unloaded or removed. [ME]

un·sight·ly (un sīt′lē), *adj.* distasteful or unpleasant to look at: *an unsightly wound; unsightly disorder.* —**un·sight′li·ness,** *n.* —**Syn.** unattractive, ugly, hideous. —**Ant.** beautiful.

un·skilled (un skild′), *adj.* **1.** of or pertaining to workers who lack technical training or skill. **2.** not demanding special training or skill: *unskilled occupations.* **3.** exhibiting a marked lack of skill or competence. **4.** not skilled or expert: *He was unskilled in the art of rhetoric.*

un′skilled la′bor, 1. work that requires practically no training or experience for its adequate or competent performance. **2.** the labor force employed for such work.

un·skill·ful (un skil′fəl), *adj.* not skillful; clumsy or bungling. Also, *esp. Brit.*, **un·skil′ful.** [ME *unskylful*] —**un·skill′ful·ly;** *esp. Brit.*, **un·skil′ful·ly,** *adv.* —**un·skill′ful·ness;** *esp. Brit.*, **un·skil′ful·ness,** *n.* —**Syn.** untrained, maladroit, inept.

un·sling (un sling′), *v.t.* **1.** to remove (something) from a slung position: *to unsling a rifle from one's shoulder.* **2.** *Naut.* to take off the slings of; release from slings.

un·sol·der (un sod′ər), *v.t.* **1.** to separate (something soldered). **2.** to disunite; sunder.

un·so·phis·ti·cat·ed (un′sə fis′tə kā′tid), *adj.* **1.** not sophisticated; simple; artless. **2.** without complexity or refinements. **3.** unadulterated; pure; genuine. **4.** not complex or intricate. —**un′so·phis′ti·cat′ed·ly,** *adv.* —**un′so·phis′ti·cat′ed·ness, un′so·phis′ti·ca′tion,** *n.* —**Syn. 1.** ingenuous, guileless, naïve.

un·sound (un sound′), *adj.* **1.** not sound; diseased, as the body or mind. **2.** decayed or impaired, as timber, foods, etc.; defective. **3.** not solid or firm, as foundations. **4.** not well-founded or valid; fallacious: *an unsound argument.* **5.** easily broken; light: *unsound slumber.* **6.** not financially strong; unreliable: *an unsound corporation.* [ME] —**un·sound′ly,** *adv.* —**un·sound′ness,** *n.* —**Syn. 1.** infirm, sick, ill. **2.** rotten, unwholesome. **4.** false, faulty.

un·spar·ing (un spâr′ing), *adj.* **1.** not sparing; liberal or profuse; excessive. **2.** unmerciful; harsh; severe. —**un·spar′ing·ly,** *adv.* —**un·spar′ing·ness,** *n.* —**Syn. 1.** generous, lavish, bountiful. **2.** merciless, unrelenting, relentless.

un·speak (un spēk′), *v.t.*, **-spoke, -spo·ken, -speak·ing.** *Obs.* to recant; retract; unsay.

un·speak·a·ble (un spē′kə bəl), *adj.* **1.** not speakable; that may not be spoken. **2.** exceeding the power of speech; inexpressible; indescribable. **3.** inexpressibly bad or objectionable. [ME *unspekeabill*] —**un·speak′a·ble·ness,** *n.* —**un·speak′a·bly,** *adv.* —**Syn. 2.** ineffable, undescribable.

un·spent (un spent′), *adj.* **1.** not spent or used, as money. **2.** not used up or consumed: *unspent energy.* [ME]

un·spo·ken (un spō′kən), *adj.* **1.** implied or understood without being spoken or uttered. **2.** not addressed (usually fol. by *to*). **3.** not talking; silent. [ME *unspokyn*]

un·spot·ted (un spot′id), *adj.* **1.** having no spots or stains; without spots; spotless. **2.** having no moral blemish or stigma. [ME] —**un·spot′ted·ness,** *n.*

un·sta·ble (un stā′bəl), *adj.* **1.** not stable; not firm or firmly fixed; unsteady. **2.** liable to fall, change, or cease. **3.** unsteadfast; inconstant; wavering. **4.** marked by emotional instability. **5.** irregular in movement. **6.** *Chem.* noting compounds that readily decompose or change into other compounds. [ME] —**un·sta′ble·ness,** *n.* —**un·sta′bly,** *adv.* —**Syn. 2.** precarious. **2, 3.** See **unsettled. 3.** vacillating.

un·stain·a·ble (un stā′nə bəl), *adj.* **1.** that cannot be spotted or stained, as garments. **2.** that cannot be morally reprehensible.

un·stained (un stānd′), *adj.* **1.** not stained or spotted; unsoiled. **2.** without moral blemish.

un·state (un stāt′), *v.t.*, **-stat·ed, -stat·ing. 1.** *Archaic.* to deprive (a person) of status, dignity, or rank. **2.** *Obs.* to deprive (a nation, government, etc.) of the character or dignity of a state.

un·stead·y (un sted′ē), *adj.*, *v.*, **-stead·ied, -stead·y·ing.** —*adj.* **1.** not steady or firm; unstable; shaky. **2.** fluctuating or wavering. **3.** irregular or uneven: *an unsteady development.* —*v.t.* **4.** to make unsteady. —**un·stead′i·ly,** *adv.* —**un·stead′i·ness,** *n.* —**Syn. 1.** See **unsettled. 2.** vacillating, flickering.

un·step (un step′), *v.t.*, **-stepped, -step·ping.** to lift from a step, as a mast.

un·stick (un stik′), *v.t.*, **-stuck, -stick·ing.** to free, as one thing stuck to another.

un·stop (un stop′), *v.t.*, **-stopped, -stop·ping. 1.** to remove the stopper from. **2.** to free from any obstruction; open. **3.** *Music.* to draw out the stops of (an organ). [ME *unstoppen*] —**un·stop′pa·ble,** *adj.* —**un·stop′pa·bly,** *adv.*

un·strained (un strānd′), *adj.* **1.** not under strain or tension. **2.** not passed through a strainer; not separated or cleared by straining. [ME]

un·strap (un strap′), *v.t.*, **-strapped, -strap·ping.** to take off or slacken the strap of.

un·stress (un′stres′), *n.* a syllable lacking in phonetic emphasis and having comparatively weak stress.

un·stressed (un strest′), *adj.* without stress or emphasis, as a syllable in a word.

un·string (un string′), *v.t.*, **-strung, -string·ing. 1.** to deprive of a string or strings. **2.** to take from a string: *to unstring beads.* **3.** to loosen the string or strings of: *to unstring a bow.* **4.** to relax the tension of. **5.** to relax unduly or weaken (the nerves). **6.** to weaken the nerves of.

un·striped (un strīpt′, -strī′pid), *adj.* not striped; nonstriated, as muscular tissue.

un·strung (un strung′), *v.* **1.** pt. and pp. of **unstring.** —*adj.* **2.** having the string or strings loosened or removed. **3.** weakened or nervously upset, as a person or his nerves.

un·stuck (un stuk′), *v.* **1.** a pt. and a pp. of **unstick.** —*adj.* **2.** freed or loosened from being fastened or stuck. **3.** out of order, control, or coherence, esp. as implying a loss of cohesiveness; undone.

un·stud·ied (un stud′ēd), *adj.* **1.** not studied; not premeditated or labored; natural; unaffected. **2.** not having

un·seared′, *adj.*
un·sea′wor′thi·ness, *n.*
un·sea′wor′thy, *adj.*
un′se·clud′ed, *adj.*
un·sec′ond·ed, *adj.*
un·sed′en·tar′y, *adj.*
un′se·duced′, *adj.*
un·see′a·ble, *adj.*
un·see′ing, *adj.*; **-ly,** *adv.*
un·seg′ment·ed, *adj.*
un′se·lect′ed, *adj.*
un′se·lec′tive, *adj.*
un′self-con′scious, *adj.*
un·sen′si·ble, *adj.*
un·sen′si·tive, *adj.*
un·sent′, *adj.*
un′sen·ti·men′tal, *adj.*
un·served′, *adj.*
un·ser′vice·a·ble, *adj.*
un·set′, *adj.*
un·sewn′, *adj.*
un·shad′owed, *adj.*
un·shak′a·ble, *adj.*
un·sha′ken, *adj.*
un·shamed′, *adj.*
un·shape′ly, *adj.*
un·shared′, *adj.*
un·shaved′, *adj.*
un·sheared′, *adj.*
un·shed′, *adj.*
un·shelled′, *adj.*
un·shel′tered, *adj.*
un·shield′ed, *adj.*
un·shod′, *adj.*
un·shorn′, *adj.*
un·shrink′a·ble, *adj.*
un·shrink′ing, *adj.*; **-ly,** *adv.*
un·shut′, *adj.*
un·sift′ed, *adj.*
un·sight′ed, *adj.*
un·signed′, *adj.*
un·si′lenced, *adj.*
un·sin′ful, *adj.*
un·sing′a·ble, *adj.*
un·sink′a·ble, *adj.*
un·sis′ter·ly, *adj.*
un·slaked′, *adj.*
un·sleep′ing, *adj.*
un·smil′ing, *adj.*; **-ly,** *adv.*
un·so′cia·ble, *adj.*
un·so′cial, *adj.*; **-ly,** *adv.*
un·soiled′, *adj.*
un·sold′, *adj.*
un·sol′dier·like′, *adj.*
un′so·lic′it·ed, *adj.*
un′so·lic′i·tous, *adj.*
un·sol′id, *adj.*
un·solv′a·ble, *adj.*
un·solved′, *adj.*
un·soothed′, *adj.*
un·sought′, *adj.*
un·spe′cial·ized′, *adj.*
un′spe·cif′ic, *adj.*
un′spe·cif′i·cal·ly, *adv.*
un·spec′i·fied′, *adj.*
un′spec·tac′u·lar, *adj.*
un·spec′u·la′tive, *adj.*
un·spir′i·tu·al, *adj.*
un·spoiled′, *adj.*
un·sports′man·like′, *adj.*
un·squan′dered, *adj.*
un·stamped′, *adj.*
un·stand′ard·ized′, *adj.*
un·sta′pled, *adj.*
un·starched′, *adj.*
un·starred′, *adj.*
un·states′man·like′, *adj.*
un·stead′fast′, *adj.*
un·stemmed′, *adj.*
un·ster′ile, *adj.*
un·ster′i·lized′, *adj.*
un·stint′ed, *adj.*
un·stop′per, *v.t.*
un·strat′i·fied, *adj.*

studied; not possessing knowledge in a specific field; unversed. [ME]

un·sub·stan·tial (un′səb stan′shəl), *adj.* **1.** not substantial; having no foundation in fact; fanciful; insubstantial. **2.** without material substance. **3.** lacking material substance; materially paltry. **4.** lacking strength or solidity; flimsy. [ME] —**un·sub·stan·ti·al·i·ty** (un′səb stan′shē al′i tē), *n.* —**un′sub·stan′tial·ly,** *adv.*

un·suc·cess·ful (un′sək ses′fəl), *adj.* not achieving or not attended with success. —**un′suc·cess′ful·ly,** *adv.* —**un′suc·cess′ful·ness,** *n.*

un·suit·a·ble (un so͞o′tə bəl), *adj.* not suitable; inappropriate; unbecoming. —**un′suit·a·bil′i·ty, un·suit′a·ble·ness,** *n.* —**un·suit′a·bly,** *adv.*

un·sung (un sung′), *adj.* **1.** not sung; not uttered or rendered by singing. **2.** not celebrated in song or verse; not praised or acclaimed.

un·sus·pect·ed (un′sə spek′tid), *adj.* **1.** not regarded with suspicion. **2.** not imagined to exist. —**un′sus·pect′ed·ly,** *adv.* —**un′sus·pect′ed·ness,** *n.*

un·sus·tain·a·ble (un′sə stā′nə bəl), *adj.* not sustainable; not able to be supported, maintained, upheld, or corroborated.

un·swear (un swâr′), *v.t.*, **-swore, -sworn, -swear·ing.** to retract (something sworn or sworn to); recant by a subsequent oath; abjure.

un·tack (un tak′), *v.t.* **1.** to unfasten (something tacked). **2.** to loose or detach by removing a tack or tacks.

un·tan·gle (un tang′gəl), *v.t.*, **-gled, -gling.** **1.** to bring out of a tangled state; disentangle; unsnarl. **2.** to straighten out or clear up (anything confused or perplexing).

un·taught (un tôt′), *v.t.* **1.** pt. and pp. of **unteach.** —*adj.* **2.** not taught; not acquired by teaching; natural. **3.** not educated; naïve; ignorant. [ME]

un·teach (un tēch′), *v.t.*, **-taught, -teach·ing. 1.** to cause to be forgotten or disbelieved, as by contrary teaching. **2.** to cause to forget or disbelieve something previously taught.

un·ten·a·ble (un ten′ə bəl), *adj.* **1.** incapable of being defended, as an argument, thesis, etc.; indefensible. **2.** not fit to be occupied or lived in. —**un′ten·a·bil′i·ty, un·ten′a·ble·ness,** *n.*

Un·ter·mey·er (un′tər mī′ər), *n.* **Louis,** 1885–1977, U.S. poet, critic, and editor.

un·think (un thingk′), *v.*, **-thought, -think·ing.** —*v.i.* **1.** to end one's thought or reverse the process of thought. —*v.t.* **2.** to dispel from the mind.

un·think·a·ble (un thing′kə bəl), *adj.* **1.** inconceivable; unimaginable. **2.** not to be considered; out of the question. [ME] —**un·think′a·bil′i·ty, un·think′a·ble·ness,** *n.* —**un·think′a·bly,** *adv.*

un·think·ing (un thing′king), *adj.* **1.** thoughtless; heedless; inconsiderate. **2.** indicating lack of thought or reflection. **3.** not endowed with the faculty of thought: *unthinking matter.* **4.** not exercising thought; not given to reflection. **5.** not thinking; unmindful. —**un·think′ing·ly,** *adv.*

un·thread (un thred′), *v.t.* **1.** to draw out or take out the thread from. **2.** to thread one's way through or out of, as a densely wooded forest. **3.** to disentangle; separate out of a raveled or confused condition.

un·throne (un thrōn′), *v.t.*, **-throned, -thron·ing.** to dethrone or remove as if by dethroning.

un·ti·dy (un tī′dē), *adj.*, **-di·er, -di·est,** *v.*, **-died, -dy·ing.** —*adj.* **1.** not tidy or neat; slovenly; disordered. **2.** not well-organized or carried out: *an untidy plan.* —*v.t.* **3.** to mess up; disorder; disarrange. [ME] —**un·ti′di·ly,** *adv.* —**un·ti′di·ness,** *n.*

un·tie (un tī′), *v.*, **-tied, -ty·ing.** —*v.t.* **1.** to loose or unfasten (anything tied); let or set loose by undoing a knot. **2.** to undo the string or cords of. **3.** to undo, as a cord or a knot; unknot. **4.** to free from restraint. **5.** to resolve, as perplexities. —*v.i.* **6.** to become untied. [ME *untye(n),* OE *untīegan*]

un·til (un til′), *conj.* **1.** up to the time that or when; till. **2.** before (usually used in negative constructions): *He did not come until the meeting was half over.* —*prep.* **3.** onward to or till (a specified time or occurrence): *He worked until 6 P.M. The children sat in class until recess.* **4.** before (usually used in negative constructions): *He did not go until night.* [ME *untill* = *un-* (< Scand; cf. OIcel *unz* up to, as far as) + *till* TILL[1]]

un·time·ly (un tīm′lē), *adj.* **1.** not timely; not occurring at a suitable time or season; ill-timed or inopportune. **2.** premature. —*adv.* **3.** unseasonably. **4.** prematurely. [ME *untimliche*] —**un·time′li·ness,** *n.* —**Syn. 1.** unseasonable, inappropriate.

un·time·ous (un tī′məs), *adj. Scot.* untimely.

un·tinged (un tinjd′), *adj.* **1.** not colored, as by paint, the sun, etc. **2.** not biased or partial; objective.

un·ti·tled (un tīt′əld), *adj.* **1.** without a title: *an untitled nobleman; an untitled book.* **2.** having no right or claim.

un·to (un′to͞o; *unstressed* un′tə), *prep. Archaic.* **1.** to (in its various uses, except as the accompaniment of the infinitive). **2.** until; till. [ME; modeled on UNTIL]

un·told (un tōld′), *adj.* **1.** not told; not related; not revealed. **2.** not numbered or enumerated; uncounted. **3.** inexpressible; incalculable: *untold suffering.* [ME; OE *unteald*]

un·touch·a·bil·i·ty (un′tuch ə bil′i tē), *n. Hinduism.* the quality or condition of being an untouchable, ascribed in the Vedic tradition to persons of low caste or to persons excluded from the caste system.

un·touch·a·ble (un tuch′ə bəl), *adj.* **1.** that may not be touched; not palpable; intangible. **2.** too distant to be touched. **3.** vile or loathsome to the touch. **4.** beyond criticism, control, or suspicion. —*n.* **5.** a member of a lower caste in India whose touch was formerly believed to defile a high-caste Hindu. **6.** a person who is beyond reproach as to honesty, diligence, etc. —**un·touch′a·bly,** *adv.*

un·touched (un tucht′), *adj.* **1.** not touched or handled, as material. **2.** not explored or visited: *untouched lands.* **3.** not eaten or drunk. **4.** remaining in a pristine state; unchanged. **5.** not injured or hurt; undamaged. **6.** not affected or altered: *She was untouched by the life around her.* **7.** emotionally unmoved; indifferent. **8.** not mentioned or described, as in conversation, a book, etc. [ME]

un·to·ward (un tōrd′, -tôrd′), *adj.* **1.** unfavorable or unfortunate: *Untoward circumstances forced him into bankruptcy.* **2.** improper: *untoward social behavior.* **3.** *Archaic.* froward; perverse. **4.** *Obs.* awkward; uncouth. —**un·to′ward·ly,** *adv.* —**un·to′ward·ness,** *n.*

un·trav·eled (un trav′əld), *adj.* **1.** not having traveled, esp. to distant places. **2.** not traveled through or over; not frequented by travelers. Also, *esp. Brit.,* **un·trav′elled.**

un·tread (un tred′), *v.t.*, **-trod, -trod·den** or **-trod, -tread·ing.** to go back through in the same steps; retrace.

un·tried (un trīd′), *adj.* **1.** not tried; not attempted. **2.** not proved or tested. **3.** not yet tried at law.

un·trimmed (un trimd′), *adj.* **1.** not trimmed. **2.** *Bookbinding.* (of gathered sections of a book) having the bolts not yet trimmed. —**un·trimmed′ness,** *n.*

un·true (un tro͞o′), *adj.* **1.** not true, as to a person or a cause, to fact, or to a standard. **2.** unfaithful; false. **3.** incorrect or inaccurate. —**un·true′ness,** *n.*

un·truss (un trus′), *v.t., v.i.* **1.** *Archaic.* to loose from or as from a truss. **2.** *Obs.* to undress. [ME]

un·truth (un tro͞oth′), *n., pl.* **-truths** (-tro͞othz, -tro͞oths). **1.** the state or character of being untrue. **2.** want of veracity; divergence from truth. **3.** something untrue; a falsehood or lie. **4.** *Archaic.* unfaithfulness; disloyalty. [ME; OE *untrēowth*] —**Syn. 3.** fiction, story, tale, fable, fabrication, invention. See **falsehood.**

un·truth·ful (un tro͞oth′fəl), *adj.* not truthful; wanting in veracity; diverging from or contrary to the truth; not corresponding with fact or reality. —**un·truth′ful·ly,** *adv.* —**un·truth′ful·ness,** *n.*

un·tune (un to͞on′, -tyo͞on′), *v.t.*, **-tuned, -tun·ing. 1.** to cause to become out of tune. **2.** to discompose; upset, as the mind or emotions.

un·tu·tored (un to͞o′tərd, -tyo͞o′-), *adj.* not tutored; untaught.

un·used (un yo͞ozd′ *for 1, 2;* un yo͞ost′ *for 3*), *adj.* **1.** not used; not put to use. **2.** never having been used. **3.** not accustomed. [ME]

un·u·su·al (un yo͞o′zho͞o əl), *adj.* not usual, common, or ordinary; uncommon in amount or degree; exceptional. —**un·u′su·al·ly,** *adv.* —**un·u′su·al·ness,** *n.* —**Syn.** extraordinary, rare, strange, remarkable, singular, curious, queer, odd.

un·ut·ter·a·ble (un ut′ər ə bəl), *adj.* **1.** not utterable; not pronounceable: *an unutterable foreign word.* **2.** not communicable by utterance; unspeakable: *unutterable joy.* —**un·ut′ter·a·bly,** *adv.*

un·var·nished (un vär′nisht), *adj.* **1.** straightforward; without vagueness or subterfuge; frank: *the unvarnished truth.* **2.** not coated with or as with varnish.

un·veil (un vāl′), *v.t.* **1.** to remove a veil or other covering from; display; reveal: *to unveil oneself.* **2.** to reveal or dis-

un·stuffed′, *adj.*
un′sub·dued′, *adj.*
un′sub·mis′sive, *adj.;* **-ly,** *adv.*
un′sub·mit′ted, *adj.*
un′sub·stan′ti·at′ed, *adj.*
un·sub′tle, *adj.*
un′sug·ges′tive, *adj.*
un·suit′ed, *adj.*
un·sul′lied, *adj.*
un·su′per·vised′, *adj.*
un′sup·port′a·ble, *adj.*
un′sup·port′ed, *adj.;* **-ly,** *adv.*
un′sup·pressed′, *adj.*
un′sup·press′i·ble, *adj.*
un·sure′, *adj.;* **-ly,** *adv.;* **-ness,** *n.*
un′sur·mount′a·ble, *adj.*
un′sur·pass′a·ble, *adj.*
un′sur·passed′, *adj.*
un′sur·prised′, *adj.*
un′sus·cep′ti·ble, *adj.*
un′sus·pect′ing, *adj.;* **-ly,** *adv.*
un′sus·pi′cious, *adj.;* **-ly,** *adv.*
un′sus·tained′, *adj.*
un·swayed′, *adj.*
un·sweet′ened, *adj.*
un·swerv′ing, *adj.*
un·sworn′, *adj.*
un′sym·met′ri·cal, *adj.;* **-ly,** *adv.*
un′sym·pa·thet′ic, *adj.*
un′sym·pa·thet′i·cal·ly, *adv.*
un·sym′pa·thiz′ing, *adj.;* **-ly,** *adv.*
un′sys·tem·at′ic, *adj.*
un′sys·tem·at′i·cal, *adj.;* **-ly,** *adv.*
un·sys′tem·a·tized′, *adj.*
un·tact′ful, *adj.;* **-ly,** *adv.*
un·taint′ed, *adj.*
un·tal′ent·ed, *adj.*
un·tam′a·ble, *adj.*
un·tame′, *adj.*
un·tame′a·ble, *adj.*
un·tamed′, *adj.*
un·tan′gi·ble, *adj.*
un·tanned′, *adj.*
un·tapped′, *adj.*
un·tar′nished, *adj.*
un·tast′ed, *adj.*
un·taste′ful, *adj.*
un·teach′a·ble, *adj.*
un·tem′pered, *adj.*
un·tempt′ed, *adj.*
un·tempt′ing, *adj.*
un·ten′ant·ed, *adj.*
un·tend′ed, *adj.*
un·ter′mi·nat′ed, *adj.*
un·ter′ri·fied′, *adj.*
un·test′ed, *adj.*
un·teth′ered, *adj.*
un·thanked′, *adj.*
un·thought′, *adj.*
un·thought′ful, *adj.;* **-ly,** *adv.*
un·threat′en·ing, *adj.*
un·thrift′y, *adj.*
un·thwart′ed, *adj.*
un·till′a·ble, *adj.*
un·tilled′, *adj.*
un·tired′, *adj.*
un·tir′ing, *adj.;* **-ly,** *adv.*
un·trace′a·ble, *adj.*
un·traced′, *adj.*
un·tracked′, *adj.*
un·trac′ta·ble, *adj.*
un·trained′, *adj.*
un·tram′meled, *adj.*
un′trans·fer′a·ble, *adj.*
un′trans·ferred′, *adj.*
un′trans·formed′, *adj.*
un′trans·lat′a·ble, *adj.*
un′trans·lat′ed, *adj.*
un·trav′ersed, *adj.*
un·treat′ed, *adj.*
un·tri′a·ble, *adj.*
un·trod′, *adj.*
un·trod′den, *adj.*
un·trou′bled, *adj.*
un·trust′ful, *adj.*
un·trust′wor′thy, *adj.*
un·tuck′, *v.t.*
un·tuft′ed, *adj.*
un·turned′, *adj.*
un·twist′, *v.*
un·typ′i·cal, *adj.;* **-ly,** *adv.*
un·us′a·ble, *adj.*
un·u′ti·lized′, *adj.*
un·ut′tered, *adj.*
un·vac′ci·nat′ed, *adj.*
un·vac′il·lat·ing, *adj.*
un·val′ued, *adj.*
un·van′quished, *adj.*
un·var′ied, *adj.*
un·var′y·ing, *adj.;* **-ly,** *adv.*
un·ve′he·ment, *adj.*
un·veined′, *adj.*
un·ven′ti·lat′ed, *adj.*
un·ven′ture·some, *adj.*

close, esp. for the first time, by or as by removing a veil or covering: *to unveil a monument.*

un·vo·cal (un vō′kəl), *adj.* **1.** not outspoken; reserved; not eloquent in speech; inarticulate. **2.** not mellifluous, as the speaking voice. **3.** not melodious, unmusical.

un·voice (un vois′), *v.t.*, **-voiced, -voic·ing.** *Phonet.* to deprive (an ordinarily voiced speech sound) of a part or all of its tonal vibration in pronouncing; devoice.

un·voiced (un voist′), *adj.* **1.** not voiced; not uttered: *unvoiced complaints.* **2.** *Phonet.* voiceless; without voice; surd.

un·warped (un wôrpt′), *adj.* **1.** not warped. **2.** impartial; undistorted: *an unwarped point of view.*

un·war·y (un wâr′ē), *adj.* not wary; not cautious or watchful, as against danger; rash or heedless. **—un·war′i·ly,** *adv.* **—un·war′i·ness,** *n.* **—Syn.** incautious, indiscreet.

un·washed (un wosht′, -wôsht′), *adj.* **1.** not cleaned or purified by or as by washing. **2.** lacking in good manners, respect, etc.; plebeian. **—***n.* **3.** an ignorant or lower-class group; rabble (usually prec. by *the*).

un·weave (un wēv′), *v.t.*, **-wove, -wo·ven, -weav·ing.** to undo, take apart, or separate (something woven); unravel.

un·weighed (un wād′), *adj.* **1.** not weighed, as for poundage. **2.** not carefully thought about, as opinions. [ME]

un·weight·ed (un wā′tid), *adj.* **1.** not burdened or encumbered with a heavy load or with mental or emotional matters, problems, etc. **2.** not considered important or significant, as one's opinions, sources, etc.: *an unweighted argument.*

un·well (un wel′), *adj.* not well; ailing; ill.

un·wept (un wept′), *adj.* **1.** not wept for; unmourned: *an unwept loss.* **2.** not wept or shed, as tears.

un·whole·some (un hōl′səm), *adj.* **1.** not wholesome; unhealthful; deleterious to physical or mental health. **2.** not sound in health; unhealthy, esp. in appearance; suggestive of disease: *an unwholesome pallor.* **3.** morally harmful; depraved: *unwholesome activities.* [ME] **—un·whole′some·ly,** *adv.* **—un·whole′some·ness,** *n.*

un·wield·y (un wēl′dē), *adj.* not wieldy; wielded with difficulty; not readily handled or managed in use or action, as from size, shape, or weight; awkward; ungainly. Also, **unwield′ly.** [ME *unweldy*] **—un·wield′i·ly,** *adv.* **—un·wield′i·ness,** *n.* **—Syn.** bulky, unmanageable, clumsy.

un·willed (un wild′), *adj.* involuntary; unintentional.

un·will·ing (un wil′ing), *adj.* **1.** not willing; reluctant; loath; averse. **2.** opposed; offering resistance; stubborn or obstinate; refractory. **—un·will′ing·ly,** *adv.* **—un·will′ing·ness,** *n.*

un·wind (un wīnd′), *v.*, **-wound, -wind·ing.** **—***v.t.* **1.** to undo or loosen from or as from a coiled condition. **2.** to relieve of tension; relax (usually used reflexively). **3.** to disentangle or disengage; untwist. **—***v.i.* **4.** to become unwound. **5.** to become relieved of tension; relax. [ME] **—un·wind′a·ble,** *adj.* **—un·wind′er,** *n.*

un·wise (un wīz′), *adj.* not wise; foolish; imprudent; lacking in good sense. [ME; OE *unwīs*] **—un·wise′ly,** *adv.*

un·wish (un wish′), *v.t.* **1.** to cease to wish for. **2.** *Obs.* to wish away.

un·wished (un wisht′), *adj.* not wished for; undesired; unwelcome.

un·wit (un wit′), *v.t.*, **-wit·ted, -wit·ting.** to render devoid of wit; derange.

un·wit·nessed (un wit′nist), *adj.* **1.** not perceived by the senses; not noticed or observed. **2.** lacking the signature of a witness. [ME]

un·wit·ting (un wit′ing), *adj.* **1.** not knowing; unaware; unconscious. **2.** inadvertent; unintentional. [ME] **—un·wit′ting·ly,** *adv.* **—un·wit′ting·ness,** *n.*

un·wont·ed (un wōn′tid, -wôn′-, -wun′-), *adj.* **1.** not customary, habitual, or usual; rare. **2.** *Archaic.* unaccustomed or unused. **—un·wont′ed·ly,** *adv.* **—un·wont′ed·ness,** *n.*

un·world·ly (un wûrld′lē), *adj.* **1.** not worldly; not seeking material advantage or gain; spiritually minded. **2.** naive; unsophisticated; provincial. **3.** not terrestrial; unearthly. **—un·world′li·ness,** *n.*

un·wor·thy (un wûr′thē), *adj.*, *n.*, *pl.* **-thies.** **—***adj.* **1.** not worthy; lacking worth or excellence. **2.** not commendable or creditable. **3.** not of adequate merit or character. **4.** of a kind not worthy (often fol. by *of*). **5.** beneath the dignity (usually fol. by *of*): *behavior unworthy of a king.* **6.** undeserving. **—***n.* **7.** an unworthy person. [ME] **—un·wor′thi·ly,** *adv.* **—un·wor′thi·ness,** *n.*

un·wound (un wound′), *v.* pt. and pp. of **unwind.**

un·wrap (un rap′), *v.*, **-wrapped, -wrap·ping.** **—***v.t.* **1.** to remove or open the wrapping of. **2.** to open (something wrapped). **—***v.i.* **3.** to become unwrapped. [ME]

un·writ·ten (un rit′ən), *adj.* **1.** not written; not put in writing or print; oral. **2.** not actually formulated or expressed; customary; traditional. **3.** containing no writing; blank. [ME, OE *unwriten*]

unwrit′ten law′, **1.** a law whose authority rests on custom, judicial decision, etc., rather than on statute. **2.** **the unwritten law,** the supposed principle of the right of the individual to avenge wrongs against personal or family honor.

un·yoke (un yōk′), *v.*, **-yoked, -yok·ing.** **—***v.t.* **1.** to free from or as from a yoke. **2.** to part or disjoin, as by removing a yoke. **—***v.i. Obs.* **3.** to remove a yoke. **4.** to cease work. [ME *unyoke(n)*, OE *ungeocian*]

un·zip (un zip′), *v.*, **-zipped, -zip·ping.** **—***v.t.* **1.** to open the zipper of. **—***v.i.* **2.** to become unzipped.

U. of S. Afr., Union of South Africa.

up (up), *adv.*, *prep.*, *adj.*, *n.*, *v.*, **upped, up·ping.** **—***adv.* **1.** to, toward, or in a more elevated position. **2.** to or in an erect position: *to stand up.* **3.** out of bed: *to get up.* **4.** above the horizon: *The moon is up.* **5.** to or at any point that is considered higher. **6.** to or at a source, origin, center, or the like: *to follow a stream up to its source.* **7.** to or at a higher point or degree, as of rank, size, value, pitch, etc. **8.** to or at a point of equal advance, extent, etc.: *to catch up in a race.* **9.** ahead; in a leading position in a competition. **10.** in continuing contact, esp. as reflecting continuing awareness, knowledge, etc. **11.** into or in activity, operation, etc.: *to set up vibrations; to be up in arms.* **12.** in a state of emotional agitation or distress: *His insults left her all worked up.* **13.** into existence, visible form, etc.: *His sample was worked up in the studio.* **14.** into view, prominence, or consideration: *The lost papers have turned up.* **15.** into or in a place of safekeeping, storage, retirement, etc.: *to lay up riches; to put up preserves.* **16.** into or in a state of union, contraction, etc.: *to add up a column of figures; to fold up.* **17.** to the required or final point: *to pay up one's debts; to be used up.* **18.** to a state of completion; to an end: *He finished it all up.* **19.** to a halt: *The horsemen reined up and dismounted.* **20.** *Baseball.* being the player or team batting; at bat. **21.** (used imperatively or hortatively with a verb implied): *Up, men, and fight! Up with the true king and down with the usurper!* **22.** ahead of an opponent or opponents, as in points or games. **23.** each; apiece: *The score was seven up in the final quarter.* **24.** *Naut.* toward the wind: *Put the helm up.* **25.** **all up with,** at or approaching the end; with defeat or ruin imminent: *He realized it was all up with him when the search party began to close in.* **26.** **up against,** *Informal.* faced or confronted with. **27.** **up against it,** *Informal.* in a difficult situation, esp. in financial straits. **28.** **up and around,** recovered from an illness; able to leave one's bed. Also, **up and about.** **29.** **up to,** **a.** as far as or approaching a certain part, degree, point, etc. **b.** in full realization of; making full use of: *He could not live up to their expectations.* **c.** as many as; to the limit of: *up to five men.* **d.** *Informal.* having adequate powers or ability for; capable of; equal to: *to be up to the job.* **e.** *Informal.* having the duty or responsibility; incumbent upon: *It's up to you to break the news to him.* **f.** engaged in; doing: *What have you been up to lately?*

—*prep.* **30.** to, toward, or at an elevated place on or in: *He is going up the stairs. The cat is up the tree.* **31.** to, toward, or at a high or higher station, condition, or rank on or in. **32.** at or to a farther point or higher place on or in: *He is up the street. He is going up the street.* **33.** toward the source, origin, etc., of: *up the stream.* **34.** toward a particular direction or in the interior of a region, territory, etc.: *The explorers were up north.* **35.** in a course or direction contrary to that of.

—*adj.* **36.** moving in or related to a direction that is up or is regarded as up. **37.** *Informal.* informed; familiar; aware (usually fol. by *on* or *in*): *He is up on current events.* **38.** concluded; ended: *The game is up. His hour is up.* **39.** going on or happening: *What's up over there?* **40.** in a condition, position, or station that is high or is considered high: *to be up on the social scale.* **41.** in an erect, vertical, or raised position: *The tent is up.* **42.** above the earth or ground: *The corn is up and ready to be harvested.* **43.** in the air; aloft. **44.** (of heavenly bodies) risen above the horizon. **45.** awake or out of bed. **46.** mounted on horseback. **47.** (of water in natural bodies) high with relation to the banks or shore: *The tide is up.* **48.** built; constructed. **49.** facing upward: *He is resting and his face is up.* **50.** (of roads, highways, etc.) having the surface broken or removed (usually used in combination): *a torn-up road.* **51.** in a state of agitation. **52.** in a mood of confidence and high spirits. **53.** wrong; amiss: *Her nervous manner told me that something was up.* **54.** ready, as by emotional or physical fitness or disposition (usually fol. by *to*): *Since her illness she has not been up to going out much.* **55.** bound; on the way: *She was on a ship up for Australia.* **56.** arrived at an unfavorable or undesired end: *They knew that their game was up.* **57.** higher than formerly in amount, degree, etc.: *The price of meat was up.* **58.** (of age) advanced (usually fol. by *in*): *to be up in years.* **59.** active: *The captain wished to set sail as soon as the wind was up.* **60.** in a legal proceeding as defendant: *He is up for murder.* **61.** in operation or ready for use: *The theater's lights are up.* **62.** (of points or other standards used to determine the winner in a competition) ahead; in advance: *He's two sets up already.* **63.** (used with a preceding numeral to indicate that a score is tied): *It was 10-up at the end of the first half.* **64.** considered or under consideration: *a candidate up for reelection.* **65.** wagered; bet: *He won all the money up in the game.* **66.** living or located inland or on elevated ground: *He lives two miles up from the coast.* **67.** left to the decision of: *It's up to you.*

—*n.* **68.** an upward movement; ascent. **69.** a rise of fortune, mood, etc.: *He has had more ups than downs in his time.* **70.** an upward slope; elevation. **71.** an upward course or rise, as in price or value. **72.** *Slang.* upper (def. 10). **73.** **on the up and up,** *Informal.* frank; honest; sincere. Also, **on the up-and-up.**

—*v.t. Informal.* **74.** to make larger; step up: *to up output.* **75.** to raise; go better than (a preceding wager).

—*v.i.* **76.** *Informal.* to start up; begin something abruptly (usually fol. by *and* and another verb): *Then he upped and ran away from home.* [ME, OE; c. OFris *up*, OS *up*, OIcel *upp*, MD *up, op;* akin to OHG *ūf* (> G *auf*), Goth *iup*]

UP, United Press. Also, **U.P.**

up-, a combining form of **up:** *upland; upshot; upheaval.* [ME and OE]

up., upper.

un·ver′i·fi′able, *adj.*
un·ver′i·fied′, *adj.*
un·versed′, *adj.*
un·vexed′, *adj.*
un·vi′a·ble, *adj.*
un·vis′it·ed, *adj.*
un·wak′ened, *adj.*
un·want′ed, *adj.*
un·war′like′, *adj.*
un·warmed′, *adj.*
un·warned′, *adj.*
un·war′rant·ed, *adj.*
un·watch′a·ble, *adj.*
un·watched′, *adj.*
un·wa′ver·ing, *adj.;* **-ly,** *adv.*
un·waxed′, *adj.*
un·weak′ened, *adj.*
un·weaned′, *adj.*
un·wear′a·ble, *adj.*
un·wea′ry, *adj.*
un·wea′ry·ing, *adj.*
un·wed′, *adj.*
un·wed′ded, *adj.*
un·wel′come, *adj.*
un·whipped′, *adj.*
un·wife′ly, *adj.*
un·wished′-for, *adj.*
un·wom′an·ly, *adj.*
un·won′, *adj.*
un·wood′ed, *adj.*
un·wooed′, *adj.*
un·work′a·ble, *adj.*
un·worked′, *adj.*
un·work′ing, *adj.*
un·worn′, *adj.*
un·wor′ried, *adj.*
un·wrin′kle, *v.t.*, **-kled, -kling.**
un·yield′ing, *adj.;* **-ly,** *adv.*
un·zeal′ous, *adj.;* **-ly,** *adv.*

up·an·chor (up′aṅg′kər, up′aṅg′-), *v.i.* to weigh anchor.
up-and-com·ing (up′ən kum′iṅg), *adj.* *U.S.* likely to succeed; bright and industrious: *an up-and-coming young executive.*
up-and-down (up′ən doun′), *adj.* **1.** moving alternately up and down. **2.** having an uneven surface: *up-and-down countryside.* **3.** changeable: *up-and-down luck.* **4.** perpendicular or nearly so: *a straight up-and-down hillside.*
U·pan·i·shad (o͞o pan′i shad′, o͞o pä′ni shäd′), *n.* *Hinduism.* any of a class of speculative treatises, usually in dialogue form, composed between the 8th and 6th centuries B.C. and first written A.D. c1300. [< Skt *upaniṣād* = *upa* near to + *ni-ṣād* a sitting or lying down]
u·pas (yo͞o′pəs), *n.* **1.** the poisonous milky sap of a large moraceous tree, *Antiaris toxicaria*, of Java, used for arrow poison. **2.** the tree. [< Malay: poison]
up·bear (up bâr′), *v.t.*, **-bore, -borne, -bear·ing.** to raise aloft; support. [ME *upbere(n)*] —**up·bear′er,** *n.*
up·beat (up′bēt′), *n.* *Music.* **1.** an unaccented beat, esp. immediately preceding a downbeat. **2.** the upward stroke with which a conductor indicates such a beat. —*adj.* **3.** *Informal.* optimistic; happy.
up·bow (up′bō′), *n.* (in bowing on a stringed instrument) a stroke toward the heel of the bow: indicated in scores by the symbol V (opposed to *down-bow*).
up·braid (up brād′), *v.t.* **1.** to find fault with or reproach severely; censure. **2.** (of things) to bring reproach on; serve as a reproach to. —*v.i.* **3.** *Archaic.* to utter reproaches. [ME; OE *upbregd(an)*] —**up·braid′er,** *n.* —**Syn. 1.** blame.
up·bring·ing (up′briṅg′iṅg), *n.* the care and training of the young or a particular type of such care and training: *the proper upbringing of young people; His religious upbringing fitted him to be a missionary.* [ME]
up·build (up bild′), *v.t.*, **-built, -build·ing.** to build up, as with the result of establishing, increasing, enlarging, or fortifying. —**up·build′er,** *n.*
UPC, the series of short black lines of varied thickness on a package that indicate price, product classification, etc., thus expediting electronic checkout, inventory control, etc., as in a supermarket. [U(NIVERSAL) P(RODUCT) C(ODE)]
up·cast (up′kast′, -käst′), *n.*, *adj.*, *v.*, **-cast, -cast·ing.** —*n.* **1.** something that is cast or thrown up, as soil or earth in digging. **2.** a shaft or passage up which air passes, as from a mine (opposed to *downcast*). —*adj.* **3.** cast up; turned, directed, or thrown upward: *The child looked at her father with upcast eyes.* —*v.t.* **4.** to cast up or upward. [ME *upcast(en)*]
up·chuck (up′chuk′), *v.i.*, *v.t.* *Slang.* to vomit.
up·com·ing (up′kum′iṅg), *adj.* about to take place, appear, or be presented: *the upcoming spring fashions.* [ME]
up·coun·try (up′kun′trē), *adj.* **1.** of, relating to, residing in, or situated in the interior of a region or country; inland: *an upcountry dialect; an upcountry town.* —*n.* **2.** the interior of a region or country. —*adv.* **3.** toward, into, or in the interior of a country: *The explorers trekked upcountry.*
up·crop·ping (up′krop′iṅg), *n.* an act of cropping up; appearance; growth: *an upcropping of corn.*
up·date (up dāt′, up′dāt′), *v.* **-dat·ed, -dat·ing,** *n.* —*v.t.* **1.** to bring (a book, figures, or the like) up to date, as by adding new information, making corrections, etc. —*n.* **2.** *Computer Technol.* current information for use by a computer. —**up′dat′er,** *n.*
Up·dike (up′dīk′), *n.* **John,** born 1932, U.S. novelist and short-story writer.
up·draft (up′draft′, -dräft′), *n.* the movement upward of air or other gas.
up·end (up end′), *v.t.* **1.** to set on end, as a barrel, ship, etc. **2.** *Informal.* to affect drastically or radically, as tastes, opinions, reputations, or systems. **3.** *Informal.* to defeat in competition, as in boxing, business, etc. —*v.i.* **4.** to become upended.
up-front (up′frunt′), *adj.* *Informal.* **1.** invested or paid in advance of actual earnings. **2.** conspicuous; prominent.
up·gath·er (up gath′ər), *v.t.* to gather up or together.
up·grade (*n.* up′grād′; *adj., adv.* up′grād′; *v.* up′grād′), *n.*, *adj.*, *adv.*, *v.*, **-grad·ed, -grad·ing.** —*n.* **1.** an incline going up in the direction of movement. **2.** an increase or improvement (usually prec. by *on the*): *Production is on the upgrade.* —*adj.* **3.** uphill; of, pertaining to, on, or along an upgrade. —*adv.* **4.** up a slope. —*v.t.* **5.** to augment the grade of, as in rank, position, importance, quality, value, etc.: *to upgrade laborers to managerial positions.*
up·growth (up′grōth′), *n.* **1.** the process of growing up; development. **2.** that which grows up, esp. a normal organic growth or process.
up·heav·al (up hē′vəl), *n.* **1.** an act of upheaving, esp. of a part of the earth's crust. **2.** the state of being upheaved. **3.** strong or violent change or disturbance, as in a society. **4.** *Geol.* an upward warping of a part of the earth's crust, forcing areas into a relatively higher position than before.
up·heave (up hēv′), *v.*, **-heaved** or **-hove, -heav·ing.** —*v.t.* **1.** to heave or lift up; raise up or aloft. —*v.i.* **2.** to rise upward. [ME *upheve(n)*]
up·held (up held′), *v.* pt. and pp. of **uphold.**
up·hill (up′hil′), *adv.* **1.** up or as if up the slope of a hill or other incline; upward: *The soldiers marched uphill.* —*adj.* **2.** going or tending upward on or as if on a hill: *an uphill road.* **3.** at a high place or point: *an uphill village.* **4.** laboriously fatiguing or difficult: *an uphill struggle to become wealthy.* —*n.* **5.** a rising terrain; ascent.
up·hold (up hōld′), *v.t.*, **-held, -hold·ing.** **1.** to lift upward; raise. **2.** to keep up or keep from sinking; support: *Stout columns upheld the building's heavy roof. Her faith upheld her in that time of sadness.* **3.** to support or defend, as against opposition or criticism: *The high court upheld the lower court's decision.* [ME *up hold(en)*] —**up·hold′er,** *n.* —**Syn. 3.** See **support.**
up·hol·ster (up hōl′stər, ə pōl′-), *v.t.* to provide (chairs, sofas, etc.) with coverings, cushions, stuffing, springs, etc. [back formation from UPHOLSTERER]
up·hol·ster·er (up hōl′stər ər, ə pōl′-), *n.* a person whose business it is to upholster furniture. [earlier *upholster* (see UPHOLD, -STER) + -ER[1]]
up·hol·ster·y (up hōl′stə rē, ə pōl′-), *n.*, *pl.* **-ster·ies.** **1.** the material supplied by an upholsterer, as cushions or furniture coverings. **2.** the business of an upholsterer.
UPI, United Press International. Also, **U.P.I.**
up·keep (up′kēp′), *n.* **1.** the process or activity of providing an establishment, machine, person, etc., with necessary or proper maintenance, repairs, support, or the like. **2.** the total costs or expenses for this.
up·land (up′lənd, -land′), *n.* **1.** land elevated above other land. **2.** the higher ground of a region or district; an elevated region. **3.** land or an area of land lying above the level where water flows or where flooding occurs. —*adj.* **4.** of or pertaining to uplands or elevated regions.
Up·land (up′lənd), *n.* a city in S California. 32,551 (1970).
up′land cot′ton, a short-staple cotton of the SE United States. Also, **Up′land cot′ton.**
up′land plov′er, a large, field-inhabiting sandpiper, *Bartramia longicauda*, of eastern North America, resembling a plover.
up·lift (*v.* up lift′; *n.* up′lift′), *v.t.* **1.** to lift up; raise; elevate. **2.** to improve socially, culturally, morally, or the like. **3.** to exalt emotionally or spiritually. —*v.i.* **4.** to become uplifted. —*n.* **5.** an act of lifting up or raising; elevation. **6.** the process or work of improving, as socially, intellectually, morally, or the like. **7.** emotional or spiritual exaltation. **8.** a brassiere. **9.** *Geol.* an upheaval. [ME *uplift(en)*] —**up·lift′er,** *n.* —**up·lift′ment,** *n.*
up·most (up′mōst′ *or, esp. Brit.,* -məst), *adj.* uppermost.
U·po·lu (o͞o pō′lo͞o), *n.* an island in Western Samoa, in the S Pacific: the home of R. L. Stevenson for last five years of his life. 82,479 (1961) with adjacent islands; 435 sq. mi.
up·on (ə pon′, ə pôn′), *prep.* **1.** up and on; upward so as to get or be on: *He climbed upon his horse and rode off.* **2.** in an elevated position on. **3.** in or into complete or approximate contact with, as an attacker or an important or pressing occasion: *The enemy was upon us. The Christmas holiday will soon be upon us.* **4.** on the occasion of, at the time of, or immediately after: *She went into mourning upon her husband's death. She was joyful upon seeing her child take his first steps.* **5.** on (in any of various senses, used as an equivalent of *on* with no added idea of ascent or elevation, and preferred in certain cases only for euphonic or metrical reasons). [ME]
up·per (up′ər), *adj.* **1.** higher, as in place, position, pitch, or in a scale: *the upper stories of a house; the upper register of a singer's voice.* **2.** superior, as in rank, dignity, or station. **3.** (of places) at a higher level, more northerly, or farther from the sea: *upper New York State.* **4.** (*often cap.*) *Stratig.* denoting a later division of a period, system, or the like: *the Upper Devonian.* —*n.* **5.** the part of a shoe or boot above the sole, comprising the quarter, vamp, counter, and lining. **6.** an upper berth. **7.** a gaiter made of cloth. Cf. **gaiter** (def. 1). **8.** Usually, **uppers. a.** an upper dental plate. **b.** an upper tooth. **9.** *Informal.* the higher of two bunks or berths. **10.** *Slang.* a stimulant drug, esp. an amphetamine. **11.** *Slang.* a stimulating or elating experience, person, or thing. [ME]
up′per air′, *Meteorol.* the atmosphere above the lower portion of the troposphere. Cf. **upper atmosphere.**
Up′per Ar′lington, a city in central Ohio, near Columbus. 38,630 (1970).
up′per at′mosphere, *Meteorol.* the portion of the atmosphere above the troposphere. Cf. **upper air.**
Up′per Aus′tria, a province in N Austria. 1,131,218 (1961); 4631 sq. mi. *Cap.:* Linz.
Up′per Can′ada, a former British province in Canada 1791–1840: now the S part of Ontario province.
up′per case′, *Print.* See under **case**[2] (def. 8).
up·per-case (up′ər kās′), *adj.*, *v.*, **-cased, -cas·ing,** *n.* —*adj.* **1.** (of an alphabetical character) capital. **2.** *Print.* pertaining to or belonging in the upper case. —*v.t.* **3.** to print or write with an upper-case letter or letters. —*n.* **4.** a capital letter. Cf. **lower-case.**
up′per cham′ber. See **upper house.**
Up′per Chinook′, a Chinookan language of the Columbia River valley from the Deschutes River to the estuary.
up·per-class (up′ər klas′, -kläs′), *adj.* relating to or typical of a high-ranking class in society.
up·per·class·man (up′ər klas′mən, -kläs′-), *n.*, *pl.* **-men.** *U.S.* a junior or senior in a secondary school or college.
up′per crust′, *Informal.* the highest social class.
up·per·cut (up′ər kut′), *n.*, *v.*, **-cut, -cut·ting.** —*n.* **1.** a swinging blow directed upward, as to an adversary's chin. —*v.t.* **2.** to strike (an opponent) with an uppercut. —*v.i.* **3.** to deliver an uppercut.
Up′per Dar′by, a town in SE Pennsylvania, near Philadelphia. 95,910 (1970).
Up′per E′gypt. See under **Egypt** (def. 1).
up′per hand′, the dominating or controlling position; the advantage: *to fight to get the upper hand.*
up′per house′, one of two branches of a legislature generally smaller and less representative than the lower branch.
Up′per Mich′igan. See **Upper Peninsula.**
up·per·most (up′ər mōst′ *or, esp. Brit.,* -məst), *adj.* Also, **upmost. 1.** highest in place, order, rank, power, etc. **2.** topmost; predominant: *a subject of uppermost importance.* —*adv.* **3.** in or into the highest place or rank.
Up′per Palat′inate. See under **Palatinate** (def. 1).
Up′per Penin′sula, the peninsula between lakes Superior and Michigan constituting the N part of Michigan. Also called **Upper Michigan, Northern Michigan.**
up′per school′, a scholastic division, esp. in a private school, including the terminal secondary grades.
Up′per Sile′sia, a highly industrialized region divided between Germany and Poland after World War I.
Up′per Tun·gus′ka (to͝on go͞os′kä, -kə, to͞oṅg-), the lower course of the Angara River. Cf. **Angara.**
Up′per Vol′ta, a republic in W Africa: formerly part of French West Africa. Official name, **Burkina Faso.** —**Up′per Vol′tan,** *adj.*, *n.*
up·pish (up′ish), *adj.* *Informal.* arrogant; presumptuous; uppity. —**up′pish·ly,** *adv.* —**up′pish·ness,** *n.*
up·pi·ty (up′i tē), *adj.* *Informal.* haughty; snobbish. [prob. UP + *-ity*, extended form of -Y[1]]

Upp·sa·la (up′sä lə, -sə-; *Swed.* ŏŏp′sä′lä′), *n.* a city in SE Sweden: university. 138,116. Also, **Upsala.**

up·raise (up rāz′), *v.t.*, **-raised, -rais·ing.** **1.** to raise up; lift or elevate. **2.** to raise from a depressed or dejected humor; cheer. [ME *upreise(n)*] —**up·rais′er,** *n.*

up·rear (up rēr′), *v.t.* **1.** to raise up; lift. **2.** to build; erect. **3.** to elevate the dignity of; exalt. **4.** to bring up; rear. —*v.i.* **5.** to rise. [ME *uprere(n)*]

up·right (up′rīt′, up rīt′), *adj.* **1.** erect or vertical, as in position or posture. **2.** raised or directed vertically or upward. **3.** adhering to rectitude; righteous, honest, or just: *an upright person.* **4.** in accord with what is right: *upright dealings.* —*n.* **5.** the state of being upright or vertical. **6.** something standing erect or vertical, as a piece of timber. **7.** an upright piano. **8.** Usually, **uprights.** *Chiefly Football.* the goal posts. —*adv.* **9.** in an upright position or direction; vertically. —*v.t.* **10.** to render upright. [ME, OE *upriht* (c. G *aufrecht*)] —**up′right′ly,** *adv.* —**up′right′ness,** *n.*
—**Syn. 1.** plumb. UPRIGHT, ERECT, VERTICAL, PERPENDICULAR imply that something is in the posture of being straight upward, not leaning. That which is UPRIGHT is in a position corresponding to that of a man standing up: *a decaying tree no longer standing upright.* ERECT emphasizes the straightness of position or posture: *proud and erect.* VERTICAL esp. suggests upward direction along the shortest line from the earth to a level above it: *the vertical edge of a door; ornamented by vertical lines.* PERPENDICULAR, a term frequently interchangeable with VERTICAL, is esp. used in mathematics: *the perpendicular side of a right triangle.*

up′right pian′o, a piano with an upright rectangular body. Cf. **spinet** (def. 1).

up·rise (*v.* up rīz′; *n.* up′rīz′), *v.*, **-rose, -ris·en, -ris·ing,** *n.* —*v.i.* **1.** to rise up; get up, as from a lying or sitting posture. **2.** to rise into view. **3.** to rise in revolt. **4.** to come into existence or prominence. **5.** to move upward; mount up; ascend. **6.** to come above the horizon. **7.** to slope upward. **8.** to swell or grow, as a sound. —*n.* **9.** an act of rising up. [ME *uprise(n)*] —**up′ris′er,** *n.*

up·ris·ing (up′rī′zing, up rī′zing), *n.* **1.** an insurrection or revolt. **2.** an act of rising up. **3.** an ascent or acclivity.

up·roar (up′rōr′, -rôr′), *n.* **1.** a state of violent and noisy disturbance; turmoil. **2.** an instance of this. [< D *oproer* tumult; c. MHG *ūfruor*, G *Aufruhr;* sense and spelling affected by *roar*] —**Syn. 1.** tumult, commotion, hubbub.

up·roar·i·ous (up rōr′ē əs, -rôr′-), *adj.* **1.** characterized by or in a state of uproar; tumultuous. **2.** making an uproar; confused and noisy, as an assembly, person, etc. **3.** very funny, as a person, situation, etc. **4.** very loud, as sounds, utterances, etc. **5.** expressed by or producing uproar. —**up·roar′i·ous·ly,** *adv.* —**up·roar′i·ous·ness,** *n.*

up·root (up ro͞ot′, -ro͝ot′), *v.t.* **1.** to pull out by or as if by the roots. **2.** to remove violently or tear away from a native place or environment: *The industrial revolution uprooted large segments of the rural population.* **3.** to destroy or eradicate as if by pulling out roots. **4.** to displace or tear away, as from a home, country, customs, etc. —*v.i.* **5.** to become uprooted. —**up·root′ed·ness,** *n.* —**up·root′er,** *n.*

up·rouse (up rouz′), *v.t.*, **-roused, -rous·ing.** to rouse up; arouse; awake.

Up·sa·la (up′sä lə, -sə-; *Swed.* ŏŏp′sä′lä′), *n.* Uppsala.

ups′ and downs′, rise and fall of fortune; good and bad times: *Every business has its ups and downs.*

up·scale (up′skāl′), *adj.*, *v.*, **-scaled, -scal·ing.** *Informal.* —*adj.* **1.** located at or moving toward the upper end of a social or economic scale: *The fashionable store caters to upscale young career people.* **2.** luxurious, costly, or elegant. —*v.t.* **3.** to improve the quality or value of: *a five-year plan to upscale the neighborhood.*

up·set (*v.*, *adj.* up set′; *n.* up′set′), *v.*, **-set, -set·ting,** *n.*, *adj.* —*v.t.* **1.** to overturn: *to upset a pitcher of milk.* **2.** to disturb mentally or emotionally; perturb: *The incident upset her.* **3.** to disturb or derange completely; put out of order; throw into disorder: *to upset a system.* **4.** to disturb physically: *It upset his stomach.* **5.** to defeat or overthrow an opponent that is considered more formidable, as in war, politics, sports, etc. **6.** *Metalworking.* to thicken the end of (a piece of heated metal) by hammering on the end against the length of the piece. —*v.i.* **7.** to become upset or overturned. —*n.* **8.** an upsetting or instance of being upset; overturn; overthrow. **9.** the unexpected defeat of a person or group that is considered more formidable. **10.** a nervous, irritable state of mind. **11.** a disordered or confused arrangement. **12.** *Metalworking.* **a.** a tool used for upsetting. **b.** that which is upset, as a bar end. —*adj.* **13.** overturned: *an upset milk pail.* **14.** disordered; disorganized: *The house is upset.* **15.** distressed; disturbed: *He is emotionally upset. She had an upset stomach.* **16.** *Archaic.* raised up. [ME] —**up·set′ta·ble,** *adj.* —**up·set′ter,** *n.* —**up·set′ting·ly,** *adv.* —**Syn. 2.** unnerve, disconcert, fluster.

up′set price′, the lowest price at which a person is permitted to bid for something being sold at auction.

up·shot (up′shot′), *n.* **1.** the final issue, the conclusion, or the result: *The upshot of the disagreement was a new bylaw.* **2.** the gist, as of an argument or thesis. [UP (in sense of termination) + SHOT[1]]

up·side (up′sīd′), *n.* the upper side or part.

up′side down′, **1.** with the upper part undermost. **2.** in or into complete disorder; mixed up; topsy-turvy. —**up′side-down′,** *adj.* —**up′side-down′ness,** *n.*

up′side-down′ cake′, a cake that is baked on a layer of fruit, then turned before serving so that the fruit is on top.

up·si·lon (yo͞op′sə lon′, up′-; *Brit.* yo͞op sī′lən), *n.* the 20th letter of the Greek alphabet (Υ, υ). [< MGk *u psilón*, lit., simple *u* (to distinguish it from the digraph *oi*, pronounced the same in LGk)]

up·spring (*v.* up spring′; *n.* up′spring′), *v.*, **-sprang** or **-sprung, -sprung, -spring·ing,** *n.* —*v.i.* **1.** to spring up. **2.** to come into being or existence; arise. —*n.* *Archaic.* **3.** growth or development. **4.** origin. [ME *upspring(en)*]

up·stage (up′stāj′), *adv.*, *adj.*, *v.*, **-staged, -stag·ing,** *n.* —*adv.* **1.** on or toward the back of the stage. —*adj.* **2.** of or pertaining to the back of the stage. —*v.t.* **3.** to move upstage of (another actor), forcing him to act with back to the audience and thereby overshadowing his performance. **4.** to outdo professionally, socially, etc. —*n.* **5.** the rear half of the stage. **6.** any stage position to the rear of another.

up·stairs (up′stârz′), *adv.*, *adj.*, *n.*, *pl.* **-stairs.** —*adv.* **1.** up the stairs; to or on an upper floor. **2.** *Informal.* in the mind: *She's a little weak upstairs.* **3.** *Mil. Slang.* at or to a higher level in the air. **4. kick upstairs,** *Informal.* to promote to a higher position that actually carries little responsibility so as to be rid of (a person). —*adj.* **5.** Also, **up′stair′.** of, pertaining to, or situated on an upper floor: *an upstairs window; an upstairs apartment.* —*n.* **6.** (*usually construed as sing.*) an upper story or stories; the part of a building or house that is above the ground floor.

up·stand·ing (up stan′ding), *adj.* **1.** standing erect; erect and tall. **2.** of a fine, vigorous type. **3.** upright; honorable; straightforward. [ME] —**up·stand′ing·ness,** *n.*

up·start (*n.*, *adj.* up′stärt′; *v.* up stärt′), *n.* **1.** a person who has risen suddenly from a humble position to wealth, power, or a position of consequence. **2.** a presumptuous and objectionable person who has so risen; parvenu. —*adj.* **3.** being, resembling, or characteristic of an upstart. —*v.i.* **4.** to start up; spring up, as to one's feet. **5.** to spring into existence or into view. —*v.t.* **6.** to cause to start up.

up·state (up′stāt′), *U.S.* —*n.* **1.** the part of a state that is farther north or farther from a chief city. —*adj.* **2.** of or coming from such an area. —**up′stat′er,** *n.*

up·stream (up′strēm′), *adv.* **1.** toward or in the higher part of a stream; against the current. —*adj.* **2.** directed or situated upstream.

up·stretched (up strecht′), *adj.* stretched upward, as the arms.

up·stroke (up′strōk′), *n.* an upward stroke, esp. of a pen or pencil, or of a piston in a vertical cylinder.

up·surge (*v.* up sûrj′; *n.* up′sûrj′), *v.*, **-surged, -surg·ing,** *n.* —*v.i.* **1.** to surge up; increase; rise. —*n.* **2.** act of surging up; rapid or large increase: *an upsurge in sales.*

up·sweep (*v.* up swēp′; *n.* up′swēp′), *v.*, **-swept, -sweep·ing,** *n.* —*v.t.* **1.** to sweep upward. —*v.i.* **2.** to be arranged in an upsweep. —*n.* **3.** a sweeping upward, as an increase in elevation or a steep slope. **4.** a hairdo produced by having the hair combed or brushed upward to the top of the head. **5.** a strongly pronounced rise in activity, as in business. **6.** a curved shape of the lower jaw of some animals.

up·swell (up swel′), *v.i.*, *v.t.*, **-swelled, -swelled** or **-swol·len, -swell·ing.** to swell up. [ME]

up·swept (up′swept′), *adj.* **1.** curved or sloped upward: *upswept automobile fenders.* **2.** combed or brushed upward to the top of the head.

up·swing (*n.* up′swing′; *v.* up swing′), *n.*, *v.*, **-swung, -swing·ing.** —*n.* **1.** an upward swing or swinging movement, as of a pendulum. **2.** a marked increase or improvement: *an upswing in prices.* —*v.i.* **3.** to make or undergo an upswing.

up·sy-dai·sy (up′sē dā′zē), *interj.* *Informal.* (used to comfort a baby at the moment of lifting him up.) [baby talk based on UP]

up·take (up′tāk′), *n.* **1.** apprehension; understanding or comprehension; mental grasp: *quick on the uptake.* **2.** an act or instance of taking up; a lifting. **3.** a pipe or passage leading upward from below, as for conducting smoke or a current of air. [ME]

up·tear (up târ′), *v.t.*, **-tore, -torn, -tear·ing.** to wrench or tear out by or as if by the roots or foundations; destroy.

up·throw (*n.* up′thrō′; *v.* up thrō′), *n.*, *v.*, **-threw, -thrown, -throw·ing.** —*n.* **1.** an upheaval, as of the earth's surface. **2.** *Geol.* an upward displacement of rock on one side of a fault. —*v.t.* **3.** to throw or cast up or upward.

up·thrust (up′thrust′), *n.* **1.** a thrust in an upward direction. **2.** *Geol.* an upheaval.

up·tick (up′tik′), *n.* **1.** a rise or improvement in business activity, in mood, etc. **2.** *Stock Exchange.* a selling price that is higher than the last previous different price.

up·tight (up′tīt′), *adj.* *Slang.* **1.** tense, nervous, or jittery. **2.** fine, excellent, or perfect. Also, **up′-tight′, up′ tight′.**

up·tilt (up tilt′), *v.t.* to tilt up.

up-to-date (up′tə dāt′), *adj.* **1.** extending to the present time; current; including the latest information: *an up-to-date report.* **2.** in accordance with the latest or modern ideas, techniques, styles, etc. **3.** keeping up with the times, as in outlook, ideas, appearance, etc. —**up′-to-date′ly,** *adv.* —**up′-to-date′ness,** *n.*

up·torn (up tôrn′), *v.* pp. of **uptear.**

up·town (*adv.*, *n.* up′toun′; *adj.* up′toun′), *adv.* **1.** toward, to, or in the upper part of a town or city: *He rode uptown on the bus.* —*adj.* **2.** moving toward, situated in, or pertaining to the upper part of a town: *uptown train.* —*n.* **3.** the uptown section of a town or city. —**up′town′er,** *n.*

up·trend (up′trend′), *n.* a tendency upward or toward growth, esp. in economic development.

up·turn (*v.* up tûrn′; *n.* up′tûrn′), *v.t.* **1.** to turn up or over. **2.** to cause disorder; upheave. **3.** to direct or turn upward. —*v.i.* **4.** to turn up or upward. —*n.* **5.** chaos or extreme disorder, as in society; an upheaval. **6.** an upward turn, or a changing and rising movement, as in prices, business, etc.

UPU, Universal Postal Union.

up·ward (up′wərd), *adv.* Also, **up′wards.** **1.** toward a higher place or position. **2.** toward a higher or more distinguished condition, rank, level, etc. **3.** more: *fourscore and upward.* **4.** toward a large city, the source or origin of a stream, or the interior of a country or region. **5.** in the upper parts; above. **6. upward** or **upwards of,** more than; above: *His vacation cost him upwards of a thousand dollars.* —*adj.* **7.** moving or tending upward; directed at or situated in a higher place or position. [ME; OE *upweard* (c. D *opwaart*)] —**up′ward·ly,** *adv.* —**up′ward·ness,** *n.*

up′ward mobil′ity. See under **vertical mobility** (def. 1).

up·wind (*adv.*, *adj.* up′wind′; *n.* up′wind′), *adv.* **1.** toward or against the wind or the direction from which it is blowing. —*adj.* **2.** moving or situated toward or in the direction from which the wind is blowing. —*n.* **3.** a wind that blows against one's course or up a slope.

Ur (ûr), *n.* an ancient Sumerian city on the Euphrates, in S Iraq. See map at **Chaldea.**

ur-, var. of **uro-**[1]: *uranalysis.*

u·ra·cil (yŏŏr′ə sil), *n.* *Biochem.* a crystalline solid, $C_4H_4N_2O_2$, used in biochemical research. [UR-[1] + AC(ET-IC) + -IL]

U, Uraeus

u·rae·mi·a (yŏŏ rē′mē ə), *n.* *Pathol.* uremia. —**u·rae′mic,** *adj.*

u·rae·us (yŏŏ rē′əs), *n., pl.* **-us·es.** the sacred asp as represented upon the headdress of divinities and royal personages of ancient Egypt. [< NL < Gk *ouraîos,* repr. Egypt word for cobra, perh. influenced by Gk *ouraîos* of the tail; see URO-[2]]

U·ral (yŏŏr′əl), *n.* **1.** a river in the Soviet Union, flowing S from the S Ural Mountains to the Caspian Sea. 1400 mi. long. —*adj.* **2.** of or pertaining to the Ural Mountains or the Ural River.

U·ral-Al·ta·ic (yŏŏr′əl al tā′ik), *adj.* **1.** of or pertaining to the Ural Mountains, on the border between the Soviet Union in Europe and Siberia, and the Altai Mountains, in S Siberia and NW Mongolia, or the country or peoples around them. **2.** speaking a Ural-Altaic language. —*n.* **3.** a highly conjectural language family consisting of the Uralic and Altaic languages.

U·ra·li·an (yŏŏ rā′lē ən), *adj.* **1.** of or pertaining to the Ural Mountains or their inhabitants. **2.** Uralic (def. 2).

Ura′lian em′erald, demantoid: not a true emerald.

U·ral·ic (yŏŏ ral′ik), *n.* **1.** a family of languages that comprises Hungarian, Finnish, and Estonian and Finno-Ugric and Samoyed as subfamilies. —*adj.* **2.** Also, **Uralian.** of or pertaining to Uralic.

u·ral·ite (yŏŏr′ə līt′), *n.* *Mineral.* hornblende formed by the hydrothermal alteration of pyroxene. [< G *Uralit,* named after URAL MOUNTAINS where found; see -ITE[1]] —**u·ral·it·ic** (yŏŏr′ə lit′ik), *adj.*

U′ral Moun′tains, a mountain range in the W Soviet Union, extending N and S from the Arctic Ocean to near the Caspian Sea, forming a natural boundary between Europe and Asia. Highest peak, Mt. Telpos, 5540 ft. Also called **U′rals.**

u·ra·nal·y·sis (yŏŏr′ə nal′i sis), *n., pl.* **-ses** (-sēz′). urinalysis.

U·ra·ni·a (yŏŏ rā′nē ə), *n.* **1.** *Class. Myth.* the Muse of astronomy. **2.** Aphrodite, as representing spiritual love.

U·ra·ni·an (yŏŏ rā′nē ən), *adj.* pertaining to the planet Uranus. [URAN(US) + -IAN]

u·ran·ic[1] (yŏŏ ran′ik), *adj.* *Chem.* **1.** of or containing uranium, esp. in the tetravalent state. **2.** containing uranium in a valence state higher than the corresponding uranous compound. [URAN(IUM) + -IC]

u·ran·ic[2] (yŏŏ ran′ik), *adj.* of or pertaining to the heavens; celestial; astronomical: *uranic principles.* [< Gk *ouran(ós)* heaven + -IC]

u·ran·i·nite (yŏŏ ran′ə nīt′), *n.* a mineral, probably originally uranium dioxide, UO_2, but altered by radioactive decay, and usually containing uranium trioxide, lead, radium, and helium, occurring in several varieties, including pitchblende: the most important ore of uranium. [URAN(IUM) + -IN[2] + -ITE[1]]

u·ra·nite (yŏŏr′ə nīt′), *n.* *Mineral.* any of the uranium phosphates, as autunite or torbernite. [< G *Uranit.* See URANIUM, -ITE[1]] —**u·ra·nit·ic** (yŏŏr′ə nit′ik), *adj.*

u·ra·ni·um (yŏŏ rā′nē əm), *n.* *Chem.* a radioactive, metallic element, used chiefly in atomic and hydrogen bombs and as a nuclear fuel in power reactors. *Symbol:* U; *at. wt.:* 238.03; *at. no.:* 92; *sp. gr.:* 19.07. [< NL; see URAN(US), -IUM]

uranium 235, *Chem.* the uranium isotope having a mass number of 235, comprising 0.715 percent of natural uranium. Also called **U-235, U 235.**

uranium 238, *Chem.* the uranium isotope having a mass number 238, comprising 99.28 percent of natural uranium: used chiefly in nuclear reactors. Also called **U-238, U 238**

ura′nium hex·a·flu′o·ride (hek′sə flŏŏ′ə rīd′, -flŏŏr′-īd, -flôr′-, -flōr′-), *Chem.* a volatile solid, UF_6, used in its gaseous state in separating uranium 235 from uranium.

ura′nium se′ries, *Chem.* the radioactive series that starts with uranium 238 and ends with a stable isotope of lead of mass number 206. Also called **u·ra′ni·um-ra′di·um se′ries** (yŏŏ rā′nē əm rā′dē əm).

urano-, a learned borrowing from Greek meaning "heavens," used in the formation of compound words: *uranography; uranometry.* [< Gk, comb. form of *ouranós* heavens]

u·ra·nog·ra·phy (yŏŏr′ə nog′rə fē), *n.* the branch of astronomy concerned with the description and mapping of the heavens, and esp. of the fixed stars. Also called **uranology.** [< Gk *ouranographía*] —**u′ra·nog′ra·pher, u′ra·nog′ra·phist,** *n.* —**u·ra·no·graph·ic** (yŏŏr′ə nə graf′ik), **u′ra·no·graph′i·cal,** *adj.*

u·ra·nol·o·gy (yŏŏr′ə nol′ə jē), *n., pl.* **-gies.** *Astron.* **1.** uranography. **2.** a treatise on the celestial bodies. —**u·ra·no·log·i·cal** (yŏŏr′ə nəloj′i kəl), *adj.*

u·ra·nom·e·try (yŏŏr′ə nom′i trē), *n.* *Astron.* **1.** a chart of the positions of the heavenly bodies on the celestial sphere. **2.** the measurement of the positions of heavenly bodies. —**u·ra·no·met·ri·cal** (yŏŏr′ə nə me′tri kəl), *adj.*

u·ra·nous (yŏŏr′ə nəs), *adj.* *Chem.* containing trivalent uranium.

U·ra·nus (yŏŏr′ə nəs, yŏŏ rā′-), *n.* **1.** *Class. Myth.* the personification of Heaven and ruler of the world, son and husband of Gaea (Earth) and father of the Titans, the Cyclopes, etc., who confined his children in Tartarus and was dethroned by his son Cronus, youngest of the Titans, at the instigation of Gaea. **2.** *Astron.* the planet seventh in order from the sun, having a diameter of 30,880 miles, a mean distance from the sun of 1,783,000,000 miles, a period of revolution of 84.02 years, and having five satellites.

u·ra·nyl (yŏŏr′ə nil), *n.* *Chem.* the bivalent ion, UO_2^{+2}, or group, UO_2, which forms salts with acids. [URAN(IUM) + -YL] —**u′ra·nyl′ic,** *adj.*

u·ra·ri (yŏŏ rär′ē), *n.* curare. [< Carib]

u·rase (yŏŏr′ās, -āz), *n.* *Biochem.* urease.

u·rate (yŏŏr′āt), *n.* *Chem.* a salt of uric acid. [URO-[1] + -ATE[2]] —**u·rat·ic** (yŏŏ rat′ik), *adj.*

ur·ban (ûr′bən), *adj.* **1.** of, pertaining to, or comprising a city or town. **2.** living in a city or cities. **3.** characteristic of or accustomed to cities; citified. [< L *urbān(us)* = *urb-* (s. of *urbs*) city + *-ānus* -AN]

Ur·ban I (ûr′bən), **Saint,** pope A.D. 222–230.

Urban II, (*Odo* or *Otho*) c1042–99, French ecclesiastic: pope 1088–99.

Urban III, (*Uberto Crivelli*) died 1187, Italian ecclesiastic: pope 1185–87.

Urban IV, (*Jacques Pantaléon*) died 1264, French ecclesiastic: pope 1261–64.

Urban V, (*Guillaume de Grimoard*) c1310–70, French ecclesiastic: pope 1362–70.

Urban VI, (*Bartolomeo Prignano*) c1318–89, Italian ecclesiastic: pope 1378–89.

Urban VII, (*Giovanni Battista Castagna*) 1521–90, Italian ecclesiastic: pope 1590.

Urban VIII, (*Maffeo Barberini*) 1568–1644, Italian ecclesiastic: pope 1623–44.

Ur·ban·a (ûr ban′ə), *n.* a city in E Illinois. 32,800 (1970).

ur′ban dis′trict, a minor administrative division in England, Wales, and Northern Ireland, with a district council, but lacking the charter of a borough.

ur·bane (ûr bān′), *adj.* **1.** having the polish and suavity regarded as characteristic of sophisticated social life in major cities: *an urbane manner.* **2.** reflecting elegance, sophistication, etc., esp. in expression: *He maintained an urbane tone in his letters.* [< L *urbānus.* See URBAN] —**ur·bane′ly,** *adv.* —**ur·bane′ness,** *n.*

ur·ban·ise (ûr′bə nīz′), *v.t.,* **-ised, -is·ing.** *Chiefly Brit.* urbanize. —**ur′ban·i·sa′tion,** *n.*

ur·ban·ism (ûr′bə niz′əm), *n.* the way of life of persons who live in a large city; urbanization. [URBAN + -ISM, modeled on F *urbanisme*]

ur·ban·ist (ûr′bə nist), *n.* a person who is a specialist in urban planning. [URBAN + -IST]

ur·ban·ite (ûr′bə nīt′), *n.* a resident of a city; a person who lives in an urban community.

ur·ban·i·ty (ûr ban′i tē), *n., pl.* **-ties.** **1.** quality of being urbane; refined or elegant courtesy or politeness; suavity. **2. urbanities,** civilities or amenities. [< L *urbānitās*]

ur·ban·ize (ûr′bə nīz′), *v.t.,* **-ized, -iz·ing.** to render urban, as a locality. Also, *esp. Brit.,* **urbanise.** —**ur′ban·i·za′tion,** *n.*

ur·ban·ol·o·gy (ûr′bən ol′ə jē), *n.* the study of urban problems, esp. as a social science. —**ur·ban·ol·o·gist** (ûr′bən ol′ə jist), *n.*

ur′ban renew′al, the art or process of rehabilitating city areas by demolishing, remodeling, or repairing existing structures or laying out new housing, public buildings, parks, etc., on cleared sites in accordance with comprehensive plans. Also called **ur′ban redevel′opment.**

ur·bi·cul·ture (ûr′bə kul′chər), *n.* the way of life characteristic of cities. [< L *urbi-* (s. of *urbs* city) + CULTURE]

ur·bi et or·bi (ŏŏR′bē et ôR′bē), *Latin.* to the city (Rome) and the world: the form of address of papal bulls.

ur·ce·o·late (ûr′sē ə lit, -lāt′), *adj.* shaped like a pitcher; swelling out like the body of a pitcher and contracted at the orifice, as a corolla. [< NL *urceolāt(us)* = L *urceol(us),* dim. of *urce(us)* pitcher + *-ātus* -ATE[1]]

ur·chin (ûr′chin), *n.* **1.** a mischievous boy or any small boy or youngster. **2.** See **sea urchin.** **3.** *Chiefly Brit. Dial.* a hedgehog. **4.** *Obs.* an elf or mischievous sprite. [ME *urchun, urchon* hedgehog < ONF *(h)erichon,* OF *heriçun* < VL **hēriciōn-* (s. of **hēriciō*), m. L *ēricius* hedgehog]

Urd (ŏŏrd), *n.* *Scand. Myth.* a giantess personifying the past: one of the three Norns that developed from Urdar. Cf. **Skuld, Verdandi.**

Ur·dar (ŏŏr′där), *n.* *Scand. Myth.* a giantess personifying fate: the original Norn. Cf. **Skuld, Urd, Verdandi.**

Ur·du (ŏŏr′dŏŏ, ûr′-, ŏŏr dŏŏ′, ûr-), *n.* one of the official languages of Pakistan, a language derived from Hindustani, used by Muslims, and written with Persian-Arabic letters.

-ure, an abstract-noun suffix of action, result, and instrument, occurring in loan words from French: *pressure; legislature.* [< F *-ure* < L *-ūra*]

u·re·a (yŏŏ rē′ə, yŏŏr′ē ə), *n.* **1.** *Biochem.* a compound, $CO(NH_2)_2$, occurring in urine and other body fluids as a product of protein metabolism. **2.** *Chem.* a commercial form of this compound used as a fertilizer, animal feed, and in organic synthesis. [< NL < F *urée.* See UR-[1], -EE] —**u·re′al, u·re′ic,** *adj.*

u·re′a-form·al′de·hyde res′in (yŏŏ rē′ə fôr mal′də-hīd′, yŏŏr′ē ə-), *Chem.* any of a group of resins formed by the interaction of urea and formaldehyde: used chiefly in the manufacture of buttons, baking enamels, and for making fabrics wrinkle-resistant.

u·re·ase (yŏŏr′ē ās′, -āz′), *n.* *Biochem.* an enzyme that changes urea into ammonium carbonate, found in bacteria, fungi, etc. [URE(A) + -ASE]

u·re·din·i·um (yŏŏr′i din′ē əm), *n., pl.* **-din·i·a** (-din′ē ə). *Bot.* (formerly) uredium. [< NL = *ūrēdin-* (s. of L *ūrēdō;* see UREDO) + *-ium* -IUM] —**u′re·din′i·al,** *adj.*

u·re·di·um (yŏŏ rē′dē əm), *n., pl.* **-di·a** (-dē ə). *Bot.* the fructification of the rust fungi, bearing uredospores. [< NL; see UREDO, -IUM] —**u·re′di·al,** *adj.*

u·re·do (yŏŏ rē′dō), *n.* *Pathol.* a skin irritation; hives; urticaria. [< L *ūrēdō* blast, blight, burning itch = *ūr(ere)* to burn + *-ēdō* n. suffix]

u·re·ide (yŏŏr′ē īd′, -id), *n.* *Chem.* any of a group of substances derived from urea in which at least one hydrogen atom has been replaced by an acyl group. [URE(A) + -IDE]

u·re·mi·a (yŏŏ rē′mē ə), *n.* *Pathol.* a condition resulting from the retention in the blood of constituents normally excreted in the urine. Also, **uraemia.** [< NL] —**u·re′mic,** *adj.*

-uret, *Chem.* **1.** a suffix meaning "combine or impregnate with": *carburet.* **2.** a suffix formerly used to form names of compounds, equivalent to **-ide.** [< NL *-urētum* < F *-ure* -ide]

u·re·ter (yŏŏ rē′tər), *n.* *Anat., Zool.* a muscular duct or tube conveying the urine from a kidney to the bladder or cloaca. [< NL < Gk *ourētḗr* = *ourē-* (verbid s. of *ourein* to

URINATE) + -*tēr* n. suffix] —**u·re′ter·al, u·re·ter·ic** (yŏŏr′i-ter′ik), *adj.*

u·re·thane (yŏŏr′ə thān′, yŏŏ reth′ān), *n.* *Chem.* **1.** any derivative of carbamic acid having the formula NH_2COOR. **2.** a powder, $NH_2COOC_2H_5$, used chiefly as a solvent, in organic synthesis, and as a fungicide and pesticide. **3.** polyurethane: *urethane foam.* Also, **u·re·than** (yŏŏr′ə than′). [UR(EA) + ETHANE]

urethr-, var. of **urethro-** before a vowel: *urethritis.*

u·re·thra (yŏŏ rē′thrə), *n., pl.* **-thrae** (-thrē), **-thras.** *Anat.* the membranous tube that extends from the urinary bladder to the exterior and that in the male conveys semen as well as urine. [< LL < Gk *ourḗthra* = *ourē-* (see URETER) + *-thra* n. suffix] —**u·re′thral,** *adj.*

u·re·thri·tis (yŏŏr′ə thrī′tis), *n.* *Pathol.* inflammation of the urethra. [< NL] —**u·re·thrit·ic** (yŏŏr′ə thrit′ik), *adj.*

urethro-, a combining form of **urethra:** *urethroscope.* Also, *esp. before a vowel,* **urethr-.**

u·re·thro·scope (yŏŏ rē′thrə skōp′), *n.* *Med.* an apparatus for observing the urethra. —**u·re·thro·scop·ic** (yŏŏ rē′-thrə skop′ik), *adj.* —**u·re·thros·co·py** (yŏŏr′ə thros′-kə pē), *n.*

u·ret·ic (yŏŏ ret′ik), *adj.* of, pertaining to, or occurring in the urine. [< LL *urēticus* < Gk *ourētikós* = *ourē-* (see URETER) + *-tikos* -TIC]

U·rey (yŏŏr′ē), *n.* **Harold Clay·ton** (klāt′ᵊn), 1893–1981, U.S. chemist and cosmologist: Nobel prize for chemistry 1934.

Ur·fa (ŏŏr fä′), *n.* a city in SE Turkey, E of the Euphrates River: on the site of ancient Edessa. 132,982.

Ur·ga (ŏŏr′gä), *n.* former name of **Ulan Bator.**

urge (ûrj), *v.,* **urged, urg·ing,** *n.* —*v.t.* **1.** to push or force along; impel with force or vigor: *to urge the cause along.* **2.** to drive with incitement to speed or effort: *to urge dogs on with shouts.* **3.** to press, push, or hasten (the course, activities, etc.): *to urge one's flight.* **4.** to impel, constrain, or move to some action: *urged by necessity.* **5.** to endeavor to induce or persuade, as by entreaties or earnest recommendations; entreat or exhort earnestly: *to urge a person to greater caution.* **6.** to press (something) upon the attention: *to urge a claim.* **7.** to insist on, allege, or assert with earnestness: *to urge the need of haste.* **8.** to press by persuasion or recommendation, as for acceptance, performance, or use; recommend or advocate earnestly. —*v.i.* **9.** to exert a driving or impelling force; give an impulse to haste or action. **10.** to make entreaties or earnest recommendations. **11.** to press arguments or allegations, as against a person. —*n.* **12.** an act of urging; impelling action, influence, or force; impulse. **13.** an involuntary, natural, or instinctive impulse. [< L *urg(ēre)* (to) press, force, drive, urge] —**urg′er,** *n.* —**urg′ing·ly,** *adv.* —**Syn. 4.** goad, spur. —**Ant. 1–3.** deter.

ur·gen·cy (ûr′jən sē), *n., pl.* **-cies. 1.** urgent character; imperativeness. **2. urgencies,** urgent requirements or needs. [< LL *urgentia* pressure = L *urgent-* (see URGENT) + *-ia;* see -ENCY]

ur·gent (ûr′jənt), *adj.* **1.** pressing; compelling or requiring immediate action or attention; imperative: *an urgent matter.* **2.** insistent or earnest in solicitation; importunate, as a person: *an urgent pleader.* **3.** expressed with insistence, as requests or appeals: *an urgent tone of voice.* [< L *urgent-* (s. of *urgēns*) = *urg-* URGE + *-ent-* -ENT] —**ur′gent·ly,** *adv.*

-urgy, an element occurring in loan words from Greek where it meant "work" (*dramaturgy*); on this model, used in the formation of compound words (*metallurgy*). [< Gk *-urgia* < *érgon,* c. WORK]

-uria, a word element meaning "urine," used in the formation of compound words: *dysuria.* [< Gk *-ouría.* See URO-¹, -IA]

U·ri′ah the Hit′tite (yŏŏ rī′ə), *n.* the husband of Bathsheba and an officer in David's army. II Sam. 11.

u·ric (yŏŏr′ik), *adj.* of, pertaining to, contained in, or derived from urine. [UR-¹ + -IC]

u′ric ac′id, *Biochem.* a compound, $C_5H_4N_4O_3$, present in urine, which in the form of its salts is found in the joints in gout and as the major constituent of kidney stones. —**u′ric-ac′id,** *adj.*

U·ri·el (yŏŏr′ē əl), *n.* one of the archangels. II Esdras 4.

U·rim and Thum·mim (yŏŏr′im; thum′im), *Judaism.* objects worn on the breastplate of the high priest, used, perhaps like lots, to determine God's response to a question answerable by "yes" or "no." Ex. 28:30. [part. trans. of Heb. *ūrīm wĕthummīm*]

urin-, var. of **urino-** before a vowel: *urinalysis.*

u·ri·nal (yŏŏr′ə nᵊl), *n.* **1.** a building, enclosure, or bathroom fixture where a person may urinate. **2.** a receptacle to receive the urine of a person with urinary incontinence or of a bedridden person. [ME < OF < LL, L *ūrīnāl(e)* of urine. See URIN-, -AL²]

u·ri·nal·y·sis (yŏŏr′ə nal′i sis), *n., pl.* **-ses** (-sēz′). analysis of urine chemically or microscopically. Also, **uranalysis.** [< NL; see URIN-, (AN)ALYSIS]

u·ri·nar·y (yŏŏr′ə ner′ē), *adj., n., pl.* **-nar·ies.** —*adj.* **1.** of or pertaining to urine. **2.** pertaining to the organs secreting and discharging urine. —*n. Archaic.* **3.** a reservoir for the reception of urine or the like. **4.** urinal (def. 1). [< NL *ūrīnāri(us)*]

u′rinary blad′der, *Anat., Zool.* a distensible, muscular and membranous sac in which the urine is retained until it is discharged from the body.

u′rinary cal′culus, *Pathol.* a calcareous concretion in the urinary tract.

u·ri·nate (yŏŏr′ə nāt′), *v.i.,* **-nat·ed, -nat·ing.** to pass or discharge urine. [< ML *ūrīnāt(us),* ptp. of *ūrīn(āre)*] —**u′ri·na′tion,** *n.* —**u′ri·na′tive,** *adv.*

u·rine (yŏŏr′in), *n.* the liquid-to-semisolid waste matter excreted by the kidneys, in man being a yellowish, slightly acid, watery fluid. [ME < OF < L *ūrīn(a);* akin to Gk *oûron* urine]

u′rine anal′ysis, urinalysis.

u·ri·nif·er·ous (yŏŏr′ə nif′ər əs), *adj.* conveying urine.

urino-, a combining form of **urine:** *urinoscopy.* Also, *esp. before a vowel,* **urin-.** [< L = *ūrīn(a)* urine + *-o-* -o-]

u·ri·no·gen·i·tal (yŏŏr′ə nō jen′i tᵊl), *adj.* genitourinary.

u·ri·nos·co·py (yŏŏr′ə nos′kə pē), *n.* *Med.* uroscopy.

u·ri·nous (yŏŏr′ə nəs), *adj.* of, pertaining to, resembling, or having the odor or qualities of urine. Also, **u·ri·nose** (yŏŏr′ə nōs′). [< NL *ūrīnōs(us)*]

Ur·mi·a (ŏŏr′mē ə), *n.* **Lake,** a salt lake in NW Iran. ab. 2000 sq. mi. Also called **Lake Urumiyeh.**

urn (ûrn), *n.* **1.** a large or decorative vase, esp. one with an ornamental foot or pedestal. **2.** a vase for holding the ashes of the cremated dead. **3.** a container with a valve, used for making tea or coffee in quantity. **4.** *Bot.* the spore-bearing part of the capsule of a moss, between lid and seta. [ME *urne* < L *ūrna* earthen vessel for ashes, water, etc., akin to *urceus* pitcher, Gk *hýrchē* jar] —**urn′like′,** *adj.*

uro-¹, a learned borrowing from Greek meaning "urine," used in the formation of compound words: *urology.* Also, *esp. before a vowel,* **ur-.** [< Gk, comb. form of *oûron* urine]

uro-², a learned borrowing from Greek meaning "tail," used in the formation of compound words: *uropod.* [comb. form repr. Gk *ourá*]

u·ro·chord (yŏŏr′ə kôrd′), *n.* *Zool.* the notochord of an ascidian or tunicate, found mostly in the larva, or being more conspicuous in the larva than in the adult, and confined chiefly to the caudal region. —**u′ro·chor′dal,** *adj.*

Ur′ of the Chal·dees′ (kal dēz′; kal′dēz), the city where Abraham was born, sometimes identified with the Sumerian city of Ur. Gen. 11:28, 31; 15:7; Neh. 9:7.

u·ro·gen·i·tal (yŏŏr′ō jen′i tᵊl), *adj.* genitourinary.

u·rog·e·nous (yŏŏ roj′ə nəs), *adj.* *Physiol.* **1.** secreting or producing urine. **2.** contained in urine.

u·ro·lith (yŏŏr′ə lith), *n.* *Pathol.* a urinary calculus. —**u′ro-lith′ic,** *adj.*

u·rol·o·gy (yŏŏ rol′ə jē), *n.* the scientific, clinical, and esp. surgical aspects of the study of the genitourinary tract in men and the urinary tract in women. —**u·ro·log·ic** (yŏŏr′ə-loj′ik), **u′ro·log′i·cal,** *adj.* —**u·rol′o·gist,** *n.*

u·ro·pod (yŏŏr′ə pod′), *n.* an abdominal limb of an arthropod, esp. one of those on either side of the telson, as in a lobster. —**u·rop·o·dal** (yŏŏ rop′ə dᵊl), **u·rop′o·dous,** *adj.*

u·ro·pyg·i·al (yŏŏr′ə pij′ē əl), *adj.* *Ornith.* of or pertaining to the uropygium. [UROPYGI(UM) + -AL¹]

uropyg′ial gland′, *Ornith.* a gland opening on the back at the base of the tail in most birds that secretes an oily fluid used by the bird in preening its feathers.

u·ro·pyg·i·um (yŏŏr′ə pij′ē əm), *n.* *Ornith.* the projecting terminal portion of a bird's body, from which the tail feathers spring. [< NL < Gk *ouropýgion* tail or tail feathers (sp. var. of *orropýgion*) = *ouro-* URO-² + *pyg(ḗ)* rump, buttocks + L *-ium* -IUM]

u·ros·co·py (yŏŏ ros′kə pē), *n.* *Med.* inspection or analysis of the urine as a means of diagnosis. Also, **urinoscopy.** —**u·ro·scop·ic** (yŏŏr′ə skop′ik), *adj.* —**u·ros′co·pist,** *n.*

u·ro·xan·thin (yŏŏr′ə zan′thin), *n.* *Biochem.* a yellow pigment, occurring in normal human urine, that on oxidation is converted to indigo blue. [< G]

Ur·quhart (ûr′kərt), *n.* **Sir Thomas,** 1611–60, Scottish author and translator.

Ur·sa Ma·jor (ûr′sə mā′jər), *gen.* **Ur·sae Ma·jor·is** (ûr′sē mə jôr′is, -jōr′-). *Astron.* the Great Bear, the most prominent northern constellation, containing the seven stars that form the Big Dipper.

Ur·sa Mi·nor (ûr′sə mī′nər), *gen.* **Ur·sae Mi·nor·is** (ûr′sē mi nōr′is, -nôr′-). *Astron.* the Little or Lesser Bear, the most northern constellation containing the stars that form the Little Dipper, the outermost of which, at the end of the handle, is Polaris.

ur·si·form (ûr′sə fôrm′), *adj.* having the form of a bear; bear-shaped. [< L *urs(us)* a bear + -I- + -FORM]

ur·sine (ûr′sīn, -sin), *adj.* **1.** of or pertaining to a bear or bears. **2.** bearlike. [< L *ursīn(us)* = *urs(us)* a bear + *-īnus* -INE¹]

ur′sine das′yure. See **Tasmanian devil.**

ur′sine howl′er, the red howling monkey, *Alouatta seniculus,* of northern South America.

Ur·spra·che (ŏŏr′shprä′KHə; *Ger.* ŌŌR′shPRÄ′KHə), *n.* a hypothetically reconstructed parent language, as Proto-Germanic. [< G: original speech]

Ur·su·la (ûr′sə lə, ûrs′yŏŏ-), *n.* **Saint,** a legendary British princess who, with 11,000 virgins, is said to have been martyred by the Huns at Cologne.

Ur·su·line (ûr′sə lin, -līn′, ûrs′yŏŏ-), *n.* **1.** *Rom. Cath. Ch.* a member of an order of nuns founded at Brescia, Italy, about 1537, devoted to teaching. —*adj.* **2.** of or pertaining to the Ursulines.

ur·ti·ca·ceous (ûr′tə kā′shəs), *adj.* belonging to the *Urticaceae,* or nettle family of plants. [< NL *Urtīcāce(ae)* = L *urtīc(a)* nettle (< *ūr(ere)* (to) burn, sting) + NL *-āceae* -ACEAE + -OUS]

ur·ti·cant (ûr′tə kənt), *adj.* urticating. [< F < ML *urtīcant-* (s. of *urtīcāns*), prp. of *urtīc(āre)* (to) sting. See URTICATE]

ur·ti·car·i·a (ûr′tə kâr′ē ə), *n.* *Pathol.* a transient condition of the skin, usually caused by an allergic reaction and characterized by pale, irregular, elevated patches and severe itching; nettle rash; hives. [< NL = L *urtīca* nettle + *-āria* -ARIA] —**ur′ti·car′i·al,** *adj.*

ur·ti·cate (ûr′tə kāt′), *v.,* **-cat·ed, -cat·ing.** —*v.t.* **1.** to sting with or as if with nettles. **2.** to whip with or as if with nettles, esp. so as to produce a stinging sensation; flog; lash. —*v.i.* **3.** to sting in the manner of a nettle. [< ML *urtīcāt(us)* (ptp. of *urtīcāre* to sting) = L *urtīc(a)* nettle + *-ātus* -ATE¹]

ur·ti·ca·tion (ûr′tə kā′shən), *n.* *Pathol.* the development or eruption of urticaria. [< ML *urtīcātiōn-* (s. of *urtīcātiō*) a stinging]

Uru., Uruguay.

U·ru·guay (yŏŏr′ə gwā′; *Sp.* ōō′RŌŌ gwī′), *n.* **1.** a republic in SE South America. 2,763,964; 72,172 sq. mi. *Cap.:* Montevideo. **2.** a river in SE South America, flowing from S Brazil along the boundary of E Argentina into the Río de la Plata. 981 mi. long. —**U·ru·guay·an** (yŏŏr′ə-gwā′ən, -gwī′ən), *adj., n.*

U·rum·chi (ōō rōōm′chē), *n.* a city in and the capital of Sinkiang, in NW China. 500,000. Also, **U·rum·tsi** (ōō rōōm′chē). Also called **Tihwa.**

U·ru·mi·yeh (o͝o ro͞o′mē ye), *n.* **Lake.** See **Urmia, Lake.**

U·run·di (o͝o ro͞on′dē), *n.* former name of **Burundi.** Cf. **Ruanda-Urundi.**

u·rus (yo͝or′əs), *n., pl.* **u·rus·es.** the aurochs. [< L *ūrus* a kind of wild ox (c. Gk *oûros*) < Gmc *ūr-;* cf. OE, OHG *ūr*]

u·ru·shi·ol (o͝or′o͞o shē ōl′, -ôl′, -ol′), *n.* a toxic, liquid, catechol derivative, the active irritant principle in several species of the plant genus *Rhus,* as in poison ivy. [< Jap *urushi* lacquer + -OL]

us (us), *pron.* **1.** the objective case of **we,** as direct or indirect object: *Will you come with us? They took us to the circus. She asked us the way.* **2.** *Informal.* (used in place of the pronoun *our* in gerundive constructions): *Do you know about us moving to town?* [ME, OE; c. G, Goth *uns*] **—Usage. 2.** See **me.**

U.S., 1. United Service. **2.** See **United States.**

u.s., 1. where mentioned above. [< L *ubi supra*] **2.** as above: a formula in judicial acts, directing that what precedes be reviewed. [< L *ut supra*]

USA, 1. See **United States Army. 2.** See **United States of America.**

U.S.A., 1. Union of South Africa. **2.** See **United States Army. 3.** See **United States of America.**

us·a·ble (yo͞o′zə bəl), *adj.* **1.** that is available for use. **2.** convenient and capable of being used. Also, **useable.** [ME < MF] **—us′a·bil′i·ty, us′a·ble·ness,** *n.* **—us′a·bly,** *adv.*

USAF, See **United States Air Force.** Also, **U.S.A.F.**

us·age (yo͞o′sij, -zij), *n.* **1.** customary way of doing something; a custom or practice: *the usages of the last 50 years.* **2.** the customary manner in which a language or a form of a language is spoken or written. **3.** a particular instance of this: *a usage borrowed from French.* **4.** manner of doing or handling something; treatment: *rough usage.* **5.** an act of using or employing; use. [ME < AF, OF < ML *ūsātic(um)* = L *ūs(us)* (see USE) + *-āticum* -AGE]

us·ance (yo͞o′zəns), *n.* **1.** *Com.* a length of time allowed by custom or usage for the payment of foreign bills of exchange. **2.** *Archaic.* **a.** use. **b.** custom; habit. **3.** *Obs.* usury. [ME *usaunce* < OF *usance,* prob. < ML *ūsantia* < L *ūsant-* (s. of *ūsāns*), prp. of *ūsāre* to USE; see -ANCE]

USAR, United States Army Reserve.

Us·beg (o͝os′beg, us′-), *n., pl.* **-begs,** (*esp. collectively*) **-beg.** Uzbek.

Us·bek (o͝os′bek, us′-), *n., pl.* **-beks,** (*esp. collectively*) **-bek.** Uzbek.

U.S.C., United States of Colombia. Also, **USC**

U.S.C.&G.S., United States Coast and Geodetic Survey.

U.S.C.G., United States Coast Guard. Also, **USCG**

USDA, United States Department of Agriculture. Also, **U.S.D.A.**

use (*v.* yo͞oz; *n.* yo͞os), *v.,* **used, us·ing,** *n.* **—***v.t.* **1.** to employ for some purpose; put into service; make use of: *to use a knife.* **2.** to avail oneself of; apply to one's own purposes: *May I use your telephone?* **3.** to expend or consume in use: *We have used the money provided.* **4.** to treat or behave toward: *He did not use his employees with much consideration.* **5.** to habituate or accustom. **6.** *Archaic.* to practice habitually or customarily. **—***v.i.* **7.** to be accustomed, wont, or customarily found (used with an infinitive expressed or understood, and, except in archaic use, now only in the past): *He used to go every day.* **8. use up, a.** to consume entirely. **b.** to exhaust of vigor or usefulness; finish. **—***n.* **9.** the act of employing, using, or putting into service: *the use of tools.* **10.** the state of being employed or used. **11.** an instance or way of employing or using something: *the painter's use of color.* **12.** a way of being employed or used; a purpose for which something is used. **13.** the power, right, or privilege of employing or using something: *to lose the use of the right eye.* **14.** service or advantage in or for being employed or used; utility or usefulness: *of no practical use.* **15.** help; profit; resulting good: *What's the use?* **16.** occasion or need, as for something to be employed or used: *Have you any use for another calendar?* **17.** continued, habitual, or customary employment or practice; custom; practice. **18.** *Law.* **a.** the enjoyment of property, as by the employment, occupation, or exercise of it. **b.** the benefit or profit of lands and tenements in the possession of another who simply holds them for the beneficiary. **c.** the equitable ownership of land to which the legal title is vested in another. **19.** *Liturgy.* the distinctive form of ritual or of any liturgical observance used in a particular church, diocese, community, etc. **20.** *Obs.* usual experience. **21. have no use for, a.** to have no occasion or need for. **b.** to refuse to tolerate; dislike: *He had no use for laggards.* **22. make use of,** to use for one's own purposes; employ. **23. put to use,** to apply; employ to advantage. [(v.) ME *use(n)* < OF *use(r)* < L *ūs(us),* ptp. of *ūtī* to use; (n.) ME *us* < OF < L *ūsus*]
—Syn. 1. USE, UTILIZE mean to make something serve one's purpose: USE is the general word: *to use a saw and other tools; to use one's eyes; to use milk or eggs in cooking.* (What is USED often has depreciated or been diminished, sometimes completely consumed: *a used automobile; All the butter has been used.*) As applied to persons, USE implies some selfish or sinister purpose: *to use another to advance oneself.* UTILIZE implies practical or profitable use: *to utilize the means at hand, a modern lighting system.* **3.** exhaust. **10.** employment, utilization, application. **11.** handling.

use·a·ble (yo͞o′zə bəl), *adj.* usable. **—use′a·bil′i·ty, use′a·ble·ness,** *n.* **—use′a·bly,** *adv.*

used (yo͞ozd), *adj.* **1.** having former ownership; secondhand: *a used car.* **2.** showing wear or being worn out. **3.** employed for a purpose; utilized. **4.** being accustomed to; established through usage. [ME]

use·ful (yo͞os′fəl), *adj.* **1.** being of use or service; serving some purpose; serviceable, advantageous, helpful, or of good effect: *a useful member of society.* **2.** of practical use, as for doing work; producing material results; supplying common needs. **—use′ful·ly,** *adv.* **—use′ful·ness,** *n.* **—Syn.** profitable, beneficial. **—Ant.** useless.

use·less (yo͞os′lis), *adj.* **1.** of no use; not serving the purpose or any purpose; unavailing. **2.** without useful qualities; of no practical good. **—use′less·ly,** *adv.* **—use′less·ness,** *n.* **—Syn. 1.** fruitless, profitless, worthless, inutile. USELESS, FUTILE, INEFFECTUAL refer to that which is unavailing. USELESS suggests something which is unavailing because of the circumstances of the case or some inherent defect: *It is useless to cry over spilt milk.* FUTILE suggests wasted effort and failure to attain a desired end: *All attempts were futile.* That which is INEFFECTUAL weakly applies energy in an ill-advised way and does not produce a desired effect: *an ineffectual effort.* **2.** unserviceable, unusable.

us·er[1] (yo͞o′zər), *n.* a person or thing that uses. [ME *usere*]

user[2] (yo͞o′zər), *n.* *Law.* the exercise of a right to the enjoyment of property. [n. use of AF *user* to USE]

us·er-friend·ly (yo͞o′zər frend′lē), *adj.* (of software, computers, etc.) easy to use or familiarize oneself with, as by someone without technical training.

USES, United States Employment Service. Also, **U.S.E.S.**

U.S.G.A., United States Golf Association. Also, **USGA**

Ush·ant (ush′ənt), *n.* an island off the NW coast of France: naval battles 1778, 1794. 1940 (1962); 4½ mi. long. French, **Ouessant.**

U-shaped (yo͞o′shāpt′), *adj.* being in the form of a **U.**

Ush·as (o͞osh′əs, o͞o shäs′), *n.* Dawn, a Vedic deity, daughter of Sky and sister of Night. [< Skt]

ush·er (ush′ər), *n.* **1.** a person who escorts people to seats in a church, theater, etc. **2.** an officer or servant having charge of an entrance door; doorkeeper. **3.** an officer whose business it is to introduce strangers or to walk before a person of rank. **—***v.t.* **4.** to act as an usher to; lead, introduce, or show (usually fol. by *in, into, out,* or *to*): *He ushered the ladies to their seats.* **5.** to precede or herald (usually fol. by *in*): *They ushered in the new theater season.* **—***v.i.* **6.** to act as an usher: *He ushered at the banquet.* [ME *uscher* < AF *usser,* OF *(h)uissier* doorman, officer of justice < VL **ustiārius* = L *ōsti(um)* door + *-ārius* -ER[1]] **—ush′er·ship′,** *n.*

Ush·er (ush′ər), *n.* **James.** See **Ussher, James.**

ush·er·ette (ush′ə ret′), *n.* a female who escorts persons to seats in a church, theater, etc.

USIA, See **United States Information Agency.** Also, **U.S.I.A.**

USIS, United States Information Service. Also, **U.S.I.S.**

Usk (usk), *n.* a river flowing from SE Wales through SW England into the Severn estuary. 60 mi. long.

Us·küb (ʏs kʏp′), *n.* Turkish name of **Skoplje.** Also, **Us·küp′.**

Us·kü·dar (ʏs′kʏ däʀ′), *n.* Turkish name of **Scutari.**

U.S.L.T.A., United States Lawn Tennis Association. Also, **USLTA**

USM, underwater-to-surface missile.

U.S.M., 1 United States Marines. **2.** United States Mint. Also, **USM**

U.S.M.A., United States Military Academy. Also, **USMA**

USMC, 1. See **United States Marine Corps. 2.** United States Maritime Commission. Also, **U.S.M.C.**

USN, See **United States Navy.** Also, **U.S.N.**

U.S.N.A., 1. United States National Army. **2.** United States Naval Academy. Also, **USNA**

U.S.N.G., United States National Guard. Also, **USNG**

U.S.N.R., United States Naval Reserve. Also, **USNR**

U.S.N.R.F., United States Naval Reserve Force. Also, **USNRF**

USO, United Service Organizations. Also, **U.S.O.**

U.S.P., United States Pharmacopeia. Also, **U.S. Pharm.**

Us·pal·la′ta Pass′ (o͞os′pä yä′tə; *Sp.* o͞os′pä yä′tä), a mountain pass in S South America, in the Andes, connecting Mendoza, Argentina and Santiago, Chile. ab. 12,600 ft. high. Also called **La Cumbre.**

U.S.P.H.S., United States Public Health Service. Also, **USPHS**

U.S.P.O., United States Post Office. Also, **USPO**

us·que·baugh (us′kwi bô′, -bä′), *n.* (in Scotland and Ireland) whiskey. [< Ir and ScotGael: lit., water of life]

U.S.R., United States Reserves. Also, **USR**

U.S.R.C., United States Reserve Corps. Also, **USRC**

U.S.S., 1. United States Senate. **2.** United States Senator. **3.** United States Service. **4.** United States Ship. **5.** United States Steamer. **6.** United States Steamship. Also, **USS**

U.S.S.Ct., United States Supreme Court.

Ussh·er (ush′ər), *n.* **James,** 1581–1656, Irish prelate and scholar. Also, **Usher.**

U.S.S.R., See **Union of Soviet Socialist Republics.** Also, **USSR**

U.S.S.S., United States Steamship. Also, **USSS**

Us·su·ri (o͞o so͞o′rē), *n.* a river forming part of the boundary between E Manchuria and the SE Soviet Union in Asia, flowing N to the Amur River. 500 mi. long.

us·tu·late (us′chə lit, -lāt′), *adj.* colored or blackened as if scorched. [< L *ustulāt(us)* scorched, burned (ptp. of *ustulāre*) = *ust(us)* burned (ptp. of *ūrere*) + *-ul-* dim. suffix + *-ātus* -ATE[1]]

us·tu·la·tion (us′chə lā′shən), *n.* the act of scorching or burning. [< ML *ustulātiōn-* (s. of *ustulātiō*) a scorching = L *ustulāt(us)* (see USTULATE) + *-iōn-* -ION]

usu., 1. usual. **2.** usually.

u·su·al (yo͞o′zho͞o əl, -zhwəl), *adj.* **1.** expected by reason of previous experience with the same occurrence, situation, person, etc.: *his usual skill.* **2.** commonly met with or observed in experience; ordinary: *the usual January weather.* **3.** commonplace; everyday: *He says the usual things.* **4. as usual,** in the customary or usual manner. **—***n.* **5.** that which is usual. [ME < LL *ūsuāl(is)* = L *ūs(us)* (see USE) + *-ālis* -AL[1]; cf. OF *usuel*] **—u′su·al·ly,** *adv.* **—u′su·al·ness,** *n.*
—Syn. 1. accustomed. USUAL, CUSTOMARY, HABITUAL refer to a settled and constant practice. USUAL indicates that which is to be expected by reason of previous experience, which shows it to occur more often than not: *There were the usual crowds at the celebration.* That which is CUSTOMARY is in accordance with prevailing usage or individual practice: *It is customary to finish up with dessert and coffee.* That which is HABITUAL has become settled or constant as the result of habit on the part of the individual: *The merchants wore habitual smiles throughout the season.* **2.** general, prevailing, familiar, expected. **—Ant. 1.** unexpected, extraordinary.

u·su·fruct (yo͞o′zo͝o frukt′, -so͝o-, yo͞oz′yo͝o-, yo͞os′-), *n.* *Roman and Civil Law.* the right of enjoying all the advantages derivable from the use of something which belongs to another. [< LL *ūsūfrūct(us)* = L *ūsu(s)* (see USE) + *frūctus* (see FRUIT)]

u·su·fruc·tu·ar·y (yo͞o′zo͝o fruk′cho͞o er′ē, -so͝o-, yo͞oz′yo͝o-, yo͞os′-), *adj., n., pl.* **-ar·ies.** *Roman and Civil Law.* —*adj.* **1.** of, pertaining to, or of the nature of usufruct. —*n.* **2.** a person who has a usufructuary property. [< LL *ūsūfrūctuārius.* See USUFRUCT, -ARY]

U·sum·bu·ra (o͞o′so͞om bo͝or′ə), *n.* former name of **Bujumbura.**

u·su·rer (yo͞o′zhər ər), *n.* **1.** a person who lends money, esp. at an exorbitant or unlawful interest rate. **2.** *Obs.* a person who lends money at interest; moneylender. [ME < AF < ML *ūsūrār(ius)* = L *ūsūri(a)* USURY + L *-ārius* -ARY]

u·su·ri·ous (yo͞o zho͝or′ē əs), *adj.* **1.** practicing usury; charging illegal or exorbitant interest rates for the use of money. **2.** constituting or characterized by usury. —**u·su′ri·ous·ly,** *adv.* —**u·su′ri·ous·ness,** *n.*

u·surp (yo͞o sûrp′, -zûrp′), *v.t.* **1.** to seize and hold (a position, office, power, etc.) by force or without legal right. —*v.i.* **2.** to commit forcible or illegal seizure of an office, power, etc.; encroach. **3.** to use without authority or right; employ wrongfully. [ME < L *ūsūrp(āre)* (to) take possession through use = *ūsū* (abl. of *ūsus* use) + *rapere* to seize] —**u·surp′a·tive,** *adj.* —**u·surp′er,** *n.* —**u·surp′ing·ly,** *adv.*

u·sur·pa·tion (yo͞o′sər pā′shən, -zər-), *n.* **1.** an act of usurping; wrongful or illegal encroachment, infringement, or seizure. **2.** illegal seizure and occupation of a throne. [ME < L *ūsūrpātiōn-* (s. of *ūsūrpātiō*) = *ūsūrpāt(us)* (ptp. of *ūsūrpāre* (to) USURP) + *-iōn-* -ION] —**u·sur·pa·tive** (yo͞o sûr′pə tiv), **u·sur·pa·to·ry** (yo͞o sûr′pə tôr′ē, -tōr′ē), *adj.*

u·su·ry (yo͞o′zhə rē), *n., pl.* **-ries.** **1.** an exorbitant amount or rate of interest, esp. in excess of the legal rate. **2.** the lending or practice of lending money at an exorbitant interest rate. **3.** *Obs.* interest paid for the use of money. [ME *usurie* < ML *ūsūria* (cf. L *ūsūra*) = < L *ūs(us)* (see USE) + *-ur-* -URE + *-ia* -Y[3]]

USW, ultrashort wave. Also, **usw**

UT, Utah (approved esp. for use with zip code).

ut (ut, o͞ot), *n.* *Music.* (formerly) do[2]. Cf. **sol-fa.** [see GAMUT]

Ut., Utah.

u·ta (yo͞o′tə), *n.* any of several large lizards of the genus *Uta,* of the western U.S. and northern Mexico. [< NL, named after UTE]

U·tah (yo͞o′tô, yo͞o′tä), *n.* a state in the W United States. 1,059,273 (1970); 84,916 sq. mi. *Cap.:* Salt Lake City. *Abbr.:* Ut., UT —**U′tah·an, U′tahn,** *adj., n.*

ut dict., (in prescriptions) as directed. [< L *ut dictum*]

Ute (yo͞ot, yo͞o′tē), *n., pl.* **Utes,** (*esp. collectively*) **Ute.** **1.** a member of an important tribe of the Shoshonean stock of North American Indians, now in Utah and Colorado. **2.** their language, of the Uto-Aztecan family of languages.

u·ten·sil (yo͞o ten′səl), *n.* **1.** any of the instruments or vessels commonly used in a kitchen, dairy, etc.: *baking utensils.* **2.** any instrument, vessel, or tool serving a useful purpose: *farming utensils.* [ME: household articles < MF *utensile* < L *ūtēnsilia* neut. pl. of *ūtēnsilis* useful < *ūt(ī)* (to) use] —**Syn. 2.** See **tool.**

uter-, a combining form of **uterus:** *uterine.*

u·ter·ine (yo͞o′tər in, -tə rīn′), *adj.* **1.** of or pertaining to the uterus or womb. **2.** maternally related but having a different father. [late ME < LL *uterīn(us)* of, pertaining to the uterus]

u·ter·us (yo͞o′tər əs), *n., pl.* **u·ter·i** (yo͞o′tə rī′). *Anat., Zool.* the portion of the oviduct in which the fertilized ovum implants itself and develops or rests during prenatal development; the womb of certain mammals. [< L: the womb, matrix; akin to Skt *udāra* belly]

Ut·gard (o͞ot′gärd), *n.* *Scand. Myth.* a part of Jotunheim sometimes identified with all Jotunheim.

U Thant (o͞o′ thänt′, tänt′, thant′, yo͞o′), 1909–74, Burmese statesman: secretary-general of the United Nations 1962–71.

U·ther (yo͞o′thər), *n.* *Arthurian Romance.* king of Britain and father of Arthur. Also called **U′ther Pendrag′on.**

U·ti·ca (yo͞o′ti kə), *n.* **1.** a city in central New York, on the Mohawk River. 91,611 (1970). **2.** an ancient city on the N coast of Africa, NW of Carthage.

u·tile (yo͞o′til), *adj.* *Obs.* useful. [< OF < L *ūtil(is)* = *ūt(ī)* (to) use + *-ilis* -ILE]

u·ti·lise (yo͞ot′əlīz′), *v.t.,* **-lised, -lis·ing.** *Chiefly Brit.* utilize. —**u′ti·lis′a·ble,** *adj.* —**u′ti·li·sa′tion,** *n.* —**u′ti·lis′er,** *n.*

u·til·i·tar·i·an (yo͞o til′i târ′ē ən), *adj.* **1.** pertaining to or consisting in utility. **2.** having regard to usefulness rather than beauty, ornamentation, etc. **3.** of, pertaining to, or adhering to the doctrine of utilitarianism. —*n.* **4.** an adherent of utilitarianism. [UTILIT(Y) + -ARIAN]

u·til·i·tar·i·an·ism (yo͞o til′i târ′ē ə niz′əm), *n.* the ethical doctrine that virtue is based on utility, and that conduct should be directed toward promoting the greatest happiness of the greatest number of people.

u·til·i·ty (yo͞o til′i tē), *n., pl.* **-ties,** *adj.* —*n.* **1.** the state or quality of being useful; usefulness. **2.** something useful. **3.** a public service, as a streetcar or railroad line, a telephone or electric-light system, or the like. **4.** Often, **utilities.** a useful or advantageous factor or feature. **5.** *Econ.* the capacity of a commodity or a service to satisfy some human want. **6.** the principle and end of utilitarian ethics; well-being or happiness; that which is conducive to the happiness and well-being of the greatest number of people. **7. utilities,** stocks or bonds of public utilities. —*adj.* **8.** (of domestic animals) raised or kept to constitute an economically profitable product rather than for show or as pets: *utility breeds.* **9.** having or made for a number of useful or practical purposes rather than a single, specialized one: *a utility knife.* **10.** designed chiefly for use or service rather than beauty, high quality, or the like: *utility furniture.* [ME *utilite* < OF *utelite* < L *ūtilitāt-* (s. of *ūtilitās*) = *ūtil(is)* useful (see UTILE) + *-itāt-* -ITY]

util′ity pole′, one of a series of large upright poles used to support telephone wires, electric cables, or the like. Also called **telephone pole.**

util′ity room′, a room containing appliances needed for the upkeep of an establishment.

u·ti·lize (yo͞ot′əlīz′), *v.t.,* **-lized, -liz·ing.** to put to use; turn to profitable account. Also, *esp. Brit.,* **utilise.** [< F *utilis(er)* = *utile* useful (see UTILE) + *-iser* -IZE] —**u′ti·liz′a·ble,** *adj.* —**u′ti·li·za′tion,** *n.* —**u′ti·liz′er,** *n.* —**Syn.** See **use.**

ut in·fra (o͝ot in′frä; *Eng.* ut in′frə), *Latin.* as (stated or shown) below: used in a book, text, etc.

ut·most (ut′mōst′ *or, esp. Brit.,* -məst), *adj.* **1.** of the greatest or highest degree, quantity, or the like; greatest: *of the utmost importance.* **2.** being at the farthest point or extremity; farthest. —*n.* **3.** Also, **uttermost.** the greatest degree or amount: *The hotel provides the utmost in comfort.* **4.** the most or best of one's abilities, powers, etc.: *He did his utmost to benefit mankind.* **5.** the extreme limit or extent. [ME *utmest,* OE *ūtemest*]

U·to-Az·tec·an (yo͞o′tō az′tek ən), *n.* **1.** an American Indian linguistic stock, widespread from Idaho to the Isthmus of Tehuantepec, and from the Rocky Mountains to the Pacific: this stock includes Hopi, Ute, Shoshone, Comanche, Nahuatl, Pima, and other languages. —*adj.* **2.** of or pertaining to Uto-Aztecan.

U·to·pi·a (yo͞o tō′pē ə), *n.* **1.** an imaginary island described in Sir Thomas More's *Utopia* (1516) as enjoying the utmost perfection in law, politics, etc. **2.** (*sometimes l.c.*) **a.** a place or state of political or social perfection. **b.** any visionary system of political or social perfection. [< NL < Gk *ou* not + *tóp(os)* a place + *-ia* n. suffix]

U·to·pi·an (yo͞o tō′pē ən), *adj.* **1.** of, pertaining to, or resembling Utopia. **2.** (*sometimes l.c.*) **a.** founded upon or involving imaginary political or social perfection. **b.** given to dreams or schemes of such perfection. —*n.* **4.** an inhabitant of Utopia. [< NL *Utopiān(us)*]

uto′pian so′cialism, (*sometimes cap.*) an economic system based on the premise that if capital voluntarily surrendered its ownership of the means of production to the state or the workers, unemployment and poverty would be abolished. Cf. **socialism.**

U·trecht (yo͞o′trekt; *Du.* Y′TREKHT), *n.* a city in the central Netherlands: treaties ending the War of the Spanish Succession signed here 1714. 278,966 (1970).

u·tri·cle (yo͞o′tri kəl), *n.* **1.** a small sac or baglike body, as an air-filled cavity in a seaweed. **2.** *Bot.* a thin bladderlike pericarp or seed vessel. **3.** *Anat.* the larger of two sacs in the membranous labyrinth of the internal ear. Cf. **saccule** (def. 1). [< L *utricul(us),* dim. of *uter* bag; see -CLE]

u·tric·u·lar (yo͞o trik′yə lər), *adj.* **1.** pertaining to or of the nature of a utricle; baglike. **2.** having a utricle or utricles. [< L *utricul(us)* UTRICLE + -AR[1]]

u·tric·u·late (yo͞o trik′yə lit, -lāt′), *adj.* *Archaic.* having a utricle; utricular; baglike. [UTRICUL(AR) + -ATE[1]]

u·tric·u·li·tis (yo͞o trik′yə lī′tis), *n.* *Pathol.* inflammation of the utricle. [< NL; see UTRICLE, -ITIS]

u·tric·u·lus (yo͞o trik′yə ləs), *n., pl.* **-li** (-lī′). utricle.

U·tril·lo (yo͞o tril′ō, o͞o-; *Fr.* Y TRĒ YŌ′), *n.* **Mau·rice** (mō rēs′; *Fr.* mō RĒS′), 1883–1955, French painter.

U·tsu·no·mi·ya (o͝o tso͝o′nô mē′yä), *n.* a city in central Honshu, in central Japan. 255,748 (1964).

ut su·pra (*Lat.* o͝ot so͞o′PRÄ; *Eng.* ut so͞o′prə), *Latin.* See **u.s.** (def. 2).

Ut·tar Pra·desh (o͝ot′ər prə dāsh′), a state in N India: a former province of British India. 73,746,401 (1961); 113,409 sq. mi. *Cap.:* Lucknow. Formerly, **United Provinces.** Former official name, **United Provinces of Agra and Oudh.**

ut·ter[1] (ut′ər), *v.t.* **1.** to give audible expression to; speak or pronounce. **2.** to give forth (cries, notes, etc.) with the voice: *to utter a sigh.* **3.** to express (oneself), esp. in words. **4.** to give forth (a sound) otherwise than with the voice: *The engine uttered a shriek.* **5.** to express by written or printed words. **6.** to make publicly known; publish: *to utter a libel.* **7.** to put into circulation, as coins, notes, etc., and esp. counterfeit money, forged checks, etc. **8.** *Archaic.* to expel; emit. **9.** *Obs.* to sell. [ME *outre* (see OUT, -ER[6]); c. G *äussern* to declare] —**ut′ter·a·ble,** *adj.* —**ut′ter·er,** *n.* —**ut′ter·less,** *adj.*

ut·ter[2] (ut′ər), *adj.* **1.** complete; total; absolute: *her utter abandonment to grief.* **2.** unconditional; unqualified: *an utter denial.* [ME; OE *uttra, ūtera* outer. See OUT, -ER[4]] —**ut′ter·ness,** *n.* —**Syn. 1.** See **absolute.**

ut·ter·ance[1] (ut′ər əns), *n.* **1.** something uttered; a word or words uttered. **2.** an act of uttering; vocal expression. **3.** a manner of speaking; power of speaking: *His very utterance was spellbinding.* **4.** a cry, animal's call, or the like. **5.** *Linguistics.* any speech sequence consisting of one or more words and preceded and followed by silence: it may be coextensive with a sentence. **6.** *Obs.* a public sale of goods. [ME; see UTTER[1], -ANCE]

ut·ter·ance[2] (ut′ər əns), *n.* *Archaic.* the utmost extremity, esp. death. [ME < OF *outrance, oultrance* = *oultr(er)* (to) pass beyond (< L *ultrā* beyond) + *-ance* -ANCE]

ut′ter bar′. See **outer bar.**

ut·ter·ly (ut′ər lē), *adv.* in an utter manner; completely; absolutely. [ME]

ut·ter·most (ut′ər mōst′ *or, esp. Brit.,* -məst), *adj.* **1.** utmost; most remote or outermost: *the uttermost stars of the galaxy.* **2.** of the greatest or highest degree, quantity, etc.; greatest. —*n.* **3.** utmost. [ME]

U·tu (o͞o′to͞o), *n.* the Sumerian sun god: the counterpart of the Akkadian Shamash.

U-turn (yo͞o′tûrn′), *n.* a U-shaped turn as made by an automobile to change direction.

UUM, underwater-to-underwater missile.

U.V., ultraviolet. Also, **UV**

u·va·rov·ite (o͞o vär′ə vīt′, yo͞o-), *n.* a variety of garnet colored emerald-green by the presence of chromium. [< G, named after Count S. S. *Uvarov* (1785–1855), president of St. Petersburg Academy; see -ITE[1]]

u·ve·a (yōō′vē ə), *n.* *Anat.* the vascular tunic of the eye, comprising the iris, choroid coat, and ciliary body. [< ML *ūvea*, var. of L *ūva* the fruit of the vine, a grape] —**u′ve·al, u′ve·ous,** *adj.*

Uve·dale (yōōd′əl, yōōv′dāl), *n.* **Nicholas.** See **Udall, Nicholas.**

u·ve·i·tis (yōō′vē ī′tis), *n.* *Pathol.* inflammation of the uvea. [< NL] —**u·ve·it·ic** (yōō′vē it′ik), *adj.*

u·vu·la (yōō′vyə lə), *n., pl.* **-las, -lae** (-lē′). *Anat.* the small, fleshy, conical body projecting downward from the middle of the soft palate. [< ML *ūvula* = L *ūv(a)* grape + *-ula* -ULE]

u·vu·lar (yōō′vyə lər), *adj.* **1.** of or pertaining to the uvula. **2.** *Phonet.* articulated with the back of the tongue held close to or touching the uvula, as in the *r*-sound of Parisian French. —*n.* **3.** *Phonet.* a uvular sound. —**u′vu·lar·ly,** *adv.*

u·vu·lec·to·my (yōō′vyə lek′tə mē), *n., pl.* **-mies.** *Surg.* excision of the uvula.

U/W, underwriter. Also, **u/w**

ux., wife. Also, **ux** [< L *uxor*]

Ux·mal (ōōs mäl′), *n.* an ancient ruined city in SE Mexico, in Yucatán: a center of later Mayan civilization.

ux·o·ri·al (uk sōr′ē əl, -sôr′-, ug zōr′-, -zôr′-), *adj.* of or pertaining to a wife; typical of or befitting a wife. [< L *ūxor* wife + -IAL] —**ux·o′ri·al·ly,** *adv.*

ux·o·ri·cide (uk sōr′i sīd′, -sôr′-, ug zōr′-, -zôr′-), *n.* **1.** the act of murdering one's wife. **2.** a man who murders his wife. [< L *ūxor* wife + -I- + -CIDE] —**ux·o′ri·cid′al,** *adj.*

ux·o·ri·lo·cal (uk sōr′ə lō′kəl, -sôr′-, ug zōr′-, -zôr′-), *adj.* matrilocal. [< L *ūxor* wife + -I- + LOCAL]

ux·o·ri·ous (uk sōr′ē əs, -sôr′-, ug zōr′-, -zôr′-), *adj.* doting upon, foolishly fond of, or affectionately oversubmissive toward one's wife. [< L *ūxōrius* = *ūxor* wife + *-ius* -IOUS] —**ux·o′ri·ous·ly,** *adv.* —**ux·o′ri·ous·ness,** *n.*

Uz·beg (ŏŏz′beg, uz′-), *n., pl.* **-begs,** (*esp. collectively*) **-beg.** Uzbek.

Uz·bek (ŏŏz′bek, uz′-), *n., pl.* **-beks,** (*esp. collectively*) **-bek.** **1.** a member of a town-dwelling, Turkic people of Turkestan and Uzbekistan. **2.** the Turkic language of the Uzbeks. Also, **Usbeg, Usbek, Uzbeg.**

Uz·bek·i·stan (ŏŏz bek′i stan′, -stän′, uz-), *n.* a constituent republic of the Soviet Union, in S central Asia. 10,100,000 (est. 1965). 158,500 sq. mi. *Cap.:* Tashkent. Official name **Uz′bek So′viet So′cialist Repub′lic.**

DEVELOPMENT OF MAJUSCULE							
NORTH SEMITIC	GREEK	ETR.	LATIN		MODERN GOTHIC	MODERN ITALIC	MODERN ROMAN
SEE LETTER U		V	V	V	𝔙	*V*	V

DEVELOPMENT OF MINUSCULE					
ROMAN CURSIVE	ROMAN UNCIAL	CAROL. MIN.	MODERN GOTHIC	MODERN ITALIC	MODERN ROMAN
SEE U	Y	—	𝔳	*v*	v

The twenty-second letter of the English alphabet originated in Etruscan, where it signified the *u*-sound. The use of V for the *v*-sound dates from the end of the Middle Ages. (See also **U.**)

V, v (vē), *n., pl.* **V's** or **Vs, v's** or **vs.** **1.** the 22nd letter of the English alphabet, a consonant. **2.** any spoken sound represented by the letter *V* or *v*, as in *very, oval,* or *shove.* **3.** something having the form of a V. **4.** a written or printed representation of the letter *V* or *v.* **5.** a device, as a printer's type, for reproducing the letter *V* or *v.*

V, **1.** *Math.* vector. **2.** velocity. **3.** victory. **4.** *Elect.* volt, volts.

V, **1.** the 22nd in order or in a series, or, if *I* is omitted, the 21st. **2.** the Roman numeral for 5. Cf. **Roman numerals.** **3.** *Chem.* vanadium.

v, **1.** velocity. **2.** vicinal. **3.** victory. **4.** *Elect.* volt, volts.

V., **1.** valve. **2.** Venerable. **3.** verb. **4.** verse. **5.** Version. **6.** versus. **7.** very. **8.** Vicar. **9.** Vice. **10.** see. [< L *vide*] **11.** village. **12.** violin. **13.** Virgin. **14.** Viscount. **15.** vision. **16.** visual acuity. **17.** vocative. **18.** Volume.

v., **1.** valve. **2.** (in personal names) van. **3.** vector. **4.** vein. **5.** ventral. **6.** verb. **7.** verse. **8.** version. **9.** verso. **10.** versus. **11.** very. **12.** vicar. **13.** vice. **14.** see. [< L *vide*] **15.** village. **16.** violin. **17.** vision. **18.** vocative. **19.** voice. **20.** volt. **21.** voltage. **22.** volume. **23.** (in personal names) von.

V-1, a robot bomb developed by the Germans in World War II and launched from bases on the ground, chiefly against England. [< G (*Vergeltungswaffe*) retaliation weapon]

V-2, a liquid-fueled rocket developed and used as a ballistic missile by the Germans toward the end of World War II, mainly against London.

V-8. See **V-eight.**

VA, **1.** See **Veterans Administration.** **2.** Virginia (approved esp. for use with zip code). **3.** volt-ampere.

va, volt-ampere.

Va., Virginia.

V.A., **1.** See **Veterans Administration.** **2.** Vicar Apostolic. **3.** Vice Admiral. **4.** (Order of) Victoria and Albert.

v.a., **1.** verb active. **2.** verbal adjective.

Vaal (väl), *n.* a river in S Africa, in the Republic of South Africa, flowing SW from the Transvaal to the Orange River. 700 mi. long.

Vaa·sa (vä′sä), *n.* a seaport in W Finland, on the Gulf of Bothnia. 46,533 (est. 1965).

vac (vak), *n. Informal.* See **vacuum cleaner.** [by shortening]

va·can·cy (vā′kən sē), *n., pl.* **-cies.** **1.** the state of being vacant; emptiness. **2.** a vacant or unoccupied place, esp. one for rent. **3.** a gap; opening; breach. **4.** an unoccupied position or office. **5.** lack of thought or intelligence; vacuity. **6.** *Obs.* unoccupied or leisure time. [< ML *vacantia.* See VACANT, -ANCY]

va·cant (vā′kənt), *adj.* **1.** having no contents; empty. **2.** not occupied or taken: *a vacant job.* **3.** not in use: *a vacant chair.* **4.** lacking in thoughtfulness or intelligence: *a vacant expression.* **5.** free from work, business, or care: *vacant hours.* **6.** *Law.* **a.** idle or unutilized, as land. **b.** without an incumbent; having no heir or claimant: *a vacant estate.* [ME < L *vacant-* (s. of *vacāns*), prp. of *vacāre* to be empty; see -ANT] —**va′cant·ly,** *adv.* —**va′cant·ness,** *n.* —**Syn. 1, 2.** See **empty. 4.** blank, vacuous, inane.

va·cate (vā′kāt), *v.,* **-cat·ed, -cat·ing.** —*v.t.* **1.** to cause to be empty or unoccupied; make vacant. **2.** to give up possession or occupancy of. **3.** to render inoperative; deprive of validity; void; annul: *to vacate a legal judgment.* —*v.i.* **4.** to withdraw from occupancy or surrender possession. [< L *vacāt(us)* emptied, ptp. of *vacāre* to be empty; see -ATE[1]] —**va′cat·a·ble,** *adj.*

va·ca·tion (vā kā′shən, və-), *n.* **1.** a period of suspension of regular work, study, or other activity (often prec. by *on*): *School children are on vacation now.* **2.** an act or instance of vacating. —*v.i.* **3.** to take or have a vacation. [< L *vacātiōn-* (s. of *vacātiō*) freedom from something (see VACATE, -ION); r. ME *vacacioun* < AF]

va·ca·tion·ist (vā kā′shə nist, və-), *n.* a person who is taking a vacation or holiday. Also, **va·ca′tion·er.**

va·ca·tion·land (vā kā′shən land′, və-), *n.* an area having recreational facilities, historic or picturesque sights, etc., that attract vacationists.

vac·ci·nal (vak′sə nᵊl), *adj.* of, pertaining to, or caused by vaccine or vaccination. [VACCIN(ATION) + -AL[1]; cf. F *vaccinal*]

vac·ci·nate (vak′sə nāt′), *v.,* **-nat·ed, -nat·ing.** *Med.* —*v.t.* **1.** to inoculate with the vaccine of cowpox so as to render immune to smallpox. **2.** to inoculate with the modified virus of any of various other diseases, as a preventive measure. —*v.i.* **3.** to perform or practice vaccination. [back formation from VACCINATION] —**vac′ci·na′tor,** *n.*

vac·ci·na·tion (vak′sə nā′shən), *n. Med.* act or practice of vaccinating; inoculation with vaccine.

vac·cine (vak sēn′, vak′sēn, -sin), *n.* **1.** the virus of cowpox, used in vaccination, obtained from the vesicles of a cow or person having the disease. **2.** the modified virus of any of various other diseases, used for preventive inoculation. —*adj.* **3.** of or pertaining to vaccination. **4.** of or pertaining to vaccinia. [< medical L (*variolae*) *vaccīnae* cowpox (in title of Dr. E. Jenner's treatise of 1798) = *vacc(a)* cow + *-īnae,* fem. pl. of *-īnus* -INE[1]]

vac·cin·i·a (vak sin′ē ə), *n.* cowpox. [< NL; see VACCINE, -IA] —**vac·cin′i·al,** *adj.*

vac·cin·i·a·ceous (vak sin′ē ā′shəs), *adj.* belonging to the *Vacciniaceae,* a family of plants usually included in the *Ericaceae,* comprising the blueberry, whortleberry, huckleberry, cranberry, etc. [< L *vaccīni(um)* blueberry + -ACEOUS]

vac·il·lant (vas′ə lənt), *adj.* wavering; hesitant; indecisive; vacillating. [< L *vacillant-* (s. of *vacillāns*), prp. of *vacillāre* to VACILLATE; see -ANT]

vac·il·late (vas′ə lāt′), *v.i.,* **-lat·ed, -lat·ing.** **1.** to waver in decision or opinion. **2.** to sway unsteadily. **3.** to oscillate or fluctuate. [< L *vacillāt(us)* (ptp. of *vacillāre*) to sway to and fro; see -ATE[1]] —**vac′il·la′tor,** *n.* —**Syn. 1.** hesitate. See **waver. 2.** reel.

vac·il·lat·ing (vas′ə lā′ting), *adj.* **1.** not resolute; wavering; indecisive. **2.** oscillating; swaying; fluctuating. Also, **vacillant.** —**vac′il·lat′ing·ly,** *adv.*

vac·il·la·tion (vas′ə lā′shən), *n.* **1.** the act or state of a person who vacillates. **2.** an instance of vacillating. **3.** unsteady movement; fluctuation. [< L *vacillātiōn-* (s. of *vacillātiō*) a swaying]

vac·il·la·to·ry (vas′ə lə tōr′ē, -tôr′ē), *adj.* marked by or displaying vacillation.

Vá·clav (vä′tsläf), *n.* Wenceslaus.

vac·u·a (vak′yo͞o ə), *n.* a pl. of **vacuum.**

va·cu·i·ty (va kyo͞o′i tē), *n., pl.* **-ties.** **1.** the state of being vacuous. **2.** an empty space; void. **3.** a vacuum. **4.** absence or lack of something specified. **5.** absence of thought or intelligence. **6.** something, as a statement, revealing such absence. [< L *vacuitās.* See VACUOUS, -ITY]

vac·u·o·late (vak′yo͞o ə lit, -lāt′), *adj.* having a vacuole or vacuoles. Also, **vac′u·o·lat′ed.**

vac·u·o·la·tion (vak′yo͞o ə lā′shən), *n.* **1.** the formation of vacuoles. **2.** the state of being vacuolate. **3.** a system of vacuoles.

vac·u·ole (vak′yo͞o ōl′), *n. Biol.* **1.** a cavity within a cell, often containing a watery liquid or secretion. **2.** a minute cavity or vesicle in organic tissue. [< F < L *vacu(us)* empty + *-olum* dim. suffix] —**vac·u·o·lar** (vak′yo͞o ō′lər, vak′yo͞o ə-, vak′yə lər), *adj.*

vac·u·ous (vak′yo͞o əs), *adj.* **1.** without contents; empty. **2.** lacking in or showing a lack of ideas or intelligence: *a vacuous mind; a vacuous book.* **3.** purposeless; idle: *a vacuous way of life.* [< L *vacuus* empty; see -OUS] —**vac′u·ous·ly,** *adv.* —**vac′u·ous·ness,** *n.*

vac·u·um (vak′yo͞o əm, -yo͞om), *n., pl.* **vac·u·ums** for 1, 2, 4, 5; **vac·u·a** (vak′yo͞o ə) for 1, 2, 4; *adj.; v.* —*n.* **1.** a space entirely devoid of matter. **2.** an enclosed space from which matter, esp. air, has been partially removed (opposed to *plenum*). **3.** the state or degree of exhaustion in such a space. **4.** anything suggesting an exhausted place or void. **5.** See **vacuum cleaner.** —*adj.* **6.** of, pertaining to, employing, or producing a vacuum. **7.** (of a hollow container) partly exhausted of gas or air. —*v.t.* **8.** to clean with a vacuum cleaner. —*v.i.* **9.** to use a vacuum cleaner. [< L, neut. of *vacuus* empty]

vac′uum bot′tle, a bottle or flask having a double wall enclosing a vacuum to retard heat transfer; thermos.

vac′uum clean′er, an electrical apparatus for cleaning carpets, floors, furniture, etc., by suction. Also called **vac′uum sweep′er.**

vac′uum distilla′tion, *Chem.* a process of distillation employing a vacuum to permit a liquid to volatilize at a lower temperature than normal.

vac·u·um-packed (vak′yo͞o əm pakt′, vak′yo͞om-), *adj.* packed in a container, usually of metal, with as much air as possible evacuated before sealing, chiefly to keep freshness.

vac′uum tube′, an electron tube the envelope of which is evacuated to a high vacuum. Also called, *Brit.,* **valve, vac′uum valve′, thermionic valve.**

va·de me·cum (vā′dē mē′kəm, vä′-), *pl.* **va·de me·cums.** **1.** something a person carries with him for frequent or regular use. **2.** a book for ready reference; manual; handbook. [< L: lit., go with me]

va·dose (vā′dōs), *adj. Geol.* found or located above the water table: *vadose water; vadose zone.* [< L *vadōs(us)* shallow = *vad(um)* shoal, ford + *-ōsus* -OSE[1]]

Va·duz (fä do͞ots′), *n.* a city in and the capital of Liechtenstein, on the upper Rhine. 7500.

vae vic·tis (wī′ wik′tēs; *Eng.* vē′ vik′tis), *Latin.* woe to the vanquished.

vag·a·bond (vag′ə bond′), *adj.* **1.** wandering from place to place without any settled home; nomadic. **2.** leading an unsettled or carefree life. **3.** disreputable; worthless; shiftless. **4.** of, pertaining to, or characteristic of a vagabond. —*n.* **5.** a person, usually without a permanent home, who wanders from place to place; nomad. **6.** an idle wanderer without a permanent home or visible means of support; tramp; vagrant. **7.** a carefree, worthless, or irresponsible person. [late ME *vagabound* < L *vagābund(us)* = *vagā(rī)* (to) wander + *-bundus* adj. suffix] —**vag′a·bond′ish,** *adj.* —**Syn. 6.** hobo, loafer. See **vagrant.**

vag·a·bond·age (vag′ə bon′dij), *n.* **1.** the state of being a vagabond. **2.** (collectively) vagabonds. Also called **vag′a·bond′ism.**

va·gal (vā′gəl), *adj.* of or pertaining to a vagus nerve. [VAG(US) + -AL[1]]

va·gar·i·ous (və gâr′ē əs), *adj.* **1.** characterized by vagaries; erratic; capricious. **2.** roving; wandering. —**va·gar′i·ous·ly,** *adv.*

va·gar·y (və gâr′ē, vā′gə rē), *n., pl.* **-gar·ies. 1.** an unpredictable, capricious, or erratic action or occurrence. **2.** a whimsical, wild, or unusual idea or action. [appar. < L *vagārī* to wander] —**Syn. 2.** caprice, whim, quirk.

va·gi·na (və jī′nə), *n., pl.* **-nas, -nae** (-nē). **1.** *Anat.* **a.** the passage leading from the uterus to the vulva in certain female mammals. Cf. **oviduct. b.** a sheathlike part or organ. **2.** *Bot.* the sheath formed by the basal part of certain leaves where they embrace the stem. [special use of L: sheath]

A, Vaginate culm; B, Vaginate leaf

vag·i·nal (vaj′ə nᵊl), *adj.* **1.** *Anat.* pertaining to the vagina. **2.** pertaining to or resembling a sheath.

vag·i·na·lec·to·my (vaj′ə nᵊlek′tə mē), *n., pl.* **-mies.** *Surg.* vaginectomy (def. 2).

vag·i·nate (vaj′ə nit, -nāt′), *adj.* *Bot.* having a vagina or sheath; sheathed. [< NL *vāgīnāt(us).* See VAGINA, -ATE[1]]

vag·i·nec·to·my (vaj′ə nek′tə mē), *n., pl.* **-mies.** *Surg.* **1.** excision of part or all of the vagina. **2.** Also, **vaginalectomy.** excision of the serous membrane that surrounds the testes.

vag·i·ni·tis (vaj′ə nī′tis), *n.* *Pathol.* inflammation of the vagina.

va·gran·cy (vā′grən sē), *n., pl.* **-cies. 1.** the state or condition of being a vagrant. **2.** the conduct of a vagrant. **3.** mental wandering; reverie.

va·grant (vā′grənt), *n.* **1.** a person who wanders about with no permanent home; vagabond. **2.** *Law.* an idle person without visible means of support, as a tramp or beggar. —*adj.* **3.** wandering or roaming from place to place; nomadic. **4.** wandering idly without visible means of support. **5.** of, pertaining to, or characteristic of a vagrant: *the vagrant life.* **6.** (of plants) straggling in growth. [late ME *vag(a)raunt* < prp. of AF *vagrer, perh. < ME *vagren, b. *vagen* (< L *vagārī* to wander) + *walchren* (< OF *wa(u)crer*) = *walc-* (see WALK) + *-r-* freq. suffix + *-en* inf. suffix] —**va′grant·ly,** *adv.* —**Syn. 1, 2.** VAGRANT, VAGABOND describe an idle, disreputable person who lacks a fixed abode. VAGRANT suggests the idea of a tramp, a person with no settled abode or livelihood, an idle and disorderly person: *picked up by police as a vagrant.* VAGABOND esp. emphasizes the idea of worthless living, often by trickery, thieving, or other disreputable means: *Actors were once classed with rogues and vagabonds.*

va·grom (vā′grəm), *adj.* *Archaic.* vagrant. [illiterate var. of VAGRANT]

vague (vāg), *adj.,* **va·guer, va·guest. 1.** not expressed, known, or understood in a clear or specific way: *a vague agreement.* **2.** not clearly perceptible: *vague silhouettes; a vague odor.* **3.** (of persons) not clear or definite in thought, understanding, or expression. **4.** showing lack of clear perception or understanding: *a vague stare.* [< L *vag(us)* wandering] —**vague′ly,** *adv.* —**vague′ness,** *n.* —**Syn. 1.** unspecific, imprecise. **2.** obscure, hazy, shadowy.

va·gus (vā′gəs), *n., pl.* **-gi** (-jī). See **vagus nerve.** [< L: wandering]

va′gus nerve′, *pl.* **vagus nerves.** *Anat.* either one of the tenth pair of cranial nerves, consisting of motor fibers that innervate the muscles of the pharynx, larynx, heart, and thoracic and abdominal viscera, and of sensory fibers that conduct impulses from these structures to the brain.

vail[1] (vāl), *v.t.* **1.** to let sink; lower. **2.** *Archaic.* to take off or doff (one's hat), as in respect or submission. [ME *vale(n),* aph. var. of *avalen* (now obs.) < MF *aval(er)* (to) move down = phrase *a val* down (lit., to the valley) (*a* to (< L *ad*) + *val* VALE) + *-er* inf. suffix]

vail[2] (vāl), *Archaic.* —*v.i., v.t.* **1.** to be of use or profit; avail. —*n.* **2.** a tip; gratuity. [late ME; aph. var. of AVAIL]

vail[3] (vāl), *Obs.* —*n.* **1.** a veil. —*v.t.* **2.** to veil.

vain (vān), *adj.* **1.** without real significance, value, or importance. **2.** excessively proud of or concerned about one's own appearance, qualities, achievements, etc. **3.** proceeding from or showing personal vanity. **4.** ineffectual or unsuccessful; futile. **5.** *Archaic.* senseless or foolish. **6. in vain, a.** without effect or avail; to no purpose. **b.** in an improper or irreverent manner: *to take God's name in vain.* [ME < OF < L *vān(us)* empty, vain] —**vain′ly,** *adv.* —**vain′ness,** *n.* —**Syn. 1.** unimportant, trivial, trifling, nugatory. **2.** egotistical, vainglorious, arrogant. **4.** fruitless, unavailing. —**Ant. 1.** useful. **2.** humble.

vain·glo·ri·ous (vān glōr′ē əs, -glôr′-), *adj.* **1.** filled with or given to vainglory. **2.** characterized by or proceeding from vainglory. —**vain·glo′ri·ous·ly,** *adv.* —**vain·glo′ri·ous·ness,** *n.*

vain·glo·ry (vān′glōr′ē, -glôr′ē, vān glōr′ē, -glôr′ē), *n.* **1.** excessive elation or pride over one's own achievements, abilities, etc.; boastful vanity. **2.** empty pomp or show. [ME *vaingloriе,* trans. of ML *vāna glōria*]

vair (vâr), *n.* **1.** a fur much used for lining and trimming medieval garments, generally regarded as a variety of squirrel with a gray back and white belly. Cf. **miniver** (def. 1). **2.** *Heraldry.* a fur represented by a pattern of escutcheon- or bell-shaped figures, each outlining the adjacent sides of those beside it so that the figures alternate vertically and horizontally both in position and in tinctures, of which argent and azure are common. [ME < OF < L *var(ium)* something parti-colored; see VARIOUS]

Vaish·na·va (vīsh′nə və), *n.* *Hinduism.* a Bhakti sect devoted to Vishnu. —**Vaish′na·vism,** *n.*

Vais·ya (vīs′yə, vīsh′-), *n.* a member of the Hindu mercantile and professional caste, above the Sudras and below the Kshatriyas. Cf. **Brahman** (def. 1). [< Skt *vaiśya* settler]

va·keel (və kēl′), *n.* *Anglo-Indian.* a native lawyer. Also, **va·kil′.** [< Hindi *vakēl* < Ar *wakīl*]

Val (val), *n.* Valenciennes (def. 2).

val., 1. valentine. **2.** valuation. **3.** value.

Va·la·don (VA lA dôN′), *n.* **Su·zanne** (SY ZAN′), 1865–1938, French painter (mother of Maurice Utrillo).

val·ance (val′əns, vā′ləns), *n.* **1.** a short curtain or piece of drapery that is hung from the edge of a canopy, from the frame of a bed, etc. **2.** a short ornamental piece of drapery placed across the top of a window. [? after VALENCE, French city noted for cloth manufacture] —**val′anced,** *adj.*

Val·cour′ Is′land (val ko͝or′), an island in NE New York, in Lake Champlain: battle 1776.

Val·dai′ Hills′ (väl dī′), a region of hills and plateaus in the W Soviet Union in Europe, at the source of the Volga River: highest point, 1140 ft.

Val·de·mar I (väl′də mär′). See **Waldemar I.**

Val·di·via (bäl dē′vyä), *n.* a seaport in S Chile. 71,490 (1963).

Val·dos·ta (val dos′tə), *n.* a city in S Georgia. 32,303 (1970).

vale (vāl), *n.* a valley. [ME < OF *val* < L *vall(is)* valley]

va·le (wä′lā; *Eng.* vä′lā, vā′lē), *interj., n.* *Latin.* good-by; farewell.

val·e·dic·tion (val′i dik′shən), *n.* **1.** an act of bidding farewell or taking leave. **2.** an utterance made in bidding farewell or taking leave; valedictory. [< L *valedictiōn-* (s. of *valedictiō*) = *valedict(us),* ptp. of *valedīcere* (*vale* farewell + *dictus;* see DICTUM) + *-iōn-* -ION]

val·e·dic·to·ri·an (val′i dik tōr′ē ən, -tôr′-), *n.* (in colleges and schools) a student, usually the one ranking highest academically in the graduating class, who delivers the valedictory at the commencement exercises.

val·e·dic·to·ry (val′i dik′tə rē), *adj., n., pl.* **-ries.** —*adj.* **1.** bidding good-by; saying farewell: *a valedictory speech.* **2.** of or pertaining to an occasion of leave-taking: *a valedictory ceremony.* —*n.* **3.** an address or oration delivered at the commencement exercises of a college or school on behalf of the graduating class. **4.** any farewell address or oration. [*valedict-* (see VALEDICTION) + -ORY[1]]

va·lence (vā′ləns), *n.* *Chem.* **1.** the quality that determines the number of atoms or groups with which any single atom or group will unite chemically. **2.** the relative combining capacity of an atom or group compared with that of the standard hydrogen atom. Also, **valency.** [< L *valentia* strength, worth = *val-* (s. of *valēre* to be strong) + *-entia* -ENCE]

Va·lence (VA läNs′), *n.* a city in SE France. 55,023 (1962).

Va·len·ci·a (və len′shē ə, -chə, -sē ə; *Sp.* bä len′thyä), *n.* **1.** a region in E Spain: formerly a Moorish kingdom. 1,440,761 (est. 1960); 9085 sq. mi. **2.** a seaport in E Spain. 571,452 (est. 1960). **3.** a city in N Venezuela. 183,505 (est. 1964).

Va·len·ci·ennes (və len′sē enz′; *Fr.* VA läN syen′), *n.* **1.** a city in N France, SE of Lille. 46,643 (1962). **2.** Also called **Valen′ciennes′ lace′, Val, Val lace.** *Textiles.* **a.** a flat bobbin lace of linen, worked in one piece with the same thread forming the ground and the motif. **b.** a cotton imitation of it.

va·len·cy (vā′lən sē), *n., pl.* **-cies.** *Chem.* valence.

Va·lens (vā′lənz), *n.* **Fla·vi·us** (flā′vē əs), A.D. c328–378, emperor of the Eastern Roman Empire 364–378.

-valent, a suffix meaning "having worth or value," used esp. in scientific terminology to refer to valence: *quadrivalent.* [< L *valent-* (s. of *valēns,* prp. of *valēre* to be strong) = *val-* strong + *-ent-* -ENT]

val·en·tine (val′ən tīn′), *n.* **1.** a card or message, usually amatory or sentimental, or a gift sent by one person to another on St. Valentine's Day. **2.** a sweetheart chosen or greeted on St. Valentine's Day. [late ME, after the feast of St. VALENTINE]

Val·en·tine (val′ən tīn′), *n.* **1. Saint,** died A.D. c270, Christian martyr at Rome. **2.** Also, **Val′en·ti′nus.** pope A.D. 827.

Val′entine Day′. See **Saint Valentine's Day.** Also, **Val′entine's Day′.**

Val·en·tin·i·an I (val′ən tin′ē ən), A.D. 321?–375, emperor of Western Roman Empire 364–375. Also, **Val·en·tin·i·a·nus I** (val′ən tin′ē ā′nəs).

Valentinian II, A.D. c371–392, emperor of the Western Roman Empire 375–392. Also, **Valentinianus II.**

Valentinian III, A.D. 419?–455, emperor of the Western Roman Empire 425–455. Also, **Valentinianus III.**

Val·en·ti·no (val′ən tē′nō), *n.* **Rudolph** (*Rodolpho d'Antonguolla*), 1895–1926, U.S. motion-picture actor, born in Italy.

Va·le·ra (və lâr′ə, -lēr′ə; *Irish* vä lā′Rə), **Ea·mon De** (ā′mon de). See **De Valera, Eamon.**

va·le·ri·an (və lēr′ē ən), *n.* **1.** Also called **allheal.** any herb of the genus *Valeriana,* as *V. officinalis,* having white or pink flowers and a root that is used medicinally. **2.** a drug consisting of or made from the root, formerly used as a nerve sedative and antispasmodic. [< ML *valeriān(a)* (herb) of *Valeria* (old Roman province, where plant is said to have been common); see -AN]

Va·le·ri·an (və lēr′ē ən), *n.* (*Publius Licinius Valerianus*) died A.D. c260, Roman emperor 253–260.

va·le·ri·a·na·ceous (və lēr′ē ə nā′shəs), *adj.* belonging to the *Valerianaceae,* a family of plants comprising valerian, spikenard, etc.

va·ler·ic (və ler′ik, -lēr′-), *adj.* pertaining to or derived from valerian. Also, **va·le·ri·an·ic** (və lēr′ē an′ik).

valer′ic ac′id, *Chem.* any of several isomeric organic acids having the formula C_4H_9COOH, the common one being a liquid of pungent odor obtained from valerian roots: used chiefly as an intermediate in perfumery.

Va·lé·ry (VA lā Rē′), *n.* **Paul** (pôl), 1871–1945, French poet and philosopher.

val·et (val′it, val′ā, va lā′; *Fr.* VA le′), *n., v.,* **-et·ed, -et·ing.** —*n.* **1.** a male servant who attends to the personal needs of his employer, as by taking care of clothing; manservant. **2.** a man who is employed to care for the clothing of patrons of a hotel, passengers on a ship, etc. **3.** a stand or rack for holding coats, hats, etc. —*v.t., v.i.* **4.** to serve as a valet. [< F; MF *va(s)let* squire = *vas-* (< ML *vassus* servant) + *-let* -LET; see VASSAL]

va·let de cham·bre (VA le də shäN′bRᵊ), *pl.* **valets de cham·bre** (VA le də shäN′bRᵊ). *French.* valet (def. 1).

val·e·tu·di·nar·i·an (val′i to͞od′ᵊnâr′ē ən, -tyo͞od′-), *n.* **1.** an invalid. **2.** a person who is excessively concerned about his poor health or ailments. —*adj.* **3.** in poor health; sickly; invalid. **4.** excessively concerned about one's poor health or ailments. **5.** of, pertaining to, or characterized by invalidism. —**val′e·tu′di·nar′i·an·ism,** *n.*

val·e·tu·di·nar·y (val′i to͞od′ᵊner′ē, -tyo͞od′-), *n., pl.* **-nar·ies.** valetudinarian. [< L *valētūdinārī(us)* sickly = *valētūdin-* (s. of *valētūdō*) good or bad state of health (*valē(re)* (to) be well + *-tūdō* -TUDE) + *-ārius* -ARY]

val·gus (val′gəs), *n., pl.* **-gus·es.** *Pathol.* —*n.* **1.** an abnormally turned position of a part of the bone structure of a human being, esp. of the leg. —*adj.* **2.** of or in such a position; bowlegged, knock-kneed, or the like. [< L: bowlegged]

Val·hal·la (val hal′ə, val′hal ə), *n.* *Teutonic Myth.* the hall of Odin into which the souls of heroes slain in battle and others who have died bravely are received. Also, **Val·hall** (val hal′, val′hal), **Walhalla, Walhall.** [Latinized form of Icel *valhöll* = *val(r)* slaughter (c. OE *wæl*) + *höll* HALL]

val·ian·cy (val′yən sē), *n.* valiant nature or quality; valor; bravery; courage. Also, **val′iance.**

val·iant (val′yənt), *adj.* **1.** boldly courageous; brave; stout-hearted: *a valiant soldier.* **2.** marked by or showing bravery or valor; heroic. **3.** worthy; excellent. [ME *valia(u)nt* < AF (= MF *vaillant,* prp. of *valoir* to be of worth < L *valēre*) = *vali-* strong, worthy + *-ant-* -ANT] —**val′iant·ly,** *adv.* —**Syn. 1.** valorous, dauntless. See **brave.**

val·id (val′id), *adj.* **1.** sound; just; well-founded: *a valid objection.* **2.** producing the desired result; effective: *a valid remedy.* **3.** having force, weight, or cogency; authoritative. **4.** *Logic.* (of an argument) so constructed that if the premises are jointly asserted the conclusion cannot be denied without contradiction. **5.** *Archaic.* robust; healthy. [< L *valid(us)* strong = *val(ēre)* (to) be strong + *-idus* -ID⁴] —**val′id·ly,** *adv.* —**val′id·ness,** *n.* —**Syn. 3.** substantial. **4.** logical.

val·i·date (val′i dāt′), *v.t.,* **-dat·ed, -dat·ing. 1.** to make valid; substantiate; confirm. **2.** to give legal force to; legalize. **3.** to give official confirmation or approval to. [< ML *validāt(us)* (ptp. of *validāre* to make valid). See VALID, -ATE¹] —**val′i·da′tion,** *n.* —**val·i·da·to·ry** (val′i-də tōr′ē, -tôr′ē), *adj.* —**Syn. 1.** authenticate, verify.

va·lid·i·ty (və lid′i tē), *n.* **1.** the state or quality of being valid. **2.** legal soundness or force. [< LL *validitāt-* (s. of *validitās*). See VALID, -ITY]

va·lise (və lēs′), *n.* a small piece of luggage that can be carried by hand. [< F (cf. ML *valisia*) < It *valigia* < ?]

Va·li·um (val′ē əm), *n.* *Pharm., Trademark,* diazepam.

Val·kyr·ie (val kēr′ē, -kī′rē, val′kēr ē), *n.* *Teutonic Myth.* any of the beautiful maidens attendant upon Odin who bring souls to Valhalla. Also, **Walkyrie.** [< Icel *valkyrja* chooser of the slain (c. OE *wælcyrie* witch) = *val(r)* slaughter (c. OE *wæl*) + *kyrja* chooser (c. OE *cyrie*); akin to CHOOSE]

Val′ lace′, Valenciennes (def. 2).

Va·lla·do·lid (bä′lyä dô lēth′), *n.* a city in N Spain, NW of Madrid: Columbus died here 1506. 132,526 (est. 1960).

val·late (val′āt), *adj.* bordered by a ridge, raised edge, or the like. [< L *vallāt(us)* (ptp. of *vallāre* to surround with a wall) = *vall(um)* rampart + *-atus* -ATE¹]

val·la·tion (və lā′shən), *n.* *Fort.* **1.** a rampart or entrenchment. **2.** the process or technique of constructing ramparts. [< LL *vallātiōn-* (s. of *vallātiō*)]

val·lec·u·la (və lek′yə lə), *n., pl.* **-lae** (-lē′). *Anat., Bot.* a furrow or depression. [< LL; see VALLEY, -CULE] —**val·lec′u·lar,** *adj.* —**val·lec′u·late′,** *adj.*

Val·le d'A·o·sta (väl′le dä ô′stä), a region in NW Italy. 99,754 (1961); 1259 sq. mi.

Val·le·jo (və lā′hō), *n.* a city in W California, on San Pablo Bay, NE of San Francisco. 71,710 (1970).

Val·let·ta (väl let′tä), *n.* a seaport in and the capital of Malta, on the NE coast. 14,049.

val·ley (val′ē), *n., pl.* **-leys. 1.** an elongated depression between uplands, hills, or mountains, often following the course of a stream. **2.** an extensive, more or less flat, and relatively low region drained by a great river system. **3.** any depression suggesting a valley. **4.** *Archit.* a depression or angle formed by the meeting of two inclined sides of a roof. **5.** the lower phase of a horizontal wave motion. [ME *valeie, valey* < OF *valee* = *val* VALE + *-ee* fem. n. suffix]

Val′ley Forge′, a village in SE Pennsylvania: winter quarters of Washington's army 1777–78.

Val′ley of Ten′ Thou′sand Smokes′, a volcanic area in SW Alaska, in Katmai National Monument.

Val′ley of the Kings′, a valley on the west bank of the Nile near the site of Thebes, in the United Arab Republic: necropolis of many rulers of ancient Egypt. Also called **Val′ley of the Tombs′.**

Val′ley Stream′, a village on W Long Island, in SE New York. 40,413 (1970).

Val·lom·bro·sa (väl′lôm brô′sä), *n.* a village in central Italy, near Florence: famous abbey; resort.

Va·lois (VA LWA′), *n.* **1.** a member of a ruling family of France that reigned from 1328 to 1589. **2.** a country in the Île de France, united to the French crown in 1167 and established as a duchy in 1406.

Va·lo·na (vä lô′nä), *n.* a seaport in SW Albania. 46,905 (est. 1964). Also called **Avlona.**

va·lo·ni·a (və lō′nē ə), *n.* acorn cups of an oak, *Quercus Aegilops,* used in tanning, dyeing, and making ink. [< It *vallonia* < ModGk *balánia,* pl. of *baláni* acorn]

val·or (val′ər), *n.* boldness or determination in facing great danger, as in battle. Also, *esp. Brit.,* **val′our.** [ME *valo(u)r* < AF (MF *valeur*) < LL *valor* worth = L *val(ēre)* (to) be of worth + *-or* -OR¹] —**Syn.** See **courage.**

val·or·ise (val′ə rīz′), *v.t.,* **-ised, -is·ing.** *Chiefly Brit.* valorize. —**val′or·i·sa′tion,** *n.*

val·or·ize (val′ə rīz′), *v.t.,* **-ized, -iz·ing.** to fix and provide for the maintaining of the price of (a commodity), esp. by a government, as by purchasing the commodity at a fixed price or by making special loans to the producers. [< LL *valor* worth (see VALOR) + -IZE] —**val′or·i·za′tion,** *n.*

val·or·ous (val′ər əs), *adj.* having or showing valor; courageous; valiant; brave. [< ML *valorōs(us)* valiant. See VALOR, -OUS] —**val′or·ous·ly,** *adv.*

Val·pa·rai·so (val′pə rī′sō, -zō), *n.* a seaport in central Chile. 251,000 (est. 1970). Spanish, **Val·pa·ra·í·so** (bäl′pä-RÄ ē′sô).

valse (VAls), *n., pl.* **valses** (VAls). *French.* waltz.

val·u·a·ble (val′yo͞o ə bəl, -yə bəl), *adj.* **1.** having considerable monetary worth. **2.** of considerable use, service, worth, or importance. —*n.* **3.** Usually, **valuables.** articles of considerable monetary worth, as jewelry or money. —**val′u·a·ble·ness,** *n.* —**val′u·a·bly,** *adv.*
—**Syn. 1, 2.** VALUABLE, PRECIOUS refer to that which has pecuniary or other value. VALUABLE applies to whatever has value, but esp. to what has considerable monetary value or is especially useful, rare, etc.: *a valuable watch.* That which is PRECIOUS has a very high intrinsic value or is very dear for its own sake, associations, or the like: *a precious jewel, friendship.* —**Ant. 1, 2.** worthless.

val·u·ate (val′yo͞o āt′), *v.t.,* **-at·ed, -at·ing.** to set a value on; appraise. [back formation from VALUATION]

val·u·a·tion (val′yo͞o ā′shən), *n.* **1.** the act of estimating or setting the value of something; appraisal. **2.** an estimated value or worth. [VALUE + -ATION; cf. MF *valuation*] —**val′u·a′tion·al,** *adj.* —**val′u·a′tion·al·ly,** *adv.*

val·u·a·tor (val′yo͞o ā′tər), *n.* a person who estimates worth or value; appraiser.

val·ue (val′yo͞o), *n., v.,* **-ued, -u·ing.** —*n.* **1.** attributed or relative worth, merit, or usefulness: *the value of a college education; to set great value on an idea.* **2.** monetary worth: *an increase in value.* **3.** equivalent worth or return: *to expect value for money.* **4.** denomination, as of a monetary issue or postage stamp. **5.** *Math.* **a.** magnitude; quantity; number represented by a figure, symbol, or the like: *the value of* x. **b.** a point in the range of a function; a point in the range corresponding to a given point in the domain of a function: *The value of* x^2 *at 2 is 4.* **6.** import or meaning, as of a word or expression. **7. values,** ideals, customs, institutions, etc. that arouse an emotional response, for or against them, in a given society or a given person. **8.** *Ethics.* any object or quality desirable as a means or as an end in itself. **9.** *Fine Arts.* **a.** degree of lightness or darkness in a color. **b.** the relation of light and shade in a painting, drawing, etc. **10.** *Music.* the relative length or duration of a tone signified by a note. **11.** *Phonet.* **a.** quality. **b.** the phonetic equivalent of a letter, as the sound of *a* in *hat, sang,* etc. —*v.t.* **12.** to calculate or reckon the monetary value of; assess; appraise. **13.** to consider with respect to worth, excellence, usefulness, or importance. **14.** to regard or esteem highly. [ME < OF, n. use of ptp. fem. of *valoir* < L *valēre* to be worth]
—**Syn. 1.** utility. VALUE, WORTH imply intrinsic excellence or desirability. VALUE is the quality of anything that renders it desirable or useful: *the value of sunlight or good books.* WORTH implies esp. spiritual qualities of mind and character, or moral excellence: *Few knew his true worth.* **2.** cost, price. **12.** evaluate. **14.** prize. See **appreciate.**

val′ue-add′ed tax′, a sales tax based on the addition to the value of consumer goods or services at each stage of production or distribution: rebatable if exported.

val·ued (val′yo͞od), *adj.* **1.** highly regarded or esteemed. **2.** estimated; appraised: *a loss of jewels valued at $100,000.* **3.** having value of a specified kind: *a many-valued position.*

val′ue judg′ment, an estimate of the worth or goodness of something or someone.

val·ue·less (val′yo͞o lis), *adj.* without worth or value. —**val′ue·less·ness,** *n.*

val·u·er (val′yo͞o ər), *n.* **1.** *Brit.* an appraiser. **2.** a person who values.

val·val (val′vəl), *adj.* valvular. Also, **val·var** (val′vər). [VALVE + -AL¹]

val·vate (val′vāt), *adj.* **1.** furnished with or opening by a valve or valves. **2.** serving as or resembling a valve. **3.** *Bot.* **a.** opening by valves, as certain capsules and anthers. **b.** meeting without overlapping, as the parts of certain buds. **c.** composed of or characterized by such parts. [< L *valvāt(us)* with folding doors. See VALVE, -ATE¹]

valve (valv), *n., v.,* **valved, valv·ing.** —*n.* **1.** any device for controlling the flow of a fluid. **2.** a movable part that closes or modifies the passage in such a device. **3.** *Anat.* a membranous fold or other structure that controls the flow of a fluid, as one that permits blood to flow in one direction only. **4.** (in musical wind instruments of the trumpet class) a device for changing the length of the air column to alter the pitch of a tone. **5.** *Zool.* **a.** one of the two or more separable pieces composing certain shells. **b.** either half of the silicified shell of a diatom. **6.** *Bot.* **a.** one of the segments into which a capsule dehisces. **b.** a flap or lidlike part of certain anthers. **7.** *Electronics Brit.* See **vacuum tube. 8.** *Archaic.* one of the leaves of a double or folding door. —*v.t.* **9.** to provide with a means of controlling the flow of liquid, gas, etc., by inserting a valve. [late ME < L *valva* leaf of a door] —**valve′less,** *adj.* —**valve′like′,** *adj.*

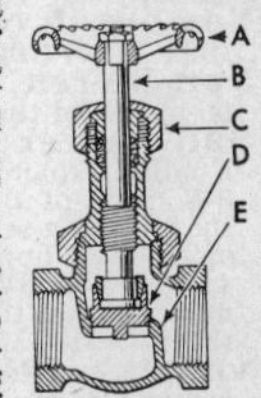

Globe valve
A, Wheel
B, Spindle
C, Stuffing nut
D, Disk
E, Valve seat

valve′ gear′, (in a reciprocating engine) the mechanism for opening and closing the valves at certain points in each stroke.

valve·let (valv′lit), *n.* a small valve; valvule.

valve′ trombone′, a trombone equipped with three or four valves in place of a slide.

val·vu·lar (val′vyə lər), *adj.* **1.** having the form or function of a valve. **2.** operating by a valve or valves. **3.** of or pertaining to a valve or valves, esp. of the heart. Also called **valval, valvar.** [< NL *valvulār(is).* See VALVULE, -AR¹]

val·vule (val′vyo͞ol), *n.* a small valve or a part resembling a valve. [< NL *valvula*]

val·vu·li·tis (val′vyə lī′tis), *n.* *Pathol.* inflammation of a cardiac valve, caused by an acute infectious process, usually rheumatic fever or syphilis.

vam·brace (vam′brās), *n.* *Armor.* **1.** a piece of plate armor for the forearm. **2.** plate armor for the whole arm. [ME *va(u)mbras* < AF *(a)vantbras* = *avant-* fore- (see AVAUNT) + *bras* arm (see BRACE)] —**vam′braced,** *adj.*

va·moose (va mo͞os′), *v.i.,* **-moosed, -moos·ing.** *U.S.*

Slang. to leave hurriedly or quickly; decamp. [< Sp *vamos* let us go, impv. 1st pers. pl. (< L *vādere* to go fast) of *ir* to go]

va·mose (va mōs′), *v.i.*, **-mosed, -mos·ing.** *U.S. Slang.* vamoose.

vamp[1] (vamp), *n.* **1.** the portion of a shoe or boot upper that covers the instep and toes. **2.** something patched up or pieced together. **3.** *Jazz.* an accompaniment, usually improvised, consisting of a succession of simple chords. **—*v.t.*** **4.** to furnish or repair with a vamp. **5.** to concoct or invent (often fol. by *up*). **6.** *Jazz.* to improvise (an accompaniment or the like). **—*v.i.*** **7.** *Jazz.* to improvise an accompaniment, tune, etc. [ME *vampe* < AF; MF *avant-pie* = *avant-* fore- (see AVAUNT) + *pie* foot (F *pied;* see -PED)] **—vamp′er,** *n.* **—vamp′ish,** *adj.*

vamp[2] (vamp), *n.* **1.** a seductive, often unscrupulous woman. **—*v.t.*** **2.** to use one's feminine charms upon; seduce. **—*v.i.*** **3.** to act as a vamp. [short for VAMPIRE]

vam·pire (vam′pīər), *n.* **1.** a preternatural being, commonly believed to be a reanimated corpse, that is said to suck the blood of sleeping persons at night. **2.** a person who preys ruthlessly upon others. **3.** a woman who exploits or ruins the men she seduces. **4.** Also called **vam′pire bat′.** *Zool.* **a.** any of several Central and South American bats of the genera *Desmodus, Diphylla,* and *Diaemus* that feed on the blood of man and other vertebrates. **b.** any of several large South American bats of the genera *Phyllostomus* and *Vampyrus,* erroneously believed to feed on blood. **c.** any of various false vampires. [< F < G *Vampir* < Slav; cf. Serbian *vampir,* Russ *upyr*] **—vam·pir·ic** (vam pir′ik), **vam·pir·ish** (vam pīər′ish), *adj.*

vam·pir·ism (vam′pīər iz′əm, -pə riz′-), *n.* **1.** belief in the existence of vampires. **2.** the acts or practices of vampires.

van[1] (van), *n.* **1.** the foremost or front division of a military or naval force. **2.** the forefront of any movement, course of progress, or the like. [short for VANGUARD]

van[2] (van), *n.* **1.** a covered vehicle, usually a large truck or trailer, used for moving furniture, goods, animals, etc. **2.** *Brit.* **a.** a railway baggage car. **b.** a covered, boxlike railway car. **c.** a small, horse-drawn wagon or a small truck, as one used by tradesmen to carry light goods. [short for CARAVAN]

van[3] (van; *Du.* vän), *prep.* (*often cap.*) from; of (used in Dutch personal names, originally to indicate place of origin). [c. VON]

van[4] (van), *n. Archaic.* a wing. [var. of FAN[1]]

Van (vän), *n.* **1. Lake,** a salt lake in E Turkey. 1454 sq. mi. **2.** a town on this lake. 42,881 (1960).

van·a·date (van′ə dāt′), *n. Chem.* a salt or ester of a vanadic acid. Also, **va·na·di·ate** (və nā′dē āt′). [VANAD(IUM) + -ATE[2]]

va·nad·ic (və nad′ik, -nā′dik), *adj. Chem.* of or containing vanadium, esp. in the trivalent or pentavalent state.

vanad′ic ac′id, *Chem.* any of certain acids containing vanadium, esp. one having the formula H_3VO_4.

va·nad·i·nite (və nad′ənīt′), *n.* a mineral, $Pb_5(VO_4)_3Cl$, an ore of lead and vanadium. [VANAD(IUM) + -IN[2] + -ITE[1]]

va·na·di·um (və nā′dē əm), *n. Chem.* a metallic element obtained as a light-gray powder with a silvery luster or as a ductile metal: used as a toughening ingredient of steel. *Symbol:* V; *at. wt.:* 50.942; *at. no.:* 23; *sp. gr.:* 5.96. [< NL < Icel *Vanad(ís)* epithet of Freya (*Vana,* gen. of VANIR + *dís* goddess) + -IUM]

vana′dium steel′, an alloy steel containing vanadium.

van·a·dous (van′ə dəs), *adj. Chem.* containing divalent or trivalent vanadium. Also, **va·na·di·ous** (və nā′dē əs).

Van Al·len (van al′ən), **James Alfred,** born 1914, U.S. physicist.

Van Al′len belt′, *Physics.* either of two regions of high-energy, charged particles surrounding the earth, the inner region centered at an altitude of 2,000 miles and the outer region at an altitude between 9,000 and 12,000 miles. Also called **Van Al′len radia′tion belt′.** [named after J. A. VAN ALLEN]

Van·brugh (van brōō′ *or, esp. Brit.,* van′brə), *n.* **John,** 1664–1726, English dramatist and architect.

Van Bu·ren (van byŏŏr′ən), **Martin,** 1782–1862, 8th president of the U.S. 1837–41.

Van·cou·ver (van kōō′vər), *n.* **1. George,** 1758–98, English explorer. **2.** a large island in SW Canada, off the SW coast of British Columbia. 215,000 (est. 1961); 12,408 sq. mi. **3.** a seaport in SW British Columbia, on the Strait of Georgia opposite SE Vancouver island. 384,522 (1961). **4.** a city in SW Washington. 41,859 (1970). **5. Mount,** a mountain on the boundary between Alaska and Canada, in the St. Elias Mountains. 15,700 ft.

van·da (van′də), *n.* any of several epiphytic orchids of the genus *Vanda,* of tropical regions of the Eastern Hemisphere, having large white, lilac, blue, or greenish flowers. [< NL < Hindi *vandā* mistletoe < Skt: parasitic plant]

Van·dal (van′dəl), *n.* **1.** a member of a Germanic people who in the 5th century A.D. ravaged Gaul and Spain, settled in Africa, and in A.D. 455 sacked Rome. **2.** (*l.c.*) a person who willfully destroys or mars public or private property. **—*adj.*** **3.** of or pertaining to the Vandals. **4.** (*l.c.*) imbued with or characterized by vandalism. [< LL *Vandal(us),* Latinized tribal name] **—Van·dal·ic** (van dal′ik), *adj.*

van·dal·ism (van′dəliz′əm), *n.* **1.** mischievous or malicious destruction or damage of property. **2.** an act of such destruction. **3.** the conduct or spirit characteristic of the Vandals. [VANDAL + -ISM; cf. F *vandalisme*] **—van′dal·is′tic, van′dal·ish,** *adj.*

van·dal·ize (van′dəlīz′), *v.t.*, **-ized, -iz·ing.** to destroy or damage by vandalism.

Van′ de Graaff′ gen′erator (van′ də graf′), *Physics, Elect.* a device for producing high-voltage static electricity, consisting of a hollow, spherical conductor atop a hollow, insulating column through which a movable belt runs between a terminal with high negative potential at the base of the column and a terminal with high positive potential in the spherical conductor, the voltage in the conductor often being used to accelerate particles. Also called **electrostatic generator.** [named after R. J. *Van de Graaff* (1901–67), American physicist]

Van·den·berg (van′dən bûrg′), *n.* **Arthur Hen·drick** (hen′drik), 1884–1951, U.S. statesman.

Van·der·bilt (van′dər bilt), *n.* **Cornelius** ("*Commodore Vanderbilt*"), 1794–1877, U.S. industrialist and financier.

van der Roh·e (van dər rō′ə, fän), **Lud·wig Mies** (lud′wig mēz′, mēs′). See **Mies van der Rohe, Ludwig.**

van′ der Waals′′ forc′es, *Physical Chem.* weak, nonspecific forces between molecules. Also, **van′ der Waals′ forc′es.** [named after J. D. *van der Waals* (1837–1923), Dutch scientist]

Van Die′men's Land′ (van dē′mənz), former name of **Tasmania.**

Vandyke beard

Van Do·ren (van dōr′ən, dôr′-), **Mark,** 1894–1972, U.S. writer and critic.

Van Dyck (van dīk′; *Flem.* vän dīk′), **Sir Anthony,** 1599–1641, Flemish painter. Also, **Vandyke.**

Van·dyke (van dīk′), *n.* **1. Sir Anthony.** See **Van Dyck, Sir Anthony. 2.** (*sometimes l.c.*) See **Vandyke beard. 3.** (*sometimes l.c.*) See **Vandyke collar.**

Vandyke′ beard′, a short, pointed beard. Also called **Vandyke, vandyke.**

Vandyke′ col′lar, a wide collar of lace and linen with the edge formed into scallops or deep points. Also, **vandyke′ col′lar.** Also called **Vandyke, vandyke.**

vane (vān), *n.* **1.** Also called **weather vane, wind vane.** a device rotating freely in a horizontal plane and so mounted and formed as to point into the wind. **2.** any of various bladelike devices mounted on the rotors of windmills, turbines, pumps, etc., to impart or receive kinetic energy to or from a fluid. **3.** *Rocketry.* any fixed or movable plane surface on the outside of a rocket or guided missile, providing directional control while the missile is within the atmosphere. **4.** *Ornith.* the web of a feather. **5.** *Navig., Survey.* either of two fixed projections for sighting an alidade or the like. **6.** *Archery.* feather (def. 7). [ME; OE *fana* flag; c. G *Fahne* flag, Goth *fana* segment of cloth; see GONFALON] **—vaned,** *adj.*

Vane (vān), *n.* **Sir Henry** (*Sir Harry Vane*), 1613–62, British statesman: governor of Massachusetts Bay Colony 1636–37.

Vä·nern (ven′ərn; *Swed.* ve′nərn), *n.* a lake in SW Sweden. 2141 sq. mi. Also, **Vä·ner** (ven′ər), **Vener.**

Van Fleet (van flēt′), **James Al·ward** (al′wərd), born 1892, U.S. army general.

vang (vang), *n. Naut.* a rope extending from the peak of a gaff to the ship's rail or to a mast, used to steady the gaff. [dial. var. of FANG[1], but perh. < D cognate *vang*]

Van Gogh (van gō′, gôkh′; *Du.* vän khôkh′), **Vin·cent** (vin′sənt; *Du.* vin sent′), 1853–90, Dutch painter. Also, **van Gogh′.**

van·guard (van′gärd′), *n.* **1.** the foremost division or the front part of an army; advance guard; van. **2.** the forefront of any movement, activity, etc., or those forming such a forefront. **3.** (*cap.*) *U.S.* a three-stage, satellite-launching rocket. [late ME *van(d)gard(e)* < MF *avangarde,* var. of *avant-garde.* See AVAUNT, GUARD]

Va·nier (van yā′; *Fr.* va nyā′), *n.* **Georges P.** (jôrj; *Fr.* zhôrzh), 1888–1967, Canadian soldier and diplomat: governor-general 1959–67.

va·nil·la (və nil′ə, -nel′-), *n.* **1.** any tropical, climbing orchid of the genus *Vanilla,* esp. *V. planifolia,* bearing podlike fruit yielding an extract used in flavoring food, in perfumery, etc. **2.** Also called **vanil′la bean′.** the fruit or bean of this orchid. **3.** the extract of this fruit. [< NL < Sp *vainilla* little pod, dim. of *vaina* sheath < L *vāgīna*]

Vanilla, *Vanilla planifolia* A, Flowering branch; B, Fruit (Length to 10 in.)

va·nil·lic (və nil′ik), *adj.* pertaining to, derived from, or resembling vanilla or vanillin.

van·il·lin (van′əlin, və nil′in), *n. Chem.* a solid, $(CH_3O)(OH)C_6H_3CHO$, obtained from the vanilla bean or prepared synthetically: used chiefly as a flavoring agent and in perfumery. Also, **van·il·line** (van′əlin, -əlēn′, və nil′in, -ēn). Also called **vanil′lic al′dehyde.** [VANILL(A) + -IN[2]]

Va·nir (vä′nir), *n.pl.* (*often l.c.*) *Scand Myth.* a race of gods, of whom Niord, Frey, and Freya were members.

van·ish (van′ish), *v.i.* **1.** to disappear from sight, esp. quickly; become invisible. **2.** to depart, esp. furtively or mysteriously. **3.** to cease to exist, as a feeling or condition. **4.** *Math.* (of a number, quantity, or function) to become zero. **—*v.t.*** **5.** to cause to disappear. **—*n.*** **6.** *Phonet.* the last part of a vowel sound when it differs noticeably in quality from the main sound, as the faint (ē) at the end of the (ā) in the pronunciation of *pain.* [ME *vanisshe(n), vanissen* < MF (*e*)*vaniss-* (s. of *e(s)vanir*) < L *ex-* EX-[1] + *vānesce(re)* (to) pass away = *vān(us)* VAIN + *-escere* -ESCE] **—van′ish·er,** *n.* **—van′ish·ing·ly,** *adv.* **—van′ish·ment,** *n.* **—Syn. 1.** evanesce. See **disappear. —Ant. 1.** appear.

van′ishing cream′, a cosmetic similar to cold cream, applied usually to the face as a base for powder.

van′ishing point′, **1.** a point of disappearance, cessation, or extinction. **2.** *Fine Arts.* (in perspective) that point toward which receding parallel lines appear to converge.

va·ni·tas va·ni·ta·tum (wä′ni täs wä′ni tä′tōōm; *Eng.* van′i tas′ van′i tā′təm), *Latin.* vanity of vanities.

van·i·to·ry (van′i tôr′ē, -tōr′ē), *n.* a combined dressing table and lavatory basin. [formerly trademark: VANI(TY) + (LAVA)TORY]

van·i·ty (van′i tē), *n., pl.* **-ties. 1.** excessive pride in one's appearance, qualities, achievements, etc.; conceit. **2.** an instance or display of this. **3.** something about which one is vain. **4.** lack of real value; triviality or worthlessness: *the vanity of a selfish life.* **5.** something worthless, trivial, or pointless. **6.** See **vanity case. 7.** See **dressing table. 8.** compact[1] (def. 9). [ME *vanite* < OF < L *vānitāt-* (s. of *vānitās*). See VAIN, -ITY] **—van′i·tied,** *adj.* **—Syn. 1.** egotism, ostentation. See **pride. —Ant. 1.** humility.

van′ity case′, a small luggage bag or case for holding cosmetics or toiletries, used or carried by women. Also called **van′ity bag′, van′ity box′.**

van′ity fair′, (*sometimes caps.*) a place or group characterized by or displaying a preoccupation with idle pleasures or ostentation. [after a fair in the town of Vanity in Bunyan's 1678 allegory *Pilgrim's Progress*]
van′ity press′, a printing house that specializes in publishing books for which the authors pay all or most of the costs. Also called **van′ity pub′lisher.**
van Ley·den (vän līd′ən). See **Leyden, Lucas van.**
van′ line′, *U.S.* a transportation company that uses large motor vans for the long-distance moving of household effects.
van·quish (vang′kwish, van′-), *v.t.* **1.** to conquer or subdue by superior force, as in battle. **2.** to defeat or overcome after a contest or struggle: *to vanquish a competitor; to vanquish one's fears.* [ME *vencusche(n), -quisshe(n)* < OF *vencus* ptp. and *venquis* pt. of *veintre* < L *vincere* to overcome] —**van′quish·a·ble,** *adj.* —**van′quish·er,** *n.* —**van′quish·ment,** *n.* —**Syn. 1.** overpower, subjugate, suppress, crush.
Van Rens·se·laer (van ren′sə lər, -lēr′), **Stephen** ("*the Patroon*"), 1765–1839, U.S. political leader and major general.
van·tage (van′tij, vän′-), *n.* **1.** a position, condition, or place affording some advantage, as for action. **2.** an advantage or superiority: *a position of vantage.* [ME < AF, aph. var. of *avantage* ADVANTAGE]
van′tage point′, a position or place that affords a wide or advantageous perspective or view.
van't Hoff (vänt hof′), **Ja·co·bus Hen·dri·cus** (yä kō′bœs hen drē′kœs), 1852–1911, Dutch chemist: Nobel prize 1901.
Va·nu·a Le·vu (vä no͞o′ä le′vo͞o), an island in the S Pacific, one of the Fiji Islands. 94,000; 2137 sq. mi.
Va·nu·a·tu (və no͞o′ə to͞o′), *n.* official name of **New Hebrides.**
Van Vech·ten (van vek′tən), **Carl,** 1880–1964, U.S. author.
van·ward (van′wərd), *adj., adv.* toward or in the van or front.
Van·zet·ti (van zet′ē; *It.* vän dzet′tē), *n.* **Bar·to·lo·me·o** (bär′tô lô me′ô), 1888–1927, Italian anarchist, in U.S. after 1908. Cf. **Sacco, Nicola.**
vap·id (vap′id), *adj.* **1.** lacking life or flavor; insipid. **2.** without liveliness or spirit; dull or tedious. [< L *vapid(us)*; akin to VAPOR] —**va·pid′i·ty, vap′id·ness,** *n.* —**vap′id·ly,** *adv.* —**Syn. 1, 2.** lifeless, spiritless, prosaic.
va·por (vā′pər), *n.* **1.** a quantity of visible matter diffused through or suspended in the air, as fog or smoke. **2.** *Physics.* a gas at a temperature below its critical temperature. **3.** matter brought to a gaseous state. **4.** *Archaic.* a strange, senseless, or fantastic notion. **5.** *Archaic.* something insubstantial or transitory. **6. vapors,** *Archaic.* **a.** mental depression, hypochondria, or low spirits. **b.** injurious exhalations formerly supposed to be produced within the body, esp. in the stomach. —*v.t.* **7.** to cause to rise or pass off in, or as in, vapor; vaporize. —*v.i.* **8.** to rise or pass off in the form of vapor. **9.** to emit vapor or exhalations. **10.** to talk or act grandiloquently or boastfully; bluster. Also, *esp. Brit.,* **vapour.** [late ME < L: steam] —**va′por·a·ble,** *adj.* —**va′por·er,** *n.* —**va′por·less,** *adj.* —**va′por·like′,** *adj.*
va·por·es·cence (vā′pə res′əns), *n.* production or formation of vapor. Also, *esp. Brit.,* **vapourescence.** —**va′por·es′cent,** *adj.*
va·por·if·ic (vā′pə rif′ik), *adj.* **1.** producing vapor; tending or causing to form vapor. **2.** of, pertaining to, or of the nature of vapor; vaporous. Also, *esp. Brit.,* **vapourific.**
va·por·im·e·ter (vā′pə rim′i tər), *n.* an instrument for measuring vapor pressure or volume.
va·por·ing (vā′pər ing), *adj.* **1.** that gives forth vapor. **2.** boastful; bragging. —*n.* **3.** the act or instance of bragging or blustering; boastful talk. Also, *esp. Brit.,* **vapouring.** —**va′por·ing·ly,** *adv.*
va·por·ise (vā′pə rīz′), *v.t., v.i.,* **-ised, -is·ing.** *Chiefly Brit.* vaporize. —**va′por·is′a·ble,** *adj.*
va·por·is·er (vā′pə rī′zər), *n.* *Chiefly Brit.* vaporizer.
va·por·ish (vā′pər ish), *adj.* **1.** of the nature of or resembling vapor. **2.** *Archaic.* inclined to or affected by depression or low spirits. Also, *esp. Brit.,* **vapourish.** —**va′por·ish·ness,** *n.*
va·por·i·za·tion (vā′pər i zā′shən *or, esp. Brit.,* -pə rī-), *n.* **1.** the act of vaporizing. **2.** the state of being vaporized. Also, *esp. Brit.,* **va′por·i·sa′tion.**
va·por·ize (vā′pə rīz′), *v.,* **-ized, -iz·ing.** —*v.t.* **1.** to cause to change into vapor. —*v.i.* **2.** to become converted into vapor. **3.** to indulge in boastful talk. Also, *esp. Brit.,* **vaporise.** —**va′por·iz′a·ble,** *adj.*
va·por·iz·er (vā′pə rī′zər), *n.* **1.** a person or thing that vaporizes. **2.** a device for turning liquid into vapor, as an atomizer, esp. one that converts a medicinal substance into a vapor that is inhaled for respiratory relief. Also, *esp. Brit.,* **vaporiser.**
va′por lock′, an obstruction to the flow of fuel to a gasoline engine, caused by the formation of bubbles in the gasoline as a result of overheating.
va·por·ous (vā′pər əs), *adj.* **1.** having the form of vapor. **2.** abounding in or giving off vapor; foggy; misty. **3.** dimmed or obscured with vapor. **4.** unsubstantial; diaphanous; airy. Also, *esp. Brit.,* **vapourous.** —**va′por·ous·ly,** *adv.* —**va′por·ous·ness, va·por·os·i·ty** (vā′pə ros′i tē), *n.*
va′por pres′sure, the pressure exerted by the molecules of a vapor, esp. that part of the total pressure exerted by vapor in a mixture of gases, as by water vapor in air.
va′por ten′sion, 1. See **vapor pressure. 2.** the maximum vapor pressure possible, at a given temperature, in a system composed of a liquid or solid substance in contact with the vapor of that substance.
va′por trail′, contrail.
va·por·y (vā′pə rē), *adj.* **1.** vaporous. **2.** vaporish. Also, *esp. Brit.,* **vapoury.**
va·pour (vā′pər), *n., v.t., v.i.* *Chiefly Brit.* vapor. —**va′pour·a·ble,** *adj.* —**va′pour·er,** *n.* —**va′pour·less,** *adj.* —**va′pour·like′,** *adj.*
va·pour·es·cence (vā′pə res′əns), *n.* *Chiefly Brit.* vaporescence. —**va′pour·es′cent,** *adj.*
va·pour·if·ic (vā′pə rif′ik), *adj.* *Chiefly Brit.* vaporific.
va·pour·ing (vā′pər ing), *adj., n.* *Chiefly Brit.* vaporing. —**va′pour·ing·ly,** *adv.*
va·pour·ish (vā′pər ish), *adj.* *Chiefly Brit.* vaporish. —**va′pour·ish·ness,** *n.*
va·pour·ous (vā′pər əs), *adj.* *Chiefly Brit.* vaporous. —**va′pour·ous·ly,** *adv.* —**va′pour·ous·ness, va·pour·os·i·ty** (vā′pə ros′i tē), *n.*
va·pour·y (vā′pə rē), *adj.* *Chiefly Brit.* vapory.
va·que·ro (vä kâr′ō; *Sp.* bä ke′rô), *n., pl.* **-que·ros** (-kâr′ōz; *Sp.* -ke′rôs). *Southwestern U.S.* a cowboy or herdsman. [< Sp = *vac(a)* cow + *-ero* -ARY]
VAR, visual aural range.
var., 1. variant. **2.** variation. **3.** variety. **4.** variometer. **5.** various.
va·ra (vär′ə; *Sp.* bä′rä; *Port.* vä′rə), *n., pl.* **va·ras** (vär′əz; *Sp.* bä′räs; *Port.* vä′rəsh). **1.** a unit of length in Spanish- and Portuguese-speaking countries, varying from about 32 to 43 inches. **2.** the square of this unit, used as a unit of area. [< Sp < L: forked pole, n. use of fem. of *vārus* crooked, bent]
Va·ra·na·si (və rä′nə sē), *n.* Benares.
Va·ran·gi·an (və ran′jē ən), *n.* any of the Northmen who, under Rurik, established a dynasty in Russia in the 9th century.
Var·dar (vär′där), *n.* a river in S Europe, flowing from SE Yugoslavia through N Greece into the Gulf of Salonika. 200 mi. long.
Va·re·se (vä re′se), *n.* a city in N Italy, NW of Milan. 90,011.
Va·rèse (vä rez′), *n.* **Ed·gard** (ed gar′), 1885–1965, U.S. composer, born in France.
Var·gas (vär′gəs), *n.* **Ge·tú·lio Dor·nel·les** (zhə to͞o′lyo͝o do͝or ne′lis), 1883–1954, Brazilian statesman: president 1934–45.
var·i·a (vâr′ē ə), *n.pl.* miscellaneous items, esp. a miscellany of literary works. [< NL, L, neut. pl. of *varius* VARIOUS]
var·i·a·ble (vâr′ē ə bəl), *adj.* **1.** apt or liable to vary or change; changeable. **2.** capable of being varied or changed; alterable. **3.** inconstant; fickle. **4.** *Biol.* deviating from the usual type. **5.** *Astron.* (of a star) changing in brightness. **6.** *Meteorol.* (of wind) tending to change in direction. **7.** *Math.* having the nature or characteristics of a variable. —*n.* **8.** something that may or does vary. **9.** *Math.* **a.** a quantity or function that may assume any given value or set of values. **b.** a symbol that represents this. **10.** *Meteorol.* a variable wind. [late ME < L *variābil(is)*] —**var′i·a·bil′i·ty, var′i·a·ble·ness,** *n.* —**var′i·a·bly,** *adv.* —**Ant. 1, 3.** constant.
Var′iable Zone′. See **Temperate Zone.**
var·i·ance (vâr′ē əns), *n.* **1.** the state, quality, or fact of being variable, divergent, different, or deviate. **2.** an instance of varying. **3.** *Statistics.* the square of the standard deviation. **4.** *Physics, Chem.* the number of degrees of freedom of a system. **5.** *Law.* a difference between two steps of a legal proceeding which must agree to be effectual, as a discrepancy between a writ and a declaration. **6.** an official permit to do something normally forbidden by regulations. **7.** a disagreement, dispute, or quarrel. **8. at variance,** in a state of difference or disagreement. [ME < L *variantia*]
var·i·ant (vâr′ē ənt), *adj.* **1.** exhibiting variety or diversity; varying. **2.** differing, esp. from something of the same general kind. —*n.* **3.** something that varies. **4.** something that differs from the standard or usual form of its kind. [late ME < L *variant-* (s. of *variāns,* prp. of *variāre*)]
var·i·ate (vâr′ē it), *n.* **1.** *Statistics.* a variable quantity associated with a probability distribution; random variable. **2.** variant. [< L *variāt(us)* (ptp. of *variāre* to VARY); see -ATE[1]]
var·i·a·tion (vâr′ē ā′shən), *n.* **1.** the act, process, or accident of varying, as in condition, character, or degree. **2.** an instance of this. **3.** the amount or rate of this. **4.** a different form of something; variant. **5.** *Music.* **a.** the transformation of a melody or theme with changes or elaborations in harmony, rhythm, and melody. **b.** a varied form of a melody or theme, esp. one of a series of such forms developing the capacities of the subject. **6.** *Ballet.* a solo dance, esp. one forming a section of a pas de deux. **7.** *Astron.* **a.** any deviation from the mean orbit of a heavenly body, esp. of a planetary or satellite orbit. **b.** an inequality in the moon's motion, having a period of one-half month. **8.** Also called **magnetic declination, magnetic variation.** *Navig.* the angle between the geographic and the magnetic meridian at a given point. Cf. **deviation** (def. 4). **9.** *Biol.* **a.** a deviation in the structure or character of an organism from that of others of the same species or group, or that of the parents. **b.** an organism exhibiting such deviation; variety. [< L *variātiōn-* (s. of *variātiō;* see VARIATE, -ION); r. ME *variacioun* < AF] —**var′i·a′tion·al, var·i·a·tive** (vâr′ē ā′tiv, -ə tiv), *adj.* —**var′i·a′tion·al·ly, var′i·a′tive·ly,** *adv.* —**Syn. 1.** mutation, modification; deviation, divergence.
var·i·cel·la (var′i sel′ə), *n.* *Pathol.* See **chicken pox.** [< NL, dim. of *variola* VARIOLA] —**var′i·cel′lar,** *adj.*
var·i·cel·late (var′i sel′it, -āt), *adj.* having small varices, as certain shells. [< NL *varicell(a)* (r. L *varicula,* dim. of *varix* varicose vein) + -ATE[1]]
var·i·cel·loid (var′i sel′oid), *adj.* resembling varicella.
var·i·ces (vâr′i sēz′), *n.* pl. of **varix.**
varico-, a word element meaning "varicose veins," used in the formation of compound words: *varicocele.* Also, *esp. before a vowel,* **varic-.** [< L *varic-* (s. of *varix*) + -o-. See VARIX]
var·i·co·cele (var′ə kō sēl′), *n.* *Pathol.* a varicose condition of the spermatic veins of the scrotum.
var·i·col·ored (vâr′i kul′ərd), *adj.* having various colors; variegated; motley. Also, *esp. Brit.,* **var′i·col′oured.**
var·i·cose (var′ə kōs′, vâr′-), *adj.* **1.** abnormally or unusually enlarged or swollen: *a varicose vein.* **2.** pertaining to or affected with varices, which often affect the superficial portions of the lower limbs. [< L *varicōs(us)*]
var·i·co·sis (var′ə kō′sis), *n.* *Pathol.* **1.** the formation of varices. **2.** varicosity.
var·i·cos·i·ty (var′ə kos′i tē), *n., pl.* **-ties.** *Pathol.* **1.** the state or condition of being varicose. **2.** varix (def. 1).
var·i·cot·o·my (var′ə kot′ə mē), *n., pl.* **-mies.** *Surg.* an operation for treating varicose veins by subcutaneous incision.
var·ied (vâr′ēd), *adj.* **1.** characterized by or exhibiting

variety; various; diverse. **2.** changed; altered. **3.** having several different colors; variegated.

var·i·e·gate (vâr′ē ə gāt′, vâr′ə gāt′), *v.t.*, **-gat·ed, -gat·ing.** **1.** to make varied in appearance, as by adding different colors. **2.** to give variety to; diversify. [< LL *variegāt(us)* (ptp. of *variegāre* to make (something) look varied) = L *vari(us)* VARIOUS + *-eg-* (var. of *-ag-*, root of *agere* to do; see AGENT) + *-ātus* -ATE]

var·i·e·gat·ed (vâr′ē ə gā′tid, vâr′ə gā′-), *adj.* **1.** varied in appearance or color; marked with patches or spots of different colors. **2.** varied; diversified; diverse.

var·i·e·ga·tion (vâr′ē ə gā′shən, vâr′ə gā′-), *n.* **1.** the act of variegating. **2.** the state or condition of being variegated; varied coloration.

var·i·er (vâr′ē ər), *n.* a person or thing that varies.

va·ri·e·tal (və rī′i təl), *adj.* **1.** of, pertaining to, designating, or characteristic of a variety. **2.** constituting a variety. [VARIET(Y) + -AL[1]] —**va·ri′e·tal·ly,** *adv.*

va·ri·e·ty (və rī′i tē), *n., pl.* **-ties.** **1.** the state or quality of being varied or diversified. **2.** difference; discrepancy. **3.** a number of different types of things, esp. ones in the same general category: *a variety of fruits.* **4.** a kind or sort: *a variety of plum.* **5.** a category within a species, based on some hereditary difference. **6.** a type of animal or plant produced by artificial selection. **7.** Also called **vari′ety show′.** *Theat.* entertainment consisting of a number of brief, unrelated performances or acts, as of singing, dancing, acrobatic exhibitions, skits, etc. Cf. **vaudeville** (def. 1). [< L *varietās.* See VARIOUS, -ITY] —**Syn. 1.** diversity, multiplicity. **3.** assortment, collection, group. **4.** class, species.

vari′ety meat′, edible meat other than the usual flesh, esp. organs, as tongue, liver, etc.

vari′ety store′, a retail store carrying a large variety of goods, esp. low-priced ones.

var·i·form (vâr′ə fôrm′), *adj.* varied in form; having various forms. —**var′i·form′ly,** *adv.*

va·ri·o·la (və rī′ə lə), *n. Pathol.* smallpox. [< ML, dim. of *varius* speckled. See VARIOUS]

va·ri·o·lar (və rī′ə lər), *adj.* variolous.

var·i·ole (vâr′ē ōl′), *n.* **1.** a shallow pit or depression like the mark left by a smallpox pustule; foveola. **2.** *Petrog.* any of the spherules of variolite. [< F: smallpox < ML *variola* VARIOLA]

var·i·o·lite (vâr′ē ə līt′), *n. Petrog.* any of certain fine-grained, basic igneous rocks containing light-colored spherules that give them a pockmarked appearance, esp. on weathered surfaces. [VARIOL(A) + -ITE[1]]

var·i·o·lit·ic (vâr′ē ə lit′ik), *adj.* **1.** *Petrog.* of or resembling variolite, esp. in texture. **2.** spotted.

var·i·o·loid (vâr′ē ə loid′), *adj.* **1.** resembling smallpox. **2.** of or pertaining to a mild case of smallpox. —*n.* **3.** a mild smallpox, esp. in persons who have been vaccinated or have previously had smallpox.

va·ri·o·lous (və rī′ə ləs), *adj.* of, pertaining to, or characteristic of smallpox. Also, **variolar.**

var·i·om·e·ter (vâr′ē om′i tər), *n.* **1.** *Elect.* a variable inductor, consisting essentially of two coils whose relative position may be changed to vary the inductance. **2.** an instrument for indicating a change in a component of a magnetic field vector, esp. one related to the earth's magnetic field. [*vari-* (see VARIOUS) + -O- + -METER]

var·i·o·rum (vâr′ē ôr′əm, -ōr′-), *adj.* **1.** containing different versions of a certain text. **2.** containing notes and commentaries by a number of scholars or critics: *a variorum text of Cicero.* —*n.* **3.** a variorum edition or text. [short for L *ēditiō cum notīs variōrum* edition with the notes of various persons]

var·i·ous (vâr′ē əs), *adj.* **1.** being different ones, or ones of different kinds of the same general thing: *various remedies.* **2.** presenting or having many different qualities or aspects: *a man of various talent.* **3.** variegated. **4.** numerous; many: *various persons.* [< L *varius* manifold, diversified, diverse; see -OUS] —**var′i·ous·ly,** *adv.*

—**Syn. 1.** VARIOUS, DIFFERENT, DISTINCT are applied to things sufficiently unlike to be perceivably of more than one kind. VARIOUS refers to several kinds of the same general thing: *various types of seaweed.* DIFFERENT is applied either to a single thing differing in identity or character from another, or to two or more things differing thus from one another: *a different story; two different stories concerning an event.* DISTINCT, however, implies want of connection between things that may possibly be alike or similar: *two distinct accounts that coincide.* **2.** diversified, varied. —**Ant. 1.** identical, same, uniform, similar.

var·i·type (vâr′i tīp′), *v.,* **-typed, -typ·ing.** —*v.i.* **1.** to operate a Varityper. —*v.t.* **2.** to set (type) on a Varityper. [back formation from VARITYPER] —**var′i·typ′ist,** *n.*

Var·i·typ·er (vâr′i tī′pər), *n. Trademark.* a typewriter-like machine with interchangeable typefaces, for composing justified matter.

var·ix (vâr′iks), *n., pl.* **var·i·ces** (vâr′i sēz′). **1.** Also called **varicosity.** *Pathol.* a permanent abnormal dilation and lengthening of a vein, usually accompanied by some tortuosity; a varicose vein. **2.** *Zool.* a mark or scar on the surface of a shell at a former position of the lip of the aperture. [< L: varicose vein]

var·let (vär′lit), *n. Archaic.* **1.** an attendant or servant. **2.** a page who serves a knight. **3.** a knavish person; rascal. [late ME < MF; var. of VALET]

var·man·nie (vär mä′nē), *n.* (in India) a method of self-defense similar to jujitsu. [?]

var·mint (vär′mənt), *n. Dial.* **1.** vermin. **2.** an objectionable or undesirable animal, usually predatory, as a coyote, bobcat, etc. **3.** a despicable, obnoxious, or annoying person. Also, **var′ment.**

var·na (vär′nə, vur′-), *n.* any of the four main Hindu social classes; caste. [< Skt *varṇa,* lit., cover, color, hence sort, class]

Var·na (vär′nə), *n.* a seaport in NE Bulgaria, on the Black Sea. 175,352 (1964). Formerly, **Stalin.**

var·nish (vär′nish), *n.* **1.** a preparation for finishing or coating wood, cloth, etc., consisting of resinous matter, as copal or lac, dissolved in an oil, alcohol, or other volatile liquid. **2.** the sap of certain trees, used for the same purpose. **3.** any of various other preparations similarly used. **4.** something resembling or suggesting a coat of varnish; gloss. **5.** *Brit.* nail polish. —*v.t.* **6.** to apply varnish to. **7.** to give a superficially pleasing appearance to, esp. in order to deceive: *to varnish the truth.* [ME *varnisch* < MF *vernis, verniz* < ML *vernicium* sandarac < MGk *berníkē,* syncopated var. of Gk *Berenī́kē,* city in Cyrenaica] —**var′nish·er,** *n.*

var′nish tree′, any of various trees yielding sap or other substances used for varnish, as *Rhus verniciflua,* of Japan.

Var·ro (var′ō), *n.* **Marcus Te·ren·ti·us** (tə ren′shē əs), c116–27? B.C., Roman scholar and author.

var·si·ty (vär′si tē), *n., pl.* **-ties,** *adj.* —*n.* **1.** any first-string team, esp. in sports, that represents a school, college, or the like: *He is on the varsity in tennis and in debating.* **2.** *Chiefly Brit. Informal.* university. —*adj.* **3.** of or pertaining to a university or school team, activity, or competition: *a varsity debater.* [var. of (UNI)VERSITY]

Var·u·na (vur′ŏŏ nə, vär′ə-), *n. Hinduism.* the Vedic god of natural and moral law, probably originally a sky god.

var·us (vâr′əs), *n. Pathol.* abnormal angulation of a bone or joint, with the angle pointing away from the midline. [< L: crooked, bent]

varve (värv), *n.* (in certain geological formations) an annual deposit usually consisting of two layers, one of fine materials and the other of coarse. [< Sw *varv* a round, (complete) turn]

var·y (vâr′ē), *v.,* **var·ied, var·y·ing.** —*v.t.* **1.** to change or alter, as in form, appearance, character, or substance. **2.** to give variety to. —*v.i.* **3.** to be different from one instance to the next: *Opinions vary on the outcome.* **4.** to change according to some other changing thing: *The demand varies with the season.* **5.** to diverge; deviate (usually fol. by *from*): *to vary from the norm.* **6.** *Math.* to be subject to change. **7.** *Biol.* to exhibit variation. [ME *varie(n)* < L *variā(re)* < *vari(us)* diverse] —**var′i·er,** *n.* —**var′y·ing·ly,** *adv.*

vas (vas), *n., pl.* **va·sa** (vā′sə). *Biol.* a vessel or duct. [< L: vessel]

vas-, var. of **vaso-** before a vowel: *vasectomy.*

Va·sa·ri (və zär′ē, -sär′ē; *It.* vä zä′rē), *n.* **Gior·gio** (jôr′jô), 1511–74, Italian painter, architect, and art historian.

Vas·co da Ga·ma (väs′kō də gam′ə, gä′mə; *Port.* väsh′kŏŏ də gä′mə). See **Gama, Vasco da.**

vas·cu·lar (vas′kyə lər), *adj. Biol.* pertaining to, composed of, or provided with vessels or ducts that convey fluids, as blood, lymph, or sap. Also, **vas·cu·lose** (vas′kyə-lōs′), **vas·cu·lous** (vas′kyə ləs). [< NL *vāsculār(is).* See VASCULUM, -AR[1]] —**vas′cu·lar′i·ty,** *n.* —**vas′cu·lar·ly,** *adv.*

vas′cular bun′dle, bundle (def. 4).

vas′cular ray′, *Bot.* a radiate band of parenchyma in the secondary xylem extending into the secondary phloem of the stems of certain vascular plants, formed by the cambium and serving for the storage of food and the conduction of nutriments.

vas′cular tis′sue, *Bot.* plant tissue consisting of ducts or vessels that, in the higher plants, form the system by which sap is conveyed through the plant.

vas·cu·lum (vas′kyə ləm), *n., pl.* **-la** (-lə), **-lums.** a kind of case or box used by botanists for carrying specimens as they are collected. [< L: little vessel. See VAS, -CULE]

vas de·fe·rens (vas def′ə renz′), *pl.* **va·sa de·fe·ren·ti·a** (vā′sə def′ə ren′shē ə). *Anat., Zool.* the deferent duct of the testis that transports the sperm from the epididymis to the penis. [< NL, L *vās* vessel + *deferēns* carrying off. See VASE, DEFERENT[2]]

vase (vās, vāz *or, esp. Brit.,* väz), *n.* a hollow container, as of glass, porcelain, or earthenware, usually higher than it is wide, used chiefly to hold cut flowers or for decoration. [< F < L *vās* vessel]

va·sec·to·my (va sek′tə mē), *n., pl.* **-mies.** *Surg.* excision of the vas deferens, or of a portion of it.

Vas·e·line (vas′ə lēn′, vas′ə lēn′), *n. Trademark.* petrolatum.

Vash·ti (vash′tī), *n.* the queen of Ahasuerus, banished for refusing to appear before his guests. Esther 1:9–22.

vaso-, a learned borrowing from Latin meaning "vessel," used in the formation of compound words: *vasoconstrictor.* Also, *esp. before a vowel,* **vas-.** [< L *vās* vessel + -O-]

vas·o·con·stric·tion (vas′ō kən strik′shən), *n. Physiol.* constriction of the blood vessels, as by the action of a nerve. —**vas′o·con·stric′tive,** *adj.*

vas·o·con·stric·tor (vas′ō kən strik′tər), *n. Physiol.* a nerve or drug that causes vasoconstriction.

vas·o·dil·a·ta·tion (vas′ō dil′ə tā′shən, -dī′lə-), *n. Physiol.* dilatation of the blood vessels, as by the action of a nerve. Also, **vas·o·di·la·tion** (vas′ō dī lā′shən, -di-).

vas·o·di·la·tor (vas′ō dī lā′tər, -di-), *n. Physiol.* a nerve or drug that causes vasodilatation.

vas·o·in·hib·i·tor (vas′ō in hib′i tər), *n.* an agent, as a drug, that inhibits the action of the vasomotor nerves. —**vas·o·in·hib·i·to·ry** (vas′ō in hib′i tôr′ē, -tōr′ē), *adj.*

vas·o·mo·tor (vas′ō mō′tər), *adj. Physiol.* regulating the diameter of blood vessels, as certain nerves.

vas·sal (vas′əl), *n.* **1.** (in the feudal system) a person granted the use of land, in return for homage, fealty, and usually military service or its equivalent. **2.** a person owing homage or fealty to a superior, as a subject or subordinate. **3.** a servant or slave. —*adj.* **4.** of, pertaining to, or characteristic of a vassal. **5.** having the status of a vassal. [ME < MF < ML *vassall(us)* = *vass(us)* servant (< Celt; cf. Welsh *gwas* young man, Ir *foss* servant) + *-allus* n. suffix]

vas·sal·age (vas′ə lij), *n.* **1.** the state or condition of a vassal. **2.** homage or service required of a vassal. **3.** a territory held by a vassal. **4.** *Hist.* (collectively) vassals. **5.** dependence or servitude. [ME < MF]

vast (vast, väst), *adj.* **1.** of very great area or extent. **2.** of very great size or quantity. **3.** very great in degree, intensity, etc.: *of vast importance.* —*n.* **4.** *Archaic or Poetic.* an immense or boundless expanse or space. [< L *vast(us)* empty, immense] —**vast′ly,** *adv.* —**vast′ness,** *n.*

Väs·ter·ås (ves′tər ôs′), *n.* a city in central Sweden. 85,007 (1964).

vas·ti·tude (vas′ti to͞od′, -tyo͞od′, vä′sti-), *n.* **1.** vastness; immensity. **2.** a vast expanse or space. [< L *vastitūdō.* See VAST, -I-, -TUDE]

vas·ti·ty (vas′ti tē, vä′sti-), *n. Archaic.* immensity; vastness. [< L *vastitās.* See VAST, -ITY]

vast·y (vas′tē, vä′stē), *adj.*, **vast·i·er, vast·i·est.** *Archaic.* vast; immense.

vat (vat), *n., v.,* **vat·ted, vat·ting.** —*n.* **1.** a large container, as a tub or tank, used for storing or holding liquids: *a wine vat.* **2.** *Chem.* **a.** a preparation containing an insoluble dye converted by reduction into a soluble leuco base. **b.** a vessel containing such a preparation. —*v.t.* **3.** to put into or treat in a vat. [ME (south); OE *fæt* vessel; c. Icel *fat* vessel, G *Fass* keg]

VAT, See **value-added tax.**

Vat., Vatican.

vat′ dye′, *Chem.* an insoluble dye impregnated into textile fibers by reduction into soluble leuco bases that regenerate the insoluble dye on oxidation.

vat·ic (vat′ik), *adj.* of, pertaining to, or characteristic of a prophet. Also, **vat′i·cal.** [< L *vāt(ēs)* seer + -IC]

Vat·i·can (vat′i kən), *n.* **1.** Also called **Vat′ican Pal′ace.** the chief residence of the popes in Vatican City. **2.** the authority and government of the pope. [< L *Vāticān(us)* (*mons*) Vatican (hill)]

Vat′ican Cit′y, an independent state within the city of Rome, on the right bank of the Tiber. Established in 1929, it is ruled by the Pope and includes St. Peter's Church and the Vatican. 1000 (est. 1970); 109 acres. Italian, **Città del Vaticano.**

vat·i·cide (vat′i sīd′), *n.* **1.** a person who kills a prophet. **2.** the act of killing a prophet. [< L *vāti-* (s. of *vātēs*) seer + -CIDE]

va·tic·i·nal (və tis′ə nᵊl), *adj.* of, pertaining to, or characterized by prophecy; prophetic. [< L *vāticin(us)* prophetic (*vāticin(ārī)* (to) prophesy + *-us* adj. suffix) + -AL¹]

va·tic·i·nate (və tis′ə nāt′), *v.t., v.i.,* **-nat·ed, -nat·ing.** to prophesy. [< L *vāticināt(us)* (ptp. of *vāticinārī* to prophesy) = *vāti-* (s. of *vātēs*) seer + *-cin-* (var. of *can-*, root of *canere* to sing, prophesy) + *-ātus* -ATE¹] —**va·tic′i·na′tor,** *n.*

vat·i·ci·na·tion (vat′i sə nā′shən), *n.* **1.** the act of prophesying. **2.** a prophecy. [< L *vāticinātiōn-* (s. of *vāticinātiō*)]

Vat·tel (*Ger.* fät′ᵊl), *n.* **Em·me·rich** (*Ger.* em′ə RIKH), 1714–67, Swiss jurist and diplomat.

Vät·ter (vet′təR), *n.* a lake in S Sweden. 80 mi. long; 733 sq. mi. Also, **Vät·tern** (vet′təRN), **Vetter.**

Vau·ban (vō bäN′), *n.* **Sé·bas·tien le Pres·tre de** (sā bAs tyaN′ lə pRe′tRᵊ də), 1633–1707, French military engineer and marshal.

Vaud (vō), *n.* a canton in W Switzerland. 521,600; 1239 sq. mi. *Cap.:* Lausanne. German, **Waadt.**

vaude·ville (vôd′vil, vōd′-, vô′də-), *n.* **1.** *Chiefly U.S.* theatrical entertainment consisting of a number of individual performances, acts, or mixed numbers. Cf. **variety** (def. 7). **2.** a theatrical piece of light or amusing character, interspersed with songs and dances. **3.** a satirical cabaret song. [< F, shortened alter. of MF *chanson du vau de Vire* song of the vale of Vire, a valley of Calvados, France, noted for satirical folksong]

vaude·vil·lian (vôd vil′yən, vōd-, vô′də-), *n.* **1.** Also, **vaude′vil·list.** a person who performs in vaudeville or writes or produces vaudeville shows. —*adj.* **2.** of, pertaining to, or characteristic of vaudeville.

Vau·dois (vō dwä′), *n., pl.* **-dois** for **1.** **1.** a native or inhabitant of Vaud. **2.** the dialect of French spoken in Vaud. [< F; MF *Vaudeis.* See VAUD, -ESE]

Vau·dois (vō dwä′), *n.pl.* Waldenses.

Vaughan (vôn), *n.* **Henry,** 1622–95, English poet and mystic.

Vaughan Wil·liams (vôn wil′yəmz), **Ralph,** 1872–1958, English composer.

vault¹ (vôlt), *n.* **1.** a construction for covering an area of considerable depth, built or affecting to be built on the principle of the arch. **2.** a chamber or passage surrounded by heavy masonry or earth and usually vaulted. **3.** a strongly built chamber for preserving money or valuable goods. **4.** a burial chamber. **5.** *Anat.* an arched roof of a cavity. **6.** something resembling an arched roof: *the vault of heaven.* —*v.t.* **7.** to construct or cover with a vault. **8.** to make in the form of a vault; arch. —*v.i.* **9.** to curve or bend in the form of a vault. [alter. of late ME *vout(e)* < MF *voute, volte* < VL **volta* a turn (cf. It *volta*), n. use of fem. ptp. **vol(vi)ta* (r. L *volūta*) of L *volvere* to turn; see REVOLVE] —**vault′like′,** *adj.*

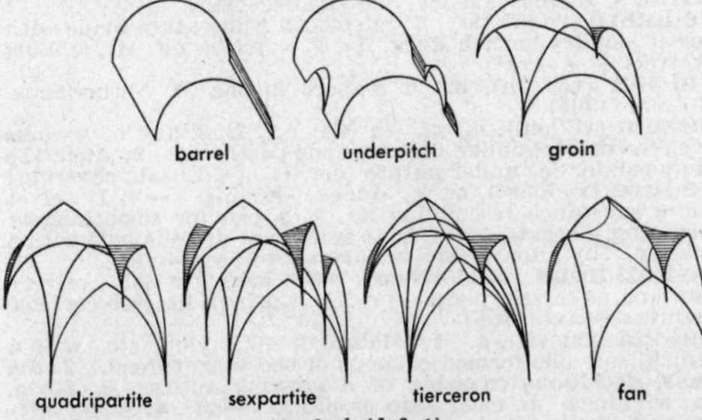

Vaults¹ (def. 1)

vault² (vôlt), *v.i.* **1.** to leap or spring, as to or from a position or over something. **2.** to leap with the hands supported on something, as on a pole. **3.** to arrive at or achieve something as if by a spring or leap: *to vault into prominence.* —*v.t.* **4.** to leap or spring over: *to vault a fence.* —*n.* **5.** act of vaulting. **6.** a leap of a horse; curvet. [< MF *volt(er)* (to) leap, turn < It *voltare* to turn < *volta* a turn (see VAULT¹)] —**vault′er,** *n.* —**Syn. 1.** See **jump.**

vault·ed (vôl′tid), *adj.* **1.** constructed or covered with a vault. **2.** provided with a vault or vaults. **3.** resembling an arched roof: *the vaulted sky.*

vault·ing¹ (vôl′ting), *n.* **1.** the act or process of constructing vaults. **2.** the structure forming a vault or vaults. [VAULT¹ + -ING¹]

vault·ing² (vôl′ting), *adj.* **1.** leaping up or over. **2.** used in vaulting: *a vaulting pole.* **3.** exaggerated; high-flown: *vaulting ambition.* [VAULT² + -ING²]

vault·y (vôl′tē), *adj.* having the appearance or characteristics of a vault; arching: *the vaulty rows of elm trees.* [VAULT¹ + -Y¹]

vaunt (vônt, vänt), *v.t.* **1.** to speak vaingloriously of; boast of: *to vaunt one's achievements.* —*v.i.* **2.** *Archaic.* to speak vaingloriously or boastfully; brag. —*n.* **3.** a boastful action or utterance. [ME *vaunte(n)* < MF *vante(r)* (to) boast < LL *vānitāre,* freq. of **vānāre* < *vān(us)* VAIN] —**vaunt′er,** *n.* —**vaunt′ing·ly,** *adv.*

vaunt-cour·i·er (vônt′ko͝or′ē ər, vänt′-), *n.* *Archaic.* a person who goes in advance, as a herald. [< F *avant-courrier* forerunner, herald. See AVAUNT, COURIER]

v. aux., auxiliary verb.

vav (vôv; *Heb.* väv), *n.* the sixth letter of the Hebrew alphabet. [< Heb *wāw* a hook]

vav·a·sor (vav′ə sôr′, -sôr′), *n.* (in the feudal system) a vassal or feudal tenant of a peer, ranking just below a baron. Also, **vav·a·sour** (vav′ə so͝or′). [ME *vavasour* < OF, perh. < ML *va(ssus) vassōr(um)* vassal of vassals; see VASSAL]

va·ward (vä′wôrd′, vou′ôrd), *n.* *Archaic.* vanguard. [late ME var. of *va(u)mwarde* < AF *van(t)warde*]

vb., **1.** verb. **2.** verbal.

V.C., **1.** Vice Chairman. **2.** Vice Chancellor. **3.** Vice Consul. **4.** See **Victoria Cross.** **5.** Vietcong.

VCR, See **videocassette recorder.**

V.D., See **venereal disease.** Also, **VD**

v.d., various dates.

V-Day (vē′dā′), *n.* a day of final military victory, esp. during World War II. [short for *Victory Day*]

VDT, See **video display terminal.**

've, contraction of *have: I've got it. We've been there before.*

Ve·a·dar (vē′ə där′; *Heb.* vē ä däR′), *n.* See **Adar Sheni.** [< Heb *we* and, additional + ADAR]

veal (vēl), *n.* **1.** Also, **veal·er** (vē′lər). a calf raised for its meat, usually a milk-fed animal less than three months old. **2.** the flesh of the calf as used for food. [ME *ve(e)l* < AF *vel* (OF *veel, veal*) < L *vitellus,* dim. of *vitulus* calf]

veal′ cut′let, a thin slice of veal dipped in egg and a mixture of bread crumbs or flour and seasonings, and sautéed, broiled, or baked.

Veb·len (veb′lən), *n.* **Thor·stein** (thôr′stīn, -stən), 1857–1929, U.S. economist and sociologist.

vec·tor (vek′tər), *n.* **1.** *Math.* **a.** a quantity possessing both magnitude and direction, represented by an arrow the direction of which indicates the direction of the quantity and the length of which is proportional to the magnitude. Cf. **scalar** (def. 3). **b.** any generalization of this quantity. **2.** the direction or course followed by an airplane, missile, or the like. **3.** *Biol.* an insect or other organism that transmits a pathogenic fungus, virus, bacterium, etc. [< L = *vect(us)* (ptp. of *vehere* to carry) + *-or* -OR²] —**vec·to·ri·al** (vek tôr′ē əl, -tôr′-), *adj.* —**vec·to′ri·al·ly,** *adv.*

A P X B
XA, XB, Vectors
XP, Resultant

vec′tor anal′ysis, the branch of calculus that deals with vectors and processes involving vectors.

vec·tor·car·di·o·gram (vek′tər kär′dē ə gram′), *n.* the graphic record produced by vectorcardiography.

vec·tor·car·di·og·ra·phy (vek′tər kär′dē og′rə fē), *n.* a method of determining the direction and magnitude of the electrical forces of the heart. —**vec·tor·car·di·o·graph·ic** (vek′tər kär′dē ə graf′ik), *adj.*

vec′tor field′, *Math., Physics.* a region, domain, set, etc., with a vector assigned at each point.

vec′tor prod′uct, *Math.* a vector perpendicular to two given vectors and having magnitude equal to the product of their magnitudes multiplied by the sine of the angle between them. Also called **cross product, outer product.** Cf. **scalar product.**

vec′tor sum′, *Math.* the vector, obtained by vector addition, that is equivalent in magnitude and direction to two or more given vectors.

Ve·da (vā′də, vē′-), *n.* *Hinduism.* **1.** Sometimes, **Vedas.** the entire body of Hindu sacred writings, chief among which are four books, the Rig-Veda, the Sama-Veda, the Atharva-Veda, and the Yajur-Veda. **2.** Also called **Samhita.** each of these four books. **3.** **Vedas,** these four books with the Brahmanas and Upanishads. [< Skt: knowledge] —**Ve·da·ic** (vi dā′ik), *adj.*

Ve·dan·ta (vi dän′tə, -dan′-), *n.* the chief Hindu philosophy, dealing mainly with the Upanishadic doctrine of the identity of Brahman and Atman. [< Skt = *vēd(a)* VEDA + *ánta* END] —**Ve·dan′tic,** *adj.* —**Ve·dan′tism,** *n.* —**Ve·dan′tist,** *n.*

V-E Day, May 8, 1945, the day of victory in Europe for the Allies in World War II.

Ved·da (ved′ə), *n.* an aborigine from Sri Lanka. Also, **Ved′dah.** [< Singhalese: bowman, hunter]

ve·dette (və det′), *n.* **1.** Also called **vedette′ boat′.** (formerly) a small naval launch used for scouting. **2.** (formerly) a mounted sentry in advance of the outposts of an army. Also, **vidette.** [< F < It *vedetta* outlook where a sentinel is posted = *ved(ere)* (to) see (< L *vidēre*) + *-etta* -ETTE]

Ve·dic (vā′dik, vē′-), *adj.* **1.** of or pertaining to the Veda or Vedas. **2.** of or pertaining to the Aryans who settled in India c1500 B.C., or to their culture. —*n.* **3.** Also called **Ve′dic San′skrit.** the language of the Vedas, closely related to classical Sanskrit.

vee (vē), *adj.* **1.** shaped like the letter *V: a vee neckline.* —*n.* **2.** anything shaped like or suggesting a *V.*

veep (vēp), *n.* *U.S. Informal.* a vice president, esp. of a country. Also called **vee·pee** (vē′pē′). [from V.P.]

veer¹ (vēr), *v.i.* **1.** to change direction or turn about or aside. **2.** (of the wind) **a.** to change direction clockwise (opposed to *back*). **b.** *Naut.* to shift to a direction more nearly astern (opposed to *haul*). —*v.t.* **3.** to alter the direction or course of; turn. **4.** *Naut.* to turn (a vessel) away from the wind; wear. —*n.* **5.** a change of direction, position, course, etc. [< MF *virer* to turn] —**veer′ing·ly,** *adv.* —**Syn. 1.** deviate, swerve, diverge.

veer[2] (vēr), *v.t.* *Naut.* to slacken or let out: *to veer chain.* [late ME *vere* < MD *viere(n)* to let out; c. MLG *vīren* to slacken, OHG *fieren* to give direction to]

veer·y (vēr′ē), *n.*, *pl.* **veer·ies.** a thrush, *Hylocichla fuscescens,* common in the eastern U.S., noted for its song. [? so called from its flight]

veg (vej), *n.*, *pl.* **veg.** *Brit. Informal.* a vegetable or dish of vegetables: *a dinner with two veg.* [by shortening]

Ve·ga (vē′gə), *n.* *Astron.* a star of the first magnitude in the constellation Lyra. [< ML < Ar *wāki′* falling]

Ve·ga (vā′gə; *Sp.* be′gä), *n.* **Lo·pe de** (lô′pe t͟he), (*Lope Félix de Vega Carpio*), 1562–1635, Spanish dramatist and poet.

veg·e·ta·ble (vej′tə bəl, vej′i tə-), *n.* **1.** any herbaceous plant whose fruit, seeds, roots, tubers, bulbs, stems, leaves, or flower parts are used as food. **2.** the edible part of such a plant. **3.** any member of the vegetable kingdom; plant. **4.** a dull, spiritless, and uninteresting person. —*adj.* **5.** of, consisting of, or made from edible vegetables. **6.** of, pertaining to, or characteristic of plants: *the vegetable kingdom.* **7.** derived from plants or some part of plants: *vegetable oils.* **8.** consisting of or containing the substance or remains of plants: *vegetable matter.* [late ME (adj.) < LL *vegetābil(is)* able to live and grow = *veget(āre)* (to) quicken (see VEGETATE) + *-ābilis* -ABLE] —**veg′e·ta·bly,** *adv.*

veg′etable but′ter, any of various vegetable fats having the consistency of butter, as cocoa butter.

veg′etable i′vory, ivory (def. 7).

veg′etable king′dom. See **plant kingdom.**

veg′etable mar′row, any of various summer squashes, as the zucchini.

veg′etable oil′, any of a large group of oils that are esters of fatty acids and glycerol, obtained from the leaves, fruit, or seeds of plants.

veg′etable sponge′, luffa (def. 2).

veg′etable tal′low, any of several tallowlike substances of vegetable origin, used in making candles, soap, etc., and as lubricants.

veg·e·tal (vej′i tᵊl), *adj.* **1.** of, pertaining to, or of the nature of plants or vegetables. **2.** vegetative (def. 2). [late ME < L *veget(āre)* to quicken (see VEGETATE) + -AL[1]]

veg·e·tar·i·an (vej′i târ′ē ən), *n.* **1.** a person who refuses to eat meat, fish, fowl, or, in some cases, any food derived from animal life for health reasons or because of moral opposition to the killing of animals. —*adj.* **2.** of or pertaining to vegetarianism or vegetarians. **3.** consisting solely of vegetables: *vegetarian vegetable soup.* [VEGET(ABLE) + -ARIAN] —**veg′e·tar′i·an·ism,** *n.*

veg·e·tate (vej′i tāt′), *v.i.*, **-tat·ed, -tat·ing.** **1.** to grow in or as in the manner of a plant. **2.** to live in an inactive, passive, or unthinking way. **3.** *Pathol.* to grow, or increase by growth, as an excrescence. [< L *vegetāt(us)* (ptp. of *vegetāre* to quicken, enliven) = *veget(us)* lively (*vegē-*, s. of *vegēre* to excite + *-tus* adj. suffix) + *-ātus* -ATE[1]]

veg·e·ta·tion (vej′i tā′shən), *n.* **1.** all the plants or plant life of a place. **2.** the act or process of vegetating. **3.** a dull or passive existence. **4.** *Pathol.* a morbid growth or excrescence. [< ML *vegetātiōn-* (s. of *vegetātiō*) = *vegetāt-* (see VEGETATE) + *-iōn-* -ION] —**veg′e·ta′tion·al,** *adj.*

veg·e·ta·tive (vej′i tā′tiv), *adj.* **1.** growing or developing as or like plants; vegetating. **2.** of, pertaining to, or concerned with vegetation or the plant kingdom. **3.** noting the parts of a plant not specialized for reproduction. **4.** (of reproduction) asexual. **5.** noting or pertaining to unconscious or involuntary bodily functions. **6.** having the power to produce or support growth in plants: *vegetative mold.* **7.** inactive or passive: *a vegetative existence.* Also, **veg·e·tive** (vej′i tiv). [late ME < ML *vegetātīv(us).* See VEGETATE, -IVE] —**veg′e·ta′tive·ly,** *adv.* —**veg′e·ta′tive·ness,** *n.*

ve·he·mence (vē′ə məns), *n.* **1.** the quality of being vehement. **2.** vigorous impetuosity; violence; fury. Also, **ve′he·men·cy.** [< L *vehementia* = *vehement-* VEHEMENT + *-ia* -Y[3]; see -ENCE] —**Syn. 1.** eagerness, verve, zeal, enthusiasm, fervency. **2.** passion. —**Ant. 1, 2.** apathy.

ve·he·ment (vē′ə mənt), *adj.* **1.** intense; ardent; impassioned. **2.** characterized by rancor or anger: *vehement opposition.* **3.** marked by great energy: *vehement clapping.* [late ME < L *vehement-* (s. of *vehemēns*) = *vehe(re)* to move, carry + *-ment-* prp. suffix] —**ve′he·ment·ly,** *adv.* —**Syn. 1.** earnest, fervent, fervid. —**Ant. 1, 2.** dispassionate.

ve·hi·cle (vē′i kəl), *n.* **1.** any means in or by which someone or something is carried or conveyed: *a motor vehicle; space vehicles.* **2.** a conveyance moving on wheels, runners, etc. **3.** a means of transmission or passage: *Air is the vehicle of sound.* **4.** a medium of communication, expression, or display. **5.** a means of accomplishing a purpose. **6.** *Pharm.* a substance, usually fluid, used as a medium for active remedies. **7.** *Painting.* a liquid, as oil, in which a pigment is mixed before being applied to a surface. **8.** *Theat., Movies.* a play or screenplay having a role unusually suited to display the talents of a particular performer. [< L *vehicul(um)* = *vehe(re)* to convey + *-culum* -CLE]

ve·hic·u·lar (vē hik′yə lər), *adj.* **1.** of, pertaining to, or for vehicles: *a vehicular tunnel.* **2.** serving as a vehicle. **3.** caused by a vehicle or vehicles: *vehicular deaths.* [< LL *vehiculār(is).* See VEHICLE, -AR[1]]

V-eight (vē′āt′), *adj.* noting an internal-combustion engine having two banks of four cylinders, each inclined so that the axes of the cylinders form an acute angle as seen from the end of the engine. Also, **V-8.**

Ve·ii (vē′yī), *n.* an ancient Etruscan city in Central Italy, in Etruria, near Rome: destroyed by the Romans 396 B.C.

veil (vāl), *n.* **1.** a piece of opaque or transparent material worn over the face. **2.** a piece of material worn so as to fall over the head and shoulders on each side of the face, forming a part of the headdress of a nun. **3.** something that covers, separates, screens, or conceals. **4.** *Bot., Anat., Zool.* a velum. **5.** *Dial.* a caul. **6. take the veil,** to become a nun. **7. the veil,** the life or vows of a nun. —*v.t.* **8.** to cover or conceal with or as with a veil. —*v.i.* **9.** to don or wear a veil. [ME *veile* < AF < VL *vēla,* fem. sing. (orig. neut. pl.) of L *vēlum* covering] —**veil′like′,** *adj.*

veiled (vāld), *adj.* **1.** having or wearing a veil. **2.** not openly or directly revealed or expressed: *a veiled threat.* —**veil·ed·ly** (vā′lid lē), *adv.*

veil·ing (vā′ling), *n.* **1.** the act of covering with or as with a veil. **2.** a veil. **3.** thin material for veils.

vein (vān), *n.* **1.** one of the system of branching vessels or tubes conveying blood from various parts of the body to the heart. **2.** (loosely) any blood vessel. **3.** one of the riblike thickenings that form the framework of the wing of an insect. **4.** one of the strands or bundles of vascular tissue forming the principal framework of a leaf. **5.** a distinct body or mass of igneous rock, deposited mineral, or the like; lode. **6.** a natural channel or watercourse beneath the surface of the earth. **7.** a streak or marking, as in marble. **8.** a condition, mood, or manner: *conversation in a serious vein.* —*v.t.* **9.** to furnish with veins. **10.** to mark with lines or streaks suggesting veins. [ME *veine* < OF < L *vēna*] —**vein′al,** *adj.* —**vein′less,** *adj.* —**vein′like′,** *adj.*

vein·ing (vā′ning), *n.* **1.** the act or process of forming veins. **2.** a vein or a pattern of veins or markings suggesting veins.

vein·let (vān′lit), *n.* a small vein.

vein·stone (vān′stōn′), *n.* gangue.

vein·ule (vān′yo͞ol), *n.* venule. Also, **vein·u·let** (vān′yə lit).

vein·y (vā′nē), *adj.*, **vein·i·er, vein·i·est.** full of veins; veined: *a veiny hand.*

vel., vellum.

ve·la (vē′lə), *n.* pl. of **velum.**

ve·la·men (və lā′min), *n.*, *pl.* **-lam·i·na** (-lam′ə nə). **1.** *Anat.* a membranous covering; velum. **2.** *Bot.* the spongy integument covering the aerial roots of epiphytic orchids. [< L = *vēlā(re)* (to) cover + *-men* n. suffix]

ve·lar (vē′lər), *adj.* **1.** of or pertaining to a velum, esp. the soft palate. **2.** *Phonet.* articulated with the back of the tongue held close to or touching the soft palate. —*n.* **3.** *Phonet.* a velar sound. [< L *vēlār(is).* See VELUM, -AR[1]]

ve·lar·ize (vē′lə rīz′), *v.t.*, **-ized, -iz·ing.** *Phonet.* to pronounce with velar articulation. —**ve′lar·i·za′tion,** *n.*

ve·lar·ized (vē′lə rīzd′), *adj.* *Phonet.* pronounced with velar articulation.

ve·late (vē′lit, -lāt), *adj.* *Bot., Zool.* having a velum. [< NL *vēlāt(us).* See VELUM, -ATE[1]]

Ve·láz·quez (və läs′kās, -kəs; *Sp.* be läth′keth), *n.* **Die·go Ro·drí·guez de Sil·va y** (dye′gô rô ᵺrē′geth ᵺe sēl′vä ē), 1599–1660, Spanish painter. Also, **Ve·lás·quez** (və läs′kās, -kəs; *Sp.* be läs′keth).

veld (velt, felt), *n.* the open country, bearing grass, bushes, or shrubs, or thinly forested, characteristic of parts of S Africa. Also, **veldt.** [< SAfrD: FIELD]

ve·li·tes (vē′li tēz′), *n.pl.* lightly-armed foot soldiers of ancient Rome. [< L, pl. of *vēles* light-armed infantryman, skirmisher]

vel·le·i·ty (və lē′i tē), *n.*, *pl.* **-ties.** **1.** volition in its weakest form. **2.** a mere wish, unaccompanied by an effort to obtain it. [< NL *velleitās* = L *velle* to be willing + *-itās* -ITY]

vel·lum (vel′əm), *n.* **1.** calfskin, lambskin, kidskin, etc., treated for use as a writing surface. **2.** a manuscript on vellum. **3.** a texture of paper or cloth suggesting vellum. —*adj.* **4.** made of or resembling vellum. **5.** bound in vellum. [late ME *velum, velim* < MF *ve(e)lin* of calf. See VEAL, -IN[1]]

ve·lo·ce (ve lô′che), *adv.* played at a fast tempo (used as a musical direction). [< It < L *vēlōci-*, s. of *vēlōx* quick]

ve·loc·i·pede (və los′ə pēd′), *n.* **1.** a vehicle, usually having two or three wheels, that is propelled by the rider. **2.** a light, pedal-driven vehicle used for carrying one person on a railroad track. [< F *vélocipède* bicycle = *vēloci-* (< L, s. of *vēlōx* quick) + *-pède* -PED] —**ve·loc′i·ped′ist,** *n.*

ve·loc·i·ty (və los′i tē), *n.*, *pl.* **-ties.** **1.** rapidity of motion or operation; swiftness; speed: *to measure the velocity of the wind.* **2.** *Mech.* the time rate of change of position of a body in a specified direction. [< L *vēlōcitās* speed. See VELOCIPEDE, -TY[2]] —**Syn. 1.** See **speed.**

ve·lo·drome (vē′lə drōm′, vel′ə-), *n.* a sports arena equipped with a banked track for cycling. [< F; see VELOCIPEDE, -DROME]

ve·lour (və lo͝or′), *n.* **1.** a velvetlike fabric of rayon, wool, or other fiber, for outerwear and upholstery. **2.** a velvety fur felt, as of beaver, for hats. Also, **ve·lours** (və lo͝or′; *Fr.* və lo͞or′). [< F, MF *velour(s),* OF *velo(u)s* < OPr *velos* velvet < L *villōsus* hairy. See VILLUS, -OSE[1]]

ve·lou·té (və lo͞o tā′), *n.* a smooth white sauce made with meat, poultry, or fish stock. [< F = *velout-* (cf. ML *velūtum* velvet) + *-é* -ATE[1]]

Vel·sen (vel′sən), *n.* a seaport in the W Netherlands. 67,806 (1965).

ve·lum (vē′ləm), *n.*, *pl.* **-la** (-lə). **1.** *Biol.* any of various veillike or curtainlike membranous partitions. **2.** *Anat.* the soft palate. See under **palate** (def. 1). [< L: sail, covering]

ve·lure (və lo͝or′), *n.*, *v.*, **-lured, -lur·ing.** —*n.* **1.** velvet or a substance resembling it. **2.** a pad for smoothing or dressing silk hats. —*v.t.* **3.** to smooth or dress (a hat) with a velure. [by alter. < MF *velour* VELOUR; see -URE]

ve·lu·ti·nous (və lo͞ot′ᵊnəs), *adj.* having a soft, velvety surface, as certain plants. [< NL *velūtīnus,* lit., velvety. See VELVET, -INE[1], -OUS]

vel·vet (vel′vit), *n.* **1.** a fabric of silk, nylon, etc., with a thick, soft pile formed of loops of the warp thread. **2.** the soft, deciduous covering of a growing antler. **3.** *Slang.* **a.** winnings. **b.** clear gain or profit. —*adj.* **4.** Also, **vel′vet·ed.** made of or covered with velvet. **5.** Also, **vel′vet·like′.** resembling velvet; smooth; soft. [ME < ML *velvet(um),* var. of *velūtum,* n. use of neut. of **velūtus* shaggy = *vel-* (see VILLUS) + *-ūtus* adj. suffix]

vel·vet·een (vel′vi tēn′), *n.* **1.** a cotton fabric with short pile, resembling velvet. **2. velveteens,** trousers of this fabric. —*adj.* **3.** made of velveteen. [VELVET + *-een,* var. of -INE[2]]

vel′vet glove′, an outwardly gentle or friendly manner used to disguise one's firm or ruthless determination.

vel′vet sponge′, a large commercial sponge, *Hippospongia gossypina,* of the West Indies.

vel·vet·y (vel′vi tē), *adj.* suggestive of or resembling velvet; smooth; soft. —**vel′vet·i·ness,** *n.*

Ven., Venerable.

ve·na (vē′nə), *n., pl.* **-nae** (-nē). *Anat.* a vein. [late ME < L *vēna* VEIN]

ve·na ca·va (vē′nə kā′və), *pl.* **ve·nae ca·vae** (vē′nē kā′vē). *Anat.* either of two large veins discharging blood into the right atrium of the heart. [< L: hollow vein]

ve·nal (vēn′əl), *adj.* **1.** open to bribery: *a venal judge.* **2.** able to be purchased, as something not rightfully offered for sale: *venal acquittals.* **3.** associated with or characterized by bribery: *a venal agreement.* [< L *vēnāl(is)* = *vēn(um)* for sale (see VEND) + *-ālis* -AL[1]] —**ve·nal·i·ty** (vē nal′i tē, və-), *n.* —**ve′nal·ly,** *adv.* —**Syn. 1.** bribable, mercenary, corruptible. See **corrupt.** —**Ant. 1.** incorruptible.

ve·nat·ic (vē nat′ik), *adj.* of or pertaining to hunting. Also, **ve·nat′i·cal.** [< L *vēnātic(us)* = *vēnāt(us)* (ptp. of *vēnārī* to hunt) + *-icus* -IC] —**ve·nat′i·cal·ly,** *adv.*

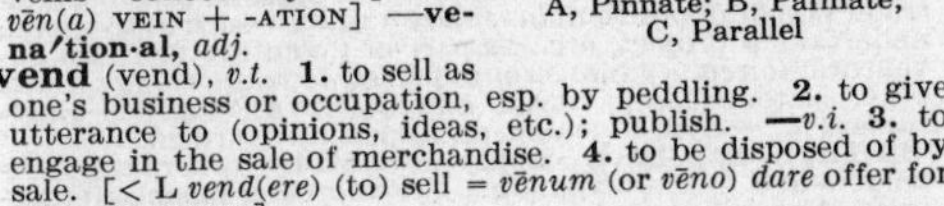

Venation of leaves
A, Pinnate; B, Palmate;
C, Parallel

ve·na·tion (vē nā′shən, və-), *n.* **1.** the arrangement of veins, as in a leaf or in the wing of an insect. **2.** these veins collectively. [< L *vēn(a)* VEIN + -ATION] —**ve·na′tion·al,** *adj.*

vend (vend), *v.t.* **1.** to sell as one's business or occupation, esp. by peddling. **2.** to give utterance to (opinions, ideas, etc.); publish. —*v.i.* **3.** to engage in the sale of merchandise. **4.** to be disposed of by sale. [< L *vend(ere)* (to) sell = *vēnum* (or *vēno*) *dare* offer for sale; see VENAL]

ven·dace (ven′dis, -dās), *n., pl.* **-dac·es,** (*esp. collectively*) **-dace.** a whitefish, *Coregonus vandesius,* found in several lakes in Scotland and England. [? *ven* white (< Celt; cf. OIr *fin(d)* white) + DACE]

Ven·de·an (ven dē′ən), *adj.* **1.** of or pertaining to the Vendée or its inhabitants. —*n.* **2.** a native or inhabitant of the Vendée, esp. one who participated in the royalist revolt in 1793. Also, **Ven·dé′an.**

vend·ee (ven dē′), *n.* *Chiefly Law.* the person to whom a thing is sold.

Ven·dée, the (vän dā′), a region in W France, on the Atlantic: royalist revolt 1793–95.

Ven·del·i·nus (ven del′ə nəs), *n.* an elliptical walled plain in the fourth quadrant of the face of the moon. ab. 100 mi. long.

Ven·dé·miaire (vän dā myer′), *n.* (in the French Revolutionary calendar) the first month of the year, extending from September 22 to October 21. [< F = *vendémi-* (< L *vindēmia* vintage) + *-aire* -ARY]

vend·er (ven′dər), *n.* vendor.

ven·det·ta (ven det′ə), *n.* **1.** a private feud, as formerly in Corsica and Italy, in which the family of a murdered person seeks to kill the murderer or members of his family. **2.** any prolonged and bitter feud, rivalry, contention, etc. [< It < L *vindicta* vengeance; see VINDICTIVE] —**ven·det′tist,** *n.*

vend·i·ble (ven′də bəl), *adj.* **1.** capable of being vended; salable: *vendible commodities.* **2.** *Obs.* mercenary; venal. —*n.* **3.** Usually, **vendibles.** vendible articles. [late ME < L *vendibil(is)*] —**vend′i·bil′i·ty,** *n.* —**vend′i·bly,** *adv.*

vend′ing machine′, a machine for storing a quantity of a small article, as candy bars, soft drinks, or packs of cigarettes, and dispensing one when a coin or coins are inserted.

ven·di·tion (ven dish′ən), *n.* the act of vending; sale. [< L *venditiōn-* (s. of *venditiō*) = *vendit(us)* (ptp. of *vendere* to VEND; see -ITE[2]) + *-iōn-* -ION]

Ven·dôme (vän dōm′), *n.* **Lou·is Jo·seph de** (lo͞o ē′ zhô-zef′ də), 1654–1712, French general and marshal.

ven·dor (ven′dər, ven dôr′), *n.* a person or agency that sells. Also, **vender.** [< AF *vendo(u)r* < L *venditor*]

ven·due (ven do͞o′, -dyo͞o′), *n.* a public auction. [< D *vendu* < MF *vendue* sale, n. use of fem. of *vendu,* ptp. of *vendre* to sell; see VEND]

ve·neer (və nēr′), *n.* **1.** a very thin layer of wood or other material for facing or inlaying wood. **2.** any of the thin layers of wood glued together to form plywood. **3.** *Building Trades.* a facing of a certain material applied to a different one or to a type of construction not ordinarily associated with it. **4.** a superficially valuable or pleasing appearance. —*v.t.* **5.** to overlay or face (wood, etc.) with thin sheets of some material. **6.** to give a superficially valuable or pleasing appearance to. [earlier *fineer* by dissimilation < G *furni(e)ren* to FURNISH] —**ve·neer′er,** *n.*

ve·neer·ing (və nēr′ing), *n.* **1.** the process, act, or craft of applying veneers. **2.** material applied as a veneer. **3.** a superficial appearance; veneer.

ven·e·nose (ven′ə nōs′), *adj.* *Archaic.* poisonous. [< LL *venēnōs(us)* = L *venēn(um)* drug, poison + *-ōsus* -OSE[1]]

ven·e·punc·ture (ven′ə pungk′chər, vē′nə-), *n.* *Med.* venipuncture. [< ML *vēnē* (L *vēnae*), gen. sing. of *vēna* VEIN + PUNCTURE]

Ve·ner (ven′ər), *n.* Vänern.

ven·er·a·ble (ven′ər ə bəl), *adj.* **1.** commanding respect or interest because of great age. **2.** worthy of veneration, as because of high office or noble character. [late ME < L *venerābil(is)* = *venerā(rī)* (to) VENERATE + *-bilis* -BLE] —**ven′er·a·bil′i·ty, ven′er·a·ble·ness,** *n.* —**ven′er·a·bly,** *adv.*

ven·er·ate (ven′ə rāt′), *v.t.,* **-at·ed, -at·ing.** to regard or treat with reverence; revere. [< L *venerāt(us)* (ptp. of *venerārī* to worship, revere) = *vener-* (s. of *venus*) loveliness + *-ātus* -ATE[1]] —**ven′er·a′tor,** *n.*

ven·er·a·tion (ven′ə rā′shən), *n.* **1.** the act or feeling of a person who venerates. **2.** an expression of this feeling. **3.** the state of being venerated; awe; reverence: *to be held in veneration.* [late ME < L *venerātiōn-* (s. of *venerātiō*) = *venerāt(us)* (see VENERATE) + *-iōn-* -ION] —**ven′er·a′tion·al,** *adj.* —**ven′er·a′tive,** *adj.* —**ven′er·a′tive·ly,** *adv.* —**ven′er·a′tive·ness,** *n.* —**Syn. 3.** awe. See **respect.**

ve·ne·re·al (və nēr′ē əl), *adj.* **1.** (of an infection, disease, etc.) characteristically arising from or transmitted through sexual intercourse. **2.** pertaining to diseases so arising. **3.** infected with or suffering from venereal disease: *a venereal patient.* **4.** of or pertaining to sexual desire or intercourse. **5.** serving or tending to excite sexual desire; aphrodisiac. [late ME < L *venere(us)* of sexual love (< *vener-,* s. of *venus* VENUS) + -AL[1]]

vene′real disease′, *Pathol.* any disease characteristically transmitted by sexual intercourse. *Abbr.:* V.D., VD Cf. **gonorrhea, syphilis.**

ve·ne·re·ol·o·gy (və nēr′ē ol′ə jē), *n.* the branch of medicine dealing with the study and treatment of venereal diseases. Also, **ven·er·ol·o·gy** (ven′ə rol′ə jē). [< L *venere(us)* VENEREAL + -O- + -LOGY] —**ve·ne′re·ol′o·gist,** *n.*

ven·er·y[1] (ven′ə rē), *n.* *Archaic.* love-making; sexual intercourse. [< L *vener-* (s. of *venus* VENUS) + -Y[3]]

ven·er·y[2] (ven′ə rē), *n.* *Archaic.* the practice or sport of hunting; the chase. [ME *venerie* hunting < MF = *ven(er)* (to) hunt (< L *vēnārī*) + *-erie* -ERY]

ven·e·sec·tion (ven′i sek′shən, vē′ni-), *n.* *Surg.* phlebotomy. Also, **venisection.** [< ML *vēnē* (see VENEPUNCTURE) + SECTION]

Ve·ne·ti·a (və nē′shē ə, -shə), *n.* **1.** an ancient district in NE Italy: later a Roman province bounded by the Alps, the Po River, and the Adriatic Sea. **2.** Venezia (def. 1).

Ve·ne·tian (və nē′shən), *adj.* **1.** of or pertaining to Venice or its inhabitants. —*n.* **2.** a native or inhabitant of Venice. **3.** (*l.c.*) *Informal.* See **Venetian blind.** [< ML *Venetiān(us)* = *Veneti(a)* Venice + *-ānus* -AN; r. ME *Venicien* < MF]

Vene′tian blind′, a blind, as for a window, having overlapping horizontal slats that may be opened or closed, esp. one in which the slats may be raised and drawn together above the window by pulling a cord.

Vene′tian glass′, ornamental glassware of the type made at Venice, esp. that from the island of Murano.

Vene′tian red′, a dark shade of orangish red.

Ve·net·ic (və net′ik), *n.* an Italic language of NE Italy, known from inscriptions from the 4th to 2nd centuries B.C. [< L *venetic(us)* = *Venet(i)* name of the tribe + *-icus* -IC]

Ve·ne·to (*It.* ve′ne tō), *n.* Venezia (def. 1).

Venez., Venezuela.

Ve·ne·zia (ve ne′tsyä), *n.* **1.** Also, **Venetia.** Also called **Veneto.** a region in NE Italy. 4,305,393; 7095 sq. mi. **2.** Italian name of **Venice.**

Vene′zia Giu′lia (jo͞o′lyä), a former region of NE Italy, at the N end of the Adriatic. The larger part, including the area surrounding the Free Territory of Trieste, was ceded to Yugoslavia 1947; the part remaining in Italy merged with Udine to form Friuli-Venezia Giulia.

Vene′zia Tri·den·ti′na (trē′den tē′nä), a former department in N Italy, now forming the greater part of the region of Trentino-Alto Adige.

Ven·e·zue·la (ven′i zwā′lə, -zwē′-; *Sp.* be′ne swe′lä), *n.* a republic in N South America. 12,300,000; 352,143 sq. mi. *Cap.:* Caracas. —**Ven′e·zue′lan,** *adj., n.*

venge (venj), *v.t.,* **venged, veng·ing.** *Archaic.* to avenge. [ME *venge(n)* < OF *veng(i)er* < L *vindicāre*; see VINDICATE]

venge·ance (ven′jəns), *n.* **1.** infliction of injury, harm, humiliation, or the like, on a person by another who has been harmed by him; violent revenge. **2.** an opportunity for or an instance of this. **3.** the desire for revenge: *He was full of vengeance.* **4.** *Obs.* hurt; injury. **5.** *Obs.* curse; imprecation. **6. with a vengeance, a.** with force or violence. **b.** to an unreasonable, excessive, or surprising degree. [ME < OF = *vengi(er)* to avenge (see VENGE) + *-ance* -ANCE] —**Syn. 1.** requital, retaliation. **1, 2.** See **revenge.** —**Ant. 1.** forgiveness.

venge·ful (venj′fəl), *adj.* **1.** desiring or seeking vengeance; vindictive. **2.** characterized by or showing a vindictive spirit: *a vengeful act.* [(RE)VENGEFUL] —**venge′ful·ly,** *adv.* —**venge′ful·ness,** *n.* —**Syn. 1.** revengeful, spiteful.

ve·ni·al (vē′nē əl, vēn′yəl), *adj.* **1.** able to be forgiven or pardoned, as a sin (opposed to *mortal*). **2.** excusable: *a venial error; a venial offense.* [ME < ML *veniāl(is)* = L *veni(a)* grace, favor, indulgence (*ven(us)* love + *-ia* -Y[3]) + *-ālis* -AL[1]] —**ve′ni·al′i·ty, ve′ni·al·ness,** *n.* —**ve′ni·al·ly,** *adv.*

ve′nial sin′, *Rom. Cath. Ch.* a transgression against the law of God that does not deprive the soul of divine grace either because it is a minor offense or because it was committed without full understanding of its seriousness or without full consent of the will. Cf. **mortal sin.**

Ven·ice (ven′is), *n.* **1.** Italian, **Venezia.** a seaport in NE Italy, built on numerous small islands in the Lagoon of Venice. 361,722. **2. Gulf of,** the N arm of the Adriatic Sea. **3. Lagoon of,** an inlet of the Gulf of Venice.

ven·in (ven′in, vē′nin), *n.* *Biochem.* any of several poisonous substances found in snake venom. Also, **ven·ine** (ven′ēn). [< F, taken as VEN(OM) + -IN[2]]

ven·i·punc·ture (ven′ə pungk′chər, vē′nə-), *n.* *Med.* the puncture of a vein for surgical or therapeutic purposes or for collecting blood specimens for analysis. Also, **venepuncture.** [var. of VENEPUNCTURE]

ve·ni·re fa·ci·as (vi nī′rē fā′shē as′), *Law.* **1.** a writ or precept directed to the sheriff, requiring him to summon qualified citizens to act as jurors. **2.** the entire jury panel from which a trial jury is selected. Also called **ve·ni′re.** [< L: lit., make come]

ve·ni·re·man (vi nī′rē mən), *n., pl.* **-men.** *Law.* a person summoned under a venire facias. [*venire* (see VENIRE FACIAS) + MAN[1]]

ven·i·sec·tion (ven′ə sek′shən, vē′nə-), *n.* *Surg.* phlebotomy. Also, **venesection.**

ven·i·son (ven′i sən, -zən *or, esp. Brit.,* ven′zən), *n.* the flesh of a deer or similar animal as used for food. [ME *ven(a)ison* < OF *veneison, venaison* < L *vēnātiōn-* (s. of *vēnātiō* hunting) = *vēnāt(us)* (see VENATIC) + *-iōn-* -ION]

Ve·ni·te (vi nī′tē), *n.* **1.** the 95th Psalm (94th in the Vulgate and the Douay Bible), used as a canticle at matins or morning prayers. **2.** a musical setting of this psalm. [< L: come ye; so called from the first word of Vulgate text]

ve·ni, vi·di, vi·ci (wā′nē, wē′dē, wē′kē; *Eng.* vē′nī, vī′dī, vī′sī, ven′ē, vē′dē, vē′chē, -sē), *Latin.* I came, I saw, I conquered.

Ven·lo (ven′lō), *n.* a city in the SE Netherlands. 57,705 (1962). Also, **Ven·loo** (ven′lō).

Venn′ di′agram (ven), *Math., Symbolic Logic.* a diagram that uses circles to represent sets and their relationships. [named after John *Venn* (1834–1923), English logician]

ven·om (ven′əm), *n.* **1.** the poisonous fluid that some animals, as certain snakes or spiders, secrete and introduce into the bodies of their victims by biting, stinging, etc. **2.** something suggesting this, as malice or jealousy. **3.** *Archaic.* poison in general. —*v.t.* **4.** *Archaic.* to make venomous; envenom. [var. of ME *venim* < AF; OF *venim, venin* < VL **venīmen*, by metathesis, etc., for L *venēnum* poison, love potion = *ven(us)* love (see VENUS) + *-ēnum*, neut. of *-ēnus* -ENE] —**Syn. 1.** See **poison. 2.** malignity, acrimony.

ven·om·ous (ven′ə məs), *adj.* **1.** (of an animal) capable of inflicting a poisoned bite, sting, or wound: *a venomous snake.* **2.** full of or containing venom; poisonous: *a venomous wound; venomous potion.* **3.** spiteful; malignant. [ME *venim(o)us* < AF *venimus* (OF *venimeux*)] —**ven′om·ous·ly,** *adv.* —**ven′om·ous·ness, ven′om·ness,** *n.*

ve·nose (vē′nōs), *adj.* **1.** having many or prominent veins. **2.** venous. [< L *vēnōs(us)* = *vēn(a)* VEIN + *-ōsus* -OSE[1]]

ve·nos·i·ty (vi nos′i tē), *n.* *Physiol.* the state or quality of being venous.

ve·nous (vē′nəs), *adj.* **1.** of, pertaining to, or of the nature of a vein or veins. **2.** having, characterized by, or composed of veins. **3.** pertaining to the blood in the pulmonary artery, right side of the heart, and most veins, that has become deoxygenated and charged with carbon dioxide during its passage through the body. [var. of VENOSE; see -OUS]

vent[1] (vent), *n.* **1.** an opening, as in a wall, serving as an outlet for air, smoke, fumes, or the like. **2.** the small opening at the breech of a gun by which fire is communicated to the charge. **3.** *Zool.* the anal or excretory opening of animals, esp. of those below mammals, as birds and reptiles. **4.** a means of exit or escape; an outlet, as from confinement. [prob. VENT[2] + VENT[3]]

vent[2] (vent), *n.* **1.** expression; utterance: *to give vent to one's emotions.* **2.** *Obs.* an emission or discharge. —*v.t.* **3.** to give free play or expression to (an emotion, passion, etc.): *She vented her rage on her associates.* **4.** to relieve (a feeling) with such expression: *to vent one's disappointment.* **5.** to release or discharge (liquid, smoke, etc.). **6.** to furnish or provide with a vent or vents. —*v.i.* **7.** to be relieved of pressure or discharged by means of a vent. **8.** (of an otter or other animal) to rise to the surface of the water to breathe. [late ME *vente(n)*, by aphesis < MF *e(s)venter* = *es-* EX-[1] + *venter* to blow < *vent* < L *ventus* WIND[1]]

vent[3] (vent), *n.* a slit in the back or sometimes at the side of a coat or jacket. [late ME *vente;* r. ME *fente* < MF < *fendre* to slit < L *findere* to split]

vent·age (ven′tij), *n.* a small hole or vent, as one of the finger holes of a flute.

ven·tail (ven′tāl), *n.* *Armor.* a defense for the lower part of the face, esp. the pivoted middle element of a face defense of a close helmet. Also, **aventail.** [ME < MF *ventaille* = *vent* (< L *ventus* WIND[1]) + *-aille* -AL[2]]

ven·ter (ven′tər), *n.* **1.** *Anat., Zool.* **a.** the abdomen or belly. **b.** a bellylike cavity or concavity. **c.** a bellylike protuberance. **2.** *Law.* the womb, or a wife or mother, as a source of offspring. [< L *venter* belly, womb]

ven·ti·duct (ven′ti dukt′), *n.* a duct, pipe, or passage for wind or air, as for ventilating apartments. [*venti-* (comb. form of L *ventus* WIND[1]) + DUCT]

ven·ti·late (ven′tᵊlāt′), *v.t.,* **-lat·ed, -lat·ing. 1.** to provide (a room or other enclosed space) with fresh or cool air. **2.** to provide with a means of access for such air. **3.** to submit (a question, problem, etc.) to open, full examination and discussion. **4.** to give utterance or expression to (an opinion, complaint, etc.). [< L *ventilāt(us)* (ptp. of *ventilāre* to fan) = **ventil(us)*, var. of *ventulus* mild breeze (*vent(us)* wind + *-ulus* dim. suffix) + *-ātus* -ATE[1]] —**ven′ti·la·ble,** *adj.*

ven·ti·la·tion (ven′tᵊlā′shən), *n.* **1.** the act of ventilating. **2.** the state of being ventilated. **3.** facilities or equipment for providing ventilation. [< L *ventilātiōn-* (s. of *ventilātiō*) = *ventilāt(us)* (see VENTILATE) + *-iōn-* -ION] —**ven′ti·la′tive,** *adj.* —**ven·ti·la·to·ry** (ven′tᵊlə tōr′ē, -tôr′ē), *adj.*

ven·ti·la·tor (ven′tᵊlā′tər), *n.* **1.** a person or thing that ventilates. **2.** a contrivance or opening for replacing foul or stagnant air with fresh air.

Ven·tôse (väɴ tōz′), *n.* (in the French Revolutionary calendar) the sixth month of the year, extending from February 19 to March 20. [< F < L *ventōsus* windy. See VENT[2], -OSE[1]]

ventr-, var. of **ventri-** before a vowel.

ven·tral (ven′trəl), *adj.* **1.** of or pertaining to the venter or belly; abdominal. **2.** situated on the abdominal side of the body. **3.** of, pertaining to, or situated on the anterior or lower side or surface, as of an organ or part. **4.** *Bot.* of or designating the lower or inner surface, as of a petal, leaf, etc. —*n.* **5.** See **pelvic fin.** [< L *ventrāl(is)* = *vent(e)r* VENTR- + *-ālis* -AL[1]] —**ven′tral·ly,** *adv.*

ven′tral fin′. See **pelvic fin.**

ventri-, a learned borrowing from Latin meaning "abdomen," used in the formation of compound words: *ventriloquy.* [comb. form of L *venter* belly, womb]

ven·tri·cle (ven′tri kəl), *n.* **1.** any of various hollow organs or parts in an animal body. **2.** *Anat.* **a.** either of the two lower chambers on each side of the heart that receive blood from the atria and in turn force it into the arteries. **b.** one of a series of connecting cavities of the brain. [< L *ventricul(us)* (little) belly, ventricle]

ven·tri·cose (ven′trə kōs′), *adj.* **1.** swollen, esp. on one side or unequally; protuberant. **2.** having a large abdomen. [< NL *ventricōs(us)*] —**ven·tri·cos·i·ty** (ven′trə kos′i tē), *n.*

ven·tric·u·lar (ven trik′yə lər), *adj.* **1.** of, pertaining to, or of the nature of a ventricle. **2.** of or pertaining to a belly or to something resembling one. [< L *ventricul(us)* (see VENTRICLE) + -AR[1]]

ven·tric·u·lus (ven trik′yə ləs), *n., pl.* **-li** (-lī′). **1.** the stomach of an insect. **2.** the muscular portion of a bird's stomach; gizzard. [< L; see VENTRICLE]

ven·tril·o·quise (ven tril′ə kwīz′), *v.i., v.t.,* **-quised, -quis·ing.** *Chiefly Brit.* ventriloquize.

ven·tril·o·quism (ven tril′ə kwiz′əm), *n.* the art or practice of speaking so that the voice does not appear to come from the speaker but from another source. Also called **ventriloquy.** —**ven·tri·lo·qui·al** (ven′trə lō′kwē əl), **ven·tril′o·qual,** *adj.* —**ven′tri·lo′qui·al·ly,** *adv.*

ven·tril·o·quist (ven tril′ə kwist), *n.* a person who performs or is skilled in ventriloquism. —**ven·tril′o·quis′tic,** *adj.*

ven·tril·o·quize (ven tril′ə kwīz′), *v.i., v.t.,* **-quized, -quiz·ing.** to speak or produce sounds in the manner of a ventriloquist. Also, *esp. Brit.,* **ventriloquise.**

ven·tril·o·quy (ven tril′ə kwē), *n.* ventriloquism. [< ML *ventriloqui(um)* = LL *ventriloqu(us)* belly speaker (*ventri-* VENTRI- + *-loquus* < *loquī* to speak) + *-ium* -Y[3]]

Ven·tris (ven′tris), *n.* **Michael George Francis,** 1922–56, English architect and linguist.

Ven·tu·ra (ven tŏŏr′ə), *n.* See **San Buenaventura.**

ven·ture (ven′chər) *n., v.,* **-tured, -tur·ing.** —*n.* **1.** an undertaking involving risk or uncertainty. **2.** a business enterprise in which loss is risked in the hope of profit. **3.** the money or property risked in such an enterprise. **4.** *Obs.* hazard or risk. **5. at a venture,** according to chance; at random: *A successor was chosen at a venture.* —*v.t.* **6.** to expose to hazard; risk. **7.** to take the risk of: *to venture a voyage.* **8.** to undertake to express, in spite of possible contradiction or opposition: *to venture a guess.* —*v.i.* **9.** to travel, undertake a project, etc., as part of a venture or as an adventure: *to venture into strange places; to venture upon a new plan.* [late ME, aph. var. of *aventure* ADVENTURE] —**ven′tur·er,** *n.* —**Syn. 6.** endanger, imperil, jeopardize.

ven′ture cap′ital, money invested by owners or stockholders in a new or expanding but unproven business enterprise. Also called **risk capital.**

ven·ture·some (ven′chər səm), *adj.* **1.** having or showing a disposition to undertake ventures; adventurous. **2.** attended with risk; hazardous. —**ven′ture·some·ly,** *adv.* —**ven′ture·some·ness,** *n.*

Ven·tu′ri tube′ (ven tŏŏr′ē), a device for measuring the flow of a fluid, consisting of a tube with a short, narrowed center section, so that a fluid flowing through the center section at a higher velocity than through an end section creates a pressure differential that is a measure of the flow of the fluid. [named after G. B. *Venturi* (1746–1822), Italian physicist whose work led to its invention]

ven·tur·ous (ven′chər əs), *adj.* **1.** ready or inclined to face risky situations; bold; daring; adventurous. **2.** hazardous; risky; dangerous: *a venturous voyage.* [VENTURE + -OUS; see ADVENTUROUS] —**ven′tur·ous·ly,** *adv.* —**ven′tur·ous·ness,** *n.* —**Syn. 1.** enterprising, rash. **2.** perilous.

ven·ue (ven′ōō, ven′yōō), *n.* **1.** *Law.* **a.** the place of a crime or cause of action. **b.** the county or place where the jury is gathered and the cause tried. **2.** the scene or locale of any action or event. **3.** the position taken by a person engaged in argument or debate; ground. [ME *venue* an attack < MF (lit., a coming), OF *venue* (ptp. fem. of *venir* < L *venīre* to come) < VL **venūta* (r. L *venta*) = *venu-* (VL ptp. s.) + *-ta* (VL, L fem. ptp. suffix)]

ven·ule (ven′yōōl), *n.* **1.** a small vein. **2.** one of the branches of a vein in the wing of an insect. Also, **veinule, veinulet.** [< L *vēnula* little vein. See VEIN, -ULE] —**ven′u·lar,** *adj.* —**ven·u·lose** (ven′yə lōs), **ven·u·lous** (ven′yə ləs), *adj.*

Ve·nus (vē′nəs), *n., pl.* **-us·es** for 2. **1.** an ancient Italian goddess of gardens and spring, identified by the Romans with Aphrodite as the goddess of love and beauty. **2.** an exceptionally beautiful woman. **3.** *Astron.* the planet second in order from the sun, having a diameter of 7700 miles, a mean distance from the sun of 67,000,000 miles, a period of revolution of 225 days, and no satellites. It is the most brilliant planet in the solar system.

Ve·nus·berg (vē′nəs bûrg′; *Ger.* vā′nŏŏs berk′), *n.* a mountain in central Germany in the caverns of which, according to medieval legend, Venus held court.

Venus's-flytrap (Height about 1 ft.)

Ve·nu·si·an (və nōō′sē ən, -shē ən, -shən, -nyōō′-), *adj.* **1.** of or pertaining to the planet Venus. —*n.* **2.** a supposed being inhabiting or coming from Venus.

Ve·nus's-fly·trap (vē′nə siz flī′trap′), *n.* a plant, *Dionaea muscipula,* native to North and South Carolina, having leaves with two lobes that close like a trap when certain delicate hairs on them are touched, as by a fly. Also called **Ve′nus fly′trap.**

Ve·nus's-gir·dle (vē′nə siz gûr′dᵊl), *n.* an iridescent blue and green ctenophore, *Cestum veneris,* having a ribbon-shaped, gelatinous body.

Ve·nus's-hair (vē′nə siz hâr′), *n.* a delicate maidenhair fern, *Adiantum Capillus-Veneris.*

ver., **1.** verse; verses. **2.** version.

ve·ra·cious (və rā′shəs), *adj.* **1.** habitually speaking the truth; truthful. **2.** characterized by truthfulness: *a veracious account.* [VERACI(TY) + -OUS] —**ve·ra′cious·ly,** *adv.* —**ve·ra′cious·ness,** *n.* —**Ant.** mendacious.

ve·rac·i·ty (və ras′i tē), *n., pl.* **-ties. 1.** personal truthfulness. **2.** conformity to truth or fact; accuracy. **3.** something veracious; a truth. [< ML *vērācitāt-* (s. of *vērācitās*) = L *vērāci-* (s. of *vērax*) true + *-tāt-* -TY[2]] —**Syn. 1.** honesty.

Ver·a·cruz (ver′ə krōōz′; *Sp.* be′rä krōōs′), *n.* **1.** a state in E Mexico, on the Gulf of Mexico. 2,727,899 (1960); 27,759 sq. mi. *Cap.:* Jalapa. **2.** a seaport in this state: the chief port of Mexico. 173,350 (est. 1965). Formerly, **Ver′a Cruz′.**

ve·ran·da (və ran′də), *n.* a porch, sometimes partly enclosed; portico or gallery. Also, **ve·ran′dah.** [< Pg *varanda* railing < Hindi; ? akin to L *vārus* crooked (see VARA)] —**ve·ran′daed, ve·ran′dahed,** *adj.*

ver·a·trine (ver′ə trēn′, -trin), *n.* *Chem.* a poisonous mixture of alkaloids obtained by extraction from the seeds of the sabadilla: formerly used as a counterirritant in the treatment of rheumatism and neuralgia. Also, **ve·ra·tri·a** (və rā′trē ə, -ra′-), **ver·a·trin** (ver′ə trin), **ver·a·tri·na** (ver′ə trī′nə). [< F < L *vērātr(um)* hellebore + F *-ine* -INE[2]]

verb (vûrb), *n.* any member of a class of words that function as the main elements of predicates, typically express action or state, may be inflected for tense, aspect, voice, and mood, and show agreement with subject or object. [late ME < L *verb(um)* verb, word] —**verb′less,** *adj.*

ver·bal (vûr′bəl), *adj.* **1.** of or pertaining to words: *verbal ability.* **2.** consisting of or in the form of words: *verbal imagery.* **3.** expressed in spoken words: *a verbal agreement.* **4.** pertaining to or concerned with words only: *a purely verbal distinction between two concepts.* **5.** corresponding word for word; verbatim: *a verbal translation.* **6.** *Gram.* of, pertaining to, or derived from a verb. —*n.* **7.** *Gram.* a word, particularly a noun or adjective, derived from a verb. [late ME < L *verbāl(is).* See VERB, -AL¹] —**ver′bal·ly,** *adv.* —**Syn. 3.** spoken. See **oral.**

ver′bal ad′jective, *Gram.* an adjective derived from a verb, as, in English, *smiling face,* or, in Greek, *batós,* going, moving, derived from *baínein,* to go, move.

ver′bal auxil′iary. See **auxiliary verb.**

ver·bal·ise (vûr′bə līz′), *v.t., v.i.,* **-ised, -is·ing.** *Chiefly Brit.* verbalize. —**ver′bal·i·sa′tion,** *n.* —**ver′bal·is′er,** *n.*

ver·bal·ism (vûr′bə liz′əm), *n.* **1.** a verbal expression, as a word or phrase. **2.** the way in which something is worded. **3.** a phrase or sentence having little or no meaning. **4.** a use of words considered as obscuring ideas or reality; verbiage.

ver·bal·ist (vûr′bə list), *n.* **1.** a person skilled in the use of words. **2.** a person who concerns himself more with words than with ideas or reality. —**ver′bal·is′tic,** *adj.*

ver·bal·ize (vûr′bə līz′), *v.,* **-ized, -iz·ing.** —*v.t.* **1.** to express in words. **2.** *Gram.* to convert into a verb. —*v.i.* **3.** to use many words; be verbose. **4.** to express something verbally. Also, *esp. Brit.,* **verbalise.** —**ver′bal·i·za′tion,** *n.* —**ver′bal·iz′er,** *n.*

ver′bal noun′, *Gram.* a noun derived from a verb, as the gerund *smoking,* in *Smoking is forbidden.*

ver·ba·tim (vər bā′tim), *adv., adj.* in exactly the same words; word for word. [late ME < ML = *verb(um)* word + *-ātim* adv. suffix]

ver·ba·tim et lit·te·ra·tim (weʀ bä′tim et lē′te ʀä′tim; *Eng.* vər bā′tim et lit′ə rā′tim), *Latin.* word for word and letter for letter; in exactly the same words.

ver·be·na (vər bē′nə), *n.* any plant of the genus *Verbena,* comprising the vervains. [< ML; see VERVAIN]

ver·be·na·ceous (vûr′bə nā′shəs), *adj.* belonging to the *Verbenaceae,* or verbena family of plants, comprising also the lantana, teak, etc.

ver·bi·age (vûr′bē ij), *n.* **1.** overabundance or superfluity of words. **2.** a manner or style of verbal expression. [< F < MF *verbi(er)* (to) gabble (< L *verbium* wording) + *-age* -AGE]

ver·bid (vûr′bid), *Gram.* —*n.* **1.** a nonfinite verb form; a verbal; an infinitive, participle, or gerund. —*adj.* **2.** of or pertaining to a verbid.

ver·bi·fy (vûr′bə fī′), *v.t.,* **-fied, -fy·ing.** to change into or employ as a verb. —**verb′i·fi·ca′tion,** *n.*

ver·bose (vər bōs′), *adj.* expressed in or characterized by the use of many or too many words; wordy. [< L *verbōs(us).* See VERB, -OSE¹] —**ver·bose′ly,** *adv.* —**ver·bos·i·ty** (vər bos′i tē), **ver·bose′ness,** *n.* —**Syn.** prolix; turgid, bombastic; talkative, loquacious. —**Ant.** laconic.

ver·bo·ten (fəʀ bōt′ᵊn; *Eng.* vər bōt′ᵊn), *adj. German.* forbidden, as by law; prohibited.

verb′ phrase′, *Gram.* a phrase in which a verb is accompanied by an auxiliary verb or verbs (as *shall have gone* in *We shall have gone*) or is combined with an adverb (as *make up* in *They make up the deficit*).

ver·bum sap (vûr′bəm sap′), a word to the wise is sufficient. Also, **verb. sap.** (vûrb′ sap′), **ver·bum sat** (vûr′bəm sat′). [short for L *verbum sapienti sat est*]

Ver·cel·li (veʀ chel′lē), *n.* a city in NW Italy, W of Milan. 51,136 (1961).

Ver·cin·get·o·rix (vûr′sin jet′ə riks, -get′-), *n.* died 45? B.C., Gallic chieftain conquered by Caesar.

Ver·dan·di (ver′dan dē), *n. Scand. Myth.* a Norn personifying the present. Cf. **Skuld, Urd.** [< Icel *verthandi,* prp. of *vertha* to become; see WORTH²]

ver·dant (vûr′dᵊnt), *adj.* **1.** green with vegetation. **2.** of the color green: *a verdant coat.* **3.** inexperienced; unsophisticated. [VERD(URE) + -ANT] —**ver′dan·cy,** *n.* —**ver′dant·ly,** *adv.*

verd′ antique′ (vûrd), **1.** a green, mottled or impure serpentine, sold as a marble and much used for decorative purposes. **2.** any of various similar green stones. Also, **verde′ antique′.** [< F < It *verde antico* green of old. See VERDURE, ANTIQUE]

Verde (vûrd), *n.* **Cape,** a cape in Senegal, near Dakar: the westernmost point of Africa.

ver·der·er (vûr′dər ər), *n. Eng. Forest Law.* a judicial officer in the royal forests. Also, **ver′de·ror.** [< AF *verderer* = *verder* (< L *viridārium* garden: *virid(is)* green + *-ārium* -ER²) + *-er* -ER¹]

Ver·di (vâr′dē; *It.* veʀ′de), *n.* **Giu·sep·pe** (jo͞o zep′pe), 1813–1901, Italian operatic composer.

ver·dict (vûr′dikt), *n.* **1.** *Law.* the finding or answer of a jury concerning a matter submitted to their judgment. **2.** any judgment or decision. [ME < ML *vērdict(um),* var. of *vērēdictum,* lit., something said truly; r. ME *verdit* < AF < L *vērum dictum* true word]

ver·di·gris (vûr′də grēs′, -gris), *n.* a green or bluish patina formed on copper, brass, or bronze surfaces, consisting principally of basic copper sulfate. [< MF *ver(t) de gris;* r. ME *ver(t) de Gres* < AF, OF *ver(t) de Grece* green of Greece] —**ver′di·gris′y,** *adj.*

ver·din (vûr′din), *n.* a small, yellow-headed titmouse, *Auriparus flaviceps,* of arid regions of the southwestern U.S. and Mexico, that builds a compact, spherical nest of thorny twigs. [< F *verdin* yellowhammer]

Ver·dun (vâr dun′, vûr-; *Fr.* veʀ dœN′), *n.* **1.** a fortress city in NE France, on the Meuse River: battle, 1916. 25,238 (1962). **2.** a city in S Quebec, in SE Canada. 78,317 (1961).

ver·dure (vûr′jər), *n.* **1.** green vegetation, esp. grass or herbage. **2.** greenness, esp. of fresh, flourishing vegetation. **3.** freshness in general; flourishing condition; vigor. [late ME < MF = *verd* green (see VERT) + *-ure* -URE] —**ver′dured,** *adj.*

ver·dur·ous (vûr′jər əs), *adj.* rich in or consisting of verdure; verdant.

ver·e·cund (ver′ə kund′), *adj. Archaic.* bashful; modest. [< L *verēcund(us)* = *verē(rī)* (to) fear + *-cundus* adj. suffix]

Ve·ree·ni·ging (fə rē′ni kiŋ), *n.* a city in the E Republic of South Africa, S of Johannesburg. 74,574 (1960).

verge¹ (vûrj), *n., v.,* **verged, verg·ing.** —*n.* **1.** the edge or border of something: *the verge of a desert.* **2.** the limit or point beyond which something begins or occurs; brink: *on the verge of a nervous breakdown.* **3.** a limiting belt, strip, or border of something. **4.** a rod, wand, or staff, esp. one carried as an emblem of authority. **5.** *Print.* a triggerlike device for releasing the matrices of a Linotype machine. **6.** *Horol.* **a.** a palletlike lever formerly used in inexpensive pendulum clocks. **b.** See under **verge escapement.** **7.** *Obs.* a stick or wand held in the hand of a person swearing fealty to the lord on being admitted as a tenant. —*v.i.* **8.** to be on the verge or border: *The situation verged on disaster. Our property verges on theirs.* —*v.t.* **9.** to serve as the verge or border of. [late ME < MF < L *virga* rod] —**Syn. 1.** brim, lip, brink.

verge² (vûrj), *v.i.,* **verged, verg·ing.** **1.** to incline; tend (usually fol. by *to* or *toward*): *The economy verges toward inflation.* **2.** to slope or sink. [< L *verge(re)* to turn, bend, be inclined]

verge·board (vûrj′bōrd′, -bôrd′), *n.* bargeboard.

verge′ escape′ment, a clock escapement, formerly in use, having pallets fixed to a vertically mounted, horizontally oscillating rod **(verge).**

ver·ger (vûr′jər), *n.* **1.** *Chiefly Brit.* a church official who serves as sacristan, caretaker, usher, and general attendant. **2.** *Brit.* an official who carries the verge or other symbol of office before a bishop, dean, or other dignitary. [late ME]

Ver·gil (vûr′jil), *n.* (*Publius Vergilius Maro*) 70–19 B.C., Roman poet: author of the *Aeneid,* an epic poem recounting the adventure of Aeneas after the fall of Troy. Also, **Virgil.** —**Ver·gil·i·an** (vər jil′ē ən, -jil′yən), *adj.*

ver·glas (ver glä′), *n., pl.* **-glases** (-glä′, -gläz′). glaze (def. 14). [< F, MF; OF *verre-glaz,* lit., glass-ice = *verre* glass (< L *vitrum*) + *glaz* ice (< LL *glacia* ice; see GLACIAL)]

ve·rid·i·cal (və rid′i kəl), *adj.* **1.** truthful; veracious. **2.** corresponding to facts; actual; genuine. Also, **ve·rid′ic.** [< L *vēridic(us)* (*vēr(us)* true + *-i-* -I- + *-dicus* speaking) + -AL¹] —**ve·rid′i·cal′i·ty,** *n.* —**ve·rid′i·cal·ly,** *adv.*

ver·i·est (ver′ē ist), *adj.* **1.** utmost; most complete: *the veriest stupidity.* **2.** superlative of **very.**

ver·i·fi·ca·tion (ver′ə fə kā′shən), *n.* **1.** the act or process of verifying. **2.** the state of being verified. **3.** evidence that verifies something. **4.** a formal assertion of the truth of something. [< ML *vērificātiōn-* (s. of *vērificātiō*) = *vērificāt(us)* (ptp. of *vērificāre;* see VERIFY, -ATE¹) + *-iōn-* -ION] —**ver′i·fi·ca′tive, ver′i·fi·ca′to·ry,** *adj.*

ver·i·fy (ver′ə fī′), *v.t.,* **-fied, -fy·ing.** **1.** to prove the truth of; confirm. **2.** to ascertain the truth, authenticity, or correctness of. **3.** to act as ultimate proof or evidence of; serve to confirm. **4.** *Law.* to substantiate (an allegation or pleading) by oath. [ME *verifie(n)* < MF *verifier* < ML *vērificāre.* See VERIDICAL, -FY] —**ver′i·fi′a·bil′i·ty,** *n.* —**ver′i·fi′a·ble,** *adj.* —**ver′i·fi′er,** *n.*

ver·i·ly (ver′ə lē), *adv. Archaic.* in truth; really; indeed. [ME; see VERY, -LY]

ver·i·sim·i·lar (ver′i sim′ə lər), *adj.* having the appearance of truth; likely; probable: *a verisimilar tale.* [< L *vērīsimil(is)* (*vērī-,* gen. sing. of *vērus* true + *similis* like) + -AR¹] —**ver′i·sim′i·lar·ly,** *adv.*

ver·i·si·mil·i·tude (ver′i si mil′i to͞od′, -tyo͞od′), *n.* **1.** the appearance or semblance of truth; likelihood; probability. **2.** something, as a statement, having merely the appearance of truth. [< L *vērīsimilitūdō* = *vērī-* (gen. sing. of *vērus* true) + *similitūdō* SIMILITUDE]

ver·ism (vēr′iz əm, ver-), *n.* the theory that strict representation of truth and reality is essential to art and literature. [< L *vēr(us)* true + -ISM. Cf. It *verismo*] —**ver′ist,** *n., adj.* —**ve·ris′tic,** *adj.*

ver·i·ta·ble (ver′i tə bəl), *adj.* **1.** being truly or very much so; genuine or real: *a veritable triumph.* **2.** *Obs.* true, as a statement or tale. [late ME < AF, MF; see VERITY, -ABLE] —**ver′i·ta·ble·ness,** *n.* —**ver′i·ta·bly,** *adv.*

ver·i·ty (ver′i tē), *n., pl.* **-ties** for 2. **1.** the state or quality of being true. **2.** something that is true, as a principle, belief, or statement. [late ME < L *vēritās* = *vēr(us)* true + *-itās* -ITY]

ver·juice (vûr′jo͞os′), *n.* **1.** an acid liquor made from the sour juice of crab apples, unripe grapes, etc. **2.** sourness, as of temper, expression, etc. —*adj.* Also, **ver′juiced′.** **3.** of or pertaining to verjuice. **4.** sour in temper, expression, etc. [ME *verjuis* < MF *ver(t)jus* = *vert* green (< L *viridis*) + *jus* JUICE]

Ver·laine (veʀ len′), *n.* **Paul** (pôl), 1844–96, French poet.

Ver·meer (vər mēr′; *Du.* vəʀ mār′), *n.* **Jan** (yän), (*Jan van der Meer van Delft*), 1632–75, Dutch painter.

ver·meil (vûr′mil *or, esp. for 2,* vər mā′), *n.* **1.** vermilion red. **2.** metal, as silver or bronze, that has been gilded. —*adj.* **3.** of the color vermilion. [late ME < MF < LL *vermicul(us)* kermes (insect and dye), L little worm; see VERMI-, -CULE]

vermi-, a learned borrowing from Latin meaning "worm," used in the formation of compound words: *vermifuge.* [comb. form of L *vermis* worm]

ver·mi·cel·li (vûr′mi sel′ē, -chel′ē), *n.* a kind of pasta in the form of long, slender, solid threads, resembling spaghetti but thinner. Cf. **macaroni** (def. 1). [< It, pl. of *vermicello* little worm = *vermi-* VERMI- + *-cello* dim. suffix]

ver·mi·cide (vûr′mi sīd′), *n.* a substance or agent used to kill worms, esp. a drug used to kill parasitic intestinal worms. —**ver′mi·cid′al,** *adj.*

ver·mic·u·lar (vər mik′yə lər), *adj.* **1.** of, pertaining to, or done by worms. **2.** consisting of or characterized by sinuous or wavy outlines, tunnels, or markings resembling the form or tracks of a worm. [< ML *vermiculār(is)* = L *vermicul(us)* (see VERMI-, -CULE) + *-āris* -AR¹] —**ver·mic′u·lar·ly,** *adv.*

ver·mic·u·late (*v.* vər mik′yə lāt′; *adj.* vər mik′yə lit, -lāt′), *v.*, **-lat·ed, -lat·ing,** *adj.* —*v.t.* **1.** to work or ornament with vermicular markings. —*adj.* Also, **ver·mic·u·lat·ed** (vər mik′yə lā′tid). **2.** worm-eaten, or appearing as if worm-eaten. **3.** vermicular. [< L *vermiculāt(us)* (ptp. of *vermiculārī* to be worm-eaten)] —**ver·mic′u·la′tion,** *n.*

Vermiculation

ver·mic·u·lite (vər mik′yə-līt′), *n.* any of a group of platy minerals, hydrous silicates of aluminum, magnesium, and iron, that expand markedly on being heated: used in the expanded state for heat insulation. [VERMICUL(AR) + -ITE[1]]

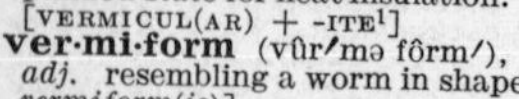

ver·mi·form (vûr′mə fôrm′), *adj.* resembling a worm in shape; long and slender. [< ML *vermiform(is)*]

ver′miform appen′dix, *Anat., Zool.* a narrow, blind tube protruding from the cecum, and situated in man in the lower right-hand part of the abdomen.

ver·mi·fuge (vûr′mə fyōōj′), *adj.* **1.** serving to expel worms or other animal parasites from the intestines, as a medicine. —*n.* **2.** a vermifuge medicine or agent.

ver·mil·ion (vər mil′yən), *n.* **1.** a brilliant scarlet red. **2.** a bright-red, water-insoluble pigment consisting of mercuric sulfide. Also, **ver·mil′lion.** [ME *vermilioun* < AF, MF *verm(e)illon* = *vermeil* VERMEIL + *-on* aug. suffix]

ver·min (vûr′min), *n., pl.* **ver·min.** (*usually construed as pl.*) **1.** noxious or objectionable animals or insects, esp. those of small size. **2.** objectionable or obnoxious persons. **3.** animals that prey upon game, as coyotes, weasels, etc. [ME *vermyne* < AF, MF *vermin(e)* < VL **verminum,* neut. of **verminus* wormy = L *vermi(s)* worm + *-nus* adj. suffix]

ver·mi·nate (vûr′mi nāt′), *v.i.,* **-nat·ed, -nat·ing. 1.** to be infested with vermin, esp. parasitic vermin. **2.** *Archaic.* to produce vermin. [< L *vermināt(us)* ptp. of *vermināre* to have worms] —**ver′mi·na′tion,** *n.*

ver·min·ous (vûr′mə nəs), *adj.* **1.** of the nature of or resembling vermin. **2.** of, pertaining to, or caused by vermin: *verminous diseases.* **3.** infested with vermin. [< L *verminōs(us)*] —**ver′min·ous·ly,** *adv.* —**ver′min·ous·ness,** *n.*

ver·mis (vûr′mis), *n., pl.* **-mes** (-mēz). *Anat.* the median lobe or division of the cerebellum. [< NL < L: worm]

Ver·mont (vər mont′), *n.* a state of the NE United States: a part of New England. 444,732 (1970); 9609 sq. mi. *Cap.:* Montpelier. *Abbr.:* Vt., VT —**Ver·mont′er,** *n.*

ver·mouth (vər mōōth′; *Fr.* ver mōōt′), *n.* an aromatized white wine in which herbs, roots, barks, bitters, and other flavorings have been steeped. [< F (now *vermout*) < G *Wermuth* (now *Wermut*) absinthe, WORMWOOD]

ver·nac·u·lar (vər nak′yə lər), *adj.* **1.** (of language) native or indigenous (opposed to *literary* or *learned*). **2.** of, pertaining to, or employing a vernacular language. **3.** employing the ordinary, everyday language of a people. **4.** noting or pertaining to the common name for an animal or plant. —*n.* **5.** the native speech or language of a place. **6.** the language or vocabulary peculiar to a class or profession. **7.** the ordinary, everyday language of a people: *a poem in the vernacular.* **8.** the common name of an animal or plant as distinguished from its Latin scientific name. [< L *vernācul(us)* native, lit., pertaining to a *verna* (slave born in master's house, native slave; see -CULE) + -AR[1]] —**ver·nac′u·lar·ly,** *adv.*

ver·nac·u·lar·ise (vər nak′yə lə rīz′), *v.t.,* **-ised, -is·ing.** *Chiefly Brit.* vernacularize. —**ver·nac′u·lar·i·sa′tion,** *n.*

ver·nac·u·lar·ism (vər nak′yə lə riz′əm), *n.* **1.** a vernacular word or expression. **2.** the use of the vernacular.

ver·nac·u·lar·ize (vər nak′yə lə rīz′), *v.t.,* **-ized, -iz·ing.** to translate into the vernacular. Also, *esp. Brit.,* **vernacularise.** —**ver·nac′u·lar·i·za′tion,** *n.*

ver·nal (vûr′nᵊl), *adj.* **1.** of, pertaining to, or occurring in spring. **2.** appropriate to or suggesting spring. **3.** youthful. [< L *vernāl(is)* = *vern(us)* of spring (*vēr* spring, c. Icel *vār,* + *-nus* adj. suffix) + *-ālis* -AL[1]] —**ver′nal·ly,** *adv.*

ver′nal e′quinox, 1. See under **equinox** (def. 1). **2.** Also called **ver′nal point′.** the position of the sun at the time of the vernal equinox.

ver·nal·ise (vûr′nᵊlīz′), *v.t.,* **-ized, -iz·ing.** *Chiefly Brit.* vernalize. —**ver′nal·i·sa′tion,** *n.*

ver·nal·ize (vûr′nᵊlīz′), *v.t.,* **-ized, -iz·ing.** to shorten the growth period before the blossoming and fruit or seed bearing of (a plant) by chilling its seed or bulb. —**ver′nal·i·za′tion,** *n.*

ver·na·tion (vər nā′shən), *n. Bot.* the arrangement of the foliage leaves within the bud. [< NL *vernātiōn-* (s. of *vernātiō*) = L *vernāt(us)* (ptp. of *vernāre* to be verdant; see VERNAL, -ATE[1]) + *-iōn-* -ION]

Verne (vûrn; *Fr.* vern), *n.* **Jules** (jōōlz; *Fr.* zhyl), 1828–1905, French novelist.

Ver·ner (vûr′nər; *Dan.* ver′nər), *n.* **Karl A·dolph** (kärl ä′dolf), 1846–96, Danish linguist.

Ver′ner's law′, *Linguistics.* the statement by K. Verner of a regularity behind some apparent exceptions in the Germanic languages to Grimm's law, namely, that Proto-Germanic, noninitial, voiceless fricatives became voiced when between voiced sounds if the immediately following vowel was accented in Proto-Indo-European.

ver·ni·er (vûr′nē ər), *n.* **1.** Also called **ver′nier scale′.** a small, movable, graduated scale running parallel to the fixed graduated scale of a sextant, or other graduated instrument, and used for measuring a fractional part of one of the divisions of the fixed scale. **2.** *Mach.* an auxiliary device for giving a piece of apparatus a higher adjustment accuracy. —*adj.* **3.** equipped with a vernier. [named after Pierre *Vernier* (1580–1637), French mathematician and inventor]

ver′nier cal′iper, a caliper formed of two pieces sliding across one another, one having a graduated scale and the other a vernier. Also called **ver′nier microm′eter.**

ver·nis·sage (vûr′ni säzh′; *Fr.* ver nē säzh′), *n.* **1.** the opening day of an art exhibit. **2.** the day before this, reserved for painters to varnish or touch up their paintings. [< F: lit., a varnishing, touching up (of paintings). See VARNISH, -AGE]

Ver·no·le·ninsk (*Russ.* ver′no le nēnsk′), *n.* former name of **Nikolaev.**

Ver·non (vûr′nən), *n.* **1. Edward** ("*Old Grog*"), 1684–1757, British admiral. **2.** a city in N Connecticut. 27,237 (1970).

Ve·ro·na (və rō′nə; *It.* ve rô′nä), *n.* a city in N Italy, on the Adige River. 221,138 (1961).

Ver·o·nal (ver′ə nᵊl), *n. Pharm., Trademark.* barbital.

Ve·ro·ne·se (ve′rô ne′ze), *n.* **Pa·o·lo** (pä′ô lô), (*Paolo Cagliari*), 1528–88, Venetian painter.

Ver·o·nese (ver′ə nēz′, -nēs′), *adj., n., pl.* **-nese.** —*adj.* **1.** of or pertaining to the city or town of Verona. —*n.* **2.** a native or inhabitant of Verona.

ve·ron·i·ca[1] (və ron′ə kə), *n.* **1.** any scrophulariaceous plant of the genus *Veronica,* as the speedwell. **2.** (*sometimes cap.*) *Eccles.* **a.** a handkerchief said to have been given to Christ, while on the way to Calvary, by St. Veronica, and to have borne the image of His face thereafter. **b.** any handkerchief, veil, or cloth bearing a representation of the face of Christ. [< ML, appar. named after St. *Veronica* (but cf. MGk plant name *berenīkion* = *Berenīk(ē)* proper name + *-ion* dim. suffix)]

ve·ron·i·ca[2] (və ron′ə kə), *n.* (in bullfighting) a pass in which the matador stands still while slowly swinging the open cape away from the charging bull. [special use of *Veronica* girl's name]

Ve·ron·i·ca (və ron′ə kə), *n.* **Saint,** a woman of Jerusalem, who wiped the brow of Christ as He carried His cross to Calvary.

Ver·ra·za·no (ver′ə zä′nō; *It.* ver′rä tsä′nô), *n.* **Gio·van·ni da** (jô vän′nē dä), c1480–1527?, Italian navigator and explorer. Also, **Ver·raz·za·no** (ver′rät tsä′nô), **Ver·ra·za·ni** (ver′rä tsä′nē).

Ver·roc·chio (və rō′kē ō′; *It.* ver rôk′kyô), *n.* **An·dre·a del** (än dre′ä del), 1435–88, Italian goldsmith, sculptor, and painter.

ver·ru·ca (və rōō′kə, ve-), *n., pl.* **-cae** (-sē). **1.** *Med.* a wart. **2.** *Zool.* a small, flattish, wartlike prominence. [< L]

ver·ru·cose (ver′ə kōs′), *adj.* studded with wartlike excrescences or elevations. [VERRUC(A) + -OSE[1]]

ver·ru·cous (ver′ə kəs), *adj.* of, pertaining to, marked by, or like a wart or warts. [var. of VERRUCOSE; see -OUS]

Ver·sailles (ver sī′, -sālz′; *Fr.* ver sä′yᵊ), *n.* a city in N France, about 12 mi. SW of Paris: palace of the French kings; peace treaty between the Allies and Germany 1919. 95,149 (1962).

ver·sant (vûr′sənt), *n.* **1.** a slope of a mountain or mountain chain. **2.** the general slope of a country or region. [< F, n. use of prp. of *verser* to turn < L *versāre.* See REVERSE, -ANT]

ver·sa·tile (vûr′sə til *or, esp. Brit.,* -tīl′), *adj.* **1.** capable of or adapted for turning easily from one to another of various tasks, fields of endeavor, etc. **2.** having or capable of many uses or applications: *a versatile new plastic.* **3.** *Bot.* attached at or near the middle so as to swing freely, as an anther. **4.** *Zool.* turning either forward or backward: *a versatile toe.* [< L *versātilis* revolving, many-sided = *versāt(us)* (ptp. of *versāre,* freq. of *vertere* to turn; see REVERSE, -ATE[1]) + *-ilis* -ILE] —**ver′sa·tile·ly,** *adv.* —**ver′sa·til′i·ty,** *n.* —**Syn. 1, 2.** adaptable.

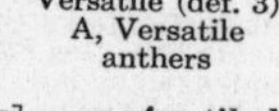

Versatile (def. 3)
A, Versatile anthers

vers de so·cié·té (ver də sô syā tā′; *Eng.* vər′ di sō′sē i tā′), *French.* humorous light verse dealing with fashions and foibles of the time.

verse (vûrs), *n., adj., v.,* **versed, vers·ing.** —*n.* **1.** (not in technical use) a stanza. **2.** a succession of metrical feet written, printed, or orally composed as one line; one of the lines of a poem. **3.** a particular type of metrical line: *a hexameter verse.* **4.** a poem or a piece of poetry. **5.** metrical composition; poetry, esp. as involving metrical form. **6.** a particular type of poetry: *elegiac verse.* **7.** a short division of a chapter in the Bible, usually consisting of one sentence or part of a long sentence. **8.** *Music.* **a.** the part of a song that follows the introduction and precedes the chorus. **b.** a part of a song designed to be sung by a solo voice. —*adj.* **9.** of, pertaining to, or written in verse. —*v.t.* **10.** to express in verse. —*v.i.* **11.** *Rare.* to versify. [ME, OE *vers* < L *versus* a row, line (of poetry), lit., a turning = *vers-* (ptp. s. of *vertere* to turn) + *-us* n. suffix (4th decl.)]
—**Syn. 1, 2.** VERSE, STANZA, STROPHE, STAVE are terms for a metrical grouping in poetic composition. VERSE is often mistakenly used for STANZA, but is properly only a single metrical line. A STANZA is a succession of lines (verses) commonly bound together by a rhyme scheme, and usually forming one of a series of similar groups which constitute a poem. STROPHE (originally the section of a Greek choral ode sung while the chorus was moving from right to left) is in English poetry practically equivalent to "section"; a STROPHE may be unrhymed or without strict form, but may be a stanza: *Strophes are divisions of odes.* A STAVE is a stanza set to music: *a stave of a hymn.*

versed (vûrst), *adj.* experienced or practiced; skilled; learned (usually fol. by *in*): *to be versed in Greek and Latin.* [< L *versāt(us)* busied, engaged (see VERSATILE), with -ED[2] for L *-ātus*]

versed′ sine′, *Trig.* one minus the cosine of a given angle or arc.

ver·si·cle (vûr′si kəl), *n.* **1.** a little verse. **2.** *Eccles.* one of a series of short sentences, or parts of sentences, usually from the Psalms, said or sung by the officiant, as distinguished from the response of the choir or congregation. Cf. **response** (def. 3a). [late ME < L *versicul(us).* See VERSE, -I-, -CLE]

ver·si·col·or (vûr′si kul′ər), *adj.* **1.** changeable in color. **2.** of various colors; parti-colored. Also, *esp. Brit.,* **ver′si·col′our.** [< L; see REVERSE, -I-, COLOR]

ver·si·fi·ca·tion (vûr′sə fə kā′shən), *n.* **1.** the act or art of versifying. **2.** verse form; metrical structure. **3.** a metrical version of something. [< L *versificātiōn-* (s. of *versificātiō*) = *versificāt(us)* (ptp. of *versificāre* to VERSIFY; see -ATE[1]) + *-iōn-* -ION]

ver·si·fy (vûr′sə fī′), *v.,* **-fied, -fy·ing.** —*v.t.* **1.** to put into verse. —*v.i.* **2.** to compose verses. [late ME *versifie(n)* < OF *versifier* < L *versificāre.* See VERSE, -IFY] **—ver′si·fi′er,** *n.*

ver·sion (vûr′zhən, -shən), *n.* **1.** a personal or particular account of something, possibly inaccurate or biased. **2.** a particular form or variety of something: *a modern version of an antique lamp.* **3.** a translation. **4.** *Med.* the act of turning a child in the uterus so as to bring it into a more favorable position for delivery. **5.** *Pathol.* an abnormal direction of the axis of the uterus or other organ. [< L *versiōn-* (s. of *versiō* a turning) = *vers(us)* (ptp. of *vertere* to turn) + *-iōn-* -ION] **—ver′sion·al,** *adj.*

vers li·bre (VER lē′BRᵊ), *French.* See **free verse.**

ver·so (vûr′sō), *n., pl.* **-sos.** *Print.* a left-hand page of a book or manuscript (opposed to *recto*). [short for L *versō foliō* on the turned leaf]

verst (vûrst, verst), *n.* a Russian measure of distance equivalent to 3500 feet or 0.6629 miles or 1.067 kilometers. Also, **verste.** [< Russ *versta* (in part through F *verste* and G *Werst*) line, linear measure; akin to VERSE]

ver·sus (vûr′səs), *prep.* **1.** against (used esp. to join the names of parties in a legal case or in any contest): *Regina versus Wilde; Army versus Navy.* **2.** as compared to; in contrast with: *traveling by plane versus traveling by train. Abbr.:* v., vs. [< L: towards, i.e., turned so as to face (something), opposite, over against; see VERSE]

vert (vûrt), *n.* **1.** *Eng. Forest Law.* **a.** vegetation bearing green leaves in a forest and capable of serving as a cover for deer. **b.** the right to cut such trees or shrubs. **2.** *Heraldry.* the tincture or color green. **—***adj.* **3.** *Heraldry.* of the tincture, or color, green: *a lion vert.* [ME *verte* < AF, MF *vert, verd* < L *viridis* green = *vir-* (root of *virēre* to be green) + *-idis* adj. suffix]

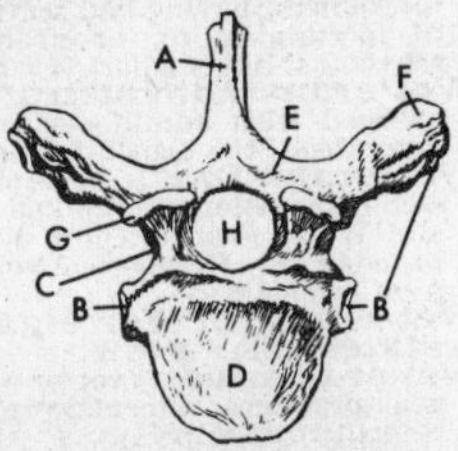

Vertebra
A, Spinous process; B, Facet of rib; C, Pedicel; D, Body; E, Lamina; F, Transverse process; G, Articular process; H, Spinal canal

vert., vertical.

vertebr-, a combining form of **vertebra:** *vertebral.*

ver·te·bra (vûr′tə brə), *n., pl.* **-brae** (-brē′), **-bras.** *Anat., Zool.* any of the bones or segments composing the spinal column, in man and higher animals consisting typically of a cylindrical body and an arch with various processes, forming a foramen through which the spinal cord passes. [< L: (spinal) joint = *verte(re)* (to) turn + *-bra* n. suffix]

ver·te·bral (vûr′tə brəl), *adj.* **1.** of or pertaining to a vertebra or the vertebrae; spinal. **2.** resembling a vertebra. **3.** composed of or having vertebrae. **—ver′te·bral·ly,** *adv.*

ver′tebral col′umn. See **spinal column.**

Ver·te·bra·ta (ver′tə brā′tə, -brä′-), *n.* the subphylum comprising the vertebrate animals. [NL; neut. pl. of *vertebrāt(us)* VERTEBRATE]

ver·te·brate (vûr′tə brāt′, -brit), *adj.* **1.** having vertebrae; having a backbone or spinal column. **2.** belonging or pertaining to the *Vertebrata* (or *Craniata*), a subphylum of chordate animals, comprising those having a brain enclosed in a skull or cranium and a segmented spinal column, including mammals, birds, reptiles, amphibians, and fishes. **—***n.* **3.** a vertebrate animal. [< L *vertebrāt(us)* jointed]

ver·te·bra·tion (vûr′tə brā′shən), *n.* vertebrate formation.

ver·tex (vûr′teks), *n., pl.* **-tex·es, -ti·ces** (-ti sēz′). **1.** the highest point of something; apex. **2.** *Anat., Zool.* the crown or top of the head. **3.** *Math.* **a.** the point farthest from the base. **b.** a point in a geometrical solid common to three or more sides. **c.** the intersection of two sides of a plane figure. [< L: a whirl, top (of the head) < *vert(ere)* (to) turn]

ver·ti·cal (vûr′ti kəl), *adj.* **1.** being in a position or direction perpendicular to the plane of the horizon; upright; plumb. **2.** of, pertaining to, or situated at a vertex. **3.** *Bot.* **a.** (of a leaf) having the blade in a perpendicular plane, so that neither of the surfaces can be called upper or lower. **b.** being in the same direction as the axis; lengthwise. **4.** *Econ.* of or pertaining to the consolidation of businesses or industries that are closely related in the manufacture or sale of a certain commodity. **—***n.* **5.** something that is vertical. **6.** the vertical or upright position. [< L *verticāl(is)* = *vertic-* (s. of *vertex*) VERTEX + *-ālis* -AL[1]] **—ver′ti·cal′i·ty, ver′ti·cal·ness,** *n.* **—ver′ti·cal·ly,** *adv.* **—Syn. 1.** See **upright. —Ant. 1.** horizontal.

ver′tical cir′cle, *Astron.* a great circle on the celestial sphere passing through the zenith.

ver′tical file′, 1. a collection of pamphlets, folders, and other printed materials stored upright, as in a filing cabinet. **2.** a cabinet for this.

ver′tical mobil′ity, *Sociol.* **1.** movement from one social level to a higher one **(upward mobility)** or a lower one **(downward mobility),** as by changing jobs, marrying, etc. **2.** cultural diffusion from one social level to another, as the adoption by one economic class of the fashions or mores of another class. Cf. **horizontal mobility.**

ver′tical sta′bilizer, *Aeron.* the fixed vertical surface of an aircraft empennage, to which the rudder is hinged. Also called **fin.**

ver′tical un′ion. See **industrial union.**

ver·ti·ces (vûr′ti sēz′), *n.* a pl. of **vertex.**

ver·ti·cil (vûr′ti sil), *n. Bot., Zool.* a whorl or circle, as of leaves, hairs, etc., arranged around a point on an axis. [< L *verticill(us)* = *vertic-* (s. of *vertex*) VERTEX + *-illus* dim. suffix]

Verticils

ver·ti·cil·las·ter (vûr′ti si las′tər), *n. Bot.* an inflorescence in which the flowers are arranged in a seeming whorl, consisting in fact of a pair of opposite axillary, usually sessile, cymes, as in many mints. [< L *verticill(us)* VERTICIL + -ASTER[1]] **—ver·ti·cil·las·trate** (vûr′ti si las′trāt, -trit), *adj.*

ver·tic·il·late (vər tis′ə lit, -lāt′, vûr′ti sil′āt), *adj. Bot., Zool.* **1.** disposed in or forming verticils or whorls, as flowers, hairs, etc. **2.** having flowers, hairs, etc., so arranged or disposed. Also, **ver·tic′il·lat′ed.** [< L *verticill(us)* VERTICIL + -ATE[1]] **—ver·tic′il·la′tion,** *n.*

ver·tig·i·nous (vər tij′ə nəs), *adj.* **1.** whirling or spinning; rotary: *the vertiginous action of a top.* **2.** affected with vertigo; dizzy. **3.** liable or threatening to cause vertigo: *a vertiginous staircase.* [< L *vertīginōs(us)* dizzy = *vertīgin-* (s. of *vertīgō*) VERTIGO + *-ōsus* -OUS] **—ver·tig′i·nous·ly,** *adv.* **—ver·tig′i·nous·ness,** *n.*

ver·ti·go (vûr′tə gō′), *n., pl.* **ver·ti·goes, ver·tig·i·nes** (vər tij′ə nēz′). *Pathol.* a disordered condition in which a person feels that he or his surroundings are whirling about. [< L: a turning or whirling around = *vert(ere)* (to) turn = *-īgō* (gen. *-īginis*) n. suffix]

ver·tu (vər to͞o′, vûr′to͞o), *n.* virtu.

Ver·tum·nus (vər tum′nəs), *n.* the ancient Roman god of gardens, orchards, and the changing seasons. Also, **Vortumnus.** [< L = *vert(ere)* (to) turn, change + *-umnus* n. suffix (< Etruscan)]

ver·vain (vûr′vān), *n.* any plant of the genus *Verbena,* having elongated or flattened spikes of sessile flowers. [late ME *vervaine* < AF, MF *verveine* < L *verbēna* holy bough carried by priests]

verve (vûrv), *n.* **1.** vivacity or liveliness; animation. **2.** *Archaic.* talent. [< F: enthusiasm, fancy < L *verba* mere words, talk, pl. of *verbum* word; see VERB]

ver·vet (vûr′vit), *n.* an African monkey, *Cercopithecus aethiops pygerythrus,* allied to the green monkey and the grivet, but distinguished by a rusty patch at the root of the tail. [< F = *ver(t)* green (see VERT) + *(gri)vet* GRIVET]

Ver·woerd (fər vo͝ort′), *n.* **Hen·drik Frensch** (hen′dRik fRens), 1901–1966, South African political leader, born in the Netherlands: prime minister 1958–1966.

ver·y (ver′ē), *adv., adj.,* **ver·i·er, ver·i·est. —***adv.* **1.** in a high degree: *It is very gracious of you to do this.* **2.** (used as an intensive emphasizing superlatives or stressing identity or oppositeness): *the very best thing to be done; in the very same place as before.* **—***adj.* **3.** precise; particular: *That is the very item we have been looking for.* **4.** mere: *The very thought of it is distressing.* **5.** sheer; utter: *She wept from the very joy of knowing he was safe.* **6.** actual: *He was caught in the very act of stealing.* **7.** being such in the extreme: *the very heart of the matter.* **8.** true; genuine: *a very fool.* **9.** *Obs.* rightful or legitimate. [ME < AF, OF *verai* (*vrai*) < VL **vērācus,* alter. of L *vērax* truthful = *vēr(us)* true (c. OE *wǣr,* G *wahr* true, correct) + *-āc-, -ax* adj. suffix]

ver′y high′ fre′quency, any frequency ranging from 30 to 300 megacycles. *Abbr.:* VHF **—ver′y-high′-fre′quen·cy,** *adj.*

Ver′y lights′ (ver′ē), colored signal flares, fired from a special pistol **(Ver′y pis′tol).** [named after E. W. *Very* (1847–1907), American inventor]

ver′y low′ fre′quency, *Radio.* any frequency between 10 and 30 kilocycles per second. *Abbr.:* VLF

Ve·sa·li·us (vi sā′lē əs), *n.* **An·dre·as** (än dRe′äs), 1514–1564, Flemish anatomist.

ve·si·ca (və sī′kə), *n., pl.* **-cae** (-sē). *Anat.* a bladder. [< L: bladder, blister]

ves·i·cal (ves′i kəl), *adj.* **1.** of or pertaining to a vesica or bladder, esp. the urinary bladder. **2.** resembling a bladder; elliptical. [< ML *vēsīcāl(is).* See VESICA, -AL[1]]

ves·i·cant (ves′ə kənt), *adj.* **1.** producing a blister or blisters, as a medicinal substance; vesicating. **—***n.* **2.** a vesicant agent or substance. [< NL *vēsīcant-* (s. of *vēsīcāns,* prp. of *vēsīcāre* to VESICATE); see -ANT]

ves·i·cate (ves′ə kāt′), *v.t.,* **-cat·ed, -cat·ing.** to raise vesicles or blisters on; blister. [< NL *vēsīcāt(us)* (ptp. of *vēsīcāre* to blister) = *vēsīc-* (see VESICA) + *-ātus* -ATE[1]] **—ves′i·ca′tion,** *n.*

ves·i·ca·to·ry (ves′ə kə tōr′ē, -tôr′ē, və sik′ə-), *adj., n., pl.* **-ries.** vesicant. [< NL *vēsīcātōri(us).* See VESICATE, -ORY[1]]

ves·i·cle (ves′i kəl), *n.* **1.** a small sac or cyst. **2.** *Anat., Zool.* a small bladderlike cavity, esp. one filled with fluid. **3.** *Pathol.* a circumscribed elevation of the epidermis containing serous fluid; blister. **4.** *Bot.* a small bladder or bladderlike air cavity. **5.** *Geol.* a small, usually spherical cavity in a rock or mineral, due to gas or vapor. [< L *vēsīcula* little bladder. See VESICA, -ULE]

ve·sic·u·lar (və sik′yə lər), *adj.* **1.** of or pertaining to a vesicle or vesicles. **2.** having the form of a vesicle. **3.** characterized by or consisting of vesicles. [< NL *vēsīculār(is)* = L *vēsīcul(a)* VESICLE + *-āris* -AR[1]] **—ve·sic′u·lar·ly,** *adv.*

ve·sic·u·late (*adj.* və sik′yə lit, -lāt′; *v.* və sik′yə lāt′), *adj., v.,* **-lat·ed, -lat·ing. —***adj.* **1.** characterized by or covered with vesicles. **2.** of the nature of a vesicle. **—***v.t., v.i.* **3.** to make or become vesicular. [< NL *vēsīculāt(us)* = L *vēsīcul(a)* VESICLE + *-ātus* -ATE[1]] **—ve·sic′u·la′tion,** *n.*

Ves·pa·si·an (ve spā′zhē ən, -zhən), *n.* (*Titus Flavius Sabinus Vespasianus*) A.D. 9–79, Roman emperor 70–79.

ves·per (ves′pər), *n.* **1.** (*cap.*) the evening star, esp. Venus; Hesperus. **2.** Also called **ves′per bell′.** a bell rung at evening. **3. vespers,** (*sometimes cap.*) *Eccles.* **a.** a religious service in the late afternoon or the evening; the sixth of the seven canonical hours. **b.** evensong. **c.** *Rom. Cath. Ch.* a part of the office to be said in the afternoon or evening. **4.** *Archaic.* evening. **—***adj.* **5.** of or pertaining to vespers. [late ME < L: evening (star); c. Gk *hésperos;* akin to WEST]

ves·per·al (ves′pər əl), *n. Eccles.* **1.** the part of an antiphonary containing the chants for vespers. **2.** a cloth used between offices to cover the altar cloth. [< LL *vesperāl(is)*]

ves·per·tide (ves′pər tīd′), *n.* the period of vespers; evening.

ves·per·tine (ves′pər tin, -tīn′), *adj.* **1.** of, pertaining to, or occurring in the evening: *vespertine stillness.* **2.** *Bot.* opening or expanding in the evening, as certain flowers. **3.** *Zool.* appearing or flying in the early evening; crepuscular. Also, **ves·per·ti·nal** (ves′pər tīn′ᵊl). [< L *vespertīn(us)* = *vesper* VESPER + formative *-t-* + *-īnus* -INE[1]]

ves·pi·ar·y (ves′pē er′ē), *n., pl.* **-ar·ies.** a nest of social wasps. [< L *vesp(a)* WASP + (AP)IARY]

ves·pid (ves′pid), *n.* **1.** any of numerous hymenopterous insects of the family *Vespidae*, comprising social and solitary wasps, as the yellowjackets and hornets. —*adj.* **2.** belonging or pertaining to the family *Vespidae*. [< NL *Vespid(ae)* = L *vesp(a)* WASP + *-idae* -ID²]

ves·pine (ves′pīn, -pin), *adj.* **1.** of or pertaining to a wasp or wasps. **2.** resembling a wasp. [< L *vesp(a)* WASP + -INE¹]

Ves·puc·ci (ve spo͞o′chē, -spyo͞o′-; *It.* ves po͞ot′chē), *n.* **A·me·ri·go** (ə mer′ə gō′; *It.* ä′me ʀē′gō), (*Americus Vespucius*), 1451–1512, Italian merchant, adventurer, and explorer after whom America was named.

ves·sel (ves′əl), *n.* **1.** a craft for traveling on water, esp. a fairly large one, having a hull or hulls. **2.** a hollow utensil used esp. for holding liquids. **3.** *Anat., Zool.* a tube or duct, as an artery or vein, containing or conveying blood or some other body fluid. **4.** *Bot.* a duct formed in the xylem, composed of connected cells that have lost their intervening partitions, for conducting water and mineral nutrients. Cf. **tracheid. 5.** a person regarded as a holder or receiver of a particular trait or quality: *a vessel of wrath.* [ME < AF, OF *vessel, va(i)ssel* < L *vascell(um)* = *vas* (see VASE) + *-cellum* dim. suffix] —**ves′seled;** *esp. Brit.,* **ves′selled,** *adj.*

vest (vest), *n.* **1.** a close-fitting, waist-length, sleeveless garment for men, designed to be worn under a jacket. **2.** a similar garment, or the simulation of the front of such a garment, worn by women. Cf. **dickey** (def. 2), **vestee. 3.** *Brit.* an undervest or undershirt. —*v.t.* **4.** to clothe; dress; robe. **5.** to place or settle in the possession or control of a person or persons (usually fol. by *in*): *to vest authority in a new official.* **6.** to invest or endow with something, esp. with powers or functions: *to vest a committee with power to contract debts.* —*v.i.* **7.** to put on vestments. **8.** to become vested in a person or persons, as a right. **9.** to devolve upon a person as his possession. [(n.) < It *veste* robe, dress < L *vestis* garment; (v.) < MF *vest(ir)* < L *vestīre* to clothe]

Ves·ta (ves′tə), *n.* the ancient Roman goddess of the hearth: identified with the Greek Hestia. [akin to Gk *hestía* hearth, household]

ves·tal (ves′tᵊl), *adj.* **1.** of or pertaining to the goddess Vesta. **2.** of, pertaining to, or characteristic of a vestal virgin; chaste; pure. —*n.* **3.** See **vestal virgin. 4.** a chaste unmarried woman; virgin. [< L *vestāl(is)*]

ves′tal vir′gin, (in ancient Rome) one of the virgins consecrated to Vesta and to the service of tending the sacred fire kept burning in the temple where she was worshiped.

vest·ed (ves′tid), *adj.* **1.** held completely, permanently, and inalienably: *vested rights.* **2.** protected or established, as by law or by right. **3.** clothed or robed, esp. in ecclesiastical vestments: *a vested priest.*

vest′ed in′terest, 1. a special interest in an existing system, arrangement, or institution for particular personal reasons. **2.** a permanent right given to an employee under a pension plan. **3. vested interests,** the persons, groups, etc., who dominate the business or financial activities of a nation.

vest·ee (ves tē′), *n.* a decorative front piece worn under a woman's jacket or blouse. Cf. **dickey** (def. 2), **vest** (def. 2). [VEST (n.) + *-ee* dim. suffix]

ves·ti·ar·y (ves′tē er′ē), *adj.* of garments or vestments. [ME *vestiarie* < ML *vestiāri(us).* See VEST (n.), -ARY]

ves·ti·bule (ves′tə byo͞ol′), *n., v.,* **-buled, -bul·ing.** —*n.* **1.** a passage, hall, or antechamber between the outer door and the interior parts of a house or building. **2.** *Railroads.* an enclosed entrance at the end of a passenger car. **3.** *Anat., Zool.* any of various cavities or hollows regarded as forming an approach or entrance to another cavity or space, as that of the internal ear. —*v.t.* **4.** to provide with a vestibule or vestibules. [< L *vestibul(um)* forecourt, entrance]

ves·tige (ves′tij), *n.* **1.** a mark, trace, or visible evidence of something that is no longer present or in existence. **2.** *Biol.* a degenerate or imperfectly developed organ or structure having little or no utility, but which in an earlier stage of the individual or in preceding organisms performed a useful function. **3.** *Archaic.* a footprint; track. [< F < L *vestīgium* footprint]

ves·tig·i·al (ve stij′ē əl), *adj.* of, pertaining to, or of the nature of a vestige: *a vestigial tail.* [VESTIGI(UM) + -AL¹] —**ves·tig′i·al·ly,** *adv.*

ves·tig·i·um (ve stij′ē əm), *n., pl.* **ves·tig·i·a** (ve stij′ē ə). *Anat.* a vestigial structure of any kind; vestige. [< L: footprint, trace]

vest·ing (vest′ing), *n.* the granting to an eligible employee of the right to specified pension benefits, regardless of discontinued employment status, usually after a fixed period of employment.

vest·ment (vest′mənt), *n.* **1.** a garment, esp. an outer garment. **2. vestments,** *Chiefly Literary.* attire; clothing. **3.** an official or ceremonial robe. **4.** *Eccles.* one of the garments worn by the clergy and their assistants, choristers, etc., during divine service and on other occasions. [syncopated var. of ME *vestiment* < ML *vestīment(um)* priestly robe, L: garment. See VEST (n.), -MENT] —**vest′ment·al,** *adj.* —**vest′ment·ed,** *adj.*

vest-pock·et (vest′pok′it), *adj.* **1.** designed to be carried in, or as in, the pocket of the vest: *a vest-pocket dictionary.* **2.** contained in a small space; miniature: *a vest-pocket park.*

ves·try (ves′trē), *n., pl.* **-tries. 1.** a room in or a building attached to a church, in which the vestments, and sometimes liturgical objects, are kept; sacristy. **2.** (in some churches) a room in or a building attached to a church, used as a chapel, for prayer meetings, for the Sunday school, etc. **3.** *Prot. Episc. Ch.* a committee serving with the churchwardens in managing the temporal affairs of the church. **4.** *Ch. of Eng.* a meeting of parishioners or of a committee of parishioners to discuss official business. [late ME *vestrie, vestrye.* See VEST (v.), -ERY] —**ves′tral,** *adj.*

ves·try·man (ves′trē mən), *n., pl.* **-men.** a member of a church vestry.

ves·ture (ves′chər), *n., v.,* **-tured, -tur·ing.** *Archaic.* —*n.* **1.** clothing; garments. **2.** something that covers like a garment; covering. —*v.t.* **3.** to clothe or cover. [late ME < AF; OF *vest(e)ure* < VL **vestītūra* = L *vestīt(us)* (ptp. of *vestīre*; see VEST, v.) + *-ūra* -URE] —**ves′tur·al,** *adj.*

Ve·su·vi·an (və so͞o′vē ən), *adj.* **1.** of, pertaining to, or resembling Mount Vesuvius. —*n.* **2.** (*l.c.*) vesuvianite.

ve·su·vi·an·ite (və so͞o′vē ə nīt′), *n.* a mineral, chiefly a hydrous silicate of calcium and aluminum; idocrase. Also called **vesuvian.** [VESUVIAN + -ITE¹]

Ve·su·vi·us (və so͞o′vē əs), *n.* **Mount,** an active volcano in SW Italy, near Naples: its eruption destroyed the ancient cities of Pompeii and Herculaneum A.D. 79. ab. 3900 ft.

vet¹ (vet), *n., v.,* **vet·ted, vet·ting.** *Informal.* —*n.* **1.** veterinarian. —*v.t.* **2.** to examine or treat in the manner of a veterinarian or doctor. **3.** *Informal.* to appraise, verify, or check for accuracy, authenticity, etc.: *An expert vetted the manuscript before publication.* [short for VETERINARIAN]

vet² (vet), *n., adj.* *Informal.* veteran (defs. 2, 4). [short form]

vet., 1. veteran. **2.** veterinarian. **3.** veterinary.

vetch (vech), *n.* **1.** any of several mostly climbing, leguminous herbs of the genus *Vicia*, as *V. sativa*, cultivated for forage and soil improvement. **2.** any of various allied plants, as *Lathyrus sativus*, of Europe, cultivated for its edible seeds and as a forage plant. **3.** the beanlike seed or fruit of any such plant. [ME *ve(c)che* < AF = OF *vecce* (F *vesce*) < L *vicia* name of plant]

vetch·ling (vech′ling), *n.* any leguminous plant of the genus *Lathyrus*.

vet·er·an (vet′ər ən, ve′trən), *n.* **1.** a person who has had long service or experience in an occupation or office. **2.** a person who has served in a military force, esp. in a war. —*adj.* **3.** experienced through long service or practice. **4.** (of soldiers) having had service or experience in warfare. **5.** of, pertaining to, or characteristic of veterans. [< L *veterān(us)* old (soldier) = *veter-* (s. of *vetus*) old + *-ānus* -AN]

Vet′erans Administra′tion, *U.S.* the federal agency charged with administering benefits provided by law for veterans of the armed forces. *Abbr.:* VA, V.A.

Vet′erans Day′, November 11, a holiday in the U.S. in commemoration of the end of hostilities in World War I and World War II: now officially observed on the fourth Monday in October. Also, **Vet′erans' Day′.** Formerly, **Armistice Day.**

Vet′erans of For′eign Wars′ of the Unit′ed States′. See **V.F.W.**

vet·er·i·nar·i·an (vet′ər ə nâr′ē ən, ve′trə-), *n.* a person who practices veterinary medicine or surgery. [< L *veterīnāri(us)* VETERINARY + -AN]

vet·er·i·nar·y (vet′ər ə ner′ē, ve′trə-), *n., pl.* **-nar·ies,** *adj.* —*n.* **1.** a veterinarian. —*adj.* **2.** noting or pertaining to the medical and surgical treatment of animals, esp. domesticated animals. [< L *veterīnāri(us)* = *veterīn(ae)* beasts of burden (pl. of *veterīnus*, adj. pertaining to such beasts = *veter-*, s. of *vetus* old, i.e., grown, able to take a load + *-īnus* -INE¹) + *-ārius* -ARY]

vet′erinary med′icine, the branch of medicine dealing with the study, prevention, and treatment of animal diseases, esp. in domesticated animals.

vet·i·ver (vet′ə vər), *n.* **1.** the long, fibrous, aromatic roots of an East Indian grass, *Vetiveria zizanoides*, used for making hangings and screens and yielding an oil used in perfumery. **2.** the grass itself. [< Tamil *vetti-vēr* = *vetti* name of the plant + *vēr* root]

vet. med., veterinary medicine.

ve·to (vē′tō), *n., pl.* **-toes,** *v.,* **-toed, -to·ing.** —*n.* **1.** the power vested in one branch of a government to cancel or postpone the decisions, enactments, etc., of another branch, esp., the right of a chief executive to reject bills passed by the legislature. **2.** the exercise of this right. **3.** Also called **ve′to mes′sage.** a document exercising such right and setting forth the reasons for such action. **4.** a nonconcurring vote by which one of the five permanent members of the Security Council can overrule the actions or decisions of the meeting on matters other than procedural. **5.** an emphatic prohibition of any sort. —*v.t.* **6.** to reject (a proposed bill or enactment) by a veto. **7.** to prohibit emphatically. Also called **ve′to pow′er** (for defs. 1, 4). [< L: I forbid]

Vet·ter (vet′ər), *n.* Vätter.

vex (veks), *v.t.* **1.** to irritate; annoy; provoke. **2.** to torment; trouble; worry. **3.** to dispute or make subject to dispute. [late ME *vexe(n)* < OF *vexer* < L *vexāre* to shake, jolt, harass, annoy, freq. of *vehere* to carry, convey] —**vex′er,** *n.* —**vex′ing·ly,** *adv.* —**Syn. 1.** anger, irk, nettle.

vex·a·tion (vek sā′shən), *n.* **1.** the act of vexing. **2.** the state of being vexed; irritation; annoyance. **3.** something that vexes; a cause of annoyance. [< L *vexātiōn-* = *vexāt(us)* (ptp. of *vexāre* to VEX; see -ATE¹) + *-iōn-* -ION]

vex·a·tious (vek sā′shəs), *adj.* **1.** causing vexation; troublesome; annoying: *a vexatious situation.* **2.** *Law.* (of legal actions) instituted without sufficient grounds in order to cause annoyance to the defendant. —**vex·a′tious·ly,** *adv.*

vexed (vekst), *adj.* **1.** irritated; annoyed. **2.** much discussed or disputed: *a vexed question.* **3.** *Literary.* tossed about, as waves. [late ME] —**vex·ed·ly** (vek′sid lē), *adv.*

vex·il·lar·y (vek′sə ler′ē), *adj.* of or pertaining to a vexillum. [< L *vexillāri(us)* standard-bearer. See VEXILLUM, -ARY]

vex·il·late (vek′sə lit, -lāt′), *adj.* having a vexillum or vexilla. [VEXILL(UM) + -ATE¹]

vex·il·lum (vek sil′əm), *n., pl.* **vex·il·la** (vek sil′ə). **1.** a military standard or flag carried by ancient Roman troops. **2.** a group of men serving under such a standard. **3.** Also, **vex·il** (vek′sil). *Bot.* the large upper petal of a papilionaceous flower; banner; standard. **4.** *Ornith. Rare.* the web or vane of a feather. [< L: standard, flag < ?]

V.F.W., Veterans of Foreign Wars: a society composed of veterans of the U.S. armed forces who have served overseas during wartime. Also, **VFW**

V.G., Vicar-General.

v.g., for example. [< L *verbi gratia*]

VHF, See **very high frequency.** Also, **vhf, V.H.F.**

VI, Virgin Islands (approved esp. for use with zip code).

V.I., 1. Vancouver Island. **2.** Virgin Islands.

v.i., 1. verb intransitive. **2.** see below. [< L *vide infra*]

vi·a (vī′ə, vē′ə), *prep.* **1.** by a route that touches or passes through; by way of. **2.** by the agency or instrumentality of. [< L *viā*, abl. of *via* way]

vi·a·ble (vī′ə bəl), *adj.* **1.** capable of living, growing, and developing, as an infant, seed, plant, etc. **2.** (of a fetus) sufficiently developed so as to be capable of living outside the uterus. **3.** practicable; workable: *a viable plan.* **4.**

having the ability to grow or develop, as a country. [< F = *vie* life (< L *vīta*) + *-able* -ABLE] —**vi′a·bil′i·ty,** *n.*

Vi′a Dol·o·ro′sa (dol′ə rō′sə, dō′lə-), Christ's route to Golgotha. [< L: lit., sorrowful road]

vi·a·duct (vī′ə dukt′), *n.* a bridge for carrying a road, railroad, etc., over a valley or the like, consisting of a number of short spans. [< L *via* way + (AQUE)DUCT]

vi·al (vī′əl, vīl), *n.* a small container, as of glass, for holding liquids. Also, **phial.** [late ME *viole,* var. of *fiole* PHIAL]

vi·a me·di·a (wē′ä me′di ä′; *Eng.* vī′ə mē′dē ə), *Latin.* a middle way, as between extreme courses.

vi·and (vī′ənd), *n.* **1.** an article of food. **2. viands,** articles or dishes of food, now usually of a choice or delicate kind. [late ME *viaunde* < MF *viande* < VL **vivanda,* var. of L *vīvenda* things to be lived on, ger. neut. pl. of *vīvere* to live]

vi·at·i·cum (vī at′ə kəm), *n., pl.* **-ca** (-kə), **-cums. 1.** *Eccles.* the Eucharist or Communion as given to a person dying or in danger of death. **2.** (among the ancient Romans) a provision or travel allowance given to officials on public missions. **3.** money or necessities for any journey. [< L, neut. of *viāticus* = *viāt(us)* (ptp. of *viāre* to travel; see VIA, -ATE[1]) + *-icus* -IC]

vi·a·tor (vī ā′tôr), *n., pl.* **vi·a·to·res** (vī′ə tōr′ēz, -tôr′-). a wayfarer; traveler. [< L = *viāt(us)* (see VIATICUM) + *-or* -OR[2]]

vibes[1] (vībz), *n.pl. Informal.* vibraharp. [short form] —**vib′ist,** *n.*

vibes[2] (vībz), *n. Slang.* vibration (def. 6). [short form]

Vi·borg (vē′bôʀ/yᵊ), *n.* Swedish name of **Vyborg.**

vi·brac·u·lum (vī brak′yə ləm), *n., pl.* **-la** (-lə). one of the modified polyps of certain bryozoans, having a long, whiplike appendage. [< NL = L *vibrā(re)* (to) shake + *-culum* -CULE] —**vi·brac′u·lar,** *adj.* —**vi·brac′u·loid′,** *adj.*

vi·bra·harp (vī′brə härp′), *n.* a musical percussion instrument resembling the marimba but having metal instead of wooden bars and a set of electrically powered resonators for sustaining the tone or creating a vibrato. [< L *vibrā(re)* (to) shake + HARP]

vi·brant (vī′brənt), *adj.* **1.** moving to and fro rapidly; vibrating. **2.** (of sounds) characterized by perceptible vibration; resonant; resounding. **3.** pulsating with vigor and energy. **4.** exciting or stimulating; lively. **5.** *Phonet.* made with tonal vibration of the vocal cords; voiced. —*n.* **6.** *Phonet.* a vibrant sound (opposed to *surd*). [< L *vibrant-* (s. of *vibrāns,* prp. of *vibrāre* to shake, move to and fro); see -ANT] —**vi′bran·cy, vi′brance,** *n.* —**vi′brant·ly,** *adv.*

vi·bra·phone (vī′brə fōn′), *n.* vibraharp. [< L *vibrā(re)* (to) shake + -PHONE] —**vi·bra·phon·ist** (vī′brə fō′nist, vī brof′ə-), *n.*

vi·brate (vī′brāt), *v.,* **-brat·ed, -brat·ing.** —*v.i.* **1.** to move rhythmically and steadily to and fro, as a pendulum; oscillate. **2.** to move to and fro or up and down quickly and repeatedly. **3.** (of sounds) to produce or have a quivering or vibratory effect; resound. **4.** to thrill, as in emotional response. **5.** to move between alternatives; vacillate. —*v.t.* **6.** to cause to move rhythmically and steadily to and fro, swing, or oscillate. **7.** to cause to quiver or tremble. **8.** to give forth or emit by or as by vibration. [< L *vibrāt(us)* (ptp. of *vibrāre* to move to and fro); see -ATE[1]] —**vi′brat·ing·ly,** *adv.* —**Syn. 2.** See **shake. 3.** echo.

vi·bra·tile (vī′brə til, -tīl′), *adj.* **1.** capable of vibrating or of being vibrated. **2.** having a vibratory motion. **3.** of, pertaining to, or of the nature of vibration. —**vi·bra·til·i·ty** (vī′brə til′i tē), *n.*

vi·bra·tion (vī brā′shən), *n.* **1.** the act of vibrating. **2.** the state of being vibrated. **3.** *Physics.* **a.** the oscillating, reciprocating, or other periodic motion of a rigid or elastic body or medium forced from a position or state of equilibrium. **b.** the analogous motion of the particles of a mass of air or the like, whose state of equilibrium has been disturbed, as in transmitting sound. **4.** an instance of vibratory motion; oscillation; quiver; tremor. **5.** a supernatural emanation that is sensed by or revealed to those attuned to the occult. **6. vibrations,** *Slang.* general emotional feelings one has from another person, a place, situation, etc. [< L *vibrātiōn-* (s. of *vibrātiō*)] —**vi·bra′tion·al,** *adj.*

vi·bra·to (vi brä′tō, vī-), *n., pl.* **-tos.** *Music.* a pulsating effect, produced in singing by the rapid reiteration of emphasis on a tone, and on bowed instruments by a rapid change of pitch corresponding to the vocal tremolo. [< It < L *vibrātus* (ptp.); see VIBRATE]

vi·bra·tor (vī′brā tər), *n.* **1.** a person or thing that vibrates. **2.** any of various machines or devices causing a vibratory motion or action, esp. one used in vibratory massage. **3.** *Elect.* **a.** a device in which, by continually repeated impulses, a steady current is changed into an oscillating current. **b.** a device for producing electric oscillations.

vi·bra·to·ry (vī′brə tōr′ē, -tôr′ē), *adj.* **1.** capable of or producing vibration. **2.** vibrating. **3.** of the nature of or consisting in vibration. **4.** of or pertaining to vibration. Also, **vi′bra·tive.**

vib·ri·o (vib′rē ō), *n., pl.* **-ri·os.** *Bacteriol.* any of several comma- or S-shaped bacteria of the genus *Vibrio,* certain species of which are pathogenic for man and animals. [< NL = *vibr(āre)* (to) shake + *-iō* n. suffix] —**vib·ri·oid** (vib′rē oid′), *adj.*

vi·bris·sa (vī bris′ə), *n., pl.* **-bris·sae** (-bris′ē). **1.** one of the stiff, bristly hairs growing about the mouth of certain animals, as a whisker of a cat. **2.** one of the long, slender, bristlelike feathers growing along the side of the mouth in many birds. [< L = *vibr(āre)* (to) shake + *-issa* n. suffix] —**vi·bris′sal,** *adj.*

vi·bur·num (vī bûr′nəm), *n.* **1.** any caprifoliaceous shrub or tree of the genus *Viburnum,* certain species of which, as the cranberry bush, *V. Opulus,* or snowball, are cultivated for ornament. **2.** the dried bark of various species of *Viburnum,* used in medicine. [< L: wayfaring tree]

Vic., 1. Vicar. **2.** Vicarage. **3.** Victoria.

vic·ar (vik′ər), *n.* **1.** *Ch. of Eng.* **a.** a person acting as priest of a parish in place of the rector. **b.** the priest of a parish whose tithes are impropriated and who receives only the smaller tithes or a salary. **2.** *Prot. Episc. Ch.* **a.** a clergyman whose charge is a chapel in a parish. **b.** a bishop's assistant in charge of a church or mission. **3.** *Rom. Cath. Ch.* an ecclesiastic representing the pope or a bishop. **4.** a person who is authorized to perform the functions of another; deputy: *God's vicar on earth.* [ME < AF *vicare* = OF *vicaire* < L *vicār(ius)* a substitute, n. use of adj.; see VICARIOUS] —**vic′ar·ly,** *adj.* —**vic′ar·ship′,** *n.*

vic·ar·age (vik′ər ij), *n.* **1.** the residence of a vicar. **2.** the benefice, office, or duties of a vicar. [late ME]

vic′ar apostol′ic, *pl.* **vicars apostolic.** *Rom. Cath. Ch.* a titular bishop serving in a district without an espicopal see.

vic′ar fo·rane′ (fō rān′, fô-), *pl.* **vicars forane.** *Rom. Cath. Ch.* dean[1] (def. 2b). [*forane* < L *forāne(us)* living away; see FOREIGN]

vic·ar-gen·er·al (vik′ər jen′ər əl), *n., pl.* **vic·ars-gen·er·al. 1.** *Rom. Cath. Ch.* a priest deputized by a bishop to assist him in the administration of a diocese. **2.** *Ch. of Eng.* an ecclesiastical officer who assists a bishop or an archbishop. **3.** a deputy, as of a king, with extensive power or jurisdiction. [ME] —**vic′ar-gen′er·al·ship′,** *n.*

vi·car·i·al (vī kâr′ē əl), *adj.* **1.** of or pertaining to a vicar or vicars. **2.** delegated or vicarious: *vicarial powers.* [< L *vicāri(us)* VICAR + -AL[1]]

vi·car·i·ate (vī kâr′ē it, -āt′, vi-), *n.* **1.** the office or authority of a vicar. **2.** the district presided over by a vicar. Also, **vic·ar·ate** (vik′ər it, -ə rāt′). [< ML *vicāriāt(us)* = L *vicāri(us)* VICAR + *-ātus* -ATE[1]]

vi·car·i·ous (vī kâr′ē əs, vi-), *adj.* **1.** performed, exercised, received, or suffered in place of another. **2.** taking the place of another person or thing. **3.** felt or enjoyed through imagined participation in the experience of others: *a vicarious thrill.* **4.** *Physiol.* noting or pertaining to the performance by one organ of part of the functions normally performed by another. [< L *vicārius* substituting = *vic-,* akin to **vicis* (inter)change (see VICE[3]), + *-ārius* -ARIOUS] —**vi·car′i·ous·ly,** *adv.* —**vi·car′i·ous·ness,** *n.*

Vic′ar of Christ′, *Rom. Cath. Ch.* the pope. Also called **Vic′ar of Je′sus Christ′.**

vice[1] (vīs), *n.* **1.** an immoral habit or practice. **2.** immoral conduct; depraved or degrading behavior: *a life of crime and vice.* **3.** sexual immorality, esp. prostitution. **4.** a fault, defect, shortcoming, or imperfection. **5.** a physical defect, flaw, or infirmity. **6.** a bad habit, as in a horse. [ME < AF, OF < L *vitium* a fault, defect, vice] —**vice′less,** *adj.* —**Syn. 2.** depravity, sin, wickedness, corruption. —**Ant. 1, 2.** virtue.

vice[2] (vīs), *n., v.t.,* **viced, vic·ing.** vise.

vi·ce[3] (vī′sē), *prep.* instead of; in the place of. [< L: instead of, abl. of **vicis* (inter)change]

vice-, a learned borrowing from Latin meaning "deputy," used in the formation of compound words: *viceroyalty.* [ME << L *vice* VICE[3]]

vice′ ad′miral, a naval officer next in rank below an admiral and above a rear admiral. —**vice′ ad′miralty.**

vice′ chair′man, a deputy or assistant chairman.

vice-chair·man (vīs′châr′mən), *n., pl.* **-men.** See **vice chairman.**

vice′ chan′cellor, 1. a substitute, deputy, or subordinate chancellor. **2.** a chancery judge acting in place of a chancellor. Cf. **chancellor** (def. 4). [late ME] —**vice′ chan′cellorship′.**

vice′ con′sul, a consular officer of a grade below that of consul. Also, **vice′-con′sul.** —**vice′-con′su·lar,** *adj.* —**vice′ con′sulate.** —**vice′-con′su·late,** *n.* —**vice′ con′sulship′.** —**vice′-con′sul·ship′,** *n.*

vice·ge·ren·cy (vīs jēr′ən sē), *n., pl.* **-cies. 1.** the position, government, or office of a vicegerent. **2.** the territory or district under a vicegerent. [VICEGER(ENT) + -ENCY]

vice·ge·rent (vīs jēr′ənt), *n.* **1.** an officer appointed by a sovereign or supreme chief as his deputy. **2.** a deputy in general. —*adj.* **3.** exercising delegated powers. [< NL *vicegerent-* (s. of *vicegerēns* managing instead of) = L *vice* (see VICE[3]) + *gerent-* (s. of *gerēns,* prp. of *gerere* to carry on, conduct); see -ENT]

vic·e·nar·y (vis′ə ner′ē), *adj.* of, pertaining to, or consisting of twenty. [< L *vīcēnāri(us)* = *vīcēn(ī)* twenty each + *-ārius* -ARY]

vi·cen·ni·al (vī sen′ē əl), *adj.* **1.** of or for twenty years. **2.** occurring every twenty years. [< L *vīcenni(um)* twenty-year period = *vīc(ēnī)* twenty each + *-enni(um)* yearly period (< *annus* year) + -AL[1]]

Vi·cen·za (vē chen′dzä), *n.* a city in central Venezia, in NE Italy. 97,617 (1961).

vice pres., vice president. Also, **Vice Pres.**

vice′ pres′ident, 1. an officer next in rank to a president. **2.** (*often caps.*) *U.S. Govt.* the officer of this rank who is elected at the same time as the President and who succeeds to the presidency on the resignation, removal, death, or disability of the President. Also, **vice′-pres′ident.** —**vice′ pres′idency.** —**vice′-pres′i·den·cy,** *n.* —**vice′-pres·i·den′tial,** *adj.*

vice·re·gal (vīs rē′gəl), *adj.* of or pertaining to a viceroy. —**vice·re′gal·ly,** *adv.*

vice-re·gent (*n.* vīs′rē′jənt; *adj.* vīs rē′jənt), *n.* **1.** a deputy regent. —*adj.* **2.** of, pertaining to, or occupying the position of a vice-regent. —**vice′-re′gen·cy,** *n.*

vice·reine (vīs′rān), *n.* the wife of a viceroy. [< F = *vice-* VICE- + *reine* < L *rēgīna* queen (*rēg-,* base of *rex* king + *-īna* fem. n. suffix)]

vice·roy (vīs′roi), *n.* **1.** a person appointed to rule a country or province as the deputy of the sovereign. **2.** an American butterfly, *Limenitis archippus,* closely mimicking the monarch butterfly in coloration. [< MF = *vice-* VICE- + *roy* < L *rēgi-,* s. of *rex* king] —**vice′roy·ship′,** *n.*

vice·roy·al·ty (vīs roi′əl tē, vīs′roi′-), *n., pl.* **-ties.** the dignity, office, or period of office of a viceroy. [VICE- + ROYALTY, modeled on F *vice-royauté*]

vice′ squad′, a police squad charged with enforcing laws dealing with gambling, prostitution, and other forms of vice.

vi·ce ver·sa (vī′sə vûr′sə, vī′sē, vīs′), in reverse order from that of a preceding statement; conversely: *She dislikes me, and vice versa.* [< L = *vice* abl. sing. of **vicis* change + *versā* abl. sing. fem. of *versus,* ptp. of *vertere* to turn]

Vi·chy (vish′ē; *Fr.* vē shē′), *n.* a city in central France: provisional capital of unoccupied France 1940–42; hot springs. 32,251.

vi·chy·ssoise (vish′ē-swäz′), *n.* a cream soup of potatoes and leeks, usually served chilled. [< F = VICHY + -ss- (< ?) + *-oise*, fem. of *-ois* -ESE]

Vi′chy wa′ter (vish′ē), **1.** a natural mineral water from springs at Vichy, used in the treatment of digestive disturbances, gout, etc. **2.** any mineral water resembling this. Also, **vi′chy wa′ter.** Also called **Vi′chy, vi′chy.**

vic·i·nage (vis′ə nij), *n.* **1.** the region near or about a place; vicinity. **2.** a particular neighborhood or district, or the people belonging to it. **3.** proximity. [< L *vīcīn(us)* near (see VICINITY) + -AGE; r. ME *vesinage* < MF]

vic·i·nal (vis′ə nəl), *adj.* **1.** of, pertaining to, or belonging to a neighborhood or district. **2.** neighboring; adjacent. **3.** *Crystall.* noting a plane whose position varies very little from that of a fundamental plane of the form. [< L *vīcīnāl(is)* = *vīcīn(us)* near + *-ālis* -AL[1]; see VICINITY]

vi·cin·i·ty (vi sin′i tē), *n., pl.* **-ties. 1.** the area or region near or about a place. **2.** the state or fact of being near; proximity; propinquity. [< L *vīcīnitās* = *vīcīn(us)* near (*vīc(us)* village + *-īnus* -INE[1]) + *-itās* -ITY]

vi·cious (vish′əs), *adj.* **1.** addicted to or characterized by vice; depraved; profligate. **2.** given or readily disposed to evil: *a vicious criminal.* **3.** spiteful; malicious. **4.** characterized or marred by faults or defects; unsound: *vicious reasoning.* **5.** savage; ferocious. [ME (< AF) < L *vitiōsus* = *viti(um)* fault, vice + *-ōsus* -OSE[1], -OUS] —**vi′cious·ly,** *adv.* —**vi′cious·ness,** *n.* —**Syn. 3.** malevolent.

vi′cious cir′cle, 1. a situation in which effort to solve a given problem results in the aggravation of the problem or the creation of a worse one. **2.** *Logic.* **a.** (in demonstration) the use of each of two propositions to establish the other. **b.** (in definition) the use of each of two terms to define the other.

vi·cis·si·tude (vi sis′i to͞od′, -tyo͞od′), *n.* **1.** a change or variation occurring in the course of something. **2.** interchange or alternation, as of states or things. **3. vicissitudes,** successive, alternating, or changing phases or conditions, as of life or fortune; ups and downs. **4.** change; mutation or mutability. [< L *vicissitūdō* = *vicissi-* (comb. form of **vicis* a turn) + *-tūdō* -TUDE] —**vi·cis·si·tu·di·nar·y** (vi sis′i to͞od′ənər′ē, -tyo͞od′-), **vi·cis′si·tu′di·nous,** *adj.*

Vicks·burg (viks′bûrg), *n.* a city in W Mississippi, on the Mississippi River: Civil War siege and Confederate surrender 1863. 25,478 (1970).

Vi·co (vik′ō; *It.* vē′kō), *n.* **Gio·van·ni Bat·tis·ta** (jō vän′nē bät tēs′tä), 1668–1744, Italian philosopher and jurist.

vi·comte (vē kônt′), *n., pl.* **-comtes** (-kônt′). a French viscount. [see VISCOUNT]

Vict., 1. Victoria. **2.** Victorian.

vic·tim (vik′tim), *n.* **1.** a person who suffers from a destructive or injurious action or agency: *war victims.* **2.** a person who is deceived or cheated. **3.** a living being sacrificed in religious rites. [< L *victim(a)* sacrificial beast]

vic·tim·ise (vik′tə mīz′), *v.t.,* **-ised, -is·ing.** *Chiefly Brit.* victimize. —**vic′tim·i·sa′tion,** *n.* —**vic′tim·is′er,** *n.*

vic·tim·ize (vik′tə mīz′), *v.t.,* **-ized, -iz·ing. 1.** to make a victim of. **2.** to dupe, swindle, or cheat. **3.** to slay as or like a sacrificial victim. —**vic′tim·i·za′tion,** *n.* —**vic′tim·iz′er,** *n.* —**Syn. 2.** defraud, hoodwink. See **cheat.**

vic·tor (vik′tər), *n.* **1.** a person who has overcome or defeated an adversary; conqueror. **2.** a winner in any struggle or contest. **3.** (*cap.*) a word used in communications to represent the letter *V.* [ME < L = *vict(us)* + *-or* -OR[2]]

Vic·tor I (vik′tər), **Saint,** pope A.D. 189–198.

Victor II, (*Gebhard*) 1018–57, German ecclesiastic: pope 1055–57.

Victor III, (*Dauferius*) 1027–87, Italian ecclesiastic: pope 1086–87.

Victor Em·man·u·el I (i man′yo͞o əl), 1759–1824, king of Sardinia 1802–21.

Victor Emmanuel II, 1820–78, king of Sardinia 1849–1878; first king of Italy 1861–78.

Victor Emmanuel III, 1869–1947, king of Italy 1900–46.

Vic·to·ri·a (vik tôr′ē ə, -tōr′-), *n.* **1.** 1819–1901, queen of Great Britain 1837–1901; empress of India 1876–1901. **2.** the ancient Roman goddess of victory, identified with the Greek goddess Nike. **3.** a state in SE Australia. 3,443,800; 87,884 sq. mi. *Cap.:* Melbourne. **4.** Also called **Hong Kong.** a seaport in and the capital of Hong Kong colony, on the SE coast of China. 520,932. **5.** a seaport in and the capital of British Columbia, on Vancouver Island, in SW Canada. 62,551. **6.** a city in S Texas. 41,349 (1970). **7. Lake.** Also called **Victoria Nyanza.** a lake in E Africa, in Uganda, Tanzania, and Kenya: second largest fresh-water lake in the world. 26,828 sq. mi. **8. Mount,** a mountain in SE New Guinea, in the Owen Stanley Range. 13,240 ft. **9.** (*l.c.*) a low, light, four-wheeled carriage with a calash top, a seat for two passengers, and a perch in front for the driver. **10.** (*l.c.*) a water lily, *Victoria regia* (or *amazonica*), having leaves often over 6 feet in diameter, and white to rose, nocturnal flowers 12 to 18 inches across.

Victoria (def. 9)

Victo′ria Cross′, a British decoration awarded to members of the British armed forces for acts of conspicuous bravery in the presence of the enemy. *Abbr.:* V. C.

Victo′ria Day′, (in Canada) the first Monday preceding May 25, observed as a national holiday.

Victo′ria Des′ert. See **Great Victoria Desert.**

Victo′ria Falls′, 1. falls of the Zambezi River in S Africa, between Zambia and Zimbabwe, near Livingstone. 420 ft. high; more than a mile wide. **2.** See **Iguassú Falls.**

Victo′ria Is′land, an island off the coast of N Canada, in the Arctic Ocean. 80,340 sq. mi.

Victo′ria Land′, a region in Antarctica, bordering on the Ross Sea, mainly in Ross Dependency.

Vic·to·ri·an (vik tôr′ē ən, -tōr′-), *adj.* **1.** of or pertaining to Queen Victoria or the period of her reign: *Victorian poets.* **2.** having the characteristics usually attributed to the Victorians, esp. prudery or stuffiness. **3.** noting or pertaining to the architecture, furnishings, and decoration of English-speaking countries during the reign of Queen Victoria, characterized chiefly by massive, elaborate, and often ostentatious workmanship. —*n.* **4.** a person, esp. an author or other famous person, who lived or flourished during the Victorian period.

Victorian sideboard

Vic·to·ri·an·ism (vik tôr′ē ə niz′əm, -tōr′-), *n.* **1.** a set of mental attitudes characteristic of those of the Victorians. **2.** a statement, action, etc., suggesting such attitudes.

Victo′ria Ny·an·za (nī an′zə, nyän′zä), Victoria (def. 7)

vic·to·ri·ous (vik tôr′ē əs, -tōr′-), *adj.* **1.** having achieved a victory; conquering; triumphant: *our victorious army.* **2.** of, pertaining to, or characterized by victory. [late ME; see VICTORY, -OUS] —**vic·to′ri·ous·ly,** *adv.*

vic·to·ry (vik′tə rē), *n., pl.* **-ries. 1.** a success or triumph over an enemy in battle or war. **2.** the ultimate and decisive superiority in any battle or contest. [ME *victorie* < L *victōria.* See VICTOR, -Y[3]]

vic′tory gar′den, a vegetable garden cultivated during World War II to increase food production.

Vic′tory Med′al, a bronze medal awarded to all who served in the U.S. armed forces during World War I or II.

Vic·tro·la (vik trō′lə), *n. Trademark.* an acoustical-disc phonograph with an internal horn.

vict·ual (vit′əl), *n., v.,* **-ualed, -ual·ing** or (*esp. Brit.*) **-ualled, -ual·ling.** —*n.* **1. victuals,** food supplies; provisions, esp. for human beings. —*v.t.* **2.** to supply with victuals. —*v.i.* **3.** to take or obtain victuals. **4.** *Archaic.* to eat or feed. [ME *vitaille* < AF, MF *vitail(l)e,* OF *vituaille* < LL *victuālia* provisions, n. use of neut. pl. of L *victuālis* pertaining to food = *victu(s)* nourishment, way of living (*vict-*, ptp. s. of *vīvere* to live + *-us* 4th decl. n. suffix) + *-ālis* -AL[1]; mod. sp. < L]

vict·ual·age (vit′əlij), *n.* food; provisions; victuals.

vict·ual·er (vit′ələr), *n.* **1.** a person who furnishes victuals, esp. a sutler. **2.** a supply ship. **3.** *Brit.* the keeper of an inn or tavern, esp. one licensed to sell liquor. Also, *esp. Brit.,* **vict′ual·ler.** [late ME *vitailler* < AF = MF *vitail(l)ier.* See VICTUAL, -ER[2]]

vi·cu·ña (vi ko͞o′nə, -kyo͞o′-, və-, və ko͞o′nyə), *n.* **1.** a wild South American ruminant, *Lama vicugna,* of the Andes, related to the guanaco but smaller, and yielding a soft, delicate wool. **2.** a fabric of this wool or of some substitute, usually twilled and finished with a soft nap. **3.** a garment, esp. an overcoat, of vicuña. Also, **vicu′na.** [< Sp *vicuña* < Quechuan *wikūña*]

Vicuña, *Lama vicugna* (2½ ft. high at shoulder; length 5½ ft.)

vi·de (wē′de; *Eng.* vī′dē), *v. Latin.* see (used esp. to refer a reader to a specified part or parts of a text).

vi·de an·te (wē′de än′te; *Eng.* vī′dē an′tē), *Latin.* see before (used esp. to refer a reader to parts of a text).

vi·de in·fra (wē′de in′frä; *Eng.* vī′dē in′frə), *Latin.* see below (used esp. to refer a reader to parts of a text).

vi·de·li·cet (wi dā′li ket′; *Eng.* vi del′i sit), *adv. Latin.* that is to say; namely *Abbr.:* viz.

vid·e·o (vid′ē ō′), *n.* **1.** the visual elements of television (distinguished from *audio*). **2.** television as an entertainment medium. —*adj.* **3.** of or pertaining to television, esp. its visual elements. [< L *vidē(re)* (to) see + *-o* as in *audio*]

vid·e·o·cas·sette (vid′ē ō′ka set′, -kə-), *n.* cassette (def. 2).

vid′eocassette record′er, an electronic apparatus for connecting to a television set to record television programs on videotape cassettes for later playing. Also called **vid′e·o·re·cord′er, VCR.**

vid·e·o·disc (vid′ē ō disk′), *n.* a disk on which motion pictures and sound are recorded for later reproduction on a player, esp. on an ordinary television screen. Also, **vid′e·o·disk′.**

vid′eo display′ ter′minal, a computer terminal consisting of a cathode-ray tube or similar screen on which data can be displayed, with a keyboard for entering data. *Abbr.:* VDT

vid′eo game′, any electronic game, usually operated through a television set, in which changing patterns and moving objects appear on a screen and can be controlled by the player or players to score points based on quick reflexes or ingenuity.

vid·e·o·tape (vid′ē ō tāp′), *n., v.,* **-taped, -tap·ing.** —*n.* **1.** a type of magnetic tape for picture recording or reproduction, usually accompanied by a sound track. —*v.t.* **2.** to record on videotape. Also, **vid′e·o·tape′.**

vid·e·o·tex (vid′ē ō teks′), *n.* **1.** an information transmission and retrieval system that provides interactive communication via telephone or television for such purposes as data acquisition and dissemination and electronic banking and shopping. **2.** the information transmitted through such a system. Also, **vid′e·o·text′.** [VIDEO + TEX(T)]

vi·de post (wē′de pōst; *Eng.* vī′dē pōst′), *Latin.* see after or further (used esp. to refer a reader to parts of a text).

vi·de su·pra (wē′de sōō′prä; *Eng.* vī′dē sōō′prə), *Latin.* see above (used esp. to refer a reader to parts of a text).

vi·dette (vi det′), *n.* vedette.

vi·de ut su·pra (wē′de ŏŏt sōō′prä; *Eng.* vī′dē ut sōō′prə), *Latin.* see as (stated) above (used esp. to refer a reader to parts of a text).

vie (vī), *v.*, **vied, vy·ing.** —*v.i.* **1.** to strive in competition or rivalry with another; contend for superiority. —*v.t.* **2.** *Archaic.* to put forward in competition or rivalry. **3.** *Obs.* to stake in card playing. [by aphesis < MF *envier* to raise the stake (at cards), OF: challenge < L *invītāre* INVITE]

Vi·en·na (vē en′ə), *n.* a port in and the capital of Austria, in the NE part, on the Danube. 1,614,841. German, **Wien.**

Vien′na Interna′tional, a socialist organization, formed in Vienna in 1921. Cf. **international** (def. 5).

Vienne (vyen), *n.* a city in SE France, on the Rhone River, S of Lyons: Roman ruins. 28,753.

Vi·en·nese (vē′ə nēz′, -nēs′), *adj., n., pl.* **-nese.** —*adj.* **1.** of, pertaining to, or characteristic of Vienna. —*n.* **2.** a native or inhabitant of Vienna.

Vien·tiane (vyen tyän′), *n.* a city in and the capital of Laos, in the NW part, on the Mekong River. 176,637.

Vi·et (vē et′, vyet), *Informal.* —*n.* **1.** Vietnam. —*adj.* **2.** Vietnamese.

Vi·et·cong (vē′et kông′, vē et′-, vyet′-), *n., pl.* **-cong,** *adj.* —*n.* **1.** a Communist-led army and guerrilla force in South Vietnam, during the Vietnam War, supported largely by North Vietnam. **2.** a member or supporter of this force. —*adj.* **3.** of or pertaining to this force or one of its members or supporters. Also, **Vi′et Cong′.** [short for Vietnamese *Viet Nam Cong San* Vietnamese Communist]

Vi·et·minh (vē′et min′, vē et′-, vyet′-), *n.* **1.** a Communist-led Vietnamese organization whose forces fought against the Japanese and esp. against the French in Indochina: officially in existence 1941–51. **2.** (*construed as pl.*) the leaders, supporters, and fighters of this organization. —*adj.* **3.** of or pertaining to the Vietminh. Also, **Vi′et Minh.** [short for Vietnamese *Viet Nam Doc Lap Dong Minh Hoi* Vietnam Independence League]

Vi·et·nam (vē′et näm′, -nam′, vē et′-, vyet′-), *n.* a country in SE Asia, comprising the former states of Annam, Tonkin, and Cochin-China: formerly part of French Indochina; divided into North Vietnam and South Vietnam during the Vietnam War but now reunified. 49,200,000; 126,104 sq. mi. *Cap.:* Hanoi. Also, **Vi′et Nam′.**

Vi·et·nam·ese (vē et′nä mēz′, -mēs′, -nə-, vyet′-), *n., pl.* **-ese,** *adj.* —*n.* **1.** a native or inhabitant of Vietnam. **2.** Formerly, **Annamese, Annamite.** an Austroasiatic language that is the official language of Vietnam. —*adj.* **3.** of or pertaining to Vietnam or its inhabitants.

Vi′etnam′ War′, a conflict, starting in 1954 and ending in 1975, between South Vietnam, later aided by the U.S., South Korea, Australia, the Philippines, Thailand, and New Zealand, and the Vietcong and North Vietnam, receiving military supplies from Communist China, the U.S.S.R., and other nations.

view (vyōō), *n.* **1.** the act or an instance of looking at or making a visual inspection of something. **2.** the range of one's sight: *into view.* **3.** an unobstructed sight of a specified object or in a specified direction. **4.** a picture or photograph of something. **5.** the act of contemplating a subject of thought. **6.** a personal attitude or opinion. **7.** an aim or purpose. **8.** a general survey or summary. **9. in view, a.** within range of vision. **b.** under consideration. **10. in view of,** in consideration of; on account of. **11. on view,** in a place for public inspection; on exhibition. **12. with a view to, a.** with the aim or intention of. **b.** with the expectation or hope of. —*v.t.* **13.** to see; behold. **14.** to look at; survey; inspect. **15.** to contemplate mentally; consider. **16.** to regard in a particular light or as specified. [late ME *v(i)ewe* < AF < MF *veue* sight < VL **vidūta,* n. use of fem. of **vidūtus,* r. L *vīsus,* ptp. of *vidēre* to see] —**view′a·ble,** *adj.* —**Syn. 3.** VIEW, PROSPECT, SCENE, VISTA refer to a landscape or perspective. VIEW is a general word, referring to whatever lies open to sight: *a fine view of the surrounding country.* PROSPECT suggests a sweeping and often distant view, as from a place of vantage: *a beautiful prospect to the south.* SCENE suggests an organic unity in the details such as is to be found in a picture: *a woodland scene.* VISTA suggests a long, narrow view, as along an avenue between rows of trees: *a pleasant vista.* **6.** belief, judgment. See **opinion.**

view·er (vyōō′ər), *n.* **1.** a person or thing that views. **2.** a person who watches television. **3.** any optical apparatus to facilitate viewing, as of a photographic transparency. **4.** *Informal.* an eyepiece or viewfinder.

view·er·ship (vyōō′ər ship′), *n.* **1.** the people who watch a particular television program. **2.** the estimated number of such people.

view·find·er (vyōō′fīn′dər), *n.* *Photog.* finder (def. 2).

view·less (vyōō′lis), *adj.* **1.** giving no view: *a viewless window.* **2.** without an opinion or opinions. **3.** *Obs.* that cannot be seen; invisible. —**view′less·ly,** *adv.*

view·point (vyōō′point′), *n.* **1.** a place affording a view of something. **2.** an attitude of mind, or the circumstances of an individual that conduce to such an attitude. [alter. of *point of view,* modeled on *standpoint*]

vi·ges·i·mal (vī jes′ə məl), *adj.* **1.** of, pertaining to, or based on twenty. **2.** twentieth. **3.** proceeding by twenties. [< L *vīgēsim(us),* var. (with *g* of *vīgintī* twenty) of *vīcēsimus, vīcensimus* twentieth + -AL[1]]

vig·il (vij′əl), *n.* **1.** a period of watchfulness or wakefulness, maintained esp. during the normal hours for sleeping. **2.** *Eccles.* **a.** a devotional watch during the customary hours of sleep. **b.** Sometimes, **vigils.** a nocturnal devotional exercise or service, esp. on the eve before a church festival. **c.** the eve, or day and night, before a church festival, esp. an eve that is a fast. [ME *vigil(i)e* < AF < ML *vigilia* eve of a holy day, special use of L *vigilia* watchfulness = *vigil-* watchful + *-ia* -Y[3]]

vig·i·lance (vij′ə ləns), *n.* **1.** the state or quality of being vigilant; watchfulness. **2.** *Pathol.* insomnia. [alter. (-ANCE for -ANCY) of obs. *vigilancy* < L *vigilantia* = *vigil-* (base of *vigilāre* to be watchful) + *-antia* -ANCY]

vig′ilance commit′tee, *U.S.* an extralegal group of citizens that summarily punishes criminals.

vig·i·lant (vij′ə lənt), *adj.* **1.** keenly watchful to detect danger or trouble. **2.** ever awake and alert; sleeplessly watchful. [< L *vigilant-* (s. of *vigilāns*), prp. of *vigilāre* to be watchful] —**vig′i·lant·ly,** *adv.* —**Syn. 2.** See **alert.**

vig·i·lan·te (vij′ə lan′tē), *n.* **1.** a person who takes the law into his or her own hands, as by avenging a crime, esp. when law-enforcement agencies are perceived as powerless or inadequate. **2.** *U.S.* a member of a vigilance committee. [< Sp: vigilant]

vig·i·lan·tism (vij′ə lən tiz′əm), *n.* a form of conduct or set of attitudes characteristic of or suggestive of vigilantes, esp. in being militant and full of suspicions.

Vi·gil·i·us (vi jil′ē əs), *n.* died A.D. 555, pope 537–555.

vig′il light′, **1.** a small candle in a church to be lighted as a devotional act. **2.** a candle or small light kept burning before a shrine, icon, etc.

vi·gnette (vin yet′), *n., v.,* **-gnet·ted, -gnet·ting.** —*n.* **1.** a decorative design or small illustration used on the title page of a book or at the beginning or end of a chapter. **2.** an engraving, drawing, photograph, or the like, that is shaded off gradually at the edges so as to leave no definite line at the border. **3.** a decorative design representing branches, leaves, grapes, or the like, as in a manuscript. **4.** any small, pleasing picture or view. **5.** a short graceful literary sketch. —*v.t.* **6.** *Photog.* to finish (a picture, photograph, etc.) in the manner of a vignette. [< F: lit., little vine (see VINE); from vinelike decorations in early books] —**vig·nett′ist,** *n.*

Vi·gno·la (vē nyô′lä), *n.* **Gia·co·mo da** (jä′kô mô dä), (*Giacomo Barocchio* or *Barozzi*), 1507–73, Italian architect.

Vi·gny (vē nyē′), *n.* **Al·fred Vic·tor de** (al fred′ vēk tôr′ də), 1797–1863, French poet, novelist, and dramatist.

Vi·go (vē′gō; *Sp.* bē′gô), **1. Bay of,** an inlet of the Atlantic, in NW Spain. 19 mi. long. **2.** a seaport on this bay: naval battle 1702. 146,320 (est. 1960).

vig·or (vig′ər), *n.* **1.** active strength or force. **2.** healthy physical or mental energy or power; vitality. **3.** energetic activity; energy; intensity. **4.** healthy growth in any living matter or organism, as a plant. **5.** effective force, esp. as having legal validity. Also, *esp. Brit.,* **vig′our.** [late ME *vigo(u)r* < AF (MF *vigeur*) < L *vigor* force, energy]

vig·or·ish (vig′ər ish), *n.* *Slang.* **1.** a charge paid on a bet, as to a bookie. **2.** interest paid to a moneylender. [?]

vi·go·ro·so (vig′ə rō′sō; *It.* vē′gô rô′zô), *adj.* vigorous or spirited in manner (used as a musical direction). [< It; c. VIGOROUS]

vig·or·ous (vig′ər əs), *adj.* **1.** full of or characterized by vigor: *a vigorous effort.* **2.** strong or active; robust. **3.** energetic; forceful. **4.** powerful in action or effect. **5.** growing well, as a plant. [ME < OF < ML *vigorōs(us)*] —**vig′or·ous·ly,** *adv.* —**Syn. 2.** sturdy, sound, healthy. See **active.**

Vii·pu·ri (vē′pŏŏ rē′), *n.* Finnish name of **Vyborg.**

Vi·king (vī′king), *n.* (*sometimes l.c.*) **1.** any of the Scandinavian pirates who plundered the northern and western coasts of Europe from the 8th to 10th centuries. **2.** a searoving bandit; pirate. **3.** *Informal.* a Scandinavian. [< Scand; cf. Icel *víkingr;* r. OE *wīcing* pirate; etym. disputed]

vil., village.

vile (vīl), *adj.,* **vil·er, vil·est.** **1.** wretchedly bad: *vile weather; a vile odor.* **2.** morally debased, depraved, or despicable. **3.** foul; filthy: *vile language.* **4.** degraded; ignominious: *vile servitude.* **5.** of little value or account; paltry: *a vile recompense.* [ME *vil* < OF < L *vīlis* of little worth, base, cheap] —**vile′ly,** *adv.* —**Syn. 1.** See **mean**[2]. **2.** vicious, evil, iniquitous. **3.** vulgar, obscene.

vil·i·fy (vil′ə fī′), *v.t.,* **-fied, -fy·ing.** **1.** to defame or slander. **2.** *Obs.* to make vile. [late ME < LL *vīlificāre.* See VILE, -FY] —**vil′i·fi·ca′tion,** *n.* —**Syn. 1.** disparage.

vil·i·pend (vil′ə pend′), *v.t.* **1.** to regard or treat as of little value or account. **2.** to vilify. [< LL *vīlipend(ere)* = L *vīli(s)* cheap (see VILE) + *pendere* to consider (see PEND)]

vil·la (vil′ə), *n.* **1.** a country residence or estate, esp. one that is large and imposing. **2.** *Brit.* a detached or semidetached dwelling house, usually suburban. [< It or L: a country house, farm, dim. of *vīcus* WICK[3]]

Vi·lla (vē′ə; *Sp.* bē′yä), *n.* **Fran·cis·co** (frän sēs′kô), (*Doroteo Arango,* "*Pancho Villa*"), 1877–1923, Mexican general and revolutionist.

Vi·lla Cis·ne·ros (bē′lyä thēs ne′rôs, bē′yä sēs ne′rôs), **1.** Formerly, **Río de Oro.** the S part of Spanish Sahara: formerly a Spanish colony. ab. 70,000 sq. mi. **2.** a seaport in and the capital of this part.

vil·lage (vil′ij), *n.* **1.** a small community or group of houses in a rural area, usually smaller than a town and sometimes incorporated as a municipality. **2.** the inhabitants of such a community, taken as a whole. **3.** a group of animal dwellings resembling a village. —*adj.* **4.** of or characteristic of a village. [late ME < MF << L *villāticum.* See VILLA, -AGE] —**Syn. 1.** See **community.**

vil′lage commu′nity, an early form of economic organization in which the land was owned in common by members of a village.

vil·lag·er (vil′i jər), *n.* an inhabitant of a village.

Vi·lla·her·mo·sa (bē′yä er mô′sä), *n.* a city in and the capital of Tabasco, in E Mexico. 52,262 (1960).

vil·lain (vil′ən), *n.* **1.** a cruelly malicious person; scoundrel. **2.** a character in a play, novel, or the like, who constitutes an important evil agency in the plot. **3.** villein. Also, *referring to a woman,* **vil′lain·ess.** [ME *vilein, vilain* < MF < LL *villān(us)* a farm servant. See VILLA, -AN] —**Syn. 1.** knave, rascal, rogue.

vil·lain·age (vil′ə nij), *n.* villeinage. Also, **vil′lan·age.**

vil·lain·ous (vil′ə nəs), *adj.* **1.** having a cruel, malicious nature or character. **2.** of, pertaining to, or befitting a villain. **3.** very objectionable or unpleasant: *a villainous storm.* [late ME] —**vil′lain·ous·ly,** *adv.* —**vil′lain·ous·ness,** *n.*

vil·lain·y (vil′ə nē), *n., pl.* **-lain·ies.** **1.** the actions or conduct of a villain; outrageous wickedness. **2.** a villainous act or deed. **3.** *Obs.* villeinage. [ME *vile(i)nie, vilainie* < OF]

Vil·la-Lo·bos (vē′lä lō′bôs, -bōs, vil′ə-; *Port.* vē′lyä lô′bŏŏs), *n.* **Hei·tor** (ā′tŏŏr), 1881–1959, Brazilian composer.

vil·la·nel·la (vil′ə nel′ə; *It.* vēl′lä nel′lä), *n., pl.* **-nel·le** (-nel′ē; *It.* -nel′le). a rustic Italian part song without accompaniment. [< It, fem. of *villanello* rural, rustic = *villan(o)* peasant, boor (see VILLAIN) + *-ello* adj. suffix]

vil·la·nelle (vil′ə nel′), *n. Pros.* a short poem of fixed form, written in five tercets, followed by a final quatrain, and charactized by refrains and the use of two rhymes. [< F < It; see VILLANELLA]

Vil′la Park′ (vil′ə), a city in NE Illinois, near Chicago. 25,891 (1970).

Vil·lard (vi lär′, -lärd′), *n.* **Oswald Garrison,** 1872–1949, U.S. journalist and author.

Vil·lars (vē lar′), *n.* **Claude Louis Hec·tor de** (klōd lwē ek tôr′ də), 1653–1734, marshal of France.

vil·lat·ic (vi lat′ik), *adj.* of or pertaining to the country or to a farm; rural. [< L *villātic(us).* See VILLA, -ATE[1], -IC]

Vi·lla·vi·cen·cio (bē′yä vē sen′syô), *n.* a city in central Colombia. 43,000 (1962).

vil·lein (vil′ən), *n.* (in the feudal system) a member of a class of persons who were serfs with respect to the lord but had the rights and privileges of freemen with respect to others. Also, **villain.** [ME; see VILLAIN]

vil·lein·age (vil′ə nij), *n.* **1.** the tenure by which a villein held land and tenements from his lord. **2.** the condition or status of a villein. Also, **villainage, villanage, vil′len·age.** [ME *vilenage* < AF, OF. See VILLEIN, -AGE]

Ville·neuve (vēl nœv′), *n.* **Pierre Charles Jean Bap·tiste Sil·ves·tre de** (pyer sharl zhän ba tēst′ sēl ves′trə də), 1763–1806, French admiral.

Ville·ur·banne (vēl yr ban′), *n.* a city in E France, near Lyons. 107,630 (1962).

vil·li·form (vil′ə fôrm′), *adj.* **1.** having the form of a villus. **2.** shaped and set so as to resemble the pile of velvet, as the teeth of certain fishes. [< NL *villiform(is).* See VILLUS, -FORM]

Vil·lon (vē yôn′), *n.* **1. Fran·çois** (frän swa′), 1431–63?, French poet. **2. Jacques** (zhäk), (*Gaston Duchamp*), 1875–1963, French painter.

vil·los·i·ty (vi los′i tē), *n., pl.* **-ties.** **1.** a villous surface or coating. **2.** a number of villi together. **3.** a villus. [< L *villōs(us)* shaggy (see VILLUS, -OSE[1]) + -ITY]

vil·lous (vil′əs), *adj.* **1.** covered with or of the nature of villi. **2.** having villiform processes. **3.** *Bot.* pubescent with long and soft hairs which are not interwoven. Also, **vil·lose** (vil′ōs). [< L *villōs(us)* shaggy; see -OUS] —**vil′lous·ly,** *adv.*

vil·lus (vil′əs), *n., pl.* **vil·li** (vil′ī). **1.** *Anat.* one of the minute, wormlike, vascular processes on certain membranes, esp. on the mucous membrane of the small intestine, where they serve in absorbing nutriment. **2.** *Bot.* one of the long, soft, straight hairs covering parts of certain plants. [< L: shaggy hair]

Vil·na (vil′nə; *Russ.* vēl′nä), *n.* a city in and the capital of Lithuania, in W Soviet Union in Europe: formerly in Poland. 293,000 (1965). Polish, **Wilno.** Lithuanian, **Vil·ni·us** (vil′nē ŏŏs′).

vim (vim), *n.* lively or energetic spirit; enthusiasm; vitality. [< L, acc. of *vīs* energy, force]

VIM (vim), *n.* a system of using electronically controlled conveyors to speed delivery and pickup of mail for skyscraper office tenants. [*V(ertical) I(mproved) M(ail)*]

vi·men (vī′men), *n., pl.* **vim·i·na** (vim′ə nə). *Bot.* a long, flexible shoot of a plant. [< L: osier, withe, twig] —**vim·i·nal** (vim′ə nəl), *adj.*

Vim·i·nal (vim′ə nəl), *n.* one of the seven hills on which ancient Rome was built.

vi·min·e·ous (vi min′ē əs), *adj. Bot.* **1.** of, like, or producing long, flexible shoots. **2.** of or made of twigs. [< L *vīmineus* made of osiers = *vīmin-* (s. of *vīmen*) osier + *-eus* -EOUS]

v. imp., verb impersonal.

Vi·my (vē mē′), *n.* a town in N France, N of Arras: battle 1917. 3009 (1962).

vin (van), *n., pl.* **vins** (van). *French.* wine.

vin-, var. of **vini-,** esp. before a vowel.

vi·na (vē′nä), *n.* a musical stringed instrument of India, consisting of a long, hollow, fretted stick to which one, two, or three gourds are attached to increase the resonance. [< Skt; cf. Hindi *bīnā*]

Vina

vi·na·ceous (vī nā′shəs), *adj.* **1.** of, pertaining to, or resembling wine or grapes. **2.** of the color of red wine: *a vinaceous rose.* [< L *vīnāceus*]

Vi·ña del Mar (bē′nyä del mär′), a city in central Chile, near Valparaiso: seaside resort. 135,782 (est. 1963).

vin·ai·grette (vin′ə gret′), *n.* **1.** a small, ornamental bottle or box for holding aromatic vinegar, smelling salts, or the like. —*adj.* **2.** (of a food) served with vinegar or vinaigrette sauce. [< F; see VINEGAR, -ETTE]

vinaigrette′ sauce′, a tart sauce of oil, vinegar, and seasonings, usually served cold with salads.

Vin·cennes (vin senz′; *Fr.* van sen′), *n.* a city in N France, near Paris: castle; park. 50,499 (1962).

Vin·cent (vin′sənt), *n.* **Saint,** died A.D. 304, Spanish martyr: patron saint of winegrowers.

Vin·cent de Paul (vin′sənt də pôl′; *Fr.* van sän′ də pôl′), **Saint,** 1576–1660, French Roman Catholic priest noted for his work to aid the poor.

Vin′cent's angi′na, *Pathol.* a disease characterized by ulceration of the mucosa of the tonsils, pharynx, and mouth, and by the development of a membrane, caused by a bacillus and spirillum. Also called **Vin′cent's infec′tion, Vin′cent's disease′, trench mouth.** [named after J. H. *Vincent* (1862–1950), French physician]

Vin·ci (vin′chē; *It.* vēn′chē), *n.* **Le·o·nar·do da** (lē′ə när′dō də, lā′-; *It.* le′ô när′dô dä), 1452–1519, Italian painter, sculptor, architect, musician, engineer, mathematician, and scientist.

vin·ci·ble (vin′sə bəl), *adj.* capable of being conquered or overcome: *vincible fears.* [< L *vincibil(is)* = *vinc(ere)* (to) overcome + *-ibilis* -IBLE]

vin·cit om·ni·a ve·ri·tas (wing′kit ōm′ni ä′ we′ri tās′; *Eng.* vin′sit om′nē ə ver′i tas′), *Latin.* truth conquers all things.

vin·cu·lum (ving′kyə ləm), *n., pl.* **-la** (-lə). **1.** a bond signifying union or unity; tie. **2.** *Math.* a stroke or brace drawn over a quantity consisting of several members or terms, as $\overline{a + b}$, in order to show that they are to be considered together. [< L: fetter = *vinc(īre)* to bind + *-ulum* n. suffix]

Vin′dhya Hills′ (vind′yä), a mountain range in central India, N of the Narbada River.

Vin′dhya Pra′desh (prä′desh), a former state in central India: now part of Madhya Pradesh.

vin·di·ca·ble (vin′də kə bəl), *adj.* capable of being vindicated. [< ML *vindicābil(is)* = L *vindicā(re)* (see VINDICATE) + *-bilis* -BLE]

vin·di·cate (vin′də kāt′), *v.t.,* **-cat·ed, -cat·ing.** **1.** to clear, as from an accusation or suspicion. **2.** to afford justification for; justify. **3.** to uphold or justify by argument or evidence. **4.** to maintain or defend against opposition. **5.** to claim for oneself or another. **6.** to get revenge for; avenge. **7.** *Obs.* to deliver from; liberate. [< L *vindicāt(us)* (ptp. of *vindicāre* to lay legal claim to (property), to free (someone) from servitude (by claiming him as free), to protect, avenge, punish) = *vindic-* (s. of *vindex* claimant, protector, avenger) + *-ātus* -ATE[1]] —**vin′di·ca′tor,** *n.* —**Syn. 1.** exonerate.

vin·di·ca·tion (vin′də kā′shən), *n.* **1.** the act of vindicating. **2.** the state of being vindicated. **3.** an excuse or justification. **4.** something that vindicates. [< L *vindicātiōn-* (s. of *vindicātiō*)]

vin·di·ca·to·ry (vin′də kə tôr′ē, -tôr′ē), *adj.* **1.** tending or serving to vindicate. **2.** punitive; retributive. Also, **vin·dic·a·tive** (vin dik′ə tiv, vin′də kā′-).

vin·dic·tive (vin dik′tiv), *adj.* **1.** disposed or inclined to revenge; vengeful. **2.** proceeding from or showing a revengeful spirit. [< L *vindict(a)* vengeance, fem. of **vindictus* (ptp. of **vindīcere* for *vindicāre;* see VINDICATE) + -IVE] —**vin·dic′tive·ly,** *adv.* —**vin·dic′tive·ness,** *n.* —**Syn. 1.** unforgiving. See **spiteful.** —**Ant. 1.** forgiving.

vine (vīn), *n.* **1.** any plant having a long, slender stem that trails or creeps on the ground or climbs by winding itself about a support or holding fast with tendrils or claspers. **2.** the stem of any such plant. **3.** a grape plant. [ME < OF *vi(g)ne* < L *vīnea* vine(yard) = *vīn(um)* WINE + *-ea,* fem. of *-eus* -EOUS] —**vined,** *adj.*

vine·dress·er (vīn′dres′ər), *n.* a person who tends or cultivates vines, esp. grapevines.

vin·e·gar (vin′ə gər), *n.* **1.** a sour liquid consisting of dilute and impure acetic acid, obtained by acetous fermentation from wine, cider, beer, ale, or the like: used as a condiment, preservative, etc. **2.** *Pharm.* a solution of a medicinal substance in dilute acetic acid or vinegar. [ME *vinegre* < OF = *vin* WINE + *egre, aigre* sour (see EAGER)] —**vin′a·ger·ish,** *adj.*

vin′egar eel′, a minute nematode worm, *Anguillula aceti,* found in vinegar, fermenting paste, etc. Also called **vin′egar worm′.**

vin·e·gar·roon (vin′ə gə rōōn′), *n.* a large whip scorpion, *Mastigoproctus giganteus,* of the southern U.S. and Mexico, that when disturbed, emits a volatile fluid having a vinegary odor. [< MexSp *vinagrón* = Sp *vinagr(e)* vinegar + *-ón* aug. suffix]

Vinegarroon (Length 2½ in.)

vin·e·gar·y (vin′ə gə rē), *adj.* **1.** of the nature of or resembling vinegar; sour; acid: *a vinegary taste.* **2.** having a disagreeable character or manner; crabbed; ill-tempered; bitter.

Vine·land (vīn′lənd), *n.* **1.** a city in S New Jersey. 47,399 (1970). **2.** Vinland.

vin·er·y (vī′nə rē), *n., pl.* **-er·ies.** **1.** a place or enclosure in which vines, esp. grapevines, are grown. **2.** vines collectively. [VINE + -ERY, r. ME *vinary* < ML *vīnāri(um),* n. use of neut. of L *vīnārius* of WINE; see -ARY]

vine·yard (vin′yərd), *n.* **1.** a plantation of grapevines, esp. one producing wine grapes. **2.** a sphere of activity, esp. on a high spiritual plane. [ME (see VINE, YARD[2]); r. *win(e)yard,* OE *wīngeard*]

vingt-et-un (*Fr.* van tā œn′), *n. Cards.* twenty-one (def. 2). [< F]

vini-, a learned borrowing from Latin meaning "wine," used in the formation of compound words: *viniculture.* Also, **vin-, vino-.** [< L, comb. form of *vīnum*]

vi·nic (vī′nik, vin′ik), *adj.* of, pertaining to, found in, or derived from wine: *a vinic odor.*

vin·i·cul·ture (vin′ə kul′chər), *n.* the science or study of making wines. —**vin′i·cul′tur·al,** *adj.* —**vin′i·cul′tur·ist,** *n.*

vi·nif·er·a (vī nif′ər ə), *adj.* **1.** of, pertaining to, or derived from a European grape, *Vitis vinifera,* cultivated in the western U.S. for table use and for making wine and raisins. —*n.* **2.** a vinifera grape. [< NL, fem. of L *vīnifer* wine-producing. See VINI-, -FER]

vi·nif·er·ous (vī nif′ər əs), *adj.* suitable for or productive of wine. [< L *vīnifer* (see VINI-, -FER) + -OUS]

Vin·land (vin′lənd), *n.* a region in E North America, somewhere between Newfoundland and Virginia: visited and described by Norsemen ab. A.D. 1000. Also, **Vineland.**

Vin·ni·tsa (vēn′i tsä), *n.* a city in the central Ukraine, in the SW Soviet Union in Europe, on the Bug River. 144,000 (est. 1964).

vino-, var. of **vini-.**

vin or·di·naire (van ôr dē ner′), *pl.* **vins or·di·naires** (van zôr dē ner′). *French.* inexpensive table wine. [lit., ordinary wine]

vi·nos·i·ty (vī nos′i tē), *n.* the collective characteristics of a wine, including its flavor, color, etc. [< LL *vīnōsitās* = L *vīnōs(us)* VINOUS + *-itās* -ITY]

vi·nous (vī′nəs), *adj.* **1.** of, pertaining to, or characteristic of wine. **2.** produced by, indicative of, or given to indulgence in wine. **3.** wine-colored; vinaceous. [< L *vīnōs(us)* = *vīn(um)* WINE + *-ōsus* -OSE[1], -OUS]

Vin·son (vin′sən), *n.* **Frederick Moore,** 1890–1953, U.S. jurist: Chief Justice of the U.S. 1946–53.

vin·tage (vin′tij), *n.* **1.** the wine from a particular harvest or crop. **2.** the annual produce of a grape harvest, esp. with reference to the wine obtained. **3.** an exceptionally fine wine from the crop of a good year. **4.** the time of harvesting grapes or of making wine. **5.** the act or process of producing wine; wine making. **6.** the class of dated or old-fashioned objects with reference to when they were made or in use: *a car of 1917 vintage.* **—***adj.* **7.** of or pertaining to wines or wine making. **8.** being of a specified vintage. **9.** being or having the best of its kind. **10.** being dated, old-fashioned, or of some antiquity. [late ME < AF = *vint(er)* VINTNER + *-age* -AGE; r. ME *vindage, vendage* < AF, by dissimilation of OF *vendange* < L *vindēmia* grape gathering = *vīn(um)* grape, WINE + *-dēmia* a taking away (*dēm(ere)* (to) take from: *dē-* DE- + *em(ere)* (to) buy, take + *-ia* -Y[3])]

vin·tag·er (vin′tə jər), *n.* a person who helps in the harvest of grapes for wine making.

vint·ner (vint′nər), *n.* a person who makes or sells wine. [ME *vint(e)ner* < *vin(e)ter* < AF; OF *vinetier* < ML *vīnētārius* = L *vīnēt(um)* vineyard (*vīn(um)* WINE + *-ētum* collective suffix) + *-ārius* -ARY]

vin·y (vī′nē), *adj.*, **vin·i·er, vin·i·est. 1.** of, pertaining to, of the nature of, or resembling vines. **2.** abounding in or producing vines.

vi·nyl (vī′nil, vīn′əl, vin′il, vin′əl), *adj.* **1.** *Chem.* containing the vinyl group. **—***n.* **2.** any resin formed by polymerization of compounds containing the vinyl group or plastics made from such resins. [VIN- + -YL]

vi·nyl·a·cet·y·lene (vī′nil ə set′əlēn′, vīn′əl ə-, vin′il-, vin′əl ə-), *n.* *Chem.* a volatile liquid, $H_2C{=}CHC{\equiv}CH$, used chiefly in the manufacture of neoprene.

vi·nyl·ben·zene (vī′nil ben′zēn, -ben zēn′, vīn′əl-, vin′il-, vin′əl-), *n.* *Chem.* styrene.

vi·nyl·eth·yl·ene (vī′nil eth′ə lēn′, vīn′əl-, vin′il-, vin′əl-), *n.* *Chem.* butadiene.

vi′nyl group′, *Chem.* the univalent group, $CH_2{=}CH{-}$, derived from ethylene. Also called **vi′nyl rad′ical.**

vi·nyl·i·dene (vī nil′i dēn′), *adj.* *Chem.* containing the vinylidene group. [VINYL + -ID[3] + -ENE]

vinyl′idene group′, *Chem.* the bivalent group, $H_2C{=}C{=}$, derived from ethylene. Also called **vinyl′idene rad′ical.**

Vi·nyl·ite (vīn′əlīt′, vin′-), *n.* *Trademark.* any of a series of thermoplastic, nontoxic, acid-resistant, vinyl resins or plastics: used in coatings, adhesives, film, molded ware, and phonograph records.

vi′nyl pol′ymer, *Chem.* any of a group of compounds derived by polymerization from vinyl compounds, as styrene.

vi′nyl res′in, *Chem.* See **polyvinyl resin.**

vi·ol (vī′əl), *n.* a bowed musical instrument, differing from the violin in having deeper ribs, sloping shoulders, a greater number of strings, usually six, and frets: common in the 16th and 17th centuries in various sizes from the treble viol to the bass viol. [< MF *viole* < OPr *viola, viula* (see VIOLA[1]); r. ME *viele* < AF (OF *viel(l)e*)]

vi·o·la[1] (vē ō′lə, vī-), *n.* a four-stringed musical instrument of the violin class, but slightly larger than the violin. [< It *viola,* prob. < OPr *viola, viula* of uncert. orig.; cf. VL *vīdula, vītula,* perh. connected with L *vītulārī* to be joyful, celebrate a festival]

vi·o·la[2] (vī′ə lə, vī ō′-), *n.* **1.** any plant of the genus *Viola,* esp. a cultivated variety. Cf. **pansy** (def. 1), **violet** (def. 1). **2.** a pansy, *V. cornuta,* cultivated as a garden plant. [< L: violet]

vi·o·la·ble (vī′ə lə bəl), *adj.* capable of being violated: *a violable precept.* [< L *violābil(is)* = *violā(re)* (to) VIOLATE + *-bilis* -BLE] **—vi′o·la·bil′i·ty,** *n.* **—vi′o·la·bly,** *adv.*

vi·o·la·ceous (vī′ə lā′shəs), *adj.* **1.** belonging to the *Violaceae,* or violet family of plants. **2.** of a violet color; bluish-purple. [< L *violāceus* violet-colored. See VIOLA[2], -ACEOUS]

vio′la clef′, *Music.* See **alto clef.**

vi·o·la da brac·cio (vē ō′lə də brä′chō, vī-), *pl.* **viola da braccios.** an old musical instrument, the alto of the viol family, held against the shoulder like a violin. [< It: lit., viola for the arm]

vi·o·la da gam·ba (vē ō′lə də gäm′bə, -gam′-, vī-), *pl.* **viola da gambas.** an old musical instrument of the viol family, held on or between the knees; bass viol. [< It: lit., viol for the leg]

Viola da gamba

vi·o·la d'a·mo·re (vē ō′lə dä mōr′ā, -môr′ā, vī-), *pl.* **viola d'amores.** a treble viol with numerous sympathetic strings and several gut strings, producing a resonant sound. [< It: lit., viol of love]

vi·o·late (vī′ə lāt′), *v.t.*, **-lat·ed, -lat·ing. 1.** to break, infringe, or transgress (a law, agreement, etc.). **2.** to disturb (a condition of peace or harmony). **3.** to act in unlawful or improper disregard of the sacred or established nature of: *to violate a church; to violate a right.* **4.** to molest sexually, esp. to rape (a woman). [late ME < L *violāt(us)* (ptp. of *violāre* to treat with violence) = *viol(entus)* VIOLENT + *-ātus* -ATE[1]] **—vi′o·la′tor, vi′o·lat′er,** *n.*

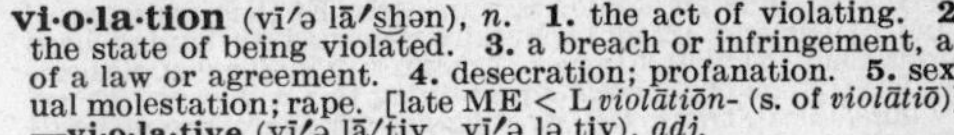

vi·o·la·tion (vī′ə lā′shən), *n.* **1.** the act of violating. **2.** the state of being violated. **3.** a breach or infringement, as of a law or agreement. **4.** desecration; profanation. **5.** sexual molestation; rape. [late ME < L *violātiōn-* (s. of *violātiō*)] **—vi·o·la·tive** (vī′ə lā′tiv, vī′ə lə tiv), *adj.*

vi·o·lence (vī′ə ləns), *n.* **1.** swift and intense force. **2.** rough or injurious physical force, action, or treatment: *to die by violence.* **3.** an unjust or unwarranted exertion of force or power. **4.** a violent act or proceeding. **5.** rough or immoderate vehemence, as of feeling or language. **6.** injury, as from distortion of meaning or fact: *to do violence to a translation.* [ME < AF, OF < L *violentia* = *violent(us)* VIOLENT + *-ia* -Y[3]; see -ENCE]

vi·o·lent (vī′ə lənt), *adj.* **1.** acting with or characterized by extreme force. **2.** characterized by or arising from injurious or destructive force: *a violent death.* **3.** roughly or immoderately vehement or impetuous. **4.** of, pertaining to, or constituting a distortion of meaning or fact. [ME < L *violent(us)* appar. = *vio-* (comb. form of *vīs* force) + *-lentus* adj. suffix] **—vi′o·lent·ly,** *adv.*

vi·o·les·cent (vī′ə les′ənt), *adj.* tending to a violet color. [< L *viol(a)* violet + -ESCENT]

vi·o·let (vī′ə lit), *n.* **1.** any chiefly low, stemless or leafy-stemmed herb of the genus *Viola,* having purple, blue, yellow, white, or variegated flowers. **2.** the flower of any native, wild species of violet, as distinguished from the pansy: the state flower of Illinois, New Jersey, and Rhode Island. **3.** bluish purple. **—***adj.* **4.** of the color violet; bluish-purple. [ME < OF *violete* = *viole* (< L *viola* violet) + *-ete* -ET]

vi′olet ray′, light of the shortest visible wavelength.

vi·o·lin (vī′ə lin′), *n.* the treble instrument of the violin family, held nearly horizontal by the player's arm and with the lower part supported against the collarbone or shoulder. [< It *violino* = *viol(a)* (see VIOLA[1]) + *-ino* dim. suffix]

Violin

violin′ clef′, *Music.* See **treble clef.**

vi·o·lin·ist (vī′ə lin′ist), *n.* a person who plays the violin. [< It *violinist(a)*]

vi·ol·ist[1] (vī′ə list), *n.* a person who plays the viol. [VIOL + -IST]

vi·o·list[2] (vē ō′list, vī-), *n.* a person who plays the viola. [VIOL(A)[1] + -IST]

Viol·let-le-Duc (vyô le′lə dʏk′), *n.* **Eu·gène Em·ma·nu·el** (œ zhen′ e mA nʏ el′), 1814–79, French architect and writer.

vi·o·lon·cel·list (vē′ə lən chel′ist), *n.* cellist.

vi·o·lon·cel·lo (vē′ə lən chel′ō), *n., pl.* **-los.** cello. [< It = *violon(e)* (*viol(a)* bass viol + *-one* aug. suffix) + *-cello* dim. suffix]

vi·os·ter·ol (vī os′tə rōl′, -rôl′, -rol′), *n.* *Biochem.* a vitamin D preparation produced by the irradiation of ergosterol. [(ULTRA)VI(OLET) + (ERG)OSTEROL]

VIP, *Informal.* very important person. Also, **V.I.P.**

vi·per (vī′pər), *n.* **1.** any of several venomous Old World snakes of the genus *Vipera,* esp. *V. berus.* **2.** any venomous Old World snake of the family *Viperidae,* characterized by erectile, venom-conducting fangs. **3.** See **pit viper. 4.** any of various venomous or supposedly venomous snakes. **5.** a malignant or spiteful person. [ME, OE *vīpere* < L *vīpera* contr. of **vī(vi)pera;* the ancients thought it was VIVIPAROUS]

vi·per·ine (vī′pər in, -pə rīn′), *adj.* of, pertaining to, or resembling a viper; venomous. [< L *vīperīn(us)*]

vi·per·ish (vī′pər ish), *adj.* viperous. **—vi′per·ish·ly,** *adv.*

vi·per·ous (vī′pər əs), *adj.* **1.** characteristic of or resembling a viper; venomous. **2.** of or pertaining to vipers. **—vi′per·ous·ly,** *adv.*

vi′per's bu′gloss, the blueweed.

vi·ra·go (vi rā′gō, vī-), *n., pl.* **-goes, -gos. 1.** a loud, ill-tempered, scolding woman; shrew. **2.** *Archaic.* a woman of masculine strength or spirit. [ME, OE < L = *vir* man + *-āgō* suffix expressing association of some kind, here resemblance]

vi·ral (vī′rəl), *adj.* of, pertaining to, or caused by a virus. [VIR(US) + -AL[1]]

Vi·ra Sai·va (vir′ə sī′və), *Hinduism.* Lingayata. [< Skt = *vīra* man + *śaiva* votary of Shiva]

vir·e·lay (vir′ə lā′), *n.* *Pros.* **1.** an old French form of short poem, composed of short lines running on two rhymes and having two opening lines recurring at intervals. **2.** any of various similar forms of poem. Also, **vir′e·lai′.** [late ME < OF *virelai,* alter. (see LAY[4]) of *vireli, virli* jingle used as the refrain of a song]

vir·e·o (vir′ē ō′), *n., pl.* **vir·e·os.** any of several small, insectivorous, American birds of the family *Vireonidae,* having the plumage usually olive-green or gray above and white or yellow below. [< L: ? greenfinch; cf. *virēre* to be green]

Vireo,
Vireo olivaceus
(Length 6 in.)

vi·res (wī′rās; *Eng.* vī′rēz), *n.* *Latin.* pl. of **vis.**

vi·res·cence (vī res′əns), *n.* *Bot.* the state of becoming somewhat green, due to the abnormal presence of chlorophyll. [VIRESC(ENT) + -ENCE]

vi·res·cent (vī res′ənt), *adj.* **1.** turning green. **2.** greenish. [< L *virescent-* (s. of *virescēns,* prp. of *virescere* to become green) = *vir-* green (see VIREO) + *-escent-* -ESCENT]

Virg., Virginia.

vir·ga (vûr′gə), *n.* (*construed as sing. or pl.*) *Meteorol.* streaks of water drops or ice particles falling out of a cloud and evaporating before reaching the ground. [< L: rod, streak]

vir·gate[1] (vûr′git, -gāt), *adj.* shaped like a rod or wand; long, slender, and straight. [< L *virgāt(us);* see VIRGATE[2]]

vir·gate[2] (vûr′git, -gāt), *n.* an early English measure of land of varying extent, generally regarded as having been equivalent to about 30 acres. [< ML *virgāta (terrae)* measure (of land), fem. of L *virgātus* pertaining to a rod = *virg(a)* rod + *-ātus* -ATE[1]; trans. OE *gierd landes* yard-measure of land]
Vir·gil (vûr′jəl), *n.* Vergil. —**Vir·gil·i·an** (vər jil′ē ən, -jil′yən), *adj.*
vir·gin (vûr′jin), *n.* **1.** a person, esp. a girl or woman, who has never had sexual intercourse. **2.** an unmarried girl or woman. **3. the Virgin,** Mary, the mother of Christ. **4.** a female animal that has never copulated. **5.** an unfertilized insect. **6.** (*cap.*) *Astron., Astrol.* the constellation or sign of Virgo. —*adj.* **7.** being a virgin. **8.** of, pertaining to, or characteristic of a virgin. **9.** pure; unsullied: *virgin snow.* **10.** without alloy or modification: *virgin gold.* **11.** not previously exploited or used: *virgin timberlands.* **12.** *Zool.* not fertilized. **13.** (of vegetable oil) obtained by the first pressing without the application of heat. [ME *virgine* < AF, OF < L *virgin-*, s. of *virgō* maiden, virgin] —**Syn. 2.** maid, maiden. **9.** chaste, unpolluted. **10.** unalloyed, unadulterated. **11.** fresh, new, maiden.
vir·gin·al[1] (vûr′jə nəl), *adj.* **1.** of, pertaining to, characteristic of, or befitting a virgin. **2.** continuing in a state of virginity. **3.** pure; unsullied; untouched. **4.** *Zool.* not fertilized. [late ME < L *virginālis*]. See VIRGIN, -AL[1]]
vir·gin·al[2] (vûr′jən əl), *n.* Often, **virginals.** a rectangular harpsichord with the strings stretched parallel to the keyboard, the earlier types placed on a table: popular in the 16th and 17th centuries. [appar. special use of VIRGINAL[1]] —**vir′gin·al·ist,** *n.*

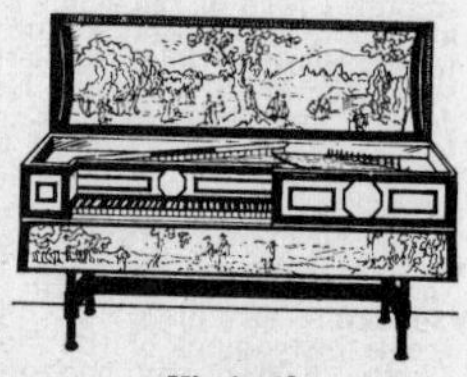
Virginal[2]

vir′gin birth′, **1.** *Theol.* the doctrine or dogma that the conception and birth of Christ did not impair the virginity of Mary. **2.** *Zool.* parthenogenesis; parturition by a female who has not copulated.
Vir·gin·ia (vər jin′yə), *n.* a state in the E United States, on the Atlantic coast. 4,648,494 (1970); 40,815 sq. mi. *Cap.:* Richmond. *Abbr.:* Va., VA —**Vir·gin′ian,** *adj., n.*
Virgin′ia Beach′, a city in SE Virginia: resort. 172,106 (1970).
Virgin′ia Cit′y, a mining town in W Nevada: famous for the discovery of the rich Comstock silver lode 1859.
Virgin′ia cow′slip, a wild, boraginaceous herb, *Mertensia virginica,* of the eastern U.S., grown as a garden perennial for its handsome clustered blue flowers. Also called **Virgin′ia blue′bell.**
Virgin′ia creep′er, a climbing, vitaceous plant, *Parthenocissus quinquefolia,* of North America, having palmate leaves, usually with five leaflets, and bluish-black berries. Also called **American ivy.**
Virgin′ia deer′, **1.** the common white-tailed deer, *Odocoileus virginianus,* of eastern North America. See illus. at **deer. 2.** any related variety of white-tailed deer.
Virgin′ia ham′, a ham from a razorback hog, cured in hickory smoke.
Virgin′ia reel′, an American country dance in which the partners start by facing each other in two lines and perform various steps together.
Virgin′ia trum′pet flow′er. See **trumpet creeper.**
Vir′gin Is′lands, a group of islands in the West Indies, E of Puerto Rico: comprises the Virgin Islands of the United States and the British Virgin Islands.
Vir′gin Is′lands of the Unit′ed States′, a group of U.S. islands in the West Indies, including St. Thomas, St. John, and St. Croix: purchased from Denmark 1917. 62,468 (1970); 132 sq. mi. *Cap.:* Charlotte Amalie. Formerly, **Danish West Indies.**
vir·gin·i·ty (vər jin′i tē), *n.* **1.** the state or condition of being a virgin. **2.** the state or condition of being pure, fresh, or unused. [ME *virginite* < AF, OF < L *virginitāt-* (s. of *virginitās*)]
Vir′gin Mar′y, Mary (def. 1).
Vir′gin Queen′, Queen Elizabeth I of England.
vir·gin's-bow·er (vûr′jinz bou′ər), any of several climbing varieties of clematis having small, white flowers in large panicles, as *Clematis Vitalba,* of Europe, or *C. virginiana,* of the U.S.
vir′gin wool′, wool that has not previously been spun, woven, or used. Cf. **reprocessed wool.**
Vir·go (vûr′gō), *n., gen.* **Vir·gi·nis** (vûr′jə nis), for 1. **1.** *Astron.* the Virgin, a zodiacal constellation between Leo and Libra, containing the bright star Spica. **2.** *Astrol.* the sixth sign of the zodiac. See diag. at **zodiac.** [< L: maiden]
vir·gu·late (vûr′gyə lit, -lāt′), *adj.* rod-shaped; virgate. [< L *virgul(a)* (*virg(a)* rod + *-ula* -ULE) + -ATE[1]]
vir·gule (vûr′gyōōl), *n.* *Print.* **1.** an oblique stroke (/) used between two words to show that the appropriate one may be chosen to complete the sense of the text: *The defendant and/or his attorney must appear in court.* **2.** a dividing line, as in dates, fractions, a run-in passage of poetry to show verse division, etc. Also called **diagonal, shilling mark, slant, slash, solidus;** *esp. Brit.,* **stroke.** [< F *virgule* comma, little rod < L *virgula;* see VIRGULATE]
vir·i·des·cent (vir′i des′ənt), *adj.* slightly green; greenish. [< LL *viridescent-* (s. of *viridescēns,* prp. of *viridescere* to become green) = *virid-* green + *-escent-* -ESCENT] —**vir′i·des′cence,** *n.*
vi·rid·i·an (və rid′ē ən), *n.* a long-lasting, bluish-green pigment, consisting of a hydrated oxide of chromium. [< L *viridi(s)* green + -AN]
vi·rid·i·ty (və rid′i tē), *n.* greenness; verdancy; verdure. [late ME < L *viriditāt-* (s. of *viriditās*) = *viridi(s)* green + *-tāt-* -TY[2]]
vir·ile (vir′əl *or, esp. Brit.,* -īl), *adj.* **1.** of, pertaining to, characteristic of, or befitting a man; masculine. **2.** having or exhibiting masculine strength. **3.** characterized by a vigorous, masculine spirit. **4.** capable of procreation. [< L *virīlis* manly = *vir* man + *-īlis* -ILE] —**Syn. 2.** vigorous. —**Ant. 1–3.** effeminate.
vir·i·lism (vir′ə liz′əm), *n.* the development of male secondary sex characteristics in a female.
vi·ril·i·ty (və ril′i tē), *n.* **1.** the state or quality of being virile. **2.** the power of procreation. [< L *virīlitās*]
vir·i·lo·cal (vir′ə lō′kəl), *adj.* patrilocal. [< L *viri-* (comb. form of *vir* man) + LOCAL] —**vir′i·lo′cal·ly,** *adv.*
vi·rol·o·gy (vī rol′ə jē, vi-), *n.* the science dealing with the study of viruses and the diseases caused by them. [*viro-* (comb. form of VIRUS) + -LOGY] —**vi·ro·log·i·cal** (vī′rə loj′i kəl), *adj.* —**vi·rol′o·gist,** *n.*
v. irr., verb irregular.
vir·tu (vər tōō′, vûr′tōō), *n.* **1.** excellence or merit in objects of art, curios, and the like. **2.** (*construed as pl.*) such objects or articles collectively. **3.** a taste for or knowledge of such objects. Also, **vertu.** [< It *virtù* VIRTUE]
vir·tu·al (vûr′chōō əl), *adj.* **1.** being such in force or effect, though not actually or expressly such: *reduced to virtual poverty.* **2.** *Archaic.* having the inherent power to produce certain effects. [late ME < ML *virtuāl(is).* See VIRTUE, -AL[1]]
vir·tu·al·ly (vûr′chōō ə lē), *adv.* **1.** for the most part; almost wholly. **2.** *Obs.* essentially, although not formally or actually. [ME]
vir·tue (vûr′chōō), *n.* **1.** moral excellence; goodness; righteousness. **2.** conformity in life and conduct to moral and ethical principles. **3.** chastity, esp. in a girl or woman. **4.** a particular moral excellence. Cf. **cardinal virtues, natural virtue, theological virtue. 5.** a good or admirable quality, as of a person, thing, etc. **6.** inherent power to produce effects; potency. **7. virtues,** an order of angels. Cf. **angel** (def. 1). **8.** *Archaic.* manly excellence; valor. **9. by** or **in virtue of,** by reason of; because of. [alter. (with *i* < L) of ME *vertu* < AF, OF < L *virtūt-* (s. of *virtūs*) maleness, worth, virtue < *vir* man] —**vir′tue·less,** *adj.* —**Syn. 1.** See **goodness. 2.** integrity. **3.** virginity, purity. —**Ant. 1.** vice.
vir·tu·os·i·ty (vûr′chōō os′i tē), *n.* **1.** the character, ability, or skill of a virtuoso. **2.** a fondness for or interest in virtu. [VIRTUOS(O) + -ITY]
vir·tu·o·so (vûr′chōō ō′sō), *n., pl.* **-sos, -si** (-sē), *adj.* —*n.* **1.** a person who has special knowledge or skill in a field, esp. in musical technique. **2.** a person who has a cultivated appreciation of artistic excellence. —*adj.* **3.** of, pertaining to, or characteristic of a virtuoso. [< It: versed, skilled < LL *virtuōsus* VIRTUOUS]
vir·tu·ous (vûr′chōō əs), *adj.* **1.** conforming to moral and ethical principles; morally excellent; upright. **2.** chaste, as a person. **3.** *Archaic.* able to produce effects; potent. [alter. (with *i* < L) of ME *vertuous* < AF < LL *virtuōsus.* See VIRTUE, -OUS] —**vir′tu·ous·ly,** *adv.* —**Syn. 1.** good, pure. —**Ant. 1.** vicious.
vir·tu·te et ar·mis (wiʀ tōō′te et är′mēs; *Eng.* vər tōō′tē et är′mis, vər tyōō′tē), *Latin.* by virtue and arms: motto of Mississippi.
vir·u·lence (vir′yə ləns, vir′ə-), *n.* **1.** the quality of being virulent. **2.** *Bacteriol.* the relative ability of a microorganism to cause disease. Also, **vir′u·len·cy.** [< LL *vīrulentia* stench = *vīrulent-* VIRULENT + *-ia* -Y[3]; see -ENCE]
vir·u·lent (vir′yə lənt, vir′ə-), *adj.* **1.** actively poisonous; intensely noxious; venomous. **2.** *Med.* highly infective; malignant or deadly. **3.** *Bacteriol.* of the nature of an organism causing specific or general clinical symptoms. **4.** intensely bitter, spiteful, or malicious. [< L *vīrulent(us)* = *vīru(s)* poison (see VIRUS) + *-lentus* adj. suffix] —**vir′u·lent·ly,** *adv.*
vi·rus (vī′rəs), *n., pl.* **-rus·es. 1.** an infectious agent, esp. any of a group of ultramicroscopic, infectious agents that reproduce only in living cells. **2.** See **virus disease. 3.** the venom of a poisonous animal. [< L: slime, poison; akin to OOZE[2]] —**Syn. 1.** See **poison.**
vi′rus disease′, any disease caused by a virus.
vis (wēs; *Eng.* vis), *n., pl.* **vi·res** (wē′ʀes; *Eng.* vī′rēz). *Latin.* strength; force or power.
Vis., **1.** Viscount. **2.** Viscountess.
vi·sa (vē′zə), *n., pl.* **-sas,** *v.,* **-saed, -sa·ing.** —*n.* **1.** *Govt.* a permit entered on the passport of a national of one country by the consular officer of another, allowing the bearer entry into or transit through the country issuing the permit. —*v.t.* **2.** to give a visa to; approve a visa for. **3.** to put a visa on (a passport). Also, **visé.** [< F, short for L *carta vīsa* the document (has been) examined; *vīsa* ptp. fem. of *vīsere* to look into, see to, freq. of *vidēre* to see]
vis·age (viz′ij), *n.* **1.** the face, esp. of a human being, usually with reference to shape, features, expression, etc.; countenance. **2.** aspect; appearance. [ME < AF, OF < LL, L *vīs(us)* (LL: face, L: sight, appearance, n. use of *vīsus,* ptp. of *vidēre* to see) + F *-age* -AGE] —**vis′aged,** *adj.* —**Syn. 1.** physiognomy. See **face.**
Vi·sa·kha·pat·nam (vi sä′kə put′nəm), *n.* a seaport in E India, on the Bay of Bengal. 182,000 (1961).
Vi·sa·lia (vi sāl′yə), *n.* a city in central California. 27,268 (1970).
vis·ard (viz′ərd), *n.* vizard.
vis-à-vis (vē′zə vē′; *Fr.* vē zA vē′), *adv., adj., prep., n., pl.* **-vis.** —*adv., adj.* **1.** face-to-face. —*prep.* **2.** in relation to; as compared with: *income vis-à-vis expenditures.* **3.** facing; opposite. —*n.* **4.** a person face-to-face with or situated opposite to another. **5.** a carriage in which the occupants sit face-to-face. [< F; see VISAGE]
Vi·sa·yan (vi sī′ən), *n., pl.* **-yans,** (*esp. collectively*) **-yan. 1.** one of a Malay people, the most numerous native race of the Philippines. **2.** the language of this people, an Indonesian language of the Malayo-Polynesian family. Also, **Bisayan.**
Visa′yan Is′lands, a group of islands in the central Philippines, including Panay, Negros, Cebú, Bohol, Leyte, Samar, Masbate, and smaller islands. Spanish, **Bisayas.**
Vis·by (vēs′bʏ), *n.* a seaport on the Swedish island of Gotland, in the Baltic: formerly an important member of the Hanseatic League. 53,662 (1964). German, **Wisby.**
Visc., **1.** Viscount. **2.** Viscountess.
vis·ca·cha (vis kä′chə), *n.* **1.** a burrowing rodent, *Lagostomus trichodactylus,* inhabiting the pampas of Paraguay and Argentina, allied to the chinchilla. **2.** a related rodent of the genus *Lagidium,* of the Andes, having long, rabbitlike ears and a squirrellike tail. Also, **vizcacha.** [< Sp < Quechuan *wiskácha*]

vis·cer·a (vis′ər ə), *n.pl., sing.* **vis·cus** (vis′kəs). **1.** *Anat., Zool.* the organs in the cavities of the body, esp. those in the abdominal cavity. **2.** (not in technical use) the intestines; bowels. [< L: internal organs, pl. of *viscus* flesh]

vis·cer·al (vis′ər əl), *adj.* **1.** of, pertaining to, or affecting the viscera. **2.** characterized by or proceeding from instinctive rather than intellectual motivation. [< ML *viscerāl(is)*] —**vis′cer·al·ly,** *adv.*

vis·cid (vis′id), *adj.* **1.** having a glutinous consistency; sticky; adhesive; viscous. **2.** *Bot.* covered by a sticky substance, as a leaf. [< LL *viscid(us)* = *visc(um)* birdlime + *-idus* -ID[4]; see VISCOUS] —**vis·cid′i·ty, vis′cid·ness,** *n.*

vis·coid (vis′koid), *adj.* somewhat viscous. Also, **vis·coi′dal.** [VISC(OUS) + -OID]

vis·com·e·ter (vi skom′i tər), *n.* a device for measuring viscosity. [syncopated var. of VISCOSIMETER] —**vis·co·met·ric** (vis′kə me′trik), *adj.* —**vis·com′e·try,** *n.*

Vis·con·ti (vēs kôn′tē), *n.* an Italian family that ruled Milan and Lombardy from 1277 to 1447.

vis·cose (vis′kōs), *n.* **1.** a viscous solution prepared by treating cellulose with caustic soda and carbon bisulfide: used in manufacturing regenerated cellulose fibers, sheets, or tubes, as rayon or cellophane. **2.** viscose rayon. —*adj.* **3.** of, pertaining to, or made from viscose. **4.** viscous. [< L *viscōs(us)* VISCOUS]

vis·co·sim·e·ter (vis′kō sim′i tər), *n.* viscometer. [VISCOSI(TY) + -METER] —**vis·co·si·met·ric** (vis′kō si me′trik, vi skos′i-), *adj.*

vis·cos·i·ty (vi skos′i tē), *n., pl.* **-ties. 1.** the state or quality of being viscous. **2.** *Physics.* **a.** the property of a fluid that resists the force tending to cause the fluid to flow. **b.** the measure of the extent to which a fluid possesses this property. [late ME < ML *viscōsitāt-* (s. of *viscōsitās*)]

vis·count (vī′kount′), *n.* **1.** a nobleman next below an earl or count and next above a baron. **2.** *Hist.* a deputy of a count or earl. **3.** (in England) a sheriff. [late ME *viscounte* < AF (OF *visconte*) = *vis* VICE[3] + *counte* COUNT[2], trans. ML *vicecomes*]

vis·count·cy (vī′kount′sē), *n.* the rank, title, or status of a viscount. Also, **vis′count·ship′.**

vis·count·ess (vī′koun′tis), *n.* **1.** the wife or widow of a viscount. **2.** a woman holding in her own right a rank equivalent to that of a viscount.

vis·count·y (vī′koun′tē), *n., pl.* **-count·ies. 1.** viscountcy. **2.** *Hist.* the jurisdiction of a viscount or the territory under his authority.

vis·cous (vis′kəs), *adj.* **1.** of a glutinous nature or consistency; sticky; thick; adhesive. **2.** having the property of viscosity. Also, **viscose.** [late ME < L *viscōs(us)* = *visc(um)* mistletoe, birdlime (made with mistletoe berries) + *-ōsus* -OUS] —**vis′cous·ly,** *adv.*

Visct., 1. Viscount. **2.** Viscountess.

vis·cus (vis′kəs), *n.* sing. of **viscera.**

vise (vīs), *n., v.,* **vised, vis·ing.** —*n.* **1.** any of various devices, usually having two jaws that may be brought together or separated by means of a screw, lever, or the like, used to hold an object firmly while work is being done on it. —*v.t.* **2.** to hold, press, or squeeze with or as with a vise. Also, **vice.** [ME *vis* < OF *vis* a screw < L *vītis* vine (spiral form gave rise to later meaning)] —**vise′like′,** *adj.*

Vise

vi·sé (vē′zā, vē zā′), *n., v.t.,* **vi·séed, vi·sé·ing.** visa. [< F, ptp. of *viser* to inspect, check; see VISA]

Vish·nu (vish′no͞o), *n. Hinduism.* **1.** (in popular Hinduism) a deity believed to have descended from heaven to earth in several incarnations. His most important human incarnation is the Krishna of the Bhagavad-Gita. **2.** (in later Hinduism) "the Preserver," the second member of the Trimurti, along with Brahma the Creator and Shiva the Destroyer. [< Skt: lit., the everywhere-active one] —**Vish′nu·ism,** *n.*

vis·i·bil·i·ty (viz′ə bil′i tē), *n.* **1.** the state or fact of being visible. **2.** the relative ability to be seen under given conditions of distance, light, atmosphere, etc.: *The pilot made an instrument landing because of low visibility.* [< LL *vīsibilitāt-* (s. of *vīsibilitās*). See VISIBLE, -TY[2]]

vis·i·ble (viz′ə bəl), *adj.* **1.** that can be seen; perceptible to the eye. **2.** apparent; manifest; obvious: *a man with no visible means of support.* **3.** noting or pertaining to a system of keeping records or information on cards or sheets in such a way that the desired reference can be brought instantly to view: *a visible file; a visible index.* [ME < L *vīsibil(is)* = *vīs-* (see VISION) + *-ibilis* -IBLE] —**vis′i·bly,** *adv.*

vis′ible hori′zon, horizon (def. 1).

vis′ible spec′trum, *Physics.* the range of electromagnetic radiations that are normally visible, having wavelengths of between 3800 and 7600 angstrom units.

vis′ible speech′, *Phonet.* the representation in graphic or pictorial form of characteristics of speech, as by means of sound spectrograms.

Vis·i·goth (viz′ə goth′), *n.* a member of the westerly division of the Goths, which formed a monarchy about A.D. 418, maintaining it in southern France until 507 and in Spain until 711. Cf. **Ostrogoth.** [< LL *Visigothī* (pl.)] —**Vis′i·goth′ic,** *adj.*

vi·sion (vizh′ən), *n.* **1.** the act or power of sensing with the eyes; sight. **2.** the act or power of anticipating that which will or may come to be: *the vision of an entrepreneur.* **3.** an experience in which a personage, thing, or event appears vividly or credibly to the mind, although not actually present, under the influence of a divine or other agency: *a vision of the millennium.* Cf. **hallucination** (def. 1). **4.** something seen or otherwise perceived during such an experience: *The Holy Grail appeared to him in the form of a vision.* **5.** a vivid, imaginative conception or anticipation: *to have visions of wealth and glory.* **6.** something seen; an object of sight. **7.** a scene, person, etc., of extraordinary beauty: *She was a vision of delight.* —*v.t.* **8.** to envision: *He tried to vision himself in a past century.* [ME < L *vīsiōn-* (s. of *vīsiō*) a seeing, view = *vīs(us)*, ptp. of *vidēre* to see + *-iōn-* -ION] —**vi′sion·less,** *adj.* —**Syn. 2.** perception, discernment. **4.** apparition.

vi·sion·al (vizh′ə nəl), *adj.* **1.** of or pertaining to visions. **2.** belonging to or seen in a vision. —**vi′sion·al·ly,** *adv.*

vi·sion·ar·y (vizh′ə ner′ē), *adj., n., pl.* **-ar·ies.** —*adj.* **1.** given to or characterized by fanciful or unpractical ideas, views, or schemes: *a visionary enthusiast.* **2.** given to or concerned with seeing visions. **3.** belonging to or seen in a vision. **4.** unreal; imaginary: *visionary evils.* **5.** purely idealistic or speculative: *a visionary scheme.* —*n.* **6.** a person who sees visions. **7.** a person who is given to audacious, highly speculative, or impractical ideas or schemes; dreamer. —**Syn. 1.** impractical, impracticable. **4.** fancied, illusory, chimerical. **5.** romantic. —**Ant. 1.** practical.

vis·it (viz′it), *v.t.* **1.** to go to and stay with (a person or family) or at (a place) for a short time. **2.** to stay with as a guest. **3.** to go to for the purpose of official inspection or examination. **4.** to come upon; assail; afflict: *The plague visited London in 1665.* **5.** to inflict, as punishment, vengeance, etc. (often fol. by *on* or *upon*). —*v.i.* **6.** to make a visit or visits. **7.** to spend a while in company with another person. **8.** to inflict punishment. —*n.* **9.** an instance of visiting: *a nice, long visit.* **10.** the act of calling upon a person, place, etc. **11.** a stay or sojourn as a guest. **12.** the act of going to a place to make an official inspection or examination. [ME *visite(n)* (cf. OF *visiter*) < L *vīsitāre,* freq. of *vīsere* to go to see, itself freq. of *vidēre* to see] —**vis′it·a·ble,** *adj.*

vis·i·tant (viz′i tənt), *n.* **1.** someone or something that makes a visit. **2.** a being believed to come from the spirit world: *a ghostly visitant.* **3.** a migratory bird that comes to and stays in a place or region for a temporary period. —*adj.* **4.** *Archaic.* visiting; paying a visit. [< L *vīsitant-* (s. of *vīsitāns*)] —**Syn. 1.** See **visitor.**

vis·it·a·tion (viz′i tā′shən), *n.* **1.** the act of visiting. **2.** a visit for the purpose of making an official examination or inspection. **3.** (*usually cap.*) the visit of the Virgin Mary to her cousin Elizabeth. Luke 1:36–56. **4.** (*cap.*) a church festival, held on July 2, in commemoration of this visit. **5.** the administration of comfort or aid, or of affliction or punishment: *a visitation of the plague.* **6.** the appearance or coming of a supernatural influence or spirit. [< L *vīsitātiōn-* (s. of *vīsitātiō*) = *vīsitāt(us)* (ptp. of *vīsitāre;* see VISIT, -ATE[1]) + *-iōn-* -ION; r. ME *visitacioun* < AF] —**vis′it·a′tion·al,** *adj.*

vis·it·a·to·ri·al (viz′i tə tôr′ē əl, -tōr′-), *adj.* **1.** of or pertaining to an official visitor or official visitation. **2.** having the power of visitation. [< ML *vīsitātōri(us)* (see VISITATION, -ORY[1]) + -AL[1]]

vis′iting card′, *Chiefly Brit.* See **calling card.**

vis′iting fire′man, *U.S. Informal.* **1.** an influential person accorded special treatment while visiting an organization, industry, city, etc. **2.** a visitor, as a tourist or vacationer, in a city, presumed to be a big spender.

vis′iting nurse′, a registered nurse employed by a social service agency to give medical care to the sick in their homes or to implement other public health programs.

vis′iting profes′sor, a professor invited to teach at a university or college other than his own for a limited period, usually for a semester or one academic year.

vis·i·tor (viz′i tər), *n.* a person who pays a visit. [late ME *visitour* < AF; OF *visiteor* < LL *vīsitātor* = L *vīsitāt(us)* (ptp. of *vīsitāre* to VISIT) + *-or* -OR[2]] —**Syn.** VISITOR, CALLER, GUEST, VISITANT are terms for a person who comes to spend time with or stay with others, or in a place. A VISITOR often stays some time, for social pleasure, for business, sightseeing, etc.: *a visitor at our neighbor's house, in San Francisco.* A CALLER comes for a brief, usually formal, visit: *The caller merely left her card.* A GUEST is anyone receiving hospitality, and the word has been extended to include a person who pays for meals and lodging: *a welcome guest; a paying guest.* VISITANT applies esp. to a migratory bird or to a supernatural being: *a warbler as a visitant.*

vis ma·jor (vis mā′jər), *Law.* See **force majeure.** [< L: lit., greater force]

vi·sor (vī′zər, viz′ər), *n.* **1.** *Armor.* **a.** (on a close helmet) a piece having slits or holes for vision, situated above and pivoted with a beaver or a ventail and beaver. **b.** a similar piece of plate having holes or slits for vision and breathing, attached to or used with any of various other helmets. **2.** the projecting front brim of a cap. **3.** a rigid, adjustable flap over the windshield for shielding the eyes of the driver of an automobile from direct sunlight or glare. —*v.t.* **4.** to protect or mask with a visor; shield. Also, **vizor.** [ME *viser* < AF (cf. OF *visiere*) = *vis* face (see VISAGE) + *-er* -ER[2]]

vis·ta (vis′tə), *n.* **1.** a view or prospect, esp. one seen through a long, narrow avenue or passage. **2.** a mental view extending over a long period of time. [< It: a view, n. use of fem. of *visto* (ptp. of *vedere* < L *vidēre* to see) < L *vīs(us)* (ptp. of *vidēre*) + It *-to* < L *-tus* ptp. suffix] —**vis·taed** (vis′təd), *adj.* —**Syn. 1.** See **view.**

VISTA (vis′tə), *n. U.S.* a national program, sponsored by the Office of Economic Opportunity, for sending volunteers into poor areas to teach various job skills. [*V(olunteers) i(n) S(ervice) t(o) A(merica)*]

Vis·tu·la (vis′cho͝o lə), *n.* a river in Poland, flowing N from the Carpathian Mountains past Warsaw into the Baltic near Danzig. ab. 650 mi. long. Polish, **Wisła.** German, **Weichsel.**

vis·u·al (vizh′o͞o əl), *adj.* **1.** of or pertaining to seeing or sight: *a visual image.* **2.** used in seeing: *the visual sense.* **3.** optical. **4.** perceptible by the sense of sight; visible. **5.** perceptible by the mind: *a visual impression captured in a line of verse.* **6.** of or involving the use of projected or displayed pictures, charts, maps, models, etc., for educational or informative purposes, usually to accompany printed or spoken material: *visual aids.* —*n.* **7. visuals,** the picture elements, as distinguished from the sound elements, in films, television, etc. [late ME < LL *vīsuāl(is)* = *vīsu(s)* sight (see VISION) + *-ālis* -AL[1]]

vis′ual acu′ity, *Ophthalm.* acuteness of the vision as determined by a comparison with the normal ability to define certain optical letters at a given distance, usually 20 feet.

vis′ual field′. See **field of vision.**
vis·u·al·ise (vizh′o͞o ə līz′), *v.i., v.t.*, **-ised, -is·ing.** *Chiefly Brit.* visualize. —**vis′u·al·i·sa′tion,** *n.*
vis·u·al·ize (vizh′o͞o ə līz′), *v.*, **-ized, -iz·ing.** —*v.i.* **1.** to recall or form mental images or pictures. —*v.t.* **2.** to form a mental image of. —**vis′u·al·i·za′tion,** *n.*
vis·u·al·ly (vizh′o͞o ə lē), *adv.* **1.** in a visual manner; by sight. **2.** with respect to sight: *The design is visually pleasing.*
vis′ual pur′ple, *Biochem.* rhodopsin.
vi·ta (vī′tə; *Lat.* wē′tä), *n., pl.* **vi·tae** (vī′tē; *Lat.* wē′tī). See **curriculum vitae** (def. 1). Also, **vi·tae** (vī′tē). [< L: life]
vi·ta·ceous (vī tā′shəs), *adj.* belonging to the *Vitaceae,* or grape family of plants, including Japanese ivy, Virginia creeper, etc. [< NL *Vīt(is)* genus name (< L *vītis* vine) + -ACEOUS]
vi·tal (vīt′əl), *adj.* **1.** of, pertaining to, or necessary to life: *vital processes.* **2.** energetic, lively, or forceful: *a vital leader.* **3.** necessary to the existence, continuance, or well-being of something; indispensable; essential. **4.** of critical importance: *vital decisions.* **5.** destructive to life; deadly: *a vital wound.* [late ME < L *vītāl(is)* = *vīt(a)* life + *-ālis* -AL¹] —**vi′tal·ly,** *adv.* —**Syn. 3.** critical. —**Ant. 3.** unimportant.
vi′tal force′, the force that animates and perpetuates living beings and organisms. Also called **vital principle.**
Vi·tal·ian (vi tāl′yən, -tā′lē ən), *n.* died A.D. 672, pope 657–672.
vi·tal·ise (vīt′əlīz′), *v.t.*, **-ised, -is·ing.** *Chiefly Brit.* vitalize. —**vi′tal·i·sa′tion,** *n.*
vi·tal·ism (vīt′əliz′əm), **1.** the doctrine that phenomena are only partly controlled by mechanical forces, and are in some measure self-determining. Cf. **dynamism** (def. 1), **mechanism** (def. 8). **2.** *Biol.* the doctrine that ascribes the functions of a living organism to a vital principle distinct from chemical and physical forces. —**vi′tal·ist,** *n., adj.* —**vi′tal·is′tic,** *adj.*
vi·tal·i·ty (vī tal′i tē), *n., pl.* **-ties. 1.** exuberant physical strength or mental vigor: *a person of great vitality.* **2.** capacity for survival or for the continuation of a meaningful or purposeful existence: *the vitality of an institution.* **3.** power to live or grow. **4.** vital force or principle. [< L *vītālitāt-* (s. of *vītālitās*)]
vi·tal·ize (vīt′əlīz′), *v.t.*, **-ized, -iz·ing. 1.** to give life to; make vital. **2.** to give vitality or vigor to; animate. Also, *esp. Brit.,* **vitalise.** —**vi′tal·i·za′tion,** *n.*
vi′tal prin′ciple. See **vital force.**
vi·tals (vī′təlz), *n.pl.* **1.** the bodily organs that are essential to life, as the brain, heart, liver, lungs, and stomach. **2.** the essential parts of something. [trans. of L *vītālia;* see VITAL]
vi′tal statis′tics, 1. statistics concerning human life or the conditions affecting human life and the maintenance of population, as deaths, births, and marriages. **2.** *Facetious.* measurement (def. 5).
vi·ta·min (vī′tə min), *n. Biochem.* any of a group of organic substances essential in small quantities to normal metabolism and health, found in natural foodstuffs and also produced synthetically. Also, **vi·ta·mine** (vī′tə min, -mēn′). [< L *vīt(a)* life + AMIN(E); coined by C. Funk, who thought they were amines] —**vi′ta·min′ic,** *adj.*
vitamin A, *Biochem.* a terpene alcohol, obtained from carotene and found in green and yellow vegetables, egg yolk, etc.: essential to growth, the protection of epithelial tissue, and the prevention of night blindness.
vitamin B_1, *Biochem.* thiamine.
vitamin B_2, *Biochem.* riboflavin.
vitamin B_6, *Biochem.* pyridoxine.
vitamin B_{12}, *Biochem.* a solid, $C_{63}H_{90}N_{14}O_{14}PCo$, obtained from liver, milk, eggs, fish, oysters, and clams: used chiefly in the treatment of pernicious anemia and sprue, and as a growth factor for hogs, dogs, and chickens. Also called **cyanocobalamin.**
vitamin B complex, *Biochem.* an important group of vitamins containing vitamin B_1, vitamin B_2, etc.
vitamin C, *Biochem.* See **ascorbic acid.**
vitamin D, *Biochem.* any of the antirachitic vitamins D_1, D_2, D_3, found in milk and fish-liver oils or obtained by irradiating provitamin D with ultraviolet light.
Vitamin D_1, *Biochem.* a mixture of sterol and calciferol, obtained by ultraviolet irradiation of ergosterol.
vitamin D_2, *Biochem.* calciferol.
vitamin D_3, *Biochem.* the naturally occurring D vitamin, $C_{27}H_{43}OH$, found in fish-liver oils, differing from vitamin D_2 by slight structural differences in the molecule. Also called **cholecalciferol.**
vitamin E, *Biochem.* a viscous fluid, found in wheat-germ oil, that promotes fertility, prevents abortion, and is active in maintaining the involuntary nervous system, vascular system, and involuntary muscles. Cf. **tocopherol.**
vitamin G, *Biochem.* riboflavin.
vitamin H, *Biochem.* biotin.
vitamin K_1, *Biochem.* a viscous liquid, $C_{31}H_{56}O_2$, occurring in leafy vegetables, rice, bran, hog liver, etc., that is obtained esp. from alfalfa or putrefied sardine meat, or synthesized. It promotes blood clotting.
vitamin K_2, *Biochem.* a solid, $C_{41}H_{56}O_2$, having properties similar to those of vitamin K_1.
vitamin P, *Biochem.* a vitamin, present in citrus fruits, rose hips, and paprika, that maintains the resistance of cell and capillary walls to permeation and change of pressure.
Vi·tebsk (vē′tepsk), *n.* a city in NE Byelorussia, in the W Soviet Union, on the Dvina River. 181,000 (est. 1964).
vi·tel·lin (vi tel′in, vī-), *n. Biochem.* a phosphoprotein in the yolk of eggs. [VITELL(US) + -IN²]
vi·tel·line (vi tel′in, -ēn, -īn, vī-), *adj.* **1.** of or pertaining to the egg yolk. **2.** having a yellow color resembling that of an egg yolk. [late ME < ML *vitellīn(us).* See VITELLUS, -INE¹]
vi·tel·lus (vi tel′əs, vī-), *n., pl.* **-lus·es.** the yolk of an egg. [< L = *vit(ulus)* calf + *-ellus* dim. suffix]
vi·ti·ate (vish′ē āt′), *v.t.*, **-at·ed, -at·ing. 1.** to impair the quality of; spoil; mar. **2.** to debase; corrupt; pervert. **3.** to make legally defective or invalid; invalidate. [< L *vitiāt(us)* (ptp. of *vitiāre* to spoil) = *viti(um)* defect, blemish + *-ātus* -ATE¹] —**vi′ti·a·ble,** *adj.* —**vi′ti·a′tion,** *n.*
vit·i·cul·ture (vit′ə kul′chər, vī′tə-), *n.* the culture or cultivation of grapevines; grape growing. [< L *vīti(s)* vine + CULTURE] —**vit′i·cul′tur·al,** *adj.* —**vit′i·cul′tur·er,** **vit′i·cul′tur·ist,** *n.*
Vi·ti Le·vu (vē′tē le′vo͞o), the largest of the Fiji Islands, in the S Pacific. 400,000 (1971); 4053 sq. mi. *Cap.:* Suva.
vit·i·li·go (vit′əlē′gō), *n. Pathol.* a skin disease characterized by smooth, white patches on various parts of the body, caused by the loss of the natural pigment. Also called **leukoderma, leucoderma, piebald skin.** [< L: tetter, appar. **vitil(is)* defective (*vit(ium)* blemish + *-ilis* -ILE) + *-īgō* n. suffix]
Vi·to·ria (vi tôr′ē ə, -tōr′-; *Sp.* bē tô′ryä), *n.* a city in N Spain: decisive defeat of the French forces in Spain 1813. 82,223 (est. 1963).
Vi·tó·ria (vi tôr′ē ə, -tōr′-; *Port.* vē tô′ryə), *n.* a seaport in E Brazil. 83,900 (1960).
vit·re·ous (vi′trē əs), *adj.* **1.** of the nature of or resembling glass, as in transparency, brittleness, hardness, glossiness, etc. **2.** of or pertaining to glass. **3.** obtained from or containing glass. [< L *vitreus* = *vitr(um)* glass + *-eus* -EOUS] —**vit′re·ous·ness, vit·re·os·i·ty** (vi′trē os′i tē), *n.*
vit′reous hu′mor, *Anat.* the transparent gelatinous substance filling the eyeball behind the crystalline lens. Also called **vit′reous bod′y.**
vi·tres·cent (vi tres′ənt), *adj.* **1.** becoming glass. **2.** tending to become glass. **3.** capable of being formed into glass. [< L *vitr(um)* glass + -ESCENT] —**vi·tres′cence,** *n.*
vitri-, a learned borrowing from Latin meaning "glass," used in the formation of compound words: *vitriform.* [comb. form of L *vitrum*]
vit·ric (vi′trik), *adj.* **1.** of or pertaining to glass. **2.** of the nature of or resembling glass.
vit·ri·fi·ca·tion (vi′trə fə kā′shən), *n.* **1.** the act or process of vitrifying. **2.** the state of being vitrified. **3.** something vitrified. Also, **vit·ri·fac·tion** (vi′trə fak′shən).
vit·ri·form (vi′trə fôrm′), *adj.* having the form or appearance of glass.
vit·ri·fy (vi′trə fī′), *v.t., v.i.*, **-fied, -fy·ing. 1.** to convert or be converted into glass. **2.** to make or become vitreous. —**vit′ri·fi′a·bil′i·ty,** *n.* —**vit′ri·fi′a·ble,** *adj.*
vit·ri·ol (vi′trē əl), *n., v.*, **-oled, -ol·ing** or (*esp. Brit.*) **-olled, -ol·ling.** —*n.* **1.** *Chem.* any of certain metallic sulfates of glassy appearance, as copper sulfate or blue vitriol. **2.** oil of vitriol; sulfuric acid. **3.** something highly caustic or severe in effect, as criticism. —*v.t.* **4.** to treat with or as with vitriol. [late ME < ML *vitriol(um)* = *vitri-* VITRI- + *-olum,* neut. of *-olus* adj. suffix]
vit·ri·ol·ic (vi′trē ol′ik), *adj.* **1.** of, pertaining to, obtained from, or resembling vitriol. **2.** severely caustic; scathing: *vitriolic criticism.*
Vi·tru·vi·us Pol·li·o (vi tro͞o′vē əs pol′ē ō′), **Marcus,** fl. 1st century B.C., Roman architect, engineer, and author. —**Vi·tru′vi·an,** *adj.*
vit·ta (vit′ə), *n., pl.* **vit·tae** (vit′ē). **1.** *Bot.* a tube or receptacle for oil, found in the fruits of most umbelliferous plants. **2.** *Zool., Bot.* a streak or stripe, as of color. [< L: ribbon, fillet, akin to *viēre* to weave together]
vit·tate (vit′āt), *adj.* **1.** provided with or having a vitta or vittae. **2.** striped longitudinally. [< L *vittāt(us)* = *vitt(a)* fillet + *-ātus* -ATE¹]
vi·tu·per·ate (vī to͞o′pə rāt′, -tyo͞o′-, vi-), *v.t.*, **-at·ed, -at·ing.** to find fault with; censure harshly or abusively; revile. [< L *vituperāt(us)* (ptp. of *vituperāre* to spoil, blame) = *vituper-* (*vitu-,* var. of *viti-,* s. of *vitium* blemish + *-per-,* var. of *-par-,* root of *parāre;* see PREPARE) + *-ātus* -ATE¹] —**vi·tu′per·a′tor,** *n.* —**Syn.** vilify, berate.
vi·tu·per·a·tion (vī to͞o′pə rā′shən, -tyo͞o′-, vi-), *n.* **1.** the act of vituperating. **2.** verbal abuse or castigation. [< L *vituperātiōn-* (s. of *vituperātiō*)] —**Syn. 2.** censure, vilification, defamation, aspersion. —**Ant. 1, 2.** praise.
vi·tu·per·a·tive (vī to͞o′pə rā′tiv, -pər ə tiv, -tyo͞o′-, vi-), *adj.* characterized by or of the nature of vituperation: *vituperative remarks.* —**vi·tu′per·a′tive·ly,** *adv.*
vi·va¹ (vē′və, -vä), *interj.* **1.** (*italics*) *Italian, Spanish.* Long live (the person named)! (used as an exclamation of acclaim or approval). —*n.* **2.** a shout of "*viva!*" [lit.: may he live! 3rd pers. sing. pres. subj. of It *vivere,* Sp *vivir* < L *vīvere* to live; see REVIVE]
vi·va² (vī′və), *n.* See **viva voce** (def. 2).
vi·va·ce (vi vä′chā; *It.* vē vä′che), *adj.* vivacious; lively (used as a musical direction). [< It < L *vīvax, -ācis* long-lived, lively; see VIVACITY]
vi·va·cious (vi vā′shəs, vī-), *adj.* **1.** lively or animated; sprightly. **2.** *Archaic.* long-lived, or tenacious of life. [VIVACI(TY) + -OUS] —**vi·va′cious·ly,** *adv.* —**vi·va′cious·ness,** *n.* —**Syn. 1.** spirited. —**Ant. 1.** languid.
vi·vac·i·ty (vi vas′i tē, vī-), *n.* **1.** the quality or state of being vivacious. **2.** liveliness; animation; sprightliness. [late ME < L *vīvācitāt-* (s. of *vīvācitās*) = *vīvāci-* (s. of *vīvax* long-lived, lively = *vīv(us)* alive + *-āci-* adj. suffix) + *-tāt-* -TY²]
Vi·val·di (vi väl′dē; *It.* vē väl′dē), *n.* **An·to·nio** (an-tō′nē ō′; *It.* än tô′nyô), c1675–1741, Italian violinist and composer.
vi·var·i·um (vī vâr′ē əm), *n., pl.* **-var·i·ums, -var·i·a** (-vâr′ē ə). a place, such as a laboratory, where animals or plants are kept alive under conditions simulating their natural environment. [< L = *vīv(us)* living + *-ārium* -ARY]
vi·va vo·ce (vī′və vō′sē), **1.** by word of mouth; orally. **2.** Also called **viva.** an oral examination or the oral part of an examination in British universities. [< ML: with living voice, L, abl. of *vīva vox*] —**vi′va-vo′ce,** *adj.*
vive (vēv), *interj. French.* Long live (the person or notion named)! (used as an exclamation of acclaim or approval): *Vive l'amour!*
vi·ver·rine (vī ver′īn, -in, vi-), *adj.* **1.** of or pertaining to the *Viverridae,* a family of small carnivorous mammals including the civets, genets, etc. —*n.* **2.** a viverrine animal. [< NL *viverrīn(us)* = L *viverr(a)* ferret + *-īnus* -INE¹]
vi·vers (vē′vərz), *n. pl. Chiefly Scot.* victuals; foodstuffs. [< MF *vivres,* pl. of *vivre* food, n. use of *vivre* to live < L *vīvere;* see VIAND]
vi·ve va·le·que (wē′we wä le′kwe; *Eng.* vī′vē və-

lē′kwē), *Latin.* live and keep well (used at the end of letters).

vivi-, a learned borrowing from Latin meaning "living," "alive," used in the formation of compound words: *vivisection.* [< L *vīvi-*, comb. form of *vīvus*]

Viv·i·an (viv′ē ən), *n.* *Arthurian Romance.* an enchantress, the mistress of Merlin: known as the Lady of the Lake. Also, **Viv′i·en.**

viv·id (viv′id), *adj.* **1.** strikingly bright or intense, as color or light. **2.** full of life; lively; animated: *a vivid personality.* **3.** presenting the appearance, freshness, spirit, etc., of life: *a vivid painting; a vivid street scene.* **4.** strong, distinct, or clearly perceptible: *a vivid impression.* **5.** forming distinct and striking mental images: *a vivid imagination.* [< L *vīvid(us)* lively = *vīv(ere)* (to) live + *-idus* -ID[4]] **—viv′id·ly,** *adv.* **—viv′id·ness,** *n.* **—Syn. 1.** brilliant, intense. **2.** spirited, vivacious. **4.** discernible, apparent.

viv·i·fy (viv′ə fī′), *v.t.*, **-fied, -fy·ing.** **1.** to give life to; animate. **2.** to enliven; brighten; sharpen. [alter. (with *-fy* for *-ficate*) of late ME *vivificate* < L *vīvificāt(us)* (ptp. of *vīvificāre*). See VIVI-, -FIC, -ATE[1]] **—viv′i·fi·ca′tion,** *n.*

vi·vip·a·ra (vi vip′ər ə), *n.pl.* viviparous animals. [< NL, L, neut. pl. of *vīviparus* VIVIPAROUS]

vi·vip·ar·ous (vī vip′ər əs), *adj.* **1.** *Zool.* bringing forth living young rather than eggs, as most mammals and some reptiles and fishes. **2.** *Bot.* producing seeds that germinate on the plant. [< L *vīviparus* bringing forth living young. See VIVI-, -PAROUS] **—viv·i·par·i·ty** (viv′ə par′i tē), *n.* **—vi·vip′a·rous·ly,** *adv.*

viv·i·sect (viv′i sekt′, viv′i sekt′), *v.t.* **1.** to dissect the living body of (an animal). **—***v.i.* **2.** to practice vivisection. [back formation from VIVISECTION] **—viv′i·sec′tor,** *n.*

viv·i·sec·tion (viv′i sek′shən), *n.* **1.** the action of cutting into or dissecting a living body. **2.** the practice of subjecting living animals to cutting operations, esp. in order to advance physiological and pathological knowledge. **—viv′i·sec′tion·al,** *adj.* **—viv′i·sec′tion·al·ly,** *adv.*

viv·i·sec·tion·ist (viv′i sek′shə nist), *n.* **1.** a person who vivisects. **2.** a person who favors the practice of vivisection.

vix·en (vik′sən), *n.* **1.** a female fox. **2.** an ill-tempered or quarrelsome woman. [dial. var. of ME *fixen* she-fox = OE *fyxen* (adj.) pertaining to a fox (by confusion of suffixes: adj. suffix *-en* was taken to be fem. suffix *-en*] **—vix′en·ish,** *adj.*

Vi·yel·la (vi yel′ə), *n.* *Trademark.* a fabric made of cotton and wool in twill weave.

viz., videlicet.

viz·ard (viz′ərd), *n.* **1.** a mask. **2.** *Obs.* a visor of a helmet. Also, **visard.** [var. of VISOR; see -ARD]

viz·ca·cha (vis kä′chə), *n.* viscacha.

vi·zier (vi zēr′, viz′yər), *n.* (formerly) a high official in certain Muslim countries and caliphates, esp. a minister of state. Also, **vi·zir′.** Cf. **grand vizier.** [< Turk *vezīr* < Ar *wazīr* burden bearer < *wazara* to carry, bear burdens] **—vi·zier·ate, vi·zir·ate** (vi zēr′it, -āt, viz′yər it, -yə rāt′), **vi·zier′ship, vi·zir′ship,** *n.* **—vi·zier′i·al, vi·zir′i·al,** *adj.*

vi·zor (vī′zər, viz′ər), *n., v.t.* visor.

V-J Day, August 15, 1945, the day Japan accepted the Allied surrender terms in World War II. [V-J: victory over Japan]

VL, Vulgar Latin.

Vlaar·ding·en (vlär′ding ən), *n.* a city in the W Netherlands, at the mouth of the Rhine. 70,404 (1962).

Vla·di·kav·kaz (vlä′di käf käs′), *n.* former name of **Ordzhonikidze.**

Vlad·i·mir (vlad′ə mir′; *Russ.* vlä dē′mir), *n.* **1.** Also, **Wladimir. Saint.** Also called **Vladimir I.** (*Vladimir the Great*) A.D. c956–1015, first Christian grand prince of Russia 980–1015. **2.** a city in the W RSFSR, in the central part of the Soviet Union in Europe, E of Moscow. 188,000 (est. 1964).

Vla·di·vos·tok (vlad′ə vos′tok; *Russ.* vlä di vos tôk′), *n.* a seaport in the SE RSFSR, in the SE Soviet Union in Asia, on the Sea of Japan: eastern terminus of the Trans-Siberian Railroad. 353,000 (est. 1964).

Vla·minck (vlᴀ maɴk′), *n.* **Mau·rice de** (mō ʀēs′ də), 1876–1958, French painter.

VLF, See **very low frequency.** Also, **vlf**

Vlis·sing·en (vlis′ing ən), *n.* Dutch name of **Flushing.**

Vl·ta·va (vəl′tä vä), *n.* Czech name of the **Moldau.**

V-mail (vē′māl′), *n.* a mail system, used by U.S. armed forces during World War II, in which a microfilm of a letter was forwarded for printing in full size on photographic paper before delivery. [V: victory]

V.M.D., Doctor of Veterinary Medicine. [< L *Veterinariae Medicinae Doctor*]

v.n., verb neuter.

V neck, a neckline V-shaped in front.

vo., verso.

V.O., very old (used esp. to indicate the age of whiskey or brandy).

VOA, 1. See **Voice of America. 2.** See **Volunteers of America.**

voc., vocative.

vocab., vocabulary.

vo·ca·ble (vō′kə bəl), *n.* **1.** a word; term; name. **2.** a word considered only as a combination of certain sounds or letters, without regard to meaning. **—***adj.* **3.** capable of being spoken. [< L *vocābul(um)* a word, a name = *vocā(re)* to call + *-bulum* n. suffix] **—vo′ca·bly,** *adv.*

vo·cab·u·lar·y (vō kab′yə ler′ē), *n., pl.* **-lar·ies. 1.** the stock of words used by or known to a particular person or group of persons. **2.** a list or collection of the words or phrases of a language, technical field, etc., usually arranged in alphabetical order and defined. **3.** the words of a language. **4.** any more or less specific group of forms characteristic of an artist, a style of art, architecture, or the like. [< ML *vocābulāri(um)*, neut. of *vocābulārius* of words. See VOCABLE, -ARY]

vocab′ulary en′try, a word, phrase, abbreviation, symbol, affix, name, etc., listed in a dictionary, with its definition or explanation in alphabetical order or listed for identification after the word from which it is derived or to which it is related.

vo·cal (vō′kəl), *adj.* **1.** of, pertaining to, or uttered with the voice: *vocal criticism.* **2.** rendered by or intended for singing: *vocal music.* **3.** giving forth sound with or as with a voice. **4.** inclined to express oneself in words, esp. copiously or insistently: *a vocal advocate of reform.* **5.** *Phonet.* **a.** vocalic (def. 1). **b.** voiced. **—***n.* **6.** a vocal sound. **7.** the part of a composition sung or intended to be sung in popular music. [late ME < L *vōcāl(is)* = *vōc-* (s. of *vōx*) voice + *-ālis* -AL[1]] **—vo′cal·ly,** *adv.* **—Syn. 4.** vociferous.

vo′cal cords′, *Anat.* either of the two pairs of folds of mucous membrane projecting into the cavity of the larynx, functioning in the production of vocal sound.

vo·cal·ic (vō kal′ik), *adj.* **1.** of, pertaining to, or resembling a vowel or vowels. **2.** consisting of, characterized by, or containing vowels.

vo·cal·ise (vō′kə līz′), *v.t., v.i.*, **-ised, -is·ing.** *Chiefly Brit.* vocalize. **—vo′cal·i·sa′tion,** *n.* **—vo′cal·is′er,** *n.*

vo·cal·ism (vō′kə liz′əm), *n.* **1.** *Phonet.* **a.** the nature of one or more given vowels. **b.** the system of vowels of a particular language. **2.** the use of the voice, as in speech or song. **3.** the act, principles, or art of singing.

vo·cal·ist (vō′kə list), *n.* a singer.

vo·cal·ize (vō′kə līz′), *v.*, **-ized, -iz·ing. —***v.t.* **1.** to make vocal; utter; articulate; sing. **2.** to endow with a voice; cause to utter. **3.** *Phonet.* **a.** to voice. **b.** to change into a vowel. **4.** (of Hebrew, Arabic, and other writing systems that do not usually indicate vowels) to furnish with vowel points. **—***v.i.* **5.** to use the voice, as in speech or song. **6.** *Phonet.* to become changed into a vowel. Also, *esp. Brit.,* **vocalise. —vo′cal·i·za′tion,** *n.* **—vo′cal·iz′er,** *n.*

vocat., vocative.

vo·ca·tion (vō kā′shən), *n.* **1.** a particular occupation, business, or profession; calling. **2.** a strong impulse or inclination to follow a particular activity or career. **3.** a function or station in life to which a person is called by God. [late ME *vocacio(u)n* < L *vocātiōn-* (s. of *vocātiō*) a call, summons = *vocāt(us)* ptp. (*voc-*, s. of *vocāre* to call + *-ātus* -ATE[1]) + *-iōn-* -ION] **—Syn. 1.** employment.

vo·ca·tion·al (vō kā′shə nəl), *adj.* **1.** of, pertaining to, or connected with a vocation or occupation: *a vocational aptitude; a vocational school.* **2.** of, pertaining to, or noting instruction or guidance in an occupation or profession chosen as a career or in the choice of a career: *a vocational counselor.* **—vo·ca′tion·al·ly,** *adv.*

voca′tional educa′tion, educational training that provides a student with practical experience in a particular occupational field.

voc·a·tive (vok′ə tiv), *adj.* **1.** *Gram.* (in certain inflected languages, as Latin) noting or pertaining to a case used to indicate that a noun refers to a person or thing being addressed. **2.** of, pertaining to, or used in calling, specifying, or addressing. **—***n.* *Gram.* **3.** the vocative case. **4.** a word in the vocative, as Latin *Pāule* "O Paul." [late ME < L *vocātīv(us)* (*cāsus*) calling (case) = *vocāt(us)* (see VOCATION) + *-īvus* -IVE] **—voc′a·tive·ly,** *adv.*

vo·cif·er·ance (vō sif′ər əns), *n.* vociferant utterance; vociferation. [VOCIFER(ANT) + -ANCE]

vo·cif·er·ant (vō sif′ər ənt), *adj.* **1.** vociferating; noisy. **—***n.* **2.** a person who vociferates. [< L *vōciferant-* (s. of *vōciferāns*) = *vōcifer-* (see VOCIFERATE) + *-ant-* -ANT]

vo·cif·er·ate (vō sif′ə rāt′), *v.i., v.t.*, **-at·ed, -at·ing.** to speak or cry out loudly or noisily; shout; bawl. [< L *vōciferāt(us)* (ptp. of *vōciferāre* to shout) = *vōcifer-* (*vōci-*, s. of *vōx* voice + *-fer-*, root of *ferre* to bring forth) + *-ātus* -ATE[1]] **—vo·cif′er·a′tor,** *n.*

vo·cif·er·a·tion (vō sif′ə rā′shən), *n.* noisy outcry; clamor. [late ME < L *vōciferātiōn-* (s. of *vōciferātiō*)]

vo·cif·er·ous (vō sif′ər əs), *adj.* **1.** crying out noisily; clamorous. **2.** characterized by or uttered with vociferation. [VOCIFER(ANT) + -OUS] **—vo·cif′er·ous·ly,** *adv.* **—vo·cif′er·ous·ness,** *n.* **—Syn. 1.** loud, noisy, vocal.

vod·ka (vod′kə), *n.* an unaged, colorless, distilled spirit, originally made in Russia. [< Russ *vod(a)* WATER + *-ka* hypocoristic suffix]

vogue (vōg), *n.* **1.** the fashion, as at a particular time. **2.** a period of popular currency, acceptance, or favor; popularity: *The book had a great vogue.* [< MF: wave or course of success < OIt *voga* a rowing < *vogare* to row, sail < ?] **—Syn. 1.** mode. See **fashion.**

Vo·gul (vō′go͝ol), *n.* a Finno-Ugric language of the Ugric group, spoken E of the Ural Mountains.

voice (vois), *n., v.*, **voiced, voic·ing. —***n.* **1.** the sound or sounds uttered through the mouth of living creatures, esp. of human beings in speaking, shouting, singing, etc. **2.** the faculty of uttering sounds through the mouth by the controlled expulsion of air. **3.** a range of such sounds distinctive to one person, or to a type of person or animal. **4.** the ability to speak or sing, or condition of effectiveness of speaking or singing: *to lose one's voice; to be in poor voice.* **5.** expression in words or uttered sounds: *to give voice to one's feelings.* **6.** the right or power to present and receive consideration of one's desires or opinions: *a voice in local affairs.* **7.** an expressed will or desire: *the voice of the people.* **8.** a quality that seems to proceed from a will or personality: *the voice of nature.* **9.** a singer or singers: *a score for voice and orchestra.* **10.** any of the vocal parts in a musical score. **11.** *Phonet.* the audible result of phonation and resonance. **12.** *Gram.* **a.** a set of categories for which the verb is inflected in some languages, as Latin, and which is typically used to indicate the relation of the verbal action to the subject as performer, undergoer, or beneficiary of its action. **b.** a set of syntactic devices in some languages, as English, that is similar to this set in function. **c.** any of the categories of these sets: *the English passive voice; the Greek middle voice.* **13.** *Obs.* rumor. **—***v.t.* **14.** to give utterance or expression to; declare; proclaim. **15.** *Music.* to regulate the tone of, as the pipes of an organ. **16.** to utter with the voice. **17.** *Phonet.* to pronounce with glottal vibration. [ME < AF *voiz, voice* (OF *voiz, vois*) < L *vōci-, vōce-*, s. of *vōx*] **—voic′er,** *n.*

voice′ box′, the larynx.

voiced (voist), *adj.* **1.** having a voice of a specified kind (usually used in combination): *gruff-voiced; shrill-voiced.* **2.** expressed vocally: *his voiced opinion.* **3.** *Phonet.* pronounced with glottal vibrations; phonated (contrasted with *voiceless*): *"B," "v," and "z" are voiced.*

voice·ful (vois′fəl), *adj.* having a voice, esp. a loud voice; sounding; sonorous.

voice·less (vois′lis), *adj.* **1.** having no voice; mute; dumb. **2.** uttering no words; silent. **3.** having an unmusical voice. **4.** unspoken; unuttered: *voiceless sympathy.* **5.** having no vote or right of choice. **6.** *Phonet.* (of a speech sound) **a.** without voice; unvoiced; aphonic (contrasted with *voiced*): *"P," "f," and "s" are voiceless.* **b.** uttered without phonation. —**voice′less·ly,** *adv.* —**voice′less·ness,** *n.* —**Syn. 1.** See **dumb.**

Voice′ of Amer′ica, the division of the United States Information Agency that makes shortwave radio broadcasts to listeners around the world. *Abbr.:* VOA

voice-o·ver (vois′ō′vər), *n.* **1.** a voice heard without a narrator being seen on the sound screen, as in some television commercials. —*adj.* **2.** of, involving, or performing a voice-over or voice-overs.

voice·print (vois′print′), *n.* See **sound spectrogram.**

voice′ vote′, a vote based on estimation of the relative strength of ayes and noes called out rather than on a counting of individual ballots, a roll call, or a division.

void (void), *adj.* **1.** *Law.* having no legal force or effect; not legally binding or enforceable. **2.** useless; ineffectual; vain. **3.** devoid; destitute (usually fol. by *of*): *a life void of meaning.* **4.** without contents; empty. **5.** without an incumbent, as an office. —*n.* **6.** an empty space; emptiness. **7.** a gap or opening, as in a wall. **8.** *Typography.* counter[3] (def. 8). —*v.t.* **9.** to make ineffectual; invalidate; nullify: *to void a check.* **10.** to empty; discharge; evacuate: *to void excrement.* **11.** to clear or empty (often fol. by *of*): *to void a chamber of occupants.* **12.** *Archaic.* to depart from; vacate. **13.** *Obs.* **a.** to avoid. **b.** to send away; dismiss; expel. [ME *void(e)* < AF, OF < VL **vocita,* fem. of **vocitus,* dissimilated var. of L *vocīvus,* var. of *vac(ī)vus* empty; see VACUUM] —**void′er,** *n.* —**void′ness,** *n.* —**Syn. 5.** vacant.

void·a·ble (voi′də bəl), *adj.* **1.** capable of being nullified or invalidated. **2.** *Law.* capable of being made or adjudged void.

void·ance (void′ᵊns), *n.* **1.** the act of voiding. **2.** vacancy, as of a benefice. [aph. var. of AVOIDANCE]

void·ed (voi′did), *adj.* **1.** having a void. **2.** having been made void. **3.** *Heraldry.* (of a charge) depicted as if the center had been removed so as to leave only an outline.

voi·là (vwa lä′), *interj. French.* There it is! Look! See! (usually used interjectionally to express success or satisfaction).

voile (voil; *Fr.* vwal), *n.* a dress fabric of wool, silk, rayon, or cotton, with an open, canvaslike weave. [< F, AF *veile* VEIL]

voir dire (vwär′ dēr′; *Fr.* vwar dēr′), *Law.* **1.** an oath administered to a proposed witness or juror by which he is sworn to speak the truth in an examination to ascertain his competence. **2.** the examination itself. [< AF = OF *voir* true, truly + *dire* to say]

voix cé·leste (vwä sā lest′), an organ stop having for each note two pipes tuned to slightly different pitches and producing a wavering gentle tone. [< F: heavenly voice]

vol., **1.** volcano. **2.** volume. **3.** volunteer.

vo·lant (vō′lənt), *adj.* **1.** engaged in or having the power of flight. **2.** moving lightly; nimble. [< F, prp. of *voler* < L *volāre* to fly; see -ANT]

vo·lan·te (vō län′tā; *It.* vô län′te), *adv., adj. Music.* moving lightly and quickly. [< It = *vol-,* s. of *volare* to fly (< L *volāre*) + *-ante* -ANT]

Vo·la·pük (vō′lə pyk′), *n.* one of the earliest of the artificially constructed international auxiliary languages, invented about 1879. Also, **Vo·la·puk** (vol′ə po͝ok′). [*vol,* repr. WO(R)L(D) + *-a-* + *pük,* repr. (S)PEAK]

vo·lar[1] (vō′lər), *adj.* of or pertaining to the palm of the hand or the sole of the foot. [< L *vol(a)* palm of hand, sole of foot + -AR[1]]

vo·lar[2] (vō′lər), *adj.* pertaining to or used for flight. [< L *vol(āre)* to fly + -AR[1]]

vol·a·tile (vol′ə til, -tᵊl *or, esp. Brit.,* -tīl′), *adj.* **1.** evaporating rapidly; passing off readily in the form of vapor. **2.** tending or threatening to break out into open violence; explosive: *a volatile political situation.* **3.** changeable; mercurial; flighty: *a volatile disposition.* **4.** fleeting; transient: *volatile beauty.* **5.** noting or subject to constant or sharp fluctuation, esp. in prices: *a volatile stock market.* **6.** *Archaic.* able or accustomed to fly, as winged creatures. [ME < L *volātilis* = *volāt(us)* (ptp. of *volāre* to fly; see -ATE[1]) + *-ilis* -ILE] —**vol·a·til·i·ty** (vol′ə til′i tē), *n.*

vol′atile oil′, a distilled oil, esp. one obtained from plant tissue, as distinguished from glyceride oils by their volatility and failure to saponify.

vol′atile salt′, **1.** See **ammonium carbonate.** **2.** See **sal volatile** (def. 2).

vol·a·til·ise (vol′ə tᵊlīz′), *v.i., v.t.,* **-ised, -is·ing.** *Chiefly Brit.* volatilize. —**vol′a·til·i·sa′tion,** *n.*

vol·a·til·ize (vol′ə tᵊlīz′), *v.,* **-ized, -iz·ing.** —*v.i.* **1.** to become volatile; pass off as vapor. —*v.t.* **2.** to make volatile; cause to pass off in the form of vapor. —**vol′a·til·i·za′tion,** *n.*

vol-au-vent (vō lō väN′), *n. Cookery.* a large shell of light, flaky pastry for filling with vegetable, fish, or meat mixtures, usually with a sauce. [< F: lit., flight on the wind]

vol·can·ic (vol kan′ik), *adj.* **1.** of or pertaining to a volcano or volcanoes. **2.** discharged from or produced by volcanoes: *volcanic mud.* **3.** characterized by the presence of volcanoes. Also, **vulcanian.** [VOLCAN(O) + -IC; cf. F *volcanique*] —**vol·can′i·cal·ly,** *adv.* —**vol·can·ic·i·ty** (vol′kə nis′i tē), *n.*

volcan′ic glass′, a natural glass produced when molten lava cools very rapidly; obsidian.

volcan′ic tuff′, tuff.

vol·can·ism (vol′kə niz′əm), *n. Geol.* the phenomena connected with volcanoes and volcanic activity. Also, **vulcanism.** —**vol′can·ist,** *n.*

vol·ca·no (vol kā′nō), *n., pl.* **-noes, -nos.** **1.** a vent in the earth's crust through which lava, steam, ashes, etc., are expelled, either continuously or at irregular intervals. **2.** a mountain or hill, usually having a cuplike crater at the summit, formed around such a vent from the ash and lava expelled through it. [< It *volcano* < L *Volcānus,* var. of *Vulcānus* VULCAN]

Volca′no Is′lands, three islands in the W Pacific, belonging to Japan. Cf. **Iwo Jima.**

vol·can·ol·o·gy (vol′kə nol′ə jē), *n.* the scientific study of volcanoes and volcanic phenomena. Also, **vulcanology.** —**vol·can·o·log·i·cal** (vol′kə nᵊloj′i kəl), **vol′can·o·log′ic,** *adj.* —**vol′can·ol′o·gist,** *n.*

vole[1] (vōl), *n.* any of several mouselike rodents of the genus *Microtus* and related genera, having short limbs and a short tail. [short for *volemouse* field mouse; *vole* < Norw *voll* field; see WOLD[1]]

Vole, *Microtus pennsylvanicus* (Total length 7 in.; tail 2 in.)

vole[2] (vōl), *n. Cards.* the winning by one player of all the tricks of a deal. [< F < *vol(er)* (to) fly < L *volāre*]

Vol·ga (vol′gə; *Russ.* vôl′gä), *n.* a river flowing from the Valdai Hills in the W Soviet Union E and then S to the Caspian Sea: the longest river in Europe. 2325 mi.

Vol·go·grad (vol′gə grad′; *Russ.* vôl′go grät′), *n.* a city in the SW RSFSR, in the S Soviet Union in Europe, on the Volga River: battles in World War II, September 1942–February 1943. 700,000 (est. 1965). Formerly, **Stalingrad, Tsaritsyn.**

vol·i·ta·tion (vol′i tā′shən), *n.* the act or power of flying. [< ML *volitātiōn-* (s. of *volitātiō*) = L *volitāt(us)* (ptp. of *volitāre* to flutter: *vol-* root of *volāre* to fly + *-it-* freq. suffix; see -ATE[1]) + *-iōn-* -ION] —**vol′i·ta′tion·al,** *adj.*

vo·li·tion (vō lish′ən), *n.* **1.** the act of willing, choosing, or resolving; exercise of willing: *He offered to help us of his own volition.* **2.** the power of willing; will. **3.** a choice or decision made by the will. [< ML *volitiōn-* (s. of *volitiō*) = *vol-* (root of L *volō* I will) + *-itiōn-* -ITION] —**vo·li′tion·al, vo·li·tion·ar·y** (vō lish′ə ner′ē), *adj.* —**Syn. 1.** discretion, choice. See **will**[2].

vol·i·tive (vol′i tiv), *adj.* **1.** of, pertaining to, or characterized by volition. **2.** *Gram.* expressing a wish or permission: *a volitive construction.* [VOLIT(ION) + -IVE]

vol·ley (vol′ē), *n., pl.* **-leys,** *v.,* **-leyed, -ley·ing.** —*n.* **1.** the simultaneous discharge of a number of missiles or firearms. **2.** the missiles so discharged. **3.** a burst or outpouring of many things at once or in quick succession: *a volley of protests.* **4.** *Tennis.* **a.** the flight of the ball before it hits the ground. **b.** the return of the ball before it hits the ground. **5.** *Soccer.* a kick of the football before it bounces on the ground. **6.** *Cricket.* a ball bowled so that it hits the wicket before it touches the ground. —*v.t.* **7.** to discharge in or as in a volley. **8.** *Tennis.* to return (the ball) before it hits the ground. **9.** *Soccer.* to kick (the ball) before it bounces on the ground. **10.** *Cricket.* to bowl (a ball) in such a manner that it is pitched near the top of the wicket. [< MF *volee* flight, n. use of fem. ptp. of *voler* to fly < L *volāre*]

vol·ley·ball (vol′ē bôl′), *n.* **1.** a game for two teams in which the object is to keep a large ball in motion, from side to side over a high net, by striking it with the hands before it touches the ground. **2.** the ball used in this game.

Vo·log·da (vô′log dä), *n.* a city in the W RSFSR, in the central Soviet Union in Europe, NE of Moscow. 156,000 (est. 1964).

Vo·los (vô′lôs), *n.* a seaport in E Thessaly, in E Greece: ancient ruins. 67,000 (est. 1971).

vo·lost (vō′lost), *n.* **1.** (formerly) a small administrative peasant division in Russia. **2.** a rural soviet. [< Russ]

vol·plane (vol′plān′), *v.i.,* **-planed, -plan·ing.** to glide in an airplane. [< F *vol plané* glided flight = *vol* flight (back formation from *voler* < L *volāre* to fly) + *plané,* ptp. of *planer* to glide (see PLANE[1])]

vols., volumes.

Vol·sci (vol′sī), *n.pl.* an ancient people of Latium who were conquered by the Romans at the end of the 4th century B.C.

Vol·scian (vol′shən), *adj.* **1.** of or pertaining to the Volsci or to their language. —*n.* **2.** one of the Volsci. [< L *Volsc(us)* of the VOLSCI + -IAN]

Vol·stead (vol′sted), *n.* **Andrew Joseph,** 1860–1946, U.S. legislator.

Vol′stead Act′, an act of Congress, introduced in 1919 by Andrew J. Volstead to implement the Eighteenth Amendment of the Constitution, which forbade the sale of alcoholic beverages.

Vol·sung (vol′so͝ong), *n.* (in the *Volsunga Saga*) a grandson of Odin and the father of Sigmund and Signy.

Vol·sun·ga Sa·ga (vol′so͝ong gə sä′gə), an Icelandic saga of the late 13th century, concerning the family of the Volsungs, the theft of the cursed treasure of Andvari, the adventures of Sigurd, his wooing of Brynhild, his enchantment and marriage to Gudrun, and his eventual murder. Also, **Vol′sung·a·sa′ga.** Cf. **Nibelungenlied.**

volt[1] (vōlt), *n. Elect.* the meter-kilogram-second unit of electromotive force or potential difference, equal to the electromotive force or potential difference that will cause a current of one ampere to flow through a conductor with a resistance of one ohm. *Abbr.:* V, v [named after A. VOLTA]

volt[2] (vōlt), *n. Manège.* a gait in which a horse going sideways turns around a center, with the head turned outward. [< F *volte* < It *volta* < VL **volvita* a turn; see VAULT[1]]

Vol·ta (vōl′tə *or, It.,* vôl′tä *for 1;* vol′tə *for 2*), *n.* **1.** Count **A·les·san·dro** (ä′les sän′drō), 1745–1827, Italian physicist. **2.** a river in W Africa, in Ghana, formed by the confluence of the Black Volta and the White Volta and flowing S into the Bight of Benin. ab. 250 mi. long; with branches, ab. 1240 mi. long.

volt·age (vōl′tij), *n. Elect.* electromotive force or potential difference expressed in volts.

volt′age divid′er, *Elect.* a resistor or series of resistors connected to a voltage source and used to provide voltages which are fractions of the voltage of the source.

vol·ta·ic (vol tā′ik), *adj. Elect.* noting or pertaining to electricity or electric currents, esp. when produced by chemical action, as in a cell; galvanic. [named after A. VOLTA; see -IC]

volta′ic bat′tery, *Elect.* an electric battery consisting of several voltaic cells connected together. Also called **galvanic battery.**

volta′ic cell′, *Elect.* a cell consisting of two electrodes of different metals immersed in a solution such that chemical action produces an electromotive force.

volta′ic cou′ple, *Elect.* a pair of substances, as two different metals, which when placed in a proper solution produces an electromotive force by chemical action.

vol·ta′ic pile′, *Elect.* a cell that consists of several metal disks, each made of one of two dissimilar metals, arranged in an alternating series, and separated by pads moistened with an electrolyte. Also called **galvanic pile.**

Vol·taire (vol târ′, vōl-; *Fr.* vôl teʀ′), *n.* (pen name of *François Marie Arouet*) 1694–1778, French philosopher, historian, dramatist, and essayist.

vol·ta·ism (vol′tə iz′əm), *n.* the branch of electrical science that deals with the chemical production of electricity or electric currents. [named after A. VOLTA; see -ISM]

vol·tam·e·ter (vol tam′i tər), *n.* a device for measuring the quantity of electricity passing through a conductor by the amount of electrolytic decomposition it produces, or for measuring the strength of a current by the amount of such decomposition in a given time. —**vol·ta·met·ric** (vol′tə me′trik), *adj.*

volt·am·me·ter (vōlt′am′mē′tər), *n.* an instrument for measuring voltage or amperage. [VOLT-AM(PERE) + -METER]

volt-am·pere (vōlt′am′pēr), *n.* *Elect.* an electric measurement unit, equal to the product of one volt and one ampere, equivalent to one watt for direct current systems and a unit of apparent power for alternating current systems. *Abbr.:* VA, va

volt·me·ter (vōlt′mē′tər), *n.* *Elect.* a calibrated instrument for measuring the potential difference between two points.

Vol·tur·no (vôl to͞oʀ′nô), *n.* a river in S central Italy, flowing from the Apennines into the Tyrrhenian Sea. 110 mi. long.

Vol·tur·nus (vol tûr′nəs), *n.* the ancient Roman personification of the east or southeast wind. Cf. **Eurus.**

vol·u·ble (vol′yə bəl), *adj.* characterized by a ready and continuous flow of words; fluent; talkative. [< L *volūbil(is)* which turns easily, hence rapid (of speech) = *volū(tus)* ptp. of *volvere* to turn + *-bilis* -BLE] —**vol′u·bil′i·ty,** *n.* —**vol′u·bly,** *adv.* —**Syn.** loquacious. See **fluent.** —**Ant.** taciturn.

vol·ume (vol′yo͞om, -yəm), *n.* **1.** a collection of written or printed sheets bound together and constituting a book. **2.** one book of a related set or series. **3.** *Hist.* a roll of papyrus, parchment, or the like, or of manuscript. **4.** the amount of space, measured in cubic units, that an object or substance occupies. **5.** a mass or quantity, esp. a large one: *a volume of mail.* **6.** amount; total: *the volume of sales.* **7.** the degree of sound intensity or audibility; loudness: *to turn up the volume on a radio.* **8.** fullness or quantity of tone. [late ME *volum(e)* < MF < L *volūmen* roll (of sheets) = *volū(tus)* (ptp. of *volvere* to roll) + *-men* n. suffix] —**Syn. 4.** See **size**[1].

vol·umed (vol′yo͞omd, -yəmd), *adj.* **1.** consisting of a volume or volumes (usually used in combination): *a many-volumed work.* **2.** in volumes of rolling or rounded masses, as smoke.

vol·u·met·ric (vol′yə me′trik), *adj.* of or pertaining to measurement by volume. Also, **vol′u·met′ri·cal.** [VOLU(ME) + -METR(Y) + -IC] —**vol′u·met′ri·cal·ly,** *adv.* —**vo·lu·me·try** (və lo͞o′mi trē), *n.*

volumet′ric anal′ysis, *Chem.* **1.** analysis by volume, esp. by titration. **2.** determination of the volume of gases or changes in their volume during combination. Cf. **gravimetric analysis.**

vo·lu·mi·nous (və lo͞o′mə nəs), *adj.* **1.** amounting to a large quantity; copious. **2.** (of writing) sufficient to fill many volumes. **3.** writing or speaking at great length; prolix. **4.** disposed in many folds or loops: *voluminous petticoats.* [< LL *volūminōs(us)* full of folds = L *volūmin-* (s. of *volūmen*) VOLUME + *-ōsus* -OUS] —**vo·lu′mi·nous·ly,** *adv.*

Vö·lund (vœ′lo͝ond), *n.* *Scand. Myth.* Wayland.

vol·un·ta·rism (vol′ən tə riz′əm), *n.* **1.** *Philos.* any of various theories regarding the will rather than the intellect as the fundamental agency or principle. **2.** voluntaryism. —**vol′un·ta·rist,** *n., adj.* —**vol′un·ta·ris′tic,** *adj.*

vol·un·tar·y (vol′ən ter′ē), *adj., n., pl.* **-tar·ies.** —*adj.* **1.** done, made, brought about, undertaken, etc., of one's own accord or by free choice: *a voluntary contribution.* **2.** exercising free choice; free. **3.** done or operating by means of volunteers rather than by hired personnel or conscripts: *a voluntary service.* **4.** of, pertaining to, or depending on voluntary action: *voluntary hospitals.* **5.** *Law.* **a.** acting or done without compulsion or obligation; unconstrained by interference. **b.** done by intention, and not by accident: *voluntary manslaughter.* **c.** made without payment or valuable consideration. **6.** *Physiol.* subject to or controlled by the will: *voluntary muscles.* **7.** proceeding from a natural impulse; spontaneous: *voluntary laughter.* —*n.* **8.** a piece of music, frequently spontaneous, performed as a prelude. [late ME < L *voluntāri(us)* = *volunt(ās)* willingness, inclination + *-ārius* -ARY] —**vol·un·tar·i·ly** (vol′ən ter′ə lē, vol′ən târ′-), *adv.* —**Syn. 1.** considered, purposeful, planned, intended, designed. **7.** unforced, natural, unconstrained.

vol·un·tar·y·ism (vol′ən ter′ē iz′əm), *n.* the principle or system of supporting churches, schools, etc., by voluntary contributions or aid, independently of the state. Also, **voluntarism.** —**vol′un·tar′y·ist,** *n.*

vol·un·teer (vol′ən tēr′), *n.* **1.** a person who offers himself for a service without obligation to do so. **2.** a person who performs a service willingly and without pay. **3.** *U.S.* a person who enlists in the military service. **4.** *Law.* **a.** a person whose actions are not founded on any legal obligation. **b.** a person to whom a conveyance is made or promise given without valuable consideration. **5.** *Agric.* a volunteer plant. **6.** (*cap.*) a native or inhabitant of Tennessee (the **Volunteer State**) (used as a nickname). —*adj.* **7.** of, pertaining to, employing, or being a volunteer or volunteers. **8.** *Agric.* growing without being seeded, planted, or cultivated by a person; springing up spontaneously. —*v.i.* **9.** to offer oneself for some service or undertaking. **10.** *U.S.* to enlist in the military service. —*v.t.* **11.** to offer (oneself or one's services) for some undertaking or purpose. **12.** to give, bestow, or perform without being asked: *to volunteer a song.* **13.** to say, tell, or communicate voluntarily: *to volunteer an explanation.* [< F *volontaire* < L *voluntāri(us)* VOLUNTARY, with -EER for F *-aire*]

Volunteers′ in Ser′vice to Amer′ica. See **VISTA.**

Vol′unteers′ of Amer′ica, a religious reform and relief organization, similar to the Salvation Army, founded in New York City in 1896 by Ballington Booth. *Abbr.:* VOA

Vol′unteer′ State′, Tennessee (used as a nickname).

vo·lup·tu·ar·y (və lup′cho͞o er′ē), *n., pl.* **-ar·ies,** *adj.* —*n.* **1.** a person whose life is devoted to the pursuit and enjoyment of sensual pleasure. —*adj.* **2.** of, pertaining to, or characterized by preoccupation with luxury and sensual pleasure. [< LL *voluptuāri(us)* (r. L *voluptārius*) pertaining to (sensual) pleasure = *volupt(ās)* pleasure + *-u-* (see VOLUPTUOUS) + *-ārius* -ARY]

vo·lup·tu·ous (və lup′cho͞o əs), *adj.* **1.** full of, characterized by, or ministering to indulgence in luxury, pleasure, and sensuous enjoyment: *a voluptuous life.* **2.** derived from gratification of the senses: *voluptuous pleasure.* **3.** directed toward or concerned with sensuous enjoyment or sensual pleasure. **4.** sensuously pleasing or delightful: *voluptuous beauty.* [late ME < L *voluptuōsus* = *volupt(ās)* pleasure + *-u-* (< ?) + *-ōsus* -OUS] —**vo·lup′tu·ous·ly,** *adv.* —**vo·lup′tu·ous·ness, vo·lup·tu·os·i·ty** (və lup′cho͞o os′i tē), *n.*

vo·lute (və lo͞ot′), *n.* **1.** a spiral or twisted formation or object. **2.** *Archit.* a spiral ornament, found esp. on the capitals of the Ionic, Corinthian, and Composite orders. **3.** *Carpentry.* a horizontal scrolled termination to the handrail of a stair. **4.** *Zool.* **a.** a turn or whorl of a spiral shell. **b.** any tropical marine gastropod of the family *Volutidae,* many species of which have shells prized for their beautiful coloration. —*adj.* **5.** having a volute or rolled-up form. [< L *volūta,* fem. of *volūtus* turned, rolled, ptp. of *volvere.* See REVOLVE] —**vo·lut′ed,** *adj.* —**vo·lu′tion,** *n.*

V, Volute (on an Ionic capital)

volute′ spring′, a coil spring, conical in shape, extending in the direction of the axis of the coil. See illus. at **spring.**

vol·va (vol′və), *n.* *Bot.* the membranous envelope which encloses various immature or button mushrooms. [< L: covering, akin to *volvere* to roll, wrap] —**vol·vate** (vol′vit, -vāt), *adj.*

vol·vox (vol′voks), *n.* any colonial, fresh-water flagellate of the genus *Volvox* that forms a hollow, greenish sphere of flagellated cells, and is usually considered to be a green alga. [< NL = L *volv(ere)* to turn, roll + *-ox* (as in *ferox*)]

vol·vu·lus (vol′vyə ləs), *n., pl.* **-lus·es.** *Pathol.* a torsion or twisting of the intestine, causing intestinal obstruction. [< NL = L *volv(ere)* to turn, twist + *-ulus* -ULE]

vo·mer (vō′mər), *n.* *Anat.* a bone of the skull in most vertebrates, in man forming a large part of the septum between the right and left cavities of the nose. [< L: plowshare] —**vo·mer·ine** (vō′mə rīn′, -mər in, vom′ə rīn′, -ər in), *adj.*

vom·it (vom′it), *v.i.* **1.** to eject the contents of the stomach through the mouth; regurgitate; throw up. **2.** to be ejected or come out with force or violence. —*v.t.* **3.** to eject from the stomach through the mouth; spew. **4.** to cast out or eject as if from the stomach; send out forcefully or violently: *The volcano vomited flames and molten rock.* —*n.* **5.** the act of vomiting. **6.** the matter ejected in vomiting. [late ME *vomite(n)* < L *vomitāre,* freq. of *vomere* to discharge, vomit] —**vom′it·er,** *n.* —**vom′i·tive, vom′i·tous,** *adj.*

vom·i·to (vom′i tō′, vō′mi-), *n.* *Pathol.* the black vomit of yellow fever. [< Sp *vómito* < L *vomitus* (see VOMITUS)]

vom·i·to·ri·um (vom′i tōr′ē əm, -tôr′-), *n., pl.* **-to·ri·a** (-tōr′ē ə, -tôr′-). vomitory (def. 5). [< LL]

vom·i·to·ry (vom′i tōr′ē, -tôr′ē), *adj., n., pl.* **-ries.** —*adj.* **1.** inducing vomiting; emetic. **2.** of or pertaining to vomiting. —*n.* **3.** an emetic. **4.** an opening through which something is ejected or discharged. **5.** Also called **vomitorium.** (in ancient Roman amphitheaters) one of the large, archlike entrances connecting with a main aisle, permitting large numbers of people to enter or leave. [< L *vomitōri(us)* = *vomit(us)* ptp. of *vomere* to vomit + *-ōrius* -ORY[1]]

vom·i·tu·ri·tion (vom′i cho͞o rish′ən), *n.* *Med.* **1.** ineffectual efforts to vomit. **2.** the vomiting of small amounts of matter. [< NL *vomiturītiōn-* (s. of *vomiturītiō*) nausea, alter. of L *vomitiōn-* (s. of *vomitiō*) a vomiting, by inserting *-turi-,* desiderative infix; L *vomitiōn-* = *vomit(us)* (ptp. of *vomere* to discharge) + *-iōn-* -ION]

vom·i·tus (vom′i təs), *n., pl.* **-tus·es.** *Med.* **1.** the act of vomiting. **2.** vomited matter. [< L (4th decl.): a vomiting; see VOMIT]

von (von; *Ger.* fôn, *unstressed* fən), *prep.* from; of (used in German and Austrian personal names, originally to indicate place of origin and later to indicate nobility): *Paul von Hindenburg.*

Von Bé·ké·sy (von bā′ke shē), **Ge·org** (gā′ôrg), 1899–1972, U.S. physicist, born in Hungary: Nobel prize for medicine 1961.

von Braun (von broun′; *Ger.* fən bʀoun′), **Wern·her** (vâr′-ner, vûr′-, wûr′-; *Ger.* veʀ′nəʀ). See **Braun, Wernher von.**

Von Kár·mán (von kär′män, -mən), **Theodore,** 1881–1963, U.S. scientist and aeronautical engineer, born in Hungary.

Von Neu·mann (von noi′män, -mən), **John,** 1903–57 U.S. mathematician, born in Hungary.

Von Stro·heim (von strō′hīm, shtrō′-; *Ger.* fən shtʀō′-hīm), **E·rich** (er′ik; *Ger.* e′ʀiкн), 1885–1957, U.S. actor and director, born in Austria.

voo·doo (vo͞o′do͞o), *n., pl.* **-doos,** *adj., v.,* **-dooed, -doo·ing.** —*n.* **1.** a class of religious rites or practices, as sorcery or witchcraft, prevalent among the Negroes of the West Indies: probably of West African origin. **2.** a person who practices such rites. **3.** a fetish or other object of voodoo worship. **4.** a group of magical and ecstatic rites associated with voodoo. **5.** black magic; sorcery. —*adj.* **6.** of, pertaining to, associated with, or practicing voodoo. —*v.t.* **7.** to affect by voodoo sorcery or conjuration. [< Creole F *voudou* << some WAfr tongue; cf. Ewe *vodu* demon]

voo·doo·ism (vōō′dōō iz′əm), *n.* **1.** the voodoo religious rites and practices. **2.** the practice of sorcery. —**voo′doo·ist,** *n.* —**voo′doo·is′tic,** *adj.*

-vora, a combination of **-vore** and **-a,** used as a final element esp. in names of zoological orders: *Carnivora.* [< L, neut. pl. of *-vorus* -VOROUS]

vo·ra·cious (vō rā′shəs, vô-, və-), *adj.* **1.** craving or consuming large quantities of food. **2.** eager to absorb, possess, or consume; insatiable: *voracious readers.* [VORACI(TY) + -OUS] —**vo·ra′cious·ly,** *adv.* —**Syn. 1.** See **ravenous.**

vo·rac·i·ty (vō ras′i tē, vô-, və-), *n.* the condition or quality of being voracious. [< L *vorācitās* = *vorāci-* (s. of *vorāx*) gluttonous + *-tās* -TY[2]]

Vor·arl·berg (fōr′ärl′berk′), *n.* a province in W Austria. 226,323 (1961); 1004 sq. mi. *Cap.:* Bregenz.

-vore, a learned borrowing from Latin meaning "eating," used in the formation of compound words: *carnivore.* Cf. **-vora, -vorous.** [< F < L *-vorus* -VOROUS]

Vo·ro·nezh (vo rô′nesh), *n.* a city in the SW RSFSR, in the central Soviet Union in Europe. 577,000 (1965).

Vo·ro·shi·lov (vo ro shē′lof), *n.* **Kli·ment E·fre·mo·vich** (klē′ment e fre′mo vich), 1881–1969, Russian general: president of the Soviet Union 1953–60.

Vo·ro·shi·lov·grad (vo ro shē′lof grät′), *n.* former name of **Lugansk.**

Vo·ro·shi·lovsk (vo ro shē′lofsk), *n.* former name of **Stavropol.**

-vorous, a combination of **-vore** and **-ous,** used in the formation of adjectives from nouns with stems in **-vora** and **-vore:** *carnivorous.* [< L *-vorus* devouring]

Vor·ster (fôr′stər), *n.* **Bal·tha·zar Jo·han·nes** (bäl′thə zär′ yō hä′nis), 1915–83, South African political leader: prime minister 1966–78.

vor·tex (vôr′teks), *n., pl.* **-tex·es, -ti·ces** (-ti sēz′). **1.** a whirling mass of water, as a whirlpool. **2.** a whirling mass of air, fire, etc. **3.** a state of affairs likened to a whirlpool for violent activity, irresistible attraction, etc. [< L, var. of *vertex* VERTEX]

vor·ti·cal (vôr′ti kəl), *adj.* **1.** of, pertaining to, or resembling a vortex. **2.** moving in a vortex. [< L *vortic-* (s. of *vortex*) + -AL[1]]

vor·ti·ces (vôr′ti sēz′), *n.* a pl. of **vortex.**

vor·ti·cose (vôr′tə kōs′), *adj.* vortical; whirling. [< L *vorticōs(us)* eddying. See VORTICAL, -OSE[1]]

vor·tig·i·nous (vôr tij′ə nəs), *adj.* resembling a vortex; whirling; vortical. [var. of VERTIGINOUS]

Vor·tum·nus (vôr tum′nəs), *n.* Vertumnus.

Vosges (vōzh), *n.* a range of low mountains in NE France: highest peak, 4668 ft.

Vos·tok (vôs′tok; *Russ.* vos tôk′), *n.* one of a series of manned satellites orbited by the Soviet Union. [lit., east]

vot·a·ble (vō′tə bəl), *adj.* capable of being voted upon; subject to a vote: *a votable issue.* Also, **voteable.**

vo·ta·ry (vō′tə rē), *n., pl.* **-ries,** *adj.* —*n.* Also, **vo′ta·rist;** *referring to a woman,* **vo·ta·ress** (vō′tər is). **1.** a person who is bound by solemn religious vows, as a monk or a nun. **2.** a devoted worshiper of God, a saint, etc. **3.** a person who is devoted to some person, subject, or pursuit. —*adj.* **4.** consecrated by a vow. **5.** of or pertaining to a vow. [< L *vōt(um)* a vow + -ARY]

vote (vōt), *n., v.,* **vot·ed, vot·ing.** —*n.* **1.** a formal expression of opinion or choice made by an individual or body of individuals. **2.** the means by which such expression is made, as a ballot, ticket, etc. **3.** the right to such expression: *to give women the vote.* **4.** the decision reached by voting, as by a majority of ballots cast: *Was the vote for or against the resolution?* **5.** a collective expression of will or attitude as inferred from a number of votes: *the labor vote.* —*v.i.* **6.** to express or signify will or choice in a matter, as by casting a ballot. —*v.t.* **7.** to enact, elect, establish, or determine by vote. **8.** to support by one's vote. **9.** to advocate by or as by one's vote. **10.** to declare or decide by general consent: *They voted the trip a success.* [late ME < L *vōt(um)* a vow]

vote·a·ble (vō′tə bəl), *adj.* votable.

vote·less (vōt′lis), *adj.* **1.** lacking or without a vote. **2.** denied the right to vote, esp. in political elections.

vot·er (vō′tər), *n.* **1.** a person who votes. **2.** a person who has the right to vote; elector.

vot′ing machine′, a mechanical apparatus used in a polling place to register and count the votes.

vo·tive (vō′tiv), *adj.* **1.** offered, given, dedicated, etc., in accordance with a vow: *a votive offering.* **2.** performed, undertaken, etc., in consequence of a vow. [< L *vōtīv(us)* = *vōt(um)* a vow + *-īvus* -IVE] —**vo′tive·ly,** *adv.*

vo′tive Mass′, *Rom. Cath. Ch.* a Mass that does not correspond with the office of the day but is said at the choice of the celebrant for a special intention.

Vo·ty·ak (vō′tē ak′), *n.* a Uralic language of the Permian branch.

vouch (vouch), *v.i.* **1.** to support someone or something as being true, certain, reliable, etc. (usually fol. by *for*): *His record in office vouches for his integrity.* **2.** to attest, guarantee, or certify someone or something (usually fol. by *for*): *to vouch for someone in a business transaction.* —*v.t.* **3.** to warrant; attest to; confirm. **4.** to sustain or uphold by, or as by, practical proof or demonstration. **5.** to support or authenticate with vouchers. **6.** (formerly) to call or summon (a person) into court to make good a warranty of title. —*n.* **7.** *Obs.* a vouching; an assertion. [ME *vouche(n)* < AF, MF *vo(u)cher,* OF *(a)vochier* < L *(ad)vocare;* see ADVOCATE]

vouch·er (vou′chər), *n.* **1.** a person or thing that vouches. **2.** a document, receipt, or the like, which gives evidence of an expenditure. **3.** *Accounting.* a printed form authorizing a disbursement, showing the payee, account number, authorization, etc. —*v.t.* **4.** *Accounting.* to prepare a voucher for. [< AF *voucher* to vouch; orig. F inf. used as n. but now taken as VOUCH + -ER]

vouch′er sys′tem, 1. *Accounting.* a procedure for controlling disbursements by means of vouchers. **2.** Also called **vouch′er plan′.** *U.S. Educ.* a plan, undergoing development in some school districts, in which each school-age child receives a publicly funded entitlement worth a fixed amount of money with which his parents can select a participating public or private school.

vouch·safe (vouch sāf′), *v.,* **-safed, -saf·ing.** —*v.t.* **1.** to grant or give, as by favor, graciousness, or condescension. **2.** to allow or permit, as by favor or graciousness: *They vouchsafed his return to his own country.* —*v.i.* **3.** to condescend; deign. [ME phrase *vouche sauf*] —**vouch·safe′ment,** *n.* —**Syn. 1.** bestow, confer, accord.

vous·soir (vōō swär′), *n.* *Archit.* any of the pieces, in the shape of a truncated wedge, that form an arch or vault. [< F; r. ME *vousor(i)e* < AF < OF *volsoir* < VL **volsōr(ium)* = *vols(us)* (r. L *volūtus,* ptp. of *volvere* to turn) + *-ōrium* -ORY[2]]

Vou·vray (vōōv rā′; *Fr.* vōō vre′), *n.* **1.** a town in W central France, E of Tours: noted for fine wines. 2753 (1962). **2.** a medium-dry white wine of this region.

vow (vou), *n.* **1.** a solemn promise, pledge, or personal commitment: *marriage vows; a vow of secrecy.* **2.** a solemn promise made to God or to any deity or saint committing oneself to an act, service, or condition. **3.** a solemn or earnest declaration. **4. take vows,** to enter a religious order. —*v.t.* **5.** to make a vow of; promise by a vow, as to God or a saint. **6.** to pledge or resolve solemnly to do, make, give, observe, etc.: *They vowed revenge.* **7.** to declare solemnly or earnestly; assert emphatically (often fol. by a clause as object): *She vowed that she would take the matter to court.* **8.** to dedicate or devote by a vow. —*v.i.* **9.** to make a vow. **10.** to make a solemn declaration. [ME < AF, OF *vo(u)* < L *vōtum,* neut. of *vōtus,* ptp. of *vovēre* to vow] —**vow′less,** *adj.*

vow·el (vou′əl), *n.* **1.** *Phonet.* **a.** (in English articulation) a speech sound produced without occluding, diverting, or obstructing the flow of air from the lungs (opposed to *consonant*). **b.** (in a syllable) the sound of greatest sonority, as *i* in *grill.* **c.** (in linguistic function) a concept empirically determined as a phonological element in structural contrast with consonant, as the (ē) of *be* (bē), *we* (wē), and *yeast* (yēst). **2.** a letter representing or usually representing a vowel, as, in English, *a, e, i, o, u, w, y.* —*adj.* **3.** of or pertaining to a vowel or vowels. [ME < OF *vouel* < L *vōcāl(is)* adj.; see VOCAL] —**vow′el·less,** *adj.* —**vow′el·like′,** *adj.*

vow·el·ize (vou′ə līz′), *v.t.,* **-ized, -iz·ing.** to provide (a Hebrew, Arabic, etc., text) with vowel points. —**vow′el·i·za′tion,** *n.*

vow′el point′, any of a group of auxiliary symbols, as small lines and dots, placed above or below consonant symbols to indicate vowels in a writing system, as that of Hebrew or Arabic, in which vowels are otherwise not written.

vox an·gel·i·ca (voks′ an jel′i kə), a pipe-organ stop producing delicate, wavering tones. [< L: angelic voice]

vox hu·ma·na (voks′ hyōō mā′nə), a pipe-organ stop designed to produce tones resembling those of the human voice. [< L: human voice]

vox pop., See **vox populi.**

vox po·pu·li (voks′ pop′yə lī′), the voice of the people; popular opinion. *Abbr.:* vox pop. [< L]

voy·age (voi′ij), *n., v.,* **-aged, -ag·ing.** —*n.* **1.** a course of travel or passage, esp. by water or air. **2.** a long journey or one full of adventures. **3.** Often, **voyages.** a series of journeys or travels as the subject of a written account, or the account itself: *the voyages of Marco Polo.* **4.** *Obs.* an enterprise or undertaking. —*v.i.* **5.** to make or take a voyage; travel; journey. —*v.t.* **6.** to traverse by a voyage. [ME *ve(i)age, viage, voyage* < AF, OF < L *viāticum* travel money; see VIATICUM] —**voy′ag·er,** *n.* —**Syn. 1.** See **trip.**

vo·ya·geur (vwä′yä zhûr′, voi ə-; *Fr.* vwa ya zhœr′), *n., pl.* **-geurs** (-zhûrz′; *Fr.* -zhœr′). (in Canada) a man employed by fur companies to transport supplies to and from their distant stations. [< F: traveler = *voyag(er)* (to) travel (< *voyage* journey; see VOYAGE) + *-eur* -OR[2]]

vo·yeur (vwä yûr′, voi-; *Fr.* vwa yœr′), *n., pl.* **-yeurs** (-yûrz′; *Fr.* -yœr′). a person who compulsively engages in the practice of obtaining sexual gratification by looking at sexual objects or acts, esp. secretively. [< F = *voi(r)* (to) see (< L *vidēre*) + *-eur* -OR[2]] —**vo·yeur′ism,** *n.* —**voy·eur·is·tic** (vwä′yə ris′tic, voi′ə-), *adj.*

V.P., Vice President. Also, **V. Pres.**

v.p., verb passive.

V.R., Queen Victoria. [< L *Victoria Regina*]

v.r., verb reflexive.

V. Rev., Very Reverend.

Vries (vrēs), *n.* **Hu·go de** (hʏ′gō də). See **De Vries, Hugo.**

vs., **1.** verse. **2.** versus.

V.S., Veterinary Surgeon.

v.s., vide supra.

V-shaped (vē′shāpt′), *adj.* having the shape of the letter V: *a V-shaped flying formation.*

V sign, a sign of victory formed by the raised index and middle fingers.

V.S.O., very superior old (used esp. to indicate the age of brandy, usually 12 to 17 years old).

V.S.O.P., very superior old pale (used esp. to indicate the age of brandy, usually 20 to 25 years old).

vss., versions.

V/STOL (vē′stôl′), *n.* vertical/short takeoff and landing.

VT, Vermont (approved esp. for use with zip code).

Vt., Vermont.

v.t., verb transitive.

Vte., Vicomte.

VT fuze, a variable time fuze.

VTO, *Aeron.* vertical takeoff.

VTOL (vē′tôl′), *n.* *Aeron.* a convertiplane capable of taking off and landing vertically, having forward speeds comparable to those of conventional aircraft. [*v(ertical) t(ake)o(ff and) l(anding)*]

V′-type en′gine (vē′tīp′), *Auto.* an engine having the cylinders aligned in two banks at an angle to each other, forming a V.

vu, volume unit. Also, **VU**

vug (vug, vōōg), *n.* *Mining.* a small cavity in a rock or lode, often lined with crystals. Also, **vugg, vugh.** [< Cornish *vooga* cave; cf. L *fovea* pit, pitfall]

Vuil·lard (vwē yar′), *n.* **(Jean) É·douard** (zhän ā-dwar′), 1868–1940, French painter.

Vul., Vulgate.

Vul·can (vul′kən), *n.* the ancient Roman god of fire and metalworking, identified with the Greek Hephaestus. [< L *Vulcān(us)*]

Vul·ca·ni·an (vul kā′nē ən), *adj.* **1.** of, pertaining to, or associated with Vulcan. **2.** (*l.c.*) volcanic. **3.** (*l.c.*) of or pertaining to metalworking. [< L *Vulcāni(us)* of Vulcan + -AN]

vul·can·ise (vul′kə nīz′), *v.t.*, **-ised, -is·ing.** *Chiefly Brit.* vulcanize. —**vul′can·i·sa′tion,** *n.* —**vul′can·is′er,** *n.*

vul·can·ism (vul′kə niz′əm), *n. Geol.* volcanism. —**vul′-can·ist,** *n.*

vul·can·ite (vul′kə nīt′), *n.* a hard, readily cut and polished rubber, obtained by vulcanizing rubber with a large amount of sulfur, used in the manufacture of combs, buttons, and for electric insulation; ebonite.

vul·can·ize (vul′kə nīz′), *v.t.*, **-ized, -iz·ing.** **1.** to treat (rubber) under heat with sulfur or some compound of sulfur in order to render it nonplastic and give greater elasticity, durability, etc. **2.** to subject (a substance other than rubber) to some analogous process, as to harden it. Also, *esp. Brit.*, **vulcanise.** —**vul′can·i·za′tion,** *n.* —**vul′can·iz′er,** *n.*

vul·can·ol·o·gy (vul′kə nol′ə jē), *n.* volcanology. —**vul-can·o·log·i·cal** (vul′kə nᵊloj′i kəl), *adj.* —**vul′can·ol′o-gist,** *n.*

Vulg., Vulgate.

vulg., **1.** vulgar. **2.** vulgarly.

vul·gar (vul′gər), *adj.* **1.** characterized by ignorance of or lack of good breeding or taste; unrefined; crude. **2.** indecent; obscene; lewd. **3.** of, pertaining to, or constituting the ordinary people in a society: *the vulgar masses.* **4.** current; popular; common: *a vulgar success.* **5.** spoken by, or being in the language spoken by, the people generally; vernacular: *a vulgar translation of the Greek text of the New Testament.* —*n.* **6.** *Archaic.* the common people. **7.** *Obs.* the vernacular. [late ME < L *vulgār(is)* = *vulg(us)* the general public + *-āris* -AR¹] —**vul′gar·ly,** *adv.* —**vul′gar·ness,** *n.* —**Syn. 1.** inelegant, low. See **common. 5.** colloquial.

vul·gar·i·an (vul gâr′ē ən), *n.* a person having vulgar tastes or manners.

vul·gar·ise (vul′gə rīz′), *v.t.*, **-ised, -is·ing.** *Chiefly Brit.* vulgarize. —**vul′gar·i·sa′tion,** *n.* —**vul′gar·is′er,** *n.*

vul·gar·ism (vul′gə riz′əm), *n.* **1.** vulgar behavior or character; vulgarity. **2.** a vulgar word or phrase used only in common colloquial, and esp. in coarse, speech.

vul·gar·i·ty (vul gar′i tē), *n., pl.* **-ties** for 2. **1.** the state or quality of being vulgar. **2.** something vulgar, as an act or expression. [< LL *vulgāritās* the common herd]

vul·gar·ize (vul′gə rīz′), *v.t.*, **-ized, -iz·ing.** to make vulgar; cause to conform to vulgar tastes; debase. Also, *esp. Brit.*, **vulgarise.** —**vul′gar·i·za′tion,** *n.* —**vul′gar·iz′er,** *n.*

Vul′gar Lat′in, popular Latin, as distinguished from literary or standard Latin, esp. those spoken forms of Latin from which the Romance languages developed. *Abbr.:* VL

Vul·gate (vul′gāt, -git), *n.* **1.** the Latin version of the Bible, prepared chiefly by St. Jerome at the end of the 4th century A.D., and used as the authorized version in liturgical services of the Roman Catholic Church. **2.** (*l.c.*) any commonly recognized text or version of a work. **3.** (*l.c.*) common, informal, or substandard speech. —*adj.* **4.** of or pertaining to the Vulgate. **5.** (*l.c.*) commonly used or accepted; common. [< LL *vulgāta (editiō)* popular edition (of the Bible); *vulgāta* fem. ptp. of *vūlgāre* to make common, publish < *vulgus* the public. See VULGAR, -ATE¹]

vul·ner·a·ble (vul′nər ə bəl), *adj.* **1.** capable of or susceptible to being wounded or hurt, as by a weapon. **2.** open to criticism, temptation, etc.: *an argument vulnerable to refutation; He has proved himself vulnerable to bribery.* **3.** (of a place) open to attack or assault. **4.** *Bridge.* having won one of the games of a rubber. [< LL *vulnerābil(is)* = L *vulnerā(re)* to wound + *-bilis* -BLE; see VULNERARY] —**vul′ner·a·bil′-i·ty, vul′ner·a·ble·ness,** *n.* —**vul′ner·a·bly,** *adv.*

vul·ner·ar·y (vul′nə rer′ē), *adj., n., pl.* **-ar·ies.** —*adj.* **1.** used to promote the healing of wounds, as herbs or other remedies. —*n.* **2.** a remedy for wounds. [< L *vulnerāri(us)* = *vulner-* (s. of *vulnus*) wound + *-ārius* -ARY]

Turkey vulture, *Cathartes aura* (Length 2½ ft.; wingspread to 6 ft.)

vul·pec·u·lar (vul pek′yə lər), *adj.* pertaining to or resembling a fox; vulpine. [< LL *vulpēculār(is)* = L *vulpēcula* (dim. of *vulpēs* fox; see -CULE) + *-āris* -AR¹]

vul·pine (vul′pīn, -pin), *adj.* pertaining to, like, or characteristic of a fox. [< L *vulpīn(us)* = *vulp(i)-* (s. of *vulpēs* fox) + *-īnus* -INE¹]

vul·ture (vul′chər), *n.* **1.** any of several large, primarily carrion-eating Old World birds of prey of the family *Accipitridae*, related to the hawks and eagles. **2.** any of several superficially similar New World birds of the family *Cathartidae.* [late ME < L *vultur*]

vul·tur·ine (vul′chə rīn′, -chər in), *adj.* **1.** of, pertaining to, or characteristic of a vulture or vultures. **2.** resembling a vulture, esp. in rapacious or predatory qualities: *a vulturine critic.* Also, **vul·tur·ous** (vul′chər əs). [< L *vulturin(us).* See VULTURE, -INE¹]

vul·va (vul′və), *n., pl.* **-vae** (-vē), **-vas.** *Anat.* the external female genitalia. [< L: covering] —**vul′val, vul′var,** *adj.* —**vul·vi·form** (vul′və fôrm′), **vul·vate** (vul′vāt, -vit), *adj.*

vv., **1.** verses. **2.** *Music.* violins.

v.v., vice versa.

V.W., Very Worshipful.

Vyat·ka (vyät′kä), *n.* former name of **Kirov.**

Vy·borg (vē′bôrg), *n.* a seaport in the NW RSFSR, in the NW Soviet Union in Europe, on the Gulf of Finland: formerly in Finland. 51,000 (1959). Finnish, **Viipuri.** Swedish, **Viborg.**

Vy·cor (vī′kôr), *n. Trademark.* a durable, highly heat-resistant glass containing approximately 96 percent silica, used chiefly for making laboratory vessels.

Vyer·nyi (vyer′nē), *n.* former name of **Alma-Ata.**

vy·ing (vī′ing), *adj.* **1.** competing; contending. —*v.* **2.** ppr. of vie.

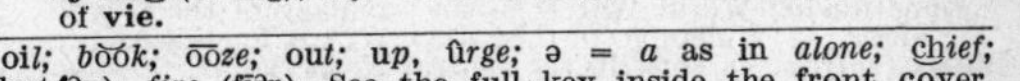
act, āble, dâre, ärt; ebb, ēqual; if, īce; hot, ōver, ôrder; oil; bo͝ok; o͞oze; out; up, ûrge; ə = *a* as in *alone;* chief; sing; shoe; thin; that; zh as in *measure;* ᵊ as in *button* (but′ᵊn), *fire* (fīᵊr). See the full key inside the front cover.

DEVELOPMENT OF MAJUSCULE						
NORTH SEMITIC	GREEK	ETR.	LATIN	MODERN		
				GOTHIC	ITALIC	ROMAN
SEE LETTERS F AND U				𝔚	*W*	W

DEVELOPMENT OF MINUSCULE					
ROMAN CURSIVE	ROMAN UNCIAL	CAROL. MIN.	MODERN		
			GOTHIC	ITALIC	ROMAN
—	ɯ	—	𝔴	*w*	w

The twenty-third letter of the English alphabet, called "double-u," created about the 11th century A.D. by the Norman scribes to represent the English sound for which they had no need in their own language, and to distinguish two U's from a U and a V. (See also **U** and **V.**) The *w*-sound was represented in North Semitic by *waw,* which in the Greek alphabet became *digamma* (ϝ) and *upsilon* (υ). (See **F.**) The Anglo-Saxons used a special character (ƿ, *wyn)* for the *w*-sound, but rather than use a foreign letter in their alphabet, the Norman French preferred to double one of their own characters.

W, w (dub′əl yo͞o′), *n., pl.* **W's** or **Ws, w's** or **ws. 1.** the 23rd letter of the English alphabet, a semivowel. **2.** any spoken sound represented by the letter *W* or *w,* as in *way, coward,* or *owe.* **3.** a written or printed representation of the letter *W* or *w.* **4.** a device, as a printer's type, for reproducing the letter *W* or *w.*

W, 1. watt; watts. **2.** west. **3.** western. **4.** withdrew.

W, 1. the 23rd in order or in a series, or, when *I* is omitted, the 22nd. **2.** *Chem.* tungsten. [< G WOLFRAM]

w, 1. *Elect.* watt; watts. **2.** withdrawn; withdrew.

W., 1. Wales. **2.** warden. **3.** warehouse. **4.** Washington. **5.** *Elect.* watt; watts. **6.** Wednesday. **7.** weight. **8.** Welsh. **9.** west. **10.** western. **11.** width. **12.** *Physics.* work.

w., 1. warden. **2.** warehouse. **3.** *Elect.* watt; watts. **4.** week; weeks. **5.** weight. **6.** west. **7.** western. **8.** wide. **9.** width. **10.** wife. **11.** with. **12.** won. **13.** *Physics.* work.

w/, with.

W-2 (dub′əl yə to͞o′), a prescribed form of statement showing the total wages paid to an earner and the taxes withheld during a specific calendar year: required by the U.S. Internal Revenue Service to be prepared by an employer for his employees. Also called **W-2′ form′.**

WA, Washington (approved esp. for use with zip code).

W.A., 1. West Africa. **2.** Western Australia.

WAAC (wak), *n.* **1.** *U.S.* **a.** Women's Army Auxiliary Corps: founded during World War II. **b.** a member of this. Cf. **Wac. 2.** *Brit.* **a.** Women's Army Auxiliary Corps: founded in 1917. **b.** a member of this. Cf. **WRAC.** Also, **W.A.A.C.**

Waadt (vät), *n.* German name of **Vaud.**

Waaf (waf), *n. Brit.* **1.** Women's Auxiliary Air Force: formed during World War II as an auxiliary of the Royal Air Force. **2.** a member of this. Also, **W.A.A.F., WAAF**

Waal (väl), *n.* a river in the central Netherlands, flowing W to the Meuse River. 52 mi. long.

Wa·bash (wô′bash), *n.* a river flowing from W Ohio through Indiana into the Ohio River. 475 mi. long.

wab·ble (wob′əl), *v.i., v.t.,* **-bled, -bling.** wobble. **—wab′bler,** *n.* **—wab′bling·ly,** *adv.*

wab·bly (wob′lē), *adj.,* **-bli·er, -bli·est.** wobbly. **—wab′bli·ness,** *n.*

Wac (wak), *n.* a member of the Women's Army Corps, an auxiliary of the U.S. Army.

Wace (wās, wäs; *Fr.* WAS), *n.* **Ro·bert** (rob′ərt; *Fr.* RÔ BER′), ("*Wace of Jersey*"), c1100–c1180, Anglo-Norman poet, born on the Channel Island of Jersey.

wack·e (wak′ə), *n.* a soft rock of fine texture, derived from disintegrated basaltic rocks. [< G: a kind of stone]

wack·y (wak′ē), *adj.,* **wack·i·er, wack·i·est.** *Slang.* odd or irrational; crazy. Also, **whacky.** [nonsense formation; cf. *icky* not a member of the group; prob. akin to WHACK] **—wack′i·ly,** *adv.* **—wack′i·ness,** *n.*

Wa·co (wā′kō), *n.* a city in central Texas, on the Brazos River. 95,326 (1970).

wad[1] (wod), *n., v.,* **wad·ded, wad·ding.** **—***n.* **1.** a small mass, lump, or ball of something. **2.** a small mass of cotton, wool, or other fibrous or soft material, used for stuffing, padding, packing, etc. **3.** a roll of something, esp. of bank notes. **4.** a plug of wadding for a gun or cartridge. **5.** *Slang.* a comparatively large quantity of something, esp. money. **6.** *Brit. Dial.* a bundle, esp. a small one, of hay, straw, etc. **—***v.t.* **7.** to form (material) into a wad. **8.** to roll tightly (often fol. by *up*). **9.** to hold in place by a wad. **10.** to put a wad into; stuff or fill out with wadding; pad. [< AL *wadda* ? < Arab *bāṭa′in* lining of a garment]

wad[2] (wod), *n.* a soft, earthy, black to dark-brown mass of manganese oxide minerals. [?]

wad[3] (wäd, wəd), *v. Scot.* would.

Wa·dai (wä dī′), *n.* a former independent sultanate of the Sudan, in N central Africa: now part of the Republic of Chad.

wad·ding (wod′ing), *n.* **1.** any fibrous or soft material for stuffing, padding, packing, etc., esp. carded cotton. **2.** material used as wads for guns, cartridges, etc. **3.** a wad.

wad·dle (wod′əl), *v.,* **-dled, -dling,** *n.* **—***v.i.* **1.** to walk with short steps, swaying or rocking from side to side, as a duck does. **2.** to move in any slow, rocking manner. **—***n.* **3.** the act or an instance of waddling. **4.** a waddling gait. [WADE + -LE; c. G *watteln*] **—wad′dler,** *n.* **—wad′dling·ly,** *adv.* **—wad′dly,** *adj.*

wad·dy (wod′ē), *n., pl.* **-dies.** *Australian.* a heavy, wooden war club of the Australian aborigines. [< native Austral]

wade (wād), *v.,* **wad·ed, wad·ing,** *n.* **—***v.i.* **1.** to walk partly immersed or sunken, as in water, snow, or mud. **2.** to play in shallow water, as a child does. **3.** to make progress slowly or laboriously: *to wade through a dull book.* **4.** *Obs.* to go or proceed. **—***v.t.* **5.** to pass through or cross by wading; ford: *to wade a stream.* **6. wade in** or **into,** *Informal.* **a.** to begin energetically. **b.** to attack vigorously. **—***n.* **7.** the act or an instance of wading. [ME; OE *wad(an)* (to) go; c. Icel *vatha,* G *waten;* akin to OE *wæd* ford, sea, L *vadum* shoal, ford, *vādere* to go, rush] **—wad′a·ble, wade′a·ble,** *adj.*

wad·er (wā′dər), *n.* **1.** a person or thing that wades. **2.** any of various long-legged birds that wade in water in search of food. **3. waders,** high waterproof boots used for wading, as by fishermen, duck hunters, etc.

wa·di (wä′dē), *n., pl.* **-dis.** (in Arabia, Syria, northern Africa, etc.) **1.** a stream or watercourse that is dry except during periods of rainfall. **2.** a valley. [< Ar *wādī*]

wad·mal (wod′məl), *n.* a bulky woolen fabric formerly used in durable winter garments. Also, **wad′maal, wad′mel, wad′mol, wad′moll.** [late ME < Scand; cf. Icel *vathmāl* kind of cloth = *vath-* (< ?) + *māl* -MEAL]

Wad Me·da·ni (wäd mə dä′nē, med′ənē), a city in the E Sudan, on the Blue Nile. 57,000 (est. 1964).

wa·dy (wä′dē), *n., pl.* **-dies.** wadi.

wae (wā), *n. Scot. and North Eng.* woe. [OE *wā* WOE]

wae·sucks (wā′suks), *interj. Scot.* alas. Also, **wae·suck** (wā′suk). [WAE + *sucks,* var. of SAKE[2]]

Waf (waf), *n.* a member of the Women in the Air Force, an auxiliary of the U.S. Air Force.

wa·fer (wā′fər), *n.* **1.** a thin, crisp cake or biscuit, often sweetened and flavored. **2.** a thin disk of unleavened bread, used in the Eucharist. **3.** a thin disk of dried paste, gelatin, adhesive paper, or the like, used for sealing letters, attaching papers, etc. **4.** *Med.* a thin, circular sheet of dry paste or the like, or a pair of such sheets, used to wrap or enclose a powder to be swallowed. **5.** any small, thin disk, as a washer, piece of insulation, etc. **6.** *Electronics.* a slice of thin monocrystalline silicon, germanium, or the like used as a base material on which single transistors or integrated-circuit components are formed. **—***v.t.* **7.** to seal, close, or attach by means of a wafer or wafers. [late ME *wafre* < MD *wafer,* var. of *wafel* WAFFLE; cf. F *gaufre* (OF *walfre*)] **—wa′fer-like′, wa′fer·y,** *adj.*

waff (waf, wäf), *n. Scot. and North Eng.* **1.** a puff or blast of air, wind, etc. **2.** a brief view; glance. [var. of WAVE]

waf·fle[1] (wof′əl), *n.* **1.** a thin batter cake baked in a heated appliance **(waf′fle i′ron),** whose parts, hinged to enclose the batter, leave a deep, gridlike, indented pattern on it. **—***adj.* **2.** Also, **waf′fled.** having a gridlike or indented lattice shape or design: *a waffle weave.* [< D *wafel* = *waf-* (cf. OHG *waba* honeycomb) + *-el* -LE; akin to WEB]

waf·fle[2] (wof′əl), *v.i.,* **-fled, -fl·ing.** to waver or vacillate: *to waffle on an important issue.* **—waf·fl·er,** *n.* **—waf·fl·ing,** *adj., n.*

W. Afr., 1. West Africa. **2.** West African.

waft (waft, wäft), *v.t.* **1.** to carry lightly and smoothly through the air or over water. **2.** *Obs.* to signal to, summon, or direct by waving. **—***v.i.* **3.** to float or be carried, esp. by the air. **—***n.* **4.** a sound, odor, etc., faintly perceived. **5.** a wafting movement; light current or gust: *a waft of air.* **6.** the act of wafting. **7.** *Naut.* waif (def. 4). [back formation from obs. *wafter,* late ME *waughter* armed escort vessel < D or LG *wachter* guard] **—waft′er,** *n.*

waft·age (waf′tij, wäf′-), *n. Archaic.* **1.** the act of wafting. **2.** the state of being wafted.

waf·ture (waf′chər, wäf′-), *n.* **1.** the act of wafting. **2.** something wafted: *waftures of incense.*

wag (wag), *v.,* **wagged, wag·ging,** *n.* **—***v.t.* **1.** to move from side to side, up and down, etc., esp. rapidly and repeatedly: *a dog wagging his tail.* **2.** to move (the tongue) as in idle or indiscreet chatter. **3.** to shake (a finger) at someone, as in reproach. **4.** to move or nod (the head). **—***v.i.* **5.** to move with a wagging motion. **6.** (of the tongue) to move constantly, as in gossip. **7.** *Brit. Slang.* to play truant; play hooky. **—***n.* **8.** the act or an instance of wagging. **9.** a person given to droll or mischievous humor. [ME *wagge* < Scand; cf. Icel *vagga* to rock] **—wag′ger,** *n.*

wage (wāj), *n., v.,* **waged, wag·ing.** **—***n.* **1.** Often, **wages.** money that is paid or received for work or services, as by the hour, day, or week. **2.** Usually, **wages.** *Econ.* the share of the products of industry received by labor for its work. **3.** Usually, **wages.** (*construed as sing. or pl.*) recompense or return: *The wages of sin is death.* **4.** *Obs.* a pledge or security. **—***v.t.* **5.** to carry on (a conflict, argument, etc.). **6.** *Chiefly Brit. Dial.* to hire. **7.** *Obs.* **a.** to stake or wager. **b.** to pledge. **—***v.i.* **8.** *Obs.* to contend; struggle. [ME < AF; OF *gauge* GAGE[1] < VL **wadium* < Gmc; see WED] **—Syn. 1.** earnings, compensation, remuneration. See **pay**[1].

wa·ger (wā′jər), *n.* **1.** something risked or staked on an uncertain event; bet. **2.** the act of betting. **3.** the subject or terms of a bet. **—***v.t.* **4.** to risk (something) on the issue of a contest or any uncertain event or matter; bet. **—***v.i.* **5.** to make or offer a wager; bet. [ME *wajour, wager* < AF *wageure.* See WAGE, -URE] **—wa′ger·er,** *n.*

wage′ scale′, 1. a schedule of wages paid workers performing related tasks in an industry or shop. **2.** a particular employer's wage schedule.

wage′ slave′, *Often Facetious.* a person who works for a meager wage, esp. at disagreeable tasks.

wage·work·er (wāj′wûr′kər), *n.* a member of the laboring class; a person who works for wages. **—wage′work′ing,** *adj., n.*

wag·ger·y (wag′ə rē), *n., pl.* **-ger·ies.** **1.** the action, spirit, or language of a wag; roguish or droll humor. **2.** a waggish act; jest or joke.

wag·gish (wag′ish), *adj.* **1.** like a wag; roguish in merriment and good humor. **2.** characteristic of or befitting a wag. —**wag′gish·ly,** *adv.* —**wag′gish·ness,** *n.* —**Syn. 1.** jocund, merry, jocose. See **humorous.**

wag·gle (wag′əl), *v.,* **-gled, -gling,** *n.* —*v.i.* **1.** to wobble or shake, esp. while in motion. —*v.t.* **2.** to move with a short wagging motion. —*n.* **3.** a waggling motion. —**wag′gling·ly,** *adv.*

wag·gly (wag′lē), *adj.* waggling; unsteady.

wag·gon (wag′ən), *n., v.t., v.i. Chiefly Brit.* wagon.

wag·gon·age (wag′ə nij), *n. Chiefly Brit.* wagonage.

wag·gon·load (wag′ən lōd′), *n. Chiefly Brit.* wagonload.

Wag·ner (wag′nər *for 1, 3, 4;* väg′nər *or Ger.* väg′nəʀ *for 2*), *n.* **1. Ho·nus** (hō′nəs), (*John Peter*), 1874–1955, U.S. baseball player. **2. Rich·ard** (rich′ərd; *Ger.* ʀɪᴋʜ′äʀt), 1813–83, German composer. **3. Robert F(erdinand),** 1877–1953, U.S. politician. **4.** his son, **Robert F(erdinand), Jr.,** born 1910, U.S. politician: mayor of New York City 1954–65.

Wag·ne·ri·an (väg nēr′ē ən), *adj.* **1.** of, pertaining to, or characteristic of Richard Wagner or his works. —*n.* **2.** Also, **Wag·ner·ite** (väg′nə rīt′). a follower or admirer of the music or theories of Richard Wagner.

wag·on (wag′ən), *n.* **1.** a small, open, four-wheeled vehicle with a handle, used by a child in play. **2.** a horse-drawn vehicle used for hauling some bulky or heavy load. **3.** any of various light vehicles for transporting passengers or goods. **4.** *Brit.* a railway freight car or flatcar. **5.** a police van for transporting prisoners; patrol wagon. **6.** See **station wagon. 7.** *Obs.* a chariot. **8. hitch one's wagon to a star,** to have a high ambition, ideal, or purpose. **9. on the wagon,** *Slang.* abstaining from alcoholic beverages. Also, **on the water wagon;** *Brit.* **on the water cart.** —*v.t.* **10.** to transport by wagon. —*v.i.* **11.** to proceed or transport goods by wagon. Also, *esp. Brit.,* **waggon.** [< D *wagen;* c. OE *wægn* ᴡᴀɪɴ] —**Syn. 1, 3.** cart, van, wain, truck.

wag·on·age (wag′ə nij), *n. Archaic.* **1.** transportation by wagon. **2.** money paid for this. **3.** a group of wagons; wagon train. Also, *esp. Brit.,* **waggonage.**

wag·on·er (wag′ə nər), *n.* **1.** a person who drives a wagon. **2.** (*cap.*) *Astron.* the northern constellation Auriga.

wag·on·ette (wag′ə net′), *n.* a light carriage, with or without a top, having a crosswise seat in front and two lengthwise seats facing each other at the back.

wa·gon-lit (ᴠᴀ gôɴ lē′), *n., pl.* **wa·gons-lits** (ᴠᴀ gôɴ lē′). *French.* (in continental European usage) a railroad sleeping car. [< F: lit., bed car = *wagon* railway coach (< E) + *lit* bed (< L *lectus*)]

wag·on·load (wag′ən lōd′), *n.* the load carried by a wagon. Also, *esp. Brit.,* **waggonload.**

wag′on sol′dier, *Mil. Slang.* a field-artillery soldier.

wag′on train′, a train of wagons and horses, as one carrying military supplies.

Wa·gram (vä′gʀäm), *n.* a village in NE Austria: Napoleon defeated the Austrians here in 1809.

wag·tail (wag′tāl′), *n.* **1.** any of numerous small, chiefly Old World birds of the family *Motacillidae,* having a slender body with a long, narrow tail that is habitually wagged up and down. **2.** any of several similar birds, as the water thrushes of the genus *Seiurus.*

Wah·ha·bi (wə hä′bē, wä-), *n., pl.* **-bis.** *Islam.* **1.** a strict Islamic sect, founded by Abd-al-Wahhab in the 18th century in Arabia and revived by Abdul-Aziz ibn-Saud in the 20th century, that opposes all practices not sanctioned by the Koran. **2.** a member of this sect. Also, **Wa·ha′bi, Wa·ha·bite** (wä hä′bīt), **Wah·ha′bee, Wah·ha′bite.** [< Ar = *Wahhāb* + *-ī* suffix of appurtenance]

Wah·ha·bism (wə hä′biz əm, wä-), *n.* the group of doctrines or practices of the Wahhabis. Also, **Wah·ha·bi·ism** (wə hä′bē iz′əm, wä-), **Wa·ha′bism.**

wa·hoo[1] (wä ho͞o′, wä′ho͞o), *n., pl.* **-hoos.** any of various American shrubs or small trees, as an elm, *Ulmus alata,* or a linden, *Tilia heterophylla.* [< Creek *uhawhu* kind of elm]

wa·hoo[2] (wä ho͞o′, wä′ho͞o), *n., pl.* **-hoos.** a shrub or small tree, *Euonymus atropurpureus,* of North America. [< Dakota *wāhu* arrowwood]

wa·hoo[3] (wä ho͞o′, wä′ho͞o), *n., pl.* **-hoos,** (*esp. collectively*) **-hoo.** a large, swift game fish, *Acanthocybium solandri,* of the high seas. [?]

waif (wāf), *n.* **1.** a person who has no home or friends, esp. a child. **2.** something that is found and whose owner is not known, esp. a stray animal. **3.** a stray item or article: *to gather waifs of gossip.* **4.** Also, **waft.** *Naut.* a signaling, or a signal given, by a flag rolled and stopped or fastened. [ME < AF, orig. adj., lost, stray, unclaimed; (OF *guaif* stray beast) < Scand; cf. Icel *veif* movement to and fro; see ᴡᴀɪᴠᴇ]

Wai·ki·ki (wī′kē kē′, wī′kē kē′), *n.* a beach on SE Oahu, in Hawaii: part of Honolulu.

wail (wāl), *v.i.* **1.** to utter a prolonged, inarticulate, mournful cry, usually high-pitched or clear sounding, as in grief or suffering: *to wail with pain.* **2.** to make mournful sounds, as music, the wind, etc. **3.** to lament or mourn bitterly. —*v.t.* **4.** to express deep sorrow for; bewail. **5.** to express in wailing. —*n.* **6.** the act of wailing. **7.** a wailing cry or any similar mournful sound. [ME *weile;* perh. < OE *weilā-(wei)* ᴡᴇʟʟᴀᴡᴀʏ; cf. OE *wǣlan* to torment, Icel *wǣla* to wail] —**wail′er,** *n.* —**wail′ing·ly,** *adv.*

wail·ful (wāl′fəl), *adj.* mournful; plaintive. —**wail′ful·ly,** *adv.*

Wail′ing Wall′, a wall in Jerusalem where Jews, on certain occasions, assemble for prayer and lamentation. It is traditionally believed to be the remains of the west wall of the Temple which was built by Herod and destroyed by Titus in 70 ᴀ.ᴅ. Also called **Wail′ing Wall′ of the Jews′.**

wail·some (wāl′səm), *adj. Archaic.* wailful.

wain (wān), *n.* a farm wagon or cart. [ME; OE *wægn;* c. G *Wagen,* D *wagen.* See ᴡᴇɪɢʜ]

wain·scot (wān′skət, -skot), *n., v.,* **-scot·ed, -scot·ing** or (*esp. Brit.*) **-scot·ted, -scot·ting.** —*n.* **1.** a dado, esp. of wood, lining an interior wall. —*v.t.* **2.** to line the walls of (a room, hallway, etc.) with or as with woodwork. [ME < MLG or MD *wagenschot* = *wagen* ᴡᴀɪɴ + *schot* (?)]

wain·scot·ing (wān′skō ting), *n.* **1.** paneling or woodwork with which rooms, hallways, etc., are wainscoted. **2.** wainscots collectively. Also, *esp. Brit.,* **wain·scot·ting** (wān′skət ing, -skot-).

wain·wright (wān′rīt′), *n.* a wagon maker. [OE *wægn-wyrhta*]

Wain·wright (wān′rīt′), *n.* **Jonathan May·hew** (mā′hyo͞o), 1883–1953, U.S. general.

waist (wāst), *n.* **1.** the narrowed part of the body in man between the ribs and the hips. **2.** the part of a garment covering this part of the body. **3.** blouse (def. 1). **4.** the part of a one-piece garment covering the body from the neck or shoulders to the waistline. **5.** a child's undergarment to which other articles of apparel may be attached. **6.** the part of an object, esp. a central or middle part, that resembles or is analogous to the human waist: *the waist of a violin; the waist of a ship.* **7.** the constricted portion of the abdomen of certain insects, as a wasp. [late ME *wast,* apocopated var. of *wastum,* OE *wæstm* growth, form, figure; akin to ᴡᴀx[2]] —**waist′less,** *adj.*

waist·band (wāst′band′, -bənd), *n.* a band encircling the waist, esp. as a part of a skirt, pair of trousers, etc.

waist·cloth (wāst′klôth′, -kloth′), *n., pl.* **-cloths** (-klôthz′, -klothz′, -klôths′, -kloths′). a loincloth.

waist·coat (wes′kət, wāst′kōt′), *n.* **1.** *Chiefly Brit.* vest (def. 1). **2.** a garment for women that is similar to a man's vest. **3.** a body garment for men, formerly worn under the doublet. —**waist′coat·ed,** *adj.*

waist-deep (wāst′dēp′), *adj.* being at or rising to the level of the waist.

waist·ed (wā′stid), *adj.* **1.** having a waist of a specified kind (usually used in combination): *long-waisted.* **2.** shaped like a waist; having concave sides: *a waisted vase.*

waist-high (wāst′hī′), *adj.* extending up to the waist.

waist·line (wāst′līn′), *n.* **1.** the encircling boundary of the narrowest part of the waist. **2.** the juncture point of the skirt and waist of a garment, as a dress.

wait (wāt), *v.i.* **1.** to hold oneself ready for an arrival or occurrence (often fol. by *for, till,* or *until*): *Let's wait for a bus.* **2.** to be in expectation or hope of something. **3.** to await one's attention: *There's a parcel waiting for you.* **4.** to be delayed or postponed. **5.** to serve as a waiter or waitress. —*v.t.* **6.** to be in patient expectation of; await patiently: *Wait your turn!* **7.** to cause to be postponed: *Did you wait supper for me?* **8. wait on** or **upon, a.** to perform the duties of an attendant or servant for. **b.** to supply the wants of a customer or master. **c.** to call upon or visit formally. **d.** *Dial.* to wait for; await. **9. wait table.** See **table** (def. 16). **10. wait up,** *Informal.* **a.** to postpone going to bed to await someone or something. **b.** to halt and wait for another to catch up, as when running or walking. —*n.* **11.** the act or an instance or period of waiting or awaiting; delay; pause. **12.** *Brit.* **a.** one of a band of musicians employed by a city or town to play music in parades, for official functions, etc. **b.** one of a band of carolers or street musicians. **13. lie in wait,** to wait in ambush. [early ME *waite(n)* < AF *waitie(r)* (OF *guaitier*) < Gmc, c. OHG *wahtēn* to watch < *wahta* a watch]
—**Syn. 1.** await, linger, remain, abide, delay. Wᴀɪᴛ, ᴛᴀʀʀʏ imply pausing to linger and thereby putting off further activity until later. Wᴀɪᴛ usually implies staying for a limited time and for a definite purpose, that is, for something expected: *to wait for a traffic light to turn green.* Tᴀʀʀʏ suggests lingering, perhaps aimlessly delaying, or pausing (briefly) in a journey: *to tarry on the way home.*

wait-a-bit (wāt′ə bit′), *n.* any of various plants bearing thorns or prickly appendages, as a procumbent herb, *Harpagophytum procumbens,* of southern Africa, or the greenbrier. [trans. of SAfrD *wacht-een-beetje*]

Waite (wāt), *n.* **Morrison Rem·ick** (rem′ik), 1816–88, U.S. jurist: Chief Justice of the U.S. 1874–88.

wait·er (wā′tər), *n.* **1.** a man who waits on table, as in a restaurant. **2.** a tray for carrying dishes, a tea service, etc.; salver. **3.** a person who waits or awaits. **4.** *Obs.* an attendant. [ME]

wait·ing (wā′ting), *n.* **1.** a period of waiting; pause, interval, or delay. **2. in waiting,** in attendance, as upon a royal personage. —*adj.* **3.** serving or being in attendance. [ME (n.); see ᴡᴀɪᴛ, -ɪɴɢ[1], -ɪɴɢ[2]]

wait′ing game′, a stratagem in which action on a matter is postponed to a more advantageous time.

wait′ing list′, a list of persons waiting, as for something in limited supply.

wait′ing room′, a room to accommodate persons waiting, as in a railroad station, a physician's office, etc.

wait·ress (wā′tris), *n.* a woman who waits on table, as in a restaurant. —**wait′ress·less,** *adj.*

waive (wāv), *v.t.,* **waived, waiv·ing. 1.** to refrain from claiming or insisting on (a right or privilege). **2.** *Law.* to relinquish (a known right, interest, etc.) intentionally. **3.** to put aside for the time; defer; postpone. **4.** to put aside or dismiss from consideration. [ME *weyve(n)* < AF *weyve(r)* (to) make a ᴡᴀɪғ (of someone) by forsaking or outlawing (him)] —**Syn. 1.** resign, renounce, surrender, give up. —**Ant. 1.** demand.

waiv·er (wā′vər), *n. Law.* **1.** an intentional relinquishment of some right, interest, or the like. **2.** an express or written statement of such relinquishment. [< AF *weyver* to ᴡᴀɪᴠᴇ used as n.; see -ᴇʀ[3]]

Wa·kash·an (wä kash′ən, wô′kə shan′), *n.* a family of American-Indian languages spoken in British Columbia and Washington and including Kwakiutl and Nootka. [< Nootka *Wa(u)kash* (lit., good) + -ᴀɴ]

Wa·ka·ya·ma (wä′kä yä′mä), *n.* a seaport on S Honshu, in S Japan. 312,000 (est. 1963).

wake[1] (wāk), *v.,* **waked** or **woke, waked** or **wok·en, wak·ing,** *n.* —*v.i.* **1.** to become roused from sleep; awake; (often fol. by *up*). **2.** to be or continue to be awake: *Waking or sleeping, I think of you.* **3.** to become roused from mental inactivity. **4.** to become aware of something: *to wake to the true situation.* **5.** *Dial.* to hold a wake over a corpse. **6.** *Chiefly Dial.* to keep watch or vigil. —*v.t.* **7.** to rouse from sleep; awaken; waken (often fol. by *up*). **8.** to rouse from inactivity, lethargy, apathy, etc. (often fol. by *up*). **9.** *Chiefly Dial.* to keep watch or vigil over. —*n.* **10.** a watching, or a watch kept, esp. for some solemn or ceremonial purpose. **11.** a watch or vigil by the body of a dead person before burial. **12.** a local annual festival in England, formerly held in honor of the patron saint of a church. [ME *wake(n)* to watch, be or become awake, OE *wacian;* ME *wakede* (past tense), OE *wacode;* ME *wook* (past tense), OE *wōc,* past of *wæcnan* to WAKEN; akin to D *waken,* G *wachen,* Icel *vaka*] —**wak′er,** *n.* —**Syn. 7.** arouse. **8.** activate, animate. —**Ant. 1.** sleep.

wake² (wāk), *n.* **1.** the track of waves left by a ship or other object moving through the water. **2.** the path or course of anything that has passed: *the wake of a storm.* **3. in the wake of, a.** as a result of: *an investigation in the wake of a scandal.* **b.** succeeding; following: *in the wake of the pioneers.* [< Scand; cf. Icel *vök* hole in the ice]

Wake·field (wāk′fēld′), *n.* **1.** a city in S Yorkshire, in N England: battle 1460. 61,591 (1961). **2.** a town in E Massachusetts, near Boston. 25,402 (1970).

wake·ful (wāk′fəl), *adj.* **1.** unable or indisposed to sleep. **2.** characterized by absence of sleep: *a wakeful night.* **3.** watchful; alert; vigilant. —**wake′ful·ly,** *adv.* —**wake′ful·ness,** *n.* —**Syn. 1, 2.** sleepless, restless.

Wake′ Is′land, an island in the N Pacific, belonging to the U.S.: air base. 3 sq. mi.

wake·less (wāk′lis), *adj.* (of sleep) sound; deep; undisturbed. [WAKE¹ + -LESS]

wak·en (wā′kən), *v.t.* **1.** to rouse from sleep; wake; awaken. **2.** to rouse from inactivity or apathy. —*v.i.* **3.** to wake or become awake; awaken. [ME; OE *wæcnan;* c. Icel *vakna;* cf. WAKE¹] —**wak′en·er,** *n.* —**Syn. 1, 2.** arouse.

wak·en·ing (wā′kə ning), *n.* awakening. [ME]

wake·rife (wāk′rīf′), *adj. Scot. and North Eng.* wakeful. [WAKE¹ + RIFE] —**wake′rife′ness,** *n.*

wake-rob·in (wāk′rob′in), *n.* **1.** the cuckoopint. **2.** any of various other arums or araceous plants, as the jack-in-the-pulpit. **3.** *U.S.* any of various liliaceous plants of the genus *Trillium,* as *T. erectum,* having rank-smelling, purple, pink, or white flowers.

Waks·man (waks′mən), *n.* **Sel·man Abraham** (sel′mən), 1888–1973, U.S. microbiologist: Nobel prize for medicine 1952.

Wal., 1. Wallachian. **2.** Walloon.

Wa·la·chi·a (wo lā′kē ə), *n.* Wallachia. —**Wa·la′chi·an,** *adj., n.*

Wał·brzych (väl′bzhiкн), *n.* a city in SW Poland, in Silesia. 122,000 (est. 1963). German, **Wal·den·burg** (väl′dən bo͝ork′).

Wal·che·ren (wäl′кнə rən), *n.* an island in the SW Netherlands, in Zeeland. 77,839. 82 sq. mi.

Wald (wôld), *n.* **Lillian,** 1867–1940, U.S. social worker.

Wal·de·mar I (väl′də mär′), (*"the Great"*) 1131–82, king of Denmark 1157–82. Also, **Valdemar I.**

Wal′den Pond′ (wôl′dən), a pond in NE Massachusetts, near Concord: site of Thoreau's cottage and inspiration for his book of philosophical observations, *Walden, or Life in the Woods* (1854).

Wal·den·ses (wol den′sēz), *n.pl.* members of a Christian sect that arose after 1170 in southern France, under the leadership of Peter Waldo, and joined the Reformation movement in the 16th century. [pl. of ME *Waldensis* < ML, trans. of F *Vaudois;* see -ESE] —**Wal·den·si·an** (wol den′sē ən, -shən), *adj., n.*

Wald·heim (wôld′hīm′; *Ger.* vält′hīm′), *n.* **Kurt** (kûrt; *Ger.* ko͝ort), born 1918, Austrian diplomat: secretary-general of the United Nations 1972–82.

Wal·do (wôl′dō, wol′-), *n.* **Peter,** d. 1217, merchant of Lyons, mendicant preacher: founder of the Waldensians.

Wal′dorf sal′ad (wôl′dôrf), a salad of celery, diced apples, nuts, and mayonnaise. [named after *Waldorf-Astoria* Hotel in New York City]

Wald·stein (*Ger.* vält′shtīn′), *n.* **Al·brecht von** (äl′brекнt fən). See **Wallenstein, Albrecht.**

wale¹ (wāl), *n., v.,* **waled, wal·ing.** —*n.* **1.** a mark made on the skin by the stroke of a rod or whip; welt. **2.** the vertical rib in knit goods or a chain of loops running lengthwise in knit fabric (opposed to *course*). **3.** the texture or weave of a fabric. **4.** *Naut.* **a.** any of certain strakes of thick outside planking on the sides of a wooden ship. **b.** gunwale. **5.** a ridge on the outside of a horse collar. —*v.t.* **6.** to mark with wales. **7.** to weave with wales. [ME; OE *walu* ridge, rib, weal; c. Icel *vǫlr,* Goth *walus* rod, wand]

wale² (wāl), *n., v.,* **waled, wal·ing.** *Scot. and North Eng.* —*n.* **1.** something that is selected as the best; choice. —*v.t.* **2.** to choose; select. [ME *wal(e)* < Scand; cf. Icel *val* choice; c. G *Wahl;* cf. VALHALLA]

Wa·ler (wā′lər), *n.* a horse bred in New South Wales, Australia, as a military saddle horse.

Wales (wālz), *n.* a division of the United Kingdom, in SW Great Britain. 2,640,632 (1961); 8016 sq. mi. Medieval, **Cambria.**

Wa·łe·sa (və wen′sə), *n.* **Lech** (lek), born 1943, Polish labor leader: Nobel peace prize 1983.

Wal′fish Bay (wôl′fish). See **Walvis Bay.**

Wal·hal·la (wal hal′ə, val-, wäl hä′lə, väl-), *n.* Valhalla. Also, **Wal·hall** (wal hal′, wal′hal).

walk (wôk), *v.i.* **1.** to advance on foot at a moderate pace; proceed by steps; move by a coordinated activity of the feet. **2.** to move about in this way for exercise or pleasure. **3.** to move about in visible form, as a ghost. **4.** (of things) to move in a manner suggestive of walking: *He typed so hard that the lamp walked right off the desk.* **5.** to follow a particular way or pattern of life: *He walked in sorrow.* **6.** *Baseball.* to receive a base on balls. —*v.t.* **7.** to move through, over, or upon by walking: *to walk the floor.* **8.** to cause or help to walk. **9.** to conduct or accompany on a walk: *He walked them about the park.* **10.** to move (a box, trunk, or other object) in a manner suggestive of walking, as by a rocking motion. **11.** *Baseball.* (of a pitcher) to give a base on balls to (a batter). **12.** to examine, measure, etc., by walking. **13. walk off,** to get rid of by walking: *to walk off a headache.* **14. walk off** or **away with, a.** to remove illegally; steal. **b.** to win or attain, as in a competition: *to walk off with the first prize; to walk away with all the honors.* **15. walk out,** *Informal.* **a.** to go on strike. **b.** to leave in protest: *to walk out of a committee meeting.* **16. walk out on,** *Informal.* to leave unceremoniously; desert; forsake: *to walk out on one's family.* **17. walk out with,** *Brit.* to court or be courted by. **18. walk over,** *Informal.* to treat inconsiderately or contemptuously. **19. walk the plank.** See **plank** (def. 5). **20.** *Theat.* **walk through,** to give a perfunctory performance, as at a first rehearsal. —*n.* **21.** the act or an instance of walking. **22.** a distance walked or to be walked, often in terms of the time required: *not more than ten minutes' walk from town.* **23.** a characteristic or individual manner of walking. **24.** a particular form of activity, occupation, status, etc.: *in every walk of life.* **25.** a place or path for walking. **26.** *Baseball.* See **base on balls. 27.** *Sports.* a walking race. **28.** an enclosed area where domestic animals are fed and left to exercise. **29.** a ropewalk. **30.** (in the West Indies) a plantation of trees, esp. coffee trees. **31.** a group, company, or congregation, esp. of snipes. **32.** *Brit.* the route of a street vender, tradesman, or the like. [ME; OE *wealc(a)n* (to) roll, toss, *gewealcan* to go; c. D, G *walken* to full (cloth), Icel *vālka* to toss] —**walk′a·ble,** *adj.* —**Syn. 1.** step. **2, 21.** stroll, tramp, hike.

walk·a·thon (wôk′ə thon′), *n.* a long-distance walking race for testing endurance. [WALK + -*athon,* modeled on *marathon*]

walk·a·way (wôk′ə wā′), *n.* an easy victory or conquest.

walk-down (wôk′doun′), *n.* a store or apartment below street level.

walk·er (wô′kər), *n.* **1.** a person who walks or likes to walk. **2.** an enclosing framework on casters or wheels for supporting a baby who is learning to walk. **3.** a similar lightweight structure, sometimes having wheels or gliders and arm supports, used by invalids, the handicapped, or the aged in walking. [ME]

Walk·er (wô′kər), *n.* **James John** (*"Jimmy"*), 1881–1946, U.S. politician: mayor of New York City 1925–32.

walk·ie-talk·ie (wô′kē tô′kē), *n. Radio.* a combined transmitter and receiver carried by one person.

walk-in (wôk′in′), *adj.* **1.** large enough to be walked into. **2.** having a private entrance directly from the street rather than through a lobby. —*n.* **3.** something large enough to be walked into, as a closet. **4.** an assured victory in an election or other contest.

walk·ing (wô′king), *adj.* **1.** that walks or is capable of walking. **2.** used in walking, esp. out of doors: *walking shoes.* **3.** living; human: *a walking encyclopedia.* **4.** suitable for or accomplished by walking: *a walking tour.* —*n.* **5.** the act or action of a person or thing that walks. **6.** the manner or way in which one walks. **7.** the conditions encountered in walking. [ME]

walk′ing beam′, an overhead pivoted lever for reversing the direction of thrusts between reciprocating machine parts.

walk′ing del′egate, (formerly) an official appointed by a trade union to represent it in various places.

walk′ing fern′, a fern, *Camptosorus rhizophyllus,* having simple fronds tapering into a prolongation that often takes root at the apex.

walk′ing leaf′. See **leaf insect.**

walk′ing pa′pers, *Informal.* a notification of dismissal.

walk′ing stick′, 1. a stick held in the hand and used to help support oneself while walking. **2.** any of several orthopterous insects of the family *Phasmidae,* having a long, slender, twiglike body.

Walking stick, *Diapheromera femorata* (Length 2 to 3 in.)

walk-on (wôk′on′, -ôn′), *n.* a small part in a play or other entertainment, esp. one without speaking lines. Also called **walk′ing part′.** Cf. **bit²** (def. 4).

walk·out (wôk′out′), *n.* **1.** a strike by workers. **2.** the act of leaving or being absent from a meeting, esp. as an expression of protest.

walk·o·ver (wôk′ō′vər), *n.* **1.** *Racing.* a walking or trotting over the course by a contestant who is the only starter. **2.** an unopposed or easy victory, as in a sports contest, election, etc.

walk-through (wôk′thro͞o′), *n. Theat.* a perfunctory performance of a script.

walk-up (wôk′up′), *n.* **1.** an apartment above the ground floor in a building that has no elevator. **2.** the building itself.

walk·way (wôk′wā′), *n.* a passage for walking; path; walk.

Wal·kyr·ie (wal kēr′ē, val-), *n.* Valkyrie.

walk·y-talk·y (wô′kē tô′kē), *n., pl.* **-talk·ies.** walkie-talkie.

wall (wôl), *n.* **1.** any upright structure having a length much greater than its thickness, used for support, enclosure, etc., as a side of a room that connects floor and ceiling, or a solid fence of masonry. **2.** Usually, **walls.** a rampart raised for defensive purposes. **3.** something that suggests a wall in its enclosing or protecting function: *the wall of a blood cell.* **4.** something that suggests a wall in being impenetrable or opaque: *a wall of fire; a wall of secrecy.* **5.** an embankment raised to confine or exclude water; sea wall. **6. drive** or **push to the wall,** to force into a desperate situation, as humiliation, defeat, or ruin. **7. go to the wall, a.** to be defeated; yield. **b.** to fail in business, esp. to become bankrupt. —*adj.* **8.** of or pertaining to a wall: *wall space.* **9.** located in or on a wall: *a wall safe.* —*v.t.* **10.** to protect, confine, or divide with or as with a wall: *to wall off part of a space.* **11.** to fill (an opening) with solid construction. **12.** to seal or entomb within a wall. [ME, OE < L *vall(um)* palisade < *vall(us)* stake; see WALE¹] —**wall′-like′,** *adj.*

wal·la (wä′lä), *n.* wallah.

wal·la·by (wol′ə bē), *n., pl.* **-bies,** (*esp. collectively*) **-by.** any of various small and medium-sized kangaroos of the genera *Macropus, Thylogale, Petrogale,* etc., some of which are no larger than rabbits. [< native Austral *wolabā*]

Wal·lace (wol′is, wô′lis), *n.* **1. Alfred Russel,** 1823–1913, English naturalist, explorer, and author. **2. George Cor·ley** (kôr′lē, kôr′-), born 1919, U.S. politician: governor of Alabama 1963–67, 1971–79, and 1983–87. **3. Henry (A·gard)** (ā′gärd), 1888–1965, U.S. agriculturalist, author, and statesman: Secretary of Agriculture 1933–40; vice president of the U.S. 1941–45; Secretary of Commerce 1945–46. **4. Lewis** (“*Lew*”), 1827–1905, U.S. general and novelist. **5. Sir William,** 1272?–1305, Scottish military leader and patriot.

Wal·la·chi·a (wo lā′kē ə), *n.* a former principality in SE Europe: united with Moldavia to form Rumania in 1861. 29,569 sq. mi. *Cap.:* Bucharest. Also, **Walachia.** —**Wal·la′chi·an,** *adj., n.*

wal·lah (wä′lä), *n. Anglo-Indian.* a person concerned with a specified thing: *a ticket wallah.* Also, **walla.** [< Hindi *-wālā* suffix of relation]

wal·la·roo (wol′ə ro͞o′), *n., pl.* **-roos,** (*esp. collectively*) **-roo.** any of several large kangaroos of the genus *Osphranter,* of the grassy plains of Australia. [< native Austral *wolarū*]

Wal·la·sey (wol′ə sē), *n.* a city in NW Cheshire, in NW England, on the Mersey estuary, near Liverpool. 103,213 (1961).

wall·board (wôl′bōrd′, -bôrd′), *n.* a material manufactured in large sheets for use in making or covering walls, ceilings, etc.

wall·cov·er·ing (wôl′kuv′ə ring), *n.* a sized flexible sheet of paper, fabric, plastic, etc., usually laminated and decoratively printed, for pasting on and covering a wall, ceiling, etc.

walled′ plain′, a circular or almost circular area on the moon, sometimes with a floor that is depressed, usually partially enclosed by walls that are lower than those of a crater; ring; ring formation. Also called **ringed plain.**

Wal·len·stein (wol′ən stīn′; *Ger.* väl′ən shtīn′), *n.* **Al·brecht Wen·zel Eu·se·bi·us von** (äl′brekht ven′tsəl oi-zā′bē o͝os′ fən), **Duke of Fried·land** (frēd′land′, -lənd; *Ger.* frēt′länt′), 1583–1634, Austrian general in the Thirty Years' War, born in Bohemia. Also, **Waldstein.**

Wal·ler (wol′ər, wô′lər), *n.* **1. Edmund,** 1607–87, English poet. **2. Thomas** (“*Fats*”), 1904–43, U.S. jazz pianist.

wal·let (wol′it, wô′lit), *n.* **1.** a flat, folding pocketbook, esp. one for paper money, personal papers, etc. **2.** *Chiefly Brit.* a knapsack or rucksack. [ME *walet* < ?]

wall·eye (wôl′ī), *n., pl.* **-eyes,** (*esp. collectively for 1, 2*) **-eye. 1.** a large game fish, *Stizostedion vitreum,* found in the lakes and rivers of northeastern North America; pikeperch. **2.** any of various other fishes having large, staring eyes. **3.** the eye of a walleyed person or animal, or one resembling it. [back formation from WALLEYED]

wall·eyed (wôl′īd), *adj.* **1.** having eyes showing an abnormal amount of the white because of divergent strabismus. **2.** having eyes showing little or no color, as the result of a light-colored or white iris or of white opacity of the cornea. **3.** having large, staring eyes, as some fishes. **4.** marked by excited or agitated staring of the eyes, as in fear, rage, or frenzy. [alter. of OE *waldenige* = *wal(e)de* streaked (see WALE[1], -ED[3]) + *-n-* (< ?) + *-ige* -eyed (see EYE); cf. ME *wawileghed,* Icel *vagleygr* (*vagl* film + *eygr* eyed)]

wall′eye pol′lack, a cod, *Theragra chalcogrammus,* found in the northern Pacific, that is related to and resembles the pollack.

wall′ fern′, the polypody, *Polypodium vulgare* or *P. virginianum.*

wall·flow·er (wôl′flou′ər), *n.* **1.** a European plant, *Cheiranthus Cheiri,* that grows wild on walls, cliffs, etc., and has sweet-scented, usually yellow or orange flowers. **2.** any brassicaceous plant of the genera *Cheiranthus* and *Erysimum.* **3.** a young woman who remains at the side at a party or dance because she is shy, unpopular, or has no partner.

Wal·ling·ford (wol′ing fərd), *n.* a town in S Connecticut. 35,714 (1970).

Wal·loon (wo lo͞on′), *n.* **1.** one of a people inhabiting chiefly the southern and southeastern parts of Belgium and adjacent regions in France. **2.** the French dialect spoken by the Walloons. [< F *Wallon* = *wall* (<< Gmc **walh-* foreign(er); see WALNUT) + *-on* n. suffix]

wal·lop (wol′əp), *v.t. Informal.* **1.** to beat soundly; thrash. **2.** to strike vigorously: *He walloped the ball right out of the park.* **3.** to defeat thoroughly, as in a game. **4.** *Chiefly Scot.* to flutter, wobble, or flop about. —*v.i.* **5.** (of a liquid) to boil violently. **6.** *Obs.* to gallop. —*n.* **7.** *Informal.* a vigorous blow. **8.** the ability to create a powerful effect: *That ad packs a wallop.* **9.** *Obs.* a gallop. [ME *wal(l)op* (n.), late ME *walopen* (v.) < AF < ?] —**wal′lop·er,** *n.*

wal·lop·ing (wol′ə ping), *Informal.* —*n.* **1.** a sound beating or thrashing. —*adj.* **2.** impressively big or good; whopping. [ME]

wal·low (wol′ō), *v.i.* **1.** to roll about or lie in water, mud, etc., for pleasure. **2.** to indulge oneself in a state of mind or way of life: *to wallow in sentimentality.* **3.** to move clumsily or with difficulty. —*n.* **4.** the act or an instance of wallowing. **5.** a place in which animals wallow. [ME *walwe,* OE *wealwi(an)* (to) roll; c. Goth *walwjan,* L *volvere*] —**wal′low·er,** *n.* —**Syn. 1.** welter.

wall·pa·per (wôl′pā′pər), *n.* **1.** a type of wallcovering made of paper. —*v.t.* **2.** to put wallpaper on (a wall, ceiling, etc.) or to furnish (a room, house, etc.) with wallpaper.

wall′ pel′litory, a small, bushy, Old World, urticaceous plant, *Parietaria officinalis,* growing on walls, and said to be a diuretic and refrigerant.

wall′ plate′, *Building Trades.* a horizontal member built into or laid along the top of a wall to support and distribute the pressure from joists, rafters, etc.

Walls·end (wôlz′end′), *n.* a city in SE Northumberland, NE England, on the Tyne. 49,785 (1961).

wall′ sock′et, socket (def. 2b).

Wall′ Street′, 1. a street in New York City, in S Manhattan: the major financial center of the U.S. **2.** the money market or the financiers of the U.S.

wall-to-wall (wôl′tə wôl′), *adj.* covering the entire floor of a room: *a wall-to-wall carpet.*

wal·ly (wā′lē), *adj. Scot.* fine; splendid. [WALE[2] + -Y[1]]

wal·ly·drag (wā′lē drag′, -dräg′, wol′ē-), *n. Scot.* a feeble, dwarfed animal or person. Also called **wal·ly·drai·gle** (wā′lē drā′gəl, wol′ē-). [? *wally* (var. of WALLOW) + DRAG]

wal·nut (wôl′nut′, -nət), *n.* **1.** the edible nut of trees of the genus *Juglans,* of the North Temperate zone. **2.** a tree bearing this nut. See illus. at **monoecious. 3.** the wood of such a tree. **4.** *Northeastern U.S.* the hickory nut. **5.** any of various fruits or trees resembling the walnut. **6.** a somewhat reddish shade of brown, as that of the heartwood of the black walnut tree. [ME; OE *wealh-hnutu,* lit., foreign nut. See WELSH, NUT]

Wal′nut Creek′, a city in W California. 39,844 (1970).

Wal·pole (wôl′pōl′, wol′-), *n.* **1. Horace, 4th Earl of Or·ford** (ôr′fərd), (*Horatio Walpole*), 1717–97, English novelist and essayist (son of Sir Robert Walpole). **2. Sir Hugh Seymour,** 1884–1941, English novelist, born in New Zealand. **3. Sir Robert, 1st Earl of Or·ford** (ôr′fərd), 1676–1745, British statesman: prime minister 1715–17; 1721–42.

Wal·pur·gis (väl po͝or′gis), *n.* **Saint,** A.D. c710–780, English missionary and abbess in Germany: feast day May 1st. Also, **Wal·pur·ga** (väl po͝or′gä).

Wal·pur′gis Night′, the evening preceding May 1st, the feast day of St. Walpurgis, on which, according to a formerly popular German superstition, witches held a sabbath, esp. on the Brocken. German, **Wal·pur·gis·nacht** (väl po͝or′gis näkht′).

wal·rus (wôl′rəs, wol′-), *n., pl.* **-rus·es,** (*esp. collectively*) **-rus.** either of two large marine mammals of the genus *Odobenus,* of arctic seas, related to the seals, and having flippers, a pair of large tusks, and a thick, tough skin. [< D: lit., whale horse; c. G *Walross,* Dan *hvalros;* cf. OE *horshwæl* horse whale]

Walrus, *Odobenus rosmarus* (Tusks to 3 ft.; length to 11 ft.)

wal′rus mustache′, a thick, shaggy mustache hanging down loosely at both ends.

Wal·sall (wôl′sôl), *n.* a city in S Staffordshire, in central England near Birmingham. 117,836 (1961).

Wal·sing·ham (wôl′sing əm), *n.* **Sir Francis,** c1530–90, English statesman: Secretary of State 1573–90.

Wal·ter (väl′tər *for 1;* wôl′tər *for 2*), *n.* **1. Bru·no** (bro͞o′nō), (*Bruno Schlesinger*), 1876–1962, German opera and symphony conductor, in U.S. after 1939. **2. Thomas U·stick** (yo͞o′stik), 1804–87, U.S. architect.

Wal·tham (wôl′thəm), *n.* a city in E Massachusetts. 61,582 (1970).

Wal·tham·stow (wôl′təm stō′, -thəm-), *n.* a city in SW Essex, in SE England, near London. 108,788 (1961).

Wal·ther von der Vo·gel·wei·de (väl′tər fôn dər fō′gəl vī′də), c1170–c1230, German minnesinger and poet.

Wal·ton (wôl′tən), *n.* **1. Ernest Thomas Sin·ton** (sin′tən), born 1903, Irish physicist: Nobel prize 1951. **2. I·zaak** (ī′zək), 1593–1683, English writer. **3. Sir William Turner,** 1902–83, English composer.

waltz (wôlts), *n.* **1.** a ballroom dance, in moderately fast triple meter, in which the dancers revolve in perpetual circles, taking one step to each beat. **2.** a piece of music for, or in the rhythm of, this dance. —*adj.* **3.** of, pertaining to, or characteristic of the waltz. —*v.i.* **4.** to dance a waltz. **5.** *Informal.* **a.** to move breezily or casually. **b.** to progress easily or successfully (often fol. by *through*): *to waltz through an exam.* —*v.t.* **6.** to lead (a partner) in dancing a waltz. **7.** *Informal.* to move or lead briskly. [back formation from G *Walzer* (taken as *walz* + -ER[1]) < *walze(n)* (to) roll, dance; cf. obs. E *walt* unsteady, and dial. *walter* to roll] —**waltz′er,** *n.*

waltz′ time′. See **three-quarter time.**

Wal′vis Bay′ (wôl′vis), **1.** a bay in S Africa, on the coast of South-West Africa. **2.** an exclave of the Republic of South Africa around this bay: administered by South-West Africa. 12,100 (est. 1960); 374 sq. mi. Also, **Walfish Bay.**

wam·ble (wom′əl, wam′-), *v.,* **-bled, -bling,** *n.* —*v.i.* **1.** *Chiefly Dial.* to move unsteadily. **2.** *Obs.* **a.** to feel nausea. **b.** (of the stomach) to turn over in nausea. —*n. Chiefly Dial.* **3.** an unsteady or rolling movement. **4.** a feeling of nausea. [ME *wamle,* nasalized var. of WOBBLE; cf. Norw *vamla* to stagger] —**wam′bli·ness,** *n.* —**wam′bling·ly,** *adv.* —**wam′bly,** *adj.*

wame (wām), *n. Scot. and North Eng.* the abdomen; belly. [var. of WOMB]

wam·pum (wom′pəm, wôm′-), *n.* beads made from shells, usually cylindrical in shape, pierced and strung, and used by North American Indians as money and for ornaments. [short for *wampumpeag* < Narraganset = *wamp(an)* shiny + *anpi* string of beads + *-ag* pl. suffix]

wan (won), *adj.,* **wan·ner, wan·nest,** *v.,* **wanned, wan·ning.** —*adj.* **1.** of an unnatural or sickly pallor: *a wan face.* **2.** showing or suggesting ill health, fatigue, unhappiness, etc.: *a wan look; a wan smile.* **3.** lacking in forcefulness, competence, or effectiveness: *wan efforts.* **4.** *Archaic.* **a.** dark or gloomy. **b.** pale in color or hue. —*v.i., v.t.* **5.** *Archaic.* to become or make wan. [ME; OE *wann* dark, gloomy; c. G *Wahn* madness] —**wan′ly,** *adv.* —**wan′ness,** *n.* —**Syn. 1.** pallid, ashen. See **pale**[1]. —**Ant. 1.** ruddy.

Wan·a·ma·ker (won′ə mā′kər), *n.* **John,** 1838–1922, U.S. merchant and philanthropist.

Wan·chüan (wän′chyän′), *n.* a city in NW Hopeh, in NE China: capital of the former Chahar province. 229,300 (est. 1957). Formerly, **Kalgan.**

wand (wond), *n.* **1.** a slender stick or rod. **2.** a rod or staff carried as an emblem of authority. **3.** a slender shoot, stem, or branch of a shrub or tree. **4.** *U.S. Archery.* a slat 6 feet by 2 inches, used as a target. [ME, prob. < Scand; cf. Icel *vǫndr,* c. Goth *wandus;* akin to WEND]

wan·der (won′dər), *v.i.* **1.** to move about without a definite purpose or objective; roam. **2.** to move or extend in an irregular line or course. **3.** to abandon interest in or concentration on something. **4.** to go astray; become lost. **5.** to deviate in conduct, belief, etc.; err; go astray. —*v.t.* **6.** to travel about, on, or through: *He wandered the streets.* [ME *wandre(n),* OE *wandrian* (c. G *wandern*), freq. of *wendan* to

WEND; see -ER[6]] —**wan′der·er,** *n.* —**Syn. 1.** range, stroll. **4, 5.** stray.

wan·der·ing (won′dər ing), *adj.* **1.** moving aimlessly from place to place. **2.** having no permanent residence; nomadic. **3.** meandering; winding: *a wandering river.* —*n.* **4.** the act of a person or thing that wanders. **5.** Usually, **wanderings. a.** aimless travels; meanderings. **b.** disordered thoughts or utterances. [ME (n., adj.), OE *wandrigende* (adj.). See WANDER, -ING[2], -ING[1]] —**wan′der·ing·ly,** *adv.*

wan′dering al′batross, a large albatross, *Diomedea exulans,* of southern waters, having the plumage mostly white with dark markings on the upper parts. See illus. at **albatross.**

Wan′dering Jew′, **1.** a legendary character condemned to roam without rest because he struck Christ on the day of the Crucifixion. **2.** Also, **wan′dering Jew′, Wan′der·ing-jew′.** any of various trailing or creeping plants, as *Zebrina pendula* or *Tradescantia fluminensis.*

Wan·der·jahr (vän′dər yär′), *n., pl.* **-jah·re** (-yä′rə). *German.* **1.** a year or period of travel. **2.** (formerly) a year in which an apprentice traveled and improved his skills before settling down to the practice of his trade.

wan·der·lust (wän′dər lust′; *Ger.* vän′dər lo͞ost′), *n.* an instinctive impulse or a great desire to rove or travel about. [< G]

wan·der·oo (won′də ro͞o′), *n., pl.* **-der·oos. 1.** any of several langurs of Ceylon. **2.** a macaque, *Macacus silenus,* of southern India. [< Sinhalese *wanduru* (pl.) < Skt *vānara* monkey]

Wands·worth (wonz′wərth), *n.* a borough of SW London, England. 284,600.

wane (wān), *v.,* **waned, wan·ing,** *n.* —*v.i.* **1.** (of the moon) to decrease periodically in the extent of its illuminated portion after the full moon. Cf. **wax**[2] (def. 2). See diag. at **moon. 2.** to decline in power, prosperity, etc. **3.** to decrease in strength, intensity, etc. **4.** to draw to a close; approach an end: *Summer is waning.* —*n.* **5.** a gradual decrease or decline, as in strength or intensity. **6.** the drawing to a close of life, an era, a period, etc. **7.** the waning of the moon. **8.** a period of waning. **9.** a defect in a board that has insufficient wood at a corner edge. **10. on the wane,** decreasing; diminishing: *Prosperity is on the wane.* [ME; OE *wan(ian)* (to) lessen; c. MD, MHG *wanen,* Icel *vana*] —**Syn. 2, 3.** diminish, fail, sink. **5.** diminution; failure, decay.

wane·y (wā′nē), *adj.,* **wan·i·er, wan·i·est. 1.** wany (def. 1). **2.** (of a timber) having a wane or wanes.

wan·gle (wang′gəl), *v.t.,* **-gled, -gling.** *Informal.* to bring about, accomplish, or obtain by contrivance, scheming, or underhand methods. [b. WAG (the tongue) and DANGLE (about someone, i.e., hang around him, court his favor)] —**wan′gler,** *n.*

Wan·hsien (wän′shyen′), *n.* a city in E Szechwan, in central China, on the Yangtze. 175,000.

wan·i·gan (won′ə gən), *n.* (in the Pacific Northwest and W Canada) **1.** a lumber camp's supply chest. **2.** a small, portable house, used as an office or shelter in temporary lumber camps. Also, **wan·gan, wan·gun** (wang′gən), **wan′-ni·gan.** [< Algonquian]

wan·ion (won′yən), *n. Archaic.* curse; vengeance. [ME *waniand,* prp. of *wanien* to WANE]

Wan′kel en′gine (vän′kəl, wän′-), an internal-combustion rotary engine that utilizes a triangular rotor which revolves in a chamber (rather than a conventional piston that moves up and down in a cylinder): it has fewer moving parts and is generally smaller and lighter for a given horsepower. Also called **Wan′kel.** [named after Felix *Wankel* (b. 1902), German inventor]

Wan·ne-Eick·el (vä′nə ī′kəl), *n.* a city in W West Germany. 98,800.

want (wont, wônt), *v.t.* **1.** to feel a need or a desire for; wish for: *to want one's dinner; always wanting something new.* **2.** to wish, need, crave, demand, or desire (often fol. by an infinitive): *I want to see you. He wants to be notified.* **3.** to be without or be deficient in: *to want judgment.* **4.** to require or need: *The house wants painting.* **5.** to seek or hunt: *They want the man for murder.* —*v.i.* **6.** to feel inclined; wish: *We can stay home if you want.* **7.** to be deficient, or to feel or have a need (sometimes fol. by *for*): *He did not want for abilities.* **8.** to be in a state of need. **9.** to be lacking or absent, as a part or thing necessary to completeness: *All that wants is his signature.* **10. want in** or **out, a.** *Informal.* to desire to enter or leave: *The cat wants in.* **b.** *Slang.* to desire to join or leave an undertaking. —*n.* **11.** something wanted or needed; necessity: *My wants are few.* **12.** absence or deficiency; lack: *plants dying for want of rain.* **13.** the state of being without something wanted or needed; need: *to be in want of an assistant.* **14.** the state of being without the necessaries of life; destitution; poverty: *a country where want is virtually unknown.* **15.** a sense of lack or need of something: *to feel a vague want.* [ME *wante* < Scand; cf. Icel *vanta* to lack] —**want′er,** *n.* —**Syn. 1.** require, need. See **wish. 3.** lack, need. **12.** dearth, scarcity, inadequacy. **14.** privation, penury, indigence, straits. See **poverty.**

want′ ad′. See **classified ad.**

want·ing (won′ting, wôn′-), *adj.* **1.** lacking or absent. **2.** deficient in some respect. —*prep.* **3.** lacking; without: *a box wanting a lid.* **4.** less; minus: *a century, wanting three years.* [ME; see WANT, -ING[2]]

want′ list′, a list of desired items circulated among dealers.

wan·ton (won′tən), *adj.* **1.** malicious and unjustifiable: *a wanton attack.* **2.** without adequate motive or provocation; headstrong; willful. **3.** without regard for what is right, humane, etc. **4.** sexually lawless or unrestrained; loose. **5.** extravagantly or excessively luxurious, as a person or his manner of living. **6.** *Archaic.* **a.** luxuriant, as vegetation. **b.** sportive or frolicsome, as children, young animals, etc. —*n.* **7.** a wanton or lascivious person, esp. a woman. —*v.i.* **8.** to behave in a wanton manner; become wanton. —*v.t.* **9.** to squander, esp. in pleasure (often fol. by *away*): *to wanton away one's inheritance.* [ME *wantowen,* lit., undisciplined, ill-reared, OE *wan-* not + *togen* disciplined, reared, ptp. of *tēon,* c. G *ziehen,* L *dūcere* to lead; akin to TOW[1]] —**wan′-ton·ly,** *adv.* —**wan′ton·ness,** *n.* —**Syn. 3.** heedless, inconsiderate. **4.** licentious, dissolute, immoral, libidinous, lustful. **5.** prodigal. **9.** waste. —**Ant. 3.** careful, considerate.

wan·y (wā′nē), *adj.,* **wan·i·er, wan·i·est. 1.** Also, **waney.** waning; decreasing; diminished in part. **2.** waney (def. 2).

wap (wap, wop), *v.,* **wapped, wap·ping,** *n. Brit. Dial.* —*v.t.* **1.** to wrap. —*n.* **2.** something that wraps, as a turn of string. [late ME *wappe(n)* < ?]

wap·en·take (wop′ən tāk′, wap′-), *n.* (formerly in N England and the Midlands) a subdivision of a shire or county corresponding to a hundred. [ME < Scand; cf. Icel *vāpnatak* (OE *wǣpen-getæc*) show of weapons at public voting = *vāpna* (gen. pl. of *vāpn* WEAPON) + *tak* taking; see TAKE]

wap·i·ti (wop′i tē), *n., pl.* **-tis,** (*esp. collectively*) **-ti.** elk (def. 2). [< Shawnee: lit., white rump]

wap·pen·shaw (wop′ən shô′, wap′-), *n.* a periodic muster or review of troops or persons under arms formerly held in certain districts of Scotland. Also, **wap′in·schaw′, wap′pen·shaw′ing.** [short for *wappenshawing* (Scot) = *wappen* (OE *wǣpna,* gen. pl. of *wǣp(e)n* WEAPON) + *shawing* showing (see SHOW); cf. D *wapenschouwing*]

wap·per·jaw (wop′ər jô′), *n. Brit. Dial.* a crooked mouth. [*wapper* (< ?) + JAW] —**wap′per·jawed′,** *adj.*

war (wôr), *n., v.,* **warred, war·ring,** *adj.* —*n.* **1.** a major armed conflict between nations or between organized parties within a state. **2.** the state of being engaged in such a conflict. **3.** the science, art, or profession of military operations. **4.** any conflict or competition suggesting active hostility: *a war of words.* **5.** *Archaic.* a battle. —*v.i.* **6.** to make or carry on war; fight. **7.** to be in conflict or in a state of strong opposition: *to war against vice.* —*adj.* **8.** of, belonging to, used in, or due to war: *war preparations; war hysteria.* [ME, late OE *werre* < OF (Norman dial.) < Gmc, c. OHG *werra* strife]

war′ ba′by, a child born or conceived in wartime.

War·beck (wôr′bek), *n.* **Per·kin** (pûr′kin), 1474–99, Flemish imposter who pretended to the throne of England.

War′ Between′ the States′, the American Civil War: used esp. in the former Confederate States.

war·ble[1] (wôr′bəl), *v.,* **-bled, -bling,** *n.* —*v.i.* **1.** to sing or whistle with trills, quavers, or melodic embellishments. **2.** *U.S.* to yodel. **3.** (of electronic equipment) to produce a continuous sound varying regularly in pitch and frequency. —*v.t.* **4.** to sing (an aria or other selection) with trills, quavers, or melodious turns. —*n.* **5.** a warbled song or succession of melodic trills, quavers, etc. **6.** the act of warbling. [late ME *werble* a tune < MF (northeast dial.) < Gmc, c. OHG *werbel* something that turns]

war·ble[2] (wôr′bəl), *n. Vet. Pathol.* **1.** a small, hard tumor on a horse's back, produced by the galling of the saddle. **2.** a lump in the skin of an animal's back, containing the larva of a warble fly. [?; cf. obs. Sw *varbulde* boil] —**war′bled,** *adj.*

war′ble fly′, any of several dipterous insects of the family *Hypodermatidae,* the larvae of which produce warbles in cattle and other animals.

war·bler (wôr′blər), *n.* **1.** a person or thing that warbles. **2.** any of several small, chiefly Old World songbirds of the family *Sylviidae.* **3.** Also called **wood warbler.** any of numerous small, insectivorous, New World birds of the family *Parulidae,* many species of which are brightly colored. [WARBLE[1] + -ER[1]]

war′ bon′net, an American-Indian headdress consisting of a headband with a tail of ornamental feathers.

War·burg (vär′bo͝ork′; *Eng.* wôr′bərg), *n.* **Ot·to Hein·rich** (ôt′ō hīn′riкн), 1883–1970, German physiologist: Nobel prize for medicine 1931.

war′ chest′, money set aside or scheduled for a particular purpose or activity, as for a political campaign or organizational drive.

war′ cloud′, something that threatens war; a harbinger of conflict.

war′ correspon′dent, a reporter or commentator assigned to send news or opinions from battle areas.

war′ crime′, Usually, **war crimes.** crimes committed against an enemy, captives, or subjects in wartime that violate international agreements or are offenses against humanity. —**war′ crim′inal.**

war′ cry′, **1.** a word, phrase, etc., shouted in charging or in rallying to attack. **2.** a slogan, phrase, or motto used to unite a political party, rally support for a cause, etc.

ward (wôrd), *n.* **1.** an administrative division or district of a city or town. **2.** one of the districts into which certain English and Scottish boroughs are divided. **3.** a division, floor, or room of a hospital for a particular class or group of patients. **4.** any of the separate divisions of a prison. **5.** *Mormon Ch.* one of the subdivisions of a stake, presided over by a bishop. **6.** *Fort.* an open space within or between the walls of a castle or fortified place. **7.** *Law.* **a.** a person, esp. a minor, who has been legally placed under the care of a guardian or a court. **b.** the state of having a legal guardian. **c.** legal guardianship, as over a minor. **8.** the state of being under restraining guard or in custody. **9.** a person who is under the protection or control of another. **10.** a movement or posture of defense, as in fencing. **11.** a metal fitting inside a lock that opposes the turning of any key not of the proper form. **12.** a slot in the bit of a key that permits it to pass along this fitting. **13.** the act of keeping guard or protective watch: *watch and ward.* **14.** *Archaic.* a company of guards or a garrison. —*v.t.* **15.** to avert, repel, or turn aside (danger, harm, an attack, an assailant, etc.) (usually fol. by *off*). **16.** *Archaic.* to protect; guard. [(n.) ME *warde,* OE *weard;* (v.) ME, OE *weardian;* c. MD *waerden,* G *warten;* cf. GUARD] —**Syn. 1.** precinct. **9.** protégé. **15.** parry, prevent.

Ward (wôrd), *n.* **1. Ar·te·mas** (är′tə məs), 1727–1800, American general in the American Revolution. **2. Ar·te·mus** (är′tə məs), (*Charles Farrar Browne*), 1834–67, U.S. humorist. **3. Barbara** (*Lady Barbara Jackson*), 1914–81, English economist and author. **4. Mrs. Humphry** (*Mary Augusta Arnold*), 1851–1920, English novelist, born in Tasmania. **5. Sir Joseph George,** 1856–1930, New Zealand statesman, born in Australia: Prime Minister 1906–12, 1928–30.

-ward, a native English suffix indicating spatial or temporal direction: *toward; seaward; afterward; backward.* Also, **-wards.** [ME; OE *-weard* towards; c. G *-wärts*]

war′ dance′, (among primitive peoples) a dance prior to waging war or in celebration of a victory.

ward·ed (wôr′did), *adj.* having notches, slots, or wards, as in locks and keys.

war·den (wôr′dᵊn), *n.* **1.** a person charged with the care or custody of persons, animals, or things; keeper. **2.** the chief administrative officer in charge of a prison. **3.** a public official charged with superintendence, as over a port, wildlife, etc. **4.** See **air raid warden.** **5.** See **fire warden.** **6.** (in Connecticut) the chief executive officer of a borough. **7.** (formerly) the principal official in a region, town, etc. **8.** *Brit.* **a.** (*cap.*) a traditional title of the president or governor of certain schools and colleges. **b.** a member of a livery company of the City of London. **9.** *Canadian.* the head of certain county or local councils. **10.** a member of the governing body of a guild. **11.** a churchwarden. **12.** *Archaic.* a gatekeeper. [ME *wardein* < OF (northeast dial.) = *ward-* (root of *warder* to GUARD) + *-ein,* var. of *-ien, -enc* < G *-ing* -ING[1]] **—ward′en·ship′,** *n.* **—Syn. 1.** warder, guardian, guard, custodian, caretaker, superintendent.

ward·er[1] (wôr′dər), *n.* **1.** a person who guards something, as a watchman, caretaker, etc. **2.** a soldier or other person set to guard an entrance. **3.** *Chiefly Brit.* an official having charge of prisoners in a jail. [late ME *warder(e)* (see WARD, -ER[1]); cf. AF *wardere* < ME] **—ward′er·ship′,** *n.*

ward·er[2] (wôr′dər), *n.* a truncheon or staff of office or authority, used in giving signals. [late ME < ?]

ward′ heel′er, *U.S.* a minor politician who canvasses voters and does other chores for a political machine or party boss.

ward·ress (wôr′dris), *n.* *Chiefly Brit.* a female warder. [WARD(E)R[1] + -ESS]

ward·robe (wôr′drōb), *n.* **1.** a collection or stock of clothes or costumes. **2.** a piece of furniture for holding clothes, now usually a tall, upright cabinet. **3.** a room or place in which to keep clothes or costumes. **4.** the department of a royal or other great household charged with the care of wearing apparel. [late ME *warderobe* < AF, OF (northeast dial). See WARD, ROBE]

ward′robe trunk′, a large, upright trunk, usually with space on one side for hanging clothes and drawers or compartments on the other for small articles, shoes, etc.

ward·room (wôrd′ro͞om′, -ro͝om′), *n.* (on a warship) **1.** the area serving as the living quarters for all commissioned officers except the commanding officer. **2.** the dining saloon and lounge for these officers. **3.** these officers collectively.

-wards, var. of **-ward:** *towards; afterwards.* [ME; OE *-weardes* = *-weard* toward + *-es* -S[1]]

ward·ship (wôrd′ship), *n.* guardianship; custody.

ware[1] (wâr), *n.* **1.** Usually, **wares. a.** articles of merchandise or manufacture; goods. **b.** anything that a person tries to sell or exploit, esp. talents or personal accomplishments. **2.** a specified kind or class of merchandise or of manufactured article (usually used in combination): *silverware; glassware.* **3.** pottery, or a particular kind of pottery: *Delft ware.* [ME; OE *waru;* c. G *Ware*]

ware[2] (wâr), *adj., v.,* **wared, war·ing.** *Archaic.* **—adj. 1.** watchful, wary, or cautious. **2.** aware; conscious. **—v.t. 3.** to beware of (usually used in the imperative). [ME; OE *wær;* c. G *(ge)wahr* aware, Icel *varr*]

ware[3] (wâʀ), *v.t.,* **wared, war·ing.** *Scot. and North Eng.* to spend or expend (money, time, worry, etc.). [ME < Scand; cf. Icel *verja* to spend, invest; c. OE *werian* to WEAR]

ware·house (*n.* wâr′hous′; *v.* wâr′houz′, -hous′), *n., pl.* **-hous·es** (-hou′ziz), *v.,* **-housed, -hous·ing. —n. 1.** Also called, *esp. Brit.,* **repository.** a building, or a part of one, for the storage of goods, merchandise, etc. **2.** *Brit.* a large retail store. **3.** a building, or a part of one, in which wholesalers display and sell merchandise. **—v.t. 4.** to place, deposit, or store in a warehouse.

ware·house·man (wâr′hous′mən), *n., pl.* **-men. 1.** a person who stores goods for others for pay. **2.** a person who is employed in or who manages a warehouse.

ware·room (wâr′ro͞om′, -ro͝om′), *n.* a room in which goods are stored or are displayed for sale.

war·fare (wôr′fâr′), *n.* the act or process of engaging in war.

war·fa·rin (wôr′fə rin), *n.* *Chem.* a colorless, crystalline, water-insoluble, poisonous solid, $C_{19}H_{16}O_4$, used chiefly for killing rodents. [*W(isconsin) A(lumni) R(esearch) F(oundation)* (owners of patent) + (COUM)ARIN]

war′ game′, *Mil.* a simulated military operation, carried out to test the validity of a war plan or operational concept.

war′ ham′mer. See **pole hammer.**

war′ hawk′, hawk[1] (def. 4).

war·head (wôr′hed′), *n.* the forward section of a self-propelled missile, bomb, torpedo, or the like, containing the destructive charge.

war-horse (wôr′hôrs′), *n.* **1.** a horse used in war; charger. **2.** *Informal.* a veteran, as a soldier or politician, of many struggles and conflicts. **3.** a musical composition, play, etc., that has been seen, heard, or performed excessively.

war·i·ly (wâr′ə lē), *adv.* in a wary manner.

war·i·ness (wâr′ē nis), *n.* the state or quality of being wary.

war·i·son (war′i sən), *n.* a note sounded as a signal for assault. [ME: defense, possessions < AF, OF (northeast dial.) = *waris-* (s. of *warir* to defend, possess < Gmc; cf. OE *warian* to defend, possess) + *-on* n. suffix]

war·like (wôr′līk′), *adj.* **1.** fit, qualified, or ready for war; martial. **2.** threatening or indicating war. **3.** of or pertaining to war. [ME] **—Syn. 2.** belligerent, hostile. **—Ant. 2.** peaceful.

war·lock (wôr′lok′), *n.* **1.** a man aided by the devil in practicing magic arts; sorcerer. **2.** a fortuneteller or conjurer. [ME *warloghe, -lach,* OE *wǣrloga* oath breaker, devil = *wǣr* covenant + *-loga* betrayer (< *l(ē)ogan* to lie)]

war′ lord′, 1. a military leader, esp. of a warlike nation. **2.** a military commander who has seized power, esp. in one section of a country. **3.** tuchun. Also, **war·lord** (wôr′lôrd′).

warm (wôrm), *adj.* **1.** having or giving out moderate heat, as perceived by the senses: *a warm bath.* **2.** characterized by considerable heat: *a warm summer.* **3.** having a sensation of bodily heat: *to be warm from running.* **4.** maintaining or preserving warmth: *warm clothing.* **5.** (of colors) suggesting warmth, as red or yellow tones. **6.** friendly, kindly, or affectionate. **7.** characterized by or showing lively feelings, emotions, etc.: *warm interest.* **8.** heated, irritated, or angry: *to become warm when contradicted.* **9.** lively or vigorous: *a warm debate.* **10.** strong or fresh: *a warm scent.* **11.** *Informal.* close to something sought, as in a child's game. **—v.t. 12.** to make warm; heat (often fol. by *up*). **13.** to excite enthusiasm, cheerfulness, or vitality in (someone). **14.** to inspire with genial emotions. **15.** to fill (a person, crowd, etc.) with strong feelings, as hatred, resentment, etc. **—v.i. 16.** to become warm or warmer (often fol. by *up*). **17.** to become ardent, enthusiastic, animated, etc. (often fol. by *up* or *to*): *The speaker quickly warmed to his subject.* **18.** to grow kindly, friendly, or sympathetically disposed (often fol. by *to* or *toward*). **19. warm up,** to prepare for a game or other activity by practice or exercise beforehand. [ME; OE *wearm;* c. G *warm,* Icel *varmr,* Gk *thermós* hot, L *formus* warm] **—warm′er,** *n.* **—warm′ish,** *adj.* **—warm′ly,** *adv.* **—warm′ness,** *n.* **—Syn. 1.** tepid, heated. **7.** hearty, enthusiastic, fervent. **8.** annoyed, vexed, irate, furious. **9.** vehement. **13.** animate, excite, waken, stir, rouse, arouse.

warm-blood·ed (wôrm′blud′id), *adj.* **1.** designating or pertaining to animals, as mammals and birds, whose normal blood temperature ranges from about 98° to 112°F and remains relatively constant, irrespective of the temperature of the surrounding medium; homoiothermal. **2.** ardent, impetuous, or passionate. **—warm′-blood′ed·ness,** *n.*

warmed-o·ver (wôrmd′ō′vər), *adj.* **1.** (of cooked foods) heated again. **2.** unimaginatively reworked or repeated, as an artistic idea.

warmed-up (wôrmd′up′), *adj.* warmed-over (def. 1).

warm′ front′, *Meteorol.* a transition zone between a mass of warm air and the colder air it is replacing.

warm-heart·ed (wôrm′här′tid), *adj.* having or showing sympathy, affection, cordiality, etc. Also, **warm′heart′ed. —warm′-heart′ed·ly, warm′heart′ed·ly,** *adv.* **—warm′-heart′ed·ness, warm′heart′ed·ness,** *n.* **—Syn.** sympathetic, compassionate, kind.

warm′ing pan′, a long-handled, covered pan, usually of brass, filled with live coals, hot water, etc., formerly used for warming beds.

war·mong·er (wôr′mung′gər, -mong′-), *n.* a person who advocates, wants, or tries to precipitate war.

war·mon·ger·ing (wôr′mung′gər ing, -mong′-), *n.* the practices and principles of a warmonger.

warm′ sec′tor, *Meteorol.* the region bounded by the cold and warm fronts of a cyclone

Warm′ Springs′, a town in W Georgia: resort; site of foundation for treatment of poliomyelitis. 523 (1970).

warmth (wôrmth), *n.* **1.** the quality or state of being warm; moderate or gentle heat. **2.** the sensation of moderate heat. **3.** liveliness of feelings, emotions, or sympathies. **4.** affection or kindliness. **5.** an effect of cheerfulness, coziness, etc., achieved by the use of warm colors. **6.** the ability to produce or retain a sensation of heat. **7.** slight anger or irritation. [ME *wermth*]

warm-up (wôrm′up′), *n.* the act or an instance of warming up.

warn (wôrn), *v.t.* **1.** to inform plainly and strongly of possible trouble. **2.** to advise (a person) that a certain act, negligence, etc., on his part will lead to opposition or reprisal. **3.** to inform of something requiring care or attention. **4.** to notify to go, keep at a distance, etc. (often fol. by *away, off,* etc.): *A sign warns trespassers off the grounds.* **—v.i. 5.** to give a warning or warnings; caution. [ME; OE *warn(ian);* c. G *warnen.* Cf. WARE[2]] **—warn′er,** *n.*

—Syn. 1. forewarn. WARN, CAUTION, ADMONISH imply attempting to prevent another from running into danger or getting into unpleasant or undesirable circumstances. To WARN is to speak plainly and usually in strong terms: *to warn him about danger and possible penalties.* To CAUTION is to advise about necessary precautions, to put a person on his guard about or against some possibly harmful circumstance or condition, thus emphasizing the avoidance of penalties (usually less serious): *to caution him against trying to go.* ADMONISH suggests giving earnest, authoritative advice, with only tacit references to danger or penalty: *to admonish a person for neglecting duties.*

War′ner Rob′ins, a city in central Georgia. 33,491 (1970).

warn·ing (wôr′ning), *n.* **1.** the act or utterance of a person or thing that warns. **2.** something that serves to warn, as a notice or signal. **—adj. 3.** serving to warn, advise, caution. [ME (n.); OE *war(e)nung* (n.). See WARN, -ING[1], -ING[2]] **—warn′ing·ly,** *adv.* **—Syn. 2.** caution, admonition, advice.

War′ of Amer′ican Independ′ence, *Brit.* See **American Revolution.**

War of 1812, the war between the United States and Great Britain from 1812 to 1815.

War′ of Independ′ence. See **American Revolution.**

war′ of nerves′, a conflict using psychological techniques in order to confuse, thwart, or intimidate an enemy.

War′ of the Aus′trian Succes′sion, the war (1740–1748) in which Austria, England, and Holland opposed Prussia, France, and Spain over the selection of rulers for territories within the Austrian Empire. Cf. **King George's War.**

War′ of the Grand′ Alli′ance, the war (1689–97) in which England, the Netherlands, Spain, Sweden, and the Holy Roman Empire, in league with Bavaria, Brandenburg, Savoy, and the Palatinate, opposed France. Cf. **King William's War.**

War′ of the Span′ish Succes′sion, the war (1701–1714) fought by Austria, England, Holland, and Prussia against France and Spain.

warp (wôrp), *v.t.* **1.** to bend or twist out of shape, esp. from a straight or flat form. **2.** to bend or turn from the natural or true direction or course. **3.** to distort or cause to distort so as to lose truth or objectivity. **4.** *Naut.* to move (a vessel) by hauling on a rope that has been fastened to something fixed. **—v.i. 5.** to become bent or twisted out of shape, esp. out of a straight or flat form. **6.** to lose mental objectivity. **7.** *Naut.* **a.** to warp a ship or boat into position. **b.** (of a ship or boat) to move by being warped. **—n. 8.** a bend, twist, or variation from a straight or flat form. **9.** a mental twist, bias, or quirk. **10.** the set of yarns placed lengthwise in the loom, crossed by and interlaced with the weft, and forming the lengthwise threads in a woven fabric. **11.** *Naut.* a rope for warping or hauling a ship or boat along or into position. [(v.) ME *werpe(n)*, OE *weorpan* to throw; c. G *werfen*, Icel *verpa*, Goth *wairpan*; (n.) ME *warpe*, OE *wearp*; c. G *Warf*, Icel *varp*] **—warp′age,** *n.* **—warp′er,** *n.* **—Syn. 1.** turn, contort, distort, spring. **2.** swerve, deviate. **—Ant. 1, 5.** straighten.

war′ paint′, paint applied by American Indians to their faces and bodies before going to war.

war·path (wôr′path′, -päth′), *n., pl.* **-paths** (-pathz′, -päthz′, -paths′, -päths′). **1.** the path or course taken by American Indians on a warlike expedition. **2. on the warpath, a.** seeking, preparing for, or engaged in war. **b.** in a state of anger or indignation; hostile.

warp′ beam′, (in a loom) a roller on which the warp ends are wound. Also called **warp′ roll′.**

warp′ knit′, a fabric or garment so constructed that runs do not occur: knitted from a warp beam that feeds yarn to the knitting frame.

war·plane (wôr′plān′), *n.* an airplane designed for or used in warfare.

warp·wise (wôrp′wīz′), *adv. Textiles.* in a vertical direction; at right angles to the filling; lengthwise.

war·rant (wôr′ənt, wor′-), *n.* **1.** authorization, sanction, or justification. **2.** something that serves as a guarantee, pledge, or security. **3.** a writing or document certifying or authorizing something. **4.** *Law.* an instrument, issued by a magistrate, authorizing an officer to make an arrest, seize property, make a search, or execute a judgment. **5.** the certificate of authority or appointment issued to an officer of the armed forces below the rank of a commissioned officer. **6.** a written authorization for the payment or receipt of money. **—*v.t.* 7.** to give authority to; authorize. **8.** to give adequate reason or justification for. **9.** to declare with conviction: *You'll be glad for a rest, I'll warrant!* **10.** to give a formal assurance or guarantee of: *to warrant safe delivery.* **11.** to guarantee (something sold) to be as represented. **12.** to guarantee (a purchase) against loss. **13.** *Law.* to guarantee title of an estate (to a grantee). [ME *warant* < AF (var. of OF *guarant*) < Gmc; cf. MLG *warend*, *-ent* warranty, n. use of prp. of *waren* to warrant; see GUARANTY] **—war′rant·less,** *adj.* **—Syn. 2.** warranty, surety. **3.** permit, voucher, writ, order, chit.

war·rant·a·ble (wôr′ən tə bəl, wor′-), *adj.* **1.** capable of being warranted. **2.** (of deer) of a legal age for hunting. **—war′rant·a·ble·ness,** *n.*

war·ran·tee (wôr′ən tē′, wor′-), *n.* a person to whom a warranty is made; the recipient of a warranty. [WARRANT(Y) or WARRANT(OR) + -EE]

war′rant of′ficer, *U.S.* an officer in the armed forces holding one of four grades ranking above enlisted men and below commissioned officers.

war·ran·tor (wôr′ən tôr′, wor′-), *n.* a person who warrants or makes a warranty; the giver or granter of a warranty. Also, **war′rant·er.**

war·ran·ty (wôr′ən tē, wor′-), *n., pl.* **-ties. 1.** the act or an instance of warranting. **2.** *Law.* **a.** a stipulation, express or implied, in assurance of some particular in connection with a contract, as of sale. **b.** a covenant in a deed **(war′ranty deed′)** to land assuring the grantee that he will enjoy the premises free from interference by any person claiming under a superior title. **c.** (in the law of insurance) a statement or promise, made by the party insured, and included as an essential part of the contract. **d.** a judicial document, as a warrant or writ. **3.** a written guarantee given to a purchaser, usually specifying that the manufacturer will make any repairs or replace defective parts free of charge for a stated period of time. [ME *warantie* < AF (var. of OF *guarantie*)]

war·ren (wôr′ən, wor′-), *n.* **1.** a place where rabbits breed or abound. **2.** a building or district containing many persons in limited or crowded quarters. [late ME *warenne* < AF (var. of OF *g(u)arenne*) < Gmc **warinne* game park = *war-* (root of *warjan* to defend) + *-inne* fem. n. suffix]

War·ren (wôr′ən, wor′-), *n.* **1. Earl,** 1891–1974, U.S. lawyer and political leader: Chief Justice of the U.S. 1953–69. **2. Joseph,** 1741–75, American physician, statesman, and patriot. **3. Robert Penn,** born 1905, U.S. novelist and poet. **4.** a city in SE Michigan, near Detroit. 179,260 (1970). **5.** a city in NE Ohio, NW of Youngstown. 63,494 (1970).

War·ring·ton (wôr′ing tən, wor′-), *n.* a city in S Lancashire, in NW England. 75,533 (1961).

war·ri·or (wôr′ē ər, wôr′yər, wor′ē ər, wor′yər), *n.* **1.** a man engaged or experienced in warfare; soldier. **2.** a person who has shown great vigor, courage, or aggressiveness, as in politics. [early ME *werreieor* < ONF = *werr(e)* WAR + *-ei-* v. suffix + *-eor* -OR[2]] **—war′ri·or·like′,** *adj.*

warrty., warranty.

war·saw (wôr′sô), *n.* a large grouper, *Epinephelus nigritus,* found in the warmer waters of the Atlantic Ocean. Also called **war′saw group′er.** [m. Sp *guasa*]

War·saw (wôr′sô), *n.* a city in and the capital of Poland, in the E central part, on the Vistula River. 1,436,000. Polish, **Warszawa.**

War′saw Trea′ty Organiza′tion, an organization formed in Warsaw, Poland (1955), comprising Albania, (withdrawn in 1968), Bulgaria, Czechoslovakia, East Germany, Hungary, Poland, Rumania, and the U.S.S.R., for collective defense under a joint military command. Also called **War′saw Pact′.** Cf. **NATO.**

war·ship (wôr′ship′), *n.* a ship built or armed for combat purposes.

war·sle (wär′səl), *v.i., v.t.,* **-sled, -sling,** *n. Chiefly Scot.* wrestle. [ME; OE **wǣrstlian*, metathetic var. (cf. OE *wǣrstlic* of wrestling) of *wrǣstlian* to WRESTLE] **—war′sler,** *n.*

Wars′ of the Ros′es, *Eng. Hist.* the conflict (1455–85), between the Lancastrians and the Yorkists ending with the accession of Henry VII and the union of the two houses. Cf. **red rose, white rose.**

war·stle (wär′səl), *v.i., v.t.,* **-stled, -stling,** *n. Chiefly Scot.* wrestle. [var. of WARSLE] **—war′stler,** *n.*

War·sza·wa (vär shä′vä), *n.* Polish name of **Warsaw.**

wart (wôrt), *n.* **1.** a small, usually hard, abnormal elevation on the skin, caused by a filterable virus. **2.** any small protuberance, as on the surface of certain plants, the skin of certain animals, etc. [ME; OE *wearte*; c. G *Warze*, Icel *varta*; akin to L *verrūca* wart] **—wart′ed,** *adj.* **—wart′like′,** *adj.*

War·ta (vär′tä), *n.* a river in Poland, flowing NW and W into the Oder. 445 mi. long. German, **War·the** (vär′tə).

Wart·burg (värt′bo͝ork), *n.* a castle in East Germany, in Thuringia, near Eisenach: Luther translated the New Testament here 1521–22.

Wart hog (2½ ft. high at shoulder; total length 6 ft.; tail 1½ ft.)

wart′ hog′, an African wild swine, *Phacochoerus aethiopicus,* having large tusks and warty excrescences on the face.

war·time (wôr′tīm′), *n.* **1.** a time or period of war. **—*adj.* 2.** caused by, characteristic of, or occurring during such a period.

wart·y (wôr′tē), *adj.,* **wart·i·er, wart·i·est. 1.** having warts; covered with or as with warts. **2.** resembling or like a wart.

war′ whoop′, a yell uttered in making an attack.

War·wick (wôr′ik, wor′- *or, for 2,* wôr′wik), *n.* **1. Earl of** (*Richard Neville, Earl of Salisbury*) (*"the Kingmaker"*), 1428–71, English military leader and statesman. **2.** a city in E Rhode Island. 83,694 (1970). **3.** a town in and the county seat of Warwickshire in central England: castle. 16,032 (1961). **4.** Warwickshire.

War·wick·shire (wôr′ik shēr′, -shər, wor′-), *n.* a county in central England. 2,023,289 (1961); 983 sq. mi. *Co. seat:* Warwick. Also called **Warwick.**

war·y (wâr′ē), *adj.,* **war·i·er, war·i·est. 1.** watchful, or on one's guard, esp. habitually. **2.** arising from or characterized by caution: *a wary look.* [WARE[2] + -Y[1]] **—Syn. 1.** alert, vigilant, guarded, prudent.

war′ zone′, 1. a zone in which hostile operations are conducted during a war. **2.** a combat area in which the rights of neutrals are suspended during wartime, as on the high seas.

was (wuz, woz; *unstressed* wəz), *v.* 1st and 3rd pers. sing. pt. indic. of **be.** [ME; OE *wæs*, past tense sing. of *wesan* to be; c. Goth, OHG, OFris *was*, Icel *var*; see WASSAIL]

Wa′satch Range′ (wô′sach), a mountain range in N Utah and SE Idaho. Highest peak, Mt. Timpanogos, 12,008 ft.

wash (wosh, wôsh), *v.t.* **1.** to free of dirt or other matter by application of or immersion in a liquid, esp. water or a solution of soap and water: *to wash a dress.* **2.** to remove (dirt or other matter) by this method: *She washed the mud off her dress.* **3.** to cleanse from defilement or guilt; purify. **4.** to move by means of water or other liquid: *The storm washed our boat ashore.* **5.** to wet or moisten, as with water. **6.** to wear or erode by the flow of a liquid, esp. water: *The storm washed gulleys in the mountain.* **7.** to cover with a thin layer, as of paint or metal.
—*v.i.* 8. to wash oneself. **9.** to wash clothes. **10.** to cleanse anything with or in water or other liquid. **11.** to undergo washing without injury, esp. shrinking or fading. **12.** *Chiefly Brit. Informal.* to stand being put to the proof: *That story won't wash.* **13.** to be carried or driven by water: *The boat had washed ashore in the night.* **14.** to move along in or as in waves, or with a rushing movement, as water. **15.** to be removed by the action of water (often fol. by *away*): *This topsoil tends to wash away.* **16. wash down, a.** to clean completely by washing: *to wash down a car.* **b.** to facilitate the swallowing of (food) by drinking water or other liquid: *to wash chicken down with wine.* **17. wash out, a.** to be removed by washing: *This stain didn't wash out.* **b.** to demolish by the action of water: *The embankment was washed out by the storm.* **c.** *Slang.* to fail to qualify or continue; be eliminated: *He washed out after one semester.* **18. wash up, a.** to wash one's face and hands. **b.** to wash (dishes, pots, etc.): *I'll wash up the dishes.* **c.** to end, esp. ignominiously (usually in the passive): *He's all washed up in Wall Street.*
—*n.* 19. the act or process of washing with water or other liquid: *to give the car a wash.* **20.** a quantity of things washed together. **21.** the flow, sweep, dash, or breaking of water. **22.** water moving along in waves or with a rushing movement. **23.** the rough or broken water or air left behind a moving ship, wing, propeller, etc. **24.** any of various liquids for grooming or cosmetic purposes: *a hair wash.* **25.** a lotion or other liquid having medicinal properties (often used in combination): *to apply wash to a skinned knee; eyewash.* **26.** a thin coating, as of paint or metal. **27.** a tract of land washed by the action of the sea or a river. **28.** a marsh, fen, or bog. **29.** a small stream or shallow pool. **30.** a shallow arm of the sea or a shallow part of a river. **31.** a depression or channel formed by flowing water. **32.** *Geol.* alluvial matter transferred and deposited by flowing water. **33.** Also called **dry wash.** *Western U.S.* the dry bed of an intermittent stream. **34.** waste liquid matter, refuse food, etc., from the kitchen, as for hogs; swill (often used in combination): *hogwash.* **35. come out in the wash,** to become known eventually.
—*adj.* 36. capable of being washed without shrinking, fading, etc.; washable: *a wash dress.* [ME; OE *wasc(an)* (c. D *wasschen*, G *waschen*, Icel *vaska*) < Gmc **watskan* = *wat-* (see WATER) + *-sk-* v. suffix + *-an* inf. suffix]
—Syn. 1, 2, 10. clean, rinse, launder, scrub, mop. **5.** bedew, bathe. **19.** ablution, cleansing, bathing. **28.** swamp, morass.

Wash (wosh, wôsh), *n.* **The,** a shallow bay of the North Sea, on the coast of E England. 20 mi. long; 15 mi. wide.

Wash., Washington (defs. 4, 5).

wash·a·ble (wosh′ə bəl, wô′shə-), *adj.* capable of being washed without shrinking, fading, or the like. **—wash′a·bil′i·ty,** *n.*

wash-and-wear (wosh′ən wâr′, wôsh′-), *adj.* noting or pertaining to a garment that can be washed, that dries quickly, and that requires little or no ironing; drip-dry.

wash·board (wosh′bōrd′, -bôrd′, wôsh′-), *n.* **1.** a rectangular board or frame, typically with a corrugated metallic surface, on which clothes are rubbed in the process of washing. **2.** a baseboard around the walls of a room. **3.** Also called **splashboard.** *Naut.* a thin, broad plank fastened to and projecting above the gunwale or side of a boat to keep out spray.

wash·bowl (wosh′bōl′, wôsh′-), *n.* a large bowl or basin used for washing one's hands and face, small articles of clothing, etc. Also called **wash·ba·sin** (wosh′bā′sin, wôsh′-).

wash·cloth (wosh′klôth′, -kloth′, wôsh′-), *n., pl.* **-cloths** (-klôthz′, -klothz′, -klôths′, -kloths′). a small cloth for washing one's face or body.

wash·day (wosh′dā′, wôsh′-), *n.* the day set apart in a household for washing clothes.

washed-out (wosht′out′, wôsht′-), *adj.* **1.** faded, esp. from washing. **2.** *Informal.* **a.** weary; exhausted. **b.** tired-looking; wan.

washed-up (wosht′up′, wôsht′-), *adj.* *Informal.* done for; having failed completely.

wash·er (wosh′ər, wô′shər), *n.* **1.** a person or thing that washes. **2.** a machine or apparatus for washing. **3.** a flat ring or perforated piece of leather, rubber, metal, etc., used to give tightness to a joint, to prevent leakage, to distribute pressure, etc. [ME]

wash·er·man (wosh′ər mən, wô′shər-), *n., pl.* **-men.** a man who washes clothes, linens, etc., for hire; laundryman.

wash·er·wom·an (wosh′ər wo͝om′ən, wô′shər-), *n., pl.* **-wom·en.** a woman who washes clothes, linens, etc., for hire; laundress.

wash′ goods′, textiles that will not fade or become weakened by washing.

wash·ing (wosh′ing, wô′shing), *n.* **1.** the act of a person or thing that washes; ablution. **2.** clothes, linens, etc., washed at one time; wash. **3.** material obtained by washing. **4.** a thin coating or covering applied in liquid form: *a washing of gold.* [ME *wasschunge*]

wash′ing machine′, an apparatus, esp. a household appliance, for washing clothing, linens, etc.

wash′ing so′da. See **sodium carbonate** (def. 2).

Wash·ing·ton (wosh′ing tən, wô′shing-), *n.* **1. Book·er T(al·ia·ferro)** (bo͝ok′ər tol′ə vər), 1856–1915, U.S. Negro reformer, educator, author, and lecturer. **2. George,** 1732–99, U.S. general and statesman: 1st president of the U.S. 1789–97. **3. Martha** (*Martha Dandridge*), 1732–1802, wife of George. **4.** Also called **Washington, D.C.** the capital of the United States, on the Potomac between Maryland and Virginia: coextensive with the District of Columbia. 637,651 (1980). *Abbr.:* Wash. **5.** Also called **Washington State.** a state in the NW United States, on the Pacific coast. 4,130,163 (1980); 68,192 sq. mi. *Cap.:* Olympia. *Abbr.:* WA, Wash. **6. Mount,** a mountain in N New Hampshire, in the White Mountains: highest peak in the NE United States. 6,293 ft. **7. Lake,** a lake in W Washington, near Seattle. 20 mi. long.

Wash·ing·to·ni·an (wosh′ing tō′nē ən, wô′shing-), *adj.* **1.** living in or coming from Washington, D.C., or the state of Washington. —*n.* **2.** a native or inhabitant of Washington, D.C., or the state of Washington.

Wash′ington's Birth′day, February 22, the date of birth of George Washington, now officially observed as a legal holiday in most states of the U.S. on the third Monday in February.

Wash′ington State′, the state of Washington, esp. as distinguished from Washington, D.C.

wash·out (wosh′out′, wôsh′-), *n.* **1.** a washing out of earth, gravel, etc., by the action of water. **2.** *Informal.* an utter failure.

wash·rag (wosh′rag′, wôsh′-), *n.* washcloth.

wash·room (wosh′ro͞om′, -ro͝om′, wôsh′-), *n.* a room having washbowls and other toilet facilities.

wash′ sale′, **1.** a sale of a stock at a loss and repurchase of the same or substantially identical stock within thirty days, for which the capital loss is disallowed for tax purposes. **2.** an illegal sale on the stock exchange in which securities appear falsely to change ownership in order to give the appearance of wide market activity and interest in a stock.

wash·stand (wosh′stand′, wôsh′-), *n.* a fixture or piece of furniture designed to hold water for use in washing one's hands and face.

wash·tub (wosh′tub′, wôsh′-), *n.* a tub for use in washing clothes, linens, etc.

wash-up (wosh′up′, wôsh′-), *n.* the act of washing or cleaning.

wash·wom·an (wosh′wo͝om′ən, wôsh′-), *n., pl.* **-wom·en** (-wim′en). washerwoman.

wash·y (wosh′ē, wô′shē), *adj.,* **wash·i·er, wash·i·est.** **1.** diluted too much; weak: *washy coffee.* **2.** pale, thin, or weak in coloring, as if from excessive dilution; pallid: *washy pink flowers.* —**wash′i·ness,** *n.*

was·n't (wuz′ənt, woz′-), contraction of *was not.*

wasp (wosp), *n.* any of numerous social or solitary, hymenopterous insects of *Vespidae, Sphecidae,* and allied families, generally having a long, slender body and narrow waist. [ME *waspe,* OE *wæsp,* metathetic var. of *wæps* < *wæfs* (by dissimilation) = *wæf-* (see WEAVE) + suffixal *-s;* akin to D *wesp,* G *Wespe,* L *vespa*]

Wasp, *Eumenes fraternus* (Length ½ in.)

WASP (wosp), *n.* *U.S.* **1.** an American of British or northern European ancestry who belongs to the Protestant church. **2.** *Often Disparaging.* such an American considered to be a member of the conservative, wealthy and privileged upper class that formerly dominated U.S. society. Also, **Wasp.** [*w(hite) A(nglo-)S(axon) P(rotestant)*] —**WASP·ish, Wasp·ish** (wŏsp′ish), *adj.*

wasp·ish (wos′pish), *adj.* **1.** quick to resent a trifling affront or injury; snappish. **2.** irascibly or petulantly spiteful. —**wasp′ish·ly,** *adv.* —**wasp′ish·ness,** *n.*

wasp′ waist′, a slender waistline, esp. when the result of tight corseting. —**wasp′-waist′ed,** *adj.*

wasp·y (wos′pē), *adj.,* **wasp·i·er, wasp·i·est.** resembling a wasp; waspish. —**wasp′i·ly,** *adv.* —**wasp′i·ness,** *n.*

was·sail (wos′əl, -āl, was′-, wo sāl′), *n.* **1.** a salutation to a person, used in England in early times when presenting a cup of drink or when drinking to a person's health. **2.** a festivity or revel with drinking of healths. **3.** liquor, esp. spiced ale, for drinking healths on festive occasions. **4.** *Archaic.* a song sung in wassailing. —*v.i.* **5.** to drink healths; revel with drinking. —*v.t.* **6.** to drink to the health or success of; toast. [ME *was-hail* = *was* be (OE *wæs,* var. of *wes,* impv. of *wesan* to be) + *hail* HALE[1] (i.e., in good health) < Scand (cf. Icel *heill* hale); r. OE *wæs hāl* be hale or whole. See HEAL] —**was′sail·er,** *n.*

Was·ser·mann (wä′sər mən; *Ger.* väs′ər män′), *n.* **1. Au·gust von** (ou′go͝ost fən), 1866–1925, German physician and bacteriologist. **2. Ja·kob** (yä′kôp), 1873–1934, German novelist.

Was′sermann reac′tion, a diagnostic test for syphilis using the fixation of a complement by the serum of a syphilitic individual. Also called **Was′ser·mann test′.** [named after A. von WASSERMANN]

wast (wost; *unstressed* wəst), *v.* *Archaic.* a 2nd pers. sing. pt. indic. of **be.**

wast·age (wā′stij), *n.* **1.** loss by use, wear, decay, etc. **2.** loss or losses as the result of wastefulness. **3.** the action or process of wasting: *the steady wastage of erosion.* **4.** that which is wasted; waste or waste materials.

waste (wāst), *v.,* **wast·ed, wast·ing,** *n., adj.* —*v.t.* **1.** to consume, spend, or employ uselessly or without adequate return. **2.** to fail or neglect to use: *to waste an opportunity.* **3.** to destroy or consume gradually; wear away. **4.** to wear down or reduce in bodily substance, health, or strength. **5.** to destroy, devastate, or ruin. —*v.i.* **6.** to be consumed, spent, or employed uselessly or without being fully utilized or appreciated. **7.** to become gradually consumed, used up, or worn away. **8.** to become emaciated or enfeebled. **9.** to diminish gradually; dwindle, as wealth, power, etc. **10.** to pass gradually, as time. —*n.* **11.** useless consumption or expenditure. **12.** neglect, instead of use: *waste of opportunity.* **13.** gradual destruction, impairment, or decay. **14.** devastation or ruin, as from war, fire, etc. **15.** a region or place that is devastated or ruined. **16.** anything unused, unproductive, or not properly utilized. **17.** an uncultivated tract of land. **18.** a wild or desolate region. **19.** (*construed as sing. or pl.*) anything left over or superfluous, as from a manufacturing process. **20.** *Phys. Geog.* material derived by mechanical and chemical disintegration of rock. **21.** garbage; refuse. **22. wastes,** excrement. **23. lay waste,** to devastate; destroy. —*adj.* **24.** not used or in use; wasted. **25.** (of land, regions, etc.) wild, barren, or uninhabited; desert. **26.** (of regions, towns, etc.) in a state of desolation and ruin. **27.** left over or superfluous: *waste products of manufacture.* **28.** rejected as useless or worthless; refuse: *to salvage waste products.* **29.** *Physiol.* pertaining to material unused by or unusable to the organism. **30.** designed or used to receive, hold, or carry away waste (often in combination): *a waste pipe; waste pile.* **31.** *Obs.* excessive; needless. [(adj., n.) ME *wast* < AF (OF *guast*) < L *vastus* empty, waste; (v.) ME *wasten* < AF *waster* (OF *guaster*) < L *vastāre* to lay waste; AF and OF forms influenced by Gmc root **wōst-* (cf. OHG *wuosti* empty, waste, c. L *vastus*)] —**wast′a·ble,** *adj.*
—**Syn. 1.** misspend, dissipate. **5.** ravage, sack. **18.** See **desert**[1]. **23.** See **ravage.** —**Ant. 1.** save.

waste·bas·ket (wāst′bas′kit, -bä′skit), *n.* a basket for small items of trash. Also called **waste′paper bas′ket.**

waste·ful (wāst′fəl), *adj.* **1.** given to or characterized by useless consumption or expenditure. **2.** devastating or destructive: *wasteful war.* [late ME] —**waste′ful·ly,** *adv.* —**waste′ful·ness,** *n.*

waste·land (wāst′land′), *n.* **1.** land that is uncultivated or barren. **2.** a devastated area. **3.** something, as a period of history, locality, etc., that is considered spiritually or intellectually barren.

waste·ness (wāst′nis), *n.* the state or condition of being waste, desolate, or the like. [late ME]

waste·pa·per (wāst′pā′pər), *n.* paper thrown away as useless.

waste′ prod′uct, **1.** material discarded as useless in the process of producing something. **2.** feces, urine, and other excreted material.

wast·er (wā′stər), *n.* **1.** a person or thing that wastes any resource. **2.** a spendthrift or wastrel. **3.** a person who destroys; vandal. **4.** *Chiefly Brit.* wastrel (def. 2). [ME < AF *wastere*]

wast·ing (wā′sting), *adj.* **1.** gradually reducing the fullness and strength of the body: *a wasting disease.* **2.** laying waste; devastating; despoiling: *a wasting war.* [ME] —**wast′ing·ly,** *adv.*

wast·rel (wā′strəl), *n.* **1.** a wasteful person; spendthrift. **2.** *Chiefly Brit.* **a.** refuse; waste. **b.** a waif; abandoned child. **c.** an idler or good-for-nothing. [WASTE + -REL]

wast·ry (wā′strē), *n.* *Scot. and North Eng.* wastefulness; reckless extravagance. Also, **waste′ry, wast′rie.**

wat (wät), *n.* a Buddhist temple or monastery in Thailand or Cambodia. [< Thai < Skt *vāṭa* enclosure]

watch (woch), *v.i.* **1.** to look attentively, or observe, as to see what is done, happens, etc. **2.** to look or wait attentively and expectantly (usually fol. by *for*): *to watch for a signal.* **3.** to maintain a guard or vigil. **4.** to be careful or cautious: *Watch when you cross the street.* —*v.t.* **5.** to look at attentively or with sustained interest. **6.** to keep under surveillance: *Watch the kettle, would you? The police are watching him.* **7.** to look or wait attentively and expectantly for: *to watch one's opportunity.* **8. watch oneself, a.** to be careful. **b.** to practice discretion or self-restraint. **9. watch out,** to be on one's guard; be cautious. **10. watch over,** to care for, safekeep, or guard protectively. —*n.* **11.** a continuous act of looking or waiting for something that may or is expected to appear or happen. **12.** constant or frequent observation, as to guard or protect; vigil: *to keep watch over a sickbed; a watch over a suspect.* **13.** a period of wakefulness, as in order to guard. **14.** a period of time for watching or keeping guard. **15.** a small, portable timepiece. **16.** a chronometer. **17.**

Naut. **a.** a period of time, usually four hours, during which one part of a ship's crew is on duty, taking turns with another part. **b.** the part of a ship's crew that is on duty during this time. **18.** one of the periods into which the night was divided in ancient times. **19. on the watch,** vigilant; alert. **20.** a person or persons appointed to keep watch. [ME *wacche,* OE *wæcc(an),* doublet of *wacian* to WAKE[1]]
—Syn. 1. WATCH, LOOK, SEE imply being aware of things around one by perceiving them through the eyes. To WATCH is to be a spectator, to look on or observe, or to fix the attention upon during passage of time: *to watch while a procession passes.* To LOOK is to direct the gaze with the intention of seeing, to use the eyesight with attention: *to look for violets in the spring; to look at articles displayed for sale.* To SEE is to perceive with the eyes, to obtain a visual impression, with or without fixing the attention: *animals able to see in the dark.* **7.** await. **11.** inspection, attention. **20.** sentry.

watch′ and ward′, a continuous watch or vigil, by or as by night and by day, esp. for the purpose of guarding.

watch·band (woch′band′), *n.* a metal, fabric, or leather bracelet attached to a wrist watch to hold it on the wrist.

watch′ cap′, *U.S. Navy.* a knitted woolen cap worn by enlisted men on duty in cold weather.

watch·case (woch′kās′), *n.* the case or outer covering for the works of a watch.

watch′ chain′, a chain, frequently of gold or silver, often attached to a pocket watch, serving as an ornament and, when passed through a buttonhole in the vest, as a guard against loss or theft of the watch.

watch·cry (woch′krī′), *n., pl.* **-cries.** watchword.

watch·dog (woch′dôg′, -dog′), *n.* **1.** a dog kept to guard property. **2.** any watchful guardian.

watch·er (woch′ər), *n.* a person who watches or who keeps watch.

watch′ fire′, a fire maintained during the night as a signal and for providing light and warmth for guards.

watch·ful (woch′fəl), *adj.* **1.** vigilant or alert; closely observant. **2.** *Archaic.* wakeful. **—watch′ful·ly,** *adv.* **—watch′ful·ness,** *n.* **—Syn. 1.** cautious, wary. See **alert.**

watch′ guard′, a short chain, cord, or ribbon for securing a watch when worn on the person.

watch·less (woch′lis), *adj.* **1.** not watchful or alert. **2.** having no watchman or guard.

watch·mak·er (woch′mā′kər), *n.* a man whose occupation it is to make and repair watches. **—watch′mak′ing,** *n.*

watch·man (woch′mən), *n., pl.* **-men. 1.** a person who keeps guard over a building at night, to protect it from fire or thieves. **2.** (formerly) a person who guards or patrols the streets at night. [late ME] **—watch′man·ly,** *adj.*

watch′ meet′ing, a religious meeting or service on watch night, terminating on the arrival of the new year. Also called **watch′-night serv′ice** (woch′nīt′).

watch′ night′, **1.** the last night of the year, observed in a watch meeting. **2.** See **watch meeting.**

watch·out (woch′out′), *n.* the act of looking out for or anticipating something; lookout.

watch′ pock′et, a small pocket in a garment, as in a vest or trousers, for holding a pocket watch, change, etc.

watch′ tack′le, a small tackle used for hauling, as a luff tackle, esp. on the decks of vessels.

watch·tow·er (woch′tou′ər), *n.* a tower on which a sentinel keeps watch.

watch·word (woch′wûrd′), *n.* **1.** a word or short phrase to be communicated, on challenge, to a sentinel or guard; password or countersign. **2.** a word or phrase expressive of a principle or rule of action; slogan. [late ME]

wa·ter (wô′tər, wot′ər), *n.* **1.** a transparent, odorless, tasteless liquid, a compound of hydrogen and oxygen, H_2O, freezing at 32°F or 0°C and boiling at 212°F or 100°C, which in a more or less impure state constitutes rain, oceans, lakes, rivers, etc.: it contains 11.188 percent hydrogen and 88.812 percent oxygen, by weight. **2.** a special form or variety of this liquid: *mineral water.* **3.** the surface of a body of this substance: *below the water.* **4. waters, a.** the water of a river or lake. **b.** an area of the sea: *Japanese waters.* **5.** Often, **waters.** the water of a mineral spring. **6.** a stage or level of water: *Low water will be at 6:12 a.m.* **7.** a liquid solution or preparation: *lavender water; ammonia water.* **8.** any liquid or aqueous organic secretion, exudation, humor, etc. **9.** *Finance.* fictitious assets or the inflated values they give to the stock of a corporation. **10.** a wavy, lustrous pattern or marking, as on silk fabrics, etc. **11.** *Jewelry.* the degree of transparency and brilliancy of a diamond or other precious stone. **12. above water,** out of embarrassment or trouble, esp. of a financial nature. **13. by water,** by ship or boat. **14. hold water,** to be logical, defensible, or valid, as a statement or argument. **15. in deep water,** *Slang.* in great distress or difficulty. **16. in hot water.** See **hot water.**
—*v.t.* **17.** to sprinkle, moisten, or drench with water. **18.** to furnish with a supply of water. **19.** to dilute, weaken, soften, or adulterate with, or as with, water (often fol. by *down*): *to water soup; to water down an unfavorable report.* **20.** *Finance.* to issue or increase the par value of (shares of stock) without having the assets to warrant doing so (often fol. by *down*). **21.** to produce a wavy, lustrous pattern, marking, or finish on (fabrics, metals, etc.)
—*v.i.* **22.** to discharge, fill with, or secrete water or liquid, as the eyes. **23.** to drink or take in a supply of water.
—*adj.* **24.** of or pertaining to water. **25.** holding or capable of holding water: *a water jug.* **26.** worked or powered by water: *a water turbine.* **27.** used in or on water: *water skis.* **28.** containing or prepared with water. **29.** pertaining to natural bodies of water, their shores, or their navigation: *a water deity; a water town; a water journey.* [ME; OE *wæter;* c. G *Wasser,* D *water;* akin to Icel *vatn,* Goth *wato,* Hittite *watar*] **—wa′ter·er,** *n.* **—wa′ter·like′,** *adj.*

wa′ter bal·let′, an entertainment consisting of synchronized movements, forming patterns and other visual effects, performed in the water by swimmers before an audience, usually to a musical accompaniment.

wa′ter bath′, **1.** a system for the control of temperature in which a vessel that contains material to be heated is set into one that contains water and is in direct contact with a heat source. **2.** a bath of water.

Wa′ter Bear′er, *Astron., Astrol.* Aquarius.

wat·er·bed (wô′tər bed′), *n.* a vinyl mattress-shaped bag filled with water and placed on a bedframe, for making the surface conform to the sleeper's body in any position.

wa′ter bee′tle, any of various aquatic beetles, as a predaceous diving beetle.

wa′ter bird′, aquatic bird; swimming or wading bird.

wa′ter bis′cuit, a crackerlike biscuit prepared from flour and water.

wa′ter blis′ter, a blister containing clear, serous fluid, as distinguished from a blood blister in which the fluid is sanguineous.

wa·ter·borne (wô′tər bōrn′, -bôrn′, wot′ər-), *adj.* **1.** floating or moving on water. **2.** transported by ship or boat. **3.** communicated by water, esp. drinking water: *waterborne diseases.*

wa′ter bot′tle, *Chiefly Brit.* canteen (def. 1).

wa′ter boy′, a person who carries drinking water to those too occupied to fetch it, as to soldiers, laborers, football players, etc.

wa·ter·brain (wô′tər brān′, wot′ər-), *n. Vet. Pathol.* gid, in sheep.

wa′ter brash′, *Pathol.* heartburn (def. 1).

Waterbuck, *Kobus ellipsiprymnus* (4 ft. high at shoulder; horns 2½ ft.; total length 6 ft.; tail 10 in.)

wa·ter·buck (wô′tər buk′, wot′ər-), *n.* any of several large African antelopes of the genus *Kobus,* frequenting marshes and reedy places, esp. *K. ellipsiprymnus,* of southern and central Africa.

wa′ter buf′falo, a buffalo, *Bubalus bubalis,* of the Old World tropics, having large, flattened, curved horns. Also called **water ox.**

wa′ter bug′, **1.** any of various aquatic hemipterous insects, as of the family *Belostomatidae.* **2.** (loosely) a cockroach.

Water buffalo (5½ ft. high at shoulder; length 9 ft.)

Wa·ter·bur·y (wô′tər ber′ē, -bə rē, wot′ər-), *n.* a city in W Connecticut. 108,033 (1970).

wa′ter chest′nut, **1.** any aquatic plant of the genus *Trapa,* bearing an edible, nutlike fruit, esp. *T. natans,* of the Old World. **2.** the fruit itself. Also called **wa′ter cal′trop.**

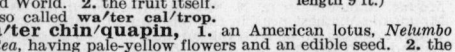

wa′ter chin′quapin, **1.** an American lotus, *Nelumbo lutea,* having pale-yellow flowers and an edible seed. **2.** the seed itself, similar in flavor to the chinquapin.

wa′ter clock′, a device, as a clepsydra, for measuring time by the flow of water.

wa′ter clos′et, **1.** a flush toilet. **2.** a room or compartment for this. **3.** *Dial.* a privy or bathroom.

wa·ter·col·or (wô′tər kul′ər, wot′ər-), *n.* **1.** a pigment for which water is used as a vehicle. **2.** the art or technique of painting with such pigments. **3.** a painting or design executed by this technique. Also, *esp. Brit.,* **wa′ter·col′our. —wa′ter·col′or;** *esp. Brit.,* **wa′ter·col′our,** *adj.* **—wa′ter·col′or·ist;** *esp. Brit.,* **wa′ter·col′our·ist,** *n.*

wa·ter-cool (wô′tər kōōl′, wot′ər-), *v.t.* to cool by means of water, esp. by water circulating in pipes or a water jacket, as in an engine, machine gun, etc.

wa′ter cool′er, a device for cooling and dispensing drinking water.

wa·ter·course (wô′tər kōrs′, -kôrs′, wot′ər-), *n.* **1.** a stream of water, as a river or brook. **2.** the bed of a stream that flows only seasonally. **3.** a natural or man-made channel conveying water.

wa·ter·craft (wô′tər kraft′, -kräft′, wot′ər-), *n.* **1.** skill in boating and water sports. **2.** any boat or ship. **3.** boats and ships collectively.

wa′ter crake′, *Brit. Dial.* the water ouzel, *Cinclus aquaticus.*

wa·ter·cress (wô′tər kres′, wot′ər-), *n.* **1.** a perennial cress, *Rorippa Nasturtium officinale,* usually growing in clear, running water, and having pungent leaves. **2.** the leaves, used for salads, soups, and as a garnish. [ME; c. MD, MLG *waterkerse*]

wa′ter cure′, hydropathy; hydrotherapy.

wa′ter dog′, a dog that swims well or is trained to retrieve waterfowl in hunting.

wa·ter·dog (wô′tər dôg′, -dog′, wot′ər-), *n.* any of several large salamanders, as a mudpuppy or hellbender.

wa·tered-down (wô′tərd doun′, wot′ərd-), *adj.* made weaker or less effective from or as from dilution with water.

wa′tered steel′, hand-wrought steel, made from parts of a bloom of heterogeneous composition, repeatedly folded over and welded and finally etched to reveal the resulting grain: esp. for sword blades. Also called **Damascus steel.**

Wa·ter·ee (wô′tə rē′, wot′ə-), *n.* a river flowing from W North Carolina into South Carolina, joining the Congaree River to form the Santee River. Cf. **Catawba** (def. 2).

wa·ter·fall (wô′tər fôl′, wot′ər-), *n.* a steep fall or flow of water in a watercourse from a height, as over a precipice; cascade. [ME; OE *wætergefeall*]

wa·ter-fast (wô′tər fast′, -fäst′, wot′ər-), *adj.* (of a color or dye) resistant to the effects caused by water; not changed or faded by the action of water.

wa′ter flea′, any of various small crustaceans that move about in the water like fleas, as *Daphnia.*

Wa·ter·ford (wô′tər fərd, wot′ər-), *n.* **1.** a county in Munster province, in S Republic of Ireland. 71,439 (1961); 710 sq. mi. **2.** its county seat: seaport. 28,216 (1961).

wa′ter foun′tain, a drinking fountain, water cooler, or other apparatus supplying drinking water.

wa·ter·fowl (wô′tər foul′, wot′ər-), *n., pl.* **-fowls,** (*esp. collectively*) **-fowl.** a water bird, esp. a swan, goose, or duck. [ME; c. G *Wasservogel*]

wa·ter·front (wô′tər frunt′, wot′ər-), *n.* **1.** land on the edge of a body of water. **2.** a part of a city or town on such land.

wa′ter gap′, a transverse gap in a mountain ridge, cut by and giving passage to a stream.

wa′ter gas′, a toxic gaseous mixture consisting chiefly of carbon monoxide and hydrogen, prepared from steam and incandescent coke: used in organic synthesis and as an illuminant and fuel. Also called **blue gas.** —**wa′ter-gas′,** *adj.*

wa′ter gate′, **1.** a gate for halting or controlling the flow of water in a watercourse; floodgate. **2.** a gateway leading to the edge of a body of water, as at a landing. [late ME]

Wa·ter·gate (wô′tər gāt′, wo′tər-), *n.* **1.** an illegal break-in at Democratic party headquarters in Washington, D.C., during the presidential campaign of 1972, allegedly by Republican campaign employees for political espionage and sabotage. **2.** any political activity that is grossly illegal or unethical, usually involving unfair tactics, concealed contributions, special-interest deals, and abuse of governmental trust for partisan advantage. [from the name of the building in which the break-in occurred]

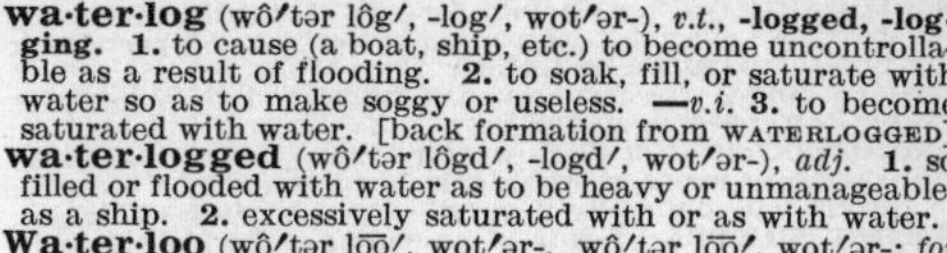

Water gauge for boiler
A, Water level
B, Upper cock
C, Lower cock

wa′ter gauge′, any device for indicating the height of water in a reservoir, tank, boiler, or other vessel.

wa′ter glass′, **1.** a drinking glass; tumbler. **2.** a glass container for holding water, as for growing bulbs, plants, or the like. **3.** a glass tube used to indicate water level, as in a boiler. **4.** a device for observing objects beneath the surface of the water, consisting essentially of an open tube or box with a glass bottom. **5.** See **sodium silicate.** Also, **wa′ter-glass′.**

wa′terglass paint′ing, stereochromy.

wa′ter gum′, **1.** (in the U.S.) a tupelo, *Nyssa sylvatica biflora,* of the southern states. **2.** (in Australia) any of several myrtaceous trees growing near water.

wa′ter ham′mer, **1.** the concussion that results when a moving volume of water in a pipe is suddenly stopped. **2.** a tube or other container partially filled with water and exhausted of air, the shaking of which causes the water to produce a hammering sound.

wa′ter hem′lock, any poisonous, umbelliferous plant of the genus *Cicuta,* as *C. virosa* of Europe, and *C. maculata* of North America, growing in swamps and marshy places.

wa′ter hen′, **1.** the moorhen or gallinule, *Gallinula chloropus,* of Europe. **2.** the coot, *Fulica americana.*

wa′ter hole′, **1.** a depression in the surface of the ground, containing water. **2.** a source of drinking water, as a spring, well, etc., in the desert. **3.** a pond; pool. **4.** a hole in the frozen surface of a body of water.

wa′ter ice′, **1.** ice formed by direct freezing of fresh or salt water, and not by compacting of snow. **2.** a frozen dessert made of water, sweetener, and flavorings.

wa·ter-inch (wô′tər inch′, wot′ər-), *n. Hydraulics.* the quantity of water (approx. 500 cubic feet) discharged in 24 hours through a circular opening of 1 inch diameter leading from a reservoir in which the water is constantly only high enough to cover the orifice.

wa·ter·i·ness (wô′tə rē nis, wot′ə-), *n.* the state or condition of being watery or diluted.

wa′tering place′, **1.** *Brit.* a seaside or lakeside vacation resort. **2.** *Chiefly Brit.* a health resort near mineral springs, a lake, or the sea. **3.** a place where drinking water may be obtained by men or animals, as a spring, water hole, etc. [late ME *watrynge place*]

wa′tering pot′, a container for water, typically of metal and having a spout with a perforated end, for watering or sprinkling plants, flowers, etc. Also called **wa′tering can′.**

wa·ter·ish (wô′tər ish, wot′ər-), *adj.* somewhat or tending to be watery. —**wa′ter·ish·ly,** *adv.* —**wa′ter·ish·ness,** *n.*

wa′ter jack′et, a casing or compartment containing water, placed about something to keep it cool or otherwise regulate its temperature, as around the cylinder or cylinders of an internal-combustion engine.

wa′ter jump′, any small body of water that a horse must jump over, as in a steeplechase.

wa·ter-laid (wô′tər lād′, wot′ər-), *adj. Ropemaking.* noting a rope laid left-handed from three or four plain-laid ropes.

wa·ter·less (wô′tər lis, wot′ər-), *adj.* **1.** devoid of water; dry. **2.** needing no water, as for cooking. [ME *waterlees,* OE *wæterlēas*] —**wa′ter·less·ly,** *adv.*

wa′terless cook′er, **1.** a tight-lidded kitchen utensil in which food can be cooked using only a small amount of water or only the juices emitted while cooking. **2.** See **pressure cooker.**

wa′ter lev′el, **1.** the surface level of any body of water. **2.** the level to which a vessel is immersed; water line.

wa′ter lil′y, **1.** Also called **water nymph.** any aquatic plant of the genus *Nymphaea,* species of which have large, disklike, floating leaves and showy, fragrant flowers, esp. *N. odorata,* of America or *N. alba,* of Europe. **2.** any plant of the genus *Nuphar.* **3.** any nymphaeaceous plant. **4.** the flower of any such plant.

Water lily, *Nymphaea odorata*

wa′ter line′, **1.** the line in which water at its surface borders upon a floating body. **2.** See **water level** (def. 1). **3.** Also called **watermark.** a line indicating the former level or passage of water. **4.** a pipe, hose, tube, or other line for conveying water. **5.** *Naval Archit.* any of a series of lines on the hull plans of a vessel representing the intersection of a series of parallel horizontal planes with the form of the hull. Also, **wa′ter·line′.**

wa·ter·locked (wô′tər lokt′, wot′ər-), *adj.* enclosed entirely, or almost entirely, by water: *a waterlocked nation.*

wa·ter·log (wô′tər lôg′, -log′, wot′ər-), *v.t.,* **-logged, -logging.** **1.** to cause (a boat, ship, etc.) to become uncontrollable as a result of flooding. **2.** to soak, fill, or saturate with water so as to make soggy or useless. —*v.i.* **3.** to become saturated with water. [back formation from WATERLOGGED]

wa·ter·logged (wô′tər lôgd′, -logd′, wot′ər-), *adj.* **1.** so filled or flooded with water as to be heavy or unmanageable, as a ship. **2.** excessively saturated with or as with water.

Wa·ter·loo (wô′tər lo͞o′, wot′ər-, wô′tər lo͞o′, wot′ər-; *for 1 also Flem.* vä′tər lō′), *n.* **1.** a village in central Belgium, south of Brussels: Napoleon decisively defeated here on June 18, 1815. **2.** a decisive or crushing defeat. **3.** a city in E Iowa. 75,533 (1970).

wa′ter main′, a main pipe or conduit in a system for conveying water.

wa·ter·man (wô′tər mən, wot′ər-), *n., pl.* **-men.** a boatman or oarsman. [late ME] —**wa′ter·man·ship′,** *n.*

wa·ter·mark (wô′tər märk′, wot′ər-), *n.* **1.** a mark indicating the height to which water rises or has risen, as in a river, inlet, etc. **2.** See **water line** (def. 3). **3.** *Papermaking.* a figure or design impressed in the paper. —*v.t.* **4.** to mark with a watermark.

wa·ter·mel·on (wô′tər mel′ən, wot′ər-), *n.* **1.** the large, roundish or elongated fruit of a trailing cucurbitaceous vine, *Citrullus vulgaris,* having a hard, green rind and a sweet, juicy, usually pink or red pulp. **2.** the plant or vine.

wa′ter mil′foil, any of various aquatic plants, chiefly of the genus *Myriophyllum,* the submersed leaves of which are very finely divided.

wa′ter mill′, a mill with machinery driven by water. [late ME]

wa′ter moc′casin, **1.** cottonmouth. **2.** any of various similar but harmless snakes, as a water snake of the genus *Natrix.*

wa′ter mo′tor, any form of prime mover or motor that is operated by the kinetic energy, pressure, or weight of water.

wa′ter nymph′, **1.** a nymph of the water, as a naiad, a Nereid, or an Oceanid. **2.** See **water lily** (def. 1). **3.** any aquatic plant of the genus *Najas.* [late ME]

wa′ter oak′, **1.** an oak, *Quercus nigra,* of the southern U.S., growing chiefly along streams and swamps. **2.** any of several other American oaks.

wa′ter of crystalliza′tion, *Chem.* water of hydration, formerly thought necessary to crystallization.

wa′ter of hydra′tion, *Chem.* the portion of a hydrate that is represented as, or can be expelled as, water: now usually regarded as being in true molecular combination with the other atoms of the compound, and not existing in the compound as water.

wa′ter ou′zel, any of several stocky, aquatic birds of the family *Cinclidae,* related to the thrushes, esp. *Cinclus aquaticus,* of Europe, and *C. mexicanus,* of western North America, having dense, oily plumage, and noted for the habit of jerking the body when perching and walking.

wa′ter ox′. See **water buffalo.**

wa′ter part′ing, a watershed or divide.

wa′ter pep′per, any of several polygonaceous plants of the genus *Polygonum,* growing in wet places, esp. the smartweed, *P. Hydropiper.*

Wa′ter Pik′, *Trademark.* a small, electrically operated appliance that uses a jet stream of water to remove food particles between teeth, stimulate the gums, etc.

wa′ter pim′pernel, **1.** the brookweed. **2.** the pimpernel, *Anagallis arvensis.*

wa′ter pipe′, a smoking apparatus, as a hookah or narghile, in which the smoke is drawn through a container of water and cooled before reaching the mouth. [late ME]

wa′ter pis′tol, a toy gun that shoots a stream of liquid. Also called **squirt gun.**

wa′ter plan′tain, any aquatic herb of the genus *Alisma,* esp. *A. Plantago-aquatica,* growing in shallow water and having leaves suggesting those of the common plantain.

wa′ter plug′, a fireplug; hydrant.

wa′ter po′lo, an aquatic game in which two teams of seven swimmers each attempt to push, carry, or pass an inflated ball across each other's goal line. Also called **polo.**

wa′ter pow′er, the power of water when used to drive machinery, turbines, etc. Also, **wa′ter·pow′er.**

wa′ter pox′, *Pathol.* See **chicken pox.**

wa·ter·proof (wô′tər pro͞of′, wot′ər-), *adj.* **1.** impervious to water. —*n.* **2.** *Chiefly Brit.* a raincoat or other outer coat impervious to water. **3.** any of several coated or rubberized fabrics that are impervious to water. —*v.t.* **4.** to make waterproof. —**wa′ter·proof′er,** *n.* —**wa′ter·proof′ness,** *n.*

wa·ter·proof·ing (wô′tər pro͞o′fing, -pro͞o′-, wot′ər-), *n.* **1.** a substance by which something is made waterproof. **2.** the act or process of making something waterproof.

wa′ter rat′, **1.** any of various rodents having aquatic habits. **2.** the muskrat, *Ondatra zibethica.* **3.** (in Australia and New Guinea) any of the aquatic rats of the subfamily *Hydromyinae,* esp. of the genus *Hydromys.*

wa·ter-re·pel·lent (wô′tər ri pel′ənt, wot′ər-), *adj.* having a water-resistant finish.

wa·ter-re·sist·ant (wô′tər ri zis′tənt, -zis′-, wot′ər-), *adj.* resisting though not entirely preventing the penetration of water.

wa′ter right′, the right to make use of the water from a particular stream, lake, or irrigation canal.

wa′ter sap′phire, a transparent variety of cordierite sometimes used as a gem.

wa·ter·scape (wô′tər skāp′, wot′ər-), *n.* a picture or view of the sea or other body of water. [WATER + (LAND)SCAPE]

wa·ter·shed (wô′tər shed′, wot′ər-), *n.* **1.** the ridge or crest line dividing two drainage areas; divide. **2.** the region or area drained by a river, stream, etc.; drainage area. **3.** a point of division, as between two periods of history.

wa′ter shield′, **1.** an aquatic plant, *Brasenia Schreberi,* having purple flowers, floating leaves, and a jellylike coating on the underwater stems and roots. **2.** a fanwort, esp. *Cabomba caroliniana.*

wa·ter-sick (wô′tər sik′, wot′ər-), *adj. Agric.* excessively watered, esp. by irrigation, so that tilling and planting cannot be done. [OE *wæter seoc* dropsical]

wa·ter·side (wô′tər sīd′, wot′ər-), *n.* **1.** the margin, bank, or shore of a river, lake, ocean, etc. —*adj.* **2.** of, pertaining to, or situated at the waterside. [late ME]
wa′ter ski′, a short, broad ski designed to plane over water in water-skiing.
wa·ter-ski (wô′tər skē′, wot′ər-), *v.i.*, **-skied, -ski·ing.** to plane over water on water skis or a water ski by grasping a towing rope pulled by a speedboat. —**wa′ter-ski′er,** *n.*
wa′ter snake′, **1.** any of numerous and widely distributed harmless, colubrid snakes of the genus *Natrix*, found in or near fresh water. **2.** any of various other snakes living in or frequenting water.
wa·ter-sol·u·ble (wô′tər sol′yə bəl, wot′ər-), *adj.* capable of dissolving in water.
wa′ter span′iel, a large, heavy-coated spaniel of a breed adapted to retrieve water fowl, as the Irish water spaniel.

Irish water spaniel (2 ft. high at shoulder)

wa·ter·spout (wô′tər spout′, wot′ər-), *n.* **1.** a spout or pipe for discharging water, esp. rainwater; downspout. **2.** a funnel-shaped or tubular portion of a cloud that touches and draws upon the surface of the ocean or other body of water, mixing spray and mist to resemble a column of water. Cf. **tornado** (def. 1). [late ME]
wa′ter sprite′, a sprite or spirit inhabiting the water, as an undine.
wa′ter strid′er, any of several hemipterous insects of the family *Gerridae*, having long, slender legs enabling them to dart about on the surface of water.
wa′ter sys′tem, **1.** a river and all its branches. **2.** a system of supplying water, as throughout a metropolitan area.
wa′ter ta′ble, the depth below which the ground is saturated with water. [late ME]
wa′ter thrush′, **1.** either of two North American warblers, *Seirus noveboracensis* or *S. motacilla*, usually found near streams. **2.** *Brit.* the water ouzel, *Cinclus aquaticus.*
wa·ter·tight (wô′tər tīt′, wot′ər-), *adj.* **1.** constructed or fitted so tightly as to be impervious to water. **2.** so devised or planned as to be impossible to evade or nullify: *a watertight alibi.* [late ME] —**wa′ter·tight′ness,** *n.*
wa′ter ton′, a unit of volume equal to 224 British imperial gallons.
wa′ter tow′er, **1.** a vertical pipe or tower for storing enough water at a height sufficient to maintain a given pressure. **2.** a fire-extinguishing apparatus for spraying water at a great height.
Wa·ter·town (wô′tər toun′, wot′ər-), *n.* **1.** a town in E Massachusetts, on the Charles River, near Boston. 39,307 (1970). **2.** a city in N New York. 30,787 (1970).
wa′ter trap′, *Golf.* a pond, stream, or the like, that serves as a trap in a golf course.
wa′ter treat′ment, the act or process of making water more potable or useful, as by purifying, softening, etc.
wa′ter va′por, gaseous water, esp. when diffused and below its boiling point, as distinguished from steam.
Wa·ter·ville (wô′tər vil′, wot′ər-), *n.* a city in SW Maine. 18,192 (1970).
wa′ter wag′on, **1.** a wagon used to transport water, as in military field operations, a construction site, etc. **2. on the water wagon.** See **wagon** (def. 9).
wa·ter·ward (wô′tər wərd, wot′ər-), *adv.* in the direction of water or a body of water. Also, **wa′ter·wards.** [ME]
wa·ter·way (wô′tər wā′, wot′ər-), *n.* a river, canal, or other navigable channel as a route or way of travel or transport. [ME; OE *wæterweg*]
wa·ter·weed (wô′tər wēd′, wot′ər-), *n.* **1.** an aquatic plant without special use or beauty. **2.** a plant, *Anacharis* (*Elodea*) *canadensis*, of North America, common in fresh-water streams and ponds.
wa′ter wheel′, **1.** a wheel or turbine turned by the weight or momentum of water and used to operate machinery. **2.** a wheel with buckets for raising or drawing water, as a noria. [late ME]
wa′ter wings′, an inflated contrivance, shaped like a pair of wings, worn for keeping afloat while learning to swim.
wa′ter witch′, **1.** Also, **wa′ter witch′er.** a person skilled at water witching; dowser. **2.** a witch believed to haunt lakes, ponds, etc.
wa′ter witch′ing, the supposed discovering of subterranean streams by means of a divining rod.
wa·ter·works (wô′tər wûrks′, wot′ər-), *n., pl.* **-works.** (*construed as sing. or pl.*) a complete system for the collection, storage, purification, and distribution of water.
wa·ter·worn (wô′tər wôrn′, wot′ər-), *adj.* worn or smoothed by the action of moving water.
wa·ter·y (wô′tə rē, wot′ə-), *adj.* **1.** pertaining to or connected with water. **2.** containing much or too much water. **3.** tearful, as the eyes. **4.** of the nature of water: *watery vapor.* **5.** resembling water in appearance or color. **6.** resembling water in fluidity and absence of viscosity. **7.** consisting of water: *a watery grave.* **8.** discharging, filled with, or secreting a waterlike, morbid substance. [OE *wæterig*]
Wat′kins Glen′, a village in W New York, on Seneca Lake: gorge and cascades; automobile races. 2,716 (1970).
Wat′ling Is′land (wot′ling). See **San Salvador** (def. 1).
WATS (wots), Wide Area Telecommunications Service (for unlimited long-distance telephone calls for a flat monthly charge).
Wat·son (wot′sən), *n.* **1. James Dewey,** born 1928, U.S. biologist: Nobel prize for medicine 1962. **2. John Broa·dus** (brô′dəs), 1878–1958, U.S. psychologist. **3. Thomas John,** 1874–1956, U.S. industrialist.
Watson-Watt, (wot′sən wot′), *n.*, **Sir Robert Alexander,** 1892–1972, Scottish physicist.
watt (wot), *n.* the meter-kilogram-second unit of power, equivalent to one joule per second and equal to the power in a circuit in which a current of one ampere flows across a potential difference of one volt. *Abbr.:* W, w, W., w. [named after James WATT]
Watt (wot), *n.* **James,** 1736–1819, Scottish engineer and inventor.
watt·age (wot′ij), *n.* **1.** power, as measured in watts. **2.** the amount of power required to operate an electrical appliance or device.
Wat·teau (wo tō′; *Fr.* VA tō′), *n.* **Jean An·toine** (zhäN äN twAN′), 1684–1721, French painter.
Wat′teau back′, a loose, full back of a woman's gown, held in, in folds, at the neck and slightly below.
watt-hour (wat′our′, -ou′ər), *n.* a unit of work equal to the power of one watt operating for one hour, equivalent to 3600 joules. *Abbr.:* Wh Also, **watt′hour′.**
wat·tle (wot′əl), *n., v.*, **-tled, -tling,** *adj.* —*n.* **1.** Often, **wattles.** *Chiefly Brit.* a number of rods or stakes interwoven with twigs or tree branches for making fences, walls, etc. **2.** *Ornith.* a fleshy lobe or appendage hanging down from the throat or chin of certain birds. —*v.t.* **3.** to bind, wall, frame, etc., with wattles. **4.** to form into a basketwork; interweave; interlace. —*adj.* **5.** built or roofed with wattle or wattles. [ME *wattel*, OE *watul* covering, var. of *wætla* bandage]
wat′tle and daub′, a building technique employing wattles plastered with clay and mud.
wat·tle·bird (wot′əl bûrd′), *n.* an Australian honey eater, *Anthochaera paradoxa*, having a wattle on each side of the throat.
watt·me·ter (wot′mē′tər), *n.* *Elect.* a calibrated instrument for measuring electric power in watts.
Watts (wots), *n.* **Isaac,** 1674–1748, English theologian and hymnist.
Wa·tu·si (wä to͞o′sē), *n., pl.* **-sis,** (*esp. collectively*) **-si.** a member of a tall, slender, originally Hamitic people of Rwanda and Burundi.
Wa·tut·si (wä to͞ot′sē), *n., pl.* **-sis,** (*esp. collectively*) **-si.** Watusi.
Waugh (wô), *n.* **Ev·e·lyn (Arthur St. John)** (ē′və lin, ēv′-lin), 1903–66, English novelist, satirist, and biographer.
waught (*Scot.* wäкнt, wôкнt; *Eng. Dial.* wäft), *Scot. and North Eng.* —*n.* **1.** a copious draft. —*v.t., v.i.* **2.** to drink fully. [?]
Wau·ke·gan (wô kē′gən), *n.* a city in NE Illinois, on Lake Michigan, N of Chicago. 65,269 (1970).
Wau·ke·sha (wô′ki shô′), *n.* a city in SE Wisconsin, W of Milwaukee. 40,274 (1970).
waul (wôl), *v.i.* to cry like a cat or a newborn infant; squall. Also, **wawl.** [? < Scand; cf. Icel *vāla* to wail. See CATERWAUL]
Wau·sau (wô′sô), *n.* a city in central Wisconsin. 32,806 (1970).
Wau·wa·to·sa (wô′wə tō′sə), *n.* a city in SE Wisconsin, near Milwaukee. 58,676 (1970).
wave (wāv), *n., v.*, **waved, wav·ing.** —*n.* **1.** a disturbance on the surface of a liquid body, as the sea or a lake, in the form of a moving ridge or swell. **2.** something that suggests this action, as an overwhelming feeling, a rapidly growing trend, or a spreading condition: *a wave of anger; a wave of installment buying; a heat wave.* **3.** a mass movement, as of settlers, migrating birds, etc. **4.** an outward curve in a surface or line; undulation. **5.** the act or an instance of waving, as a flag or the hand. **6.** waviness, as of the hair. **7.** a special treatment to impart waviness. **8.** *Physics.* a progressive disturbance propagated from point to point in a medium or space without progress or advance by the points themselves, as in the transmission of sound or light. **9.** *Archaic.* **a.** a body of water. **b.** the sea. —*v.i.* **10.** to move to and fro, as a hand in salutation or a branch or flag stirred by the wind. **11.** to move the hand to and fro as a signal or gesture. **12.** to curve alternately in opposite directions. —*v.t.* **13.** to cause to flutter or move to and fro. **14.** to signify by waving the hand or something held in the hand: *to wave goodbye.* **15.** to direct as specified by waving: *to wave a train to a halt.* **16.** to form in a series of alternating curves. **17.** to give a wavy appearance or pattern to, as silk. **18.** to impart a wave to (the hair). [ME; OE *wafian*; c. MHG *waben.* See WAVER[1]] —**wave′less,** *adj.* —**wave′like′,** *adj.*
—**Syn. 1.** undulation, sea. WAVE, BREAKER, SURF refer to a ridge or swell on the surface of water. WAVE is the general word: *waves in a high wind.* A BREAKER is a wave breaking, or about to break, upon the shore or upon rocks: *the roar of breakers.* SURF is the collective name for breakers: *Heavy surf makes bathing dangerous.*
Wave (wāv), *n.* an enlisted member of the Waves. Also, **WAVE.** [see WAVES]
waved (wāvd), *adj.* having a form, outline, or appearance resembling waves; undulating.
wave′ front′, *Physics.* a surface, real or imaginary, that is the locus of all adjacent points at which the phase of oscillation is the same.
wave′ func′tion, *Physics.* **1.** a solution of a wave equation. **2.** the solution of the Schrödinger wave equation: the square of the absolute value of its amplitude represents the probability of finding a given particle in a given element of volume.
wave′ guide′, *Electronics.* a piece of hollow, conducting tubing, usually rectangular or circular in cross section, used as a conductor or directional transmitter for microwaves propagated through its interior.
wave·length (wāv′lengkth′), *n.* *Physics.* the distance, measured in the direction of propagation of a wave, between two successive points in the wave that are characterized by the same phase of oscillation. Also, **wave′ length′.**
wave·let (wāv′lit), *n.* a small wave; ripple.
wa·vell·ite (wā′və līt′), *n.* a hydrous aluminum fluorophosphate occurring as a white to yellowish-green or brown mineral, often in radiating fibers. [named after W. *Wavell* (d. 1829), English physician, its discoverer; see -ITE[1]]
wave′ mechan′ics, *Physics.* the part of quantum mechanics that describes elementary particles by means of their wavelike properties.
wave·me·ter (wāv′mē′tər), *n.* a device for measuring the wavelength or frequency of a radio wave.
wave′ num′ber, the number of waves in one centimeter of light in a given wavelength.
wa·ver[1] (wā′vər), *v.i.* **1.** to sway to and fro; flutter. **2.** to flicker or quiver, as light. **3.** to become unsteady; begin to fail. **4.** shake or tremble, as the hands or voice. **5.** to hesitate between choices; feel or show doubt, indecision, etc. **6.** (of things) to fluctuate or vary. —*n.* **7.** an act of wavering, fluttering, or vacillating. [ME (see WAVE, -ER[6]); c.

dial. G *wabern* to move about, Icel *vafra* to toddle] —**wa′ver·er,** *n.* —**wa′ver·ing·ly,** *adv.*
—**Syn. 4.** quiver. **5.** WAVER, FLUCTUATE, VACILLATE refer to an alternation or hesitation between one direction and another. WAVER means to hesitate between choices: *to waver between two courses of action.* FLUCTUATE suggests irregular change from one side to the other or up and down: *The prices of stocks fluctuate when there is bad news followed by good.* VACILLATE is to make up one's mind and change it again suddenly; to be undecided as to what to do: *We must not vacillate but must set a day.*

wav·er[2] (wā′vər), *n.* **1.** a person who waves or causes something to flutter or have a waving motion. **2.** a person who specializes in waving hair. **3.** something, as a curling iron, used for waving hair. [WAVE + -ER[1]]

Waves (wāvz), *n.* (*construed as sing. or pl.*) Women's Reserve, U.S. Naval Reserve. Also, **WAVES.** [*W*(*omen's*) *A*(*ppointed*) *V*(*olunteer*) *E*(*mergency*) *S*(*ervice*)]

wave′ the′ory, *Physics.* the theory that light is transmitted as a wave, similar to oscillations in magnetic and electric fields. Also called **undulatory theory.** Cf. **corpuscular theory.**

wave′ train′, *Physics.* a series of successive waves spaced at regular intervals.

wav·y (wā′vē), *adj.*, **wav·i·er, wav·i·est.** **1.** curving alternately in opposite directions; undulating. **2.** abounding or characterized by waves: *the wavy sea.* **3.** resembling or suggesting waves: *a cotton material with a wavy pattern.* **4.** *Bot.* **a.** bending with successive curves in opposite directions, as a margin. **b.** having such a margin, as a leaf. **5.** *Heraldry.* noting a partition line or ordinary formed in a series of S-curves. Cf. **undé. 6.** vibrating or tremulous; unsteady; wavering. —**wav′i·ly,** *adv.* —**wav′i·ness,** *n.*

wawl (wôl), *v.i. Chiefly Scot.* waul.

wax[1] (waks), *n.* **1.** Also called **beeswax.** a solid, yellowish substance secreted by bees, plastic when warm and melting at about 145°F, used by bees in constructing their honeycomb. **2.** any of various similar substances, as spermaceti, and the secretions of certain insects and plants. **3.** any of a group of substances composed of hydrocarbons, alcohols, fatty acids, and esters that are solid at ordinary temperatures. **4.** cerumen; earwax. **5.** a resinous substance used by shoemakers for rubbing thread. **6.** See **sealing wax.** —*v.t.* **7.** to rub, smear, stiffen, polish, etc., with wax: *to wax the kitchen floor.* —*adj.* **8.** made of, pertaining to, or resembling wax. [ME; OE *weax;* c. D *was,* G *Wachs,* Icel *vax*] —**wax′er,** *n.* —**wax′like′,** *adj.*

wax[2] (waks), *v.i.*, **waxed; waxed** or (*Archaic*) **wax·en; wax·ing.** **1.** to increase in extent, quantity, intensity, power, etc.: *Discord waxed at an alarming rate.* **2.** (of the moon) to increase in the extent of its visible illuminated portion. Cf. **wane** (def. 1). See diag. at **moon. 3.** to grow or become: *He waxed angry at the insinuation.* [ME; OE *weaxan;* c. G *wachsen;* akin to WAIST]

wax[3] (waks), *n. Chiefly Brit.* a fit of anger; rage. [? special use of WAX[2]]

wax′ bean′, **1.** a variety of string bean bearing yellowish, waxy pods. **2.** the pod of this plant, used for food.

wax·ber·ry (waks′ber′ē, -bə rē), *n., pl.* **-ries.** **1.** the wax myrtle, or the bayberry. **2.** the snowberry.

wax·bill (waks′bil′), *n.* any of several Old World weaverbirds, esp. of the genus *Estrilda,* having white, pink, or red bills of waxy appearance, often kept as pets.

waxed′ pa′per. See **wax paper.**

wax·en[1] (wak′sən), *adj.* **1.** made of or covered, polished, or treated with wax. **2.** resembling or suggesting wax: *Illness gave his face a waxen appearance.* **3.** weak, manageable, or impressionable, as a person or his characteristics. [ME]

waxen[2] (wak′sən), *v. Archaic.* a pp. of **wax**[2].

wax′ myr′tle, a shrub or tree of the genus *Myrica,* as *M. cerifera,* bearing small berries coated with wax that is sometimes used in making candles.

wax′ palm′, **1.** a tall, pinnate-leaved palm, *Ceroxylon andicola,* of the Andes, whose stem and leaves yield a resinous wax. **2.** Also called **carnauba.** a palmate-leaved palm, *Copernicia cerifera,* of Brazil, having leaves coated with a hard wax.

wax′ pa′per, a whitish, translucent wrapping paper made moistureproof by a paraffin coating. Also, **waxed paper.**

wax·plant (waks′plant′, -plänt′), *n.* any climbing or trailing, asclepiadaceous plant of the genus *Hoya,* of tropical Asia and Australia, having glossy leaves and umbels of pink, white, or yellowish, waxy flowers.

wax·weed (waks′wēd′), *n.* an American lythraceous herb, *Cuphea* (or *Parsonsia*) *petiolata,* having a viscid pubescence and purple flowers.

wax·wing (waks′wing′), *n.* any of several passerine birds of the family *Bombycillidae,* having a showy crest and secondaries tipped with a red, waxy material.

wax·work (waks′wûrk′), *n.* **1.** an artistic object made of wax, as a figurine or ornament. **2.** a life-size, lifelike representation of a human being, made of wax.

wax·works (waks′wûrks′), *n., pl.* **-works.** (*usually construed as sing.*) an exhibition of or a museum for displaying wax figures, ornaments, etc.

wax·y[1] (wak′sē), *adj.*, **wax·i·er, wax·i·est.** **1.** resembling wax in appearance or characteristics. **2.** abounding in, covered with, or made of wax. **3.** *Pathol.* pertaining to or suffering from a degeneration caused by deposits of an insoluble waxlike material in an organ. [WAX[1] + -Y[1]] —**wax′i·ly,** *adv.* —**wax′i·ness,** *n.*

wax·y[2] (wak′sē), *adj.*, **wax·i·er, wax·i·est.** *Chiefly Brit.* angry. [WAX[3] + -Y[1]]

way (wā), *n.* **1.** manner, mode, or fashion: *a new way of looking at a matter; to reply in a polite way.* **2.** characteristic or habitual manner: *He has many strange ways.* **3.** a method, plan, or means for attaining a goal: *a way to reduce costs.* **4.** a respect or particular: *The plan is defective in several ways.* **5.** a direction: *Look this way.* **6.** a vicinity: *We're having a drought out our way.* **7.** passage or progress to a definite goal: *to find one's way.* **8.** distance: *They've come a long way.* **9.** a path or course to a place: *What's the shortest way to town?* **10.** an ancient Roman road: *the Appian Way.* **11.** *Chiefly Brit.* a minor street in a town: *He lives in Stepney Way.* **12.** a means of passage or movement (usually used in combination): *highway; doorway.* **13.** course or mode of procedure that one chooses or wills: *She always has her own way.* **14.** the method or manner of acting that one advocates: *We'll do it your way.* **15.** a person's intended path or course of action: *He won't let scruples stand in his way.* **16.** Often, **ways.** habits or customs: *I don't like his ways at all.* **17.** condition, as to health, prosperity, or the like: *to be in a bad way.* **18.** the scope of a person's experience or notice: *the best device that ever came in my way.* **19.** a course of life, action, or experience: *The way of transgressors is hard.* **20.** *Law.* a right of way. **21.** *Naut.* **a. ways,** groundways down which a hull slides in being launched. **b.** movement or speed through the water. **22.** *Mach.* a guide for something that slides. **23. by the way,** incidentally (used to introduce a question or comment): *By the way, have you received that letter yet?* **24. by way of, a.** by the route of; through; via. **b.** as a method or means of: *to number articles by way of distinguishing them.* **c.** *Chiefly Brit.* in the state or position of; ostensibly (being, doing, etc.): *He is by way of being an authority on the subject.* **25. come one's way,** to come to one; befall one. **26. give way, a.** to withdraw or retreat. **b.** to collapse; yield. **27. give way to, a.** to yield to. **b.** to lose control of (one's temper, emotions, etc.): *to give way to anger.* **28. go out of one's way, a.** make an unusual effort to do something. **b.** to do something deliberately or maliciously. **29. lead the way, a.** to act as a guide. **b.** to take the initiative; set the example. **30. make one's way, a.** to go forward; proceed. **b.** to achieve worldly recognition or success. **31. make way,** to allow to pass; clear the way. **32. out of the way, a.** in a state or condition so as not to obstruct or annoy: *I feel better, now that problem is out of the way.* **b.** at a distance from the usual route. **c.** improper; amiss. **d.** extraordinary; unusual. **33. under way, a.** in motion. **b.** in progress, as an enterprise.
—*adv.* **34.** Also, **'way.** away; from this or that place: *Go way.* **35.** to a great degree or at quite a distance; far: *way too heavy; way down the road.* [ME; OE *weg;* c. D, G *Weg,* Icel *vegr,* Goth *wigs*]
—**Syn. 3.** scheme. See **method.**

way·bill (wā′bil′), *n.* a list of goods sent by a common carrier, as a railroad, with shipping directions.

way·far·er (wā′fâr′ər), *n.* a traveler, esp. on foot. [ME *weyfarere.* See WAY, FARE, -ER[1]]

way·far·ing (wā′fâr′ing), *adj., n.* traveling, esp. on foot. [ME; OE *wegfarende.* See WAY, FARE, -ING[1], -ING[2]]

way·go·ing (wā′gō′ing), *Chiefly Scot. and North Eng.* —*adj.* **1.** going away; departing. **2.** of or pertaining to a person who goes away. —*n.* **3.** the act of leaving; departure.

Way·land (wā′lənd), *n.* (in N European folklore) the king of the elves, a smith and artificer: known in Scandinavia as Völund and in Germany as Wieland.

way·lay (wā lā′), *v.t.*, **-laid, -lay·ing.** to intercept or attack from ambush, as in order to rob, seize, or slay. [WAY + LAY[1], after MLG, MD *wegelagen* to lie in wait < *wegelage* a lying in wait] —**way·lay′er,** *n.*

way·less (wā′lis), *adj.* lacking a way, road, or path; trackless: *wayless countryside.* [ME; OE *wegleas*]

Wayne (wān), *n.* **1. Anthony** ("*Mad Anthony*"), 1745–96, American Revolutionary War general. **2.** a township in N New Jersey. 49,141 (1970). **3.** a city in SE Michigan, near Detroit. 21,054 (1970).

way′ out′, **1.** the means by which a predicament, dilemma, etc., may be solved. **2.** *Chiefly Brit.* an exit or exit door, as in a theater.

way-out (wā′out′), *adj. Informal.* exotic or esoteric in character. [(A)WAY + OUT]

way′ point′, **1.** a place or point between major points on a route. **2.** See **way station.**

-ways, a suffix appearing in native English adverbs: *always; sideways.* [ME, comb. form of *weyes,* OE *weges, gen.* sing. of *weg* WAY]

ways′ and means′, **1.** legislation and methods for raising revenue for public expense. **2.** methods and means of accomplishing or paying for something. [late ME]

way·side (wā′sīd′), *n.* **1.** the side of the way; land immediately adjacent to a road, highway, path, etc.; roadside. —*adj.* **2.** being, situated, or found at or along the wayside: *a wayside inn.* [late ME]

way′ sta′tion, *U.S.* a station intermediate between principal stations, as on a railroad.

way′ train′, a train that stops at every station along a route; local train.

way·ward (wā′wərd), *adj.* **1.** turned or turning away from what is right or proper; willful; disobedient. **2.** swayed or prompted by caprice; capricious. **3.** turning or changing irregularly; irregular: *a wayward stream.* [ME, aph. var. of *awayward.* See AWAY, -WARD] —**way′ward·ly,** *adv.* —**way′ward·ness,** *n.* —**Syn. 1.** headstrong, unruly. See **willful.**

way·worn (wā′wōrn′, -wôrn′), *adj.* worn or wearied by travel.

Wa·zir·a·bad (wə zēr′ä bäd′), *n.* Balkh.

Wa·zir·i·stan (wä zēr′i stän′), *n.* a mountainous region in Pakistan, on the border of Afghanistan.

Wb, weber; webers.

W/B, waybill. Also, **W.B.**

w.b., **1.** warehouse book. **2.** water ballast. **3.** waybill. **4.** westbound.

WbN, See **west by north.**

WbS, See **west by south.**

w.c., **1.** water closet. **2.** without charge.

W.C.T.U., Woman's Christian Temperance Union.

wd., **1.** ward. **2.** word.

W.D., War Department.

we (wē), *pron. pl.; possessive* **our** or **ours,** *objective* **us.** **1.** nominative pl. of **I. 2.** (used to denote oneself and another or others that are mentioned or implied): *the world we live in; we doctors; We have two children.* **3.** I (used where an impersonal quality is desirable, as in royal proclamations or editorials). **4.** you (used familiarly, often with the implication of mild condescension or sarcasm): *We know that's naughty, don't we?* [ME, OE; c. D *wij*, G *wir*, Icel *vēr*, Goth *weis*]

weak (wēk), *adj.* **1.** liable to yield, break, or collapse under moderate pressure or strain. **2.** lacking in vigor or ability, as a person, his mind, or a part of his body, due to being very young, very old, sick, etc. **3.** lacking in courage, resolution, authority, etc. **4.** unable to satisfy a critical mind, as an argument or an artistic composition. **5.** deficient, as in attainment or resources: *I am weak in spelling.* **6.** of little force, intensity, flavor, etc.: *a weak pulse; weak sunlight; weak tea.* **7.** revealing weakness of body, mind, character, etc.: *a weak smile; a weak compromise.* **8.** unstressed, as a syllable, vowel, or word. **9.** *Gram.* **a.** (of Germanic verbs) inflected with suffixes, without inherited change of the root vowel, as English *walk, walked.* **b.** (of Germanic nouns and adjectives) inflected with endings originally appropriate to stems terminating in *-n*, as *alte* in German *der alte Mann* ("the old man") is a weak adjective. **10.** *Com.* characterized by a decline in prices. [ME *weik* < Scand (cf. Icel *veikr*); c. OE *wāc*, D *week*, G *weich;* akin to OE *wīcan* to yield, give way, Icel *vīkja* to move, turn, draw back, G *weichen* to yield] **—weak′ish,** *adj.* **—weak′ish·ly,** *adv.* **—weak′ish·ness,** *n.*

—Syn. 1. fragile, frail, delicate. **2.** sickly, unwell, invalid. WEAK, DECREPIT, FEEBLE, WEAKLY imply a lack of strength or of good health. WEAK means not physically strong, because of extreme youth, old age, illness, etc.: *weak after an attack of fever.* DECREPIT means old and broken in health to a marked degree: *decrepit and barely able to walk.* FEEBLE denotes much the same as WEAK, but connotes being pitiable or inferior: *feeble and almost senile.* WEAKLY suggests a long-standing sickly condition, a state of chronic bad health: *A weakly child may become a strong man.* **3.** ineffective, ineffectual; vacillating, irresolute. **4.** unsound, ineffective, inadequate. **5.** wanting, short, lacking. **—Ant.** strong.

weak·en (wē′kən), *v.t., v.i.* to make or become weak or weaker. **—weak′en·er,** *n.* **—Syn.** enfeeble, debilitate, enervate, deplete, diminish. **—Ant.** strengthen.

weak′er sex′, the female sex; women.

weak·fish (wēk′fish′), *n., pl.* (*esp. collectively*) **-fish,** (*esp. referring to two or more kinds or species*) **-fish·es.** any sciaenoid food fish of the genus *Cynoscion*, as *C. regalis*, found along the Atlantic and Gulf coasts of the U.S. [< D *weekvis* (obs.) = *week* soft (see WEAK) + *vis* FISH]

weak-head·ed (wēk′hed′id), *adj.* **1.** easily intoxicated by alcoholic beverages. **2.** prone to dizziness or giddiness. **3.** weak-minded. **—weak′-head′ed·ly,** *adv.* **—weak′-head′ed·ness,** *n.*

weak-heart·ed (wēk′här′tid), *adj.* without courage or fortitude; fainthearted. **—weak′heart′ed·ly,** *adv.* **—weak′heart′ed·ness,** *n.*

weak-kneed (wēk′nēd′), *adj.* yielding readily to opposition, pressure, intimidation, etc. **—weak′-kneed′ly,** *adv.* **—weak′-kneed′ness,** *n.*

weak·ling (wēk′ling), *n.* **1.** a person who is physically or morally weak. **—***adj.* **2.** weak; not strong.

weak·ly (wēk′lē), *adj.*, **-li·er, -li·est,** *adv.* **—***adj.* **1.** weak or feeble in constitution; not robust; sickly. **—***adv.* **2.** in a weak manner. [ME *weekely*] **—weak′li·ness,** *n.* **—Syn. 1.** See **weak.**

weak-mind·ed (wēk′mīn′did), *adj.* **1.** having or showing a lack of mental firmness. **2.** having or showing mental feebleness. **—weak′-mind′ed·ly,** *adv.* **—weak′-mind′ed·ness,** *n.*

weak·ness (wēk′nis), *n.* **1.** the state or quality of being weak; lack of strength, firmness, vigor, etc. **2.** an inadequate or defective quality, as in a person's character. **3.** a self-indulgent liking or special fondness, as for a particular object: *a weakness for opera.* **4.** an object of such liking or fondness. [ME *weikenes*] **—Syn. 1.** fragility. **2.** failing, flaw. See **fault. —Ant. 1.** strength.

weak′ sis′ter, *Slang.* a vacillating person; coward.

weal[1] (wēl), *n.* **1.** *Archaic.* well-being, prosperity, or happiness. **2.** *Obs.* wealth or riches. **3.** *Obs.* the body politic; the state. [ME *wele*, OE *wela;* cf. WELL[1]]

weal[2] (wēl), *n.* wheal. [var. of WALE[1], with *ea* of WHEAL]

weald (wēld), *n.* wooded or uncultivated country. [ME *weeld*, OE *weald* forest; c. G *Wald;* cf. WOLD[1]]

Weald (wēld), *n.* **the,** a region in SE England, in Kent, Surrey, and Essex counties: once a forest area; now an agricultural region.

wealth (welth), *n.* **1.** a great quantity or store of money or property of value. **2.** a plentiful amount: *a wealth of detail.* **3.** *Econ.* **a.** all goods that have a monetary or exchange value. **b.** anything that has utility and is capable of being appropriated or exchanged. **4.** rich or valuable contents or produce: *the wealth of the soil.* **5.** the state of being rich; prosperity; affluence: *persons of wealth and standing.* **6.** *Obs.* happiness. [ME *welth* (see WELL[1], -TH[1]); modeled on *health*] **—wealth′less,** *adj.* **—Syn. 3a.** possessions, assets, goods, property, money. **5.** opulence, fortune. **—Ant. 5.** poverty.

wealth·y (wel′thē), *adj.*, **wealth·i·er, wealth·i·est. 1.** having great wealth; rich; affluent. **2.** having any stated or implied thing in abundance. [late ME] **—wealth′i·ly,** *adv.* **—wealth′i·ness,** *n.* **—Syn. 1.** prosperous, well-to-do, moneyed. See **rich. —Ant. 1.** poor.

wean (wēn), *v.t.* **1.** to accustom (a child or young animal) to food other than its mother's milk. **2.** to free (a person or his feelings) from a habit, attitude, etc., regarded as undesirable. [ME *wene*, OE *wen(ian);* c. D *wennen*, G *(ge)wöhnen*, Icel *venja* to accustom] **—wean·ed·ness** (wē′nid nis, wēnd′-), *n.*

wean·ling (wēn′ling), *n.* **1.** a child or animal newly weaned. **—***adj.* **2.** newly weaned.

weap·on (wep′ən), *n.* **1.** any instrument or device for attack or defense in a fight. **2.** anything used against an opponent, adversary, or victim: *the weapon of satire.* **3.** *Zool.* any part or organ serving for attack or defense, as claws, horns, teeth, stings, etc. [ME *wepen*, OE *wǣpen;* c. Icel *vāpn*, Goth *wēpna* (pl.), G *Waffe*] **—weap′oned,** *adj.*

weap·on·ry (wep′ən rē), *n.* **1.** weapons or weaponlike instruments collectively. **2.** the invention and production of weapons.

wear (wâr), *v.*, **wore, worn, wear·ing,** *n.* **—***v.t.* **1.** to carry upon or have fitted to one's body or clothing as a covering, support, or ornament: *to wear a dress; to wear a brace; to wear a medal.* **2.** to modify one's appearance with: *to wear a disguise; to wear a smile.* **3.** to cause gradual deterioration in, as from prolonged strain or friction: *to wear a sock through.* **4.** to create (a hole, depression, etc.) in something through such deterioration. **5.** to harass, weaken, or fatigue. **6.** to pass (time) gradually or tediously. **7.** *Naut.* to bring (a vessel) on another tack by turning her head away from the wind until the wind is on her stern, and then bringing her head up toward the wind on the other side. **—***v.i.* **8.** to deteriorate, as from prolonged strain or friction. **9.** to admit of being worn or subjected to wear. **10.** to respond to wear or strain in a specified way: *to wear thin.* **11.** (of time) to pass, esp. slowly or tediously. **12.** *Naut.* (of a vessel) to be worn. **13. wear down, a.** to reduce or impair by long wearing. **b.** to make weary; tire. **c.** to prevail over by persistence; overcome: *to wear down the opposition.* **14. wear off,** to diminish gradually, as in effect; disappear: *The drug began to wear off.* **15. wear out, a.** to make or become unfit or useless through wear. **b.** to exhaust, as by continued strain; weary. **—***n.* **16.** the act of wearing; use, as of a garment: *articles for winter wear.* **17.** the state of being worn, as on the person. **18.** clothing (often used in combination): *travel wear; sportswear.* **19.** gradual deterioration as from prolonged strain or friction: *The carpet shows wear.* **20.** the quality of resisting deterioration with use; durability. **21.** *Naut.* the maneuver of wearing a vessel. [ME *were*, OE *wer(ian);* c. Icel *verja*, Goth *wasjan* to clothe] **—wear′a·ble,** *adj.* **—wear′er,** *n.*

wear·a·bil·i·ty (wâr′ə bil′i tē), *n.* the durability of clothing under normal wear.

wear·a·ble (wâr′ə bəl), *adj.* capable of being worn; suitable or ready for wearing.

wear′ and tear′ (târ), damage or deterioration resulting from ordinary use; normal depreciation.

wea·ri·ful (wēr′ē fəl), *adj.* **1.** full of weariness. **2.** causing weariness; tedious; tiresome. [late ME] **—wea′ri·ful·ly,** *adv.* **—wea′ri·ful·ness,** *n.*

wea·ri·less (wēr′ē lis), *adj.* unwearying; tireless. [late ME] **—wea′ri·less·ly,** *adv.*

wear·ing (wâr′ing), *adj.* **1.** pertaining to or made for wear. **2.** tiring; wearying. **—wear′ing·ly,** *adv.*

wear′ing appar′el, clothing; garments.

wea·ri·some (wēr′ē səm), *adj.* **1.** causing weariness; fatiguing. **2.** tiresome or tedious. [late ME *werysom*] **—wea′ri·some·ly,** *adv.* **—wea′ri·some·ness,** *n.* **—Syn. 1.** tiring. **2.** boring, monotonous, dull. **—Ant. 2.** interesting.

wear·proof (wâr′pro͞of′), *adj.* resistant to damage or deterioration by normal use or wear.

wea·ry (wēr′ē), *adj.*, **-ri·er, -ri·est,** *v.*, **-ried, -ry·ing. —***adj.* **1.** physically or mentally exhausted by hard work, strain, etc.; fatigued. **2.** characterized by or causing fatigue: *a weary journey.* **3.** impatient or dissatisfied with something (often fol. by *of*): *weary of excuses.* **—***v.t., v.i.* **4.** to make or become weary; fatigue or tire: *The long hours of work have wearied me.* **5.** to make or grow impatient or dissatisfied with something or at having too much of something (often fol. by *of*): *We had quickly wearied of such witless entertainment.* [ME *wery*, OE *wērig;* c. OS *-wōrig;* akin to OE *wōrian* to crumble, break down, totter] **—wea′ri·ly,** *adv.* **—wea′ri·ness,** *n.* **—wea′ry·ing·ly,** *adv.* **—Syn. 1.** See **tired**[1]. **4.** exhaust.

wea·sand (wē′zənd), *n. Archaic.* **1.** throat. **2.** esophagus; gullet. **3.** trachea; windpipe. Also, *esp. Scot.*, **weazand, wessand.** [ME *wesand*, OE *wǣsend*, var. of *wāsend* gullet; c. OFris *wāsande* windpipe]

wea·sel (wē′zəl), *n., pl.* **-sels,** (*esp. collectively*) **-sel,** *v.* **—***n.* **1.** any small carnivore of the genus *Mustela*, of the family *Mustelidae*, having a long, slender body and feeding chiefly on small rodents. **2.** any of various similar animals of the family *Mustelidae.* **3.** a cunning, sneaky person. **—***v.i.* **4.** to evade an obligation, duty, or the like; renege (often fol. by *out*): *He tried to weasel out of the agreement.* [ME *wesele*, OE *wesle, weosule;* c. OHG *wisula*, G *Wiesel*]

Weasel,
Mustela frenata
(Total length 16 in.; tail 6 in.)

wea′sel words′, statements that are evasive, indirect, or intentionally misleading or ambiguous. **—wea′sel-word′ed,** *adj.*

weath·er (weth′ər), *n.* **1.** the state of the atmosphere with respect to wind, temperature, cloudiness, moisture, pressure, etc. **2.** a strong wind or storm or strong winds and storms collectively: *We've had some real weather this spring.* **3. under the weather,** *Informal.* **a.** somewhat ailing; ill. **b.** suffering from a hangover. **c.** more or less drunk. **—***v.t.* **4.** to expose to the weather; dry, season, or otherwise affect by exposure to the air or atmosphere: *to weather lumber before marketing it.* **5.** to discolor, disintegrate, or affect injuriously, as by the effects of weather: *These crumbling stones have been weathered by the centuries.* **6.** to bear up against and come safely through (a storm, danger, trouble, etc.). **7.** *Naut.* (of a ship, mariner, etc.) to pass or sail to the windward of: *to weather a cape.* **—***v.i.* **8.** to undergo change, esp. disintegration or change of color, as the result of exposure to atmospheric conditions. **9.** to endure or resist exposure to the weather. [ME, OE *weder;* c. D *weder*, G *Wetter*, Icel *vethr*] **—weath′er·a·bil′i·ty,** *n.* **—weath′er·er,** *n.*

weath·er-beat·en (weth′ər bēt′ᵊn), *adj.* **1.** bearing evidences of wear or damage as a result of exposure to the weather. **2.** showing signs of a life in the open: *a weather-beaten face.*

weath·er·board (weth′ər bōrd′, -bôrd′), *n.* **1.** a type of board used as a siding for a building, having parallel faces with a rabbet in the upper edge and so laid that the lower edge of each board overlaps the upper edge of the board below and fits within the rabbet. **2.** *Naut.* the side of a vessel toward the wind. **—***v.t.* **3.** to cover or furnish with weatherboards.

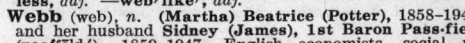

weath·er·board·ing (weth′ər bōr′ding, -bôr′-), *n.* a covering or facing of weatherboards.
weath·er-bound (weth′ər bound′), *adj.* delayed or shut in by bad weather, as a ship or an airplane.
Weath′er Bu′reau, former name of **National Weather Service.**
weath·er·cock (weth′ər kok′), *n.* **1.** a weather vane decorated with the figure of a cock. **2.** (loosely) any weather vane. [ME *wedercoc*]
weath′er deck′, (of a ship) the uppermost continuous deck exposed to the weather.
weath′er eye′, **1.** sensitivity and alertness to signs of change in the weather. **2.** a careful watch for change, as in circumstance, condition, status, etc.
weath·er·glass (weth′ər glas′, -gläs′), *n.* any of various instruments, as a barometer, that indicates the state of the atmosphere.
weath·er·ize (weth′ə rīz′), *v.t.* **-ized, -iz·ing.** to prepare (a house or other building) so as to protect against severe weather, esp. against winter cold, as with insulation, heating, and storm windows. **—weath′er·i·za′tion,** *n.*
weath·er·ly (weth′ər lē), *adj. Naut.* (of a ship or boat) making very little leeway when close-hauled.
weath·er·man (weth′ər man′), *n., pl.* **-men.** a person who forecasts or reports weather conditions, as an employee of the U.S. Weather Bureau or a radio or television announcer who broadcasts weather reports.
weath′er map′, a map or chart showing weather conditions over a wide area at a particular time.
weath·er·proof (weth′ər pro͞of′), *adj.* **1.** able to withstand exposure to all kinds of weather. **—*v.t.* 2.** to make (something) weatherproof. **—weath′er·proof′ness,** *n.*
weath′er report′, a summary of weather conditions, often including predicted conditions, for an area.
weath′er sta′tion, an installation equipped and used for the making of meteorological observations.
weath·er-strip (weth′ər strip′), *v.t.,* **-stripped, -strip·ping.** to apply weather stripping to (something).
weath′er strip′ping, **1.** Also, **weath′er strip′.** a narrow strip of metal, wood, rubber, etc., placed between a door or window sash and its frame to exclude rain, air, etc. **2.** such strips collectively.
weath·er·tight (weth′ər tīt′), *adj.* secure against wind, rain, etc. **—weath′er·tight′ness,** *n.*
weath′er vane′, vane (def. 1).
weath·er-wise (weth′ər wīz′), *adj.* **1.** skillful in predicting weather. **2.** skillful in predicting reactions, opinions, etc.: *weather-wise political experts.* [late ME *wederwise*]
weath·er·worn (weth′ər wōrn′, -wôrn′), *adj.* weather-beaten.
weave (wēv), *v.,* **wove** or (*Rare*) **weaved; wo·ven** or **wove; weav·ing;** *n.* **—*v.t.* 1.** to interlace (threads, yarns, strips, fibrous material, etc.) so as to form a fabric or material. **2.** to form by such interlacing: *to weave a basket; to weave cloth.* **3.** (of a spider or larva) to form (a web); spin. **4.** to form by combining various elements or details into a connected whole: *to weave a tale; to weave a plan.* **5.** to introduce as an element or detail into a connected whole (usually fol. by *in* or *into*): *to weave a melody into a musical composition.* **6.** to move (someone or something) along in a winding or zigzag course; move from side to side, esp. to avoid obstructions: *to weave one's way through traffic.* **—*v.i.* 7.** to form or construct something, as fabric, by interlacing threads, yarns, strips, etc. **8.** to compose a connected whole by combining various elements or details. **9.** to move or proceed from side to side or in a zigzag course: *dancers weaving in time to the music.* **—*n.* 10.** a pattern of or method for interlacing yarns. [ME *weve,* OE *wefan;* c. Icel *vefa,* G *weben;* see WEB]

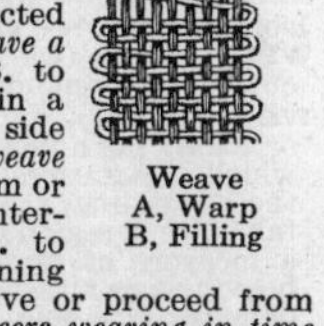

Weave
A, Warp
B, Filling

weav·er (wē′vər), *n.* **1.** a person who weaves. **2.** a person whose occupation is weaving. **3.** a weaverbird. [late ME *wevere*]
Wea·ver (wē′vər), *n.* **Robert (Clifton),** born 1907, U.S. economist and government official: first Secretary of Housing and Urban Development 1966–68.
weav·er·bird (wē′vər bûrd′), *n.* any of numerous, chiefly African and Asian, passerine birds of the family *Ploceidae,* that build elaborately woven nests. Also called **weav′er finch′.**
wea′ver's hitch′. See **sheet bend.** Also called **weav′er's knot′.**
wea·zand (wē′zənd), *n. Chiefly Scot.* weasand.

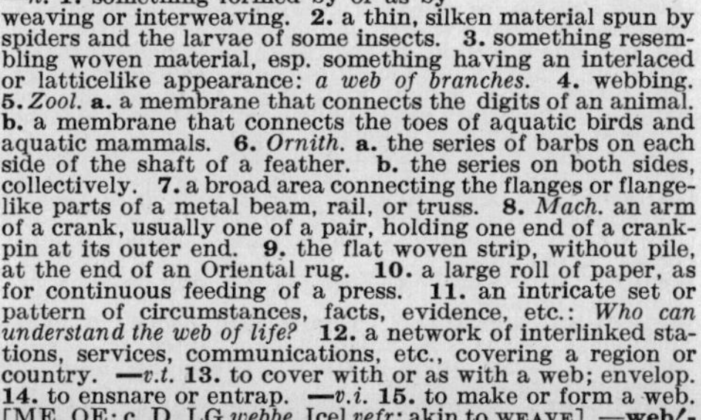
Weaverbird, *Ploceus cucullatus* (Length 7 in.)

web (web), *n., v.,* **webbed, web·bing.** **—*n.* 1.** something formed by or as by weaving or interweaving. **2.** a thin, silken material spun by spiders and the larvae of some insects. **3.** something resembling woven material, esp. something having an interlaced or latticelike appearance: *a web of branches.* **4.** webbing. **5.** *Zool.* **a.** a membrane that connects the digits of an animal. **b.** a membrane that connects the toes of aquatic birds and aquatic mammals. **6.** *Ornith.* **a.** the series of barbs on each side of the shaft of a feather. **b.** the series on both sides, collectively. **7.** a broad area connecting the flanges or flangelike parts of a metal beam, rail, or truss. **8.** *Mach.* an arm of a crank, usually one of a pair, holding one end of a crankpin at its outer end. **9.** the flat woven strip, without pile, at the end of an Oriental rug. **10.** a large roll of paper, as for continuous feeding of a press. **11.** an intricate set or pattern of circumstances, facts, evidence, etc.: *Who can understand the web of life?* **12.** a network of interlinked stations, services, communications, etc., covering a region or country. **—*v.t.* 13.** to cover with or as with a web; envelop. **14.** to ensnare or entrap. **—*v.i.* 15.** to make or form a web. [ME, OE; c. D, LG *webbe,* Icel *vefr;* akin to WEAVE] **—web′less,** *adj.* **—web′like′,** *adj.*

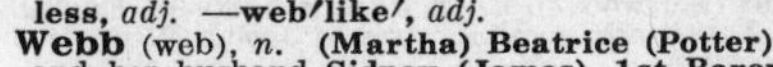

Webb (web), *n.* **(Martha) Beatrice (Potter),** 1858–1943, and her husband **Sidney (James), 1st Baron Pass·field** (pas′fēld′), 1859–1947, English economists, social reformers, socialists, and authors.
webbed (webd), *adj.* having the fingers or toes connected by a web or membrane.
Web·be She·be·li (web′ā shi bā′lē). See **Webi Shebeli.** Also, **Web′be Shi·be′li.**
web·bing (web′ing), *n.* **1.** a strong, woven material of hemp, cotton, or jute, used for belts, carrying straps, harnesses, etc., and under springs or upholstery, for support. **2.** *Zool.* the membrane forming a web or webs. **3.** something resembling this, as the leather thongs or piece connecting the thumb and forefinger of a baseball glove or mitt. **4.** any material or part formed from interlaced threads, thongs, branches, etc., or having a latticelike appearance, as the face of a tennis racket or a snowshoe. [late ME]
web·by (web′ē), *adj.,* **-bi·er, -bi·est.** **1.** pertaining to, of the nature of, or resembling a web. **2.** webbed.
web·er (web′ər), *n. Elect.* the meter-kilogram-second unit of magnetic flux and magnetic pole strength, equal to a flux that produces an electromotive force of one volt in a single turn of wire when the flux is uniformly reduced to zero in a period of one second; 10^8 maxwells. *Abbr.:* Wb [named after W. E. WEBER]
We·ber (vā′bər; *Ger.* vā′bər), *n.* **1. Ernst Hein·rich** (ernst hīn′riKH), 1795–1878, German physiologist. **2. Baron Karl Ma·ri·a Frie·drich Ernst von** (kärl mä rē′ä frē′driKH ernst fən), 1786–1826, German pianist, conductor, and composer. **3. Max** (maks; *Ger.* mäks), 1864–1920, German sociologist and political economist. **4. Wil·helm E·du·ard** (vil′helm ā′do͞o ärt′), 1804–91, German physicist (brother of Ernst Heinrich).
We·bern (vā′bərn; *Ger.* vā′bərn), *n.* **An·ton von** (än′tōn fən), 1883–1945, Austrian composer.
web′ foot′, *Furniture.* a pad foot having the appearance of toes joined by a web. Also called **duck foot.**
web·foot (web′fo͝ot′), *n., pl.* **-feet.** **1.** a foot with the toes joined by a web. **2.** an animal with webfeet. **—web′-foot′ed,** *adj.*
We·bi She·be·li (wā′bē shi bā′lē), a river in E Africa, flowing SE from central Ethiopia to the Juba River, in the Somali Republic. ab. 700 mi. long. Also, **Webbe Shebeli, Webbe Shibeli, We′bi Shi·be′li.**
web′ press′, *Print.* a press into which paper is fed automatically from a large roll. Also called **web′-fed press′.**
web·ster (web′stər), *n. Archaic.* a weaver. [ME; OE *webbestre.* See WEB, -STER]
Web·ster (web′stər), *n.* **1. Daniel** 1782–1852, U.S. statesman and orator. **2. John,** c1580–1625?, English dramatist. **3. Noah,** 1758–1843, U.S. lexicographer. **—Web·ste·ri·an** (web stēr′ē ən), *adj.*
Web′ster Groves′, a city in E Missouri, near St. Louis. 27,455 (1970).
web-toed (web′tōd′), *adj.* web-footed.
wed (wed), *v.,* **wed·ded** or **wed, wed·ding.** **—*v.t.* 1.** to marry (another person) in a formal ceremony; take as one's husband or wife. **2.** to unite (a couple) in marriage or wedlock; marry. **3.** to bind by close or lasting ties; attach firmly: *He wedded himself to the cause of the poor.* **4.** to blend together or unite perfectly, as two sometimes discordant elements. **—*v.i.* 5.** to contract marriage; marry. **6.** to become united or to blend: *a building that will wed with the landscape.* [ME *wedde,* OE *wedd(ian)* (to) pledge; c. G *wetten* to bet, Icel *vethja* pledge]
we'd (wēd), contraction of *we had, we should,* or *we would.*
Wed., Wednesday.
wed·ded (wed′id), *adj.* **1.** united in matrimony; married: *the wedded couple.* **2.** of or pertaining to marriage or to those married: *wedded happiness.* [ME; OE *geweddodan*]
Wed′dell Sea′ (wed′əl), an arm of the Atlantic, E of Antarctic Peninsula.
wed·ding (wed′ing), *n.* **1.** the act or ceremony of marrying; marriage; nuptials. **2.** the anniversary of a marriage, or its celebration: *a silver wedding.* **3.** the act or an instance of harmonious blending or association: *a perfect wedding of words and music.* [ME; OE *weddung*] **—Syn. 1.** See **marriage.**
wed′ding cake′, a cake, traditionally prepared for a bride and groom and their wedding guests, that is usually white or yellow in tiered layers and covered with white icing and decorated.
wed′ding chest′, an ornamented chest for a trousseau.
wed′ding day′, **1.** the day of a wedding. **2.** the anniversary of a wedding.
wed′ding ring′, **1.** a ring, usually of gold, platinum, or silver, given to the bride by the groom during a marriage ceremony. **2.** a ring similarly given to the groom by the bride. [ME]
wedge (wej), *n., v.,* **wedged, wedg·ing.** **—*n.* 1.** a piece of hard material with two principal faces meeting in a sharply acute angle, the narrow end of which may be driven between two objects or parts to split, separate, lift, or hold them. **2.** anything in the form of an isosceles triangle: *a wedge of pie.* **3.** a cuneiform character or stroke of this shape. **4.** something that serves to create disunity. **5.** a military formation generally in the form of a V with the point toward the enemy. **6.** a means of initiation: *to use letters of introduction as a wedge for entering a group.* **7.** *Golf.* a club with an iron head the face of which is nearly horizontal, for lofting the ball, esp. out of sand traps and high grass. **—*v.t.* 8.** to separate or split with or as with a wedge (often fol. by *open, apart,* etc.). **9.** to pack, secure, or fix tightly by driving in a wedge or wedges. **10.** to thrust into or through a narrow space. **—*v.i.* 11.** to force a way into or through a narrow space. [ME *wegge,* OE *wecg;* c. dial. G *Weck* (OHG *wecki*), Icel *veggr*] **—wedge′like′,** *adj.*

Wedge

wedged (wejd), *adj.* having the shape of a wedge.
Wedg·ie (wej′ē), *n. Trademark.* a shoe having a wedge heel.

Wedg·wood (wej′wo͝od′), *n.* **1.** **Josiah,** 1730–95, English potter. **2.** *Trademark.* ceramic ware of Josiah Wedgwood and his successors.

wedg·y (wej′ē), *adj.,* **wedg·i·er, wedg·i·est.** resembling a wedge; wedgelike.

wed·lock (wed′lok), *n.* the state of marriage; matrimony. [ME *wedlok,* OE *wedlāc,* lit., a pledging = *wed* pledge (see WED) + *-lāc* verbal n. suffix]

Wednes·day (wenz′dē, -dā), *n.* the fourth day of the week, following Tuesday. [ME *Wednesdai,* OE **Wēdnesdæg,* mutated var. of *Wōdnesdæg* Woden's day; c. D *Woensdag,* Dan *onsdag;* trans. of L *Mercuriī diēs* day of Mercury]

Wednes·days (wenz′dēz, -dāz), *adv.* on or during Wednesdays; every Wednesday.

wee (wē), *adj.,* **we·er, we·est,** *n.* —*adj.* **1.** little; very small. **2.** very early: *in the wee hours of the morning.* —*n. Scot.* **3.** a little bit. **4.** a short space of time. [ME *we,* var. of *wei* (small) quantity, OE *wēg,* var. of *wǣge* weight, akin to *wegan* to WEIGH[1]] —**Syn. 1.** tiny, diminutive; minuscule.

weed[1] (wēd), *n.* **1.** a valueless, troublesome, or noxious plant growing wild, esp. one that grows profusely or on cultivated ground to the exclusion or injury of the desired crop. **2.** *Slang.* a cigarette or cigar. **3.** a thin, ungainly person or animal. **4.** **the weed,** *Informal.* tobacco. —*v.t.* **5.** to free from weeds or troublesome plants: *to weed a garden.* **6.** to root out or remove (a weed or weeds), as from a garden or lawn (often fol. by *out*). **7.** to remove as being undesirable, inefficient, or superfluous (often fol. by *out*): *to weed out inexperienced players.* —*v.i.* **8.** to remove weeds or the like. [ME *wede,* OE *wēod;* c. OS *wiod* weed, MD *wiet* fern] —**weed′er,** *n.* —**weed′less,** *adj.* —**weed′like′,** *adj.*

weed[2] (wēd), *n.* **1.** **weeds,** mourning garments: *widow's weeds.* **2.** a mourning band of black crepe or cloth, as worn on a man's hat or coat sleeve. **3.** *Archaic.* **a.** a garment: *clad in rustic weeds.* **b.** clothing. [ME *wede,* OE *wǣd,* *(ge)wǣde* garment, clothing; c. OS *wād, gewādi,* OHG *wāt, gewāti* clothing]

Weed (wēd), *n.* **Thur·low** (thûr′lō), 1797–1882, U.S. journalist and politician.

weed-kill·er (wēd′kil′ər), *n.* an herbicide.

weed·y (wē′dē), *adj.,* **weed·i·er, weed·i·est.** **1.** full of or abounding in weeds. **2.** consisting of or pertaining to weeds. **3.** (of a plant, flower, etc.) growing poorly or in a straggling manner. **4.** (of a person or animal) thin, ungainly, or scrawny. [late ME] —**weed′i·ly,** *adv.* —**weed′i·ness,** *n.*

week (wēk), *n.* **1.** a period of seven successive days, usually understood as beginning with Sunday and ending with Saturday. **2.** a period of seven successive days that begins with or includes an indicated day: *the week of June 3; Christmas week.* **3.** (*often cap.*) a period of seven successive days devoted to a particular celebration, honor, cause, etc.: *National Book Week.* **4.** the working days or working portion of such a period; workweek: *a five-day week; a 35-hour week.* —*adv.* **5.** *Brit.* seven days before or after a specified day: *I shall come Tuesday week.* [ME *weke,* OE *wice;* c. D *week,* Icel *vika* week, Goth *wikō* turn, L *vicis* change]

week·day (wēk′dā′), *n.* **1.** any day of the week except the Sabbath. —*adj.* **2.** of or on a weekday: *weekday occupations.* [ME; OE *wicdæg*]

week·days (wēk′dāz′), *adv.* every day, esp. Monday through Friday, during the workweek.

week·end (wēk′end′), *n.* **1.** the end of a week, esp. the period of time between Friday evening and Monday morning. —*adj.* **2.** of, for, or on a weekend: *a weekend excursion.* —*v.i.* **3.** to spend a weekend as a period of leisure.

week·end·er (wēk′en′dər), *n.* **1.** a person who goes on a weekend vacation. **2.** a weekend guest. **3.** a traveling bag large enough to carry the clothing and personal articles needed for a weekend trip.

week·ends (wēk′endz′), *adv.* every weekend; on or during weekends.

Week·ley (wēk′lē), *n.* **Ernest,** 1865–1954, English etymologist and lexicographer.

week·ly (wēk′lē), *adj., adv., n., pl.* **-lies.** —*adj.* **1.** happening or appearing once every week: *a weekly appointment.* **2.** computed or determined by the week: *a weekly rate.* **3.** of, pertaining to, or happening within any given week: *weekly labors.* —*adv.* **4.** once a week; by the week: *to pay rent weekly.* —*n.* **5.** a periodical appearing once a week. [late ME]

Weems (wēmz), *n.* **Mason Locke,** 1759–1825, U.S. clergyman and biographer.

ween (wēn), *v.t., v.i. Archaic.* to think; suppose. [ME *wene(n),* OE *wēnan* to expect; c. Goth *wēnjan,* Icel *væna* to hope, expect, G *wähnen* to imagine]

wee·nie (wē′nē), *n. Informal.* a wiener. Also, **wienie.**

weep[1] (wēp), *v.,* **wept, weep·ing,** *n.* —*v.i.* **1.** to express grief, sorrow, or any overpowering emotion by shedding tears; shed tears; cry: *to weep for joy; to weep with rage.* **2.** to let fall drops of water or other liquid; drip; leak. **3.** to exude water or liquid, as soil, rock, a plant stem, a sore, etc. —*v.t.* **4.** to weep for (someone or something): *He wept his dead brother.* **5.** to shed (tears). **6.** to exude or drip (any liquid). **7.** to bring to a specified condition by weeping: *to weep oneself to sleep.* —*n.* **8.** *Informal.* weeping, or a fit of weeping. **9.** exudation of water or liquid. [ME *wepe(n),* OE *wēpan* to wail; c. Goth *wōpjan* to call, Icel *æpa* to cry out] —**Syn. 1.** sob; wail, lament. **4.** bewail, bemoan, lament. —**Ant. 1.** laugh.

weep[2] (wēp), *n. Brit. Dial.* the lapwing. [so called from its cry]

weep·er (wē′pər), *n.* **1.** a person who weeps. **2.** (formerly) a hired mourner at a funeral. **3.** something worn as a badge of mourning, as a widow's black veil. **4.** any of various loose-hanging, streamerlike objects, as a tendril of moss hanging from a tree. [late ME]

weep·ing (wē′ping), *adj.* **1.** expressing grief, sorrow, or any overwhelming emotion by shedding tears: *weeping multitudes.* **2.** dripping or oozing liquid. **3.** (of trees, shrubs, etc.) having slender, drooping branches. [ME; OE *wepende*] —**weep′ing·ly,** *adv.*

weep′ing wil′low, an Asian willow, *Salix babylonica,* characterized by the drooping habit of its branches: grown as an ornamental.

weep·y (wē′pē), *adj.,* **weep·i·er, weep·i·est.** **1.** of or like weeping; tearful. **2.** easily moved to tears. **3.** exuding water or other moisture; leaky; seepy. —**weep′i·ness,** *n.*

wee·ver (wē′vər), *n.* **1.** either of two small, European marine fishes of the genus *Trachinus, T. draco* or *T. vipera,* having highly poisonous dorsal spines. **2.** any fish of the same family, *Trachinidae.* [? ME **wēver,* OE *wifer* arrow (c. Icel *vifr* sword); modern meaning by assoc. with obs. *wiver* viper; see WYVERN]

wee·vil (wē′vəl), *n.* **1.** Also called **snout beetle.** any of numerous beetles of the family *Curculionidae,* which have the head prolonged into a snout, and which are destructive to grain, fruit, cotton bolls, nuts, etc. **2.** any of several related beetles of the family *Mylabridae,* the larvae of which live and feed in seeds, esp. those of legumes. [ME *wevel,* OE *wifel;* c. OHG *wibil* beetle; akin to WAVE]

wee·vil·y (wē′və lē), *adj.* infested with weevils. Also, **wee′vil·ly, wee·viled, wee·villed** (wē′vəld).

wee·wee (wē′wē′), *n., v.,* **-weed, -wee·ing.** *Baby Talk.* —*n.* **1.** urine. —*v.i.* **2.** to urinate.

weft (weft), *n.* **1.** *Textiles.* filling (def. 4). **2.** a woven fabric or garment. [ME, OE; see WEAVE]

weft·wise (weft′wīz′), *adv. Textiles.* in a horizontal direction; from selvage to selvage; crosswise.

Wehr·macht (vâr′mäKHt′), *n.* the German armed forces prior to and during World War II. [< G = *Wehr* defense + *Macht* force]

Weich·sel (vīk′səl), *n.* German name of the **Vistula.**

Weid·man (wīd′mən), *n.* **Jerome,** born 1913, U.S. author.

wei·ge·la (wī gē′lə, -jē′-, wī′gə lə), *n.* any of various shrubby, caprifoliaceous plants of the genus *Weigela,* of eastern Asia, having funnel-shaped, white, pink, or crimson flowers. Also, **wei·ge·li·a** (wī gē′lē ə, -jē′-). [< NL; named after C. E. *Weigel* (1748–1831), German physician]

weigh (wā), *v.t.* **1.** to ascertain the force that gravitation exerts upon (a person or thing) by use of a balance, scale, or other mechanical device: *to weigh oneself; to weigh potatoes.* **2.** to measure, separate, or apportion (a certain quantity of something) according to weight (usually fol. by *out*): *to weigh out five pounds of sugar.* **3.** to make heavy; increase the weight or bulk of; weight: *We weighed the drapes to make them hang properly.* **4.** to evaluate in the mind; consider carefully in order to reach an opinion, decision or choice: *to weigh the facts.* **5.** *Archaic.* to raise, lift, or hoist (something). —*v.i.* **6.** to have weight or a specified amount of weight: *to weigh less; to weigh a ton.* **7.** to have importance or influence: *My plea weighed in his favor.* **8.** to bear down as a weight or burden (usually fol. by *on* or *upon*): *Responsibility weighed upon him.* **9.** to consider carefully or judicially: *to weigh well before deciding.* **10.** **weigh anchor,** *Naut.* to raise a ship's anchor from the bottom in preparation for getting under way. **11.** **weigh down, a.** to be or cause to become heavy. **b.** to cause to bend beneath a weight. **c.** to lower the spirits of; burden; depress: *weighed down with care.* **12.** **weigh in,** *Sports.* **a.** (of a boxer or wrestler) to be weighed officially by a medical examiner on the day of a bout. **b.** (of a jockey) to be weighed officially with the saddle and weights after a race. [ME *weghe,* OE *wega(n)* (to) carry, weigh; c. D *wegen,* G *wägen,* Icel *vega,* L *vehere*] —**weigh′a·ble,** *adj.* —**weigh′er,** *n.* —**Syn. 4.** ponder, contemplate. See **study.**

weigh·man (wā′mən), *n., pl.* **-men.** a person whose occupation is weighing goods, produce, etc.

weight (wāt), *n.* **1.** the amount or quantity of heaviness or mass; the amount a thing weighs. **2.** *Physics.* the force which gravitation exerts upon a body, equal to the mass of the body times the local acceleration of gravity: commonly taken, in a region of constant gravitational acceleration, as a measure of mass. **3.** a system of units for expressing heaviness or mass: *avoirdupois weight.* **4.** a unit of heaviness or mass: *The pound is a common weight in English-speaking countries.* **5.** a standard body of determinate mass, as of metal, for using on a balance or scale in weighing objects, substances, etc. **6.** a specific quantity of a substance which is determined by weighing or which weighs a fixed amount: *a half-ounce weight of gold dust.* **7.** any heavy load, mass, or object: *Put down that weight and rest your arms.* **8.** an object useful because of its heaviness: *A weight held the door open.* **9.** a mental or moral burden, as of care, sorrow, or responsibility: *the weight of cares.* **10.** importance or influence: *an opinion of great weight.* **11.** *Statistics.* a measure of the relative importance of an item in a statistical population. **12.** (of clothing, textiles, etc.) relative heaviness or thickness as related to warmth, seasonal use, or purpose (often used in combination): *a winter-weight jacket.* **13.** *Print.* (of type) the degree of blackness or boldness. **14.** (in boxing and the like) a division or class to which a contestant belongs according to how much he weighs. **15.** the total amount the jockey, saddle, and leads must weigh on a racehorse during a race, according to the conditions of the race. **16.** *Gymnastics.* a metal disc of standard determined mass for lifting in competition or for exercise. Cf. **weight lifting.** **17.** the stress or accent value given a sound, syllable, or word. **18.** **carry weight,** to have importance or influence: *His opinion is certain to carry weight.* **19.** **pull one's weight,** to contribute one's rightful share of work to a project or job. Also, **pull one's own weight.** **20.** **throw one's weight around** or **about,** to use one's power and influence, esp. unduly. —*v.t.* **21.** to add weight to; load with additional weight. **22.** to burden with or as with weight: *to be weighted with years.* **23.** *Statistics.* to give a statistical weight to. **24.** to bias or slant toward a particular goal or direction, as in order to favor someone or something. [ME; OE *wiht* (c. D *wicht,* G *(Ge)wicht*) = *wih-* (see WEIGH) + *-t* -TH[1]] —**weight′er,** *n.* —**Syn. 10.** effect, power, significance.

weight′ den′sity, the weight per unit volume of a substance or object.

weight·ed (wā′tid), *adj.* **1.** burdened; loaded. **2.** having additional weight. **3.** adjusted or adapted to a representative value, as a statistic. —**weight′ed·ly,** *adv.* —**weight′ed·ness,** *n.*

weight·less (wāt′lis), *adj.* being without apparent weight, as a freely falling body or a body acted upon by a force that neutralizes gravitation. —**weight′less·ly,** *adv.* —**weight′less·ness,** *n.*

weight′ lift′ing, the act, art, or sport of lifting standard weights in a prescribed manner, as a competitive event or conditioning exercise. —**weight′ lift′er.**

weight·y (wā′tē), *adj.*, **weight·i·er, weight·i·est. 1.** having considerable weight. **2.** burdensome or troublesome. **3.** important or momentous: *weighty negotiations.* **4.** having or exerting influence, power, etc.; influential. [late ME] —**weight′i·ly,** *adv.* —**weight′i·ness,** *n.* —**Syn. 3.** significant, serious. See **heavy.** —**Ant. 1.** light.

Wei·hai·wei (wā′hī′wā′), *n.* a seaport in NE Shantung, in NE China: district leased to Great Britain 1898–1930. 175,000 (est. 1950); 285 sq. mi.

Weill (wīl; *Ger.* vīl), *n.* **Kurt** (kûrt; *Ger.* ko͝ort), 1900–50, German composer, in the U.S. after 1935.

Wei·mar (vī′mär), *n.* a city in SW East Germany. 66,675 (est. 1955). —**Wei·mar′i·an,** *adj.*, *n.*

Wei·mar·an·er (vī′mə rä′nər, wī′mə rā′-), *n.* one of a German breed of large hunting dogs having a smooth silver-gray to dark-gray coat, a cropped tail, and blue-gray or amber eyes. [< G, after WEIMAR; see -AN, -ER[1]]

Wei′mar Repub′lic, the German republic (1919–33), founded at Weimar.

weir (wēr), *n.* **1.** a small dam in a river or stream **2.** a fence, as of brush, set in a stream, channel, etc., for catching fish. [ME, OE < *wer(ian)* (to) defend, dam up]

weird (wērd), *adj.* **1.** involving or suggesting the supernatural; unearthly or eerie: *a weird sound.* **2.** fantastic; bizarre: *a weird hat.* **3.** *Archaic.* concerned with or controlling fate or destiny. —*n. Chiefly Scot.* **4.** fate; destiny. **5.** fate (def. 6). [ME *werd,* OE *wyrd;* akin to WORTH[2]] —**weird′ly,** *adv.* —**weird′ness,** *n.*

—**Syn. 1.** unnatural, preternatural. WEIRD, EERIE, UNEARTHLY, UNCANNY refer to that which is mysterious and apparently outside natural law. WEIRD refers to that which is suggestive of the fateful intervention of supernatural influences in human affairs: *the weird adventures of a group lost in the jungle.* EERIE refers to that which, by suggesting the ghostly, makes one's flesh creep: *an eerie moaning.* UNEARTHLY refers to that which seems by its nature to belong to another world: *an unearthly light which preceded the storm.* UNCANNY refers to that which is mysterious because of its apparent defiance of the laws established by experience: *an uncanny ability to recall numbers.*

weird·o (wēr′dō), *n., pl.* **weird·os.** *Slang.* an odd, eccentric, or abnormal person or thing. Also, **weird′ie, weird′y** (wēr′dē).

weird′ sis′ters, 1. the Fates. **2.** *Scand. Myth.* the Norns.

Weir·ton (wēr′tən), *n.* a city in N West Virginia, on the Ohio River. 27,131 (1970).

weis·en·heim·er (wī′zən hī′mər), *n.* wisenheimer.

Weis·mann (vīs′män′), *n.* **Au·gust** (ou′go͝ost), 1834–1914, German biologist. —**Weis′mann·i·an,** *adj.*, *n.*

Weis·mann·ism (vīs′män iz′əm), *n. Biol.* the theories of heredity as expounded by Weismann, esp. the theory that all inheritable characters are carried in the germ plasm which passes from one generation to another and which is isolated from the soma, and that acquired characters are not and cannot be inherited.

Weiss·horn (vīs′hôrn′), *n.* a mountain in S Switzerland, in the Alps. 14,804 ft.

Weiz·mann (vīts′män′; *Eng.* wīts′mən, wīz′-), *n.* **Cha·im** (KHī′im), 1874–1952, Israeli chemist and Zionist leader, born in Russia: 1st president of Israel 1948–52.

we·ka (wā′kä, wē′kə), *n.* any of several large, flightless, New Zealand rails of the genus *Gallirallus.* [< Maori]

welch (welch, welsh), *v.i. Slang.* welsh. —**welch′er,** *n.*

Welch (welch, welsh), *adj.*, *n.* Welsh.

Welch (welch, welsh), *n.* **Robert, Jr.,** 1899–1985, U.S. businessman: founder of the John Birch Society.

Welch·man (welch′mən, welsh′-), *n., pl.* **-men.** Welshman.

wel·come (wel′kəm), *interj.*, *n.*, *v.*, **-comed, -com·ing,** *adj.* —*interj.* **1.** (a word of kindly greeting, as to a person whose arrival gives pleasure): *Welcome, stranger!* —*n.* **2.** a kindly greeting or reception: *to give someone a warm welcome.* **3. wear out one's welcome,** to make one's visits so frequent or so long as to be annoying. —*v.t.* **4.** to greet the arrival of (a person, guests, etc.) with pleasure or kindly courtesy. **5.** to receive or accept with pleasure: *to welcome a change.* **6.** to meet, accept, or receive (an action, challenge, person, etc.) in a specified, esp. unfriendly, manner: *They welcomed him with hisses and catcalls.* —*adj.* **7.** gladly received, as a person whose arrival gives pleasure: *a welcome visitor.* **8.** agreeable, as something arriving, occurring, or experienced: *a welcome rest.* **9.** given permission (to use or enjoy): *He is welcome to try it.* **10.** without obligation for the courtesy or favor received (used as a conventional response to expressions of thanks): *You're quite welcome.* [ME < Scand; cf. Icel *velkominn* = *vel* WELL[1] + *kominn* come (ptp.); r. OE *wilcuma* = *wil-* welcome (see WILL[2]) + *cuma* comer] —**wel′come·ly,** *adv.* —**wel′come·ness,** *n.* —**wel′com·er,** *n.*

wel′come wag′on, 1. a vehicle which carries information about the community, gifts, and sample products of local merchants to newcomers in an area. **2.** Also, **Wel′come Wag′on.** the group sponsoring such a service.

weld[1] (weld), *v.t.* **1.** to unite or fuse, as pieces of metal, by hammering, compressing, or the like, esp. after rendering soft or pasty by heat, sometimes with the addition of fusible material. **2.** to bring into complete union, harmony, agreement, etc. —*v.i.* **3.** to undergo welding; be capable of being welded: *a metal that welds easily.* —*n.* **4.** a welded junction or joint. **5.** the act of welding or the state of being welded. [var. of WELL[2]] —**weld′a·bil′i·ty,** *n.* —**weld′a·ble,** *adj.* —**weld′er, wel′dor,** *n.* —**weld′less,** *adj.*

weld[2] (weld), *n.* **1.** a mignonette, *Reseda Luteola,* of southern Europe, yielding a yellow dye. **2.** the dye. [ME *welde;* c. MLG *walde,* MD *woude*]

wel·fare (wel′fâr′), *n.* **1.** the good fortune, health, happiness, prosperity, etc., of a person, group, or organization; well-being. **2.** See **welfare work. 3.** (*cap.*) *Informal.* a governmental agency that provides funds and aid to people in need, esp. those who are unable to work. **4. on welfare,** receiving financial aid from the government or from a private organization because of hardship and need. [ME, from phrase *wel fare*] —**Syn. 1.** success, weal, benefit, profit.

wel′fare fund′, a fund set up by a union or employer, providing benefits to workers during a period of unemployment or disablement.

Wel′fare Is′land, an island in the East River, in New York City: hospitals.

wel′fare state′, a state in which the welfare of the people in such matters as social security, health, education, housing, and working conditions is the responsibility of the government.

wel′fare work′, the efforts or programs of an agency, community, business organization, etc., to improve living conditions, increase job opportunities, secure hospitalization, and the like, for needy persons within its jurisdiction. —**wel′fare work′er.**

wel·far·ism (wel′fâr′iz əm, -fâ riz′-), *n.* the set of attitudes and policies characterizing, or tending toward the establishment of, a welfare state.

wel·kin (wel′kin), *n. Chiefly Literary.* the sky; the vault of heaven. [ME *welken(e),* OE *welcn,* var. of *wolcen* cloud, sky; c. G *Wolke;* akin to OE *wlaco* tepid]

well[1] (wel), *adv.*, *adj.*, *compar.* **bet·ter,** *superl.* **best,** *interj.*, *n.* —*adv.* **1.** in a good or satisfactory manner: *Things are going well.* **2.** in a careful or thorough manner: *Listen well. Shake well before using.* **3.** in a moral or proper manner: *to behave well.* **4.** commendably, meritoriously, or excellently: *a difficult task well done.* **5.** with propriety, justice, or reason: *I could not well refuse.* **6.** favorably: *to think well of someone.* **7.** to a considerable extent or degree: *a sum well over the amount fixed.* **8.** with great or intimate knowledge: *I knew him well. I know all too well what you mean.* **9.** without being unduly upset: *He took the news well.* **10.** advantageously: *You're well out of that place!* **11. as well,** in addition; also; too. **12. as well as,** as much or as truly as; equally as: *She was good as well as beautiful.* —*adj.* **13.** in good health; sound in body and mind: *He is not a well man.* **14.** satisfactory, pleasing, or good: *All is well with us.* **15.** proper, fitting, or gratifying: *It is well that you didn't go.* **16.** in a satisfactory position; well-off: *I am very well as I am.* **17. leave well enough alone,** not to change what is satisfactory. —*interj.* **18.** (used to express surprise, reproof, etc.): *Well! There's no need to shout.* **19.** (used to introduce a sentence, resume a conversation, etc.): *Well, I'd better be getting on now.* —*n.* **20.** well-being; good fortune; success: *to wish well to someone.* [ME, OE *wel(l);* c. D *wel,* G *wohl,* Icel *vel,* Goth *waila*] —**Syn. 1.** properly, correctly, efficiently. **13.** healthy, hale. **15.** suitable, befitting. —**Ant. 1.** poorly, badly. **13.** ill, sick. —**Usage.** See **good.**

well[2] (wel), *n.* **1.** a hole drilled or bored into the earth, as to obtain water, petroleum, natural gas, brine, or sulfur. **2.** a spring or natural source of water. **3.** a container for a fluid, as ink. **4.** any sunken or deep enclosed space, as a shaft for air or light, stairs, elevator, etc., extending vertically through the floors of a building. **5.** a hollow compartment, recessed area, or depression for holding a specific item or items, as to hold fish in the bottom of a boat, the retracted wheels of an airplane in flight, etc. **6.** something that suggests a well in depth or abundance: *a well of compassion.* —*v.i.* **7.** to rise, spring, or gush from the earth or some other source, as water (often fol. by *up, out,* or *forth*): *Tears welled up in her eyes.* —*v.t.* **8.** to send welling up or forth: *a fountain welling its pure water.* —*adj.* **9.** like, of, resembling, or used in connection with a well. [(n.) ME, OE; c. G *Welle* wave; (v.) ME *welle(n),* OE *wellan* (c. D *wellen,* Icel *vella*), var. of *wiellan,* causative of *weallan* to boil]

we'll (wēl), contraction of *we will* or *we shall.*

well-ad·vised (wel′ad vīzd′), *adj.* **1.** acting with caution, care, or wisdom: *He would be well-advised to sell the stock now.* **2.** based on or showing wise consideration: *a well-advised delay.* [ME *well avysed*]

Wel′land Canal′ (wel′ənd), a ship canal in S Canada, in Ontario, connecting Lakes Erie and Ontario: 8 locks. 25 mi.

well·a·way (wel′ə wā′), *interj. Archaic.* an exclamation of sorrow. Also, **well·a·day** (wel′ə dā′). [ME *welawei,* r. ME, OE *weilāwei* (*wei* < Scand; cf. Icel *vei* woe), r. OE *wā lā wā* woe! lo! woe!]

well-bal·anced (wel′bal′ənst), *adj.* **1.** rightly balanced, adjusted, or regulated: *a well-balanced diet.* **2.** sensible; sane: *a well-balanced mind.*

well-be·ing (wel′bē′ing), *n.* a good or satisfactory condition of existence; a state characterized by health, happiness, and prosperity; welfare: *to look after the well-being of one's children.*

well-be·lov·ed (wel′bi luv′id, -luvd′), *adj.* **1.** loved deeply and sincerely. **2.** highly respected and honored: *our well-beloved speaker.* —*n.* **3.** a well-beloved person or persons. [ME *wel biloved*]

well·born (wel′bôrn′), *adj.* born of a good, noble, or highly esteemed family. [ME; OE *welboren*]

well-bred (wel′bred′), *adj.* **1.** showing good breeding, as in behavior or manners. **2.** (of animals) of a desirable breed or pedigree.

well-con·di·tioned (wel′kən dish′ənd), *adj.* **1.** being in good physical condition. **2.** characterized by proper behavior or disposition.

well′-ac·cept′ed, *adj.*
well′-ac·com′plished, *adj.*
well′-ac·cus′tomed, *adj.*
well′-ac·knowl′edged, *adj.*
well′-ac·quaint′ed, *adj.*
well′-act′ed, *adj.*
well′-a·dapt′ed, *adj.*
well′-ad·just′ed, *adj.*
well′-ad·min′is·tered, *adj.*
well′-ad′ver·tised′, *adj.*
well′-aged′, *adj.*
well′-aimed′, *adj.*
well′-aired′, *adj.*
well′-ap·plied′, *adj.*
well′-ar′gued, *adj.*
well′-armed′, *adj.*
well′-ar·ranged′, *adj.*
well′-as·sumed′, *adj.*
well′-at·tend′ed, *adj.*
well′-at·test′ed, *adj.*
well′-at·tired′, *adj.*
well′-au·then′ti·cat′ed, *adj.*
well′-a·ware′, *adj.*
well′-be·haved′, *adj.*
well′-blessed′, *adj.*
well′-built′, *adj.*
well′-cal′cu·lat′ed, *adj.*
well′-cho′sen, *adj.*
well′-clothed′, *adj.*
well′-coached′, *adj.*
well′-com′pen·sat′ed, *adj.*
well′-con·cealed′, *adj.*

well-de·fined (wel′di fīnd′), *adj.* sharply or clearly stated, outlined, described, etc.: *a well-defined boundary.*

well-dis·posed (wel′di spōzd′), *adj.* **1.** favorably, sympathetically, or kindly disposed: *The sponsors are well-disposed toward our plan.* **2.** of pleasant disposition. [ME]

well·do·er (wel′do͞o′ər), *n. Obs.* **1.** a person who does well or acts rightly. **2.** a doer of good deeds. [late ME]

well·do·ing (wel′do͞o′ing), *n.* good conduct or action. [late ME]

well-done (wel′dun′), *adj.* **1.** performed with skill and efficiency. **2.** (of meat) thoroughly cooked, esp. until all redness is gone. [late ME]

well-dressed (wel′drest′), *adj.* attired in clothing that is of good quality, is properly fitted, and is appropriate and becoming.

Welles (welz), *n.* **1. (George) Orson,** 1915–85, U.S. actor, director, and producer. **2. Gideon,** 1802–78, U.S. journalist, legislator, and government official: Secretary of the Navy 1861–69. **3. Sumner,** 1892–1961, U.S. diplomat and government official.

Welles·ley (welz′lē), *n.* **1. Arthur.** See **Wellington, 1st Duke of. 2.** his brother **Robert Col·ley** (kol′ē), **1st Marquis,** 1760–1842, British statesman and administrator, born in Ireland: governor general of India 1797–1805. **3.** a town in E Massachusetts, near Boston. 28,051 (1970).

well-es·tab·lished (wel′e stab′lisht), *adj.* permanently founded; settled; firmly set: *a well-established business: a well-established habit.*

well-fa·vored (wel′fā′vərd), *adj.* of pleasing appearance; good-looking; pretty or handsome. Also, *esp. Brit.,* **well′-fa′voured.** [late ME] —**well′-fa′vored·ness;** *esp. Brit.,* **well′-fa′voured·ness,** *n.*

well-fed (wel′fed′), *adj.* properly nourished, esp. so as to be fat or plump. [ME *wel fedde*]

well-fixed (wel′fikst′), *adj. Informal.* well-off, esp. with regard to money or possessions.

well-found (wel′found′), *adj.* well-furnished with supplies, necessaries, etc.: *a well-found ship.*

well-found·ed (wel′foun′did), *adj.* based on good reasons, information, etc.: *well-founded suspicions.* [late ME]

well-groomed (wel′gro͞omd′), *adj.* **1.** having the hair, skin, etc., well cared for; clean, neat, and well-dressed: *a well-groomed young man.* **2.** (of an animal) tended, cleaned, combed, etc., with great care. **3.** carefully cared for; neat; tidy: *a well-groomed lawn.*

well-ground·ed (wel′groun′did), *adj.* **1.** based on good reasons; well-founded. **2.** well or thoroughly instructed in the basic principles of a subject: *He is well-grounded in mathematics.* [late ME]

well-han·dled (wel′han′dəld), *adj.* **1.** having been handled or used much: *a sale of well-handled goods.* **2.** treated, managed, or directed with efficiency: *a well-handled campaign.* **3.** treated with taste, discretion, etc.

well·head (wel′hed′), *n.* **1.** a fountainhead; source. **2.** Also called **wellhouse.** a shelter for a well. [ME *welleheved*]

well-heeled (wel′hēld′), *adj. Informal.* well-off; rich.

well·hole (wel′hōl′), *n.* the shaft of a well.

well·house (wel′hous′), *n., pl.* **-hous·es** (-hou′ziz). wellhead (def. 2).

well-in·formed (wel′in fôrmd′), *adj.* having extensive knowledge or information, as in one particular subject or in a variety of subjects. [late ME]

Wel·ling·ton (wel′ing tən), *n.* **1. 1st Duke of** (*Arthur Wellesley*) ("*the Iron Duke*"), 1769–1852, British general and statesman, born in Ireland: prime minister 1828–30. **2.** a seaport in and the capital of New Zealand, on S North Island. 349,628. **3.** (*sometimes l.c.*) See **Wellington boot.**

Wel′lington boot′, **1.** a leather boot with the front part of the top extending above the knee. **2.** a loose rubber boot extending to the calf. Also, **wel′lington boot′, Wellington.**

well-in·ten·tioned (wel′in ten′shənd), *adj.* well-meaning.

well-knit (wel′nit′), *adj.* closely or carefully joined together or related: *a well-knit plot.* [late ME]

well-known (wel′nōn′), *adj.* **1.** clearly or fully known. **2.** familiarly known; familiar: *a well-known face.* **3.** generally or widely known: *a well-known painting.* [late ME]

well′-made play′ (wel′mād′), a play characterized by careful construction and having a conventional and sometimes contrived plot.

well-man·nered (wel′man′ərd), *adj.* polite; courteous.

well-mean·ing (wel′mē′ning), *adj.* **1.** meaning or intending well; having good intentions: *a well-meaning but tactless person.* **2.** Also, **well-meant** (wel′ment′). proceeding from good intentions: *well-meaning words.* [late ME]

well-met (wel′met′), *adj. Archaic.* (used as a salutation in indicating pleasure at seeing someone.) Also, **well′ met′.**

well-nigh (wel′nī′), *adv.* very nearly; almost: *It's well-nigh bedtime.* [ME *wel ne(ig)h,* OE *wel nēah*]

well-off (wel′ôf′, -of′), *adj.* **1.** in a satisfactory, favorable, or good position or condition. **2.** having sufficient money or possessions.

well-or·dered (wel′ôr′dərd), *adj.* arranged or planned in a desirable way.

well-pre·served (wel′pri zûrvd′), *adj.* **1.** having been maintained in good condition. **2.** *Informal.* preserving a youthful appearance.

well-read (wel′red′), *adj.* well-informed through reading.

well-round·ed (wel′roun′did), *adj.* **1.** having desirably varied abilities or attainments. **2.** desirably varied: *a well-rounded curriculum.* **3.** fully-developed; well-balanced.

Wells (welz), *n.* **1. H(erbert) G(eorge),** 1866–1946, English novelist and historian. **2.** a historic town in E Somersetshire, in SW England: cathedral. 6691 (1961).

wells·ite (wel′zīt), *n.* a mineral, hydrous silicate of calcium, barium, potassium, sodium, and aluminum, occurring in colorless or white crystals. [named after H. L. *Wells* (1855–1924), American chemist; see -ITE[1]]

well-spo·ken (wel′spō′kən), *adj.* **1.** speaking well, fittingly, or pleasingly: *The new chairwoman was very well-spoken.* **2.** spoken in an apt, fitting, or pleasing manner: *a few well-spoken words on civic pride.* [late ME]

well·spring (wel′spring′), *n.* **1.** the head or source of a stream; fountainhead. **2.** an abundant source or supply of anything: *a wellspring of affection.* [ME, OE]

well′ sweep′, sweep[1] (def. 24).

well-thought-of (wel′thôt′uv′, -ov′), *adj.* highly esteemed; of good reputation.

well-timed (wel′tīmd′), *adj.* fittingly or appropriately timed; opportune; timely.

well-to-do (wel′tə do͞o′), *adj.* prosperous; rich. —**Syn.** affluent, moneyed, well-fixed, well-off.

well-turned (wel′tûrnd′), *adj.* **1.** smoothly or gracefully shaped; well-formed: *a well-turned ankle.* **2.** gracefully and concisely expressed: *a well-turned phrase.*

well-wish·er (wel′wish′ər), *n.* a person who wishes well to another person, a cause, etc. —**well′-wish′ing,** *adj., n.*

well-worn (wel′wōrn′, -wôrn′), *adj.* **1.** showing the effects of extensive use or wear. **2.** trite; hackneyed: *a well-worn saying.* **3.** fittingly or becomingly worn or borne: *a well-worn reserve.*

welsh (welsh, welch), *v.i. Slang.* **1.** to cheat by failing to pay a gambling debt. **2.** to fail deliberately to meet one's obligations: *to welsh on one's promise.* Also, **welch.** [? special use of WELSH] —**welsh′er,** *n.*

Welsh (welsh, welch), *adj.* **1.** of or pertaining to Wales, its people, or their language. —*n.* **2.** the inhabitants of Wales and their descendants elsewhere. **3.** Also called **Cymric, Kymric.** the Celtic language of Wales. Also, **Welch.** [ME *Welische,* OE *Welisc* < *Walh* Briton, foreigner (cf. L *Volcae* a Gallic tribe); c. G *welsch* foreign, Italian]

Welsh corgi
(1 ft. high at shoulder)

Welsh′ cor′gi (kôr′gē), one of either of two Welsh breeds of dogs having short legs, erect ears, and a foxlike head.

Welsh·man (welsh′mən, welch′-), *n., pl.* **-men.** a native or inhabitant of Wales. Also, **Welchman.** [ME, OE]

Welsh′ po′ny, one of a breed of small, sturdy ponies raised originally in the mountains of Wales.

Welsh′ rab′bit, a dish consisting of melted cheese, usually mixed with ale or beer, milk, and spices, served over toast. Also, **Welsh′ rare′bit.** [prob. of jocular orig.]

Welsh′ spring′er span′iel, one of a Welsh breed of springer spaniels having a red and white coat.

Welsh′ ter′rier, one of a Welsh breed of terriers having a wiry, black-and-tan coat, resembling an Airedale but smaller.

Welsh terrier
(15 in. high at shoulder)

welt (welt), *n.* **1.** a ridge or wale on the surface of the body, as from a blow of a stick or whip. **2.** a blow producing such a ridge or wale. **3.** *Shoemaking.* **a.** a strip, as of leather, set in between the outsole of a shoe and the edges of its insole and upper, through which these parts are joined by stitching or stapling. **b.** a strip, usually of leather, that ornaments a shoe. **4.** a strengthening or ornamental finish along a seam, the edge of a garment, etc. —*v.t.* **5.** to beat soundly, as with a stick or whip. **6.** to furnish or supply

well′-con·firmed′, *adj.*
well′-con·nect′ed, *adj.*
well′-con·sid′ered, *adj.*
well′-con·struct′ed, *adj.*
well′-con·tent′ed, *adj.*
well′-con·trolled′, *adj.*
well′-cooked′, *adj.*
well′-cul′ti·vat′ed, *adj.*
well′-de·fend′ed, *adj.*
well′-dem′on·strat′ed, *adj.*
well′-de·scribed′, *adj.*
well′-de·served′, *adj.*
well′-de·vel′oped, *adj.*
well′-de·vised′, *adj.*
well′-di·gest′ed, *adj.*
well′-dis′ci·plined, *adj.*
well′-doc′u·ment′ed, *adj.*
well′-earned′, *adj.*
well′-ed′u·cat′ed, *adj.*
well′-em·ployed′, *adj.*
well′-en·dowed′, *adj.*
well′-e·quipped′, *adj.*
well′-es·teemed′, *adj.*
well′-fi·nanced′, *adj.*
well′-fin′ished, *adj.*
well′-fit′ted, *adj.*
well′-formed′, *adj.*
well′-for′ti·fied′, *adj.*
well′-fought′, *adj.*
well′-fur′nished, *adj.*
well′-gov′erned, *adj.*
well′-guard′ed, *adj.*
well′-hid′den, *adj.*
well′-housed′, *adj.*
well′-il′lus·trat′ed, *adj.*
well′-in·clined′, *adj.*
well′-jus′ti·fied′, *adj.*
well′-kept′, *adj.*
well′-liked′, *adj.*
well′-loved′, *adj.*
well′-man′aged, *adj.*
well′-marked′, *adj.*
well′-matched′, *adj.*
well′-mer′it·ed, *adj.*
well′-mixed′, *adj.*
well′-mo′ti·vat′ed, *adj.*
well′-not′ed, *adj.*
well′-paid′, *adj.*
well′-placed′, *adj.*
well′-planned′, *adj.*
well′-played′, *adj.*
well′-pleased′, *adj.*
well′-prac′ticed, *adj.*
well′-pre·pared′, *adj.*
well′-pro·por′tioned, *adj.*
well′-pro·tect′ed, *adj.*
well′-pro·vid′ed, *adj.*
well′-qual′i·fied′, *adj.*
well′-rea′soned, *adj.*
well′-re·ceived′, *adj.*
well′-rec′og·nized′, *adj.*
well′-rec′om·mend′ed, *adj.*
well′-re·gard′ed, *adj.*
well′-reg′u·lat′ed, *adj.*
well′-re·hearsed′, *adj.*
well′-re·mem′bered, *adj.*
well′-rep′re·sent′ed, *adj.*
well′-re·spect′ed, *adj.*
well′-re·viewed′, *adj.*
well′-ri′pened, *adj.*
well′-sat′is·fied′, *adj.*
well′-schooled′, *adj.*
well′-sea′soned, *adj.*
well′-se·cured′, *adj.*
well′-sit′u·at′ed, *adj.*
well′-spent′, *adj.*
well′-stat′ed, *adj.*
well′-stocked′, *adj.*
well′-suit′ed, *adj.*
well′-sup·plied′, *adj.*
well′-sup·port′ed, *adj.*
well′-sus·tained′, *adj.*
well′-taught′, *adj.*
well′-trained′, *adj.*
well′-trav′eled, *adj.*
well′-trav′elled, *adj.*
well′-treat′ed, *adj.*
well′-un′der·stood′, *adj.*
well′-used′, *adj.*
well′-ver′i·fied′, *adj.*
well′-word′ed, *adj.*
well′-wrought′, *adj.*

with a welt or welts. [late ME *welte, walt* shoemaker's welt, OE *wælt* (thigh) sinew, var. of *weald* groin (basic meaning: that which holds things together)]

Welt·an·schau·ung (velt′än shou′o͝ong), *n. German.* a comprehensive conception or image of civilization and of the universe and of man's relation to it. [lit., manner of looking at the world]

Welt·an·sicht (velt′än′zikнt), *n. German.* a world view; an attitude toward, or interpretation of, reality.

wel·ter (wel′tər), *v.i.* **1.** to roll, toss, or heave, as waves, the sea, etc. **2.** to roll or writhe; wallow, as animals (often fol. by *about*): *pigs weltering about in the mud.* **3.** to lie bathed in or be drenched in something, esp. blood. **4.** to become deeply or extensively involved, associated, entangled, etc.: *to welter in confusion.* —*n.* **5.** a confused mass or accumulation; jumble; muddle. **6.** a state of commotion, turmoil, or upheaval. **7.** a rolling, tossing, or tumbling motion, as of the sea. [ME, freq. (see -ER[6]) of obs. *welt* to roll, OE *weltan;* c. MD *welteren,* LG *weltern* to roll]

wel·ter·weight (wel′tər wāt′), *n.* a boxer or other contestant intermediate in weight between a lightweight and a middleweight, esp. a professional boxer weighing up to 147 pounds.

Welt·schmerz (velt′shmerts′), *n. German.* sorrow which one feels and accepts as his necessary portion in life; sentimental pessimism. [lit., world-pain]

Wel·ty (wel′tē), *n.* **Eu·do·ra** (yo͞o dôr′ə, -dôr′ə), born 1909, U.S. short-story writer and novelist.

Wem·bley (wem′blē), *n.* a city in E Middlesex, in SE England, near London: tennis matches. 124,843 (1961).

Wemyss (wēmz), *n.* a parish in central Fife, in E Scotland, on the Firth of Forth: castle. 10,593.

wen[1] (wen), *n. Pathol.* a benign encysted tumor of the skin, esp. on the scalp, containing sebaceous matter; a sebaceous cyst. [ME, OE *wenn;* c. D *wen*]

wen[2] (wen), *n.* wynn.

We·natch·ee (wə nach′ē), *n.* a city in central Washington. 16,912 (1970).

Wen·ces·laus (wen′sis lôs′), *n.* **1.** Also, **Wen′ces·las′.** 1361–1419, emperor of the Holy Roman Empire 1378–1400; as Wenceslaus IV, king of Bohemia 1378–1419. **2. Saint** ("*Good King Wenceslaus*"), A.D. 903?–c935, duke of Bohemia 928–935. German, **Wenzel.** Czech, **Václav.**

wench (wench), *n.* **1.** a girl or young woman. **2.** *Archaic.* a strumpet. —*v.i.* **3.** to associate, esp. habitually, with promiscuous women. [ME, back formation from *wenchel,* OE *wencel* child, akin to *wancol* tottering; cf. G *wankeln* to totter] —**wench′er,** *n.*

Wen·chow (wen′chou′; *Chin.* wun′jō′), *n.* former name of **Yungkia.**

wend (wend), *v.,* **wend·ed** or (*Archaic*) **went; wend·ing.** —*v.t.* **1.** to pursue or direct (one's way). —*v.i.* **2.** *Archaic.* to proceed or go. [ME; OE *wend(an);* c. D, G *wenden,* Goth *wandjan,* causative of *windan* to wind]

Wend (wend), *n.* a member of a Slavic people in Saxony and adjoining parts of Prussia; Sorb. [< G *Wende;* c. OE *Winedas* (pl.); cf. L *Venedī* Slavs < Gmc (basic sense: dwellers in a watery, swampy region)]

Wend·ish (wen′dish), *adj.* **1.** of or pertaining to the Wends or their language; Sorbian. —*n.* **2.** Sorbian (def. 2). [< G *wendisch*]

went (went), *v.* **1.** pt. of **go. 2.** *Archaic.* a pt. and pp. of **wend.**

wen·tle·trap (wen′tᵊl trap′), *n.* any of several marine gastropods of the family *Scalariidae,* having a whitish, spiraled shell. [< D *wenteltrap* winding stairway, spiral shell = *wentel,* earlier *wendel* (akin to OE *windel* winding staircase; see WIND[2]) + *trap* tread, step, stair, akin to OE *treppan* to tread]

Went·worth (went′wûrth′), *n.* **1. Thomas, 1st Earl of Strafford.** See **Strafford, 1st Earl of. 2. William Charles,** 1793–1872, Australian political leader, author, and journalist.

Wen·zel (*Ger.* ven′tsəl), *n.* Wenceslaus.

wept (wept), *v.* pt. and pp. of **weep**[1].

were (wûr *or, esp. Brit.,* wâr; *unstressed* wər), *v.* a 2nd pers. sing. past indic., pl. past indic., and past subj. of **be.** [ME; OE *wǣre* past subj., *wǣre* past ind. 2nd pers. sing. and *wǣron* past ind. pl. of *wesan* to be; c. D, G *waren,* Dan *var,* etc. See WAS]

we're (wēr), contraction of *we are.*

were·n't (wûrnt, wûr′ənt), contraction of *were not.*

were·wolf (wēr′wo͝olf′, wûr′-, wâr′-), *n., pl.* **-wolves** (-wo͝olvz′). (in folklore and superstition) a human being that has changed or been changed into a wolf, or is capable of assuming the form of a wolf, while retaining human intelligence. Also, **werwolf.** [ME *werwolf,* OE *werwulf* = *wer* man (c. Goth *wair,* L *vir*) + *wulf* WOLF; c. MD *weerwolf,* OHG *werwolf*]

Wer·fel (*Ger.* veʀ′fəl), *n.* **Franz** (*Ger.* fʀänts), 1890–1945, Austrian novelist, poet, and dramatist, born in Czechoslovakia: in the U.S. after 1939.

wer·gild (wûr′gild, wer′-), *n.* (in Anglo-Saxon England and medieval Germanic countries) **1.** money paid to the relatives of a murder victim in compensation for loss and to prevent a blood feud. **2.** money paid as compensation for the murder or disablement of a person. Also, **wer′geld, were′gild.** [ME (Scot) *weregylt,* OE *wer(e)gild* = *wer* man (see WEREWOLF) + *gild* GELD[2]; c. MD *weergelt,* OHG *wergelt;* see YIELD]

wer·ner·ite (wûr′nə rīt′), *n.* a variety of scapolite. [named after A. G. *Werner* (1750–1817), German mineralogist; see -ITE[1]]

wert (wûrt; *unstressed* wərt), *v. Archaic.* a 2nd pers. sing. pt. indic. and subj. of **be.**

Wer·the·ri·an (ver tēr′ē ən), *adj.* of, pertaining to, or characteristic of Werther, the morbidly sentimental hero of Goethe's romantic novel *The Sorrows of Werther* (1774).

wer·wolf (wēr′wo͝olf′, wûr′-, wâr′-), *n., pl.* **-wolves** (-wo͝olvz′). werewolf.

We·ser (vā′zər), *n.* a river flowing through N West Germany into the North Sea. ab. 300 mi. long.

We·ser·mün·de (*Ger.* vā′zəʀ myn′də), *n.* former name of **Bremerhaven.**

wes·kit (wes′kit), *n.* a vest or waistcoat, esp. one worn by women. [alter. of WAISTCOAT]

Wes·ley (wes′lē *or, esp. Brit.,* wez′-), *n.* **1. Charles,** 1707–88, English evangelist and hymnist. **2.** his brother **John,** 1703–91, English theologian and evangelist: founder of Methodism.

Wes·ley·an (wes′lē ən *or, esp. Brit.,* wez′-), *adj.* **1.** of or pertaining to John Wesley, founder of Methodism. **2.** pertaining to Methodism. —*n.* **3.** a follower of John Wesley. **4.** *Chiefly Brit.* a member of the denomination founded by him; Methodist.

Wes·ley·an·ism (wes′lē ə niz′əm *or, esp. Brit.,* wez′-), *n.* the evangelical principles taught by John Wesley; Methodism. Also, **Wes′ley·ism.**

wes·sand (wē′zənd), *n. Chiefly Scot.* weasand.

Wes·sex (wes′iks), *n.* (in the Middle Ages) a kingdom, later an earldom, in S England. *Cap.:* Winchester. See map at **Mercia.** [OE *Westseaxe, -seaxan* West Saxons]

west (west), *n.* **1.** a cardinal point of the compass, 90° to the left when facing north, corresponding to the point where the sun is seen to set. *Abbr.:* W **2.** the direction in which this point lies. **3.** (*often cap.*) a region or territory situated in this direction. **4.** (*usually cap.*) the western part of the U.S. **5.** (*usually cap.*) the western part of the world, as distinguished from the East or Orient; the Occident. **6.** (*cap.*) the noncommunist countries of Western Europe and the Americas. —*adj.* **7.** lying toward or situated in the west: *the west end of town.* **8.** in the direction of or toward the west. **9.** coming from the west, as a wind. —*adv.* **10.** to, toward, or in the west: *heading west.* **11.** from the west. **12. go west,** *Informal.* to die. [ME, OE; c. D, G *west,* Icel *vestr;* cf. F *ouest* < OE]

West (west), *n.* **1. Benjamin,** 1738–1820, U.S. painter, in England after 1763. **2. Mae,** 1892–1980, U.S. actress. **3. Nathanael** (pen name of *Nathan Wallenstein Weinstein*), 1902?–40, U.S. novelist. **4. Dame Rebecca** (pen name of *Cicily Isabel Fairfield Andrews*), 1892–1983, English novelist and critic, born in Ireland.

West., western. Also, **west.**

West′ Al′lis (al′is), a city in SE Wisconsin, near Milwaukee. 71,649 (1970).

West′ Bank′, an area in the Middle East, between the W bank of the Jordan River and the E frontier of Israel: occupied in 1967 and subsequently claimed by Israel.

West′ Ben·gal′, a state in E India: formerly part of the province of Bengal. 34,926,279 (1961); 33,805 sq. mi. *Cap.:* Calcutta. Cf. **Bengal** (def. 1).

West′ Ber·lin′. See under **Berlin** (def. 2).

west·bound (west′bound′), *adj.* proceeding or headed west.

West′ Brom′wich (brum′ij, -ich, brom′-), a city in S Staffordshire, in central England. 95,909 (1961).

west′ by north′, *Navig., Survey.* a point on the compass 11°15′ north of west. *Abbr.:* WbN

west′ by south′, *Navig., Survey.* a point on the compass 11°15′ south of west. *Abbr.:* WbS

West′ Co·vi′na, a city in SW California.

West′ End′, a fashionable section of London, England: noted for theaters.

west·er[1] (wes′tər), *n.* a wind or storm coming from the west. [WEST + -ER[1]]

west·er[2] (wes′tər), *v.i.* **1.** (of heavenly bodies) to move or tend westward. **2.** to shift or veer toward the west. [late ME; see WEST, -ER[6]]

west·er·ing (wes′tər ing), *adj.* moving or shifting toward the west.

west·er·ly (wes′tər lē), *adj., adv., n., pl.* **-lies.** —*adj.* **1.** of, pertaining to, or situated in the west. **2.** in the direction of or toward the west. **3.** coming from the west, as a wind. —*adv.* **4.** toward the west. **5.** from the west, as a wind. —*n.* **6.** a westerly wind. —**west′er·li·ness,** *n.*

west·ern (wes′tərn), *adj.* **1.** lying toward or situated in the west. **2.** directed or proceeding toward the west; westward. **3.** coming or originating from the west, as a wind. **4.** (*often cap.*) of, pertaining to, living in, or characteristic of the West, esp. the western U.S. **5.** (*usually cap.*) Occidental: *to adopt Western dress.* **6.** (*usually cap.*) of or pertaining to the noncommunist countries of Europe and the Americas: *Western trade agreements.* **7.** (*cap.*) of or pertaining to the Western Church. —*n.* **8.** a person living in a western region or country. **9.** (*often cap.*) a story, movie, television play, etc., about the U.S. West of the 19th century, esp. about cowboys, the westward migration, Indian wars, etc. **10.** See **western omelet. 11.** See **western sandwich.** [ME, OE *westerne*]

West′ern Aus·tral′ia, a state in W Australia. 736,629 (1961); 975,920 sq. mi. *Cap.:* Perth.

West′ern Church′, 1. the Roman Catholic Church, sometimes with the Anglican Church, or, more broadly, the Christian churches of the West. **2.** the Christian church in the countries that were once part of the Western Roman Empire and in countries evangelized from them.

West′ern Em′pire. See **Western Roman Empire.**

West·ern·er (wes′tər nər), *n.* (*sometimes l.c.*) a native or inhabitant of the West, esp. of the western U.S.

West′ern Ghats′, a low mountain range in W India, along the W margin of the Deccan plateau and bordering on the Arabian Sea. ab. 1000 mi. long.

West′ern Hem′i·sphere, 1. the western part of the terrestrial globe, including North and South America, their islands, and the surrounding waters. **2.** that half of the earth traversed in passing westward from the prime meridian to 180° longitude.

west′ern hem′lock, a hemlock, *Tsuga heterophylla,* of western North America: the state tree of Washington.

West′ern Is′lands, Hebrides.

west·ern·ism (wes′tər niz′əm), *n.* (*often cap.*) a word, idiom, or practice characteristic of people of the Occident or of the western U.S.

west·ern·ize (wes′tər nīz′), *v.t.,* **-ized, -iz·ing.** to influence with ideas, customs, practices, etc., characteristic of the Occident or of the western U.S. Also, *esp. Brit.,* **west′ern·ise′.** —**west′ern·i·za′tion,** *n.*

west·ern·most (wes′tərn mōst′ *or, esp. Brit.*, -məst), *adj.* most western or westerly; farthest west.
West′ern O′cean, the Atlantic Ocean in ancient geography, as lying to the west of the known world.
west′ern om′elet, an omelet prepared with diced green peppers, onions, and ham.
West′ern Reserve′, a tract of land in NE Ohio reserved by Connecticut (1786) when its rights to other land in the western U.S. were ceded to the federal government: relinquished in 1800.
West′ern Ro′man Em′pire, the western division of the Roman Empire after A.D. 395: became extinct after the fall of Rome A.D. 476. Also called **Western Empire.** Cf. **Eastern Roman Empire.**
West′ern sad′dle, a heavy saddle having a deep seat, high cantle and pommel, pommel horn, wide leather flaps for protecting the rider's legs, and little padding. See illus. at **saddle.**
West′ern Samo′a, an independent country comprising the W part of Samoa: formerly a trust territory of New Zealand. 152,000; 1133 sq. mi. *Cap.:* Apia. Cf. **American Samoa, Samoa.** —**West′ern Samo′an.**
west′ern sand′wich, a sandwich with a western omelet for a filling.
West′ern Slavs′. See under **Slav** (def. 1).
West′ern Thrace′. See under **Thrace** (def. 2).
West·fa·len (vest fä′lən), *n.* German name of **Westphalia.**
West·field (west′fēld′), *n.* **1.** a city in NE New Jersey. 33,720 (1970). **2.** a city in SW Massachusetts. 31,433 (1970).
West′ Flan′ders, a province in W Belgium. 1,071,604; 1249 sq. mi. *Cap.:* Bruges.
West′ Flem′ish, Flemish as used in West Flanders. *Abbr.:* WFlem
West′ Fri′sian, Frisian as used in the western part of Friesland. *Abbr.:* WFris
West′ German′ic, 1. a subbranch of Germanic that includes English, Frisian, Flemish, Dutch, Plattdeutsch, Yiddish, and German. *Abbr.:* WGmc, W.Gmc., W.Ger. **2.** of or pertaining to this subbranch of Germanic.
West′ Ger′many, a republic in central Europe: created in 1949 by the coalescing of the British, French, and U.S. zones of occupied Germany established in 1945. 61,644,600; 94,905 sq. mi. *Cap.:* Bonn. Official name, **Federal Republic of Germany.** —**West′ Ger′man.**
West′ Goth′, a Visigoth. [(erroneous) trans. of VISIGOTH]
West′ Ham′ (ham), a city in SW Essex, in SE England, near London. 157,186 (1961).
West′ Hart′ford, a town in central Connecticut. 68,031 (1970).
West′ Har′tle·pool (här′tᵊl po͞ol′), a seaport in E Durham, in NE England. 77,073 (1961).
West′ Ha′ven, a town in S Connecticut, near New Haven. 52,851 (1970).
West′ Hol′lywood′, a town in S California, W of Los Angeles. 34,625 (1970).
West′ In′dies, 1. Also called **the Indies.** an archipelago in the N Atlantic between North and South America, comprising the Greater Antilles, the Lesser Antilles, and the Bahamas. **2. Federation of.** Also called **West′ In′dies Federa′tion.** a former federation (1958–62) of the British islands in the Caribbean, comprising Barbados, Jamaica, Trinidad, Tobago, and the Windward and Leeward island colonies. —**West′ In′dian.**
West′ In′dies Asso′ciated States′, the two island states of Antigua and St. Kitts-Nevis-Anguilla in the E West Indies; in association with Great Britain since 1967: former associated islands included Dominica, Grenada, St. Lucia, and St. Vincent.
west·ing (wes′ting), *n.* **1.** *Navig.* the distance due west made good on any course tending westward. **2.** *Survey.* a distance west from a north-south reference line.
West·ing·house (wes′ting hous′), *n.* **George,** 1846–1914, U.S. inventor and manufacturer.
West′ I′ri·an (ēr′ē än′), the W part of the island of New Guinea, formerly a Dutch territory: a province of Indonesia since 1963. 957,000; ab. 159,000 sq. mi. Also called **Irian Jaya, West New Guinea.** Formerly, **Netherlands New Guinea, Dutch New Guinea.**
West·land (west′lənd), *n.* a city in SE Michigan, W of Detroit. 86,749 (1970).
West′ Lo′thi·an (lō′thē ən, -thē-), a county in S Scotland. 92,764 (1961); 120 sq. mi. *Co. seat:* Linlithgow. Formerly, **Linlithgow.**
Westm., Westminster.
West·meath (west′mēth′, -mēth′), *n.* a county in Leinster in the N central Republic of Ireland. 53,570; 681 sq. mi. *Co. seat:* Mullingar.
West′ Mem′phis, a city in E Arkansas, on the Mississippi. 26,070 (1970).
West′ Miff′lin, a city in W Pennsylvania, on the Monongahela River. 28,070 (1970).
West·min·ster (west′min′stər), *n.* **1.** a central borough (officially a city) of London, England: Westminster Abbey, Houses of Parliament, Buckingham Palace. 214,000. **2.** a city in SW California, SE of Los Angeles. 59,874 (1970).
West′minster Ab′bey, a Gothic church in London, England: burial place of English sovereigns.
West·mont (west′mont), *n.* a town in SW California, E of Los Angeles. 29,310 (1970).
West·more·land (west′mōr′lənd, -môr′-; *for 1 also* west′mōr′lənd, -môr′-; *for 2 also Brit.* west′mər lənd), *n.* **1. William (Childs)** (chīldz), born 1914, U.S. general: commander of U.S. forces in the Vietnam War 1964–68. **2.** a county in NW England, partially in the Lake District. 67,222 (1961); 789 sq. mi. *Co. seat:* Appleby.
west·most (west′mōst′ *or, esp. Brit.*, -məst), *adj.* westernmost. [ME; r. ME, OE *westmest;* see -MOST]
West′ New′ Guin′ea. See **West Irian.**
West′ New′ York′, a town in NE New Jersey, across the Hudson from New York City. 40,627 (1970).
west-north·west (west′nôrth′west′; *Naut.* west′nôr′-west′), *n.* **1.** a point on the compass midway between west and northwest. —*adj.* **2.** in the direction of or toward this point. **3.** from this point, as a wind. —*adv.* **4.** toward this point. **5.** from this point. *Abbr.:* WNW
West′ Or′ange, a town in NE New Jersey, near Newark. 43,715 (1970).
West′ Pak′istan, the former W section of Pakistan, N of the Arabian Sea: now known as Pakistan.
West′ Palm′ Beach′, a city in SE Florida: winter resort. 57,375 (1970).
West·pha·li·a (west fā′lē ə, -fāl′yə), *n.* a former province in NW Germany, now a part of North Rhine-Westphalia. German, **Westfalen.** —**West·pha′li·an,** *adj., n.*
West′ Point′, a military reservation in SE New York, on the Hudson: U.S. Military Academy.
West·port (west′pōrt′, -pôrt′), *n.* a town in SW Connecticut. 27,414 (1970).
West′ Prus′sia, a former province of Prussia, now in Poland. German, **West·preus·sen** (vest′proi′sən). —**West′ Prus′sian.**
West′ Punjab′, a region in E Pakistan, formerly the W part of the Indian province of Punjab.
West′ Rid′ing (rī′ding), an administrative division of Yorkshire, England. 3,641,228 (1961); 2790 sq. mi. *Co. seat:* Wakefield.
West′ Sax′on, a Saxon living in Wessex before the Norman Conquest. [late ME, alter. of OE *Westseaxan* WESSEX]
west-south·west (west′south′west′; *Naut.* west′sou′-west′), *n.* **1.** a point on the compass midway between west and southwest. —*adj.* **2.** in the direction of or toward this point. **3.** from this point, as a wind. —*adv.* **4.** toward this point. **5.** from this point. *Abbr.:* WSW
West′ Spring′field, a city in SE Massachusetts. 28,461 (1970).
West′ Suf′folk, an administrative division of Suffolk, in E England. 129,969 (1961); 611 sq. mi. *Co. seat:* Bury St. Edmonds.
West′ Sus′sex, an administrative division of Sussex, in SE England. 623,100; 628 sq. mi. *Co. seat:* Chichester.
West′ Virgin′ia, a state in the E United States. 1,744,237 (1970); 24,181 sq. mi. *Cap.:* Charleston. *Abbr.:* W.Va., WV —**West′ Virgin′ian.**
West·wall (west′wôl′; *Ger.* vest′väl′), *n.* See **Siegfried line.**
west·ward (west′wərd), *adj.* **1.** moving, facing, or situated toward the west. —*adv.* **2.** Also, **west′wards.** toward the west. —*n.* **3.** the west. [ME; OE *westweard*]
west·ward·ly (west′wərd lē), *adj., adv.* toward the west.
wet (wet), *adj.*, **wet·ter, wet·test,** *n., v.*, **wet** or **wet·ted, wet·ting.** —*adj.* **1.** moistened, covered, or soaked, with water or some other liquid. **2.** in a liquid form or state: *wet paint.* **3.** characterized by the presence or use of water or other liquids. **4.** *U.S.* allowing or favoring the sale of alcoholic beverages: *a wet town.* **5.** preserved in a liquid, as food in syrup, a specimen in alcohol, etc. **6.** characterized by the presence or frequent occurrence of rain, mist, etc.: *a wet climate.* **7.** laden with a comparatively high percent of moisture or vapor, esp. water vapor: *There was a wet breeze from the west.* **8. all wet,** *Slang.* completely mistaken; in error. **9. wet behind the ears,** *Informal.* immature; naïve. —*n.* **10.** wetness; moisture. **11.** damp weather; rain: *Stay out of the wet as much as possible.* **12.** *U.S.* a person in favor of allowing the manufacture and sale of alcoholic beverages. —*v.t.* **13.** to make (something) wet, as by moistening or soaking: *Wet your hands before soaping them.* **14.** to urinate on or in: *The dog had wet the carpet.* —*v.i.* **15.** to become wet (sometimes fol. by *through*): *My jacket has wet through.* **16.** (of animals and children) to urinate. **17. wet one's whistle.** See **whistle** (def. 11). [ME *wett,* ptp. of *weten,* OE *wǣtan* to wet; r. ME *weet,* OE *wǣt,* c. OFris *wēt,* Icel *vātr;* see WATER] —**wet′ly,** *adv.* —**wet′ness,** *n.* —**wet′ter,** *n.* —**wet′tish,** *adj.*
—**Syn. 1.** damped, drenched. **10.** humidity, dampness, dankness. **13.** WET, DRENCH, SATURATE, SOAK imply moistening something thoroughly. To WET is to moisten in any manner with water or other liquid: *to wet or dampen a cloth.* DRENCH suggests wetting completely, as by a downpour: *A heavy rain drenched the fields.* SATURATE implies wetting to the limit of absorption: *to saturate a sponge.* To SOAK is to keep covered by a liquid for a time: *to soak beans before baking.* —**Ant. 1.** dry.
wet·back (wet′bak′), *n.* *Often Disparaging.* a Mexican laborer who enters the U.S. illegally.
wet′ bar′, a small bar with a running water sink, as in a recreation room.
wet′ blan′ket, a person or thing that dampens enthusiasm or enjoyment or has a discouraging or depressing effect.
wet′-bulb′ thermom′eter (wet′bulb′), a thermometer having a bulb that is kept moistened when humidity determinations are being made with a psychrometer. Cf. **dry-bulb thermometer.**
wet′ cell′, *Elect.* a cell whose electrolyte is in liquid form and free to flow.
wet′ chinook′. See under **Chinook** (def. 4).
wet′ dream′, an erotic dream leading to involuntary ejaculation or orgasm.
wet′ fly′, *Angling.* an artificial fly designed for below the surface of the water. Cf. **dry fly.**
weth·er (weth′ər), *n.* a castrated male sheep. [OE; c. OS *withar,* OHG *widar,* Icel *vethr,* Goth *withrus*]
Weth·ers·field (weth′ərz fēld′), *n.* a town in central Connecticut. 26,662 (1970).
wet′ nurse′, a woman hired to suckle another's infant.
wet-nurse (wet′nûrs′), *v.t.*, **-nursed, -nurs·ing. 1.** to act as a wet nurse to (an infant). **2.** *Informal.* to give excessive care or attention to; treat as if helpless.
wet′ pack′, *Med.* a type of bath in which wet sheets are applied to the patient.
wet·proof (wet′pro͞of′), *adj.* waterproof.
wet′ strength′, *Papermaking.* the relative resistance of paper to tearing when wet.
wet·ta·bil·i·ty (wet′ə bil′i tē), *n.* **1.** the condition of being wettable. **2.** the degree or extent to which something absorbs or can be made to absorb moisture.
wet·ta·ble (wet′ə bəl), *adj.* **1.** able to be wetted. **2.** made soluble or receptive to moisture, as by the addition of a chemical agent.

Wet·ter·horn (vet′ər hôrn′), *n.* a mountain in S Switzerland, in the Bernese Alps. 12,149 ft.

wet′ting a′gent, *Chem.* any admixture to a liquid for increasing its ability to penetrate, or spread over the surface of, a given material, esp. cloth, paper, or leather.

wet′ wash′, laundry that has been washed but not dried or ironed. Cf. **dry wash** (def. 1).

we've (wēv), contraction of *we have.*

Wex·ford (weks′fərd), *n.* **1.** a county in Leinster province, in the SE Republic of Ireland. 83,308 (1961); 908 sq. mi. **2.** its county seat: a seaport. 11,328 (1961).

Wey·den (vīd′ən), *n.* **Roger** or **Ro·gier** (*Flem.* rô gēr′) **van der** (van dər; *Flem.* vän dər), 1400?–64, Flemish painter.

Wey·gand (vā gäN′), *n.* **Ma·xime** (mak sēm′), 1867–1965, French general.

Weyl (vīl), *n.* **Her·mann** (hûr′mən; *Ger.* her′män), 1885–1955, German mathematician, in the U.S. after 1933.

Wey·mouth (wā′məth), *n.* a town in E Massachusetts, S of Boston. 54,610 (1970).

wf, *Print.* See **wrong font.** Also, **w.f.**

WFlem, West Flemish.

WFris, West Frisian.

WFTU, World Federation of Trade Unions. Also, **W.F.T.U.**

W.G., **1.** water gauge. **2.** weight guaranteed. **3.** wire gauge. Also, **w.g.**

W.Ger., **1.** West Germanic. **2.** West Germany.

WGmc, West Germanic. Also, **W.Gmc.**

Wh, *Elect.* watt-hour; watt-hours. Also, **wh, whr**

whack (hwak, wak), *Informal.* —*v.t.* **1.** to strike with a smart, resounding blow or blows. —*v.i.* **2.** to strike a smart, resounding blow or blows. —*n.* **3.** a smart, resounding blow. **4.** a trial or attempt: *to take a whack at a job.* **5.** a portion or share. **6. out of whack,** in poor condition; out of order: *My stomach's out of whack.* [var. of THWACK] —**whack′er,** *n.*

whack·ing (hwak′ing, wak′-), *adj. Chiefly Brit. Informal.* large.

whack·y (hwak′ē, wak′ē), *adj.,* **whack·i·er, whack·i·est.** wacky.

whale[1] (hwāl, wāl), *n., pl.* **whales,** (*esp. collectively*) **whale,** *v.,* **whaled, whal·ing.** —*n.* **1.** any of the larger marine mammals of the order *Cetacea,* esp. as distinguished from the smaller dolphins and porpoises, having a fishlike body, forelimbs modified into flippers, and a head that is horizontally flattened. **2.** *Slang.* something extraordinarily big, great, or fine of its kind: *a whale of a lot of money.* —*v.i.* **3.** to engage in whaling or whale fishing. [ME; OE *hwæl;* c. G. *Wal(fisch),* Icel *hvalr;* akin to L *squalus* kind of fish = movable *s-* + *-qualus*]

Whale[1], *Physeter catodon* (Length to 65 ft.)

whale[2] (hwāl, wāl), *v.t.,* **whaled, whal·ing.** *Informal.* to hit, thrash, or beat soundly. [var. of WALE[1]]

whale·boat (hwāl′bōt′, wāl′-), *n.* a long, narrow boat designed for quick turning and use in rough seas: formerly used in whaling, now mainly for sea rescue.

whale·bone (hwāl′bōn′, wāl′-), *n.* **1.** an elastic, horny substance growing in place of teeth in the upper jaw of certain whales, forming a series of thin, parallel plates on each side of the palate for filtering plankton from the water; baleen. **2.** a thin strip of this substance, for stiffening a corset.

whale′bone whale′, any whale of the suborder *Mysticeti,* having plates of whalebone on the sides of the upper jaw. Also called **baleen whale.** Cf. **toothed whale.**

whale·man (hwāl′mən, wāl′-), *n., pl.* **-men.** a man whose occupation is whaling; whaler.

whal·er (hwā′lər, wā′-), *n.* a person or vessel employed in whaling.

Whales (hwālz, wālz), *n.* **Bay of,** an inlet of the Ross Sea, in Antarctica: location of Little America.

whal·ing (hwā′ling, wā′-), *n.* the work or industry of capturing and rendering whales; whale fishing.

wham (hwam, wam), *n.* **1.** a loud sound produced by an explosion or sharp impact. **2.** a forcible impact. [imit.]

wham·my (hwam′ē, wam′ē), *n., pl.* **-mies.** *Slang.* the evil eye; jinx. [WHAM + -Y[2], one of the methods of putting a whammy on someone being to strike the fist into the palm]

whang (hwang, wang), *n.* **1.** *Informal.* the sound produced by a resounding blow: *the whang of gongs and cymbals.* **2.** *Dial.* **a.** a thong, esp. of leather. **b.** Also called **thong leather.** leather used to make thongs, lacing, etc.; rawhide. —*v.i.* **3.** *Informal.* to resound with a blow. [alter. of *thwang,* early form of THONG; cf. WHITTLE, WHACK]

wharf (hwôrf, wôrf), *n., pl.* **wharves** (hwôrvz, wôrvz), **wharfs,** *v.* —*n.* **1.** a structure built on the shore or projecting into the water so that vessels may be moored along its side; a pier or quay. —*v.t.* **2.** to provide with a wharf or wharves. **3.** to place or store on a wharf. **4.** to accommodate at or bring to a wharf. —*v.i.* **5.** to tie up at a wharf; dock. [ME; OE *hwearf* embankment; c. MLG *warf;* akin to G *Werf* pier]

wharf·age (hwôr′fij, wôr′-), *n.* **1.** the use of a wharf. **2.** a charge or payment for the use of a wharf.

wharf·in·ger (hwôr′fin jər, wôr′-), *n.* a person who owns or has charge of a wharf. [WHARFAGE + -ER[1], with *-n-* as in *passenger, messenger,* etc.]

wharf′ rat′, **1.** a large brown rat that is commonly found on wharves. **2.** a person who lives or loiters near wharves.

Whar·ton (hwôr′tən, wôr′-), *n.* **Edith (New·bold Jones)** (no͞o′bōld, nyo͞o′-), 1862–1937, U.S. novelist.

wharve (hwôrv, wôrv), *n. Spinning.* a wheel or round piece of wood on a spindle, serving as a flywheel or as a pulley. [ME *wherve,* OE *hweorfa* < *hwerfan* to revolve]

wharves (hwôrvz, wôrvz), *n.* a pl. of **wharf.**

what (hwut, hwot, wut, wot; *unstressed* hwət, wət), *pron., pl.* **what,** *n., adj., adv., interj., conj.* —*pron.* **1.** (used interrogatively as a request for specific information): *What is the matter? What is your name?* **2.** (used interrogatively to inquire about the character, occupation, etc., of a person): *What does he do? What does she take me for?* **3.** (used interrogatively to inquire as to the origin, identity, etc., of something): *What is that bird?* **4.** (used interrogatively to inquire as to the worth, usefulness, force, or importance of something): *What is wealth without friends?* **5.** (used interrogatively to request a repetition of words or information not fully understood, usually used in elliptical constructions): *You need what?* **6.** (used interrogatively to inquire the reason or purpose of something, usually used in elliptical constructions): *What of it? What for?* **7.** (used relatively to indicate that which): *This is what he says.* **8.** whatever; anything that: *Come what may.* **9.** how much?: *What does it cost?* **10.** the kind of thing or person that: *He said what everyone expected he would.* **11.** as much or as many as: *Everyone should give what he can.* **12.** the thing or fact that (used in parenthetic clauses): *He went to the meeting and, what was worse, insisted on speaking.* **13.** (used to indicate more to follow, additional possibilities, alternatives, etc.): *You know what? Shall we go or what?* **14.** *Brit.* don't you agree?: *An unusual chap, what?* **15.** (used as an intensifier in exclamatory phrases, often fol. by an indefinite article): *What luck! What an idea!* **16.** *Nonstandard.* that; which; who: *She's the one what told me.* **17. so what?** *Informal.* See **so**[1] (def. 19). **18. what have you,** *Informal.* and other things of the same kind; and so forth: *money, jewels, stocks, and what have you.* **19. what if,** what would be the outcome if; suppose that: *What if everyone who was invited comes?* **20. what it takes,** *Informal.* that which enables one to achieve success or attain a desired end: *to have what it takes.* **21. what's what,** *Informal.* the true situation; all the facts: *Ask someone who knows what's what.* —*n.* **22.** the true nature or identity of something: *a lecture on the what and how of crop rotation.* —*adj.* **23.** (used interrogatively before nouns and pronouns): *What clothes shall I pack?* **24.** whatever: *Take what supplies you need.* —*adv.* **25.** to what extent or degree?; how much?: *What does it matter?* **26. what with,** with the attending circumstance of: *A slow trip, what with the foul weather, isn't it?* —*interj.* **27.** (used in exclamatory expressions, often fol. by a question): *What, no salt?* —*conj.* **28.** *Dial.* as much as; as far as: *He helps me what he can.* [ME; OE *hwæt;* c. G *was,* D *wat,* Icel *hvat,* Goth *hwa,* L *quod,* etc.]

what'd (hwut′id, hwot′-, wut′-, wot′-; hwud, wud), contraction of *what did: What'd you say?*

what·e'er (hwut âr′, hwot-, wut-, wot-, hwət-, wət-), *pron., adj. Literary.* whatever.

what·ev·er (hwut ev′ər, hwot-, wut-, wot-, hwət-, wət-), *pron.* **1.** anything that (usually used in relative clauses): *Do whatever you like.* **2.** (used relatively to indicate a quantity of a specified or implied antecedent): *Take whatever you like of these.* **3.** no matter what: *He'll do it, whatever happens.* **4.** any or any one of a number of things whether specifically known or not: *papers, magazines, or whatever.* **5.** what (used interrogatively): *Whatever do you mean?* —*adj.* **6.** in any amount; to any extent: *whatever merit the work has.* **7.** no matter what: *whatever rebuffs he might receive.* **8.** being what or who it may be: *Whatever the reason, he refuses to go.* **9.** of any kind (used as an intensifier following the noun or pronoun it modifies): *any person whatever.* [ME]

what'll (hwut′əl, hwot′-, wut′-, wot′-), contraction of *what shall* or *what will: What'll she say?*

what·not (hwut′not′, hwot′-, wut′-, wot′-), *n.* **1.** a stand with shelves for bric-a-brac, books, etc. **2.** anything of the same or similar kind: *sheets, napkins, and whatnot.*

what's (hwuts, hwots, wuts, wots; *unstressed* hwəts, wəts), **1.** contraction of *what is* or *what has.* **2.** *Informal.* contraction of *what does: What's the man say?*

what·so·e'er (hwut′sō âr′, hwot′-, wut′-, wot′-), *pron., adj. Literary.* whatsoever.

what·so·ev·er (hwut′sō ev′ər, hwot′-, wut′-, wot′-), *pron., adj.* (an intensive form of **whatever**): *whatsoever it be; in any place whatsoever.* [ME = *what so* (OE *swā hwæt swā*) + *ever* EVER]

what've (hwut′əv, hwot′-, wut′-, wot′-), contraction of *what have: What've you done with the money?*

wheal (hwēl, wēl), *n.* **1.** a small burning or itching swelling on the skin, as from a mosquito bite or from hives. **2.** a wale or welt. Also, **weal.** [akin to WHELK[2] and to obs. *wheal* (v.), OE *hwelian* to suppurate, develop weals]

wheat (hwēt, wēt), *n.* **1.** the grain of any cereal grass of the genus *Triticum,* esp. *T. aestivum* (*T. sativum*), used in the form of flour for making bread, cake, pastry, etc. **2.** the plant which bears this grain. [ME *whete,* OE *hwǣte;* c. Icel *hveiti,* Goth *hwaiteis,* G *Weizen*]

wheat′ cake′, a pancake made of wheat flour.

wheat·en (hwēt′ən, wēt′-), *adj.* **1.** made of wheat flour or grain. **2.** of or pertaining to wheat. [ME *wheten,* OE *hwǣten*]

wheat′ germ′, the embryo or nucleus of the wheat kernel, used in or on foods as a concentrated source of vitamins.

Whea·ton (hwēt′ən, wēt′-), *n.* **1.** a town in central Maryland. 66,247 (1970). **2.** a city in NE Illinois, W of Chicago. 31,138 (1970).

Wheat′ Ridge′, a city in central Colorado, near Denver. 29,795 (1970).

wheat′ rust′, *Plant Pathol.* any of several diseases of wheat caused by several rust fungi of the genus *Puccinia.*

Wheat·stone (hwēt′stōn′, wēt′- *or, esp. Brit.,* wēt′stən, hwēt′-), *n.* **Sir Charles,** 1802–75, English physicist and inventor.

Wheat′stone bridge′, *Elect.* a circuit for measuring an unknown resistance by comparing it with known resistances. Also, **Wheat′stone's bridge′.** Cf. **bridge** (def. 9). [named after C. WHEATSTONE]

whee·dle (hwēd′əl, wēd′-), *v.,* **-dled, -dling.** —*v.t.* **1.** to endeavor to influence (a person) by flattering or beguiling words or acts. **2.** to persuade (a person) by such words or acts: *She wheedled him into going to the theater with her.* **3.** to obtain (something) by artful persuasions: *She wheedled a new car out of her father.* —*v.i.* **4.** to use flattery or coaxing on someone as a means of persuasion: *There's no need to wheedle if you really need something.* [? aspirated var. of *weedle, OE *wǣdlian* to beg < *wǣdla* beggar = *wǣth-* wandering +

-*la* masc. n. suffix] —**whee′dler,** *n.* —**whee′dling·ly,** *adv.* —**Syn. 1.** flatter, cajole. **2.** coax, beguile, inveigle.

wheel (hwēl, wēl), *n.* **1.** a circular frame or disk arranged to revolve on an axis, as on or in vehicles, machinery, etc. **2.** any machine, apparatus, instrument, etc., shaped like this or having a circular frame, disk, or revolving drum as an essential feature: *a potter's wheel; roulette wheel.* **3.** See **steering wheel. 4.** a circular frame with an axle connecting to the rudder of a ship, for steering: *He took the wheel during the storm.* **5.** *Informal.* a bicycle. **6.** a circular instrument of torture on which the victim was stretched until disjointed. **7.** a round object, decoration, etc.: *a wheel of cheese.* **8. a. wheels,** moving, propelling, or animating agencies: *the wheels of commerce.* **b.** *Slang.* a personal means of transportation, esp. a car. **9.** a wheeling or circular movement: *the intricate wheels of the folk dances.* **10.** (formerly) a movement of troops, ships, etc., drawn up in line, as if turning on a pivot. **11.** *Naut.* **a.** a paddle wheel. **b.** a propeller. **12.** *Slang.* an active and influential person. **13. at the wheel, a.** at the steering wheel of a ship, motor vehicle, etc. **b.** in command or control. **14. wheels within wheels,** an involved interaction of motives or agencies operating to produce a final result. —*v.t.* **15.** to cause to turn, rotate, or revolve, as on an axis. **16.** to perform (a movement) in a circular or curving direction. **17.** to move, roll, or convey on wheels, casters, etc.: *The servants wheel out the tables.* **18.** to provide (a vehicle, machine, etc.) with a wheel or wheels. —*v.i.* **19.** to turn on or as on an axis or about a center; revolve, rotate, or pivot. **20.** *Brit., Mil.* to turn: *Right wheel!* **21.** to move in a circular or curving course: *pigeons wheeling above.* **22.** to turn so as to face in a different direction (often fol. by *about* or *around*): *He wheeled about and faced his opponent squarely.* **23.** to roll along on or as on wheels; travel along smoothly: *The car wheeled along the highway.* **24. wheel and deal,** *Slang.* to operate without restraint by using personal or financial power in big business, politics, etc. [ME, OE *hwēol, hweohl;* c. D *wiel,* Icel *hjōl,* Gk *kýklos;* see CYCLE] —**wheel′less,** *adj.*

wheel′ and ax′le, a simple machine consisting, in its typical form, of a cylindrical drum to which a wheel concentric with the drum is firmly fastened: ropes are so applied that as one unwinds from the wheel, another rope is wound on to the drum.

wheel′ an′imalcule, a rotifer.

wheel·bar·row (hwēl′bar′ō, wēl′-), *n.* **1.** a frame or box for conveying a load, supported at one end by a wheel or wheels, and lifted and pushed at the other by two horizontal shafts. —*v.t.* **2.** to move or convey in a wheelbarrow. [ME]

wheel·base (hwēl′bās′, wēl′-), *n.* *Auto.* the distance measured in inches from the center of the front-wheel spindle to the center of the rear-wheel axle.

wheel′ bug′, an assassin bug, *Arilus cristatus,* that has a toothed, semicircular crest on the pronotum, and preys on other insects.

wheel·chair (hwēl′châr′, wēl′-), *n.* a chair mounted on large wheels for use by invalids and convalescents.

wheeled (hwēld, wēld), *adj.* equipped with or using wheels (often used in combination): *a four-wheeled carriage.*

wheel·er (hwē′lər, wē′-), *n.* **1.** a person or thing that wheels. **2.** a person who makes wheels; wheelwright. **3.** something provided with a wheel or wheels (usually used in combination): *a four-wheeler; a stern-wheeler.* **4.** See **wheel horse** (def. 1).

Wheel·er (hwē′lər, wē′-), *n.* **1. Burton K(endall),** 1882–1975, U.S. political leader. **2. William Al·mon** (al′mən, ôl′-), 1819–1887, vice president of the U.S. 1877–81.

wheel·er-deal·er (hwē′lər dē′lər, wē′-), *n.* *Slang.* a person who wheels and deals. Also, **wheel′er and deal′er.**

wheel′ horse′, **1.** a horse, or one of the horses, harnessed behind others and nearest the front wheels of a vehicle. **2.** a reliable, diligent, and strong worker.

wheel·house (hwēl′hous′, wēl′-), *n., pl.* **-hous·es** (-hou′ziz). pilothouse.

Wheel·ing (hwē′ling, wē′-), *n.* a city in N West Virginia, on the Ohio River. 48,188 (1970).

wheel′ lock′, an old type of gunlock in which sparks are produced by the friction of a small steel wheel against a piece of iron pyrites.

wheel·man (hwēl′mən, wēl′-), *n., pl.* **-men.** a helmsman or steersman. Also, **wheelsman.**

wheel′ of for′tune, **1.** a wheel in allegory whose spinnings represent the uncertainty of fate. **2.** a disklike gambling device that is rotated or spun to determine the winners of prizes.

wheels·man (hwēlz′mən, wēlz′-), *n., pl.* **-men.** wheelman.

wheel′ win′dow, a rose window having prominent radiating mullions.

wheel·work (hwēl′wûrk′, wēl′-), *n.* a train of gears, as in a timepiece.

wheel·wright (hwēl′rīt′, wēl′-), *n.* a person whose trade it is to make or repair wheels, wheeled carriages, etc. [ME]

wheeze (hwēz, wēz), *v.,* **wheezed, wheez·ing,** *n.* —*v.i.* **1.** to breathe with difficulty and with a whistling sound: *His asthma was causing him to wheeze.* **2.** to make a sound resembling difficult breathing. —*n.* **3.** a wheezing breath or sound. **4.** an old and frequently used joke or saying. [late ME *whese,* OE **hwǣs(an)* (to) blow (whence *hwǣst* blowing); c. Icel *hvǣsa* to hiss] —**wheez′er,** *n.* —**wheez′ing·ly,** *adv.*

wheez·y (hwē′zē, wē′-), *adj.,* **wheez·i·er, wheez·i·est.** afflicted with or characterized by wheezing. —**wheez′i·ly,** *adv.* —**wheez′i·ness,** *n.*

whelk¹ (hwelk, welk), *n.* any of several large, edible, spiral-shelled, marine gastropods of the family *Buccinidae,* esp. *Buccinum undatum.* [aspirated var. of ME *welk,* OE *weoloc*]

Whelk, *Buccinum undatum* (Length 3 in.)

whelk² (hwelk, welk), *n.* a pimple or pustule. [ME *whelke,* OE *hwylca, hwelca;* see WHEAL]

whelm (hwelm, welm), *v.t.* **1.** to submerge; engulf. **2.** to overwhelm. [ME *whelme;* appar. b. (dial.) *whelve* (OE *gehwelfan* to bend over) + HELM²]

whelp (hwelp, welp), *n.* **1.** the young of the dog, or of the

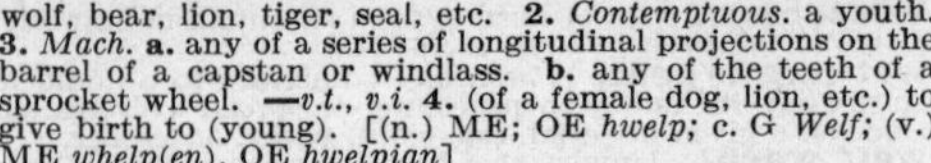

wolf, bear, lion, tiger, seal, etc. **2.** *Contemptuous.* a youth. **3.** *Mach.* **a.** any of a series of longitudinal projections on the barrel of a capstan or windlass. **b.** any of the teeth of a sprocket wheel. —*v.t., v.i.* **4.** (of a female dog, lion, etc.) to give birth to (young). [(n.) ME; OE *hwelp;* c. G *Welf;* (v.) ME *whelp(en),* OE *hwelpian*]

when (hwen, wen), *adv.* **1.** at what time or period?; how long ago?; how soon?: *When are they to arrive? When did the Roman Empire exist?* **2.** under what circumstances?; upon what occasion?: *When is a letter of condolence in order? When did you ever see such a crowd?* —*conj.* **3.** at what time: *to know when to be silent.* **4.** at the time or in the event that: *when we were young; when the noise stops.* **5.** upon or after which; and then: *We had just fallen asleep when the bell rang.* **6.** while on the contrary; considering that; whereas: *Why are you here when you should be in school?* —*pron.* **7.** what time: *Since when is that allowed? 'Till when is the store open?* **8.** which time: *They left on Monday, since when we have heard nothing.* —*n.* **9.** the time of anything: *the when and the where of an act.* [ME *when(ne),* OE *hwenne;* c. G *wann* when, *wenn* if, when (cf. Goth *hwan* when, how); akin to WHO, WHAT] —**Usage.** See **where.**

when·as (hwen az′, wen-), *conj.* **1.** *Archaic.* **a.** when. **b.** inasmuch as. **2.** *Obs.* whereas. [late ME]

whence (hwens, wens), *adv.* **1.** from what place?: *Whence comest thou?* **2.** from what source, origin, or cause?: *Whence has he wisdom?* —*conj.* **3.** from what place, source, cause, etc.: *He told whence he came.* [ME *whennes, whannes* = *whanne* (by syncope from OE *hwanone* whence) + *-s* -s¹] —**Usage.** Since WHENCE means "from what place?" it should not be preceded by "from": *Whence did he come?* (not *From whence did he come?*)

whence·so·ev·er (hwens′sō ev′ər, wens′-), *adv., conj.* from whatsoever place, source, or cause.

when·e'er (hwen âr′, wen-), *conj.* *Literary.* whenever (def. 1).

when·ev·er (hwen ev′ər, wen-), *conj.* **1.** at whatever time; at any time when: *Come whenever you like.* **2.** when? (used emphatically): *Whenever did he say that?* [late ME]

when's (hwenz, wenz), **1.** contraction of *when is: When's the wedding to be?* **2.** contraction of *when has: When's that ever been the case?*

when·so·ev·er (hwen′sō ev′ər, wen′-), *adv., conj.* at whatsoever time. [ME = *whenso* (modeled on *whereso*) + *ever* EVER]

where (hwâr, wâr), *adv.* **1.** in or at what place?: *Where is he?* **2.** in what position or circumstances?: *Where do you stand on this question?* **3.** in what particular respect, way, etc.?: *Where does this affect us?* **4.** to what place, point, or end?; whither?: *Where are you going?* **5.** from what source?; whence?: *Where did you get such a notion?* —*conj.* **6.** in or at what place, part, point, etc.: *Find where he is.* **7.** in or at the place, part, point, etc., in or at which: *The book is where you left it.* **8.** in a position, case, etc., in which: *Where ignorance is bliss, 'tis folly to be wise.* **9.** to what or whatever place; wherever: *I will go where you go.* **10.** in or at which place; and there: *They came to the town, where they lodged for the night.* —*pron.* **11.** what place?: *Where did you come from?* **12.** the place in which; point at which: *This is where the boat docks. That was where the phone rang.* —*n.* **13.** the place in which something is located or occurs: *the wheres and hows of job hunting.* [ME *wher,* OE *hwǣr;* c. D *waar,* OHG *hwār;* akin to Icel *hvar,* Goth *hwar*]

—**Usage.** In careful English, WHERE is not used in place of WHEN: *A holiday is where we have time off* should be rewritten as: *A holiday is an occasion when we have time off.* WHERE should not be used to replace THAT: *I see by the papers that* (not *where*) *he has retired.* The phrases WHERE AT and WHERE TO are generally considered too informal to be used in good writing, and are also to be avoided in speech: *Where is she?* (not *Where is she at?*); *Where are you going?* (not *Where are you going to?*).

where·a·bouts (hwâr′ə bouts′, wâr′-), *adv.* **1.** about where?; where? —*conj.* **2.** near or in what place: *trying to find whereabouts in the world we were.* —*n.* **3.** (*construed as sing. or pl.*) the place where a person or thing is; the locality of a person or thing: *There is no clue as to his whereabouts.* [late ME *whereaboutes* = ME *wheraboute* (see WHERE, ABOUT) + *-s* -s¹]

where·as (hwâr az′, wâr-), *conj.* **1.** while on the contrary: *One arrived promptly, whereas the others were late.* **2.** it being the case that, or considering that (used esp. in formal preambles). [ME *wheras*]

where·at (hwâr at′, wâr-), *adv., conj.* **1.** at which: *a reception whereat many were present.* **2.** to which, or in reference to which; whereupon: *a remark whereat he quickly angered.* [ME *wherat*]

where·by (hwâr bī′, wâr-), *conj., adv.* **1.** by what or by which. **2.** *Obs.* by what?; how? [ME *wherby*]

where'd (hwârd, wârd), **1.** contraction of *where did: Where'd you go on your holiday?* **2.** a contraction of *where had: Where'd he been?*

wher·e'er (hwâr âr′, wâr-), *conj., adv.* *Literary.* wherever.

where·fore (hwâr′fōr, -fôr, wâr′-), *adv.* **1.** for what?; why? —*conj.* **2.** for what or which cause or reason: *Wherefore let us be grateful.* —*n.* **3.** the cause or reason: *to study the whys and wherefores of a situation.* [ME] —**Syn. 2.** See **therefore.**

where·from (hwâr frum′, -from′, wâr-), *conj., adv.* from which; whence.

where·in (hwâr in′, wâr-), *conj.* **1.** in what or in which. —*adv.* **2.** in what way or respect? [ME *wherin*]

where·in·to (hwâr in′to͞o, wâr-; hwâr′in to͞o′, wâr′-), *conj.* into which.

where'll (hwârl, wârl), contraction of *where shall* or *where will: Where'll I be ten years from now?*

where·of (hwâr uv′, -ov′, wâr-), *adv., conj.* of what, which, or whom. [ME *wherof*]

where·on (hwâr on′, -ôn′, wâr-), *conj.* **1.** on what or which. —*adv.* **2.** *Archaic.* on what? [ME *wheron*]

where're (hwâr′ər, wâr′-, hwâr, wâr), contraction of *where are: Where're you going?*

where's (hwârz, wârz), **1.** contraction of *where is: Where's my share?* **2.** *Informal.* contraction of *where has: Where's he been all night?*

where·so·e'er (hwâr′sō âr′, wâr′-), *conj.* *Literary.* wheresoever.

where·so·ev·er (hwâr′sō ev′ər, wâr′-), *conj.* in or to whatsoever place; wherever. [ME = *whereso* (OE (*swā*) *hwǣr swā*) + *ever* EVER]

where·through (hwâr thro͞o′, wâr-), *conj.* through, during, or because of which. [ME *hwerthrough*]

where·to (hwâr to͞o′, wâr-), *conj., adv.* **1.** to what or what place or end. **2.** to which. [ME *wherto*]

where·un·to (hwâr un′to͞o, wâr-), *conj., adv.* whereto. [late ME]

where·up·on (hwâr′ə pon′, -pôn′, wâr′-), *conj.* **1.** upon what or upon which: *the shelf whereupon the book rests.* **2.** at or after which; as a consequence: *The flag passed, whereupon he saluted.* **3.** *Archaic.* upon what? [ME *wherupon*]

where've (hwârv, wârv, hwâr′əv, wâr′-), contraction of *where have: Where've you seen this before?*

wher·ev·er (hwâr ev′ər, wâr-), *conj.* **1.** in, at, or to whatever place. **2.** in any case or condition: *wherever it is heard of.* —*adv.* **3.** where? (used emphatically): *Wherever did you find that?* [ME; OE *hwǣr ǣfre*]

where·with (hwâr with′, -wit͟h′, wâr-), *adv.* **1.** with which; by means of which. **2.** *Archaic.* **a.** with what? **b.** because of which; by reason of which. **c.** whereupon; at which. —*pron.* **3.** that by which; that with which. —*n.* **4.** *Rare.* wherewithal. [ME *wherwith*]

where·with·al (hwâr′wit͟h ôl′, wâr′-), *n.* **1.** that wherewith to do something; means or supplies for the purpose or need, esp. money: *the wherewithal to pay my rent.* —*adv.* **2.** by means of which; out of which. **3.** *Archaic.* wherewith. —*pron.* **4.** wherewith. [WHERE + WITHAL]

wher·ry (hwer′ē, wer′ē), *n., pl.* **-ries,** *v.,* **-ried, -ry·ing.** —*n.* **1.** a light rowboat for one person; skiff. **2.** any of various barges, fishing vessels, etc., used locally in England. **3.** (in England) a light rowboat used for carrying passengers and goods on rivers. —*v.t., v.i.* **4.** to use, or transport in, a wherry. [late ME *whery* < ?]

whet (hwet, wet), *v.,* **whet·ted, whet·ting,** *n.* —*v.t.* **1.** to sharpen (a knife, tool, etc.) by grinding or friction. **2.** to make keen or eager; stimulate: *to whet the appetite.* —*n.* **3.** the act of whetting. **4.** something that whets; appetizer. [ME *whette,* OE *hwett(an)* (< *hwæt* bold); c. G *wetzen,* Icel *hvetja,* Goth *gahwatjan* to incite] —**whet′ter,** *n.*

wheth·er (hwet͟h′ər, wet͟h′-), *conj.* **1.** (used to introduce the first of two or more alternatives, and sometimes repeated before the second or later alternative, usually with the correlative *or*): *It matters little whether we go or stay. Whether we go or whether we stay, the result is the same.* **2.** (used to introduce a single alternative, the other being implied or understood, or some clause or element not involving alternatives): *See whether he has come.* **3. whether or no,** under whatever circumstances; regardless: *He threatens to go whether or no.* —*pron. Archaic.* **4.** which (of two)? **5.** (used to introduce a question presenting alternatives, usually with the correlative *or*). [ME; OE *hwether, hwæther* = *hwe-, hwa-* (see WHO) + *-ther* comp. suffix; c. Icel *hvatharr,* Goth *hwathar*] —**Usage.** See **if.**

whet·stone (hwet′stōn′, wet′-), *n.* a stone for sharpening cutlery or tools by friction. [ME *whetston,* OE *hwetstān*]

whew (hwyo͞o), *interj.* (a whistling exclamation or sound expressing astonishment, relief, etc.)

whey (hwā, wā), *n.* a milk serum, separating as a watery liquid from the curd after coagulation, as in the making of cheese. [ME *wheye,* OE *hwǣg;* c. D, LG *wei*] —**whey′ey,** *adj.*

whey·face (hwā′fās′, wā′-), *n.* a face that or a person who is pallid, as from fear. —**whey′faced′,** *adj.*

which (hwich, wich), *pron.* **1.** what one?: *Which of these do you want?* **2.** whichever: *Choose which appeals to you.* **3.** (used relatively in restrictive and nonrestrictive clauses to represent a specified antecedent): *The book, which I read last night, was exciting. The lawyer represented five families, of which our family was the largest.* **4.** (used relatively in restrictive clauses having *that* as the antecedent): *Damaged goods constituted part of that which was sold at the auction.* **5.** (used after a preposition to represent a specified antecedent): *the horse on which I rode.* **6.** (used relatively to represent a specified or implied antecedent) the one that; a particular one that: *You may choose which you like.* **7.** (used in parenthetic clauses) the thing or fact that: *He hung around for hours and, which was worse, kept me from doing my work.* —*adj.* **8.** what one of (a certain number or group mentioned or implied)?: *Which book do you want?* **9.** whichever: *Use which method you prefer.* **10.** being previously mentioned: *It stormed all day, during which time the ship broke up.* [ME; OE *hwilc* = *hwi-* (see WHO) + *-līc* body, shape, kind (see LIKE[1]); c. D *welk,* G *welch,* Goth *hwileiks,* lit., of what form]
—**Usage.** Teachers of English and many good writers and stylists have long maintained that the distinction between WHICH and THAT in relative clauses is a useful one that should be kept. The traditional rule is that THAT is used to introduce restrictive relative clauses and WHICH to introduce nonrestrictive relative clauses. In *The house that has green shutters has been sold,* the relative clause is restrictive, hence is introduced by THAT. (That is, "It was the house with green shutters that was sold," not any other house.) In *The house, which has green shutters, has been sold,* the relative clause is descriptive or parenthetical, hence is introduced by WHICH. In practice, however, this distinction is made more often in careful writing than in ordinary speech—where stress can often serve to express the restrictiveness or nonrestrictiveness of a clause—and many excellent writers regularly fail to treat THAT and WHICH differently. On the other hand, WHICH is used regularly in referring to inanimate objects and, usually, animals and never, in modern usage, to individual persons, while THAT can be used for either. WHO, in its various forms, is used only in referring to people or to animals having proper names: *The man whom* (or *that*) *you saw is my father.* WHO can be either restrictive or nonrestrictive.

which·ev·er (hwich ev′ər, wich-), *pron.* **1.** (of a certain number or group specified or implied) any one that: *Take whichever you like.* **2.** no matter which: *Whichever you choose, the others will be offended.* —*adj.* **3.** (of an indicated number) no matter which: *whichever day.* [late ME]

which·so·ev·er (hwich′sō ev′ər, wich′-), *pron., adj.* whichever. [late ME = *whichso* (modeled on *whatso*) + *ever* EVER]

whid·ah (hwid′ə, wid′ə), *n.* whydah.

whiff (hwif, wif), *n.* **1.** a slight gust or puff of wind, air, smoke, or the like: *a whiff of fresh air.* **2.** a slight trace of odor or smell: *a whiff of onions.* **3.** a single inhalation or exhalation. **4.** a slight outburst: *a little whiff of temper.* —*v.i.* **5.** to blow or come in whiffs or puffs, as wind, smoke, etc. **6.** to inhale or exhale whiffs, as in smoking tobacco. —*v.t.* **7.** to blow or drive with a whiff or puff, as the wind does. **8.** to inhale or exhale (air, tobacco smoke, etc.) in whiffs. **9.** to smoke (a pipe, cigar, etc.). [aspirated var. of ME *weffe* whiff (of steam or vapor)] —**whiff′er,** *n.*

whif·fet (hwif′it, wif′-), *n. U.S. Informal.* an insignificant person; whippersnapper. [WHIFF + -ET, modeled on *whippet*]

whif·fle (hwif′əl, wif′-), *v.,* **-fled, -fling.** —*v.i.* **1.** to blow in light or shifting gusts or puffs, as the wind. **2.** to shift about; vacillate; be fickle. —*v.t.* **3.** to blow with light, shifting gusts. [WHIFF + -LE]

whif·fler[1] (hwif′lər, wif′-), *n.* **1.** a person who frequently shifts his opinions, attitudes, interests, etc. **2.** a person who is vacillating or evasive in an argument. [WHIFFLE + -ER[1]]

whif·fler[2] (hwif′lər, wif′-), *n. Hist.* an attendant who clears the way for a procession. [earlier *wiffler* armed attendant = *wiffle* (var. of ME *wifle,* OE *wifel* battle-ax) + -ER[1]]

W, Whiffletrees
D, Doubletree

whif·fle·tree (hwif′əl trē′, wif′-), *n.* a crossbar, pivoted at the middle, to which the traces of a harness are fastened for pulling a cart, carriage, plow, etc. Also called **whippletree, singletree, swingletree.** Cf. **doubletree.** [var. of WHIPPLETREE]

Whig (hwig, wig), *n.* **1.** *Amer. Hist.* **a.** a member of the patriotic party during the Revolutionary period; supporter of the Revolution. **b.** a member of a political party (c1834–1855) that was formed in opposition to the Democratic party, and favored organized economic expansion and a high protective tariff, while opposing the strength of the presidency. **2.** *Brit. Politics.* a member of a major political party (1679–1832) in Great Britain that held liberal principles and favored reforms: later called the Liberal party. —*adj.* **3.** of, pertaining to, or characteristic of the Whigs. [short for *whiggamore* (member of band of Scottish rebels that marched on Edinburgh in 1648) = *whig* + (BLACK)AMOOR; first element *whig* akin to WHEY]

Whig·gish (hwig′ish, wig′-), *adj.* inclined to Whiggism. —**Whig′gish·ly,** *adv.* —**Whig′gish·ness,** *n.*

Whig·gism (hwig′iz əm, wig′-), *n.* the principles or practices of Whigs. Also, **Whig′ger·y.**

whig·ma·lee·rie (hwig′mə lēr′ē, wig′-), *n.* **1.** a whim; notion. **2.** a fanciful ornament or contrivance. [?]

while (hwīl, wīl), *n., conj., prep., v.,* **whiled, whil·ing.** —*n.* **1.** a period or interval of time: *to wait a long while.* **2.** *Archaic.* a particular time or occasion. **3. all the while,** during this entire time; all along. **4. worth one's while,** worth one's time, trouble, or expense; worthwhile. —*conj.* **5.** during or in the time that. **6.** throughout the time that; as long as: *while rivers run downhill.* **7.** although; even though: *While flattered, I must decline to accept.* **8.** at the same time that (showing an analogous or corresponding action or state): *Books strewed the floor, while magazines covered the tables.* —*prep.* **9.** *Archaic.* until. —*v.t.* **10.** to cause (time) to pass, esp. in some easy or pleasant manner (usually fol. by *away*). [ME; OE *hwīl;* c. D *wijl,* G *weile,* Goth *hweila,* Icel *hvīla*]

whiles (hwīlz, wīlz), *adv.* **1.** *Chiefly Scot.* at times. **2.** *Obs.* in the meantime. —*conj.* **3.** *Archaic.* while. [ME]

whil·li·kers (hwil′ə kərz, wil′-), *interj. Informal.* (used as an intensive after *gee* or *golly* to express astonishment, delight, etc.) Also, **whil·li·kins** (hwil′ə kinz, wil′-). [?]

whi·lom (hwī′ləm, wī′-), *adv. Archaic.* at one time; formerly. [ME; OE *hwīlom* at times, dat. pl. of *hwīl* WHILE (n.)]

whilst (hwīlst, wīlst), *conj. Chiefly Brit.* while. [late ME *whilest* (see WHILES); inorganic *-t,* as in *amongst, amidst,* etc.]

whim (hwim, wim), *n.* **1.** an odd or capricious idea, notion, or desire. **2.** capricious humor: *to be swayed by whim.* **3.** *Mining Obs.* a vertical drum, usually horse-operated, for winding in a hoisting rope. [short for WHIM-WHAM] —**Syn. 1.** whimsy, humor, caprice.

Whim (def. 3)

whim·brel (hwim′brəl, wim′-), *n.* a curlew, *Numenius phaeopus,* of both the New and Old Worlds. [*whim* (? imit.) + intrusive *-b-* + -REL]

whim·per (hwim′pər, wim′-), *v.i.* **1.** to cry with low, plaintive, broken sounds. —*v.t.* **2.** to utter in a whimper. —*n.* **3.** a whimpering cry or sound. [obs. *whimp* to whine + -ER[6]] —**whim′per·er,** *n.* —**whim′per·ing·ly,** *adv.* —**Syn. 1.** whine, weep, sob. **3.** whine, sob.

whim·sey (hwim′zē, wim′-), *n., pl.* **-seys.** whimsy.

whim·si·cal (hwim′zi kəl, wim′-), *adj.* **1.** given to whimsy or fanciful notions; capricious; erratic. **2.** of the nature of or proceeding from whimsy, as thoughts or actions. —**whim′si·cal·ly,** *adv.* —**Syn. 1.** notional.

whim·si·cal·i·ty (hwim′zi kal′i tē, wim′-), *n., pl.* **-ties** for 2. **1.** Also, **whim′si·cal·ness.** whimsical quality or character. **2.** a whimsical notion, speech, or act.

whim·sy (hwim′zē, wim′-), *n., pl.* **-sies. 1.** capricious humor or disposition; extravagant, fanciful, or excessively playful expression: *a play likely to please those with a strong tolerance for whimsy.* **2.** an odd or fanciful notion. **3.** anything odd or fanciful; whim. Also, **whimsey.** [WHIM(-WHAM) + FANTA)SY] —**Syn. 2.** caprice, whim, humor, quirk.

whim-wham (hwim′hwam′, wim′wam′), *n.* **1.** any odd or fanciful object or thing; gimcrack. **2. whim-whams,** *Informal.* nervousness; jitters. [cf. *flimflam, jim-jam,* etc.]

whin·chat (hwin′chat′, win′-), *n.* a small, Old World thrush, *Saxicola rubetra,* having a buff-colored breast and white at the base of the tail. [*whin* thorny shrub + CHAT]

whine (hwīn, wīn), *v.,* **whined, whin·ing,** *n.* —*v.i.* **1.** to utter a low, usually nasal, complaining cry or sound: *The puppies were whining from hunger.* **2.** to snivel or complain in a peevish, self-pitying way. —*v.t.* **3.** to utter with or as if with a whine. —*n.* **4.** a whining utterance, sound, or tone. **5.** a feeble, peevish complaint. [ME; OE *hwīna(n)* (to) whiz; c. Icel *hvīna*] —**whin′er,** *n.* —**whin′ing·ly,** *adv.* —**Syn. 1.** moan, whimper. **2.** See **complain.**

whin·ny (hwin′ē, win′ē), *v.,* **-nied, -ny·ing,** *n.* —*v.i.* **1.** to utter the characteristic cry of a horse; neigh. —*v.t.* **2.** to express by whinnying. —*n.* **3.** a neigh. [imit.; cf. earlier *whrinny,* L *hinnīre*]

whin·stone (hwin′stōn′, win′-), *n.* any of the dark-colored, fine-grained rocks such as dolerite and basalt trap. Also called **whin** (hwin, win). [?]

whin·y (hwī′nē, wī′-), *adj.,* **whin·i·er, whin·i·est.** complaining; fretful; cranky. Also, **whin′ey.**

whip (hwip, wip), *v.,* **whipped** or **whipt, whip·ping,** *n.* —*v.t.* **1.** to strike with quick, repeated strokes of something slender and flexible; lash. **2.** to beat with a strap, lash, rod, or the like, esp. by way of punishment or chastisement; flog; thrash: *Criminals used to be whipped for minor offenses.* **3.** to drive with or as with a whip. **4.** to train or organize forcefully: *to whip recruits into shape.* **5.** *Informal.* to outdo or defeat decisively, as in an athletic contest. **6.** to hoist or haul by means of a whip. **7.** to pull suddenly (usually fol. by *out, in, into,* etc.): *He whipped his gun out of its holster.* **8.** to fish (a stream, lake, etc.) with rod and line, esp. by making repeated casts. **9.** to overlay or cover (cord, rope, etc.) with windings, cord, thread, or the like. **10.** to wind (cord, twine, thread, etc.) about something: *The tailor whipped the seams with heavy thread.* **11.** to beat (eggs, cream, etc.) with an eggbeater, whisk, fork, or other implement in order to mix in air and cause to expand and thicken. —*v.i.* **12.** to move or go quickly and suddenly; dart; whisk (usually fol. by *around, into, off,* etc.): *She whipped into the store for a bottle of milk.* **13.** to beat or lash about, as a pennant in the wind. **14.** to fish with rod and line, esp. by casting the line frequently. **15. whip up,** *Informal.* **a.** to plan or assemble quickly: *to whip up a delicious dinner.* **b.** to incite; arouse; stir: *The crowd was whipped up to a frenzy.* —*n.* **16.** an instrument for striking, as in driving animals or in punishing, typically consisting of a long flexible lash with a rigid handle. **17.** a whipping or lashing stroke or motion. **18.** *Chiefly Brit.* a person who uses a whip as part of his work, as a coachman. **19.** *Politics.* **a.** Also called **party whip.** a party manager in a legislative body who secures attendance for voting and directs other members. **b.** *Eng.* a written call made on members of a party to be in attendance for voting. **20.** a tackle consisting of a fall rove through a single standing block **(single whip),** or of a fall secured at one end and rove through a single running and a single standing block **(double whip).** See diag. at **tackle. 21.** the wrapping around the end of a whipped cord or the like. **22.** a dish made of cream or egg whites whipped to a froth with flavoring, often with fruit pulp or the like: *prune whip.* [ME *whippe,* aspirated var. of *wippe(n)*; c. D *wippen* to swing, oscillate; cf. LG *wip(pe)* quick movement] —**whip′like′,** *adj.* —**whip′per,** *n.* —**Syn. 2.** scourge.

whip·cord (hwip′kôrd′, wip′-), *n.* **1.** a cotton, woolen, or worsted fabric with a steep, diagonally ribbed surface. **2.** a strong, hard-twisted cord, sometimes used for the lashes of whips. [ME *wyppe-cord*]

whip′ hand′, 1. the hand that holds the whip, in driving. **2.** a position of dominance.

whip·lash (hwip′lash′, wip′-), *n.* **1.** the lash of a whip. **2.** Also called **whip′lash in′jury.** a neck injury caused by a sudden jerking backward, forward, or backward and forward of the head as during an automobile accident.

whip·per·snap·per (hwip′ər snap′ər, wip′-), *n.* an unimportant but offensively presumptuous person, esp. a young one. [jingling extension of *whipsnapper* a cracker of whips]

whip·pet (hwip′it, wip′-), *n.* a small, swift dog resembling a greyhound, used for hunting rabbits and for racing. [? alter. of phrase *whip it* move briskly]

Whippet (22 in. high at shoulder)

whip′ping boy′, 1. a person who is made to bear the blame for another's mistake; scapegoat. **2.** (formerly) a boy educated along with and taking punishment in place of a young prince or nobleman.

whip′ping cream′, *Cookery.* cream that contains enough butterfat to allow it to be whipped.

whip′ping post′, a post to which persons are tied to undergo whipping as a legal penalty.

whip·ple·tree (hwip′əl trē′, wip′-), *n.* whiffletree. [*whipple* (see WHIP, -LE) + TREE]

whip·poor·will (hwip′ər wil′, wip′-, hwip′ər wil′, wip′-), *n.* a nocturnal, North American goatsucker, *Caprimulgus vociferus,* having a variegated plumage of gray, black, white, and tawny. [imit.]

whip·ray (hwip′rā′, wip′-), *n.* any ray having a long, whiplike tail, esp. a stingray.

whip·saw (hwip′sô′, wip′-), *n., v.,* **-sawed, -sawed** or **-sawn, -saw·ing.** —*n.* **1.** a saw for cutting small curves, esp. one having a blade in a frame. **2.** a saw for two persons, used to divide timbers lengthwise. —*v.t.* **3.** to cut with a whipsaw. **4.** to win two bets from (a person) at one turn or play, as at faro. **5.** to defeat or worst in two ways at once.

whip′ scor′pion, any of numerous arachnids of the order *Pedipalpi,* of tropical and warm temperate regions, resembling a scorpion but having an abdomen that ends in a slender, nonvenomous whip.

whip·snake (hwip′snāk′, wip′-), *n.* **1.** any of several long, slender New World snakes of the genus *Masticophis,* the tail of which resembles a whip. **2.** any of various similar colubrid snakes. Also, **whip′ snake′.**

whip·stall (hwip′stôl′, wip′-), *Aeron.* —*n.* **1.** a stall during a vertical climb in which the nose of the airplane falls forward and downward in a whiplike movement. —*v.t.* **2.** to cause (an aircraft) to undergo whipstall. —*v.i.* **3.** to whipstall an aircraft.

whip·stitch (hwip′stich′, wip′-), *v.t.* **1.** to sew with stitches passing over an edge, in joining, finishing, or gathering. —*n.* **2.** one such stitch. **3.** *Informal.* a little while.

whip·stock (hwip′stok′, wip′-), *n.* the handle of a whip.

whip·worm (hwip′wûrm′, wip′-), *n.* any of several parasitic nematodes of the genus *Trichuris,* having a long, slender, whiplike anterior end.

whir (hwûr, wûr), *v.,* **whirred, whir·ring,** *n.* —*v.i.* **1.** to move quickly with a humming or buzzing sound. —*n.* **2.** the act or sound of whirring. Also, **whirr.** [ME *quirre* (Scot) < Scand; cf. Dan *hvirre,* Norw *kvirra.* See WHIRL]

whirl (hwûrl, wûrl), *v.i.* **1.** to turn around, spin, or rotate rapidly: *the fan blades whirled in the hot room.* **2.** to face about quickly: *He whirled and faced his pursuers.* **3.** to move, travel, or be carried along rapidly. **4.** to feel as though spinning rapidly; reel as from dizziness: *My head began to whirl.* —*v.t.* **5.** to cause to turn around, spin, or rotate rapidly. **6.** to send, drive, or carry in a circular or curving course. **7.** to drive, send, or carry along with great or dizzying rapidity. **8.** *Obs.* to hurl. —*n.* **9.** the act of whirling. **10.** a whirling movement; quick turn or swing. **11.** a short drive, run, walk, or the like. **12.** something that whirls; a whirling current or mass. **13.** a rapid round of events, affairs, etc.: *Her life was a whirl of parties.* **14.** a state marked by a dizzying succession or mingling of feelings, thoughts, etc. **15.** a state of dizziness: *Her head was in a whirl from fatigue.* **16.** an attempt or trial: *to give a plan a whirl.* [ME *whirle* < Scand; cf. Icel *hvirfla* to whirl, akin to OE *hwyrflung* turning, revolving, *hwyrfel* circuit, etc. See WHORL] —**whirl′er,** *n.* —**whirl′ing·ly,** *adv.* —**Syn. 1.** gyrate, pirouette. **1, 5.** revolve, twirl, wheel. **10.** spin, revolution.

whirl·a·bout (hwûrl′ə bout′, wûrl′-), *n.* **1.** a whirling about. **2.** a whirligig. —*adj.* **3.** whirling about.

whirl·i·cote (hwûr′lə kōt′, wûrl′-), *n.* a large, heavy coach or carriage. [appar. miswritten for late ME *whirlecole.* See WHIRL, -CULE]

whirl·i·gig (hwûr′lə gig, wûr′-), *n.* **1.** something that whirls. **2.** a whirling or giddy motion or course. **3.** a merry-go-round. **4.** a carrousel. **5.** a toy for whirling or spinning, as a top. [late ME *whirlegigge.* See WHIRL, GIG[1]]

whirl′igig bee′tle, any of numerous aquatic beetles of the family *Gyrinidae,* commonly seen circling rapidly about in large numbers on the surface of the water.

whirl′ing der′vish, *Islam.* a dervish whose actions include ecstatic whirling, dancing, chanting, etc.

whirl·pool (hwûrl′pōōl′, wûrl′-), *n.* a whirling eddy or current, as in a river or the sea. [WHIRL + POOL[1]; cf. OE *hwyrfepōl*]

whirl′pool bath′, a therapeutic bath in which a part or parts of the body are immersed in whirling hot water.

whirl·wind (hwûrl′wind′, wûrl′-), *n.* **1.** any of several relatively small masses of air rotating rapidly around an advancing, more or less vertical axis, as a dust devil, tornado, or waterspout. **2.** anything resembling a whirlwind, as in violent action or destructive force. **3. reap the whirlwind,** to suffer the penalties for one's misdeeds. Hos. 8:7. [ME < Scand; cf. Icel *hvirfilvindr;* c. G *Wirbelwind*]

whirl·y·bird (hwûr′lē bûrd′, wûr′-), *n.* *Informal.* helicopter. [*whirly* (see WHIRL, -Y[1]) + BIRD]

whirr (hwûr, wûr), *v.i., v.t., n.* whir.

whir·ry (hwûr′ē, wûr′ē), *v.i.,* **-ried, -ry·ing.** *Scot.* to hurry; go rapidly. [perh. b. WHIR and HURRY]

whish (hwish, wish), *v.i.* **1.** to make, or move with, a whiz or swish. —*n.* **2.** a whishing sound. [imit.]

whisht (hwist, wist, hwisht, wisht), *interj., adj.* whist[2]. [cf. OE *hwiscettung* squeaking (said of mice)]

whisk[1] (hwisk, wisk), *v.t.* **1.** to sweep (dust, crumbs, etc., or a surface) with light strokes, as with a whisk broom, brush, or the like. **2.** to move with a rapid, sweeping stroke: *She whisked everything off the table with her arm.* **3.** to draw, snatch, carry, etc., lightly and rapidly: *He whisked the money into his pocket.* **4.** to carry or move with haste; transport speedily: *The limousine whisked her home.* —*v.i.* **5.** to sweep, pass, or go lightly and rapidly. —*n.* **6.** the act or an instance of whisking. [late ME *quhiske* (Scot) < Scand (aspiration from E); cf. Dan *viske* to wipe, c. G *wischen*]

whisk[2] (hwisk, wisk), *v.t.* **1.** to whip (eggs, cream, etc.) to a froth. —*n.* **2.** a small bunch of grass, straw, or the like, esp. for use in brushing. **3.** See **whisk broom. 4.** an implement, usually a bunch of wire loops held together in a handle, for beating or whipping eggs, cream, etc. [aspirated var. of ME *wisk* < Scand; cf. Icel *visk* wisp, c. G *Wisch* wisp of straw]

whisk′ broom′, a small short-handled broom used chiefly to brush clothes.

whisk·er (hwis′kər, wis′-), *n.* **1.** Usually, **whiskers.** the hair growing on the side of a man's face, esp. when worn long and with the chin clean-shaven. **2. whiskers,** the beard generally. **3.** a single hair of the beard. **4.** *Archaic.* a mustache. **5.** one of the long, stiff, bristly hairs growing about the mouth of certain animals, as the cat, rat, etc.; vibrissa. **6.** Also called **whisk′er boom′, whisk′er pole′.** *Naut.* any spar for extending the clew or clews of a sail so that it can catch more wind. [late ME] —**whisk′er·y,** *adj.*

whisk·ered (hwis′kərd, wis′-), *adj.* having, wearing, or covered with whiskers.

whis·key (hwis′kē, wis′-), *n., pl.* **-keys,** *adj.* —*n.* **1.** a distilled alcoholic liquor made from grain, as barley, rye, corn, etc., usually consisting of from 40 to 50 percent alcohol. **2.** a drink of whiskey. **3.** a word used in communications to represent the letter W. —*adj.* **4.** made of, relating to, or resembling whiskey. Also, **whisky.** [short for *whiskybae* < Gael *uisgebeatha* USQUEBAUGH]

whis′key sour′, a cocktail made with whiskey, lemon juice, and sugar, usually garnished with an orange slice.

whis·ky (hwis′kē, wis′-), *n., pl.* **-kies,** *adj.* whiskey, esp. Scotch or Canadian whiskey.

whis·per (hwis′pər, wis′pər), *v.i.* **1.** to speak with soft, hushed sounds, using the breath, lips, etc., but with no vibration of the vocal cords. **2.** to talk softly and privately (often implying gossip, slander, plotting, or the like): *The* *king knew that the courtiers were whispering.* **3.** (of trees, water, breezes, etc.) to make a soft, rustling sound. —*v.t.* **4.** to utter in whispers. **5.** to say or tell in a whisper; to tell privately. **6.** to speak to or tell (a person) in a whisper, or privately. —*n.* **7.** the mode of utterance, or the voice, of a person who whispers. **8.** something uttered by whispering. **9.** a soft, rustling sound like a whisper: *the whisper of leaves in the wind.* [ME *whispere(n),* OE *hwisprian;* c. G *wispern;* akin to Icel *hviskra* to whisper, *hvīsla* to whistle. See WHINE]

whis·per·er (hwis′pər ər, wis′-), *n.* **1.** a person or thing that whispers. **2.** a gossip, talebearer or rumor-monger.

whis·per·ing (hwis′pər ing, wis′-), *n.* **1.** whispered talk or conversation. **2.** rumor, hearsay, or gossip. **3.** a whispered sound. —*adj.* **4.** that whispers; making a sound like a whisper. **5.** given to whispering; gossipy. **6.** conversing in whispers. [ME (n.), OE *hvisprunge* (n.). See WHISPER, -ING[2], -ING[1]] —**whis′per·ing·ly,** *adv.*

whis′pering campaign′, the organized spreading by word of mouth of insinuations, rumors, or charges meant to destroy the reputation of a person, organization, cause, etc.

whis·per·y (hwis′pə rē, wis′-), *adj.* **1.** like a whisper. **2.** abounding in whispers or other soft, mysterious sounds.

whist[1] (hwist, wist), *n.* a card game, an early form of bridge, usually played by four players, two against two, with 52 cards. [special use of WHIST[2]; r. *whisk* earlier name of game < ?]

whist[2] (hwist, wist), *interj.* **1.** hush! silence! be still! —*adj.* **2.** *Archaic.* hushed; silent; still. Also, **whisht.** [imit.; cf. SHH, SHUSH, etc.]

whis·tle (hwis′əl, wis′-), *v.,* **-tled, -tling,** *n.* —*v.i.* **1.** to make a clear musical sound, a series of such sounds, or a high-pitched, warbling sound by the forcible expulsion of the breath through the pursed lips. **2.** to make such a sound or series of sounds otherwise, as by blowing on some device. **3.** (of a device) to produce a similar sound when actuated by steam or the like: *This teakettle will whistle when it boils.* **4.** to emit similar sounds from the mouth, as birds do. **5.** to move, go, pass, etc., with a whistling or whizzing sound, as a bullet, the wind, etc. —*v.t.* **6.** to produce by whistling: *He can whistle any tune.* **7.** to call, direct, or signal by or as by whistling. **8. whistle for,** to attempt to summon or obtain as unsuccessfully as by whistling: *to whistle for a wind; He said we could go whistle for our money.* —*n.* **9.** an instrument for producing whistling sounds by means of the breath, steam, etc., as a small wooden or tin tube; a pipe. **10.** a sound produced by whistling. **11. blow the whistle,** *Slang.* **a.** to stop (a person, organization, etc., from continuing a specific activity). **b.** to betray or turn informer. **c.** to expose or make public: *to blow the whistle on a conspiracy.* **12. wet one's whistle,** *Informal.* to take a drink. [ME; OE *hwistl(ian);* akin to Icel *hvīsla* to whistle, *hviskra* to whisper. See WHINE]

whis·tler (hwis′lər, wis′-), *n.* **1.** a person or thing that whistles. **2.** any of various birds whose wings whistle in flight, esp. the goldeneye and European widgeon. **3.** a large marmot, *Marmota caligata,* of mountainous northwestern North America, closely related to the woodchuck. [ME; OE *hwistlere*]

Whis·tler (hwis′lər, wis′-), *n.* **James (Abbott) Mc·Neill** (mək nēl′), 1834–1903, U.S. painter and etcher, in France and England after 1855. —**Whis·tle·ri·an** (hwis lēr′ē ən, wis-), *adj.*

whis′tle stop′, **1.** a small, unimportant town along a railroad line. **2.** a brief appearance, single performance, or the like, in a small town, as during a political campaign, theatrical tour, etc.

whis·tle-stop (hwis′əl stop′, wis′-), *v.i.,* **-stopped, -stopping.** to campaign for political office by traveling around the country and stopping at towns to give brief speeches.

whis′tling (hwis′ling, wis′-), *n.* **1.** the act or sound of a person or thing that whistles. **2.** *Vet. Pathol.* a form of roaring characterized by a peculiarly shrill sound. [ME; OE *hwistlung*] —**whis′tling·ly,** *adv.*

whis′tling swan′, a large, white, North American swan, *Olor columbianus,* having black feet and a small yellow spot at the base of the black bill, noted for its whistling cry.

whit (hwit, wit), *n.* a particle; bit; jot (used esp. in negative phrases): *not a whit better.* [appar. scribal metathetic var. of ME, OE *wiht* WIGHT[1]]

Whit·by (hwit′bē, wit′-), *n.* a seaport in NE Yorkshire, in NE England: church council A.D. 664. 12,717.

white (hwīt, wīt), *adj.,* **whit·er, whit·est,** *n., v.,* **whit·ed, whit·ing.** —*adj.* **1.** of the color of pure snow, of the margins of this page, etc.; reflecting nearly all the rays of sunlight or a similar light: *Her white dress was dazzling in the sun.* **2.** (of human beings) marked by very slight pigmentation of the skin, as many Caucasoids. **3.** dominated by or including only Caucasoids: *a white school.* **4.** pallid or pale, as from fear or other emotions. **5.** silvery, as hair. **6.** snowy: *a white Christmas.* **7.** lacking color; transparent: *white glass.* **8.** politically ultraconservative. **9.** blank, as an unoccupied space in printed matter: *Fill in the white space below.* **10.** *Armor.* composed entirely of polished and exposed steel plates. **11.** wearing white clothing: *a white friar.* **12.** *Slang.* honest; decent: *That's very white of you.* **13.** auspicious or fortunate. **14.** morally pure; innocent. **15.** without malice; harmless: *white magic.* **16.** (of wines) light-colored or yellowish, as opposed to red. **17.** *Brit.* (of coffee) containing milk or cream. —*n.* **18.** a color without hue at one extreme end of the scale of grays, opposite to black. **19.** the quality or state of being white; whiteness: *The white of the snow was marred by the traffic.* **20.** lightness of skin pigment. **21.** a white material, area, etc. **22.** *Biol.* a pellucid viscous fluid which surrounds the yolk of an egg; albumen. **23.** the white part of the eyeball. **24.** *Informal.* a white person; a member of the Caucasoid race. **25. whites, a.** (*construed as sing.*) *Pathol.* leukorrhea. **b.** white or nearly white clothing. **c.** top-grade white flour. **26.** white wine. **27.** See **white bread. 28.** a type or breed that is white in color. **29.** *Archery.* **a.** the outermost ring of the butt. **b.** an arrow that hits this ring. **c.** the central part of the butt or target. **30.** *Chess, Checkers.* the men or pieces that are light-colored. **31.** (*often cap.*) a member of a royalist, conservative, or reactionary political party. —*v.t.* **32.** to make white; whiten. [ME *whit(e),* OE *hwīt;* c. G *weiss,* Icel *hvītr*]

White (hwīt, wīt), *n.* **1. Byron R(aymond),** born 1917, U.S. jurist: associate justice of the U.S. Supreme Court since 1962. **2. E(l·wyn) B(rooks)** (el′win), 1899–1985, U.S. humorist and poet. **3. Gilbert,** 1720–93, English clergyman, naturalist, and writer. **4. Stan·ford** (stan′fərd), 1853–1906, U.S. architect. **4. T(erence) H(an·bur·y)** (han′bə rē), 1896–1964, English novelist. **5. William Allen,** 1868–1944, U.S. journalist.

white′ alert′, (in military or civilian defense) an all-clear signal, directive, etc., indicating that the danger of air raid no longer exists.

white′ al′kali, **1.** *Agric.* a whitish layer of mineral salts, esp. sodium sulfate, sodium chloride, and magnesium sulfate, often found on top of soils under low rainfall. **2.** refined soda ash.

white′ ant′, termite.

white′ ash′. See under **ash[2]** (def. 1).

white·bait (hwīt′bāt′, -wīt′-), *n., pl.* **-bait.** any small, delicate fish cooked whole without being cleaned, esp. the sprat. [so called from use as bait]

white′ bass′ (bas), an edible, fresh-water serranid fish, *Roccus chrysops,* of the Great Lakes and Mississippi River drainage, silvery with yellow below and having the sides streaked with blackish lines.

white′ bear′. See **polar bear.**

white′ belt′, *Judo.* **1.** a white waistband worn by a beginner with his judo costume. **2.** a beginning judo player or the rank of beginner. Cf. **black belt** (def. 2), **brown belt.**

white′ birch′, **1.** the European birch, *Betula pendula,* yielding a hard wood. **2.** See **paper birch.**

white′ blood′ cell′, a leukocyte. Also called **white′ blood′ cor′puscle.**

white′ book′, an official report issued by a government, formerly often bound in white.

white′ bread′, any white or light-colored bread made from finely ground, usually bleached, flour. [ME *whit bre(e)d;* r. OE *hwītehlāf*]

white·cap (whīt′kap′, wīt′-), *n.* a wave with a broken and foaming white crest.

white′ ce′dar, **1.** a coniferous tree, *Chamaecyparis thyoides,* of the swamps of the eastern U.S. **2.** the wood of this tree, used in the construction of boxes, crates, wooden utensils, etc. **3.** the arborvitae, *Thuja occidentalis.* **4.** a pinaceous tree, *Chamaecyparis lawsoniana,* grown for its timber and as an ornamental.

white′ clo′ver, a clover, *Trifolium repens,* having white flowers, common in pastures and meadows. See illus. at **clover.** [ME *white clovere* (*clavere*), OE *hwiteclǣfre*]

white′ coal′, water, as of a stream, used for power.

white-col·lar (hwīt′kol′ər, wīt′-), *adj.* belonging or pertaining to the salaried or professional workers whose jobs generally do not involve manual labor. Cf. **blue-collar.**

white′ crap′pie. See under **crappie.**

whit·ed (hwī′tid, wī′-), *adj.* **1.** made white; bleached. **2.** covered with whitewash, whiting, or the like. [ME]

white′ damp′, a poisonous coal-mine gas composed chiefly of carbon monoxide.

whit′ed sep′ulcher, an evil person who feigns goodness; hypocrite. Matt. 23:27.

white′ dwarf′, *Astron.* a star having average mass and very small volume and of which the density may be a ton per cubic inch.

white′ el′ephant, **1.** an albino elephant. **2.** a possession entailing great expense or trouble out of proportion to its usefulness or value to the owner. **3.** a possession unwanted by the owner but difficult to dispose of.

white′ en′sign, the British naval ensign, consisting of the red cross of St. George on a white field, with the British union in the upper quarter along the hoist.

white·face (hwīt′fās′, wīt′-), *n.* **1.** a Hereford. **2.** white facial makeup, as for a clown.

white-faced (hwīt′fāst′, wīt′-), *adj.* **1.** having a white or pale face. **2.** marked with white on the front of the head, as a horse.

white′ feath′er, **1.** a symbol of cowardice. **2. show the white feather,** to behave in a cowardly manner. [orig. from a white feather in a gamecock's tail, taken as a sign of inferior breeding and hence of poor fighting qualities]

White·field (hwīt′fēld′, wīt′-), *n.* **George,** 1714–70, English Methodist evangelist. —**White′field′i·an, White′field·ite′,** *n.*

white·fish (hwīt′fish′, wīt′-), *n., pl.* (*esp. collectively*) **-fish,** (*esp. referring to two or more kinds or species*) **-fish·es.** **1.** any of several fishes of the family *Coregonidae,* found in northern waters of North America and Eurasia, similar to the trout but having a smaller mouth and larger scales. **2.** a marine food fish of California, *Caulolatilus princeps.* **3.** any of various silvery fishes of the minnow or carp family. **4.** the beluga, *Delphinapterus leucas.* [late ME]

white′ flag′, a white flag or piece of cloth, used as a symbol of surrender or truce.

white′ fox′. See **arctic fox.**

White′ Fri′ar, a Carmelite friar: so called from the distinctive white cloak worn. [late ME]

White·fri·ars (hwīt′frī′ərz, wīt′-), *n.* a district in central London, England.

white′ frost′, a heavy coating of frost.

white′ gold′, any of several gold alloys colored white by the presence of nickel or platinum.

white′ goods′, **1.** household goods, as bed sheets, tablecloths, towels, etc., formerly bleached and finished in white but now often patterned and colored. **2.** large household appliances, as refrigerators, stoves, and washers.

White·hall (hwīt′hôl′, wīt′-), *n.* **1.** Also called **White′hall Pal′ace.** a former palace in central London, England: execution of Charles I, 1649. **2.** a city in central Ohio, near Columbus. 25,263 (1970). **3.** the British government or its policies, so called from location of government Ministries on *Whitehall Street,* London.

White·head (hwīt′hed′, wīt′-), *n.* **Alfred North,** 1861–

1947, English philosopher and mathematician, in the U.S. after 1924.

white-head·ed (hwīt′hed′id, wīt′-), *adj.* having white hair.

white′ heat′, **1.** an intense heat at which a substance glows white. **2.** a stage of intense activity, excitement, feeling, etc.

white′ hope′, a person who is expected to be a major source of benefit to his profession, place of work, etc.

White·horse (hwīt′hôrs′, wīt′-), *n.* a town in and the capital of the Yukon Territory, in NW Canada. 5031 (1961).

white-hot (hwīt′hot′, wīt′-), *adj.* **1.** showing white heat. **2.** exceedingly enthusiastic, ardent, angry, devoted, etc.

White′ House′, the, **1.** Also called **Executive Mansion.** the official residence of the President of the United States, at Washington, D.C. **2.** *U.S.* the executive branch of the federal government.

white′ lead′ (led), **1.** a white powder, $2PbCO_3 \cdot Pb(OH)_2$, used as a pigment, in putty, and in ointments for burns. **2.** the putty made from this substance in oil. **3.** white lead ore; cerussite. [late ME]

white′ lead′ ore′, *Mineral.* cerussite.

white′ leath′er, leather treated with chemicals, as alum, salt, etc.; tawed leather. Also, **whitleather.**

white′ leg′, *Pathol.* See **milk leg.**

white′ lie′, a minor lie uttered from polite, amiable, or pardonable motives; a polite or harmless fib.

white′ line′, a solid stripe of paint, tiles, or the like, down the center of a road, for directing traffic.

white-liv·ered (hwīt′liv′ərd, wīt′-), *adj.* **1.** lacking courage; cowardly; lily-livered. **2.** lacking in vitality or spirit; pale; unhealthy.

white·ly (hwīt′lē, wīt′-), *adv.* with a white hue or color. [late ME]

white′ man's′ bur′den, the alleged duty of the white race to care for subject peoples of other races in its colonial possessions. [from the title of a poem by Rudyard Kipling]

white′ mat′ter, *Anat.* nerve tissue, esp. of the brain and spinal cord, which contains fibers only and is nearly white in color. Cf. **gray matter** (def. 1).

white′ meat′, **1.** any meat that is light-colored before cooking, as veal. Cf. **red meat.** **2.** any meat that is light-colored after cooking, as breast of chicken. Cf. **dark meat.** Also called **light meat.** [late ME]

white′ met′al, any of various light-colored alloys, as Babbitt metal or Britannia metal.

White′ Moun′tains, a mountain range in N New Hampshire, part of the Appalachian Mountains. Highest peak, Mt. Washington, 6293 ft.

white′ mus′tard. See under **mustard** (def. 2).

whit·en (hwīt′ᵊn, wīt′-), *v.t., v.i.* to make or become white. [ME; see WHITE, -EN[1]]

—Syn. WHITEN, BLANCH, BLEACH mean to make or become white. To WHITEN implies giving a white color or appearance to by putting a substance of some kind on the outside: *to whiten shoes.* To BLANCH implies taking away natural or original color throughout: *to blanch celery by growing it in the dark.* To BLEACH implies making white by placing in sunlight or by using chemicals: *to bleach linen, hair.* **—Ant.** blacken.

whit·en·er (hwīt′ᵊnər, wīt′-), *n.* **1.** a person or thing that whitens. **2.** a preparation for making something white, as a bleach, dye, polish, or the like.

white·ness (hwīt′nis, wīt′-), *n.* **1.** the quality or state of being white. **2.** paleness. **3.** something that is white. [ME *whitenes,* OE *hwītnes*]

White′ Nile′, the part of the Nile SW of Khartoum. ab. 500 mi. long. Cf. **Nile.**

whit·en·ing (hwīt′ᵊning, wīt′-), *n.* **1.** the act or process of making or turning white. **2.** a preparation for making something white; whiting.

white′ oak′, **1.** an oak, *Quercus alba,* of eastern North America, having a light-gray to white bark and yielding a hard, durable wood: the state tree of Connecticut and Maryland. **2.** an oak, *Quercus petraea,* of England. **3.** any of several other species of oak, as *Q. Garryana* or *Q. lobata,* of western North America, or *Q. Robur,* of Great Britain. **4.** the wood of any of these trees.

white′ pa′per, **1.** paper bleached white. **2.** an official governmental report. **3.** an authoritative report issued by any organization: *The TV station presented its white paper on Vietnam.* Cf. **blue book** (def. 3), **white book.**

White′ Pass′, a mountain pass in SE Alaska, near Skagway. 2888 ft. high.

white′ pep′per, a condiment prepared from the husked dried berries of the pepper plant, used either whole or ground.

white′ perch′, **1.** a small game fish, *Morone americana,* found in streams along the Atlantic coast of the U.S. **2.** See **silver perch** (def. 2).

white′ pine′, **1.** a pine, *Pinus Strobus,* of eastern North America, yielding a light-colored, soft, light wood of great commercial importance. **2.** the wood itself. **3.** any of various similar species of pine or their woods.

white′ plague′, *Pathol.* tuberculosis, esp. pulmonary tuberculosis.

White′ Plains′, a city in SE New York, near New York City: battle 1776. 50,346 (1970).

white′ pop′lar, **1.** an Old World poplar, *Populus alba,* widely cultivated in the U.S., having the underside of the leaves covered with a dense silvery-white down. **2.** the soft, straight-grained wood of the tulip tree.

white′ pota′to, potato (def. 1).

white′ race′, (loosely) Caucasoid people.

white′ rain′bow, fogbow.

white′ rat′, an albino variety of the Norway rat, *Rattus norvegicus,* used in biological experiments.

White′ Riv′er, a river flowing SE from NW Arkansas into the Mississippi River. 690 mi. long.

White′ Rock′, one of a variety of white Plymouth Rock chickens.

white′ rose′, *Eng. Hist.* the emblem of the royal house of York. Cf. **red rose, Wars of the Roses.**

White′ Rus′sia, Byelorussia.

White′ Rus′sian, **1.** a Russian who fought against the Bolsheviks in the Russian civil war. **2.** Byelorussian.

White′ Rus′sian So′viet So′cialist Repub′lic, Byelorussia (def. 1).

white′ sale′, a sale of sheets, pillowcases, and other white goods.

white′ sap′phire, *Mineral.* a colorless variety of corundum, used as a gemstone.

white′ sauce′, a sauce made of butter, flour, seasonings, and milk or sometimes chicken or veal stock; béchamel.

White′ Sea′, an arm of the Arctic Ocean, in the NW Soviet Union in Europe. ab. 36,000 sq. mi.

white′ slave′, a girl or woman who is sold or forced into prostitution. **—white′-slave′,** *adj.*

White′ Slave′ Act′. See **Mann Act.**

white′ slav′ery, the condition of or traffic in white slaves. **—white′ slav′er.**

white·smith (hwīt′smith′, wīt′-), *n.* a tinsmith. [ME, modeled on *blacksmith*]

white′ spruce′, **1.** a spruce, *Picea glauca,* of northern North America, having bluish-green leaves and silvery-brown bark. **2.** the light, soft wood of this tree.

white′ stork′, a large, Eurasian stork, *Ciconia ciconia,* having white plumage with black in the wings and a red bill: the bird in legend that delivers newborn babies. See illus. at **stork.**

white′ suprem′acist, a person who advocates or supports the theory of white supremacy.

white′ suprem′acy, the belief, theory, or doctrine that the white man has a natural superiority over the Negro and must keep him subordinated.

white′-tailed deer′ (hwīt′tāld′, wīt′-), a common North American deer, *Odocoileus virginianus,* having a tail with a white underside. Also, **white′tail deer′, white′tail′.**

white·throat (hwīt′thrōt′, wīt′-), *n.* any of several small songbirds having white throats, esp. an Old World warbler, *Sylvia communis.*

white′ tie′, **1.** a white bow tie for men, worn with formal evening dress. **2.** formal evening dress for men (distinguished from *black tie*).

white′ trash′, *Derogatory.* **1.** a member of the class of poor whites, esp. in the southern U.S. **2.** poor whites collectively.

white′ tur′nip, the turnip, *Brassica Rapa.*

White′ Vol′ta, a river in W Africa, in Ghana: a branch of the Volta River. ab. 550 mi. long. Cf. **Volta** (def. 2).

white·wall (hwīt′wôl′, wīt′-), *n.* a rubber tire having a sidewall with a white band on it. Also called **white′wall tire′.** [WHITE + (SIDE)WALL]

white·wash (hwīt′wosh′, -wôsh′, wīt′-), *n.* **1.** a composition, as of lime and water, or of whiting, size, and water, used for whitening walls, woodwork, etc. **2.** anything, as deceptive words or actions, used in an attempt to absolve a person or organization from blame, excuse a scandal, cover up defects, gloss over faults, etc.: *The report was a whitewash of the scandal.* **3.** *Informal.* (in sports) a defeat in which the loser fails to score. **—*v.t.*** **4.** to whiten with whitewash. **5.** to protect from blame by means of a whitewash. **6.** *Informal.* (in sports) to defeat in a whitewash. **—white′wash′er,** *n.*

white′ wa′ter, **1.** frothy water, as in whitecaps, rapids, etc. **2.** light-colored sea water over a shoal, sandy bottom, or the like.

white′ whale′, beluga (def. 2).

white′ wine′, wine having a yellowish to amber color derived from the light-colored grapes used in production, or from dark grapes with the skins, pulp, and seeds removed. [ME; cf. F *vin blanc*]

white·wood (hwīt′wo͝od′, wīt′-), *n.* **1.** any of numerous trees, as the tulip tree or the linden, yielding a white or light-colored wood. **2.** the wood. **3.** a cottonwood of the genus *Populus.*

whit·ey (hwī′tē, wī′-), *n.* *Slang.* a white person or white people collectively (used derogatively by American Negroes). Also, **White′y, whity.**

whith·er (hwith′ər, with′-), *Archaic.* **—*adv.*** **1.** to what place?; where? **2.** to what end, point, action, or the like?; to what? **—*conj.*** **3.** to which place. [ME, var. of ME, OE *hwider,* alter. of *hwæder* (c. Goth *hwadre*), modeled on *hider* HITHER]

whith·er·so·ev·er (hwith′ər sō ev′ər, with′-), *conj.* *Archaic.* to whatsoever place. [ME = *whitherso* (OE *swā hwider swā*) + *ever* EVER]

whith·er·ward (hwith′ər wərd, with′-), *adv.* *Archaic.* toward what place?; in what direction? Also, **whith′erwards.** [ME]

whit·ing[1] (hwī′ting, wī′-), *n., pl.* (*esp. collectively*) **-ing,** (*esp. referring to two or more kinds or species*) **-ings.** **1.** a slender food fish of the genus *Menticirrhus,* of the croaker family, found along the Atlantic coast of North America. **2.** the hake, *Merluccius bilinearis.* **3.** any of several European fishes of the cod family, esp. *Merlangus merlangus.* [late ME, perh. alter. of OE *hwītling* kind of fish; cf. MD *witinc,* of which the E may be a trans.: *whit-* for *wit-, -ing* for *-inc*]

whit·ing[2] (hwī′ting, wī′-), *n.* pure white chalk, or calcium carbonate, that has been ground and washed: used in making putty, whitewash, silver polish, etc. [ME; OE *hwīting-* (in *hwītingmelu;* see MEAL[2])]

whit·ish (hwī′tish, wī′-), *adj.* somewhat white; tending to white. [late ME] **—whit′ish·ness,** *n.*

whit·leath·er (hwit′leth′ər, wit′-), *n.* See **white leather.** [late ME *whitlether*]

whit·low (hwit′lō, wit′-), *n.* *Pathol.* an inflammation of the deeper tissues of a finger or toe, esp. of the terminal phalanx, usually terminating in suppuration. Also called **agnail.** [ME *whit(f)lowe, whitflawe.* See WHITE, FLAW[1]]

Whit·man (hwit′mən, wit′-), *n.* **1. Marcus,** 1802–47, U.S. missionary and pioneer. **2. Walt(er),** 1819–92, U.S. poet.

Whit·mon·day (hwit′mun′dē, -dā, wit′-), *n.* the Monday following Whitsunday. [modeled on WHITSUNDAY]

Whit·ney (hwit′nē, wit′-), *n.* **1. Eli,** 1765–1825, U.S. manufacturer and inventor. **2. John Hay,** 1904–82, U.S. diplomat and newspaper publisher. **3. Mount,** a mountain in E California, in the Sierra Nevada Mountains. 14,495 ft.

Whit·sun (hwit′sən, wit′-), *adj.* **1.** of or pertaining to Whitsunday or Whitsuntide. —*n.* **2.** Whitsunday or Whitsuntide. [ME *Whitsone(n)* < *Whitsonenday* by apocope. See WHITSUNDAY]

Whit·sun·day (hwit′sun′dē, -dā, wit′-; hwit′sən dā′, wit′-), *n.* the seventh Sunday after Easter, celebrated as a festival in commemoration of the descent of the Holy Spirit on the day of Pentecost. [ME *whitsonenday*, OE *Hwīta Sunnandæg* white Sunday; generally thought to come from the white baptismal robes worn on that day]

Whit·sun·tide (hwit′sən tīd′, wit′-), *n.* the week beginning with Whitsunday, esp. the first three days of this week. [ME *whitsone(n)tide.* See WHITSUN, TIDE¹]

Whit·ti·er (hwit′ē ər, wit′-), *n.* **1. John Green·leaf** (grēn′lēf′), 1807–92, U.S. poet. **2.** a city in SW California, E of Los Angeles. 72,863 (1970).

Whit·ting·ton (hwit′ing tən, wit′-), *n.* **Richard** ("*Dick Whittington*"), 1358?–1423, English merchant and philanthropist: Lord Mayor of London 1398, 1406–07, 1419–20.

whit·tle (hwit′ᵊl, wit′-), *v.*, **-tled, -tling,** *n.* —*v.t.* **1.** to cut, trim, or shape (a stick, piece of wood, or the like) by taking off bits with a knife. **2.** to remove (bits or slivers) from a stick, piece of wood, or the like, in this way. **3.** to reduce the amount of, as if by whittling; pare down (usually fol. by *down, away,* etc.): *to whittle down expenses.* —*v.i.* **4.** to cut bits from a piece of wood or the like with a knife, as in shaping something or as a mere aimless diversion. **5.** *Dial.* to tire oneself or another by worrying or fussing. —*n.* **6.** *Brit. Dial.* a knife, esp. a large one, as a carving knife or a butcher knife. [late ME, alter. of *thwitel* knife, OE *thwīt(an)* (to) cut + *-el* -LE] —**whit′tler,** *n.*

Whit·tle (hwit′ᵊl, wit′-), *n.* **Sir Frank,** born 1907, English engineer and inventor.

whit·tling (hwit′ling, wit′-), *n.* **1.** the act of one who whittles. **2.** a bit or chip whittled off.

Whit·tues·day (hwit′tōōz′dē, -dā, -tyōōz′-, wit′-), the day following Whitmonday. [modeled on WHITSUNDAY]

whit·y (hwī′tē, wī′-), *n. Slang.* whitey.

whiz¹ (hwiz, wiz), *v.*, **whizzed, whiz·zing,** *n.* —*v.i.* **1.** to make a humming, buzzing, or hissing sound, as an object passing rapidly through the air. **2.** to move or rush with such a sound: *The angry hornets whizzed by in a cloud.* —*v.t.* **3.** to cause to whiz. —*n.* **4.** the sound of a whizzing object. **5.** a swift movement producing such a sound. **6.** *Informal.* a person who is expert at a particular activity: *He's a whiz at math.* Also, **whizz.** [imit.; cf. FIZZ] —**whiz′zing·ly,** *adv.*

whiz² (hwiz, wiz), *n.* wizard (def. 3).

whiz-bang (*n.* hwiz′bang′, wiz′-; *adj.* hwiz′bang′, wiz′-), *n.* **1.** *Mil.* a small, high-speed shell whose sound as it flies through the air arrives almost at the same instant as its explosion. **2.** a firecracker with a similar effect. —*adj.* **3.** *Informal.* excellent; first-rate; topnotch: *a whiz-bang navigator.* Also, **whizz′-bang′.** [orig. imit.]

who (hōō), *pron.; possessive* **whose;** *objective* **whom.** **1.** what person?: *Who did it? Whose is this? To whom did you write?* **2.** (of a person) of what character, origin, position, importance, etc.: *Who does she think she is?* **3.** the person that or any person that (used relatively to represent a specified or implied antecedent): *It was who you thought. Ask whom you like.* **4.** (used relatively in restrictive and nonrestrictive clauses to represent a specified antecedent, the antecedent being a person or sometimes an animal or personified thing): *Any boy who wants to can learn to swim. Mrs. Johnson, of whom I spoke yesterday, came to tea today.* **5.** *Informal.* (used, esp. in speech, in the interrogative in lieu of the objective form "whom"): *Who are you looking for?* **6.** *Archaic.* the person or persons who. **7. as who should say,** *Archaic.* in a manner of speaking; so to say. [ME; OE *hwā;* c. Goth *hwas,* OHG *hwer,* L *quis,* etc.] —**Usage.** See **which.**

WHO, See **World Health Organization.**

whoa (hwō, wō), *interj.* stop! (used esp. to horses). [dial. var. of HO]

who'd (hōōd), contraction of *who would: Who'd have thought it!*

who·dun·it (hōō dun′it), *n. Informal.* a detective story. [jocular formation from question *Who done it?* (for standard E *Who did it?*)]

who·e'er (hōō âr′), *pron. Literary.* whoever.

who·ev·er (hōō ev′ər), *pron.; possessive* **whos·ev·er;** *objective* **whom·ev·er.** **1.** whatever person; anyone that: *Whoever did it should be proud. Tell it to whomever you like.* **2.** no matter who: *I won't do it, whoever asks.* **3.** who?; what person? (used to express astonishment, disbelief, disdain, etc.): *Whoever is that? Whoever told you such a thing?* [ME]

whole (hōl), *adj.* **1.** comprising the full quantity, amount, extent, number, etc., without diminution or exception; entire, full, or total: *He ate the whole pie? They ran the whole distance.* **2.** containing all the elements properly belonging; complete: *a whole set of antique china.* **3.** undivided; in one piece: *to swallow a thing whole.* **4.** *Math.* integral, or not fractional. **5.** uninjured, undamaged, or unbroken; sound; intact: *He was surprised to find himself whole after the accident.* **6.** being fully or entirely as specified; not adulterated or refined: *whole grain.* **7.** pertaining to all aspects of human nature, esp. with reference to physical, intellectual, and spiritual development: *education for the whole man.* **8. out of whole cloth,** without foundation in fact; fictitious: *a story made out of whole cloth.* —*n.* **9.** all the amount or every part of something: *We have used up the whole of our food supply.* **10.** a thing complete in itself, or comprising all its parts or elements. **11.** an assemblage of parts associated or viewed together as one thing; a unitary system. **12. as a whole,** all things included or considered; altogether: *As a whole, the relocation seems to have been beneficial.* **13. on** or **upon the whole, a.** in view of all the circumstances; after consideration. **b.** disregarding minor exceptions; in general. [ME *hole, hool,* OE *hāl;* c. D *heel,* G *heil,* Icel *heill;* see HALE¹, HEAL; sp. with *w* reflects dial. speech] —**whole′ness,** *n.*
—**Syn. 1.** undiminished, undivided, integral, complete. **9.** totality, aggregate. WHOLE, TOTAL mean the entire or complete sum or amount. The WHOLE is all there is; every part, member, aspect; the complete sum, amount, quantity of anything, not divided; the entirety: *the whole of one's property, family.* TOTAL also means whole, complete amount, or number, but conveys the idea of something added up: *The total of his gains amounted to millions.* —**Ant. 1.** partial.

whole′ blood′, **1.** human blood as taken directly from the body, from which none of the elements have been removed, used in transfusions. **2.** relationship between persons through both parents. Cf. **half blood.** [ME]

whole′ broth′er, a brother whose parents are the same as one's own.

whole′ gale′, *Meteorol.* (on the Beaufort scale) a wind of 55–63 miles per hour.

whole·heart·ed (hōl′här′tid), *adj.* fully or completely sincere, enthusiastic, energetic, etc. —**whole′heart′ed·ly,** *adv.* —**whole′heart′ed·ness,** *n.*

whole′ hog′, *Slang.* **1.** the furthest extent; everything. **2. go whole hog,** to do something completely or thoroughly. Also, **go the whole hog.**

whole-length (hōl′lengkth′, -length′), *adj.* **1.** extended to or having its entire length; not shortened or abridged: *a whole-length report.* **2.** portraying or accommodating the full length of the human figure: *a whole-length sofa; a whole-length portrait of the general.* —*n.* **3.** a portrait or statue showing the full length of its subject.

whole′ milk′, milk containing all its constituents as received from the cow or other milk-giving animal.

whole′ note′, *Music.* a note equivalent in duration to four quarter notes. See illus. at **note.**

whole′ num′ber, an integral.

whole′ rest′, *Music.* a rest equal in value to a whole note. See illus. at **rest¹.**

whole·sale (hōl′sāl′), *n., adj., adv., v.,* **-saled, -sal·ing.** —*n.* **1.** the sale of goods in large amounts, as to retailers or jobbers rather than to consumers directly (opposed to *retail*). —*adj.* **2.** of, pertaining to, or engaged in sale by wholesale. **3.** extensive; broadly indiscriminate: *wholesale discharge of workers.* —*adv.* **4.** on wholesale terms: *I can get it for you wholesale.* —*v.t., v.i.* **5.** to sell by wholesale. [late ME, from the phrase (*by*) *hole sale* in gross] —**whole′sal′er,** *n.* —**Syn. 3.** far-reaching, comprehensive, thorough.

whole′ sis′ter, a sister whose parents are the same as one's own.

whole·some (hōl′səm), *adj.* **1.** conducive to moral or general well-being; salutary; beneficial: *wholesome recreation.* **2.** conducive to bodily health; healthful; salubrious: *wholesome food.* **3.** suggestive of physical or mental health, esp. in appearance. **4.** healthy or sound. [ME *ho(o)lsom,* OE **hālsum* (see WHOLE, -SOME¹): c. Icel *heilsamr,* OHG *heilsam*] —**whole′some·ly,** *adv.* —**whole′some·ness,** *n.* —**Syn. 1.** good. **2, 3.** See **healthy.**

whole-souled (hōl′sōld′), *adj.* wholehearted; hearty.

whole′ step′, *Music.* an interval of two semitones, as A–B or B–C♯; a major second. Also called **whole′ tone′.**

whole′-tone scale′ (hōl′tōn′), *Music.* a scale progressing entirely by whole tones, as C, D, E, F♯, G♯, A♯, C.

whole-wheat (hōl′hwēt′, -wēt′), *adj.* prepared with the complete wheat kernel: *whole-wheat bread.*

who·lism (hō′liz əm), *n.* holism. —**who·lis′tic,** *adj.*

who'll (hōōl), contraction of *who will* or *who shall.*

whol·ly (hō′lē, hōl′lē), *adv.* **1.** entirely; totally; altogether. **2.** to the whole amount, extent, etc. **3.** so as to comprise or involve all. [ME *holliche,* OE **hāllīche*]

whom (hōōm), *pron.* the objective case of **who,** both as direct and indirect object: *Whom did you call? With whom did you stay? You gave whom the book?* [ME; OE *hwām,* dat. of *hwā* WHO]

whom·ev·er (hōōm ev′ər), *pron.* the objective case of **whoever:** *She questioned whomever she met.* [ME]

whomp (hwomp, womp), *Informal.* —*n.* **1.** a loud, heavy blow, slap, bang, or the like. —*v.t.* **2.** to defeat (a person, opposing team, etc.) decisively. **3.** to slap or strike. [imit.]

whom·so·ev·er (hōōm′sō ev′ər), *pron.* the objective case of **whosoever:** *Ask whomsoever you like.* [late ME = *whomso* (early ME (*swā*) *hwām swā;* see WHOM, SO¹) + *ever* EVER]

whoop (hōōp, hwōōp, wōōp), *n.* **1.** a cry or shout, as of hunters, warriors, etc. **2.** the whooping sound characteristic of whooping cough. **3. not worth a whoop,** *Informal.* to be worthless: *Her promises aren't worth a whoop.* —*v.i.* **4.** to utter a loud cry or shout in expressing enthusiasm, excitement, etc. **5.** to cry as an owl, crane, or certain other birds. **6.** to make the characteristic sound accompanying the deep intake of air that follows a series of coughs in whooping cough. —*v.t.* **7.** to utter with or as with a whoop or whoops. **8.** to call, urge, pursue, or drive with whoops: *to whoop dogs on.* **9. whoop it up,** *Slang.* **a.** to raise a disturbance, as in noisy celebration. **b.** to arouse enthusiasm for; promote: *Every spring they whoop it up for the circus.* —*interj.* **10.** (used as a cry to attract attention from afar, or to show excitement, encouragement, enthusiasm, etc.) [ME *whope(n),* OE *hwōpan* to threaten; c. Goth *hwopan* to boast] —**whoop′er,** *n.*

whoop-de-do (wōōp′dē dōō′, -dōō′, hwōōp′-, hōōp′-) *n., pl.* **-dos.** *Informal.* **1.** lively and noisy festivities. **2.** heated discussion or debate, esp. in public. **3.** extravagant publicity. Also, **whoop′-de-doo′.** [irreg.; see WHOOP]

whoop·ee (*n.* hwŏŏp′ē, wŏŏp′ē, hwōōp′pē, wōō′-; *interj.* hwŏŏp′ē′, wŏŏp′ē′, hwōōp′pē′, wōō′-), *Informal.* —*n.* **1. make whoopee,** to engage in uproarious merrymaking. —*interj.* **2.** (used as a shout of exuberant joy.) [WHOOP + *-ee* intensive suffix]

whoop′ing cough′ (hōō′ping, hŏŏp′ing), *Pathol.* an infectious disease of the respiratory mucous membrane, esp. of children, characterized by a series of short, convulsive coughs followed by a deep inspiration accompanied by a whooping sound. Also called **chincough, pertussis.**

whoop′ing crane′ (hōō′ping, hwōō′-, wōō′-), a large, white, nearly extinct, North American crane, *Grus americana,* having a loud, whooping call. See illus. at **crane.**

whoops (hwŏŏps, wŏŏps, hwōōps, wōōps), *interj.* (used to express surprise, mild embarrassment, etc., or as a casual apology.) [WHOOP + *-s* intensive suffix]

whoosh (hwŏŏsh, wŏŏsh, hwōōsh, wōōsh), *n.* **1.** a loud, rushing noise, as of air or water. —*v.i., v.t.* **2.** to move swiftly with a gushing or hissing noise. Also, **woosh.** [imit.]

who·sis (hōō′zis), *n., pl.* **-sis·es.** *Informal.* an object or person whose name is not known or cannot be recalled: *It's the whoosis next to the volume control.* Also, **whosis.** [? alter. of phrase *who's this*]

whop (hwop, wop), *v.,* **whopped, whop·ping,** *n. Informal.* —*v.t.* **1.** to strike forcibly. **2.** to defeat soundly. —*n.* **3.** a forcible blow. [late ME, aspirated form of *wap* < ?]

whop·per (hwop′ər, wop′-), *n. Informal.* **1.** something uncommonly large of its kind. **2.** a big lie. [WHOP + -ER[1]]

whop·ping (hwop′ing, wop′-), *adj. Informal.* very large of its kind: *We caught four whopping trout.* [WHOP + -ING[2]]

whore (hōr, hôr *or, often,* hŏŏr), *n., v.,* **whored, whor·ing.** —*n.* **1.** a woman who engages in promiscuous sexual intercourse for money; prostitute; harlot; strumpet. **2.** *Slang.* any promiscuous woman. —*v.i.* **3.** to act as a whore. **4.** to consort with whores. —*v.t.* **5.** *Obs.* to make a whore of; corrupt; debauch. [ME, OE *hōre;* c. Icel *hōra,* G *Hure,* Goth *hors* harlot, L *cārus* dear]

who're (hōō′ər, hŏŏr), contraction of *who are.*

whore·dom (hōr′dəm, hôr′- *or, often,* hŏŏr′-), *n.* **1.** the activity or state of whoring. **2.** *Bible.* idolatry. [ME *hordom* = OE *hōr* adultery + *-dōm* -DOM; cf. Icel *hōrdōmr*]

whore·house (hōr′hous′, hôr′- *or, often,* hŏŏr′-), *n., pl.* **-hous·es** (-hou′ziz). a house or apartment in which prostitutes are available for hire; house of prostitution; brothel. [ME *hoore-hows*]

whore·mong·er (hōr′mung′gər, -mong′-, hôr′- *or, often,* hŏŏr′-), *n.* a man who consorts with whores; a lecher or pander. Also called **whore·mas·ter** (hōr′mas′tər, -mä′stər, hôr′- *or, often,* hŏŏr′-). —**whore′mon′ger·ing,** *n.*

whore·son (hōr′sən, hôr′- *or, often,* hŏŏr′-), *Archaic.* —*n.* **1.** a bastard. **2.** wretch; scoundrel. —*adj.* **3.** wretched; scurvy. [ME *horeson;* cf. Icel *hōruson(r)*]

whor·ish (hōr′ish, hôr′- *or, often,* hŏŏr′-), *adj.* having the character of a whore; lewd; unchaste. —**whore′ish·ly,** *adv.* —**whore′ish·ness,** *n.*

whorl (hwûrl, wûrl, hwôrl, wôrl), *n.* **1.** a circular arrangement of like parts, as leaves, flowers, etc., round a point on an axis; verticil. **2.** one of the turns or volutions of a spiral shell. **3.** anything shaped like a coil. **4.** one of the central ridges of a fingerprint, forming at least one complete circle. **5.** *Textiles.* a flywheel or pulley, as for a spindle. [late ME *whorle, whorvil,* etc., OE *hwyrfel* = *hweorfa* whorl of a spindle + *-el* -LE]

whorled (hwûrld, wûrld, hwôrld, wôrld), *adj.* **1.** having a whorl or whorls. **2.** arranged in a whorl, as leaves.

whort (hwûrt, wûrt), *n.* the whortleberry. Also, **whor·tle** (hwûr′tᵊl, wûr′-). [dial. var. of ME *hurte,* OE *horte* WHORTLEBERRY]

whor·tle·ber·ry (hwûr′tᵊl ber′ē, wûr′-), *n., pl.* **-ries.** **1.** the edible, black berry of an ericaceous shrub, *Vaccinium Myrtillus,* of Europe and Siberia. **2.** the shrub itself. Also, **hurtleberry.** [dial. var. of ME *hurtilberye* = *hurte* (see WHORT) + *-l* (< ?) + *berye* BERRY]

who's (hōōz), **1.** contraction of *who is: Who's there?* **2.** contraction of *who has: Who's seen it?*

whose (hōōz), *pron.* **1.** (the possessive case of **who** used as an adjective): *Whose umbrella did I take? Whose is this one?* **2.** (the possessive case of **which** used as an adjective): *a word whose meaning escapes me; an animal whose fur changes color.* **3.** the one belonging to what person: *Whose won the third prize?* [ME *whos,* early ME *hwās;* r. *hwas,* OE *hwæs,* gen. of *hwā* WHO]

whose·so·ev·er (hōōz′sō ev′ər), *pron.* **1.** (the possessive case of **whosoever** used as an attributive adjective): *Whosesoever books are overdue will be fined.* **2.** the one or ones belonging to whomsoever: *Whosesoever are left here will be confiscated.* [earlier *whoseso* (see WHOSE, SO[1]) + EVER]

whos·ev·er (hōō zev′ər), *pron.* **1.** (the possessive case of **whoever** used as an adjective): *Whosever wagon this is, get it out of here. Whosever is this ridiculous hat?* **2.** the one or ones belonging to whomever: *Whosever will win, do you think?*

who·sis (hōō′zis), *n. Informal.* whoosis.

who·so (hōō′sō), *pron.* whosoever; whoever. [ME, early ME *hwa swa,* OE (*swā*) *hwā swā*]

who·so·ev·er (hōō′sō ev′ər), *pron.; possessive* **whose·so·ev·er,** *objective* **whom·so·ev·er.** whoever; whatever person: *Whosoever wants to apply should write to the bureau.* [ME]

whr., watt-hour.

whse., warehouse.

whsle., wholesale.

why (hwī, wī), *adv., conj., n., pl.* **whys,** *interj.* —*adv.* **1.** for what; for what reason, cause, or purpose?: *Why did you behave so badly?* —*conj.* **2.** for what cause or reason: *I don't know why he is leaving.* **3.** for which; on account of which (usually after *reason* to introduce a relative clause): *the reason why he refused to go.* **4.** the reason for which: *That is why he returned.* —*n.* **5.** a question concerning the cause or reason of something: *a child's unending hows and whys.* **6.** the cause or reason: *the whys and wherefores of a troublesome situation.* —*interj.* **7.** (used as an expression of surprise, hesitation, etc., or sometimes an expletive): *Why, it's all gone!* [ME; OE *hwī, hwȳ,* instr. case of *hwæt* WHAT; c. OIcel *hvī*]

whyd·ah (hwid′ə, wid′ə), *n.* any of several small, African weaverbirds of the subfamily *Viduinae,* the males of which have elongated, drooping tail feathers during the breeding season. Also, **whidah.** Also called **widow bird.** [alter. of WIDOW (BIRD) to make name agree with that of a town in Dahomey, West Africa, one of its haunts]

WI, Wisconsin (approved esp. for use with zip code).

W.I., **1.** West Indian. **2.** West Indies.

w.i., (of securities) when issued: used to indicate a transaction to be completed when the security is issued at a later date.

Wi·ak (wē yäk′), *n.* Biak.

Wich·i·ta (wich′i tô′), *n.* a city in S Kansas, on the Arkansas River. 276,554 (1970).

Wich′ita Falls′, a city in N Texas. 96,265 (1970).

wick[1] (wik), *n.* a bundle or loose twist or braid of soft threads, or a woven strip or tube, as of cotton or asbestos, which in a candle, lamp, oil stove, cigarette lighter, or the like, serves to draw up melted tallow or wax or oil or other flammable liquid to be burned at its outer edge. [ME *wicke, weke,* OE *wice, wēoc(e);* c. OHG *wiohha* lint, wick (G *Wieke* lint), MD *wiecke,* MLG *wêke;* akin to OE *wōci(g)e,* Skt *vāgurā* noose]

wick[2] (wik), *n. Curling.* a narrow opening in the field, bounded by other players' stones. [?]

wick[3] (wik), *n. Archaic.* a village; hamlet. [ME *wik, wich,* OE *wīc* house, village (= OS *wīc,* OHG *wīch*) < L *vīcus* village, estate, c. Gk *oîkos* house]

Wick (wik), *n.* a town in and the county seat of Caithness, in N Scotland: herring fisheries. 7545 (est. 1964).

wick·ed (wik′id), *adj.* **1.** evil or morally bad in principle or practice; sinful; iniquitous. **2.** mischievous or malicious. **3.** causing or threatening great injury, discomfort, or annoyance: *a wicked hailstorm.* **4.** going beyond justifiable limits; unreasonable or extreme: *wicked prices; a wicked exam.* **5.** *Slang.* excellent; masterly: *He plays a wicked trumpet.* [ME *wikked* = *wikke* bad (? OE *wicca* wizard, used as adj.) + *-ed* -ED[3]. See WITCH] —**wick′ed·ly,** *adv.* —**Syn. 1.** ungodly, impious, profane; immoral, corrupt, depraved; heinous; infamous, vile, villainous. See **bad**[1]. —**Ant. 1.** good.

wick·ed·ness (wik′id nis), *n.* **1.** the quality or state of being wicked. **2.** wicked conduct or practices. **3.** a wicked act or thing. [ME]

wick·er (wik′ər), *n.* **1.** a slender, pliant twig; osier; withe. **2.** plaited or woven twigs or osiers as the material of baskets, chairs, etc.; wickerwork. —*adj.* **3.** consisting or made of wicker: *a wicker basket.* **4.** covered with wicker: *a wicker jug.* [ME < Scand; cf. dial. Sw *vikker* willow. See WEAK]

wick·er·work (wik′ər wûrk′), *n.* anything made of wicker.

wick·et (wik′it), *n.* **1.** a small door or gate, esp. one beside, or forming part of, a larger one. **2.** a small window or opening, often closed by a grating or the like, as in a door, or forming a place of communication in a ticket office, a teller's cage in a bank, etc. **3.** a gate by which a flow of water is regulated, as in a canal lock. **4.** *Cricket.* **a.** either of the two frameworks, each consisting of three stumps with two bails in grooves across the tops, at which the bowler aims the ball. **b.** the area between the wickets; the playing field. **c.** a batsman's turn or inning at the wicket. **d.** the period during which two men bat together. **5.** *Croquet.* any of the hoops through which a ball must be hit in playing the game. **6.** a turnstile in an entrance. **7. to be on, have, or bat a sticky wicket,** *Brit. Slang.* to be at or have a disadvantage. [ME *wiket* < AF (OF *guischet*) < Gmc; cf. MD *wiket* wicket = *wik-* (akin to OE *wīcan* to yield; see WEAK) + *-et* n. suffix]

wick·et·keep·er (wik′it kē′pər), *n. Cricket.* the player on the fielding side who stands immediately behind the wicket to stop balls that pass it.

wick·i·up (wik′ē up′), *n.* **1.** (in Nevada, Arizona, etc.) an American Indian hut made of brushwood or covered with mats. **2.** *Western U.S.* any rude hut. Also, **wick′y·up′, wikiup.** [prob. < Algonquian (Sac-Fox-Kickapoo) *wikiyapi* lodge, dwelling. See WIGWAM]

Wick·liffe (wik′lif), *n.* **John.** See **Wycliffe, John.** Also, **Wic′lif.**

Wick·low (wik′lō), *n.* **1.** a county in Leinster province, in the E Republic of Ireland. 58,473 (1961); 782 sq. mi. **2.** a town in and the county seat of this county.

wic·o·py (wik′ə pē), *n., pl.* **-pies.** **1.** the leatherwood, *Dirca palustris.* **2.** any of various willow herbs, as *Chamænerion angustifolium.* **3.** basswood. [< Algonquian *wik'pi, wighebi,* etc., inner bark]

wid·der (wid′ər), *n. Dial.* widow.

wide (wīd), *adj.,* **wid·er, wid·est,** *adv., n.* —*adj.* **1.** having considerable or great extent from side to side; broad: *a wide boulevard.* **2.** having a certain or specified extent from side to side: *three feet wide.* **3.** of great horizontal extent; extensive; vast; spacious: *the wide plains of the West.* **4.** of great range or scope; embracing a great number or variety of subjects, cases, etc.: *wide reading; wide experience.* **5.** open to the full or a great extent; expanded; distended: *to stare with wide eyes.* **6.** full, ample, or roomy, as clothing: *He wore wide, flowing robes.* **7.** apart or remote from a specified point or object (often fol. by *of*): *a shot wide of the mark; a guess wide of the truth.* **8.** *Phonet.* lax (def. 6). **9.** *Baseball. Informal.* outside (def. 10). —*adv.* **10.** to a considerable or great extent from side to side: *The river runs wide here.* **11.** over an extensive space or region, or far abroad: *scattered far and wide.* **12.** to the full extent of opening: *Open your mouth wide.* **13.** to the utmost, or fully: *to be wide awake.* **14.** away from or to one side of a point, mark, purpose, or the like; aside; astray: *The shot went wide.* —*n.* **15.** *Cricket.* a bowled ball that goes wide of the wicket, and counts as a run for the side batting. **16.** *Archaic.* a wide space or expanse. [ME; OE *wīd;* c. D *wijd,* G *weit,* Icel *vīthr*] —**wide′ness,** *n.*
—**Syn. 1.** WIDE, BROAD refer to dimensions. They are often interchangeable, but WIDE esp. applies to things of which the length is much greater than the width: *a wide road, piece of ribbon.* BROAD is more emphatic, and applies to things of considerable or great width, esp. to surfaces extending laterally: *a broad valley.* —**Ant. 1, 4, 5, 10.** narrow.

wide-an·gle (wīd′ang′gəl), *adj. Photog.* **1.** noting or pertaining to a lens having an angle of view of 60° or more, and a focal length of less than the diagonal of the film used with it. **2.** employing or made with such a lens.

wide-a·wake (wīd′ə wāk′), *adj.* **1.** fully awake; with the eyes wide open. **2.** alert, keen, or knowing. —**wide′-a·wake′ness,** *n.* —**Syn. 2.** sharp, quick, astute.

wide-eyed (wīd′īd′), *adj.* with the eyes open wide, as in amazement, innocence, sleeplessness, etc.

wide·ly (wīd′lē), *adv.* **1.** to a wide extent. **2.** over a wide space or area: *a widely distributed plant.* **3.** by or among a large number of persons: *a man who is widely known.* **4.** in many or various subjects, cases, etc.: *to be widely read.* **5.** by a great amount: *two widely differing accounts of an incident.*

wide·mouthed (wīd′mouthd′, -moutht′), *adj.* **1.** having a wide mouth: *a widemouthed river; a widemouthed person.* **2.** having the mouth opened wide, as in astonishment.

wid·en (wīd′ᵊn), *v.t., v.i.* to make or become wide or wider; broaden; expand. —**wid′en·er,** *n.*

wide-o·pen (wīd′ō′pən), *adj.* **1.** opened to the full extent: *a wide-open window.* **2.** having no effective laws or enforcement of laws regulating liquor sales, vice, gambling, etc.: *a wide-open town.* [late ME]

wide-rang·ing (wīd′rān′jing), *adj.* **1.** extending over a large area. **2.** extensive or diversified in scope.

wide-screen (wīd′skrēn′), *adj.* of or pertaining to motion

pictures projected on a screen having greater width than height, usually in a ratio of 1 to 2.5.
wide·spread (wīd′spred′), *adj.* **1.** distributed or extended over a wide area. **2.** opened or extended to full width.
wide-spread·ing (wīd′spred′ing), *adj.* spreading over or affecting a broad area.
widg·eon (wij′ən), *n., pl.* **-eons,** (*esp. collectively*) **-eon** for 1. **1.** any of several fresh-water ducks between the mallard and teal in size, as *Anas penelope,* of the Old World, having a reddish-brown head with a buff crown. **2.** *Obs.* a fool. Also, **wigeon.** [? < AF *wigeon, var. of F *vigeon* < VL *vībiōn-,* s. of *vībiō;* cf. ML *vīpiō* kind of crane (< *wip-* imit. of bird's cry)]
widg·et (wij′it), *n.* a small mechanical device, as a knob, switch, etc., esp. one whose name is not known or cannot be recalled; gadget. [alter. of GADGET]
wid·ish (wī′dish), *adj.* rather wide.
wid·ow (wid′ō), *n.* **1.** a woman who has lost her husband by death and has not married again. **2.** *Cards.* an additional hand or part of a hand, as one dealt to the table. **3.** *Print.* a short last line, as of a paragraph. **4.** *Slang.* a woman often left alone because her husband devotes his free time to a hobby or sport (used in combination): *a poker widow.* —*v.t.* **5.** to make (someone) a widow: *She was widowed by the war.* [ME *wid(e)we,* OE *widuwe;* c. Goth *widuwo,* G *Witwe,* L *vidua* (fem. of *viduus* bereaved), Skt *vidhavā* widow. See DIVIDE] —**wid′ow·hood′,** *n.*
wid′ow bird′, whydah. [trans. of NL *Vidua* name of the genus (L: lit., widow). See WHYDAH]
wid·ow·er (wid′ō ər), *n.* a man who has lost his wife by death and has not married again. [late ME (see WIDOW, -ER[1]); r. *widow* (now dial.), OE *widuwa*] —**wid′ow·ered,** *adj.* —**wid′ow·er·hood′,** *n.*
wid′ow's mite′, a small contribution given cheerfully by a person who can ill afford it. Mark 12:41–44.
wid′ow's peak′, a point formed by the hairline in the center of the forehead.
wid′ow's walk′, a platform or walk atop a roof, as on certain coastal New England houses of the 18th and early 19th centuries: often used as a lookout for incoming ships.
width (width *or, often,* with), *n.* **1.** extent from side to side; breadth; wideness. **2.** a piece of the full wideness, as of cloth. [WID(E) + -TH[1], modeled on *breadth*]
width·wise (width′wīz′ *or, often,* with′-), *adv.* in the direction of the width.
Wi·du·kind (vē′dōō kint′), *n.* Wittekind.
wie geht's (vē gāts′), *German.* how are you?
Wie·land (vē′länt), *n.* **1.** *German Myth.* Wayland. **2.** **Chris·toph Mar·tin** (kris′tôf mär′tēn), 1733–1813, German poet, novelist, and critic.
wield (wēld), *v.t.* **1.** to exercise (power, authority, influence, etc.), as in ruling or dominating. **2.** to handle or use (a weapon, instrument, etc.). **3.** *Obs.* to govern. [ME *welde(n),* OE *wieldan* to control, for *wealdan* to rule; c. G *walten,* Icel *valda,* Goth *waldan;* akin to L *valēre* to be strong, prevail] —**wield′a·ble,** *adj.* —**wield′er,** *n.*
wield·y (wēl′dē), *adj.,* **wield·i·er, wield·i·est.** readily wielded or managed, as in use or action. [late ME]
Wien (vēn), *n.* **1.** **Wil·helm** (vil′helm), 1864–1928, German physicist: Nobel prize 1911. **2.** German name of **Vienna.**
wie·ner (wē′nər), *n. U.S.* frankfurter. Also, **wie·ner·wurst** (wē′nər wûrst′). [< G, short for *Wiener Wurst* Viennese sausage]
Wie·ner (wē′nər), *n.* **Nor·bert** (nôr′bərt), 1894–1964, U.S. mathematician; pioneer in cybernetics.
Wie·ner schnit·zel (vē′nər shnit′səl, shnit′səl), a thick breaded veal cutlet, variously seasoned or garnished. [< G = *Wiener* Viennese + *Schnitzel* cutlet, chop]
wie·nie (wē′nē), *n.* weenie.
Wies·ba·den (vēs′bäd′ən), *n.* a city in W West Germany: health resort; mineral springs. 258,000 (est. 1963).
Wie·sel (wi zel′), *n.* **El·ie** (el′ē), (*Eliezer*), born 1928, U.S. author, born in Rumania: Nobel peace prize 1986.
wife (wīf), *n., pl.* **wives** (wīvz), *v.,* **wifed, wif·ing.** —*n.* **1.** a woman joined in marriage to a man; a woman considered in relation to her husband; spouse. **2.** a woman (*archaic* or *dial.,* except in combination): *midwife; fishwife.* **3. take to wife,** to marry (a woman). —*v.i., v.t.* **4.** *Rare.* wive. [ME, OE *wīf* woman; c. D *wijf,* G *Weib,* Icel *vīf*] —**wife′dom,** *n.* —**wife′less,** *adj.*
wife·hood (wīf′ho͝od), *n.* **1.** the state of being a wife. **2.** wifely character or quality; wifeliness. [ME *wifhood,* OE *wīfhād*]
wife·like (wīf′līk′), *adj.* **1.** wifely. —*adv.* **2.** in a manner befitting a wife.
wife·ly (wīf′lē), *adj.,* **-li·er, -li·est.** of, like, or befitting a wife. [ME *wifly,* OE *wīflīc*] —**wife′li·ness,** *n.*
wig (wig), *n., v.,* **wigged, wig·ging.** —*n.* **1.** an artificial covering of hair for the head, worn to conceal baldness, as part of official attire, as a fashionable adornment, etc. —*v.t.* **2.** to furnish with a wig or wigs. **3.** *Brit. Informal.* to reprimand or reprove severely. [short for PERIWIG] —**wig′less,** *adj.* —**wig′like′,** *adj.*
wig·an (wig′ən), *n.* a stiff, canvaslike fabric for stiffening parts of garments. [after WIGAN, where originally produced]
Wig·an (wig′ən), *n.* a city in S Lancashire, in NW England. 78,702 (1961).
wig·eon (wij′ən), *n., pl.* **-eons,** (*esp. collectively*) **-eon.** widgeon.
wig·ger·y (wig′ə rē), *n., pl.* **-ger·ies.** **1.** wigs or a wig; false hair. **2.** the wearing of wigs.
Wig·gin (wig′in), *n.* **Kate Douglas,** 1856–1923, U.S. writer.
wig·gle (wig′əl), *v.,* **-gled, -gling,** *n.* —*v.i.* **1.** to move or go with short, quick, movements from side to side. **2.** to wriggle. —*v.t.* **3.** to cause to wiggle. **4.** to wriggle. —*n.* **5.** a wiggling movement or course. **6.** a wiggly line. **7.** a wriggle. [ME *wigle(n),* freq. of dial. *wig* to wag; akin to OE *wegan* to move, *wēg* motion, *wicga* insect; cf. Norw *vigla* to totter, freq. of *vigga* to rock oneself, D, LG *wiggelen*]
wig·gler (wig′lər), *n.* **1.** a person or thing that wiggles. **2.** wriggler.
Wig·gles·worth (wig′əlz wûrth′), *n.* **Michael,** 1631–1705, U.S. theologian and author, born in England.
wig·gly (wig′lē), *adj.,* **-gli·er, -gli·est.** **1.** wiggling; wriggling: *a wiggly child.* **2.** undulating; wavy: *a wiggly line.*
wight[1] (wīt), *n.* **1.** *Archaic.* a human being. **2.** *Obs.* any living being; a creature. [ME, OE *wiht;* c. G *Wicht,* Icel *vættr,* Goth *waiht*]
wight[2] (wīt), *adj. Brit. Dial.* strong and brave, esp. in war. [ME < Scand; cf. Icel *vīgt,* neut. of *vīgr* able to fight]
Wight (wīt), *n.* **Isle of,** an island off the S coast of England, forming an administrative division of Hampshire. 95,479 (1961); 147 sq. mi. *Co. seat:* Newport.
wig·mak·er (wig′mā′kər), *n.* a person who makes or sells wigs.
Wig·ner (wig′nər), *n.* **Eugene Paul,** born 1902, U.S. physicist, born in Hungary: Nobel prize 1963.
Wig·town (wig′tən, -toun′), *n.* **1.** a county in SW Scotland. 28,524 (est. 1965); 487 sq. mi. **2.** a town in and the county seat of this county. Also called **Wig·town·shire** (wig′tən-shēr′, -shər, -toun′-).
wig·wag (wig′wag′), *v.,* **-wagged, -wag·ging,** *n.* —*v.t., v.i.* **1.** to move to and fro. **2.** *Naut.* to signal by movements of two flags or the like waved according to a code. —*n.* *Naut.* **3.** the act or process of sending messages by the movements of two flags or the like waved according to a code. **4.** a message so signaled. [*wig* to wag (now dial.; see WIGGLE) + WAG; repetitive compound with gradation, parallel to ZIGZAG, etc.] —**wig′wag′ger,** *n.*
wig·wam (wig′wom, -wôm), *n.* an American Indian hut or lodge, usually of rounded or oval shape, formed of poles overlaid with bark, mats, or skins. [< Abnaki (Algonquian): their abode]

Wigwam

wik·i·up (wik′ē up′), *n.* wickiup.
Wil·ber·force (wil′bər fōrs′, -fôrs′), *n.* **William,** 1759–1833, British statesman, philanthropist, and writer.
Wil·bur (wil′bər), *n.* **Richard,** born 1921, U.S. poet.
wil·co (wil′kō), *interj.* (esp. in radio transmission) an indication that the message just received will be complied with. [short for *will comply*]
Wil·cox (wil′koks), *n.* **Ella Wheeler,** 1850–1919, U.S. poet and journalist.
wild (wīld), *adj.* **1.** living in a state of nature; not tamed or domesticated: *a wild animal.* **2.** growing or produced without cultivation or the care of man, as plants, flowers, fruit, honey, etc.: *wild cherries.* **3.** uncultivated, uninhabited, or waste: *This is still wild country.* **4.** uncivilized or unaffected by civilization: *wild Indians.* **5.** of great violence, fury, intensity, etc.; violent; furious: *a wild storm.* **6.** characterized by or indicating violent feelings or excitement. **7.** frantic; distracted, crazy, or mad: *to drive someone wild.* **8.** violently or uncontrollably affected: *wild with rage.* **9.** undisciplined, unruly, lawless, or turbulent: *a gang of wild boys.* **10.** unrestrained or unbridled: *wild enthusiasm.* **11.** disregardful of moral restraints as to pleasurable indulgence: *He repented his wild youth.* **12.** unrestrained by reason or prudence: *wild schemes.* **13.** extravagant or fantastic: *wild fancies.* **14.** disorderly or disheveled: *wild hair.* **15.** wide of the mark: *He scored on a wild throw.* **16.** *Informal.* intensely eager or enthusiastic: *wild about the new styles.* **17.** *Cards.* (of a card) having its value decided by the wishes of the players. —*adv.* **18.** in a wild manner; wildly. **19. run wild, a.** to grow unchecked: *The rambler roses are running wild.* **b.** to show lack of restraint or control: *Those children are allowed to run wild.* —*n.* **20.** Often, **wilds.** an uncultivated, uninhabited, or desolate region or tract; wilderness; desert. **21. the wild,** the wilderness; uncultivated areas: *the lure of the wild.* [ME, OE *wilde;* c. D, G *wild,* Goth *wiltheis,* Icel *villr,* Sw *vild*] —**wild′ly,** *adv.* —**wild′ness,** *n.* —**Syn. 1.** untamed, savage, unbroken, ferocious. **5.** tempestuous, turbulent. **7.** insane. **9.** self-willed, ungoverned, unrestrained, uncontrolled, riotous. **12.** reckless, rash, extravagant, impracticable. **13.** bizarre, fanciful, strange. **14.** unkempt. —**Ant. 1.** tame.
wild′ all′spice, the spicebush.
wild′ boar′, a wild, Old World swine, *Sus scrofa,* from which most of the domestic hogs are believed to be derived.

Wild boar
(3 ft. high at shoulder; total length 4½ ft.; tail 6 in.)

wild′ car′rot, an umbelliferous weed, *Daucus carota,* having a thin and woody root, common in fields and waste places: the wild form of the cultivated carrot.
wild·cat (wīld′kat′), *n., pl.,* **-cats,** for 1–4, (*esp. collectively*) **-cat,** *adj., v.,* **-cat·ted, -cat·ting.** —*n.* **1.** any of several North American felines of the genus *Lynx.* Cf. **lynx. 2.** a yellowish-gray, black-striped, European feline, *Felis sylvestris,* resembling and closely related to the domestic cat with which it interbreeds freely. **3.** a similar feline, *Felis libyca,* of northern Africa, believed to be the chief ancestor of the domestic cat. **4.** any of several other of the smaller felines, as the serval, ocelot, etc. **5.** a quick-tempered or savage person. **6.** an exploratory oil or gas well. **7.** a reckless or unsound enterprise, business, etc. —*adj.* **8.** characterizied by or proceeding from reckless or unsafe business methods: *wildcat companies.* **9.** (of a labor strike) originating spontaneously without a formal vote or decision or without the sanction of the union. —*v.i.* **10.** to search an area of unknown or doubtful productivity for oil, ore, or the like, esp. as an independent prospector. —*v.t.* **11.** to search (an area of unknown or doubtful productivity) for oil, ore, or the like. [late ME *wilde cat;* cf. MLG *wildkatte*]
wild·cat·ter (wīld′kat′ər), *n. Informal.* an oil prospector.
wild′ cel′ery. See **tape grass.**
wild′ cher′vil, a honewort, *Cryptotaenia canadensis,* of North America.
Wilde (wīld), *n.* **Oscar (Fin·gal O'Fla·her·tie Wills)**

(fiṅg′gəl ō fla′hər tē wilz, ō flâr′tē), 1854–1900, Irish poet, dramatist, novelist, essayist, and critic.

wil·de·beest (wil′də bēst′; *Du.* vil′də bāst′), *n., pl.* **-beests,** (*esp. collectively*) **-beest,** *Du.* **-bees·te** (-bās′tə). gnu. [< SAfrD: lit., wild beast]

wil·der[1] (wil′dər), *Archaic.* —*v.t.* **1.** to cause to lose one's way. **2.** to bewilder. —*v.i.* **3.** to lose one's way. **4.** to be bewildered. [freq. formation based on WILD; cf. Icel *villr* astray, *villst* to go astray] —**wil′der·ment,** *n.*

wild·er[2] (wīl′dər), *adj.* comparative of **wild.** [WILD + -ER[4]]

Wil·der (wīl′dər), *n.* **Thorn·ton (Niv·en)** (thôrn′tən niv′ən), 1897–1975, U.S. novelist and playwright.

wil·der·ness (wil′dər nis), *n.* **1.** a wild, comparatively uninhabited, and uncultivated region, as of forest or desert; a tract of wasteland. **2.** any desolate tract, as of open sea. **3.** a bewildering mass or collection. [ME, OE *wilder(en)* wild (*wildor, wilder* wild beast + *-en* -EN[1]) + -NESS, the n. suffix r. adj. one] —**Syn. 1.** See **desert**[1].

Wil·der·ness (wil′dər nis), *n.* a wooded area in NE Virginia: several battles fought here in 1864 between Grant and Lee.

wild-eyed (wīld′īd′), *adj.* **1.** having an angry, insane, or distressed expression in the eyes. **2.** extremely irrational, senseless, or radical: *a wild-eyed plan.*

wild·fire (wīld′fīər′), *n.* **1.** a highly flammable composition, as Greek fire, difficult to extinguish when ignited, formerly used in warfare. **2.** sheet lightning, unaccompanied by thunder. **3.** the ignis fatuus or a similar light. **4.** *Pathol. Obs.* erysipelas or some similar disease. **5. like wildfire,** over a large area, distance, etc., in a very short period of time; very fast: *The rumor spread like wildfire. He ran like wildfire to avoid the police.* [ME *wildefire,* OE *wildfȳr*]

wild′ flow′er, **1.** the flower of a plant that normally grows in fields, forests, etc., without cultivation. **2.** the plant itself. Also, **wild′flow′er.**

wild·fowl (wīld′foul′), *n.* a game bird, esp. a duck, goose, or swan. [ME *wilde foul,* OE *wildefugl*]

wild′-goose′ chase′ (wīld′gōōs′), a wild or absurd search for something nonexistent or unobtainable.

wild′ hy′acinth, **1.** a camass, *Camassia scilloides,* of eastern North America. **2.** the harebell, *Scilla nonscripta,* of Europe.

wild′ in′digo, any American, leguminous plant of the genus *Baptisia,* esp. *B. tinctoria,* having yellow flowers.

wild·ing (wīl′diṅg), *n.* **1.** a wild apple tree. **2.** its fruit. **3.** any plant that grows wild. **4.** *Bot.* an escape. **5.** a wild animal. —*adj.* **6.** *Archaic.* not cultivated or domesticated.

wild′ let′tuce, any of various uncultivated species of lettuce, growing as weeds in fields and waste places.

wild·life (wīld′līf′), *n.* wild animals.

wild·ling (wīld′liṅg), *n.* a wild plant, flower, or animal.

wild′ mad′der, **1.** madder[1] (defs. 1, 2). **2.** either of two bedstraws, *Galium Mollugo* or *G. tinctorium.*

wild′ man′, **1.** an uncivilized or savage person. **2.** a man of violent temper, erratic behavior, etc.

wild′ mus′tard, the charlock.

wild′ oat′, **1.** any uncultivated species of *Avena,* esp. a common weedy grass, *A. fatua,* resembling the cultivated oat. **2. sow one's wild oats,** to lead a dissolute and indiscreet life in one's youth.

wild′ pars′ley, any of several umbelliferous plants resembling the parsley in shape and structure.

wild′ pars′nip, an umbelliferous weed, *Pastinaca sativa,* having an inedible acrid root, common in fields and waste places: the wild form of the cultivated parsnip.

wild′ pink′, an American catchfly, *Silene pennsylvanica.*

wild′ pitch′, *Baseball.* a pitched ball that the catcher misses and could not be expected to catch, resulting in a base runner's or runners' advancing one or more bases or the batter's reaching first base safely. Cf. **passed ball.**

wild′ rice′, **1.** a tall, aquatic grass, *Zizania aquatica,* of northeastern North America. **2.** the grain of this plant, used for food.

wild′ rose′, any native species of rose, usually having a single flower with the corolla consisting of one circle of roundish, spreading petals.

wild′ rye′, any grass of the genus *Elymus,* somewhat resembling rye.

wild′ silk′, **1.** tussah. **2.** *Brit.* See **raw silk.**

wild′ vanil′la, a composite plant, *Trilisa odoratissima,* of the southeastern U.S., having leaves with a persistent, vanillalike fragrance.

Wild′ West′, the western frontier of the U.S., during the 19th century, before the establishment of stable government.

Wild′ West′ show′, a show featuring scenes and events from the early western U.S. and displaying feats of marksmanship, horsemanship, rope twirling, and the like.

wild·wood (wīld′wo͝od′), *n.* a wood growing in the wild or natural state; forest. [ME *wilde wode,* OE *wilde wudu*]

wile (wīl), *n., v.,* **wiled, wil·ing.** —*n.* **1.** a trick, artifice, or stratagem meant to fool, trap, or entice. **2. wiles,** artful or beguiling behavior. **3.** deceitful cunning; trickery. —*v.t.* **4.** to beguile, entice, or lure (*away, from, into,* etc.): *The music wiled him from his study.* **5. wile away,** to spend or pass (time), esp. in a leisurely or pleasurable fashion. [ME, OE *wigle* divination; akin to Icel *vēl* artifice; see GUILE] —**Syn. 1.** deception, maneuver, device. **3.** chicanery, fraud.

wil·ful (wil′fəl), *adj.* willful. —**wil′ful·ly,** *adv.* —**wil′ful·ness,** *n.*

Wil·helm I (wil′helm; *Ger.* vil′helm). See **William I** (def. 3).

Wilhelm II. See **William II** (def. 2).

Wil·hel·mi·na I (wil′ə mē′nə, wil′hel-; *Du.* vil′hel mē′nä), (*Wilhelmina Helena Pauline Maria of Orange-Nassau*) 1880–1962, queen of the Netherlands 1890–1948 (mother of Juliana).

Wil·helms·ha·ven (vil′helms hä′fən), *n.* a seaport in N West Germany, on the North Sea. 100,400 (1963).

Wil·helm·stras·se (vil′helm shträ′sə), *n.* a street in the center of Berlin, Germany: former location of the German foreign office and other government buildings.

Wilkes (wilks), *n.* **1. Charles,** 1798–1877, U.S. rear admiral and explorer. **2. John,** 1727–97, English political leader and journalist.

Wilkes-Bar·re (wilks′bar′ē, -bar′ə, -bâr′), *n.* a city in E Pennsylvania, on the Susquehanna River. 58,856 (1970).

Wilkes′ Land′, a coastal region of Antarctica, S of Australia.

Wil·kins (wil′kinz), *n.* **1. Sir George Hubert,** 1888–1958, Australian antarctic explorer, aviator, and aerial navigator. **2. Roy,** 1901–81, U.S. journalist and civil-rights leader: executive secretary of the NAACP 1955–76.

Wil·kins·burg (wil′kinz bûrg′), *n.* a borough in SW Pennsylvania, near Pittsburgh. 26,780 (1970).

will[1] (wil), *v.* and *auxiliary v., pres. sing. 1st pers.* **will,** *2nd* **will** or (*Archaic*) **wilt,** *3rd* **will,** *pres. pl.* **will;** *past sing. 1st pers.* **would,** *2nd* **would** or (*Archaic*) **wouldst,** *3rd* **would,** *past pl.* **would;** *past part.* (*Obs.*) **wold** or **would;** *imperative, infinitive, and pres. participle lacking.* —*auxiliary verb.* **1.** am (is, are, etc.) about or going to (in future constructions, sometimes noting in the first person promise or determination, in the second and third persons mere futurity): *I will come right over. She will see you at dinner. It will rain tomorrow.* **2.** am (is, are, etc.) disposed or willing to: *People will do right. The doctor will see you now.* **3.** am (is, are, etc.) expected or required to: *You will report to the principal at once.* **4.** may be expected or supposed to: *You will not have forgotten him. This will be right.* **5.** am (is, are, etc.) determined or sure to (used emphatically): *You would do it. People will talk.* **6.** am (is, are, etc.) accustomed to, or do usually or often: *You will often see him sitting there. He would write for hours at a time.* **7.** am (is, are, etc.) habitually disposed or inclined to: *Boys will be boys. After dinner he would smoke his pipe.* **8.** am (is, are, etc.) capable of; can: *This tree will live without water for three months.* —*v.t., v.i.* **9.** to wish; desire; like: *Go where you will. Ask, if you will, who the owner is.* [ME; OE *wyll(an)*; c. D *willen,* G *wollen,* Icel *vilja,* Goth *wiljan,* L *velle* to wish] —**Usage.** See **shall.**

will[2] (wil), *n., v.,* **willed, will·ing.** —*n.* **1.** the faculty of conscious and particularly of deliberate action; the power of control the mind has over its own actions: *the freedom of the will.* **2.** power of choosing one's own actions: *to have a strong will.* **3.** the act or process of using or asserting one's choice; volition: *My hands are obedient to my will.* **4.** wish or desire: *to submit against one's will.* **5.** purpose or determination, often hearty or stubborn determination; willfulness: *to have the will to succeed.* **6.** the wish or purpose as carried out, or to be carried out: *to work one's will.* **7.** disposition, whether good or ill, toward another. **8.** *Law.* a legal declaration of a person's wishes as to the disposition of his property or estate after his death. **9. at will,** at one's discretion or pleasure; as one desires: *to wander at will through the countryside.* —*v.t.* **10.** to decide upon, bring about, or attempt to effect or bring about by an act of will: *He can walk if he wills it.* **11.** to purpose, determine on, or elect, by act of will: *If he wills success, he can find it.* **12.** to give by will or testament; bequeath or devise. **13.** to influence by exerting will power: *She was willed to walk the tightrope by the hypnotist.* —*v.i.* **14.** to exercise one's will: *To will is not enough; one must do.* **15.** to decide or determine: *Others debate, but the king wills.* [(n.) ME, OE (also ME *wille,* OE *willa*); c. D *wil,* G *Wille,* Icel *vili,* Goth *wilja;* (v.) OE *willian*] —**will′er,** *n.*

—**Syn. 1, 4.** pleasure, disposition, inclination. **5.** resolution, decision. WILL, VOLITION refer to conscious choice of action or thought. WILL denotes fixed and persistent intent or purpose: *Where there's a will there's a way.* VOLITION is the power of forming an intention or the incentive for using the will: *to exercise one's volition in making a decision.* **10.** determine. **12.** leave.

will·a·ble (wil′ə bəl), *adj.* capable of being willed or fixed by will. [late ME]

Wil·lam·ette (wi lam′it), *n.* a river flowing N through NW Oregon into the Columbia River at Portland. ab. 290 mi. long.

Wil·lard (wil′ərd), *n.* **1. Emma (Hart),** 1787–1870, U.S. educator and poet. **2. Frances Elizabeth Caroline,** 1839–1898. U.S. educator, reformer, and author. **3. Jess,** 1883–1968, U.S. boxer: world heavyweight champion 1915–19.

will-call (wil′kôl′), *adj.* noting a department in a store where goods ordered by a customer are held until called for.

willed (wild), *adj.* having a will (usually used in combination): *strong-willed; weak-willed.* [ME]

Wil·lem I (vil′əm). See **William I** (def. 2).

wil·lem·ite (wil′ə mīt′), *n.* a mineral, a zinc silicate, Zn_2SiO_4, a minor ore of zinc. [named after King WILLEM I; see -ITE[1]]

Wil·lem·stad (wil′əm stät′), *n.* a seaport on the island of Curaçao, in the S West Indies: capital of the Netherlands Antilles. 43,547 (1960).

Willes·den (wilz′dən), *n.* a city in E Middlesex, in SE England, near London. 170,835 (1961).

wil·let (wil′it), *n., pl.* **-lets,** (*esp. collectively*) **-let.** a large North American shorebird, *Catoptrophorus semipalmatus,* having a striking black and white wing pattern. [short for *pill-will-willet,* conventional imit. of bird's cry]

will·ful (wil′fəl), *adj.* **1.** deliberate, voluntary, or intentional: *willful murder.* **2.** perversely obstinate; unreasonably stubborn. Also, **wilful.** [ME; OE *wilful* willing] —**will′ful·ly,** *adv.* —**will′ful·ness,** *n.*

—**Syn. 1.** volitional. **2.** contrary, refractory, pigheaded, inflexible, obdurate, adamant. WILLFUL, HEADSTRONG, PERVERSE, WAYWARD refer to a person who stubbornly insists upon doing as he pleases. WILLFUL suggests a stubborn persistence in doing what one wishes, esp. in opposition to those whose wishes or commands ought to be respected or obeyed: *a willful child who disregarded his parents' advice.* A person who is HEADSTRONG is often foolishly, and sometimes violently, self-willed: *reckless and headstrong youths.* The PERVERSE person is unreasonably or obstinately intractable or contrary, often with the express intention of being disagreeable: *perverse out of sheer spite.* WAYWARD in this sense has the connotation of rash wrong-headedness which gets a person into trouble: *a reform school for wayward boys.* —**Ant. 2.** obedient, tractable.

Wil·liam I (wil′yəm), **1.** (*"the Conqueror"*) 1027–87, duke of Normandy 1035–87; king of England 1066–87 (son of Robert I, duke of Normandy). **2.** Also, **Willem I.** (*William I of Orange*) (*"the Silent"*) 1533–84, Dutch leader, statesman, and revolutionary leader born in Germany: prince of Orange 1544–84; count of Nassau 1559–84; 1st stadholder of the United Provinces of the Netherlands 1578–84. **3.** Also, **Wilhelm I.** (*Wilhelm Friedrich Ludwig*) 1797–1888, King of Prussia 1861–88; emperor of Germany 1871–88 (brother of Frederick William IV).

William II, 1. (*William Rufus*) ("*the Red*") 1056?–1100, King of England 1087–1100 (son of William I, duke of Normandy). **2.** Also, **Wilhelm II.** (*Frederick Wilhem Viktor Albert*) 1859–1941, king of Prussia and emperor of Germany 1888–1918.

William III, (*William III of Orange*) 1650–1702, stadholder of the United Provinces of the Netherlands 1672–1702; king of England 1689–1702, joint ruler with his wife Mary II.

William IV, ("*the Sailor-King*") 1765–1837, king of Great Britain and Ireland 1830–37 (brother of George IV).

Wil′liam of Malmes′bur·y (mämz′ber′ē, -bə rē, -brē), c1090–1143?, English historian.

Wil·liams (wil′yəmz), *n.* **1. Roger,** 1603?–83, English clergyman in America: founder of Rhode Island colony 1636. **2. Tennessee** (pen name of *Thomas Lanier Williams*), 1914–83, U.S. dramatist. **3. William Car·los** (kär′lōs), 1883–1963, U.S. poet, novelist, and physician.

Wil·liams·burg (wil′yəmz bûrg′), *n.* a city in SE Virginia: colonial capital of Virginia; now restored to its original pre-Revolutionary style. 9069 (1970).

Wil·liams·port (wil′yəmz pōrt′, -pôrt′), *n.* a city in central Pennsylvania, on the Susquehanna River. 37,918 (1970).

Wil′liam Tell′, a legendary Swiss patriot forced by the Austrian governor to shoot an apple off his son's head with bow and arrow.

Wil′liam the Con′queror. See **William I** (def. 1).

wil·lies (wil′ēz), *n.pl. Slang.* nervousness or fright; jitters; creeps (usually prec. by *the*): *That horror movie gave me the willies.* [?]

will·ing (wil′ing), *adj.* **1.** disposed or consenting; inclined: *I am willing to go despite her attitude.* **2.** cheerfully consenting or ready: *He is a willing worker.* **3.** done, given, borne, used, etc., with cheerful readiness. [ME; OE *willend-*] —**will′ing·ly,** *adv.* —**will′ing·ness,** *n.*

Wil·ling·bor·o (wil′ing bûr′ō), *n.* a township in SW New Jersey. 43,386 (1970).

wil·li·waw (wil′ə wô′), *n.* a violent squall that moves seaward down a mountainous coast, esp. in the Strait of Magellan. Also, **wil′lie-wa′, wil′li·wau′, willy-waa, willywaw.** [var. of *willy-willy* < native Austral]

Will·kie (wil′kē), *n.* **Wen·dell Lewis** (wen′dᵊl), 1892–1944, U.S. executive, lawyer, and political leader.

will-less (wil′lis), *adj.* **1.** having or exerting no will. **2.** done or occurring without the will; involuntary. **3.** leaving no will; intestate: *to die will-less.* —**will′-less·ly,** *adv.* —**will′-less·ness,** *n.*

will-o'-the-wisp (wil′ə thə wisp′), *n.* **1.** See **ignis fatuus** (def. 1). **2.** anything that deludes or misleads by luring on. [orig. *Will* (i.e., William) *with the wisp;* see WISP] —**will′-o'-the-wisp′ish,** *adj.*

wil·low (wil′ō), *n.* **1.** any tree or shrub of the genus *Salix,* many species of which have tough, pliable twigs or branches used for wickerwork, etc. **2.** the wood of any of these trees. **3.** *Informal.* something, esp. a cricket bat, made of willow wood. [ME *wilwe,* var. of *wilghe,* OE *welig;* c. D *wilg,* LG *wilge,* Gk *helíkē* (aspirated var. of *elíkē* convolution < prehistoric **welikā*)] —**wil′low·like′,** *adj.*

Wil·low·brook (wil′ō bro͝ok′), *n.* a town in S California, S of Los Angeles. 28,705 (1970).

wil′low herb′, **1.** an onagraceous plant, *Epilobium* (*Chamaenerion*) *angustifolium,* having narrow, willowlike leaves and racemes of purple flowers. **2.** any plant of this genus. **3.** the purple loosestrife, *Lythrum Salicaria.*

wil′low oak′, an oak, *Quercus Phellos,* of the southwestern U.S., having entire, lanceolate leaves, yielding a hard, heavy wood used in the construction of buildings.

wil′low pat′tern, a decorative design in English ceramics, derived from Chinese sources, usually executed in blue and white and depicting a willow tree, small bridge, and two birds.

wil′low war′bler, any of several usually grayish-green leaf warblers, esp. *Phylloscopus trochilus,* of Europe.

wil·low·ware (wil′ō wâr′), *n.* china using the willow pattern.

wil·low·y (wil′ō ē), *adj.* **1.** pliant; lithe. **2.** gracefully slender and supple. **3.** abounding with willows.

will′ pow′er, strength of one's will, esp. in the exercise of self-control.

wil·ly-nil·ly (wil′ē nil′ē), *adv.* **1.** willingly or unwillingly: *He'll have to do it willy-nilly.* —*adj.* **2.** shilly-shallying; vacillating. [from the phrase *will ye, nill ye.* See WILL[1], NILL]

wil·ly-waa (wil′ē wô′), *n.* williwaw. Also, **wil′ly·waw′.**

Wil·mette (wil met′), *n.* a city in NE Illinois, near Chicago. 32,134 (1970).

Wil·ming·ton (wil′ming tən), *n.* **1.** a seaport in N Delaware, on the Delaware River. 80,386 (1970). **2.** a seaport in SE North Carolina, on the Cape Fear River. 46,169 (1970).

Wil·no (vēl′nō), *n.* Polish name of **Vilna.**

Wil·son (wil′sən), *n.* **1. Edmund,** 1895–1972, U.S. literary and social critic. **2. Henry** (*Jeremiah Jones Colbath*), 1812–1875, U.S. politician: vice president of the U.S. 1873–75. **3. (James) Harold,** born 1916, British statesman: prime minister 1964–70, 1974–76. **4. John** ("*Christopher North*"), 1785–1854, Scottish poet, journalist, and critic. **5. (Thomas) Wood·row** (wo͝od′rō), 1856–1924, 28th president of the U.S. 1913–21: Nobel peace prize 1919. **6. Mount,** a mountain in SW California. 5710 ft. **7.** a city in E North Carolina. 29,347.

Wil′son cloud′ cham′ber, *Physics.* See **cloud chamber.** Also called **Wil′son cham′ber.** [named after Charles T. R. *Wilson* (1869–1959), Scottish physicist]

Wil·so·ni·an (wil sō′nē ən), *adj.* of, pertaining to, or characteristic of Woodrow Wilson.

Wil′son's snipe′, an American snipe, *Capella delicata,* having reddish-brown, black, and white plumage. See illus. at **snipe.** [named after Alexander *Wilson* (1766–1813), Scottish-American ornithologist]

wilt[1] (wilt), *v.i.* **1.** to become limp and drooping, as a fading flower; wither. **2.** to lose strength, vigor, assurance, etc. —*v.t.* **3.** to cause to wilt. —*n.* **4.** the act of wilting. **5.** the state of being wilted. **6.** *Plant Pathol.* **a.** the drying out, drooping, and withering of the leaves of a plant due to inadequate water supply, excessive transpiration, or vascular disease. **b.** a disease so characterized. **7.** a virus disease of various caterpillars, characterized by the liquefaction of body tissues. Also called **wilt′ disease′** (for defs. 6b, 7). [dial. var. of *wilk* to wither, itself a var. of *welk,* ME *welke(n)* < MD; akin to WELKIN, G *welk* faded (orig., moist)]

wilt[2] (wilt), *v. Archaic.* second pers. sing. pres. ind. of **will**[1].

Wil·ton (wil′tᵊn), *n.* Also called **Wil′ton car′pet, Wil′ton rug′.** a carpet woven on a Jacquard loom, having the loops cut to form a velvet pile. [named after *Wilton,* town of Wiltshire, England]

Wilt·shire (wilt′shēr, -shər), *n.* **1.** Also called **Wilts** (wilts). a county in S England. 422,753 (1961); 1345 sq. mi. *Co. seat:* Salisbury. **2.** one of an English breed of white sheep having long, spiral horns.

wil·y (wī′lē), *adj.,* **wil·i·er, wil·i·est.** full of, marked by, or proceeding from wiles; crafty; cunning. [ME] —**wil′i·ly,** *adv.* —**wil′i·ness,** *n.* —**Syn.** artful, sly, designing, foxy.

wim·ble (wim′bəl), *n., v.,* **-bled, -bling.** —*n.* **1.** any of various instruments for boring. —*v.t.* **2.** to bore or perforate with or as with a wimble. [ME < MD or MLG *wimmel* auger; see GIMLET]

Wim·ble·don (wim′bəl dən), *n.* a city in N Surrey, in SE England, near London: international tennis tournaments. 56,994 (1961).

wimp (wimp), *n. Slang,* a passive, ineffective, often self-pitying person. [? fr. *Wimpy,* name of a character in *Popeye,* a popular comic strip] —**wimp′y,** *adj.*

wim·ple (wim′pəl), *n., v.,* **-pled, -pling.** —*n.* **1.** a woman's headcloth drawn in folds about the chin, formerly worn out of doors, and still in use by nuns. **2.** *Chiefly Scot.* **a.** a fold or wrinkle, as in cloth. **b.** a curve, bend, or turn, as in a road or river. —*v.t.* **3.** to cover or muffle with or as with a wimple. **4.** to cause to ripple or undulate, as water. **5.** *Archaic.* to veil or enwrap. —*v.i.* **6.** to ripple, as water. **7.** *Archaic.* to lie in folds, as a veil. **8.** *Chiefly Scot.* to follow a curving course, as a road or river. [ME, var. of ME, OE *wimpel;* c. D, LG *wimpel,* Icel *vimpill*]

Wimple

win[1] (win), *v.,* **won** or (*Obs.*) **wan; won; win·ning;** *n.* —*v.i.* **1.** to finish first in a race, contest, or the like. **2.** to succeed by striving or effort (sometimes fol. by *out*): *He applied for a scholarship and won. His finer nature won out.* **3.** to gain the victory; overcome an adversary: *The home team won.* —*v.t.* **4.** to succeed in reaching (a place, condition, etc.), esp. by great effort: *They won the shore through a violent storm.* **5.** to get by effort, as through labor, competition, or conquest: *He won his post after years of striving.* **6.** to gain (a prize, fame, etc.): *He won the prize by being the first to finish the race.* **7.** to be successful in (a game, battle, etc.). **8.** to make (one's way), as by effort, ability, etc. **9.** to attain or reach (a point, goal, etc.). **10.** to gain (favor, love, consent, etc.) as by qualities or influence. **11.** to gain the favor, regard, or adherence of. **12.** to gain the consent or support of; persuade (often fol. by *over*): *The speech won him over to our side.* **13.** to persuade to marry; gain in marriage. —*n.* **14.** a victory, as in a game or horse race. **15.** *U.S.* the position of the competitor who comes in first in a horse race, harness race, etc. Cf. **place** (def. 26), **show** (def. 28). [ME *winne(n),* OE *winnan* to work, fight, bear; c. G *(ge)winnen,* Goth *winnan,* Icel *vinna*] —**win′na·ble,** *adj.* —**Syn. 5.** obtain, acquire, achieve. See **gain**[1]. **12.** convince.

win[2] (win), *v.t.,* **winned, win·ning.** *Scot. and North Eng.* to dry (hay, wood, etc.) by exposure to air and sun. [? var. of WINNOW]

wince (wins), *v.,* **winced, winc·ing,** *n.* —*v.i.* **1.** to shrink, as in pain or from a blow; start; flinch. —*n.* **2.** a wincing or shrinking movement; a slight start. [ME *winse(n),* var. of *winchen, wenchen* to kick < AF **wenc(h)ier* (OF *guenc(h)ier*) < Gmc (? OE). Cf. WENCH, WINCH] —**winc′er,** *n.* —**winc′ing·ly,** *adv.* —**Syn. 1.** blench, quail.

winch (winch), *n.* **1.** the crank or handle of a revolving machine. **2.** a windlass turned by a crank, for hoisting or hauling. —*v.t.* **3.** to hoist or haul by means of a winch. [ME *winche,* OE *wince* pulley; akin to WENCH, WINCE]

Win·ches·ter (win′ches′tər, -chi stər), *n.* **1.** a city in and the county seat of Hampshire, in S England: cathedral; capital of medieval England. 46,230 (1961). **2.** See **Winchester rifle.**

Win′chester bush′el. See under **bushel**[1] (def. 1). [named after WINCHESTER, England]

Win′chester ri′fle, a type of repeating rifle with a tubular magazine under the barrel, first made about 1866. [after D. F. *Winchester* (1810–80), U S. manufacturer]

Winck·el·mann (ving′kəl män′), *n.* **Jo·hann Jo·a·chim** (yō′hän yō′ä KHim), 1717–68, German archaeologist and art historian.

wind[1] (*n.* wind, *Poetic* wīnd; *v.* wind), *n.* **1.** air in natural motion, as along the earth's surface. **2.** a gale; storm; hurricane. **3.** any stream of air, as that produced by a bellows, fan, etc. **4.** air that is blown or forced to produce a musical sound in singing or playing an instrument. **5.** a wind instrument. **6.** wind instruments collectively. **7. the winds,** the members of an orchestra or band who play the wind instruments. **8.** breath or breathing: *to catch one's wind.* **9.** the power of breathing freely, as during continued exertion: *Smoking affected his wind.* **10.** any influential force or trend: *strong winds of public opinion.* **11.** a hint or intimation: *to catch wind of a stock split.* **12.** air carrying an animal's odor or scent. **13.** empty talk; mere words. **14.** gas generated in the stomach and intestines. **15.** any direction of the compass. **16. break wind,** to expel gas from the stomach and bowels through the anus. **17. how the wind blows** or **lies,** what the tendency or probability is: *Try to find out how the wind blows.* Also, **which way the wind blows. 18. in the teeth of the wind,** sailing directly into the wind; against the wind. Also, **in the eye of the wind, in the wind's eye. 19. in the wind,** about to occur; impending: *There's good news in the wind.* **20. off the wind, a.** away from the wind; with the wind at one's back. **b.** (of a sailing vessel) headed into the wind with sails shaking or aback. **21. sail close to the wind,** to sail as nearly as possible in the direction from which the wind is blowing. **22. take the wind out of one's sails,** to destroy a person's self-assurance, as by unexpectedly disproving his argument; disconcert; deflate; frustrate. **—***v.t.* **23.** to expose to wind or air. **24.** to follow by the scent. **25.** to make short of wind or breath, as by vigorous exercise. **26.** to let recover breath, as by resting after exertion. **—***v.i.* **27.** to catch the scent or odor of game. [ME, OE; c. D, G *Wind,* Icel *vindr,* Goth *winds,* L *ventus*]

—Syn. 1. WIND, AIR, ZEPHYR, BREEZE, BLAST, GUST refer to a quantity of air set in motion naturally. WIND applies to any such air in motion, blowing with whatever degree of gentleness or violence. AIR, usually literary, applies to a very gentle motion of the air. ZEPHYR, also literary, refers to an air characterized by its soft, mild quality. A BREEZE is usually a light wind of moderate temperature. BLAST and GUST apply to quick, forceful winds of short duration; BLAST implies a violent rush of air, often a cold one, whereas a GUST can be little more than a flurry.

wind[2] (wīnd), *v.,* **wound** or (*Rare*) **wind·ed; wind·ing;** *n.* **—***v.i.* **1.** to change direction; bend; turn; take a frequently bending course: *The river winds through the forest.* **2.** to have a circular or spiral course or direction. **3.** to coil or twine about something. **4.** to be twisted or warped, as a board. **5.** to proceed circuitously or indirectly. **6.** to undergo winding, or winding up. **—***v.t.* **7.** to encircle or wreathe, as with something twined, wrapped, or placed about. **8.** to roll or coil (thread, string, etc.) into a ball, on a spool, or the like (often fol. by *up*). **9.** to remove or take off by unwinding (usually fol. by *off* or *from*): *She wound the thread off the bobbin.* **10.** to coil, fold, wrap, or place about something. **11.** to impart power to (a mechanism) by turning a key or crank (often fol. by *up*): *to wind a clock.* **12.** to haul or hoist by means of a winch, windlass, or the like (often fol. by *up*). **13.** to make (one's or its way) in a winding or frequently bending course: *The stream winds its way through the woods.* **14.** to make (one's or its way into) by indirect, stealthy, or devious manner: *to wind one's way into another's confidence.* **15. wind up, a.** to bring to a state of great tension; excite: *He was all wound up before the game.* **b.** to bring or come to a conclusion: *to wind up the campaign.* **c.** to settle or arrange in order to conclude: *to wind up one's affairs.* **d.** *Baseball.* (of a pitcher) to execute a windup. **—***n.* **16.** act of winding. **17.** a single turn, twist, or bend of something wound: *If you give it another wind, you'll break the mainspring.* [ME; OE *wind(an)*; c. D, G *winden,* Icel *vinda,* Goth *-windan;* akin to WEND, WANDER]

wind[3] (wīnd, wind), *v.t.,* **wind·ed** or **wound, wind·ing. 1.** to blow (a horn, a blast, etc.). **2.** to sound by blowing. [special use of WIND[1]]

WInd, West Indian. Also, **W.Ind.**

wind·a·ble (wīn′də bəl), *adj.* that can be wound.

wind·age (win′dij), *n.* **1.** the influence of the wind in deflecting a missile. **2.** the amount of such deflection. **3.** the degree to which a gunsight must be adjusted to correct for this. **4.** the amount by which the diameter of a projectile must be smaller than that of the gun bore to allow for the escape of gas and to prevent friction. **5.** *Naut.* the portion of a vessel's surface upon which the wind acts.

wind·bag (wind′bag′), *n.* **1.** *Slang.* an empty, voluble, pretentious talker. **2.** the bag of a bagpipe. [late ME]

wind-bell (wind′bel′), *n.* **1.** a bell sounded by the action of the wind. **2.** Usually, **wind-bells.** a group of small pieces of glass, metal, etc., hanging freely and rustling against each other to be sounded by the action of the wind.

wind·blown (wind′blōn′), *adj.* **1.** blown or as if blown by the wind: *windblown hair.* **2.** (of trees) growing in a certain shape because of strong prevailing winds.

wind-borne (wind′bōrn′, -bôrn′), *adj.* carried by the wind, as pollen or seed.

wind·bound (wind′bound′), *adj.* (of a sailing ship, sailboat, or the like) kept from sailing by a strong or contrary wind.

wind·break (wind′brāk′), *n.* a growth of trees, a structure of boards, or the like, serving as a shelter from the wind.

Wind·break·er (wind′brā′kər), *n. Trademark.* a waist-length or slightly longer, lightweight, wind-resistant jacket of fabric or leather, often having a collar, for sports or other outdoor wear.

wind-bro·ken (wind′brō′kən), *adj. Vet. Med.* (of horses) having the breathing impaired; affected with heaves.

wind·burn (wind′bûrn′), *n.* an inflammation of the skin caused by overexposure to the wind. —**wind′burned′,** *adj.*

wind·chest (wind′chest′), *n.* a chamber receiving and regulating the air supply for an organ.

wind′ chill′, the coldness felt on the exposed human flesh by a combination of temperature and wind velocity. Also called **chill factor.** —**wind′-chill′,** *adj.*

wind′ cone′ (wind), windsock.

wind·ed (win′did), *adj.* **1.** having wind or breath of a specified kind (usually used in combination): *short-winded; broken-winded.* **2.** out of breath. [late ME] —**wind′ed·ness,** *n.*

wind·er (wīn′dər), *n.* **1.** a person or thing that winds. **2.** a step in a spiral staircase that is wider at one end than the other. Cf. **flier** (def. 7). **3.** a plant that coils or twines itself about something. **4.** an instrument or a machine for winding thread or the like.

Win·der·mere (win′dər mēr′), *n.* **Lake,** a lake in NW England, between Westmorland and Lancashire: the largest lake in England. 10½ mi. long; 5⅔ sq. mi.

wind·fall (wind′fôl′), *n.* **1.** something blown down by the wind, as fruit. **2.** an unexpected gain, piece of good fortune, or the like. [late ME]

wind·flaw (wind′flô′), *n.* flaw[2] (def. 1).

wind·flow·er (wind′flou′ər), *n.* any plant of the genus *Anemone.* [trans. of ANEMONE]

wind·gall (wind′gôl′), *n. Vet. Med.* a puffy distention of the synovial bursa at the fetlock joint. —**wind′galled′,** *adj.*

wind′ gauge′ (wind), **1.** anemometer. **2.** a scale on the rear sight of a rifle by which the sight is adjusted to correct for windage.

wind′ harp′ (wind). See **aeolian harp.**

Wind·hoek (*Du.* vint′ho͝ok′), *n.* a city in and the capital of South-West Africa, in the central part. 62,000.

wind·hov·er (wind′huv′ər, -hov′-), *n.* the kestrel, *Falco tinnunculus.* [WIND[1] + HOVER; from its hovering flight, head to the wind]

wind·ing (wīn′ding), *n.* **1** the act of a person or thing that winds. **2.** a bend or turn. **3.** a whole turn of something that is wound or coiled. **4.** *Elect.* **a.** a symmetrically laid, electrically conducting current path in any device. **b.** the manner of such coiling or of its connection: *a series winding.* **—***adj.* **5.** bending or turning; sinuous. **6.** helical, as stairs. [ME (n.), OE *windung* (n.). See WIND[2], -ING[1], -ING[2]] —**wind′ing·ly,** *adv.* —**wind′ing·ness** *n.*

wind′ing frame′, a machine on which yarn or thread is wound.

wind′ing sheet′, a sheet in which a corpse is wrapped for burial. [late ME]

wind′ in′strument (wind), a musical instrument sounded by the breath or the force of air, as the clarinet, flute, trumpet, trombone, etc.

wind·jam·mer (wind′jam′ər, win′-), *n. Informal.* **1.** any large sailing ship. **2.** a member of its crew. [WIND[1] + *jammer* (see JAM[1], -ER[1]); so called in contempt]

wind·lass (wind′ləs), *n.* **1.** a device for hauling or hoisting, commonly having a horizontal drum on which a rope attached to the load is wound; winch. **—***v.t.* **2.** to raise, haul, or move by means of a windlass. [ME *windelas* = *windel(en),* freq. of *winden* to WIND[2] + *-as* pole (< Scand; cf. Icel *āss* beam, pole)]

Windlass (Hand operated)

wind·less (wind′lis), *adj.* **1.** free from wind; calm: *a windless day.* **2.** out of breath. [late ME] —**wind′less·ly,** *adv.* —**wind′less·ness,** *n.*

win·dle·straw (win′dəl strô′, win′əl-), *n. Brit. Dial.* **1.** a withered stalk of any of various grasses. **2.** any tall, thin person. [OE *windelstrēaw* = *windel* box, basket, container (akin to WIND[2]) + *strēaw* STRAW]

wind·mill (wind′mil′), *n.* **1.** any of various machines for grinding, pumping, etc., driven by the force of the wind acting upon a number of vanes or sails. **2.** an imaginary opponent, wrong, etc. (in allusion to Cervantes' romance *Don Quixote de la Mancha* (1605 and 1615) in which the hero fights a windmill): *to tilt at windmills.* **—***v.t.* **3.** *Aeron.* (of a propeller engine or turbojet engine) to rotate solely under the force of a passing airstream. [ME]

Windmill

win·dow (win′dō), *n.* **1.** an opening in a wall or the like for the admission of light, air, or both, or for the purpose of looking in or out. **2.** the glazing and fittings of such an opening. **3.** a pane of such glazing: *to break a window.* **4.** anything likened to a window in appearance or function, as a transparent section in an envelope, displaying the address. **—***v.t.* **5.** to furnish with a window or windows. [ME *windoge, windowe* < Scand; cf. Icel *vindauga* = *vindr* wind + *auga* eye] —**win′dow·less,** *adj.*

win′dow box′, a box for growing plants, placed at or in a window.

win′dow dress′er, a person employed to decorate the display windows of a store, as with merchandise offered for sale.

win′dow dress′ing, 1. the work of a window dresser. **2.** misrepresentation of facts so as to give a favorable impression.

win·dow·pane (win′dō pān′), *n.* a plate of glass for filling a window sash within the frame.

win′dow sash′, the frame holding the pane or panes of a window.

win′dow seat′, 1. a seat built beneath the sill of a recessed or other window. **2.** a seat immediately adjacent to a window, as in a car, train, airplane, etc.: *Please reserve a window seat for me.*

win′dow shade′, a shade or blind for a window, as a sheet of sturdy, sized cloth or paper on a spring roller.

win·dow-shop (win′dō shop′), *v.i.,* **-shopped, -shop·ping.** to look at articles in the windows of stores without making any purchases. —**win′dow-shop′per,** *n.*

win′dow sill′, the sill under a window.

wind·pipe (wind′pīp′), *n.* the trachea of an air-breathing vertebrate.

wind-pol·li·nat·ed (wind′pol′ə nā′tid), *adj. Bot.* being pollinated by air-borne pollen. —**wind′-pol′li·na′tion,** *n.*

wind·proof (wind′pro͞of′), *adj.* resisting wind, as fabric, a jacket, coat, etc.

Wind′ Riv′er Range′ (wind), a mountain range in W Wyoming, part of the Rocky Mountains. Highest peak, Gannett Peak, 13,785 ft.

wind′ rose′ (wind), a map symbol showing, for a given locality or area, the frequency and strength of the wind from various directions.

wind·row (wind′rō′, win′-), *n.* **1.** a row or line of hay, sheaves of grain, etc., left to dry. **2.** a row of dry leaves, dust, etc., swept together by the wind. **—***v.t.* **3.** to arrange in a windrow or windrows.

wind′ sail′ (wind), *Naut.* a sail rigged over a hatchway, ventilator, or the like, to divert moving air downward into the vessel.
wind′ scale′ (wind), a numerical scale, as the Beaufort scale, for designating relative wind intensities.
wind·screen (wind′skrēn′, win′-), *n. Chiefly Brit.* windshield.
wind′ shear′ (wind), a condition, dangerous to aircraft, in which the speed or direction of the wind is subject to abrupt, unpredictable changes.
wind·shield (wind′shēld′, win′-), *n.* a shield of glass projecting above and across the dashboard of an automobile, motorcycle, or the like.
wind′shield wip′er, an automatic device consisting of a squeegee connected to a mechanical arm attached to a windshield, used to maintain clarity of vision by wiping rain, snow, etc., off the windshield.
wind·sock (wind′sok′), *n.* a tapered, tubular, cloth vane, open at both ends and having at the larger end a fixed ring pivoted to swing freely at the top of a pole or stanchion to catch the wind, installed at airports or elsewhere to indicate wind direction and approximate intensity.
Wind·sor (win′zər), *n.* **1.** (since 1917) a member of the present British royal family. Cf. **Saxe-Coburg-Gotha** (def. 1). **2. Duke of.** See **Edward VIII. 3.** Also called **New Windsor.** a city in E Berkshire, in S England, on the Thames: the site of the residence **(Wind′sor Cas′tle)** of English sovereigns since William I. 30,065. **4.** a city in S Ontario, in SE Canada, opposite Detroit, Michigan. 203,300.

Windsor chairs

Wind′sor chair′, (*sometimes l.c.*) a wooden chair having a spindle back and legs slanting outward: common in 18th-century England and in the American colonies.
Wind′sor knot′, a wide, triangular knot sometimes used in tying a four-in-hand necktie.
Wind′sor tie′, a wide, soft necktie of black silk tied at the neck in a loose bow.
wind·storm (wind′stôrm′), *n.* a storm with heavy wind, but little or no precipitation.
wind-suck·ing (wind′suk′ing), *n. Vet. Med.* cribbing (def. 1).
wind·surf·ing (wind′sûrf′ing), *n.* a form of sailing in which a flexible sail, free to move in any direction, is mounted on a surfboard and the craft guided by the standing rider.
wind-swept (wind′swept′), *adj.* open or exposed to the wind: *a wind-swept beach.*
wind′ tee′ (wind), a large, T-shaped weather vane on or near an airfield.
wind′ tun′nel (wind), *Aeron.* a tubular interior through which air can be sent at controlled speeds and which is equipped with devices for measuring and recording forces and moments on scale models of complete aircraft or of their parts or, sometimes, on full-scale aircraft or their parts.
wind·up (wīnd′up′), *n.* **1.** the conclusion of any activity; end or close. **2.** *Baseball.* the preparatory arm, body, and leg movements performed by a pitcher before pitching a ball.
wind′ vane′ (wind), vane (def. 1).
wind·ward (wind′wərd), *adv.* **1.** toward the wind; toward the point from which the wind blows. **—***adj.* **2.** pertaining to, situated in, or moving toward the point from which the wind blows (opposed to *leeward*). **—***n.* **3.** the point or quarter from which the wind blows. **4.** the side toward the wind.
Wind′ward Is′lands, **1.** a group of islands in the SE West Indies, consisting of the S part of the Lesser Antilles: includes British and French territories. **2.** a group of British islands in the SE West Indies, consisting of Dominica, St. Lucia, Grenada, and St. Vincent, and their dependencies. 732,000; 821 sq. mi.
Wind′ward Pas′sage, a strait in the West Indies, between Cuba and Haiti. 50 mi. wide.
wind·y (win′dē), *adj.,* **wind·i·er, wind·i·est.** **1.** accompanied or characterized by wind: *a windy day.* **2.** exposed to or swept by the wind: *a windy hill.* **3.** consisting of or resembling wind: *a windy tempest of activity.* **4.** characterized by or given to prolonged, empty talk; verbose; bombastic: *a windy speaker; a windy speech.* [ME; OE *windig*] **—wind′i·ly,** *adv.* **—wind′i·ness,** *n.*
Wind′y Cit′y, Chicago, Ill. (usually prec. by *the*) (used as a nickname).
wine (wīn), *n., adj., v.,* **wined, win·ing.** **—***n.* **1.** fermented juice of the grape, made in many varieties such as red, white, sweet, dry, still, and sparkling, for use as a beverage, in cookery, religious rites, etc., and usually having an alcoholic content of 14 percent or less. **2.** a particular variety of such fermented grape juice: *port and sherry wines.* **3.** the juice, fermented or unfermented, of various other fruits or plants, used as a beverage, sauce, etc.: *currant wine.* **4.** a dark reddish color, as of red wines. **5. new wine in old bottles,** something new placed in or superimposed on an old or existing form, system, etc. Matt. 9:17. **—***adj.* **6.** dark red in color. **—***v.t.* **7.** to supply or treat with wine. **—***v.i.* **8.** to drink wine. **9. wine and dine,** to entertain lavishly. [ME, OE *wīn* (c. G *Wein,* D *wijn,* Icel *vīn,* Goth *wein*) << L *vīnum,* c. Gk *oînos* < ?] **—wine′less,** *adj.* **—win′ish,** *adj.*
wine·bib·ber (wīn′bib′ər), *n.* a person who drinks much wine. **—wine′bib′bing,** *n., adj.*
wine′ cel′lar, **1.** a cellar for the storage of wine. **2.** a store or stock of wines.
wine·glass (wīn′glas′, -gläs′), *n.* a glass for serving wine, usually having the form of a small goblet.
wine·glass·ful (wīn′glas′fo͝ol′, -gläs′-), *n., pl.* **-fuls.** the capacity of a wineglass, commonly considered as equal to 2 fluid ounces or ¼ cup.
wine·grow·er (wīn′grō′ər), *n.* a person who owns or works in a vineyard or winery. **—wine′grow′ing,** *n.*
wine′ meas′ure, a former English system of measures for wine, in which the gallon was equal to 231 cubic inches.
wine′ palm′, any of various palms yielding toddy. Cf. toddy (def. 2).
wine′ press′, a machine in which the juice is pressed from grapes for wine. Also, **wine′ press′er.**
win·er·y (wī′nə rē), *n., pl.* **-er·ies.** an establishment for making wine.
Wine·sap (wīn′sap′), *n.* **1.** a red variety of apple that ripens in the autumn. **2.** the tree bearing this fruit.
wine·shop (wīn′shop′), *n.* a shop where wine is sold.
wine·skin (wīn′skin′), *n.* a vessel made of the skin of a goat or the like, used for holding wine.
wing (wing), *n.* **1.** either of the two anterior extremities or appendages of the scapular arch or shoulder girdle of most birds and of bats, which constitute the forelimbs, correspond to the human arms, and are adapted for flight. **2.** either of two corresponding parts in flightless birds, which may be rudimentary, as in certain ratite birds, or adapted for swimming, as in penguins. **3.** any of certain other winglike structures of other animals, as the patagium of a flying squirrel. **4.** one of the paired, thin, lateral extensions of the body wall of an insect, located on the mesothorax and the metathorax, by means of which it flies. **5.** any of various objects or parts whose position suggests the wing of a bird. **6.** *Informal.* an arm of a human being, esp. a baseball player's pitching or throwing arm. **7.** a means or instrument of flight, travel, or progress. **8.** the act or manner of flying. **9.** *Aeron.* **a.** the portion of a main supporting surface confined to one side of an airplane. **b.** both portions taken collectively. **10.** *Archit.* a part of a building projecting on one side of, or subordinate to, a central or main part. **11.** *Furniture.* either of two forward extensions of the sides of the back of an easy chair. **12.** *Mil.* either of the two side portions of an army or fleet, usually called right wing and left wing, and distinguished from the center; flank units. **13.** *U.S.* an administrative and tactical unit of the Air Force consisting of two or more groups, headquarters, and certain supporting and service units. **14.** (in flight formation) noting a position to the side and just to the rear of another airplane. **15.** *Sports.* **a.** (in some team games) any one of the positions, or a player in such a position, on the far side of the center position: known as the left and right wings with reference to the direction of the opposite goal. **b.** such a position or player in the first line of a team. **16.** *Theat.* the platform or space on the right or left of the stage proper. **17.** *Anat.* an ala: *the wings of the sphenoid.* **18.** *Bot.* **a.** any leaflike expansion, as of a samara. **b.** one of the two side petals of a papilionaceous flower. **19.** either of the parts of a double door, screen, etc. **20.** the feather of an arrow. **21.** a political group, or a number of such groups, considered with respect to their radicalism or conservatism. Cf. **left wing, right wing. 22. on the wing,** in flight, or flying. **23. take wing,** to begin to fly; take to the air. **24. under one's wing,** under one's protection, care, or patronage. **—***v.t.* **25.** to equip with wings. **26.** to enable to fly, move rapidly, etc.; lend speed or celerity to. **27.** to transport on or as on wings. **28.** to perform or accomplish by wings. **29.** to wound or disable in the wing: *to wing a bird.* **30.** to wound (a person) in an arm or other nonvital part. **—***v.i.* **31.** to travel on or as on wings; fly. [ME *wenge* (pl.) < Scand; cf. Icel *vængir* (pl.)] **—wing′like′,** *adj.*
wing·back (wing′bak′), *n. Football.* **1.** an offensive back who lines up outside of an end. **2.** the position played by this back.
wing′ bolt′, a bolt with a head shaped like a wing nut.
wing′ bow′ (bō), (of poultry) the distinctively colored feathers on the shoulder or bend of the wing of a bird.
wing′ chair′, a large upholstered chair having a back with wings.

Wing chair

wing′ col′lar, a stand-up collar having the front edges or corners folded down, worn by men for formal or evening dress.
wing′ command′er, **1.** an officer in the Royal Air Force equivalent in rank to a lieutenant colonel in the U.S. Air Force. **2.** an officer of the U.S. Navy or Air Force who commands a wing.
wing′ cov′erts, *Ornith.* the feathers that cover the bases of the quill feathers of the wing in birds, divided into greater, middle, and primary coverts.
wing′ dam′, a jetty for diverting the current of a stream.
wing-ding (wing′ding′), *n. Slang.* a noisy, exciting celebration or party. [rhyming formation, perh. < *whing* a sharp ringing sound + DING]
winged (wingd *or, esp. Poetic,* wing′id), *adj.* **1.** having wings. **2.** having a winglike part or parts: *a winged seed.* **3.** rapid or swift. **4.** elevated or lofty: *winged sentiments.* **5.** disabled in the wing, as a bird. **6.** wounded in an arm or other nonvital part. [late ME] **—wing′ed·ly,** *adv.*
wing′ flat′, *Theat.* a flat, esp. a hinged two-panel unit, usually forming part of a unit of four panels of painted scenery. Also called **coulisse.**
wing-foot·ed (wing′fo͝ot′id), *adj.* **1.** having winged feet. **2.** swift.
wing·less (wing′lis), *adj.* **1.** having no wings. **2.** having only rudimentary wings, as an apteryx. **—wing′less·ness,** *n.*
wing·let (wing′lit), *n.* **1.** a little wing. **2.** *Zool.* alula.
wing′ nut′, a nut having two flat, widely projecting pieces such that it can be readily tightened with the thumb and forefinger.
wings (wingz), *n.* **1.** *Mil. Informal.* a badge bearing the image of a spread pair of bird's wings, awarded to an aircrewman on completion of certain requirements. **2.** a similar badge awarded to a member of a commercial airline crew.
wing′ shoot′ing, *Hunting.* the act or practice of shooting at birds moving through the air.
wing′ shot′, *Hunting.* **1.** a shot taken at a bird moving through the air. **2.** an expert in wing shooting.
wing·span (wing′span′), *n.* the distance between the wing tips of an airplane.

wing·spread (wiṅg′spred′), *n.* (of a winged creature or object) the distance between the tips of the wings when they are extended as far as possible.

wing′ tip′, **1.** the extreme outer edge of an airplane wing, wing of a bird, or the like. **2.** a shoe toecap, esp. one with a perforated pattern, having a point at the center and a piece at each side extending back along the top and sides. **3.** a style of shoe with such a toe.

wink[1] (wiṅgk), *v.i.* **1.** to close and open the eyes quickly. **2.** to close and open one eye quickly as a hint or signal. **3.** (of the eyes) to close and open thus; blink. **4.** to shine with little flashes of light; twinkle: *The city lights winked in the distance.* **—***v.t.* **5.** to close and open (the eyes or an eye) quickly. **6.** to drive or force by winking or blinking (usually fol. by *back* or *away*): *to wink back tears.* **7.** to signal or convey by a wink. **8. wink at,** to ignore deliberately, as to avoid the necessity of taking action: *It is time for public-spirited citizens to stop winking at the misappropriation of tax money.* **—***n.* **9.** the act of winking. **10.** a winking movement, esp. of one eye, as in giving a hint or signal. **11.** a hint or signal given by winking. **12.** the time required for winking once; an instant or twinkling: *I'll be there in a wink.* **13.** a little flash of light; a twinkle. **14.** the least bit: *I didn't sleep a wink last night because of the thunderstorm.* [ME *winke(n),* OE *wincian;* c. G *winken* to wave, signal] **—Syn. 1, 2.** WINK, BLINK refer to rapid motions of the eyelid. To WINK is to close and open either one or both eyelids voluntarily and with a rapid motion. To BLINK suggests a sleepy, dazed, or dazzled condition in which it is difficult to focus the eyes or see clearly: *Bright sun makes one blink.*

wink[2] (wiṅgk), *n.* *Games.* a disk or similar small object used in tiddlywinks. [(TIDDLY)WINK(S)]

Win·kel·ried (*Ger.* viṅg′kəl ʀēt′), *n.* **Ar·nold von** (*Ger.* äʀ′nôlt fən), died 1386?, Swiss hero in the battle of Sempach, 1386.

wink·er (wiṅg′kər), *n.* **1.** a person or thing that winks. **2.** a blinker or blinder for a horse.

win·kle (wiṅg′kəl), *n., v.,* **-kled, -kling.** *Brit.* **—***n.* **1.** any of various marine gastropods; periwinkle. **—***v.t.* **2.** *Informal.* to pry (something) out of a place or out of hiding. [short for PERIWINKLE]

Win·ne·ba·go (win′ə bā′gō), *n., pl.* **-gos,** (*esp. collectively*) **-go. 1.** a member of a North American Indian tribe speaking a Siouan language closely related to Assiniboin, Teton, and Mandan, now living in Green Bay, Wisconsin, and NE Nebraska. **2. Lake,** a lake in E Wisconsin. 30 mi. long.

Win·ne·pe·sau·kee (win′ə pə sô′kē), *n.* **Lake,** a lake in central New Hampshire: summer resort. 25 mi. long.

win·ner (win′ər), *n.* a person or thing that wins; victor. [ME]

win′ner's cir′cle, a small, usually circular area or enclosure at a race track where awards are bestowed on winning mounts and their jockeys.

win·ning (win′iṅg), *n.* **1.** the act of a person or thing that wins. **2.** Usually, **winnings.** that which is won, esp. money. **—***adj.* **3.** successful or victorious, as in a contest. **4.** charming; engaging; pleasing: *a winning smile.* [ME] **—win′-ning·ly,** *adv.* **—win′ning·ness,** *n.* **—Syn. 4.** captivating, attractive, winsome. **—Ant. 1, 3.** losing.

win′ning gal′lery, *Court Tennis.* a winning opening on the hazard side. Cf. **dedans** (def. 1), **grille** (def. 4).

win′ning haz′ard. See under **hazard** (def. 9).

Win·ni·peg (win′ə peg′), *n.* **1.** a city in and the capital of Manitoba, in S Canada, on the Red River. 265,429 (1961). **2. Lake,** a lake in S Canada, in Manitoba. ab. 260 mi. long; ab. 9300 sq. mi. **3.** a river in S Canada, flowing NW from the Lake of the Woods to Lake Winnipeg. ab. 200 mi. long. **—Win′ni·peg′ger,** *n.*

Win·ni·pe·go·sis (win′ə pə gō′sis), *n.* **Lake,** a lake in S Canada, in W Manitoba, W of Lake Winnipeg. 2086 sq. mi.

win·now (win′ō), *v.t.* **1.** to free (grain) from the lighter particles of chaff, dirt, etc., esp. by throwing it into the air and allowing the wind or a current of air to blow away the impurities. **2.** to drive or blow (chaff, dirt, etc.) away by fanning. **3.** to blow upon; fan. **4.** to subject to some process of critical analysis or separation. **—***v.i.* **5.** to free grain from chaff by wind or driven air. **—***n.* **6.** a device or contrivance used for winnowing. **7.** the act of winnowing. [ME *win(d)-we(n),* OE *windwian* (see WIND[1]); cf. L *ventilāre* < *vent(us)* wind] **—win′now·er,** *n.*

win·o (wī′nō), *n., pl.* **win·os.** *Slang.* a person, usually a derelict, who keeps himself intoxicated on cheap wine. [WINE + *-o* suffix of association]

Wi·no·na (wi nō′nə), *n.* a city in SE Minnesota, on the Mississippi. 26,438 (1970).

Wins·low (winz′lō), *n.* **Edward,** 1595–1655, English colonist and author in America: governor of the Plymouth Colony 1633, 1639, 1644.

win·some (win′səm), *adj.* winning, engaging, or charming: *a winsome smile.* [ME *winsom,* OE *wynsum* = *wyn* joy + *-sum* -SOME[1]] **—win′some·ly,** *adv.* **—win′some·ness,** *n.*

Win·sor (win′zər), *n.* **Justin,** 1831–97, U.S. librarian and historian.

Win·ston-Sa·lem (win′stən sā′ləm), *n.* a city in N North Carolina. 134,676 (1970).

win·ter (win′tər), *n.* **1.** the cold season between autumn and spring: in the Northern Hemisphere from the winter solstice to the vernal equinox; in the Southern Hemisphere from the summer solstice to the autumnal equinox. **2.** cold weather: *a touch of winter.* **3.** the colder half of the year. **4.** a whole year as represented by this season: *a man of sixty winters.* **5.** a period like winter, as the last or final period of life, a period of decline, decay, inertia, dreariness, or adversity: *the winter of our discontent.* **—***adj.* **6.** of, pertaining to, or characteristic of winter. **7.** planted in the autumn to be harvested in the spring or early summer. **8.** (of fruit and vegetables) of a kind that may be kept for use during the winter. **—***v.i.* **9.** to spend or pass the winter: *We plan to winter in Italy.* **10.** to keep, feed, or manage during the winter, as plants or cattle: *The cows are wintering in the barn.* [ME, OE; c. G *Winter,* Icel *vetr,* Goth *wintrus;* akin to WET, WATER] **—win′ter·er,** *n.* **—win′ter·ish,** *adj.* **—win′ter·less,** *adj.*

win′ter ac′onite, a small, ranunculaceous Old World herb, *Eranthis hyemalis,* cultivated for its yellow flowers.

win′ter bar′ley, barley that is planted in the autumn to be harvested in the spring or early summer.

win·ter·ber·ry (win′tər ber′ē), *n., pl.* **-ries.** any of several North American hollies of the genus *Ilex,* having red berries that are persistent through the winter.

win·ter·bourne (win′tər bōrn′, -bŏŏrn′), *n.* a channel filled only at a time of excessive rainfall. [OE *winterburna*]

win·ter·feed (win′tər fēd′), *v.,* **-fed, -feed·ing,** *n.* **—***v.t.* **1.** to feed (cattle, sheep, etc.) during the winter when pasturage is not available: *He winterfed the animals.* **2.** to supply (grain, hay, etc.) to livestock in winter: *We winterfed corn and oats to the animals.* **—***v.i.* **3.** to provide feed for livestock, as in winter. **—***n.* **4.** the feed given to livestock during the winter.

win′ter floun′der, a flounder, *Pseudopleuronectes americanus,* found along the Atlantic coast of North America, used as food, esp. in winter. See illus. at **flounder.**

win·ter·green (win′tər grēn′), *n.* **1.** a small, creeping, evergreen, ericaceous shrub, *Gaultheria procumbens,* common in eastern North America, having white, bell-shaped flowers, a bright-red, berrylike fruit, and aromatic leaves that yield a volatile oil. **2.** the oil of this shrub. **3.** the flavor of this oil, or something having this flavor. **4.** any of various small evergreen herbs of the genera *Pyrola* and *Chimaphila.* [trans. of D *wintergroen* or G *Wintergrün*]

win′tergreen oil′. See **methyl salicylate.**

win·ter·ize (win′tə rīz′), *v.t.,* **-ized, -iz·ing.** to prepare for cold weather, as by adding antifreeze to an automobile engine or insulation in a building: *to winterize an air conditioner.* **—win′ter·i·za′tion,** *n.*

win·ter·kill (win′tər kil′), *v., n.* *U.S.* **—***v.t., v.i.* **1.** to kill by or die from exposure to the cold of winter, as wheat. **—***n.* **2.** the act or an instance of winterkilling. **3.** death resulting from winterkilling. **—win′ter·kill′ing,** *adj., n.*

win′ter lamb′, a lamb born in the fall or early winter and sold for slaughter prior to May 20.

win′ter mel′on, a variety of late-keeping muskmelon, *Cucumis melo inodorus,* having a sweet, edible flesh.

win′ter sa′vory. See under **savory**[2].

win′ter sol′stice, *Astron.* the solstice on or about December 21st that marks the beginning of winter in the Northern Hemisphere.

win′ter squash′, any of several squashes of the varieties *Cucurbita maxima* or *C. moschata* that mature in late autumn and are used as a vegetable.

win·ter·tide (win′tər tīd′), *n.* *Literary.* wintertime. [ME; OE *wintertīd*]

win·ter·time (win′tər tīm′), *n.* the season of winter. [ME; r. ME, OE *wintertīd* WINTERTIDE]

win′ter wheat′, wheat that is planted in the autumn to be harvested in the spring or early summer.

win·ter·y (win′tə rē), *adj.,* **-ter·i·er, -ter·i·est.** wintry.

Win·throp (win′thrəp), *n.* **1. John,** 1588–1649, English colonist in America: 1st governor of the Massachusetts Bay colony. **2.** his son, **John,** 1606–76, English colonist in America: colonial governor of Connecticut 1657, 1659–76. **3. John** or **Fitz-John** (fits′jon′), 1638–1707, American soldier and statesman: colonial governor of Connecticut 1698–1707 (son of the younger John Winthrop).

win·tle (win′tᵊl), *v.i.,* **-tled, -tling.** *Scot.* to roll or swing back and forth. [< D or Flem; cf. MD *wentelen,* Flem *windtelen* to roll; appar. freq. of *winden* to WIND[2]]

win·try (win′trē), *adj.,* **-tri·er, -tri·est.** pertaining to, characteristic of, or suggesting winter: *wintry skies.* Also, **wintery.** [OE *wint(e)rig*] **—win′tri·ly,** *adv.* **—win′tri·ness,** *n.*

win·y (wī′nē), *adj.,* **win·i·er, win·i·est. 1.** of, like, or characteristic of wine. **2.** affected by wine.

winze[1] (winz), *n.* *Mining.* a vertical or inclined shaft driven downward from a drift into a body of ore. [earlier *winds,* appar. WIND[1]]

winze[2] (winz), *n.* *Scot.* a curse. [< MD *wens(ch)* WISH]

wipe (wīp), *v.,* **wiped, wip·ing,** *n.* **—***v.t.* **1.** to rub lightly with or on a cloth, towel, paper, the hand, etc., in order to clean or dry the surface of: *He wiped the furniture with a damp cloth.* **2.** to remove by rubbing with or on something (usually fol. by *away, off, out,* etc.): *Wipe the dirt off your shoes. Wipe the dust from the pictures.* **3.** to remove as if by rubbing (usually fol. by *away, off,* etc.): *Wipe that smile off your face!* **4.** to erase, as from existence or memory (often fol. by *from*): *to wipe a thought from one's mind.* **5.** to rub or draw (something) over a surface, as in cleaning or drying. **6. wipe out, a.** to destroy completely; demolish: *The entire city was wiped out.* **b.** *Informal.* to murder; kill: *They wiped him out to keep him from appearing as a witness.* **—***n.* **7.** act of wiping: *She gave a few quick wipes to the furniture.* **8.** a rub, as of one thing over another. **9.** a sweeping stroke or blow. [ME; OE *wīp(ian);* c. OHG *wīfan* to wind round, Goth *weipan* to crown, L *vibrāre* to move to and fro]

wip·er (wī′pər), *n.* **1.** a person or thing that wipes. **2.** something used for wiping, as a towel, handkerchief, squeegee, etc. **3.** *Elect.* that portion of a selector or other similar device that makes contact with the terminals of a bank. **4.** *Mach.* a projection or partial cam, as on a rotating shaft, moving to lift or dislodge another part, esp. so as to let it drop when released.

wire (wīᵊr), *n., adj., v.,* **wired, wir·ing.** **—***n.* **1.** a slender, stringlike piece or filament of metal. **2.** material woven from such pieces, used for fences, cages, or the like. **3.** a length of such material, consisting either of a single filament or of several filaments woven or twisted together and usually insulated with a dielectric material, used as a conductor of electricity. **4.** a long wire or cable used in cable, telegraph, or telephone systems. **5.** *Naut.* a wire rope. **6.** a telegram. **7.** *Informal.* the telegraphic system: *to send a message by wire.* **8.** a metallic string of a musical instrument. **9.** *Horse Racing.* the finish line. **10.** the woven wire mesh over which the wet pulp is spread in a papermaking machine. **11. pull wires,** *Informal.* to use one's position or influence to obtain a desired result; pull strings. **12. the wire,** the telephone: *There's someone on the wire for you.* **13. under the wire,** just within the limit or deadline. **—***v.t.* **14.** to furnish with wires. **15.** to install an electric system of wiring as for lighting, etc. **16.** to fasten or bind with wire: *He wired the halves together.* **17.** *Informal.* to send by telegraph, as a message: *Please wire the money at once.* **18.** *Informal.* to send a telegraphic message to: *She wired him to come at* *once.* —*v.i.* **19.** *Informal.* to send a telegraphic message; telegraph. [ME, OE *wīr;* c. LG *wīr,* Icel *vīra-* wire, OHG *wiara* fine gold work, Gk *îris* (< **wiris*) rainbow; akin to L *vi(ēre)* (to) weave together] —**wire′like′,** *adj.*

wire′ cloth′, a material of wires of moderate fineness, used for making strainers, manufacturing paper, etc. —**wire′-cloth′,** *adj.*

wire′ cut′ter, any of various devices designed to cut wire, as heavy shears.

wired (wīərd), *adj.* **1.** equipped with wires, as for electricity, telephone service, etc. **2.** consisting of or constructed with wires: *a wired barrier.* **3.** tied or secured with wires. [late ME]

wire·danc·er (wīər′dan′sər, -dän′-), *n.* a person who dances or performs other feats on a high wire. —**wire′-danc′ing,** *n.*

wire·draw (wīər′drô′), *v.t.,* **-drew, -drawn, -draw·ing.** to draw (metal) out into wire, esp. forcibly through a series of dies. [back formation from WIREDRAWER] —**wire′-draw′er,** *n.*

wire′ gauge′, a gauge calibrated for determining the diameter of wire.

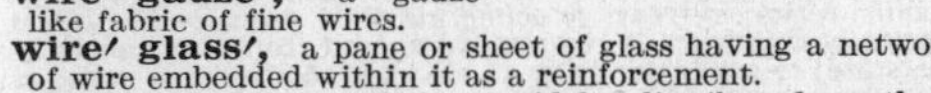

Wire gauge

wire′ gauze′, a gauze-like fabric of fine wires.

wire′ glass′, a pane or sheet of glass having a network of wire embedded within it as a reinforcement.

wire′ grass′, **1.** *U.S.* a widely distributed southern grass, *Cynodon Dactylon,* used for pasture and turf. **2.** any of various similar grasses with spreading habit, that may be a pest in cultivated fields.

wire·hair (wīər′hâr′), *n.* a fox terrier having a wiry coat. Also called **wire′-haired ter′rier.**

Wirehair (15 in. high at shoulder)

wire-haired (wīər′hârd′), *adj.* having coarse, stiff, wirelike hair.

wire′-haired point′ing grif′fon, griffon[1] (def. 2).

wire·less (wīər′lis), *adj.* **1.** having no wire. **2.** noting or pertaining to any of various devices that are operated with or actuated by electromagnetic waves. **3.** *Chiefly Brit.* radio. —*n.* **4.** wireless telegraphy or telephony. **5.** a wireless telegraph or telephone, or the like. **6.** a wireless message. **7.** *Chiefly Brit.* **a.** a radio receiving set. **b.** a radio broadcast or program. —*v.t., v.i.* **8.** to telegraph or telephone by wireless. —**wire′less·ly,** *adv.* —**wire′less·ness,** *n.*

wire′less tel′egraph, radiotelegraph.

wire′less tel′ephone, radiotelephone.

wire·man (wīər′mən), *n., pl.* **-men.** a person who installs and maintains electric wiring.

Wire·pho·to (wīər′fō′tō), *n., pl.* **-tos. 1.** *Trademark.* a device for transmitting photographs over distances by wire. **2.** a photograph so transmitted.

wire·pull·er (wīər′po͝ol′ər), *n.* **1.** a person or thing that pulls wires. **2.** a person who uses influence to direct and control the actions of others.

wire·pull·ing (wīər′po͝ol′ing), *n.* **1.** the act of pulling wires. **2.** the use of influence to manipulate persons or organizations.

wire′ record′er, a device for recording and playing back sound on a magnetized steel wire. —**wire′ record′ing.**

wire′ room′, a bookmaking establishment.

wire′ rope′, a rope made of or containing strands of wire twisted together.

wire′ serv′ice, an agency or business organization that syndicates news, the latest stock-market prices, etc., by telegraph wire to its subscribers or members.

wire·tap (wīər′tap′), *n., v.,* **-tapped, -tap·ping,** *adj.* —*n.* **1.** an act or the technique of tapping telephone or telegraph wires for evidence or other information. —*v.t.* **2.** to obtain (information, evidence, etc.) by a wiretap. **3.** to listen in on by means of a wiretap. —*v.i.* **4.** to tap telephone or telegraph wires for evidence, information, etc. —*adj.* **5.** pertaining to or obtained by wiretap. [back formation from WIRETAPPER] —**wire′tap′per,** *n.*

wire wheel (wīər′ hwēl′, wēl′ *for 1;* wīər′ hwēl′, wēl′ *for 2*), **1.** a wheellike brush having stiff wire bristles, used esp. for finishing or cleaning metal. **2.** a wheel having wire spokes.

wire·work (wīər′wûrk′), *n.* **1.** work consisting of wire. **2.** fabrics or articles made of wire.

wire·works (wīər′wûrks′), *n., pl.* **-works.** (*construed as sing. or pl.*) an establishment where wire is made or put to some industrial use. —**wire′work′er,** *n.*

wire·worm (wīər′wûrm′), *n.* **1.** any of the slender, hard-bodied larvae of click beetles, many of which live underground and feed on the roots of plants. **2.** any of various small myriapods. **3.** See **stomach worm.**

wire-wove (wīər′wōv′), *adj.* **1.** made of woven wire. **2.** noting fine glazed paper used esp. as letter paper.

wir·ing (wīər′ing), *n.* **1.** the act of a person who wires. **2.** *Elect.* the aggregate of wires in a lighting system, switchboard, radio, etc. —*adj.* **3.** that installs or is used in wiring.

wir·ra (wir′ə), *interj. Irish Eng.* (an exclamation of sorrow or lament). [short for Ir *a Muire* O Mary, a call to the Virgin]

Wirtz (wûrts), *n.* **W(illiam) Willard,** born 1912, U.S. lawyer and government official: Secretary of Labor 1962–68.

wir·y (wīər′ē), *adj.,* **wir·i·er, wir·i·est. 1.** made of wire. **2.** in the form of wire. **3.** resembling wire, as in slenderness or stiffness. **4.** lean and sinewy; vigorous; strong: *a wiry little man.* —**wir′i·ly,** *adv.* —**wir′i·ness,** *n.*

wis (wis), *v.t., v.i. Archaic.* to know. [by false analysis of IWIS as *I wis* I know; see WIT[2]]

Wis., Wisconsin. Also, **Wisc.**

Wis·by (viz′bē; *Eng.* wiz′bē), *n.* German name of **Visby.**

Wis·con·sin (wis kon′sən), *n.* **1.** a state in the N central United States: a part of the Midwest. 4,417,933 (1970); 56,154 sq. mi. *Cap.:* Madison. *Abbr.:* WI, Wis., Wisc. **2.** a river flowing SW from N Wisconsin to the Mississippi. 430 mi. long. **3.** the fourth stage of the glaciation of North America during the Pleistocene. Cf. **Würm.** —**Wis·con′sin·ite′,** *n.*

Wisd., Wisdom of Solomon.

wis·dom (wiz′dəm), *n.* **1.** the quality or state of being wise; knowledge of what is true or right coupled with good judgment. **2.** scholarly knowledge or learning. **3.** wise sayings or teachings. **4.** (*cap.*) *Douay Bible.* See **Wisdom of Solomon.** [ME, OE; c. Icel *vīsdōmr,* G *Weistum.* See WISE[1], -DOM] —**Syn. 1.** discretion, judgment, understanding, sagacity. See **information.** —**Ant. 1.** stupidity, foolishness. **2.** ignorance.

Wis′dom of Je′sus, Son′ of Si′rach (sī′rak), Ecclesiasticus.

Wis′dom of Sol′omon, a book of the Apocrypha. Also called, *Douay Bible,* **Wisdom.**

wis′dom tooth′, **1.** the third molar on each side of the upper and lower jaws: the last tooth to erupt. **2. cut one's wisdom teeth,** to attain maturity.

wise[1] (wīz), *adj.,* **wis·er, wis·est,** *v.,* **wised, wis·ing.** —*adj.* **1.** having the power of discerning and judging properly as to what is true or right; possessing discernment, judgment, or discretion. **2.** characterized by or showing such power: *a wise decision.* **3.** possessed of or characterized by scholarly knowledge or learning; learned; erudite: *wise in the law.* **4.** *Slang.* **a.** informed; in the know. **b.** insolent; impertinent. **5. be** or **get wise to,** *Slang.* to be or become cognizant of; learn. **6. get wise,** *Slang.* **a.** to become informed. **b.** to be or become presumptuous or impertinent: *Don't get wise with me, young man!* **7. put someone wise,** *U.S. Slang.* to inform a person, esp. with regard to something generally known to others. —*v.i., v.t.* **8. wise up,** *U.S. Slang.* to make or become aware of something generally known to others, as a fact, situation, attitude, etc.: *He never wised up to the fact that the joke was on him.* [ME, OE *wīs;* c. D *wijs,* G *weise,* Icel *vīss,* Goth *-weis;* akin to WIT[1]] —**wise′ly,** *adv.* —**Syn. 1, 2.** discerning, sage, sagacious, intelligent, penetrating. —**Ant. 1, 2.** foolish.

wise[2] (wīz), *n.* way of proceeding; manner; fashion (usually used in combination or in certain phrases): *otherwise; lengthwise; in any wise; in no wise.* [ME, OE: way, manner, etc.; melody (OE); c. D *wijze,* G *Weise* manner, melody, Icel *vīsa* short poem, Dan *vise* ballad]

wise[3] (wīz), *v.t.,* **wised, wis·ing.** *Scot.* to direct the course of; cause to turn. [ME *wise(n),* OE *wīsian* to show the way, guide, direct < *wīs* WISE[1]; c. OHG *wīsan,* Icel *vīsa* in same sense]

Wise (wīz), *n.* **Stephen Samuel,** 1874–1949, U.S. rabbi, theologian, and Zionist leader; born in Hungary.

-wise, a suffixal use of **wise** in adverbs denoting manner, position, direction, reference, etc.: *clockwise; nowise; timewise; edgewise; sidewise.* Cf. **-ways.**

wise·a·cre (wīz′ā′kər), *n.* **1.** See **wise guy. 2.** a person who possesses or affects to possess great wisdom. [< MD *wijsseggher* soothsayer]

wise·crack (wīz′krak′), *Informal.* —*n.* **1.** a smart or facetious remark. —*v.i.* **2.** to make wisecracks. —*v.t.* **3.** to say as a wisecrack. —**wise′crack′er,** *n.* —**Syn. 1.** witticism, quip.

wise′ guy′, *Slang.* a cocksure, conceited, and often insolent person; wiseacre; smart aleck.

Wise·man (wīz′mən), *n.* **Nicholas Patrick Stephen,** 1802–65, Irish cardinal and author, born in Spain.

wis·en·heim·er (wī′zən hī′mər), *n.* a wiseacre or smart aleck. Also, **weisenheimer.** [WISE[1] + *-enheimer* (abstracted from names of German origin, such as *Oppenheimer*)]

wi·sent (vē′zənt), *n.* bison (def. 2). [< G; OHG *wisunt.* See BISON]

wish (wish), *v.t.* **1.** to feel an impulse toward attainment or possession of something; to want, desire, or long for (usually fol. by an infinitive or a clause): *I wish to travel. I wish that it were morning.* **2.** to desire (a person or thing) to be (as specified): *to wish the problem settled.* **3.** to entertain wishes, favorably or otherwise, for: *to wish one well; to wish one ill.* **4.** to bid, as in greeting or leave-taking: *to wish one a good morning.* **5.** to command: *I wish him to come.* **6.** to entertain (wishes), favorably or otherwise (usually fol. by *to*): *to wish well to a person.* —*v.i.* **7.** to desire; long; yearn (often fol. by *for*): *Mother says I may go if I wish. I wished for a book.* **8.** to make a wish: *She wished so much she believed her dreams would come true.* **9. wish on, a.** to force or impose: *I wouldn't wish that awful job on my worst enemy.* **b.** Also, **wish upon.** to make a wish using some object as a magical talisman: *to wish on a star.* —*n.* **10.** a distinct mental inclination toward the doing, obtaining, attaining, etc., of something; a desire felt or expressed: *to disregard the wishes of others.* **11.** an expression of a wish, often one of a kindly or courteous nature: *to send one's best wishes.* **12.** that which is wished: *He got his wish, a new car.* [ME *wisshe(n),* OE *wȳscan;* c. G *wünschen,* Icel *æskja;* akin to OE *wynn* joy, L *venus* loveliness] —**wish′er,** *n.* —**wish′less,** *adj.*

—**Syn. 1.** crave. WISH, DESIRE, WANT indicate a longing for something. To WISH is to feel an impulse toward attainment or possession of something; the strength of the feeling may be of greater or less intensity: *I wish I could go home.* DESIRE, a more formal word, suggests a strong wish: *They desire a new regime.* WANT suggests a feeling of lack or need which imperatively demands fulfillment: *People all over the world want peace.*

wish·bone (wish′bōn′), *n.* a forked bone, formed by the fusion of the two clavicles, in front of the breastbone in most birds; furcula.

wish·ful (wish′fəl), *adj.* having or showing a wish; desirous. —**wish′ful·ly,** *adv.* —**wish′ful·ness,** *n.*

wish′ful think′ing, interpretation of facts, actions, words, etc., as one would like them to be rather than as they really are. —**wish′ful think′er.**

wish·y-wash·y (wish′ē wosh′ē, -wô′shē), *adj.* **1.** washy or watery, as a liquid; thin and weak. **2.** lacking in decisiveness; without strength or character; feeble. [gradational compound based on WASHY] —**wish′y-wash′i·ly,** *adv.* —**wish′y-wash′i·ness,** *n.*

Wi·sła (vē′swä), *n.* Polish name of the **Vistula.**

Wis·mar (vis′mär), *n.* a seaport in N East Germany, on the Baltic. 54,834 (est. 1955).

wisp (wisp), *n.* **1.** a handful or small bundle of straw, hay, or the like. **2.** any small or thin tuft, lock, mass, etc.: *wisps of hair.* **3.** a person or thing that is small, delicate, or barely discernible: *a mere wisp of a girl.* **4.** *Chiefly Brit. Dial.* **a.** a pad or twist of straw, as used to rub down a horse. **b.** a twisted bit of straw used as a torch. **5.** a will-o'-the-wisp or ignis fatuus. —*v.t.* **6.** to twist into a wisp. [ME *wisp, wips;* akin to WIPE] —**wisp′like′,** *adj.*

wisp·y (wis′pē), *adj.,* **wisp·i·er, wisp·i·est.** being a wisp or in wisps; wisplike: *a wispy plant.* Also, **wisp′ish.** —**wisp′i·ly,** *adv.* —**wisp′i·ness,** *n.*

Wiss·ler (wis′lər), *n.* **Clark,** 1870–1947, U.S. anthropologist.

wist (wist), *v.* pt. and pp. of **wit**[2].

Wis·ter (wis′tər), *n.* **Owen,** 1860–1938, U.S. novelist.

wis·te·ri·a (wi stēr′ē ə), *n.* any climbing, leguminous shrub of the genus *Wisteria,* having showy, pendent racemes of blue-violet, white, purple, or rose flowers. Also, **wis·tar·i·a** (wi stēr′ē ə, -stâr′-). [named after C. *Wistar* (1761–1818), American anatomist]

wist·ful (wist′fəl), *adj.* **1.** characterized by melancholy; longing; yearning. **2.** pensive, esp. in a melancholy way. [obs. *wist* quiet, silent, attentive (var. of WHIST[2]) + -FUL] —**wist′ful·ly,** *adv.* —**wist′ful·ness,** *n.*

wit[1] (wit), *n.* **1.** the keen perception and cleverly apt expression of amusing words or ideas or of those connections between ideas which awaken amusement and pleasure. **2.** speech or writing expressing such perception. **3.** a person having or noted for such perception and expression. **4.** understanding, intelligence, or sagacity. **5.** Usually, **wits. a.** shrewdness or ingenuity: *to live by one's wits.* **b.** the power of reasoning: *to lose one's wits.* **6. keep** or **have one's wits about one,** to remain alert and observant. [ME, OE; c. G *Witz,* Icel *vit;* akin to WIT[2]] —**Syn. 1.** See **humor. 4.** sense, mind.

wit[2] (wit), *v.t., v.i., pres. sing. 1st pers.* **wot,** *2nd* **wost,** *3rd* **wot,** *pres. pl.* **wit** or **wite;** *past* and *past part.* **wist;** *pres. part.* **wit·ting. 1.** *Archaic.* to know. **2. to wit,** that is to say; namely: *a grievous crime, to wit, homicide.* [ME *wit(en),* OE *witan;* c. D *weten,* G *wissen,* Icel *vita,* Goth *witan* to know, L *vidēre,* Gk *idein* to see. See WOT]

wit·an (wit′ən), *n. Early Eng. Hist.* **1.** the members of the national council or witenagemot. **2.** (*construed as sing.*) the witenagemot. [OE, pl. of *wita* one who knows, councilor; see WIT[2]]

witch (wich), *n.* **1.** a person, esp. a woman, who professes or is supposed to practice magic, esp. black magic; sorceress. Cf. **warlock. 2.** *Slang.* an ugly or malignant woman; hag. **3.** a person who uses a divining rod; dowser. —*v.t.* **4.** to affect by or as by witchcraft; bewitch; charm. [ME *wicche,* OE *wicce.* See WICKED] —**witch′hood,** *n.*

witch·craft (wich′kraft′, -kräft′), *n.* **1.** the art or practices of a witch; sorcery; magic. **2.** magical influence; witchery. [ME *wicchecraft,* OE *wiccecræft*]

witch′ doc′tor, (in some primitive societies) a man who attempts to cure sickness and to exorcise evil spirits by the use of magic.

witch-elm (wich′elm′), *n.* wych-elm.

witch·er·y (wich′ə rē), *n., pl.* **-er·ies. 1.** witchcraft; magic. **2.** fascination; charm.

witch·es'-broom (wich′iz brōōm′, -brŏŏm′), *n. Plant Pathol.* an abnormal, brushlike growth of small thin branches on woody plants, caused esp. by fungi, viruses, and mistletoes.

witch′ grass′, a panic grass, *Panicum capillare,* having a bushlike compound panicle, common as a weed in North America. [see QUITCH GRASS]

witch′ ha′zel, 1. a shrub, *Hamamelis virginiana,* of eastern North America. **2.** a liquid extraction from the leaves or bark of this plant, containing water and alcohol, used externally as an embrocation for inflammations and bruises and as an astringent. [*witch,* var. of *wych* (see WYCH-ELM)]

witch′ hunt′, an intensive effort to discover and expose disloyalty, subversion, dishonesty, or the like, usually based on slight, doubtful, or irrelevant evidence. Also, **witch′-hunt′.** —**witch′ hunt′er.** —**witch′-hunt′ing.** *n.*

witch·ing (wich′ing), *n.* **1.** the use or practice of witchcraft. **2.** fascination; charm; enchantment. —*adj.* **3.** of, characterized by, or suitable for sorcery or black magic: *the witching hour of midnight.* [late ME < obs. *witch* to use witchcraft, OE *wiccian*]

witch′ moth′, any of several large noctuid moths of the genus *Erebus,* esp. the blackish *E. odora.*

wite[1] (wīt), *n.* (in Anglo-Saxon law) **1.** a fine imposed by a king or lord on a subject who committed a serious crime. **2.** a fee demanded for granting a special privilege. Also, **wyte.** [ME, OE: penalty; c. OHG *wīzi,* Icel *vīti;* akin to OE *witan* to blame]

wite[2] (wīt), *v.* a pres. pl. of **wit**[2].

wit·e·na·ge·mot (wit′ənə gə mōt′), *n. Early Eng. Hist.* the assembly of the witan; the national council attended by the king, aldermen, bishops, and nobles. [OE = *witena,* gen. pl. of *wita* councilor (see WITAN) + *gemōt* MOOT]

with (with, with), *prep.* **1.** accompanied by; accompanying: *I will go with you. He fought with his brother against the enemy.* **2.** in some particular relation to (esp. implying interaction, company, association, conjunction, or connection): *I dealt with the problem. She agreed with me.* **3.** characterized by or having: *a man with initiative.* **4.** (of means or instrument) by the use of: *to line a coat with silk; to cut with a knife.* **5.** (of manner) using or showing: *to work with diligence.* **6.** in correspondence, comparison, or proportion to: *Their power increased with their number. How does their plan compare with ours?* **7.** in regard to: *to be pleased with a gift.* **8.** (of cause) owing to: *to die with pneumonia; to pale with fear.* **9.** in the region, sphere, or view of: *It is day with us while it is night with the Chinese.* **10.** (of separation) from: *to part with a thing.* **11.** against, as in opposition or competition: *He fought with his brother over the inheritance.* **12.** in the keeping or service of: *to leave something with a friend.* **13.** in affecting the judgment, estimation, or consideration of: *Her argument carried a lot of weight with the trustees.* **14.** at the same time as or immediately after; upon: *And with that last remark, she turned and left.* **15.** of the same opinion or conviction as: *Are you with me in thinking he's right?* **16.** in the same locality or vicinity as: *He can't live with her, and he can't live without her.* **17. in with.** See **in** (def. 21). **18. with child,** pregnant. [ME, OE (c. Icel *vith*), appar. short var. of OE *wither* against; c. OS *withar,* OHG *widar,* Icel *vithr,* Goth *withra* = *wi-* + comp. suffix (see FARTHER)]

with-, a combining form of **with,** having a separative or opposing force: *withstand; withdraw.* [ME, OE]

with·al (with ôl′, with-), *Archaic.* —*adv.* **1.** with it all; as well; besides. **2.** in spite of all; nevertheless. **3.** with that; therewith. —*prep.* **4.** with (used after its object). [ME phrase *with al(le);* r. OE *mid ealle, mid eallum*]

with·draw (with drô′, with-), *v.,* **-drew, -drawn, -draw·ing.** —*v.t.* **1.** to draw back, away, or aside; take back; remove: *She withdrew her hand from his. He withdrew his savings from the bank.* **2.** to retract or recall: *to withdraw an untrue charge.* —*v.i.* **3.** to go or move back, away, or aside; retire; retreat: *to withdraw from reality; The others tactfully withdrew.* **4.** to remove oneself from some activity or state: *to withdraw from an election.* **5.** to cease using or consuming an addictive narcotic (fol. by *from*): *to withdraw from heroin.* **6.** *Parl. Proc.* to remove an amendment, motion, etc., from consideration. [ME *withdrawe(n)*] —**with·draw′a·ble,** *adj.* —**with·draw′er,** *n.* —**Syn. 2.** revoke, rescind, disavow. **3.** See **depart.**

with·draw·al (with drô′əl, with-), *n.* the act or condition of withdrawing. Also, **with·draw′ment.**

withdraw′al symp′tom, any physical or psychological disturbance, as sweating or depression, experienced by a user of an addictive substance, as a drug, when deprived of it.

withdraw′ing room′, *Archaic.* a room to withdraw or retire to; drawing room.

with·drawn (with drôn′, with-), *v.* **1.** pp. of **withdraw.** —*adj.* **2.** removed from circulation, contact, etc. **3.** shy; retiring. —**with·drawn′ness,** *n.*

with·drew (with drōō′, with-), *v.* pt. of **withdraw.**

withe (with, with, wīth), *n., v.,* **withed, with·ing.** —*n.* **1.** a willow twig or osier. **2.** any tough, flexible twig or stem suitable for binding things together. **3.** an elastic handle for a tool, to lessen shock occurring in use. —*v.t.* **4.** to bind with withes. [ME, OE *withthe;* akin to Icel *vith* WITHY, Goth *(kuna)wida* chain, L *vi(ēre)* (to) weave together]

with·er (with′ər), *v.i.* **1.** to dry up and shrink, wilt, or fade; decay: *The grapes had withered on the vine.* **2.** to lose freshness or vitality, as with age (often fol. by *away*). —*v.t.* **3.** to cause to lose freshness, bloom, vigor, etc.: *The drought withered the buds.* **4.** to affect harmfully; blight: *Reputations were withered by the scandal.* **5.** to abash, as by a scathing glance. [ME; ? var. of WEATHER] —**with′ered·ness,** *n.* —**with′er·er,** *n.* —**with′er·ing·ly,** *adv.*

—**Syn. 1.** wrinkle, shrink, dry, decline, languish, wilt, waste. WITHER, SHRIVEL imply a shrinking, wilting, and wrinkling. WITHER (of plants and flowers) is to dry up, shrink, wilt, fade, whether as a natural process or as the result of exposure to excessive heat or drought: *Plants withered in the hot sun.* SHRIVEL, used of thin, flat objects and substances, such as leaves, the skin, etc., means to curl, roll up, become wrinkled: *The leaves shrivel in cold weather. Paper shrivels in fire.*

With·er (with′ər), *n.* **George,** 1588–1667, English poet and pamphleteer. Also, **With·ers** (with′ərz).

with·er·ite (with′ə rīt′), *n.* a mineral, barium carbonate, $BaCO_3$, a minor ore of barium. [named after W. *Withering* (1741–99), who first described it; see -ITE[1]]

withe′ rod′, either of two North American viburnums, *Viburnum cassinoides* or *V. nudum,* having tough, osierlike shoots.

with·ers (with′ərz), *n.* (*construed as pl.*) the highest part of the back at the base of the neck of a horse, cow, sheep, etc. [?]

With·er·spoon (with′ər spōōn′), *n.* **John,** 1723–94, U.S. theologian and statesman, born in Scotland.

with·hold (with hōld′, with-), *v.,* **-held, -hold·ing.** —*v.t.* **1.** to hold back; restrain or check. **2.** to refrain from giving or granting: *to withhold payment.* —*v.i.* **3.** to hold back; refrain. [ME *withholde(n)*] —**with·hold′er,** *n.* —**Syn. 1, 2.** suppress, repress. See **keep.** —**Ant. 1, 2.** advance.

withhold′ing tax′, the part of an employee's income tax liability that is withheld by the employer from wages or salary and paid directly to the government. Also called **withholding.**

with·in (with in′, with-), *adv.* **1.** in or into the interior or inner part; inside. **2.** in or into a house, building, etc.; indoors: *The fire was burning on the hearth within.* **3.** on or as regards the inside; internally. **4.** inside an enclosed place, area, room, etc.: *He was startled by a cry from within.* **5.** in the mind, heart, or soul; inwardly. —*prep.* **6.** in or into the interior of or the parts or space enclosed by: *within a city.* **7.** inside of; in. **8.** in the compass or limits of; not beyond or exceeding: *to live within one's income.* **9.** at or to some point not beyond, as in length or distance; not farther than: *within a radius of a mile.* **10.** at or to some amount or degree not exceeding: *within two degrees of freezing.* **11.** in the course or period of, as in time: *within one's lifetime; within one's memory; within three minutes.* **12.** inside of the limits fixed or required by; not transgressing: *within the law; within reason.* **13.** in the field, sphere, or scope of: *within the family; within one's power.* —*n.* **14.** the inside of a place, space, or building. [ME *withinne,* OE *withinnan* = *with* WITH + *innan* (from) within = *in* IN + *-an* suffix of motion from]

with·in·doors (with in′dôrz′, -dôrz′, with-), *adv.* into or inside the house.

with·in-named (wiŧħ in′nāmd′, with-), *adj.* that is named herein.

with-it (wiŧħ′it′, with′-), *adj. Slang.* up-to-date, modern, or smart: *a with-it boutique.* —**with-it-ness** (wiŧħ′it nis′, with′), *n.*

with·out (wiŧħ out′, with-), *prep.* **1.** with the absence, omission, or avoidance of; not with; with no or none of; lacking: *without help; without him to help; without shoes.* **2.** free from; excluding: *a world without hunger.* **3.** at, on, or to the outside of; outside of: *both within and without the house.* **4.** beyond the limits or scope of (now used chiefly in opposition to *within*): *whether within or without the law.* —*adv.* **5.** in or into an exterior or outer place; outside. **6.** outside a house, building, etc.: *The carriage awaits without.* **7.** lacking something implied or understood: *We must take this or go without.* **8.** as regards the outside; externally. —*n.* **9.** outside of a place: *We heard a cry from the without.* —*conj.* **10.** *Chiefly Dial.* unless. [ME *withoute(n)*, OE *withūtan* = *with* WITH + *-ūtan* (from) without = *ūt* OUT + *-an* suffix of motion from]

with·out·doors (wiŧħ out′dōrz′, -dôrz′, with-), *adv. Archaic.* out of doors.

with·stand (with stand′, wiŧħ-), *v.*, **-stood, -stand·ing.** —*v.t.* **1.** to resist or oppose, esp. successfully: *to withstand rust; to withstand the invaders; to withstand temptation.* —*v.i.* **2.** to stand in opposition. [ME *withstande(n)*, OE *withstandan* (see WITH-, STAND); c. Icel *vithstanda;* akin to G *widerstehen*] —**Syn. 1.** confront, face. See **oppose.**

with·y (wiŧħ′ē, with′ē), *n., pl.* **with·ies.** *Chiefly Brit.* **1.** a willow. **2.** a pliable branch or twig, esp. a withe. [ME; OE *wīthig* (see WITHE); akin to Icel *vīth(i)r*, OHG *wīda*, Gk *eitéa* (< **weitea*) willow, L *vītis* vine]

wit·less (wit′lis), *adj.* lacking wit or intelligence; stupid. [ME; OE *witlēas*] —**wit′less·ly,** *adv.* —**wit′lessness,** *n.*

wit·ling (wit′ling), *n.* a person who affects wittiness.

wit·ness (wit′nis), *v.t.* **1.** to see or know by personal presence and perception: *to witness an accident.* **2.** to be present at (an occurrence) as a formal witness, spectator, bystander, etc.: *She witnessed our wedding.* **3.** to bear witness to; testify to; give or afford evidence of. **4.** to attest by one's signature: *He witnessed her will.* —*v.i.* **5.** to bear witness; testify; give or afford evidence. —*n.* **6.** a person who is present at an occurrence, esp. one who is able to attest as to what took place. **7.** the formal testimony of such a person: *to bear false witness.* **8.** a person who gives testimony, as in a court of law. **9.** a person who signs a document in attestation of the genuineness of its execution. [ME, OE *witnes*] —**wit′ness·a·ble,** *adj.* —**wit′ness·er,** *n.* —**Syn. 1.** perceive, watch, mark, note. See **observe.**

wit·ness-box (wit′nis boks′), *n. Chiefly Brit.* See **witness stand.**

wit′ness stand′, the place occupied by a person giving testimony in a court.

wit·ted (wit′id), *adj.* having intelligence or wits (usually used in combination): *quick-witted; slow-witted; dull-witted.* [late ME] —**wit′ted·ness,** *n.*

Wit·te·kind (vit′ə kint), *n.* died A.D. 807?, Westphalian chief: leader of the Saxons against Charlemagne. Also, **Widukind.**

Wit·ten·berg (wit′ᵊn bûrg′; *Ger.* vit′ᵊn berk′), *n.* a city in central East Germany, on the Elbe: Luther taught in the university here; beginnings of the Reformation 1517. 48,132 (est. 1955).

Witt·gen·stein (vit′gən shtīn′, -stīn′), *n.* **Lud·wig (Jo·sef Jo·hann)** (lo͞ot′viKH yō′zef yō′hän, lo͞od′-), 1889–1951, Austrian philosopher.

wit·ti·cism (wit′i siz′əm), *n.* a witty remark or sentence. [< WITTY, modeled on *criticism*] —**Syn.** joke, jest, quip.

wit·ting (wit′ing), *adj.* **1.** knowing; aware; conscious. —*n.* **2.** *Chiefly Dial.* knowledge. [late ME *witing*] —**wit′-ting·ly,** *adv.*

wit·tol (wit′ᵊl), *n. Archaic.* a man who knows of and tolerates his wife's infidelity. [ME *wetewold* = *wete* WIT² + *-wold*, modeled on *cokewold* CUCKOLD]

wit·ty (wit′ē), *adj.*, **-ti·er, -ti·est.** **1.** possessing wit in speech or writing; amusingly clever in perception and expression. **2.** characterized by wit: *a witty remark.* **3.** *Brit. Dial.* intelligent; clever. [ME; OE *wittig*] —**wit′ti·ly,** *adv.* —**wit′ti·ness,** *n.* —**Syn. 1, 2.** droll, funny, original. See **humorous.** —**Ant. 1.** dull, stupid.

Wit·wa·ters·rand (wit wô′tərz rand′, -wot′ərz-), *n.* a rocky ridge in S Africa, in the Republic of South Africa, near Johannesburg. Also called **The Rand.**

wive (wīv), *v.*, **wived, wiv·ing.** *Obs.* —*v.i.* **1.** to take a wife; marry. —*v.t.* **2.** to take as wife; marry. **3.** to provide with a wife. [ME; OE *wīfian;* see WIFE]

wi·vern (wī′vərn), *n. Heraldry.* wyvern.

wives (wīvz), *n.* pl. of **wife.**

wiz·ard (wiz′ərd), *n.* **1.** a man who professes to practice magic; a magician or sorcerer. **2.** a conjurer or juggler. **3.** Also called **whiz, wiz** (wiz). *Informal.* a person of amazing skill or accomplishment: *a wizard at chemistry.* —*adj.* **4.** of or pertaining to a wizard. **5.** *Brit. Slang.* superb; excellent; wonderful. [late ME *wisard.* See WISE¹, -ARD] —**wiz′-ard·like′,** *adj.* —**Syn. 1.** enchanter, necromancer, diviner.

wiz·ard·ly (wiz′ərd lē), *adj.* of, like, or befitting a wizard.

wiz·ard·ry (wiz′ər drē), *n.* the art or practices of a wizard; sorcery; magic.

wiz·en (wiz′ən; *Dial.* wē′zən), *Brit. Dial.* —*v.i., v.t.* **1.** to wither; shrivel; dry up. —*adj.* **2.** wizened. [ME *wisen*, OE *wisnian;* c. Icel *visna* to wither]

wiz·ened (wiz′ənd; *Dial.* wē′zənd), *adj.* withered; shriveled: *a wizened old man.*

wk., **1.** week. **2.** work.

wkly., weekly.

w.l., **1.** water line. **2.** wave length.

Wla·di·mir (vlad′ə mēr′; *Russ.* vlä dē′miR), *n.* See **Vladimir, Saint.**

wmk., watermark.

WNW, west-northwest.

wo (wō), *n., pl.* **wos,** *interj. Archaic.* woe.

w/o, without.

W.O., **1.** War Office. **2.** warrant officer.

woad (wōd), *n.* **1.** a European, brassicaceous plant, *Isatis tinctoria*, formerly cultivated for a blue dye extracted from its leaves. **2.** the dye extracted. [ME *wode*, OE *wād* (c. G *Waid*); akin to F *guède*, ML *waizda* < Gmc]

woad·ed (wō′did), *adj.* dyed or colored blue with woad.

woad·wax·en (wōd′wak′sən), *n.* an ornamental, leguminous shrub, *Genista tinctoria*, whose flowers yield a yellow dye formerly used with woad to make a permanent green dye. Also, **woad′wax′, woodwaxen, woodwax.** Also called **dyer's-broom.** [ME *wodewaxen* = *wode* WOOD¹ + *waxen* grown (ptp. of *waxen* to WAX²); r. ME *wodewax*, OE *wuduweax*]

wob·ble (wob′əl), *v.*, **-bled, -bling,** *n.* —*v.i.* **1.** to incline to one side and to the other alternately, as an improperly balanced wheel. **2.** to move unsteadily with a side-to-side motion. **3.** to show unsteadiness; tremble; quaver: *His voice wobbled.* **4.** to vacillate; waver. —*n.* **5.** a wobbling movement. Also, **wabble.** [< LG *wabbel(n)*; akin to Icel *vafla* to toddle, MHG *wabelen* to waver, OE *wæflian* to speak incoherently] —**wob′bler,** *n.*

wob·bly (wob′lē), *adj.*, **-bli·er, -bli·est.** shaky; unsteady. Also, **wabbly.**

Wob·bly (wob′lē), *n., pl.* **-blies.** *Informal.* a member of the Industrial Workers of the World. [orig. uncert.]

wo·be·gone (wō′bi gôn′, -gon′), *adj. Archaic.* woebegone.

Wo·burn (wō′bərn, wo͞o′-), *n.* a city in E Massachusetts, N of Boston. 37,406 (1970).

Wode·house (wo͝od′hous′), *n.* **P(el·ham) G(ren·ville)** (pel′əm gren′vil) 1881–1975, U.S. writer, born in England.

Wo·den (wōd′ᵊn), *n.* the chief god of the pagan Anglo-Saxons, identified with the Scandinavian Odin. Also, **Wo′dan.** [ME, OE (c. G *Wotan*, Icel *Othinn*) = *wōd* WOOD² + *-en* n. suffix]

woe (wō), *n.* **1.** grievous distress, affliction, or trouble. **2.** an affliction: *She suffered a fall, among her other woes.* —*interj.* **3.** an exclamation of grief, distress, or lamentation. [ME *wo*, OE *wā*, interj. (cf. WELLAWAY); c. G *Weh*, D *wee*, Icel *vei*, L *vae*] —**Syn. 1.** tribulation, trial.

woe·be·gone (wō′bi gôn′, -gon′), *adj.* **1.** beset with woe. **2.** showing or indicating woe: *a woebegone look.* [ME *wo begon* woe (has or had) surrounded (someone) = *wo* WOE + *begon* ptp. of *bego*, OE *begān* to surround, besiege (see BE-, GO)] —**woe′be·gone′ness,** *n.*

woe·ful (wō′fəl), *adj.* **1.** full of woe; wretched; unhappy: *Hers is a woeful situation.* **2.** affected with, characterized by, or indicating woe. **3.** of wretched quality; sorry; poor: *a woeful collection of paintings.* Also, **wo′ful.** [ME] —**woe′-ful·ly, wo′ful·ly,** *adv.* —**woe′ful·ness, wo′ful·ness,** *n.*

woe·some (wō′səm), *adj. Archaic.* woeful.

Wof·fing·ton (wof′ing tən), *n.* **Margaret** ("*Peg Woffington*"), 1714–60, Irish actress in England.

wok (wok), *n.* a large, bowl-shaped metal pan widely used in cooking Chinese food. [< Chin]

woke (wōk), *v.* a pt. of **wake.**

wok·en (wō′kən), *v.* a pp. of **wake.**

wold¹ (wōld), *n.* **1.** an elevated tract of open country. **2.** Often, **wolds.** an open, hilly district, esp. in England, as in Yorkshire or Lincolnshire. [ME; OE *w(e)ald* forest; c. G *Wald;* akin to Icel *vǫllr* plain, and to WILD]

wold² (wōld), *v. Obs.* a pp. of **will**¹.

Wolf, *Canis lupus* (3 ft. high at shoulder; total length 5½ ft.; tail 1½ ft.)

wolf (wo͝olf), *n., pl.* **wolves** (wo͝olvz), *v.* —*n.* **1.** any of several large, carnivorous mammals of the genus *Canis*, of the family *Canidae*, esp. *C. lupus*, usually hunting in packs. **2.** the fur of such an animal. **3.** any of various wolflike animals of different families, as the thylacine. **4.** the larva of any of various small insects infesting granaries. **5.** *Informal.* a man who makes amorous advances to many women. **6.** *Music.* **a.** the harsh discord heard in certain chords of keyboard instruments, esp. the organ, when tuned on some system of unequal temperament. **b.** (in bowed instruments) a harsh sound produced by a string caused by a defect in the instrument. **7. cry wolf,** to raise a false alarm. **8. keep the wolf from the door,** to avert poverty or starvation. **9. wolf in sheep's clothing,** a person who conceals his true evil intentions or character beneath an innocent exterior. —*v.t.* **10.** *Informal.* to devour voraciously (often fol. by *down*). —*v.i.* **11.** to hunt for wolves. [ME; OE *wulf;* c. G *Wolf*, Icel *ulfr*, Goth *wulfs*, L *lupus*, Gk *lýkos*, Skt *vṛka*] —**wolf′like′,** *adj.*

Wolf (vôlf), *n.* **1. Christian von, Baron.** See **Wolff, Christian von.** **2. Frie·drich Au·gust** (frē′driKH ou′go͝ost), 1759–1824, German classical scholar. **3. Hugo** (ho͞o′gō), 1860–1903, Austrian composer.

wolf·ber·ry (wo͝olf′ber′ē, -bə rē), *n., pl.* **-ries.** a caprifoliaceous shrub, *Symphoricarpos occidentalis*, of northern North America, bearing white berries.

wolf′ call′, a whistle, shout, or the like, uttered by a male in admiration of a female's appearance.

wolf-child (wo͝olf′chīld′), *n., pl.* **-chil·dren.** a child, esp. a boy, who is thought to have been suckled or nurtured by wolves.

wolf′ cub′, *Brit.* a member of the junior division, for boys from 8 to 11, of the Boy Scouts; cub scout.

wolf′ dog′, **1.** a cross between a wolf and a domestic dog. **2.** an Eskimo dog.

Wolfe (wo͝olf), *n.* **1. James,** 1727–59, English general. **2. Thomas (Clay·ton)** (klāt′ᵊn), 1900–38, U.S. novelist.

Wolff (vôlf; *Eng.* wo͝olf), *n.* **1.** Also, **Wolf. Chris·ti·an von** (kRis′tē än′ fən), **Baron.** 1679–1754, German philosopher and mathematician. **2. Kas·par Frie·drich** (käs′pär frē′driKH), 1733–94, German anatomist and physiologist.

Wolff′ian bod′y, *Embryol.* the mesonephros. [named after K. F. WOLFF; see -IAN]

wolf·fish (wo͝olf′fish′), *n., pl.* (*esp. collectively*) **-fish,** (*esp. referring to two or more kinds or species*) **-fish·es.** a large acanthopterygian fish of the genus *Anarrhichas*, as *A. lupus* of the northern Atlantic, allied to the blenny, and noted for its ferocious habits.

wolf·hound (wo͝olf′hound′), *n.* any of several large dogs used in hunting wolves. Cf. **borzoi, Irish wolfhound.**

wolf·ish (wo͝ol′fish), *adj.* **1.** resembling a wolf, as in form or characteristics. **2.** characteristic of or befitting a wolf; fiercely rapacious. **—wolf′ish·ly,** *adv.* **—wolf′ish·ness,** *n.*

wolf′ note′ wolf (def. 6).

wolf′ pack′, 1. a group of wolves hunting together. **2.** a group of submarines operating together in hunting down and attacking enemy convoys.

wolf·ram (wo͝ol′frəm), *n.* **1.** *Chem.* tungsten. **2.** *Mineral.* wolframite. [< G; orig. man's name = *Wolf* WOLF + *Ram(n)* RAVEN[1]]

wolf·ram·ite (wo͝ol′frə mīt′, vôl′-), *n.* a mineral, iron manganese tungstate, (Fe,Mn)WO_4, an important ore of tungsten. Also, **wolfram.** [WOLFRAM + -ITE[1]]

wolf·ra·mi·um (wo͝ol frā′mē əm, vôl-), *n.* tungsten.

Wolf·ram von Esch·en·bach (vôl′främ fən esh′ən-bäkh′), c1170–c1220, German poet.

wolfs·bane (wo͝olfs′bān′), *n.* any of several plants of the genus *Aconitum*, esp. *A. lycoctonum*, having yellow flowers.

wolf′ spi′der, any of numerous spiders of the family *Lycosidae*, that hunt their prey instead of snaring it in a web.

wolf′ whis′tle, a wolf call made by whistling, often characterized by a sliding sound from a high to a low note.

wol·las·ton·ite (wo͝ol′ə stə nīt′), *n.* a mineral, calcium silicate, $CaSiO_3$. [named after W. H. *Wollaston* (1766–1828), English chemist; see -ITE[1]]

Wol·lon·gong (wo͝ol′ən gông′, -gong′), *n.* a seaport in E New South Wales, in E Australia. 131,754 (1961).

Wo·lof (wō′lof), *n.* a language of Senegal, a Niger-Congo language closely related to Fulani.

Wol·sey (wo͝ol′zē), *n.* **Thomas,** 1475?–1530, English cardinal and statesman.

wolv·er (wo͝ol′vər), *n.* a person who hunts wolves.

Wol·ver·hamp·ton (wo͝ol′vər hamp′tən), *n.* a city in S Staffordshire, in W England. 150,385 (1961).

wol·ver·ine (wo͝ol′və rēn′, wo͝ol′və rēn′), *n.* **1.** Also called **carcajou.** a stocky, carnivorous, North American mammal, *Gulo luscus*, of the weasel family, having blackish, shaggy hair with white markings. **2.** (*cap.*) a native or inhabitant of Michigan (the **Wolverine State**) (used as a nickname). [*wolvering* (with -INE for -ING[1]) = *wolver* wolflike creature (*wolv-* + *-er* < ?) + -ING[1]]

Wolverine (14 in. high at shoulder; total length 3½ ft.; tail 9 in.)

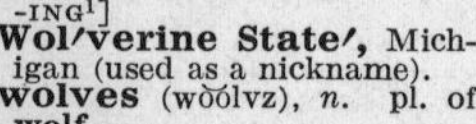

Wol′verine State′, Michigan (used as a nickname).

wolves (wo͝olvz), *n.* pl. of **wolf.**

wom·an (wo͝om′ən), *n., pl.* **wom·en** (wim′in), *adj.* **—n. 1.** the female human being (distinguished from *man*). **2.** an adult female person. **3.** feminine nature, characteristics, or feelings: *There's not much of the woman about her.* **4.** a sweetheart or paramour; mistress. **5.** a female person who cleans house, cooks, etc.; housekeeper: *The woman will be in to clean today.* **6.** women collectively: *Woman is fickle.* **—adj. 7.** of women; womanly. **8.** female: *a woman plumber.* [ME *womman, wimman,* OE *wīfman* = *wīf* female + *man* human being. See WIFE, MAN[1]]
—Syn. 2. WOMAN, FEMALE, LADY apply to the adult of the human race correlative with man. WOMAN is the general term: *a woman nearing middle age.* FEMALE was formerly used interchangeably with WOMAN, but now sometimes has a contemptuous implication: *a strong-minded female.* LADY implies family or social position, but is now also used conventionally for any woman (esp. as a courteous term for one engaged in menial tasks): *a highborn lady; a scrub lady.*

wom·an-chas·er (wo͝om′ən chā′sər), *n.* a man who is excessively attentive to women in hope of receiving their attention, affection, etc.

wom·an-hat·er (wo͝om′ən hā′tər), *n.* a person, esp. a man, who dislikes women; misogynist.

wom·an·hood (wo͝om′ən ho͝od′), *n.* **1.** the state of being a woman; womanly character or qualities. **2.** women collectively. [late ME]

wom·an·ise (wo͝om′ə nīz′), *v.t., v.i.,* **-ised, -is·ing.** *Chiefly Brit.* womanize.

wom·an·ish (wo͝om′ə nish), *adj.* **1.** womanlike or feminine. **2.** weakly feminine; effeminate. [late ME] **—wom′an·ish·ly,** *adv.* **—wom′an·ish·ness,** *n.* **—Syn. 2.** See **womanly.**

wom·an·ize (wo͝om′ə nīz′), *v.,* **-ized, -iz·ing.** **—v.t. 1.** to make effeminate. **—v.i. 2.** to pursue or court women habitually. Also, *esp. Brit.,* **womanise.**

wom·an·iz·er (wo͝om′ə nī′zər), *n.* a woman-chaser, esp. a philanderer.

wom·an·kind (wo͝om′ən kīnd′), *n.* women, as distinguished from men; the female sex. [late ME]

wom·an·like (wo͝om′ən līk′), *adj.* like a woman; womanly. [late ME] **—Syn.** See **womanly.**

wom·an·ly (wo͝om′ən lē), *adj.* **1.** like or befitting a woman; feminine; not masculine or girlish. **—adv. 2.** in the manner of, or befitting, a woman. [ME *wommanlich(e)*] **—wom′an·li·ness, wom′an·ness,** *n.*
—Syn. 1. WOMANLY, WOMANLIKE, WOMANISH mean resembling a woman. WOMANLY implies resemblance in appropriate, fitting ways: *womanly decorum, modesty.* WOMANLIKE, a neutral synonym, may suggest mild disapproval or, more rarely, disgust: *Womanlike, she (he) burst into tears.* WOMANISH usually implies an inappropriate resemblance and suggests weakness or effeminacy: *womanish petulance.*

wom′an of the house′. See **lady of the house.**

wo′man of the streets′, a prostitute; a streetwalker. Also, **wom′an of the street′.**

wom′an of the world′, a woman experienced and sophisticated in the ways and manners of the world.

wom′an's rights′. See **women's rights.**

wom′an suf′frage, the right of women to vote; female suffrage. **—wom′an-suf′frage,** *adj.* **—wom′an-suf′fra·gist,** *n.*

womb (wo͞om), *n.* **1.** the uterus of the human female and certain higher female mammals. **2.** the place in which anything is formed or produced: *the womb of time.* **3.** the interior of anything. **4.** *Obs.* the belly. [ME, OE: belly, womb; c. D *wam,* G *Wamme,* Goth *wamba* belly] **—wombed,** *adj.*

wom·bat (wom′bat), *n.* any of several burrowing, herbivorous marsupials of the family *Vombatidae*, of Australia, about the size of a badger. [< native Austral]

Wombat, *Vombatus hirsutus* (Length 3 ft.)

wom·en (wim′in), *n.* pl. of **woman.**

wom·en·folk (wim′in fōk′), *n.* (*construed as pl.*) **1.** women in general; all women. **2.** a particular group of women. Also, **wom′en-folks′.**

wo′men's lib′, *Sometimes Derogatory.* See **women's liberation.** **—wo′men's lib′ber.**

wo′men's libera′tion, a modern movement to gain full educational, social, and economic opportunities for women equal to those which men are traditionally understood to have. Also called **wo′men's libera′tion move′ment.**

wom′en's rights′, the political, legal, and social rights equal to those of men, claimed by and for women. Also, **woman's rights.**

wom·mer·a (wom′ər ə), *n.* *Australian.* boomerang. [< native Austral]

won[1] (wun), *v.* a pt. and pp. of **win.**

won[2] (wun, wo͞on, wōn), *v.i.,* **wonned, won·ning.** *Archaic.* to dwell; abide; stay. [ME *wone,* OE *wun(ian)*; c. G *wohnen;* see WONT]

won[3] (won), *n., pl.* **won.** a paper money and monetary unit of South Korea. [< Korean]

won·der (wun′dər), *v.i.* **1.** to think or speculate curiously: *to wonder about the origin of the solar system.* **2.** to be filled with admiration, amazement, or awe; marvel (often fol. by *at*): *He wondered at her composure in such a crisis.* **—v.t. 3.** to speculate curiously or be curious about: *I wonder what happened.* **4.** to feel wonder at: *I wonder that you went.* **—n. 5.** something that causes surprise, astonishment, or admiration. **6.** the emotion excited by what is strange, admirable, or surprising. **7.** a miracle; miraculous deed or event. [ME; OE *wundor;* c. D *wonder,* G *Wunder,* Icel *undr*] **—won′der·er,** *n.* **—won′der·less,** *adj.* **—Syn. 1.** meditate, ponder, question. **6.** surprise, astonishment, amazement, awe, admiration.

won′der drug′, any drug noted for its startling curative effect, as an antibiotic or sulfa drug.

won·der·ful (wun′dər fəl), *adj.* exciting wonder; marvelous; extraordinary; remarkable. [ME; OE *wundorful;* c. G *wundervoll*] **—won′der·ful·ly,** *adv.* **—won′der·ful·ness,** *n.* **—Syn.** awesome, wondrous, miraculous, astonishing, amazing, astounding. **—Ant.** ordinary.

won·der·land (wun′dər land′), *n.* **1.** a land of wonders or marvels. **2.** a wonderful country or region.

won·der·ment (wun′dər mənt), *n.* **1.** an expression or state of wonder. **2.** a cause or occasion of wonder.

won·der-strick·en (wun′dər strik′ən), *adj.* struck or affected with wonder. Also, **won′der-struck′.**

won·der·work (wun′dər wûrk′), *n.* a wonderful work; marvel. [OE *wundorweorc*]

won·der-work·er (wun′dər wûr′kər), *n.* a worker or performer of wonders or marvels. **—won′der-work′ing,** *adj.*

won·drous (wun′drəs), *adj.* **1.** *Literary.* wonderful; remarkable. **—adv. 2.** *Archaic.* wonderfully; remarkably. [metathetic var. of ME *wonders* (gen. of WONDER) wonderful; sp. conformed to -OUS; c. G *Wunders*] **—won′drous·ly,** *adv.* **—won′drous·ness,** *n.*

won·ky (wong′kē), *adj.* *Brit. Slang.* **1.** shaky; wobbly. **2.** unreliable. [var. of dial. *wanky* = *wank(le)* (ME *wankel,* OE *wancol;* see WENCH) + -Y[1]]

Wŏn·san (wœn′sän′), *n.* a seaport in E North Korea. 112,952 (1949). Japanese, **Gensan.**

wont (wônt, wōnt, wunt), *adj., n., v.,* **wont, wont** or **wont·ed, wont·ing.** **—adj. 1.** accustomed; used (usually fol. by an infinitive): *He was wont to rise at dawn.* **—n. 2.** custom; habit; practice: *It was her wont to lie abed till noon.* **—v.t.** *Archaic.* **3.** to accustom (a person), as to a thing. **4.** to render (a thing) customary or usual (usually used passively). **—v.i. 5.** *Archaic.* to be wont; to be accustomed. [ME *woned,* OE *(ge)wunod,* ptp. of *(ge)wunian* to be used to (see WON[2]); c. G *(ge)wöhnt*]

won't (wōnt, wunt), contraction of *will not.*

wont·ed (wôn′tid, wōn′-, wun′-), *adj.* *Archaic.* **1.** accustomed; habituated; used. **2.** customary, habitual, or usual. **—wont′ed·ly,** *adv.* **—wont′ed·ness,** *n.* **—Syn. 1.** wont.

won ton (won′ ton′), (in Chinese cooking) **1.** a dumpling filled with minced pork and spices, usually boiled in and served with soup, but sometimes fried as a side dish. **2.** Also called **won′ ton′ soup′.** a soup containing this. [< Chin (Cantonese dial.) *wan t'an,* lit., pastry]

woo (wo͞o), *v.t.* **1.** to seek the favor, affection, or love of, esp. with a view to marriage. **2.** to seek to win: *to woo fame.* **3.** to invite (consequences, whether good or bad) by one's action: *to woo one's own destruction.* **4.** to seek to persuade (a person, group, etc.), as to do something; solicit; importune. **—v.i. 5.** to court a woman: *He went wooing.* [ME *wowe,* OE *wōgian*] **—woo′ing·ly,** *adv.*

wood[1] (wo͝od), *n.* **1.** the hard, fibrous substance composing most of the stem and branches of a tree or shrub, and lying beneath the bark; xylem. **2.** the trunks or main stems of trees as suitable for architectural and other purposes; timber or lumber. **3.** firewood. **4.** the cask, barrel, or keg, as distinguished from the bottle: *aged in the wood.* **5.** *Music.* **a.** a woodwind instrument. **b. woods,** such instruments collectively in a band or orchestra. **6.** Usually, **woods.** a large and thick collection of growing trees; a grove or forest: *They picnicked in the woods.* **7.** *Golf.* a club with a wooden head, as a driver, brassie, or spoon, for hitting long shots. Cf. **iron** (def. 6). **8. out of the woods,** out of a dangerous, perplexing, or difficult situation; secure; safe. **—adj. 9.**

made of wood; wooden. **10.** used to store, work, or carry wood: *a wood chisel.* **11.** dwelling or growing in woods: *wood bird.* **—*v.t.* 12.** to cover or plant with trees. **13.** to supply with wood; get supplies of wood for. **—*v.i.* 14.** to take in or get supplies of wood (often fol. by *up*): *to wood up before the approach of winter.* [ME; OE *wudu,* earlier *widu;* c. Icel *vithr,* OHG *witu,* OIr *fid*] **—Syn. 6.** See **forest.**

wood[2] (wo͝od), *adj. Archaic.* wild, as with rage or excitement. [ME; OE *wōd;* c. Icel *ōthr;* akin to G *Wut,* rage, OE *wōth* song, L *vātēs* seer]

Wood (wo͝od), *n.* **1. Grant,** 1892–1942, U.S. painter. **2. Leonard,** 1860–1927, U.S. military doctor and political administrator.

wood′ al′cohol. See **methyl alcohol.**

wood′ anem′one, any of several anemones, esp. *Anemone nemorosa,* of the Old World, or *A. quinquefolia,* of the U.S.

wood′ bet′ony, 1. a betony. **2.** a scrophylariaceous herb, *Pedicularis canadensis,* of eastern North America.

wood·bine (wo͝od′bīn′), *n.* **1.** a European honeysuckle, *Lonicera Periclymenum.* **2.** any of various other honeysuckles. **3.** *U.S.* the Virginia creeper, *Parthenocissus quinquefolia.* [ME *wodebinde,* OE *wudubind* = *wudu* WOOD[1] + *bind* binding; see BIND]

wood′ block′, 1. a block of wood engraved in relief, for use in printing; woodcut. **2.** a print or impression from such a block. **—wood′-block′,** *adj.*

wood·bor·er (wo͝od′bōr′ər, -bôr′-), *n. Entomol.* borer (def. 3).

Wood·bridge (wo͝od′brij′), *n.* a town in NE New Jersey. 98,944 (1970).

Wood·bridge-Ma·rums·co (wo͝od′brij′mə rumz′kō), *n.* a town in E Virginia. 25,412 (1970).

wood-carv·er (wo͝od′kär′vər), *n.* a person whose craft is wood carving.

wood′ carv′ing, 1. the art or technique of carving objects by hand from wood or of carving decorations into wood. **2.** a carving or decoration made by this art or technique.

wood·chat (wo͝od′chat′), *n.* **1.** Also called **wood′chat shrike′.** a shrike, *Lanius senator,* of Europe and northern Africa, having a black forehead and a chestnut crown, nape, and mantle. **2.** *Rare.* any of various Asiatic thrushes, esp. of the genus *Larvivora.*

wood·chop·per (wo͝od′chop′-ər), *n. U.S.* a person who chops wood, esp. one who chops down trees. **—wood′chop′ping,** *n.*

wood·chuck (wo͝od′chuk′), *n.* a stocky, burrowing North American marmot, *Marmota monax,* that hibernates in the winter. Also called **ground hog.** [alter. of Cree *wuchak* fisher, marten, weasel]

Woodchuck (Total length 2 ft.; tail 7 in.)

wood′ clamp′. See **hand screw.**

wood′ coal′, 1. brown coal; lignite. **2.** charcoal.

wood·cock (wo͝od′kok′), *n., pl.* **-cocks,** (*esp. collectively*) **-cock. 1.** an Old World, snipelike game bird, *Scolopax rusticola,* having a long bill, short legs, and large eyes placed far back on the head. **2.** a similar and closely related but smaller bird, *Philohela minor,* of eastern North America. **3.** *Archaic.* a simpleton. [ME *wodecok,* OE *wuducoc*]

wood·craft (wo͝od′kraft′, -kräft′), *n.* **1.** skill in anything that pertains to the woods or forest, esp. in making one's way through the woods, or in hunting, trapping, etc. **2.** forestry (def. 1). **3.** the art of making or carving wooden objects. [late ME]

wood·crafts·man (wo͝od′krafts′mən, -kräfts′-), *n., pl.* **-men.** a person skilled in woodcraft.

wood·cut (wo͝od′kut′), *n.* **1.** a carved block of wood from which prints are made. **2.** a print or impression from such a block.

wood·cut·ter (wo͝od′kut′ər), *n.* a person who cuts down trees for firewood. **—wood′cut′ting,** *n.*

wood′ duck′, a North American duck, *Aix sponsa,* that nests in trees, the male of which has a long crest and black, chestnut, green, purple, and white plumage.

wood·ed (wo͝od′id), *adj.* covered with or abounding in woods or trees.

wood·en (wo͝od′ᵊn), *adj.* **1.** consisting or made of wood: *a wooden ship.* **2.** stiff, ungainly, or awkward: *a wooden gait.* **3.** without spirit, animation, or awareness: *a wooden stare.* **4.** indicating the fifth event of a series, as a wedding anniversary. **—wood′en·ly,** *adv.* **—wood′en·ness,** *n.*

wood′ engrav′ing, 1. the art or process of engraving designs in relief with a burin on the end grain of wood, for printing. **2.** a block of wood so engraved. **3.** a print or impression from it. **—wood′ engrav′er.**

wood·en·head (wo͝od′ᵊn hed′), *n. Informal.* a stupid person; blockhead.

wood·en-head·ed (wo͝od′ᵊn hed′id), *adj. Informal.* thick-headed, dull; stupid. **—wood′en-head′ed·ness,** *n.*

Wood′en Horse′. See **Trojan Horse** (def. 1).

wood′en In′dian, a carved wooden statue of a standing American Indian, formerly placed before a cigar store as an advertisement.

wood′en shoe′, sabot (def. 1).

wood·en·ware (wo͝od′ᵊn wâr′), *n.* vessels, utensils, etc., made of wood.

wood·house (wo͝od′hous′), *n., pl.* **-hous·es** (-hou′ziz). a house or shed in which wood is stored. [late ME]

wood′ hy′acinth, an Old World squill, *Scilla nonscripta,* having drooping flowers.

wood′ i′bis, any of several storks of the subfamily *Mycteriinae,* having chiefly white plumage and a featherless head and resembling the true ibises in having curved bills, esp. *Mycteria americana,* of the warm parts of America, and *Ibis ibis,* of Africa.

wood·land (*n.* wo͝od′land′, -lənd; *adj.* wo͝od′lənd), *n.* **1.** land covered with woods or trees. **—*adj.* 2.** of, pertaining to, or inhabiting the woods; sylvan: *a woodland nymph.* [OE *wuduland*] **—wood′land·er,** *n.*

Wood·lawn-Wood·moor (wo͝od′lôn wo͝od′mo͝or), *n.* a town in central Maryland, near Baltimore. 28,821 (1970).

wood′ louse′, *Zool.* any of certain small, terrestrial isopod crustaceans of the genera *Oniscus, Armadillidium,* etc., having a flattened, elliptical body.

wood·man (wo͝od′mən), *n., pl.* **-men.** woodsman (def. 1). [ME *wodeman,* OE *wudumann*] **—wood·man·craft** (wo͝od′mən-kraft′, -kräft′), *n.*

wood·note (wo͝od′nōt′), *n.* a wild or natural musical tone, as that of a forest bird.

wood′ nymph′, 1. (esp. in legend) a nymph of the woods; dryad. **2.** a brown satyr butterfly, *Minois alope,* having a broad yellow band marked with black and white eyespots across each front wing.

wood·peck·er (wo͝od′pek′ər), *n.* any of numerous scansorial birds of the family *Picidae,* having a hard, chisellike bill which it hammers repeatedly into wood in search of insects, stiff tail feathers to assist in climbing, and usually more or less boldly patterned plumage.

Woodpecker, *Dryocopus pileatus* (Length 17 to 19½ in.)

wood′ pe′wee, a small American flycatcher, *Contopus virens.*

wood·pile (wo͝od′pīl′), *n.* a pile or stack of firewood.

wood′ pitch′, the final product of the destructive distillation of wood.

wood·print (wo͝od′print′), *n.* woodcut.

wood′ pulp′, wood reduced to pulp through mechanical and chemical treatment for use in the manufacture of certain kinds of paper.

wood′ rat′. See **pack rat** (def. 1).

wood·ruff (wo͝od′rəf, -ruf′), *n.* a low, aromatic, rubiaceous herb, *Asperula odorata,* of the Old World, having small, sweet-scented, white flowers. [ME *woderove,* OE *wudurōfe* = *wudu* WOOD[1] + *rōfe,* var. of *rīfe* (< **ryfe*), c. G *Rübe* carrot]

Woods (wo͝odz), *n.* **Lake of the.** See **Lake of the Woods.**

wood·shed (wo͝od′shed′), *n.* a shed for keeping firewood.

wood·si·a (wo͝od′zē ə), *n.* any rock-inhabiting fern of the genus *Woodsia,* of temperate and cold regions. [named after J. *Woods* (d. 1864), English botanist; see -IA]

woods·man (wo͝odz′mən), *n., pl.* **-men. 1.** Also, **woodman.** a person accustomed to life in the woods and skilled in the arts of the woods, as hunting, trapping, etc. **2.** a lumberman.

wood′ sor′rel, any of numerous herbs of the genus *Oxalis,* esp. *O. Acetosella,* of Europe and North America, having heart-shaped, trifoliolate leaves, and white, pink-veined flowers. [after F *sorrel de bois;* r. *woodsour* (so called from sour taste of the leaves)]

wood′ spir′it. See **methyl alcohol.**

wood′ sug′ar, *Chem.* a water-soluble powder, $C_5H_{10}O_5$, the dextrorotatory form of xylose: used chiefly in dyeing and tanning.

woods·y (wo͝od′zē), *adj.,* **woods·i·er, woods·i·est.** *U.S.* of, or characteristic or suggestive of, the woods.

wood′ tar′, a dark viscid product obtained from wood by distillation or by slow burning without flame, used to preserve timber, rope, etc., or subjected to further distillation to yield creosote, oils, and wood pitch.

wood′ thrush′, a large thrush, *Hylocichla mustelina,* common in woodlands of eastern North America. See illus. at **thrush.**

wood′ turn′ing, the forming of wood articles upon a lathe. **—wood′tur′ner,** *n.* **—wood′-turn′ing,** *adj.*

wood′ vin′egar. See **pyroligneous acid.**

wood′ war′bler, warbler (def. 3).

wood·wax·en (wo͝od′wak′sən), *n.* woadwaxen. Also, **wood·wax** (wo͝od′waks′).

wood·wind (wo͝od′wind′), *n.* **1.** a musical wind instrument of the group comprising the flutes, clarinets, oboes, bassoons, and sometimes the saxophones. **2. woodwinds,** the section of an orchestra or band comprising the woodwind instruments. **—*adj.* 3.** of or relating to woodwinds.

wood·work (wo͝od′wûrk′), *n.* **1.** objects or parts made of wood. **2.** the interior wooden fittings, esp. of a house, as doors, stairways, moldings, etc.

wood·work·er (wo͝od′wûr′kər), *n.* a worker in wood, as a carpenter, joiner, or cabinetmaker.

wood·work·ing (wo͝od′wûr′king), *n.* **1.** the act or art of working wood. **—*adj.* 2.** of or used for shaping wood.

wood·worm (wo͝od′wûrm′), *n.* a worm or larva that breeds in or bores in wood.

wood·y (wo͝od′ē), *adj.,* **wood·i·er, wood·i·est. 1.** abounding with woods; wooded. **2.** belonging or pertaining to the woods; sylvan. **3.** consisting of or containing wood; ligneous. **4.** resembling wood, as in appearance, texture, or toughness. [late ME] **—wood′i·ness,** *n.*

woo·er (wo͞o′ər), *n.* a person who woos, as a suitor or lover. [ME *wowere, wower,* OE *wōgere*]

woof[1] (wo͝of, wo͞of), *n.* **1.** filling (def. 4). **2.** *Brit.* warp (def. 10). **3.** texture; fabric. [ME *oof, owf,* OE *ōwef, āwef* (cf. *gewef*) = *ō-, ā-* (< ?) + *wef* (akin to WEB, etc.); modern *w-* from WEFT, WARP, etc.]

woof[2] (wo͝of), *interj.* (used to express the bark of a dog.)

woof·er (wo͝of′ər), *n.* a loudspeaker designed for the reproduction of low-frequency sounds. [WOOF + -ER[1]]

wool (wo͝ol), *n.* **1.** the fine, soft, curly hair that forms the fleece of sheep and certain other animals, characterized by minute, overlapping surface scales that give it its felting property. **2.** fabrics and garments of sheep's wool. **3.** yarn made of sheep's wool. **4.** any of various substances used commercially as substitutes for the wool of sheep or other animals. **5.** any finely fibrous or filamentous matter suggestive of the wool of sheep: *glass wool; steel wool.* **6.** any coating of short, fine hairs or hairlike processes, as on a caterpillar or a plant; pubescence. **7.** *Informal.* the human hair, esp. when short, thick, and crisp. **8. all wool and a**

yard wide, genuine; excellent; sincere: *He was a real friend, all wool and a yard wide.* **9. dyed in the wool,** inveterate; confirmed: *a sinner who was dyed in the wool.* **10. pull the wool over someone's eyes,** to deceive or delude someone. [ME *wolle,* OE *wull(e);* c. D *wol,* G *Wolle,* Icel *ull,* Goth *wulla;* akin to L *vellus* fleece, Gk *oûlos* woolly, etc.] —**wool′-like′,** *adj.*

wool·en (wŏŏl′ən), *n.* **1.** any cloth of carded wool yarn of which the fibers vary in length: bulkier, looser, less regular, and of greater twist than worsted. **2. woolens,** wool cloth or clothing. —*adj.* **3.** made or consisting of wool: *woolen cloth.* **4.** of or pertaining to wool or woolen fabrics. Also, *esp. Brit.,* **woollen.** [ME *wollen,* OE *wullen,* var. of *wyllen*]

wool·er (wŏŏl′ər), *n.* a domestic animal raised for its wool.

Woolf (wŏŏlf), *n.* **(Adeline) Virginia,** nee **Stephen,** 1882–1941, English novelist, essayist, and critic.

wool′ fat′, lanolin.

wool·fell (wŏŏl′fel′), *n.* the skin of a wool-bearing animal with the fleece still on it. [ME *wolle fell*]

wool·gath·er·ing (wŏŏl′gath′ər ing), *n.* indulgence in daydreaming; absentmindedness. —**wool′gath′er·er,** *n.*

wool·grow·er (wŏŏl′grō′ər), *n.* a person who raises sheep or other animals for the production of wool. —**wool′-grow′ing,** *n.*

Wooll·cott (wŏŏl′kət), *n.* **Alexander,** 1887–1943, U.S. essayist and journalist.

wool·len (wŏŏl′ən), *n., adj. Chiefly Brit.* woolen.

Wool·ley (wŏŏl′ē), *n.* **Sir (Charles) Leonard,** 1880–1960, English archaeologist and explorer.

wool·ly (wŏŏl′ē), *adj.,* **-li·er, -li·est,** *n., pl.* **-lies.** —*adj.* **1.** consisting of wool: *a woolly fleece.* **2.** resembling wool, as in being warm, fuzzy, thick, etc. **3.** clothed or covered with wool or something resembling it: *a woolly caterpillar.* **4.** *Bot.* covered with a pubescence of soft hairs resembling wool. **5.** *Informal.* like the rough, vigorous atmosphere of the early West in America: *wild and woolly.* **6.** unclear; disorganized; fuzzy: *woolly thinking.* —*n.* **7.** *Western U.S.* a woolbearing animal; sheep. **8.** Usually, **woollies.** *Informal.* a knitted undergarment of wool or other fiber. Also, **wooly.** —**wool′li·ness,** *n.*

wool′ly bear′, the caterpillar of any of several moths, as a tiger moth, having a dense coat of woolly hairs.

wool·man (wŏŏl′mən), *n., pl.* **-men.** a person who buys and sells wool; wool dealer.

wool·pack (wŏŏl′pak′), *n.* **1.** the package in which wool was formerly done up, as for transportation. **2.** something resembling such a package, as a fleecy cumulus cloud.

wool·sack (wŏŏl′sak′), *n.* **1.** a sack or bag of wool. **2.** *Brit.* **a.** (in the House of Lords) one of a number of cloth-covered seats or divans stuffed with wool, for the use of judges, esp. one for the Lord Chancellor. **b.** the Lord Chancellor's office.

wool·shed (wŏŏl′shed′), *n.* a building in which sheep are sheared and wool is gathered and prepared for market.

wool′sort·ers disease′ (wŏŏl′sôr′tərz), *Pathol.* pulmonary anthrax in man, caused by inhaling the spores of *Bacillus anthracis.*

wool′ sponge′, a commercial sponge, *Hippiospongia lachne,* of Florida and the West Indies, the surface of which resembles the fleece of a sheep.

wool′ sta′pler, 1. a dealer in wool. **2.** a person who sorts wool, according to the staple or fiber. —**wool′sta′-pling,** *adj.*

Wool·wich (wŏŏl′ij, -ich), *n.* a borough of E London, England: royal military academy. 146,397 (1961).

Wool·worth (wŏŏl′wûrth′), *n.* **F(rank) W(in·field)** (win′-fēld′), 1852–1919, U.S. merchant.

wool·y (wŏŏl′ē), *adj.,* **wool·i·er, wool·i·est,** *n., pl.* **wool·ies.** woolly. —**wool′i·ness,** *n.*

woo·mer·a (wōō′mər ə), *n.* womera.

Woon·sock·et (wōōn sok′it), *n.* a city in NE Rhode Island. 46,820 (1970).

woo·ra·li (wŏŏ rä′lē), *n.* curare.

woosh (wōōsh, wŏŏsh), *n., v.i., v.t.* whoosh.

Woos·ter (wŏŏs′tər), *n.* **David,** 1711–77, American Revolutionary War general.

wooz·y (wōō′zē, wŏŏz′ē), *adj.,* **wooz·i·er, wooz·i·est.** *Informal.* **1.** stupidly confused; muddled: *woozy from a blow on the head.* **2.** physically out of sorts, as with dizziness, faintness, or slight nausea: *He felt woozy after the flu.* **3.** drunken. [? short for *boozy-woozy,* rhyming compound based on BOOZY] —**wooz′i·ly,** *adv.* —**wooz′i·ness,** *n.*

wop (wop), *n. Disparaging and Offensive.* an Italian or a person of Italian descent. [? It (south) *guappo* dandy]

Worces·ter (wŏŏs′tər), *n.* **1. Joseph Emerson,** 1784–1865, U.S. lexicographer. **2.** a city in central Massachusetts. 176,572 (1970). **3.** a city in and the county seat of Worcestershire, in W England, on the Severn: cathedral; Cromwell's defeat of the Scots 1651. 65,865 (1961). **4.** Worcestershire.

Worces′ter chi′na, a soft-paste porcelain containing little or no clay, made at Worcester, England, since 1751. Also called **Royal Worcester, Worces′ter por′celain.**

Worces·ter·shire (wŏŏs′tər shēr′, -shər), *n.* a county in W central England. 568,642 (1961); 699 sq. mi. *Co. seat:* Worcester. Also called **Worcester.**

Worces′tershire sauce′, a sharp sauce made with soy, vinegar, spices, etc., originally made in Worcester, England.

word (wûrd), *n.* **1.** a unit of language, consisting of one or more spoken sounds or their written representation, that functions as a principal carrier of meaning, is separated from other such units in writing and speech, is composed of one or more morphemes with relative freedom to enter into syntactic constructions, and is either the smallest unit susceptible of independent use or consists of two or three such units combined under certain linking conditions, as with the loss of primary accent which distinguishes *black′-bird′* from *black′ bird′.* **2. words, a.** speech or talk, esp. when insincere or vacuous: *Words mean little when action is called for.* **b.** the text or lyrics of a song as distinguished from the music. **c.** contentious or angry speech; a quarrel: *to have words with someone.* **3.** a short talk or conversation: *I'd like a word with you.* **4.** an expression or utterance: *a word of praise.* **5.** warrant, assurance, or promise: *to keep one's word.* **6.** news; tidings; information: *We received word of his death.* **7.** a verbal signal, as a password, watchword, or countersign. **8.** an authoritative utterance, or command: *His word was law.* **9.** (*cap.*) Also called **the Word, the Word of God. a.** the Scriptures; the Bible. **b.** the Logos. **c.** the message of the gospel of Christ. **10.** *Archaic.* a proverb or motto. **11. be as good as one's word,** to keep one's promises. **12. eat one's words,** to admit humbly that something one has said was wrong. **13. have no words for,** to be unable to describe. **14. in a word,** in summary; in short: *In a word, there was no comparison.* Also, **in one word. 15. in so many words,** literally; explicitly: *He told them in so many words to get out.* **16. man of his word** or **woman of her word,** a person who keeps his or her word. **17. of few words,** laconic; taciturn: *a man of few words.* **18. put in a good word for,** to speak favorably of; commend. Also, **put in a word for. 19. take one at one's word,** to accept someone's promise or assertion as sincere or true. **20. take the words out of one's mouth,** to say exactly what another person was about to say. **21. word of mouth.** See **mouth** (def. 14). —*v.t.* **22.** to express in words; put into words. —*interj.* **23. my word!** or **upon my word!** *Chiefly Brit.* (used as an exclamation of surprise or astonishment.) [ME, OE; c. D *woord,* G *Wort,* Icel *orth,* Goth *waurd;* akin to OPruss *wirds,* L *verbum* word, Lith *vardas* name] —**Syn. 4.** statement, declaration. **5.** pledge. **8.** order.

word′ ac′cent, *Phonet.* See **word stress.**

word·age (wûr′dij), *n.* **1.** words collectively. **2.** quantity or amount of words. **3.** verbiage; wordiness. **4.** choice of words; wording.

word′ blind′ness, alexia.

word·book (wûrd′bŏŏk′), *n.* a book of words, usually with definitions, explanations, etc.; dictionary.

word′ class′, *Gram.* a group of words all of which are members of the same form class or part of speech.

word-for-word (wûrd′fər wûrd′), *adj.* **1.** in exactly the same words; verbatim. **2.** one word at a time, without regard for the sense of the whole: *a word-for-word translation.*

word′ game′, any game involving skill in using, forming, guessing, or changing words or expressions.

word·ing (wûr′ding), *n.* **1.** the act or manner of expressing in words; phrasing. **2.** the form of words in which a thing is expressed. —**Syn.** See **diction.**

word·less (wûrd′lis), *adj.* **1.** speechless, silent, or mute. **2.** unexpressed or unexpressible in words. **3.** communicating or communicated by a means other than words. [ME] —**word′less·ly,** *adv.* —**word′less·ness,** *n.*

word′ of hon′or, a pledge of one's honor that a specified condition, bargain, etc., will be fulfilled; oath; promise.

word-of-mouth (wûrd′əv mouth′), *adj.* spread or made known by verbal communication: *The producers rely on word-of-mouth advertising.*

word′ or′der, the way in which words are arranged in sequence in a sentence or smaller constructions.

word·play (wûrd′plā′), *n.* **1.** clever or subtle repartee; verbal wit. **2.** a play on words; pun.

S	A	T	E	D
A	T	O	N	E
T	O	A	S	T
E	N	S	U	E
D	E	T	E	R

Word square

word′ proc′essing, a computerized system programmed for rapid, efficient production and editing of letters, reports, business records, etc., usually including a keyboard, a video display, memory storage on tapes or disks, and a high-speed printer. —**word′ proc′essor.**

word′ square′, a set of words such that when arranged one beneath another in the form of a square they read alike horizontally and vertically.

word′ stress′, the stress pattern or patterns associated with the words of a particular language when they are considered in isolation. Also called **word accent.** Cf. **sentence stress.**

Words·worth (wûrdz′wûrth′), *n.* **William,** 1770–1850, English poet. —**Words·worth′i·an,** *adj., n.*

word·y (wûr′dē), *adj.,* **word·i·er, word·i·est. 1.** characterized by or given to the use of many, or too many, words; verbose. **2.** pertaining to or consisting of words; verbal. [ME; OE *wordig*] —**word′i·ly,** *adv.* —**word′i·ness,** *n.*

wore (wōr, wôr), *v.* pt. of **wear.**

work (wûrk), *n., adj., v.,* **worked** or **wrought, work·ing.** —*n.* **1.** exertion or effort directed to produce or accomplish something; labor; toil. **2.** that on which exertion or labor is expended; a task or undertaking. **3.** employment, as in some form of industry, esp. as a means of earning one's livelihood: *to look for work.* **4.** materials, things, etc., on which one is working or is to work. **5.** the result of exertion, labor, or activity; a deed or performance. **6.** a product of exertion, labor, or activity: *a work of art; literary works.* **7.** an engineering structure, as a building or bridge. **8.** a building, wall, trench, or the like, made as a means of fortification. **9. works, a.** (*construed as sing. or pl.*) a place or establishment for manufacturing (often used in combination): *ironworks.* **b.** the working parts of a machine: *the works of a watch.* **c.** *Theol.* righteous deeds. **10.** *Physics.* the transference of energy equal to the product of the component of a force that acts in the direction of the motion of the point of application of the force and the distance through which the point of application moves. **11. at work, a.** working, as at one's job: *He's always at work in the afternoons.* **b.** in action or operation: *to watch machines at work.* **12. shoot the works,** *Slang.* to make an intense or unsparing effort, spend all one's resources, etc.: *Let's shoot the works and order the crêpe suzettes.* **13. the works,** *Slang.* **a.** everything; all related items or matters: *a hamburger with the works.* **b.** harsh or cruel treatment: *to give someone the works.* —*adj.* **14.** of, for, or concerning work: *work clothes.* —*v.i.* **15.** to do work; labor. **16.** to be employed, esp. as a means of earning one's livelihood. **17.** to be in operation, as a machine. **18.** to act or operate effectively: *This plan will not work.* **19.** to attain a specified condition, as if by repeated movement (often fol. by *up, loose,* etc.): *The nails worked loose.* **20.** to have an effect or influence, as on a person or on the mind or feelings of a person. **21.** to move in agitation, as the features under strong emotion. **22.** to make way with effort or under stress: *The ship works to windward.* **23.** to give slightly at the joints, as a vessel

under strain at sea. **24.** to undergo treatment by labor in a given way: *This dough works slowly.* **25.** to ferment, as a liquid.
—*v.t.* **26.** to use or manage (an apparatus, contrivance, etc.). **27.** to bring about (any result) by or as by work or effort. **28.** to manipulate or treat by labor: *to work butter.* **29.** to carry on operations in (a district or region). **30.** to achieve by work or effort: *to work one's passage.* **31.** to keep (a person, a horse, etc.) at work: *She works her employees hard.* **32.** *Informal.* to exploit (someone) to advantage. **33.** to make or decorate by needlework or embroidery: *She worked a needlepoint cushion.* **34.** to cause a strong emotion or specific reaction in: *to work a crowd into a frenzy.* **35.** to cause to move in emotional agitation: *to work one's features.* **36.** to cause fermentation in. **37. work off, a.** to lose or dispose of, as by exercise or labor: *to work off excess weight.* **b.** to pay or fulfill by working: *to work off a debt.* **38. work on** or **upon,** to exercise influence or persuasion on. **39. work out, a.** to bring about by careful thought or calculation: *to work out a solution to a problem.* **b.** to solve, as a problem. **c.** to have a result or outcome (often fol. by *to*): *Things have worked out badly. The bill works out to $300.* **d.** to evolve; elaborate. **e.** to prove feasible: *I hope this works out.* **f.** to practice, exercise, or train, as for an athletic sport. **40. work up, a.** to move or stir the feelings of; excite. **b.** to prepare; elaborate: *Work up some plans.* [(n.) ME *worke,* OE *worc;* (v). ME *worke,* v. use of *worke* (n.); r. ME *wyrche,* OE *wyrcean*] **—work′less,** *adj.* **—work′less·ness,** *n.*
—Syn. 1. WORK, DRUDGERY, LABOR, TOIL refer to exertion of body or mind in performing or accomplishing something. WORK is the general word, and may apply to exertion that is either easy or hard: *heavy work; part-time work; outdoor work.* DRUDGERY suggests continuous, dreary, and dispiriting work, esp. of a menial or servile kind: *the drudgery of household tasks.* LABOR particularly denotes hard manual work: *labor on a farm, in a steel mill.* TOIL suggests wearying or exhausting labor: *toil that breaks down the worker's health.*

work·a·ble (wûr′kə bəl), *adj.* **1.** practicable or feasible: *a workable arrangement.* **2.** capable of or suitable for being worked. **—work′a·bil′i·ty, work′a·ble·ness,** *n.*

work·a·day (wûr′kə dā′), *adj.* **1.** of or befitting working days; characteristic of a workday and its occupations. **2.** ordinary; commonplace; humdrum; prosaic. [ME *werkeday* < Scand; cf. Icel *virkidagr* working day, weekday]

work·a·hol·ic (wûrk′ə hô′lik, -hol′ik), *n. Informal.* a person obsessively occupied with work at the expense of normal leisure, human relationships, etc. [WORK + A(LCO)-HOLIC] **—work′a·hol′ism,** *n.*

work·bag (wûrk′bag′), *n.* a bag for holding implements and materials for work, esp. needlework.

work·bench (wûrk′bench′), *n.* a sturdy table at which an artisan works.

work·book (wûrk′bo͝ok′), *n.* **1.** a manual of operating instructions. **2.** a book designed to guide the work of a student by inclusion of some instructional material, and usually providing questions, exercises, etc. **3.** a book in which a record is kept of work completed or planned.

work·box (wûrk′boks′), *n.* a box to hold instruments and materials for work, esp. needlework.

work′ camp′, 1. a camp for prisoners sentenced to labor, esp. to outdoor labor. **2.** a volunteer project in aid of some worthy cause.

work·day (wûrk′dā′), *n.* **1.** a day on which work is done, esp. a fixed number of hours for obligatory, salaried work, as a weekday that is not a holiday. **2.** the part of a day during which one works: *a seven-hour workday.*

worked (wûrkt), *adj.* that has undergone working.
—Syn. WORKED, WROUGHT both apply to something on which effort has been applied. WORKED implies expended effort of almost any kind: *a worked silver mine.* WROUGHT implies fashioning, molding, or making, esp., by hand: *a wrought-iron railing.*

worked-up (wûrkt′up′), *adj.* wrought-up.

work·er (wûr′kər), *n.* **1.** a person or thing that works. **2.** a laborer or employee: *steel workers.* **3.** a person engaged in a particular field, activity, or cause: *a worker in psychological research; a worker for the Republican party.* **4.** *Entomol.* a sterile or infertile female ant, bee, wasp, or termite. [late ME *werker, worcher*] **—work′er·less,** *adj.*

work′ eth′ic, a belief in the moral benefit and importance of work and its inherent ability to strengthen character.

work·fare (wûrk′fâr′), *n.* a governmental plan under which employable welfare recipients are required to accept public-service jobs or to participate in manpower training. [WORK + (WEL)FARE]

work′ farm′, a farm to which juvenile offenders are sent for a period to work, for punishment or rehabilitation.

work·folk (wûrk′fōk′), *n.pl.* people who work for a wage, salary, commission, etc., esp. rural or agricultural employees. Also, **work′folks′.** [late ME]

work′ force′, 1. the total number of workers in a specific undertaking. **2.** the total number of persons employed or employable: *a sharp increase in the nation's work force.*

work′ func′tion, *Physics.* the least energy necessary to free an electron from a metal surface.

work·horse (wûrk′hôrs′), *n.* **1.** a horse used for plowing, hauling, and other heavy labor. **2.** a person who works tirelessly at a task, assumes extra duties, etc.

work·house (wûrk′hous′), *n., pl.* **-hous·es** (-hou′ziz). **1.** *U.S.* a house of correction. **2.** *Brit.* (formerly) a poorhouse in which paupers were given work. **3.** *Obs.* a workshop. [ME *werkhous,* OE *weorchūs* workshop]

work·ing (wûr′king), *n.* **1.** act of a person or thing that works. **2.** operation; action: *the involuted workings of his mind.* **3.** the process of shaping a material: *The working of clay is easy when it's damp.* **4.** Usually, **workings.** a part of a mine, quarry, or the like, in which work is carried on. **5.** the process of fermenting, as of yeasts. **6.** repeated movement or strain tending to loosen a structural assembly or part. **7.** disturbed or twisting motions, as of a part of the body: *The working of his limbs revealed his disease.* **—*adj.*** **8.** that works. **9.** doing some form of work or labor, esp. manual, mechanical, or industrial work, as for a living: *a working man.* **10.** operating; producing effects, results, etc. **11.** pertaining to, connected with, or used in operating or working. **12.** serving to permit or facilitate work, development, communication, etc.: *a working model; a working majority; a working knowledge of Spanish.* [ME *werking*]

work′ing as′set, *Accounting.* invested capital that is comparatively liquid.

work′ing cap′ital, 1. the amount of capital needed to carry on a business. **2.** *Accounting.* current assets minus current liabilities. **3.** liquid capital assets as distinguished from fixed capital assets.

work′ing class′, the class of persons working for wages, esp. in manual labor. **—work′ing-class′,** *adj.*

work′ing day′, workday.

work′ing draw′ing, an accurately measured and detailed drawing of a structure, machine, etc., or of any part of one, used as a guide in construction.

work′ing hypoth′esis. See under **hypothesis** (def. 1).

work·ing·man (wûr′king man′), *n., pl.* **-men.** a man of the working class.

work′ing pa′pers, 1. legal papers often required for employment, as by an alien. **2.** *U.S.* legal papers enabling a minor to work under specific conditions.

work′ing sub′stance, a substance, usually a fluid, that undergoes changes in pressure, temperature, volume, or form as part of a process for accomplishing work.

work·ing·wom·an (wûr′king wo͝om′ən), *n., pl.* **-wom·en.** a woman who is regularly employed.

work′ load′, 1. the amount of work that a machine, employee, or group of employees can be or is expected to perform. **2.** the number of hours that a machine, worker, teacher, etc., is required to work during any specific period.

work·man (wûrk′mən), *n., pl.* **-men. 1.** a man employed or skilled in some form of manual, mechanical, or industrial work. **2.** a male worker. [ME *werkman,* OE *weorcman*]

work·man·like (wûrk′mən līk′), *adj.* **1.** like or befitting a workman. **2.** skillful; well-executed: *a workmanlike piece of writing.* Also, **work′man·ly.** [late ME *werkmanlike*]

work·man·ship (wûrk′mən ship′), *n.* **1.** the art or skill of a workman. **2.** the quality or mode of execution, as of a thing made. **3.** the product or result of the labor and skill of a workman; work executed. [late ME *werkmanschipe*]

work′men's compensa′tion insur′ance, insurance required by law from employers for the protection of employees while engaged in the employer's business.

work′ of art′, 1. a piece of creative work in the arts, esp. a painting or a piece of sculpture. **2.** a process or product that gives aesthetic pleasure and that can be judged separately from any utilitarian considerations.

work·out (wûrk′out′), *n.* **1.** a trial or practice session in athletics, as in running, boxing, or football. **2.** a period of physical exercise.

work·peo·ple (wûrk′pē′pəl), *n.pl.* people employed at work or labor; workers; employees.

work·piece (wûrk′pēs′), *n.* a piece of work being machined.

work·place (wûrk′plās′), *n.* **1.** a person's place of employment. **2.** any or all places where people are employed: *a bill to set safety standards for the workplace.*

Work′ Pro′jects Administra′tion. See **WPA.**

work·room (wûrk′ro͞om′, -ro͝om′), *n.* a room in which work is carried on.

works′ coun′cil, *Chiefly Brit.* **1.** an elected body of employee representatives that deals with management regarding grievances, working conditions, wages, etc. **2.** a joint committee representing employer and employees that discusses similar matters within a plant or business.

work′ sheet′, 1. a sheet of paper on which work schedules, working time, special instructions, etc., are recorded. **2.** a piece or scrap of paper on which problems, ideas, or the like, are set down in tentative form.

work·shop (wûrk′shop′), *n.* **1.** a room, group of rooms, or building in which work, esp. mechanical work, is carried on. **2.** a seminar, discussion group, or the like, which emphasizes exchange of ideas and the demonstration and application of techniques, skills, etc.: *a theater workshop.*

work′ sta′tion, a work or office area assigned to one person, esp. a desk with modular units that accommodate a computer terminal, modem, or other electronic equipment.

work·ta·ble (wûrk′tā′bəl), *n.* a table at which a person works, often with drawers for materials, tools, etc.

work′ train′, a train that transports railroad workers, building materials, etc., to assignments on the line.

work·week (wûrk′wēk′), *n.* the total number of regular working hours or days in a week.

work·wom·an (wûrk′wo͝om′ən), *n., pl.* **-wom·en. 1.** a female worker. **2.** a woman employed or skilled in some manual, mechanical, or industrial work.

world (wûrld), *n.* **1.** the earth or globe, considered as a planet. **2.** a particular division of the earth: *the New World.* **3.** the earth or the total known part of it, with its inhabitants, affairs, etc., during a particular period: *the ancient world.* **4.** mankind; the human race; humanity: *The world must eliminate war and poverty.* **5.** the public generally: *The whole world knows it.* **6.** the class of persons devoted to the affairs, interests, or pursuits of this life: *The world worships success.* **7.** a particular class of mankind, with common interests, aims, etc.: *the fashionable world.* **8.** any sphere, realm, or domain, with all pertaining to it: *woman's world; the world of dreams; the insect world.* **9.** everything that exists; the entire system of created things; the universe. **10.** any complex whole conceived as resembling the universe: *A microcosm is conceived of as a world in miniature.* **11.** this or some specified other existence: *this world; the world to come.* **12.** a very great quantity or extent: *a world of good.* **13.** any heavenly body: *the starry worlds.* **14. for all the world, a.** for any consideration, however great: *She wouldn't come to visit us for all the world.* **b.** in every respect; precisely: *You look for all the world like my Aunt Mary.* **15. in the world, a.** at all; ever: *I never in the world would have believed such an obvious lie.* **b.** from among all possibilities: *Where in the world did you find that hat?* **16. out of this** or **the world,** *Informal.* wonderfully good; exceptional; fine: *She bakes an* *apple pie that is out of this world.* **17. set the world on fire,** to achieve fame and success. **18. think the world of,** to like or admire greatly. **19. world without end,** for all eternity; for always: *forever and ever, world without end.* [ME, OE, var. of OE *weorold;* c. D *wereld,* G *Welt,* Icel *veröld,* all < Gmc **wer-ald-,* lit., man-era]

World′ Bank′, an international bank established in 1944 to assist in the reconstruction and development of member nations, esp. through the guaranteeing of loans: a specialized agency of the United Nations. Official name, **International Bank for Reconstruction and Development.**

world·beat·er (wûrld′bē′tər), *n.* a person or thing that surpasses all others of like kind, as in quality, endurance, etc.

World′ Coun′cil of Church′es, an ecumenical organization formed in 1948 in Amsterdam, The Netherlands, comprising more than 160 Protestant and Eastern churches in over 48 countries, for the purpose of cooperative, coordinated action in theological, ecclesiastical, and secular matters.

World′ Court′, the chief judicial agency of the United Nations, reorganized from the similar body of the League of Nations in 1945, to decide disputes arising between nations. Official name, **International Court of Justice.**

World′ Health′ Organiza′tion, an agency of the United Nations, established in 1948, concerned with improving the health of the world's people and preventing or controlling communicable diseases on a world-wide basis through various technical projects and programs. *Abbr.:* WHO

world·ling (wûrld′ling), *n.* a person devoted to the interests and pleasures of this world; a worldly person.

world·ly (wûrld′lē), *adj.,* **-li·er, -li·est,** *adv.* —*adj.* **1.** of or pertaining to this world as contrasted with heaven, spiritual life, etc.; earthly; mundane. **2.** devoted to, directed toward, or connected with the affairs, interests, or pleasures of this world. **3.** of or pertaining to the people or laity; secular. **4.** knowledgeable in the ways of the world; sophisticated. **5.** *Obs.* of, pertaining to, or existing on earth: *ants, flies, and other worldly insects.* —*adv.* **6.** in a worldly manner (archaic except in combination): *worldly-minded.* [ME; OE *wor(u)ldlic*] —**world′li·ness,** *n.* —**Syn. 1.** temporal. See **earthly. 4.** urbane, cosmopolitan. —**Ant. 1.** spiritual.

world·ly-wise (wûrld′lē wīz′), *adj.* wise as to the affairs of this world.

world′ pow′er, a nation, organization, or institution capable of influencing world events.

World′ Se′ries, *Baseball.* an annual series of games played in the fall between the winning teams of the two major leagues. Also, **World's′ Se′ries.**

world's′ fair′, a large fair or exposition in which various nations participate with exhibitions of their arts, crafts, industrial and agricultural products, scientific achievements, etc.

world-shak·ing (wûrld′shā′king), *adj.* of sufficient size, importance, or magnitude to affect the entire world: *the world-shaking discoveries of modern science.*

world's old′est profes′sion, prostitution.

world′ soul′, the animating principle or the moving force of the universe; world spirit.

world′ spir′it, 1. God. **2.** See **world soul.**

world′ war′, a war that is waged in many parts of the world and involves most of the principal nations of the world.

World War I, the war fought mainly in Europe and the Middle East between the Central Powers and the Allies, beginning on July 28, 1914, and ending on November 11, 1918, with the collapse of the Central Powers. Also called **Great War.**

World War II, the war between the Axis and the Allies beginning on September 1, 1939, with the German invasion of Poland and ending with the surrender of Germany on May 8, 1945, and of Japan on August 14, 1945.

World War III, a hypothetical world war of the future, often conceived of as a war waged with nuclear weapons and resulting in the near or total destruction of mankind.

world-wea·ry (wûrld′wēr′ē), *adj.* weary of the world; bored with existence, material pleasures, etc. —**world′-wea′ri·ness,** *n.*

world-wide (wûrld′wīd′), *adj.* extending or spread throughout the world. Also, **world′wide′.**

worm (wûrm), *n.* **1.** *Zool.* any of numerous long, slender, soft-bodied, legless, bilateral invertebrates including the flatworms, roundworms, acanthocephalans, nemerteans, gordiaceans, and annelids. **2.** (loosely) any of numerous small creeping animals with more or less slender, elongated bodies, and without limbs or with very short ones, including individuals of widely differing kinds, as earthworms, tapeworms, insect larvae, adult forms of some insects, etc. **3.** something resembling or suggesting such a creature, as in appearance or movement. **4.** *Slang.* a groveling, abject, or contemptible person. **5.** the spiral pipe in which the vapor is condensed in a still. **6.** See **screw conveyor. 7.** a rotating cylinder or shaft, cut with one or more helical threads, that engages with and drives a worm gear. **8.** something that penetrates, injures, or consumes slowly or insidiously, like a gnawing worm. **9. worms,** (*construed as sing.*) *Pathol., Vet. Pathol.* any disease or disorder arising from the presence of parasitic worms in the intestines or other tissues. **10.** the lytta of a dog or other carnivorous animal. —*v.i.* **11.** to move or act like a worm; creep, crawl, or advance slowly or stealthily. **12.** to get by insidious procedure (usually fol. by *into*): *to worm into another's favor.* —*v.t.* **13.** to cause to move or advance in a devious or stealthy manner. **14.** to get by persistent, insidious efforts (usually fol. by *out* or *from*): *to worm a secret out of a person.* **15.** to insinuate (oneself) or make (one's way) with devious or stealthy persistence (usually fol. by *into*). **16.** to free from worms: *He wormed the puppies.* **17.** *Naut.* to wind yarn or the like spirally around (a rope) so as to fill the spaces between the strands and render the surface smooth. [ME; OE *wyrm* worm, serpent; c. D *worm,* G *Wurm,* Icel *ormr,* L *vermis;* cf. VERMIN, VARMINT] —**worm′er,** *n.* —**worm′like′, worm′ish,** *adj.*

worm′ drive′, *Mach.* a drive mechanism utilizing a worm gear.

worm-eat·en (wûrm′ēt′ən), *adj.* **1.** eaten into or gnawed by worms. **2.** impaired by time, decayed, or antiquated. [late ME *wormeten* (see WORM, EAT); r. ME *wormete,* OE *wyrmǣte* worm-eaten (state)]

worm′ fence′. See **snake fence.**

worm′ gear′, 1. a mechanism consisting of a worm engaging with and driving a gear wheel, the two axes usually being at right angles to each other. **2.** Also called **worm wheel.** a gear wheel driven by a worm. Also, **worm′-gear′.**

Worm gear (def. 2)

worm·hole (wûrm′hōl′), *n.* a hole made by a burrowing or gnawing worm, as in timber, nuts, etc.

wor·mil (wôr′mil), *n.* *Vet. Pathol.* warble[2] (def. 2). [alter. of *warnel,* OE *wernægel,* lit., man-nail (i.e., horny place made by man). See WEREWOLF, NAIL]

worm′ liz′ard, any of numerous burrowing, legless lizards of the family *Amphisbaenidae,* that are found chiefly in Africa and South America and that resemble an earthworm in shape and habits.

worm·root (wûrm′ro͞ot′, -ro͝ot′), *n.* pinkroot.

Worms (wûrmz; *Ger.* vôʀms), *n.* **1.** a city in E Rhineland-Palatinate, in W West Germany. 63,100 (1963). **2. Diet of,** the council or diet held here (1521) at which Luther was condemned as a heretic.

worm·seed (wûrm′sēd′), *n.* **1.** the dried, unexpanded flower heads of a wormwood, *Artemisia Cina* (**Levant wormseed**), or the fruit of certain goosefoots, esp. *Chenopodium anthelminticum,* the Mexican tea or American wormseed, used as an anthelmintic drug. **2.** any of these plants. [late ME *wyrmsed*]

worm′ snake′, any of several small, wormlike snakes, esp. *Carphophis amoenus,* of the eastern and central U.S.

worm′ wheel′. See **worm gear** (def. 2).

worm·wood (wûrm′wo͝od′), *n.* **1.** any composite herb or low shrub of the genus *Artemisia.* **2.** a bitter, aromatic herb, *A. Absinthium,* of the Old World, used as a vermifuge and a tonic and as an ingredient of absinthe. **3.** something bitter, grievous, or extremely unpleasant. [late ME *wormwode* (see WORM, WOOD[1]); r. ME *wermode,* OE *wermōd,* c. G *Wermut;* see VERMOUTH]

worm·y (wûr′mē), *adj.,* **worm·i·er, worm·i·est. 1.** containing a worm or worms. **2.** damaged or bored into by worms; worm-eaten. **3.** wormlike; groveling; low. [late ME] —**worm′i·ness,** *n.*

worn (wōrn, wôrn), *v.* **1.** pp. of **wear.** —*adj.* **2.** diminished in value or usefulness through wear, use, handling, etc.: *worn clothing; worn tires.* **3.** wearied; exhausted. —**worn′ness,** *n.*

worn-out (wōrn′out′, wôrn′-), *adj.* **1.** worn or used until no longer fit for use. **2.** depleted of energy, strength, enthusiasm, or the like; exhausted; fatigued.

wor·ri·ment (wûr′ē mənt, wur′-), *n.* *Informal.* **1.** trouble; annoyance. **2.** worry; anxiety.

wor·ri·some (wûr′ē səm, wur′-), *adj.* **1.** worrying, annoying, or disturbing; causing worry: *a worrisome problem.* **2.** inclined to worry. —**wor′ri·some·ly,** *adv.*

wor·ry (wûr′ē, wur′ē), *v.,* **-ried, -ry·ing,** *n., pl.* **-ries.** —*v.i.* **1.** to feel uneasy or anxious; fret; torment oneself with or suffer from disturbing thoughts. **2.** to move with effort: *an old car worrying uphill.* —*v.t.* **3.** to make uneasy or anxious; trouble; torment with annoyances, cares, anxieties, etc.; plague, pester, or bother: *His debts worried him.* **4.** to seize, esp. by the throat, with the teeth and shake or mangle, as one animal does another. **5.** to harass, as by repeated biting or snapping. **6. worry along** or **through,** *Informal.* to progress or succeed by constant effort, despite difficulty: *To others the situation seemed intolerable, but with luck and persistence she worried through.* —*n.* **7.** a worried condition or feeling; uneasiness or anxiety. **8.** a cause of uneasiness or anxiety; trouble. **9.** the act of worrying. [ME *wory,* var. of *wery, wiry,* OE *wyrgan* to strangle; c. G *würgen*] —**wor′ri·er,** *n.* —**wor′ry·ing·ly,** *adv.*

—**Syn. 3.** harry, hector, disquiet. WORRY, ANNOY, HARASS all mean to disturb or interfere with someone's comfort or peace of mind. To WORRY is to cause anxiety, apprehension, or care: *to worry one's parents.* To ANNOY is to vex or irritate by continued repetition of interferences: *to annoy the neighbors.* HARASS implies long-continued worry and annoyance: *Cares of office harass a president.* **7.** apprehension, disquiet, misgiving, fear. See **concern.**

wor·ry·wart (wûr′ē wôrt′, wur′-), *n.* a person who tends to worry habitually and often needlessly.

worse (wûrs), *adj., comparative of* **bad** *and* **ill. 1.** bad, ill, or unsatisfactory in a greater or higher degree; inferior in excellence, quality, or character. **2.** more unfavorable or injurious. **3.** in less good condition; in poorer health. —*n.* **4.** that which is worse. —*adv.* **5.** in a more evil, wicked, severe, or disadvantageous manner. **6.** with more severity, intensity, etc.; in a greater degree. [ME; OE *wiersa;* c. Icel *verri,* Goth *wairsiza*]

wors·en (wûr′sən), *v.t., v.i.* to make or become worse. [ME *worsene(n)*]

wors·er (wûr′sər), *adj., adv.* *Dial.* worse.

wor·ship (wûr′ship), *n., v.,* **-shiped, -ship·ing** or (*esp. Brit.*) **-shipped, -ship·ping.** —*n.* **1.** reverent honor and homage paid to God or a sacred personage, or to any object regarded as sacred. **2.** formal or ceremonious rendering of such honor and homage: *They attended worship this morning.* **3.** adoring reverence or regard: *excessive worship of business success.* **4.** the object of adoring reverence or regard. **5.** (*sometimes cap.*) *Chiefly Brit.* a title of honor used in addressing or mentioning certain magistrates and others of high rank or station (usually prec. by *his* or *your*). **6.** *Archaic.* honorable character or standing: *men of worship.* —*v.t.* **7.** to render religious reverence and homage to. **8.** to feel an adoring reverence or regard for (any person or thing). —*v.i.* **9.** to render religious reverence and homage, as to a deity. **10.** to attend services of divine worship. **11.** to feel an adoring reverence or regard. [ME *wors(c)hipe,* OE *worthscipe,* var. of *weorthscipe.* See WORTH[1], -SHIP] —**wor′ship·er;** *esp. Brit.,* **wor′ship·per,** *n.* —**wor′ship·ing·ly;** *esp. Brit.,* **wor′ship·ping·ly,** *adv.* —**Syn. 3.** honor, adoration, idolatry. **8.** honor, venerate, revere, glorify, idolize, adulate. —**Ant. 8.** detest.

wor·ship·ful (wûr′ship fəl), *adj.* **1.** given to the worship of something. **2.** (*sometimes cap.*) *Chiefly Brit.* a formal title of honor used in announcing or mentioning certain highly regarded or respected persons or groups (usually prec. by *the*). [ME] —**wor′ship·ful·ly,** *adv.* —**wor′ship·ful·ness,** *n.*

worst (wûrst), *adj., superlative of* **bad** *and* **ill.** **1.** bad or ill in the highest, greatest, or most extreme degree: *the worst person.* **2.** most faulty, unsatisfactory, or objectionable: *the worst paper submitted.* **3.** most unfavorable or injurious. **4.** in the poorest condition: *the worst house on the block.* **5.** most unpleasant, unattractive, or disagreeable: *the worst personality I've ever known.* **6.** most lacking in skill; least skilled: *the worst typist in the group.* **7. in the worst way,** *Informal.* in an extreme degree; very much: *She wanted a doll for Christmas in the worst way.* Also, **the worst way.** —*n.* **8.** that which is worst. **9. at worst,** if the worst happens; under the worst conditions: *He will be expelled from school, at worst.* Also, **at the worst.** **10. get the worst of something,** to be defeated; lose: *to get the worst of a fight.* **11. if worst comes to worst,** if the very worst happens: *If worst comes to worst, we still have some money in reserve.* —*adv.* **12.** in the most evil, wicked, severe, or disadvantageous manner. **13.** with the most severity, intensity, etc.; in the greatest degree. —*v.t.* **14.** to give (one) the worst of a contest or struggle; defeat; beat: *He worsted him easily.* [ME *worste,* OE *wur(re)sta,* var. of *wyr(re)sta, wer(re)sta;* c. Icel *verstr*]

wor·sted (wo͝os′tid, wûr′stid), *n.* **1.** firmly twisted yarn or thread spun from combed, stapled wool fibers of the same length, for weaving, knitting, etc. Cf. **woolen.** **2.** wool cloth woven from such yarns, having a hard, smooth surface and no nap. —*adj.* **3.** consisting or made of worsted. [ME *worsted(e)* special use of *Worstede* (OE *Wurthestede,* now *Worstead*), name of parish in Norfolk (England) where the cloth was made]

wort[1] (wûrt), *n.* the unfermented or fermenting infusion of malt which after fermentation becomes beer or mash. [ME; OE *wyrt* root, plant; c. G *Würze* spice; see WORT[2]]

wort[2] (wûrt), *n.* a plant, herb, or vegetable (usually used in combination). [ME; OE *wyrt* root, plant; c. OHG *wurz,* Icel *urt* herb, Goth *waurts* root; akin to ROOT[1]]

worth[1] (wûrth), *prep.* **1.** good or important enough to justify (what is specified): *advice worth taking; a place worth visiting.* **2.** having a value of, or equal in value to, as in money: *This vase is worth twelve dollars.* **3.** having property to the value or amount of: *He is worth millions.* —*n.* **4.** excellence of character or quality as commanding esteem: *men of worth.* **5.** usefulness or importance, as to the world, to a person, or for a purpose: *His worth to the world is inestimable.* **6.** value, as in money. **7.** a quantity of something of a specified value: *ten cents' worth of candy.* **8.** wealth; riches; property or possessions: *net worth.* **9. for all one is worth,** *Informal.* with one's best effort; to the utmost: *He ran for all he was worth.* **10. put in one's two cents worth,** *Slang.* to offer one's opinion in a dispute or discussion. Also, **put in one's two cents.** [ME; OE *w(e)orth;* c. G *Wert* (OHG *werd*), Icel *verthr,* Goth *wairths*] —**Syn. 1.** deserving, meriting, justifying. **6.** See **value.**

worth[2] (wûrth), *v.i. Archaic.* to happen or betide: *woe worth the day.* [ME *worthe(n),* OE *wurthan, weorthan;* c. Icel *vertha,* G *werden,* Goth *wairthan* to become, L *vertere* to turn]

worth·less (wûrth′lis), *adj.* without worth; of no use, importance, or value; good-for-nothing. —**worth′less·ly,** *adv.* —**worth′less·ness,** *n.*

worth·while (wûrth′hwīl′, -wīl′), *adj.* such as to repay one's time, attention, interest, work, trouble, etc.: *a worthwhile book.* Also, *esp. Brit.,* **worth′-while′.**

wor·thy (wûr′thē), *adj.,* **-thi·er, -thi·est,** *n., pl.* **-thies.** —*adj.* **1.** having adequate or great merit, character, or value: *a worthy successor.* **2.** of commendable excellence or merit; deserving (usually fol. by *of* or an infinitive): *a book worthy of praise; a man worthy to lead.* —*n.* **3.** a person of eminent worth, merit, or position: *The town worthies included the doctor and the lawyer.* [ME] —**wor′thi·ly,** *adv.* —**wor′thi·ness,** *n.* —**Syn. 2.** meritorious, worthwhile, excellent, exemplary, righteous, upright, honest.

wot (wot), *v. Archaic.* first and third pers. sing. pres. of **wit**[2]. [ME *woot,* OE *wāt;* c. Icel *veit,* G *weiss,* Goth *wait,* Gk *oîda,* Skt *veda;* see WIT[2]]

Wo·tan (vō′tän, vō-), a Germanic god corresponding to the Scandinavian Odin.

Wot·ton (wot′ən), *n.* **Henry,** 1568–1639, English poet and diplomat.

would (wo͝od; *unstressed* wəd), *v.* **1.** a pt. and pp. of **will**[1]. **2.** (used to express a wish): *I would it were true. Would he were here!* **3.** (used in place of *will,* to make a statement or form a question less direct or blunt): *Would you be so kind?* [ME, OE *wolde.* See WILL[1]]

would-be (wo͝od′bē′), *adj.* **1.** wishing or pretending to be: *a would-be wit.* **2.** intended to be: *a would-be kindness.*

would·n't (wo͝od′ənt), contraction of *would not.*

wouldst (wo͝odst), *v. Archaic.* second pers. sing. pt. of **will**[1].

wound[1] (wo͞ond; *Archaic and Literary* wound), *n.* **1.** an injury to an organism, usually one involving division of tissue or rupture of the integument or mucous membrane, due to external violence or some mechanical agency rather than disease. **2.** a similar injury to the tissue of a plant. **3.** an injury or hurt to feelings, sensibilities, reputation, etc. —*v.t.* **4.** to inflict a wound upon; injure; hurt. —*v.i.* **5.** to inflict a wound or wounds. [ME; OE *wund;* c. OHG *wunta,* Icel *und,* Goth *wunds*] —**wound′ing·ly,** *adv.* —**Syn. 1.** cut, stab, laceration, lesion, trauma. See **injury.** **3.** insult, grief, anguish. **4.** harm, damage; cut, stab, lacerate.

wound[2] (wound), *v.* a pt. and pp. of **wind**[2] and **wind**[3].

wound·ed (wo͞on′did), *adj.* **1.** suffering injury or bodily harm, as a laceration, bullet wound, or the like: *to bandage a wounded hand.* **2.** suffering or revealing that one suffers from a slight, insult, etc. —*n.* **3.** wounded persons collectively (often prec. by *the*): *emergency treatment for the wounded.* [ME; OE *gewundode*]

wound·wort (wo͞ond′wûrt′), *n.* See **kidney vetch.**

wove (wōv), *v.* a pt. and pp. of **weave.**

wo·ven (wō′vən), *v.* a pp. of **weave.**

wove′ pa′per, paper that exhibits a pattern of fine mesh when held up to the light. Cf. **laid paper.**

wow[1] (wou), *v.t.* **1.** *Slang.* to gain an enthusiastic response from; thrill. —*n.* **2.** *Slang.* an extraordinary success. —*interj.* **3.** *Informal.* (an exclamation of surprise, wonder, pleasure, or the like): *Wow! Look at that!*

wow[2] (wou, wō), *n.* a slow variation or distortion in the pitch fidelity of reproduced sound, caused by fluctuations in the speed of a component in the sound-reproducing system. [imit.]

wow·ser (wou′zər), *n. Australian.* an excessively puritanical person. [?]

wp., *Baseball.* wild pitch; wild pitches.

WPA, Work Projects Administration: the former federal agency (1935–43) charged with instituting and administering public works in order to relieve national unemployment.

WPB, War Production Board. Also, **W.P.B.**

wpm, words per minute.

WRAC, (rak), *Brit.* Women's Royal Army Corps. Also, **W.R.A.C.**

wrack[1] (rak), *n.* ruin or destruction: *gone to wrack and ruin.* [ME *wrak;* OE *wræc* vengeance, misery, akin to *wracu* vengeance, misery, *wrecan* to WREAK]

wrack[2] (rak), *n.* **1.** wreck or wreckage. **2.** a remnant of something destroyed: *leaving not a wrack behind.* **3.** seaweed or other marine vegetation cast on the shore. **4.** rack[4]. —*v.i.* **5.** rack[4]. [var. of RACK[4]]

WRAF (raf), *Brit.* Women's Royal Air Force. Also, **W.R.A.F.**

wraith (rāth), *n.* **1.** an apparition of a living person supposed to portend his death. **2.** a visible spirit; ghost. [?] —**wraith′like′,** *adj.*

Wran·gel (rang′gəl; *Russ.* VRÄN gel′yə), *n.* a Russian island in the Arctic Ocean, off the coast of the NE Soviet Union in Asia. ab. 2000 sq. mi.

Wran·gell (rang′gəl), *n.* **Mount,** an active volcano in SE Alaska, in the Wrangell Mountains. 14,006 ft.

Wran′gell Moun′tains, a mountain range in SE Alaska. Highest peak, Mt. Bona, 16,420 ft.

wran·gle (rang′gəl), *v.,* **-gled, -gling,** *n.* —*v.i.* **1.** to argue or dispute, esp. in a noisy or angry manner. —*v.t.* **2.** to argue or dispute. **3.** to get by wrangling. **4.** to bring or put into some condition by wrangling (usually fol. by *away* or *into*): *He wrangled his wife into agreement.* **5.** *U.S.* to tend or round up (cattle, horses, or other livestock). —*n.* **6.** a noisy or angry dispute; controversy; altercation. [late ME, appar. < LG *wrangeln,* freq. of *wrangen* to struggle, make uproar; akin to WRING] —**wran′gler,** *n.* —**Syn. 1.** quarrel, bicker. **6.** argument, quarrel.

wrap (rap), *v.,* **wrapped** or **wrapt, wrap·ping,** *n.* —*v.t.* **1.** to enclose in something wound or folded about (often fol. by *up*): *She wrapped her head in a scarf.* **2.** to enclose and make fast (an article, bundle, etc.) within a covering of paper or the like (often fol. by *up*): *He wrapped up the package in brown paper.* **3.** to wind, fold, or bind around an object, as in order to cover it: *He wrapped brown paper around the package.* **4.** to protect with coverings, outer garments, etc. (usually fol. by *up*). **5.** to surround, envelop, shroud, or hide. **6.** to fold or roll up. —*v.i.* **7.** to wrap oneself, as with clothing (usually fol. by *up*). **8.** to become wrapped, as about something; fold. **9. wrapped up in,** intensely absorbed in: *wrapped up in one's work.* **10. wrap up,** *Informal.* to conclude (an activity). —*n.* **11.** something to be wrapped about the person, esp. in addition to the usual indoor clothing, as a shawl, scarf, mantle, sweater, jacket, etc.: *evening wrap.* **12. wraps,** outdoor garments; coverings, furs, etc. [ME; b. obs. *wry* (OE *wrēon* to cover, clothe, hide) and LAP[2]; cf. ME var. *wlappe,* with only *w* of *wry*]

wrap·a·round (rap′ə round′), *adj.* **1.** overlapping or appearing to overlap another part, as a skirt that wraps around the body and overlaps at a full-length opening: *a wraparound dress; a wraparound windshield.* —*n.* **2.** a wraparound object. **3.** outsert. Also, **wrap′-a-round′.**

wrap·per (rap′ər), *n.* **1.** a person or thing that wraps. **2.** something in which a thing is wrapped. **3.** a long, loose garment, as a woman's bathrobe. **4.** *Brit.* See **book jacket.** **5.** the tobacco leaf used for covering a cigar. [late ME]

wrap·ping (rap′ing), *n.* Often, **wrappings.** that in which something is wrapped; wrapper. [late ME]

wrap′ping pa′per, heavy paper used for wrapping packages, parcels, etc.

wrapt (rapt), *v.* a pt. and pp. of **wrap.**

wrap-up (rap′up′), *n. Informal.* a report that summarizes something, esp. recent news.

wrasse (ras), *n.* any of various marine fishes of the family *Labridae,* esp. of the genus *Labrus,* having thick, fleshy lips, powerful teeth, and usually a brilliant color, certain species being valued as food fishes. [< Cornish *wrach,* var. (by lenition) of *gwrach*]

wras·tle (ras′əl), *v.i., v.t.,* **-tled, -tling,** *n. Dial.* wrestle. [ME *wrastle(n)* to WRESTLE; see WARSLE]

wrath (rath, räth *or, esp. Brit.,* rôth), *n.* **1.** strong, stern, or fierce anger; deeply resentful indignation; ire. **2.** vengeance or punishment motivated by anger. —*adj.* **3.** *Archaic.* wroth. [ME *wraththe,* OE *wrǣththo.* See WROTH, -TH[1]] —**Syn. 1.** rage, resentment, passion.

wrath·ful (rath′fəl, räth′- *or, esp. Brit.,* rôth′-), *adj.* full of or expressing wrath. [ME] —**wrath′ful·ly,** *adv.* —**wrath′ful·ness,** *n.* —**Syn.** irate, furious, resentful, indignant, enraged.

wrath·y (rath′ē, rä′thē *or, esp. Brit.,* rô′thē), *adj.,* **wrath·i·er, wrath·i·est.** *Informal.* wrathful; angry. —**wrath′i·ly,** *adv.* —**wrath′i·ness,** *n.*

wreak (rēk), *v.t.* **1.** to inflict or execute (punishment, vengeance, etc.): *They wreaked havoc on the enemy.* **2.** to carry out the promptings of (one's rage, ill humor, will, desire, etc.), as on a victim or object: *He wreaked his anger on the workmen.* [ME *wreke(n),* OE *wrecan;* c. G *rächen* to avenge, Icel *reka* to drive, avenge, Goth *wrikan* to persecute, L *urgēre* to drive, push] —**wreak′er,** *n.*

wreath (rēth), *n., pl.* **wreaths** (rēthz), *v.* —*n.* **1.** something twisted or bent into a circular form; a circular band of flowers, foliage, or any ornamental work, for a decorative purpose; garland. **2.** any ringlike, curving, or curling mass or formation: *a wreath of clouds.* **3.** *Heraldry.* torse. **—*v.t., v.i.*** **4.** to wreathe. [ME *wrethe,* OE *wrǣth* (c. *wrǣd*), cf. *writha* thong, collar, and see WRITHE] **—wreath′less,** *adj.* **—wreath′like′,** *adj.*

wreathe (rēth), *v.,* **wreathed; wreathed** or (*Archaic*) **wreath·en; wreath·ing.** **—*v.t.*** **1.** to encircle or adorn with or as with a wreath or wreaths. **2.** to form as a wreath by twisting, twining, or otherwise. **3.** to surround in curving or curling masses or form. **4.** to envelop: *a face wreathed in smiles.* **—*v.i.*** **5.** to take the form of a wreath or wreaths. **6.** to move in curving or curling masses, as smoke. [WREATH; in some senses, back formation from late ME *wrethen* (WREATH + -EN[2])]

wreck (rek), *n.* **1.** any structure or object reduced to a state of ruin. **2.** wreckage, goods, etc., remaining above water after a shipwreck, esp. when cast ashore. **3.** the ruin or destruction of a vessel in the course of navigation; shipwreck. **4.** a vessel in a state of ruin from disaster at sea, on rocks, etc. **5.** the ruin or destruction of anything: *the wreck of one's hopes.* **6.** a person of ruined health; someone in bad shape physically or mentally: *The strain of his work left him a complete wreck.* **—*v.t.*** **7.** to cause the wreck of (a vessel), as in navigation; shipwreck. **8.** to involve in a wreck. **9.** to cause the ruin or destruction of: *to wreck a car.* **—*v.i.*** **10.** to be involved in a wreck; become wrecked: *The trains wrecked at the crossing.* **11.** to act as a wrecker; engage in wrecking. [ME *wrek* < Scand; cf. Icel *rek* < *wrek (AF *wrec* < ME)] **—Syn. 5.** devastation, desolation. **9.** destroy, devastate.

wreck·age (rek′ij), *n.* **1.** the act of wrecking. **2.** the state of being wrecked. **3.** remains or fragments of something that has been wrecked.

wreck·er (rek′ər), *n.* **1.** a person or thing that wrecks. **2.** a person, car, or train employed in removing wreckage, debris, etc., as from railroad tracks. **3.** Also called **tow car, tow truck.** a vehicle equipped with a mechanical apparatus for hoisting and pulling, used to tow wrecked or disabled automobiles. **4.** Also called **housewrecker.** a person whose business it is to demolish and remove houses or other buildings, as in clearing sites for other use. **5.** a person or vessel employed in recovering salvage from wrecked or disabled vessels. **6.** a person who plunders wrecks, esp. after exhibiting false signals in order to cause shipwrecks.

wreck′ing bar′. See **pinch bar.**

wren (ren), *n.* **1.** any of numerous small, active, passerine birds of the family *Troglodytidae,* esp. *Troglodytes troglodytes,* of the Northern Hemisphere, having dark brown plumage barred with black. **2.** any of various similar, unrelated birds, esp. any of several Old World warblers. [ME, OE *wrenna;* cf. OHG *wrendilo,* Icel *rindill*]

Wren, *Troglodytes aedon* (Length 5 in.)

Wren (ren), *n.* **Sir Christopher,** 1632–1723, English architect: built St. Paul's Cathedral and other London landmarks.

Wren (ren), *n.* (*sometimes l.c.*) *Chiefly Brit. Informal.* a member of the Wrens.

wrench (rench), *v.t.* **1.** to twist suddenly and forcibly; pull, jerk, or force by a violent twist: *He wrenched the prisoner's wrist.* **2.** to overstrain or injure (the ankle, knee, etc.) by a sudden, violent twist. **3.** to affect distressingly as if by twisting. **4.** to wrest, as from the right use or meaning. **—*v.i.*** **5.** to twist, turn, or move suddenly aside. **6.** to give a wrench or twist at something. **—*n.*** **7.** a tool for gripping and turning or twisting the head of a bolt, a nut, a pipe, or the like, commonly consisting of a bar of metal with fixed or adjustable jaws. **8.** a wrenching movement; a sudden, violent twist. **9.** a painful, straining twist, as of the ankle or wrist. **10.** sudden and sharp emotional strain or anguish. [ME *wrenche(n),* OE *wrencan* to twist, turn; c. G *renken*]

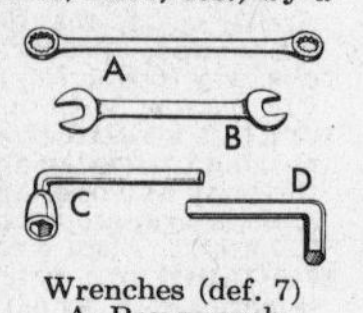

Wrenches (def. 7)
A, Box wrench
B, Open-end wrench
C, Socket wrench
D, Allen wrench

Wrens (renz), *n.* (*construed as sing. or pl.*) *Informal.* the Women's Royal Naval Service: established in Great Britain in 1917 as an auxiliary to the Royal Navy. [*WRNS,* with *E* put in to give the sequence a vowel]

wrest (rest), *v.t.* **1.** to twist or turn with force. **2.** to take away by force: *to wrest a knife from a child.* **3.** to get by effort: *to wrest a living from the soil.* **4.** to twist or turn from the proper application, meaning, or the like. **—*n.*** **5.** a twist or wrench. **6.** a key or small wrench for tuning stringed musical instruments, as the harp or piano. [ME *wreste(n),* OE *wrǣstan;* c. Icel *reista;* akin to WRIST] **—wrest′er,** *n.* **—Syn. 3.** See **extract. 4.** wrench.

wres·tle (res′əl), *v.,* **-tled, -tling,** *n.* **—*v.i.*** **1.** to engage in wrestling. **2.** to contend, as in a struggle for mastery; grapple: *to wrestle with a problem.* **—*v.t.*** **3.** to contend with in wrestling. **4.** to force by or as if by wrestling. **5.** *U.S.* to throw (a calf or other animal) for branding. **—*n.*** **6.** an act of or a bout at wrestling. **7.** a struggle. [ME; OE **wrǣstlian* (cf. OE *wrǣstlere* wrestler), freq. of *wrǣstan* to WREST] **—wres′tler,** *n.*

wres·tling (res′ling), *n.* **1.** a sport in which two opponents struggle hand to hand, as in order to pin or press each other's shoulders to the ground. **2.** the act of a person who wrestles. [ME; OE *wrǣstlung*]

wrest′ pin′, peg (def. 2).

wretch (rech), *n.* **1.** a deplorably unfortunate or unhappy person. **2.** a person of despicable or base character. [ME *wrecche,* OE *wrecca* exile, adventurer; c. G *Recke* warrior, hero, Icel *rekkr* man; akin to WREAK]

wretch·ed (rech′id), *adj.* **1.** very unfortunate in condition or circumstances; miserable; pitiable. **2.** characterized by or attended with misery and sorrow. **3.** despicable, contemptible, or mean: *a wretched little liar.* **4.** poor, sorry, or pitiful; worthless: *a wretched job of sewing.* [ME *wrecchede.* See WRETCH, -ED[3]] **—wretch′ed·ly,** *adv.* **—wretch′ed·ness,** *n.* **—Syn. 1.** distressed, afflicted, woeful, woebegone. **3.** base, vile. **—Ant. 1.** comfortable, enviable.

wri·er (rī′ər), *adj.* comparative of **wry.**

wri·est (rī′ist), *adj.* superlative of **wry.**

wrig·gle (rig′əl), *v.,* **-gled, -gling,** *n.* **—*v.i.*** **1.** to twist from side to side; writhe; squirm. **2.** to move along by twisting and turning the body, as a worm or snake. **3.** to make one's way by shifts or expedients (often fol. by *out*): *to wriggle out of a difficulty.* **—*v.t.*** **4.** to cause to wriggle: *to wriggle one's hips.* **5.** to bring, get, make, etc., by wriggling: *to wriggle one's way through a narrow opening.* **—*n.*** **6.** act of wriggling; a wriggling movement. [< MLG *wriggele(n)* (c. D *wriggelen*), freq. of **wriggen* to twist, turn, akin to OE *wrigian* to twist; see WRY] **—wrig′gling·ly,** *adv.*

wrig·gler (rig′lər), *n.* **1.** a person or thing that wriggles. **2.** the larva of a mosquito. Also called **wiggler.**

wrig·gly (rig′lē), *adj.,* **-gli·er, -gli·est.** **1.** twisting; writhing; squirming. **2.** evasive; shifty: *a wriggly character.*

wright (rīt), *n.* a workman, esp. a constructive workman (used chiefly in combination): *a wheelwright; a playwright.* [ME; OE *wryhta,* metathetic var. of *wyrhta* worker; see WORK]

Wright (rīt), *n.* **1. Frances** or **Fanny,** 1795–1852, U.S. abolitionist and social reformer, born in Scotland. **2. Frank Lloyd,** 1869–1959, U.S. architect. **3. Or·ville** (ôr′vil), 1871–1948, and his brother **Wilbur,** 1867–1912, U.S. aeronautical inventors. **4. Richard,** 1908–60, U.S. novelist. **5. Russel,** 1904–76, U.S. industrial designer.

wring (ring), *v.,* **wrung** or (*Rare*) **wringed; wring·ing;** *n.* **—*v.t.*** **1.** to twist forcibly. **2.** to twist or compress in order to force out water or other liquid (often fol. by *out*): *to wring clothes.* **3.** to extract or expel by or as by twisting or compression (usually fol. by *out* or *from*): *to wring water out of clothes.* **4.** to affect painfully by or as if by some contorting or compressing action. **5.** to clasp tightly with or without twisting: *to wring one's hands.* **6.** to force (usually fol. by *off*) by twisting. **—*v.i.*** **7.** to perform the action of wringing something. **—*n.*** **8.** a wringing; forcible twist or squeeze. [ME; OE *wring(an);* c. G *ringen* to wrestle; base *wring-* nasalized var. of *wrig-;* see WRIGGLE] **—Syn. 6.** wrest.

wring·er (ring′ər), *n.* **1.** a person or thing that wrings. **2.** an apparatus or machine for squeezing liquid out of anything wet, as two rollers through which an article of wet clothing may be squeezed. [ME]

wrin·kle[1] (ring′kəl), *n., v.,* **-kled, -kling.** **—*n.*** **1.** a ridge or furrow on a surface, due to contraction, folding, rumpling, aging, or the like. **—*v.t.*** **2.** to form a wrinkle or wrinkles in: *Don't wrinkle your dress.* **—*v.i.*** **3.** to become wrinkled. [late ME, back formation from *wrinkled,* OE *gewrinclod,* ptp. of *gewrinclian* to wind round; perh. akin to WRENCH] **—wrin′kle·less,** *adj.*

wrin·kle[2] (ring′kəl), *n.* *Informal.* an ingenious trick or device; a clever innovation: *a new advertising wrinkle.* [late ME = *wrinc* trick (OE *wrenc;* see WRENCH) + *-le* -LE]

wrin·kly (ringk′lē), *adj.,* **-kli·er, -kli·est.** having wrinkles or tending to wrinkle; creased: *a wrinkly material impossible to keep pressed.*

wrist (rist), *n.* **1.** the carpus or lower part of the forearm where it joins the hand. **2.** the joint or articulation between the forearm and the hand. **3.** the part of an article of clothing that fits around the wrist. [ME, OE; c. G *Rist* back of hand, Icel *rist* instep; akin to WRITHE]

wrist·band (rist′band′), *n.* the band of a sleeve, esp. that of a shirt sleeve, that covers the wrist.

wrist·let (rist′lit), *n.* **1.** a band worn around the wrist, esp. to protect it from cold. **2.** a bracelet.

wrist·lock (rist′lok′), *n.* *Wrestling.* a hold in which an opponent's wrist is grasped and twisted.

wrist′ pin′, *Mach.* a pin joining the end of a connecting rod to a trunk piston or the end of a piston rod.

wrist′ watch′, a watch for wearing on the wrist by means of a strap or band. Also, **wrist′watch′.**

writ[1] (rit), *n.* **1.** *Law.* a formal order under seal, issued in the name of a sovereign, government, court, or other authority, enjoining the officer or other person to whom it is issued to do or refrain from some specified act. **2.** something written; a writing: *sacred writ.* **3.** a formal document under seal expressing the order or command of an English sovereign. [ME, OE; c. Icel *rit* writing, Goth *writs* letter. See WRITE]

writ[2] (rit), *v.* *Archaic.* a pt. and pp. of **write.**

write (rīt), *v.,* **wrote** or (*Archaic*) **writ; writ·ten** or (*Archaic*) **writ; writ·ing.** **—*v.t.*** **1.** to form (characters, letters, words, etc.) on the surface of some material, as with a pen, pencil, typewriter, or other instrument or means; inscribe: *Write your name on the board.* **2.** to express or communicate in writing; give a written account of. **3.** to fill in the blank spaces of (a printed form) with writing: *to write a check.* **4.** to execute or produce by setting down words, figures, etc.: *to write two copies of a letter.* **5.** to compose and produce in words or characters duly set down: *to write a letter to a friend.* **6.** to produce as author or composer: *to write a sonnet; to write a symphony.* **7.** to trace significant characters on, or mark or cover with writing. **8.** to impress the marks or indications of: *Honesty is written on his face.* **9.** *Computer Technol.* to record (information) in a memory unit. **10.** to underwrite: *What company wrote your insurance?* **—*v.i.*** **11.** to form characters, words, etc., with a pen, pencil, typewriter, or other instrument or means, or as a pen or the like does: *He writes with a pen. This pen writes well.* **12.** to write as a profession or occupation: *He writes for the daily newspaper. He used to write for the musical theater.* **13.** to express ideas in writing. **14.** to write a letter or letters, or communicate by letter: *Write if you get work.* **15.** to compose or work as a writer or author. **16. write down, a.** to set down in writing; record; note. **b.** to direct one's efforts in writing to a lower level, as to a less intelligent reader or audience: *He writes down to the public.* **17. write off, a.** to cancel an entry in an account, as an unpaid and uncollectable debt. **b.** to regard as worthless, lost, obsolete, etc.; decide to forget: *They decided to write off their attempt at pioneering and return to civilization.* **c.** to amortize: *The new equipment was written off in three years.* **18. write oneself out,** to exhaust one's store of ideas for things to write. **19. write out, a.** to put into writing. **b.** to write in full form; state completely. **20. write up,** to put into writing, esp. in full detail: *to write up a report.* [ME; OE *wrītan;* c. G *reissen* to tear, draw, Icel *rīta* to write] **—writ′a·ble,** *adj.*

write-in (rīt′in′), *n.* **1.** a candidate or vote for a candidate not listed on the printed ballot but written onto the ballot by the voter. —*adj.* **2.** being or pertaining to such a candidate or vote or a ballot so marked.

write-off (rīt′ôf′, -of′), *n.* **1.** a cancellation from the accounts as a loss. **2.** a reduction in book value; depreciation.

writ·er (rī′tər), *n.* **1.** a person engaged in writing, esp. as an occupation or profession; an author or journalist. **2.** a clerk, scribe, or the like. **3.** a person who writes or is able to write. **4. the writer,** I; me (used to avoid use of the first person in written text). [ME, OE *writere*]

writ′er's cramp′, *Pathol.* spasmodic contractions of the muscles of the thumb and forefinger during writing, sometimes accompanied by pain.

write-up (rīt′up′), *n.* a written description or account, as in a newspaper or magazine.

writhe (rīth), *v.*, **writhed, writh·ing,** *n.* —*v.i.* **1.** to squirm or twist the body about, as in pain or with violent effort. **2.** to shrink mentally, as in acute discomfort. —*v.t.* **3.** to twist or bend, as in pain or with violent effort. —*n.* **4.** a writhing movement. [ME; OE *wrīthan* (to) twist, wind; c. Icel *rītha* to knit, twist; akin to WREATH, WRY] —**writh′er,** *n.* —**writh′ing·ly,** *adv.*

writh·en (rith′ən), *adj. Archaic.* twisted. [ME]

writ·ing (rī′ting), *n.* **1.** the act of a person or thing that writes. **2.** state of being written; written form: *to commit one's thoughts to writing.* **3.** a meaningful group of written characters or symbols; that which is written. **4.** something indicated or expressed through such a group, esp. a literary composition. **5.** the typical or distinctive form of the symbols or characters written by hand by one person or within a culture. **6.** literary or musical style, form, quality, technique, etc.: *His writing shows a keen knowledge of history.* **7.** the profession of a writer: *He turned to writing at an early age.* **8. writing on the wall.** See **handwriting** (def. 4). [ME, OE]

writ′ing desk′, a piece of furniture with a surface for writing upon.

writ′ing pa′per, 1. paper on which to write. **2.** stationery; notepaper.

writ′ of extent′, *Eng. Law.* extent (def. 4a).

writ·ten (rit′ən), *v., adj.* —*v.* **1.** a pp. of **write.** —*adj.* **2.** expressed in writing (opposed to *spoken*).

W.R.N.S., *Brit.* Women's Royal Naval Service. Cf. **Wrens.**

wrnt., warrant.

Wro·cław (vrô′tsläf), *n.* Polish name of **Breslau.**

wrong (rông, rong), *adj.* **1.** not in accordance with what is morally right or good: *a wrong deed.* **2.** deviating from truth or fact: *a wrong answer.* **3.** not correct in action, judgment, or method: *You are wrong to blame him.* **4.** not proper or usual; not in accordance with requirements or recommended practice: *the wrong way to hold a golf club.* **5.** out of order; awry; amiss: *Something is wrong with the machine.* **6.** not suitable or appropriate: *He always says the wrong thing.* —*n.* **7.** something that is unjust: *to suffer many wrongs.* **8.** whatever would be incorrect or immoral to do, choose, or act upon: *not to know right from wrong.* **9.** *Law.* **a.** an invasion of another's right, to his damage. **b.** a tort. **10. get in wrong,** *Slang.* to come into disfavor with someone. **11. in the wrong,** in error: *He knew he was in the wrong, but refused to concede the point.* —*adv.* **12.** in a wrong manner; not rightly; awry; amiss: *You did it wrong again.* **13. go wrong, a.** to go amiss; fail: *Everything is going wrong today.* **b.** to pursue an immoral course: *It is sad that one so young should go wrong.* —*v.t.* **14.** to do wrong to; treat unfairly or unjustly. **15.** to impute evil to (someone) unjustly; malign. [ME, OE, perh. < Scand; cf. Dan *vrang* wrong, Icel *rangr* awry; c. D *wrang* acid, tart; akin to WRING] —**wrong′er,** *n.* —**wrong′ly,** *adv.* —**wrong′ness,** *n.*
—**Syn. 1.** bad, evil, wicked, sinful, immoral. **2.** inaccurate, incorrect, false, untrue, mistaken. **6.** improper, unsuitable. **8.** misdoing, wickedness, sin, vice. **14.** maltreat, defraud.

wrong·do·er (rông′do͞o′ər, -do͞o′-, rong′-), *n.* **1.** a person who does wrong, esp. a sinner or transgressor. **2.** *Law.* a person guilty of violating the legal right of another.

wrong·do·ing (rông′do͞o′ing, -do͞o′-, rong′-), *n.* **1.** behavior or action that is wrong, evil, or blameworthy. **2.** an act that is wrong, evil, or blameworthy.

wrong′ font′, *Print.* the improper font, or size and style of type, for its place. *Abbr.:* wf, w.f.

wrong·ful (rông′fəl, rong′-), *adj.* **1.** full of or characterized by wrong; unjust or unfair. **2.** having no legal right; unlawful. [ME] —**wrong′ful·ly,** *adv.* —**wrong′ful·ness,** *n.*

wrong-head·ed (rông′hed′id, rong′-), *adj.* perversely wrong in judgment or opinion; misguided and stubborn. Also, **wrong′head′ed.** —**wrong′-head′ed·ly, wrong′head′ed·ly,** *adv.* —**wrong′-head′ed·ness, wrong′head′ed·ness,** *n.*

wrong′ num′ber, 1. (in telephoning) **a.** a call made to a number other than the one intended, as by an error in dialing or not remembering the correct number. **b.** the number or person reached through such a call. **2.** *Slang.* **a.** the wrong person for a particular task, role, or situation: *Me fight the champ?—You've got the wrong number!* **b.** an inadequate, disagreeable, or unpopular person: *She's O.K., but her sister's a wrong number.*

wrote (rōt), *v.* a pt. of **write.**

wroth (rôth, roth *or, esp. Brit.,* rōth), *adj.* angry; wrathful (usually used predicatively): *He was wroth to see the damage to his home.* [ME; OE *wrāth;* c. D *wreed* cruel, Icel *reithr* angry. See WRITHE]

wrought (rôt), *v.* **1.** a pt. and pp. of **work.** —*adj.* **2.** worked. **3.** elaborated; embellished. **4.** not rough or crude. **5.** (of metal objects) produced or shaped by beating with a hammer. —**Syn. 2.** See **worked.**

wrought′ i′ron, a comparatively pure form of iron, almost entirely free of carbon and having a fibrous structure, that is readily forged and welded. —**wrought′-i′ron,** *adj.*

wrought-up (rôt′up′), *adj.* excited; perturbed: *She's all wrought-up about nothing.* Also, **worked-up.**

W.R.S.S.R., White Russian Soviet Socialist Republic.

wrung (rung), *v.* a pt. and pp. of **wring.**

wry (rī), *adj.*, **wri·er, wri·est. 1.** produced or characterized by a distortion or lopsidedness of the facial features: *a wry grin.* **2.** devious in course or purpose; misdirected. **3.** contrary; perverse. **4.** distorted or perverted, as in meaning. **5.** bitterly or disdainfully ironic: *wry humor.* [adj. use of *wry* (v.), ME *wrye(n),* OE *wrīgian* to go forward, swerve; c. D *wrijgen* to twist; akin to OE *wrigels,* L *rīcula* evil, Gk *rhoikós* crooked] —**wry′ly,** *adv.* —**wry′ness,** *n.*

wry·neck (rī′nek′), *n. Informal.* **1.** torticollis. **2.** a person having torticollis.

W.S., West Saxon.

WSW, west-southwest. Also, **W.S.W.**

wt., weight.

Wu·chang (wo͞o′chäng′), *n.* a former city in E China: now a part of Wuhan.

wud (wo͝od), *adj. Chiefly Scot.* wood; mad. [see WOOD[2]]

Wu·han (wo͞o′hän′), *n.* the extensive metropolitan area formed by the former cities of Hankow, Hanyang, and Wuchang in E China at the junction of the Han and Yangtze rivers. 2,146,000 (est. 1957). Also called **Han Cities.**

Wu·hsien (wo͞o′shyen′), *n.* a city in S Kiangsu, in E China. 633,000 (est. 1957). Formerly, **Soochow.**

Wu·hu (wo͞o′ho͞o′), *n.* a port in E Anhwei in E China, on the Yangtze River. 242,100 (est. 1957).

wul·fen·ite (wo͝ol′fə nīt′), *n.* a mineral consisting of lead molybdate. [named after F. X. von *Wulfen* (1728–1805), Austrian scientist; see -ITE[1]]

Wul·fi·la (wo͝ol′fə lə), *n.* Ulfilas.

Wun·der·kind (vo͝on′dər kint′; *Eng.* vo͝on′dər kind′, wun′-), *n., pl.* **-kin·der** (-kin′dər), *Eng.* **-kinds.** *German.* a wonder child or child prodigy.

Wup·per·tal (vo͝op′ər täl′), *n.* a city in W West Germany, in the Ruhr Valley: formed by the union of Barmen, Elberfeld, and smaller communities in 1929. 422,900 (1963).

Würm (vo͝orm, wo͝orm, wûrm; *Ger.* vyrm), *n.* the fourth stage of the glaciation of Eurasia during the Pleistocene. Cf. **Wisconsin** (def. 3). [after a district in the Alps; name chosen as *Würm* is representative of the last stage of extreme cold]

wurst (wûrst, wo͝orst), *n.* sausage (def. 1). [< G: lit., mixture; akin to WORSE]

Würt·tem·berg (wûr′təm bûrg′; *Ger.* vyr′təm berk′), *n.* a former state in SW West Germany: now part of Baden-Württemberg.

Würz·burg (wûrts′bûrg; *Ger.* vyrts′bo͝ork′), *n.* a city in NW Bavaria, in S West Germany, on the Main River. 120,798 (est. 1964).

Wu·sih (wo͞o′sē′, -shē′), *n.* a city in S Kiangsu, in E China. 613,000 (est. 1957).

WV, West Virginia (approved esp. for use with zip code).

W.Va., West Virginia.

W.V.S., *Brit.* Women's Voluntary Service.

WW, World War.

WY, Wyoming (approved esp. for use with zip code).

Wy., Wyoming.

Wy·an·dot (wī′ən dot′), *n., pl.* **-dots,** (*esp. collectively*) **-dot** for 1. **1.** an Indian of the former Huron confederacy. **2.** a dialect of the Huron language, esp. as used by those elements of the Huron tribe regrouped in Oklahoma. Also, **Wyandotte.**

Wy·an·dotte (wī′ən dot′), *n., pl.* **-dottes** for 2, 3; (*esp. collectively for 3*) **-dotte. 1.** a city in SE Michigan, on the Detroit River. 41,061 (1970). **2.** one of an American breed of chickens, raised for meat and eggs. **3.** Wyandot.

Wy·att (wī′ət), *n.* **1. James,** 1746–1813, English architect. **2.** Also, **Wy′at. Sir Thomas,** 1503?–42, English poet and diplomat.

wych-elm (wich′elm′), *n.* an elm, *Ulmus glabra,* of northern and western Europe. Also, **witch-elm.** [*wych* (ME *wyche,* OE *wice* wych-elm) + ELM]

Wych·er·ley (wich′ər lē), *n.* **William,** c1640–1716, English dramatist and poet.

Wyc·liffe (wik′lif), *n.* **John,** c1320–84, English theologian, religious reformer, and Biblical translator. Also, **Wyc′lif, Wickliffe, Wiclif.** —**Wyc′liff·ism, Wyc′lif·ism,** *n.*

Wyc·lif·fite (wik′li fīt′), *adj.* **1.** of or pertaining to Wycliffe or the Wycliffites. —*n.* **2.** a follower of John Wycliffe; Lollard. Also, **Wyc′lif·ite′.**

wye (wī), *n., pl.* **wyes.** the letter Y, or something having a similar shape.

Wye (wī), *n.* a river flowing from central Wales through SW England into the Severn estuary. 130 mi. long.

Wy·eth (wī′əth), *n.* **1. Andrew New·ell** (no͞o′əl, nyo͞o′-), born 1917, U.S. painter. **2.** his father, **N(ewell) C(on·vers)** (kon′vərz), 1882–1945, U.S. illustrator and painter.

Wy·lie (wī′lē), *n.* **Elinor (Morton),** nee **Hoyt** (hoit), 1885–1928, U.S. poet and novelist.

wy·lie·coat (wī′lē kōt′), *n. Scot. and North Eng.* a woolen or flannel undergarment, as a warm undershirt. [ME (Scot) *wyle cot = wyle* (< ?) + *cot* COAT]

wynn (win), *n.* the rune for *w.* Also, **wen.** [OE: lit., joy]

Wyo., Wyoming.

Wy·o·ming (wī ō′ming), *n.* **1.** a state in the NW United States. 332,416 (1970); 97,914 sq. mi. *Cap.:* Cheyenne. *Abbr.:* WY, Wyo., Wy. **2.** a city in W Michigan, near Grand Rapids. 56,560 (1970). —**Wy·o·ming·ite** (wī ō′ming īt′), *n.*

Wyo′ming Val′ley, a valley in NE Pennsylvania, along the Susquehanna River: Indian massacre 1778.

wyte (wīt), *v.*, **wyt·ed, wyt·ing,** *n. Chiefly Scot.* wite[1].

Wythe (with), *n.* **George,** 1729–1806, U.S. jurist and statesman.

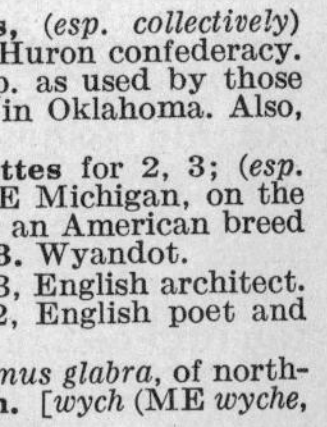

Wyvern

wy·vern (wī′vərn), *n. Heraldry.* a two-legged winged dragon having the hinder part of a serpent with a barbed tail. Also, **wivern.** [ME *wyvre* < AF *wivre* (OF *guivre*) << OHG *wīpera* < L *vīpera* VIPER; modern *-n* unexplained]

DEVELOPMENT OF MAJUSCULE								
NORTH SEMITIC	GREEK		ETR.	LATIN		MODERN		
						GOTHIC	ITALIC	ROMAN
—	—	X	—	—	X	X	*X*	X

DEVELOPMENT OF MINUSCULE					
ROMAN CURSIVE	ROMAN UNCIAL	CAROL. MIN.	MODERN		
			GOTHIC	ITALIC	ROMAN
x	x	x		*x*	x

The twenty-fourth letter of the English alphabet originated in form with a variant of North Semitic *taw,* where it signified the *t*-sound. It was adopted by Classical Greek for the KH-sound (as in Scottish *loch*) and in some local scripts for the *ks*-sound. In the latter representation it passed from Latin into English and has been maintained, despite its redundancy, for the letter-combination KS.

X, x (eks), *n., pl.* **X's** or **Xs, x's** or **xs. 1.** the 24th letter of the English alphabet, a consonant. **2.** any spoken sound represented by the letter *X* or *x,* as in *xylene, box,* or *Xerxes.* **3.** something having the shape of an X. **4.** a written or printed representation of the letter *X* or *x.* **5.** a person, thing, agency, factor, etc., of unknown identity.

X (eks), *v.t.,* **x-ed** or **x'd** (ekst), **x-ing** or **x'ing** (ek′sing). **1.** to cross out or mark with or as with an *x* (often fol. by *out*): *to x out an error.* **2.** to indicate with or as with an *x,* as a choice (often fol. by *in*).

X, 1. the 24th in order or in a series, or, when *I* is omitted, the 23rd. **2.** (*sometimes l.c.*) the Roman numeral for 10. Cf. **Roman numerals. 3.** Christ. **4.** Christian. **5.** *Elect.* reactance. **6.** *U.S.* a designation by the motion-picture industry for films no one under 17 years of age may attend. **7.** *Chem. Obs.* xenon.

x, 1. an unknown quantity or a variable. **2.** ex[1] (def. 1). **3.** experimental. **4.** a sign used to indicate x-ray or x-rays. **5.** a sign used at the end of letters, telegrams, etc., to indicate a kiss. **6.** a sign indicating multiplication; times: $8 \times 8 = 64$. **7.** a sign used between figures indicating dimensions: 3″ × 4″ (read: "three by four inches"). **8.** power of magnification: *50x telescope.* **9.** (used as a signature by an illiterate person.) **10.** crossed with. **11.** out of; foaled by: *a colt by Flag-a-way x Merrylegs.* **12.** (used to indicate choice, as on a ballot, examination, etc.) **13.** (used to indicate an error, as on a test.) **14.** *Math.* (in Cartesian coordinates) the *x*-axis. **15.** a person or thing of unknown identity.

xanth-, var. of **xantho-** before a vowel: *xanthate; xanthous.*

xan·thate (zan′thāt), *n. Chem.* a salt or ester of xanthic acid. —**xan·tha′tion,** *n.*

xan·the·in (zan′thē in), *n.* the part of the coloring matter in yellow flowers that is soluble in water. [< F *xanthéine* = *xanth-* XANTH- + *-éine* n. suffix to distinguish it from F *xanthine* XANTHIN]

xan·thic (zan′thik), *adj.* **1.** of or pertaining to a yellow or yellowish color. **2.** *Bot.* yellow. **3.** *Chem.* of or derived from xanthine or xanthic acid. [< F *xanthique*]

xan′thic ac′id, *Chem.* an unstable organic acid with the type formula ROCSSH where R is a group.

xan·thin (zan′thin), *n.* **1.** the part of the coloring matter in yellow flowers that is insoluble. Cf. **xanthein. 2.** a yellow coloring matter in madder. [< F *xanthine,* or < G *Xanthin*]

xan·thine (zan′thēn, -thin), *n. Biochem., Chem.* **1.** a crystalline nitrogenous compound, $C_5H_4N_4O_2$, related to uric acid, found in urine, blood, and certain animal and vegetable tissues. **2.** any derivative of this compound. [< F]

Xan·thip·pe (zan tip′ē), *n.* **1.** fl. late 5th century B.C., wife of Socrates. **2.** a shrewish, ill-tempered woman. Also, **Xan·tip′pe.**

xantho-, a learned borrowing from Greek meaning "yellow," used in the formation of compound words: *xanthophyll.* Also, *esp. before a vowel,* **xanth-.** [comb. form of Gk *xanthós*]

xan·tho·chroid (zan′thə kroid′), *Ethnol.* —*adj.* **1.** belonging to or pertaining to the light-complexioned or light-haired peoples of the Caucasian race. —*n.* **2.** a person having xanthochroid characteristics. [NL *xanthochr(oi)* pale yellow ones < Gk *xanth-* XANTH- + *ōchroí* (pl. of *ōchrós* pale) + -OID]

xan·tho·phyll (zan′thə fil), *n. Biochem.* lutein (def. 1). Also, **xan′tho·phyl.** [< F *xanthophylle*] —**xan′tho·phyll′ous,** *adj.*

xan·thous (zan′thəs), *adj.* **1.** yellow. **2.** yellowish.

Xan·thus (zan′thəs), *n.* an ancient city of Lycia, in SW Asia Minor, near the mouth of the Xanthus River.

Xa·vi·er (zā′vē ər, zav′ē-, zā′vyər), *n.* **Saint Francis** (*Francisco Javier*) ("*the Apostle of the Indies*"), 1506–52, Spanish Jesuit missionary, esp. in India and Japan.

x-ax·is (eks′ak′sis), *n., pl.* **x-ax·es** (eks′ak′sēz). *Math.* **1.** (in a plane Cartesian coordinate system) the axis, usually horizontal, along which the abscissa is measured and from which the ordinate is measured. **2.** (in a three-dimensional Cartesian coordinate system) the axis along which values of *x* are measured and at which both *y* and *z* equal zero.

X chromosome, *Biol.* a sex chromosome carrying genes that produce female characteristics in humans and most other mammals and that usually occurs in pairs in a female and singly in males. Cf. **Y chromosome.**

xd, *Stock Exchange.* without dividends. Also, **xdiv.**

Xe, *Chem.* xenon.

xe·bec (zē′bek), *n.* a small three-masted vessel of the Mediterranean, formerly much used by corsairs, now employed to some extent in commerce. Also, **zebec, zebeck.** [< Catalan *xabec* or Sp *xabeque* (now *jabeque*), both < Ar *shabbāk;* first *e* < var. *chebec* < F]

Xebec

xe·ni·a (zē′nē ə), *n. Bot.* the influence or effect of the pollen on structures other than the embryo, as the seed or fruit. [< NL < Gk *xenía.* See XEN-, -IA] —**xe′ni·al,** *adj.*

Xe·ni·a (zē′nē ə, zēn′yə), *n.* a city in W Ohio. 25,373 (1970).

xeno-, a learned borrowing from Greek meaning "alien," "strange," "guest," used in the formation of compound words: *xenolith.* Also, *esp. before a vowel,* **xen-.** [comb. form of Gk *xénos*]

Xe·noc·ra·tes (zə nok′rə tēz′), *n.* 396–314 B.C., Greek philosopher.

xen·o·gen·e·sis (zen′ə jen′i sis), *n. Biol.* **1.** the supposed generation of offspring completely and permanently different from the parent. **2.** heterogenesis (def. 1). Also, **xe·nog·e·ny** (zə noj′ə nē). —**xen·o·ge·net·ic** (zen′ō jə net′ik), **xen′o·gen′ic,** *adj.*

xen·o·lith (zen′ᵊlith), *n. Petrog.* a rock fragment foreign to the igneous rock in which it is embedded. —**xen′o·lith′ic,** *adj.*

xen·o·mor·phic (zen′ə môr′fik), *adj. Petrog.* noting or pertaining to a mineral constituent of a rock whose crystalline form is forced upon it by other constituents of the rock. —**xen′o·mor′phi·cal·ly,** *adv.*

xe·non (zē′non, zen′on), *n. Chem.* a chemically inactive gaseous element present in the atmosphere in the proportion of one volume in 170,000,000 volumes of air: used for filling luminescent and electron tubes. *Symbol:* Xe; *at. wt.:* 131.30; *at. no.:* 54; *weight of one liter of the gas at 0°C and at 760 mm pressure:* 5.887 g. [< Gk, neut. of *xénos* strange]

Xe·noph·a·nes (zə nof′ə nēz′), *n.* c570–c480 B.C., Greek philosopher and poet. —**Xe·noph′a·ne′an,** *adj.*

xen·o·phobe (zen′ə fōb′), *n.* a person who fears or hates foreigners, foreign customs, or the like.

xen·o·pho·bi·a (zen′ə fō′bē ə), *n.* an unreasonable fear or hatred of foreigners or strangers or of that which is foreign or strange. —**xen′o·pho′bic,** *adj.*

Xen·o·phon (zen′ə fən, -fon′), *n.* 434?–355? B.C., Greek historian and essayist.

xe·rarch (zēr′ärk), *adj. Ecol.* (of a sere) originating in a dry habitat.

Xe·res (*Sp.* he′res, *older* she′res), *n.* former name of **Jerez.**

xe·ric (zēr′ik), *adj.* of, pertaining to, or adapted to a dry environment. —**xe′ri·cal·ly,** *adv.*

xero-, a learned borrowing from Greek meaning "dry," used in the formation of compound words: *xerophyte.* Also, *esp. before a vowel,* **xer-.** [comb. form of Gk *xērós*]

xe·rog·ra·phy (zi rog′rə fē), *n.* a copying process in which areas on a sheet of plain paper corresponding to those on the original that are to be reproduced are sensitized by static electricity and then sprinkled with colored resin that adheres and is fused permanently to the paper. —**xe·ro·graph·ic** (zēr′ə graf′ik), *adj.* —**xe′ro·graph′i·cal·ly,** *adv.*

xe·roph·i·lous (zi rof′ə ləs), *adj.* **1.** *Bot.* growing in or adapted to dry, esp. dry and hot, regions. **2.** *Zool.* living in dry situations. —**xe·roph′i·ly,** *n.*

xe·roph·thal·mi·a (zēr′of thal′mē ə), *n. Ophthalm.* abnormal dryness of the eyeball characterized by conjunctivitis, caused by a deficiency of tears and attributed to a lack of vitamin A. —**xe′roph·thal′mic,** *adj.*

xe·ro·phyte (zēr′ə fīt′), *n.* a plant adapted for growth under dry conditions. —**xe·ro·phyt·ic** (zēr′ə fit′ik), *adj.* —**xe′ro·phyt′i·cal·ly,** *adv.* —**xe·ro·phyt·ism** (zēr′ə fī′tiz əm, -fī tiz′-), *n.*

Xer·ox (zēr′oks), *n.* **1.** *Trademark.* a process for reproducing printed, written, or pictorial matter by xerography. —*v.t., v.i.* **2.** (*l.c.*) to print or reproduce by xerography.

Xerx·es I (zûrk′sēz), 519?–465 B.C., king of Persia 486?–465 (son of Darius I).

xi (zī, sī; *Gk* ksē), *n., pl.* **xis.** the 14th letter of the Greek alphabet (Ξ, ξ).

Xi·me·nes (hē me′neth), *n.* See **Jiménez de Cisneros.**

x in, *Stock Exchange.* without interest. Also, **x in., x-i., x.i., xint, x-int., x. int.**

Xin·gú (shing gōō′), *n.* a river flowing N through central Brazil to the Amazon. 1300 mi. long.

-xion, *Chiefly Brit.* var. of **-tion:** *connexion; inflexion.*

Xi′ par′ticle, *Physics.* hyperon.

xiph·i·ster·num (zif′i stûr′nəm), *n., pl.* **-na** (-nə). *Anat.* the lowermost of the three segments of the sternum. Cf. **gladiolus** (def. 2), **manubrium** (def. 2a). [< NL *xiphi-* (comb. form of Gk *xíphos* sword) + STERNUM] —**xiph′i·ster′nal,** *adj.*

xiph·oid (zif′oid), *adj.* **1.** *Anat., Zool.* sword-shaped; ensiform. —*n.* **2.** the xiphisternum. [< NL *xiphoīd(ēs)* < Gk *xiphoeidḗs* swordlike = *xipho(s)* sword + *-eidēs* -OID]

xiph·o·su·ran (zif′ə sŏŏr′ən), *adj.* **1.** belonging or pertaining to the order *Xiphosura,* comprising the horseshoe crabs. —*n.* **2.** an arthropod of the order *Xiphosura;* a horseshoe crab. [< NL *xiphosūr(a)* (< Gk *xíphos* sword + *ourá* tail) + -AN]

XL, extra large.

Xmas, Christmas.

Xn., Christian.

Xnty., Christianity.

XP (kī′rō′, kē′rō′), *n.* the Christian monogram made from the first two letters of the Greek word for Christ. [< Gk XP(IΣTOΣ) CHRIST]

xr, *Stock Exchange.* without rights. Also, **x rts**

x-ray (eks′rā′), *n.* Also, **x ray. 1.** Often, **x-rays.** a form of electromagnetic radiation, similar to light but of shorter wavelength and capable of penetrating solids and of ionizing gases. **2.** a radiograph made by x-rays. **3.** a word in communications to represent the letter *X*. **—*v.t.* 4.** to examine or treat by means of x-rays. **—*adj.* 5.** of or pertaining to x-rays. Also, **X′-ray′.** [trans. of G *X-strahl*]

x′-ray tube′, an electronic tube for producing x-rays, essentially a cathode-ray tube in which a metal target is bombarded with high-energy electrons.

Xt., Christ.

Xtian., Christian.

Xty., Christianity.

x-u·nit (eks′yo͞o′nit), *n.* a unit used to express the wavelength of x-rays or gamma rays, equal to approximately 10^{-11} centimeter or 10^{-3} angstrom. *Abbr.:* Xu, XU

Xu·thus (zo͞o′thəs), *n.* *Class. Myth.* a son of Hellen and the husband of Creusa.

xw, *Stock Exchange.* without warrant.

xyl-, var. of **xylo-** before a vowel: *xylene.*

xy·lan (zī′lan), *n.* *Chem.* the pentosan occurring in woody tissue that hydrolyzes to xylose: used as the source of furfural.

xy·lem (zī′ləm, -lem), *n.* *Bot.* the part of a vascular bundle consisting of tracheids, vessels, parenchyma cells, and fibers, and forming the woody tissue of a plant. [XYL- + *-em* -EME]

xy·lene (zī′lēn), *n.* *Chem.* any of three flammable, toxic, isomeric liquids having the formula $C_6H_4(CH_3)_2$, used chiefly in the manufacture of dyes. Also, **xylol.**

xy·li·dine (zī′li dēn′, -din, zil′i-), *n.* **1.** any of six isomeric compounds that have the formula $(CH_3)_2C_6H_3NH_2$, derivatives of xylene, used in dye manufacture. **2.** an oily liquid consisting of a mixture of certain of these compounds, used commercially in making dyes. [XYL- + -ID[2] + -INE[2]]

xylo-, a learned borrowing from Greek meaning "wood," used in the formation of compound words: *xylotomy.* Also, *esp. before a vowel,* **xyl-.** [comb. form of Gk *xýlon*]

xy·lo·graph (zī′lə graf′, -gräf′), *n.* an engraving on wood.

xy·log·ra·phy (zī log′rə fē), *n.* the art of engraving on wood or of printing from such engravings. [< F *xylographie*] **—xy·log′ra·pher,** *n.* **—xy·lo·graph·ic** (zī′lə graf′ik), **xy′lo·graph′i·cal,** *adj.*

xy·loid (zī′loid), *adj.* resembling wood; ligneous.

xy·lol (zī′lōl, -lol), *n.* xylene.

xy·loph·a·gous (zī lof′ə gəs), *adj.* **1.** feeding on wood, as the larvae of certain insects. **2.** perforating or destroying timber, as certain mollusks, crustaceans, and fungi. [< Gk *xylophágos*]

xy·lo·phone (zī′lə fōn′), *n.* a musical instrument consisting of a graduated series of wooden bars, usually sounded by striking with small wooden hammers. **—xy·lo·phon·ic** (zī′lə fon′ik), *adj.* **—xy·lo·phon·ist** (zī′lə fō′nist, zī lof′ə-nist, zi-), *n.*

xy·lose (zī′lōs), *n.* *Chem.* a crystalline aldopentose, $C_5H_{10}O_5$.

xy·lot·o·mous (zī lot′ə məs), *adj.* boring into or cutting wood, as certain insects.

xy·lot·o·my (zī lot′ə mē), *n.* the art of cutting sections of wood, as with a microtome, for microscopic examination. **—xy·lot′o·mist,** *n.*

xys·ter (zis′tər), *n.* a surgical instrument for scraping bones. [< NL < Gk: scraping tool = *xys-* (s. of *xýein* to scrape) + *-tēr* instrument or agent n. suffix]

Xys·tus I (zis′təs). See **Sixtus I.**

Xystus II. See **Sixtus II.**

Xystus III. See **Sixtus III.**

Y

DEVELOPMENT OF MAJUSCULE						
NORTH SEMITIC	GREEK	ETR.	LATIN	MODERN		
				GOTHIC	ITALIC	ROMAN
SEE LETTER U			Y	𝔜	*Y*	Y

DEVELOPMENT OF MINUSCULE					
ROMAN CURSIVE	ROMAN UNCIAL	CAROL. MIN.	MODERN		
			GOTHIC	ITALIC	ROMAN
y	y	—	𝔶	*y*	y

The twenty-fifth letter of the English alphabet, as a consonant, developed from North Semitic *yodh,* whence it was adopted into Greek as a vowel (*iota*) and became English I. (See **I.**) The Y-form goes back to Greek Y, a variant of North Semitic *waw.* (See **U, V, W.**) After the conquest of Greece by the Romans in the 1st century B.C., it was used in Latin for transliterating the Greek Y-sound (as in French *pure,* German *über*) in such words as *zephyros.*

Y, y (wī), *n., pl.* **Y's** or **Ys, y's** or **ys. 1.** the 25th letter of the English alphabet, a semivowel. **2.** any spoken sound represented by the letter *Y* or *y,* as in *yet, city,* or *rhythm.* **3.** something having the shape of a Y, as a roof or a highway intersection; wye. **4.** a written or printed representation of the letter *Y* or *y.* **5.** a device, as a printer's type, for reproducing the letter *Y* or *y.*

Y, (in Japan) yen; yen.

Y, 1. the 25th in order or in a series, or, when *I* is omitted, the 24th. **2.** *Elect.* admittance. **3.** *Chem.* yttrium.

y, *Math.* **1.** a symbol frequently used to indicate an unknown quantity. **2.** *Math.* (in Cartesian coordinates) the *y*-axis.

y-, an inflective prefix occurring in certain obsolete words (*ywis*) and esp. in archaic past participles: *yclad.* [ME *y-, i-,* OE *ge-* prefix of uncertain meaning, sometimes of perfective or intensifying force; c. OFris, OS *ge-, gi-,* Goth *ga-,* G *ge-,* perh. L *com-* together]

-y¹, a native English suffix of adjectives meaning "characterized by or inclined to" the substance or action of the word or stem to which the suffix is attached: *juicy; grouchy.* Also, **-ey.** [OE *-ig;* c. G *-ig,* perh. L *-ic(us),* Gk *-ik(os)*]

-y², a hypocoristic suffix common in names: *pussy; Billy; Whitey.* Also, **-ey, -ie.** [ME; often through Scot influence]

-y³, a suffix of various origins used in the formation of action nouns from verbs (*inquiry*), also found in other abstract nouns: *carpentry; infamy.* [repr. L *-ia, -ium;* Gk *-ia, -eia, -ion;* F *-ie;* G *-ie*]

Y., 1. Young Men's Christian Association. **2.** Young Men's Hebrew Association. **3.** Young Women's Christian Association. **4.** Young Women's Hebrew Association.

y., 1. yard; yards. **2.** year; years.

ya (yə), *pron. Eye Dialect.* **1.** you: *Hey, ya dope!* **2.** your: *Ya father's moustache!*

yab·ber (yab′ər), *n. Australian.* jabber. [< native Austral *yabba* language, akin to *ya* to speak]

Ya·blo·noi′ Moun′tains (yä′blo noi′), a mountain range in the SE Soviet Union in Asia, E of Lake Baikal. Also called **Ya·blo·no·voi** (yä′blo no voi′).

yacht (yot), *n.* **1.** a vessel used for private cruising, racing, or other noncommercial purposes. **—***v.i.* **2.** to sail, voyage, or race in a yacht. [var. of *yaught* < earlier D *jaght* (short for *jaghtschip* ship for chasing) = *jag(en)* (to) chase (c. G *jagen* to hunt) + *-t* n. suffix]

yacht·ing (yot′ing), *n.* the practice or sport of sailing or voyaging in a yacht.

yachts·man (yots′mən), *n., pl.* **-men.** a person, esp. a man, who owns or sails a yacht. **—yachts′man·ship′, yacht′man·ship′,** *n.*

yachts·wom·an (yots′wŏŏm′ən), *n., pl.* **-wom·en.** a woman who owns or sails a yacht, or who is devoted to yachting.

yack·e·ty-yak (yak′i tē yak′), *n., v.,* **-yakked, -yak·king.** *Slang.* **—***n.* **1.** uninterrupted, often idle or gossipy, talk. **—***v.i.* **2.** to talk, esp. pointlessly and uninterruptedly. Also, **yack′ety-yack′, yakety-yak, yakity-yak.** Also called **yak.** [? imit.]

Yad·kin (yad′kin), *n.* a part of the Pee Dee River that flows SE through central North Carolina.

Ya·fo (yä fô′), *n.* Jaffa.

Ya′gi anten′na (yä′gē, yag′ē), *Radio.* a sharply directional antenna array, consisting of one or two dipoles connected to the transmitting or receiving circuit and several insulated dipoles all parallel and about equally spaced in a line: used chiefly to improve television reception in outlying areas. [named after Hidetsugu *Yagi* (b. 1886), Japanese electrical engineer]

yah (yä, yâ), *interj.* (an exclamation of impatience or derision.)

Ya·ha·ta (yä′hä tä′), *n.* Yawata.

Ya·hoo (yä′hōō, yā′-, yä hōō′), *n., pl.* **-hoos. 1.** (in Swift's novel *Gulliver's Travels,* 1726) one of a race of manlike brutes, ruled by the Houyhnhnms. **2.** (*l.c.*) a coarse, uncouth person. [name coined by Swift] **—ya′hoo·ism,** *n.*

Yahr·zeit (yôr′tsīt), *n. Judaism.* the anniversary of the death of a parent or other close relative, observed by lighting a memorial light and reciting the *Kaddish* at specified times. Also, **Jahrzeit.** [< Yiddish, special use of MHG *jārzīt* anniversary (lit., year time). See YEAR, TIDE¹]

Yah·weh (yä′we), *n.* a name of God, transliterated by scholars from the Tetragrammaton and commonly rendered Jehovah. Also, **Yah′we, Yah·veh, Yah·ve** (yä′ve), **Jahveh, Jahve, Jahweh, Jahwe.** [modern rendering of YHVH; the vowels supplied are conjectural and not attested in Heb]

Yah·wism (yä′wiz əm), *n.* the worship of Yahweh or the religious system based on such worship. Also, **Yah·vism** (yä′viz əm), **Jahwism, Jahvism.**

Yah·wist (yä′wist), *n.* the writer of the earliest major source of the Hexateuch, in which God is characteristically referred to as Yahweh rather than Elohim. Also, **Yah·vist** (yä′vist), **Jahvist, Jahwist.** Cf. **Elohist. —Yah·wis′tic, Yah·vis·tic** (yä vis′tik), *adj.*

Yaj·ur-Ve·da (yuj′ŏŏr vā′də, -vē′-), *n. Hinduism.* a Samhita, containing a collection of sacrificial formulas. Cf. **Veda.** [< Skt *yajur* sacred, holy (c. HAGIO-) + *veda* VEDA]

yak¹ (yak), *n.* **1.** a stocky, shaggy-haired wild ox, *Poephagus grunniens,* of the Tibetan highlands. **2.** a domesticated variety of this animal. [< Tibetan *gyag*]

Yak¹,
Poephagus grunniens
(6 ft. high at shoulder; total length to 14 ft.; tail 3 ft.)

yak² (yak), *n., v.i.,* **yakked, yak·king.** *Slang.* yackety-yak. [prob. imit.]

yak·e·ty-yak (yak′i tē-yak′), *n., v.i.,* **-yakked, -yak·king.** yackety-yak. Also, **yak′ity-yak′.**

Yak·i·ma (yak′ə mə), *n.* a city in S Washington. 45,588 (1970).

ya·ki·to·ri (yä kē′tôr′′ē, -tôr′-), *n.* a Japanese dish of barbecued chicken, usually skewered and boneless. [< Jap = *yaki* broiled + *tori* chicken]

Ya·kut (yä kŏŏt′), *n.* a Turkic language of northeastern Siberia.

Yakut′ Auton′omous So′viet So′cialist Repub′lic, an administrative division of the RSFSR, in the NE Soviet Union in Asia. 631,000 (est. 1966). 1,170,200 sq. mi. *Cap.:* Yakutsk.

Ya·kutsk (yä kutsk′), *n.* a city in the NE Soviet Union in Asia, on the Lena River. 92,000 (est. 1966).

Yale (yāl), *n.* **El·i·hu** (el′ə hyōō′), 1648–1721, English colonial official, born in America: principal benefactor of Yale University.

Yal·ta (yôl′tə; *Russ.* yäl′tä), *n.* a seaport in the S Ukraine, in the SW Soviet Union in Europe, on the Black Sea: wartime conference of Roosevelt, Churchill, and Stalin February 4–12, 1945. 47,100 (1959).

Ya·lu (yä′lōō′; *Chin.* yä′lʏ′), *n.* a river in E Asia, forming part of the boundary between China and North Korea and flowing SW to the Yellow Sea. 300 mi. long.

yam (yam), *n.* **1.** the starchy, tuberous root of any of various climbing vines of the genus *Dioscorea,* cultivated for food in tropical regions. **2.** any of these plants. **3.** *Southern U.S.* the sweet potato. [prob. < Pg *inhame* or Sp *(i)ñame* << WAfr; akin to Senegal *nyami* to eat]

Ya·ma·mo·to (yä′mä mô′tô), *n.* **I·so·ro·ku** (ē′sô rô′kŏŏ), 1884–1943, Japanese admiral.

Ya·ma·shi·ta (yä′mä shē′tä), *n.* **To·mo·yu·ki** (tô′mô yōō′-kē), ("*the Tiger of Malaya*"), 1885–1946, Japanese general.

ya·men (yä′mən), *n.* (in the Chinese Empire) the residence or office of a public official. [var. of *yamun* < Chin *ya* office + *mên* gate]

yam·mer (yam′ər), *Informal.* **—***v.i.* **1.** to whine or complain. **2.** to talk loudly and persistently. **—***v.t.* **3.** to utter clamorously or complainingly. **—***n.* **4.** the act or noise of yammering. [late ME *yamur, yamer* < MD *jammer(en);* r. ME *yomer,* OE *geōmr(ian)* (to) complain < *geōmor* sad; akin to G *Jammer* lamentation] **—yam′mer·er,** *n.*

Yang (yäng, yang), *n.* See under **Yin and Yang.**

Yang·kü (*Chin.* yäng′kʏ′), *n.* former name of **Taiyüan.**

Yang·tze (yang′sē; *Chin.* yäng′tse′), *n.* a river in E Asia, flowing from the Tibetan plateau through central China to the East China Sea. ab. 3200 mi. long. Also called **Yang·tze-Kiang** (yang′sē kyang′; *Chin.* yäng′tse′gyäng′).

yank (yangk), *v.t., v.i.* **1.** to pull or remove abruptly and vigorously. **—***n.* **2.** an abrupt, vigorous pull; jerk. [?]

Yank (yangk), *n., adj. Slang.* Yankee. [shortened form]

Yan·kee (yang′kē), *n.* **1.** a native or inhabitant of New England. **2.** a native or inhabitant of a northern U.S. state, esp. of one of the states siding with the Union in the American Civil War. **3.** a native or inhabitant of the United States. **4.** a word used in communications to represent the letter *Y.* **—***adj.* **5.** of, pertaining to, or characteristic of a Yankee or Yankees: *Yankee ingenuity.* [? back formation from D *Jan Kees* John Cheese, nickname (mistaken for plural) applied by the Dutch of colonial New York to English settlers in Connecticut]

Yan·kee·dom (yang′kē dəm), *n.* **1.** the region inhabited by Yankees. **2.** Yankees collectively.

Yan·kee·ism (yang′kē iz′əm), *n.* **1.** Yankee character or characteristics. **2.** a Yankee peculiarity, as of speech.

yan·qui (yäng′kē), *n., pl.* **-quis** (-kēs). (*often cap.*) *Spanish.* (in Latin America) Yankee; a U.S. citizen.

Yao (you), *n.* a legendary emperor of China who, with his successor **(Shun),** was a paragon of good government.

Ya·oun·dé (*Fr.* ya ōōn dā′), *n.* a city in and the capital of Cameroon, in the SW part. 180,000. Also, **Yaunde.**

yap (yap), *v.,* **yapped, yap·ping,** *n.* **—***v.i.* **1.** to bark shrilly; yelp. **—***n.* **2.** a shrill bark; yelp. **3.** *Slang.* the mouth. [imit.] **—yap′per,** *n.* **—yap′ping·ly,** *adv.*

Yap (yăp, yap), *n.* one of the Caroline Islands, in the W Pacific: U.S. cable station. 7625 including adjacent islands (1970); 83 sq. mi.

ya·pon (yô′pon), *n.* yaupon.

Ya·pu·rá (*Sp.* yä′po͞o rä′), *n.* Japurá.

Ya·qui (yä′kē), *n., pl.* **-quis,** (*esp. collectively*) **-qui** for 1. **1.** a member of a Pima Indian people of Sonora, Mexico. **2.** the language of the Yaqui Indians. **3.** a river in NW Mexico, flowing into the Gulf of California. 420 mi. long.

yar (yâr), *n.* yare (defs. 1, 2).

Yar·bor·ough (yär′bûr′ō, -bur′ō *or, esp. Brit.,* -bər ə), *n. Whist, Bridge.* a hand in which none of the cards is higher than a nine. [named after the 2nd Earl of *Yarborough* (d. 1897), said to have bet 1000 to 1 against its occurrence]

yard[1] (yärd), *n.* **1.** a common unit of linear measure in English-speaking countries, equal to 3 feet or 36 inches, and equivalent to 0.9144 meter. **2.** *Naut.* a long spar, supported more or less at its center, to which the head of a square sail, lateen sail, or lugsail is bent. [ME *yerd(e),* OE (Anglian) *gerd;* c. D *gard,* G *Gerte* rod]

yard[2] (yärd), *n.* **1.** an area, usually planted with grass, adjacent to a house. **2.** a partially or wholly paved open area adjacent to or enclosed by a building or buildings. **3.** a relatively open area containing various structures and used for work or storage purposes (often used in combination): *brickyard; railroad yard.* **4.** a pen or other enclosure for livestock. **5.** the winter pasture of moose and deer. **6. the Yard,** *Brit. Informal.* See **Scotland Yard.** —*v.t.* **7.** to put into or enclose in a yard. [ME *yerd,* OE *geard* enclosure; c. D *gaard* garden, Icel *garthr* yard, Goth *gards* house (OSlav *grad,* Russ *gorod* town, prob. < Gmc), L *hortus* garden, OIr *gort* field; akin to GARDEN]

yard·age[1] (yär′dij), *n.* measurement, or the amount measured in yards. [YARD[1] + -AGE]

yard·age[2] (yär′dij), *n.* **1.** the use of a yard or enclosure, as in loading or unloading cattle or other livestock at a railroad station. **2.** the charge for such use. [YARD[2] + -AGE]

yard·arm (yärd′ärm′), *n. Naut.* either of the outer portions of the yard of a square sail.

yard·bird (yärd′bûrd′), *n. Slang.* **1.** an army recruit or inductee, esp. one assigned to menial tasks at a training center. **2.** a convict.

yard′ goods′. See **piece goods.**

yard′ grass′, a coarse annual grass, *Eleusine indica,* of the Old World, common in dooryards and fields.

yard·man (yärd′mən), *n., pl.* **-men.** a man who works in a railroad yard, shipyard, or the like.

yard·mas·ter (yärd′mas′tər, -mä′stər), *n.* a person who superintends all or part of a railroad yard.

yard·stick (yärd′stik′), *n.* **1.** a measuring stick a yard long. **2.** any standard of measurement or judgment: *Test scores are not the only yardstick of academic achievement.*

yare (yâr *or, esp. for 1, 2,* yär), *adj.,* **yar·er, yar·est. 1.** quick; agile; lively. **2.** (of a ship) quick to the helm; easily handled or maneuvered. **3.** *Archaic.* **a.** ready; prepared. **b.** nimble; quick. Also, **yar** (for defs. 1, 2). [ME; OE *gearu, gearo* = *ge-* Y- + *earu* ready; c. D *gaar,* G *gar* done, dressed (as meat)] —**yare′ly,** *adv.*

Yar·kand (yär′kand′), *n.* Soche.

Yar·mouth (yär′məth), *n.* **1.** a seaport in SW Nova Scotia, in SE Canada: summer resort. 8636 (1961). **2. Great.** See **Great Yarmouth.**

Yar·muk (yär mo͞ok′), *n.* a river in NW Jordan, flowing W into the Jordan River. 50 mi. long.

yar·mul·ke (yär′məl kə, yä′məl-), *n. Judaism.* a man's skullcap, worn esp. during prayer and religious study. Also, **yar′mel·ke.** [< Yiddish << Turk *yağmurluk* raincoat]

yarn (yärn), *n.* **1.** thread made of natural or synthetic fibers and used for knitting or weaving. **2.** a continuous strand or thread made from glass, metal, plastic, etc. **3.** the thread, in the form of a loosely twisted aggregate of fibers, as of hemp, of which rope is made. **4.** *Informal.* a tale, esp. a long story of adventure or incredible happenings. —*v.i.* **5.** *Informal.* to spin a yarn; tell stories. [ME; OE *gearn;* c. G *Garn;* akin to Icel *görn* gut, Gk *chordē* intestine, chord, Lith *žarnà* entrails, L *hernia* a rupture, Skt *hirā* vein]

yarn-dyed (yärn′dīd′), *adj.* (of fabrics) woven from yarns previously dyed (opposed to *piece-dyed*).

Ya·ro·slavl (yä ro släv′lᵊ), *n.* a city in the W RSFSR, in the central Soviet Union in Europe, on the Volga. 467,000 (est. 1964).

yar·row (yar′ō), *n.* **1.** an asteraceous plant, *Achillea millefolium,* of Europe and America, having finely divided leaves and whitish flowers, sometimes used in medicine as a tonic and astringent. **2.** any of various other plants of the genus *Achillea.* [ME *yar(o)we,* OE *gearwe;* c. G *Garbe* sheaf]

yash·mak (yäsh mäk′, yash′mak), *n.* the veil worn by Muslim women in public. Also, **yash·mac′.** [< Turk *yaşmak*]

Yas·sy (yä′sē), *n.* Jassy.

yat·a·ghan (yat′ə gan′, -gən; *Turk.* yä′tä gän′), *n.* a Turkish saber having a doubly curved blade, concave toward the hilt, and a hilt with a prominent pommel and no guard. Also, **ataghan, yat′a·gan′.** [< Turk *yātāghan*]

yauld (yôd, yôld, yäd, yäld), *adj. Scot. and North Eng.* active; vigorous. [?]

Yaun·de (youn′dā), *n.* Yaoundé.

yaup (yôp, yäp), *v.i., n.* yawp. —**yaup′er,** *n.*

yau·pon (yô′pən), *n.* a holly shrub or small tree, *Ilex vomitoria,* of the southern U.S., having leaves that are sometimes used as a substitute for tea. Also, **yapon.** [< Catawba *yopun* = *yop* shrub, bush, tree + *-un* dim. suffix]

yaw (yô), *v.i.* **1.** to deviate temporarily from a straight course, as a vessel. **2.** (of an aircraft) to have a motion about its vertical axis. **3.** (of a rocket or guided missile) to deviate from a stable flight attitude by oscillation of the longitudinal axis in the horizontal plane. —*v.t.* **4.** to cause to yaw. —*n.* **5.** the movement of yawing. [?]

Ya·wa·ta (yä′wä tä′), *n.* a former city, now part of Kitakyushu, on N Kyushu, in SW Japan: steel industry. Also, **Yahata.**

yawl[1] (yôl), *n.* **1.** a ship's small boat, manned by four or six oarsmen. **2.** a two-masted, fore-and-aft-rigged sailing vessel having a large mainmast and a smaller jiggermast or mizzenmast stepped abaft the sternpost. Cf. **ketch.** [< D *jol* kind of boat < ?]

Yawl[1] (def. 2)

yawl[2] (yôl), *n., v.i., v.t. Brit. Dial.* yowl; howl. [akin to YOWL]

yawn (yôn), *v.i.* **1.** to open the mouth involuntarily with a prolonged, deep inhalation of air, as from drowsiness or weariness. **2.** to extend or stretch wide, as an open and deep space or a widely gaping aperture. —*n.* **3.** the act of yawning. **4.** an opening; open space; chasm. [ME *yane(n), yone(n),* OE *geonian;* akin to OE *gānian, gīnan,* Icel *gīna,* G *gähnen,* L *hiāre* to gape] —**yawn′er,** *n.* —**Syn. 1.** gape.

yawp (yôp, yäp), *v.i.* **1.** *Informal.* to utter a loud, harsh cry; yelp, squawk, or bawl. **2.** *Slang.* to talk noisily and foolishly. —*n.* **3.** *Informal.* a harsh cry. **4.** raucous or querulous speech. Also, **yaup.** [ME *yolp(en);* akin to YELP] —**yawp′er,** *n.*

yaws (yôz), *n.* (*construed as sing.*) *Pathol.* a disease occurring in certain tropical regions, caused by the organism *Treponema pertenue,* and characterized by an eruption of raspberrylike excrescences on the skin. Also called **frambesia, pian.** [< Carib dial.]

y-ax·is (wī′ak′sis), *n., pl.* **y-ax·es** (wī′ak′sēz). *Math.* **1.** (in a plane Cartesian coordinate system) the axis, usually vertical, along which the ordinate is measured and from which the abscissa is measured. **2.** (in a three-dimensional Cartesian coordinate system) the axis along which values of *y* are measured and at which both *x* and *z* equal zero.

Yaz·oo (yaz′o͞o), *n.* a river flowing SW from N Mississippi into the Mississippi River at Vicksburg. 188 mi. long.

Yb, *Chem.* ytterbium.

Y chromosome, *Biol.* a sex chromosome carrying genes that produce male characteristics in humans and most mammals and that occurs singly and only in males. Cf. **X chromosome.**

y·clept (ē klept′), *v.* a pp. of **clepe.** Also, **y·cleped′.** [ME *ycleped,* OE *geclypod,* ptp. of *clypian, cleopian,* to CLEPE]

yd., yard; yards.

yds., yards.

ye[1] (yē), *pron. Archaic, Literary, or Brit. Dial.* **1.** (used nominatively as the plural of **thou**): *O ye of little faith; ye brooks and hills.* **2.** (used nominatively for the second person singular.) **3.** (used objectively in the second person singular or plural.) [ME; OE *gē;* c. D *gij,* G *ihr,* Icel *ēr,* Goth *jus*]

ye[2] (t͟hē; *spelling pron.* yē), *definite article. Archaic.* the[1].

yea (yā), *adv.* **1.** yes (used in affirmation or assent). **2.** *Archaic.* **a.** indeed: *Yea, and he did come.* **b.** not only this but even: *a good, yea, a noble man.* —*n.* **3.** an affirmative reply or vote; affirmation. **4.** a person who votes in the affirmative: *The yeas outnumbered those who voted against the bill.* [ME *ye, ya,* OE *gēa;* c. D, G, Icel, Goth *ja*]

yeah (yâ), *adv. Informal.* yes. [var. of YEA or YES]

yean (yēn), *v.i.* (of a sheep or goat) to bring forth young. [ME *yene(n),* OE *geēanian* to bring forth young; akin to EWE]

yean·ling (yēn′ling), *n.* **1.** the young of a sheep or a goat; a lamb or a kid. —*adj.* **2.** just born; infant.

year (yēr), *n.* **1.** a period of 365 or 366 days, now commonly divided into 12 calendar months and reckoned as beginning Jan. 1 and ending Dec. 31 **(calendar year).** Cf. **common year, leap year. 2.** a period of approximately this length: *It happened five years ago.* **3.** *Astron.* **a.** Also called **lunar year.** a division of time equal to 12 lunar months. **b.** Also called **astronomical year, equinoctial year, solar year, tropical year.** a division of time equal to the interval between one vernal equinox and the next. **c.** Also called **sidereal year.** a division of time representing the time required for the earth to complete one revolution around the sun, measured with relation to the fixed stars. **4.** the time in which any planet completes a revolution around the sun: *the Martian year.* **5.** a period out of every 12 months devoted to a certain pursuit, activity, or the like: *the academic year.* **6. years, a.** age. **b.** old age: *a man of years.* **7. year in and year out,** regularly through the years; continually. Also, **year in, year out.** [ME *yeer,* OE *gēar;* c. D *jaar,* G *Jahr,* Icel *ār,* Goth *jēr,* Gk *hôros* a year, *hôra* a season of the year, part of a day, hour]

year-a·round (yēr′ə round′), *adj.* year-round.

year·book (yēr′bo͝ok′), *n.* **1.** a book published annually, containing information about the past year. **2.** a book published by the graduating class of a high school or college, containing photographs of class members and commemorating school activities, studies, etc.

year-end (yēr′end′), *n.* **1.** the end of a calendar year. —*adj.* **2.** taking place or done at the year-end.

year·ling (yēr′ling), *n.* **1.** an animal in its second year. **2.** a horse one year old, dating from January 1 of the year after the year of foaling. —*adj.* **3.** being a year old. **4.** of a year's duration or standing. [late ME; c. G *Jährling*]

year·long (yēr′lông′, -long′), *adj.* lasting for a year.

year·ly (yēr′lē), *adj., adv., n., pl.* **-lies.** —*adj.* **1.** pertaining to a year or to each year. **2.** occurring, arriving, etc., once a year or each year. —*adv.* **3.** once a year; annually. —*n.* **4.** a publication appearing once a year. [ME *yeerly,* OE *gēarlīc*]

yearn (yûrn), *v.i.* **1.** to have an earnest or strong desire. **2.** to feel tenderness or affection. [ME *yerne(n),* OE *giernan* < *georn* eager; akin to Icel *girna* to desire (perh. L *hortārī* to urge), OIr *(to)-gairim* I desire; Gk *chaír(ein)* to rejoice, Skt *háryati* he desires] —**yearn′er,** *n.* —**Syn. 1.** aspire.

yearn·ing (yûr′ning), *n.* deep longing, esp. when accompanied by tenderness or sadness. [ME; OE *gierninge*] —**yearn′ing·ly,** *adv.* —**Syn. 1.** See **desire.**

year′ of grace′, any year of the Christian era.

year-round (yēr′round′), *adj.* continuing, active, etc., throughout the year. Also, **year-around.**

yeast (yēst), *n.* **1.** a yellowish, somewhat viscid, semifluid froth or sediment consisting of the cells of certain minute fungi, used to induce fermentation in the manufacture of alcoholic beverages, esp. beer, as a leaven in dough, and in medicine. **2.** any minute, unicellular, ascomycetous fungus of the genus *Saccharomyces*, and related genera. **3.** spume; foam. **4.** ferment; agitation. —*v.i.* **5.** to ferment. **6.** to be covered with froth. [ME *ye(e)st*, OE *gist, gyst;* c. D *gist*, G *Gischt* yeast, foam, Icel *jöstr, jastr* yeast, Gk *zestós* boiled]

yeast′ plant′, yeast. (def. 2.)

yeast·y (yē′stē), *adj.*, **yeast·i·er, yeast·i·est. 1.** of, containing, or resembling yeast. **2.** frothy; foamy. **3.** youthful; exuberant; ebullient. —**yeast′i·ly,** *adv.* —**yeast′i·ness,** *n.*

Yeats (yāts), *n.* **William Butler,** 1865–1939, Irish poet, dramatist, and essayist: Nobel prize 1923.

Ye·do (ye′dō′), *n.* a former name of **Tokyo.** Also, **Yed′do′.**

yegg (yeg), *n. Slang.* **1.** an itinerant burglar, esp. one whose thefts are insignificant. **2.** a thug. [? var. of *yekk* beggar, a term once popular in California Chinatowns; ? the surname of an American burglar]

Yeisk (āsk), *n.* a seaport in the SW RSFSR, in the SW Soviet Union in Europe, on the Sea of Azov. 64,418. Also, **Eisk, Eysk.**

yelk (yelk), *n. Dial.* yolk.

yell (yel), *v.i.* **1.** to cry out with a strong, loud, clear sound. **2.** to scream with pain, fright, etc. —*v.t.* **3.** to utter with a yell. —*n.* **4.** a cry uttered by yelling. **5.** *U.S.* a set of words or syllables yelled as a cheer, as in a school or college. [ME *yelle(n)*, OE *gellan, giellan*] —**yell′er,** *n.*

yel·low (yel′ō), *adj.* **1.** of a bright color like that of butter, lemons, etc.; between green and orange in the spectrum. **2.** noting or pertaining to the Mongoloid race. **3.** *Often Disparaging.* having the yellowish skin of a mulatto or dark-skinned quadroon. **4.** of sallow complexion. **5.** *Informal.* cowardly. **6.** (of journalism, a newspaper, etc.) sensational, esp. morbidly or offensively so. —*n.* **7.** a hue between green and orange in the spectrum. **8.** the yolk of an egg. **9.** a yellow pigment or dye. —*v.t., v.i.* **10.** to make or become yellow. [ME *yelou*, OE *geolo, geolu*] —**yel′low·ness,** *n.*

yel′low-bellied sap′sucker, a sapsucker, *Sphyrapicus varius*, of eastern North America, having a red patch on the forehead and black and white plumage with a pale-yellow abdomen. Also called **yel′low-bellied wood′pecker.**

yel·low·bel·ly (yel′ō bel′ē), *n., pl.* **-lies.** *Slang.* a person without courage, fortitude, or nerve; coward. —**yel′low-bel′lied,** *adj.*

yel′low bile′, *Old Physiol.* a humor regarded as causing anger; choler.

yel·low·bird (yel′ō bûrd′), *n.* **1.** *Brit. Dial.* any of various yellow or golden birds, as the golden oriole of Europe. **2.** *U.S. Dial.* **a.** any of several American goldfinches. **b.** See **yellow warbler.**

yel·low·cake (yel′ō kāk′), *n.* the powdered raw material extracted from a uranium oxide and used esp. in nuclear reactors.

yel′low dai′sy, the black-eyed Susan, *Rudbeckia hirta.*

yel′low dog′, a cowardly, despicable person.

yel′low-dog′ con′tract (yel′ō dôg′, -dog′), a contract between a worker and an employer in which the worker agrees not to remain in or join a union.

Yel′low Em′peror. See **Huang Ti.**

yel′low fe′ver, *Pathol.* an acute, often fatal, infectious, febrile disease of warm climates, caused by a filterable virus transmitted by a mosquito, *Aedes aegypti*, and characterized by jaundice, vomiting, hemorrhages, etc. Also called **yellow jack.**

yel′low-fe′ver mosqui′to (yel′ō fē′vər), a mosquito, *Aedes aegypti*, that transmits yellow fever and dengue.

yel·low·ham·mer (yel′ō ham′ər), *n.* **1.** a common European bunting, *Emberiza citrinella*, the male of which is marked with bright yellow. **2.** *U.S. Dial.* the flicker, *Colaptes auratus.* [b. earlier *yellow-ham* (OE *geolu* YELLOW + *hama* covering; i.e., yellow-feathered bird) and *yelambre* (OE *geolu* + *ambre;* c. G *Ammer* bunting)]

yel′low hon′eysuckle, a spreading, twining vine, *Lonicera flava*, of the southern and eastern U.S., having leaves that are blue-green on the underside and fragrant, tubular, orange-yellow flowers.

yel·low·ish (yel′ō ish), *adj.* somewhat yellow; tending to yellow; tinged with yellow. [ME]

yel′low jack′, *pl.*, (*esp. collectively*) **jack,** (*esp. referring to two or more kinds or species*) **jacks** for 2. **1.** *Pathol.* See **yellow fever. 2.** any carangoid fish, esp. a Caribbean food fish, *Caranx bartholomaei.*

yel·low·jack·et (yel′ō jak′it), *n.* any of several social wasps of the family *Vespidae*, having a black body with bright yellow markings.

yel·low·legs (yel′ō legz′), *n.* (*construed as sing.*) either of two American shore birds having yellow legs, *Totanus melanoleucus* **(greater yellowlegs),** or *T. flavipes* **(lesser yellowlegs).**

yel′low met′al, 1. a yellow alloy of about 60 percent copper and about 40 percent zinc. **2.** gold.

yel′low pag′es, *U.S.* the classified section of a telephone directory, listing subscribers by the type of business or service they offer.

yel′low per′il, the alleged threat of the populous yellow race to the white race and Western civilization.

yel′low pine′, 1. any of several North American pines yielding a strong, yellowish wood. **2.** the wood of any such tree.

yel′low pop′lar, the tulip tree, *Liriondendron Tulipifera.*

yel′low race′, (loosely) Mongoloid peoples, esp. the Chinese.

Yel′low Riv′er. See **Hwang Ho.**

Yel′low Sea′, an arm of the Pacific N of the East China Sea, between China and Korea. Chinese, **Hwang Hai.**

yel′low spot′, *Anat.* a small, circular, yellowish area on the retina, opposite the pupil.

Yel·low·stone (yel′ō stōn′), *n.* a river flowing from NW Wyoming through Yellowstone Lake and NE through Montana into the Missouri River in W North Dakota. 671 mi. long.

Yel′lowstone Na′tional Park′, a park in NW Wyoming and adjacent parts of Montana and Idaho: geysers, hot springs, falls, lake, canyon. 3458 sq. mi.

yel′low streak′, *Informal.* a trait of cowardice in one's character.

yel·low·tail (yel′ō tāl′), *n., pl.* **-tails,** (*esp. collectively*), **-tail. 1.** a game fish, *Seriola dorsalis*, of California. **2.** Also called **yel′lowtail snap′per.** a small West Indian snapper, *Ocyurus chrysurus*, a game fish. **3.** See **yellowtail flounder. 4.** any of several other fishes with a yellow or yellowish caudal fin.

yel′lowtail floun′der, a flounder, *Limanda ferruginea*, found along the Atlantic coast of North America, having a yellowish tail fin and rusty-red spots on the body.

yel·low·throat (yel′ō thrōt′), *n.* any of several American warblers of the genus *Geothlypis*, having a yellow throat.

yel′low war′bler, a small American warbler, *Dendroica petechia*, the male of which has yellow plumage.

yel·low·weed (yel′ō wēd′), *n.* **1.** *U.S. Dial.* any of certain coarse species of goldenrod. **2.** the European ragwort, *Senecio Jacobaea.*

yel·low·wood (yel′ō wo͝od′), *n.* **1.** the hard, yellow wood of a fabaceous tree, *Cladrastis lutea*, of the southern U.S. **2.** the tree itself, having showy, white flowers and yielding a yellow dye. **3.** any of various other yellow woods, as that of a small tree, *Schaefferia frutescens*, of southern Florida. **4.** any of the trees yielding these woods.

yelp (yelp), *v.i.* **1.** to give a quick, sharp, shrill cry, as a dog or fox. —*v.t.* **2.** to utter or express by or as by yelping. —*n.* **3.** a quick, sharp bark or cry. [ME *yelpe(n)*, OE *gelpan* to boast; c. LG *galpen* to croak] —**yelp′er,** *n.*

Yem·en (yem′ən), *n.* **1.** Official name, **Peo′ple's Democrat′ic Repub′lic of Yem′en.** Formerly, **South Yemen, Southern Yemen.** a republic in S Arabia, formed in 1967 from the Federation of South Arabia and the Eastern Aden Protectorate. 1,900,000; ab. 112,000 sq. mi. *Cap.:* Aden. **2.** Official name, **Yem′en Ar′ab Repub′lic.** a republic in SW Arabia, on the Red Sea. 5,800,000; ab. 75,000 sq. mi. *Cap.:* San'a. —**Yem·en·ite** (yem′ə nīt′), **Yem·e·ni** (yem′ə nē), *adj., n.*

yen[1] (yen), *n., pl.* **yen.** an aluminum coin and monetary unit of Japan. *Abbr.:* Y; *Symbol.:* ¥ [< Jap < Chin *yüan* a round thing, a dollar]

yen[2] (yen), *n., v.*, **yenned, yen·ning.** *Informal.* —*n.* **1.** a desire or craving. —*v.i.* **2.** to have a craving; yearn. [? < Chin (slang) *yan* craving]

Yen·an (yen′än′), *n.* a city in N Shensi, in NE China: the capital of Communist China prior to the capture of the city by Nationalist forces in 1947. 45,000. Also called **Fushih.**

Ye·ni·se·i (yen′i sā′; *Russ.* ye ni sā′yᵊ), *n.* a river in the Soviet Union in Asia, flowing N from Tuva Republic to the Arctic Ocean. 2800 mi. long.

Yen·tai (yen′tī′), *n.* Chefoo.

yeo·man (yō′mən), *n., pl.* **-men,** *adj.* —*n.* **1.** *U.S. Navy.* a petty officer having chiefly clerical duties. **2.** *Brit.* a farmer who cultivates his own land. **3.** *Archaic.* **a.** an attendant or subordinate official in a royal or noble household. **b.** an assistant. **4.** *Archaic or Hist.* one of a class of freeholders, below the gentry, who cultivated their own land. —*adj.* **5.** of, pertaining to, composed of, or characteristic of yeomen. **6.** performed or rendered in a valiant or workmanlike manner. [ME *yeman, yoman* = *ye, yo* (? < *geng, gong*, variants of *young*) + *man* MAN[1]]

yeo·man·ly (yō′mən lē), *adj.* **1.** of the condition or rank of a yeoman. **2.** pertaining to or befitting a yeoman. —*adv.* **3.** like or as befits a yeoman. [ME *yemanly*]

yeo′man of the guard′, a member of the bodyguard of the English sovereign, instituted in 1485, which now consists of 100 men, including officers, having purely ceremonial duties. Also called **Yeo′man of the Roy′al Guard′.**

yeo·man·ry (yō′mən rē), *n.* yeomen collectively. [ME]

yeo′man's serv′ice, good, useful, or workmanlike service. Also, **yeo′man serv′ice.**

yep (yep), *adv. Informal.* yes.

-yer, var. of **-er**[2] after *w: lawyer; sawyer.*

Yer·ba Bue·na (yâr′bə bwā′nə, yûr′bə), **1.** an island in San Francisco Bay between Oakland and San Francisco, California. **2.** (*l.c.*) a labiate herb, *Satureia Douglasii*, of the Pacific coast of North America, used formerly in medicine. **3.** (*l.c.*) a trailing, perennial herb, *Micromeria chamissonis*, of the western coast of North America, having hairy leaves, solitary white flowers, and branches that root at the tips.

Ye·re·van (*Armenian.* ye re vän′), *n.* Erivan.

yerk (yûrk), *Chiefly Brit. Dial.* —*v.t.* **1.** to strike or whip. —*n.* **2.** a blow or stroke. [late ME < ?]

yes (yes), *adv., n., pl.* **yes·es.** —*adv.* **1.** (used to express affirmation or assent or to mark the addition of something emphasizing and amplifying a previous statement): *Do you want that? Yes, I do.* **2.** (used to express an emphatic contradiction): *You say I can't, but I say yes I can.* **3.** (used, usually interrogatively, to express uncertainty, curiosity, etc.): *"Yes?" he said as he opened the door. That was a marvelous show! Yes?* **4.** (used to express polite attentiveness.) —*n.* **5.** an affirmative reply. [ME *yes, yis*, OE *gēse*, prob. = *gēa* YEA + *sī* be it (pres. subj. sing. of *bēon* to be)]

ye·shi·va (yə shē′və; *Heb.* yi shē vä′), *n., pl. Eng.* **-vahs,** *Heb.* **-voth** (-vōt′). **1.** an Orthodox Jewish school for the religious and secular education of children of elementary school age. **2.** an Orthodox Jewish school of higher instruction in Jewish learning. [< Heb: academy, orig., sitting (i.e., a place to sit)]

ye·shi·vah (yə shē′və; *Heb.* yi shē vä′), *n., pl. Eng.* **-vahs,** *Heb.* **-voth** (-vôt′). yeshiva.

yes′ man′, *Informal.* a man who always agrees with his superior; a sycophant.

yes·ter (yes′tər), *adj.* *Archaic.* of or pertaining to yesterday. [back formation from YESTERDAY, etc.]

yester-, a native English prefix indicating the previous occurrence of the time referred to by the word to which the prefix is attached: *yesterday; yesterweek.* [comb. form repr. OE *geostran, giestron;* c. G *gestern,* D *gisteren,* L *hesternus*]

yes·ter·day (yes′tər dē, -dā′), *adv.* **1.** on the day preceding this day. **2.** in the recent past. **—***n.* **3.** the day preceding this day. **4.** the recent past. **5.** Usually, **yesterdays.** time past: *the dim yesterdays of mankind.* **—***adj.* **6.** belonging or pertaining to the day before or to a time in the recent past: *yesterday morning.* [ME; OE *geostran dæg*]

yes·ter·eve·ning (yes′tər ēv′ning), *Archaic.* **—***n.* **1.** yesterday evening. **—***adv.* **2.** on or during yesterday evening.

yes·ter·morn·ing (yes′tər môr′ning), *Archaic.* **—***n.* **1.** yesterday morning. **—***adv.* **2.** on yesterday morning.

yes·tern (yes′tərn), *adj.* *Archaic.* yester. [YESTER + -*(e)n* adj. suffix (? -EN[2], but cf. OE *geostran*)]

yes·ter·night (yes′tər nīt′), *Archaic.* **—***n.* **1.** the night last past. **—***adv.* **2.** during last night. [ME; OE *gystran niht*]

yes·ter·noon (yes′tər no͞on′), *Archaic.* **—***n.* **1.** yesterday noon. **—***adv.* **2.** at noon yesterday.

yes·ter·week (yes′tər wēk′), *Archaic.* **—***n.* **1.** last week. **—***adv.* **2.** in or during the last week.

yes·ter·year (yes′tər yēr′), *n.* **1.** last year; time not long past. **—***adv.* **2.** during time not long past.

yes·treen (ye strēn′), *adv.* *Scot.* yesterday evening; last evening. [YEST(E)R- + E(V)EN[2]]

yet (yet), *adv.* **1.** up until or at the present time or the time specified: *Is anyone here yet?* **2.** just now; so soon: *Don't go yet.* **3.** in the time remaining; eventually: *There is yet time. We'll get there yet!* **4.** In addition; besides: *yet further triumphs to come.* **5.** nevertheless: *strange, yet true.* **6.** moreover: *I've never read it nor yet intend to.* **7. as yet.** See **as**[1] (def. 23). **—***conj.* **8.** though; nevertheless: *It is good, yet it could be improved.* [ME *yet(e),* OE *gīet(a);* c. MHG *ieze* yet, now < G *jetzt* now] **—Syn.** See **but**[1].

yet·i (yet′ē), *n.* (*sometimes cap.*) See **Abominable Snowman.** [< Tibetan]

Yev·tu·shen·ko (yev′to͞o sheng′kō; *Russ.* yef to͝o shen′kọ), *n.* **Yev·ge·ny A·le·xan·dro·vich** (yev ge′nē ä′le ksän′drọ vich), born 1933, Russian poet. Also, **Evtushenko.**

yew[1] (yo͞o), *n.* **1.** any of several evergreen, coniferous trees and shrubs of the genus *Taxus,* of the Old World, North America, and Japan. **2.** the fine-grained, elastic wood of any of these trees. **3.** an archer's bow made of this wood. **4.** this tree or its branches as a symbol of sorrow, death, or resurrection. [ME *ew(e),* OE *ēow, ī(o)w;* c. Icel *ȳr,* OHG *īga, īwa* (MHG *īwe,* G *Eibe*), OIr *ibar* (MIr *eo*)]

yew[2] (yo͞o, *unstressed* yo͝o), *pron.* *Eye Dialect.* you.

Ye·zo (ye′zô), *n.* former name of **Hokkaido.**

Ygg·dra·sil (ig′drə sil, yg′-), *n.* *Scand. Myth.* an evergreen ash tree, the three roots of which bind together Asgard, Midgard, and Niflheim. Also, **Yg′dra·sil.**

YHA, Youth Hostels Association.

YHVH, a transliteration of the Tetragrammaton. Also, **YHWH, JHVH, JHWH** [< Heb]

yid (yid), *n.* *Offensive.* a Jew. [short for YIDDISH, or < Yiddish *yid* a JEW (< MHG *Jude, Jüde*)]

Yid·dish (yid′ish), *n.* **1.** a language consisting of a group of closely similar High German dialects, with vocabulary admixture from Hebrew and Slavic, written in Hebrew letters and spoken mainly by Jews in countries E of Germany and by Jewish emigrants from these regions. **—***adj.* **2.** of, pertaining to, or characteristic of Yiddish. [< Yiddish *yidish* < MHG *jüdisch* (*diutsch*) Jewish (German) = *Jüde* JEW + -*isch* -ISH[1]]

yield (yēld), *v.t.* **1.** to produce or give forth (a product or quantity of a product) by a natural process or by cultivation: *The farm yields hay and tobacco. The tree yields six bushels of apples. The cow yields milk twice a day.* **2.** to earn or furnish (profit, interest, etc.). **3.** to concede, surrender, or relinquish. **4.** to render, as homage or thanks. **—***v.i.* **5.** to be productive or rewarding, as a farm, mine, or investment. **6.** to concede or surrender, as to a superior force. **7.** to give oneself up, as to temptation or strong emotion. **8.** to be influenced or dissuaded by another person, arguments, etc. **9.** to collapse, as under pressure. **10.** to surrender voluntarily one's right, privilege, etc. **—***n.* **11.** the act of yielding or producing. **12.** something that is yielded. **13.** *Chem.* the quantity of product formed in a reaction: generally expressed as a percentage of the quantity obtained to that theoretically obtainable. [ME *yelde(n),* OE *g(i)eldan* to pay; c. G *gelten* to be worth, apply to] **—yield′a·ble,** *adj.* **—yield′er,** *n.*
—Syn. 1. furnish, bear. **3.** abandon, forgo. YIELD, SUBMIT, SURRENDER mean to give way or give up to someone or something. To YIELD is to concede under some degree of pressure, but not necessarily to surrender totally: *to yield ground to an enemy.* To SUBMIT is to give up more completely to authority, superior force, etc., and to cease opposition, although usually with reluctance: *to submit to control.* To SURRENDER is to give up complete possession of, relinquish, and cease claim to: *to surrender a fortress, one's freedom, rights.* **4.** impart, bestow. **8.** bend, bow.

yield·ing (yēl′ding), *adj.* **1.** inclined to surrender or submit. **2.** tending to give way, esp. under pressure. **3.** (of a crop, soil, etc.) producing a yield; productive. [ME] **—yield′ing·ly,** *adv.* **—yield′ing·ness,** *n.*

Yig·dal (yēg däl′), *n.* *Judaism.* a liturgical prayer, or hymn, expressing the faith of Israel in God. [< Heb: lit., becomes great]

yill (yil), *n.* *Scot.* ale.

Yin (yin), *n.* See under **Yin and Yang.**

Yin and Yang

Yin and Yang (yin′ and yäng′, yang′), (in Chinese philosophy and religion) two principles, one negative, dark, and feminine **(Yin),** and one positive, bright, and masculine **(Yang),** whose interaction influences the destinies of creatures and things.

Ying·kow (ying′kou′), *n.* a port in NE China, near the Gulf of Liaotung: the major port of Manchuria. 131,400 (1953). Also called **Newchwang.**

yip (yip), *v.,* **yipped, yip·ping,** *n.* **—***v.i.* **1.** to bark sharply, as a young dog. **—***n.* **2.** a sharp bark; yelp. [late ME *yippe,* ? alter. of *yilpe* YELP]

yipe (yīp), *interj.* (an expression or exclamation of fright, surprise, pain, etc.) [? var. of YAP]

yip·pee (yip′ē), *interj.* (used as an exclamation of joy, exultation, or the like.)

Yip·pie (yip′ē), *n.* a member of a group of ecstatically rebellious students opposed to the Vietnam War. Also, **yip′pie.** [*Y(outh) I(nternational) P(arty);* modeled on HIPPIE]

yird (yûrd), *n.* *Scot. and North Eng.* earth.

yirr (yûr), *Scot.* **—***v.i.* **1.** to snarl or growl, as a dog does. **—***n.* **2.** a growl or snarl, as of a dog. [? OE *georr(an)* to make a harsh sound]

Yiz·kor (yēz kôr′; *Eng.* yis′kər), *n.* *Hebrew.* the Jewish service for commemorating the dead. [lit., be mindful]

-yl, *Chem.* a suffix used in the names of radicals: *ethyl.* [comb. form repr. Gk *hȳlē* matter, wood, substance]

y·lang-y·lang (ē′läng ē′läng), *n.* **1.** an aromatic tree, *Carangium odoratum* (or *Cananga odorata*), of the Philippines, Java, etc., having fragrant, drooping flowers that yield a volatile oil used in perfumery. **2.** the oil or perfume. Also, **ilang-ilang.** [< Tagalog *ilang-ilang*]

Y.M.C.A., Young Men's Christian Association.

Y.M.H.A., Young Men's Hebrew Association.

Y·mir (ē′mir, y′mir), *n.* *Scand. Myth.* the earliest being and the progenitor of the giants, killed by Odin and his brothers. From his flesh the earth was made, from his blood the waters, and from his skull the heavens. Also, **Y·mer** (ē′mər).

y.o., 1. year old. **2.** years old.

yod (yo͝od; *Heb.* yôd), *n.* the 10th letter of the Hebrew alphabet. [< Heb: hand]

yo·del (yōd′əl), *v.,* **-deled, -del·ing,** or (*esp. Brit.*) **-delled, -del·ling,** *n.* **—***v.t., v.i.* **1.** to sing or call out with frequent changes from the ordinary voice to falsetto and back again. **—***n.* **2.** a song, refrain, etc., so sung or called out. [< G *jodeln*] **—yo′del·er;** *esp. Brit.,* **yo′del·ler,** *n.*

yo·dle (yōd′əl), *v.t., v.i.,* **-dled, -dling,** *n.* yodel. **—yo′dler,** *n.*

Yo·ga (yō′gə), *n.* (*sometimes l.c.*) *Indian Philosophy.* **1.** freedom of the self from its noneternal or impermanent elements or states. **2.** any of the methods or disciplines by which such freedom is attained, as certain exercises. **3.** these exercises practiced for any reason. [< Hind < Skt: union; akin to YOKE[1]] **—Yo·gic** (yō′gik), *adj.* **—Yo′gism,** *n.*

yogh (yōкн), *n.* the letter ȝ used in the writing of Middle English to represent a palatal fricative, as in *ȝung* (Modern English "young"), or a velar fricative, as in *litȝliche* (Modern English "lightly"). [ME]

yo·ghurt (yō′gərt), *n.* yogurt. Also, **yo′ghourt.**

yo·gi (yō′gē), *n., pl.* **-gis** (-gēz). a person who practices Yoga. Also, **yo·gin** (yō′gin). [< Hind *yogī* < Skt *yogin* < *yoga* YOGA]

yo·gi·ni (yō′gə nē), *n.* a woman who practices Yoga. [< Hind *yogin*]

yo·gurt (yō′gərt), *n.* a prepared food having the consistency of custard, made from milk curdled by the action of cultures, sometimes sweetened or flavored. Also, **yoghurt, yoghourt.** [< Turk *yōghurt*]

yo-heave-ho (yō′hēv′hō′), *interj.* (used formerly as a chant by sailors when hauling on a rope.)

yo-ho (yō hō′), *interj., v.,* **-hoed, -ho·ing.** **—***interj.* **1.** (used as a call or shout to attract attention, accompany effort, etc.) **—***v.i.* **2.** to shout "yo-ho!"

yoicks (hīk; *spelling pron.* yoiks), *interj.* huic.

yoke[1] (yōk), *n., pl.* **yokes** for 1, 3–11, **yoke** for 2; *v.,* **yoked, yok·ing.** **—***n.* **1.** a contrivance for joining together a pair of draft animals, esp. oxen, usually consisting of a crosspiece with two bow-shaped pieces, each enclosing the head of an animal. Cf. **harness** (def. 1). **2.** a pair of draft animals fastened together by a yoke: *five yoke of oxen.* **3.** something resembling a yoke in form or use. **4.** a frame fitting the neck and shoulders of a person, for carrying a pair of buckets or the like, one at each end. **5.** *Mach.* a viselike piece gripping two parts firmly together. **6.** *Naut.* a crossbar on the head of the rudder to permit the steering of the boat from forward. **7.** a fitting for the neck of a draft animal for suspending the tongue of a cart, carriage, etc., from a harness. **8.** a shaped piece in a garment, fitted about or below the neck and shoulders or about the hips, from which the rest of the garment hangs. **9.** an emblem or symbol of subjection, as an archway under which prisoners of war were compelled to pass. **10.** oppressive domination, as by a state. **11.** something that couples or binds together; bond or tie. **—***v.t.* **12.** to put a yoke on. **13.** to attach (a draft animal) to a plow or vehicle. **14.** to harness a draft animal to (a plow or vehicle). **15.** to join or link. **—***v.i.* **16.** to be or become joined, linked, or united. [ME *yok(e),* OE *geoc;* c. D *juk,* G *Joch,* Icel *ok,* L *jugum,* Gk *zygón,* Hittite *yugan,* Skt *yuga*] **—yoke′less,** *adj.* **—Syn. 2.** See **pair.**

Y, Yoke

yoke[2] (yōk), *n.* yolk.

yo·kel (yō′kəl), *n.* a rustic; a country bumpkin. [?] **—yo′kel·ish,** *adj.*

Yok·ka·i·chi (yô′kä ē′chē), *n.* a city on W central Honshu, in S Japan. 210,359 (1964).

Yo·ko·ha·ma (yō′kə hä′mə; *Jap.* yô′kô hä′mä), *n.* a seaport on SE Honshu, in central Japan, on Tokyo Bay. 1,639,307 (1964).

Yo·ko·su·ka (yō′kə so͞o′kə, yə ko͝os′kə; *Jap.* yô′kô so͞o′kä), *n.* a seaport on SE Honshu, in central Japan, on Tokyo Bay: naval base. 310,229 (1964).

Yo·kuts (yō′kuts), *n.* a Penutian family of languages.

yolk (yōk, yōlk), *n.* **1.** the yellow and principal substance of an egg, as distinguished from the white. **2.** *Biol.* the part of the contents of the egg of an animal that enters directly into the formation of the embryo, together with any material that nourishes the embryo during its formation. **3.** a natural grease exuded from the skin of sheep. Also, **yoke.** [ME *yolke, yelke,* OE *geoloca* (*geolu* yellow + *-ca* n. suffix)] **—yolk′y,** *adj.*

Yom Kip·pur (yom kip′ər; *Heb.* yôm′ kē po͞or′), a Jewish high holy day observed on the 10th day of Tishri by fasting and the daylong recitation of prayers expressing repentance in the synagogue. Also called **Day of Atonement.** [< Heb = *yōm* day + *kippur* atonement]

yon (yon), *Chiefly Dial.* **—***adj., adv.* **1.** yonder. **—***pron.* **2.** that or those yonder. [ME; OE *geon;* akin to D *gene,* G *jener,* Goth *jains* that, Icel *enn, inn* the]

yond (yond), *adv., adj. Archaic.* yonder. [ME; OE *geond;* akin to D *ginds,* Goth *jaind.* See YON]

yon·der (yon′dər), *adj.* **1.** being over there: *Do you see yonder hut?* **—***adv.* **2.** over there: *Look yonder!* [ME *yonder, yender* (with *-er* as in HITHER, THITHER); akin to D *ginder,* Goth *jaindre*]

yo·ni (yō′nē), *n.* (in Shaktism) the external female genitals regarded as the symbol of Shakti. Cf. **linga** (def. 2). [< Skt]

Yon·kers (yong′kərz), *n.* a city in SE New York, on the Hudson near New York City. 204,297 (1970).

yoo-hoo (yo͞o′ho͞o′), *interj.* **1.** (used as an exclamation to get someone's attention, in calling to another person, or the like.) **—***v.i.* **2.** to get or attempt to get someone's attention by or as by calling "yoo-hoo." [imit.]

yore (yōr, yôr), *n.* **1.** *Chiefly Literary.* time past: *knights of yore.* **—***adv.* **2.** *Obs.* of old; long ago. [ME; OE *geāra,* appar. akin to *gēar* YEAR]

York (yôrk), *n.* **1.** a member of the royal house of England that ruled from 1461 to 1485. **2. 1st Duke of** (*Edmund of Langley*), 1341–1402, progenitor of the house of York (son of Edward III). **3. Alvin Cul·lum** (kul′əm) (*Sergeant York*), 1887–1964, U.S. soldier and hero of World War I. **4.** Yorkshire (def. 1). **5.** Ancient, **Eboracum.** a city and the county seat of Yorkshire, in NE England: the capital of Roman Britain; cathedral. 104,468 (1961). **6.** a city in SE Pennsylvania: meeting of the Continental Congress 1777–78. 50,335 (1970). **7.** an estuary in E Virginia, flowing SE into Chesapeake Bay. 40 mi. long. **8. Cape,** a cape at the NE extremity of Australia.

York·ist (yôr′kist), *n.* **1.** an adherent or member of the royal house of York, esp. in the Wars of the Roses. **—***adj.* **2.** belonging or pertaining to the English royal house of York. **3.** of or pertaining to the Yorkists.

York′ rite′, one of the two advanced divisions of Masonic membership leading to the Knights Templar degree. Cf. **Scottish rite.**

York·shire (yôrk′shēr, -shər), *n.* **1.** Also called **York, Yorks** (yôrks). a county in N England, comprising the administrative counties of East Riding, North Riding, and West Riding. 3,722,561 (1961); 6089 sq. mi. *Co. seat:* York. **2.** one of an English breed of white hogs having erect ears.

Yorkshire terrier (8 in. high at shoulder)

York′shire pud′ding, an unsweetened batter of flour, salt, eggs, and milk, baked in meat drippings.

York′shire ter′rier, one of an English breed of toy terriers having a long, silky, straight coat that is dark steel-blue from the back of the skull to the tail and is tan on the head, chest, and legs.

York·town (yôrk′toun′), *n.* a village in SE Virginia: surrender (October 19, 1781) of Cornwallis to Washington.

Yo·ru·ba (yor′o͝o bə, -bä′, yôr′-), *n., pl.* **-bas,** (*esp. collectively*) **-ba** for 1. **1.** a member of a numerous West African coastal Negro people. **2.** the language of the Yoruba; Kwa. —**Yo′ru·ban,** *adj.*

Yo·sem·i·te (yō sem′i tē), *n.* a valley in E California, in the Sierra Nevada Mountains: a part of Yosemite National Park. 7 mi. long.

Yosem′ite Falls′, a series of three major scenic falls in Yosemite National Park. Total height of the three (including rapids), 2526 ft.

Yosem′ite Na′tional Park′, a national park in E California. 1182 sq. mi.

Yosh·kar-O·la (*Russ.* yosh-kär′o lä′), *n.* Ioshkar-Ola.

you (yo͞o; *unstressed* yo͝o), *pron., poss.* **your** or **yours,** *obj., both as direct and indirect object,* **you. 1.** the pronoun of the second person singular or plural: *Did you do that? What happened to you? Did it hurt you?* **2.** one; anyone; people in general: *a tiny animal you can't even see.* **3.** *Informal.* (used in place of the pronoun *your* with a gerund): *I heard about you being elected.* **4.** *Archaic.* **a.** yourself; yourselves: *Get you home.* **b.** a pl. form of the pronoun *ye.* [ME; OE *ēow* (dat., acc. of *gē* YE[1]); c. D *u,* OHG *iu*] **—Usage. 3.** See **me.**

you-all (yo͞o ôl′, yôl), *pron. Chiefly Southern U.S.* you (used in direct address when referring to two or more persons): *Tell your mother it's time you-all came to visit us.*

you'd (yo͞od), contraction of *you had* or *you would.*

you'll (yo͞ol; *unstressed* yo͝ol), contraction of *you will* or *you shall.*

young (yung), *adj.* **young·er** (yung′gər), **young·est** (yung′gist), *n.* **—***adj.* **1.** being in the first or early stage of life or growth: *Once, she too was a young girl.* **2.** having the appearance, freshness, vigor, or other qualities of youth. **3.** of or pertaining to youth: *in one's young days.* **4.** not far advanced in years or experience in comparison with another or others. **5.** junior: *the young Mr. Smith.* **6.** being in an early stage, as of maturity or development: *a young wine.* **—***n.* **7.** young persons collectively: *a game for young and old.* **8.** young offspring: *a mother hen and her young.* **9. with young,** pregnant. [ME *yong(e),* OE *geong;* c. D *jong,* G *jung,* Icel *ungr,* Goth *jungs;* akin to L *juvenis*]
—Syn. 1. growing. YOUNG, YOUTHFUL, JUVENILE all refer to lack of age. YOUNG is the general word for that which is undeveloped, immature, and in process of growth: *a young colt, child; young shoots of wheat.* YOUTHFUL has connotations suggesting the favorable characteristics of youth, such as vigor, enthusiasm, and hopefulness: *youthful sports, energy, outlook.* JUVENILE may suggest less desirable characteristics, such as childishness, petulance, idleness, selfishness, or heedlessness (*juvenile behavior*), or it may refer simply to the years, up to the later teens, before legal responsibility: *juvenile delinquency; juvenile books.* **—Ant. 1.** mature, old.

Young (yung), *n.* **1. Brig·ham** (brig′əm), 1801–77, U.S. Mormon leader. **2. Owen D.,** 1874–1962, U.S. lawyer, industrialist, government administrator, and financier. **3. Thomas,** 1773–1829, English physician, physicist, mathematician, and Egyptologist. **4. Whitney M., Jr.,** 1921–71, U.S. social worker and educator: executive director of the National Urban League 1961–71.

young·ber·ry (yung′ber′ē, -bə rē), *n., pl.* **-ries.** *Hort.* the large, dark-purple, sweet fruit of a trailing blackberry in the southwest U.S., a cross between several blackberries. [named after B. M. *Young,* American hybridizer, who developed it c1900]

young′ blood′, youth, or its ideas, practices, etc.

young′ hy′son. See under **hyson.**

young′ la′dy, 1. a young, usually unmarried woman or refinement. **2.** any young girl. **3.** a girl friend; sweetheart; fiancée: *Has his young lady met the family?* [late ME]

young·ling (yung′ling), *n.* **1.** a young person or animal. **2.** a novice; a beginner. [ME *yongling,* OE *geongling;* c. D *jongeling,* G *Jüngling*]

young′ man′, 1. a male in early manhood. **2.** a boyfriend; sweetheart; fiancé: *She introduced us to her young man.* [ME *yongmon*]

young one (yung′ ən, wən), *Informal.* a child or young animal; offspring.

Young′ Pretend′er. See **Stuart, Charles Edward.**

young·ster (yung′stər), *n.* **1.** a young person. **2.** a young horse or other animal. **3.** (in the U.S. Naval Academy) a midshipman in his second year. **—Syn. 1.** youth, lad.

Youngs·town (yungz′toun′), *n.* a city in NE Ohio. 140,909 (1970).

Young′ Turk′, any person aggressively advocating reform within an organization. Also, **young′ Turk′.**

youn·ker (yung′kər), *n. Obs.* a young noble or gentleman. [< MD *jonckher* = *jonc* YOUNG + *here* lord; c. G *Junker*]

your (yo͝or, yōr, yôr; *unstressed* yər), *pron.* **1.** (a form of the possessive case of **you** used as an attributive adjective): *I like your idea.* Cf. **yours. 2.** (used informally to indicate all members of a group, occupation, etc., or things of a particular type): *Take your factory worker, for instance.* **3.** (used to indicate that one belonging to oneself or to any person). **4.** of or pertaining to people in general; one's: *As you go down the hill, the library is on your left.* [ME; OE *ēower* (gen. of *gē* YE[1]); c. G *euer*] **—Usage.** See **me.**

you're (yo͝or; *unstressed* yər), contraction of *you are.*

your'n (yo͝orn, yōrn, yôrn), *pron. Dial.* yours. Also, **yourn.** [YOUR + *-n* as in MINE[1]]

yours (yo͝orz, yōrz, yôrz), *pron.* **1.** (a form of the possessive case of **you** used as a predicate adjective): *Which cup is yours? Is she a friend of yours?* **2.** that which belongs to you: *Yours was the first face I recognized.* [YOUR + *-s* as in HIS]

your·self (yo͝or self′, yōr-, yôr-, yər-), *n., pl.* **-selves** (-selvz′). **1.** (an emphatic appositive of **you** or **ye**): *a letter you yourself wrote.* **2.** (a reflexive form of **you**): *Did you ever ask yourself "why"?* **3.** (used as the object of a preposition or as the direct or indirect object of a verb): *People like yourself often feel that way.* **4.** your normal or customary self: *You'll soon be yourself again.* **5.** oneself: *The surest way is to do it yourself.* **—Usage.** See **myself.**

yours′ tru′ly, 1. a conventional phrase used at the end of a letter. **2.** *Informal.* I; myself; me: *I'm only in business to profit yours truly.*

youse (yo͞oz; *unstressed* yəz), *pron. Nonstandard.* you (usually used in addressing two or more people).

youth (yo͞oth), *n., pl.* **youths** (yo͞oths, yo͞othz), (*collectively*) **youth. 1.** the condition of being young. **2.** the vitality characteristic of the young. **3.** the time of being young; early life. **4.** the first or early period of anything. **5.** young persons collectively. **6.** a young person, esp. a young man. [ME *youthe,* OE *geoguth;* c. D *jeugd,* G *Jugend*] **—Syn. 3.** minority, immaturity. **6.** youngster, lad, boy.

youth·en (yo͞o′thən), *v.t.* to make youthful; to restore youth or its semblance to (someone or something): *She youthened her appearance with make-up.*

youth·ful (yo͞oth′fəl), *adj.* **1.** characterized by youth; young. **2.** of, pertaining to, or suggesting youth or its vitality. **3.** *Phys. Geog.* (of topographical features) having undergone erosion to a slight extent only. **—youth′ful·ly,** *adv.* **—youth′ful·ness,** *n.* **—Syn. 2.** See **young.**

youth′ hos′tel, hostel (def. 1).

you've (yo͞ov; *unstressed* yo͝ov), contraction of *you have.*

yow (you), *interj., n.* (an exclamation or shout of pain, dismay, etc.) [imit.]

yowl (youl), *v.i.* **1.** to utter a long distressful or dismal cry, as an animal or a person; howl. **—***n.* **2.** a yowling cry; a howl. [ME *yuhele, yule, youle,* appar from a cry of pain or distress *yuhele.* Cf. OE *geoh-* (in *geohthu* grief), *wā lā* alas] **—yowl′er,** *n.*

yo-yo (yō′yō), *n., pl.* **-yos.** a toy, consisting of two round, flat-sided blocks of wood, plastic, or metal connected by a dowel pin in the center, around which a string is wound. The yo-yo is spun out and reeled in by the string, one end of which is looped around the player's finger. [formerly trademark]

y·per·ite (ē′pə rīt′), *n. Chem.* See **mustard gas.** [< F *ypérite,* named after YPRES; see -ITE[1]]

Y·pres (ē′prᴇᵊ), *n.* a town in W Belgium: battles 1914–18. 18,358 (est. 1964). Flemish, **Ieper.**

Yp·si·lan·ti (ip′sə lan′tē), *n.* **1. Alexander,** 1792–1828, and his brother **De·me·tri·os** (di mē′trē əs; *Gk.* t͟hē mē′trē-ôs), 1793–1832, Greek patriots and revolutionary leaders. **2.** a city in SE Michigan, W of Detroit. 29,538 (1970). Also, **Yp·si·lan·tis** (*Gk.* ē′psē län′dēs) (for def. 1).

yr., **1.** year; years. **2.** your.

yrs., **1.** years. **2.** yours.

Y·ser (*Fr.* ē zᴇʀ′), *n.* a river flowing from N France through NW Belgium into the North Sea: battles 1914–18. 55 mi. long.

Y·seult (i so͞olt′), *n.* Iseult. German, **Y·sol·de** (ē zôl′də).

Ys·pa·da·den Pen·kawr (is pa dad′ᵊn pen′kour), *Welsh Legend.* the father of Olwen.

Yt, *Chem.* yttrium.

Y.T., Yukon Territory.

yt·ter·bi·a (i tûr′bē ə), *n.* *Chem.* a colorless mass, Yb_2O_3, used in alloys and ceramics. Also called **ytter′bium ox′ide.** [< NL, named after *Ytterby,* a quarry near Stockholm, Sweden, where found; see -ɪᴀ]

yt·ter·bite (i tûr′bīt), *n.* gadolinite. [*Ytterb*(*y*) (see ʏᴛᴛᴇʀʙɪᴀ) + -ɪᴛᴇ¹]

yt·ter·bi·um (i tûr′bē əm), *n.* *Chem.* a rare metallic element. *Symbol:* Yb; *at. wt.:* 173.04; *at. no.:* 70; *sp. gr.:* 6.96. [< NL; see ʏᴛᴛᴇʀʙɪᴛᴇ, -ɪᴜᴍ] —**yt·ter′bic, yt·ter′bous,** *adj.*

ytter′bium met′al, *Chem.* See **yttrium metal.**

yt·tri·a (i′trē ə), *n.* *Chem.* a powder, Y_2O_3, used chiefly in incandescent gas and acetylene mantles. Also called **yt′trium ox′ide.** [< NL, named after *Ytt*(*e*)*r*(*by*). See ʏᴛᴛᴇʀʙɪᴀ]

yt·tri·um (i′trē əm), *n.* *Chem.* a rare, trivalent metallic element. *Symbol:* Y, Yt; *at. wt.:* 88.905; *at. no.:* 39; *sp. gr.:* 4.47. [< NL, named after *Ytt*(*e*)*r*(*by*). See ʏᴛᴛᴇʀʙɪᴀ, -ɪᴜᴍ] —**yt′tric,** *adj.*

yt′trium met′al, *Chem.* any of a subgroup of rare-earth metals, of which the cerium and terbium metals comprise the other two subgroups. Cf. **rare-earth element.**

Yü (ʏʏ), *n.* a legendary Chinese emperor who drained the land and made the mountains.

yu·an (yo͞o än′; *Chin.* ʏʏän), *n., pl.* **-an. 1.** a paper money and monetary unit of the Republic of China, equal to 100 cents; dollar. **2.** jên-min-piao. [< Chin]

Yü·an (yo͞o än′; *Chin.* ʏʏän), *n.* (*sometimes l.c.*) (in the Republic of China) a department of government; council.

Yu·ca·tán (yo͞o′kə tan′; *Sp.* yo͞o′kä-tän′), *n.* **1.** a peninsula in SE Mexico and N Central America comprising parts of SE Mexico, N Guatemala, and Belize. **2.** a state in SE Mexico, in N Yucatán Peninsula. 904,000; 14,868 sq. mi. *Cap.:* Mérida. Also, **Yu·ca·tan** (yo͞o′kə tan′).

Yu·ca·tec (yo͞o′kə tek′), *n., pl.* **-tecs,** (*esp. collectively*) **-tec. 1.** a member of an American-Indian people of Yucatán, Mexico. **2.** the Mayan dialect of these people. —**Yu′ca·tec′an,** *adj.*

Yucca,
Yucca gloriosa
(Height about 8 ft.)

yuc·ca (yuk′ə), *n.* any liliaceous plant of the genus *Yucca,* of the warmer regions of America, having pointed, usually rigid leaves and panicles of white, waxy flowers: the state flower of New Mexico. [< AmerSp *yuca* << native Indian name]

yuch·y (yuk′ē), *adj.,* **yuch·i·er, yuch·i·est.** yucky.

yuck (yuk), *interj.* *Slang.* (used as an expression of disgust or repugnance.) Also, **yuch** (yuk, ʏᴜᴋʜ).

yuck·y (yuk′ē), *adj.,* **yuck·i·er, yuck·i·est.** *Slang.* thoroughly unappetizing, disgusting, or repugnant: *a yucky mixture of Brussels sprouts, raisins, and stewed tomatoes.*

Yü·en (yo͞o en′; *Chin.* ʏʏen), *n.* a river in S China, flowing NE to Tungting. 540 mi. long. Also, **Yü·an** (yo͞o än′; *Chin.* ʏʏän).

Yu·ga (yo͝og′ə), *n.* *Hinduism.* **1.** an age of time. **2.** any of four ages, each worse than the last, forming a single cycle due to be repeated. [< Skt: age, orig. yoke]

Yugo., Yugoslavia.

Yu·go·slav (yo͞o′gō släv′, -slav′), *n.* **1.** a native or inhabitant of Yugoslavia. **2.** a southern Slav; a member of the southern group of Slavic peoples. Cf. **Slav.** —*adj.* **3.** of or pertaining to the Yugoslavs. Also, **Yu′go-Slav′, Jugoslav, Jugo-Slav.** [earlier *Jugo-Slav* < G *Jugoslawe* < Serb *jug* south (< OSlav *jugŭ*) + *-o-* -o- + G *Slawe* Sʟᴀᴠ]

Yu·go·sla·vi·a (yo͞o′gō slä′vē ə), *n.* a republic in S Europe comprised of Bosnia and Herzegovina, Croatia, Macedonia, Montenegro, Serbia, and Slovenia. 21,352,000; 98,725 sq. mi. (1945). *Cap.:* Belgrade. Also, **Jugoslavia.** Formerly (1918–29), **Kingdom of the Serbs, Croats, and Slovenes.** —**Yu′go·sla′vi·an,** *adj., n.* —**Yu′go·sla′vic,** *adj.*

Yu·ka·wa (yo͞o kä′wä), *n.* **Hi·de·ki** (hē′de kē), 1907–81, Japanese physicist: Nobel prize 1949.

Yu·kon (yo͞o′kon), *n.* **1.** a river flowing NW and then SW from NW Canada through central Alaska to the Bering Sea. ab. 2000 mi. long. **2.** a territory in NW Canada. 21,392; 207,076 sq. mi. *Cap.:* Whitehorse. —**Yu′kon·er,** *n.*

Yu′kon time′. See under **standard time.**

yule (yo͞ol), *n.* Christmas, or the Christmas season. [ME *yole,* OE *geōl*(*a*) Christmastide; c. Icel *jōl;* akin to Goth *jiuleis*]

yule′ log′, a large log of wood that traditionally formed the backlog of the fire at Christmas. Also called **yule′ block′, yule′ clog′.**

yule·tide (yo͞ol′tīd′), *n.* **1.** the Christmas season. —*adj.* **2.** of or pertaining to the Christmas season.

Yu·ma (yo͞o′mə), *n., pl.* **-mas,** (*esp. collectively*) **-ma** for 1. **1.** a member of an American-Indian people of Arizona. **2.** the Yuman dialect of the Yuma Indians, mutually intelligible with the dialect of the Mohave Indians. **3.** a city in SW Arizona, on the Colorado River. 29,007 (1970).

Yu·man (yo͞o′mən), *n.* **1.** a group comprising the language shared by the Yuma and Mohave Indians and several other languages of the lower valley of the Colorado River. —*adj.* **2.** of or pertaining to Yuman.

yum·my (yum′ē), *adj.,* **-mi·er, -mi·est.** *Informal.* pleasing to the senses, esp. to the taste; delicious. [*yum* exclamation of pleasure + -ʏ¹]

Yung·kia (yo͝ong′kyä′), *n.* a seaport in SE Chekiang, in E China. 250,000. Formerly, **Wenchow.**

Yung·ning (yo͝ong′ning′), *n.* former name of **Nanning.**

Yün·nan (yo͞o nan′; *Chin.* ʏʏn′nän′), *n.* **1.** a province in SW China. 20,510,000; 168,417 sq. mi. *Cap.:* Kunming. **2.** Kunming.

Yup·pie (yup′ē), *n.* (*often l.c.*) a young, ambitious, educated, usually urban professional with an affluent life style. Also, **Yup′py.** [*y*(*oung*) *u*(*rban*) *p*(*rofessional*) + -ɪᴇ]

Yur·ev (yo͝oʀ′yef), *n.* Russian name of **Tartu.**

yurt (yo͝ort), *n.* a circular, portable dwelling used by Mongol and Turkic peoples of central Asia. [< Turkic: dwelling]

Yu·zov·ka (*Russ.* yo͞o′zof kä′), *n.* former name of **Donetsk.**

Y.W.C.A., Young Women's Christian Association.

Y.W.H.A., Young Women's Hebrew Association.

y·wis (i wis′), *adv.* *Archaic.* iwis.

Z

DEVELOPMENT OF MAJUSCULE								
NORTH SEMITIC	GREEK		ETR.	LATIN		MODERN		
						GOTHIC	ITALIC	ROMAN
I	I	Z	I	—	Z	Z	Z	Z

DEVELOPMENT OF MINUSCULE					
ROMAN CURSIVE	ROMAN UNCIAL	CAROL. MIN.	MODERN		
			GOTHIC	ITALIC	ROMAN
z	Z	—	z	z	z

The twenty-sixth and last letter of the English alphabet developed from the seventh letter of the North Semitic alphabet, *zayin.* Adopted into Greek as *zeta* (ζ), it passed on to the Etruscans. The Romans dropped it because there is no *z*-sound in Latin, giving its seventh position to the new letter G. The letter Z does not reappear in Latin until after the conquest of Greece by the Romans in the 1st century B.C., when it was adopted to transliterate the Greek *z*-sound in words like *zeugma* and *zephyros.* Placed at the end of the alphabet together with Greek-derived Y, it passed to all West-European alphabets in this position.

Z, z (zē *or, esp. Brit.,* zed; *Archaic.* iz′ərd), *n., pl.* **Z's** or **Zs, z's** or **zs.** **1.** the 26th letter of the English alphabet, a consonant. **2.** any spoken sound represented by the letter *Z* or *z,* as in *zero, zigzag,* or *fuzz.* **3.** something having the shape of a Z. **4.** a written or printed representation of the letter *Z* or *z.*

Z, 1. *Astron.* zenith distance. **2.** Zone.

Z, 1. the 26th in order or in a series, or, when *I* is omitted, the 25th. **2.** *Chem., Physics.* See **atomic number. 3.** *Elect.* impedance.

z, 1. an unknown quantity or variable. **2.** zone. **3.** the z-axis.

z., 1. zero. **2.** zinc.

za·ba·glio·ne (zä′bəl yō′nē; *It.* dzä′bä lyô′ne), *n. Italian Cookery.* a custardlike dessert of beaten egg yolks, sugar, and Marsala wine. Also, **za·ba·io·ne, za·ba·jo·ne** (zä′bə-yō′nē; *It.* dzä′bä yô′ne). [< It, var. of *zabaione,* perh. < LL *sabai(a)* an Illyrian drink + It *-one* aug. suffix]

Zab·rze (zäb′zhe), *n.* a city in SW Poland: formerly in Germany. 203,000. German, **Hindenburg.**

Za·ca·te·cas (sä′kä te′käs), *n.* a state in central Mexico. 1,097,000; 28,125 sq. mi.

Zach·a·ri·ah (zak′ə rī′ə), *n.* the father of John the Baptist. Luke 1:5. Also, **Zacharias.**

Zach·a·ri·as (zak′ə rī′əs), *n.* **1. Saint.** Also, **Zachary.** died 752, Greek ecclesiastic, born in Italy: pope 741–752. **2.** Zachariah.

Zach·a·ry (zak′ə rē), *n.* Zacharias (def. 1).

Za·cyn·thus (zə kin′thəs), *n.* Latin name of **Zante.**

Za·dar (zä′där), *n.* a seaport in W Yugoslavia, on the Dalmatian coast: formerly, with surrounding territory, an exclave of Italy. 43,000. Formerly, **Zara.**

zad·dik (tsä dēk′; *Eng.* tsä′dik), *n., pl.* **zad·di·kim** (tsä dē-kēm′; *Eng.* tsä dē′kim, -dik′im). *Hebrew.* a person of outstanding virtue and piety. Also, **tzaddik.** [lit., righteous]

Za·ga·zig (zä′gä zēg′), *n.* a city in the NE Arab Republic of Egypt, on the Nile delta. 195,100 (1975). Also, **Zaqaziq.**

Za·greb (zä′greb), *n.* a city in and the capital of Croatia, in NW Yugoslavia. 566,084. German, **Agram.**

Zag·re·us (zag′rē əs), *n.* a child deity in Orphic mythology, later identified with Dionysus, whom Hera ordered the Titans to slay.

Zag′ros Moun′tains (zag′rəs), a mountain range in S and SW Iran, extending along the borders of Turkey and Iraq. Highest peak, Zardeh Kuh, 14,912 ft.

zai·ba·tsu (zī′bä′tso͞o), *n.* (*construed as sing. or pl.*) the great industrial or financial combinations of Japan. [< Jap: lit., wealth family]

za·ire (zä ēr′, zä′ēr), *n., pl.* **zaire.** the monetary unit of Zaïre, equal to 100 makuta. [named after ZAÏRE]

Za·ïre (zä ēr′, zä′ēr), *n.* **1.** Formerly, **Belgian Congo, Democratic Republic of the Congo.** a republic in central Africa: a former Belgian colony. 24,800,000; 905,328 sq. mi. *Cap.:* Kinshasa. **2.** Formerly, **Congo River.** a river in central Africa, flowing from SE Zaïre to the Atlantic. ab. 3000 mi. long. —**Za·ir′e·an,** *n., adj.*

Za·kyn·thos (zä′kēn thôs′; *Eng.* zə kin′thəs), *n.* Greek name of **Zante.**

Za·ma (zā′mə, zä′mä), *n.* an ancient town in N Africa, SW of Carthage: the Romans defeated Hannibal near here in the final battle of the second Punic War, 202 B.C.

Zam·be·zi (zam bē′zē), *n.* a river in S Africa, flowing S and E from Zambia into the Mozambique Channel of the Indian Ocean: Victoria Falls. 1650 mi. long. —**Zam·be′zi·an,** *adj.*

Zam·bi·a (zam′bē ə, zäm′-), *n.* a republic in S Africa: a former British protectorate and part of the Federation of Rhodesia and Nyasaland; gained independence October 24, 1964; a member of the British Commonwealth of Nations. 5,500,000; 288,130 sq. mi. *Cap.:* Lusaka. Formerly, **Northern Rhodesia.** —**Zam′bi·an,** *adj., n.*

Zam·bo·an·ga (säm′bô äng′gä), *n.* a seaport on SW Mindanao, in the Philippines. 128,981 (est. 1960).

za·mi·a (zā′mē ə), *n.* any cycadaceous plant of the genus *Zamia,* having a tuberous stem and a crown of palmlike, pinnate leaves. [< NL, special use of L *zamiae* (pl.), misreading of Pliny's (*nucēs*) *azāniae* pine (nuts)]

za·min·dar (zə mēn där′), *n.* (formerly in India) a landlord or farmer required to pay a land tax. [< Hindi < Pers *zamīndār* landholder = *zamīn* earth, land + *-dār* holding]

zan·der (zan′dər), *n., pl.* **-ders,** (*esp. collectively*) **-der.** a pikeperch, *Stizostedion lucioperca,* found in the fresh waters of central Europe. [< G, ? < Slav]

Zanes·ville (zānz′vil), *n.* a city in SE Ohio. 33,045 (1970).

Zang·will (zang′wil), *n.* **Israel,** 1865–1926, English novelist and playwright.

Zan·te (zän′tē, -tā, zan′-), *n.* a Greek island, off the W coast of Greece: southernmost of the Ionian Islands. 35,509 (1961); 157 sq. mi. Greek, **Zakynthos.** Latin, **Zacynthus.**

zan·thox·y·lum (zan thok′sə ləm), *n.* the bark of any of several shrubs or trees of the genus *Zanthoxylum,* esp. the prickly ash and the Hercules'-club. [< NL = Gk *xantho-* XANTHO- + *xýlon;* see XYL-]

za·ny (zā′nē), *adj.,* **-ni·er, -ni·est,** *n., pl.* **-nies.** —*adj.* **1.** ludicrously or whimsically comical; clownishly crazy. —*n.* **2.** an apish buffoon; clown. **3.** a silly person; simpleton. [< It *zan(n)i,* Venetian and Lombardic var. of *Gianni* for *Giovanni* John] —**za′ni·ly,** *adv.* —**za′ni·ness,** *n.* —**za′ny·ish,** *adj.*

Zan·zi·bar (zan′zə bär′, zan′zə bär′), *n.* **1.** an island off the E coast of Africa: with Pemba and adjacent small islands formerly comprised a British protectorate that became independent in 1963; now part of Tanzania. 421,000; 640 sq. mi. **2.** a seaport on W Zanzibar. 68,000. —**Zan′zi·ba′ri,** *adj. n.*

zap (zap), *v.,* **zapped, zap·ping,** *n. Slang.* —*v.t.* **1.** to kill or shoot. **2.** to attack, damage, or destroy. **3.** to bombard with x-rays, laser beams, etc. —*n.* **4.** force, energy, or drive. **5.** a jolt or charge, as of electricity. [imit. of the sound of gunfire]

Za·pa·ta (sä pä′tä), *n.* **E·mi·lia·no** (e′mē lyä′nô), 1877?–1919, Mexican revolutionist: guerrilla leader 1911–16.

Za·po·rozh·ye (zä′po rôzh′ye), *n.* a city in the SE Ukraine, in the SW Soviet Union in Europe, on the Dnieper River. 784,000. Formerly, **Aleksandrovsk.**

Za·qa·ziq (zä′kä zēk′), *n.* Zagazig.

Za·ra (zä′rä; *It.* dzä′rä), *n.* former name of **Zadar.**

Za·ra·go·za (thä′rä gô′thä, sä′rä gô′sä), *n.* Spanish name of **Saragossa.**

Zar·a·thus·tra (zar′ə tho͞o′strə), *n.* Zoroaster. —**Zar·a·thus·tri·an** (zar′ə tho͞o′strē ən), *adj., n.* —**Zar′a·thus′tric,** *adj.*

Zar·deh Kuh (zär′də ko͞o′), a mountain in W Iran: the highest peak of the Zagros Mountains, 14,921 ft. Also, **Zard Kuh** (zärd′ ko͞o′).

za·re·ba (zə rē′bə), *n.* (in the Sudan and adjoining regions) a protective enclosure, as of thorn bushes. Also, **za·ree′ba.** [< Ar *zarībah* pen]

zarf (zärf), *n.* (in the Levant) a holder, usually of ornamental metal, for a coffee cup without a handle. [< Ar *zarf* vessel, sheath]

Z, Zarf

zar·zue·la (zär zwā′lə, -zwē′-; *Sp.* thär-thwe′lä, sär swe′-), *n., pl.* **-las** (-ləz; *Sp.* -läs). a Spanish opera having spoken dialogue and often a satirically treated, topical theme. [< Sp, after *La Zarzuela,* palace near Madrid where first performance took place (1629)]

z-ax·is (zē′ak′sis), *n., pl.* **z-ax·es** (zē′ak′sēz). *Math.* (in a three-dimensional Cartesian coordinate system) the axis along which values of *z* are measured and at which both *x* and *y* equal zero.

za·yin (zä′yin; *Heb.* zä′yēn), *n.* the seventh letter of the Hebrew alphabet. [< Heb]

za·zen (zä′zen′), *n. Zen.* meditation in a prescribed, cross-legged posture. [< Jap; see ZEN]

Z-bar (zē′bär′), *n.* a metal bar with a Z-shaped section. See illus. at **shape.**

Ze·a (zē′ä, zē′ə), *n.* Keos.

zeal (zēl), *n.* fervor for a person, cause, or object; eager desire or endeavor; enthusiastic diligence. [late ME *zele* < L *zēl(us)* < Gk *zêlos*] —**Syn.** passion. —**Ant.** apathy.

Zea·land (zē′lənd), *n.* the largest island of Denmark: Copenhagen is located here. 2,055,040; 2709 sq. mi. Also, **Seeland.** Danish, **Sjaelland.** —**Zea′land·er,** *n.*

zeal·ot (zel′ət), *n.* **1.** a person who shows zeal. **2.** an excessively zealous person; fanatic. **3.** (*cap.*) *Judaism.* a member of an ancient radical group in Judea, that advocated the overthrow of Roman rule. [< LL *zēlōtēs* < Gk = *zēlō-* (var. s. of *zēloûn* to be zealous; see ZEAL) + *-tēs* agent suffix]

zeal·ot·ry (zel′ə trē), *n.* undue or excessive zeal; fanaticism.

zeal·ous (zel′əs), *adj.* full of, characterized by, or resulting from zeal; ardently active, devoted, or diligent. [< ML *zēlōs(us)*] —**zeal′ous·ly,** *adv.* —**zeal′ous·ness,** *n.* —**Syn.** fervent, intense.

ze·bec (zē′bek), *n.* xebec. Also, **ze′beck.**

Zeb·e·dee (zeb′i dē′), *n.* the father of the apostles James and John. Matt. 4:21.

Zebra, *Equus burchelli* (4 ft. high at shoulder; total length 8½ ft.; tail 1½ ft.)

ze·bra (zē′brə; *esp. Brit.,* zeb′rə), *n., pl.* **-bras,** (*esp. collectively*) **-bra.** any of several horselike, African mammals of the genus *Equus,* having a characteristic pattern of black or dark-brown stripes on a whitish background. [< Pg < OSp: wild ass, prob. < VL **eciferus,* L *equiferus* wild horse = *equi-* (s. of *equus* horse) + *ferus* wild] —**ze′bra·like′, ze·bra·ic** (zi brā′ik), *adj.* —**ze·brine** (zē′brīn, -brin), *adj.*

ze·bra·fish (zē′brə fish′), *n., pl.* **-fish·es,** (*esp. collectively*) **-fish.** an oviparous fish, *Brachydanio rerio,* having zebra-like stripes, often kept in aquariums.

ze·bra-plant (zē′brə plant′), *n.* a foliage plant, *Calathea zebrina*, of Brazil, having leaves that are striped with yellow-green and olive-green.
ze·brass (zē′bras), *n.* the offspring of a zebra and an ass. [ZEBR(A) + ASS[1]]
ze·bra·wood (zē′brə wo͝od′), *n.* **1.** any of several trees, esp. *Connarus guianensis*, of tropical America, yielding a striped, hard wood used for making furniture. **2.** the wood of any of these trees.
ze·bu (zē′byo͞o), *n.* a domesticated, Asiatic, bovine animal, *Bos indicus*, having a large hump over the shoulders and a large dewlap. [< F *zébu*, perh. < Tibetan]
Zeb·u·lun (zeb′yo͝o lən, zə byo͞o′lən), *n.* **1.** a son of Jacob and Leah. Gen. 30:20. **2.** one of the 12 tribes of Israel.
Zech·a·ri·ah (zek′ə rī′ə), *n.* **1.** a Minor Prophet of the 6th century B.C. **2.** a book of the Bible bearing his name.
zed (zed), *n.* *Chiefly Brit.* the letter *Z* or *z*. [ME < MF *zede* < L *zēta* < Gk]

Zebu
(6 ft. high at shoulder)

Zed·e·ki·ah (zed′ə kī′ə), *n.* the last king of Judah. II Kings 24, 25; Jer. 52:1–11.
zee (zē), *n.* **1.** *Chiefly U.S.* the letter *Z* or *z*. **2.** something resembling the letter *Z* in shape.
Zee·brug·ge (zē′bro͝og′ə; *Flemish.* zā′brœкн′ə), *n.* a seaport in NW Belgium: part of the city of Bruges; German submarine base in World War I.
Zee·land (zē′lənd; *Du.* zā′länt), *n.* a province in SW Netherlands, consisting largely of islands. 332,286; 1041 sq. mi. *Cap.:* Middelburg. —**Zee′land·er,** *n.*
ze·in (zē′in), *n.* *Biochem.* a yellow powder obtained from corn, used chiefly in the manufacture of fibers, plastics, and paper coatings. [< NL *zē(a)* maize (L *zēa* spelt < Gk *zeiá* barley, wheat; c. Skt *yáva* grain) + -IN[2]]
Zeist (zīst), *n.* a city in the central Netherlands. 58,630.
Zeit·geist (tsīt′gīst′), *n.* *German.* the spirit of the time; general trend of thought or feeling of an era.
zem·stvo (zemst′vō; *Russ.* zyem′stfo), *n., pl.* **zem·stvos** (zemst′vōz; *Russ.* zyem′stfoz). *Russ. Hist.* a system of elected local assemblies founded in 1864 by Alexander II to replace the abolished authority of the nobles: it became the core of the liberal movement from 1905 to 1917. [< Russ = *zem(lya)* land, earth + *-stvo* n. suffix]
Zen (zen), *n.* **1.** Chinese, **Ch'an.** *Buddhism.* a Mahayana movement, introduced into China in the 6th century A.D. and into Japan in the 12th century, whose emphasis is upon enlightenment by means of direct, intuitive insights. Cf. **mondo. 2.** the discipline and practice of this sect. [< Jap < Chin *ch'an* < Pali *jhāna* < Skt *dhyāna* religious meditation] —**Zen′ic,** *adj.* —**Zen′ist,** *n.*
ze·na·na (ze nä′nə), *n.* (in India) **1.** the part of the house in which the women and girls of a family are secluded. **2.** its occupants collectively. —*adj.* **3.** of or pertaining to the zenana or its occupants. [< Hindi < Pers *zanāna* < *zan* woman; c. Skt *jani* woman, wife, Gk *gynē*, OSlav *žena*, OE *cwēn* woman, wife; see QUEEN]
Zend (zend), *n.* *Zoroastrianism.* an exposition of the Avesta in Pahlavi. [< Pers: interpretation, commentary] —**Zend′ic,** *adj.*
Zend-A·ves·ta (zend′ə ves′tə), *n.* *Zoroastrianism.* the Avesta together with the Zend. [< Parsee, var. of *Avesta'-va-zend* AVESTA with commentary]
Zeng·er (zeng′ər, -gər), *n.* **John Peter,** 1697–1746, American journalist, printer, and publisher, born in Germany.
ze·nith (zē′nith *or, esp. Brit.,* zen′ith), *n.* **1.** the point on the celestial sphere vertically above a given position or observer. Cf. **nadir. 2.** highest point or state; culmination. [ME *cenith* < ML < OSp *zenit*, scribal error for *zemt* < Ar *samt* road (cf. Ar *samt ar-rās* road above (over) one's head, the opposite of *nadir*)] —**Syn. 2.** apex, summit. —**Ant. 1, 2.** nadir.
ze·nith·al (zē′nə thəl *or, esp. Brit.,* zen′ə-), *adj.* **1.** of or pertaining to the zenith; situated at or near the zenith. **2.** (of a map) drawn to indicate the actual direction of any point from the center point. [ZENITH + -AL[1]]
ze′nithal equidis′tant projec′tion. See **azimuthal equidistant projection.**
Ze·no (zē′nō), *n.* **1.** See **Zeno of Citium. 2.** See **Zeno of Elea.**
Ze·no·bi·a (zə nō′bē ə), *n.* (*Septimia Bathzabbai*) queen of Palmyra in Syria A.D. 267–272.
Ze′no of Ci′ti·um (sish′ē əm), c340–c265 B.C., Greek philosopher, born in Cyprus. Also called **Zeno, Ze′no the Sto′ic.**
Ze′no of E′lea, c490–c430 B.C., Greek philosopher. Also called **Zeno.**
ze·o·lite (zē′ə līt′), *n.* any of a group of hydrated silicates of aluminum with alkali metals. [< Gk *ze(in)* (to) boil + -o- + -LITE] —**ze·o·lit·ic** (zē′ə lit′ik), *adj.*
Zeph., Zephaniah.
Zeph·a·ni·ah (zef′ə nī′ə), *n.* **1.** a Minor Prophet of the 7th century B.C. **2.** a book of the Bible bearing his name.
zeph·yr (zef′ər), *n.* **1.** a gentle, mild breeze. **2.** (*cap.*) *Literary.* the west wind personified. **3.** any of various things of fine, light quality, as fabric, yarn, etc. [< L *zephyr(us)* < Gk *zéphyros* the west wind] —**Syn. 1.** See **wind**[1].
zeph′yr cloth′, a lightweight worsted cloth.
zeph·yr·e·an (zef′ə rē′ən), *adj.* of, pertaining to, or like a zephyr; full of or containing light breezes. Also, **ze·phyr·i·an** (zi fēr′ē ən), **zeph·yr·ous** (zef′ər əs).
Zeph·y·ri·nus (zef′ə rī′nəs), *n.* **Saint,** pope A.D. 198?–217.
Zeph·y·rus (zef′ər əs), *n.* *Class. Myth.* the west wind personified.
zeph′yr wor′sted, lightweight worsted yarn.
zeph′yr yarn′, any of various soft, lightweight yarns.
Zep·pe·lin (zep′ə lin; *for 1 also Ger.* tsep′ə lēn′), *n.* **1.** Count **Fer·di·nand von** (fer′di nänt′ fən), 1838–1917, German general and aeronautical designer. **2.** (*sometimes l.c.*) a long, rigid dirigible balloon.
Zer·matt (*Ger.* tser mät′), *n.* a village in S Switzerland, near the Matterhorn: resort. 3101.
ze·ro (zēr′ō), *n., pl.* **-ros, -roes,** *v.,* **-roed, -ro·ing,** *adj.* —*n.* **1.** the figure or symbol 0, which in the Arabic notation for numbers stands for the absence of quantity; cipher. **2.** the origin of any kind of measurement, positive or negative, on a scale. **3.** a mathematical value intermediate between positive and negative values. **4.** naught; nothing. **5.** the lowest point or degree. **6.** *Linguistics.* the absence of a linguistic element, as a phoneme or morpheme in a position in which one previously existed or might by analogy be expected to exist. —*v.t.* **7.** to adjust (an instrument or apparatus) to zero point or to an arbitrary reading from which other readings are to be measured. **8. zero in,** to aim (a rifle, etc.) at the precise center or range of a target. **9. zero in on, a.** to direct fire at the precise center or range of (a target). **b.** to concentrate upon (an object, solving a problem, etc.). —*adj.* **10.** having a value of zero: *a zero population growth.* **11.** without change or inflection: *a zero plural.* **12.** *Meteorol.* **a.** (of an atmospheric ceiling) pertaining to or limiting vertical visibility to 50 feet or less. **b.** of, pertaining to, or limiting horizontal visibility to 165 feet or less. [< It < ML *zephirum* < Ar *sifr* CIPHER]
ze′ro-base budg′eting (zēr′ō bās′), a process in government and corporate finance of justifying an overall budget at each fiscal year or each review period rather than dealing only with proposed changes from a previous budget.
ze′ro grav′ity, *Physics.* the condition in which the apparent effect of gravity is zero, as on a body in orbit.
ze′ro hour′, 1. *Mil.* the time set for the beginning of an attack. **2.** *Informal.* **a.** the time set for the beginning of any event, action, etc. **b.** a decisive or critical time.
ze·ro-ze·ro (zēr′ō zēr′ō), *adj.* *Meteorol.* (of atmospheric conditions) having or characterized by zero visibility in both horizontal and vertical directions.
zest (zest), *n.* **1.** keen relish; hearty enjoyment; gusto. **2.** an agreeable or piquant flavor imparted to something. **3.** anything added to impart flavor, cause relish, etc. **4.** piquancy; interest; charm. [< F *zest* (now *zeste*) orange or lemon peel used for flavoring < ?] —**zest′y,** *adj.*
zest·ful (zest′fəl), *adj.* **1.** full of zest. **2.** characterized by keen relish, hearty enjoyment, etc. —**zest′ful·ly,** *adv.* —**zest′ful·ness,** *n.*
ze·ta (zā′tə, zē′-), *n.* the sixth letter of the Greek alphabet (Z, ζ). [< Gk *zêta* < Sem; cf. Heb *ṣādhē*]
Ze·thus (zē′thəs), *n.* *Class. Myth.* a son of Zeus and twin brother of Amphion, whom he assisted in building the walls of Thebes.
Zet·land (zet′lənd), *n.* See **Shetland Islands.**
zeug·ma (zo͞og′mə), *n.* *Gram., Rhet.* the use of a verb with two subjects or objects, or of an adjective with two nouns, although appropriate to only one of the two, as in *to wage war and peace.* [< Gk: a yoking = *zeug(nýnai)* (to) yoke + *-ma* n. suffix] —**zeug·mat·ic** (zo͞og mat′ik), *adj.* —**zeug·mat′i·cal·ly,** *adv.*
Zeus (zo͞os), *n.* the supreme deity of the ancient Greeks, a son of Cronus and Rhea, brother of Demeter, Hades, Hera, Hestia, and Poseidon, and father of Apollo, Athena, and other gods, demigods, and mortals; the god of the heavens, identified by the Romans with Jupiter. [< Gk (gen. *Diós*)]
Zeux·is (zo͞ok′sis), *n.* fl. c430–c400 B.C., Greek painter.
Zhda·nov (zhdä′nəf), *n.* a city in the SE Ukraine, in the SW Soviet Union in Europe, on the Sea of Azov. 480,000. Formerly, **Mariupol.**
Zhi·to·mir (zhi tô′mir), *n.* a city in the central Ukraine, in the SW Soviet Union, W of Kiev. 244,000.
zib·el·ine (zib′ə līn′, -lin), *adj.* **1.** of or pertaining to the sable. —*n.* **2.** the fur of the sable. **3.** a thick woolen cloth with a flattened hairy nap. Also, **zib′el·line′.** [< MF < It *zibellino* = *zibel-* (<< Slav; see SABLE) + *-ino* n. suffix; r. *sibelin* < OF]
zib·et (zib′it), *n.* a civet, *Viverra zibetha*, of India, the Malay Peninsula, and other parts of Asia. [< ML *zibethum* or It *zibetto* < Ar *zabād*]
Zieg·feld (zig′feld), *n.* **Flor·enz** (flôr′ənz, flor′-), 1867–1932, U.S. theatrical producer.
Zif (zif; *Heb.* zēv), *n.* *Chiefly Biblical.* Ziv.
zig·gu·rat (zig′o͝o rat′), *n.* (among the ancient Babylonians and Assyrians) a temple of Sumerian origin in the form of a pyramidal tower presenting the appearance of a series of terraces. Also, **zik·ku·rat, zik·u·rat** (zik′o͝o rat′). [< Assyrian *ziqqurratu* height]
zig·zag (zig′zag′), *n., adj., adv., v.,* **-zagged, -zag·ging.** —*n.* **1.** a line, course, or progression characterized by sharp turns first to one side and then to the other. **2.** a pair of such turns, as in a line or path. —*adj.* **3.** proceeding or formed in a zigzag. —*adv.* **4.** in a zigzag manner. —*v.t.* **5.** to make (something) zigzag. —*v.i.* **6.** to proceed in a zigzag line or course. [< F; r. earlier *ziczac* < F < G *zickzack*, gradational compound based on *Zacke* TACK[1]] —**zig′zag′ged·ness,** *n.*
zig·zag·ger (zig′zag′ər), *n.* **1.** a person or thing that zigzags. **2.** an attachment on a sewing machine for making zigzag stitches.
zilch (zilch), *n.* *Slang.* zero; nothing. [orig. uncert.; perh. humorous alter. of ZERO]
zil·lah (zil′ə), *n.* (formerly in British India) any of the administrative districts making up a province. [< Hindi *ḍilah* < Ar *ḍil'* part]
zil·lion (zil′yən), *n., pl.* **-lions,** (*as after a numeral*) **-lion,** *adj.* *Informal.* —*n.* **1.** an extremely large, indeterminate number. —*adj.* **2.** of, pertaining to, or amounting to a zillion. [z + *-illion*, modeled on *million*]
Zim·ba·bwe (zim bä′bwā), *n.* **1.** a republic in S Africa: a former British colony; declared independence as Rhodesia 1965; officially recognized as a republic under present name 1980. 7,734,000; 150,338 sq. mi. *Cap.:* Harare. **2.** an archaeological site, discovered c1870, in Rhodesia.

zinc (zingk), *n.*, *v.*, **zincked** or **zinced** (zingkt), **zinck·ing** or **zinc·ing** (zing′king). —*n.* **1.** *Chem.* a metallic element resembling magnesium in its chemical relations: used in making galvanized iron, alloys, and as an element in voltaic cells. *Symbol:* Zn; *at. wt.:* 65.37; *at. no.:* 30; *sp. gr.:* 7.14 at 20°C. —*v.t.* **2.** to coat or cover with zinc. [< G *Zink*, ? < *Zinn* TIN] —**zinc′ic, zinc′ous, zinc′oid,** *adj.*

zinc·ate (zing′kāt), *n.* *Chem.* a salt derived from H_2ZnO_2, the acid form of amphoteric zinc hydroxide.

zinc′ blende′, *Mineral.* sphalerite.

zinc′ chlo′ride, *Chem.* a poisonous solid, $ZnCl_2$, used chiefly as a wood preservative and antiseptic, and in the manufacture of paper and soldering fluxes.

zinc·if·er·ous (zing kif′ər əs, zin sif′-), *adj.* yielding or containing zinc.

zinc·i·fy (zing′kə fī′), *v.t.*, **-fied, -fy·ing.** to cover or impregnate with zinc. —**zinc′i·fi·ca′tion,** *n.*

zinc·ite (zing′kīt), *n.* a mineral, native zinc oxide, ZnO, an important ore of zinc.

zinck·en·ite (zing′kə nīt′), *n.* *Mineral.* zinkenite.

zin·cog·ra·phy (zing kog′rə fē), *n.* the art or process of producing a printing surface on a zinc plate. —**zin·cog′ra·pher,** *n.* —**zin·co·graph·ic** (zing′kə graf′ik), **zin′co·graph′i·cal,** *adj.*

zinc′ oint′ment, *Pharm.* an ointment containing 20 percent of zinc oxide, used chiefly in the treatment of skin conditions.

zinc′ ox′ide, *Chem., Pharm.* a powder, ZnO, used chiefly as a pigment, as an ingredient of cosmetics, dental cements, matches, and opaque glass, and as an astringent and antiseptic. Also called **zinc′ white′.**

zinc′ ste′arate, *Chem.* a powder, $Zn(C_{18}H_{35}O_2)_2$, used in the manufacture of cosmetics, ointments, and lacquers, as a drying agent for rubber, and as a waterproofing agent.

zinc′ sul′fate, *Chem.* a powder, $ZnSO_4{\cdot}7H_2O$, used for preserving skins and wood, electrodeposition of zinc, in the bleaching of paper, as a mordant in calico printing, and as an astringent, styptic, and emetic. Also called **zinc′ vit′riol.**

zin·fan·del (zin′fən del′), *n.* **1.** a black grape, grown in California. **2.** a dry red wine made from this grape in California. [?]

zing (zing), *n.* **1.** vitality; animation. **2.** a sharp, singing or whining noise, as of a bullet passing through the air. —*interj.* **3.** (used to imitate the rapid movement of an object through the air.) —*v.i.* **4.** to move or proceed with a sharp, singing or whining noise. [imit.]

zin·ga·ra (tsēng′gä rä′), *n.*, *pl.* **-re** (-re′). *Italian.* a female Gypsy.

zin·ga·ro (tsēng′gä rō′), *n.*, *pl.* **-ri** (-rē′). *Italian.* a Gypsy.

zin·gi·ber·a·ceous (zin′jə bə rā′shəs), *adj.* belonging to the *Zingiberaceae*, or ginger, family of plants. [< NL *zingiber* genus name (see GINGER) + -ACEOUS]

Zin·jan·thro·pus (zin jan′thrə pəs), *n.* a tentative genus of Australopithecines based on a skull and other skeletal remains found at the Olduvai Gorge in Tanzania. [< NL < Ar *Zinj* East Africa + Gk *ánthrōpos* man]

zin·ken·ite (zing′kə nīt′), *n.* a steel-gray mineral with metallic luster, lead antimony sulfide, $PbSb_2S_4$. Also, **zinckenite.** [< G *Zinkenit*, named after J. K. L. *Zincken* (1790–1862), German mineralogist and mining director; see -ITE[1]]

zin·ni·a (zin′ē ə), *n.* **1.** any composite plant of the genus *Zinnia* (*Crassina*), found in Mexico and the U.S. **2.** a zinnia, *Z. elegans:* the state flower of Indiana. [< NL, named after J. G. *Zinn* (1727–59), German botanist; see -IA]

Zi·nov·ievsk (zi nôf′yəfsk), *n.* former name of **Kirovograd.**

Zins·ser (zin′sər), *n.* **Hans** (hanz, hänz), 1878–1940, U.S. bacteriologist.

Zin·zen·dorf (tsin′tsən dôrf′), *n.* **Count Ni·ko·laus Lud·wig von** (nē′kô lous lo͞ot′vikh fən, lo͞od′-), 1700–60, German religious leader: reformer and organizer of the Moravian Church.

Zi·on (zī′ən), *n.* **1.** a hill in Jerusalem, on which the Temple was built. **2.** the Jewish people. **3.** Palestine as the Jewish homeland and symbol of Judaism. **4.** heaven as the final gathering place of true believers. Also, **Sion.** [< Heb *tsīyōn* (*z* repr. *ts* as in G); r. ME, OE *Sion* < LL (Vulgate) < Gk (Septuagint) < Heb, as above]

Zi·on·ism (zī′ə niz′əm), *n.* a world-wide Jewish movement for the establishment in Palestine of a national homeland for the Jews. —**Zi′on·ist,** *n.*, *adj.* —**Zi′on·is′tic,** *adj.*

Zi′on Na′tional Park′, a park in SW Utah. 148 sq. mi.

zip[1] (zip), *n.*, *v.*, **zipped, zip·ping.** *Informal.* —*n.* **1.** a sudden, brief hissing sound, as of a bullet. **2.** energy; vim; vigor. —*v.i.* **3.** to act or move with speed or energy. —*v.t.* **4.** to add vitality or zest to (usually fol. by *up*). [imit.]

zip[2] (zip), *v.*, **zipped, zip·ping.** —*v.t.* **1.** to fasten or unfasten with a zipper. —*v.i.* **2.** to be fastened or unfastened by means of a zipper. [back formation from ZIPPER]

zip[3] (zip), *n.*, *v.*, **zipped, zip·ping.** *Slang.* —*n.* **1.** zero or nothing, esp. as a sports score. —*v.t.* **2.** to beat or defeat by keeping an opponent from scoring.

zip′ code′, *U.S.* a five-digit code written directly after the address, esp. on something to be mailed, the first three digits indicating the state and place of delivery, the last two digits the post office or postal zone; used to expedite the delivery of mail. Also, **ZIP code, Zip code.** Also called **zip, ZIP, Zip.** [*z*(*one*) *i*(*mprovement*) *p*(*rogram*)]

zip-code (zip′kōd′), *v.t.*, **-cod·ed, -cod·ing.** to use a zip code on or in: *to zip-code addresses on envelopes.* Also, **ZIP′-code′.**

zip′ fas′tener, *Brit.* a zipper.

zip′ gun′, a homemade pistol, typically consisting of a metal tube taped to a wooden stock and firing a .22-caliber bullet.

zip·per (zip′ər), *n.* **1.** a person or thing that zips. **2.** Also called **slide fastener.** a device for joining two pieces of cloth, plastic, etc., consisting of two parallel rows of parts interlocked or parted by the motion of a slide. —*v.t.*, *v.i.* **3.** zip[2]. [formerly trademark]

zip·py (zip′ē), *adj.*, **-pi·er, -pi·est.** *Informal.* lively; peppy. [ZIP[1] + -Y[1]]

zir·con (zûr′kon), *n.* a common mineral, zirconium silicate, Zr_2SiO_4, used as a refractory when opaque and as a gem when transparent. [< G *Zirkon;* r. JARGON[2]]

zir·con·ate (zûr′kə nāt′), *n.* *Chem.* a salt of the acid form of zirconium hydroxide.

zir·co·ni·a (zər kō′nē ə), *n.* *Chem.* a water-insoluble powder, ZrO_2, used chiefly as a pigment for paints, an abrasive, and in the manufacture of refractory crucibles. Also called **zirco′nium ox′ide, zirco′nium diox′ide.** [< NL]

zir·co·ni·um (zər kō′nē əm), *n.* *Chem.* a metallic element resembling titanium in its chemical reactions: used in steel metallurgy, as a scavenger, as a refractory, and as an opacifier in vitreous enamels. *Symbol:* Zr; *at. wt.:* 91.22; *at. no.:* 40; *sp. gr.:* 6.49 at 20°C. [< NL; see ZIRCON, -IUM] —**zir·con·ic** (zər kon′ik), *adj.*

Zis·ka (zis′kə; *Ger.* tsis′kä), *n.* **John** or **Jo·hann** (*Ger.* yō′hän). See **Žižka, Jan.**

zit (zit), *n. Slang.* pimple; skin blemish. [?]

zith·er (zith′ər), *n.* a musical instrument, consisting of a flat sounding box, usually with 30 to 40 strings stretched over it, which is placed on a horizontal surface and played with a plectrum and the fingertips. [< G < L *cithara* < Gk *kithára*] —**zith′er·ist,** *n.*

Zither

Ziv (ziv; *Heb.* zēv), *n.* *Chiefly Biblical.* a month equivalent to Iyar of the modern Jewish calendar. I Kings 6:1. [Heb: lit., radiance]

zi·zith (tsit′sis; *Heb.* tsē tsēt′), *n.* (*construed as sing. or pl.*) *Judaism.* the fringes, or tassels, of entwined threads at the four corners of the tallith. Also, **tzitzith.** [< Heb: fringe]

Žiž·ka (*Czech.* zhish′kä), **Jan** (yän), c1370–1424, Bohemian Hussite military leader. Also, **Ziska.**

Zl., zloty; zlotys.

Zla·to·ust (zlä to o͞ost′), *n.* a city in the W RSFSR, in the W Soviet Union in Asia, in the Ural Mountains. 198,000.

zlo·ty (zlô′tē), *n.*, *pl.* **-tys,** (*collectively*) **-ty.** a nickel coin and monetary unit of Poland, equal to 100 groszy. *Abbr.:* Zl. [< Pol: golden]

Zn, *Chem.* zinc.

zo-, var. of **zoo-** before a vowel: *zooid.*

zo·a (zō′ə), *n.* pl. of **zoon.**

-zoa, a plural combining form occurring as the final element in names of zoological groups: *Protozoa.* [pl. comb. form of NL *zōon* < Gk *zôion* animal]

Zo·an (zō′an), *n.* Biblical name of **Tanis.**

zod., zodiac.

zo·di·ac (zō′dē ak′), *n.* **1.** an imaginary belt of the heavens, centering on the ecliptic, within which are the apparent paths of the sun, moon, and principal planets. It is divided into 12 constellations and signs of the zodiac. **2.** a circular or elliptical diagram representing this belt, usually containing pictures of the beings and objects associated with the constellations and signs. [< L *zōdiac*(*us*) < Gk *zōidiakós* (*kýklos*) signal (circle) = *zōidi*(*on*) animal sign (*zôi*(*on*) animal + *-dion* dim. suffix) + *-akos* -AC] —**zo·di·a·cal** (zō dī′ə kəl), *adj.*

Zodiac

zodi′acal light′, a luminous tract in the sky, seen in the west after sunset or in the east before sunrise and thought to be the light reflected from a cloud of meteoric matter revolving around the sun.

Zo·har (zō′här), *n.* a medieval mystical work on the Pentateuch: the definitive work of Jewish cabala.

Zo·la (zō′lə; *Fr.* zô lä′), n. **É·mile** (ā mēl′), 1840–1902, French novelist.

Zoll·ver·ein (tsôl′fer īn′), *n.* See **customs union.** [< G = *Zoll* custom, duty, tariff + *Verein* union]

Zom·ba (zom′bə), *n.* a city in and the former capital (until 1975) of Malawi, in the S part. 15,705.

zom·bi (zom′bē), *n.*, *pl.* **-bis.** **1.** the python god among certain West Africans. **2.** the snake god worshiped in the voodoo ceremonies in the West Indies and certain parts of the southern U.S. **3.** a supernatural force that brings a corpse to physical life. **4.** zombie (defs. 1, 2). Also, **zombie** (for defs. 1–3). [< WAfr: fetish]

zom·bie (zom′bē), *n.* **1.** the body of a dead person given the semblance of life by a supernatural force. **2.** a tall drink made typically with several kinds of rum, citrus juice, and often apricot liqueur. **3.** zombi (defs. 1–3). **4.** *Slang.* a person who is extremely unperceptive, unresponsive, and apathetic. Also, **zombi** (for defs. 1, 2). [var. of ZOMBI]

zon·al (zōn′əl), *adj.* **1.** of or pertaining to a zone or zones. **2.** of the nature of a zone. Also, **zon·a·ry** (zō′nə rē). —**zon′al·ly,** *adv.*

zon·ate (zō′nāt), *adj.* **1.** marked with a zone or zones, as of color, texture, or the like. **2.** arranged in a zone or zones. Also, **zo′nat·ed.**

zo·na·tion (zō nā′shən), *n.* **1.** the state or condition of being zonate. **2.** arrangement or distribution in zones.

zone (zōn), *n., v.,* **zoned, zon·ing.** —*n.* **1.** an area that is divided off or somehow differentiated from other areas. **2.** *Geog.* any of five great divisions of the earth's surface, bounded by lines parallel to the equator, and named according to the prevailing temperature. Cf. **North Frigid Zone, North Temperate Zone, South Frigid Zone, South Temperate Zone, Torrid Zone. 3.** *Biogeog.* an area characterized by a particular set of organisms, whose presence is determined by environmental conditions. **4.** *Geol.* a horizon. **5.** *Geom.* a part of the surface of a sphere included between two parallel planes. **6.** a specific district, area, etc., within which a uniform charge is made for transportation or other service. **7.** an area or district in a city or town under special restrictions as to the type of buildings that may be erected. **8.** See **time zone. 9.** Also called **postal delivery zone.** (in the U.S. postal system) any of the numbered districts into which a city is divided for expediting mail delivery. **10.** *Sports.* a particular portion of a playing area: *end zone; defensive zone.* **11.** *Archaic.* a girdle or belt; cincture. —*v.t.* **12.** to mark with zones or bands. **13.** to divide into zones. **14.** to divide (an urban area) into zones in order to enforce building restrictions. **15.** to encircle or surround with a zone. —*v.i.* **16.** to be formed into a zone or zones. [< L *zōna* < Gk *zṓnē* belt] —**Syn. 1.** region. See **belt. 15.** gird, band.

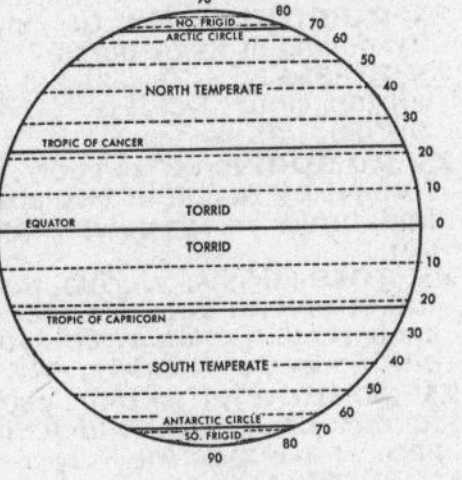

Terrestrial zones

zone′ defense′, *Sports.* a method of defense, esp. in basketball and football, in which each member of the defensive team guards a specified portion of the playing area. Cf. **man-to-man defense.**

zonked (zoŋkt, zôŋkt), *adj.* *Slang.* **1.** under the influence of a drug, such as marijuana. **2.** intoxicated or drunk.

zon·ule (zōn′yo͞ol), *n.* a little zone, belt, band, etc. [< NL *zōnula.* See ZONE, -ULE] —**zon·u·lar** (zōn′yə lər), *adj.*

zoo (zo͞o), *n., pl.* **zoos.** See **zoological garden.** [first two syllables of ZOOLOGICAL GARDEN taken as one syllable]

zoo-, a learned borrowing from Greek meaning "living being," "animal," used in the formation of compound words: *zoometry; zooplankton.* Also, *esp. before a vowel,* **zo-.** [comb. form repr. Gk *zôion* animal]

zoochem., zoochemistry.

zo·o·chem·is·try (zō′ə kem′i strē), *n.* the branch of chemistry dealing with the constituents of the animal body. Also, **zo′ö·chem′is·try.** —**zo·o·chem·i·cal, zo·ö·chem·i·cal** (zō′ə kem′i kəl), *adj.*

zoogeog., zoogeography. Also, **zoögeog.**

zo·o·ge·og·ra·phy (zō′ə jē og′rə fē), *n.* **1.** the science dealing with the geographical distribution of animals. **2.** the study of the causes, effects, and other relations involved in such distributions. Also, **zo′ö·ge·og′ra·phy.** —**zo′o·ge·og′ra·pher, zo′ö·ge·og′ra·pher,** *n.* —**zo·o·ge·o·graph·ic, zo·ö·ge·o·graph·ic** (zō′ə jē′ə graf′ik), **zo′o·ge′o·graph′i·cal, zo′ö·ge′o·graph′i·cal,** *adj.* —**zo′o·ge′o·graph′i·cal·ly, zo′ö·ge′o·graph′i·cal·ly,** *adv.*

zo·o·gloe·a (zō′ə glē′ə), *n.* *Bacteriol.* a jellylike mass of microorganisms. Also, **zo′ö·gloe′a.** [zoo- + NL *gloea* gum < Gk *gloía* glue] —**zo′o·gloe′al, zo′ö·gloe′al, zo′o·gle′al, zo′ö·gle′al,** *adj.*

zo·o·graft·ing (zō′ə graf′tiŋ, -gräf′-), *n.* zooplasty. Also, **zo′ö·graft′ing.**

zo·og·ra·phy (zō og′rə fē), *n.* the branch of zoology dealing with the description of animals. Also, **zo·ög′ra·phy.** —**zo·og′ra·pher, zo·ög′ra·pher,** *n.* —**zo·o·graph·ic, zo·ö·graph·ic** (zō′ə graf′ik), **zo′o·graph′i·cal, zo′ö·graph′i·cal,** *adj.*

zo·oid (zō′oid), *n.* **1.** *Biol.* any organic body or cell capable of spontaneous movement and of an existence more or less apart from or independent of the parent organism. **2.** *Zool.* **a.** any animal organism or individual capable of separate existence, and produced by fission, gemmation, or some method other than direct sexual reproduction. **b.** one of the individuals, as certain free-swimming medusas, that, in the alternation of generations, are produced asexually. **c.** any one of the recognizably distinct individuals or elements of a compound or colonial animal, whether detached, detachable, or not. —*adj.* **3.** Also, **zo·oi′dal, zo·öi′dal.** pertaining to, resembling, or of the nature of an animal. Also, **zo′öid.**

zool., 1. zoological. **2.** zoologist. **3.** zoology. Also, **zoöl.**

zo·ol·a·try (zō ol′ə trē), *n.* the worship of or excessive attention to animals. Also, **zo·öl′a·try.** —**zo·ol′a·ter, zo·öl′a·ter,** *n.* —**zo·ol′a·trous, zo·öl′a·trous,** *adj.*

zo·o·log·i·cal (zō′ə loj′i kəl), *adj.* **1.** of or pertaining to zoology. **2.** relating to or concerned with animals. Also, **zo′ö·log′i·cal, zo′o·log′ic, zo′ö·log′ic.** —**zo′o·log′i·cal·ly, zo′ö·log′i·cal·ly,** *adv.*

zo′olog′ical gar′den, a park or other large enclosure in which live animals are kept for public exhibition. Also called **zoo.**

zo·ol·o·gist (zō ol′ə jist), *n.* a specialist in zoology. Also, **zo·öl′o·gist.**

zo·ol·o·gy (zō ol′ə jē), *n., pl.* **-gies. 1.** the science or branch of biology dealing with animals. **2.** a treatise on zoology. **3.** the animal life of a particular region. Also, **zo·öl′o·gy.**

zoom (zo͞om), *v.i.* **1.** to move quickly or suddenly with a loud humming or buzzing sound. **2.** to fly an airplane suddenly and sharply upward at great speed for a short distance. **3.** *Photog.* to change the magnification of an image while maintaining the subject in focus. —*v.t.* **4.** to cause (an airplane) to zoom. —*n.* **5.** the act or process of zooming. **6.** a zooming sound. **7.** See **zoom lens.** [imit.]

zo·om·e·try (zō om′i trē), *n.* measurement of the proportional lengths or sizes of the parts of animals. Also, **zo·öm′e·try.** —**zo·o·met·ric, zo·ö·met·ric** (zō′ə me′trik), **zo′o·met′ri·cal, zo′ö·met′ri·cal,** *adj.*

zoom′ lens′, (in a camera or motion-picture projector) a lens assembly whose focal length can be adjusted continuously to provide various degrees of magnification with no loss of focus.

zo·o·mor·phic (zō′ə môr′fik), *adj.* **1.** of or pertaining to the ascription of animal form or attributes to beings or things not animal. **2.** characterized by a highly conventionalized representation of animal forms as an artistic or symbolic style. **3.** representing or using animal forms. Also, **zo′ö·mor′phic.** —**zo′o·morph′, zo′ö·morph′,** *n.*

zo·o·mor·phism (zō′ə môr′fiz əm), *n.* **1.** zoomorphic representation, as in ornament. **2.** zoomorphic conception, as of a deity. Also, **zo′ö·mor′phism.**

zo·on (zō′on), *n., pl.* **zo·a** (zō′ə). *Zool. Rare.* **1.** any individual, or the individuals collectively, produced from a single egg. **2.** zooid (def. 2). Also, **zo′ön.** [< NL *zōon* < Gk *zôion* animal] —**zo·on′al, zo·ön′al,** *adj.*

-zoon, a combining form of **zoon:** *protozoon.*

zo·on·o·sis (zō on′ə sis, zō′ə nō′sis), *n.* *Pathol.* a disease of animals communicable to man. Also, **zo·ön′o·sis.**

zo·oph·i·lous (zō of′ə ləs), *adj.* **1.** *Bot.* adapted to pollination by animals. **2.** having an affinity for animals. Also, **zo·öph′i·lous, zo·o·phil·ic, zo·ö·phil·ic** (zō′ə fil′ik).

zo·o·pho·bi·a (zō′ə fō′bē ə), *n.* abnormal fear of animals. Also, **zo′ö·pho′bi·a.** —**zo·oph·o·bous, zo·öph·o·bous** (zō of′ə bəs), *adj.*

zo·o·phyte (zō′ə fīt′), *n.* any of various invertebrate animals resembling a plant, as a coral, sea anemone, etc. Also, **zo′ö·phyte′.** [< NL *zōophyton* < Gk *zōiόphyton*] —**zo·o·phyt·ic, zo·ö·phyt·ic** (zō′ə fit′ik), **zo′o·phyt′i·cal, zo′ö·phyt′i·cal,** *adj.*

zo·o·plank·ton (zō′ə plaŋk′tən), *n.* the animal organisms in plankton. Also, **zo′ö·plank′ton.** Cf. **phytoplankton.**

zo·o·plas·ty (zō′ə plas′tē), *n.* *Surg.* the transplantation of living tissue from a lower animal to the human body. Also, **zo′ö·plas′ty.** Also called **zoografting.** —**zo′o·plas′tic, zo′ö·plas′tic,** *adj.*

zo·o·sperm (zō′ə spûrm′), *n.* *Bot. Obs.* zoospore. Also, **zo′ö·sperm′.** —**zo·o·sper·mat·ic, zo·ö·sper·mat·ic** (zō′ə spər mat′ik), *adj.*

zo·o·spo·ran·gi·um (zō′ə spə ran′jē əm), *n., pl.* **-gi·a** (-jē ə). *Bot.* a sporangium or spore case in which zoospores are produced. Also, **zo′ö·spo·ran′gi·um.** —**zo′o·spo·ran′gi·al, zo′ö·spo·ran′gi·al,** *adj.*

zo·o·spore (zō′ə spōr′, -spôr′), *n.* **1.** *Bot.* an asexual spore produced by certain algae and some fungi, capable of moving about by means of flagella. **2.** *Zool.* any of the minute motile flagelliform or amoeboid bodies that issue from the sporocyst of certain protozoans. Also, **zo′ö·spore′.** —**zo·o·spor·ic, zo·ö·spor·ic** (zō′ə spôr′ik, -spor′-), **zo·os·por·ous, zo·ös·por·ous** (zō os′pər əs, zō′ə spōr′-, -spôr′-), *adj.*

zo·ot·o·my (zō ot′ə mē), *n.* **1.** the anatomy, esp. the comparative anatomy, of animals. **2.** the dissection of animals. Also, **zo·öt′o·my.** [< NL *zōotomia.* See ZOO-, -TOMY] —**zo·o·tom·ic, zo·ö·tom·ic** (zō′ə tom′ik), **zo′o·tom′i·cal, zo′ö·tom′i·cal,** *adj.* —**zo′o·tom′i·cal·ly, zo′ö·tom′i·cal·ly,** *adv.* —**zo·ot′o·mist, zo·öt′o·mist,** *n.*

zoot′ suit′, a suit with baggy, tight-cuffed pants and an oversized coat. [rhyming compound based on SUIT] —**zoot′-suit′er,** *n.*

Zo·rach (zôr′äk, -ak, zôr′-), *n.* **William,** 1887–1966, U.S. sculptor and painter, born in Lithuania.

zor·il (zôr′il, zor′-), *n.* **1.** a weasellike, African animal, *Ictonyx striatus,* resembling a skunk in coloration and habits. **2.** any of various similar African animals of related genera. **3.** any of various skunks of S North America and South America. Also, **zo·ril·la** (zə ril′ə), **zo·rille** (zə ril′), **zo·ril·lo** (zə ril′ō). [var. of *zorille* < F < Sp *zorrilla, -o* = *zorra, -o* fox + *-illa, -o* dim. suffix]

Zo·ro·as·ter (zōr′ō as′tər, zôr′-), *n.* fl. 6th century B.C., Persian religious teacher. Also called **Zarathustra.**

Zo·ro·as·tri·an (zōr′ō as′trē ən, zôr′-), *adj.* **1.** of or pertaining to Zoroaster or to Zoroastrianism. —*n.* **2.** one of the adherents of Zoroastrianism, now chiefly represented by the Gabars of Iran and the Parsees of India. [< L *Zōroastr(ēs)* < Gk (< Avestan ZARATHUSTRA) + -IAN]

Zo·ro·as·tri·an·ism (zōr′ō as′trē ə niz′əm, zôr′-), *n.* an Iranian religion, supposedly founded by Zoroaster, postulating existence of a supreme deity, Ahura Mazda, and a cosmic struggle between a spirit of good, Spenta Mainyu, and a spirit of evil, Angra Mainyu. Also, **Zo′ro·as′trism.** Also called **Mazdaism.**

Zo·si·mus (zō′sə məs), *n.* **Saint,** pope A.D. 417–418.

zos·ter (zos′tər), *n.* *Pathol.* shingles. [< L < Gk *zōstḗr* girdle]

Zou·ave (zo͞o äv′, zwäv), *n.* **1.** (*sometimes l.c.*) one of a former body of infantry in the French army, composed originally of Algerians, distinguished by their picturesque Oriental uniforms. **2.** a member of any body of soldiers adopting a similar dress and drill, esp. any of certain volunteers in the American Civil War. [< F < *Zwāwa* Kabyle tribal name]

zounds (zoundz), *interj.* *Archaic.* (used as a mild oath.) [(*God*)'*s* (*w*)*ounds*]

zow·ie (zou′ē), *interj.* (used to express keen pleasure, surprise, approval, etc.)

zoy·si·a (zoi′sē ə), *n.* any hardy perennial grass of the genus *Zoysia*, native to Eastern Asia. [< NL, var. of *zoisia;* named after Karl von *Zois* (d. 1800), German botanist; see -IA]
ZPG, zero population growth.
Zr, *Chem.* zirconium.
zuc·chet·to (zo͞o ket′ō; *It.* tso͞ok ket′tô), *n., pl.* **-tos,** *It.* **-ti** (-tē). a small, round skullcap worn by Roman Catholic ecclesiastics. [< It, var. of *zucchetta* = *zucc(a)* gourd, head (var. of *cucuzza;* cf. L *cucurbita*) + *-etta* -ETTE]
zuc·chi·ni (zo͞o kē′nē), *n., pl.* **-ni, -nis.** a variety of summer squash shaped like a cucumber and having a smooth, dark-green skin. [< It, pl. of *zucchino* = *zucc(a)* gourd (see ZUCCHETTO) + *-ino* dim. suffix]
Zug (tso͞okh), *n.* **1.** a city in central Switzerland, on the lake of Zug. 19,792 (1960). **2. Lake of,** a lake in central Switzerland. 15 sq. mi.
Zui·der Zee (zī′dər zē′; *Du.* zœi′dər zā′), a former shallow inlet of the North Sea in central Netherlands: now Ijssel Lake. Also, **Zuyder Zee.**
Zu′l·hij·jah (zo͞ol hij′ä), *n.* the 12th month of the Islamic calendar.
Zu′l·ka·dah (zo͞ol′kə dä′), *n.* the 11th month of the Islamic calendar.
Zu·lu (zo͞o′lo͞o), *n., pl.* **-lus,** (*esp. collectively*) **-lu,** *adj.* **—***n.* **1.** a people of SE Africa, inhabiting the coastal region between Natal and Lourenço Marques. **2.** a member of the Zulu people. **3.** the language of the Zulus, a Bantu language. **4.** a word used in communications to represent the letter *Z.* **—***adj.* **5.** of or pertaining to the Zulus or their language.
Zu·lu·land (zo͞o′lo͞o land′), *n.* a territory in NE Natal, in the Republic of South Africa.
Zu·ñi (zo͞o′nyē, -nē, so͞o′-), *n., pl.* **-ñis,** (*esp. collectively*) **-ñi** for 1. **1.** a member of a tribe of North American Indians inhabiting the largest of the Indian pueblos, in western New Mexico. **2.** the language of the Zuñi tribe, of uncertain linguistic affinity. [< Sp < a native name] **—Zu′ñi·an,** *adj., n.*
Zur·ba·rán (tho͞or′bä rän′), *n.* **Fran·cis·co de** (frän thēs′kô the), 1598–1663?, Spanish painter.
Zu·rich (zo͝or′ik), *n.* **1.** a canton in N Switzerland. 952,304 (1960); 668 sq. mi. **2.** the capital of this canton, on the Lake of Zurich. 440,000 (est. 1964). **3. Lake of,** a lake in N Switzerland. 25 mi. long; 34 sq. mi. German, **Zü·rich** (tsʏ′rikh) (for defs. 1, 2).
Zuy·der Zee (zī′dər zē′; *Du.* zœi′dər zā′). See **Zuider Zee.**
Zweig (zwīg, swīg; *Ger.* tsvīkh), *n.* **Ste·fan** (stef′ən, -än; *Ger.* shte′fän), 1881–1942, Austrian dramatist, critic, biographer, and novelist.
Zwick·au (tsvik′ou), *n.* a city in W Saxony, in S East Germany. 128,505 (1964).
zwie·back (zwī′bak′, -bäk′, zwē′-, swī′-; *Ger.* tsvē′bäk′), *n.* a special egg bread made into rusks. [< G: twice-baked = *zwie* twice + *backen* to bake. See TWI-, BAKE[1]; cf. BISCUIT]
Zwing·li (zwing′lē, swing′-; *Ger.* tsving′lē), *n.* **Ul·rich** (o͝ol′rikh) or **Hul·dreich** (ho͝ol′drīkh), 1484–1531, Swiss Protestant reformer. **—Zwing′li·an,** *adj., n.*
zwit·ter·i·on (tsvit′ər ī′ən), *n.* *Physical Chem.* an ion with both a positive and a negative charge. Also, **zwit′ter-i′on.** [< G *Zwitter* half-breed + ION] **—zwit·ter·i·on·ic** (tsvit′ər ī on′ik), *adj.*
Zwol·le (zwôl′ə), *n.* a city in the central Netherlands. 56,779 (1962).
zyg·a·poph·y·sis (zig′ə pof′i sis, zī′gə-), *n., pl.* **-ses** (-sēz′). *Anat., Zool.* one of the articular processes upon the neural arch of a vertebra, usually occurring in two pairs, one anterior and the other posterior, and serving to interlock each vertebra with the ones above and below. **—zyg·ap·o·phys·e·al, zyg·ap·o·phys·i·al** (zig′ap ə fiz′ē əl), *adj.*
zygo-, a learned borrowing from Greek meaning "yoke," "yoked," "yoke-shaped," used in the formation of compound words: *zygomorphic.* Also, *esp. before a vowel,* **zyg-.** [comb. form of Gk *zygón* YOKE]
zy·go·dac·tyl (zī′gə dak′til, zig′ə-), *adj.* **1.** Also, **zy′go·dac′ty·lous.** (of a bird) having the toes of each foot arranged in pairs, with two toes in front and two behind. **—***n.* **2.** a zygodactyl bird. **—zy′go·dac′tyl·ism,** *n.*

Zygodactyl foot

zy·go·ma (zī gō′mə, zi-), *n., pl.* **-ma·ta** (-mə tə). *Anat.* **1.** See **zygomatic arch. 2.** the zygomatic process of the temporal bone. **3.** See **zygomatic bone.** [< NL < Gk = *zygo(ûn)* (to) yoke (see ZYGO-) + *-ma* n. suffix]
zy·go·mat·ic (zī′gə mat′ik, zig′ə-), *Anat.* **—***adj.* **1.** of, pertaining to, or situated near the zygoma. **—***n.* **2.** See **zygomatic bone.** [*zygomat-* (comb. form of ZYGOMA) + -IC]
zy′gomat′ic arch′, *Anat.* the bony arch below the orbit of the skull.
zy′gomat′ic bone′, *Anat.* a bone on each side of the face below the eye, forming the prominence of the cheek and part of the orbit. Also called **malar, malar bone, cheekbone.**
zy′gomat′ic proc′ess, *Anat.* any of several bony processes that articulate with the zygomatic bone.
zy·go·mor·phic (zī′gə môr′fik, zig′ə-), *adj.* *Bot., Zool.* having bilateral symmetry; divisible into similar or symmetrical halves by one plane only. Also, **zy′go·mor′phous.** **—zy′go·mor′phism, zy′go·mor′phy,** *n.*
zy·go·phyl·la·ceous (zī′gō fə lā′shəs, zig′ō-), *adj.* belonging to the *Zygophyllaceae,* or bean caper family of plants. [< NL *zygophyll(um)* genus name (see ZYGO-, -PHYLL) + -ACEOUS]
zy·go·phyte (zī′gə fīt′, zig′ə-), *n.* a plant that reproduces by means of zygospores.
zy·go·sis (zī gō′sis, zi-), *n.* *Biol.* the union of two gametes; conjugation. [< NL < Gk: a yoking] **—zy·gose** (zī′gōs, zig′ōs), *adj.*
zy·go·spore (zī′gə spōr′, -spôr′, zig′ə-), *n.* *Bot.* a cell formed by fusion of two similar gametes, as in certain algae and fungi. **—zy·go·spor·ic** (zī′gə spôr′ik, -spor′-, zig′ə-), *adj.*
zy·gote (zī′gōt, zig′ōt), *n.* *Biol.* **1.** the cell produced by the union of two gametes. **2.** the individual developing from such a cell. [< Gk *zygōtós* yoked] **—zy·got·ic** (zī got′ik, zi-), *adj.* **—zy·got′i·cal·ly,** *adv.*
zy·go·tene (zī′gə tēn′, zig′ə-), *n.* *Biol.* the synaptic stage in meiosis, during which homologous chromosomes conjugate. [< F *zygotène* = *zygo-* ZYGO- + *-tène* < L *taenia* < Gk *tainía* fillet]
zy·mase (zī′mās), *n.* *Biochem.* an enzyme in yeast that causes the decomposition of sugar into alcohol and carbon dioxide, obtainable in the form of an extract.
zymo-, a learned borrowing from Greek meaning "ferment," "leaven," used in the formation of compound words: *zymology.* Also, *esp. before a vowel,* **zym-.** [comb. form repr. Gk *zýmē* leaven]
zy·mo·gen (zī′mə jən), *n.* *Biochem.* any of various substances that may change into an enzyme because of some internal change. [< G]
zy·mo·gen·e·sis (zī′mə jen′i sis) *n.* *Biochem.* the change of a zymogen into an enzyme.
zy·mo·gen·ic (zī′mə jen′ik), *adj.* *Biochem.* **1.** of or pertaining to a zymogen. **2.** causing fermentation. Also, **zy·mog·e·nous** (zī moj′ə nəs).
zy·mol·o·gy (zī mol′ə jē), *n.* *Biochem.* the science dealing with fermentation and the action of enzymes; enzymology. **—zy·mo·log·ic** (zī′mə loj′ik), *adj.* **—zy·mol′o·gist,** *n.*
zy·mol·y·sis (zī mol′i sis), *n.* *Biochem.* **1.** the digestive and fermentative action of enzymes. **2.** fermentation or other hydrolytic reactions produced by an enzyme. **—zy·mo·lyt·ic** (zī′mə lit′ik), *adj.*
zy·mom·e·ter (zī mom′i tər), *n.* an instrument for ascertaining the degree of fermentation.
zy·mo·plas·tic (zī′mō plas′tik), *adj.* producing enzymes.
zy·mo·sis (zī mō′sis), *n., pl.* **-ses** (-sēz). **1.** an infectious or contagious disease. **2.** *Obs.* a process analogous to fermentation, by which certain infectious and contagious diseases were supposed to be produced. [< NL < Gk]
zy·mos·then·ic (zī′məs then′ik), *adj.* increasing the activity of an enzyme.
zy·mot·ic (zī mot′ik), *adj.* **1.** pertaining to or caused by or as by fermentation. **2.** of or pertaining to zymosis or to zymotic diseases. [< Gk *zymōtik(ós)* causing fermentation] **—zy·mot′i·cal·ly,** *adv.*
zy·mur·gy (zī′mûr jē), *n.* the branch of chemistry dealing with fermentation, as in winemaking, brewing, etc.
Zyr·i·an (zir′ē ən), *n.* a Uralic language belonging to the Permian branch and having written documents from the 14th century to the present. Also called **Komi.**
Zz., ginger. [< L *zingiber*] Also, **zz.**
ZZZ, (used to represent the sound of a person snoring.) Also, **zzz**

SIGNS AND SYMBOLS

ASTRONOMY

ASTRONOMICAL BODIES

☉ **1.** the sun. **2.** Sunday.

☾ ☽ ● } **1.** the moon. **2.** Monday.

● } new moon.

☽) } the moon, first quarter.

○ } full moon.

☾ (} the moon, last quarter.

☿ **1.** Mercury. **2.** Wednesday.

♀ **1.** Venus. **2.** Friday.

⊕ ♁ ⊖ } Earth.

♂ **1.** Mars. **2.** Tuesday.

♃ **1.** Jupiter. **2.** Thursday.

♄ **1.** Saturn. **2.** Saturday.

⛢ ♅ } Uranus.

♆ Neptune.

♇ Pluto.

Asteroids, or minor planets, are each designated by a number within a circle, as ① Ceres, ② Pallas, ③ Juno, ④ Vesta.

✳ ✱ } star.

☄ comet.

α, β, etc. the first, second, etc., star in a specified constellation (followed by the Latin name of the constellation in the genitive); as: α Orionis.

ASPECTS AND NODES

☌ conjunction; having the same longitude or right ascension.

⚹ sextile; differing by 60° in longitude or right ascension.

Q } quintile; differing by 72° in longitude or right ascension.

□ quadrature; differing by 90° in longitude or right ascension.

△ trine; differing by 120° in longitude or right ascension.

☍ opposition; differing by 180° in longitude or right ascension.

☊ ascending node.

☋ descending node.

♈ vernal equinox.

♎ autumnal equinox.

SIGNS OF THE ZODIAC

Spring Signs

♈ Aries, the Ram.

♉ Taurus, the Bull.

♊ II } Gemini, the Twins.

Summer Signs

♋ } Cancer, the Crab.

♌ Leo, the Lion.

♍ Virgo, the Virgin.

Autumn Signs

♎ Libra, the Balance.

♏ Scorpio, the Scorpion.

♐ Sagittarius, the Archer.

Winter Signs

♑ } Capricorn, the Goat.

♒ Aquarius, the Water Bearer.

♓ Pisces, the Fishes.

QUANTITIES, UNITS, ETC.

α R.A. } right ascension.

β celestial latitude.

△ distance from Earth.

δ declination.

ε obliquity of the ecliptic.

θ equation of light.

λ longitude.

μ proper motion.

ρ density.

☊ longitude of the ascending node.

ω angle between ascending node and the perihelion.

☉ the sun's longitude.

☽ the moon's longitude.

E. east.

h ʰ } hour(s); as in: 2h; 4^h.

m ᵐ } minute(s) of time; as in: 8m; 15^m.

N. + } north.

S. − } south.

s ˢ } second(s) of time; as in: 6s; 20^s.

W. west.

° degree(s) of arc.

′ minute(s) of arc.

″ second(s) of arc.

BIOLOGY

♂ male; a male organism, organ, or cell; a staminate flower or plant, or the staminate parent of a hybrid.

♀ female; a female organism, organ, or cell; a pistillate flower or plant, or the seed-bearing parent of a hybrid.

□ (in genealogical and inheritance charts) a male.

○ (in genealogical and inheritance charts) a female.

P parent or parental generation; the first generation in a specified line of descent.

F filial generation; any generation following a parental generation.

F_1, F_2, F_3, etc. the first, second, third, etc., filial generations.

× **1.** magnified by. **2.** crossed with; denoting a sexual hybrid.

+ **1.** denoting a graft hybrid (asexual hybrid). **2.** denoting the presence of a specified characteristic or trait.

— denoting the absence of a specified characteristic or trait.

○ ⊙ ① } annual plant.

⊙⊙ ② } biennial plant.

♃ perennial herb or plant.

△ evergreen plant.

° ′ ″ } feet, inches, lines, respectively.

′ ″ ‴ } used by some authors in place of °, ′, ″.

$\underline{*}$ northern hemisphere.

$\overline{*}$ southern hemisphere.

|✱ Old World.

✱| New World.

CHEMISTRY

ELEMENTS

Each of the chemical elements is represented by a symbol, derived from the initial letter or from an abbreviation of the English or Latin name. For example: H (hydrogen), O (oxygen), Na (sodium, for Latin *natrium*), etc.

Isotopes are often indicated by a superior number, indicating the atomic mass, as in: U^{235} or ^{235}U, meaning the uranium isotope of atomic mass 235. See **Periodic Table of the Elements** on page 428.

COMPOUNDS

Compounds are represented by combinations of the symbols of their constituent elements, with an inferior number to the right of each symbol indicating the number of atoms of the element entering into the compound (number 1 is, however, omitted). Thus, in some simple cases, NaCl (sodium chloride, or common salt) is a compound containing one atom of sodium and one of chlorine, H_2O (water) contains two atoms of hydrogen and one of oxygen, H_2O_2 (hydrogen peroxide, or common peroxide) contains two atoms each of hydrogen and oxygen. A molecule may also consist entirely of atoms of a single element, as O_3 (ozone), which consists of three atoms of oxygen. Other symbols used in the formulas of molecules and compounds are:

· **1.** denoting free radicals; as in: $CH_3\cdot$ (methyl); $C_6H_5\cdot$ (phenyl). **2.** denoting water of crystallization (or hydration); as in: $Na_2CO_3\cdot 10H_2O$ (washing soda).

( ) denoting a radical within a compound; as in: $(C_2H_5)_2O$ (ether).

[ ] denoting a complex grouping in a coordination formula; as in: $[Co(NH_3)_6]Cl_3$, indicating a complex molecule containing a complex cation, made up of one atom of cobalt and six molecules of ammonia, which as a unit does not possess properties characteristic of either constituent, and three chlorine atoms which maintain their characteristic properties.

1, 2, 3, etc. (before a symbol or formula) denoting a multiplication of the symbol or formula; as in: 3H, indicating three atoms of hydrogen; $6H_2O$, indicating six molecules of water.

1-, 2-, 3-, etc. (in names of compounds) denoting one of several possible positions of substituted atoms or groups; as in: 1-propanol.

α, β, etc. (in names of compounds) denoting one of several possible positions of substituted atoms or groups.

$^+$ denoting dextrorotation; as in: $^+120°$.

$^-$ denoting levorotation; as in: $^-120°$.

R (in structural formulas) denoting a radical.

VALENCE AND ELECTRIC CHARGE

$^-$, $^=$, $^\equiv$, etc. *a.* (in the superior position) denoting a negative charge of one, two, three, etc.; as in: Cl^-; $(SO_4)^=$. *b.* denoting a single, double, triple, etc., bond; as in: $H-O-H$; $Ca=O$.

$^{-1}$, $^{-2}$, $^{-3}$, etc. same as $^-$, $^=$, $^\equiv$, etc. (def. a); as in: Cl^{-1}; $(SO_4)^{-2}$.

$^+$, $^{++}$, $^{+++}$, etc. denoting a positive charge of one, two, three, etc.; as in: K^+, Ca^{++}.

$^{+1}$, $^{+2}$, $^{+3}$, etc. same as $^+$, $^{++}$, $^{+++}$, etc.; as in: K^{+1}; Ca^{+2}.

$'$, $''$, $'''$, etc. *a.* denoting a valence of one, two, three, etc.; as in: Cu$'$, indicating univalent copper; Cu$''$, indicating bivalent copper. *b.* denoting a charge, esp. a negative charge, of one, two, three, etc.; as in: I$'$, used in place of I^- or I^{-1}, indicating that the iodine ion has a single negative charge.

·, :, ⋮, etc. denoting a single, double, triple, etc., bond; as in: H·O·H; Ca:O. The symbol : is also used in electronic formulas in place of · or – to indicate a single bond (paired electrons).

CHEMICAL REACTIONS

+ added to; together with.

= form; are equal to; as in: $H+H+O=H_2O$.

$\rightarrow$ $\leftarrow$ denoting a reaction in the direction indicated; as in: $3H_2+N_2\rightarrow 2NH_3$.

$\rightleftarrows$ denoting a reversible reaction, i.e., a reaction which proceeds simultaneously in both directions; as in: $H_2O+Cl_2\rightleftarrows HCl+HClO$.

$\downarrow$ (after a symbol or formula) denoting the precipitation of a specified substance; as in: $AgNO_3+HCl\rightarrow AgCl\downarrow +HNO_3$.

$\uparrow$ (after a symbol or formula) denoting that a specified substance passes off as a gas; as in: $FeS+2HCl\rightarrow H_2S\uparrow +FeCl_2$.

$\equiv$ $\Leftrightarrow$ (in a quantitative equation) denoting the quantities of specified substances which will enter completely into a reaction, without leaving excess material.

CHESS

	WHITE	BLACK	
K	♔	♚	king.
Q	♕	♛	queen.
R	♖	♜	rook.
B	♗	♝	bishop.
N or Kt	♘	♞	knight.
P	♙	♟	pawn.

Chess notation, in which each move is recorded as a particular piece moving to a particular square, employs the following designations for the several squares:

BLACK

QR1 QR8	QN1 QN8	QB1 QB8	Q1 Q8	K1 K8	KB1 KB8	KN1 KN8	KR1 KR8
QR2 QR7	QN2 QN7	QB2 QB7	Q2 Q7	K2 K7	KB2 KB7	KN2 KN7	KR2 KR7
QR3 QR6	QN3 QN6	QB3 QB6	Q3 Q6	K3 K6	KB3 KB6	KN3 KN6	KR3 KR6
QR4 QR5	QN4 QN5	QB4 QB5	Q4 Q5	K4 K5	KB4 KB5	KN4 KN5	KR4 KR5
QR5 QR4	QN5 QN4	QB5 QB4	Q5 Q4	K5 K4	KB5 KB4	KN5 KN4	KR5 KR4
QR6 QR3	QN6 QN3	QB6 QB3	Q6 Q3	K6 K3	KB6 KB3	KN6 KN3	KR6 KR3
QR7 QR2	QN7 QN2	QB7 QB2	Q7 Q2	K7 K2	KB7 KB2	KN7 KN2	KR7 KR2
QR8 QR1	QN8 QN1	QB8 QB1	Q8 Q1	K8 K1	KB8 KB1	KN8 KN1	KR8 KR1

WHITE

Note that each square is known by two designations, one from the vantage point of White, the other from that of Black. In the above diagram, the letter designations are:

QR queen rook.
QN queen knight.
QB queen bishop.
KB king bishop.
KN king knight.
KR king rook.

In addition, the following are used:

x captures; as in: QxP=queen takes pawn.

— moves to; as in: R—KB5 =rook moves to king bishop five.

ch check; as in: B—KR4 ch =bishop moves to king rook four giving check.

dis ch discovered check.

dbl ch double check.

e.p. en passant.

mate checkmate.

O—O castles, king-side.

O—O—O castles, queen-side.

! good move; as in: RxP!

!! very good move.

!!! outstanding move.

? bad move.

!? good (or bad) move depending on opponent's response.

COMMERCE

@ **1.** at; as in: eggs @ 60¢ per dozen. **2.** to; as in: woolen cloth per yard $5.00 @ $8.50.

a/c account.

B/E bill of exchange.

B/L bill of lading.

B/S bill of sale.

c/d *Bookkeeping.* carried down.

c/f *Bookkeeping.* carried forward.

c.&f. cost and freight.

C/L carload lot.

c/o **1.** care of. **2.** *Bookkeeping.* carried over.

c/s cases.

L/C letter of credit.

O/S out of stock.

P&L **1.** profit and loss. **2.** *Bookkeeping.* a summary account to which are transferred the balances of accounts showing either a profit or loss.

w/ with.

w/o without.

1. (before a figure or figures) number; numbered; as in: #40 thread. **2.** (after a figure or figures) pound(s); as in: 20#.

% **1.** percent; per hundred. **2.** order of.

℔ per; as in: apples $3 ℔ bushel.

MATHEMATICS

ARITHMETIC AND ALGEBRA

+ **1.** plus; add. **2.** positive; positive value; as: +64. **3.** denoting underestimated approximate accuracy, with some figures omitted at the end; as in: $\pi = 3.14159+$.

− **1.** minus; subtract. **2.** negative; negative value; as: −64. **3.** denoting overestimated approximate accuracy, with some figures omitted at the end; as in: $\pi = 3.1416-$.

± **1.** plus or minus; add or subtract; as in: $4 \pm 2 = 6$ or 2. **2.** positive or negative; as in: $\sqrt{a^2} = \pm a$. **3.** denoting the probable error associated with a figure derived by experiment and observation, approximate calculation, etc.

∓ **1.** minus or plus. Cf. – (def. 1). **2.** negative or positive, used where ± has appeared previously; as in: $(a \pm b)(a^2 \mp ab + b^2) = (a^3 \pm b^3)$, upper signs or lower signs to be taken consistently throughout.

× } times; multiplied by; as in:
· } $2 \times 4 = 2 \cdot 4$.

Note: multiplication may also be indicated by writing the algebraic symbols for multiplicand(s) and multiplier(s) close together without any sign; as in: *xy*; $a(a + b) = a^2 + ab$.

÷ / — } divided by; as in: $8 \div 2 = 8/2 = \frac{8}{2} = 4$.

: / — } denoting the ratio of (in proportion).

= equals; is equal to.

:: equals; is equal to (in proportion); as in: 6 : 3 :: 8 : 4.

≠ ≠ } is not equal to.

≡ is identical with.

≢ ≢ } is not identical with.

≈ is approximately equal to.

∼ **1.** is equivalent to. **2.** is similar to.

> is greater than.

≫ is much greater than.

< is less than.

≪ is much less than.

≯ is not greater than.

≮ is not less than.

≥ ≧ ⩾ } is equal to or greater than.

≤ ≦ ⩽ } is equal to or less than.

∝ varies directly as; is directly proportional to; as in: $x \propto y$.

→ approaches as a limit.

$^1, ^2, ^3$, etc. (at the right of a symbol, figure, etc.) exponents, indicating the quantity is raised to the first, second, third, etc., power; as in: $(ab)^2 = a^2b^2$; $4^3 = 64$.

√ √ } the radical sign, indicating the square root of; as in: $\sqrt{81} = 9$.

∛, ∜, $\sqrt[5]{}$, etc. the radical sign used with indexes, indicating the third, fourth, fifth, etc., root; as in: $\sqrt[3]{125} = 5$.

$^{\frac{1}{2}}, ^{\frac{1}{3}}, ^{\frac{1}{4}}$, etc. fractional exponents used to indicate roots, and equal to √, ∛, ∜, etc.; as in: $9^{\frac{1}{2}} = \sqrt{9} = 3$; $a^{\frac{3}{4}} = a^{\frac{1}{4}} \times a^{\frac{1}{2}} = \sqrt[4]{a^3}$.

$^{-1}, ^{-2}, ^{-3}$, etc. negative exponents, used to indicate the reciprocal of the same quantity with a positive exponent; as in:

$$9^{-2} = \frac{1}{9^2} = \frac{1}{81}; a^{-\frac{1}{2}} = \frac{1}{\sqrt{a}}.$$

( ) parentheses; as in: $2(a + b)$.

[ ] brackets; as in: $4 + 3[a(a + b)]$.

{ } braces; as in: $5 + b\{(a + b)[2 - a(a + b)] - 3\}$.

—— vinculum; as in: $\overline{a + b}$.

Note: Parentheses, brackets, braces, and vincula are used with quantities consisting of more than one member or term, to group them and show they are to be considered together.

! ⌊ } factorial of; as in: $4! = \underline{4|} = 4 \cdot 3 \cdot 2 \cdot 1 = 24$.

∞ infinity.

| | absolute value of the quantity within the bars.

′, ″, ‴, etc. prime, double prime, triple prime, etc., used to indicate: *a.* constants, as distinguished from the variable denoted by a letter alone. *b.* a variable under different conditions, at different times, etc.

f, F, φ, etc. function of; as in: $f(x)$ = a function of *x*. *Note:* in addition to φ, other symbols (esp. letters from the Greek alphabet) may be used to indicate functions, as ψ or γ.

GEOMETRY

∠ angle; as in: ∠ ABC, (*pl.* ∠s).

⊥ **1.** a perpendicular (*pl.* ⊥s). **2.** is perpendicular to; as in: AB ⊥ CD.

∥ **1.** a parallel (*pl.* ∥s). **2.** is parallel to; as in: AB∥CD.

△ triangle; as in: △ABC, (*pl.* △s).

▭ rectangle; as in: ▭ABCD.

□ square; as in: □ABCD.

▱ parallelogram; as in: ▱ABCD.

○ circle (*pl.* Ⓢ).

≅ ≡ } is congruent to; as in: △ABD ≅ △CEF.

∼ is similar to; as in: △ACE∼△BDF.

∴ therefore; hence.

∵ since; because.

π the Greek letter pi, representing the ratio (3.14159+) of the circumference of a circle to its diameter.

⌒ (over a group of letters) indicating an arc of a circle; as: $\overset{\frown}{GH}$, the arc between points G and H.

° degree(s) of arc; as in: 90°.

′ minute(s) of arc; as in: 90°30′.

″ second(s) of arc; as in: 90°30′15″.

CALCULUS

△ an increment; as: △*y* = an increment of *y*.

d differential operator; as: *dx* = differential of *x*.

Σ summation operator.

$\prod_{1}^{n}$ product of *n* terms.

∫ integral sign; as in: $\int f(x)\,dx$, the integral of $f(x)$ with respect to *x*.

$\int_a^b$ definite integral, giving limits; as in: $\int_a^b f(x)\,dx$, the definite integral of $f(x)$ between limits *a* and *b*.

MEDICINE AND PHARMACY

+ **1.** excess of. **2.** acid reaction. **3.** positive reaction (to a clinical or diagnostic test).

– **1.** deficiency of. **2.** alkaline reaction. **3.** negative reaction (to a clinical or diagnostic test).

℈ scruple.

℈ss half a scruple.

℈i one scruple.

℈iss a scruple and a half.

℈ij two scruples.

ʒ dram.

ʒss half a dram.

ʒi one dram.

ʒiss a dram and a half.

ʒij two drams.

℥ ounce.

℥ss half an ounce.

℥i one ounce.

℥iss an ounce and a half.

℥ij two ounces.

Apothecaries' Measures

♏ minim.

fʒ fluid dram.

f℥ fluid ounce.

O. pint (L. *octarius*).

C. gallon (L. *congius*).

℞ take (L. *recipe*).

MISCELLANEOUS

& & } the ampersand, meaning *and*. Cf. **ampersand.**

&c. et cetera; and others; and so forth; and so on. Cf. **et cetera.**

′ foot; feet; as in: 6′ = six feet.

″ inch; inches; as in: 6′2″ = six feet, two inches.

× **1.** by: used in stating dimensions; as in: 2′×4′×1′; a 2″×4″ board. **2.** a sign (the cross) made in place of a signature by a person who cannot write; as in:

his
John × Jones
mark.

♠ *Cards.* spade.

♥ *Cards.* heart.

♦ *Cards.* diamond.

♣ *Cards.* club.

† died: used esp. in genealogical tables.

* born: used esp. in genealogical tables.

© copyright; copyrighted.

® registered; registered trademark.

¶ paragraph mark.

§ section mark.

" ditto; indicating the same as the aforesaid: used in charts, lists, etc.

MONETARY

$ } 1. dollar(s), in the United States, Canada, Hong Kong, Liberia, etc. **2.** peso(s), in Colombia, Mexico, etc. **3.** cruzeiro(s), in Brazil (Cr$ is also used). **4.** escudo(s), in Portugal.

VN$ Vietnamese piaster(s).

C$ cordoba(s), in Nicaragua.

M$N paper peso(s), in Argentina.

¢ cent(s), in the United States, Canada, etc.

£ pound(s), in United Kingdom, Ireland, etc.

p new penny (new pence), in United Kingdom, Ireland, etc.

/ } s. } (formerly) shilling(s), in United Kingdom, Ireland, etc.

d. (formerly) penny (pence), in United Kingdom, Ireland, etc.

B/ balboa(s), in Panama.

₡ colon(es), in Costa Rica and El Salvador.

₱ peso(s), in the Philippines.

S/ **1.** sucre(s), in Ecuador. **2.** sol(s), in Peru.

¥ yen (yen), in Japan.

MUSIC

G clef; treble clef: indicates that the second line of the staff corresponds to the G next above middle C.

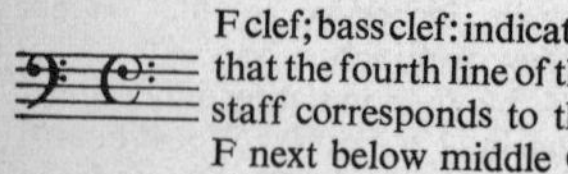

F clef; bass clef: indicates that the fourth line of the staff corresponds to the F next below middle C.

♯ sharp: indicates that the note it precedes is raised one half step.

♭ flat: indicates that the note it precedes is lowered one half step.

♮ natural: indicates the natural note, canceling the effect of a previous sharp or flat.

× double sharp: indicates that the note it precedes is raised two half steps.

♭♭ double flat: indicates that the note it precedes is lowered two half steps.

♮♯ indicates a single sharp when used after a double sharp.

♮♭ indicates a single flat when used after a double flat.

𝅜, 𝅜 breve; double whole note.

𝅝 whole note; semibreve.

𝅗𝅥, 𝅗𝅥 half note; minim.

♩, ♩ quarter note; crochet.

♪, ♪ eighth note; quaver.

𝅘𝅥𝅯, 𝅘𝅥𝅯 sixteenth note; semiquaver.

𝅘𝅥𝅰, 𝅘𝅥𝅰 thirty-second note; demisemiquaver.

𝅘𝅥𝅱, 𝅘𝅥𝅱 sixty-fourth note; hemidemisemiquaver.

⌒ ⌒ tie; a short curved line connecting two successive notes of the same pitch, indicating a tone duration of their combined values. Thus,

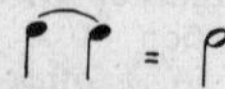

Dots placed after notes add additional value to them:

𝅗𝅥. , ♩. , ♪., etc.

The single dot placed after the note adds to it one half of its value. Thus,

♪. = ♪ 𝅘𝅥𝅯

The double dot adds one half plus one quarter of the note's value. Thus,

♩.. = ♩ ♪ 𝅘𝅥𝅯

Rests indicate intervals of silence between tones. Rest values are:

𝄺 double whole rest.

𝄻 whole rest.

𝄼 half rest.

𝄽, ×, 𝄾 quarter rest.

𝄾 eighth rest.

𝄿 sixteenth rest.

𝅀 thirty-second rest.

𝅁 sixty-fourth rest.

Dots placed after rests have the same meaning as dots placed after notes, adding additional value to them; for example:

𝄽. = 𝄽 𝄾

𝄾. = 𝄾 𝄿

PHYSICS

GENERAL

α angular acceleration.

ε permitivity; dielectric constant.

λ wavelength.

μ permeability.

ν frequency.

ρ resistivity.

PARTICLES

α alpha particle.

γ photon.

Λ lambda particle.

μ muon.

ν neutrino.

Ξ xi particle.

π pion.

Σ sigma particle.

A bar over the symbol for a particle indicates its antiparticle. Thus, $\bar{\nu}$ is the symbol for the antineutrino.

RELIGION

† the cross: a symbol or emblem of Christianity.

☩ Celtic cross: used esp. as a symbol of the Presbyterian Church.

☦ three-barred cross; Russian cross: used esp. as a symbol of the Russian Orthodox Church.

✠ Greek cross: used esp. as a symbol of the Greek Orthodox Church.

✠ } ✚ } **1.** a modification of the cross used by the pope and by Roman Catholic archbishops and bishops before their names. **2.** an indication inserted at those points in the service at which the sign of the cross is made.

✡ star of David: a symbol of Judaism and the Jewish people.

☪ crescent: a symbol or emblem of Islam.

℟ response: used in prayer books, esp. of the Roman Catholic Church.

✳ an indication used in Roman Catholic service books to separate a verse of a psalm into two parts, showing where the response begins.

℣ } V' } an indication used in service books to show the point at which a versicle begins.

DIRECTORY OF COLLEGES AND UNIVERSITIES

This alphabetical list of colleges and universities in the United States is followed by a similar list of Canadian institutions providing higher education leading to university degrees, or non-degree postsecondary education. Both lists also contain basic information about the institutions. Unless otherwise indicated, all colleges and universities listed are coeducational and predominantly offer four-year bachelor's degrees, or higher degrees. In the U.S. list, branches or affiliates of large university or college systems are given either separate or combined listings according to each institution's own customary style; in the Canada list, universities authorized by provincial governments to grant degrees are given as main entries, with the colleges affiliated with them for degree-granting purposes given as subordinate entries.

Basic information for each college or university is given in this order:

mailing address, including city or town, state or provincial abbreviation, and zip or postal code (street addresses are not needed for colleges and universities).

sponsorship. Private, religious, federal, state, or local sponsorship is shown for U.S. colleges and universities, and specific religious sponsorship for Canadian institutions.

level. The abbreviation "jr" is given for U.S. two-year or junior colleges; all others offer four-year bachelor's degrees.

year founded. The original year of founding is given, even though the date a school received its present name or status may have occurred later.

coeducational status. Schools "for men" or "for women" only are so identified; all other institutions are coeducational.

accreditation. A "*" is shown for U.S. institutions with full regional accreditation and for Canadian institutions which are members of the Association of Universities and Colleges of Canada.

selected professional and paraprofessional fields in which an institution offers degree programs or study programs are given (see the list of abbreviations below).

graduate studies offered, identifying the highest such degree granted, as master's or doctorate.

approximate size of the institution's total full-time and part-time enrollment. This is shown by the abbreviations S, M, and L (explained in the abbreviations list below).

Abbreviations used in the listings are as follows:

*	institution holds full accreditation by the appropriate U.S. regional accrediting association or is a member of the Association of Universities and Colleges of Canada
A&M	Agricultural and Mechanical
aflt.	affiliated with
a-nurs	nursing (associate degree)
arch	architecture
art	fine or visual arts
assoc.	associated with
Bapt	Baptist
beyond Mst	highest graduate study offering is for a form of certification beyond the master's degree but below the doctorate
bus	business administration
C.	College
Comm.	Community
D	highest degree offering is the doctorate
dent	dentistry (doctorate)
dent-a	dental assistant
dent-h	dental hygienist
ed	education
engr	engineering
engr-t	engineering technology
fed.	federated with
Inst.	Institute
jr	institution offers programs predominantly on the level of the first two college years
L	large size, with over 10,000 enrollment
law	law
lib	librarianship (master's degree)
M	medium size, with enrollment of 3,000–10,000
med	medicine (doctorate)
med-a	medical assistant
med-rec-t	medical record technician
Meth	Methodist
Mst	highest degree offering is the master's
mus	music
Presb	Presbyterian
Prot	sponsorship by one or more Protestant denominations
pvt	private, nonprofit institution with independent or nonsectarian sponsorship
RC	Roman Catholic
resp-ther	respiratory therapist
resp-ther-t	respiratory therapy technician
S	small size, with under 3,000 enrollment
U.	University
x-ray-t	radiologic or x-ray technology

United States

Abilene Christian U., Abilene, TX 79699; pvt; 1906; *; ed, mus; beyond Mst; M
Abilene Christian U. at Dallas, Garland, TX 75041; pvt; jr; 1971; *; S
Abraham Baldwin Agricultural C., Tifton, GA 31793; state; jr; 1924; *; S
Academy of Aeronautics, Flushing, NY 11371; pvt; jr; 1932; *; engr-t; S
Academy of the New Church, Bryn Athyn, PA 19009; Prot; 1876; *; S
Adams State C., Alamosa, CO 81102; state; jr; 1921; *; ed; S
Adelphi U., Garden City, NY 11530; pvt; 1896; *; D; L
Adirondack Comm. C., Glens Falls, NY 12801; state/local; jr; 1960; *; S
Adrian C., Adrian, MI 49221; Meth; 1859; *; ed; S
Agnes Scott C., Decatur, GA 30030; pvt; 1889; for women; *; S
Agricultural and Technical C. at Alfred (see under **State U. of New York**)
Agricultural and Technical C. at Canton (see under **State U. of New York**)
Agricultural and Technical C. at Cobleskill (see under **State U. of New York**)
Agricultural and Technical C. at Delhi (see under **State U. of New York**)
Agricultural and Technical C. at Farmingdale (see under **State U. of New York**)
Agricultural and Technical C. at Morrisville (see under **State U. of New York**)
Aiken Technical C., Aiken, SC 29801; state; jr; 1972; *; S
Aims Comm. C., Greeley, CO 80631; local; 1967; *; resp-ther, x-ray-t; M
Akron, U. of, Akron, OH 44325; state; 1870; *; art, bus, ed, engr, engr-t, law, mus; L
Akron, U. of, Wayne General and Technical C., Orrville, OH 44667; state; jr; 1972; *; S
Alabama A&M U., Normal, AL 35762; state; 1875; *; lib; beyond Mst; M
Alabama Christian C., Montgomery, AL 36109; Prot; jr; 1942; *; S
Alabama in Birmingham, U. of, Birmingham, AL 35294; state; 1966; *; D; L
Alabama in Huntsville, U. of, Huntsville, AL 35899; state; 1950; *; engr; D; M
Alabama State U., Montgomery, AL 36195; state; 1874; *; beyond Mst; M
Alabama, U. of, University, AL 35486; state; 1831; *; law, lib, mus; D; L
Alameda, C. of, Alameda, CA 94501; state/local; jr; 1964; *; dent-a; M
Alaska Bible C., Glenallen, AK 99588; pvt; 1966; S
Alaska, U. of, Anchorage Campus, Anchorage, AK 99504; state; 1970; *; Mst; M
Alaska, U. of, Anchorage Comm. C, Anchorage, AK 99504; state; jr; 1954; *; dent-a, dent-h; M
Alaska, U. of, Fairbanks Campus, Fairbanks, AK 99701; state; 1917; *; D; M
Alaska, U. of, Juneau, Juneau, AK 99802; state; 1956; beyond Mst; S
Alaska, U. of, Kenai Peninsula Comm. C., Soldotna, AK 99669; state; jr; 1964; *; S
Alaska, U. of, Ketchikan Comm. C., Ketchikan, AK 99901; state; jr; 1954; *; S
Alaska, U. of, Kodiak Comm. C., Kodiak, AK 99615; state; jr; 1968; *; S
Alaska, U. of, Kuskokwim Comm. C., Bethel, AK 99559; state; jr; 1972; *; S
Alaska, U. of, Sitka Comm. C., Sitka, AK 99835; state; jr; 1962; S
Alaska, U. of, Tanana Valley Comm. C., Fairbanks, AK 99701; state; jr; 1974; S
Albany Junior C., Albany, GA 31707; state; jr; 1963; *; dent-h; S
Albany Junior C. of New York (see **Russell Sage Junior C. of Albany**)
Albany Medical C., Albany, NY 12208; pvt; 1839; *; med; D, grad only; S
Albany State C., Albany, GA 31705; state; 1903; *; ed; S
Albemarle, C. of the, Elizabeth City, NC 27909; state/local; jr; 1960; *; S
Albertus Magnus C., New Haven, CT 06511; RC; 1925; *; S
Albion C., Albion, MI 49224; Meth; 1835; *; mus; S
Albright C., Reading, PA 19603; Meth; 1856; *; S
Albuquerque, U. of, Albuquerque, NM 87140; pvt; 1920; *; x-ray-t; S
Alcorn State U., Lorman, MS 39096; state; 1871; *; ed; Mst; S
Alderson Broaddus C., Philippi, WV 26416; Bapt; 1871; *; S
Alexander City State Junior C., Alexander City, AL 35010; state; jr; 1963; *; S
Alfred U., Alfred, NY 14802; pvt; 1836; *; art, engr; D; S
Alice Lloyd C., Pippa Passes, KY 41844; pvt; 1921; *; S
Allan Hancock C., Santa Maria, CA 93454; state/local; jr; 1920; *; dent-a; M
Allegany Comm. C., Cumberland, MD 21502; local; jr; 1961; *; S
Allegheny C., Meadville, PA 16335; pvt; 1815; *; Mst; S
Allegheny County, Comm. C. of, Allegheny Campus, Pittsburgh, PA 15212; local; jr; 1966; *; med-a, med-rec-t, resp-ther, resp-ther-t; M
Allen County Comm. Junior C., Iola, KS 66749; state/local; jr; 1923; *; S
Allen U., Columbia, SC 29204; African Methodist Episcopal; 1870; S
Allentown C. of Saint Francis de Sales, Center Valley, PA 18034; RC; 1964; *; S
Alliance C., Cambridge Springs, PA 16403; pvt; 1912; *; S
Alma C., Alma, MI 48801; pvt; 1886; *; ed; S
Alpena Comm. C., Alpena, MI 49707; local; jr; 1952; *; S
Alvernia C., Reading, PA 19607; RC; 1958; *; S
Alverno C., Milwaukee, WI 53215; pvt; 1936; *; ed, mus; S
Alvin Comm. C., Alvin, TX 77511; local; jr; 1948; *; resp-ther-t; S
Amarillo C., Amarillo, TX 79178; state/local; jr; 1929; *; a-nurs, dent-a; M
American Academy of Dramatic Arts—West, Pasadena, CA 91107; pvt; jr; 1974; S
American C., Bryn Mawr, PA 19010; pvt; 1927; *; beyond M; S
American Graduate School of International Management, Glendale, AZ 85306; pvt; 1946; *; Mst, grad only; S
American International C., Springfield, MA 01109; pvt; 1885; *; Mst; S
American River C., Sacramento, CA 95841; state/local; jr; 1955; *; resp-ther; L
American Samoa Comm. C., Pago Pago, AS 96799; state; jr; 1970; *; S
American Technological U., Killeen, TX 76541; pvt; 1973; *; Mst; S
American U., Washington, DC 20016; Meth; 1893; *; ed, law, mus; D; L
Amherst C., Amherst, MA 01002; pvt; 1821; *; S
Ancilla C., Donaldson, IN 46513; RC; jr; 1937; *; S
Anderson C., Anderson, IN 46011; Church of God; 1917; *; a-nurs, ed, mus; S
Anderson C., Anderson, SC 29621; Bapt; jr; 1911; *; S
Andrew C., Cuthbert, GA 31740; Meth; jr; 1854; *; S
Andrews U., Berrien Springs, MI 49104; Prot; 1874; *; ed, mus; D; S
Angelina C., Lufkin, TX 75901; state/local; jr; 1968; *; a-nurs; S
Angelo State U., San Angelo, TX 76901; state; 1926; *; a-nurs; Mst; M
Anna Maria C., Paxton, MA 01612; RC; 1946; *; mus; S
Anne Arundel Comm. C., Arnold, MD 21012; state/local; jr; 1961; *; a-nurs; M
Anoka-Ramsey Comm. C., Coon Rapids, MN 55433; state; jr; 1965; *; M
Antelope Valley C., Lancaster, CA 93534; state/local; jr; 1929; *; M
Antillian C., Mayaguez, PR 00708; Seventh-Day Adventists; 1922; *; S
Antioch U., Yellow Springs, OH 45387; pvt; 1852; *; law; Mst; M
Appalachian State U., Boone, NC 28608; state; 1899; *; bus; beyond Mst; L
Aquinas C., Grand Rapids, MI 49506; RC; 1923; *; Mst; S
Aquinas Junior C., Nashville, TN 32705; RC; jr; 1961; *; x-ray-t; S
Arapahoe Comm. C., Littleton, CO 80120; state; jr; 1965; *; med-a; M
Arizona C. of the Bible, Phoenix, AZ 85021; pvt; 1971; S
Arizona State U., Tempe, AZ 85281; state; 1885; *; arch, law, mus; D; L
Arizona, U. of, Tucson, AZ 85721; state; 1885; *; arch, med, mus; D; L
Arizona Western C., Yuma, AZ 85364; state/local; jr; 1963; *; a-nurs; M
Arkansas C., Batesville, AR 72501; Presb; 1872; *; ed; S
Arkansas State U., State University, AR 72467; state; 1909; *; Mst; M
Arkansas State U., Beebe Branch, Beebe, AR 72012; state; jr; 1927; *; S
Arkansas Technical U., Russellville, AR 72801; state; 1909; *; Mst; S
Arkansas, U. of, Fayetteville, AR 72701; state; 1871; *; engr, law, mus; D; L
Arkansas at Little Rock, U. of, Little Rock, AR 72204; state; 1927; *; Mst; L
Arkansas, U. of, Medical Sciences Campus, Little Rock, AR 72205; state; 1879; med, x-ray-t; D; S

Arkansas at Monticello, U. of, Monticello, AR 71655; state; 1909; *; ed; S
Arkansas at Pine Bluff, U. of, Pine Bluff, AR 71601; state; 1873; *; ed; S
Armstrong C., Berkeley, CA 94704; prop; 1918; *; Mst; S
Armstrong State C., Savannah, GA 31406; state; 1935; *; a-nurs; Mst; S
Art Center C. of Design, Pasadena, CA 91103; pvt; 1930; *; art; Mst; S
Art Inst. of Chicago, School of the, Chicago, IL 60603; pvt; 1866; *; Mst; S
Asbury C., Wilmore, KY 40390; pvt; 1890; *; mus; S
Ashland C., Ashland, OH 44805; Brethren Church; 1878; *; ed, mus; D; S
Asnuntuck Comm. C., Enfield, CT 06082; state; jr; 1972; *; S
Assumption C., Worcester, MA 01609; RC; 1904; *; beyond Mst; S
Athens State C., Athens, AL 35611; state; 1822; *; S
Atlanta Christian C., East Point, GA 30344; Interdenominational; 1937; S
Atlanta C. of Art, Atlanta, GA 30309; pvt; 1928; *; art; S
Atlanta Junior C., Atlanta, GA 30310; state; jr; 1974; S
Atlantic Christian C., Wilson, NC 27893; Prot; 1902; *; ed; S
Atlantic, C. of the, Bar Harbor, ME 04609; pvt; 1969; *; S
Atlantic Comm. C., Mays Landing, NJ 08330; state/local; jr; 1964; *; M
Atlantic Union C., South Lancaster, MA 01561; Prot; 1882; *; ed; S
Auburn U., Auburn, AL 36849; state; 1856; *; arch, art, bus, engr; D; L
Auburn U. at Montgomery, Montgomery, AL 36109; state; 1967; *; Mst; M
Augsburg C., Minneapolis, MN 55454; Prot; 1869; *; ed; S
Augusta C., Augusta, GA 30910; state; 1925; *; a-nurs, ed, mus; Mst; M
Augustana C., Rock Island, IL 61201; Prot; 1860; *; ed, mus; Mst; S
Augustana C., Sioux Falls, SD 57197; American Lutheran; 1860; *; ed, mus; S
Aurora C., Aurora, IL 60507; pvt; 1893; *; Mst; S
Austin C., Sherman, TX 75090; Presb; 1849; *; Mst; S
Austin Comm. C., Austin, MN 55912; state; jr; 1940; *; a-nurs; S
Austin Comm. C., Austin, TX 78768; state/local; jr; 1972; *; L
Austin Peay State U., Clarksville, TN 37040; state; 1927; *; beyond Mst; M
Averett C., Danville, VA 24541; Bapt; 1859; *; Mst; S
Avila C., Kansas City, MO 64145; RC; 1916; *; Mst; S
Azusa Pacific C., Azusa, CA 91702; pvt; 1899; *; Mst; S
Babson C., Babson Park, MA 02157; pvt; 1919; *; bus; Mst; S
Bacone C., Muskogee, OK 74401; pvt; jr; 1880; *; a-nurs; S
Bainbridge Junior C., Bainbridge, GA 31717; state; jr; 1970; *; S
Baker U., Baldwin City, KS 66006; Meth; 1858; *; ed; Mst; S
Bakersfield C., Bakersfield, CA 93305; state/local; jr; 1913; *; x-ray-t; L
Baldwin-Wallace C., Berea, OH 44017; Meth; 1845; *; ed, mus; Mst; M
Ball State U., Muncie, IN 47306; state; 1918; *; arch, bus, ed, lib, mus; D; L
Baltimore, Comm. C. of, Baltimore, MD 21215; local; jr; 1947; *; a-nurs; M
Baltimore Hebrew C., Baltimore, MD 21215; pvt; 1919; *; Mst; S
Baltimore, U. of, Baltimore, MD 21201; state; 1925; *; Mst; M
Bank Street C. of Education, New York, NY 10025; pvt; 1916; *; Mst; S
Baptist Bible C., Springfield, MO 65803; Bapt; 1950; S
Baptist Bible C. of Denver, Broomsfield, CO 80020; pvt; 1952; Mst; S
Baptist Bible C. of Pennsylvania, Clarks Summit, PA 18411; Bapt; 1932; Mst; S
Baptist C. at Charleston, Charleston, SC 29411; Bapt; 1960; *; S
Barat C., Lake Forest, IL 60045; pvt; 1858; *; S
Barber-Scotia C., Concord, NC 28025; Presb; 1867; *; S
Bard C., Annandale-on-Hudson, NY 12504; pvt; 1860; *; S
Barnard C., New York, NY 10027; pvt; 1889; for women; *; S
Barrington C., Barrington, RI 02806; pvt; 1900; *; mus; S
Barry C., Miami, FL 33161; RC; 1940; *; Mst; S
Barstow C., Barstow, CA 92311; state/local; jr; 1959; *; S
Bartlesville Wesleyan C., Bartlesville, OK 74003; Wesleyan Church; 1907; *; S
Barton County Comm. C., Great Bend, KS 67530; local; jr; 1965; *; S
Bates C., Lewiston, ME 04240; pvt; 1864; *; S
Bay de Noc Comm. C., Escabana, MI 49829; local; jr; 1962; *; S
Bay Path Junior C., Longmeadow, MA 01106; pvt; jr; 1897; *; S
Bayamon Central U., Bayamon, PR 00619; RC; 1961; *; S
Baylor U., Waco, TX 76706; Bapt; 1845; *; bus, law, mus, x-ray-t; L
Beacon C., Washington, DC 20009; pvt; 1971; Mst; S
Beal C., Bangor, ME 04401; prop; jr; 1891; S
Beaufort County Comm. C., Washington, NC 27889; state/local; jr; 1968; *; S
Beaver C., Glenside, PA 19038; Presb; 1853; *; art; beyond Mst; S
Beaver County, Comm. C. of, Monaca, PA 15061; state/local; jr; 1966; *; S
Becker Junior C., Worcester, Worcester, MA 01609; pvt; jr; 1887; *; S
Bee County C., Beeville, TX 78102; state/local; jr; 1965; *; dent-h; S
Belhaven C., Jackson, MS 39202; Presb; 1883; *; mus; S
Bellarmine C., Louisville, KY 40205; RC; 1950; *; x-ray-t; Mst; S
Belleville Area C., Belleville, IL 62221; state/local; jr; 1946; *; x-ray-t; M
Bellevue C., Bellevue, NE 68005; pvt; 1965; *; S
Bellevue Comm. C., Bellevue, WA 98007; state; jr; 1965; *; a-nurs, x-ray-t; M
Belmont Abbey C., Belmont, NC 28012; RC; 1876; *; S
Belmont C., Nashville, TN 32703; Bapt; 1951; *; a-nurs, mus; S
Belmont Technical C., Saint Clairsville, OH 43950; state; jr; 1969; *; S
Beloit C., Beloit, WI 53511; pvt; 1846; *; Mst; S
Bemidji State U., Bemidji, MN 56601; state; 1913; *; ed; Mst; M
Benedict C., Columbia, SC 29204; pvt; 1870; *; S
Benedictine C., Atchison, KS 66002; pvt; 1858; *; ed, mus; S
Bennett C., Greensboro, NC 27420; Meth; 1873; for women; *; S
Bennington C., Bennington, VT 05201; pvt; 1925; *; Mst; S
Bentley C., Waltham, MA 02154; pvt; 1917; *; M
Berea C., Berea, KY 40404; pvt; 1855; *; ed, mus; S
Bergen Comm. C., Paramus, NJ 07652; state/local; jr; 1965; *; x-ray-t; L
Berklee C. of Music, Boston, MA 02215; pvt; 1945; *; S
Berkshire Comm. C., Pittsfield, MA 01201; state; jr; 1960; *; a-nurs; M
Berry C., Mount Berry, GA 30149; pvt; 1902; *; ed, mus; Mst; S
Bethany Bible C., Santa Cruz, CA 95066; Prot; 1919; *; S
Bethany C., Lindsborg, KS 67456; Prot; 1881; *; ed, mus; S
Bethany C., Bethany, WV 26032; Prot; 1840; *; a-nurs, engr-t; S
Bethany Lutheran C., Mankato, MN 56001; Prot; jr; 1911; *; S
Bethany Nazarene C., Bethany, OK 73008; Prot; 1899; *; Mst; S
Bethel C., Mishawaka, IN 46544; Missionary Church Inc.; 1947; *; S
Bethel C., North Newton, KS 67117; Prot; 1887; *; S
Bethel C., Saint Paul, MN 55112; Bapt; 1871; *; ed; S
Bethel C., McKenzie, TN 38201; Presb; 1842; *; S
Bethune Cookman C., Daytona Beach, FL 32015; Meth; 1904; *; S
Big Bend Comm. C., Moses Lake, WA 98837; state; jr; 1962; *; S
Biola C., La Mirada, CA 90639; pvt; 1908; *; mus; M
Birmingham Southern C., Birmingham, AL 35254; Meth; 1856; *; ed, mus; S
Biscayne C., Miami, FL 33054; RC; 1962; *; S
Bishop C., Dallas, TX 75241; Bapt; 1881; *; S
Bismarck Junior C., Bismarck, ND 58501; local; jr; 1939; *; S
Black Hawk C. East Campus, Kewanee, IL 61443; state/local; jr; 1967; *; S
Black Hawk C. Quad-Cities Campus, Moline, IL 61265; local; jr; 1946; *; M
Black Hills State C., Spearfish, SD 57783; state; 1883; *; ed; Mst; M
Blackburn C., Carlinville, IL 62626; Presb; 1857; *; S
Blackhawk Technical Inst., Janesville, WI 53545; state/local; jr; 1912; *; S
Bladen Technical Inst., Dublin, NC 28332; state; jr; 1967; *; S
Blinn C., Brenham, TX 77833; state/local; jr; 1883; *; S
Bloomfield C., Bloomfield, NJ 07003; Presb; 1868; *; S
Bloomsburg State C., Bloomsburg, PA 17815; state; 1839; *; ed; Mst; M
Blue Hills Regional Technical Inst., Canton, MA 02021; local; jr; 1963; *; S
Blue Mountain C., Blue Mountain, MS 38610; Bapt; 1873; *; S
Blue Mountain Comm. C., Pendleton, OR 97801; state/local; jr; 1962; *; S
Blue Ridge Comm. C., Weyers Cave, VA 24486; state; jr; 1965; *; S
Blue Ridge Technical C., Flat Rock, NC 28731; state/local; jr; 1969; *; S
Bluefield C., Bluefield, VA 24605; Bapt; 1920; *; S
Bluefield State C., Bluefield, WV 24701; state; 1895; *; a-nurs, engr-t; S
Bluffton C., Bluffton, OH 45817; Mennonite Church; 1899; *; mus; S
Boca Raton, C. of, Boca Raton, FL 33431; pvt; jr; 1963; *; S
Boise State U., Boise, ID 83725; state; 1932; *; resp-ther, x-ray-t; Mst; L
Boricua C., New York, NY 10032; pvt; 1974; *; S
Borromeo C. of Ohio, Wickliffe, OH 44092; RC; 1954; *; S
Boston C., Chestnut Hill, MA 02167; RC; 1863; *; bus, law, ed; D; L
Boston Conservatory of Music, Boston, MA 02115; pvt; 1867; *; mus; Mst; S
Boston State C., Boston, MA 02115; state; 1852; *; M
Boston U., Boston, MA 02215; pvt; 1869; *; bus, dent, law, med, mus; D; L
Bowdoin C., Brunswick, ME 04011; pvt; 1794; *; S
Bowie State C., Bowie, MD 20715; state; 1865; *; ed; Mst; S
Bowling Green State U., Bowling Green, OH 43403; state; 1910; *; D; L
Bradford C., Bradford, MA 01830; pvt; 1803; *; S
Bradley U., Peoria, IL 61625; pvt; 1897; *; bus, ed, engr; beyond M; M
Brainerd Comm. C., Brainerd, MN 56401; state; jr; 1938; *; S
Brandeis U., Waltham, MA 02254; pvt; 1947; *; D; M
Brandywine C., of Widener U., Wilmington, DE 19803; pvt; jr; 1965; *; S
Brazosport C., Lake Jackson, TX 77566; local; jr; 1948; *; M
Brenau C., Gainesville, GA 30501; pvt; 1878; *; S
Brescia C., Owensboro, KY 42301; RC; 1878; *; S
Brevard C., Brevard, NC 28712; Meth; jr; 1853; *; S
Brevard Comm. C., Cocoa, FL 32922; local; jr; 1960; *; dent-a, x-ray-t; L
Brewer State Junior C., Fayette, AL 35555; state; jr; 1969; *; S
Brewton-Parker C., Mount Vernon, GA 30445; Bapt; jr; 1904; *; S
Briar Cliff C., Sioux City, IA 51104; RC; 1929; *; S
Bridgeport Engineering Inst., Bridgeport, CT 06606; pvt; 1924; *; S
Bridgeport, U. of, Bridgeport, CT 06602; pvt; 1927; *; engr, mus; D; M
Bridgewater C., Bridgewater, VA 22812; Church of the Brethren; 1880; *; S
Bridgewater State C., Bridgewater, MA 02324; state; 1840; *; ed; Mst; M
Brigham Young U., Provo, UT 84602; Prot; 1875; *; D; L
Brigham Young U., Hawaii Campus, Laie, Oahu, HI 96762; Prot; 1955; *; S
Bristol C., Bristol, TN 37620; prop; 1895; S
Bristol Comm. C., Fall River, MA 02720; state; jr; 1965; *; a-nurs, dent-h; M
Brockport, C. at (see under **State U. of New York**)
Bronx Comm. C. (see under **City U. of New York**)
Brookdale Comm. C., Lincroft, NJ 07738; state/local; jr; *; a-nurs, resp-ther; M
Brookhaven C., Farmers Branch, TX 75234; state/local; jr; 1965; *; M
Brooklyn Center, New York (see under **Long Island U.**)
Brooklyn C. (see under **City U. of New York**)
Brooklyn Law School, Brooklyn, NY 11201; pvt; 1901; law; grad only; S
Brooks Inst., Santa Barbara, CA 93108; prop; 1945; *; Mst; S
Broome Comm. C., Binghamton, NY 13902; state/local; jr; 1946; *; M
Broward Comm. C., Fort Lauderdale, FL 33301; local; jr; 1959; *; L
Brown U., Providence, RI 02912; pvt; 1764; *; engr, med; D; M
Brunswick Junior C., Brunswick, GA 31520; state; jr; 1961; *; x-ray-t; S
Bryan C., Dayton, TN 37321; pvt; 1930; *; S
Bryant C. of Business Admininstration, Smithfield, RI 02917; pvt; 1863; *; M
Bryn Mawr C., Bryn Mawr, PA 19010; pvt; 1880; for women; *; D; S
Bucknell U., Lewisburg, PA 17837; pvt; 1846; *; engr, mus; Mst; M
Bucks County Comm. C., Newtown, PA 18940; local; jr; 1964; *; a-nurs; M
Buena Vista C., Store Lake, IA 50588; Presb; 1891; *; ed; S
Bunker Hill Comm. C., Boston, MA 02129; state; jr; 1973; *; a-nurs, x-ray-t; M
Burlington County C., Pemberton, NJ 08068; state/local; jr; 1966; *; M
Butler County Comm. C., El Dorado, KS 67042; local; jr; 1927; *; S
Butler County Comm. C., Butler, PA 16001; local; jr; 1965; *; S
Butler U., Indianapolis, IN 46208; pvt; 1855; *; x-ray-t; beyond Mst; M
Butte C., Oroville, CA 95965; state/local; jr; 1966; *; resp-ther; M
Cabrillo C., Aptos, CA 95003; state/local; jr; 1959; *; dent-a, dent-h, x-ray-t; M
Cabrini C., Radnor, PA 19087; RC; 1957; *; S
Caldwell C., Caldwell, NJ 07006; RC; 1939; *; S
Caldwell Comm. C. and Technical Inst., Lenoir, NC 28638; state/local; jr; 1964; *; x-ray-t; S
California Baptist C., Riverside, CA 92504; Bapt; 1950; *; S
California C. of Arts and Crafts, Oakland, CA 94618; pvt; 1907; *; art; S
California C. of Podiatric Medicine, San Francisco, CA 94115; pvt; 1914; *; S
California Inst. of the Arts, Valencia, CA 91355; pvt; 1964; *; art, mus; Mst; S
California Inst. of Technology, Pasadena, CA 91125; pvt; 1891; *; engr; D; S
California Lutheran C., Thousand Oaks, CA 91360; Prot; 1959; *; Mst; S
California Maritime Academy, Vallejo, CA 94590; state; 1929; *; engr-t; S
California Polytechnic State U.—San Luis Obispo, San Luis Obispo, CA 93407; state; 1901; *; arch, engr, engr-t; Mst; L
California State C., California, PA 15419; state; 1852; *; ed; beyond Mst; M
California State C.—Bakersfield, Bakersfield, CA 93309; state; 1965; *; M
California State C.—San Bernardino, San Bernardino, CA 92407; state; 1960; *; Mst; M
California State C.—Stanislaus, Turlock, CA 95380; state; 1957; *; Mst; M
California State Polytechnic U., Pomona, CA 91768; state; 1938; *; Mst; L
California State U.—Chico, Chico, CA 95929; state; 1887; *; Mst; L
California State U.—Dominguez Hills, Carson, CA 90747; state; 1960; *; M
California State U.—Fresno, Fresno, CA 93740; state; 1911; *; mus; Mst; L
California State U.—Fullerton, Fullerton, CA 92634; state; 1957; *; Mst; L
California State U.—Hayward, Hayward, CA 94542; state; 1957; *; Mst; L
California State U.—Long Beach, Long Beach, CA 90840; state; 1948; *; Mst; L
California State U.—Los Angeles, Los Angeles, CA 90032; state; 1947; *; D; L
California State U.—Northridge, Northridge, CA 91330; state; 1959; *; Mst; L
California State U.—Sacramento, Sacramento, CA 95819; state; 1947; *; Mst; L
California-Berkeley, U. of, Berkeley, CA 94720; state; 1868; *; lib; D; L
California-Davis, U. of, Davis, CA 95616; state; 1905; *; engr, law, med; D; L
California-Irvine, U. of, Irvine, CA 92717; state; 1964; *; engr, med; D; L
California-Los Angeles, U. of, Los Angeles, CA 90024; state; 1919; *; D; L
California-Riverside, U. of, Riverside, CA 92521; state; 1954; *; D; M
California-San Diego, U. of, La Jolla, CA 92093; state; 1912; *; med; D; L
California-San Francisco, U. of, San Francisco, CA 94122; state; 1864; *; D; M
California-Santa Barbara, U. of, Santa Barbara, CA 93106; state; 1898; *; engr; D; L
California-Santa Cruz, U. of, Santa Cruz, CA 95064; state; 1962; *; D; M
Calumet C., Whiting, IN 46394; RC; 1951; *; S
Calvin C., Grand Rapids, MI 49506; Prot; 1876; *; ed; Mst; M
Camden County C., Blackwood, NJ 08012; state/local; jr; 1977; *; a-nurs; M
Cameron U., Lawton, OK 73505; state; 1909; *; a-nurs, mus; M
Campbell U., Buies Creek, NC 27506; Bapt; 1887; *; ed, law; Mst; S
Campbellsville C., Campbellsville, KY 42718; Bapt; 1906; *; S
Canada C., Redwood City, CA 94061; state/local; jr; 1968; *; x-ray-t; M
Canisius C., Buffalo, NY 14208; pvt; 1870; *; bus, ed; beyond Mst; M
Canyons, C. of the, Valencia, CA 91355; state/local; jr; 1967; *; M
Cape Cod Comm. C., West Barnstable, MA 02668; state; jr; 1961; *; S
Capital U., Columbus, OH 43209; American Lutheran; 1850; *; Mst; S
Cardinal Glennon C., St. Louis, MO 63119; RC; 1898; for men; *; S
Cardinal Stritch C., Milwaukee, WI 53217; RC; 1937; *; ed; S
Caribbean U. C., Bayamon, PR 00619; pvt; 1969; *; S
Carl Sandburg C., Galesburg, IL 61401; state/local; jr; 1966; *; M
Carleton C., Northfield, MN 55057; pvt; 1866; *; art, ed; S
Carlow C., Pittsburgh, PA 15213; RC; 1929; for women; *; S
Carnegie-Mellon U., Pittsburgh, PA 15213; pvt; 1900; *; arch, mus; D; M
Carroll C., Helena, MT 59601; RC; 1909; *; S
Carroll C., Waukesha, WI 53186; Presb; 1846; *; S
Carson-Newman C., Jefferson City, TN 37760; Bapt; 1851; *; ed, mus; S
Carthage C., Kenosha, WI 53141; Prot; 1846; *; mus; Mst; S
Case Western Reserve U., Cleveland, OH 44106; pvt; 1826; *; bus; D; M
Casper C., Casper, WY 82601; local; jr; 1945; *; a-nurs, x-ray-t; M
Castleton State C., Castleton, VT 05735; state; 1869; *; a-nurs; Mst; S
Catawba C., Salisbury, NC 28144; United Church of Christ; 1851; *; S
Catawba Valley Technical C., Hickory, NC 28601; state/local; jr; 1960; *; S
Catholic U. of America, Washington, DC 20064; RC; 1887; *; arch; D; M
Catholic U. of Puerto Rico, Ponce, PR 00731; RC; 1948; *; law; Mst; L
Catonsville Comm. C., Catonsville, MD 21228; local; jr; 1956; *; L
Cayey U. C. (see under **Puerto Rico, U. of**)
Cayuga County Comm. C., Auburn, NY 13021; state/local; jr; 1953; *; M

Cazenovia C., Cazenovia, NY 13035; pvt; jr; 1824; *; S
Cecil Comm. C., North East, MD 21901; state/local; jr; 1968; *; S
Cedar Crest C., Allentown, PA 18104; Prot; 1867; for women; *; S
Cedar Valley C., Lancaster, TX 75134; state; jr; 1974; *; S
Cedarville C., Cedarville, OH 45314; Bapt; 1887; *; S
Centenary C., Hackettstown, NJ 07840; pvt; 1867; for women; *; S
Centenary C. of Louisiana, Shreveport, LA 71104; Meth; 1825; *; mus; Mst; S
Center for Creative Studies, Detroit, MI 48202; pvt; 1926; *; art; S
Center for Early Education, Los Angeles, CA 90048; pvt; 1939; *; Mst; S
Central Arizona C., Coolidge, AZ 85228; local; jr; 1962; *; a-nurs; M
Central Arkansas, U. of, Conway, AR 72032; state; 1907; *; beyond Mst; M
Central C., Pella, IA 50219; Reformed Church in America, 1853; *; ed; S
Central C., McPherson, KS 67460; Meth; jr; 1884; *; S
Central Connecticut State C., New Britain, CT 06050; state; 1849; *; ed; L
Central Florida Comm. C., Ocala, FL 32670; local; jr; 1957; *; x-ray-t; S
Central Florida, U. of, Orlando, FL 32816; state; 1963; *; bus, engr; Mst; L
Central Methodist C., Fayette, MO 65248; Meth; 1853; *; ed, mus; S
Central Michigan U., Mount Pleasant, MI 48859; state; 1892; *; ed, mus; D; L
Central Missouri State U., Warrensburg, MO 64093; state; 1871; *; Mst; M
Central New England C., Worcester, MA 01610; pvt; 1971; *; S
Central Oregon Comm. C., Bend, OR 97701; local; jr; 1949; *; med-rec-t; S
Central Piedmont Comm. C., Charlotte, NC 28204; state/local; jr; 1963; *; L
Central State U., Wilberforce, OH 45384; state; 1887; *; ed; S
Central State U., Edmond, OK 73034; state; 1890; *; ed; Mst; L
Central Technical Comm. C., Grand Island, NE 68801; local; jr; 1966; M
Central Texas C., Killeen, TX 76541; local; jr; 1965; *; a-nurs; M
Central Virginia Comm. C., Lynchburg, VA 24502; state; jr; 1966; *; M
Central Washington U., Ellensburg, WA 98926; state; 1890; *; ed, mus; M
Central Wesleyan C., Central, SC 29630; Wesleyan Church; 1906; *; S
Central Wyoming C., Riverton, WY 82501; local; jr; 1966; *; S
Central Y.M.C.A. Comm. C., Chicago, IL 60606; pvt; jr; 1960; *; x-ray-t; M
Centralia C., Centralia, WA 98531; state; jr; 1925; *; M
Centre C. of Kentucky, Danville, KY 40422; pvt; 1819; *; S
Cerritos C., Norwalk, CA 90650; state/local; jr; 1955; *; dent-a, dent-h; L
Cerro Coso Comm. C., Ridgecrest, CA 93555; state/local; jr; 1973; *; M
Chabot C., Hayward, CA 94545; state/local; jr; 1961; *; dent-a, dent-h; L
Chadron State C., Chadron, NE 69337; state; 1911; *; ed; S
Chaffey C., Alta Loma, CA 91701; state/local; jr; 1883; *; a-nurs, dent-a; L
Chaminade U. of Honolulu, Honolulu, HI 96816; pvt; 1955; *; Mst; S
Champlain C., Burlington, VT 05401; pvt; jr; 1956; *; dent-a; S
Chapman C., Orange, CA 92666; pvt; 1918; *; Mst; M
Charles County Comm. C., La Plata, MD 20646; local; jr; 1958; *; M
Charles S. Mott Comm. C., Flint, MI 48503; local; jr; 1923; *; med-a; M
Charleston, C. of, Charleston, SC 29401; state; 1770; *; Mst; M
Charleston, U. of, Charleston, WV 25304; pvt; 1888; *; a-nurs, x-ray-t; Mst; S
Chatham C., Pittsburgh, PA 15232; pvt; 1869; for women; *; S
Chattahoochee Valley Comm. C., Phenix City, AL 36867; state; jr; 1974; *; S
Chemeketa Comm. C., Salem, OR 97309; local; jr; 1962; *; a-nurs, med-a; M
Chesapeake C., Wye Mills, MD 21679; state/local; jr; 1965; *; S
Chestnut Hill C., Philadelphia, PA 19118; RC; 1924; for women; *; Mst; S
Cheyney State C., Cheyney, PA 19319; state; 1837; *; ed; Mst; S
Chicago State U., Chicago, IL 60628; state; 1867; *; ed; Mst; M
Chicago, U. of, Chicago, IL 60637; pvt; 1890; *; bus, law, lib, med; D; M
Chowan C., Murfreesboro, NC 27855; Bapt; jr; 1848; *; S
Christian Brothers C., Memphis, TN 38104; RC; 1871; *; engr; S
Christopher Newport C., Newport News, VA 23606; state; 1960; *; M
Cincinnati, U. of, Cincinnati, OH 45221; state; 1819; *; arch, engr; D; L
Cincinnati, U. of, Raymond Walters C., Cincinnati, OH 45246; state; jr; 1819; *; a-nurs, dent-h; M
Cisco Junior C., Cisco, TX 76437; state; jr; 1940; *; S
Citadel, The, Charleston, SC 29409; state; 1842; for men; *; beyond Mst; M
Citrus C., Azusa, CA 91702; state/local; *; dent-a; M
City C. of San Francisco, San Francisco, CA 94112; state/local; jr; 1935; *; L
City Colleges of Chicago, Chicago City-Wide C., Chicago, IL 60601; local; jr; 1975; *; M
City Colleges of Chicago, Kennedy-King C., Chicago, IL 60621; state/local; jr; 1934; *; M
City Colleges of Chicago, Loop C., Chicago, IL 60601; state/local; jr; 1962; *; M
City Colleges of Chicago, Malcolm X C., Chicago, IL 60612; state/local; jr; 1911; *; resp-ther, x-ray-t; M
City Colleges of Chicago, Olive-Harvey C., Chicago, IL 60628; state/local; jr; 1970; *; M
City Colleges of Chicago, Richard J. Daley C., Chicago, IL 60652; state/local; jr; 1960; *; M
City Colleges of Chicago, Truman C., Chicago, IL 60630; state/local; jr; 1956; *; M
City Colleges of Chicago, Wright C., Chicago, IL 60634; state/local; jr; 1934; *; x-ray-t; M
City U. of New York, Bernard Baruch C., New York, NY 10010; state/local; jr; 1919; *; bus; D; L
City U. of New York, Borough of Manhattan Comm. C., New York, NY 10019; state/local; jr; 1963; *; a-nurs, med-rec-t, resp-ther; M
City U. of New York, Bronx Comm. C., Bronx, NY 10453; state/local; jr; 1957; *; a-nurs, engr-t; M
City U. of New York, Brooklyn C., Brooklyn, NY 11210; state/local; 1930; *; ed; D; L
City U. of New York, City C., New York, NY 10031; state/local; 1847; *; ed, engr; beyond Mst; L
City U. of New York, C. of Staten Island, Staten Island, NY 10301; state/local; 1955; a-nurs; beyond Mst; L
City U. of New York Graduate School and U. Center, New York, NY 10036; state/local; 1961; *; D, grad only; S
City U. of New York, Herbert H. Lehman C., Bronx, NY 10468; state/local; 1931; *; ed; D; M
City U. of New York, Hostos Comm. C., Bronx, NY 10451; state/local; jr; 1970; *; x-ray-t; S
City U. of New York, Hunter C., New York, NY 10021; state/local; 1870; *; ed; beyond Mst; L
City U. of New York, John Jay C. of Criminal Justice, New York, NY 10019; state/local; 1964; *; D; M
City U. of New York, Kingsborough Comm. C., Brooklyn, NY 11235; state/local; jr; 1963; *; a-nurs; M
City U. of New York, La Guardia Comm. C., Long Island City, NY 11101; state/local; jr; 1970; *; M
City U. of New York, Medgar Evers C., Brooklyn, NY 11225; state/local; 1969; *; S
City U. of New York, Queens C., Flushing, NY 11367; state/local; 1937; *; lib; beyond Mst; L
City U. of New York, Queensborough Comm. C., New York, NY 11364; state/local; jr; 1958; *; a-nurs, engr-t; L
City U. of New York, York C., Jamaica, NY 11451; state/local; 1966; *; M
Clackamas Comm. C., Oregon City, OR 97045; local; jr; 1966; *; M
Claflin C., Orangeburg, SC 29115; Meth; 1869; *; S
Claremont-McKenna C., Claremont, CA 91711; pvt; 1946; *; S
Claremore Junior C., Claremore, OK 74017; state; jr; 1907; *; S
Clarendon C., Clarendon, TX 79226; state/local; jr; 1898; *; S
Clarion State C., Clarion, PA 16214; state; 1867; *; ed, lib; Mst; M
Clark C., Atlanta, GA 30314; Meth; 1869; *; ed; S
Clark C., Vancouver, WA 98663; state; jr; 1933; *; M
Clark County Comm. C., Las Vegas, NV 89030; state; jr; 1971; *; dent-h; M
Clark U., Worcester, MA 01610; pvt; 1887; *; D; M
Clarke C., Dubuque, IA 52001; RC; 1843; *; ed; Mst; S
Clarke C., Newton, MS 39345; Bapt; jr; 1908; *; S
Clarkson C. of Technology, Potsdam, NY 13676; pvt; 1896; *; bus, engr; D; M
Clatsop Comm. C., Astoria, OR 97103; local; jr; 1958; *; S
Clayton Junior C., Morrow, GA 30260; state; jr; 1965; *; a-nurs, dent-h; S
Clemson U., Clemson, SC 29631; state; 1889; *; a-nurs, arch, bus, ed, engr, engr-t; D; L
Cleveland Inst. of Art, Cleveland, OH 44106; pvt; 1882; *; art; S
Cleveland State Comm. C., Cleveland, TN 37311; state; jr; 1967; *; M
Cleveland State U., Cleveland, OH 44115; state; 1964; *; engr, law; D; L
Clinton Comm. C., Clinton, IA 52732; state/local; jr; 1946; *; S
Clinton Comm. C., Plattsburgh, NY 12901; state/local; jr; 1966; *; S
Cloud County Comm. C., Concordia, KS 66901; local; jr; 1965; *; a-nurs; S
Coahoma Junior C., Clarksdale, MS 38614; state/local; jr; 1949; *; S
Coastal Carolina Comm. C., Jacksonville, NC 28540; state/local; jr; 1964; *; S
Coastline Comm. C., Fountain Valley, CA 92708; state/local; jr; 1976; *; L
Cochise C., Douglas, AZ 85607; local; jr; 1962; *; M
Coe C., Cedar Rapids, IA 52402; pvt; 1851; *; mus; S
Coffeyville Comm. C., Coffeyville, KS 67337; state/local; jr; 1923; *; S
Cogswell C., San Francisco, CA 94108; pvt; 1887; *; engr-t; S
Coker C., Harstville, SC 29550; pvt; 1908; *; mus; S
Colby C., Waterville, ME 04901; pvt; 1813; *; S
Colby Comm. C., Colby, KS 67701; state/local; jr; 1964; *; S
Colby-Sawyer C., New London, NH 03257; pvt; 1837; *; S
Colegio Universitario del Turabo, Caguas, PR 00625; pvt; 1972; *; M
Coleman C., San Diego, CA 92110; pvt; 1963; S
Colgate Rochester Divinity School-Bexley Hall-Crozer Theological Seminary, Rochester, NY 14620; pvt; 1817; D, grad only; S
Colgate U., Hamilton, NY 13346; pvt; 1819; *; S
C. Misericordia, Dallas, PA 18612; RC; 1924; *; mus, x-ray-t; S
Colorado C., Colorado Springs, CO 80903; pvt; 1874; *; mus; Mst; S
Colorado Mountain C., Glenwood Springs, CO 81601; local; jr; 1965; *; M
Colorado Northwestern Comm. C., Rangely, CO 81648; local; jr; 1962; *; S
Colorado School of Mines, Golden, CO 80401; state; 1869; *; engr; D; S
Colorado State U., Fort Collins, CO 80523; state; 1870; *; bus, mus; D; L
Colorado at Boulder, U. of, Boulder, CO 80309; state; 1876; *; arch; D; L
Colorado at Denver, U. of, Denver, CO 80202; state; 1956; *; D; M
Colorado Women's C., Denver, CO 80220; pvt; 1888; for women; *; ed; S
Columbia Basin Comm. C., Pasco, WA 99301; state; jr; 1955; *; M
Columbia Christian C., Portland, OR 97220; pvt; 1949; *; S
Columbia C., Columbia, CA 95310; state/local; jr; 1968; *; S
Columbia C., Chicago, IL 60605; pvt; 1890; *; M
Columbia C., Columbia, MO 65216; Prot; 1851; *; S
Columbia C., Columbia, SC 29203; Meth; 1854; *; ed, mus; S
Columbia-Greene Comm. C., Hudson, NY 12534; state/local; jr; 1966; *; S
Columbia State Comm. C., Columbia, TN 38401; state; jr; 1966; *; a-nurs; S
Columbia Union C., Takoma Park, MD 20012; Prot; 1904; *; resp-ther; S
Columbia U., New York, NY 10027; pvt; 1754; *; arch, bus, med; D; L
Columbia U. Teachers C., New York, NY 10027; pvt; 1887; *; ed; D, grad only; M
Columbus C., Columbus, GA 31907; state; 1958; *; a-nurs, dent-h; Mst; M
Compton Comm. C., Compton, CA 90221; state/local; jr; 1927; *; resp-ther; M
Concord C., Athens, WV 24712; state; 1872; *; ed; S
Concordia C., River Forest, IL 60305; Lutheran Church; 1864; *; ed; Mst; S
Concordia C., Ann Arbor, MI 48105; Lutheran Church; 1962; *; S
Concordia C., Bronxville, NY 10708; Lutheran Church; 1881; *; S
Concordia C., Portland, OR 97211; Lutheran Church, 1905; *; S
Concordia C., Milwaukee, WI 53208; Lutheran Church; 1881; *; S
Concordia C.: Moorhead, Moorhead, MN 56560; American Lutheran; 1891; *; S
Concordia C.: Saint Paul, Saint Paul, MN 55104; Lutheran Church; 1893; *; S
Concordia Lutheran C., Austin, TX 78705; Lutheran Church; 1926; *; S
Concordia Teachers C., Seward, NE 68434; Lutheran Church; 1894; *; S
Connecticut C., New London, CT 06320; pvt; 1911; *; Mst; S
Connecticut, U. of, Storrs, CT 06268; state; 1881; *; bus, ed, law, mus; D; L
Connors State C., Warner, OK 74469; state; jr; 1908; *; S
Conservatory of Music of Puerto Rico, San Juan, PR 00936; state; 1959; *; S
Contra Costa C., San Pablo, CA 94806; state/local; jr; 1948; *; dent-a; M
Converse C., Spartansburg, SC 29301; pvt; 1889; *; mus; Mst; S
Cooper Union, New York, NY 10003; pvt; 1859; *; arch, art, engr; S
Copiah-Lincoln Junior C., Wesson, MS 39191; state; jr; 1915; *; S
Coppin State C., Baltimore, MD 21216; state; 1900; *; ed; Mst; S
Cornell C., Mount Vernon, IA 52314; pvt; 1853; *; mus; S
Cornell U., Ithaca, NY 14853; pvt/state; 1865; *; arch, bus, engr, law; D; L
Cornell U. Medical Center, New York, NY 10021; pvt; 1898; med; D, grad only; S
Corning Comm. C., Corning, NY 14830; state/local; jr; 1956; *; a-nurs; S
Corpus Christi State U., Corpus Christi, TX 78412; state; 1971; *; Mst; S
Cortland, C. at (see under **State U. of New York**)
Cosumnes River C., Sacramento, CA 95823; state/local; jr; 1970; *; M
Cottey C., Nevada, MO 64772; pvt; jr; 1884; *; S
County C. of Morris, Randolph, NJ 07869; state/local; jr; 1965; *; a-nurs; L
Covenant C., Lookout Mountain, TN 37350; Presb; 1955; *; S
Cowley County Comm. C., Arkansas City, KS 67005; state/local; jr; 1935; *; S
Crafton Hills C., Yucaipa, CA 92399; state/local; jr; 1972; *; resp-ther; S
Cranbrook Academy of Art, Bloomfield Hills, MI 48013; pvt; 1932; *; art; Mst, grad only; S
Craven Comm. C., New Bern, NC 28560; state/local; jr; 1965; *; S
Creighton U., Omaha, NE 68178; pvt; 1878; *; bus, dent, ed, law, med; D; M
Crowder C., Neosho, MO 64850; local; jr; 1963; *; S
Crowley's Ridge C., Paragould, AR 72450; Churches of Christ; 1973; S
Cuesta C., San Luis Obispo, CA 93406; state/local; jr; 1964; *; M
Culver-Stockton C., Canton, MO 63435; Prot; 1853; *; S
Cumberland C., Williamsburg, KY 40769; Bapt; 1889; *; a-nurs, mus; S
Cumberland C. of Tennessee, Lebanon, TN 37087; pvt; jr; 1842; *; S
Cumberland County C., Vineland, NJ 08360; state/local; jr; 1963; *; a-nurs; S
Curry C., Milton, MA 02186; pvt; 1879; *; S
Curtis Inst. of Music, Philadelphia, PA 19103; pvt; 1924; mus; Mst; S
Cuyahoga Comm. C. District, Cleveland, OH 44115; state/local; jr; 1962; *; L
Cypress C., Cypress, CA 90630; state/local; jr; 1966; *; dent-a, dent-h; L
D-Q U., Davis, CA 95616; pvt; jr; 1971; *; S
Dabney S. Lancaster Comm. C., Clifton Forge, VA 24422; state; jr; 1967; *; S
Daemen C., Amherst, NY 14226; pvt; 1947; *; S
Dakota State C., Madison, SD 57042; state; 1881; *; ed, med-rec-t; S
Dakota Wesleyan U., Davison, SD 57301; Meth; 1885; *; a-nurs, x-ray-t; S
Dallas Baptist C., Dallas, TX 75236; Bapt; 1965; *; S
Dallas Theological Seminary, Dallas, TX 75204; pvt; 1924; *; D, grad only; S
Dallas, U. of, Irving, TX 75061; RC; 1956; *; D; S
Dana C., Blair, NE 68008; American Lutheran; 1884; *; ed; S
Daniel Webster C., Nashua, NH 03063; pvt; 1965; *; S
Danville Area Comm. C., Danville, IL 61832; state/local; jr; 1946; *; M
Dartmouth C., Hanover, NH 03755; pvt; 1769; *; bus, engr, med; D; M
David Lipscomb C., Nashville, TN 37203; Churches of Christ; 1891; *; ed; S
Davidson C., Davidson, NC 28036; Presb; 1837; *; S
Davis and Elkins C., Elkins, WV 26241; Presb; 1904; *; S
Dawson Comm. C., Glendive, MT 59330; state/local; jr; 1940; *; S
Dayton, U. of, Dayton, OH 45469; RC; 1850; *; ed, engr, law, mus; D; L
Daytona Beach Comm. C., Daytona Beach, FL 32015; local; jr; 1958; *; M
De Anza C., Cupertino, CA 95014; state/local; jr; 1967; *; L
De Lourdes C., Des Plaines, IL 60016; RC; 1927; for women; S
De Paul U., Chicago, IL 60604; RC; 1898; *; bus, ed, law, mus, x-ray-t; D; L
De Pauw U., Greencastle, IN 46135; Meth; 1837; *; ed, mus; Mst; S
Dean Junior C., Franklin, MA 02038; pvt; jr; 1865; *; S
Deep Springs C., Dyer, NV 89010; pvt; jr; 1917; for men; *; S
Defiance C., Defiance, OH 43512; United Church of Christ; 1850; *; S
Dekalb Comm. C., Clarkston, GA 30021; local; jr; 1963; *; a-nurs, dent-h; L
Del Mar C., Corpus Christi, TX 78404; local; jr; 1935; *; a-nurs, dent-h; M
Delaware County, Comm. C. of, Media, PA 19063; state/local; jr; 1967; *; M
Delaware State C., Dover, DE 19901; state; 1891; *; S
Delaware Technical and Comm. C., Southern Campus, Georgetown, DE 19947; state; jr; 1967; *; S
Delaware, U. of, Newark, DE 19711; state-related; 1833; *; bus, engr; D; L

Delaware Valley C. of Science and Agriculture, Doylestown, PA 18901; pvt; 1896; *; S
Delgado Comm. C., New Orleans, LA 70119; state/local; jr; 1921; *; M
Delta C., University Center, MI 48710; local; jr; 1957; *; a-nurs, engr-t; L
Delta State U., Cleveland, MS 38732; state; 1924; *; ed, mus; beyond Mst; M
Denison U., Granville, OH 43023; pvt; 1831; *; mus; S
Denver, Comm. C. of, Auraria Campus, Denver, CO 80204; state; jr; 1970; *; M
Denver, U. of, Denver, CO 80208; Meth; 1864; *; art, bus, ed, engr, law, mus; D; M
Des Moines Area Comm. C., Ankeny, IA 50021; state/local; jr; 1966; *; M
Desert, C. of the, Palm Desert, CA 92260; state/local; jr; 1958; *; a-nurs; M
Detroit Inst. of Technology, Detroit, MI 48201; pvt; 1877; *; S
Detroit, U. of, Detroit, MI 48221; pvt; 1877; *; arch, bus, engr, law; D; M
Dickinson C., Carlisle, PA 17013; pvt; 1773; *; S
Dickinson State C., Dickinson, ND 58601; state; 1918; *; a-nurs, ed; S
Dillard U., New Orleans, LA 70122; Prot; 1869; *; mus; S
District of Columbia, U. of the, Washington, DC 20004; local; 1975; *; Mst; L
Dixie C., Saint George, UT 84770; state; jr; 1911; *; S
Doane C., Crete, NE 68333; United Church of Christ; 1872; *; S
Dr. Martin Luther C., New Ula, MN 56073; Lutheran; 1884; *; S
Dodge City Comm. C., Dodge City, KS 67801; state/local; jr; 1935; *; S
Dominican C. of Blauvelt, Orangeburg, NY 10962; pvt; 1952; *; S
Dominican C. of San Rafael, San Rafael, CA 94901; pvt; 1889; *; Mst; S
Don Bosco C., Newton, NJ 07860; RC; 1928; for men; *; S
Donnelly C., Kansas City, KS 66102; RC; jr; 1949; *; S
Dordt C., Sioux Center, IA 51250; Christian Reformed Church; 1955; *; S
Dowling C., Oakdale, NY 11769; pvt; 1959; *; Mst; S
Drake U., Des Moines, IA 50311; pvt; 1881; *; art, bus, ed, law, mus; D; M
Draughon's Junior C. of Business, Savannah, GA 31406; prop; jr; 1899; S
Drew U., Madison, NJ 07940; pvt; 1866; *; D; S
Drexel U., Philadelphia, PA 19104; pvt; 1891; *; arch, bus, engr, lib; D; L
Dropsie U., the, Philadelphia, PA 19132; pvt; 1907; *; D, grad only; S
Drury C., Springfield, MO 68502; pvt; 1873; *; ed; Mst; S
Du Page, C. of, Glen Ellyn, IL 60137; state/local; jr; 1966; *; resp-ther-t; L
Dubuque, U. of, Dubuque, IA 52001; Presb; 1852; *; ed; Mst; S
Duke U., Durham, NC 27706; pvt; 1838; *; bus, ed, engr, law, med; D; M
Duquesne U., Pittsburgh, PA 15219; RC; 1878; *; bus, law, mus; D; M
Dutchess Comm. C., Poughkeepsie, NY 12601; state/local; jr; 1957; *; a-nurs; M
Dyke C., Cleveland, OH 44114; pvt; 1848; *; S
D'Youville C., Buffalo, NY 14201; pvt; 1908; *; S
Earlham C., Richmond, IN 47374; Friends; 1847; *; Mst; S
East Arkansas Comm. C., Forrest City, AR 72335; local; jr; 1973; *; S
East Carolina U., Greenville, NC 27834; state; 1907; *; art, bus, ed, mus; D; L
East Central Junior C., Decatur, MS 39327; local; jr; 1928; *; S
East Central Junior C., Union, MO 63084; local; jr; 1968; *; dent-a; S
East Central Oklahoma State U., Ada, OK 74820; state; 1909; *; ed; Mst; M
East Los Angeles C., East Los Angeles, CA 90022; local; jr; 1945; *; L
East Mississippi Junior C., Scooba, MS 39358; state/local; jr; 1927; *; S
East Stroudsburg State C., East Stroudsburg, PA 18301; state; 1893; *; Mst; M
East Tennessee State U., Johnson City, TN 37601; state; 1911; *; D; L
East Texas Baptist C., Marshall, TX 75670; Bapt; 1912; *; mus; S
East Texas State U., Commerce, TX 75428; state; 1917; *; bus, ed; D; M
Eastern Arizona C., Thatcher, AZ 85552; state/local; jr; 1888; *; M
Eastern C., Saint Davids, PA 19087; Bapt; 1952; *; S
Eastern Connecticut State C., Willimantic, CT 06226; state; 1889; *; ed; Mst; S
Eastern Illinois U., Charleston, IL 61920; state; 1895; *; beyond Mst; L
Eastern Kentucky U., Richmond, KY 40475; state; 1906; *; beyond Mst; L
Eastern Michigan U., Ypsilanti, MI 48197; state; 1849; *; beyond Mst; L
Eastern Montana C., Billings, MT 59101; state; 1927; *; ed, mus; Mst; M
Eastern Nazarene C., Wollaston, MA 02170; Prot; 1900; *; Mst; S
Eastern New Mexico U., Portales, NM 88130; state; 1927; *; beyond Mst; M
Eastern Oklahoma State C., Wilburton, OK 74578; state; jr; 1909; *; a-nurs; S
Eastern Oregon State C., La Grande, OR 57850; state; 1929; *; Mst; S
Eastern Shore Comm. C., Melfa, VA 23410; state; jr; 1971; *; S
Eastern Utah, C. of, Price, UT 84501; state; jr; 1937; *; S
Eastern Washington U., Cheney, WA 99004; state; 1890; *; beyond Mst; M
Eastern Wyoming C., Torrington, WY 82240; local; jr; 1948; *; S
Eastfield C., Mesquite, TX 75150; state/local; jr; 1970; *; M
Eckerd C., Saint Petersburg, FL 33733; Presb; 1959; *; S
Edgewood C., Madison, WI 53711; RC; 1927; *; ed; S
Edinboro State C., Edinboro, PA 16444; state; 1857; *; ed; beyond Mst; M
Edison Comm. C., Fort Myers, FL 33907; local; jr; 1961; *; M
Edmonds Comm. C., Lynnwood, WA 98036; state; jr; 1967; *; dent-a; M
Edward Waters C., Jacksonville, FL 32209; Prot; 1866; *; S
El Camino C., Torrance, CA 90506; state/local; jr; 1947; *; med-a, resp-ther; L
El Centro C., Dallas, TX 75202; state/local; jr; 1966; *; a-nurs, dent-a; M
El Paso County Comm. C., El Paso, TX 79998; local; jr; 1969; *; a-nurs; L
El Reno Junior C., El Reno, OK 73036; state/local; jr; 1938; *; S
Elgin Comm. C., Elgin, IL 60120; local; jr; 1949; *; a-nurs, dent-a; M
Elizabeth City State U., Elizabeth City, NC 27909; state; 1891; *; S
Elizabeth Seton C., Yonkers, NY 10701; pvt; jr; 1960; *; S
Elizabethtown C., Elizabethtown, PA 17022; Prot; 1899; *; mus; S
Ellsworth Comm. C., Iowa Falls, IA 50126; state/local; jr; 1890; *; S
Elmhurst C., Elmhurst, IL 60126; United Church of Christ; 1871; *; ed; M
Elmira C., Elmira, NY 14901; pvt; 1853; *; resp-ther; Mst; S
Elon C., Elon College, NC 27244; United Church of Christ; 1889; *; S
Emanuel County Junior C., Swainsboro, GA 30401; jr; 1970; *; S
Embry-Riddle Aeronautical U., Daytona Beach, FL 32014; pvt; 1926; *; Mst; M
Emerson C., Boston, MA 02116; pvt; 1880; *; Mst; S
Emmanuel C., Franklin Springs, GA 30639; Prot; jr; 1919; *; S
Emmanuel C., Boston, MA 02115; RC; 1919; for women; *; Mst; S
Emory and Henry C., Emory, VA 24327; Meth; 1839; *; S
Emory U., Atlanta, GA 30322; Meth; 1836; *; bus, law, lib, med; D; M
Empire State C. (see under **State U. of New York**)
Emporia State U., Emporia, KS 66801; state; 1863; *; beyond Mst; M
Endicott C., Beverly, MA 01915; pvt; jr; 1939; for women; *; S
Enterprise State Junior C., Enterprise, AL 36331; state; jr; 1963; *; S
Erie Comm. C., North Campus, Williamsville, NY 14221; state/local; jr; 1946; *; dent-h, engr-t, resp-ther, x-ray-t; L
Erskine C. and Seminary, Due West, SC 29639; Presb; 1836; *; Mst; S
Essex Comm. C., Baltimore County, MD 21237; local; jr; 1957; *; a-nurs; M
Essex County C., Newark, NJ 07102; state/local; jr; 1966; *; a-nurs, x-ray-t; M
Eureka C., Eureka, IL 61530; Christian Church (Disciples of Christ); 1855; *; S
Evangel C., Springfield, MO 65802; Assemblies of God Church; 1955; *; S
Evansville, U. of, Evansville, IN 47702; Meth; 1854; *; a-nurs, ed; Mst; M
Everett Comm. C., Everett, WA 98201; state; jr; 1941; *; a-nurs; L
Evergreen State C., Olympia, WA 98505; state; 1967; *; S
Evergreen Valley C., San Jose, CA 95135; state/local; jr; 1975; *; a-nurs; M
Fairfield U., Fairfield, CT 06430; pvt; 1942; *; beyond Mst; M
Fairleigh Dickinson U., Florham-Madison Campus, Madison, NJ 07940; pvt; 1958; *; resp-ther; D; M
Fairleigh Dickinson U., Rutherford Campus, Rutherford, NJ 07070; pvt; 1942; *; D; M
Fairleigh Dickinson U., Teaneck Campus, Teaneck, NJ 07666; pvt; 1954; *; dent, dent-h, engr; D; M
Fairmont State C., Fairmont, WV 26554; state; 1865; *; med-rec-t; M
Faith Baptist Bible C., Ankeny, IA 50021; pvt; 1921; S
Fashion Inst. of Technology, New York, NY 10001; state/local; 1944; *; M
Fayetteville State U., Fayetteville, NC 28301; state; 1867; *; ed; Mst; S
Felician C., Chicago, IL 60659; RC; jr; 1926; *; S
Felician C., Lodi, NJ 07644; RC; 1935; for women; *; a-nurs; S
Ferris State C., Big Rapids, MI 49307; state; 1884; *; dent-a, x-ray-t; L
Ferrum C., Ferrum, VA 24088; Meth; 1913; *; S
Findlay C., Findlay, OH 45840; Church of God; 1882; *; S
Fisher Junior C., Boston, MA 02116; pvt; jr; 1903; *; M
Fisk U., Nashville, TN 37203; pvt; 1867; *; mus; Mst; S
Fitchburg State C., Fitchburg, MA 01420; state; 1894; *; ed; Mst; M
Flagler C., Saint Augustine, FL 32084; pvt; 1963; *; S
Flaming Rainbow U., Tahlequah, OK 74454; pvt; 1972; S
Flathead Valley Comm. C., Kalispell, MT 59901; local; jr; 1967; *; S
Florida A&M U., Tallahassee, FL 32307; state; 1887; *; ed, engr-t; Mst; M
Florida Atlantic U., Boca Raton, FL 33431; state; 1961; *; bus; D; M
Florida C., Temple Terrace, FL 33617; pvt; jr; 1944; *; S
Florida Inst. of Technology, Melbourne, FL 32901; pvt; 1958; *; engr; D; M
Florida International U., Miami, FL 33199; state; 1965; *; engr-t; Mst; L
Florida Junior C. at Jacksonville, Jacksonville, FL 32202; local; jr; 1963; *; L
Florida Keys Comm. C., Key West, FL 33040; state/local; jr; 1963; *; S
Florida Memorial C., Miami, FL 33054; pvt; 1879; *; S
Florida Southern C., Lakeland, FL 33802; Meth; 1885; *; S
Florida State U., Tallahassee, FL 32306; state; 1851; *; bus, ed, law; D; L
Florida, U. of, Gainesville, FL 32611; state; 1853; *; engr, law, med; D; L
Floyd Junior C., Rome, GA 30161; state; jr; 1968; *; a-nurs; S
Fontbonne C., Saint Louis, MO 63105; RC; 1917; *; ed, mus; Mst; S
Foothill C., Los Altos Hills, CA 94022; state/local; jr; 1958; *; dent-h; L
Fordham U., Bronx, NY 10458; pvt; 1841; *; bus, ed, law; D; L
Fort Hays State U., Hays, KS 67601; state; 1902; *; beyond Mst; M
Fort Lauderdale C., Fort Lauderdale, FL 33301; pvt; 1940; S
Fort Lewis C., Durango, CO 81301; state; 1911; *; bus, ed; M
Fort Scott Comm. C., Fort Scott, KS 66701; state/local; jr; 1919; *; S
Fort Valley State C., Fort Valley, GA 31030; state; 1895; *; ed; Mst; S
Fort Wright C., Spokane, WA 99204; RC; 1907; *; S
Framingham State C., Framingham, MA 01701; state; 1839; *; ed; Mst; M
Francis Marion C., Florence, SC 29501; state; 1970; *; Mst; S
Franklin and Marshall C., Lancaster, PA 17604; pvt; 1787; *; Mst; S
Franklin C. of Indiana, Franklin, IN 46131; Bapt; 1834; *; S
Franklin Pierce C., Rindge, NH 03461; pvt; 1962; *; S
Franklin U., Columbus, OH 43215; pvt; 1902; *; engr-t; M
Frederick Comm. C., Frederick, MD 21701; local; jr; 1957; *; dent-a; S
Fredonia, C. at (see under **State U. of New York**)
Free Will Baptist Bible C., Nashville, TN 37205; Bapt; 1942; S
Freed-Hardeman C., Henderson, TN 38340; Churches of Christ; 1869; *; S
Fresno City C., Fresno, CA 93741; state/local; jr; 1910; *; dent-h, x-ray-t; L
Fresno Pacific C., Fresno, CA 93702; Prot; 1944; *; Mst; S
Friends U., Wichita, KS 67213; Friends; 1898; *; ed, mus; S
Friends World C., Huntington, NY 11743; pvt; 1965; S
Frostburg State C., Frostburg, MD 21532; state; 1898; *; ed; Mst; M
Fullerton C., Fullerton, CA 92634; state/local; jr; 1913; *; L
Fulton-Montgomery Comm. C., Johnstown, NY 12095; local; jr; 1963; *; S
Furman U., Greenville, SC 29613; Bapt; 1826; *; mus; Mst; M
Gadsden State Junior C., Gadsden, AL 39503; state; jr; 1963; *; x-ray-t; M
Gainesville Junior C., Gainesville, FL 30503; state; jr; 1964; *; S
Gallaudet C., Washington, DC 20002; pvt; 1857; *; ed; D; S
Galveston C., Galveston, TX 77550; state/local; jr; 1966; *; a-nurs, x-ray-t; S
Ganado, C. of, Ganado, AZ 86505; pvt; jr; 1970; *; S
Gannon U., Erie, PA 16541; RC; 1944; *; ed, engr, med-a, x-ray-t; Mst; M
Garden City Comm. C., Garden City, KS 67846; local; jr; 1919; *; S
Gardner-Webb C., Boiling Springs, NC 28017; Bapt; 1905; *; a-nurs; Mst; S
Garrett Comm. C., McHenry, MD 21541; local; jr; 1971; *; S
Gaston C., Dallas, NC 28034; state/local; jr; 1963; *; engr-t; M
Gavilan C., Gilroy, CA 95020; state/local; jr; 1919; *; S
General Motors Inst., Flint, MI 48502; pvt; 1919; *; engr; S
Genesee Comm. C., Batavia, NY 14020; state/local; jr; 1966; *; a-nurs; S
Geneseo, C. at (see under **State U. of New York**)
Geneva C., Beaver Falls, PA 15010; Presb; 1848; *; S
George Corley Wallace State Comm. C. at Selma, Selma, AL 36701; state; jr; 1963; *; S
George Fox C., Newberg, OR 97132; Prot; 1891; *; S
George Mason U., Fairfax, VA 22030; state; 1957; *; ed; D; L
George Washington U., Washington, DC 20052; pvt; 1821; *; bus; D; L
George Williams C., Downers Grove, IL 60515; pvt; 1886; *; Mst; S
Georgetown C., Georgetown, KY 40324; Bapt; 1829; *; Mst; S
Georgetown U., Washington, DC 20057; RC; 1789; *; dent, law, med; D; L
Georgia C., Milledgeville, GA 31061; state; 1889; *; mus; beyond Mst; M
Georgia Inst. of Technology, Atlanta, GA 30332; state; 1885; *; engr; D; L
Georgia Military C., Milledgeville, GA 31061; pvt; jr; 1879; *; S
Georgia Southern C., Statesboro, GA 30460; state; 1906; *; beyond Mst; M
Georgia Southwestern C., Americus, GA 31709; state; 1906; *; Mst; S
Georgia State U., Atlanta, GA 30303; state; 1913; *; art, bus, mus; D; L
Georgia, U. of, Athens, GA 30602; state; 1785; *; art, bus, engr, law; D; L
Georgian Court C., Lakewood, NJ 08701; RC; 1908; for women; *; Mst; S
Gettysburg C., Gettysburg, PA 17235; pvt; 1832; *; S
Glassboro State C., Glassboro, NJ 08028; state; 1923; *; ed, mus; Mst; L
Glen Oaks Comm. C., Centreville, MI 49032; local; jr; 1965; *; S
Glendale Comm. C., Glendale, AZ 85302; state/local; jr; 1965; *; engr-t; L
Glendale Comm. C., Glendale, CA 91208; state/local; jr; 1927; *; M
Glenville State C., Glenville, WV 26351; state; 1872; *; ed; S
Gloucester County C., Sewell, NJ 08080; state/local; jr; 1966; *; a-nurs; S
Goddard C., Plainfield, VT 05667; pvt; 1938; *; Mst; S
Gogebic Comm. C., Ironwood, MI 49938; local; jr; 1931; *; S
Golden Gate U., San Francisco, CA 94105; pvt; 1901; *; law; D; M
Golden Valley Lutheran C., Minneapolis, MN 55422; pvt; jr; 1967; *; S
Golden West C., Huntington Beach, CA 92647; state/local; jr; 1966; *; L
Goldey Beacom C., Wilmington, DE 19808; pvt; 1886; *; S
Gonzaga U., Spokane, WA 99258; RC; 1887; *; ed, law; D; M
Gordon C., Wenham, MA 01984; pvt; 1889; *; mus; S
Gordon Junior C., Barnesville, GA 30204; state; jr; 1972; *; a-nurs; S
Goshen C., Goshen, IN 46526; Mennonite Church; 1894; *; ed; S
Goucher C., Towson, MD 21204; pvt; 1885; for women; *; Mst; S
Governors State U., Park Forest South, IL 60466; state; 1969; *; Mst; M
Grace C., Winona Lake, IN 46590; Brethren Church; 1948; *; S
Graceland C., Lamoni, IA 50140; Prot; 1895; *; ed; S
Grambling State U., Grambling, LA 71245; state; 1901; *; ed, mus; Mst; M
Grand Canyon C., Phoenix, AZ 85061; Bapt; 1949; *; S
Grand Rapids Baptist C. and Seminary, Grand Rapids, MI 49505; Bapt; 1941; *; Mst; S
Grand Rapids Junior C., Grand Rapids, MI 49502; local; jr; 1914; *; M
Grand Valley State Colleges, Allendale, MI 49401; state; 1960; *; mus; Mst; M
Grand View C., Des Moines, IA 50316; Prot; 1896; *; S
Grays Harbor C., Aberdeen, WA 98520; state/local; jr; 1930; *; M
Grayson County C., Denison, TX 75020; state/local; jr; 1963; *; a-nurs; M
Great Falls, C. of, Great Falls, MT 59405; RC; 1932; *; S
Great Lakes Bible C., Lansing, MI 48901; Christian Churches; 1949; S
Greater Hartford Comm. C., Hartford, CT 06105; state; jr; 1967; *; med-a; S
Green Mountain C., Poultney, VT 05764; pvt; 1834; *; dent-a; S
Green River Comm. C., Auburn, WA 98002; state; jr; 1965; *; M
Greensboro C., Greensboro, NC 27420; Meth; 1838; *; mus; S
Greenville C., Greenville, IL 62246; Meth; 1892; *; ed; S
Griffin C., Seattle, WA 98121; prop; 1909; S
Grinnell C., Grinnell, IA 50112; pvt; 1846; *; S
Grossmont C., El Cajon, CA 92020; state/local; jr; 1961; *; resp-ther; L
Grove City C., Grove City, PA 16127; pvt; 1876; *; S
Gruss Girls Seminary, Spring Valley, NY 10977; pvt; 1976; for women; S
Guam, U. of, Mangilao, GU 96913; territory; 1952; *; Mst; M
Guilford C., Greensboro, NC 27410; Friends; 1837; *; S
Gulf Coast Comm. C., Panama City, FL 32401; local; jr; 1957; *; dent-a; M
Gustavus Adolphus C., Saint Peter, MN 56082; Prot; 1862; *; ed, mus; S
Gwynedd-Mercy C., Gwynedd Valley, PA 19437; pvt; 1948; *; a-nurs; S
Hagerstown Junior C., Hagerstown, MD 21740; state/local; jr; 1946; *; S
Hahnemann Medical C. and Hospital, Philadelphia, PA 19102; pvt; 1848; *; a-nurs, med, resp-ther, x-ray-t; D; S
Halifax Comm. C., Weldon, NC 27890; state/local; jr; 1967; *; S

Hamilton C., Clinton, NY 13323; pvt; 1812; *; S
Hamline U., Saint Paul, MN 55104; Meth; 1854; *; ed, mus; S
Hampden-Sydney C., Hampden-Sydney, VA 23943; Presb; 1776; for men; *; S
Hampshire C., Amherst, MA 01002; pvt; 1965; *; S
Hampton Inst., Hampton, VA 23668; pvt; 1868; *; arch, ed, mus; Mst; M
Hannibal-La Grange C., Hannibal, MO 63401; Bapt; 1858; *; S
Hanover C., Hanover, IN 47243; Presb; 1827; *; S
Hardin-Simmons U., Abilene, TX 79601; Bapt; 1891; *; ed, mus; Mst; S
Harding U., Searcy, AR 72143; Churches of Christ; 1924; *; ed; Mst; M
Harford Comm. C., Bel Air, MD 21014; local; jr; 1957; *; a-nurs; M
Harris-Stowe State C., Saint Louis, MO 63103; state; 1857; *; ed; S
Harrisburg Area Comm. C., Harrisburg, PA 17110; state/local; jr; 1964; *; M
Hartford, U. of, West Hartford, CT 06117; pvt; 1877; *; art, ed, engr; D; L
Hartnell C., Salinas, CA 93901; state/local; jr; 1920; *; M
Hartwick C., Oneonta, NY 13820; pvt; 1928; *; S
Harvard U., Cambridge, MA 02138; pvt; 1636; *; arch, bus, law, med; D; L
Harvey Mudd C., Claremont, CA 91711; pvt; 1955; *; engr; Mst; S
Haskell Indian Junior C., Lawrence, KS 66044; federal; jr; 1884; *; dent-a; S
Hastings C., Hastings, NE 68901; Presb; 1882; *; ed, mus; S
Haverford C., Haverford, PA 19041; pvt; 1833; *; S
Hawaii Loa C., Kaneohe, HI 96744; Prot; 1963; *; S
Hawaii Pacific C., Honolulu, HI 96813; pvt; 1965; *; S
Hawaii at Hilo, U. of, Hilo, HI 96720; state; 1947; *; M
Hawaii, U. of, Honolulu Comm. C., Honolulu, HI 96817; state; jr; 1920; *; M
Hawaii, U. of, Kapiolani Comm. C., Honolulu, HI 96814; state; jr; 1957; *; M
Hawaii, U. of, Kauai Comm. C., Lihur, HI 96766; state; jr; 1926; *; S
Hawaii, U. of, Leeward Comm. C., Pearl City, HI 96782; state; jr; 1968; *; M
Hawaii at Manoa, U. of, Honolulu, HI 96822; state; 1907; *; med, mus; D; L
Hawaii, U. of, Maui Comm. C., Kahului, HI 96732; state; jr; 1972; *; S
Hawaii, U. of, West Oahu C., Aiea, HI 96701; state; 1973; S
Hawaii, U. of, Windward Comm. C., Kaneohe, HI 96817; state; jr; 1972; *; S.
Hazard Comm. C., Hazard, KY 41701; state; jr; 1968; *; S
Hebrew Union C., Cincinnati, OH 45220; Jewish; 1875; *; grad only; D; S
Hebrew Union C., California Branch, Los Angeles, CA 90007; Jewish; 1954; D, grad only; S
Hebrew Union C., New York Branch, New York, NY 10012; Jewish; 1922; *; D; S
Heidelberg C., Seneca, OH 44883; United Church of Christ; 1850; *; mus; S
Henderson State U., Arkadelphia, AR 71923; state; 1890; *; ed, mus; Mst; M
Hendrix C., Conway, AR 72032; Meth; 1876; *; ed, mus; S
Henry Ford Comm. C., Dearborn, MI 48128; local; jr; 1938; *; a-nurs; L
Herkimer County Comm. C., Herkimer, NY 13350; state/local; jr; 1966; *; S
Hesston C., Hesston, KS 67062; Mennonite Church; jr; 1909; *; a-nurs; S
High Point C., High Point, NC 27262; Meth; 1924; *; ed; S
Highland Comm. C., Highland, KS 66035; local; jr; 1857; *; S
Highland Park Comm. C., Highland Park, MI 48203; local; jr; 1918; *; S
Highline Comm. C., Midway, WA 98031; state; jr; 1961; *; a-nurs; M
Hilbert C., Hamburg, NY 14075; pvt; jr; 1957; *; S
Hillsborough Comm. C., Tampa, FL 33622; state; jr; 1968; *; x-ray-t; L
Hillsdale C., Hillsdale, MI 49242; pvt; 1844; *; S
Hinds Junior C., Raymond, MS 39154; state/local; jr; 1917; *; a-nurs; M
Hiram C., Hiram, OH 44234; pvt; 1850; *; ed, mus; S
Hiwassee C., Madisonville, TN 37354; Meth; jr; 1849; *; S
Hobart-William Smith Colleges, Geneva, NY 14456; pvt; 1822; *; S
Hofstra U., Hempstead, NY 11550; pvt; 1935; *; bus, ed, engr, law; D; L
Hollins C., Hollins College, VA 24020; pvt; 1842; for women; *; mus; S
Holmes Junior C., Goodman, MS 39079; local; jr; 1925; *; S
Holy Cross, C. of the, Worcester, MA 01610; RC; 1843; *; Mst; S
Holy Family C., Philadelphia, PA 19114; RC; 1954; *; S
Holy Names C., Oakland, CA 94619; pvt; 1868; *; mus; Mst; S
Holyoke Comm. C., Holyoke, MA 01040; state; jr; 1946; *; a-nurs, med-rec-t; M
Honolulu Comm. C. (see under **Hawaii, U. of**)
Hood C., Frederick, MD 21701; pvt; 1893; for women; *; x-ray-t; Mst; S
Hope C., Holland, MI 49423; pvt; 1862; *; art, ed, mus; S
Hopkinsville Comm. C., Hopkinsville, KY 42240; state; jr; 1965; *; S
Hostos Comm. C. (see under **City U. of New York**)
Houghton C., Houghton, NY 14744; Wesleyan Church; 1883; *; mus; S
Housatonic Comm. C., Bridgeport, CT 06608; state; jr; 1966; *; S
Houston Baptist U., Houston, TX 77074; Bapt; 1960; *; Mst; S
Houston Comm. C., Houston, TX 77007; state; jr; 1971; *; x-ray-t; L
Houston, U. of, Houston, TX 77004; state; 1927; *; arch, bus, law, mus; D; L
Houston at Clear Lake City, U. of, Houston, TX 77058; state; 1971; *; Mst; M
Howard Comm. C., Columbia, MD 21044; state/local; jr; 1966; *; a-nurs; S
Howard Payne U., Brownwood, TX 76801; Bapt; 1889; *; S
Howard U., Washington, DC 20059; pvt; 1867; *; bus, engr, law, med; D; L
Hudson Valley Comm. C., Troy, NY 12180; state/local; jr; 1953; *; a-nurs, dent-a, med-a; M
Humacao U.C. (see under **Puerto Rico, U. of**)
Humboldt State U., Arcata, CA 95521; state; 1913; *; mus; Mst; M
Humphreys C., Stockton, CA 95207; pvt; jr; 1896; *; S
Hunter C. (see under **City U. of New York**)
Huntingdon C., Montgomery, AL 36106; Meth; 1854; *; S
Huntington C., Huntington, IN 46750; Prot; 1897; *; Mst; S
Huron C., Huron, SD 57350; Presb; 1883; *; S
Husson C., Bangor, ME 04401; pvt; 1898; *; Mst; S
Huston-Tillotson C., Austin, TX 78702; Prot; 1876; *; S
Hutchinson Comm. C., Hutchinson, KS 67501; state/local; jr; 1928; *; S
Idaho, C. of, Caldwell, ID 83605; pvt; 1891; *; Mst; S
Idaho State U., Pocatello, ID 83209; state; 1901; *; bus, dent-h, ed; D; M
Idaho, U. of, Moscow, ID 83843; state; 1889; *; arch, ed, engr, law, mus; D; M
Illinois Benedictine C., Lisle, IL 60532; RC; 1887; *; Mst; S
Illinois Central C., East Peoria, IL 61635; state/local; jr; 1966; *; a-nurs; L
Illinois C., Jacksonville, IL 62650; pvt; 1829; *; S
Illinois C. of Optometry, Chicago, IL 60616; pvt; 1872; *; S
Illinois Eastern Comm. Colleges, Wabash Valley C., Mount Carmel, IL 62863; state/local; jr; 1960; *; M
Illinois Inst. of Technology, Chicago, IL 60616; pvt; 1940; *; arch, law; D; M
Illinois State U., Normal, IL 61761; state; 1857; *; art, ed, mus; D; L
Illinois, U. of, Chicago Circle Campus, Chicago, IL 60680; state; 1965; *; D; L
Illinois Medical Center at Chicago, U. of, Chicago, IL 60612; state; 1896; D; M
Illinois, U. of, Urbana-Champaign Campus, Urbana, IL 61801; state; 1867; * arch, art, bus, ed, engr, law, lib, mus; D; L
Illinois Valley Comm. C., Oglesby, IL 61348; local; jr; 1966; *; dent-a; M
Illinois Wesleyan U, Bloomington, IL 61701; Meth; 1850; *; ed, mus; S
Immaculata C., Immaculata, PA 19345; RC; 1920; for women; *; S
Imperial Valley C., Imperial, CA 92251; local; jr; 1922; *; a-nurs; M
Incarnate Word C., San Antonio, TX 78209; RC; 1881; *; ed; Mst; S
Independence Comm. C., Independence, KS 67301; local; jr; 1925; *; S
Indian Hills Comm. C., Ottumwa, IA 52501; state/local; jr; 1966; *; S
Indian River Comm. C., Fort Pierce, FL 33450; local; jr; 1960; *; a-nurs; M
Indian Valley Colleges, Novato, CA 94947; state/local; jr; 1971; *; S
Indiana Central U., Indianapolis, IN 46227; Meth; 1902; *; a-nurs, ed; Mst; M
Indiana Inst. of Technology, Fort Wayne, IN 46803; pvt; 1930; *; S
Indiana State U., Terre Haute, IN 47809; state; 1865; *; bus, ed, mus; D; L
Indiana State U., Evansville Campus, Evansville, IN 47712; state; 1965; *; M
Indiana U., Bloomington, IN 47405; state; 1820; *; bus, ed, law, mus; D; L
Indiana U. Northwest, Gary, IN 46408; state; 1921; *; a-nurs; Mst; M
Indiana U. of Pennsylvania, Indiana, PA 15705; state; 1875; *; D; L
Indiana U.—Purdue U. at Fort Wayne, Fort Wayne, IN 46805; state; 1964; *; M
Indiana U.—Purdue U. at Indianapolis, Indianapolis, IN 46202; state; 1969; *; L
Indiana U. at South Bend, South Bend, IN 46615; state; 1940; *; Mst; M
Indiana U. Southeast, New Albany, IN 47150; state; 1941; *; Mst; M
Indiana Vocational Technical C.—Central Indiana, Indianapolis, IN 46202; state; jr; 1966; *; resp-ther-t, x-ray-t; M
Indiana Vocational Technical C.—Columbus, Columbus IN 47201; state; jr; 1967; *; S
Indiana Vocational Technical C.—Eastcentral, Muncie, IN 47302; state; jr; 1968; *; med-a; S
Indiana Vocational Technical C.—Kokomo, Kokomo, IN 46901; state; jr; 1968; *; med-a; S
Indiana Vocational Technical C.—Lafayette, Lafayette, IN 47905; state; jr; 1968; dent-a, resp-ther-t; S
Indiana Vocational Technical C.—Northcentral, South Bend, IN 46619; state; jr; 1967; *; med-a; S
Indiana Vocational Technical C.—Northeast, Fort Wayne, IN 46803; state; jr; 1968; *; med-a, resp-ther-t; S
Indiana Vocational Technical C.—Northwest, Gary, IN 46409; state; jr; 1968; *; med-a, resp-ther-t; S
Indiana Vocational Technical C.—Southcentral, Sellersburg, IN 47172; state; jr; 1968; *; med-a; S
Indiana Vocational Technical C.—Southeast, Madison, IN 47250; state; jr; 1971; *; med-a; S
Indiana Vocational Technical C.—Southwest, Evansville, IN 47710; state; jr; 1968; *; S
Indiana Vocational Technical C.—Wabash Valley, Terre Haute, IN 47802; state; jr; 1966; *; med-a; S
Insurance, C. of, New York, NY 10038; pvt; 1929; *; Mst; S
Inter American U. of Puerto Rico, Metropolitan Campus, Hato Rey, PR 00924; pvt; 1960; *; Mst; L
Inter American U. of Puerto Rico, San German Campus, San German, PR 00753; pvt; 1912; *; Mst; M
International C., Los Angeles, CA 90024; pvt; 1970; D; S
International Fine Arts C., Miami, FL 33132; prop; jr; 1965; *; S
International Inst. of the Americas of World U., Hato Rey, PR 00917; pvt; 1965; *; Mst; M
Inver Hills Comm. C., Inver Grove Heights, MN 55075; state; jr; 1967; *; M
Iona C., New Rochelle, NY 10801; pvt; 1940; *; beyond Mst; M
Iowa Central Comm. C., Fort Dodge, IA 50501; local; jr; 1966; *; dent-a; med-a; S
Iowa Lakes Comm. C., Estherville, IA 51334; state/local; jr; 1924; *; S
Iowa State U., Ames, IA 50011; state; 1858; *; arch, ed, engr, mus; D; L
Iowa, U. of, Iowa City, IA 52242; state; 1847; *; ed, bus, law, lib, med; D; L
Iowa Wesleyan C., Mount Pleasant, IA 52641; Meth; 1842; *; ed; S
Iowa Western Comm. C., Council Bluffs, IA 51502; state/local; jr; 1966; *; S
Isothermal Comm. C., Spindale, NC 28160; state/local; jr; *; 1964; S
Itasca Comm. C., Grand Rapids, MN 55744; state; jr; 1922; *; S
Itawamba Junior C., Fulton, MS 38843; local; jr; 1948; *; resp-ther-t; S
Ithaca C., Ithaca, NY 14850; pvt; 1892; *; ed, mus; Mst; M
J. Sargeant Reynolds Comm. C., Richmond, VA 23241; state; jr; 1972; *; M
Jackson Comm. C., Jackson, MI 49201; local; jr; 1928; *; M
Jackson State Comm. C., Jackson, TN 38301; state; jr; 1965; *; S
Jackson State U., Jackson, MS 39217; state; 1877; *; ed; beyond Mst; M
Jacksonville C., Jacksonville, TX 75766; Bapt; jr; 1899; *; S
Jacksonville State U., Jacksonville, AL 36265; state; 1883; *; ed; Mst; M
Jacksonville U., Jacksonville, FL 32211; pvt; 1934; *; mus; Mst; S
James H. Faulkner State Junior C., Bay Minette, AL 36507; state; jr; 1965; *; S
James Madison U., Harrisonburg, VA 22807; state; 1908; *; ed, mus; Mst; M
James Sprunt Technical C., Kenansville, NC 28349; state; jr; 1964; *; S
Jamestown C., Jamestown, ND 58401; Presb; 1883; *; S
Jamestown Comm. C., Jamestown, NY 14701; state/local; jr; 1950; *; a-nurs; M
Jarvis Christian C., Hawkins, TX 75765; Prot; 1912; *; S
Jefferson C., Hillsboro, MO 63050; state/local; jr; 1963; *; S
Jefferson Comm. C., Louisville, KY 40201; state; jr; 1967; *; a-nurs; S
Jefferson Comm. C., Watertown, NY 13601; state/local; jr; 1961; *; a-nurs; S
Jefferson Davis State Junior C., Brewton, AL 36426; state; jr; 1965; *; S
Jefferson State Junior C., Birmingham, AL 35215; state; jr; 1963; *; M
Jersey City State C., Jersey City, NJ 07305; state; 1927; *; art, ed, mus; Mst; M
Jewish Theological Seminary of America, New York, NY 10027; Jewish; 1886; *; D; S
John A. Gupton C., Nashville, TN 37203; pvt; jr; 1946; *; S
John A. Logan C., Carterville, IL 62918; state/local; jr; 1967; *; S
John Brown U., Siloam Springs, AR 72761; pvt; 1919; *; ed; S
John C. Calhoun State Comm. C., Decatur, AL 35602; state; jr; 1963; *; M
John Carroll U., Cleveland, OH 44118; RC; 1886; *; bus, ed; Mst; M
John F. Kennedy U., Orinda, CA 94563; pvt; 1964; *; Mst; S
John Jay C. of Criminal Justice (see under **City U. of New York**)
John Tyler Comm. C., Chester VA 23831; state; jr; 1967; *; M
John Wood Comm. C., Quincy, IL 62301; state/local; jr; 1974; *; S
Johns Hopkins U., Baltimore, MD 21218; pvt; 1876; *; engr; med; D; M
Johnson Bible C., Knoxville, TN 37920; pvt; 1893; *; S
Johnson C. Smith U., Charlotte, NC 28216; Presb; 1867; *; S
Johnson County Comm. C., Overland Park, KS 66210; local; jr; 1967; *; M
Johnson State C., Johnson, VT 05656; state; 1828; *; Mst; S
Johnston Technical C., Smithfield, NC 27577; state/local; jr; 1969; *; x-ray-t; S
Joliet Junior C., Joliet, IL 60436; local; jr; 1901; *; a-nurs; M
Jones County Junior C., Ellisville, MS 39437; state/local; jr; 1927; *; S
Judaism, U. of, Los Angeles, CA 90024; pvt; 1947; *; beyond Mst; S
Judson Baptist C., The Dalles, OR 97058; Bapt; jr; 1956; *; S
Judson C., Marion, AL 36756; Bapt; 1838; for women; *; mus; S
Judson C., Elgin, IL 60120; Bapt; 1963; *; S
Juilliard School, the, New York, NY 10023; pvt; 1905; *; D; S
Juniata C., Huntingdon, PA 16652; pvt; 1876; *; S
Kalamazoo C., Kalamazoo, MI 49007; Bapt; 1833; *; S
Kalamazoo Valley Comm. C., Kalamazoo, MI 49009; local; jr; 1966; *; M
Kankakee Comm. C., Kankakee, IL 60901; state/local; jr; 1966; *; M
Kansas City Art Inst., Kansas City, MO 64111; pvt; 1885; *; art; S
Kansas City Kansas Comm. C., Kansas City, KS 66112; local; jr; 1923; *; M
Kansas Newman C., Wichita, KS 67213; RC; 1933; *; S
Kansas State U., Manhattan, KS 66506; state; 1863; *; arch, bus, mus; D; L
Kansas, U. of, Lawrence, KS 66045; state; 1865; *; engr, law, mus; D; L
Kansas, U. of, Health Sciences and Hospital, Kansas City, KS 66103; state; 1905; med, resp-ther, x-ray-t; D; S
Kansas Wesleyan, Salina, KS 67401; Meth; 1885; *; S
Kapiolani C. (see under **Hawaii, U. of**)
Kaskaskia C., Centralia, IL 62801; state/local; jr; 1940; *; a-nurs, x-ray-t; S
Kauai Comm. C. (see under **Hawaii, U. of**)
Kean C. of New Jersey, Union, NJ 07083; state; 1855; *; ed; beyond Mst; L
Kearney State C., Kearney, NE 68847; state; 1903; *; ed; beyond Mst; M
Keene State C. (see under **New Hampshire, U. of**)
Kellogg Comm. C., Battle Creek, MI 49016; local; jr; 1956; *; x-ray-t; M
Kemper Military School and C., Boonville, MO 65233; pvt/ jr; 1923; *; S
Kenai Peninsula Comm. C. (see under **Alaska, U. of**)
Kendall C., Evanston, IL 60201; Meth; 1934; *; S
Kennedy-King C. (see under **City Colleges of Chicago**)
Kennesaw C., Marietta, GA 30061; state; 1966; *; a-nurs; M
Kent State U., Kent, OH 44242; state; 1910; *; arch, art, bus, ed, lib; D; L
Kentucky State U., Frankfort, KY 40601; state; 1886; *; a-nurs; Mst; S
Kentucky, U. of, Lexington, KY 40506; state; 1865; *; arch, bus; D; L
Kentucky Wesleyan C., Owensboro, KY 42301; Meth; 1860; *; S
Kenyon C., Gambier, OH 43022; pvt; 1824; *; S
Ketchikan Comm. C. (see under **Alaska, U. of**)
Kettering C. of Medical Arts, Kettering, OH 45429; Prot; jr; 1967; *; S
Keuka C., Keuka Park, NY 14478; pvt; 1890; for women; *; S
Keystone Junior C., La Plume, PA 18440; pvt; jr; 1868; *; S
Kilgore C., Kilgore, TX 75662; local; jr; 1935; *; a-nurs; M
King C., Bristol, TN 37620; Presb; 1867; *; S
King's C., Briarcliff Manor, NY 10510; pvt; 1938; *; S
King's C., Wilkes-Barre, PA 18711; pvt; 1946; *; ed; S
Kingsborough Comm. C. (see under **City U. of New York**)
Kirkwood Comm. C., Cedar Rapids, IA 52406; local; jr; 1966; *; resp-ther; M
Kirtland Comm. C., Roscommon, MI 48653; local; jr; 1966; *; S

Kishwaukee C., Malta, IL 60150; state/local; jr; 1967; *; x-ray-t; S
Knox C., Galesburg, IL 61401; pvt; 1837; *; ed; S
Knoxville C., Knoxville, TN 37921; Presb; 1875; *; S
Kodiak Comm. C. (see under **Alaska, U. of**)
Kuskokwim Comm. C. (see under **Alaska, U. of**)
Kutztown State C., Kutztown, PA 19530; state; 1866; *; ed; Mst; M
La Grange C., La Grange, GA 30240; Meth; 1831; *; a-nurs; Mst; S
La Roche C., Pittsburgh, PA 15237; RC; 1963; *; Mst; S
La Salle C., Philadelphia, PA 19141; RC; 1863; *; Mst; M
La Verne, U. of, La Verne, CA 91750; Church of the Brethren; 1891; *; D; M
Labette Comm. C., Parsons, KS 67357; local; jr; 1923; *; a-nurs; S
Laboure Junior C., Boston, MA 02124; RC; jr; 1971; *; a-nurs; S
Lackawanna Junior C., Scranton, PA 18503; pvt; jr; 1894; *; S
Lafayette C., Easton, PA 18042; Presb; 1826; *; engr; S
Lake City Comm. C., Lake City, FL 32055; state; jr; 1947; *; S
Lake County, C. of, Grayslake, IL 60030; local; jr; 1967; *; a-nurs, x-ray-t; L
Lake Erie C., Painesville, OH 44077; pvt; 1856; *; Mst; S
Lake Forest C., Lake Forest, IL 60045; pvt; 1857; *; Mst; S
Lake Land C., Mattoon, IL 61938; state/local; jr; 1966; *; dent-a, dent-h; M
Lake Michigan C., Benton Harbor, MI 49022; local; jr; 1946; *; x-ray-t; M
Lake Region Junior C., Devils Lake, ND 58301; state/local; jr; 1941; *; S
Lake-Sumter Comm. C., Leesburg, FL 32748; state/local; jr; 1962; *; S
Lake Superior State C., Sault Ste Marie, MI 49783; state; 1946; *; engr-t; S
Lake Tahoe Comm. C., S. Lake Tahoe, CA 95702; state/local; jr; 1975; *; S
Lakeland C., Sheboygan, WI 53081; United Church of Christ; 1862; *; S
Lakeland Comm. C., Mentor, OH 44060; state/local; jr; 1967; *; dent-h, resp-ther; M
Lakewood Comm. C., White Bear Lake, MN 55110; state; jr; 1967; *; M
Lamar Comm. C., Lamar, CO 81052; state; jr; 1937; *; S
Lamar U., Beaumont, TX 77710; state; 1923; *; bus, dent-h, ed, engr; D; L
Lambuth C., Jackson, TN 38301; Meth; 1843; *; S
Lander C., Greenwood, SC 29646; state; 1872; *; a-nurs; S
Lane C., Jackson, TN 38301; Christian Methodist Episcopal; 1882; *; S
Lane Comm. C., Eugene, OR 97405; local; jr; 1964; *; a-nurs, resp-ther; M
Laney C., Oakland, CA 94607; state/local; jr; 1953; *; M
Langston U., Langston, OK 73050; state; 1897; *; ed; S
Lansing Comm. C., Lansing, MI 48914; local; jr; 1957; *; a-nurs; L
Laramie County Comm. C., Cheyenne, WY 82001; state/local; 1968; *; S
Laredo Junior C., Laredo, TX 78040; local; jr; 1946; *; a-nurs, x-ray-t; S
Laredo State U., Laredo, TX 78040; state; 1969; *; Mst; S
Lasell Junior C., Newton, MA 92166; pvt; jr; 1851; for women; *; S
Lassen C., Susanville, CA 96130; state/local; jr; 1925; *; S
Lawrence Inst. of Technology, Southfield, MI 48075; pvt; 1932; *; engr; M
Lawrence U., Appleton, WI 54911; pvt; 1847; *; mus; S
Lawson State Comm. C., Birmingham, AL 35211; state; jr; 1965; *; S
LDS Business C., Salt Lake City, UT 84111; Latter-Day Saints; jr; 1886; *; S
Le Moyne C., Syracuse, NY 13214; RC; 1946; *; S
Le Moyne-Owen C., Memphis, TN 38126; Prot; 1862; *; S
Le Tourneau C., Longview, TX 75607; pvt; 1946; *; engr; S
Lebanon Valley C., Annville, PA 17003; Meth; 1866; *; mus; S
Lee C., Cleveland, TN 37311; Church of God; 1918; *; S
Lee C., Baytown, TX 77520; state/local; jr; 1934; *; M
Lees Junior C., Jackson, KY 41339; Presb; jr; 1883; *; S
Lees-McRae C., Banner Elk, NC 28604; Presb; 1900; *; S
Leeward Comm. C. (see under **Hawaii, U. of**)
Lehigh County Comm. C., Schencksville, PA 18078; state/local; jr; 1966; *; M
Lehigh U., Bethlehem, PA 18015; pvt; 1865; *; bus, ed, engr; D; M
Lenoir Comm. C., Kinston, NC 28501; state/local; jr; 1958; *; S
Lenoir-Rhyne C., Hickory, NC 28603; Prot; 1891; *; ed; Mst; S
Lesley C., Cambridge, MA 02238; pvt; 1909; *; S
Lewis and Clark C., Portland, OR 97219; pvt; 1867; *; ed, law, mus; Mst; M
Lewis and Clark Comm. C., Godfrey, IL 62035; state/local; jr; 1970; *; M
Lewis-Clark State C., Lewiston, ID 83501; state; 1893; *; a-nurs, ed; S
Lewis C. of Business, Detroit, MI 48235; pvt; jr; 1874; *; S
Lewis U., Romeoville, IL 60441; pvt; 1934; *; Mst; S
Liberty Baptist C., Lynchburg, VA 24506; Bapt; 1971; *; S
Limestone C., Gaffney, SC 29340; pvt; 1845; *; mus; S
Lincoln C., Lincoln, IL 62656; pvt; jr; 1865; *; S
Lincoln Land Comm. C., Springfield, IL 62708; local; jr; 1967; *; a-nurs; M
Lincoln Memorial U., Harrogate, TN 37752; pvt; 1897; *; S
Lincoln U., San Francisco, CA 94118; pvt; 1919; *; Mst; S
Lincoln U., Jefferson City, MO 65101; state; 1866; * ed; mus; Mst; S
Lincoln U., Lincoln University, PA 19352; state-related; 1845; *; Mst; S
Lindenwood C., Saint Charles, MO 63301; pvt; 1827; *; ed; Mst; S
Lindsey Wilson C., Columbia, KY 42728; Meth; jr; 1903; *; S
Linfield C., McMinnville, OR 97128; Bapt; 1849; *; mus; Mst; S
Linn-Benton Comm. C., Albany, OR 97321; state/local; jr; 1966; *; a-nurs; M
Livingston U., Livingston, AL 35470; state; 1835; *; a-nurs; ed; beyond Mst; S
Livingstone C., Salisbury, NC 28144; Prot; 1879; *; S
Lock Haven State C., Lock Haven, PA 17745; state; 1870; *; ed; S
Loma Linda U., Loma Linda, CA 92515; Seventh-Day Adventists; 1905; *; M
Lon Morris C., Jacksonville, TX 75766; Meth; jr; 1873; *; S
Long Beach City C., Long Beach, CA 90808; state/local; jr; 1927; *; L
Long Island C. Hospital School of Nursing, Brooklyn, NY 11201; pvt; jr; 1883; S
Long Island Seminary of Jewish Studies for Women, Far Rockaway, NY 11691; pvt; 1967; for women; S
Long Island U., Brooklyn Center, Brooklyn, NY 11201; pvt; 1926; *; D; M
Long Island U., C. W. Post Center, Greenvale, NY 11548; pvt; 1954; *; L
Long Island U., Southampton Center, Southampton, NY 11968; pvt; 1963; *; S
Longview Comm. C., Lee's Summit, MO 64063; local; jr; 1968; *; engr-t; M
Longwood C., Farmville, VA 23901; state; 1839; *; ed; Mst; S
Loop C. (see under **City Colleges of Chicago**)
Lorain County Comm. C., Elyria, OH 44035; state/local; jr; 1963; *; M
Loras C., Dubuque, IA 52001; RC; 1839; *; ed; Mst; S
Lord Fairfax Comm. C., Middletown, VA 22645; state; jr; 1969; *; S
Loretto Heights C., Denver, CO 80236; pvt; 1918; *; ed, mus; S
Los Angeles Baptist C., Newhall, CA 91322; Bapt; 1927; *; S
Los Angeles City C., Los Angeles, CA 90029; state/local; jr; 1929; *; L
Los Angeles Harbor C., Wilmington, CA 90744; state/local; jr; 1949; *; L
Los Angeles Pierce C., Woodland Hills, CA 91371; state/local; jr; 1947; *; L
Los Angeles Southwest C., Los Angeles, CA 90047; state/local; jr; 1967; *; M
Los Angeles Trade-Technical C., Los Angeles, CA 90015; local; jr; 1925; *; L
Los Angeles Valley C., Van Nuys, CA 91401; state/local; jr; 1949; *; L
Los Medanos C., Pittsburg, CA 94565; state/local; jr; 1973; *; M
Louisburg C., Louisburg, NC 27549; Meth; jr; 1787; *; S
Louisiana C., Pineville, LA 71360; Bapt; 1906; *; S
Louisiana State U. and A&M C., Baton Rouge, LA 70803; state; 1855; *; D; L
Louisiana State U. in Shreveport, Shreveport, LA 71115; state; 1965; *; Mst; M
Louisiana Technical U., Ruston, LA 71272; state; 1894; *; arch, mus; D; M
Louisville, U. of, Louisville, KY 40292; state; 1798; *; dent, dent-a, engr, law, med; D; L
Lowell, U. of, Lowell, MA 01854; state; 1894; *; ed, engr, engr-t, mus; D; L
Lower Columbia C., Longview, WA 98632; state; jr; 1934; *; a-nurs; M
Loyola C., Baltimore, MD 21210; RC; 1852; *; bus; beyond Mst; M
Loyola Marymount U., Los Angeles, CA 90045; RC; 1911; *; engr, law; M
Loyola U. of Chicago, Chicago, IL 60611; RC; 1870; *; bus, dent, dent-a, law, med; D; L
Loyola U. in New Orleans, New Orleans, LA 70118; RC; 1912; *; Mst; M
Lubbock Christian C., Lubbock, TX 79407; Churches of Christ; 1957; *; S
Lurleen B. Wallace State Junior C., Andalusia, AL 36420; state; jr; 1967; *; S
Luther C., Decorah, IA 52101; American Lutheran; 1861; *; ed, mus; S
Luzerne County Comm. C., Nanticoke, PA 18634; local; jr; 1966; *; a-nurs; M
Lycoming C., Williamsport, PA 17701; Meth; 1812; *; S
Lynchburg C., Lynchburg, VA 24501; pvt; 1903; *; beyond Mst; S
Lyndon State C., Lyndonville, VT 05851; state; 1911; *; Mst; S
Macalester C., Saint Paul, MN 55105; Presb; 1874; *; ed, mus; S
MacCormac Junior C., Chicago, IL 60604; pvt; jr; 1904; *; S
MacMurray C., Jacksonville, IL 62650; Meth; 1846; *; mus; S
Macomb County Comm. C., Center Campus, Mt. Clemens, MI 48044; local; jr; 1954; *; a-nurs, dent-a; M
Macon Junior C., Macon, GA 31206; state; jr; 1965; *; a-nurs, dent-h; S
Madisonville Comm. C., Madisonville, KY 42431; state; jr; 1968; *; S
Madonna C., Livonia, MI 48150; RC; 1947; *; ed; M
Maharishi International University, Fairfield, IA 52556; pvt; 1971; *; Mst; S
Maine Maritime Academy, Castine, ME 04421; state; 1941; *; S
Maine at Augusta, U. of, Augusta, ME 04330; state; jr; 1965; *; a-nurs; M
Maine at Orono, U. of, Orono, ME 04469; state; 1865; *; art, bus; D; L
Mainland, C. of the, Texas City, TX 77590; local; jr; 1966; *; a-nurs; S
Malcolm X C. (see under **City Colleges of Chicago**)
Malone C., Canton, OH 44709; Friends; 1892; *; S.
Manatee Junior C., Bradenton, FL 33507; local; jr; 1957; *; a-nurs; M
Manchester C., North Manchester, IN 46962; Prot; 1889; *; ed, mus; S
Manchester Comm. C., Manchester, CT 06040; state; jr; 1963; *; resp-ther; M
Manhattan C., Bronx, NY 10471; pvt; 1853; *; engr; Mst; M
Manhattan School of Music, New York, NY 10027; pvt; 1917; *; mus; D; S
Manhattanville C., Purchase, NY 10577; pvt; 1841; *; mus; Mst; S
Mankato State U., Mankato, MN 56001; state; 1866; *; art; beyond Mst; L
Mannes C. of Music, New York, NY 10021; pvt; 1916; *; Mst; S
Manor Junior C., Jenkintown, PA 19046; pvt; jr; 1947; *; dent-a; S
Mansfield State C., Mansfield, PA 16933; state; 1854; *; Mst; S
Maple Woods Comm. C., Kansas City, MO 64156; local; jr; 1968; *; S
Maria C. of Albany, Albany, NY 12208; pvt; jr; 1958; *; a-nurs; S
Maria Regina C., Syracuse, NY 13208; pvt; jr; 1961; for women; *; S
Marian C., Indianapolis, IN 46222; RC; 1851; *; ed; S
Marian C. of Fond du Lac, Fond du Lac, WI 54935; RC; 1936; *; ed; S
Maricopa Technical Comm. C., Phoenix, AZ 85004; state/local; jr; 1968; *; M
Marietta C., Marietta, OH 45750; pvt; 1834; *; Mst; S
Marin, C. of, Kentfield, CA 94904; state/local; jr; 1926; *; a-nurs, dent-a; M
Marion C., Marion, IN 46952; Wesleyan Church; 1920; *; Mst; S
Marion Military Inst., Marion, AL 36756; pvt; jr; 1842; for men; *; S
Marist C., Poughkeepsie, NY 12601; pvt; 1946; *; Mst; S
Maritime C. (see under **State U. of New York**)
Marlboro C., Marlboro, VT 05344; pvt; 1946; *; S
Marquette U., Milwaukee, WI 53233; RC; 1864; *; bus, dent, engr, law; L
Mars Hill C., Mars Hill, NC 28754; Bapt; 1856; *; mus; S
Marshall U., Huntington, WV 25701; state; 1837; *; ed, mus; beyond Mst; L
Marshalltown Comm. C., Marshalltown, IA 50158; state/local; jr; 1927; *; S
Martin Center C., Indianapolis, IN 46205; pvt; 1977; S
Martin C., Pulaski, TN 38478; Meth; jr; 1870; *; S
Martin Comm. C., Williamstown, NC 27892; state; jr; 1967; *; S
Mary Baldwin C., Staunton, VA 24401; Presb; 1842; for women; *; S
Mary C., Bismarck, ND 58501; RC; 1955; *; S
Mary Hardin-Baylor, U. of, Belton, TX 76513; Bapt; 1845; *; S
Mary Holmes C., West Point, MS 39773; Presb; 1892; *; S
Mary Washington C., Fredericksburg, VA 22401; state; 1908; *; mus; Mst; S
Marycrest C., Davenport, IA 52804; RC; 1939; *; ed; Mst; S
Marygrove C., Detroit, MI 48221; RC; 1910; *; ed; Mst; S
Maryland Inst. C. of Art, Baltimore, MD 21217; pvt; 1826; *; art; Mst; S
Maryland, U. of, Baltimore County Campus, Catonsville, MD 21228; state; 1963; *; D; M
Maryland, U. of, Baltimore Professional Schools, Baltimore, MD 21201; state; 1807; *; dent, dent-h, law, med, x-ray-t; D; M
Maryland, U. of, College Park Campus, College Park, MD 20742; state; 1856; *; arch, bus, ed, engr, lib, mus; D; L
Maryland: Eastern Shore, U. of, Princess Anne, MD 21853; state; 1886; *; D; S
Marylhurst C. for Lifelong Learning, Marylhurst, OR 97036; RC; 1893; *; S
Marymount C., Tarrytown, NY 10591; pvt; 1919; for women; *; S
Marymount C. of Kansas, Salina, KS 67401; RC; 1922; *; ed, mus; S
Marymount C. of Virginia, Arlington, VA 22207; RC; 1950; for women; *; S
Marymount Manhattan C., New York, NY 10021; pvt; 1937; for women; *; S
Marymount Palos Verdes C., Rancho Palos Verdes, CA 90274; RC; jr; 1967; *; S
Maryville C., Maryville, TN 37801; Presb; 1819; *; mus; S
Maryville C.—Saint Louis, Saint Louis, MO 63141; pvt; 1872; *; Mst; S
Marywood C., Scranton, PA 18509; RC; 1915; for women; *; ed, mus; Mst; M
Massachusetts Bay Comm. C., Wellesley, MA 02181; state; jr; 1961; *; M
Massachusetts C. of Art, Boston, MA 02215; state; 1873; *; art; Mst; S
Massachusetts C. of Pharmacy and Allied Health Sciences, Boston, MA 02115; pvt; 1823; *; D; S
Massachusetts Inst. of Technology, Cambridge, MA 02139; pvt; 1861; *; D; M
Massachusetts Maritime Academy, Buzzards Bay, MA 02532; state; 1891; *; S
Massachusetts, U. of, Amherst Campus, Amherst, MA 01003; state; 1863; *; D; L
Massachusetts, U. of, Boston Campus, Boston, MA 02125; state; 1965; *; M
Massasoit Comm. C., Brockton, MA 02402; state; jr; 1966; *; resp-ther; M
Mater Dei C., Ogdensburg, NY 13669; pvt; jr; 1960; *; S
Mattatuck Comm. C., Waterbury, CT 06708; state; jr; 1967; *; x-ray-t; M
Mayo Medical School, Rochester, MN 55901; pvt; 1971; med; grad only; S
Maysville Comm. C., Maysville, KY 41056; state; jr; 1968; *; S
Mayville State C., Mayville, ND 58257; state; 1889; *; ed; S
McCook Comm. C., McCook, NE 69001; state/local; jr; 1926; *; S
McHenry County C., Crystal Lake, IL 60014; state/local; jr; 1967; *; M
McKendree C., Lebanon, IL 62254; Meth; 1828; *; S.
McLennan Comm. C., Waco, TX 76708; state/local; jr; 1965; *; a-nurs; M
McMurry C., Abilene, TX 79697; Meth; 1923; *; ed; S
McNeese State U., Lake Charles, LA 70609; state; 1938; *; beyond Mst; M
McPherson C., McPherson, KS 67460; Church of the Brethren; 1887; *; S
Meadville-Lombard Theological School, Chicago, IL 61602; pvt; 1844; D, grad only; S
Medaille C., Buffalo, NY 14214; pvt; 1875; *; S
Medger Evers C. (see under **City U. of New York**)
Medical C. of Georgia, Augusta, GA 30912; state; 1828; *; dent, med; D; S
Medical C. of Pennsylvania, The, Philadelphia, PA 19129; pvt; 1850; med, x-ray-t; D; S
Medical U. of South Carolina, Charleston, SC 29401; state; 1824; *; D; S
Medicine and Dentistry of New Jersey at Newark, C. of, Newark, NJ 07103; state; 1954; *; dent, med; D, grad only; S
Meharry Medical C., Nashville, TN 37208; pvt; 1876; *; dent-h, med; D; S
Memphis Academy of the Arts, Memphis, TN 38112; pvt; 1936; *; art; S
Memphis State U., Memphis, TN 38152; state; 1912; *; law, mus; D; L
Mendocino C., Ukiah, CA 95482; state/local; jr; 1973; *; S
Menlo C., Menlo Park, CA 94025; pvt; 1927; *; S
Merced C., Merced, CA 95340; state/local; jr; 1962; *; dent-a, x-ray-t; M
Mercer County Comm. C., Trenton, NJ 08690; state/local; jr; 1966; *; M
Mercer U., Macon, GA 31207; Bapt; 1833; *; ed, law; Mst; S
Mercer U. in Atlanta, Atlanta, GA 30341; Bapt; 1964; *; Mst; S
Mercer U. Southern School of Pharmacy, Atlanta, GA 30312; Bapt; 1903; *; S
Mercy C., Dobbs Ferry, NY 10522; pvt; 1950; *; M
Mercy C. of Detroit, Detroit, MI 48219; RC; 1941; *; med-rec-t; Mst; S
Mercyhurst C., Erie, PA 16546; RC; 1926; *; dent-a; Mst; S
Meredith C., Raleigh, NC 27611; Bapt; 1891; *; mus; S
Meridian Junior C., Meridian, MS 39301; local; jr; 1937; *; x-ray-t; S
Merrimack C., North Andover, MA 01845; RC; 1947; *; ed, engr; M
Merritt C., Oakland, CA 94619; state/local; jr; 1953; *; x-ray-t; M
Mesa C., Grand Junction, CO 81501; state; 1925; *; a-nurs, x-ray-t; M
Mesa Comm. C., Mesa, AZ 85202; state/local; jr; 1965;*; a-nurs; L
Mesabi Comm. C., Virginia, MN 55792; state; jr; 1918; *; S
Messiah C., Grantham, PA 17027; Brethren in Christ Church; 1909; *; S
Methodist C., Fayetteville, NC 28301; Meth; 1956; *; S
Metropolitan State C., Denver, CO 80204; state; 1963; *; ed, engr-t; L
Metropolitan State U., Saint Paul, MN 55101; state; 1971; *; S

Metropolitan U.C., Rio Piedras, PR 00928; pvt; jr; 1949; *; resp-ther; M
Miami-Dade Comm. C., Miami, FL 33176; state; jr; 1959; *; a-nurs; L
Miami, U. of, Coral Gables, FL 33124; pvt; 1925; *; arch, med, mus; D; L
Miami U., Oxford Campus, Oxford, OH 45056; state; 1809; *; mus; D; L
Michigan Christian C., Rochester, MI 48063; pvt; jr; 1959; *; S
Michigan State U., East Lansing, MI 48824; state; 1855; *; D; L
Michigan Technological U., Houghton, MI 49931; state; 1885; *; engr; D; M
Michigan—Ann Arbor, U. of, Ann Arbor, MI 48109; state; 1817; *; D; L
Michigan—Dearborn, U. of, Dearborn, MI 48128; state; 1959; *; engr; Mst; M
Michigan—Flint, U. of, Flint, MI 48503; state; 1956; *; ed; Mst; M
Micronesia, Comm. C. of, Ponape Island, Trust Territory of the Pacific Islands, Eastern Caroline Islands 96941; territory; jr; 1963; *; S
Mid-America Nazarene C., Olathe, KS 66061; Church of Nazarene; 1966; *; S
Mid Michigan Comm. C., Harrison, MI 48625; state/local; jr; 1965; *; S
Mid Plains Comm. C., North Platte, NE 69101; state/local; jr; 1964; S
Middle Georgia C., Cochran, GA 31014; state; jr; 1884; *; S
Middle Tennessee State U., Murfreesboro, TN 37132; state; 1911; *; D; L
Middlebury C., Middlebury, VT 05753; pvt; 1800; *; D; S
Middlesex Comm. C., Middletown, CT 06457; state; jr; 1966; *; x-ray-t; M
Middlesex Comm. C., Bedford, MA 01730; state; jr; 1969; *; a-nurs, med-a; M
Middlesex County C., Edison, NJ 08818; state/local; jr; 1964; *; x-ray-t; L
Midland C., Midland, TX 79701; local; jr; 1969; *; S
Midland Lutheran C., Fremont, NE 68025; Prot; 1883; *; resp-ther; S
Midway C., Midway, KY 40347; pvt; jr; 1847; for women; *; a-nurs; S
Midwest C. of Engineering, Lombard, IL 60148; pvt; 1967; *; Mst; S
Midwestern State U., Wichita Falls, TX 76308; state; 1922; *; Mst; M
Miles C., Birmingham, AL 35208; Christian Methodist Episcopal; 1905; *; S
Miles Comm. C., Miles City, MT 59301; state/local; jr; 1939; *; S
Millersville State C., Millersville, PA 17551; state; 1852; *; beyond Mst; M
Milligan C., Milligan College, TN 37682; pvt; 1866; *; ed; S
Millikin U., Decatur, IL 62522; Presb; 1901; *; mus; S
Mills C., Oakland, CA 94613; pvt; 1852; for women; *; Mst; S
Millsaps C., Jackson, MS 39210; Meth; 1890; *; Mst; S
Milton C., Milton, WI 53563; pvt; 1844; *; S
Milwaukee School of Engineering, Milwaukee, WI 53201; pvt; 1903; *; Mst; S
Mineral Area C., Flat River, MO 63601; local; jr; 1965; *; dent-a; S
Minneapolis C. of Art and Design, Minneapolis, MN 55404; pvt; 1886; *; art; S
Minneapolis Comm. C., Minneapolis, MN 55403; state; jr; 1965; *; a-nurs; S
Minnesota at Duluth, U. of, Duluth, MN 55812; state; 1947; *; beyond Mst; M
Minnesota at Morris, U. of, Morris, MN 56267; state; 1959; *; ed; S
Minnesota: Twin Cities, U. of, Minneapolis, MN 55455; state; 1851; *; D; L
Minot State C., Minot, ND 58701; state; 1913; *; ed, mus; Mst; S
Mira Costa C., Oceanside, CA 92054; state/local; jr; 1934; *; M
Mission C., Santa Clara, CA 95054; state/local; jr; 1975; *; M
Mississippi C., Clinton, MS 39058; Bapt; 1836; *; ed, mus; beyond Mst; M
Mississippi County Comm. C., Blytheville, AR 72315; state/local; jr; 1974; *; S
Mississippi Delta Junior C., Moorhead, MS 38761; local; jr; 1911; *; S
Mississippi Gulf Coast Junior C., Perkinston, MS 39573; local; jr; 1911; *; M
Mississippi State U., Mississippi State, MS 39762; state; 1878; *; engr; D; L
Mississippi, U. of, University, MS 38677; state; 1844; *; bus, med; D; M
Mississippi Medical Center, U. of, Jackson, MS 39216; state; 1955; *; D; S
Mississippi U. for Women, Columbus, MS 39701; state; 1884; for women; *; a-nurs, ed, mus; beyond Mst; S
MIssissippi Valley State U., Itta Bena, MS 38941; state; 1946; *; Mst; S
Missouri Baptist C., Saint Louis, MO 63141; Bapt; 1963; *; S
Missouri Southern State C., Joplin, MO 64801; state; 1965; *; ed, x-ray-t; M
Missouri—Columbia, U. of, Columbia, MO 65211; state; 1839; *; D; L
Missouri—Kansas City, U. of, Kansas City, MO 64110; state; 1929; *; D; L
Missouri—Rolla, U. of, Rolla, MO 65401; state; 1870; *; engr; D; M
Missouri—Saint Louis, U. of, Saint Louis, MO 63121; state; 1963; *; D; L
Missouri Valley C., Marshall, MO 65340; Presb; 1888; *; S.
Missouri Western State C., Saint Joseph, MO 64507; state 1915; *; ed; M
Mitchell C., New London, CT 06320 pvt; jr; 1938; *; S
Mitchell Comm. C., Statesville, NC 28677; state; jr; 1852; *; S
Moberly Junior C., Moberly, MO 65270; state/local; jr; 1927; *; S
Mobile C., Mobile, AL 36613; Bapt; 1961; *; a-nurs; S
Modesto Junior C., Modesto, CA 95350; state/local; jr; 1921; *; med-a; L
Mohave Comm. C., Kingman, AZ 86401; state/local; jr; 1971; M
Mohawk Valley Comm. C., Utica, NY 13501; state/local; jr; 1946; *; M
Mohegan Comm. C., Norwich, CT 06360; state; jr; 1970; *; a-nurs; S
Molloy C., Rockville Centre, NY 11570; RC; 1955; for women; *; S
Monmouth C., Monmouth, IL 61462; pvt; 1886; S
Monmouth C., West Long Branch, NJ 07764; pvt; 1933; *; engr; Mst; M
Monroe Comm. C., Rochester, NY 14623; state/local; jr; 1960; *; a-nurs; L
Monroe County Comm. C., Monroe, MI 48161; local; jr; 1964; *; S
Montana C. of Mineral Science and Technology, Butte, MT 59701; state; 1893; *; engr; Mst; S
Montana State, U., Bozeman, MT 59717; state; 1893; *; arch, engr-t; D; L
Montana, U. of, Missoula, MT 59812; state; 1893; *; bus, ed, law, mus; D; M
Montcalm Comm. C., Sidney, MI 48885; local; jr; 1965; *; S
Montclair State C., Upper Montclair, NJ 07043; state; 1908; *; Mst; L
Monterey Inst. of International Studies, Monterey, CA 93940; pvt; 1955; *; S
Monterey Peninsula C., Monterey, CA 93940; state/local; jr; 1947; *; dent-a; M
Montevallo, U. of, Montevallo, AL 35115; state; 1896; *; beyond Mst; S
Montgomery C.: Takoma Park Campus, Takoma Park, MD 20012; local; jr; 1946; *; a-nurs, dent-a, x-ray-t; M
Montgomery County Comm. C., Blue Bell, PA 19422; local; jr; 1964; *; M
Montreat-Anderson C., Montreat, NC 28757; Presb; jr; 1916; *; S
Moody Bible Inst., Chicago, IL 60610; pvt; 1886; S
Moore C. of Art, Philadelphia, PA 19103; pvt; 1844; for women; *; art; S
Moorhead State U., Moorhead, MN 56560; state; 1885; *; ed, mus; Mst; M
Moorpark C., Moorpark, CA 93021; state/local; jr; 1963; *; M
Moraine Valley Comm. C., Palos Hills, IL 60465; state/local; jr; 1968; *; M
Moravian C., Bethelehem, PA 18018; Moravian Church; 1782; *; S
Morehead State U., Morehead, KY 40351; state; 1923; *; beyond Mst; M
Morehouse C., Atlanta, GA 30314; pvt; 1867; *; S
Morgan State U., Baltimore, MD 21239; state; 1867; *; art, ed, mus; D; M
Morningside C., Sioux City, IA 51106; Meth; 1893; *; ed, mus: Mst; S
Morris Brown C., Atlanta, GA 30314; African Methodist Episcopal; 1881; *; S
Morris C., Sumter, SC 29150; Bapt; 1908; *; S
Morristown C., Morristown, TN 37814; Meth; jr; 1881; *; S
Morton C., Cicero, IL 60650; state/local; jr; 1924; *; dent-a; M
Motlow State Comm. C., Tullahoma, TN 37388; state; jr; 1965; *; S
Mount Aloysius Junior C., Cresson, PA 16630; pvt; jr; 1939; *; a-nurs; S
Mount Holyoke C., South Hadley, MA 01075; pvt; 1837; for women; *; Mst; S
Mount Hood Comm. C., Gresham, OR 97030; local; jr; 1965; *; resp-ther; L
Mount Ida Junior C., Newton Centre, MA 02159; pvt; jr; 1899; *; dent-a; S
Mount Marty C., Yankton, SD 57078; RC; 1936; *; ed, resp-ther; S
Mount Mary C., Milwaukee, WI 53222; RC; 1877; for women; *; ed; S
Mount Mercy C., Cedar Rapids, IA 52402; RC; 1928; *; S
Mount Olive C., Mount Olive, NC 28365; Bapt; jr; 1951; *; S
Mount Sacred Heart C., Hamden, CT 06514; RC; jr; 1954; for women; S
Mount Saint Clare C., Clinton, IA 52732; RC; 1895; *; S
Mount Saint Joseph on the Ohio, C. of, Mount Saint Joseph, OH 45051; RC; 1920; for women; *; resp-ther; S
Mount Saint Mary C., Newburgh, NY 12550; pvt; 1954; *; S
Mount Saint Mary's C., Los Angeles, CA 90049; RC; 1925; for women; *; S
Mount Saint Mary's C., Emmitsburg, MD 21727; RC; 1808; *; Mst; S
Mount Saint Vincent, C. of, Riverdale, NY 10471; pvt; 1847; *; S
Mount San Antonio C., Walnut, CA 91789; state/local; jr; 1945; *; L
Mount San Jacinto C., San Jacinto, CA 92383; state/local; jr; 1962; *; S
Mount Senario C., Ladysmith, WI 54848; pvt; 1962; *; S
Mount Union C., Alliance, OH 44601; Meth; 1846; *; mus; S
Mount Vernon C., Washington, DC 20007; pvt; 1875; *; S
Mount Vernon Nazarene C., Mount Vernon, OH 43050; Prot; 1966; *; S
Mount Wachusett Comm. C., Gardner, MA 01440; state; jr; 1963; *; a-nurs; M
Mountain Empire Comm. C., Big Stone Gap, VA 24219; state; jr; 1970; *; S
Mountain View C., Dallas, TX 75211; state/local; jr; 1970; *; M
Muhlenberg C., Allentown, PA 18104; pvt; 1869; *; ed; S
Mundelein C., Chicago, IL 60660; pvt; 1929; for women; *; ed; Mst; S
Murray State C., Tishomingo, OK 73460; state; jr; 1908; *; a-nurs; S
Murray State U., Murray, KY 42071; state; 1922; *; beyond Mst; M
Muscatine Comm. C., Muscatine, IA 52761; state/local; jr; 1929; *; S
Museum Art School, Portland, OR 97205; pvt; 1909; *; art; S
Museum of Fine Arts—Boston, School of the, Boston, MA 02115; pvt; 1876; art; Mst; S
Muskegon Comm. C., Muskegon, MI 49442; local; jr; 1926; *; dent-a; M
Muskingum C., New Concord, OH 43762; Presb; 1837; *; mus; S
Napa C., Napa, CA 94558; state/local; jr; 1940; *; resp-ther; M
Naropa Inst., Boulder, CO 80302; pvt; 1974; Mst; S
Nassau Comm. C., Garden City, NY 11530; state/local; jr; 1959; *; L
Nasson C., Springvale, ME 04083; pvt; 1909; *; S
Nathaniel Hawthorne C., Antrim, NH 03440; pvt; 1962; *; S
National C., Rapid City, SD 57709; pvt; 1941; S
National C. of Education, Evanston, IL 60201; pvt; 1886; *; ed; S
National U., San Diego, CA 92108; pvt; 1971; *; D; M
Native American Educational Services, Chicago, IL 60640; pvt; 1974; S
Navajo Comm. C. Tsaile, AZ 86556; local; jr; 1968; *; S
Navarro C., Corsicana, TX 75110; local; jr; 1946; *; S
Nazareth C., Nazareth, MI 49074; RC; 1924; *; ed; S
Nazareth C. of Rochester, Rochester, NY 14610; pvt; 1924; *; Mst; S
Nebraska-Lincoln, U. of, Lincoln, NE 68588; state; 1869; *; law, mus; D; L
Nebraska Medical Center, U. of, Omaha, NE 68105; state; 1869; *; D; S
Nebraska at Omaha, U. of, Omaha, NE 68182; state; 1908; *; D; L
Nebraska Wesleyan U., Lincoln, NE 68504; pvt; 1887; *; ed, mus; S
Nebraska Western C., Scotts Bluff, NE 69361; state/local; jr;. 1926; *; S
Neosho County Comm. C., Chanute, KS 66720; local; jr; 1935; *; S
Neumann C., Aston, PA 19014; RC; 1962; *; S
Nevada—Las Vegas, U. of, Las Vegas, NV 89154; state; 1955; *; x-ray-t; D; M
Nevada—Reno, U. of, Reno, NV 89557; state; 1864; *; med; D; M
New C. of California, San Francisco, CA 94110; pvt; 1971; *; Mst; S
New England C., Henniker, NH 03242; pvt; 1946; *; Mst; S
New England C. of Optometry, Boston, MA 02115; pvt; 1894; *; S
New England Conservatory of Music, Boston, MA 02115; pvt; 1867; *; S
New England, U. of, Biddeford, ME 04005; pvt; 1943; *; S
New Hampshire C., Manchester, NH 03104; pvt; 1932; *; Mst; M
New Hampshire, U. of, Durham, NH 03824; state; 1866; *; ed, engr, mus; D; L
New Hampshire, U. of, Keene State C., Keene, NH 03431; state; 1909; *; M
New Hampshire, U. of, Plymouth State C., Plymouth NH 03264; state; 1871; *; ed; Mst; M
New Haven, U. of, West Haven, CT 06516; pvt; 1920; *; engr; Mst; M
New Jersey Inst. of Technology, Newark, NJ 07102; state/local; 1881; *; arch, engr, engr-t; D; M
New Mexico Highlands U., Las Vegas, NM 87701; state; 1893; *; Mst; S
New Mexico Inst. of Mining and Technology, Socorro, NM 87801; state; 1889; *; engr; D; S
New Mexico Junior C., Hobbs, NM 88240; local; jr; 1965; *; a-nurs; S
New Mexico Military Inst., Roswell, NM 88201; state; jr; 1891; *; S
New Mexico State U., Las Cruces, NM 88003; state; 1888; *; D; L
New Mexico, U. of, Albuquerque, NM 87131; state; 1889; *; med, mus; D; L
New Orleans, U. of, New Orleans, LA 70122; state; 1956; *; mus; D; L
New Paltz, C. at (see under **State U. of New York**)
New River Comm. C., Dublin, VA 24084; state; jr; 1966; *; S
New Rochelle, C. of, New Rochelle, NY 10801; pvt; 1898; *; Mst; M
New School for Social Research, New York, NY 10011; pvt; 1919; *; D; M
New School of Music, Philadelphia, PA 19103; pvt; 1945; *; S
New York City Comm. C. (see under **City U. of New York**)
New York, City U. of (see **City U. of New York**)
New York Inst. of Technology, Old Westbury, NY 11568; pvt; 1955; *; M
New York State C. of Ceramics at Alfred U., Alfred, NY 14802; state; 1900; S
New York, State U. of (see **U. of New York**)
New York U., New York, NY 10003; pvt; 1831; *; bus, law, med; D; L
Newberry C., Newberry, SC 29108; Prot; 1856; *; ed, mus; S
Newbury Junior C., Boston, MA 02115; pvt; jr; 1962; *; resp-ther-t, x-ray-t; S
Niagara County Comm. C., Sanborn, NY 14132; state/local; jr; 1962; *; M
Niagara U., Niagara U., NY 14109; RC; 1856; *; beyond Mst; M
Nicholls State U., Thibodaux, LA 70310; state; 1948; *; beyond Mst; M
Nichols C., Dudley, MA 01570; pvt; 1931; *; Mst; S
Nicolet C. and Technical Inst., Rhinelander, WI 54501; state; jr; 1967; *; S
Norfolk State U., Norfolk, VA 23504; state; 1935; *; a-nurs, ed, mus; Mst; M
Normandale Comm. C., Bloomington, MN 55431; state; jr; 1965; *; a-nurs; M
North Adams State C., North Adams, MA 01247; state; 1894; *; ed; Mst; S
North Alabama, U. of, Florence, AL 36530; state; 1872; *; ed; beyond Mst; M
North Arkansas Comm. C., Harrison, AR 72601; state/local; jr; 1974; *; S
North Carolina Agricultural and Technical State U., Greensboro, NC 27411; state; 1891; *; bus, engr, ed; beyond Mst; M
North Carolina Central U., Durham, NC 27707; state; 1910; *; Mst; M
North Carolina School of the Arts, Winston-Salem, NC 27107; state; 1963; *; S
North Carolina State U. at Raleigh, Raleigh, NC 27650; state; 1887; *; D; L
North Carolina at Chapel Hill, U. of, Chapel Hill, NC 27514; state; 1789; *; bus, dent, dent-a, dent-h, ed, engr, law, lib, med, x-ray-t; D; L
North Carolina Wesleyan C., Rocky Mount, NC 27801; Meth; 1956; *; S
North Central C., Naperville, IL 60566; Meth; 1861; *; S
North Central Michigan C., Petoskey, MI 49770; local; jr; 1958; *; S
North Country Comm. C., Saranac Lake, NY 12983; state/local; jr; 1967; *; S
North Dakota State School of Science, Wahpeton, ND 58075; state; jr; 1903; *; dent-a, dent-h; M
North Dakota State U., Fargo, ND 58105; state; 1890; *; a-nurs, arch, ed, engr, mus; D; M
North Dakota, U. of, Grand Forks, ND 58202; state; 1884; *; law, med; D; M
North Florida Junior C., Madison, FL 32340; local; jr; 1958; *; S
North Florida, U. of, Jacksonville, FL 32216; state; 1965; *; bus; Mst; M
North Georgia C., Dahlonega, GA 30597; state; 1872; *; a-nurs, ed; Mst; S
North Greenville C., Tigerville, SC 29688; Bapt; jr; 1892; *; S
North Harris County C., Houston, TX 77073; state/local; jr; 1972; *; M
North Hennepin Comm. C., Brooklyn Park, MN 55445; state; jr; 1966; *; M
North Idaho C., Coeur d'Alene, ID 83814; local; jr; 1933; *; a-nurs; S
North Iowa Area Comm. C., Mason City, IA 50401; state/local; jr; 1917; *; S
North Lake C., Irving, TX 75062; local; jr; 1965; *; M
North Park C. and Theological Seminary, Chicago, IL 60625; Evangelical Covenant Church of America; 1891; *; mus; S
North Seattle Comm. C., Seattle, WA 98103; state; jr; 1970; *; M
North Shore Comm. C., Beverly, MA 01915; state; jr; 1965; *; a-nurs; S
North Texas State U., Denton, TX 76203; state; 1890; *; bus, mus; D; L
Northampton County Area Comm. C., Behlehem, PA 18017; state/local; jr; 1966; *; a-nurs, dent-a, dent-h, x-ray-t; M
Northeast Alabama State Junior C., Rainsville, AL 35986; state; jr; 1963; *; S
Northeast Louisiana U., Monroe, LA 71209; state; 1931; *; bus; D; M
Northeast Mississippi Junior C., Booneville, MS 38829; local; jr; 1941; *; S
Northeast Missouri State U., Kirksville, MO 63501; state; 1867; *; Mst; M
Northeastern Bible C., Essex Falls, NJ 07021; Interdenominational; 1950; *; S
Northeastern Christian Junior C., Villanova, PA 19085; Church of Christ (Scientist); Jr; 1956; *: S
Northeastern Illinois U., Chicago, IL 60625; state; 1961; *; ed; Mst; L
Northeastern Junior C., Sterling, CO 80751; local; jr; 1941; *; S
Northeastern Oklahoma A&M C., Miami, OK 74354; state; jr; 1919; *; S
Northeastern Oklahoma State U., Tahlequah, OK 74464; state; 1851; *; Mst; M

Northeastern U., Boston, MA 02117; pvt; 1898; *; a-nurs, bus; D; L
Northern Arizona U., Flagstaff, AZ 86011; state; 1899; *; mus, x-ray-t; D; L
Northern Colorado, U. of, Greeley, CO 80639; state; 1889; *; ed, mus; D; L
Northern Essex Comm. C., Haverhill, MA 01830; state; jr; 1960; *; M
Northern Illinois U., De Kalb, IL 60115; state; 1895; *; art, bus, ed, lib; D; L
Northern Iowa, U. of, Cedar Falls, IA 50613; state; 1876; *; ed, mus; D; L
Northern Kentucky U., Highland Heights, KY 41076; state; 1968; *; Mst; M
Northern Michigan U., Marquette, MI 49855; state; 1899; *; beyond Mst; M
Northern Montana C., Havre, MT 59501; state; 1929; *; Mst; S
Northern Nevada Comm. C., Elko, NV 89801; state; jr; 1967; *; S
Northern Oklahoma C., Tonkawa, OK 74653; state; jr; 1901; *; a-nurs; S
Northern State C., Aberdeen, SD 57401; state; 1901; *; ed, mus; Mst; S
Northern Virginia Comm. C., Annandale, VA 22003; state; 1965; jr; *; L
Northland C., Ashland, WI 54806; pvt; 1892; *; S
Northland Comm. C., Thief River Falls, MN 56701; state; jr; 1965; *; S
Northrop U., Inglewood, CA 90306; pvt; 1942; *; engr, engr-t; Mst; S
Northwest Alabama State Junior C., Phil Campbell, AL 35581; state; jr; 1961; *; a-nurs; S
Northwest Christian C., Eugene, OR 97401; Christian Church; 1895; *; S
Northwest C. of the Assemblies of God, Kirkland, WA 98033; Assemblies of God Church; 1934; *; S
Northwest Comm. C., Powell, WY 82435; state/local; jr; 1946; *; S
Northwest Iowa Technical C., Sheldon, IA 51201; state/local; jr; 1966; *; S
Northwest Mississippi Junior C., Senatobia, MS 38668; state; jr; 1927; *; S
Northwest Missouri State U., Kirksville, MO 63501; state; 1867; *; Mst; M
Northwest Nazarene C., Nampa, ID 83651; Prot; 1913; *; ed; Mst; S
Northwestern C., Orange City, IA 51041; Prot; 1882; *; ed; S
Northwestern C., Roseville, MN 55113; pvt; 1902; *; S
Northwestern Connecticut Comm. C., Winsted, CT 06098; state; jr; 1965; *; S
Northwestern Michigan C., Traverse City, MI 49684; local; jr; 1951; *; S
Northwestern Oklahoma State U., Alva, OK 73717; state; 1897; *; ed; Mst; S
Northwestern State U. of Louisiana, Natchitoches, LA 71457; state; 1884; *; D; M
Northwestern U., Evanston, IL 60201; pvt; 1851; *; engr, law, med; D; L
Northwood Inst., Midland, MI 48640; pvt; 1959; *; S
Norwalk Comm. C., Norwalk, CT 06854; state; jr; 1961; *; a-nurs; S
Norwich U., Northfield, VT 05663; pvt; 1819; *; engr; Mst; S
Notre Dame C., Manchester, NH 03104; RC; 1950; for women; *; S
Notre Dame, C. of, Belmont, CA 94002; pvt; 1868; *; ed, mus; Mst; S
Notre Dame C. of Ohio, Cleveland, OH 44121; RC; 1922; for women; *; S
Notre Dame of Maryland, C. of, Baltimore, MD 21210; RC; 1873; for women; *; S
Notre Dame, U. of, Notre Dame, IN 46556; RC; 1842; *; law; D; M
Nova U., Fort Lauderdale, FL 33314; pvt; 1964; *; D; M
Nyack C., Nyack, NY 10960; Prot; 1882; *; mus; Mst; S
Oakland City C., Oakland City, IN 47660; Bapt; 1885; *; S
Oakland Comm. C., Bloomfield Hills, MI 48013; state/local; jr; 1964; *; dent-a, dent-h, resp-ther; L
Oakland U., Rochester, MI 48063; state; 1957; *; ed, engr; D; L
Oakton Comm. C., Des Plaines, IL 60016; state/local; jr; 1969; *; x-ray-t; L
Oakwood C., Huntsville, AL 35806; Seventh-Day Adventists; 1896; *; S
Oberlin C., Oberlin, OH 44074; pvt; 1833; *; art, mus; Mst; S
Oblate C., Washington, DC 20017; RC; 1926; for men; *; Mst; S
Occidental C., Los Angeles, CA 90041; pvt; 1887; *; Mst; S
Ocean County C., Toms River, NJ 08753; state/local; jr; 1964; *; engr-t; M
Odessa C., Odessa, TX 79760; local; jr; 1946; *; a-nurs, resp-ther, x-ray-t; M
Oglethorpe U., Atlanta, GA 30319; pvt; 1835; *; Mst; S
Ohio Dominican C., Columbus, OH 43219; RC; 1911; *; S
Ohio Northern U., Ada, OH 45810; Meth; 1871; *; engr, law, mus; S
Ohio State U., Columbus, OH 43210; state; 1870; *; arch, bus, dent; D; L
Ohio U., Athens, OH 45701; state; 1804; *; bus, ed, engr, mus; D; L
Ohio Valley C., Parkersburg, WV 26101; Prot; jr; 1958; *; S
Ohio Wesleyan U., Delaware, OH 43015; Meth; 1842; *; mus; S
Ohlone C., Fremont, CA 94538; state/local; jr; 1966; *; a-nurs; M
Okaloosa-Walton Junior C., Niceville, FL 32578; local; jr; 1963; *; M
Oklahoma Baptist U., Shawnee, OK 74801; Bapt; 1910; *; ed, mus; S
Oklahoma Christian C., Oklahoma City, OK 73111; pvt; 1950; *; ed; S
Oklahoma City Southwestern C., Oklahoma City, OK 73127; Prot; 1946; *; S
Oklahoma City U., Oklahoma City, OK 73106; Meth; 1901; *; law; Mst; S
Oklahoma Panhandle State U., Goodwell, OK 73939; state; 1909; *; ed; S
Oklahoma State U., Stillwater, OK 74078; state; 1890; *; arch, bus; D; L
Oklahoma Health Sciences Center, U. of, Oklahoma City, OK 73190; state; 1900; dent, dent-h, med, resp-ther, x-ray-t; D; S
Oklahoma Norman Campus, U. of, Norman, OK 73019; state; 1890; *; D; L
Old Dominion U., Norfolk, VA 23508; state; 1930; *; bus, engr; D; L
Olivet C., Olivet, MI 49076; pvt; 1844; *; Mst; S
Olivet Nazarene C., Kankakee, IL 60901; Prot; 1907; *; ed; Mst; S
Olympic C., Brewerton, WA 98310; state; jr; 1946; *; M
Oneonta, C. at (see under **State U. of New York**)
Onondaga Comm. C., Syracuse, NY 13215; state/local; 1962; *; a-nurs; M
Oral Roberts U., Tulsa, OK 74171; pvt; 1965; *; Mst; M
Orange Coast C., Costa Mesa, CA 92626; state/local; jr; 1947; *; x-ray-t; L
Orange County Comm. C., Middletown, NY 10940; state/local; jr; *; dent-h; M
Oregon C. of Education, Monmouth, OR 97361; state; 1856; *; Mst; M
Oregon Health Sciences Center, U. of, Portland, OR 97201; state; 1974; D; S
Oregon Inst. of Technology, Klamath Falls, OR 97601; state; 1946; *; S
Oregon State U., Corvallis, OR 97331; state; 1850; *; bus, ed, engr; D; L
Oregon, U. of, Eugene, OR 97403; state; 1876; *; arch, bus, ed, law, mus; D; L
Oscar Rose Junior C., Midwest City, OK 73110; state/local; jr; 1968; *; M
Oswego, C. at (see under **State U. of New York**)
Otero Junior C., La Junta, CO 81050; state; jr; 1941; *; S
Otis Art Inst. of Parsons School of Design, Los Angeles, CA 90057; pvt; 1918; *; art; Mst; S
Ottawa U., Ottawa, KS 66067; Bapt; 1865; *; S
Otterbein C., Westerville, OH 43081; Meth; 1847; *; ed, mus; S
Ouachita Baptist U., Arkadelphia, AR 71923; Bapt; 1886; *; ed, mus; Mst; S
Our Lady of the Elms, C. of, Chicopee, MA 01013; RC; 1928; for women; *; S
Our Lady of Holy Cross C., New Orleans, LA 70114; RC; 1922; *; S
Our Lady of the Lake U., San Antonio, TX 78285; RC; 1911; *; Mst; S
Oxnard C., Oxnard, CA 93032; state/local; jr; 1975; *; M
Ozarks, C. of the, Clarksville, AR 72830; Presb; 1834; *; S
Ozarks, School of the, Point Lookout, MS 65726; pvt; 1906; *; ed, mus; S
Pace U., New York Campus, New York, NY 10038; pvt; 1906; *; D; L
Pace U., Pleasantville-Briarcliff Campus, Pleasantville, NY 10570; pvt; 1963; *; a-nurs; D; M
Pace U., White Plains Campus, White Plains, NY 10603; pvt; 1923; *; law; S
Pacific Christian C., Fullerton, CA 92631; pvt; 1928; *; Mst; S
Pacific Lutheran U., Tacoma, WA 98447; Prot; 1890; *; bus, ed; Mst; M
Pacific Oaks C., Pasadena, CA 91103; pvt; 1951; *; Mst; S
Pacific Union C., Angwin, CA 94508; Prot; 1882; *; a-nurs, mus; Mst; S
Pacific U., Forest Grove, OR 97116; Prot; 1849; *; mus; Mst; S
Pacific, U. of the, Stockton, CA 95211; pvt; 1851; *; dent, ed, engr, law; D; M
Paducah Comm. C., Paducah, KY 42001; state; jr; 1968; a-nurs; S
Paine C., Augusta, GA 30910; Prot; 1822; *; S
Palm Beach Atlantic C., West Palm Beach, FL 33401; Bapt; 1968; *; S
Palm Beach Junior C., Lake Worth, FL 33461; local; jr; 1933; *; dent-a; M
Palo Verde C., Blythe, CA 92225; state/local; jr; 1947; *; S
Palomar C., San Marcos, CA 92069; state/local; jr; 1946; *; a-nurs, dent-a; L
Pamlico Technical C., Grantsboro, NC 28529; state/local; jr; 1962; *; S
Pan American U., Edinburg, TX 78539; state; 1927; *; a-nurs, bus, ed; Mst; M
Panama Canal C., Panama Region, Former Canal Zone 34002; federal; 1934; *; S
Panola Junior C., Carthage, TX 75633; local; jr; 1947; *; S
Paris Junior C., Paris, TX 75460; state/local; jr; 1924; *; a-nurs; S
Park C., Parkville, MO 64152; Prot; 1875; *; M
Parkersburg Comm. C., Parkersburg, WV 26101; state; jr; 1971; *; a-nurs; M
Parkland C., Champaign, IL 61820; state/local; jr; 1966; *; x-ray-t; M
Parsons School of Design, New York, NY 10011; pvt; 1896; *; art; Mst; S
Pasadena City C., Pasadena, CA 91106; state/local; jr; 1924; *; x-ray-t; L
Pasco-Hernando Comm. C., Dade City, FL 33525; local; jr; 1972; *; S
Passaic County Comm. C., Paterson, NJ 07509; state/local; jr; 1968; *; M
Patrick Henry Comm. C., Martinsville, VA 24112; state; jr; 1962; *; S
Patrick Henry State Junior C., Monroeville, AL 36460; state; jr; 1965; *; S
Patten C., Oakland, CA 94601; Prot; 1945; *; S
Paul D. Camp Comm. C., Franklin, VA 23851; state; jr; 1970; *; S
Paul Quinn C., Waco, TX 76704; African Methodist Episcopal; 1872; *; S
Paul Smith's C. of Arts and Sciences, Paul Smith's, NY 12970; pvt; jr; 1937; *; S
Peabody Inst. of Johns Hopkins U., Baltimore, MD 21202; pvt; 1857; *; D; S
Peace C., Raleigh, NC 27604; Presb; jr; 1857; *; S
Pearl River Junior C., Poplarville, MS 39470; state/local; jr; 1921; *; S
Peirce Junior C., Philadelphia, PA 19102; pvt; jr; 1865; *; S
Pembroke State U., Pembroke, NC 28372; state; 1887; *; ed, mus; Mst; S
Peninsula C., Port Angeles, WA 98362; state/local; jr; 1961; *; M
Penn Valley Comm. C., Kansas City, MO 64111; local; jr; 1915; *; M
Pennsylvania C. of Optometry, Philadelphia, PA 19141; pvt; 1919; *; S
Pennsylvania State U., University Park, PA 16802; state-related; 1855; *; arch, bus, ed, engr, mus; D; L
Pennsylvania State U., Behrend College, Erie, PA 16510; state-related; 1926; *; engr-t; Mst; S
Pennsylvania, U. of, Philadelphia, PA 19104; pvt; 1740; *; arch, bus, dent, engr, law, med; D; L
Pensacola Junior C., Pensacola, FL 32504; local; jr; 1948; *; resp-ther-t; M
Pepperdine U., Malibu, CA 90265; pvt; 1937; *; law, mus; D; M
Peru State C., Peru, NE 68421; state; 1867; *; ed; S
Pfeiffer C., Misenheimer, NC 28109; Meth; 1885; *; mus; S
Philadelphia C. of Art, Philadelphia, PA 19102; pvt; 1876; *; art; S
Philadelphia C. of Bible, Langhorne, PA 19047; pvt; 1913; *; S
Philadelphia C. of the Performing Arts, Philadelphia, PA 19102; pvt; 1870; *; S
Philadelphia C. of Pharmacy and Science, Philadelphia, PA 19104; pvt; 1821; *; D; S
Philadelphia C. of Textiles and Science, Philadelphia, PA 19144; pvt; 1884; *; S
Philadelphia, Comm. C. of, Philadelphia, PA 19107; state/local; jr; 1965; *; L
Philander Smith C., Little Rock, AR 72206; Meth; 1877; *; S
Phillips County Comm. C., Helena, AR 72342; state/local; jr; 1965; *; S
Phillips U., Enid, OK 73701; Christian Church; 1907; *; mus; D; S
Phoenix C., Phoenix, AZ 85013; state/local; jr; 1920; *; a-nurs, engr-t; L
Piedmont C., Demorest, GA 30535; pvt; 1897; *; S
Piedmont Virginia Comm. C., Charlottesville, VA 22901; state; jr; 1969; *; M
Pikes Peak Comm. C., Colorado Springs, CO 80906; state; jr; 1967; *; M
Pikeville C., Pikeville, KY 41501; Presb; 1889; *; S
Pima Comm. C., Tucson, AZ 85709; state/local; jr; 1966; *; x-ray-t; L
Pine Manor C., Chestnut Hill, MA 02167; pvt; 1911; *; S
Pioneer Comm. C., Kansas City, MO 64111; local; jr; 1976; *; S
Pitt Comm. C., Greenville, NC 27834; state; jr; 1961; *; x-ray-t; S
Pittsburg State U., Pittsburg, KS 66762; state; 1903; *; engr-t, ed, mus; beyond Mst; M
Pittsburgh, U. of, Pittsburgh, PA 15260; state-related; 1787; *; bus, med; D; L
Pittsburgh, U. of, Bradford Campus, Bradford, PA 16701; state-related; 1963; *; S
Pittsburgh, U. of, Greensburg Campus, Greensburg, PA 15601; state-related; jr; 1963; *; S
Pittsburgh, U. of, Johnstown Campus, Johnstown, PA 15904; state-related; 1927; *; engr-t; S
Pittsburgh, U. of, Titusville Campus, Titusville, PA 16354; state-related; jr; 1963; *; S
Pitzer C., Claremont, CA 91711; pvt; 1963; *; S
Plattsburgh, C. at (see under **State U. of New York**)
Plymouth State C. (see under **New Hampshire, U. of**)
Point Loma C., San Diego, CA 92106; Church of Nazarene; 1902; *; Mst; S
Point Park C., Pittsburgh, PA 15222; pvt; 1960; *; S
Polk Comm. C., Winter Haven, FL 33880; local; jr; 1963; *; M
Polytechnic Inst. of New York, Brooklyn, NY 11201; pvt; 1854; *; engr; D; M
Pomona C., Claremont, CA 91711; pvt; 1887; *; S
Pontifical C. Josephinum, Columbus, OH 43085; RC; 1892; for men; *; Mst; S
Pope John XXIII National Seminary, Weston, MA 02193; RC; 1964; for men; Mst; S
Porterville C., Porterville, CA 93257; state/local; jr; 1927; *; S
Portland Comm. C., Portland, OR 97219; local; jr; 1961; *; x-ray-t; L
Portland School of Art, Portland, ME 04101; pvt; 1882; *; art; S
Portland State U., Portland, OR 97207; state; 1946; *; bus, ed, engr; D; L
Portland, U. of, Portland, OR 97203; pvt; 1901; *; bus, engr; Mst; S
Post C., Waterbury, CT 06708; pvt; 1890; *; S
Potomac State C., Keyser, WV 26726; state; jr; 1901; *; S
Potsdam, C. at (see under **State U. of New York**)
Prairie State C., Chicago Heights, IL 60411; state/local; jr; 1957; *; dent-h; M
Prairie View A&M U., Prairie View, TX 77445; state; 1876; *; engr; Mst; M
Pratt Comm. C., Pratt, KS 67124; state/local; jr; 1938; *; S
Pratt Inst., Brooklyn, NY 11205; pvt; 1887; *; arch, art, engr, lib; Mst; M
Presbyterian C., Clinton, SC 29325; Presb; 1880; *; S
Prescott Center C., Prescott, AZ 86301; pvt; 1975; S
Presentation C., Aberdeen, SD 57401; RC; jr; 1951; *; a-nurs; S
Prestonburg Comm. C., Prestonburg, KY 41653; state; jr; 1964; *; S
Prince Georges Comm. C., Largo, MD 20870; local; jr; 1958; *; a-nurs; L
Princeton Theological Seminary, Princeton, NJ 08540; Presb; 1812; *; D, grad only; S
Princeton U., Princeton, NJ 08544; pvt; 1746; *; arch, engr; D; M
Principia C., Elsah, IL 62028; pvt; 1898; *; S
Providence C., Providence, RI 02918; RC; 1917; *; D; M
Pueblo Vocational Comm. C., Pueblo, CO 81004; state; jr; 1979; *; x-ray-t; S
Puerto Rico Regional Colleges Administration, Rio Piedras, PR 00931; public; jr; 1967; *; a-nurs (Arecibo Campus only); L
Puerto Rico, U. of, Cayey U. C., Cayey, PR 00633; public; 1967; *; S
Puerto Rico, U. of, Humacao U. C., Humacao, PR 00661; public; 1962; *; a-nurs; M
Puerto Rico, U. of, Mayaguez Campus, Mayaguez, PR 00708; public; 1911; *; a-nurs, engr; D; M
Puerto Rico, U. of, Medical Sciences Campus, San Juan, PR 00936; public; 1950; *; dent, dent-a, dent-h, med, med-rec-t; D; S
Puerto Rico, U. of, Rio Piedras Campus, Rio Piedras, PR 00931; public; 1903; *; arch, ed, law; D; L
Puget Sound, U. of, Tacoma, WA 98416; Meth; 1888; *; ed, law, mus; Mst; M
Purchase, C. at (see under **State U. of New York**)
Purdue U., West Lafayette, IN 47907; state; 1869; *; bus, ed, engr; D; L
Purdue U., Calumet Campus, Hammond IN 46323; state; 1943; *; a-nurs, ed, engr-t; beyond Mst; M
Purdue U., North Central Campus, Westville, IN 46391; state; 1943; *; a-nurs; S
Queens C. (see under **City U. of New York**)
Queens C., Charlotte, NC 28274; Presb; 1857; *; mus; Mst; S
Queensborough Comm. C. (see under **City U. of New York**)
Quincy C., Quincy, IL 62301; RC; 1859; *; mus; S
Quinebaug Valley Comm. C., Danielson, CT 06239; state; jr; 1971; *; S
Quinnipiac C., Hamden, CT 06518; pvt; 1929; *; a-nurs, x-ray-t; M
Quinsigamond Comm. C., Worcester, MA 01606; state; jr; 1963; *; dent-h; M
Rabbinical Seminary of America, New York, NY 11375; Jewish; 1933; for men; S
Radford U., Radford, VA 24142; state; 1910; *; ed; beyond Mst; M
Rainy River Comm. C., International Falls, MN 56649; state; jr; 1967; *; S
Ramapo C. of New Jersey, Mahwah, NJ 07430; state; 1969; *; M
Rand Graduate Inst. of Policy Studies, Santa Monica, CA 90406; pvt; 1970; *; D; S
Randolph-Macon C., Ashland, VA 23005; Meth; 1830; *; S
Randolph-Macon Women's C., Lynchburg, VA 24503; Meth; 1891; for women; *; S
Ranger Junior C., Ranger, TX 76470; local; jr; 1926; *; S
Rappahannock Comm. C., Glenns, VA 23149; state; jr; 1970; *; S
Raymond Walters C. (see under **Cincinnati, U. of**)
Reading Area Comm. C., Reading, PA 19603; state/local; jr; 1971; *; S
Redlands, U. of, Redlands, CA 92373; pvt; 1907; *; mus; Mst; M
Redwoods, C. of the, Eureka, CA 95501; state/local; jr; 1964; *; dent-a; M

Reed C., Portland, OR 97202; pvt; 1909; *; Mst; S
Regents External Degree Program of the U. of the State of New York, Albany, NY 12230; state; 1784; *; a-nurs; L
Regis C., Denver, CO 80221; RC; 1877; *; Mst; S
Regis C., Weston, MA 02193; pvt; 1927; for women; *; Mst; S
Reinhardt C., Waleska, GA 30183; Meth; jr; 1883; S
Rend Lake C., Ina, IL 62846; state/local; jr; 1955; *; M
Rensselaer Polytechnic Inst., Troy, NY 12181; pvt; 1824; *; engr; D; M
Rhode Island C., Providence, RI 02908; state; 1854; *; art, ed, mus; Mst; M
Rhode Island, Comm. C. of, Warwick, RI 02886; state; jr; 1960; *; x-ray-t; L
Rhode Island School of Design, Providence, RI 02903; pvt; 1877; *; Mst; S
Rhode Island, U. of, Kingston, RI 02881; state; 1888; *; engr, lib, mus; D; L
Rice U., Houston, TX 77001; pvt; 1891; *; arch, engr; D; M
Richard Bland C., Petersburg, VA 23803; state; jr; 1960; *; S
Richard J. Daley C. (see under **City Colleges of Chicago**)
Richland C., Dallas, TX 75243; state/local; jr; 1972; *; L
Richland Comm. C., Decatur, IL 62523; state/local; jr; 1971; *; S
Richmond Technical Inst., Hamlet, NC 28345; state/local; jr; 1964; *; S
Richmond, U. of, Richmond, VA 23173; Bapt; 1830; *; bus, law, mus; Mst; M
Ricks C., Rexburg, ID 83440; Latter-Day Saints; jr; 1888; *; a-nurs, engr-t; M
Rider C., Lawrenceville, NJ 08648; pvt; 1865; *; ed; Mst; M
Ringling School of Art and Design, Sarasota, FL 33580; pvt; 1931; *; S
Rio Grande C. and Comm. C., Rio Grande, OH 45674; pvt; 1876; *; S
Rio Hondo C., Whittier, CA 90608; state/local; jr; 1960; *; resp-ther; L
Ripon C., Ripon, WI 54971; pvt; 1851; *; S
Riverside City C., Riverside, CA 92506; state/local; jr; 1916; *; L
Rivier C., Nashua, NH 03060; RC; 1933; for women; *; Mst; S
Roane State Comm. C., Harriman, TN 37748; state; jr; 1970; *; x-ray-t; M
Roanoke-Chowan Technical Inst., Ahoskie, NC 27910; state/local; jr; 1967; *; S
Roanoke C., Salem, VA 24153; Lutheran Church in America; 1842; *; S
Robert Morris C., Coraopolis, PA 15108; pvt; 1921; *; x-ray-t; Mst; M
Roberts Wesleyan C., Rochester, NY 14624; Meth; 1866; *; S
Rochester Comm. C., Rochester, MN 55901; state; jr; 1915; *; resp-ther; S
Rochester Inst. of Technology, Rochester, NY 14623; pvt; 1849; *; Mst; L
Rochester, U. of, Rochester, NY 14627; pvt; 1850; *; bus, engr, med; D; M
Rock Valley C., Rockford, IL 61101; local; jr; 1964; *; resp-ther-t; M
Rockefeller U., New York, NY 10021; pvt; 1901; D, grad only; S
Rockford C., Rockford, IL 61101; pvt; 1847; *; Mst; S
Rockhurst C., Kansas City, MO 64110; RC; 1910; *; Mst; M
Rockingham Comm. C., Wentworth, NC 27375; state/local; jr; 1963; *; S
Rockland Comm. C., Suffern, NY 10901; state/local; jr; 1957; *; a-nurs; M
Rockmont C., Denver, CO 80226; pvt; 1914; S
Rocky Mountain C., Billings, MT 59102; Interdenominational; 1878; *; S
Roger Williams C., Bristol, RI 02809; pvt; 1945; *; engr-t; S
Roger Williams C., Providence Branch, Providence, RI 02903; pvt; 1945; *; S
Rogue Comm. C., Grants Pass, OR 97526; local; jr; 1970; *; resp-ther; S
Rollins C., Winter Park, FL 32789; pvt; 1885; *; mus; beyond Mst; M
Roosevelt U., Chicago, IL 60605; pvt; 1945; *; bus, ed, mus; beyond Mst; M
Rosary C., River Forest, IL 60305; pvt; 1901; *; lib, mus; Mst; S
Rose-Hulman Inst. of Technology, Terre Haute, IN 47803; pvt; 1874; *; Mst; S
Rosemont C., Rosemont, PA 19010; pvt; 1921; for women; *; S
Roxbury Comm. C., Roxbury, MA 02186; state; jr; 1972; S
Rush U., Chicago, IL 60612; pvt; 1969; *; med; D; S
Russell Sage C., Troy, NY 12180; pvt; 1916; for women; *; Mst; M
Russell Sage Junior C. of Albany, Albany, NY 12208; pvt; jr; 1957; *; S
Rust C., Holly Springs, MS 38635; Meth; 1866; *; S
Rutgers the State U. of New Jersey: Camden Campus, Camden, NJ 08102; state; 1927; *; ed, law; D; M
Rutgers the State U. of New Jersey: New Brunswick Campus, New Brunswick, NJ 08903; state; 1766; *; ed, engr, lib, mus; D; L
Rutgers the State U. of New Jersey: Newark Campus, Newark, NJ 07102; state; 1892; *; bus, ed, law; D; L
S. D. Bishop State Junior C., Mobile, AL 36690; state; jr; 1965; *; a-nurs; S
Sacramento City C., Sacramento, CA 95822; state/local; jr; 1916; *; a-nurs; L
Sacred Heart C., Belmont, NC 28012; RC; 1892; *; S
Sacred Heart U., Bridgeport, CT 06606; pvt; 1963; *; Mst; M
Sacred Heart, U. of the, Santurce, PR 00914; RC; 1935; *; M
Saddleback Comm. C., Mission Viejo, CA 92692; state/local; jr; 1967; *; L
Saginaw Valley State C., University Center, MI 48710; state; 1963; *; Mst; M
Saint Alphonsus C., Suffield, CT 06078; RC; 1963; for men; *; S
Saint Ambrose C., Davenport, IA 52803; RC; 1882; *; Mst; S
Saint Andrew's Presbyterian C., Laurinburg, NC 28352; Presb; 1958; *; mus; S
Saint Anselm C., Manchester, NH 03102; RC; 1889; *; S
Saint Augustine's C., Raleigh, NC 27611; Protestant Episcopal; 1867; *; S
Saint Benedict, C. of, Saint Joseph, MN 56374; RC; 1913; *; ed; S
Saint Bonaventure U., Saint Bonaventure, NY 14778; pvt; 1858; *; D; S
Saint Catharine C., Saint Catharine, KY 40061; RC; jr; 1931; *; S
Saint Catherine, C. of, Saint Paul, MN 55105; RC; 1905; for women; *; S
Saint Clair County Comm. C., Port Huron, MI 48060; local; jr; 1923; *; M
Saint Cloud State U., Saint Cloud, MN 56301; state; 1869; *; beyond Mst; L
Saint Edward's U., Austin, TX 78704; pvt; 1885; *; Mst; S
Saint Elizabeth, C. of, Convent Station, NJ 07961; RC; 1899; for women; *; S
Saint Francis C., Fort Wayne, IN 46808; RC; 1890; *; ed; beyond Mst; S
Saint Francis C., Brooklyn, NY 11201; pvt; 1859; *; M
Saint Francis C., Loretto, PA 15940; RC; 1847; *; Mst; S
Saint Francis, C. of, Joliet, IL 60435; RC; 1925; *; Mst; M
Saint Francis de Sales C., Milwaukee, WI 53207; RC; 1856; for men; *; S
Saint Francis Seminary School of Pastoral Ministry, Milwaukee, WI 53207; RC; 1856; *; Mst, grad only; S
Saint Gregory's C., Shawnee, OK 74801; RC; jr; 1875; *; S
Saint John Fisher C., Rochester, NY 14618; pvt; 1948; *; S
Saint John's C., Camarillo, CA 93010; RC; 1939; for men; *; Mst; S
Saint John's C., Winfield, KS 67156; RC; 1923; for women; *; ed, mus; S
Saint John's C., Annapolis, MD 21404; pvt; 1784; *; Mst; S
Saint John's C., Santa Fe, NM 87501; pvt; 1964; *; Mst; S
Saint John's Provincial Seminary, Plymouth, MI 48170; RC; 1949; *; grad only; S
Saint Johns River Comm. C., Palatka, FL 32077; state/local; jr; 1957; *; S
Saint John's Seminary C., Brighton, MA 02135; RC; 1883; for men; *; Mst; S
Saint John's U., Collegeville, MN 56321; RC; 1977; *; Mst; S
Saint John's U., Jamaica, NY 14439; RC; 1870, *; bus, law, lib; D; L
Saint Joseph C., West Hartford, CT 06117; pvt; 1932; for women; *; Mst; S
Saint Joseph the Provider, C. of, Rutland, VT 05701; pvt; 1954; *; S
Saint Joseph Seminary C., Saint Benedict, LA 70457; RC; 1891; *; S
Saint Joseph's C., Rensselaer, IN 47978; RC; 1889; *; ed; Mst; S
Saint Joseph's C., North Windham, ME 04062; RC; 1915; *; S
Saint Joseph's C., Brooklyn, NY 11205; pvt; 1916; *; S
Saint Joseph's C., Suffolk Campus, Patchogue, NY 11772; pvt; 1916; S
Saint Joseph's Seminary and C., Yonkers, NY 10704; RC; 1896; for men; *; grad only; S
Saint Joseph's U., Philadelphia, PA 19131; RC; 1851; *; Mst; M
Saint Lawrence U., Canton, NY 13617; pvt; 1856; *; Mst; S
Saint Leo C., Saint Leo, FL 33574; RC; 1889; *; M
Saint Louis Christian C., Florissant, MO 63033; Christian Churches-Churches of Christ; 1956; S
Saint Louis C. of Pharmacy, Saint Louis, MO 63110; pvt; 1864; *; S
Saint Louis Comm. C. at Forest Park, Saint Louis, MO 63110; local; jr; 1962; *; a-nurs, dent-a, dent-h, resp-ther, resp-ther-t, x-ray-t; M
Saint Louis U., Saint Louis, MO 63103; RC; 1818; *; bus, ed, law, med; D; M
Saint Martin's C., Lacey, WA 98503; RC; 1895; *; engr; Mst; S
Saint Mary C., Leavenworth, KS 66048; RC; 1923; for women; *; ed, mus; S
Saint Mary, C. of, Omaha, NE 68124; pvt; 1923; for women; *; resp-ther; S
Saint Mary of the Plains C., Dodge City, KS 67801; RC; 1952; *; ed; S
Saint Mary-of-the-Woods C., Saint Mary-of-the-Woods, IN 47876; RC; 1841; for women; *; mus; S
Saint Mary's C., Notre Dame, IN 46556; RC; 1844; for women; *; art, ed; S
Saint Mary's C., Orchard Lake, MI 48033; pvt; 1885; *; S
Saint Mary's C., Winona, MN 55987; RC; 1912; *; Mst; S
Saint Mary's C., Raleigh, NC 27611; Prot; jr; 1842; for women; *; S
Saint Mary's C. of California, Moraga, CA 94575; RC; 1863; *; Mst; S
Saint Mary's C. of Maryland, Saint Mary's City, MD 20686; state; 1839; *; S
Saint Mary's C. of O'Fallon, O'Fallon, MO 63366; RC; jr; 1921; *; a-nurs; S
Saint Mary's Dominican C., New Orleans, LA 70118; RC; 1908; for women; *; S
Saint Mary's Junior C., Minneapolis, MN 55454; RC; jr; 1964; *; a-nurs; S
Saint Mary's Seminary and U., Baltimore, MD 21210; RC; 1791; *; S
Saint Mary's U. of San Antonio; San Antonio, TX 78284; RC; 1852; *; law; M
Saint Meinrad C., Saint Meinrad, IN 47577; RC; 1857; for men; *; S
Saint Michael's C., Winooski, VT 05404; RC; 1903; *; Mst; S
Saint Norbert C., De Pere, WI 54115; RC; 1898; *; ed; S
Saint Olaf C., Northfield, MN 55057; American Lutheran; 1874; *; ed, mus; M
Saint Patrick's C., Mountain View, CA 94042; RC; 1898; for men; *; S
Saint Paul Bible C., Bible College, MN 55375; Prot;1916; *; S
Saint Paul's C., Concordia, MO 64020; Lutheran Church; jr; 1883; *; S
Saint Paul's C., Lawrenceville, VA 23868; Protestant Episcopal; 1888; *; S
Saint Peter's C., Jersey City, NJ 07306; RC; 1872; *; M
Saint Petersburg Junior C., Saint Petersburg, FL 33733; local; jr; 1927; *; L
Saint Philip's C., San Antonio, TX 78203; local; jr; 1927; *; x-ray-t; M
Saint Rose, C. of, Albany, NY 12203; pvt; 1920; *; Mst; S
Saint Scholastica, C. of, Duluth, MN 55811; RC; 1912; *; Mst; S
Saint Teresa, C. of, Winona, MN 55987; RC; 1907; for women; *; ed; S
Saint Thomas Aquinas C., Sparkill, NY 10968; pvt; 1952; *; S
Saint Thomas, C. of, Saint Paul, MN 55105; RC; 1885; *; ed; beyond Mst; M
Saint Thomas, U. of, Houston, TX 77006; RC; 1947; *; Mst; S
Saint Vincent C., Latrobe, PA 15650; RC; 1846; for men; *; S
Saint Vincent Seminary, Latrobe, PA 15650; RC; 1846; for men; *; Mst, grad only; S
Saint Xavier C., Chicago, IL 60655; RC; 1847; *; Mst; S
Salem C., Winston-Salem, NC 27108; Prot; 1772; for women; *; ed, mus; S
Salem C., Salem, WV 26426; pvt; 1888; *; Mst; S
Salem Comm. C., Penns Grove, NJ 08069; state/local; jr; 1972; *; S
Salem State C., Salem, MA 01970; state; 1854; *; ed; Mst; S
Salisbury State C., Salisbury, MD 21801; state; 1925; *; ed; Mst; M
Salve Regina—the Newport C., Newport, RI 02840; RC; 1934; *; Mst; S
Sam Houston State U., Huntsville, TX 77341; state; 1879; *; ed, mus; D; L
Samford U., Birmingham, AL 35229; Bapt; 1841; *; a-nurs, ed, law; Mst; M
Sampson Technical C., Clinton, NC 28328; state/local; jr; 1965; *; S
San Antonio C., San Antonio, TX 78284; local; jr; 1925; *; med-a; L
San Bernardino Valley C., San Bernardino, CA 92410; local; jr; 1926; *; L
San Diego City C., San Diego, CA 92101; state/local; jr; 1914; *; M
San Diego Mesa C., San Diego, CA 92111; state/local; jr; 1962; *; x-ray-t; M
San Diego State U., San Diego, CA 92182; state; 1897; *; bus, engr, mus; D; L
San Diego, U. of, San Diego, CA 92110; RC; 1949; *; bus, law; D; M
San Francisco Art Inst., San Francisco, CA 94133; pvt; 1871; *; art; Mst; S
San Francisco Conservatory of Music, San Francisco, CA 94122; pvt; 1917; *; S
San Francisco State U., San Francisco, CA 94132; state; 1899; *; bus; D; L
San Francisco Theological Seminary, San Anselmo, CA 94960; Presb; 1871; *; D, grad only; S
San Francisco, U. of, San Francisco, CA 94117; RC; 1855; *; bus, law; D; M
San Jacinto C., Pasadena, TX 77505; local; jr; 1960; *; resp-ther-t; L
San Joaquin Delta C., Stockton, CA 95207; state/local; jr; 1935; *; a-nurs; L
San Jose City C., San Jose, CA 95128; state/local; jr; 1921; *; L
San Jose State U., San Jose, CA 95192; state; 1857; *; engr, lib, mus; Mst; L
San Juan Technological Comm. C., Hato Rey, PR 00907; local; jr; 1972; *; S
San Mateo, C. of, San Mateo, CA 94402; state/local; jr; 1922; *; dent-a; L
Sandhills Comm. C., Carthage, NC 28327; state; jr; 1963; *; a-nurs, x-ray-t; S
Sangamon State U., Springfield, IL 62708; state; 1969; *; Mst; M
Santa Ana C., Santa Ana, CA 92706; state/local; 1915; *; L
Santa Barbara City C., Santa Barbara, CA 93109; state/local; jr; 1946; *; M
Santa Clara, U. of, Santa Clara, CA 95053; RC; 1851; *; bus, engr, law; D; M
Santa Fe, C. of, Santa Fe, NM 87501; pvt; 1947; *; a-nurs; S
Santa Fe Comm. C., Gainesville, FL 32601; local; jr; 1965; *; dent-h, x-ray-t; M
Santa Monica C., Santa Monica, CA 90405; state/local; jr; 1929; *; L
Santa Rosa Junior C., Santa Rosa, CA 95401; state/local; jr; 1918; *; x-ray-t; L
Sarah Lawrence C., Bronxville, NY 10708; pvt; 1926; *; Mst; S
Sarasota, U. of, Sarasota, FL 33577; pvt; 1974; D; S
Sauk Valley C., Dixon, IL 61021; state; jr; 1965; *; x-ray-t; M
Savannah State C., Savannah, GA 31404; state; 1890; *; engr-t; Mst; S
Scarritt C., Nashville, TN 37203; Meth; 1892; *; Mst; S
Schenectady County Comm. C., Schenectady, NY 12305; state/local; 1967; *; S
School for International Training, Brattleboro, VT 05301; pvt; 1964; *; Mst; S
Schoolcraft C., Livonia, MI 48152; local; jr; 1961; *; med-rec-t; M
Schreiner C., Kerrville, TX 78028; Presb; jr; 1923; *; S
Science and Arts of Oklahoma, U. of, Chickasha, OK 73018; state; 1908; *; S
Scott Comm. C., Bettendorf, IA 52722; state/local; jr; 1966; *; x-ray-t; S
Scottsdale Comm. C., Scottsdale, AZ 85253; state/local; jr; 1969; *; a-nurs; M
Scranton, U. of, Scranton, PA 18510; RC; 1888; *; ed; Mst; M
Scripps C., Claremont, CA 91711; pvt; 1926; for women; *; S
Seattle Comm. C., Central Campus, Seattle, WA 98122; state; jr; 1966; *; L
Seattle Pacific U., Seattle, WA 98119; Meth; 1891; *; ed, mus; beyond Mst; S
Seattle U., Seattle, WA 98122; RC; 1891; *; bus, ed, engr; D; M
Selma U., Selma, AL 36701; Bapt; 1878; S
Seminole Comm. C., Sanford, FL 32771; local; jr; 1965; *; resp-ther-t; M
Seminole Junior C., Seminole, OK 74868; state/local; jr; 1931; *; a-nurs; S
Sequoias, C. of the, Visalia, CA 93277; state/local; jr; 1925; *; M
Seton Hall U., South Orange, NJ 07079; RC; 1856; *; bus, ed, law; D; L
Seton Hill C., Greensburg, PA 15601; RC; 1883; for women; *; mus; S
Seward County Comm. C., Liberal, KS 67901; state/local; jr; 1967; *; S
Shasta C., Redding, CA 96099; state/local; jr; 1948; *; L
Shaw C. at Detroit, Detroit, MI 48202; pvt; 1936; S
Shaw U., Raleigh, NC 27611; Bapt; 1865; *; S
Shawnee C., Ullin, IL 62992; local; jr; 1967; *; x-ray-t; S
Shawnee State Comm. C., Portsmouth, OH 45662; state; jr; 1975; *; dent-h; S
Shelby State Comm. C., Memphis, TN 38104; state; jr; 1969; *; x-ray-t; M
Sheldon Jackson C., Sitka, AK 99835; pvt; 1878; *; S
Shenandoah C. and Conservatory of Music, Winchester, VA 22601; Meth; 1875; *; a-nurs, mus, resp-ther; Mst; S
Shepherd C., Shepherdstown, WV 25443; state; 1871; *; ed; S
Sheridan C., Sheridan, WY 82801; local; jr; 1948; *; dent-a, dent-h; S
Shimer C., Waukegan, IL 60085; pvt; 1853; *; S
Shippensburg State C., Shippensburg, PA 17257; state; 1871; *; ed; Mst; M
Shoreline Comm. C., Seattle, WA 98133; state; jr; 1963; *; a-nurs, dent-h, med-rec-t; M
Shorter C., Rome, GA 30161; Bapt; 1873; *; mus; S
Siena C., Loudonville, NY 12211; pvt; 1937; *; M
Siena Heights C., Adrian, MI 49221; RC; 1919; *; Mst; S
Sierra C., Rocklin, CA 95677; state/local; jr; 1914; *; M
Sierra Nevada C., Incline Village, NV 89450; pvt; 1969; *; S
Silver Lake C., Manitowoc, WI 54220; RC; 1935; *; ed; S
Simmons C., Boston, MA 02115; pvt; 1899; *; lib; D; S
Simon's Rock Early C., Great Barrington, MA 01230; pvt; 1964; *; S
Simpson C., San Francisco, CA 94134; Prot; 1921; *; S
Simpson C., Indianola, IA 50125; Meth; 1960; *; ed, mus; S
Sinclair Comm. C., Dayton, OH 45402; local; jr; 1887; *; x-ray-t; L
Sioux Falls C., Sioux Falls, SD 57101; Bapt; 1883; *; ed; S
Siskiyous, C. of the, Weed, CA 96094; state/local; jr; 1957; *; S
Sitka Comm. C. (see under **Alaska, U. of**)
Skagit Valley C., Mount Vernon, WA 98273; state; jr; 1926; *; resp-ther-t; M
Skidmore C., Saratoga Springs, NY 12866; pvt; 1922; *; art; S
Skyline C., San Bruno, CA 94066; state/local; jr; 1969; *; resp-ther; M
Slippery Rock State C., Slippery Rock, PA 16057; state; 1889; *; ed; M

Smith C., Northampton, MA 01063; pvt; 1871; for women; *; D; M
Snead State Junior C., Boaz, AL 35957; state; jr; 1898; *; S
Snow C., Ephraim, UT 84627; state; jr; 1888; *; S
Sojourner-Douglas C., Baltimore, MD 21205; pvt; 1980; *; S
Solano Comm. C., Suisun City, CA 94585; state/local; jr; 1945; *; M
Somerset County C., Somerville, NJ 08876; state/local; jr; 1966; *; a-nurs; M
Sonoma State U., Rohnert Park, CA 94928; state; 1960; *; mus; Mst; M
South Alabama, U. of, Mobile, AL 36688; state; 1963; *; engr, med; D; M
South Carolina State C., Orangeburg, SC 29117; state; 1896; *; ed; Mst; M
South Carolina at Columbia, U. of, Columbia, SC 29208; state; 1801; *; D; L
South Central Comm. C., New Haven, CT 06511; state; jr; 1968; x-ray-t; S
South Dakota School of Mines and Technology, Rapid City, SD 57701; state; 1885; *; engr; D; S
South Dakota State U., Brookings, SD 57007; state; 1881; *; ed, engr; D; M
South Dakota, U. of, Vermillion, SD 57069; state; 1862; *; law, med; D; M
South Florida Junior C., Avon Park, FL 33825; local; jr; 1965; *; resp-ther; M
South Florida, U. of, Tampa, FL 33620; state; 1956; *; bus, ed, engr, lib; D; L
South Georgia C., Douglas, GA 31533; state; jr; 1906; *; a-nurs; S
South Oklahoma City Junior C., Oklahoma City, OK 73159; state/local; jr; 1969; *; a-nurs; M
South Plains C., Levelland, TX 79336; state; jr; 1957; *; x-ray-t; S
South, U. of the, Sewanee, TN 37375; Protestant Episcopal; 1860; *; Mst; S
Southeast Comm. C., Milford Campus, Milford, NE 68405; local; jr; 1941; *; S
Southeast Missouri State U., Cape Girardeau, MO 63701; state; 1873; *; ed; M
Southeastern Comm. C., West Burlington, IA 52655; state/local; jr; 1966; *; S
Southeastern Comm. C., Whiteville, NC 28472; state; jr; 1964; *; S
Southeastern Illinois C., Harrisburg, IL 62946; state/local; jr; 1960; *; S
Southeastern Louisiana U., Hammond, LA 70402; state; 1925; *; Mst; M
Southeastern Massachusetts U., North Dartmouth, MA 02747; state; 1895; *; M
Southeastern Oklahoma State U., Durant, OK 74701; state; 1909; *; ed; Mst; M
Southeastern U., Washington, DC 20024; pvt; 1864; *; Mst; S
Southern Arkansas U., Magnolia, AR 71753; state; 1909; *; a-nurs; Mst; S
Southern Baptist C., Walnut Ridge, AR 72476; Bapt; jr; 1941; *; S
Southern California C., Costa Mesa, CA 92626; Prot; 1920; *; S
Southern California C. of Optometry, Fullerton, CA 92631; pvt; 1904; *; S
Southern California, U. of, Los Angeles, CA 90007; pvt; 1880; *; med; D; L
Southern Colorado, U. of, Pueblo, CO 81001; state; 1933; *; mus; Mst; M
Southern Connecticut State C., New Haven, CT 06515; state; 1893; *; lib; L
Southern Idaho, C. of, Twin Falls, ID 83301; local; jr; 1964; *; a-nurs; M
Southern Illinois U. at Carbondale, Carbondale, IL 62901; state; 1869; *; D; L
Southern Illinois U. at Edwardsville, Edwardsville, IL 62026; state; 1965; *; L
Southern Maine, U. of, Portland ME 04103; state; 1878; *; ed, law; Mst; M
Southern Methodist U., Dallas, TX 75275; Meth; 1911; *; engr, law, mus; D; M
Southern Missionary C., Collegedale, TN 37315; Prot; 1892; *; a-nurs; S
Southern Mississippi, U. of, Hattiesburg, MS 39401; state; 1910; *; D; L
Southern Oregon State C., Ashland, OR 97520; state; 1926; *; Mst; M
Southern Union State Junior C., Wadley, AL 36276; state; jr; 1922; *; S
Southern U. and A&M C., Baton Rouge, LA 70813; state; 1880; *; Mst; M
Southern U. in New Orleans, New Orleans, LA 70126; state; 1956; *; S
Southern Utah State C., Cedar City, UT 84720; state; 1897; *; ed; S
Southern Vermont C., Bennington, VT 05201; pvt; 1926; *; S
Southern West Virginia Comm. C., Holden, WV 25625; state; jr; 1971; *; S
Southside Virginia Comm. C., Alberta, VA 23821; state; jr; 1968; *; S
Southwest Baptist C., Bolivar, MO 65613; Bapt; 1878; *; mus; S
Southwest, C. of the, Hobbs, NM 88240; pvt; 1956; *; S
Southwest Mississippi Junior C., Summit, MS 39666; local; jr; 1918; *; S
Southwest Missouri State U., Springfield, MO 65802; state; 1906; *; Mst; L
Southwest State U., Marshall, MN 56258; state; 1963; *; S
Southwest Texas Junior C., Uvalde, TX 78801; local; jr; 1946; *; S
Southwest Texas State U., San Marcos, TX 78666; state; 1899; *; Mst; L
Southwest Virginia Comm. C., Richlands, VA 24641; state; jr; 1967; *; S
Southwestern Adventist C., Keene, TX 76059; Prot; 1893; *; a-nurs; S
Southwestern at Memphis, Memphis, TN 38112; Presb; 1848; *; mus; S
Southwestern Christian C., Terrell, TX 75160; Prot; jr; 1949; *; S
Southwestern C., Chula Vista, CA 92010; state/local; jr; 1961; *; L
Southwestern C., Winfield, KS 67156; Meth; 1885; *; mus; S
Southwestern Comm. C., Creston, IA 50801; state; jr; 1966; *; S
Southwestern Junior C., Waxahachie, TX 75165; Prot; jr; 1927; *; S
Southwestern Louisiana, U. of, Lafayette, LA 70504; state; 1898; *; D; L
Southwestern Michigan C., Dowagiac, MI 49047; state/local; jr; 1964; *; S
Southwestern Oklahoma State U., Weatherford, OK 73096; state; 1901; *; Mst; M
Southwestern Oregon Comm. C., Coos Bay, OR 97420; local; jr; 1961; *; M
Southwestern Technical C., Sylva, NC 28779; state/local; jr; 1964; *; S
Southwestern U., Georgetown, TX 78626; Meth; 1840; *; mus; S
Spalding C., Louisville, KY 40203; pvt; 1814; *; beyond Mst; S
Spartanburg Methodist C., Spartanburg, SC 29301; Meth; jr; 1911; *; S
Spelman C., Atlanta, GA 30314; pvt; 1881; for women; *; 1881; S
Spertus C. of Judaica, Chicago, IL 60605; pvt; 1925; *; Mst; S
Spokane Comm. C., Spokane, WA 99202; state; jr; 1963; *; resp-ther; L
Spokane Falls Comm. C., Spokane, WA 99204; state; jr; 1967; *; L
Spoon River C., Canton, IL 61520; local; jr; 1959; *; S
Spring Arbor C., Spring Arbor, MI 49283; Meth; 1873; *; S
Spring Garden C., Chestnut Hill, PA 19118; pvt; 1851; *; S
Spring Hill C., Mobile, AL 36608; RC; 1830; *; S
Springfield C., Springfield, MA 01109; pvt; 1885; *; D; S
Springfield C. in Illinois, Springfield, IL 62702; RC; jr; 1929; *; S
Stanford U., Stanford, CA 94305; pvt; 1885; *; bus, engr, law, med; D; L
Starr King School for the Ministry, Berkeley, CA 94709; Unitarian Universalist; 1904; Mst, grad only; S
State Comm. C., East Saint Louis, IL 62201; state; jr; 1969; *; S
State Fair Comm. C., Sedalia, MO 65301; local; jr; 1966; *; resp-ther-t; S
State U. of New York, Agricultural and Technical C. at Alfred, Alfred, NY 14802; state; jr; 1908; *; a-nurs, engr-t, med-rec-t; M
State U. of New York, Agricultural and Technical C. at Canton, Canton, NY 13617; state; jr; 1906; *; a-nurs, engr-t; S
State U. of New York, Agricultural and Technical C. at Cobleskill, Cobleskill, NY 12043; state; jr; 1911; *; S
State U. of New York, Agricultural and Technical C. at Delhi, Delhi, NY 13753; state; jr; 1913; *; S
State U. of New York, Agricultural and Technical C. at Farmingdale, Farmingdale, NY 11735; state; jr; 1912; *; a-nurs, engr-t; L
State U. of New York, Agricultural and Technical C. at Morrisville, Morrisville, NY 13408; state; jr; 1908; *; a-nurs; M
State U. of New York at Albany, Albany, NY 12222; state; 1844; *; D; L
State U. of New York at Binghamton, Binghamton, NY 13901; state; 1946; *; L
State U. of New York at Buffalo, Buffalo, NY 14214; state; 1846; *; D; L
State U. of New York C. at Brockport, Brockport, NY 14420; state; 1867; *; M
State U. of New York C. at Buffalo, Buffalo, NY 14222; state; 1867; *; L
State U. of New York C. at Cortland, Cortland, NY 13045; state; 1866; *; Mst; M
State U. of New York C. of Environmental Science and Forestry, Syracuse, NY 13210; state; 1911; *; D; S
State U. of New York C. at Fredonia, Fredonia, NY 14063; state; 1867; *; M
State U. of New York C. at Geneseo, Geneseo, NY 14454; state; 1867; *; Mst; M
State U. of New York C. at New Paltz, New Paltz, NY 12562; state; 1828; *; M
State U. of New York C. at Old Westbury, Old Westbury, NY 11568; state; 1967; *; S
State U. of New York C. at Oneonta, Oneonta, NY 13820; state; 1887; *; Mst; M
State U. of New York C. of Optometry, New York, NY 10010; state; 1971; *; S
State U. of New York C. at Plattsburgh, Plattsburgh, NY 12901; state; 1889; *; M
State U. of New York C. at Potsdam, Potsdam, NY 13676; state; 1816; *; M
State U. of New York C. at Purchase, Purchase, NY 10577; state; 1967; *; M
State U. of New York C. of Technology at Utica-Rome, Utica, NY 13502; state; 1966; *; Mst; M
State U. of New York Downstate Medical Center, Brooklyn, NY 11203; state; 1858; *; med; D; S
State U. of New York Empire State C., Saratoga Springs, NY 12866; state; 1971; *; M
State U. of New York Maritime C., Bronx, NY 10465; state; 1874; *; Mst; S
State U. of New York at Oswego, Oswego, NY 13126; state; 1961; *; M
State U. of New York at Stony Brook, Stony Brook, NY 11794; state; 1957; *; L
State U. of New York Upstate Medical Center, Syracuse, NY 13210; state; 1834; *; med, resp-ther, x-ray-t; D; S
Staten Island, C. of (see under **City U. of New York**)
Stephen F. Austin State U., Nacogdoches, TX 75962; state; 1921; *; D; L
Stephens C., Columbia, MO 65215; pvt; 1833; *; S
Sterling C., Sterling, KS 67579; Presb; 1887; *; ed; S
Stetson U., Deland, FL 32720; Bapt; 1883; *; law, mus; beyond Mst; S
Steubenville, U. of, Steubenville, OH 43952; RC; 1946; *; S
Stevens Inst. of Technology, Hoboken, NJ 07030; pvt; 1870; *; engr; D; S
Stillman C., Tuscaloosa, AL 35401; Presb; 1876; *; S
Stockton State C., Pomona, NJ 08240; state; 1969; *; M
Stonehill C., North Easton, MA 02356; RC; 1948; *; ed; S
Sue Bennett C., London, KY 40741; Meth; jr; 1897; *; S
Suffolk County Comm. C., Selden, NY 11784; state/local; jr; 1959; *; a-nurs; L
Suffolk U., Boston, MA 02114; pvt; 1906; *; law; M
Sul Ross State U., Alpine, TX 79830; state; 1917; *; beyond Mst; S
Sullivan County Comm. C., Loch Sheldrake, NY 12759; local; jr; 1962; *; S
Suomi C., Hancock, MI 49930; Lutheran Church in America; jr; 1896; *; S
Surry Comm. C., Dobson, NC 27017; state; jr; 1964; *; S
Susquehanna U., Selinsgrove, PA 17870; Prot; 1858; *; mus; S
Swarthmore C., Swarthmore, PA 19081; pvt; 1864; *; engr; Mst; S
Sweet Briar C., Sweet Briar, VA 24595; pvt; 1901; for women; *; S
Syracuse U., Syracuse, NY 13210; pvt; 1870; *; ed, engr, law, lib, mus; D; L
Tabor C., Hillsboro, KS 67063; Mennonite Brethren Church; 1908; *; mus; S
Tacoma Comm. C., Tacoma, WA 98465; state; jr; 1965; *; resp-ther-t, x-ray-t; M
Taft C., Taft, CA 93268; state/local; jr; 1922; *; S
Talladega C., Talladega, AL 35160; pvt; 1867; *; S
Tallahassee Comm. C., Tallahassee, FL 32304; local; jr; 1965; *; x-ray-t; M
Tampa, U. of, Tampa, FL 33606; pvt; 1931; *; mus; S
Tanana Valley Comm. C. (see under **Alaska, U. of**)
Tarkio C., Tarkio, MO 64491; Presb; 1883; *; S
Tarleton State U., Stephenville, TX 76402; state; 1899; *; ed; Mst; M
Tarrant County Junior C., Fort Worth, TX 76102; state/local; jr; 1965; *; L
Taylor U., Upland, IN 46989; pvt; 1846; *; ed, mus; S
Temple Junior C., Temple, TX 76501; local; jr; 1926; *; resp-ther; S
Temple U., Philadelphia, PA 19122; state-related; 1888; *; bus, law, med; D; L
Tennessee Center for the Health Sciences, U. of, Memphis, TN 38163; state; 1911; *; dent, dent-h, med; D; S
Tennessee at Chattanooga, U. of, Chattanooga, TN 37401; state; 1886; *; engr, ed, mus; Mst; M
Tennessee at Knoxville, U. of, Knoxville, TN 37516; state; 1794; *; arch, bus, ed, engr, law, lib. mus, x-ray-t; D; L
Tennessee at Martin, U. of, Martin, TN 38238, state; 1927; *; a-nurs, ed, engr-t, mus; Mst; M
Tennessee State U., Nashville, TN 37203; state; 1912; *; engr, mus; Mst; M
Tennessee Technological U., Cookeville, TN 38501; state; 1915; *; bus, ed; D; M
Tennessee Wesleyan C., Athens, TN 37303; Meth; 1857; *; S
Texarkana Comm. C., Texarkana, TX 75501; local; jr; 1927; *; a-nurs; M
Texas A&I U., Kingsville, TX 78363; state; 1917; *; ed, engr, mus; D; M
Texas A&M U., College Station, TX 77843; state; 1876; *; engr, engr-t; D; L
Texas Christian U., Fort Worth, TX 76129; Christian Church; 1873; *; bus; D; M
Texas C., Tyler, TX 75702; Christian Methodist Episcopal; 1894; *; S
Texas Lutheran C., Seguin, TX 78155; American Lutheran; 1891; *; S
Texas Southern U. Houston, TX 77004; state; 1947; *; bus, law; D; M
Texas Southmost C., Brownsville, TX 78520; state/local; jr; 1926; *; M
Texas Tech U., Lubbock, TX 79409; state; 1923; *; bus, law, med; D; L
Texas at Arlington, U. of, Arlington, TX 76019; state; 1895; *; arch, bus, engr, mus; D; L
Texas at Austin, U. of, Austin, TX 78712; state; 1881; *; arch, bus, ed, engr, law, lib, mus; D; L
Texas at Dallas, U. of, Richardson, TX 75080; state; 1969; *; D; M
Texas at El Paso, U. of, El Paso, TX 79968; state; 1913; *; engr, mus; D; L
Texas Health Science Center at Dallas, U. of, Dallas, TX 75235; state; 1943; *; med; D; S
Texas Health Science Center at Houston, U. of, Houston, TX 77025; state; 1972; *; dent, dent-a, dent-h, med; D; S
Texas Health Science Center at San Antonio, U. of, San Antonio, TX 78285; state; 1959; *; dent, dent-a, dent-h, med; D; S
Texas Medical Branch at Galveston, U. of, Galveston, TX 77550; state; 1881; *; med, resp-ther, x-ray-t; D; S
Texas of the Permian Basin, U. of, Odessa, TX 79762; state; 1969; *; Mst; S
Texas at Tyler, U. of, Tyler, TX 75701; state; 1971; *; Mst; S
Texas Wesleyan C., Fort Worth, TX 76105; Meth; 1890; *; ed, mus; Mst; S
Texas Woman's U., Denton, TX 76204; state; 1901; for women; *; lib, mus; D; M
Theology at Claremont, School of, Claremont, CA 91711; Prot; 1885; *; D, grad only; S
Thiel C., Greenville, PA 16125; Lutheran Church in America; 1866; *; S
Thomas A. Edison C., Trenton, NJ 08625; state/local; 1972; *; M
Thomas C., Waterville, ME 04901; pvt; 1894; *; Mst; S
Thomas County Comm. C., Thomasville, GA 31792; pvt; jr; 1950; *; S
Thomas Jefferson U., Philadelphia, PA 19107; pvt; 1824; *; med; D; S
Thomas More C., Fort Mitchell, KY 41017; RC; 1921; *; S
Thomas Nelson Comm. C., Hampton, VA 23670; state; jr; 1967; *; M
Thornton Comm. C., South Holland, IL 60473; state/local; jr; 1927; *; M
Three Rivers Comm. C., Poplar Bluff, MO 63901; state; jr; 1966; *; dent-a; S
Tidewater Comm. C., Portsmouth, VA 23703; state; jr; 1968; *; a-nurs; L
Tiffin U., Tiffin, OH 44883; pvt; 1918; S
Tift C., Forsyth, GA 31029; Bapt; 1849; *; S
Toccoa Falls C., Toccoa Falls, GA 30598; pvt; 1907; S
Toledo, U. of, Toledo, OH 43606; state; 1872; *; bus, ed, engr, law; D; L
Tompkins-Cortland Comm. C., Dryden, NY 13053; state/local; jr; 1968; *; S
Tougaloo C., Tougaloo, MS 39174; United Church of Christ; 1869; *; S
Touro C., New York, NY 10036; pvt; 1970; *; Mst; S
Towson State U., Baltimore, MD 21204; state; 1866; *; ed; Mst; L
Transylvania U., Lexington, KY 40508; pvt; 1780; *; S
Treasure Valley Comm. C., Ontario, OR 97914; local; jr; 1961; *; S
Trenton State C., Trenton, NJ 08625; state; 1855; *; ed, engr-t, beyond Mst; L
Trevecca Nazarene C., Nashville, TN 37210; Church of Nazarene; 1901; *; S
Tri-County Comm. C., Murphy, NC 28906; state; jr; 1964; *; S
Tri-State U., Angola, IN 46703; pvt; 1884; *; engr; S
Trinidad State Junior C., Trinidad, CO 81082; state; jr; 1925; *; S
Trinity Christian C., Palos Heights, IL 60463; pvt; 1956; *; S
Trinity C., Hartford, CT 06106; pvt; 1823; *; Mst; S
Trinity C., Washington, DC 20017; RC; 1897; *; beyond Mst; S
Trinity C., Deerfield, IL 60015; pvt; 1897; *; S
Trinity C., Burlington, VT 05401; RC; 1925; for women; *; S
Trinity U., San Antonio, TX 78284; pvt; 1869; *; ed, engr; Mst; M
Triton C., River Grove, IL 60171; local; jr; 1964; *; a-nurs, x-ray-t; L
Trocaire C., Buffalo, NY 14220; pvt; jr; 1958; *; a-nurs, x-ray-t; S
Troy State U., Troy, AL 36081; state; 1887; *; ed; beyond Mst; M
Truckee Meadows Comm. C., Sparks, NE 89431; state; jr; 1971; *; dent-a; M
Truett McConnell C., Cleveland, GA 30528; Bapt; jr; 1946; *; mus; S
Truman C. (see under **City Colleges of Chicago**)
Tufts U., Medford, MA 02155; pvt; 1852; *; dent, dent-a, engr, med; D; M
Tulane U. of Louisiana, New Orleans, LA 70118; pvt; 1834; *; law, med; D; L
Tulsa Junior C., Tulsa, OK 74119; state, jr; 1968; *; a-nurs, med-a, x-ray-t; M
Tulsa, U. of, Tulsa, OK 74104; pvt; 1894; *; bus, ed, engr, law, mus; D; M
Tunxis Comm. C., Farmington, CT 06032; state; jr; 1969; *; dent-a, dent-h; M

Tusculum C., Greeneville, TN 37743; Presb; 1794; *; S
Tuskegee Inst., Tuskegee Institute, AL 36088; pvt; 1881; *; engr; Mst; M
Tyler Junior C., Tyler, TX 75701; state/local; jr; 1926; *; resp-ther, x-ray-t; M
Ulster County Comm. C., Stone Ridge, NY 12484; state/local; jr; 1961; *; S
Umpqua Comm. C., Roseburg, OR 97470; local; jr; 1964; *; S
Union C., Barbourville, KY 40906; Meth; 1879; *; x-ray-t; beyond Mst; S
Union C., Lincoln, NE 68506; Seventh-Day Adventists; 1889; *; ed, mus; S
Union C., Cranford, NJ 07016; pvt; jr; 1933; *; M
Union C., Schenectady, NY 12308; pvt; 1795; *; engr; D; M
Union Theological Seminary, New York, NY 10027; pvt; 1836; *; D, grad only; S
Union Theological Seminary in Virginia, Richmond, VA 23227; Presb; 1812; *; D, grad only; S
Union U., Jackson, TN 38301; Bapt; 1825; *; a-nurs, mus; S
United States Air Force Academy, US Air Force Academy, CO 80840; federal; 1954; *; engr; M
United States Army Command and General Staff C., Fort Leavenworth, KS 66027; federal; 1881; *; Mst; S
United States Coast Guard Academy, New London, CT 06320; federal; 1876; *; engr; S
United States International U., San Diego, CA 92131; pvt; 1952; *; D; S
United States Merchant Marine Academy, Kings Point, NY 11024; federal; 1938; *; S
United States Military Academy, West Point, NY 10996; federal; 1802; *; M
United States Naval Academy, Annapolis, MD 21402; federal; 1845; *; engr; M
Unity C., Unity, ME 04988; pvt; 1966; *; S
Universidad de Ponce, Ponce, PR 00731; prop; jr; 1973; S
Universidad Politecnica de Puerto Rico, Hato Rey, PR 00918; pvt; 1977; S
Upper Iowa U., Fayette, IA 52142; pvt; 1857; *; S
Upsala C., East Orange, NJ 07019; Prot; 1893; *; Mst; S
Upstate Medical Center (see under **State U. of New York**)
Urbana C., Urbana, OH 43078; pvt; 1850; *; S
Ursinus C., Collegeville, PA 19426; pvt; 1869; *; S
Ursuline C., Cleveland, OH 44124; pvt; 1871; for women; *; S
Utah State U., Logan, UT 84322; state; 1888; *; bus, ed, engr; D; M
Utah, U. of, Salt Lake City, UT 84112; state; 1850; *; law, med; D; L
Utica C. of Syracuse U., Utica, NY 13502; pvt; 1946; *; S
Utica Junior C., Utica, MS 39175; state; jr; 1903; *; S
Valdosta State C., Valdosta, GA 31601; state; 1906; *; ed; beyond Mst; M
Valencia Comm. C., Orlando, FL 32802; local; jr; 1967; *; a-nurs, resp-ther; M
Valley City State C., Valley City, ND 58072; state; 1889; *; ed; S
Valley Forge Christian C., Phoenixville, PA 19460; Assemblies of God Church; 1938; S
Valley Forge Military Junior C., Wayne, PA 19087; pvt; jr; 1938; for men; *; S
Valparaiso U., Valparaiso, IN 46383; Lutheran Church; 1859; *; law; Mst; M
Vance-Granville Comm. C., Henderson, NC 27536; state-related; jr; 1969; *; S
Vanderbilt U., Nashville, TN 37212; pvt; 1873; *; bus, engr, law, med; D; M
Vandercook C. of Music, Chicago, IL 60616; pvt; 1909; *; mus; Mst; S
Vassar C., Poughkeepsie, NY 12601; pvt; 1861; *; Mst; S
Ventura C., Ventura, CA 93003; local; jr; 1925; *; resp-ther; L
Vermilion Comm. C., Ely, MN 55731; state; jr; 1922; *; S
Vermont C., Montpelier, VT 05602; pvt; 1834; a-nurs; Mst; S
Vermont, Comm. C. of, Montpelier, VT 05602; state; jr; 1970; *; S
Vermont, U. of, Burlington, VT 05405; state; 1791; *; engr, med; D; L
Vernon Regional Junior C., Vernon, TX 76384; state/local; jr; 1970; *; S
Victor Valley C., Victorville, CA 92392; state/local; jr; 1960; *; a-nurs; M
Victoria C., Victoria, TX 77901; local jr; 1925; *; resp-ther-t; S
Villa Julie C., Stevenson, MD 21553; pvt; 1947; *; S
Villa Maria C., Erie, PA 16505; RC; 1925; for women; *; S
Villa Maria C. of Buffalo, Buffalo, NY 14225; pvt; jr; 1960; *; S
Villanova U., Villanova, PA 19085; RC; 1842; *; bus, engr, law; D; M
Vincennes U., Vincennes, IN 47591; state; 1801; *; a-nurs, resp-ther; M
Virgin Islands, C. of the, Saint Thomas, VI 00801; state; 1962; *; Mst; S
Virginia Commonwealth U., Richmond, VA 23284; state; 1838; *; D; L
Virginia Highlands Comm. C., Abington, VA 24210; state; 1967; a-nurs; S
Virginia Intermont C., Briston, VA 24201; pvt; 1884; *; S
Virginia Military Inst., Lexington, VA 24450; state; 1839; for men; *; engr; S
Virginia Polytechnic Inst. and State U., Blacksburg, VA 24061; state; 1872; *; L
Virginia State U., Petersburg, VA 23803; state; 1882; *; ed, mus; Mst; M
Virginia Union U., Richmond, VA 23220; Bapt; 1865; *; S
Virginia, U. of, Charlottesville, VA 22903; state; 1819; *; law, med; D; L
Virginia Wesleyan C., Norfolk, VA 23502; Meth; 1961; *; S
Virginia Western Comm. C., Roanoke, VA 24015; state; jr; 1966; *; a-nurs; M
Visual Arts, School of, New York, NY 10010; prop; 1947; *; M
Viterbo C., La Crosse, WI 54601; RC; 1890; *; ed, mus; S
Volunteer State Comm. C., Gallatin, TN 37066; state; jr; 1970; *; dent-a; M
Voorhees C., Denmark, SC 29042; Protestant Episcopal; 1897; *; S
Wabash C., Crawfordsville, IN 47933; pvt; 1832; for men; *; S
Wagner C., Staten Island, NY 10301; Lutheran Church in America; 1883; *; S
Wake Forest U., Winston-Salem, NC 27109; Bapt; 1834; *; ed, law, med; D; M
Waldorf C., Forest City, IA 50436; American Lutheran; jr; 1903; *; S
Walker C., Jasper, AL 35501; pvt; jr; 1938; *; S
Walla Walla C., College Place, WA 99324; Prot; 1892; *; engr, mus; Mst; S
Walla Walla Comm. C., Walla Walla, WA 99362; state; jr; 1967; *; a-nurs; M
Wallace State Comm. C. at Hanceville, Hanceville, AL 35077; state; jr; 1966; *; S
Walsh C., North Canton, OH 44720; RC; 1958; *; S
Walsh C. of Accountancy and Business Administration, Troy, MI 48084; pvt; 1968; *; Mst; S
Walters State Comm. C., Morristown, TN 37814; state; jr; 1969; *; M
Warner Pacific C., Portland, OR 97215; Church of God; 1937; *; Mst; S
Warner Southern C., Lake Wales, FL 33853; Church of God; 1964; *; S
Warren Wilson C., Swannanoa, NC 28778; Presb; 1894; *; S
Wartburg C., Waverly, IA 50677; American Lutheran; 1852; *; mus; S
Wartburg Theological Seminary, Dubuque, IA 52001; American Lutheran; 1854; *; beyond Mst; S
Washburn U. of Topeka, Topeka, KS 66621; local; 1865; *; law; Mst; M
Washington and Jefferson C., Washington, PA 15301; pvt; 1781; *; Mst; S
Washington and Lee U., Lexington, VA 24450; pvt; 1749; for men; *; law; S
Washington C., Chestertown, MD 21620; pvt; 1782; *; Mst; S
Washington International C., Washington, DC 20006; pvt; 1970; S
Washington State U., Pullman, WA 99164; state; 1890; *; arch, bus, engr; D; L
Washington Technical C., Marietta WA 45750; state; jr; 1971; *; S
Washington Theological Union, Silver Spring, MD 20910; pvt; 1969; *; Mst, grad only; S
Washington U., Saint Louis, MO 63130; pvt; 1853; *; arch, art, bus, dent, ed, engr, law, med, x-ray-t; D; L
Washington, U. of, Seattle, WA 98195; state; 1861; *; arch, art, bus, dent-h, ed, engr, law, lib, mus; D; L
Washtenaw Comm. C., Ann Arbor, MI 48106; local; jr; 1965; *; x-ray-t; M
Waterbury State Technical C., Waterbury, CT 06708; state; jr; 1964; *; S
Watterson C., Louisville, KY 40218; prop; jr; 1963; *; S
Waubonsee Comm. C., Sugar Grove, IL 60554; local; jr; 1966; *; M
Waukesha County Technical Inst., Pewaukee, WI 53072; state/local; jr; 1923; *; a-nurs; med-a; M
Waycross Junior C., Waycross, GA 31501; state; jr; 1970; *; S
Wayland Baptist C., Plainview, TX 79072; Bapt; 1908; *; S
Wayne Comm. C., Goldsboro, NC 27530; state/local; jr; 1957; *; dent-h; S
Wayne County Comm. C., Detroit, MI 48201; state/local; jr; 1966; *; L
Wayne State C., Wayne, NE 68787; state; 1909; *; ed; Mst; S
Wayne State U., Detroit, MI 48202; state; 1868; *; bus, ed, engr, law, lib, med, mus, x-ray-t; D; L
Waynesburg C., Waynesburg, PA 15370; Presb; 1849; *; S
Weatherford C., Weatherford, TX 76086; local; jr; 1869; *; S
Webb Inst. of Naval Architecture, Glen Cove, NY 11542; pvt; 1889; *; engr; S
Webber C., Babson Park, FL 33827; pvt; 1927; *; S
Weber State C., Ogden, UT 84408; state; 1889; *; a-nurs, ed, engr-t, resp-ther, x-ray-t; Mst; M
Webster C., Saint Louis, MO 63119; pvt; 1915; *; mus; M
Wellesley C., Wellesley, MA 02181; pvt; 1875; for women; *; S
Wells C., Aurora, NY 13026; pvt; 1868; for women; *; S
Wenatchee Valley C., Wenatchee, WA 98801; state; jr; 1939; *; M
Wentworth Inst. of Technology, Boston, MA 02115; pvt; 1904; *; engr-t; S
Wentworth Military Academy, Lexington, MO 64067; pvt; jr; 1880; for men; *; S
Wesley C., Dover, DE 19901; Meth; 1873; *; a-nurs; S
Wesley C., Florence, MS 39073; Prot; 1972; S
Wesleyan C., Macon, GA 31297; Meth; 1836; for women; *; mus; S
Wesleyan U., Middletown, CT 06457; pvt; 1831; *; D; S
West Chester State C., West Chester, PA 19380; state; 1871; *; Mst; M
West Coast Bible C., Fresno, CA 93710; Church of God; 1949; *; S
West Coast U., Los Angeles, CA 90020; pvt; 1909; *; Mst; S
West Coast U., Orange County Center, Orange, CA 92668; pvt; 1963; Mst; S
West Florida, U. of, Pensacola, FL 32504; state; 1963; *; mus; Mst; M
West Georgia C., Carrollton, GA 30118; state; 1933; *; beyond Mst; M
West Hills C., Coalinga, CA 93210; state/local; jr; 1932; *; S
West Liberty State C., West Liberty, WV 26074; state; 1837; *; ed, mus; S
West Los Angeles C., Culver City, CA 90230; local; jr; 1968; *; L
West Los Angeles, U. of, Culver City, CA 90230; pvt; 1966; Mst; S
West Shore Comm. C., Scottville, MI 49454; local; jr; 1967; *; S
West Texas State U., Canyon, TX 79016; state; 1909; *; beyond Mst; M
West Valley C., Saratoga, CA 95070; state/local; jr; 1963; *; med-a; L
West Virginia C. of Graduate Studies, Institute, WV 25112; state; 1972; *; ed; beyond Mst; M
West Virginia Inst. of Technology, Montgomery, WV 25136; state; 1895; *; dent-h, ed, engr, engr-t, med-rec-t; Mst; M
West Virginia Northern Comm. C., Wheeling, WV 26003; state; jr; 1972; *; a-nurs, resp-ther; M
West Virginia State C., Institute, WV 25112; state; 1891; *; ed; M
West Virginia U., Morgantown, WV 26506; state; 1867; *; art, bus, dent, dent-h, ed, engr, law, med, mus, x-ray-t; D; L
West Virginia Wesleyan C., Buckhannon, WV 26201; Meth; 1890; *; mus; Mst; S
Westark Comm. C., Fort Smith, AR 72913; state/local; jr; 1928; *; a-nurs; M
Westbrook C., Portland, ME 04103; pvt; 1831; *; a-nurs, dent-h; S
Westchester Comm. C., Valhalla, NY 10595; state/local; 1946; *; resp-ther, x-ray-t; M
Western Baptist C., Salem, OR 97302; Bapt; 1936; *; S
Western Carolina U., Cullowhee, NC 28723; state; 1889; *; ed; beyond Mst; M
Western Connecticut State C., Danbury, CT 06810; state; 1903; *; ed; beyond Mst; M
Western Illinois U., Macomb, IL 61455; state; 1899; *; bus, ed, mus; beyond Mst; L
Western Iowa Tech Comm. C., Sioux City, IA 51102; state/local; jr; 1966; *; dent-a; S
Western Kentucky U., Bowling Green, KY 42101; state; 1906; *; a-nurs, dent-h, ed, engr-t, med-rec-t, mus; beyond Mst; L
Western Maryland C., Westminster, MD 21157; pvt; 1867; *; mus; Mst; S
Western Michigan U., Kalamazoo, MI 49008; state; 1903; *; art, bus, ed, engr, lib, mus; D; L
Western Montana C., Dillon, MT 59725; state; 1893; *; Mst; S
Western Nevada Comm. C., Carson City, NV 89701; state; jr; 1971; *; M
Western New England C., Springfield, MA 01119; pvt; 1919; *; engr, law; Mst; M
Western New Mexico U., Silver City, NM 88061; state; 1893; *; Mst; S
Western Oklahoma State C., Altus, OK 73521; state; jr; 1926; *; S
Western Piedmont Comm. C., Morgantown, NC 28655; state; jr; 1964; *; S
Western State C. of Colorado, Gunnison, CO 81230; state; 1911; *; ed; Mst; M
Western State U. C. of Law, Orange County, Fullerton, CA 92631; prop; 1966; *; S
Western State U. C. of Law of San Diego, San Diego, CA 92101; prop; 1969; *; S
Western Texas C., Snyder, TX 79549; state; 1909; *; ed, mus; beyond Mst; M
Western Washington U., Bellingham, WA 98225; state; 1899; *; ed; Mst; L
Western Wisconsin Technical Inst., La Crosse, WI 54601; state/local; jr; 1912; *; a-nurs, dent-a, med-a, med-rec-t; M
Western Wyoming Comm. C., Rock Springs, WY 82901; state/local; jr; 1959; *; resp-ther-t, x-ray-t; S
Westfield State C., Westfield, MA 01085; state; 1838; *; ed; beyond Mst; M
Westmar C., Le Mars, IA 51031; Meth; 1890; *; S
Westminster Choir C., Princeton, NJ 08540; pvt; 1926; *; mus; Mst; S
Westminster C., Fulton, MO 65251; pvt; 1849; *; S
Westminster C., New Wilmington, PA 16142; Presb; 1852; *; mus; Mst; S
Westminster C., Salt Lake City, UT 84105; pvt; 1875; *; Mst; S
Westmont C., Santa Barbara, CA 93108; pvt; 1940; *; S
Westmoreland County Comm. C., Youngwood, PA 15697; local; jr; 1970; *; S
Wharton County Junior C., Wharton, TX 77488; local; jr; 1946; *; med-rec-t; S
Whatcom Comm. C., Bellingham, WA 98225; state; jr; 1970; *; S
Wheaton C., Wheaton, IL 60187; pvt; 1860; *; ed, mus; Mst; S
Wheaton C., Norton, MA 02766; pvt; 1834; for women; *; S
Wheeling C., Wheeling, WV 26003; RC; 1954; *; Mst; S
Wheelock C., Boston, MA 02215; pvt; 1889; *; ed; beyond Mst; S
White Pines C., Chester, NH 03036; pvt; jr; 1965; *; S
White Plains, C. of (see under **Pace U.**)
Whitman C., Walla Walla, WA 99362; pvt; 1859; *; mus; S
Whittier C., Whittier, CA 90608; pvt; 1901; *; D; S
Whitworth C., Spokane, WA 99251; Presb; 1890; *; ed; Mst; S
Wichita State U., Wichita, KS 67208; state; 1892; *; bus, dent-h, ed, engr, mus, resp-ther; D; L
Widener C. of Widener U., Chester, PA 19013; pvt; 1821; *; engr, law; Mst; M
Wilberforce U., Wilberforce, OH 45384; Prot; 1856; *; S
Wiley C., Marshall, TX 75670; Meth; 1873; *; S
Wilkes C., Wilkes-Barre, PA 18703; pvt; 1933; *; Mst; S
Wilkes Comm. C., Wilkesboro, NC 28697; state; jr; 1965; *; S
Willamette U., Salem, OR 97301; pvt; 1842; *; law, mus; Mst; S
William and Mary, C. of, Williamsburg, VA 23185; state; 1693; *; bus, ed, law; D; M
William Carey C., Hattiesburg, MS 39401; Bapt; 1906; *; mus; beyond Mst; S
William Carey International U., Pasadena, CA 91104; pvt; 1977; S
William Jewell C., Liberty, MO 64068; Bapt; 1849; *; S
William Paterson C., Wayne, NJ 07470; state; 1855; *; ed; Mst; L
William Penn C., Oskaloosa, IA 52577; Friends; 1873; *; ed; S
William Rainey Harper C., Palatine, IL 60067; state/local; jr; 1965; *; L
William Woods C., Fulton, MO 65251; pvt; 1870; for women; *; ed; S
Williams C., Williamstown, MA 01267; pvt; 1793; *; Mst; S
Williamsburg Technical C., Kingstree, SC 29556; state/local; jr; 1969; *; S
Williamsport Area Comm. C., Williamsport, PA 17701; local; jr; 1965; *; M
Willmar Comm. C., Willmar, MN 56201; state; jr; 1961; *; S
Wilmington C., New Castle, DE 19720; pvt; 1967; *; Mst; S
Wilmington C., Wilmington, OH 45177; Friends United Meeting; 1870; *; S
Wilson C., Chambersburg, PA 17201; pvt; 1869; for women; *; S
Wilson County Technical Inst., Wilson, NC 27893; state; jr; 1959; *; S
Windward Comm. C. (see under **Hawaii, U. of**)
Wingate C., Wingate, NC 28174; Bapt; 1896; *; mus; S
Winona State U., Winona MN 55987; state; 1858; *; ed; beyond Mst; M
Winston-Salem State U., Winston-Salem, NC 27102; state; 1892; *; ed, mus; S
Winthrop C., Rock Hill, SC 29733; state; 1886; *; bus; beyond Mst; M
Wisconsin Indianhead Vocational Technical and Adult Education District, Shell Lake, WI 54871; state; jr; 1968; *; med-a; M
Wisconsin—Eau Claire, U. of, Eau Claire, WI 54701; state; 1916; *; Mst; L
Wisconsin—Green Bay, U. of, Green Bay, WI 54302; state; 1965; *; Mst; M
Wisconsin—La Crosse, U. of, La Crosse, WI 54601; state; 1909; *; ed; Mst; M
Wisconsin—Madison, U. of, Madison, WI 53706; state; 1849; *; bus, ed, engr, law, lib, med, mus, x-ray-t; D; L
Wisconsin—Milwaukee, U. of, Milwaukee, WI 53201; state; 1955; *; arch, bus, ed, engr, lib, mus; D; L
Wisconsin—Oshkosh, U. of, Oshkosh, WI 54901; state; 1871; *; bus, ed, mus; Mst; L
Wisconsin—Parkside, U. of, Kenosha, WI 53141; state; 1965; *; Mst; M
Wisconsin—Platteville, U. of, Platteville, WI 53818; state; 1866; *; ed, engr; Mst; M

Wisconsin—River Falls, U. of, River Falls, WI 54022; state; 1874; *; ed; Mst; M
Wisconsin—Stevens Point, U. of, Stevens Point, WI 54481; state; 1894; *; ed, mus; Mst; M
Wisconsin—Stout, U. of, Menomonie, WI 54751; state; 1893; *; ed; beyond Mst; M
Wisconsin—Superior, U. of, Superior, WI 54860; state; 1893; *; ed; beyond Mst; S
Wisconsin—Whitewater, U. of, Whitewater, WI 53190; state; 1868; *; Mst; M
Wittenberg U., Springfield, OH 45501; Prot; 1845; *; ed, mus, x-ray-t; Mst; S
Wofford C., Spartanburg, SC 29301; Meth; 1854; *; S
Wood Junior C., Mathiston, MS 39752; Meth; jr; 1886; *; S
Woodbury U., Los Angeles, CA 90017; pvt; 1884; *; Mst; S
Wooster, C. of Wooster, OH 44691; pvt; 1866; *; art, mus; S
Wor-Wic Technical Comm. C., Salisbury, MD 21801; local; jr; 1975; *; S
Worcester Junior C., Worcester, MA 01610; pvt; jr; 1905; *; S
Worcester Polytechnic Inst./ Worcester, MA 01609; pvt; 1865; *; engr; D; M
Worcester State C., Worcester, MA 01602; state; 1874; *; ed; beyond Mst; M
World C. West, San Rafael, CA 94902; pvt; 1971; S
Worthington Comm. C., Worthington, MN 56187; state; jr; 1935; *; S
Wright C. (see under **City Colleges of Chicago**)
Wright State U., Dayton, OH 45435; state; 1964; *; bus, ed, engr, med, mus; Mst; L
Wright State U., Western Ohio Branch, Celina, OH 45822; state; jr; 1969; *; S
Wyoming, U. of, Laramie, WY 82071; state; 1886; *; bus, ed, engr, law, mus; D; M
Wytheville Comm. C., Wytheville, VA 24382; state; jr; 1962; *; a-nurs, dent-a; S
Xavier U., Cincinnati, OH 45207; RC; 1831; *; x-ray-t; Mst; M
Xavier U. of Louisiana, New Orleans, LA 70125; RC; 1915; *; mus; Mst; S
Yakima Valley Comm. C., Yakima, WA 98902; state; jr; 1928; *; a-nurs, dent-h, x-ray-t; M
Yale U., New Haven, CT 06520; pvt; 1701; *; arch, engr, law, med, mus; D; M
Yankton C., Yankton, SD 57078; United Church of Christ; 1881; *; mus; S
Yavapai C., Prescott, AZ 86301; local; jr; 1966; *; M
Yeshiva U., New York, NY 10033; pvt; 1886; *; med; D; M
York C., York, NE 68467; pvt; jr; 1956; *; S
York C. (see under **City U. of New York**)
York C. of Pennsylvania, York, PA 17405; pvt; 1941; *; resp-ther; Mst; M
York Technical C., Rock Hill, SC 29730; state; jr; 1962; *; S
Young Harris C., Young Harris, GA 30582; Meth; 1886; jr; *; S
Youngstown State U., Youngstown, OH 44555; state; 1908; *; a-nurs, dent-h, ed, engr, engr-t, mus, resp-ther; Mst; L
Yuba C., Marysville, CA 95901; state/local; jr; 1927; *; M

Canada

Acadia Divinity C. (see under **Acadia U.**)
Acadia U., Wolfville, N.S. B0P 1X0; 1828; *; bus, ed, mus; Mst; M
  Acadia Divinity C., 1968
Ahuntsic, C., Montreal, Que. H2M 1Y8; 514-389-5921; non-degree
Alberta, U. of, Edmonton, Alta. T6G 2E5; 1906; *; law, lib, med, mus; D; L
  Camrose Lutheran C., Camrose, Alta. T4V 2R3; Lutheran; 1959
  Canadian Union C., Lacombe, Alta, T0C 0Z0; Prot; 1907
  Concordia Lutheran C., Edmonton, Alta, T5B 4E4; Lutheran; 1921
  St. Joseph's C., Edmonton, Alta. T6G 2M7; RC; 1926
  St. Stephens's C., Edmonton, Alta. T6G 2M7; United Church; 1927
Algoma U.C. (see under **Laurentian U. of Sudbury**)
Algonquin C. of Applied Arts and Technology, Nepean, Ont. K2G 1V8; 613-725-7432; non-degree
André-Laurendeau, C., Lasalle, Que. H8N 2J4; 514-364-3320; non-degree
Assiniboine Comm. C., Brandon, Man. R7A 5Z9; 204-725-4530; non-degree
Assumption U. (see **Windsor, U. of**)
Athabasca U., Edmonton, Alta. T5V 1G9; 1970; * (provisional); M
Atlantic School of Theology (see under **King's C., U. of**)
Bay St. George Comm. C., Stephenville, Nfld. A2N 2Z6; 709-643-5161; non-degree
Bishop's U., Lennoxville, Que. J1M 1Z7; 1843; *; bus, ed; Mst; S
  Thomas More Inst. for Adult Education, Montreal, Que. H3G 1X7
Bois de Boulogne C., Montreal, Que. H4N 1L3; 514-332-3000; non-degree
Brandon U., Brandon, Man. R7A 6A9; 1899; *; ed, mus; Mst; S
Brescia C., London, Ont. N6G 1H2; RC; 1919; for women; *; S
British Columbia Inst. of Technology, Burnaby, B.C. V5G 3H2; 604-434-5734; non-degree
British Columbia Mining School, Rossland, B.C. V0G 1Y0; 604-362-5377; non-degree
British Columbia, U. of, Vancouver, B.C. V6T 1W5; 1908; *; law, med; D; L
  Carey Hall, Vancouver, B.C. V6T 1J6; Baptist; for men
  Regent C., Vancouver, B.C. V6T 1W6
  St. Andrew's Hall, Vancouver, B.C. V6T 1J6; Presb; for men
  St. Mark's C., Vancouver, B.C. V6T 1J7: RC; for men
  Vancouver School of Theology, Vancouver, B.C. V6T 1L4
Brock U., St. Catherines, Ont. L2S 3A1; 1964; *; bus, ed; Mst; M
Calgary, U. of, Calgary, Alta. T2N 1N4; 1945; *; engr, law, med, mus; D; L
  Medicine Hat C., Medicine Hat, Alta. T1A 4G5; 1945
  Mt. Royal C., Calgary, Alta. T3E 6K6; 1910
Cambrian C. of Applied Arts and Technology, Sudbury, Ont. P3A 3V8; 705-566-8101; non-degree
Camosun C., Victoria, B.C. V8P 5J2; 604-592-1281; non-degree
Campion C. (fed. **Regina, U. of**), Regina, Sask. S4S 0A2; RC; 1917; *; S
Camrose Lutheran C. (see under **Alberta, U. of**)
Canadian Theological C. (see under **Regina, U. of**)
Canadian Union C. (see under **Alberta, U. of**)
Canadore C. of Applied Arts and Technology, North Bay, Ont. P1B 8K9; 705-474-7600; non-degree
Canterbury C. (see under **Windsor, U. of**)
Cape Breton, C. of, Sydney, N.S. B1P 6L2; 1974; *; bus; S
Capilano C., North Vancouver, B.C. V7J 3H5; 604-986-1911; non-degree
Carey Hall (see under **British Columbia, U. of**)
Cariboo C., Kamloops, B.C. V2C 5N3; 604-374-0123; non-degree
Carleton U., Ottawa, Ont. K1S 5B6; 1942; *; arch, bus, engr; D; L
Carlton Trail Comm. C., Humboldt, Sask. S0K 2A0; 306-682-2623; non-degree
Centennial C. of Applied Arts and Technology, Scarborough, Ont. M1K 5E9; 416-694-3241; non-degree
Champlain Regional C., Sherbrooke, Que. J1H 5N1; 819-563-9661; non-degree
Christian Brothers C. (see under **Memorial U. of Newfoundland**)
Concordia Lutheran C. (see under **Alberta, U. of**)
Concordia U., Montreal, Que. H3G 1M8; 1974; *; art, bus, engr; D; L
Conestoga C. of Applied Arts and Technology, Kitchener, Ont. N2G 4M4; 519-653-2511; non-degree
Confederation C. of Applied Arts and Technology, Thunder Bay, Ont. P7C 4W1; 807-475-6110; non-degree
Conrad Grebel C. (see under **Waterloo, U. of**)
Coteau Range Comm. C., Moose Jaw, Sask. S6H 4R3; 306-692-6431; non-degree
Crafts Training School, St. John's, Nfld. A1B 3T1; 709-737-3038; non-degree
Cumberland Comm. C., Nipawin, Sask. S0E 1E0; 306-862-4653; non-degree
Cypress Hills Comm. C., Swift Current, Sask. S9H 0T7; 306-773-1531; non-degree
Dalhousie U., Halifax, N.S. B3H 3J5; 1818; *; law, lib, med, mus; D; M
Dawson C., Westmount, Que. H3Z 1W7; 514-931-8731; non-degree
Dominican College of Philosophy and Theology (Collège Dominicain de Philosophie et de Théologie), Ottawa, Ont. K1R 7G2; RC; 1900; D; S
Douglas C., New Westminster, B.C. V3L 5B2; 604-521-4851; non-degree
Drummondville, C. de, Drummondville, Que. J2B 1J3; 819-478-4671; non-degree
Durham C. of Applied Arts and Technology, Oshawa, Ont. L1H 7L7; 416-576-0210; non-degree
East Kootenay Comm. C., Cranbrook, B.C. V1C 5L7; 604-489-2751; non-degree
Edouard-Montpetit, C., Longueuil, Que. J4H 3M6; 514-679-2630; non-degree
Emily Carr C. of Art and Design, Vancouver, B.C. V6H 3R9; 604-687-2345; non-degree
Emmanuel and St. Chad, C. of (see under **Saskatchewan, U. of**)
Emmanuel C. of Victoria U. (see under **Toronto, U. of**)
Fairview C., Fairview, Alta. T0H 1L0; 403-835-2213; non-degree
Fanshawe C. of Applied Arts and Technology, London, Ont. N5W 5H1; 519-452-4100; non-degree
Fisheries, Navigation, Marine Engineering and Electronics, C. of, St. John's, Nfld. A1C 5R3; 709-726-5272; non-degree
François-Xavier-Garneau, C., Sillery, Que. G1T 2S5; 418-688-8310; non-degree
Fraser Valley C., Chilliwack, B.C. V2P 6T4; 604-792-0025; non-degree
George Brown C. of Applied Arts and Technology, Toronto, Ont. M5T 2T9; 416-967-1212; non-degree
Georgian C. of Applied Arts and Technology, Barrie, Ont. L4M 3X9; 705-728-1951; non-degree
Granby, C. de, Granby, Que. J2G 6T6; 514-372-6614; non-degree
Grande Prairie Regional C., Grande Prairie, Alta. T8V 4C4; 403-532-8830; non-degree
Grant MacEwan Comm. C., Edmonton, Alta. T5J 2P2; 403-425-8810; non-degree
Guelph, U. of, Guelph, Ont. N1G 2W1; 1862; *; engr; D; L
Hauterive, C. de, Hauterive, Que. G5C 2B2; 418-589-5707; non-degree
Hearst, U.C. of (see under **Laurentian U. of Sudbury**)
Higher Commercial Studies, School of (see under **Montreal, U. of**)
Holland C., Charlottetown, P.E.I. C1A 4J9; 902-892-4278; non-degree
Holy Redeemer C. (see under **Windsor, U. of**)
Humber C. of Applied Arts and Technology, Rexdale, Ont. M9W 5L7; 416-675-3111; non-degree
Huntington U. (see under **Laurentian U. of Sudbury**)
Huron C., London, Ont. N6G 1H3; 1863; *; bus; Mst; S
Ignatius C. (see under **St. Mary's U.**)
Iona C. (see under **Windsor, U. of**)
John Abbot C., Ste.-Anne-de-Bellevue, Que. H9X 3L9; 514-457-6610; non-degree
Joliette, C. de, Joliette, Que. J6E 4T1: 514-759-1661; non-degree
Keewatin Comm. C., The Pas, Man. R9A 1M7; 204-623-3416; non-degree
Kelsay Inst. of Applied Arts and Sciences, Saskatoon, Sask. S7K 3R5; 306-664-6424; non-degree
Keyano C., Fort McMurray, Alta. T9H 2H7; 403-791-2213; non-degree
King's C. (aflt. **Western Ontario, U. of**), London, Ont. N6A 2M3; RC; 1955; *; S
King's C., U. of (fed. **Dalhousie U.**), Halifax, N.S. B3H 2A1; 1789; *; Mst; S
  Atlantic School of Theology, Halifax, N.S. B3H 3B5; 1971
Knox C. (see under **Toronto, U. of**)
La Gaspésie, C. de, Gaspé, Que. G0C 1R0; 418-368-2201; non-degree
La Pocatière, C. de, La Pocatière, Que. G0R 1Z0: 418-856-1525; non-degree
La Région de l'Amiante, C. de, Thetford Mines, Que. G6G 1N1; 418-338-8591; non-degree
La Ronge Region Comm. C., La Ronge, Sask. S0J 1L0; 306-425-2480; non-degree
Lakehead U., Thunder Bay, Ont. P7B 5E1; 1946; *; bus, ed, engr; Mst; M
Lakeland C., Lloydminster, Alta. T9V 0W2; 403-875-8828; non-degree
Lambton C. of Applied Arts and Technology, Sarnia, Ont. N7T 7K4; 519-542-7751; non-degree
Laurentian U. of Sudbury, Sudbury, Ont. P3E 2C6; 1960; *; engr; Mst; M
  Algoma U.C., Sault Ste. Marie, Ont. P6A 2G4; 1965
  Hearst, U.C. of, Hearst, Ont. P0L 1N0; 1953
  Huntington U., Sudbury, Ont. P3E 2C6; United Church; 1960
  Nipissing U.C., North Bay, Ont. P1B 8L7; 1961
  Thorneloe U., Sudbury, Ont. P3E 2C6; Anglican; 1961
Laval U. (Université Laval), Quebec City, Que. G1K 7P4; 1663; *; D; L
Lethbridge Comm. C., Lethbridge, Alta. T1K 1L6; 403-320-3200; non-degree
Lethbridge, U. of, Lethbridge, Alta. T1K 3M4; 1967; *; art, bus, ed, mus; S
Lévis-Lauzon, C. de, Lauzon, Que. G6V 6Z9; 418-833-5110; non-degree
Limoilou, C. de, Quebec City, Que. G1K 7H3; 418-694-2193; non-degree
Lionel Groulx C., Ste. Therèse, Que. J7E 3G6; 514-430-3120; non-degree
L'Outaouais, C. de, Hull, Que. J8Y 6M5; 819-770-4012; non-degree
Loyalist C. of Applied Arts and Technology, Bellevue, Ont. K8N 5B9; 613-962-9501; non-degree
Luther C. (fed. **Regina, U. of**), Regina, Sask. S4S 0A2; Lutheran; 1913; *; mus; S
Lutheran Theological Seminary (see under **Saskatchewan, U. of**)
Maisonneuve, C. de, Montreal, Que. H1X 2A2; 514-254-7131; non-degree
Malaspina C., Nanaimo, B.C. V9R 5S4; 604-753-3245; non-degree
Manitoba, U. of, Winnipeg, Man. R3T 2N2; 1877; *; engr, law, med, mus; D; L
  St. Andrew's C., Winnipeg, Man. R3T 2M7; 1946
  St. Boniface, U.C. of, Winnipeg, Man. R2H 0H7; 1818
Maritime Forest Ranger School (see under **New Brunswick, U. of**)
Matane, C. de, Matane, Que. G4W 3P7; 418-562-1240; non-degree
McGill U., Montreal, Que. H3A 2T5; 1821; *; engr, law, lib, med, mus; D; L
  Montreal Diocesan Theological C., Montreal, Que. H3A 2A8; 1873
  Presbyterian C. of Montreal, Montreal, Que. H3A 2A8; 1865
  United Theological C. of Montreal, Montreal, Que. H3A 2A9; 1926
McMaster Divinity C. (see under **McMaster U.**)
McMaster U., Hamilton, Ont. L8S 4L8; 1887; *; bus, engr, med, mus; D; L
  McMaster Divinity C., Hamilton, Ont. L8S 4K1; Bapt; 1957
Medicine Hat C. (see under **Calgary, U. of**)
Memorial U. of Newfoundland, St. John's, Nfld. A1C 5S7; 1925; *; D; L
  Christian Brothers C., Mono Mills, Ont. L9W 2Z2; RC; for men
  Sir Wilfred Grenfell C., Corner Brook, Nfld. A2H 6P9
Mennonite Brethren C. of Arts (see under **Winnipeg, U. of**)
Mistikwa Comm. C., North Battleford, Sask. S9A 0Z9; 306-445-6288; non-degree
Mohawk C. of Applied Arts and Technology, Hamilton, Ont. L8N 3T2; 416-389-4461; non-degree
Moncton, U. of, Moncton, N.B. E1A 3E9; 1864; *; engr, law, mus; Mst; M
Montmorency, C., Laval, Que. H7N 5H9; 514-667-5100; non-degree
Montreal Diocesan Theological C. (see under **McGill, U. of**)
Montreal, U. of, Montreal, Que. H3C 3J7; 1876; *; ed, engr, law; D; L
  Higher Commercial Studies, School of, Montreal, Que. H3T 1V6; 1907
  Polytechnic School (École Polytechnique), Montreal, Que. H3C 3A7; 1873
Mt. Allison U., Sackville, N.B. E0A 3C0; United Church; 1843; *; Mst; S
Mt. Royal C. (see under **Calgary, U. of**)
Mt. St. Vincent U., Halifax, N.S. B3M 2J6; RC; 1914; bus, ed; Mst; S
Natonum Comm C., Prince Albert, Sask. S6V 6K1; 306-764-6671; non-degree
New Brunswick Comm. C., Moncton Campus, Moncton, N.B. E1C 8H9; 506-384-9121; non-degree
New Brunswick, U. of, Fredericton, N.B. E3B 5A3; 1785; *; engr, law; D; M
  Maritime Forest Ranger School, Fredericton, N.B. E3B 4X6
New Caledonia, C. of, Prince George, B.C. V2N 1P8; 604-562-2131; non-degree
Newfoundland and Labrador C. of Trades and Technology, St. John's, Nfld. A1C 5P7; 709-753-9360; non-degree
Niagara C. of Applied Arts and Technology, Welland, Ont. L3B 5S2; 416-735-2211; non-degree
Nipissing U.C. (see under **Laurentian U. of Sudbury**)
Nord-Ouest, C. du, Rouyn, Que. J9X 5E5; 819-762-0931; non-degree
North Island C., Comox, B.C. V9N 6P7; 604-339-5551; non-degree

Northern Alberta Inst. of Technology, Edmonton, Alta. T5G 2R1; 403-427-9300; non-degree
Northern C. of Applied Arts and Technology, South Porcupine, Ont. P0N 1H0; 705-235-3211; non-degree
Northern Lights C., Dawson Creek, B.C. V1G 4G2; 604-782-5251; non-degree
Northwest Comm C., Terrace, B.C. V8G 4C2; 604-635-6511; non-degree
Nova Scotia Agricultural C., Truro, N.S. B2N 5E3; 1905; *; S
Nova Scotia C. of Art and Design, Halifax, N.S. B3J 3J6; 1887; *; art; Mst; S
Nova Scotia Inst. of Technology, Halifax, N.S. B3J 3C4; 902-454-7451; non-degree
Nova Scotia Land Survey Inst., Lawrencetown, N.S. B0S 1M0; 902-584-2226; non-degree
Okanagan C., Kelowna, B.C. V1Y 4X8; 604-762-5445; non-degree
Olds C., Olds, Alta. T0M 1P0; 403-556-8281; non-degree
Ontario Inst. for Studies in Education (aflt. **Toronto, U. of**), Toronto, Ont. M5S 1V6; 1965; *; ed; D; S
Open Learning Inst., Richmond, B.C. V6X 1Z9; 604-270-4131; non-degree
Ottawa, U. of, Ottawa, Ont. K1N 6N5; 1848; *; bus, ed, engr, law, med; D; L
Pacific Marine Training Inst., Vancouver, B.C. V5L 1J5; 604-254-0741; non-degree
Pacific Vocational Inst., Burnaby, B.C. V5G 3H1; 604-434-5711; non-degree
Parkland Comm. C., Melville, Sask. S0A 2P0; 306-728-4471; non-degree
Polytechnic School (see under **Montreal, U. of**)
Prairie West Comm. C., Biggar, Sask. S0K 0M0; 306-948-3363; non-degree
Presbyterian C. of Montreal (see under **McGill U.**)
Prince Edward Island, U. of, Charlottetown, P.E.I. C1A 4P3; 1969; *; engr; S
Quebec, U. of, Quebec City, Que. G1V 2M3; 1968; *; engr, law, mus; D; L
  Télé-université, Quebec City, Que. G1N 4M6
  Université du Québec à Chicoutimi, Chicoutimi, Que. G7H 2B1
  Université du Québec à Montréal, Montreal, Que. H3C 3P8
  Université du Québec à Rimouski, Rimouski, Que. G5L 3A1
  Université du Québec à Trois Rivières, Trois Rivières, Que. G9A 5H7
Queen's Theological C. (see under **Queen's U. at Kingston**)
Queen's U. at Kingston, Kingston, Ont. K7L 3N6; 1841; *; med, mus; D; L
  Queen's Theological C., Kingston, Ont. K7L 3N6; 1912
Red Deer C., Red Deer, Alta. T4N 5H5; 403-342-3200; non-degree
Red River Comm. C., Winnipeg, Man. R3H 0J9; 204-632-2380; non-degree
Regent C. (see under **British Columbia, U. of**)
Regina Plains Comm. C., Regina, Sask. S4P 1X7; 306-569-3811; non-degree
Regina, U. of, Regina, Sask. S4S 0A2; 1907; *; art, bus, ed, engr; D; M
  Canadian Theological C., Regina, Sask. S4T 0H8
  Saskatchewan Indian Federated C., Regina, Sask. S4S 0A2
Regis C. (see under **Toronto, U. of**)
Renison C. (see under **Waterloo, U. of**)
Rimouski, C. de, Rimouski, Que. G5L 4H6; 418-723-1880; non-degree
Rivière du Loup, C. de, Rivière du Loup, Que. G5R 1S8; 418-862-6903; non-degree
Rosemont, C. de, Montreal, Que. H1X 2S9; 514-376-1620
Royal Conservatory of Music (see under **Toronto, U. of**)
Royal Military C. of Canada, Kingston, Ont. K7L 2W3; 1874; *; engr; Mst; S
Royal Military C. of St. Jean, Saint-Jean, Que. J0J 1R0; 1952; S
Royal Roads Military C., Victoria, B.C. V0S 1B0; 1942; S
Ryerson Polytechnical Inst., Toronto, Ont. M5B 1E8; 1948; *; art, bus; L
Saguenay-Lac-St.-Jean, C. Régional du, Jonquière, Que. G7S 4R8; 418-548-7191; non-degree
St. Andrew's C. (Man.; see under **Manitoba, U. of**)
St. Andrew's C. (Sask.; see under **Saskatchewan, U. of**)
St. Andrew's Hall (see under **British Columbia, U. of**)
St. Anne U., Church Point, N.S. B0W 1M0; RC; 1890; *; bus, ed; S
St. Augustine's Seminary (see under **St. Paul U.**)
St. Boniface, U.C. of (see under **Manitoba, U. of**)
St. Clair C. of Applied Arts and Technology, Windsor, Ont. N9A 6S4; 519-966-1656; non-degree
St. Francis Xavier U., Antigonish, N.S. B2G 1C0; RC; 1853; *; Mst; S
Saint-Hyacinthe, C. de, Saint-Hyacinthe, Que. J2S 7G7; 514-773-6800; non-degree
Saint-Jean-Sur-Richelieu, C., Saint-Jean, Que. J3B 7B1; 514-347-5301; non-degree
Saint-Jérôme, C. de, St. Jérôme, Que. J7Z 4V2; 514-436-1580; non-degree
St. Jerome's C., U. of, Waterloo, Ont. N2L 3G3; RC; 1864; S
St. John's C., Winnipeg, Man. R3T 2M5; Anglican; 1849; Mst; S
St. Joseph's C. (see under **Alberta, U. of**)
Saint-Laurent, C. de, Montreal, Que. H4L 3X7: 514-747-6521; non-degree
St. Lawrence C. of Applied Arts and Technology, Kingston, Ont. K7L 5A6; 613-544-5400; non-degree
St. Mark's C. (see under **British Columbia, U. of**)
St. Mary's U., Halifax, N.S. B3H 3C3; 1802; *; bus, ed, engr; Mst; M
  Ignatius C., Guelph, Ont. N1H 6N6; RC; 1913; for men
St. Michael's C., U. of, Toronto, Ont. M5J 1J4; RC; 1852; *; bus; D; S
St. Paul U., Ottawa, Ont. K1S 1C4; RC; 1848; D; S
  St. Augustine's Seminary, Scarborough, Ont. M1M 1M3; RC
St. Paul's C., Winnipeg, Man. R3T 2M6; RC; 1926; Mst; S
St. Paul's C. (see under **Waterloo, U. of**)
St. Peter's C. (see under **Saskatchewan, U. of**)
St. Stephen's C. (see under **Alberta, U. of**)
St. Thomas More C., Saskatoon, Sask. S7N 0W6; RC; 1936; *; art, mus; S
St. Thomas U., Fredericton, N.B. E3B 5G3; RC; 1910; ed; S
Sainte-Foy, C. de, Sainte-Foy, Que. G1V 1T3; 418-657-3511; non-degree
Saskatchewan Indian Comm. C., Saskatoon, Sask. S7K 3S9: 306-244-4444; non-degree
Saskatchewan Indian Federated C. (see under **Regina, U. of**)
Saskatchewan Technical Inst., Moose Jaw, Sask. S6H 4R4; 306-693-8222; non-degree
Saskatchewan, U. of, Saskatoon, Sask. S7N 0W0; 1907; *; med, mus; D; L
  Emmanuel and St. Chad, C. of, Saskatoon, Sask. S7N 0W6; Anglican; 1879
  Lutheran Theological Seminary, Saskatoon, Sask. S7N 0X3; 1965
  St. Andrew's C., Saskatoon, Sask. S7N 0W3; United Church; 1912
  St. Peter's C., Muenster, Sask. S0K 2Y0; RC; 1924
Saskatoon Region Comm. C., Saskatoon, Sask. S7K 0J4; 306-244-1114; non-degree
Sault C. of Applied Arts and Technology, Sault Ste. Marie, Ont. P6A 5L3; 705-494-2050; non-degree
Selkirk C., Castelgar, B.C. V1N 3J1; 604-365-7292; non-degree
Seneca C. of Applied Arts and Technology, Willowdale, Ont. M2J 2X5; 416-491-5050; non-degree
Sept-Îles, C. de, Sept-Îles, Que. G4R 1H2; 418-962-9848; non-degree
Shawinigan, C. de, Shawinigan, Que. G9N 6V8; 819-539-6401; non-degree
Sherbrooke, C. de, Sherbrooke, Que. J1H 5M7; 819-563-3150; non-degree
Sherbrooke, U. of, Sherbrooke, Que. J1K 2R1; 1954; *; law, med; D; L
Sheridan C. of Applied Arts and Technology, Oakville, Ont. L6H 2L1; 416-845-9430; non-degree
Simon Fraser U., Burnaby, B.C. V5A 1S6; 1963; *; bus, ed; D; L
Sir Sandford Fleming C. of Applied Arts and Technology, Peterborough, Ont. K9H 2X8; 705-743-5620; non-degree
Sir Wilfred Grenfell C. (see under **Memorial U. of Newfoundland**)
Sorel-Tracy, C. de, Sorel, Que. J3P 1J6; 514-742-4557; non-degree
South East Region Comm. C., Weyburn, Sask. S4H 2L1; 306-842-7417; non-degree
Southern Alberta Inst. of Technology, Calgary, Alta. T2M 0L4; 403-284-8841; non-degree
Sudbury, U. of, Sudbury, Ont. P3E 2C6; RC; 1913; S
Technical U. of Nova Scotia, Halifax, N.S. B3J 2X4; 1907; *; arch, engr; D; S
Tele-University (Télé-université; see under Quebec, U. of)
Thomas More Inst. for Adult Education (see under **Bishop's U.**)
Thorneloe U. (see under **Laurentian U. of Sudbury**)
Trent U., Peterborough, Ont. K9J 7B8; 1963; *; Mst; M
Trinity C., U. of (fed. **Toronto, U. of**), Toronto, Ont. M5S 1H8; 1852; *; D; S
Toronto School of Theology (see under **Toronto, U. of**)
Toronto, U. of, Toronto, Ont. M5S 1A1; 1827; *; law, lib, med, mus; D; L
  Royal Conservatory of Music, Toronto, Ont. M5S 1W2; 1886
  Toronto School of Theology, Toronto, Ont. M5S 2B8; 1969; includes six colleges federated with U. of Toronto (Emmanuel C. of Victoria U., Knox C., Regis C., St. Michael's C. theology faculty, Trinity C. divinity faculty, Wycliffe C.)
Trois-Rivières, C. de, Trois-Rivières, Que. G9A 5E6; 818-376-1721; non-degree
United Theological C. of Montreal (see under **McGill U.**)
Valleyfield, C. de, Salaberry-de-Valleyfield, Que. J6T 1X6; 514-373-9441; non-degree
Vancouver Comm. C., Vancouver, B.C. V6B !N2; 604-688-1111; non-degree
Vancouver School of Theology (see under **British Columbia, U. of**)
Vanier C., St. Laurent, Que. H4L 3X9; 514-333-3811; non-degree
Victoria U. (fed. **Toronto, U. of**), Toronto, Ont. M5S 1K7; 1836; *; bus; D; M
Victoria, U. of, Victoria, B.C. V8W 2Y2; 1903; *; art, ed, law, mus; D; M
Victoriaville, C. de, Victoriaville, Que. G6P 4B3; 819-758-6401; non-degree
Vieux Montréal, C. du, Montreal, Que. H2X 3M8; 514-284-7255; non-degree
Wascana Inst. of Applied Arts and Sciences, Regina, Sask. S4P 3A3; 306-565-4356; non-degree
Waterloo Lutheran Seminary (see under **Wilfrid Laurier U.**)
Waterloo, U. of, Waterloo, Ont. N2L 3G1; 1957; *; arch, engr; D; L
  Conrad Grebel C., Waterloo, Ont. N2L 3G6; Mennonite; 1961
  Renison C., Waterloo, Ont. N2L 3G4; Anglican; 1959
  St. Paul's C., Waterloo, Ont. N2L 3G1; United Church 1963
West Side Comm C., Beuval, Sask. S0M 0G0; 306-288-2113; non-degree
Western Ontario, U. of, London, Ont. N6A 3K7; 1878; *; med, mus; D; L
Wilfrid Laurier U., Waterloo, Ont. N2L 3C5; 1911; *; bus, mus; Mst; M
  Waterloo Lutheran Seminary, Waterloo, Ont. N2L 3C5; 1911
Windsor, U. of, Windsor, Ont. N9B 3P4; 1857; *; engr, law, mus; Mst; L
  Assumption U., Windsor, Ont. N9B 3P4; 1857
  Canterbury C., Windsor, Ont. N9B 3P4; Anglican; 1957
  Holy Redeemer C., Windsor, Ont. N9B 3P4; RC; 1956; for men
  Iona C., Windsor, Ont. N9B 3P4; United Church; 1964
Winnipeg, U. of, Winnipeg, Man. R3B 2E9; 1871; *; ed; Mst; M
  Mennonite Brethren C. of Arts, Winnipeg, Man. R2L 1L1; 1944
Wycliffe C. (see under **Toronto, U. of**)
York U., Downsview, Ont. M3J 1P3; 1959; *; art, bus, law; D; L

ENGLISH GIVEN NAMES

Masculine Names

A

Aar·on (âr′ən, ar′-) < Heb: ? light.
Abe (āb), short for *Abraham.*
A·bel (ā′bəl) < Heb, of uncert. meaning.
Ab·ner (ab′nər) < Heb: of light.
A·bra·ham (ā′brə ham′, -həm) < Heb: father of the people.
A·bram (ā′brəm) < Heb: exalted father. Also, **Avram.**
Ab·sa·lom (ab′sə ləm) < Heb: father of peace.
Ad·am (ad′əm) < Heb: earth.
Ad·olf (ad′olf, ā′dolf; *Ger.* ä′dôlf) < Gmc: noble + wolf. Also, **Ad·olph** (ad′olf, ā′dolf), **A·dol·phus** (ə dol′fəs).
A·dri·an (ā′drē ən) < L: of the Adriatic Sea.
Al (al), short for *Albert.*
Al·an (al′ən) < Celt: ? harmony. Also, **Al′lan, Al′len.**
Al·as·tair (al′ə stər, -stâr′), Scot form of *Alexander.* Also, **Al·is·ter** (al′i stər).
Al·ban (ôl′bən, al′-) < L: man of Alba. Also, **Al·ben** (al′bən), **Al·bin** (al′bin).
Al·bert (al′bərt) < F or L < Gmc: noble + bright.
Al·den (ôl′dᵊn) < OE: old + friend. Also, **Ald·win** (ôld′win).
Al·do (ôl′dō, al′-, äl′-) < It < Gmc: rich + old.
Al·ec (al′ik), short for *Alexander.* Also, **Al′eck.**
Al·ex (al′iks), short for *Alexander.*
Al·ex·an·der (al′ig zan′dər, -zän′-) < Gk: helper of men.
A·lex·is (ə lek′sis) < Gk: helper.
Al·fie (al′fē), shortened dim. of *Alfred.* Also, **Alf.**
Al·fred (al′frid) < OE: elf + counsel.
Al·ger·non (al′jər nən) < ONF: whiskered.
A·lon·so (ə lon′zō; *Sp.* ä lôn′sô), Sp var. of *Alphonso.* Also, **A·lon′zo.**
Al·o·y·sius (al′ō ish′əs) < L < Gmc: famous warrior.
Al·phon·so (al fon′sō, -zō) < Sp < Gmc: noble + ready. Also, **Al·phonse** (al′fons; *Fr.* al fôɴs′).
Al·vin (al′vin) < OE: elf + friend. Also, **Al·win** (al′win), **Al·van** (al′vən).
Am·brose (am′brōz) < Gk: immortal.
A·mos (ā′məs) < Heb: burden.
An·a·tole (an′ə tōl′; *Fr.* a na tôl′) < Gk: sunrise.
An·dré (äɴ dʀe′), F form of *Andrew.*
An·drew (an′drōō) < Gk: manly.
An·dy (an′dē), shortened dim. of *Andrew.*
An·gus (ang′gəs) < Celt: ? one choice.
An·selm (an′selm) < Gmc: god + helmet.
An·tho·ny (an′thə nē, an′tə-) < L *Antonius,* Roman family name. Also, **An·to·ny** (an′tə nē).
An·toine (an′twän; *Fr.* äɴ twaɴ′), F form of *Anthony.*
Ar·chi·bald (är′chə bôld′, -bəld) < Gmc: distinguished + bold.
Ar·chie (är′chē), shortened dim. of *Archibald.*
Ar·mand (är′mənd; *Fr.* ar mäɴ′), F form of *Herman.*
Ar·nold (är′nᵊld) < Gmc: eagle + power.
Art (ärt), short for *Arthur.* Also, **Art·ie** (är′tē).
Ar·thur (är′thər), of uncert. orig. and meaning.
Au·brey (ô′brē) < F < Gmc: elf + ruler.
Au·gus·tine (ô′gə stēn′, ô gus′tin), dim. of *Augustus.*
Au·gus·tus (ô gus′təs) < L: venerable, majestic. Also, **Au′gust.**
Aus·tin (ôs′tin), var. of *Augustine.*
A·ver·y (ā′və rē) < OE: elf + favor.
A·vram (ā′vrəm), var. of **Abram.**
Ayl·mer (āl′mər) < OE: noble + famous.

B

Bald·win (bôld′win) < OE: bold + friend.
Bar·na·bas (bär′nə bəs) < Heb: son of exhortation. Also, **Bar·na·by** (bär′nə bē).
Bar·ney (bär′nē), shortened dim. of *Barnabas* or *Bernard.*
Bar·rett (bar′it) < Gmc: bear + rule. Also, **Bar′ret.**
Bar·ry (bar′ē) < Ir: spear.
Bar·thol·o·mew (bär thol′ə myōō′) < Heb: son of Talmai.
Bas·il (baz′əl, bas′-) < Gk: royal.
Bay·ard (bā′ərd), F family name, ? *bay* brown + suffix *-ard.*
Ben (ben), short for *Benjamin.* Also, **Ben·ny** (ben′ē).
Ben·e·dict (ben′i dikt) < L: blessed.
Ben·ja·min (ben′jə min) < Heb: son of the right.
Ben·nett (ben′it), var. of *Benedict.* Also, **Ben′net.**
Ber·nard (bûr′nərd, bər närd′) < Gmc: bear + hardy. Also, **Bar·nard** (bär′nərd).
Bert (bûrt), short for *Albert, Herbert, Bertram.* Also, **Bert·ie** (bûr′tē), **Burt.**
Ber·tram (bûr′trəm) < Gmc: bright + raven.
Ber·trand (bûr′trənd; *Fr.* ber träɴ′), F var. of *Bertram.*
Bev·er·ley (bev′ər lē) < OE: (dweller at the) beaver meadow.
Bill (bil), short for *William.* Also, **Bil·ly, Bil·lie** (bil′ē).
Blair (blâr) < Celt: (dweller near the) field.
Bob (bob), short for *Robert.* Also, **Bob·by, Bob·bie** (bob′ē).
Bon·i·face (bon′ə fās′) < L: doer of good.
Bo·ris (bōr′is, bôr′-) < Slav: fighter.
Boyd (boid), family name < Gael: light.
Brett (bret) < OE: a Breton, native of Brittany.
Bri·an (brī′ən) ? < Celt, of uncert. meaning. Also, **Bry′an, Bry·ant** (brī′ənt).
Brice (brīs) ? < Celt, of uncert. meaning. Also, **Bryce.**
Bruce (brōōs), Norman family name *de Bruce,* after *Brieuse* in Normandy.
Bru·no (brōō′nō) < It < Gmc: brown.
Burl (bûrl), short for *Burleigh.*
Bur·leigh (bûr′lē) < OE: hill + field.
Burt (bûrt), var. of *Bert.*
Butch (bŏŏch), boy's nickname of unknown orig.
By·ron (bī′rən), a family name < OF: a cowman.

C

Cad·wal·la·der (kad wol′ə dər) < Welsh: arranger of battle.
Cae·sar (sē′zər), Roman family name.
Ca·leb (kā′ləb) < Heb: dog.
Cal·vin (kal′vin) < L: bald.
Carl (kärl), var. of *Charles.* Also, **Karl.**
Car·lyle (kär līl′) < OE, of uncert. meaning.
Car·roll (kar′əl) < Roman family name *Carolus,* L form of *Charles.* Also, **Car′ol.**
Car·y (kâr′ē, kar′ē), a family name. Also, **Car′ey.**
Cas·ey (kā′sē) < Ir: brave. Also, **Case.**
Cas·par (kas′pər), one of the Three Wise Men; < ? Also, **Cas′per.**
Ce·cil (sē′səl *or, esp. Brit.,* ses′əl) < *Caecilius,* Roman family name.
Ced·ric (sed′rik, sē′drik) < Celt: chief.
Chad (chad), of uncert. orig. and meaning.
Charles (chärlz; *Fr.* sharl) < F < Gmc: man.
Chaun·cey (chôn′sē, chän′-) < F, of uncert. meaning.
Ches·ter (ches′tər) < OE: family name < L *castra* camp.
Chris·tian (kris′chən) < L < Gk: Christian.
Chris (kris), short for *Christopher.*
Chris·to·pher (kris′tə fər) < Gk: Christ-bearer.
Chuck (chuk), var. of *Charles.*
Clar·ence (klar′əns) < L: clear one.
Claude (klôd; *Fr.* klōd) < *Claudius,* Roman family name. Also, **Claud, Clau·di·us** (klô′dē əs).
Clay·ton (klā′tən) < OE place-name: clay town.
Clem·ent (klem′ənt) < OF < L: kind, merciful. Also, **Clem.**
Clif·ford (klif′ərd) < OE place-name: cliff crossing. Also, **Cliff.**
Clif·ton (klif′tən) < OE place-name: cliff town.
Clin·ton (klin′tᵊn) < OE: (dweller in the) hill town. Also, **Clint.**
Clive (klīv) < OE family name: cliff.
Clyde (klīd) < Scot family name, after the river *Clyde.*
Col·in (kol′in, kō′lin), Scot var. of *Colum,* ? < L: dove.
Con·rad (kon′rad) < Gmc: bold + counsel. Also, **Konrad.**
Con·roy (kon′roi) < OF: wise king.
Con·stan·tine (kon′stən tēn′, -tīn′) < L: constant, steadfast.
Cor·ey (kōr′ē, kôr′ē), of uncert. meaning and orig. Also, **Cor′y.**
Cor·nel·ius (kôr nēl′yəs), Roman family name.
Cos·mo (koz′mō; *It.* kôz′mô) < It < L < Gk: order, adornment.
Craig (krāg) < Scot family name: crag.
Cur·tis (kûr′tis) < OF: courteous.
Cuth·bert (kuth′bərt) < OE: famous + bright.
Cy (sī), short for *Cyrus.*
Cyr·il (sir′əl) < Gk: lord.
Cy·rus (sī′rəs), name of Persian king.

D

Dan·iel (dan′yəl) < Heb: the Lord is my judge.
Dan·ny (dan′ē), shortened dim. of *Daniel.* Also, **Dan.**
Da·ri·us (də rī′əs, dar′ē əs) < L < Gk < Pers: possessing wealth.
Dar·rell (dar′əl) < OE: dear. Also, **Dar′yl.**
Da·vid (dā′vid) < Heb: beloved.
Da·vy (dā′vē), dim. of *David.* Also, **Da′vey, Dave.**
Dean (dēn) < OE family name: valley. Also, **Deane.**
De·me·tri·us (də mē′trē əs) < Gk: of Demeter, goddess of fertility and harvests.
Den·nis (den′is) < OF < Gk: of Dionysus (god of wine). Also, **Den′is, Den·ny** (den′ē).
Der·ek (der′ik), short for *Theodoric.*
De·Witt (də wit′) < Flem family name: white.
Dex·ter (dek′stər) < L: on the right.
Dick (dik), short for *Richard.*
Dirk (dûrk), var. of *Derek.* Also, **Dirck.**
Dom·i·nick (dom′ə nik) < L: of the Lord. Also, **Dom′i·nic.**
Don (don), short for *Donald.* Also, **Don·nie** (don′ē).
Don·ald (don′ᵊld) < Celt: world + power.
Do·ri·an (dōr′ē ən, dôr′-) < Gk: a Dorian.
Doug·las (dug′ləs) < Scot: black water.
Drew (drōō) < OF < Gmc: trusty.
Dud·ley (dud′lē) < OE place-name: dry field.
Duke (dōōk, dyōōk) < L: leader.
Dun·can (dung′kən) < Scot: brown soldier.
Dun·stan (dun′stən) < OE: stone hill.
Dwight (dwīt) < OE, of uncert. meaning.

E

Earl (ûrl) < OE: noble.
Eb·en (eb′ən), short for *Ebenezer.*
Eb·en·e·zer (eb′ə nē′zər) < Heb: stone of help.
Ed (ed), short for *Edward, Edgar, Edwin.* Also, **Ed·die** (ed′ē).

Ed·gar (ed′gər) < OE: rich, happy + spear.
Ed·mond (ed′mənd) < OE: rich, happy + protection. Also, **Ed′mund.**
Ed·sel (ed′səl) < OE: rich + hall.
Ed·ward (ed′wərd) < OE: rich, happy + guardian.
Ed·win (ed′win) < OE: rich, happy + friend.
Eg·bert (eg′bərt) < OE: bright sword.
Ei·nar (ī′nər, ī′när) < Gmc: warrior chief.
El·bert (el′bərt), var. of *Albert.*
El·dred (el′drid) < OE: old in counsel.
E·li (ē′lī) < Heb: height. Also, **E′ly.**
E·li·as (i lī′əs), Gk form of *Elijah.*
El·i·hu (el′ə hyo͞o, i lī′hyo͞o) < Heb: the Lord is God.
E·li·jah (i lī′jə), var. of *Elihu.*
El·i·ot (el′ē ət, el′yət), var. of *Elias.* Also, **El′li·ott, El′li·ot.**
E·li·sha (i lī′shə) < Heb: the Lord is salvation.
El·lis (el′is), var. of *Elias.*
El·mer (el′mər), var. of *Aylmer.*
E·man·u·el (i man′yo͞o əl) < Heb: God is with us. Also, **Em·man′u·el, Im·manuel.**
Em·er·y (em′ə rē) < Gmc: industrious ruler. Also, **Em·er·ic** (em′ər ik).
É·mile (ā mēl′; *Fr.* ā mēl′) < F < Gmc < L: industrious. Also, **Em·il** (em′il, ē′mil, ā′mil; *Ger.* ā′mēl).
E·noch (ē′nək) < Heb: teacher.
En·ri·co (en rē′kō; *It.* en ʀē′kô), It form of *Henry.*
Eph·raim (ef′rəm, ē′frē əm, ē′frəm) < Heb: very fruitful.
E·ras·mus (i raz′məs) < Gk: beloved.
E·ras·tus (i ras′təs) < Gk: lovable.
Er·ic (er′ik) < Scand, of uncert. meaning. Also, **Er′ik.**
Er·nest (ûr′nist) < OE: vigor, intent. Also, **Er·nie** (ûr′nē).
Er·win (ûr′win), var. of *Irving.*
E·than (ē′thən) < Heb: strength.
Eth·el·bert (eth′əl bûrt′) < OE: noble + bright.
Eth·el·red (eth′əl red′) < OE: noble + counsel.
Eu·gene (yo͞o jēn′, yo͞o′jēn) < Gk: wellborn.
Eus·tace (yo͞o′stis) < L, prob. < Gk: steadfast.
Ev·an (ev′ən), Welsh form of *John.*
Ev·er·ard (ev′ə rärd′) < Gmc: boar + hard.
Ev·er·ett (ev′ər it, ev′rit), var. of *Everard.*
Ew·an (yo͞o′ən), var. of *Evan.*
E·ze·ki·el (i zē′kē əl) < Heb: God strengthens.
Ez·ra (ez′rə) < Heb: help.

F

Fe·lix (fē′liks) < L: happy, lucky.
Fer·di·nand (fûr′dᵊnand′) < Sp < Gmc: bold peace.
Floyd (floid), var. of *Lloyd.*
Fran·cis (fran′sis) < OF: Frenchman.
Frank (frangk), short for *Francis.*
Frank·lin (frangk′lin) < Gmc: freeholder.
Fred (fred), short for *Frederick.* Also, **Fred·dy, Fred·die** (fred′ē).
Fred·er·ick (fred′rik, -ər ik) < Gmc: peace + ruler. Also, **Fred′er·ic.**
Fritz (frits), G dim. of *Friedrich* (= *Frederick*).

G

Ga·bri·el (gā′brē əl) < Heb: man of God. Also, **Gabe.**
Ga·ma·li·el (gə mā′lē əl, -māl′yəl) < Heb: the Lord is my reward.
Gard·ner (gärd′nər) < ME < OF: gardener.
Gar·rett (gar′it) < OE: powerful with the spear.
Garth (gärth) < ME < ON: protector of the garden.
Gar·y (gar′ē) < OE: spear bearer. Also, **Gar′ry.**
Gas·ton (gas′tən; *Fr.* gas tôn′) < F, of uncert. meaning.
Gene (jēn), short for *Eugene.*
Geof·frey (jef′rē) < OF < Gmc: divine peace. Also, **Jeffrey.**
George (jôrj) < Gk: farmer.
Ger·ald (jer′əld) < Gmc: spear + rule.
Ge·rard (jə rärd′), var. of *Gerald.*
Ger·ry (jer′ē), shortened dim. of *Gerald.*
Gid·e·on (gid′ē ən) < Heb: great destroyer.
Gif·ford (gif′ərd) < Gmc: ? brave gift.
Gil·bert (gil′bərt) < ONF < Gmc: pledge + bright.
Giles (jīlz) < F < L *Aegidius* < Gk: shieldbearer.
Glen (glen) < Celt: (dweller in the) glen.
God·frey (god′frē) < ONF < Gmc: god + peace.
God·win (god′win) < OE: good friend.
Gor·don (gôr′dən) < Scot family name < OE: round hill.
Gra·ham (grā′əm), a family name, prob. < OE: gray home.
Grant (grant, gränt) < ONF < L: large, great.
Greg·o·ry (greg′ə rē) < Gk: watchful. Also, **Greg.**
Grif·fin (grif′in) < Welsh, ? ult. from Roman name *Rufus:* red. Also, **Grif·fith** (grif′ith).
Gus (gus), short for *Augustus.*
Gus·ta·vus (gus tā′vəs, -tä′-) < L < Gmc: staff of God. Also, **Gus·taf** (*Swed.* gus′täv; *Ger.* go͝os′täf), **Gus·tave** (*Fr.* gʏs tav′).
Guy (gī; *Fr.* gē) < F < Gmc: woods.

H

Hal (hal), short for *Henry, Harold.*
Hank (hangk), short for *Henry.*
Han·ni·bal (han′ə bəl) < L < Sem: grace of Baal.
Har·old (har′əld) < OE < ON: army + power.
Har·ry (har′ē), var. of *Henry, Harold.*
Har·vey (här′vē) < OE < Gmc: army + battle.
Hec·tor (hek′tər) < Gk: ? holding fast.
Hen·ry (hen′rē) < OE < Gmc: home + kingdom.
Her·bert (hûr′bərt) < OE: army + bright.
Her·man (hûr′mən) < OE: army + man. Also, **Herm.**
Hew·ett (hyo͞o′it) < OE: clearing, cutting.
Hil·a·ry (hil′ə rē) < L: cheerful.
Hi·ram (hī′rəm) < Heb: noble.
Hodge (hoj), var. of *Roger.*
Ho·mer (hō′mər), name of Gk epic poet.
Hor·ace (hôr′is, hor′-) < *Horatius,* Roman family name.
Ho·ra·tio (hə rā′shē ō′, hō-, hô-), var. of *Horace.*
How·ard (hou′ərd) < OF < Gmc: brave heart. Also, **How·ie** (hou′ē).
Hoyt (hoit) < Gmc: glee.
Hu·bert (hyo͞o′bərt) < Gmc: mind + bright.
Hugh (hyo͞o) < ONF < Gmc: heart, mind.
Hu·go (hyo͞o′gō), var. of *Hugh.*
Hum·bert (hum′bərt) < Gmc: high + bright.
Hum·phrey (hum′frē) < ONF < Gmc: high + peace.
Hun·ting·ton (hun′ting tən) < OE family name: hunting estate.
Hy (hī), short for *Hyman.*
Hy·man (hī′mən), var. of Heb *Chaim:* life.

I

I·an (ē′ən, ē′än, ī′ən), Scot form of *John.*
Ich·a·bod (ik′ə bod′) < Heb: without honor.
Ig·na·tius (ig nā′shəs) < L < Gk: fiery. Also, **Ig·nace** (ig′näts; *Fr.* ē nyas′).
Im·man·u·el (i man′yo͞o əl), var. of *Emanuel.*
In·gram (ing′grəm) < Gmc, of uncert. meaning.
I·ra (ī′rə) < Heb: watchful.
Ir·ving (ûr′ving), a family name < a place name in Ayrshire or Dumfriesshire. Also, **Ir·vin** (ûr′vin).
Ir·win (ûr′win), var. of *Irving.*
I·saac (ī′zək) < Heb: laughter.
I·sai·ah (ī zā′ə, ī zī′ə) < Heb: the Lord's salvation.
Is·i·dore (iz′ə dōr′, -dôr′) < Gk: gift of Isis.
Is·ra·el (iz′rē əl, -rēl) < Heb: he who strives with God.
I·van (ī′vən; *Russ.* ē vän′), Russ form of *John.*
I·vor (ē′vər, ī′vər) < Scot: ? one who carries the bow.

J

Ja·bez (jā′biz) < Heb, of uncert. meaning.
Jack (jak), short for *Jacob;* var. of *John.*
Jack·son (jak′sən), son of Jack.
Ja·cob (jā′kəb) < Heb: supplanter.
Jacques (zhäk), F form of *Jack.*
James (jāmz), var. of *Jacob* < OF *Jacomus* < L *Jacobus* < Heb.
Jar·vis (jär′vis) < ONF < Gmc: spear + vassal. Also, **Jer·vis** (jûr′vis).
Ja·son (jā′sən) < Gk, of uncert. orig. and meaning.
Jas·per (jas′pər), var. of *Caspar.*
Jay (jā), short for *Jacob, James.*
Jed (jed), short for *Jedediah.*
Je·de·di·ah (je′di dī′ə) < Heb: God is my friend.
Jeff (jef), short for *Jeffrey.*
Jef·frey (jef′rē), var. of *Geoffrey.*
Je·hu (jē′hyo͞o) < Heb: He is God.
Jeph·thah (jef′thə) < Heb: opposer.
Jer·e·mi·ah (jer′ə mī′ə) < Heb: God is high. Also, **Jer·e·my** (jer′ə mē).
Je·rome (jə rōm′) < Gk: sacred name.
Jer·ry (jer′ē), shortened dim. of *Gerald, Gerard, Jeremiah, Jerome.*
Jes·se (jes′ē) < Heb: God exists. Also, **Jess** (jes).
Jim (jim), short for *James.* Also, **Jim·my, Jim·mie** (jim′ē).
Job (jōb) < Heb: persecuted.
Jock (jok), Scot form of *Jack.*
Joe (jō), short for *Joseph.*
Jo·el (jō′əl) < Heb: the Lord is God.
John (jon) < Heb: God is gracious. Also, **John·ny, John·nie** (jon′ē).
Jo·nah (jō′nə) < Heb: dove. Also, **Jo·nas** (jō′nəs).
Jon·a·than (jon′ə thən) < Heb: God gave.
Jo·seph (jō′zəf, -səf) < Heb: increaser.
Josh·u·a (josh′o͞o ə) < Heb: God is salvation. Also, **Josh.**
Jo·si·ah (jō sī′ə) < Heb: God supports.
Ju·dah (jo͞o′də) < Heb: praised.
Jude (jo͞od) < Heb: praise. Also, **Ju·das** (jo͞o′dəs).
Jul·ian (jo͞ol′yən), var. of *Julius.*
Jul·ius (jo͞ol′yəs), a Roman family name. Also, **Jules** (jo͞olz; *Fr.* zhʏl).
Jus·tin (jus′tin) < L: just.

K

Karl (kärl; *Ger.* käʀl), G var. of *Charles.* Also, **Carl.**
Kay (kā), of uncert. meaning and orig.
Keith (kēth) < Scot place name < ?
Ken·neth (ken′ith) < Ir: handsome. Also, **Ken.**
Kent (kent) < OE name of a county in England.
Kev·in (kev′in) ? var. of *Kenneth.*
Kirk (kûrk) < Scot: church.
Kit (kit), short for *Christopher.*
Kon·rad (kon′rad), var. of *Conrad.*
Kyle (kīl) < Welsh: narrow channel.

L

Lam·bert (lam′bərt) < OF < Gmc: land + bright.
Lance (lans) < Gmc: of the land.
Lan·ce·lot (lan′sə lət, -lot′, län′-), F dim. of *Lance.*
Lane (lān), from common noun.
Lar·ry (lar′ē), shortened dim. of *Lawrence.*
Law·rence (lôr′əns, lor′-) < L: a man of Laurentium. Also, **Lau′rence.**
Lee (lē) < OE family name: field, lea.
Leigh (lē), var. of *Lee.*
Lem·u·el (lem′yo͞o əl) < Heb: devoted to God.
Le·o (lē′ō) < L < Gk: lion.
Le·on (lē′on), var. of *Leo.*
Leon·ard (len′ərd) < Gmc: lion + hardy.
Le·on·i·das (lē on′i dəs) < Gk: lionlike.
Le·o·pold (lē′ə pōld′) < Gmc: people + bold.
Le·roy (lə roi′, lē′roi) < OFr: the king. Also, **Le Roy.**
Les·lie (les′lē, lez′-) < Scot place-name < ? Also, **Les′ley.**
Les·ter (les′tər), var. of *Leicester,* place-name in England.
Le·vi (lē′vī) < Heb: a joining.
Lew (lo͞o), short for *Louis.* Also, **Lou.**
Lew·is (lo͞o′is), var. of *Louis.*
Li·nus (lī′nəs) < Gk: flaxen (hair).
Li·o·nel (lī′ə nəl, -nel′), dim. of *Leon.*
Llew·el·lyn (lo͞o el′in) < Welsh: lionlike, leader.
Lloyd (loid) < Welsh: gray.
Lou (lo͞o), short for *Louis.*
Lou·is (lo͞o′is, lo͞o′ē; *Fr.* lwē) < F < Gmc: loud battle. Also, **Lewis.**
Low·ell (lō′əl) < F < Gmc: little wolf. Also, **Lov·ell** (luv′əl).
Lu·cas (lo͞o′kəs), var. of *Luke.*
Lu·cian (lo͞o′shən) < L < Gk, of uncert. meaning. Confused with *Lucius.*
Lu·cius (lo͞o′shəs) < L: bringing light.
Lud·wig (lud′wig; *Ger.* lo͞ot′viᴋʜ, lo͞od′-) < Gmc: famous warrior.
Luke (lo͞ok) < Gk: man of Lucania.
Lu·ther (lo͞o′thər) < Gmc: famous + army.
Lyle (līl) < ME < MF: (man of) the island.
Lynn (lin) < Welsh place-name: lake.

M

Mac (mak) < Gael: son. Also, **Mack.**
Mal·colm (mal′kəm) < Gael: disciple of St. Columba.
Mar·cus (mär′kəs) < L, prob. < *Mars* (the god).
Ma·ri·o (mar′ē ō′, mär′-; It. mä′ʀyô) < Roman family name *Marius.*
Mar·i·on (mar′ē ən, mâr′-), masc. var. of *Mary.*
Mark (märk), var. of *Marcus.* Also, **Marc.**
Mar·ma·duke (mär′mə do͞ok′, -dyo͞ok′) < Celt: ? servant of Madoc.
Mar·shall (mär′shəl), from the noun in sense of "farrier." Also, **Mar′shal.**
Mar·tin (mär′tin) < L < *Mars* (the god). Also, **Mar·ty** (mär′tē).
Mar·vin (mär′vin) < Celt: sea friend.
Ma·son (mā′sən), from the common noun.
Matt (mat), short for *Matthew.* Also, **Mat·ty** (mat′ē).
Mat·thew (math′yo͞o) < Heb: gift of God.
Mau·rice (mô rēs′, môr′is, mor′-; *Fr.* mō ʀēs′) < F < L: the Moor.
Max (maks), short for *Maximilian.*
Max·i·mil·ian (mak′sə mil′yən) < Gmc < L *Maximus* + *Aemilianus.*
May·nard (mā′nərd, -närd) < Gmc: strong + hardy.
Mer·e·dith (mer′i dith) < Welsh, of uncert. meaning.
Mer·vin (mûr′vin), var. of *Marvin.*
Mi·cah (mī′kə), var. of *Michael.*
Mi·chael (mī′kəl) < Heb: Who is like the Lord?
Mick·ey (mik′ē), shortened dim. of *Michael.* Also, **Mick′y.**
Mike (mīk), short for *Michael.*
Miles (mīlz) < F < Gmc: merciful.
Mil·ton (mil′tᵊn), a family name, from a place-name: mill town.
Mitch·ell (mich′əl), var. of *Michael.*
Mon·roe (mən rō′), a family name < Celt: ? red swamp.
Mon·ta·gue (mon′tə gyo͞o′) < ONF family name < *Mont Aigu* in Normandy.
Mont·gom·er·y (mont gum′ə rē) < ONF family name < *Montgomerie* in Normandy.
Mor·gan (môr′gən) < Celt: ? sea dweller.
Mor·ris (môr′is, mor′-), var. of *Maurice.*
Mor·ti·mer (môr′tə mər) < ONF family name < *Mortimer* in Normandy.
Mor·ton (môr′tən), a family name, from a place-name: town on the moor. Also, **Mort, Mor·ty** (môr′tē).
Mose (mōz), short for *Moses.*
Mo·ses (mō′ziz, -zis) < Heb, of uncert. meaning.
Moss (môs, mos), var. of *Moses.*
Mur·doch (mûr′dok) < Gael: sea man.
Mur·ray (mûr′ē, mur′ē) < Scot family name < *Moray* in Scotland.
My·ron (mī′rən) < Gk: pleasant.

N

Na·hum (nā′həm) < Heb: comforter.
Nat (nat), short for *Nathan, Nathaniel.*
Na·than (nā′thən) < Heb: gift.
Na·than·iel (nə than′yəl) < Heb: gift of God. Also **Na·than′ael.**
Ned (ned), short for *Edward.*
Neil (nēl) ? < Ir: champion, or var. of *Nigel.* Also, **Neal.**
Ne·ro (nēr′ō), a Roman family name.
Nev·ille (nev′il) < ONF family name < *Neville* in Normandy. Also, **Nev′il.**
New·ton (no͞o′tᵊn, nyo͞o′-), a family name, from a place-name: new town.
Nich·o·las (nik′ə ləs) < Gk: victory + people.
Nick (nik), short for *Nicholas.* Also, **Nic, Nick·y** (nik′e).
Ni·gel (nī′jəl) < L *Nigellus:* black, dark.
No·ah (nō′ə) < Heb: rest.
No·am (nō′əm), var. of *Noah.*
No·el (nō′əl) < OF < L: birthday, Christmas Day.
Nor·man (nôr′mən) < OE: Northman.
Nor·ton (nôr′tᵊn) < OE family name < a place-name: north town.

O

O·ba·di·ah (ō′bə dī′ə) < Heb: servant of God.
Oc·ta·vi·us (ok tā′vē əs), Roman family name < L *octavus* eighth.
O·laf (ō′ləf; *Dan., Norw.* ō′läf; *Swed.* o͞o′läf, -läv) < Scand: forefather + offspring or heirloom.
Ol·i·ver (ol′ə vər) < F: ? olive tree.
O·mar (ō′mär) < Ar: builder, most high, richness, life.
Or·lan·do (ôr lan′dō; *It.* ôʀ län′dô), It form of *Roland.*
Or·son (ôr′sən) < Gmc: bearlike.
Os·bert (oz′bərt) < OE: god + bright.
Os·car (os′kər) < OE: god + spear.
Os·wald (oz′wəld) < OE: god + power.
Ot·to (ot′ō; *Ger.* ô′tō) < Gmc: rich.
Ow·en (ō′in) < Welsh: youth, young warrior, ? < L *Eugenius* (= *Eugene*).

P

Pat (pat), short for *Patrick.*
Pat·rick (pa′trik) < L: patrician.
Paul (pôl) < L: little.
Per·ci·val (pûr′sə vəl) < OF: pierce + valley. Also, **Per′ce·val.**
Per·cy (pûr′sē) < ONF family name < *Perci* in Normandy.
Per·ry (per′ē), a family name < ME *pery* pear tree.
Pete (pēt), short for *Peter.*
Pe·ter (pē′tər) < Gk: a stone.
Phil (fil), short for *Philip.*
Phil·ip (fil′ip) < Gk: lover of horses. Also, **Phil′lip.**
Phin·e·as (fin′ē əs) < Heb: serpent's mouth or oracle.
Pierce (pērs), var. of *Peter.* Also, **Pearce.**
Pip (pip), short for *Philip.*

Q

Quen·tin (kwen′tᵊn) < F < L *quintus* fifth. Also, **Quen′ton.**
Quin·cy (kwin′sē) < OF < L *quintus* fifth.

R

Ralph (ralf) < Scand: counsel + wolf.
Ram·sey (ram′zē) < Scand: wooded island.
Ran·dall (ran′dᵊl) < OE: shield + wolf. Also, **Ran′dal.**
Ran·dolph (ran′dolf, -dəlf), var. of *Randall.*
Ran·dy (ran′dē), shortened dim. of *Randolph.*
Ra·oul (ʀᴀ o͞ol′), F form of *Ralph.*
Ra·pha·el (raf′ē əl, rā′fēl, rä′fä el′) < Heb: healing of the Lord.
Ray (rā), short for *Raymond.*
Ray·mond (rā′mənd) < OF < Gmc: counsel + protection.
Reg·i·nald (rej′ə nəld) < OE: counsel + rule.
Reid (rēd) < OE: red. Also, **Read.**
Reu·ben (ro͞o′bin) < Heb: behold a son.
Rex (reks) < L: king.
Rey·nold (ren′əld), var. of *Reginald.*
Rich·ard (rich′ərd) < OF < Gmc: powerful + hard.
Rob (rob), short for *Robert.* Also, **Robbie** (rob′ē).
Rob·ert (rob′ərt) < OF < Gmc: glory + bright.
Rob·in (rob′in), shortened dim. of *Robert.*
Rod·er·ick (rod′ər ik, rod′rik) < Gmc: glory + ruler.
Rod·ney (rod′nē) < OE family name < *Rodney Stoke* in Somerset.
Rog·er (roj′ər) < ONF < Gmc: fame + spear.
Ro·land (rō′lənd) < OF < Gmc: glory + land.
Rolf (rolf) < Scand: glory + wolf. Also, **Rolph.**
Rol·lo (rol′ō), var. of *Rolf.*
Ron·ald (ron′əld) < Scand: counsel + rule.
Ros·coe (ros′kō) < Gmc: swift horse.
Ross (rôs, ros) < Welsh family name: ? hill.
Roy (roi) < Gael: red; confused with F *roi* king.
Ru·dolf (ro͞o′dolf; *Ger.* ʀo͞o′dôlf), G form of *Rolf.* Also, **Ru·dolph** (ro͞o′dolf).
Rud·yard (rud′yərd) < OF < Gmc: red + guarded.
Ru·fus (ro͞o′fəs) < L: red-headed.
Ru·pert (ro͞o′pərt), var. of *Robert* (through G *Rupprecht*).
Rus·sell (rus′əl) < OF, dim. of *roux* red.
Rus·ty (rus′tē), dim. of *Rust,* from OF *Rousset* red-headed.
Ruth·er·ford (ruth′ər fərd, ruth′-) < OE: (dweller near the) cattle crossing.

S

Sam (sam), short for *Samuel.*
Sam·son (sam′sən) < Heb: like the sun.
Sam·u·el (sam′yo͞o əl) < Heb: name of God.
Sand·er (san′dər), Scot var. of *Alexander.* Also, **San′dor.**
San·dy (san′dē), Scot dim. of *Alexander.*
Saul (sôl) < Heb: asked for.
Scott (skot) < OE family name: the Scot.
Sean (shôn), Ir form of *John.*
Se·bas·tian (si bas′chən) < L: man of Sebastia (in Pontus).
Se·lig (sē′lig, sel′ig; *Ger.* zā′liᴋʜ), var. of *Zelig.*
Seth (seth) < Heb: substitute.
Sey·mour (sē′mōr, -môr) < ONF family name < *St. Maur* in Normandy.
Shawn (shôn), Ir form of *John.*
Shel·don (shel′dən, -dᵊn) < OF family name < a place-name: level-top hill.
Sher·lock (shûr′lok) < OE: fair-haired.
Sid·ney (sid′nē), a family name, contr. of F *Saint Denis.* Also, **Sid.**
Sig·mund (sig′mənd; *Ger.* zēᴋʜ′mo͝ont) < Gmc: victory + protection.
Si·las (sī′ləs) < Gk, of uncert. meaning.
Sil·ves·ter (sil ves′tər) < L: of the woodland. Also, **Syl·ves′ter.**
Sim·e·on (sim′ē ən) < Heb: hear.
Si·mon (sī′mən), Gk form of *Simeon;* but confused with a Gk name: snub-nosed.
Sin·clair (sin klâr′), a family name, contr. of F *St. Clair.*
Sol·o·mon (sol′ə mən) < Heb: peaceful.
Spen·cer (spen′sər) < OE < L: dispenser (of provisions). Also, **Spence.**
Stan·ley (stan′lē) < OE family name < a place-name: stone field.
Ste·phen (stē′vən) < Gk: crown. Also, **Ste′ven.**
Steve (stēv), short for *Stephen.*
Stu·art (sto͞o′ərt, styo͞o′-) < OE: steward. Also, **Stew′art.**
Sum·ner (sum′nər) < ME < OF: summoner.

T

Ted (ted), short for *Edward;* but often used as short for *Theodore.*
Ter·ence (ter′əns), from a Roman family name; of uncert. meaning.
Ter·rel (ter′əl) < ME < OF: draw.
Ter·ry (ter′ē), short for *Terence.*
Thad·de·us (thad′ē əs) < Aram: praise.
The·o·dore (thē′ə dōr, -dôr) < Gk: gift of God.
The·od·o·ric (thē od′ə rik) < Gmc: people's rule.
Thom·as (tom′əs) < Aram: twin.
Thurs·ton (thûrs′tən) < Dan: Thor + stone.
Tim (tim), short for *Timothy.*
Tim·o·thy (tim′ə thē) < Gk: honor + God.
Ti·tus (tī′təs), a Roman first name; of uncert. meaning.
To·bi·as (tō bī′əs) < Heb: God is good. Also, **To·by** (tō′bē).
Tod (tod) < ME: fox.
Tom (tom), short for *Thomas.* Also, **Tom·my, Tom·mie** (tom′ē).
To·ny (tō′nē), short for *Anthony.*
Tris·tan (tris′tən, -tan; *Ger.* tʀis′tän) < Celt: ? herald. Also, **Tris·tram** (tris′trəm).

U

U·lys·ses (yo͞o lis′ēz), L form of Gk *Odysseus,* hero of the "Odyssey."
Up·ton (up′tən) < OE: upper town.
U·ri·ah (yo͝o rī′ə) < Heb: God is light.

V

Va·chel (vā′chəl) < OF < L: little cow.
Val·en·tine (val′ən tīn′) < L: strong.
Van (van), a family name, var. of *fan* or *fen;* but also abstracted from Dutch family names.
Vaughn (vôn) < Welsh: small.
Ver·gil (vûr′jəl) < L *Vergilius,* Roman family name. Also, **Vir′gil.**
Ver·non (vûr′nən) < ONF family name < L: springlike.
Vic·tor (vik′tər) < L: conqueror.
Vin·cent (vin′sənt) < L: conquering.
Viv·i·an (viv′ē ən) < L: alive. Also, **Viv′i·en.**

W

Wal·do (wôl′dō, wol′-) < Gmc: rule.
Wal·lace (wol′is), Scot family name: Welshman, foreigner.
Wal·ter (wôl′tər) < ONF < Gmc: rule + army. Also, **Walt.**
Ward (wôrd) < OE: guard.

War·ren (wôr′in, wor′-) < Gmc: protection.
Wayne (wān) < OE: wagon (maker).
Wes·ley (wes′lē *or, esp. Brit.,* wez′lē), a family name from a place-name < OE: west field. Also, **Wes** (wes).
Wil·bur (wil′bər) < OE: wild boar.
Wil·fred (wil′frid) < OE: will + peace.
Will (wil), short for *William.* Also, **Wil·lie** (wil′ē).
Wil·lard (wil′ərd) < Gmc: will + hardy.
Wil·liam (wil′yəm) < ONF < Gmc: will + helmet.
Wil·lis (wil′is), var. of *William.*
Win·fred (win′frid) < OE: peaceful friend.
Win·ston (win′stən) < OE: friendly stone.
Win·throp (win′thrəp) < OE: friendly village.
Wy·att (wī′ət), var. of *Guy.*
Wys·tan (wis′tən) < OE: battle + stone.

X

Xa·vi·er (zā′vē ər, zav′ē-, zā′vyər) < Sp < Ar: ? bright.

Y

Yale (yāl), of uncert. meaning and orig.
Yan·cey (yan′sē), AmerInd rendering of *Yankee.*

Z

Zach·a·ri·ah (zak′ə rī′ə) < Heb: God is renowned. Also, **Zach·a·ri·as** (zak′ə rī′əs), **Zach·a·ry** (zak′ə rē).
Zack (zak), short for *Zachariah.* Also, **Zach, Zak.**
Ze·lig (zē′lig, zel′ig; *Ger.* tse′liKH) < Gmc: blessed. Also, **Selig.**

Feminine Names

A

Ab·by (ab′ē), shortened dim. of *Abigail.*
Ab·i·gail (ab′ə gāl′) < Heb: my father's joy.
A·da (ā′də) < Gmc: noble; confused with *Adah;* also short for *Adelaide.*
A·dah (ä′də) < Heb: ornament.
Ad·die (ad′ē), shortened dim. of *Adeline, Adelaide.*
Ad·e·laide (ad′ᵊlād′) < Gmc: nobility.
A·dele (ə del′) < F < Gmc: noble. Also, **A·del·a** (ə del′ə, ad′ᵊlə), **A·dèle** (*Fr.* A del′).
Ad·e·line (ad′ᵊlīn′; *Dan.* ä′də lē′nə; *Fr.* Adᵊlēn′; *Ger.* ä′dā lē′nə), dim. of *Adele.*
A·di·na (ə dē′nə) < Heb: gentle.
A·dri·enne (ā′drē en′; *Fr.* A drē en′) < F, fem. of *Adrian.*
Ag·a·tha (ag′ə thə) < Gk: good.
Ag·gie (ag′ē), shortened dim. of *Agatha* or *Agnes.*
Ag·nes (ag′nis) < Gk: chaste.
Ai·leen (ā lēn′; *Irish.* ī lēn′), Ir form of *Helen.* Also **A·lene** (ə lēn′), **Eileen.**
A·layne (ə lān′), fem. of *Alan;* also var. of *Helen, Elaine.*
Al·ber·ta (al bûr′tə), fem. of *Albert.*
Al·ber·tine (al′bər tēn′; *Fr.* Al bER·tēn′; *Ger.* äl′beR tē′nə), fem. dim. of *Albert.*
Al·bi·na (al bī′nə, -bē′-), fem. of *Albin.*
Al·e·the·a (al′ə thē′ə) < Gk: truth.
Al·ex·an·dra (al′ig zan′drə; -zän′-), fem. of *Alexander.*
Al·fre·da (al frē′də), fem. of *Alfred.*
Al·ice (al′is; *Fr.* A lēs′; *Ger.* ä lē′sə) < F < Gmc: of noble rank.
A·li·cia (ə lish′ə, ə lish′ē ə; ə lē′shə, ə lē′shē ə; *It.* ä lē′chē ä; *Sp.* ä lē′thyä, -syä), var. of *Alice.*
A·line (ə lēn′, al′ēn), var. of *Adeline.*
Al·i·son (al′i sən), var. of *Alice.* Also, **Al′li·son, Al′ly·son.**
A·lis·sa (ə lis′ə) < Heb: joy. Also, **A·li·sa** (ə lē′sə).
Al·ma (al′mə; *Ger., Sp.* äl′mä) < L: kind.
Al·ta (al′tə) < L: high, tall; also < Gmc: old.
Al·the·a (al thē′ə) < Gk: wholesome.
Al·ve·ra (al vēr′ə), var. of *Elvira.* Also, **Al·vi·ra** (al vī′rə, -vēr′ə).
Al·vi·na (al vī′nə), fem. of *Alvin.*
A·man·da (ə man′də) < L: beloved.
A·mel·ia (ə mēl′yə; *It., Sp.* ä me′lyä) < Gmc: industrious. Also, **A·mé·lie** (*Fr.* A mā lē′).
A·my (ā′mē) < OF < L: beloved. Also, **Ai·mée** (ā′mē, *Fr.* e mā′).
An·a·sta·sia (an′ə stā′zhə, än′ə stä′shə) < Gk: resurrection.
An·dre·a (an′drē ə, än′-), Latinized fem. form of *Andrew.*
An·dri·ette (an′drē et′), fem. dim. of *André.*
An·ge·la (an′jə lə) < Gk: messenger.
An·gel·i·ca (an jel′i kə; *It.* än je′lē kä), var. of *Angela.* Also, **An·gé·lique** (an′jə lēk′; *Fr.* äN zhā lēk′).
An·ge·li·na (an′jə lē′nə, -lī′-; *It.* än′je·lē′nä), dim. of *Angela.* Also, **An·gé·line** (an′jə lēn′; *Fr.* äN zhā lēn′).
A·ni·ta (ə nē′tə; *Sp.* ä nē′tä) < Sp, dim. of *Anna.*
An·na (an′ə; *Du., Ger., Sp.* ä′nä; *Fr.* A nA′; *It.* än′nä) < Gk < Heb: grace. Cf. **Hannah.**
An·na·bel (an′ə bel′) < Scot, of uncert. meaning. Also, **An′na·belle′, An·na·bel·la** (an′ə bel′ə).
Anne (an; *Fr.* An) < F, var. of *Anna.* Also, **Ann** (an).
Anne·ma·rie (an′mə rē′), *Anne* + *Marie.*
An·nette (ə net′; *Fr.* A net′), F dim. of *Anne.*
An·nie (an′ē), dim. of *Anna.*
An·the·a (an′thē ə) < Gk: flowery.
An·toi·nette (an′twə net′; *Fr.* äN twA·net′) < F, fem. dim. of *Anthony.*
An·to·ni·a (an tōn′ē ə; -tōn′yə; *It., Sp.* än tô′nyä) < It, fem. of *Anthony.*
A·pril (ā′prəl) < L: name of the month.
Ar·a·bel (ar′ə bel′; *Fr.* A RA bel′), var. of *Annabel.* Also, **Ar·a·bel·la** (ar′ə·bel′ə).
Ar·lene (är lēn′), of uncert. orig. and meaning.
As·trid (as′trid; *Norw.* äs′tRē) < Scand: divine + strength.
Au·drey (ô′drē) < OE: noble + strength.
Au·gus·ta (ô gus′tə; *Ger.* ou gŏŏs′tä), fem. of *Augustus.*
Au·re·lia (ô rēl′yə; *Du., Ger.* ou·RA′lē ə; *It., Sp.* ou RE′lyä) < L, fem. of a Roman family name, ? < *aurum* gold.
Au·ro·ra (ô rōr′ə, ô rôr′ə, ə rōr′ə, ə rôr′ə) < L: dawn.
Av·e·line (av′ə lēn′, -līn′; *Fr.* ä vᵊlēn′) < F: hazel.
A·vis (ā′vis) < L: bird. Also, **A′vice.**
A·vi·va (ə vē′və; *Heb.* ä vē′vä) < Heb: spring.

B

Ba·bette (ba bet′; *Fr.* bA bet′) < F, shortened dim. of *Elizabeth.*
Babs (babz), short for *Barbara, Babette.*
Bar·ba·ra (bar′bər ə; -brə; *Du., Ger., It., Sp.* bäR′bä rä′) < Gk: foreign, exotic.
Bath·she·ba (bath shē′bə, bath′·shə-; *Heb.* bät shə′bä) < Heb: daughter of the oath.
Bea (bē), short for *Beatrice.*
Be·a·trice (bē′ə tris, bē′tris; *It.* be′ä·tRē′che) < L: one who brings joy. Also, **Be·a·trix** (bē′ə triks; *Fr.* be ä·tRēs′; *Dan., Du., Ger., Swed.* bā ä′·tRiks).
Beck·y (bek′ē), shortened dim. of *Rebecca.*
Be·lin·da (bə lin′də) < OSp: beautiful.
Bel·la (bel′ə), short for *Isabella.*
Belle (bel), var. of *Bella.*
Ber·e·ni·ce (ber′ə nī′sē, ber′ə nēs′) < Gk: bringer of victory. Also, **Bé·ré·nice** (*Fr.* bā RA nēs′). Also, **Ber·nice** (bûr nēs′).
Ber·na·dette (bûr′nə det′; *Fr.* beR nA·det′) < F, fem. dim. of *Bernard.*
Ber·na·dine (bûr′nə dēn′, bûr′nə·dēn′) < F, fem. dim. of *Bernard.* Also, **Ber·nar·dine** (bûr′nər dēn′; *Fr.* beR NAR dēn′).
Ber·tha (bûr′thə) < Gmc: bright.
Ber·tie (bûr′tē), shortened dim. of *Bertha.*
Ber·yl (ber′əl) < Gk: name of a precious stone.
Bess (bes), short for *Elizabeth.* Also, **Bes′sie.**
Beth (beth), short for *Elizabeth.*
Beth·el (beth′əl) < Heb: house of God.
Bet·sy (bet′sē), shortened dim. of *Elizabeth.*
Bet·ti·na (be tē′nə; *It.* bet tē′nä) < It, dim. of *Elizabeth.*
Bet·ty (bet′ē), shortened dim. of *Elizabeth.*
Beu·lah (byŏŏ′lə) < Heb: married.
Bev·er·ly (bev′ər lē) < OE: (dweller at the) beaver meadow.
Bi·an·ca (byäng′kə, bē ang′kə; *It., Sp.* byäng′kä) < It: white.
Bid·dy (bid′ē), shortened dim. of *Bridget.*
Blanche (blanch, blänch; *Fr.* bläNsh) < F < Gmc: white.
Bob·bie (bob′ē), shortened dim. of *Barbara, Roberta.* Also, **Bob′by.**
Bo·bette (bo bet′), fem. dim. of *Bob.*
Bon·nie (bon′ē) < F < L: good.
Bren·da (bren′də) < Gmc: flame or sword.
Brid·get (brij′it) < Celt: strength.
Brid·ie (brī′dē), shortened dim. of *Bridget.* Also, **Brid′ey.**
Brun·hil·de (brŏŏn hil′də) < Gmc: breastplate + battle. Also, **Brun·hil′da.**
Bun·ny (bun′ē), shortened dim. of *Bernice.* Also, **Bun′nie.**

C

Ca·mel·lia (kə mēl′yə) ? < L: flower name.
Ca·mil·la (kə mil′ə) < L: a noble maiden in Vergil's *Aeneid.* Also, **Camille** (kə mēl′; *Fr.* kA mē′yᵊ).
Can·dace (kan′dis, kan′də sē′, kan·dā′sē) < L < Gk: glowing. Also, **Candice** (kan′dis, kan dēs′, kan′di sē′).
Can·di·da (kan′di də) < L: gleaming white.
Can·dy (kan′dē), shortened dim. of *Candace.* Also, **Can′die.**
Car·a (kar′ə) < It: dear one.
Car·en (kar′ən), var. of *Karen.*
Car·la (kär′lə), fem. of *Carl.*
Car·lot·ta (kär lot′ə; *It.* käR lôt′tä), var. of *Charlotte.* Also, **Car·lot·a** (kär·lot′ə; *Sp.* käR lô′tä).
Car·mel (kär′mel) < Heb: garden.
Car·mel·a (kär mel′ə; *Sp., It.* käR·me′lä), var. of Carmel. Also, **Car·mel·la** (kär mel′ə).
Car·me·li·ta (käR′me lē′ta), dim. of *Carmela.*
Car·men (kär′mən; *Sp.* käR′men) < L: song.
Car·ol (kar′əl), fem. of *Carol.* Also, **Car′ole, Karol.**
Car·o·la (kar′ə lə, kə rō′lə), var. of *Carol.*
Car·o·line (kar′ō līn′, -lin; *Fr.* kA Rô·lēn′), dim. of *Carol.* Also, **Car·o·lyn** (kar′ə lin), **Car·o·li·na** (kar′ə lī′nə; *It., Sp.* kä′Rô lē′nä).
Car·rie (kar′ē), shortened dim. of *Caroline.*
Cass (kas), shortened dim. of *Cassandra.* Also, **Cas·sie** (kas′ē).
Cas·san·dra (kə san′drə) < Gk: helper of men.
Cath·er·ine (kath′ər in, kath′rin), var. of *Katherine.* Also, **Cath′ar·ine.**
Cath·leen (kath lēn′, kath′lēn), var. of *Kathleen.*
Cath·y (kath′ē), shortened dim. of *Catherine.* Also, **Cath′ie, Kathy, Kathie.**
Ce·cile (si sēl′), var. of *Cecilia.* Also, **Cé·cile** (*Fr.* sā sēl′).
Ce·cil·ia (si sēl′yə), fem. of *Cecil.* Also, **Cec·i·ly** (ses′ə lē).
Ce·leste (sə lest′) < L: heavenly. Also, **Cé·leste** (*Fr.* sā lest′).
Cel·es·tine (sel′i stīn′, -stēn′, si les′·tin, -tīn′), dim. of *Celeste.*
Cel·ia (sēl′yə), short for *Cecilia.*
Char·i·ty (char′i tē) < the abstract noun.
Char·lene (shär lēn′), fem. of *Charles.*
Char·lotte (shär′lət; *Fr.* shAR lôt′; *Ger.* shäR lô′tə) < F, fem. dim. of *Charles.*
Char·mi·an (chär′mē ən) < Gk: source of joy.
Cher·ry (cher′ē), shortened dim. of *Charity.*
Cher·yl (sher′əl), var. of *Charlotte.* Also, **Sheryl.**
Chi·qui·ta (chə kē′tə; *Sp.* chē kē′tä) < Sp: small.
Chlo·e (klō′ē) < Gk: blooming.
Chlo·ette (klō et′; *Fr.* klô et′) < F, dim. of *Chloe.*
Chris (kris), short for *Christiana, Christine.*
Chris·ta·bel (kris′tə bel′), *Christ* + L *bel(la)* beautiful.
Chris·ti·an·a (kris′tē an′ə), fem. of *Christian.*
Chris·tine (kri stēn′), fem. var. of *Christian.* Also, **Chris·ti·na** (kri·stēn′ə).

Cic·e·ly (sis′ə lē), var. of *Cecilia.*
Cin·dy (sin′dē), shortened dim. of *Cynthia.*
Clar·a (klar′ə, klâr′ə) < L: clear, bright. Also, **Clare** (klâr), **Claire** (klâr; *Fr.* kleʀ).
Clar·i·bel (klar′ə bel′, klâr′-), *Clara* + *-bel,* as in *Christabel.*
Clar·ice (klar′is, klə rēs′; *Fr.* klᴀ ʀēs′), dim. of *Clara.*
Cla·rin·da (klə rin′də), var. of *Clara.*
Cla·ris·sa (klə ris′ə), var. of *Clara.* Also, **Cla·risse** (klə rēs′; *Fr.* klᴀ-ʀēs′).
Claud·ette (klô det′; *Fr.* klō det′) < F, dim. of *Claudia.*
Clau·di·a (klô′dē ə), fem. of **Claude.**
Clau·dine (klô dēn′; *Fr.* klō dēn′), dim. of *Claudia.*
Clem·en·tine (klem′ən tīn′, -tēn′; *Fr.* kle mᴀɴ tēn′) < F, fem. dim. of *Clement.* Also, **Cle·men·ti·na** (klem′ən tē′nə; *It.* kle′men tē′nä).
Clem·mie (klem′ē), shortened dim. of *Clementine.*
Cle·o (klē′ō), short for *Cleopatra.*
Cle·o·pat·ra (klē′ō pa′trə, -pä′-, -pā′-) < Gk: fame + father.
Cli·o (klī′ō) < Gk: muse presiding over history.
Clo·til·da (klō til′də) < Gmc: famous + battle. Also, **Clo·thilde** (*Fr.* klō-tēld′), **Clo·thil·de** (klō til′də).
Co·lette (kō let′, ko-; *Fr.* kô let′), short for *Nicolette.*
Col·leen (kol′ēn, ko lēn′, kə-) < Ir: girl.
Con·chi·ta (kən chē′tə; *Sp.* kôn chē′tä) < Sp, shortened dim. of *Concepción.*
Con·cor·di·a (kən kôr′dē ə, kəng-, kon-, kong-) < L: harmony.
Con·nie (kon′ē), shortened dim. of *Constance.*
Con·stance (kon′stəns; *Fr.* kôɴ-stäɴs′) < L: constancy. Also, **Con·stan·tia** (kon stan′shə, -shē′ə).
Con·sue·la (kon swā′lə; *It., Sp.* kôn-swe′lä) < Sp: consolation. Also, **Con·sue·lo** (kon swā′lō; *It., Sp.* kôn-swe′lô).
Cook·ie (ko͝ok′ē) < the common noun.
Co·ra (kōr′ə, kôr′ə) < Gk: maid.
Cor·del·ia (kôr dēl′yə) < Welsh: jewel of the sea.
Co·rin·na (kō rin′ə, -rē′nə, kô-, kə-), dim. of *Cora.* Also, **Co·rinne** (kō rin′, -rēn′, kô-, kə-).
Cor·nel·ia (kôr nēl′yə), fem. of *Cornelius.*
Cor·y (kōr′ē, kôr′ē), dim. of *Cora, Cornelia.*
Crys·tal (kris′tᵊl) < the common noun.
Cyn·thi·a (sin′thē ə) < Gk: (of Mount) Cynthos; epithet of Artemis.

D

Dag·mar (dag′mär; *Dan.* däg′mäʀ) < Dan: day + glory.
Dai·sy (dā′zē), flower name.
Dale (dāl) < the common noun. Also, **Dayle.**
Dan·iel·a (dan yel′ə), fem. of *Daniel.* Also, **Dan·ielle** (dan yel′; *Fr.* dᴀɴ-yel′).
Daph·ne (daf′nē) < Gk: laurel.
Dar·la (där′lə), var. of *Darlene.*
Dar·lene (där lēn′) < OE: darling. Also, **Dar·leen′.**
Da·vi·da (də vē′də), fem. of *David.*
Dawn (dôn) < the common noun.
De·an·na (dē an′ə), var. of *Diana.*
Deb·by (deb′ē), shortened dim. of *Deborah.* Also, **Deb′bie, Deb.**
Deb·o·rah (deb′ə rə, deb′rə) < Heb: bee. Also, **Deb′o·ra, Deb·ra** (deb′rə).
Dee (dē), shortened dim. of *Diana, Delia, Deirdre.*
Deir·dre (dēr′drē, -drə; *Irish.* dâʀ′-dʀā) < Ir: sorrow.
Del·ia (dēl′yə) < Gk: of Delos; epithet of Artemis.
De·li·lah (di lī′lə) < Heb: delicate. Also, **De·li′la.**
Del·la (del′ə), var. of *Delia.* Also, **Dell.**
De·lo·res (də lōr′is, -lôr′-), var. of *Dolores.*
Del·phine (del′fēn) < F < Gk: of Delphi. Also, **Del·phin·i·a** (del fin′-ē ə).
De·nise (də nēs′, -nēz′), fem. of *Denis.*
Des·de·mo·na (dez′də mō′nə) < Gk: unhappiness.
Dé·si·rée (dez′ə rā′; *Fr.* dā zē ʀā′) < F: desired.
Di·an·a (dī an′ə) < L: goddess of the moon. Also, **Di·ane** (dī an′; *Fr.* dē ᴀɴ′).
Di·do (dī′dō) < Gk mythology.
Di·na (dē′nə), var. of *Dinah.*
Di·nah (dī′nə) < Heb: vindicated.
Dol·ly (dol′ē), shortened dim. of *Dorothy.* Also, **Doll.**
Do·lo·res (də lōr′is, -lôr′-; *Sp.* dô lô′-ʀes) < Sp < L: sorrows.
Dom·i·nique (dom′ə nēk′; *Fr.* dô mē-nēk′) < F < L: of the Lord. Also, **Dom·i·ni·ca** (dom′ə nē′kə, də min′-ə kə).
Don·na (don′ə; *It.* dôn′nä) < It: lady.
Do·ra (dōr′ə, dôr′ə) < Gk: gifts.
Do·reen (dō rēn′, dô-, dōr′ēn, dôr′-) < Ir: serious. Also, **Do·rene′.**
Do·ris (dôr′is, dor′-) < Gk: bountiful.
Dor·o·thy (dôr′ə thē, dor′-) < Gk: gift of God. Also, **Dor·o·the·a** (dôr′ə-thē′ə, dor′-).
Dot·ty (dot′ē), shortened dim. of *Dorothy.* Also, **Dot′tie, Dot.**
Dul·cie (dul′sē) < L: sweet.
Dul·cin·e·a (dul sin′ē ə, dul′sə nā′ə, -nē′ə; *Sp.* do͞ol′thē ne′ä, -sē-) < Sp, var. of *Dulcie.*

E

E·die (ē′dē), shortened dim. of *Edith.*
E·dith (ē′dith) < OE: rich, happy + war. Also, **E′dyth.**
Ed·na (ed′nə) < Heb: renewal, rebirth.
Ed·wi·na (ed wē′nə, -win′ə), fem. of *Edwin.*
Ef·fie (ef′ē), shortened dim. of *Euphemia.*
Ei·leen (ī lēn′, ā lēn′) < Ir, var. of *Helen.*
E·laine (i lān′), var. of *Helen.*
El·ber·ta (el bûr′tə), fem. of *Elbert.*
El·ea·nor (el′ə nər, -nôr′), var. of *Helen.* Also, **El′i·nor, El·ea·no·ra** (el′ə nōr′ə, -nôr′ə, el′ē ə-).
E·le·na (ə lā′nə, el′ə nə; *It.* e le′nä), It var. of *Helen.*
E·lise (i lēs′, i lēz′; *Ger.* e lē′zə), short for *Elizabeth.* Also, **É·lise** (*Fr.* ā lēs′).
E·li·za (i lī′zə), short for *Elizabeth.*
E·liz·a·beth (i liz′ə beth) < Heb: oath of God. Also, **E·lis′a·beth.**
El·la (el′ə) < OE: elf.
El·len (el′ən), var. of *Helen.*
El·lie (el′ē), shortened dim. of *Eleanor, Helen.*
El·o·ise (el′ə wēz′, el′ə wēz′) < F < Gmc: healthy + ample.
El·sa (el′sə), short for *Elizabeth.* Also, **El·se** (el′sə; *Ger.* el′zə).
El·sie (el′sē) < Scot, shortened dim. of *Elizabeth.*
El·speth (el′speth, -spəth), Scot var. of *Elizabeth.*
El·va (el′və) < OE: elf.
El·vi·ra (el vīr′ə, -vēr′ə; *Sp.* el vē′ʀä) < Sp < Gmc: elf counsel.
Em·i·ly (em′ə lē) < Gmc < L: industrious. Also, **E·mil·ia** (*Du., It., Sp.* e mē′lyä), **É·mi·lie** (em′ə lē; *Fr.* ā mē lē′).
Em·ma (em′ə), var. of *Erma, Irma.*
Em·me·line (em′ə lēn′, -līn′), dim. of *Amelia.*
E·nid (ē′nid, *Welsh.* en′id) < OE: pure.
Er·i·ca (er′i kə), fem. of *Eric.* Also, **Er′i·ka.**
Er·ma (ûr′mə), shortened dim. of *Ermengarde.*
Er·men·garde (ûr′mən gärd′) < Gmc: immense + protection.
Er·men·trude (ûr′mən tro͞od′) < Gmc: immense + protector.
Er·na (ûr′nə) < OE: eagle.
Er·nes·tine (ûr′ni stēn′), fem. dim. of *Ernest.*
Es·me (ez′mē), ? short for *Esmeralda.*
Es·me·ral·da (ez′mə ral′də; *Sp.* es′-me ʀäl′dä) < Sp < Gk: emerald.
Es·sie (es′ē), shortened dim. of *Esther.*
Es·telle (e stel′, i stel′) < L: star. Also, **Es·tel·la** (e stel′ə, i stel′ə).
Es·ther (es′tər) < Heb < Pers: star.
Eth·el (eth′əl) < Gmc: noble.
Eth·e·lind (eth′ə lind) < OE: noble + shield. Also, **Eth·lyn** (eth′lin).
Et·ta (et′ə), short for *Henrietta.*
Eu·gen·i·a (yo͞o jē′nē ə) < Gk: nobility. Also, **Eu·gé·nie** (*Fr.* œ zhā nē′).
Eu·la·lie (*Fr.* œ lᴀ lē′) < Gk: speaking well.
Eu·nice (yo͞o′nis) < Gk: good victory.
Eu·phe·mi·a (yo͞o fē′mē ə) < Gk: good speech, good repute.
E·van·ge·line (i van′jə lēn′, -līn′, -lin), name invented by H. W. Longfellow.
Eve (ēv) < Heb: life. Also, **E·va** (ē′və).
Ev·e·lyn (ev′ə lin; *Brit.* ēv′lin), dim. of *Eve.* Also, **Ev·a·li·na** (ev′ə lī′nə, -lē′-).
E·vi·ta (e vē′tä), Sp dim. of *Eva.*

F

Faith (fāth) < the abstract noun.
Fan·ny (fan′ē), shortened dim. of *Frances.* Also, **Fan′nie, Fan.**
Faus·ti·na (fô stī′nə, -stē′-) < L: fortunate. Also, **Fau·stine** (fô stēn′; *Fr.* fō stēn′; *Ger.* fou stē′nə).
Fay (fā), short for *Faith.* Also, **Faye.**
Fe·lice (fə lēs′), var. of *Felicia.* Also, **Fé·lice** (*Fr.* fā lēs′).
Fe·li·cia (fə lē′shə, -lish′ə, -lish′ē ə, -lis′ē ə) < L: happy.
Fe·li·pa (fe lē′pä) < Sp, var. of *Philippa.*
Fer·di·nan·da (fûr′də nan′də), fem. of *Ferdinand.*
Fern (fûrn) plant name.
Fer·nan·da (fûr nan′də; *Sp.* feʀ-nän′dä) < Sp, var. of *Ferdinanda.*
Fi·del·ia (fi dēl′yə) < L: faithful.
Fi·fi (fē′fē′) < F, shortened dim. of *Josephine.*
Fi·fine (fi fēn′), dim. of *Fifi.*
Fleu·rette (flû ret′, flo͝o-; *Fr.* flœ-ʀet′) < F, dim. of *fleur* flower. Also, **Flo·rette** (flō ret′, flô-).
Flo (flō), short for *Florence.*
Flo·ra (flōr′ə, flôr′ə) < L: flower.
Flor·ence (flôr′əns, flor′-) < F < L: flowery.
Flor·rie (flôr′ē, flor′ē), shortened dim. of *Florence.* Also, **Flos·sie** (flos′ē).
Fran (fran), short for *Frances.*
Fran·ces (fran′sis), fem. of *Francis.*
Fran·ces·ca (fran ches′kə; frän-; *It.* fʀän che′skä) < It, fem. of *Francis.*
Fran·cine (fran sēn′), dim. of *Frances.* Also, **Fran·cene′.**
Fred·e·ri·ca (fred′ə rē′kə, fre drē′-), fem. of *Frederick.*
Frie·da (frē′də), fem. of *Fred.* Also, **Fre·da** (frē′də, fred′ə).
Ful·vi·a (fo͝ol′vē ə) < L, fem. of a Roman family name < *fulvus* tawny.

G

Ga·bri·elle (gā′brē el′, gab′rē-; *Fr.* gᴀ bʀē el′), F fem. of *Gabriel.*
Gail (gāl) < Heb: joy. Also, **Gale, Gayle.**
Gay (gā) < the adj. Also, **Gaye.**
Gen·e·vieve (jen′ə vēv′; *Fr.* zhə-nᵊvyev′) < F < Celt, of uncert. meaning.
Ge·nev·ra (jə nev′rə), var. of *Genevieve.* Also, **Ge·ne·va** (jə nē′və), **Gi·nev·ra** (*It.* jē nev′ʀä).
Geor·gette (jôr jet′) < F, fem. of *George.*
Geor·gia (jôr′jə), fem. of *George.*
Geor·gi·an·a (jôr′jē an′ə), var. of *Georgia.*
Geor·gi·na (jôr jē′nə), dim. of *Georgia.*
Ger·al·dine (jer′əl dēn′), fem. dim. of *Gerald.*
Ger·maine (jer mān′; *Fr.* zheʀ men′) < F < L < Gmc: German.
Ger·tie (gûr′tē), shortened dim. of Gertrude. Also, **Gur′ty.**
Ger·trude (gûr′tro͞od; *Fr.* zheʀ tʀo͞od′; *It.* jeʀ tʀo͞o′de) < Gmc: spear + strength.
Gil·ber·ta (gil bûr′tə), fem. of *Gilbert.* Also, **Gil·berte** (*Fr.* zhēl beʀt′).
Gil·ber·tine (gil′bər tēn′), dim. of *Gilberta.*
Gil·da (gil′də) < OE: golden.
Gil·li·an (jil′ē ən, -yən), var. of *Juliana.*
Gi·na (jē′nə, jin′ə; *It.* jē′nä), short for *Regina, Giovannina, Angelina, Luigina.*
Gin·ger (jin′jər), short for *Virginia.*
Gin·ny (jin′ē), shortened dim. of *Virginia.*
Gio·van·na (jô vän′nä) < It, fem. of *John.*
Gi·selle (ji zel′; *Fr.* zhē zel′) < F, short for *Elizabeth.* Also, **Gi·sele′, Gi·se·la** (*Ger.* gē′zə lə).
Glad·ys (glad′is) < Welsh, fem. form of *Claude.*
Glo·ri·a (glōr′ē ə, glôr′-) < L: glory. Also, **Glo·ri** (glōr′ē, glôr′ē).
Go·di·va (gə dī′və) < OE: God + gift.
Grace (grās) < L: grace. Also, **Gra′cie, Gra·cia** (grā′shə, -shē ə).
Gret·a (gret′ə; *Ger.* gʀā′tə), short for *Margaret.*
Gret·chen (grech′ən; *Ger.* gʀāt′shən) < G, shortened dim. of *Margaret.*
Gri·sel·da (gri zel′də) < Gmc: gray + battle. Also, **Gris·sel** (gris′əl).
Guen·e·vere (gwen′ə vēr′) < Welsh: white, fair. Also, **Guin·e·vere** (gwin′ə-vēr′).
Gu·nil·la (gə nil′ə; *Swed.* go͞o′nē lä′) < Scand: battlemaid.
Gus·sie (gus′ē), shortened dim. of *Augusta.*
Gwen (gwen), short for *Gwendolyn.*
Gwen·do·lyn (gwen′də lin) < Welsh: white.

H

Han·nah (han′ə; *Heb.* ᴋʜä nä′) < Gk < Heb: grace. Also, **Han′na.**
Har·ri·et (har′ē it), fem. of *Harry.*
Hat·ty (hat′ē), shortened dim. of *Harriet.*

Hay·ley (hā′lē), ? from surname *Hailey.*
Ha·zel (hā′zəl), plant name.
Heath·er (heth′ər), plant name.
Hed·da (hed′ə) < Gmc: strife.
Hed·wig (hed′wig) < Gmc: war + holy. Also, **Hed·vig** (hed′vig; *Ger.* hed′vɪᴋʜ).
Hed·y (hed′ē) < Gk: pleasing.
Hei·di (hī′dē), shortened dim. of *Adalheid,* G form of *Adelaide.*
He·laine (hə lān′), var. of *Helen.*
Hel·en (hel′ən) < Gk: light. Also, **He·le·na** (hə lē′nə, -lā′-, hel′ə nə), **He·lene** (hə lēn′).
Hel·ga (hel′gə) < Gmc: holy.
Hé·lo·ise (ā lō ēz′), F var. of *Eloise.* Also, **Hel·o·ise** (hel′ə wēz′).
Hen·ri·et·ta (hen′rē et′ə), fem. of *Henry.*
Heph·zi·bah (hef′zə bə, hep′-) < Heb: my desire is in her.
Her·mi·a (hûr′mē ə), var. of *Hermione.*
Her·mi·o·ne (hûr mī′ə nē′) < Gk, fem. < *Hermes* messenger of the gods.
Her·tha (hûr′thə) < OE: goddess of earth.
Hes·ter (hes′tər), var. of *Esther.*
Het·ty (het′ē), shortened dim. of *Esther, Hester.*
Hil·a·ry (hil′ə rē), fem. of *Hilary.* Also, **Hil′la·ry.**
Hil·da (hil′də) < Gmc: (maid of) battle.
Hil·de·garde (hil′də gärd′) < Gmc: battle + protector.
Hol·ly (hol′ē), plant name.
Ho·no·ri·a (hō nōr′ē ə, -nôr′-) < L: honorable.
Hope (hōp) < the abstract noun.
Ho·ra·ti·a (hə rā′shē ə, -shə, hō-, hô-), fem. of *Horatio.*
Hor·tense (hôr′tens; *Fr.* ôʀ täɴs′) < F < L: (of the) garden. Also, **Hor·ten·si·a** (hôr ten′sē ə).
Hul·da (hul′də) < Scand: amiable, lovely.
Hy·a·cinth (hī′ə sinth), flower name.

I

I·an·the (ī an′thē) < Gk: violet flower.
I·da (ī′də) < Gmc: happy.
Il·se (il′sə; *Ger.* il′zə), G dim. of *Elizabeth.*
Im·o·gene (im′ə jēn′), of uncert. orig. and meaning. Also, **Im·o·gen** (im′ə-jen′).
I·na (ī′nə), of uncert. orig. and meaning.
I·nez (ī′nez, ī nez′, ē′nez, ē nez′; *Sp.* ē neth′, ē nes′), Sp form of *Agnes.*
I·rene (ī rēn′) < Gk: peace.
I·ris (ī′ris) < Gk: rainbow; but usually directly from the flower name.
Ir·ma (ûr′mə), var. of *Erma.*
Is·a·bel (iz′ə bel′), var. of *Elizabeth.* Also, **Is·a·bel·la** (iz′ə bel′ə), **Is′o·bel′, Is·a·belle** (iz′ə bel′; *Fr.* ē sä bel′).
Is·a·do·ra (iz′ə dōr′ə, -dôr′ə), fem. of *Isidore.*
I·vy (ī′vē), plant name.

J

Jack·ie (jak′ē), shortened dim. of *Jacqueline.*
Jac·que·line (jak′ə lin, -lēn′, jak′wə-; *Fr.* zhäkᵊlēn′), F fem. var. of *Jack.*
Jac·quette (jə ket′; *Fr.* zhä ket′), var. of *Jacqueline.*
Jan (jan), short for *Jane, Janet.*
Jane (jān), fem. of *John.*
Jan·et (jan′it), dim. of *Jane.*
Jan·ice (jan′is), var. of *Jane.* Also, **Jan′is.**
Jean (jēn), Scot form of *Jane.* Also, **Jeanne** (jēn; *Fr.* zhän).
Jean·nette (jə net′), F dim. of *Jean.*
Jean·ine (jə nēn′), dim. of *Jean.* Also, **Jean·nine** (jə nēn′; *Fr.* zhə nēn′).
Je·mi·ma (jə mī′mə) < Heb: dove.
Jen·ni·fer (jen′ə fər), var. of *Guenevere.*
Jen·ny (jen′ē), shortened dim. of *Jennifer.* Also, **Jen′nie.**
Jes·si·ca (jes′ə kə), var. of *Jessie.*
Jes·sie (jes′ē), Scot dim. of *Janet;* now used as fem. of *Jesse.*
Jew·el (jo͞o′əl) < the common noun.
Jill (jil′), short for *Juliana.*
Jo (jō), short for *Josephine, Joan.*
Joan (jōn), fem. of *John.*
Joc·e·lyn (jos′ə lin), var. of *Joyce.* Also, **Joc′e·lyne.**
Jo·dy (jō′dē), shortened dim. of *Judith.* Also, **Jo′di, Jo′die.**
Jo·han·na (jō han′ə), var. of *Joan.* Also, **Jo·an·na** (jō an′ə), **Jo·anne** (jō an′).
Jo·se·phine (jō′zə fēn′, -sə-; *Fr.* zhō-ze fēn′), fem. of *Joseph.*
Joy (joi) < the abstract noun.
Joyce (jois) < F: joy.
Jua·na (wä′nə; *Sp.* hwä′nä), Sp fem. of *John.*
Juan·i·ta (wä nē′tə; *Sp.* hwä nē′tä), dim. of *Juana.*
Ju·dith (jo͞o′dith), fem. of *Judah.*
Ju·dy (jo͞o′dē), shortened dim. of *Judith.*
Jul·ia (jo͞ol′yə), fem. of *Julius.* Also, **Ju·lie** (jo͞o′lē; *Fr.* zhʏ lē′).
Ju·li·an·a (jo͞o′lē an′ə; -än′ə), dim. of *Julia.* Also, **Ju·li·a·ne** (*Ger.* yo͞o′lē-än′ə), **Ju·lienne** (*Fr.* zhʏ lyen′).
Ju·li·et (jo͞o′lē ət, jo͞o′lē et′, jo͞ol′-yət), dim. of *Julia.*
June (jo͞on) < the name of the month.
Jus·ti·na (jə stē′nə), fem. of *Justin.* Also, **Jus·tine** (jə stēn′, ju-; *Fr.* zhʏ-stēn′).

K

Kar·en (kar′ən; *Dan.* kä′ʀən), Dan form of *Katharine.*
Kar·ol (kar′əl), var. of *Carol.*
Kate (kāt), short for *Katherine.* Also, **Ka′tie, Ka′ty.**
Kath·er·ine (kath′ə rin, kath′rin) < Gk: ? pure. Also, **Catherine, Kath′-ar·ine, Kath·ryn** (kath′rin).
Kath·leen (kath lēn′, kath′lēn), Ir form of *Katherine.* Also, **Cathleen.**
Kath·y (kath′ē), shortened dim. of *Katherine.* Also, **Cathy, Cathie, Kath′ie.**
Ka·tri·na (kə trē′nə), var. of *Katherine.* Also, **Kat·rine** (kat′rin, -rēn).
Kay (kā), short for *Katherine.* Also, **Kaye.**
Kir·sten (kûr′stən, kēr′-; *Norw.* ᴋʜish′tən, ᴋʜiʀ′stən), Scand form of *Christine.*
Kit·ty (kit′ē), shortened dim. of *Katherine.* Also, **Kit′tie, Kit.**

L

Lan·a (lan′ə, lä′nə), var. of *Helen.*
Lar·a (lar′ə, lä′rə), var. of *Laura.*
Lau·ra (lôr′ə) < L: laurel.
Lau·rie (lôr′ē), dim. of *Laura.*
Lau·ret·ta (lô ret′ə), dim. of *Laura.* Also, **Lau·rette′, Loretta.**
La·verne (lə vûrn′), var. of *Verna.*
La·vin·i·a (lə vin′ē ə) < L, a princess in Vergil's *Aeneid.*
Le·ah (lē′ə; *Heb.* lā′ä) < Heb: weary.
Lee (lē), var. of *Leah, Lena.* Also, **Lea.**
Lei·la (lē′lə, lī′-), < Heb: night.
Le·na (lē′nə), short for *Helena.*
Lé·o·nie (lē′ə nē; *Fr.* lā ō nē′), F fem. of *Leon.*
Le·o·no·ra (lē′ə nōr′ə, -nôr′ə; *It.* le′ô-nô′rä), var. of *Eleanor.* Also, **Le·o·nore** (lē′ə nōr′, -nôr′; *Ger.* lā′ō-nō′ʀə), **Le·nore** (lə nōr′, -nôr′; *Ger.* le nō′ʀə).
Les·lie (les′lē, lez′-), fem. of *Leslie.* Also, **Les′ley.**
Le·ti·tia (li tish′ə) < L: gladness.
Let·ty (let′ē), shortened dim. of *Letitia.* Also, **Let′tie.**
Lib·by (lib′ē), shortened dim. of *Elizabeth.*
Li·la (lī′lə), var. of *Leila.*
Lil·ith (lil′ith) < Heb: from the night.
Lil·li·an (lil′ē ən, -yən), ? dim. of *Elizabeth.* Also, **Lil′i·an.**
Lil·y (lil′ē), var. of *Lillian;* later, flower name. Also, **Lil′lie, Lil′ly.**
Lin·da (lin′də) < Sp: pretty.
Li·sa (lē′sə, -zə), short for *Elizabeth.* Also, **Li·se** (lē′sə, -zə; *Ger.* lē′zə).
Li·za (lī′zə), short for *Elizabeth.*
Liz·beth (liz′bəth), var. of *Elizabeth.*
Liz·zie (liz′ē), shortened dim. of *Elizabeth.* Also, **Liz′zy, Liz.**
Lo·is (lō′is), prob. < Gk; of uncert. meaning.
Lo·la (lō′lə; *Sp.* lô′lä) < Sp, short for *Dolores* and *Carlota* (= *Charlotte*).
Lo·li·ta (lō lē′tə; *Sp.* lô lē′tä), Sp dim. of *Lola.*
Lol·ly (lol′ē), dim. of *Laura.*
Lo·na (lō′nə) < Gmc: solitary.
Lo·ret·ta (lô ret′ə), var. of *Lauretta.*
Lor·na (lôr′nə), name invented by R. D. Blackmore.
Lor·raine (lô rān′, lə-) < Fr: (girl) of Lorraine.
Lor·rie (lôr′ē), shortened dim. of *Lorraine.*
Lot·tie (lot′ē), shortened dim. of *Charlotte.* Also, **Lot′ty.**
Lou (lo͞o), short for *Louise.* Also, **Lu.**
Lou·ise (lo͞o ēz′; *Fr.* lwēz′; *Ger.* lo͞o-ē′zə), F fem. of *Louis.* Also, **Lou·i·sa** (lo͞o ē′zə).
Lu·cia (lo͞o′shə, -shē ə, -sē ə; *Ger.* lo͞o-tsē′ä; *It.* lo͞o chē′ä), fem. of *Lucius.*
Lu·cille (lo͞o sēl′), fem. dim. of *Lucius.*
Lu·cin·da (lo͞o sin′də), var. of *Lucy.*
Lu·cy (lo͞o′sē), var. of *Lucia.* Also, **Lu′ci.**
Lu·lu (lo͞o′lo͞o′), var. of *Louise.*
Lyd·i·a (lid′ē ə) < Gk: (woman) of Lydia.
Lynn (lin), var. of *Linda.* Also, **Lynne, Lyn.**

M

Ma·bel (mā′bəl), short for *Amabel* < L: lovable.
Mad·e·leine (mad′ᵊlin; *Fr.* mᴀdᵊ len′), F form of *Magdalene.* Also, **Mad·e·lin** (mad′ᵊlin).
Madge (maj), short for *Margaret.*
Mae (mā), var. of *May.*
Mag·da (mag′də; *Ger.* mäg′dä) < G, short for *Magdalene.*
Mag·da·lene (mag′də lēn′, mag′də-lē′nē) < Heb: (woman) of Magdala. Also, **Mag·da·len** (mag′də lən).
Mag·gie (mag′ē), shortened dim. of *Margaret.* Also, **Mag.**
Mai·sie (mā′zē), Scot dim. of *Margaret.*
Mal·vi·na (mal vī′nə, -vē′-), ? < Gael: smooth snow. Also, **Mal′vine.**
Ma·mie (mā′mē), dim. of *Margaret, Mary.*
Mar·cel·la (mär sel′ə), It fem. dim. of *Marcus.* Also, **Mar·celle′.**
Mar·cia (mär′shə), fem. of *Marcus.* Also, **Marsha.**
Mar·ga·ret (mär′gə rit, -grit) < L < Gk: pearl. Also, **Mar·ga·ri·ta** (mär′-gə rē′tə; *It.* mäʀ′gä ʀē′tä).
Marge (märj), short for *Margaret.* Also, **Mar·gie** (mär′jē), **Marj.**
Mar·got (mär′gō, -gət; *Fr.* mäʀ gō′), F dim. of *Margaret.*
Mar·gue·rite (mär′gə rēt′; *Fr.* mᴀʀ-gə ʀēt′), F form of *Margaret.*
Ma·ri·a (mə rē′ə, -rī′ə; *Du., Ger., It., Sp.* mä ʀē′ä), var. of *Mary.*
Mar·i·an (mâr′ē ən, mar′-), *Mary* + *Anne.* Also, **Mar·i·anne** (mâr′ē an′, mar′-; *Fr.* mᴀ ʀē ᴀɴ′), **Mar·y·anne** (mâr′ē an′, mar′-), **Mar′i·on.**
Ma·rie (mə rē′; *Fr.* mᴀ ʀē′), F form of *Mary.*
Mar·i·et·ta (mâr′ē et′ə, mar′-; *It.* mä′ʀe et′tä), dim. of *Maria.*
Mar·i·gold (mar′ə gōld′), flower name.
Mar·i·lyn (mar′ə lin), var. of *Mary.* Also, **Mar′y·lynne.**
Ma·ri·na (mə rē′nə), ? < L: of the sea.
Mar·is (mar′is) < L: of the sea.
Mar·jo·rie (mär′jə rē), var. of *Margaret.* Also, **Mar′jo·ry, Mar′ge·ry.**
Mar·la (mär′lə), var. of *Mary.*
Mar·sha (mär′shə), var. of *Marcia.*
Mar·tha (mär′thə) < Aram: lady.
Mar·y (mâr′ē) < Heb: bitter.
Ma·thil·da (mə til′də) < Gmc: might + battle. Also, **Ma·til′da.**
Mat·ty (mat′ē), shortened dim. of *Matilda.* Also, **Mat′tie.**
Maud (môd), var. of *Matilda.* Also, **Maude.**
Mau·ra (mô′rə), Ir form of *Mary.* Also, **Moira.**
Mau·reen (mô rēn′), Ir dim. of *Mary.*
Ma·vis (mā′vis) < obs. noun meaning "thrush."
Max·ine (mak sēn′, mak′sēn), F fem. dim. of *Max.*
May (mā), dim. of *Mary* or from name of month. Also, **Mae.**
Meg (meg), short for *Margaret.*
Me·het·a·bel (mə het′ə bəl) < Heb: favored by God. Also, **Me·hit·a·bel** (mə hit′ə bəl).
Mel·a·nie (mel′ə nē) < Gk: black, dark.
Me·lis·sa (mə lis′ə) < Gk: bee.
Mel·o·dy (mel′ə dē) < the common noun. Also, **Mel′o·die.**
Mer·ce·des (mər sā′dēz, -sē′-, mûr′-si dēz′; *Sp.* meʀ the′des, -se′-) < Sp: (Our Lady of) Mercies.
Mi·a (mē′ə), prob. short for *Maria* or names ending in *-mia.*
Mi·chelle (mi shel′; *Fr.* mē shel′), F fem. of *Michael.* Also, **Mi·chele** (mi-shel′).
Mi·gnon (min yon′, -yun′, min′yon, -yən; *Fr.* mē nyôɴ′) < F: little, dainty. Also, **Mi·gnonne′.**
Mil·dred (mil′drid) < OE: mild + strength.
Mil·li·cent (mil′i sənt) < Gmc: work + strong.
Mil·lie (mil′ē), shortened dim. of *Mildred.* Also, **Mil′ly.**
Mim·i (mim′ē, mē′mē; *Fr.* mē mē′), shortened dim. of *Miriam.*
Mi·na (mē′nə), short for *Wilhelmina.*
Min·dy (min′dē), var. of *Minna.*
Mi·ner·va (mə nûr′və) < L: goddess of wisdom.
Min·na (min′ə) < Gmc: memory, love.
Min·nie (min′ē), Scot dim. of *Mary.*
Mi·ran·da (mə ran′də; *Sp.* mē-ʀän′dä) < L: to be admired.
Mir·i·am (mir′ē əm) < Heb, older form of *Mary.*
Moi·ra (moi′rə), Ir form of *Mary.* Also, **Maura.**
Mol·ly (mol′ē), dim. of *Mary.* Also, **Mol′lie, Moll.**
Mo·na (mō′nə) < Ir: noble.
Mon·i·ca (mon′ə kə) < L, of uncert. meaning.
Mor·na (môr′nə) < Gael: beloved.

Mu·ri·el (myŏŏr′ē əl), ? < Gael: ? sea + bright.
My·ra (mī′rə) < L: wonderful. Also, **Mi′ra.**
Myr·na (mûr′nə) < Gael, of uncert. meaning.
Myr·tle (mûr′tᵊl), plant name.

N

Na·dine (nā dēn′, nə-; *Fr.* nᴀ dēn′) < F < Russ: hope.
Nan (nan), short for *Anna, Anne,* etc. Also, **Nan·ny, Nan·nie** (nan′ē).
Na·nanne (nə nan′; *Fr.* nᴀ nᴀɴ′), F dim. of *Anne.*
Nan·cy (nan′sē), dim. of *Anna, Anne,* etc.
Na·nette (nə net′), dim. of *Anne.*
Na·o·mi (nā ō′mē; *Heb.* nä ä mē′) < Heb: pleasant
Nat·a·lie (nat′ᵊlē; *Fr.* nᴀ tᴀ lē′) < L: birthday, Christmas. Also, **Nath′a·lie.**
Nell (nel), short for *Helen.* Also, **Nel·lie, Nel·ly** (nel′ē).
Net·tie (net′ē), Scot dim. of *Janet.* Also, **Net·ta** (net′ə).
Nick·y (nik′ē), shortened dim. of *Nicole.* Also, **Nik′ki.**
Ni·cole (ni kōl′; *Fr.* nē kôl′), F fem. of *Nicholas.*
Ni·co·lette (nik′ə let′; *Fr.* nē kô let′), F dim. of *Nicole.*
Ni·na (nē′nə, nī′-; *Russ.* nē′nä), Russ dim. of *Anna.*
Ni·ta (nē′tə) < Sp, short for *Juanita.*
No·elle (nō el′, nō′əl), fem. of *Noel.*
No·la (nō′lə) < Celt: noble or famous.
No·na (nō′nə) < L: ninth.
No·ra (nōr′ə, nôr′ə), var. of *Honoria.*
No·reen (nôr′ēn, nō rēn′), Ir dim. of *Nora.* Also, **No′rene.**
Nor·ma (nôr′mə), fem. of *Norman.*

O

Oc·ta·vi·a (ok tā′vē ə), fem. of *Octavius.*
O·dette (ō det′; *Fr.* ô det′), F dim. of *Odille.* Also, **O·det·ta** (ō det′ə).
O·dille (ō dil′) < F < Gmc: from the fatherland.
Ol·ga (ol′gə; *Russ.* ôl′gä) < Russ < Scand: holy.
Ol·ive (ol′iv) < L: olive.
O·liv·i·a (ō liv′ē ə), var. of *Olive.*
O·lym·pi·a (ō lim′pē ə) < Gk: of Olympus.
Oo·na (o͞o′nə), var. of *Una.*
O·pal (ō′pəl), name of precious stone.
O·phel·ia (ō fēl′yə), prob. < Gk: help.
O·ri·an·a (ōr′e ān′ə, ôr′-) < OF, ? < L *orīrī* to rise.

P

Pam·e·la (pam′ə lə), invented name. Also, **Pam.**
Pan·sy (pan′zē), flower name.
Pat (pat), short for *Patricia.*
Pa·tience (pā′shəns) < the abstract noun.
Pa·tri·cia (pə trish′ə, -trē′shə) < L, fem. of *Patrick.* Also, **Pa·trice** (pə trēs′).
Pat·ty (pat′ē), shortened dim. of *Patricia* or *Patience.* Also, **Pat′tie.**
Pau·la (pô′lə), G fem. of *Paul.*
Pau·lette (pô let′), F fem. dim. of *Paul.*
Pau·line (pô lēn′; *Fr.* pō lēn′; *Ger.* pou lē′nə), F fem. dim. of *Paul.*
Pearl (pûrl), name of the gem.
Peg (peg), short for *Margaret.* Also, **Peg·gy** (peg′ē).
Pe·nel·o·pe (pə nel′ə pē) < Gk: ? weaver.
Pen·ny (pen′ē), shortened dim. of *Penelope.* Also, **Pen′nie.**
Per·sis (pûr′sis) < Gk: a Persian woman.
Phi·lip·pa (fə lip′ə), fem. of *Philip.*
Phil·li·da (fil′ə də), var. of *Phyllis.*
Phil·o·me·na (fil′ə mē′nə) < Gk: friend + power.
Phoe·be (fē′bē) < Gk: the shining one.
Phyl·lis (fil′is) < Gk: green leaf.
Pol·ly (pol′ē), var. of *Molly.*
Pris·cil·la (pri sil′ə), L fem. dim. of Roman name *Priscus.*
Pru·dence (pro͞od′dəns) < the abstract noun.
Prue (pro͞o), short for *Prudence.* Also, **Pru.**

Q

Queen·ie (kwē′nē), dim. of noun *queen.*

R

Ra·chel (rā′chəl) < Heb: lamb.
Rae (rā), short for *Rachel.* Also, **Ray, Raye.**
Ra·mo·na (rə mō′nə) < Sp, fem. of *Raymond.*
Ran·dy (ran′dē), fem. dim. of *Randolph.* Also, **Ran′die.**
Re·bec·ca (rə bek′ə) < Heb: binding.
Re·gi·na (rə jē′nə) < L: queen.
Re·na (rē′nə), short for *Marina.* Also, **Ri′na.**
Rho·da (rō′də) < Gk: rose.
Rhon·da (ron′də) < Welsh place-name.
Ri·ta (rē′tə) < It, short for *Margarita.*
Ro·ber·ta (rə bûr′tə, rō-), Scot fem. of *Robert.*
Rob·in (rob′in), fem. dim. of *Robert.* Also, **Rob′yn.**
Ro·chelle (rə shel′) < F: small rock.
Ro·mo·la (rə mō′lə; *It.* rô′mô lä) < It, fem. of L. *Romulus.*
Ro·sa (rō′zə; *It.* rô′zä; *Sp.* rô′sä), var. of *Rose.*
Ros·a·bel (rō′zə bel′), invented name < *Rosa* + *-bel,* as in *Christabel.*
Ro·sa·lie (rō′zə lē′, roz′ə-; *Fr.* rô zᴀ lē′) < F < L: the festival of roses.
Ros·a·lind (roz′ə lind), prob. coined by Spenser, but associated with Sp *rosa linda* beautiful rose.
Ro·sa·mund (rō′zə mənd, roz′ə-) < Gmc: horse + protection. Also, **Ro′sa·mond.**
Rose (rōz) < L: rose.
Rose·an·na (rō zan′ə), *Rose* + *Anna.* Also, **Rose·anne′, Ros·an′na Ros′anne.**
Rose·mar·y (rōz′mâr′ē, -mə rē′), plant name. Also, **Rose·ma·rie** (rōz′mə rē′).
Ro·set·ta (rō zet′ə), dim. of *Rose.* Also, **Ro·sette′.**
Ro·sie (rō′zē), dim. of *Rose.* Also, **Ro′sy.**
Ro·si·na (rō zē′nə; *It.* rô zē′nä), It dim. of *Rose.*
Ro·si·ta (rō zē′tə; *Sp.* rô sē′tä), Sp dim. of *Rose.*
Ros·lyn (roz′lin), var. of *Rosalind.*
Ro·we·na (rō wē′nə), of uncert. orig. and meaning.
Rox·anne (rok san′) < Pers, of uncert. meaning. Also, **Rox·an·a** (rok san′ə), **Rox·an′na, Rox·ane** (rok san′; *Fr.* rôk sᴀɴ′).
Ru·by (ro͞o′bē), name of precious stone.
Ruth (ro͞oth) < Heb, of uncert. meaning.

S

Sa·bi·na (sə bī′nə, -bē′-) < L: a Sabine woman.
Sa·bri·na (sə brē′nə) < L: Severn (the river).
Sa·die (sā′dē), dim. of *Sarah.*
Sal·ly (sal′ē), dim. of *Sarah.* Also, **Sal′lie.**
Sa·lo·me (sə lō′me, sal′ə mā′) < Heb: peace.
Sa·man·tha (sə man′thə) < Heb, of uncert. meaning.
San·dra (san′drə, son′-) < It, fem. var. of *Alexander.* Also, **Saun·dra** (sôn′drə, son′-), **Son·dra** (son′drə).
San·dy (san′dē), dim. of *Alexandra.*
Sar·ah (sâr′ə) < Heb: princess. Also, **Sar′a.**
Sel·ma (sel′mə) < Celt: fair.
Shar·on (shar′ən) < Heb: a plain in western Israel.
Sheil·a (shē′lə), Ir form of *Celia.* Also, **Sheil′ah.**
Sher·ry (sher′ē), var. of *Charlotte.*
Sher·yl (sher′əl), var. of *Cheryl.*
Shir·ley (shir′lē), a family name, from a place-name.
Sib·yl (sib′əl) < Gk: prophetess. Also, **Syb′yl.**
Sid·ney (sid′nē), var. of *Sidony.* Also, **Syd′ney.**
Sid·o·ny (sid′ᵊnē) < name of ancient Phoenician city *Sidon.* Also, **Si·do·nie** (*Fr.* sē dô nē′), **Si·don·ia** (si dōn′yə).
Sig·rid (sē′grid, sig′rid; *Ger.* zē′grit, -grēt; *Norw.* si′gri; *Swed.* sē′grid) < Scand: victory.
Sil·vi·a (sil′vē ə) < L: girl of the forest. Also, **Syl′vi·a.**
So·nia (sōn′yə), Russ dim. of *Sophia.*
So·phi·a (sō fē′ə) < Gk: wisdom. Also, **So·phie** (sō′fē; *Fr.* sô fē′), **So·fi·a** (sō fē′ə; *It.* sô fē′ä).
Sta·cy (stā′sē), shortened dim. of *Anastasia.*
Stel·la (stel′ə) < L: star.
Steph·a·nie (stef′ə nē; *Fr.* ste fᴀ nē′), fem. of *Stephen.* Also, **Stef·a·nie** (stef′ə nē).
Sue (so͞o), short for *Susan, Susannah.*
Su·san (so͞o′zən), var. of *Susannah.*
Su·san·nah (so͞o zan′ə) < Heb: lily. Also, **Su·san′na.**
Su·sie (so͞o′zē), shortened dim. of *Susan, Susannah.* Also, **Su′zy.**
Su·zanne (so͞o zan′; *Fr.* so͞o zᴀɴ′), form of *Susannah.*

T

Tab·i·tha (tab′ə thə) < Aram: gazelle.
Ta·mar·a (tə mar′ə, -mä′rə) < Heb: date palm. Also, **Ta·mar** (tə mär′; *Heb.* tä mäʀ′).
Tam·my (tam′ē), shortened dim. of *Tamara.* Also, **Tam′mie.**
Ter·ry (ter′ē), shortened dim. of *Theresa.* Also, **Ter′ri.**
Tess (tes), short for *Theresa.* Also, **Tes·sie** (tes′ē).
Thel·ma (thel′mə), invented name.
The·o·do·ra (thē′ə dōr′ə; -dôr′ə), fem. of *Theodore.*
The·o·do·sia (thē′ə dō′shə, -shē ə) < Gk: god-given.
The·re·sa (tə rē′sə), of uncert. orig. and meaning. Also, **Te·re·sa** (tə-rē′sə; *It.* te ʀe′zä; *Sp.* te ʀe′sä), **Thé·rèse** (*Fr.* tā ʀez′), **The·rese′.**
Til·da (til′də), short for *Matilda.*
Til·ly (til′ē), shortened dim. of *Matilda.* Also, **Til′lie.**
Ti·na (tē′nə), short for *Albertine, Christine, Ernestine, Justina.*
Trix·ie (trik′sē), shortened dim. of *Beatrix.*
Tru·dy (tro͞o′dē), shortened dim. of *Gertrude.*

U

U·na (o͞o′nə) < L: one. Also Latinization of Irish *Unagh.* Also, **Oona.**
Ur·su·la (ûr′sə lə) < L, dim. of *Ursa* she-bear.

V

Val·e·rie (val′ə rē) < L, fem. of a Roman family name. Also, **Val′e·ry, Va·lé·rie** (*Fr.* vᴀ lā ʀē′).
Va·nes·sa (və nes′ə), invented name.
Ve·ra (vēr′ə; *Russ.* ve′ʀä) < Russ: faith.
Ver·na (vûr′nə), ? fem. of *Vernon.*
Ver·on·i·ca (və ron′ə kə) < LL: true image.
Vick·y (vik′ē), shortened dim. of *Victoria.* Also, **Vick′ie.**
Vic·to·ri·a (vik tōr′ē ə, -tôr′-) < L: victory.
Vi·da (vē′də), short for *Davida.*
Vi·o·la (vī ō′lə, vē-; vī′ə lə, vē′-) < L: violet.
Vi·o·let (vī′ə lit) < F, dim. of *Viola.*
Vir·gin·ia (vûr gin′yə) < L, fem. of a Roman family name; but also after the state.
Viv·i·an (viv′ē ən) < L: full of life.

W

Wan·da (won′də) < Gmc: stock, stem.
Wen·dy (wen′dē), ? shortened dim. of *Gwendolyn.*
Wil·hel·mi·na (wil′ə mē′nə, wil′hel-; *Du.* vil′hel mē′nä) < G, fem. of *William.*
Wil·ma (wil′mə), short for *Wilhelmina.*
Win·i·fred (win′ə frid), E var. of Welsh *Gwenfrewi* (var. of *Guenevere*).
Win·nie (win′ē), shortened dim. of *Winifred.*

X

Xe·ni·a (zē′nē ə, zēn′yə), var. of *Zenia.*

Y

Yo·lan·de (yō lan′də; *Fr.* yô länd′) < OF, ? var. of *Violante,* var. of *Viola.* Also, **Yo·lan·da** (yō lan′də).
Y·vette (i vet′, ē vet′; *Fr.* ē vet′), dim. of *Yvonne.*
Y·vonne (i von′, ē von′; *Fr.* ē vôn′) < F, of uncert. meaning.

Z

Ze·ni·a (zē′nē ə, zēn′yə) < Gk: hospitable. Also, **Xenia.**
Zoe (zō, zō′ē) < Gk: life.

BASIC MANUAL OF STYLE

In this concise manual, not every acceptable alternative has been included. Every suggestion here, however, can be used with confidence. The style practices described here are those prevalent in the United States.

Punctuation

PERIOD (.)

Use a period:

1. To end a declarative or imperative sentence (but not an exclamatory sentence).

    The meeting was amicable and constructive.
    Please pass the salt.
    Read the next two chapters before Friday.

2. To end an indirect question.

    Tell us when the plane is leaving.

3. To follow most abbreviations.

ELLIPSIS (. . . or . . . .)

Use an ellipsis mark (three or four consecutive periods) to indicate that part of a quoted sentence has been omitted.

1. If the omission occurs at the beginning or in the middle of the sentence, use three periods in the ellipsis.

    ". . . the book is lively . . . and well written."

2. If the last part of the sentence is omitted or if entire sentences are omitted, add a fourth period to the ellipsis to mark the end of the sentence.

    "He left his home . . . . Years later he returned to find that everything had changed . . . ."

QUESTION MARK (?)

Use a question mark:

1. To end a sentence, clause, or phrase (or after a single word) that asks a question.

    Who invited him to the party?
    "Is something wrong?" she asked.
    Who said "When?"
    Whom shall we elect? Smith? Jones?

2. To indicate doubt or uncertainty.

    The manuscript dates back to 560? B.C.

EXCLAMATION POINT (!)

Use an exclamation point to end a sentence, clause, or phrase (or after a single word) that indicates strong emotion or feeling, especially surprise, command, admiration, etc.

Go away!
What a day this has been!
"Hey, there!" he shouted.
"Wow!"

COMMA (,)

Use a comma:

1. To separate words, phrases, and clauses that are part of a series of three or more items.

    The Danes are an industrious, friendly, generous, and hospitable people.
    The chief agricultural products of Denmark are butter, eggs, potatoes, beets, wheat, barley, and oats.

    It is permissible to omit the final comma before the *and* in a series of words as long as the absence of a comma does not interfere with clarity of meaning. The final commas in the examples above, while desirable, are not essential.

    In many cases, however, the inclusion or omission of a comma before the conjunction can materially affect the meaning. In the following sentence, omission of the final comma might indicate that the tanks were amphibious.

    Their equipment included airplanes, helicopters, artillery, amphibious vehicles, and tanks.

    Do not use commas to separate two items treated as a single unit within a series.

    For breakfast he ordered orange juice, bread and butter, coffee, and bacon and eggs.

    But

    At the supermarket he bought orange juice, bread, butter, bacon, and eggs.

2. Do not use commas to separate adjectives which are so closely related that they appear to form a single element with the noun they modify. Adjectives which refer to the number, age (*old, young, new*), size, color, or location of the noun often fall within this category. A simple test can usually determine the appropriateness of a comma in such instances: If *and* can not replace the comma without creating a clumsy, almost meaningless effect, it is safe to conclude that a comma is also out of place.

    twenty happy little youngsters
    a dozen large blue dresses
    several dingy old Western mining towns
    beautiful tall white birches

    But commas must be used in the following cases where clarity demands separation of the items in a series:

    a dozen large blue, red, yellow, and green dresses
    twenty old, young, and middle-aged spectators

    In a series of phrases or dependent clauses, place a comma before the conjunction.

    He sold his business, rented his house, gave up his car, paid his creditors, and set off for Africa.
    They strolled along the city streets, browsed in the bookshops, and dined at their favorite café.

3. To separate independent clauses joined by the coordinating conjunctions *and, but, yet, for, or, nor.*

    Almost any man knows how to earn money, but not one in a million knows how to spend it.

    The comma may be omitted in sentences consisting of two short independent clauses.

    We missed the train but we caught the bus in time.

4. To separate a long introductory phrase or subordinate clause from the rest of the sentence.

    Having rid themselves of their former rulers, the people now disagreed on the new leadership.
    Although the details have not been fully developed, scientists are confident of man's reaching the moon.

5. To set off words of direct address, interjections, or transitional words used to introduce a sentence (*oh, yes, no, however, nevertheless, still, anyway, well, why, frankly, really, moreover, incidentally,* etc.).

    Jim, where have you been?
    Oh, here's our new neighbor.
    Why, you can't mean that!
    Still, you must agree that he knows his business.
    Fine, we'll get together.
    Well, can you imagine that!

6. To set off an introductory modifier (adjective, adverb, participle, participial phrase) even if it consists of only one word or a short phrase.

    Politically, our candidate has proved to be inept.
    Hurt, she left the room quickly.
    Pleased with the result, he beamed at his painting.

7. To set off a nonrestrictive clause or phrase (an element which is not essential to the basic meaning of the sentence). Place commas both before and after the nonrestrictive portion.

    Our professor did not agree that corporations should be protected as "persons" under the Fourteenth Amendment, although the Supreme Court had held that they were.
    The old hotel, which had housed visiting celebrities for almost a century, remained outwardly unchanged.

8. To set off appositives or appositive phrases. Place commas both before and after the appositive.

    March, the month of crocuses, can still bring snow and ice.

One of our major problems, narcotics, remains unsolved.
Mr. Case, a member of the committee, refused to comment.

9. To set off parenthetical words and phrases and words of direct address.
   You may, if you insist, demand a retraction.
   The use of pesticides, however, has its disadvantages.
   He knew, nevertheless, that all was lost.
   Mr. Brown, far younger in spirit than his seventy years, delighted in his grandchildren.
   You realize, Mary, that we may never return to Paris.
10. To set off quoted matter from the rest of the sentence. (See *Quotation Marks* below.)
11. To set off items in dates and titles of individuals.
    Both John Adams and Thomas Jefferson died on July 4, 1826, just fifty years after the Declaration of Independence.

    A comma may or may not be used when only two items are given in a date.
    Washington was born in February, 1732, in Virginia.
    or
    Washington was born in February 1732, in Virginia.
12. To set off elements in addresses and geographical locations when the items are written on the same line.
    35 Fifth Avenue, New York, N.Y.
    1515 Halsted Street, Chicago, Illinois.
    He lived in Lima, Peru, for fifteen years.
13. To set off titles of individuals.
    Dr. Martin Price, Dean of Admissions
    Mr. John Winthrop, President
14. To set off the salutation in a personal letter.
    Dear Sam,
15. To set off the closing in a letter.
    Sincerely yours,
    Very truly yours,
16. To denote an omitted word or words in one or more parallel constructions within a sentence.
    John is studying Greek; George, Latin.

SEMICOLON (;)

Use a semicolon:

1. To separate independent clauses not joined by a conjunction.
   The house burned down; it was the last shattering blow.
   The war must continue; we must be satisfied only with victory.
2. To separate independent clauses that are joined by such conjunctive adverbs as *hence, however, therefore,* etc.
   The funds are inadequate; therefore, the project will close down.
   Enrollments exceed all expectations; however, there is a teacher shortage.
3. To separate long or possibly ambiguous items in a series, especially when the items already include commas.
   The elected officers are Jonathan Crane, president; Frances Glenn, vice president; Edward Morrell, treasurer; and Susan Stone, secretary.
4. To separate elements that are closely related but cannot be joined unambiguously.
   Poverty is unbearable; luxury, insufferable.
5. To precede an abbreviation or word that introduces an explanatory or summarizing statement.
   On the advice of his broker, after much deliberation, he chose to invest in major industries; i.e., steel, automobiles, and oil.
   She organized her work well; for example, by putting correspondence in folders of different colors to indicate degrees of urgency.

COLON (:)

Use a colon:

1. To introduce a series or list of items, examples, or the like.
   The three committees are as follows: membership, finance, and nominations.
   He named his five favorite poets: Byron, Keats, Tennyson, Hardy, and Auden.
2. To introduce a long formal statement, quotation, or question.
   This I believe: All men are created equal and must enjoy equally the rights that are inalienably theirs.
   Richards replied: "You are right. There can be no unilateral peace just as there can be no unilateral war. No one will contest that view."
   This is the issue: Can an employer dismiss a man simply because he laughs loudly?

   Note that the first word of the sentence following the colon is capitalized.
3. To follow a formal salutation, as in a letter or speech.
   Dear Mr. Chadwin:
   My Fellow Americans:
   To Whom It May Concern:
4. To follow the name of the speaker in a play.
   Ghost: Revenge his foul and most unnatural murder.
   Hamlet: Murder?
5. To separate parts of a citation.
   Genesis 3:2.
   Journal of Astronomy 15:261–327.
6. To separate hours from minutes in indicating time.
   1:30 p.m.
7. To indicate that an initial clause in a sentence will be further explained or illustrated by the material which follows the colon. In effect, the colon is a substitute for such phrases as "for example," or "namely."
   It was a city notorious for its inadequacies: its schools were antiquated, its administration was corrupt, and everyone felt the burden of its taxes.

APOSTROPHE (')

Use an apostrophe:

1. To denote the omission of letters, figures, or numerals.
   a. The contraction of a word:

nat'l	m'f'g	ne'er
ma'am	couldn't	won't
I'm	you're	he's
she's	we're	they're

      Do not confuse *it's* (contraction of *it is*) with the possessive *its*, which does not contain an apostrophe.
   b. The contraction of a number, usually a date:
      the Spirit of '76
      the Class of '48
   c. The omission of letters in quoting dialect:
      "I ain't goin' back 'cause I'm doin' mighty fine now."
2. To denote the possessive case of nouns.
   a. To form the possessive of most singular and plural nouns or of indefinite pronouns not ending in *s*, add an apostrophe and an *s*.

the city's industries	someone's car
the women's clubs	bachelor's degree

   b. To form the possessive of singular nouns (both common and proper) ending in *s* or the sound of *s*, add an apostrophe and an *s* in most instances.

the horse's mane	Kansas's schools
the bus's signal light	Texas's governor
Tennessee Williams's plays	the class's average
	Francis's promotion

      But if the addition of an *s* would produce an awkward or unpleasant sound or visual effect, add only an apostrophe.

Socrates' concepts	for goodness' sake
Aristophanes' comedies	for old times' sake

      In some cases either form is acceptable.
      Mr. Jones's or Jones' employees
      Keats's or Keats' poetry
   c. To form the possessive of plural nouns (both common and proper) ending in *s*, add only an apostrophe.

farmers' problems	judges' opinions
students' views	the Smiths' travels
critics' reviews	the Joneses' relatives
two weeks' vacation	three months' delay

      Note, however, that plurals not ending in *s* form their possessive by adding the apostrophe and *s*.
      men's clothing
      women's hats

d. To denote possession in most compound constructions, add the apostrophe and *s* to the last word of the compound.

anyone else's property
one another's books
brother-in-law's job
the attorney general's office

e. To denote joint possession by two or more proper names, add the apostrophe and *s* to the last name only.

Brown, Ross and King's law firm
Japan and Germany's agreement
Lewis and Clark's expedition

f. To denote individual ownership by two or more proper names, add the apostrophe and an *s* to both names.

John's and Mary's skis.

3. To form the plurals of letters or figures add an apostrophe and an *s*.

Dot the i's and cross the t's.

33 r.p.m.'s	+'s and −'s	C.O.'s
figure 8's	the 1890's (or 1890s)	V.I.P.'s
t's	PX's	GI's

QUOTATION MARKS (" ")

Use quotation marks:

1. To distinguish spoken words from other matter, as in reporting dialogue.

"God bless us every one!" said Tiny Tim.

2. To mark single words, sentences, paragraphs, or poetic stanzas which are quoted verbatim from the original.

Portia's speech on "the quality of mercy" is one of the most quoted passages from Shakespeare.

It was Shaw who wrote: "All great truths begin as blasphemies."

3. To enclose a quotation within a quotation, in which case a single quotation mark is used.

Reading Jill's letter, Pat said, "Listen to this! 'I've just received notice that I made Dean's list.' Isn't that great?"

4. To enclose titles of newspaper and magazine articles, essays, stories, poems, and chapters of books. The quotation marks are designed to distinguish such literary pieces from the books or periodicals (these are italicized) in which they appear.

Our anthology contains such widely assorted pieces as Bacon's essay "Of Studies," Poe's "The Gold Bug," Keats's "Ode to a Nightingale," and an article on criticism from *The Saturday Review*.

5. To enclose titles of short musical compositions and songs as distinct from symphonies and operas which are italicized.

Our national anthem is "The Star-Spangled Banner."

Even the youngsters laughed at the "Figaro" aria from *The Barber of Seville*.

6. To enclose titles of works of art such as paintings, drawings, photographs, and sculpture.

Most people recognize Da Vinci's "Mona Lisa" or Rodin's "The Thinker."

7. To enclose titles of radio and television programs.

"Meet the Press"
"What's My Line?"

8. To enclose titles of plays *only* if they are referred to as part of a larger collection. Referred to as single volumes, they are italicized.

"The Wild Duck" is the Ibsen play included in this edition of *Modern European Plays*.

9. To enclose names of ships and airplanes. Italics may also be used for this purpose.

Lindbergh flew across the Atlantic in the "Spirit of St. Louis."

We sailed on the "Queen Elizabeth."

10. To emphasize a word or phrase which is itself the subject of discussion.

The words "imply" and "infer" are not synonymous.

Such Freudian terms as the "ego," the "superego," the "id," and the "libido" are now considered part of the English language.

11. To draw attention to an uncommon word or phrase, a technical term, or a usage very different in style (dialect, extreme slang) from the context. Italics are often used for the same purpose.

Teachers need not be dismayed when students smirk at "square" traditions.

In glass blowing, the molten glass is called "metal."

12. To suggest ironic use of a word or phrase.

The radio blasting forth John's favorite "music" is to his grandfather an instrument of torture.

Bob's skiing "vacation" consisted of three weeks with his leg in a cast.

NOTE: The placement of quotation marks is determined by certain arbitrary rules and varies with different marks of punctuation.

1. Use quotation marks both before and after a quoted word, phrase, or longer passage.

2. Use a comma between the quoted matter and such phrases as "according to the speaker," "he said," "she replied," "they asked," whenever these phrases introduce a quotation, are used parenthetically, or follow a quotation which, in its original form, would end with a period.

According to the Declaration of Independence, "all men are created equal."

"Well," announced John's father, "we are going to the zoo next week."

John asked, "Why not this week?"

"We're going to visit Grandpa," replied his father.

3. Whenever such phrases as "he said," "he replied," or "he asked" follow a question or an exclamation, use the corresponding punctuation before the end quotation mark.

"Why can't we go this week?" asked John.

"We simply can't. And that's final!" replied his father.

4. Always place the end quotation mark *before* a colon or semicolon.

He remembered that the boys had always called Tom "the champ"; he began to wonder if the reputation endured.

There were several reasons why Tom was acknowledged as "the champ": physical strength, intellectual superiority, and qualities of leadership.

5. Place the end quotation mark *after* a question mark or exclamation point only when the question or exclamation is part of the quoted passage.

"Hurry, please, before it's too late!" she cried.

"Is there any hope of recovering the property?" he asked.

In all other cases, place the quotation mark *before* the exclamation point or question mark.

Did Pangloss really mean it when he said, "This is the best of all possible worlds"?

How absurd of him to say "This is the best of all possible worlds"!

6. If a quotation consists of two or more consecutive paragraphs, use quotation marks at the beginning of each paragraph, but place them at the end of the last paragraph only.

PARENTHESES ( )

Use parentheses:

1. To enclose material that is not part of the main sentence but is too relevant to omit.

Faulkner's novels (published by Random House) were selected as prizes.

Mr. Johnson (to the chairman): Will you allow that question to pass unanswered?

The data (see Table 13) was very impressive.

2. To enclose part of a sentence that, if enclosed by commas, would be confusing.

The authors he advised (none other than Hemingway, Lewis, and Cather) would have been delighted to honor him today.

3. To enclose an explanatory item that is not part of the statement or sentence.

He wrote to *The Paris* (Illinois) *News*.

4. To enclose numbers or letters that designate each item in a series.

   The project is (1) too time-consuming, (2) too expensive, and (3) poorly staffed.

   He was required to take courses in (a) mathematics, (b) English, (c) history, and (d) geology.

5. To enclose a numerical figure used to confirm a spelled-out number which precedes it.

   Enclosed is a check for ten dollars ($10.00) to cover the cost of the order.

BRACKETS [ ]

Brackets are used in pairs to enclose figures, phrases, or sentences that are meant to be set apart from the context—usually a direct quotation.

Use brackets:

1. To set off a notation, explanation, or editorial comment that is inserted in quoted material and is not part of the original text.

   According to the Globe critic, "This [*Man and Superman*] is one of Shaw's greatest plays."

   Or substitute the bracketed proper name for the pronoun: "[*Man and Superman*] is one of Shaw's . . . ."

   "As a result of the Gemini V mission [the flight by astronauts Cooper and Conrad in August 1965], we have proof that man can withstand the eight days in space required for a round trip to the moon."

   "Young as they are," he writes, "these students are afflicted with cynicism, world-weariness, and *a total disregard for tradition and authority*." [Emphasis is mine.]

2. To correct an error in a quotation.

   "It was on April 25, 1944 [1945—Ed.] that delegates representing forty-six countries met in San Francisco."

3. To indicate that an error in fact, spelling, punctuation, or language usage is quoted deliberately in an effort to reproduce the original statement with complete accuracy. The questionable fact or expression is followed by the Latin word *sic*, meaning "thus," which is enclosed in brackets.

   "George Washington lived during the seventeenth [sic] century."

   "The governor of Missisipi [sic] addressed the student body."

4. To enclose stage directions in plays. Parentheses may also be used for this purpose.

   Juliet: [Snatching Romeo's dagger] . . . O happy dagger! This is thy sheath; [Stabs herself] there rest and let me die.

5. To enclose comments made on a verbatim transcription of a speech, debate, or testimony.

   Sen. Eaton: The steady rise in taxes must be halted. [Applause]

6. To substitute for parentheses within material already enclosed by parentheses. Although it is not seen frequently, this device is sometimes used in footnotes.

   [1]See "René Descartes" (M. C. Beardsley, *The European Philosophers from Descartes to Nietzsche* [New York, 1960]).

7. To enclose the publication date, inserted by the editor, of an item appearing in an earlier issue of a periodical. This device is used in letters to the editor or in articles written on subjects previously reported. Parentheses may also be used for this purpose.

   Dear Sir: Your excellent article on China [April 15] brings to mind my recent experience . . .

   When removing old wallpaper [*Homeowners' Monthly*, March 1965] some do-it-yourselfers neglect to . . .

DASH (—)

Use a dash:

1. To mark an abrupt change in thought or grammatical construction in the middle of a sentence.

   He won the game—but I'm getting ahead of the story.

2. To suggest halting or hesitant speech.

   "Well—er—ah—it's hard to explain," he faltered.

3. To indicate a sudden break or interruption before a sentence is completed.

   "Harvey, don't climb up that—." It was too late.

4. To add emphasis to parenthetical material or to mark an emphatic separation between parenthetical material and the rest of a sentence.

   His influence—he was a powerful figure in the community—was a deterrent to effective opposition.

   The excursions for school groups—to museums, zoos, and theaters—are less expensive.

   The car he was driving—a gleaming red convertible—was the most impressive thing about him.

5. To set off an appositive or an appositive phrase when a comma would provide less than the desired emphasis on the appositive or when the use of commas might result in confusion with commas within the appositive phrase.

   The premier's promise of changes—land reform, higher wages, reorganization of industry—was not easily fulfilled.

6. To replace an offensive word or part of one.

   Where the h— is he?

   Where's that son of a —?

HYPHEN (-)

The hyphenation of compound nouns and modifiers is often arbitrary, inconsistent, and subject to change. Practices vary. To determine current usage as well as traditional forms, it is best to consult the dictionary.

Use a hyphen:

1. To spell out a word or name.

   r-e-a-s-o-n
   G-a-e-l-i-c

2. To divide a word into syllables.

   hal-lu-ci-na-tion

3. To mark the division of a word of more than one syllable at the end of a line, indicating that the word is to be completed on the following line.

   It is difficult to estimate the damaging psychological effects of poverty.

4. To separate the parts (when spelling out numerals) of a compound number from twenty-one to ninety-nine.

   thirty-six inches to the yard
   Fifty-second Street
   nineteen hundred and forty-three

5. To express decades in words.

   the nineteen-twenties
   the eighteen-sixties

6. To separate (when spelling out numerals) the numerator from the denominator of a fraction, especially a fraction which is used as an adjective.

   One-half cup of milk
   a two-thirds majority

   While some authorities avoid hyphenating fractions used as nouns, the practice is not uncommon.

   Three fourths (or three-fourths) of his constituents
   One fifth (or one-fifth) of the class

   Do not use a hyphen to indicate a fraction if either the numerator or denominator is already hyphenated.

   one thirty-second
   forty-five hundredths
   twenty-one thirty-sixths

7. To form certain compound nouns.

   a. Nouns consisting of two or more words which show the combination of two or more constituents, qualities, or functions in one person or thing.

secretary-treasurer	city-state
teacher-counselor	AFL-CIO

   b. Nouns made up of two or more words, including other parts of speech.

cease-fire	editor-in-chief
coat-of-arms	fourth-grader
court-martial	hand-me-down
cure-all	has-been
do-gooder	jack-in-the-pulpit
do-it-yourselfer	post-mortem
	teen-ager

   Do not hyphenate compound nouns denoting chemical terms, military rank, or certain governmental positions.

hydrogen sulfide	sergeant at arms
sodium chloride	brigadier general

carbon tetrachloride
vice admiral
lieutenant governor
justice of the peace
lieutenant junior grade
attorney general
private first class

8. To connect the elements of a compound modifier when used *before* the noun it modifies. In most cases, the same modifier is not hyphenated if it *follows* the noun it modifies.

   They engaged in hand-to-hand combat.
   They fought hand to hand.
   They endured a hand-to-mouth existence.
   They lived hand to mouth.
   a well-known expert
   an expert who is well known

   Do not hyphenate a compound modifier which includes an adverb ending in *ly* even when it is used before the noun.

   his loose-fitting jacket
   his loosely fitting jacket
   a well-guarded secret
   a carefully guarded secret

9. To distinguish a less common pronunciation or meaning of a word from its more customary usage.

COMMON FORM:	HYPHENATED FORM:
a recreation hall	re-creation of a scene
to recover from an illness	re-cover the couch
to reform a sinner	re-form their lines

10. To prevent possible confusion in pronunciation if a prefix results in the doubling of a letter, especially a vowel.

    anti-inflationary, co-ordinate, pre-eminent, re-election, co-op, pre-empt, re-enact, re-entry

    The dieresis is sometimes, but less frequently, used over *e* and *o* to accomplish the same result:

    coöp   reëntry

11. To join the following prefixes with *proper* nouns or adjectives.

anti	anti-American, anti-British
mid	mid-Victorian, mid-Atlantic, mid-August
neo	neo-Nazi, neo-Darwinism
non	non-European, non-Asian, non-Christian
pan	Pan-American, Pan-Slavic, Pan-African
pro	pro-French, pro-American
un	un-American, un-British

With few exceptions, these prefixes are joined to common nouns without hyphenation:

anticlimax, midsummer, proslavery, nonintervention, neoclassic, unambiguous

12. To join the following prefixes and suffixes with the main word of a compound.

co-	co-chairman, co-worker, co-author
ex-	ex-sergeant, ex-mayor, ex-wife, ex-premier
self-	self-preservation, self-defeating, self-explanatory, self-educated
-elect	president-elect, governor-elect

13. To form most compound nouns and adjectives which begin with the word elements listed below. For words not listed, it is best to consult the dictionary.

cross-	cross-examine	cross-fertilize
	cross-purposes	cross-stitch
double-	double-breasted	double-edged
	doubled-jointed	double-park
great-	(always used in family relationships)	
	great-grandfather	great-grandchild
	great-hearted	
heavy-	heavy-handed	heavy-hearted
	heavy-duty (but heavyweight)	
ill-	ill-disposed	ill-organized
	ill-timed	
light-	light-fingered	light-footed
	light-hearted	light-year
single-	single-breasted	single-handed
	single-minded	
well-	well-behaved	well-balanced
	well-preserved	well-wisher

Division of Words

The division of a word at the end of a line should be avoided. If it is necessary to divide a word, follow the syllabification shown in the dictionary.

Do not syllabify a word so that only one letter stands alone at the end or beginning of a line. Do not divide a one-syllable word, including words ending in *-ed* (such as *walked, saved, hurled*). Avoid the division of a word that carries only two letters over to the next line. The following terminal parts of words should never be divided: *-able, -ible, -cial, -sial, -tial; -cion, -sion, -tion; -gion; -ceous, -cious, -tious; -geous.*

If a word that already has a hyphen must be broken, hyphenate only at the hyphen.

mother-
in-law

mother-in-
law

but not

moth-
er-in-law

Abbreviation

In standard academic, scientific, business or other organizational reports and correspondence, abbreviations are generally avoided unless they are the commonly required ones and are specifically known and accepted terms within a particular discipline or trade.

Some abbreviations that are acceptable in journalistic or business writing may not be appropriate in extremely formal announcements or invitations in which even dates are spelled out.

Abbreviations are often used in ordering and billing, catalogs, tabulations, telephone books, classified advertising, and similar cases where brevity is essential.

In some cases, the decision to use an abbreviation is a matter of individual preference. When in doubt, it is usually prudent to use the spelled-out form. Do not, however, spell out a word in one sentence or paragraph only to use the abbreviated form elsewhere. As in all writing, it is most important to maintain consistency of usage within any single written document, whether it be a letter or a treatise.

Use abbreviations in writing:

1. The following titles and forms of address whenever they precede a proper name: *Mr., Mrs., Dr., Mme., Mlle., M.* Do not spell out these titles even in the most formal situations.

   Mlle. Modiste   Dr. Kildare
   Mr. Carl Sandburg   Mme. Curie

2. Except in an extremely formal context, titles of the clergy, government officials, officers of organizations, military and naval personnel, provided that the title is followed by a first name or initial as well as a surname. If the title is followed only by a surname, it must be spelled out.

Gen. Curtis Le May	General Le May
Sgt. Leon Greene	Sergeant Greene
Prof. Samuel Page	Professor Page
Gov. Nelson Rockefeller	Governor Rockefeller
Rev. John McDermott	The Reverend John McDermott *or* The Reverend Dr. (*or* Mr.) McDermott
Hon. Jacob Javits	The Honorable Jacob Javits *or* The Honorable Mr. Javits

   Note above that in very formal writing, the titles *Honorable* and *Reverend* are spelled out and are preceded by *The.* When the first name or initial is omitted, the title Mr. or Dr. is substituted.

3. *Jr.* or *Sr.* following a name. These abbreviations should be added only when the names preceding them include a first name or initial.

4. *Esq.* following a name. Not a common usage in the United States, this abbreviation should not be used with any other title.
5. Academic degrees: *B.A.* (Bachelor of Arts); *M.A.* (Master of Arts); *M.S.* (Master of Science); *Ph.D.* (Doctor of Philosophy); *M.D.* (Doctor of Medicine), etc. When a name is followed by a scholastic degree or by the abbreviations of religious or fraternal orders (BPOE) it should not be preceded by *Mr., Miss, Dr.*, or any other title.
6. The terms used to describe business firms (*Co., Corp., Inc., Bro.* or *Bros., Ltd., R.R.* or *Ry.*) only when these abbreviations are part of the legally authorized name. In all other cases (except for brevity in tables, etc.), *Company, Corporation, Incorporated, Brothers,* and *Limited* should be spelled out.
7. Except in formal writing, the names ot states, territories, or possessions that immediately follow the name of a city, mountain, airport, or other identifiable geographic locations. Check the dictionary for all such abbreviations.

   Detroit, Mich.
   San Juan, P.R.
8. Certain foreign expressions:

   i.e. (*id est*), that is
   e.g. (*exempli gratia*), for example
   et al. (*et alii*), and others
   etc. (*et cetera*), and so forth

Do not abbreviate:

1. Names of countries, except:
   a. The U.S.S.R. (Union of Soviet Socialist Republics) because of its exceptional length.
   b. U.S. (United States) when preceding the name of an American ship. The abbreviation U.S. may also be used in tables, footnotes, etc., when modifying a Government agency: *U.S. Congress, U.S. Post Office*, etc.
2. The words *street, avenue, boulevard, drive, square, road*, and *court*, except in lists requiring brevity.
3. The days of the week and the months of the year except in the most informal situations or in tables.
4. Weights and measures except in lists of items, technical writing, etc.

   She had hoped to lose ten pounds.
   We used ten yards of cloth.

Do not use a period after the following abbreviations or shortened forms:

1. After a contraction, which is not to be confused with an abbreviation. Contractions contain apostrophes which indicate omitted letters; they never end with a period.

   sec't'y or sec'y — sec.
   Nat'l — natl.
2. After chemical symbols.

   H_2O — NaCl
3. After *percent*
4. After initials of military services and specific military terms.

USA	United States Army
USAF	United States Air Force
USMC	United States Marine Corps
USN	United States Navy
USNR	United States Naval Reserve
USCG	United States Coast Guard
USNG	United States National Guard
MP	military police
SP	shore patrol
POW	prisoner of war
PX	post exchange
GI	government issue
APO	Army post office

5. After the initials of certain governmental agencies or call letters of television and radio stations.

   NATO, SEATO, UNICEF, CIA, CARE, OES, CAP, WQXR, WINS
6. After letters that are used as symbols rather than initials.

   Let us assume that A and B are playing opposite C and D.
7. After listed items (as in catalogs, outlines, or syllabuses), if none of the items is a complete sentence. If the list includes only one complete sentence, use a period after this and all other items on the list, including those which are not complete sentences. Consistency is essential: a period after each item or no end punctuation whatever.
8. Points of the compass.

   NE — SW
   ESE — E by NE

Capitalization

Many writers have a tendency to use capitals unnecessarily. When in doubt, one can usually learn whether a particular word is generally capitalized by consulting the dictionary. A safe guideline is to capitalize only when there is specific need or reason to do so.

Capitalize the first word of a sentence. Capitalize, also, any word (or the first word of a phrase) that stands independently as though it were a sentence.

He is the new president of the club.
Where is the chess set?
Hurrah! No school!

Capitalize the first word of each line of poetry (unless the poet specifically avoided capitals in such instances).

Her pretty feet
Like snails did creep
A little out, and then,
As if they started at Bo-Peep,
Did soon draw in again.

Capitalize the first word of a direct quotation within a sentence (unless the quotation is a fragment).

He replied, "He prefers to enter in the fall."
"George," she asked, "don't you want to join us for dinner?"
He denied that he was "a neurotic editor."

Always capitalize the interjection *O* or the pronoun *I*. None of the other pronouns are capitalized unless they occur at the beginning of a sentence or refer to the Deity.

Here I am. — Exult, O Shores!

Capitalize all proper nouns and adjectives:

Italians	Scottish
Emily Dickinson	Edwardian
the Cabot family	Germanic
Australia	Shavian
Chicago	Chaucerian

The German *von* and the Dutch *van* in proper names are commonly not printed with a capital when part of a name, but usage varies.

Paul von Hindenburg — Vincent van Gogh

The French particles *de* and *du* and the Italian *di* and *da* are commonly written in lower case when they are preceded by a first name or title. Without title or first name, the particle is sometimes dropped, sometimes capitalized.

Marquis de Lafayette	Count de Mirabeau
(De) Lafayette	(De) Mirabeau

In English or American names these particles are commonly capitalized in all positions:

William De Morgan	Lee De Forest
De Morgan	De Forest

Do not capitalize words derived from proper nouns but now having a special meaning distinct from the proper name:

antimacassar	china
pasteurize	macadam

Capitalize recognized geographical names:

Ohio River	Strait of Juan de Fuca
Cascade Mountains	Gulf of Mexico

Capitalize the following when they follow a single proper name and are written in the singular:

Butte	County	Delta
Canyon	Creek	Gap

Glacier Ocean Range
Harbor Peninsula River
Head Plateau Valley

For example, the *Sacramento River*, but the *Tennessee and Cumberland rivers.*

Capitalize the following in the singular and plural when they follow a proper name:

Hill Mountain
Island Narrows

Capitalize the following in the singular whether placed before or after the name. Capitalize in the plural when they come before the name and sometimes following a single name:

Bay Sea Gulf Mount
Point Cape Isle Peak
Strait Desert Lake Plain

For example, *Lakes George and Champlain* but *Malheur and Goose lakes.*

Capitalize compass directions when they designate particular regions. Capitalize also the nicknames or special names for regions or districts:

East Tennessee — the South
Middle Atlantic States — the Near East
the New World — the Dust Bowl

Exception: Do not capitalize merely directional parts of states or countries.

eastern Washington — southern Indiana

Capitalize the names of streets, parks, buildings, etc.:

Fifth Avenue — Central Park
Metropolitan Opera House — Empire State Building

Exceptions: Do not capitalize such categories of buildings as *library, post office*, or *museum*, written without a proper name, unless local custom makes the classification equivalent to a proper name.

Capitalize the various names of God or the Christian Trinity, both nouns and adjectives, and all pronouns clearly referring to the Deity. Capitalize also words that refer to the Bible or other sacred writings.

the Word — Holy Bible
the Savior — the Koran
the Messiah — Ten Commandments
the Almighty — the Virgin Mary

Capitalize all personifications.

Come, gentle Death!

Capitalize the names of organizations, institutions, political parties, alliances, movements, classes, religious groups, nationalities, races, etc.:

Democratic party — Royalist Spain
Labor party — Axis powers
Republicans — Soviet Russia
Protestants — University of Wisconsin
United Nations — Lutherans
American Legion — Dutch Treat Club
Negroes — Caucasians

Capitalize divisions, departments, and offices of government, when the official name is used. Do not capitalize incomplete or roundabout designations:

Department of Commerce
Circuit Court of Marion County
Bureau of Labor Statistics
Congress
Senate
House of Burgesses
United States Army
Board of Aldermen
the council
the lower house (of Congress)
the bureau
the legislature

Capitalize the names of wars, battles, treaties, documents, prizes, and important periods or events:

The Battle of the Bulge
Declaration of Independence
Pulitzer Prize
Revolutionary War
Congress of Vienna
Black Death
War of 1812
Golden Age of Pericles
Middle Ages
Treaty of Versailles

Do no[illegible]italize *war* or *treaty* when used without the disting[illegible]ng name.

Capitalize the numerals used with kings, dynasties, or organizations. Numerals preceding the name are ordinarily spelled out; those following the name are commonly put in Roman numerals:

Second World War — World War II
Nineteenth Amendment — Third Army
Forty-eighth Congress — Henry IV

Capitalize titles, military or civil ranks of honor, academic degrees, decorations, etc., when written with the name, and all titles of honor or rank when used for specific persons in place of the name:

General Bradley
the Senator from Ohio
the Earl of Rochester
King George
the Archbishop of Canterbury
Your Highness

Capitalize the main words (nouns, verbs, adjectives, adverbs) of the titles of books, articles, poems, plays, musical compositions, etc., as well as the first word:

The House of the Seven Gables
All's Well That Ends Well
The Kreutzer Sonata

Titles of chapters in a book are usually capitalized. Capitalize also any sections of a specific book, such as *Bibliography*, *Index*, *Table of Contents*, etc.

In expressions of time, *A.M.*, *P.M.*, *A.D.*, and *B.C.* are usually written or typed in capitals without space between them.

9:40 A.M. — 6:10 P.M.
12 P.M. — A.D. 1491
42 B.C.

It is equally acceptable to show *a.m.* and *p.m.* in lower-case letters. When A.M., P.M., A.D., and B.C. are to be typeset, one may mark them with double-underlining to indicate that small capitals are to be used.

Italics

Italics (indicated by underlining in manuscript) are occasionally used to emphasize a particular word, phrase, or statement. Done with restraint, this use of italics can be effective. Done to excess, it reduces the text to a flickering mass.

Italics are used when referring to the titles of books, magazines, newspapers, motion pictures and plays, longer musical compositions, works of art, ships, aircraft, and book-length poems.

The Catcher in the Rye — *Mona Lisa*
Harper's Magazine — Rodin's *The Thinker*
the *New York Post* — the *Queen Mary*
High Noon — the *Zeppelin*
Hamlet — *Paradise Lost*
Beethoven's *Ninth Symphony* — *The Faerie Queen*

Foreign words and phrases that are used in English texts should always be italicized.

In his younger days he was quite a *bon vivant.*
I'll be there, *deo volente.*

Use italics when referring to a letter, number, word, or expression as such. Quotation marks are sometimes used instead of italics.

The word *fantastic* is her favorite adjective.
Do not pronounce the final *e* in *Hecate*.
She drew a large *4* on the blackboard.

Use italics for parenthesized stage directions in a play.

HEIDI [*turning to* ANITA]: Did he call me?
ANITA: I didn't hear him. [*She picks up a magazine.*]

Numerals

In general, numbers that can be stated in only one or two words are spelled out.

There were twelve girls and twenty-six boys there.
The sweater cost twenty-five dollars.
He gave one-tenth of his income to charity.

Other numbers are usually shown in figures.

> There are 392 members in the association.
> The radio cost him $136.50.
> The population of Chicago in 1950 was 3,620,962.

The numeral at the beginning of a sentence is usually spelled out. If this is awkward or difficult to read, rewrite the sentence to avoid beginning with a numeral.

> Three hundred and sixty students attended the dance.
> Twenty-six million votes were cast for him.
> Six thousand dollars was stolen from the safe.

It is important to be consistent in the treatment of numbers when they appear in the same series or in the same sentence or paragraph. Do not spell some out and use figures for others.

> The three chairs are 36, 72, and 122 years old.
> He spent $100 on rent, $30 on food, and $265 on clothes.

Use figures (generally) for dates, pages, dimensions, decimals, percentages, measures, statistical data, exact amounts of money, designations of time when followed by A.M. or P.M., and addresses.

June 24, 1945	0.9631	96.8°
124 B.C.	23 percent	86%
p. 263	75 pounds	8:30 A.M.
p. xxvi	93 miles	3:20 P.M.
2′ x 4′	$369.27	4262 Brush
10 ft. 3 in.	£5.9s.6d	Street

Spell out ordinal numbers whenever possible.

sixteenth century	Fifth Avenue
Eighty-second Congress	Third Republic
Third Assembly District	Twenty-third Psalm

Manuscript Preparation

The manuscript should be typewritten, double-spaced, on white medium-weight paper. The sheets should be of the standard 8½″ x 11″ size and of good enough quality to permit clear markings in ink. Margins should be about one inch on each side and at the top and bottom. All pages should be numbered consecutively, preferably at the top, throughout the entire work.

A quotation that will run three lines or more is usually set off as a single-spaced, double-indented paragraph.

It is not advantageous to submit the manuscript in any special ornamental binder. If assembled neatly in a folder, envelope, or cardboard box, the manuscript will be more in keeping with the practice of most professional writers and with the preference of most editors.

IMPORTANT: The author should always retain a complete carbon copy of the manuscript, not only to facilitate correspondence between the editor and author, but to serve as insurance against loss of the original copy. Publishers are usually very careful not to lose or damage a manuscript, but their legal responsibility does not extend beyond "reasonable care."

Footnotes

Footnotes serve a variety of purposes: to indicate the source of a fact, opinion, or quotation; to provide additional or explanatory material which, although relevant, would interrupt the smooth flow of the main text; and to cross-refer the reader to another part of the text. Excessive use of footnotes, however, is usually distracting; it is the sign, generally, of spurious scholarship and pedantry.

Material in the text to which footnotes are to be keyed should be numbered with superscript Arabic numerals ([1], [2], [3], [4], etc.). These numerals are usually placed without intervening space at the close of the sentence, quotation, or paragraph, unless doing so would cause confusion or ambiguity (in which case the numeral is placed after the specific word, phrase, or name to which it refers). The superscripts should be free of periods, slashes, parentheses or other unnecessary marks.

Footnote numbers should continue consecutively throughout an article or chapter, usually numbering anew in each chapter.

Occasionally a writer will prefer to number the footnotes anew on each page. Because this causes many problems in typesetting, it is preferably avoided. Similarly, some writers prefer to use special symbols (*, †, ‡, §, ‖, ¶, etc.) instead of superscript numerals. Because this system of symbols is limited and confusing, it too is preferably avoided.

Footnotes are placed at the bottom of the page under a straight line that extends from the left to the right margins. (Some style manuals suggest that this line extend only two or three inches in from the left margin.) One line of space is left blank above this separation line and two lines of space are left blank below it. The footnote, which begins with the appropriate superscript number without a space after it, is usually typed single-space. The first line of the footnote is the same indention used throughout the text itself; subsequent lines are typed to the same margins as the text itself. Avoid carrying footnotes onto a following page, if at all possible.

BOOKS: FIRST FOOTNOTE REFERENCES

When a book is first mentioned in a footnote, the bibliographical information should be as complete as possible. The information should appear in the following order:

1. AUTHOR'S NAME OR AUTHORS' NAMES. The given name or initials are given first, using the form in which the name is generally encountered, the surname being followed by a comma.
2. TITLE OF THE CHAPTER OR PART. When reference is made to an article in a collection, symposium, or the like, the title of the article appears within quotation marks, the final quotation mark being preceded by a comma.
3. TITLE OF THE BOOK. The title is underlined (to indicate italics) and followed by a comma unless the next information is in parentheses; in such a case, the comma follows the closing parenthesis. If the title is exceptionally long, it may be shortened by omissions (indicated by three periods in each case). The title should be taken as it is shown on the title page.
4. EDITOR'S OR TRANSLATOR'S NAME. The name of the editor or translator, given in its full and normal form, is preceded by "ed." or "trans." It is followed by a comma unless the next material is in parentheses (in which case the comma follows the closing parenthesis).
5. EDITION USED. If the edition is other than the first one, the edition is identified in Arabic numerals, followed by a comma unless the next material is in parentheses (in which case the comma follows the closing parenthesis).
6. SERIES TITLE. The name of the series is shown without underlining or quotation marks. It is followed by the specific number of the work in the series, preceded and followed by commas. If the next material is in parentheses, the second comma is placed after the closing parenthesis.
7. NUMBER OF VOLUMES. If there is more than one volume in the work and it appears relevant to indicate this fact, the number is shown in Arabic numerals.
8. PLACE OF PUBLICATION. This information, plus the name of the publisher and date of publication, is shown within one set of parentheses. The place of publication is usually found on the title page; if more than one city is shown, it is necessary only to show the publisher's main place of activity. If the city is not well known or if it might be confused with another of the same name, add the state or nation. It is followed by a colon.
9. NAME OF THE PUBLISHER. The name of the company, institution, etc., that published the work is shown next, followed by a comma.
10. DATE OF PUBLICATION. The date of publication is usually found on the copyright page. If no date is shown on the title page or copyright page, write "n.d." (without quotation marks) to indicate "no date." The parentheses containing the place of publication, publisher's name, and date of publication is followed by a comma.